THE OFFICIAL®

2008 PRICE GUIDE TO

BASEBALL CARDS

DR. JAMES BECKETT

TWENTY-EIGHTH EDITION

House of Collectibles
New York

Important Notice: All of the information, including valuations, in this book has been compiled from reliable sources, and efforts have been made to eliminate errors and questionable data. Nevertheless, the possibility of error, in a work of such immense scope, always exists. The publisher will not be held responsible for losses that may occur in the purchase, sale, or other transaction of items because of information contained herein. Readers who feel they have discovered errors are invited to *write* and inform us, so they may be corrected in subsequent editions. Those seeking further information on the topics covered in this book are advised to refer to the complete line of *Official Price Guides* published by the House of Collectibles.

House of Collectibles and colophon are trademarks of Random House, Inc.

www.houseofcollectibles.com

Manufactured in the United States of America

ISSN: 1062-7138

ISBN: 978-0-375-72292-9

10 9 8 7 6 5 4 3 2 1

Twenty-Eighth Edition: April 2008

Table of Contents

About the Author

Jim Beckett, the leading authority on sports card values in the United States, maintains a wide range of activities in the world of sports. He possesses one of the finest collections of sports cards and autographs in the world, has made numerous appearances on radio and television, and has been frequently cited in many national publications. He was awarded the first "Special Achievement Award" for Contributions to the Hobby by the National Sports Collectors Convention in 1980, the "Jock Jaspersen Award" for Hobby Dedication in 1983, and the "Buck Barker, Spirit of the Hobby" award in 1991.

Dr. Beckett is the author of *Beckett Baseball Card Price Guide, The Official Price Guide to Baseball Cards, Price Guide to Baseball Collectibles, The Sport Americana Baseball Memorabilia and Autograph Price Guide, Beckett Almanac of Baseball Cards and Collectibles, Beckett Football Card Price Guide, The Official Price Guide to Football Cards, Beckett Hockey Card Price Guide, The Official Price Guide to Hockey Cards, Beckett Basketball Card Price Guide, The Official Price Guide to Basketball Cards, The Beckett Baseball Card Alphabetical Checklist, The Beckett Basketball Card Alphabetical Checklist,* and *The Beckett Football Card Alphabetical Checklist.* In addition, he is the founder, publisher, and editor of *Beckett Baseball Card Monthly, Beckett Basketball Monthly, Beckett Football Card Monthly, Beckett Hockey Collector, Beckett Sports Collectibles,* and *Beckett Racing and Motorsports Marketplace.*

Jim Beckett received his Ph.D. in Statistics from Southern Methodist University in 1975. Prior to starting Beckett Publications in 1984, Dr. Beckett served as an Associate Professor of Statistics at Bowling Green State University and as a vice president of a consulting firm in Dallas, Texas.

How to Use This Book

Isn´t it great? Every year this book gets better with all the new sets coming out. But even more exciting is that every year there are more options in collecting the cards we love so much. This edition has been enhanced and expanded from the previous edition. The cards you collect — who appears on them, what they look like, where they are from, and (most important to most of you) what their current values are — are enumerated within. Many of the features contained in the other *Beckett Price Guides* have been incorporated into this volume since condition grading, terminology, and many other aspects of collecting are common to the card hobby in general. We hope you find the book both interesting and useful in your collecting pursuits.

The Beckett Guide has been successful where other attempts have failed because it is complete, current, and valid. This price guide contains not just one, but three prices by condition for all the baseball cards listed. The prices were added to the card lists just prior to printing and reflect not the author´s opinions or desires but the going retail prices for each card, based on the marketplace (sports memorabilia conventions and shows, sports card shops, hobby papers, current mail-order catalogs, local club meetings, auction results, and other firsthand reportings of actually realized prices).

What is the best price guide available on the market today? Of course, card sellers prefer the price guide with the highest prices, while card buyers naturally prefer the one with the lowest prices. Accuracy, however, is the true test. Use the price guide trusted by more collectors and dealers than all the others combined. Look for the Beckett® name. I won´t put my name on anything I won´t stake my reputation on. Not the lowest and not the highest — but the most accurate, with integrity.

To facilitate your use of this book, read the complete introductory section on the following pages before going to the pricing pages. Every collectible field has its own terminology; we´ve tried to capture most of these terms and definitions in our glossary. Please read carefully the section on grading and the condition of your cards, as you cannot determine which price column is appropriate for a given card without first knowing its condition.

Welcome to the world of baseball cards.

How to Collect

Each collection is personal and reflects the individuality of its owner. There are no set rules on how to collect cards. Since card collecting is a hobby or leisure pastime, what you collect, how much you collect, and how much time and money you spend collecting are entirely up to you. The funds you have available for collecting and your own personal taste should determine how you collect. Information and ideas presented here are intended to help you get the most enjoyment from this hobby.

It is impossible to collect every card ever produced. Therefore, beginners as well as intermediate and advanced collectors usually specialize in some way. One of the reasons this hobby is popular is that individual collectors can define and tailor their collecting methods to match their own tastes. To give you some idea of the various approaches to collecting, we will list some of the more popular areas of specialization.

Many collectors select complete sets from particular years. For example, they may concentrate on assembling complete sets from all the years since their birth or since they became avid sports fans. They may try to collect a card for every player during that specified period of time.

Many others wish to acquire only certain players. Usually such players are the superstars of the sport, but occasionally collectors will specialize in all the cards of players who attended a particular college or came from a certain town. Some collectors are interested in only the first cards or Rookie Cards of certain players. A handy guide for collectors interested in pursuing the hobby this way is *The Sport Americana Baseball Card Alphabetical Checklist.*

Another fun way to collect cards is by team. Most fans have a favorite team, and it is natural for that loyalty to be translated into a desire for cards of the players on that favorite team. For most of the recent years, team sets (all the cards from a given team for that year) are readily available at a reasonable price. *The Sport Americana Team Baseball Card Checklist* will open up this field to the collector.

Obtaining Cards

Several avenues are open to card collectors. Cards still can be purchased in the traditional way: by the pack at the local candy, grocery, drug, or major discount store.

But there are also thousands of card shops across the country that specialize in selling cards individually or by the pack, box, or set. Another alternative is the thousands of card shows held each month around the country, which feature anywhere from 8 to 800 tables of sports cards and memorabilia for sale.

For many years, it has been possible to purchase complete sets of baseball cards through mail-order advertisers found in traditional sports media publications, such as the *Sporting News, Baseball Digest*, and, *Street & Smith* yearbooks. These sets also are advertised in the card collecting periodicals. Many collectors will begin by subscribing to at least one of the hobby periodicals, all with good up-to-date information. In fact, subscription offers can be found in the advertising section of this book.

Most serious card collectors obtain old (and new) cards from one or more of several main sources: (1) trading or buying from other collectors or dealers; (2) responding to sale or auction ads in the hobby publications; (3) buying at a local hobby store; (4) attending sports collectibles shows or conventions; and (5) purchasing cards over the Internet.

We advise that you try all five methods since each has its own distinct advantages: (1) trading is a great way to make new friends; (2) hobby periodicals help you keep up with what's going on in the hobby (including when and where the conventions are happening); (3) stores provide the opportunity to enjoy personalized service and consider a great diversity of material in a relaxed sports-oriented atmosphere; (4) shows allow you to choose from multiple dealers and thousands of cards under one roof in a competitive situation; and (5) the Internet allows one to purchase cards in a convenient manner from almost anywhere in the world.

Preserving Your Cards

Cards are fragile. They must be handled properly in order to retain their value. Careless handling can easily result in creased or bent cards. It is, however, not recommended that tweezers or tongs be used to pick up your cards since such utensils might mar or indent card surfaces and thus reduce those cards´ conditions and values.

In general, your cards should be handled directly as little as possible. This is sometimes easier to say than to do.

Although there are still many who use custom boxes, storage trays, or even shoe boxes, plastic sheets are the preferred method of many collectors for storing cards.

A collection stored in plastic pages in a three-ring album allows you to view your collection at any time without the need to touch the cards themselves. Cards can also be kept in single holders (of various types and thicknesses) designed for the enjoyment of each card individually.

For a large collection, some collectors may use a combination of the above methods. When purchasing plastic sheets for your cards, be sure that you find the pocket size that fits the cards snugly. Don´t put your 1951 Bowman in a sheet designed to fit 1981 Topps.

Most hobby and collectibles shops and virtually all collectors´ conventions will have these plastic pages available in quantity for the various sizes offered, or you can purchase them directly from the advertisers in this book.

Also, remember that pocket size isn´t the only factor to consider when looking for plastic sheets. Other factors such as safety, economy, appearance, availability, or personal preference also may influence which types of sheets a collector may want to buy.

Damp, sunny, and/or hot conditions — no, this is not a weather forecast — are three elements to avoid in extremes if you are interested in preserving your collection. Too much (or too little) humidity can cause the gradual deterioration of a card. Direct, bright sun (or fluorescent light) over time will bleach out the color of a card. Extreme heat accelerates the decomposition of the card. On the other hand, many cards have lasted more than 75 years without much scientific intervention. So be cautious, even if the above factors typically present a problem only when present in the extreme. It never hurts to be prudent.

Collecting vs. Investing

Collecting individual players and collecting complete sets are both popular vehicles for investment and speculation.

Most investors and speculators stock up on complete sets or on quantities of players they think have good investment potential.

There is obviously no guarantee in this book, or anywhere else for that matter, that cards will outperform the stock market or other investment alternatives in the future. After all, baseball cards do not pay quarterly dividends and cards cannot be sold at their "current values" as easily as stocks or bonds.

Nevertheless, investors have noticed a favorable long-term trend in the past performance of baseball and other sports collectibles, and certain cards and sets have outperformed just about any other investment in some years.

Many hobbyists maintain that the best investment is and always will be the building of a collection, which traditionally has held up better than outright speculation.

Some of the obvious questions are: Which cards? When to buy? When to sell? The best investment you can make is in your own education.

The more you know about your collection and the hobby, the more informed the decisions you will be able to make. We´re not selling investment tips. We´re selling information about the current value of baseball cards. It´s up to you to use that information to your best advantage.

Terminology

Each hobby has its own language to describe its area of interest. The nomenclature traditionally used for trading cards is derived from the American Card Catalog, published in 1960 by Nostalgia Press. That catalog, written by Jefferson Burdick (who is called the "Father of Card Collecting" for his pioneering work), uses letter and number designations for each separate set of cards. The letter used in the ACC designation refers to the generic type of card. While both sport and nonsport issues are classified in the ACC, we shall confine ourselves to the sport issues. The following list defines the letters and their meanings as used by the American Card Catalog.

(none) or N - 19th Century U.S. Tobacco.
B - Blankets.
D - Bakery Inserts Including Bread.
E - Early Candy and Gum.
F - Food Inserts.
H - Advertising.
M - Periodicals.
PC - Postcards.
R - Candy and Gum since 1930.
T - Tobacco.

Following the letter prefix and an optional hyphen are one-, two-, or three-digit numbers, R(-)999. These typically represent the company or entity issuing the cards. In several cases, the ACC number is extended by an additional hyphen and another one- or two-digit numerical suffix. For example, the 1957 Topps regular-series baseball card issue carries an ACC designation of R414-11. The "R" indicates a Candy or Gum card produced since 1930. The "414" is the ACC designation for Topps Chewing Gum baseball card issues, and the "11" is the ACC designation for the 1957 regular issue (Topps´ eleventh baseball set). Like other traditional methods of identification, this system provides order to the process of cataloging cards; however, most serious collectors learn the ACC designation of the popular sets by repetition and familiarity, rather than by attempting to "figure out" what they might or should be. From 1948 forward, collectors and dealers commonly refer to all sets by their year, maker, type of issue, and any other distinguishing characteristic. For example, such a characteristic could be an unusual issue or one of several regular issues put out by a specific maker in a single year. Regional issues are usually referred to by year, maker, and sometimes by title or theme of the set.

Glossary/Legend

Our glossary defines terms used in the card collecting hobby and in this book. Many of these terms are also common to other types of sports memorabilia collecting. Some terms may have several meanings depending on use and context.

ACETATE—A transparent plastic.

AS—All-Star card. A card portraying an All-Star Player of the previous year that says "All-Star" on its face.

ATG—All-Time Great card.

ATL—All-Time Leaders card.

AU(TO)—Autographed card.

AW—Award Winner.

BB—Building Blocks.

BC—Bonus Card.

BF—Bright Futures.

BL—Blue Letters.

BNR—Banner Season.

BOX CARD—Card issued on a box (e.g., 1987 Topps Box Bottoms).

BRICK—A group of 50 or more cards having common characteristics that is intended to be bought, sold, or traded as a unit.

CABINETS—Popular and highly valuable photographs on thick card stock produced in the 19th and early 20th centuries.

CC—Curtain Call.

CG—Cornerstones of the Game.

CHECKLIST—A list of the cards contained in a particular set. The list is always in numerical order if the cards are numbered. Some unnumbered sets are artificially numbered in alphabetical order, by team and alphabetically within the team, or by uniform number for convenience.

CL—Checklist card. A card that lists in order the cards and players in the set or series. Older checklist cards in Mint condition that have not been marked are very desirable and command premiums.

CO—Coach.

COMM—Commissioner.

COMMON CARD—The typical card of any set; it has no premium value accruing from subject matter, numerical scarcity, popular demand, or anomaly.

CONVENTION—A gathering of dealers and collectors at a single location for the purpose of buying, selling, and trading sports memorabilia items. Conventions are open to the public and sometimes feature autograph guests, door prizes, contests, seminars, etc. They are frequently referred to simply as "shows."

COOP—Cooperstown.

COR—Corrected card.

CP—Changing Places.

CT—Cooperstown.

CY—Cy Young Award.

DD—Decade of Dominance.

DEALER—A person who engages in buying, selling, and trading sports collectibles or supplies. A dealer may also be a collector, but as a dealer, his main goal is to earn a profit.

DIE-CUT—A card with part of its stock partially cut, allowing one or more parts to be folded or removed. After removal or appropriate folding, the remaining part of the card can frequently be made to stand up.

DK—Diamond King.

DL—Division Leaders.

DP—Double Print (a card that was printed in double the quantity compared to the other cards in the same series) or a Draft Pick card.

DT—Dream Team.

DUFEX—A method of card manufacturing technology patented by Pinnacle Brands, Inc. It involves a refractive quality to a card with a foil coating.

ERA—Earned Run Average.

ERR—Error card. A card with erroneous information, spelling, or depiction on either side of the card. Most errors are not corrected by the producing card company.

FC—Fan Club.

FDP—First or First-Round Draft Pick.

FF—Future Foundation.

FOIL—Foil embossed stamp on card.

FOLD—Foldout.

FP—Franchise Player.

FR—Franchise.

FS—Father/son card.

FS—Future Star.

FUN—Fun cards.

FY—First Year.

GL—Green Letters.

GLOSS—A card with luster; a shiny finish as in a card with UV coating.

HG—Heroes of the Game.

HH—Hometown Heroes.

HIGH NUMBER—The cards in the last series of numbers in a year in which such higher-numbered cards were printed or distributed in significantly lesser amounts than the lower-numbered cards. The high-number designation refers to a scarcity of the high-numbered cards. Not all years have high numbers in terms of this definition.
HL—Highlight card.
HOF—Hall of Fame, or a card that portrays a Hall of Famer (HOFer).
HOLOGRAM—A three-dimensional photographic image.
HOR—Horizontal pose on card as opposed to the standard vertical orientation found on most cards.
IA—In Action card.
IF—Infielder.
INSERT—A card of a different type or any other sports collectible (typically a poster or sticker) contained and sold in the same package along with a card or cards of a major set. An insert card is either unnumbered or not numbered in the same sequence as the major set. Sometimes the inserts are randomly distributed and are not found in every pack.
INTERACTIVE—A concept that involves collector participation.
IRT—International Road Trip.
ISSUE—Synonymous with set, but usually used in conjunction with a manufacturer, e.g., a Topps issue.
JSY—Jersey.
KM—K-Men.
LHP—Left-handed pitcher.
LL—League Leaders or large letters on card.
LUM—Lumberjack.
MAJOR SET—A set produced by a national manufacturer of cards containing a large number of cards. Usually 100 or more different cards constitute a major set.
MB—Master Blasters.
MEM—Memorial card. For example, the 1990 Donruss and Topps Bart Giamatti cards.
METALLIC—A glossy design method that enhances card features.
MG—Manager.
MI—Maximum Impact.
MINI—A small card; for example, a 1975 Topps card of identical design but smaller dimensions than the regular Topps issue of 1975.
ML—Major League.
MM—Memorable Moments.
MULTI-PLAYER CARD—A single card depicting two or more players (but not a team card).
MVP—Most Valuable Player.
NAU—No autograph on card.
NG—Next Game.
NH—No-Hitter.
NNOF—No name on front.
NOF—Name on front.
NOTCHING—The grooving of the card, usually caused by fingernails, rubber bands, or bumping card edges against other objects.
NT—Now and Then.
NV—Novato.
OF—Outfield or Outfielder.
OLY—Olympics Card.
P—Pitcher or Pitching pose.

P1—First Printing.
P2—Second Printing.
P3—Third Printing.
PACKS—A means by which cards are issued in terms of pack type (wax, cello, foil, rack, etc.) and channel of distribution (hobby, retail, etc.).
PARALLEL— A card that is similar in design to its counterpart from a basic set but that has a distinguishing quality.
PF—Profiles.
PG—Postseason Glory.
PLASTIC SHEET—A clear, plastic page that is punched for insertion into a binder (with standard three-ring spacing) containing pockets for displaying cards. Many different styles of sheets exist with pockets of varying sizes to hold the many differing card formats. Also called a display sheet or storage sheet.
PLATINUM—A metallic element used in the process of creating a glossy card.
PP—Power Passion.
PR—Printed name on back.
PREMIUM—A card, sometimes on photographic stock, that is purchased or obtained in conjunction with, or redemption for, another card or product. The premium is not packaged in the same unit as the primary item.
PRES—President.
PRISMATIC/PRISM—A glossy or bright design that refracts or disperses light.
PS—Pace Setters.
PT—Power Tools.
PUZZLE CARD—A card whose back contains a part of a picture which, when joined correctly with other puzzle cards, forms the completed picture.
PUZZLE PIECE—A die-cut piece designed to interlock with similar pieces (e.g., early 1980s Donruss).
PVC—Polyvinyl chloride, a substance used to make many of the popular card display protective sheets. Non-PVC sheets are considered preferable for long-term storage of cards by many.
RARE—A card or series of cards of very limited availability. Unfortunately, "rare" is a subjective term frequently used indiscriminately to hype value. "Rare" cards are harder to obtain than "scarce" cards.
RB—Record Breaker.
RC—Rookie Card.
REDEMPTION—A program established by multiple card manufacturers that allows collectors to mail in a special card (usually a random insert) in return for special cards, sets, or other prizes not available through conventional channels.
REFRACTOR—A card that features a design element that enhances (distorts) its color/appearance through deflecting light.
REV NEG—Reversed or flopped photo side of the card. This is a major type of error card, but only some are corrected.
RHP—Right-handed pitcher.
RHW—Rookie Home Whites.
RIF—Rifleman.
RPM—Rookie Premiere Materials.
RR—Rated Rookie.
ROO—Rookie.
ROY—Rookie of the Year.
RP—Relief pitcher.
RTC—Rookie True Colors.
SA—Super Action card.
SASE—Self-Addressed, Stamped Envelope.

SB—Scrapbook.
SB—Stolen Bases.
SCARCE—A card or series of cards of limited availability. This subjective term is sometimes used indiscriminately to hype value. "Scarce" cards are not as difficult to obtain as "rare" cards.
SCR—Script name on back.
SD—San Diego Padres.
SEMI-HIGH—A card from the next-to-last series of a sequentially issued set. It has more value than an average card and generally less value than a high number. A card is not called a semi-high unless the next-to-last series in which it exists has an additional premium attached to it.
SERIES—The entire set of cards issued by a particular producer in a particular year; e.g., the 1971 Topps series. Also, within a particular set, series can refer to a group of (consecutively numbered) cards printed at the same time, e.g., the first series of the 1957 Topps issue (#1 through #88).
SET—One each of the entire run of cards of the same type produced by a particular manufacturer during a single year. In other words, if you have a complete set of 1976 Topps then you have every card from #1 up to and including #660; i.e., all the different cards that were produced.
SF—Starflics.
SH—Season Highlight.
SHEEN—Brightness or luster emitted by card.
SKIP-NUMBERED—A set that has many unissued card numbers between the lowest number in the set and the highest number in the set, e.g., the 1948 Leaf baseball set contains ninety-eight cards skip-numbered from #1 to #168. A major set in which a few numbers were not printed is not considered to be skip-numbered.
SP—Single or Short Print (a card that was printed in lesser quantity compared to the other cards in the same series; see also DP and TP).
SPECIAL CARD—A card that portrays something other than a single player or team, for example, a card that portrays the previous year's statistical leaders or the results from the previous year's World Series.
SS—Shortstop.
STANDARD SIZE—Most modern sports cards measure 2-1/2 by 3-1/2 inches. Exceptions are noted in card descriptions throughout this book.
STAR CARD—A card that portrays a player of some repute, usually determined by his ability; but sometimes referring to sheer popularity.
STOCK—The cardboard or paper on which the card is printed.
SUPERIMPOSED—Affixed on top of something; i.e., a player photo over a solid background.
SUPERSTAR CARD—A card that portrays a superstar, e.g., a Hall of Famer or player with strong Hall of Fame potential.
TC—Team Checklist.
TEAM CARD—A card that depicts an entire team.
THREE-DIMENSIONAL (3D)—A visual image that provides an illusion of depth and perspective.
TOPICAL—A subset or group of cards that have a common theme (e.g., MVP award winners).
TP—Triple Print (a card that was printed in triple the quantity compared to the other cards in the same series).
TR—Trade reference on card.
TRANSPARENT—Clear, see-through.
UDCA—Upper Deck Classic Alumni.
UER—Uncorrected Error.
UMP—Umpire.

USA—Team USA.
UV—Ultraviolet, a glossy coating used in producing cards.
VAR—Variation card. One of two or more cards from the same series with the same number (or player with identical pose if the series is unnumbered) differing from one another by some aspect, the different feature stemming from the printing or stock of the card. This can be caused when the manufacturer of the cards notices an error in one or more of the cards, makes the changes, and then resumes the print run. In this case there will be two versions or variations of the same card. Sometimes one of the variations is relatively scarce.
VERT—Vertical pose on card.
WAS—Washington National League (1974 Topps).
WC—What´s the Call?
WL—White letters on front.
WS—World Series card.
YL—Yellow letters on front.
YT—Yellow team name on front.
*—to denote multi-sport sets.

Understanding Card Values

Determining Value

Why are some cards more valuable than others? Obviously, the economic laws of supply and demand are applicable to card collecting just as they are to any other field where a commodity is bought, sold, or traded in a free, unregulated market.

Supply (the number of cards available on the market) is less than the total number of cards originally produced since attrition diminishes that original quantity. Each year a percentage of cards is typically thrown away, destroyed, or otherwise lost to collectors. This percentage is much, much smaller today than it was in the past because more and more people have become increasingly aware of the value of their cards.

For those who collect only Mint condition cards, the supply of older cards can be quite small indeed. Until recently, collectors were not so conscious of the need to preserve the condition of their cards. For this reason, it is difficult to know exactly how many 1953 Topps are currently available, Mint or otherwise. It is generally accepted that there are fewer 1953 Topps available than 1963, 1973, or 1983 Topps cards. If demand were equal for each of these sets, the law of supply and demand would increase the price for the least available sets. Demand, however, is never equal for all sets, so price correlations can be complicated. The demand for a card is influenced by many factors. These include: (1) the age of the card; (2) the number of cards printed; (3) the player(s) portrayed on the card; (4) the attractiveness and popularity of the set; and (5) the physical condition of the card.

In general, (1) the older the card, (2) the fewer the number of the cards printed, (3) the more famous, popular, and talented the player, (4) the more attractive and popular the set, and (5) the better the condition of the card, the higher the value of the card will be. There are exceptions to all but one of these factors: the condition of the card. Given two cards similar in all respects except condition, the one in the best condition will always be valued higher.

While those guidelines help to establish the value of a card, the countless exceptions and peculiarities make any simple, direct mathematical formula to determine card values impossible.

Regional Variation

Since the market varies from region to region, prices may be higher. This is known as a regional premium. How significant the premium is — and if there is any premium at all — depends on the local popularity of the team and the player.

The largest regional premiums usually do not apply to superstars, who often are so well known nationwide that the prices of their key cards are too high for local dealers to realize a premium.

Lesser stars often command the strongest premiums. Their popularity is concentrated in their home regions, creating local demand that greatly exceeds overall demand.

Regional premiums can apply to popular retired players and sometimes can be found in the areas where the players grew up or starred in college.

A regional discount is the converse of a regional premium. Regional discounts occur when a player has been so popular in his region for so long that local collectors and dealers have accumulated quantities of his key cards. The abundant supply may make the cards available in that area at the lowest prices anywhere.

Set Prices

A somewhat paradoxical situation exists regarding the price of a complete set versus the combined cost of the individual cards in the set. In nearly every case, the sum of the prices for the individual cards is higher than the cost for the complete set. This especially true of cards from the last few years. The reasons for this apparent anomaly stem from the habits of collectors and from the carrying costs to dealers. Today, each card in a set normally is produced in the same quantity as all other cards in its set.

Many collectors pick up only stars, superstars, and particular teams. As a result, the dealer is left with a shortage of certain player cards and an abundance of others. He therefore incurs an expense in simply "carrying" these less desirable cards in stock. On the other hand, if he sells a complete set, he gets rid of large numbers of cards at one time. For this reason, he generally is willing to receive less money for a complete set. By doing this, he recovers all of his costs and also makes a profit.

The disparity between the price of the complete set and the sum of the prices of the individual cards also has been influenced by the fact that some of the major manufacturers now are pre-collating card sets. Since "pulling" individual cards from the sets involves a specific type of labor (and cost), the singles or star card market is not affected significantly by pre-collation.

Set prices also do not include rare card varieties, unless specifically stated. Of course, the prices for sets do include one example of each type for the given set, but this is the least expensive variety.

Scarce Series

Scarce series occur because cards issued before 1974 were made available to the public each year in several series of finite numbers of cards, rather than all cards of the set being available for purchase at one time. At some point during the year, usually toward the end of the baseball season, interest in current year baseball cards waned. Consequently, the manufacturers produced smaller numbers of these later-series cards.

Nearly all nationwide issues from post–World War II manufacturers (1948 to 1973) exhibit these series variations. In the past, Topps, for example, may have issued series consisting of many different numbers of cards, including 55, 66, 80, 88, and others. Recently, Topps has settled on what is now its standard sheet size of 132 cards, six of which constitute its 792-card set.

While the number of cards within a given series is usually the same as the number of cards on one printed sheet, this is not always the case. For example, Bowman used 36 cards on its standard printed sheets, but in 1948 substituted 12 cards during later print runs of that year's baseball cards. Twelve of the cards from the initial sheet of 36 cards were removed and replaced by 12 different cards, giving, in effect, a first series of 36 cards and a second series of 12 new cards. This replacement produced a scarcity of 24 cards — the 12 cards removed from the original sheet and the 12 new cards added to the sheet. A full sheet of 1948 Bowman cards (second printing) shows that card numbers 37 through 48 have replaced 12 of the cards on the first printing sheet.

The Topps Company also has created scarcities and/or excesses of certain cards in many of its sets. Topps, however, has most frequently gone the other direction by double printing some of the cards. Double printing causes in abundance of cards of the players who are on the same sheet more than one time. During the years 1978 to 1981, Topps double printed 66 cards out of its large 726-card set. The Topps practice of double printing cards in earlier years is the most logical explanation for the known scarcities of particular cards in some of these Topps sets.

From 1988 through 1990, Donruss short printed and double printed certain cards in its major sets. Ostensibly this was because of its addition of bonus team MVP cards in its regular-issue wax packs.

We are always looking for information about or photographs of printing sheets of cards for research. Each year, we try to update the hobby´s knowledge of distribution anomalies. Please let us know at the address in this book if you have firsthand knowledge that would be helpful in this pursuit.

Grading Your Cards

Each hobby — stamps, coins, comic books, record collecting, etc. — has its own grading terminology. Collectors of sports cards are no exception. The one invariable criterion for determining the value of a card is its condition: The better the condition of the card, the more valuable it is. Condition grading, however, is subjective. Individual card dealers and collectors differ in the strictness of their grading, but the stated condition of a card should be determined without regard to whether it is being bought or sold.

No allowance is made for age. A 1952 card is judged by the same standards as a 1992 card. But there are specific sets and cards that are condition-sensitive (marked with "!" in the Price Guide) because of their border color, consistently poor centering, etc. Such cards and sets sometimes command premiums above the listed percentages in Mint condition.

Centering

Current centering terminology uses numbers representing the percentage of border on either side of the main design. Obviously, centering is diminished in importance for borderless cards such as Stadium Club.

Slightly Off-Center (60/40): A slightly off-center card is one that, upon close inspection, is found to have one border bigger than the opposite border. This degree once was offensive only to purists, but now some hobbyists try to avoid cards that are anything other than perfectly centered.

Off-Center (70/30): An off-center card has one border that is noticeably more than twice as wide as the opposite border.

Badly Off-Center (80/20 or worse): A badly off-center card has virtually no border on one side of the card.

Miscut: A miscut card actually shows part of the adjacent card in its larger border and consequently a corresponding amount of its card is cut off.

Corner Wear

Corner wear is the most scrutinized grading criteria in the hobby. These are the major categories of corner wear:

Corner with a slight touch of wear: The corner still is sharp, but there is a slight touch of wear showing. On a dark-bordered card, this shows as a dot of white.

Fuzzy corner: The corner still comes to a point, but the point has just begun to fray. A slightly "dinged" corner is considered the same as a fuzzy corner.

Slightly rounded corner: The fraying of the corner has increased to where there is only a hint of a point. Mild layering may be evident. A "dinged" corner is considered the same as a slightly rounded corner.

Rounded corner: The point is completely gone. Some layering is noticeable.

Badly rounded corner: The corner is completely round and rough. Severe layering is evident.

Creases

A third common defect is the crease. The degree of creasing in a card is difficult to show in a drawing or picture. On giving the specific condition of an expensive card for sale, the seller should note any creases additionally. Creases can be categorized as to severity according to the following scale:

Light Crease: A light crease is a crease that is barely noticeable upon close inspection. In fact, when cards are in plastic sheets or holders, a light crease may not be seen (until the card is taken out of the holder). A light crease on the front is much more serious than a light crease on the card back only.

Medium Crease: A medium crease is noticeable when held and studied at arm´s length by the naked eye, but does not overly detract from the appearance of the card. It is an obvious crease, but not one that breaks the picture surface of the card.

Heavy Crease: A heavy crease is one that has torn or broken through the card´s picture surface; i.e., puts a tear in the photo surface.

Alterations

Deceptive Trimming: This occurs when someone alters the card in order (1) to shave off edge wear, (2) to improve the sharpness of the corners, or (3) to improve centering — obviously their objective is to falsely increase the perceived value of the card to an unsuspecting buyer. The shrinkage usually is evident only if the trimmed card is compared to an adjacent full-size card or if the trimmed card is itself measured.

Obvious Trimming: Obvious trimming is noticeable and unfortunate. It is usually performed by noncollectors who give no thought to the present or future value of their cards.

Deceptively Retouched Borders: This occurs when the borders (especially on those cards with dark borders) are touched up on the edges and corners with magic marker or crayons of appropriate color in order to make the card appear Mint.

Categorization of Defects—Miscellaneous Flaws

The following are common minor flaws that, depending on severity, lower a card´s condition by one to four grades and often render it no better than Excellent-Mint: bubbles (lumps in surface), gum and wax stains, diamond cutting (slanted borders), notching, off-centered backs, paper wrinkles, scratched-off cartoons or puzzles on back, rubber band marks, scratches, surface impressions, and warping.

The following are common serious flaws that, depending on severity, lower a card´s condition at least four grades and often render it no better than Good: chemical or sun fading, erasure marks, mildew, miscutting (severe off-centering), holes, bleached or retouched borders, tape marks, tears, trimming, water or coffee stains, and writing.

Condition Guide

Grades

Mint (Mt)—A card with no flaws or wear. The card has four perfect corners, 60/40 or better centering from top to bottom and from left to right, original gloss, smooth edges, and original color borders. A Mint card does not have print spots or color or focus imperfections.

Near Mint-Mint (NrMt-Mt)—A card with one minor flaw. Any one of the following would lower a Mint card to Near Mint-Mint: one corner with a slight touch of wear, barely noticeable print spots, or color or focus imperfections. The card must have

60/40 or better centering in both directions, original gloss, smooth edges, and original color borders.

Near Mint (NrMt)—A card with one minor flaw. Any one of the following would lower a Mint card to Near Mint: one fuzzy corner or two to four corners with slight touches of wear, 70/30 to 60/40 centering, slightly rough edges, minor print spots, color or focus imperfections. The card must have original gloss and original color borders.

Excellent-Mint (ExMt)—A card with two or three fuzzy, but not rounded, corners and centering no worse than 80/20. The card may have no more than two of the following: slightly rough edges, very slightly discolored borders, minor print spots, color or focus imperfections. The card must have original gloss.

Excellent (Ex)—A card with four fuzzy but definitely not rounded corners and centering no worse than 80/20. The card may have a small amount of original gloss lost, rough edges, slightly discolored borders, and minor print spots or color or focus imperfections.

Very Good (Vg)—A card that has been handled but not abused: slightly rounded corners with slight layering, slight notching on edges, a significant amount of gloss lost from the surface (but no scuffing) and moderate discoloration of borders. The card may have a few light creases.

Good (G), Fair (F), Poor (P)—A well-worn, mishandled, or abused card: badly rounded and layered corners, scuffing, most or all original gloss missing, seriously discolored borders, moderate or heavy creases, and one or more serious flaws. The grade of Good, Fair, or Poor depends on the severity of wear and flaws. Good, Fair, and Poor cards generally are used only as fillers.

The most widely used grades are defined above. Obviously, many cards will not perfectly fit one of the definitions.

Therefore, categories between the major grades known as in-between grades are used, such as Good to Very Good (G-Vg), Very Good to Excellent (VgEx), and Excellent-Mint to Near Mint (ExMt-NrMt). Such grades indicate a card with all qualities of the lower category but with at least a few qualities of the higher category.

Beckett Baseball Card Price Guide lists each card and set in two grades, with the middle grade valued at about 40%–45% of the top grade.

The value of cards that fall between the listed columns can also be calculated using a percentage of the top grade. For example, a card that falls between the top and middle grades (Ex, ExMt, or NrMt in most cases) will generally be valued at anywhere from 50% to 90% of the top grade.

Similarly, a card that falls between the middle and bottom grades (G-Vg, Vg, or VgEx in most cases) will generally be valued at anywhere from 20%–40% of the top grade.

There are also cases where cards are in better condition than the top grade or worse than the bottom grade. Cards that grade worse than the lowest grade are generally valued at 5%–10% of the top grade.

When a card exceeds the top grade by one — such as NrMt-Mt when the top grade is NrMt, or Mint when the top grade is NrMt-Mt — a premium of up to 50% is possible, with 10%–20% the usual norm.

When a card exceeds the top grade by two — such as Mint when the top grade is NrMt, or NrMt-Mt when the top grade is ExMt — a premium of 25%–50% is the usual norm. But certain condition-sensitive cards or sets, particularly those from the pre-war era, can bring premiums of up to 100% or even more.

Unopened packs, boxes, and factory-collated sets are considered Mint in their unknown (and presumed perfect) state. Once opened, however, each card can be graded (and valued) in its own right by taking into account any defects that may be present in spite of the fact that the card has never been handled.

Selling Your Cards

Just about every collector sells cards or will sell cards eventually. Someday you may be interested in selling your duplicates or maybe even your whole collection. You may sell to other collectors, friends, or dealers. You may even sell cards you purchased from a certain dealer back to that same dealer. In any event, it helps to know some of the mechanics of the typical transaction between buyer and seller.

Dealers will buy cards in order to resell them to other collectors who are interested in the cards. Dealers will always pay a higher percentage for items that (in their opinion) can be resold quickly, and a much lower percentage for those items that are perceived as having low demand and hence are slow moving. In either case, dealers must buy at a price that allows for the expense of doing business and a margin for profit.

If you have cards for sale, the best advice we can give is that you get several offers for your cards — either from card shops or at a card show — and take the best offer, all things considered. Note, the "best" offer may not be the one for the highest amount. And remember, if a dealer really wants your cards, he won't let you get away without making his best competitive offer. Another alternative is to place your cards in an auction as one or several lots.

Many people think nothing of going into a department store and paying $15 for an item of clothing for which the store paid $5. But if you were selling your $15 card to a dealer and he offered you $5 for it, you might consider his markup unreasonable. To complete the analogy: Most department stores (and card dealers) that consistently pay $10 for $15 items eventually go out of business. An exception is when the dealer has lined up a willing buyer for the item(s) you are attempting to sell, or if the cards are so hot that it's likely he'll have to hold the cards for just a short period of time.

In those cases, an offer of up to 75% of book value still will allow the dealer to make a reasonable profit considering the short time he will need to hold the merchandise. In general, however, most cards and collections will bring offers in the range of 25%–50% of retail price. Also consider that most material from the last five to ten years is plentiful. If that's what you're selling, don't be surprised if your best offer is well below that range.

Interesting Notes

The first card numerically of an issue is the single card most likely to obtain excessive wear.

Consequently, you typically will find the price on the #1 card (in NrMt or Mint condition) somewhat higher than might otherwise be the case.

Similarly, but to a lesser extent (because normally the less important, reverse side of the card is the one exposed), the last card numerically in an issue also is prone to abnormal wear. This extra wear and tear occurs because the first and last cards are exposed to the elements (human element included) more than any of the other cards. They are generally end cards in any brick formations and are subject to rubber bandings, stackings on wet surfaces, and like activities.

Sports cards have no intrinsic value. The value of a card, like the value of other collectibles, can be determined only by you and your enjoyment in viewing and possessing these cardboard treasures.

Remember, the buyer ultimately determines the price of each baseball card. You are the determining price factor because you have the ability to say "No" to the price of any card by not exchanging your hard-earned money for a given issue. When the cost of a trading card exceeds the enjoyment you will receive from it, your answer should be "No." We assess and report the prices. You set them!

We are always interested in receiving the price input of collectors and dealers. We happily credit major contributors.

We welcome your opinions, since your contributions assist us in ensuring a better guide each year.

If you would like to join our survey list for the next editions of this book and others authored by Dr. Beckett, please send your name and address to Dr. James Beckett, 15850 Dallas Parkway, Dallas, TX 75248.

History of Baseball Cards

Today's version of the baseball card, with its colorful and oftentimes high-tech front and back, is a far cry from its earliest predecessors. The issue remains cloudy as to which was the very first baseball card ever produced, but the institution of base-

Centering

Well-centered

Slightly Off-centered

Off-centered

Badly Off-centered

Miscut

ball cards dates from the latter half of the 19th century, more than 100 years ago. Early issues, generally printed on heavy cardboard, were of poor quality, with photographs, drawings, and printing far short of today's standards.

Goodwin & Co., of New York, makers of Gypsy Queen, Old Judge, and other cigarette brands, is considered by many to be the first issuer of baseball and other sports cards. Its issues, predominantly sized 1-1/2 by 2-1/2 inches, generally consisted of photographs of baseball players, boxers, wrestlers, and other subjects mounted on stiff cardboard. More than 2,000 different photos of baseball players alone have been identified. These "Old Judges," a collective name commonly used for the Goodwin & Co. cards, were issued from 1886 to 1890 and are treasured parts of many collections today.

Among the other cigarette companies that issued baseball cards still attracting attention today are Allen & Ginter, D. Buchner & Co. (Gold Coin Chewing Tobacco), and P. H. Mayo & Brother. Cards from the first two companies bear colored line drawings, while the Mayos are sepia photographs on black cardboard. In addition to the small-size cards from this era, several tobacco companies issued cabinet-size baseball cards. These "cabinets" were considerably larger than the small cards, usually about 4-1/4 by 6-1/2 inches, and were printed on heavy stock. Goodwin & Co.'s Old Judge cabinets and the National Tobacco Works' "Newsboy" baseball photos are two that remain popular today.

By 1895, the American Tobacco Company began to dominate its competition. They discontinued baseball card inserts in their cigarette packages (actually slide boxes in those days). The lack of competition in the cigarette market had made these inserts unnecessary. This marked the end of the first era of baseball cards. At the dawn of the 20th century, few baseball cards were being issued. But once again, it was the cigarette companies, particularly, the American Tobacco Company, followed to a lesser extent by the candy and gum makers that revived the practice of including baseball cards with their products. The bulk of these cards, identified in the American Card Catalog (designated hereafter as ACC) as T or E cards for 20th century "Tobacco" or "Early Candy and Gum" issues, respectively, were released from 1909 to 1915.

This romantic and popular era of baseball card collecting produced many desirable items. The most outstanding is the fabled T-206 Honus Wagner card. Other perennial favorites among collectors are the T-206 Eddie Plank card, and the T-206 Magee error card. The former was once the second most valuable card and only recently relinquished that position to a more distinctive and aesthetically pleasing Napoleon Lajoie card from the 1933–34 Goudey Gum series. The latter misspells the player's name as "Magie"; the most famous and most valuable blooper card.

The ingenuity and distinctiveness of this era has yet to be surpassed. Highlights include:

- The T-202 Hassan triple-folders, one of the best looking and the most distinctive cards ever issued;
- The durable T-201 Mecca double-folders, one of the first sets with players' records on the reverse;
- The T-3 Turkey Reds, the hobby's most popular cabinet card;
- The E-145 Cracker Jacks, the only major set containing Federal League player cards; and
- The T-204 Ramlys, with their distinctive black-and-white oval photos and ornate gold borders.

These are but a few of the varieties issued during this period.

Increasing Popularity

While the American Tobacco Company dominated the field, several other tobacco companies, as well as clothing manufacturers, newspapers and periodicals, game makers, and companies whose identities remain anonymous, also issued cards during this period. In fact, the Collins-McCarthy Candy Company, makers of Zeenuts Pacific Coast League baseball cards, issued cards yearly from 1911 to 1938. Its record for continuous annual card production has been exceeded only by the Topps Chewing Gum Company. The era of the tobacco card issues closed with the onset of World War I, with the exception of the Red Man chewing tobacco sets produced from 1952 to 1955.

Corner Wear

The partial cards here have been photographed at 300%. This was done in order to magnify each card's corner wear to such a degree that differences could be shown on a printed page.

The 1962 Topps Mickey Mantle card definitely has a rounded corner. Some may say that this card is badly rounded, but that is a judgment call.

The 1962 Topps Hank Aaron card has a slightly rounded corner. Note that there is definite corner wear evident by the fraying and that the corner no longer sports a sharp point.

The 1962 Topps Gil Hodges card has corner wear; it is slightly better than the Aaron card above. Nevertheless, some collectors might classify this Hodges corner as slightly rounded.

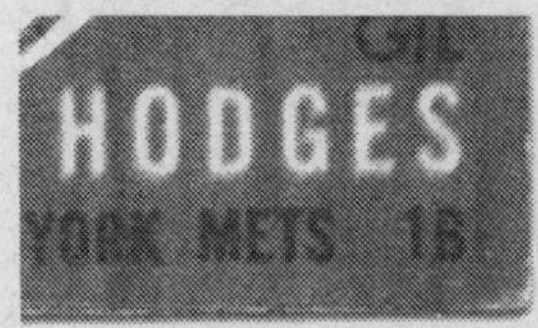

The 1962 Topps Manager's Dream card showing Mantle and Mays has slight corner wear. This is not a fuzzy corner as very slight wear is noticeable on the card's photo surface.

The 1962 Topps Don Mossi card has very slight corner wear such that it might be called a fuzzy corner. A close look at the original card shows the corner is not perfect, but almost. However, note that the issue of corner wear is somewhat academic with respect to this card. As you can plainly see, the heavy crease going across his name breaks through the photo surface.

The next flurry of card issues came in the roaring and prosperous 1920s, the era of the E card. The caramel companies (National Caramel, American Caramel, York Caramel) were the leading distributors of these E cards. In addition, the strip card, a continuous strip with several cards divided by dotted lines or other sectioning features, flourished during this time. While the E cards and the strip cards generally are considered less imaginative than the T cards or the recent candy and gum issues, they still are pursued by many advanced collectors.

Another significant event of the 1920s was the introduction of the arcade card. Taking its designation from its issuer, the Exhibit Supply Company of Chicago, it is usually known as the "Exhibit" card. Once a trademark of the penny arcades, amusement parks, and county fairs across the country, Exhibit machines dispensed nearly postcard-size photos on thick stock for one penny. These picture cards bore likenesses of a favorite cowboy, actor, actress, or baseball player. Exhibit Supply and its associated companies produced baseball cards during a longer time span, although discontinuous, than any other manufacturer. Its first cards appeared in 1921, while its last issue was in 1966. In 1979, the Exhibit Supply Company was bought and somewhat revived by a collector/dealer who has since reprinted Exhibit photos of the past.

If the T card period, from 1909 to 1915, can be designated the "Golden Age" of baseball card collecting, then perhaps the "Silver Age" commenced with the introduction of the Big League Gum series of 239 cards in 1933 (a 240th card was added in 1934). These are the forerunners of today's baseball gum cards, and the Goudey Gum Company of Boston is responsible for their success. This era spanned the period from the Depression days of 1933 to America's formal involvement in World War II in 1941.

Goudey's attractive designs, with full-color line drawings on thick card stock, greatly influenced other cards being issued at that time. As a result, the most attractive and popular vintage cards in history were produced in this "Silver Age." The 1933 Goudey Big League Gum series also owes its popularity to the more than forty Hall of Fame players in the set. These include four cards of Babe Ruth and two of Lou Gehrig. Goudey's reign continued in 1934, when it issued a 96-card set in color, together with the single remaining card from the 1933 series, #106, the Napoleon Lajoie card.

In addition to Goudey, several other bubblegum manufacturers issued baseball cards during this era. DeLong Gum Company issued an extremely attractive set in 1933. National Chicle Company's 192-card "Batter-Up" series of 1934-36 became the largest die-cut set in card history. In addition, that company offered the popular "Diamond Stars" series during the same period. Other popular sets included the "Tattoo Orbit" set of sixty color cards issued in 1933 and Gum Products' 75-card "Double Play" set, featuring sepia depictions of two players per card.

In 1939, Gum Inc., which later became Bowman Gum, replaced Goudey Gum as the leading baseball card producer. In 1939 and the following year, it issued two important sets of black-and-white cards. In 1939, its "Play Ball America" set consisted of 162 cards. The larger, 240-card "Play Ball" set of 1940 still is considered by many to be the most attractive black-and-white cards ever produced. That firm introduced its only color set in 1941, consisting of 72 cards titled "Play Ball Sports Hall of Fame." Many of these were colored repeats of poses from the black-and-white 1940 series.

In addition to regular gum cards, many manufacturers distributed premium issues during the 1930s. These premiums were printed on paper or photographic stock, rather than card stock. They were much larger than the regular cards and were sold for a penny across the counter with gum (which was packaged separately from the premium). They often were redeemed at the store or through the mail in exchange for the wrappers of previously purchased gum cards, like proof-of-purchase box-top premiums today. The gum premiums are scarcer than the card issues of the 1930s and in most cases no manufacturer's name is present.

World War II brought an end to this popular era of card collecting when paper and rubber shortages curtailed the production of bubblegum baseball cards. They were resurrected again in 1948 by the Bowman Gum Company (the direct descendent of Gum Inc.). This marked the beginning of the modern era of card collecting.

In 1948, Bowman Gum issued a 48-card set in black and white consisting of one card and one slab of gum in every 1-cent pack. That same year, the Leaf Gum Company also issued a set of cards. Although rather poor in quality, these cards were issued in color. A squabble over the rights to use players´ pictures developed between Bowman and Leaf. Eventually Leaf dropped out of the card market, but not before it had left a lasting heritage to the hobby by issuing some of the rarest cards now in existence. Leaf´s baseball card series of 1948-49 contained 98 cards, skip numbered to #168 (not all numbers were printed). Of these 98 cards, 49 are relatively plentiful; the other 49, however, are rare and quite valuable.

Bowman continued its production of cards in 1949 with a color series of 240 cards. Because there are many scarce "high numbers," this series remains the most difficult Bowman regular issue to complete. Although the set was printed in color and commands great interest due to its scarcity, it is considered aesthetically inferior to the Goudey and National Chicle issues of the 1930s. In addition to the regular issue of 1949, Bowman also produced a set of 36 Pacific Coast League players. Although this was not a regular issue, it still is prized by collectors. In fact, it has become the most valuable Bowman series.

In 1950 (representing Bowman´s one-year monopoly of the baseball card market), the company began a string of top-quality cards that continued until its demise in 1955. The 1950 series was itself something of an oddity because the low numbers, rather than the traditional high numbers, were the more difficult cards to obtain.

The year 1951 marked the beginning of the most competitive and perhaps the highest quality period of baseball card production. In that year, Topps Chewing Gum Company of Brooklyn entered the market. Topps´ 1951 series consisted of two sets of 52 cards each, one set with red backs and the other with blue backs. In addition, Topps also issued 31 insert cards, three of which remain the rarest Topps cards ("Current All-Stars" Konstanty, Roberts, and Stanky). The 1951 Topps cards were unattractive and paled in comparison to the 1951 Bowman issues. They were successful, however, and Topps has continued to produce cards ever since.

Intensified Competition

Topps issued a larger and more attractive card set in 1952. This larger size became standard for the next five years. (Bowman followed with larger-size baseball cards in 1953.) This 1952 Topps set has become, like the 1933 Goudey series and the T-206 white border series, the classic set of its era. The 407-card set is a collector´s dream of scarcities, rarities, errors, and variations. It also contains the first Topps issues of Mickey Mantle and Willie Mays.

As with Bowman and Leaf in the late 1940s, competition over player rights arose. Ensuing court battles occurred between Topps and Bowman. The market split due to stiff competition, and in January 1956, Topps bought out Bowman. (Topps, using the Bowman name, resurrected Bowman as a label in 1989.) Topps remained essentially unchallenged as the primary producer of baseball cards through 1980. So, the story of major baseball card sets from 1956 through 1980 is by and large the story of Topps´ issues. Notable exceptions include the small sets produced by Fleer Gum in 1959, 1960, 1961, and 1963, and the Kellogg´s Cereal and Hostess Cakes baseball cards issued to promote their products.

A court decision in 1980 paved the way for two other large gum companies to enter (or reenter, in Fleer´s case) the baseball card arena. Fleer, which had last made photo cards in 1963, and the Donruss Company (then a division of General Mills) secured rights to produce baseball cards of current players, thus breaking Topps´ monopoly. Each company issued major card sets in 1981 with bubblegum products.

Then a higher court decision in that year overturned the lower court ruling against Topps. It appeared that Topps had regained its sole position as a producer of baseball cards. Undaunted by the revocation ruling, Fleer and Donruss continued to issue cards in 1982 but without bubblegum or any other edible product. Fleer issued its current player baseball cards with "team logo stickers," while Donruss issued its cards with a piece of a baseball jigsaw puzzle.

Sharing the Pie

Since 1981, these three major baseball card producers all have thrived, sharing relatively equal recognition. Each has steadily increased its involvement in terms of numbers of issues per year. To the delight of collectors, their competition has generated novel, and in some cases exceptional, issues of current Major League Baseball players. Collectors also eagerly accepted the debut efforts of Score (1988) and Upper Deck (1989). These five companies were about to embark on a wild ride through the 1990s.

Upper Deck's successful entry into the market turned out to be very important. The company's card stock, photography, packaging, and marketing gave baseball cards a new standard for quality and began the "premium card" trend that continues today. The second premium baseball card set to be issued was the 1990 Leaf set, named for and issued by the parent company of Donruss. To gauge the significance of the premium card trend, one need only note that two of the most valuable post-1986 regular-issue cards in the hobby are the 1989 Upper Deck Ken Griffey Jr. and 1990 Leaf Frank Thomas Rookie Cards.

The impressive debut of Leaf in 1990 was followed by those of Studio, Ultra, and Stadium Club in 1991. Of those, Stadium Club with its dramatic borderless photos and un-coated card fronts made the biggest impact. In 1992, Bowman and Pinnacle joined the premium fray. In 1992, Donruss and Fleer abandoned the traditional 50-cent pack market and instead produced premium sets comparable to (and presumably designed to compete against) Upper Deck's set. Those moves, combined with the almost instantaneous spread of premium cards to the other major team sports cards, serve as strong indicators that premium cards were here to stay. Bowman had been a lower-level product from 1989 to 1991.

In 1993, Fleer, Topps, and Upper Deck produced the first "super premium" cards with Flair, Finest, and SP, respectively. The success of all three products was an indication the baseball card market was headed toward even higher price levels, and that turned out to be the case in 1994 with the introduction of Bowman's Best (a Topps hybrid of prospect-oriented Bowman and the superpremium Finest) and Leaf Limited. Other 1994 debuts included Upper Deck's entry-level Collector's Choice and Pinnacle's hobby-only Select.

Overall, inserts continued to dominate the hobby scene. Specifically, the parallel chase cards introduced in 1992 with Topps Gold became the latest major hobby trend. Topps Gold was followed by 1993 Finest Refractors (at the time the scarcest insert ever produced and still a landmark set) and the one-per-box Stadium Club First Day Issue.

Of course, the biggest on-field news of 1994 was the owner-provoked players' strike that halted the season prematurely. While the baseball card hobby suffered noticeably from the strike, there was no catastrophic market crash as some had feared. However, the strike drastically slowed down a market that was both strong and growing and contributed to a serious hobby contraction that continues to this day.

By 1995, parallel insert sets were commonplace and had taken on a new complexion: the most popular ones were those that had announced (or at least suspected) print runs of 500 or less, such as Finest Refractors and Select Artist's Proofs.

This trend continued in 1996, with several parallel inserts that were printed in quantities of 250 or less, such as Finest Gold Refractors, Fleer Circa Rave, Studio Silver Press Proofs, and three of the six Select Certified parallels. It could be argued that the high price tags on these extremely limited parallel cards (many exceeded the $1,000 plateau) were driving many single-player collectors to frustration, and even completely out of the hobby. At the same time, average pack prices soared while average number of cards per pack dropped, making the baseball card hobby increasingly expensive.

On the positive side, two trends from 1996 clearly brought in new collectors: Topps' Mickey Mantle retrospective inserts in both series of Topps and Stadium Club and Leaf's Signature Series, which included one certified autograph per pack. Although the Mantle craze following his passing seemed to be a short-term phenomenon, the inclusion of autographs in packs seemed to have more long-term significance.

In 1997 the print runs in selected sets got even lower. Both Fleer/SkyBox and Pinnacle brands issued cards of which only one exists.

The growth in popularity of autographs also continued. Many products had autographed cards in their packs. A very positive trend was a return to basics. Many collectors bought Rookie Cards, as they understood that concept, and worked on finishing sets.

There was also an increase in international players collecting. Hideo Nomo was incredibly popular in Japan while Chan Ho Park was in demand in Korea. This bodes well for an international growth in the hobby.

Clearly, 1998 was a year of rebirth and growth for the hobby. The big boost came from the home run chase being conducted by Mark McGwire and Sammy Sosa, as well as the continued brilliance of stalwarts like Ken Griffey Jr. and Roger Clemens. The baseball card hobby received a great deal of positive publicity from the renewed interest in the game.

Rookie Cards of the key players of 1998 made significant gains in value as the hobby once again turned to Rookie Cards as the collectible of choice. Also, cards professionally graded by companies such as PSA and SGC were becoming more heavily traded in both older and newer material.

In addition, the Internet and various services such as eBay contributed to the strong growth in collecting interest over the year.

There were downsides in 1998, though. Pinnacle Brands folded, leaving a legacy of innovation and promotions not seen by other companies. In addition, there still was the problem of collectors being frustrated by the extremely short printed cards of their favorite players, making set completion almost impossible.

During 1998, Pacific received a full baseball license and added many innovations to the card market. Their 1998 OnLine set is the most comprehensive set issued in the last five years and many veteran collectors applauded Pacific's continuing attempts to get as many players as possible into their sets.

In the last couple of years, card companies have been printing specific subsets (usually young players or Rookie Cards) in shorter supply than the regular cards. This is not in every set, but in many sets produced since 1998.

In 1999, many of the trends of the last couple of years continued to gain strength. Buying, selling, and trading cards over the Internet became a dominant factor in the secondary market. Beckett Media LP began its own Marketplace, offering the collectors a chance to search across inventory from many of the finest dealers nationwide in one comprehensive on-line database; eBay continued to flourish, while many other parties began to reap the benefits of the burgeoning online auction market. The Barry Halper collection was auctioned off, bringing many museum quality items to the market and giving the older memorabilia market a significant boost as many treasures were made available to collectors.

Also, the boom in Internet trading created a perfect fit for professionally graded cards, as buyers and sellers traded cards sight unseen with the confidence established by a third-party grader.

From a field of almost a dozen contenders, three companies emerged in 1999 to dominate the field of professional grading, BGS (Beckett Grading Services), PSA (Professional Sports Authenticator), and SGC (Sportscard Guaranty L.L.C.). In 1999 these companies made dramatic expansions in on-site grading and submissions at card shows throughout the nation. In response to the widespread acceptance of graded cards, the line of monthly Beckett Price Guides each added a separate section within the price guide area for professionally graded cards.

Similar to 1998, four licensed manufacturers (Fleer/SkyBox, Pacific, Topps, and Upper Deck) produced slightly more than fifty different products for 1999.

Perhaps the biggest hit of the 1999 card season was created by Topps. Card #220 within the basic issue first series 1999 Topps brand featured Home Run King Mark McGwire in 70 variations, one for each homer he slugged in 1998, and many collectors went after the whole set. Continuing a legacy as strong as the Yankees, the basic Topps issue was one of the most popular sets released in 1999.

Closely trailing the Topps McGwire promotion was Upper Deck's dynamic A Piece of History bat card promotion. The card that kicked off the frenzy was the Babe Ruth A Piece of History distributed in 1999 Upper Deck series 1 packs. Upper Deck actually purchased a cracked game-used Babe Ruth bat for $24,000 and proceeded to cut it up into approximately 350-400 chips of wood to create the now famous Ruth bat card. The card instantly created polar opposites of opinion among hobbyists. Traditional collectors howled at the sacrilegious act of destroying such a historic piece of memorabilia while more open-minded collectors jumped at the opportunity to chase such an important card. The Ruth card was followed up by the cross-brand "500 Club" bat card promotion, whereby UD produced bat cards from every major league ballplayer who hit 500 or more home runs in their career (except for Mark McGwire, who hit his 500th in the midst of the 1999 season and promptly stated that he did not support Upper Deck's promotion).

More memorabilia cards than ever were offered to collectors in 1999 as Fleer/SkyBox kicked up their efforts to match the standards set by Upper Deck in previous years. Batting gloves, hats, and shoes joined the typical bats and jerseys as pieces of game-used equipment to be featured on trading cards. Sets like E-X Century Authen-Kicks and Fleer Mystique Feel the Game typified the new offerings.

Topps only dabbled with memorabilia cards in 1999, but continued to offer some of the hottest autographed inserts, highlighted by the Topps Stars Rookie Reprint Autographs and the Topps Nolan Ryan Autographs.

Pacific made a clear decision to steer free of memorabilia and autograph inserts, instead focusing on offering collectors a wide selection of beautifully designed insert and parallel cards. Those themes worked beautifully with their established presence for making comprehensive sets, providing collectors with the necessary challenge to pursue regional stars and a favorite team in addition to the typical superstars.

An astounding total of 264 players made their first appearance on a major league licensed trading card in 1999. What may go down as the deepest class of Rookie Cards of all time features a cornucopia of talented youngsters led by Rick Ankiel, Josh Beckett, Pat Burrell, Josh Hamilton, Eric Munson, Corey Patterson, and Alfonso Soriano.

As in years past, Topps continued to provide collectors with a fistful of Rookie Cards within their Bowman, Bowman Chrome, and Bowman's Best brands. In a trend established in 1998 by Fleer when they released their Fleer Update set (fueled largely by a J. D. Drew Rookie Card), hobbyists enjoyed a bevy of late-season sets chock full of RC's. Fleer/SkyBox made an all-out effort by stuffing more than 100 Rookie Cards into their 1999 Fleer Update set. Topps produced their first boxed Traded set since 1994. Each 1999 Topps Traded set contained 1 of 75 different cards autographed by a rookie prospect. Considering how much wider the selection of Rookie Cards became in 1999, it's amazing to see that so few of these RC's were serial numbered. When one looks at the success established with serial numbered Rookie Cards in the basketball and football card markets with brands like SP Authentic and SPx Finite, one can only scratch his head when realizing that Fleer Mystique was the only brand to offer baseball collectors serial numbered RC's. Thus, it's not surprising to see that despite having twenty-five different Rookie Cards issued in 1999, Pat Burrell's Fleer Mystique RC (#'d of 2,999) had been established as his "best" RC by year's end.

Youngsters weren't the only players in the limelight in 1999 as retired stars and Hall of Famers were featured on more cards than any other year during the 1990s. Upper Deck's Century Legends brand, featuring the top fifty active and top fifty retired players of the decade as chosen by the Sporting News was a runaway hit.

Perhaps the most popular insert set of the year, outpacing all of the dazzling high-dollar memorabilia cards, was Topps Gallery Heritage. Utilizing the design and painting style of artist Gerry Dvorak from the classic 1953 Topps set, these modern masterpieces proved that insert cards can still be a hot commodity in the secondary market, albeit assuming they're well conceived and well made, an unfortunate rarity these days.

The spate of basic issue sets with short-printed subsets continued across many brands in 1999. In reaction to many frustrated dealers and collectors struggling to complete these sets, Fleer/SkyBox created dual versions of each prospect card for the 1999 SkyBox Premium set, an action shot was short-printed and a posed shot was seeded at the same rate as other basic issue cards. The idea was well received by collectors but enjoyed a surprisingly short-lived period of active trading in the secondary market.

The year 2000 was marked by several major developments that would continue shaping the future of our hobby. First off, Pacific decided to forfeit their baseball card license on January 1st, 2000, in an effort to more sharply focus their production expenditures into football and hockey.

In a separate development, Wizards of the Coast (primarily known for their non-sport gaming cards) was granted a license to produce baseball trading cards and debuted their MLB Showdown brand. The cards proved to be quite successful in that they were collected as a set by veteran collectors and played as a game by children (and some adults) both inside and outside of the typical collecting community.

By year's end, Fleer fazed out their SkyBox and Flair brand names in an effort to take full advantage of the historic significance and brand recognition of their flagship Fleer sets issued sporadically during the late 1950s-1970s and consistently from 1981 to the present.

Almost sixty brands of MLB-licensed cards, issued by five manufacturers, were produced in 2000. In addition, Just Minors and Team Best produced a variety of attractive minor league products. Most shop owners continued to generate their income primarily through the sales of packs and boxes of new product, and, as in years past, they had to make careful decisions as to what to keep in stock for customers and what to pass up in fear of a low sell through.

Vintage (or retro-themed) sets dominated the market highlighted by Fleer Greats of the Game, Upper Deck Yankees Legends, and the run of 3,000 hit club and Joe DiMaggio game-used cards issued by Fleer and Upper Deck. In 2001, Topps Heritage (mimicking the style of the classic '52 Topps cards), Upper Deck Vintage (in an homage to '63 Topps baseball), and the return of Topps Archives (after a six-year hiatus) added fuel to the fire.

Using the vintage-theme to tap into a base of wealthy consumers, Upper Deck rolled out their line of Master Collection products (which debuted in basketball a year prior with a Michael Jordan set). Both the Yankees Master Collection and Brooklyn Dodgers Master Collection sets carried initial SRP's of $4,000 or more, marking the most expensive "factory set" of all-time. Each of these sets was serial numbered (500 Yankees and 250 Dodgers), came in a stylish wood box and contained an assortment of game-used and autograph cards from legends of days gone by.

Game-used memorabilia cards became more abundant in all products to the point where a few early 2001 releases (2001 Pacific Private Stock and 2001 SP Game Bat Edition both carrying SRP's in the $15-$20 range) included them at a rate of one per pack. Both products enjoyed a dynamic sell through and proved to be very popular in the secondary market. The result, however, on the secondary market values of game-used memorabilia cards has been dramatic. An Alex Rodriguez or Ken Griffey Jr. game bat or game jersey card that sold for $200+ in 1999 could be had for as little as $25-$50 in early 2001.

Patch cards (a swatch of jersey that contains part of a multi-colored patch) really caught on by year's end as the market formalized premium values on these cards. Upper Deck was the first to create separate "super-premium" jersey Patch inserts within 2000 Upper Deck 1 and 2000 Upper Deck Game Jersey Edition (aka series 2). Pacific followed suit with their Game Gear patch subset within the invincible brand.

By early 2001, Major League Baseball Properties had gotten involved with the trading card autograph and memorabilia programs. From 2001 on, all MLB-licensed trading cards produced by the manufacturers that involved an autograph or game-used memorabilia item had to have the procurement of the item witnessed by a representative of Andersen Consulting, a firm hired by MLB to oversee this historic program. Never before had the league and manufacturers made such an effort to offer autographed or game-used memorabilia trading cards of such authentic provenance.

Short-printed subset cards, a trend started in 1999, continued to be a common element in most basic sets. The trend, however, evolved to the point where these short prints were now being serial numbered, autographed by the player, or incorporating an element of game-used material onto the card. The result was higher values on the key singles, but lower odds of actually finding a good RC in a pack. By year's end, a general sentiment of frustration over not being able to pull good Rookie Cards from a box was beginning to be heard more and more often from collectors.

Rookie Cards incorporating game-used material debuted at year's end in 2000 Black Diamond Rookie Edition. Also, Rookie Cards signed by the player, introduced within the basketball and football card markets in 1999 (with Upper Deck's SPx brand), made their baseball debut in 2000 SPx. Serial-numbered Rookie Cards grew in total usage, but shrank in print run numbers as production figures reached an all-time low of 999 copies for a basic issue RC within the 2000 Pacific Omega set.

Year-end boxed sets, a trend brought back from a four-year hiatus by Fleer in 1998 with it's Fleer Update set, continued to expand as Topps issued it's Bowman Draft Picks and Bowman Chrome Draft Picks sets to cap the now single-series accompanying standard Bowman and Bowman Chrome products.

Fleer broke new ground by blending a 1980s "old-school" concept with some postmodern angles in their 2000 Fleer Glossy boxed set. Harkening back to the run of Glossy parallel factory sets produced from 1987 to 1989, the 2000 Fleer Glossy set included a parallel version of the complete 400-card basic 2000 Fleer set. In addition, 50 new cards (card #'s 401-450, each serial numbered to 1,000 copies) featuring a selection of prospects and rookies were created. Each Glossy factory set contained 5 of the 50 new cards, making it a real challenge to complete the Glossy set.

In a first of its kind for the baseball market, Upper Deck issued a product in December 2000 called Rookie Update that incorporated new cards for three separate popular brands (SP Authentic, SPx, and UD Pros and Prospects) into each pack of cards.

Upper Deck came to terms with Major League Baseball for a license to produce cards featuring members of past and present Team USA squads (bringing back a run of cards last seen in 1993 Topps Traded). That allowed Upper Deck the opportunity to radically expand their production of "true" Rookie Cards in year-end 2000 products, adding a spate of cards featuring heroes from the Olympics in Sydney, Australia, like Ben Sheets. Not surprisingly, the number of prospects making their Rookie Card debut in 2000 sets jumped from about 280 players in 1999 to slightly more than 350 players in 2000.

The influence of sports card dealers and collectors from the Far East (and most noticeably Japan) continued to grow in 2000 as stateside buying approached frenzied levels over scarce Hideo Nomo and Kazuhiro Sasaki cards. A much-traveled starter these days, Nomo's first-ever certified autograph card (issued within the Fleer Mystique Fresh Ink insert set) was the hottest card in the hobby for two months (initially trading for as much as $600-$800).

Not all trends were met with success this year. In particular, low-end products geared towards the youth audience (like 2000 Impact by Fleer) were roundly ignored. The hobby still faces a tough road ahead to keep new waves of collectors involved from generation to generation. Part of the Catch-22 with creating affordable brands catered to youths is that the same customers are most interested in the high-end, expensive material.

Also, Upper Deck's PowerDeck product faced an indifferent audience for a second year in a row, as collectors and even general sports enthusiasts outside the hobby failed to get excited over the CD-ROM cards. More success was met by UD's e-Card insert program, whereby collectors who pulled an e-Card from a pack of UD cards had to go to UD's Website and check the serial number printed on the card to see whether it could evolve into an autograph, game jersey, or game jersey autograph exchange.

The Internet continued to have profound ramifications on shaping the destiny of sports card collecting. By 2000, nearly every dealer (and hard-core collector) was buying or selling cards to some degree in on-line auctions. Auction sales had become so prolific that they were now having a strong effect on the secondary market sales levels of trading cards in arenas entirely outside of cyberspace, like shops, shows, and mail order.

The eBay site continued to dominate the on-line auction action, introducing what appears to be a popular "Buy It Now" option to their already established auction format. The Pit.com opened in mid-year with their concept of buying and selling a portfolio of professionally graded sports cards through their Web site. The concept is based almost exactly upon the methodology used for buying and selling stocks through a brokerage house, with daily ebbs and flows in posted buy and sell prices on your inventory.

Beckett.com made radical improvements to their Marketplace search engines and expanded their inventory of sports cards to the point where they were providing both a wider and a deeper selection of trading cards than any site on the Internet. In addition, a company-wide effort to provide daily news content on their site (coupled with a weekly newsletter sent to over 400,000 collectors) began at year's end, and the hobby has reaped the benefits ever since.

As the 2001 season approached, hobbyists waited with bated breath for seven-time Japanese batting champ Ichiro Suzuki to make his debut in the Seattle Mariner's outfield. And what a stunning debut it was. Ichiro led the league in hitting, led the Mariners to their best record ever, and walked off with the A.L. Rookie of the Year and Most Valuable Player awards. Upper Deck obtained the exclusive rights to produce his autograph cards and they hit a grand slam in midsummer by releasing his SPx Rookie Card, featuring a game jersey swatch and a cut signature autograph. In a year studded with notable cards, this one was likely the most memorable.

In the National League, 37-year-old San Francisco Giants superstar Barry Bonds captivated the nation by bashing a jaw-dropping 73 home runs, shattering Mark McGwire's 1998 single-season home run record.

Cardinals' rookie Albert Pujols emerged out of the low minor leagues to become an instant hobby superstar and walk away with N.L. Rookie of the Year honors.

The year 2001 was a tumultuous one for sports cards. Topps started the year off with a bang by celebrating their 50th anniversary producing baseball cards. Pacific forfeited its license to make baseball cards after an eight-year run to focus on football and hockey cards. Playoff, a company based out of Grand Prairie, Texas, that had earned its stripes by producing football cards in the late 1990s, purchased the rights to the much-hallowed Donruss corporate name and became a formal MLB licensee in the spring of 2001. Their entrance into the baseball card market heralded the return of benchmark brands like Donruss, Donruss Signature, and Leaf.

Competition was fiercer than ever amongst the four primary licensees (Donruss-Playoff, Fleer, Topps, and Upper Deck) as they cranked out almost 80 different products over the course of 2001.

Of all these, likely the most historically important product, Upper Deck Prospect Premieres, was widely overlooked upon release. In a bold move, Upper Deck created a set of 102 prospects, none of which had played a day in the majors. Each player was pictured, however, in the major league uniforms of their parent ballclubs and signed to individual contracts. Because no active major leaguers were featured, Upper Deck did not have to include licensing rights from the MLB Players Association, though they did get licensing from Major League Properties. The industry had never seen a major release featuring active ballplayers marketed to the mainstream audience that lacked licensing from the MLBPA. Because of its lack of historical predecessors and a mixed reception from collectors, the cards were tagged by Beckett Baseball Card Monthly as XRC's (or Extended Rookie Cards), a term that had not been used since 1989.

UD's Prospect Premieres was the first major effort by a manufacturer to level the playing field between Topps and everyone else in that Topps has exclusive rights from the MLBPA to include minor leaguers in their basic brands.

Rookie Cards continued to fascinate collectors, especially in a year with talents like Ichiro and Albert Pujols. The number of players featured on Rookie Cards in 2001 ballooned to an almost absurd figure of 505.

Exchange cards became more prevalent than ever, as manufacturers expanded their use from autograph cards that didn't get returned in time for pack out to slots within basic sets left open in brands released early in the year to fill in with late-season rookie call-ups.

Certified autograph cards remained a huge player in how brands were structured, but the quality of the players suffered greatly as autograph fees continued to spiral out of control. Signatures from superstars like Barry Bonds and Derek Jeter were now being featured on cards with miniscule print runs of 25 or 50 copies while unknown (and often aging and talentless) prospects signed their serial-numbered

Rookies Cards by the hundred count.

More serial-numbered Rookie Cards were produced than ever before, but the quantities produced kept sinking lower and lower as companies tried to create secondary market value by simply limiting supply, a dangerous move to say the least. Donruss-Playoff produced the scarcest Rookie Cards of the year, a handful of Game Base cards (including Ichiro) each serial #'d to a scant 100 copies, within their Leaf Limited set.

After a six-month delay, Topps released their much awaited e-Topps program, a product sold entirely on their Web site whereby trading is conducted in a similar fashion to the buying and selling of stocks, in September.

Several products incorporated non-card memorabilia such as signed caps, bobbing head dolls, and signed baseballs with mixed results.

Memorabilia cards continued their slide into mediocrity as the number of cards featuring various bits and pieces of balls, bases, bats, jerseys, pants, shoes, seats, and whatever else could be dreamt up continued to be offered to consumers, who found the cards less appealing with each passing month. To battle consumer apathy, companies often started to offer combination memorabilia cards featuring notable teammates or several pieces of equipment from a notable star.

Retro-themed cards continued to grow in popularity, and some of the innovations seen in these sets were remarkable. Of particular note was Upper Deck's SP Legendary Cuts Autographs set, featuring 84 deceased players. The set required UD to purchase more than 3,300 autograph cuts, which were then incorporated into a windowpane card design. The result was the first certified autograph cards for legends like Roger Maris, Satchell Paige, and Jackie Robinson. Also, Topps Tribute released at year's end and carrying a hefty $40 per pack suggested retail was widely hailed as one of the most beautiful retro-themed cards ever designed, with their crystal-board fronts encasing full-color, razor-sharp photos.

Pack prices continued to escalate, but surprisingly, the public did not balk as long as they delivered value. The most notable high-end product to hit the market in 2001 was Upper Deck Ultimate Collection with a suggested retail of $100 per pack.

September 11th, 2001, is a day that will go down as one of the most devastating in the history of the United States of America. The game of baseball and the hobby of collecting sports cards were rightfully cast aside as the nation mourned the tragic loss of lives in New York, Pennsylvania, and Washington, D.C. America's economy tumbled as airline traveling ground to a near halt and threats of anthrax crippled the mail system. An economy threatening to slip into recession at the beginning of the year dove headlong into it. The sports card market, along with many other industries, felt the hit for several months. Slowly, Americans looked to move past the grief and the sports card industry, steeped in American nostalgia, provided an ideal retreat for many.

The Arizona Diamondbacks beat the New York Yankees in one of the finest World Series ever played, a much-needed diversion for a grief-stricken nation and a calling card for the dramatic power and glory of our National Pastime.

2002 was a relatively quiet one for baseball cards. Dodger's rookie pitcher Kazuhisa Ishii got off to a blazing first half start and his cards carried many releases through to the All-Star break. Ishii stumbled badly in the second half and no notable rookies were in place to pick up market interest. Cubs hurler Mark Prior created a stir, and his 2001 Rookie Cards were red hot at mid-season. For the second straight season, Barry Bonds was the most dominant star in our sport. His early cards continued to outpace all others in volume trading and professional grading submissions.

The number of players featured on Rookie Cards (or Extended Rookie Cards) reached an all-time high of 524 in 2002 as the manufacturers continued to push the envelope toward more immediate coverage of the current year draft. Though few collectors took notice at the time of release, Upper Deck's incorporation of collegiate Team USA athletes into several year-end brands may take hold and grow into a more prominent position in our industry for collegiate ballplayers. The results of these trends, however, are cards that feature a lot of talented youngsters whom most collectors, unfortunately, have never heard of and won't see in a major league uniform for several years.

To make up for the void in excitement generated by rookies and prospects, the manufacturers made some interesting innovations in product distribution and brand development. In general, base sets got noticeably bigger (including Upper Deck's 1,182 card 40-Man brand and Topps 990-card Topps Total brand). In addition, brands like Topps 206, Leaf Rookies and Stars, and Fleer Fall Classics started to incorporate variations of the base cards directly into the basic issue set (different images, switched out teams, etc.).

One of the bigger surprise hits of the year was the aforementioned Topps 206 brand, which borrowed design elements and set composition from the legendary T-206 tobacco set. Other brands continued to successfully mine from cards and eras long since passed.

Donruss continued to push the creative envelope by incorporating 8½" by 11" framed signature pieces directly into boxes of their Playoff Absolute brand. After a four-year hiatus, Fleer brought back their eponymous "Fleer" name brand with a 540-card set. Donruss introduced their wildly successful Diamond Kings brand, which featured a 150-card painted set. Fleer's Box Score brand was also a popular debut utilizing a unique box-inside-a-box distribution concept. Popular brands like SP Legendary Cuts, Leaf Certified, Topps Heritage, and Topps Tribute all received warm welcomes for their follow-ups to their successes achieved the prior year.

The 2004 season continued to bring us again a growing number of sets with price points ranging from $1.29 to $150. There were also many new heroes during the 2003 season as players such as Josh Beckett, Miguel Cabrera, and Dontrelle Willis of the World Champion Florida Marlins were very strong sellers.

Hideki Matsui, who was the most anticipated rookie for the 2003 season, had a very fine year for the American League Champion Yankees but did not draw the same interest from collectors as Ichiro Suzuki did during the 2001 season.

The 2005 season was most notable for the departure of both Fleer and Donruss/Playoff from the ranks of major manufacturers. One of the issues in recent years has been the staggering amount of sets as well as the complexities of those sets. With some direction from the licensors, the baseball card market was reduced and a maximum of 40 products are expected to be released during the 2006 calendar year.

Despite the struggles the sport of baseball has endured; in recent years, the baseball card market has stepped back to the forefront of the card-collecting hobby, outpacing football, basketball, hockey, golf, and motor sports in volume dollars. As the hobby of collecting baseball cards evolves, we continue to face a market that is blessed with bold creativity and superlative quality; and also challenged with the need to reach new consumers both in mass retail and in cyberspace to continue its growth.

Additional Reading

Each year Beckett Media LP produces comprehensive annual price guides for several sports: *Beckett Baseball Card Price Guide, Beckett Basketball Card Price Guide, Beckett Football Card Price Guide, Beckett Hockey Card Price Guide, Beckett Racing Price Guide,* and a line of *Beckett Alphabetical Checklists* books have been released as well. The aim of these annual guides is to provide information and accurate pricing on a wide array of sports cards, ranging from main issues by the major card manufacturers to various regional, promotional, and food issues. Alphabetical checklist books are published to assist the collector in identifying all the cards of any particular player. The seasoned collector will find these tools valuable sources of information that will enable him to pursue his hobby interests.

In addition, abridged editions of the *Beckett Price Guides* have been published for each of these major sports as part of the House of Collectibles series: *The Official Price Guide to Baseball Cards, The Official Price Guide to Football Cards,* and *The Official Price Guide to Basketball Cards.* Published in a convenient mass-market paperback format, these price guides provide information and accurate pricing on all the main issues by the major card manufacturers.

Prices in This Guide

Prices found in this guide reflect current retail rates just prior to the printing of this book. They do not reflect the FOR SALE prices of the author, the publisher, the distributors, the advertisers, or any card dealers associated with this guide. No one is obligated in any way to buy, sell, or trade his or her cards based on these prices. The price listings were compiled by the author from actual buy/sell transactions at sports conventions, sports card shops, buy/sell advertisements in the hobby papers, for sale prices from dealer catalogs and price lists, and discussions with leading hobbyists in the United States and Canada. All prices are in U.S. dollars.

Acknowledgments

A great deal of diligence, hard work, and dedicated effort went into this year's volume. However, the high standards to which we hold ourselves could not have been met without the expert input and generous amount of time contributed by many people. Our sincere thanks are extended to each and every one of you.

A complete list of these invaluable contributors appears after the **Price Guide** section.

2005 Artifacts

❑ COMP.SET w/o SP's (100) 40.00 15.00
❑ COMMON CARD (1-100) .50 .20
❑ COMMON CARD (101-150) 3.00 1.25
❑ COMMON CARD (151-200) 3.00 1.25
❑ COMMON CARD (201-285) 3.00 1.25
❑ 201-285 ISSUED IN 05 UD UPDATE PACKS
❑ 201-285: ONE #'d CARD OR AU PER PACK
❑ 201-285 PRINT RUN 799 SERIAL #'d SETS
❑ 1 Adam Dunn .50 .20
❑ 2 Adrian Beltre .50 .20
❑ 3 Albert Pujols 2.50 1.00
❑ 4 Alex Rodriguez 2.00 .75
❑ 5 Alfonso Soriano .50 .20
❑ 6 Andruw Jones .75 .30
❑ 7 Andy Pettitte .75 .30
❑ 8 Aramis Ramirez .50 .20
❑ 9 Aubrey Huff .50 .20
❑ 10 Barry Larkin .75 .30
❑ 11 Ben Sheets .50 .20
❑ 12 Bernie Williams .75 .30
❑ 13 Bobby Abreu .50 .20
❑ 14 Brad Penny .50 .20
❑ 15 Bret Boone .50 .20
❑ 16 Brian Giles .50 .20
❑ 17 Carl Crawford .50 .20
❑ 18 Carl Pavano .50 .20
❑ 19 Carlos Beltran .50 .20
❑ 20 Carlos Delgado .50 .20
❑ 21 Carlos Guillen .50 .20
❑ 22 Carlos Lee .50 .20
❑ 23 Carlos Zambrano .50 .20
❑ 24 Chipper Jones 1.25 .50
❑ 25 Craig Biggio .75 .30
❑ 26 Craig Wilson .50 .20
❑ 27 Curt Schilling .75 .30
❑ 28 David Ortiz 1.25 .50
❑ 29 Derek Jeter 2.50 1.00
❑ 30 Eric Chavez .50 .20
❑ 31 Eric Gagne .50 .20
❑ 32 Frank Thomas 1.25 .50
❑ 33 Garret Anderson .50 .20
❑ 34 Gary Sheffield .50 .20
❑ 35 Greg Maddux 2.00 .75
❑ 36 Hank Blalock .50 .20
❑ 37 Hideki Matsui 2.00 .75
❑ 38 Ichiro Suzuki 2.50 1.00
❑ 39 Ivan Rodriguez .75 .30
❑ 40 J.D. Drew .50 .20
❑ 41 Jake Peavy .50 .20
❑ 42 Jason Kendall .50 .20
❑ 43 Jason Schmidt .50 .20
❑ 44 Jeff Bagwell .75 .30
❑ 45 Jeff Kent .50 .20
❑ 46 Jim Edmonds .50 .20
❑ 47 Jim Thome .75 .30
❑ 48 Joe Mauer 1.25 .50
❑ 49 Johan Santana 1.25 .50
❑ 50 John Smoltz .75 .30
❑ 51 Jose Reyes .50 .20
❑ 52 Jose Vidro .50 .20
❑ 53 Josh Beckett .50 .20
❑ 54 Ken Griffey Jr. 2.00 .75
❑ 55 Kerry Wood .50 .20
❑ 56 Kevin Brown .50 .20
❑ 57 Lance Berkman .50 .20
❑ 58 Larry Walker .75 .30
❑ 59 Livan Hernandez .50 .20
❑ 60 Luis Gonzalez .50 .20
❑ 61 Lyle Overbay .50 .20
❑ 62 Magglio Ordonez .50 .20
❑ 63 Manny Ramirez .75 .30
❑ 64 Mark Mulder .50 .20
❑ 65 Mark Prior .75 .30
❑ 66 Mark Teixeira .75 .30
❑ 67 Melvin Mora .50 .20
❑ 68 Michael Young .50 .20
❑ 69 Miguel Cabrera .75 .30
❑ 70 Miguel Tejada .50 .20
❑ 71 Mike Lowell .50 .20
❑ 72 Mike Mussina .75 .30
❑ 73 Mike Piazza 1.25 .50
❑ 74 Mike Sweeney .50 .20
❑ 75 Nomar Garciaparra 1.25 .50
❑ 76 Oliver Perez .50 .20
❑ 77 Paul Konerko .50 .20
❑ 78 Pedro Martinez .75 .30
❑ 79 Preston Wilson .50 .20
❑ 80 Rafael Furcal .50 .20
❑ 81 Rafael Palmeiro .75 .30
❑ 82 Randy Johnson 1.25 .50
❑ 83 Richie Sexson .50 .20
❑ 84 Roger Clemens 2.00 .75
❑ 85 Roy Halladay .50 .20
❑ 86 Roy Oswalt .50 .20
❑ 87 Sammy Sosa 1.25 .50
❑ 88 Scott Podsednik .50 .20
❑ 89 Scott Rolen .75 .30
❑ 90 Shawn Green .50 .20
❑ 91 Steve Finley .50 .20
❑ 92 Tim Hudson .50 .20
❑ 93 Todd Helton .75 .30
❑ 94 Tom Glavine .75 .30
❑ 95 Torii Hunter .50 .20
❑ 96 Travis Hafner .50 .20
❑ 97 Troy Glaus .50 .20
❑ 98 Vernon Wells .50 .20
❑ 99 Victor Martinez .50 .20
❑ 100 Vladimir Guerrero 1.25 .50
❑ 101 Aaron Rowand FS 3.00 1.25
❑ 102 Adam LaRoche FS 3.00 1.25
❑ 103 Adrian Gonzalez FS 3.00 1.25
❑ 104 Alexis Rios FS 3.00 1.25
❑ 105 Angel Guzman FS 3.00 1.25
❑ 106 B.J. Upton FS 3.00 1.25
❑ 107 Bobby Crosby FS 3.00 1.25
❑ 108 Bobby Madritsch FS 3.00 1.25
❑ 109 Brandon Claussen FS 3.00 1.25
❑ 110 Bucky Jacobsen FS 3.00 1.25
❑ 111 Casey Kotchman FS 3.00 1.25
❑ 112 Chad Cordero FS 3.00 1.25
❑ 113 Chase Utley FS 4.00 1.50
❑ 114 Chris Burke FS 3.00 1.25
❑ 115 Dallas McPherson FS 3.00 1.25
❑ 116 Daniel Cabrera FS 3.00 1.25
❑ 117 David DeJesus FS 3.00 1.25
❑ 118 David Wright FS 8.00 3.00
❑ 119 Eddy Rodriguez FS 3.00 1.25
❑ 120 Edwin Jackson FS 3.00 1.25
❑ 121 Gabe Gross FS 3.00 1.25
❑ 122 Garrett Atkins FS 3.00 1.25
❑ 123 Gavin Floyd FS 3.00 1.25
❑ 124 Gerald Laird FS 3.00 1.25
❑ 125 Guillermo Quiroz FS 3.00 1.25
❑ 126 J.D. Closser FS 3.00 1.25
❑ 127 Jason Bay FS 3.00 1.25
❑ 128 Jason DuBois FS 3.00 1.25
❑ 129 Jason Lane FS 3.00 1.25
❑ 130 Jayson Werth FS 3.00 1.25
❑ 131 Jeff Francis FS 3.00 1.25
❑ 132 Jesse Crain FS 3.00 1.25
❑ 133 Joe Blanton FS 3.00 1.25
❑ 134 Joe Mauer FS 5.00 2.00
❑ 135 Jose Capellan FS 3.00 1.25
❑ 136 Kevin Youkilis FS 3.00 1.25
❑ 137 Khalil Greene FS 4.00 1.50
❑ 138 Laynce Nix FS 3.00 1.25
❑ 139 Nick Swisher FS 3.00 1.25
❑ 140 Oliver Perez FS 3.00 1.25
❑ 141 Rickie Weeks FS 3.00 1.25
❑ 142 Robb Quinlan FS 3.00 1.25
❑ 143 Roman Colon FS 3.00 1.25
❑ 144 Ryan Howard FS 5.00 2.00
❑ 145 Ryan Wagner FS 3.00 1.25
❑ 146 Scott Kazmir FS 3.00 1.25
❑ 147 Scott Proctor FS 3.00 1.25
❑ 148 Wily Mo Pena FS 3.00 1.25
❑ 149 Yhency Brazoban FS 3.00 1.25
❑ 150 Zack Greinke FS 3.00 1.25
❑ 151 Al Kaline LGD 4.00 1.50
❑ 152 Babe Ruth LGD 10.00 4.00
❑ 153 Billy Williams LGD 3.00 1.25
❑ 154 Bob Feller LGD 3.00 1.25
❑ 155 Bob Gibson LGD 3.00 1.25
❑ 156 Bob Lemon LGD 3.00 1.25
❑ 157 Bobby Doerr LGD 3.00 1.25
❑ 158 Brooks Robinson LGD 3.00 1.25
❑ 159 Cal Ripken LGD 10.00 4.00
❑ 160 Christy Mathewson LGD 4.00 1.50
❑ 161 Cy Young LGD 4.00 1.50
❑ 162 Dizzy Dean LGD 3.00 1.25
❑ 163 Don Drysdale LGD 3.00 1.25
❑ 164 Eddie Mathews LGD 4.00 1.50
❑ 165 Enos Slaughter LGD 3.00 1.25
❑ 166 Ernie Banks LGD 4.00 1.50
❑ 167 Fergie Jenkins LGD 3.00 1.25
❑ 168 George Sisler LGD 3.00 1.25
❑ 169 Harmon Killebrew LGD 4.00 1.50
❑ 170 Honus Wagner LGD 4.00 1.50
❑ 171 Jackie Robinson LGD 4.00 1.50
❑ 172 Jimmie Foxx LGD 4.00 1.50
❑ 173 Joe DiMaggio LGD 5.00 2.00
❑ 174 Joe Morgan LGD 3.00 1.25
❑ 175 Juan Marichal LGD 3.00 1.25
❑ 176 Lou Brock LGD 3.00 1.25
❑ 177 Lou Gehrig LGD 5.00 2.00
❑ 178 Luis Aparicio LGD 3.00 1.25
❑ 179 Mel Ott LGD 3.00 1.25
❑ 180 Mickey Cochrane LGD 3.00 1.25
❑ 181 Mickey Mantle LGD 15.00 6.00
❑ 182 Mike Schmidt LGD 5.00 2.00
❑ 183 Nolan Ryan LGD 8.00 3.00
❑ 184 Pee Wee Reese LGD 3.00 1.25
❑ 185 Phil Rizzuto LGD 3.00 1.25
❑ 186 Ralph Kiner LGD 3.00 1.25
❑ 187 Rogers Hornsby LGD 3.00 1.25
❑ 188 Roy Campanella LGD 4.00 1.50
❑ 189 Satchel Paige LGD 4.00 1.50
❑ 190 Stan Musial LGD 4.00 1.50
❑ 191 Rick Ferrell LGD 3.00 1.25
❑ 192 Thurman Munson LGD 4.00 1.50
❑ 193 Tom Seaver LGD 3.00 1.25
❑ 194 Ty Cobb LGD 4.00 1.50
❑ 195 Walter Johnson LGD 4.00 1.50
❑ 196 Warren Spahn LGD 3.00 1.25
❑ 197 Whitey Ford LGD 3.00 1.25
❑ 198 Willie McCovey LGD 3.00 1.25
❑ 199 Willie Stargell LGD 3.00 1.25
❑ 200 Yogi Berra LGD 4.00 1.50
❑ 201 Adam Shabala FS RC 3.00 1.25
❑ 202 Ambiorix Burgos FS RC 3.00 1.25
❑ 203 Ambiorix Concepcion FS RC 3.00 1.25
❑ 204 Anibal Sanchez FS RC 8.00 3.00
❑ 205 Bill McCarthy FS RC 3.00 1.25
❑ 206 Brandon McCarthy FS RC 4.00 1.50
❑ 207 Brian Burres FS RC 3.00 1.25
❑ 208 Carlos Ruiz FS RC 3.00 1.25
❑ 209 Casey Rogowski FS RC 4.00 1.50
❑ 210 Chad Orvella FS RC 3.00 1.25
❑ 211 Chris Resop FS RC 3.00 1.25
❑ 212 Chris Roberson FS RC 3.00 1.25
❑ 213 Chris Seddon FS RC 3.00 1.25
❑ 214 Colter Bean FS RC 3.00 1.25
❑ 215 Dae-Sung Koo FS RC 3.00 1.25
❑ 216 Dave Gassner FS RC 3.00 1.25
❑ 217 Brian Anderson FS RC 4.00 1.50
❑ 218 D.J. Houlton FS RC 3.00 1.25
❑ 219 Derek Wathan FS RC 3.00 1.25
❑ 220 Devon Lowery FS RC 3.00 1.25
❑ 221 Enrique Gonzalez FS RC 3.00 1.25
❑ 222 Eude Brito FS RC 3.00 1.25
❑ 223 Francisco Butto FS RC 3.00 1.25
❑ 224 Franquelis Osoria FS RC 3.00 1.25
❑ 225 Garrett Jones FS RC 3.00 1.25
❑ 226 Geovany Soto FS RC 3.00 1.25
❑ 227 Hayden Penn FS RC 4.00 1.50
❑ 228 Ismael Ramirez FS RC 3.00 1.25
❑ 229 Jared Gothreaux FS RC 3.00 1.25
❑ 230 Jason Hammel FS RC 3.00 1.25

❑ 231 Jeff Miller FS RC 3.00 1.25
❑ 232 Jeff Niemann FS RC 4.00 1.50
❑ 233 Joel Peralta FS RC 3.00 1.25
❑ 234 John Hattig FS RC 3.00 1.25
❑ 235 Jorge Campillo FS RC 3.00 1.25
❑ 236 Juan Morillo FS RC 3.00 1.25
❑ 237 Justin Verlander FS RC 10.00 4.00
❑ 238 Ryan Garko FS RC 5.00 2.00
❑ 239 Keiichi Yabu FS RC 3.00 1.25
❑ 240 Kendry Morales FS RC 5.00 2.00
❑ 241 Luis Hernandez FS RC 3.00 1.25
❑ 242 Luis Pena FS RC 3.00 1.25
❑ 243 Luis O.Rodriguez FS RC 3.00 1.25
❑ 244 Luke Scott FS RC 5.00 2.00
❑ 245 Marcos Carvajal FS RC 3.00 1.25
❑ 246 Mark Woodyard FS RC 3.00 1.25
❑ 247 Matt A.Smith FS RC 3.00 1.25
❑ 248 Matthew Lindstrom FS RC 3.00 1.25
❑ 249 Miguel Negron FS RC 4.00 1.50
❑ 250 Mike Morse FS RC 3.00 1.25
❑ 251 Nate McLouth FS RC 4.00 1.50
❑ 252 Nelson Cruz FS RC 5.00 2.00
❑ 253 Nick Masset FS RC 3.00 1.25
❑ 254 Oscar Robles FS RC 3.00 1.25
❑ 255 Paulino Reynoso FS RC 3.00 1.25
❑ 256 Pedro Lopez FS RC 3.00 1.25
❑ 257 Pete Orr FS RC 3.00 1.25
❑ 258 Philip Humber FS RC 4.00 1.50
❑ 259 Prince Fielder FS RC 10.00 4.00
❑ 260 Randy Messenger FS RC 3.00 1.25
❑ 261 Randy Williams FS RC 3.00 1.25
❑ 262 Raul Tablado FS RC 3.00 1.25
❑ 263 Ronny Paulino FS RC 4.00 1.50
❑ 264 Russ Rohlicek FS RC 3.00 1.25
❑ 265 Russell Martin FS RC 6.00 2.50
❑ 266 Scott Baker FS RC 4.00 1.50
❑ 267 Scott Munter FS RC 3.00 1.25
❑ 268 Sean Thompson FS RC 3.00 1.25
❑ 269 Sean Tracey FS RC 3.00 1.25
❑ 270 Shane Costa FS RC 3.00 1.25
❑ 271 Stephen Drew FS RC 10.00 4.00
❑ 272 Steve Schmoll FS RC 3.00 1.25
❑ 273 Tadahito Iguchi FS RC 5.00 2.00
❑ 274 Tony Giarratano FS RC 3.00 1.25
❑ 275 Tony Pena FS RC 3.00 1.25
❑ 276 Travis Bowyer FS RC 3.00 1.25
❑ 277 Ubaldo Jimenez FS RC 6.00 2.50
❑ 278 Wladimir Balentien FS RC 4.00 1.50
❑ 279 Yorman Bazardo FS RC 3.00 1.25
❑ 280 Yuniesky Betancourt FS RC 5.00 2.00
❑ 281 Ryan Zimmerman FS RC 15.00 6.00
❑ 282 Chris Denorfia FS RC 4.00 1.50
❑ 283 Dana Eveland FS RC 3.00 1.25
❑ 284 Jermaine Van Buren FS 3.00 1.25
❑ 285 Mark McLemore FS RC 3.00 1.25

2006 Artifacts

❑ COMPLETE SET (100) 40.00 15.00
❑ COMMON CARD (1-100) .50 .20
❑ COMMON ROOKIE .75 .30
❑ 1 Luis Gonzalez .50 .20
❑ 2 Conor Jackson (RC) 1.25 .50
❑ 3 Joey Devine RC .75 .30
❑ 4 Andruw Jones .75 .30
❑ 5 Chipper Jones 1.25 .50
❑ 6 John Smoltz .75 .30
❑ 7 Jeff Francoeur 1.25 .50
❑ 8 Brian Roberts .50 .20
❑ 9 Miguel Tejada .50 .20
❑ 10 Nick Markakis (RC) 1.25 .50
❑ 11 Curt Schilling .75 .30
❑ 12 David Ortiz 1.25 .50
❑ 13 Johnny Damon .75 .30
❑ 14 Manny Ramirez .75 .30
❑ 15 Jonathan Papelbon (RC) 4.00 1.50
❑ 16 Aramis Ramirez .50 .20
❑ 17 Carlos Zambrano .50 .20
❑ 18 Derrek Lee .50 .20
❑ 19 Greg Maddux 2.00 .75
❑ 20 Mark Prior .75 .30
❑ 21 Mark Buehrle .50 .20
❑ 22 Paul Konerko .50 .20
❑ 23 Adam Dunn .50 .20
❑ 24 Ken Griffey Jr. 2.00 .75
❑ 25 Travis Hafner .50 .20
❑ 26 Victor Martinez .50 .20
❑ 27 Todd Helton .75 .30
❑ 28 Ivan Rodriguez .75 .30
❑ 29 Jeremy Bonderman .50 .20
❑ 30 Jeremy Hermida (RC) .75 .30
❑ 31 Carlos Delgado .50 .20
❑ 32 Dontrelle Willis .50 .20
❑ 33 Josh Beckett .50 .20
❑ 34 Miguel Cabrera .75 .30
❑ 35 Craig Biggio .75 .30
❑ 36 Lance Berkman .50 .20
❑ 37 Roger Clemens 2.50 1.00
❑ 38 Roy Oswalt .50 .20
❑ 39 Josh Willingham (RC) .75 .30
❑ 40 Hanley Ramirez (RC) 2.00 .75
❑ 41 Prince Fielder (RC) 3.00 1.25
❑ 42 Zack Greinke .50 .20
❑ 43 Francisco Rodriguez .50 .20
❑ 44 Vladimir Guerrero 1.25 .50
❑ 45 Tim Hamulack (RC) .75 .30
❑ 46 Jeff Kent .50 .20
❑ 47 Ben Sheets .50 .20
❑ 48 Rickie Weeks .50 .20
❑ 49 Francisco Liriano (RC) 4.00 1.50
❑ 50 Joe Mauer .75 .30
❑ 51 Johan Santana .75 .30
❑ 52 Justin Morneau .50 .20
❑ 53 Torii Hunter .50 .20
❑ 54 Carlos Beltran .50 .20
❑ 55 David Wright 2.00 .75
❑ 56 Jose Reyes 1.25 .50
❑ 57 Mike Piazza 1.25 .50
❑ 58 Pedro Martinez .75 .30
❑ 59 Alex Rodriguez 2.00 .75
❑ 60 Derek Jeter 3.00 1.25
❑ 61 Hideki Matsui 1.25 .50
❑ 62 Randy Johnson 1.25 .50
❑ 63 Justin Verlander (RC) 3.00 1.25
❑ 64 Bobby Crosby .50 .20
❑ 65 Eric Chavez .50 .20
❑ 66 Brian Anderson (RC) .75 .30
❑ 67 Bobby Abreu .50 .20
❑ 68 Pat Burrell .50 .20
❑ 69 Jason Bay .50 .20
❑ 70 Oliver Perez .50 .20
❑ 71 Chuck James (RC) 1.25 .50
❑ 72 Brian Giles .50 .20
❑ 73 Jake Peavy .50 .20
❑ 74 Khalil Greene .75 .30
❑ 75 Jason Schmidt .50 .20
❑ 76 Kenji Johjima RC 4.00 1.50
❑ 77 Jeremy Accardo RC .75 .30
❑ 78 Adrian Beltre .50 .20
❑ 79 Ichiro Suzuki 2.00 .75
❑ 80 Jeff Harris RC .75 .30
❑ 81 Felix Hernandez .75 .30
❑ 82 Albert Pujols 2.50 1.00
❑ 83 Chris Carpenter .50 .20
❑ 84 Jim Edmonds .75 .30
❑ 85 Scott Rolen .75 .30
❑ 86 Mike Jacobs (RC) .75 .30
❑ 87 Carl Crawford .50 .20
❑ 88 Anderson Hernandez (RC) .75 .30
❑ 89 Scott Kazmir .75 .30
❑ 90 Josh Rupe (RC) .75 .30
❑ 91 Scott Feldman RC .75 .30
❑ 92 Alfonso Soriano .50 .20
❑ 93 Hank Blalock .50 .20
❑ 94 Mark Teixeira .75 .30
❑ 95 Michael Young .50 .20
❑ 96 Roy Halladay .50 .20
❑ 97 Vernon Wells .50 .20
❑ 98 Jason Bergmann RC .75 .30
❑ 99 Ryan Zimmerman (RC) 5.00 2.00
❑ 100 Jose Vidro .50 .20

2007 Artifacts

❑ COMPLETE SET (100) 40.00 15.00
❑ COMMON CARD (1-70) .40 .15
❑ COMMON ROOKIE (71-100) .75 .30
❑ 1 Miguel Tejada .40 .15
❑ 2 David Ortiz 1.00 .40
❑ 3 Manny Ramirez .60 .25
❑ 4 Curt Schilling .60 .25
❑ 5 Jim Thome .60 .25
❑ 6 Paul Konerko .40 .15
❑ 7 Jermaine Dye .40 .15
❑ 8 Travis Hafner .40 .15
❑ 9 Victor Martinez .40 .15
❑ 10 Grady Sizemore .60 .25
❑ 11 Ivan Rodriguez .60 .25
❑ 12 Magglio Ordonez .40 .15
❑ 13 Justin Verlander 1.00 .40
❑ 14 Mark Teahen .40 .15
❑ 15 Vladimir Guerrero 1.00 .40
❑ 16 Jered Weaver .60 .25
❑ 17 Justin Morneau .40 .15
❑ 18 Joe Mauer .60 .25
❑ 19 Torii Hunter .40 .15
❑ 20 Johan Santana .60 .25
❑ 21 Derek Jeter 2.50 1.00
❑ 22 Alex Rodriguez 1.50 .60
❑ 23 Johnny Damon .60 .25
❑ 24 Huston Street .40 .15
❑ 25 Nick Swisher .40 .15
❑ 26 Ichiro Suzuki 1.50 .60
❑ 27 Richie Sexson .40 .15
❑ 28 Carl Crawford .40 .15
❑ 29 Scott Kazmir .60 .25
❑ 30 Michael Young .40 .15
❑ 31 Mark Teixeira .60 .25
❑ 32 Vernon Wells .40 .15
❑ 33 Roy Halladay .40 .15
❑ 34 Brandon Webb .40 .15
❑ 35 Stephen Drew .60 .25
❑ 36 Chipper Jones 1.00 .40
❑ 37 Andruw Jones .60 .25
❑ 38 Derrek Lee .40 .15
❑ 39 Aramis Ramirez .40 .15
❑ 40 Ken Griffey Jr. 1.50 .60
❑ 41 Adam Dunn .40 .15
❑ 42 Todd Helton .60 .25
❑ 43 Matt Holliday .50 .20
❑ 44 Miguel Cabrera .60 .25
❑ 45 Hanley Ramirez .60 .25
❑ 46 Dontrelle Willis .40 .15
❑ 47 Lance Berkman .40 .15
❑ 48 Roy Oswalt .40 .15
❑ 49 Craig Biggio .60 .25
❑ 50 Nomar Garciaparra 1.00 .40
❑ 51 Derek Lowe .40 .15
❑ 52 Prince Fielder 1.00 .40
❑ 53 Rickie Weeks .40 .15
❑ 54 Jose Reyes 1.00 .40
❑ 55 David Wright 1.50 .60
❑ 56 Carlos Beltran .40 .15
❑ 57 Ryan Howard 1.50 .60

❑ 58 Chase Utley 1.00 .40
❑ 59 Jimmy Rollins .40 .15
❑ 60 Jason Bay .40 .15
❑ 61 Freddy Sanchez .40 .15
❑ 62 Trevor Hoffman .40 .15
❑ 63 Adrian Gonzalez .40 .15
❑ 64 Omar Vizquel .60 .25
❑ 65 Matt Cain .60 .25
❑ 66 Albert Pujols 2.00 .75
❑ 67 Jim Edmonds .60 .25
❑ 68 Chris Carpenter .40 .15
❑ 69 David Eckstein .40 .15
❑ 70 Ryan Zimmerman 1.00 .40
❑ 71 Alexi Casilla RC 1.25 .50
❑ 72 Andrew Miller RC 5.00 2.00
❑ 73 Andy Cannizaro RC .75 .30
❑ 74 Brian Stokes (RC) .75 .30
❑ 75 Carlos Maldonado (RC) .75 .30
❑ 76 Cesar Jimenez RC .75 .30
❑ 77 Daisuke Matsuzaka RC 8.00 3.00
❑ 78 Delmon Young (RC) 1.25 .50
❑ 79 Delwyn Young (RC) .75 .30
❑ 80 Fred Lewis (RC) 1.25 .50
❑ 81 Glen Perkins (RC) .75 .30
❑ 82 Jeff Baker (RC) .75 .30
❑ 83 Jeff Fiorentino (RC) .75 .30
❑ 84 Jeff Salazar (RC) .75 .30
❑ 85 Jerry Owens (RC) .75 .30
❑ 86 Josh Fields (RC) .75 .30
❑ 87 Juan Perez RC .75 .30
❑ 88 Juan Salas (RC) .75 .30
❑ 89 Justin Hampson (RC) .75 .30
❑ 90 Kevin Kouzmanoff (RC) .75 .30
❑ 91 Michael Bourn (RC) .75 .30
❑ 92 Miguel Montero (RC) .75 .30
❑ 93 Mike Rabelo RC .75 .30
❑ 94 Oswaldo Navarro RC .75 .30
❑ 95 Philip Humber (RC) .75 .30
❑ 96 Ryan Braun RC .75 .30
❑ 97 Ryan Sweeney (RC) .75 .30
❑ 98 Sean Henn (RC) .75 .30
❑ 99 Jose Reyes RC .75 .30
❑ 100 Troy Tulowitzki (RC) 2.00 .75

2006 Bazooka

❑ COMPLETE SET (220) 40.00 15.00
❑ COMMON CARD (1-200) .40 .15
❑ COMMON CARD (201-220) .40 .15
❑ 1 Josh Gibson 1.50 .60
❑ 2 Scott Podsednik .40 .15
❑ 3 Sammy Sosa 1.00 .40
❑ 4 Ivan Rodriguez .60 .25
❑ 5 Derek Jeter 2.50 1.00
❑ 6 Manny Ramirez .60 .25
❑ 7 Nook Logan .40 .15
❑ 8 Adam Dunn .40 .15
❑ 9 Travis Hafner .40 .15
❑ 10 Felix Hernandez .60 .25
❑ 11 Larry Bigbie .40 .15
❑ 12 Magglio Ordonez .40 .15
❑ 13 Josh Beckett .40 .15
❑ 14 Mike Sweeney .40 .15
❑ 15 Mickey Mantle 5.00 2.00
❑ 16 Grady Sizemore .60 .25
❑ 17 Brian Fuentes .40 .15
❑ 18 Wily Mo Pena .40 .15
❑ 19 Morgan Ensberg .40 .15
❑ 20 Tim Hudson .40 .15
❑ 21 Justin Verlander 1.50 .60
❑ 22 Jermaine Dye .40 .15
❑ 23 Miguel Cabrera .40 .15
❑ 24 Greg Maddux 1.50 .60
❑ 25 Jason Giambi .40 .15
❑ 26 Ben Sheets .40 .15
❑ 27 Brad Radke .40 .15
❑ 28 Torii Hunter .40 .15
❑ 29 Mike Piazza 1.00 .40
❑ 30 Jason Kendall .40 .15
❑ 31 Pat Burrell .40 .15
❑ 32 Khalil Greene .60 .25
❑ 33 Brian Roberts .40 .15
❑ 34 C.C. Sabathia .40 .15
❑ 35 Mike Mussina .60 .25
❑ 36 Bob Wickman .40 .15
❑ 37 Dmitri Young .40 .15
❑ 38 Dontrelle Willis .40 .15
❑ 39 David DeJesus .40 .15
❑ 40 J.D. Drew .40 .15
❑ 41 Chad Tracy .40 .15
❑ 42 Joe Mauer 1.00 .40
❑ 43 Melvin Mora .40 .15
❑ 44 Carlos Zambrano .40 .15
❑ 45 Mariano Rivera 1.00 .40
❑ 46 Coco Crisp .40 .15
❑ 47 Derrek Lee .60 .25
❑ 48 Cliff Floyd .40 .15
❑ 49 Willy Taveras .40 .15
❑ 50 Albert Pujols 2.00 .75
❑ 51 Aaron Boone .40 .15
❑ 52 Mark Mulder .40 .15
❑ 53 Brad Wilkerson .40 .15
❑ 54 Hank Blalock .40 .15
❑ 55 Hideki Matsui 1.00 .40
❑ 56 Victor Martinez .40 .15
❑ 57 Jeremy Bonderman .40 .15
❑ 58 Felipe Lopez .40 .15
❑ 59 Paul Lo Duca .40 .15
❑ 60 Derek Lowe .40 .15
❑ 61 Luis Gonzalez .40 .15
❑ 62 Paul Konerko .40 .15
❑ 63 Miguel Tejada .40 .15
❑ 64 Jeromy Burnitz .40 .15
❑ 65 Orlando Hernandez .40 .15
❑ 66 Curt Schilling .60 .25
❑ 67 Joe Nathan .40 .15
❑ 68 Jose Reyes .40 .15
❑ 69 David Wright 1.00 .40
❑ 70 Eric Chavez .40 .15
❑ 71 Rich Harden .40 .15
❑ 72 A.J. Pierzynski .40 .15
❑ 73 Trevor Hoffman .40 .15
❑ 74 Adrian Beltre .40 .15
❑ 75 Alex Rodriguez 1.50 .60
❑ 76 Jonathan Papelbon 2.00 .75
❑ 77 Jorge Cantu .40 .15
❑ 78 Mark Teixeira .60 .25
❑ 79 Chien-Ming Wang 1.50 .60
❑ 80 Jeff Francoeur 1.00 .40
❑ 81 Ichiro Suzuki 1.50 .60
❑ 82 Jhonny Peralta .40 .15
❑ 83 Todd Helton .60 .25
❑ 84 Brad Penny .40 .15
❑ 85 Shawn Chacon .40 .15
❑ 86 Billy Wagner .40 .15
❑ 87 Jason Schmidt .40 .15
❑ 88 Austin Kearns .40 .15
❑ 89 Chris Carpenter .40 .15
❑ 90 Chipper Jones 1.00 .40
❑ 91 Shawn Green .40 .15
❑ 92 A.J. Burnett .40 .15
❑ 93 Joe Crede .40 .15
❑ 94 Mark Prior .60 .25
❑ 95 Andy Pettitte .60 .25
❑ 96 Edgar Renteria .40 .15
❑ 97 Roy Halladay .40 .15
❑ 98 Eric Milton .40 .15
❑ 99 Craig Biggio .60 .25
❑ 100 Barry Bonds 2.50 1.00
❑ 101 Troy Glaus .40 .15
❑ 102 Aaron Rowand .40 .15
❑ 103 Aramis Ramirez .40 .15
❑ 104 Nomar Garciaparra 1.00 .40
❑ 105 Randy Johnson 1.00 .40
❑ 106 David Ortiz 1.00 .40
❑ 107 Vinny Castilla .40 .15
❑ 108 Carl Crawford .40 .15
❑ 109 Zach Duke .40 .15
❑ 110 Barry Zito .40 .15
❑ 111 Darin Erstad .40 .15
❑ 112 Chris Capuano .40 .15
❑ 113 Javy Lopez .40 .15
❑ 114 Lew Ford .40 .15
❑ 115 Robinson Cano .60 .25
❑ 116 Ronnie Belliard .40 .15
❑ 117 Placido Polanco .40 .15
❑ 118 Rickie Weeks .40 .15
❑ 119 Brad Lidge .40 .15
❑ 120 Andruw Jones .60 .25
❑ 121 Nick Swisher .40 .15
❑ 122 Bartolo Colon .40 .15
❑ 123 Juan Pierre .40 .15
❑ 124 Johan Santana 1.00 .40
❑ 125 Jorge Posada .60 .25
❑ 126 Jeff Francis .40 .15
❑ 127 Matt Holliday .50 .20
❑ 128 Carlos Delgado .40 .15
❑ 129 Zack Greinke .40 .15
❑ 130 Lyle Overbay .40 .15
❑ 131 Conor Jackson .40 .15
❑ 132 Mark Buehrle .40 .15
❑ 133 Chone Figgins .40 .15
❑ 134 Pedro Martinez .60 .25
❑ 135 Roger Clemens 2.00 .75
❑ 136 Raul Ibanez .40 .15
❑ 137 Jim Edmonds .40 .15
❑ 138 Michael Young .40 .15
❑ 139 Preston Wilson .40 .15
❑ 140 Rafael Furcal .40 .15
❑ 141 Bobby Abreu .40 .15
❑ 142 Tadahito Iguchi .40 .15
❑ 143 B.J. Ryan .40 .15
❑ 144 Francisco Rodriguez .40 .15
❑ 145 J.T. Snow .40 .15
❑ 146 Aubrey Huff .40 .15
❑ 147 Mike Morse .40 .15
❑ 148 Jason Bay .40 .15
❑ 149 Roy Oswalt .40 .15
❑ 150 Carlos Beltran .40 .15
❑ 151 Carlos Lee .40 .15
❑ 152 Emil Brown .40 .15
❑ 153 Craig Monroe .40 .15
❑ 154 Kris Benson .40 .15
❑ 155 Gary Sheffield .40 .15
❑ 156 Jake Peavy .40 .15
❑ 157 David Eckstein .40 .15
❑ 158 Tom Glavine .60 .25
❑ 159 Jeff Kent .40 .15
❑ 160 Livan Hernandez .40 .15
❑ 161 Orlando Hudson .40 .15
❑ 162 Randy Winn .40 .15
❑ 163 Jimmy Rollins .40 .15
❑ 164 Luis Castillo .40 .15
❑ 165 Nick Johnson .40 .15
❑ 166 Johnny Damon .60 .25
❑ 167 Eric Gagne .40 .15
❑ 168 Geoff Jenkins .40 .15
❑ 169 Mike Cameron .40 .15
❑ 170 Marcus Giles .40 .15
❑ 171 Huston Street .40 .15
❑ 172 Moises Alou .40 .15
❑ 173 Scott Rolen .60 .25
❑ 174 Jose Vidro .40 .15
❑ 175 Alfonso Soriano .40 .15
❑ 176 Toby Hall .40 .15
❑ 177 Orlando Cabrera .40 .15
❑ 178 Brian Giles .40 .15
❑ 179 Erubiel Durazo .40 .15
❑ 180 Matt Morris .40 .15
❑ 181 Jack Wilson .40 .15
❑ 182 Brady Clark .40 .15
❑ 183 Shannon Stewart .40 .15
❑ 184 Kerry Wood .40 .15
❑ 185 Carl Pavano .40 .15
❑ 186 Chase Utley .60 .25
❑ 187 Omar Vizquel .60 .25
❑ 188 Vladimir Guerrero 1.00 .40
❑ 189 Richie Sexson .40 .15
❑ 190 John Smoltz .60 .25
❑ 191 Garret Anderson .40 .15
❑ 192 Jon Garland .40 .15

❑ 193 Julio Lugo	.40	.15
❑ 194 Rocco Baldelli	.40	.15
❑ 195 Jaret Wright	.40	.15
❑ 196 Matt Clement	.40	.15
❑ 197 Vernon Wells	.40	.15
❑ 198 Sean Casey	.40	.15
❑ 199 Lance Berkman	.40	.15
❑ 200 Justin Morneau	.40	.15
❑ 201 Shaun Marcum (RC)	.40	.15
❑ 202 Chuck James (RC)	.40	.15
❑ 203 Hong-Chih Kuo (RC)	1.00	.40
❑ 204 Darrell Rasner (RC)	.40	.15
❑ 205 Anthony Reyes (RC)	.60	.25
❑ 206 Francisco Liriano (RC)	2.00	.75
❑ 207 Joe Saunders (RC)	.40	.15
❑ 208 Fausto Carmona (RC)	.40	.15
❑ 209 Charlton Jimerson (RC)	.40	.15
❑ 210 Bryan Bullington (RC)	.40	.15
❑ 211 Tom Gorzelanny (RC)	.40	.15
❑ 212 Anderson Hernandez (RC)	.40	.15
❑ 213 Ryan Garko (RC)	.40	.15
❑ 214 John Koronka (RC)	.40	.15
❑ 215 Chris Denorfia (RC)	.40	.15
❑ 216 Jeff Mathis (RC)	.40	.15
❑ 217 Jose Bautista (RC)	.40	.15
❑ 218 Danny Sandoval RC	.40	.15
❑ 219 Robert Andino RC	.40	.15
❑ 220 Justin Huber (RC)	.40	.15

1948 Bowman

❑ COMPLETE SET (48)	5000.00	3000.00
❑ COMMON CARD (1-36)	20.00	10.00
❑ COMMON CARD (37-48)	30.00	15.00
❑ WRAPPER (5-CENT)	700.00	600.00
❑ WRAPPER (1-CENT)		
❑ 1 Bob Elliott RC	125.00	75.00
❑ 2 Ewell Blackwell RC	60.00	35.00
❑ 3 Ralph Kiner RC	250.00	150.00
❑ 4 Johnny Mize RC	125.00	75.00
❑ 5 Bob Feller RC	250.00	150.00
❑ 6 Yogi Berra RC	800.00	500.00
❑ 7 Pete Reiser SP RC	125.00	75.00
❑ 8 Phil Rizzuto SP RC	350.00	200.00
❑ 9 Walker Cooper RC	20.00	10.00
❑ 10 Buddy Rosar RC	20.00	10.00
❑ 11 Johnny Lindell RC	25.00	12.50
❑ 12 Johnny Sain RC	80.00	50.00
❑ 13 Willard Marshall SP RC	40.00	20.00
❑ 14 Allie Reynolds RC	60.00	35.00
❑ 15 Eddie Joost	20.00	10.00
❑ 16 Jack Lohrke SP RC	40.00	20.00
❑ 17 Enos Slaughter RC	100.00	60.00
❑ 18 Warren Spahn RC	300.00	175.00
❑ 19 Tommy Henrich	60.00	35.00
❑ 20 Buddy Kerr SP RC	40.00	20.00
❑ 21 Ferris Fain RC	40.00	20.00
❑ 22 Floyd Bevens SP RC	50.00	30.00
❑ 23 Larry Jansen RC	25.00	12.50
❑ 24 Dutch Leonard SP	40.00	20.00
❑ 25 Barney McCosky	20.00	10.00
❑ 26 Frank Shea SP RC	50.00	30.00
❑ 27 Sid Gordon RC	25.00	12.50
❑ 28 Emil Verban SP RC	40.00	20.00
❑ 29 Joe Page SP RC	80.00	50.00
❑ 30 Whitey Lockman SP RC	50.00	30.00
❑ 31 Bill McCahan RC	20.00	10.00
❑ 32 Bill Rigney RC	20.00	10.00
❑ 33 Bill Johnson RC	25.00	12.50
❑ 34 Sheldon Jones SP RC	40.00	20.00
❑ 35 Snuffy Stirnweiss RC	40.00	20.00
❑ 36 Stan Musial RC	800.00	500.00
❑ 37 Clint Hartung RC	30.00	15.00
❑ 38 Red Schoendienst RC	200.00	125.00
❑ 39 Augie Galan RC	30.00	15.00
❑ 40 Marty Marion RC	80.00	50.00
❑ 41 Rex Barney RC	60.00	35.00
❑ 42 Ray Poat RC	30.00	15.00
❑ 43 Bruce Edwards RC	40.00	20.00
❑ 44 Johnny Wyrostek RC	30.00	15.00
❑ 45 Hank Sauer RC	60.00	35.00
❑ 46 Herman Wehmeier RC	30.00	15.00
❑ 47 Bobby Thomson RC	100.00	60.00
❑ 48 Dave Koslo RC	80.00	50.00

1949 Bowman

❑ COMP. MASTER SET (252)	16000.00	10000.00
❑ COMPLETE SET (240)	15000.00	10000.00
❑ COMMON CARD (1-144)	15.00	7.50
❑ COMMON CARD (145-240)	50.00	30.00
❑ WRAPPER (1-CENT,Rd,Wh,Bl)		
❑ WRAPPER (5-CENT, GR.)	250.00	200.00
❑ WRAPPER (5-CENT, BL.)	200.00	150.00
❑ 1 Vern Bickford RC	125.00	75.00
❑ 2 Whitey Lockman	40.00	20.00
❑ 3 Bob Porterfield RC	15.00	7.50
❑ 4A Jerry Priddy NNOF RC	15.00	7.50
❑ 4B Jerry Priddy NOF	50.00	30.00
❑ 5 Hank Sauer	40.00	20.00
❑ 6 Phil Cavarretta RC	40.00	20.00
❑ 7 Joe Dobson RC	15.00	7.50
❑ 8 Murry Dickson RC	15.00	7.50
❑ 9 Ferris Fain	40.00	20.00
❑ 10 Ted Gray RC	15.00	7.50
❑ 11 Lou Boudreau MG RC	80.00	50.00
❑ 12 Cass Michaels RC	15.00	7.50
❑ 13 Bob Chesnes RC	15.00	7.50
❑ 14 Curt Simmons RC	40.00	20.00
❑ 15 Ned Garver RC	15.00	7.50
❑ 16 Al Kozar RC	15.00	7.50
❑ 17 Earl Torgeson RC	15.00	7.50
❑ 18 Bobby Thomson	40.00	20.00
❑ 19 Bobby Brown RC	60.00	35.00
❑ 20 Gene Hermanski RC	15.00	7.50
❑ 21 Frank Baumholtz RC	25.00	12.50
❑ 22 Peanuts Lowrey RC	15.00	7.50
❑ 23 Bobby Doerr	80.00	50.00
❑ 24 Stan Musial	600.00	350.00
❑ 25 Carl Scheib RC	15.00	7.50
❑ 26 George Kell RC	80.00	50.00
❑ 27 Bob Feller	300.00	200.00
❑ 28 Don Kolloway RC	15.00	7.50
❑ 29 Ralph Kiner	125.00	75.00
❑ 30 Andy Seminick	40.00	20.00
❑ 31 Dick Kokos RC	15.00	7.50
❑ 32 Eddie Yost RC	60.00	35.00
❑ 33 Warren Spahn	200.00	125.00
❑ 34 Dave Koslo	15.00	7.50
❑ 35 Vic Raschi RC	60.00	35.00
❑ 36 Pee Wee Reese	200.00	125.00
❑ 37 Johnny Wyrostek	15.00	7.50
❑ 38 Emil Verban	15.00	7.50
❑ 39 Billy Goodman RC	25.00	12.50
❑ 40 George Munger RC	15.00	7.50
❑ 41 Lou Brissie RC	15.00	7.50
❑ 42 Hoot Evers RC	15.00	7.50
❑ 43 Dale Mitchell RC	40.00	20.00
❑ 44 Dave Philley RC	15.00	7.50
❑ 45 Wally Westlake RC	15.00	7.50
❑ 46 Robin Roberts RC	250.00	150.00
❑ 47 Johnny Sain	60.00	35.00
❑ 48 Willard Marshall	15.00	7.50
❑ 49 Frank Shea	25.00	12.50
❑ 50 Jackie Robinson RC	1500.00	900.00
❑ 51 Herman Wehmeier	15.00	7.50
❑ 52 Johnny Schmitz RC	15.00	7.50
❑ 53 Jack Kramer RC	15.00	7.50
❑ 54 Marty Marion	60.00	35.00
❑ 55 Eddie Joost	15.00	7.50
❑ 56 Pat Mullin RC	15.00	7.50
❑ 57 Gene Bearden RC	40.00	20.00
❑ 58 Bob Elliott	40.00	20.00
❑ 59 Jack Lohrke	15.00	7.50
❑ 60 Yogi Berra	300.00	175.00
❑ 61 Rex Barney	40.00	20.00
❑ 62 Grady Hatton RC	15.00	7.50
❑ 63 Andy Pafko RC	40.00	20.00
❑ 64 Dom DiMaggio	60.00	35.00
❑ 65 Enos Slaughter	80.00	50.00
❑ 66 Elmer Valo RC	15.00	7.50
❑ 67 Alvin Dark RC	40.00	20.00
❑ 68 Sheldon Jones	15.00	7.50
❑ 69 Tommy Henrich	40.00	20.00
❑ 70 Carl Furillo RC	150.00	90.00
❑ 71 Vern Stephens RC	15.00	7.50
❑ 72 Tommy Holmes RC	40.00	20.00
❑ 73 Billy Cox RC	40.00	20.00
❑ 74 Tom McBride RC	15.00	7.50
❑ 75 Eddie Mayo RC	15.00	7.50
❑ 76 Bill Nicholson RC	25.00	12.50
❑ 77 Ernie Bonham RC	15.00	7.50
❑ 78A Sam Zoldak NNOF RC	15.00	7.50
❑ 78B Sam Zoldak NOF	50.00	30.00
❑ 79 Ron Northey RC	15.00	7.50
❑ 80 Bill McCahan	15.00	7.50
❑ 81 Virgil Stallcup RC	15.00	7.50
❑ 82 Joe Page	60.00	35.00
❑ 83A Bob Scheffing NNOF RC	15.00	7.50
❑ 83B Bob Scheffing NOF	50.00	30.00
❑ 84 Roy Campanella RC	800.00	500.00
❑ 85A Johnny Mize NNOF	100.00	60.00
❑ 85B Johnny Mize NOF	150.00	90.00
❑ 86 Johnny Pesky RC	60.00	35.00
❑ 87 Randy Gumpert RC	15.00	7.50
❑ 88A Bill Salkeld NNOF RC	15.00	7.50
❑ 88B Bill Salkeld NOF	50.00	30.00
❑ 89 Mizell Platt RC	15.00	7.50
❑ 90 Gil Coan RC	15.00	7.50
❑ 91 Dick Wakefield RC	15.00	7.50
❑ 92 Willie Jones RC	40.00	20.00
❑ 93 Ed Stevens RC	15.00	7.50
❑ 94 Mickey Vernon RC	40.00	20.00
❑ 95 Howie Pollet RC	15.00	7.50
❑ 96 Taft Wright	15.00	7.50
❑ 97 Danny Litwhiler RC	15.00	7.50
❑ 98A Phil Rizzuto NNOF	200.00	125.00
❑ 98B Phil Rizzuto NOF	250.00	150.00
❑ 99 Frank Gustine RC	15.00	7.50
❑ 100 Gil Hodges RC	250.00	150.00
❑ 101 Sid Gordon	15.00	7.50
❑ 102 Stan Spence RC	15.00	7.50
❑ 103 Joe Tipton RC	15.00	7.50
❑ 104 Eddie Stanky RC	40.00	20.00
❑ 105 Bill Kennedy RC	15.00	7.50
❑ 106 Jake Early RC	15.00	7.50
❑ 107 Eddie Lake RC	15.00	7.50
❑ 108 Ken Heintzelman RC	15.00	7.50
❑ 109A Ed Fitzgerald SCR RC	15.00	7.50
❑ 109B Ed Fitzgerald PR	60.00	35.00
❑ 110 Early Wynn RC	150.00	90.00
❑ 111 Red Schoendienst	100.00	60.00
❑ 112 Sam Chapman	40.00	20.00
❑ 113 Ray LaManno RC	15.00	7.50
❑ 114 Allie Reynolds	60.00	35.00
❑ 115 Dutch Leonard	15.00	7.50
❑ 116 Joe Hatten RC	15.00	7.50
❑ 117 Walker Cooper	15.00	7.50
❑ 118 Sam Mele RC	15.00	7.50
❑ 119 Floyd Baker RC	15.00	7.50
❑ 120 Cliff Fannin RC	15.00	7.50
❑ 121 Mark Christman RC	15.00	7.50
❑ 122 George Vico RC	15.00	7.50
❑ 123 Johnny Blatnik	15.00	7.50

❑ 124A D.Murtaugh SCR RC 40.00 20.00
❑ 124B D.Murtaugh PR 60.00 35.00
❑ 125 Ken Keltner RC 25.00 12.50
❑ 126A Al Brazle SCR RC 15.00 7.50
❑ 126B Al Brazle PR 60.00 35.00
❑ 127A Hank Majeski SCR RC 15.00 7.50
❑ 127B Hank Majeski PR 60.00 35.00
❑ 128 Johnny VanderMeer 60.00 35.00
❑ 129 Bill Johnson 40.00 20.00
❑ 130 Harry Walker RC 15.00 7.50
❑ 131 Paul Lehner RC 15.00 7.50
❑ 132A Al Evans SCR RC 15.00 7.50
❑ 132B Al Evans PR 60.00 35.00
❑ 133 Aaron Robinson RC 15.00 7.50
❑ 134 Hank Borowy RC 15.00 7.50
❑ 135 Stan Rojek RC 15.00 7.50
❑ 136 Hank Edwards RC 15.00 7.50
❑ 137 Ted Wilks RC 15.00 7.50
❑ 138 Buddy Rosar 15.00 7.50
❑ 139 Hank Arft RC 15.00 7.50
❑ 140 Ray Scarborough RC 15.00 7.50
❑ 141 Tony Lupien RC 15.00 7.50
❑ 142 Eddie Waitkus RC 40.00 20.00
❑ 143A Bob Dillinger SCR RC 25.00 12.50
❑ 143B Bob Dillinger PR 60.00 35.00
❑ 144 Mickey Haefner RC 15.00 7.50
❑ 145 Sylvester Donnelly RC 50.00 30.00
❑ 146 Mike McCormick RC 50.00 30.00
❑ 147 Bert Singleton RC 50.00 30.00
❑ 148 Bob Swift RC 50.00 30.00
❑ 149 Roy Partee RC 50.00 30.00
❑ 150 Allie Clark RC 50.00 30.00
❑ 151 Mickey Harris RC 50.00 30.00
❑ 152 Clarence Maddern RC 50.00 30.00
❑ 153 Phil Masi RC 50.00 30.00
❑ 154 Clint Hartung 60.00 35.00
❑ 155 Mickey Guerra RC 50.00 30.00
❑ 156 Al Zarilla RC 50.00 30.00
❑ 157 Walt Masterson RC 50.00 30.00
❑ 158 Harry Brecheen RC 60.00 35.00
❑ 159 Glen Moulder RC 50.00 30.00
❑ 160 Jim Blackburn RC 50.00 30.00
❑ 161 Jocko Thompson RC 50.00 30.00
❑ 162 Preacher Roe RC 125.00 75.00
❑ 163 Clyde McCullough RC 50.00 30.00
❑ 164 Vic Wertz RC 80.00 50.00
❑ 165 Snuffy Stirnweiss 80.00 50.00
❑ 166 Mike Tresh RC 50.00 30.00
❑ 167 Babe Martin RC 50.00 30.00
❑ 168 Doyle Lade RC 50.00 30.00
❑ 169 Jeff Heath RC 60.00 35.00
❑ 170 Bill Rigney 60.00 35.00
❑ 171 Dick Fowler RC 50.00 30.00
❑ 172 Eddie Pellagrini RC 50.00 30.00
❑ 173 Eddie Stewart RC 50.00 30.00
❑ 174 Terry Moore RC 80.00 50.00
❑ 175 Luke Appling 150.00 90.00
❑ 176 Ken Raffensberger RC 50.00 30.00
❑ 177 Stan Lopata RC 60.00 35.00
❑ 178 Tom Brown RC 60.00 35.00
❑ 179 Hugh Casey 80.00 50.00
❑ 180 Connie Berry 50.00 30.00
❑ 181 Gus Niarhos RC 50.00 30.00
❑ 182 Hal Peck RC 50.00 30.00
❑ 183 Lou Stringer RC 50.00 30.00
❑ 184 Bob Chipman RC 50.00 30.00
❑ 185 Pete Reiser 80.00 50.00
❑ 186 Buddy Kerr 50.00 30.00
❑ 187 Phil Marchildon RC 50.00 30.00
❑ 188 Karl Drews RC 50.00 30.00
❑ 189 Earl Wooten RC 50.00 30.00
❑ 190 Jim Hearn RC 50.00 30.00
❑ 191 Joe Haynes RC 50.00 30.00
❑ 192 Harry Gumbert 50.00 30.00
❑ 193 Ken Trinkle RC 50.00 30.00
❑ 194 Ralph Branca RC 100.00 60.00
❑ 195 Eddie Bockman RC 50.00 30.00
❑ 196 Fred Hutchinson RC 60.00 35.00
❑ 197 Johnny Lindell 60.00 35.00
❑ 198 Steve Gromek RC 50.00 30.00
❑ 199 Tex Hughson RC 50.00 30.00
❑ 200 Jess Dobernic RC 50.00 30.00
❑ 201 Sibby Sisti RC 50.00 30.00
❑ 202 Larry Jansen 60.00 35.00
❑ 203 Barney McCosky 50.00 30.00
❑ 204 Bob Savage RC 50.00 30.00
❑ 205 Dick Sisler RC 60.00 35.00
❑ 206 Bruce Edwards 50.00 30.00
❑ 207 Johnny Hopp RC 50.00 30.00
❑ 208 Dizzy Trout 60.00 35.00
❑ 209 Charlie Keller 80.00 50.00
❑ 210 Joe Gordon RC 80.00 50.00
❑ 211 Boo Ferriss RC 50.00 30.00
❑ 212 Ralph Hamner RC 50.00 30.00
❑ 213 Red Barrett RC 50.00 30.00
❑ 214 Richie Ashburn RC 600.00 350.00
❑ 215 Kirby Higbe 50.00 30.00
❑ 216 Schoolboy Rowe 60.00 35.00
❑ 217 Marino Pieretti RC 50.00 30.00
❑ 218 Dick Kryhoski RC 50.00 30.00
❑ 219 Virgil Trucks RC 60.00 35.00
❑ 220 Johnny McCarthy 50.00 30.00
❑ 221 Bob Muncrief RC 50.00 30.00
❑ 222 Alex Kellner RC 50.00 30.00
❑ 223 Bobby Hofman RC 50.00 30.00
❑ 224 Satchel Paige RC 1500.00 1000.00
❑ 225 Jerry Coleman RC 80.00 50.00
❑ 226 Duke Snider RC 1000.00 600.00
❑ 227 Fritz Ostermueller 50.00 30.00
❑ 228 Jackie Mayo RC 50.00 30.00
❑ 229 Ed Lopat RC 150.00 90.00
❑ 230 Augie Galan 60.00 35.00
❑ 231 Earl Johnson RC 50.00 30.00
❑ 232 George McQuinn 60.00 35.00
❑ 233 Larry Doby RC 300.00 175.00
❑ 234 Rip Sewell RC 50.00 30.00
❑ 235 Jim Russell RC 50.00 30.00
❑ 236 Fred Sanford RC 50.00 30.00
❑ 237 Monte Kennedy RC 50.00 30.00
❑ 238 Bob Lemon RC 200.00 125.00
❑ 239 Frank McCormick 50.00 30.00
❑ 240 Babe Young UER 100.00 60.00

1950 Bowman

❑ COMPLETE SET (252) 8500.00 6000.00
❑ COMMON CARD (1-72) 50.00 30.00
❑ COMMON CARD (73-252) 15.00 7.50
❑ WRAPPER (1-CENT) 250.00 200.00
❑ WRAPPER (5-CENT) 250.00 200.00
❑ 1 Mel Parnell RC 150.00 90.00
❑ 2 Vern Stephens 60.00 35.00
❑ 3 Dom DiMaggio 80.00 50.00
❑ 4 Gus Zernial RC 60.00 35.00
❑ 5 Bob Kuzava RC 50.00 30.00
❑ 6 Bob Feller 300.00 175.00
❑ 7 Jim Hegan 60.00 35.00
❑ 8 George Kell 80.00 50.00
❑ 9 Vic Wertz 60.00 35.00
❑ 10 Tommy Henrich 80.00 50.00
❑ 11 Phil Rizzuto 300.00 175.00
❑ 12 Joe Page 80.00 50.00
❑ 13 Ferris Fain 60.00 35.00
❑ 14 Alex Kellner 50.00 30.00
❑ 15 Al Kozar 50.00 30.00
❑ 16 Roy Sievers RC 80.00 50.00
❑ 17 Sid Hudson 50.00 30.00
❑ 18 Eddie Robinson RC 50.00 30.00
❑ 19 Warren Spahn 300.00 175.00
❑ 20 Bob Elliott 60.00 35.00
❑ 21 Pee Wee Reese 300.00 175.00
❑ 22 Jackie Robinson 1200.00 700.00
❑ 23 Don Newcombe RC 150.00 90.00
❑ 24 Johnny Schmitz 50.00 30.00
❑ 25 Hank Sauer 60.00 35.00
❑ 26 Grady Hatton 50.00 30.00
❑ 27 Herman Wehmeier 50.00 30.00
❑ 28 Bobby Thomson 80.00 50.00
❑ 29 Eddie Stanky 60.00 35.00
❑ 30 Eddie Waitkus 60.00 35.00
❑ 31 Del Ennis 80.00 50.00
❑ 32 Robin Roberts 150.00 90.00
❑ 33 Ralph Kiner 100.00 60.00
❑ 34 Murry Dickson 50.00 30.00
❑ 35 Enos Slaughter 100.00 60.00
❑ 36 Eddie Kazak RC 60.00 35.00
❑ 37 Luke Appling 80.00 50.00
❑ 38 Bill Wight RC 50.00 30.00
❑ 39 Larry Doby 100.00 60.00
❑ 40 Bob Lemon 80.00 50.00
❑ 41 Hoot Evers 50.00 30.00
❑ 42 Art Houtteman RC 50.00 30.00
❑ 43 Bobby Doerr 80.00 50.00
❑ 44 Joe Dobson 50.00 30.00
❑ 45 Al Zarilla 50.00 30.00
❑ 46 Yogi Berra 400.00 250.00
❑ 47 Jerry Coleman 80.00 50.00
❑ 48 Lou Brissie 50.00 30.00
❑ 49 Elmer Valo 50.00 30.00
❑ 50 Dick Kokos 50.00 30.00
❑ 51 Ned Garver 60.00 35.00
❑ 52 Sam Mele 50.00 30.00
❑ 53 Clyde Vollmer RC 50.00 30.00
❑ 54 Gil Coan 50.00 30.00
❑ 55 Buddy Kerr 50.00 30.00
❑ 56 Del Crandall RC 60.00 35.00
❑ 57 Vern Bickford 50.00 30.00
❑ 58 Carl Furillo 80.00 50.00
❑ 59 Ralph Branca 80.00 50.00
❑ 60 Andy Pafko 60.00 35.00
❑ 61 Bob Rush RC 50.00 30.00
❑ 62 Ted Kluszewski 125.00 75.00
❑ 63 Ewell Blackwell 60.00 35.00
❑ 64 Alvin Dark 60.00 35.00
❑ 65 Dave Koslo 50.00 30.00
❑ 66 Larry Jansen 60.00 35.00
❑ 67 Willie Jones 60.00 35.00
❑ 68 Curt Simmons 60.00 35.00
❑ 69 Wally Westlake 50.00 30.00
❑ 70 Bob Chesnes 50.00 30.00
❑ 71 Red Schoendienst 80.00 50.00
❑ 72 Howie Pollet 50.00 30.00
❑ 73 Willard Marshall 15.00 7.50
❑ 74 Johnny Antonelli RC 60.00 35.00
❑ 75 Roy Campanella 300.00 175.00
❑ 76 Rex Barney 40.00 20.00
❑ 77 Duke Snider 300.00 175.00
❑ 78 Mickey Owen 25.00 12.50
❑ 79 Johnny VanderMeer 40.00 20.00
❑ 80 Howard Fox RC 15.00 7.50
❑ 81 Ron Northey 15.00 7.50
❑ 82 Whitey Lockman 25.00 12.50
❑ 83 Sheldon Jones 15.00 7.50
❑ 84 Richie Ashburn 125.00 75.00
❑ 85 Ken Heintzelman 15.00 7.50
❑ 86 Stan Rojek 15.00 7.50
❑ 87 Bill Werle RC 15.00 7.50
❑ 88 Marty Marion 40.00 20.00
❑ 89 George Munger 15.00 7.50
❑ 90 Harry Brecheen 40.00 20.00
❑ 91 Cass Michaels 15.00 7.50
❑ 92 Hank Majeski 15.00 7.50
❑ 93 Gene Bearden 40.00 20.00
❑ 94 Lou Boudreau MG 60.00 35.00
❑ 95 Aaron Robinson 15.00 7.50
❑ 96 Virgil Trucks 25.00 12.50
❑ 97 Maurice McDermott RC 15.00 7.50
❑ 98 Ted Williams 1000.00 600.00
❑ 99 Billy Goodman 25.00 12.50
❑ 100 Vic Raschi 60.00 35.00
❑ 101 Bobby Brown 60.00 35.00
❑ 102 Billy Johnson 25.00 12.50
❑ 103 Eddie Joost 15.00 7.50
❑ 104 Sam Chapman 15.00 7.50
❑ 105 Bob Dillinger 15.00 7.50
❑ 106 Cliff Fannin 15.00 7.50
❑ 107 Sam Dente RC 15.00 7.50
❑ 108 Ray Scarborough 15.00 7.50
❑ 109 Sid Gordon 15.00 7.50
❑ 110 Tommy Holmes 25.00 12.50
❑ 111 Walker Cooper 15.00 7.50
❑ 112 Gil Hodges 125.00 75.00
❑ 113 Gene Hermanski 15.00 7.50

❑ 114 Wayne Terwilliger RC	15.00	7.50
❑ 115 Roy Smalley	15.00	7.50
❑ 116 Virgil Stallcup	15.00	7.50
❑ 117 Bill Rigney	15.00	7.50
❑ 118 Clint Hartung	15.00	7.50
❑ 119 Dick Sisler	25.00	12.50
❑ 120 John Thompson	15.00	7.50
❑ 121 Andy Seminick	25.00	12.50
❑ 122 Johnny Hopp	25.00	12.50
❑ 123 Dino Restelli RC	15.00	7.50
❑ 124 Clyde McCullough	15.00	7.50
❑ 125 Del Rice RC	15.00	7.50
❑ 126 Al Brazle	15.00	7.50
❑ 127 Dave Philley	15.00	7.50
❑ 128 Phil Masi	15.00	7.50
❑ 129 Joe Gordon	25.00	12.50
❑ 130 Dale Mitchell	25.00	12.50
❑ 131 Steve Gromek	15.00	7.50
❑ 132 Mickey Vernon	25.00	12.50
❑ 133 Don Kolloway	15.00	7.50
❑ 134 Paul Trout	15.00	7.50
❑ 135 Pat Mullin	15.00	7.50
❑ 136 Buddy Rosar	15.00	7.50
❑ 137 Johnny Pesky	25.00	12.50
❑ 138 Allie Reynolds	60.00	35.00
❑ 139 Johnny Mize	80.00	50.00
❑ 140 Pete Suder RC	15.00	7.50
❑ 141 Joe Coleman RC	25.00	12.50
❑ 142 Sherman Lollar RC	40.00	20.00
❑ 143 Eddie Stewart	15.00	7.50
❑ 144 Al Evans	15.00	7.50
❑ 145 Jack Graham RC	15.00	7.50
❑ 146 Floyd Baker	15.00	7.50
❑ 147 Mike Garcia RC	40.00	20.00
❑ 148 Early Wynn	80.00	50.00
❑ 149 Bob Swift	15.00	7.50
❑ 150 George Vico	15.00	7.50
❑ 151 Fred Hutchinson	25.00	12.50
❑ 152 Ellis Kinder RC	15.00	7.50
❑ 153 Walt Masterson	15.00	7.50
❑ 154 Gus Niarhos	15.00	7.50
❑ 155 Frank Shea	25.00	12.50
❑ 156 Fred Sanford	25.00	12.50
❑ 157 Mike Guerra	15.00	7.50
❑ 158 Paul Lehner	15.00	7.50
❑ 159 Joe Tipton	15.00	7.50
❑ 160 Mickey Harris	15.00	7.50
❑ 161 Sherry Robertson RC	15.00	7.50
❑ 162 Eddie Yost	25.00	12.50
❑ 163 Earl Torgeson	15.00	7.50
❑ 164 Sibby Sisti	15.00	7.50
❑ 165 Bruce Edwards	15.00	7.50
❑ 166 Joe Hatton	15.00	7.50
❑ 167 Preacher Roe	60.00	35.00
❑ 168 Bob Scheffing	15.00	7.50
❑ 169 Hank Edwards	15.00	7.50
❑ 170 Dutch Leonard	15.00	7.50
❑ 171 Harry Gumbert	15.00	7.50
❑ 172 Peanuts Lowrey	15.00	7.50
❑ 173 Lloyd Merriman RC	15.00	7.50
❑ 174 Hank Thompson RC	40.00	20.00
❑ 175 Monte Kennedy	15.00	7.50
❑ 176 Sylvester Donnelly	15.00	7.50
❑ 177 Hank Borowy	15.00	7.50
❑ 178 Ed Fitzgerald	15.00	7.50
❑ 179 Chuck Diering RC	15.00	7.50
❑ 180 Harry Walker	25.00	12.50
❑ 181 Marino Pieretti	15.00	7.50
❑ 182 Sam Zoldak	15.00	7.50
❑ 183 Mickey Haefner	15.00	7.50
❑ 184 Randy Gumpert	15.00	7.50
❑ 185 Howie Judson RC	15.00	7.50
❑ 186 Ken Keltner	25.00	12.50
❑ 187 Lou Stringer	15.00	7.50
❑ 188 Earl Johnson	15.00	7.50
❑ 189 Owen Friend RC	15.00	7.50
❑ 190 Ken Wood RC	15.00	7.50
❑ 191 Dick Starr RC	15.00	7.50
❑ 192 Bob Chipman	15.00	7.50
❑ 193 Pete Reiser	40.00	20.00
❑ 194 Billy Cox	60.00	35.00
❑ 195 Phil Cavarretta	40.00	20.00
❑ 196 Doyle Lade	15.00	7.50
❑ 197 Johnny Wyrostek	15.00	7.50
❑ 198 Danny Litwhiler	15.00	7.50
❑ 199 Jack Kramer	15.00	7.50
❑ 200 Kirby Higbe	25.00	12.50
❑ 201 Pete Castiglione RC	15.00	7.50
❑ 202 Cliff Chambers RC	15.00	7.50
❑ 203 Danny Murtaugh	25.00	12.50
❑ 204 Granny Hamner RC	40.00	20.00
❑ 205 Mike Goliat RC	15.00	7.50
❑ 206 Stan Lopata	25.00	12.50
❑ 207 Max Lanier RC	15.00	7.50
❑ 208 Jim Hearn	15.00	7.50
❑ 209 Johnny Lindell	15.00	7.50
❑ 210 Ted Gray	15.00	7.50
❑ 211 Charlie Keller	40.00	20.00
❑ 212 Jerry Priddy	15.00	7.50
❑ 213 Carl Scheib	15.00	7.50
❑ 214 Dick Fowler	15.00	7.50
❑ 215 Ed Lopat	60.00	35.00
❑ 216 Bob Porterfield	25.00	12.50
❑ 217 Casey Stengel MG	125.00	75.00
❑ 218 Cliff Mapes RC	25.00	12.50
❑ 219 Hank Bauer RC	100.00	60.00
❑ 220 Leo Durocher MG	60.00	35.00
❑ 221 Don Mueller RC	40.00	20.00
❑ 222 Bobby Morgan RC	15.00	7.50
❑ 223 Jim Russell	15.00	7.50
❑ 224 Jack Banta RC	15.00	7.50
❑ 225 Eddie Sawyer MG RC	25.00	12.50
❑ 226 Jim Konstanty RC	60.00	35.00
❑ 227 Bob Miller RC	25.00	12.50
❑ 228 Bill Nicholson	25.00	12.50
❑ 229 Frankie Frisch MG	60.00	35.00
❑ 230 Bill Serena RC	15.00	7.50
❑ 231 Preston Ward RC	15.00	7.50
❑ 232 Al Rosen RC	60.00	35.00
❑ 233 Allie Clark	15.00	7.50
❑ 234 Bobby Shantz RC	60.00	35.00
❑ 235 Harold Gilbert RC	15.00	7.50
❑ 236 Bob Cain RC	15.00	7.50
❑ 237 Bill Salkeld	15.00	7.50
❑ 238 Nippy Jones RC	15.00	7.50
❑ 239 Bill Howerton RC	15.00	7.50
❑ 240 Eddie Lake	15.00	7.50
❑ 241 Neil Berry RC	15.00	7.50
❑ 242 Dick Kryhoski	15.00	7.50
❑ 243 Johnny Groth RC	15.00	7.50
❑ 244 Dale Coogan RC	15.00	7.50
❑ 245 Al Papai RC	15.00	7.50
❑ 246 Walt Dropo RC	40.00	20.00
❑ 247 Irv Noren RC	25.00	12.50
❑ 248 Sam Jethroe RC	60.00	35.00
❑ 249 Snuffy Stirnweiss	25.00	12.50
❑ 250 Ray Coleman RC	15.00	7.50
❑ 251 Les Moss RC	15.00	7.50
❑ 252 Billy DeMars RC	60.00	35.00
❑ 252A Billy DeMars NC		

1951 Bowman

❑ COMPLETE SET (324)	20000.00	15000.00
❑ COMMON CARD (1-252)	20.00	10.00
❑ COMMON CARD (253-324)	50.00	30.00
❑ WRAPPER (1-CENT)	200.00	150.00
❑ WRAPPER (5-CENT)	250.00	200.00
❑ 1 Whitey Ford RC	2500.00	1500.00
❑ 2 Yogi Berra	400.00	250.00
❑ 3 Robin Roberts	100.00	60.00
❑ 4 Del Ennis	25.00	12.50
❑ 5 Dale Mitchell	25.00	12.50
❑ 6 Don Newcombe	60.00	35.00
❑ 7 Gil Hodges	125.00	75.00
❑ 8 Paul Lehner	20.00	10.00
❑ 9 Sam Chapman	20.00	10.00
❑ 10 Red Schoendienst	60.00	35.00
❑ 11 George Munger	20.00	10.00
❑ 12 Hank Majeski	20.00	10.00
❑ 13 Eddie Stanky	25.00	12.50
❑ 14 Alvin Dark	40.00	20.00
❑ 15 Johnny Pesky	25.00	12.50
❑ 16 Maurice McDermott	20.00	10.00
❑ 17 Pete Castiglione	20.00	10.00
❑ 18 Gil Coan	20.00	10.00
❑ 19 Sid Gordon	20.00	10.00
❑ 20 Del Crandall UER	25.00	12.50
❑ 21 Snuffy Stirnweiss	25.00	12.50
❑ 22 Hank Sauer	25.00	12.50
❑ 23 Hoot Evers	20.00	10.00
❑ 24 Ewell Blackwell	40.00	20.00
❑ 25 Vic Raschi	60.00	35.00
❑ 26 Phil Rizzuto	150.00	90.00
❑ 27 Jim Konstanty	25.00	12.50
❑ 28 Eddie Waitkus	20.00	10.00
❑ 29 Allie Clark	20.00	10.00
❑ 30 Bob Feller	125.00	75.00
❑ 31 Roy Campanella	300.00	175.00
❑ 32 Duke Snider	250.00	150.00
❑ 33 Bob Hooper RC	20.00	10.00
❑ 34 Marty Marion MG	40.00	20.00
❑ 35 Al Zarilla	20.00	10.00
❑ 36 Joe Dobson	20.00	10.00
❑ 37 Whitey Lockman	40.00	20.00
❑ 38 Al Evans	20.00	10.00
❑ 39 Ray Scarborough	20.00	10.00
❑ 40 Gus Bell RC	60.00	35.00
❑ 41 Eddie Yost	25.00	12.50
❑ 42 Vern Bickford	20.00	10.00
❑ 43 Billy DeMars	20.00	10.00
❑ 44 Roy Smalley	20.00	10.00
❑ 45 Art Houtteman	20.00	10.00
❑ 46 George Kell UER	60.00	35.00
❑ 47 Grady Hatton	20.00	10.00
❑ 48 Ken Raffensberger	20.00	10.00
❑ 49 Jerry Coleman	25.00	12.50
❑ 50 Johnny Mize	80.00	50.00
❑ 51 Andy Seminick	20.00	10.00
❑ 52 Dick Sisler	40.00	20.00
❑ 53 Bob Lemon	60.00	35.00
❑ 54 Ray Boone RC	40.00	20.00
❑ 55 Gene Hermanski	20.00	10.00
❑ 56 Ralph Branca	60.00	35.00
❑ 57 Alex Kellner	20.00	10.00
❑ 58 Enos Slaughter	60.00	35.00
❑ 59 Randy Gumpert	20.00	10.00
❑ 60 Chico Carrasquel RC	60.00	35.00
❑ 61 Jim Hearn	25.00	12.50
❑ 62 Lou Boudreau MG	60.00	35.00
❑ 63 Bob Dillinger	20.00	10.00
❑ 64 Bill Werle	20.00	10.00
❑ 65 Mickey Vernon	40.00	20.00
❑ 66 Bob Elliott	25.00	12.50
❑ 67 Roy Sievers	25.00	12.50
❑ 68 Dick Kokos	20.00	10.00
❑ 69 Johnny Schmitz	20.00	10.00
❑ 70 Ron Northey	20.00	10.00
❑ 71 Jerry Priddy	20.00	10.00
❑ 72 Lloyd Merriman	20.00	10.00
❑ 73 Tommy Byrne RC	20.00	10.00
❑ 74 Billy Johnson	25.00	12.50
❑ 75 Russ Meyer RC	25.00	12.50
❑ 76 Stan Lopata	25.00	12.50
❑ 77 Mike Goliat	20.00	10.00
❑ 78 Early Wynn	60.00	35.00
❑ 79 Jim Hegan	25.00	12.50
❑ 80 Pee Wee Reese	200.00	125.00
❑ 81 Carl Furillo	60.00	35.00
❑ 82 Joe Tipton	20.00	10.00
❑ 83 Carl Scheib	20.00	10.00
❑ 84 Barney McCosky	20.00	10.00
❑ 85 Eddie Kazak	20.00	10.00
❑ 86 Harry Brecheen	25.00	12.50
❑ 87 Floyd Baker	20.00	10.00
❑ 88 Eddie Robinson	20.00	10.00
❑ 89 Hank Thompson	25.00	12.50
❑ 90 Dave Koslo	20.00	10.00
❑ 91 Clyde Vollmer	20.00	10.00
❑ 92 Vern Stephens	25.00	12.50

❑ 93	Danny O'Connell RC	20.00	10.00
❑ 94	Clyde McCullough	20.00	10.00
❑ 95	Sherry Robertson	20.00	10.00
❑ 96	Sandy Consuegra RC	20.00	10.00
❑ 97	Bob Kuzava	20.00	10.00
❑ 98	Willard Marshall	20.00	10.00
❑ 99	Earl Torgeson	20.00	10.00
❑ 100	Sherm Lollar	25.00	12.50
❑ 101	Owen Friend	20.00	10.00
❑ 102	Dutch Leonard	20.00	10.00
❑ 103	Andy Pafko	40.00	20.00
❑ 104	Virgil Trucks	25.00	12.50
❑ 105	Don Kolloway	20.00	10.00
❑ 106	Pat Mullin	20.00	10.00
❑ 107	Johnny Wyrostek	20.00	10.00
❑ 108	Virgil Stallcup	20.00	10.00
❑ 109	Allie Reynolds	60.00	35.00
❑ 110	Bobby Brown	40.00	20.00
❑ 111	Curt Simmons	25.00	12.50
❑ 112	Willie Jones	20.00	10.00
❑ 113	Bill Nicholson	20.00	10.00
❑ 114	Sam Zoldak	20.00	10.00
❑ 115	Steve Gromek	20.00	10.00
❑ 116	Bruce Edwards	20.00	10.00
❑ 117	Eddie Miksis RC	20.00	10.00
❑ 118	Preacher Roe	60.00	35.00
❑ 119	Eddie Joost	20.00	10.00
❑ 120	Joe Coleman	25.00	12.50
❑ 121	Gerry Staley RC	20.00	10.00
❑ 122	Joe Garagiola RC	100.00	60.00
❑ 123	Howie Judson	20.00	10.00
❑ 124	Gus Niarhos	20.00	10.00
❑ 125	Bill Rigney	25.00	12.50
❑ 126	Bobby Thomson	60.00	35.00
❑ 127	Sal Maglie RC	60.00	35.00
❑ 128	Ellis Kinder	20.00	10.00
❑ 129	Matt Batts	20.00	10.00
❑ 130	Tom Saffell RC	20.00	10.00
❑ 131	Cliff Chambers	20.00	10.00
❑ 132	Cass Michaels	20.00	10.00
❑ 133	Sam Dente	20.00	10.00
❑ 134	Warren Spahn	150.00	90.00
❑ 135	Walker Cooper	20.00	10.00
❑ 136	Ray Coleman	20.00	10.00
❑ 137	Dick Starr	20.00	10.00
❑ 138	Phil Cavarretta	25.00	12.50
❑ 139	Doyle Lade	20.00	10.00
❑ 140	Eddie Lake	20.00	10.00
❑ 141	Fred Hutchinson	25.00	12.50
❑ 142	Aaron Robinson	20.00	10.00
❑ 143	Ted Kluszewski	80.00	50.00
❑ 144	Herman Wehmeier	20.00	10.00
❑ 145	Fred Sanford	25.00	12.50
❑ 146	Johnny Hopp	25.00	12.50
❑ 147	Ken Heintzelman	20.00	10.00
❑ 148	Granny Hamner	20.00	10.00
❑ 149	Bubba Church RC	20.00	10.00
❑ 150	Mike Garcia	25.00	12.50
❑ 151	Larry Doby	60.00	35.00
❑ 152	Cal Abrams RC	20.00	10.00
❑ 153	Rex Barney	25.00	12.50
❑ 154	Pete Suder	20.00	10.00
❑ 155	Lou Brissie	20.00	10.00
❑ 156	Del Rice	20.00	10.00
❑ 157	Al Brazle	20.00	10.00
❑ 158	Chuck Diering	20.00	10.00
❑ 159	Eddie Stewart	20.00	10.00
❑ 160	Phil Masi	20.00	10.00
❑ 161	Wes Westrum RC	20.00	10.00
❑ 162	Larry Jansen	25.00	12.50
❑ 163	Monte Kennedy	20.00	10.00
❑ 164	Bill Wight	20.00	10.00
❑ 165	Ted Williams UER	800.00	500.00
❑ 166	Stan Rojek	20.00	10.00
❑ 167	Murry Dickson	20.00	10.00
❑ 168	Sam Mele	20.00	10.00
❑ 169	Sid Hudson	20.00	10.00
❑ 170	Sibby Sisti	20.00	10.00
❑ 171	Buddy Kerr	20.00	10.00
❑ 172	Ned Garver	20.00	10.00
❑ 173	Hank Arft	20.00	10.00
❑ 174	Mickey Owen	25.00	12.50
❑ 175	Wayne Terwilliger	20.00	10.00
❑ 176	Vic Wertz	40.00	20.00
❑ 177	Charlie Keller	25.00	12.50
❑ 178	Ted Gray	20.00	10.00
❑ 179	Danny Litwhiler	20.00	10.00
❑ 180	Howie Fox	20.00	10.00
❑ 181	Casey Stengel MG	80.00	50.00
❑ 182	Tom Ferrick RC	20.00	10.00
❑ 183	Hank Bauer	60.00	35.00
❑ 184	Eddie Sawyer MG	40.00	20.00
❑ 185	Jimmy Bloodworth	20.00	10.00
❑ 186	Richie Ashburn	100.00	60.00
❑ 187	Al Rosen	40.00	20.00
❑ 188	Bobby Avila RC	25.00	12.50
❑ 189	Erv Palica RC	20.00	10.00
❑ 190	Joe Hatten	20.00	10.00
❑ 191	Billy Hitchcock RC	20.00	10.00
❑ 192	Hank Wyse RC	20.00	10.00
❑ 193	Ted Wilks	20.00	10.00
❑ 194	Peanuts Lowrey	20.00	10.00
❑ 195	Paul Richards MG	25.00	12.50
❑ 196	Billy Pierce RC	60.00	35.00
❑ 197	Bob Cain	20.00	10.00
❑ 198	Monte Irvin RC	125.00	75.00
❑ 199	Sheldon Jones	20.00	10.00
❑ 200	Jack Kramer	20.00	10.00
❑ 201	Steve O'Neill MG RC	20.00	10.00
❑ 202	Mike Guerra	20.00	10.00
❑ 203	Vern Law RC	60.00	35.00
❑ 204	Vic Lombardi RC	20.00	10.00
❑ 205	Mickey Grasso RC	20.00	10.00
❑ 206	Conrado Marrero RC	20.00	10.00
❑ 207	Billy Southworth MG RC	20.00	10.00
❑ 208	Blix Donnelly	20.00	10.00
❑ 209	Ken Wood	20.00	10.00
❑ 210	Les Moss	20.00	10.00
❑ 211	Hal Jeffcoat RC	20.00	10.00
❑ 212	Bob Rush	20.00	10.00
❑ 213	Neil Berry	20.00	10.00
❑ 214	Bob Swift	20.00	10.00
❑ 215	Ken Peterson	20.00	10.00
❑ 216	Connie Ryan RC	20.00	10.00
❑ 217	Joe Page	25.00	12.50
❑ 218	Ed Lopat	60.00	35.00
❑ 219	Gene Woodling RC	60.00	35.00
❑ 220	Bob Miller	20.00	10.00
❑ 221	Dick Whitman RC	20.00	10.00
❑ 222	Thurman Tucker RC	20.00	10.00
❑ 223	Johnny VanderMeer	40.00	20.00
❑ 224	Billy Cox	25.00	12.50
❑ 225	Dan Bankhead RC	40.00	20.00
❑ 226	Jimmie Dykes MG	20.00	10.00
❑ 227	Bobby Shantz UER	25.00	12.50
❑ 228	Cloyd Boyer RC	25.00	12.50
❑ 229	Bill Howerton	20.00	10.00
❑ 230	Max Lanier	20.00	10.00
❑ 231	Luis Aloma RC	20.00	10.00
❑ 232	Nellie Fox RC	250.00	150.00
❑ 233	Leo Durocher MG	60.00	35.00
❑ 234	Clint Hartung	25.00	12.50
❑ 235	Jack Lohrke	20.00	10.00
❑ 236	Buddy Rosar	20.00	10.00
❑ 237	Billy Goodman	25.00	12.50
❑ 238	Pete Reiser	40.00	20.00
❑ 239	Bill MacDonald RC	20.00	10.00
❑ 240	Joe Haynes	20.00	10.00
❑ 241	Irv Noren	25.00	12.50
❑ 242	Sam Jethroe	25.00	12.50
❑ 243	Johnny Antonelli	25.00	12.50
❑ 244	Cliff Fannin	20.00	10.00
❑ 245	John Berardino RC	60.00	35.00
❑ 246	Bill Serena	20.00	10.00
❑ 247	Bob Ramazzotti RC	20.00	10.00
❑ 248	Johnny Klippstein RC	20.00	10.00
❑ 249	Johnny Groth	20.00	10.00
❑ 250	Hank Borowy	20.00	10.00
❑ 251	Willard Ramsdell RC	20.00	10.00
❑ 252	Dixie Howell RC	20.00	10.00
❑ 253	Mickey Mantle RC	8000.00	5000.00
❑ 254	Jackie Jensen RC	100.00	60.00
❑ 255	Milo Candini RC	50.00	30.00
❑ 256	Ken Silvestri RC	50.00	30.00
❑ 257	Birdie Tebbetts RC	60.00	35.00
❑ 258	Luke Easter RC	60.00	35.00
❑ 259	Chuck Dressen MG	60.00	35.00
❑ 260	Carl Erskine RC	100.00	60.00
❑ 261	Wally Moses	60.00	35.00
❑ 262	Gus Zernial	60.00	35.00
❑ 263	Howie Pollet	60.00	35.00
❑ 264	Don Richmond RC	50.00	30.00
❑ 265	Steve Bilko RC	50.00	30.00
❑ 266	Harry Dorish RC	50.00	30.00
❑ 267	Ken Holcombe RC	50.00	30.00
❑ 268	Don Mueller	60.00	35.00
❑ 269	Ray Noble RC	50.00	30.00
❑ 270	Willard Nixon RC	50.00	30.00
❑ 271	Tommy Wright RC	50.00	30.00
❑ 272	Billy Meyer MG RC	50.00	30.00
❑ 273	Danny Murtaugh	60.00	35.00
❑ 274	George Metkovich RC	50.00	30.00
❑ 275	Bucky Harris MG	80.00	50.00
❑ 276	Frank Quinn RC	50.00	30.00
❑ 277	Roy Hartsfield RC	50.00	30.00
❑ 278	Norman Roy RC	50.00	30.00
❑ 279	Jim Delsing RC	50.00	30.00
❑ 280	Frank Overmire	50.00	30.00
❑ 281	Al Widmar RC	50.00	30.00
❑ 282	Frankie Frisch MG	100.00	60.00
❑ 283	Walt Dubiel RC	50.00	30.00
❑ 284	Gene Bearden	60.00	35.00
❑ 285	Johnny Lipon RC	50.00	30.00
❑ 286	Bob Usher RC	50.00	30.00
❑ 287	Jim Blackburn	50.00	30.00
❑ 288	Bobby Adams	50.00	30.00
❑ 289	Cliff Mapes	60.00	35.00
❑ 290	Bill Dickey CO	150.00	90.00
❑ 291	Tommy Henrich CO	80.00	50.00
❑ 292	Eddie Pellagrini	50.00	30.00
❑ 293	Ken Johnson RC	50.00	30.00
❑ 294	Jocko Thompson	50.00	30.00
❑ 295	Al Lopez MG RC	125.00	75.00
❑ 296	Bob Kennedy RC	60.00	35.00
❑ 297	Dave Philley	50.00	30.00
❑ 298	Joe Astroth RC	50.00	30.00
❑ 299	Clyde King RC	50.00	30.00
❑ 300	Hal Rice RC	50.00	30.00
❑ 301	Tommy Glaviano RC	50.00	30.00
❑ 302	Jim Busby RC	50.00	30.00
❑ 303	Marv Rotblatt RC	50.00	30.00
❑ 304	Al Gettell RC	50.00	30.00
❑ 305	Willie Mays RC	2500.00	1800.00
❑ 306	Jimmy Piersall RC	125.00	75.00
❑ 307	Walt Masterson	50.00	30.00
❑ 308	Ted Beard RC	50.00	30.00
❑ 309	Mel Queen RC	50.00	30.00
❑ 310	Erv Dusak RC	50.00	30.00
❑ 311	Mickey Harris	50.00	30.00
❑ 312	Gene Mauch RC	60.00	35.00
❑ 313	Ray Mueller RC	50.00	30.00
❑ 314	Johnny Sain	80.00	50.00
❑ 315	Zack Taylor MG	50.00	30.00
❑ 316	Duane Pillette RC	50.00	30.00
❑ 317	Smoky Burgess RC	80.00	50.00
❑ 318	Warren Hacker RC	50.00	30.00
❑ 319	Red Rolfe MG	60.00	35.00
❑ 320	Hal White RC	50.00	30.00
❑ 321	Earl Johnson	50.00	30.00
❑ 322	Luke Sewell MG	60.00	35.00
❑ 323	Joe Adcock RC	80.00	50.00
❑ 324	Johnny Pramesa RC	125.00	75.00

1952 Bowman

❑ COMPLETE SET (252)	8500.00	5500.00
❑ COMMON CARD (1-216)	15.00	7.50
❑ COMMON CARD (217-252)	60.00	35.00
❑ WRAPPER (1-CENT)	200.00	150.00
❑ WRAPPER (5-CENT)	100.00	75.00
❑ 1 Yogi Berra	600.00	350.00

❑ 2 Bobby Thomson 40.00 20.00
❑ 3 Fred Hutchinson 25.00 12.50
❑ 4 Robin Roberts 80.00 50.00
❑ 5 Minnie Minoso RC 125.00 75.00
❑ 6 Virgil Stallcup 15.00 7.50
❑ 7 Mike Garcia 25.00 12.50
❑ 8 Pee Wee Reese 150.00 90.00
❑ 9 Vern Stephens 25.00 12.50
❑ 10 Bob Hooper 15.00 7.50
❑ 11 Ralph Kiner 60.00 35.00
❑ 12 Max Surkont RC 15.00 7.50
❑ 13 Cliff Mapes 15.00 7.50
❑ 14 Cliff Chambers 15.00 7.50
❑ 15 Sam Mele 15.00 7.50
❑ 16 Turk Lown RC 15.00 7.50
❑ 17 Ed Lopat 40.00 20.00
❑ 18 Don Mueller 25.00 12.50
❑ 19 Bob Cain 15.00 7.50
❑ 20 Willie Jones 15.00 7.50
❑ 21 Nellie Fox 100.00 60.00
❑ 22 Willard Ramsdell 15.00 7.50
❑ 23 Bob Lemon 60.00 35.00
❑ 24 Carl Furillo 40.00 20.00
❑ 25 Mickey McDermott 15.00 7.50
❑ 26 Eddie Joost 15.00 7.50
❑ 27 Joe Garagiola 40.00 20.00
❑ 28 Roy Hartsfield 15.00 7.50
❑ 29 Ned Garver 15.00 7.50
❑ 30 Red Schoendienst 60.00 35.00
❑ 31 Eddie Yost 25.00 12.50
❑ 32 Eddie Miksis 15.00 7.50
❑ 33 Gil McDougald RC 80.00 50.00
❑ 34 Alvin Dark 25.00 12.50
❑ 35 Granny Hamner 15.00 7.50
❑ 36 Cass Michaels 15.00 7.50
❑ 37 Vic Raschi 25.00 12.50
❑ 38 Whitey Lockman 25.00 12.50
❑ 39 Vic Wertz 25.00 12.50
❑ 40 Bubba Church 15.00 7.50
❑ 41 Chico Carrasquel 25.00 12.50
❑ 42 Johnny Wyrostek 15.00 7.50
❑ 43 Bob Feller 150.00 90.00
❑ 44 Roy Campanella 250.00 150.00
❑ 45 Johnny Pesky 25.00 12.50
❑ 46 Carl Scheib 15.00 7.50
❑ 47 Pete Castiglione 15.00 7.50
❑ 48 Vern Bickford 15.00 7.50
❑ 49 Jim Hearn 15.00 7.50
❑ 50 Gerry Staley 15.00 7.50
❑ 51 Gil Coan 15.00 7.50
❑ 52 Phil Rizzuto 150.00 90.00
❑ 53 Richie Ashburn 125.00 75.00
❑ 54 Billy Pierce 25.00 12.50
❑ 55 Ken Raffensberger 15.00 7.50
❑ 56 Clyde King 25.00 12.50
❑ 57 Clyde Vollmer 15.00 7.50
❑ 58 Hank Majeski 15.00 7.50
❑ 59 Murry Dickson 15.00 7.50
❑ 60 Sid Gordon 15.00 7.50
❑ 61 Tommy Byrne 15.00 7.50
❑ 62 Joe Presko RC 15.00 7.50
❑ 63 Irv Noren 15.00 7.50
❑ 64 Roy Smalley 15.00 7.50
❑ 65 Hank Bauer 40.00 20.00
❑ 66 Sal Maglie 25.00 12.50
❑ 67 Johnny Groth 15.00 7.50
❑ 68 Jim Busby 15.00 7.50
❑ 69 Joe Adcock 25.00 12.50
❑ 70 Carl Erskine 40.00 20.00
❑ 71 Vern Law 25.00 12.50
❑ 72 Earl Torgeson 15.00 7.50
❑ 73 Jerry Coleman 25.00 12.50
❑ 74 Wes Westrum 25.00 12.50
❑ 75 George Kell 60.00 35.00
❑ 76 Del Ennis 25.00 12.50
❑ 77 Eddie Robinson 15.00 7.50
❑ 78 Lloyd Merriman 15.00 7.50
❑ 79 Lou Brissie 15.00 7.50
❑ 80 Gil Hodges 100.00 60.00
❑ 81 Billy Goodman 25.00 12.50
❑ 82 Gus Zernial 25.00 12.50
❑ 83 Howie Pollet 15.00 7.50
❑ 84 Sam Jethroe 25.00 12.50
❑ 85 Marty Marion CO 25.00 12.50
❑ 86 Cal Abrams 15.00 7.50
❑ 87 Mickey Vernon 25.00 12.50
❑ 88 Bruce Edwards 15.00 7.50
❑ 89 Billy Hitchcock 15.00 7.50
❑ 90 Larry Jansen 25.00 12.50
❑ 91 Don Kolloway 15.00 7.50
❑ 92 Eddie Waitkus 25.00 12.50
❑ 93 Paul Richards MG 25.00 12.50
❑ 94 Luke Sewell MG 25.00 12.50
❑ 95 Luke Easter 25.00 12.50
❑ 96 Ralph Branca 25.00 12.50
❑ 97 Willard Marshall 15.00 7.50
❑ 98 Jimmie Dykes MG 25.00 12.50
❑ 99 Clyde McCullough 15.00 7.50
❑ 100 Sibby Sisti 15.00 7.50
❑ 101 Mickey Mantle 2500.00 1500.00
❑ 102 Peanuts Lowrey 15.00 7.50
❑ 103 Joe Haynes 15.00 7.50
❑ 104 Hal Jeffcoat 15.00 7.50
❑ 105 Bobby Brown 25.00 12.50
❑ 106 Randy Gumpert 15.00 7.50
❑ 107 Del Rice 15.00 7.50
❑ 108 George Metkovich 15.00 7.50
❑ 109 Tom Morgan RC 15.00 7.50
❑ 110 Max Lanier 15.00 7.50
❑ 111 Hoot Evers 15.00 7.50
❑ 112 Smoky Burgess 25.00 12.50
❑ 113 Al Zarilla 15.00 7.50
❑ 114 Frank Hiller RC 15.00 7.50
❑ 115 Larry Doby 60.00 35.00
❑ 116 Duke Snider 200.00 125.00
❑ 117 Bill Wight 15.00 7.50
❑ 118 Ray Murray RC 15.00 7.50
❑ 119 Bill Howerton 15.00 7.50
❑ 120 Chet Nichols RC 15.00 7.50
❑ 121 Al Corwin RC 15.00 7.50
❑ 122 Billy Johnson 15.00 7.50
❑ 123 Sid Hudson 15.00 7.50
❑ 124 Birdie Tebbetts 15.00 7.50
❑ 125 Howie Fox 15.00 7.50
❑ 126 Phil Cavarretta 25.00 12.50
❑ 127 Dick Sisler 15.00 7.50
❑ 128 Don Newcombe 60.00 35.00
❑ 129 Gus Niarhos 15.00 7.50
❑ 130 Allie Clark 15.00 7.50
❑ 131 Bob Swift 15.00 7.50
❑ 132 Dave Cole RC 15.00 7.50
❑ 133 Dick Kryhoski 15.00 7.50
❑ 134 Al Brazle 15.00 7.50
❑ 135 Mickey Harris 15.00 7.50
❑ 136 Gene Hermanski 15.00 7.50
❑ 137 Stan Rojek 15.00 7.50
❑ 138 Ted Wilks 15.00 7.50
❑ 139 Jerry Priddy 15.00 7.50
❑ 140 Ray Scarborough 15.00 7.50
❑ 141 Hank Edwards 15.00 7.50
❑ 142 Early Wynn 60.00 35.00
❑ 143 Sandy Consuegra 15.00 7.50
❑ 144 Joe Hatton 15.00 7.50
❑ 145 Johnny Mize 60.00 35.00
❑ 146 Leo Durocher MG 60.00 35.00
❑ 147 Marlin Stuart RC 15.00 7.50
❑ 148 Ken Heintzelman 15.00 7.50
❑ 149 Howie Judson 15.00 7.50
❑ 150 Herman Wehmeier 15.00 7.50
❑ 151 Al Rosen 25.00 12.50
❑ 152 Billy Cox 15.00 7.50
❑ 153 Fred Hatfield RC 15.00 7.50
❑ 154 Ferris Fain 25.00 12.50
❑ 155 Billy Meyer MG 15.00 7.50
❑ 156 Warren Spahn 125.00 75.00
❑ 157 Jim Delsing 15.00 7.50
❑ 158 Bucky Harris MG 40.00 20.00
❑ 159 Dutch Leonard 15.00 7.50
❑ 160 Eddie Stanky 25.00 12.50
❑ 161 Jackie Jensen 40.00 20.00
❑ 162 Monte Irvin 60.00 35.00
❑ 163 Johnny Lipon 15.00 7.50
❑ 164 Connie Ryan 15.00 7.50
❑ 165 Saul Rogovin RC 15.00 7.50
❑ 166 Bobby Adams 15.00 7.50
❑ 167 Bobby Avila 25.00 12.50
❑ 168 Preacher Roe 25.00 12.50
❑ 169 Walt Dropo 25.00 12.50
❑ 170 Joe Astroth 15.00 7.50
❑ 171 Mel Queen 15.00 7.50
❑ 172 Ebba St.Claire RC 15.00 7.50
❑ 173 Gene Bearden 15.00 7.50
❑ 174 Mickey Grasso 15.00 7.50
❑ 175 Randy Jackson RC 15.00 7.50
❑ 176 Harry Brecheen 25.00 12.50
❑ 177 Gene Woodling 25.00 12.50
❑ 178 Dave Williams RC 25.00 12.50
❑ 179 Pete Suder 15.00 7.50
❑ 180 Ed Fitzgerald 15.00 7.50
❑ 181 Joe Collins RC 25.00 12.50
❑ 182 Dave Koslo 15.00 7.50
❑ 183 Pat Mullin 15.00 7.50
❑ 184 Curt Simmons 25.00 12.50
❑ 185 Eddie Stewart 15.00 7.50
❑ 186 Frank Smith RC 15.00 7.50
❑ 187 Jim Hegan 25.00 12.50
❑ 188 Chuck Dressen MG 25.00 12.50
❑ 189 Jimmy Piersall 25.00 12.50
❑ 190 Dick Fowler 15.00 7.50
❑ 191 Bob Friend RC 40.00 20.00
❑ 192 John Cusick RC 15.00 7.50
❑ 193 Bobby Young RC 15.00 7.50
❑ 194 Bob Porterfield 15.00 7.50
❑ 195 Frank Baumholtz 15.00 7.50
❑ 196 Stan Musial 500.00 300.00
❑ 197 Charlie Silvera RC 15.00 7.50
❑ 198 Chuck Diering 15.00 7.50
❑ 199 Ted Gray 15.00 7.50
❑ 200 Ken Silvestri 15.00 7.50
❑ 201 Ray Coleman 15.00 7.50
❑ 202 Harry Perkowski RC 15.00 7.50
❑ 203 Steve Gromek 15.00 7.50
❑ 204 Andy Pafko 25.00 12.50
❑ 205 Walt Masterson 15.00 7.50
❑ 206 Elmer Valo 15.00 7.50
❑ 207 George Strickland RC 15.00 7.50
❑ 208 Walker Cooper 15.00 7.50
❑ 209 Dick Littlefield RC 15.00 7.50
❑ 210 Archie Wilson RC 15.00 7.50
❑ 211 Paul Minner RC 15.00 7.50
❑ 212 Solly Hemus RC 15.00 7.50
❑ 213 Monte Kennedy 15.00 7.50
❑ 214 Ray Boone 15.00 7.50
❑ 215 Sheldon Jones 15.00 7.50
❑ 216 Matt Batts 15.00 7.50
❑ 217 Casey Stengel MG 150.00 90.00
❑ 218 Willie Mays 1500.00 900.00
❑ 219 Neil Berry 60.00 35.00
❑ 220 Russ Meyer 60.00 35.00
❑ 221 Lou Kretlow RC 60.00 35.00
❑ 222 Dixie Howell 60.00 35.00
❑ 223 Harry Simpson RC 60.00 35.00
❑ 224 Johnny Schmitz 60.00 35.00
❑ 225 Del Wilber RC 60.00 35.00
❑ 226 Alex Kellner 60.00 35.00
❑ 227 Clyde Sukeforth CO RC 60.00 35.00
❑ 228 Bob Chipman 60.00 35.00
❑ 229 Hank Arft 60.00 35.00
❑ 230 Frank Shea 60.00 35.00
❑ 231 Dee Fondy RC 60.00 35.00
❑ 232 Enos Slaughter 100.00 60.00
❑ 233 Bob Kuzava 60.00 35.00
❑ 234 Fred Fitzsimmons CO 60.00 35.00
❑ 235 Steve Souchock RC 60.00 35.00
❑ 236 Tommy Brown 60.00 35.00
❑ 237 Sherm Lollar 60.00 35.00
❑ 238 Roy McMillan RC 60.00 35.00
❑ 239 Dale Mitchell 60.00 35.00
❑ 240 Billy Loes RC 60.00 35.00
❑ 241 Mel Parnell 60.00 35.00
❑ 242 Everett Kell RC 60.00 35.00
❑ 243 George Munger 60.00 35.00
❑ 244 Lew Burdette RC 80.00 50.00
❑ 245 George Schmees RC 60.00 35.00
❑ 246 Jerry Snyder RC 60.00 35.00
❑ 247 Johnny Pramesa 60.00 35.00
❑ 248 Bill Werle Full Name 60.00 35.00
❑ 248A Bill Werle No W 60.00 35.00
❑ 249 Hank Thompson 60.00 35.00
❑ 250 Ike Delock RC 60.00 35.00
❑ 251 Jack Lohrke 60.00 35.00
❑ 252 Frank Crosetti CO 125.00 75.00

1953 Bowman Black and White

❑ COMPLETE SET (64)	3000.00	2000.00
❑ WRAPPER (1-CENT)	350.00	300.00
❑ 1 Gus Bell	125.00	75.00
❑ 2 Willard Nixon	40.00	25.00
❑ 3 Bill Rigney	40.00	25.00
❑ 4 Pat Mullin	40.00	25.00
❑ 5 Dee Fondy	40.00	25.00
❑ 6 Ray Murray	40.00	25.00
❑ 7 Andy Seminick	40.00	25.00
❑ 8 Pete Suder	40.00	25.00
❑ 9 Walt Masterson	40.00	25.00
❑ 10 Dick Sisler	60.00	35.00
❑ 11 Dick Gernert	40.00	25.00
❑ 12 Randy Jackson	40.00	25.00
❑ 13 Joe Tipton	40.00	25.00
❑ 14 Bill Nicholson	60.00	35.00
❑ 15 Johnny Mize	125.00	75.00
❑ 16 Stu Miller RC	60.00	35.00
❑ 17 Virgil Trucks	60.00	35.00
❑ 18 Billy Hoeft	40.00	25.00
❑ 19 Paul LaPalme	40.00	25.00
❑ 20 Eddie Robinson	40.00	25.00
❑ 21 Clarence Podbielan	40.00	25.00
❑ 22 Matt Batts	40.00	25.00
❑ 23 Wilmer Mizell	60.00	35.00
❑ 24 Del Wilber	40.00	25.00
❑ 25 Johnny Sain	80.00	50.00
❑ 26 Preacher Roe	80.00	50.00
❑ 27 Bob Lemon	175.00	100.00
❑ 28 Hoyt Wilhelm	125.00	75.00
❑ 29 Sid Hudson	40.00	25.00
❑ 30 Walker Cooper	40.00	25.00
❑ 31 Gene Woodling	80.00	50.00
❑ 32 Rocky Bridges	40.00	25.00
❑ 33 Bob Kuzava	40.00	25.00
❑ 34 Ebba St.Claire	40.00	25.00
❑ 35 Johnny Wyrostek	40.00	25.00
❑ 36 Jimmy Piersall	80.00	50.00
❑ 37 Hal Jeffcoat	40.00	25.00
❑ 38 Dave Cole	40.00	25.00
❑ 39 Casey Stengel MG	350.00	200.00
❑ 40 Larry Jansen	60.00	35.00
❑ 41 Bob Ramazzotti	40.00	25.00
❑ 42 Howie Judson	40.00	25.00
❑ 43 Hal Bevan ERR RC	40.00	25.00
❑ 43A Hal Bevan COR	40.00	25.00
❑ 44 Jim Delsing	40.00	25.00
❑ 45 Irv Noren	60.00	35.00
❑ 46 Bucky Harris MG	80.00	50.00
❑ 47 Jack Lohrke	40.00	25.00
❑ 48 Steve Ridzik RC	40.00	25.00
❑ 49 Floyd Baker	40.00	25.00
❑ 50 Dutch Leonard	40.00	25.00
❑ 51 Lew Burdette	80.00	50.00
❑ 52 Ralph Branca	80.00	50.00
❑ 53 Morrie Martin	40.00	25.00
❑ 54 Bill Miller	40.00	25.00
❑ 55 Don Johnson	40.00	25.00
❑ 56 Roy Smalley	40.00	25.00
❑ 57 Andy Pafko	60.00	35.00
❑ 58 Jim Konstanty	60.00	35.00
❑ 59 Duane Pillette	40.00	25.00
❑ 60 Billy Cox	80.00	50.00
❑ 61 Tom Gorman RC	40.00	25.00
❑ 62 Keith Thomas RC	40.00	25.00
❑ 63 Steve Gromek	40.00	25.00
❑ 64 Andy Hansen	80.00	50.00

1953 Bowman Color

❑ COMPLETE SET (160)	15000.00	9000.00
❑ COMMON CARD (1-112)	40.00	20.00
❑ COMMON CARD (113-128)	80.00	50.00
❑ COMMON CARD (129-160)	75.00	45.00
❑ WRAPPER (1-CENT)	400.00	300.00
❑ WRAPPER (5-CENT)	300.00	250.00
❑ 1 Davey Williams	175.00	100.00
❑ 2 Vic Wertz	50.00	30.00
❑ 3 Sam Jethroe	50.00	30.00
❑ 4 Art Houtteman	40.00	20.00
❑ 5 Sid Gordon	40.00	20.00
❑ 6 Joe Ginsberg	40.00	20.00
❑ 7 Harry Chiti RC	40.00	20.00
❑ 8 Al Rosen	50.00	30.00
❑ 9 Phil Rizzuto	225.00	150.00
❑ 10 Richie Ashburn	150.00	90.00
❑ 11 Bobby Shantz	50.00	30.00
❑ 12 Carl Erskine	60.00	35.00
❑ 13 Gus Zernial	50.00	30.00
❑ 14 Billy Loes	50.00	30.00
❑ 15 Jim Busby	40.00	20.00
❑ 16 Bob Friend	50.00	30.00
❑ 17 Gerry Staley	40.00	20.00
❑ 18 Nellie Fox	150.00	90.00
❑ 19 Alvin Dark	50.00	30.00
❑ 20 Don Lenhardt	40.00	20.00
❑ 21 Joe Garagiola	60.00	35.00
❑ 22 Bob Porterfield	40.00	20.00
❑ 23 Herman Wehmeier	40.00	20.00
❑ 24 Jackie Jensen	60.00	35.00
❑ 25 Hoot Evers	40.00	20.00
❑ 26 Roy McMillan	50.00	30.00
❑ 27 Vic Raschi	60.00	35.00
❑ 28 Smoky Burgess	50.00	30.00
❑ 29 Bobby Avila	50.00	30.00
❑ 30 Phil Cavarretta	50.00	30.00
❑ 31 Jimmy Dykes MG	50.00	30.00
❑ 32 Stan Musial	600.00	350.00
❑ 33 Pee Wee Reese	1000.00	500.00
❑ 34 Gil Coan	40.00	20.00
❑ 35 Maurice McDermott	40.00	20.00
❑ 36 Minnie Minoso	80.00	50.00
❑ 37 Jim Wilson	40.00	20.00
❑ 38 Harry Byrd RC	40.00	20.00
❑ 39 Paul Richards MG	50.00	30.00
❑ 40 Larry Doby	100.00	60.00
❑ 41 Sammy White	40.00	20.00
❑ 42 Tommy Brown	40.00	20.00
❑ 43 Mike Garcia	50.00	30.00
❑ 44 Bauer/Berra/Mantle	800.00	500.00
❑ 45 Walt Dropo	50.00	30.00
❑ 46 Roy Campanella	350.00	200.00
❑ 47 Ned Garver	40.00	20.00
❑ 48 Hank Sauer	50.00	30.00
❑ 49 Eddie Stanky MG	50.00	30.00
❑ 50 Lou Kretlow	40.00	20.00
❑ 51 Monte Irvin	80.00	50.00
❑ 52 Marty Marion MG	50.00	30.00
❑ 53 Del Rice	40.00	20.00
❑ 54 Chico Carrasquel	40.00	20.00
❑ 55 Leo Durocher MG	80.00	50.00
❑ 56 Bob Cain	40.00	20.00
❑ 57 Lou Boudreau MG	80.00	50.00
❑ 58 Willard Marshall	40.00	20.00
❑ 59 Mickey Mantle	2000.00	1200.00
❑ 60 Granny Hamner	40.00	20.00
❑ 61 George Kell	80.00	50.00
❑ 62 Ted Kluszewski	100.00	60.00
❑ 63 Gil McDougald	80.00	50.00
❑ 64 Curt Simmons	50.00	30.00
❑ 65 Robin Roberts	125.00	75.00
❑ 66 Mel Parnell	50.00	30.00
❑ 67 Mel Clark RC	40.00	20.00
❑ 68 Allie Reynolds	60.00	35.00
❑ 69 Charlie Grimm MG	50.00	30.00
❑ 70 Clint Courtney RC	40.00	20.00
❑ 71 Paul Minner	40.00	20.00
❑ 72 Ted Gray	40.00	20.00
❑ 73 Billy Pierce	50.00	30.00
❑ 74 Don Mueller	50.00	30.00
❑ 75 Saul Rogovin	40.00	20.00
❑ 76 Jim Hearn	40.00	20.00
❑ 77 Mickey Grasso	40.00	20.00
❑ 78 Carl Furillo	60.00	35.00
❑ 79 Ray Boone	50.00	30.00
❑ 80 Ralph Kiner	100.00	60.00
❑ 81 Enos Slaughter	100.00	60.00
❑ 82 Joe Astroth	40.00	20.00
❑ 83 Jack Daniels RC	40.00	20.00
❑ 84 Hank Bauer	60.00	35.00
❑ 85 Solly Hemus	40.00	20.00
❑ 86 Harry Simpson	40.00	20.00
❑ 87 Harry Perkowski	40.00	20.00
❑ 88 Joe Dobson	40.00	20.00
❑ 89 Sandy Consuegra	40.00	20.00
❑ 90 Joe Nuxhall	50.00	30.00
❑ 91 Steve Souchock	40.00	20.00
❑ 92 Gil Hodges	300.00	175.00
❑ 93 P.Rizzuto/B.Martin	300.00	175.00
❑ 94 Bob Addis	40.00	20.00
❑ 95 Wally Moses CO	50.00	30.00
❑ 96 Sal Maglie	50.00	30.00
❑ 97 Eddie Mathews	350.00	200.00
❑ 98 Hector Rodriguez RC	40.00	20.00
❑ 99 Warren Spahn	350.00	200.00
❑ 100 Bill Wight	40.00	20.00
❑ 101 Red Schoendienst	80.00	50.00
❑ 102 Jim Hegan	50.00	30.00
❑ 103 Del Ennis	50.00	30.00
❑ 104 Luke Easter	50.00	30.00
❑ 105 Eddie Joost	40.00	20.00
❑ 106 Ken Raffensberger	40.00	20.00
❑ 107 Alex Kellner	40.00	20.00
❑ 108 Bobby Adams	40.00	20.00
❑ 109 Ken Wood	40.00	20.00
❑ 110 Bob Rush	40.00	20.00
❑ 111 Jim Dyck RC	40.00	20.00
❑ 112 Toby Atwell	40.00	20.00
❑ 113 Karl Drews	80.00	50.00
❑ 114 Bob Feller	500.00	350.00
❑ 115 Cloyd Boyer	80.00	50.00
❑ 116 Eddie Yost	100.00	60.00
❑ 117 Duke Snider	600.00	350.00
❑ 118 Billy Martin	400.00	250.00
❑ 119 Dale Mitchell	100.00	60.00
❑ 120 Marlin Stuart	80.00	50.00
❑ 121 Yogi Berra	800.00	500.00
❑ 122 Bill Serena	80.00	50.00
❑ 123 Johnny Lipon	80.00	50.00
❑ 124 Chuck Dressen MG	100.00	60.00
❑ 125 Fred Hatfield	80.00	50.00
❑ 126 Al Corwin	80.00	50.00
❑ 127 Dick Kryhoski	80.00	50.00
❑ 128 Whitey Lockman	100.00	60.00
❑ 129 Russ Meyer	75.00	45.00
❑ 130 Cass Michaels	75.00	45.00
❑ 131 Connie Ryan	75.00	45.00
❑ 132 Fred Hutchinson	90.00	60.00
❑ 133 Willie Jones	75.00	45.00
❑ 134 Johnny Pesky	90.00	60.00
❑ 135 Bobby Morgan	75.00	45.00
❑ 136 Jim Brideweser RC	75.00	45.00
❑ 137 Sam Dente	75.00	45.00
❑ 138 Bubba Church	75.00	45.00
❑ 139 Pete Runnels	90.00	60.00
❑ 140 Al Brazle	75.00	45.00
❑ 141 Frank Shea	75.00	45.00
❑ 142 Larry Miggins RC	75.00	45.00
❑ 143 Al Lopez MG	110.00	70.00
❑ 144 Warren Hacker	75.00	45.00

❑ 145 George Shuba 90.00 60.00
❑ 146 Early Wynn 200.00 125.00
❑ 147 Clem Koshorek 75.00 45.00
❑ 148 Billy Goodman 90.00 60.00
❑ 149 Al Corwin 75.00 45.00
❑ 150 Carl Scheib 75.00 45.00
❑ 151 Joe Adcock 110.00 70.00
❑ 152 Clyde Vollmer 75.00 45.00
❑ 153 Whitey Ford 800.00 500.00
❑ 154 Turk Lown 75.00 45.00
❑ 155 Allie Clark 75.00 45.00
❑ 156 Max Surkont 75.00 45.00
❑ 157 Sherm Lollar 90.00 60.00
❑ 158 Howard Fox 75.00 45.00
❑ 159 Mickey Vernon UER 90.00 60.00
❑ 160 Cal Abrams 500.00 300.00

1954 Bowman

❑ COMPLETE SET (224) 4000.00 2500.00
❑ WRAP.(1-CENT, DATED) 150.00 100.00
❑ WRAP.(1-CENT, UNDAT) 200.00 150.00
❑ WRAP.(5-CENT, DATED) 150.00 100.00
❑ WRAP.(5-CENT, UNDAT) 60.00 50.00
❑ 1 Phil Rizzuto 175.00 100.00
❑ 2 Jackie Jensen 30.00 15.00
❑ 3 Marion Fricano 12.00 6.00
❑ 4 Bob Hooper 12.00 6.00
❑ 5 Billy Hunter 12.00 6.00
❑ 6 Nellie Fox 80.00 50.00
❑ 7 Walt Dropo 20.00 10.00
❑ 8 Jim Busby 12.00 6.00
❑ 9 Dave Williams 12.00 6.00
❑ 10 Carl Erskine 20.00 10.00
❑ 11 Sid Gordon 12.00 6.00
❑ 12 Roy McMillan 20.00 10.00
❑ 13 Paul Minner 12.00 6.00
❑ 14 Gerry Staley 12.00 6.00
❑ 15 Richie Ashburn 80.00 50.00
❑ 16 Jim Wilson 12.00 6.00
❑ 17 Tom Gorman 12.00 6.00
❑ 18 Hoot Evers 12.00 6.00
❑ 19 Bobby Shantz 20.00 10.00
❑ 20 Art Houtteman 12.00 6.00
❑ 21 Vic Wertz 20.00 10.00
❑ 22 Sam Mele 12.00 6.00
❑ 23 Harvey Kuenn RC 30.00 15.00
❑ 24 Bob Porterfield 12.00 6.00
❑ 25 Wes Westrum 20.00 10.00
❑ 26 Billy Cox 20.00 10.00
❑ 27 Dick Cole RC 12.00 6.00
❑ 28 Jim Greengrass 12.00 6.00
❑ 29 Johnny Klippstein 12.00 6.00
❑ 30 Del Rice 12.00 6.00
❑ 31 Smoky Burgess 20.00 10.00
❑ 32 Del Crandall 20.00 10.00
❑ 33A Vic Raschi NTR 20.00 10.00
❑ 33B Vic Raschi TR 30.00 15.00
❑ 34 Sammy White 12.00 6.00
❑ 35 Eddie Joost 12.00 6.00
❑ 36 George Strickland 12.00 6.00
❑ 37 Dick Kokos 12.00 6.00
❑ 38 Minnie Minoso 30.00 15.00
❑ 39 Ned Garver 12.00 6.00
❑ 40 Gil Coan 12.00 6.00
❑ 41 Alvin Dark 20.00 10.00
❑ 42 Billy Loes 20.00 10.00
❑ 43 Bob Friend 20.00 10.00
❑ 44 Harry Perkowski 12.00 6.00
❑ 45 Ralph Kiner 50.00 25.00
❑ 46 Rip Repulski 12.00 6.00
❑ 47 Granny Hamner 12.00 6.00
❑ 48 Jack Dittmer 12.00 6.00
❑ 49 Harry Byrd 12.00 6.00
❑ 50 George Kell 50.00 25.00
❑ 51 Alex Kellner 12.00 6.00
❑ 52 Joe Ginsberg 12.00 6.00
❑ 53 Don Lenhardt 12.00 6.00
❑ 54 Chico Carrasquel 12.00 6.00
❑ 55 Jim Delsing 12.00 6.00
❑ 56 Maurice McDermott 12.00 6.00
❑ 57 Hoyt Wilhelm 50.00 25.00
❑ 58 Pee Wee Reese 80.00 50.00
❑ 59 Bob Schultz 12.00 6.00
❑ 60 Fred Baczewski RC 12.00 6.00
❑ 61 Eddie Miksis 12.00 6.00
❑ 62 Enos Slaughter 50.00 25.00
❑ 63 Earl Torgeson 12.00 6.00
❑ 64 Eddie Mathews 80.00 50.00
❑ 65 Mickey Mantle 1500.00 900.00
❑ 66A Ted Williams 3000.00 1800.00
❑ 66B Jimmy Piersall 80.00 50.00
❑ 67 Carl Scheib 12.00 6.00
❑ 68 Bobby Avila 20.00 10.00
❑ 69 Clint Courtney 12.00 6.00
❑ 70 Willard Marshall 12.00 6.00
❑ 71 Ted Gray 12.00 6.00
❑ 72 Eddie Yost 20.00 10.00
❑ 73 Don Mueller 20.00 10.00
❑ 74 Jim Gilliam 30.00 15.00
❑ 75 Max Surkont 12.00 6.00
❑ 76 Joe Nuxhall 20.00 10.00
❑ 77 Bob Rush 12.00 6.00
❑ 78 Sal Yvars 12.00 6.00
❑ 79 Curt Simmons 20.00 10.00
❑ 80 Johnny Logan 12.00 6.00
❑ 81 Jerry Coleman 20.00 10.00
❑ 82 Billy Goodman 20.00 10.00
❑ 83 Ray Murray 12.00 6.00
❑ 84 Larry Doby 50.00 25.00
❑ 85 Jim Dyck 12.00 6.00
❑ 86 Harry Dorish 12.00 6.00
❑ 87 Don Lund 12.00 6.00
❑ 88 Tom Umphlett RC 12.00 6.00
❑ 89 Willie Mays 500.00 300.00
❑ 90 Roy Campanella 150.00 90.00
❑ 91 Cal Abrams 12.00 6.00
❑ 92 Ken Raffensberger 12.00 6.00
❑ 93 Bill Serena 12.00 6.00
❑ 94 Solly Hemus 12.00 6.00
❑ 95 Robin Roberts 50.00 25.00
❑ 96 Joe Adcock 20.00 10.00
❑ 97 Gil McDougald 20.00 10.00
❑ 98 Ellis Kinder 12.00 6.00
❑ 99 Pete Suder 12.00 6.00
❑ 100 Mike Garcia 20.00 10.00
❑ 101 Don Larsen RC 80.00 50.00
❑ 102 Billy Pierce 20.00 10.00
❑ 103 Steve Souchock 12.00 6.00
❑ 104 Frank Shea 12.00 6.00
❑ 105 Sal Maglie 20.00 10.00
❑ 106 Clem Labine 20.00 10.00
❑ 107 Paul LaPalme 12.00 6.00
❑ 108 Bobby Adams 12.00 6.00
❑ 109 Roy Smalley 12.00 6.00
❑ 110 Red Schoendienst 50.00 25.00
❑ 111 Murry Dickson 12.00 6.00
❑ 112 Andy Pafko 20.00 10.00
❑ 113 Allie Reynolds 20.00 10.00
❑ 114 Willard Nixon 12.00 6.00
❑ 115 Don Bollweg 12.00 6.00
❑ 116 Luke Easter 20.00 10.00
❑ 117 Dick Kryhoski 12.00 6.00
❑ 118 Bob Boyd 12.00 6.00
❑ 119 Fred Hatfield 12.00 6.00
❑ 120 Mel Hoderlein RC 12.00 6.00
❑ 121 Ray Katt RC 12.00 6.00
❑ 122 Carl Furillo 30.00 15.00
❑ 123 Toby Atwell 12.00 6.00
❑ 124 Gus Bell 20.00 10.00
❑ 125 Warren Hacker 12.00 6.00
❑ 126 Cliff Chambers 12.00 6.00
❑ 127 Del Ennis 20.00 10.00
❑ 128 Ebba St.Claire 12.00 6.00
❑ 129 Hank Bauer 30.00 15.00
❑ 130 Milt Bolling 12.00 6.00
❑ 131 Joe Astroth 12.00 6.00
❑ 132 Bob Feller 80.00 50.00
❑ 133 Duane Pillette 12.00 6.00
❑ 134 Luis Aloma 12.00 6.00
❑ 135 Johnny Pesky 20.00 10.00
❑ 136 Clyde Vollmer 12.00 6.00
❑ 137 Al Corwin 12.00 6.00
❑ 138 Gil Hodges 80.00 50.00
❑ 139 Preston Ward 12.00 6.00
❑ 140 Saul Rogovin 12.00 6.00
❑ 141 Joe Garagiola 30.00 15.00
❑ 142 Al Brazle 12.00 6.00
❑ 143 Willie Jones 12.00 6.00
❑ 144 Ernie Johnson RC 30.00 15.00
❑ 145 Billy Martin 80.00 50.00
❑ 146 Dick Gernert 12.00 6.00
❑ 147 Joe DeMaestri 12.00 6.00
❑ 148 Dale Mitchell 20.00 10.00
❑ 149 Bob Young 12.00 6.00
❑ 150 Cass Michaels 12.00 6.00
❑ 151 Pat Mullin 12.00 6.00
❑ 152 Mickey Vernon 20.00 10.00
❑ 153 Whitey Lockman 20.00 10.00
❑ 154 Don Newcombe 30.00 15.00
❑ 155 Frank Thomas RC 20.00 10.00
❑ 156 Rocky Bridges 12.00 6.00
❑ 157 Turk Lown 12.00 6.00
❑ 158 Stu Miller 20.00 10.00
❑ 159 Johnny Lindell 12.00 6.00
❑ 160 Danny O'Connell 12.00 6.00
❑ 161 Yogi Berra 175.00 100.00
❑ 162 Ted Lepcio 12.00 6.00
❑ 163A Dave Philley NTR 20.00 10.00
❑ 163B Dave Philley TR 30.00 15.00
❑ 164 Early Wynn 50.00 25.00
❑ 165 Johnny Groth 12.00 6.00
❑ 166 Sandy Consuegra 12.00 6.00
❑ 167 Billy Hoeft 12.00 6.00
❑ 168 Ed Fitzgerald 12.00 6.00
❑ 169 Larry Jansen 20.00 10.00
❑ 170 Duke Snider 250.00 150.00
❑ 171 Carlos Bernier 12.00 6.00
❑ 172 Andy Seminick 12.00 6.00
❑ 173 Dee Fondy 12.00 6.00
❑ 174 Pete Castiglione 12.00 6.00
❑ 175 Mel Clark 12.00 6.00
❑ 176 Vern Bickford 12.00 6.00
❑ 177 Whitey Ford 100.00 60.00
❑ 178 Del Wilber 12.00 6.00
❑ 179 Morrie Martin 12.00 6.00
❑ 180 Joe Tipton 12.00 6.00
❑ 181 Les Moss 12.00 6.00
❑ 182 Sherm Lollar 20.00 10.00
❑ 183 Matt Batts 12.00 6.00
❑ 184 Mickey Grasso 12.00 6.00
❑ 185 Daryl Spencer RC 12.00 6.00
❑ 186 Russ Meyer 12.00 6.00
❑ 187 Vern Law 20.00 10.00
❑ 188 Frank Smith 12.00 6.00
❑ 189 Randy Jackson 12.00 6.00
❑ 190 Joe Presko 12.00 6.00
❑ 191 Karl Drews 12.00 6.00
❑ 192 Lew Burdette 20.00 10.00
❑ 193 Eddie Robinson 12.00 6.00
❑ 194 Sid Hudson 12.00 6.00
❑ 195 Bob Cain 12.00 6.00
❑ 196 Bob Lemon 50.00 25.00
❑ 197 Lou Kretlow 12.00 6.00
❑ 198 Virgil Trucks 12.00 6.00
❑ 199 Steve Gromek 12.00 6.00
❑ 200 Conrado Marrero 12.00 6.00
❑ 201 Bobby Thomson 30.00 15.00
❑ 202 George Shuba 20.00 10.00
❑ 203 Vic Janowicz 20.00 10.00
❑ 204 Jack Collum RC 12.00 6.00
❑ 205 Hal Jeffcoat 12.00 6.00
❑ 206 Steve Bilko 12.00 6.00
❑ 207 Stan Lopata 12.00 6.00
❑ 208 Johnny Antonelli 20.00 10.00
❑ 209 Gene Woodling 12.00 6.00
❑ 210 Jimmy Piersall 30.00 15.00
❑ 211 Al Robertson RC 12.00 6.00
❑ 212 Owen Friend 12.00 6.00
❑ 213 Dick Littlefield 12.00 6.00
❑ 214 Ferris Fain 20.00 10.00

❑ 215 Johnny Bucha 12.00 6.00
❑ 216 Jerry Snyder 12.00 6.00
❑ 217 Hank Thompson 20.00 10.00
❑ 218 Preacher Roe 20.00 10.00
❑ 219 Hal Rice 12.00 6.00
❑ 220 Hobie Landrith RC 12.00 6.00
❑ 221 Frank Baumholtz 12.00 6.00
❑ 222 Memo Luna RC 12.00 6.00
❑ 223 Steve Ridzik 12.00 6.00
❑ 224 Bill Bruton 50.00 25.00

1955 Bowman

❑ COMPLETE SET (320) 6000.00 3500.00
❑ COMMON CARD (1-96) 12.00 6.00
❑ COM. CARD (97-224) 10.00 5.00
❑ COM. CARD (225-320) 15.00 7.50
❑ COM. UMPIRE (225-320) 30.00 18.00
❑ WRAPPER (1-CENT) 60.00 50.00
❑ WRAPPER (5-CENT) 60.00 50.00
❑ 1 Hoyt Wilhelm 100.00 60.00
❑ 2 Alvin Dark 15.00 7.50
❑ 3 Joe Coleman 15.00 7.50
❑ 4 Eddie Waitkus 15.00 7.50
❑ 5 Jim Robertson 12.00 6.00
❑ 6 Pete Suder 12.00 6.00
❑ 7 Gene Baker RC 12.00 6.00
❑ 8 Warren Hacker 12.00 6.00
❑ 9 Gil McDougald 20.00 10.00
❑ 10 Phil Rizzuto 125.00 75.00
❑ 11 Bill Bruton 15.00 7.50
❑ 12 Andy Pafko 15.00 7.50
❑ 13 Clyde Vollmer 12.00 6.00
❑ 14 Gus Keriazakos RC 12.00 6.00
❑ 15 Frank Sullivan RC 12.00 6.00
❑ 16 Jimmy Piersall 20.00 10.00
❑ 17 Del Ennis 15.00 7.50
❑ 18 Stan Lopata 12.00 6.00
❑ 19 Bobby Avila 15.00 7.50
❑ 20 Al Smith 15.00 7.50
❑ 21 Don Hoak 12.00 6.00
❑ 22 Roy Campanella 125.00 75.00
❑ 23 Al Kaline 150.00 90.00
❑ 24 Al Aber 12.00 6.00
❑ 25 Minnie Minoso 30.00 15.00
❑ 26 Virgil Trucks 15.00 7.50
❑ 27 Preston Ward 12.00 6.00
❑ 28 Dick Cole 12.00 6.00
❑ 29 Red Schoendienst 30.00 15.00
❑ 30 Bill Sami 12.00 6.00
❑ 31 Johnny Temple RC 15.00 7.50
❑ 32 Wally Post 15.00 7.50
❑ 33 Nellie Fox 50.00 30.00
❑ 34 Clint Courtney 12.00 6.00
❑ 35 Bill Tuttle RC 12.00 6.00
❑ 36 Wayne Belardi RC 12.00 6.00
❑ 37 Pee Wee Reese 100.00 60.00
❑ 38 Early Wynn 30.00 15.00
❑ 39 Bob Darnell RC 15.00 7.50
❑ 40 Vic Wertz 15.00 7.50
❑ 41 Mel Clark 12.00 6.00
❑ 42 Bob Greenwood RC 12.00 6.00
❑ 43 Bob Buhl 15.00 7.50
❑ 44 Danny O'Connell 12.00 6.00
❑ 45 Tom Umphlett 12.00 6.00
❑ 46 Mickey Vernon 15.00 7.50
❑ 47 Sammy White 12.00 6.00
❑ 48A Milt Bolling ERR 20.00 10.00
❑ 48B Milt Bolling COR 20.00 10.00
❑ 49 Jim Greengrass 12.00 6.00
❑ 50 Hobie Landrith 12.00 6.00
❑ 51 Elvin Tappe RC 12.00 6.00
❑ 52 Hal Rice 12.00 6.00
❑ 53 Alex Kellner 12.00 6.00
❑ 54 Don Bollweg 12.00 6.00
❑ 55 Cal Abrams 12.00 6.00
❑ 56 Billy Cox 15.00 7.50
❑ 57 Bob Friend 15.00 7.50
❑ 58 Frank Thomas 15.00 7.50
❑ 59 Whitey Ford 100.00 60.00
❑ 60 Enos Slaughter 30.00 15.00
❑ 61 Paul LaPalme 12.00 6.00
❑ 62 Royce Lint RC 12.00 6.00
❑ 63 Irv Noren 15.00 7.50
❑ 64 Curt Simmons 15.00 7.50
❑ 65 Don Zimmer RC 20.00 10.00
❑ 66 George Shuba 20.00 10.00
❑ 67 Don Larsen 20.00 10.00
❑ 68 Elston Howard RC 80.00 50.00
❑ 69 Billy Hunter 12.00 6.00
❑ 70 Lew Burdette 20.00 10.00
❑ 71 Dave Jolly 12.00 6.00
❑ 72 Chet Nichols 12.00 6.00
❑ 73 Eddie Yost 15.00 7.50
❑ 74 Jerry Snyder 12.00 6.00
❑ 75 Brooks Lawrence RC 12.00 6.00
❑ 76 Tom Poholsky 12.00 6.00
❑ 77 Jim McDonald RC 12.00 6.00
❑ 78 Gil Coan 12.00 6.00
❑ 79 Willie Miranda 12.00 6.00
❑ 80 Lou Limmer 12.00 6.00
❑ 81 Bobby Morgan 12.00 6.00
❑ 82 Lee Walls RC 12.00 6.00
❑ 83 Max Surkont 12.00 6.00
❑ 84 George Freese RC 12.00 6.00
❑ 85 Cass Michaels 12.00 6.00
❑ 86 Ted Gray 12.00 6.00
❑ 87 Randy Jackson 12.00 6.00
❑ 88 Steve Bilko 12.00 6.00
❑ 89 Lou Boudreau MG 30.00 15.00
❑ 90 Art RC 12.00 6.00
❑ 91 Dick Marlowe RC 12.00 6.00
❑ 92 George Zuverink 12.00 6.00
❑ 93 Andy Seminick 12.00 6.00
❑ 94 Hank Thompson 15.00 7.50
❑ 95 Sal Maglie 15.00 7.50
❑ 96 Ray Narleski RC 12.00 6.00
❑ 97 Johnny Podres 30.00 15.00
❑ 98 Jim Gilliam 20.00 10.00
❑ 99 Jerry Coleman 15.00 7.50
❑ 100 Tom Morgan 10.00 5.00
❑ 101A Don Johnson ERR 20.00 10.00
❑ 101B Don Johnson COR 20.00 10.00
❑ 102 Bobby Thomson 15.00 7.50
❑ 103 Eddie Mathews 80.00 50.00
❑ 104 Bob Porterfield 10.00 5.00
❑ 105 Johnny Schmitz 10.00 5.00
❑ 106 Del Rice 10.00 5.00
❑ 107 Solly Hemus 10.00 5.00
❑ 108 Lou Kretlow 10.00 5.00
❑ 109 Vern Stephens 15.00 7.50
❑ 110 Bob Miller 10.00 5.00
❑ 111 Steve Ridzik 10.00 5.00
❑ 112 Granny Hamner 10.00 5.00
❑ 113 Bob Hall RC 10.00 5.00
❑ 114 Vic Janowicz 15.00 7.50
❑ 115 Roger Bowman RC 10.00 5.00
❑ 116 Sandy Consuegra 10.00 5.00
❑ 117 Johnny Groth 10.00 5.00
❑ 118 Bobby Adams 10.00 5.00
❑ 119 Joe Astroth 10.00 5.00
❑ 120 Ed Burtschy RC 10.00 5.00
❑ 121 Rufus Crawford RC 10.00 5.00
❑ 122 Al Corwin 10.00 5.00
❑ 123 Marv Grissom RC 10.00 5.00
❑ 124 Johnny Antonelli 15.00 7.50
❑ 125 Paul Giel RC 15.00 7.50
❑ 126 Billy Goodman 15.00 7.50
❑ 127 Hank Majeski 10.00 5.00
❑ 128 Mike Garcia 15.00 7.50
❑ 129 Hal Naragon RC 10.00 5.00
❑ 130 Richie Ashburn 50.00 30.00
❑ 131 Willard Marshall 10.00 5.00
❑ 132A Harvey Kueen ERR 50.00 30.00
❑ 132B Harvey Kuenn COR 30.00 15.00
❑ 133 Charles King RC 10.00 5.00
❑ 134 Bob Feller 80.00 50.00
❑ 135 Lloyd Merriman 10.00 5.00
❑ 136 Rocky Bridges 10.00 5.00
❑ 137 Bob Talbot 10.00 5.00
❑ 138 Davey Williams 15.00 7.50
❑ 139 W.Shantz/B.Shantz 15.00 7.50
❑ 140 Bobby Shantz 15.00 7.50
❑ 141 Wes Westrum 15.00 7.50
❑ 142 Rudy Regalado RC 10.00 5.00
❑ 143 Don Newcombe 30.00 15.00
❑ 144 Art Houtteman 10.00 5.00
❑ 145 Bob Nieman RC 10.00 5.00
❑ 146 Don Liddle 10.00 5.00
❑ 147 Sam Mele 10.00 5.00
❑ 148 Bob Chakales 10.00 5.00
❑ 149 Cloyd Boyer 10.00 5.00
❑ 150 Billy Klaus RC 10.00 5.00
❑ 151 Jim Brideweser 10.00 5.00
❑ 152 Johnny Klippstein 10.00 5.00
❑ 153 Eddie Robinson 10.00 5.00
❑ 154 Frank Lary RC 15.00 7.50
❑ 155 Gerry Staley 10.00 5.00
❑ 156 Jim Hughes 15.00 7.50
❑ 157A Ernie Johnson ERR 20.00 10.00
❑ 157B Ernie Johnson COR 20.00 10.00
❑ 158 Gil Hodges 50.00 30.00
❑ 159 Harry Byrd 10.00 5.00
❑ 160 Bill Skowron 20.00 10.00
❑ 161 Matt Batts 10.00 5.00
❑ 162 Charlie Maxwell 10.00 5.00
❑ 163 Sid Gordon 15.00 7.50
❑ 164 Toby Atwell 10.00 5.00
❑ 165 Maurice McDermott 10.00 5.00
❑ 166 Jim Busby 10.00 5.00
❑ 167 Bob Grim RC 20.00 10.00
❑ 168 Yogi Berra 125.00 75.00
❑ 169 Carl Furillo 30.00 15.00
❑ 170 Carl Erskine 20.00 10.00
❑ 171 Robin Roberts 50.00 30.00
❑ 172 Willie Jones 10.00 5.00
❑ 173 Chico Carrasquel 10.00 5.00
❑ 174 Sherm Lollar 15.00 7.50
❑ 175 Wilmer Shantz RC 10.00 5.00
❑ 176 Joe DeMaestri 10.00 5.00
❑ 177 Willard Nixon 10.00 5.00
❑ 178 Tom Brewer RC 10.00 5.00
❑ 179 Hank Aaron 250.00 150.00
❑ 180 Johnny Logan 15.00 7.50
❑ 181 Eddie Miksis 10.00 5.00
❑ 182 Bob Rush 10.00 5.00
❑ 183 Ray Katt 10.00 5.00
❑ 184 Willie Mays 250.00 150.00
❑ 185 Vic Raschi 10.00 5.00
❑ 186 Alex Grammas 10.00 5.00
❑ 187 Fred Hatfield 10.00 5.00
❑ 188 Ned Garver 10.00 5.00
❑ 189 Jack Collum 10.00 5.00
❑ 190 Fred Baczewski 10.00 5.00
❑ 191 Bob Lemon 30.00 15.00
❑ 192 George Strickland 10.00 5.00
❑ 193 Howie Judson 10.00 5.00
❑ 194 Joe Nuxhall 15.00 7.50
❑ 195A Erv Palica 15.00 7.50
❑ 195B Erv Palica TR 40.00 20.00
❑ 196 Russ Meyer 15.00 7.50
❑ 197 Ralph Kiner 30.00 15.00
❑ 198 Dave Pope RC 10.00 5.00
❑ 199 Vern Law 15.00 7.50
❑ 200 Dick Littlefield 10.00 5.00
❑ 201 Allie Reynolds 20.00 10.00
❑ 202 Mickey Mantle UER 800.00 500.00
❑ 203 Steve Gromek 10.00 5.00
❑ 204A Frank Bolling ERR RC 20.00 10.00
❑ 204B Frank Bolling COR 20.00 10.00
❑ 205 Rip Repulski 10.00 5.00
❑ 206 Ralph Beard RC 10.00 5.00
❑ 207 Frank Shea 10.00 5.00
❑ 208 Ed Fitzgerald 10.00 5.00
❑ 209 Smoky Burgess 15.00 7.50
❑ 210 Earl Torgeson 10.00 5.00
❑ 211 Sonny Dixon RC 10.00 5.00
❑ 212 Jack Dittmer 10.00 5.00
❑ 213 George Kell 30.00 15.00
❑ 214 Billy Pierce 15.00 7.50
❑ 215 Bob Kuzava 10.00 5.00

❑ 216 Preacher Roe	20.00	10.00
❑ 217 Del Crandall	15.00	7.50
❑ 218 Joe Adcock	15.00	7.50
❑ 219 Whitey Lockman	15.00	7.50
❑ 220 Jim Hearn	10.00	5.00
❑ 221 Hector Brown	10.00	5.00
❑ 222 Russ Kemmerer RC	10.00	5.00
❑ 223 Hal Jeffcoat	10.00	5.00
❑ 224 Dee Fondy	10.00	5.00
❑ 225 Paul Richards MG	15.00	7.50
❑ 226 Bill McKinley UMP	30.00	18.00
❑ 227 Frank Baumholtz	15.00	7.50
❑ 228 John Phillips RC	15.00	7.50
❑ 229 Jim Brosnan RC	20.00	10.00
❑ 230 Al Brazle	15.00	7.50
❑ 231 Jim Konstanty	20.00	10.00
❑ 232 Birdie Tebbetts MG	20.00	10.00
❑ 233 Bill Serena	15.00	7.50
❑ 234 Dick Bartell CO	20.00	10.00
❑ 235 Joe Paparella UMP	30.00	18.00
❑ 236 Murry Dickson	15.00	7.50
❑ 237 Johnny Wyrostek	15.00	7.50
❑ 238 Eddie Stanky MG	20.00	10.00
❑ 239 Edwin Rommel UMP	40.00	20.00
❑ 240 Billy Loes	20.00	10.00
❑ 241 Johnny Pesky	20.00	10.00
❑ 242 Ernie Banks	350.00	200.00
❑ 243 Gus Bell	20.00	10.00
❑ 244 Duane Pillette	15.00	7.50
❑ 245 Bill Miller	15.00	7.50
❑ 246 Hank Bauer	30.00	15.00
❑ 247 Dutch Leonard CO	15.00	7.50
❑ 248 Harry Dorish	15.00	7.50
❑ 249 Billy Gardner RC	20.00	10.00
❑ 250 Larry Napp UMP	30.00	18.00
❑ 251 Stan Jok	15.00	7.50
❑ 252 Roy Smalley	15.00	7.50
❑ 253 Jim Wilson	15.00	7.50
❑ 254 Bennett Flowers RC	15.00	7.50
❑ 255 Pete Runnels	20.00	10.00
❑ 256 Owen Friend	15.00	7.50
❑ 257 Tom Alston RC	15.00	7.50
❑ 258 John Stevens UMP	30.00	18.00
❑ 259 Don Mossi RC	30.00	15.00
❑ 260 Edwin Hurley UMP	30.00	18.00
❑ 261 Walt Moryn RC	20.00	10.00
❑ 262 Jim Lemon FBC	15.00	7.50
❑ 263 Eddie Joost	15.00	7.50
❑ 264 Bill Henry RC	15.00	7.50
❑ 265 Al Barlick UMP	80.00	50.00
❑ 266 Mike Fornieles	15.00	7.50
❑ 267 J.Honochick UMP	80.00	50.00
❑ 268 Roy Lee Hawes RC	15.00	7.50
❑ 269 Joe Amalfitano RC	20.00	10.00
❑ 270 Chico Fernandez RC	20.00	10.00
❑ 271 Bob Hooper	15.00	7.50
❑ 272 John Flaherty UMP	30.00	18.00
❑ 273 Bubba Church	15.00	7.50
❑ 274 Jim Delsing	15.00	7.50
❑ 275 William Grieve UMP	30.00	18.00
❑ 276 Ike Delock	15.00	7.50
❑ 277 Ed Runge UMP	30.00	18.00
❑ 278 Charlie Neal RC	40.00	20.00
❑ 279 Hank Soar UMP	40.00	20.00
❑ 280 Clyde McCullough	15.00	7.50
❑ 281 Charles Berry UMP	40.00	20.00
❑ 282 Phil Cavarretta MG	20.00	10.00
❑ 283 Nestor Chylak UMP	80.00	50.00
❑ 284 Bill Jackowski UMP	30.00	18.00
❑ 285 Walt Dropo	20.00	10.00
❑ 286 Frank Secory UMP	30.00	18.00
❑ 287 Ron Mrozinski RC	15.00	7.50
❑ 288 Dick Smith RC	15.00	7.50
❑ 289 Arthur Gore UMP	30.00	18.00
❑ 290 Hershell Freeman RC	15.00	7.50
❑ 291 Frank Dascoli UMP	30.00	18.00
❑ 292 Marv Blaylock RC	15.00	7.50
❑ 293 Thomas Gorman UMP	40.00	20.00
❑ 294 Wally Moses CO	15.00	7.50
❑ 295 Lee Ballanfant UMP	30.00	18.00
❑ 296 Bill Virdon RC	30.00	15.00
❑ 297 Dusty Boggess UMP	30.00	18.00
❑ 298 Charlie Grimm	20.00	10.00
❑ 299 Lon Warneke UMP	40.00	20.00
❑ 300 Tommy Byrne	20.00	10.00
❑ 301 William Engeln UMP	30.00	18.00
❑ 302 Frank Malzone RC	30.00	15.00
❑ 303 Jocko Conlan UMP	80.00	50.00
❑ 304 Harry Chiti	15.00	7.50
❑ 305 Frank Umont UMP	30.00	18.00
❑ 306 Bob Cerv	20.00	10.00
❑ 307 Babe Pinelli UMP	40.00	20.00
❑ 308 Al Lopez MG	50.00	30.00
❑ 309 Hal Dixon UMP	30.00	18.00
❑ 310 Ken Lehman RC	15.00	7.50
❑ 311 Lawrence Goetz UMP	30.00	18.00
❑ 312 Bill Wight	15.00	7.50
❑ 313 Augie Donatelli UMP	50.00	30.00
❑ 314 Dale Mitchell	20.00	10.00
❑ 315 Cal Hubbard UMP	80.00	50.00
❑ 316 Marion Fricano	15.00	7.50
❑ 317 William Summers UMP	20.00	10.00
❑ 318 Sid Hudson	15.00	7.50
❑ 319 Al Schroll RC	15.00	7.50
❑ 320 George Susce RC	50.00	30.00

1989 Bowman

❑ COMPLETE SET (484)	25.00	10.00
❑ COMP.FACT.SET (484)	25.00	10.00
❑ 1 Oswald Peraza	.05	.01
❑ 2 Brian Holton	.05	.01
❑ 3 Jose Bautista RC	.10	.02
❑ 4 Pete Harnisch RC	.25	.08
❑ 5 Dave Schmidt	.05	.01
❑ 6 Gregg Olson RC	.25	.08
❑ 7 Jeff Ballard	.05	.01
❑ 8 Bob Melvin	.05	.01
❑ 9 Cal Ripken	.75	.30
❑ 10 Randy Milligan	.05	.01
❑ 11 Juan Bell RC	.10	.02
❑ 12 Billy Ripken	.05	.01
❑ 13 Jim Traber	.05	.01
❑ 14 Pete Stanicek	.05	.01
❑ 15 Steve Finley RC	.75	.30
❑ 16 Larry Sheets	.05	.01
❑ 17 Phil Bradley	.05	.01
❑ 18 Brady Anderson RC	.40	.15
❑ 19 Lee Smith	.10	.02
❑ 20 Tom Fischer	.05	.01
❑ 21 Mike Boddicker	.05	.01
❑ 22 Rob Murphy	.05	.01
❑ 23 Wes Gardner	.05	.01
❑ 24 John Dopson	.05	.01
❑ 25 Bob Stanley	.05	.01
❑ 26 Roger Clemens	1.00	.40
❑ 27 Rich Gedman	.05	.01
❑ 28 Marty Barrett	.05	.01
❑ 29 Luis Rivera	.05	.01
❑ 30 Jody Reed	.05	.01
❑ 31 Nick Esasky	.05	.01
❑ 32 Wade Boggs	.15	.05
❑ 33 Jim Rice	.10	.02
❑ 34 Mike Greenwell	.05	.01
❑ 35 Dwight Evans	.15	.05
❑ 36 Ellis Burks	.10	.02
❑ 37 Chuck Finley	.10	.02
❑ 38 Kirk McCaskill	.05	.01
❑ 39 Jim Abbott RC	1.00	.40
❑ 40 Bryan Harvey RC *	.25	.08
❑ 41 Bert Blyleven	.10	.02
❑ 42 Mike Witt	.05	.01
❑ 43 Bob McClure	.05	.01
❑ 44 Bill Schroeder	.05	.01
❑ 45 Lance Parrish	.10	.02
❑ 46 Dick Schofield	.05	.01
❑ 47 Wally Joyner	.10	.02
❑ 48 Jack Howell	.05	.01
❑ 49 Johnny Ray	.05	.01
❑ 50 Chili Davis	.10	.02
❑ 51 Tony Armas	.10	.02
❑ 52 Claudell Washington	.05	.01
❑ 53 Brian Downing	.10	.02
❑ 54 Devon White	.10	.02
❑ 55 Bobby Thigpen	.05	.01
❑ 56 Bill Long	.05	.01
❑ 57 Jerry Reuss	.05	.01
❑ 58 Shawn Hillegas	.05	.01
❑ 59 Melido Perez	.05	.01
❑ 60 Jeff Bittiger	.05	.01
❑ 61 Jack McDowell	.10	.02
❑ 62 Carlton Fisk	.15	.05
❑ 63 Steve Lyons	.05	.01
❑ 64 Ozzie Guillen	.10	.02
❑ 65 Robin Ventura RC	.75	.30
❑ 66 Fred Manrique	.05	.01
❑ 67 Dan Pasqua	.05	.01
❑ 68 Ivan Calderon	.05	.01
❑ 69 Ron Kittle	.05	.01
❑ 70 Daryl Boston	.05	.01
❑ 71 Dave Gallagher	.05	.01
❑ 72 Harold Baines	.10	.02
❑ 73 Charles Nagy RC	.25	.08
❑ 74 John Farrell	.05	.01
❑ 75 Kevin Wickander	.05	.01
❑ 76 Greg Swindell	.05	.01
❑ 77 Mike Walker	.05	.01
❑ 78 Doug Jones	.05	.01
❑ 79 Rich Yett	.05	.01
❑ 80 Tom Candiotti	.05	.01
❑ 81 Jesse Orosco	.05	.01
❑ 82 Bud Black	.05	.01
❑ 83 Andy Allanson	.05	.01
❑ 84 Pete O'Brien	.05	.01
❑ 85 Jerry Browne	.05	.01
❑ 86 Brook Jacoby	.05	.01
❑ 87 Mark Lewis RC	.25	.08
❑ 88 Luis Aguayo	.05	.01
❑ 89 Cory Snyder	.05	.01
❑ 90 Oddibe McDowell	.05	.01
❑ 91 Joe Carter	.10	.02
❑ 92 Frank Tanana	.10	.02
❑ 93 Jack Morris	.10	.02
❑ 94 Doyle Alexander	.05	.01
❑ 95 Steve Searcy	.05	.01
❑ 96 Randy Bockus	.05	.01
❑ 97 Jeff M. Robinson	.05	.01
❑ 98 Mike Henneman	.05	.01
❑ 99 Paul Gibson	.05	.01
❑ 100 Frank Williams	.05	.01
❑ 101 Matt Nokes	.05	.01
❑ 102 Rico Brogna RC	.40	.15
❑ 103 Lou Whitaker	.10	.02
❑ 104 Al Pedrique	.05	.01
❑ 105 Alan Trammell	.10	.02
❑ 106 Chris Brown	.05	.01
❑ 107 Pat Sheridan	.05	.01
❑ 108 Chet Lemon	.10	.02
❑ 109 Keith Moreland	.05	.01
❑ 110 Mel Stottlemyre Jr.	.05	.01
❑ 111 Bret Saberhagen	.10	.02
❑ 112 Floyd Bannister	.05	.01
❑ 113 Jeff Montgomery	.05	.01
❑ 114 Steve Farr	.05	.01
❑ 115 Tom Gordon UER RC	.40	.15
❑ 116 Charlie Leibrandt	.05	.01
❑ 117 Mark Gubicza	.05	.01
❑ 118 Mike Macfarlane RC *	.25	.08
❑ 119 Bob Boone	.10	.02
❑ 120 Kurt Stillwell	.05	.01
❑ 121 George Brett	.60	.25
❑ 122 Frank White	.10	.02
❑ 123 Kevin Seitzer	.05	.01
❑ 124 Willie Wilson	.10	.02
❑ 125 Pat Tabler	.05	.01
❑ 126 Bo Jackson	.25	.08
❑ 127 Hugh Walker RC	.10	.02
❑ 128 Danny Tartabull	.05	.01
❑ 129 Teddy Higuera	.05	.01
❑ 130 Don August	.05	.01
❑ 131 Juan Nieves	.05	.01

❑ 132 Mike Birkbeck .05 .01
❑ 133 Dan Plesac .05 .01
❑ 134 Chris Bosio .05 .01
❑ 135 Bill Wegman .05 .01
❑ 136 Chuck Crim .05 .01
❑ 137 B.J. Surhoff .10 .02
❑ 138 Joey Meyer .05 .01
❑ 139 Dale Sveum .05 .01
❑ 140 Paul Molitor .10 .02
❑ 141 Jim Gantner .05 .01
❑ 142 Gary Sheffield RC 1.50 .60
❑ 143 Greg Brock .05 .01
❑ 144 Robin Yount .40 .15
❑ 145 Glenn Braggs .05 .01
❑ 146 Rob Deer .05 .01
❑ 147 Fred Toliver .05 .01
❑ 148 Jeff Reardon .10 .02
❑ 149 Allan Anderson .05 .01
❑ 150 Frank Viola .10 .02
❑ 151 Shane Rawley .05 .01
❑ 152 Juan Berenguer .05 .01
❑ 153 Johnny Ard .05 .01
❑ 154 Tim Laudner .05 .01
❑ 155 Brian Harper .05 .01
❑ 156 Al Newman .05 .01
❑ 157 Kent Hrbek .10 .02
❑ 158 Gary Gaetti .10 .02
❑ 159 Wally Backman .05 .01
❑ 160 Gene Larkin .05 .01
❑ 161 Greg Gagne .05 .01
❑ 162 Kirby Puckett .25 .08
❑ 163 Dan Gladden .05 .01
❑ 164 Randy Bush .05 .01
❑ 165 Dave LaPoint .05 .01
❑ 166 Andy Hawkins .05 .01
❑ 167 Dave Righetti .10 .02
❑ 168 Lance McCullers .05 .01
❑ 169 Jimmy Jones .05 .01
❑ 170 Al Leiter .25 .08
❑ 171 John Candelaria .05 .01
❑ 172 Don Slaught .05 .01
❑ 173 Jamie Quirk .05 .01
❑ 174 Rafael Santana .05 .01
❑ 175 Mike Pagliarulo .05 .01
❑ 176 Don Mattingly .60 .25
❑ 177 Ken Phelps .05 .01
❑ 178 Steve Sax .05 .01
❑ 179 Dave Winfield .10 .02
❑ 180 Stan Jefferson .05 .01
❑ 181 Rickey Henderson .25 .08
❑ 182 Bob Brower .05 .01
❑ 183 Roberto Kelly .05 .01
❑ 184 Curt Young .05 .01
❑ 185 Gene Nelson .05 .01
❑ 186 Bob Welch .10 .02
❑ 187 Rick Honeycutt .05 .01
❑ 188 Dave Stewart .10 .02
❑ 189 Mike Moore .05 .01
❑ 190 Dennis Eckersley .15 .05
❑ 191 Eric Plunk .05 .01
❑ 192 Storm Davis .05 .01
❑ 193 Terry Steinbach .10 .02
❑ 194 Ron Hassey .05 .01
❑ 195 Stan Royer RC .10 .02
❑ 196 Walt Weiss .05 .01
❑ 197 Mark McGwire 1.00 .40
❑ 198 Carney Lansford .10 .02
❑ 199 Glenn Hubbard .05 .01
❑ 200 Dave Henderson .05 .01
❑ 201 Jose Canseco .25 .08
❑ 202 Dave Parker .10 .02
❑ 203 Scott Bankhead .05 .01
❑ 204 Tom Niedenfuer .05 .01
❑ 205 Mark Langston .05 .01
❑ 206 Erik Hanson RC .25 .08
❑ 207 Mike Jackson .05 .01
❑ 208 Dave Valle .05 .01
❑ 209 Scott Bradley .05 .01
❑ 210 Harold Reynolds .10 .02
❑ 211 Tino Martinez RC 2.00 .75
❑ 212 Rich Renteria .05 .01
❑ 213 Rey Quinones .05 .01
❑ 214 Jim Presley .05 .01
❑ 215 Alvin Davis .05 .01
❑ 216 Edgar Martinez .25 .08
❑ 217 Darnell Coles .05 .01
❑ 218 Jeffrey Leonard .05 .01
❑ 219 Jay Buhner .10 .02
❑ 220 Ken Griffey Jr. RC 6.00 2.50
❑ 221 Drew Hall .05 .01
❑ 222 Bobby Witt .05 .01
❑ 223 Jamie Moyer .10 .02
❑ 224 Charlie Hough .10 .02
❑ 225 Nolan Ryan 1.00 .40
❑ 226 Jeff Russell .05 .01
❑ 227 Jim Sundberg .10 .02
❑ 228 Julio Franco .10 .02
❑ 229 Buddy Bell .10 .02
❑ 230 Scott Fletcher .05 .01
❑ 231 Jeff Kunkel .05 .01
❑ 232 Steve Buechele .05 .01
❑ 233 Monty Fariss .05 .01
❑ 234 Rick Leach .05 .01
❑ 235 Ruben Sierra .10 .02
❑ 236 Cecil Espy .05 .01
❑ 237 Rafael Palmeiro .25 .08
❑ 238 Pete Incaviglia .05 .01
❑ 239 Dave Stieb .10 .02
❑ 240 Jeff Musselman .05 .01
❑ 241 Mike Flanagan .05 .01
❑ 242 Todd Stottlemyre .05 .01
❑ 243 Jimmy Key .10 .02
❑ 244 Tony Castillo RC .10 .02
❑ 245 Alex Sanchez RC .05 .01
❑ 246 Tom Henke .05 .01
❑ 247 John Cerutti .05 .01
❑ 248 Ernie Whitt .05 .01
❑ 249 Bob Brenly .05 .01
❑ 250 Rance Mulliniks .05 .01
❑ 251 Kelly Gruber .05 .01
❑ 252 Ed Sprague RC .25 .08
❑ 253 Fred McGriff .15 .05
❑ 254 Tony Fernandez .05 .01
❑ 255 Tom Lawless .05 .01
❑ 256 George Bell .10 .02
❑ 257 Jesse Barfield .10 .02
❑ 258 Roberto Alomar w/Dad .15 .05
❑ 259 Ken Griffey Sr./Jr. 1.00 .40
❑ 260 Cal Ripken Sr./Jr. .25 .08
❑ 261 M.Stottlemyre Jr./Sr. .05 .01
❑ 262 Zane Smith .05 .01
❑ 263 Charlie Puleo .05 .01
❑ 264 Derek Lilliquist RC .10 .02
❑ 265 Paul Assenmacher .05 .01
❑ 266 John Smoltz RC 1.50 .60
❑ 267 Tom Glavine .25 .08
❑ 268 Steve Avery RC .25 .08
❑ 269 Pete Smith .05 .01
❑ 270 Jody Davis .05 .01
❑ 271 Bruce Benedict .05 .01
❑ 272 Andres Thomas .05 .01
❑ 273 Gerald Perry .05 .01
❑ 274 Ron Gant .10 .02
❑ 275 Darrell Evans .10 .02
❑ 276 Dale Murphy .15 .05
❑ 277 Dion James .05 .01
❑ 278 Lonnie Smith .05 .01
❑ 279 Geronimo Berroa .05 .01
❑ 280 Steve Wilson RC .10 .02
❑ 281 Rick Sutcliffe .10 .02
❑ 282 Kevin Coffman .05 .01
❑ 283 Mitch Williams .05 .01
❑ 284 Greg Maddux .50 .20
❑ 285 Paul Kilgus .05 .01
❑ 286 Mike Harkey RC .10 .02
❑ 287 Lloyd McClendon .05 .01
❑ 288 Damon Berryhill .05 .01
❑ 289 Ty Griffin .05 .01
❑ 290 Ryne Sandberg .40 .15
❑ 291 Mark Grace .25 .08
❑ 292 Curt Wilkerson .05 .01
❑ 293 Vance Law .05 .01
❑ 294 Shawon Dunston .05 .01
❑ 295 Jerome Walton RC .25 .08
❑ 296 Mitch Webster .05 .01
❑ 297 Dwight Smith RC .25 .08
❑ 298 Andre Dawson .10 .02
❑ 299 Jeff Sellers .05 .01
❑ 300 Jose Rijo .10 .02
❑ 301 John Franco .10 .02
❑ 302 Rick Mahler .05 .01
❑ 303 Ron Robinson .05 .01
❑ 304 Danny Jackson .05 .01
❑ 305 Rob Dibble RC .40 .15
❑ 306 Tom Browning .05 .01
❑ 307 Bo Diaz .05 .01
❑ 308 Manny Trillo .05 .01
❑ 309 Chris Sabo RC * .40 .15
❑ 310 Ron Oester .05 .01
❑ 311 Barry Larkin .15 .05
❑ 312 Todd Benzinger .05 .01
❑ 313 Paul O'Neill .15 .05
❑ 314 Kal Daniels .05 .01
❑ 315 Joel Youngblood .05 .01
❑ 316 Eric Davis .10 .02
❑ 317 Dave Smith .05 .01
❑ 318 Mark Portugal .05 .01
❑ 319 Brian Meyer .05 .01
❑ 320 Jim Deshaies .05 .01
❑ 321 Juan Agosto .05 .01
❑ 322 Mike Scott .10 .02
❑ 323 Rick Rhoden .05 .01
❑ 324 Jim Clancy .05 .01
❑ 325 Larry Andersen .05 .01
❑ 326 Alex Trevino .05 .01
❑ 327 Alan Ashby .05 .01
❑ 328 Craig Reynolds .05 .01
❑ 329 Bill Doran .05 .01
❑ 330 Rafael Ramirez .05 .01
❑ 331 Glenn Davis .05 .01
❑ 332 Willie Ansley RC .10 .02
❑ 333 Gerald Young .05 .01
❑ 334 Cameron Drew .05 .01
❑ 335 Jay Howell .05 .01
❑ 336 Tim Belcher .05 .01
❑ 337 Fernando Valenzuela .10 .02
❑ 338 Ricky Horton .05 .01
❑ 339 Tim Leary .05 .01
❑ 340 Bill Bene .05 .01
❑ 341 Orel Hershiser .10 .02
❑ 342 Mike Scioscia .10 .02
❑ 343 Rick Dempsey .05 .01
❑ 344 Willie Randolph .10 .02
❑ 345 Alfredo Griffin .05 .01
❑ 346 Eddie Murray .25 .08
❑ 347 Mickey Hatcher .05 .01
❑ 348 Mike Sharperson .05 .01
❑ 349 John Shelby .05 .01
❑ 350 Mike Marshall .05 .01
❑ 351 Kirk Gibson .10 .02
❑ 352 Mike Davis .05 .01
❑ 353 Bryn Smith .05 .01
❑ 354 Pascual Perez .05 .01
❑ 355 Kevin Gross .05 .01
❑ 356 Andy McGaffigan .05 .01
❑ 357 Brian Holman RC * .10 .02
❑ 358 Dave Wainhouse RC .10 .02
❑ 359 Dennis Martinez .10 .02
❑ 360 Tim Burke .05 .01
❑ 361 Nelson Santovenia .05 .01
❑ 362 Tim Wallach .05 .01
❑ 363 Spike Owen .05 .01
❑ 364 Rex Hudler .05 .01
❑ 365 Andres Galarraga .10 .02
❑ 366 Otis Nixon .05 .01
❑ 367 Hubie Brooks .05 .01
❑ 368 Mike Aldrete .05 .01
❑ 369 Tim Raines .10 .02
❑ 370 Dave Martinez .05 .01
❑ 371 Bob Ojeda .05 .01
❑ 372 Ron Darling .10 .02
❑ 373 Wally Whitehurst RC .10 .02
❑ 374 Randy Myers .10 .02
❑ 375 David Cone .10 .02
❑ 376 Dwight Gooden .10 .02
❑ 377 Sid Fernandez .05 .01
❑ 378 Dave Proctor .05 .01
❑ 379 Gary Carter .10 .02
❑ 380 Keith Miller .05 .01
❑ 381 Gregg Jefferies .05 .01
❑ 382 Tim Teufel .05 .01
❑ 383 Kevin Elster .05 .01
❑ 384 Dave Magadan .05 .01
❑ 385 Keith Hernandez .10 .02
❑ 386 Mookie Wilson .10 .02
❑ 387 Darryl Strawberry .10 .02
❑ 388 Kevin McReynolds .05 .01
❑ 389 Mark Carreon .05 .01

❑ 390 Jeff Parrett .05 .01
❑ 391 Mike Maddux .05 .01
❑ 392 Don Carman .05 .01
❑ 393 Bruce Ruffin .05 .01
❑ 394 Ken Howell .05 .01
❑ 395 Steve Bedrosian .05 .01
❑ 396 Floyd Youmans .05 .01
❑ 397 Larry McWilliams .05 .01
❑ 398 Pat Combs RC * .10 .02
❑ 399 Steve Lake .05 .01
❑ 400 Dickie Thon .05 .01
❑ 401 Ricky Jordan RC * .25 .08
❑ 402 Mike Schmidt .50 .20
❑ 403 Tom Herr .05 .01
❑ 404 Chris James .05 .01
❑ 405 Juan Samuel .05 .01
❑ 406 Von Hayes .05 .01
❑ 407 Ron Jones .10 .02
❑ 408 Curt Ford .05 .01
❑ 409 Bob Walk .05 .01
❑ 410 Jeff D. Robinson .05 .01
❑ 411 Jim Gott .05 .01
❑ 412 Scott Medvin .05 .01
❑ 413 John Smiley .05 .01
❑ 414 Bob Kipper .05 .01
❑ 415 Brian Fisher .05 .01
❑ 416 Doug Drabek .05 .01
❑ 417 Mike LaValliere .05 .01
❑ 418 Ken Oberkfell .05 .01
❑ 419 Sid Bream .05 .01
❑ 420 Austin Manahan .05 .01
❑ 421 Jose Lind .05 .01
❑ 422 Bobby Bonilla .10 .02
❑ 423 Glenn Wilson .05 .01
❑ 424 Andy Van Slyke .15 .05
❑ 425 Gary Redus .05 .01
❑ 426 Barry Bonds 1.50 .60
❑ 427 Don Heinkel .05 .01
❑ 428 Ken Dayley .05 .01
❑ 429 Todd Worrell .05 .01
❑ 430 Brad DuVall .05 .01
❑ 431 Jose DeLeon .05 .01
❑ 432 Joe Magrane .05 .01
❑ 433 John Ericks .05 .01
❑ 434 Frank DiPino .05 .01
❑ 435 Tony Pena .05 .01
❑ 436 Ozzie Smith .40 .15
❑ 437 Terry Pendleton .10 .02
❑ 438 Jose Oquendo .05 .01
❑ 439 Tim Jones .05 .01
❑ 440 Pedro Guerrero .10 .02
❑ 441 Milt Thompson .05 .01
❑ 442 Willie McGee .10 .02
❑ 443 Vince Coleman .05 .01
❑ 444 Tom Brunansky .05 .01
❑ 445 Walt Terrell .05 .01
❑ 446 Eric Show .05 .01
❑ 447 Mark Davis .05 .01
❑ 448 Andy Benes RC .40 .15
❑ 449 Ed Whitson .05 .01
❑ 450 Dennis Rasmussen .05 .01
❑ 451 Bruce Hurst .05 .01
❑ 452 Pat Clements .05 .01
❑ 453 Benito Santiago .10 .02
❑ 454 Sandy Alomar Jr. RC .40 .15
❑ 455 Garry Templeton .10 .02
❑ 456 Jack Clark .10 .02
❑ 457 Tim Flannery .05 .01
❑ 458 Roberto Alomar .25 .08
❑ 459 Carmelo Martinez .05 .01
❑ 460 John Kruk .10 .02
❑ 461 Tony Gwynn .30 .10
❑ 462 Jerald Clark RC .10 .02
❑ 463 Don Robinson .05 .01
❑ 464 Craig Lefferts .05 .01
❑ 465 Kelly Downs .05 .01
❑ 466 Rick Reuschel .10 .02
❑ 467 Scott Garrelts .05 .01
❑ 468 Wil Tejada .05 .01
❑ 469 Kirt Manwaring .05 .01
❑ 470 Terry Kennedy .05 .01
❑ 471 Jose Uribe .05 .01
❑ 472 Royce Clayton RC .40 .15
❑ 473 Robby Thompson .05 .01
❑ 474 Kevin Mitchell .10 .02
❑ 475 Ernie Riles .05 .01
❑ 476 Will Clark .15 .05
❑ 477 Donell Nixon .05 .01
❑ 478 Candy Maldonado .05 .01
❑ 479 Tracy Jones .05 .01
❑ 480 Brett Butler .10 .02
❑ 481 Checklist 1-121 .05 .01
❑ 482 Checklist 122-242 .05 .01
❑ 483 Checklist 243-363 .05 .01
❑ 484 Checklist 364-484 .05 .01

1990 Bowman

❑ COMPLETE SET (528) 25.00 10.00
❑ COMP.FACT.SET (528) 25.00 10.00
❑ 1 Tommy Greene RC .10 .02
❑ 2 Tom Glavine .15 .05
❑ 3 Andy Nezelek .05 .01
❑ 4 Mike Stanton RC .25 .08
❑ 5 Rick Luecken RC .05 .01
❑ 6 Kent Mercker RC .25 .08
❑ 7 Derek Lilliquist .05 .01
❑ 8 Charlie Leibrandt .05 .01
❑ 9 Steve Avery .05 .01
❑ 10 John Smoltz .25 .08
❑ 11 Mark Lemke .05 .01
❑ 12 Lonnie Smith .05 .01
❑ 13 Oddibe McDowell .05 .01
❑ 14 Tyler Houston RC .25 .08
❑ 15 Jeff Blauser .05 .01
❑ 16 Ernie Whitt .05 .01
❑ 17 Alexis Infante .05 .01
❑ 18 Jim Presley .05 .01
❑ 19 Dale Murphy .15 .05
❑ 20 Nick Esasky .05 .01
❑ 21 Rick Sutcliffe .10 .02
❑ 22 Mike Bielecki .05 .01
❑ 23 Steve Wilson .05 .01
❑ 24 Kevin Blankenship .05 .01
❑ 25 Mitch Williams .05 .01
❑ 26 Dean Wilkins RC .05 .01
❑ 27 Greg Maddux .40 .15
❑ 28 Mike Harkey .05 .01
❑ 29 Mark Grace .15 .05
❑ 30 Ryne Sandberg .40 .15
❑ 31 Greg Smith RC .05 .01
❑ 32 Dwight Smith .05 .01
❑ 33 Damon Berryhill .05 .01
❑ 34 Earl Cunningham UER RC .10 .02
❑ 35 Jerome Walton .05 .01
❑ 36 Lloyd McClendon .05 .01
❑ 37 Ty Griffin .05 .01
❑ 38 Shawon Dunston .05 .01
❑ 39 Andre Dawson .10 .02
❑ 40 Luis Salazar .05 .01
❑ 41 Tim Layana RC .05 .01
❑ 42 Rob Dibble .10 .02
❑ 43 Tom Browning .05 .01
❑ 44 Danny Jackson .05 .01
❑ 45 Jose Rijo .05 .01
❑ 46 Scott Scudder .05 .01
❑ 47 Randy Myers UER (Career ERA .274, should be 2.74 .10 .02
❑ 48 Brian Lane RC .10 .02
❑ 49 Paul O'Neill .15 .05
❑ 50 Barry Larkin .15 .05
❑ 51 Reggie Jefferson RC .25 .08
❑ 52 Jeff Branson RC .10 .02
❑ 53 Chris Sabo .05 .01
❑ 54 Joe Oliver .05 .01
❑ 55 Todd Benzinger .05 .01
❑ 56 Rolando Roomes .05 .01
❑ 57 Hal Morris .05 .01
❑ 58 Eric Davis .10 .02
❑ 59 Scott Bryant RC .05 .01
❑ 60 Ken Griffey Sr. .10 .02
❑ 61 Darryl Kile RC .50 .20
❑ 62 Dave Smith .05 .01
❑ 63 Mark Portugal .05 .01
❑ 64 Jeff Juden RC .10 .02
❑ 65 Bill Gullickson .05 .01
❑ 66 Danny Darwin .05 .01
❑ 67 Larry Andersen .05 .01
❑ 68 Jose Cano RC .05 .01
❑ 69 Dan Schatzeder .05 .01
❑ 70 Jim Deshaies .05 .01
❑ 71 Mike Scott .05 .01
❑ 72 Gerald Young .05 .01
❑ 73 Ken Caminiti .10 .02
❑ 74 Ken Oberkfell .05 .01
❑ 75 Dave Rohde RC .05 .01
❑ 76 Bill Doran .05 .01
❑ 77 Andujar Cedeno RC .10 .02
❑ 78 Craig Biggio .25 .08
❑ 79 Karl Rhodes RC .25 .08
❑ 80 Glenn Davis .05 .01
❑ 81 Eric Anthony RC .10 .02
❑ 82 John Wetteland .25 .08
❑ 83 Jay Howell .05 .01
❑ 84 Orel Hershiser .10 .02
❑ 85 Tim Belcher .05 .01
❑ 86 Kiki Jones RC .05 .01
❑ 87 Mike Hartley RC .05 .01
❑ 88 Ramon Martinez .05 .01
❑ 89 Mike Scioscia .05 .01
❑ 90 Willie Randolph .10 .02
❑ 91 Juan Samuel .05 .01
❑ 92 Jose Offerman RC .25 .08
❑ 93 Dave Hansen RC .25 .08
❑ 94 Jeff Hamilton .05 .01
❑ 95 Alfredo Griffin .05 .01
❑ 96 Tom Goodwin RC .25 .08
❑ 97 Kirk Gibson .10 .02
❑ 98 Jose Vizcaino RC .25 .08
❑ 99 Kal Daniels .05 .01
❑ 100 Hubie Brooks .05 .01
❑ 101 Eddie Murray .25 .08
❑ 102 Dennis Boyd .05 .01
❑ 103 Tim Burke .05 .01
❑ 104 Bill Sampen RC .05 .01
❑ 105 Brett Gideon .05 .01
❑ 106 Mark Gardner RC .10 .02
❑ 107 Howard Farmer RC .05 .01
❑ 108 Mel Rojas RC .10 .02
❑ 109 Kevin Gross .05 .01
❑ 110 Dave Schmidt .05 .01
❑ 111 Dennis Martinez .10 .02
❑ 112 Jerry Goff RC .05 .01
❑ 113 Andres Galarraga .10 .02
❑ 114 Tim Wallach .05 .01
❑ 115 Marquis Grissom RC .50 .20
❑ 116 Spike Owen .05 .01
❑ 117 Larry Walker RC 1.00 .40
❑ 118 Tim Raines .10 .02
❑ 119 Delino DeShields RC .25 .08
❑ 120 Tom Foley .05 .01
❑ 121 Dave Martinez .05 .01
❑ 122 Frank Viola UER (Career ERA .384 should be 3.84 .05 .01
❑ 123 Julio Valera RC .05 .01
❑ 124 Alejandro Pena .05 .01
❑ 125 David Cone .10 .02
❑ 126 Dwight Gooden .10 .02
❑ 127 Kevin D. Brown RC .05 .01
❑ 128 John Franco .10 .02
❑ 129 Terry Bross RC .05 .01
❑ 130 Blaine Beatty RC .05 .01
❑ 131 Sid Fernandez .05 .01
❑ 132 Mike Marshall .05 .01
❑ 133 Howard Johnson .05 .01
❑ 134 Jaime Roseboro RC .05 .01
❑ 135 Alan Zinter RC .10 .02
❑ 136 Keith Miller .05 .01
❑ 137 Kevin Elster .05 .01

❑	138	Kevin McReynolds	.05	.01
❑	139	Barry Lyons	.05	.01
❑	140	Gregg Jefferies	.10	.02
❑	141	Darryl Strawberry	.10	.02
❑	142	Todd Hundley RC	.25	.08
❑	143	Scott Service	.05	.01
❑	144	Chuck Malone RC	.05	.01
❑	145	Steve Ontiveros	.05	.01
❑	146	Roger McDowell	.05	.01
❑	147	Ken Howell	.05	.01
❑	148	Pat Combs	.05	.01
❑	149	Jeff Parrett	.05	.01
❑	150	Chuck McElroy RC	.10	.02
❑	151	Jason Grimsley RC	.10	.02
❑	152	Len Dykstra	.10	.02
❑	153	Mickey Morandini RC	.25	.08
❑	154	John Kruk	.10	.02
❑	155	Dickie Thon	.05	.01
❑	156	Ricky Jordan	.05	.01
❑	157	Jeff Jackson RC	.10	.02
❑	158	Darren Daulton	.10	.02
❑	159	Tom Herr	.05	.01
❑	160	Von Hayes	.05	.01
❑	161	Dave Hollins RC	.25	.08
❑	162	Carmelo Martinez	.05	.01
❑	163	Bob Walk	.05	.01
❑	164	Doug Drabek	.05	.01
❑	165	Walt Terrell	.05	.01
❑	166	Bill Landrum	.05	.01
❑	167	Scott Ruskin RC	.05	.01
❑	168	Bob Patterson	.05	.01
❑	169	Bobby Bonilla	.10	.02
❑	170	Jose Lind	.05	.01
❑	171	Andy Van Slyke	.15	.05
❑	172	Mike LaValliere	.05	.01
❑	173	Willie Greene RC	.10	.02
❑	174	Jay Bell	.10	.02
❑	175	Sid Bream	.05	.01
❑	176	Tom Prince	.05	.01
❑	177	Wally Backman	.05	.01
❑	178	Moises Alou RC	.75	.30
❑	179	Steve Carter	.05	.01
❑	180	Gary Redus	.05	.01
❑	181	Barry Bonds	1.00	.40
❑	182	Don Slaught UER (Card back shows headings for a	.05	.01
❑	183	Joe Magrane	.05	.01
❑	184	Bryn Smith	.05	.01
❑	185	Todd Worrell	.05	.01
❑	186	Jose DeLeon	.05	.01
❑	187	Frank DiPino	.05	.01
❑	188	John Tudor	.05	.01
❑	189	Howard Hilton RC	.05	.01
❑	190	John Ericks	.05	.01
❑	191	Ken Dayley	.05	.01
❑	192	Ray Lankford RC	.50	.20
❑	193	Todd Zeile	.10	.02
❑	194	Willie McGee	.10	.02
❑	195	Ozzie Smith	.40	.15
❑	196	Milt Thompson	.05	.01
❑	197	Terry Pendleton	.10	.02
❑	198	Vince Coleman	.05	.01
❑	199	Paul Coleman RC	.10	.02
❑	200	Jose Oquendo	.05	.01
❑	201	Pedro Guerrero	.05	.01
❑	202	Tom Brunansky	.05	.01
❑	203	Roger Smithberg RC	.05	.01
❑	204	Eddie Whitson	.05	.01
❑	205	Dennis Rasmussen	.05	.01
❑	206	Craig Lefferts	.05	.01
❑	207	Andy Benes	.10	.02
❑	208	Bruce Hurst	.05	.01
❑	209	Eric Show	.05	.01
❑	210	Rafael Valdez RC	.05	.01
❑	211	Joey Cora	.10	.02
❑	212	Thomas Howard	.05	.01
❑	213	Rob Nelson	.05	.01
❑	214	Jack Clark	.10	.02
❑	215	Garry Templeton	.05	.01
❑	216	Fred Lynn	.05	.01
❑	217	Tony Gwynn	.30	.10
❑	218	Benito Santiago	.10	.02
❑	219	Mike Pagliarulo	.05	.01
❑	220	Joe Carter	.10	.02
❑	221	Roberto Alomar	.15	.05
❑	222	Bip Roberts	.05	.01
❑	223	Rick Reuschel	.05	.01
❑	224	Russ Swan RC	.05	.01
❑	225	Eric Gunderson RC	.05	.01
❑	226	Steve Bedrosian	.05	.01
❑	227	Mike Remlinger RC	.05	.01
❑	228	Scott Garrelts	.05	.01
❑	229	Ernie Camacho	.05	.01
❑	230	Andres Santana RC	.10	.02
❑	231	Will Clark	.15	.05
❑	232	Kevin Mitchell	.05	.01
❑	233	Robby Thompson	.05	.01
❑	234	Bill Bathe	.05	.01
❑	235	Tony Perezchica	.05	.01
❑	236	Gary Carter	.10	.02
❑	237	Brett Butler	.10	.02
❑	238	Matt Williams	.10	.02
❑	239	Earnie Riles	.05	.01
❑	240	Kevin Bass	.05	.01
❑	241	Terry Kennedy	.05	.01
❑	242	Steve Hosey RC	.10	.02
❑	243	Ben McDonald RC	.25	.08
❑	244	Jeff Ballard	.05	.01
❑	245	Joe Price	.05	.01
❑	246	Curt Schilling	1.00	.40
❑	247	Pete Harnisch	.05	.01
❑	248	Mark Williamson	.05	.01
❑	249	Gregg Olson	.10	.02
❑	250	Chris Myers RC	.05	.01
❑	251A	David Segui ERR	.50	.20
❑	251B	David Segui COR RC	.50	.20
❑	252	Joe Orsulak	.05	.01
❑	253	Craig Worthington	.05	.01
❑	254	Mickey Tettleton	.05	.01
❑	255	Cal Ripken	.75	.30
❑	256	Bill Ripken	.05	.01
❑	257	Randy Milligan	.05	.01
❑	258	Brady Anderson	.10	.02
❑	259	Chris Hoiles RC	.25	.08
❑	260	Mike Devereaux	.05	.01
❑	261	Phil Bradley	.05	.01
❑	262	Leo Gomez RC	.10	.02
❑	263	Lee Smith	.10	.02
❑	264	Mike Rochford	.05	.01
❑	265	Jeff Reardon	.10	.02
❑	266	Wes Gardner	.05	.01
❑	267	Mike Boddicker	.05	.01
❑	268	Roger Clemens	1.00	.40
❑	269	Rob Murphy	.05	.01
❑	270	Mickey Pina RC	.05	.01
❑	271	Tony Pena	.05	.01
❑	272	Jody Reed	.05	.01
❑	273	Kevin Romine	.05	.01
❑	274	Mike Greenwell	.05	.01
❑	275	Mo Vaughn RC	1.00	.40
❑	276	Danny Heep	.05	.01
❑	277	Scott Cooper RC	.10	.02
❑	278	Greg Blosser RC	.10	.02
❑	279	Dwight Evans UER (* by "1990 Team Breakdown")	.15	.05
❑	280	Ellis Burks	.15	.05
❑	281	Wade Boggs	.15	.05
❑	282	Marty Barrett	.05	.01
❑	283	Kirk McCaskill	.05	.01
❑	284	Mark Langston	.05	.01
❑	285	Bert Blyleven	.10	.02
❑	286	Mike Fetters RC	.25	.08
❑	287	Kyle Abbott RC	.05	.01
❑	288	Jim Abbott	.15	.05
❑	289	Chuck Finley	.10	.02
❑	290	Gary DiSarcina RC	.25	.08
❑	291	Dick Schofield	.05	.01
❑	292	Devon White	.10	.02
❑	293	Bobby Rose	.05	.01
❑	294	Brian Downing	.05	.01
❑	295	Lance Parrish	.05	.01
❑	296	Jack Howell	.05	.01
❑	297	Claudell Washington	.05	.01
❑	298	John Orton RC	.10	.02
❑	299	Wally Joyner	.10	.02
❑	300	Lee Stevens	.10	.02
❑	301	Chili Davis	.10	.02
❑	302	Johnny Ray	.05	.01
❑	303	Greg Hibbard RC	.10	.02
❑	304	Eric King	.05	.01
❑	305	Jack McDowell	.05	.01
❑	306	Bobby Thigpen	.05	.01
❑	307	Adam Peterson	.05	.01
❑	308	Scott Radinsky RC	.25	.08
❑	309	Wayne Edwards RC	.05	.01
❑	310	Melido Perez	.05	.01
❑	311	Robin Ventura	.25	.08
❑	312	Sammy Sosa RC	3.00	1.25
❑	313	Dan Pasqua	.05	.01
❑	314	Carlton Fisk	.15	.05
❑	315	Ozzie Guillen	.10	.02
❑	316	Ivan Calderon	.05	.01
❑	317	Daryl Boston	.05	.01
❑	318	Craig Grebeck RC	.25	.08
❑	319	Scott Fletcher	.05	.01
❑	320	Frank Thomas RC	2.00	.75
❑	321	Steve Lyons	.05	.01
❑	322	Carlos Martinez	.05	.01
❑	323	Joe Skalski	.05	.01
❑	324	Tom Candiotti	.05	.01
❑	325	Greg Swindell	.05	.01
❑	326	Steve Olin RC	.25	.08
❑	327	Kevin Wickander	.05	.01
❑	328	Doug Jones	.05	.01
❑	329	Jeff Shaw	.05	.01
❑	330	Kevin Bearse RC	.05	.01
❑	331	Dion James	.05	.01
❑	332	Jerry Browne	.05	.01
❑	333	Albert Belle	.25	.08
❑	334	Felix Fermin	.05	.01
❑	335	Candy Maldonado	.05	.01
❑	336	Cory Snyder	.05	.01
❑	337	Sandy Alomar Jr.	.10	.02
❑	338	Mark Lewis	.05	.01
❑	339	Carlos Baerga RC	.25	.08
❑	340	Chris James	.05	.01
❑	341	Brook Jacoby	.05	.01
❑	342	Keith Hernandez	.10	.02
❑	343	Frank Tanana	.05	.01
❑	344	Scott Aldred RC	.05	.01
❑	345	Mike Henneman	.05	.01
❑	346	Steve Wapnick RC	.05	.01
❑	347	Greg Gohr RC	.10	.02
❑	348	Eric Stone RC	.05	.01
❑	349	Brian DuBois RC	.05	.01
❑	350	Kevin Ritz RC	.05	.01
❑	351	Rico Brogna	.25	.08
❑	352	Mike Heath	.05	.01
❑	353	Alan Trammell	.10	.02
❑	354	Chet Lemon	.05	.01
❑	355	Dave Bergman	.05	.01
❑	356	Lou Whitaker	.10	.02
❑	357	Cecil Fielder UER	.10	.02
❑	358	Milt Cuyler RC	.10	.02
❑	359	Tony Phillips	.05	.01
❑	360	Travis Fryman RC	.50	.20
❑	361	Ed Romero	.05	.01
❑	362	Lloyd Moseby	.05	.01
❑	363	Mark Gubicza	.05	.01
❑	364	Bret Saberhagen	.10	.02
❑	365	Tom Gordon	.10	.02
❑	366	Steve Farr	.05	.01
❑	367	Kevin Appier	.10	.02
❑	368	Storm Davis	.05	.01
❑	369	Mark Davis	.05	.01
❑	370	Jeff Montgomery	.10	.02
❑	371	Frank White	.10	.02
❑	372	Brent Mayne RC	.25	.08
❑	373	Bob Boone	.10	.02
❑	374	Jim Eisenreich	.05	.01
❑	375	Danny Tartabull	.05	.01
❑	376	Kurt Stillwell	.05	.01
❑	377	Bill Pecota	.05	.01
❑	378	Bo Jackson	.25	.08
❑	379	Bob Hamelin RC	.25	.08
❑	380	Kevin Seitzer	.05	.01
❑	381	Rey Palacios	.05	.01
❑	382	George Brett	.60	.25
❑	383	Gerald Perry	.05	.01
❑	384	Teddy Higuera	.05	.01
❑	385	Tom Filer	.05	.01
❑	386	Dan Plesac	.05	.01
❑	387	Cal Eldred RC	.25	.08
❑	388	Jaime Navarro	.05	.01
❑	389	Chris Bosio	.05	.01
❑	390	Randy Veres	.05	.01

❑ 391 Gary Sheffield .25 .08
❑ 392 George Canale RC .05 .01
❑ 393 B.J. Surhoff .10 .02
❑ 394 Tim McIntosh RC .05 .01
❑ 395 Greg Brock .05 .01
❑ 396 Greg Vaughn .05 .01
❑ 397 Darryl Hamilton .05 .01
❑ 398 Dave Parker .10 .02
❑ 399 Paul Molitor .10 .02
❑ 400 Jim Gantner .05 .01
❑ 401 Rob Deer .05 .01
❑ 402 Billy Spiers .05 .01
❑ 403 Glenn Braggs .05 .01
❑ 404 Robin Yount .40 .15
❑ 405 Rick Aguilera .10 .02
❑ 406 Johnny Ard .05 .01
❑ 407 Kevin Tapani RC .25 .08
❑ 408 Park Pittman RC .05 .01
❑ 409 Allan Anderson .05 .01
❑ 410 Juan Berenguer .05 .01
❑ 411 Willie Banks RC .10 .02
❑ 412 Rich Yett .05 .01
❑ 413 Dave West .05 .01
❑ 414 Greg Gagne .05 .01
❑ 415 Chuck Knoblauch RC .50 .20
❑ 416 Randy Bush .05 .01
❑ 417 Gary Gaetti .10 .02
❑ 418 Kent Hrbek .10 .02
❑ 419 Al Newman .05 .01
❑ 420 Danny Gladden .05 .01
❑ 421 Paul Sorrento RC .25 .08
❑ 422 Derek Parks RC .10 .02
❑ 423 Scott Leius RC .10 .02
❑ 424 Kirby Puckett .25 .08
❑ 425 Willie Smith .05 .01
❑ 426 Dave Righetti .05 .01
❑ 427 Jeff D. Robinson .05 .01
❑ 428 Alan Mills RC .10 .02
❑ 429 Tim Leary .05 .01
❑ 430 Pascual Perez .05 .01
❑ 431 Alvaro Espinoza .05 .01
❑ 432 Dave Winfield .10 .02
❑ 433 Jesse Barfield .05 .01
❑ 434 Randy Velarde .05 .01
❑ 435 Rick Cerone .05 .01
❑ 436 Steve Balboni .05 .01
❑ 437 Mel Hall .05 .01
❑ 438 Bob Geren .05 .01
❑ 439 Bernie Williams RC 1.50 .60
❑ 440 Kevin Maas RC .25 .08
❑ 441 Mike Blowers RC .10 .02
❑ 442 Steve Sax .05 .01
❑ 443 Don Mattingly .60 .25
❑ 444 Roberto Kelly .05 .01
❑ 445 Mike Moore .05 .01
❑ 446 Reggie Harris RC .10 .02
❑ 447 Scott Sanderson .05 .01
❑ 448 Dave Otto .05 .01
❑ 449 Dave Stewart .10 .02
❑ 450 Rick Honeycutt .05 .01
❑ 451 Dennis Eckersley .10 .02
❑ 452 Carney Lansford .10 .02
❑ 453 Scott Hemond RC .10 .02
❑ 454 Mark McGwire 1.00 .40
❑ 455 Felix Jose .05 .01
❑ 456 Terry Steinbach .05 .01
❑ 457 Rickey Henderson .25 .08
❑ 458 Dave Henderson .05 .01
❑ 459 Mike Gallego .05 .01
❑ 460 Jose Canseco .15 .05
❑ 461 Walt Weiss .05 .01
❑ 462 Ken Phelps .05 .01
❑ 463 Darren Lewis RC .10 .02
❑ 464 Ron Hassey .05 .01
❑ 465 Roger Salkeld RC .10 .02
❑ 466 Scott Bankhead .05 .01
❑ 467 Keith Comstock .05 .01
❑ 468 Randy Johnson .50 .20
❑ 469 Erik Hanson .05 .01
❑ 470 Mike Schooler .05 .01
❑ 471 Gary Eave RC .05 .01
❑ 472 Jeffrey Leonard .05 .01
❑ 473 Dave Valle .05 .01
❑ 474 Omar Vizquel .25 .08
❑ 475 Pete O'Brien .05 .01
❑ 476 Henry Cotto .05 .01
❑ 477 Jay Buhner .10 .02
❑ 478 Harold Reynolds .10 .02
❑ 479 Alvin Davis .05 .01
❑ 480 Darnell Coles .05 .01
❑ 481 Ken Griffey Jr. .75 .30
❑ 482 Greg Briley .05 .01
❑ 483 Scott Bradley .05 .01
❑ 484 Tino Martinez .50 .20
❑ 485 Jeff Russell .05 .01
❑ 486 Nolan Ryan 1.00 .40
❑ 487 Robb Nen RC .50 .20
❑ 488 Kevin Brown .10 .02
❑ 489 Brian Bohanon RC .10 .02
❑ 490 Ruben Sierra .10 .02
❑ 491 Pete Incaviglia .05 .01
❑ 492 Juan Gonzalez RC 1.00 .40
❑ 493 Steve Buechele .05 .01
❑ 494 Scott Coolbaugh .05 .01
❑ 495 Geno Petralli .05 .01
❑ 496 Rafael Palmeiro .15 .05
❑ 497 Julio Franco .10 .02
❑ 498 Gary Pettis .05 .01
❑ 499 Donald Harris RC .05 .01
❑ 500 Monty Fariss .05 .01
❑ 501 Harold Baines .10 .02
❑ 502 Cecil Espy .05 .01
❑ 503 Jack Daugherty RC .05 .01
❑ 504 Willie Blair RC .10 .02
❑ 505 Dave Stieb .10 .02
❑ 506 Tom Henke .05 .01
❑ 507 John Cerutti .05 .01
❑ 508 Paul Kilgus .05 .01
❑ 509 Jimmy Key .10 .02
❑ 510 John Olerud RC 1.00 .40
❑ 511 Ed Sprague .10 .02
❑ 512 Manuel Lee .05 .01
❑ 513 Fred McGriff .25 .08
❑ 514 Glenallen Hill .05 .01
❑ 515 George Bell .05 .01
❑ 516 Mookie Wilson .10 .02
❑ 517 Luis Sojo RC .25 .08
❑ 518 Nelson Liriano .05 .01
❑ 519 Kelly Gruber .05 .01
❑ 520 Greg Myers .05 .01
❑ 521 Pat Borders .05 .01
❑ 522 Junior Felix .05 .01
❑ 523 Eddie Zosky RC .10 .02
❑ 524 Tony Fernandez .05 .01
❑ 525 Checklist 1-132 UER (No copyright mark on the ba .05 .01
❑ 526 Checklist 133-264 .05 .01
❑ 527 Checklist 265-396 .05 .01
❑ 528 Checklist 397-528 .05 .01

1991 Bowman

❑ COMPLETE SET (704) 40.00 15.00
❑ COMP.FACT.SET (704) 40.00 15.00
❑ 1 Rod Carew I .15 .05
❑ 2 Rod Carew II .15 .05
❑ 3 Rod Carew III .15 .05
❑ 4 Rod Carew IV .15 .05
❑ 5 Rod Carew V .15 .05
❑ 6 Willie Fraser .05 .01
❑ 7 John Olerud .10 .02
❑ 8 William Suero RC .05 .01
❑ 9 Roberto Alomar .15 .05
❑ 10 Todd Stottlemyre .05 .01
❑ 11 Joe Carter .10 .02
❑ 12 Steve Karsay RC .50 .20
❑ 13 Mark Whiten .05 .01
❑ 14 Pat Borders .05 .01
❑ 15 Mike Timlin RC .50 .20
❑ 16 Tom Henke .05 .01
❑ 17 Eddie Zosky .05 .01
❑ 18 Kelly Gruber .05 .01
❑ 19 Jimmy Key .10 .02
❑ 20 Jerry Schunk RC .05 .01
❑ 21 Manuel Lee .05 .01
❑ 22 Dave Stieb .05 .01
❑ 23 Pat Hentgen RC .50 .20
❑ 24 Glenallen Hill .05 .01
❑ 25 Rene Gonzales .05 .01
❑ 26 Ed Sprague .05 .01
❑ 27 Ken Dayley .05 .01
❑ 28 Pat Tabler .05 .01
❑ 29 Denis Boucher RC .15 .05
❑ 30 Devon White .10 .02
❑ 31 Dante Bichette .10 .02
❑ 32 Paul Molitor .10 .02
❑ 33 Greg Vaughn .05 .01
❑ 34 Dan Plesac .05 .01
❑ 35 Chris George RC .15 .05
❑ 36 Tim McIntosh .05 .01
❑ 37 Franklin Stubbs .05 .01
❑ 38 Bo Dodson RC .15 .05
❑ 39 Ron Robinson .05 .01
❑ 40 Ed Nunez .05 .01
❑ 41 Greg Brock .05 .01
❑ 42 Jaime Navarro .05 .01
❑ 43 Chris Bosio .05 .01
❑ 44 B.J. Surhoff .10 .02
❑ 45 Chris Johnson RC .05 .01
❑ 46 Willie Randolph .10 .02
❑ 47 Narciso Elvira RC .05 .01
❑ 48 Jim Gantner .05 .01
❑ 49 Kevin Brown .05 .01
❑ 50 Julio Machado .05 .01
❑ 51 Chuck Crim .05 .01
❑ 52 Gary Sheffield .10 .02
❑ 53 Angel Miranda RC .15 .05
❑ 54 Ted Higuera .05 .01
❑ 55 Robin Yount .40 .15
❑ 56 Cal Eldred .05 .01
❑ 57 Sandy Alomar Jr. .05 .01
❑ 58 Greg Swindell .05 .01
❑ 59 Brook Jacoby .05 .01
❑ 60 Efrain Valdez RC .05 .01
❑ 61 Ever Magallanes RC .05 .01
❑ 62 Tom Candiotti .05 .01
❑ 63 Eric King .05 .01
❑ 64 Alex Cole .05 .01
❑ 65 Charles Nagy .05 .01
❑ 66 Mitch Webster .05 .01
❑ 67 Chris James .05 .01
❑ 68 Jim Thome RC 4.00 1.50
❑ 69 Carlos Baerga .05 .01
❑ 70 Mark Lewis .05 .01
❑ 71 Jerry Browne .05 .01
❑ 72 Jesse Orosco .05 .01
❑ 73 Mike Huff .05 .01
❑ 74 Jose Escobar RC .05 .01
❑ 75 Jeff Manto .05 .01
❑ 76 Turner Ward RC .15 .05
❑ 77 Doug Jones .05 .01
❑ 78 Bruce Egloff RC .05 .01
❑ 79 Tim Costo RC .15 .05
❑ 80 Beau Allred .05 .01
❑ 81 Albert Belle .10 .02
❑ 82 John Farrell .05 .01
❑ 83 Glenn Davis .05 .01
❑ 84 Joe Orsulak .05 .01
❑ 85 Mark Williamson .05 .01
❑ 86 Ben McDonald .05 .01
❑ 87 Billy Ripken .05 .01
❑ 88 Leo Gomez .05 .01
❑ 89 Bob Melvin .05 .01
❑ 90 Jeff M. Robinson .05 .01
❑ 91 Jose Mesa .05 .01
❑ 92 Gregg Olson .05 .01
❑ 93 Mike Devereaux .05 .01
❑ 94 Luis Mercedes RC .15 .05
❑ 95 Arthur Rhodes RC .50 .20
❑ 96 Juan Bell .05 .01

❑	97	Mike Mussina RC	4.00	1.50
❑	98	Jeff Ballard	.05	.01
❑	99	Chris Hoiles	.05	.01
❑	100	Brady Anderson	.10	.02
❑	101	Bob Milacki	.05	.01
❑	102	David Segui	.05	.01
❑	103	Dwight Evans	.15	.05
❑	104	Cal Ripken	.75	.30
❑	105	Mike Linskey RC	.05	.01
❑	106	Jeff Tackett RC	.15	.05
❑	107	Jeff Reardon	.10	.02
❑	108	Dana Kiecker	.05	.01
❑	109	Ellis Burks	.10	.02
❑	110	Dave Owen	.05	.01
❑	111	Danny Darwin	.05	.01
❑	112	Mo Vaughn	.10	.02
❑	113	Jeff McNeely RC	.15	.05
❑	114	Tom Bolton	.05	.01
❑	115	Greg Blosser	.05	.01
❑	116	Mike Greenwell	.05	.01
❑	117	Phil Plantier RC	.15	.05
❑	118	Roger Clemens	.75	.30
❑	119	John Marzano	.05	.01
❑	120	Jody Reed	.05	.01
❑	121	Scott Taylor RC	.15	.05
❑	122	Jack Clark	.10	.02
❑	123	Derek Livernois RC	.05	.01
❑	124	Tony Pena	.05	.01
❑	125	Tom Brunansky	.05	.01
❑	126	Carlos Quintana	.05	.01
❑	127	Tim Naehring	.05	.01
❑	128	Matt Young	.05	.01
❑	129	Wade Boggs	.15	.05
❑	130	Kevin Morton RC	.05	.01
❑	131	Pete Incaviglia	.05	.01
❑	132	Rob Deer	.05	.01
❑	133	Bill Gullickson	.05	.01
❑	134	Rico Brogna	.05	.01
❑	135	Lloyd Moseby	.05	.01
❑	136	Cecil Fielder	.10	.02
❑	137	Tony Phillips	.05	.01
❑	138	Mark Leiter RC	.15	.05
❑	139	John Cerutti	.05	.01
❑	140	Mickey Tettleton	.05	.01
❑	141	Milt Cuyler	.05	.01
❑	142	Greg Gohr	.05	.01
❑	143	Tony Bernazard	.05	.01
❑	144	Dan Gakeler RC	.05	.01
❑	145	Travis Fryman	.10	.02
❑	146	Dan Petry	.05	.01
❑	147	Scott Aldred	.05	.01
❑	148	John DeSilva RC	.05	.01
❑	149	Rusty Meacham RC	.15	.05
❑	150	Lou Whitaker	.10	.02
❑	151	Dave Haas RC	.05	.01
❑	152	Luis de los Santos	.05	.01
❑	153	Ivan Cruz RC	.05	.01
❑	154	Alan Trammell	.10	.02
❑	155	Pat Kelly RC	.05	.01
❑	156	Carl Everett RC	1.50	.60
❑	157	Greg Cadaret	.05	.01
❑	158	Kevin Maas	.05	.01
❑	159	Jeff Johnson RC	.05	.01
❑	160	Willie Smith	.05	.01
❑	161	Gerald Williams RC	.50	.20
❑	162	Mike Humphreys RC	.15	.05
❑	163	Alvaro Espinoza	.05	.01
❑	164	Matt Nokes	.05	.01
❑	165	Wade Taylor RC	.05	.01
❑	166	Roberto Kelly	.05	.01
❑	167	John Habyan	.05	.01
❑	168	Steve Farr	.05	.01
❑	169	Jesse Barfield	.05	.01
❑	170	Steve Sax	.05	.01
❑	171	Jim Leyritz	.05	.01
❑	172	Robert Eenhoorn RC	.15	.05
❑	173	Bernie Williams	.25	.08
❑	174	Scott Lusader	.05	.01
❑	175	Torey Lovullo	.05	.01
❑	176	Chuck Cary	.05	.01
❑	177	Scott Sanderson	.05	.01
❑	178	Don Mattingly	.60	.25
❑	179	Mel Hall	.05	.01
❑	180	Juan Gonzalez	.25	.08
❑	181	Hensley Meulens	.05	.01
❑	182	Jose Offerman	.05	.01
❑	183	Jeff Bagwell RC	3.00	1.25
❑	184	Jeff Conine RC	1.00	.40
❑	185	Henry Rodriguez RC	.50	.20
❑	186	Jimmy Reese CO	.10	.02
❑	187	Kyle Abbott	.05	.01
❑	188	Lance Parrish	.10	.02
❑	189	Rafael Montalvo RC	.05	.01
❑	190	Floyd Bannister	.05	.01
❑	191	Dick Schofield	.05	.01
❑	192	Scott Lewis RC	.05	.01
❑	193	Jeff D. Robinson	.05	.01
❑	194	Kent Anderson	.05	.01
❑	195	Wally Joyner	.10	.02
❑	196	Chuck Finley	.10	.02
❑	197	Luis Sojo	.05	.01
❑	198	Jeff Richardson RC	.05	.01
❑	199	Dave Parker	.10	.02
❑	200	Jim Abbott	.15	.05
❑	201	Junior Felix	.05	.01
❑	202	Mark Langston	.05	.01
❑	203	Tim Salmon RC	1.50	.60
❑	204	Cliff Young	.05	.01
❑	205	Scott Bailes	.05	.01
❑	206	Bobby Rose	.05	.01
❑	207	Gary Gaetti	.10	.02
❑	208	Ruben Amaro RC	.15	.05
❑	209	Luis Polonia	.05	.01
❑	210	Dave Winfield	.10	.02
❑	211	Bryan Harvey	.05	.01
❑	212	Mike Moore	.05	.01
❑	213	Rickey Henderson	.25	.08
❑	214	Steve Chitren RC	.05	.01
❑	215	Bob Welch	.05	.01
❑	216	Terry Steinbach	.05	.01
❑	217	Earnest Riles	.05	.01
❑	218	Todd Van Poppel RC	.50	.20
❑	219	Mike Gallego	.05	.01
❑	220	Curt Young	.05	.01
❑	221	Todd Burns	.05	.01
❑	222	Vance Law	.05	.01
❑	223	Eric Show	.05	.01
❑	224	Don Peters RC	.05	.01
❑	225	Dave Stewart	.10	.02
❑	226	Dave Henderson	.05	.01
❑	227	Jose Canseco	.15	.05
❑	228	Walt Weiss	.05	.01
❑	229	Dann Howitt	.05	.01
❑	230	Willie Wilson	.05	.01
❑	231	Harold Baines	.10	.02
❑	232	Scott Hemond	.05	.01
❑	233	Joe Slusarski RC	.05	.01
❑	234	Mark McGwire	.75	.30
❑	235	Kirk Dressendorfer RC	.15	.05
❑	236	Craig Paquette RC	.50	.20
❑	237	Dennis Eckersley	.10	.02
❑	238	Dana Allison RC	.05	.01
❑	239	Scott Bradley	.05	.01
❑	240	Brian Holman	.05	.01
❑	241	Mike Schooler	.05	.01
❑	242	Rich DeLucia RC	.05	.01
❑	243	Edgar Martinez	.15	.05
❑	244	Henry Cotto	.05	.01
❑	245	Omar Vizquel	.15	.05
❑	246	Ken Griffey Jr.	.50	.20
❑	247	Jay Buhner	.10	.02
❑	248	Bill Krueger	.05	.01
❑	249	Dave Fleming RC	.15	.05
❑	250	Patrick Lennon RC	.05	.01
❑	251	Dave Valle	.05	.01
❑	252	Harold Reynolds	.10	.02
❑	253	Randy Johnson	.30	.10
❑	254	Scott Bankhead	.05	.01
❑	255	Ken Griffey Sr. UER 246	.05	.01
❑	256	Greg Briley	.05	.01
❑	257	Tino Martinez	.25	.08
❑	258	Alvin Davis	.05	.01
❑	259	Pete O'Brien	.05	.01
❑	260	Erik Hanson	.05	.01
❑	261	Bret Boone RC	1.50	.60
❑	262	Roger Salkeld	.05	.01
❑	263	Dave Burba RC	.50	.20
❑	264	Kerry Woodson RC	.15	.05
❑	265	Julio Franco	.10	.02
❑	266	Dan Peltier RC	.15	.05
❑	267	Jeff Russell	.05	.01
❑	268	Steve Buechele	.05	.01
❑	269	Donald Harris	.05	.01
❑	270	Robb Nen	.15	.05
❑	271	Rich Gossage	.10	.02
❑	272	Ivan Rodriguez RC	4.00	1.50
❑	273	Jeff Huson	.05	.01
❑	274	Kevin Brown	.10	.02
❑	275	Dan Smith RC	.15	.05
❑	276	Gary Pettis	.05	.01
❑	277	Jack Daugherty	.05	.01
❑	278	Mike Jeffcoat	.05	.01
❑	279	Brad Arnsberg	.05	.01
❑	280	Nolan Ryan	1.00	.40
❑	281	Eric McCray RC	.05	.01
❑	282	Scott Chiamparino	.05	.01
❑	283	Ruben Sierra	.10	.02
❑	284	Geno Petralli	.05	.01
❑	285	Monty Fariss	.05	.01
❑	286	Rafael Palmeiro	.15	.05
❑	287	Bobby Witt	.05	.01
❑	288	Dean Palmer UER	.10	.02
❑	289	Tony Scruggs RC	.05	.01
❑	290	Kenny Rogers	.10	.02
❑	291	Bret Saberhagen	.10	.02
❑	292	Brian McRae RC	.50	.20
❑	293	Storm Davis	.05	.01
❑	294	Danny Tartabull	.05	.01
❑	295	David Howard RC	.05	.01
❑	296	Mike Boddicker	.05	.01
❑	297	Joel Johnston RC	.15	.05
❑	298	Tim Spehr RC	.05	.01
❑	299	Hector Wagner RC	.05	.01
❑	300	George Brett	.60	.25
❑	301	Mike Macfarlane	.05	.01
❑	302	Kirk Gibson	.10	.02
❑	303	Harvey Pulliam RC	.15	.05
❑	304	Jim Eisenreich	.05	.01
❑	305	Kevin Seitzer	.05	.01
❑	306	Mark Davis	.05	.01
❑	307	Kurt Stillwell	.05	.01
❑	308	Jeff Montgomery	.05	.01
❑	309	Kevin Appier	.10	.02
❑	310	Bob Hamelin	.05	.01
❑	311	Tom Gordon	.05	.01
❑	312	Kerwin Moore RC	.15	.05
❑	313	Hugh Walker	.05	.01
❑	314	Terry Shumpert	.05	.01
❑	315	Warren Cromartie	.05	.01
❑	316	Gary Thurman	.05	.01
❑	317	Steve Bedrosian	.05	.01
❑	318	Danny Gladden	.05	.01
❑	319	Jack Morris	.10	.02
❑	320	Kirby Puckett	.25	.08
❑	321	Kent Hrbek	.10	.02
❑	322	Kevin Tapani	.05	.01
❑	323	Denny Neagle RC	.50	.20
❑	324	Rich Garces RC	.15	.05
❑	325	Larry Casian RC	.05	.01
❑	326	Shane Mack	.05	.01
❑	327	Allan Anderson	.05	.01
❑	328	Junior Ortiz	.05	.01
❑	329	Paul Abbott RC	.15	.05
❑	330	Chuck Knoblauch	.10	.02
❑	331	Chili Davis	.10	.02
❑	332	Todd Ritchie RC	.50	.20
❑	333	Brian Harper	.05	.01
❑	334	Rick Aguilera	.10	.02
❑	335	Scott Erickson	.05	.01
❑	336	Pedro Munoz RC	.15	.05
❑	337	Scott Leius	.05	.01
❑	338	Greg Gagne	.05	.01
❑	339	Mike Pagliarulo	.05	.01
❑	340	Terry Leach	.05	.01
❑	341	Willie Banks	.05	.01
❑	342	Bobby Thigpen	.05	.01
❑	343	Roberto Hernandez RC	.50	.20
❑	344	Melido Perez	.05	.01
❑	345	Carlton Fisk	.15	.05
❑	346	Norberto Martin RC	.05	.01
❑	347	Johnny Ruffin RC	.15	.05
❑	348	Jeff Carter	.05	.01
❑	349	Lance Johnson	.05	.01
❑	350	Sammy Sosa	.25	.08
❑	351	Alex Fernandez	.05	.01
❑	352	Jack McDowell	.05	.01
❑	353	Bob Wickman RC	1.50	.60
❑	354	Wilson Alvarez	.05	.01

❑ 355 Charlie Hough .10 .02
❑ 356 Ozzie Guillen .10 .02
❑ 357 Cory Snyder .05 .01
❑ 358 Robin Ventura .10 .02
❑ 359 Scott Fletcher .05 .01
❑ 360 Cesar Bernhardt RC .05 .01
❑ 361 Dan Pasqua .05 .01
❑ 362 Tim Raines .10 .02
❑ 363 Brian Drahman RC .05 .01
❑ 364 Wayne Edwards .05 .01
❑ 365 Scott Radinsky .05 .01
❑ 366 Frank Thomas .25 .08
❑ 367 Cecil Fielder SLUG .05 .01
❑ 368 Julio Franco SLUG .05 .01
❑ 369 Kelly Gruber SLUG .05 .01
❑ 370 Alan Trammell SLUG .10 .02
❑ 371 Rickey Henderson SLUG .15 .05
❑ 372 Jose Canseco SLUG .10 .02
❑ 373 Ellis Burks SLUG .05 .01
❑ 374 Lance Parrish SLUG .05 .01
❑ 375 Dave Parker SLUG .05 .01
❑ 376 Eddie Murray SLUG .15 .05
❑ 377 Ryne Sandberg SLUG .25 .08
❑ 378 Matt Williams SLUG .05 .01
❑ 379 Barry Larkin SLUG .10 .02
❑ 380 Barry Bonds SLUG .50 .20
❑ 381 Bobby Bonilla SLUG .05 .01
❑ 382 Darryl Strawberry SLUG .05 .01
❑ 383 Benny Santiago SLUG .05 .01
❑ 384 Don Robinson SLUG .05 .01
❑ 385 Paul Coleman .05 .01
❑ 386 Milt Thompson .05 .01
❑ 387 Lee Smith .10 .02
❑ 388 Ray Lankford .10 .02
❑ 389 Tom Pagnozzi .05 .01
❑ 390 Ken Hill .05 .01
❑ 391 Jamie Moyer .10 .02
❑ 392 Greg Carmona RC .05 .01
❑ 393 John Ericks .05 .01
❑ 394 Bob Tewksbury .05 .01
❑ 395 Jose Oquendo .05 .01
❑ 396 Rheal Cormier RC .15 .05
❑ 397 Mike Milchin RC .05 .01
❑ 398 Ozzie Smith .40 .15
❑ 399 Aaron Holbert RC .15 .05
❑ 400 Jose DeLeon .05 .01
❑ 401 Felix Jose .05 .01
❑ 402 Juan Agosto .05 .01
❑ 403 Pedro Guerrero .10 .02
❑ 404 Todd Zeile .05 .01
❑ 405 Gerald Perry .05 .01
❑ 406 Donovan Osborne UER RC .15 .05
❑ 407 Bryn Smith .05 .01
❑ 408 Bernard Gilkey .05 .01
❑ 409 Rex Hudler .05 .01
❑ 410 Thomson/Branca FOIL .25 .08
❑ 411 Lance Dickson RC .15 .05
❑ 412 Danny Jackson .05 .01
❑ 413 Jerome Walton .05 .01
❑ 414 Sean Cheetham RC .05 .01
❑ 415 Joe Girardi .05 .01
❑ 416 Ryne Sandberg .40 .15
❑ 417 Mike Harkey .05 .01
❑ 418 George Bell .05 .01
❑ 419 Rick Wilkins RC .15 .05
❑ 420 Earl Cunningham .05 .01
❑ 421 Heathcliff Slocumb RC .15 .05
❑ 422 Mike Bielecki .05 .01
❑ 423 Jessie Hollins RC .15 .05
❑ 424 Shawon Dunston .05 .01
❑ 425 Dave Smith .05 .01
❑ 426 Greg Maddux .40 .15
❑ 427 Jose Vizcaino .05 .01
❑ 428 Luis Salazar .05 .01
❑ 429 Andre Dawson .10 .02
❑ 430 Rick Sutcliffe .10 .02
❑ 431 Paul Assenmacher .05 .01
❑ 432 Erik Pappas RC .05 .01
❑ 433 Mark Grace .15 .05
❑ 434 Dennis Martinez .10 .02
❑ 435 Marquis Grissom .10 .02
❑ 436 Wil Cordero RC .50 .20
❑ 437 Tim Wallach .05 .01
❑ 438 Brian Barnes RC .05 .01
❑ 439 Barry Jones .05 .01
❑ 440 Ivan Calderon .05 .01
❑ 441 Stan Spencer RC .05 .01
❑ 442 Larry Walker .25 .08
❑ 443 Chris Haney RC .15 .05
❑ 444 Hector Rivera RC .05 .01
❑ 445 Delino DeShields .10 .02
❑ 446 Andres Galarraga .10 .02
❑ 447 Gilberto Reyes .05 .01
❑ 448 Willie Greene .05 .01
❑ 449 Greg Colbrunn RC .50 .20
❑ 450 Rondell White RC 1.00 .40
❑ 451 Steve Frey .05 .01
❑ 452 Shane Andrews RC .15 .05
❑ 453 Mike Fitzgerald .05 .01
❑ 454 Spike Owen .05 .01
❑ 455 Dave Martinez .05 .01
❑ 456 Dennis Boyd .05 .01
❑ 457 Eric Bullock .05 .01
❑ 458 Reid Cornelius RC .15 .05
❑ 459 Chris Nabholz .05 .01
❑ 460 David Cone .10 .02
❑ 461 Hubie Brooks .05 .01
❑ 462 Sid Fernandez .05 .01
❑ 463 Doug Simons RC .05 .01
❑ 464 Howard Johnson .05 .01
❑ 465 Chris Donnels RC .05 .01
❑ 466 Anthony Young RC .15 .05
❑ 467 Todd Hundley .05 .01
❑ 468 Rick Cerone .05 .01
❑ 469 Kevin Elster .05 .01
❑ 470 Wally Whitehurst .05 .01
❑ 471 Vince Coleman .05 .01
❑ 472 Dwight Gooden .10 .02
❑ 473 Charlie O'Brien .05 .01
❑ 474 Jeromy Burnitz RC 1.00 .40
❑ 475 John Franco .10 .02
❑ 476 Daryl Boston .05 .01
❑ 477 Frank Viola .10 .02
❑ 478 D.J. Dozier .05 .01
❑ 479 Kevin McReynolds .05 .01
❑ 480 Tom Herr .05 .01
❑ 481 Gregg Jefferies .05 .01
❑ 482 Pete Schourek RC .15 .05
❑ 483 Ron Darling .05 .01
❑ 484 Dave Magadan .05 .01
❑ 485 Andy Ashby RC .50 .20
❑ 486 Dale Murphy .15 .05
❑ 487 Von Hayes .05 .01
❑ 488 Kim Batiste RC .15 .05
❑ 489 Tony Longmire RC .15 .05
❑ 490 Wally Backman .05 .01
❑ 491 Jeff Jackson .05 .01
❑ 492 Mickey Morandini .05 .01
❑ 493 Darrel Akerfelds .05 .01
❑ 494 Ricky Jordan .05 .01
❑ 495 Randy Ready .05 .01
❑ 496 Darrin Fletcher .05 .01
❑ 497 Chuck Malone .05 .01
❑ 498 Pat Combs .05 .01
❑ 499 Dickie Thon .05 .01
❑ 500 Roger McDowell .05 .01
❑ 501 Len Dykstra .10 .02
❑ 502 Joe Boever .05 .01
❑ 503 John Kruk .10 .02
❑ 504 Terry Mulholland .05 .01
❑ 505 Wes Chamberlain RC .15 .05
❑ 506 Mike Lieberthal RC 1.00 .40
❑ 507 Darren Daulton .10 .02
❑ 508 Charlie Hayes .05 .01
❑ 509 John Smiley .05 .01
❑ 510 Gary Varsho .05 .01
❑ 511 Curt Wilkerson .05 .01
❑ 512 Orlando Merced RC .15 .05
❑ 513 Barry Bonds 1.00 .40
❑ 514 Mike LaValliere .05 .01
❑ 515 Doug Drabek .05 .01
❑ 516 Gary Redus .05 .01
❑ 517 William Pennyfeather RC .15 .05
❑ 518 Randy Tomlin RC .05 .01
❑ 519 Mike Zimmerman RC .15 .05
❑ 520 Jeff King .05 .01
❑ 521 Kurt Miller RC .15 .05
❑ 522 Jay Bell .10 .02
❑ 523 Bill Landrum .05 .01
❑ 524 Zane Smith .05 .01
❑ 525 Bobby Bonilla .10 .02
❑ 526 Bob Walk .05 .01
❑ 527 Austin Manahan .05 .01
❑ 528 Joe Ausanio RC .05 .01
❑ 529 Andy Van Slyke .15 .05
❑ 530 Jose Lind .05 .01
❑ 531 Carlos Garcia RC .15 .05
❑ 532 Don Slaught .05 .01
❑ 533 Gen.Colin Powell .50 .20
❑ 534 Frank Bolick RC .15 .05
❑ 535 Gary Scott RC .05 .01
❑ 536 Nikco Riesgo RC .05 .01
❑ 537 Reggie Sanders RC 1.50 .60
❑ 538 Tim Howard RC .15 .05
❑ 539 Ryan Bowen RC .15 .05
❑ 540 Eric Anthony .05 .01
❑ 541 Jim Deshaies .05 .01
❑ 542 Tom Nevers RC .15 .05
❑ 543 Ken Caminiti .10 .02
❑ 544 Karl Rhodes .05 .01
❑ 545 Xavier Hernandez .05 .01
❑ 546 Mike Scott .05 .01
❑ 547 Jeff Juden .05 .01
❑ 548 Darryl Kile .10 .02
❑ 549 Willie Ansley .05 .01
❑ 550 Luis Gonzalez RC 1.50 .60
❑ 551 Mike Simms RC .05 .01
❑ 552 Mark Portugal .05 .01
❑ 553 Jimmy Jones .05 .01
❑ 554 Jim Clancy .05 .01
❑ 555 Pete Harnisch .05 .01
❑ 556 Craig Biggio .15 .05
❑ 557 Eric Yelding .05 .01
❑ 558 Dave Rohde .05 .01
❑ 559 Casey Candaele .05 .01
❑ 560 Curt Schilling .25 .08
❑ 561 Steve Finley .10 .02
❑ 562 Javier Ortiz .05 .01
❑ 563 Andujar Cedeno .05 .01
❑ 564 Rafael Ramirez .05 .01
❑ 565 Kenny Lofton RC 1.50 .60
❑ 566 Steve Avery .05 .01
❑ 567 Lonnie Smith .05 .01
❑ 568 Kent Mercker .05 .01
❑ 569 Chipper Jones RC 6.00 2.50
❑ 570 Terry Pendleton .10 .02
❑ 571 Otis Nixon .05 .01
❑ 572 Juan Berenguer .05 .01
❑ 573 Charlie Leibrandt .05 .01
❑ 574 David Justice .10 .02
❑ 575 Keith Mitchell RC .15 .05
❑ 576 Tom Glavine .15 .05
❑ 577 Greg Olson .05 .01
❑ 578 Rafael Belliard .05 .01
❑ 579 Ben Rivera RC .15 .05
❑ 580 John Smoltz .15 .05
❑ 581 Tyler Houston .05 .01
❑ 582 Mark Wohlers RC .50 .20
❑ 583 Ron Gant .10 .02
❑ 584 Ramon Caraballo RC .15 .05
❑ 585 Sid Bream .05 .01
❑ 586 Jeff Treadway .05 .01
❑ 587 Javy Lopez RC 3.00 1.25
❑ 588 Deion Sanders .15 .05
❑ 589 Mike Heath .05 .01
❑ 590 Ryan Klesko RC 1.00 .40
❑ 591 Bob Ojeda .05 .01
❑ 592 Alfredo Griffin .05 .01
❑ 593 Raul Mondesi RC 1.00 .40
❑ 594 Greg Smith .05 .01
❑ 595 Orel Hershiser .10 .02
❑ 596 Juan Samuel .05 .01
❑ 597 Brett Butler .10 .02
❑ 598 Gary Carter .10 .02
❑ 599 Stan Javier .05 .01
❑ 600 Kal Daniels .05 .01
❑ 601 Jamie McAndrew RC .15 .05
❑ 602 Mike Sharperson .05 .01
❑ 603 Jay Howell .05 .01
❑ 604 Eric Karros RC 1.50 .60
❑ 605 Tim Belcher .05 .01
❑ 606 Dan Opperman RC .05 .01
❑ 607 Lenny Harris .05 .01
❑ 608 Tom Goodwin .05 .01
❑ 609 Darryl Strawberry .10 .02
❑ 610 Ramon Martinez .05 .01
❑ 611 Kevin Gross .05 .01
❑ 612 Zakary Shinall RC .05 .01

❑ 613	Mike Scioscia	.05	.01
❑ 614	Eddie Murray	.25	.08
❑ 615	Ronnie Walden RC	.15	.05
❑ 616	Will Clark	.15	.05
❑ 617	Adam Hyzdu RC	.50	.20
❑ 618	Matt Williams	.10	.02
❑ 619	Don Robinson	.05	.01
❑ 620	Jeff Brantley	.05	.01
❑ 621	Greg Litton	.05	.01
❑ 622	Steve Decker RC	.05	.01
❑ 623	Robby Thompson	.05	.01
❑ 624	Mark Leonard RC	.05	.01
❑ 625	Kevin Bass	.05	.01
❑ 626	Scott Garrelts	.05	.01
❑ 627	Jose Uribe	.05	.01
❑ 628	Eric Gunderson	.05	.01
❑ 629	Steve Hosey	.05	.01
❑ 630	Trevor Wilson	.05	.01
❑ 631	Terry Kennedy	.05	.01
❑ 632	Dave Righetti	.10	.02
❑ 633	Kelly Downs	.05	.01
❑ 634	Johnny Ard	.05	.01
❑ 635	Eric Christopherson RC	.15	.05
❑ 636	Kevin Mitchell	.05	.01
❑ 637	John Burkett	.05	.01
❑ 638	Kevin Rogers RC	.15	.05
❑ 639	Bud Black	.05	.01
❑ 640	Willie McGee	.10	.02
❑ 641	Royce Clayton	.05	.01
❑ 642	Tony Fernandez	.05	.01
❑ 643	Ricky Bones RC	.15	.05
❑ 644	Thomas Howard	.05	.01
❑ 645	Dave Staton RC	.15	.05
❑ 646	Jim Presley	.05	.01
❑ 647	Tony Gwynn	.30	.10
❑ 648	Marty Barrett	.05	.01
❑ 649	Scott Coolbaugh	.05	.01
❑ 650	Craig Lefferts	.05	.01
❑ 651	Eddie Whitson	.05	.01
❑ 652	Oscar Azocar	.05	.01
❑ 653	Wes Gardner	.05	.01
❑ 654	Bip Roberts	.05	.01
❑ 655	Robbie Beckett RC	.15	.05
❑ 656	Benito Santiago	.10	.02
❑ 657	Greg W.Harris	.05	.01
❑ 658	Jerald Clark	.05	.01
❑ 659	Fred McGriff	.15	.05
❑ 660	Larry Andersen	.05	.01
❑ 661	Bruce Hurst	.05	.01
❑ 662	Steve Martin UER RC	.15	.05
❑ 663	Rafael Valdez	.05	.01
❑ 664	Paul Faries RC	.05	.01
❑ 665	Andy Benes	.05	.01
❑ 666	Randy Myers	.05	.01
❑ 667	Rob Dibble	.10	.02
❑ 668	Glenn Sutko RC	.05	.01
❑ 669	Glenn Braggs	.05	.01
❑ 670	Billy Hatcher	.05	.01
❑ 671	Joe Oliver	.05	.01
❑ 672	Freddie Benavides RC	.15	.05
❑ 673	Barry Larkin	.15	.05
❑ 674	Chris Sabo	.05	.01
❑ 675	Mariano Duncan	.05	.01
❑ 676	Chris Jones RC	.05	.01
❑ 677	Gino Minutelli RC	.05	.01
❑ 678	Reggie Jefferson	.05	.01
❑ 679	Jack Armstrong	.05	.01
❑ 680	Chris Hammond	.05	.01
❑ 681	Jose Rijo	.05	.01
❑ 682	Bill Doran	.05	.01
❑ 683	Terry Lee RC	.05	.01
❑ 684	Tom Browning	.05	.01
❑ 685	Paul O'Neill	.15	.05
❑ 686	Eric Davis	.10	.02
❑ 687	Dan Wilson RC	.50	.20
❑ 688	Ted Power	.05	.01
❑ 689	Tim Layana	.05	.01
❑ 690	Norm Charlton	.05	.01
❑ 691	Hal Morris	.05	.01
❑ 692	Rickey Henderson RB	.15	.05
❑ 693	Sam Militello RC	.15	.05
❑ 694	Matt Mieske RC	.15	.05
❑ 695	Paul Russo RC	.15	.05
❑ 696	Domingo Mota MVP	.05	.01
❑ 697	Todd Guggiana RC	.15	.05
❑ 698	Marc Newfield RC	.15	.05
❑ 699	Checklist 1-122	.05	.01
❑ 700	Checklist 123-244	.05	.01
❑ 701	Checklist 245-366	.05	.01
❑ 702	Checklist 367-471	.05	.01
❑ 703	Checklist 472-593	.05	.01
❑ 704	Checklist 594-704	.05	.01

1992 Bowman

❑	COMPLETE SET (705)	150.00	75.00
❑ 1	Ivan Rodriguez	1.25	.50
❑ 2	Kirk McCaskill	.50	.20
❑ 3	Scott Livingstone	.50	.20
❑ 4	Salomon Torres RC	.50	.20
❑ 5	Carlos Hernandez	.50	.20
❑ 6	Dave Hollins	.50	.20
❑ 7	Scott Fletcher	.50	.20
❑ 8	Jorge Fabregas RC	.50	.20
❑ 9	Andujar Cedeno	.50	.20
❑ 10	Howard Johnson	.50	.20
❑ 11	Trevor Hoffman RC	10.00	4.00
❑ 12	Roberto Kelly	.50	.20
❑ 13	Gregg Jefferies	.50	.20
❑ 14	Marquis Grissom	.50	.20
❑ 15	Mike Ignasiak	.50	.20
❑ 16	Jack Morris	.50	.20
❑ 17	William Pennyfeather	.50	.20
❑ 18	Todd Stottlemyre	.50	.20
❑ 19	Chito Martinez	.50	.20
❑ 20	Roberto Alomar	.75	.30
❑ 21	Sam Militello	.50	.20
❑ 22	Hector Fajardo RC	.50	.20
❑ 23	Paul Quantrill RC	.50	.20
❑ 24	Chuck Knoblauch	.50	.20
❑ 25	Reggie Jefferson	.50	.20
❑ 26	Jeremy McGarity RC	.50	.20
❑ 27	Jerome Walton	.50	.20
❑ 28	Chipper Jones	10.00	4.00
❑ 29	Brian Barber RC	.50	.20
❑ 30	Ron Darling	.50	.20
❑ 31	Roberto Petagine RC	.50	.20
❑ 32	Chuck Finley	.50	.20
❑ 33	Edgar Martinez	.75	.30
❑ 34	Napoleon Robinson	.50	.20
❑ 35	Andy Van Slyke	.75	.30
❑ 36	Bobby Thigpen	.50	.20
❑ 37	Travis Fryman	.50	.20
❑ 38	Eric Christopherson	.50	.20
❑ 39	Terry Mulholland	.50	.20
❑ 40	Darryl Strawberry	.50	.20
❑ 41	Manny Alexander RC	.50	.20
❑ 42	Tracy Sanders RC	.50	.20
❑ 43	Pete Incaviglia	.50	.20
❑ 44	Kim Batiste	.50	.20
❑ 45	Frank Rodriguez	.50	.20
❑ 46	Greg Swindell	.50	.20
❑ 47	Delino DeShields	.50	.20
❑ 48	John Ericks	.50	.20
❑ 49	Franklin Stubbs	.50	.20
❑ 50	Tony Gwynn	1.50	.60
❑ 51	Clifton Garrett RC	.50	.20
❑ 52	Mike Gardella	.50	.20
❑ 53	Scott Erickson	.50	.20
❑ 54	Gary Caraballo RC	.50	.20
❑ 55	Jose Oliva RC	.50	.20
❑ 56	Brook Fordyce	.50	.20
❑ 57	Mark Whiten	.50	.20
❑ 58	Joe Slusarski	.50	.20
❑ 59	J.R. Phillips RC	.50	.20
❑ 60	Barry Bonds	4.00	1.50
❑ 61	Bob Milacki	.50	.20
❑ 62	Keith Mitchell	.50	.20
❑ 63	Angel Miranda	.50	.20
❑ 64	Raul Mondesi	.50	.20
❑ 65	Brian Koelling RC	.50	.20
❑ 66	Brian McRae	.50	.20
❑ 67	John Patterson RC	.50	.20
❑ 68	John Wetteland	.50	.20
❑ 69	Wilson Alvarez	.50	.20
❑ 70	Wade Boggs	.75	.30
❑ 71	Darryl Ratliff RC	.50	.20
❑ 72	Jeff Jackson	.50	.20
❑ 73	Jeremy Hernandez RC	.50	.20
❑ 74	Darryl Hamilton	.50	.20
❑ 75	Rafael Belliard	.50	.20
❑ 76	Rick Trlicek RC	.50	.20
❑ 77	Felipe Crespo RC	.50	.20
❑ 78	Carney Lansford	.50	.20
❑ 79	Ryan Long RC	.50	.20
❑ 80	Kirby Puckett	1.25	.50
❑ 81	Earl Cunningham	.50	.20
❑ 82	Pedro Martinez	10.00	4.00
❑ 83	Scott Hatteberg RC	1.00	.40
❑ 84	Juan Gonzalez	.75	.30
❑ 85	Robert Nutting RC	.50	.20
❑ 86	Pokey Reese RC	1.00	.40
❑ 87	Dave Silvestri	.50	.20
❑ 88	Scott Ruffcorn RC	.50	.20
❑ 89	Rick Aguilera	.50	.20
❑ 90	Cecil Fielder	.50	.20
❑ 91	Kirk Dressendorfer	.50	.20
❑ 92	Jerry DiPoto RC	.50	.20
❑ 93	Mike Felder	.50	.20
❑ 94	Craig Paquette	.50	.20
❑ 95	Elvin Paulino RC	.50	.20
❑ 96	Donovan Osborne	.50	.20
❑ 97	Hubie Brooks	.50	.20
❑ 98	Derek Lowe RC	4.00	1.50
❑ 99	David Zancanaro	.50	.20
❑ 100	Ken Griffey Jr.	2.00	.75
❑ 101	Todd Hundley	.50	.20
❑ 102	Mike Trombley RC	.50	.20
❑ 103	Ricky Gutierrez RC	1.00	.40
❑ 104	Braulio Castillo	.50	.20
❑ 105	Craig Lefferts	.50	.20
❑ 106	Rick Sutcliffe	.50	.20
❑ 107	Dean Palmer	.50	.20
❑ 108	Henry Rodriguez	.50	.20
❑ 109	Mark Clark RC	1.00	.40
❑ 110	Kenny Lofton	.75	.30
❑ 111	Mark Carreon	.50	.20
❑ 112	J.T. Bruett	.50	.20
❑ 113	Gerald Williams	.50	.20
❑ 114	Frank Thomas	1.25	.50
❑ 115	Kevin Reimer	.50	.20
❑ 116	Sammy Sosa	1.25	.50
❑ 117	Mickey Tettleton	.50	.20
❑ 118	Reggie Sanders	.50	.20
❑ 119	Trevor Wilson	.50	.20
❑ 120	Cliff Brantley	.50	.20
❑ 121	Spike Owen	.50	.20
❑ 122	Jeff Montgomery	.50	.20
❑ 123	Alex Sutherland	.50	.20
❑ 124	Brien Taylor RC	1.00	.40
❑ 125	Brian Williams RC	.50	.20
❑ 126	Kevin Seitzer	.50	.20
❑ 127	Carlos Delgado RC	12.00	5.00
❑ 128	Gary Scott	.50	.20
❑ 129	Scott Cooper	.50	.20
❑ 130	Domingo Jean RC	.50	.20
❑ 131	Pat Mahomes RC	1.00	.40
❑ 132	Mike Boddicker	.50	.20
❑ 133	Roberto Hernandez	.50	.20
❑ 134	Dave Valle	.50	.20
❑ 135	Kurt Stillwell	.50	.20
❑ 136	Brad Pennington RC	.50	.20
❑ 137	Jermaine Swinton RC	.50	.20
❑ 138	Ryan Hawblitzel RC	.50	.20
❑ 139	Tito Navarro RC	.50	.20
❑ 140	Sandy Alomar Jr.	.50	.20
❑ 141	Todd Benzinger	.50	.20
❑ 142	Danny Jackson	.50	.20
❑ 143	Melvin Nieves RC	.50	.20
❑ 144	Jim Campanis	.50	.20
❑ 145	Luis Gonzalez	.50	.20

❑ 146	Dave Doorneweerd RC	.50	.20
❑ 147	Charlie Hayes	.50	.20
❑ 148	Greg Maddux	2.00	.75
❑ 149	Brian Harper	.50	.20
❑ 150	Brent Miller RC	.50	.20
❑ 151	Shawn Estes RC	1.00	.40
❑ 152	Mike Williams RC	1.00	.40
❑ 153	Charlie Hough	.50	.20
❑ 154	Randy Myers	.50	.20
❑ 155	Kevin Young RC	1.00	.40
❑ 156	Rick Wilkins	.50	.20
❑ 157	Terry Shumpert	.50	.20
❑ 158	Steve Karsay	.50	.20
❑ 159	Gary DiSarcina	.50	.20
❑ 160	Deion Sanders	.75	.30
❑ 161	Tom Browning	.50	.20
❑ 162	Dickie Thon	.50	.20
❑ 163	Luis Mercedes	.50	.20
❑ 164	Riccardo Ingram	.50	.20
❑ 165	Tavo Alvarez RC	.50	.20
❑ 166	Rickey Henderson	1.25	.50
❑ 167	Jaime Navarro	.50	.20
❑ 168	Billy Ashley RC	.50	.20
❑ 169	Phil Dauphin RC	.50	.20
❑ 170	Ivan Cruz	.50	.20
❑ 171	Harold Baines	.50	.20
❑ 172	Bryan Harvey	.50	.20
❑ 173	Alex Cole	.50	.20
❑ 174	Curtis Shaw RC	.50	.20
❑ 175	Matt Williams	.50	.20
❑ 176	Felix Jose	.50	.20
❑ 177	Sam Horn	.50	.20
❑ 178	Randy Johnson	1.25	.50
❑ 179	Ivan Calderon	.50	.20
❑ 180	Steve Avery	.50	.20
❑ 181	William Suero	.50	.20
❑ 182	Bill Swift	.50	.20
❑ 183	Howard Battle RC	.50	.20
❑ 184	Ruben Amaro	.50	.20
❑ 185	Jim Abbott	.75	.30
❑ 186	Mike Fitzgerald	.50	.20
❑ 187	Bruce Hurst	.50	.20
❑ 188	Jeff Juden	.50	.20
❑ 189	Jeromy Burnitz	.50	.20
❑ 190	Dave Burba	.50	.20
❑ 191	Kevin Brown	.50	.20
❑ 192	Patrick Lennon	.50	.20
❑ 193	Jeff McNeely	.50	.20
❑ 194	Wil Cordero	.50	.20
❑ 195	Chili Davis	.50	.20
❑ 196	Milt Cuyler	.50	.20
❑ 197	Von Hayes	.50	.20
❑ 198	Todd Revenig RC	.50	.20
❑ 199	Joel Johnston	.50	.20
❑ 200	Jeff Bagwell	1.25	.50
❑ 201	Alex Fernandez	.50	.20
❑ 202	Todd Jones RC	2.50	1.00
❑ 203	Charles Nagy	.50	.20
❑ 204	Tim Raines	.50	.20
❑ 205	Kevin Maas	.50	.20
❑ 206	Julio Franco	.50	.20
❑ 207	Randy Velarde	.50	.20
❑ 208	Lance Johnson	.50	.20
❑ 209	Scott Leius	.50	.20
❑ 210	Derek Lee	.50	.20
❑ 211	Joe Sondrini RC	.50	.20
❑ 212	Royce Clayton	.50	.20
❑ 213	Chris George	.50	.20
❑ 214	Gary Sheffield	.50	.20
❑ 215	Mark Gubicza	.50	.20
❑ 216	Mike Moore	.50	.20
❑ 217	Rick Huisman RC	.50	.20
❑ 218	Jeff Russell	.50	.20
❑ 219	D.J. Dozier	.50	.20
❑ 220	Dave Martinez	.50	.20
❑ 221	Alan Newman RC	.50	.20
❑ 222	Nolan Ryan	4.00	1.50
❑ 223	Teddy Higuera	.50	.20
❑ 224	Damon Buford RC	.50	.20
❑ 225	Ruben Sierra	.50	.20
❑ 226	Tom Nevers	.50	.20
❑ 227	Tommy Greene	.50	.20
❑ 228	Nigel Wilson RC	.50	.20
❑ 229	John DeSilva	.50	.20
❑ 230	Bobby Witt	.50	.20
❑ 231	Greg Cadaret	.50	.20
❑ 232	John Vander Wal RC	1.00	.40
❑ 233	Jack Clark	.50	.20
❑ 234	Bill Doran	.50	.20
❑ 235	Bobby Bonilla	.50	.20
❑ 236	Steve Olin	.50	.20
❑ 237	Derek Bell	.50	.20
❑ 238	David Cone	.50	.20
❑ 239	Victor Cole	.50	.20
❑ 240	Rod Bolton RC	.50	.20
❑ 241	Tom Pagnozzi	.50	.20
❑ 242	Rob Dibble	.50	.20
❑ 243	Michael Carter RC	.50	.20
❑ 244	Don Peters	.50	.20
❑ 245	Mike LaValliere	.50	.20
❑ 246	Joe Perona RC	.50	.20
❑ 247	Mitch Williams	.50	.20
❑ 248	Jay Buhner	.50	.20
❑ 249	Andy Benes	.50	.20
❑ 250	Alex Ochoa RC	.50	.20
❑ 251	Greg Blosser	.50	.20
❑ 252	Jack Armstrong	.50	.20
❑ 253	Juan Samuel	.50	.20
❑ 254	Terry Pendleton	.50	.20
❑ 255	Ramon Martinez	.50	.20
❑ 256	Rico Brogna	.50	.20
❑ 257	John Smiley	.50	.20
❑ 258	Carl Everett	.75	.30
❑ 259	Tim Salmon	.75	.30
❑ 260	Will Clark	.75	.30
❑ 261	Ugueth Urbina RC	1.00	.40
❑ 262	Jason Wood RC	.50	.20
❑ 263	Dave Magadan	.50	.20
❑ 264	Dante Bichette	.50	.20
❑ 265	Jose DeLeon	.50	.20
❑ 266	Mike Neill RC	1.00	.40
❑ 267	Paul O'Neill	.75	.30
❑ 268	Anthony Young	.50	.20
❑ 269	Greg W. Harris	.50	.20
❑ 270	Todd Van Poppel	.50	.20
❑ 271	Pedro Castellano RC	.50	.20
❑ 272	Tony Phillips	.50	.20
❑ 273	Mike Gallego	.50	.20
❑ 274	Steve Cooke RC	.50	.20
❑ 275	Robin Ventura	.50	.20
❑ 276	Kevin Mitchell	.50	.20
❑ 277	Doug Linton RC	.50	.20
❑ 278	Robert Eenhoorn	.50	.20
❑ 279	Gabe White RC	.50	.20
❑ 280	Dave Stewart	.50	.20
❑ 281	Mo Sanford	.50	.20
❑ 282	Greg Perschke	.50	.20
❑ 283	Kevin Flora RC	.50	.20
❑ 284	Jeff Williams RC	1.00	.40
❑ 285	Keith Miller	.50	.20
❑ 286	Andy Ashby	.50	.20
❑ 287	Doug Dascenzo	.50	.20
❑ 288	Eric Karros	.50	.20
❑ 289	Glenn Murray RC	.50	.20
❑ 290	Troy Percival RC	3.00	1.25
❑ 291	Orlando Merced	.50	.20
❑ 292	Peter Hoy	.50	.20
❑ 293	Tony Fernandez	.50	.20
❑ 294	Juan Guzman	.50	.20
❑ 295	Jesse Barfield	.50	.20
❑ 296	Sid Fernandez	.50	.20
❑ 297	Scott Cepicky	.50	.20
❑ 298	Garret Anderson RC	5.00	2.00
❑ 299	Cal Eldred	.50	.20
❑ 300	Ryne Sandberg	2.50	1.00
❑ 301	Jim Gantner	.50	.20
❑ 302	Mariano Rivera RC	25.00	10.00
❑ 303	Ron Lockett RC	.50	.20
❑ 304	Jose Offerman	.50	.20
❑ 305	Dennis Martinez	.50	.20
❑ 306	Luis Ortiz RC	.50	.20
❑ 307	David Howard	.50	.20
❑ 308	Russ Springer RC	1.00	.40
❑ 309	Chris Howard	.50	.20
❑ 310	Kyle Abbott	.50	.20
❑ 311	Aaron Sele RC	1.00	.40
❑ 312	David Justice	.50	.20
❑ 313	Pete O'Brien	.50	.20
❑ 314	Greg Hansell RC	.50	.20
❑ 315	Dave Winfield	.50	.20
❑ 316	Lance Dickson	.50	.20
❑ 317	Eric King	.50	.20
❑ 318	Vaughn Eshelman RC	.50	.20
❑ 319	Tim Belcher	.50	.20
❑ 320	Andres Galarraga	.50	.20
❑ 321	Scott Bullett RC	.50	.20
❑ 322	Doug Strange	.50	.20
❑ 323	Jerald Clark	.50	.20
❑ 324	Dave Righetti	.50	.20
❑ 325	Greg Hibbard	.50	.20
❑ 326	Eric Hillman RC	.50	.20
❑ 327	Shane Reynolds RC	1.00	.40
❑ 328	Chris Hammond	.50	.20
❑ 329	Albert Belle	.50	.20
❑ 330	Rich Becker RC	.50	.20
❑ 331	Ed Williams	.50	.20
❑ 332	Donald Harris	.50	.20
❑ 333	Dave Smith	.50	.20
❑ 334	Steve Fireovid	.50	.20
❑ 335	Steve Buechele	.50	.20
❑ 336	Mike Schooler	.50	.20
❑ 337	Kevin McReynolds	.50	.20
❑ 338	Hensley Meulens	.50	.20
❑ 339	Benji Gil RC	1.00	.40
❑ 340	Don Mattingly	3.00	1.25
❑ 341	Alvin Davis	.50	.20
❑ 342	Alan Mills	.50	.20
❑ 343	Kelly Downs	.50	.20
❑ 344	Leo Gomez	.50	.20
❑ 345	Tarrik Brock RC	.50	.20
❑ 346	Ryan Turner RC	.50	.20
❑ 347	John Smoltz	.75	.30
❑ 348	Bill Sampen	.50	.20
❑ 349	Paul Byrd RC	3.00	1.25
❑ 350	Mike Bordick	.50	.20
❑ 351	Jose Lind	.50	.20
❑ 352	David Wells	.50	.20
❑ 353	Barry Larkin	.75	.30
❑ 354	Bruce Ruffin	.50	.20
❑ 355	Luis Rivera	.50	.20
❑ 356	Sid Bream	.50	.20
❑ 357	Julian Vasquez RC	.50	.20
❑ 358	Jason Bere RC	1.00	.40
❑ 359	Ben McDonald	.50	.20
❑ 360	Scott Stahoviak RC	.50	.20
❑ 361	Kirt Manwaring	.50	.20
❑ 362	Jeff Johnson	.50	.20
❑ 363	Rob Deer	.50	.20
❑ 364	Tony Pena	.50	.20
❑ 365	Melido Perez	.50	.20
❑ 366	Clay Parker	.50	.20
❑ 367	Dale Sveum	.50	.20
❑ 368	Mike Scioscia	.50	.20
❑ 369	Roger Salkeld	.50	.20
❑ 370	Mike Stanley	.50	.20
❑ 371	Jack McDowell	.50	.20
❑ 372	Tim Wallach	.50	.20
❑ 373	Billy Ripken	.50	.20
❑ 374	Mike Christopher	.50	.20
❑ 375	Paul Molitor	.50	.20
❑ 376	Dave Stieb	.50	.20
❑ 377	Pedro Guerrero	.50	.20
❑ 378	Russ Swan	.50	.20
❑ 379	Bob Ojeda	.50	.20
❑ 380	Donn Pall	.50	.20
❑ 381	Eddie Zosky	.50	.20
❑ 382	Darnell Coles	.50	.20
❑ 383	Tom Smith RC	.50	.20
❑ 384	Mark McGwire	3.00	1.25
❑ 385	Gary Carter	.50	.20
❑ 386	Rich Amaral RC	.50	.20
❑ 387	Alan Embree RC	1.00	.40
❑ 388	Jonathan Hurst RC	.50	.20
❑ 389	Bobby Jones RC	1.00	.40
❑ 390	Rico Rossy	.50	.20
❑ 391	Dan Smith	.50	.20
❑ 392	Terry Steinbach	.50	.20
❑ 393	Jon Farrell RC	.50	.20
❑ 394	Dave Anderson	.50	.20
❑ 395	Benny Santiago	.50	.20
❑ 396	Mark Wohlers	.50	.20
❑ 397	Mo Vaughn	.50	.20
❑ 398	Randy Kramer	.50	.20
❑ 399	John Jaha RC	1.00	.40
❑ 400	Cal Ripken	4.00	1.50
❑ 401	Ryan Bowen	.50	.20
❑ 402	Tim McIntosh	.50	.20
❑ 403	Bernard Gilkey	.50	.20

❑	404	Junior Felix	.50	.20
❑	405	Cris Colon RC	.50	.20
❑	406	Marc Newfield	.50	.20
❑	407	Bernie Williams	.75	.30
❑	408	Jay Howell	.50	.20
❑	409	Zane Smith	.50	.20
❑	410	Jeff Shaw	.50	.20
❑	411	Kerry Woodson	.50	.20
❑	412	Wes Chamberlain	.50	.20
❑	413	Dave Mlicki RC	1.00	.40
❑	414	Benny Distefano	.50	.20
❑	415	Kevin Rogers	.50	.20
❑	416	Tim Naehring	.50	.20
❑	417	Clemente Nunez RC	.50	.20
❑	418	Luis Sojo	.50	.20
❑	419	Kevin Ritz	.50	.20
❑	420	Omar Olivares	.50	.20
❑	421	Manuel Lee	.50	.20
❑	422	Julio Valera	.50	.20
❑	423	Omar Vizquel	.75	.30
❑	424	Darren Burton RC	.50	.20
❑	425	Mel Hall	.50	.20
❑	426	Dennis Powell	.50	.20
❑	427	Lee Stevens	.50	.20
❑	428	Glenn Davis	.50	.20
❑	429	Willie Greene	.50	.20
❑	430	Kevin Wickander	.50	.20
❑	431	Dennis Eckersley	.50	.20
❑	432	Joe Orsulak	.50	.20
❑	433	Eddie Murray	1.25	.50
❑	434	Matt Stairs RC	1.00	.40
❑	435	Wally Joyner	.50	.20
❑	436	Rondell White	.50	.20
❑	437	Rob Maurer	.50	.20
❑	438	Joe Redfield	.50	.20
❑	439	Mark Lewis	.50	.20
❑	440	Darren Daulton	.50	.20
❑	441	Mike Henneman	.50	.20
❑	442	John Cangelosi	.50	.20
❑	443	Vincent Moore RC	.50	.20
❑	444	John Wehner	.50	.20
❑	445	Kent Hrbek	.50	.20
❑	446	Mark McLemore	.50	.20
❑	447	Bill Wegman	.50	.20
❑	448	Robby Thompson	.50	.20
❑	449	Mark Anthony RC	.50	.20
❑	450	Archi Cianfrocco RC	.50	.20
❑	451	Johnny Ruffin	.50	.20
❑	452	Javy Lopez	2.00	.75
❑	453	Greg Gohr	.50	.20
❑	454	Tim Scott	.50	.20
❑	455	Stan Belinda	.50	.20
❑	456	Darrin Jackson	.50	.20
❑	457	Chris Gardner	.50	.20
❑	458	Esteban Beltre	.50	.20
❑	459	Phil Plantier	.50	.20
❑	460	Jim Thome	8.00	3.00
❑	461	Mike Piazza RC	25.00	10.00
❑	462	Matt Sinatro	.50	.20
❑	463	Scott Servais	.50	.20
❑	464	Brian Jordan RC	2.00	.75
❑	465	Doug Drabek	.50	.20
❑	466	Carl Willis	.50	.20
❑	467	Bret Barberie	.50	.20
❑	468	Hal Morris	.50	.20
❑	469	Steve Sax	.50	.20
❑	470	Jerry Willard	.50	.20
❑	471	Dan Wilson	.50	.20
❑	472	Chris Hoiles	.50	.20
❑	473	Rheal Cormier	.50	.20
❑	474	John Morris	.50	.20
❑	475	Jeff Reardon	.50	.20
❑	476	Mark Leiter	.50	.20
❑	477	Tom Gordon	.50	.20
❑	478	Kent Bottenfield RC	1.00	.40
❑	479	Gene Larkin	.50	.20
❑	480	Dwight Gooden	.50	.20
❑	481	B.J. Surhoff	.50	.20
❑	482	Andy Stankiewicz	.50	.20
❑	483	Tino Martinez	.75	.30
❑	484	Craig Biggio	.75	.30
❑	485	Denny Neagle	.50	.20
❑	486	Rusty Meacham	.50	.20
❑	487	Kal Daniels	.50	.20
❑	488	Dave Henderson	.50	.20
❑	489	Tim Costo	.50	.20
❑	490	Doug Davis	.50	.20
❑	491	Frank Viola	.50	.20
❑	492	Cory Snyder	.50	.20
❑	493	Chris Martin	.50	.20
❑	494	Dion James	.50	.20
❑	495	Randy Tomlin	.50	.20
❑	496	Greg Vaughn	.50	.20
❑	497	Dennis Cook	.50	.20
❑	498	Rosario Rodriguez	.50	.20
❑	499	Dave Staton	.50	.20
❑	500	George Brett	3.00	1.25
❑	501	Brian Barnes	.50	.20
❑	502	Butch Henry RC	.50	.20
❑	503	Harold Reynolds	.50	.20
❑	504	David Nied RC	.50	.20
❑	505	Lee Smith	.50	.20
❑	506	Steve Chitren	.50	.20
❑	507	Ken Hill	.50	.20
❑	508	Robbie Beckett	.50	.20
❑	509	Troy Afenir	.50	.20
❑	510	Kelly Gruber	.50	.20
❑	511	Bret Boone	.75	.30
❑	512	Jeff Branson	.50	.20
❑	513	Mike Jackson	.50	.20
❑	514	Pete Harnisch	.50	.20
❑	515	Chad Kreuter	.50	.20
❑	516	Joe Vitko RC	.50	.20
❑	517	Orel Hershiser	.50	.20
❑	518	John Doherty RC	.50	.20
❑	519	Jay Bell	.50	.20
❑	520	Mark Langston	.50	.20
❑	521	Dann Howitt	.50	.20
❑	522	Bobby Reed RC	.50	.20
❑	523	Bobby Munoz RC	.50	.20
❑	524	Todd Ritchie	.50	.20
❑	525	Bip Roberts	.50	.20
❑	526	Pat Listach RC	1.00	.40
❑	527	Scott Brosius RC	2.00	.75
❑	528	John Roper RC	.50	.20
❑	529	Phil Hiatt RC	.50	.20
❑	530	Denny Walling	.50	.20
❑	531	Carlos Baerga	.50	.20
❑	532	Manny Ramirez RC	25.00	10.00
❑	533	Pat Clements UER	.50	.20
❑	534	Ron Gant	.50	.20
❑	535	Pat Kelly	.50	.20
❑	536	Bill Spiers	.50	.20
❑	537	Darren Reed	.50	.20
❑	538	Ken Caminiti	.50	.20
❑	539	Butch Huskey RC	.50	.20
❑	540	Matt Nokes	.50	.20
❑	541	John Kruk	.50	.20
❑	542	John Jaha FOIL	.50	.20
❑	543	Justin Thompson RC	.50	.20
❑	544	Steve Hosey	.50	.20
❑	545	Joe Kmak	.50	.20
❑	546	John Franco	.50	.20
❑	547	Devon White	.50	.20
❑	548	Elston Hansen FOIL SP RC	.50	.20
❑	549	Ryan Klesko	.50	.20
❑	550	Danny Tartabull	.50	.20
❑	551	Frank Thomas FOIL	1.25	.50
❑	552	Kevin Tapani	.50	.20
❑	553	Willie Banks	.50	.20
❑	554	B.J.Wallace FOIL RC	.50	.20
❑	555	Orlando Miller RC	.50	.20
❑	556	Mark Smith RC	.50	.20
❑	557	Tim Wallach FOIL	.50	.20
❑	558	Bill Gullickson	.50	.20
❑	559	Derek Bell FOIL	.50	.20
❑	560	Joe Randa FOIL RC	3.00	1.25
❑	561	Frank Seminara RC	.50	.20
❑	562	Mark Gardner	.50	.20
❑	563	Rick Greene FOIL RC	.50	.20
❑	564	Gary Gaetti	.50	.20
❑	565	Ozzie Guillen	.50	.20
❑	566	Charles Nagy FOIL	.50	.20
❑	567	Mike Milchin	.50	.20
❑	568	Ben Shelton RC	.50	.20
❑	569	Chris Roberts FOIL	.50	.20
❑	570	Ellis Burks	.50	.20
❑	571	Scott Scudder	.50	.20
❑	572	Jim Abbott FOIL	.75	.30
❑	573	Joe Carter	.50	.20
❑	574	Steve Finley	.50	.20
❑	575	Jim Olander FOIL	.50	.20
❑	576	Carlos Garcia	.50	.20
❑	577	Gregg Olson	.50	.20
❑	578	Greg Swindell FOIL	.50	.20
❑	579	Matt Williams FOIL	.50	.20
❑	580	Mark Grace	.75	.30
❑	581	Howard House FOIL RC	.50	.20
❑	582	Luis Polonia	.50	.20
❑	583	Erik Hanson	.50	.20
❑	584	Salomon Torres FOIL	.50	.20
❑	585	Carlton Fisk	.75	.30
❑	586	Bret Saberhagen	.50	.20
❑	587	Chad McConnell FOIL RC	.50	.20
❑	588	Jimmy Key	.50	.20
❑	589	Mike Macfarlane	.50	.20
❑	590	Barry Bonds FOIL	4.00	1.50
❑	591	Jamie McAndrew	.50	.20
❑	592	Shane Mack	.50	.20
❑	593	Kerwin Moore	.50	.20
❑	594	Joe Oliver	.50	.20
❑	595	Chris Sabo	.50	.20
❑	596	Alex Gonzalez RC	1.00	.40
❑	597	Brett Butler	.50	.20
❑	598	Mark Hutton RC	.50	.20
❑	599	Andy Benes FOIL	.50	.20
❑	600	Jose Canseco	.75	.30
❑	601	Darryl Kile	.50	.20
❑	602	Matt Stairs FOIL	.50	.20
❑	603	Rob Butler FOIL RC	.50	.20
❑	604	Willie McGee	.50	.20
❑	605	Jack McDowell FOIL	.50	.20
❑	606	Tom Candiotti	.50	.20
❑	607	Ed Martel RC	.50	.20
❑	608	Matt Mieske FOIL	.50	.20
❑	609	Darrin Fletcher	.50	.20
❑	610	Rafael Palmeiro	.75	.30
❑	611	Bill Swift FOIL	.50	.20
❑	612	Mike Mussina	1.25	.50
❑	613	Vince Coleman	.50	.20
❑	614	Scott Cepicky COR	.50	.20
❑	614A	Scott Cepicky FOIL UER	.50	.20
❑	615	Mike Greenwell	.50	.20
❑	616	Kevin McGehee RC	.50	.20
❑	617	Jeffrey Hammonds FOIL	.50	.20
❑	618	Scott Taylor	.50	.20
❑	619	Dave Otto	.50	.20
❑	620	Mark McGwire FOIL	3.00	1.25
❑	621	Kevin Tatar RC	.50	.20
❑	622	Steve Farr	.50	.20
❑	623	Ryan Klesko FOIL	.50	.20
❑	624	Dave Fleming	.50	.20
❑	625	Andre Dawson	.50	.20
❑	626	Tino Martinez FOIL SP	.75	.30
❑	627	Chad Curtis RC	1.00	.40
❑	628	Mickey Morandini	.50	.20
❑	629	Gregg Olson FOIL SP	.50	.20
❑	630	Lou Whitaker	.50	.20
❑	631	Arthur Rhodes	.50	.20
❑	632	Brandon Wilson RC	.50	.20
❑	633	Lance Jennings RC	.50	.20
❑	634	Allen Watson RC	.50	.20
❑	635	Len Dykstra	.50	.20
❑	636	Joe Girardi	.50	.20
❑	637	Kiki Hernandez FOIL RC	.50	.20
❑	638	Mike Hampton RC	2.00	.75
❑	639	Al Osuna	.50	.20
❑	640	Kevin Appier	.50	.20
❑	641	Rick Helling FOIL	.50	.20
❑	642	Jody Reed	.50	.20
❑	643	Ray Lankford	.50	.20
❑	644	John Olerud	.50	.20
❑	645	Paul Molitor FOIL	.50	.20
❑	646	Pat Borders	.50	.20
❑	647	Mike Morgan	.50	.20
❑	648	Larry Walker	.75	.30
❑	649	Pedro Castellano FOIL	.50	.20
❑	650	Fred McGriff	.75	.30
❑	651	Walt Weiss	.50	.20
❑	652	Calvin Murray FOIL RC	1.00	.40
❑	653	Dave Nilsson	.50	.20
❑	654	Greg Pirkl RC	.50	.20
❑	655	Robin Ventura FOIL	.50	.20
❑	656	Mark Portugal	.50	.20
❑	657	Roger McDowell	.50	.20
❑	658	Rick Hirtensteiner FOIL RC	.50	.20
❑	659	Glenallen Hill	.50	.20
❑	660	Greg Gagne	.50	.20

❑ 661 Charles Johnson FOIL .50 .20
❑ 662 Brian Hunter .50 .20
❑ 663 Mark Lemke .50 .20
❑ 664 Tim Belcher FOIL SP .50 .20
❑ 665 Rich DeLucia .50 .20
❑ 666 Bob Walk .50 .20
❑ 667 Joe Carter FOIL .50 .20
❑ 668 Jose Guzman .50 .20
❑ 669 Otis Nixon .50 .20
❑ 670 Phil Nevin FOIL .50 .20
❑ 671 Eric Davis .50 .20
❑ 672 Damion Easley RC 1.00 .40
❑ 673 Will Clark FOIL .75 .30
❑ 674 Mark Kiefer RC .50 .20
❑ 675 Ozzie Smith 2.00 .75
❑ 676 Manny Ramirez FOIL 12.00 5.00
❑ 677 Gregg Olson .50 .20
❑ 678 Cliff Floyd RC 3.00 1.25
❑ 679 Duane Singleton RC .50 .20
❑ 680 Jose Rijo .50 .20
❑ 681 Willie Randolph .50 .20
❑ 682 Michael Tucker FOIL RC 1.00 .40
❑ 683 Darren Lewis .50 .20
❑ 684 Dale Murphy .75 .30
❑ 685 Mike Pagliarulo .50 .20
❑ 686 Paul Miller RC .50 .20
❑ 687 Mike Robertson RC .50 .20
❑ 688 Mike Devereaux .50 .20
❑ 689 Pedro Astacio RC 1.00 .40
❑ 690 Alan Trammell .50 .20
❑ 691 Roger Clemens 2.50 1.00
❑ 692 Bud Black .50 .20
❑ 693 Turk Wendell RC 1.00 .40
❑ 694 Barry Larkin FOIL .75 .30
❑ 695 Todd Zeile .50 .20
❑ 696 Pat Hentgen .50 .20
❑ 697 Eddie Taubensee RC 1.00 .40
❑ 698 Guillermo Velasquez RC .50 .20
❑ 699 Tom Glavine .75 .30
❑ 700 Robin Yount 2.00 .75
❑ 701 Checklist 1-141 .50 .20
❑ 702 Checklist 142-282 .50 .20
❑ 703 Checklist 283-423 .50 .20
❑ 704 Checklist 424-564 .50 .20
❑ 705 Checklist 565-705 .50 .20

1993 Bowman

❑ COMPLETE SET (708) 40.00 15.00
❑ 1 Glenn Davis .15 .05
❑ 2 Hector Roa RC .25 .08
❑ 3 Ken Ryan RC .25 .08
❑ 4 Derek Wallace RC .25 .08
❑ 5 Jorge Fabregas .15 .05
❑ 6 Joe Oliver .15 .05
❑ 7 Brandon Wilson .15 .05
❑ 8 Mark Thompson RC .25 .08
❑ 9 Tracy Sanders .15 .05
❑ 10 Rich Renteria .15 .05
❑ 11 Lou Whitaker .30 .10
❑ 12 Brian L. Hunter RC .50 .20
❑ 13 Joe Vitiello .15 .05
❑ 14 Eric Karros .30 .10
❑ 15 Joe Kmak .15 .05
❑ 16 Tavo Alvarez .15 .05
❑ 17 Steve Dunn RC .25 .08
❑ 18 Tony Fernandez .15 .05
❑ 19 Melido Perez .15 .05
❑ 20 Mike Lieberthal .30 .10
❑ 21 Terry Steinbach .15 .05
❑ 22 Stan Belinda .15 .05
❑ 23 Jay Buhner .30 .10
❑ 24 Allen Watson .15 .05
❑ 25 Daryl Henderson RC .25 .08
❑ 26 Ray McDavid RC .25 .08
❑ 27 Shawn Green 1.00 .40
❑ 28 Bud Black .15 .05
❑ 29 Sherman Obando RC .25 .08
❑ 30 Mike Hostetler RC .25 .08
❑ 31 Nate Minchey RC .25 .08
❑ 32 Randy Myers .15 .05
❑ 33 Brian Grebeck .15 .05
❑ 34 John Roper .15 .05
❑ 35 Larry Thomas .15 .05
❑ 36 Alex Cole .15 .05
❑ 37 Tom Kramer RC .25 .08
❑ 38 Matt Whisenant RC .25 .08
❑ 39 Chris Gomez RC .50 .20
❑ 40 Luis Gonzalez .30 .10
❑ 41 Kevin Appier .30 .10
❑ 42 Omar Daal RC .25 .08
❑ 43 Duane Singleton .15 .05
❑ 44 Bill Risley .15 .05
❑ 45 Pat Meares RC .50 .20
❑ 46 Butch Huskey .15 .05
❑ 47 Bobby Munoz .15 .05
❑ 48 Juan Bell .15 .05
❑ 49 Scott Lydy RC .25 .08
❑ 50 Dennis Moeller .15 .05
❑ 51 Marc Newfield .15 .05
❑ 52 Tripp Cromer RC .25 .08
❑ 53 Kurt Miller .15 .05
❑ 54 Jim Pena .15 .05
❑ 55 Juan Guzman .15 .05
❑ 56 Matt Williams .30 .10
❑ 57 Harold Reynolds .30 .10
❑ 58 Donnie Elliott RC .25 .08
❑ 59 Jon Shave RC .25 .08
❑ 60 Kevin Roberson RC .25 .08
❑ 61 Hilly Hathaway RC .25 .08
❑ 62 Jose Rijo .15 .05
❑ 63 Kerry Taylor RC .15 .05
❑ 64 Ryan Hawblitzel .15 .05
❑ 65 Glenallen Hill .15 .05
❑ 66 Ramon D. Martinez RC .25 .08
❑ 67 Travis Fryman .30 .10
❑ 68 Tom Nevers .15 .05
❑ 69 Phil Hiatt .15 .05
❑ 70 Tim Wallach .15 .05
❑ 71 B.J. Surhoff .30 .10
❑ 72 Rondell White .30 .10
❑ 73 Denny Hocking RC .50 .20
❑ 74 Mike Oquist RC .25 .08
❑ 75 Paul O'Neill .50 .20
❑ 76 Willie Banks .15 .05
❑ 77 Bob Welch .15 .05
❑ 78 Jose Sandoval RC .25 .08
❑ 79 Bill Haselman .15 .05
❑ 80 Rheal Cormier .15 .05
❑ 81 Dean Palmer .30 .10
❑ 82 Pat Gomez RC .25 .08
❑ 83 Steve Karsay .15 .05
❑ 84 Carl Hanselman RC .25 .08
❑ 85 T.R. Lewis RC .25 .08
❑ 86 Chipper Jones .75 .30
❑ 87 Scott Hatteberg .15 .05
❑ 88 Greg Hibbard .15 .05
❑ 89 Lance Painter RC .25 .08
❑ 90 Chad Mottola RC .50 .20
❑ 91 Jason Bere .15 .05
❑ 92 Dante Bichette .30 .10
❑ 93 Sandy Alomar Jr. .15 .05
❑ 94 Carl Everett .30 .10
❑ 95 Danny Bautista RC .50 .20
❑ 96 Steve Finley .30 .10
❑ 97 David Cone .30 .10
❑ 98 Todd Hollandsworth .15 .05
❑ 99 Matt Mieske .15 .05
❑ 100 Larry Walker .30 .10
❑ 101 Shane Mack .15 .05
❑ 102 Aaron Ledesma RC .25 .08
❑ 103 Andy Pettitte RC 8.00 3.00
❑ 104 Kevin Stocker .15 .05
❑ 105 Mike Mohler RC .25 .08
❑ 106 Tony Menendez .15 .05
❑ 107 Derek Lowe .30 .10
❑ 108 Basil Shabazz .15 .05
❑ 109 Dan Smith .15 .05
❑ 110 Scott Sanders RC .50 .20
❑ 111 Todd Stottlemyre .15 .05
❑ 112 Benji Simonton RC .25 .08
❑ 113 Rick Sutcliffe .30 .10
❑ 114 Lee Heath RC .25 .08
❑ 115 Jeff Russell .15 .05
❑ 116 Dave Stevens RC .25 .08
❑ 117 Mark Holzemer RC .25 .08
❑ 118 Tim Belcher .15 .05
❑ 119 Bobby Thigpen .15 .05
❑ 120 Roger Bailey RC .25 .08
❑ 121 Tony Mitchell RC .25 .08
❑ 122 Junior Felix .15 .05
❑ 123 Rich Robertson RC .25 .08
❑ 124 Andy Cook RC .25 .08
❑ 125 Brian Bevil RC .25 .08
❑ 126 Darryl Strawberry .30 .10
❑ 127 Cal Eldred .15 .05
❑ 128 Cliff Floyd .30 .10
❑ 129 Alan Newman .15 .05
❑ 130 Howard Johnson .15 .05
❑ 131 Jim Abbott .50 .20
❑ 132 Chad McConnell .15 .05
❑ 133 Miguel Jimenez RC .25 .08
❑ 134 Brett Backlund RC .25 .08
❑ 135 John Cummings RC .25 .08
❑ 136 Brian Barber .15 .05
❑ 137 Rafael Palmeiro .50 .20
❑ 138 Tim Worrell RC .25 .08
❑ 139 Jose Pett RC .25 .08
❑ 140 Barry Bonds 2.00 .75
❑ 141 Damon Buford .15 .05
❑ 142 Jeff Blauser .15 .05
❑ 143 Frankie Rodriguez .15 .05
❑ 144 Mike Morgan .15 .05
❑ 145 Gary DiSarcina .15 .05
❑ 146 Pokey Reese .15 .05
❑ 147 Johnny Ruffin .15 .05
❑ 148 David Nied .15 .05
❑ 149 Charles Nagy .15 .05
❑ 150 Mike Myers RC .25 .08
❑ 151 Kenny Carlyle RC .25 .08
❑ 152 Eric Anthony .15 .05
❑ 153 Jose Lind .15 .05
❑ 154 Pedro Martinez 1.50 .60
❑ 155 Mark Kiefer .15 .05
❑ 156 Tim Laker RC .25 .08
❑ 157 Pat Mahomes .15 .05
❑ 158 Bobby Bonilla .30 .10
❑ 159 Domingo Jean .15 .05
❑ 160 Darren Daulton .30 .10
❑ 161 Mark McGwire 2.00 .75
❑ 162 Jason Kendall RC 2.00 .75
❑ 163 Desi Relaford .15 .05
❑ 164 Ozzie Canseco .15 .05
❑ 165 Rick Helling .15 .05
❑ 166 Steve Pegues RC .25 .08
❑ 167 Paul Molitor .30 .10
❑ 168 Larry Carter RC .15 .05
❑ 169 Arthur Rhodes .15 .05
❑ 170 Damon Hollins RC .50 .20
❑ 171 Frank Viola .30 .10
❑ 172 Steve Trachsel RC 1.00 .40
❑ 173 J.T.Snow RC 1.00 .40
❑ 174 Keith Gordon RC .25 .08
❑ 175 Carlton Fisk .50 .20
❑ 176 Jason Bates RC .25 .08
❑ 177 Mike Crosby RC .25 .08
❑ 178 Benny Santiago .30 .10
❑ 179 Mike Moore .15 .05
❑ 180 Jeff Juden .15 .05
❑ 181 Darren Burton .15 .05
❑ 182 Todd Williams RC .50 .20
❑ 183 John Jaha .15 .05
❑ 184 Mike Lansing RC .50 .20
❑ 185 Pedro Grifol RC .25 .08
❑ 186 Vince Coleman .15 .05
❑ 187 Pat Kelly .15 .05
❑ 188 Clemente Alvarez RC .25 .08
❑ 189 Ron Darling .15 .05
❑ 190 Orlando Merced .15 .05
❑ 191 Chris Bosio .15 .05
❑ 192 Steve Dixon RC .25 .08

❑ 193 Doug Dascenzo .15 .05
❑ 194 Ray Holbert RC .25 .08
❑ 195 Howard Battle .15 .05
❑ 196 Willie McGee .30 .10
❑ 197 John O'Donoghue RC .25 .08
❑ 198 Steve Avery .15 .05
❑ 199 Greg Blosser .15 .05
❑ 200 Ryne Sandberg 1.25 .50
❑ 201 Joe Grahe .15 .05
❑ 202 Dan Wilson .30 .10
❑ 203 Domingo Martinez RC .25 .08
❑ 204 Andres Galarraga .30 .10
❑ 205 Jamie Taylor RC .25 .08
❑ 206 Darrell Whitmore RC .25 .08
❑ 207 Ben Blomdahl RC .25 .08
❑ 208 Doug Drabek .15 .05
❑ 209 Keith Miller .15 .05
❑ 210 Billy Ashley .15 .05
❑ 211 Mike Farrell RC .25 .08
❑ 212 John Wetteland .30 .10
❑ 213 Randy Tomlin .15 .05
❑ 214 Sid Fernandez .15 .05
❑ 215 Quilvio Veras RC .50 .20
❑ 216 Dave Hollins .15 .05
❑ 217 Mike Neill .15 .05
❑ 218 Andy Van Slyke .50 .20
❑ 219 Bret Boone .30 .10
❑ 220 Tom Pagnozzi .15 .05
❑ 221 Mike Welch RC .25 .08
❑ 222 Frank Seminara .15 .05
❑ 223 Ron Villone .15 .05
❑ 224 D.J.Thielen RC .25 .08
❑ 225 Cal Ripken 2.50 1.00
❑ 226 Pedro Borbon Jr. RC .25 .08
❑ 227 Carlos Quintana .15 .05
❑ 228 Tommy Shields .15 .05
❑ 229 Tim Salmon .50 .20
❑ 230 John Smiley .15 .05
❑ 231 Ellis Burks .30 .10
❑ 232 Pedro Castellano .15 .05
❑ 233 Paul Byrd .30 .10
❑ 234 Bryan Harvey .15 .05
❑ 235 Scott Livingstone .15 .05
❑ 236 James Mouton RC .25 .08
❑ 237 Joe Randa .30 .10
❑ 238 Pedro Astacio .15 .05
❑ 239 Darryl Hamilton .15 .05
❑ 240 Joey Eischen RC .25 .08
❑ 241 Edgar Herrera RC .25 .08
❑ 242 Dwight Gooden .30 .10
❑ 243 Sam Militello .15 .05
❑ 244 Ron Blazier RC .25 .08
❑ 245 Ruben Sierra .30 .10
❑ 246 Al Martin .15 .05
❑ 247 Mike Felder .15 .05
❑ 248 Bob Tewksbury .15 .05
❑ 249 Craig Lefferts .15 .05
❑ 250 Luis Lopez RC .25 .08
❑ 251 Devon White .30 .10
❑ 252 Will Clark .50 .20
❑ 253 Mark Smith .15 .05
❑ 254 Terry Pendleton .30 .10
❑ 255 Aaron Sele .15 .05
❑ 256 Jose Viera RC .25 .08
❑ 257 Damion Easley .15 .05
❑ 258 Rod Lofton RC .25 .08
❑ 259 Chris Snopek RC .25 .08
❑ 260 Quinton McCracken RC .50 .20
❑ 261 Mike Matthews RC .25 .08
❑ 262 Hector Carrasco RC .25 .08
❑ 263 Rick Greene .15 .05
❑ 264 Chris Holt RC .50 .20
❑ 265 George Brett 2.00 .75
❑ 266 Rick Gorecki RC .25 .08
❑ 267 Francisco Gamez RC .25 .08
❑ 268 Marquis Grissom .30 .10
❑ 269 Kevin Tapani UER .15 .05
❑ 270 Ryan Thompson .15 .05
❑ 271 Gerald Williams .15 .05
❑ 272 Paul Fletcher RC .25 .08
❑ 273 Lance Blankenship .15 .05
❑ 274 Marty Neff RC .25 .08
❑ 275 Shawn Estes .15 .05
❑ 276 Rene Arocha RC .50 .20
❑ 277 Scott Eyre RC .25 .08
❑ 278 Phil Plantier .15 .05
❑ 279 Paul Spoljaric RC .25 .08
❑ 280 Chris Gambs .15 .05
❑ 281 Harold Baines .30 .10
❑ 282 Jose Oliva .15 .05
❑ 283 Matt Whiteside RC .25 .08
❑ 284 Brant Brown RC .50 .20
❑ 285 Russ Springer .15 .05
❑ 286 Chris Sabo .15 .05
❑ 287 Ozzie Guillen .30 .10
❑ 288 Marcus Moore RC .25 .08
❑ 289 Chad Ogea .15 .05
❑ 290 Walt Weiss .15 .05
❑ 291 Brian Edmondson .15 .05
❑ 292 Jimmy Gonzalez .15 .05
❑ 293 Danny Miceli RC .50 .20
❑ 294 Jose Offerman .15 .05
❑ 295 Greg Vaughn .15 .05
❑ 296 Frank Bolick .15 .05
❑ 297 Mike Maksudian RC .25 .08
❑ 298 John Franco .30 .10
❑ 299 Danny Tartabull .15 .05
❑ 300 Len Dykstra .30 .10
❑ 301 Bobby Witt .15 .05
❑ 302 Trey Beamon RC .25 .08
❑ 303 Tino Martinez .50 .20
❑ 304 Aaron Holbert .15 .05
❑ 305 Juan Gonzalez .30 .10
❑ 306 Billy Hall RC .25 .08
❑ 307 Duane Ward .15 .05
❑ 308 Rod Beck .15 .05
❑ 309 Jose Mercedes RC .25 .08
❑ 310 Otis Nixon .15 .05
❑ 311 Gettys Glaze RC .25 .08
❑ 312 Candy Maldonado .15 .05
❑ 313 Chad Curtis .15 .05
❑ 314 Tim Costo .15 .05
❑ 315 Mike Robertson .15 .05
❑ 316 Nigel Wilson .15 .05
❑ 317 Greg McMichael RC .50 .20
❑ 318 Scott Pose RC .25 .08
❑ 319 Ivan Cruz .15 .05
❑ 320 Greg Swindell .15 .05
❑ 321 Kevin McReynolds .15 .05
❑ 322 Tom Candiotti .15 .05
❑ 323 Rob Wishnevski RC .25 .08
❑ 324 Ken Hill .15 .05
❑ 325 Kirby Puckett .75 .30
❑ 326 Tim Bogar RC .25 .08
❑ 327 Mariano Rivera 2.50 1.00
❑ 328 Mitch Williams .15 .05
❑ 329 Craig Paquette .15 .05
❑ 330 Jay Bell .30 .10
❑ 331 Jose Martinez RC .25 .08
❑ 332 Rob Deer .15 .05
❑ 333 Brook Fordyce .15 .05
❑ 334 Matt Nokes .15 .05
❑ 335 Derek Lee .15 .05
❑ 336 Paul Ellis RC .25 .08
❑ 337 Desi Wilson RC .25 .08
❑ 338 Roberto Alomar .50 .20
❑ 339 Jim Tatum FOIL RC .25 .08
❑ 340 J.T.Snow FOIL 1.00 .40
❑ 341 Tim Salmon FOIL .50 .20
❑ 342 Russ Davis FOIL RC .50 .20
❑ 343 Javy Lopez FOIL .50 .20
❑ 344 Troy O'Leary FOIL RC .50 .20
❑ 345 Marty Cordova FOIL RC .50 .20
❑ 346 Bubba Smith RC FOIL .25 .08
❑ 347 Chipper Jones FOIL .75 .30
❑ 348 Jessie Hollins FOIL .15 .05
❑ 349 Willie Greene FOIL .15 .05
❑ 350 Mark Thompson FOIL .15 .05
❑ 351 Nigel Wilson FOIL .15 .05
❑ 352 Todd Jones FOIL .30 .10
❑ 353 Raul Mondesi FOIL .30 .10
❑ 354 Cliff Floyd FOIL .30 .10
❑ 355 Bobby Jones FOIL .30 .10
❑ 356 Kevin Stocker FOIL .15 .05
❑ 357 Midre Cummings FOIL .15 .05
❑ 358 Allen Watson FOIL .15 .05
❑ 359 Ray McDavid FOIL .15 .05
❑ 360 Steve Hosey FOIL .15 .05
❑ 361 Brad Pennington FOIL .15 .05
❑ 362 Frankie Rodriguez FOIL .15 .05
❑ 363 Troy Percival FOIL .50 .20
❑ 364 Jason Bere FOIL .15 .05
❑ 365 Manny Ramirez FOIL 1.25 .50
❑ 366 Justin Thompson FOIL .15 .05
❑ 367 Joe Vitiello FOIL .15 .05
❑ 368 Tyrone Hill FOIL .15 .05
❑ 369 David McCarty FOIL .15 .05
❑ 370 Brien Taylor FOIL .15 .05
❑ 371 Todd Van Poppel FOIL .15 .05
❑ 372 Marc Newfield FOIL .15 .05
❑ 373 Terrell Lowery FOIL RC .50 .20
❑ 374 Alex Gonzalez FOIL .15 .05
❑ 375 Ken Griffey Jr. 1.25 .50
❑ 376 Donovan Osborne .15 .05
❑ 377 Ritchie Moody RC .25 .08
❑ 378 Shane Andrews .15 .05
❑ 379 Carlos Delgado .75 .30
❑ 380 Bill Swift .15 .05
❑ 381 Leo Gomez .15 .05
❑ 382 Ron Gant .30 .10
❑ 383 Scott Fletcher .15 .05
❑ 384 Matt Walbeck RC .50 .20
❑ 385 Chuck Finley .30 .10
❑ 386 Kevin Mitchell .15 .05
❑ 387 Wilson Alvarez UER .15 .05
❑ 388 John Burke RC .25 .08
❑ 389 Alan Embree .15 .05
❑ 390 Trevor Hoffman .75 .30
❑ 391 Alan Trammell .30 .10
❑ 392 Todd Jones .30 .10
❑ 393 Felix Jose .15 .05
❑ 394 Orel Hershiser .30 .10
❑ 395 Pat Listach .15 .05
❑ 396 Gabe White .15 .05
❑ 397 Dan Serafini RC .25 .08
❑ 398 Todd Hundley .15 .05
❑ 399 Wade Boggs .50 .20
❑ 400 Tyler Green .15 .05
❑ 401 Mike Bordick .15 .05
❑ 402 Scott Bullett .15 .05
❑ 403 LaGrande Russell RC .25 .08
❑ 404 Ray Lankford .30 .10
❑ 405 Nolan Ryan 3.00 1.25
❑ 406 Robbie Beckett .15 .05
❑ 407 Brent Bowers RC .25 .08
❑ 408 Adell Davenport RC .25 .08
❑ 409 Brady Anderson .30 .10
❑ 410 Tom Glavine .50 .20
❑ 411 Doug Hecker RC .25 .08
❑ 412 Jose Guzman .15 .05
❑ 413 Luis Polonia .15 .05
❑ 414 Brian Williams .15 .05
❑ 415 Bo Jackson .75 .30
❑ 416 Eric Young .15 .05
❑ 417 Kenny Lofton .30 .10
❑ 418 Orestes Destrade .15 .05
❑ 419 Tony Phillips .15 .05
❑ 420 Jeff Bagwell .50 .20
❑ 421 Mark Gardner .15 .05
❑ 422 Brett Butler .30 .10
❑ 423 Graeme Lloyd RC .50 .20
❑ 424 Delino DeShields .15 .05
❑ 425 Scott Erickson .15 .05
❑ 426 Jeff Kent .75 .30
❑ 427 Jimmy Key .30 .10
❑ 428 Mickey Morandini .15 .05
❑ 429 Marcos Armas RC .25 .08
❑ 430 Don Slaught .15 .05
❑ 431 Randy Johnson .75 .30
❑ 432 Omar Olivares .15 .05
❑ 433 Charlie Leibrandt .15 .05
❑ 434 Kurt Stillwell .15 .05
❑ 435 Scott Brow RC .25 .08
❑ 436 Robby Thompson .15 .05
❑ 437 Ben McDonald .15 .05
❑ 438 Deion Sanders .50 .20
❑ 439 Tony Pena .15 .05
❑ 440 Mark Grace .50 .20
❑ 441 Eduardo Perez .15 .05
❑ 442 Tim Pugh RC .25 .08
❑ 443 Scott Ruffcorn .15 .05
❑ 444 Jay Gainer RC .25 .08
❑ 445 Albert Belle .30 .10
❑ 446 Bret Barberie .15 .05
❑ 447 Justin Mashore .15 .05
❑ 448 Pete Harnisch .15 .05
❑ 449 Greg Gagne .15 .05
❑ 450 Eric Davis .30 .10

❑ 451 Dave Micki .15 .05
❑ 452 Moises Alou .30 .10
❑ 453 Rick Aguilera .15 .05
❑ 454 Eddie Murray .75 .30
❑ 455 Bob Wickman .15 .05
❑ 456 Wes Chamberlain .15 .05
❑ 457 Brent Gates .15 .05
❑ 458 Paul Wagner .15 .05
❑ 459 Mike Hampton .30 .10
❑ 460 Ozzie Smith 1.25 .50
❑ 461 Tom Henke .15 .05
❑ 462 Ricky Gutierrez .15 .05
❑ 463 Jack Morris .30 .10
❑ 464 Joel Chimelis .15 .05
❑ 465 Gregg Olson .15 .05
❑ 466 Javy Lopez .50 .20
❑ 467 Scott Cooper .15 .05
❑ 468 Willie Wilson .15 .05
❑ 469 Mark Langston .15 .05
❑ 470 Barry Larkin .50 .20
❑ 471 Rod Bolton .15 .05
❑ 472 Freddie Benavides .15 .05
❑ 473 Ken Ramos RC .25 .08
❑ 474 Chuck Carr .15 .05
❑ 475 Cecil Fielder .30 .10
❑ 476 Eddie Taubensee .15 .05
❑ 477 Chris Eddy RC .25 .08
❑ 478 Greg Hansell .15 .05
❑ 479 Kevin Reimer .15 .05
❑ 480 Dennis Martinez .30 .10
❑ 481 Chuck Knoblauch .30 .10
❑ 482 Mike Draper .15 .05
❑ 483 Spike Owen .15 .05
❑ 484 Terry Mulholland .15 .05
❑ 485 Dennis Eckersley .30 .10
❑ 486 Blas Minor .15 .05
❑ 487 Dave Fleming .15 .05
❑ 488 Dan Cholowsky .15 .05
❑ 489 Ivan Rodriguez .50 .20
❑ 490 Gary Sheffield .30 .10
❑ 491 Ed Sprague .15 .05
❑ 492 Steve Hosey .15 .05
❑ 493 Jimmy Haynes RC .50 .20
❑ 494 John Smoltz .50 .20
❑ 495 Andre Dawson .30 .10
❑ 496 Rey Sanchez .15 .05
❑ 497 Ty Van Burkleo .15 .05
❑ 498 Bobby Ayala RC .25 .08
❑ 499 Tim Raines .30 .10
❑ 500 Charlie Hayes .15 .05
❑ 501 Paul Sorrento .15 .05
❑ 502 Richie Lewis RC .25 .08
❑ 503 Jason Pfaff RC .25 .08
❑ 504 Ken Caminiti .30 .10
❑ 505 Mike Macfarlane .15 .05
❑ 506 Jody Reed .15 .05
❑ 507 Bobby Hughes RC .25 .08
❑ 508 Wil Cordero .15 .05
❑ 509 George Tsamis RC .25 .08
❑ 510 Bret Saberhagen .30 .10
❑ 511 Derek Jeter RC 25.00 10.00
❑ 512 Gene Schall .15 .05
❑ 513 Curtis Shaw .15 .05
❑ 514 Steve Cooke .15 .05
❑ 515 Edgar Martinez .50 .20
❑ 516 Mike Milchin .15 .05
❑ 517 Billy Ripken .15 .05
❑ 518 Andy Benes .15 .05
❑ 519 Juan de la Rosa RC .25 .08
❑ 520 John Burkett .15 .05
❑ 521 Alex Ochoa .15 .05
❑ 522 Tony Tarasco RC .50 .20
❑ 523 Luis Ortiz .15 .05
❑ 524 Rick Wilkins .15 .05
❑ 525 Chris Turner RC .25 .08
❑ 526 Rob Dibble .30 .10
❑ 527 Jack McDowell .15 .05
❑ 528 Daryl Boston .15 .05
❑ 529 Bill Wertz RC .25 .08
❑ 530 Charlie Hough .30 .10
❑ 531 Sean Bergman .15 .05
❑ 532 Doug Jones .15 .05
❑ 533 Jeff Montgomery .15 .05
❑ 534 Roger Cedeno RC .50 .20
❑ 535 Robin Yount 1.25 .50
❑ 536 Mo Vaughn .30 .10
❑ 537 Brian Harper .15 .05
❑ 538 Juan Castillo RC .15 .05
❑ 539 Steve Farr .15 .05
❑ 540 John Kruk .30 .10
❑ 541 Troy Neel .15 .05
❑ 542 Danny Clyburn RC .25 .08
❑ 543 Jim Converse RC .25 .08
❑ 544 Gregg Jefferies .15 .05
❑ 545 Jose Canseco .50 .20
❑ 546 Julio Bruno RC .25 .08
❑ 547 Rob Butler .15 .05
❑ 548 Royce Clayton .15 .05
❑ 549 Chris Hoiles .15 .05
❑ 550 Greg Maddux 1.25 .50
❑ 551 Joe Ciccarella RC .25 .08
❑ 552 Ozzie Timmons .15 .05
❑ 553 Chili Davis .30 .10
❑ 554 Brian Koelling .15 .05
❑ 555 Frank Thomas .75 .30
❑ 556 Vinny Castilla .75 .30
❑ 557 Reggie Jefferson .15 .05
❑ 558 Rob Natal .15 .05
❑ 559 Mike Henneman .15 .05
❑ 560 Craig Biggio .50 .20
❑ 561 Billy Brewer .15 .05
❑ 562 Dan Melendez .15 .05
❑ 563 Kenny Felder RC .25 .08
❑ 564 Miguel Batista RC 1.00 .40
❑ 565 Dave Winfield .30 .10
❑ 566 Al Shirley .15 .05
❑ 567 Robert Eenhoorn .15 .05
❑ 568 Mike Williams .15 .05
❑ 569 Tanyon Sturtze RC .50 .20
❑ 570 Tim Wakefield .75 .30
❑ 571 Greg Pirkl .15 .05
❑ 572 Sean Lowe RC .25 .08
❑ 573 Terry Burrows RC .25 .08
❑ 574 Kevin Higgins .15 .05
❑ 575 Joe Carter .30 .10
❑ 576 Kevin Rogers .15 .05
❑ 577 Manny Alexander .15 .05
❑ 578 David Justice .30 .10
❑ 579 Brian Conroy RC .25 .08
❑ 580 Jessie Hollins .15 .05
❑ 581 Ron Watson RC .25 .08
❑ 582 Bip Roberts .15 .05
❑ 583 Tom Urbani RC .25 .08
❑ 584 Jason Hutchins RC .25 .08
❑ 585 Carlos Baerga .15 .05
❑ 586 Jeff Mutis .15 .05
❑ 587 Justin Thompson .15 .05
❑ 588 Orlando Miller .15 .05
❑ 589 Brian McRae .15 .05
❑ 590 Ramon Martinez .15 .05
❑ 591 Dave Nilsson .15 .05
❑ 592 Jose Vidro RC 2.00 .75
❑ 593 Rich Becker .15 .05
❑ 594 Preston Wilson RC 1.50 .60
❑ 595 Don Mattingly 2.00 .75
❑ 596 Tony Longmire .15 .05
❑ 597 Kevin Seitzer .15 .05
❑ 598 Midre Cummings RC .25 .08
❑ 599 Omar Vizquel .50 .20
❑ 600 Lee Smith .30 .10
❑ 601 David Hulse RC .25 .08
❑ 602 Darrell Sherman RC .25 .08
❑ 603 Alex Gonzalez .15 .05
❑ 604 Geronimo Pena .15 .05
❑ 605 Mike Devereaux .15 .05
❑ 606 Sterling Hitchcock RC .50 .20
❑ 607 Mike Greenwell .15 .05
❑ 608 Steve Buechele .15 .05
❑ 609 Troy Percival .50 .20
❑ 610 Roberto Kelly .15 .05
❑ 611 James Baldwin RC .50 .20
❑ 612 Jerald Clark .15 .05
❑ 613 Albie Lopez RC .25 .08
❑ 614 Dave Magadan .15 .05
❑ 615 Mickey Tettleton .15 .05
❑ 616 Sean Runyan RC .25 .08
❑ 617 Bob Hamelin .15 .05
❑ 618 Raul Mondesi .30 .10
❑ 619 Tyrone Hill .15 .05
❑ 620 Darrin Fletcher .15 .05
❑ 621 Mike Trombley .15 .05
❑ 622 Jeromy Burnitz .30 .10
❑ 623 Bernie Williams .50 .20
❑ 624 Mike Farmer RC .25 .08
❑ 625 Rickey Henderson .75 .30
❑ 626 Carlos Garcia .15 .05
❑ 627 Jeff Darwin RC .25 .08
❑ 628 Todd Zeile .15 .05
❑ 629 Benji Gil .15 .05
❑ 630 Tony Gwynn 1.00 .40
❑ 631 Aaron Small RC 1.00 .40
❑ 632 Joe Rosselli RC .25 .08
❑ 633 Mike Mussina .50 .20
❑ 634 Ryan Klesko .30 .10
❑ 635 Roger Clemens 1.50 .60
❑ 636 Sammy Sosa .75 .30
❑ 637 Orlando Palmeiro RC .25 .08
❑ 638 Willie Greene .15 .05
❑ 639 George Bell .15 .05
❑ 640 Garvin Alston RC .25 .08
❑ 641 Pete Janicki RC .25 .08
❑ 642 Chris Sheff RC .25 .08
❑ 643 Felipe Lira RC .25 .08
❑ 644 Roberto Petagine .15 .05
❑ 645 Wally Joyner .30 .10
❑ 646 Mike Piazza 3.00 1.25
❑ 647 Jaime Navarro .15 .05
❑ 648 Jeff Hartsock .15 .05
❑ 649 David McCarty .15 .05
❑ 650 Bobby Jones .30 .10
❑ 651 Mark Hutton .15 .05
❑ 652 Kyle Abbott .15 .05
❑ 653 Steve Cox RC .25 .08
❑ 654 Jeff King .15 .05
❑ 655 Norm Charlton .15 .05
❑ 656 Mike Gulan RC .25 .08
❑ 657 Julio Franco .30 .10
❑ 658 Cameron Cairncross RC .25 .08
❑ 659 John Olerud .30 .10
❑ 660 Salomon Torres .15 .05
❑ 661 Brad Pennington .15 .05
❑ 662 Melvin Nieves .15 .05
❑ 663 Ivan Calderon .15 .05
❑ 664 Turk Wendell .15 .05
❑ 665 Chris Pritchett .15 .05
❑ 666 Reggie Sanders .30 .10
❑ 667 Robin Ventura .30 .10
❑ 668 Joe Girardi .15 .05
❑ 669 Manny Ramirez 1.25 .50
❑ 670 Jeff Conine .30 .10
❑ 671 Greg Gohr .15 .05
❑ 672 Andujar Cedeno .15 .05
❑ 673 Les Norman RC .25 .08
❑ 674 Mike James RC .25 .08
❑ 675 Marshall Boze RC .25 .08
❑ 676 B.J.Wallace .15 .05
❑ 677 Kent Hrbek .30 .10
❑ 678 Jack Voigt RC .25 .08
❑ 679 Brien Taylor .15 .05
❑ 680 Curt Schilling .30 .10
❑ 681 Todd Van Poppel .15 .05
❑ 682 Kevin Young .30 .10
❑ 683 Tommy Adams .15 .05
❑ 684 Bernard Gilkey .15 .05
❑ 685 Kevin Brown .30 .10
❑ 686 Fred McGriff .50 .20
❑ 687 Pat Borders .15 .05
❑ 688 Kirt Manwaring .15 .05
❑ 689 Sid Bream .15 .05
❑ 690 John Valentin .15 .05
❑ 691 Steve Olsen RC .25 .08
❑ 692 Roberto Mejia RC .25 .08
❑ 693 Carlos Delgado FOIL .75 .30
❑ 694 Steve Gibralter FOIL RC .25 .08
❑ 695 Gary Mota FOIL RC .25 .08
❑ 696 Jose Malave FOIL RC .25 .08
❑ 697 Larry Sutton FOIL RC .25 .08
❑ 698 Dan Frye FOIL RC .25 .08
❑ 699 Tim Clark FOIL RC .25 .08
❑ 700 Brian Rupp FOIL RC .25 .08
❑ 701 Felipe/Moises Alou FOIL .30 .10
❑ 702 Barry/Bobby Bonds FOIL 1.00 .40
❑ 703 Ken Griffey Jr./Sr. FOIL .75 .30
❑ 704 Brian/Hal McRae FOIL .15 .05
❑ 705 Checklist 1 .15 .05
❑ 706 Checklist 2 .15 .05
❑ 707 Checklist 3 .15 .05
❑ 708 Checklist 4 .15 .05

1994 Bowman

❑ COMPLETE SET (682)	60.00	30.00
❑ 1 Joe Carter	.40	.15
❑ 2 Marcus Moore	.25	.08
❑ 3 Doug Creek RC	.40	.15
❑ 4 Pedro Martinez	1.00	.40
❑ 5 Ken Griffey Jr.	1.50	.60
❑ 6 Greg Swindell	.25	.08
❑ 7 J.J. Johnson	.25	.08
❑ 8 Homer Bush RC	.40	.15
❑ 9 Arquimedez Pozo RC	.40	.15
❑ 10 Bryan Harvey	.25	.08
❑ 11 J.T. Snow	.40	.15
❑ 12 Alan Benes RC	1.00	.40
❑ 13 Chad Kreuter	.25	.08
❑ 14 Eric Karros	.40	.15
❑ 15 Frank Thomas	1.00	.40
❑ 16 Bret Saberhagen	.40	.15
❑ 17 Terrell Lowery	.25	.08
❑ 18 Rod Bolton	.25	.08
❑ 19 Harold Baines	.40	.15
❑ 20 Matt Walbeck	.25	.08
❑ 21 Tom Glavine	.60	.25
❑ 22 Todd Jones	.25	.08
❑ 23 Alberto Castillo RC	.40	.15
❑ 24 Ruben Sierra	.40	.15
❑ 25 Don Mattingly	2.50	1.00
❑ 26 Mike Morgan	.25	.08
❑ 27 Jim Musselwhite RC	.40	.15
❑ 28 Matt Brunson RC	.40	.15
❑ 29 Adam Meinershagen RC	.40	.15
❑ 30 Joe Girardi	.25	.08
❑ 31 Shane Halter	.25	.08
❑ 32 Jose Paniagua RC	1.00	.40
❑ 33 Paul Perkins RC	.40	.15
❑ 34 John Hudek RC	.40	.15
❑ 35 Frank Viola	.40	.15
❑ 36 David Lamb RC	.40	.15
❑ 37 Marshall Boze	.25	.08
❑ 38 Jorge Posada RC	8.00	3.00
❑ 39 Brian Anderson RC	1.00	.40
❑ 40 Mark Whiten	.25	.08
❑ 41 Sean Bergman	.25	.08
❑ 42 Jose Parra RC	.40	.15
❑ 43 Mike Robertson	.25	.08
❑ 44 Pete Walker RC	.40	.15
❑ 45 Juan Gonzalez	.40	.15
❑ 46 Cleveland Ladell RC	.40	.15
❑ 47 Mark Smith	.25	.08
❑ 48 Kevin Jarvis RC UER	.40	.15
❑ 49 Amaury Telemaco RC	.40	.15
❑ 50 Andy Van Slyke	.60	.25
❑ 51 Rikkert Faneyte RC	.40	.15
❑ 52 Curtis Shaw	.25	.08
❑ 53 Matt Drews RC	.40	.15
❑ 54 Wilson Alvarez	.25	.08
❑ 55 Manny Ramirez	1.00	.40
❑ 56 Bobby Munoz	.25	.08
❑ 57 Ed Sprague	.25	.08
❑ 58 Jamey Wright RC	1.00	.40
❑ 59 Jeff Montgomery	.25	.08
❑ 60 Kirk Rueter	.25	.08
❑ 61 Edgar Martinez	.60	.25
❑ 62 Luis Gonzalez	.40	.15
❑ 63 Tim Vanegmond RC	.40	.15
❑ 64 Bip Roberts	.25	.08
❑ 65 John Jaha	.25	.08
❑ 66 Chuck Carr	.25	.08
❑ 67 Chuck Finley	.40	.15
❑ 68 Aaron Holbert	.25	.08
❑ 69 Cecil Fielder	.40	.15
❑ 70 Tom Engle RC	.40	.15
❑ 71 Ron Karkovice	.25	.08
❑ 72 Joe Orsulak	.25	.08
❑ 73 Duff Brumley RC	.40	.15
❑ 74 Craig Clayton RC	.40	.15
❑ 75 Cal Ripken	3.00	1.25
❑ 76 Brad Fullmer RC	1.00	.40
❑ 77 Tony Tarasco	.25	.08
❑ 78 Terry Farrar RC	.40	.15
❑ 79 Matt Williams	.40	.15
❑ 80 Rickey Henderson	1.00	.40
❑ 81 Terry Mulholland	.25	.08
❑ 82 Sammy Sosa	1.00	.40
❑ 83 Paul Sorrento	.25	.08
❑ 84 Pete Incaviglia	.25	.08
❑ 85 Darren Hall RC	.40	.15
❑ 86 Scott Klingenbeck	.25	.08
❑ 87 Dario Perez RC	.40	.15
❑ 88 Ugueth Urbina	.25	.08
❑ 89 Dave Vanhof RC	.40	.15
❑ 90 Domingo Jean	.25	.08
❑ 91 Otis Nixon	.25	.08
❑ 92 Andres Berumen	.25	.08
❑ 93 Jose Valentin	.25	.08
❑ 94 Edgar Renteria RC	5.00	2.00
❑ 95 Chris Turner	.25	.08
❑ 96 Ray Lankford	.40	.15
❑ 97 Danny Bautista	.25	.08
❑ 98 Chan Ho Park RC	1.50	.60
❑ 99 Glenn DiSarcina RC	.40	.15
❑ 100 Butch Huskey	.25	.08
❑ 101 Ivan Rodriguez	.60	.25
❑ 102 Johnny Ruffin	.25	.08
❑ 103 Alex Ochoa	.25	.08
❑ 104 Torii Hunter RC	5.00	2.00
❑ 105 Ryan Klesko	.40	.15
❑ 106 Jay Bell	.40	.15
❑ 107 Kurt Peltzer RC	.40	.15
❑ 108 Miguel Jimenez	.25	.08
❑ 109 Russ Davis	.25	.08
❑ 110 Derek Wallace	.25	.08
❑ 111 Keith Lockhart RC	1.00	.40
❑ 112 Mike Lieberthal	.40	.15
❑ 113 Dave Stewart	.40	.15
❑ 114 Tom Schmidt	.25	.08
❑ 115 Brian McRae	.25	.08
❑ 116 Moises Alou	.40	.15
❑ 117 Dave Fleming	.25	.08
❑ 118 Jeff Bagwell	.60	.25
❑ 119 Luis Ortiz	.25	.08
❑ 120 Tony Gwynn	1.25	.50
❑ 121 Jaime Navarro	.25	.08
❑ 122 Benito Santiago	.40	.15
❑ 123 Darrell Whitmore	.25	.08
❑ 124 John Mabry RC	1.00	.40
❑ 125 Mickey Tettleton	.25	.08
❑ 126 Tom Candiotti	.25	.08
❑ 127 Tim Raines	.40	.15
❑ 128 Bobby Bonilla	.40	.15
❑ 129 John Dettmer	.25	.08
❑ 130 Hector Carrasco	.25	.08
❑ 131 Chris Hoiles	.25	.08
❑ 132 Rick Aguilera	.25	.08
❑ 133 David Justice	.40	.15
❑ 134 Esteban Loaiza RC	1.50	.60
❑ 135 Barry Bonds	2.50	1.00
❑ 136 Bob Welch	.25	.08
❑ 137 Mike Stanley	.25	.08
❑ 138 Roberto Hernandez	.25	.08
❑ 139 Sandy Alomar Jr.	.25	.08
❑ 140 Darren Daulton	.40	.15
❑ 141 Angel Martinez RC	.40	.15
❑ 142 Howard Johnson	.25	.08
❑ 143 Bob Hamelin	.25	.08
❑ 144 J.J.Thobe RC	.40	.15
❑ 145 Roger Salkeld	.25	.08
❑ 146 Orlando Miller	.25	.08
❑ 147 Dmitri Young	.40	.15
❑ 148 Tim Hyers RC	.40	.15
❑ 149 Mark Loretta RC	5.00	2.00
❑ 150 Chris Hammond	.25	.08
❑ 151 Joel Moore RC	.40	.15
❑ 152 Todd Zeile	.25	.08
❑ 153 Wil Cordero	.25	.08
❑ 154 Chris Smith	.25	.08
❑ 155 James Baldwin	.25	.08
❑ 156 Edgardo Alfonzo RC	1.00	.40
❑ 157 Kym Ashworth RC	.40	.15
❑ 158 Paul Bako RC	.40	.15
❑ 159 Rick Krivda RC	.40	.15
❑ 160 Pat Mahomes	.25	.08
❑ 161 Damon Hollins	.25	.08
❑ 162 Felix Martinez RC	.40	.15
❑ 163 Jason Myers RC	.40	.15
❑ 164 Izzy Molina RC	.40	.15
❑ 165 Brien Taylor	.25	.08
❑ 166 Kevin Orie RC	.40	.15
❑ 167 Casey Whitten RC	.40	.15
❑ 168 Tony Longmire	.25	.08
❑ 169 John Olerud	.40	.15
❑ 170 Mark Thompson	.25	.08
❑ 171 Jorge Fabregas	.25	.08
❑ 172 John Wetteland	.40	.15
❑ 173 Dan Wilson	.25	.08
❑ 174 Doug Drabek	.25	.08
❑ 175 Jeff McNeely	.25	.08
❑ 176 Melvin Nieves	.25	.08
❑ 177 Doug Glanville RC	1.00	.40
❑ 178 Javier De La Hoya RC	.40	.15
❑ 179 Chad Curtis	.25	.08
❑ 180 Brian Barber	.25	.08
❑ 181 Mike Henneman	.25	.08
❑ 182 Jose Offerman	.25	.08
❑ 183 Robert Ellis RC	.40	.15
❑ 184 John Franco	.40	.15
❑ 185 Benji Gil	.25	.08
❑ 186 Hal Morris	.25	.08
❑ 187 Chris Sabo	.25	.08
❑ 188 Blaise Ilsley RC	.40	.15
❑ 189 Steve Avery	.25	.08
❑ 190 Rick White RC	.40	.15
❑ 191 Rod Beck	.25	.08
❑ 192 Mark McGwire UER NNO	2.50	1.00
❑ 193 Jim Abbott	.60	.25
❑ 194 Randy Myers	.25	.08
❑ 195 Kenny Lofton	.40	.15
❑ 196 Mariano Duncan	.25	.08
❑ 197 Lee Daniels RC	.40	.15
❑ 198 Armando Reynoso	.25	.08
❑ 199 Joe Randa	.40	.15
❑ 200 Cliff Floyd	.40	.15
❑ 201 Tim Harkrider RC	.40	.15
❑ 202 Kevin Gallaher RC	.40	.15
❑ 203 Scott Cooper	.25	.08
❑ 204 Phil Stidham RC	.40	.15
❑ 205 Jeff D'Amico RC	.40	.15
❑ 206 Matt Whisenant	.25	.08
❑ 207 De Shawn Warren	.25	.08
❑ 208 Rene Arocha	.25	.08
❑ 209 Tony Clark RC	1.50	.60
❑ 210 Jason Jacome RC	.40	.15
❑ 211 Scott Christman RC	.40	.15
❑ 212 Bill Pulsipher	.40	.15
❑ 213 Dean Palmer	.40	.15
❑ 214 Chad Mottola	.25	.08
❑ 215 Manny Alexander	.25	.08
❑ 216 Rich Becker	.25	.08
❑ 217 Andre King RC	.40	.15
❑ 218 Carlos Garcia	.25	.08
❑ 219 Ron Pezzoni RC	.40	.15
❑ 220 Steve Karsay	.25	.08
❑ 221 Jose Musset RC	.40	.15
❑ 222 Karl Rhodes	.25	.08
❑ 223 Frank Cimorelli RC	.40	.15
❑ 224 Kevin Jordan RC	.40	.15
❑ 225 Duane Ward	.25	.08
❑ 226 John Burke	.25	.08
❑ 227 Mike Macfarlane	.25	.08
❑ 228 Mike Lansing	.25	.08
❑ 229 Chuck Knoblauch	.40	.15
❑ 230 Ken Caminiti	.40	.15
❑ 231 Gar Finnvold RC	.40	.15
❑ 232 Derrek Lee RC	8.00	3.00
❑ 233 Brady Anderson	.40	.15
❑ 234 Vic Darensbourg RC	.40	.15
❑ 235 Mark Langston	.25	.08
❑ 236 T.J.Mathews RC	.40	.15
❑ 237 Lou Whitaker	.40	.15

❑ 238 Roger Cedeno .25 .08
❑ 239 Alex Fernandez .25 .08
❑ 240 Ryan Thompson .25 .08
❑ 241 Kerry Lacy RC .40 .15
❑ 242 Reggie Sanders .40 .15
❑ 243 Brad Pennington .25 .08
❑ 244 Bryan Eversgerd RC .40 .15
❑ 245 Greg Maddux 1.50 .60
❑ 246 Jason Kendall .40 .15
❑ 247 J.R. Phillips .25 .08
❑ 248 Bobby Witt .25 .08
❑ 249 Paul O'Neill .60 .25
❑ 250 Ryne Sandberg 1.50 .60
❑ 251 Charles Nagy .25 .08
❑ 252 Kevin Stocker .25 .08
❑ 253 Shawn Green 1.00 .40
❑ 254 Charlie Hayes .25 .08
❑ 255 Donnie Elliott .25 .08
❑ 256 Rob Fitzpatrick RC .40 .15
❑ 257 Tim Davis .25 .08
❑ 258 James Mouton .25 .08
❑ 259 Mike Greenwell .25 .08
❑ 260 Ray McDavid .25 .08
❑ 261 Mike Kelly .25 .08
❑ 262 Andy Larkin RC .40 .15
❑ 263 Marquis Riley UER .25 .08
❑ 264 Bob Tewksbury .25 .08
❑ 265 Brian Edmondson .25 .08
❑ 266 Eduardo Lantigua RC .40 .15
❑ 267 Brandon Wilson .25 .08
❑ 268 Mike Welch .25 .08
❑ 269 Tom Henke .25 .08
❑ 270 Pokey Reese .25 .08
❑ 271 Gregg Zaun RC 1.00 .40
❑ 272 Todd Ritchie .25 .08
❑ 273 Javier Lopez .40 .15
❑ 274 Kevin Young .25 .08
❑ 275 Kirt Manwaring .25 .08
❑ 276 Bill Taylor RC .40 .15
❑ 277 Robert Eenhoorn .25 .08
❑ 278 Jessie Hollins .25 .08
❑ 279 Julian Tavarez RC 1.00 .40
❑ 280 Gene Schall .25 .08
❑ 281 Paul Molitor .40 .15
❑ 282 Neifi Perez RC 1.00 .40
❑ 283 Greg Gagne .25 .08
❑ 284 Marquis Grissom .40 .15
❑ 285 Randy Johnson 1.00 .40
❑ 286 Pete Harnisch .25 .08
❑ 287 Joel Bennett RC .40 .15
❑ 288 Derek Bell .25 .08
❑ 289 Darryl Hamilton .25 .08
❑ 290 Gary Sheffield .40 .15
❑ 291 Eduardo Perez .25 .08
❑ 292 Basil Shabazz .25 .08
❑ 293 Eric Davis .40 .15
❑ 294 Pedro Astacio .25 .08
❑ 295 Robin Ventura .40 .15
❑ 296 Jeff Kent .60 .25
❑ 297 Rick Helling .25 .08
❑ 298 Joe Oliver .25 .08
❑ 299 Lee Smith .40 .15
❑ 300 Dave Winfield .40 .15
❑ 301 Deion Sanders .60 .25
❑ 302 Ravelo Manzanillo RC .40 .15
❑ 303 Mark Portugal .25 .08
❑ 304 Brent Gates .25 .08
❑ 305 Wade Boggs .60 .25
❑ 306 Rick Wilkins .25 .08
❑ 307 Carlos Baerga .25 .08
❑ 308 Curt Schilling .40 .15
❑ 309 Shannon Stewart 1.00 .40
❑ 310 Darren Holmes .25 .08
❑ 311 Robert Toth RC .40 .15
❑ 312 Gabe White .25 .08
❑ 313 Mac Suzuki RC 1.00 .40
❑ 314 Alvin Morman RC .40 .15
❑ 315 Mo Vaughn .40 .15
❑ 316 Bryce Florie RC .40 .15
❑ 317 Gabby Martinez RC .40 .15
❑ 318 Carl Everett .40 .15
❑ 319 Kerwin Moore .25 .08
❑ 320 Tom Pagnozzi .25 .08
❑ 321 Chris Gomez .25 .08
❑ 322 Todd Williams .25 .08
❑ 323 Pat Hentgen .25 .08
❑ 324 Kirk Presley RC .40 .15
❑ 325 Kevin Brown .40 .15
❑ 326 Jason Isringhausen RC 3.00 1.25
❑ 327 Rick Forney RC .40 .15
❑ 328 Carlos Pulido RC .40 .15
❑ 329 Terrell Wade RC .40 .15
❑ 330 Al Martin .25 .08
❑ 331 Dan Carlson RC .40 .15
❑ 332 Mark Acre RC .40 .15
❑ 333 Sterling Hitchcock .25 .08
❑ 334 Jon Ratliff RC .40 .15
❑ 335 Alex Ramirez RC .40 .15
❑ 336 Phil Geisler RC .25 .08
❑ 337 Eddie Zambrano FOIL RC .40 .15
❑ 338 Jim Thome FOIL .60 .25
❑ 339 James Mouton FOIL .25 .08
❑ 340 Cliff Floyd FOIL .40 .15
❑ 341 Carlos Delgado FOIL .60 .25
❑ 342 Roberto Petagine FOIL .25 .08
❑ 343 Tim Clark FOIL .25 .08
❑ 344 Bubba Smith FOIL .25 .08
❑ 345 Randy Curtis FOIL RC .40 .15
❑ 346 Joe Biasucci FOIL RC .40 .15
❑ 347 D.J. Boston FOIL RC .40 .15
❑ 348 Ruben Rivera FOIL RC .40 .15
❑ 349 Bryan Link FOIL RC .40 .15
❑ 350 Mike Bell FOIL RC .40 .15
❑ 351 Marty Watson FOIL RC .40 .15
❑ 352 Jason Myers FOIL .25 .08
❑ 353 Chipper Jones FOIL 1.00 .40
❑ 354 Brooks Kieschnick FOIL .40 .15
❑ 355 Pokey Reese FOIL .25 .08
❑ 356 John Burke FOIL .25 .08
❑ 357 Kurt Miller FOIL .25 .08
❑ 358 Orlando Miller FOIL .25 .08
❑ 359 Todd Hollandsworth FOIL .25 .08
❑ 360 Rondell White FOIL .40 .15
❑ 361 Bill Pulsipher FOIL .40 .15
❑ 362 Tyler Green FOIL .25 .08
❑ 363 Midre Cummings FOIL .25 .08
❑ 364 Brian Barber FOIL .25 .08
❑ 365 Melvin Nieves FOIL .25 .08
❑ 366 Salomon Torres FOIL .25 .08
❑ 367 Alex Ochoa FOIL .25 .08
❑ 368 Frankie Rodriguez FOIL .25 .08
❑ 369 Brian Anderson FOIL .40 .15
❑ 370 James Baldwin FOIL .25 .08
❑ 371 Manny Ramirez FOIL 1.00 .40
❑ 372 Justin Thompson FOIL .25 .08
❑ 373 Johnny Damon FOIL .60 .25
❑ 374 Jeff D'Amico FOIL .40 .15
❑ 375 Rich Becker FOIL .25 .08
❑ 376 Derek Jeter FOIL 3.00 1.25
❑ 377 Steve Karsay FOIL .25 .08
❑ 378 Mac Suzuki FOIL .40 .15
❑ 379 Benji Gil FOIL .25 .08
❑ 380 Alex Gonzalez FOIL .25 .08
❑ 381 Jason Bere FOIL .25 .08
❑ 382 Brett Butler FOIL .40 .15
❑ 383 Jeff Conine FOIL .40 .15
❑ 384 Darren Daulton FOIL .40 .15
❑ 385 Jeff Kent FOIL .60 .25
❑ 386 Don Mattingly FOIL 2.50 1.00
❑ 387 Mike Piazza FOIL 2.00 .75
❑ 388 Ryne Sandberg FOIL 1.50 .60
❑ 389 Rich Amaral .25 .08
❑ 390 Craig Biggio .60 .25
❑ 391 Jeff Suppan RC 2.00 .75
❑ 392 Andy Benes .25 .08
❑ 393 Cal Eldred .25 .08
❑ 394 Jeff Conine .40 .15
❑ 395 Tim Salmon .60 .25
❑ 396 Ray Suplee RC .40 .15
❑ 397 Tony Phillips .25 .08
❑ 398 Ramon Martinez .25 .08
❑ 399 Julio Franco .40 .15
❑ 400 Dwight Gooden .40 .15
❑ 401 Kevin Loman RC .40 .15
❑ 402 Jose Rijo .25 .08
❑ 403 Mike Devereaux .25 .08
❑ 404 Mike Zolecki RC .40 .15
❑ 405 Fred McGriff .60 .25
❑ 406 Danny Clyburn .25 .08
❑ 407 Robby Thompson .25 .08
❑ 408 Terry Steinbach .25 .08
❑ 409 Luis Polonia .25 .08
❑ 410 Mark Grace .60 .25
❑ 411 Albert Belle .40 .15
❑ 412 John Kruk .40 .15
❑ 413 Scott Spiezio RC 1.00 .40
❑ 414 Ellis Burks UER .40 .15
❑ 415 Joe Vitiello .25 .08
❑ 416 Tim Costo .25 .08
❑ 417 Marc Newfield .25 .08
❑ 418 Oscar Henriquez RC .40 .15
❑ 419 Matt Perisho RC .40 .15
❑ 420 Julio Bruno .25 .08
❑ 421 Kenny Felder .25 .08
❑ 422 Tyler Green .25 .08
❑ 423 Jim Edmonds 1.00 .40
❑ 424 Ozzie Smith 1.50 .60
❑ 425 Rick Greene .25 .08
❑ 426 Todd Hollandsworth .25 .08
❑ 427 Eddie Pearson RC .40 .15
❑ 428 Quilvio Veras .25 .08
❑ 429 Kenny Rogers .40 .15
❑ 430 Willie Greene .25 .08
❑ 431 Vaughn Eshelman .25 .08
❑ 432 Pat Meares .25 .08
❑ 433 Jermaine Dye RC 6.00 2.50
❑ 434 Steve Cooke .25 .08
❑ 435 Bill Swift .25 .08
❑ 436 Fausto Cruz RC .40 .15
❑ 437 Mark Hutton .25 .08
❑ 438 Brooks Kieschnick RC .40 .15
❑ 439 Yorkis Perez .25 .08
❑ 440 Len Dykstra .40 .15
❑ 441 Pat Borders .25 .08
❑ 442 Doug Walls RC .40 .15
❑ 443 Wally Joyner .40 .15
❑ 444 Ken Hill .25 .08
❑ 445 Eric Anthony .25 .08
❑ 446 Mitch Williams .25 .08
❑ 447 Cory Bailey RC .40 .15
❑ 448 Dave Staton .25 .08
❑ 449 Greg Vaughn .25 .08
❑ 450 Dave Magadan .25 .08
❑ 451 Chili Davis .40 .15
❑ 452 Gerald Santos RC .40 .15
❑ 453 Joe Perona .25 .08
❑ 454 Delino DeShields .25 .08
❑ 455 Jack McDowell .25 .08
❑ 456 Todd Hundley .25 .08
❑ 457 Ritchie Moody .25 .08
❑ 458 Bret Boone .40 .15
❑ 459 Ben McDonald .25 .08
❑ 460 Kirby Puckett 1.00 .40
❑ 461 Gregg Olson .25 .08
❑ 462 Rich Aude RC .40 .15
❑ 463 John Burkett .25 .08
❑ 464 Troy Neel .25 .08
❑ 465 Jimmy Key .40 .15
❑ 466 Ozzie Timmons .25 .08
❑ 467 Eddie Murray 1.00 .40
❑ 468 Mark Tranberg RC .40 .15
❑ 469 Alex Gonzalez .25 .08
❑ 470 David Nied .25 .08
❑ 471 Barry Larkin .60 .25
❑ 472 Brian Looney RC .40 .15
❑ 473 Shawn Estes .25 .08
❑ 474 A.J.Sager RC .40 .15
❑ 475 Roger Clemens 2.00 .75
❑ 476 Vince Moore .25 .08
❑ 477 Scott Karl RC .40 .15
❑ 478 Kurt Miller .25 .08
❑ 479 Garret Anderson 1.00 .40
❑ 480 Allen Watson .25 .08
❑ 481 Jose Lima RC 1.00 .40
❑ 482 Rick Gorecki .25 .08
❑ 483 Jimmy Hurst RC .40 .15
❑ 484 Preston Wilson .40 .15
❑ 485 Will Clark .60 .25
❑ 486 Mike Ferry RC .40 .15
❑ 487 Curtis Goodwin RC .40 .15
❑ 488 Mike Myers .25 .08
❑ 489 Chipper Jones 1.00 .40
❑ 490 Jeff King .25 .08
❑ 491 W.VanLandingham RC .40 .15
❑ 492 Carlos Reyes RC .40 .15
❑ 493 Andy Pettitte 1.00 .40
❑ 494 Brant Brown .25 .08
❑ 495 Daron Kirkreit .25 .08

❑ 496 Ricky Bottalico RC	.40	.15
❑ 497 Devon White	.40	.15
❑ 498 Jason Johnson RC	1.00	.40
❑ 499 Vince Coleman	.25	.08
❑ 500 Larry Walker	.40	.15
❑ 501 Bobby Ayala	.25	.08
❑ 502 Steve Finley	.40	.15
❑ 503 Scott Fletcher	.25	.08
❑ 504 Brad Ausmus	.60	.25
❑ 505 Scott Talanoa RC	.40	.15
❑ 506 Orestes Destrade	.25	.08
❑ 507 Gary DiSarcina	.25	.08
❑ 508 Willie Smith RC	.40	.15
❑ 509 Alan Trammell	.40	.15
❑ 510 Mike Piazza	2.00	.75
❑ 511 Ozzie Guillen	.40	.15
❑ 512 Jeromy Burnitz	.40	.15
❑ 513 Darren Oliver RC	1.00	.40
❑ 514 Kevin Mitchell	.25	.08
❑ 515 Rafael Palmeiro	.60	.25
❑ 516 David McCarty	.25	.08
❑ 517 Jeff Blauser	.25	.08
❑ 518 Trey Beamon	.25	.08
❑ 519 Royce Clayton	.25	.08
❑ 520 Dennis Eckersley	.40	.15
❑ 521 Bernie Williams	.60	.25
❑ 522 Steve Buechele	.25	.08
❑ 523 Dennis Martinez	.40	.15
❑ 524 Dave Hollins	.25	.08
❑ 525 Joey Hamilton	.25	.08
❑ 526 Andres Galarraga	.40	.15
❑ 527 Jeff Granger	.25	.08
❑ 528 Joey Eischen	.25	.08
❑ 529 Desi Relaford	.25	.08
❑ 530 Roberto Petagine	.25	.08
❑ 531 Andre Dawson	.40	.15
❑ 532 Ray Holbert	.25	.08
❑ 533 Duane Singleton	.25	.08
❑ 534 Kurt Abbott RC	.40	.15
❑ 535 Bo Jackson	1.00	.40
❑ 536 Gregg Jefferies	.25	.08
❑ 537 David Mysel	.25	.08
❑ 538 Raul Mondesi	.40	.15
❑ 539 Chris Snopek	.25	.08
❑ 540 Brook Fordyce	.25	.08
❑ 541 Ron Frazier RC	.40	.15
❑ 542 Brian Koelling	.25	.08
❑ 543 Jimmy Haynes	.25	.08
❑ 544 Marty Cordova	.25	.08
❑ 545 Jason Green RC	.40	.15
❑ 546 Orlando Merced	.25	.08
❑ 547 Lou Pote RC	.40	.15
❑ 548 Todd Van Poppel	.25	.08
❑ 549 Pat Kelly	.25	.08
❑ 550 Turk Wendell	.25	.08
❑ 551 Herbert Perry RC	.40	.15
❑ 552 Ryan Karp RC	.40	.15
❑ 553 Juan Guzman	.25	.08
❑ 554 Bryan Rekar RC	.40	.15
❑ 555 Kevin Appier	.40	.15
❑ 556 Chris Schwab RC	.40	.15
❑ 557 Jay Buhner	.40	.15
❑ 558 Andujar Cedeno	.25	.08
❑ 559 Ryan McGuire RC	.40	.15
❑ 560 Ricky Gutierrez	.25	.08
❑ 561 Keith Kimsey RC	.40	.15
❑ 562 Tim Clark	.25	.08
❑ 563 Damion Easley	.25	.08
❑ 564 Clint Davis RC	.40	.15
❑ 565 Mike Moore	.25	.08
❑ 566 Orel Hershiser	.40	.15
❑ 567 Jason Bere	.25	.08
❑ 568 Kevin McReynolds	.25	.08
❑ 569 Leland Macon RC	.40	.15
❑ 570 John Courtright RC	.40	.15
❑ 571 Sid Fernandez	.25	.08
❑ 572 Chad Roper	.25	.08
❑ 573 Terry Pendleton	.40	.15
❑ 574 Danny Miceli	.25	.08
❑ 575 Joe Rosselli	.25	.08
❑ 576 Mike Bordick	.25	.08
❑ 577 Danny Tartabull	.25	.08
❑ 578 Jose Guzman	.25	.08
❑ 579 Omar Vizquel	.60	.25
❑ 580 Tommy Greene	.25	.08
❑ 581 Paul Spoljaric	.25	.08
❑ 582 Walt Weiss	.25	.08
❑ 583 Oscar Jimenez RC	.40	.15
❑ 584 Rod Henderson	.25	.08
❑ 585 Derek Lowe	.40	.15
❑ 586 Richard Hidalgo RC	1.00	.40
❑ 587 Shayne Bennett RC	.40	.15
❑ 588 Tim Belk RC	.40	.15
❑ 589 Matt Mieske	.25	.08
❑ 590 Nigel Wilson	.25	.08
❑ 591 Jeff Knox RC	.40	.15
❑ 592 Bernard Gilkey	.25	.08
❑ 593 David Cone	.40	.15
❑ 594 Paul LoDuca RC	5.00	2.00
❑ 595 Scott Ruffcorn	.25	.08
❑ 596 Chris Roberts	.25	.08
❑ 597 Oscar Munoz RC	.40	.15
❑ 598 Scott Sullivan RC	.40	.15
❑ 599 Matt Jarvis RC	.40	.15
❑ 600 Jose Canseco	.60	.25
❑ 601 Tony Graffanino RC	1.50	.60
❑ 602 Don Slaught	.25	.08
❑ 603 Brett King RC	.40	.15
❑ 604 Jose Herrera RC	.40	.15
❑ 605 Melido Perez	.25	.08
❑ 606 Mike Hubbard RC	.40	.15
❑ 607 Chad Ogea	.25	.08
❑ 608 Wayne Gomes RC	1.00	.40
❑ 609 Roberto Alomar	.60	.25
❑ 610 Angel Echevarria RC	.40	.15
❑ 611 Jose Lind	.25	.08
❑ 612 Darrin Fletcher	.25	.08
❑ 613 Chris Bosio	.25	.08
❑ 614 Darryl Kile	.40	.15
❑ 615 Frankie Rodriguez	.25	.08
❑ 616 Phil Plantier	.25	.08
❑ 617 Pat Listach	.25	.08
❑ 618 Charlie Hough	.40	.15
❑ 619 Ryan Hancock RC	.40	.15
❑ 620 Darrel Deak RC	.40	.15
❑ 621 Travis Fryman	.40	.15
❑ 622 Brett Butler	.40	.15
❑ 623 Lance Johnson	.25	.08
❑ 624 Pete Smith	.25	.08
❑ 625 James Hurst RC	.40	.15
❑ 626 Roberto Kelly	.25	.08
❑ 627 Mike Mussina	.60	.25
❑ 628 Kevin Tapani	.25	.08
❑ 629 John Smoltz	.60	.25
❑ 630 Midre Cummings	.25	.08
❑ 631 Salomon Torres	.25	.08
❑ 632 Willie Adams	.25	.08
❑ 633 Derek Jeter	3.00	1.25
❑ 634 Steve Trachsel	.25	.08
❑ 635 Albie Lopez	.25	.08
❑ 636 Jason Moler	.25	.08
❑ 637 Carlos Delgado	.60	.25
❑ 638 Roberto Mejia	.25	.08
❑ 639 Darren Burton	.25	.08
❑ 640 B.J. Wallace	.25	.08
❑ 641 Brad Clontz RC	.40	.15
❑ 642 Billy Wagner RC	4.00	1.50
❑ 643 Aaron Sele	.25	.08
❑ 644 Cameron Cairncross	.25	.08
❑ 645 Brian Harper	.25	.08
❑ 646 Marc Valdes UER NNO	.25	.08
❑ 647 Mark Ratekin	.25	.08
❑ 648 Terry Bradshaw RC	.40	.15
❑ 649 Justin Thompson	.25	.08
❑ 650 Mike Busch RC	.40	.15
❑ 651 Joe Hall RC	.40	.15
❑ 652 Bobby Jones	.25	.08
❑ 653 Kelly Stinnett RC	1.00	.40
❑ 654 Rod Steph RC	.40	.15
❑ 655 Jay Powell RC	1.00	.40
❑ 656 Keith Garagozzo RC	.40	.15
❑ 657 Todd Dunn	.25	.08
❑ 658 Charles Peterson RC	.40	.15
❑ 659 Darren Lewis	.25	.08
❑ 660 John Wasdin RC	.40	.15
❑ 661 Tate Seefried RC	.40	.15
❑ 662 Hector Trinidad RC	.40	.15
❑ 663 John Carter RC	.25	.08
❑ 664 Larry Mitchell	.25	.08
❑ 665 David Catlett RC	.40	.15
❑ 666 Dante Bichette	.40	.15
❑ 667 Felix Jose	.25	.08
❑ 668 Rondell White	.40	.15
❑ 669 Tino Martinez	.60	.25
❑ 670 Brian L.Hunter	.25	.08
❑ 671 Jose Malave	.25	.08
❑ 672 Archi Cianfrocco	.25	.08
❑ 673 Mike Matheny RC	1.50	.60
❑ 674 Bret Barberie	.25	.08
❑ 675 Andrew Lorraine RC	.40	.15
❑ 676 Brian Jordan	.40	.15
❑ 677 Tim Belcher	.25	.08
❑ 678 Antonio Osuna RC	.40	.15
❑ 679 Checklist	.25	.08
❑ 680 Checklist	.25	.08
❑ 681 Checklist	.25	.08
❑ 682 Checklist	.25	.08

1995 Bowman

❑ COMPLETE SET (439)	150.00	90.00
❑ 1 Billy Wagner	.75	.30
❑ 2 Chris Widger	.25	.08
❑ 3 Brent Bowers	.25	.08
❑ 4 Bob Abreu RC	8.00	3.00
❑ 5 Lou Collier RC	1.00	.40
❑ 6 Juan Acevedo RC	.50	.20
❑ 7 Jason Kelley RC	.50	.20
❑ 8 Brian Sackinsky	.25	.08
❑ 9 Scott Christman	.25	.08
❑ 10 Damon Hollins	.25	.08
❑ 11 Willis Otanez RC	.50	.20
❑ 12 Jason Ryan RC	.50	.20
❑ 13 Jason Giambi	.75	.30
❑ 14 Andy Taulbee RC	.50	.20
❑ 15 Mark Thompson	.25	.08
❑ 16 Hugo Pivaral RC	.50	.20
❑ 17 Brien Taylor	.25	.08
❑ 18 Antonio Osuna	.25	.08
❑ 19 Edgardo Alfonzo	.25	.08
❑ 20 Carl Everett	.50	.20
❑ 21 Matt Drews	.25	.08
❑ 22 Bartolo Colon RC	4.00	1.50
❑ 23 Andruw Jones RC	25.00	10.00
❑ 24 Robert Person RC	1.00	.40
❑ 25 Derrek Lee	1.25	.50
❑ 26 John Ambrose RC	.50	.20
❑ 27 Eric Knowles RC	.50	.20
❑ 28 Chris Roberts	.25	.08
❑ 29 Don Wengert	.25	.08
❑ 30 Marcus Jensen RC	1.00	.40
❑ 31 Brian Barber	.25	.08
❑ 32 Kevin Brown C	.50	.20
❑ 33 Benji Gil	.25	.08
❑ 34 Mike Hubbard	.25	.08
❑ 35 Bart Evans RC	.50	.20
❑ 36 Enrique Wilson RC	.50	.20
❑ 37 Brian Buchanan RC	.50	.20
❑ 38 Ken Ray RC	.50	.20
❑ 39 Micah Franklin RC	.50	.20
❑ 40 Ricky Otero RC	.50	.20
❑ 41 Jason Kendall	.50	.20
❑ 42 Jimmy Hurst	.25	.08
❑ 43 Jerry Wolak RC	.50	.20
❑ 44 Jayson Peterson RC	.50	.20
❑ 45 Allen Battle RC	.50	.20
❑ 46 Scott Stahoviak	.25	.08
❑ 47 Steve Schrenk RC	.50	.20
❑ 48 Travis Miller RC	.50	.20
❑ 49 Eddie Rios RC	.50	.20
❑ 50 Mike Hampton	.50	.20

❑ 51 Chad Frontera RC .50 .20
❑ 52 Tom Evans .25 .08
❑ 53 C.J. Nitkowski .25 .08
❑ 54 Clay Caruthers RC .50 .20
❑ 55 Shannon Stewart .50 .20
❑ 56 Jorge Posada 1.25 .50
❑ 57 Aaron Holbert .25 .08
❑ 58 Harry Berrios RC .50 .20
❑ 59 Steve Rodriguez .25 .08
❑ 60 Shane Andrews .25 .08
❑ 61 Will Cunnane RC .50 .20
❑ 62 Richard Hidalgo .25 .08
❑ 63 Bill Selby RC .50 .20
❑ 64 Jay Cranford RC .50 .20
❑ 65 Jeff Suppan .50 .20
❑ 66 Curtis Goodwin .25 .08
❑ 67 John Thomson RC 1.00 .40
❑ 68 Justin Thompson .25 .08
❑ 69 Troy Percival .50 .20
❑ 70 Matt Wagner RC .50 .20
❑ 71 Terry Bradshaw .25 .08
❑ 72 Greg Hansell .25 .08
❑ 73 John Burke .25 .08
❑ 74 Jeff D'Amico .25 .08
❑ 75 Ernie Young .25 .08
❑ 76 Jason Bates .25 .08
❑ 77 Chris Stynes .25 .08
❑ 78 Cade Gaspar RC .50 .20
❑ 79 Melvin Nieves .25 .08
❑ 80 Rick Gorecki .25 .08
❑ 81 Felix Rodriguez RC .50 .20
❑ 82 Ryan Hancock .25 .08
❑ 83 Chris Carpenter RC 8.00 3.00
❑ 84 Ray McDavid .25 .08
❑ 85 Chris Wimmer .25 .08
❑ 86 Doug Glanville .25 .08
❑ 87 DeShawn Warren .25 .08
❑ 88 Damian Moss RC .50 .20
❑ 89 Rafael Orellano RC .50 .20
❑ 90 Vladimir Guerrero RC ! 40.00 20.00
❑ 91 Raul Casanova RC .50 .20
❑ 92 Karim Garcia RC .50 .20
❑ 93 Bryce Florie .25 .08
❑ 94 Kevin Orie .25 .08
❑ 95 Ryan Nye RC .50 .20
❑ 96 Matt Sachse RC .50 .20
❑ 97 Ivan Arteaga RC .50 .20
❑ 98 Glenn Murray .25 .08
❑ 99 Stacy Hollins RC .50 .20
❑ 100 Jim Pittsley .25 .08
❑ 101 Craig Mattson RC .50 .20
❑ 102 Neifi Perez .25 .08
❑ 103 Keith Williams .25 .08
❑ 104 Roger Cedeno .25 .08
❑ 105 Tony Terry RC .50 .20
❑ 106 Jose Malave .25 .08
❑ 107 Joe Rosselli .25 .08
❑ 108 Kevin Jordan .25 .08
❑ 109 Sid Roberson RC .50 .20
❑ 110 Alan Embree .25 .08
❑ 111 Terrell Wade .25 .08
❑ 112 Bob Wolcott .25 .08
❑ 113 Carlos Perez RC 1.00 .40
❑ 114 Mike Bovee RC .50 .20
❑ 115 Tommy Davis RC .50 .20
❑ 116 Jeremey Kendall RC .50 .20
❑ 117 Rich Aude .25 .08
❑ 118 Rick Huisman .25 .08
❑ 119 Tim Belk .25 .08
❑ 120 Edgar Renteria .50 .20
❑ 121 Calvin Maduro RC .50 .20
❑ 122 Jerry Martin RC .50 .20
❑ 123 Ramon Fermin RC .50 .20
❑ 124 Kimera Bartee RC .50 .20
❑ 125 Mark Farris .25 .08
❑ 126 Frank Rodriguez .25 .08
❑ 127 Bob Higginson RC 2.00 .75
❑ 128 Bret Wagner .25 .08
❑ 129 Edwin Diaz RC .50 .20
❑ 130 Jimmy Haynes .25 .08
❑ 131 Chris Weinke RC QB 1.00 .40
❑ 132 Damian Jackson RC .50 .20
❑ 133 Felix Martinez .25 .08
❑ 134 Edwin Hurtado RC .50 .20
❑ 135 Matt Raleigh RC .50 .20
❑ 136 Paul Wilson .25 .08
❑ 137 Ron Villone .25 .08
❑ 138 Eric Stuckenschneider RC .50 .20
❑ 139 Tate Seefried .25 .08
❑ 140 Rey Ordonez RC 2.00 .75
❑ 141 Eddie Pearson .25 .08
❑ 142 Kevin Gallaher .25 .08
❑ 143 Torii Hunter .75 .30
❑ 144 Daron Kirkreit .25 .08
❑ 145 Craig Wilson .25 .08
❑ 146 Ugueth Urbina .25 .08
❑ 147 Chris Snopek .25 .08
❑ 148 Kym Ashworth .25 .08
❑ 149 Wayne Gomes .25 .08
❑ 150 Mark Loretta .50 .20
❑ 151 Ramon Morel RC .50 .20
❑ 152 Trot Nixon .50 .20
❑ 153 Desi Relaford .25 .08
❑ 154 Scott Sullivan .25 .08
❑ 155 Marc Barcelo .25 .08
❑ 156 Willie Adams .25 .08
❑ 157 Derrick Gibson RC .50 .20
❑ 158 Brian Meadows RC .50 .20
❑ 159 Julian Tavarez .25 .08
❑ 160 Bryan Rekar .25 .08
❑ 161 Steve Gibralter .25 .08
❑ 162 Esteban Loaiza .25 .08
❑ 163 John Wasdin .25 .08
❑ 164 Kirk Presley .25 .08
❑ 165 Mariano Rivera 1.50 .60
❑ 166 Andy Larkin .25 .08
❑ 167 Sean Whiteside RC .50 .20
❑ 168 Matt Apana RC .50 .20
❑ 169 Shawn Senior RC .50 .20
❑ 170 Scott Gentile .25 .08
❑ 171 Quilvio Veras .25 .08
❑ 172 Eli Marrero RC 1.50 .60
❑ 173 Mendy Lopez RC .50 .20
❑ 174 Homer Bush .25 .08
❑ 175 Brian Stephenson RC .50 .20
❑ 176 Jon Nunnally .25 .08
❑ 177 Jose Herrera .25 .08
❑ 178 Corey Avrard RC .50 .20
❑ 179 David Bell .25 .08
❑ 180 Jason Isringhausen .50 .20
❑ 181 Jamey Wright .25 .08
❑ 182 Lonell Roberts RC .25 .08
❑ 183 Marty Cordova .25 .08
❑ 184 Amaury Telemaco .25 .08
❑ 185 John Mabry .25 .08
❑ 186 Andrew Vessel RC .50 .20
❑ 187 Jim Cole RC .50 .20
❑ 188 Marquis Riley .25 .08
❑ 189 Todd Dunn .25 .08
❑ 190 John Carter .25 .08
❑ 191 Donnie Sadler RC 1.00 .40
❑ 192 Mike Bell .25 .08
❑ 193 Chris Cumberland RC .50 .20
❑ 194 Jason Schmidt 1.25 .50
❑ 195 Matt Brunson .25 .08
❑ 196 James Baldwin .25 .08
❑ 197 Bill Simas RC .50 .20
❑ 198 Gus Gandarillas .25 .08
❑ 199 Mac Suzuki .25 .08
❑ 200 Rick Holifield RC .50 .20
❑ 201 Fernando Lunar RC .50 .20
❑ 202 Kevin Jarvis .25 .08
❑ 203 Everett Stull .25 .08
❑ 204 Steve Wojciechowski .25 .08
❑ 205 Shawn Estes .25 .08
❑ 206 Jermaine Dye .50 .20
❑ 207 Marc Kroon .25 .08
❑ 208 Peter Munro RC 1.00 .40
❑ 209 Pat Watkins .25 .08
❑ 210 Matt Smith .25 .08
❑ 211 Joe Vitiello .25 .08
❑ 212 Gerald Witasick Jr. .25 .08
❑ 213 Freddy Adrian Garcia RC .50 .20
❑ 214 Glenn Dishman RC .50 .20
❑ 215 Jay Canizaro RC .50 .20
❑ 216 Angel Martinez .25 .08
❑ 217 Yamil Benitez RC .50 .20
❑ 218 Fausto Macey RC .50 .20
❑ 219 Eric Owens .25 .08
❑ 220 Checklist .25 .08
❑ 221 Dwayne Hosey FOIL RC .50 .20
❑ 222 Brad Woodall FOIL RC .50 .20
❑ 223 Billy Ashley FOIL .25 .08
❑ 224 Mark Grudzielanek FOIL RC 2.00 .75
❑ 225 Mark Johnson FOIL RC 1.00 .40
❑ 226 Tim Unroe FOIL RC .50 .20
❑ 227 Todd Greene FOIL .25 .08
❑ 228 Larry Sutton FOIL .25 .08
❑ 229 Derek Jeter FOIL 4.00 1.50
❑ 230 Sal Fasano FOIL RC .50 .20
❑ 231 Ruben Rivera FOIL .25 .08
❑ 232 Chris Truby FOIL RC .50 .20
❑ 233 John Donati FOIL .25 .08
❑ 234 Decomba Conner FOIL RC .50 .20
❑ 235 Sergio Nunez FOIL RC .50 .20
❑ 236 Ray Brown FOIL RC .50 .20
❑ 237 Juan Melo FOIL RC .50 .20
❑ 238 Hideo Nomo FOIL RC 5.00 2.00
❑ 239 Jaime Bluma RC FOIL .50 .20
❑ 240 Jay Payton FOIL RC 2.00 .75
❑ 241 Paul Konerko FOIL 4.00 1.50
❑ 242 Scott Elarton FOIL RC 1.00 .40
❑ 243 Jeff Abbott FOIL RC 1.00 .40
❑ 244 Jim Brower FOIL RC .50 .20
❑ 245 Geoff Blum FOIL RC 2.00 .75
❑ 246 Aaron Boone FOIL RC 2.00 .75
❑ 247 J.R. Phillips FOIL .25 .08
❑ 248 Alex Ochoa FOIL .25 .08
❑ 249 Nomar Garciaparra FOIL 4.00 1.50
❑ 250 Garret Anderson FOIL .50 .20
❑ 251 Ray Durham FOIL .50 .20
❑ 252 Paul Shuey FOIL .25 .08
❑ 253 Tony Clark FOIL .25 .08
❑ 254 Johnny Damon FOIL .75 .30
❑ 255 Duane Singleton FOIL .25 .08
❑ 256 LaTroy Hawkins FOIL .25 .08
❑ 257 Andy Pettitte FOIL .75 .30
❑ 258 Ben Grieve FOIL .25 .08
❑ 259 Marc Newfield FOIL .25 .08
❑ 260 Terrell Lowery FOIL .25 .08
❑ 261 Shawn Green FOIL .50 .20
❑ 262 Chipper Jones FOIL 1.25 .50
❑ 263 Brooks Kieschnick FOIL .25 .08
❑ 264 Pokey Reese FOIL .25 .08
❑ 265 Doug Million FOIL .25 .08
❑ 266 Marc Valdes FOIL .25 .08
❑ 267 Brian L.Hunter FOIL .25 .08
❑ 268 Todd Hollandsworth FOIL .25 .08
❑ 269 Rod Henderson FOIL .25 .08
❑ 270 Bill Pulsipher FOIL .25 .08
❑ 271 Scott Rolen FOIL RC 12.00 5.00
❑ 272 Trey Beamon FOIL .25 .08
❑ 273 Alan Benes FOIL .25 .08
❑ 274 Dustin Hermanson FOIL .25 .08
❑ 275 Ricky Bottalico .25 .08
❑ 276 Albert Belle .50 .20
❑ 277 Deion Sanders .75 .30
❑ 278 Matt Williams .50 .20
❑ 279 Jeff Bagwell .75 .30
❑ 280 Kirby Puckett 1.25 .50
❑ 281 Dave Hollins .25 .08
❑ 282 Don Mattingly 3.00 1.25
❑ 283 Joey Hamilton .25 .08
❑ 284 Bobby Bonilla .50 .20
❑ 285 Moises Alou .50 .20
❑ 286 Tom Glavine .75 .30
❑ 287 Brett Butler .50 .20
❑ 288 Chris Hoiles .25 .08
❑ 289 Kenny Rogers .50 .20
❑ 290 Larry Walker .50 .20
❑ 291 Tim Raines .50 .20
❑ 292 Kevin Appier .50 .20
❑ 293 Roger Clemens 2.50 1.00
❑ 294 Chuck Carr .25 .08
❑ 295 Randy Myers .25 .08
❑ 296 Dave Nilsson .25 .08
❑ 297 Joe Carter .50 .20
❑ 298 Chuck Finley .50 .20
❑ 299 Ray Lankford .50 .20
❑ 300 Roberto Kelly .25 .08
❑ 301 Jon Lieber .25 .08
❑ 302 Travis Fryman .50 .20
❑ 303 Mark McGwire 3.00 1.25
❑ 304 Tony Gwynn 1.50 .60
❑ 305 Kenny Lofton .50 .20
❑ 306 Mark Whiten .25 .08
❑ 307 Doug Drabek .25 .08
❑ 308 Terry Steinbach .25 .08

❑ 309	Ryan Klesko	.50	.20
❑ 310	Mike Piazza	2.00	.75
❑ 311	Ben McDonald	.25	.08
❑ 312	Reggie Sanders	.50	.20
❑ 313	Alex Fernandez	.25	.08
❑ 314	Aaron Sele	.25	.08
❑ 315	Gregg Jefferies	.25	.08
❑ 316	Rickey Henderson	1.25	.50
❑ 317	Brian Anderson	.25	.08
❑ 318	Jose Valentin	.25	.08
❑ 319	Rod Beck	.25	.08
❑ 320	Marquis Grissom	.50	.20
❑ 321	Ken Griffey Jr.	2.00	.75
❑ 322	Bret Saberhagen	.50	.20
❑ 323	Juan Gonzalez	.50	.20
❑ 324	Paul Molitor	.50	.20
❑ 325	Gary Sheffield	.50	.20
❑ 326	Darren Daulton	.50	.20
❑ 327	Bill Swift	.25	.08
❑ 328	Brian McRae	.25	.08
❑ 329	Robin Ventura	.50	.20
❑ 330	Lee Smith	.50	.20
❑ 331	Fred McGriff	.75	.30
❑ 332	Delino DeShields	.25	.08
❑ 333	Edgar Martinez	.75	.30
❑ 334	Mike Mussina	.75	.30
❑ 335	Orlando Merced	.25	.08
❑ 336	Carlos Baerga	.25	.08
❑ 337	Wil Cordero	.25	.08
❑ 338	Tom Pagnozzi	.25	.08
❑ 339	Pat Hentgen	.25	.08
❑ 340	Chad Curtis	.25	.08
❑ 341	Darren Lewis	.25	.08
❑ 342	Jeff Kent	.50	.20
❑ 343	Bip Roberts	.25	.08
❑ 344	Ivan Rodriguez	.75	.30
❑ 345	Jeff Montgomery	.25	.08
❑ 346	Hal Morris	.25	.08
❑ 347	Danny Tartabull	.25	.08
❑ 348	Raul Mondesi	.50	.20
❑ 349	Ken Hill	.25	.08
❑ 350	Pedro Martinez	.75	.30
❑ 351	Frank Thomas	1.25	.50
❑ 352	Manny Ramirez	.75	.30
❑ 353	Tim Salmon	.75	.30
❑ 354	W. VanLandingham	.25	.08
❑ 355	Andres Galarraga	.50	.20
❑ 356	Paul O'Neill	.75	.30
❑ 357	Brady Anderson	.50	.20
❑ 358	Ramon Martinez	.25	.08
❑ 359	John Olerud	.50	.20
❑ 360	Ruben Sierra	.50	.20
❑ 361	Cal Eldred	.25	.08
❑ 362	Jay Buhner	.50	.20
❑ 363	Jay Bell	.50	.20
❑ 364	Wally Joyner	.50	.20
❑ 365	Chuck Knoblauch	.50	.20
❑ 366	Len Dykstra	.50	.20
❑ 367	John Wetteland	.50	.20
❑ 368	Roberto Alomar	.75	.30
❑ 369	Craig Biggio	.75	.30
❑ 370	Ozzie Smith	2.00	.75
❑ 371	Terry Pendleton	.50	.20
❑ 372	Sammy Sosa	1.25	.50
❑ 373	Carlos Garcia	.25	.08
❑ 374	Jose Rijo	.25	.08
❑ 375	Chris Gomez	.25	.08
❑ 376	Barry Bonds	3.00	1.25
❑ 377	Steve Avery	.25	.08
❑ 378	Rick Wilkins	.25	.08
❑ 379	Pete Harnisch	.25	.08
❑ 380	Dean Palmer	.50	.20
❑ 381	Bob Hamelin	.25	.08
❑ 382	Jason Bere	.25	.08
❑ 383	Jimmy Key	.50	.20
❑ 384	Dante Bichette	.50	.20
❑ 385	Rafael Palmeiro	.75	.30
❑ 386	David Justice	.50	.20
❑ 387	Chili Davis	.50	.20
❑ 388	Mike Greenwell	.25	.08
❑ 389	Todd Zeile	.25	.08
❑ 390	Jeff Conine	.50	.20
❑ 391	Rick Aguilera	.25	.08
❑ 392	Eddie Murray	1.25	.50
❑ 393	Mike Stanley	.25	.08
❑ 394	Cliff Floyd UER	.50	.20
❑ 395	Randy Johnson	1.25	.50
❑ 396	David Nied	.25	.08
❑ 397	Devon White	.50	.20
❑ 398	Royce Clayton	.25	.08
❑ 399	Andy Benes	.25	.08
❑ 400	John Hudek	.25	.08
❑ 401	Bobby Jones	.25	.08
❑ 402	Eric Karros	.50	.20
❑ 403	Will Clark	.75	.30
❑ 404	Mark Langston	.25	.08
❑ 405	Kevin Brown	.50	.20
❑ 406	Greg Maddux	2.00	.75
❑ 407	David Cone	.50	.20
❑ 408	Wade Boggs	.75	.30
❑ 409	Steve Trachsel	.25	.08
❑ 410	Greg Vaughn	.25	.08
❑ 411	Mo Vaughn	.50	.20
❑ 412	Wilson Alvarez	.25	.08
❑ 413	Cal Ripken	4.00	1.50
❑ 414	Rico Brogna	.25	.08
❑ 415	Barry Larkin	.75	.30
❑ 416	Cecil Fielder	.50	.20
❑ 417	Jose Canseco	.75	.30
❑ 418	Jack McDowell	.25	.08
❑ 419	Mike Lieberthal	.50	.20
❑ 420	Andrew Lorraine	.25	.08
❑ 421	Rich Becker	.25	.08
❑ 422	Tony Phillips	.25	.08
❑ 423	Scott Ruffcorn	.25	.08
❑ 424	Jeff Granger	.25	.08
❑ 425	Greg Pirkl	.25	.08
❑ 426	Dennis Eckersley	.50	.20
❑ 427	Jose Lima	.25	.08
❑ 428	Russ Davis	.25	.08
❑ 429	Armando Benitez	.25	.08
❑ 430	Alex Gonzalez	.25	.08
❑ 431	Carlos Delgado	.50	.20
❑ 432	Chan Ho Park	.50	.20
❑ 433	Mickey Tettleton	.25	.08
❑ 434	Dave Winfield	.50	.20
❑ 435	John Burkett	.25	.08
❑ 436	Orlando Miller	.25	.08
❑ 437	Rondell White	.50	.20
❑ 438	Jose Oliva	.25	.08
❑ 439	Checklist	.25	.08

1996 Bowman

❑	COMPLETE SET (385)	50.00	20.00
❑ 1	Cal Ripken	2.50	1.00
❑ 2	Ray Durham	.30	.10
❑ 3	Ivan Rodriguez	.50	.20
❑ 4	Fred McGriff	.50	.20
❑ 5	Hideo Nomo	.75	.30
❑ 6	Troy Percival	.30	.10
❑ 7	Moises Alou	.30	.10
❑ 8	Mike Stanley	.30	.10
❑ 9	Jay Buhner	.30	.10
❑ 10	Shawn Green	.30	.10
❑ 11	Ryan Klesko	.30	.10
❑ 12	Andres Galarraga	.30	.10
❑ 13	Dean Palmer	.30	.10
❑ 14	Jeff Conine	.30	.10
❑ 15	Brian L.Hunter	.30	.10
❑ 16	J.T. Snow	.30	.10
❑ 17	Larry Walker	.30	.10
❑ 18	Barry Larkin	.50	.20
❑ 19	Alex Gonzalez	.30	.10
❑ 20	Edgar Martinez	.50	.20
❑ 21	Mo Vaughn	.30	.10
❑ 22	Mark McGwire	2.00	.75
❑ 23	Jose Canseco	.50	.20
❑ 24	Jack McDowell	.30	.10
❑ 25	Dante Bichette	.30	.10
❑ 26	Wade Boggs	.50	.20
❑ 27	Mike Piazza	1.25	.50
❑ 28	Ray Lankford	.30	.10
❑ 29	Craig Biggio	.50	.20
❑ 30	Rafael Palmeiro	.50	.20
❑ 31	Ron Gant	.30	.10
❑ 32	Javy Lopez	.30	.10
❑ 33	Brian Jordan	.30	.10
❑ 34	Paul O'Neill	.50	.20
❑ 35	Mark Grace	.50	.20
❑ 36	Matt Williams	.30	.10
❑ 37	Pedro Martinez	.50	.20
❑ 38	Rickey Henderson	.75	.30
❑ 39	Bobby Bonilla	.30	.10
❑ 40	Todd Hollandsworth	.30	.10
❑ 41	Jim Thome	.50	.20
❑ 42	Gary Sheffield	.75	.30
❑ 43	Tim Salmon	.50	.20
❑ 44	Gregg Jefferies	.30	.10
❑ 45	Roberto Alomar	.50	.20
❑ 46	Carlos Baerga	.30	.10
❑ 47	Mark Grudzielanek	.30	.10
❑ 48	Randy Johnson	.75	.30
❑ 49	Tino Martinez	.50	.20
❑ 50	Robin Ventura	.30	.10
❑ 51	Ryne Sandberg	1.25	.50
❑ 52	Jay Bell	.30	.10
❑ 53	Jason Schmidt	.50	.20
❑ 54	Frank Thomas	.75	.30
❑ 55	Kenny Lofton	.30	.10
❑ 56	Ariel Prieto	.30	.10
❑ 57	David Cone	.30	.10
❑ 58	Reggie Sanders	.30	.10
❑ 59	Michael Tucker	.30	.10
❑ 60	Vinny Castilla	.30	.10
❑ 61	Len Dykstra	.30	.10
❑ 62	Todd Hundley	.30	.10
❑ 63	Brian McRae	.30	.10
❑ 64	Dennis Eckersley	.30	.10
❑ 65	Rondell White	.30	.10
❑ 66	Eric Karros	.30	.10
❑ 67	Greg Maddux	1.25	.50
❑ 68	Kevin Appier	.30	.10
❑ 69	Eddie Murray	.75	.30
❑ 70	John Olerud	.30	.10
❑ 71	Tony Gwynn	1.00	.40
❑ 72	David Justice	.30	.10
❑ 73	Ken Caminiti	.30	.10
❑ 74	Terry Steinbach	.30	.10
❑ 75	Alan Benes	.30	.10
❑ 76	Chipper Jones	.75	.30
❑ 77	Jeff Bagwell	.50	.20
❑ 78	Barry Bonds	2.00	.75
❑ 79	Ken Griffey Jr.	1.50	.60
❑ 80	Roger Cedeno	.30	.10
❑ 81	Joe Carter	.30	.10
❑ 82	Henry Rodriguez	.30	.10
❑ 83	Jason Isringhausen	.30	.10
❑ 84	Chuck Knoblauch	.30	.10
❑ 85	Manny Ramirez	.50	.20
❑ 86	Tom Glavine	.50	.20
❑ 87	Jeffrey Hammonds	.30	.10
❑ 88	Paul Molitor	.30	.10
❑ 89	Roger Clemens	1.50	.60
❑ 90	Greg Vaughn	.30	.10
❑ 91	Marty Cordova	.30	.10
❑ 92	Albert Belle	.30	.10
❑ 93	Mike Mussina	.50	.20
❑ 94	Garret Anderson	.30	.10
❑ 95	Juan Gonzalez	.30	.10
❑ 96	John Valentin	.30	.10
❑ 97	Jason Giambi	.30	.10
❑ 98	Kirby Puckett	.75	.30
❑ 99	Jim Edmonds	.30	.10
❑ 100	Cecil Fielder	.30	.10
❑ 101	Mike Aldrete	.30	.10
❑ 102	Marquis Grissom	.30	.10
❑ 103	Derek Bell	.30	.10
❑ 104	Raul Mondesi	.30	.10
❑ 105	Sammy Sosa	.75	.30
❑ 106	Travis Fryman	.30	.10

❑ 107 Rico Brogna .30 .10
❑ 108 Will Clark .50 .20
❑ 109 Bernie Williams .50 .20
❑ 110 Brady Anderson .30 .10
❑ 111 Torii Hunter .30 .10
❑ 112 Derek Jeter 2.00 .75
❑ 113 Mike Kusiewicz RC .50 .20
❑ 114 Scott Rolen .75 .30
❑ 115 Ramon Castro .30 .10
❑ 116 Jose Guillen RC 3.00 1.25
❑ 117 Wade Walker RC .50 .20
❑ 118 Shawn Senior .30 .10
❑ 119 Onan Masaoka RC 1.00 .40
❑ 120 Marlon Anderson RC 1.00 .40
❑ 121 Katsuhiro Maeda RC 1.00 .40
❑ 122 Garrett Stephenson RC .50 .20
❑ 123 Butch Huskey .30 .10
❑ 124 D'Angelo Jimenez RC 1.00 .40
❑ 125 Tony Mounce RC .50 .20
❑ 126 Jay Canizaro .30 .10
❑ 127 Juan Melo .30 .10
❑ 128 Steve Gibralter .30 .10
❑ 129 Freddy Adrian Garcia .30 .10
❑ 130 Julio Santana .30 .10
❑ 131 Richard Hidalgo .30 .10
❑ 132 Jermaine Dye .30 .10
❑ 133 Willie Adams .30 .10
❑ 134 Everett Stull .30 .10
❑ 135 Ramon Morel .30 .10
❑ 136 Chan Ho Park .30 .10
❑ 137 Jamey Wright .30 .10
❑ 138 Luis R.Garcia RC .50 .20
❑ 139 Dan Serafini .30 .10
❑ 140 Ryan Dempster RC 2.00 .75
❑ 141 Tate Seefried .30 .10
❑ 142 Jimmy Hurst .30 .10
❑ 143 Travis Miller .30 .10
❑ 144 Curtis Goodwin .30 .10
❑ 145 Rocky Coppinger RC .50 .20
❑ 146 Enrique Wilson .30 .10
❑ 147 Jaime Bluma .30 .10
❑ 148 Andrew Vessel .30 .10
❑ 149 Damian Moss .30 .10
❑ 150 Shawn Gallagher RC .50 .20
❑ 151 Pat Watkins .30 .10
❑ 152 Jose Paniagua .30 .10
❑ 153 Danny Graves .30 .10
❑ 154 Bryon Gainey RC .50 .20
❑ 155 Steve Soderstrom .30 .10
❑ 156 Cliff Brumbaugh RC .50 .20
❑ 157 Eugene Kingsale RC .50 .20
❑ 158 Lou Collier .30 .10
❑ 159 Todd Walker .30 .10
❑ 160 Kris Detmers RC .50 .20
❑ 161 Josh Booty RC .50 .20
❑ 162 Greg Whiteman RC .50 .20
❑ 163 Damian Jackson .30 .10
❑ 164 Tony Clark .30 .10
❑ 165 Jeff D'Amico .30 .10
❑ 166 Johnny Damon .50 .20
❑ 167 Rafael Orellano .30 .10
❑ 168 Ruben Rivera .30 .10
❑ 169 Alex Ochoa .30 .10
❑ 170 Jay Powell .30 .10
❑ 171 Tom Evans .30 .10
❑ 172 Ron Villone .30 .10
❑ 173 Shawn Estes .30 .10
❑ 174 John Wasdin .30 .10
❑ 175 Bill Simas .30 .10
❑ 176 Kevin Brown .30 .10
❑ 177 Shannon Stewart .30 .10
❑ 178 Todd Greene .30 .10
❑ 179 Bob Wolcott .30 .10
❑ 180 Chris Snopek .30 .10
❑ 181 Nomar Garciaparra 1.50 .60
❑ 182 Cameron Smith RC .50 .20
❑ 183 Matt Drews .30 .10
❑ 184 Jimmy Haynes .30 .10
❑ 185 Chris Carpenter .50 .20
❑ 186 Desi Relaford .30 .10
❑ 187 Ben Grieve .30 .10
❑ 188 Mike Bell .30 .10
❑ 189 Luis Castillo RC 1.50 .60
❑ 190 Ugueth Urbina .30 .10
❑ 191 Paul Wilson .30 .10
❑ 192 Andruw Jones 1.25 .50
❑ 193 Wayne Gomes .30 .10
❑ 194 Craig Counsell RC 1.50 .60
❑ 195 Jim Cole .30 .10
❑ 196 Brooks Kieschnick .30 .10
❑ 197 Trey Beamon .30 .10
❑ 198 Marino Santana RC .50 .20
❑ 199 Bob Abreu .75 .30
❑ 200 Pokey Reese .30 .10
❑ 201 Dante Powell .30 .10
❑ 202 George Arias .30 .10
❑ 203 Jorge Velandia RC .50 .20
❑ 204 George Lombard RC .50 .20
❑ 205 Byron Browne RC .50 .20
❑ 206 John Frascatore .30 .10
❑ 207 Terry Adams .30 .10
❑ 208 Wilson Delgado RC .50 .20
❑ 209 Billy McMillon .30 .10
❑ 210 Jeff Abbott .30 .10
❑ 211 Trot Nixon .30 .10
❑ 212 Amaury Telemaco .30 .10
❑ 213 Scott Sullivan .30 .10
❑ 214 Justin Thompson .30 .10
❑ 215 Decomba Conner .30 .10
❑ 216 Ryan McGuire .30 .10
❑ 217 Matt Luke .30 .10
❑ 218 Doug Million .30 .10
❑ 219 Jason Dickson RC .50 .20
❑ 220 Ramon Hernandez RC 2.00 .75
❑ 221 Mark Bellhorn RC 2.00 .75
❑ 222 Eric Ludwick RC .50 .20
❑ 223 Luke Wilcox RC .50 .20
❑ 224 Marty Malloy RC .50 .20
❑ 225 Gary Coffee RC .50 .20
❑ 226 Wendell Magee RC .50 .20
❑ 227 Brett Tomko RC 1.00 .40
❑ 228 Derek Lowe .30 .10
❑ 229 Jose Rosado RC .50 .20
❑ 230 Steve Bourgeois RC .50 .20
❑ 231 Neil Weber RC .50 .20
❑ 232 Jeff Ware .30 .10
❑ 233 Edwin Diaz .30 .10
❑ 234 Greg Norton .30 .10
❑ 235 Aaron Boone .30 .10
❑ 236 Jeff Suppan .30 .10
❑ 237 Bret Wagner .30 .10
❑ 238 Elieser Marrero .30 .10
❑ 239 Will Cunnane .30 .10
❑ 240 Brian Barkley RC .50 .20
❑ 241 Jay Payton .30 .10
❑ 242 Marcus Jensen .30 .10
❑ 243 Ryan Nye .30 .10
❑ 244 Chad Mottola .30 .10
❑ 245 Scott McClain RC .50 .20
❑ 246 Jesse Ibarra RC .50 .20
❑ 247 Mike Darr RC .50 .20
❑ 248 Bobby Estalella RC .50 .20
❑ 249 Michael Barrett .30 .10
❑ 250 Jamie Lopiccolo RC .50 .20
❑ 251 Shane Spencer RC 1.00 .40
❑ 252 Ben Petrick RC .50 .20
❑ 253 Jason Bell RC .50 .20
❑ 254 Arnold Gooch RC .50 .20
❑ 255 T.J. Mathews .30 .10
❑ 256 Jason Ryan .30 .10
❑ 257 Pat Cline RC .50 .20
❑ 258 Rafael Carmona RC .50 .20
❑ 259 Carl Pavano RC 2.00 .75
❑ 260 Ben Davis .30 .10
❑ 261 Matt Lawton RC 1.00 .40
❑ 262 Kevin Sefcik RC .50 .20
❑ 263 Chris Fussell RC .50 .20
❑ 264 Mike Cameron RC 1.50 .60
❑ 265 Marty Janzen RC .50 .20
❑ 266 Livan Hernandez RC 2.00 .75
❑ 267 Raul Ibanez RC 2.00 .75
❑ 268 Juan Encarnacion .30 .10
❑ 269 David Yocum RC .50 .20
❑ 270 Jonathan Johnson RC .50 .20
❑ 271 Reggie Taylor .30 .10
❑ 272 Danny Buxbaum RC .50 .20
❑ 273 Jacob Cruz .30 .10
❑ 274 Bobby Morris RC .50 .20
❑ 275 Andy Fox RC .50 .20
❑ 276 Greg Keagle .30 .10
❑ 277 Charles Peterson .30 .10
❑ 278 Derrek Lee .50 .20
❑ 279 Bryant Nelson RC .50 .20
❑ 280 Antone Williamson .30 .10
❑ 281 Scott Elarton .30 .10
❑ 282 Shad Williams RC .50 .20
❑ 283 Rich Hunter RC .50 .20
❑ 284 Chris Sheff .30 .10
❑ 285 Derrick Gibson .30 .10
❑ 286 Felix Rodriguez .30 .10
❑ 287 Brian Banks RC .50 .20
❑ 288 Jason McDonald .30 .10
❑ 289 Glendon Rusch RC 1.00 .40
❑ 290 Gary Rath .30 .10
❑ 291 Peter Munro .30 .10
❑ 292 Tom Fordham .30 .10
❑ 293 Jason Kendall .30 .10
❑ 294 Russ Johnson .30 .10
❑ 295 Joe Long .30 .10
❑ 296 Robert Smith RC .50 .20
❑ 297 Jarrod Washburn RC 1.50 .60
❑ 298 Dave Coggin RC .50 .20
❑ 299 Jeff Yoder RC .50 .20
❑ 300 Jed Hansen RC .50 .20
❑ 301 Matt Morris RC 2.50 1.00
❑ 302 Josh Bishop RC .50 .20
❑ 303 Dustin Hermanson .30 .10
❑ 304 Mike Gulan .30 .10
❑ 305 Felipe Crespo .30 .10
❑ 306 Quinton McCracken .30 .10
❑ 307 Jim Bonnici RC .50 .20
❑ 308 Sal Fasano .30 .10
❑ 309 Gabe Alvarez RC .50 .20
❑ 310 Heath Murray RC .50 .20
❑ 311 Javier Valentin RC .50 .20
❑ 312 Bartolo Colon .75 .30
❑ 313 Olmedo Saenz .30 .10
❑ 314 Norm Hutchins RC .50 .20
❑ 315 Chris Holt .30 .10
❑ 316 David Doster RC .50 .20
❑ 317 Robert Person .30 .10
❑ 318 Donne Wall RC .50 .20
❑ 319 Adam Riggs RC .50 .20
❑ 320 Homer Bush .30 .10
❑ 321 Brad Rigby RC .50 .20
❑ 322 Lou Merloni RC .50 .20
❑ 323 Neifi Perez .30 .10
❑ 324 Chris Cumberland .30 .10
❑ 325 Alvie Shepherd RC .50 .20
❑ 326 Jarrod Patterson RC .50 .20
❑ 327 Ray Ricken RC .50 .20
❑ 328 Danny Klassen RC .50 .20
❑ 329 David Miller RC .50 .20
❑ 330 Chad Alexander RC .50 .20
❑ 331 Matt Beaumont .30 .10
❑ 332 Damon Hollins .30 .10
❑ 333 Todd Dunn .30 .10
❑ 334 Mike Sweeney RC 2.00 .75
❑ 335 Richie Sexson .50 .20
❑ 336 Billy Wagner .30 .10
❑ 337 Ron Wright RC .50 .20
❑ 338 Paul Konerko .75 .30
❑ 339 Tommy Phelps RC .50 .20
❑ 340 Karim Garcia .30 .10
❑ 341 Mike Grace RC .50 .20
❑ 342 Russell Branyan RC 1.00 .40
❑ 343 Randy Winn RC 1.50 .60
❑ 344 A.J. Pierzynski RC 4.00 1.50
❑ 345 Mike Busby RC .50 .20
❑ 346 Matt Beech RC .50 .20
❑ 347 Jose Cepeda RC .50 .20
❑ 348 Brian Stephenson .30 .10
❑ 349 Rey Ordonez .30 .10
❑ 350 Rich Aurilia RC 1.00 .40
❑ 351 Edgard Velazquez RC .50 .20
❑ 352 Raul Casanova .30 .10
❑ 353 Carlos Guillen RC 2.00 .75
❑ 354 Bruce Aven RC .50 .20
❑ 355 Ryan Jones RC .50 .20
❑ 356 Derek Aucoin RC .50 .20
❑ 357 Brian Rose RC .50 .20
❑ 358 Richard Almanzar RC .50 .20
❑ 359 Fletcher Bates RC .50 .20
❑ 360 Russ Ortiz RC 1.50 .60
❑ 361 Wilton Guerrero RC .50 .20
❑ 362 Geoff Jenkins RC 1.50 .60
❑ 363 Pete Janicki .30 .10
❑ 364 Yamil Benitez .30 .10

❑ 365	Aaron Holbert	.30	.10
❑ 366	Tim Belk	.30	.10
❑ 367	Terrell Wade	.30	.10
❑ 368	Terrence Long	.30	.10
❑ 369	Brad Fullmer	.30	.10
❑ 370	Matt Wagner	.30	.10
❑ 371	Craig Wilson RC	.50	.20
❑ 372	Mark Loretta	.30	.10
❑ 373	Eric Owens	.30	.10
❑ 374	Vladimir Guerrero	1.50	.60
❑ 375	Tommy Davis	.30	.10
❑ 376	Donnie Sadler	.30	.10
❑ 377	Edgar Renteria	.30	.10
❑ 378	Todd Helton	1.50	.60
❑ 379	Ralph Milliard RC	.50	.20
❑ 380	Darin Blood RC	.50	.20
❑ 381	Shayne Bennett	.30	.10
❑ 382	Mark Redman	.30	.10
❑ 383	Felix Martinez	.30	.10
❑ 384	Sean Watkins RC	.50	.20
❑ 385	Oscar Henriquez	.30	.10
❑ M20	52 Bowman Mantle	5.00	2.00
❑ NNO	Unnumbered Checklists	.30	.10

1997 Bowman

❑	COMPLETE SET (441)	60.00	25.00
❑	COMPLETE SERIES 1 (221)	30.00	12.50
❑	COMPLETE SERIES 2 (220)	30.00	12.50
❑ 1	Derek Jeter	2.00	.75
❑ 2	Edgar Renteria	.30	.10
❑ 3	Chipper Jones	.75	.30
❑ 4	Hideo Nomo	.75	.30
❑ 5	Tim Salmon	.50	.20
❑ 6	Jason Giambi	.30	.10
❑ 7	Robin Ventura	.30	.10
❑ 8	Tony Clark	.30	.10
❑ 9	Barry Larkin	.50	.20
❑ 10	Paul Molitor	.30	.10
❑ 11	Bernard Gilkey	.30	.10
❑ 12	Jack McDowell	.30	.10
❑ 13	Andy Benes	.30	.10
❑ 14	Ryan Klesko	.30	.10
❑ 15	Mark McGwire	2.00	.75
❑ 16	Ken Griffey Jr.	1.25	.50
❑ 17	Robb Nen	.30	.10
❑ 18	Cal Ripken	2.50	1.00
❑ 19	John Valentin	.30	.10
❑ 20	Ricky Bottalico	.30	.10
❑ 21	Mike Lansing	.30	.10
❑ 22	Ryne Sandberg	1.25	.50
❑ 23	Carlos Delgado	.30	.10
❑ 24	Craig Biggio	.50	.20
❑ 25	Eric Karros	.30	.10
❑ 26	Kevin Appier	.30	.10
❑ 27	Mariano Rivera	.75	.30
❑ 28	Vinny Castilla	.30	.10
❑ 29	Juan Gonzalez	.30	.10
❑ 30	Al Martin	.30	.10
❑ 31	Jeff Cirillo	.30	.10
❑ 32	Eddie Murray	.75	.30
❑ 33	Ray Lankford	.30	.10
❑ 34	Manny Ramirez	.50	.20
❑ 35	Roberto Alomar	.50	.20
❑ 36	Will Clark	.50	.20
❑ 37	Chuck Knoblauch	.30	.10
❑ 38	Harold Baines	.30	.10
❑ 39	Trevor Hoffman	.30	.10
❑ 40	Edgar Martinez	.50	.20
❑ 41	Geronimo Berroa	.30	.10
❑ 42	Rey Ordonez	.30	.10
❑ 43	Mike Stanley	.30	.10
❑ 44	Mike Mussina	.50	.20
❑ 45	Kevin Brown	.30	.10
❑ 46	Dennis Eckersley	.30	.10
❑ 47	Henry Rodriguez	.30	.10
❑ 48	Tino Martinez	.50	.20
❑ 49	Eric Young	.30	.10
❑ 50	Bret Boone	.30	.10
❑ 51	Raul Mondesi	.30	.10
❑ 52	Sammy Sosa	.75	.30
❑ 53	John Smoltz	.50	.20
❑ 54	Billy Wagner	.30	.10
❑ 55	Jeff D'Amico	.30	.10
❑ 56	Ken Caminiti	.30	.10
❑ 57	Jason Kendall	.30	.10
❑ 58	Wade Boggs	.50	.20
❑ 59	Andres Galarraga	.30	.10
❑ 60	Jeff Brantley	.30	.10
❑ 61	Mel Rojas	.30	.10
❑ 62	Brian L. Hunter	.30	.10
❑ 63	Bobby Bonilla	.30	.10
❑ 64	Roger Clemens	1.50	.60
❑ 65	Jeff Kent	.30	.10
❑ 66	Matt Williams	.30	.10
❑ 67	Albert Belle	.30	.10
❑ 68	Jeff King	.30	.10
❑ 69	John Wetteland	.30	.10
❑ 70	Deion Sanders	.50	.20
❑ 71	Bubba Trammell RC	.60	.25
❑ 72	Felix Heredia RC	.40	.15
❑ 73	Billy Koch RC	1.00	.40
❑ 74	Sidney Ponson RC	1.00	.40
❑ 75	Ricky Ledee RC	.60	.25
❑ 76	Brett Tomko	.30	.10
❑ 77	Braden Looper RC	.40	.15
❑ 78	Damian Jackson	.30	.10
❑ 79	Jason Dickson	.30	.10
❑ 80	Chad Green RC	.40	.15
❑ 81	R.A. Dickey RC	.40	.15
❑ 82	Jeff Liefer	.30	.10
❑ 83	Matt Wagner	.30	.10
❑ 84	Richard Hidalgo	.30	.10
❑ 85	Adam Riggs	.30	.10
❑ 86	Robert Smith	.30	.10
❑ 87	Chad Hermansen RC	.40	.15
❑ 88	Felix Martinez	.30	.10
❑ 89	J.J. Johnson	.30	.10
❑ 90	Todd Dunwoody	.30	.10
❑ 91	Katsuhiro Maeda	.30	.10
❑ 92	Darin Erstad	.30	.10
❑ 93	Elieser Marrero	.30	.10
❑ 94	Bartolo Colon	.30	.10
❑ 95	Chris Fussell	.30	.10
❑ 96	Ugueth Urbina	.30	.10
❑ 97	Josh Paul RC	.40	.15
❑ 98	Jaime Bluma	.30	.10
❑ 99	Seth Greisinger RC	.40	.15
❑ 100	Jose Cruz Jr. RC	.60	.25
❑ 101	Todd Dunn	.30	.10
❑ 102	Joe Young RC	.40	.15
❑ 103	Jonathan Johnson	.30	.10
❑ 104	Justin Towle RC	.40	.15
❑ 105	Brian Rose	.30	.10
❑ 106	Jose Guillen	.30	.10
❑ 107	Andruw Jones	.50	.20
❑ 108	Mark Kotsay RC	1.50	.60
❑ 109	Wilton Guerrero	.30	.10
❑ 110	Jacob Cruz	.30	.10
❑ 111	Mike Sweeney	.30	.10
❑ 112	Julio Mosquera	.30	.10
❑ 113	Matt Morris	.30	.10
❑ 114	Wendell Magee	.30	.10
❑ 115	John Thomson	.30	.10
❑ 116	Javier Valentin	.30	.10
❑ 117	Tom Fordham	.30	.10
❑ 118	Ruben Rivera	.30	.10
❑ 119	Mike Drumright RC	.40	.15
❑ 120	Chris Holt	.30	.10
❑ 121	Sean Maloney	.30	.10
❑ 122	Michael Barrett	.30	.10
❑ 123	Tony Saunders RC	.40	.15
❑ 124	Kevin Brown C	.30	.10
❑ 125	Richard Almanzar	.30	.10
❑ 126	Mark Redman	.30	.10
❑ 127	Anthony Sanders RC	.40	.15
❑ 128	Jeff Abbott	.30	.10
❑ 129	Eugene Kingsale	.30	.10
❑ 130	Paul Konerko	.50	.20
❑ 131	Randall Simon RC	.60	.25
❑ 132	Andy Larkin	.30	.10
❑ 133	Rafael Medina	.30	.10
❑ 134	Mendy Lopez	.30	.10
❑ 135	Freddy Adrian Garcia	.30	.10
❑ 136	Karim Garcia	.30	.10
❑ 137	Larry Rodriguez RC	.40	.15
❑ 138	Carlos Guillen	.30	.10
❑ 139	Aaron Boone	.30	.10
❑ 140	Donnie Sadler	.30	.10
❑ 141	Brooks Kieschnick	.30	.10
❑ 142	Scott Spiezio	.30	.10
❑ 143	Everett Stull	.30	.10
❑ 144	Enrique Wilson	.30	.10
❑ 145	Milton Bradley RC	2.00	.75
❑ 146	Kevin Orie	.30	.10
❑ 147	Derek Wallace	.30	.10
❑ 148	Russ Johnson	.30	.10
❑ 149	Joe Lagarde RC	.40	.15
❑ 150	Luis Castillo	.30	.10
❑ 151	Jay Payton	.30	.10
❑ 152	Joe Long	.30	.10
❑ 153	Livan Hernandez	.30	.10
❑ 154	Vladimir Nunez RC	.60	.25
❑ 155	Pokey Reese UER	.30	.10
❑ 156	George Arias	.30	.10
❑ 157	Homer Bush	.30	.10
❑ 158	Chris Carpenter UER	.30	.10
❑ 159	Eric Milton RC	.60	.25
❑ 160	Richie Sexson	.30	.10
❑ 161	Carl Pavano	.30	.10
❑ 162	Chris Gissell RC	.40	.15
❑ 163	Mac Suzuki	.30	.10
❑ 164	Pat Cline	.30	.10
❑ 165	Ron Wright	.30	.10
❑ 166	Dante Powell	.30	.10
❑ 167	Mark Bellhorn	.30	.10
❑ 168	George Lombard	.30	.10
❑ 169	Pee Wee Lopez RC	.40	.15
❑ 170	Paul Wilder RC	.40	.15
❑ 171	Brad Fullmer	.30	.10
❑ 172	Willie Martinez RC	.40	.15
❑ 173	Dario Veras RC	.40	.15
❑ 174	Dave Coggin	.30	.10
❑ 175	Kris Benson RC	1.00	.40
❑ 176	Torii Hunter	.30	.10
❑ 177	D.T. Cromer	.30	.10
❑ 178	Nelson Figueroa RC	.40	.15
❑ 179	Hiram Bocachica RC	.40	.15
❑ 180	Shane Monahan	.30	.10
❑ 181	Jimmy Anderson RC	.40	.15
❑ 182	Juan Melo	.30	.10
❑ 183	Pablo Ortega RC	.40	.15
❑ 184	Calvin Pickering RC	.40	.15
❑ 185	Reggie Taylor	.30	.10
❑ 186	Jeff Farnsworth RC	.40	.15
❑ 187	Terrence Long	.30	.10
❑ 188	Geoff Jenkins	.30	.10
❑ 189	Steve Rain RC	.40	.15
❑ 190	Nerio Rodriguez RC	.40	.15
❑ 191	Derrick Gibson	.30	.10
❑ 192	Darin Blood	.30	.10
❑ 193	Ben Davis	.30	.10
❑ 194	Adrian Beltre RC	3.00	1.25
❑ 195	Damian Sapp RC UER	.40	.15
❑ 196	Kerry Wood RC	5.00	2.00
❑ 197	Nate Rolison RC	.40	.15
❑ 198	Fernando Tatis RC	.40	.15
❑ 199	Brad Penny RC	3.00	1.25
❑ 200	Jake Westbrook RC	1.00	.40
❑ 201	Edwin Diaz	.30	.10
❑ 202	Joe Fontenot RC	.60	.25
❑ 203	Matt Halloran RC	.40	.15
❑ 204	Blake Stein RC	.40	.15
❑ 205	Onan Masaoka	.30	.10
❑ 206	Ben Petrick	.30	.10
❑ 207	Matt Clement RC	1.00	.40
❑ 208	Todd Greene	.30	.10
❑ 209	Ray Ricken	.30	.10
❑ 210	Eric Chavez RC	4.00	1.50
❑ 211	Edgard Velazquez	.30	.10
❑ 212	Bruce Chen RC	1.00	.40

❑ 213 Danny Patterson .30 .10
❑ 214 Jeff Yoder .30 .10
❑ 215 Luis Ordaz RC .40 .15
❑ 216 Chris Widger .30 .10
❑ 217 Jason Brester .30 .10
❑ 218 Carlton Loewer .30 .10
❑ 219 Chris Reitsma RC .60 .25
❑ 220 Neifi Perez .30 .10
❑ 221 Hideki Irabu RC .60 .25
❑ 222 Ellis Burks .30 .10
❑ 223 Pedro Martinez .50 .20
❑ 224 Kenny Lofton .30 .10
❑ 225 Randy Johnson .75 .30
❑ 226 Terry Steinbach .30 .10
❑ 227 Bernie Williams .50 .20
❑ 228 Dean Palmer .30 .10
❑ 229 Alan Benes .30 .10
❑ 230 Marquis Grissom .30 .10
❑ 231 Gary Sheffield .30 .10
❑ 232 Curt Schilling .30 .10
❑ 233 Reggie Sanders .30 .10
❑ 234 Bobby Higginson .30 .10
❑ 235 Moises Alou .30 .10
❑ 236 Tom Glavine .50 .20
❑ 237 Mark Grace .50 .20
❑ 238 Ramon Martinez .30 .10
❑ 239 Rafael Palmeiro .50 .20
❑ 240 John Olerud .30 .10
❑ 241 Dante Bichette .30 .10
❑ 242 Greg Vaughn .30 .10
❑ 243 Jeff Bagwell .50 .20
❑ 244 Barry Bonds 2.00 .75
❑ 245 Pat Hentgen .30 .10
❑ 246 Jim Thome .50 .20
❑ 247 Jermaine Allensworth .30 .10
❑ 248 Andy Pettitte .50 .20
❑ 249 Jay Bell .30 .10
❑ 250 John Jaha .30 .10
❑ 251 Jim Edmonds .30 .10
❑ 252 Ron Gant .30 .10
❑ 253 David Cone .30 .10
❑ 254 Jose Canseco .50 .20
❑ 255 Jay Buhner .30 .10
❑ 256 Greg Maddux 1.25 .50
❑ 257 Brian McRae .30 .10
❑ 258 Lance Johnson .30 .10
❑ 259 Travis Fryman .30 .10
❑ 260 Paul O'Neill .50 .20
❑ 261 Ivan Rodriguez .50 .20
❑ 262 Gregg Jefferies .30 .10
❑ 263 Fred McGriff .50 .20
❑ 264 Derek Bell .30 .10
❑ 265 Jeff Conine .30 .10
❑ 266 Mike Piazza 1.25 .50
❑ 267 Mark Grudzielanek .30 .10
❑ 268 Brady Anderson .30 .10
❑ 269 Marty Cordova .30 .10
❑ 270 Ray Durham .30 .10
❑ 271 Joe Carter .30 .10
❑ 272 Brian Jordan .30 .10
❑ 273 David Justice .30 .10
❑ 274 Tony Gwynn 1.00 .40
❑ 275 Larry Walker .30 .10
❑ 276 Cecil Fielder .30 .10
❑ 277 Mo Vaughn .30 .10
❑ 278 Alex Fernandez .30 .10
❑ 279 Michael Tucker .30 .10
❑ 280 Jose Valentin .30 .10
❑ 281 Sandy Alomar Jr. .30 .10
❑ 282 Todd Hollandsworth .30 .10
❑ 283 Rico Brogna .30 .10
❑ 284 Rusty Greer .30 .10
❑ 285 Roberto Hernandez .30 .10
❑ 286 Hal Morris .30 .10
❑ 287 Johnny Damon .50 .20
❑ 288 Todd Hundley .30 .10
❑ 289 Rondell White .30 .10
❑ 290 Frank Thomas .75 .30
❑ 291 Don Denbow RC .40 .15
❑ 292 Derrek Lee .50 .20
❑ 293 Todd Walker .30 .10
❑ 294 Scott Rolen .50 .20
❑ 295 Wes Helms .30 .10
❑ 296 Bob Abreu .50 .20
❑ 297 John Patterson RC 1.50 .60
❑ 298 Alex Gonzalez RC 1.00 .40
❑ 299 Grant Roberts RC .40 .15
❑ 300 Jeff Suppan .30 .10
❑ 301 Luke Wilcox .30 .10
❑ 302 Marlon Anderson .30 .10
❑ 303 Ray Brown .30 .10
❑ 304 Mike Caruso RC .40 .15
❑ 305 Sam Marsonek RC .40 .15
❑ 306 Brady Raggio RC .40 .15
❑ 307 Kevin McGlinchy RC .60 .25
❑ 308 Roy Halladay RC 5.00 2.00
❑ 309 Jeremi Gonzalez RC .40 .15
❑ 310 Aramis Ramirez RC 4.00 1.50
❑ 311 Dee Brown RC .40 .15
❑ 312 Justin Thompson .30 .10
❑ 313 Jay Tessmer RC .40 .15
❑ 314 Mike Johnson RC .40 .15
❑ 315 Danny Clyburn .30 .10
❑ 316 Bruce Aven .30 .10
❑ 317 Keith Foulke RC 1.50 .60
❑ 318 Jimmy Osting RC .60 .25
❑ 319 Valerio De Los Santos RC .40 .15
❑ 320 Shannon Stewart .30 .10
❑ 321 Willie Adams .30 .10
❑ 322 Larry Barnes RC .40 .15
❑ 323 Mark Johnson RC .40 .15
❑ 324 Chris Stowers RC .40 .15
❑ 325 Brandon Reed .30 .10
❑ 326 Randy Winn .30 .10
❑ 327 Steve Chavez RC .40 .15
❑ 328 Nomar Garciaparra 1.25 .50
❑ 329 Jacque Jones RC 1.50 .60
❑ 330 Chris Clemons .30 .10
❑ 331 Todd Helton .75 .30
❑ 332 Ryan Brannan RC .40 .15
❑ 333 Alex Sanchez RC .60 .25
❑ 334 Arnold Gooch .30 .10
❑ 335 Russell Branyan .30 .10
❑ 336 Daryle Ward .40 .15
❑ 337 John LeRoy RC .40 .15
❑ 338 Steve Cox .30 .10
❑ 339 Kevin Witt .30 .10
❑ 340 Norm Hutchins .30 .10
❑ 341 Gabby Martinez .30 .10
❑ 342 Kris Detmers .30 .10
❑ 343 Mike Villano RC .40 .15
❑ 344 Preston Wilson .30 .10
❑ 345 James Manias RC .40 .15
❑ 346 Deivi Cruz RC .60 .25
❑ 347 Donzell McDonald RC .40 .15
❑ 348 Rod Myers RC .40 .15
❑ 349 Shawn Chacon RC 1.00 .40
❑ 350 Elvin Hernandez RC .60 .25
❑ 351 Orlando Cabrera RC 1.50 .60
❑ 352 Brian Banks .30 .10
❑ 353 Robbie Bell .40 .15
❑ 354 Brad Rigby .30 .10
❑ 355 Scott Elarton .30 .10
❑ 356 Kevin Sweeney RC .40 .15
❑ 357 Steve Soderstrom .30 .10
❑ 358 Ryan Nye .30 .10
❑ 359 Marlon Allen RC .40 .15
❑ 360 Donny Leon RC .40 .15
❑ 361 Garrett Neubart RC .60 .25
❑ 362 Abraham Nunez RC .60 .25
❑ 363 Adam Eaton RC 1.00 .40
❑ 364 Octavio Dotel RC .60 .25
❑ 365 Dean Crow RC .40 .15
❑ 366 Jason Baker RC .40 .15
❑ 367 Sean Casey 1.00 .40
❑ 368 Joe Lawrence RC .40 .15
❑ 369 Adam Johnson RC .40 .15
❑ 370 Scott Schoeneweis RC .60 .25
❑ 371 Gerald Witasick Jr. .30 .10
❑ 372 Ronnie Belliard RC 1.25 .50
❑ 373 Russ Ortiz .30 .10
❑ 374 Robert Stratton RC .60 .25
❑ 375 Bobby Estalella .30 .10
❑ 376 Corey Lee RC .40 .15
❑ 377 Carlos Beltran 2.00 .75
❑ 378 Mike Cameron .30 .10
❑ 379 Scott Randall RC .40 .15
❑ 380 Corey Erickson RC .40 .15
❑ 381 Jay Canizaro .30 .10
❑ 382 Kerry Robinson RC .40 .15
❑ 383 Todd Noel RC .40 .15
❑ 384 A.J. Zapp RC .40 .15
❑ 385 Jarrod Washburn .30 .10
❑ 386 Ben Grieve .30 .10
❑ 387 Javier Vazquez RC 1.50 .60
❑ 388 Tony Graffanino .30 .10
❑ 389 Travis Lee RC .60 .25
❑ 390 DaRond Stovall .30 .10
❑ 391 Dennis Reyes RC .60 .25
❑ 392 Danny Buxbaum .30 .10
❑ 393 Marc Lewis RC .40 .15
❑ 394 Kelvim Escobar RC 1.00 .40
❑ 395 Danny Klassen .30 .10
❑ 396 Ken Cloude RC .40 .15
❑ 397 Gabe Alvarez .30 .10
❑ 398 Jaret Wright RC .60 .25
❑ 399 Raul Casanova .30 .10
❑ 400 Clayton Bruner RC .40 .15
❑ 401 Jason Marquis RC 1.00 .40
❑ 402 Marc Kroon .30 .10
❑ 403 Jamey Wright .30 .10
❑ 404 Matt Snyder RC .40 .15
❑ 405 Josh Garrett RC .40 .15
❑ 406 Juan Encarnacion .30 .10
❑ 407 Heath Murray .30 .10
❑ 408 Brett Herbison RC .60 .25
❑ 409 Brent Butler RC .40 .15
❑ 410 Danny Peoples RC .40 .15
❑ 411 Miguel Tejada RC 6.00 2.50
❑ 412 Damian Moss .30 .10
❑ 413 Jim Pittsley .30 .10
❑ 414 Dmitri Young .30 .10
❑ 415 Glendon Rusch .30 .10
❑ 416 Vladimir Guerrero .75 .30
❑ 417 Cole Liniak RC .60 .25
❑ 418 Ramon Hernandez .30 .10
❑ 419 Cliff Politte RC .40 .15
❑ 420 Mel Rosario RC .40 .15
❑ 421 Jorge Carrion RC .40 .15
❑ 422 John Barnes RC .40 .15
❑ 423 Chris Stowe RC .40 .15
❑ 424 Vernon Wells RC 5.00 2.00
❑ 425 Brett Caradonna RC .40 .15
❑ 426 Scott Hodges RC .60 .25
❑ 427 Jon Garland RC 2.50 1.00
❑ 428 Nathan Haynes RC .40 .15
❑ 429 Geoff Goetz RC .40 .15
❑ 430 Adam Kennedy RC 1.00 .40
❑ 431 T.J. Tucker RC .40 .15
❑ 432 Aaron Akin RC .40 .15
❑ 433 Jayson Werth RC 1.00 .40
❑ 434 Glenn Davis RC .40 .15
❑ 435 Mark Mangum RC .40 .15
❑ 436 Troy Cameron RC .40 .15
❑ 437 J.J. Davis RC .40 .15
❑ 438 Lance Berkman RC 8.00 3.00
❑ 439 Jason Standridge RC .40 .15
❑ 440 Jason Dellaero RC .60 .25
❑ 441 Hideki Irabu .60 .25

1998 Bowman

❑ COMPLETE SET (441) 50.00 20.00
❑ COMPLETE SERIES 1 (221) 25.00 10.00
❑ COMPLETE SERIES 2 (220) 25.00 10.00
❑ 1 Nomar Garciaparra 1.25 .50
❑ 2 Scott Rolen .50 .20
❑ 3 Andy Pettitte .50 .20
❑ 4 Ivan Rodriguez .50 .20
❑ 5 Mark McGwire 2.00 .75
❑ 6 Jason Dickson .30 .10

❑ 7 Jose Cruz Jr.	.30	.10
❑ 8 Jeff Kent	.30	.10
❑ 9 Mike Mussina	.50	.20
❑ 10 Jason Kendall	.30	.10
❑ 11 Brett Tomko	.30	.10
❑ 12 Jeff King	.30	.10
❑ 13 Brad Radke	.30	.10
❑ 14 Robin Ventura	.30	.10
❑ 15 Jeff Bagwell	.50	.20
❑ 16 Greg Maddux	1.25	.50
❑ 17 John Jaha	.30	.10
❑ 18 Mike Piazza	1.25	.50
❑ 19 Edgar Martinez	.50	.20
❑ 20 David Justice	.30	.10
❑ 21 Todd Hundley	.30	.10
❑ 22 Tony Gwynn	1.00	.40
❑ 23 Larry Walker	.30	.10
❑ 24 Bernie Williams	.50	.20
❑ 25 Edgar Renteria	.30	.10
❑ 26 Rafael Palmeiro	.50	.20
❑ 27 Tim Salmon	.50	.20
❑ 28 Matt Morris	.30	.10
❑ 29 Shawn Estes	.30	.10
❑ 30 Vladimir Guerrero	.75	.30
❑ 31 Fernando Tatis	.30	.10
❑ 32 Justin Thompson	.30	.10
❑ 33 Ken Griffey Jr.	1.25	.50
❑ 34 Edgardo Alfonzo	.30	.10
❑ 35 Mo Vaughn	.30	.10
❑ 36 Marty Cordova	.30	.10
❑ 37 Craig Biggio	.50	.20
❑ 38 Roger Clemens	1.50	.60
❑ 39 Mark Grace	.50	.20
❑ 40 Ken Caminiti	.30	.10
❑ 41 Tony Womack	.30	.10
❑ 42 Albert Belle	.30	.10
❑ 43 Tino Martinez	.50	.20
❑ 44 Sandy Alomar Jr.	.30	.10
❑ 45 Jeff Cirillo	.30	.10
❑ 46 Jason Giambi	.30	.10
❑ 47 Darin Erstad	.30	.10
❑ 48 Livan Hernandez	.30	.10
❑ 49 Mark Grudzielanek	.30	.10
❑ 50 Sammy Sosa	.75	.30
❑ 51 Curt Schilling	.30	.10
❑ 52 Brian Hunter	.30	.10
❑ 53 Neifi Perez	.30	.10
❑ 54 Todd Walker	.30	.10
❑ 55 Jose Guillen	.30	.10
❑ 56 Jim Thome	.50	.20
❑ 57 Tom Glavine	.50	.20
❑ 58 Todd Greene	.30	.10
❑ 59 Rondell White	.30	.10
❑ 60 Roberto Alomar	.50	.20
❑ 61 Tony Clark	.30	.10
❑ 62 Vinny Castilla	.30	.10
❑ 63 Barry Larkin	.50	.20
❑ 64 Hideki Irabu	.30	.10
❑ 65 Johnny Damon	.50	.20
❑ 66 Juan Gonzalez	.30	.10
❑ 67 John Olerud	.30	.10
❑ 68 Gary Sheffield	.30	.10
❑ 69 Raul Mondesi	.30	.10
❑ 70 Chipper Jones	.75	.30
❑ 71 David Ortiz	2.50	1.00
❑ 72 Warren Morris RC	.40	.15
❑ 73 Alex Gonzalez	.30	.10
❑ 74 Nick Bierbrodt	.30	.10
❑ 75 Roy Halladay	.30	.10
❑ 76 Danny Buxbaum	.30	.10
❑ 77 Adam Kennedy	.30	.10
❑ 78 Jared Sandberg	.30	.10
❑ 79 Michael Barrett	.30	.10
❑ 80 Gil Meche	.60	.25
❑ 81 Jayson Werth	.30	.10
❑ 82 Abraham Nunez	.30	.10
❑ 83 Ben Petrick	.30	.10
❑ 84 Brett Caradonna	.30	.10
❑ 85 Mike Lowell RC	2.50	1.00
❑ 86 Clayton Bruner	.30	.10
❑ 87 John Curtice RC	.60	.25
❑ 88 Bobby Estalella	.30	.10
❑ 89 Juan Melo	.30	.10
❑ 90 Arnold Gooch	.30	.10
❑ 91 Kevin Millwood RC	1.50	.60
❑ 92 Richie Sexson	.30	.10
❑ 93 Orlando Cabrera	.30	.10
❑ 94 Pat Cline	.30	.10
❑ 95 Anthony Sanders	.30	.10
❑ 96 Russ Johnson	.30	.10
❑ 97 Ben Grieve	.30	.10
❑ 98 Kevin McGlinchy	.30	.10
❑ 99 Paul Wilder	.30	.10
❑ 100 Russ Ortiz	.30	.10
❑ 101 Ryan Jackson RC	.40	.15
❑ 102 Heath Murray	.30	.10
❑ 103 Brian Rose	.30	.10
❑ 104 Ryan Radmanovich RC	.40	.15
❑ 105 Ricky Ledee	.30	.10
❑ 106 Jeff Wallace RC	.40	.15
❑ 107 Ryan Minor RC	.40	.15
❑ 108 Dennis Reyes	.30	.10
❑ 109 James Manias	.30	.10
❑ 110 Chris Carpenter	.30	.10
❑ 111 Daryle Ward	.30	.10
❑ 112 Vernon Wells	.30	.10
❑ 113 Chad Green	.30	.10
❑ 114 Mike Stoner RC	.40	.15
❑ 115 Brad Fullmer	.30	.10
❑ 116 Adam Eaton	.30	.10
❑ 117 Jeff Liefer	.30	.10
❑ 118 Corey Koskie RC	1.00	.40
❑ 119 Todd Helton	.50	.20
❑ 120 Jaime Jones RC	.40	.15
❑ 121 Mel Rosario	.30	.10
❑ 122 Geoff Goetz	.30	.10
❑ 123 Adrian Beltre	.30	.10
❑ 124 Jason Dellaero	.30	.10
❑ 125 Gabe Kapler RC	1.00	.40
❑ 126 Scott Schoeneweis	.30	.10
❑ 127 Ryan Brannan	.30	.10
❑ 128 Aaron Akin	.30	.10
❑ 129 Ryan Anderson RC	.40	.15
❑ 130 Brad Penny	.30	.10
❑ 131 Bruce Chen	.30	.10
❑ 132 Eli Marrero	.30	.10
❑ 133 Eric Chavez	.30	.10
❑ 134 Troy Glaus RC	4.00	1.50
❑ 135 Troy Cameron	.30	.10
❑ 136 Brian Sikorski RC	.40	.15
❑ 137 Mike Kinkade RC	.40	.15
❑ 138 Braden Looper	.30	.10
❑ 139 Mark Mangum	.30	.10
❑ 140 Danny Peoples	.30	.10
❑ 141 J.J. Davis	.30	.10
❑ 142 Ben Davis	.30	.10
❑ 143 Jacque Jones	.30	.10
❑ 144 Derrick Gibson	.30	.10
❑ 145 Bronson Arroyo	1.50	.60
❑ 146 Luis De Los Santos RC	.40	.15
❑ 147 Jeff Abbott	.30	.10
❑ 148 Mike Cuddyer RC	1.50	.60
❑ 149 Jason Romano	.30	.10
❑ 150 Shane Monahan	.30	.10
❑ 151 Ntema Ndungidi RC	.40	.15
❑ 152 Alex Sanchez	.30	.10
❑ 153 Jack Cust RC	2.00	.75
❑ 154 Brent Butler	.30	.10
❑ 155 Ramon Hernandez	.30	.10
❑ 156 Norm Hutchins	.30	.10
❑ 157 Jason Marquis	.30	.10
❑ 158 Jacob Cruz	.30	.10
❑ 159 Rob Burger RC	.40	.15
❑ 160 Dave Coggin	.30	.10
❑ 161 Preston Wilson	.30	.10
❑ 162 Jason Fitzgerald RC	.40	.15
❑ 163 Dan Serafini	.30	.10
❑ 164 Peter Munro	.30	.10
❑ 165 Trot Nixon	.30	.10
❑ 166 Homer Bush	.30	.10
❑ 167 Dermal Brown	.30	.10
❑ 168 Chad Hermansen	.30	.10
❑ 169 Julio Moreno RC	.40	.15
❑ 170 John Roskos RC	.40	.15
❑ 171 Grant Roberts	.30	.10
❑ 172 Ken Cloude	.30	.10
❑ 173 Jason Brester	.30	.10
❑ 174 Jason Conti	.30	.10
❑ 175 Jon Garland	.30	.10
❑ 176 Robbie Bell	.30	.10
❑ 177 Nathan Haynes	.30	.10
❑ 178 Ramon Ortiz RC	.60	.25
❑ 179 Shannon Stewart	.30	.10
❑ 180 Pablo Ortega	.30	.10
❑ 181 Jimmy Rollins RC	5.00	2.00
❑ 182 Sean Casey	.30	.10
❑ 183 Ted Lilly RC	1.00	.40
❑ 184 Chris Enochs RC	.40	.15
❑ 185 Maggio Ordonez UER RC	5.00	2.00
❑ 186 Mike Drumright	.30	.10
❑ 187 Aaron Boone	.30	.10
❑ 188 Matt Clement	.30	.10
❑ 189 Todd Dunwoody	.30	.10
❑ 190 Larry Rodriguez	.30	.10
❑ 191 Todd Noel	.30	.10
❑ 192 Geoff Jenkins	.30	.10
❑ 193 George Lombard	.30	.10
❑ 194 Lance Berkman	.30	.10
❑ 195 Marcus McCain	.30	.10
❑ 196 Ryan McGuire	.30	.10
❑ 197 Jhensy Sandoval	.30	.10
❑ 198 Corey Lee	.30	.10
❑ 199 Mario Valdez	.30	.10
❑ 200 Robert Fick RC	.60	.25
❑ 201 Donnie Sadler	.30	.10
❑ 202 Marc Kroon	.30	.10
❑ 203 David Miller	.30	.10
❑ 204 Jarrod Washburn	.30	.10
❑ 205 Miguel Tejada	.75	.30
❑ 206 Raul Ibanez	.30	.10
❑ 207 John Patterson	.30	.10
❑ 208 Calvin Pickering	.30	.10
❑ 209 Felix Martinez	.30	.10
❑ 210 Mark Redman	.30	.10
❑ 211 Scott Elarton	.30	.10
❑ 212 Jose Amado RC	.40	.15
❑ 213 Kerry Wood	.30	.10
❑ 214 Dante Powell	.30	.10
❑ 215 Aramis Ramirez	.30	.10
❑ 216 A.J. Hinch	.30	.10
❑ 217 Dustin Carr RC	.40	.15
❑ 218 Mark Kotsay	.30	.10
❑ 219 Jason Standridge	.30	.10
❑ 220 Luis Ordaz	.30	.10
❑ 221 Orlando Hernandez RC	2.00	.75
❑ 222 Cal Ripken	2.50	1.00
❑ 223 Paul Molitor	.30	.10
❑ 224 Derek Jeter	2.00	.75
❑ 225 Barry Bonds	2.00	.75
❑ 226 Jim Edmonds	.30	.10
❑ 227 John Smoltz	.50	.20
❑ 228 Eric Karros	.30	.10
❑ 229 Ray Lankford	.30	.10
❑ 230 Rey Ordonez	.30	.10
❑ 231 Kenny Lofton	.30	.10
❑ 232 Alex Rodriguez	1.25	.50
❑ 233 Dante Bichette	.30	.10
❑ 234 Pedro Martinez	.50	.20
❑ 235 Carlos Delgado	.30	.10
❑ 236 Rod Beck	.30	.10
❑ 237 Matt Williams	.30	.10
❑ 238 Charles Johnson	.30	.10
❑ 239 Rico Brogna	.30	.10
❑ 240 Frank Thomas	.75	.30
❑ 241 Paul O'Neill	.50	.20
❑ 242 Jaret Wright	.30	.10
❑ 243 Brant Brown	.30	.10
❑ 244 Ryan Klesko	.30	.10
❑ 245 Chuck Finley	.30	.10
❑ 246 Derek Bell	.30	.10
❑ 247 Delino DeShields	.30	.10
❑ 248 Chan Ho Park	.30	.10
❑ 249 Wade Boggs	.50	.20
❑ 250 Jay Buhner	.30	.10
❑ 251 Butch Huskey	.30	.10
❑ 252 Steve Finley	.30	.10
❑ 253 Will Clark	.50	.20
❑ 254 John Valentin	.30	.10
❑ 255 Bobby Higginson	.30	.10
❑ 256 Darryl Strawberry	.30	.10
❑ 257 Randy Johnson	.75	.30
❑ 258 Al Martin	.30	.10
❑ 259 Travis Fryman	.30	.10
❑ 260 Fred McGriff	.50	.20
❑ 261 Jose Valentin	.30	.10
❑ 262 Andruw Jones	.50	.20
❑ 263 Kenny Rogers	.30	.10
❑ 264 Moises Alou	.30	.10

❑ 265 Denny Neagle	.30	.10
❑ 266 Ugueth Urbina	.30	.10
❑ 267 Derrek Lee	.50	.20
❑ 268 Ellis Burks	.30	.10
❑ 269 Mariano Rivera	.75	.30
❑ 270 Dean Palmer	.30	.10
❑ 271 Eddie Taubensee	.30	.10
❑ 272 Brady Anderson	.30	.10
❑ 273 Brian Giles	.30	.10
❑ 274 Quinton McCracken	.30	.10
❑ 275 Henry Rodriguez	.30	.10
❑ 276 Andres Galarraga	.30	.10
❑ 277 Jose Canseco	.50	.20
❑ 278 David Segui	.30	.10
❑ 279 Bret Saberhagen	.30	.10
❑ 280 Kevin Brown	.50	.20
❑ 281 Chuck Knoblauch	.30	.10
❑ 282 Jeromy Burnitz	.30	.10
❑ 283 Jay Bell	.30	.10
❑ 284 Manny Ramirez	.50	.20
❑ 285 Rick Helling	.30	.10
❑ 286 Francisco Cordova	.30	.10
❑ 287 Bob Abreu	.30	.10
❑ 288 J.T. Snow	.30	.10
❑ 289 Hideo Nomo	.75	.30
❑ 290 Brian Jordan	.30	.10
❑ 291 Javy Lopez	.30	.10
❑ 292 Travis Lee	.30	.10
❑ 293 Russell Branyan	.30	.10
❑ 294 Paul Konerko	.30	.10
❑ 295 Masato Yoshii RC	.60	.25
❑ 296 Kris Benson	.30	.10
❑ 297 Juan Encarnacion	.30	.10
❑ 298 Eric Milton	.30	.10
❑ 299 Mike Caruso	.30	.10
❑ 300 Ricardo Aramboles RC	.40	.15
❑ 301 Bobby Smith	.30	.10
❑ 302 Billy Koch	.30	.10
❑ 303 Richard Hidalgo	.30	.10
❑ 304 Justin Baughman RC	.40	.15
❑ 305 Chris Gissell	.30	.10
❑ 306 Donnie Bridges RC	.40	.15
❑ 307 Nelson Lara RC	.40	.15
❑ 308 Randy Wolf RC	.60	.25
❑ 309 Jason LaRue RC	.60	.25
❑ 310 Jason Gooding RC	.40	.15
❑ 311 Edgard Clemente	.30	.10
❑ 312 Andrew Vessel	.30	.10
❑ 313 Chris Reitsma	.30	.10
❑ 314 Jesus Sanchez RC	.40	.15
❑ 315 Buddy Carlyle RC	.40	.15
❑ 316 Randy Winn	.30	.10
❑ 317 Luis Rivera RC	.40	.15
❑ 318 Marcus Thames RC	2.50	1.00
❑ 319 A.J. Pierzynski	.30	.10
❑ 320 Scott Randall	.30	.10
❑ 321 Damian Sapp	.30	.10
❑ 322 Ed Yarnall RC	.40	.15
❑ 323 Luke Allen RC	.40	.15
❑ 324 J.D. Smart	.30	.10
❑ 325 Willie Martinez	.30	.10
❑ 326 Alex Ramirez	.30	.10
❑ 327 Eric DuBose RC	.40	.15
❑ 328 Kevin Witt	.30	.10
❑ 329 Dan McKinley RC	.40	.15
❑ 330 Cliff Politte	.30	.10
❑ 331 Vladimir Nunez	.30	.10
❑ 332 John Halama RC	.40	.15
❑ 333 Nerio Rodriguez	.30	.10
❑ 334 Desi Relaford	.30	.10
❑ 335 Robinson Checo	.30	.10
❑ 336 John Nicholson	.50	.20
❑ 337 Tom LaRosa RC	.40	.15
❑ 338 Kevin Nicholson RC	.40	.15
❑ 339 Javier Vazquez	.30	.10
❑ 340 A.J. Zapp	.30	.10
❑ 341 Tom Evans	.30	.10
❑ 342 Kerry Robinson	.30	.10
❑ 343 Gabe Gonzalez RC	.40	.15
❑ 344 Ralph Milliard	.30	.10
❑ 345 Enrique Wilson	.30	.10
❑ 346 Elvin Hernandez	.30	.10
❑ 347 Mike Lincoln RC	.40	.15
❑ 348 Cesar King RC	.40	.15
❑ 349 Cristian Guzman RC	.60	.25
❑ 350 Donzell McDonald	.30	.10
❑ 351 Jim Parque RC	.40	.15
❑ 352 Mike Saipe RC	.40	.15
❑ 353 Carlos Febles RC	.60	.25
❑ 354 Dernell Stenson RC	.40	.15
❑ 355 Mark Osborne RC	.40	.15
❑ 356 Odalis Perez RC	1.50	.60
❑ 357 Jason Dewey RC	.40	.15
❑ 358 Joe Fontenot	.30	.10
❑ 359 Jason Grilli RC	.40	.15
❑ 360 Kevin Haverbusch RC	.40	.15
❑ 361 Jay Yennaco RC	.40	.15
❑ 362 Brian Buchanan	.30	.10
❑ 363 John Barnes	.30	.10
❑ 364 Chris Fussell	.30	.10
❑ 365 Kevin Gibbs RC	.40	.15
❑ 366 Joe Lawrence	.30	.10
❑ 367 DaRond Stovall	.30	.10
❑ 368 Brian Fuentes RC	.40	.15
❑ 369 Jimmy Anderson	.30	.10
❑ 370 Lariel Gonzalez RC	.40	.15
❑ 371 Scott Williamson RC	.40	.15
❑ 372 Milton Bradley	.30	.10
❑ 373 Jason Halper RC	.40	.15
❑ 374 Brent Billingsley RC	.40	.15
❑ 375 Joe DePastino RC	.40	.15
❑ 376 Jake Westbrook	.30	.10
❑ 377 Octavio Dotel	.30	.10
❑ 378 Jason Williams RC	.40	.15
❑ 379 Julio Ramirez RC	.40	.15
❑ 380 Seth Greisinger	.30	.10
❑ 381 Mike Judd RC	.40	.15
❑ 382 Ben Ford RC	.40	.15
❑ 383 Tom Bennett RC	.40	.15
❑ 384 Adam Butler RC	.40	.15
❑ 385 Wade Miller RC	1.00	.40
❑ 386 Kyle Peterson RC	.40	.15
❑ 387 Tommy Peterman RC	.40	.15
❑ 388 Onan Masaoka	.30	.10
❑ 389 Jason Rakers RC	.40	.15
❑ 390 Rafael Medina	.30	.10
❑ 391 Luis Lopez RC	.40	.15
❑ 392 Jeff Yoder	.30	.10
❑ 393 Vance Wilson RC	.40	.15
❑ 394 Fernando Seguignol RC	.40	.15
❑ 395 Ron Wright	.30	.10
❑ 396 Ruben Mateo RC	.40	.15
❑ 397 Steve Lomasney RC	.60	.25
❑ 398 Damian Jackson	.30	.10
❑ 399 Mike Jerzembeck RC	.40	.15
❑ 400 Luis Rivas RC	1.00	.40
❑ 401 Kevin Burford RC	.40	.15
❑ 402 Glenn Davis	.30	.10
❑ 403 Robert Luce RC	.40	.15
❑ 404 Cole Liniak	.30	.10
❑ 405 Matt LeCroy RC	.60	.25
❑ 406 Jeremy Giambi RC	.60	.25
❑ 407 Shawn Chacon	.30	.10
❑ 408 Dewayne Wise RC	.40	.15
❑ 409 Steve Woodard	.30	.10
❑ 410 Francisco Cordero RC	1.00	.40
❑ 411 Damon Minor RC	.40	.15
❑ 412 Lou Collier	.30	.10
❑ 413 Justin Towle	.30	.10
❑ 414 Juan LeBron	.30	.10
❑ 415 Michael Coleman	.30	.10
❑ 416 Felix Rodriguez	.30	.10
❑ 417 Paul Ah Yat RC	.40	.15
❑ 418 Kevin Barker RC	.40	.15
❑ 419 Brian Meadows	.30	.10
❑ 420 Darnell McDonald RC	.40	.15
❑ 421 Matt Kinney RC	.40	.15
❑ 422 Mike Vavrek RC	.40	.15
❑ 423 Courtney Duncan RC	.40	.15
❑ 424 Kevin Millar RC	1.50	.60
❑ 425 Ruben Rivera	.30	.10
❑ 426 Steve Shoemaker RC	.40	.15
❑ 427 Dan Reichert RC	.40	.15
❑ 428 Carlos Lee RC	3.00	1.25
❑ 429 Rod Barajas	1.00	.40
❑ 430 Pablo Ozuna RC	.60	.25
❑ 431 Todd Belitz RC	.40	.15
❑ 432 Sidney Ponson	.30	.10
❑ 433 Steve Carver RC	.40	.15
❑ 434 Esteban Yan RC	.60	.25
❑ 435 Cedrick Bowers	.30	.10
❑ 436 Marlon Anderson	.30	.10
❑ 437 Carl Pavano	.30	.10
❑ 438 Jae Weong Seo RC	.60	.25
❑ 439 Jose Taveras RC	.40	.15
❑ 440 Matt Anderson RC	.40	.15
❑ 441 Darron Ingram RC	.40	.15
❑ NNO S.Hasegawa '91 BBM	10.00	4.00
❑ NNO H.Irabu '91 BBM	10.00	4.00
❑ NNO H.Nomo '91 BBM	25.00	10.00

1999 Bowman

❑ COMPLETE SET (440)	80.00	30.00
❑ COMPLETE SERIES 1 (220)	30.00	12.50
❑ COMPLETE SERIES 2 (220)	50.00	20.00
❑ 1 Ben Grieve	.30	.10
❑ 2 Kerry Wood	.30	.10
❑ 3 Ruben Rivera	.30	.10
❑ 4 Sandy Alomar Jr.	.30	.10
❑ 5 Cal Ripken	2.50	1.00
❑ 6 Mark McGwire	2.00	.75
❑ 7 Vladimir Guerrero	.75	.30
❑ 8 Moises Alou	.30	.10
❑ 9 Jim Edmonds	.30	.10
❑ 10 Greg Maddux	1.25	.50
❑ 11 Gary Sheffield	.30	.10
❑ 12 John Valentin	.30	.10
❑ 13 Chuck Knoblauch	.30	.10
❑ 14 Tony Clark	.30	.10
❑ 15 Rusty Greer	.30	.10
❑ 16 Al Leiter	.30	.10
❑ 17 Travis Lee	.30	.10
❑ 18 Jose Cruz Jr.	.30	.10
❑ 19 Pedro Martinez	.50	.10
❑ 20 Paul O'Neill	.50	.10
❑ 21 Todd Walker	.30	.10
❑ 22 Vinny Castilla	.30	.10
❑ 23 Barry Larkin	.50	.10
❑ 24 Curt Schilling	.30	.10
❑ 25 Jason Kendall	.30	.10
❑ 26 Scott Erickson	.30	.10
❑ 27 Andres Galarraga	.30	.10
❑ 28 Jeff Shaw	.30	.10
❑ 29 John Olerud	.30	.10
❑ 30 Orlando Hernandez	.30	.10
❑ 31 Larry Walker	.30	.10
❑ 32 Andruw Jones	.50	.10
❑ 33 Jeff Cirillo	.30	.10
❑ 34 Barry Bonds	2.00	.75
❑ 35 Manny Ramirez	.50	.10
❑ 36 Mark Kotsay	.30	.10
❑ 37 Ivan Rodriguez	.50	.10
❑ 38 Jeff King	.30	.10
❑ 39 Brian Hunter	.30	.10
❑ 40 Ray Durham	.30	.10
❑ 41 Bernie Williams	.50	.10
❑ 42 Darin Erstad	.30	.10
❑ 43 Chipper Jones	.75	.30
❑ 44 Pat Hentgen	.30	.10
❑ 45 Eric Young	.30	.10
❑ 46 Jaret Wright	.30	.10
❑ 47 Juan Guzman	.30	.10
❑ 48 Jorge Posada	.50	.10
❑ 49 Bobby Higginson	.30	.10
❑ 50 Jose Guillen	.30	.10
❑ 51 Trevor Hoffman	.30	.10
❑ 52 Ken Griffey Jr.	1.25	.50
❑ 53 David Justice	.30	.10
❑ 54 Matt Williams	.30	.10
❑ 55 Eric Karros	.30	.10

❑ 56 Derek Bell	.30	.10
❑ 57 Ray Lankford	.30	.10
❑ 58 Mariano Rivera	.75	.30
❑ 59 Brett Tomko	.30	.10
❑ 60 Mike Mussina	.50	.10
❑ 61 Kenny Lofton	.30	.10
❑ 62 Chuck Finley	.30	.10
❑ 63 Alex Gonzalez	.30	.10
❑ 64 Mark Grace	.50	.10
❑ 65 Raul Mondesi	.30	.10
❑ 66 David Cone	.30	.10
❑ 67 Brad Fullmer	.30	.10
❑ 68 Andy Benes	.30	.10
❑ 69 John Smoltz	.50	.10
❑ 70 Shane Reynolds	.30	.10
❑ 71 Bruce Chen	.30	.10
❑ 72 Adam Kennedy	.30	.10
❑ 73 Jack Cust	.30	.10
❑ 74 Matt Clement	.30	.10
❑ 75 Derrick Gibson	.30	.10
❑ 76 Darnell McDonald	.30	.10
❑ 77 Adam Everett RC	1.00	.40
❑ 78 Ricardo Aramboles	.30	.10
❑ 79 Mark Quinn RC	.40	.15
❑ 80 Jason Rakers	.30	.10
❑ 81 Seth Etherton RC	.40	.15
❑ 82 Jeff Urban RC	.60	.25
❑ 83 Manny Aybar	.30	.10
❑ 84 Mike Nannini RC	.40	.15
❑ 85 Onan Masaoka	.30	.10
❑ 86 Rod Barajas	.30	.10
❑ 87 Mike Frank	.30	.10
❑ 88 Scott Randall	.30	.10
❑ 89 Justin Bowles RC	.40	.15
❑ 90 Chris Haas	.30	.10
❑ 91 Arturo McDowell RC	.40	.15
❑ 92 Matt Belisle RC	.40	.15
❑ 93 Scott Elarton	.30	.10
❑ 94 Vernon Wells	.30	.10
❑ 95 Pat Cline	.30	.10
❑ 96 Ryan Anderson	.30	.10
❑ 97 Kevin Barker	.30	.10
❑ 98 Ruben Mateo	.30	.10
❑ 99 Robert Fick	.30	.10
❑ 100 Corey Koskie	.30	.10
❑ 101 Ricky Ledee	.30	.10
❑ 102 Rick Elder RC	.40	.15
❑ 103 Jack Cressend RC	.40	.15
❑ 104 Joe Lawrence	.30	.10
❑ 105 Mike Lincoln	.30	.10
❑ 106 Kit Pellow RC	.40	.15
❑ 107 Matt Burch RC	.60	.25
❑ 108 Cole Liniak	.30	.10
❑ 109 Jason Dewey	.30	.10
❑ 110 Cesar King	.30	.10
❑ 111 Julio Ramirez	.30	.10
❑ 112 Jake Westbrook	.30	.10
❑ 113 Eric Valent RC	.60	.25
❑ 114 Roosevelt Brown RC	.40	.15
❑ 115 Choo Freeman RC	.60	.25
❑ 116 Juan Melo	.30	.10
❑ 117 Jason Grilli	.30	.10
❑ 118 Jared Sandberg	.30	.10
❑ 119 Glenn Davis	.30	.10
❑ 120 David Riske RC	.40	.15
❑ 121 Jacque Jones	.30	.10
❑ 122 Corey Lee	.30	.10
❑ 123 Michael Barrett	.30	.10
❑ 124 Lariel Gonzalez	.30	.10
❑ 125 Mitch Meluskey	.30	.10
❑ 126 F.Adrian Garcia	.30	.10
❑ 127 Tony Torcato RC	.40	.15
❑ 128 Jeff Liefer	.30	.10
❑ 129 Ntema Ndungidi	.30	.10
❑ 130 Andy Brown RC	.40	.15
❑ 131 Ryan Mills RC	.40	.15
❑ 132 Andy Abad RC	.40	.15
❑ 133 Carlos Febles	.30	.10
❑ 134 Jason Tyner RC	.40	.15
❑ 135 Mark Osborne	.30	.10
❑ 136 Phil Norton RC	.40	.15
❑ 137 Nathan Haynes	.30	.10
❑ 138 Roy Halladay	.30	.10
❑ 139 Juan Encarnacion	.30	.10
❑ 140 Brad Penny	.30	.10
❑ 141 Grant Roberts	.30	.10
❑ 142 Aramis Ramirez	.30	.10
❑ 143 Cristian Guzman	.30	.10
❑ 144 Mamon Tucker RC	.40	.15
❑ 145 Ryan Bradley	.30	.10
❑ 146 Brian Simmons	.30	.10
❑ 147 Dan Reichert	.30	.10
❑ 148 Russ Branyan	.30	.10
❑ 149 Victor Valencia RC	.50	.20
❑ 150 Scott Schoeneweis	.30	.10
❑ 151 Sean Spencer RC	.40	.15
❑ 152 Odalis Perez	.30	.10
❑ 153 Joe Fontenot	.30	.10
❑ 154 Milton Bradley	.30	.10
❑ 155 Josh McKinley RC	.40	.15
❑ 156 Terrence Long	.30	.10
❑ 157 Danny Klassen	.30	.10
❑ 158 Paul Hoover RC	.60	.25
❑ 159 Ron Belliard	.30	.10
❑ 160 Armando Rios	.30	.10
❑ 161 Ramon Hernandez	.30	.10
❑ 162 Jason Conti	.30	.10
❑ 163 Chad Hermansen	.30	.10
❑ 164 Jason Standridge	.30	.10
❑ 165 Jason Dellaero	.30	.10
❑ 166 John Curtice	.30	.10
❑ 167 Clayton Andrews RC	.40	.15
❑ 168 Jeremy Giambi	.30	.10
❑ 169 Alex Ramirez	.30	.10
❑ 170 Gabe Molina RC	.40	.15
❑ 171 Mario Encarnacion RC	.40	.15
❑ 172 Mike Zywica RC	.40	.15
❑ 173 Chip Ambres RC	.40	.15
❑ 174 Trot Nixon	.30	.10
❑ 175 Pat Burrell RC	3.00	1.25
❑ 176 Jeff Yoder	.30	.10
❑ 177 Chris Jones RC	.40	.15
❑ 178 Kevin Witt	.30	.10
❑ 179 Keith Luuloa RC	.40	.15
❑ 180 Billy Koch	.30	.10
❑ 181 Damaso Marte RC	.40	.15
❑ 182 Ryan Glynn RC	.40	.15
❑ 183 Calvin Pickering	.30	.10
❑ 184 Michael Cuddyer	.30	.10
❑ 185 Nick Johnson RC	2.00	.75
❑ 186 Doug Mientkiewicz RC	1.00	.40
❑ 187 Nate Cornejo RC	.40	.15
❑ 188 Octavio Dotel	.30	.10
❑ 189 Wes Helms	.30	.10
❑ 190 Nelson Lara	.30	.10
❑ 191 Chuck Abbott RC	.40	.15
❑ 192 Tony Armas Jr.	.30	.10
❑ 193 Gil Meche	.30	.10
❑ 194 Ben Petrick	.30	.10
❑ 195 Chris George RC	.40	.15
❑ 196 Scott Hunter RC	.40	.15
❑ 197 Ryan Brannan	.30	.10
❑ 198 Amaury Garcia RC	.60	.25
❑ 199 Chris Gissell	.30	.10
❑ 200 Austin Kearns RC	3.00	1.25
❑ 201 Alex Gonzalez	.30	.10
❑ 202 Wade Miller	.30	.10
❑ 203 Scott Williamson	.30	.10
❑ 204 Chris Enochs	.30	.10
❑ 205 Fernando Seguignol	.30	.10
❑ 206 Marlon Anderson	.30	.10
❑ 207 Todd Sears RC	.40	.15
❑ 208 Nate Bump RC	.40	.15
❑ 209 J.M. Gold RC	.40	.15
❑ 210 Matt LeCroy	.30	.10
❑ 211 Alex Hernandez	.30	.10
❑ 212 Luis Rivera	.30	.10
❑ 213 Troy Cameron	.30	.10
❑ 214 Alex Escobar RC	.60	.25
❑ 215 Jason LaRue	.30	.10
❑ 216 Kyle Peterson	.30	.10
❑ 217 Brent Butler	.30	.10
❑ 218 Dernell Stenson	.30	.10
❑ 219 Adrian Beltre	.30	.10
❑ 220 Daryle Ward	.30	.10
❑ 221 Jim Thome	.50	.10
❑ 222 Cliff Floyd	.30	.10
❑ 223 Rickey Henderson	.75	.30
❑ 224 Garret Anderson	.30	.10
❑ 225 Ken Caminiti	.30	.10
❑ 226 Bret Boone	.30	.10
❑ 227 Jeromy Burnitz	.30	.10
❑ 228 Steve Finley	.30	.10
❑ 229 Miguel Tejada	.30	.10
❑ 230 Greg Vaughn	.30	.10
❑ 231 Jose Offerman	.30	.10
❑ 232 Andy Ashby	.30	.10
❑ 233 Albert Belle	.30	.10
❑ 234 Fernando Tatis	.30	.10
❑ 235 Todd Helton	.50	.10
❑ 236 Sean Casey	.30	.10
❑ 237 Brian Giles	.30	.10
❑ 238 Andy Pettitte	.50	.10
❑ 239 Fred McGriff	.50	.10
❑ 240 Roberto Alomar	.50	.10
❑ 241 Edgar Martinez	.50	.10
❑ 242 Lee Stevens	.30	.10
❑ 243 Shawn Green	.30	.10
❑ 244 Ryan Klesko	.30	.10
❑ 245 Sammy Sosa	.75	.30
❑ 246 Todd Hundley	.30	.10
❑ 247 Shannon Stewart	.30	.10
❑ 248 Randy Johnson	.75	.30
❑ 249 Rondell White	.30	.10
❑ 250 Mike Piazza	1.25	.50
❑ 251 Craig Biggio	.50	.10
❑ 252 David Wells	.30	.10
❑ 253 Brian Jordan	.30	.10
❑ 254 Edgar Renteria	.30	.10
❑ 255 Bartolo Colon	.30	.10
❑ 256 Frank Thomas	.75	.30
❑ 257 Will Clark	.50	.10
❑ 258 Dean Palmer	.30	.10
❑ 259 Dmitri Young	.30	.10
❑ 260 Scott Rolen	.50	.10
❑ 261 Jeff Kent	.30	.10
❑ 262 Dante Bichette	.30	.10
❑ 263 Nomar Garciaparra	1.25	.50
❑ 264 Tony Gwynn	1.00	.40
❑ 265 Alex Rodriguez	1.25	.50
❑ 266 Jose Canseco	.50	.10
❑ 267 Jason Giambi	.30	.10
❑ 268 Jeff Bagwell	.50	.10
❑ 269 Carlos Delgado	.30	.10
❑ 270 Tom Glavine	.50	.10
❑ 271 Eric Davis	.30	.10
❑ 272 Edgardo Alfonzo	.30	.10
❑ 273 Tim Salmon	.50	.10
❑ 274 Johnny Damon	.50	.10
❑ 275 Rafael Palmeiro	.50	.10
❑ 276 Denny Neagle	.30	.10
❑ 277 Neifi Perez	.30	.10
❑ 278 Roger Clemens	1.50	.60
❑ 279 Brant Brown	.30	.10
❑ 280 Kevin Brown	.50	.10
❑ 281 Jay Bell	.30	.10
❑ 282 Jay Buhner	.30	.10
❑ 283 Matt Lawton	.30	.10
❑ 284 Robin Ventura	.30	.10
❑ 285 Juan Gonzalez	.30	.10
❑ 286 Mo Vaughn	.30	.10
❑ 287 Kevin Millwood	.30	.10
❑ 288 Tino Martinez	.50	.10
❑ 289 Justin Thompson	.30	.10
❑ 290 Derek Jeter	2.00	.75
❑ 291 Ben Davis	.30	.10
❑ 292 Mike Lowell	.30	.10
❑ 293 Calvin Murray	.30	.10
❑ 294 Micah Bowie RC	.40	.15
❑ 295 Lance Berkman	.30	.10
❑ 296 Jason Marquis	.30	.10
❑ 297 Chad Green	.30	.10
❑ 298 Dee Brown	.30	.10
❑ 299 Jerry Hairston Jr.	.30	.10
❑ 300 Gabe Kapler	.30	.10
❑ 301 Brent Stentz RC	.60	.25
❑ 302 Scott Mullen RC	.40	.15
❑ 303 Brandon Reed	.30	.10
❑ 304 Shea Hillenbrand RC	1.50	.60
❑ 305 J.D. Closser RC	.60	.25
❑ 306 Gary Matthews Jr.	.30	.10
❑ 307 Toby Hall RC	.60	.25
❑ 308 Jason Phillips RC	.40	.15
❑ 309 Jose Macias RC	.40	.15
❑ 310 Jung Bong RC	.40	.15
❑ 311 Ramon Soler RC	.40	.15
❑ 312 Kelly Dransfeldt RC	.40	.15
❑ 313 Carlos E. Hernandez RC	.60	.25

❑ 314 Kevin Haverbusch .30 .10
❑ 315 Aaron Myette RC .40 .15
❑ 316 Chad Harville RC .40 .15
❑ 317 Kyle Farnsworth RC .60 .25
❑ 318 Gookie Dawkins RC .60 .25
❑ 319 Willie Martinez .30 .10
❑ 320 Carlos Lee .30 .10
❑ 321 Carlos Pena RC .75 .30
❑ 322 Peter Bergeron RC .40 .15
❑ 323 A.J. Burnett RC 1.50 .60
❑ 324 Bucky Jacobsen RC .60 .25
❑ 325 Mo Bruce RC .40 .15
❑ 326 Reggie Taylor .30 .10
❑ 327 Jackie Rexrode .30 .10
❑ 328 Alvin Morrow RC .40 .15
❑ 329 Carlos Beltran .50 .10
❑ 330 Eric Chavez .30 .10
❑ 331 John Patterson .30 .10
❑ 332 Jayson Werth .30 .10
❑ 333 Richie Sexson .30 .10
❑ 334 Randy Wolf .30 .10
❑ 335 Eli Marrero .30 .10
❑ 336 Paul LoDuca .30 .10
❑ 337 J.D Smart .30 .10
❑ 338 Ryan Minor .30 .10
❑ 339 Kris Benson .30 .10
❑ 340 George Lombard .30 .10
❑ 341 Troy Glaus .50 .10
❑ 342 Eddie Yarnall .30 .10
❑ 343 Kip Wells RC .60 .25
❑ 344 C.C. Sabathia RC 2.50 1.00
❑ 345 Sean Burroughs RC 1.00 .40
❑ 346 Felipe Lopez RC 2.50 1.00
❑ 347 Ryan Rupe RC .40 .15
❑ 348 Orber Moreno RC .40 .15
❑ 349 Rafael Roque RC .40 .15
❑ 350 Alfonso Soriano RC 8.00 3.00
❑ 351 Pablo Ozuna .30 .10
❑ 352 Corey Patterson RC 1.50 .60
❑ 353 Braden Looper .30 .10
❑ 354 Robbie Bell .30 .10
❑ 355 Mark Mulder RC 2.50 1.00
❑ 356 Angel Pena .30 .10
❑ 357 Kevin McGlinchy .30 .10
❑ 358 Michael Restovich RC .60 .25
❑ 359 Eric DuBose .30 .10
❑ 360 Geoff Jenkins .30 .10
❑ 361 Mark Harriger RC .40 .15
❑ 362 Junior Herndon RC .40 .15
❑ 363 Tim Raines Jr. RC .40 .15
❑ 364 Rafael Furcal RC 2.00 .75
❑ 365 Marcus Giles RC 1.50 .60
❑ 366 Ted Lilly .30 .10
❑ 367 Jorge Toca RC .60 .25
❑ 368 David Kelton RC .40 .15
❑ 369 Adam Dunn RC 5.00 2.00
❑ 370 Guillermo Mota RC .40 .15
❑ 371 Brett Laxton RC .40 .15
❑ 372 Travis Harper RC .60 .25
❑ 373 Tom Davey RC .40 .15
❑ 374 Darren Blakely RC .40 .15
❑ 375 Tim Hudson RC 4.00 1.50
❑ 376 Jason Romano .30 .10
❑ 377 Dan Reichert .30 .10
❑ 378 Julio Lugo RC 1.00 .40
❑ 379 Jose Garcia RC .40 .15
❑ 380 Erubiel Durazo RC .60 .25
❑ 381 Jose Jimenez .30 .10
❑ 382 Chris Fussell .30 .10
❑ 383 Steve Lomasney .30 .10
❑ 384 Juan Pena RC .60 .25
❑ 385 Allen Levrault RC .40 .15
❑ 386 Juan Rivera RC 1.50 .60
❑ 387 Steve Colyer RC .40 .15
❑ 388 Joe Nathan RC 2.00 .75
❑ 389 Ron Walker RC .40 .15
❑ 390 Nick Bierbrodt .30 .10
❑ 391 Luke Prokopec RC .40 .15
❑ 392 Dave Roberts RC 1.00 .40
❑ 393 Mike Darr .30 .10
❑ 394 Abraham Nunez RC .60 .25
❑ 395 Giuseppe Chiaramonte RC .40 .15
❑ 396 Jermaine Van Buren RC .40 .15
❑ 397 Mike Kusiewicz .30 .10
❑ 398 Matt Wise RC .40 .15
❑ 399 Joe McEwing RC .60 .25
❑ 400 Matt Holliday RC 6.00 2.50
❑ 401 Willi Mo Pena RC 5.00 2.00
❑ 402 Ruben Quevedo RC .40 .15
❑ 403 Rob Ryan RC .40 .15
❑ 404 Freddy Garcia RC 1.50 .60
❑ 405 Kevin Eberwein RC .40 .15
❑ 406 Jesus Colome RC .40 .15
❑ 407 Chris Singleton .30 .10
❑ 408 Bubba Crosby RC 1.00 .40
❑ 409 Jesus Cordero RC .40 .15
❑ 410 Donny Leon .30 .10
❑ 411 Goefrey Tomlinson RC .60 .25
❑ 412 Jeff Winchester RC .40 .15
❑ 413 Adam Piatt RC .40 .15
❑ 414 Robert Stratton .30 .10
❑ 415 T.J. Tucker .30 .10
❑ 416 Ryan Langerhans RC 1.00 .40
❑ 417 Anthony Shumaker RC .40 .15
❑ 418 Matt Miller RC .40 .15
❑ 419 Doug Clark RC .40 .15
❑ 420 Kory DeHaan RC .40 .15
❑ 421 David Eckstein RC 3.00 1.25
❑ 422 Brian Cooper RC .40 .15
❑ 423 Brady Clark RC 1.50 .60
❑ 424 Chris Magruder RC .60 .25
❑ 425 Bobby Seay RC .40 .15
❑ 426 Aubrey Huff RC 2.00 .75
❑ 427 Mike Jerzembeck .30 .10
❑ 428 Matt Blank RC .60 .25
❑ 429 Benny Agbayani RC .60 .25
❑ 430 Kevin Beirne RC .40 .15
❑ 431 Josh Hamilton RC 5.00 2.00
❑ 432 Josh Girdley RC .40 .15
❑ 433 Kyle Snyder RC .40 .15
❑ 434 Mike Paradis RC .40 .15
❑ 435 Jason Jennings RC 1.00 .40
❑ 436 David Walling RC .40 .15
❑ 437 Omar Ortiz RC .60 .25
❑ 438 Jay Gehrke RC .60 .25
❑ 439 Casey Burns RC .60 .25
❑ 440 Carl Crawford RC 6.00 2.50

2000 Bowman

❑ COMPLETE SET (440) 60.00 25.00
❑ 1 Vladimir Guerrero .75 .30
❑ 2 Chipper Jones .75 .30
❑ 3 Todd Walker .30 .10
❑ 4 Barry Larkin .50 .20
❑ 5 Bernie Williams .50 .20
❑ 6 Todd Helton .50 .20
❑ 7 Jermaine Dye .30 .10
❑ 8 Brian Giles .30 .10
❑ 9 Freddy Garcia .30 .10
❑ 10 Greg Vaughn .30 .10
❑ 11 Alex Gonzalez .30 .10
❑ 12 Luis Gonzalez .30 .10
❑ 13 Ron Belliard .30 .10
❑ 14 Ben Grieve .30 .10
❑ 15 Carlos Delgado .30 .10
❑ 16 Brian Jordan .30 .10
❑ 17 Fernando Tatis .30 .10
❑ 18 Ryan Rupe .30 .10
❑ 19 Miguel Tejada .30 .10
❑ 20 Mark Grace .50 .20
❑ 21 Kenny Lofton .30 .10
❑ 22 Eric Karros .30 .10
❑ 23 Cliff Floyd .30 .10
❑ 24 John Halama .30 .10
❑ 25 Cristian Guzman .30 .10
❑ 26 Scott Williamson .30 .10
❑ 27 Mike Lieberthal .30 .10
❑ 28 Tim Hudson .30 .10
❑ 29 Warren Morris .30 .10
❑ 30 Pedro Martinez .50 .20
❑ 31 John Smoltz .50 .20
❑ 32 Ray Durham .30 .10
❑ 33 Chad Allen .30 .10
❑ 34 Tony Clark .30 .10
❑ 35 Tino Martinez .50 .20
❑ 36 J.T. Snow .30 .10
❑ 37 Kevin Brown .30 .10
❑ 38 Bartolo Colon .30 .10
❑ 39 Rey Ordonez .30 .10
❑ 40 Jeff Bagwell .50 .20
❑ 41 Ivan Rodriguez .50 .20
❑ 42 Eric Chavez .30 .10
❑ 43 Eric Milton .30 .10
❑ 44 Jose Canseco .50 .20
❑ 45 Shawn Green .30 .10
❑ 46 Rich Aurilia .30 .10
❑ 47 Roberto Alomar .50 .20
❑ 48 Brian Daubach .30 .10
❑ 49 Maggio Ordonez .30 .10
❑ 50 Derek Jeter 2.00 .75
❑ 51 Kris Benson .30 .10
❑ 52 Albert Belle .30 .10
❑ 53 Rondell White .30 .10
❑ 54 Justin Thompson .30 .10
❑ 55 Nomar Garciaparra 1.25 .50
❑ 56 Chuck Finley .30 .10
❑ 57 Omar Vizquel .50 .20
❑ 58 Luis Castillo .30 .10
❑ 59 Richard Hidalgo .30 .10
❑ 60 Barry Bonds 2.00 .75
❑ 61 Craig Biggio .50 .20
❑ 62 Doug Glanville .30 .10
❑ 63 Gabe Kapler .30 .10
❑ 64 Johnny Damon .50 .20
❑ 65 Pokey Reese .30 .10
❑ 66 Andy Pettitte .50 .20
❑ 67 B.J. Surhoff .30 .10
❑ 68 Richie Sexson .30 .10
❑ 69 Javy Lopez .30 .10
❑ 70 Raul Mondesi .30 .10
❑ 71 Darin Erstad .30 .10
❑ 72 Kevin Millwood .30 .10
❑ 73 Ricky Ledee .30 .10
❑ 74 John Olerud .30 .10
❑ 75 Sean Casey .30 .10
❑ 76 Carlos Febles .30 .10
❑ 77 Paul O'Neill .50 .20
❑ 78 Bob Abreu .30 .10
❑ 79 Neifi Perez .30 .10
❑ 80 Tony Gwynn 1.00 .40
❑ 81 Russ Ortiz .30 .10
❑ 82 Matt Williams .30 .10
❑ 83 Chris Carpenter .30 .10
❑ 84 Roger Cedeno .30 .10
❑ 85 Tim Salmon .50 .20
❑ 86 Billy Koch .30 .10
❑ 87 Jeromy Burnitz .30 .10
❑ 88 Edgardo Alfonzo .30 .10
❑ 89 Jay Bell .30 .10
❑ 90 Manny Ramirez .50 .20
❑ 91 Frank Thomas .75 .30
❑ 92 Mike Mussina .50 .20
❑ 93 J.D. Drew .30 .10
❑ 94 Adrian Beltre .30 .10
❑ 95 Alex Rodriguez 1.25 .50
❑ 96 Larry Walker .30 .10
❑ 97 Juan Encarnacion .30 .10
❑ 98 Mike Sweeney .30 .10
❑ 99 Rusty Greer .30 .10
❑ 100 Randy Johnson .75 .30
❑ 101 Jose Vidro .30 .10
❑ 102 Preston Wilson .30 .10
❑ 103 Greg Maddux 1.25 .50
❑ 104 Jason Giambi .30 .10
❑ 105 Cal Ripken 2.50 1.00
❑ 106 Carlos Beltran .30 .10
❑ 107 Vinny Castilla .30 .10
❑ 108 Mariano Rivera .75 .30
❑ 109 Mo Vaughn .30 .10
❑ 110 Rafael Palmeiro .50 .20

❑ 111 Shannon Stewart .30 .10
❑ 112 Mike Hampton .30 .10
❑ 113 Joe Nathan .30 .10
❑ 114 Ben Davis .30 .10
❑ 115 Andruw Jones .50 .20
❑ 116 Robin Ventura .30 .10
❑ 117 Damion Easley .30 .10
❑ 118 Jeff Cirillo .30 .10
❑ 119 Kerry Wood .30 .10
❑ 120 Scott Rolen .50 .20
❑ 121 Sammy Sosa .75 .30
❑ 122 Ken Griffey Jr. 1.25 .50
❑ 123 Shane Reynolds .30 .10
❑ 124 Troy Glaus .30 .10
❑ 125 Tom Glavine .50 .20
❑ 126 Michael Barrett .30 .10
❑ 127 Al Leiter .30 .10
❑ 128 Jason Kendall .30 .10
❑ 129 Roger Clemens 1.50 .60
❑ 130 Juan Gonzalez .30 .10
❑ 131 Corey Koskie .30 .10
❑ 132 Curt Schilling .30 .10
❑ 133 Mike Piazza 1.25 .50
❑ 134 Gary Sheffield .30 .10
❑ 135 Jim Thome .50 .20
❑ 136 Orlando Hernandez .30 .10
❑ 137 Ray Lankford .30 .10
❑ 138 Geoff Jenkins .30 .10
❑ 139 Jose Lima .30 .10
❑ 140 Mark McGwire 2.00 .75
❑ 141 Adam Piatt .30 .10
❑ 142 Pat Manning RC .30 .10
❑ 143 Marcos Castillo RC .30 .10
❑ 144 Lesli Brea RC .30 .10
❑ 145 Humberto Cota RC .50 .20
❑ 146 Ben Petrick .30 .10
❑ 147 Kip Wells .30 .10
❑ 148 Wily Pena .30 .10
❑ 149 Chris Wakeland RC .30 .10
❑ 150 Brad Baker RC .30 .10
❑ 151 Robbie Morrison RC .30 .10
❑ 152 Reggie Taylor .30 .10
❑ 153 Matt Ginter RC .30 .10
❑ 154 Peter Bergeron .30 .10
❑ 155 Roosevelt Brown .30 .10
❑ 156 Matt Cepicky RC .30 .10
❑ 157 Ramon Castro .30 .10
❑ 158 Brad Baisley RC .30 .10
❑ 159 Jeff Goldbach RC .30 .10
❑ 160 Mitch Meluskey .30 .10
❑ 161 Chad Harville .30 .10
❑ 162 Brian Cooper .30 .10
❑ 163 Marcus Giles .30 .10
❑ 164 Jim Morris .75 .30
❑ 165 Geoff Goetz .30 .10
❑ 166 Bobby Bradley RC .30 .10
❑ 167 Rob Bell .30 .10
❑ 168 Joe Crede 1.50 .60
❑ 169 Michael Restovich .30 .10
❑ 170 Quincy Foster RC .30 .10
❑ 171 Enrique Cruz RC .30 .10
❑ 172 Mark Quinn .30 .10
❑ 173 Nick Johnson .30 .10
❑ 174 Jeff Liefer .30 .10
❑ 175 Kevin Mench RC 2.00 .75
❑ 176 Steve Lomasney .30 .10
❑ 177 Jayson Werth .30 .10
❑ 178 Tim Drew .30 .10
❑ 179 Chip Ambres .30 .10
❑ 180 Ryan Anderson .30 .10
❑ 181 Matt Blank .30 .10
❑ 182 Giuseppe Chiaramonte .30 .10
❑ 183 Corey Myers RC .30 .10
❑ 184 Jeff Yoder .30 .10
❑ 185 Craig Dingman RC .30 .10
❑ 186 Jon Hamilton RC .30 .10
❑ 187 Toby Hall .30 .10
❑ 188 Russell Branyan .30 .10
❑ 189 Brian Falkenborg RC .30 .10
❑ 190 Aaron Harang RC 2.50 1.00
❑ 191 Juan Pena .30 .10
❑ 192 Travis Thompson RC .30 .10
❑ 193 Alfonso Soriano .75 .30
❑ 194 Alejandro Diaz RC .30 .10
❑ 195 Carlos Pena .30 .10
❑ 196 Kevin Nicholson .30 .10
❑ 197 Mo Bruce .30 .10
❑ 198 C.C. Sabathia .30 .10
❑ 199 Carl Crawford .30 .10
❑ 200 Rafael Furcal .30 .10
❑ 201 Andrew Beinbrink RC .30 .10
❑ 202 Jimmy Osting .30 .10
❑ 203 Aaron McNeal RC .30 .10
❑ 204 Brett Laxton .30 .10
❑ 205 Chris George .30 .10
❑ 206 Felipe Lopez .30 .10
❑ 207 Ben Sheets RC 2.50 1.00
❑ 208 Mike Meyers RC .50 .20
❑ 209 Jason Conti .30 .10
❑ 210 Milton Bradley .30 .10
❑ 211 Chris Mears RC .30 .10
❑ 212 Carlos Hernandez RC .75 .30
❑ 213 Jason Romano .30 .10
❑ 214 Geofrey Tomlinson .30 .10
❑ 215 Jimmy Rollins .30 .10
❑ 216 Pablo Ozuna .30 .10
❑ 217 Steve Cox .30 .10
❑ 218 Terrence Long .30 .10
❑ 219 Jeff DaVanon RC .50 .20
❑ 220 Rick Ankiel .30 .10
❑ 221 Jason Standridge .30 .10
❑ 222 Tony Armas Jr. .30 .10
❑ 223 Jason Tyner .30 .10
❑ 224 Ramon Ortiz .30 .10
❑ 225 Daryle Ward .30 .10
❑ 226 Enger Veras RC .30 .10
❑ 227 Chris Jones .30 .10
❑ 228 Eric Cammack RC .30 .10
❑ 229 Ruben Mateo .30 .10
❑ 230 Ken Harvey RC .50 .20
❑ 231 Jake Westbrook .30 .10
❑ 232 Rob Purvis RC .30 .10
❑ 233 Choo Freeman .30 .10
❑ 234 Aramis Ramirez .30 .10
❑ 235 A.J. Burnett .30 .10
❑ 236 Kevin Barker .30 .10
❑ 237 Chance Caple RC .30 .10
❑ 238 Jarrod Washburn .30 .10
❑ 239 Lance Berkman .30 .10
❑ 240 Michael Wenner RC .30 .10
❑ 241 Alex Sanchez .30 .10
❑ 242 Pat Daneker .30 .10
❑ 243 Grant Roberts .30 .10
❑ 244 Mark Ellis RC .50 .20
❑ 245 Donny Leon .30 .10
❑ 246 David Eckstein .30 .10
❑ 247 Dicky Gonzalez RC .30 .10
❑ 248 John Patterson .30 .10
❑ 249 Chad Green .30 .10
❑ 250 Scot Shields RC .30 .10
❑ 251 Troy Cameron .30 .10
❑ 252 Jose Molina .30 .10
❑ 253 Rob Pugmire RC .30 .10
❑ 254 Rick Elder .30 .10
❑ 255 Sean Burroughs .30 .10
❑ 256 Josh Kalinowski RC .30 .10
❑ 257 Matt LeCroy .30 .10
❑ 258 Alex Graman RC .30 .10
❑ 259 Tomo Ohka RC .50 .20
❑ 260 Brady Clark .30 .10
❑ 261 Rico Washington RC .30 .10
❑ 262 Gary Matthews Jr. .30 .10
❑ 263 Matt Wise .30 .10
❑ 264 Keith Reed RC .30 .10
❑ 265 Santiago Ramirez RC .30 .10
❑ 266 Ben Broussard RC 1.25 .50
❑ 267 Ryan Langerhans .30 .10
❑ 268 Juan Rivera .30 .10
❑ 269 Shawn Gallagher .30 .10
❑ 270 Jorge Toca .30 .10
❑ 271 Brad Lidge .50 .20
❑ 272 Leoncio Estrella RC .30 .10
❑ 273 Ruben Quevedo .30 .10
❑ 274 Jack Cust .30 .10
❑ 275 T.J. Tucker .30 .10
❑ 276 Mike Colangelo .30 .10
❑ 277 Brian Schneider .30 .10
❑ 278 Calvin Murray .30 .10
❑ 279 Josh Girdley .30 .10
❑ 280 Mike Paradis .30 .10
❑ 281 Chad Hermansen .30 .10
❑ 282 Ty Howington RC .30 .10
❑ 283 Aaron Myette .30 .10
❑ 284 D'Angelo Jimenez .30 .10
❑ 285 Dernell Stenson .30 .10
❑ 286 Jerry Hairston Jr. .30 .10
❑ 287 Gary Majewski RC .50 .20
❑ 288 Derrin Ebert .30 .10
❑ 289 Steve Fish RC .30 .10
❑ 290 Carlos E. Hernandez .30 .10
❑ 291 Allen Levrault .30 .10
❑ 292 Sean McNally RC .30 .10
❑ 293 Randey Dorame RC .30 .10
❑ 294 Wes Anderson RC .30 .10
❑ 295 B.J. Ryan .30 .10
❑ 296 Alan Webb RC .30 .10
❑ 297 Brandon Inge RC 2.00 .75
❑ 298 David Walling .30 .10
❑ 299 Sun Woo Kim RC .30 .10
❑ 300 Pat Burrell .30 .10
❑ 301 Rick Guttormson RC .30 .10
❑ 302 Gil Meche .30 .10
❑ 303 Carlos Zambrano RC 5.00 2.00
❑ 304 Eric Byrnes UER RC .50 .20
❑ 305 Robb Quinlan RC .50 .20
❑ 306 Jackie Rexrode .30 .10
❑ 307 Nate Bump .30 .10
❑ 308 Sean DePaula RC .30 .10
❑ 309 Matt Riley .30 .10
❑ 310 Ryan Minor .30 .10
❑ 311 J.J. Davis .30 .10
❑ 312 Randy Wolf .30 .10
❑ 313 Jason Jennings .30 .10
❑ 314 Scott Seabol RC .30 .10
❑ 315 Doug Davis .30 .10
❑ 316 Todd Moser RC .30 .10
❑ 317 Rob Ryan .30 .10
❑ 318 Bubba Crosby .30 .10
❑ 319 Lyle Overbay RC 1.25 .50
❑ 320 Mario Encarnacion .30 .10
❑ 321 Francisco Rodriguez RC 2.50 1.00
❑ 322 Michael Cuddyer .30 .10
❑ 323 Ed Yarnall .30 .10
❑ 324 Cesar Saba RC .30 .10
❑ 325 Gookie Dawkins .30 .10
❑ 326 Alex Escobar .30 .10
❑ 327 Julio Zuleta RC .30 .10
❑ 328 Josh Hamilton .50 .20
❑ 329 Nick Neugebauer RC .30 .10
❑ 330 Matt Belisle .30 .10
❑ 331 Kurt Ainsworth RC .30 .10
❑ 332 Tim Raines Jr. .30 .10
❑ 333 Eric Munson .30 .10
❑ 334 Donzell McDonald .30 .10
❑ 335 Larry Bigbie RC .75 .30
❑ 336 Matt Watson RC .30 .10
❑ 337 Aubrey Huff .30 .10
❑ 338 Julio Ramirez .30 .10
❑ 339 Jason Grabowski RC .30 .10
❑ 340 Jon Garland .30 .10
❑ 341 Austin Kearns .30 .10
❑ 342 Josh Pressley RC .30 .10
❑ 343 Miguel Olivo RC .75 .30
❑ 344 Julio Lugo .30 .10
❑ 345 Roberto Vaz .30 .10
❑ 346 Ramon Soler .30 .10
❑ 347 Brandon Phillips RC 1.50 .60
❑ 348 Vince Faison RC .30 .10
❑ 349 Mike Venafro .30 .10
❑ 350 Rick Asadoorian RC .50 .20
❑ 351 B.J. Garbe RC .30 .10
❑ 352 Dan Reichert .30 .10
❑ 353 Jason Stumm RC .30 .10
❑ 354 Ruben Salazar RC .30 .10
❑ 355 Francisco Cordero .30 .10
❑ 356 Juan Guzman RC .30 .10
❑ 357 Mike Bacsik RC .30 .10
❑ 358 Jared Sandberg .30 .10
❑ 359 Rod Barajas .30 .10
❑ 360 Junior Brignac RC .30 .10
❑ 361 J.M. Gold .30 .10
❑ 362 Octavio Dotel .30 .10
❑ 363 David Kelton .30 .10
❑ 364 Scott Morgan .30 .10
❑ 365 Wascar Serrano RC .30 .10
❑ 366 Wilton Veras .30 .10
❑ 367 Eugene Kingsale .30 .10
❑ 368 Ted Lilly .30 .10

❑ 369 George Lombard	.30	.10
❑ 370 Chris Haas	.30	.10
❑ 371 Wilton Pena RC	.30	.10
❑ 372 Vernon Wells	.30	.10
❑ 373 Jason Royer RC	.30	.10
❑ 374 Jeff Heaverlo RC	.30	.10
❑ 375 Calvin Pickering	.30	.10
❑ 376 Mike Lamb RC	.75	.30
❑ 377 Kyle Snyder	.30	.10
❑ 378 Javier Cardona RC	.30	.10
❑ 379 Aaron Rowand RC	2.00	.75
❑ 380 Dee Brown	.30	.10
❑ 381 Brett Myers RC	1.50	.60
❑ 382 Abraham Nunez	.30	.10
❑ 383 Eric Valent	.30	.10
❑ 384 Jody Gerut RC	.50	.20
❑ 385 Adam Dunn	.75	.30
❑ 386 Jay Gehrke	.30	.10
❑ 387 Omar Ortiz	.30	.10
❑ 388 Darnell McDonald	.30	.10
❑ 389 Tony Schrager RC	.30	.10
❑ 390 J.D. Closser	.30	.10
❑ 391 Ben Christensen RC	.30	.10
❑ 392 Adam Kennedy	.30	.10
❑ 393 Nick Green RC	.30	.10
❑ 394 Ramon Hernandez	.30	.10
❑ 395 Roy Oswalt RC	12.00	5.00
❑ 396 Andy Tracy RC	.30	.10
❑ 397 Eric Gagne	.75	.30
❑ 398 Michael Tejera RC	.30	.10
❑ 399 Adam Everett	.30	.10
❑ 400 Corey Patterson	.30	.10
❑ 401 Gary Knotts RC	.30	.10
❑ 402 Ryan Christianson RC	.30	.10
❑ 403 Eric Ireland RC	.30	.10
❑ 404 Andrew Good RC	.30	.10
❑ 405 Brad Penny	.30	.10
❑ 406 Jason LaRue	.30	.10
❑ 407 Kit Pellow	.30	.10
❑ 408 Kevin Beirne	.30	.10
❑ 409 Kelly Dransfeldt	.30	.10
❑ 410 Jason Grilli	.30	.10
❑ 411 Scott Downs RC	.30	.10
❑ 412 Jesus Colome	.30	.10
❑ 413 John Sneed RC	.30	.10
❑ 414 Tony McKnight	.30	.10
❑ 415 Luis Rivera	.30	.10
❑ 416 Adam Eaton	.30	.10
❑ 417 Mike MacDougal RC	.50	.20
❑ 418 Mike Nannini	.30	.10
❑ 419 Barry Zito RC	4.00	1.50
❑ 420 DeWayne Wise	.30	.10
❑ 421 Jason Dellaero	.30	.10
❑ 422 Chad Moeller	.30	.10
❑ 423 Jason Marquis	.30	.10
❑ 424 Tim Redding RC	.50	.20
❑ 425 Mark Mulder	.30	.10
❑ 426 Josh Paul	.30	.10
❑ 427 Chris Enochs	.30	.10
❑ 428 Wilfredo Rodriguez RC	.30	.10
❑ 429 Kevin Witt	.30	.10
❑ 430 Scott Sobkowiak RC	.30	.10
❑ 431 McKay Christensen	.30	.10
❑ 432 Jung Bong	.30	.10
❑ 433 Keith Evans RC	.30	.10
❑ 434 Garry Maddox Jr. RC	.30	.10
❑ 435 Ramon Santiago RC	.30	.10
❑ 436 Alex Cora	.30	.10
❑ 437 Carlos Lee	.30	.10
❑ 438 Jason Repko RC	.75	.30
❑ 439 Matt Burch	.30	.10
❑ 440 Shawn Sonnier RC	.30	.10

2000 Bowman Draft Picks

❑ COMP.FACT.SET (111)	40.00	20.00
❑ COMPLETE SET (110)	25.00	10.00
❑ 1 Pat Burrell	.30	.10
❑ 2 Rafael Furcal	.30	.10
❑ 3 Grant Roberts	.30	.10
❑ 4 Barry Zito	1.50	.60
❑ 5 Julio Zuleta	.30	.10
❑ 6 Mark Mulder	.30	.10
❑ 7 Rob Bell	.30	.10
❑ 8 Adam Piatt	.30	.10
❑ 9 Mike Lamb	.60	.25

❑ 10 Pablo Ozuna	.30	.10
❑ 11 Jason Tyner	.30	.10
❑ 12 Jason Marquis	.30	.10
❑ 13 Eric Munson	.30	.10
❑ 14 Seth Etherton	.30	.10
❑ 15 Milton Bradley	.30	.10
❑ 16 Nick Green	.30	.10
❑ 17 Chin-Feng Chen RC	.60	.25
❑ 18 Matt Boone RC	.30	.10
❑ 19 Kevin Gregg RC	.30	.10
❑ 20 Eddy Garabito RC	.30	.10
❑ 21 Aaron Capista RC	.30	.10
❑ 22 Esteban German RC	.30	.10
❑ 23 Derek Thompson RC	.30	.10
❑ 24 Phil Merrell RC	.30	.10
❑ 25 Brian O'Connor RC	.30	.10
❑ 26 Yamid Haad	.30	.10
❑ 27 Hector Mercado RC	.30	.10
❑ 28 Jason Woolf RC	.30	.10
❑ 29 Eddy Furniss RC	.30	.10
❑ 30 Cha Sueng Baek RC	.30	.10
❑ 31 Colby Lewis RC	.30	.10
❑ 32 Pasqual Coco RC	.30	.10
❑ 33 Jorge Cantu RC	2.50	1.00
❑ 34 Erasmo Ramirez RC	.30	.10
❑ 35 Bobby Kielty RC	.40	.15
❑ 36 Joaquin Benoit RC	.30	.10
❑ 37 Brian Esposito RC	.30	.10
❑ 38 Michael Wenner	.30	.10
❑ 39 Juan Rincon RC	.30	.10
❑ 40 Yorvit Torrealba RC	6.00	.25
❑ 41 Chad Durham RC	.30	.10
❑ 42 Jim Mann RC	.30	.10
❑ 43 Shane Loux RC	.30	.10
❑ 44 Luis Rivas	.30	.10
❑ 45 Ken Chenard RC	.30	.10
❑ 46 Mike Lockwood RC	.30	.10
❑ 47 Yovanny Lara RC	.30	.10
❑ 48 Bubba Carpenter RC	.30	.10
❑ 49 Ryan Dittfurth RC	.30	.10
❑ 50 John Stephens RC	.30	.10
❑ 51 Pedro Feliz RC	1.00	.40
❑ 52 Kenny Kelly RC	.30	.10
❑ 53 Neil Jenkins RC	.30	.10
❑ 54 Mike Glendenning RC	.30	.10
❑ 55 Bo Porter	.30	.10
❑ 56 Eric Byrnes	.30	.10
❑ 57 Tony Alvarez RC	.30	.10
❑ 58 Kazuhiro Sasaki RC	.60	.25
❑ 59 Chad Durbin RC	.30	.10
❑ 60 Mike Bynum RC	.30	.10
❑ 61 Travis Wilson RC	.30	.10
❑ 62 Jose Leon RC	.30	.10
❑ 63 Ryan Vogelsong RC	.30	.10
❑ 64 Geraldo Guzman RC	.30	.10
❑ 65 Craig Anderson RC	.30	.10
❑ 66 Carlos Silva RC	.40	.15
❑ 67 Brad Thomas RC	.30	.10
❑ 68 Chin-Hui Tsao RC	2.00	.75
❑ 69 Mark Buehrle RC	4.00	1.50
❑ 70 Juan Salas RC	.30	.10
❑ 71 Denny Abreu RC	.30	.10
❑ 72 Keith McDonald RC	.30	.10
❑ 73 Chris Richard RC	.30	.10
❑ 74 Tomas De la Rosa RC	.30	.10
❑ 75 Vicente Padilla RC	.40	.15
❑ 76 Justin Brunette RC	.30	.10
❑ 77 Scott Linebrink RC	.30	.10
❑ 78 Jeff Sparks RC	.30	.10
❑ 79 Tike Redman RC	.60	.25
❑ 80 John Lackey RC	2.50	1.00
❑ 81 Joe Strong RC	.30	.10
❑ 82 Brian Tollberg RC	.30	.10
❑ 83 Steve Sisco RC	.30	.10
❑ 84 Chris Clapinski RC	.30	.10
❑ 85 Augie Ojeda RC	.30	.10
❑ 86 Adrian Gonzalez RC	3.00	1.25
❑ 87 Mike Stodolka RC	.30	.10
❑ 88 Adam Johnson RC	.30	.10
❑ 89 Matt Wheatland RC	.30	.10
❑ 90 Corey Smith RC	.30	.10
❑ 91 Rocco Baldelli RC	2.00	.75
❑ 92 Keith Bucktrot RC	.30	.10
❑ 93 Adam Wainwright RC	1.25	.50
❑ 94 Blaine Boyer RC	.30	.10
❑ 95 Aaron Herr RC	.40	.15
❑ 96 Scott Thorman RC	1.00	.40
❑ 97 Bryan Digby RC	.30	.10
❑ 98 Josh Shortslef RC	.50	.20
❑ 99 Sean Smith RC	.30	.10
❑ 100 Alex Cruz RC	.30	.10
❑ 101 Marc Love RC	.30	.10
❑ 102 Kevin Lee RC	.30	.10
❑ 103 Victor Ramos RC	.30	.10
❑ 104 Jason Kaanoi RC	.30	.10
❑ 105 Luis Escobar RC	.30	.10
❑ 106 Tripper Johnson RC	.30	.10
❑ 107 Phil Dumatrait RC	.30	.10
❑ 108 Bryan Edwards RC	.30	.10
❑ 109 Grady Sizemore RC	15.00	6.00
❑ 110 Thomas Mitchell RC	.30	.10

2001 Bowman

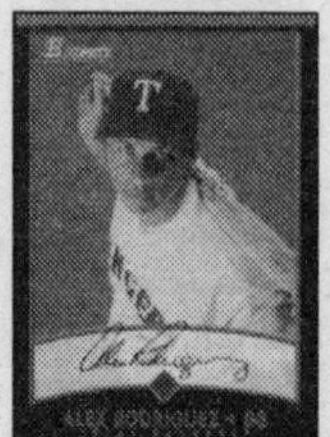

❑ COMPLETE SET (440)	150.00	90.00
❑ COMMON CARD (1-440)	.30	.10
❑ COMMON RC	.40	.15
❑ 1 Jason Giambi	.30	.10
❑ 2 Rafael Furcal	.30	.10
❑ 3 Rick Ankiel	.30	.10
❑ 4 Freddy Garcia	.30	.10
❑ 5 Magglio Ordonez	.30	.10
❑ 6 Bernie Williams	.50	.20
❑ 7 Kenny Lofton	.30	.10
❑ 8 Al Leiter	.30	.10
❑ 9 Albert Belle	.30	.10
❑ 10 Craig Biggio	.50	.20
❑ 11 Mark Mulder	.30	.10
❑ 12 Carlos Delgado	.30	.10
❑ 13 Darin Erstad	.30	.10
❑ 14 Richie Sexson	.30	.10
❑ 15 Randy Johnson	.75	.30
❑ 16 Greg Maddux	1.25	.50
❑ 17 Cliff Floyd	.30	.10
❑ 18 Mark Buehrle	.50	.20
❑ 19 Chris Singleton	.30	.10
❑ 20 Orlando Hernandez	.30	.10
❑ 21 Javier Vazquez	.30	.10
❑ 22 Jeff Kent	.30	.10
❑ 23 Jim Thome	.50	.20
❑ 24 John Olerud	.30	.10
❑ 25 Jason Kendall	.30	.10
❑ 26 Scott Rolen	.50	.20
❑ 27 Tony Gwynn	1.00	.40
❑ 28 Edgardo Alfonzo	.30	.10
❑ 29 Pokey Reese	.30	.10
❑ 30 Todd Helton	.50	.20

❑ 31 Mark Quinn .30 .10
❑ 32 Dan Tosca RC .40 .15
❑ 33 Dean Palmer .30 .10
❑ 34 Jacque Jones .30 .10
❑ 35 Ray Durham .30 .10
❑ 36 Rafael Palmeiro .50 .20
❑ 37 Carl Everett .30 .10
❑ 38 Ryan Dempster .30 .10
❑ 39 Randy Wolf .30 .10
❑ 40 Vladimir Guerrero .75 .30
❑ 41 Livan Hernandez .30 .10
❑ 42 Mo Vaughn .30 .10
❑ 43 Shannon Stewart .30 .10
❑ 44 Preston Wilson .30 .10
❑ 45 Jose Vidro .30 .10
❑ 46 Fred McGriff .50 .20
❑ 47 Kevin Brown .30 .10
❑ 48 Peter Bergeron .30 .10
❑ 49 Miguel Tejada .30 .10
❑ 50 Chipper Jones .75 .30
❑ 51 Edgar Martinez .50 .20
❑ 52 Tony Batista .30 .10
❑ 53 Jorge Posada .50 .20
❑ 54 Ricky Ledee .30 .10
❑ 55 Sammy Sosa .75 .30
❑ 56 Steve Cox .30 .10
❑ 57 Tony Armas Jr. .30 .10
❑ 58 Gary Sheffield .30 .10
❑ 59 Bartolo Colon .30 .10
❑ 60 Pat Burrell .30 .10
❑ 61 Jay Payton .30 .10
❑ 62 Sean Casey .30 .10
❑ 63 Larry Walker .30 .10
❑ 64 Mike Mussina .50 .20
❑ 65 Nomar Garciaparra 1.25 .50
❑ 66 Darren Dreifort .30 .10
❑ 67 Richard Hidalgo .30 .10
❑ 68 Troy Glaus .30 .10
❑ 69 Ben Grieve .30 .10
❑ 70 Jim Edmonds .30 .10
❑ 71 Raul Mondesi .30 .10
❑ 72 Andruw Jones .50 .20
❑ 73 Luis Castillo .30 .10
❑ 74 Mike Sweeney .30 .10
❑ 75 Derek Jeter 2.00 .75
❑ 76 Ruben Mateo .30 .10
❑ 77 Carlos Lee .30 .10
❑ 78 Cristian Guzman .30 .10
❑ 79 Mike Hampton .30 .10
❑ 80 J.D. Drew .30 .10
❑ 81 Matt Lawton .30 .10
❑ 82 Moises Alou .30 .10
❑ 83 Terrence Long .30 .10
❑ 84 Geoff Jenkins .30 .10
❑ 85 Manny Ramirez Sox .50 .20
❑ 86 Johnny Damon .50 .20
❑ 87 Barry Larkin .50 .20
❑ 88 Pedro Martinez .50 .20
❑ 89 Juan Gonzalez .30 .10
❑ 90 Roger Clemens 1.50 .60
❑ 91 Carlos Beltran .30 .10
❑ 92 Brad Radke .30 .10
❑ 93 Orlando Cabrera .30 .10
❑ 94 Roberto Alomar .50 .20
❑ 95 Barry Bonds 2.00 .75
❑ 96 Tim Hudson .30 .10
❑ 97 Tom Glavine .50 .20
❑ 98 Jeromy Burnitz .30 .10
❑ 99 Adrian Beltre .30 .10
❑ 100 Mike Piazza 1.25 .50
❑ 101 Kerry Wood .30 .10
❑ 102 Steve Finley .30 .10
❑ 103 Alex Cora .30 .10
❑ 104 Bob Abreu .30 .10
❑ 105 Neifi Perez .30 .10
❑ 106 Mark Redman .30 .10
❑ 107 Paul Konerko .30 .10
❑ 108 Jermaine Dye .30 .10
❑ 109 Brian Giles .30 .10
❑ 110 Ivan Rodriguez .50 .20
❑ 111 Vinny Castilla .30 .10
❑ 112 Adam Kennedy .30 .10
❑ 113 Eric Chavez .30 .10
❑ 114 Billy Koch .30 .10
❑ 115 Shawn Green .30 .10
❑ 116 Matt Williams .30 .10
❑ 117 Greg Vaughn .30 .10
❑ 118 Gabe Kapler .30 .10
❑ 119 Jeff Cirillo .30 .10
❑ 120 Frank Thomas .75 .30
❑ 121 David Justice .30 .10
❑ 122 Cal Ripken 2.50 1.00
❑ 123 Rich Aurilia .30 .10
❑ 124 Curt Schilling .30 .10
❑ 125 Barry Zito .50 .20
❑ 126 Brian Jordan .30 .10
❑ 127 Chan Ho Park .30 .10
❑ 128 J.T. Snow .30 .10
❑ 129 Kazuhiro Sasaki .30 .10
❑ 130 Alex Rodriguez 1.25 .50
❑ 131 Mariano Rivera .75 .30
❑ 132 Eric Milton .30 .10
❑ 133 Andy Pettitte .50 .20
❑ 134 Scott Elarton .30 .10
❑ 135 Ken Griffey Jr. 1.25 .50
❑ 136 Bengie Molina .30 .10
❑ 137 Jeff Bagwell .50 .20
❑ 138 Kevin Millwood .30 .10
❑ 139 Tino Martinez .50 .20
❑ 140 Mark McGwire 2.00 .75
❑ 141 Larry Barnes .30 .10
❑ 142 John Buck RC 1.00 .40
❑ 143 Freddie Bynum RC .40 .15
❑ 144 Abraham Nunez .30 .10
❑ 145 Felix Diaz RC .40 .15
❑ 146 Horacio Estrada .30 .10
❑ 147 Ben Diggins .30 .10
❑ 148 Tsuyoshi Shinjo RC 1.00 .40
❑ 149 Rocco Baldelli .30 .10
❑ 150 Rod Barajas .30 .10
❑ 151 Luis Terrero .30 .10
❑ 152 Milton Bradley .30 .10
❑ 153 Kurt Ainsworth .30 .10
❑ 154 Russell Branyan .30 .10
❑ 155 Ryan Anderson .30 .10
❑ 156 Mitch Jones RC .60 .25
❑ 157 Chip Ambres .30 .10
❑ 158 Steve Bennett RC .40 .15
❑ 159 Ivanon Coffie .30 .10
❑ 160 Sean Burroughs .30 .10
❑ 161 Keith Bucktrot .30 .10
❑ 162 Tony Alvarez .30 .10
❑ 163 Joaquin Benoit .30 .10
❑ 164 Rick Asadoorian .30 .10
❑ 165 Ben Broussard .30 .10
❑ 166 Ryan Madson RC 1.25 .50
❑ 167 Dee Brown .30 .10
❑ 168 Sergio Contreras RC .60 .25
❑ 169 John Barnes .30 .10
❑ 170 Ben Washburn RC .40 .15
❑ 171 Erick Almonte RC .40 .15
❑ 172 Shawn Fagan RC .40 .15
❑ 173 Gary Johnson RC .40 .15
❑ 174 Brady Clark .30 .10
❑ 175 Grant Roberts .30 .10
❑ 176 Tony Torcato .30 .10
❑ 177 Ramon Castro .30 .10
❑ 178 Esteban German .30 .10
❑ 179 Joe Hamer RC .60 .25
❑ 180 Nick Neugebauer .30 .10
❑ 181 Dernell Stenson .30 .10
❑ 182 Yhency Brazoban RC 1.00 .40
❑ 183 Aaron Myette .30 .10
❑ 184 Juan Sosa .30 .10
❑ 185 Brandon Inge .30 .10
❑ 186 Domingo Guante RC .40 .15
❑ 187 Adrian Brown .30 .10
❑ 188 Deivi Mendez RC .40 .15
❑ 189 Luis Matos .30 .10
❑ 190 Pedro Liriano RC .60 .25
❑ 191 Donnie Bridges .30 .10
❑ 192 Alex Cintron .30 .10
❑ 193 Jace Brewer .30 .10
❑ 194 Ron Davenport RC .60 .25
❑ 195 Jason Belcher RC .40 .15
❑ 196 Adrian Hernandez RC .40 .15
❑ 197 Bobby Kielty .30 .10
❑ 198 Reggie Griggs RC .60 .25
❑ 199 Reggie Abercrombie RC 1.00 .40
❑ 200 Troy Farnsworth RC .60 .25
❑ 201 Matt Belisle .30 .10
❑ 202 Miguel Villilo RC .60 .25
❑ 203 Adam Everett .30 .10
❑ 204 John Lackey .30 .10
❑ 205 Pasqual Coco .30 .10
❑ 206 Adam Wainwright .30 .10
❑ 207 Matt White RC .60 .25
❑ 208 Chin-Feng Chen .30 .10
❑ 209 Jeff Andra RC .40 .15
❑ 210 Willie Bloomquist .30 .10
❑ 211 Wes Anderson .30 .10
❑ 212 Enrique Cruz .30 .10
❑ 213 Jerry Hairston Jr. .30 .10
❑ 214 Mike Bynum .30 .10
❑ 215 Brian Hitchcox RC .40 .15
❑ 216 Ryan Christianson .30 .10
❑ 217 J.J. Davis .30 .10
❑ 218 Jovanny Cedeno .30 .10
❑ 219 Elvin Nina .30 .10
❑ 220 Alex Graman .30 .10
❑ 221 Arturo McDowell .30 .10
❑ 222 Deivis Santos RC .40 .15
❑ 223 Jody Gerut .30 .10
❑ 224 Sun Woo Kim .30 .10
❑ 225 Jimmy Rollins .30 .10
❑ 226 Ntema Ndungidi .30 .10
❑ 227 Ruben Salazar .30 .10
❑ 228 Josh Girdley .30 .10
❑ 229 Carl Crawford .30 .10
❑ 230 Luis Montanez RC .60 .25
❑ 231 Ramon Carvajal RC .60 .25
❑ 232 Matt Riley .30 .10
❑ 233 Ben Davis .30 .10
❑ 234 Jason Grabowski .30 .10
❑ 235 Chris George .30 .10
❑ 236 Hank Blalock RC 5.00 2.00
❑ 237 Roy Oswalt .75 .30
❑ 238 Eric Reynolds RC .40 .15
❑ 239 Brian Cole .30 .10
❑ 240 Denny Bautista RC 1.00 .40
❑ 241 Hector Garcia RC .40 .15
❑ 242 Joe Thurston RC .60 .25
❑ 243 Brad Cresse .30 .10
❑ 244 Corey Patterson .30 .10
❑ 245 Brett Evert RC .40 .15
❑ 246 Elpidio Guzman RC .40 .15
❑ 247 Vernon Wells .30 .10
❑ 248 Roberto Miniel RC .60 .25
❑ 249 Brian Bass RC .40 .15
❑ 250 Mark Burnett RC .60 .25
❑ 251 Juan Silvestre .30 .10
❑ 252 Pablo Ozuna .30 .10
❑ 253 Jayson Werth .30 .10
❑ 254 Russ Jacobson .30 .10
❑ 255 Chad Hermansen .30 .10
❑ 256 Travis Hafner RC 10.00 4.00
❑ 257 Brad Baker .30 .10
❑ 258 Gookie Dawkins .30 .10
❑ 259 Michael Cuddyer .30 .10
❑ 260 Mark Buehrle .50 .20
❑ 261 Ricardo Aramboles .30 .10
❑ 262 Esix Snead RC .40 .15
❑ 263 Wilson Betemit RC 3.00 1.25
❑ 264 Albert Pujols RC 80.00 40.00
❑ 265 Joe Lawrence .30 .10
❑ 266 Ramon Ortiz .30 .10
❑ 267 Ben Sheets .50 .20
❑ 268 Luke Lockwood RC .60 .25
❑ 269 Toby Hall .30 .10
❑ 270 Jack Cust .30 .10
❑ 271 Pedro Feliz .30 .10
❑ 272 Noel Devarez RC .60 .25
❑ 273 Josh Beckett .50 .20
❑ 274 Alex Escobar .30 .10
❑ 275 Doug Gredvig RC .40 .15
❑ 276 Marcus Giles .30 .10
❑ 277 Jon Rauch .30 .10
❑ 278 Brian Schmitt RC .40 .15
❑ 279 Seung Song RC .60 .25
❑ 280 Kevin Mench .30 .10
❑ 281 Adam Eaton .30 .10
❑ 282 Shawn Sonnier .30 .10
❑ 283 Andy Van Hekken RC .40 .15
❑ 284 Aaron Rowand .30 .10
❑ 285 Tony Blanco RC .60 .25
❑ 286 Ryan Kohlmeier .30 .10
❑ 287 C.C. Sabathia .30 .10
❑ 288 Bubba Crosby .30 .10

❑ 289 Josh Hamilton .30 .10
❑ 290 Dee Haynes RC .40 .15
❑ 291 Jason Marquis .30 .10
❑ 292 Julio Zuleta .30 .10
❑ 293 Carlos Hernandez .30 .10
❑ 294 Matt Lecroy .30 .10
❑ 295 Andy Beal RC .40 .15
❑ 296 Carlos Pena .30 .10
❑ 297 Reggie Taylor .30 .10
❑ 298 Bob Keppel RC .40 .15
❑ 299 Miguel Cabrera 1.50 .60
❑ 300 Ryan Franklin .30 .10
❑ 301 Brandon Phillips .30 .10
❑ 302 Victor Hall RC .60 .25
❑ 303 Tony Pena Jr. .30 .10
❑ 304 Jim Journell RC .60 .25
❑ 305 Cristian Guerrero .30 .10
❑ 306 Miguel Olivo .30 .10
❑ 307 Jin Ho Cho .30 .10
❑ 308 Choo Freeman .30 .10
❑ 309 Danny Borrell RC .40 .15
❑ 310 Doug Mientkiewicz .30 .10
❑ 311 Aaron Herr .30 .10
❑ 312 Keith Ginter .30 .10
❑ 313 Felipe Lopez .30 .10
❑ 314 Jeff Goldbach .30 .10
❑ 315 Travis Harper .30 .10
❑ 316 Paul LoDuca .30 .10
❑ 317 Joe Torres .30 .10
❑ 318 Eric Byrnes .30 .10
❑ 319 George Lombard .30 .10
❑ 320 Dave Krynzel .30 .10
❑ 321 Ben Christensen .30 .10
❑ 322 Aubrey Huff .30 .10
❑ 323 Lyle Overbay .30 .10
❑ 324 Sean McGowan .30 .10
❑ 325 Jeff Heaverlo .30 .10
❑ 326 Timo Perez .30 .10
❑ 327 Octavio Martinez RC .60 .25
❑ 328 Vince Faison .30 .10
❑ 329 David Parrish RC .40 .15
❑ 330 Bobby Bradley .30 .10
❑ 331 Jason Miller RC .40 .15
❑ 332 Corey Spencer RC .40 .15
❑ 333 Craig House .30 .10
❑ 334 Maxim St. Pierre RC .60 .25
❑ 335 Adam Johnson .30 .10
❑ 336 Joe Crede .75 .30
❑ 337 Greg Nash RC .40 .15
❑ 338 Chad Durbin .30 .10
❑ 339 Pat Magness RC .60 .25
❑ 340 Matt Wheatland .30 .10
❑ 341 Julio Lugo .30 .10
❑ 342 Grady Sizemore 1.50 .60
❑ 343 Adrian Gonzalez .30 .10
❑ 344 Tim Raines Jr. .30 .10
❑ 345 Ranier Olmedo RC .60 .25
❑ 346 Phil Dumatrait .30 .10
❑ 347 Brandon Mims RC .40 .15
❑ 348 Jason Jennings .30 .10
❑ 349 Phil Wilson RC .60 .25
❑ 350 Jason Hart .30 .10
❑ 351 Cesar Izturis .30 .10
❑ 352 Matt Butler RC .60 .25
❑ 353 David Kelton .30 .10
❑ 354 Luke Prokopec .30 .10
❑ 355 Corey Smith .30 .10
❑ 356 Joel Pineiro .60 .25
❑ 357 Ken Chenard .30 .10
❑ 358 Keith Reed .30 .10
❑ 359 David Walling .30 .10
❑ 360 Alexis Gomez RC .40 .15
❑ 361 Justin Morneau RC 12.00 5.00
❑ 362 Josh Fogg RC .60 .25
❑ 363 J.R. House .30 .10
❑ 364 Andy Tracy .30 .10
❑ 365 Kenny Kelly .30 .10
❑ 366 Aaron McNeal .30 .10
❑ 367 Nick Johnson .30 .10
❑ 368 Brian Esposito .30 .10
❑ 369 Charles Frazier RC .40 .15
❑ 370 Scott Heard .30 .10
❑ 371 Pat Strange .30 .10
❑ 372 Mike Meyers .30 .10
❑ 373 Ryan Ludwick RC .60 .25
❑ 374 Brad Wilkerson .30 .10
❑ 375 Allen Levrault .30 .10
❑ 376 Seth McClung RC .60 .25
❑ 377 Joe Nathan .30 .10
❑ 378 Rafael Soriano RC .60 .25
❑ 379 Chris Richard .30 .10
❑ 380 Jared Sandberg .30 .10
❑ 381 Tike Redman .30 .10
❑ 382 Adam Dunn .50 .20
❑ 383 Jared Abruzzo RC .40 .15
❑ 384 Jason Richardson RC .40 .15
❑ 385 Matt Holliday .40 .15
❑ 386 Darwin Cubillan RC .40 .15
❑ 387 Mike Nannini .30 .10
❑ 388 Blake Williams RC .40 .15
❑ 389 Valentino Pascucci RC .60 .25
❑ 390 Jon Garland .30 .10
❑ 391 Josh Pressley .30 .10
❑ 392 Jose Ortiz .30 .10
❑ 393 Ryan Hannaman RC .60 .25
❑ 394 Steve Smyth RC .60 .25
❑ 395 John Patterson .30 .10
❑ 396 Chad Petty RC .40 .15
❑ 397 Jake Peavy UER RC 6.00 2.50
❑ 398 Onix Mercado RC .60 .25
❑ 399 Jason Romano .30 .10
❑ 400 Luis Torres RC .60 .25
❑ 401 Casey Fossum RC .40 .15
❑ 402 Eduardo Figueroa RC .40 .15
❑ 403 Bryan Barnowski RC .40 .15
❑ 404 Tim Redding .30 .10
❑ 405 Jason Standridge .30 .10
❑ 406 Marvin Seale RC .60 .25
❑ 407 Todd Moser .30 .10
❑ 408 Alex Gordon .30 .10
❑ 409 Steve Smitherman RC .60 .25
❑ 410 Ben Petrick .30 .10
❑ 411 Eric Munson .30 .10
❑ 412 Luis Rivas .30 .10
❑ 413 Matt Ginter .30 .10
❑ 414 Alfonso Soriano .50 .20
❑ 415 Rafael Boitel RC .40 .15
❑ 416 Dany Morban RC .40 .15
❑ 417 Justin Woodrow RC .60 .25
❑ 418 Wilfredo Rodriguez .30 .10
❑ 419 Derrick Van Dusen RC .40 .15
❑ 420 Josh Spoerl RC .60 .25
❑ 421 Juan Pierre .30 .10
❑ 422 J.C. Romero .30 .10
❑ 423 Ed Rogers RC .40 .15
❑ 424 Tomo Ohka .30 .10
❑ 425 Ben Hendrickson RC .40 .15
❑ 426 Carlos Zambrano .50 .20
❑ 427 Brett Myers .30 .10
❑ 428 Scott Seabol .30 .10
❑ 429 Thomas Mitchell .30 .10
❑ 430 Jose Reyes RC 25.00 10.00
❑ 431 Kip Wells .30 .10
❑ 432 Donzell McDonald .30 .10
❑ 433 Adam Pettyjohn RC .40 .15
❑ 434 Austin Kearns .30 .10
❑ 435 Rico Washington .30 .10
❑ 436 Doug Nickle RC .40 .15
❑ 437 Steve Lomasney .30 .10
❑ 438 Jason Jones RC .40 .15
❑ 439 Bobby Seay .30 .10
❑ 440 Justin Wayne RC .60 .25
❑ ROYR Sasaki/Furcal ROY Jsy 15.00 6.00
❑ NNO Sean Burroughs Ball/80 15.00 6.00

2001 Bowman Draft Picks

❑ COMP.FACT.SET (112) 40.00 20.00
❑ COMPLETE SET (110) 30.00 15.00
❑ BDP1 Alfredo Amezaga RC .30 .10
❑ BDP2 Andrew Good .30 .10
❑ BDP3 Kelly Johnson RC 3.00 1.25
❑ BDP4 Larry Bigbie .30 .10
❑ BDP5 Matt Thompson RC .40 .15
❑ BDP6 Wilton Chavez RC .40 .15
❑ BDP7 Joe Borchard RC .40 .15
❑ BDP8 David Espinosa .30 .10
❑ BDP9 Zach Day RC .40 .15
❑ BDP10 Brad Hawpe RC 2.50 1.00
❑ BDP11 Nate Cornejo .30 .10
❑ BDP12 Matt Cooper RC .40 .15
❑ BDP13 Brad Lidge .30 .10
❑ BDP14 Angel Berroa RC .60 .25
❑ BDP15 Lamont Matthews RC .40 .15
❑ BDP16 Jose Garcia .30 .10
❑ BDP17 Grant Balfour RC .30 .10
❑ BDP18 Ron Chiavacci RC .30 .10
❑ BDP19 Jae Seo .30 .10
❑ BDP20 Juan Rivera .30 .10
❑ BDP21 D'Angelo Jimenez .30 .10
❑ BDP22 Juan A.Pena RC .40 .15
❑ BDP23 Marlon Byrd RC .40 .15
❑ BDP24 Sean Burnett .30 .10
❑ BDP25 Josh Pearce RC .40 .15
❑ BDP26 Brandon Duckworth RC .30 .10
❑ BDP27 Jack Taschner RC .30 .10
❑ BDP28 Marcus Thames .30 .10
❑ BDP29 Brent Abernathy .30 .10
❑ BDP30 David Elder RC .30 .10
❑ BDP31 Scott Cassidy RC .40 .15
❑ BDP32 Dennis Tankersley RC .30 .10
❑ BDP33 Denny Stark .30 .10
❑ BDP34 Dave Williams RC .30 .10
❑ BDP35 Boof Bonser RC .30 .10
❑ BDP36 Kris Foster RC .30 .10
❑ BDP37 Luis Garcia RC .40 .15
❑ BDP38 Shawn Chacon .30 .10
❑ BDP39 Mike Rivera RC .40 .15
❑ BDP40 Will Smith RC .40 .15
❑ BDP41 Morgan Ensberg RC 2.00 .75
❑ BDP42 Ken Harvey .30 .10
❑ BDP43 Ricardo Rodriguez RC .40 .15
❑ BDP44 Jose Mieses RC .40 .15
❑ BDP45 Luis Maza RC .30 .10
❑ BDP46 Julio Perez RC .40 .15
❑ BDP47 Dustan Mohr RC .40 .15
❑ BDP48 Randy Flores RC .30 .10
❑ BDP49 Covelli Crisp RC 5.00 2.00
❑ BDP50 Kevin Reese RC .40 .15
❑ BDP51 Brad Thomas UER .30 .10
❑ BDP52 Xavier Nady .30 .10
❑ BDP53 Ryan Vogelsong .30 .10
❑ BDP54 Carlos Silva .30 .10
❑ BDP55 Dan Wright .30 .10
❑ BDP56 Brent Butler .30 .10
❑ BDP57 Brandon Knight RC .30 .10
❑ BDP58 Brian Reith RC .30 .10
❑ BDP59 Mario Valenzuela RC .40 .15
❑ BDP60 Bobby Hill RC .40 .15
❑ BDP61 Rich Rundles RC .40 .15
❑ BDP62 Rick Elder .30 .10
❑ BDP63 J.D. Closser .30 .10
❑ BDP64 Scot Shields .30 .10
❑ BDP65 Miguel Olivo .30 .10
❑ BDP66 Stubby Clapp RC .30 .10
❑ BDP67 Jerome Williams RC .60 .25
❑ BDP68 Jason Lane RC .60 .25
❑ BDP69 Chase Utley RC 15.00 6.00
❑ BDP70 Erik Bedard RC 5.00 2.00
❑ BDP71 Alex Herrera UER RC .30 .10
❑ BDP72 Juan Cruz RC .40 .15
❑ BDP73 Billy Martin RC .30 .10
❑ BDP74 Ronnie Merrill RC .40 .15
❑ BDP75 Jason Kinchen RC .30 .10
❑ BDP76 Wilkin Ruan RC .40 .15
❑ BDP77 Cody Ransom RC .30 .10
❑ BDP78 Bud Smith RC .30 .10
❑ BDP79 Wily Mo Pena .30 .10
❑ BDP80 Jeff Nettles RC .40 .15
❑ BDP81 Jamal Strong RC .30 .10

❑ BDP82 Bill Ortega RC	.30	.10
❑ BDP83 Mike Bell	.30	.10
❑ BDP84 Ichiro Suzuki RC	8.00	3.00
❑ BDP85 Fernando Rodney RC	.30	.10
❑ BDP86 Chris Smith RC	.30	.10
❑ BDP87 John VanBenschoten RC	.40	.15
❑ BDP88 Bobby Crosby RC	4.00	1.50
❑ BDP89 Kenny Baugh RC	.30	.10
❑ BDP90 Jake Gautreau RC	.30	.10
❑ BDP91 Gabe Gross RC	.60	.25
❑ BDP92 Kris Honel RC	.40	.15
❑ BDP93 Dan Denham RC	.30	.10
❑ BDP94 Aaron Heilman RC	.40	.15
❑ BDP95 Irvin Guzman RC	4.00	1.50
❑ BDP96 Mike Jones RC	.60	.25
❑ BDP97 John-Ford Griffin RC	.40	.15
❑ BDP98 Macay McBride RC	1.00	.40
❑ BDP99 John Rheinecker RC	1.00	.40
❑ BDP100 Bronson Sardinha RC	.30	.10
❑ BDP101 Jason Weintraub RC	.30	.10
❑ BDP102 J.D. Martin RC	.30	.10
❑ BDP103 Jayson Nix RC	.40	.15
❑ BDP104 Noah Lowry RC	2.50	1.00
❑ BDP105 Richard Lewis RC	.40	.15
❑ BDP106 Brad Hennessey RC	.60	.25
❑ BDP107 Jeff Mathis RC	.60	.25
❑ BDP108 Jon Skaggs RC	.40	.15
❑ BDP109 Justin Pope RC	.40	.15
❑ BDP110 Josh Burrus RC	.40	.15

2002 Bowman

❑ COMPLETE SET (440)	80.00	40.00
❑ COMMON CARD (1-110)	.30	.10
❑ COMMON CARD (111-440)	.30	.10
❑ 1 Adam Dunn	.30	.10
❑ 2 Derek Jeter	2.00	.75
❑ 3 Alex Rodriguez	1.25	.50
❑ 4 Miguel Tejada	.30	.10
❑ 5 Nomar Garciaparra	1.25	.50
❑ 6 Toby Hall	.30	.10
❑ 7 Brandon Duckworth	.30	.10
❑ 8 Paul LoDuca	.30	.10
❑ 9 Brian Giles	.30	.10
❑ 10 C.C. Sabathia	.30	.10
❑ 11 Curt Schilling	.30	.10
❑ 12 Tsuyoshi Shinjo	.30	.10
❑ 13 Ramon Hernandez	.30	.10
❑ 14 Jose Cruz Jr.	.30	.10
❑ 15 Albert Pujols	1.50	.60
❑ 16 Joe Mays	.30	.10
❑ 17 Javy Lopez	.30	.10
❑ 18 J.T. Snow	.30	.10
❑ 19 David Segui	.30	.10
❑ 20 Jorge Posada	.50	.20
❑ 21 Doug Mientkiewicz	.30	.10
❑ 22 Jerry Hairston Jr.	.30	.10
❑ 23 Bernie Williams	.50	.20
❑ 24 Mike Sweeney	.30	.10
❑ 25 Jason Giambi	.30	.10
❑ 26 Ryan Dempster	.30	.10
❑ 27 Ryan Klesko	.30	.10
❑ 28 Mark Quinn	.30	.10
❑ 29 Jeff Kent	.30	.10
❑ 30 Eric Chavez	.30	.10
❑ 31 Adrian Beltre	.30	.10
❑ 32 Andruw Jones	.50	.20
❑ 33 Alfonso Soriano	.30	.10
❑ 34 Aramis Ramirez	.30	.10
❑ 35 Greg Maddux	1.25	.50
❑ 36 Andy Pettitte	.50	.20
❑ 37 Bartolo Colon	.30	.10
❑ 38 Ben Sheets	.30	.10
❑ 39 Bobby Higginson	.30	.10
❑ 40 Ivan Rodriguez	.50	.20
❑ 41 Brad Penny	.30	.10
❑ 42 Carlos Lee	.30	.10
❑ 43 Damion Easley	.30	.10
❑ 44 Preston Wilson	.30	.10
❑ 45 Jeff Bagwell	.50	.20
❑ 46 Eric Milton	.30	.10
❑ 47 Rafael Palmeiro	.50	.20
❑ 48 Gary Sheffield	.30	.10
❑ 49 J.D. Drew	.30	.10
❑ 50 Jim Thome	.50	.20
❑ 51 Ichiro Suzuki	1.50	.60
❑ 52 Bud Smith	.30	.10
❑ 53 Chan Ho Park	.30	.10
❑ 54 D'Angelo Jimenez	.30	.10
❑ 55 Ken Griffey Jr.	1.25	.50
❑ 56 Wade Miller	.30	.10
❑ 57 Vladimir Guerrero	.75	.30
❑ 58 Troy Glaus	.30	.10
❑ 59 Shawn Green	.30	.10
❑ 60 Kerry Wood	.30	.10
❑ 61 Jack Wilson	.30	.10
❑ 62 Kevin Brown	.30	.10
❑ 63 Marcus Giles	.30	.10
❑ 64 Pat Burrell	.30	.10
❑ 65 Larry Walker	.30	.10
❑ 66 Sammy Sosa	.75	.30
❑ 67 Raul Mondesi	.30	.10
❑ 68 Tim Hudson	.30	.10
❑ 69 Lance Berkman	.30	.10
❑ 70 Mike Mussina	.50	.20
❑ 71 Barry Zito	.30	.10
❑ 72 Jimmy Rollins	.30	.10
❑ 73 Barry Bonds	2.00	.75
❑ 74 Craig Biggio	.50	.20
❑ 75 Todd Helton	.50	.20
❑ 76 Roger Clemens	1.50	.60
❑ 77 Frank Catalanotto	.30	.10
❑ 78 Josh Towers	.30	.10
❑ 79 Roy Oswalt	.30	.10
❑ 80 Chipper Jones	.75	.30
❑ 81 Cristian Guzman	.30	.10
❑ 82 Darin Erstad	.30	.10
❑ 83 Freddy Garcia	.30	.10
❑ 84 Jason Tyner	.30	.10
❑ 85 Carlos Delgado	.30	.10
❑ 86 Jon Lieber	.30	.10
❑ 87 Juan Pierre	.30	.10
❑ 88 Matt Morris	.30	.10
❑ 89 Phil Nevin	.30	.10
❑ 90 Jim Edmonds	.30	.10
❑ 91 Magglio Ordonez	.30	.10
❑ 92 Mike Hampton	.30	.10
❑ 93 Rafael Furcal	.30	.10
❑ 94 Richie Sexson	.30	.10
❑ 95 Luis Gonzalez	.30	.10
❑ 96 Scott Rolen	.50	.20
❑ 97 Tim Redding	.30	.10
❑ 98 Moises Alou	.30	.10
❑ 99 Jose Vidro	.30	.10
❑ 100 Mike Piazza	1.25	.50
❑ 101 Pedro Martinez	.50	.20
❑ 102 Geoff Jenkins	.30	.10
❑ 103 Johnny Damon Sox	.50	.20
❑ 104 Mike Cameron	.30	.10
❑ 105 Randy Johnson	.75	.30
❑ 106 David Eckstein	.30	.10
❑ 107 Javier Vazquez	.30	.10
❑ 108 Mark Mulder	.30	.10
❑ 109 Robert Fick	.30	.10
❑ 110 Roberto Alomar	.50	.20
❑ 111 Wilson Betemit	.30	.10
❑ 112 Chris Tritle RC	.30	.10
❑ 113 Ed Rogers	.30	.10
❑ 114 Juan Pena	.30	.10
❑ 115 Josh Beckett	.40	.15
❑ 116 Juan Cruz	.30	.10
❑ 117 Noochie Varner RC	.40	.15
❑ 118 Taylor Buchholz RC	.60	.25
❑ 119 Mike Rivera	.30	.10
❑ 120 Hank Blalock	.60	.25
❑ 121 Hansel Izquierdo RC	.40	.15
❑ 122 Orlando Hudson	.30	.10
❑ 123 Bill Hall	.40	.15
❑ 124 Jose Reyes	.60	.25
❑ 125 Juan Rivera	.30	.10
❑ 126 Eric Valent	.30	.10
❑ 127 Scotty Layfield RC	.40	.15
❑ 128 Austin Kearns	.30	.10
❑ 129 Nic Jackson RC	.40	.15
❑ 130 Chris Baker RC	.40	.15
❑ 131 Chad Qualls RC	.50	.20
❑ 132 Marcus Thames	.30	.10
❑ 133 Nathan Haynes	.30	.10
❑ 134 Brett Evert	.30	.10
❑ 135 Joe Borchard	.30	.10
❑ 136 Ryan Christianson	.30	.10
❑ 137 Josh Hamilton	.30	.10
❑ 138 Corey Patterson	.30	.10
❑ 139 Travis Wilson	.30	.10
❑ 140 Alex Escobar	.30	.10
❑ 141 Alexis Gomez	.30	.10
❑ 142 Nick Johnson	.40	.15
❑ 143 Kenny Kelly	.30	.10
❑ 144 Marlon Byrd	.30	.10
❑ 145 Kory DeHaan	.30	.10
❑ 146 Matt Belisle	.30	.10
❑ 147 Carlos Hernandez	.30	.10
❑ 148 Sean Burroughs	.30	.10
❑ 149 Angel Berroa	.30	.10
❑ 150 Aubrey Huff	.40	.15
❑ 151 Travis Hafner	.40	.15
❑ 152 Brandon Berger	.30	.10
❑ 153 David Krynzel	.30	.10
❑ 154 Ruben Salazar	.30	.10
❑ 155 J.R. House	.30	.10
❑ 156 Juan Silvestre	.30	.10
❑ 157 Dewon Brazelton	.30	.10
❑ 158 Jayson Werth	.30	.10
❑ 159 Larry Barnes	.30	.10
❑ 160 Elvis Pena	.30	.10
❑ 161 Ruben Gotay RC	.50	.20
❑ 162 Tommy Marx RC	.40	.15
❑ 163 John Suomi RC	.40	.15
❑ 164 Javier Colina	.30	.10
❑ 165 Greg Sain RC	.40	.15
❑ 166 Robert Cosby RC	.40	.15
❑ 167 Angel Pagan RC	.50	.20
❑ 168 Ralph Santana RC	.40	.15
❑ 169 Joe Orloski RC	.40	.15
❑ 170 Shayne Wright RC	.40	.15
❑ 171 Jay Caligiuri RC	.40	.15
❑ 172 Greg Montalbano RC	.40	.15
❑ 173 Rich Harden RC	3.00	1.25
❑ 174 Rich Thompson RC	.40	.15
❑ 175 Fred Bastardo RC	.40	.15
❑ 176 Alejandro Giron RC	.40	.15
❑ 177 Jesus Medrano RC	.40	.15
❑ 178 Kevin Deaton RC	.40	.15
❑ 179 Mike Rosamond RC	.40	.15
❑ 180 Jon Guzman RC	.40	.15
❑ 181 Gerard Oakes RC	.40	.15
❑ 182 Francisco Liriano RC	8.00	3.00
❑ 183 Matt Allegra RC	.40	.15
❑ 184 Mike Snyder RC	.40	.15
❑ 185 James Shanks RC	.40	.15
❑ 186 Anderson Hernandez RC	.40	.15
❑ 187 Dan Trumble RC	.40	.15
❑ 188 Luis DePaula RC	.40	.15
❑ 189 Randall Shelley RC	.40	.15
❑ 190 Richard Lane RC	.40	.15
❑ 191 Antwon Rollins RC	.40	.15
❑ 192 Ryan Bukvich RC	.40	.15
❑ 193 Derrick Lewis	.30	.10
❑ 194 Eric Miller RC	.40	.15
❑ 195 Justin Schuda RC	.40	.15
❑ 196 Brian West RC	.40	.15
❑ 197 Adam Roller RC	.40	.15
❑ 198 Neal Frendling RC	.40	.15
❑ 199 Jeremy Hill RC	.40	.15
❑ 200 James Barrett RC	.40	.15
❑ 201 Brett Kay RC	.40	.15
❑ 202 Ryan Mottl RC	.40	.15
❑ 203 Brad Nelson RC	.40	.15
❑ 204 Juan M. Gonzalez RC	.40	.15
❑ 205 Curtis Legendre RC	.40	.15
❑ 206 Ronald Acuna RC	.40	.15

❑ 207	Chris Flinn RC	.40	.15
❑ 208	Nick Alvarez RC	.40	.15
❑ 209	Jason Ellison RC	.75	.30
❑ 210	Blake McGinley RC	.40	.15
❑ 211	Dan Phillips RC	.40	.15
❑ 212	Demetrius Heath RC	.40	.15
❑ 213	Eric Bruntlett RC	.40	.15
❑ 214	Joe Jiannetti RC	.40	.15
❑ 215	Mike Hill RC	.40	.15
❑ 216	Ricardo Cordova RC	.40	.15
❑ 217	Mark Hamilton RC	.40	.15
❑ 218	David Mattox RC	.40	.15
❑ 219	Jose Morban RC	.40	.15
❑ 220	Scott Wiggins RC	.30	.10
❑ 221	Steve Green	.30	.10
❑ 222	Brian Rogers	.30	.10
❑ 223	Chin-Hui Tsao	.40	.15
❑ 224	Kenny Baugh	.30	.10
❑ 225	Nate Teut	.30	.10
❑ 226	Josh Wilson RC	.40	.15
❑ 227	Christian Parker	.30	.10
❑ 228	Tim Raines Jr.	.30	.10
❑ 229	Anastacio Martinez RC	.40	.15
❑ 230	Richard Lewis	.30	.10
❑ 231	Tim Kalita RC	.40	.15
❑ 232	Edwin Almonte RC	.40	.15
❑ 233	Hee-Seop Choi	.30	.10
❑ 234	Ty Howington	.30	.10
❑ 235	Victor Alvarez RC	.40	.15
❑ 236	Morgan Ensberg	.40	.15
❑ 237	Jeff Austin RC	.40	.15
❑ 238	Luis Terrero	.30	.10
❑ 239	Adam Wainwright	.30	.10
❑ 240	Clint Weibl RC	.30	.10
❑ 241	Eric Cyr	.30	.10
❑ 242	Marlyn Tisdale RC	.40	.15
❑ 243	John VanBenschoten	.30	.10
❑ 244	Ryan Raburn RC	.40	.15
❑ 245	Miguel Cabrera	1.50	.60
❑ 246	Jung Bong	.30	.10
❑ 247	Raul Chavez RC	.30	.10
❑ 248	Erik Bedard	.40	.15
❑ 249	Chris Snelling RC	.60	.25
❑ 250	Joe Rogers RC	.40	.15
❑ 251	Nate Field RC	.40	.15
❑ 252	Matt Herges RC	.30	.10
❑ 253	Matt Childers RC	.40	.15
❑ 254	Erick Almonte	.30	.10
❑ 255	Nick Neugebauer	.30	.10
❑ 256	Ron Calloway RC	.40	.15
❑ 257	Seung Song	.30	.10
❑ 258	Brandon Phillips	.30	.10
❑ 259	Cole Barthel RC	.30	.10
❑ 260	Jason Lane	.40	.15
❑ 261	Jae Seo	.30	.10
❑ 262	Randy Flores	.30	.10
❑ 263	Scott Chiasson	.30	.10
❑ 264	Chase Utley	2.50	1.00
❑ 265	Tony Alvarez	.30	.10
❑ 266	Ben Howard RC	.40	.15
❑ 267	Nelson Castro RC	.40	.15
❑ 268	Mark Lukasiewicz	.30	.10
❑ 269	Eric Glaser RC	.40	.15
❑ 270	Rob Henkel RC	.40	.15
❑ 271	Jose Valverde RC	.40	.15
❑ 272	Ricardo Rodriguez	.30	.10
❑ 273	Chris Smith	.30	.10
❑ 274	Mark Prior	.60	.25
❑ 275	Miguel Olivo	.30	.10
❑ 276	Ben Broussard	.30	.10
❑ 277	Zach Sorensen	.30	.10
❑ 278	Brian Mallette RC	.30	.10
❑ 279	Brad Wilkerson	.30	.10
❑ 280	Carl Crawford	.40	.15
❑ 281	Chone Figgins RC	1.50	.60
❑ 282	Jimmy Alvarez RC	.40	.15
❑ 283	Gavin Floyd RC	1.00	.40
❑ 284	Josh Bonifay RC	.40	.15
❑ 285	Garrett Guzman RC	.40	.15
❑ 286	Blake Williams	.30	.10
❑ 287	Matt Holliday	.30	.10
❑ 288	Ryan Madson	.30	.10
❑ 289	Luis Torres	.30	.10
❑ 290	Jeff Verplancke RC	.40	.15
❑ 291	Nate Espy RC	.40	.15
❑ 292	Jeff Lincoln RC	.40	.15
❑ 293	Ryan Snare RC	.40	.15
❑ 294	Jose Ortiz	.30	.10
❑ 295	Eric Munson	.30	.10
❑ 296	Denny Bautista	.30	.10
❑ 297	Willy Aybar	.40	.15
❑ 298	Kelly Johnson	.60	.25
❑ 299	Justin Morneau	.40	.15
❑ 300	Derrick Van Dusen	.30	.10
❑ 301	Chad Petty	.30	.10
❑ 302	Mike Restovich	.30	.10
❑ 303	Shawn Fagan	.30	.10
❑ 304	Yurendell DeCaster RC	.40	.15
❑ 305	Justin Wayne	.30	.10
❑ 306	Mike Peeples RC	.30	.10
❑ 307	Joel Guzman	1.00	.40
❑ 308	Ryan Vogelsong	.30	.10
❑ 309	Jorge Padilla RC	.40	.15
❑ 310	Grady Sizemore	1.00	.40
❑ 311	Joe Jester RC	.40	.15
❑ 312	Jim Journell	.30	.10
❑ 313	Bobby Seay	.30	.10
❑ 314	Ryan Church RC	1.00	.40
❑ 315	Grant Balfour	.30	.10
❑ 316	Mitch Jones	.30	.10
❑ 317	Travis Foley RC	.40	.15
❑ 318	Bobby Crosby	1.00	.40
❑ 319	Adrian Gonzalez	.30	.10
❑ 320	Ronnie Merrill	.30	.10
❑ 321	Joel Pineiro	.30	.10
❑ 322	John-Ford Griffin	.30	.10
❑ 323	Brian Forystek RC	.40	.15
❑ 324	Sean Douglass	.30	.10
❑ 325	Manny Delcarmen RC	.50	.20
❑ 326	Donnie Bridges	.30	.10
❑ 327	Jim Kavourias RC	.40	.15
❑ 328	Gabe Gross	.30	.10
❑ 329	Jon Rauch	.30	.10
❑ 330	Bill Ortega	.30	.10
❑ 331	Joey Hammond RC	.40	.15
❑ 332	Ramon Moreta RC	.40	.15
❑ 333	Ron Davenport	.30	.10
❑ 334	Brett Myers	.40	.15
❑ 335	Carlos Pena	.30	.10
❑ 336	Ezequiel Astacio RC	.40	.15
❑ 337	Edwin Yan RC	.40	.15
❑ 338	Josh Girdley	.30	.10
❑ 339	Shaun Boyd	.30	.10
❑ 340	Juan Rincon	.30	.10
❑ 341	Chris Duffy RC	.50	.20
❑ 342	Jason Kinchen	.30	.10
❑ 343	Brad Thomas	.30	.10
❑ 344	David Kelton	.30	.10
❑ 345	Rafael Soriano	.30	.10
❑ 346	Colin Young RC	.40	.15
❑ 347	Eric Byrnes	.30	.10
❑ 348	Chris Narveson RC	.50	.20
❑ 349	John Rheinecker	.30	.10
❑ 350	Mike Wilson RC	.40	.15
❑ 351	Justin Sherrod RC	.40	.15
❑ 352	Deivi Mendez	.30	.10
❑ 353	Wily Mo Pena	.40	.15
❑ 354	Brett Roneberg RC	.40	.15
❑ 355	Trey Lunsford RC	.40	.15
❑ 356	Jimmy Gobble RC	.40	.15
❑ 357	Brent Butler	.30	.10
❑ 358	Aaron Heilman	.30	.10
❑ 359	Wilkin Ruan	.30	.10
❑ 360	Brian Wolfe RC	.40	.15
❑ 361	Cody Ransom	.30	.10
❑ 362	Koyie Hill	.30	.10
❑ 363	Scott Cassidy	.30	.10
❑ 364	Tony Fontana RC	.40	.15
❑ 365	Mark Teixeira	1.50	.60
❑ 366	Doug Sessions RC	.40	.15
❑ 367	Victor Hall	.30	.10
❑ 368	Josh Cisneros RC	.40	.15
❑ 369	Kevin Mench	.30	.10
❑ 370	Tike Redman	.30	.10
❑ 371	Jeff Heaverlo	.30	.10
❑ 372	Carlos Brackley RC	.40	.15
❑ 373	Brad Hawpe	.30	.10
❑ 374	Jesus Colome	.30	.10
❑ 375	David Espinosa	.30	.10
❑ 376	Jesse Foppert RC	.50	.20
❑ 377	Ross Peeples RC	.40	.15
❑ 378	Alex Requena RC	.40	.15
❑ 379	Joe Mauer RC	12.00	5.00
❑ 380	Carlos Silva	.30	.10
❑ 381	David Wright RC	30.00	12.50
❑ 382	Craig Kuzmic RC	.40	.15
❑ 383	Pete Zamora RC	.40	.15
❑ 384	Matt Parker RC	.40	.15
❑ 385	Keith Ginter	.30	.10
❑ 386	Gary Cates Jr. RC	.40	.15
❑ 387	Justin Reid RC	.40	.15
❑ 388	Jake Mauer RC	.40	.15
❑ 389	Dennis Tankersley	.30	.10
❑ 390	Josh Barfield RC	2.50	1.00
❑ 391	Luis Maza	.30	.10
❑ 392	Henry Pichardo RC	.40	.15
❑ 393	Michael Floyd RC	.40	.15
❑ 394	Clint Nageotte RC	.50	.20
❑ 395	Raymond Cabrera RC	.40	.15
❑ 396	Mauricio Lara RC	.40	.15
❑ 397	Alejandro Cadena RC	.40	.15
❑ 398	Jonny Gomes RC	2.50	1.00
❑ 399	Jason Bulger RC	.40	.15
❑ 400	Bobby Jenks RC	1.50	.60
❑ 401	David Gil RC	.40	.15
❑ 402	Joel Crump RC	.40	.15
❑ 403	Kazuhisa Ishii RC	.75	.30
❑ 404	So Taguchi RC	.75	.30
❑ 405	Ryan Doumit RC	.60	.25
❑ 406	Macay McBride	.40	.15
❑ 407	Brandon Claussen	.30	.10
❑ 408	Chin-Feng Chen	.40	.15
❑ 409	Josh Phelps	.30	.10
❑ 410	Freddie Money RC	.50	.20
❑ 411	Cliff Bartosh RC	.40	.15
❑ 412	Josh Pearce	.30	.10
❑ 413	Lyle Overbay	.30	.10
❑ 414	Ryan Anderson	.30	.10
❑ 415	Terrance Hill RC	.40	.15
❑ 416	John Rodriguez RC	.50	.20
❑ 417	Richard Stahl	.30	.10
❑ 418	Brian Specht	.30	.10
❑ 419	Chris Latham RC	.30	.10
❑ 420	Carlos Cabrera RC	.40	.15
❑ 421	Jose Bautista RC	1.00	.40
❑ 422	Kevin Frederick RC	.40	.15
❑ 423	Jerome Williams	.30	.10
❑ 424	Napoleon Calzado RC	.40	.15
❑ 425	Benito Baez	.30	.10
❑ 426	Xavier Nady	.30	.10
❑ 427	Jason Botts RC	.60	.25
❑ 428	Steve Bechler RC	.40	.15
❑ 429	Reed Johnson RC	1.00	.40
❑ 430	Mark Outlaw RC	.40	.15
❑ 431	Billy Sylvester	.30	.10
❑ 432	Luke Lockwood	.30	.10
❑ 433	Jake Peavy	.60	.25
❑ 434	Alfredo Amezaga	.30	.10
❑ 435	Aaron Cook RC	.40	.15
❑ 436	Josh Shaffer RC	.40	.15
❑ 437	Dan Wright	.30	.10
❑ 438	Ryan Gripp RC	.40	.15
❑ 439	Alex Herrera	.30	.10
❑ 440	Jason Bay RC	5.00	2.00

2002 Bowman Draft

❑	COMPLETE SET (165)	50.00	25.00
❑ BDP1	Clint Everts RC	.50	.20
❑ BDP2	Fred Lewis RC	.40	.15
❑ BDP3	Jon Broxton RC	1.00	.40

❑ BDP4 Jason Anderson RC	.40	.15
❑ BDP5 Mike Eusebio RC	.40	.15
❑ BDP6 Zack Greinke RC	4.00	1.50
❑ BDP7 Joe Blanton RC	2.00	.75
❑ BDP8 Sergio Santos RC	.50	.20
❑ BDP9 Jason Cooper RC	.40	.15
❑ BDP10 Delwyn Young RC	1.00	.40
❑ BDP11 Jeremy Hermida RC	5.00	2.00
❑ BDP12 Dan Ortmeier RC	.50	.20
❑ BDP13 Kevin Jepsen RC	.50	.20
❑ BDP14 Russ Adams RC	.50	.20
❑ BDP15 Mike Nixon RC	.40	.15
❑ BDP16 Nick Swisher RC	5.00	2.00
❑ BDP17 Cole Hamels RC	15.00	6.00
❑ BDP18 Brian Dopirak RC	1.00	.40
❑ BDP19 James Loney RC	6.00	2.50
❑ BDP20 Denard Span RC	.50	.20
❑ BDP21 Billy Petrick RC	.40	.15
❑ BDP22 Jared Doyle RC	.40	.15
❑ BDP23 Jeff Francoeur RC	15.00	6.00
❑ BDP24 Nick Bourgeois RC	.40	.15
❑ BDP25 Matt Cain RC	6.00	2.50
❑ BDP26 John McCurdy RC	.40	.15
❑ BDP27 Mark Kiger RC	.40	.15
❑ BDP28 Bill Murphy RC	.40	.15
❑ BDP29 Matt Craig RC	.50	.20
❑ BDP30 Mike Megrew RC	.40	.15
❑ BDP31 Ben Crockett RC	.40	.15
❑ BDP32 Luke Hagerty RC	.40	.15
❑ BDP33 Matt Whitney RC	.40	.15
❑ BDP34 Dan Meyer RC	.50	.20
❑ BDP35 Jeremy Brown RC	.40	.15
❑ BDP36 Doug Johnson RC	.40	.15
❑ BDP37 Steve Obenchain RC	.40	.15
❑ BDP38 Matt Clanton RC	.40	.15
❑ BDP39 Mark Teahen RC	1.00	.40
❑ BDP40 Tom Carrow RC	.40	.15
❑ BDP41 Micah Schilling RC	.40	.15
❑ BDP42 Blair Johnson RC	.40	.15
❑ BDP43 Jason Pridie RC	.40	.15
❑ BDP44 Joey Votto RC	3.00	1.25
❑ BDP45 Taber Lee RC	.40	.15
❑ BDP46 Adam Peterson RC	.40	.15
❑ BDP47 Adam Donachie RC	.40	.15
❑ BDP48 Josh Murray RC	.40	.15
❑ BDP49 Brent Clevlen RC	2.00	.75
❑ BDP50 Chad Pleiness RC	.40	.15
❑ BDP51 Zach Hammes RC	.40	.15
❑ BDP52 Chris Snyder RC	.50	.20
❑ BDP53 Chris Smith RC	.40	.15
❑ BDP54 Justin Maureau RC	.40	.15
❑ BDP55 David Bush RC	1.00	.40
❑ BDP56 Tim Gilhooly RC	.40	.15
❑ BDP57 Blair Barbier RC	.40	.15
❑ BDP58 Zach Segovia RC	.40	.15
❑ BDP59 Jeremy Reed RC	1.00	.40
❑ BDP60 Matt Pender RC	.40	.15
❑ BDP61 Eric Thomas RC	.40	.15
❑ BDP62 Justin Jones RC	.50	.20
❑ BDP63 Brian Slocum RC	.40	.15
❑ BDP64 Larry Broadway RC	.40	.15
❑ BDP65 Bo Flowers RC	.40	.15
❑ BDP66 Scott White RC	.40	.15
❑ BDP67 Steve Stanley RC	.40	.15
❑ BDP68 Alex Merricks RC	.40	.15
❑ BDP69 Josh Womack RC	.40	.15
❑ BDP70 Dave Jensen RC	.40	.15
❑ BDP71 Curtis Granderson RC	5.00	2.00
❑ BDP72 Pat Osborn RC	.40	.15
❑ BDP73 Nic Carter RC	.40	.15
❑ BDP74 Mitch Talbot RC	.40	.15
❑ BDP75 Don Murphy RC	.40	.15
❑ BDP76 Val Majewski RC	.40	.15
❑ BDP77 Javy Rodriguez RC	.40	.15
❑ BDP78 Fernando Pacheco RC	.40	.15
❑ BDP79 Steve Russell RC	.40	.15
❑ BDP80 Jon Slack RC	.40	.15
❑ BDP81 John Baker RC	.40	.15
❑ BDP82 Aaron Coonrod RC	.40	.15
❑ BDP83 Josh Johnson RC	5.00	2.00
❑ BDP84 Jake Blalock RC	.50	2.00
❑ BDP85 Alex Hart RC	.40	.15
❑ BDP86 Wes Bankston RC	2.00	.75
❑ BDP87 Josh Rupe RC	.40	.15
❑ BDP88 Dan Cevette RC	.40	.15
❑ BDP89 Kiel Fisher RC	.50	.20
❑ BDP90 Alan Rick RC	.40	.15
❑ BDP91 Charlie Morton RC	.40	.15
❑ BDP92 Chad Spann RC	.40	.15
❑ BDP93 Kyle Boyer RC	.40	.15
❑ BDP94 Bob Malek RC	.40	.15
❑ BDP95 Ryan Rodriguez RC	.40	.15
❑ BDP96 Jordan Renz RC	.40	.15
❑ BDP97 Randy Frye RC	.40	.15
❑ BDP98 Rich Hill RC	5.00	2.00
❑ BDP99 B.J. Upton RC	5.00	2.00
❑ BDP100 Dan Christensen RC	.40	.15
❑ BDP101 Casey Kotchman RC	1.00	.40
❑ BDP102 Eric Good RC	.30	.10
❑ BDP103 Mike Fontenot RC	.40	.15
❑ BDP104 John Webb RC	.40	.15
❑ BDP105 Jason Dubois RC	.50	.20
❑ BDP106 Ryan Kibler RC	.40	.15
❑ BDP107 Jhonny Peralta RC	2.50	1.00
❑ BDP108 Kirk Saarloos RC	.40	.15
❑ BDP109 Rhett Parrott RC	.40	.15
❑ BDP110 Jason Grove RC	.40	.15
❑ BDP111 Colt Griffin RC	.40	.15
❑ BDP112 Dallas McPherson RC	1.00	.40
❑ BDP113 Oliver Perez RC	1.00	.40
❑ BDP114 Marshall McDougall RC	.40	.15
❑ BDP115 Mike Wood RC	.40	.15
❑ BDP116 Scott Hairston RC	.50	.20
❑ BDP117 Jason Simontacchi RC	.40	.15
❑ BDP118 Taggert Bozied RC	.50	.20
❑ BDP119 Shelley Duncan RC	3.00	1.25
❑ BDP120 Dontrelle Willis RC	5.00	2.00
❑ BDP121 Sean Burnett	.30	.10
❑ BDP122 Aaron Cook	.30	.10
❑ BDP123 Brett Evert	.30	.10
❑ BDP124 Jimmy Journell	.30	.10
❑ BDP125 Brett Myers	.30	.10
❑ BDP126 Brad Baker	.30	.10
❑ BDP127 Billy Traber RC	.40	.15
❑ BDP128 Adam Wainwright	.30	.10
❑ BDP129 Jason Young RC	.30	.10
❑ BDP130 John Buck	.30	.10
❑ BDP131 Kevin Cash RC	.40	.15
❑ BDP132 Jason Stokes RC	.50	.20
❑ BDP133 Drew Henson	.30	.10
❑ BDP134 Chad Tracy RC	1.00	.40
❑ BDP135 Orlando Hudson	.30	.10
❑ BDP136 Brandon Phillips	.30	.10
❑ BDP137 Joe Borchard	.30	.10
❑ BDP138 Marlon Byrd	.30	.10
❑ BDP139 Carl Crawford	.30	.10
❑ BDP140 Michael Restovich	.30	.10
❑ BDP141 Corey Hart RC	1.50	.60
❑ BDP142 Edwin Almonte	.30	.10
❑ BDP143 Francis Beltran RC	.40	.15
❑ BDP144 Jorge De La Rosa RC	.40	.15
❑ BDP145 Gerardo Garcia RC	.40	.15
❑ BDP146 Franklyn German RC	.40	.15
❑ BDP147 Francisco Liriano	3.00	1.25
❑ BDP148 Francisco Rodriguez	.30	.10
❑ BDP149 Ricardo Rodriguez	.30	.10
❑ BDP150 Seung Song	.30	.10
❑ BDP151 John Stephens	.30	.10
❑ BDP152 Justin Huber RC	.75	.30
❑ BDP153 Victor Martinez	.75	.30
❑ BDP154 Hee Seop Choi	.30	.10
❑ BDP155 Justin Morneau	.30	.10
❑ BDP156 Miguel Cabrera	1.25	.50
❑ BDP157 Victor Diaz RC	.75	.30
❑ BDP158 Jose Reyes	.50	.20
❑ BDP159 Omar Infante	.30	.10
❑ BDP160 Angel Berroa	.30	.10
❑ BDP161 Tony Alvarez	.30	.10
❑ BDP162 Shin Soo Choo RC	.75	.30
❑ BDP163 Wily Mo Pena	.30	.10
❑ BDP164 Andres Torres	.30	.10
❑ BDP165 Jose Lopez RC	2.00	.75

2003 Bowman

❑ COMPLETE SET (330)	60.00	25.00
❑ COMMON CARD (1-155)	.30	.10
❑ COMMON CARD (156-330)	.30	.10
❑ 1 Garret Anderson	.30	.10
❑ 2 Derek Jeter	2.00	.75
❑ 3 Gary Sheffield	.30	.10
❑ 4 Matt Morris	.30	.10
❑ 5 Derek Lowe	.30	.10
❑ 6 Andy Van Hekken	.30	.10
❑ 7 Sammy Sosa	.75	.30
❑ 8 Ken Griffey Jr.	1.25	.50
❑ 9 Omar Vizquel	.50	.20
❑ 10 Jorge Posada	.50	.20
❑ 11 Lance Berkman	.30	.10
❑ 12 Mike Sweeney	.30	.10
❑ 13 Adrian Beltre	.30	.10
❑ 14 Richie Sexson	.30	.10
❑ 15 A.J. Pierzynski	.30	.10
❑ 16 Bartolo Colon	.30	.10
❑ 17 Mike Mussina	.50	.20
❑ 18 Paul Byrd	.30	.10
❑ 19 Bobby Abreu	.30	.10
❑ 20 Miguel Tejada	.30	.10
❑ 21 Aramis Ramirez	.30	.10
❑ 22 Edgardo Alfonzo	.30	.10
❑ 23 Edgar Martinez	.50	.20
❑ 24 Albert Pujols	1.50	.60
❑ 25 Carl Crawford	.30	.10
❑ 26 Eric Hinske	.30	.10
❑ 27 Tim Salmon	.50	.20
❑ 28 Luis Gonzalez	.30	.10
❑ 29 Jay Gibbons	.30	.10
❑ 30 John Smoltz	.50	.20
❑ 31 Tim Wakefield	.30	.10
❑ 32 Mark Prior	.50	.20
❑ 33 Magglio Ordonez	.30	.10
❑ 34 Adam Dunn	.30	.10
❑ 35 Larry Walker	.30	.10
❑ 36 Luis Castillo	.30	.10
❑ 37 Wade Miller	.30	.10
❑ 38 Carlos Beltran	.30	.10
❑ 39 Odalis Perez	.30	.10
❑ 40 Alex Sanchez	.30	.10
❑ 41 Torii Hunter	.30	.10
❑ 42 Cliff Floyd	.30	.10
❑ 43 Andy Pettitte	.50	.20
❑ 44 Francisco Rodriguez	.30	.10
❑ 45 Eric Chavez	.30	.10
❑ 46 Kevin Millwood	.30	.10
❑ 47 Dennis Tankersley	.30	.10
❑ 48 Hideo Nomo	.75	.30
❑ 49 Freddy Garcia	.30	.10
❑ 50 Randy Johnson	.75	.30
❑ 51 Aubrey Huff	.30	.10
❑ 52 Carlos Delgado	.30	.10
❑ 53 Troy Glaus	.30	.10
❑ 54 Junior Spivey	.30	.10
❑ 55 Mike Hampton	.30	.10
❑ 56 Sidney Ponson	.30	.10
❑ 57 Aaron Boone	.30	.10
❑ 58 Kerry Wood	.30	.10
❑ 59 Runelvys Hernandez	.30	.10
❑ 60 Nomar Garciaparra	1.25	.50
❑ 61 Todd Helton	.50	.20
❑ 62 Mike Lowell	.30	.10
❑ 63 Roy Oswalt	.30	.10
❑ 64 Raul Ibanez	.30	.10
❑ 65 Brian Jordan	.30	.10
❑ 66 Geoff Jenkins	.30	.10
❑ 67 Jermaine Dye	.30	.10
❑ 68 Tom Glavine	.50	.20
❑ 69 Bernie Williams	.50	.20
❑ 70 Vladimir Guerrero	.75	.30
❑ 71 Mark Mulder	.30	.10
❑ 72 Jimmy Rollins	.30	.10

- ❑ 73 Oliver Perez .30 .10
- ❑ 74 Rich Aurilia .30 .10
- ❑ 75 Joel Pineiro .30 .10
- ❑ 76 J.D. Drew .30 .10
- ❑ 77 Ivan Rodriguez .50 .20
- ❑ 78 Josh Phelps .30 .10
- ❑ 79 Darin Erstad .30 .10
- ❑ 80 Curt Schilling .30 .10
- ❑ 81 Paul Lo Duca .30 .10
- ❑ 82 Marty Cordova .30 .10
- ❑ 83 Manny Ramirez .50 .20
- ❑ 84 Bobby Hill .30 .10
- ❑ 85 Paul Konerko .30 .10
- ❑ 86 Austin Kearns .30 .10
- ❑ 87 Jason Jennings .30 .10
- ❑ 88 Brad Penny .30 .10
- ❑ 89 Jeff Bagwell .50 .20
- ❑ 90 Shawn Green .30 .10
- ❑ 91 Jason Schmidt .30 .10
- ❑ 92 Doug Mientkiewicz .30 .10
- ❑ 93 Jose Vidro .30 .10
- ❑ 94 Bret Boone .30 .10
- ❑ 95 Jason Giambi .30 .10
- ❑ 96 Barry Zito .30 .10
- ❑ 97 Roy Halladay .30 .10
- ❑ 98 Pat Burrell .30 .10
- ❑ 99 Sean Burroughs .30 .10
- ❑ 100 Barry Bonds 2.00 .75
- ❑ 101 Kazuhiro Sasaki .30 .10
- ❑ 102 Fernando Vina .30 .10
- ❑ 103 Chan Ho Park .30 .10
- ❑ 104 Andruw Jones .50 .20
- ❑ 105 Adam Kennedy .30 .10
- ❑ 106 Shea Hillenbrand .30 .10
- ❑ 107 Greg Maddux 1.25 .50
- ❑ 108 Jim Edmonds .30 .10
- ❑ 109 Pedro Martinez .50 .20
- ❑ 110 Moises Alou .30 .10
- ❑ 111 Jeff Weaver .30 .10
- ❑ 112 C.C. Sabathia .30 .10
- ❑ 113 Robert Fick .30 .10
- ❑ 114 A.J. Burnett .30 .10
- ❑ 115 Jeff Kent .30 .10
- ❑ 116 Kevin Brown .30 .10
- ❑ 117 Rafael Furcal .30 .10
- ❑ 118 Cristian Guzman .30 .10
- ❑ 119 Brad Wilkerson .30 .10
- ❑ 120 Mike Piazza 1.25 .50
- ❑ 121 Alfonso Soriano .30 .10
- ❑ 122 Mark Ellis .30 .10
- ❑ 123 Vicente Padilla .30 .10
- ❑ 124 Eric Gagne .30 .10
- ❑ 125 Ryan Klesko .30 .10
- ❑ 126 Ichiro Suzuki 1.50 .60
- ❑ 127 Tony Batista .30 .10
- ❑ 128 Roberto Alomar .50 .20
- ❑ 129 Alex Rodriguez 1.25 .50
- ❑ 130 Jim Thome .50 .20
- ❑ 131 Jarrod Washburn .30 .10
- ❑ 132 Orlando Hudson .30 .10
- ❑ 133 Chipper Jones .75 .30
- ❑ 134 Rodrigo Lopez .30 .10
- ❑ 135 Johnny Damon .50 .20
- ❑ 136 Matt Clement .30 .10
- ❑ 137 Frank Thomas .75 .30
- ❑ 138 Ellis Burks .30 .10
- ❑ 139 Carlos Pena .30 .10
- ❑ 140 Josh Beckett .30 .10
- ❑ 141 Joe Randa .30 .10
- ❑ 142 Brian Giles .30 .10
- ❑ 143 Kazuhisa Ishii .30 .10
- ❑ 144 Corey Koskie .30 .10
- ❑ 145 Orlando Cabrera .30 .10
- ❑ 146 Mark Buehrle .30 .10
- ❑ 147 Roger Clemens 1.50 .60
- ❑ 148 Tim Hudson .30 .10
- ❑ 149 Randy Wolf .30 .10
- ❑ 150 Josh Fogg .30 .10
- ❑ 151 Phil Nevin .30 .10
- ❑ 152 John Olerud .30 .10
- ❑ 153 Scott Rolen .50 .20
- ❑ 154 Joe Kennedy .30 .10
- ❑ 155 Rafael Palmeiro .50 .20
- ❑ 156 Chad Hutchinson .30 .10
- ❑ 157 Quincy Carter XRC .40 .15
- ❑ 158 Hee Seop Choi .30 .10
- ❑ 159 Joe Borchard .30 .10
- ❑ 160 Brandon Phillips .30 .10
- ❑ 161 Wily Mo Pena .30 .10
- ❑ 162 Victor Martinez .50 .20
- ❑ 163 Jason Stokes .30 .10
- ❑ 164 Ken Harvey .30 .10
- ❑ 165 Juan Rivera .30 .10
- ❑ 166 Jose Contreras RC 1.50 .60
- ❑ 167 Dan Haren RC 1.00 .40
- ❑ 168 Michel Hernandez RC .40 .15
- ❑ 169 Eider Torres RC .40 .15
- ❑ 170 Chris De La Cruz RC .40 .15
- ❑ 171 Ramon Nivar-Martinez RC .40 .15
- ❑ 172 Mike Adams RC .40 .15
- ❑ 173 Justin Arneson RC .40 .15
- ❑ 174 Jamie Athas RC .40 .15
- ❑ 175 Dwaine Bacon RC .40 .15
- ❑ 176 Clint Barmes RC 1.00 .40
- ❑ 177 B.J. Barns RC .40 .15
- ❑ 178 Tyler Johnson RC .40 .15
- ❑ 179 Bobby Basham RC .40 .15
- ❑ 180 T.J. Bohn RC .40 .15
- ❑ 181 J.D. Durbin RC .40 .15
- ❑ 182 Brandon Bowe RC .40 .15
- ❑ 183 Craig Brazell RC .40 .15
- ❑ 184 Dusty Brown RC .40 .15
- ❑ 185 Brian Bruney RC .50 .20
- ❑ 186 Greg Bruso RC .40 .15
- ❑ 187 Jaime Bubela RC .40 .15
- ❑ 188 Bryan Bullington RC .40 .15
- ❑ 189 Brian Burgamy RC .40 .15
- ❑ 190 Eny Cabreja RC 1.25 .50
- ❑ 191 Daniel Cabrera RC .75 .30
- ❑ 192 Ryan Cameron RC .40 .15
- ❑ 193 Lance Caracciolí RC .40 .15
- ❑ 194 David Cash RC .40 .15
- ❑ 195 Bernie Castro RC .40 .15
- ❑ 196 Ismael Castro RC .50 .20
- ❑ 197 Daryl Clark RC .40 .15
- ❑ 198 Jeff Clark RC .40 .15
- ❑ 199 Chris Colton RC .40 .15
- ❑ 200 Dexter Cooper RC .40 .15
- ❑ 201 Callix Crabbe RC .50 .20
- ❑ 202 Chien-Ming Wang RC 6.00 2.50
- ❑ 203 Eric Crozier RC .50 .20
- ❑ 204 Nook Logan RC .50 .20
- ❑ 205 David DeJesus RC .75 .30
- ❑ 206 Matt DeMarco RC .40 .15
- ❑ 207 Chris Duncan RC 4.00 1.50
- ❑ 208 Eric Eckenstahler .30 .10
- ❑ 209 Willie Eyre RC .40 .15
- ❑ 210 Evel Bastida-Martinez RC .40 .15
- ❑ 211 Chris Fallon RC .40 .15
- ❑ 212 Mike Flannery RC .40 .15
- ❑ 213 Mike Oâ ™Keefe RC .40 .15
- ❑ 214 Ben Francisco RC .40 .15
- ❑ 215 Kason Gabbard RC .40 .15
- ❑ 216 Mike Gallo RC .40 .15
- ❑ 217 Jairo Garcia RC .50 .20
- ❑ 218 Angel Garcia RC .50 .20
- ❑ 219 Michael Garciaparra RC .30 .10
- ❑ 220 Joey Gomes RC .40 .15
- ❑ 221 Dusty Gomon RC .50 .20
- ❑ 222 Bryan Grace RC .40 .15
- ❑ 223 Tyson Graham RC .40 .15
- ❑ 224 Henry Guerrero RC .40 .15
- ❑ 225 Franklin Gutierrez RC 1.00 .40
- ❑ 226 Carlos Guzman RC .50 .20
- ❑ 227 Matthew Hagen RC .40 .15
- ❑ 228 Josh Hall RC .40 .15
- ❑ 229 Rob Hammock RC .40 .15
- ❑ 230 Brendan Harris RC .50 .20
- ❑ 231 Gary Harris RC .40 .15
- ❑ 232 Clay Hensley RC .40 .15
- ❑ 233 Michael Hinckley RC .50 .20
- ❑ 234 Luis Hodge RC .40 .15
- ❑ 235 Donnie Hood RC .50 .20
- ❑ 236 Travis Ishikawa RC 1.00 .40
- ❑ 237 Edwin Jackson RC .50 .20
- ❑ 238 Ardley Jansen RC .50 .20
- ❑ 239 Ferenc Jongejan RC .40 .15
- ❑ 240 Matt Kata RC .40 .15
- ❑ 241 Kazuhiro Takeoka RC .40 .15
- ❑ 242 Beau Kemp RC .40 .15
- ❑ 243 Il Kim RC .40 .15
- ❑ 244 Brennan King RC .40 .15
- ❑ 245 Chris Kroski RC .40 .15
- ❑ 246 Jason Kubel RC 2.00 .75
- ❑ 247 Pete LaForest RC .40 .15
- ❑ 248 Wil Ledezma RC .40 .15
- ❑ 249 Jeremy Bonderman RC 3.00 1.25
- ❑ 250 Gonzalo Lopez RC .40 .15
- ❑ 251 Brian Luderer RC .40 .15
- ❑ 252 Ruddy Lugo RC .40 .15
- ❑ 253 Wayne Lydon RC .40 .15
- ❑ 254 Mark Malaska RC .40 .15
- ❑ 255 Andy Marte RC 3.00 1.25
- ❑ 256 Tyler Martin RC .40 .15
- ❑ 257 Branden Florence RC .40 .15
- ❑ 258 Aneudis Mateo RC .40 .15
- ❑ 259 Derell McCall RC .40 .15
- ❑ 260 Brian McCann RC 8.00 3.00
- ❑ 261 Mike McNutt RC .40 .15
- ❑ 262 Jacabo Meque RC .40 .15
- ❑ 263 Derek Michaelis RC .40 .15
- ❑ 264 Aaron Miles RC .50 .20
- ❑ 265 Jose Morales RC .40 .15
- ❑ 266 Dustin Moseley RC .40 .15
- ❑ 267 Adrian Myers RC .40 .15
- ❑ 268 Dan Neil RC .40 .15
- ❑ 269 Jon Nelson RC .50 .20
- ❑ 270 Mike Neu RC .40 .15
- ❑ 271 Leigh Neuage RC .40 .15
- ❑ 272 Wes O'Brien RC .40 .15
- ❑ 273 Trent Oeltjen RC .50 .20
- ❑ 274 Tim Olson RC .40 .15
- ❑ 275 David Pahucki RC .40 .15
- ❑ 276 Nathan Panther RC .40 .15
- ❑ 277 Arnie Munoz RC .40 .15
- ❑ 278 Dave Pember RC .40 .15
- ❑ 279 Jason Perry RC .50 .20
- ❑ 280 Matthew Peterson RC .40 .15
- ❑ 281 Ryan Shealy RC 2.50 1.00
- ❑ 282 Jorge Piedra RC .50 .20
- ❑ 283 Simon Pond RC .40 .15
- ❑ 284 Aaron Rakers RC .40 .15
- ❑ 285 Hanley Ramirez RC 5.00 2.00
- ❑ 286 Manuel Ramirez RC .50 .20
- ❑ 287 Kevin Randel RC .40 .15
- ❑ 288 Darrell Rasner RC .40 .15
- ❑ 289 Prentice Redman RC .40 .15
- ❑ 290 Eric Reed RC .40 .15
- ❑ 291 Wilton Reynolds RC .50 .20
- ❑ 292 Eric Riggs RC .50 .20
- ❑ 293 Carlos Rijo RC .40 .15
- ❑ 294 Rajai Davis RC .40 .15
- ❑ 295 Aron Weston RC .40 .15
- ❑ 296 Arturo Rivas RC .40 .15
- ❑ 297 Kyle Roat RC .40 .15
- ❑ 298 Bubba Nelson RC .50 .20
- ❑ 299 Levi Robinson RC .40 .15
- ❑ 300 Ray Sadler RC .40 .15
- ❑ 301 Gary Schneidmiller RC .40 .15
- ❑ 302 Jon Schuerholz RC .40 .15
- ❑ 303 Corey Shafer RC .40 .15
- ❑ 304 Brian Shackelford RC .40 .15
- ❑ 305 Bill Simon RC .40 .15
- ❑ 306 Haj Turay RC .30 .10
- ❑ 307 Sean Smith RC .50 .20
- ❑ 308 Ryan Spataro RC .40 .15
- ❑ 309 Jemel Spearman RC .40 .15
- ❑ 310 Keith Stamler RC .40 .15
- ❑ 311 Luke Steidlmayer RC .40 .15
- ❑ 312 Adam Stern RC .30 .10
- ❑ 313 Jay Sitzman RC .40 .15
- ❑ 314 Thomari Story-Harden RC .50 .20
- ❑ 315 Terry Tiffee RC .40 .15
- ❑ 316 Nick Trzesniak RC .40 .15
- ❑ 317 Denny Tussen RC .40 .15
- ❑ 318 Scott Tyler RC .50 .20
- ❑ 319 Shane Victorino RC .75 .30
- ❑ 320 Doug Waechter RC .50 .20
- ❑ 321 Brandon Watson RC .40 .15
- ❑ 322 Todd Wellemeyer RC .40 .15
- ❑ 323 Eli Whiteside RC .40 .15
- ❑ 324 Josh Willingham RC 1.00 .40
- ❑ 325 Travis Wong RC .50 .20
- ❑ 326 Brian Wright RC .40 .15
- ❑ 327 Kevin Youkilis RC 3.00 1.25
- ❑ 328 Andy Sisco RC .30 .10
- ❑ 329 Dustin Yount RC .50 .20

❑ 330 Andrew Dominique RC	.40	.15
❑ NNO Hinske/Jennings ROY Relic	15.00	6.00

2003 Bowman Draft

❑ COMPLETE SET (165)	50.00	20.00
❑ 1 Dontrelle Willis	.75	.30
❑ 2 Freddy Sanchez	.30	.10
❑ 3 Miguel Cabrera	.75	.30
❑ 4 Ryan Ludwick	.30	.10
❑ 5 Ty Wigginton	.30	.10
❑ 6 Mark Teixeira	.50	.20
❑ 7 Trey Hodges	.30	.10
❑ 8 Laynce Nix	.30	.10
❑ 9 Antonio Perez	.30	.10
❑ 10 Jody Gerut	.30	.10
❑ 11 Jae Weong Seo	.30	.10
❑ 12 Erick Almonte	.30	.10
❑ 13 Lyle Overbay	.30	.10
❑ 14 Billy Traber	.30	.10
❑ 15 Andres Torres	.30	.10
❑ 16 Jose Valverde	.30	.10
❑ 17 Aaron Heilman	.30	.10
❑ 18 Brandon Larson	.30	.10
❑ 19 Jung Bong	.30	.10
❑ 20 Jesse Foppert	.30	.10
❑ 21 Angel Berroa	.30	.10
❑ 22 Jeff DaVanon	.30	.10
❑ 23 Kurt Ainsworth	.30	.10
❑ 24 Brandon Claussen	.30	.10
❑ 25 Xavier Nady	.30	.10
❑ 26 Travis Hafner	.30	.10
❑ 27 Jerome Williams	.30	.10
❑ 28 Jose Reyes	.30	.10
❑ 29 Sergio Mitre RC	.50	.20
❑ 30 Bo Hart RC	.40	.15
❑ 31 Adam Miller RC	2.50	1.00
❑ 32 Brian Finch RC	.40	.15
❑ 33 Taylor Mattingly RC	.50	.20
❑ 34 Daric Barton RC	2.50	1.00
❑ 35 Chris Ray RC	1.00	.40
❑ 36 Jarrod Saltalamacchia RC	8.00	3.00
❑ 37 Dennis Dove RC	.50	.20
❑ 38 James Houser RC	.50	.20
❑ 39 Clint King RC	.50	.20
❑ 40 Lou Palmisano RC	.50	.20
❑ 41 Dan Moore RC	.40	.15
❑ 42 Craig Stansberry RC	.50	.20
❑ 43 Jo Jo Reyes RC	1.25	.50
❑ 44 Jake Stevens RC	.50	.20
❑ 45 Tom Gorzelanny RC	1.25	.50
❑ 46 Brian Marshall RC	.40	.15
❑ 47 Scott Beerer RC	.40	.15
❑ 48 Javi Herrera RC	.50	.20
❑ 49 Steve LeRud RC	.50	.20
❑ 50 Josh Banks RC	.75	.30
❑ 51 Jon Papelbon RC	12.00	5.00
❑ 52 Juan Valdes RC	.50	.20
❑ 53 Beau Vaughan RC	.50	.20
❑ 54 Matt Chico RC	.50	.20
❑ 55 Todd Jennings RC	.50	.20
❑ 56 Anthony Gwynn RC	1.25	.50
❑ 57 Matt Harrison RC	.75	.30
❑ 58 Aaron Marsden RC	.50	.20
❑ 59 Casey Abrams RC	.40	.15
❑ 60 Cory Stuart RC	.40	.15
❑ 61 Mike Wagner RC	.40	.15
❑ 62 Jordan Pratt RC	.50	.20
❑ 63 Andre Randolph RC	.50	.20
❑ 64 Blake Balkcom RC	.50	.20
❑ 65 Josh Muecke RC	.40	.15
❑ 66 Jamie D'Antona RC	.75	.30
❑ 67 Cole Seifrig RC	.40	.15
❑ 68 Josh Anderson RC	.50	.20
❑ 69 Matt Lorenzo RC	.50	.20
❑ 70 Nate Spears RC	.50	.20
❑ 71 Chris Goodman RC	.40	.15
❑ 72 Brian McFall RC	.40	.15
❑ 73 Billy Hogan RC	.50	.20
❑ 74 Jamie Romak RC	.50	.20
❑ 75 Jeff Cook RC	.50	.20
❑ 76 Brooks McNiven RC	.40	.15
❑ 77 Xavier Paul RC	.50	.20
❑ 78 Bob Zimmerman RC	.40	.15
❑ 79 Mickey Hall RC	.50	.20
❑ 80 Shaun Marcum RC	.50	.20
❑ 81 Matt Nachreiner RC	.50	.20
❑ 82 Chris Kinsey RC	.40	.15
❑ 83 Jonathan Fulton RC	.50	.20
❑ 84 Edgardo Baez RC	.50	.20
❑ 85 Robert Valido RC	.50	.20
❑ 86 Kenny Lewis RC	.50	.20
❑ 87 Trent Peterson RC	.40	.15
❑ 88 Johnny Woodard RC	.50	.20
❑ 89 Wes Littleton RC	.50	.20
❑ 90 Sean Rodriguez RC	1.50	.60
❑ 91 Kyle Pearson RC	.40	.15
❑ 92 Josh Rainwater RC	.50	.20
❑ 93 Travis Schlichting RC	.50	.20
❑ 94 Tim Battle RC	.75	.30
❑ 95 Aaron Hill RC	1.50	.60
❑ 96 Bob McCrory RC	.40	.15
❑ 97 Rick Guarno RC	.50	.20
❑ 98 Brandon Yarbrough RC	.40	.15
❑ 99 Peter Stonard RC	.40	.15
❑ 100 Darin Downs RC	.50	.20
❑ 101 Matt Bruback RC	.30	.10
❑ 102 Danny Garcia RC	.40	.15
❑ 103 Cory Stewart RC	.40	.15
❑ 104 Ferdin Tejeda RC	.40	.15
❑ 105 Kade Johnson RC	.40	.15
❑ 106 Andrew Brown RC	.50	.20
❑ 107 Aquilino Lopez RC	.40	.15
❑ 108 Stephen Randolph RC	.40	.15
❑ 109 Dave Matranga RC	.40	.15
❑ 110 Dustin McGowan RC	.50	.20
❑ 111 Juan Camacho RC	.40	.15
❑ 112 Cliff Lee	.30	.10
❑ 113 Jeff Duncan RC	.40	.15
❑ 114 C.J. Wilson	.30	.10
❑ 115 Brandon Roberson RC	.40	.15
❑ 116 David Corrente RC	.40	.15
❑ 117 Kevin Beavers RC	.40	.15
❑ 118 Anthony Webster RC	.50	.20
❑ 119 Oscar Villarreal RC	.40	.15
❑ 120 Hong-Chih Kuo RC	2.50	1.00
❑ 121 Josh Barfield	.30	.10
❑ 122 Denny Bautista	.30	.10
❑ 123 Chris Burke RC	1.25	.50
❑ 124 Robinson Cano RC	8.00	3.00
❑ 125 Jose Castillo	.30	.10
❑ 126 Neal Cotts	.30	.10
❑ 127 Jorge De La Rosa	.30	.10
❑ 128 J.D. Durbin	.40	.15
❑ 129 Edwin Encarnacion	1.00	.40
❑ 130 Gavin Floyd	.30	.10
❑ 131 Alexis Gomez	.30	.10
❑ 132 Edgar Gonzalez RC	.40	.15
❑ 133 Khalil Greene	.75	.30
❑ 134 Zack Greinke	.30	.10
❑ 135 Franklin Gutierrez	.50	.20
❑ 136 Rich Harden	.50	.20
❑ 137 J.J. Hardy RC	5.00	2.00
❑ 138 Ryan Howard RC	30.00	12.50
❑ 139 Justin Huber	.30	.10
❑ 140 David Kelton	.30	.10
❑ 141 Dave Krynzel	.30	.10
❑ 142 Pete LaForest	.40	.15
❑ 143 Adam LaRoche	.30	.10
❑ 144 Preston Larrison RC	.50	.20
❑ 145 John Maine RC	5.00	2.00
❑ 146 Andy Marte	1.25	.50
❑ 147 Jeff Mathis	.30	.10
❑ 148 Joe Mauer	.75	.30
❑ 149 Clint Nageotte	.30	.10
❑ 150 Chris Narveson	.30	.10
❑ 151 Ramon Nivar	.40	.15
❑ 152 Felix Pie RC	5.00	2.00
❑ 153 Guillermo Quiroz RC	.40	.15
❑ 154 Rene Reyes	.30	.10
❑ 155 Royce Ring	.30	.10
❑ 156 Alexis Rios	1.00	.40
❑ 157 Grady Sizemore	.75	.30
❑ 158 Stephen Smitherman	.30	.10
❑ 159 Seung Song	.30	.10
❑ 160 Scott Thorman	.30	.10
❑ 161 Chad Tracy	.30	.10
❑ 162 Chin-Hui Tsao	.30	.10
❑ 163 John VanBenschoten	.30	.10
❑ 164 Kevin Youkilis	4.00	1.50
❑ 165 Chien-Ming Wang	5.00	2.00

2004 Bowman

❑ COMPLETE SET (330)	80.00	40.00
❑ ROY ODDS 1:829 H, 1:284 HTA, 1:1632 R		
❑ 1 Garret Anderson	.30	.10
❑ 2 Larry Walker	.30	.10
❑ 3 Derek Jeter	1.50	.60
❑ 4 Curt Schilling	.50	.20
❑ 5 Carlos Zambrano	.30	.10
❑ 6 Shawn Green	.30	.10
❑ 7 Manny Ramirez	.50	.20
❑ 8 Randy Johnson	.75	.30
❑ 9 Jeremy Bonderman	.30	.10
❑ 10 Alfonso Soriano	.30	.10
❑ 11 Scott Rolen	.50	.20
❑ 12 Kerry Wood	.30	.10
❑ 13 Eric Gagne	.30	.10
❑ 14 Ryan Klesko	.30	.10
❑ 15 Kevin Millar	.30	.10
❑ 16 Ty Wigginton	.30	.10
❑ 17 David Ortiz	.75	.30
❑ 18 Luis Castillo	.30	.10
❑ 19 Bernie Williams	.50	.20
❑ 20 Edgar Renteria	.30	.10
❑ 21 Matt Kata	.30	.10
❑ 22 Bartolo Colon	.30	.10
❑ 23 Derrek Lee	.50	.20
❑ 24 Gary Sheffield	.30	.10
❑ 25 Nomar Garciaparra	1.25	.50
❑ 26 Kevin Millwood	.30	.10
❑ 27 Corey Patterson	.30	.10
❑ 28 Carlos Beltran	.30	.10
❑ 29 Mike Lieberthal	.30	.10
❑ 30 Troy Glaus	.30	.10
❑ 31 Preston Wilson	.30	.10
❑ 32 Jorge Posada	.50	.20
❑ 33 Bo Hart	.30	.10
❑ 34 Mark Prior	.50	.20
❑ 35 Hideo Nomo	.75	.30
❑ 36 Jason Kendall	.30	.10
❑ 37 Roger Clemens	1.50	.60
❑ 38 Dmitri Young	.30	.10
❑ 39 Jason Giambi	.30	.10
❑ 40 Jim Edmonds	.30	.10
❑ 41 Ryan Ludwick	.30	.10
❑ 42 Brandon Webb	.30	.10
❑ 43 Todd Helton	.50	.20
❑ 44 Jacque Jones	.30	.10
❑ 45 Jamie Moyer	.30	.10
❑ 46 Tim Salmon	.50	.20
❑ 47 Kelvim Escobar	.30	.10
❑ 48 Tony Batista	.30	.10

Card	Player	Price 1	Price 2
❑ 49	Nick Johnson	.30	.10
❑ 50	Jim Thome	.50	.20
❑ 51	Casey Blake	.30	.10
❑ 52	Trot Nixon	.30	.10
❑ 53	Luis Gonzalez	.30	.10
❑ 54	Dontrelle Willis	.50	.20
❑ 55	Mike Mussina	.50	.20
❑ 56	Carl Crawford	.30	.10
❑ 57	Mark Buehrle	.30	.10
❑ 58	Scott Podsednik	.30	.10
❑ 59	Brian Giles	.30	.10
❑ 60	Rafael Furcal	.30	.10
❑ 61	Miguel Cabrera	.50	.20
❑ 62	Rich Harden	.30	.10
❑ 63	Mark Teixeira	.50	.20
❑ 64	Frank Thomas	.75	.30
❑ 65	Johan Santana	.75	.30
❑ 66	Jason Schmidt	.30	.10
❑ 67	Aramis Ramirez	.30	.10
❑ 68	Jose Reyes	.30	.10
❑ 69	Magglio Ordonez	.30	.10
❑ 70	Mike Sweeney	.30	.10
❑ 71	Eric Chavez	.30	.10
❑ 72	Rocco Baldelli	.30	.10
❑ 73	Sammy Sosa	.75	.30
❑ 74	Javy Lopez	.30	.10
❑ 75	Roy Oswalt	.30	.10
❑ 76	Raul Ibanez	.30	.10
❑ 77	Ivan Rodriguez	.50	.20
❑ 78	Jerome Williams	.30	.10
❑ 79	Carlos Lee	.30	.10
❑ 80	Geoff Jenkins	.30	.10
❑ 81	Sean Burroughs	.30	.10
❑ 82	Marcus Giles	.30	.10
❑ 83	Mike Lowell	.30	.10
❑ 84	Barry Zito	.30	.10
❑ 85	Aubrey Huff	.30	.10
❑ 86	Esteban Loaiza	.30	.10
❑ 87	Torii Hunter	.30	.10
❑ 88	Phil Nevin	.30	.10
❑ 89	Andruw Jones	.50	.20
❑ 90	Josh Beckett	.30	.10
❑ 91	Mark Mulder	.30	.10
❑ 92	Hank Blalock	.30	.10
❑ 93	Jason Phillips	.30	.10
❑ 94	Russ Ortiz	.30	.10
❑ 95	Juan Pierre	.30	.10
❑ 96	Tom Glavine	.50	.20
❑ 97	Gil Meche	.30	.10
❑ 98	Ramon Ortiz	.30	.10
❑ 99	Richie Sexson	.30	.10
❑ 100	Albert Pujols	1.50	.60
❑ 101	Javier Vazquez	.30	.10
❑ 102	Johnny Damon	.50	.20
❑ 103	Alex Rodriguez Yanks	1.25	.50
❑ 104	Omar Vizquel	.50	.20
❑ 105	Chipper Jones	.75	.30
❑ 106	Lance Berkman	.30	.10
❑ 107	Tim Hudson	.30	.10
❑ 108	Carlos Delgado	.30	.10
❑ 109	Austin Kearns	.30	.10
❑ 110	Orlando Cabrera	.30	.10
❑ 111	Edgar Martinez	.50	.20
❑ 112	Melvin Mora	.30	.10
❑ 113	Jeff Bagwell	.50	.20
❑ 114	Marlon Byrd	.30	.10
❑ 115	Vernon Wells	.30	.10
❑ 116	C.C. Sabathia	.30	.10
❑ 117	Cliff Floyd	.30	.10
❑ 118	Ichiro Suzuki	1.50	.60
❑ 119	Miguel Olivo	.30	.10
❑ 120	Mike Piazza	1.25	.50
❑ 121	Adam Dunn	.30	.10
❑ 122	Paul Lo Duca	.30	.10
❑ 123	Brett Myers	.30	.10
❑ 124	Michael Young	.30	.10
❑ 125	Sidney Ponson	.30	.10
❑ 126	Greg Maddux	1.25	.50
❑ 127	Vladimir Guerrero	.75	.30
❑ 128	Miguel Tejada	.30	.10
❑ 129	Andy Pettitte	.50	.20
❑ 130	Rafael Palmeiro	.50	.20
❑ 131	Ken Griffey Jr.	1.25	.50
❑ 132	Shannon Stewart	.30	.10
❑ 133	Joel Pineiro	.30	.10
❑ 134	Luis Matos	.30	.10
❑ 135	Jeff Kent	.30	.10
❑ 136	Randy Wolf	.30	.10
❑ 137	Chris Woodward	.30	.10
❑ 138	Jody Gerut	.30	.10
❑ 139	Jose Vidro	.30	.10
❑ 140	Bret Boone	.30	.10
❑ 141	Bill Mueller	.30	.10
❑ 142	Angel Berroa	.30	.10
❑ 143	Bobby Abreu	.30	.10
❑ 144	Roy Halladay	.30	.10
❑ 145	Delmon Young	.50	.20
❑ 146	Jonny Gomes	.30	.10
❑ 147	Rickie Weeks	.30	.10
❑ 148	Edwin Jackson	.30	.10
❑ 149	Neal Cotts	.30	.10
❑ 150	Jason Bay	.30	.10
❑ 151	Khalil Greene	.50	.20
❑ 152	Joe Mauer	.75	.30
❑ 153	Bobby Jenks	.30	.10
❑ 154	Chin-Feng Chen	.30	.10
❑ 155	Chien-Ming Wang	1.00	.40
❑ 156	Mickey Hall	.30	.10
❑ 157	James Houser	.30	.10
❑ 158	Jay Sborz	.30	.10
❑ 159	Jonathan Fulton	.30	.10
❑ 160	Steven Lerud	.30	.10
❑ 161	Grady Sizemore	.75	.30
❑ 162	Felix Pie	.50	.20
❑ 163	Dustin McGowan	.30	.10
❑ 164	Chris Lubanski	.30	.10
❑ 165	Tom Gorzelanny	.30	.10
❑ 166	Rudy Guillen FY RC	.75	.30
❑ 167	Bobby Brownlie FY RC	1.00	.40
❑ 168	Conor Jackson FY RC	3.00	1.25
❑ 169	Matt Moses FY RC	1.00	.40
❑ 170	Ervin Santana FY RC	1.50	.60
❑ 171	Merkin Valdez FY RC	.50	.20
❑ 172	Erick Aybar FY RC	1.00	.40
❑ 173	Brad Sullivan FY RC	.50	.20
❑ 174	David Aardsma FY RC	.50	.20
❑ 175	Brad Snyder FY RC	1.00	.40
❑ 176	Alberto Callaspo FY RC	.75	.30
❑ 177	Brandon Medders FY RC	.40	.15
❑ 178	Zach Miner FY RC	1.25	.50
❑ 179	Charlie Zink FY RC	.30	.10
❑ 180	Adam Greenberg FY RC	.75	.30
❑ 181	Kevin Howard FY RC	.50	.20
❑ 182	Wanell Severino FY RC	.30	.10
❑ 183	Kevin Kouzmanoff FY RC	2.00	.75
❑ 184	Joel Zumaya FY RC	5.00	2.00
❑ 185	Skip Schumaker FY RC	.40	.15
❑ 186	Nic Ungs FY RC	.40	.15
❑ 187	Todd Self FY RC	.50	.20
❑ 188	Brian Steffek FY RC	.30	.10
❑ 189	Brock Peterson FY RC	.40	.15
❑ 190	Greg Thissen FY RC	.40	.15
❑ 191	Frank Brooks FY RC	.30	.10
❑ 192	Estee Harris FY RC	.50	.20
❑ 193	Chris Mabeus FY RC	.40	.15
❑ 194	Dan Giese FY RC	.40	.15
❑ 195	Jared Wells FY RC	.30	.10
❑ 196	Carlos Sosa FY RC	.40	.15
❑ 197	Bobby Madritsch FY	.30	.10
❑ 198	Calvin Hayes FY RC	.50	.20
❑ 199	Omar Quintanilla FY RC	.50	.20
❑ 200	Chris O'Riordan FY RC	.40	.15
❑ 201	Tim Hutting FY RC	.30	.10
❑ 202	Carlos Quentin FY RC	2.50	1.00
❑ 203	Brayan Pena FY RC	.40	.15
❑ 204	Jeff Salazar FY RC	1.00	.40
❑ 205	David Murphy FY RC	.75	.30
❑ 206	Alberto Garcia FY RC	.50	.20
❑ 207	Ramon Ramirez FY RC	.40	.15
❑ 208	Luis Bolivar FY RC	.50	.20
❑ 209	Rodney Choy Foo FY RC	.30	.10
❑ 210	Kyle Sleeth FY RC	.50	.20
❑ 211	Anthony Acevedo FY RC	.40	.15
❑ 212	Chad Santos FY RC	.40	.15
❑ 213	Jason Frasor FY RC	.40	.15
❑ 214	Jesse Roman FY RC	.30	.10
❑ 215	James Tomlin FY RC	.40	.15
❑ 216	Josh Labandeira FY RC	.40	.15
❑ 217	Joaquin Arias FY RC	.75	.30
❑ 218	Don Sutton FY UER RC	1.00	.40
❑ 219	Danny Gonzalez FY RC	.30	.10
❑ 220	Javier Guzman FY RC	.50	.20
❑ 221	Anthony Lerew FY RC	.75	.30
❑ 222	Jon Knott FY RC	.40	.15
❑ 223	Jesse English FY RC	.40	.15
❑ 224	Felix Hernandez FY RC	8.00	3.00
❑ 225	Travis Hanson FY RC	.50	.20
❑ 226	Jesse Floyd FY RC	.40	.15
❑ 227	Nick Gorneault FY RC	.50	.20
❑ 228	Craig Ansman FY RC	.40	.15
❑ 229	Wardell Starling FY RC	.40	.15
❑ 230	Carl Loadenthal FY RC	.50	.20
❑ 231	Dave Crouthers FY RC	.30	.10
❑ 232	Harvey Garcia FY RC	.30	.10
❑ 233	Casey Kopitzke FY RC	.30	.10
❑ 234	Ricky Nolasco FY RC	1.25	.50
❑ 235	Miguel Perez FY RC	.40	.15
❑ 236	Ryan Mulhern FY RC	.40	.15
❑ 237	Chris Aguila FY RC	.40	.15
❑ 238	Brooks Conrad FY RC	.50	.20
❑ 239	Damaso Espino FY RC	.30	.10
❑ 240	Jereme Milons FY RC	.50	.20
❑ 241	Luke Hughes FY RC	.30	.10
❑ 242	Kory Casto FY RC	.50	.20
❑ 243	Jose Valdez FY RC	.40	.15
❑ 244	J.T. Stotts FY RC	.30	.10
❑ 245	Lee Gwaltney FY RC	.30	.10
❑ 246	Yoann Torrealba FY RC	.30	.10
❑ 247	Omar Falcon FY RC	.40	.15
❑ 248	Jon Coutlangus FY RC	.30	.10
❑ 249	George Sherrill FY RC	.40	.15
❑ 250	John Santor FY RC	.30	.10
❑ 251	Tony Richie FY RC	.40	.15
❑ 252	Kevin Richardson FY RC	.30	.10
❑ 253	Tim Bittner FY RC	.40	.15
❑ 254	Dustin Nippert FY RC	1.25	.50
❑ 255	Jose Capellan FY RC	.50	.20
❑ 256	Donald Levinski FY RC	.30	.10
❑ 257	Jerome Gamble FY RC	.30	.10
❑ 258	Jeff Keppinger FY RC	.40	.15
❑ 259	Jason Szuminski FY RC	.30	.10
❑ 260	Akinori Otsuka FY RC	.40	.15
❑ 261	Ryan Budde FY RC	.40	.15
❑ 262	Shingo Takatsu FY RC	.75	.30
❑ 263	Jeff Allison FY RC	.40	.15
❑ 264	Hector Gimenez FY RC	.30	.10
❑ 265	Tim Frend FY RC	.40	.15
❑ 266	Tom Farmer FY RC	.40	.15
❑ 267	Shawn Hill FY RC	.40	.15
❑ 268	Lastings Milledge FY RC	5.00	2.00
❑ 269	Scott Proctor FY RC	.50	.20
❑ 270	Jorge Mejia FY RC	.40	.15
❑ 271	Terry Jones FY RC	.50	.20
❑ 272	Zach Duke FY RC	2.00	.75
❑ 273	Tim Stauffer FY RC	.75	.30
❑ 274	Luke Anderson FY RC	.30	.10
❑ 275	Hunter Brown FY RC	.30	.10
❑ 276	Matt Lemanczyk FY RC	.40	.15
❑ 277	Fernando Cortez FY RC	.30	.10
❑ 278	Vince Perkins FY RC	.50	.20
❑ 279	Tommy Murphy FY RC	.40	.15
❑ 280	Mike Gosling FY RC	.30	.10
❑ 281	Paul Bacot FY RC	.50	.20
❑ 282	Matt Capps FY RC	.40	.15
❑ 283	Juan Gutierrez FY RC	.40	.15
❑ 284	Teodoro Encarnacion FY RC	.50	.20
❑ 285	Juan Cedeno FY RC	.40	.15
❑ 286	Matt Creighton FY RC	.40	.15
❑ 287	Ryan Hankins FY RC	.30	.10
❑ 288	Leo Nunez FY RC	.40	.15
❑ 289	Dave Wallace FY RC	.40	.15
❑ 290	Rob Tejeda FY RC	.75	.30
❑ 291	Lincoln Holdzkom FY RC	.40	.15
❑ 292	Jason Hirsh FY RC	1.50	.60
❑ 293	Tydus Meadows FY RC	.40	.15
❑ 294	Khalid Ballouli FY RC	.30	.10
❑ 295	Benji DeQuin FY RC	.30	.10
❑ 296	Tyler Davidson FY RC	1.50	.60
❑ 297	Brant Colamarino FY RC	.75	.30
❑ 298	Marcus McBeth FY RC	.30	.10
❑ 299	Brad Eldred FY RC	.60	.25
❑ 300	David Pauley FY RC	1.25	.50
❑ 301	Yadier Molina FY RC	1.50	.60
❑ 302	Chris Shelton FY RC	1.25	.50
❑ 303	Travis Blackley FY RC	.40	.15
❑ 304	Jon DeVries FY RC	.40	.15
❑ 305	Sheldon Fulse FY RC	.30	.10
❑ 306	Vito Chiaravalloti FY RC	.40	.15

❑ 307 Warner Madrigal FY RC .75 .30
❑ 308 Reid Gorecki FY RC .40 .15
❑ 309 Sung Jung FY RC .30 .10
❑ 310 Pete Shier FY RC .30 .10
❑ 311 Michael Mooney FY RC .40 .15
❑ 312 Kenny Perez FY RC .40 .15
❑ 313 Michael Mallory FY RC .40 .15
❑ 314 Ben Himes FY RC .30 .10
❑ 315 Ivan Ochoa FY RC .40 .15
❑ 316 Donald Kelly FY RC .40 .15
❑ 317 Logan Kensing FY RC .40 .15
❑ 318 Kevin Davidson FY RC .30 .10
❑ 319 Brian Pilkington FY RC .30 .10
❑ 320 Alex Romero FY RC .40 .15
❑ 321 Chad Chop FY RC .40 .15
❑ 322 Dioner Navarro FY RC .75 .30
❑ 323 Casey Myers FY RC .30 .10
❑ 324 Mike Rouse FY RC .40 .15
❑ 325 Sergio Silva FY RC .30 .10
❑ 326 J.J. Furmaniak FY RC .75 .30
❑ 327 Brad Vericker FY RC .40 .15
❑ 328 Blake Hawksworth FY RC .50 .20
❑ 329 Brock Jacobsen FY RC .30 .10
❑ 330 Alec Zumwalt FY RC .30 .10
❑ BW Berroa Bat/Willis Jsy ROY 15.00 6.00

2004 Bowman Draft

❑ COMPLETE SET (165) 40.00 15.00
❑ COMMON CARD (1-165) .30 .10
❑ COMMON RC (1-165) .30 .10
❑ COMMON RC YR .30 .10
❑ PLATES ODDS 1:559 HOBBY
❑ PLATES PRINT RUN 1 SERIAL #'d SET
❑ BLACK-CYAN-MAGENTA-YELLOW EXIST
❑ NO PLATES PRICING DUE TO SCARCITY
❑ 1 Lyle Overbay .30 .10
❑ 2 David Newhan .30 .10
❑ 3 J.R. House .30 .10
❑ 4 Chad Tracy .30 .10
❑ 5 Humberto Quintero .30 .10
❑ 6 Dave Bush .30 .10
❑ 7 Scott Hairston .30 .10
❑ 8 Mike Wood .30 .10
❑ 9 Alexis Rios .30 .10
❑ 10 Sean Burnett .30 .10
❑ 11 Wilson Valdez .30 .10
❑ 12 Lew Ford .30 .10
❑ 13 Freddy Thon RC .40 .15
❑ 14 Zack Greinke .30 .10
❑ 15 Bucky Jacobsen .30 .10
❑ 16 Kevin Youkilis .30 .10
❑ 17 Grady Sizemore .75 .30
❑ 18 Denny Bautista .30 .10
❑ 19 David DeJesus .30 .10
❑ 20 Casey Kotchman .30 .10
❑ 21 David Kelton .30 .10
❑ 22 Charles Thomas RC .40 .15
❑ 23 Kazuhito Tadano RC .50 .20
❑ 24 Justin Leone RC .50 .20
❑ 25 Eduardo Villacis RC .40 .15
❑ 26 Brian Dallimore RC .30 .10
❑ 27 Nick Green .30 .10
❑ 28 Sam McConnell RC .40 .15
❑ 29 Brad Halsey RC .50 .20
❑ 30 Roman Colon RC .30 .10
❑ 31 Josh Fields RC 2.00 .75
❑ 32 Cody Bunkelman RC .50 .20
❑ 33 Jay Rainville RC 1.25 .50
❑ 34 Richie Robnett RC 1.00 .40
❑ 35 Jon Poterson RC .75 .30
❑ 36 Huston Street RC 2.00 .75
❑ 37 Erick San Pedro RC .40 .15
❑ 38 Cory Dunlap RC 1.25 .50
❑ 39 Kurt Suzuki RC 1.00 .40
❑ 40 Anthony Swarzak RC .75 .30
❑ 41 Ian Desmond RC 1.25 .50
❑ 42 Chris Covington RC .50 .20
❑ 43 Christian Garcia RC .75 .30
❑ 44 Gaby Hernandez RC 1.25 .50
❑ 45 Steven Register RC .40 .15
❑ 46 Eduardo Morlan RC .75 .30
❑ 47 Collin Balester RC .50 .20
❑ 48 Nathan Phillips RC .50 .20
❑ 49 Dan Schwartzbauer RC .50 .20
❑ 50 Rafael Gonzalez RC .40 .15
❑ 51 K.C. Herren RC .75 .30
❑ 52 William Susdorf RC .40 .15
❑ 53 Rob Johnson RC .50 .20
❑ 54 Louis Marson RC .75 .30
❑ 55 Joe Koshansky RC 2.00 .75
❑ 56 Jamar Walton RC .75 .30
❑ 57 Mark Lowe RC 1.50 .60
❑ 58 Matt Macri RC 1.00 .40
❑ 59 Donny Lucy RC .40 .15
❑ 60 Mike Ferris RC .50 .20
❑ 61 Mike Nickeas RC .50 .20
❑ 62 Eric Hurley RC 1.00 .40
❑ 63 Scott Elbert RC 1.00 .40
❑ 64 Blake DeWitt RC 1.50 .60
❑ 65 Danny Putnam RC .75 .30
❑ 66 J.P. Howell RC 1.00 .40
❑ 67 John Wiggins RC .40 .15
❑ 68 Justin Orenduff RC .75 .30
❑ 69 Ray Liotta RC 1.25 .50
❑ 70 Billy Buckner RC .50 .20
❑ 71 Eric Campbell RC 2.00 .75
❑ 72 Olin Wick RC .75 .30
❑ 73 Sean Gamble RC .50 .20
❑ 74 Seth Smith RC 1.00 .40
❑ 75 Wade Davis RC 1.50 .60
❑ 76 Joe Jacobitz RC .40 .15
❑ 77 J.A. Happ RC .75 .30
❑ 78 Eric Ridener RC .40 .15
❑ 79 Matt Tuiasosopo RC 2.00 .75
❑ 80 Brad Bergesen RC .40 .15
❑ 81 Javy Guerra RC .50 .20
❑ 82 Buck Shaw RC .50 .20
❑ 83 Paul Janish RC .75 .30
❑ 84 Sean Kazmar RC .40 .15
❑ 85 Josh Johnson RC .50 .20
❑ 86 Angel Salome RC 1.25 .50
❑ 87 Jordan Parraz RC .75 .30
❑ 88 Kelvin Vazquez RC .40 .15
❑ 89 Grant Hansen RC .40 .15
❑ 90 Matt Fox RC .40 .15
❑ 91 Trevor Plouffe RC 1.25 .50
❑ 92 Wes Whisler RC .40 .15
❑ 93 Curtis Thigpen RC .75 .30
❑ 94 Donnie Smith RC .50 .20
❑ 95 Luis Rivera RC .50 .20
❑ 96 Jesse Hoover RC .50 .20
❑ 97 Jason Vargas RC 1.50 .60
❑ 98 Clary Carlsen RC .40 .15
❑ 99 Mark Robinson RC .40 .15
❑ 100 J.C. Holt RC .50 .20
❑ 101 Chad Blackwell RC .40 .15
❑ 102 Daryl Jones RC 1.00 .40
❑ 103 Jonathan Tierce RC .40 .15
❑ 104 Patrick Bryant RC .40 .15
❑ 105 Eddie Prasch RC .50 .20
❑ 106 Mitch Einertson RC .50 .20
❑ 107 Kyle Waldrop RC 1.00 .40
❑ 108 Jeff Marquez RC .50 .20
❑ 109 Zach Jackson RC .75 .30
❑ 110 Josh Wahpepah RC .40 .15
❑ 111 Adam Lind RC 2.00 .75
❑ 112 Kyle Bloom RC .50 .20
❑ 113 Ben Harrison RC .40 .15
❑ 114 Taylor Tankersley RC .50 .20
❑ 115 Steven Jackson RC .40 .15
❑ 116 David Purcey RC .75 .30
❑ 117 Jacob McGee RC 1.00 .40
❑ 118 Lucas Harrell RC .40 .15
❑ 119 Brandon Allen RC 1.00 .40
❑ 120 Van Pope RC .50 .20
❑ 121 Jeff Francis .30 .10
❑ 122 Joe Blanton .30 .10
❑ 123 Wil Ledezma .30 .10
❑ 124 Bryan Bullington .30 .10
❑ 125 Jairo Garcia .30 .10
❑ 126 Matt Cain 1.00 .40
❑ 127 Arnie Munoz .30 .10
❑ 128 Clint Everts .30 .10
❑ 129 Jesus Cota .30 .10
❑ 130 Gavin Floyd .30 .10
❑ 131 Edwin Encarnacion .30 .10
❑ 132 Koyie Hill .30 .10
❑ 133 Ruben Gotay .30 .10
❑ 134 Jeff Mathis .30 .10
❑ 135 Andy Marte .50 .20
❑ 136 Dallas McPherson .30 .10
❑ 137 Justin Morneau .30 .10
❑ 138 Rickie Weeks .30 .10
❑ 139 Joel Guzman .50 .20
❑ 140 Shin Soo Choo .30 .10
❑ 141 Yusmeiro Petit RC 2.00 .75
❑ 142 Jorge Cortes RC .40 .15
❑ 143 Val Majewski .30 .10
❑ 144 Felix Pie .50 .20
❑ 145 Aaron Hill .30 .10
❑ 146 Jose Capellan .30 .10
❑ 147 Dioner Navarro .50 .20
❑ 148 Fausto Carmona RC 1.50 .60
❑ 149 Robinzon Diaz RC .40 .15
❑ 150 Felix Hernandez 4.00 1.50
❑ 151 Andres Blanco RC .40 .15
❑ 152 Jason Kubel .30 .10
❑ 153 Willy Taveras RC 1.00 .40
❑ 154 Merkin Valdez .50 .20
❑ 155 Robinson Cano .75 .30
❑ 156 Bill Murphy .30 .10
❑ 157 Chris Burke .30 .10
❑ 158 Kyle Sleeth .30 .10
❑ 159 B.J. Upton .50 .20
❑ 160 Tim Stauffer .50 .20
❑ 161 David Wright 2.00 .75
❑ 162 Conor Jackson 1.25 .50
❑ 163 Brad Thompson RC .75 .30
❑ 164 Delmon Young .50 .20
❑ 165 Jeremy Reed .30 .10

2005 Bowman

❑ COMPLETE SET (330) 80.00 40.00
❑ COMMON CARD (1-140) .30 .10
❑ COMMON CARD (141-165) .40 .15
❑ COMMON CARD (166-330) .40 .15
❑ PLATE ODDS 1:695 HOBBY, 1:177 HTA
❑ PLATE PRINT RUN 1 SET PER COLOR
❑ BLACK-CYAN-MAGENTA-YELLOW ISSUED
❑ NO PLATE PRICING DUE TO SCARCITY
❑ ROY ODDS 1:668 H, 1:248 HTA, 1:1535 R
❑ 1 Gavin Floyd .30 .10
❑ 2 Eric Chavez .30 .10
❑ 3 Miguel Tejada .30 .10
❑ 4 Dmitri Young .30 .10
❑ 5 Hank Blalock .30 .10
❑ 6 Kerry Wood .30 .10
❑ 7 Andy Pettitte .50 .20
❑ 8 Pat Burrell .30 .10
❑ 9 Johnny Estrada .30 .10
❑ 10 Frank Thomas .75 .30
❑ 11 Juan Pierre .30 .10

❑ 12 Tom Glavine .50 .20
❑ 13 Lyle Overbay .30 .10
❑ 14 Jim Edmonds .30 .10
❑ 15 Steve Finley .30 .10
❑ 16 Jermaine Dye .30 .10
❑ 17 Omar Vizquel .50 .20
❑ 18 Nick Johnson .30 .10
❑ 19 Brian Giles .30 .10
❑ 20 Justin Morneau .30 .10
❑ 21 Preston Wilson .30 .10
❑ 22 Wily Mo Pena .30 .10
❑ 23 Rafael Palmeiro .50 .20
❑ 24 Scott Kazmir .30 .10
❑ 25 Derek Jeter 1.50 .60
❑ 26 Barry Zito .30 .10
❑ 27 Mike Lowell .30 .10
❑ 28 Jason Bay .30 .10
❑ 29 Ken Harvey .30 .10
❑ 30 Nomar Garciaparra .75 .30
❑ 31 Roy Halladay .30 .10
❑ 32 Todd Helton .50 .20
❑ 33 Mark Kotsay .30 .10
❑ 34 Jake Peavy .30 .10
❑ 35 David Wright 1.25 .50
❑ 36 Dontrelle Willis .30 .10
❑ 37 Marcus Giles .30 .10
❑ 38 Chone Figgins .30 .10
❑ 39 Sidney Ponson .30 .10
❑ 40 Randy Johnson .75 .30
❑ 41 John Smoltz .50 .20
❑ 42 Kevin Millar .30 .10
❑ 43 Mark Teixeira .50 .20
❑ 44 Alex Rios .30 .10
❑ 45 Mike Piazza .75 .30
❑ 46 Victor Martinez .30 .10
❑ 47 Jeff Bagwell .50 .20
❑ 48 Shawn Green .30 .10
❑ 49 Ivan Rodriguez .50 .20
❑ 50 Alex Rodriguez 1.25 .50
❑ 51 Kazuo Matsui .30 .10
❑ 52 Mark Mulder .30 .10
❑ 53 Michael Young .30 .10
❑ 54 Javy Lopez .30 .10
❑ 55 Johnny Damon .50 .20
❑ 56 Jeff Francis .30 .10
❑ 57 Rich Harden .30 .10
❑ 58 Bobby Abreu .30 .10
❑ 59 Mark Loretta .30 .10
❑ 60 Gary Sheffield .30 .10
❑ 61 Jamie Moyer .30 .10
❑ 62 Garret Anderson .30 .10
❑ 63 Vernon Wells .30 .10
❑ 64 Orlando Cabrera .30 .10
❑ 65 Magglio Ordonez .30 .10
❑ 66 Ronnie Belliard .30 .10
❑ 67 Carlos Lee .30 .10
❑ 68 Carl Pavano .30 .10
❑ 69 Jon Lieber .30 .10
❑ 70 Aubrey Huff .30 .10
❑ 71 Rocco Baldelli .30 .10
❑ 72 Jason Schmidt .30 .10
❑ 73 Bernie Williams .50 .20
❑ 74 Hideki Matsui 1.25 .50
❑ 75 Ken Griffey Jr. 1.25 .50
❑ 76 Josh Beckett .30 .10
❑ 77 Mark Buehrle .30 .10
❑ 78 David Ortiz .75 .30
❑ 79 Luis Gonzalez .30 .10
❑ 80 Scott Rolen .50 .20
❑ 81 Joe Mauer .75 .30
❑ 82 Jose Reyes .30 .10
❑ 83 Adam Dunn .30 .10
❑ 84 Greg Maddux 1.25 .50
❑ 85 Bartolo Colon .30 .10
❑ 86 Bret Boone .30 .10
❑ 87 Mike Mussina .50 .20
❑ 88 Ben Sheets .30 .10
❑ 89 Lance Berkman .30 .10
❑ 90 Miguel Cabrera .50 .20
❑ 91 C.C. Sabathia .30 .10
❑ 92 Mike Maroth .30 .10
❑ 93 Andruw Jones .50 .20
❑ 94 Jack Wilson .30 .10
❑ 95 Ichiro Suzuki 1.50 .60
❑ 96 Geoff Jenkins .30 .10
❑ 97 Zack Greinke .30 .10
❑ 98 Jorge Posada .50 .20
❑ 99 Travis Hafner .30 .10
❑ 100 Barry Bonds 2.00 .75
❑ 101 Aaron Rowand .30 .10
❑ 102 Aramis Ramirez .30 .10
❑ 103 Curt Schilling .50 .20
❑ 104 Melvin Mora .30 .10
❑ 105 Albert Pujols 1.50 .60
❑ 106 Austin Kearns .30 .10
❑ 107 Shannon Stewart .30 .10
❑ 108 Carl Crawford .30 .10
❑ 109 Carlos Zambrano .30 .10
❑ 110 Roger Clemens 1.25 .50
❑ 111 Javier Vazquez .30 .10
❑ 112 Randy Wolf .30 .10
❑ 113 Chipper Jones .75 .30
❑ 114 Larry Walker .50 .20
❑ 115 Alfonso Soriano .30 .10
❑ 116 Brad Wilkerson .30 .10
❑ 117 Bobby Crosby .30 .10
❑ 118 Jim Thome .50 .20
❑ 119 Oliver Perez .30 .10
❑ 120 Vladimir Guerrero .75 .30
❑ 121 Roy Oswalt .30 .10
❑ 122 Torii Hunter .30 .10
❑ 123 Rafael Furcal .30 .10
❑ 124 Luis Castillo .30 .10
❑ 125 Carlos Beltran .30 .10
❑ 126 Mike Sweeney .30 .10
❑ 127 Johan Santana .75 .30
❑ 128 Tim Hudson .30 .10
❑ 129 Troy Glaus .30 .10
❑ 130 Manny Ramirez .50 .20
❑ 131 Jeff Kent .30 .10
❑ 132 Jose Vidro .30 .10
❑ 133 Edgar Renteria .30 .10
❑ 134 Russ Ortiz .30 .10
❑ 135 Sammy Sosa .75 .30
❑ 136 Carlos Delgado .30 .10
❑ 137 Richie Sexson .30 .10
❑ 138 Pedro Martinez .50 .20
❑ 139 Adrian Beltre .30 .10
❑ 140 Mark Prior .50 .20
❑ 141 Omar Quintanilla .40 .15
❑ 142 Carlos Quentin .50 .20
❑ 143 Dan Johnson .50 .20
❑ 144 Jake Stevens .40 .15
❑ 145 Nate Schierholtz .50 .20
❑ 146 Neil Walker .40 .15
❑ 147 Bill Bray .40 .15
❑ 148 Taylor Tankersley .40 .15
❑ 149 Trevor Plouffe .50 .20
❑ 150 Felix Hernandez 2.00 .75
❑ 151 Philip Hughes .50 .20
❑ 152 James Houser .40 .15
❑ 153 David Murphy .40 .15
❑ 154 Ervin Santana .40 .15
❑ 155 Anthony Whittington .40 .15
❑ 156 Chris Lambert .40 .15
❑ 157 Jeremy Sowers .50 .20
❑ 158 Giovanny Gonzalez .40 .15
❑ 159 Blake DeWitt .50 .20
❑ 160 Thomas Diamond .50 .20
❑ 161 Greg Golson .40 .15
❑ 162 David Aardsma .40 .15
❑ 163 Paul Maholm .40 .15
❑ 164 Mark Rogers .50 .20
❑ 165 Homer Bailey .50 .20
❑ 166 Chip Cannon FY RC 1.00 .40
❑ 167 Tony Giarratano FY RC .50 .20
❑ 168 Darren Fenster FY RC .50 .20
❑ 169 Elvys Quezada FY RC .50 .20
❑ 170 Glen Perkins FY RC 1.00 .40
❑ 171 Ian Kinsler FY RC 3.00 1.25
❑ 172 Mike Bourn FY RC 1.00 .40
❑ 173 Jeremy West FY RC .75 .30
❑ 174 Justin Verlander FY RC 5.00 2.00
❑ 175 Kevin West FY RC .50 .20
❑ 176 Luis Hernandez FY RC .50 .20
❑ 177 Matt Campbell FY RC .50 .20
❑ 178 Nate McLouth FY RC .75 .30
❑ 179 Ryan Goleski FY RC .75 .30
❑ 180 Matthew Lindstrom FY RC .50 .20
❑ 181 Matt DeSalvo FY RC .75 .30
❑ 182 Kole Strayhorn FY RC .50 .20
❑ 183 Jose Vaquedano FY RC .50 .20
❑ 184 James Jurries FY RC .75 .30
❑ 185 Ian Bladergroen FY RC .75 .30
❑ 186 Eric Nielsen FY RC .50 .20
❑ 187 Chris Vines FY RC .50 .20
❑ 188 Chris Denorfia FY RC 1.00 .40
❑ 189 Kevin Melillo FY RC 1.00 .40
❑ 190 Melky Cabrera FY RC 2.50 1.00
❑ 191 Ryan Sweeney FY RC 1.25 .50
❑ 192 Sean Marshall FY RC 2.00 .75
❑ 193 Andy LaRoche FY RC 4.00 1.50
❑ 194 Tyler Pelland FY RC .75 .30
❑ 195 Mike Morse FY RC .60 .25
❑ 196 Wes Swackhamer FY RC .50 .20
❑ 197 Wade Robinson FY RC .50 .20
❑ 198 Dan Santin FY RC .50 .20
❑ 199 Steve Doetsch FY RC .75 .30
❑ 200 Shane Costa FY RC .50 .20
❑ 201 Scott Mathieson FY RC 1.00 .40
❑ 202 Ben Jones FY RC 1.00 .40
❑ 203 Michael Rogers FY RC .50 .20
❑ 204 Matt Rogelstad FY RC .50 .20
❑ 205 Luis Ramirez FY RC .50 .20
❑ 206 Landon Powell FY RC .75 .30
❑ 207 Erik Cordier FY RC .50 .20
❑ 208 Chris Seddon FY RC .50 .20
❑ 209 Chris Roberson FY RC .50 .20
❑ 210 Thomas Oldham FY RC .50 .20
❑ 211 Dana Eveland FY RC .50 .20
❑ 212 Cody Haerther FY RC .50 .20
❑ 213 Danny Core FY RC .50 .20
❑ 214 Craig Tatum FY RC .50 .20
❑ 215 Elliot Johnson FY RC .50 .20
❑ 216 Ender Chavez FY RC .50 .20
❑ 217 Errol Simonitsch FY RC .75 .30
❑ 218 Matt Van Der Bosch FY RC .50 .20
❑ 219 Eulogio de la Cruz FY RC .50 .20
❑ 220 C.J. Smith FY RC .50 .20
❑ 221 Adam Boeve FY RC .50 .20
❑ 222 Adam Harben FY RC .75 .30
❑ 223 Baltazar Lopez FY RC .50 .20
❑ 224 Russ Martin FY RC 2.00 .75
❑ 225 Brian Bannister FY RC 1.00 .40
❑ 226 Brian Miller FY RC .50 .20
❑ 227 Casey McGehee FY RC .50 .20
❑ 228 Humberto Sanchez FY RC 2.00 .75
❑ 229 Javon Moran FY RC .50 .20
❑ 230 Brandon McCarthy FY RC 1.50 .60
❑ 231 Danny Zell FY RC .50 .20
❑ 232 Jake Postlewait FY RC .50 .20
❑ 233 Juan Tejeda FY RC .50 .20
❑ 234 Keith Ramsey FY RC .50 .20
❑ 235 Lorenzo Scott FY RC .50 .20
❑ 236 Wladimir Balentien FY RC 1.00 .40
❑ 237 Martin Prado FY RC .50 .20
❑ 238 Matt Albers FY RC 1.25 .50
❑ 239 Brian Schweiger FY RC .50 .20
❑ 240 Brian Stavisky FY RC .50 .20
❑ 241 Pat Misch FY RC .50 .20
❑ 242 Pat Osborn FY .40 .15
❑ 243 Ryan Feierabend FY RC .50 .20
❑ 244 Shaun Marcum FY .40 .15
❑ 245 Kevin Collins FY RC .50 .20
❑ 246 Stuart Pomeranz FY RC .50 .20
❑ 247 Tetsu Yofu FY RC .50 .20
❑ 248 Hernan Iribarren FY RC .75 .30
❑ 249 Mike Spidale FY RC .50 .20
❑ 250 Tony Arnerich FY RC .50 .20
❑ 251 Manny Parra FY RC .50 .20
❑ 252 Drew Anderson FY RC .50 .20
❑ 253 T.J. Beam FY RC 1.00 .40
❑ 254 Pedro Lopez FY RC .50 .20
❑ 255 Andy Sides FY RC .50 .20
❑ 256 Bear Bay FY RC .75 .30
❑ 257 Bill McCarthy FY RC .50 .20
❑ 258 Daniel Haigwood FY RC 1.00 .40
❑ 259 Brian Sprout FY RC 1.00 .40
❑ 260 Bryan Triplett FY RC .50 .20
❑ 261 Steven Bondurant FY RC .50 .20
❑ 262 Darwinson Salazar FY RC .50 .20
❑ 263 David Shepard FY RC .50 .20
❑ 264 Johan Silva FY RC .50 .20
❑ 265 J.B. Thurmond FY RC .50 .20
❑ 266 Brandon Moorhead FY RC .50 .20
❑ 267 Kyle Nichols FY RC .75 .30
❑ 268 Jonathan Sanchez FY RC 1.25 .50
❑ 269 Mike Esposito FY RC .50 .20

❑ 270 Erik Schindewolf FY RC .50 .20
❑ 271 Peeter Ramos FY RC .50 .20
❑ 272 Juan Senreiso FY RC .50 .20
❑ 273 Matthew Kemp FY RC 4.00 1.50
❑ 274 Vinny Rottino FY RC .50 .20
❑ 275 Micah Furtado FY RC .50 .20
❑ 276 George Kottaras FY RC 1.00 .40
❑ 277 Billy Butler FY RC 4.00 1.50
❑ 278 Buck Coats FY RC .50 .20
❑ 279 Kenny Durost FY RC .50 .20
❑ 280 Nick Touchstone FY RC .50 .20
❑ 281 Jerry Owens FY RC .75 .30
❑ 282 Stefan Bailie FY RC .50 .20
❑ 283 Jesse Gutierrez FY RC .50 .20
❑ 284 Chuck Tiffany FY RC 1.25 .50
❑ 285 Brendan Ryan FY RC .50 .20
❑ 286 Hayden Penn FY RC 1.00 .40
❑ 287 Shawn Bowman FY RC .75 .30
❑ 288 Alexander Smit FY RC .50 .20
❑ 289 Micah Schnurstein FY RC .50 .20
❑ 290 Jared Gothreaux FY RC .50 .20
❑ 291 Jair Jurrjens FY RC 1.50 .60
❑ 292 Bobby Livingston FY RC .50 .20
❑ 293 Ryan Speier FY RC .50 .20
❑ 294 Zach Parker FY RC .50 .20
❑ 295 Christian Colonel FY RC .50 .20
❑ 296 Scott Mitchinson FY RC .50 .20
❑ 297 Neil Wilson FY RC .50 .20
❑ 298 Chuck James FY RC 2.00 .75
❑ 299 Heath Totten FY RC .50 .20
❑ 300 Sean Tracey FY RC .50 .20
❑ 301 Ismael Ramirez FY RC .50 .20
❑ 302 Matt Brown FY RC .50 .20
❑ 303 Franklin Morales FY RC .75 .30
❑ 304 Brandon Sing FY RC .75 .30
❑ 305 D.J. Houlton FY RC .50 .20
❑ 306 Jayce Tingler FY RC .50 .20
❑ 307 Mitchell Arnold FY RC .50 .20
❑ 308 Jim Burt FY RC .50 .20
❑ 309 Jason Motte FY RC .50 .20
❑ 310 David Gassner FY RC .50 .20
❑ 311 Andy Santana FY RC .50 .20
❑ 312 Kelvin Pichardo FY RC .50 .20
❑ 313 Carlos Carrasco FY RC 1.25 .50
❑ 314 Willy Mota FY RC .50 .20
❑ 315 Frank Mata FY RC .50 .20
❑ 316 Carlos Gonzalez FY RC 4.00 1.50
❑ 317 Jeff Niemann FY RC 1.00 .40
❑ 318 Chris B.Young FY RC 2.50 1.00
❑ 319 Billy Sadler FY RC .50 .20
❑ 320 Ricky Barrett FY RC .50 .20
❑ 321 Ben Harrison FY .40 .15
❑ 322 Steve Nelson FY RC .50 .20
❑ 323 Daryl Thompson FY RC .50 .20
❑ 324 Philip Humber FY RC 1.00 .40
❑ 325 Jeremy Harts FY RC .50 .20
❑ 326 Nick Masset FY RC .50 .20
❑ 327 Mike Rodriguez FY RC .50 .20
❑ 328 Mike Garber FY RC .50 .20
❑ 329 Kennard Bibbs FY RC .50 .20
❑ 330 Ryan Garko FY RC 1.50 .60
❑ BC Bay Bat/Crosby Bat ROY 15.00 6.00

2005 Bowman Draft

❑ COMPLETE SET (165) 40.00 15.00
❑ COMMON CARD (1-165) .30 .10
❑ COMMON RC .30 .10
❑ COMMON RC YR .30 .10
❑ OVERALL PLATE ODDS 1:826 HOBBY
❑ PLATE PRINT RUN 1 SET PER COLOR
❑ BLACK-CYAN-MAGENTA-YELLOW ISSUED
❑ NO PLATE PRICING DUE TO SCARCITY
❑ 1 Rickie Weeks .30 .10
❑ 2 Kyle Davies .30 .10
❑ 3 Garrett Atkins .30 .10
❑ 4 Chien-Ming Wang 1.00 .40
❑ 5 Dallas McPherson .30 .10
❑ 6 Dan Johnson .30 .10
❑ 7 Andy Sisco .30 .10
❑ 8 Ryan Doumit .30 .10
❑ 9 J.P. Howell .30 .10
❑ 10 Tim Stauffer .30 .10
❑ 11 Willy Taveras .30 .10
❑ 12 Aaron Hill .30 .10
❑ 13 Victor Diaz .30 .10
❑ 14 Wilson Betemit .30 .10
❑ 15 Ervin Santana .30 .10
❑ 16 Mike Morse .30 .10
❑ 17 Yadier Molina .30 .10
❑ 18 Kelly Johnson .30 .10
❑ 19 Clint Barmes .30 .10
❑ 20 Robinson Cano .50 .20
❑ 21 Brad Thompson .30 .10
❑ 22 Jorge Cantu .30 .10
❑ 23 Brad Halsey .30 .10
❑ 24 Lance Niekro .30 .10
❑ 25 D.J. Houlton .30 .10
❑ 26 Ryan Church .30 .10
❑ 27 Hayden Penn .75 .30
❑ 28 Chris Young .30 .10
❑ 29 Chad Orvella RC .30 .10
❑ 30 Mark Teahen .30 .10
❑ 31 Mark McCormick FY RC .50 .20
❑ 32 Jay Bruce FY RC 2.00 .75
❑ 33 Beau Jones FY RC .50 .20
❑ 34 Tyler Greene FY RC .75 .30
❑ 35 Zach Ward FY RC .30 .10
❑ 36 Josh Bell FY RC .75 .30
❑ 37 Josh Wall FY RC .50 .20
❑ 38 Nick Webber FY RC .30 .10
❑ 39 Travis Buck FY RC 1.00 .40
❑ 40 Kyle Winters FY RC .50 .20
❑ 41 Mitch Boggs FY RC .30 .10
❑ 42 Tommy Mendoza FY RC .75 .30
❑ 43 Brad Corley FY RC .50 .20
❑ 44 Drew Butera FY RC .30 .10
❑ 45 Ryan Mount FY RC .75 .30
❑ 46 Tyler Herron FY RC .50 .20
❑ 47 Nick Weglarz FY RC .50 .20
❑ 48 Brandon Erbe FY RC 1.00 .40
❑ 49 Cody Allen FY RC .30 .10
❑ 50 Eric Fowler FY RC .30 .10
❑ 51 James Boone FY RC .50 .20
❑ 52 Josh Flores FY RC 1.25 .50
❑ 53 Brandon Monk FY RC .50 .20
❑ 54 Kieron Pope FY RC .75 .30
❑ 55 Kyle Cofield FY RC .30 .10
❑ 56 Brent Lillibridge FY RC .50 .20
❑ 57 Daryl Jones FY .30 .10
❑ 58 Eli Iorg FY RC .50 .20
❑ 59 Brett Hayes FY RC .30 .10
❑ 60 Mike Durant FY RC .75 .30
❑ 61 Michael Bowden FY RC 2.00 .75
❑ 62 Paul Kelly FY RC .50 .20
❑ 63 Andrew McCutchen FY RC 2.00 .75
❑ 64 Travis Wood FY RC 1.00 .40
❑ 65 Cesar Ramos FY RC .50 .20
❑ 66 Chaz Roe FY RC .50 .20
❑ 67 Matt Torra FY RC .50 .20
❑ 68 Kevin Slowey FY RC 1.50 .60
❑ 69 Trayvon Robinson FY RC .50 .20
❑ 70 Reid Engel FY RC .30 .10
❑ 71 Kris Harvey FY RC .50 .20
❑ 72 Craig Italiano FY RC .75 .30
❑ 73 Matt Maloney FY RC 1.00 .40
❑ 74 Sean West FY RC .75 .30
❑ 75 Henry Sanchez FY RC .50 .20
❑ 76 Scott Blue FY RC .30 .10
❑ 77 Jordan Schafer FY RC 1.00 .40
❑ 78 Chris Robinson FY RC .50 .20
❑ 79 Chris Hobdy FY RC .30 .10
❑ 80 Brandon Durden FY RC .30 .10
❑ 81 Clay Buchholz FY RC 8.00 3.00
❑ 82 Josh Geer FY RC .30 .10
❑ 83 Sam LeCure FY RC .30 .10
❑ 84 Justin Thomas FY RC .30 .10
❑ 85 Brett Gardner FY RC .50 .20
❑ 86 Tommy Manzella FY RC .30 .10
❑ 87 Matt Green FY RC .30 .10
❑ 88 Yunel Escobar FY RC 1.00 .40
❑ 89 Mike Costanzo FY RC .75 .30
❑ 90 Nick Hundley FY RC .30 .10
❑ 91 Zach Simons FY RC .30 .10
❑ 92 Jacob Marceaux FY RC .30 .10
❑ 93 Jed Lowrie FY RC .50 .20
❑ 94 Brandon Snyder FY RC 1.00 .40
❑ 95 Matt Goyen FY RC .30 .10
❑ 96 Jon Egan FY RC .50 .20
❑ 97 Drew Thompson FY RC .50 .20
❑ 98 Bryan Anderson FY RC 1.00 .40
❑ 99 Clayton Richard FY RC .30 .10
❑ 100 Jimmy Shull FY RC .50 .20
❑ 101 Mark Pawelek FY RC 1.50 .60
❑ 102 P.J. Phillips FY RC .75 .30
❑ 103 John Drennen FY RC 1.25 .50
❑ 104 Nolan Reimold FY RC 1.00 .40
❑ 105 Troy Tulowitzki FY RC 4.00 1.50
❑ 106 Kevin Whelan FY RC .40 .15
❑ 107 Wade Townsend FY RC .50 .20
❑ 108 Micah Owings FY RC 1.25 .50
❑ 109 Ryan Tucker FY RC .50 .20
❑ 110 Jeff Clement FY RC 1.50 .60
❑ 111 Josh Sullivan FY RC .30 .10
❑ 112 Jeff Lyman FY RC .50 .20
❑ 113 Brian Bogusevic FY RC .30 .10
❑ 114 Trevor Bell FY RC .50 .20
❑ 115 Brent Cox FY RC .50 .20
❑ 116 Michael Billek FY RC .30 .10
❑ 117 Garrett Olson FY RC .50 .20
❑ 118 Steven Johnson FY RC .30 .10
❑ 119 Chase Headley FY RC .75 .30
❑ 120 Daniel Carte FY RC .50 .20
❑ 121 Francisco Liriano PROS 1.50 .60
❑ 122 Fausto Carmona PROS .30 .10
❑ 123 Zach Jackson PROS .30 .10
❑ 124 Adam Loewen PROS .30 .10
❑ 125 Chris Lambert PROS .30 .10
❑ 126 Scott Mathieson FY .30 .10
❑ 127 Paul Maholm PROS .30 .10
❑ 128 Fernando Nieve PROS .30 .10
❑ 129 Justin Verlander FY 1.50 .60
❑ 130 Yusmeiro Petit PROS .50 .20
❑ 131 Joel Zumaya PROS .30 .10
❑ 132 Merkin Valdez PROS .30 .10
❑ 133 Ryan Garko FY .50 .20
❑ 134 Edison Volquez FY RC .75 .30
❑ 135 Russ Martin FY .75 .30
❑ 136 Conor Jackson PROS .30 .10
❑ 137 Miguel Montero FY RC 1.00 .40
❑ 138 Josh Barfield PROS .30 .10
❑ 139 Delmon Young PROS .50 .20
❑ 140 Andy LaRoche FY .75 .30
❑ 141 William Bergolla PROS .30 .10
❑ 142 B.J. Upton PROS .30 .10
❑ 143 Hernan Iribarren FY .30 .10
❑ 144 Brandon Wood PROS .75 .30
❑ 145 Jose Bautista PROS .30 .10
❑ 146 Edwin Encarnacion PROS .30 .10
❑ 147 Javier Herrera FY RC .75 .30
❑ 148 Jeremy Hermida PROS .75 .30
❑ 149 Frank Diaz PROS RC .30 .10
❑ 150 Chris B.Young FY 1.00 .40
❑ 151 Shin-Soo Choo PROS .30 .10
❑ 152 Kevin Thompson PROS RC .30 .10
❑ 153 Hanley Ramirez PROS .50 .20
❑ 154 Lastings Milledge PROS .30 .10
❑ 155 Luis Montanez PROS .30 .10
❑ 156 Justin Huber PROS .30 .10
❑ 157 Zach Duke PROS .50 .20
❑ 158 Jeff Francoeur PROS .75 .30
❑ 159 Melky Cabrera FY 1.00 .40
❑ 160 Bobby Jenks PROS .30 .10
❑ 161 Ian Snell PROS .30 .10
❑ 162 Fernando Cabrera PROS .30 .10
❑ 163 Troy Patton PROS .50 .20
❑ 164 Anthony Lerew PROS .30 .10
❑ 165 Nelson Cruz FY RC .75 .30

2006 Bowman

❑ COMP.SET w/o AU's (220)	40.00	15.00
❑ COMP.SET w/PROS (330)	80.00	40.00
❑ COMMON CARD (1-200)	.30	.10
❑ SEMISTARS 1-220	.50	.20
❑ UNLISTED STARS 1-220	.75	.30
❑ COMMON ROOKIE (201-220)	.40	.15
❑ ROOKIE SEMIS 201-220	.60	.25
❑ 219-220 AU ODDS 1:1150 HOBBY, 1:699 HTA		
❑ COMMON AUTO (221-231)	10.00	4.00
❑ 221-231 AU ODDS 1:82 HOBBY, 1:40 HTA		
❑ 1-220 PLATE ODDS 1:588 HOBBY, 1:575 HTA		
❑ 221-231 AU PLATES 1:15,700 H, 1:4100 HTA		
❑ PLATE PRINT RUN 1 SET PER COLOR		
❑ BLACK-CYAN-MAGENTA-YELLOW ISSUED		
❑ NO PLATE PRICING DUE TO SCARCITY		
❑ 1 Nick Swisher	.30	.12
❑ 2 Ted Lilly	.30	.12
❑ 3 John Smoltz	.50	.20
❑ 4 Lyle Overbay	.30	.12
❑ 5 Alfonso Soriano	.30	.12
❑ 6 Javier Vazquez	.30	.12
❑ 7 Ronnie Belliard	.30	.12
❑ 8 Jose Reyes	.75	.30
❑ 9 Brian Roberts	.30	.12
❑ 10 Curt Schilling	.50	.20
❑ 11 Adam Dunn	.30	.12
❑ 12 Zack Greinke	.30	.12
❑ 13 Carlos Guillen	.30	.12
❑ 14 Jon Garland	.30	.12
❑ 15 Robinson Cano	.50	.20
❑ 16 Chris Burke	.30	.10
❑ 17 Barry Zito	.30	.10
❑ 18 Russ Adams	.30	.10
❑ 19 Chris Capuano	.30	.10
❑ 20 Scott Rolen	.50	.20
❑ 21 Kerry Wood	.30	.10
❑ 22 Scott Kazmir	.50	.20
❑ 23 Brandon Webb	.30	.10
❑ 24 Jeff Kent	.30	.10
❑ 25 Albert Pujols	1.50	.60
❑ 26 C.C. Sabathia	.30	.10
❑ 27 Adrian Beltre	.30	.10
❑ 28 Brad Wilkerson	.30	.10
❑ 29 Randy Wolf	.30	.10
❑ 30 Jason Bay	.30	.10
❑ 31 Austin Kearns	.30	.10
❑ 32 Clint Barmes	.30	.10
❑ 33 Mike Sweeney	.30	.10
❑ 34 Justin Verlander	1.25	.50
❑ 35 Justin Morneau	.30	.10
❑ 36 Scott Podsednik	.30	.10
❑ 37 Jason Giambi	.30	.10
❑ 38 Steve Finley	.30	.10
❑ 39 Morgan Ensberg	.30	.10
❑ 40 Eric Chavez	.30	.10
❑ 41 Roy Halladay	.30	.10
❑ 42 Horacio Ramirez	.30	.10
❑ 43 Ben Sheets	.30	.10
❑ 44 Chris Carpenter	.30	.10
❑ 45 Andruw Jones	.50	.20
❑ 46 Carlos Zambrano	.30	.10
❑ 47 Jonny Gomes	.30	.10
❑ 48 Shawn Green	.30	.10
❑ 49 Moises Alou	.30	.10
❑ 50 Ichiro Suzuki	1.25	.50
❑ 51 Juan Pierre	.30	.10
❑ 52 Grady Sizemore	.50	.20
❑ 53 Kazuo Matsui	.30	.10
❑ 54 Jose Vidro	.30	.10
❑ 55 Jake Peavy	.30	.10
❑ 56 Dallas Mcpherson	.30	.10
❑ 57 Ryan Howard	1.25	.50
❑ 58 Zach Duke	.30	.10
❑ 59 Michael Young	.30	.10
❑ 60 Todd Helton	.50	.20
❑ 61 David Dejesus	.30	.10
❑ 62 Ivan Rodriguez	.50	.20
❑ 63 Johan Santana	.50	.20
❑ 64 Danny Haren	.30	.10
❑ 65 Derek Jeter	2.00	.75
❑ 66 Greg Maddux	1.25	.50
❑ 67 Jorge Cantu	.30	.10
❑ 68 Conor Jackson	.30	.10
❑ 69 Victor Martinez	.30	.10
❑ 70 David Wright	1.25	.50
❑ 71 Ryan Church	.30	.10
❑ 72 Khalil Greene	.50	.20
❑ 73 Jimmy Rollins	.30	.10
❑ 74 Hank Blalock	.30	.10
❑ 75 Pedro Martinez	.50	.20
❑ 76 Jon Papelbon	2.00	.75
❑ 77 Felipe Lopez	.30	.10
❑ 78 Jeff Francis	.30	.10
❑ 79 Andy Sisco	.30	.10
❑ 80 Hideki Matsui	1.25	.50
❑ 81 Ken Griffey Jr.	1.25	.50
❑ 82 Nomar Garciaparra	.75	.30
❑ 83 Kevin Millwood	.30	.10
❑ 84 Paul Konerko	.30	.10
❑ 85 A.J. Burnett	.30	.10
❑ 86 Mike Piazza	.75	.30
❑ 87 Brian Giles	.30	.10
❑ 88 Johnny Damon	.50	.20
❑ 89 Jim Thome	.50	.20
❑ 90 Roger Clemens	1.50	.60
❑ 91 Aaron Rowand	.30	.10
❑ 92 Rafael Furcal	.30	.10
❑ 93 Gary Sheffield	.30	.10
❑ 94 Mike Cameron	.30	.10
❑ 95 Carlos Delgado	.30	.10
❑ 96 Jorge Posada	.50	.20
❑ 97 Denny Bautista	.30	.10
❑ 98 Mike Maroth	.30	.10
❑ 99 Brad Radke	.30	.10
❑ 100 Alex Rodriguez	1.25	.50
❑ 101 Freddy Garcia	.30	.10
❑ 102 Oliver Perez	.30	.10
❑ 103 Jon Lieber	.30	.10
❑ 104 Melvin Mora	.30	.10
❑ 105 Travis Hafner	.30	.10
❑ 106 Matt Cain	.50	.20
❑ 107 Derek Lowe	.30	.10
❑ 108 Luis Castillo	.30	.10
❑ 109 Livan Hernandez	.30	.10
❑ 110 Tadahito Iguchi	.30	.10
❑ 111 Shawn Chacon	.30	.10
❑ 112 Frank Thomas	.75	.30
❑ 113 Josh Beckett	.30	.12
❑ 114 Aubrey Huff	.30	.10
❑ 115 Derrek Lee	.30	.10
❑ 116 Chien-Ming Wang	1.25	.50
❑ 117 Joe Crede	.30	.10
❑ 118 Torii Hunter	.30	.10
❑ 119 J.D. Drew	.30	.10
❑ 120 Troy Glaus	.30	.10
❑ 121 Sean Casey	.30	.10
❑ 122 Edgar Renteria	.30	.10
❑ 123 Craig Wilson	.30	.10
❑ 124 Adam Eaton	.30	.10
❑ 125 Jeff Francoeur	.75	.30
❑ 126 Bruce Chen	.30	.10
❑ 127 Cliff Floyd	.30	.10
❑ 128 Jeremy Reed	.30	.10
❑ 129 Jake Westbrook	.30	.10
❑ 130 Wily Mo Pena	.30	.10
❑ 131 Toby Hall	.30	.10
❑ 132 David Ortiz	.75	.30
❑ 133 David Eckstein	.30	.10
❑ 134 Brady Clark	.30	.10
❑ 135 Marcus Giles	.30	.10
❑ 136 Aaron Hill	.30	.10
❑ 137 Mark Kotsay	.30	.10
❑ 138 Carlos Lee	.30	.10
❑ 139 Roy Oswalt	.30	.10
❑ 140 Chone Figgins	.30	.10
❑ 141 Mike Mussina	.50	.20
❑ 142 Orlando Hernandez	.30	.10
❑ 143 Magglio Ordonez	.30	.10
❑ 144 Jim Edmonds	.50	.20
❑ 145 Bobby Abreu	.30	.10
❑ 146 Nick Johnson	.30	.10
❑ 147 Carlos Beltran	.30	.10
❑ 148 Jhonny Peralta	.30	.10
❑ 149 Pedro Feliz	.30	.10
❑ 150 Miguel Tejada	.30	.10
❑ 151 Luis Gonzalez	.30	.10
❑ 152 Carl Crawford	.30	.10
❑ 153 Yadier Molina	.30	.10
❑ 154 Rich Harden	.30	.10
❑ 155 Tim Wakefield	.30	.10
❑ 156 Rickie Weeks	.30	.10
❑ 157 Johnny Estrada	.30	.10
❑ 158 Gustavo Chacin	.30	.10
❑ 159 Dan Johnson	.30	.10
❑ 160 Willy Taveras	.30	.10
❑ 161 Garret Anderson	.30	.10
❑ 162 Randy Johnson	.75	.30
❑ 163 Jermaine Dye	.30	.10
❑ 164 Joe Mauer	.50	.20
❑ 165 Ervin Santana	.30	.10
❑ 166 Jeremy Bonderman	.30	.10
❑ 167 Garrett Atkins	.30	.10
❑ 168 Manny Ramirez	.50	.20
❑ 169 Brad Eldred	.30	.10
❑ 170 Chase Utley	.75	.30
❑ 171 Mark Loretta	.30	.10
❑ 172 John Patterson	.30	.10
❑ 173 Tom Glavine	.50	.20
❑ 174 Dontrelle Willis	.30	.10
❑ 175 Mark Teixeira	.50	.20
❑ 176 Felix Hernandez	.50	.20
❑ 177 Cliff Lee	.30	.10
❑ 178 Jason Schmidt	.30	.10
❑ 179 Chad Tracy	.30	.10
❑ 180 Rocco Baldelli	.30	.10
❑ 181 Aramis Ramirez	.30	.10
❑ 182 Andy Pettitte	.50	.20
❑ 183 Mark Mulder	.30	.10
❑ 184 Geoff Jenkins	.30	.10
❑ 185 Chipper Jones	.75	.30
❑ 186 Vernon Wells	.30	.10
❑ 187 Bobby Crosby	.30	.10
❑ 188 Lance Berkman	.30	.10
❑ 189 Vladimir Guerrero	.75	.30
❑ 190 Jose Capellan	.30	.10
❑ 191 Brad Penny	.30	.10
❑ 192 Jose Guillen	.30	.10
❑ 193 Brett Myers	.30	.10
❑ 194 Miguel Cabrera	.50	.20
❑ 195 Bartolo Colon	.30	.10
❑ 196 Craig Biggio	.50	.20
❑ 197 Tim Hudson	.30	.10
❑ 198 Mark Prior	.50	.20
❑ 199 Mark Buehrle	.30	.10
❑ 200 Barry Bonds	2.00	.75
❑ 201 Anderson Hernandez (RC)	.40	.15
❑ 202 Charlton Jimerson (RC)	.40	.15
❑ 203 Jeremy Accardo RC	.40	.15
❑ 204 Hanley Ramirez (RC)	1.00	.40
❑ 205 Matt Capps (RC)	.40	.15
❑ 206 John-Ford Griffin (RC)	.40	.15
❑ 207 Chuck James (RC)	.60	.25
❑ 208 Jaime Bubela (RC)	.40	.15
❑ 209 Mark Woodyard (RC)	.40	.15
❑ 210 Jason Botts (RC)	.40	.15
❑ 211 Chris Demaria RC	.40	.15
❑ 212 Miguel Perez (RC)	.40	.15
❑ 213 Tom Gorzelanny (RC)	.40	.15
❑ 214 Adam Wainwright (RC)	.40	.15
❑ 215 Ryan Garko (RC)	.40	.15
❑ 216 Jason Bergmann RC	.40	.15
❑ 217 J.J. Furmaniak (RC)	.40	.15
❑ 218 Francisco Liriano (RC)	2.00	.75
❑ 219 Kenji Johjima RC	2.00	.75
❑ 219a Kenji Johjima AU	60.00	30.00
❑ 220 Craig Hansen RC	1.50	.60
❑ 220a Craig Hansen AU	50.00	20.00
❑ 221 Ryan Zimmerman AU (RC)	50.00	20.00

❑ 222 Joey Devine AU RC	10.00	4.00
❑ 223 Scott Olsen AU (RC)	10.00	4.00
❑ 224 Darrel Rasner AU (RC)	10.00	4.00
❑ 225 Craig Breslow AU RC	10.00	4.00
❑ 226 Reggie Abercrombie AU (RC)	10.00	4.00
❑ 227 Dan Uggla AU (RC)	40.00	15.00
❑ 228 Willie Eyre AU (RC)	10.00	4.00
❑ 229 Joel Zumaya AU (RC)	30.00	12.50
❑ 230 Ricky Nolasco AU (RC)	10.00	4.00
❑ 231 Ian Kinsler AU (RC)	25.00	10.00

2006 Bowman Draft

❑ COMPLETE SET (55)	15.00	6.00
❑ COMMON RC (1-55)	.40	.15
❑ RC SEMIS 1-55	.60	.25
❑ RC UNLISTED 1-55	1.00	.40
❑ APPX. TWO PER HOBBY/RETAL PACK		
❑ ODDS INFO PROVIDED BY BECKETT		
❑ OVERALL PLATE ODDS 1:990 HOBBY		
❑ PLATE PRINT RUN 1 SET PER COLOR		
❑ BLACK-CYAN-MAGENTA-YELLOW ISSUED		
❑ NO PLATE PRICING DUE TO SCARCITY		
❑ 1 Matt Kemp (RC)	.60	.25
❑ 2 Taylor Tankersley (RC)	.40	.15
❑ 3 Mike Napoli RC	1.00	.40
❑ 4 Brian Bannister (RC)	.40	.15
❑ 5 Melky Cabrera (RC)	.60	.25
❑ 6 Bill Bray (RC)	.40	.15
❑ 7 Brian Anderson (RC)	.40	.15
❑ 8 Jered Weaver (RC)	1.25	.50
❑ 9 Chris Duncan (RC)	.60	.25
❑ 10 Boof Bonser (RC)	.60	.25
❑ 11 Mike Rouse (RC)	.40	.15
❑ 12 David Pauley (RC)	.40	.15
❑ 13 Russ Martin (RC)	.60	.25
❑ 14 Jeremy Sowers (RC)	.40	.15
❑ 15 Kevin Reese (RC)	.40	.15
❑ 16 John Rheinecker (RC)	.40	.15
❑ 17 Tommy Murphy (RC)	.40	.15
❑ 18 Sean Marshall (RC)	.40	.15
❑ 19 Jason Kubel (RC)	.40	.15
❑ 20 Chad Billingsley (RC)	.60	.25
❑ 21 Kendry Morales (RC)	.60	.25
❑ 22 Jon Lester RC	1.25	.50
❑ 23 Brandon Fahey RC	.40	.15
❑ 24 Josh Johnson (RC)	.60	.25
❑ 25 Kevin Frandsen (RC)	.40	.15
❑ 26 Casey Janssen RC	.60	.25
❑ 27 Scott Thorman (RC)	.40	.15
❑ 28 Scott Mathieson (RC)	.40	.15
❑ 29 Jeremy Hermida (RC)	.40	.15
❑ 30 Dustin Nippert (RC)	.40	.15
❑ 31 Kevin Thompson (RC)	.40	.15
❑ 32 Bobby Livingston (RC)	.40	.15
❑ 33 Travis Ishikawa (RC)	.40	.15
❑ 34 Jeff Mathis (RC)	.40	.15
❑ 35 Charlie Haeger RC	.60	.25
❑ 36 Josh Willingham (RC)	.40	.15
❑ 37 Taylor Buchholz (RC)	.40	.15
❑ 38 Joel Guzman (RC)	.40	.15
❑ 39 Zach Jackson (RC)	.40	.15
❑ 40 Howie Kendrick (RC)	1.00	.40
❑ 41 T.J. Beam (RC)	.40	.15
❑ 42 Ty Taubenheim RC	.60	.25
❑ 43 Erick Aybar (RC)	.40	.15
❑ 44 Anibal Sanchez (RC)	.60	.25
❑ 45 Michael Pelfrey RC	1.50	.60
❑ 46 Shawn Hill (RC)	.40	.15
❑ 47 Chris Roberson (RC)	.40	.15
❑ 48 Carlos Villanueva RC	.40	.15
❑ 49 Andre Ethier (RC)	1.00	.40
❑ 50 Anthony Reyes (RC)	.60	.25
❑ 51 Franklin Gutierrez (RC)	.40	.15
❑ 52 Angel Guzman (RC)	.40	.15
❑ 53 Michael O'Connor RC	.40	.15
❑ 54 James Shields RC	.40	.15
❑ 55 Nate McLouth (RC)	.40	.15

2007 Bowman

❑ COMP.SET w/o AU's (221)	50.00	20.00
❑ COMMON CARD (1-200)	.30	.12
❑ COMMON ROOKIE (201-220)	.40	.15
❑ COMMON AUTO (221-236)	10.00	4.00
❑ 219/221-236 AU ODDS 1:98 HOBBY, 1:25 HTA		
❑ BONDS ODDS 1:51 HTA, 1:610 RETAIL		
❑ 1-220 PLATE ODDS 1:1468 H, 1:212 HTA		
❑ 221-231 AU PLATES 1:8200 H, 1:1150 HTA		
❑ BONDS PLATE ODDS 1:106,000 HTA		
❑ PLATE PRINT RUN 1 SET PER COLOR		
❑ BLACK-CYAN-MAGENTA-YELLOW ISSUED		
❑ NO PLATE PRICING DUE TO SCARCITY		
❑ 1 Hanley Ramirez	.50	.20
❑ 2 Justin Verlander	.75	.30
❑ 3 Ryan Zimmerman	.75	.30
❑ 4 Jered Weaver	.50	.20
❑ 5 Stephen Drew	.50	.20
❑ 6 Jonathan Papelbon	.75	.30
❑ 7 Melky Cabrera	.30	.12
❑ 8 Francisco Liriano	.75	.30
❑ 9 Prince Fielder	.75	.30
❑ 10 Dan Uggla	.50	.20
❑ 11 Jeremy Sowers	.30	.12
❑ 12 Carlos Quentin	.30	.12
❑ 13 Chuck James	.30	.12
❑ 14 Andre Ethier	.50	.20
❑ 15 Cole Hamels UER	.50	.20
❑ 16 Kenji Johjima	.75	.30
❑ 17 Chad Billingsley	.30	.12
❑ 18 Ian Kinsler	.30	.12
❑ 19 Jason Hirsh	.30	.12
❑ 20 Nick Markakis	.50	.20
❑ 21 Jeremy Hermida	.30	.12
❑ 22 Ryan Shealy	.30	.12
❑ 23 Scott Olsen	.30	.12
❑ 24 Russell Martin	.30	.12
❑ 25 Conor Jackson	.30	.12
❑ 26 Erik Bedard	.30	.12
❑ 27 Brian McCann	.30	.12
❑ 28 Michael Barrett	.30	.12
❑ 29 Brandon Phillips	.30	.12
❑ 30 Garrett Atkins	.30	.12
❑ 31 Freddy Garcia	.30	.12
❑ 32 Mark Loretta	.30	.12
❑ 33 Craig Biggio	.50	.20
❑ 34 Jeremy Bonderman	.30	.12
❑ 35 Johan Santana	.50	.20
❑ 36 Jorge Posada	.50	.20
❑ 37 Brian Bannister	.30	.12
❑ 38 Carlos Delgado	.30	.12
❑ 39 Gary Matthews Jr.	.30	.12
❑ 40 Mike Cameron	.30	.12
❑ 41 Adrian Beltre	.30	.12
❑ 42 Freddy Sanchez	.30	.12
❑ 43 Austin Kearns	.30	.12
❑ 44 Mark Buehrle	.30	.12
❑ 45 Miguel Cabrera	.50	.20
❑ 46 Josh Beckett	.50	.20
❑ 47 Chone Figgins	.30	.12
❑ 48 Edgar Renteria	.30	.12
❑ 49 Derek Lowe	.30	.12
❑ 50 Ryan Howard	1.25	.50
❑ 51 Shawn Green	.30	.12
❑ 52 Jason Giambi	.30	.12
❑ 53 Ervin Santana	.30	.12
❑ 54 Jack Wilson	.30	.12
❑ 55 Roy Oswalt	.30	.12
❑ 56 Dan Haren	.30	.12
❑ 57 Jose Vidro	.30	.12
❑ 58 Kevin Millwood	.30	.12
❑ 59 Jim Edmonds	.50	.20
❑ 60 Carl Crawford	.30	.12
❑ 61 Randy Wolf	.30	.12
❑ 62 Paul LoDuca	.30	.12
❑ 63 Johnny Estrada	.30	.12
❑ 64 Brian Roberts	.30	.12
❑ 65 Manny Ramirez	.50	.20
❑ 66 Jose Contreras	.30	.12
❑ 67 Josh Barfield	.30	.12
❑ 68 Juan Pierre	.30	.12
❑ 69 David DeJesus	.30	.12
❑ 70 Gary Sheffield	.30	.12
❑ 71 Jon Lieber	.30	.12
❑ 72 Randy Johnson	.75	.30
❑ 73 Rickie Weeks	.30	.12
❑ 74 Brian Giles	.30	.12
❑ 75 Ichiro Suzuki	1.25	.50
❑ 76 Nick Swisher	.30	.12
❑ 77 Justin Morneau	.30	.12
❑ 78 Scott Kazmir	.50	.20
❑ 79 Lyle Overbay	.30	.12
❑ 80 Alfonso Soriano	.30	.12
❑ 81 Brandon Webb	.30	.12
❑ 82 Joe Crede	.30	.12
❑ 83 Corey Patterson	.30	.12
❑ 84 Kenny Rogers	.30	.12
❑ 85 Ken Griffey Jr	1.25	.50
❑ 86 Cliff Lee	.30	.12
❑ 87 Mike Lowell	.30	.12
❑ 88 Marcus Giles	.30	.12
❑ 89 Orlando Cabrera	.30	.12
❑ 90 Derek Jeter	2.00	.75
❑ 91 Josh Johnson	.30	.12
❑ 92 Carlos Guillen	.30	.12
❑ 93 Bill Hall	.30	.12
❑ 94 Michael Cuddyer	.30	.12
❑ 95 Miguel Tejada	.30	.12
❑ 96 Todd Helton	.50	.20
❑ 97 C.C. Sabathia	.30	.12
❑ 98 Tadahito Iguchi	.30	.12
❑ 99 Jose Reyes	.30	.12
❑ 100 David Wright	1.25	.50
❑ 101 Barry Zito	.30	.12
❑ 102 Jake Peavy	.30	.12
❑ 103 Richie Sexson	.30	.12
❑ 104 A.J. Burnett	.30	.12
❑ 105 Eric Chavez	.30	.12
❑ 106 Jorge Cantu	.30	.12
❑ 107 Grady Sizemore	.50	.20
❑ 108 Bronson Arroyo	.30	.12
❑ 109 Mike Mussina	.50	.20
❑ 110 Magglio Ordonez	.30	.12
❑ 111 Anibal Sanchez	.30	.12
❑ 112 Jeff Francoeur	.75	.30
❑ 113 Kevin Youkilis	.30	.12
❑ 114 Aubrey Huff	.30	.12
❑ 115 Carlos Zambrano	.30	.12
❑ 116 Mark Teahen	.30	.12
❑ 117 Carlos Silva	.30	.12
❑ 118 Pedro Martinez	.50	.20
❑ 119 Hideki Matsui	.75	.30
❑ 120 Mike Piazza	.75	.30
❑ 121 Jason Schmidt	.30	.12
❑ 122 Greg Maddux	1.25	.50
❑ 123 Joe Blanton	.30	.12
❑ 124 Chris Carpenter	.30	.12
❑ 125 David Ortiz	.75	.30
❑ 126 Alex Rios	.30	.12
❑ 127 Nick Johnson	.30	.12
❑ 128 Carlos Lee	.30	.12
❑ 129 Pat Burrell	.30	.12
❑ 130 Ben Sheets	.30	.12
❑ 131 Kazuo Matsui	.30	.12

❑ 132 Adam Dunn .30 .12
❑ 133 Jermaine Dye .30 .12
❑ 134 Curt Schilling .50 .20
❑ 135 Chad Tracy .30 .12
❑ 136 Vladimir Guerrero .75 .30
❑ 137 Melvin Mora .30 .12
❑ 138 John Smoltz .50 .20
❑ 139 Craig Monroe .30 .12
❑ 140 Dontrelle Willis .30 .12
❑ 141 Jeff Francis .30 .12
❑ 142 Chipper Jones .75 .30
❑ 143 Frank Thomas .75 .30
❑ 144 Brett Myers .30 .12
❑ 145 Xavier Nady .30 .12
❑ 146 Robinson Cano .50 .20
❑ 147 Jeff Kent .30 .12
❑ 148 Scott Rolen .50 .20
❑ 149 Roy Halladay .30 .12
❑ 150 Joe Mauer .50 .20
❑ 151 Bobby Abreu .30 .12
❑ 152 Matt Cain .50 .20
❑ 153 Hank Blalock .30 .12
❑ 154 Chris Capuano .30 .12
❑ 155 Jake Westbrook .30 .12
❑ 156 Javier Vazquez .30 .12
❑ 157 Garret Anderson .30 .12
❑ 158 Aramis Ramirez .30 .12
❑ 159 Mark Kotsay .30 .12
❑ 160 Matt Kemp .30 .12
❑ 161 Adrian Gonzalez .30 .12
❑ 162 Felix Hernandez .50 .20
❑ 163 David Eckstein .30 .12
❑ 164 Curtis Granderson .30 .12
❑ 165 Paul Konerko .30 .12
❑ 166 Orlando Hudson .30 .12
❑ 167 Tim Hudson .30 .12
❑ 168 J.D. Drew .30 .12
❑ 169 Chien-Ming Wang 1.25 .50
❑ 170 Jimmy Rollins .30 .12
❑ 171 Matt Morris .30 .12
❑ 172 Raul Ibanez .30 .12
❑ 173 Mark Teixeira .50 .20
❑ 174 Ted Lilly .30 .12
❑ 175 Albert Pujols 1.50 .60
❑ 176 Carlos Beltran .30 .12
❑ 177 Lance Berkman .30 .12
❑ 178 Ivan Rodriguez .50 .20
❑ 179 Torii Hunter .30 .12
❑ 180 Johnny Damon .50 .20
❑ 181 Chase Utley .75 .30
❑ 182 Jason Bay .30 .12
❑ 183 Jeff Weaver .30 .12
❑ 184 Troy Glaus .30 .12
❑ 185 Rocco Baldelli .30 .12
❑ 186 Rafael Furcal .30 .12
❑ 187 Jim Thome .50 .20
❑ 188 Travis Hafner .30 .12
❑ 189 Matt Holliday .75 .30
❑ 190 Andruw Jones .50 .20
❑ 191 Ramon Hernandez .30 .12
❑ 192 Victor Martinez .30 .12
❑ 193 Aaron Hill .30 .12
❑ 194 Michael Young .30 .12
❑ 195 Vernon Wells .30 .12
❑ 196 Mark Mulder .30 .12
❑ 197 Derrek Lee .30 .12
❑ 198 Tom Glavine .50 .20
❑ 199 Chris Young .30 .12
❑ 200 Alex Rodriguez 1.25 .50
❑ 201 Delmon Young (RC) 1.00 .40
❑ 202 Alexi Casilla RC .60 .25
❑ 203 Shawn Riggans (RC) .40 .15
❑ 204 Jeff Baker (RC) .40 .15
❑ 205 Hector Gimenez (RC) .40 .15
❑ 206 Ubaldo Jimenez (RC) .40 .15
❑ 207 Adam Lind (RC) .40 .15
❑ 208 Joaquin Arias (RC) .40 .15
❑ 209 David Murphy (RC) .40 .15
❑ 210 Daisuke Matsuzaka RC 5.00 2.00
❑ 211 Jerry Owens (RC) .40 .15
❑ 212 Ryan Sweeney (RC) .40 .15
❑ 213 Kei Igawa RC 1.50 .60
❑ 214 Fred Lewis (RC) .40 .15
❑ 215 Philip Humber (RC) .40 .15
❑ 216 Kevin Hooper (RC) .40 .15
❑ 217 Jeff Fiorentino (RC) .40 .15
❑ 218 Michael Bourn (RC) .40 .15
❑ 219 Hideki Okajima RC 2.00 .75
❑ 219b H.Okajima English AU 40.00 15.00
❑ 219c H.Okajima Japan AU 60.00 30.00
❑ 220 Josh Fields (RC) .40 .15
❑ 221 Andrew Miller AU RC 50.00 20.00
❑ 222 Troy Tulowitzki AU (RC) 30.00 12.50
❑ 223 Ryan Braun AU RC 25.00 10.00
❑ 224 Oswaldo Navarro AU RC 10.00 4.00
❑ 225 Philip Humber AU (RC) 10.00 4.00
❑ 226 Mitch Maier AU RC 10.00 4.00
❑ 227 Jerry Owens AU (RC) 10.00 4.00
❑ 228 Mike Rabelo AU RC 10.00 4.00
❑ 229 Delwyn Young AU (RC) 10.00 4.00
❑ 230 Miguel Montero AU (RC) 10.00 4.00
❑ 231 Akinori Iwamura AU RC 25.00 10.00
❑ 232 Matt Lindstrom AU (RC) 10.00 4.00
❑ 233 Josh Hamilton AU (RC) 25.00 10.00
❑ 235 Elijah Dukes AU RC 25.00 10.00
❑ 236 Sean Henn AU (RC) 10.00 4.00
❑ 237 Barry Bonds 8.00 3.00

1997 Bowman Chrome

❑ COMPLETE SET (300) 150.00 75.00
❑ 1 Derek Jeter 3.00 1.25
❑ 2 Chipper Jones 1.25 .50
❑ 3 Hideo Nomo 1.25 .50
❑ 4 Tim Salmon .75 .30
❑ 5 Robin Ventura .50 .20
❑ 6 Tony Clark .50 .20
❑ 7 Barry Larkin .75 .30
❑ 8 Paul Molitor .50 .20
❑ 9 Andy Benes .50 .20
❑ 10 Ryan Klesko .50 .20
❑ 11 Mark McGwire 3.00 1.25
❑ 12 Ken Griffey Jr. 2.00 .75
❑ 13 Robb Nen .50 .20
❑ 14 Cal Ripken 4.00 1.50
❑ 15 John Valentin .50 .20
❑ 16 Ricky Bottalico .50 .20
❑ 17 Mike Lansing .50 .20
❑ 18 Ryne Sandberg 2.00 .75
❑ 19 Carlos Delgado .50 .20
❑ 20 Craig Biggio .75 .30
❑ 21 Eric Karros .50 .20
❑ 22 Kevin Appier .50 .20
❑ 23 Mariano Rivera 1.25 .50
❑ 24 Vinny Castilla .50 .20
❑ 25 Juan Gonzalez .50 .20
❑ 26 Al Martin .50 .20
❑ 27 Jeff Cirillo .50 .20
❑ 28 Ray Lankford .50 .20
❑ 29 Manny Ramirez .75 .30
❑ 30 Roberto Alomar .75 .30
❑ 31 Will Clark .75 .30
❑ 32 Chuck Knoblauch .50 .20
❑ 33 Harold Baines .50 .20
❑ 34 Edgar Martinez .75 .30
❑ 35 Mike Mussina .75 .30
❑ 36 Kevin Brown .50 .20
❑ 37 Dennis Eckersley .50 .20
❑ 38 Tino Martinez .75 .30
❑ 39 Raul Mondesi .50 .20
❑ 40 Sammy Sosa 1.25 .50
❑ 41 John Smoltz .75 .30
❑ 42 Billy Wagner .50 .20
❑ 43 Ken Caminiti .50 .20
❑ 44 Wade Boggs .75 .30
❑ 45 Andres Galarraga .50 .20
❑ 46 Roger Clemens 2.50 1.00
❑ 47 Matt Williams .50 .20
❑ 48 Albert Belle .50 .20
❑ 49 Jeff King .50 .20
❑ 50 John Wetteland .50 .20
❑ 51 Deion Sanders .75 .30
❑ 52 Ellis Burks .50 .20
❑ 53 Pedro Martinez .75 .30
❑ 54 Kenny Lofton .50 .20
❑ 55 Randy Johnson 1.25 .50
❑ 56 Bernie Williams .75 .30
❑ 57 Marquis Grissom .50 .20
❑ 58 Gary Sheffield .50 .20
❑ 59 Curt Schilling .50 .20
❑ 60 Reggie Sanders .50 .20
❑ 61 Bobby Higginson .50 .20
❑ 62 Moises Alou .50 .20
❑ 63 Tom Glavine .75 .30
❑ 64 Mark Grace .75 .30
❑ 65 Rafael Palmeiro .75 .30
❑ 66 John Olerud .50 .20
❑ 67 Dante Bichette .50 .20
❑ 68 Jeff Bagwell .75 .30
❑ 69 Barry Bonds 3.00 1.25
❑ 70 Pat Hentgen .50 .20
❑ 71 Jim Thome .75 .30
❑ 72 Andy Pettitte .75 .30
❑ 73 Jay Bell .50 .20
❑ 74 Jim Edmonds .50 .20
❑ 75 Ron Gant .50 .20
❑ 76 David Cone .50 .20
❑ 77 Jose Canseco .75 .30
❑ 78 Jay Buhner .50 .20
❑ 79 Greg Maddux 2.00 .75
❑ 80 Lance Johnson .50 .20
❑ 81 Travis Fryman .50 .20
❑ 82 Paul O'Neill .75 .30
❑ 83 Ivan Rodriguez .75 .30
❑ 84 Fred McGriff .75 .30
❑ 85 Mike Piazza 2.00 .75
❑ 86 Brady Anderson .50 .20
❑ 87 Marty Cordova .50 .20
❑ 88 Joe Carter .50 .20
❑ 89 Brian Jordan .50 .20
❑ 90 David Justice .50 .20
❑ 91 Tony Gwynn 1.50 .60
❑ 92 Larry Walker .50 .20
❑ 93 Mo Vaughn .50 .20
❑ 94 Sandy Alomar Jr. .50 .20
❑ 95 Rusty Greer .50 .20
❑ 96 Roberto Hernandez .50 .20
❑ 97 Hal Morris .50 .20
❑ 98 Todd Hundley .50 .20
❑ 99 Rondell White .50 .20
❑ 100 Frank Thomas 1.25 .50
❑ 101 Bubba Trammell RC 1.50 .60
❑ 102 Sidney Ponson RC 2.50 1.00
❑ 103 Ricky Ledee RC 1.50 .60
❑ 104 Brett Tomko .50 .20
❑ 105 Braden Looper RC 1.00 .40
❑ 106 Jason Dickson .50 .20
❑ 107 Chad Green RC 1.00 .40
❑ 108 R.A. Dickey RC 1.00 .40
❑ 109 Jeff Liefer .50 .20
❑ 110 Richard Hidalgo .50 .20
❑ 111 Chad Hermansen RC 1.00 .40
❑ 112 Felix Martinez .50 .20
❑ 113 J.J. Johnson .50 .20
❑ 114 Todd Dunwoody .50 .20
❑ 115 Katsuhiro Maeda .50 .20
❑ 116 Darin Erstad .50 .20
❑ 117 Elieser Marrero .50 .20
❑ 118 Bartolo Colon .50 .20
❑ 119 Ugueth Urbina .50 .20
❑ 120 Jaime Bluma .50 .20
❑ 121 Seth Greisinger RC 1.00 .40
❑ 122 Jose Cruz Jr. RC 1.50 .60
❑ 123 Todd Dunn .50 .20
❑ 124 Justin Towle RC 1.00 .40
❑ 125 Brian Rose .50 .20
❑ 126 Jose Guillen .50 .20
❑ 127 Andruw Jones .75 .30
❑ 128 Mark Kotsay RC 4.00 1.50
❑ 129 Wilton Guerrero .50 .20
❑ 130 Jacob Cruz .50 .20

131	Mike Sweeney	.50	.20
132	Matt Morris	.50	.20
133	John Thomson	.50	.20
134	Javier Valentin	.50	.20
135	Mike Drumright RC	1.00	.40
136	Michael Barrett	.50	.20
137	Tony Saunders RC	1.00	.40
138	Kevin Brown	.50	.20
139	Anthony Sanders RC	1.00	.40
140	Jeff Abbott	.50	.20
141	Eugene Kingsale	.50	.20
142	Paul Konerko	.75	.30
143	Randall Simon RC	1.50	.60
144	Freddy Adrian Garcia	.50	.20
145	Karim Garcia	.50	.20
146	Carlos Guillen	.50	.20
147	Aaron Boone	.50	.20
148	Donnie Sadler	.50	.20
149	Brooks Kieschnick	.50	.20
150	Scott Spiezio	.50	.20
151	Kevin Orie	.50	.20
152	Russ Johnson	.50	.20
153	Livan Hernandez	.50	.20
154	Vladimir Nunez RC	1.00	.40
155	Pokey Reese	.50	.20
156	Chris Carpenter	.50	.20
157	Eric Milton RC	1.50	.60
158	Richie Sexson	.50	.20
159	Carl Pavano	.50	.20
160	Pat Cline	.50	.20
161	Ron Wright	.50	.20
162	Dante Powell	.50	.20
163	Mark Bellhorn	.50	.20
164	George Lombard	.50	.20
165	Paul Wilder RC	1.00	.40
166	Brad Fullmer	.50	.20
167	Kris Benson RC	2.50	1.00
168	Torii Hunter	.50	.20
169	D.T. Cromer RC	1.00	.40
170	Nelson Figueroa RC	1.00	.40
171	Hiram Bocachica RC	1.00	.40
172	Shane Monahan	.50	.20
173	Juan Melo	.50	.20
174	Calvin Pickering RC	1.00	.40
175	Reggie Taylor	.50	.20
176	Geoff Jenkins	.50	.20
177	Steve Rain RC	1.00	.40
178	Nerio Rodriguez RC	1.00	.40
179	Derrick Gibson	.50	.20
180	Darin Blood	.50	.20
181	Ben Davis	.50	.20
182	Adrian Beltre RC	8.00	3.00
183	Kerry Wood RC	12.00	5.00
184	Nate Rolison RC	1.00	.40
185	Fernando Tatis RC	1.00	.40
186	Jake Westbrook RC	2.50	1.00
187	Edwin Diaz	.50	.20
188	Joe Fontenot RC	1.00	.40
189	Matt Halloran RC	1.00	.40
190	Matt Clement RC	2.50	1.00
191	Todd Greene	.50	.20
192	Eric Chavez RC	10.00	4.00
193	Edgard Velazquez	.50	.20
194	Bruce Chen RC	2.50	1.00
195	Jason Brester	.50	.20
196	Chris Reitsma RC	1.50	.60
197	Neifi Perez	.50	.20
198	Hideki Irabu RC	1.50	.60
199	Don Denbow RC	1.00	.40
200	Derrek Lee	.75	.30
201	Todd Walker	.50	.20
202	Scott Rolen	.75	.30
203	Wes Helms	.50	.20
204	Bob Abreu	.75	.30
205	John Patterson RC	4.00	1.50
206	Alex Gonzalez RC	2.50	1.00
207	Grant Roberts RC	1.00	.40
208	Jeff Suppan	.50	.20
209	Luke Wilcox	.50	.20
210	Marlon Anderson	.50	.20
211	Mike Caruso RC	1.00	.40
212	Roy Halladay RC	12.00	5.00
213	Jeremi Gonzalez RC	1.00	.40
214	Aramis Ramirez RC	10.00	4.00
215	Dee Brown RC	1.00	.40
216	Justin Thompson	.50	.20

217	Danny Clyburn	.50	.20
218	Bruce Aven	.50	.20
219	Keith Foulke RC	4.00	1.50
220	Shannon Stewart	.50	.20
221	Larry Barnes RC	1.00	.40
222	Mark Johnson RC	1.00	.40
223	Randy Winn	.50	.20
224	Nomar Garciaparra	2.00	.75
225	Jacque Jones RC	4.00	1.50
226	Chris Clemons	.50	.20
227	Todd Helton	1.25	.50
228	Ryan Brannan RC	1.00	.40
229	Alex Sanchez RC	1.50	.60
230	Russell Branyan	.50	.20
231	Daryle Ward	1.00	.40
232	Kevin Witt	.50	.20
233	Gabby Martinez	.50	.20
234	Preston Wilson	.50	.20
235	Donzell McDonald RC	1.00	.40
236	Orlando Cabrera RC	4.00	1.50
237	Brian Banks	.50	.20
238	Robbie Bell	1.00	.40
239	Brad Rigby	.50	.20
240	Scott Elarton	.50	.20
241	Donny Leon RC	1.00	.40
242	Abraham Nunez RC	1.00	.40
243	Adam Eaton RC	2.50	1.00
244	Octavio Dotel RC	1.50	.60
245	Sean Casey	2.50	1.00
246	Joe Lawrence RC	1.00	.40
247	Adam Johnson RC	1.00	.40
248	Ronnie Belliard RC	3.00	1.25
249	Bobby Estalella	.50	.20
250	Corey Lee RC	1.00	.40
251	Mike Cameron	.50	.20
252	Kerry Robinson RC	1.00	.40
253	A.J. Zapp RC	1.00	.40
254	Jarrod Washburn	.50	.20
255	Ben Grieve	.50	.20
256	Javier Vazquez RC	4.00	1.50
257	Travis Lee RC	1.50	.60
258	Dennis Reyes RC	1.00	.40
259	Danny Buxbaum	.50	.20
260	Kelvim Escobar RC	2.50	1.00
261	Danny Klassen	.50	.20
262	Ken Cloude RC	1.00	.40
263	Gabe Alvarez	.50	.20
264	Clayton Bruner RC	1.00	.40
265	Jason Marquis RC	2.50	1.00
266	Jamey Wright	.50	.20
267	Matt Snyder RC	1.00	.40
268	Josh Garrett RC	1.00	.40
269	Juan Encarnacion	.50	.20
270	Heath Murray	.50	.20
271	Brent Butler RC	1.00	.40
272	Danny Peoples RC	1.00	.40
273	Miguel Tejada RC	20.00	8.00
274	Jim Pittsley	.50	.20
275	Dmitri Young	.50	.20
276	Vladimir Guerrero	1.25	.50
277	Cole Liniak RC	1.00	.40
278	Ramon Hernandez	.50	.20
279	Cliff Politte RC	1.00	.40
280	Mel Rosario RC	1.00	.40
281	Jorge Carrion RC	1.00	.40
282	John Barnes RC	1.00	.40
283	Chris Stowe RC	1.00	.40
284	Vernon Wells RC	12.00	5.00
285	Brett Caradonna RC	1.00	.40
286	Scott Hodges RC	1.00	.40
287	Jon Garland RC	6.00	2.50
288	Nathan Haynes RC	1.00	.40
289	Geoff Goetz RC	1.00	.40
290	Adam Kennedy RC	2.50	1.00
291	T.J. Tucker RC	1.00	.40
292	Aaron Akin RC	1.00	.40
293	Jayson Werth RC	2.50	1.00
294	Glenn Davis RC	1.00	.40
295	Mark Mangum RC	1.00	.40
296	Troy Cameron RC	1.00	.40
297	J.J. Davis RC	1.00	.40
298	Lance Berkman RC	15.00	6.00
299	Jason Standridge RC	1.00	.40
300	Jason Dellaero RC	1.00	.40

1998 Bowman Chrome

	COMPLETE SET (441)	160.00	60.00
	COMPLETE SERIES 1 (221)	80.00	30.00
	COMPLETE SERIES 2 (220)	80.00	30.00
1	Nomar Garciaparra	2.00	.75
2	Scott Rolen	.75	.30
3	Andy Pettitte	.75	.30
4	Ivan Rodriguez	.75	.30
5	Mark McGwire	3.00	1.25
6	Jason Dickson	.50	.20
7	Jose Cruz Jr.	.50	.20
8	Jeff Kent	.50	.20
9	Mike Mussina	.75	.30
10	Jason Kendall	.50	.20
11	Brett Tomko	.50	.20
12	Jeff King	.50	.20
13	Brad Radke	.50	.20
14	Robin Ventura	.50	.20
15	Jeff Bagwell	.75	.30
16	Greg Maddux	2.00	.75
17	John Jaha	.50	.20
18	Mike Piazza	2.00	.75
19	Edgar Martinez	.75	.30
20	David Justice	.50	.20
21	Todd Hundley	.50	.20
22	Tony Gwynn	1.50	.60
23	Larry Walker	.50	.20
24	Bernie Williams	.75	.30
25	Edgar Renteria	.50	.20
26	Rafael Palmeiro	.75	.30
27	Tim Salmon	.75	.30
28	Matt Morris	.50	.20
29	Shawn Estes	.50	.20
30	Vladimir Guerrero	1.25	.50
31	Fernando Tatis	.50	.20
32	Justin Thompson	.50	.20
33	Ken Griffey Jr.	2.00	.75
34	Edgardo Alfonzo	.50	.20
35	Mo Vaughn	.50	.20
36	Marty Cordova	.50	.20
37	Craig Biggio	.75	.30
38	Roger Clemens	2.50	1.00
39	Mark Grace	.75	.30
40	Ken Caminiti	.50	.20
41	Tony Womack	.50	.20
42	Albert Belle	.50	.20
43	Tino Martinez	.75	.30
44	Sandy Alomar Jr.	.50	.20
45	Jeff Cirillo	.50	.20
46	Jason Giambi	.50	.20
47	Darin Erstad	.50	.20
48	Livan Hernandez	.50	.20
49	Mark Grudzielanek	.50	.20
50	Sammy Sosa	1.25	.50
51	Curt Schilling	.50	.20
52	Brian Hunter	.50	.20
53	Neifi Perez	.50	.20
54	Todd Walker	.50	.20
55	Jose Guillen	.50	.20
56	Jim Thome	.75	.30
57	Tom Glavine	.75	.30
58	Todd Greene	.50	.20
59	Rondell White	.50	.20
60	Roberto Alomar	.75	.30
61	Tony Clark	.50	.20
62	Vinny Castilla	.50	.20
63	Barry Larkin	.75	.30

❑ 64 Hideki Irabu .50 .20
❑ 65 Johnny Damon .75 .30
❑ 66 Juan Gonzalez .50 .20
❑ 67 John Olerud .50 .20
❑ 68 Gary Sheffield .50 .20
❑ 69 Raul Mondesi .50 .20
❑ 70 Chipper Jones 1.25 .50
❑ 71 David Ortiz 6.00 2.50
❑ 72 Warren Morris RC 1.00 .40
❑ 73 Alex Gonzalez .50 .20
❑ 74 Nick Bierbrodt .50 .20
❑ 75 Roy Halladay .50 .20
❑ 76 Danny Buxbaum .50 .20
❑ 77 Adam Kennedy .50 .20
❑ 78 Jared Sandberg .50 .20
❑ 79 Michael Barrett .50 .20
❑ 80 Gil Meche 1.50 .60
❑ 81 Jayson Werth .50 .20
❑ 82 Abraham Nunez .50 .20
❑ 83 Ben Petrick .50 .20
❑ 84 Brett Caradonna .50 .20
❑ 85 Mike Lowell RC 6.00 2.50
❑ 86 Clay Bruner .50 .20
❑ 87 John Curtice RC 1.50 .60
❑ 88 Bobby Estalella .50 .20
❑ 89 Juan Melo .50 .20
❑ 90 Arnold Gooch .50 .20
❑ 91 Kevin Millwood RC 4.00 1.50
❑ 92 Richie Sexson .50 .20
❑ 93 Orlando Cabrera .50 .20
❑ 94 Pat Cline .50 .20
❑ 95 Anthony Sanders .50 .20
❑ 96 Russ Johnson .50 .20
❑ 97 Ben Grieve .50 .20
❑ 98 Kevin McGlinchy .50 .20
❑ 99 Paul Wilder .50 .20
❑ 100 Russ Ortiz .50 .20
❑ 101 Ryan Jackson RC 1.00 .40
❑ 102 Heath Murray .50 .20
❑ 103 Brian Rose .50 .20
❑ 104 Ryan Radmanovich RC 1.00 .40
❑ 105 Ricky Ledee .50 .20
❑ 106 Jeff Wallace RC 1.00 .40
❑ 107 Ryan Minor RC 1.00 .40
❑ 108 Dennis Reyes .50 .20
❑ 109 James Manias .50 .20
❑ 110 Chris Carpenter .50 .20
❑ 111 Daryle Ward .50 .20
❑ 112 Vernon Wells .50 .20
❑ 113 Chad Green .50 .20
❑ 114 Mike Stoner RC 1.00 .40
❑ 115 Brad Fullmer .50 .20
❑ 116 Adam Eaton .50 .20
❑ 117 Jeff Liefer .50 .20
❑ 118 Corey Koskie RC 2.50 1.00
❑ 119 Todd Helton .75 .30
❑ 120 Jaime Jones RC 1.00 .40
❑ 121 Mel Rosario .50 .20
❑ 122 Geoff Goetz .50 .20
❑ 123 Adrian Beltre .50 .20
❑ 124 Jason Dellaero .50 .20
❑ 125 Gabe Kapler RC 2.50 1.00
❑ 126 Scott Schoeneweis .50 .20
❑ 127 Ryan Brannan .50 .20
❑ 128 Aaron Akin .50 .20
❑ 129 Ryan Anderson RC 1.00 .40
❑ 130 Brad Penny .50 .20
❑ 131 Bruce Chen .50 .20
❑ 132 Eli Marrero .50 .20
❑ 133 Eric Chavez .50 .20
❑ 134 Troy Glaus RC 8.00 3.00
❑ 135 Troy Cameron .50 .20
❑ 136 Brian Sikorski RC 1.00 .40
❑ 137 Mike Kinkade RC 1.00 .40
❑ 138 Braden Looper .50 .20
❑ 139 Mark Mangum .50 .20
❑ 140 Danny Peoples .50 .20
❑ 141 J.J. Davis .50 .20
❑ 142 Ben Davis .50 .20
❑ 143 Jacque Jones .50 .20
❑ 144 Derrick Gibson .50 .20
❑ 145 Bronson Arroyo 4.00 1.50
❑ 146 Luis De Los Santos RC 1.00 .40
❑ 147 Jeff Abbott .50 .20
❑ 148 Mike Cuddyer RC 4.00 1.50
❑ 149 Jason Romano .50 .20
❑ 150 Shane Monahan .50 .20
❑ 151 Ntema Ndungidi RC 1.00 .40
❑ 152 Alex Sanchez .50 .20
❑ 153 Jack Cust RC 8.00 3.00
❑ 154 Brent Butler .50 .20
❑ 155 Ramon Hernandez .50 .20
❑ 156 Norm Hutchins .50 .20
❑ 157 Jason Marquis .50 .20
❑ 158 Jacob Cruz .50 .20
❑ 159 Rob Burger RC 1.00 .40
❑ 160 Dave Coggin .50 .20
❑ 161 Preston Wilson .50 .20
❑ 162 Jason Fitzgerald RC 1.00 .40
❑ 163 Dan Serafini .50 .20
❑ 164 Pete Munro .50 .20
❑ 165 Trot Nixon .50 .20
❑ 166 Homer Bush .50 .20
❑ 167 Dermal Brown .50 .20
❑ 168 Chad Hermansen .50 .20
❑ 169 Julio Moreno RC 1.00 .40
❑ 170 John Roskos RC 1.00 .40
❑ 171 Grant Roberts .50 .20
❑ 172 Ken Cloude .50 .20
❑ 173 Jason Brester .50 .20
❑ 174 Jason Conti .50 .20
❑ 175 Jon Garland .50 .20
❑ 176 Robbie Bell .50 .20
❑ 177 Nathan Haynes .50 .20
❑ 178 Ramon Ortiz RC 1.50 .60
❑ 179 Shannon Stewart .50 .20
❑ 180 Pablo Ortega .50 .20
❑ 181 Jimmy Rollins RC 8.00 3.00
❑ 182 Sean Casey .50 .20
❑ 183 Ted Lilly RC 2.50 1.00
❑ 184 Chris Enochs RC 1.00 .40
❑ 185 Magglio Ordonez UER RC 10.00 4.00
❑ 186 Mike Drumright .50 .20
❑ 187 Aaron Boone .50 .20
❑ 188 Matt Clement .50 .20
❑ 189 Todd Dunwoody .50 .20
❑ 190 Larry Rodriguez .50 .20
❑ 191 Todd Noel .50 .20
❑ 192 Geoff Jenkins .50 .20
❑ 193 George Lombard .50 .20
❑ 194 Lance Berkman .50 .20
❑ 195 Marcus McCain .50 .20
❑ 196 Ryan McGuire .50 .20
❑ 197 Jhensy Sandoval .50 .20
❑ 198 Corey Lee .50 .20
❑ 199 Mario Valdez .50 .20
❑ 200 Robert Fick RC 1.50 .60
❑ 201 Donnie Sadler .50 .20
❑ 202 Marc Kroon .50 .20
❑ 203 David Miller .50 .20
❑ 204 Jarrod Washburn .50 .20
❑ 205 Miguel Tejada 1.25 .50
❑ 206 Raul Ibanez .50 .20
❑ 207 John Patterson .50 .20
❑ 208 Calvin Pickering .50 .20
❑ 209 Felix Martinez .50 .20
❑ 210 Mark Redman .50 .20
❑ 211 Scott Elarton .50 .20
❑ 212 Jose Amado RC 1.00 .40
❑ 213 Kerry Wood .50 .20
❑ 214 Dante Powell .50 .20
❑ 215 Aramis Ramirez .50 .20
❑ 216 A.J. Hinch .50 .20
❑ 217 Dustin Carr RC 1.00 .40
❑ 218 Mark Kotsay .50 .20
❑ 219 Jason Standridge .50 .20
❑ 220 Luis Ordaz .50 .20
❑ 221 Orlando Hernandez RC 5.00 2.00
❑ 222 Cal Ripken 4.00 1.50
❑ 223 Paul Molitor .50 .20
❑ 224 Derek Jeter 3.00 1.25
❑ 225 Barry Bonds 3.00 1.25
❑ 226 Jim Edmonds .50 .20
❑ 227 John Smoltz .75 .30
❑ 228 Eric Karros .50 .20
❑ 229 Ray Lankford .50 .20
❑ 230 Rey Ordonez .50 .20
❑ 231 Kenny Lofton .50 .20
❑ 232 Alex Rodriguez 2.00 .75
❑ 233 Dante Bichette .50 .20
❑ 234 Pedro Martinez .75 .30
❑ 235 Carlos Delgado .50 .20
❑ 236 Rod Beck .50 .20
❑ 237 Matt Williams .50 .20
❑ 238 Charles Johnson .50 .20
❑ 239 Rico Brogna .50 .20
❑ 240 Frank Thomas 1.25 .50
❑ 241 Paul O'Neill .75 .30
❑ 242 Jaret Wright .50 .20
❑ 243 Brant Brown .50 .20
❑ 244 Ryan Klesko .50 .20
❑ 245 Chuck Finley .50 .20
❑ 246 Derek Bell .50 .20
❑ 247 Delino DeShields .50 .20
❑ 248 Chan Ho Park .50 .20
❑ 249 Wade Boggs .75 .30
❑ 250 Jay Buhner .50 .20
❑ 251 Butch Huskey .50 .20
❑ 252 Steve Finley .50 .20
❑ 253 Will Clark .75 .30
❑ 254 John Valentin .50 .20
❑ 255 Bobby Higginson .50 .20
❑ 256 Darryl Strawberry .50 .20
❑ 257 Randy Johnson 1.25 .50
❑ 258 Al Martin .50 .20
❑ 259 Travis Fryman .50 .20
❑ 260 Fred McGriff .75 .30
❑ 261 Jose Valentin .50 .20
❑ 262 Andruw Jones .75 .30
❑ 263 Kenny Rogers .50 .20
❑ 264 Moises Alou .50 .20
❑ 265 Denny Neagle .50 .20
❑ 266 Ugueth Urbina .50 .20
❑ 267 Derrek Lee .75 .30
❑ 268 Ellis Burks .50 .20
❑ 269 Mariano Rivera 1.25 .50
❑ 270 Dean Palmer .50 .20
❑ 271 Eddie Taubensee .50 .20
❑ 272 Brady Anderson .50 .20
❑ 273 Brian Giles .50 .20
❑ 274 Quinton McCracken .50 .20
❑ 275 Henry Rodriguez .50 .20
❑ 276 Andres Galarraga .50 .20
❑ 277 Jose Canseco .75 .30
❑ 278 David Segui .50 .20
❑ 279 Bret Saberhagen .50 .20
❑ 280 Kevin Brown .75 .30
❑ 281 Chuck Knoblauch .50 .20
❑ 282 Jeromy Burnitz .50 .20
❑ 283 Jay Bell .50 .20
❑ 284 Manny Ramirez .75 .30
❑ 285 Rick Helling .50 .20
❑ 286 Francisco Cordova .50 .20
❑ 287 Bob Abreu .50 .20
❑ 288 J.T. Snow .50 .20
❑ 289 Hideo Nomo 1.25 .50
❑ 290 Brian Jordan .50 .20
❑ 291 Javy Lopez .50 .20
❑ 292 Travis Lee .50 .20
❑ 293 Russell Branyan .50 .20
❑ 294 Paul Konerko .50 .20
❑ 295 Masato Yoshii RC 1.50 .60
❑ 296 Kris Benson .50 .20
❑ 297 Juan Encarnacion .50 .20
❑ 298 Eric Milton .50 .20
❑ 299 Mike Caruso .50 .20
❑ 300 Ricardo Aramboles RC 1.00 .40
❑ 301 Bobby Smith .50 .20
❑ 302 Billy Koch .50 .20
❑ 303 Richard Hidalgo .50 .20
❑ 304 Justin Baughman RC 1.00 .40
❑ 305 Chris Gissell .50 .20
❑ 306 Donnie Bridges RC 1.00 .40
❑ 307 Nelson Lara RC 1.00 .40
❑ 308 Randy Wolf RC 1.50 .60
❑ 309 Jason LaRue RC 1.50 .60
❑ 310 Jason Gooding RC 1.00 .40
❑ 311 Edgard Clemente .50 .20
❑ 312 Andrew Vessel .50 .20
❑ 313 Chris Reitsma .50 .20
❑ 314 Jesus Sanchez RC 1.00 .40
❑ 315 Buddy Carlyle RC 1.00 .40
❑ 316 Randy Winn .50 .20
❑ 317 Luis Rivera RC 1.00 .40
❑ 318 Marcus Thames RC 6.00 2.50
❑ 319 A.J. Pierzynski .50 .20
❑ 320 Scott Randall .50 .20
❑ 321 Damian Sapp .50 .20

❑	322 Ed Yarnall RC	1.00	.40
❑	323 Luke Allen RC	1.00	.40
❑	324 J.D. Smart	.50	.20
❑	325 Willie Martinez	.50	.20
❑	326 Alex Ramirez	.50	.20
❑	327 Eric DuBose RC	1.00	.40
❑	328 Kevin Witt	.50	.20
❑	329 Dan McKinley RC	1.00	.40
❑	330 Cliff Politte	.50	.20
❑	331 Vladimir Nunez	.50	.20
❑	332 John Halama RC	1.00	.40
❑	333 Nerio Rodriguez	.50	.20
❑	334 Desi Relaford	.50	.20
❑	335 Robinson Checo	.50	.20
❑	336 John Nicholson	.75	.30
❑	337 Tom LaRosa RC	1.00	.40
❑	338 Kevin Nicholson RC	1.00	.40
❑	339 Javier Vazquez	.50	.20
❑	340 A.J. Zapp	.50	.20
❑	341 Tom Evans	.50	.20
❑	342 Kerry Robinson	.50	.20
❑	343 Gabe Gonzalez RC	1.00	.40
❑	344 Ralph Milliard	.50	.20
❑	345 Enrique Wilson	.50	.20
❑	346 Elvin Hernandez	.50	.20
❑	347 Mike Lincoln RC	1.00	.40
❑	348 Cesar King RC	1.00	.40
❑	349 Cristian Guzman RC	1.50	.60
❑	350 Donzell McDonald	.50	.20
❑	351 Jim Parque RC	1.00	.40
❑	352 Mike Saipe RC	1.00	.40
❑	353 Carlos Febles RC	1.50	.60
❑	354 Dernell Stenson RC	1.00	.40
❑	355 Mark Osborne RC	1.00	.40
❑	356 Odalis Perez RC	4.00	1.50
❑	357 Jason Dewey RC	1.00	.40
❑	358 Joe Fontenot	.50	.20
❑	359 Jason Grilli RC	1.00	.40
❑	360 Kevin Haverbusch RC	1.00	.40
❑	361 Jay Yennaco RC	1.00	.40
❑	362 Brian Buchanan	.50	.20
❑	363 John Barnes	.50	.20
❑	364 Chris Fussell	.50	.20
❑	365 Kevin Gibbs RC	1.00	.40
❑	366 Joe Lawrence	.50	.20
❑	367 DaRond Stovall	.50	.20
❑	368 Brian Fuentes RC	1.00	.40
❑	369 Jimmy Anderson	.50	.20
❑	370 Lariel Gonzalez RC	1.00	.40
❑	371 Scott Williamson RC	1.00	.40
❑	372 Milton Bradley	.50	.20
❑	373 Jason Halper RC	1.00	.40
❑	374 Brent Billingsley RC	1.00	.40
❑	375 Joe DePastino RC	1.00	.40
❑	376 Jake Westbrook	.50	.20
❑	377 Octavio Dotel	.50	.20
❑	378 Jason Williams RC	1.00	.40
❑	379 Julio Ramirez RC	1.00	.40
❑	380 Seth Greisinger	.50	.20
❑	381 Mike Judd RC	1.00	.40
❑	382 Ben Ford RC	1.00	.40
❑	383 Tom Bennett RC	1.00	.40
❑	384 Adam Butler RC	1.00	.40
❑	385 Wade Miller RC	2.50	1.00
❑	386 Kyle Peterson RC	1.00	.40
❑	387 Tommy Peterman RC	1.00	.40
❑	388 Onan Masaoka	.50	.20
❑	389 Jason Rakers RC	1.00	.40
❑	390 Rafael Medina	.50	.20
❑	391 Luis Lopez RC	1.00	.40
❑	392 Jeff Yoder	.50	.20
❑	393 Vance Wilson RC	1.00	.40
❑	394 Fernando Seguignol RC	1.00	.40
❑	395 Ron Wright	.50	.20
❑	396 Ruben Mateo RC	1.00	.40
❑	397 Steve Lomasney RC	1.50	.60
❑	398 Damian Jackson	.50	.20
❑	399 Mike Jerzembeck RC	1.00	.40
❑	400 Luis Rivas RC	2.50	1.00
❑	401 Kevin Burford RC	1.00	.40
❑	402 Glenn Davis	.50	.20
❑	403 Robert Luce RC	1.00	.40
❑	404 Cole Liniak	.50	.20
❑	405 Matt LeCroy RC	1.50	.60
❑	406 Jeremy Giambi RC	1.50	.60
❑	407 Shawn Chacon	.50	.20
❑	408 Dewayne Wise RC	1.00	.40
❑	409 Steve Woodard	.50	.20
❑	410 Francisco Cordero RC	2.50	1.00
❑	411 Damon Minor RC	1.00	.40
❑	412 Lou Collier	.50	.20
❑	413 Justin Towle	.50	.20
❑	414 Juan LeBron	.50	.20
❑	415 Michael Coleman	.50	.20
❑	416 Felix Rodriguez	.50	.20
❑	417 Paul Ah Yat RC	1.00	.40
❑	418 Kevin Barker RC	1.00	.40
❑	419 Brian Meadows	.50	.20
❑	420 Darnell McDonald RC	1.00	.40
❑	421 Matt Kinney RC	1.00	.40
❑	422 Mike Vavrek RC	1.00	.40
❑	423 Courtney Duncan RC	1.00	.40
❑	424 Kevin Millar RC	4.00	1.50
❑	425 Ruben Rivera	.50	.20
❑	426 Steve Shoemaker RC	1.00	.40
❑	427 Dan Reichert RC	1.00	.40
❑	428 Carlos Lee RC	6.00	2.50
❑	429 Rod Barajas	2.50	1.00
❑	430 Pablo Ozuna RC	1.50	.60
❑	431 Todd Belitz RC	1.00	.40
❑	432 Sidney Ponson	.50	.20
❑	433 Steve Carver RC	1.00	.40
❑	434 Esteban Yan RC	1.50	.60
❑	435 Cedrick Bowers	.50	.20
❑	436 Marlon Anderson	.50	.20
❑	437 Carl Pavano	.50	.20
❑	438 Jae Weong Seo RC	1.50	.60
❑	439 Jose Taveras RC	1.00	.40
❑	440 Matt Anderson RC	1.00	.40
❑	441 Darron Ingram RC	1.00	.40

1999 Bowman Chrome

❑	COMPLETE SET (440)	200.00	100.00
❑	COMPLETE SERIES 1 (220)	80.00	40.00
❑	COMPLETE SERIES 2 (220)	120.00	60.00
❑	1 Ben Grieve	.50	.20
❑	2 Kerry Wood	.50	.20
❑	3 Ruben Rivera	.50	.20
❑	4 Sandy Alomar Jr.	.50	.20
❑	5 Cal Ripken	4.00	1.50
❑	6 Mark McGwire	3.00	1.25
❑	7 Vladimir Guerrero	1.25	.50
❑	8 Moises Alou	.50	.20
❑	9 Jim Edmonds	.50	.20
❑	10 Greg Maddux	2.00	.75
❑	11 Gary Sheffield	.50	.20
❑	12 John Valentin	.50	.20
❑	13 Chuck Knoblauch	.50	.20
❑	14 Tony Clark	.50	.20
❑	15 Rusty Greer	.50	.20
❑	16 Al Leiter	.50	.20
❑	17 Travis Lee	.50	.20
❑	18 Jose Cruz Jr.	.50	.20
❑	19 Pedro Martinez	.75	.30
❑	20 Paul O'Neill	.75	.30
❑	21 Todd Walker	.50	.20
❑	22 Vinny Castilla	.50	.20
❑	23 Barry Larkin	.75	.30
❑	24 Curt Schilling	.50	.20
❑	25 Jason Kendall	.50	.20
❑	26 Scott Erickson	.50	.20
❑	27 Andres Galarraga	.50	.20
❑	28 Jeff Shaw	.50	.20
❑	29 John Olerud	.50	.20
❑	30 Orlando Hernandez	.50	.20
❑	31 Larry Walker	.50	.20
❑	32 Andruw Jones	.75	.30
❑	33 Jeff Cirillo	.50	.20
❑	34 Barry Bonds	3.00	1.25
❑	35 Manny Ramirez	.75	.30
❑	36 Mark Kotsay	.50	.20
❑	37 Ivan Rodriguez	.75	.30
❑	38 Jeff King	.50	.20
❑	39 Brian Hunter	.50	.20
❑	40 Ray Durham	.50	.20
❑	41 Bernie Williams	.75	.30
❑	42 Darin Erstad	.50	.20
❑	43 Chipper Jones	1.25	.50
❑	44 Pat Hentgen	.50	.20
❑	45 Eric Young	.50	.20
❑	46 Jaret Wright	.50	.20
❑	47 Juan Guzman	.50	.20
❑	48 Jorge Posada	.75	.30
❑	49 Bobby Higginson	.50	.20
❑	50 Jose Guillen	.50	.20
❑	51 Trevor Hoffman	.50	.20
❑	52 Ken Griffey Jr.	2.00	.75
❑	53 David Justice	.50	.20
❑	54 Matt Williams	.50	.20
❑	55 Eric Karros	.50	.20
❑	56 Derek Bell	.50	.20
❑	57 Ray Lankford	.50	.20
❑	58 Mariano Rivera	1.25	.50
❑	59 Brett Tomko	.50	.20
❑	60 Mike Mussina	.75	.30
❑	61 Kenny Lofton	.50	.20
❑	62 Chuck Finley	.50	.20
❑	63 Alex Gonzalez	.50	.20
❑	64 Mark Grace	.75	.30
❑	65 Raul Mondesi	.50	.20
❑	66 David Cone	.50	.20
❑	67 Brad Fullmer	.50	.20
❑	68 Andy Benes	.50	.20
❑	69 John Smoltz	.75	.30
❑	70 Shane Reynolds	.50	.20
❑	71 Bruce Chen	.50	.20
❑	72 Adam Kennedy	.50	.20
❑	73 Jack Cust	.50	.20
❑	74 Matt Clement	.50	.20
❑	75 Derrick Gibson	.50	.20
❑	76 Darnell McDonald	.50	.20
❑	77 Adam Everett RC	2.50	1.00
❑	78 Ricardo Aramboles	.50	.20
❑	79 Mark Quinn RC	1.00	.40
❑	80 Jason Rakers	.50	.20
❑	81 Seth Etherton RC	1.00	.40
❑	82 Jeff Urban RC	1.00	.40
❑	83 Manny Aybar	.50	.20
❑	84 Mike Nannini RC	1.00	.40
❑	85 Onan Masaoka	.50	.20
❑	86 Rod Barajas	.50	.20
❑	87 Mike Frank	.50	.20
❑	88 Scott Randall	.50	.20
❑	89 Justin Bowles RC	1.00	.40
❑	90 Chris Haas	.50	.20
❑	91 Arturo McDowell RC	1.00	.40
❑	92 Matt Belisle RC	1.00	.40
❑	93 Scott Elarton	.50	.20
❑	94 Vernon Wells	.50	.20
❑	95 Pat Cline	.50	.20
❑	96 Ryan Anderson	.50	.20
❑	97 Kevin Barker	.50	.20
❑	98 Ruben Mateo	.50	.20
❑	99 Robert Fick	.50	.20
❑	100 Corey Koskie	.50	.20
❑	101 Ricky Ledee	.50	.20
❑	102 Rick Elder RC	1.00	.40
❑	103 Jack Cressend RC	1.00	.40
❑	104 Joe Lawrence	.50	.20
❑	105 Mike Lincoln	.50	.20
❑	106 Kit Pellow RC	1.00	.40
❑	107 Matt Burch RC	1.00	.40
❑	108 Cole Liniak	.50	.20
❑	109 Jason Dewey	.50	.20
❑	110 Cesar King	.50	.20
❑	111 Julio Ramirez	.50	.20
❑	112 Jake Westbrook	.50	.20
❑	113 Eric Valent RC	1.50	.60
❑	114 Roosevelt Brown RC	1.00	.40
❑	115 Choo Freeman RC	1.50	.60

❑ 116 Juan Melo .50 .20
❑ 117 Jason Grilli .50 .20
❑ 118 Jared Sandberg .50 .20
❑ 119 Glenn Davis .50 .20
❑ 120 David Riske RC 1.00 .40
❑ 121 Jacque Jones .50 .20
❑ 122 Corey Lee .50 .20
❑ 123 Michael Barrett .50 .20
❑ 124 Lariel Gonzalez .50 .20
❑ 125 Mitch Meluskey .50 .20
❑ 126 F.Adrian Garcia .50 .20
❑ 127 Tony Torcato RC 1.00 .40
❑ 128 Jeff Liefer .50 .20
❑ 129 Ntema Ndungidi .50 .20
❑ 130 Andy Brown RC 1.00 .40
❑ 131 Ryan Mills RC 1.00 .40
❑ 132 Andy Abad RC 1.00 .40
❑ 133 Carlos Febles .50 .20
❑ 134 Jason Tyner RC 1.00 .40
❑ 135 Mark Osborne .50 .20
❑ 136 Phil Norton RC 1.00 .40
❑ 137 Nathan Haynes .50 .20
❑ 138 Roy Halladay .50 .20
❑ 139 Juan Encarnacion .50 .20
❑ 140 Brad Penny .50 .20
❑ 141 Grant Roberts .50 .20
❑ 142 Aramis Ramirez .50 .20
❑ 143 Cristian Guzman .50 .20
❑ 144 Mamon Tucker RC 1.00 .40
❑ 145 Ryan Bradley .50 .20
❑ 146 Brian Simmons .50 .20
❑ 147 Dan Reichert .50 .20
❑ 148 Russell Branyan .50 .20
❑ 149 Victor Valencia RC 1.00 .40
❑ 150 Scott Schoeneweis .50 .20
❑ 151 Sean Spencer RC 1.00 .40
❑ 152 Odalis Perez .50 .20
❑ 153 Joe Fontenot .50 .20
❑ 154 Milton Bradley .50 .20
❑ 155 Josh McKinley RC 1.00 .40
❑ 156 Terrence Long .50 .20
❑ 157 Danny Klassen .50 .20
❑ 158 Paul Hoover RC 1.00 .40
❑ 159 Ron Belliard .50 .20
❑ 160 Armando Rios .50 .20
❑ 161 Ramon Hernandez .50 .20
❑ 162 Jason Conti .50 .20
❑ 163 Chad Hermansen .50 .20
❑ 164 Jason Standridge .50 .20
❑ 165 Jason Dellaero .50 .20
❑ 166 John Curtice .50 .20
❑ 167 Clayton Andrews RC 1.00 .40
❑ 168 Jeremy Giambi .50 .20
❑ 169 Alex Ramirez .50 .20
❑ 170 Gabe Molina RC 1.00 .40
❑ 171 Mario Encarnacion RC 1.00 .40
❑ 172 Mike Zywica RC 1.00 .40
❑ 173 Chip Ambres RC 1.00 .40
❑ 174 Trot Nixon .50 .20
❑ 175 Pat Burrell RC 8.00 3.00
❑ 176 Jeff Yoder .50 .20
❑ 177 Chris Jones RC 1.00 .40
❑ 178 Kevin Witt .50 .20
❑ 179 Keith Luuloa RC 1.00 .40
❑ 180 Billy Koch .50 .20
❑ 181 Damaso Marte RC 1.00 .40
❑ 182 Ryan Glynn RC 1.00 .40
❑ 183 Calvin Pickering .50 .20
❑ 184 Michael Cuddyer .50 .20
❑ 185 Nick Johnson RC 5.00 2.00
❑ 186 Doug Mientkiewicz RC 2.50 1.00
❑ 187 Nate Cornejo RC 1.00 .40
❑ 188 Octavio Dotel .50 .20
❑ 189 Wes Helms .50 .20
❑ 190 Nelson Lara .50 .20
❑ 191 Chuck Abbott RC 1.00 .40
❑ 192 Tony Armas Jr. .50 .20
❑ 193 Gil Meche .50 .20
❑ 194 Ben Petrick .50 .20
❑ 195 Chris George RC 1.00 .40
❑ 196 Scott Hunter RC 1.00 .40
❑ 197 Ryan Brannan .50 .20
❑ 198 Amaury Garcia RC 1.00 .40
❑ 199 Chris Gissell .50 .20
❑ 200 Austin Kearns RC 8.00 3.00
❑ 201 Alex Gonzalez .50 .20
❑ 202 Wade Miller .50 .20
❑ 203 Scott Williamson .50 .20
❑ 204 Chris Enochs .50 .20
❑ 205 Fernando Seguignol .50 .20
❑ 206 Marlon Anderson .50 .20
❑ 207 Todd Sears RC 1.00 .40
❑ 208 Nate Bump RC 1.00 .40
❑ 209 J.M. Gold RC 1.00 .40
❑ 210 Matt LeCroy .50 .20
❑ 211 Alex Hernandez .50 .20
❑ 212 Luis Rivera .50 .20
❑ 213 Troy Cameron .50 .20
❑ 214 Alex Escobar RC 1.50 .60
❑ 215 Jason LaRue .50 .20
❑ 216 Kyle Peterson .50 .20
❑ 217 Brent Butler .50 .20
❑ 218 Dernell Stenson .50 .20
❑ 219 Adrian Beltre .50 .20
❑ 220 Daryle Ward .50 .20
❑ 221 Jim Thome .75 .30
❑ 222 Cliff Floyd .50 .20
❑ 223 Rickey Henderson 1.25 .50
❑ 224 Garret Anderson .50 .20
❑ 225 Ken Caminiti .50 .20
❑ 226 Bret Boone .50 .20
❑ 227 Jeromy Burnitz .50 .20
❑ 228 Steve Finley .50 .20
❑ 229 Miguel Tejada .50 .20
❑ 230 Greg Vaughn .50 .20
❑ 231 Jose Offerman .50 .20
❑ 232 Andy Ashby .50 .20
❑ 233 Albert Belle .50 .20
❑ 234 Fernando Tatis .50 .20
❑ 235 Todd Helton .75 .30
❑ 236 Sean Casey .50 .20
❑ 237 Brian Giles .50 .20
❑ 238 Andy Pettitte .75 .30
❑ 239 Fred McGriff .75 .30
❑ 240 Roberto Alomar .75 .30
❑ 241 Edgar Martinez .75 .30
❑ 242 Lee Stevens .50 .20
❑ 243 Shawn Green .50 .20
❑ 244 Ryan Klesko .50 .20
❑ 245 Sammy Sosa 1.25 .50
❑ 246 Todd Hundley .50 .20
❑ 247 Shannon Stewart .50 .20
❑ 248 Randy Johnson 1.25 .50
❑ 249 Rondell White .50 .20
❑ 250 Mike Piazza 2.00 .75
❑ 251 Craig Biggio .75 .30
❑ 252 David Wells .50 .20
❑ 253 Brian Jordan .50 .20
❑ 254 Edgar Renteria .50 .20
❑ 255 Bartolo Colon .50 .20
❑ 256 Frank Thomas 1.25 .50
❑ 257 Will Clark .75 .30
❑ 258 Dean Palmer .50 .20
❑ 259 Dmitri Young .50 .20
❑ 260 Scott Rolen .75 .30
❑ 261 Jeff Kent .50 .20
❑ 262 Dante Bichette .50 .20
❑ 263 Nomar Garciaparra 2.00 .75
❑ 264 Tony Gwynn 1.50 .60
❑ 265 Alex Rodriguez 2.00 .75
❑ 266 Jose Canseco .75 .30
❑ 267 Jason Giambi .50 .20
❑ 268 Jeff Bagwell .75 .30
❑ 269 Carlos Delgado .50 .20
❑ 270 Tom Glavine .75 .30
❑ 271 Eric Davis .50 .20
❑ 272 Edgardo Alfonzo .50 .20
❑ 273 Tim Salmon .75 .30
❑ 274 Johnny Damon .75 .30
❑ 275 Rafael Palmeiro .75 .30
❑ 276 Denny Neagle .50 .20
❑ 277 Neifi Perez .50 .20
❑ 278 Roger Clemens 2.50 1.00
❑ 279 Brant Brown .50 .20
❑ 280 Kevin Brown .75 .30
❑ 281 Jay Bell .50 .20
❑ 282 Jay Buhner .50 .20
❑ 283 Matt Lawton .50 .20
❑ 284 Robin Ventura .50 .20
❑ 285 Juan Gonzalez .50 .20
❑ 286 Mo Vaughn .50 .20
❑ 287 Kevin Millwood .50 .20
❑ 288 Tino Martinez .75 .30
❑ 289 Justin Thompson .50 .20
❑ 290 Derek Jeter 3.00 1.25
❑ 291 Ben Davis .50 .20
❑ 292 Mike Lowell .50 .20
❑ 293 Calvin Murray .50 .20
❑ 294 Micah Bowie RC 1.00 .40
❑ 295 Lance Berkman .50 .20
❑ 296 Jason Marquis .50 .20
❑ 297 Chad Green .50 .20
❑ 298 Dee Brown .50 .20
❑ 299 Jerry Hairston Jr. .50 .20
❑ 300 Gabe Kapler .50 .20
❑ 301 Brent Stentz RC 1.00 .40
❑ 302 Scott Mullen RC 1.00 .40
❑ 303 Brandon Reed .50 .20
❑ 304 Shea Hillenbrand RC 4.00 1.50
❑ 305 J.D. Closser RC 1.50 .60
❑ 306 Gary Matthews Jr. .50 .20
❑ 307 Toby Hall RC 1.50 .60
❑ 308 Jason Phillips RC 1.00 .40
❑ 309 Jose Macias RC 1.00 .40
❑ 310 Jung Bong RC 1.00 .40
❑ 311 Ramon Soler RC 1.00 .40
❑ 312 Kelly Dransfeldt RC 1.00 .40
❑ 313 Carlos E. Hernandez RC 1.50 .60
❑ 314 Kevin Haverbusch .50 .20
❑ 315 Aaron Myette RC 1.00 .40
❑ 316 Chad Harville RC 1.00 .40
❑ 317 Kyle Farnsworth RC 1.50 .60
❑ 318 Gookie Dawkins RC 1.50 .60
❑ 319 Willie Martinez .50 .20
❑ 320 Carlos Lee .50 .20
❑ 321 Carlos Pena RC 2.00 .75
❑ 322 Peter Bergeron RC 1.00 .40
❑ 323 A.J. Burnett RC 4.00 1.50
❑ 324 Bucky Jacobsen RC 1.50 .60
❑ 325 Mo Bruce RC 1.00 .40
❑ 326 Reggie Taylor .50 .20
❑ 327 Jackie Rexrode .50 .20
❑ 328 Alvin Morrow RC 1.00 .40
❑ 329 Carlos Beltran .75 .30
❑ 330 Eric Chavez .50 .20
❑ 331 John Patterson .50 .20
❑ 332 Jayson Werth .50 .20
❑ 333 Richie Sexson .50 .20
❑ 334 Randy Wolf .50 .20
❑ 335 Eli Marrero .50 .20
❑ 336 Paul LoDuca .50 .20
❑ 337 J.D Smart .50 .20
❑ 338 Ryan Minor .50 .20
❑ 339 Kris Benson .50 .20
❑ 340 George Lombard .50 .20
❑ 341 Troy Glaus .75 .30
❑ 342 Eddie Yarnall .50 .20
❑ 343 Kip Wells RC 1.50 .60
❑ 344 C.C. Sabathia RC 6.00 2.50
❑ 345 Sean Burroughs RC 2.50 1.00
❑ 346 Felipe Lopez RC 6.00 2.50
❑ 347 Ryan Rupe RC 1.00 .40
❑ 348 Orber Moreno RC 1.00 .40
❑ 349 Rafael Roque RC 1.00 .40
❑ 350 Alfonso Soriano RC 25.00 10.00
❑ 351 Pablo Ozuna .50 .20
❑ 352 Corey Patterson RC 4.00 1.50
❑ 353 Braden Looper .50 .20
❑ 354 Robbie Bell .50 .20
❑ 355 Mark Mulder RC 6.00 2.50
❑ 356 Angel Pena .50 .20
❑ 357 Kevin McGlinchy .50 .20
❑ 358 Michael Restovich RC 1.50 .60
❑ 359 Eric DuBose .50 .20
❑ 360 Geoff Jenkins .50 .20
❑ 361 Mark Harriger RC 1.00 .40
❑ 362 Junior Herndon RC 1.00 .40
❑ 363 Tim Raines Jr. RC 1.00 .40
❑ 364 Rafael Furcal RC 5.00 2.00
❑ 365 Marcus Giles RC 4.00 1.50
❑ 366 Ted Lilly .50 .20
❑ 367 Jorge Toca RC 1.50 .60
❑ 368 David Kelton RC 1.00 .40
❑ 369 Adam Dunn RC 15.00 6.00
❑ 370 Guillermo Mota RC 1.00 .40
❑ 371 Brett Laxton RC 1.00 .40
❑ 372 Travis Harper RC 1.00 .40
❑ 373 Tom Davey RC 1.00 .40

❑ 374	Darren Blakely RC	1.00	.40
❑ 375	Tim Hudson RC	8.00	3.00
❑ 376	Jason Romano	.50	.20
❑ 377	Dan Reichert	.50	.20
❑ 378	Julio Lugo RC	2.50	1.00
❑ 379	Jose Garcia RC	1.00	.40
❑ 380	Erubiel Durazo RC	1.50	.60
❑ 381	Jose Jimenez	.50	.20
❑ 382	Chris Fussell	.50	.20
❑ 383	Steve Lomasney	.50	.20
❑ 384	Juan Pena RC	1.00	.40
❑ 385	Allen Levrault RC	1.00	.40
❑ 386	Juan Rivera RC	4.00	1.50
❑ 387	Steve Colyer RC	1.00	.40
❑ 388	Joe Nathan RC	5.00	2.00
❑ 389	Ron Walker RC	1.00	.40
❑ 390	Nick Bierbrodt	.50	.20
❑ 391	Luke Prokopec RC	1.00	.40
❑ 392	Dave Roberts RC	2.50	1.00
❑ 393	Mike Darr	.50	.20
❑ 394	Abraham Nunez RC	1.50	.60
❑ 395	Giuseppe Chiaramonte RC	1.00	.40
❑ 396	Jermaine Van Buren RC	1.00	.40
❑ 397	Mike Kusiewicz	.50	.20
❑ 398	Matt Wise RC	1.00	.40
❑ 399	Joe McEwing RC	1.50	.60
❑ 400	Matt Holliday RC	20.00	8.00
❑ 401	Willi Mo Pena RC	12.00	5.00
❑ 402	Ruben Quevedo RC	1.00	.40
❑ 403	Rob Ryan RC	1.00	.40
❑ 404	Freddy Garcia RC	4.00	1.50
❑ 405	Kevin Eberwein RC	1.00	.40
❑ 406	Jesus Colome RC	1.00	.40
❑ 407	Chris Singleton	.50	.20
❑ 408	Bubba Crosby RC	2.50	1.00
❑ 409	Jesus Cordero RC	1.00	.40
❑ 410	Donny Leon	.50	.20
❑ 411	Goefrey Tomlinson RC	1.00	.40
❑ 412	Jeff Winchester RC	1.00	.40
❑ 413	Adam Piatt RC	1.00	.40
❑ 414	Robert Stratton	.50	.20
❑ 415	T.J. Tucker	.50	.20
❑ 416	Ryan Langerhans RC	2.50	1.00
❑ 417	Anthony Shumaker RC	1.00	.40
❑ 418	Matt Miller RC	1.00	.40
❑ 419	Doug Clark RC	1.00	.40
❑ 420	Kory DeHaan RC	1.00	.40
❑ 421	David Eckstein RC	8.00	3.00
❑ 422	Brian Cooper RC	1.00	.40
❑ 423	Brady Clark RC	4.00	1.50
❑ 424	Chris Magruder RC	1.00	.40
❑ 425	Bobby Seay RC	1.00	.40
❑ 426	Aubrey Huff RC	5.00	2.00
❑ 427	Mike Jerzembeck	.50	.20
❑ 428	Matt Blank RC	1.00	.40
❑ 429	Benny Agbayani RC	1.50	.60
❑ 430	Kevin Beirne RC	1.00	.40
❑ 431	Josh Hamilton RC	12.00	5.00
❑ 432	Josh Girdley RC	1.00	.40
❑ 433	Kyle Snyder RC	1.00	.40
❑ 434	Mike Paradis RC	1.00	.40
❑ 435	Jason Jennings RC	2.50	1.00
❑ 436	David Walling RC	1.00	.40
❑ 437	Omar Ortiz RC	1.00	.40
❑ 438	Jay Gehrke RC	1.50	.60
❑ 439	Casey Burns RC	1.00	.40
❑ 440	Carl Crawford RC	15.00	6.00

2000 Bowman Chrome

❑	COMPLETE SET (440)	120.00	60.00
❑ 1	Vladimir Guerrero	1.25	.50
❑ 2	Chipper Jones	1.25	.50
❑ 3	Todd Walker	.50	.20
❑ 4	Barry Larkin	.75	.30
❑ 5	Bernie Williams	.75	.30
❑ 6	Todd Helton	.75	.30
❑ 7	Jermaine Dye	.50	.20
❑ 8	Brian Giles	.50	.20
❑ 9	Freddy Garcia	.50	.20
❑ 10	Greg Vaughn	.50	.20
❑ 11	Alex Gonzalez	.50	.20
❑ 12	Luis Gonzalez	.50	.20
❑ 13	Ron Belliard	.50	.20
❑ 14	Ben Grieve	.50	.20
❑ 15	Carlos Delgado	.50	.20

❑ 16	Brian Jordan	.50	.20
❑ 17	Fernando Tatis	.50	.20
❑ 18	Ryan Rupe	.50	.20
❑ 19	Miguel Tejada	.50	.20
❑ 20	Mark Grace	.75	.30
❑ 21	Kenny Lofton	.50	.20
❑ 22	Eric Karros	.50	.20
❑ 23	Cliff Floyd	.50	.20
❑ 24	John Halama	.50	.20
❑ 25	Cristian Guzman	.50	.20
❑ 26	Scott Williamson	.50	.20
❑ 27	Mike Lieberthal	.50	.20
❑ 28	Tim Hudson	.50	.20
❑ 29	Warren Morris	.50	.20
❑ 30	Pedro Martinez	.75	.30
❑ 31	John Smoltz	.75	.30
❑ 32	Ray Durham	.50	.20
❑ 33	Chad Allen	.50	.20
❑ 34	Tony Clark	.50	.20
❑ 35	Tino Martinez	.75	.30
❑ 36	J.T. Snow	.50	.20
❑ 37	Kevin Brown	.75	.30
❑ 38	Bartolo Colon	.50	.20
❑ 39	Rey Ordonez	.50	.20
❑ 40	Jeff Bagwell	.75	.30
❑ 41	Ivan Rodriguez	.75	.30
❑ 42	Eric Chavez	.50	.20
❑ 43	Eric Milton	.50	.20
❑ 44	Jose Canseco	.75	.30
❑ 45	Shawn Green	.50	.20
❑ 46	Rich Aurilia	.50	.20
❑ 47	Roberto Alomar	.75	.30
❑ 48	Brian Daubach	.50	.20
❑ 49	Magglio Ordonez	.50	.20
❑ 50	Derek Jeter	3.00	1.25
❑ 51	Kris Benson	.50	.20
❑ 52	Albert Belle	.50	.20
❑ 53	Rondell White	.50	.20
❑ 54	Justin Thompson	.50	.20
❑ 55	Nomar Garciaparra	2.00	.75
❑ 56	Chuck Finley	.50	.20
❑ 57	Omar Vizquel	.75	.30
❑ 58	Luis Castillo	.50	.20
❑ 59	Richard Hidalgo	.50	.20
❑ 60	Barry Bonds	3.00	1.25
❑ 61	Craig Biggio	.75	.30
❑ 62	Doug Glanville	.50	.20
❑ 63	Gabe Kapler	.50	.20
❑ 64	Johnny Damon	.75	.30
❑ 65	Pokey Reese	.50	.20
❑ 66	Andy Pettitte	.75	.30
❑ 67	B.J. Surhoff	.50	.20
❑ 68	Richie Sexson	.50	.20
❑ 69	Javy Lopez	.50	.20
❑ 70	Raul Mondesi	.50	.20
❑ 71	Darin Erstad	.50	.20
❑ 72	Kevin Millwood	.50	.20
❑ 73	Ricky Ledee	.50	.20
❑ 74	John Olerud	.50	.20
❑ 75	Sean Casey	.50	.20
❑ 76	Carlos Febles	.50	.20
❑ 77	Paul O'Neill	.75	.30
❑ 78	Bob Abreu	.50	.20
❑ 79	Neifi Perez	.50	.20
❑ 80	Tony Gwynn	1.50	.60
❑ 81	Russ Ortiz	.50	.20
❑ 82	Matt Williams	.50	.20
❑ 83	Chris Carpenter	.50	.20
❑ 84	Roger Cedeno	.50	.20
❑ 85	Tim Salmon	.75	.30
❑ 86	Billy Koch	.50	.20
❑ 87	Jeromy Burnitz	.50	.20
❑ 88	Edgardo Alfonzo	.50	.20
❑ 89	Jay Bell	.50	.20
❑ 90	Manny Ramirez	.75	.30
❑ 91	Frank Thomas	1.25	.50
❑ 92	Mike Mussina	.75	.30
❑ 93	J.D. Drew	.50	.20
❑ 94	Adrian Beltre	.50	.20
❑ 95	Alex Rodriguez	2.00	.75
❑ 96	Larry Walker	.50	.20
❑ 97	Juan Encarnacion	.50	.20
❑ 98	Mike Sweeney	.50	.20
❑ 99	Rusty Greer	.50	.20
❑ 100	Randy Johnson	1.25	.50
❑ 101	Jose Vidro	.50	.20
❑ 102	Preston Wilson	.50	.20
❑ 103	Greg Maddux	2.00	.75
❑ 104	Jason Giambi	.50	.20
❑ 105	Cal Ripken	4.00	1.50
❑ 106	Carlos Beltran	.50	.20
❑ 107	Vinny Castilla	.50	.20
❑ 108	Mariano Rivera	1.25	.50
❑ 109	Mo Vaughn	.50	.20
❑ 110	Rafael Palmeiro	.75	.30
❑ 111	Shannon Stewart	.50	.20
❑ 112	Mike Hampton	.50	.20
❑ 113	Joe Nathan	.50	.20
❑ 114	Ben Davis	.50	.20
❑ 115	Andruw Jones	.75	.30
❑ 116	Robin Ventura	.50	.20
❑ 117	Damion Easley	.50	.20
❑ 118	Jeff Cirillo	.50	.20
❑ 119	Kerry Wood	.50	.20
❑ 120	Scott Rolen	.75	.30
❑ 121	Sammy Sosa	1.25	.50
❑ 122	Ken Griffey Jr.	2.00	.75
❑ 123	Shane Reynolds	.50	.20
❑ 124	Troy Glaus	.50	.20
❑ 125	Tom Glavine	.75	.30
❑ 126	Michael Barrett	.50	.20
❑ 127	Al Leiter	.50	.20
❑ 128	Jason Kendall	.50	.20
❑ 129	Roger Clemens	2.50	1.00
❑ 130	Juan Gonzalez	.50	.20
❑ 131	Corey Koskie	.50	.20
❑ 132	Curt Schilling	.50	.20
❑ 133	Mike Piazza	2.00	.75
❑ 134	Gary Sheffield	.50	.20
❑ 135	Jim Thome	.75	.30
❑ 136	Orlando Hernandez	.50	.20
❑ 137	Ray Lankford	.50	.20
❑ 138	Geoff Jenkins	.50	.20
❑ 139	Jose Lima	.50	.20
❑ 140	Mark McGwire	3.00	1.25
❑ 141	Adam Piatt	.50	.20
❑ 142	Pat Manning RC	.75	.30
❑ 143	Marcos Castillo RC	.75	.30
❑ 144	Lesli Brea RC	.75	.30
❑ 145	Humberto Cota RC	1.25	.50
❑ 146	Ben Petrick	.50	.20
❑ 147	Kip Wells	.50	.20
❑ 148	Wily Pena	.50	.20
❑ 149	Chris Wakeland RC	.75	.30
❑ 150	Brad Baker RC	.75	.30
❑ 151	Robbie Morrison RC	.75	.30
❑ 152	Reggie Taylor	.50	.20
❑ 153	Matt Ginter RC	.75	.30
❑ 154	Peter Bergeron	.50	.20
❑ 155	Roosevelt Brown	.50	.20
❑ 156	Matt Cepicky RC	.75	.30
❑ 157	Ramon Castro	.50	.20
❑ 158	Brad Baisley RC	.75	.30
❑ 159	Jason Hart RC	.75	.30
❑ 160	Mitch Meluskey	.50	.20
❑ 161	Chad Harville	.50	.20
❑ 162	Brian Cooper	.50	.20
❑ 163	Marcus Giles	.50	.20
❑ 164	Jim Morris	1.25	.50
❑ 165	Geoff Goetz	.50	.20
❑ 166	Bobby Bradley RC	.75	.30
❑ 167	Rob Bell	.50	.20
❑ 168	Joe Crede	2.50	1.00
❑ 169	Michael Restovich	.50	.20

Card		
❑ 170 Quincy Foster RC	.75	.30
❑ 171 Enrique Cruz RC	.75	.30
❑ 172 Mark Quinn	.50	.20
❑ 173 Nick Johnson	.50	.20
❑ 174 Jeff Liefer	.50	.20
❑ 175 Kevin Mench RC	5.00	2.00
❑ 176 Steve Lomasney	.50	.20
❑ 177 Jayson Werth	.50	.20
❑ 178 Tim Drew	.50	.20
❑ 179 Chip Ambres	.50	.20
❑ 180 Ryan Anderson	.50	.20
❑ 181 Matt Blank	.50	.20
❑ 182 Giuseppe Chiaramonte	.50	.20
❑ 183 Corey Myers RC	.75	.30
❑ 184 Jeff Yoder	.50	.20
❑ 185 Craig Dingman RC	.75	.30
❑ 186 Jon Hamilton RC	.75	.30
❑ 187 Toby Hall	.50	.20
❑ 188 Russell Branyan	.50	.20
❑ 189 Brian Falkenborg RC	.75	.30
❑ 190 Aaron Harang RC	5.00	2.00
❑ 191 Juan Pena	.50	.20
❑ 192 Chin-Hui Tsao RC	5.00	2.00
❑ 193 Alfonso Soriano	1.25	.50
❑ 194 Alejandro Diaz RC	.75	.30
❑ 195 Carlos Pena	.50	.20
❑ 196 Kevin Nicholson	.50	.20
❑ 197 Mo Bruce	.50	.20
❑ 198 C.C. Sabathia	.50	.20
❑ 199 Carl Crawford	.50	.20
❑ 200 Rafael Furcal	.50	.20
❑ 201 Andrew Beinbrink RC	.75	.30
❑ 202 Jimmy Osting	.50	.20
❑ 203 Aaron McNeal RC	.75	.30
❑ 204 Brett Laxton	.50	.20
❑ 205 Chris George	.50	.20
❑ 206 Felipe Lopez	.50	.20
❑ 207 Ben Sheets RC	6.00	2.50
❑ 208 Mike Meyers RC	1.25	.50
❑ 209 Jason Conti	.50	.20
❑ 210 Milton Bradley	.50	.20
❑ 211 Chris Mears RC	.75	.30
❑ 212 Carlos Hernandez RC	1.25	.50
❑ 213 Jason Romano	.50	.20
❑ 214 Geofrey Tomlinson	.50	.20
❑ 215 Jimmy Rollins	.50	.20
❑ 216 Pablo Ozuna	.50	.20
❑ 217 Steve Cox	.50	.20
❑ 218 Terrence Long	.50	.20
❑ 219 Jeff DaVanon RC	1.25	.50
❑ 220 Rick Ankiel	.50	.20
❑ 221 Jason Standridge	.50	.20
❑ 222 Tony Armas Jr.	.50	.20
❑ 223 Jason Tyner	.50	.20
❑ 224 Ramon Ortiz	.50	.20
❑ 225 Daryle Ward	.50	.20
❑ 226 Enger Veras RC	.75	.30
❑ 227 Chris Jones	.50	.20
❑ 228 Eric Cammack RC	.75	.30
❑ 229 Ruben Mateo	.50	.20
❑ 230 Ken Harvey RC	1.25	.50
❑ 231 Jake Westbrook	.50	.20
❑ 232 Rob Purvis RC	.75	.30
❑ 233 Choo Freeman	.50	.20
❑ 234 Aramis Ramirez	.50	.20
❑ 235 A.J. Burnett	.50	.20
❑ 236 Kevin Barker	.50	.20
❑ 237 Chance Caple RC	.75	.30
❑ 238 Jarrod Washburn	.50	.20
❑ 239 Lance Berkman	.50	.20
❑ 240 Michael Wenner RC	.75	.30
❑ 241 Alex Sanchez	.50	.20
❑ 242 Pat Daneker	.50	.20
❑ 243 Grant Roberts	.50	.20
❑ 244 Mark Ellis RC	1.25	.50
❑ 245 Donny Leon	.50	.20
❑ 246 David Eckstein	.50	.20
❑ 247 Dicky Gonzalez RC	.75	.30
❑ 248 John Patterson	.50	.20
❑ 249 Chad Green	.50	.20
❑ 250 Scot Shields RC	.75	.30
❑ 251 Troy Cameron	.50	.20
❑ 252 Jose Molina	.50	.20
❑ 253 Rob Pugmire RC	.75	.30
❑ 254 Rick Elder	.50	.20
❑ 255 Sean Burroughs	.50	.20
❑ 256 Josh Kalinowski RC	.75	.30
❑ 257 Matt LeCroy	.50	.20
❑ 258 Alex Graman RC	.75	.30
❑ 259 Juan Silvestre RC	.75	.30
❑ 260 Brady Clark	.50	.20
❑ 261 Rico Washington RC	.75	.30
❑ 262 Gary Matthews Jr.	.50	.20
❑ 263 Matt Wise	.50	.20
❑ 264 Keith Reed RC	.75	.30
❑ 265 Santiago Ramirez RC	.75	.30
❑ 266 Ben Broussard RC	3.00	1.25
❑ 267 Ryan Langerhans	.50	.20
❑ 268 Juan Rivera	.50	.20
❑ 269 Shawn Gallagher	.50	.20
❑ 270 Jorge Toca	.50	.20
❑ 271 Brad Lidge	.75	.30
❑ 272 Leoncio Estrella RC	.75	.30
❑ 273 Ruben Quevedo	.50	.20
❑ 274 Jack Cust	.50	.20
❑ 275 T.J. Tucker	.50	.20
❑ 276 Mike Colangelo	.50	.20
❑ 277 Brian Schneider	.50	.20
❑ 278 Calvin Murray	.50	.20
❑ 279 Josh Girdley	.50	.20
❑ 280 Mike Paradis	.50	.20
❑ 281 Chad Hermansen	.50	.20
❑ 282 Ty Howington RC	.75	.30
❑ 283 Aaron Myette	.50	.20
❑ 284 D'Angelo Jimenez	.50	.20
❑ 285 Dernell Stenson	.50	.20
❑ 286 Jerry Hairston Jr.	.50	.20
❑ 287 Gary Majewski RC	1.25	.50
❑ 288 Derrin Ebert	.50	.20
❑ 289 Steve Fish RC	.75	.30
❑ 290 Carlos E. Hernandez	.50	.20
❑ 291 Allen Levrault	.50	.20
❑ 292 Sean McNally RC	.75	.30
❑ 293 Randey Dorame RC	.75	.30
❑ 294 Wes Anderson RC	.75	.30
❑ 295 B.J. Ryan	.50	.20
❑ 296 Alan Webb RC	.75	.30
❑ 297 Brandon Inge RC	5.00	2.00
❑ 298 David Walling	.50	.20
❑ 299 Sun Woo Kim RC	.75	.30
❑ 300 Pat Burrell	.50	.20
❑ 301 Rick Guttormson RC	.75	.30
❑ 302 Gil Meche	.50	.20
❑ 303 Carlos Zambrano RC	12.00	5.00
❑ 304 Eric Byrnes UER RC	1.00	.40
❑ 305 Robb Quinlan RC	1.25	.50
❑ 306 Jackie Rexrode	.50	.20
❑ 307 Nate Bump	.50	.20
❑ 308 Sean DePaula RC	.75	.30
❑ 309 Matt Riley	.50	.20
❑ 310 Ryan Minor	.50	.20
❑ 311 J.J. Davis	.50	.20
❑ 312 Randy Wolf	.50	.20
❑ 313 Jason Jennings	.50	.20
❑ 314 Scott Seabol RC	.75	.30
❑ 315 Doug Davis	.50	.20
❑ 316 Todd Moser RC	.75	.30
❑ 317 Rob Ryan	.50	.20
❑ 318 Bubba Crosby	.50	.20
❑ 319 Lyle Overbay RC	3.00	1.25
❑ 320 Mario Encarnacion	.50	.20
❑ 321 Francisco Rodriguez RC	6.00	2.50
❑ 322 Michael Cuddyer	.50	.20
❑ 323 Ed Yarnall	.50	.20
❑ 324 Cesar Saba RC	.75	.30
❑ 325 Gookie Dawkins	.50	.20
❑ 326 Alex Escobar	.50	.20
❑ 327 Julio Zuleta RC	.75	.30
❑ 328 Josh Hamilton	.75	.30
❑ 329 Carlos Urquiola RC	.75	.30
❑ 330 Matt Belisle	.50	.20
❑ 331 Kurt Ainsworth RC	.75	.30
❑ 332 Tim Raines Jr.	.50	.20
❑ 333 Eric Munson	.50	.20
❑ 334 Donzell McDonald	.50	.20
❑ 335 Larry Bigbie RC	2.00	.75
❑ 336 Matt Watson RC	.75	.30
❑ 337 Aubrey Huff	.50	.20
❑ 338 Julio Ramirez	.50	.20
❑ 339 Jason Grabowski RC	.75	.30
❑ 340 Jon Garland	.50	.20
❑ 341 Austin Kearns	.50	.20
❑ 342 Josh Pressley RC	.75	.30
❑ 343 Miguel Olivo RC	2.00	.75
❑ 344 Julio Lugo	.50	.20
❑ 345 Roberto Vaz	.50	.20
❑ 346 Ramon Soler	.50	.20
❑ 347 Brandon Phillips RC	4.00	1.50
❑ 348 Vince Faison RC	.75	.30
❑ 349 Mike Venafro	.50	.20
❑ 350 Rick Asadoorian RC	1.25	.50
❑ 351 B.J. Garbe RC	.75	.30
❑ 352 Dan Reichert	.50	.20
❑ 353 Jason Stumm RC	.75	.30
❑ 354 Ruben Salazar RC	.75	.30
❑ 355 Francisco Cordero	.50	.20
❑ 356 Juan Guzman RC	.75	.30
❑ 357 Mike Bacsik RC	.75	.30
❑ 358 Jared Sandberg	.50	.20
❑ 359 Rod Barajas	.50	.20
❑ 360 Junior Brignac RC	.75	.30
❑ 361 J.M. Gold	.50	.20
❑ 362 Octavio Dotel	.50	.20
❑ 363 David Kelton	.50	.20
❑ 364 Scott Morgan	.50	.20
❑ 365 Wascar Serrano RC	.75	.30
❑ 366 Wilton Veras	.50	.20
❑ 367 Eugene Kingsale	.50	.20
❑ 368 Ted Lilly	.50	.20
❑ 369 George Lombard	.50	.20
❑ 370 Chris Haas	.50	.20
❑ 371 Wilton Pena RC	.75	.30
❑ 372 Vernon Wells	.50	.20
❑ 373 Keith Ginter RC	.75	.30
❑ 374 Jeff Heaverlo RC	.75	.30
❑ 375 Calvin Pickering	.50	.20
❑ 376 Mike Lamb RC	2.00	.75
❑ 377 Kyle Snyder	.50	.20
❑ 378 Javier Cardona RC	.75	.30
❑ 379 Aaron Rowand RC	5.00	2.00
❑ 380 Dee Brown	.50	.20
❑ 381 Brett Myers RC	4.00	1.50
❑ 382 Abraham Nunez	.50	.20
❑ 383 Eric Valent	.50	.20
❑ 384 Jody Gerut RC	1.25	.50
❑ 385 Adam Dunn	1.25	.50
❑ 386 Jay Gehrke	.50	.20
❑ 387 Omar Ortiz	.50	.20
❑ 388 Darnell McDonald	.50	.20
❑ 389 Tony Schrager RC	.75	.30
❑ 390 J.D. Closser	.50	.20
❑ 391 Ben Christensen RC	.75	.30
❑ 392 Adam Kennedy	.50	.20
❑ 393 Nick Green RC	.75	.30
❑ 394 Ramon Hernandez	.50	.20
❑ 395 Roy Oswalt RC	25.00	10.00
❑ 396 Andy Tracy RC	.75	.30
❑ 397 Eric Gagne	1.25	.50
❑ 398 Michael Tejera RC	.75	.30
❑ 399 Adam Everett	.50	.20
❑ 400 Corey Patterson	.50	.20
❑ 401 Gary Knotts RC	.75	.30
❑ 402 Ryan Christianson RC	.75	.30
❑ 403 Eric Ireland RC	.75	.30
❑ 404 Andrew Good RC	.75	.30
❑ 405 Brad Penny	.50	.20
❑ 406 Jason LaRue	.50	.20
❑ 407 Kit Pellow	.50	.20
❑ 408 Kevin Beirne	.50	.20
❑ 409 Kelly Dransfeldt	.50	.20
❑ 410 Jason Grilli	.50	.20
❑ 411 Scott Downs RC	.75	.30
❑ 412 Jesus Colome	.50	.20
❑ 413 John Sneed RC	.75	.30
❑ 414 Tony McKnight	.50	.20
❑ 415 Luis Rivera	.50	.20
❑ 416 Adam Eaton	.50	.20
❑ 417 Mike MacDougal RC	1.25	.50
❑ 418 Mike Nannini	.50	.20
❑ 419 Barry Zito RC	10.00	4.00
❑ 420 DeWayne Wise	.50	.20
❑ 421 Jason Dellaero	.50	.20
❑ 422 Chad Moeller	.50	.20
❑ 423 Jason Marquis	.50	.20
❑ 424 Tim Redding RC	1.25	.50
❑ 425 Mark Mulder	.50	.20
❑ 426 Josh Paul	.50	.20
❑ 427 Chris Enochs	.50	.20

❑ 428 Wilfredo Rodriguez RC	.75	.30
❑ 429 Kevin Witt	.50	.20
❑ 430 Scott Sobkowiak RC	.75	.30
❑ 431 McKay Christensen	.50	.20
❑ 432 Jung Bong	.50	.20
❑ 433 Keith Evans RC	.75	.30
❑ 434 Garry Maddox Jr. RC	.75	.30
❑ 435 Ramon Santiago RC	.75	.30
❑ 436 Alex Cora	.50	.20
❑ 437 Carlos Lee	.50	.20
❑ 438 Jason Repko RC	2.00	.75
❑ 439 Matt Burch	.50	.20
❑ 440 Shawn Sonnier RC	.75	.30

2000 Bowman Chrome Draft Picks

❑ COMP.FACT.SET (110)	50.00	20.00
❑ 1 Pat Burrell	.50	.20
❑ 2 Rafael Furcal	.50	.20
❑ 3 Grant Roberts	.50	.20
❑ 4 Barry Zito	4.00	1.50
❑ 5 Julio Zuleta	.50	.20
❑ 6 Mark Mulder	.50	.20
❑ 7 Rob Bell	.50	.20
❑ 8 Adam Piatt	.50	.20
❑ 9 Mike Lamb	.75	.30
❑ 10 Pablo Ozuna	.50	.20
❑ 11 Jason Tyner	.50	.20
❑ 12 Jason Marquis	.50	.20
❑ 13 Eric Munson	.50	.20
❑ 14 Seth Etherton	.50	.20
❑ 15 Milton Bradley	.50	.20
❑ 16 Nick Green	.50	.20
❑ 17 Chin-Feng Chen RC	1.50	.60
❑ 18 Matt Boone RC	.50	.20
❑ 19 Kevin Gregg RC	.50	.20
❑ 20 Eddy Garabito RC	.50	.20
❑ 21 Aaron Capista RC	.50	.20
❑ 22 Esteban German RC	.50	.20
❑ 23 Derek Thompson RC	.50	.20
❑ 24 Phil Merrell RC	.50	.20
❑ 25 Brian O'Connor RC	.50	.20
❑ 26 Yamid Haad	.50	.20
❑ 27 Hector Mercado RC	.50	.20
❑ 28 Jason Woolf RC	.50	.20
❑ 29 Eddy Furniss RC	.50	.20
❑ 30 Cha Sueng Baek RC	.50	.20
❑ 31 Colby Lewis RC	.50	.20
❑ 32 Pasqual Coco RC	.50	.20
❑ 33 Jorge Cantu RC	5.00	2.00
❑ 34 Erasmo Ramirez RC	.50	.20
❑ 35 Bobby Kielty RC	1.00	.40
❑ 36 Joaquin Benoit RC	.50	.20
❑ 37 Brian Esposito RC	.50	.20
❑ 38 Michael Wenner	.50	.20
❑ 39 Juan Rincon RC	.50	.20
❑ 40 Yorvit Torrealba RC	1.00	.40
❑ 41 Chad Durham RC	.50	.20
❑ 42 Jim Mann RC	.50	.20
❑ 43 Shane Loux RC	.50	.20
❑ 44 Luis Rivas	.50	.20
❑ 45 Ken Chenard RC	.50	.20
❑ 46 Mike Lockwood RC	.50	.20
❑ 47 Yovanny Lara RC	.50	.20
❑ 48 Bubba Carpenter RC	.50	.20
❑ 49 Ryan Dittfurth RC	.50	.20
❑ 50 John Stephens RC	.50	.20
❑ 51 Pedro Feliz RC	2.50	1.00
❑ 52 Kenny Kelly RC	.50	.20
❑ 53 Neil Jenkins RC	.50	.20
❑ 54 Mike Glendenning RC	.50	.20
❑ 55 Bo Porter	.50	.20
❑ 56 Eric Byrnes	.50	.20
❑ 57 Tony Alvarez RC	.50	.20
❑ 58 Kazuhiro Sasaki RC	1.50	.60
❑ 59 Chad Durbin RC	.50	.20
❑ 60 Mike Bynum RC	.50	.20
❑ 61 Travis Wilson RC	.50	.20
❑ 62 Jose Leon RC	.50	.20
❑ 63 Ryan Vogelsong RC	.50	.20
❑ 64 Geraldo Guzman RC	.50	.20
❑ 65 Craig Anderson RC	.50	.20
❑ 66 Carlos Silva RC	1.00	.40
❑ 67 Brad Thomas RC	.50	.20
❑ 68 Chin-Hui Tsao	1.50	.60
❑ 69 Mark Buehrle RC	8.00	3.00
❑ 70 Juan Salas RC	.50	.20
❑ 71 Denny Abreu RC	.50	.20
❑ 72 Keith McDonald RC	.50	.20
❑ 73 Chris Richard RC	.50	.20
❑ 74 Tomas De la Rosa RC	.50	.20
❑ 75 Vicente Padilla RC	1.00	.40
❑ 76 Justin Brunette RC	.50	.20
❑ 77 Scott Linebrink RC	.50	.20
❑ 78 Jeff Sparks RC	.50	.20
❑ 79 Tike Redman RC	1.50	.60
❑ 80 John Lackey RC	5.00	2.00
❑ 81 Joe Strong RC	.50	.20
❑ 82 Brian Tollberg RC	.50	.20
❑ 83 Steve Sisco RC	.50	.20
❑ 84 Chris Clapinski RC	.50	.20
❑ 85 Augie Ojeda RC	.50	.20
❑ 86 Adrian Gonzalez RC	6.00	2.50
❑ 87 Mike Stodolka RC	.50	.20
❑ 88 Adam Johnson RC	.50	.20
❑ 89 Matt Wheatland RC	.50	.20
❑ 90 Corey Smith RC	.50	.20
❑ 91 Rocco Baldelli RC	5.00	2.00
❑ 92 Keith Bucktrot RC	.50	.20
❑ 93 Adam Wainwright RC	2.50	1.00
❑ 94 Blaine Boyer RC	.50	.20
❑ 95 Aaron Herr RC	1.00	.40
❑ 96 Scott Thorman RC	2.50	1.00
❑ 97 Bryan Digby RC	.50	.20
❑ 98 Josh Shortslef RC	.50	.20
❑ 99 Sean Smith RC	.50	.20
❑ 100 Alex Cruz RC	.50	.20
❑ 101 Marc Love RC	.50	.20
❑ 102 Kevin Lee RC	.50	.20
❑ 103 Timo Perez RC	1.00	.40
❑ 104 Alex Cabrera RC	1.00	.40
❑ 105 Shane Heams RC	.50	.20
❑ 106 Tripper Johnson RC	.50	.20
❑ 107 Brent Abernathy RC	.50	.20
❑ 108 John Cotton RC	.50	.20
❑ 109 Brad Wilkerson RC	2.50	1.00
❑ 110 Jon Rauch RC	.50	.20

2001 Bowman Chrome

❑ COMP.SET w/o SP's (220)	50.00	20.00
❑ COMMON (1-110/201-310)	.50	.20
❑ COM.REF (111-200/311-330)	5.00	2.00
❑ COMMON AU REF (331-350)	50.00	20.00
❑ 1 Jason Giambi	.50	.20
❑ 2 Rafael Furcal	.50	.20
❑ 3 Bernie Williams	.75	.30
❑ 4 Kenny Lofton	.50	.20
❑ 5 Al Leiter	.50	.20
❑ 6 Albert Belle	.50	.20
❑ 7 Craig Biggio	.75	.30
❑ 8 Mark Mulder	.50	.20
❑ 9 Carlos Delgado	.50	.20
❑ 10 Darin Erstad	.50	.20
❑ 11 Richie Sexson	.50	.20
❑ 12 Randy Johnson	1.25	.50
❑ 13 Greg Maddux	2.00	.75
❑ 14 Orlando Hernandez	.50	.20
❑ 15 Javier Vazquez	.50	.20
❑ 16 Jeff Kent	.50	.20
❑ 17 Jim Thome	.75	.30
❑ 18 John Olerud	.50	.20
❑ 19 Jason Kendall	.50	.20
❑ 20 Scott Rolen	.75	.30
❑ 21 Tony Gwynn	1.50	.60
❑ 22 Edgardo Alfonzo	.50	.20
❑ 23 Pokey Reese	.50	.20
❑ 24 Todd Helton	.75	.30
❑ 25 Mark Quinn	.50	.20
❑ 26 Dean Palmer	.50	.20
❑ 27 Ray Durham	.50	.20
❑ 28 Rafael Palmeiro	.75	.30
❑ 29 Carl Everett	.50	.20
❑ 30 Vladimir Guerrero	1.25	.50
❑ 31 Livan Hernandez	.50	.20
❑ 32 Preston Wilson	.50	.20
❑ 33 Jose Vidro	.50	.20
❑ 34 Fred McGriff	.75	.30
❑ 35 Kevin Brown	.50	.20
❑ 36 Miguel Tejada	.50	.20
❑ 37 Chipper Jones	1.25	.50
❑ 38 Edgar Martinez	.75	.30
❑ 39 Tony Batista	.50	.20
❑ 40 Jorge Posada	.75	.30
❑ 41 Sammy Sosa	1.25	.50
❑ 42 Gary Sheffield	.50	.20
❑ 43 Bartolo Colon	.50	.20
❑ 44 Pat Burrell	.50	.20
❑ 45 Jay Payton	.50	.20
❑ 46 Mike Mussina	.75	.30
❑ 47 Nomar Garciaparra	2.00	.75
❑ 48 Darren Dreifort	.50	.20
❑ 49 Richard Hidalgo	.50	.20
❑ 50 Troy Glaus	.50	.20
❑ 51 Ben Grieve	.50	.20
❑ 52 Jim Edmonds	.50	.20
❑ 53 Raul Mondesi	.50	.20
❑ 54 Andruw Jones	.75	.30
❑ 55 Mike Sweeney	.50	.20
❑ 56 Derek Jeter	3.00	1.25
❑ 57 Ruben Mateo	.50	.20
❑ 58 Cristian Guzman	.50	.20
❑ 59 Mike Hampton	.50	.20
❑ 60 J.D. Drew	.50	.20
❑ 61 Matt Lawton	.50	.20
❑ 62 Moises Alou	.50	.20
❑ 63 Terrence Long	.50	.20
❑ 64 Geoff Jenkins	.50	.20
❑ 65 Manny Ramirez Sox	.75	.30
❑ 66 Johnny Damon	.75	.30
❑ 67 Pedro Martinez	.75	.30
❑ 68 Juan Gonzalez	.50	.20
❑ 69 Roger Clemens	2.50	1.00
❑ 70 Carlos Beltran	.50	.20
❑ 71 Roberto Alomar	.75	.30
❑ 72 Barry Bonds	3.00	1.25
❑ 73 Tim Hudson	.50	.20
❑ 74 Tom Glavine	.75	.30
❑ 75 Jeromy Burnitz	.50	.20
❑ 76 Adrian Beltre	.50	.20
❑ 77 Mike Piazza	2.00	.75
❑ 78 Kerry Wood	.50	.20
❑ 79 Steve Finley	.50	.20
❑ 80 Bob Abreu	.50	.20
❑ 81 Neifi Perez	.50	.20
❑ 82 Mark Redman	.50	.20
❑ 83 Paul Konerko	.50	.20
❑ 84 Jermaine Dye	.50	.20
❑ 85 Brian Giles	.50	.20
❑ 86 Ivan Rodriguez	.75	.30
❑ 87 Adam Kennedy	.50	.20
❑ 88 Eric Chavez	.50	.20
❑ 89 Billy Koch	.50	.20

❑ 90 Shawn Green .50 .20
❑ 91 Matt Williams .50 .20
❑ 92 Greg Vaughn .50 .20
❑ 93 Jeff Cirillo .50 .20
❑ 94 Frank Thomas 1.25 .50
❑ 95 David Justice .50 .20
❑ 96 Cal Ripken 4.00 1.50
❑ 97 Curt Schilling .50 .20
❑ 98 Barry Zito .75 .30
❑ 99 Brian Jordan .50 .20
❑ 100 Chan Ho Park .50 .20
❑ 101 J.T. Snow .50 .20
❑ 102 Kazuhiro Sasaki .50 .20
❑ 103 Alex Rodriguez 2.00 .75
❑ 104 Mariano Rivera 1.25 .50
❑ 105 Eric Milton .50 .20
❑ 106 Andy Pettitte .75 .30
❑ 107 Ken Griffey Jr. 2.00 .75
❑ 108 Bengie Molina .50 .20
❑ 109 Jeff Bagwell .75 .30
❑ 110 Mark McGwire 3.00 1.25
❑ 111 Dan Tosca RC 5.00 2.00
❑ 112 Sergio Contreras RC 8.00 3.00
❑ 113 Mitch Jones RC 8.00 3.00
❑ 114 Ramon Carvajal RC 8.00 3.00
❑ 115 Ryan Madson RC 10.00 4.00
❑ 116 Hank Blalock RC 40.00 20.00
❑ 117 Ben Washburn RC 5.00 2.00
❑ 118 Erick Almonte RC 5.00 2.00
❑ 119 Shawn Fagan RC 8.00 3.00
❑ 120 Gary Johnson RC 5.00 2.00
❑ 121 Brett Evert RC 5.00 2.00
❑ 122 Joe Hamer RC 8.00 3.00
❑ 123 Yhency Brazoban RC 10.00 4.00
❑ 124 Domingo Guante RC 5.00 2.00
❑ 125 Deivi Mendez RC 5.00 2.00
❑ 126 Adrian Hernandez RC 5.00 2.00
❑ 127 Reggie Abercrombie RC 10.00 4.00
❑ 128 Steve Bennett RC 5.00 2.00
❑ 129 Matt White RC 8.00 3.00
❑ 130 Brian Hitchcox RC 5.00 2.00
❑ 131 Deivis Santos RC 5.00 2.00
❑ 132 Luis Montanez RC 8.00 3.00
❑ 133 Eric Reynolds RC 5.00 2.00
❑ 134 Denny Bautista RC 10.00 4.00
❑ 135 Hector Garcia RC 5.00 2.00
❑ 136 Joe Thurston RC 8.00 3.00
❑ 137 Tsuyoshi Shinjo RC 10.00 4.00
❑ 138 Elpidio Guzman RC 5.00 2.00
❑ 139 Brian Bass RC 5.00 2.00
❑ 140 Mark Burnett RC 8.00 3.00
❑ 141 Russ Jacobson UER 5.00 2.00
❑ 142 Travis Hafner RC 50.00 20.00
❑ 143 Wilson Betemit RC 15.00 6.00
❑ 144 Luke Lockwood RC 8.00 3.00
❑ 145 Noel Devarez RC 8.00 3.00
❑ 146 Doug Gredvig RC 5.00 2.00
❑ 147 Seung Song RC 8.00 3.00
❑ 148 Andy Van Hekken RC 5.00 2.00
❑ 149 Ryan Kohlmeier 5.00 2.00
❑ 150 Dee Haynes RC 5.00 2.00
❑ 151 Jim Journell RC 8.00 3.00
❑ 152 Chad Petty RC 5.00 2.00
❑ 153 Danny Borrell RC 5.00 2.00
❑ 154 Dave Krynzel 5.00 2.00
❑ 155 Octavio Martinez RC 8.00 3.00
❑ 156 David Parrish RC 5.00 2.00
❑ 157 Jason Miller RC 5.00 2.00
❑ 158 Corey Spencer RC 5.00 2.00
❑ 159 Maxim St. Pierre RC 8.00 3.00
❑ 160 Pat Magness RC 8.00 3.00
❑ 161 Ranier Olmedo RC 8.00 3.00
❑ 162 Brandon Mims RC 5.00 2.00
❑ 163 Phil Wilson RC 8.00 3.00
❑ 164 Jose Reyes RC 175.00 125.00
❑ 165 Matt Butler RC 8.00 3.00
❑ 166 Joel Pineiro 8.00 3.00
❑ 167 Ken Chenard 5.00 2.00
❑ 168 Alexis Gomez RC 5.00 2.00
❑ 169 Justin Morneau RC 80.00 40.00
❑ 170 Josh Fogg RC 8.00 3.00
❑ 171 Charles Frazier RC 5.00 2.00
❑ 172 Ryan Ludwick RC 8.00 3.00
❑ 173 Seth McClung RC 8.00 3.00
❑ 174 Justin Wayne RC 8.00 3.00
❑ 175 Rafael Soriano RC 8.00 3.00
❑ 176 Jared Abruzzo RC 5.00 2.00
❑ 177 Jason Richardson RC 5.00 2.00
❑ 178 Darwin Cubillan RC 5.00 2.00
❑ 179 Blake Williams RC 5.00 2.00
❑ 180 Valentino Pascucci RC 8.00 3.00
❑ 181 Ryan Hannaman RC 8.00 3.00
❑ 182 Steve Smyth RC 8.00 3.00
❑ 183 Jake Peavy RC 60.00 30.00
❑ 184 Onix Mercado RC 8.00 3.00
❑ 185 Luis Torres RC 8.00 3.00
❑ 186 Casey Fossum RC 5.00 2.00
❑ 187 Eduardo Figueroa RC 5.00 2.00
❑ 188 Bryan Barnowski RC 5.00 2.00
❑ 189 Jason Standridge 5.00 2.00
❑ 190 Marvin Seale RC 8.00 3.00
❑ 191 Steve Smitherman RC 8.00 3.00
❑ 192 Rafael Boitel RC 5.00 2.00
❑ 193 Dany Morban RC 5.00 2.00
❑ 194 Justin Woodrow RC 8.00 3.00
❑ 195 Ed Rogers RC 5.00 2.00
❑ 196 Ben Hendrickson RC 5.00 2.00
❑ 197 Thomas Mitchell 5.00 2.00
❑ 198 Adam Pettyjohn RC 5.00 2.00
❑ 199 Doug Nickle RC 5.00 2.00
❑ 200 Jason Jones RC 5.00 2.00
❑ 201 Larry Barnes .50 .20
❑ 202 Ben Diggins .50 .20
❑ 203 Dee Brown .50 .20
❑ 204 Rocco Baldelli .50 .20
❑ 205 Luis Terrero .50 .20
❑ 206 Milton Bradley .50 .20
❑ 207 Kurt Ainsworth .50 .20
❑ 208 Sean Burroughs .50 .20
❑ 209 Rick Asadoorian .50 .20
❑ 210 Ramon Castro .50 .20
❑ 211 Nick Neugebauer .50 .20
❑ 212 Aaron Myette .50 .20
❑ 213 Luis Matos .50 .20
❑ 214 Donnie Bridges .50 .20
❑ 215 Alex Cintron .50 .20
❑ 216 Bobby Kielty .50 .20
❑ 217 Matt Belisle .50 .20
❑ 218 Adam Everett .50 .20
❑ 219 John Lackey .50 .20
❑ 220 Adam Wainwright .50 .20
❑ 221 Jerry Hairston Jr. .50 .20
❑ 222 Mike Bynum .50 .20
❑ 223 Ryan Christianson .50 .20
❑ 224 J.J. Davis .50 .20
❑ 225 Alex Graman .50 .20
❑ 226 Abraham Nunez .50 .20
❑ 227 Sun Woo Kim .50 .20
❑ 228 Jimmy Rollins .50 .20
❑ 229 Ruben Salazar .50 .20
❑ 230 Josh Girdley .50 .20
❑ 231 Carl Crawford .50 .20
❑ 232 Ben Davis .50 .20
❑ 233 Jason Grabowski .50 .20
❑ 234 Chris George .50 .20
❑ 235 Roy Oswalt 1.25 .50
❑ 236 Brian Cole .50 .20
❑ 237 Corey Patterson .50 .20
❑ 238 Vernon Wells .50 .20
❑ 239 Brad Baker .50 .20
❑ 240 Gookie Dawkins .50 .20
❑ 241 Michael Cuddyer .50 .20
❑ 242 Ricardo Aramboles .50 .20
❑ 243 Ben Sheets .75 .30
❑ 244 Toby Hall .50 .20
❑ 245 Jack Cust .50 .20
❑ 246 Pedro Feliz .50 .20
❑ 247 Josh Beckett .75 .30
❑ 248 Alex Escobar .50 .20
❑ 249 Marcus Giles .50 .20
❑ 250 Jon Rauch .50 .20
❑ 251 Kevin Mench .50 .20
❑ 252 Shawn Sonnier .50 .20
❑ 253 Aaron Rowand .50 .20
❑ 254 C.C. Sabathia .50 .20
❑ 255 Bubba Crosby .50 .20
❑ 256 Josh Hamilton .50 .20
❑ 257 Carlos Hernandez .50 .20
❑ 258 Carlos Pena .50 .20
❑ 259 Miguel Cabrera 4.00 1.50
❑ 260 Brandon Phillips .50 .20
❑ 261 Tony Pena Jr. .50 .20
❑ 262 Cristian Guerrero .50 .20
❑ 263 Jin Ho Cho .50 .20
❑ 264 Aaron Herr .50 .20
❑ 265 Keith Ginter .50 .20
❑ 266 Felipe Lopez .50 .20
❑ 267 Travis Harper .50 .20
❑ 268 Joe Torres .50 .20
❑ 269 Eric Byrnes .50 .20
❑ 270 Ben Christensen .50 .20
❑ 271 Aubrey Huff .50 .20
❑ 272 Lyle Overbay .50 .20
❑ 273 Vince Faison .50 .20
❑ 274 Bobby Bradley .50 .20
❑ 275 Joe Crede 1.25 .50
❑ 276 Matt Wheatland .50 .20
❑ 277 Grady Sizemore 2.00 .75
❑ 278 Adrian Gonzalez .50 .20
❑ 279 Tim Raines Jr. .50 .20
❑ 280 Phil Dumatrait .50 .20
❑ 281 Jason Hart .50 .20
❑ 282 David Kelton .50 .20
❑ 283 David Walling .50 .20
❑ 284 J.R. House .50 .20
❑ 285 Kenny Kelly .50 .20
❑ 286 Aaron McNeal .50 .20
❑ 287 Nick Johnson .50 .20
❑ 288 Scott Heard .50 .20
❑ 289 Brad Wilkerson .50 .20
❑ 290 Allen Levrault .50 .20
❑ 291 Chris Richard .50 .20
❑ 292 Jared Sandberg .50 .20
❑ 293 Tike Redman .50 .20
❑ 294 Adam Dunn .75 .30
❑ 295 Josh Pressley .50 .20
❑ 296 Jose Ortiz .50 .20
❑ 297 Jason Romano .50 .20
❑ 298 Tim Redding .50 .20
❑ 299 Alex Gordon .50 .20
❑ 300 Ben Petrick .50 .20
❑ 301 Eric Munson .50 .20
❑ 302 Luis Rivas .50 .20
❑ 303 Matt Ginter .50 .20
❑ 304 Alfonso Soriano .75 .30
❑ 305 Wilfredo Rodriguez .50 .20
❑ 306 Brett Myers .50 .20
❑ 307 Scott Seabol .50 .20
❑ 308 Tony Alvarez .50 .20
❑ 309 Donzell McDonald .50 .20
❑ 310 Austin Kearns .50 .20
❑ 311 Will Ohman RC 8.00 3.00
❑ 312 Ryan Soules RC 5.00 2.00
❑ 313 Cody Ross RC 5.00 2.00
❑ 314 Bill Whitecotton RC 5.00 2.00
❑ 315 Mike Burns RC 8.00 3.00
❑ 316 Manuel Acosta RC 5.00 2.00
❑ 317 Lance Niekro RC 10.00 4.00
❑ 318 Travis Thompson RC 8.00 3.00
❑ 319 Zach Sorensen RC 8.00 3.00
❑ 320 Austin Evans RC 5.00 2.00
❑ 321 Brad Stiles RC 5.00 2.00
❑ 322 Joe Kennedy RC 10.00 4.00
❑ 323 Luke Martin RC 8.00 3.00
❑ 324 Juan Diaz RC 8.00 3.00
❑ 325 Pat Hallmark RC 5.00 2.00
❑ 326 Christian Parker RC 5.00 2.00
❑ 327 Ronny Corona RC 8.00 3.00
❑ 328 Jermaine Clark RC 5.00 2.00
❑ 329 Scott Dunn RC 8.00 3.00
❑ 330 Scott Chiasson RC 8.00 3.00
❑ 331 Greg Nash AU RC 50.00 20.00
❑ 332 Brad Cresse AU 50.00 20.00
❑ 333 John Buck AU RC 80.00 40.00
❑ 334 Freddie Bynum AU RC 50.00 20.00
❑ 335 Felix Diaz AU RC 50.00 20.00
❑ 336 Jason Belcher AU RC 50.00 20.00
❑ 337 Troy Farnsworth AU RC 50.00 20.00
❑ 338 Roberto Miniel AU RC 50.00 20.00
❑ 339 Esix Snead AU RC 50.00 20.00
❑ 340 Albert Pujols AU RC 3500.00 3000.00
❑ 341 Jeff Andra AU RC 50.00 20.00
❑ 342 Victor Hall AU RC 50.00 20.00
❑ 343 Pedro Liriano AU RC 50.00 20.00
❑ 344 Andy Beal AU RC 50.00 20.00
❑ 345 Bob Keppel AU RC 50.00 20.00
❑ 346 Brian Schmitt AU RC 50.00 20.00
❑ 347 Ron Davenport AU RC 150.00 90.00

❑ 348 Tony Blanco AU RC	50.00	20.00
❑ 349 Reggie Griggs AU RC	50.00	20.00
❑ 350 Derrick Van Dusen AU RC	50.00	20.00
❑ 351A Ichiro Suzuki English RC	100.00	60.00
❑ 351B Ichiro Suzuki Japan RC	100.00	60.00

2002 Bowman Chrome

❑ COMP.RED SET (110)	40.00	15.00
❑ COMP.BLUE w/o SP's (110)	40.00	15.00
❑ COMMON RED (1-110)	.50	.20
❑ COMMON BLUE (111-383)	.75	.30
❑ COMMON AU (324B/384-405)	10.00	4.00
❑ 324B/384-405 GROUP A AUTO ODDS 1:28		
❑ 403-404 GROUP B AUTO ODDS 1:1290		
❑ 324B/384-405 OVERALL AUTO ODDS 1:27		
❑ 1 Adam Dunn	.50	.20
❑ 2 Derek Jeter	3.00	1.25
❑ 3 Alex Rodriguez	2.00	.75
❑ 4 Miguel Tejada	.50	.20
❑ 5 Nomar Garciaparra	2.00	.75
❑ 6 Toby Hall	.50	.20
❑ 7 Brandon Duckworth	.50	.20
❑ 8 Paul LoDuca	.50	.20
❑ 9 Brian Giles	.50	.20
❑ 10 C.C. Sabathia	.50	.20
❑ 11 Curt Schilling	.50	.20
❑ 12 Tsuyoshi Shinjo	.50	.20
❑ 13 Ramon Hernandez	.50	.20
❑ 14 Jose Cruz Jr.	.50	.20
❑ 15 Albert Pujols	2.50	1.00
❑ 16 Joe Mays	.50	.20
❑ 17 Javy Lopez	.50	.20
❑ 18 J.T. Snow	.50	.20
❑ 19 David Segui	.50	.20
❑ 20 Jorge Posada	.75	.30
❑ 21 Doug Mientkiewicz	.50	.20
❑ 22 Jerry Hairston Jr.	.50	.20
❑ 23 Bernie Williams	.75	.30
❑ 24 Mike Sweeney	.50	.20
❑ 25 Jason Giambi	.50	.20
❑ 26 Ryan Dempster	.50	.20
❑ 27 Ryan Klesko	.50	.20
❑ 28 Mark Quinn	.50	.20
❑ 29 Jeff Kent	.50	.20
❑ 30 Eric Chavez	.50	.20
❑ 31 Adrian Beltre	.50	.20
❑ 32 Andruw Jones	.75	.30
❑ 33 Alfonso Soriano	.50	.20
❑ 34 Aramis Ramirez	.50	.20
❑ 35 Greg Maddux	2.00	.75
❑ 36 Andy Pettitte	.75	.30
❑ 37 Bartolo Colon	.50	.20
❑ 38 Ben Sheets	.50	.20
❑ 39 Bobby Higginson	.50	.20
❑ 40 Ivan Rodriguez	.75	.30
❑ 41 Brad Penny	.50	.20
❑ 42 Carlos Lee	.50	.20
❑ 43 Damion Easley	.50	.20
❑ 44 Preston Wilson	.50	.20
❑ 45 Jeff Bagwell	.75	.30
❑ 46 Eric Milton	.50	.20
❑ 47 Rafael Palmeiro	.75	.30
❑ 48 Gary Sheffield	.50	.20
❑ 49 J.D. Drew	.50	.20
❑ 50 Jim Thome	.75	.30
❑ 51 Ichiro Suzuki	2.50	1.00
❑ 52 Bud Smith	.50	.20
❑ 53 Chan Ho Park	.50	.20
❑ 54 D'Angelo Jimenez	.50	.20
❑ 55 Ken Griffey Jr.	2.00	.75
❑ 56 Wade Miller	.50	.20
❑ 57 Vladimir Guerrero	1.25	.50
❑ 58 Troy Glaus	.50	.20
❑ 59 Shawn Green	.50	.20
❑ 60 Kerry Wood	.50	.20
❑ 61 Jack Wilson	.50	.20
❑ 62 Kevin Brown	.50	.20
❑ 63 Marcus Giles	.50	.20
❑ 64 Pat Burrell	.50	.20
❑ 65 Larry Walker	.50	.20
❑ 66 Sammy Sosa	1.25	.50
❑ 67 Raul Mondesi	.50	.20
❑ 68 Tim Hudson	.50	.20
❑ 69 Lance Berkman	.50	.20
❑ 70 Mike Mussina	.75	.30
❑ 71 Barry Zito	.50	.20
❑ 72 Jimmy Rollins	.50	.20
❑ 73 Barry Bonds	3.00	1.25
❑ 74 Craig Biggio	.75	.30
❑ 75 Todd Helton	.75	.30
❑ 76 Roger Clemens	2.50	1.00
❑ 77 Frank Catalanotto	.50	.20
❑ 78 Josh Towers	.50	.20
❑ 79 Roy Oswalt	.50	.20
❑ 80 Chipper Jones	1.25	.50
❑ 81 Cristian Guzman	.50	.20
❑ 82 Darin Erstad	.50	.20
❑ 83 Freddy Garcia	.50	.20
❑ 84 Jason Tyner	.50	.20
❑ 85 Carlos Delgado	.50	.20
❑ 86 Jon Lieber	.50	.20
❑ 87 Juan Pierre	.50	.20
❑ 88 Matt Morris	.50	.20
❑ 89 Phil Nevin	.50	.20
❑ 90 Jim Edmonds	.50	.20
❑ 91 Magglio Ordonez	.50	.20
❑ 92 Mike Hampton	.50	.20
❑ 93 Rafael Furcal	.50	.20
❑ 94 Richie Sexson	.50	.20
❑ 95 Luis Gonzalez	.50	.20
❑ 96 Scott Rolen	.75	.30
❑ 97 Tim Redding	.50	.20
❑ 98 Moises Alou	.50	.20
❑ 99 Jose Vidro	.50	.20
❑ 100 Mike Piazza	2.00	.75
❑ 101 Pedro Martinez	.75	.30
❑ 102 Geoff Jenkins	.50	.20
❑ 103 Johnny Damon Sox	.75	.30
❑ 104 Mike Cameron	.50	.20
❑ 105 Randy Johnson	1.25	.50
❑ 106 David Eckstein	.50	.20
❑ 107 Javier Vazquez	.50	.20
❑ 108 Mark Mulder	.50	.20
❑ 109 Robert Fick	.50	.20
❑ 110 Roberto Alomar	.75	.30
❑ 111 Wilson Betemit	.75	.30
❑ 112 Chris Tritle SP RC	5.00	2.00
❑ 113 Ed Rogers	.75	.30
❑ 114 Juan Pena	.75	.30
❑ 115 Josh Beckett	1.25	.50
❑ 116 Juan Cruz	.75	.30
❑ 117 Noochie Varner SP RC	5.00	2.00
❑ 118 Blake Williams	.75	.30
❑ 119 Mike Rivera	.75	.30
❑ 120 Hank Blalock	2.00	.75
❑ 121 Hansel Izquierdo SP RC	5.00	2.00
❑ 122 Orlando Hudson	.75	.30
❑ 123 Bill Hall SP	5.00	2.00
❑ 124 Jose Reyes	2.00	.75
❑ 125 Juan Rivera	.75	.30
❑ 126 Eric Valent	.75	.30
❑ 127 Scotty Layfield SP RC	5.00	2.00
❑ 128 Austin Kearns	.75	.30
❑ 129 Nic Jackson SP RC	5.00	2.00
❑ 130 Scott Chiasson	.75	.30
❑ 131 Chad Qualls SP RC	8.00	3.00
❑ 132 Marcus Thames	.75	.30
❑ 133 Nathan Haynes	.75	.30
❑ 134 Joe Borchard	.75	.30
❑ 135 Josh Hamilton	.75	.30
❑ 136 Corey Patterson	.75	.30
❑ 137 Travis Wilson	.75	.30
❑ 138 Alex Escobar	.75	.30
❑ 139 Alexis Gomez	.75	.30
❑ 140 Nick Johnson	1.25	.50
❑ 141 Marlon Byrd	.75	.30
❑ 142 Kory DeHaan	.75	.30
❑ 143 Carlos Hernandez	.75	.30
❑ 144 Sean Burroughs	.75	.30
❑ 145 Angel Berroa	.75	.30
❑ 146 Aubrey Huff	1.25	.50
❑ 147 Travis Hafner	1.25	.50
❑ 148 Brandon Berger	.75	.30
❑ 149 J.R. House	.75	.30
❑ 150 Dewon Brazelton	.75	.30
❑ 151 Jayson Werth	.75	.30
❑ 152 Larry Barnes	.75	.30
❑ 153 Ruben Gotay SP RC	8.00	3.00
❑ 154 Tommy Marx SP RC	5.00	2.00
❑ 155 John Suomi SP RC	5.00	2.00
❑ 156 Javier Colina SP	5.00	2.00
❑ 157 Greg Sain SP RC	5.00	2.00
❑ 158 Robert Cosby SP RC	5.00	2.00
❑ 159 Angel Pagan SP RC	8.00	3.00
❑ 160 Ralph Santana RC	1.25	.50
❑ 161 Joe Orloski RC	1.25	.50
❑ 162 Shayne Wright SP RC	5.00	2.00
❑ 163 Jay Caligiuri SP RC	5.00	2.00
❑ 164 Greg Montalbano SP RC	5.00	2.00
❑ 165 Rich Harden SP RC	30.00	12.50
❑ 166 Rich Thompson SP RC	5.00	2.00
❑ 167 Fred Bastardo SP RC	5.00	2.00
❑ 168 Alejandro Giron SP RC	5.00	2.00
❑ 169 Jesus Medrano SP RC	5.00	2.00
❑ 170 Kevin Deaton SP RC	5.00	2.00
❑ 171 Mike Rosamond RC	1.25	.50
❑ 172 Jon Guzman SP RC	5.00	2.00
❑ 173 Gerard Oakes SP RC	5.00	2.00
❑ 174 Francisco Liriano SP RC	40.00	15.00
❑ 175 Matt Allegra SP RC	5.00	2.00
❑ 176 Mike Snyder SP RC	5.00	2.00
❑ 177 James Shanks SP RC	5.00	2.00
❑ 178 Anderson Hernandez SP RC	5.00	2.00
❑ 179 Dan Trumble SP RC	5.00	2.00
❑ 180 Luis DePaula SP RC	5.00	2.00
❑ 181 Randall Shelley SP RC	5.00	2.00
❑ 182 Richard Lane SP RC	5.00	2.00
❑ 183 Antwon Rollins SP RC	5.00	2.00
❑ 184 Ryan Bukvich SP RC	5.00	2.00
❑ 185 Derrick Lewis SP	5.00	2.00
❑ 186 Eric Miller SP RC	5.00	2.00
❑ 187 Justin Schuda SP RC	5.00	2.00
❑ 188 Brian West SP RC	5.00	2.00
❑ 189 Brad Wilkerson	.75	.30
❑ 190 Neal Frendling SP RC	5.00	2.00
❑ 191 Jeremy Hill SP RC	5.00	2.00
❑ 192 James Barrett SP RC	5.00	2.00
❑ 193 Brett Kay SP RC	5.00	2.00
❑ 194 Ryan Mottl SP RC	5.00	2.00
❑ 195 Brad Nelson SP RC	5.00	2.00
❑ 196 Juan M. Gonzalez SP RC	5.00	2.00
❑ 197 Curtis Legendre SP RC	5.00	2.00
❑ 198 Ronald Acuna SP RC	5.00	2.00
❑ 199 Chris Flinn SP RC	5.00	2.00
❑ 200 Nick Alvarez SP RC	5.00	2.00
❑ 201 Jason Ellison SP RC	10.00	4.00
❑ 202 Blake McGinley SP RC	5.00	2.00
❑ 203 Dan Phillips SP RC	5.00	2.00
❑ 204 Demetrius Heath SP RC	5.00	2.00
❑ 205 Eric Bruntlett SP RC	5.00	2.00
❑ 206 Joe Jiannetti SP RC	5.00	2.00
❑ 207 Mike Hill SP RC	5.00	2.00
❑ 208 Ricardo Cordova SP RC	5.00	2.00
❑ 209 Mark Hamilton SP RC	5.00	2.00
❑ 210 David Mattox SP RC	5.00	2.00
❑ 211 Jose Morban SP RC	5.00	2.00
❑ 212 Scott Wiggins SP RC	5.00	2.00
❑ 213 Steve Green	.75	.30
❑ 214 Brian Rogers SP	5.00	2.00
❑ 215 Kenny Baugh	.75	.30
❑ 216 Anastacio Martinez SP RC	5.00	2.00
❑ 217 Richard Lewis	.75	.30
❑ 218 Tim Kalita SP RC	5.00	2.00
❑ 219 Edwin Almonte SP RC	5.00	2.00
❑ 220 Hee Seop Choi	.75	.30
❑ 221 Ty Howington	.75	.30
❑ 222 Victor Alvarez SP RC	5.00	2.00
❑ 223 Morgan Ensberg	1.25	.50
❑ 224 Jeff Austin SP RC	5.00	2.00
❑ 225 Clint Weibl SP RC	5.00	2.00

❑ 226 Eric Cyr	.75	.30
❑ 227 Marlyn Tisdale SP RC	5.00	2.00
❑ 228 John VanBenschoten	.75	.30
❑ 229 David Krynzel	.75	.30
❑ 230 Raul Chavez SP RC	5.00	2.00
❑ 231 Brett Evert	.75	.30
❑ 232 Joe Rogers SP RC	5.00	2.00
❑ 233 Adam Wainwright	.75	.30
❑ 234 Matt Herges RC	.75	.30
❑ 235 Matt Childers SP RC	5.00	2.00
❑ 236 Njck Neugebauer	.75	.30
❑ 237 Carl Crawford	1.25	.50
❑ 238 Seung Song	.75	.30
❑ 239 Randy Flores	.75	.30
❑ 240 Jason Lane	1.25	.50
❑ 241 Chase Utley	8.00	3.00
❑ 242 Ben Howard SP RC	5.00	2.00
❑ 243 Eric Glaser SP RC	5.00	2.00
❑ 244 Josh Wilson RC	1.25	.50
❑ 245 Jose Valverde SP RC	5.00	2.00
❑ 246 Chris Smith	.75	.30
❑ 247 Mark Prior	2.00	.75
❑ 248 Brian Mallette SP RC	5.00	2.00
❑ 249 Chone Figgins SP RC	8.00	3.00
❑ 250 Jimmy Alvarez SP RC	5.00	2.00
❑ 251 Luis Terrero	.75	.30
❑ 252 Josh Bonifay SP RC	5.00	2.00
❑ 253 Garrett Guzman SP RC	5.00	2.00
❑ 254 Jeff Verplancke SP RC	5.00	2.00
❑ 255 Nate Espy SP RC	5.00	2.00
❑ 256 Jeff Lincoln SP RC	5.00	2.00
❑ 257 Ryan Snare SP RC	5.00	2.00
❑ 258 Jose Ortiz	.75	.30
❑ 259 Denny Bautista	.75	.30
❑ 260 Willy Aybar	.75	.30
❑ 261 Kelly Johnson	3.00	1.25
❑ 262 Shawn Fagan	.75	.30
❑ 263 Yurendell DeCaster SP RC	5.00	2.00
❑ 264 Mike Peeples SP RC	5.00	2.00
❑ 265 Joel Guzman	3.00	1.25
❑ 266 Ryan Vogelsong	.75	.30
❑ 267 Jorge Padilla SP RC	5.00	2.00
❑ 268 Joe Jester SP RC	5.00	2.00
❑ 269 Ryan Church SP RC	10.00	4.00
❑ 270 Mitch Jones	.75	.30
❑ 271 Travis Foley SP RC	5.00	2.00
❑ 272 Bobby Crosby	3.00	1.25
❑ 273 Adrian Gonzalez	.75	.30
❑ 274 Ronnie Merrill	.75	.30
❑ 275 Joel Pineiro	.75	.30
❑ 276 John-Ford Griffin	.75	.30
❑ 277 Brian Forystek SP RC	5.00	2.00
❑ 278 Sean Douglass	.75	.30
❑ 279 Manny Delcarmen SP RC	8.00	3.00
❑ 280 Jim Kavourias SP RC	5.00	2.00
❑ 281 Gabe Gross	.75	.30
❑ 282 Bill Ortega	.75	.30
❑ 283 Joey Hammond SP RC	5.00	2.00
❑ 284 Brett Myers	1.25	.50
❑ 285 Carlos Pena	.75	.30
❑ 286 Ezequiel Astacio SP RC	5.00	2.00
❑ 287 Edwin Yan SP RC	5.00	2.00
❑ 288 Chris Duffy SP RC	8.00	3.00
❑ 289 Jason Kinchen	.75	.30
❑ 290 Rafael Soriano	.75	.30
❑ 291 Colin Young RC	5.00	2.00
❑ 292 Eric Byrnes	.75	.30
❑ 293 Chris Narveson SP RC	8.00	3.00
❑ 294 John Rheinecker	.75	.30
❑ 295 Mike Wilson SP RC	5.00	2.00
❑ 296 Justin Sherrod SP RC	5.00	2.00
❑ 297 Deivi Mendez	.75	.30
❑ 298 Wily Mo Pena	1.25	.50
❑ 299 Brett Roneberg SP RC	5.00	2.00
❑ 300 Trey Lunsford SP RC	5.00	2.00
❑ 301 Christian Parker	.75	.30
❑ 302 Brent Butler	.75	.30
❑ 303 Aaron Heilman	.75	.30
❑ 304 Wilkin Ruan	.75	.30
❑ 305 Kenny Kelly	.75	.30
❑ 306 Cody Ransom	.75	.30
❑ 307 Koyie Hill SP	5.00	2.00
❑ 308 Tony Fontana SP RC	5.00	2.00
❑ 309 Mark Teixeira	5.00	2.00
❑ 310 Doug Sessions SP RC	5.00	2.00
❑ 311 Josh Cisneros SP RC	5.00	2.00
❑ 312 Carlos Brackley SP RC	5.00	2.00
❑ 313 Tim Raines Jr.	.75	.30
❑ 314 Ross Peeples SP RC	5.00	2.00
❑ 315 Alex Requena SP RC	5.00	2.00
❑ 316 Chin-Hui Tsao	1.25	.50
❑ 317 Tony Alvarez	.75	.30
❑ 318 Craig Kuzmic SP RC	5.00	2.00
❑ 319 Pete Zamora SP RC	5.00	2.00
❑ 320 Matt Parker SP RC	5.00	2.00
❑ 321 Keith Ginter	.75	.30
❑ 322 Gary Cates Jr. SP RC	5.00	2.00
❑ 323 Matt Belisle	.75	.30
❑ 324A Ben Broussard	.75	.30
❑ 324B Jake Mauer AU A RC	10.00	4.00
❑ 325 Dennis Tankersley	.75	.30
❑ 326 Juan Silvestre	.75	.30
❑ 327 Henry Pichardo SP RC	5.00	2.00
❑ 328 Michael Floyd SP RC	5.00	2.00
❑ 329 Clint Nageotte SP RC	8.00	3.00
❑ 330 Raymond Cabrera SP RC	5.00	2.00
❑ 331 Mauricio Lara SP RC	5.00	2.00
❑ 332 Alejandro Cadena SP RC	5.00	2.00
❑ 333 Jonny Gomes SP RC	15.00	6.00
❑ 334 Jason Bulger SP RC	5.00	2.00
❑ 335 Nate Teut	.75	.30
❑ 336 David Gil SP RC	5.00	2.00
❑ 337 Joel Crump SP RC	5.00	2.00
❑ 338 Brandon Phillips	.75	.30
❑ 339 Macay McBride	1.25	.50
❑ 340 Brandon Claussen	.75	.30
❑ 341 Josh Phelps	.75	.30
❑ 342 Freddie Money SP RC	5.00	2.00
❑ 343 Cliff Bartosh SP RC	5.00	2.00
❑ 344 Terrance Hill SP RC	5.00	2.00
❑ 345 John Rodriguez SP RC	8.00	3.00
❑ 346 Chris Latham SP RC	5.00	2.00
❑ 347 Carlos Cabrera SP RC	5.00	2.00
❑ 348 Jose Bautista SP RC	10.00	4.00
❑ 349 Kevin Frederick SP RC	5.00	2.00
❑ 350 Jerome Williams	.75	.30
❑ 351 Napoleon Calzado SP RC	5.00	2.00
❑ 352 Benito Baez SP	5.00	2.00
❑ 353 Xavier Nady	.75	.30
❑ 354 Jason Botts SP RC	8.00	3.00
❑ 355 Steve Bechler SP RC	5.00	2.00
❑ 356 Reed Johnson SP RC	10.00	4.00
❑ 357 Mark Outlaw SP RC	5.00	2.00
❑ 358 Jake Peavy	2.00	.75
❑ 359 Josh Shaffer SP RC	5.00	2.00
❑ 360 Dan Wright SP	5.00	2.00
❑ 361 Ryan Gripp SP RC	5.00	2.00
❑ 362 Nelson Castro SP RC	5.00	2.00
❑ 363 Jason Bay SP RC	25.00	10.00
❑ 364 Franklyn German SP RC	5.00	2.00
❑ 365 Corwin Malone SP RC	5.00	2.00
❑ 366 Kelly Ramos SP RC	5.00	2.00
❑ 367 John Ennis SP RC	5.00	2.00
❑ 368 George Perez SP	5.00	2.00
❑ 369 Rene Reyes SP RC	5.00	2.00
❑ 370 Rolando Viera SP RC	5.00	2.00
❑ 371 Earl Snyder SP RC	5.00	2.00
❑ 372 Kyle Kane SP RC	5.00	2.00
❑ 373 Mario Ramos SP RC	5.00	2.00
❑ 374 Tyler Yates SP RC	5.00	2.00
❑ 375 Jason Young SP RC	5.00	2.00
❑ 376 Chris Bootcheck SP RC	5.00	2.00
❑ 377 Jesus Cota SP RC	5.00	2.00
❑ 378 Corky Miller SP	5.00	2.00
❑ 379 Matt Erickson SP RC	5.00	2.00
❑ 380 Justin Huber SP RC	10.00	4.00
❑ 381 Felix Escalona SP RC	5.00	2.00
❑ 382 Kevin Cash SP RC	5.00	2.00
❑ 383 J.J. Putz SP RC	8.00	3.00
❑ 384 Chris Snelling AU A RC	20.00	8.00
❑ 385 David Wright AU A RC	400.00	200.00
❑ 386 Brian Wolfe AU A RC	10.00	4.00
❑ 387 Justin Reid AU A RC	10.00	4.00
❑ 389 Ryan Raburn AU A RC	10.00	4.00
❑ 390 Josh Barfield AU A RC	50.00	25.00
❑ 391 Joe Mauer AU A RC	200.00	125.00
❑ 392 Bobby Jenks AU A RC	25.00	10.00
❑ 393 Rob Henkel AU A RC	10.00	4.00
❑ 394 Jimmy Gobble AU A RC	10.00	4.00
❑ 395 Jesse Foppert AU A RC	15.00	6.00
❑ 396 Gavin Floyd AU A RC	25.00	10.00
❑ 397 Nate Field AU A RC	10.00	4.00
❑ 398 Ryan Doumit AU A RC	15.00	6.00
❑ 399 Ron Calloway AU A RC	10.00	4.00
❑ 400 Taylor Buchholz AU A RC	15.00	6.00
❑ 401 Adam Roller AU A RC	10.00	4.00
❑ 402 Cole Barthel AU A RC	10.00	4.00
❑ 403 Kazuhisa Ishii SP RC	8.00	3.00
❑ 403A Kazuhisa Ishii AU B	50.00	30.00
❑ 404 So Taguchi SP RC	8.00	3.00
❑ 404A So Taguchi AU B	50.00	30.00
❑ 405 Chris Baker AU A RC	10.00	4.00

2002 Bowman Chrome Draft

❑ COMPLETE SET (175)	350.00	200.00
❑ COMP.SET w/o AU's (165)	200.00	135.00
❑ COMMON CARD (1-165)	.40	.15
❑ COMMON CARD (166-175)	10.00	4.00
❑ 1 Clint Everts RC	1.50	.60
❑ 2 Fred Lewis RC	1.00	.40
❑ 3 Jon Broxton RC	3.00	1.25
❑ 4 Jason Anderson RC	1.00	.40
❑ 5 Mike Eusebio RC	1.00	.40
❑ 6 Zack Greinke RC	5.00	2.00
❑ 7 Joe Blanton RC	5.00	2.00
❑ 8 Sergio Santos RC	1.50	.60
❑ 9 Jason Cooper RC	1.00	.40
❑ 10 Delwyn Young RC	3.00	1.25
❑ 11 Jeremy Hermida RC	12.00	5.00
❑ 12 Dan Ortmeier RC	1.50	.60
❑ 13 Kevin Jepsen RC	1.50	.60
❑ 14 Russ Adams RC	1.50	.60
❑ 15 Mike Nixon RC	1.00	.40
❑ 16 Nick Swisher RC	15.00	6.00
❑ 17 Cole Hamels RC	40.00	15.00
❑ 18 Brian Dopirak RC	3.00	1.25
❑ 19 James Loney RC	12.00	5.00
❑ 20 Denard Span RC	1.50	.60
❑ 21 Billy Petrick RC	1.00	.40
❑ 22 Jared Doyle RC	1.00	.40
❑ 23 Jeff Francoeur RC	40.00	20.00
❑ 24 Nick Bourgeois RC	1.00	.40
❑ 25 Matt Cain RC	15.00	6.00
❑ 26 John McCurdy RC	1.00	.40
❑ 27 Mark Kiger RC	1.00	.40
❑ 28 Bill Murphy RC	1.00	.40
❑ 29 Matt Craig RC	1.50	.60
❑ 30 Mike Megrew RC	1.00	.40
❑ 31 Ben Crockett RC	1.00	.40
❑ 32 Luke Hagerty RC	1.00	.40
❑ 33 Matt Whitney RC	1.00	.40
❑ 34 Dan Meyer RC	1.50	.60
❑ 35 Jeremy Brown RC	1.00	.40
❑ 36 Doug Johnson RC	1.00	.40
❑ 37 Steve Obenchain RC	1.00	.40
❑ 38 Matt Clanton RC	1.00	.40
❑ 39 Mark Teahen RC	3.00	1.25
❑ 40 Tom Carrow RC	1.00	.40
❑ 41 Micah Schilling RC	1.00	.40
❑ 42 Blair Johnson RC	1.00	.40
❑ 43 Jason Pridie RC	1.00	.40
❑ 44 Joey Votto RC	12.00	5.00
❑ 45 Taber Lee RC	1.00	.40
❑ 46 Adam Peterson RC	1.00	.40
❑ 47 Adam Donachie RC	1.00	.40
❑ 48 Josh Murray RC	1.00	.40
❑ 49 Brent Clevlen RC	6.00	2.50
❑ 50 Chad Pleiness RC	1.00	.40
❑ 51 Zach Hammes RC	1.00	.40

❑ 52 Chris Snyder RC 1.50 .60
❑ 53 Chris Smith RC 1.00 .40
❑ 54 Justin Maureau RC 1.00 .40
❑ 55 David Bush RC 3.00 1.25
❑ 56 Tim Gilhooly RC 1.00 .40
❑ 57 Blair Barbier RC 1.00 .40
❑ 58 Zach Segovia RC 1.00 .40
❑ 59 Jeremy Reed RC 3.00 1.25
❑ 60 Matt Pender RC 1.00 .40
❑ 61 Eric Thomas RC 1.00 .40
❑ 62 Justin Jones RC 1.50 .60
❑ 63 Brian Slocum RC 1.00 .40
❑ 64 Larry Broadway RC 1.00 .40
❑ 65 Bo Flowers RC 1.00 .40
❑ 66 Scott White RC 1.00 .40
❑ 67 Steve Stanley RC 1.00 .40
❑ 68 Alex Merricks RC 1.00 .40
❑ 69 Josh Womack RC 1.00 .40
❑ 70 Dave Jensen RC 1.00 .40
❑ 71 Curtis Granderson RC 12.00 5.00
❑ 72 Pat Osborn RC 1.00 .40
❑ 73 Nic Carter RC 1.00 .40
❑ 74 Mitch Talbot RC 1.00 .40
❑ 75 Don Murphy RC 1.00 .40
❑ 76 Val Majewski RC 1.00 .40
❑ 77 Javy Rodriguez RC 1.00 .40
❑ 78 Fernando Pacheco RC 1.00 .40
❑ 79 Steve Russell RC 1.00 .40
❑ 80 Jon Slack RC 1.00 .40
❑ 81 John Baker RC 1.00 .40
❑ 82 Aaron Coonrod RC 1.00 .40
❑ 83 Josh Johnson RC 10.00 4.00
❑ 84 Jake Blalock RC 1.50 .60
❑ 85 Alex Hart RC 1.00 .40
❑ 86 Wes Bankston RC 6.00 2.50
❑ 87 Josh Rupe RC 1.00 .40
❑ 88 Dan Cevette RC 1.00 .40
❑ 89 Kiel Fisher RC 1.50 .60
❑ 90 Alan Rick RC 1.00 .40
❑ 91 Charlie Morton RC 1.00 .40
❑ 92 Chad Spann RC 1.00 .40
❑ 93 Kyle Boyer RC 1.00 .40
❑ 94 Bob Malek RC 1.00 .40
❑ 95 Ryan Rodriguez RC 1.00 .40
❑ 96 Jordan Renz RC 1.00 .40
❑ 97 Randy Frye RC 1.00 .40
❑ 98 Rich Hill RC 12.00 5.00
❑ 99 B.J. Upton RC 15.00 6.00
❑ 100 Dan Christensen RC 1.00 .40
❑ 101 Casey Kotchman RC 6.00 2.50
❑ 102 Eric Good RC 1.00 .40
❑ 103 Mike Fontenot RC 1.00 .40
❑ 104 John Webb RC 1.00 .40
❑ 105 Jason Dubois RC 1.50 .60
❑ 106 Ryan Kibler RC 1.00 .40
❑ 107 Jhonny Peralta RC 8.00 3.00
❑ 108 Kirk Saarloos RC 1.00 .40
❑ 109 Rhett Parrott RC 1.00 .40
❑ 110 Jason Grove RC 1.00 .40
❑ 111 Colt Griffin RC 1.00 .40
❑ 112 Dallas McPherson RC 3.00 1.25
❑ 113 Oliver Perez RC 3.00 1.25
❑ 114 Marshall McDougall RC 1.00 .40
❑ 115 Mike Wood RC 1.00 .40
❑ 116 Scott Hairston RC 1.50 .60
❑ 117 Jason Simontacchi RC 1.00 .40
❑ 118 Taggert Bozied RC 1.50 .60
❑ 119 Shelley Duncan RC 10.00 4.00
❑ 120 Dontrelle Willis RC 15.00 6.00
❑ 121 Sean Burnett .40 .15
❑ 122 Aaron Cook .60 .25
❑ 123 Brett Evert .40 .15
❑ 124 Jimmy Journell .40 .15
❑ 125 Brett Myers .60 .25
❑ 126 Brad Baker .40 .15
❑ 127 Billy Traber RC 1.00 .40
❑ 128 Adam Wainwright .40 .15
❑ 129 Jason Young 1.00 .40
❑ 130 John Buck .40 .15
❑ 131 Kevin Cash 1.00 .40
❑ 132 Jason Stokes RC 1.50 .60
❑ 133 Drew Henson .40 .15
❑ 134 Chad Tracy RC 5.00 2.00
❑ 135 Orlando Hudson .40 .15
❑ 136 Brandon Phillips .40 .15
❑ 137 Joe Borchard .40 .15
❑ 138 Marlon Byrd .40 .15
❑ 139 Carl Crawford .60 .25
❑ 140 Michael Restovich .40 .15
❑ 141 Corey Hart RC 5.00 2.00
❑ 142 Edwin Almonte .60 .25
❑ 143 Francis Beltran RC 1.00 .40
❑ 144 Jorge De La Rosa RC 1.00 .40
❑ 145 Gerardo Garcia RC 1.00 .40
❑ 146 Franklyn German RC 1.00 .40
❑ 147 Francisco Liriano 10.00 4.00
❑ 148 Francisco Rodriguez .60 .25
❑ 149 Ricardo Rodriguez .40 .15
❑ 150 Seung Song .40 .15
❑ 151 John Stephens .40 .15
❑ 152 Justin Huber RC 2.50 1.00
❑ 153 Victor Martinez 1.50 .60
❑ 154 Hee Seop Choi .40 .15
❑ 155 Justin Morneau .60 .25
❑ 156 Miguel Cabrera 2.50 1.00
❑ 157 Victor Diaz RC 2.50 1.00
❑ 158 Jose Reyes 1.00 .40
❑ 159 Omar Infante .40 .15
❑ 160 Angel Berroa .40 .15
❑ 161 Tony Alvarez .40 .15
❑ 162 Shin Soo Choo RC 2.50 1.00
❑ 163 Wily Mo Pena .60 .25
❑ 164 Andres Torres .40 .15
❑ 165 Jose Lopez RC 6.00 2.50
❑ 166 Scott Moore AU RC 15.00 6.00
❑ 167 Chris Gruler AU RC 10.00 4.00
❑ 168 Joe Saunders AU RC 20.00 8.00
❑ 169 Jeff Francis AU RC 50.00 20.00
❑ 170 Royce Ring AU RC 10.00 4.00
❑ 171 Greg Miller AU RC 15.00 6.00
❑ 172 Brandon Weeden AU RC 10.00 4.00
❑ 173 Drew Meyer AU RC 10.00 4.00
❑ 174 Khalil Greene AU RC 60.00 30.00
❑ 175 Mark Schramek AU RC 10.00 4.00

2003 Bowman Chrome

❑ COMPLETE SET (351) 500.00 300.00
❑ COMP.SET w/o AU's (331) 150.00 75.00
❑ COMMON CARD (1-165) .50 .20
❑ COMMON CARD (166-330) .50 .20
❑ COMMON RC (156-330) 1.00 .40
❑ COMP.SET w/o AU'S INCLUDES 351 MAYS
❑ MAYS AU IS NOT PART OF 351-CARD SET
❑ 1 Garret Anderson .50 .20
❑ 2 Derek Jeter 3.00 1.25
❑ 3 Gary Sheffield .50 .20
❑ 4 Matt Morris .50 .20
❑ 5 Derek Lowe .50 .20
❑ 6 Andy Van Hekken .50 .20
❑ 7 Sammy Sosa 1.25 .50
❑ 8 Ken Griffey Jr. 2.00 .75
❑ 9 Omar Vizquel .75 .30
❑ 10 Jorge Posada .75 .30
❑ 11 Lance Berkman .50 .20
❑ 12 Mike Sweeney .50 .20
❑ 13 Adrian Beltre .50 .20
❑ 14 Richie Sexson .50 .20
❑ 15 A.J. Pierzynski .50 .20
❑ 16 Bartolo Colon .50 .20
❑ 17 Mike Mussina .75 .30
❑ 18 Paul Byrd .50 .20
❑ 19 Bobby Abreu .50 .20
❑ 20 Miguel Tejada .50 .20
❑ 21 Aramis Ramirez .50 .20
❑ 22 Edgardo Alfonzo .50 .20
❑ 23 Edgar Martinez .75 .30
❑ 24 Albert Pujols 2.50 1.00
❑ 25 Carl Crawford .50 .20
❑ 26 Eric Hinske .50 .20
❑ 27 Tim Salmon .75 .30
❑ 28 Luis Gonzalez .50 .20
❑ 29 Jay Gibbons .50 .20
❑ 30 John Smoltz .50 .20
❑ 31 Tim Wakefield .50 .20
❑ 32 Mark Prior .75 .30
❑ 33 Magglio Ordonez .50 .20
❑ 34 Adam Dunn .50 .20
❑ 35 Larry Walker .50 .20
❑ 36 Luis Castillo .50 .20
❑ 37 Wade Miller .50 .20
❑ 38 Carlos Beltran .50 .20
❑ 39 Odalis Perez .50 .20
❑ 40 Alex Sanchez .50 .20
❑ 41 Torii Hunter .50 .20
❑ 42 Cliff Floyd .50 .20
❑ 43 Andy Pettitte .75 .30
❑ 44 Francisco Rodriguez .50 .20
❑ 45 Eric Chavez .50 .20
❑ 46 Kevin Millwood .50 .20
❑ 47 Dennis Tankersley .50 .20
❑ 48 Hideo Nomo 1.25 .50
❑ 49 Freddy Garcia .50 .20
❑ 50 Randy Johnson 1.25 .50
❑ 51 Aubrey Huff .50 .20
❑ 52 Carlos Delgado .50 .20
❑ 53 Troy Glaus .50 .20
❑ 54 Junior Spivey .50 .20
❑ 55 Mike Hampton .50 .20
❑ 56 Sidney Ponson .50 .20
❑ 57 Aaron Boone .50 .20
❑ 58 Kerry Wood .50 .20
❑ 59 Willie Harris .50 .20
❑ 60 Nomar Garciaparra 2.00 .75
❑ 61 Todd Helton .75 .30
❑ 62 Mike Lowell .50 .20
❑ 63 Roy Oswalt .50 .20
❑ 64 Raul Ibanez .50 .20
❑ 65 Brian Jordan .50 .20
❑ 66 Geoff Jenkins .50 .20
❑ 67 Jermaine Dye .50 .20
❑ 68 Tom Glavine .75 .30
❑ 69 Bernie Williams .75 .30
❑ 70 Vladimir Guerrero 1.25 .50
❑ 71 Mark Mulder .50 .20
❑ 72 Jimmy Rollins .50 .20
❑ 73 Oliver Perez .50 .20
❑ 74 Rich Aurilia .50 .20
❑ 75 Joel Pineiro .50 .20
❑ 76 J.D. Drew .50 .20
❑ 77 Ivan Rodriguez .75 .30
❑ 78 Josh Phelps .50 .20
❑ 79 Darin Erstad .50 .20
❑ 80 Curt Schilling .50 .20
❑ 81 Paul Lo Duca .50 .20
❑ 82 Marty Cordova .50 .20
❑ 83 Manny Ramirez .75 .30
❑ 84 Bobby Hill .50 .20
❑ 85 Paul Konerko .50 .20
❑ 86 Austin Kearns .50 .20
❑ 87 Jason Jennings .50 .20
❑ 88 Brad Penny .50 .20
❑ 89 Jeff Bagwell .75 .30
❑ 90 Shawn Green .50 .20
❑ 91 Jason Schmidt .50 .20
❑ 92 Doug Mientkiewicz .50 .20
❑ 93 Jose Vidro .50 .20
❑ 94 Bret Boone .50 .20
❑ 95 Jason Giambi .50 .20
❑ 96 Barry Zito .50 .20
❑ 97 Roy Halladay .50 .20
❑ 98 Pat Burrell .50 .20
❑ 99 Sean Burroughs .50 .20
❑ 100 Barry Bonds 3.00 1.25
❑ 101 Kazuhiro Sasaki .50 .20
❑ 102 Fernando Vina .50 .20
❑ 103 Chan Ho Park .50 .20
❑ 104 Andruw Jones .75 .30
❑ 105 Adam Kennedy .50 .20
❑ 106 Shea Hillenbrand .50 .20
❑ 107 Greg Maddux 2.00 .75

❑ 108 Jim Edmonds .50 .20
❑ 109 Pedro Martinez .75 .30
❑ 110 Moises Alou .50 .20
❑ 111 Jeff Weaver .50 .20
❑ 112 C.C. Sabathia .50 .20
❑ 113 Robert Fick .50 .20
❑ 114 A.J. Burnett .50 .20
❑ 115 Jeff Kent .50 .20
❑ 116 Kevin Brown .50 .20
❑ 117 Rafael Furcal .50 .20
❑ 118 Cristian Guzman .50 .20
❑ 119 Brad Wilkerson .50 .20
❑ 120 Mike Piazza 2.00 .75
❑ 121 Alfonso Soriano .50 .20
❑ 122 Mark Ellis .50 .20
❑ 123 Vicente Padilla .50 .20
❑ 124 Eric Gagne .50 .20
❑ 125 Ryan Klesko .50 .20
❑ 126 Ichiro Suzuki 2.50 1.00
❑ 127 Tony Batista .50 .20
❑ 128 Roberto Alomar .75 .30
❑ 129 Alex Rodriguez 2.00 .75
❑ 130 Jim Thome .75 .30
❑ 131 Jarrod Washburn .50 .20
❑ 132 Orlando Hudson .50 .20
❑ 133 Chipper Jones 1.25 .50
❑ 134 Rodrigo Lopez .50 .20
❑ 135 Johnny Damon .75 .30
❑ 136 Matt Clement .50 .20
❑ 137 Frank Thomas 1.25 .50
❑ 138 Ellis Burks .50 .20
❑ 139 Carlos Pena .50 .20
❑ 140 Josh Beckett .50 .20
❑ 141 Joe Randa .50 .20
❑ 142 Brian Giles .50 .20
❑ 143 Kazuhisa Ishii .50 .20
❑ 144 Corey Koskie .50 .20
❑ 145 Orlando Cabrera .50 .20
❑ 146 Mark Buehrle .50 .20
❑ 147 Roger Clemens 2.50 1.00
❑ 148 Tim Hudson .50 .20
❑ 149 Randy Wolf .50 .20
❑ 150 Josh Fogg .50 .20
❑ 151 Phil Nevin .50 .20
❑ 152 John Olerud .50 .20
❑ 153 Scott Rolen .75 .30
❑ 154 Joe Kennedy .50 .20
❑ 155 Rafael Palmeiro .75 .30
❑ 156 Chad Hutchinson .50 .20
❑ 157 Quincy Carter XRC 1.50 .60
❑ 158 Hee Seop Choi .50 .20
❑ 159 Joe Borchard .50 .20
❑ 160 Brandon Phillips .50 .20
❑ 161 Wily Mo Pena .50 .20
❑ 162 Victor Martinez .75 .30
❑ 163 Jason Stokes .50 .20
❑ 164 Ken Harvey .50 .20
❑ 165 Juan Rivera .50 .20
❑ 166 Joe Valentine RC 1.50 .60
❑ 168 Michel Hernandez RC 1.50 .60
❑ 169 Eider Torres RC 1.50 .60
❑ 170 Chris De La Cruz RC 1.50 .60
❑ 171 Ramon Nivar-Martinez RC 1.50 .60
❑ 172 Mike Adams RC 1.50 .60
❑ 173 Justin Arneson RC 1.50 .60
❑ 174 Jamie Athas RC 1.50 .60
❑ 175 Dwaine Bacon RC 1.50 .60
❑ 176 Clint Barmes RC 4.00 1.50
❑ 177 B.J. Barns RC 1.50 .60
❑ 178 Tyler Johnson RC 1.50 .60
❑ 179 Brandon Webb RC 12.00 5.00
❑ 180 T.J. Bohn RC 1.50 .60
❑ 181 Ozzie Chavez RC 1.50 .60
❑ 182 Brandon Bowe RC 1.50 .60
❑ 183 Craig Brazell RC 1.50 .60
❑ 184 Dusty Brown RC 1.50 .60
❑ 185 Brian Bruney RC 2.00 .75
❑ 186 Greg Bruso RC 1.50 .60
❑ 187 Jaime Bubela RC 1.50 .60
❑ 188 Matt Diaz RC 3.00 1.25
❑ 189 Brian Burgamy RC 1.50 .60
❑ 190 Eny Cabreja RC 5.00 2.00
❑ 191 Daniel Cabrera RC 3.00 1.25
❑ 192 Ryan Cameron RC 1.50 .60
❑ 193 Lance Caraccioli RC 1.50 .60
❑ 194 David Cash RC 1.50 .60
❑ 195 Bernie Castro RC 1.50 .60
❑ 196 Ismael Castro RC 2.00 .75
❑ 197 Cory Doyne RC 1.50 .60
❑ 198 Jeff Clark RC 1.50 .60
❑ 199 Chris Colton RC 1.50 .60
❑ 200 Dexter Cooper RC 1.50 .60
❑ 201 Callix Crabbe RC 2.00 .75
❑ 202 Chien-Ming Wang RC 15.00 6.00
❑ 203 Eric Crozier RC 2.00 .75
❑ 204 Nook Logan RC 2.00 .75
❑ 205 David DeJesus RC 3.00 1.25
❑ 206 Matt DeMarco RC 1.50 .60
❑ 207 Chris Duncan RC 12.00 5.00
❑ 208 Eric Eckenstahler .50 .20
❑ 209 Willie Eyre RC 1.50 .60
❑ 210 Evel Bastida-Martinez RC 1.50 .60
❑ 211 Chris Fallon RC 1.50 .60
❑ 212 Mike Flannery RC 1.50 .60
❑ 213 Mike Oâ ™Keefe RC 1.50 .60
❑ 214 Lew Ford RC 2.00 .75
❑ 215 Kason Gabbard RC 1.50 .60
❑ 216 Mike Gallo RC 1.50 .60
❑ 217 Jairo Garcia RC 2.00 .75
❑ 218 Angel Garcia RC 2.00 .75
❑ 219 Michael Garciaparra RC 1.50 .60
❑ 220 Jeremy Griffiths RC 1.50 .60
❑ 221 Dusty Gomon RC 2.00 .75
❑ 222 Bryan Grace RC 1.50 .60
❑ 223 Tyson Graham RC 1.50 .60
❑ 224 Henry Guerrero RC 1.50 .60
❑ 225 Franklin Gutierrez RC 4.00 1.50
❑ 226 Carlos Guzman RC 2.00 .75
❑ 227 Matthew Hagen RC 1.50 .60
❑ 228 Josh Hall RC 1.50 .60
❑ 229 Rob Hammock RC 1.50 .60
❑ 230 Brendan Harris RC 2.00 .75
❑ 231 Gary Harris RC 1.50 .60
❑ 232 Clay Hensley RC 1.50 .60
❑ 233 Michael Hinckley RC 2.00 .75
❑ 234 Luis Hodge RC 1.50 .60
❑ 235 Donnie Hood RC 2.00 .75
❑ 236 Matt Hensley RC 1.50 .60
❑ 237 Edwin Jackson RC 2.00 .75
❑ 238 Ardley Jansen RC 2.00 .75
❑ 239 Ferenc Jongejan RC 1.50 .60
❑ 240 Matt Kata RC 1.50 .60
❑ 241 Kazuhiro Takeoka RC 1.50 .60
❑ 242 Charlie Manning RC 1.50 .60
❑ 243 Il Kim RC 1.50 .60
❑ 244 Brennan King RC 1.50 .60
❑ 245 Chris Kroski RC 1.50 .60
❑ 246 David Martinez RC 1.50 .60
❑ 247 Pete LaForest RC 1.50 .60
❑ 248 Wil Ledezma RC 1.50 .60
❑ 249 Jeremy Bonderman RC 10.00 4.00
❑ 250 Gonzalo Lopez RC 1.50 .60
❑ 251 Brian Luderer RC 1.50 .60
❑ 252 Ruddy Lugo RC 1.50 .60
❑ 253 Wayne Lydon RC 1.50 .60
❑ 254 Mark Malaska RC 1.50 .60
❑ 255 Andy Marte RC 10.00 4.00
❑ 256 Tyler Martin RC 1.50 .60
❑ 257 Branden Florence RC 1.50 .60
❑ 258 Aneudis Mateo RC 1.50 .60
❑ 259 Derell McCall RC 1.50 .60
❑ 260 Elizardo Ramirez RC 2.00 .75
❑ 261 Mike McNutt RC 1.50 .60
❑ 262 Jacobo Meque RC 1.50 .60
❑ 263 Derek Michaelis RC 1.50 .60
❑ 264 Aaron Miles RC 2.00 .75
❑ 265 Jose Morales RC 1.50 .60
❑ 266 Dustin Moseley RC 1.50 .60
❑ 267 Adrian Myers RC 1.50 .60
❑ 268 Dan Neil RC 1.50 .60
❑ 269 Jon Nelson RC 2.00 .75
❑ 270 Mike Neu RC 1.50 .60
❑ 271 Leigh Neuage RC 1.50 .60
❑ 272 Wes O'Brien RC 1.50 .60
❑ 273 Trent Oeltjen RC 2.00 .75
❑ 274 Tim Olson RC 1.50 .60
❑ 275 David Pahucki RC 1.50 .60
❑ 276 Nathan Panther RC 1.50 .60
❑ 277 Arnie Munoz RC 1.50 .60
❑ 278 Dave Pember RC 1.50 .60
❑ 279 Jason Perry RC 2.00 .75
❑ 280 Matthew Peterson RC 1.50 .60
❑ 281 Greg Aquino RC 1.50 .60
❑ 282 Jorge Piedra RC 2.00 .75
❑ 283 Simon Pond RC 1.50 .60
❑ 284 Aaron Rakers RC 1.50 .60
❑ 285 Felix Sanchez RC 1.50 .60
❑ 286 Manuel Ramirez RC 2.00 .75
❑ 287 Kevin Randel RC 1.50 .60
❑ 288 Kelly Shoppach RC 3.00 1.25
❑ 289 Prentice Redman RC 1.50 .60
❑ 290 Eric Reed RC 1.50 .60
❑ 291 Wilton Reynolds RC 2.00 .75
❑ 292 Eric Riggs RC 2.00 .75
❑ 293 Carlos Rijo RC 1.50 .60
❑ 294 Tyler Adamczyk RC 1.50 .60
❑ 295 Jon-Mark Sprowl RC 1.50 .60
❑ 296 Arturo Rivas RC 1.50 .60
❑ 297 Kyle Roat RC 1.50 .60
❑ 298 Bubba Nelson RC .75 .30
❑ 299 Levi Robinson RC 1.50 .60
❑ 300 Ray Sadler RC 1.50 .60
❑ 301 Rylan Reed RC 1.50 .60
❑ 302 Jon Schuerholz RC 1.50 .60
❑ 303 Nobuaki Yoshida RC 1.50 .60
❑ 304 Brian Shackelford RC 1.50 .60
❑ 305 Bill Simon RC 1.50 .60
❑ 306 Haj Turay RC 1.00 .40
❑ 307 Sean Smith RC 2.00 .75
❑ 308 Ryan Spataro RC 1.50 .60
❑ 309 Jemel Spearman RC 1.50 .60
❑ 310 Keith Stamler RC 1.50 .60
❑ 311 Luke Steidlmayer RC 1.50 .60
❑ 312 Adam Stern RC 1.00 .40
❑ 313 Jay Sitzman RC 1.50 .60
❑ 314 Mike Wodnicki RC 1.50 .60
❑ 315 Terry Tiffee RC 1.50 .60
❑ 316 Nick Trzesniak RC 1.50 .60
❑ 317 Denny Tussen RC 1.50 .60
❑ 318 Scott Tyler RC 2.00 .75
❑ 319 Shane Victorino RC 3.00 1.25
❑ 320 Doug Waechter RC 2.00 .75
❑ 321 Brandon Watson RC 1.50 .60
❑ 322 Todd Wellemeyer RC 1.50 .60
❑ 323 Eli Whiteside RC 1.50 .60
❑ 324 Josh Willingham RC 4.00 1.50
❑ 325 Travis Wong RC 2.00 .75
❑ 326 Brian Wright RC 1.50 .60
❑ 327 Felix Pie RC 12.00 5.00
❑ 328 Andy Sisco RC .50 .20
❑ 329 Dustin Yount RC 2.00 .75
❑ 330 Andrew Dominique RC 1.50 .60
❑ 331 Brian McCann AU A RC 120.00 60.00
❑ 332 Jose Contreras AU B RC 150.00 90.00
❑ 333 Corey Shafer AU A RC 10.00 4.00
❑ 334 Hanley Ramirez AU A RC 200.00 150.00
❑ 335 Ryan Shealy AU A RC 30.00 12.50
❑ 336 Kevin Youkilis AU A RC 50.00 20.00
❑ 337 Jason Kubel AU A RC 30.00 12.50
❑ 338 Aron Weston AU A RC 10.00 4.00
❑ 338B Rajai Davis AU A ERR
❑ 339 J.D. Durbin AU A RC 10.00 4.00
❑ 340 Gary Schneidmiller AU A RC 10.004.00
❑ 341 Travis Ishikawa AU A RC 15.00 6.00
❑ 342 Ben Francisco AU A RC 10.00 4.00
❑ 343 Bobby Basham AU A RC 10.00 4.00
❑ 344 Joey Gomes AU A RC 10.00 4.00
❑ 345 Beau Kemp AU A RC 10.00 4.00
❑ 346 T.Story-Harden AU A RC 10.00 4.00
❑ 347 Daryl Clark AU A RC 10.00 4.00
❑ 348 Bryan Bullington AU A RC 10.00 4.00
❑ 349 Rajai Davis AU A RC 10.00 4.00
❑ 350 Darrell Rasner AU A RC 10.00 4.00
❑ 351 Willie Mays 2.00 .75
❑ 351AU Willie Mays AU 250.00 150.00

2003 Bowman Chrome Draft

❑ COMPLETE SET (176) 550.00 400.00
❑ COMP.SET w/o AU's (165) 100.00 50.00
❑ COMMON CARD (1-165) .40 .15
❑ 1-165 TWO PER BOWMAN DRAFT PACK
❑ COMMON CARD (166-176) 10.00 4.00
❑ 166-176 STATED ODDS 1:41 H/R
❑ LUBANSKI IS AN SP BY 1000 COPIES
❑ 1 Dontrelle Willis 1.50 .60
❑ 2 Freddy Sanchez .40 .15

❑ 3 Miguel Cabrera 1.50 .60
❑ 4 Ryan Ludwick .40 .15
❑ 5 Ty Wigginton .40 .15
❑ 6 Mark Teixeira 1.00 .40
❑ 7 Trey Hodges .40 .15
❑ 8 Laynce Nix .60 .25
❑ 9 Antonio Perez .40 .15
❑ 10 Jody Gerut .40 .15
❑ 11 Jae Weong Seo .40 .15
❑ 12 Erick Almonte .40 .15
❑ 13 Lyle Overbay .40 .15
❑ 14 Billy Traber .40 .15
❑ 15 Andres Torres .40 .15
❑ 16 Jose Valverde .40 .15
❑ 17 Aaron Heilman .40 .15
❑ 18 Brandon Larson .40 .15
❑ 19 Jung Bong .40 .15
❑ 20 Jesse Foppert .40 .15
❑ 21 Angel Berroa .40 .15
❑ 22 Jeff DaVanon .40 .15
❑ 23 Kurt Ainsworth .40 .15
❑ 24 Brandon Claussen .40 .15
❑ 25 Xavier Nady .40 .15
❑ 26 Travis Hafner .60 .25
❑ 27 Jerome Williams .40 .15
❑ 28 Jose Reyes .60 .25
❑ 29 Sergio Mitre RC 1.50 .60
❑ 30 Bo Hart RC 1.00 .40
❑ 31 Adam Miller RC 10.00 4.00
❑ 32 Brian Finch RC 1.00 .40
❑ 33 Taylor Mattingly RC 1.50 .60
❑ 34 Daric Barton RC 6.00 2.50
❑ 35 Chris Ray RC 3.00 1.25
❑ 36 Jarrod Saltalamacchia RC 15.00 6.00
❑ 37 Dennis Dove RC 1.50 .60
❑ 38 James Houser RC 1.50 .60
❑ 39 Clint King RC 1.50 .60
❑ 40 Lou Palmisano RC 1.50 .60
❑ 41 Dan Moore RC 1.00 .40
❑ 42 Craig Stansberry RC 1.50 .60
❑ 43 Jo Jo Reyes RC 3.00 1.25
❑ 44 Jake Stevens RC 1.50 .60
❑ 45 Tom Gorzelanny RC 5.00 2.00
❑ 46 Brian Marshall RC 1.00 .40
❑ 47 Scott Beerer RC 1.00 .40
❑ 48 Javi Herrera RC 1.50 .60
❑ 49 Steve LeRud RC 1.50 .60
❑ 50 Josh Banks RC 2.50 1.00
❑ 51 Jon Papelbon RC 30.00 12.50
❑ 52 Juan Valdes RC 1.50 .60
❑ 53 Beau Vaughan RC 1.50 .60
❑ 54 Matt Chico RC 1.50 .60
❑ 55 Todd Jennings RC 1.50 .60
❑ 56 Anthony Gwynn RC 4.00 1.50
❑ 57 Matt Harrison RC 2.50 1.00
❑ 58 Aaron Marsden RC 1.50 .60
❑ 59 Casey Abrams RC 1.00 .40
❑ 60 Cory Stuart RC 1.00 .40
❑ 61 Mike Wagner RC 1.00 .40
❑ 62 Jordan Pratt RC 1.50 .60
❑ 63 Andre Randolph RC 1.50 .60
❑ 64 Blake Balkcom RC 1.50 .60
❑ 65 Josh Muecke RC 1.00 .40
❑ 66 Jamie D'Antona RC 2.50 1.00
❑ 67 Cole Seifrig RC 1.00 .40
❑ 68 Josh Anderson RC 1.50 .60
❑ 69 Matt Lorenzo RC 1.50 .60
❑ 70 Nate Spears RC 1.50 .60
❑ 71 Chris Goodman RC 1.00 .40
❑ 72 Brian McFall RC 1.00 .40
❑ 73 Billy Hogan RC 1.50 .60
❑ 74 Jamie Romak RC 1.50 .60
❑ 75 Jeff Cook RC 1.50 .60
❑ 76 Brooks McNiven RC 1.00 .40
❑ 77 Xavier Paul RC 1.50 .60
❑ 78 Bob Zimmerman RC 1.00 .40
❑ 79 Mickey Hall RC 1.50 .60
❑ 80 Shaun Marcum RC 1.50 .60
❑ 81 Matt Nachreiner RC 1.50 .60
❑ 82 Chris Kinsey RC 1.00 .40
❑ 83 Jonathan Fulton RC 1.50 .60
❑ 84 Edgardo Baez RC 1.50 .60
❑ 85 Robert Valido RC 1.50 .60
❑ 86 Kenny Lewis RC 1.50 .60
❑ 87 Trent Peterson RC 1.00 .40
❑ 88 Johnny Woodard RC 1.50 .60
❑ 89 Wes Littleton RC 1.50 .60
❑ 90 Sean Rodriguez RC 5.00 2.00
❑ 91 Kyle Pearson RC 1.00 .40
❑ 92 Josh Rainwater RC 1.50 .60
❑ 93 Travis Schlichting RC 1.50 .60
❑ 94 Tim Battle RC 2.50 1.00
❑ 95 Aaron Hill RC 5.00 2.00
❑ 96 Bob McCrory RC 1.00 .40
❑ 97 Rick Guarno RC 1.50 .60
❑ 98 Brandon Yarbrough RC 1.00 .40
❑ 99 Peter Stonard RC 1.00 .40
❑ 100 Darin Downs RC 1.50 .60
❑ 101 Matt Bruback RC 1.00 .40
❑ 102 Danny Garcia RC 1.00 .40
❑ 103 Cory Stewart RC 1.00 .40
❑ 104 Ferdin Tejeda RC 1.00 .40
❑ 105 Kade Johnson RC 1.00 .40
❑ 106 Andrew Brown RC 1.50 .60
❑ 107 Aquilino Lopez RC 1.00 .40
❑ 108 Stephen Randolph RC 1.00 .40
❑ 109 Dave Matranga RC 1.00 .40
❑ 110 Dustin McGowan RC 1.50 .60
❑ 111 Juan Camacho RC 1.00 .40
❑ 112 Cliff Lee .40 .15
❑ 113 Jeff Duncan RC 1.00 .40
❑ 114 C.J. Wilson .40 .15
❑ 115 Brandon Roberson RC 1.00 .40
❑ 116 David Corrente RC 1.00 .40
❑ 117 Kevin Beavers RC 1.00 .40
❑ 118 Anthony Webster RC 1.50 .60
❑ 119 Oscar Villarreal RC 1.00 .40
❑ 120 Hong-Chih Kuo RC 8.00 3.00
❑ 121 Josh Barfield .60 .25
❑ 122 Denny Bautista .40 .15
❑ 123 Chris Burke RC 4.00 1.50
❑ 124 Robinson Cano RC 25.00 10.00
❑ 125 Jose Castillo .40 .15
❑ 126 Neal Cotts .40 .15
❑ 127 Jorge De La Rosa .40 .15
❑ 128 J.D. Durbin .50 .20
❑ 129 Edwin Encarnacion 2.00 .75
❑ 130 Gavin Floyd .40 .15
❑ 131 Alexis Gomez .40 .15
❑ 132 Edgar Gonzalez RC 1.00 .40
❑ 133 Khalil Greene 1.50 .60
❑ 134 Zack Greinke .60 .25
❑ 135 Franklin Gutierrez 1.50 .60
❑ 136 Rich Harden 1.00 .40
❑ 137 J.J. Hardy RC 10.00 4.00
❑ 138 Ryan Howard RC 60.00 30.00
❑ 139 Justin Huber .40 .15
❑ 140 David Kelton .40 .15
❑ 141 Dave Krynzel .40 .15
❑ 142 Pete LaForest .50 .20
❑ 143 Adam LaRoche .40 .15
❑ 144 Preston Larrison RC 1.00 .40
❑ 145 John Maine RC 12.00 5.00
❑ 146 Andy Marte 4.00 1.50
❑ 147 Jeff Mathis .40 .15
❑ 148 Joe Mauer 1.50 .60
❑ 149 Clint Nageotte .40 .15
❑ 150 Chris Narveson .40 .15
❑ 151 Ramon Nivar .50 .20
❑ 152 Felix Pie 5.00 2.00
❑ 153 Guillermo Quiroz RC 1.00 .40
❑ 154 Rene Reyes .40 .15
❑ 155 Royce Ring .40 .15
❑ 156 Alexis Rios 3.00 1.25
❑ 157 Grady Sizemore 1.50 .60
❑ 158 Stephen Smitherman .40 .15
❑ 159 Seung Song .40 .15
❑ 160 Scott Thorman .40 .15
❑ 161 Chad Tracy .40 .15
❑ 162 Chin-Hui Tsao .60 .25
❑ 163 John VanBenschoten .40 .15
❑ 164 Kevin Youkilis 5.00 2.00
❑ 165 Chien-Ming Wang 6.00 2.50
❑ 166 Chris Lubanski AU SP RC 40.00 20.00
❑ 167 Ryan Harvey AU RC 30.00 12.50
❑ 168 Matt Murton AU RC 30.00 12.50
❑ 169 Jay Sborz AU RC 10.00 4.00
❑ 170 Brandon Wood AU RC 100.00 70.00
❑ 171 Nick Markakis AU RC 80.00 40.00
❑ 172 Rickie Weeks AU RC 50.00 25.00
❑ 173 Eric Duncan AU RC 30.00 12.50
❑ 174 Chad Billingsley AU RC 50.00 30.00
❑ 175 Ryan Wagner AU RC 10.00 4.00
❑ 176 Delmon Young AU RC 150.00 100.00

2004 Bowman Chrome

❑ COMPLETE SET (350) 400.00 250.00
❑ COMP.SET w/o AU's (330) 120.00 60.00
❑ COMMON CARD (1-150) .50 .20
❑ COMMON CARD (151-165) .50 .20
❑ COMMON AUTO (331-350) 10.00 4.00
❑ 331-350 AU'S ARE NOT SERIAL-NUMBERED
❑ 331-350 PRINT RUN PROVIDED BY TOPPS
❑ 1 Garret Anderson .50 .20
❑ 2 Larry Walker .50 .20
❑ 3 Derek Jeter 2.50 1.00
❑ 4 Curt Schilling .75 .30
❑ 5 Carlos Zambrano .50 .20
❑ 6 Shawn Green .50 .20
❑ 7 Manny Ramirez .75 .30
❑ 8 Randy Johnson 1.25 .50
❑ 9 Jeremy Bonderman .50 .20
❑ 10 Alfonso Soriano .50 .20
❑ 11 Scott Rolen .75 .30
❑ 12 Kerry Wood .50 .20
❑ 13 Eric Gagne .50 .20
❑ 14 Ryan Klesko .50 .20
❑ 15 Kevin Millar .50 .20
❑ 16 Ty Wigginton .50 .20
❑ 17 David Ortiz 1.25 .50
❑ 18 Luis Castillo .50 .20
❑ 19 Bernie Williams .75 .30
❑ 20 Edgar Renteria .50 .20
❑ 21 Matt Kata .50 .20
❑ 22 Bartolo Colon .50 .20
❑ 23 Derrek Lee .75 .30
❑ 24 Gary Sheffield .50 .20
❑ 25 Nomar Garciaparra 2.00 .75
❑ 26 Kevin Millwood .50 .20
❑ 27 Corey Patterson .50 .20
❑ 28 Carlos Beltran .50 .20
❑ 29 Mike Lieberthal .50 .20
❑ 30 Troy Glaus .50 .20
❑ 31 Preston Wilson .50 .20
❑ 32 Jorge Posada .75 .30
❑ 33 Bo Hart .50 .20
❑ 34 Mark Prior .75 .30
❑ 35 Hideo Nomo 1.25 .50
❑ 36 Jason Kendall .50 .20
❑ 37 Roger Clemens 2.50 1.00
❑ 38 Dmitri Young .50 .20
❑ 39 Jason Giambi .50 .20

❑ 40	Jim Edmonds	.50	.20
❑ 41	Ryan Ludwick	.50	.20
❑ 42	Brandon Webb	.50	.20
❑ 43	Todd Helton	.75	.30
❑ 44	Jacque Jones	.50	.20
❑ 45	Jamie Moyer	.50	.20
❑ 46	Tim Salmon	.75	.30
❑ 47	Kelvim Escobar	.50	.20
❑ 48	Tony Batista	.50	.20
❑ 49	Nick Johnson	.50	.20
❑ 50	Jim Thome	.75	.30
❑ 51	Casey Blake	.50	.20
❑ 52	Trot Nixon	.50	.20
❑ 53	Luis Gonzalez	.50	.20
❑ 54	Dontrelle Willis	.75	.30
❑ 55	Mike Mussina	.75	.30
❑ 56	Carl Crawford	.50	.20
❑ 57	Mark Buehrle	.50	.20
❑ 58	Scott Podsednik	.50	.20
❑ 59	Brian Giles	.50	.20
❑ 60	Rafael Furcal	.50	.20
❑ 61	Miguel Cabrera	.75	.30
❑ 62	Rich Harden	.50	.20
❑ 63	Mark Teixeira	.75	.30
❑ 64	Frank Thomas	1.25	.50
❑ 65	Johan Santana	1.25	.50
❑ 66	Jason Schmidt	.50	.20
❑ 67	Aramis Ramirez	.50	.20
❑ 68	Jose Reyes	.50	.20
❑ 69	Magglio Ordonez	.50	.20
❑ 70	Mike Sweeney	.50	.20
❑ 71	Eric Chavez	.50	.20
❑ 72	Rocco Baldelli	.50	.20
❑ 73	Sammy Sosa	1.25	.50
❑ 74	Javy Lopez	.50	.20
❑ 75	Roy Oswalt	.50	.20
❑ 76	Raul Ibanez	.50	.20
❑ 77	Ivan Rodriguez	.75	.30
❑ 78	Jerome Williams	.50	.20
❑ 79	Carlos Lee	.50	.20
❑ 80	Geoff Jenkins	.50	.20
❑ 81	Sean Burroughs	.50	.20
❑ 82	Marcus Giles	.50	.20
❑ 83	Mike Lowell	.50	.20
❑ 84	Barry Zito	.50	.20
❑ 85	Aubrey Huff	.50	.20
❑ 86	Esteban Loaiza	.50	.20
❑ 87	Torii Hunter	.50	.20
❑ 88	Phil Nevin	.50	.20
❑ 89	Andruw Jones	.75	.30
❑ 90	Josh Beckett	.50	.20
❑ 91	Mark Mulder	.50	.20
❑ 92	Hank Blalock	.50	.20
❑ 93	Jason Phillips	.50	.20
❑ 94	Russ Ortiz	.50	.20
❑ 95	Juan Pierre	.50	.20
❑ 96	Tom Glavine	.75	.30
❑ 97	Gil Meche	.50	.20
❑ 98	Ramon Ortiz	.50	.20
❑ 99	Richie Sexson	.50	.20
❑ 100	Albert Pujols	2.50	1.00
❑ 101	Javier Vazquez	.50	.20
❑ 102	Johnny Damon	.75	.30
❑ 103	Alex Rodriguez	2.00	.75
❑ 104	Omar Vizquel	.75	.30
❑ 105	Chipper Jones	1.25	.50
❑ 106	Lance Berkman	.50	.20
❑ 107	Tim Hudson	.50	.20
❑ 108	Carlos Delgado	.50	.20
❑ 109	Austin Kearns	.50	.20
❑ 110	Orlando Cabrera	.50	.20
❑ 111	Edgar Martinez	.75	.30
❑ 112	Melvin Mora	.50	.20
❑ 113	Jeff Bagwell	.75	.30
❑ 114	Marlon Byrd	.50	.20
❑ 115	Vernon Wells	.50	.20
❑ 116	C.C. Sabathia	.50	.20
❑ 117	Cliff Floyd	.50	.20
❑ 118	Ichiro Suzuki	2.50	1.00
❑ 119	Miguel Olivo	.50	.20
❑ 120	Mike Piazza	2.00	.75
❑ 121	Adam Dunn	.50	.20
❑ 122	Paul Lo Duca	.50	.20
❑ 123	Brett Myers	.50	.20
❑ 124	Michael Young	.50	.20
❑ 125	Sidney Ponson	.50	.20
❑ 126	Greg Maddux	2.00	.75
❑ 127	Vladimir Guerrero	1.25	.50
❑ 128	Miguel Tejada	.50	.20
❑ 129	Andy Pettitte	.75	.30
❑ 130	Rafael Palmeiro	.75	.30
❑ 131	Ken Griffey Jr.	2.00	.75
❑ 132	Shannon Stewart	.50	.20
❑ 133	Joel Pineiro	.50	.20
❑ 134	Luis Matos	.50	.20
❑ 135	Jeff Kent	.50	.20
❑ 136	Randy Wolf	.50	.20
❑ 137	Chris Woodward	.50	.20
❑ 138	Jody Gerut	.50	.20
❑ 139	Jose Vidro	.50	.20
❑ 140	Bret Boone	.50	.20
❑ 141	Bill Mueller	.50	.20
❑ 142	Angel Berroa	.50	.20
❑ 143	Bobby Abreu	.50	.20
❑ 144	Roy Halladay	.50	.20
❑ 145	Delmon Young	.75	.30
❑ 146	Jonny Gomes	.50	.20
❑ 147	Rickie Weeks	.50	.20
❑ 148	Edwin Jackson	.50	.20
❑ 149	Neal Cotts	.50	.20
❑ 150	Jason Bay	.50	.20
❑ 151	Khalil Greene	1.00	.40
❑ 152	Joe Mauer	1.25	.50
❑ 153	Bobby Jenks	.75	.30
❑ 154	Chin-Feng Chen	.50	.20
❑ 155	Chien-Ming Wang	2.00	.75
❑ 156	Mickey Hall	.50	.20
❑ 157	James Houser	.50	.20
❑ 158	Jay Sborz	.50	.20
❑ 159	Jonathan Fulton	.50	.20
❑ 160	Steven Lerud	.50	.20
❑ 161	Grady Sizemore	1.50	.60
❑ 162	Felix Pie	2.00	.75
❑ 163	Dustin McGowan	.50	.20
❑ 164	Chris Lubanski	.75	.30
❑ 165	Tom Gorzelanny	.50	.20
❑ 166	Rudy Guillen RC	3.00	1.25
❑ 167	Aarom Baldiris RC	2.00	.75
❑ 168	Conor Jackson RC	10.00	4.00
❑ 169	Matt Moses RC	4.00	1.50
❑ 170	Ervin Santana RC	6.00	2.50
❑ 171	Merkin Valdez RC	2.00	.75
❑ 172	Erick Aybar RC	3.00	1.25
❑ 173	Brad Sullivan RC	2.00	.75
❑ 174	Joey Gathright RC	4.00	1.50
❑ 175	Brad Snyder RC	4.00	1.50
❑ 176	Alberto Callaspo RC	3.00	1.25
❑ 177	Brandon Medders RC	1.50	.60
❑ 178	Zach Miner RC	5.00	2.00
❑ 179	Charlie Zink RC	1.00	.40
❑ 180	Adam Greenberg RC	3.00	1.25
❑ 181	Kevin Howard RC	2.00	.75
❑ 182	Wanell Severino RC	1.00	.40
❑ 183	Chin-Lung Hu RC	5.00	2.00
❑ 184	Joel Zumaya RC	12.00	5.00
❑ 185	Skip Schumaker RC	1.50	.60
❑ 186	Nic Ungs RC	1.50	.60
❑ 187	Todd Self RC	2.00	.75
❑ 188	Brian Steffek RC	1.00	.40
❑ 189	Brock Peterson RC	1.50	.60
❑ 190	Greg Thissen RC	1.50	.60
❑ 191	Frank Brooks RC	1.00	.40
❑ 192	Scott Olsen RC	6.00	2.50
❑ 193	Chris Mabeus RC	1.50	.60
❑ 194	Dan Giese RC	1.50	.60
❑ 195	Jared Wells RC	1.00	.40
❑ 196	Carlos Sosa RC	1.50	.60
❑ 197	Bobby Madritsch	1.00	.40
❑ 198	Calvin Hayes RC	2.00	.75
❑ 199	Omar Quintanilla RC	2.00	.75
❑ 200	Chris O'Riordan RC	1.50	.60
❑ 201	Tim Hutting RC	1.00	.40
❑ 202	Carlos Quentin RC	10.00	4.00
❑ 203	Brayan Pena RC	1.50	.60
❑ 204	Jeff Salazar RC	4.00	1.50
❑ 205	David Murphy RC	3.00	1.25
❑ 206	Alberto Garcia RC	2.00	.75
❑ 207	Ramon Ramirez RC	1.50	.60
❑ 208	Luis Bolivar RC	1.50	.60
❑ 209	Rodney Choy Foo RC	1.00	.40
❑ 210	Fausto Carmona RC	8.00	3.00
❑ 211	Anthony Acevedo RC	1.50	.60
❑ 212	Chad Santos RC	1.50	.60
❑ 213	Jason Frasor RC	1.50	.60
❑ 214	Jesse Roman RC	1.00	.40
❑ 215	James Tomlin RC	1.50	.60
❑ 216	Josh Labandeira RC	1.50	.60
❑ 217	Ryan Meaux RC	1.50	.60
❑ 218	Don Sutton RC	4.00	1.50
❑ 219	Danny Gonzalez RC	1.00	.40
❑ 220	Javier Guzman RC	2.00	.75
❑ 221	Anthony Lerew RC	3.00	1.25
❑ 222	Jon Connolly RC	4.00	1.50
❑ 223	Jesse English RC	1.50	.60
❑ 224	Hector Made RC	3.00	1.25
❑ 225	Travis Hanson RC	2.00	.75
❑ 226	Jesse Floyd RC	1.50	.60
❑ 227	Nick Gorneault RC	2.00	.75
❑ 228	Craig Ansman RC	1.50	.60
❑ 229	Paul McAnulty RC	3.00	1.25
❑ 230	Carl Loadenthal RC	2.00	.75
❑ 231	Dave Crouthers RC	1.00	.40
❑ 232	Harvey Garcia RC	1.00	.40
❑ 233	Casey Kopitzke RC	1.00	.40
❑ 234	Ricky Nolasco RC	5.00	2.00
❑ 235	Miguel Perez RC	1.50	.60
❑ 236	Ryan Mulhern RC	1.50	.60
❑ 237	Chris Aguila RC	1.50	.60
❑ 238	Brooks Conrad RC	2.00	.75
❑ 239	Damaso Espino RC	1.00	.40
❑ 240	Jereme Milons RC	2.00	.75
❑ 241	Luke Hughes RC	1.00	.40
❑ 242	Kory Casto RC	2.00	.75
❑ 243	Jose Valdez RC	1.50	.60
❑ 244	J.T. Stotts RC	1.00	.40
❑ 245	Lee Gwaltney RC	1.00	.40
❑ 246	Yoann Torrealba RC	1.00	.40
❑ 247	Omar Falcon RC	1.50	.60
❑ 248	Jon Coutlangus RC	1.00	.40
❑ 249	George Sherrill RC	1.50	.60
❑ 250	John Santor RC	1.00	.40
❑ 251	Tony Richie RC	1.50	.60
❑ 252	Kevin Richardson RC	1.00	.40
❑ 253	Tim Bittner RC	1.50	.60
❑ 254	Chris Saenz RC	1.50	.60
❑ 255	Jose Capellan RC	2.00	.75
❑ 256	Donald Levinski RC	1.00	.40
❑ 257	Jerome Gamble RC	1.00	.40
❑ 258	Jeff Keppinger RC	1.50	.60
❑ 259	Jason Szuminski RC	1.00	.40
❑ 260	Akinori Otsuka RC	1.50	.60
❑ 261	Ryan Budde RC	1.50	.60
❑ 262	Marland Williams RC	2.00	.75
❑ 263	Jeff Allison RC	1.50	.60
❑ 264	Hector Gimenez RC	1.00	.40
❑ 265	Tim Frend RC	1.50	.60
❑ 266	Tom Farmer RC	1.50	.60
❑ 267	Shawn Hill RC	1.50	.60
❑ 268	Mike Huggins RC	1.50	.60
❑ 269	Scott Proctor RC	2.00	.75
❑ 270	Jorge Mejia RC	1.50	.60
❑ 271	Terry Jones RC	2.00	.75
❑ 272	Zach Duke RC	8.00	3.00
❑ 273	Jesse Crain RC	3.00	1.25
❑ 274	Luke Anderson RC	1.00	.40
❑ 275	Hunter Brown RC	1.00	.40
❑ 276	Matt Lemanczyk RC	1.50	.60
❑ 277	Fernando Cortez RC	1.00	.40
❑ 278	Vince Perkins RC	2.00	.75
❑ 279	Tommy Murphy RC	1.50	.60
❑ 280	Mike Gosling RC	1.00	.40
❑ 281	Paul Bacot RC	2.00	.75
❑ 282	Matt Capps RC	1.50	.60
❑ 283	Juan Gutierrez RC	1.50	.60
❑ 284	Teodoro Encarnacion RC	2.00	.75
❑ 285	Chad Bentz RC	1.50	.60
❑ 286	Kazuo Matsui RC	2.00	.75
❑ 287	Ryan Hankins RC	1.00	.40
❑ 288	Leo Nunez RC	1.50	.60
❑ 289	Dave Wallace RC	1.50	.60
❑ 290	Rob Tejeda RC	3.00	1.25
❑ 291	Paul Maholm RC	4.00	1.50
❑ 292	Casey Daigle RC	1.50	.60
❑ 293	Tydus Meadows RC	1.00	.40
❑ 294	Khalid Ballouli RC	1.00	.40
❑ 295	Benji DeQuin RC	1.00	.40
❑ 296	Tyler Davidson RC	2.00	.75
❑ 297	Brant Colamarino RC	3.00	1.25

❑ 298 Marcus McBeth RC 1.00 .40
❑ 299 Brad Eldred RC 2.00 .75
❑ 300 David Pauley RC 5.00 2.00
❑ 301 Yadier Molina RC 6.00 2.50
❑ 302 Chris Shelton RC 5.00 2.00
❑ 303 Nyjer Morgan RC 1.00 .40
❑ 304 Jon DeVries RC 1.50 .60
❑ 305 Sheldon Fulse RC 1.00 .40
❑ 306 Vito Chiaravalloti RC 1.50 .60
❑ 307 Warner Madrigal RC 3.00 1.25
❑ 308 Reid Gorecki RC 1.50 .60
❑ 309 Sung Jung RC 1.00 .40
❑ 310 Pete Shier RC 1.00 .40
❑ 311 Michael Mooney RC 1.50 .60
❑ 312 Kenny Perez RC 1.50 .60
❑ 313 Michael Mallory RC 1.50 .60
❑ 314 Ben Himes RC 1.00 .40
❑ 315 Ivan Ochoa RC 1.50 .60
❑ 316 Donald Kelly RC 1.50 .60
❑ 317 Tom Mastny RC 1.50 .60
❑ 318 Kevin Davidson RC 1.00 .40
❑ 319 Brian Pilkington RC 1.00 .40
❑ 320 Alex Romero RC 1.50 .60
❑ 321 Chad Chop RC 1.50 .60
❑ 322 Kody Kirkland RC 2.00 .75
❑ 323 Casey Myers RC 1.00 .40
❑ 324 Mike Rouse RC 1.50 .60
❑ 325 Sergio Silva RC 1.00 .40
❑ 326 J.J. Furmaniak RC 3.00 1.25
❑ 327 Brad Vericker RC 1.50 .60
❑ 328 Blake Hawksworth RC 2.00 .75
❑ 329 Brock Jacobsen RC 1.00 .40
❑ 330 Alec Zumwalt RC 1.00 .40
❑ 331 Wardell Starling AU RC 10.00 4.00
❑ 332 Estee Harris AU RC 10.00 4.00
❑ 333 Kyle Sleeth AU RC 10.00 4.00
❑ 334 Dioner Navarro AU RC 15.00 6.00
❑ 335 Logan Kensing AU RC 10.00 4.00
❑ 336 Travis Blackley AU RC 10.00 4.00
❑ 337 Lincoln Holdzkom AU RC 10.00 4.00
❑ 338 Jason Hirsh AU RC 25.00 10.00
❑ 339 Juan Cedeno AU RC 10.00 4.00
❑ 340 Matt Creighton AU RC 10.00 4.00
❑ 341 Tim Stauffer AU RC 15.00 6.00
❑ 342 Shingo Takatsu AU RC 15.00 6.00
❑ 343 Lastings Milledge AU RC 50.00 20.00
❑ 344 Dustin Nippert AU RC 10.00 4.00
❑ 345 Felix Hernandez AU RC 120.00 60.00
❑ 346 Joaquin Arias AU RC 15.00 6.00
❑ 347 Kevin Kouzmanoff AU RC 30.00 12.50
❑ 348 B.Brownlie AU RC EXCH 10.00 4.00
❑ 349 David Aardsma AU RC 10.00 4.00
❑ 350 Jon Knott AU RC 15.00 6.00

2004 Bowman Chrome Draft

❑ COMPLETE SET (175) 300.00 175.00
❑ COMP.SET w/o SP's (165) 100.00 50.00
❑ COMMON CARD (1-165) .40 .15
❑ COMMON RC YR .40 .15
❑ 1-165 TWO PER BOWMAN DRAFT PACK
❑ 166-175 ODDS 1:60 BOWMAN DRAFT HOBBY
❑ 166-175 ODDS 1:60 BOWMAN DRAFT RETAIL
❑ 166-175 STATED PRINT RUN 1695 SETS
❑ 166-175 ARE NOT SERIAL-NUMBERED
❑ 166-175 PRINT RUN PROVIDED BY TOPPS
❑ PLATES 1-165 ODDS 1:559 HOBBY
❑ PLATES 166-175 ODDS 1:18,354 HOBBY
❑ PLATES PRINT RUN 1 SERIAL #'d SET
❑ BLACK-CYAN-MAGENTA-YELLOW EXIST
❑ NO PLATES PRICING DUE TO SCARCITY
❑ 1 Lyle Overbay .40 .15
❑ 2 David Newhan .40 .15
❑ 3 J.R. House .40 .15
❑ 4 Chad Tracy .40 .15
❑ 5 Humberto Quintero .40 .15
❑ 6 Dave Bush .40 .15
❑ 7 Scott Hairston .40 .15
❑ 8 Mike Wood .40 .15
❑ 9 Alexis Rios .60 .25
❑ 10 Sean Burnett .40 .15
❑ 11 Wilson Valdez .40 .15
❑ 12 Lew Ford .40 .15
❑ 13 Freddy Thon RC 1.00 .40
❑ 14 Zack Greinke .60 .25
❑ 15 Bucky Jacobsen .40 .15
❑ 16 Kevin Youkilis .40 .15
❑ 17 Grady Sizemore 1.50 .60
❑ 18 Denny Bautista .40 .15
❑ 19 David DeJesus .40 .15
❑ 20 Casey Kotchman .60 .25
❑ 21 David Kelton .40 .15
❑ 22 Charles Thomas RC 1.00 .40
❑ 23 Kazuhito Tadano RC 1.50 .60
❑ 24 Justin Leone RC 1.50 .60
❑ 25 Eduardo Villacis RC 1.00 .40
❑ 26 Brian Dallimore RC 1.00 .40
❑ 27 Nick Green .40 .15
❑ 28 Sam McConnell RC 1.00 .40
❑ 29 Brad Halsey RC 1.50 .60
❑ 30 Roman Colon RC 1.00 .40
❑ 31 Josh Fields RC 6.00 2.50
❑ 32 Cody Bunkelman RC 1.50 .60
❑ 33 Jay Rainville RC 4.00 1.50
❑ 34 Richie Robnett RC 3.00 1.25
❑ 35 Jon Poterson RC 2.50 1.00
❑ 36 Huston Street RC 5.00 2.00
❑ 37 Erick San Pedro RC 1.00 .40
❑ 38 Cory Dunlap RC 3.00 1.25
❑ 39 Kurt Suzuki RC 3.00 1.25
❑ 40 Anthony Swarzak RC 2.50 1.00
❑ 41 Ian Desmond RC 4.00 1.50
❑ 42 Chris Covington RC 1.50 .60
❑ 43 Christian Garcia RC 2.50 1.00
❑ 44 Gaby Hernandez RC 4.00 1.50
❑ 45 Steven Register RC 1.00 .40
❑ 46 Eduardo Morlan RC 3.00 1.25
❑ 47 Collin Balester RC 1.50 .60
❑ 48 Nathan Phillips RC 1.50 .60
❑ 49 Dan Schwartzbauer RC 1.50 .60
❑ 50 Rafael Gonzalez RC 1.00 .40
❑ 51 K.C. Herren RC 2.50 1.00
❑ 52 William Susdorf RC 1.00 .40
❑ 53 Rob Johnson RC 1.50 .60
❑ 54 Louis Marson RC 2.50 1.00
❑ 55 Joe Koshansky RC 6.00 2.50
❑ 56 Jamar Walton RC 2.50 1.00
❑ 57 Mark Lowe RC 5.00 2.00
❑ 58 Matt Macri RC 3.00 1.25
❑ 59 Donny Lucy RC 1.00 .40
❑ 60 Mike Ferris RC 1.50 .60
❑ 61 Mike Nickeas RC 1.50 .60
❑ 62 Eric Hurley RC 3.00 1.25
❑ 63 Scott Elbert RC 3.00 1.25
❑ 64 Blake DeWitt RC 5.00 2.00
❑ 65 Danny Putnam RC 2.50 1.00
❑ 66 J.P. Howell RC 3.00 1.25
❑ 67 John Wiggins RC 1.00 .40
❑ 68 Justin Orenduff RC 2.50 1.00
❑ 69 Ray Liotta RC 3.00 1.25
❑ 70 Billy Buckner RC 1.50 .60
❑ 71 Eric Campbell RC 6.00 2.50
❑ 72 Olin Wick RC 2.50 1.00
❑ 73 Sean Gamble RC 1.50 .60
❑ 74 Seth Smith RC 3.00 1.25
❑ 75 Wade Davis RC 5.00 2.00
❑ 76 Joe Jacobitz RC 1.00 .40
❑ 77 J.A. Happ RC 2.50 1.00
❑ 78 Eric Ridener RC 1.00 .40
❑ 79 Matt Tuiasosopo RC 4.00 1.50
❑ 80 Brad Bergesen RC 1.00 .40
❑ 81 Javy Guerra RC 1.50 .60
❑ 82 Buck Shaw RC 1.50 .60
❑ 83 Paul Janish RC 2.00 .75
❑ 84 Sean Kazmar RC 1.00 .40
❑ 85 Josh Johnson RC 1.50 .60
❑ 86 Angel Salome RC 4.00 1.50
❑ 87 Jordan Parraz RC 2.50 1.00
❑ 88 Kelvin Vazquez RC 1.00 .40
❑ 89 Grant Hansen RC 1.00 .40
❑ 90 Matt Fox RC 1.00 .40
❑ 91 Trevor Plouffe RC 4.00 1.50
❑ 92 Wes Whisler RC 1.00 .40
❑ 93 Curtis Thigpen RC 2.50 1.00
❑ 94 Donnie Smith RC 1.50 .60
❑ 95 Luis Rivera RC 1.50 .60
❑ 96 Jesse Hoover RC 1.50 .60
❑ 97 Jason Vargas RC 4.00 1.50
❑ 98 Clary Carlsen RC 1.00 .40
❑ 99 Mark Robinson RC 1.00 .40
❑ 100 J.C. Holt RC 1.50 .60
❑ 101 Chad Blackwell RC 1.00 .40
❑ 102 Daryl Jones RC 3.00 1.25
❑ 103 Jonathan Tierce RC 1.00 .40
❑ 104 Patrick Bryant RC 1.00 .40
❑ 105 Eddie Prasch RC 1.50 .60
❑ 106 Mitch Einertson RC 2.00 .75
❑ 107 Kyle Waldrop RC 3.00 1.25
❑ 108 Jeff Marquez RC 1.50 .60
❑ 109 Zach Jackson RC 2.50 1.00
❑ 110 Josh Wahpepah RC 1.00 .40
❑ 111 Adam Lind RC 8.00 3.00
❑ 112 Kyle Bloom RC 1.50 .60
❑ 113 Ben Harrison RC 1.00 .40
❑ 114 Taylor Tankersley RC 1.50 .60
❑ 115 Steven Jackson RC 1.00 .40
❑ 116 David Purcey RC 2.50 1.00
❑ 117 Jacob McGee RC 3.00 1.25
❑ 118 Lucas Harrell RC 1.00 .40
❑ 119 Brandon Allen RC 3.00 1.25
❑ 120 Van Pope RC 1.50 .60
❑ 121 Jeff Francis .60 .25
❑ 122 Joe Blanton .60 .25
❑ 123 Wil Ledezma .40 .15
❑ 124 Bryan Bullington .40 .15
❑ 125 Jairo Garcia .40 .15
❑ 126 Matt Cain 2.00 .75
❑ 127 Arnie Munoz .40 .15
❑ 128 Clint Everts .40 .15
❑ 129 Jesus Cota .40 .15
❑ 130 Gavin Floyd .40 .15
❑ 131 Edwin Encarnacion .60 .25
❑ 132 Koyie Hill .40 .15
❑ 133 Ruben Gotay .40 .15
❑ 134 Jeff Mathis .40 .15
❑ 135 Andy Marte 1.00 .40
❑ 136 Dallas McPherson .60 .25
❑ 137 Justin Morneau .60 .25
❑ 138 Rickie Weeks .60 .25
❑ 139 Joel Guzman 1.00 .40
❑ 140 Shin Soo Choo .40 .15
❑ 141 Yusmeiro Petit RC 5.00 2.00
❑ 142 Jorge Cortes RC 1.00 .40
❑ 143 Val Majewski .40 .15
❑ 144 Felix Pie 1.00 .40
❑ 145 Aaron Hill .40 .15
❑ 146 Jose Capellan .60 .25
❑ 147 Dioner Navarro 1.00 .40
❑ 148 Fausto Carmona 2.50 1.00
❑ 149 Robinzon Diaz RC 1.00 .40
❑ 150 Felix Hernandez 15.00 6.00
❑ 151 Andres Blanco RC 1.00 .40
❑ 152 Jason Kubel .40 .15
❑ 153 Willy Taveras RC 2.50 1.00
❑ 154 Merkin Valdez 1.00 .40
❑ 155 Robinson Cano 1.50 .60
❑ 156 Bill Murphy .40 .15
❑ 157 Chris Burke .60 .25
❑ 158 Kyle Sleeth .40 .15
❑ 159 B.J. Upton 1.00 .40
❑ 160 Tim Stauffer 1.00 .40
❑ 161 David Wright 4.00 1.50
❑ 162 Conor Jackson 4.00 1.50
❑ 163 Brad Thompson RC 2.50 1.00
❑ 164 Delmon Young 1.00 .40
❑ 165 Jeremy Reed .60 .25
❑ 166 Matt Bush AU RC 25.00 10.00
❑ 167 Mark Rogers AU RC 20.00 8.00
❑ 168 Thomas Diamond AU RC 25.00 10.00
❑ 169 Greg Golson AU RC 15.00 6.00

No.	Player	Price	Price
170	Homer Bailey AU RC	100.00	50.00
171	Chris Lambert AU RC	10.00	4.00
172	Neil Walker AU RC	40.00	15.00
173	Bill Bray AU RC	10.00	4.00
174	Philip Hughes AU RC	120.00	75.00
175	Gio Gonzalez AU RC	40.00	15.00

2005 Bowman Chrome

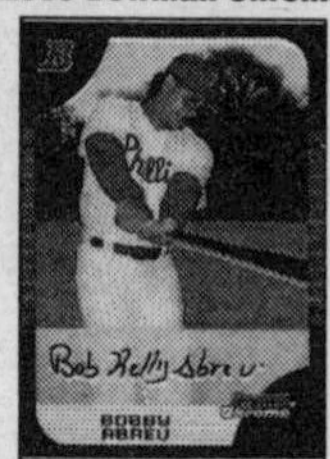

No.	Player	Price	Price
	COMP.SET w/o AU's (330)	120.00	60.00
	COMMON CARD (1-140)	.50	.20
	COMMON CARD (141-165)	.50	.20
	COMMON CARD (166-330)	1.00	.40
	COMMON AUTO (331-353)	10.00	4.00
	1-330 PLATE ODDS 1:779 HOBBY		
	331-353 AU PLATE ODDS 1:10,996 HOBBY		
	PLATE PRINT RUN 1 SET PER COLOR		
	BLACK-CYAN-MAGENTA-YELLOW ISSUED		
	NO PLATE PRICING DUE TO SCARCITY		
1	Gavin Floyd	.50	.20
2	Eric Chavez	.50	.20
3	Miguel Tejada	.50	.20
4	Dmitri Young	.50	.20
5	Hank Blalock	.50	.20
6	Kerry Wood	.50	.20
7	Andy Pettitte	.75	.30
8	Pat Burrell	.50	.20
9	Johnny Estrada	.50	.20
10	Frank Thomas	1.25	.50
11	Juan Pierre	.50	.20
12	Tom Glavine	.75	.30
13	Lyle Overbay	.50	.20
14	Jim Edmonds	.50	.20
15	Steve Finley	.50	.20
16	Jermaine Dye	.50	.20
17	Omar Vizquel	.75	.30
18	Nick Johnson	.50	.20
19	Brian Giles	.50	.20
20	Justin Morneau	.50	.20
21	Preston Wilson	.50	.20
22	Wily Mo Pena	.50	.20
23	Rafael Palmeiro	.75	.30
24	Scott Kazmir	.50	.20
25	Derek Jeter	2.50	1.00
26	Barry Zito	.50	.20
27	Mike Lowell	.50	.20
28	Jason Bay	.50	.20
29	Ken Harvey	.50	.20
30	Nomar Garciaparra	1.25	.50
31	Roy Halladay	.50	.20
32	Todd Helton	.75	.30
33	Mark Kotsay	.50	.20
34	Jake Peavy	.50	.20
35	David Wright	2.00	.75
36	Dontrelle Willis	.50	.20
37	Marcus Giles	.50	.20
38	Chone Figgins	.50	.20
39	Sidney Ponson	.50	.20
40	Randy Johnson	1.25	.50
41	John Smoltz	.75	.30
42	Kevin Millar	.50	.20
43	Mark Teixeira	.75	.30
44	Alex Rios	.50	.20
45	Mike Piazza	1.25	.50
46	Victor Martinez	.50	.20
47	Jeff Bagwell	.75	.30
48	Shawn Green	.50	.20
49	Ivan Rodriguez	.75	.30
50	Alex Rodriguez	2.00	.75
51	Kazuo Matsui	.50	.20
52	Mark Mulder	.50	.20
53	Michael Young	.50	.20
54	Javy Lopez	.50	.20
55	Johnny Damon	.75	.30
56	Jeff Francis	.50	.20
57	Rich Harden	.50	.20
58	Bobby Abreu	.50	.20
59	Mark Loretta	.50	.20
60	Gary Sheffield	.50	.20
61	Jamie Moyer	.50	.20
62	Garret Anderson	.50	.20
63	Vernon Wells	.50	.20
64	Orlando Cabrera	.50	.20
65	Magglio Ordonez	.50	.20
66	Ronnie Belliard	.50	.20
67	Carlos Lee	.50	.20
68	Carl Pavano	.50	.20
69	Jon Lieber	.50	.20
70	Aubrey Huff	.50	.20
71	Rocco Baldelli	.50	.20
72	Jason Schmidt	.50	.20
73	Bernie Williams	.75	.30
74	Hideki Matsui	2.00	.75
75	Ken Griffey Jr.	2.00	.75
76	Josh Beckett	.50	.20
77	Mark Buehrle	.50	.20
78	David Ortiz	1.25	.50
79	Luis Gonzalez	.50	.20
80	Scott Rolen	.75	.30
81	Joe Mauer	1.25	.50
82	Jose Reyes	.50	.20
83	Adam Dunn	.50	.20
84	Greg Maddux	2.00	.75
85	Bartolo Colon	.50	.20
86	Bret Boone	.50	.20
87	Mike Mussina	.75	.30
88	Ben Sheets	.50	.20
89	Lance Berkman	.50	.20
90	Miguel Cabrera	.75	.30
91	C.C. Sabathia	.50	.20
92	Mike Maroth	.50	.20
93	Andruw Jones	.75	.30
94	Jack Wilson	.50	.20
95	Ichiro Suzuki	2.50	1.00
96	Geoff Jenkins	.50	.20
97	Zack Greinke	.50	.20
98	Jorge Posada	.75	.30
99	Travis Hafner	.50	.20
100	Barry Bonds	3.00	1.25
101	Aaron Rowand	.50	.20
102	Aramis Ramirez	.50	.20
103	Curt Schilling	.75	.30
104	Melvin Mora	.50	.20
105	Albert Pujols	2.50	1.00
106	Austin Kearns	.50	.20
107	Shannon Stewart	.50	.20
108	Carl Crawford	.50	.20
109	Carlos Zambrano	.50	.20
110	Roger Clemens	2.00	.75
111	Javier Vazquez	.50	.20
112	Randy Wolf	.50	.20
113	Chipper Jones	1.25	.50
114	Larry Walker	.75	.30
115	Alfonso Soriano	.50	.20
116	Brad Wilkerson	.50	.20
117	Bobby Crosby	.50	.20
118	Jim Thome	.75	.30
119	Oliver Perez	.50	.20
120	Vladimir Guerrero	1.25	.50
121	Roy Oswalt	.50	.20
122	Torii Hunter	.50	.20
123	Rafael Furcal	.50	.20
124	Luis Castillo	.50	.20
125	Carlos Beltran	.50	.20
126	Mike Sweeney	.50	.20
127	Johan Santana	1.25	.50
128	Tim Hudson	.50	.20
129	Troy Glaus	.50	.20
130	Manny Ramirez	.75	.30
131	Jeff Kent	.50	.20
132	Jose Vidro	.50	.20
133	Edgar Renteria	.50	.20
134	Russ Ortiz	.50	.20
135	Sammy Sosa	1.25	.50
136	Carlos Delgado	.50	.20
137	Richie Sexson	.50	.20
138	Pedro Martinez	.75	.30
139	Adrian Beltre	.50	.20
140	Mark Prior	.75	.30
141	Omar Quintanilla	.50	.20
142	Carlos Quentin	.75	.30
143	Dan Johnson	.50	.20
144	Jake Stevens	.50	.20
145	Nate Schierholtz	.75	.30
146	Neil Walker	.50	.20
147	Bill Bray	.50	.20
148	Taylor Tankersley	.50	.20
149	Trevor Plouffe	.75	.30
150	Felix Hernandez	6.00	2.50
151	Philip Hughes	2.00	.75
152	James Houser	.50	.20
153	David Murphy	.50	.20
154	Ervin Santana	.75	.30
155	Anthony Whittington	.50	.20
156	Chris Lambert	.50	.20
157	Jeremy Sowers	.75	.30
158	Giovanny Gonzalez	.75	.30
159	Blake DeWitt	.75	.30
160	Thomas Diamond	.75	.30
161	Greg Golson	.75	.30
162	David Aardsma	.50	.20
163	Paul Maholm	.50	.20
164	Mark Rogers	.75	.30
165	Homer Bailey	.75	.30
166	Elvin Puello RC	1.50	.60
167	Tony Giarratano RC	1.50	.60
168	Darren Fenster RC	1.50	.60
169	Elvys Quezada RC	1.50	.60
170	Glen Perkins RC	3.00	1.25
171	Ian Kinsler RC	10.00	4.00
172	Adam Bostick RC	1.50	.60
173	Jeremy West RC	2.00	.75
174	Brett Harper RC	2.00	.75
175	Kevin West RC	1.50	.60
176	Luis Hernandez RC	1.50	.60
177	Matt Campbell RC	1.50	.60
178	Nate McLouth RC	2.00	.75
179	Ryan Goleski RC	2.00	.75
180	Matthew Lindstrom RC	1.50	.60
181	Matt DeSalvo RC	2.00	.75
182	Kole Strayhorn RC	1.50	.60
183	Jose Vaquedano RC	1.50	.60
184	James Jurries RC	2.00	.75
185	Ian Bladergroen RC	2.00	.75
186	Kila Kaaihue RC	4.00	1.50
187	Luke Scott RC	6.00	2.50
188	Chris Denorfia RC	4.00	1.50
189	Jai Miller RC	2.00	.75
190	Melky Cabrera RC	8.00	3.00
191	Ryan Sweeney RC	4.00	1.50
192	Sean Marshall RC	6.00	2.50
193	Erick Abreu RC	3.00	1.25
194	Tyler Pelland RC	2.00	.75
195	Cole Armstrong RC	1.50	.60
196	John Hudgins RC	1.50	.60
197	Wade Robinson RC	1.50	.60
198	Dan Santin RC	1.50	.60
199	Steve Doetsch RC	1.50	.60
200	Shane Costa RC	1.50	.60
201	Scott Mathieson RC	3.00	1.25
202	Ben Jones RC	2.00	.75
203	Michael Rogers RC	1.50	.60
204	Matt Rogelstad RC	1.50	.60
205	Luis Ramirez RC	1.50	.60
206	Landon Powell RC	2.00	.75
207	Erik Cordier RC	1.50	.60
208	Chris Seddon RC	1.50	.60
209	Chris Roberson RC	1.50	.60
210	Thomas Oldham RC	1.50	.60
211	Dana Eveland RC	1.50	.60
212	Cody Haerther RC	1.50	.60
213	Danny Core RC	1.50	.60
214	Craig Tatum RC	1.50	.60
215	Elliot Johnson RC	1.50	.60
216	Ender Chavez RC	1.50	.60
217	Errol Simonitsch RC	2.00	.75
218	Matt Van Der Bosch RC	1.50	.60
219	Eulogio de la Cruz RC	1.50	.60
220	Drew Toussaint RC	1.50	.60
221	Adam Boeve RC	1.50	.60
222	Adam Harben RC	2.00	.75

❑ 223 Baltazar Lopez RC	1.50	.60
❑ 224 Russ Martin RC	5.00	2.00
❑ 225 Brian Bannister RC	4.00	1.50
❑ 226 Chris Walker RC	1.50	.60
❑ 227 Casey McGehee RC	1.50	.60
❑ 228 Humberto Sanchez RC	6.00	2.50
❑ 229 Javon Moran RC	1.50	.60
❑ 230 Brandon McCarthy RC	5.00	2.00
❑ 231 Danny Zell RC	1.50	.60
❑ 232 Kevin Barry RC	1.50	.60
❑ 233 Juan Tejeda RC	1.50	.60
❑ 234 Keith Ramsey RC	1.50	.60
❑ 235 Lorenzo Scott RC	1.50	.60
❑ 236 Jon Barratt RC	1.50	.60
❑ 237 Martin Prado RC	1.50	.60
❑ 238 Matt Albers RC	4.00	1.50
❑ 239 Brian Schweiger RC	1.50	.60
❑ 240 Raul Tablado RC	1.50	.60
❑ 241 Pat Misch RC	1.50	.60
❑ 242 Pat Osborn	1.50	.60
❑ 243 Ryan Feierabend RC	1.50	.60
❑ 244 Shaun Marcum	1.00	.40
❑ 245 Kevin Collins RC	1.50	.60
❑ 246 Stuart Pomeranz RC	1.50	.60
❑ 247 Tetsu Yofu RC	1.50	.60
❑ 248 Hernan Iribarren RC	2.00	.75
❑ 249 Mike Spidale RC	1.50	.60
❑ 250 Tony Americh RC	1.50	.60
❑ 251 Manny Parra RC	2.00	.75
❑ 252 Drew Anderson RC	1.50	.60
❑ 253 T.J. Beam RC	3.00	1.25
❑ 254 Claudio Arias RC	2.00	.75
❑ 255 Andy Sides RC	1.50	.60
❑ 256 Bear Bay RC	2.00	.75
❑ 257 Bill McCarthy RC	1.50	.60
❑ 258 Daniel Haigwood RC	3.00	1.25
❑ 259 Brian Sprout RC	2.00	.75
❑ 260 Bryan Triplett RC	1.50	.60
❑ 261 Steven Bondurant RC	1.50	.60
❑ 262 Darwinson Salazar RC	1.50	.60
❑ 263 David Shepard RC	1.50	.60
❑ 264 Johan Silva RC	1.50	.60
❑ 265 J.B. Thurmond RC	1.50	.60
❑ 266 Brandon Moorhead RC	1.50	.60
❑ 267 Kyle Nichols RC	2.00	.75
❑ 268 Jonathan Sanchez RC	5.00	2.00
❑ 269 Mike Esposito RC	1.50	.60
❑ 270 Erik Schindewolf RC	1.50	.60
❑ 271 Peeter Ramos RC	1.50	.60
❑ 272 Juan Senreiso RC	1.50	.60
❑ 273 Travis Chick RC	2.00	.75
❑ 274 Vinny Rottino RC	1.50	.60
❑ 275 Micah Furtado RC	1.50	.60
❑ 276 George Kottaras RC	3.00	1.25
❑ 277 Abel Gomez RC	2.00	.75
❑ 278 Buck Coats RC	1.50	.60
❑ 279 Kenny Durost RC	1.50	.60
❑ 280 Nick Touchstone RC	1.50	.60
❑ 281 Jerry Owens RC	2.00	.75
❑ 282 Stefan Bailie RC	1.50	.60
❑ 283 Jesse Gutierrez RC	1.50	.60
❑ 284 Chuck Tiffany RC	4.00	1.50
❑ 285 Brendan Ryan RC	1.50	.60
❑ 286 Julio Pimentel RC	2.00	.75
❑ 287 Shawn Bowman RC	2.00	.75
❑ 288 Alexander Smit RC	1.50	.60
❑ 289 Micah Schnurstein RC	1.50	.60
❑ 290 Jared Gothreaux RC	1.50	.60
❑ 291 Jair Jurrjens RC	4.00	1.50
❑ 292 Bobby Livingston RC	1.50	.60
❑ 293 Ryan Speier RC	1.50	.60
❑ 294 Zach Parker RC	1.50	.60
❑ 295 Christian Colonel RC	1.50	.60
❑ 296 Scott Mitchinson RC	1.50	.60
❑ 297 Neil Wilson RC	1.50	.60
❑ 298 Chuck James RC	6.00	2.50
❑ 299 Heath Totten RC	1.50	.60
❑ 300 Sean Tracey RC	1.50	.60
❑ 301 Tadahito Iguchi RC	5.00	2.00
❑ 302 Matt Brown RC	1.50	.60
❑ 303 Franklin Morales RC	3.00	1.25
❑ 304 Brandon Sing RC	2.00	.75
❑ 305 D.J. Houlton RC	1.50	.60
❑ 306 Jayce Tingler RC	1.50	.60
❑ 307 Mitchell Arnold RC	1.50	.60
❑ 308 Jim Burt RC	1.50	.60
❑ 309 Jason Motte RC	1.50	.60
❑ 310 David Gassner RC	1.50	.60
❑ 311 Andy Santana RC	1.50	.60
❑ 312 Kelvin Pichardo RC	1.50	.60
❑ 313 Carlos Carrasco RC	5.00	2.00
❑ 314 Willy Mota RC	1.50	.60
❑ 315 Frank Mata RC	1.50	.60
❑ 316 Carlos Gonzalez RC	12.00	5.00
❑ 317 Jesse Floyd	1.00	.40
❑ 318 Chris B.Young RC	8.00	3.00
❑ 319 Billy Sadler RC	1.50	.60
❑ 320 Ricky Barrett RC	1.50	.60
❑ 321 Ben Harrison	1.50	.60
❑ 322 Steve Nelson RC	1.50	.60
❑ 323 Daryl Thompson RC	1.50	.60
❑ 324 Davis Romero RC	1.50	.60
❑ 325 Jeremy Harts RC	1.50	.60
❑ 326 Nick Masset RC	1.50	.60
❑ 327 Thomas Pauly RC	1.50	.60
❑ 328 Mike Garber RC	1.50	.60
❑ 329 Kennard Bibbs RC	1.50	.60
❑ 330 Colter Bean RC	1.50	.60
❑ 331 Justin Verlander AU RC	80.00	40.00
❑ 332 Chip Cannon AU RC	25.00	10.00
❑ 333 Kevin Melillo AU RC	15.00	6.00
❑ 334 Jake Postlewait AU RC	10.00	4.00
❑ 335 Wes Swackhamer AU RC	10.00	4.00
❑ 336 Mike Rodriguez AU RC	10.00	4.00
❑ 337 Philip Humber AU RC	40.00	15.00
❑ 338 Jeff Niemann AU RC	40.00	15.00
❑ 339 Brian Miller AU RC	10.00	4.00
❑ 340 Chris Vines AU RC	10.00	4.00
❑ 341 Andy LaRoche AU RC	50.00	20.00
❑ 342 Mike Bourn AU RC	25.00	10.00
❑ 343 Eric Nielsen AU RC	10.00	4.00
❑ 344 Wladimir Balentien AU RC	50.00	20.00
❑ 345 Ismael Ramirez AU RC	10.00	4.00
❑ 346 Pedro Lopez AU RC	10.00	4.00
❑ 347 Shawn Bowman AU	15.00	6.00
❑ 348 Hayden Penn AU RC	25.00	10.00
❑ 349 Matthew Kemp AU RC	70.00	40.00
❑ 350 Brian Stavisky AU RC	10.00	4.00
❑ 351 C.J. Smith AU RC	10.00	4.00
❑ 352 Mike Morse AU RC	10.00	4.00
❑ 353 Billy Butler AU RC	100.00	50.00

2005 Bowman Chrome Draft

❑ COMP.SET w/o SP's (165)	100.00	50.00
❑ COMMON CARD (1-165)	.40	.15
❑ COMMON RC	1.00	.40
❑ COMMON RC YR	.40	.15
❑ 1-165 TWO PER BOWMAN DRAFT PACK		
❑ 166-180 GROUP A ODDS 1:671 H, 1:643 R		
❑ 166-180 GROUP B ODDS 1:69 H, 1:69 R		
❑ 1-165 PLATE ODDS 1:826 HOBBY		
❑ 166-180 AU PLATE ODDS 1:18,411 HOBBY		
❑ PLATE PRINT RUN 1 SET PER COLOR		
❑ BLACK-CYAN-MAGENTA-YELLOW ISSUED		
❑ NO PLATE PRICING DUE TO SCARCITY		
❑ 1 Rickie Weeks	.60	.25
❑ 2 Kyle Davies	.40	.15
❑ 3 Garrett Atkins	.40	.15
❑ 4 Chien-Ming Wang	2.00	.75
❑ 5 Dallas McPherson	.40	.15
❑ 6 Dan Johnson	.60	.25
❑ 7 Andy Sisco	.40	.15
❑ 8 Ryan Doumit	.40	.15
❑ 9 J.P. Howell	.40	.15
❑ 10 Tim Stauffer	.40	.15
❑ 11 Willy Taveras	.60	.25
❑ 12 Aaron Hill	.40	.15
❑ 13 Victor Diaz	.40	.15
❑ 14 Wilson Betemit	.40	.15
❑ 15 Ervin Santana	.60	.25
❑ 16 Mike Morse	.60	.25
❑ 17 Yadier Molina	.60	.25
❑ 18 Kelly Johnson	.40	.15
❑ 19 Clint Barmes	.60	.25
❑ 20 Robinson Cano	1.00	.40
❑ 21 Brad Thompson	.40	.15
❑ 22 Jorge Cantu	.60	.25
❑ 23 Brad Halsey	.40	.15
❑ 24 Lance Niekro	.60	.25
❑ 25 D.J. Houlton	.40	.15
❑ 26 Ryan Church	.40	.15
❑ 27 Hayden Penn	1.50	.60
❑ 28 Chris Young	.40	.15
❑ 29 Chad Orvella RC	1.00	.40
❑ 30 Mark Teahen	.40	.15
❑ 31 Mark McCormick FY RC	1.50	.60
❑ 32 Jay Bruce FY RC	12.00	5.00
❑ 33 Beau Jones FY RC	2.50	1.00
❑ 34 Tyler Greene FY RC	2.50	1.00
❑ 35 Zach Ward FY RC	1.00	.40
❑ 36 Josh Bell FY RC	4.00	1.50
❑ 37 Josh Wall FY RC	1.50	.60
❑ 38 Nick Webber FY RC	1.00	.40
❑ 39 Travis Buck FY RC	4.00	1.25
❑ 40 Kyle Winters FY RC	1.50	.60
❑ 41 Mitch Boggs FY RC	1.00	.40
❑ 42 Tommy Mendoza FY RC	2.50	1.00
❑ 43 Brad Corley FY RC	1.50	.60
❑ 44 Drew Butera FY RC	1.00	.40
❑ 45 Ryan Mount FY RC	2.50	1.00
❑ 46 Tyler Herron FY RC	1.50	.60
❑ 47 Nick Weglarz FY RC	2.50	1.00
❑ 48 Brandon Erbe FY RC	4.00	1.50
❑ 49 Cody Allen FY RC	1.00	.40
❑ 50 Eric Fowler FY RC	1.00	.40
❑ 51 James Boone FY RC	1.50	.60
❑ 52 Josh Flores FY RC	4.00	1.50
❑ 53 Brandon Monk FY RC	1.50	.60
❑ 54 Kieron Pope FY RC	2.50	1.00
❑ 55 Kyle Cofield FY RC	1.00	.40
❑ 56 Brent Lillibridge FY RC	1.50	.60
❑ 57 Daryl Jones FY	1.00	.40
❑ 58 Eli Iorg FY RC	1.50	.60
❑ 59 Brett Hayes FY RC	1.00	.40
❑ 60 Mike Durant FY RC	3.00	1.25
❑ 61 Michael Bowden FY RC	5.00	2.00
❑ 62 Paul Kelly FY RC	1.50	.60
❑ 63 Andrew McCutchen FY RC	8.00	3.00
❑ 64 Travis Wood FY RC	4.00	1.50
❑ 65 Cesar Ramos FY RC	1.50	.60
❑ 66 Chaz Roe FY RC	1.50	.60
❑ 67 Matt Torra FY RC	1.50	.60
❑ 68 Kevin Slowey FY RC	6.00	2.50
❑ 69 Trayvon Robinson FY RC	1.50	.60
❑ 70 Reid Engel FY RC	1.00	.40
❑ 71 Kris Harvey FY RC	1.50	.60
❑ 72 Craig Italiano FY RC	2.50	1.00
❑ 73 Matt Maloney FY RC	3.00	1.25
❑ 74 Sean West FY RC	3.00	1.25
❑ 75 Henry Sanchez FY RC	2.50	1.00
❑ 76 Scott Blue FY RC	1.00	.40
❑ 77 Jordan Schafer FY RC	6.00	2.50
❑ 78 Chris Robinson FY RC	1.50	.60
❑ 79 Chris Hobdy FY RC	1.00	.40
❑ 80 Brandon Durden FY RC	1.00	.40
❑ 81 Clay Buchholz FY RC	20.00	8.00
❑ 82 Josh Geer FY RC	1.00	.40
❑ 83 Sam LeCure FY RC	1.00	.40
❑ 84 Justin Thomas FY RC	1.00	.40
❑ 85 Brett Gardner FY RC	1.50	.60
❑ 86 Tommy Manzella FY RC	1.00	.40
❑ 87 Matt Green FY RC	1.00	.40
❑ 88 Yunel Escobar FY RC	4.00	1.50
❑ 89 Mike Costanzo FY RC	3.00	1.25
❑ 90 Nick Hundley FY RC	1.00	.40
❑ 91 Zach Simons FY RC	1.00	.40
❑ 92 Jacob Marceaux FY RC	1.00	.40
❑ 94 Brandon Snyder FY RC	3.00	1.25
❑ 95 Matt Goyen FY RC	1.00	.40

- ❑ 96 Jon Egan FY RC 1.50 .60
- ❑ 97 Drew Thompson FY RC 1.50 .60
- ❑ 98 Bryan Anderson FY RC 4.00 1.50
- ❑ 99 Clayton Richard FY RC 1.00 .40
- ❑ 100 Jimmy Shull FY RC 1.50 .60
- ❑ 101 Mark Pawelek FY RC 6.00 2.50
- ❑ 102 P.J. Phillips FY RC 2.50 1.00
- ❑ 103 John Drennen FY RC 4.00 1.50
- ❑ 104 Nolan Reimold FY RC 5.00 2.00
- ❑ 105 Troy Tulowitzki FY RC 12.00 5.00
- ❑ 106 Kevin Whelan FY RC 1.25 .50
- ❑ 107 Wade Townsend FY RC 1.50 .60
- ❑ 108 Micah Owings FY RC 2.50 1.00
- ❑ 109 Ryan Tucker FY RC 1.50 .60
- ❑ 110 Jeff Clement FY RC 8.00 3.00
- ❑ 111 Josh Sullivan FY RC 1.00 .40
- ❑ 112 Jeff Lyman FY RC 1.50 .60
- ❑ 113 Brian Bogusevic FY RC 1.00 .40
- ❑ 114 Trevor Bell FY RC 1.50 .60
- ❑ 115 Brent Cox FY RC 1.50 .60
- ❑ 116 Michael Billek FY RC 1.00 .40
- ❑ 117 Garrett Olson FY RC 1.50 .60
- ❑ 118 Steven Johnson FY RC 1.50 .60
- ❑ 119 Chase Headley FY RC 2.50 1.00
- ❑ 120 Daniel Carte FY RC 1.50 .60
- ❑ 121 Francisco Liriano PROS 2.50 1.00
- ❑ 122 Fausto Carmona PROS .40 .15
- ❑ 123 Zach Jackson PROS .40 .15
- ❑ 124 Adam Loewen PROS .40 .15
- ❑ 125 Chris Lambert PROS .40 .15
- ❑ 126 Scott Mathieson FY .60 .25
- ❑ 127 Paul Maholm PROS .60 .25
- ❑ 128 Fernando Nieve PROS .40 .15
- ❑ 129 Justin Verlander FY 6.00 2.50
- ❑ 130 Yusmeiro Petit PROS 1.00 .40
- ❑ 131 Joel Zumaya PROS 1.50 .60
- ❑ 132 Merkin Valdez PROS .40 .15
- ❑ 133 Ryan Garko FY RC 4.00 1.50
- ❑ 134 Edison Volquez FY RC 2.50 1.00
- ❑ 135 Russ Martin FY 1.50 .60
- ❑ 136 Conor Jackson PROS .60 .25
- ❑ 137 Miguel Montero FY RC 4.00 1.50
- ❑ 138 Josh Barfield PROS .60 .25
- ❑ 139 Delmon Young PROS 1.00 .40
- ❑ 140 Andy LaRoche FY 1.50 .60
- ❑ 141 William Bergolla PROS .40 .15
- ❑ 142 B.J. Upton PROS .60 .25
- ❑ 143 Hernan Iribarren FY .60 .25
- ❑ 144 Brandon Wood PROS 1.50 .60
- ❑ 145 Jose Bautista PROS .40 .15
- ❑ 146 Edwin Encarnacion PROS .60 .25
- ❑ 147 Javier Herrera FY RC 2.50 1.00
- ❑ 148 Jeremy Hermida PROS 1.50 .60
- ❑ 149 Frank Diaz PROS RC 1.00 .40
- ❑ 150 Chris B.Young FY 3.00 1.25
- ❑ 151 Shin-Soo Choo PROS .40 .15
- ❑ 152 Kevin Thompson PROS RC 1.00 .40
- ❑ 153 Hanley Ramirez PROS 1.00 .40
- ❑ 154 Lastings Milledge PROS .60 .25
- ❑ 155 Luis Montanez PROS .40 .15
- ❑ 156 Justin Huber PROS .40 .15
- ❑ 157 Zach Duke PROS .75 .30
- ❑ 158 Jeff Francoeur PROS 1.25 .50
- ❑ 159 Melky Cabrera FY 3.00 1.25
- ❑ 160 Bobby Jenks PROS .60 .25
- ❑ 161 Ian Snell PROS .40 .15
- ❑ 162 Fernando Cabrera PROS .40 .15
- ❑ 163 Troy Patton PROS 1.00 .40
- ❑ 164 Anthony Lerew PROS .60 .25
- ❑ 165 Nelson Cruz FY RC 3.00 1.25
- ❑ 166 Stephen Drew AU A RC 80.00 40.00
- ❑ 167 Jered Weaver AU A RC 60.00 30.00
- ❑ 168 Ryan Braun AU B RC 200.00 125.00
- ❑ 169 John Mayberry Jr. AU B RC 30.00 12.50
- ❑ 170 Aaron Thompson AU B RC 15.00 6.00
- ❑ 171 Cesar Carrillo AU B RC 25.00 10.00
- ❑ 172 Jacoby Ellsbury AU B RC 150.00 75.00
- ❑ 173 Matt Garza AU B RC 50.00 30.00
- ❑ 174 Cliff Pennington AU B RC 15.00 6.00
- ❑ 175 Colby Rasmus AU B RC 80.00 50.00
- ❑ 176 Chris Volstad AU B RC 30.00 12.50
- ❑ 177 Ricky Romero AU B RC 15.00 6.00
- ❑ 178 Ryan Zimmerman AU B RC 100.00 50.00
- ❑ 179 C.J. Henry AU B RC 25.00 10.00
- ❑ 180 Eddy Martinez AU B RC 15.00 6.00

2006 Bowman Chrome

- ❑ COMP.SET w/o AU's (220) 60.00 30.00
- ❑ COMMON CARD (1-200) .50 .20
- ❑ COMMON ROOKIE (201-220) .60 .25
- ❑ 219 AU ODDS 1:2734 HOBBY, 1:6617 RETAIL
- ❑ 221-224 AU ODDS 1:27 HOBBY, 1:65 RETAIL
- ❑ 1-220 PLATE ODDS 1:836 HOBBY
- ❑ 219 AU PLATE ODDS 1:292,536 HOBBY
- ❑ 221-224 AU PLATES ODDS 1:9,000 HOBBY
- ❑ PLATE PRINT RUN 1 SET PER COLOR
- ❑ BLACK-CYAN-MAGENTA-YELLOW ISSUED
- ❑ NO PLATE PRICING DUE TO SCARCITY
- ❑ 1 Nick Swisher .50 .20
- ❑ 2 Ted Lilly .50 .20
- ❑ 3 John Smoltz .75 .30
- ❑ 4 Lyle Overbay .50 .20
- ❑ 5 Alfonso Soriano .50 .20
- ❑ 6 Javier Vazquez .50 .20
- ❑ 7 Ronnie Belliard .50 .20
- ❑ 8 Jose Reyes 1.25 .50
- ❑ 9 Brian Roberts .50 .20
- ❑ 10 Curt Schilling .75 .30
- ❑ 11 Adam Dunn .50 .20
- ❑ 12 Zack Greinke .50 .20
- ❑ 13 Carlos Guillen .50 .20
- ❑ 14 Jon Garland .50 .20
- ❑ 15 Robinson Cano .75 .30
- ❑ 16 Chris Burke .50 .20
- ❑ 17 Barry Zito .50 .20
- ❑ 18 Russ Adams .50 .20
- ❑ 19 Chris Capuano .50 .20
- ❑ 20 Scott Rolen .75 .30
- ❑ 21 Kerry Wood .50 .20
- ❑ 22 Scott Kazmir .75 .30
- ❑ 23 Brandon Webb .50 .20
- ❑ 24 Jeff Kent .50 .20
- ❑ 25 Albert Pujols 2.50 1.00
- ❑ 26 C.C. Sabathia .50 .20
- ❑ 27 Adrian Beltre .50 .20
- ❑ 28 Brad Wilkerson .50 .20
- ❑ 29 Randy Wolf .50 .20
- ❑ 30 Jason Bay .50 .20
- ❑ 31 Austin Kearns .50 .20
- ❑ 32 Clint Barmes .50 .20
- ❑ 33 Mike Sweeney .50 .20
- ❑ 34 Kevin Youkilis .50 .20
- ❑ 35 Justin Morneau .50 .20
- ❑ 36 Scott Podsednik .50 .20
- ❑ 37 Jason Giambi .50 .20
- ❑ 38 Steve Finley .50 .20
- ❑ 39 Morgan Ensberg .50 .20
- ❑ 40 Eric Chavez .50 .20
- ❑ 41 Roy Halladay .50 .20
- ❑ 42 Horacio Ramirez .50 .20
- ❑ 43 Ben Sheets .50 .20
- ❑ 44 Chris Carpenter .50 .20
- ❑ 45 Andruw Jones .75 .30
- ❑ 46 Carlos Zambrano .50 .20
- ❑ 47 Jonny Gomes .50 .20
- ❑ 48 Shawn Green .50 .20
- ❑ 49 Moises Alou .50 .20
- ❑ 50 Ichiro Suzuki 2.00 .75
- ❑ 51 Juan Pierre .50 .20
- ❑ 52 Grady Sizemore .75 .30
- ❑ 53 Kazuo Matsui .50 .20
- ❑ 54 Jose Vidro .50 .20
- ❑ 55 Jake Peavy .50 .20
- ❑ 56 Dallas McPherson .50 .20
- ❑ 57 Ryan Howard 2.00 .75
- ❑ 58 Zach Duke .50 .20
- ❑ 59 Michael Young .50 .20
- ❑ 60 Todd Helton .75 .30
- ❑ 61 David DeJesus .50 .20
- ❑ 62 Ivan Rodriguez .75 .30
- ❑ 63 Johan Santana .75 .30
- ❑ 64 Danny Haren .50 .20
- ❑ 65 Derek Jeter 3.00 1.25
- ❑ 66 Greg Maddux 2.00 .75
- ❑ 67 Jorge Cantu .50 .20
- ❑ 68 J.J. Hardy .50 .20
- ❑ 69 Victor Martinez .50 .20
- ❑ 70 David Wright 2.00 .75
- ❑ 71 Ryan Church .50 .20
- ❑ 72 Khalil Greene .75 .30
- ❑ 73 Jimmy Rollins .50 .20
- ❑ 74 Hank Blalock .50 .20
- ❑ 75 Pedro Martinez .75 .30
- ❑ 76 Chris Shelton .50 .20
- ❑ 77 Felipe Lopez .50 .20
- ❑ 78 Jeff Francis .50 .20
- ❑ 79 Andy Sisco .50 .20
- ❑ 80 Hideki Matsui 1.25 .50
- ❑ 81 Ken Griffey Jr. 2.00 .75
- ❑ 82 Nomar Garciaparra 1.25 .50
- ❑ 83 Kevin Millwood .50 .20
- ❑ 84 Paul Konerko .50 .20
- ❑ 85 A.J. Burnett .50 .20
- ❑ 86 Mike Piazza 1.25 .50
- ❑ 87 Brian Giles .50 .20
- ❑ 88 Johnny Damon .75 .30
- ❑ 89 Jim Thome .75 .30
- ❑ 90 Roger Clemens 2.50 1.00
- ❑ 91 Aaron Rowand .50 .20
- ❑ 92 Rafael Furcal .50 .20
- ❑ 93 Gary Sheffield .50 .20
- ❑ 94 Mike Cameron .50 .20
- ❑ 95 Carlos Delgado .50 .20
- ❑ 96 Jorge Posada .75 .30
- ❑ 97 Denny Bautista .50 .20
- ❑ 98 Mike Maroth .50 .20
- ❑ 99 Brad Radke .50 .20
- ❑ 100 Alex Rodriguez 2.00 .75
- ❑ 101 Freddy Garcia .50 .20
- ❑ 102 Oliver Perez .50 .20
- ❑ 103 Jon Lieber .50 .20
- ❑ 104 Melvin Mora .50 .20
- ❑ 105 Travis Hafner .50 .20
- ❑ 106 Alex Rios .50 .20
- ❑ 107 Derek Lowe .50 .20
- ❑ 108 Luis Castillo .50 .20
- ❑ 109 Livan Hernandez .50 .20
- ❑ 110 Tadahito Iguchi .50 .20
- ❑ 111 Shawn Chacon .50 .20
- ❑ 112 Frank Thomas 1.25 .50
- ❑ 113 Josh Beckett .50 .20
- ❑ 114 Aubrey Huff .50 .20
- ❑ 115 Derrek Lee .50 .20
- ❑ 116 Chien-Ming Wang 2.00 .75
- ❑ 117 Joe Crede .50 .20
- ❑ 118 Torii Hunter .50 .20
- ❑ 119 J.D. Drew .50 .20
- ❑ 120 Troy Glaus .50 .20
- ❑ 121 Sean Casey .50 .20
- ❑ 122 Edgar Renteria .50 .20
- ❑ 123 Craig Wilson .50 .20
- ❑ 124 Adam Eaton .50 .20
- ❑ 125 Jeff Francoeur 1.25 .50
- ❑ 126 Bruce Chen .50 .20
- ❑ 127 Cliff Floyd .50 .20
- ❑ 128 Jeremy Reed .50 .20
- ❑ 129 Jake Westbrook .50 .20
- ❑ 130 Wily Mo Pena .50 .20
- ❑ 131 Toby Hall .50 .20
- ❑ 132 David Ortiz 1.25 .50
- ❑ 133 David Eckstein .50 .20
- ❑ 134 Brady Clark .50 .20
- ❑ 135 Marcus Giles .50 .20
- ❑ 136 Aaron Hill .50 .20
- ❑ 137 Mark Kotsay .50 .20
- ❑ 138 Carlos Lee .50 .20
- ❑ 139 Roy Oswalt .50 .20
- ❑ 140 Chone Figgins .50 .20
- ❑ 141 Mike Mussina .75 .30

❑ 142 Orlando Hernandez	.50	.20
❑ 143 Magglio Ordonez	.50	.20
❑ 144 Jim Edmonds	.75	.30
❑ 145 Bobby Abreu	.50	.20
❑ 146 Nick Johnson	.50	.20
❑ 147 Carlos Beltran	.50	.20
❑ 148 Jhonny Peralta	.50	.20
❑ 149 Pedro Feliz	.50	.20
❑ 150 Miguel Tejada	.50	.20
❑ 151 Luis Gonzalez	.50	.20
❑ 152 Carl Crawford	.50	.20
❑ 153 Yadier Molina	.50	.20
❑ 154 Rich Harden	.50	.20
❑ 155 Tim Wakefield	.50	.20
❑ 156 Rickie Weeks	.50	.20
❑ 157 Johnny Estrada	.50	.20
❑ 158 Gustavo Chacin	.50	.20
❑ 159 Dan Johnson	.50	.20
❑ 160 Willy Taveras	.50	.20
❑ 161 Garret Anderson	.50	.20
❑ 162 Randy Johnson	1.25	.50
❑ 163 Jermaine Dye	.50	.20
❑ 164 Joe Mauer	.75	.30
❑ 165 Ervin Santana	.50	.20
❑ 166 Jeremy Bonderman	.50	.20
❑ 167 Garrett Atkins	.50	.20
❑ 168 Manny Ramirez	.75	.30
❑ 169 Brad Eldred	.50	.20
❑ 170 Chase Utley	1.25	.50
❑ 171 Mark Loretta	.50	.20
❑ 172 John Patterson	.50	.20
❑ 173 Tom Glavine	.75	.30
❑ 174 Dontrelle Willis	.50	.20
❑ 175 Mark Teixeira	.75	.30
❑ 176 Felix Hernandez	.75	.30
❑ 177 Cliff Lee	.50	.20
❑ 178 Jason Schmidt	.50	.20
❑ 179 Chad Tracy	.50	.20
❑ 180 Rocco Baldelli	.50	.20
❑ 181 Aramis Ramirez	.50	.20
❑ 182 Andy Pettitte	.75	.30
❑ 183 Mark Mulder	.50	.20
❑ 184 Geoff Jenkins	.50	.20
❑ 185 Chipper Jones	1.25	.50
❑ 186 Vernon Wells	.50	.20
❑ 187 Bobby Crosby	.50	.20
❑ 188 Lance Berkman	.50	.20
❑ 189 Vladimir Guerrero	1.25	.50
❑ 190 Coco Crisp	.50	.20
❑ 191 Brad Penny	.50	.20
❑ 192 Jose Guillen	.50	.20
❑ 193 Brett Myers	.50	.20
❑ 194 Miguel Cabrera	.75	.30
❑ 195 Bartolo Colon	.50	.20
❑ 196 Craig Biggio	.75	.30
❑ 197 Tim Hudson	.50	.20
❑ 198 Mark Prior	.75	.30
❑ 199 Mark Buehrle	.50	.20
❑ 200 Barry Bonds	2.50	1.00
❑ 201 Anderson Hernandez (RC)	.60	.25
❑ 202 Jose Capellan (RC)	.60	.25
❑ 203 Jeremy Accardo RC	.60	.25
❑ 204 Hanley Ramirez (RC)	1.50	.60
❑ 205 Matt Capps (RC)	.60	.25
❑ 206 Jonathan Papelbon (RC)	3.00	1.25
❑ 207 Chuck James (RC)	1.00	.40
❑ 208 Matt Cain (RC)	1.00	.40
❑ 209 Cole Hamels (RC)	1.50	.60
❑ 210 Jason Botts (RC)	.60	.25
❑ 211 Lastings Milledge (RC)	1.00	.40
❑ 212 Conor Jackson (RC)	1.00	.40
❑ 213 Yusmeiro Petit (RC)	.60	.25
❑ 214 Alay Soler RC	.60	.25
❑ 215 Willy Aybar (RC)	.60	.25
❑ 216 Adam Loewen (RC)	.60	.25
❑ 217 Justin Verlander (RC)	2.50	1.00
❑ 218 Francisco Liriano (RC)	3.00	1.25
❑ 219 Kenji Johjima RC	3.00	1.25
❑ 219a Kenji Johjima AU	120.00	60.00
❑ 220 Craig Hansen RC	2.50	1.00
❑ 221 Prince Fielder AU (RC)	80.00	40.00
❑ 222 Josh Barfield AU (RC)	15.00	6.00
❑ 223 Fausto Carmona AU (RC)	30.00	12.50
❑ 224 James Loney AU (RC)	40.00	15.00

2006 Bowman Chrome Draft

❑ COMPLETE SET (55)	40.00	15.00
❑ COMMON RC (1-55)	1.00	.40
❑ RC SEMIS 1-55	1.50	.60
❑ RC UNLISTED 1-55	2.50	1.00
❑ APPX. ODDS 1:2 HOBBY, 1:2 RETAIL		
❑ ODDS INFO PROVIDED BY BECKETT		
❑ OVERALL PLATE ODDS 1:990 HOBBY		
❑ PLATE PRINT RUN 1 SET PER COLOR		
❑ BLACK-CYAN-MAGENTA-YELLOW ISSUED		
❑ NO PLATE PRICING DUE TO SCARCITY		
❑ 1 Matt Kemp (RC)	1.50	.60
❑ 2 Taylor Tankersley (RC)	1.00	.40
❑ 3 Mike Napoli RC	2.50	1.00
❑ 4 Brian Bannister (RC)	1.00	.40
❑ 5 Melky Cabrera (RC)	1.50	.60
❑ 6 Bill Bray (RC)	1.00	.40
❑ 7 Brian Anderson (RC)	1.00	.40
❑ 8 Jered Weaver (RC)	3.00	1.25
❑ 9 Chris Duncan (RC)	1.50	.60
❑ 10 Boof Bonser (RC)	1.50	.60
❑ 11 Mike Rouse (RC)	1.00	.40
❑ 12 David Pauley (RC)	1.00	.40
❑ 13 Russ Martin (RC)	1.50	.60
❑ 14 Jeremy Sowers (RC)	1.00	.40
❑ 15 Kevin Reese (RC)	1.00	.40
❑ 16 John Rheinecker (RC)	1.00	.40
❑ 17 Tommy Murphy (RC)	1.00	.40
❑ 18 Sean Marshall (RC)	1.00	.40
❑ 19 Jason Kubel (RC)	1.00	.40
❑ 20 Chad Billingsley (RC)	1.50	.60
❑ 21 Kendry Morales (RC)	1.50	.60
❑ 22 Jon Lester RC	2.50	1.00
❑ 23 Brandon Fahey RC	1.00	.40
❑ 24 Josh Johnson (RC)	1.50	.60
❑ 25 Kevin Frandsen (RC)	1.00	.40
❑ 26 Casey Janssen RC	1.50	.60
❑ 27 Scott Thorman (RC)	1.00	.40
❑ 28 Scott Mathieson (RC)	1.00	.40
❑ 29 Jeremy Hermida (RC)	1.00	.40
❑ 30 Dustin Nippert (RC)	1.00	.40
❑ 31 Kevin Thompson (RC)	1.00	.40
❑ 32 Bobby Livingston (RC)	1.00	.40
❑ 33 Travis Ishikawa (RC)	1.00	.40
❑ 34 Jeff Mathis (RC)	1.00	.40
❑ 35 Charlie Haeger RC	1.50	.60
❑ 36 Josh Willingham (RC)	1.00	.40
❑ 37 Taylor Buchholz (RC)	1.00	.40
❑ 38 Joel Guzman (RC)	1.00	.40
❑ 39 Zach Jackson (RC)	1.00	.40
❑ 40 Howie Kendrick (RC)	2.50	1.00
❑ 41 T.J. Beam (RC)	1.00	.40
❑ 42 Ty Taubenheim RC	1.50	.60
❑ 43 Erick Aybar (RC)	1.00	.40
❑ 44 Anibal Sanchez (RC)	1.50	.60
❑ 45 Michael Pelfrey RC	8.00	3.00
❑ 46 Shawn Hill (RC)	1.00	.40
❑ 47 Chris Roberson (RC)	1.00	.40
❑ 48 Carlos Villanueva RC	1.00	.40
❑ 49 Andre Ethier (RC)	2.50	1.00
❑ 50 Anthony Reyes (RC)	1.50	.60
❑ 51 Franklin Gutierrez (RC)	1.00	.40
❑ 52 Angel Guzman (RC)	1.00	.40
❑ 53 Michael O'Connor RC	1.00	.40
❑ 54 James Shields RC	1.00	.40
❑ 55 Nate McLouth (RC)	1.00	.40

2007 Bowman Chrome

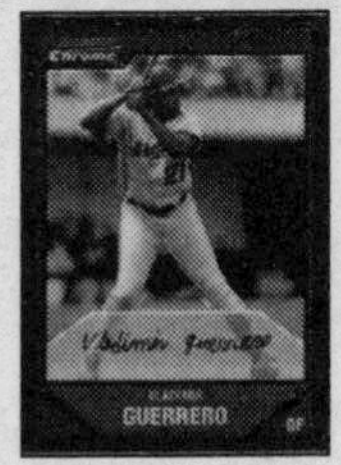

❑ COMPLETE SET (220)	60.00	30.00
❑ COMMON CARD (1-190)	.50	.20
❑ COMMON ROOKIE (191-220)	.75	.30
❑ 1-220 PLATE ODDS 1:1054 HOBBY		
❑ PLATE PRINT RUN 1 SET PER COLOR		
❑ BLACK-CYAN-MAGENTA-YELLOW ISSUED		
❑ NO PLATE PRICING DUE TO SCARCITY		
❑ 1 Hanley Ramirez	.75	.30
❑ 2 Justin Verlander	1.25	.50
❑ 3 Ryan Zimmerman	1.25	.50
❑ 4 Jered Weaver	.75	.30
❑ 5 Stephen Drew	.75	.30
❑ 6 Jonathan Papelbon	1.25	.50
❑ 7 Melky Cabrera	.50	.20
❑ 8 Francisco Liriano	1.25	.50
❑ 9 Prince Fielder	1.25	.50
❑ 10 Dan Uggla	.75	.30
❑ 11 Jeremy Sowers	.50	.20
❑ 12 Carlos Quentin	.50	.20
❑ 13 Chuck James	.50	.20
❑ 14 Andre Ethier	.75	.30
❑ 15 Cole Hamels	.75	.30
❑ 16 Kenji Johjima	1.25	.50
❑ 17 Chad Billingsley	.50	.20
❑ 18 Ian Kinsler	.50	.20
❑ 19 Jason Hirsh	.50	.20
❑ 20 Nick Markakis	.75	.30
❑ 21 Jeremy Hermida	.50	.20
❑ 22 Ryan Shealy	.50	.20
❑ 23 Scott Olsen	.50	.20
❑ 24 Russell Martin	.50	.20
❑ 25 Conor Jackson	.50	.20
❑ 26 Erik Bedard	.50	.20
❑ 27 Brian McCann	.50	.20
❑ 28 Michael Barrett	.50	.20
❑ 29 Brandon Phillips	.50	.20
❑ 30 Garrett Atkins	.50	.20
❑ 31 Freddy Garcia	.50	.20
❑ 32 Mark Loretta	.50	.20
❑ 33 Craig Biggio	.75	.30
❑ 34 Jeremy Bonderman	.50	.20
❑ 35 Johan Santana	.75	.30
❑ 36 Jorge Posada	.75	.30
❑ 37 Victor Martinez	.50	.20
❑ 38 Carlos Delgado	.50	.20
❑ 39 Gary Matthews Jr.	.50	.20
❑ 40 Mike Cameron	.50	.20
❑ 41 Adrian Beltre	.50	.20
❑ 42 Freddy Sanchez	.50	.20
❑ 43 Austin Kearns	.50	.20
❑ 44 Mark Buehrle	.50	.20
❑ 45 Miguel Cabrera	.75	.30
❑ 46 Josh Beckett	.75	.30
❑ 47 Chone Figgins	.50	.20
❑ 48 Edgar Renteria	.50	.20
❑ 49 Derek Lowe	.50	.20
❑ 50 Ryan Howard	2.00	.75
❑ 51 Shawn Green	.50	.20
❑ 52 Jason Giambi	.50	.20
❑ 53 Ervin Santana	.50	.20
❑ 54 Aaron Hill	.50	.20
❑ 55 Roy Oswalt	.50	.20
❑ 56 Dan Haren	.50	.20
❑ 57 Jose Vidro	.50	.20
❑ 58 Kevin Millwood	.50	.20
❑ 59 Jim Edmonds	.75	.30

❑ 60 Carl Crawford .50 .20
❑ 61 Randy Wolf .50 .20
❑ 62 Paul LoDuca .50 .20
❑ 63 Johnny Estrada .50 .20
❑ 64 Brian Roberts .50 .20
❑ 65 Manny Ramirez .75 .30
❑ 66 Jose Contreras .50 .20
❑ 67 Josh Barfield .50 .20
❑ 68 Juan Pierre .50 .20
❑ 69 David DeJesus .50 .20
❑ 70 Gary Sheffield .50 .20
❑ 71 Michael Young .50 .20
❑ 72 Randy Johnson 1.25 .50
❑ 73 Rickie Weeks .50 .20
❑ 74 Brian Giles .50 .20
❑ 75 Ichiro Suzuki 2.00 .75
❑ 76 Nick Swisher .50 .20
❑ 77 Justin Morneau .50 .20
❑ 78 Scott Kazmir .75 .30
❑ 79 Lyle Overbay .50 .20
❑ 80 Alfonso Soriano .50 .20
❑ 81 Brandon Webb .50 .20
❑ 82 Joe Crede .50 .20
❑ 83 Corey Patterson .50 .20
❑ 84 Kenny Rogers .50 .20
❑ 85 Ken Griffey Jr. 2.00 .75
❑ 86 Cliff Lee .50 .20
❑ 87 Mike Lowell .50 .20
❑ 88 Marcus Giles .50 .20
❑ 89 Orlando Cabrera .50 .20
❑ 90 Derek Jeter 3.00 1.25
❑ 91 Ramon Hernandez .50 .20
❑ 92 Carlos Guillen .50 .20
❑ 93 Bill Hall .50 .20
❑ 94 Michael Cuddyer .50 .20
❑ 95 Miguel Tejada .50 .20
❑ 96 Todd Helton .75 .30
❑ 97 C.C. Sabathia .50 .20
❑ 98 Tadahito Iguchi .50 .20
❑ 99 Jose Reyes 1.25 .50
❑ 100 David Wright 2.00 .75
❑ 101 Barry Zito .50 .20
❑ 102 Jake Peavy .50 .20
❑ 103 Richie Sexson .50 .20
❑ 104 A.J. Burnett .50 .20
❑ 105 Eric Chavez .50 .20
❑ 106 Vernon Wells .50 .20
❑ 107 Grady Sizemore .75 .30
❑ 108 Bronson Arroyo .50 .20
❑ 109 Mike Mussina .75 .30
❑ 110 Magglio Ordonez .50 .20
❑ 111 Anibal Sanchez .50 .20
❑ 112 Jeff Francoeur 1.25 .50
❑ 113 Kevin Youkilis .50 .20
❑ 114 Aubrey Huff .50 .20
❑ 115 Carlos Zambrano .50 .20
❑ 116 Mark Teahen .50 .20
❑ 117 Mark Mulder .50 .20
❑ 118 Pedro Martinez .75 .30
❑ 119 Hideki Matsui 1.25 .50
❑ 120 Mike Piazza 1.25 .50
❑ 121 Jason Schmidt .50 .20
❑ 122 Greg Maddux 2.00 .75
❑ 123 Joe Blanton .50 .20
❑ 124 Chris Carpenter .50 .20
❑ 125 David Ortiz 1.25 .50
❑ 126 Alex Rios .50 .20
❑ 127 Nick Johnson .50 .20
❑ 128 Carlos Lee .50 .20
❑ 129 Pat Burrell .50 .20
❑ 130 Ben Sheets .50 .20
❑ 131 Derrek Lee .50 .20
❑ 132 Adam Dunn .50 .20
❑ 133 Jermaine Dye .50 .20
❑ 134 Curt Schilling .75 .30
❑ 135 Chad Tracy .50 .20
❑ 136 Vladimir Guerrero 1.25 .50
❑ 137 Melvin Mora .50 .20
❑ 138 John Smoltz .75 .30
❑ 139 Craig Monroe .50 .20
❑ 140 Dontrelle Willis .50 .20
❑ 141 Jeff Francis .50 .20
❑ 142 Chipper Jones 1.25 .50
❑ 143 Frank Thomas 1.25 .50
❑ 144 Brett Myers .50 .20
❑ 145 Tom Glavine .75 .30
❑ 146 Robinson Cano .75 .30
❑ 147 Jeff Kent .50 .20
❑ 148 Scott Rolen .75 .30
❑ 149 Roy Halladay .50 .20
❑ 150 Joe Mauer .75 .30
❑ 151 Bobby Abreu .50 .20
❑ 152 Matt Cain .75 .30
❑ 153 Hank Blalock .50 .20
❑ 154 Chris Young .50 .20
❑ 155 Jake Westbrook .50 .20
❑ 156 Javier Vazquez .50 .20
❑ 157 Garret Anderson .50 .20
❑ 158 Aramis Ramirez .50 .20
❑ 159 Mark Kotsay .50 .20
❑ 160 Matt Kemp .50 .20
❑ 161 Adrian Gonzalez .50 .20
❑ 162 Felix Hernandez .75 .30
❑ 163 David Eckstein .50 .20
❑ 164 Curtis Granderson .50 .20
❑ 165 Paul Konerko .50 .20
❑ 166 Alex Rodriguez 2.00 .75
❑ 167 Tim Hudson .50 .20
❑ 168 J.D. Drew .50 .20
❑ 169 Chien-Ming Wang 2.00 .75
❑ 170 Jimmy Rollins .50 .20
❑ 171 Matt Morris .50 .20
❑ 172 Raul Ibanez .50 .20
❑ 173 Mark Teixeira .75 .30
❑ 174 Ted Lilly .50 .20
❑ 175 Albert Pujols 2.50 1.00
❑ 176 Carlos Beltran .50 .20
❑ 177 Lance Berkman .50 .20
❑ 178 Ivan Rodriguez .75 .30
❑ 179 Torii Hunter .50 .20
❑ 180 Johnny Damon .75 .30
❑ 181 Chase Utley 1.25 .50
❑ 182 Jason Bay .50 .20
❑ 183 Jeff Weaver .50 .20
❑ 184 Troy Glaus .50 .20
❑ 185 Rocco Baldelli .50 .20
❑ 186 Rafael Furcal .50 .20
❑ 187 Jim Thome .75 .30
❑ 188 Travis Hafner .50 .20
❑ 189 Matt Holliday 1.25 .50
❑ 190 Andruw Jones .75 .30
❑ 191 Andrew Miller RC 5.00 2.00
❑ 192 Ryan Braun RC .75 .30
❑ 193 Oswaldo Navarro RC .75 .30
❑ 194 Mike Rabelo RC .75 .30
❑ 195 Delwyn Young (RC) .75 .30
❑ 196 Miguel Montero (RC) .75 .30
❑ 197 Matt Lindstrom (RC) .75 .30
❑ 198 Josh Hamilton (RC) 2.00 .75
❑ 199 Elijah Dukes RC 1.25 .50
❑ 200 Sean Henn (RC) .75 .30
❑ 201 Delmon Young (RC) 1.25 .50
❑ 202 Alexi Casilla RC 1.25 .50
❑ 203 Hunter Pence (RC) 6.00 2.50
❑ 204 Jeff Baker (RC) .75 .30
❑ 205 Hector Gimenez (RC) .75 .30
❑ 206 Ubaldo Jimenez (RC) .75 .30
❑ 207 Adam Lind (RC) .75 .30
❑ 208 Joaquin Arias (RC) .75 .30
❑ 209 David Murphy (RC) .75 .30
❑ 210 Daisuke Matsuzaka RC 8.00 3.00
❑ 211 Jerry Owens (RC) .75 .30
❑ 212 Ryan Sweeney (RC) .75 .30
❑ 213 Kei Igawa RC 2.00 .75
❑ 214 Mitch Maier RC .75 .30
❑ 215 Philip Humber (RC) .75 .30
❑ 216 Troy Tulowitzki (RC) 2.00 .75
❑ 217 Tim Lincecum RC 10.00 4.00
❑ 218 Michael Bourn (RC) .75 .30
❑ 219 Hideki Okajima RC 4.00 1.50
❑ 220 Josh Fields (RC) .75 .30

2001 Bowman Heritage

❑ COMPLETE SET (440) 200.00 125.00
❑ COMP.SET w/o SP's (330) 50.00 20.00
❑ COMMON CARD (1-330) .40 .15
❑ COMMON RC (1-330) .40 .15
❑ COMMON CARD (331-440) 2.00 .75
❑ 1 Chipper Jones 1.00 .40
❑ 2 Pete Harnisch .40 .15
❑ 3 Brian Giles .40 .15
❑ 4 J.T. Snow .40 .15
❑ 5 Bartolo Colon .40 .15
❑ 6 Jorge Posada .60 .25
❑ 7 Shawn Green .40 .15
❑ 8 Derek Jeter 2.50 1.00
❑ 9 Benito Santiago .40 .15
❑ 10 Ramon Hernandez .40 .15
❑ 11 Bernie Williams .60 .25
❑ 12 Greg Maddux 1.50 .60
❑ 13 Barry Bonds 2.50 1.00
❑ 14 Roger Clemens 2.00 .75
❑ 15 Miguel Tejada .40 .15
❑ 16 Pedro Feliz .40 .15
❑ 17 Jim Edmonds .40 .15
❑ 18 Tom Glavine .60 .25
❑ 19 David Justice .40 .15
❑ 20 Rich Aurilia .40 .15
❑ 21 Jason Giambi .40 .15
❑ 22 Orlando Hernandez .40 .15
❑ 23 Shawn Estes .40 .15
❑ 24 Nelson Figueroa .40 .15
❑ 25 Terrence Long .40 .15
❑ 26 Mike Mussina .60 .25
❑ 27 Eric Davis .40 .15
❑ 28 Jimmy Rollins .40 .15
❑ 29 Andy Pettitte .60 .25
❑ 30 Shawon Dunston .40 .15
❑ 31 Tim Hudson .40 .15
❑ 32 Jeff Kent .40 .15
❑ 33 Scott Brosius .40 .15
❑ 34 Livan Hernandez .40 .15
❑ 35 Alfonso Soriano .60 .25
❑ 36 Mark McGwire 2.50 1.00
❑ 37 Russ Ortiz .40 .15
❑ 38 Fernando Vina .40 .15
❑ 39 Ken Griffey Jr. 1.50 .60
❑ 40 Edgar Renteria .40 .15
❑ 41 Kevin Brown .40 .15
❑ 42 Robb Nen .40 .15
❑ 43 Paul LoDuca .40 .15
❑ 44 Bobby Abreu .40 .15
❑ 45 Adam Dunn .60 .25
❑ 46 Osvaldo Fernandez .40 .15
❑ 47 Marvin Benard .40 .15
❑ 48 Mark Gardner .40 .15
❑ 49 Alex Rodriguez 1.50 .60
❑ 50 Preston Wilson .40 .15
❑ 51 Roberto Alomar .60 .25
❑ 52 Ben Davis .40 .15
❑ 53 Derek Bell .40 .15
❑ 54 Ken Caminiti .40 .15
❑ 55 Barry Zito .60 .25
❑ 56 Scott Rolen .60 .25
❑ 57 Geoff Jenkins .40 .15
❑ 58 Mike Cameron .40 .15
❑ 59 Ben Grieve .40 .15
❑ 60 Chuck Knoblauch .40 .15
❑ 61 Matt Lawton .40 .15
❑ 62 Chan Ho Park .40 .15
❑ 63 Lance Berkman .40 .15
❑ 64 Carlos Beltran .40 .15
❑ 65 Dean Palmer .40 .15
❑ 66 Alex Gonzalez .40 .15
❑ 67 Larry Walker .40 .15
❑ 68 Magglio Ordonez .40 .15
❑ 69 Ellis Burks .40 .15
❑ 70 Mark Mulder .40 .15
❑ 71 Randy Johnson 1.00 .40

❑	72	John Smoltz	.60	.25
❑	73	Jerry Hairston Jr.	.40	.15
❑	74	Pedro Martinez	.60	.25
❑	75	Fred McGriff	.60	.25
❑	76	Sean Casey	.40	.15
❑	77	C.C. Sabathia	.40	.15
❑	78	Todd Helton	.60	.25
❑	79	Brad Penny	.40	.15
❑	80	Mike Sweeney	.40	.15
❑	81	Billy Wagner	.40	.15
❑	82	Mark Buehrle	.60	.25
❑	83	Cristian Guzman	.40	.15
❑	84	Jose Vidro	.40	.15
❑	85	Pat Burrell	.40	.15
❑	86	Jermaine Dye	.40	.15
❑	87	Brandon Inge	.40	.15
❑	88	David Wells	.40	.15
❑	89	Mike Piazza	1.50	.60
❑	90	Jose Cabrera	.40	.15
❑	91	Cliff Floyd	.40	.15
❑	92	Matt Morris	.40	.15
❑	93	Raul Mondesi	.40	.15
❑	94	Joe Kennedy RC	.60	.25
❑	95	Jack Wilson RC	.60	.25
❑	96	Andruw Jones	.60	.25
❑	97	Mariano Rivera	1.00	.40
❑	98	Mike Hampton	.40	.15
❑	99	Roger Cedeno	.40	.15
❑	100	Jose Cruz	.40	.15
❑	101	Mike Lowell	.40	.15
❑	102	Pedro Astacio	.40	.15
❑	103	Joe Mays	.40	.15
❑	104	John Franco	.40	.15
❑	105	Tim Redding	.40	.15
❑	106	Sandy Alomar Jr.	.40	.15
❑	107	Bret Boone	.40	.15
❑	108	Josh Towers RC	.60	.25
❑	109	Matt Stairs	.40	.15
❑	110	Chris Truby	.40	.15
❑	111	Jeff Suppan	.40	.15
❑	112	J.C. Romero	.40	.15
❑	113	Felipe Lopez	.40	.15
❑	114	Ben Sheets	.60	.25
❑	115	Frank Thomas	1.00	.40
❑	116	A.J. Burnett	.40	.15
❑	117	Tony Clark	.40	.15
❑	118	Mac Suzuki	.40	.15
❑	119	Brad Radke	.40	.15
❑	120	Jeff Shaw	.40	.15
❑	121	Nick Neugebauer	.40	.15
❑	122	Kenny Lofton	.40	.15
❑	123	Jacque Jones	.40	.15
❑	124	Brent Mayne	.40	.15
❑	125	Carlos Hernandez	.40	.15
❑	126	Shane Spencer	.40	.15
❑	127	John Lackey	.40	.15
❑	128	Sterling Hitchcock	.40	.15
❑	129	Darren Dreifort	.40	.15
❑	130	Rusty Greer	.40	.15
❑	131	Michael Cuddyer	.40	.15
❑	132	Tyler Houston	.40	.15
❑	133	Chin-Feng Chen	.40	.15
❑	134	Ken Harvey	.40	.15
❑	135	Marquis Grissom	.40	.15
❑	136	Russell Branyan	.40	.15
❑	137	Eric Karros	.40	.15
❑	138	Josh Beckett	.60	.25
❑	139	Todd Zeile	.40	.15
❑	140	Corey Koskie	.40	.15
❑	141	Steve Sparks	.40	.15
❑	142	Bobby Seay	.40	.15
❑	143	Tim Raines Jr.	.40	.15
❑	144	Julio Zuleta	.40	.15
❑	145	Jose Lima	.40	.15
❑	146	Dante Bichette	.40	.15
❑	147	Randy Keisler	.40	.15
❑	148	Brent Butler	.40	.15
❑	149	Antonio Alfonseca	.40	.15
❑	150	Bryan Rekar	.40	.15
❑	151	Jeffrey Hammonds	.40	.15
❑	152	Larry Bigbie	.40	.15
❑	153	Blake Stein	.40	.15
❑	154	Robin Ventura	.40	.15
❑	155	Rondell White	.40	.15
❑	156	Juan Silvestre	.40	.15
❑	157	Marcus Thames	.40	.15
❑	158	Sidney Ponson	.40	.15
❑	159	Juan A. Pena RC	.40	.15
❑	160	C.J. Nitkowski	.40	.15
❑	161	Adam Everett	.40	.15
❑	162	Eric Munson	.40	.15
❑	163	Jason Isringhausen	.40	.15
❑	164	Brad Fullmer	.40	.15
❑	165	Miguel Olivo	.40	.15
❑	166	Fernando Tatis	.40	.15
❑	167	Freddy Garcia	.40	.15
❑	168	Tom Goodwin	.40	.15
❑	169	Armando Benitez	.40	.15
❑	170	Paul Konerko	.40	.15
❑	171	Jeff Cirillo	.40	.15
❑	172	Shane Reynolds	.40	.15
❑	173	Kevin Tapani	.40	.15
❑	174	Joe Crede	1.00	.40
❑	175	Omar Infante RC	.40	.15
❑	176	Jake Peavy RC	5.00	2.00
❑	177	Corey Patterson	.40	.15
❑	178	Mike Penney RC	.40	.15
❑	179	Jeromy Burnitz	.40	.15
❑	180	David Segui	.40	.15
❑	181	Marcus Giles	.40	.15
❑	182	Paul O'Neill	.60	.25
❑	183	John Olerud	.40	.15
❑	184	Andy Benes	.40	.15
❑	185	Brad Cresse	.40	.15
❑	186	Ricky Ledee	.40	.15
❑	187	Allen Levrault UER	.40	.15
❑	188	Royce Clayton	.40	.15
❑	189	Kelly Johnson RC	3.00	1.25
❑	190	Quilvio Veras	.40	.15
❑	191	Mike Williams	.40	.15
❑	192	Jason Lane RC	.60	.25
❑	193	Rick Helling	.40	.15
❑	194	Tim Wakefield	.40	.15
❑	195	James Baldwin	.40	.15
❑	196	Cody Ransom RC	.40	.15
❑	197	Bobby Kielty	.40	.15
❑	198	Bobby Jones	.40	.15
❑	199	Steve Cox	.40	.15
❑	200	Jamal Strong RC	.40	.15
❑	201	Steve Lomasney	.40	.15
❑	202	Brian Cardwell RC	.40	.15
❑	203	Mike Matheny	.40	.15
❑	204	Jeff Randazzo RC	.40	.15
❑	205	Aubrey Huff	.40	.15
❑	206	Chuck Finley	.40	.15
❑	207	Denny Bautista RC	.60	.25
❑	208	Terry Mulholland	.40	.15
❑	209	Rey Ordonez	.40	.15
❑	210	Keith Surkont RC	.40	.15
❑	211	Orlando Cabrera	.40	.15
❑	212	Juan Encarnacion	.40	.15
❑	213	Dustin Hermanson	.40	.15
❑	214	Luis Rivas	.40	.15
❑	215	Mark Quinn	.40	.15
❑	216	Randy Velarde	.40	.15
❑	217	Billy Koch	.40	.15
❑	218	Ryan Rupe	.40	.15
❑	219	Keith Ginter	.40	.15
❑	220	Woody Williams	.40	.15
❑	221	Ryan Franklin	.40	.15
❑	222	Aaron Myette	.40	.15
❑	223	Joe Borchard RC	.40	.15
❑	224	Nate Cornejo	.40	.15
❑	225	Julian Tavarez	.40	.15
❑	226	Kevin Millwood	.40	.15
❑	227	Travis Hafner RC	5.00	2.00
❑	228	Charles Nagy	.40	.15
❑	229	Mike Lieberthal	.40	.15
❑	230	Jeff Nelson	.40	.15
❑	231	Ryan Dempster	.40	.15
❑	232	Andres Galarraga	.40	.15
❑	233	Chad Durbin	.40	.15
❑	234	Timo Perez	.40	.15
❑	235	Troy O'Leary	.40	.15
❑	236	Kevin Young	.40	.15
❑	237	Gabe Kapler	.40	.15
❑	238	Juan Cruz RC	.40	.15
❑	239	Masato Yoshii	.40	.15
❑	240	Aramis Ramirez	.40	.15
❑	241	Matt Cooper RC	.40	.15
❑	242	Randy Flores RC	.40	.15
❑	243	Rafael Furcal	.40	.15
❑	244	David Eckstein	.40	.15
❑	245	Matt Clement	.40	.15
❑	246	Craig Biggio	.60	.25
❑	247	Rick Reed	.40	.15
❑	248	Jose Macias	.40	.15
❑	249	Alex Escobar	.40	.15
❑	250	Roberto Hernandez	.40	.15
❑	251	Andy Ashby	.40	.15
❑	252	Tony Armas Jr.	.40	.15
❑	253	Jamie Moyer	.40	.15
❑	254	Jason Tyner	.40	.15
❑	255	Charles Kegley RC	.40	.15
❑	256	Jeff Conine	.40	.15
❑	257	Francisco Cordova	.40	.15
❑	258	Ted Lilly	.40	.15
❑	259	Joe Randa	.40	.15
❑	260	Jeff D'Amico	.40	.15
❑	261	Albie Lopez	.40	.15
❑	262	Kevin Appier	.40	.15
❑	263	Richard Hidalgo	.40	.15
❑	264	Omar Daal	.40	.15
❑	265	Ricky Gutierrez	.40	.15
❑	266	John Rocker	.40	.15
❑	267	Ray Lankford	.40	.15
❑	268	Beau Hale RC	.40	.15
❑	269	Tony Blanco RC	.40	.15
❑	270	Derrek Lee UER	.60	.25
❑	271	Jamey Wright	.40	.15
❑	272	Alex Gordon	.40	.15
❑	273	Jeff Weaver	.40	.15
❑	274	Jaret Wright	.40	.15
❑	275	Jose Hernandez	.40	.15
❑	276	Bruce Chen	.40	.15
❑	277	Todd Hollandsworth	.40	.15
❑	278	Wade Miller	.40	.15
❑	279	Luke Prokopec	.40	.15
❑	280	Rafael Soriano RC	.40	.15
❑	281	Damion Easley	.40	.15
❑	282	Darren Oliver	.40	.15
❑	283	Brandon Duckworth RC	.40	.15
❑	284	Aaron Herr	.40	.15
❑	285	Ray Durham	.40	.15
❑	286	Wilmy Caceras RC	.40	.15
❑	287	Ugueth Urbina	.40	.15
❑	288	Scott Seabol	.40	.15
❑	289	Lance Niekro RC	.60	.25
❑	290	Trot Nixon	.40	.15
❑	291	Adam Kennedy	.40	.15
❑	292	Brian Schmitt RC	.40	.15
❑	293	Grant Roberts	.40	.15
❑	294	Benny Agbayani	.40	.15
❑	295	Travis Lee	.40	.15
❑	296	Erick Almonte RC	.40	.15
❑	297	Jim Thome	.60	.25
❑	298	Eric Young	.40	.15
❑	299	Dan Denham RC	.40	.15
❑	300	Boof Bonser RC	.40	.15
❑	301	Denny Neagle	.40	.15
❑	302	Kenny Rogers	.40	.15
❑	303	J.D. Closser	.40	.15
❑	304	Chase Utley RC	12.00	5.00
❑	305	Rey Sanchez	.40	.15
❑	306	Sean McGowan	.40	.15
❑	307	Justin Pope RC	.40	.15
❑	308	Torii Hunter	.40	.15
❑	309	B.J. Surhoff	.40	.15
❑	310	Aaron Heilman RC	.50	.20
❑	311	Gabe Gross RC	.60	.25
❑	312	Lee Stevens	.40	.15
❑	313	Todd Hundley	.40	.15
❑	314	Macay McBride RC	1.00	.40
❑	315	Edgar Martinez	.60	.25
❑	316	Omar Vizquel	.60	.25
❑	317	Reggie Sanders	.40	.15
❑	318	John-Ford Griffin RC	.40	.15
❑	319	T.Salmon UER Glaus Photo	.40	.15
❑	320	Pokey Reese	.40	.15
❑	321	Jay Payton	.40	.15
❑	322	Doug Glanville	.40	.15
❑	323	Greg Vaughn	.40	.15
❑	324	Ruben Sierra	.40	.15
❑	325	Kip Wells	.40	.15
❑	326	Carl Everett	.40	.15
❑	327	Garret Anderson	.40	.15
❑	328	Jay Bell	.40	.15
❑	329	Barry Larkin	.60	.25

❑ 330 Jeff Mathis RC .60 .25
❑ 331 Adrian Gonzalez SP 2.00 .75
❑ 332 Juan Rivera SP 2.00 .75
❑ 333 Tony Alvarez SP 2.00 .75
❑ 334 Xavier Nady SP 2.00 .75
❑ 335 Josh Hamilton SP 2.00 .75
❑ 336 Will Smith SP RC 2.00 .75
❑ 337 Israel Alcantara SP 2.00 .75
❑ 338 Chris George SP 2.00 .75
❑ 339 Sean Burroughs SP 2.00 .75
❑ 340 Jack Cust SP 2.00 .75
❑ 341 Henry Mateo SP RC 2.00 .75
❑ 342 Carlos Pena SP 2.00 .75
❑ 343 J.R. House SP 2.00 .75
❑ 344 Carlos Silva SP 2.00 .75
❑ 345 Mike Rivera SP RC 2.00 .75
❑ 346 Adam Johnson SP 2.00 .75
❑ 347 Scott Heard SP 2.00 .75
❑ 348 Alex Cintron SP 2.00 .75
❑ 349 Miguel Cabrera SP 8.00 3.00
❑ 350 Nick Johnson SP 2.00 .75
❑ 351 Albert Pujols SP RC 80.00 40.00
❑ 352 Ichiro Suzuki SP RC 30.00 12.50
❑ 353 Carlos Delgado SP 2.00 .75
❑ 354 Troy Glaus SP 2.00 .75
❑ 355 Sammy Sosa SP 3.00 1.25
❑ 356 Ivan Rodriguez SP 3.00 1.25
❑ 357 Vladimir Guerrero SP 3.00 1.25
❑ 358 Manny Ramirez Sox SP 3.00 1.25
❑ 359 Luis Gonzalez SP 2.00 .75
❑ 360 Roy Oswalt SP 3.00 1.25
❑ 361 Moises Alou SP 2.00 .75
❑ 362 Juan Gonzalez SP 2.00 .75
❑ 363 Tony Gwynn SP 4.00 1.50
❑ 364 Hideo Nomo SP 3.00 1.25
❑ 365 Tsuyoshi Shinjo SP RC 3.00 1.25
❑ 366 Kazuhiro Sasaki SP 2.00 .75
❑ 367 Cal Ripken SP 10.00 4.00
❑ 368 Rafael Palmeiro SP 3.00 1.25
❑ 369 J.D. Drew SP 2.00 .75
❑ 370 Doug Mientkiewicz SP 2.00 .75
❑ 371 Jeff Bagwell SP 3.00 1.25
❑ 372 Darin Erstad SP 2.00 .75
❑ 373 Tom Gordon SP 2.00 .75
❑ 374 Ben Petrick SP 2.00 .75
❑ 375 Eric Milton SP 2.00 .75
❑ 376 Nomar Garciaparra SP 5.00 2.00
❑ 377 Julio Lugo SP 2.00 .75
❑ 378 Tino Martinez SP 3.00 1.25
❑ 379 Javier Vazquez SP 2.00 .75
❑ 380 Jeremy Giambi SP 2.00 .75
❑ 381 Marty Cordova SP 2.00 .75
❑ 382 Adrian Beltre SP 2.00 .75
❑ 383 John Burkett SP 2.00 .75
❑ 384 Aaron Boone SP 2.00 .75
❑ 385 Eric Chavez SP 2.00 .75
❑ 386 Curt Schilling SP 2.00 .75
❑ 387 Cory Lidle UER SP 2.00 .75
❑ 388 Jason Schmidt SP 2.00 .75
❑ 389 Johnny Damon SP 3.00 1.25
❑ 390 Steve Finley SP 2.00 .75
❑ 391 Edgardo Alfonzo SP 2.00 .75
❑ 392 Jose Valentin SP 2.00 .75
❑ 393 Jose Canseco SP 3.00 1.25
❑ 394 Ryan Klesko SP 2.00 .75
❑ 395 David Cone SP 2.00 .75
❑ 396 Jason Kendall UER SP 2.00 .75
❑ 397 Placido Polanco SP 2.00 .75
❑ 398 Glendon Rusch SP 2.00 .75
❑ 399 Aaron Sele SP 2.00 .75
❑ 400 D'Angelo Jimenez SP 2.00 .75
❑ 401 Mark Grace SP 3.00 1.25
❑ 402 Al Leiter SP 2.00 .75
❑ 403 Brian Jordan SP 2.00 .75
❑ 404 Phil Nevin SP 2.00 .75
❑ 405 Brent Abernathy SP 2.00 .75
❑ 406 Kerry Wood SP 2.00 .75
❑ 407 Alex Gonzalez SP 2.00 .75
❑ 408 Robert Fick SP 2.00 .75
❑ 409 Dmitri Young UER SP 2.00 .75
❑ 410 Wes Helms SP 2.00 .75
❑ 411 Trevor Hoffman SP 2.00 .75
❑ 412 Rickey Henderson SP 3.00 1.25
❑ 413 Bobby Higginson SP 2.00 .75
❑ 414 Gary Sheffield SP 2.00 .75
❑ 415 Darryl Kile SP 2.00 .75
❑ 416 Richie Sexson SP 2.00 .75
❑ 417 Frank Menechino SP RC 2.00 .75
❑ 418 Javy Lopez SP 2.00 .75
❑ 419 Carlos Lee SP 2.00 .75
❑ 420 Jon Lieber SP 2.00 .75
❑ 421 Hank Blalock SP RC 6.00 2.50
❑ 422 Marlon Byrd SP RC .40 .15
❑ 423 Jason Kinchen SP RC 2.00 .75
❑ 424 Morgan Ensberg SP RC 5.00 2.00
❑ 425 Greg Nash SP RC 2.00 .75
❑ 426 Dennis Tankersley SP RC 2.00 .75
❑ 427 Nate Murphy SP RC 2.00 .75
❑ 428 Chris Smith SP RC 2.00 .75
❑ 429 Jake Gautreau SP RC 2.00 .75
❑ 430 John VanBenschoten SP RC 2.00 .75
❑ 431 Travis Thompson SP RC 2.00 .75
❑ 432 Orlando Hudson SP RC 3.00 1.25
❑ 433 Jerome Williams SP RC 3.00 1.25
❑ 434 Kevin Reese SP RC 2.00 .75
❑ 435 Ed Rogers SP RC 2.00 .75
❑ 436 Ryan Jamison SP RC 2.00 .75
❑ 437 Adam Pettyjohn SP RC 2.00 .75
❑ 438 Hee Seop Choi SP RC 3.00 1.25
❑ 439 Justin Morneau SP RC 12.00 5.00
❑ 440 Mitch Jones SP RC 2.00 .75

2002 Bowman Heritage

❑ COMP.SET w/o SP's (324) 50.00 25.00
❑ COMMON CARD (1-439) .40 .15
❑ COMMON SP 2.00 .75
❑ 1 Brent Abernathy .40 .15
❑ 2 Jermaine Dye .40 .15
❑ 3 James Shanks RC .40 .15
❑ 4 Chris Flinn RC .40 .15
❑ 5 Mike Peeples SP RC 2.00 .75
❑ 6 Gary Sheffield .40 .15
❑ 7 Livan Hernandez SP 2.00 .75
❑ 8 Jeff Austin RC .40 .15
❑ 9 Jeremy Giambi .40 .15
❑ 10 Adam Roller RC .40 .15
❑ 11 Sandy Alomar Jr. SP 2.00 .75
❑ 12 Matt Williams SP 2.00 .75
❑ 13 Hee Seop Choi .40 .15
❑ 14 Jose Offerman .40 .15
❑ 15 Robin Ventura .40 .15
❑ 16 Craig Biggio .60 .25
❑ 17 David Wells .40 .15
❑ 18 Rob Henkel RC .40 .15
❑ 19 Edgar Martinez .60 .25
❑ 20 Matt Morris SP 2.00 .75
❑ 21 Jose Valentin .40 .15
❑ 22 Barry Bonds 2.50 1.00
❑ 23 Justin Schuda RC .40 .15
❑ 24 Josh Phelps .40 .15
❑ 25 John Rodriguez RC .50 .20
❑ 26 Angel Pagan RC .50 .20
❑ 27 Aramis Ramirez .40 .15
❑ 28 Jack Wilson .40 .15
❑ 29 Roger Clemens 2.00 .75
❑ 30 Kazuhisa Ishii RC .50 .20
❑ 31 Carlos Beltran .40 .15
❑ 32 Drew Henson SP 2.00 .75
❑ 33 Kevin Young SP 2.00 .75
❑ 34 Juan Cruz SP 2.00 .75
❑ 35 Curtis Legendre RC .40 .15
❑ 36 Jose Morban RC .40 .15
❑ 37 Ricardo Cordova SP RC 2.00 .75
❑ 38 Adam Everett .40 .15
❑ 39 Mark Prior .60 .25
❑ 40 Jose Bautista RC 1.00 .40
❑ 41 Travis Foley RC .40 .15
❑ 42 Kerry Wood .40 .15
❑ 43 B.J. Surhoff .40 .15
❑ 44 Moises Alou .40 .15
❑ 45 Joey Hammond .40 .15
❑ 46 Eric Bruntlett RC .40 .15
❑ 47 Carlos Guillen .40 .15
❑ 48 Joe Crede .40 .15
❑ 49 Dan Phillips RC .40 .15
❑ 50 Jason LaRue .40 .15
❑ 51 Javy Lopez .40 .15
❑ 52 Larry Bigbie SP 2.00 .75
❑ 53 Chris Baker RC .40 .15
❑ 54 Marty Cordova .40 .15
❑ 55 C.C. Sabathia .40 .15
❑ 56 Mike Piazza 1.50 .60
❑ 57 Brian Giles .40 .15
❑ 58 Mike Bordick SP 2.00 .75
❑ 59 Tyler Houston SP 2.00 .75
❑ 60 Gabe Kapler .40 .15
❑ 61 Ben Broussard .40 .15
❑ 62 Steve Finley SP 2.00 .75
❑ 63 Koyie Hill .40 .15
❑ 64 Jeff D'Amico .40 .15
❑ 65 Edwin Almonte RC .40 .15
❑ 66 Pedro Martinez .60 .25
❑ 66B Nomar Garciaparra 66 1.50 .60
❑ 67 Travis Fryman SP 2.00 .75
❑ 68 Brady Clark SP 2.00 .75
❑ 69 Reed Johnson SP RC 4.00 1.50
❑ 70 Mark Grace SP 3.00 1.25
❑ 71 Tony Batista SP 2.00 .75
❑ 72 Roy Oswalt .40 .15
❑ 73 Pat Burrell SP 2.00 .75
❑ 74 Dennis Tankersley .40 .15
❑ 75 Ramon Ortiz .40 .15
❑ 76 Neal Frendling SP RC 2.00 .75
❑ 77 Omar Vizquel SP 3.00 1.25
❑ 78 Hideo Nomo 1.00 .40
❑ 79 Orlando Hernandez SP 2.00 .75
❑ 80 Andy Pettitte .60 .25
❑ 81 Cole Barthel RC .40 .15
❑ 82 Bret Boone .40 .15
❑ 83 Alfonso Soriano .40 .15
❑ 84 Brandon Duckworth .40 .15
❑ 85 Ben Grieve .40 .15
❑ 86 Mike Rosamond SP RC 2.00 .75
❑ 87 Luke Prokopec .40 .15
❑ 88 Chone Figgins RC 1.50 .60
❑ 89 Rick Ankiel SP 2.00 .75
❑ 90 David Eckstein .40 .15
❑ 91 Corey Koskie .40 .15
❑ 92 David Justice .40 .15
❑ 93 Jimmy Alvarez RC .40 .15
❑ 94 Jason Schmidt .40 .15
❑ 95 Reggie Sanders .40 .15
❑ 96 Victor Alvarez RC .40 .15
❑ 97 Brett Roneberg RC .40 .15
❑ 98 D'Angelo Jimenez .40 .15
❑ 99 Hank Blalock .60 .25
❑ 100 Juan Rivera .40 .15
❑ 101 Mark Buehrle SP 2.00 .75
❑ 102 Juan Uribe .40 .15
❑ 103 Royce Clayton SP 2.00 .75
❑ 104 Brett Kay RC .40 .15
❑ 105 John Olerud .40 .15
❑ 106 Richie Sexson .40 .15
❑ 107 Chipper Jones 1.00 .40
❑ 108 Adam Dunn .40 .15
❑ 109 Tim Salmon SP 3.00 1.25
❑ 110 Eric Karros .40 .15
❑ 111 Jose Vidro .40 .15
❑ 112 Jerry Hairston Jr. .40 .15
❑ 113 Anastacio Martinez RC .40 .15
❑ 114 Robert Fick SP 2.00 .75
❑ 115 Randy Johnson 1.00 .40
❑ 116 Trot Nixon SP 2.00 .75
❑ 117 Nick Bierbrodt SP 2.00 .75
❑ 118 Jim Edmonds .40 .15
❑ 119 Rafael Palmeiro .60 .25
❑ 120 Jose Macias .40 .15
❑ 121 Josh Beckett .40 .15
❑ 122 Sean Douglass .40 .15
❑ 123 Jeff Kent .40 .15

❑ 124 Tim Redding .40 .15
❑ 125 Xavier Nady .40 .15
❑ 126 Carl Everett .40 .15
❑ 127 Joe Randa .40 .15
❑ 128 Luke Hudson SP 2.00 .75
❑ 129 Eric Miller RC .40 .15
❑ 130 Melvin Mora .40 .15
❑ 131 Adrian Gonzalez .40 .15
❑ 132 Larry Walker SP 2.00 .75
❑ 133 Nic Jackson SP RC 2.00 .75
❑ 134 Mike Lowell SP 2.00 .75
❑ 135 Jim Thome .60 .25
❑ 136 Eric Milton .40 .15
❑ 137 Rich Thompson SP RC 2.00 .75
❑ 138 Placido Polanco SP 2.00 .75
❑ 139 Juan Pierre .40 .15
❑ 140 David Segui .40 .15
❑ 141 Chuck Finley .40 .15
❑ 142 Felipe Lopez .40 .15
❑ 143 Toby Hall .40 .15
❑ 144 Fred Bastardo RC .40 .15
❑ 145 Troy Glaus .40 .15
❑ 146 Todd Helton .60 .25
❑ 147 Ruben Gotay SP RC 3.00 1.25
❑ 148 Darin Erstad .40 .15
❑ 149 Ryan Gripp SP RC 2.00 .75
❑ 150 Orlando Cabrera .40 .15
❑ 151 Jason Young RC .40 .15
❑ 152 Sterling Hitchcock SP 2.00 .75
❑ 153 Miguel Tejada .40 .15
❑ 154 Al Leiter .40 .15
❑ 155 Taylor Buchholz RC .50 .20
❑ 156 Juan M. Gonzalez RC .40 .15
❑ 157 Damion Easley .40 .15
❑ 158 Jimmy Gobble RC .40 .15
❑ 159 Dennis Ulacia SP RC 2.00 .75
❑ 160 Shane Reynolds SP 2.00 .75
❑ 161 Javier Colina .40 .15
❑ 162 Frank Thomas 1.00 .40
❑ 163 Chuck Knoblauch .40 .15
❑ 164 Sean Burroughs .40 .15
❑ 165 Greg Maddux 1.50 .60
❑ 166 Jason Ellison RC .75 .30
❑ 167 Tony Womack .40 .15
❑ 168 Randall Shelley SP RC 2.00 .75
❑ 169 Jason Marquis .40 .15
❑ 170 Brian Jordan .40 .15
❑ 171 Vicente Padilla .40 .15
❑ 172 Barry Zito .40 .15
❑ 173 Matt Allegra SP RC 2.00 .75
❑ 174 Ralph Santana SP RC 2.00 .75
❑ 175 Carlos Lee .40 .15
❑ 176 Richard Hidalgo SP 2.00 .75
❑ 177 Kevin Deaton RC .40 .15
❑ 178 Juan Encarnacion .40 .15
❑ 179 Mark Quinn .40 .15
❑ 180 Rafael Furcal .40 .15
❑ 181 G.Anderson UER Figgins .40 .15
❑ 182 David Wright RC 20.00 8.00
❑ 183 Jose Reyes .60 .25
❑ 184 Mario Ramos SP RC 2.00 .75
❑ 185 J.D. Drew .40 .15
❑ 186 Juan Gonzalez .40 .15
❑ 187 Nick Neugebauer .40 .15
❑ 188 Alejandro Giron RC .40 .15
❑ 189 John Burkett .40 .15
❑ 190 Ben Sheets .40 .15
❑ 191 Vinny Castilla SP 2.00 .75
❑ 192 Cory Lidle .40 .15
❑ 193 Fernando Vina .40 .15
❑ 194 Russell Branyan SP 2.00 .75
❑ 195 Ben Davis .40 .15
❑ 196 Angel Berroa .40 .15
❑ 197 Alex Gonzalez .40 .15
❑ 198 Jared Sandberg .40 .15
❑ 199 Travis Lee SP 2.00 .75
❑ 200 Luis DePaula SP RC 2.00 .75
❑ 201 Ramon Hernandez SP 2.00 .75
❑ 202 Brandon Inge .40 .15
❑ 203 Aubrey Huff .40 .15
❑ 204 Mike Rivera .40 .15
❑ 205 Brad Nelson RC .40 .15
❑ 206 Colt Griffin SP RC 2.00 .75
❑ 207 Joel Pineiro .40 .15
❑ 208 Adam Pettyjohn .40 .15
❑ 209 Mark Redman .40 .15
❑ 210 Roberto Alomar SP 3.00 1.25
❑ 211 Denny Neagle .40 .15
❑ 212 Adam Kennedy .40 .15
❑ 213 Jason Arnold SP RC 2.00 .75
❑ 214 Jamie Moyer .40 .15
❑ 215 Aaron Boone .40 .15
❑ 216 Doug Glanville .40 .15
❑ 217 Nick Johnson SP 2.00 .75
❑ 218 Mike Cameron SP 2.00 .75
❑ 219 Tim Wakefield SP 2.00 .75
❑ 220 Todd Stottlemyre SP 2.00 .75
❑ 221 Mo Vaughn SP 2.00 .75
❑ 222 Vladimir Guerrero 1.00 .40
❑ 223 Bill Ortega .40 .15
❑ 224 Kevin Brown .40 .15
❑ 225 Peter Bergeron SP 2.00 .75
❑ 226 Shannon Stewart SP 2.00 .75
❑ 227 Eric Chavez .40 .15
❑ 228 Clint Weibl RC .40 .15
❑ 229 Todd Hollandsworth SP 2.00 .75
❑ 230 Jeff Bagwell .60 .25
❑ 231 Chad Qualls RC .50 .20
❑ 232 Ben Howard RC .40 .15
❑ 233 Rondell White SP 2.00 .75
❑ 234 Fred McGriff .60 .25
❑ 235 Steve Cox SP 2.00 .75
❑ 236 Chris Tritle RC .40 .15
❑ 237 Eric Valent .40 .15
❑ 238 Joe Mauer RC 8.00 3.00
❑ 239 Shawn Green .40 .15
❑ 240 Jimmy Rollins .40 .15
❑ 241 Edgar Renteria .40 .15
❑ 242 Edwin Yan RC .40 .15
❑ 243 Noochie Varner RC .40 .15
❑ 244 Kris Benson SP 2.00 .75
❑ 245 Mike Hampton .40 .15
❑ 246 So Taguchi RC .50 .20
❑ 247 Sammy Sosa 1.00 .40
❑ 248 Terrence Long .40 .15
❑ 249 Jason Bay RC 5.00 2.00
❑ 250 Kevin Millar SP 2.00 .75
❑ 251 Albert Pujols 2.00 .75
❑ 252 Chris Latham RC .40 .15
❑ 253 Eric Byrnes .40 .15
❑ 254 Napoleon Calzado SP RC 2.00 .75
❑ 255 Bobby Higginson .40 .15
❑ 256 Ben Molina .40 .15
❑ 257 Torii Hunter SP 2.00 .75
❑ 258 Jason Giambi .40 .15
❑ 259 Bartolo Colon .40 .15
❑ 260 Benito Baez .40 .15
❑ 261 Ichiro Suzuki 2.00 .75
❑ 262 Mike Sweeney .40 .15
❑ 263 Brian West RC .40 .15
❑ 264 Brad Penny .40 .15
❑ 265 Kevin Millwood SP 2.00 .75
❑ 266 Orlando Hudson .40 .15
❑ 267 Doug Mientkiewicz .40 .15
❑ 268 Luis Gonzalez SP 2.00 .75
❑ 269 Jay Caligiuri RC .40 .15
❑ 270 Nate Cornejo SP 2.00 .75
❑ 271 Lee Stevens .40 .15
❑ 272 Eric Hinske .40 .15
❑ 273 Antwon Rollins RC .40 .15
❑ 274 Bobby Jenks RC 1.50 .60
❑ 275 Joe Mays .40 .15
❑ 276 Josh Shaffer RC .40 .15
❑ 277 Jonny Gomes RC 2.50 1.00
❑ 278 Bernie Williams .60 .25
❑ 279 Ed Rogers .40 .15
❑ 280 Carlos Delgado .40 .15
❑ 281 Raul Mondesi SP 2.00 .75
❑ 282 Jose Ortiz .40 .15
❑ 283 Cesar Izturis .40 .15
❑ 284 Ryan Dempster SP 2.00 .75
❑ 285 Brian Daubach .40 .15
❑ 286 Hansel Izquierdo RC .40 .15
❑ 287 Mike Lieberthal SP 2.00 .75
❑ 288 Marcus Thames .40 .15
❑ 289 Nomar Garciaparra 1.50 .60
❑ 290 Brad Fullmer .40 .15
❑ 291 Tino Martinez .60 .25
❑ 292 James Barrett RC .40 .15
❑ 293 Jacque Jones .40 .15
❑ 294 Nick Alvarez SP RC 2.00 .75
❑ 295 Jason Grove SP RC 2.00 .75
❑ 296 Mike Wilson SP RC 2.00 .75
❑ 297 J.T. Snow .40 .15
❑ 298 Cliff Floyd .40 .15
❑ 299 Todd Hundley SP 2.00 .75
❑ 300 Tony Clark SP 2.00 .75
❑ 301 Demetrius Heath RC .40 .15
❑ 302 Morgan Ensberg .40 .15
❑ 303 Cristian Guzman .40 .15
❑ 304 Frank Catalanotto .40 .15
❑ 305 Jeff Weaver .40 .15
❑ 306 Tim Hudson .40 .15
❑ 307 Scott Wiggins SP RC 2.00 .75
❑ 308 Shea Hillenbrand SP 2.00 .75
❑ 309 Todd Walker SP 2.00 .75
❑ 310 Tsuyoshi Shinjo .40 .15
❑ 311 Adrian Beltre .40 .15
❑ 312 Craig Kuzmic RC .40 .15
❑ 313 Paul Konerko .40 .15
❑ 314 Scott Hairston RC .50 .20
❑ 315 Chan Ho Park .40 .15
❑ 316 Jorge Posada .60 .25
❑ 317 Chris Snelling RC .75 .30
❑ 318 Keith Foulke .40 .15
❑ 319 John Smoltz .60 .25
❑ 320 Ryan Church SP RC 4.00 1.50
❑ 321 Mike Mussina .60 .25
❑ 322 Tony Armas Jr. SP 2.00 .75
❑ 323 Craig Counsell .40 .15
❑ 324 Marcus Giles .40 .15
❑ 325 Greg Vaughn .40 .15
❑ 326 Curt Schilling .40 .15
❑ 327 Jeromy Burnitz .40 .15
❑ 328 Eric Byrnes .40 .15
❑ 329 Johnny Damon Sox .60 .25
❑ 330 Michael Floyd SP RC 2.00 .75
❑ 331 Edgardo Alfonzo .40 .15
❑ 332 Jeremy Hill RC .40 .15
❑ 333 Josh Bonifay RC .40 .15
❑ 334 Byung-Hyun Kim .40 .15
❑ 335 Keith Ginter .40 .15
❑ 336 Ronald Acuna SP RC 2.00 .75
❑ 337 Mike Hill SP RC 2.00 .75
❑ 338 Sean Casey .40 .15
❑ 339 Matt Anderson SP 2.00 .75
❑ 340 Dan Wright .40 .15
❑ 341 Ben Petrick .40 .15
❑ 342 Mike Sirotka SP 2.00 .75
❑ 343 Alex Rodriguez 1.50 .60
❑ 344 Einar Diaz .40 .15
❑ 345 Derek Jeter 2.50 1.00
❑ 346 Jeff Conine .40 .15
❑ 347 Ray Durham SP 2.00 .75
❑ 348 Wilson Betemit SP 2.00 .75
❑ 349 Jeffrey Hammonds .40 .15
❑ 350 Dan Trumble RC .40 .15
❑ 351 Phil Nevin SP 2.00 .75
❑ 352 A.J. Burnett .40 .15
❑ 353 Bill Mueller .40 .15
❑ 354 Charles Nagy .40 .15
❑ 355 Rusty Greer SP 2.00 .75
❑ 356 Jason Botts RC .50 .20
❑ 357 Magglio Ordonez .40 .15
❑ 358 Kevin Appier .40 .15
❑ 359 Brad Radke .40 .15
❑ 360 Chris George .40 .15
❑ 361 Chris Piersoll RC .40 .15
❑ 362 Ivan Rodriguez .60 .25
❑ 363 Jim Kavourias RC .40 .15
❑ 364 Rick Helling SP 2.00 .75
❑ 365 Dean Palmer .40 .15
❑ 366 Rich Aurilia SP 2.00 .75
❑ 367 Ryan Vogelsong .40 .15
❑ 368 Matt Lawton .40 .15
❑ 369 Wade Miller .40 .15
❑ 370 Dustin Hermanson .40 .15
❑ 371 Craig Wilson .40 .15
❑ 372 Todd Zeile SP 2.00 .75
❑ 373 Jon Guzman RC .40 .15
❑ 374 Ellis Burks .40 .15
❑ 375 Robert Cosby SP RC 2.00 .75
❑ 376 Jason Kendall .40 .15
❑ 377 Scott Rolen SP 3.00 1.25
❑ 378 Andruw Jones .60 .25
❑ 379 Greg Sain RC .40 .15
❑ 380 Paul LoDuca .40 .15
❑ 381 Scotty Layfield RC .40 .15

- ❑ 382 Tomo Ohka .40 .15
- ❑ 383 Garrett Guzman RC .40 .15
- ❑ 384 Jack Cust SP 2.00 .75
- ❑ 385 Shayne Wright RC .40 .15
- ❑ 386 Derrek Lee .60 .25
- ❑ 387 Jesus Medrano RC .40 .15
- ❑ 388 Javier Vazquez .40 .15
- ❑ 389 Preston Wilson SP 2.00 .75
- ❑ 390 Gavin Floyd RC 1.00 .40
- ❑ 391 Sidney Ponson SP 2.00 .75
- ❑ 392 Jose Hernandez .40 .15
- ❑ 393 Scott Erickson SP 2.00 .75
- ❑ 394 Jose Valverde RC .40 .15
- ❑ 395 Mark Hamilton SP RC 2.00 .75
- ❑ 396 Brad Cresse .40 .15
- ❑ 397 Danny Bautista .40 .15
- ❑ 398 Ray Lankford SP 2.00 .75
- ❑ 399 Miguel Batista SP 2.00 .75
- ❑ 400 Brent Butler .40 .15
- ❑ 401 Manny Delcarmen SP RC 3.00 1.25
- ❑ 402 Kyle Farnsworth SP 2.00 .75
- ❑ 403 Freddy Garcia .40 .15
- ❑ 404 Joe Jiannetti RC .40 .15
- ❑ 405 Josh Barfield RC 2.50 1.00
- ❑ 406 Corey Patterson .40 .15
- ❑ 407 Josh Towers .40 .15
- ❑ 408 Carlos Pena .40 .15
- ❑ 409 Jeff Cirillo .40 .15
- ❑ 410 Jon Lieber .40 .15
- ❑ 411 Woody Williams SP 2.00 .75
- ❑ 412 Richard Lane SP RC 2.00 .75
- ❑ 413 Alex Gonzalez .40 .15
- ❑ 414 Wilkin Ruan .40 .15
- ❑ 415 Geoff Jenkins .40 .15
- ❑ 416 Carlos Hernandez .40 .15
- ❑ 417 Matt Clement SP 2.00 .75
- ❑ 418 Jose Cruz Jr. .40 .15
- ❑ 419 Jake Mauer RC .40 .15
- ❑ 420 Matt Childers RC .40 .15
- ❑ 421 Tom Glavine SP 3.00 1.25
- ❑ 422 Ken Griffey Jr. 1.50 .60
- ❑ 423 Anderson Hernandez RC .40 .15
- ❑ 424 John Suomi RC .40 .15
- ❑ 425 Doug Sessions RC .40 .15
- ❑ 426 Jaret Wright .40 .15
- ❑ 427 Rolando Viera SP RC 2.00 .75
- ❑ 428 Aaron Sele .40 .15
- ❑ 429 Dmitri Young .40 .15
- ❑ 430 Ryan Klesko .40 .15
- ❑ 431 Kevin Tapani SP 2.00 .75
- ❑ 432 Joe Kennedy .40 .15
- ❑ 433 Austin Kearns .40 .15
- ❑ 434 Roger Cedeno SP 2.00 .75
- ❑ 435 Lance Berkman .40 .15
- ❑ 436 Frank Menechino .40 .15
- ❑ 437 Brett Myers .40 .15
- ❑ 438 Bob Abreu .40 .15
- ❑ 439 Shawn Estes SP 2.00 .75

2003 Bowman Heritage

- ❑ COMPLETE SET (300) 120.00 60.00
- ❑ 1 Jorge Posada .60 .25
- ❑ 2 Todd Helton .60 .25
- ❑ 3 Marcus Giles .40 .15
- ❑ 4 Eric Chavez .40 .15
- ❑ 5 Edgar Martinez .60 .25
- ❑ 6 Luis Gonzalez .40 .15
- ❑ 7 Corey Patterson .40 .15
- ❑ 8 Preston Wilson .40 .15
- ❑ 9 Ryan Klesko .40 .15
- ❑ 10 Randy Johnson 1.00 .40
- ❑ 11 Jose Guillen .40 .15
- ❑ 12 Carlos Lee .40 .15
- ❑ 13 Steve Finley .40 .15
- ❑ 14 A.J. Pierzynski .40 .15
- ❑ 15 Troy Glaus .40 .15
- ❑ 16 Darin Erstad .40 .15
- ❑ 17 Moises Alou .40 .15
- ❑ 18 Torii Hunter .40 .15
- ❑ 19 Marlon Byrd .40 .15
- ❑ 20 Mark Prior .60 .25
- ❑ 21 Shannon Stewart .40 .15
- ❑ 22 Craig Biggio .60 .25
- ❑ 23 Johnny Damon .60 .25
- ❑ 24 Robert Fick .40 .15
- ❑ 25 Jason Giambi .40 .15
- ❑ 26 Fernando Vina .40 .15
- ❑ 27 Aubrey Huff .40 .15
- ❑ 28 Benito Santiago .40 .15
- ❑ 29 Jay Gibbons .40 .15
- ❑ 30 Ken Griffey Jr. 1.50 .60
- ❑ 31 Rocco Baldelli .40 .15
- ❑ 32 Pat Burrell .40 .15
- ❑ 33 A.J. Burnett .40 .15
- ❑ 34 Omar Vizquel .60 .25
- ❑ 35 Greg Maddux 1.50 .60
- ❑ 36 Cliff Floyd .40 .15
- ❑ 37 C.C. Sabathia .40 .15
- ❑ 38 Geoff Jenkins .40 .15
- ❑ 39 Ty Wigginton .40 .15
- ❑ 40 Jeff Kent .40 .15
- ❑ 41 Orlando Hudson .40 .15
- ❑ 42 Edgardo Alfonzo .40 .15
- ❑ 43 Greg Myers .40 .15
- ❑ 44 Melvin Mora .40 .15
- ❑ 45 Sammy Sosa 1.00 .40
- ❑ 46 Russ Ortiz .40 .15
- ❑ 47 Josh Beckett .40 .15
- ❑ 48 David Wells .40 .15
- ❑ 49 Woody Williams .40 .15
- ❑ 50 Alex Rodriguez 1.50 .60
- ❑ 51 Randy Wolf .40 .15
- ❑ 52 Carlos Beltran .40 .15
- ❑ 53 Austin Kearns .40 .15
- ❑ 54 Trot Nixon .40 .15
- ❑ 55 Ivan Rodriguez .60 .25
- ❑ 56 Shea Hillenbrand .40 .15
- ❑ 57 Roberto Alomar .60 .25
- ❑ 58 John Olerud .40 .15
- ❑ 59 Michael Young .60 .25
- ❑ 60 Garret Anderson .40 .15
- ❑ 61 Mike Lieberthal .40 .15
- ❑ 62 Adam Dunn .40 .15
- ❑ 63 Raul Ibanez .40 .15
- ❑ 64 Kenny Lofton .40 .15
- ❑ 65 Ichiro Suzuki 2.00 .75
- ❑ 66 Jarrod Washburn .40 .15
- ❑ 67 Shawn Chacon .40 .15
- ❑ 68 Alex Gonzalez .40 .15
- ❑ 69 Roy Halladay .40 .15
- ❑ 70 Vladimir Guerrero 1.00 .40
- ❑ 71 Hee Seop Choi .40 .15
- ❑ 72 Jody Gerut .40 .15
- ❑ 73 Ray Durham .40 .15
- ❑ 74 Mark Teixeira .60 .25
- ❑ 75 Hank Blalock .40 .15
- ❑ 76 Jerry Hairston Jr. .40 .15
- ❑ 77 Erubiel Durazo .40 .15
- ❑ 78 Frank Catalanotto .40 .15
- ❑ 79 Jacque Jones .40 .15
- ❑ 80 Bobby Abreu .40 .15
- ❑ 81 Mike Hampton .40 .15
- ❑ 82 Zach Day .40 .15
- ❑ 83 Jimmy Rollins .40 .15
- ❑ 84 Joel Pineiro .40 .15
- ❑ 85 Brett Myers .40 .15
- ❑ 86 Frank Thomas 1.00 .40
- ❑ 87 Aramis Ramirez .40 .15
- ❑ 88 Paul Lo Duca .40 .15
- ❑ 89 Dmitri Young .40 .15
- ❑ 90 Brian Giles .40 .15
- ❑ 91 Jose Cruz Jr. .40 .15
- ❑ 92 Derek Lowe .40 .15
- ❑ 93 Mark Buehrle .40 .15
- ❑ 94 Wade Miller .40 .15
- ❑ 95 Derek Jeter 2.50 1.00
- ❑ 96 Bret Boone .40 .15
- ❑ 97 Tony Batista .40 .15
- ❑ 98 Sean Casey .40 .15
- ❑ 99 Eric Hinske .40 .15
- ❑ 100 Albert Pujols 2.00 .75
- ❑ 101 Runelvys Hernandez .40 .15
- ❑ 102 Vernon Wells .40 .15
- ❑ 103 Kerry Wood .40 .15
- ❑ 104 Lance Berkman .40 .15
- ❑ 105 Alfonso Soriano .40 .15
- ❑ 106 Bill Mueller .40 .15
- ❑ 107 Bartolo Colon .40 .15
- ❑ 108 Andy Pettitte .60 .25
- ❑ 109 Rafael Furcal .40 .15
- ❑ 110 Dontrelle Willis 1.00 .40
- ❑ 111 Carl Crawford .40 .15
- ❑ 112 Scott Rolen .60 .25
- ❑ 113 Chipper Jones 1.00 .40
- ❑ 114 Magglio Ordonez .40 .15
- ❑ 115 Bernie Williams .60 .25
- ❑ 116 Roy Oswalt .40 .15
- ❑ 117 Kevin Brown .40 .15
- ❑ 118 Cristian Guzman .40 .15
- ❑ 119 Kazuhisa Ishii .40 .15
- ❑ 120 Larry Walker .40 .15
- ❑ 121 Miguel Tejada .40 .15
- ❑ 122 Manny Ramirez .60 .25
- ❑ 123 Mike Mussina .60 .25
- ❑ 124 Mike Lowell .40 .15
- ❑ 125 Scott Podsednik .40 .15
- ❑ 126 Aaron Boone .40 .15
- ❑ 127 Carlos Delgado .40 .15
- ❑ 128 Jose Vidro .40 .15
- ❑ 129 Brad Radke .40 .15
- ❑ 130 Rafael Palmeiro .60 .25
- ❑ 131 Mark Mulder .40 .15
- ❑ 132 Jason Schmidt .40 .15
- ❑ 133 Gary Sheffield .40 .15
- ❑ 134 Richie Sexson .40 .15
- ❑ 135 Barry Zito .40 .15
- ❑ 136 Tom Glavine .60 .25
- ❑ 137 Jim Edmonds .40 .15
- ❑ 138 Andruw Jones .60 .25
- ❑ 139 Pedro Martinez .60 .25
- ❑ 140 Curt Schilling .40 .15
- ❑ 141 Phil Nevin .40 .15
- ❑ 142 Nomar Garciaparra 1.50 .60
- ❑ 143 Vicente Padilla .40 .15
- ❑ 144 Kevin Millwood .40 .15
- ❑ 145 Shawn Green .40 .15
- ❑ 146 Jeff Bagwell .60 .25
- ❑ 147 Hideo Nomo 1.00 .40
- ❑ 148 Fred McGriff .60 .25
- ❑ 149 Matt Morris .40 .15
- ❑ 150 Roger Clemens 2.00 .75
- ❑ 151 Jerome Williams .40 .15
- ❑ 152 Orlando Cabrera .40 .15
- ❑ 153 Tim Hudson .40 .15
- ❑ 154 Mike Sweeney .40 .15
- ❑ 155 Jim Thome .60 .25
- ❑ 156 Rich Aurilia .40 .15
- ❑ 157 Mike Piazza 1.50 .60
- ❑ 158 Edgar Renteria .40 .15
- ❑ 159 Javy Lopez .40 .15
- ❑ 160 Jamie Moyer .40 .15
- ❑ 161 Miguel Cabrera DI 1.00 .40
- ❑ 162 Adam Loewen DI RC 1.00 .40
- ❑ 163 Jose Reyes DI .40 .15
- ❑ 164 Zack Greinke DI .40 .15
- ❑ 165 Gavin Floyd DI .40 .15
- ❑ 166 Jeremy Guthrie DI .40 .15
- ❑ 167 Victor Martinez DI .60 .25
- ❑ 168 Rich Harden DI .60 .25
- ❑ 169 Joe Mauer DI 1.00 .40
- ❑ 170 Khalil Greene DI 1.00 .40
- ❑ 171A Willie Mays 2.00 .75
- ❑ 171B Willie Mays DI 2.00 .75
- ❑ 171C Willie Mays KN 2.00 .75
- ❑ 172A Phil Rizzuto .60 .25
- ❑ 172B Phil Rizzuto DI .60 .25
- ❑ 172C Phil Rizzuto KN .60 .25
- ❑ 173A Al Kaline 1.00 .40
- ❑ 173B Al Kaline DI 1.00 .40
- ❑ 173C Al Kaline KN 1.00 .40

❑ 174A Warren Spahn .60 .25
❑ 174B Warren Spahn DI .60 .25
❑ 174C Warren Spahn KN .60 .25
❑ 175A Jimmy Piersall .40 .15
❑ 175B Jimmy Piersall DI .40 .15
❑ 175C Jimmy Piersall KN .40 .15
❑ 176A Luis Aparicio .40 .15
❑ 176B Luis Aparicio DI .40 .15
❑ 176C Luis Aparicio KN .40 .15
❑ 177A Whitey Ford .60 .25
❑ 177B Whitey Ford DI .60 .25
❑ 177C Whitey Ford KN .60 .25
❑ 178A Harmon Killebrew 1.00 .40
❑ 178B Harmon Killebrew DI 1.00 .40
❑ 178C Harmon Killebrew KN 1.00 .40
❑ 179A Duke Snider .60 .25
❑ 179B Duke Snider DI .60 .25
❑ 179C Duke Snider KN .60 .25
❑ 180A Roberto Clemente 2.50 1.00
❑ 180B Roberto Clemente DI 2.50 1.00
❑ 180C Roberto Clemente KN 2.50 1.00
❑ 181 David Martinez KN RC .40 .15
❑ 182 Felix Pie KN RC 4.00 1.50
❑ 183 Kevin Correia KN RC .40 .15
❑ 184 Brandon Webb KN RC 2.50 1.00
❑ 185 Matt Diaz KN RC .75 .30
❑ 186 Lew Ford KN RC .50 .20
❑ 187 Jeremy Griffiths KN RC .40 .15
❑ 188 Matt Hensley KN RC .40 .15
❑ 189 Danny Garcia KN RC .40 .15
❑ 190 Elizardo Ramirez KN RC .50 .20
❑ 191 Greg Aquino KN RC .40 .15
❑ 192 Felix Sanchez KN RC .40 .15
❑ 193 Kelly Shoppach KN RC .75 .30
❑ 194 Bubba Nelson KN RC .50 .20
❑ 195 Mike Oâ ™Keefe KN RC .40 .15
❑ 196 Hanley Ramirez KN RC 4.00 1.50
❑ 197 Todd Wellemeyer KN RC .40 .15
❑ 198 Dustin Moseley KN RC .40 .15
❑ 199 Eric Crozier KN RC .50 .20
❑ 200 Ryan Shealy KN RC 2.50 1.00
❑ 201 Jeremy Bonderman KN RC 2.50 1.00
❑ 202 Bo Hart KN RC .40 .15
❑ 203 Dusty Brown KN RC .40 .15
❑ 204 Rob Hammock KN RC .40 .15
❑ 205 Jorge Piedra KN RC .50 .20
❑ 206 Jason Kubel KN RC 1.50 .60
❑ 207 Stephen Randolph KN RC .40 .15
❑ 208 Andy Sisco KN RC .40 .15
❑ 209 Matt Kata KN RC .40 .15
❑ 210 Robinson Cano KN RC 8.00 3.00
❑ 211 Ben Francisco KN RC .40 .15
❑ 212 Arnie Munoz KN RC .40 .15
❑ 213 Ozzie Chavez KN RC .40 .15
❑ 214 Beau Kemp KN RC .40 .15
❑ 215 Travis Wong KN RC .50 .20
❑ 216 Brian McCann KN RC 6.00 2.50
❑ 217 Aquilino Lopez KN RC .40 .15
❑ 218 Bobby Basham KN RC .40 .15
❑ 219 Tim Olson KN RC .40 .15
❑ 220 Nathan Panther KN RC .40 .15
❑ 221 Wil Ledezma KN RC .40 .15
❑ 222 Josh Willingham KN RC 1.00 .40
❑ 223 David Cash KN RC .40 .15
❑ 224 Oscar Villarreal KN RC .40 .15
❑ 225 Jeff Duncan KN RC .40 .15
❑ 226 Dan Haren KN RC 1.00 .40
❑ 227 Michel Hernandez KN RC .40 .15
❑ 228 Matt Murton KN RC 2.00 .75
❑ 229 Clay Hensley KN RC .40 .15
❑ 230 Tyler Johnson KN RC .40 .15
❑ 231 Tyler Martin KN RC .40 .15
❑ 232 J.D. Durbin KN RC .40 .15
❑ 233 Shane Victorino KN RC .75 .30
❑ 234 Rajai Davis KN RC .40 .15
❑ 235 Chien-Ming Wang KN RC 5.00 2.00
❑ 236 Travis Ishikawa KN RC .75 .30
❑ 237 Eric Eckenstahler KN .40 .15
❑ 238 Dustin McGowan KN RC .50 .20
❑ 239 Prentice Redman KN RC .40 .15
❑ 240 Haj Turay KN RC .40 .15
❑ 241 Matt DeMarco KN RC .40 .15
❑ 242 Lou Palmisano KN RC .50 .20
❑ 243 Eric Reed KN RC .40 .15
❑ 244 Willie Eyre KN RC .40 .15
❑ 245 Ferdin Tejeda KN RC .40 .15
❑ 246 Michael Garciaparra KN RC .40 .15
❑ 247 Michael Hinckley KN RC .50 .20
❑ 248 Branden Florence KN RC .40 .15
❑ 249 Trent Oeltjen KN RC .50 .20
❑ 250 Mike Neu KN RC .40 .15
❑ 251 Chris Lubanski KN RC 1.00 .40
❑ 252 Brandon Wood KN RC 10.00 4.00
❑ 253 Delmon Young KN RC 5.00 2.00
❑ 254 Matt Harrison KN RC .75 .30
❑ 255 Chad Billingsley KN RC 3.00 1.25
❑ 256 Josh Anderson KN RC .50 .20
❑ 257 Brian McFall KN RC .40 .15
❑ 258 Ryan Wagner KN RC .40 .15
❑ 259 Billy Hogan KN RC .50 .20
❑ 260 Nate Spears KN RC .50 .20
❑ 261 Ryan Harvey KN RC 2.00 .75
❑ 262 Wes Littleton KN RC .50 .20
❑ 263 Xavier Paul KN RC .50 .20
❑ 264 Sean Rodriguez KN RC 2.00 .75
❑ 265 Brian Finch KN RC .40 .15
❑ 266 Josh Rainwater KN RC .50 .20
❑ 267 Brian Snyder KN RC .50 .20
❑ 268 Eric Duncan KN RC 2.00 .75
❑ 269 Rickie Weeks KN RC 3.00 1.25
❑ 270 Tim Battle KN RC .75 .30
❑ 271 Scott Beerer KN RC .40 .15
❑ 272 Aaron Hill KN RC .75 .30
❑ 273 Casey Abrams KN RC .40 .15
❑ 274 Jonathan Fulton KN RC .50 .20
❑ 275 Todd Jennings KN RC .50 .20
❑ 276 Jordan Pratt KN RC .50 .20
❑ 277 Tom Gorzelanny KN RC 1.25 .50
❑ 278 Matt Lorenzo KN RC .50 .20
❑ 279 Jarrod Saltalamacchia KN RC 5.002.00
❑ 280 Mike Wagner KN RC .40 .15

2004 Bowman Heritage

❑ COMPLETE SET (351) 300.00 175.00
❑ COMP.SET w/o SP's (300) 50.00 25.00
❑ SP STATED ODDS 1:3 HOBBY, 1:3 RETAIL
❑ SP's: 2/9/13/21/25/40B/46/48B/50/55/61
❑ SP's: 77/80/87/89/95/100/104/109/127/130
❑ SP's: 132/141/183A/189/204/206/208/210
❑ SP's: 213/216/220/224/228/234/240/243
❑ SP's: 246/249/259/268/270-271/282/291
❑ SP's: 304/318/327/334/342/348
❑ PLATES STATED ODDS 1:240 HOBBY
❑ PLATES PRINT RUN 1 #'d SET PER COLOR
❑ PLATES: BLACK, CYAN, MAGENTA, YELLOW
❑ NO PLATES PRICING DUE TO SCARCITY
❑ ROOP BINDER ODDS 1:240 HOBBY
❑ ROOP BINDER EXCH.DEADLINE 12/31/05
❑ 1 Tom Glavine .60 .25
❑ 2 Mike Piazza SP 8.00 3.00
❑ 3 Sidney Ponson .40 .15
❑ 4 Jerry Hairston Jr. .40 .15
❑ 5 Jermaine Dye .40 .15
❑ 6 Bobby Crosby .40 .15
❑ 7 Carlos Zambrano .40 .15
❑ 8 Moises Alou .40 .15
❑ 9 Alex Rodriguez SP 8.00 3.00
❑ 10 Derek Jeter 2.00 .75
❑ 11 Rafael Furcal .40 .15
❑ 12 J.D. Drew .40 .15
❑ 13 Joe Mauer SP 6.00 2.50
❑ 14 Brad Radke .40 .15
❑ 15 Johnny Damon .60 .25
❑ 16 Derek Lowe .40 .15
❑ 17 Pat Burrell .40 .15
❑ 18 Mike Lieberthal .40 .15
❑ 19 Cliff Lee .40 .15
❑ 20 Ronnie Belliard .40 .15
❑ 21 Eric Gagne SP 5.00 2.00
❑ 22 Brad Penny .40 .15
❑ 23 Al Kaline RET 1.50 .60
❑ 24 Mike Maroth .40 .15
❑ 25 Magglio Ordonez SP 5.00 2.00
❑ 26 Mark Buehrle .40 .15
❑ 27 Jack Wilson .40 .15
❑ 28 Oliver Perez .40 .15
❑ 29 Red Schoendienst RET .60 .25
❑ 30 Yadier Molina FY RC 2.00 .75
❑ 31 Ryan Freel .40 .15
❑ 32 Adam Dunn .40 .15
❑ 33 Paul Konerko .40 .15
❑ 34 Esteban Loaiza .40 .15
❑ 35 Ivan Rodriguez .60 .25
❑ 36 Carlos Guillen .40 .15
❑ 37 Adrian Beltre .40 .15
❑ 38 C.C. Sabathia .40 .15
❑ 39 Hideo Nomo 1.00 .40
❑ 40A Victor Martinez .40 .15
❑ 40B V.Martinez Pedro Stats SP 5.00 2.00
❑ 41 Bobby Abreu .40 .15
❑ 42 Randy Wolf .40 .15
❑ 43 Johnny Estrada .40 .15
❑ 44 Russ Ortiz .40 .15
❑ 45 Kenny Rogers .40 .15
❑ 46 Hank Blalock SP 5.00 2.00
❑ 47 David Ortiz 1.00 .40
❑ 48A Pedro Martinez .60 .25
❑ 48B P.Martinez Victor Stats SP 8.00 3.00
❑ 49 Austin Kearns .40 .15
❑ 50 Ken Griffey Jr. SP 8.00 3.00
❑ 51 Mark Prior .60 .25
❑ 52 Kerry Wood .40 .15
❑ 53 Eric Chavez .40 .15
❑ 54 Tim Hudson .40 .15
❑ 55 Rafael Palmeiro SP 8.00 3.00
❑ 56 Javy Lopez .40 .15
❑ 57 Jason Bay .40 .15
❑ 58 Craig Wilson .40 .15
❑ 59 Whitey Ford RET 1.00 .40
❑ 60 Jason Giambi .40 .15
❑ 61 Scott Rolen SP 8.00 3.00
❑ 62 Matt Morris .40 .15
❑ 63 Javier Vazquez .40 .15
❑ 64 Jim Thome .60 .25
❑ 65 Don Zimmer RET .60 .25
❑ 66 Shawn Green .40 .15
❑ 67 Don Larsen RET 1.00 .40
❑ 68 Gary Sheffield .40 .15
❑ 69 Jorge Posada .60 .25
❑ 70 Bernie Williams .60 .25
❑ 71 Chipper Jones 1.00 .40
❑ 72 Andruw Jones .60 .25
❑ 73 John Thomson .40 .15
❑ 74 Jim Edmonds .40 .15
❑ 75 Albert Pujols 2.00 .75
❑ 76 Chris Carpenter .40 .15
❑ 77 Aubrey Huff SP 5.00 2.00
❑ 78 Carl Crawford .40 .15
❑ 79 Victor Zambrano .40 .15
❑ 80 Alfonso Soriano SP 5.00 2.00
❑ 81 Lance Berkman .40 .15
❑ 82 Mike Sweeney .40 .15
❑ 83 Ken Harvey .40 .15
❑ 84 Angel Berroa .40 .15
❑ 85 A.J. Burnett .40 .15
❑ 86 Mike Lowell .40 .15
❑ 87 Miguel Cabrera SP 8.00 3.00
❑ 88 Preston Wilson .40 .15
❑ 89 Todd Helton SP 8.00 3.00
❑ 90 Larry Walker Cards .60 .25
❑ 91 Vladimir Guerrero 1.00 .40
❑ 92 Garret Anderson .40 .15
❑ 93 Bartolo Colon .40 .15
❑ 94 Scott Hairston .40 .15
❑ 95 Richie Sexson SP 5.00 2.00
❑ 96 Sean Casey .40 .15
❑ 97 John Podres RET .60 .25
❑ 98 Andy Pettitte .60 .25
❑ 99 Roy Oswalt .40 .15
❑ 100 Roger Clemens SP 8.00 3.00

❑ 101 Scott Podsednik	.40	.15
❑ 102 Ben Sheets	.40	.15
❑ 103 Lyle Overbay	.40	.15
❑ 104 Nick Johnson SP	5.00	2.00
❑ 105 Zach Day	.40	.15
❑ 106 Jose Reyes	.40	.15
❑ 107 Khalil Greene	.60	.25
❑ 108 Sean Burroughs	.40	.15
❑ 109 David Wells SP	5.00	2.00
❑ 110 Jason Schmidt	.40	.15
❑ 111 Neifi Perez	.40	.15
❑ 112 Edgar Renteria	.40	.15
❑ 113 Rich Aurilia	.40	.15
❑ 114 Edgar Martinez	.60	.25
❑ 115 Joel Pineiro	.40	.15
❑ 116 Mark Teixeira	.60	.25
❑ 117 Michael Young	.40	.15
❑ 118 Ricardo Rodriguez	.40	.15
❑ 119 Carlos Delgado	.40	.15
❑ 120 Roy Halladay	.40	.15
❑ 121 Jose Guillen	.40	.15
❑ 122 Troy Glaus	.40	.15
❑ 123 Shea Hillenbrand	.40	.15
❑ 124 Luis Gonzalez	.40	.15
❑ 125 Horacio Ramirez	.40	.15
❑ 126 Melvin Mora	.40	.15
❑ 127 Miguel Tejada SP	5.00	2.00
❑ 128 Manny Ramirez	.60	.25
❑ 129 Tim Wakefield	.40	.15
❑ 130 Curt Schilling SP	8.00	3.00
❑ 131 Aramis Ramirez	.40	.15
❑ 132 Sammy Sosa SP	8.00	3.00
❑ 133 Matt Clement	.40	.15
❑ 134 Juan Uribe	.40	.15
❑ 135 Dontrelle Willis	.60	.25
❑ 136 Paul Lo Duca	.40	.15
❑ 137 Juan Pierre	.40	.15
❑ 138 Kevin Brown	.40	.15
❑ 139 B.Giles/M.Giles	.40	.15
❑ 140 Brian Giles	.40	.15
❑ 141 Nomar Garciaparra SP	8.00	3.00
❑ 142 Cesar Izturis	.40	.15
❑ 143 Don Newcombe RET	.60	.25
❑ 144 Craig Biggio	.60	.25
❑ 145 Carlos Beltran	.40	.15
❑ 146 Torii Hunter	.40	.15
❑ 147 Livan Hernandez	.40	.15
❑ 148 Cliff Floyd	.40	.15
❑ 149 Barry Zito	.40	.15
❑ 150 Mark Mulder	.40	.15
❑ 151 Rocco Baldelli	.40	.15
❑ 152 Bret Boone	.40	.15
❑ 153 Jamie Moyer	.40	.15
❑ 154 Ichiro Suzuki	2.00	.75
❑ 155 Brett Myers	.40	.15
❑ 156 Carl Pavano	.40	.15
❑ 157 Josh Beckett	.40	.15
❑ 158 Randy Johnson	1.00	.40
❑ 159 Trot Nixon	.40	.15
❑ 160 Dmitri Young	.40	.15
❑ 161 Jacque Jones	.40	.15
❑ 162 Lew Ford	.40	.15
❑ 163 Jose Vidro	.40	.15
❑ 164 Mark Kotsay	.40	.15
❑ 165 A.J. Pierzynski	.40	.15
❑ 166 Dewon Brazelton	.40	.15
❑ 167 Jeromy Burnitz	.40	.15
❑ 168 Johan Santana	1.00	.40
❑ 169 Greg Maddux	1.50	.60
❑ 170 Carl Erskine RET	.60	.25
❑ 171 Robin Roberts RET	.60	.25
❑ 172 Freddy Garcia	.40	.15
❑ 173 Carlos Lee	.40	.15
❑ 174 Jeff Bagwell	.60	.25
❑ 175 Jeff Kent	.40	.15
❑ 176 Kazuhisa Ishii	.40	.15
❑ 177 Orlando Cabrera	.40	.15
❑ 178 Shannon Stewart	.40	.15
❑ 179 Mike Cameron	.40	.15
❑ 180 Mike Mussina	.60	.25
❑ 181 Frank Thomas	1.00	.40
❑ 182 Jaret Wright	.40	.15
❑ 183A Alex Gonzalez Marlins SP	5.00	2.00
❑ 183B Alex Gonzalez Padres	.40	.15
❑ 184 Matt Lawton	.40	.15
❑ 185 Derrek Lee	.60	.25
❑ 186 Omar Vizquel	.60	.25
❑ 187 Jeremy Bonderman	.40	.15
❑ 188 Jake Westbrook	.40	.15
❑ 189 Zack Greinke SP	5.00	2.00
❑ 190 Chad Tracy	.40	.15
❑ 191 Rondell White	.40	.15
❑ 192 Alex Gonzalez	.40	.15
❑ 193 Geoff Jenkins	.40	.15
❑ 194 Ralph Kiner RET	1.00	.40
❑ 195 Al Leiter	.40	.15
❑ 196 Kevin Millwood	.40	.15
❑ 197 Jason Kendall	.40	.15
❑ 198 Kris Benson	.40	.15
❑ 199 Ryan Klesko	.40	.15
❑ 200 Mark Loretta	.40	.15
❑ 201 Richard Hidalgo	.40	.15
❑ 202 Reed Johnson	.40	.15
❑ 203 Luis Castillo	.40	.15
❑ 204 Jon Zeringue DP SP RC	5.00	2.00
❑ 205 Matt Bush DP RC	2.50	1.00
❑ 206 Kurt Suzuki DP SP RC	6.00	2.50
❑ 207 Mark Rogers DP RC	2.00	.75
❑ 208 Jason Vargas DP SP RC	5.00	2.00
❑ 209 Homer Bailey DP RC	4.00	1.50
❑ 210 Ray Liotta DP SP RC	5.00	2.00
❑ 211 Eric Campbell DP RC	3.00	1.25
❑ 212 Thomas Diamond DP RC	2.50	1.00
❑ 213 Gaby Hernandez DP SP RC	8.00	3.00
❑ 214 Neil Walker DP RC	2.00	.75
❑ 215 Bill Bray DP RC	.75	.30
❑ 216 Wade Davis DP SP RC	8.00	3.00
❑ 217 David Purcey DP RC	1.50	.60
❑ 218 Scott Elbert DP RC	2.00	.75
❑ 219 Josh Fields DP RC	4.00	1.50
❑ 220 Josh Johnson DP SP RC	5.00	2.00
❑ 221 Chris Lambert DP RC	1.00	.40
❑ 222 Trevor Plouffe DP RC	2.50	1.00
❑ 223 Bruce Froemming UMP	.50	.20
❑ 224 Matt Macri DP SP RC	4.00	1.50
❑ 225 Greg Golson DP RC	2.50	1.00
❑ 226 Philip Hughes DP RC	10.00	4.00
❑ 227 Kyle Waldrop DP RC	2.00	.75
❑ 228 Matt Tuiasosopo DP SP RC	8.00	3.00
❑ 229 Richie Robnett DP RC	2.00	.75
❑ 230 Taylor Tankersley DP RC	1.00	.40
❑ 231 Blake DeWitt DP RC	3.00	1.25
❑ 232 Charlie Reliford UMP	.50	.20
❑ 233 Eric Hurley DP RC	2.00	.75
❑ 234 Jordan Parraz DP SP RC	5.00	2.00
❑ 235 J.P. Howell DP RC	2.00	.75
❑ 236 Dana DeMuth UMP	.50	.20
❑ 237 Zach Jackson DP RC	1.50	.60
❑ 238 Justin Orenduff DP RC	1.50	.60
❑ 239 Brad Thompson FY RC	.75	.30
❑ 240 J.C. Holt DP SP RC	5.00	2.00
❑ 241 Matt Fox DP RC	.75	.30
❑ 242 Danny Putnam DP RC	1.50	.60
❑ 243 Daryl Jones DP SP RC	5.00	2.00
❑ 244 Jon Poterson DP RC	.75	.30
❑ 245 Gio Gonzalez DP RC	2.50	1.00
❑ 246 Lucas Harrell DP SP RC	5.00	2.00
❑ 247 Jerry Crawford UMP	.50	.20
❑ 248 Jay Rainville DP RC	2.50	1.00
❑ 249 Donnie Smith DP SP RC	5.00	2.00
❑ 250 Huston Street DP RC	3.00	1.25
❑ 251 Jeff Marquez DP RC	1.00	.40
❑ 252 Reid Brignac DP RC	3.00	1.25
❑ 253 Yusmeiro Petit FY RC	2.00	.75
❑ 254 K.C. Herren DP RC	1.50	.60
❑ 255 Dale Scott UMP	.50	.20
❑ 256 Erick San Pedro DP RC	.75	.30
❑ 257 Ed Montague UMP	.50	.20
❑ 258 Billy Buckner DP RC	1.00	.40
❑ 259 Mitch Einertson DP SP RC	5.00	2.00
❑ 260 Aarom Baldiris FY RC	.50	.20
❑ 261 Conor Jackson FY RC	3.00	1.25
❑ 262 Rick Reed UMP	.50	.20
❑ 263 Ervin Santana FY RC	2.00	.75
❑ 264 Gerry Davis UMP	.50	.20
❑ 265 Merkin Valdez FY RC	.50	.20
❑ 266 Joey Gathright FY RC	1.00	.40
❑ 267 Alberto Callaspo FY RC	.75	.30
❑ 268 Carlos Quentin FY SP RC	10.00	4.00
❑ 269 Gary Darling UMP	.50	.20
❑ 270 Jeff Salazar FY SP RC	5.00	2.00
❑ 271 Akinori Otsuka FY SP RC	5.00	2.00
❑ 272 Joe Brinkman UMP	.50	.20
❑ 273 Omar Quintanilla FY RC	.50	.20
❑ 274 Brian Runge UMP	.50	.20
❑ 275 Tom Mastny FY RC	.40	.15
❑ 276 John Hirschbeck UMP	.50	.20
❑ 277 Warner Madrigal FY RC	.75	.30
❑ 278 Joe West UMP	.50	.20
❑ 279 Paul Maholm FY RC	1.00	.40
❑ 280 Larry Young UMP	.50	.20
❑ 281 Mike Reilly UMP	.50	.20
❑ 282 Kazuo Matsui FY SP RC	5.00	2.00
❑ 283 Randy Marsh UMP	.50	.20
❑ 284 Frank Francisco FY RC	.40	.15
❑ 285 Zach Duke FY RC	2.00	.75
❑ 286 Tim McClelland UMP	.50	.20
❑ 287 Jesse Crain FY RC	.75	.30
❑ 288 Hector Gimenez FY RC	.40	.15
❑ 289 Marland Williams FY RC	.50	.20
❑ 290 Brian Gorman UMP	.50	.20
❑ 291 Jose Capellan FY SP RC	5.00	2.00
❑ 292 Tim Welke UMP	.50	.20
❑ 293 Javier Guzman FY RC	.50	.20
❑ 294 Paul McAnulty FY RC	.75	.30
❑ 295 Hector Made FY RC	.75	.30
❑ 296 Jon Connolly FY RC	1.00	.40
❑ 297 Don Sutton FY RC	1.00	.40
❑ 298 Fausto Carmona FY RC	2.00	.75
❑ 299 Ramon Ramirez FY RC	.40	.15
❑ 300 Brad Snyder FY RC	1.00	.40
❑ 301 Chin-Lung Hu FY RC	1.25	.50
❑ 302 Rudy Guillen FY RC	.75	.30
❑ 303 Matt Moses FY RC	1.00	.40
❑ 304 Brad Halsey FY SP RC	5.00	2.00
❑ 305 Erick Aybar FY RC	1.00	.40
❑ 306 Brad Sullivan FY RC	.50	.20
❑ 307 Nick Gorneault FY RC	.50	.20
❑ 308 Craig Ansman FY RC	.40	.15
❑ 309 Ricky Nolasco FY RC	1.25	.50
❑ 310 Luke Hughes FY RC	.40	.15
❑ 311 Danny Gonzalez FY RC	.40	.15
❑ 312 Josh Labandeira FY RC	.40	.15
❑ 313 Donald Levinski FY RC	.40	.15
❑ 314 Vince Perkins FY RC	.50	.20
❑ 315 Tommy Murphy FY RC	.40	.15
❑ 316 Chad Bentz FY RC	.40	.15
❑ 317 Chris Shelton FY RC	2.00	.75
❑ 318 Nyjer Morgan FY SP RC	5.00	2.00
❑ 319 Kody Kirkland FY RC	.50	.20
❑ 320 Blake Hawksworth FY RC	.50	.20
❑ 321 Alex Romero FY RC	.40	.15
❑ 322 Mike Gosling FY RC	.40	.15
❑ 323 Ryan Budde FY RC	.40	.15
❑ 324 Kevin Howard FY RC	.50	.20
❑ 325 Wanell Macia FY RC	.40	.15
❑ 326 Travis Blackley FY RC	.40	.15
❑ 327 Kazuhito Tadano FY SP RC	5.00	2.00
❑ 328 Shingo Takatsu FY RC	.75	.30
❑ 329 Joaquin Arias FY RC	.75	.30
❑ 330 Juan Cedeno FY RC	.40	.15
❑ 331 Bobby Brownlie FY RC	1.00	.40
❑ 332 Lastings Milledge FY RC	5.00	2.00
❑ 333 Estee Harris FY RC	.50	.20
❑ 334 Tim Stauffer FY SP RC	5.00	2.00
❑ 335 Jon Knott FY RC	.40	.15
❑ 336 David Aardsma FY RC	.50	.20
❑ 337 Wardell Starling FY RC	.40	.15
❑ 338 Dioner Navarro FY RC	.75	.30
❑ 339 Logan Kensing FY RC	.40	.15
❑ 340 Jason Hirsh FY RC	2.00	.75
❑ 341 Matt Creighton FY RC	.40	.15
❑ 342 Felix Hernandez FY SP RC	20.00	8.00
❑ 343 Kyle Sleeth FY RC	.50	.20
❑ 344 Dustin Nippert FY RC	.50	.20
❑ 345 Anthony Lerew FY RC	.75	.30
❑ 346 Chris Saenz FY RC	.40	.15
❑ 347 Steve Palermo SUP	1.00	.40
❑ 348 Barry Bonds SP	15.00	6.00
❑ MJ Roop Binder EXCH		

2005 Bowman Heritage

❑ COMPLETE SET (350)	300.00	175.00
❑ COMP.SET w/o SP's (300)	50.00	25.00
❑ COMMON CARD (1-300)	.40	.15
❑ COMMON RC (1-300)	.40	.15
❑ COMMON SP (301-350)	5.00	2.00

Card	Hi	Lo
❑ COM.SP RC (301-350)	5.00	2.00
❑ 301-350 SP ODDS 1:3 H, 1:3 R		
❑ PLATES STATED ODDS 1:343 HOBBY		
❑ PLATES PRINT RUN 1 #'d SET PER COLOR		
❑ PLATES: BLACK, CYAN, MAGENTA, YELLOW		
❑ NO PLATES PRICING DUE TO SCARCITY		
❑ ROOP BINDER EXCH ODDS 1:240 H		
❑ ROOP BINDER EXCH.DEADLINE 12/31/07		
❑ 1 Steven White FY RC	.40	.15
❑ 2 Jorge Posada	.60	.25
❑ 3 Brett Myers	.40	.15
❑ 4 Pat Burrell	.40	.15
❑ 5 Grady Sizemore	.60	.25
❑ 6 Jeff Weaver	.40	.15
❑ 7 Jeff Kent	.40	.15
❑ 8 Mark Kotsay	.40	.15
❑ 9 Nick Swisher	.60	.25
❑ 10 Scott Rolen	.60	.25
❑ 11 Matt Morris	.40	.15
❑ 12 Luis Castillo	.40	.15
❑ 13 Pedro Feliz	.40	.15
❑ 14 Omar Vizquel	.60	.25
❑ 15 Edgar Renteria	.40	.15
❑ 16 David Wells	.40	.15
❑ 17 Chad Cordero	.40	.15
❑ 18 Brad Wilkerson	.40	.15
❑ 19 Kelly Johnson	.40	.15
❑ 20 Johnny Estrada	.40	.15
❑ 21 Brian Roberts	.40	.15
❑ 22 Jeromy Burnitz	.40	.15
❑ 23 Magglio Ordonez	.40	.15
❑ 24 Adam Dunn	.40	.15
❑ 25 Randy Johnson	1.00	.40
❑ 26 Derek Jeter	2.00	.75
❑ 27 Jon Lieber	.40	.15
❑ 28 Jim Thome	.60	.25
❑ 29 Ronnie Belliard	.40	.15
❑ 30 Jake Westbrook	.40	.15
❑ 31 Bengie Molina	.40	.15
❑ 32 J.D. Drew	.40	.15
❑ 33 Rich Harden	.40	.15
❑ 34 David Eckstein	.40	.15
❑ 35 Scott Podsednik	.40	.15
❑ 36 Mark Buehrle	.40	.15
❑ 37 Barry Bonds	2.50	1.00
❑ 38 Brian Schneider	.40	.15
❑ 39 Tim Wakefield	.40	.15
❑ 40 Craig Wilson	.40	.15
❑ 41 Jose Vidro	.40	.15
❑ 42 Jacque Jones	.40	.15
❑ 43 Felix Hernandez	1.00	.40
❑ 44 Nomar Garciaparra	1.00	.40
❑ 45 Neifi Perez	.40	.15
❑ 46 Brandon Inge	.40	.15
❑ 47 Felipe Lopez	.40	.15
❑ 48 Ken Griffey Jr.	1.50	.60
❑ 49 Robinson Cano	.60	.25
❑ 50 Jason Giambi	.40	.15
❑ 51 Mike Lieberthal	.40	.15
❑ 52 Bobby Abreu	.40	.15
❑ 53 C.C. Sabathia	.40	.15
❑ 54 Aaron Boone	.40	.15
❑ 55 Milton Bradley	.40	.15
❑ 56 Derek Lowe	.40	.15
❑ 57 Barry Zito	.40	.15
❑ 58 Jim Edmonds	.40	.15
❑ 59 Jon Garland	.40	.15
❑ 60 Tadahito Iguchi RC	1.50	.60
❑ 61 Jason Schmidt	.40	.15
❑ 62 David Ortiz	1.00	.40
❑ 63 Matt Lawton	.40	.15
❑ 64 Zach Duke	.60	.25
❑ 65 Gary Sheffield	.40	.15
❑ 66 Chipper Jones	1.00	.40
❑ 67 Sammy Sosa	1.00	.40
❑ 68 Rafael Palmeiro	.60	.25
❑ 69 Carlos Zambrano	.40	.15
❑ 70 Aramis Ramirez	.40	.15
❑ 71 Chris Shelton	.60	.25
❑ 72 Wily Mo Pena	.40	.15
❑ 73 Mike Mussina	.60	.25
❑ 74 Chien-Ming Wang	1.50	.60
❑ 75 Randy Wolf	.40	.15
❑ 76 Jimmy Rollins	.40	.15
❑ 77 Chase Utley	.60	.25
❑ 78 Kevin Millwood	.40	.15
❑ 79 Victor Martinez	.40	.15
❑ 80 Morgan Ensberg	.40	.15
❑ 81 Bartolo Colon	.40	.15
❑ 82 Bobby Crosby	.40	.15
❑ 83 Dan Johnson	.40	.15
❑ 84 Dan Haren	.40	.15
❑ 85 Yadier Molina	.40	.15
❑ 86 Mark Mulder	.40	.15
❑ 87 Russell Branyan	.40	.15
❑ 88 Lyle Overbay	.40	.15
❑ 89 Edgardo Alfonzo	.40	.15
❑ 90 Mike Matheny	.40	.15
❑ 91 J.T. Snow	.40	.15
❑ 92 Curt Schilling	.60	.25
❑ 93 Oliver Perez	.40	.15
❑ 94 Mark Redman	.40	.15
❑ 95 Esteban Loaiza	.40	.15
❑ 96 Livan Hernandez	.40	.15
❑ 97 Ryan Church	.40	.15
❑ 98 Kyle Davies	.40	.15
❑ 99 Mike Hampton	.40	.15
❑ 100 Jeff Francoeur	1.00	.40
❑ 101 Javy Lopez	.40	.15
❑ 102 Mark Prior	.60	.25
❑ 103 Kerry Wood	.40	.15
❑ 104 Carlos Guillen	.40	.15
❑ 105 Dmitri Young	.40	.15
❑ 106 David Wright	1.50	.60
❑ 107 Cliff Floyd	.40	.15
❑ 108 Carlos Beltran	.40	.15
❑ 109 Melky Cabrera RC	2.00	.75
❑ 110 Carl Pavano	.40	.15
❑ 111 Jamie Moyer	.40	.15
❑ 112 Joel Pineiro	.40	.15
❑ 113 Adrian Beltre	.40	.15
❑ 114 Jhonny Peralta	.40	.15
❑ 115 Travis Hafner	.40	.15
❑ 116 Cesar Izturis	.40	.15
❑ 117 Brad Penny	.40	.15
❑ 118 Garret Anderson	.40	.15
❑ 119 Scott Kazmir	.40	.15
❑ 120 Aubrey Huff	.40	.15
❑ 121 Larry Walker	.60	.25
❑ 122 Albert Pujols	2.00	.75
❑ 123 Paul Konerko	.40	.15
❑ 124 Frank Thomas	1.00	.40
❑ 125 Phil Nevin	.40	.15
❑ 126 Brian Giles	.40	.15
❑ 127 Ramon Hernandez	.40	.15
❑ 128 Johnny Damon	.60	.25
❑ 129 Trot Nixon	.40	.15
❑ 130 Rocco Baldelli	.40	.15
❑ 131 Carl Crawford	.40	.15
❑ 132 Alfonso Soriano	.40	.15
❑ 133 Mark Teixeira	.60	.25
❑ 134 Gustavo Chacin	.40	.15
❑ 135 Vernon Wells	.40	.15
❑ 136 Erik Bedard	.40	.15
❑ 137 Daniel Cabrera	.40	.15
❑ 138 Michael Barrett	.40	.15
❑ 139 Greg Maddux	1.50	.60
❑ 140 Javier Vazquez	.40	.15
❑ 141 Chad Tracy	.40	.15
❑ 142 Michael Young	.40	.15
❑ 143 Kenny Rogers	.40	.15
❑ 144 Mike Piazza	1.00	.40
❑ 145 Jose Reyes	.40	.15
❑ 146 Geoff Jenkins	.40	.15
❑ 147 Carlos Lee	.40	.15
❑ 148 Brady Clark	.40	.15
❑ 149 Torii Hunter	.40	.15
❑ 150 Johan Santana	1.00	.40
❑ 151 Steve Finley	.40	.15
❑ 152 Darin Erstad	.40	.15
❑ 153 Jake Peavy	.40	.15
❑ 154 Xavier Nady	.40	.15
❑ 155 Ryan Klesko	.40	.15
❑ 156 Ichiro Suzuki	2.00	.75
❑ 157 Richie Sexson	.40	.15
❑ 158 Raul Ibanez	.40	.15
❑ 159 Freddy Garcia	.40	.15
❑ 160 Brad Hawpe	.40	.15
❑ 161 Jeff Francis	.40	.15
❑ 162 Todd Helton	.60	.25
❑ 163 Clint Barmes	.40	.15
❑ 164 Rodrigo Lopez	.40	.15
❑ 165 Melvin Mora	.40	.15
❑ 166 Brandon Webb	.40	.15
❑ 167 Shawn Green	.40	.15
❑ 168 Moises Alou	.40	.15
❑ 169 Matt Clement	.40	.15
❑ 170 John Smoltz	.60	.25
❑ 171 Rafael Furcal	.40	.15
❑ 172 Jeff Bagwell	.60	.25
❑ 173 Roger Clemens	1.50	.60
❑ 174 Dontrelle Willis	.40	.15
❑ 175 Paul Lo Duca	.40	.15
❑ 176 Zack Greinke	.40	.15
❑ 177 David DeJesus	.40	.15
❑ 178 Mike Sweeney	.40	.15
❑ 179 Ben Sheets	.40	.15
❑ 180 Doug Davis	.40	.15
❑ 181 Mike Cameron	.40	.15
❑ 182 Lance Berkman	.40	.15
❑ 183 Craig Biggio	.60	.25
❑ 184 Shannon Stewart	.40	.15
❑ 185 Joe Mauer	1.00	.40
❑ 186 Justin Morneau	.40	.15
❑ 187 Mike Maroth	.40	.15
❑ 188 Ivan Rodriguez	.60	.25
❑ 189 Luis Gonzalez	.40	.15
❑ 190 Troy Glaus	.40	.15
❑ 191 Adam Eaton	.40	.15
❑ 192 Khalil Greene	.60	.25
❑ 193 Mike Lowell	.40	.15
❑ 194 Miguel Cabrera	.60	.25
❑ 195 Roy Halladay	.40	.15
❑ 196 Ted Lilly	.40	.15
❑ 197 Alex Rios	.40	.15
❑ 198 Josh Beckett	.40	.15
❑ 199 A.J. Burnett	.40	.15
❑ 200 Juan Pierre	.40	.15
❑ 201 Marcus Giles	.40	.15
❑ 202 Craig Tatum FY RC	.40	.15
❑ 203 Hayden Penn FY RC	.75	.30
❑ 204 C.J. Smith FY RC	.40	.15
❑ 205 Matt Albers FY RC	1.00	.40
❑ 206 Jared Gothreaux FY RC	.40	.15
❑ 207 Mike Rodriguez FY RC	.40	.15
❑ 208 Hernan Iribarren FY RC	.50	.20
❑ 209 Manny Parra FY RC	.40	.15
❑ 210 Kevin Collins FY RC	.40	.15
❑ 211 Buck Coats FY RC	.40	.15
❑ 212 Jeremy West FY RC	.75	.30
❑ 213 Ian Bladergroen FY RC	.50	.20
❑ 214 Chuck Tiffany FY RC	1.00	.40
❑ 215 Andy LaRoche FY RC	3.00	1.25
❑ 216 Frank Diaz FY RC	.40	.15
❑ 217 Jai Miller FY RC	.50	.20
❑ 218 Tony Giarratano FY RC	.40	.15
❑ 219 Danny Zell FY RC	.40	.15
❑ 220 Justin Verlander FY RC	4.00	1.50
❑ 221 Ryan Sweeney FY RC	1.00	.40
❑ 222 Brandon McCarthy FY RC	1.25	.50
❑ 223 Jerry Owens FY RC	.50	.20
❑ 224 Glen Perkins FY RC	.75	.30
❑ 225 Kevin West FY RC	.40	.15
❑ 226 Billy Butler FY RC	4.00	1.50
❑ 227 Shane Costa FY RC	.40	.15
❑ 228 Erik Schindewolf FY RC	.40	.15
❑ 229 Miguel Montero FY RC	1.25	.50
❑ 230 Stephen Drew FY RC	5.00	2.00
❑ 231 Matt DeSalvo FY RC	.50	.20
❑ 232 Ben Jones FY RC	.50	.20

Card		
❑ 233 Bill McCarthy FY RC	.40	.15
❑ 234 Chuck James FY RC	1.50	.60
❑ 235 Brandon Sing FY RC	.50	.20
❑ 236 Andy Santana FY RC	.40	.15
❑ 237 Brendan Ryan FY RC	.40	.15
❑ 238 Wes Swackhamer FY RC	.40	.15
❑ 239 Jeff Niemann FY RC	.75	.30
❑ 240 Ian Kinsler FY RC	2.50	1.00
❑ 241 Micah Furtado FY RC	.40	.15
❑ 242 Ryan Mount FY RC	.75	.30
❑ 243 P.J. Phillips FY RC	.75	.30
❑ 244 Trevor Bell FY RC	.75	.30
❑ 245 Jered Weaver FY RC	5.00	2.00
❑ 246 Eddy Martinez FY RC	1.00	.40
❑ 247 Brian Bannister FY RC	.75	.30
❑ 248 Philip Humber FY RC	.75	.30
❑ 249 Michael Rogers FY RC	.40	.15
❑ 250 Landon Powell FY RC	.50	.20
❑ 251 Kennard Bibbs FY RC	.40	.15
❑ 252 Nelson Cruz FY RC	1.25	.50
❑ 253 Paul Kelly FY RC	.50	.20
❑ 254 Kevin Slowey FY RC	1.25	.50
❑ 255 Brandon Snyder FY RC	1.50	.60
❑ 256 Nolan Reimold FY RC	1.25	.50
❑ 257 Brian Stavisky FY RC	.40	.15
❑ 258 Javier Herrera FY RC	2.00	.75
❑ 259 Russ Martin FY RC	1.25	.50
❑ 260 Matthew Kemp FY RC	5.00	2.00
❑ 261 Wade Townsend FY RC	.50	.20
❑ 262 Nick Touchstone FY RC	.40	.15
❑ 263 Ryan Feierabend FY RC	.40	.15
❑ 264 Bobby Livingston FY RC	.40	.15
❑ 265 Wladimir Balentien FY RC	.75	.30
❑ 266 Keiichi Yabu FY RC	.40	.15
❑ 267 Craig Italiano FY RC	.75	.30
❑ 268 Ryan Goleski FY RC	.40	.15
❑ 269 Ryan Garko FY RC	1.25	.50
❑ 270 Mike Bourn FY RC	.75	.30
❑ 271 Scott Mathieson FY RC	.75	.30
❑ 272 Scott Mitchinson FY RC	.40	.15
❑ 273 Tyler Greene FY RC	.75	.30
❑ 274 Mark McCormick FY RC	.50	.20
❑ 275 Daryl Jones FY	.40	.15
❑ 276 Travis Chick FY RC	.50	.20
❑ 277 Luis Hernandez FY RC	.40	.15
❑ 278 Steve Doetsch FY RC	.40	.15
❑ 279 Chris Vines FY RC	.40	.15
❑ 280 Mike Costanzo FY RC	1.25	.50
❑ 281 Matt Maloney FY RC	1.00	.40
❑ 282 Matt Goyen FY RC	.40	.15
❑ 283 Jacob Marceaux FY RC	.40	.15
❑ 284 David Gassner FY RC	.40	.15
❑ 285 Ricky Barrett FY RC	.40	.15
❑ 286 Jon Egan FY RC	.50	.20
❑ 287 Scott Blue FY RC	.40	.15
❑ 288 Steven Bondurant FY RC	.40	.15
❑ 289 Kevin Melillo FY RC	.75	.30
❑ 290 Brad Corley FY RC	.50	.20
❑ 291 Brent Lillibridge FY RC	.40	.15
❑ 292 Mike Morse FY RC	.75	.30
❑ 293 Justin Thomas FY RC	.40	.15
❑ 294 Nick Webber FY RC	.40	.15
❑ 295 Mitch Boggs FY RC	.40	.15
❑ 296 Jeff Lyman FY RC	.50	.20
❑ 297 Jordan Schafer FY RC	1.00	.40
❑ 298 Ismael Ramirez FY RC	.40	.15
❑ 299 Chris B.Young FY RC	2.00	.75
❑ 300 Brian Miller FY RC	.40	.15
❑ 301 Jason Bay SP	5.00	2.00
❑ 302 Tim Hudson SP	5.00	2.00
❑ 303 Miguel Tejada SP	5.00	2.00
❑ 304 Jeremy Bonderman SP	5.00	2.00
❑ 305 Alex Rodriguez SP	8.00	3.00
❑ 306 Rickie Weeks SP	5.00	2.00
❑ 307 Manny Ramirez SP	8.00	3.00
❑ 308 Nick Johnson SP	5.00	2.00
❑ 309 Andruw Jones SP	8.00	3.00
❑ 310 Hideki Matsui SP	6.00	2.50
❑ 311 Jeremy Reed SP	5.00	2.00
❑ 312 Dallas McPherson SP	5.00	2.00
❑ 313 Vladimir Guerrero SP	8.00	3.00
❑ 314 Eric Chavez SP	5.00	2.00
❑ 315 Chris Carpenter SP	5.00	2.00
❑ 316 Aaron Hill SP	5.00	2.00
❑ 317 Derrek Lee SP	8.00	3.00
❑ 318 Mark Loretta SP	5.00	2.00
❑ 319 Garrett Atkins SP	5.00	2.00
❑ 320 Hank Blalock SP	5.00	2.00
❑ 321 Chris Young SP	5.00	2.00
❑ 322 Roy Oswalt SP	5.00	2.00
❑ 323 Carlos Delgado SP	5.00	2.00
❑ 324 Pedro Martinez SP	8.00	3.00
❑ 325 Jeff Clement FY SP RC	10.00	4.00
❑ 326 Jimmy Shull FY SP RC	5.00	2.00
❑ 327 Daniel Carte FY SP RC	5.00	2.00
❑ 328 Travis Buck FY SP RC	6.00	2.50
❑ 329 Chris Volstad FY SP RC	5.00	2.00
❑ 330 A.McCutchen FY SP RC	10.00	4.00
❑ 331 Cliff Pennington FY SP RC	5.00	2.00
❑ 332 John Mayberry Jr. FY SP RC	5.00	2.00
❑ 333 C.J. Henry FY SP RC	8.00	3.00
❑ 334 Ricky Romero FY SP RC	5.00	2.00
❑ 335 Aaron Thompson FY SP RC	5.00	2.00
❑ 336 Cesar Carrillo FY SP RC	5.00	2.00
❑ 337 Jacoby Ellsbury FY SP RC	12.00	5.00
❑ 338 Matt Garza FY SP RC	8.00	3.00
❑ 339 Colby Rasmus FY SP RC	8.00	3.00
❑ 340 Ryan Zimmerman FY SP RC	15.00	6.00
❑ 341 Ryan Braun FY SP RC	15.00	6.00
❑ 342 Brent Lillibridge FY SP	5.00	2.00
❑ 343 Jay Bruce FY SP RC	12.00	5.00
❑ 344 Matt Green FY SP RC	5.00	2.00
❑ 345 Brent Cox FY SP RC	5.00	2.00
❑ 346 Jed Lowrie FY SP RC	5.00	2.00
❑ 347 Beau Jones FY SP RC	5.00	2.00
❑ 348 Eli Iorg FY SP RC	5.00	2.00
❑ 349 Chaz Roe FY SP RC	5.00	2.00
❑ 350 Mystery Redemption SP	25.00	10.00
❑ NNO Roop Binder Redemption	15.00	6.00

2006 Bowman Heritage

Card		
❑ COMPLETE SET (300)	150.00	75.00
❑ COMP.SET w/o SP's (250)	40.00	15.00
❑ COMMON CARD (1-300)	.40	.15
❑ SEMISTARS 1-300	.60	.25
❑ UNLISTED 1-300	1.00	.40
❑ COMMON RC (1-300)	.40	.15
❑ RC UNLISTED 1-300	1.00	.40
❑ COMMON SP (202-300)	5.00	2.00
❑ SP SEMIS 202-300	8.00	3.00
❑ SP UNL 202-300	8.00	3.00
❑ COM.SP RC (202-300)	5.00	2.00
❑ SP RC SEMI 202-300	5.00	2.00
❑ SP RC UNL 202-300	5.00	2.00
❑ 202-300 SP ODDS 1:3 H, 1:3 R		
❑ SP CL: EVEN #s B/WN 202-300		
❑ OVERALL PLATE ODDS 1:497 HOBBY		
❑ PLATE PRINT RUN 1 SET PER COLOR		
❑ BLACK-CYAN-MAGENTA-YELLOW ISSUED		
❑ NO PLATE PRICING DUE TO SCARCITY		
❑ 1 David Wright	1.50	.60
❑ 2 Andruw Jones	.60	.25
❑ 3 Ryan Howard	1.50	.60
❑ 4 Jason Bay	.40	.15
❑ 5 Paul Konerko	.40	.15
❑ 6 Jake Peavy	.40	.15
❑ 7 Todd Jones	.40	.15
❑ 8 Troy Glaus	.40	.15
❑ 9 Rocco Baldelli	.40	.15
❑ 10 Rafael Furcal	.40	.15
❑ 11 Freddy Sanchez	.40	.15
❑ 12 Jermaine Dye	.40	.15
❑ 13 A.J. Burnett	.40	.15
❑ 14 Michael Cuddyer	.40	.15
❑ 15 Barry Zito	.40	.15
❑ 16 Chipper Jones	1.00	.40
❑ 17 Paul LoDuca	.40	.15
❑ 18 Mark Mulder	.40	.15
❑ 19 Raul Ibanez	.40	.15
❑ 20 Carlos Delgado	.40	.15
❑ 21 Marcus Giles	.40	.15
❑ 22 Dan Haren	.40	.15
❑ 23 Justin Morneau	.40	.15
❑ 24 Livan Hernandez	.40	.15
❑ 25 Ken Griffey Jr.	1.50	.60
❑ 26 Aaron Hill	.40	.15
❑ 27 Tadahito Iguchi	.40	.15
❑ 28 Nate Robertson	.40	.15
❑ 29 Kevin Millwood	.40	.15
❑ 30 Jim Thome	.60	.25
❑ 31 Aubrey Huff	.40	.15
❑ 32 Dontrelle Willis	.40	.15
❑ 33 Khalil Greene	.60	.25
❑ 34 Doug Davis	.40	.15
❑ 35 Ivan Rodriguez	.60	.25
❑ 36 Rickie Weeks	.40	.15
❑ 37 Jhonny Peralta	.40	.15
❑ 38 Yadier Molina	.40	.15
❑ 39 Eric Chavez	.40	.15
❑ 40 Alfonso Soriano	.40	.15
❑ 41 Pat Burrell	.40	.15
❑ 42 B.J. Ryan	.40	.15
❑ 43 Carl Crawford	.40	.15
❑ 44 Preston Wilson	.40	.15
❑ 45 Jorge Posada	.60	.25
❑ 46 Carlos Zambrano	.40	.15
❑ 47 Mark Teahen	.40	.15
❑ 48 Nick Johnson	.40	.15
❑ 49 Mark Kotsay	.40	.15
❑ 50 Derek Jeter	2.50	1.00
❑ 51 Moises Alou	.40	.15
❑ 52 Ryan Freel	.40	.15
❑ 53 Shannon Stewart	.40	.15
❑ 54 Casey Blake	.40	.15
❑ 55 Edgar Renteria	.40	.15
❑ 56 Frank Thomas	1.00	.40
❑ 57 Ty Wigginton	.40	.15
❑ 58 Jeff Kent	.40	.15
❑ 59 Chien-Ming Wang	1.50	.60
❑ 60 Josh Beckett	.40	.15
❑ 61 Chase Utley	1.00	.40
❑ 62 Gary Matthews	.40	.15
❑ 63 Torii Hunter	.40	.15
❑ 64 Bobby Jenks	.40	.15
❑ 65 Wilson Betemit	.40	.15
❑ 66 Jeremy Bonderman	.40	.15
❑ 67 Scott Rolen	.60	.25
❑ 68 Brad Penny	.40	.15
❑ 69 Jacque Jones	.40	.15
❑ 70 Jose Reyes	.40	.15
❑ 71 Brian Roberts	.40	.15
❑ 72 John Smoltz	.60	.25
❑ 73 Johnny Estrada	.40	.15
❑ 74 Ronnie Belliard	.40	.15
❑ 75 Vladimir Guerrero	1.00	.40
❑ 76 A.J. Pierzynski	.40	.15
❑ 77 Garrett Atkins	.40	.15
❑ 78 Adam LaRoche	.40	.15
❑ 79 Mark Loretta	.40	.15
❑ 80 Todd Helton	.60	.25
❑ 81 Jose Vidro	.40	.15
❑ 82 Carlos Guillen	.40	.15
❑ 83 Michael Barrett	.40	.15
❑ 84 Lyle Overbay	.40	.15
❑ 85 Travis Hafner	.40	.15
❑ 86 Shea Hillenbrand	.40	.15
❑ 87 Julio Lugo	.40	.15
❑ 88 Tim Hudson	.40	.15
❑ 89 Scott Podsednik	.40	.15
❑ 90 Roy Halladay	.40	.15
❑ 91 Bartolo Colon	.40	.15
❑ 92 Ryan Langerhans	.40	.15
❑ 93 Tom Glavine	.60	.25
❑ 94 Kenny Rogers	.40	.15
❑ 95 Robinson Cano	.60	.25
❑ 96 Mark Prior	.60	.25
❑ 97 Jason Schmidt	.40	.15
❑ 98 Bengie Molina	.40	.15
❑ 99 Jon Lieber	.40	.15
❑ 100 Alex Rodriguez	1.50	.60

❑ 101 Scott Kazmir .60 .25
❑ 102 Jeff Francoeur 1.00 .40
❑ 103 Chris Carpenter .40 .15
❑ 104 Juan Uribe .40 .15
❑ 105 Mariano Rivera 1.00 .40
❑ 106 Rich Harden .40 .15
❑ 107 Jack Wilson .40 .15
❑ 108 Austin Kearns .40 .15
❑ 109 Marcus Thames .40 .15
❑ 110 Miguel Tejada .40 .15
❑ 111 Chone Figgins .40 .15
❑ 112 Bronson Arroyo .40 .15
❑ 113 Chad Cordero .40 .15
❑ 114 Bill Hall .40 .15
❑ 115 Curt Schilling .60 .25
❑ 116 David Eckstein .40 .15
❑ 117 Ramon Hernandez .40 .15
❑ 118 Eric Byrnes .40 .15
❑ 119 Clint Barmes .40 .15
❑ 120 Bobby Abreu .40 .15
❑ 121 Joe Crede .40 .15
❑ 122 Derek Lowe .40 .15
❑ 123 Jason Marquis .40 .15
❑ 124 Erik Bedard .40 .15
❑ 125 Derrek Lee .40 .15
❑ 126 Brian McCann .40 .15
❑ 127 Magglio Ordonez .40 .15
❑ 128 Ben Sheets .40 .15
❑ 129 Brandon Inge .40 .15
❑ 130 Miguel Cabrera .60 .25
❑ 131 Jim Edmonds .60 .25
❑ 132 John Lackey .40 .15
❑ 133 Kevin Mench .40 .15
❑ 134 Adrian Beltre .40 .15
❑ 135 Curtis Granderson .40 .15
❑ 136 Shawn Green .40 .15
❑ 137 Jose Contreras .40 .15
❑ 138 Joe Nathan .40 .15
❑ 139 Bobby Crosby .40 .15
❑ 140 Johnny Damon .60 .25
❑ 141 Brad Hawpe .40 .15
❑ 142 Brandon Phillips .40 .15
❑ 143 Victor Martinez .40 .15
❑ 144 Jimmy Rollins .40 .15
❑ 145 Corey Patterson .40 .15
❑ 146 Grady Sizemore .60 .25
❑ 147 Placido Polanco .40 .15
❑ 148 Mike Lowell .40 .15
❑ 149 Francisco Rodriguez .40 .15
❑ 150 Ichiro Suzuki 1.50 .60
❑ 151 Kris Benson .40 .15
❑ 152 Scott Hatteberg .40 .15
❑ 153 Akinori Otsuka .40 .15
❑ 154 Cesar Izturis .40 .15
❑ 155 Roger Clemens 2.00 .75
❑ 156 Kerry Wood .40 .15
❑ 157 Tom Gordon .40 .15
❑ 158 Sean Casey .40 .15
❑ 159 Jose Lopez .40 .15
❑ 160 Orlando Hernandez .40 .15
❑ 161 Aramis Ramirez .40 .15
❑ 162 J.D. Drew .40 .15
❑ 163 David DeJesus .40 .15
❑ 164 Craig Biggio .60 .25
❑ 165 Brett Myers .40 .15
❑ 166 C.C. Sabathia .40 .15
❑ 167 Zach Duke .40 .15
❑ 168 Luis Castillo .40 .15
❑ 169 Hideki Matsui 1.00 .40
❑ 170 Brian Giles .40 .15
❑ 171 Coco Crisp .40 .15
❑ 172 Richie Sexson .40 .15
❑ 173 Nomar Garciaparra 1.00 .40
❑ 174 Roy Oswalt .40 .15
❑ 175 David Ortiz 1.00 .40
❑ 176 Matt Morris .40 .15
❑ 177 Felipe Lopez .40 .15
❑ 178 Garret Anderson .40 .15
❑ 179 Kevin Youkilis .40 .15
❑ 180 Alex Rios .40 .15
❑ 181 Jon Garland .40 .15
❑ 182 Luis Gonzalez .40 .15
❑ 183 Cliff Floyd .40 .15
❑ 184 Juan Encarnacion .40 .15
❑ 185 Nick Swisher .40 .15
❑ 186 Mike Cameron .40 .15
❑ 187 Jose Castillo .40 .15
❑ 188 Ray Durham .40 .15
❑ 189 Jorge Cantu .40 .15
❑ 190 Andy Pettitte .40 .15
❑ 191 Chad Tracy .40 .15
❑ 192 Adrian Gonzalez .40 .15
❑ 193 Jose Valentin .40 .15
❑ 194 Mark Buehrle .40 .15
❑ 195 Huston Street .40 .15
❑ 196 Chris Capuano .40 .15
❑ 197 Aaron Rowand .40 .15
❑ 198 Billy Wagner .40 .15
❑ 199 Orlando Cabrera .40 .15
❑ 200 Albert Pujols 2.00 .75
❑ 201 Dan Uggla (RC) 1.00 .40
❑ 202 Alay Soler SP RC 5.00 2.00
❑ 203 Matt Kemp (RC) .60 .25
❑ 204 Mike Napoli SP RC 5.00 2.00
❑ 205 Joel Zumaya (RC) 1.00 .40
❑ 206 Mike Pelfrey SP RC 8.00 3.00
❑ 207 Ian Kinsler (RC) .60 .25
❑ 208 Josh Willingham SP (RC) 5.00 2.00
❑ 209 Erick Aybar (RC) .40 .15
❑ 210 Willie Eyre SP (RC) 5.00 2.00
❑ 211 Kendry Morales (RC) .60 .25
❑ 212 Scott Thorman SP (RC) 5.00 2.00
❑ 213 Hanley Ramirez (RC) 1.00 .40
❑ 214 Boof Bonser SP (RC) 5.00 2.00
❑ 215 Anthony Reyes (RC) .60 .25
❑ 216 Justin Huber SP (RC) 5.00 2.00
❑ 217 Yusmeiro Petit (RC) .40 .15
❑ 218 Jason Bartlett SP (RC) 5.00 2.00
❑ 219 Shin-Soo Choo (RC) .60 .25
❑ 220 Francisco Liriano SP (RC) 5.00 2.00
❑ 221 Craig Hansen RC 1.50 .60
❑ 222 Ricky Nolasco SP (RC) 5.00 2.00
❑ 223 Adam Loewen (RC) .40 .15
❑ 224 Scott Olsen SP (RC) 5.00 2.00
❑ 225 Cole Hamels (RC) 1.00 .40
❑ 226 Martin Prado SP (RC) 5.00 2.00
❑ 227 James Loney (RC) .60 .25
❑ 228 Kevin Thompson SP (RC) 5.00 2.00
❑ 229 Adam Jones RC 1.25 .50
❑ 230 Josh Johnson SP (RC) 5.00 2.00
❑ 231 Anderson Hernandez (RC) .40 .15
❑ 232 Tony Gwynn Jr. SP (RC) 5.00 2.00
❑ 233 Casey Janssen RC .60 .25
❑ 234 Taylor Tankersley SP (RC) 5.00 2.00
❑ 235 Mike Thompson RC .40 .15
❑ 236 Jeremy Sowers SP (RC) 5.00 2.00
❑ 237 Anibal Sanchez (RC) .60 .25
❑ 238 Adam Wainwright SP (RC) 5.00 2.00
❑ 239 Rich Hill (RC) .40 .15
❑ 240 Russ Martin SP (RC) 5.00 2.00
❑ 241 Joe Inglett RC .40 .15
❑ 242 Tony Pena SP (RC) 5.00 2.00
❑ 243 Josh Sharpless RC .40 .15
❑ 244 Darrell Rasner SP (RC) 5.00 2.00
❑ 245 Joe Saunders (RC) .40 .15
❑ 246 Jon Lester SP RC 5.00 2.00
❑ 247 Jeremy Hermida (RC) .40 .15
❑ 248 Chad Billingsley SP (RC) 5.00 2.00
❑ 249 Bobby Livingston (RC) .40 .15
❑ 250 Justin Verlander SP (RC) 5.00 2.00
❑ 251 Mickey Mantle 8.00 3.00
❑ 252 Hank Blalock SP 5.00 2.00
❑ 253 Manny Ramirez .60 .25
❑ 254 Mike Mussina SP 8.00 3.00
❑ 255 Greg Maddux 1.50 .60
❑ 256 Jason Giambi SP 5.00 2.00
❑ 257 Mark Teixeira .60 .25
❑ 258 Carlos Beltran SP 5.00 2.00
❑ 259 Matt Holliday .50 .20
❑ 260 Pedro Martinez SP 8.00 3.00
❑ 261 Joe Mauer .60 .25
❑ 262 Melvin Mora SP 5.00 2.00
❑ 263 Mike Piazza 1.00 .40
❑ 264 B.J. Upton SP 5.00 2.00
❑ 265 Vernon Wells .40 .15
❑ 266 Gary Sheffield SP 5.00 2.00
❑ 267 Randy Johnson 1.00 .40
❑ 268 Ryan Zimmerman SP 5.00 2.00
❑ 269 Lance Berkman .40 .15
❑ 270 Johan Santana SP 8.00 3.00
❑ 271 Carlos Lee .40 .15
❑ 272 Brandon Webb SP 5.00 2.00
❑ 273 Adam Dunn .40 .15
❑ 274 Michael Young SP 5.00 2.00
❑ 275 Barry Bonds 2.00 .75
❑ 276 Jonathan Papelbon SP (RC) 5.00 2.00
❑ 277 Howie Kendrick (RC) 1.00 .40
❑ 278 Melky Cabrera SP (RC) 5.00 2.00
❑ 279 Jered Weaver (RC) 1.25 .50
❑ 280 Josh Barfield SP (RC) 5.00 2.00
❑ 281 Chuck James (RC) .60 .25
❑ 282 Lastings Milledge SP (RC) 5.00 2.00
❑ 283 Nick Markakis (RC) .60 .25
❑ 284 Jose Capellan SP (RC) 5.00 2.00
❑ 285 Prince Fielder (RC) 1.50 .60
❑ 286 Jason Botts SP (RC) 5.00 2.00
❑ 287 Eliezer Alfonzo RC .40 .15
❑ 288 Sean Marshall SP (RC) 5.00 2.00
❑ 289 Ryan Garko (RC) .40 .15
❑ 290 Stephen Drew SP (RC) 5.00 2.00
❑ 291 Joel Guzman (RC) .40 .15
❑ 292 Hong-Chih Kuo SP (RC) 5.00 2.00
❑ 293 Zach Miner (RC) .40 .15
❑ 294 Angel Guzman SP (RC) 5.00 2.00
❑ 295 Andre Ethier (RC) 1.00 .40
❑ 296 Fausto Carmona SP (RC) 5.00 2.00
❑ 297 Ronny Paulino (RC) .40 .15
❑ 298 Matt Cain SP (RC) 5.00 2.00
❑ 299 Carlos Quentin (RC) .60 .25
❑ 300 Kenji Johjima SP RC 5.00 2.00

2007 Bowman Heritage

❑ COMP.SET w/o SPs (251) 40.00 15.00
❑ COMMON CARD (1-200) .40 .15
❑ COMMON ROOKIE (201-251) .50 .20
❑ COMMON SP (180-200) 3.00 1.25
❑ COMMON SP RC (200-251) 4.00 1.50
❑ SP ODDS 1:3 HOBBY
❑ NO SIG CARDS ARE SHORT PRINTS
❑ COMP.SET INCLUDES ALL MANTLE VAR.
❑ OVERALL PLATE ODDS 1:463 HOBBY
❑ PLATE PRINT RUN 1 SET PER COLOR
❑ BLACK-CYAN-MAGENTA-YELLOW ISSUED
❑ NO PLATE PRICING DUE TO SCARCITY
❑ 1 Jeff Francoeur 1.00 .40
❑ 2 Jered Weaver .60 .25
❑ 3 Derrek Lee .40 .15
❑ 4 Todd Helton .60 .25
❑ 5 Shawn Hill .40 .15
❑ 6 Ivan Rodriguez .60 .25
❑ 7 Mickey Mantle 5.00 2.00
❑ 8 Ramon Hernandez .40 .15
❑ 9 Randy Johnson 1.00 .40
❑ 10 Jermaine Dye .40 .15
❑ 11 Brian Roberts .40 .15
❑ 12 Hank Blalock .40 .15
❑ 13 Chien-Ming Wang 1.50 .60
❑ 14 Mike Lowell .40 .15
❑ 15 Brandon Webb .40 .15
❑ 16 Kelly Johnson .40 .15
❑ 17 Nick Johnson .40 .15
❑ 18 Zach Duke .40 .15
❑ 19 Aaron Hill .40 .15
❑ 20 Miguel Tejada .40 .15
❑ 21 Mark Buehrle .40 .15
❑ 22 Michael Young .40 .15
❑ 23 Carlos Delgado .40 .15
❑ 24 Anibal Sanchez .40 .15
❑ 25 Vladimir Guerrero 1.00 .40
❑ 26 Russell Martin .40 .15

	No.	Player		
❑	27	Lance Berkman	.40	.15
❑	28	Bobby Crosby	.40	.15
❑	29	Javier Vazquez	.40	.15
❑	30	Manny Ramirez	.60	.25
❑	31	Rich Hill	.40	.15
❑	32	Mike Sweeney	.40	.15
❑	33	Jeff Kent	.40	.15
❑	34	Noah Lowry	.40	.15
❑	35	Alfonso Soriano	.40	.15
❑	36	Paul Lo Duca	.40	.15
❑	37	J.D. Drew	.40	.15
❑	38	C.C Sabathia	.40	.15
❑	39	Craig Biggio	.60	.25
❑	40	Adam Dunn	.40	.15
❑	41	Josh Beckett	.60	.25
❑	42	Carlos Guillen	.40	.15
❑	43	Jeff Francis	.40	.15
❑	44	Orlando Hudson	.40	.15
❑	45	Grady Sizmore	.60	.25
❑	46	Jason Jennings	.40	.15
❑	47	Mark Teixeira	.60	.25
❑	48	Freddy Garcia	.40	.15
❑	49	Adrian Gonzalez	.40	.15
❑	50	Albert Pujols	2.00	.75
❑	51	Tom Glavine	.60	.25
❑	52	J.J. Hardy	.40	.15
❑	53	Bobby Abreu	.40	.15
❑	54	Bartolo Colon	.40	.15
❑	55	Garrett Atkins	.40	.15
❑	56	Moises Alou	.40	.15
❑	57	Cliff Lee	.40	.15
❑	58	Michael Cuddyer	.40	.15
❑	59	Brandon Phillips	.40	.15
❑	60	Jeremy Bonderman	.40	.15
❑	61	Rickie Weeks	.40	.15
❑	62	Chris Carpenter	.40	.15
❑	63	Frank Thomas	1.00	.40
❑	64	Victor Martinez	.40	.15
❑	65	Dontrelle Willis	.40	.15
❑	66	Jim Thome	.60	.25
❑	67	Aaron Rowand	.40	.15
❑	68	Andy Pettitte	.60	.25
❑	69	Brian McCann	.40	.15
❑	70	Roger Clemens	2.00	.75
❑	71	Gary Matthews	.40	.15
❑	72	Bronson Arroyo	.40	.15
❑	73	Jeremy Hermida	.40	.15
❑	74	Eric Chavez	.40	.15
❑	75	David Ortiz	1.00	.40
❑	76	Stephen Drew	.60	.25
❑	77	Ronnie Belliard	.40	.15
❑	78	James Shields	.40	.15
❑	79	Richie Sexson	.40	.15
❑	80	Johan Santana	.60	.25
❑	81	Orlando Cabrera	.40	.15
❑	82	Aramis Ramirez	.40	.15
❑	83	Greg Maddux	1.50	.60
❑	84	Reggie Sanders	.40	.15
❑	85	Carlos Zambrano	.40	.15
❑	86	Bengie Molina	.40	.15
❑	87	David DeJesus	.40	.15
❑	88	Adam Wainwright	.40	.15
❑	89	Conor Jackson	.40	.15
❑	90	David Wright	1.50	.60
❑	91	Ryan Garko	.40	.15
❑	92	Bill Hall	.40	.15
❑	93	Marcus Giles	.40	.15
❑	94	Kenny Rogers	.40	.15
❑	95	Joe Mauer	.60	.25
❑	96	Hanley Ramirez	.60	.25
❑	97	Brian Giles	.40	.15
❑	98	Dan Haren	.40	.15
❑	99	Robinson Cano	.60	.25
❑	100	Ryan Howard	1.50	.60
❑	101	Andruw Jones	.60	.25
❑	102	Aaron Harang	.40	.15
❑	103	Hideki Matsui	1.00	.40
❑	104	Nick Swisher	.40	.15
❑	105	Pedro Martinez	.60	.25
❑	106	Felipe Lopez	.40	.15
❑	107	Erik Bedard	.40	.15
❑	108	Rafael Furcal	.40	.15
❑	109	Curt Schilling	.60	.25
❑	110	Jose Reyes	1.00	.40
❑	111	Adam LaRoche	.40	.15
❑	112	Mike Mussina	.60	.25
❑	113	Melvin Mora	.40	.15
❑	114	Zack Greinke	.40	.15
❑	115	Justin Morneau	.40	.15
❑	116	Ervin Santana	.40	.15
❑	117	Ken Griffey Jr.	1.50	.60
❑	118	David Eckstein	.40	.15
❑	119	Jamie Moyer	.40	.15
❑	120	Jorge Posada	.60	.25
❑	121	Justin Verlander	1.00	.40
❑	122	Sammy Sosa	1.00	.40
❑	123	Jason Schmidt	.40	.15
❑	124	Josh Willingham	.40	.15
❑	125	Roy Oswalt	.40	.15
❑	126	Travis Hafner	.40	.15
❑	127	John Maine	.40	.15
❑	128	Willy Taveras	.40	.15
❑	129	Maggilo Ordonez	.40	.15
❑	130	Barry Zito	.40	.15
❑	131	Prince Fielder	1.00	.40
❑	132	Michael Barrett	.40	.15
❑	133	Livan Hernandez	.40	.15
❑	134	Troy Glaus	.40	.15
❑	135	Rocco Baldelli	.40	.15
❑	136	Jason Giambi	.40	.15
❑	137	Austin Kearns	.40	.15
❑	138	Dan Uggla	.60	.25
❑	139	Pat Burrell	.40	.15
❑	140	Carlos Beltran	.40	.15
❑	141	Carlos Quentin	.40	.15
❑	142	Johnny Estrada	.40	.15
❑	143	Torii Hunter	.40	.15
❑	144	Carlos Lee	.40	.15
❑	145	Mike Piazza	1.00	.40
❑	146	Mark Teahen	.40	.15
❑	147	Juan Pierre	.40	.15
❑	148	Paul Konerko	.40	.15
❑	149	Freddy Sanchez	.40	.15
❑	150	Derek Jeter	2.50	1.00
❑	151	Orlando Hernandez	.40	.15
❑	152	Raul Ibanez	.40	.15
❑	153	John Smoltz	.60	.25
❑	154	Scott Rolen	.60	.25
❑	155	Jimmy Rollins	.40	.15
❑	156	A.J. Burnett	.40	.15
❑	157	Jason Varitek	1.00	.40
❑	158	Ben Sheets	.40	.15
❑	159	Matt Cain	.60	.25
❑	160	Carl Crawford	.40	.15
❑	161	Jeff Suppan	.40	.15
❑	162	Tadahito Iguchi	.40	.15
❑	163	Kevin Millwood	.40	.15
❑	164	Chris Duncan	.40	.15
❑	165	Rich Harden	.40	.15
❑	166	Joe Crede	.40	.15
❑	167	Chipper Jones	1.00	.40
❑	168	Gary Sheffield	.40	.15
❑	169	Cole Hamels	.60	.25
❑	170	Jason Bay	.40	.15
❑	171	Jhonny Peralta	.40	.15
❑	172	Aubrey Huff	.40	.15
❑	173	Xavier Nady	.40	.15
❑	174	Kazuo Matsui	.40	.15
❑	175	Vernon Wells	.40	.15
❑	176	Johnny Damon	.60	.25
❑	177	Jim Edmonds	.60	.25
❑	178	Jose Vidro	.40	.15
❑	179	Garret Anderson	.40	.15
❑	180	Alex Rios	.40	.15
❑	181a	Ichiro Suzuki	1.50	.60
❑	181b	Ichiro Suzuki SP	8.00	3.00
❑	182a	Jake Peavy	.40	.15
❑	182b	Jake Peavy SP	4.00	1.25
❑	183a	Ian Kinsler	.40	.15
❑	183b	Ian Kinsler SP	4.00	1.25
❑	184a	Tom Gorzelanny	.40	.15
❑	184b	Tom Gorzelanny SP	4.00	1.25
❑	185a	Miguel Cabrera	.60	.25
❑	185b	Miguel Cabrera SP	5.00	2.00
❑	186a	Scott Kazmir	.60	.25
❑	186b	Scott Kazmir SP	5.00	2.00
❑	187a	Matt Holliday	1.00	.40
❑	187b	Matt Holliday SP	5.00	2.00
❑	188a	Roy Halladay	.40	.15
❑	188b	Roy Halladay SP	4.00	1.25
❑	189a	Ryan Zimmerman	1.00	.40
❑	189b	Ryan Zimmerman SP	5.00	2.00
❑	190a	Alex Rodriguez	1.50	.60
❑	190b	Alex Rodriguez SP	8.00	3.00
❑	191a	Kenji Johjima	1.00	.40
❑	191b	Kenji Johjima SP	5.00	2.00
❑	192a	Gil Meche	.40	.15
❑	192b	Gil Meche SP	4.00	1.25
❑	193a	Chase Utley	1.00	.40
❑	193b	Chase Utley SP	5.00	2.00
❑	194a	Jeremy Sowers	.40	.15
❑	194b	Jeremy Sowers SP	3.00	1.25
❑	195a	John Lackey	.40	.15
❑	195b	John Lackey SP	3.00	1.25
❑	196a	Nick Markakis	.60	.25
❑	196b	Nick Markakis SP	5.00	2.00
❑	197a	Tim Hudson	.40	.15
❑	197b	Tim Hudson SP	3.00	1.25
❑	198a	B.J. Upton	.40	.15
❑	198b	B.J. Upton SP	3.00	1.25
❑	199a	Felix Hernandez	.60	.25
❑	199b	Felix Hernandez SP	5.00	2.00
❑	200a	Barry Bonds	2.00	.75
❑	200b	Barry Bonds SP	10.00	4.00
❑	201	Jarrod Saltalamacchia (RC)	.75	.30
❑	202	Tim Lincecum RC	5.00	2.00
❑	203	Kory Casto (RC)	.50	.20
❑	204	Sean Henn (RC)	.50	.20
❑	205	Hector Gimenez (RC)	.50	.20
❑	206	Homer Bailey (RC)	.75	.30
❑	207	Yunel Escobar (RC)	.50	.20
❑	208	Matt Lindstrom (RC)	.50	.20
❑	209	Tyler Clippard (RC)	.75	.30
❑	210	Joe Smith RC	.50	.20
❑	211	Tony Abreu RC	1.50	.60
❑	212	Billy Butler (RC)	.75	.30
❑	213	Gustavo Molina RC	.50	.20
❑	214	Brian Stokes (RC)	.50	.20
❑	215	Kevin Slowey (RC)	1.25	.50
❑	216	Curtis Thigpen (RC)	.50	.20
❑	217	Carlos Gomez RC	.75	.30
❑	218	Rick Vanden Hurk RC	.75	.30
❑	219	Michael Bourn (RC)	.50	.20
❑	220	Jeff Baker (RC)	.50	.20
❑	221	Andy LaRoche (RC)	.50	.20
❑	222	Andy Sonnanstine RC	.50	.20
❑	223	Chase Wright RC	1.25	.50
❑	224	Mark Reynolds RC	1.25	.50
❑	225	Matt Chico (RC)	.50	.20
❑	226a	Hunter Pence (RC)	3.00	1.25
❑	226b	Hunter Pence SP	8.00	3.00
❑	227a	John Danks RC	.50	.20
❑	227b	John Danks SP	4.00	1.50
❑	228a	Elijah Dukes RC	.75	.30
❑	228b	Elijah Dukes SP	6.00	2.50
❑	229a	Kei Igawa RC	1.25	.50
❑	229b	Kei Igawa SP	6.00	2.50
❑	230a	Felix Pie (RC)	.50	.20
❑	230b	Felix Pie SP	4.00	1.50
❑	231a	Jesus Flores RC	.50	.20
❑	231b	Jesus Flores SP	4.00	1.50
❑	232a	Dallas Braden RC	.75	.30
❑	232b	Dallas Braden SP	6.00	2.50
❑	233a	Akinori Iwamura RC	1.25	.50
❑	233b	Akinori Iwamura SP	6.00	2.50
❑	234a	Ryan Braun (RC)	3.00	1.25
❑	234b	Ryan Braun SP	8.00	3.00
❑	235a	Alex Gordon RC	2.50	1.00
❑	235b	Alex Gordon SP	8.00	3.00
❑	236a	Micah Owings (RC)	.50	.20
❑	236b	Micah Owings SP	4.00	1.50
❑	237a	Kevin Kouzmanoff (RC)	.50	.20
❑	237b	Kevin Kouzmanoff SP	4.00	1.50
❑	238a	Glen Perkins (RC)	.50	.20
❑	238b	Glen Perkins SP	4.00	1.50
❑	239a	Danny Putnam (RC)	.50	.20
❑	239b	Danny Putnam SP	4.00	1.50
❑	240a	Philip Hughes (RC)	2.50	1.00
❑	240b	Philip Hughes SP	8.00	3.00
❑	241a	Ryan Sweeney (RC)	.50	.20
❑	241b	Ryan Sweeney SP	4.00	1.50
❑	242a	Josh Hamilton (RC)	1.25	.50
❑	242b	Josh Hamilton SP	6.00	2.50
❑	243a	Hideki Okajima RC	2.50	1.00
❑	243b	Hideki Okajima SP	8.00	3.00
❑	244a	Adam Lind (RC)	.50	.20
❑	244b	Adam Lind SP	4.00	1.50
❑	245a	Travis Buck (RC)	.50	.20

❑ 245b Travis Buck SP 4.00 1.50
❑ 246a Miguel Montero (RC) .50 .20
❑ 246b Miguel Montero SP 4.00 1.50
❑ 247a Brandon Morrow RC .75 .30
❑ 247b Brandon Morrow SP 6.00 2.50
❑ 248a Troy Tulowitzki (RC) 1.25 .50
❑ 248b Troy Tulowitzki SP 6.00 2.50
❑ 249a Delmon Young (RC) .75 .30
❑ 249b Delmon Young SP 6.00 2.50
❑ 250a Daisuke Matsuzaka RC 5.00 2.00
❑ 250b Daisuke Matsuzaka SP 10.00 4.00
❑ 251 Joba Chamberlain RC 8.00 3.00

2004 Bowman Sterling

❑ FY ODDS APPX.TWO PER HOBBY PACK
❑ FY AU ODDS APPX.ONE PER HOBBY PACK
❑ AU-GU ODDS APPX.ONE PER HOBBY PACK
❑ AU-GU 1:2 WRAPPER ODDS IS AN ERROR
❑ GU ODDS APPX. 1.5 PER HOBBY PACK
❑ GU 1:2 WRAPPER ODDS IS AN ERROR
❑ AB Angel Berroa Bat 5.00 2.00
❑ ABA Aarom Baldiris FY RC 5.00 2.00
❑ AC Alberto Callaspo FY AU RC 20.00 8.00
❑ AD Adam Dunn Bat 5.00 2.00
❑ AER Alex Rodriguez Bat 15.00 6.00
❑ AJ Andruw Jones Jsy 8.00 3.00
❑ AK Austin Kearns Jsy 5.00 2.00
❑ ANR Aramis Ramirez Bat 5.00 2.00
❑ AP Albert Pujols Jsy 20.00 8.00
❑ AR Alex Romero FY AU RC 8.00 3.00
❑ AW Adam Wainwright AU Jsy 25.00 10.00
❑ AWH A.Whittington FY RC 5.00 2.00
❑ AZ Alec Zumwalt FY AU RC 8.00 3.00
❑ BB Brian Bixler AU Jsy RC 10.00 4.00
❑ BBR Bill Bray FY RC 4.00 1.50
❑ BBU Billy Buckner FY RC 5.00 2.00
❑ BC2 Bobby Crosby Jsy 5.00 2.00
❑ BD Blake DeWitt AU Jsy RC 30.00 12.50
❑ BE Brad Eldred FY RC 5.00 2.00
❑ BH B.Hawksworth FY AU RC 10.00 4.00
❑ BT Brad Thompson FY RC 5.00 2.00
❑ BU B.J. Upton AU Bat 25.00 10.00
❑ BW Bernie Williams Jsy 8.00 3.00
❑ CA Chris Aguila FY AU RC 8.00 3.00
❑ CB Craig Biggio Jsy 8.00 3.00
❑ CC Chad Cordero AU Jsy 15.00 6.00
❑ CG Christian Garcia AU Jsy RC 15.00 6.00
❑ CH Chin-Lung Hu FY RC 15.00 6.00
❑ CIB Carlos Beltran Bat 5.00 2.00
❑ CJ Conor Jackson FY RC 20.00 8.00
❑ CL Chris Lubanski AU Bat 10.00 4.00
❑ CLA Chris Lambert FY RC 5.00 2.00
❑ CN Chris Nelson FY RC 8.00 3.00
❑ CQ Carlos Quentin FY AU RC 15.00 6.00
❑ CT Curtis Thigpen FY RC 5.00 2.00
❑ DD David DeJesus AU Jsy 15.00 6.00
❑ DP Danny Putnam AU Jsy RC 10.00 4.00
❑ DPU David Purcey FY RC 5.00 2.00
❑ DW David Wright AU Jsy 50.00 30.00
❑ DWW Dontrelle Willis Jsy 8.00 3.00
❑ DY Delmon Young AU Bat 25.00 10.00
❑ EG Eric Gagne Jsy 5.00 2.00
❑ EH Eric Hurley FY RC 5.00 2.00
❑ ESP Erick San Pedro FY RC 4.00 1.50
❑ FC Fausto Carmona FY RC 10.00 4.00
❑ FG Freddy Guzman FY RC 4.00 1.50
❑ FH Felix Hernandez FY RC 30.00 12.50
❑ FP Felix Pie AU Jsy 25.00 10.00
❑ FT Frank Thomas Bat 8.00 3.00
❑ GG Greg Golson FY RC 8.00 3.00
❑ GH Gaby Hernandez FY RC 8.00 3.00
❑ GIG Gio Gonzalez FY RC 8.00 3.00
❑ GS Gary Sheffield Bat 5.00 2.00
❑ HB Homer Bailey AU Jsy RC 50.00 20.00
❑ HC Hee Seop Choi Bat 5.00 2.00
❑ HG Hector Gimenez FY AU RC 8.00 3.00
❑ HJB Hank Blalock Bat 5.00 2.00
❑ HM Hector Made FY RC 5.00 2.00
❑ HS Huston Street AU Jsy RC 25.00 10.00
❑ IR Ivan Rodriguez Bat 8.00 3.00
❑ JB Jeff Bagwell Jsy 8.00 3.00
❑ JC Jose Capellan FY RC 5.00 2.00
❑ JCR Jesse Crain FY RC 5.00 2.00
❑ JD Johnny Damon Bat 8.00 3.00
❑ JE Johnny Estrada Bat 5.00 2.00
❑ JFI Josh Fields FY RC 15.00 6.00
❑ JG Joey Gathright FY RC 5.00 2.00
❑ JH Jesse Hoover FY RC 5.00 2.00
❑ JK Jason Kendall Bat 5.00 2.00
❑ JM Jeff Marquez AU Jsy RC 15.00 6.00
❑ JO Justin Orenduff FY RC 5.00 2.00
❑ JP Juan Pierre Bat 5.00 2.00
❑ JPH J.P. Howell FY RC 5.00 2.00
❑ JR Jay Rainville FY AU RC 20.00 8.00
❑ JS Jeremy Sowers FY AU RC 30.00 15.00
❑ JZ Jon Zeringue FY RC 5.00 2.00
❑ KCH K.C. Herren FY RC 5.00 2.00
❑ KS Kurt Suzuki FY RC 6.00 2.50
❑ KT Kazuhito Tadano FY RC 5.00 2.00
❑ KW Kerry Wood Jsy 5.00 2.00
❑ KWA Kyle Waldrop AU Jsy RC 15.00 6.00
❑ LB Lance Berkman Jsy 5.00 2.00
❑ LC Luis Castillo Jsy 5.00 2.00
❑ LH Linc Holdzkom FY AU RC 8.00 3.00
❑ LN Laynce Nix Bat 5.00 2.00
❑ MA Moises Alou Bat 5.00 2.00
❑ MAM Mark Mulder Jsy 5.00 2.00
❑ MAR Manny Ramirez Bat 8.00 3.00
❑ MB Matt Bush AU Jsy RC 25.00 10.00
❑ MC Miguel Cabrera Bat 8.00 3.00
❑ MCT Mark Teixeira Bat 8.00 3.00
❑ ME Mitch Einertson FY RC 5.00 2.00
❑ MF Mike Ferris FY RC 5.00 2.00
❑ MFO Matt Fox FY RC 4.00 1.50
❑ MJP Mike Piazza Bat 8.00 3.00
❑ MM Matt Moses FY AU RC 15.00 6.00
❑ MMC Matt Macri FY RC 6.00 2.50
❑ MP Mark Prior Jsy 8.00 3.00
❑ MR Mike Rouse FY AU RC 8.00 3.00
❑ MRO Mark Rogers FY RC 8.00 3.00
❑ MT M.Tuiasosopo AU Bat RC 30.00 12.50
❑ MT1 Miguel Tejada Bat 5.00 2.00
❑ MT2 Miguel Tejada Jsy 5.00 2.00
❑ MW Marland Williams FY RC 5.00 2.00
❑ MY Michael Young Bat 5.00 2.00
❑ NJ Nick Johnson Bat 5.00 2.00
❑ NM Nyjer Morgan FY RC 4.00 1.50
❑ NS Nate Schierholtz FY RC 8.00 3.00
❑ NW Neil Walker FY RC 8.00 3.00
❑ OQ Omar Quintanilla FY RC 5.00 2.00
❑ PGM Paul Maholm FY RC 8.00 3.00
❑ PH Philip Hughes FY RC 25.00 10.00
❑ PL Paul LoDuca Bat 5.00 2.00
❑ PR Pokey Reese Bat 5.00 2.00
❑ RB Rocco Baldelli Bat 5.00 2.00
❑ RBR Reid Brignac FY RC 10.00 4.00
❑ RC Robinson Cano AU Jsy 50.00 20.00
❑ RH Ryan Harvey AU Bat 15.00 6.00
❑ RJH Richard Hidalgo Bat 5.00 2.00
❑ RM Ryan Meaux FY AU RC 8.00 3.00
❑ RO Russ Ortiz Jsy 5.00 2.00
❑ RP Rafael Palmeiro Bat 8.00 3.00
❑ SK Scott Kazmir AU Jsy RC 30.00 12.50
❑ SO Scott Olsen AU Jsy RC 30.00 15.00
❑ SS Sammy Sosa Jsy 8.00 3.00
❑ SSM Seth Smith FY RC 8.00 3.00
❑ TD Thomas Diamond FY RC 8.00 3.00
❑ TG Troy Glaus Bat 5.00 2.00
❑ TLH Todd Helton Bat 8.00 3.00
❑ TM Tino Martinez Bat 8.00 3.00
❑ TMG Tom Glavine Jsy 8.00 3.00
❑ TP Trevor Plouffe AU Jsy RC 15.00 6.00
❑ TT T.Tankersley AU Jsy RC 10.00 4.00
❑ VG Vladimir Guerrero Bat 8.00 3.00
❑ VP Vince Perkins FY AU RC 10.00 4.00
❑ YP Yusmeiro Petit FY RC 10.00 4.00
❑ ZD Zach Duke FY RC 10.00 4.00
❑ ZJ Zach Jackson FY RC 5.00 2.00

2005 Bowman Sterling

❑ COMMON CARD 4.00 1.50
❑ BASIC CARDS APPX.TWO PER HOBBY PACK
❑ BASIC CARDS APPX.TWO PER RETAIL PACK
❑ AU GROUP A ODDS 1:2 HOBBY
❑ AU GROUP B ODDS 1:3 HOBBY
❑ AU-GU GROUP A ODDS 1:2 H, 1:2 R
❑ AU-GU GROUP B ODDS 1:37 H, 1:37 R
❑ AU-GU GROUP C ODDS 1:11 H, 1:11 R
❑ AU-GU GROUP D ODDS 1:10 H, 1:10 R
❑ AU-GU GROUP E ODDS 1:27 H, 1:27 R
❑ AU-GU GROUP F ODDS 1:13 H, 1:13 R
❑ GU GROUP A ODDS 1:3 H, 1:3 R
❑ GU GROUP B ODDS 1:5 H, 1:5 R
❑ GU GROUP C ODDS 1:6 H, 1:6 R
❑ ACL Andy LaRoche RC 8.00 3.00
❑ AL Adam Lind AU Bat B 25.00 10.00
❑ AM A.McCutchen AU Jsy D RC 50.0020.00
❑ AP Albert Pujols Jsy B 15.00 6.00
❑ AR Alex Rodriguez Jsy B UER 15.00 6.00
❑ ARA Aramis Ramirez Bat A 5.00 2.00
❑ AS Alfonso Soriano Bat A 5.00 2.00
❑ AT Aaron Thompson AU A RC 10.00 4.00
❑ BA Brian Anderson RC 6.00 2.50
❑ BB Billy Buckner AU Jsy A 10.00 4.00
❑ BBU Billy Butler RC 12.00 5.00
❑ BC Brent Cox AU Jsy D RC 15.00 6.00
❑ BCR Brad Corley RC 5.00 2.00
❑ BE Brad Eldred AU Jsy C 10.00 4.00
❑ BH Brett Hayes RC 4.00 1.50
❑ BJ Beau Jones AU Jsy A RC 20.00 8.00
❑ BL B.Livingston AU Jsy A RC 10.00 4.00
❑ BLB Barry Bonds Jsy C 15.00 6.00
❑ BM B.McCarthy AU Jsy A RC 25.00 10.00
❑ BMU Bill Mueller Jsy C 5.00 2.00
❑ BRB Brian Bogusevic RC 4.00 1.50
❑ BS Brandon Sing AU A RC 10.00 4.00
❑ BSN Brandon Snyder RC 8.00 3.00
❑ BZ Barry Zito Uni A 5.00 2.00
❑ CB Carlos Beltran Bat A 5.00 2.00
❑ CBU Clay Buchholz RC 30.00 12.50
❑ CC Cesar Carrillo RC 6.00 2.50
❑ CD Carlos Delgado Jsy A 5.00 2.00
❑ CH C.J. Henry AU B RC 12.00 5.00
❑ CHE Chase Headley RC 8.00 3.00
❑ CI Craig Italiano RC 5.00 2.00
❑ CJ Chuck James RC 10.00 4.00
❑ CLT Chuck Tiffany RC 5.00 2.00
❑ CN Chris Nelson AU Jsy A 10.00 4.00
❑ CP Cliff Pennington AU B RC 10.00 4.00
❑ CPP C.Pignatiello AU Jsy A RC 10.00 4.00
❑ CR Colby Rasmus AU Jsy A RC 60.0030.00
❑ CRA Cesar Ramos RC 5.00 2.00
❑ CRO Chaz Roe AU Jsy A RC 15.00 6.00
❑ CS C.J. Smith AU Jsy A RC 10.00 4.00
❑ CSU Curt Schilling Jsy C 8.00 3.00
❑ CT Curtis Thigpen AU Jsy A 10.00 4.00
❑ CV Chris Volstad AU B RC 12.00 5.00
❑ DC Dan Carte RC 5.00 2.00
❑ DL Derrek Lee Bat A 8.00 3.00
❑ DO David Ortiz Bat A 8.00 3.00
❑ DP Dustin Pedroia AU Jsy A 80.00 40.00
❑ DT Drew Thompson RC 5.00 2.00

- ❑ DW Dontrelle Willis Jsy C 5.00 2.00
- ❑ EC Eric Chavez Uni B 5.00 2.00
- ❑ EI Eli Iorg AU Jsy C RC 15.00 6.00
- ❑ EM Eddy Martinez AU A RC 10.00 4.00
- ❑ GK George Kottaras AU A RC 10.00 4.00
- ❑ GM Greg Maddux Jsy C 10.00 4.00
- ❑ GO Garrett Olson AU A RC 15.00 6.00
- ❑ GS Gary Sheffield Bat A 5.00 2.00
- ❑ HAS Henry Sanchez RC 6.00 2.50
- ❑ HB Hank Blalock Bat A 5.00 2.00
- ❑ HI Hernan Iribarren RC 5.00 2.00
- ❑ HM Hideki Matsui AS Jsy C 15.00 6.00
- ❑ HS Hum Sanchez AU A RC 20.00 8.00
- ❑ IR Ivan Rodriguez Bat A 8.00 3.00
- ❑ JB Jay Bruce AU Jsy D RC 60.00 30.00
- ❑ JBE Josh Beckett Uni A 5.00 2.00
- ❑ JC Jeff Clement RC 15.00 6.00
- ❑ JCN John Nelson AU Uni A RC 10.00 4.00
- ❑ JD Johnny Damon Bat A 8.00 3.00
- ❑ JDR John Drennen RC 8.00 3.00
- ❑ JE J.Ellsbury AU Jsy E RC 120.00 60.00
- ❑ JEG Jon Egan RC 5.00 2.00
- ❑ JF Josh Fields AU Jsy A 12.00 5.00
- ❑ JG Josh Geer AU Jsy A RC 10.00 4.00
- ❑ JGI Josh Gibson Seat C 15.00 6.00
- ❑ JL Jed Lowrie AU Jsy F RC 30.00 12.50
- ❑ JLY Jeff Lyman RC 5.00 2.00
- ❑ JM John Mayberry Jr. AU A RC 15.00 6.00
- ❑ JMA Jacob Marceaux RC 4.00 1.50
- ❑ JN Jeff Niemann AU Jsy A RC 15.00 6.00
- ❑ JO Justin Olson AU Jsy A RC 10.00 4.00
- ❑ JP Jorge Posada Bat A 8.00 3.00
- ❑ JPE Jim Edmonds Jsy B 5.00 2.00
- ❑ JS John Smoltz Jsy A 8.00 3.00
- ❑ JV J.Verlander AU Jsy A RC 60.00 30.00
- ❑ JW Josh Wall RC 5.00 2.00
- ❑ JWE Jered Weaver RC 15.00 6.00
- ❑ KG Khalil Greene Jsy B 8.00 3.00
- ❑ KM Kevin Millar Bat A 5.00 2.00
- ❑ KS Kevin Slowey RC 15.00 6.00
- ❑ KW Kevin Whelan RC 5.00 2.00
- ❑ LWJ Chipper Jones Bat A 8.00 3.00
- ❑ MA Matt Albers AU A RC 10.00 4.00
- ❑ MAM Matt Maloney RC 6.00 2.50
- ❑ MB M.Bowden AU Jsy A RC 30.00 12.50
- ❑ MC Mike Conroy AU Jsy A RC 10.00 4.00
- ❑ MCA Miguel Cabrera Jsy A 8.00 3.00
- ❑ MCO Mike Costanzo RC 8.00 3.00
- ❑ MG Matt Green AU A RC 8.00 3.00
- ❑ MGA Matt Garza RC 10.00 4.00
- ❑ MGI Marcus Giles AS Jsy B 5.00 2.00
- ❑ MM Mark Mulder Uni B 5.00 2.00
- ❑ MMC Mark McCormick RC 5.00 2.00
- ❑ MP Mike Piazza Bat A 8.00 3.00
- ❑ MPR Mark Prior Jsy B 8.00 3.00
- ❑ MR Manny Ramirez Bat A 8.00 3.00
- ❑ MT Miguel Tejada Uni A 5.00 2.00
- ❑ MTE Mark Teixeira Bat A 8.00 3.00
- ❑ MTO Matt Torra RC 5.00 2.00
- ❑ MY Michael Young Bat A 5.00 2.00
- ❑ NH Nick Hundley RC 4.00 1.50
- ❑ NR Nolan Reimold RC 8.00 3.00
- ❑ NW Nick Webber RC 4.00 1.50
- ❑ PH Philip Humber AU Jsy A RC 25.0010.00
- ❑ PK Paul Kelly RC 5.00 2.00
- ❑ PL Paul Lo Duca Bat A 5.00 2.00
- ❑ PM Pedro Martinez Jsy A 8.00 3.00
- ❑ PP P.J. Phillips RC 5.00 2.00
- ❑ RB Ryan Braun AU A RC 120.00 60.00
- ❑ RBE Ronnie Belliard Bat A 5.00 2.00
- ❑ RF Rafael Furcal Jsy A 5.00 2.00
- ❑ RM Russ Martin AU Jsy F RC 40.00 15.00
- ❑ RMO Ryan Mount RC 5.00 2.00
- ❑ RR Ricky Romero RC 5.00 2.00
- ❑ RT Raul Tablado AU Jsy A RC 10.00 4.00
- ❑ RZ Ryan Zimmerman RC 25.00 10.00
- ❑ SD Stephen Drew RC 20.00 8.00
- ❑ SE Scott Elbert AU Jsy A 10.00 4.00
- ❑ SM Steve Marek AU Jsy A RC 10.00 4.00
- ❑ SR Scott Rolen Jsy B 8.00 3.00
- ❑ SS Sammy Sosa Bat A 8.00 3.00
- ❑ SW Steven White AU B RC 8.00 3.00
- ❑ TB Trevor Bell AU Jsy C RC 15.00 6.00
- ❑ TBU Travis Buck RC 8.00 3.00
- ❑ TC Travis Chick AU A RC 8.00 3.00
- ❑ TG Tyler Greene RC 5.00 2.00
- ❑ TH Torii Hunter Bat A 5.00 2.00
- ❑ THE Tyler Herron RC 5.00 2.00
- ❑ THU Tim Hudson Uni A 5.00 2.00
- ❑ TI Tadahito Iguchi RC 5.00 2.00
- ❑ TLH Todd Helton Jsy B 8.00 3.00
- ❑ TM Tyler Minges AU Jsy A RC 10.00 4.00
- ❑ TM Tino Martinez Bat A 8.00 3.00
- ❑ TN Trot Nixon Bat A 5.00 2.00
- ❑ TT Troy Tulowitzki RC 15.00 6.00
- ❑ TW Travis Wood RC 6.00 2.50
- ❑ VG Vladimir Guerrero Bat A 8.00 3.00
- ❑ VM Victor Martinez Bat A 5.00 2.00
- ❑ WT Wade Townsend RC 5.00 2.00
- ❑ YE Yunel Escobar RC 5.00 2.00
- ❑ ZS Zach Simons RC 4.00 1.50

2006 Bowman Sterling

- ❑ COMMON ROOKIE 3.00 1.25
- ❑ COMMON AUTO RC 8.00 3.00
- ❑ AU RC AUTO ODDS 1:4 HOBBY
- ❑ COMMON AU-GU RC 10.00 4.00
- ❑ AU-GU RC ODDS 1:4 HOBBY
- ❑ COMMON GU VET 6.00 2.50
- ❑ GU VET ODDS 1:4 HOBBY
- ❑ OVERALL PLATE ODDS 1:23 BOXES
- ❑ PLATE PRINT RUN 1 SET PER COLOR
- ❑ BLACK-CYAN-MAGENTA-YELLOW ISSUED
- ❑ NO PLATE PRICING DUE TO SCARCITY
- ❑ EXCHANGE DEADLINE 12/31/08
- ❑ AD Adam Dunn Jsy 6.00 2.50
- ❑ AE Andre Ethier AU (RC) 25.00 10.00
- ❑ AER Alex Rodriguez Bat 25.00 10.00
- ❑ AJ Andruw Jones Jsy 8.00 3.00
- ❑ ALR A.Reyes Jsy AU (RC) EXCH 15.006.00
- ❑ ALS Alay Soler RC 3.00 1.25
- ❑ AP Albert Pujols Jsy 20.00 8.00
- ❑ AP2 Albert Pujols Bat 20.00 8.00
- ❑ APS Alfonso Soriano Bat 10.00 4.00
- ❑ AR Aramis Ramirez Bat UER 8.00 3.00
- ❑ AS Anibal Sanchez (RC) 4.00 1.50
- ❑ BA Brian Anderson (RC) 3.00 1.25
- ❑ BB Brian Bannister (RC) 3.00 1.25
- ❑ BL B.Livingston Jsy AU (RC) 10.00 4.00
- ❑ BLB Barry Bonds Bat 15.00 6.00
- ❑ BON Boof Bonser (RC) 4.00 1.50
- ❑ BR Brian Roberts Jsy 6.00 2.50
- ❑ BZ Ben Zobrist (RC) 4.00 1.50
- ❑ CB Carlos Beltran Jsy 6.00 2.50
- ❑ CB2 Carlos Beltran Bat 6.00 2.50
- ❑ CC Chris Carpenter Jsy 10.00 4.00
- ❑ CH Cole Hamels Jsy AU (RC) 40.00 15.00
- ❑ CHJ Chuck James (RC) 4.00 1.50
- ❑ CI Chris Iannetta Jsy AU RC 20.00 8.00
- ❑ CJ Conor Jackson (RC) 4.00 1.50
- ❑ CJJ Casey Janssen RC 4.00 1.50
- ❑ CQ Carlos Quentin (RC) 4.00 1.50
- ❑ CRB Chad Billingsley (RC) 4.00 1.50
- ❑ CRH Craig Hansen RC 5.00 2.00
- ❑ CS Curt Schilling Jsy 8.00 3.00
- ❑ DG David Gassner (RC) 3.00 1.25
- ❑ DO David Ortiz Bat 10.00 4.00
- ❑ DP David Pauley (RC) 3.00 1.25
- ❑ DU Dan Uggla (RC) 5.00 2.00
- ❑ DW David Wright Jsy 15.00 6.00
- ❑ DWW Dontrelle Willis Jsy 6.00 2.50
- ❑ EC Eric Chavez Pants 6.00 2.50
- ❑ EG Enrique Gonzalez (RC) 3.00 1.25
- ❑ FG Franklin Gutierrez (RC) 3.00 1.25
- ❑ FL Francisco Liriano (RC) 6.00 2.50
- ❑ GS Grady Sizemore Jsy 10.00 4.00
- ❑ HB Hank Blalock Jsy 6.00 2.50
- ❑ HK1 Howie Kendrick (RC) 5.00 2.00
- ❑ HK2 H.Kendrick Jsy AU (RC) EXCH 20.00 8.00
- ❑ HM Hideki Matsui Bat 15.00 6.00
- ❑ HP Hayden Penn (RC) 3.00 1.25
- ❑ HR Hanley Ramirez (RC) 5.00 2.00
- ❑ IK Ian Kinsler AU (RC) 25.00 10.00
- ❑ IR Ivan Rodriguez Jsy 8.00 3.00
- ❑ IS Ichiro Suzuki Jsy 25.00 10.00
- ❑ JAS Johan Santana Jsy 10.00 4.00
- ❑ JB J.Bulger Jsy AU (RC) EXCH 10.00 4.00
- ❑ JBS Jeremy Sowers (RC) 3.00 1.25
- ❑ JCB Jason Botts AU (RC) 8.00 3.00
- ❑ JD Joey Devine RC 3.00 1.25
- ❑ JDD Johnny Damon Bat 10.00 4.00
- ❑ JHT Jim Thome Bat 10.00 4.00
- ❑ JI Joe Inglett AU RC 12.00 5.00
- ❑ JJ Josh Johnson (RC) 4.00 1.50
- ❑ JK Jeff Karstens RC 5.00 2.00
- ❑ JL James Loney (RC) 4.00 1.50
- ❑ JLB Josh Barfield AU (RC) 8.00 3.00
- ❑ JM Jeff Mathis (RC) 3.00 1.25
- ❑ JP Jonathan Papelbon (RC) 8.00 3.00
- ❑ JRH Rich Harden Jsy 6.00 2.50
- ❑ JS James Shields RC 3.00 1.25
- ❑ JT Jack Taschner Jsy AU (RC) 10.00 4.00
- ❑ JTA Jordan Tata RC 3.00 1.25
- ❑ JTL Jon Lester Jsy AU RC EXCH 40.00 15.00
- ❑ JV Justin Verlander (RC) 8.00 3.00
- ❑ JW Jered Weaver (RC) 6.00 2.50
- ❑ JZ Joel Zumaya (RC) 5.00 2.00
- ❑ KF Kevin Frandsen (RC) 3.00 1.25
- ❑ KJ Kenji Johjima RC 8.00 3.00
- ❑ KM Kendry Morales (RC) 4.00 1.50
- ❑ LB Lance Berkman Jsy 8.00 3.00
- ❑ LM Lastings Milledge AU (RC) 20.00 8.00
- ❑ LWJ Chipper Jones Jsy 10.00 4.00
- ❑ MC Miguel Cabrera Jsy 8.00 3.00
- ❑ MC2 Miguel Cabrera Bat 8.00 3.00
- ❑ MCC Melky Cabrera (RC) 4.00 1.50
- ❑ MCM Mickey Mantle Bat 100.00 50.00
- ❑ MCT Mark Teixeira Bat 8.00 3.00
- ❑ ME Morgan Ensberg Jsy 6.00 2.50
- ❑ MJP Mike Piazza Bat 10.00 4.00
- ❑ MK Matt Kemp (RC) 4.00 1.50
- ❑ MM Mark Mulder Pants 6.00 2.50
- ❑ MN Mike Napoli Jsy AU RC EXCH 15.00 6.00
- ❑ MP Martin Prado Jsy AU (RC) 20.00 8.00
- ❑ MPP Mike Pelfrey RC 15.00 6.00
- ❑ MR Manny Ramirez Jsy 10.00 4.00
- ❑ MR2 Manny Ramirez Bat 10.00 4.00
- ❑ MS Matt Smith (RC) 4.00 1.50
- ❑ MT Miguel Tejada Pants 6.00 2.50
- ❑ NM Nick Markakis (RC) 4.00 1.50
- ❑ PF Prince Fielder Jsy AU (RC) 80.00 40.00
- ❑ PK Paul Konerko Bat 8.00 3.00
- ❑ PM Pedro Martinez Pants 8.00 3.00
- ❑ RC Robinson Cano Bat 12.00 5.00
- ❑ RH Ryan Howard Jsy 20.00 8.00
- ❑ RK Ryan Garko (RC) 3.00 1.25
- ❑ RM Russ Martin (RC) 4.00 1.50
- ❑ RN Ricky Nolasco AU (RC) 8.00 3.00
- ❑ RP Ronny Paulino Jsy AU (RC) 15.00 6.00
- ❑ RZ Ryan Zimmerman (RC) 8.00 3.00
- ❑ SD Stephen Drew (RC) 5.00 2.00
- ❑ SM Scott Mathieson (RC) 3.00 1.25
- ❑ SO Scott Olsen (RC) 3.00 1.25
- ❑ SR Scott Rolen Pants 8.00 3.00
- ❑ ST S.Thorman Jsy AU (RC) EXCH 12.00 5.00
- ❑ TGJ Tony Gwynn Jr (RC) 6.00 2.50
- ❑ TH Todd Helton Jsy 8.00 3.00
- ❑ TT Taylor Tankersley (RC) 3.00 1.25
- ❑ VG Vladimir Guerrero Jsy 8.00 3.00
- ❑ WA Willy Aybar (RC) 3.00 1.25
- ❑ YP Yusmeiro Petit Jsy AU (RC) 10.00 4.00
- ❑ ZM Zach Miner AU (RC) 8.00 3.00

1914 Cracker Jack

- ❑ COMPLETE SET (144) 45000.00 27500.00
- ❑ 1 Otto Knabe 250.00 150.00
- ❑ 2 Frank Baker 400.00 250.00
- ❑ 3 Joe Tinker 400.00 250.00
- ❑ 4 Larry Doyle 175.00 100.00

❑ 5 Ward Miller 150.00 75.00
❑ 6 Eddie Plank 600.00 350.00
❑ 7 Eddie Collins 450.00 275.00
❑ 8 Rube Oldring 150.00 75.00
❑ 9 Artie Hoffman 150.00 75.00
❑ 10 John McInnis 150.00 75.00
❑ 11 George Stovall 150.00 75.00
❑ 12 Connie Mack MG 500.00 300.00
❑ 13 Art Wilson 150.00 75.00
❑ 14 Sam Crawford 300.00 175.00
❑ 15 Reb Russell 150.00 75.00
❑ 16 Howie Camnitz 150.00 75.00
❑ 17 Roger Bresnahan 350.00 200.00
❑ 18 Johnny Evers 350.00 200.00
❑ 19 Chief Bender 450.00 275.00
❑ 20 Cy Falkenberg 150.00 75.00
❑ 21 Heinie Zimmerman 150.00 75.00
❑ 22 Joe Wood 300.00 175.00
❑ 23 Charles Comiskey 350.00 200.00
❑ 24 George Mullen 150.00 75.00
❑ 25 Michael Simon 150.00 75.00
❑ 26 James Scott 150.00 75.00
❑ 27 Bill Carrigan 150.00 75.00
❑ 28 Jack Barry 150.00 75.00
❑ 29 Vean Gregg 200.00 125.00
❑ 30 Ty Cobb 6000.00 3600.00
❑ 31 Heinie Wagner 150.00 75.00
❑ 32 Mordecai Brown 350.00 200.00
❑ 33 Amos Strunk 150.00 75.00
❑ 34 Ira Thomas 150.00 75.00
❑ 35 Harry Hooper 300.00 175.00
❑ 36 Ed Walsh 300.00 175.00
❑ 37 Grover C. Alexander 800.00 500.00
❑ 38 Red Dooin 200.00 125.00
❑ 39 Chick Gandil 350.00 200.00
❑ 40 Jimmy Austin 200.00 125.00
❑ 41 Tommy Leach 150.00 75.00
❑ 42 Al Bridwell 150.00 75.00
❑ 43 Rube Marquard 350.00 200.00
❑ 44 Jeff (Charles) Tesreau 150.00 75.00
❑ 45 Fred Luderus 150.00 75.00
❑ 46 Bob Groom 150.00 75.00
❑ 47 Josh Devore 200.00 125.00
❑ 48 Harry Lord 250.00 150.00
❑ 49 John Miller 150.00 75.00
❑ 50 John Hummell 150.00 75.00
❑ 51 Nap Rucker 175.00 100.00
❑ 52 Zach Wheat 350.00 200.00
❑ 53 Otto Miller 150.00 75.00
❑ 54 Marty O'Toole 150.00 75.00
❑ 55 Dick Hoblitzel 200.00 125.00
❑ 56 Clyde Milan 175.00 100.00
❑ 57 Walter Johnson 2000.00 1200.00
❑ 58 Wally Schang 175.00 100.00
❑ 59 Harry Gessler 150.00 75.00
❑ 60 Rollie Zeider 250.00 150.00
❑ 61 Ray Schalk 300.00 175.00
❑ 62 Jay Cashion 300.00 175.00
❑ 63 Babe Adams 175.00 100.00
❑ 64 Jimmy Archer 150.00 75.00
❑ 65 Tris Speaker 700.00 450.00
❑ 66 Napoleon Lajoie 800.00 500.00
❑ 67 Otis Crandall 150.00 75.00
❑ 68 Honus Wagner 2500.00 1800.00
❑ 69 John McGraw 450.00 275.00
❑ 70 Fred Clarke 300.00 175.00
❑ 71 Chief Meyers 175.00 100.00
❑ 72 John Boehling 150.00 75.00
❑ 73 Max Carey 300.00 175.00
❑ 74 Frank Owens 150.00 75.00
❑ 75 Miller Huggins 300.00 175.00
❑ 76 Claude Hendrix 150.00 75.00
❑ 77 Hughie Jennings MG 300.00 175.00
❑ 78 Fred Merkle 200.00 125.00
❑ 79 Ping Bodie 175.00 100.00
❑ 80 Ed Ruelbach 175.00 100.00
❑ 81 Jim Delahanty 175.00 100.00
❑ 82 Gavvy Cravath 200.00 125.00
❑ 83 Russ Ford 150.00 75.00
❑ 84 Elmer E. Knetzer 150.00 75.00
❑ 85 Buck Herzog 150.00 75.00
❑ 86 Burt Shotton 150.00 75.00
❑ 87 Forrest Cady 150.00 75.00
❑ 88 Christy Mathewson 3000.00 2000.00
❑ 89 Lawrence Cheney 150.00 75.00
❑ 90 Frank Smith 150.00 75.00
❑ 91 Roger Peckinpaugh 175.00 100.00
❑ 92 Al Demaree 200.00 125.00
❑ 93 Del Pratt 250.00 150.00
❑ 94 Eddie Cicotte 325.00 175.00
❑ 95 Ray Keating 150.00 75.00
❑ 96 Beals Becker 150.00 75.00
❑ 97 John (Rube) Benton 150.00 75.00
❑ 98 Frank LaPorte 150.00 75.00
❑ 99 Frank Chance 1500.00 1000.00
❑ 100 Thomas Seaton 150.00 75.00
❑ 101 Frank Schulte 150.00 75.00
❑ 102 Ray Fisher 150.00 75.00
❑ 103 Joe Jackson 8000.00 5000.00
❑ 104 Vic Saier 150.00 75.00
❑ 105 James Lavender 150.00 75.00
❑ 106 Joe Birmingham 150.00 75.00
❑ 107 Tom Downey 150.00 75.00
❑ 108 Sherry Magee 200.00 125.00
❑ 109 Fred Blanding 150.00 75.00
❑ 110 Bob Bescher 150.00 75.00
❑ 111 Jim Callahan 300.00 175.00
❑ 112 Ed Sweeney 150.00 75.00
❑ 113 George Suggs 150.00 75.00
❑ 114 George Moriarity 175.00 100.00
❑ 115 Addison Brennan 150.00 75.00
❑ 116 Rollie Zeider 150.00 75.00
❑ 117 Ted Easterly 150.00 75.00
❑ 118 Ed Konetchy 200.00 125.00
❑ 119 George Perring 150.00 75.00
❑ 120 Mike Doolan 150.00 75.00
❑ 121 Hub Perdue 200.00 125.00
❑ 122 Owen Bush 150.00 75.00
❑ 123 Slim Sallee 150.00 75.00
❑ 124 Earl Moore 150.00 75.00
❑ 125 Bert Niehoff 200.00 125.00
❑ 126 Walter Blair 150.00 75.00
❑ 127 Butch Schmidt 150.00 75.00
❑ 128 Steve Evans 150.00 75.00
❑ 129 Ray Caldwell 150.00 75.00
❑ 130 Ivy Wingo 150.00 75.00
❑ 131 George Baumgardner 150.00 75.00
❑ 132 Les Nunamaker 150.00 75.00
❑ 133 Branch Rickey MG 450.00 275.00
❑ 134 Armando Marsans 200.00 125.00
❑ 135 Bill Killefer 150.00 75.00
❑ 136 Rabbit Maranville 350.00 200.00
❑ 137 William Rariden 150.00 75.00
❑ 138 Hank Gowdy 150.00 75.00
❑ 139 Rebel Oakes 150.00 75.00
❑ 140 Danny Murphy 150.00 75.00
❑ 141 Cy Barger 150.00 75.00
❑ 142 Eugene Packard 150.00 75.00
❑ 143 Jake Daubert 175.00 100.00
❑ 144 James C. Walsh 200.00 125.00

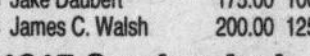

1915 Cracker Jack

❑ COMPLETE SET (176) 35000.00 20000.00
❑ COMMON CARD (1-144) 100.00 60.00
❑ COMMON CARD(145-176) 125.00 75.00
❑ 1 Otto Knabe 175.00 100.00
❑ 2 Frank Baker 350.00 200.00
❑ 3 Joe Tinker 350.00 200.00
❑ 4 Larry Doyle 100.00 60.00
❑ 5 Ward Miller 100.00 60.00
❑ 6 Eddie Plank 500.00 300.00
❑ 7 Eddie Collins 350.00 200.00
❑ 8 Rube Oldring 100.00 60.00

❑ 9 Artie Hoffman 100.00 60.00
❑ 10 John McInnis 100.00 60.00
❑ 11 George Stovall 100.00 60.00
❑ 12 Connie Mack MG 400.00 250.00
❑ 13 Art Wilson 100.00 60.00
❑ 14 Sam Crawford 300.00 175.00
❑ 15 Reb Russell 100.00 60.00
❑ 16 Howie Camnitz 100.00 60.00
❑ 17 Roger Bresnahan 300.00 175.00
❑ 18 Johnny Evers 300.00 175.00
❑ 19 Chief Bender 350.00 200.00
❑ 20 Cy Falkenberg 100.00 60.00
❑ 21 Heinie Zimmerman 100.00 60.00
❑ 22 Joe Wood 250.00 150.00
❑ 23 Charles Comiskey 300.00 200.00
❑ 24 George Mullen 100.00 60.00
❑ 25 Michael Simon 100.00 60.00
❑ 26 James Scott 100.00 60.00
❑ 27 Bill Carrigan 100.00 60.00
❑ 28 Jack Barry 100.00 60.00
❑ 29 Vean Gregg 125.00 75.00
❑ 30 Ty Cobb 4000.00 3000.00
❑ 31 Heinie Wagner 100.00 60.00
❑ 32 Mordecai Brown 300.00 175.00
❑ 33 Amos Strunk 100.00 60.00
❑ 34 Ira Thomas 100.00 60.00
❑ 35 Harry Hooper 250.00 150.00
❑ 36 Ed Walsh 300.00 175.00
❑ 37 Grover C. Alexander 600.00 350.00
❑ 38 Red Dooin 125.00 75.00
❑ 39 Chick Gandil 300.00 175.00
❑ 40 Jimmy Austin 125.00 75.00
❑ 41 Tommy Leach 100.00 60.00
❑ 42 Al Bridwell 100.00 60.00
❑ 43 Rube Marquard 350.00 200.00
❑ 44 Jeff (Charles) Tesreau 100.00 60.00
❑ 45 Fred Luderus 100.00 60.00
❑ 46 Bob Groom 100.00 60.00
❑ 47 Josh Devore 125.00 75.00
❑ 48 Steve O'Neill 125.00 75.00
❑ 49 John Miller 100.00 60.00
❑ 50 John Hummell 100.00 60.00
❑ 51 Nap Rucker 125.00 75.00
❑ 52 Zach Wheat 300.00 175.00
❑ 53 Otto Miller 100.00 60.00
❑ 54 Marty O'Toole 100.00 60.00
❑ 55 Dick Hoblitzel 125.00 75.00
❑ 56 Clyde Milan 125.00 75.00
❑ 57 Walter Johnson 1500.00 1000.00
❑ 58 Wally Schang 125.00 75.00
❑ 59 Harry Gessler 100.00 60.00
❑ 60 Oscar Dugey 125.00 75.00
❑ 61 Ray Schalk 250.00 150.00
❑ 62 Willie Mitchell 125.00 75.00
❑ 63 Babe Adams 125.00 75.00
❑ 64 Jimmy Archer 100.00 60.00
❑ 65 Tris Speaker 600.00 350.00
❑ 66 Napoleon Lajoie 600.00 350.00
❑ 67 Otis Crandall 100.00 60.00
❑ 68 Honus Wagner 1500.00 1000.00
❑ 69 John McGraw MG 300.00 175.00
❑ 70 Fred Clarke 250.00 150.00
❑ 71 Chief Meyers 100.00 60.00
❑ 72 John Boehling 100.00 60.00
❑ 73 Max Carey 250.00 150.00
❑ 74 Frank Owens 100.00 60.00
❑ 75 Miller Huggins 300.00 175.00
❑ 76 Claude Hendrix 100.00 60.00

❑ 77 Hughie Jennings MG	300.00	175.00
❑ 78 Fred Merkle	125.00	75.00
❑ 79 Ping Bodie	125.00	75.00
❑ 80 Ed Ruelbach	125.00	75.00
❑ 81 Jim Delahanty	125.00	75.00
❑ 82 Gavvy Cravath	125.00	75.00
❑ 83 Russ Ford	100.00	60.00
❑ 84 Elmer E. Knetzer	100.00	60.00
❑ 85 Buck Herzog	100.00	60.00
❑ 86 Burt Shotton	100.00	60.00
❑ 87 Forrest Cady	100.00	60.00
❑ 88 Christy Mathewson	1500.00	1000.00
❑ 89 Lawrence Cheney	100.00	60.00
❑ 90 Frank Smith	100.00	60.00
❑ 91 Roger Peckinpaugh	125.00	75.00
❑ 92 Al Demaree	125.00	75.00
❑ 93 Del Pratt	175.00	100.00
❑ 94 Eddie Cicotte	300.00	175.00
❑ 95 Ray Keating	100.00	60.00
❑ 96 Beals Becker	100.00	60.00
❑ 97 John (Rube) Benton	100.00	60.00
❑ 98 Frank LaPorte	100.00	60.00
❑ 99 Hal Chase	300.00	175.00
❑ 100 Thomas Seaton	100.00	60.00
❑ 101 Frank Schulte	100.00	60.00
❑ 102 Ray Fisher	100.00	60.00
❑ 103 Joe Jackson	8000.00	5000.00
❑ 104 Vic Saier	100.00	60.00
❑ 105 James Lavender	100.00	60.00
❑ 106 Joe Birmingham	100.00	60.00
❑ 107 Thomas Downey	100.00	60.00
❑ 108 Sherry Magee	125.00	75.00
❑ 109 Fred Blanding	100.00	60.00
❑ 110 Bob Bescher	100.00	60.00
❑ 111 Herbie Moran	125.00	75.00
❑ 112 Ed Sweeney	100.00	60.00
❑ 113 George Suggs	100.00	60.00
❑ 114 George Moriarity	125.00	75.00
❑ 115 Addison Brennan	100.00	60.00
❑ 116 Rollie Zeider	100.00	60.00
❑ 117 Ted Easterly	100.00	60.00
❑ 118 Ed Konetchy	125.00	75.00
❑ 119 George Perring	100.00	60.00
❑ 120 Mike Doolan	100.00	60.00
❑ 121 Hub Perdue	125.00	75.00
❑ 122 Owen Bush	100.00	60.00
❑ 123 Slim Sallee	100.00	60.00
❑ 124 Earl Moore	100.00	60.00
❑ 125 Bert Niehoff	125.00	75.00
❑ 126 Walter Blair	100.00	60.00
❑ 127 Butch Schmidt	100.00	60.00
❑ 128 Steve Evans	100.00	60.00
❑ 129 Ray Caldwell	100.00	60.00
❑ 130 Ivy Wingo	100.00	60.00
❑ 131 Geo. Baumgardner	100.00	60.00
❑ 132 Les Nunamaker	100.00	60.00
❑ 133 Branch Rickey MG	300.00	175.00
❑ 134 Armando Marsans	125.00	75.00
❑ 135 William Killefer	100.00	60.00
❑ 136 Rabbit Maranville	250.00	150.00
❑ 137 William Rariden	100.00	60.00
❑ 138 Hank Gowdy	100.00	60.00
❑ 139 Rebel Oakes	100.00	60.00
❑ 140 Danny Murphy	100.00	60.00
❑ 141 Cy Barger	100.00	60.00
❑ 142 Eugene Packard	100.00	60.00
❑ 143 Jake Daubert	100.00	60.00
❑ 144 James C. Walsh	100.00	60.00
❑ 145 Ted Cather	125.00	75.00
❑ 146 George Tyler	125.00	75.00
❑ 147 Lee Magee	125.00	75.00
❑ 148 Owen Wilson	125.00	75.00
❑ 149 Hal Janvrin	125.00	75.00
❑ 150 Doc Johnston	125.00	75.00
❑ 151 George Whitted	125.00	75.00
❑ 152 George McQuillen	125.00	75.00
❑ 153 Bill James	125.00	75.00
❑ 154 Dick Rudolph	125.00	75.00
❑ 155 Joe Connolly	125.00	75.00
❑ 156 Jean Dubuc	125.00	75.00
❑ 157 George Kaiserling	125.00	75.00
❑ 158 Fritz Maisel	125.00	75.00
❑ 159 Heinie Groh	125.00	75.00
❑ 160 Benny Kauff	125.00	75.00
❑ 161 Edd Roush	300.00	175.00
❑ 162 George Stallings MG	125.00	75.00
❑ 163 Bert Whaling	125.00	75.00
❑ 164 Bob Shawkey	125.00	75.00
❑ 165 Eddie Murphy	125.00	75.00
❑ 166 Joe Bush	125.00	75.00
❑ 167 Clark Griffith	300.00	175.00
❑ 168 Vin Campbell	125.00	75.00
❑ 169 Raymond Collins	125.00	75.00
❑ 170 Hans Lobert	125.00	75.00
❑ 171 Earl Hamilton	125.00	75.00
❑ 172 Erskine Mayer	125.00	75.00
❑ 173 Tilly Walker	125.00	75.00
❑ 174 Robert Veach	125.00	75.00
❑ 175 Joseph Benz	125.00	75.00
❑ 176 Hippo Vaughn	175.00	100.00

1981 Donruss

❑ COMPLETE SET (605)	50.00	20.00
❑ 1 Ozzie Smith	3.00	1.25
❑ 2 Rollie Fingers	.25	.08
❑ 3 Rick Wise	.10	.02
❑ 4 Gene Richards	.10	.02
❑ 5 Alan Trammell	.50	.20
❑ 6 Tom Brookens	.10	.02
❑ 7A Duffy Dyer P1	.25	.08
❑ 7B Duffy Dyer P2	.10	.02
❑ 8 Mark Fidrych	.25	.08
❑ 9 Dave Rozema	.10	.02
❑ 10 Ricky Peters RC	.10	.02
❑ 11 Mike Schmidt	2.50	1.00
❑ 12 Willie Stargell	.50	.20
❑ 13 Tim Foli	.10	.02
❑ 14 Manny Sanguillen	.25	.08
❑ 15 Grant Jackson	.10	.02
❑ 16 Eddie Solomon	.10	.02
❑ 17 Omar Moreno	.10	.02
❑ 18 Joe Morgan	.50	.20
❑ 19 Rafael Landestoy	.10	.02
❑ 20 Bruce Bochy	.10	.02
❑ 21 Joe Sambito	.10	.02
❑ 22 Manny Trillo	.10	.02
❑ 23A Dave Smith P1	.50	.20
❑ 23B Dave Smith P2 RC	.50	.20
❑ 24 Terry Puhl	.10	.02
❑ 25 Bump Wills	.10	.02
❑ 26A John Ellis P1 ERR	.50	.20
❑ 26B John Ellis P2 COR	.25	.08
❑ 27 Jim Kern	.10	.02
❑ 28 Richie Zisk	.10	.02
❑ 29 John Mayberry	.10	.02
❑ 30 Bob Davis	.10	.02
❑ 31 Jackson Todd	.10	.02
❑ 32 Alvis Woods	.10	.02
❑ 33 Steve Carlton	.50	.20
❑ 34 Lee Mazzilli	.25	.08
❑ 35 John Stearns	.10	.02
❑ 36 Roy Lee Jackson RC	.10	.02
❑ 37 Mike Scott	.25	.08
❑ 38 Lamar Johnson	.10	.02
❑ 39 Kevin Bell	.10	.02
❑ 40 Ed Farmer	.10	.02
❑ 41 Ross Baumgarten	.10	.02
❑ 42 Leo Sutherland RC	.10	.02
❑ 43 Dan Meyer	.10	.02
❑ 44 Ron Reed	.10	.02
❑ 45 Mario Mendoza	.10	.02
❑ 46 Rick Honeycutt	.10	.02
❑ 47 Glenn Abbott	.10	.02
❑ 48 Leon Roberts	.10	.02
❑ 49 Rod Carew	.50	.20
❑ 50 Bert Campaneris	.25	.08
❑ 51A Tom Donahue P1 ERR	.25	.08
❑ 51B Tom Donohue P2 RC	.10	.02
❑ 52 Dave Frost	.10	.02
❑ 53 Ed Halicki	.10	.02
❑ 54 Dan Ford	.10	.02
❑ 55 Garry Maddox	.10	.02
❑ 56A Steve Garvey P1 25HR	.25	.08
❑ 56B Steve Garvey P2 21HR	.25	.08
❑ 57 Bill Russell	.25	.08
❑ 58 Don Sutton	.25	.08
❑ 59 Reggie Smith	.25	.08
❑ 60 Rick Monday	.25	.08
❑ 61 Ray Knight	.25	.08
❑ 62 Johnny Bench	1.00	.40
❑ 63 Mario Soto	.25	.08
❑ 64 Doug Bair	.10	.02
❑ 65 George Foster	.25	.08
❑ 66 Jeff Burroughs	.25	.08
❑ 67 Keith Hernandez	.25	.08
❑ 68 Tom Herr	.10	.02
❑ 69 Bob Forsch	.10	.02
❑ 70 John Fulgham	.10	.02
❑ 71A Bobby Bonds P1 ERR	1.00	.40
❑ 71B Bobby Bonds P2 COR	.50	.20
❑ 72A Rennie Stennett P1	.25	.08
❑ 72B Rennie Stennett P2	.10	.02
❑ 73 Joe Strain	.10	.02
❑ 74 Ed Whitson	.10	.02
❑ 75 Tom Griffin	.10	.02
❑ 76 Billy North	.10	.02
❑ 77 Gene Garber	.10	.02
❑ 78 Mike Hargrove	.10	.02
❑ 79 Dave Rosello	.10	.02
❑ 80 Ron Hassey	.10	.02
❑ 81 Sid Monge	.10	.02
❑ 82A Joe Charboneau P1	1.00	.40
❑ 82B Joe Charboneau P2 RC	1.00	.40
❑ 83 Cecil Cooper	.25	.08
❑ 84 Sal Bando	.25	.08
❑ 85 Moose Haas	.10	.02
❑ 86 Mike Caldwell	.10	.02
❑ 87A Larry Hisle P1	.25	.08
❑ 87B Larry Hisle P2	.10	.02
❑ 88 Luis Gomez	.10	.02
❑ 89 Larry Parrish	.10	.02
❑ 90 Gary Carter	.50	.20
❑ 91 Bill Gullickson RC	.50	.20
❑ 92 Fred Norman	.10	.02
❑ 93 Tommy Hutton	.10	.02
❑ 94 Carl Yastrzemski	1.50	.60
❑ 95 Glenn Hoffman RC	.10	.02
❑ 96 Dennis Eckersley	.50	.20
❑ 97A Tom Burgmeier P1	.25	.08
❑ 97B Tom Burgmeier P2	.10	.02
❑ 98 Win Remmerswaal RC	.10	.02
❑ 99 Bob Horner	.25	.08
❑ 100 George Brett	2.50	1.00
❑ 101 Dave Chalk	.10	.02
❑ 102 Dennis Leonard	.10	.02
❑ 103 Renie Martin	.10	.02
❑ 104 Amos Otis	.25	.08
❑ 105 Graig Nettles	.25	.08
❑ 106 Eric Soderholm	.10	.02
❑ 107 Tommy John	.25	.08
❑ 108 Tom Underwood	.10	.02
❑ 109 Lou Piniella	.25	.08
❑ 110 Mickey Klutts	.10	.02
❑ 111 Bobby Murcer	.25	.08
❑ 112 Eddie Murray	1.50	.60
❑ 113 Rick Dempsey	.10	.02
❑ 114 Scott McGregor	.10	.02
❑ 115 Ken Singleton	.25	.08
❑ 116 Gary Roenicke	.10	.02
❑ 117 Dave Revering	.10	.02
❑ 118 Mike Norris	.10	.02
❑ 119 Rickey Henderson	6.00	2.50
❑ 120 Mike Heath	.10	.02
❑ 121 Dave Cash	.10	.02
❑ 122 Randy Jones	.25	.08
❑ 123 Eric Rasmussen	.10	.02
❑ 124 Jerry Mumphrey	.10	.02
❑ 125 Richie Hebner	.10	.02
❑ 126 Mark Wagner	.10	.02
❑ 127 Jack Morris	.50	.20

❑ 128 Dan Petry .10 .02
❑ 129 Bruce Robbins .10 .02
❑ 130 Champ Summers .10 .02
❑ 131 Pete Rose 3.00 1.25
❑ 131B Pete Rose P2 2.00 .75
❑ 132 Willie Stargell .50 .20
❑ 133 Ed Ott .10 .02
❑ 134 Jim Bibby .10 .02
❑ 135 Bert Blyleven .25 .08
❑ 136 Dave Parker .25 .08
❑ 137 Bill Robinson .10 .02
❑ 138 Enos Cabell .10 .02
❑ 139 Dave Bergman .10 .02
❑ 140 J.R. Richard .25 .08
❑ 141 Ken Forsch .10 .02
❑ 142 Larry Bowa UER .25 .08
❑ 143 Frank LaCorte UER .10 .02
❑ 144 Denny Walling .10 .02
❑ 145 Buddy Bell .25 .08
❑ 146 Fergie Jenkins .25 .08
❑ 147 Dannny Darwin .25 .08
❑ 148 John Grubb .10 .02
❑ 149 Alfredo Griffin .10 .02
❑ 150 Jerry Garvin .10 .02
❑ 151 Paul Mirabella RC .10 .02
❑ 152 Rick Bosetti .10 .02
❑ 153 Dick Ruthven .10 .02
❑ 154 Frank Taveras .10 .02
❑ 155 Craig Swan .10 .02
❑ 156 Jeff Reardon RC 1.00 .40
❑ 157 Steve Henderson .10 .02
❑ 158 Jim Morrison .10 .02
❑ 159 Glenn Borgmann .10 .02
❑ 160 LaMarr Hoyt RC .50 .20
❑ 161 Rich Wortham .10 .02
❑ 162 Thad Bosley .10 .02
❑ 163 Julio Cruz .10 .02
❑ 164A Del Unser P1 .25 .08
❑ 164B Del Unser P2 .10 .02
❑ 165 Jim Anderson .10 .02
❑ 166 Jim Beattie .10 .02
❑ 167 Shane Rawley .10 .02
❑ 168 Joe Simpson .10 .02
❑ 169 Rod Carew .50 .20
❑ 170 Fred Patek .10 .02
❑ 171 Frank Tanana .25 .08
❑ 172 Alfredo Martinez RC .10 .02
❑ 173 Chris Knapp .10 .02
❑ 174 Joe Rudi .25 .08
❑ 175 Greg Luzinski .25 .08
❑ 176 Steve Garvey .50 .20
❑ 177 Joe Ferguson .10 .02
❑ 178 Bob Welch .25 .08
❑ 179 Dusty Baker .25 .08
❑ 180 Rudy Law .10 .02
❑ 181 Dave Concepcion .25 .08
❑ 182 Johnny Bench 1.00 .40
❑ 183 Mike LaCoss .10 .02
❑ 184 Ken Griffey .25 .08
❑ 185 Dave Collins .10 .02
❑ 186 Brian Asselstine .10 .02
❑ 187 Garry Templeton .25 .08
❑ 188 Mike Phillips .10 .02
❑ 189 Pete Vuckovich .10 .02
❑ 190 John Urrea .10 .02
❑ 191 Tony Scott .10 .02
❑ 192 Darrell Evans .25 .08
❑ 193 Milt May .10 .02
❑ 194 Bob Knepper .10 .02
❑ 195 Randy Moffitt .10 .02
❑ 196 Larry Herndon .10 .02
❑ 197 Rick Camp .10 .02
❑ 198 Andre Thornton .25 .08
❑ 199 Tom Veryzer .10 .02
❑ 200 Gary Alexander .10 .02
❑ 201 Rick Waits .10 .02
❑ 202 Rick Manning .10 .02
❑ 203 Paul Molitor 1.00 .40
❑ 204 Jim Gantner .10 .02
❑ 205 Paul Mitchell .10 .02
❑ 206 Reggie Cleveland .10 .02
❑ 207 Sixto Lezcano .10 .02
❑ 208 Bruce Benedict .10 .02
❑ 209 Rodney Scott .10 .02
❑ 210 John Tamargo .10 .02
❑ 211 Bill Lee .25 .08
❑ 212 Andre Dawson .50 .20
❑ 213 Rowland Office .10 .02
❑ 214 Carl Yastrzemski 1.50 .60
❑ 215 Jerry Remy .10 .02
❑ 216 Mike Torrez .10 .02
❑ 217 Skip Lockwood .10 .02
❑ 218 Fred Lynn .25 .08
❑ 219 Chris Chambliss .25 .08
❑ 220 Willie Aikens .10 .02
❑ 221 John Wathan .10 .02
❑ 222 Dan Quisenberry .10 .02
❑ 223 Willie Wilson .25 .08
❑ 224 Clint Hurdle .10 .02
❑ 225 Bob Watson .10 .02
❑ 226 Jim Spencer .10 .02
❑ 227 Ron Guidry .25 .08
❑ 228 Reggie Jackson 1.00 .40
❑ 229 Oscar Gamble .10 .02
❑ 230 Jeff Cox RC .10 .02
❑ 231 Luis Tiant .25 .08
❑ 232 Rich Dauer .10 .02
❑ 233 Dan Graham .10 .02
❑ 234 Mike Flanagan .10 .02
❑ 235 John Lowenstein .10 .02
❑ 236 Benny Ayala .10 .02
❑ 237 Wayne Gross .10 .02
❑ 238 Rick Langford .10 .02
❑ 239 Tony Armas .25 .08
❑ 240A Bob Lacy P1 ERR .50 .20
❑ 240B Bob Lacey P2 COR .10 .02
❑ 241 Gene Tenace .25 .08
❑ 242 Bob Shirley .10 .02
❑ 243 Gary Lucas RC .10 .02
❑ 244 Jerry Turner .10 .02
❑ 245 John Wockenfuss .10 .02
❑ 246 Stan Papi .10 .02
❑ 247 Milt Wilcox .10 .02
❑ 248 Dan Schatzeder .10 .02
❑ 249 Steve Kemp .10 .02
❑ 250 Jim Lentine RC .10 .02
❑ 251 Pete Rose 3.00 1.25
❑ 252 Bill Madlock .25 .08
❑ 253 Dale Berra .10 .02
❑ 254 Kent Tekulve .10 .02
❑ 255 Enrique Romo .10 .02
❑ 256 Mike Easler .10 .02
❑ 257 Chuck Tanner MG .10 .02
❑ 258 Art Howe .10 .02
❑ 259 Alan Ashby .10 .02
❑ 260 Nolan Ryan 5.00 2.00
❑ 261A Vern Ruhle P1 ERR .50 .20
❑ 261B Vern Ruhle P2 COR .25 .08
❑ 262 Bob Boone .25 .08
❑ 263 Cesar Cedeno .25 .08
❑ 264 Jeff Leonard .25 .08
❑ 265 Pat Putnam .10 .02
❑ 266 Jon Matlack .10 .02
❑ 267 Dave Rajsich .10 .02
❑ 268 Billy Sample .10 .02
❑ 269 Damaso Garcia RC .10 .02
❑ 270 Tom Buskey .10 .02
❑ 271 Joey McLaughlin .10 .02
❑ 272 Barry Bonnell .10 .02
❑ 273 Tug McGraw .25 .08
❑ 274 Mike Jorgensen .10 .02
❑ 275 Pat Zachry .10 .02
❑ 276 Neil Allen .10 .02
❑ 277 Joel Youngblood .10 .02
❑ 278 Greg Pryor .10 .02
❑ 279 Britt Burns RC .10 .02
❑ 280 Rich Dotson RC .10 .02
❑ 281 Chet Lemon .25 .08
❑ 282 Rusty Kuntz RC .10 .02
❑ 283 Ted Cox .10 .02
❑ 284 Sparky Lyle .25 .08
❑ 285 Larry Cox .10 .02
❑ 286 Floyd Bannister .10 .02
❑ 287 Byron McLaughlin .10 .02
❑ 288 Rodney Craig .10 .02
❑ 289 Bobby Grich .25 .08
❑ 290 Dickie Thon .10 .02
❑ 291 Mark Clear .10 .02
❑ 292 Dave Lemanczyk .10 .02
❑ 293 Jason Thompson .10 .02
❑ 294 Rick Miller .10 .02
❑ 295 Lonnie Smith .25 .08
❑ 296 Ron Cey .25 .08
❑ 297 Steve Yeager .25 .08
❑ 298 Bobby Castillo .10 .02
❑ 299 Manny Mota .25 .08
❑ 300 Jay Johnstone .10 .02
❑ 301 Dan Driessen .10 .02
❑ 302 Joe Nolan RC .10 .02
❑ 303 Paul Householder RC .10 .02
❑ 304 Harry Spilman .10 .02
❑ 305 Cesar Geronimo .10 .02
❑ 306A Gary Mathews P1 ERR .50 .20
❑ 306B Gary Matthews P2 COR .25 .08
❑ 307 Ken Reitz .10 .02
❑ 308 Ted Simmons .25 .08
❑ 309 John Littlefield RC .10 .02
❑ 310 George Frazier .10 .02
❑ 311 Dane Iorg .10 .02
❑ 312 Mike Ivie .10 .02
❑ 313 Dennis Littlejohn .10 .02
❑ 314 Gary Lavelle .10 .02
❑ 315 Jack Clark .25 .08
❑ 316 Jim Wohlford .10 .02
❑ 317 Rick Matula .10 .02
❑ 318 Toby Harrah .25 .08
❑ 319A Dwane Kuiper P1 ERR .25 .08
❑ 319B Duane Kuiper P2 COR .10 .02
❑ 320 Len Barker .25 .08
❑ 321 Victor Cruz .10 .02
❑ 322 Dell Alston .10 .02
❑ 323 Robin Yount 1.50 .60
❑ 324 Charlie Moore .10 .02
❑ 325 Lary Sorensen .10 .02
❑ 326A Gorman Thomas P1 .50 .20
❑ 326B Gorman Thomas P2 .25 .08
❑ 327 Bob Rodgers MG .10 .02
❑ 328 Phil Niekro .25 .08
❑ 329 Chris Speier .10 .02
❑ 330A Steve Rodgers P1 .25 .08
❑ 330B Steve Rogers P2 COR .25 .08
❑ 331 Woodie Fryman .10 .02
❑ 332 Warren Cromartie .10 .02
❑ 333 Jerry White .10 .02
❑ 334 Tony Perez .50 .20
❑ 335 Carlton Fisk .50 .20
❑ 336 Dick Drago .10 .02
❑ 337 Steve Renko .10 .02
❑ 338 Jim Rice .25 .08
❑ 339 Jerry Royster .10 .02
❑ 340 Frank White .25 .08
❑ 341 Jamie Quirk .10 .02
❑ 342A Paul Spittorff P1 ERR .25 .08
❑ 342B Paul Splittorff P2 COR .10 .02
❑ 343 Marty Pattin .10 .02
❑ 344 Pete LaCock .10 .02
❑ 345 Willie Randolph .25 .08
❑ 346 Rick Cerone .10 .02
❑ 347 Rich Gossage .25 .08
❑ 348 Reggie Jackson 1.00 .40
❑ 349 Ruppert Jones .10 .02
❑ 350 Dave McKay RC .10 .02
❑ 351 Yogi Berra CO 1.00 .40
❑ 352 Doug DeCinces .10 .02
❑ 353 Jim Palmer .50 .20
❑ 354 Tippy Martinez .10 .02
❑ 355 Al Bumbry .10 .02
❑ 356 Earl Weaver MG .25 .08
❑ 357A Bob Picciolo P1 ERR .25 .08
❑ 357B Rob Picciolo P2 COR .10 .02
❑ 358 Matt Keough .10 .02
❑ 359 Dwayne Murphy .10 .02
❑ 360 Brian Kingman .10 .02
❑ 361 Bill Fahey .10 .02
❑ 362 Steve Mura .10 .02
❑ 363 Dennis Kinney RC .10 .02
❑ 364 Dave Winfield .50 .20
❑ 365 Lou Whitaker .50 .20
❑ 366 Lance Parrish .25 .08
❑ 367 Tim Corcoran .10 .02
❑ 368 Pat Underwood .10 .02
❑ 369 Al Cowens .10 .02
❑ 370 Sparky Anderson MG .25 .08
❑ 371 Pete Rose 3.00 1.25
❑ 372 Phil Garner .25 .08
❑ 373 Steve Nicosia .10 .02
❑ 374 John Candelaria .25 .08
❑ 375 Don Robinson .10 .02

- ❑ 376 Lee Lacy .10 .02
- ❑ 377 John Milner .10 .02
- ❑ 378 Craig Reynolds .10 .02
- ❑ 379A Luis Pujols P1 ERR .25 .08
- ❑ 379B Luis Pujols P2 COR .10 .02
- ❑ 380 Joe Niekro .10 .02
- ❑ 381 Joaquin Andujar .25 .08
- ❑ 382 Keith Moreland RC .10 .02
- ❑ 383 Jose Cruz .25 .08
- ❑ 384 Bill Virdon MG .10 .02
- ❑ 385 Jim Sundberg .25 .08
- ❑ 386 Doc Medich .10 .02
- ❑ 387 Al Oliver .25 .08
- ❑ 388 Jim Norris .10 .02
- ❑ 389 Bob Bailor .10 .02
- ❑ 390 Ernie Whitt .10 .02
- ❑ 391 Otto Velez .10 .02
- ❑ 392 Roy Howell .10 .02
- ❑ 393 Bob Walk RC .50 .20
- ❑ 394 Doug Flynn .10 .02
- ❑ 395 Pete Falcone .10 .02
- ❑ 396 Tom Hausman .10 .02
- ❑ 397 Elliott Maddox .10 .02
- ❑ 398 Mike Squires .10 .02
- ❑ 399 Marvis Foley RC .10 .02
- ❑ 400 Steve Trout .10 .02
- ❑ 401 Wayne Nordhagen .10 .02
- ❑ 402 Tony LaRussa MG .25 .08
- ❑ 403 Bruce Bochte .10 .02
- ❑ 404 Bake McBride .25 .08
- ❑ 405 Jerry Narron .10 .02
- ❑ 406 Rob Dressler .10 .02
- ❑ 407 Dave Heaverlo .10 .02
- ❑ 408 Tom Paciorek .10 .02
- ❑ 409 Carney Lansford .25 .08
- ❑ 410 Brian Downing .25 .08
- ❑ 411 Don Aase .10 .02
- ❑ 412 Jim Barr .10 .02
- ❑ 413 Don Baylor .25 .08
- ❑ 414 Jim Fregosi MG .10 .02
- ❑ 415 Dallas Green MG .10 .02
- ❑ 416 Dave Lopes .25 .08
- ❑ 417 Jerry Reuss .10 .02
- ❑ 418 Rick Sutcliffe .25 .08
- ❑ 419 Derrel Thomas .10 .02
- ❑ 420 Tom Lasorda MG .50 .20
- ❑ 421 Charlie Leibrandt RC .50 .20
- ❑ 422 Tom Seaver 1.00 .40
- ❑ 423 Ron Oester .10 .02
- ❑ 424 Junior Kennedy .10 .02
- ❑ 425 Tom Seaver 1.00 .40
- ❑ 426 Bobby Cox MG .25 .08
- ❑ 427 Leon Durham RC .50 .20
- ❑ 428 Terry Kennedy .10 .02
- ❑ 429 Silvio Martinez .10 .02
- ❑ 430 George Hendrick .25 .08
- ❑ 431 Red Schoendienst MG .50 .20
- ❑ 432 Johnnie LeMaster .10 .02
- ❑ 433 Vida Blue .25 .08
- ❑ 434 John Montefusco .10 .02
- ❑ 435 Terry Whitfield .10 .02
- ❑ 436 Dave Bristol MG .10 .02
- ❑ 437 Dale Murphy .50 .20
- ❑ 438 Jerry Dybzinski RC .10 .02
- ❑ 439 Jorge Orta .10 .02
- ❑ 440 Wayne Garland .10 .02
- ❑ 441 Miguel Dilone .10 .02
- ❑ 442 Dave Garcia MG .10 .02
- ❑ 443 Don Money .10 .02
- ❑ 444A Buck Martinez P1 ERR .25 .08
- ❑ 444B Buck Martinez P2 COR .10 .02
- ❑ 445 Jerry Augustine .10 .02
- ❑ 446 Ben Oglivie .25 .08
- ❑ 447 Jim Slaton .10 .02
- ❑ 448 Doyle Alexander .10 .02
- ❑ 449 Tony Bernazard .10 .02
- ❑ 450 Scott Sanderson .10 .02
- ❑ 451 David Palmer .10 .02
- ❑ 452 Stan Bahnsen .10 .02
- ❑ 453 Dick Williams MG .10 .02
- ❑ 454 Rick Burleson .10 .02
- ❑ 455 Gary Allenson .10 .02
- ❑ 456 Bob Stanley .10 .02
- ❑ 457A John Tudor ERR 1.00 .40
- ❑ 457B John Tudor RC 1.00 .40
- ❑ 458 Dwight Evans .50 .20
- ❑ 459 Glenn Hubbard .10 .02
- ❑ 460 U.L. Washington .10 .02
- ❑ 461 Larry Gura .10 .02
- ❑ 462 Rich Gale .10 .02
- ❑ 463 Hal McRae .25 .08
- ❑ 464 Jim Frey MG RC .10 .02
- ❑ 465 Bucky Dent .25 .08
- ❑ 466 Dennis Werth RC .10 .02
- ❑ 467 Ron Davis .10 .02
- ❑ 468 Reggie Jackson 1.00 .40
- ❑ 469 Bobby Brown .10 .02
- ❑ 470 Mike Davis RC .50 .20
- ❑ 471 Gaylord Perry .25 .08
- ❑ 472 Mark Belanger .10 .02
- ❑ 473 Jim Palmer .50 .20
- ❑ 474 Sammy Stewart .10 .02
- ❑ 475 Tim Stoddard .10 .02
- ❑ 476 Steve Stone .10 .02
- ❑ 477 Jeff Newman .10 .02
- ❑ 478 Steve McCatty .10 .02
- ❑ 479 Billy Martin MG .50 .20
- ❑ 480 Mitchell Page .10 .02
- ❑ 481 Steve Carlton CY .25 .08
- ❑ 482 Bill Buckner .25 .08
- ❑ 483A Ivan DeJesus P1 ERR .25 .08
- ❑ 483B Ivan DeJesus P2 COR .10 .02
- ❑ 484 Cliff Johnson .10 .02
- ❑ 485 Lenny Randle .10 .02
- ❑ 486 Larry Milbourne .10 .02
- ❑ 487 Roy Smalley .10 .02
- ❑ 488 John Castino .10 .02
- ❑ 489 Ron Jackson .10 .02
- ❑ 490A Dave Roberts P1 .25 .08
- ❑ 490B Dave Roberts P2 .10 .02
- ❑ 491 George Brett MVP 1.50 .60
- ❑ 492 Mike Cubbage .10 .02
- ❑ 493 Rob Wilfong .10 .02
- ❑ 494 Danny Goodwin .10 .02
- ❑ 495 Jose Morales .10 .02
- ❑ 496 Mickey Rivers .10 .02
- ❑ 497 Mike Edwards .10 .02
- ❑ 498 Mike Sadek .10 .02
- ❑ 499 Lenn Sakata .10 .02
- ❑ 500 Gene Michael MG .10 .02
- ❑ 501 Dave Roberts .10 .02
- ❑ 502 Steve Dillard .10 .02
- ❑ 503 Jim Essian .10 .02
- ❑ 504 Rance Mulliniks .10 .02
- ❑ 505 Darrell Porter .10 .02
- ❑ 506 Joe Torre MG .25 .08
- ❑ 507 Terry Crowley .10 .02
- ❑ 508 Bill Travers .10 .02
- ❑ 509 Nelson Norman .10 .02
- ❑ 510 Bob McClure .10 .02
- ❑ 511 Steve Howe RC .50 .20
- ❑ 512 Dave Rader .10 .02
- ❑ 513 Mick Kelleher .10 .02
- ❑ 514 Kiko Garcia .10 .02
- ❑ 515 Larry Biittner .10 .02
- ❑ 516A Willie Norwood P1 .25 .08
- ❑ 516B Willie Norwood P2 .10 .02
- ❑ 517 Bo Diaz .10 .02
- ❑ 518 Juan Beniquez .10 .02
- ❑ 519 Scot Thompson .10 .02
- ❑ 520 Jim Tracy RC 1.00 .40
- ❑ 521 Carlos Lezcano RC .10 .02
- ❑ 522 Joe Amalfitano MG .10 .02
- ❑ 523 Preston Hanna .10 .02
- ❑ 524A Ray Burris P1 .25 .08
- ❑ 524B Ray Burris P2 .10 .02
- ❑ 525 Broderick Perkins .10 .02
- ❑ 526 Mickey Hatcher .10 .02
- ❑ 527 John Goryl MG .10 .02
- ❑ 528 Dick Davis .10 .02
- ❑ 529 Butch Wynegar .10 .02
- ❑ 530 Sal Butera RC .10 .02
- ❑ 531 Jerry Koosman .25 .08
- ❑ 532A Geoff Zahn P1 .25 .08
- ❑ 532B Geoff Zahn P2 .10 .02
- ❑ 533 Dennis Martinez .25 .08
- ❑ 534 Gary Thomasson .10 .02
- ❑ 535 Steve Macko .10 .02
- ❑ 536 Jim Kaat .25 .08
- ❑ 537 G.Brett/R.Carew 1.50 .60
- ❑ 538 Tim Raines RC 2.50 1.00
- ❑ 539 Keith Smith .10 .02
- ❑ 540 Ken Macha .10 .02
- ❑ 541 Burt Hooton .10 .02
- ❑ 542 Butch Hobson .10 .02
- ❑ 543 Bill Stein .10 .02
- ❑ 544 Dave Stapleton RC .10 .02
- ❑ 545 Bob Pate RC .10 .02
- ❑ 546 Doug Corbett RC .10 .02
- ❑ 547 Darrell Jackson .10 .02
- ❑ 548 Pete Redfern .10 .02
- ❑ 549 Roger Erickson .10 .02
- ❑ 550 Al Hrabosky .25 .08
- ❑ 551 Dick Tidrow .10 .02
- ❑ 552 Dave Ford RC .10 .02
- ❑ 553 Dave Kingman .25 .08
- ❑ 554A Mike Vail P1 .25 .08
- ❑ 554B Mike Vail P2 .10 .02
- ❑ 555A Jerry Martin P1 .25 .08
- ❑ 555B Jerry Martin P2 .10 .02
- ❑ 556A Jesus Figueroa P1 .25 .08
- ❑ 556B Jesus Figueroa P2 RC .10 .02
- ❑ 557 Don Stanhouse .10 .02
- ❑ 558 Barry Foote .10 .02
- ❑ 559 Tim Blackwell .10 .02
- ❑ 560 Bruce Sutter .50 .20
- ❑ 561 Rick Reuschel .25 .08
- ❑ 562 Lynn McGlothen .10 .02
- ❑ 563A Bob Owchinko P1 .25 .08
- ❑ 563B Bob Owchinko P2 .10 .02
- ❑ 564 John Verhoeven .10 .02
- ❑ 565 Ken Landreaux .10 .02
- ❑ 566A Glen Adams P1 ERR .25 .08
- ❑ 566B Glenn Adams P2 COR .10 .02
- ❑ 567 Hosken Powell .10 .02
- ❑ 568 Dick Noles .10 .02
- ❑ 569 Danny Ainge RC 3.00 1.25
- ❑ 570 Bobby Mattick MG RC .10 .02
- ❑ 571 Joe Lefebvre RC .10 .02
- ❑ 572 Bobby Clark .10 .02
- ❑ 573 Dennis Lamp .10 .02
- ❑ 574 Randy Lerch .10 .02
- ❑ 575 Mookie Wilson RC 3.00 1.25
- ❑ 576 Ron LeFlore .25 .08
- ❑ 577 Jim Dwyer .10 .02
- ❑ 578 Bill Castro .10 .02
- ❑ 579 Greg Minton .10 .02
- ❑ 580 Mark Littell .10 .02
- ❑ 581 Andy Hassler .10 .02
- ❑ 582 Dave Stieb .25 .08
- ❑ 583 Ken Oberkfell .10 .02
- ❑ 584 Larry Bradford .10 .02
- ❑ 585 Fred Stanley .10 .02
- ❑ 586 Bill Caudill .10 .02
- ❑ 587 Doug Capilla .10 .02
- ❑ 588 George Riley RC .10 .02
- ❑ 589 Willie Hernandez .10 .02
- ❑ 590 Mike Schmidt MVP 2.50 1.00
- ❑ 591 Steve Stone CY .10 .02
- ❑ 592 Rick Sofield .10 .02
- ❑ 593 Bombo Rivera .10 .02
- ❑ 594 Gary Ward .10 .02
- ❑ 595A Dave Edwards P1 .25 .08
- ❑ 595B Dave Edwards P2 .10 .02
- ❑ 596 Mike Proly .10 .02
- ❑ 597 Tommy Boggs .10 .02
- ❑ 598 Greg Gross .10 .02
- ❑ 599 Elias Sosa .10 .02
- ❑ 600 Pat Kelly .10 .02
- ❑ 601A Checklist 1-120 P1 .25 .08
- ❑ 601B Checklist 1-120 P2 .50 .20
- ❑ 602 Checklist 121-240 NNO .25 .08
- ❑ 603A Checklist 241-360 P1 .25 .08
- ❑ 603B Checklist 241-360 P2 .25 .08
- ❑ 604A Checklist 361-480 P1 .25 .08
- ❑ 604B Checklist 361-480 P2 .25 .08
- ❑ 605A Checklist 481-600 P1 .25 .08
- ❑ 605B Checklist 481-600 P2 .25 .08

1982 Donruss

- ❑ COMPLETE SET (660) 60.00 30.00
- ❑ COMP.FACT.SET (660) 60.00 30.00
- ❑ COMP.RUTH PUZZLE 10.00 5.00
- ❑ 1 Pete Rose DK 2.50 1.00
- ❑ 2 Gary Carter DK .20 .07
- ❑ 3 Steve Garvey DK .20 .07
- ❑ 4 Vida Blue DK .20 .07

Card		
❑ 5 Alan Trammell DK	.20	.07
❑ 5A Alan Trammel DK ERR	.20	.07
❑ 6 Len Barker DK	.10	.02
❑ 7 Dwight Evans DK	.40	.15
❑ 8 Rod Carew DK	.40	.15
❑ 9 George Hendrick DK	.20	.07
❑ 10 Phil Niekro DK	.20	.07
❑ 11 Richie Zisk DK	.10	.02
❑ 12 Dave Parker DK	.20	.07
❑ 13 Nolan Ryan DK	4.00	1.50
❑ 14 Ivan DeJesus DK	.10	.02
❑ 15 George Brett DK	2.00	.75
❑ 16 Tom Seaver DK	.40	.15
❑ 17 Dave Kingman DK	.20	.07
❑ 18 Dave Winfield DK	.20	.07
❑ 19 Mike Norris DK	.10	.02
❑ 20 Carlton Fisk DK	.40	.15
❑ 21 Ozzie Smith DK	1.50	.60
❑ 22 Roy Smalley DK	.10	.02
❑ 23 Buddy Bell DK	.20	.07
❑ 24 Ken Singleton DK	.20	.07
❑ 25 John Mayberry DK	.10	.02
❑ 26 Gorman Thomas DK	.20	.07
❑ 27 Earl Weaver MG	.20	.07
❑ 28 Rollie Fingers	.20	.07
❑ 29 Sparky Anderson MG	.20	.07
❑ 30 Dennis Eckersley	.40	.15
❑ 31 Dave Winfield	.20	.07
❑ 32 Burt Hooton	.10	.02
❑ 33 Rick Waits	.10	.02
❑ 34 George Brett	2.00	.75
❑ 35 Steve McCatty	.10	.02
❑ 36 Steve Rogers	.20	.07
❑ 37 Bill Stein	.10	.02
❑ 38 Steve Renko	.10	.02
❑ 39 Mike Squires	.10	.02
❑ 40 George Hendrick	.20	.07
❑ 41 Bob Knepper	.10	.02
❑ 42 Steve Carlton	.40	.15
❑ 43 Larry Biittner	.10	.02
❑ 44 Chris Welsh	.10	.02
❑ 45 Steve Nicosia	.10	.02
❑ 46 Jack Clark	.20	.07
❑ 47 Chris Chambliss	.20	.07
❑ 48 Ivan DeJesus	.10	.02
❑ 49 Lee Mazzilli	.20	.07
❑ 50 Julio Cruz	.10	.02
❑ 51 Pete Redfern	.10	.02
❑ 52 Dave Stieb	.20	.07
❑ 53 Doug Corbett	.10	.02
❑ 54 George Bell RC	1.00	.40
❑ 55 Joe Simpson	.10	.02
❑ 56 Rusty Staub	.20	.07
❑ 57 Hector Cruz	.10	.02
❑ 58 Claudell Washington	.10	.02
❑ 59 Enrique Romo	.10	.02
❑ 60 Gary Lavelle	.10	.02
❑ 61 Tim Flannery	.10	.02
❑ 62 Joe Nolan	.10	.02
❑ 63 Larry Bowa	.20	.07
❑ 64 Sixto Lezcano	.10	.02
❑ 65 Joe Sambito	.10	.02
❑ 66 Bruce Kison	.10	.02
❑ 67 Wayne Nordhagen	.10	.02
❑ 68 Woodie Fryman	.10	.02
❑ 69 Billy Sample	.10	.02
❑ 70 Amos Otis	.20	.07
❑ 71 Matt Keough	.10	.02
❑ 72 Toby Harrah	.20	.07
❑ 73 Dave Righetti RC	1.50	.60
❑ 74 Carl Yastrzemski	1.25	.50
❑ 75 Bob Welch	.20	.07
❑ 76 Alan Trammell	.20	.07
❑ 76A Alan Trammel ERR	.20	.07
❑ 77 Rick Dempsey	.10	.02
❑ 78 Paul Molitor	.20	.07
❑ 79 Dennis Martinez	.20	.07
❑ 80 Jim Slaton	.10	.02
❑ 81 Champ Summers	.10	.02
❑ 82 Carney Lansford	.20	.07
❑ 83 Barry Foote	.10	.02
❑ 84 Steve Garvey	.20	.07
❑ 85 Rick Manning	.10	.02
❑ 86 John Wathan	.10	.02
❑ 87 Brian Kingman	.10	.02
❑ 88 Andre Dawson	.20	.07
❑ 89 Jim Kern	.10	.02
❑ 90 Bobby Grich	.20	.07
❑ 91 Bob Forsch	.10	.02
❑ 92 Art Howe	.10	.02
❑ 93 Marty Bystrom	.10	.02
❑ 94 Ozzie Smith	1.50	.60
❑ 95 Dave Parker	.20	.07
❑ 96 Doyle Alexander	.10	.02
❑ 97 Al Hrabosky	.10	.02
❑ 98 Frank Taveras	.10	.02
❑ 99 Tim Blackwell	.10	.02
❑ 100 Floyd Bannister	.10	.02
❑ 101 Alfredo Griffin	.10	.02
❑ 102 Dave Engle	.10	.02
❑ 103 Mario Soto	.20	.07
❑ 104 Ross Baumgarten	.10	.02
❑ 105 Ken Singleton	.20	.07
❑ 106 Ted Simmons	.20	.07
❑ 107 Jack Morris	.20	.07
❑ 108 Bob Watson	.10	.02
❑ 109 Dwight Evans	.40	.15
❑ 110 Tom Lasorda MG	.40	.15
❑ 111 Bert Blyleven	.20	.07
❑ 112 Dan Quisenberry	.10	.02
❑ 113 Rickey Henderson	2.50	1.00
❑ 114 Gary Carter	.20	.07
❑ 115 Brian Downing	.20	.07
❑ 116 Al Oliver	.20	.07
❑ 117 LaMarr Hoyt	.10	.02
❑ 118 Cesar Cedeno	.20	.07
❑ 119 Keith Moreland	.10	.02
❑ 120 Bob Shirley	.10	.02
❑ 121 Terry Kennedy	.10	.02
❑ 122 Frank Pastore	.10	.02
❑ 123 Gene Garber	.10	.02
❑ 124 Tony Pena	.20	.07
❑ 125 Allen Ripley	.10	.02
❑ 126 Randy Martz	.10	.02
❑ 127 Richie Zisk	.10	.02
❑ 128 Mike Scott	.20	.07
❑ 129 Lloyd Moseby	.10	.02
❑ 130 Rob Wilfong	.10	.02
❑ 131 Tim Stoddard	.10	.02
❑ 132 Gorman Thomas	.20	.07
❑ 133 Dan Petry	.10	.02
❑ 134 Bob Stanley	.10	.02
❑ 135 Lou Piniella	.20	.07
❑ 136 Pedro Guerrero	.20	.07
❑ 137 Len Barker	.10	.02
❑ 138 Rich Gale	.10	.02
❑ 139 Wayne Gross	.10	.02
❑ 140 Tim Wallach RC	1.00	.40
❑ 141 Gene Mauch MG	.10	.02
❑ 142 Doc Medich	.10	.02
❑ 143 Tony Bernazard	.10	.02
❑ 144 Bill Virdon MG	.10	.02
❑ 145 John Littlefield	.10	.02
❑ 146 Dave Bergman	.10	.02
❑ 147 Dick Davis	.10	.02
❑ 148 Tom Seaver	.75	.30
❑ 149 Matt Sinatro	.10	.02
❑ 150 Chuck Tanner MG	.10	.02
❑ 151 Leon Durham	.10	.02
❑ 152 Gene Tenace	.20	.07
❑ 153 Al Bumbry	.10	.02
❑ 154 Mark Brouhard	.10	.02
❑ 155 Rick Peters	.10	.02
❑ 156 Jerry Remy	.10	.02
❑ 157 Rick Reuschel	.20	.07
❑ 158 Steve Howe	.10	.02
❑ 159 Alan Bannister	.10	.02
❑ 160 U.L. Washington	.10	.02
❑ 161 Rick Langford	.10	.02
❑ 162 Bill Gullickson	.10	.02
❑ 163 Mark Wagner	.10	.02
❑ 164 Geoff Zahn	.10	.02
❑ 165 Ron LeFlore	.20	.07
❑ 166 Dane Iorg	.10	.02
❑ 167 Joe Niekro	.10	.02
❑ 168 Pete Rose	2.50	1.00
❑ 169 Dave Collins	.10	.02
❑ 170 Rick Wise	.10	.02
❑ 171 Jim Bibby	.10	.02
❑ 172 Larry Herndon	.10	.02
❑ 173 Bob Horner	.20	.07
❑ 174 Steve Dillard	.10	.02
❑ 175 Mookie Wilson	.20	.07
❑ 176 Dan Meyer	.10	.02
❑ 177 Fernando Arroyo	.10	.02
❑ 178 Jackson Todd	.10	.02
❑ 179 Darrell Jackson	.10	.02
❑ 180 Alvis Woods	.10	.02
❑ 181 Jim Anderson	.10	.02
❑ 182 Dave Kingman	.20	.07
❑ 183 Steve Henderson	.10	.02
❑ 184 Brian Asselstine	.10	.02
❑ 185 Rod Scurry	.10	.02
❑ 186 Fred Breining	.10	.02
❑ 187 Danny Boone	.10	.02
❑ 188 Junior Kennedy	.10	.02
❑ 189 Sparky Lyle	.20	.07
❑ 190 Whitey Herzog MG	.20	.07
❑ 191 Dave Smith	.10	.02
❑ 192 Ed Ott	.10	.02
❑ 193 Greg Luzinski	.20	.07
❑ 194 Bill Lee	.20	.07
❑ 195 Don Zimmer MG	.20	.07
❑ 196 Hal McRae	.20	.07
❑ 197 Mike Norris	.10	.02
❑ 198 Duane Kuiper	.10	.02
❑ 199 Rick Cerone	.10	.02
❑ 200 Jim Rice	.20	.07
❑ 201 Steve Yeager	.20	.07
❑ 202 Tom Brookens	.10	.02
❑ 203 Jose Morales	.10	.02
❑ 204 Roy Howell	.10	.02
❑ 205 Tippy Martinez	.10	.02
❑ 206 Moose Haas	.10	.02
❑ 207 Al Cowens	.10	.02
❑ 208 Dave Stapleton	.10	.02
❑ 209 Bucky Dent	.20	.07
❑ 210 Ron Cey	.20	.07
❑ 211 Jorge Orta	.10	.02
❑ 212 Jamie Quirk	.10	.02
❑ 213 Jeff Jones	.10	.02
❑ 214 Tim Raines	.40	.15
❑ 215 Jon Matlack	.10	.02
❑ 216 Rod Carew	.40	.15
❑ 217 Jim Kaat	.20	.07
❑ 218 Joe Pittman	.10	.02
❑ 219 Larry Christenson	.10	.02
❑ 220 Juan Bonilla RC	.15	.05
❑ 221 Mike Easler	.10	.02
❑ 222 Vida Blue	.20	.07
❑ 223 Rick Camp	.10	.02
❑ 224 Mike Jorgensen	.10	.02
❑ 225 Jody Davis	.10	.02
❑ 226 Mike Parrott	.10	.02
❑ 227 Jim Clancy	.10	.02
❑ 228 Hosken Powell	.10	.02
❑ 229 Tom Hume	.10	.02
❑ 230 Britt Burns	.10	.02
❑ 231 Jim Palmer	.20	.07
❑ 232 Bob Rodgers MG	.10	.02
❑ 233 Milt Wilcox	.10	.02
❑ 234 Dave Revering	.10	.02
❑ 235 Mike Torrez	.10	.02
❑ 236 Robert Castillo	.10	.02
❑ 237 Von Hayes RC	.50	.20
❑ 238 Renie Martin	.10	.02
❑ 239 Dwayne Murphy	.10	.02
❑ 240 Rodney Scott	.10	.02
❑ 241 Fred Patek	.10	.02
❑ 242 Mickey Rivers	.10	.02

❑	243 Steve Trout	.10	.02
❑	244 Jose Cruz	.20	.07
❑	245 Manny Trillo	.10	.02
❑	246 Lary Sorensen	.10	.02
❑	247 Dave Edwards	.10	.02
❑	248 Dan Driessen	.10	.02
❑	249 Tommy Boggs	.10	.02
❑	250 Dale Berra	.10	.02
❑	251 Ed Whitson	.10	.02
❑	252 Lee Smith RC	2.00	.75
❑	253 Tom Paciorek	.10	.02
❑	254 Pat Zachry	.10	.02
❑	255 Luis Leal	.10	.02
❑	256 John Castino	.10	.02
❑	257 Rich Dauer	.10	.02
❑	258 Cecil Cooper	.20	.07
❑	259 Dave Rozema	.10	.02
❑	260 John Tudor	.20	.07
❑	261 Jerry Mumphrey	.10	.02
❑	262 Jay Johnstone	.10	.02
❑	263 Bo Diaz	.10	.02
❑	264 Dennis Leonard	.10	.02
❑	265 Jim Spencer	.10	.02
❑	266 John Milner	.10	.02
❑	267 Don Aase	.10	.02
❑	268 Jim Sundberg	.20	.07
❑	269 Lamar Johnson	.10	.02
❑	270 Frank LaCorte	.10	.02
❑	271 Barry Evans	.10	.02
❑	272 Enos Cabell	.10	.02
❑	273 Del Unser	.10	.02
❑	274 George Foster	.20	.07
❑	275 Brett Butler RC	1.00	.40
❑	276 Lee Lacy	.10	.02
❑	277 Ken Reitz	.10	.02
❑	278 Keith Hernandez	.20	.07
❑	279 Doug DeCinces	.10	.02
❑	280 Charlie Moore	.10	.02
❑	281 Lance Parrish	.20	.07
❑	282 Ralph Houk MG	.10	.02
❑	283 Rich Gossage	.20	.07
❑	284 Jerry Reuss	.10	.02
❑	285 Mike Stanton	.10	.02
❑	286 Frank White	.20	.07
❑	287 Bob Owchinko	.10	.02
❑	288 Scott Sanderson	.10	.02
❑	289 Bump Wills	.10	.02
❑	290 Dave Frost	.10	.02
❑	291 Chet Lemon	.20	.07
❑	292 Tito Landrum	.10	.02
❑	293 Vern Ruhle	.10	.02
❑	294 Mike Schmidt	2.00	.75
❑	295 Sam Mejias	.10	.02
❑	296 Gary Lucas	.10	.02
❑	297 John Candelaria	.10	.02
❑	298 Jerry Martin	.10	.02
❑	299 Dale Murphy	.40	.15
❑	300 Mike Lum	.10	.02
❑	301 Tom Hausman	.10	.02
❑	302 Glenn Abbott	.10	.02
❑	303 Roger Erickson	.10	.02
❑	304 Otto Velez	.10	.02
❑	305 Danny Goodwin	.10	.02
❑	306 John Mayberry	.10	.02
❑	307 Lenny Randle	.10	.02
❑	308 Bob Bailor	.10	.02
❑	309 Jerry Morales	.10	.02
❑	310 Rufino Linares	.10	.02
❑	311 Kent Tekulve	.10	.02
❑	312 Joe Morgan	.20	.07
❑	313 John Urrea	.10	.02
❑	314 Paul Householder	.10	.02
❑	315 Garry Maddox	.10	.02
❑	316 Mike Ramsey	.10	.02
❑	317 Alan Ashby	.10	.02
❑	318 Bob Clark	.10	.02
❑	319 Tony LaRussa MG	.20	.07
❑	320 Charlie Lea	.10	.02
❑	321 Danny Darwin	.10	.02
❑	322 Cesar Geronimo	.10	.02
❑	323 Tom Underwood	.10	.02
❑	324 Andre Thornton	.10	.02
❑	325 Rudy May	.10	.02
❑	326 Frank Tanana	.20	.07
❑	327 Dave Lopes	.20	.07
❑	328 Richie Hebner	.10	.02
❑	329 Mike Flanagan	.10	.02
❑	330 Mike Caldwell	.10	.02
❑	331 Scott McGregor	.10	.02
❑	332 Jerry Augustine	.10	.02
❑	333 Stan Papi	.10	.02
❑	334 Rick Miller	.10	.02
❑	335 Graig Nettles	.20	.07
❑	336 Dusty Baker	.20	.07
❑	337 Dave Garcia MG	.10	.02
❑	338 Larry Gura	.10	.02
❑	339 Cliff Johnson	.10	.02
❑	340 Warren Cromartie	.10	.02
❑	341 Steve Comer	.10	.02
❑	342 Rick Burleson	.10	.02
❑	343 John Martin RC	.15	.05
❑	344 Craig Reynolds	.10	.02
❑	345 Mike Proly	.10	.02
❑	346 Ruppert Jones	.10	.02
❑	347 Omar Moreno	.10	.02
❑	348 Greg Minton	.10	.02
❑	349 Rick Mahler	.10	.02
❑	350 Alex Trevino	.10	.02
❑	351 Mike Krukow	.10	.02
❑	352A Shane Rawley ERR (Photo actually Jim Anderson)	.40	.15
❑	352B Shane Rawley COR	.10	.02
❑	353 Garth Iorg	.10	.02
❑	354 Pete Mackanin	.10	.02
❑	355 Paul Moskau	.10	.02
❑	356 Richard Dotson	.10	.02
❑	357 Steve Stone	.10	.02
❑	358 Larry Hisle	.10	.02
❑	359 Aurelio Lopez	.10	.02
❑	360 Oscar Gamble	.10	.02
❑	361 Tom Burgmeier	.10	.02
❑	362 Terry Forster	.20	.07
❑	363 Joe Charboneau	.20	.07
❑	364 Ken Brett	.10	.02
❑	365 Tony Armas	.20	.07
❑	366 Chris Speier	.10	.02
❑	367 Fred Lynn	.20	.07
❑	368 Buddy Bell	.20	.07
❑	369 Jim Essian	.10	.02
❑	370 Terry Puhl	.10	.02
❑	371 Greg Gross	.10	.02
❑	372 Bruce Sutter	.40	.15
❑	373 Joe Lefebvre	.10	.02
❑	374 Ray Knight	.20	.07
❑	375 Bruce Benedict	.10	.02
❑	376 Tim Foli	.10	.02
❑	377 Al Holland	.10	.02
❑	378 Ken Kravec	.10	.02
❑	379 Jeff Burroughs	.10	.02
❑	380 Pete Falcone	.10	.02
❑	381 Ernie Whitt	.10	.02
❑	382 Brad Havens	.10	.02
❑	383 Terry Crowley	.10	.02
❑	384 Don Money	.10	.02
❑	385 Dan Schatzeder	.10	.02
❑	386 Gary Allenson	.10	.02
❑	387 Yogi Berra CO	.75	.30
❑	388 Ken Landreaux	.10	.02
❑	389 Mike Hargrove	.10	.02
❑	390 Darryl Motley	.10	.02
❑	391 Dave McKay	.10	.02
❑	392 Stan Bahnsen	.10	.02
❑	393 Ken Forsch	.10	.02
❑	394 Mario Mendoza	.10	.02
❑	395 Jim Morrison	.10	.02
❑	396 Mike Ivie	.10	.02
❑	397 Broderick Perkins	.10	.02
❑	398 Darrell Evans	.20	.07
❑	399 Ron Reed	.10	.02
❑	400 Johnny Bench	.75	.30
❑	401 Steve Bedrosian RC	.50	.20
❑	402 Bill Robinson	.10	.02
❑	403 Bill Buckner	.20	.07
❑	404 Ken Oberkfell	.10	.02
❑	405 Cal Ripken RC	40.00	15.00
❑	406 Jim Gantner	.10	.02
❑	407 Kirk Gibson	.75	.30
❑	408 Tony Perez	.40	.15
❑	409 Tommy John	.20	.07
❑	410 Dave Stewart RC	1.50	.60
❑	411 Dan Spillner	.10	.02
❑	412 Willie Aikens	.10	.02
❑	413 Mike Heath	.10	.02
❑	414 Ray Burris	.10	.02
❑	415 Leon Roberts	.10	.02
❑	416 Mike Witt	.50	.20
❑	417 Bob Molinaro	.10	.02
❑	418 Steve Braun	.10	.02
❑	419 Nolan Ryan	4.00	1.50
❑	420 Tug McGraw	.20	.07
❑	421 Dave Concepcion	.20	.07
❑	422A Juan Eichelberger ERR (Photo actually Gary Lucas	.40	.15
❑	422B Juan Eichelberger COR	.10	.02
❑	423 Rick Rhoden	.10	.02
❑	424 Frank Robinson MG	.40	.15
❑	425 Eddie Miller	.10	.02
❑	426 Bill Caudill	.10	.02
❑	427 Doug Flynn	.10	.02
❑	428 Larry Andersen UER (Misspelled Anderson on card	.10	.02
❑	429 Al Williams	.10	.02
❑	430 Jerry Garvin	.10	.02
❑	431 Glenn Adams	.10	.02
❑	432 Barry Bonnell	.10	.02
❑	433 Jerry Narron	.10	.02
❑	434 John Stearns	.10	.02
❑	435 Mike Tyson	.10	.02
❑	436 Glenn Hubbard	.10	.02
❑	437 Eddie Solomon	.10	.02
❑	438 Jeff Leonard	.10	.02
❑	439 Randy Bass	.50	.20
❑	440 Mike LaCoss	.10	.02
❑	441 Gary Matthews	.20	.07
❑	442 Mark Littell	.10	.02
❑	443 Don Sutton	.20	.07
❑	444 John Harris	.10	.02
❑	445 Vada Pinson CO	.20	.07
❑	446 Elias Sosa	.10	.02
❑	447 Charlie Hough	.20	.07
❑	448 Willie Wilson	.20	.07
❑	449 Fred Stanley	.10	.02
❑	450 Tom Veryzer	.10	.02
❑	451 Ron Davis	.10	.02
❑	452 Mark Clear	.10	.02
❑	453 Bill Russell	.20	.07
❑	454 Lou Whitaker	.20	.07
❑	455 Dan Graham	.10	.02
❑	456 Reggie Cleveland	.10	.02
❑	457 Sammy Stewart	.10	.02
❑	458 Pete Vuckovich	.10	.02
❑	459 John Wockenfuss	.10	.02
❑	460 Glenn Hoffman	.10	.02
❑	461 Willie Randolph	.20	.07
❑	462 Fernando Valenzuela	.75	.30
❑	463 Ron Hassey	.10	.02
❑	464 Paul Splittorff	.10	.02
❑	465 Rob Picciolo	.10	.02
❑	466 Larry Parrish	.10	.02
❑	467 Johnny Grubb	.10	.02
❑	468 Dan Ford	.10	.02
❑	469 Silvio Martinez	.10	.02
❑	470 Kiko Garcia	.10	.02
❑	471 Bob Boone	.20	.07
❑	472 Luis Salazar	.10	.02
❑	473 Randy Niemann	.10	.02
❑	474 Tom Griffin	.10	.02
❑	475 Phil Niekro	.20	.07
❑	476 Hubie Brooks	.10	.02
❑	477 Dick Tidrow	.10	.02
❑	478 Jim Beattie	.10	.02
❑	479 Damaso Garcia	.10	.02
❑	480 Mickey Hatcher	.10	.02
❑	481 Joe Price	.10	.02
❑	482 Ed Farmer	.10	.02
❑	483 Eddie Murray	.75	.30
❑	484 Ben Oglivie	.20	.07
❑	485 Kevin Saucier	.10	.02
❑	486 Bobby Murcer	.20	.07
❑	487 Bill Campbell	.10	.02
❑	488 Reggie Smith	.20	.07
❑	489 Wayne Garland	.10	.02
❑	490 Jim Wright	.10	.02
❑	491 Billy Martin MG	.40	.15

❑ 492 Jim Fanning MG .10 .02
❑ 493 Don Baylor .20 .07
❑ 494 Rick Honeycutt .10 .02
❑ 495 Carlton Fisk .40 .15
❑ 496 Denny Walling .10 .02
❑ 497 Bake McBride .20 .07
❑ 498 Darrell Porter .10 .02
❑ 499 Gene Richards .10 .02
❑ 500 Ron Oester .10 .02
❑ 501 Ken Dayley .10 .02
❑ 502 Jason Thompson .10 .02
❑ 503 Milt May .10 .02
❑ 504 Doug Bird .10 .02
❑ 505 Bruce Bochte .10 .02
❑ 506 Neil Allen .10 .02
❑ 507 Joey McLaughlin .10 .02
❑ 508 Butch Wynegar .10 .02
❑ 509 Gary Roenicke .10 .02
❑ 510 Robin Yount 1.25 .50
❑ 511 Dave Tobik .10 .02
❑ 512 Rich Gedman .50 .20
❑ 513 Gene Nelson .10 .02
❑ 514 Rick Monday .20 .07
❑ 515 Miguel Dilone .10 .02
❑ 516 Clint Hurdle .10 .02
❑ 517 Jeff Newman .10 .02
❑ 518 Grant Jackson .10 .02
❑ 519 Andy Hassler .10 .02
❑ 520 Pat Putnam .10 .02
❑ 521 Greg Pryor .10 .02
❑ 522 Tony Scott .10 .02
❑ 523 Steve Mura .10 .02
❑ 524 Johnnie LeMaster .10 .02
❑ 525 Dick Ruthven .10 .02
❑ 526 John McNamara MG .10 .02
❑ 527 Larry McWilliams .10 .02
❑ 528 Johnny Ray RC .50 .20
❑ 529 Pat Tabler .10 .02
❑ 530 Tom Herr .10 .02
❑ 531A SD Chicken ERR 1.00 .40
❑ 531B SD Chicken COR 1.00 .40
❑ 532 Sal Butera .10 .02
❑ 533 Mike Griffin .10 .02
❑ 534 Kelvin Moore .10 .02
❑ 535 Reggie Jackson .40 .15
❑ 536 Ed Romero .10 .02
❑ 537 Derrel Thomas .10 .02
❑ 538 Mike O'Berry .10 .02
❑ 539 Jack O'Connor .10 .02
❑ 540 Bob Ojeda RC .50 .20
❑ 541 Roy Lee Jackson .10 .02
❑ 542 Lynn Jones .10 .02
❑ 543 Gaylord Perry .20 .07
❑ 544A Phil Garner ERR
(Reverse negative) .20 .07
❑ 544B Phil Garner COR .20 .07
❑ 545 Garry Templeton .20 .07
❑ 546 Rafael Ramirez .10 .02
❑ 547 Jeff Reardon .20 .07
❑ 548 Ron Guidry .20 .07
❑ 549 Tim Laudner .10 .02
❑ 550 John Henry Johnson .10 .02
❑ 551 Chris Bando .10 .02
❑ 552 Bobby Brown .10 .02
❑ 553 Larry Bradford .10 .02
❑ 554 Scott Fletcher RC .50 .20
❑ 555 Jerry Royster .10 .02
❑ 556 Shooty Babitt UER
(Spelled Babbitt
on front) .10 .02
❑ 557 Kent Hrbek RC 1.00 .40
❑ 558 R.Guidry/T.John .20 .07
❑ 559 Mark Bomback .10 .02
❑ 560 Julio Valdez .10 .02
❑ 561 Buck Martinez .10 .02
❑ 562 Mike A. Marshall RC .50 .20
❑ 563 Rennie Stennett .10 .02
❑ 564 Steve Crawford .10 .02
❑ 565 Bob Babcock .10 .02
❑ 566 Johnny Podres CO .20 .07
❑ 567 Paul Serna .10 .02
❑ 568 Harold Baines .20 .07
❑ 569 Dave LaRoche .10 .02
❑ 570 Lee May .10 .02
❑ 571 Gary Ward .10 .02
❑ 572 John Denny .10 .02
❑ 573 Roy Smalley .10 .02
❑ 574 Bob Brenly RC 1.00 .40
❑ 575 R.Jackson/D.Winfield .20 .07
❑ 576 Luis Pujols .10 .02
❑ 577 Butch Hobson .10 .02
❑ 578 Harvey Kuenn MG .10 .02
❑ 579 Cal Ripken Sr. CO .20 .07
❑ 580 Juan Berenguer .10 .02
❑ 581 Benny Ayala .10 .02
❑ 582 Vance Law .10 .02
❑ 583 Rick Leach .10 .02
❑ 584 George Frazier .10 .02
❑ 585 P.Rose/M.Schmidt 1.50 .60
❑ 586 Joe Rudi .20 .07
❑ 587 Juan Beniquez .10 .02
❑ 588 Luis DeLeon .10 .02
❑ 589 Craig Swan .10 .02
❑ 590 Dave Chalk .10 .02
❑ 591 Billy Gardner MG .10 .02
❑ 592 Sal Bando .20 .07
❑ 593 Bert Campaneris .20 .07
❑ 594 Steve Kemp .10 .02
❑ 595A Randy Lerch ERR
(Braves) .40 .15
❑ 595B Randy Lerch COR
(Brewers) .10 .02
❑ 596 Bryan Clark RC .15 .05
❑ 597 Dave Ford .10 .02
❑ 598 Mike Scioscia .20 .07
❑ 599 John Lowenstein .10 .02
❑ 600 Rene Lachemann MG .10 .02
❑ 601 Mick Kelleher .10 .02
❑ 602 Ron Jackson .10 .02
❑ 603 Jerry Koosman .20 .07
❑ 604 Dave Goltz .10 .02
❑ 605 Ellis Valentine .10 .02
❑ 606 Lonnie Smith .10 .02
❑ 607 Joaquin Andujar .20 .07
❑ 608 Garry Hancock .10 .02
❑ 609 Jerry Turner .10 .02
❑ 610 Bob Bonner .10 .02
❑ 611 Jim Dwyer .10 .02
❑ 612 Terry Bulling .10 .02
❑ 613 Joel Youngblood .10 .02
❑ 614 Larry Milbourne .10 .02
❑ 615 Gene Roof UER
(Name on front
is Phil Roof) .10 .02
❑ 616 Keith Drumwright .10 .02
❑ 617 Dave Rosello .10 .02
❑ 618 Rickey Keeton .10 .02
❑ 619 Dennis Lamp .10 .02
❑ 620 Sid Monge .10 .02
❑ 621 Jerry White .10 .02
❑ 622 Luis Aguayo .10 .02
❑ 623 Jamie Easterly .10 .02
❑ 624 Steve Sax RC 1.00 .40
❑ 625 Dave Roberts .10 .02
❑ 626 Rick Bosetti .10 .02
❑ 627 Terry Francona RC 3.00 1.25
❑ 628 T.Seaver/J.Bench .75 .30
❑ 629 Paul Mirabella .10 .02
❑ 630 Rance Mulliniks .10 .02
❑ 631 Kevin Hickey RC .15 .05
❑ 632 Reid Nichols .10 .02
❑ 633 Dave Geisel .10 .02
❑ 634 Ken Griffey .20 .07
❑ 635 Bob Lemon MG .40 .15
❑ 636 Orlando Sanchez .10 .02
❑ 637 Bill Almon .10 .02
❑ 638 Danny Ainge .20 .07
❑ 639 Willie Stargell .40 .15
❑ 640 Bob Sykes .10 .02
❑ 641 Ed Lynch .10 .02
❑ 642 John Ellis .10 .02
❑ 643 Fergie Jenkins .20 .07
❑ 644 Lenn Sakata .10 .02
❑ 645 Julio Gonzalez .10 .02
❑ 646 Jesse Orosco .10 .02
❑ 647 Jerry Dybzinski .10 .02
❑ 648 Tommy Davis CO .20 .07
❑ 649 Ron Gardenhire RC .50 .20
❑ 650 Felipe Alou CO .20 .07
❑ 651 Harvey Haddix CO .20 .07
❑ 652 Willie Upshaw .50 .20
❑ 653 Bill Madlock .20 .07
❑ 654A DK Checklist 1-26
ERR (Unnumbered)
(With Trammel .40 .15
❑ 654B DK Checklist 1-26
COR (Unnumbered)
(With Trammel .20 .07
❑ 655 Checklist 27-130
(Unnumbered) .20 .07
❑ 656 Checklist 131-234
(Unnumbered) .20 .07
❑ 657 Checklist 235-338
(Unnumbered) .20 .07
❑ 658 Checklist 339-442
(Unnumbered) .20 .07
❑ 659 Checklist 443-544
(Unnumbered) .20 .07
❑ 660 Checklist 545-653
(Unnumbered) .20 .07

1983 Donruss

❑ COMPLETE SET (660) 60.00 30.00
❑ COMP.FACT.SET (660) 80.00 40.00
❑ COMP.COBB PUZZLE 5.00 2.00
❑ 1 Fernando Valenzuela DK .20 .07
❑ 2 Rollie Fingers DK .20 .07
❑ 3 Reggie Jackson DK .40 .15
❑ 4 Jim Palmer DK .20 .07
❑ 5 Jack Morris DK .20 .07
❑ 6 George Foster DK .20 .07
❑ 7 Jim Sundberg DK .20 .07
❑ 8 Willie Stargell DK .40 .15
❑ 9 Dave Stieb DK .20 .07
❑ 10 Joe Niekro DK .10 .02
❑ 11 Rickey Henderson DK 1.50 .60
❑ 12 Dale Murphy DK .40 .15
❑ 13 Toby Harrah DK .20 .07
❑ 14 Bill Buckner DK .20 .07
❑ 15 Willie Wilson DK .20 .07
❑ 16 Steve Carlton DK .40 .15
❑ 17 Ron Guidry DK .20 .07
❑ 18 Steve Rogers DK .20 .07
❑ 19 Kent Hrbek DK .20 .07
❑ 20 Keith Hernandez DK .20 .07
❑ 21 Floyd Bannister DK .10 .02
❑ 22 Johnny Bench DK .75 .30
❑ 23 Britt Burns DK .10 .02
❑ 24 Joe Morgan DK .20 .07
❑ 25 Carl Yastrzemski DK .75 .30
❑ 26 Terry Kennedy DK .10 .02
❑ 27 Gary Roenicke .10 .02
❑ 28 Dwight Bernard .10 .02
❑ 29 Pat Underwood .10 .02
❑ 30 Gary Allenson .10 .02
❑ 31 Ron Guidry .20 .07
❑ 32 Burt Hooton .10 .02
❑ 33 Chris Bando .10 .02
❑ 34 Vida Blue .20 .07
❑ 35 Rickey Henderson 1.50 .60
❑ 36 Ray Burris .10 .02
❑ 37 John Butcher .10 .02
❑ 38 Don Aase .10 .02
❑ 39 Jerry Koosman .20 .07
❑ 40 Bruce Sutter .40 .15
❑ 41 Jose Cruz .20 .07
❑ 42 Pete Rose 2.50 1.00
❑ 43 Cesar Cedeno .20 .07
❑ 44 Floyd Chiffer .10 .02
❑ 45 Larry McWilliams .10 .02

❑ 46 Alan Fowlkes .10 .02
❑ 47 Dale Murphy .40 .15
❑ 48 Doug Bird .10 .02
❑ 49 Hubie Brooks .10 .02
❑ 50 Floyd Bannister .10 .02
❑ 51 Jack O'Connor .10 .02
❑ 52 Steve Senteney .10 .02
❑ 53 Gary Gaetti RC 1.00 .40
❑ 54 Damaso Garcia .10 .02
❑ 55 Gene Nelson .10 .02
❑ 56 Mookie Wilson .20 .07
❑ 57 Allen Ripley .10 .02
❑ 58 Bob Horner .20 .07
❑ 59 Tony Pena .10 .02
❑ 60 Gary Lavelle .10 .02
❑ 61 Tim Lollar .10 .02
❑ 62 Frank Pastore .10 .02
❑ 63 Garry Maddox .10 .02
❑ 64 Bob Forsch .10 .02
❑ 65 Harry Spilman .10 .02
❑ 66 Geoff Zahn .10 .02
❑ 67 Salome Barojas .10 .02
❑ 68 David Palmer .10 .02
❑ 69 Charlie Hough .20 .07
❑ 70 Dan Quisenberry .10 .02
❑ 71 Tony Armas .20 .07
❑ 72 Rick Sutcliffe .20 .07
❑ 73 Steve Balboni .10 .02
❑ 74 Jerry Remy .10 .02
❑ 75 Mike Scioscia .20 .07
❑ 76 John Wockenfuss .10 .02
❑ 77 Jim Palmer .20 .07
❑ 78 Rollie Fingers .20 .07
❑ 79 Joe Nolan .10 .02
❑ 80 Pete Vuckovich .10 .02
❑ 81 Rick Leach .10 .02
❑ 82 Rick Miller .10 .02
❑ 83 Graig Nettles .20 .07
❑ 84 Ron Cey .20 .07
❑ 85 Miguel Dilone .10 .02
❑ 86 John Wathan .10 .02
❑ 87 Kelvin Moore .10 .02
❑ 88A Bryn Smith FDC Bym .20 .07
❑ 88B Bryn Smith FDC COR .40 .15
❑ 89 Dave Hostetler .10 .02
❑ 90 Rod Carew .40 .15
❑ 91 Lonnie Smith .10 .02
❑ 92 Bob Knepper .10 .02
❑ 93 Marty Bystrom .10 .02
❑ 94 Chris Welsh .10 .02
❑ 95 Jason Thompson .10 .02
❑ 96 Tom O'Malley .10 .02
❑ 97 Phil Niekro .20 .07
❑ 98 Neil Allen .10 .02
❑ 99 Bill Buckner .20 .07
❑ 100 Ed VandeBerg .10 .02
❑ 101 Jim Clancy .10 .02
❑ 102 Robert Castillo .10 .02
❑ 103 Bruce Berenyi .10 .02
❑ 104 Carlton Fisk .40 .15
❑ 105 Mike Flanagan .10 .02
❑ 106 Cecil Cooper .20 .07
❑ 107 Jack Morris .20 .07
❑ 108 Mike Morgan .10 .02
❑ 109 Luis Aponte .10 .02
❑ 110 Pedro Guerrero .20 .07
❑ 111 Len Barker .10 .02
❑ 112 Willie Wilson .20 .07
❑ 113 Dave Beard .10 .02
❑ 114 Mike Gates .10 .02
❑ 115 Reggie Jackson .40 .15
❑ 116 George Wright RC .50 .20
❑ 117 Vance Law .10 .02
❑ 118 Nolan Ryan 4.00 1.50
❑ 119 Mike Krukow .10 .02
❑ 120 Ozzie Smith 1.25 .50
❑ 121 Broderick Perkins .10 .02
❑ 122 Tom Seaver .75 .30
❑ 123 Chris Chambliss .20 .07
❑ 124 Chuck Tanner MG .10 .02
❑ 125 Johnnie LeMaster .10 .02
❑ 126 Mel Hall RC .50 .20
❑ 127 Bruce Bochte .10 .02
❑ 128 Charlie Puleo .10 .02
❑ 129 Luis Leal .10 .02
❑ 130 John Pacella .10 .02
❑ 131 Glenn Gulliver .10 .02
❑ 132 Don Money .10 .02
❑ 133 Dave Rozema .10 .02
❑ 134 Bruce Hurst .10 .02
❑ 135 Rudy May .10 .02
❑ 136 Tom Lasorda MG .40 .15
❑ 137 Dan Spillner UER
(Photo actually
Ed Whitson) .10 .02
❑ 138 Jerry Martin .10 .02
❑ 139 Mike Norris .10 .02
❑ 140 Al Oliver .20 .07
❑ 141 Daryl Sconiers .10 .02
❑ 142 Lamar Johnson .10 .02
❑ 143 Harold Baines .20 .07
❑ 144 Alan Ashby .10 .02
❑ 145 Garry Templeton .20 .07
❑ 146 Al Holland .10 .02
❑ 147 Bo Diaz .10 .02
❑ 148 Dave Concepcion .20 .07
❑ 149 Rick Camp .10 .02
❑ 150 Jim Morrison .10 .02
❑ 151 Randy Martz .10 .02
❑ 152 Keith Hernandez .20 .07
❑ 153 John Lowenstein .10 .02
❑ 154 Mike Caldwell .10 .02
❑ 155 Milt Wilcox .10 .02
❑ 156 Rich Gedman .10 .02
❑ 157 Rich Gossage .20 .07
❑ 158 Jerry Reuss .10 .02
❑ 159 Ron Hassey .10 .02
❑ 160 Larry Gura .10 .02
❑ 161 Dwayne Murphy .10 .02
❑ 162 Woodie Fryman .10 .02
❑ 163 Steve Comer .10 .02
❑ 164 Ken Forsch .10 .02
❑ 165 Dennis Lamp .10 .02
❑ 166 David Green RC .50 .20
❑ 167 Terry Puhl .10 .02
❑ 168 Mike Schmidt 2.00 .75
❑ 169 Eddie Milner .10 .02
❑ 170 John Curtis .10 .02
❑ 171 Don Robinson .10 .02
❑ 172 Rich Gale .10 .02
❑ 173 Steve Bedrosian .10 .02
❑ 174 Willie Hernandez .10 .02
❑ 175 Ron Gardenhire .10 .02
❑ 176 Jim Beattie .10 .02
❑ 177 Tim Laudner .10 .02
❑ 178 Buck Martinez .10 .02
❑ 179 Kent Hrbek .20 .07
❑ 180 Alfredo Griffin .10 .02
❑ 181 Larry Andersen .10 .02
❑ 182 Pete Falcone .10 .02
❑ 183 Jody Davis .10 .02
❑ 184 Glenn Hubbard .10 .02
❑ 185 Dale Berra .10 .02
❑ 186 Greg Minton .10 .02
❑ 187 Gary Lucas .10 .02
❑ 188 Dave Van Gorder .10 .02
❑ 189 Bob Dernier .10 .02
❑ 190 Willie McGee RC 1.50 .60
❑ 191 Dickie Thon .10 .02
❑ 192 Bob Boone .20 .07
❑ 193 Britt Burns .10 .02
❑ 194 Jeff Reardon .20 .07
❑ 195 Jon Matlack .10 .02
❑ 196 Don Slaught RC .50 .20
❑ 197 Fred Stanley .10 .02
❑ 198 Rick Manning .10 .02
❑ 199 Dave Righetti .20 .07
❑ 200 Dave Stapleton .10 .02
❑ 201 Steve Yeager .20 .07
❑ 202 Enos Cabell .10 .02
❑ 203 Sammy Stewart .10 .02
❑ 204 Moose Haas .10 .02
❑ 205 Lenn Sakata .10 .02
❑ 206 Charlie Moore .10 .02
❑ 207 Alan Trammell .20 .07
❑ 208 Jim Rice .20 .07
❑ 209 Roy Smalley .10 .02
❑ 210 Bill Russell .20 .07
❑ 211 Andre Thornton .10 .02
❑ 212 Willie Aikens .10 .02
❑ 213 Dave McKay .10 .02
❑ 214 Tim Blackwell .10 .02
❑ 215 Buddy Bell .20 .07
❑ 216 Doug DeCinces .10 .02
❑ 217 Tom Herr .10 .02
❑ 218 Frank LaCorte .10 .02
❑ 219 Steve Carlton .40 .15
❑ 220 Terry Kennedy .10 .02
❑ 221 Mike Easler .10 .02
❑ 222 Jack Clark .20 .07
❑ 223 Gene Garber .10 .02
❑ 224 Scott Holman .10 .02
❑ 225 Mike Proly .10 .02
❑ 226 Terry Bulling .10 .02
❑ 227 Jerry Garvin .10 .02
❑ 228 Ron Davis .10 .02
❑ 229 Tom Hume .10 .02
❑ 230 Marc Hill .10 .02
❑ 231 Dennis Martinez .20 .07
❑ 232 Jim Gantner .10 .02
❑ 233 Larry Pashnick .10 .02
❑ 234 Dave Collins .10 .02
❑ 235 Tom Burgmeier .10 .02
❑ 236 Ken Landreaux .10 .02
❑ 237 John Denny .10 .02
❑ 238 Hal McRae .20 .07
❑ 239 Matt Keough .10 .02
❑ 240 Doug Flynn .10 .02
❑ 241 Fred Lynn .20 .07
❑ 242 Billy Sample .10 .02
❑ 243 Tom Paciorek .10 .02
❑ 244 Joe Sambito .10 .02
❑ 245 Sid Monge .10 .02
❑ 246 Ken Oberkfell .10 .02
❑ 247 Joe Pittman UER
(Photo actually
Juan Eichelberge .10 .02
❑ 248 Mario Soto .20 .07
❑ 249 Claudell Washington .10 .02
❑ 250 Rick Rhoden .10 .02
❑ 251 Darrell Evans .20 .07
❑ 252 Steve Henderson .10 .02
❑ 253 Manny Castillo .10 .02
❑ 254 Craig Swan .10 .02
❑ 255 Joey McLaughlin .10 .02
❑ 256 Pete Redfern .10 .02
❑ 257 Ken Singleton .20 .07
❑ 258 Robin Yount 1.25 .50
❑ 259 Elias Sosa .10 .02
❑ 260 Bob Ojeda .10 .02
❑ 261 Bobby Murcer .20 .07
❑ 262 Candy Maldonado RC .50 .20
❑ 263 Rick Waits .10 .02
❑ 264 Greg Pryor .10 .02
❑ 265 Bob Owchinko .10 .02
❑ 266 Chris Speier .10 .02
❑ 267 Bruce Kison .10 .02
❑ 268 Mark Wagner .10 .02
❑ 269 Steve Kemp .10 .02
❑ 270 Phil Garner .20 .07
❑ 271 Gene Richards .10 .02
❑ 272 Renie Martin .10 .02
❑ 273 Dave Roberts .10 .02
❑ 274 Dan Driessen .10 .02
❑ 275 Rufino Linares .10 .02
❑ 276 Lee Lacy .10 .02
❑ 277 Ryne Sandberg RC 10.00 4.00
❑ 278 Darrell Porter .10 .02
❑ 279 Cal Ripken 6.00 2.50
❑ 280 Jamie Easterly .10 .02
❑ 281 Bill Fahey .10 .02
❑ 282 Glenn Hoffman .10 .02
❑ 283 Willie Randolph .20 .07
❑ 284 Fernando Valenzuela .20 .07
❑ 285 Alan Bannister .10 .02
❑ 286 Paul Splittorff .10 .02
❑ 287 Joe Rudi .20 .07
❑ 288 Bill Gullickson .10 .02
❑ 289 Danny Darwin .10 .02
❑ 290 Andy Hassler .10 .02
❑ 291 Ernesto Escarrega .10 .02
❑ 292 Steve Mura .10 .02
❑ 293 Tony Scott .10 .02
❑ 294 Manny Trillo .10 .02
❑ 295 Greg Harris .10 .02
❑ 296 Luis DeLeon .10 .02
❑ 297 Kent Tekulve .10 .02
❑ 298 Atlee Hammaker .10 .02

❑ 299 Bruce Benedict .10 .02
❑ 300 Fergie Jenkins .20 .07
❑ 301 Dave Kingman .20 .07
❑ 302 Bill Caudill .10 .02
❑ 303 John Castino .10 .02
❑ 304 Ernie Whitt .10 .02
❑ 305 Randy Johnson .10 .02
❑ 306 Garth Iorg .10 .02
❑ 307 Gaylord Perry .20 .07
❑ 308 Ed Lynch .10 .02
❑ 309 Keith Moreland .10 .02
❑ 310 Rafael Ramirez .10 .02
❑ 311 Bill Madlock .20 .07
❑ 312 Milt May .10 .02
❑ 313 John Montefusco .10 .02
❑ 314 Wayne Krenchicki .10 .02
❑ 315 George Vukovich .10 .02
❑ 316 Joaquin Andujar .20 .07
❑ 317 Craig Reynolds .10 .02
❑ 318 Rick Burleson .10 .02
❑ 319 Richard Dotson .10 .02
❑ 320 Steve Rogers .20 .07
❑ 321 Dave Schmidt .10 .02
❑ 322 Bud Black RC .50 .20
❑ 323 Jeff Burroughs .10 .02
❑ 324 Von Hayes .10 .02
❑ 325 Butch Wynegar .10 .02
❑ 326 Carl Yastrzemski 1.25 .50
❑ 327 Ron Roenicke .10 .02
❑ 328 Howard Johnson RC 1.00 .40
❑ 329 Rick Dempsey UER (Posing as a left-handed batte .10 .02
❑ 330A Jim Slaton (Bio printed black on white) .10 .02
❑ 330B Jim Slaton (Bio printed black on yellow) .20 .07
❑ 331 Benny Ayala .10 .02
❑ 332 Ted Simmons .20 .07
❑ 333 Lou Whitaker .20 .07
❑ 334 Chuck Rainey .10 .02
❑ 335 Lou Piniella .20 .07
❑ 336 Steve Sax .20 .07
❑ 337 Toby Harrah .20 .07
❑ 338 George Brett 2.00 .75
❑ 339 Dave Lopes .20 .07
❑ 340 Gary Carter .20 .07
❑ 341 John Grubb .10 .02
❑ 342 Tim Foli .10 .02
❑ 343 Jim Kaat .20 .07
❑ 344 Mike LaCoss .10 .02
❑ 345 Larry Christenson .10 .02
❑ 346 Juan Bonilla .10 .02
❑ 347 Omar Moreno .10 .02
❑ 348 Chili Davis .20 .07
❑ 349 Tommy Boggs .10 .02
❑ 350 Rusty Staub .20 .07
❑ 351 Bump Wills .10 .02
❑ 352 Rick Sweet .10 .02
❑ 353 Jim Gott RC .50 .20
❑ 354 Terry Felton .10 .02
❑ 355 Jim Kern .10 .02
❑ 356 Bill Almon UER (Expos/Mets in 1983, not Padres/M .10 .02
❑ 357 Tippy Martinez .10 .02
❑ 358 Roy Howell .10 .02
❑ 359 Dan Petry .10 .02
❑ 360 Jerry Mumphrey .10 .02
❑ 361 Mark Clear .10 .02
❑ 362 Mike Marshall .10 .02
❑ 363 Lary Sorensen .10 .02
❑ 364 Amos Otis .20 .07
❑ 365 Rick Langford .10 .02
❑ 366 Brad Mills .10 .02
❑ 367 Brian Downing .20 .07
❑ 368 Mike Richardt .10 .02
❑ 369 Aurelio Rodriguez .10 .02
❑ 370 Dave Smith .10 .02
❑ 371 Tug McGraw .20 .07
❑ 372 Doug Bair .10 .02
❑ 373 Ruppert Jones .10 .02
❑ 374 Alex Trevino .10 .02
❑ 375 Ken Dayley .10 .02
❑ 376 Rod Scurry .10 .02
❑ 377 Bob Brenly .10 .02
❑ 378 Scot Thompson .10 .02
❑ 379 Julio Cruz .10 .02
❑ 380 John Stearns .10 .02
❑ 381 Dale Murray .10 .02
❑ 382 Frank Viola RC 1.50 .60
❑ 383 Al Bumbry .10 .02
❑ 384 Ben Oglivie .20 .07
❑ 385 Dave Tobik .10 .02
❑ 386 Bob Stanley .10 .02
❑ 387 Andre Robertson .10 .02
❑ 388 Jorge Orta .10 .02
❑ 389 Ed Whitson .10 .02
❑ 390 Don Hood .10 .02
❑ 391 Tom Underwood .10 .02
❑ 392 Tim Wallach .20 .07
❑ 393 Steve Renko .10 .02
❑ 394 Mickey Rivers .10 .02
❑ 395 Greg Luzinski .20 .07
❑ 396 Art Howe .10 .02
❑ 397 Alan Wiggins .10 .02
❑ 398 Jim Barr .10 .02
❑ 399 Ivan DeJesus .10 .02
❑ 400 Tom Lawless .10 .02
❑ 401 Bob Walk .10 .02
❑ 402 Jimmy Smith .10 .02
❑ 403 Lee Smith .40 .15
❑ 404 George Hendrick .20 .07
❑ 405 Eddie Murray .75 .30
❑ 406 Marshall Edwards .10 .02
❑ 407 Lance Parrish .20 .07
❑ 408 Carney Lansford .20 .07
❑ 409 Dave Winfield .20 .07
❑ 410 Bob Welch .20 .07
❑ 411 Larry Milbourne .10 .02
❑ 412 Dennis Leonard .10 .02
❑ 413 Dan Meyer .10 .02
❑ 414 Charlie Lea .10 .02
❑ 415 Rick Honeycutt .10 .02
❑ 416 Mike Witt .10 .02
❑ 417 Steve Trout .10 .02
❑ 418 Glenn Brummer .10 .02
❑ 419 Denny Walling .10 .02
❑ 420 Gary Matthews .20 .07
❑ 421 Charlie Leibrandt UER (Liebrandt on front of car .10 .02
❑ 422 Juan Eichelberger UER (Photo actually Joe Pittma .10 .02
❑ 423 Cecilio Guante UER (Listed as Matt on card) .10 .02
❑ 424 Bill Laskey .10 .02
❑ 425 Jerry Royster .10 .02
❑ 426 Dickie Noles .10 .02
❑ 427 George Foster .20 .07
❑ 428 Mike Moore RC .50 .20
❑ 429 Gary Ward .10 .02
❑ 430 Barry Bonnell .10 .02
❑ 431 Ron Washington .10 .02
❑ 432 Rance Mulliniks .10 .02
❑ 433 Mike Stanton .10 .02
❑ 434 Jesse Orosco .10 .02
❑ 435 Larry Bowa .20 .07
❑ 436 Biff Pocoroba .10 .02
❑ 437 Johnny Ray .10 .02
❑ 438 Joe Morgan .20 .07
❑ 439 Eric Show RC .50 .20
❑ 440 Larry Biittner .10 .02
❑ 441 Greg Gross .10 .02
❑ 442 Gene Tenace .20 .07
❑ 443 Danny Heep .10 .02
❑ 444 Bobby Clark .10 .02
❑ 445 Kevin Hickey .10 .02
❑ 446 Scott Sanderson .10 .02
❑ 447 Frank Tanana .20 .07
❑ 448 Cesar Geronimo .10 .02
❑ 449 Jimmy Sexton .10 .02
❑ 450 Mike Hargrove .10 .02
❑ 451 Doyle Alexander .10 .02
❑ 452 Dwight Evans .40 .15
❑ 453 Terry Forster .20 .07
❑ 454 Tom Brookens .10 .02
❑ 455 Rich Dauer .10 .02
❑ 456 Rob Picciolo .10 .02
❑ 457 Terry Crowley .10 .02
❑ 458 Ned Yost .10 .02
❑ 459 Kirk Gibson .20 .07
❑ 460 Reid Nichols .10 .02
❑ 461 Oscar Gamble .10 .02
❑ 462 Dusty Baker .20 .07
❑ 463 Jack Perconte .10 .02
❑ 464 Frank White .20 .07
❑ 465 Mickey Klutts .10 .02
❑ 466 Warren Cromartie .10 .02
❑ 467 Larry Parrish .10 .02
❑ 468 Bobby Grich .20 .07
❑ 469 Dane Iorg .10 .02
❑ 470 Joe Niekro .10 .02
❑ 471 Ed Farmer .10 .02
❑ 472 Tim Flannery .10 .02
❑ 473 Dave Parker .20 .07
❑ 474 Jeff Leonard .10 .02
❑ 475 Al Hrabosky .10 .02
❑ 476 Ron Hodges .10 .02
❑ 477 Leon Durham .10 .02
❑ 478 Jim Essian .10 .02
❑ 479 Roy Lee Jackson .10 .02
❑ 480 Brad Havens .10 .02
❑ 481 Joe Price .10 .02
❑ 482 Tony Bernazard .10 .02
❑ 483 Scott McGregor .10 .02
❑ 484 Paul Molitor .20 .07
❑ 485 Mike Ivie .10 .02
❑ 486 Ken Griffey .20 .07
❑ 487 Dennis Eckersley .40 .15
❑ 488 Steve Garvey .20 .07
❑ 489 Mike Fischlin .10 .02
❑ 490 U.L. Washington .10 .02
❑ 491 Steve McCatty .10 .02
❑ 492 Roy Johnson .10 .02
❑ 493 Don Baylor .20 .07
❑ 494 Bobby Johnson .10 .02
❑ 495 Mike Squires .10 .02
❑ 496 Bert Roberge .10 .02
❑ 497 Dick Ruthven .10 .02
❑ 498 Tito Landrum .10 .02
❑ 499 Sixto Lezcano .10 .02
❑ 500 Johnny Bench .75 .30
❑ 501 Larry Whisenton .10 .02
❑ 502 Manny Sarmiento .10 .02
❑ 503 Fred Breining .10 .02
❑ 504 Bill Campbell .10 .02
❑ 505 Todd Cruz .10 .02
❑ 506 Bob Bailor .10 .02
❑ 507 Dave Stieb .20 .07
❑ 508 Al Williams .10 .02
❑ 509 Dan Ford .10 .02
❑ 510 Gorman Thomas .20 .07
❑ 511 Chet Lemon .20 .07
❑ 512 Mike Torrez .10 .02
❑ 513 Shane Rawley .10 .02
❑ 514 Mark Belanger .10 .02
❑ 515 Rodney Craig .10 .02
❑ 516 Onix Concepcion .10 .02
❑ 517 Mike Heath .10 .02
❑ 518 Andre Dawson .20 .07
❑ 519 Luis Sanchez .10 .02
❑ 520 Terry Bogener .10 .02
❑ 521 Rudy Law .10 .02
❑ 522 Ray Knight .20 .07
❑ 523 Joe Lefebvre .10 .02
❑ 524 Jim Wohlford .10 .02
❑ 525 Julio Franco RC 6.00 2.50
❑ 526 Ron Oester .10 .02
❑ 527 Rick Mahler .10 .02
❑ 528 Steve Nicosia .10 .02
❑ 529 Junior Kennedy .10 .02
❑ 530A Whitey Herzog MG (Bio printed black on white) .20 .07
❑ 530B Whitey Herzog MG (Bio printed black on yellow) .20 .07
❑ 531A Don Sutton .20 .07
❑ 531B Don Sutton .20 .07
❑ 532 Mark Brouhard .10 .02
❑ 533A Sparky Anderson MG (Bio printed black on white) .20 .07

❑ 533B Sparky Anderson MG (Bio printed black on yellow) .20 .07
❑ 534 Roger LaFrancois .10 .02
❑ 535 George Frazier .10 .02
❑ 536 Tom Niedenfuer .10 .02
❑ 537 Ed Glynn .10 .02
❑ 538 Lee May .10 .02
❑ 539 Bob Kearney .10 .02
❑ 540 Tim Raines .20 .07
❑ 541 Paul Mirabella .10 .02
❑ 542 Luis Tiant .20 .07
❑ 543 Ron LeFlore .20 .07
❑ 544 Dave LaPoint .10 .02
❑ 545 Randy Moffitt .10 .02
❑ 546 Luis Aguayo .10 .02
❑ 547 Brad Lesley .15 .05
❑ 548 Luis Salazar .10 .02
❑ 549 John Candelaria .10 .02
❑ 550 Dave Bergman .10 .02
❑ 551 Bob Watson .10 .02
❑ 552 Pat Tabler .10 .02
❑ 553 Brent Gaff .10 .02
❑ 554 Al Cowens .10 .02
❑ 555 Tom Brunansky .20 .07
❑ 556 Lloyd Moseby .10 .02
❑ 557A Pascual Perez ERR Twins 2.00 .75
❑ 557B Pascual Perez COR (Braves in glove) .20 .07
❑ 558 Willie Upshaw .10 .02
❑ 559 Richie Zisk .10 .02
❑ 560 Pat Zachry .10 .02
❑ 561 Jay Johnstone .10 .02
❑ 562 Carlos Diaz RC .15 .05
❑ 563 John Tudor .20 .07
❑ 564 Frank Robinson MG .40 .15
❑ 565 Dave Edwards .10 .02
❑ 566 Paul Householder .10 .02
❑ 567 Ron Reed .10 .02
❑ 568 Mike Ramsey .10 .02
❑ 569 Kiko Garcia .10 .02
❑ 570 Tommy John .20 .07
❑ 571 Tony LaRussa MG .20 .07
❑ 572 Joel Youngblood .10 .02
❑ 573 Wayne Tolleson .10 .02
❑ 574 Keith Creel .10 .02
❑ 575 Billy Martin MG .40 .15
❑ 576 Jerry Dybzinski .10 .02
❑ 577 Rick Cerone .10 .02
❑ 578 Tony Perez .40 .15
❑ 579 Greg Brock .10 .02
❑ 580 Glenn Wilson .50 .20
❑ 581 Tim Stoddard .10 .02
❑ 582 Bob McClure .10 .02
❑ 583 Jim Dwyer .10 .02
❑ 584 Ed Romero .10 .02
❑ 585 Larry Herndon .10 .02
❑ 586 Wade Boggs RC 10.00 4.00
❑ 587 Jay Howell .10 .02
❑ 588 Dave Stewart .20 .07
❑ 589 Bert Blyleven .20 .07
❑ 590 Dick Howser MG .10 .02
❑ 591 Wayne Gross .10 .02
❑ 592 Terry Francona .20 .07
❑ 593 Don Werner .10 .02
❑ 594 Bill Stein .10 .02
❑ 595 Jesse Barfield .20 .07
❑ 596 Bob Molinaro .10 .02
❑ 597 Mike Vail .10 .02
❑ 598 Tony Gwynn RC 15.00 6.00
❑ 599 Gary Rajsich .10 .02
❑ 600 Jerry Ujdur .10 .02
❑ 601 Cliff Johnson .10 .02
❑ 602 Jerry White .10 .02
❑ 603 Bryan Clark .10 .02
❑ 604 Joe Ferguson .10 .02
❑ 605 Guy Sularz .10 .02
❑ 606A Ozzie Virgil (Green border on photo) .20 .07
❑ 606B Ozzie Virgil (Orange border on photo) .20 .07
❑ 607 Terry Harper .10 .02
❑ 608 Harvey Kuenn MG .10 .02
❑ 609 Jim Sundberg .20 .07
❑ 610 Willie Stargell .40 .15
❑ 611 Reggie Smith .20 .07
❑ 612 Rob Wilfong .10 .02
❑ 613 Niekro Brothers .20 .07
❑ 614 Lee Elia MG .10 .02
❑ 615 Mickey Hatcher .10 .02
❑ 616 Jerry Hairston .10 .02
❑ 617 John Martin .10 .02
❑ 618 Wally Backman .10 .02
❑ 619 Storm Davis RC .50 .20
❑ 620 Alan Knicely .10 .02
❑ 621 John Stuper .10 .02
❑ 622 Matt Sinatro .10 .02
❑ 623 Geno Petralli .50 .20
❑ 624 Duane Walker .10 .02
❑ 625 Dick Williams MG .10 .02
❑ 626 Pat Corrales MG .10 .02
❑ 627 Vern Ruhle .10 .02
❑ 628 Joe Torre MG .20 .07
❑ 629 Anthony Johnson .10 .02
❑ 630 Steve Howe .10 .02
❑ 631 Gary Woods .10 .02
❑ 632 LaMarr Hoyt .10 .02
❑ 633 Steve Swisher .10 .02
❑ 634 Terry Leach .10 .02
❑ 635 Jeff Newman .10 .02
❑ 636 Brett Butler .20 .07
❑ 637 Gary Gray .10 .02
❑ 638 Lee Mazzilli .20 .07
❑ 639A Ron Jackson ERR A's 20.00 8.00
❑ 639B Ron Jackson COR (Angels in glove, red border on) .10 .02
❑ 639C Ron Jackson COR (Angels in glove, green border .40 .15
❑ 640 Juan Beniquez .10 .02
❑ 641 Dave Rucker .10 .02
❑ 642 Luis Pujols .10 .02
❑ 643 Rick Monday .20 .07
❑ 644 Hosken Powell .10 .02
❑ 645 The Chicken .40 .15
❑ 646 Dave Engle .10 .02
❑ 647 Dick Davis .10 .02
❑ 648 F.Robby/V.Blue/J.Morgan .40 .15
❑ 649 Al Chambers .10 .02
❑ 650 Jesus Vega .10 .02
❑ 651 Jeff Jones .10 .02
❑ 652 Marvis Foley .10 .02
❑ 653 Ty Cobb Puzzle .75 .30
❑ 654A Dick Perez/DK CL .40 .15
❑ 654B Dick Perez/DK CL .40 .15
❑ 655 Checklist 27-130 (Unnumbered) .10 .02
❑ 656 Checklist 131-234 (Unnumbered) .10 .02
❑ 657 Checklist 235-338 (Unnumbered) .10 .02
❑ 658 Checklist 339-442 (Unnumbered) .10 .02
❑ 659 Checklist 443-544 (Unnumbered) .10 .02
❑ 660 Checklist 545-653 (Unnumbered) .10 .02

1984 Donruss

❑ COMPLETE SET (660) 120.00 70.00
❑ COMP.FACT.SET (658) 120.00 70.00
❑ COMP.SNIDER PUZZLE 5.00 2.00
❑ 1 Robin Yount DK 2.50 1.00
❑ 1A Robin Yount DK ERR 5.00 2.00
❑ 2 Dave Concepcion DK .75 .30
❑ 2A Dave Concepcion DK ERR .75 .30
❑ 3 Dwayne Murphy DK .25 .08
❑ 3A Dwayne Murphy DK ERR .25 .08
❑ 4 John Castino DK .25 .08
❑ 4A John Castino DK ERR .25 .08
❑ 5 Leon Durham DK .75 .30
❑ 5A Leon Durham DK ERR .25 .08
❑ 6 Rusty Staub DK .75 .30
❑ 6A Rusty Staub DK ERR .75 .30
❑ 7 Jack Clark DK .75 .30
❑ 7A Jack Clark DK ERR .75 .30
❑ 8 Dave Dravecky DK .25 .08
❑ 8A Dave Dravecky DK ERR .25 .08
❑ 9 Al Oliver DK .75 .30
❑ 9A Al Oliver DK ERR .75 .30
❑ 10 Dave Righetti DK .75 .30
❑ 10A Dave Righetti DK ERR .75 .30
❑ 11 Hal McRae DK .75 .30
❑ 11A Hal McRae DK ERR .75 .30
❑ 12 Ray Knight DK .75 .30
❑ 12A Ray Knight DK ERR .75 .30
❑ 13 Bruce Sutter DK 1.50 .60
❑ 13A Bruce Sutter DK ERR 1.50 .60
❑ 14 Bob Horner DK .75 .30
❑ 14A Bob Horner DK ERR .75 .30
❑ 15 Lance Parrish DK .75 .30
❑ 15A Lance Parrish DK ERR .75 .30
❑ 16 Matt Young DK .75 .30
❑ 16A Matt Young DK ERR .75 .30
❑ 17 Fred Lynn DK .75 .30
❑ 17A Fred Lynn DK ERR .75 .30
❑ 18 Ron Kittle DK .25 .08
❑ 18A Ron Kittle DK ERR .25 .08
❑ 19 Jim Clancy DK .25 .08
❑ 19A Jim Clancy DK ERR .25 .08
❑ 20 Bill Madlock DK .75 .30
❑ 20A Bill Madlock DK ERR .75 .30
❑ 21 Larry Parrish DK .25 .08
❑ 21A Larry Parrish DK ERR .25 .08
❑ 22 Eddie Murray DK 3.00 1.25
❑ 22A Eddie Murray DK ERR 3.00 1.25
❑ 23 Mike Schmidt DK 5.00 2.00
❑ 23A Mike Schmidt DK ERR 5.00 2.00
❑ 24 Pedro Guerrero DK .75 .30
❑ 24A Pedro Guerrero DK ERR .75 .30
❑ 25 Andre Thornton DK .25 .08
❑ 25A Andre Thornton DK ERR .25 .08
❑ 26 Wade Boggs DK 3.00 1.25
❑ 26A Wade Boggs DK ERR 3.00 1.25
❑ 27 Joel Skinner RC .25 .08
❑ 28 Tommy Dunbar RC .25 .08
❑ 29A Mike Stenhouse ERR RC .25 .08
❑ 29B Mike Stenhouse COR 3.00 1.25
❑ 30A Ron Darling ERR RC 2.00 .75
❑ 30B Ron Darling COR 3.00 1.25
❑ 31 Dion James RC .25 .08
❑ 32 Tony Fernandez RC 2.00 .75
❑ 33 Angel Salazar RC .25 .08
❑ 34 Kevin McReynolds RC 2.00 .75
❑ 35 Dick Schofield RC 1.00 .40
❑ 36 Brad Komminsk RC .25 .08
❑ 37 Tim Teufel RC 1.00 .40
❑ 38 Doug Frobel RC .25 .08
❑ 39 Greg Gagne RC 1.00 .40
❑ 40 Mike Fuentes RC .25 .08
❑ 41 Joe Carter RC 8.00 3.00
❑ 42 Mike C. Brown RC .25 .08
❑ 43 Mike Jeffcoat RC .25 .08
❑ 44 Sid Fernandez RC ! 2.00 .75
❑ 45 Brian Dayett RC .25 .08
❑ 46 Chris Smith RC .25 .08
❑ 47 Eddie Murray 3.00 1.25
❑ 48 Robin Yount 5.00 2.00
❑ 49 Lance Parrish 1.50 .60
❑ 50 Jim Rice .75 .30
❑ 51 Dave Winfield .75 .30
❑ 52 Fernando Valenzuela .75 .30
❑ 53 George Brett 8.00 3.00
❑ 54 Rickey Henderson 5.00 2.00
❑ 55 Gary Carter .75 .30

❑ 56 Buddy Bell .75 .30
❑ 57 Reggie Jackson 1.50 .60
❑ 58 Harold Baines .75 .30
❑ 59 Ozzie Smith 5.00 2.00
❑ 60 Nolan Ryan 15.00 6.00
❑ 61 Pete Rose 10.00 4.00
❑ 62 Ron Oester .25 .08
❑ 63 Steve Garvey .75 .30
❑ 64 Jason Thompson .25 .08
❑ 65 Jack Clark .75 .30
❑ 66 Dale Murphy 1.50 .60
❑ 67 Leon Durham .25 .08
❑ 68 Darryl Strawberry RC 8.00 3.00
❑ 69 Richie Zisk .25 .08
❑ 70 Kent Hrbek .75 .30
❑ 71 Dave Stieb .75 .30
❑ 72 Ken Schrom .25 .08
❑ 73 George Bell .75 .30
❑ 74 John Moses .25 .08
❑ 75 Ed Lynch .25 .08
❑ 76 Chuck Rainey .25 .08
❑ 77 Biff Pocoroba .25 .08
❑ 78 Cecilio Guante .25 .08
❑ 79 Jim Barr .25 .08
❑ 80 Kurt Bevacqua .25 .08
❑ 81 Tom Foley .25 .08
❑ 82 Joe Lefebvre .25 .08
❑ 83 Andy Van Slyke RC 4.00 1.50
❑ 84 Bob Lillis MG .25 .08
❑ 85 Ricky Adams .25 .08
❑ 86 Jerry Hairston .25 .08
❑ 87 Bob James .25 .08
❑ 88 Joe Altobelli MG .25 .08
❑ 89 Ed Romero .25 .08
❑ 90 John Grubb .25 .08
❑ 91 John Henry Johnson .25 .08
❑ 92 Juan Espino .25 .08
❑ 93 Candy Maldonado .25 .08
❑ 94 Andre Thornton .25 .08
❑ 95 Onix Concepcion .25 .08
❑ 96 Donnie Hill UER
(Listed as P,
should be 2B) .25 .08
❑ 97 Andre Dawson .75 .30
❑ 98 Frank Tanana .75 .30
❑ 99 Curt Wilkerson .25 .08
❑ 100 Larry Gura .25 .08
❑ 101 Dwayne Murphy .25 .08
❑ 102 Tom Brennan .25 .08
❑ 103 Dave Righetti .75 .30
❑ 104 Steve Sax .25 .08
❑ 105 Dan Petry .75 .30
❑ 106 Cal Ripken 20.00 8.00
❑ 107 Paul Molitor .75 .30
❑ 108 Fred Lynn .75 .30
❑ 109 Neil Allen .25 .08
❑ 110 Joe Niekro .25 .08
❑ 111 Steve Carlton 1.50 .60
❑ 112 Terry Kennedy .25 .08
❑ 113 Bill Madlock .75 .30
❑ 114 Chili Davis .75 .30
❑ 115 Jim Gantner .25 .08
❑ 116 Tom Seaver 3.00 1.25
❑ 117 Bill Buckner .75 .30
❑ 118 Bill Caudill .25 .08
❑ 119 Jim Clancy .25 .08
❑ 120 John Castino .25 .08
❑ 121 Dave Concepcion .75 .30
❑ 122 Greg Luzinski .75 .30
❑ 123 Mike Boddicker .25 .08
❑ 124 Pete Ladd .25 .08
❑ 125 Juan Berenguer .25 .08
❑ 126 John Montefusco .25 .08
❑ 127 Ed Jurak .25 .08
❑ 128 Tom Niedenfuer .25 .08
❑ 129 Bert Blyleven .75 .30
❑ 130 Bud Black .25 .08
❑ 131 Gorman Heimueller .25 .08
❑ 132 Dan Schatzeder .25 .08
❑ 133 Ron Jackson .25 .08
❑ 134 Tom Henke RC 2.00 .75
❑ 135 Kevin Hickey .25 .08
❑ 136 Mike Scott .75 .30
❑ 137 Bo Diaz .25 .08
❑ 138 Glenn Brummer .25 .08
❑ 139 Sid Monge .25 .08
❑ 140 Rich Gale .25 .08
❑ 141 Brett Butler .75 .30
❑ 142 Brian Harper RC 1.00 .40
❑ 143 John Rabb .25 .08
❑ 144 Gary Woods .25 .08
❑ 145 Pat Putnam .25 .08
❑ 146 Jim Acker .25 .08
❑ 147 Mickey Hatcher .25 .08
❑ 148 Todd Cruz .25 .08
❑ 149 Tom Tellmann .25 .08
❑ 150 John Wockenfuss .25 .08
❑ 151 Wade Boggs 8.00 3.00
❑ 152 Don Baylor .75 .30
❑ 153 Bob Welch .75 .30
❑ 154 Alan Bannister .25 .08
❑ 155 Willie Aikens .25 .08
❑ 156 Jeff Burroughs .25 .08
❑ 157 Bryan Little .25 .08
❑ 158 Bob Boone .75 .30
❑ 159 Dave Hostetler .25 .08
❑ 160 Jerry Dybzinski .25 .08
❑ 161 Mike Madden .25 .08
❑ 162 Luis DeLeon .25 .08
❑ 163 Willie Hernandez .25 .08
❑ 164 Frank Pastore .25 .08
❑ 165 Rick Camp .25 .08
❑ 166 Lee Mazzilli .75 .30
❑ 167 Scot Thompson .25 .08
❑ 168 Bob Forsch .25 .08
❑ 169 Mike Flanagan .25 .08
❑ 170 Rick Manning .25 .08
❑ 171 Chet Lemon .75 .30
❑ 172 Jerry Remy .25 .08
❑ 173 Ron Guidry .75 .30
❑ 174 Pedro Guerrero .75 .30
❑ 175 Willie Wilson .75 .30
❑ 176 Carney Lansford .75 .30
❑ 177 Al Oliver .75 .30
❑ 178 Jim Sundberg .75 .30
❑ 179 Bobby Grich .75 .30
❑ 180 Rich Dotson .25 .08
❑ 181 Joaquin Andujar .75 .30
❑ 182 Jose Cruz .75 .30
❑ 183 Mike Schmidt 8.00 3.00
❑ 184 Gary Redus RC 1.00 .40
❑ 185 Garry Templeton .75 .30
❑ 186 Tony Pena .25 .08
❑ 187 Greg Minton .25 .08
❑ 188 Phil Niekro .75 .30
❑ 189 Fergie Jenkins .75 .30
❑ 190 Mookie Wilson .75 .30
❑ 191 Jim Beattie .25 .08
❑ 192 Gary Ward .25 .08
❑ 193 Jesse Barfield .75 .30
❑ 194 Pete Filson .25 .08
❑ 195 Roy Lee Jackson .25 .08
❑ 196 Rick Sweet .25 .08
❑ 197 Jesse Orosco .25 .08
❑ 198 Steve Lake .25 .08
❑ 199 Ken Dayley .25 .08
❑ 200 Manny Sarmiento .25 .08
❑ 201 Mark Davis .25 .08
❑ 202 Tim Flannery .25 .08
❑ 203 Bill Scherrer .25 .08
❑ 204 Al Holland .25 .08
❑ 205 Dave Von Ohlen .25 .08
❑ 206 Mike LaCoss .25 .08
❑ 207 Juan Beniquez .25 .08
❑ 208 Juan Agosto .25 .08
❑ 209 Bobby Ramos .25 .08
❑ 210 Al Bumbry .25 .08
❑ 211 Mark Brouhard .25 .08
❑ 212 Howard Bailey .25 .08
❑ 213 Bruce Hurst .25 .08
❑ 214 Bob Shirley .25 .08
❑ 215 Pat Zachry .25 .08
❑ 216 Julio Franco 3.00 1.25
❑ 217 Mike Armstrong .25 .08
❑ 218 Dave Beard .25 .08
❑ 219 Steve Rogers .75 .30
❑ 220 John Butcher .25 .08
❑ 221 Mike Smithson .25 .08
❑ 222 Frank White .75 .30
❑ 223 Mike Heath .25 .08
❑ 224 Chris Bando .25 .08
❑ 225 Roy Smalley .25 .08
❑ 226 Dusty Baker .75 .30
❑ 227 Lou Whitaker .75 .30
❑ 228 John Lowenstein .25 .08
❑ 229 Ben Oglivie .75 .30
❑ 230 Doug DeCinces .25 .08
❑ 231 Lonnie Smith .25 .08
❑ 232 Ray Knight .75 .30
❑ 233 Gary Matthews .75 .30
❑ 234 Juan Bonilla .25 .08
❑ 235 Rod Scurry .25 .08
❑ 236 Atlee Hammaker .25 .08
❑ 237 Mike Caldwell .25 .08
❑ 238 Keith Hernandez .75 .30
❑ 239 Larry Bowa .75 .30
❑ 240 Tony Bernazard .25 .08
❑ 241 Damaso Garcia .25 .08
❑ 242 Tom Brunansky .25 .08
❑ 243 Dan Driessen .25 .08
❑ 244 Ron Kittle .25 .08
❑ 245 Tim Stoddard .25 .08
❑ 246 Bob L. Gibson RC
(Brewers Pitcher) .25 .08
❑ 247 Marty Castillo .25 .08
❑ 248 Don Mattingly RC 40.00 15.00
❑ 249 Jeff Newman .25 .08
❑ 250 Alejandro Pena RC 2.00 .75
❑ 251 Toby Harrah .75 .30
❑ 252 Cesar Geronimo .25 .08
❑ 253 Tom Underwood .25 .08
❑ 254 Doug Flynn .25 .08
❑ 255 Andy Hassler .25 .08
❑ 256 Odell Jones .25 .08
❑ 257 Rudy Law .25 .08
❑ 258 Harry Spilman .25 .08
❑ 259 Marty Bystrom .25 .08
❑ 260 Dave Rucker .25 .08
❑ 261 Ruppert Jones .25 .08
❑ 262 Jeff R. Jones
(Reds OF) .25 .08
❑ 263 Gerald Perry 1.00 .40
❑ 264 Gene Tenace .75 .30
❑ 265 Brad Wellman .25 .08
❑ 266 Dickie Noles .25 .08
❑ 267 Jamie Allen .25 .08
❑ 268 Jim Gott .25 .08
❑ 269 Ron Davis .25 .08
❑ 270 Benny Ayala .25 .08
❑ 271 Ned Yost .25 .08
❑ 272 Dave Rozema .25 .08
❑ 273 Dave Stapleton .25 .08
❑ 274 Lou Piniella .75 .30
❑ 275 Jose Morales .25 .08
❑ 276 Broderick Perkins .25 .08
❑ 277 Butch Davis RC .25 .08
❑ 278 Tony Phillips RC 2.00 .75
❑ 279 Jeff Reardon .75 .30
❑ 280 Ken Forsch .25 .08
❑ 281 Pete O'Brien RC 1.00 .40
❑ 282 Tom Paciorek .25 .08
❑ 283 Frank LaCorte .25 .08
❑ 284 Tim Lollar .25 .08
❑ 285 Greg Gross .25 .08
❑ 286 Alex Trevino .25 .08
❑ 287 Gene Garber .25 .08
❑ 288 Dave Parker .75 .30
❑ 289 Lee Smith .75 .30
❑ 290 Dave LaPoint .25 .08
❑ 291 John Shelby .25 .08
❑ 292 Charlie Moore .25 .08
❑ 293 Alan Trammell .75 .30
❑ 294 Tony Armas .75 .30
❑ 295 Shane Rawley .25 .08
❑ 296 Greg Brock .25 .08
❑ 297 Hal McRae .75 .30
❑ 298 Mike Davis .25 .08
❑ 299 Tim Raines .75 .30
❑ 300 Bucky Dent .75 .30
❑ 301 Tommy John .75 .30
❑ 302 Carlton Fisk 1.50 .60
❑ 303 Darrell Porter .25 .08
❑ 304 Dickie Thon .25 .08
❑ 305 Garry Maddox .25 .08
❑ 306 Cesar Cedeno .75 .30
❑ 307 Gary Lucas .25 .08
❑ 308 Johnny Ray .25 .08
❑ 309 Andy McGaffigan .25 .08

	Card	Price	Price
❑	310 Claudell Washington	.25	.08
❑	311 Ryne Sandberg	12.00	5.00
❑	312 George Foster	.75	.30
❑	313 Spike Owen RC	1.00	.40
❑	314 Gary Gaetti	1.50	.60
❑	315 Willie Upshaw	.25	.08
❑	316 Al Williams	.25	.08
❑	317 Jorge Orta	.25	.08
❑	318 Orlando Mercado	.25	.08
❑	319 Junior Ortiz	.25	.08
❑	320 Mike Proly	.25	.08
❑	321 Randy Johnson UER ('72-'82 stats are from Twins'	.25	.08
❑	322 Jim Morrison	.25	.08
❑	323 Max Venable	.25	.08
❑	324 Tony Gwynn	12.00	5.00
❑	325 Duane Walker	.25	.08
❑	326 Ozzie Virgil	.25	.08
❑	327 Jeff Lahti	.25	.08
❑	328 Bill Dawley	.25	.08
❑	329 Rob Wilfong	.25	.08
❑	330 Marc Hill	.25	.08
❑	331 Ray Burris	.25	.08
❑	332 Allan Ramirez	.25	.08
❑	333 Chuck Porter	.25	.08
❑	334 Wayne Krenchicki	.25	.08
❑	335 Gary Allenson	.25	.08
❑	336 Bobby Meacham	.25	.08
❑	337 Joe Beckwith	.25	.08
❑	338 Rick Sutcliffe	.75	.30
❑	339 Mark Huismann	.25	.08
❑	340 Tim Conroy	.25	.08
❑	341 Scott Sanderson	.25	.08
❑	342 Larry Biittner	.25	.08
❑	343 Dave Stewart	.75	.30
❑	344 Darryl Motley	.25	.08
❑	345 Chris Codiroli	.25	.08
❑	346 Rich Behenna	.25	.08
❑	347 Andre Robertson	.25	.08
❑	348 Mike Marshall	.25	.08
❑	349 Larry Herndon	.75	.30
❑	350 Rich Dauer	.25	.08
❑	351 Cecil Cooper	.75	.30
❑	352 Rod Carew	1.50	.60
❑	353 Willie McGee	.75	.30
❑	354 Phil Garner	.75	.30
❑	355 Joe Morgan	.75	.30
❑	356 Luis Salazar	.25	.08
❑	357 John Candelaria	.25	.08
❑	358 Bill Laskey	.25	.08
❑	359 Bob McClure	.25	.08
❑	360 Dave Kingman	.75	.30
❑	361 Ron Cey	.75	.30
❑	362 Matt Young RC	1.00	.40
❑	363 Lloyd Moseby	.25	.08
❑	364 Frank Viola	1.50	.60
❑	365 Eddie Milner	.25	.08
❑	366 Floyd Bannister	.25	.08
❑	367 Dan Ford	.25	.08
❑	368 Moose Haas	.25	.08
❑	369 Doug Bair	.25	.08
❑	370 Ray Fontenot	.25	.08
❑	371 Luis Aponte	.25	.08
❑	372 Jack Fimple	.25	.08
❑	373 Neal Heaton	.25	.08
❑	374 Greg Pryor	.25	.08
❑	375 Wayne Gross	.25	.08
❑	376 Charlie Lea	.25	.08
❑	377 Steve Lubratich	.25	.08
❑	378 Jon Matlack	.25	.08
❑	379 Julio Cruz	.25	.08
❑	380 John Mizerock	.25	.08
❑	381 Kevin Gross RC	1.00	.40
❑	382 Mike Ramsey	.25	.08
❑	383 Doug Gwosdz	.25	.08
❑	384 Kelly Paris	.25	.08
❑	385 Pete Falcone	.25	.08
❑	386 Milt May	.25	.08
❑	387 Fred Breining	.25	.08
❑	388 Craig Lefferts RC	.25	.08
❑	389 Steve Henderson	.25	.08
❑	390 Randy Moffitt	.25	.08
❑	391 Ron Washington	.25	.08
❑	392 Gary Roenicke	.25	.08
❑	393 Tom Candiotti RC	2.00	.75
❑	394 Larry Pashnick	.25	.08
❑	395 Dwight Evans	1.50	.60
❑	396 Rich Gossage	.75	.30
❑	397 Derrel Thomas	.25	.08
❑	398 Juan Eichelberger	.25	.08
❑	399 Leon Roberts	.25	.08
❑	400 Dave Lopes	.75	.30
❑	401 Bill Gullickson	.25	.08
❑	402 Geoff Zahn	.25	.08
❑	403 Billy Sample	.25	.08
❑	404 Mike Squires	.25	.08
❑	405 Craig Reynolds	.25	.08
❑	406 Eric Show	.25	.08
❑	407 John Denny	.25	.08
❑	408 Dann Bilardello	.25	.08
❑	409 Bruce Benedict	.25	.08
❑	410 Kent Tekulve	.25	.08
❑	411 Mel Hall	.75	.30
❑	412 John Stuper	.25	.08
❑	413 Rick Dempsey	.25	.08
❑	414 Don Sutton	.75	.30
❑	415 Jack Morris	.75	.30
❑	416 John Tudor	.75	.30
❑	417 Willie Randolph	.75	.30
❑	418 Jerry Reuss	.25	.08
❑	419 Don Slaught	.75	.30
❑	420 Steve McCatty	.25	.08
❑	421 Tim Wallach	.25	.08
❑	422 Larry Parrish	.25	.08
❑	423 Brian Downing	.75	.30
❑	424 Britt Burns	.25	.08
❑	425 David Green	.25	.08
❑	426 Jerry Mumphrey	.25	.08
❑	427 Ivan DeJesus	.25	.08
❑	428 Mario Soto	.75	.30
❑	429 Gene Richards	.25	.08
❑	430 Dale Berra	.25	.08
❑	431 Darrell Evans	.75	.30
❑	432 Glenn Hubbard	.25	.08
❑	433 Jody Davis	.25	.08
❑	434 Danny Heep	.25	.08
❑	435 Edwin Nunez RC	.25	.08
❑	436 Bobby Castillo	.25	.08
❑	437 Ernie Whitt	.25	.08
❑	438 Scott Ullger	.25	.08
❑	439 Doyle Alexander	.25	.08
❑	440 Domingo Ramos	.25	.08
❑	441 Craig Swan	.25	.08
❑	442 Warren Brusstar	.25	.08
❑	443 Len Barker	.25	.08
❑	444 Mike Easler	.25	.08
❑	445 Renie Martin	.25	.08
❑	446 Dennis Rasmussen RC	1.00	.40
❑	447 Ted Power	.25	.08
❑	448 Charles Hudson	.25	.08
❑	449 Danny Cox RC	.25	.08
❑	450 Kevin Bass	.25	.08
❑	451 Daryl Sconiers	.25	.08
❑	452 Scott Fletcher	.25	.08
❑	453 Bryn Smith	.25	.08
❑	454 Jim Dwyer	.25	.08
❑	455 Rob Picciolo	.25	.08
❑	456 Enos Cabell	.25	.08
❑	457 Dennis Boyd	.75	.30
❑	458 Butch Wynegar	.25	.08
❑	459 Burt Hooton	.25	.08
❑	460 Ron Hassey	.25	.08
❑	461 Danny Jackson RC	1.00	.40
❑	462 Bob Kearney	.25	.08
❑	463 Terry Francona	.75	.30
❑	464 Wayne Tolleson	.25	.08
❑	465 Mickey Rivers	.25	.08
❑	466 John Wathan	.25	.08
❑	467 Bill Almon	.25	.08
❑	468 George Vukovich	.25	.08
❑	469 Steve Kemp	.25	.08
❑	470 Ken Landreaux	.25	.08
❑	471 Milt Wilcox	.25	.08
❑	472 Tippy Martinez	.25	.08
❑	473 Ted Simmons	.75	.30
❑	474 Tim Foli	.25	.08
❑	475 George Hendrick	.75	.30
❑	476 Terry Puhl	.25	.08
❑	477 Von Hayes	.25	.08
❑	478 Bobby Brown	.25	.08
❑	479 Lee Lacy	.25	.08
❑	480 Joel Youngblood	.25	.08
❑	481 Jim Slaton	.25	.08
❑	482 Mike Fitzgerald	.25	.08
❑	483 Keith Moreland	.25	.08
❑	484 Ron Roenicke	.25	.08
❑	485 Luis Leal	.25	.08
❑	486 Bryan Oelkers	.25	.08
❑	487 Bruce Berenyi	.25	.08
❑	488 LaMarr Hoyt	.25	.08
❑	489 Joe Nolan	.25	.08
❑	490 Marshall Edwards	.25	.08
❑	491 Mike Laga	.75	.30
❑	492 Rick Cerone	.25	.08
❑	493 Rick Miller UER (Listed as Mike on card front)	.25	.08
❑	494 Rick Honeycutt	.25	.08
❑	495 Mike Hargrove	.25	.08
❑	496 Joe Simpson	.25	.08
❑	497 Keith Atherton	.25	.08
❑	498 Chris Welsh	.25	.08
❑	499 Bruce Kison	.25	.08
❑	500 Bobby Johnson	.25	.08
❑	501 Jerry Koosman	.75	.30
❑	502 Frank DiPino	.25	.08
❑	503 Tony Perez	1.50	.60
❑	504 Ken Oberkfell	.25	.08
❑	505 Mark Thurmond	.25	.08
❑	506 Joe Price	.25	.08
❑	507 Pascual Perez	.25	.08
❑	508 Marvell Wynne	1.00	.40
❑	509 Mike Krukow	.25	.08
❑	510 Dick Ruthven	.25	.08
❑	511 Al Cowens	.25	.08
❑	512 Cliff Johnson	.25	.08
❑	513 Randy Bush	.25	.08
❑	514 Sammy Stewart	.25	.08
❑	515 Bill Schroeder	.25	.08
❑	516 Aurelio Lopez	.75	.30
❑	517 Mike C. Brown	.25	.08
❑	518 Graig Nettles	.75	.30
❑	519 Dave Sax	.25	.08
❑	520 Jerry Willard	.25	.08
❑	521 Paul Splittorff	.25	.08
❑	522 Tom Burgmeier	.25	.08
❑	523 Chris Speier	.25	.08
❑	524 Bobby Clark	.25	.08
❑	525 George Wright	.25	.08
❑	526 Dennis Lamp	.25	.08
❑	527 Tony Scott	.25	.08
❑	528 Ed Whitson	.25	.08
❑	529 Ron Reed	.25	.08
❑	530 Charlie Puleo	.25	.08
❑	531 Jerry Royster	.25	.08
❑	532 Don Robinson	.25	.08
❑	533 Steve Trout	.25	.08
❑	534 Bruce Sutter	1.50	.60
❑	535 Bob Horner !	.75	.30
❑	536 Pat Tabler	.25	.08
❑	537 Chris Chambliss	.75	.30
❑	538 Bob Ojeda	.25	.08
❑	539 Alan Ashby	.25	.08
❑	540 Jay Johnstone	.25	.08
❑	541 Bob Dernier	.25	.08
❑	542 Brook Jacoby	1.00	.40
❑	543 U.L. Washington	.25	.08
❑	544 Danny Darwin	.25	.08
❑	545 Kiko Garcia	.25	.08
❑	546 Vance Law UER (Listed as P on card front)	.25	.08
❑	547 Tug McGraw	.75	.30
❑	548 Dave Smith	.25	.08
❑	549 Len Matuszek	.25	.08
❑	550 Tom Hume	.25	.08
❑	551 Dave Dravecky	.25	.08
❑	552 Rick Rhoden	.25	.08
❑	553 Duane Kuiper	.25	.08
❑	554 Rusty Staub	.75	.30
❑	555 Bill Campbell	.25	.08
❑	556 Mike Torrez	.25	.08
❑	557 Dave Henderson	.75	.30
❑	558 Len Whitehouse	.25	.08
❑	559 Barry Bonnell	.25	.08
❑	560 Rick Lysander	.25	.08
❑	561 Garth Iorg	.25	.08

❑ 562 Bryan Clark .25 .08
❑ 563 Brian Giles .25 .08
❑ 564 Vern Ruhle .25 .08
❑ 565 Steve Bedrosian .25 .08
❑ 566 Larry McWilliams .25 .08
❑ 567 Jeff Leonard UER
(Listed as P
on card front) .25 .08
❑ 568 Alan Wiggins .25 .08
❑ 569 Jeff Russell RC 1.00 .40
❑ 570 Salome Barojas .25 .08
❑ 571 Dane Iorg .25 .08
❑ 572 Bob Knepper .25 .08
❑ 573 Gary Lavelle .25 .08
❑ 574 Gorman Thomas .75 .30
❑ 575 Manny Trillo .25 .08
❑ 576 Jim Palmer .75 .30
❑ 577 Dale Murray .25 .08
❑ 578 Tom Brookens .75 .30
❑ 579 Rich Gedman .25 .08
❑ 580 Bill Doran RC 1.00 .40
❑ 581 Steve Yeager .75 .30
❑ 582 Dan Spillner .25 .08
❑ 583 Dan Quisenberry .25 .08
❑ 584 Rance Mulliniks .25 .08
❑ 585 Storm Davis .25 .08
❑ 586 Dave Schmidt .25 .08
❑ 587 Bill Russell .75 .30
❑ 588 Pat Sheridan .25 .08
❑ 589 Rafael Ramirez
UER (A's on front) .25 .08
❑ 590 Bud Anderson .25 .08
❑ 591 George Frazier .25 .08
❑ 592 Lee Tunnell .25 .08
❑ 593 Kirk Gibson 3.00 1.25
❑ 594 Scott McGregor .25 .08
❑ 595 Bob Bailor .25 .08
❑ 596 Tommy Herr .25 .08
❑ 597 Luis Sanchez .25 .08
❑ 598 Dave Engle .25 .08
❑ 599 Craig McMurtry .25 .08
❑ 600 Carlos Diaz .25 .08
❑ 601 Tom O'Malley .25 .08
❑ 602 Nick Esasky .25 .08
❑ 603 Ron Hodges .25 .08
❑ 604 Ed VandeBerg .25 .08
❑ 605 Alfredo Griffin .25 .08
❑ 606 Glenn Hoffman .25 .08
❑ 607 Hubie Brooks .25 .08
❑ 608 Richard Barnes UER
(Photo actually
Neal Heaton) .25 .08
❑ 609 Greg Walker 1.00 .40
❑ 610 Ken Singleton .75 .30
❑ 611 Mark Clear .25 .08
❑ 612 Buck Martinez .25 .08
❑ 613 Ken Griffey .75 .30
❑ 614 Reid Nichols .25 .08
❑ 615 Doug Sisk .25 .08
❑ 616 Bob Brenly .25 .08
❑ 617 Joey McLaughlin .25 .08
❑ 618 Glenn Wilson .75 .30
❑ 619 Bob Stoddard .25 .08
❑ 620 Lenn Sakata UER
(Listed as Len
on card front) .25 .08
❑ 621 Mike Young RC .25 .08
❑ 622 John Stefero .25 .08
❑ 623 Carmelo Martinez .25 .08
❑ 624 Dave Bergman .25 .08
❑ 625 Ozzie Smith/W.McGee 3.00 1.25
❑ 626 Rudy May .25 .08
❑ 627 Matt Keough .25 .08
❑ 628 Jose DeLeon RC 1.00 .40
❑ 629 Jim Essian .25 .08
❑ 630 Darnell Coles RC 1.00 .40
❑ 631 Mike Warren .25 .08
❑ 632 Del Crandall MG .25 .08
❑ 633 Dennis Martinez .75 .30
❑ 634 Mike Moore .25 .08
❑ 635 Lary Sorensen .25 .08
❑ 636 Ricky Nelson .25 .08
❑ 637 Omar Moreno .25 .08
❑ 638 Charlie Hough .75 .30
❑ 639 Dennis Eckersley ! 1.50 .60
❑ 640 Walt Terrell .25 .08
❑ 641 Denny Walling .25 .08
❑ 642 Dave Anderson RC .25 .08
❑ 643 Jose Oquendo RC 1.00 .40
❑ 644 Bob Stanley .25 .08
❑ 645 Dave Geisel .25 .08
❑ 646 Scott Garrelts .25 .08
❑ 647 Gary Pettis .25 .08
❑ 648 Duke Snider Puzzle 1.50 .60
❑ 649 Johnnie LeMaster .25 .08
❑ 650 Dave Collins .25 .08
❑ 651 The Chicken 1.50 .60
❑ 652 DK Checklist 1-26
(Unnumbered) .75 .30
❑ 653 Checklist 27-130
(Unnumbered) .25 .08
❑ 654 Checklist 131-234
(Unnumbered) .25 .08
❑ 655 Checklist 235-338
(Unnumbered) .25 .08
❑ 656 Checklist 339-442
(Unnumbered) .25 .08
❑ 657 Checklist 443-546
(Unnumbered) .25 .08
❑ 658 Checklist 547-651
(Unnumbered) .25 .08
❑ A G.Perry/R.Fingers SP 2.50 1.00
❑ B J.Bench/C.Yastrzemski SP 5.00 2.00

1985 Donruss

❑ COMPLETE SET (660) 60.00 30.00
❑ COMP.FACT.SET (660) 100.00 50.00
❑ COMP.GEHRIG PUZZLE 4.00 1.50
❑ 1 Ryne Sandberg DK 1.25 .50
❑ 2 Doug DeCinces DK .15 .05
❑ 3 Richard Dotson DK .15 .05
❑ 4 Bert Blyleven DK .40 .15
❑ 5 Lou Whitaker DK .40 .15
❑ 6 Dan Quisenberry DK .15 .05
❑ 7 Don Mattingly DK 2.50 1.00
❑ 8 Carney Lansford DK .40 .15
❑ 9 Frank Tanana DK .40 .15
❑ 10 Willie Upshaw DK .15 .05
❑ 11 Claudell Washington DK .15 .05
❑ 12 Mike Marshall DK .15 .05
❑ 13 Joaquin Andujar DK .40 .15
❑ 14 Cal Ripken DK 2.50 1.00
❑ 15 Jim Rice DK .40 .15
❑ 16 Don Sutton DK .40 .15
❑ 17 Frank Viola DK .40 .15
❑ 18 Alvin Davis DK .40 .15
❑ 19 Mario Soto DK .40 .15
❑ 20 Jose Cruz DK .40 .15
❑ 21 Charlie Lea DK .15 .05
❑ 22 Jesse Orosco DK .15 .05
❑ 23 Juan Samuel DK .15 .05
❑ 24 Tony Pena DK .15 .05
❑ 25 Tony Gwynn DK 1.25 .50
❑ 26 Bob Brenly DK .15 .05
❑ 27 Danny Tartabull RC 1.00 .40
❑ 28 Mike Bielecki RC .25 .08
❑ 29 Steve Lyons RC .50 .20
❑ 30 Jeff Reed RC .25 .08
❑ 31 Tony Brewer RC .25 .08
❑ 32 John Morris RC .25 .08
❑ 33 Daryl Boston RC .25 .08
❑ 34 Al Pulido RC .25 .08
❑ 35 Steve Kiefer RC .25 .08
❑ 36 Larry Sheets RC .25 .08
❑ 37 Scott Bradley RC .25 .08
❑ 38 Calvin Schiraldi RC .50 .20
❑ 39 Shawon Dunston RC 1.00 .40
❑ 40 Charlie Mitchell RC .25 .08
❑ 41 Billy Hatcher RC .50 .20
❑ 42 Russ Stephans RC .25 .08
❑ 43 Alejandro Sanchez RC .25 .08
❑ 44 Steve Jeltz RC .25 .08
❑ 45 Jim Traber RC .25 .08
❑ 46 Doug Loman RC .25 .08
❑ 47 Eddie Murray 1.25 .50
❑ 48 Robin Yount 2.00 .75
❑ 49 Lance Parrish .40 .15
❑ 50 Jim Rice .40 .15
❑ 51 Dave Winfield .40 .15
❑ 52 Fernando Valenzuela .40 .15
❑ 53 George Brett 3.00 1.25
❑ 54 Dave Kingman .40 .15
❑ 55 Gary Carter .40 .15
❑ 56 Buddy Bell .40 .15
❑ 57 Reggie Jackson .75 .30
❑ 58 Harold Baines .40 .15
❑ 59 Ozzie Smith 2.00 .75
❑ 60 Nolan Ryan 6.00 2.50
❑ 61 Mike Schmidt 3.00 1.25
❑ 62 Dave Parker .40 .15
❑ 63 Tony Gwynn 2.50 1.00
❑ 64 Tony Pena .15 .05
❑ 65 Jack Clark .40 .15
❑ 66 Dale Murphy .75 .30
❑ 67 Ryne Sandberg 2.50 1.00
❑ 68 Keith Hernandez .40 .15
❑ 69 Alvin Davis RC* .50 .20
❑ 70 Kent Hrbek .40 .15
❑ 71 Willie Upshaw .15 .05
❑ 72 Dave Engle .15 .05
❑ 73 Alfredo Griffin .15 .05
❑ 74A Jack Perconte
(Career Highlights
takes four line .15 .05
❑ 74B Jack Perconte
(Career Highlights
takes three lin .15 .05
❑ 75 Jesse Orosco .15 .05
❑ 76 Jody Davis .15 .05
❑ 77 Bob Horner .40 .15
❑ 78 Larry McWilliams .15 .05
❑ 79 Joel Youngblood .15 .05
❑ 80 Alan Wiggins .15 .05
❑ 81 Ron Oester .15 .05
❑ 82 Ozzie Virgil .15 .05
❑ 83 Ricky Horton .15 .05
❑ 84 Bill Doran .15 .05
❑ 85 Rod Carew .75 .30
❑ 86 LaMarr Hoyt .15 .05
❑ 87 Tim Wallach .15 .05
❑ 88 Mike Flanagan .15 .05
❑ 89 Jim Sundberg .40 .15
❑ 90 Chet Lemon .40 .15
❑ 91 Bob Stanley .15 .05
❑ 92 Willie Randolph .40 .15
❑ 93 Bill Russell .40 .15
❑ 94 Julio Franco .40 .15
❑ 95 Dan Quisenberry .15 .05
❑ 96 Bill Caudill .15 .05
❑ 97 Bill Gullickson .15 .05
❑ 98 Danny Darwin .15 .05
❑ 99 Curtis Wilkerson .15 .05
❑ 100 Bud Black .15 .05
❑ 101 Tony Phillips .15 .05
❑ 102 Tony Bernazard .15 .05
❑ 103 Jay Howell .15 .05
❑ 104 Burt Hooton .15 .05
❑ 105 Milt Wilcox .15 .05
❑ 106 Rich Dauer .15 .05
❑ 107 Don Sutton .40 .15
❑ 108 Mike Witt .15 .05
❑ 109 Bruce Sutter .40 .15
❑ 110 Enos Cabell .15 .05
❑ 111 John Denny .15 .05
❑ 112 Dave Dravecky .15 .05
❑ 113 Marvell Wynne .15 .05
❑ 114 Johnnie LeMaster .15 .05
❑ 115 Chuck Porter .15 .05
❑ 116 John Gibbons RC .15 .05
❑ 117 Keith Moreland .15 .05

❑ 118	Darnell Coles	.15	.05
❑ 119	Dennis Lamp	.15	.05
❑ 120	Ron Davis	.15	.05
❑ 121	Nick Esasky	.15	.05
❑ 122	Vance Law	.15	.05
❑ 123	Gary Roenicke	.15	.05
❑ 124	Bill Schroeder	.15	.05
❑ 125	Dave Rozema	.15	.05
❑ 126	Bobby Meacham	.15	.05
❑ 127	Marty Barrett	.15	.05
❑ 128	R.J. Reynolds	.15	.05
❑ 129	Ernie Camacho UER (Photo actually Rich Thompson)	.15	.05
❑ 130	Jorge Orta	.15	.05
❑ 131	Lary Sorensen	.15	.05
❑ 132	Terry Francona	.40	.15
❑ 133	Fred Lynn	.40	.15
❑ 134	Bob Jones	.15	.05
❑ 135	Jerry Hairston	.15	.05
❑ 136	Kevin Bass	.15	.05
❑ 137	Garry Maddox	.15	.05
❑ 138	Dave LaPoint	.15	.05
❑ 139	Kevin McReynolds	.40	.15
❑ 140	Wayne Krenchicki	.15	.05
❑ 141	Rafael Ramirez	.15	.05
❑ 142	Rod Scurry	.15	.05
❑ 143	Greg Minton	.15	.05
❑ 144	Tim Stoddard	.15	.05
❑ 145	Steve Henderson	.15	.05
❑ 146	George Bell	.40	.15
❑ 147	Dave Meier	.15	.05
❑ 148	Sammy Stewart	.15	.05
❑ 149	Mark Brouhard	.15	.05
❑ 150	Larry Herndon	.15	.05
❑ 151	Oil Can Boyd	.15	.05
❑ 152	Brian Dayett	.15	.05
❑ 153	Tom Niedenfuer	.15	.05
❑ 154	Brook Jacoby	.15	.05
❑ 155	Onix Concepcion	.15	.05
❑ 156	Tim Conroy	.15	.05
❑ 157	Joe Hesketh	.15	.05
❑ 158	Brian Downing	.40	.15
❑ 159	Tommy Dunbar	.15	.05
❑ 160	Marc Hill	.15	.05
❑ 161	Phil Garner	.40	.15
❑ 162	Jerry Davis	.15	.05
❑ 163	Bill Campbell	.15	.05
❑ 164	John Franco RC	1.00	.40
❑ 165	Len Barker	.15	.05
❑ 166	Benny Distefano	.15	.05
❑ 167	George Frazier	.15	.05
❑ 168	Tito Landrum	.15	.05
❑ 169	Cal Ripken	5.00	2.00
❑ 170	Cecil Cooper	.40	.15
❑ 171	Alan Trammell	.40	.15
❑ 172	Wade Boggs	1.25	.50
❑ 173	Don Baylor	.40	.15
❑ 174	Pedro Guerrero	.40	.15
❑ 175	Frank White	.40	.15
❑ 176	Rickey Henderson	1.50	.60
❑ 177	Charlie Lea	.15	.05
❑ 178	Pete O'Brien	.15	.05
❑ 179	Doug DeCinces	.15	.05
❑ 180	Ron Kittle	.15	.05
❑ 181	George Hendrick	.40	.15
❑ 182	Joe Niekro	.15	.05
❑ 183	Juan Samuel	.15	.05
❑ 184	Mario Soto	.40	.15
❑ 185	Goose Gossage	.40	.15
❑ 186	Johnny Ray	.15	.05
❑ 187	Bob Brenly	.15	.05
❑ 188	Craig McMurtry	.15	.05
❑ 189	Leon Durham	.15	.05
❑ 190	Dwight Gooden RC	3.00	1.25
❑ 191	Barry Bonnell	.15	.05
❑ 192	Tim Teufel	.15	.05
❑ 193	Dave Stieb	.40	.15
❑ 194	Mickey Hatcher	.15	.05
❑ 195	Jesse Barfield	.40	.15
❑ 196	Al Cowens	.15	.05
❑ 197	Hubie Brooks	.15	.05
❑ 198	Steve Trout	.15	.05
❑ 199	Glenn Hubbard	.15	.05
❑ 200	Bill Madlock	.40	.15
❑ 201	Jeff D. Robinson	.15	.05
❑ 202	Eric Show	.15	.05
❑ 203	Dave Concepcion	.40	.15
❑ 204	Ivan DeJesus	.15	.05
❑ 205	Neil Allen	.15	.05
❑ 206	Jerry Mumphrey	.15	.05
❑ 207	Mike C. Brown	.15	.05
❑ 208	Carlton Fisk	.75	.30
❑ 209	Bryn Smith	.15	.05
❑ 210	Tippy Martinez	.15	.05
❑ 211	Dion James	.15	.05
❑ 212	Willie Hernandez	.15	.05
❑ 213	Mike Easler	.15	.05
❑ 214	Ron Guidry	.40	.15
❑ 215	Rick Honeycutt	.15	.05
❑ 216	Brett Butler	.40	.15
❑ 217	Larry Gura	.15	.05
❑ 218	Ray Burris	.15	.05
❑ 219	Steve Rogers	.40	.15
❑ 220	Frank Tanana UER (Bats Left listed twice on card	.40	.15
❑ 221	Ned Yost	.15	.05
❑ 222	Bret Saberhagen RC	1.50	.60
❑ 223	Mike Davis	.15	.05
❑ 224	Bert Blyleven	.40	.15
❑ 225	Steve Kemp	.15	.05
❑ 226	Jerry Reuss	.15	.05
❑ 227	Darrell Evans UER (80 homers in 1980)	.40	.15
❑ 228	Wayne Gross	.15	.05
❑ 229	Jim Gantner	.15	.05
❑ 230	Bob Boone	.40	.15
❑ 231	Lonnie Smith	.15	.05
❑ 232	Frank DiPino	.15	.05
❑ 233	Jerry Koosman	.40	.15
❑ 234	Graig Nettles	.40	.15
❑ 235	John Tudor	.40	.15
❑ 236	John Rabb	.15	.05
❑ 237	Rick Manning	.15	.05
❑ 238	Mike Fitzgerald	.15	.05
❑ 239	Gary Matthews	.40	.15
❑ 240	Jim Presley	.50	.20
❑ 241	Dave Collins	.15	.05
❑ 242	Gary Gaetti	.40	.15
❑ 243	Dann Bilardello	.15	.05
❑ 244	Rudy Law	.15	.05
❑ 245	John Lowenstein	.15	.05
❑ 246	Tom Tellmann	.15	.05
❑ 247	Howard Johnson	.40	.15
❑ 248	Ray Fontenot	.15	.05
❑ 249	Tony Armas	.40	.15
❑ 250	Candy Maldonado	.15	.05
❑ 251	Mike Jeffcoat	.15	.05
❑ 252	Dane Iorg	.15	.05
❑ 253	Bruce Bochte	.15	.05
❑ 254	Pete Rose Expos	4.00	1.50
❑ 255	Don Aase	.15	.05
❑ 256	George Wright	.15	.05
❑ 257	Britt Burns	.15	.05
❑ 258	Mike Scott	.40	.15
❑ 259	Len Matuszek	.15	.05
❑ 260	Dave Rucker	.15	.05
❑ 261	Craig Lefferts	.15	.05
❑ 262	Jay Tibbs	.15	.05
❑ 263	Bruce Benedict	.15	.05
❑ 264	Don Robinson	.15	.05
❑ 265	Gary Lavelle	.15	.05
❑ 266	Scott Sanderson	.15	.05
❑ 267	Matt Young	.15	.05
❑ 268	Ernie Whitt	.15	.05
❑ 269	Houston Jimenez	.15	.05
❑ 270	Ken Dixon	.15	.05
❑ 271	Pete Ladd	.15	.05
❑ 272	Juan Berenguer	.15	.05
❑ 273	Roger Clemens RC	40.00	15.00
❑ 274	Rick Cerone	.15	.05
❑ 275	Dave Anderson	.15	.05
❑ 276	George Vukovich	.15	.05
❑ 277	Greg Pryor	.15	.05
❑ 278	Mike Warren	.15	.05
❑ 279	Bob James	.15	.05
❑ 280	Bobby Grich	.40	.15
❑ 281	Mike Mason RC	.25	.08
❑ 282	Ron Reed	.15	.05
❑ 283	Alan Ashby	.15	.05
❑ 284	Mark Thurmond	.15	.05
❑ 285	Joe Lefebvre	.15	.05
❑ 286	Ted Power	.15	.05
❑ 287	Chris Chambliss	.40	.15
❑ 288	Lee Tunnell	.15	.05
❑ 289	Rich Bordi	.15	.05
❑ 290	Glenn Brummer	.15	.05
❑ 291	Mike Boddicker	.15	.05
❑ 292	Rollie Fingers	.40	.15
❑ 293	Lou Whitaker	.40	.15
❑ 294	Dwight Evans	.75	.30
❑ 295	Don Mattingly	5.00	2.00
❑ 296	Mike Marshall	.15	.05
❑ 297	Willie Wilson	.40	.15
❑ 298	Mike Heath	.15	.05
❑ 299	Tim Raines	.40	.15
❑ 300	Larry Parrish	.15	.05
❑ 301	Geoff Zahn	.15	.05
❑ 302	Rich Dotson	.15	.05
❑ 303	David Green	.15	.05
❑ 304	Jose Cruz	.40	.15
❑ 305	Steve Carlton	.40	.15
❑ 306	Gary Redus	.15	.05
❑ 307	Steve Garvey	.40	.15
❑ 308	Jose DeLeon	.15	.05
❑ 309	Randy Lerch	.15	.05
❑ 310	Claudell Washington	.15	.05
❑ 311	Lee Smith	.40	.15
❑ 312	Darryl Strawberry	1.25	.50
❑ 313	Jim Beattie	.15	.05
❑ 314	John Butcher	.15	.05
❑ 315	Damaso Garcia	.15	.05
❑ 316	Mike Smithson	.15	.05
❑ 317	Luis Leal	.15	.05
❑ 318	Ken Phelps	.15	.05
❑ 319	Wally Backman	.15	.05
❑ 320	Ron Cey	.40	.15
❑ 321	Brad Komminsk	.15	.05
❑ 322	Jason Thompson	.15	.05
❑ 323	Frank Williams	.15	.05
❑ 324	Tim Lollar	.15	.05
❑ 325	Eric Davis RC	3.00	1.25
❑ 326	Von Hayes	.15	.05
❑ 327	Andy Van Slyke	.75	.30
❑ 328	Craig Reynolds	.15	.05
❑ 329	Dick Schofield	.15	.05
❑ 330	Scott Fletcher	.15	.05
❑ 331	Jeff Reardon	.40	.15
❑ 332	Rick Dempsey	.15	.05
❑ 333	Ben Oglivie	.40	.15
❑ 334	Dan Petry	.15	.05
❑ 335	Jackie Gutierrez	.15	.05
❑ 336	Dave Righetti	.40	.15
❑ 337	Alejandro Pena	.15	.05
❑ 338	Mel Hall	.15	.05
❑ 339	Pat Sheridan	.15	.05
❑ 340	Keith Atherton	.15	.05
❑ 341	David Palmer	.15	.05
❑ 342	Gary Ward	.15	.05
❑ 343	Dave Stewart	.40	.15
❑ 344	Mark Gubicza RC*	.50	.20
❑ 345	Carney Lansford	.40	.15
❑ 346	Jerry Willard	.15	.05
❑ 347	Ken Griffey	.40	.15
❑ 348	Franklin Stubbs	.15	.05
❑ 349	Aurelio Lopez	.15	.05
❑ 350	Al Bumbry	.15	.05
❑ 351	Charlie Moore	.15	.05
❑ 352	Luis Sanchez	.15	.05
❑ 353	Darrell Porter	.15	.05
❑ 354	Bill Dawley	.15	.05
❑ 355	Charles Hudson	.15	.05
❑ 356	Garry Templeton	.40	.15
❑ 357	Cecilio Guante	.15	.05
❑ 358	Jeff Leonard	.15	.05
❑ 359	Paul Molitor	.40	.15
❑ 360	Ron Gardenhire	.15	.05
❑ 361	Larry Bowa	.40	.15
❑ 362	Bob Kearney	.15	.05
❑ 363	Garth Iorg	.15	.05
❑ 364	Tom Brunansky	.15	.05
❑ 365	Brad Gulden	.15	.05
❑ 366	Greg Walker	.15	.05
❑ 367	Mike Young	.15	.05
❑ 368	Rick Waits	.15	.05
❑ 369	Doug Bair	.15	.05
❑ 370	Bob Shirley	.15	.05

Card		
❑ 371 Bob Ojeda	.15	.05
❑ 372 Bob Welch	.40	.15
❑ 373 Neal Heaton	.15	.05
❑ 374 Danny Jackson UER (Photo actually Frank Wills)	.15	.05
❑ 375 Donnie Hill	.15	.05
❑ 376 Mike Stenhouse	.15	.05
❑ 377 Bruce Kison	.15	.05
❑ 378 Wayne Tolleson	.15	.05
❑ 379 Floyd Bannister	.15	.05
❑ 380 Vern Ruhle	.15	.05
❑ 381 Tim Corcoran	.15	.05
❑ 382 Kurt Kepshire	.15	.05
❑ 383 Bobby Brown	.15	.05
❑ 384 Dave Van Gorder	.15	.05
❑ 385 Rick Mahler	.15	.05
❑ 386 Lee Mazzilli	.40	.15
❑ 387 Bill Laskey	.15	.05
❑ 388 Thad Bosley	.15	.05
❑ 389 Al Chambers	.15	.05
❑ 390 Tony Fernandez	.40	.15
❑ 391 Ron Washington	.15	.05
❑ 392 Bill Swaggerty	.15	.05
❑ 393 Bob L. Gibson	.15	.05
❑ 394 Marty Castillo	.15	.05
❑ 395 Steve Crawford	.15	.05
❑ 396 Clay Christiansen	.15	.05
❑ 397 Bob Bailor	.15	.05
❑ 398 Mike Hargrove	.15	.05
❑ 399 Charlie Leibrandt	.15	.05
❑ 400 Tom Burgmeier	.15	.05
❑ 401 Razor Shines	.15	.05
❑ 402 Rob Wilfong	.15	.05
❑ 403 Tom Henke	.40	.15
❑ 404 Al Jones	.15	.05
❑ 405 Mike LaCoss	.15	.05
❑ 406 Luis DeLeon	.15	.05
❑ 407 Greg Gross	.15	.05
❑ 408 Tom Hume	.15	.05
❑ 409 Rick Camp	.15	.05
❑ 410 Milt May	.15	.05
❑ 411 Henry Cotto RC	.25	.08
❑ 412 David Von Ohlen	.15	.05
❑ 413 Scott McGregor	.15	.05
❑ 414 Ted Simmons	.40	.15
❑ 415 Jack Morris	.40	.15
❑ 416 Bill Buckner	.40	.15
❑ 417 Butch Wynegar	.15	.05
❑ 418 Steve Sax	.15	.05
❑ 419 Steve Balboni	.15	.05
❑ 420 Dwayne Murphy	.15	.05
❑ 421 Andre Dawson	.40	.15
❑ 422 Charlie Hough	.40	.15
❑ 423 Tommy John	.40	.15
❑ 424A Tom Seaver ERR	.75	.30
❑ 424B Tom Seaver COR	10.00	4.00
❑ 425 Tommy Herr	.15	.05
❑ 426 Terry Puhl	.15	.05
❑ 427 Al Holland	.15	.05
❑ 428 Eddie Milner	.15	.05
❑ 429 Terry Kennedy	.15	.05
❑ 430 John Candelaria	.15	.05
❑ 431 Manny Trillo	.15	.05
❑ 432 Ken Oberkfell	.15	.05
❑ 433 Rick Sutcliffe	.40	.15
❑ 434 Ron Darling	.40	.15
❑ 435 Spike Owen	.15	.05
❑ 436 Frank Viola	.40	.15
❑ 437 Lloyd Moseby	.15	.05
❑ 438 Kirby Puckett RC	10.00	4.00
❑ 439 Jim Clancy	.15	.05
❑ 440 Mike Moore	.15	.05
❑ 441 Doug Sisk	.15	.05
❑ 442 Dennis Eckersley	.75	.30
❑ 443 Gerald Perry	.15	.05
❑ 444 Dale Berra	.15	.05
❑ 445 Dusty Baker	.40	.15
❑ 446 Ed Whitson	.15	.05
❑ 447 Cesar Cedeno	.40	.15
❑ 448 Rick Schu	.15	.05
❑ 449 Joaquin Andujar	.40	.15
❑ 450 Mark Bailey	.15	.05
❑ 451 Ron Romanick	.15	.05
❑ 452 Julio Cruz	.15	.05
❑ 453 Miguel Dilone	.15	.05
❑ 454 Storm Davis	.15	.05
❑ 455 Jaime Cocanower	.15	.05
❑ 456 Barbaro Garbey	.15	.05
❑ 457 Rich Gedman	.15	.05
❑ 458 Phil Niekro	.40	.15
❑ 459 Mike Scioscia	.40	.15
❑ 460 Pat Tabler	.15	.05
❑ 461 Darryl Motley	.15	.05
❑ 462 Chris Codiroli	.15	.05
❑ 463 Doug Flynn	.15	.05
❑ 464 Billy Sample	.15	.05
❑ 465 Mickey Rivers	.15	.05
❑ 466 John Wathan	.15	.05
❑ 467 Bill Krueger	.15	.05
❑ 468 Andre Thornton	.15	.05
❑ 469 Rex Hudler	.15	.05
❑ 470 Sid Bream RC	.50	.20
❑ 471 Kirk Gibson	.40	.15
❑ 472 John Shelby	.15	.05
❑ 473 Moose Haas	.15	.05
❑ 474 Doug Corbett	.15	.05
❑ 475 Willie McGee	.40	.15
❑ 476 Bob Knepper	.15	.05
❑ 477 Kevin Gross	.15	.05
❑ 478 Carmelo Martinez	.15	.05
❑ 479 Kent Tekulve	.15	.05
❑ 480 Chili Davis	.40	.15
❑ 481 Bobby Clark	.15	.05
❑ 482 Mookie Wilson	.40	.15
❑ 483 Dave Owen	.15	.05
❑ 484 Ed Nunez	.15	.05
❑ 485 Rance Mulliniks	.15	.05
❑ 486 Ken Schrom	.15	.05
❑ 487 Jeff Russell	.15	.05
❑ 488 Tom Paciorek	.15	.05
❑ 489 Dan Ford	.15	.05
❑ 490 Mike Caldwell	.15	.05
❑ 491 Scottie Earl	.15	.05
❑ 492 Jose Rijo RC	1.00	.40
❑ 493 Bruce Hurst	.15	.05
❑ 494 Ken Landreaux	.15	.05
❑ 495 Mike Fischlin	.15	.05
❑ 496 Don Slaught	.15	.05
❑ 497 Steve McCatty	.15	.05
❑ 498 Gary Lucas	.15	.05
❑ 499 Gary Pettis	.15	.05
❑ 500 Marvis Foley	.15	.05
❑ 501 Mike Squires	.15	.05
❑ 502 Jim Pankovits	.15	.05
❑ 503 Luis Aguayo	.15	.05
❑ 504 Ralph Citarella	.15	.05
❑ 505 Bruce Bochy	.15	.05
❑ 506 Bob Owchinko	.15	.05
❑ 507 Pascual Perez	.15	.05
❑ 508 Lee Lacy	.15	.05
❑ 509 Atlee Hammaker	.15	.05
❑ 510 Bob Dernier	.15	.05
❑ 511 Ed VandeBerg	.15	.05
❑ 512 Cliff Johnson	.15	.05
❑ 513 Len Whitehouse	.15	.05
❑ 514 Dennis Martinez	.40	.15
❑ 515 Ed Romero	.15	.05
❑ 516 Rusty Kuntz	.15	.05
❑ 517 Rick Miller	.15	.05
❑ 518 Dennis Rasmussen	.15	.05
❑ 519 Steve Yeager	.40	.15
❑ 520 Chris Bando	.15	.05
❑ 521 U.L. Washington	.15	.05
❑ 522 Curt Young	.15	.05
❑ 523 Angel Salazar	.15	.05
❑ 524 Curt Kaufman	.15	.05
❑ 525 Odell Jones	.15	.05
❑ 526 Juan Agosto	.15	.05
❑ 527 Denny Walling	.15	.05
❑ 528 Andy Hawkins	.15	.05
❑ 529 Sixto Lezcano	.15	.05
❑ 530 Skeeter Barnes RC	.25	.08
❑ 531 Randy Johnson	.15	.05
❑ 532 Jim Morrison	.15	.05
❑ 533 Warren Brusstar	.15	.05
❑ 534A Jeff Pendleton ERR RC	1.00	.40
❑ 534B Terry Pendleton COR	1.00	.40
❑ 535 Vic Rodriguez	.15	.05
❑ 536 Bob McClure	.15	.05
❑ 537 Dave Bergman	.15	.05
❑ 538 Mark Clear	.15	.05
❑ 539 Mike Pagliarulo	.15	.05
❑ 540 Terry Whitfield	.15	.05
❑ 541 Joe Beckwith	.15	.05
❑ 542 Jeff Burroughs	.15	.05
❑ 543 Dan Schatzeder	.15	.05
❑ 544 Donnie Scott	.15	.05
❑ 545 Jim Slaton	.15	.05
❑ 546 Greg Luzinski	.40	.15
❑ 547 Mark Salas	.15	.05
❑ 548 Dave Smith	.15	.05
❑ 549 John Wockenfuss	.15	.05
❑ 550 Frank Pastore	.15	.05
❑ 551 Tim Flannery	.15	.05
❑ 552 Rick Rhoden	.15	.05
❑ 553 Mark Davis	.15	.05
❑ 554 Jeff Dedmon	.15	.05
❑ 555 Gary Woods	.15	.05
❑ 556 Danny Heep	.15	.05
❑ 557 Mark Langston RC	1.00	.40
❑ 558 Darrell Brown	.15	.05
❑ 559 Jimmy Key RC	1.00	.40
❑ 560 Rick Lysander	.15	.05
❑ 561 Doyle Alexander	.15	.05
❑ 562 Mike Stanton	.15	.05
❑ 563 Sid Fernandez	.40	.15
❑ 564 Richie Hebner	.15	.05
❑ 565 Alex Trevino	.15	.05
❑ 566 Brian Harper	.15	.05
❑ 567 Dan Gladden RC	.50	.20
❑ 568 Luis Salazar	.15	.05
❑ 569 Tom Foley	.15	.05
❑ 570 Larry Andersen	.15	.05
❑ 571 Danny Cox	.15	.05
❑ 572 Joe Sambito	.15	.05
❑ 573 Juan Beniquez	.15	.05
❑ 574 Joel Skinner	.15	.05
❑ 575 Randy St.Claire	.15	.05
❑ 576 Floyd Rayford	.15	.05
❑ 577 Roy Howell	.15	.05
❑ 578 John Grubb	.15	.05
❑ 579 Ed Jurak	.15	.05
❑ 580 John Montefusco	.15	.05
❑ 581 Orel Hershiser RC	3.00	1.25
❑ 582 Tom Waddell	.15	.05
❑ 583 Mark Huismann	.15	.05
❑ 584 Joe Morgan	.40	.15
❑ 585 Jim Wohlford	.15	.05
❑ 586 Dave Schmidt	.15	.05
❑ 587 Jeff Kunkel	.15	.05
❑ 588 Hal McRae	.40	.15
❑ 589 Bill Almon	.15	.05
❑ 590 Carmelo Castillo	.15	.05
❑ 591 Omar Moreno	.15	.05
❑ 592 Ken Howell	.15	.05
❑ 593 Tom Brookens	.15	.05
❑ 594 Joe Nolan	.15	.05
❑ 595 Willie Lozado	.15	.05
❑ 596 Tom Nieto	.15	.05
❑ 597 Walt Terrell	.15	.05
❑ 598 Al Oliver	.40	.15
❑ 599 Shane Rawley	.15	.05
❑ 600 Denny Gonzalez	.15	.05
❑ 601 Mark Grant	.15	.05
❑ 602 Mike Armstrong	.15	.05
❑ 603 George Foster	.40	.15
❑ 604 Dave Lopes	.40	.15
❑ 605 Salome Barojas	.15	.05
❑ 606 Roy Lee Jackson	.15	.05
❑ 607 Pete Filson	.15	.05
❑ 608 Duane Walker	.15	.05
❑ 609 Glenn Wilson	.15	.05
❑ 610 Rafael Santana	.15	.05
❑ 611 Roy Smith	.15	.05
❑ 612 Ruppert Jones	.15	.05
❑ 613 Joe Cowley	.15	.05
❑ 614 Al Nipper UER (Photo actually Mike Brown)	.15	.05
❑ 615 Gene Nelson	.15	.05
❑ 616 Joe Carter	1.25	.50
❑ 617 Ray Knight	.40	.15
❑ 618 Chuck Rainey	.15	.05
❑ 619 Dan Driessen	.15	.05
❑ 620 Daryl Sconiers	.15	.05
❑ 621 Bill Stein	.15	.05
❑ 622 Roy Smalley	.15	.05

❑ 623 Ed Lynch .15 .05
❑ 624 Jeff Stone .15 .05
❑ 625 Bruce Berenyi .15 .05
❑ 626 Kelvin Chapman .15 .05
❑ 627 Joe Price .15 .05
❑ 628 Steve Bedrosian .15 .05
❑ 629 Vic Mata .15 .05
❑ 630 Mike Krukow .15 .05
❑ 631 Phil Bradley .50 .20
❑ 632 Jim Gott .15 .05
❑ 633 Randy Bush .15 .05
❑ 634 Tom Browning RC .50 .20
❑ 635 Lou Gehrig Puzzle 1.25 .50
❑ 636 Reid Nichols .15 .05
❑ 637 Dan Pasqua RC .50 .20
❑ 638 German Rivera .15 .05
❑ 639 Don Schulze .15 .05
❑ 640A Mike Jones
(Career Highlights,
takes five lines) .15 .05
❑ 640B Mike Jones
(Career Highlights,
takes four lines) .15 .05
❑ 641 Pete Rose 4.00 1.50
❑ 642 Wade Rowdon .15 .05
❑ 643 Jerry Narron .15 .05
❑ 644 Darrell Miller .15 .05
❑ 645 Tim Hulett RC .25 .08
❑ 646 Andy McGaffigan .15 .05
❑ 647 Kurt Bevacqua .15 .05
❑ 648 John Russell .15 .05
❑ 649 Ron Robinson .15 .05
❑ 650 Donnie Moore .15 .05
❑ 651A D.Mattingly/D.Winfield YL 2.00 .75
❑ 651B D.Mattingly/D.Winfield WL 5.00 2.00
❑ 652 Tim Laudner .15 .05
❑ 653 Steve Farr RC .50 .20
❑ 654 DK Checklist 1-26
(Unnumbered) .15 .05
❑ 655 Checklist 27-130
(Unnumbered) .15 .05
❑ 656 Checklist 131-234
(Unnumbered) .15 .05
❑ 657 Checklist 235-338
(Unnumbered) .15 .05
❑ 658 Checklist 339-442
(Unnumbered) .15 .05
❑ 659 Checklist 443-546
(Unnumbered) .15 .05
❑ 660 Checklist 547-653
(Unnumbered) .15 .05

1986 Donruss

❑ COMPLETE SET (660) 40.00 15.00
❑ COMP.FACT.SET (660) 40.00 15.00
❑ COMP.AARON PUZZLE 2.00 .75
❑ 1 Kirk Gibson DK .25 .08
❑ 2 Goose Gossage DK .25 .08
❑ 3 Willie McGee DK .25 .08
❑ 4 George Bell DK .25 .08
❑ 5 Tony Armas DK .25 .08
❑ 6 Chili Davis DK .25 .08
❑ 7 Cecil Cooper DK .25 .08
❑ 8 Mike Boddicker DK .15 .05
❑ 9 Dave Lopes DK .25 .08
❑ 10 Bill Doran DK .15 .05
❑ 11 Bret Saberhagen DK .25 .08
❑ 12 Brett Butler DK .25 .08
❑ 13 Harold Baines DK .25 .08
❑ 14 Mike Davis DK .15 .05
❑ 15 Tony Perez DK .50 .20
❑ 16 Willie Randolph DK .25 .08
❑ 17 Bob Boone DK .25 .08
❑ 18 Orel Hershiser DK .50 .20
❑ 19 Johnny Ray DK .15 .05
❑ 20 Gary Ward DK .15 .05
❑ 21 Rick Mahler DK .15 .05
❑ 22 Phil Bradley DK .15 .05
❑ 23 Jerry Koosman DK .25 .08
❑ 24 Tom Brunansky DK .15 .05
❑ 25 Andre Dawson DK .15 .05
❑ 26 Dwight Gooden DK .75 .30
❑ 27 Kal Daniels RC .50 .20
❑ 28 Fred McGriff RC 8.00 3.00
❑ 29 Cory Snyder .15 .05
❑ 30 Jose Guzman RC .15 .05
❑ 31 Ty Gainey RC .15 .05
❑ 32 Johnny Abrego RC .15 .05
❑ 33A Andres Galarraga RC 1.50 .60
❑ 33B Andre`s Galarraga RC 1.50 .60
❑ 34 Dave Shipanoff RC .15 .05
❑ 35 Mark McLemore RC 1.00 .40
❑ 36 Marty Clary RC .15 .05
❑ 37 Paul O'Neill RC 4.00 1.50
❑ 38 Danny Tartabull .25 .08
❑ 39 Jose Canseco RC 10.00 4.00
❑ 40 Juan Nieves RC .15 .05
❑ 41 Lance McCullers RC .15 .05
❑ 42 Rick Surhoff RC .15 .05
❑ 43 Todd Worrell RC .50 .20
❑ 44 Bob Kipper RC .15 .05
❑ 45 John Habyan RC .15 .05
❑ 46 Mike Woodard RC .15 .05
❑ 47 Mike Boddicker .15 .05
❑ 48 Robin Yount 1.25 .50
❑ 49 Lou Whitaker .25 .08
❑ 50 Oil Can Boyd .15 .05
❑ 51 Rickey Henderson .75 .30
❑ 52 Mike Marshall .15 .05
❑ 53 George Brett 2.00 .75
❑ 54 Dave Kingman .25 .08
❑ 55 Hubie Brooks .15 .05
❑ 56 Oddibe McDowell .15 .05
❑ 57 Doug DeCinces .15 .05
❑ 58 Britt Burns .15 .05
❑ 59 Ozzie Smith 1.25 .50
❑ 60 Jose Cruz .25 .08
❑ 61 Mike Schmidt 2.00 .75
❑ 62 Pete Rose 2.50 1.00
❑ 63 Steve Garvey .25 .08
❑ 64 Tony Pena .15 .05
❑ 65 Chili Davis .25 .08
❑ 66 Dale Murphy .50 .20
❑ 67 Ryne Sandberg 1.50 .60
❑ 68 Gary Carter .25 .08
❑ 69 Alvin Davis .15 .05
❑ 70 Kent Hrbek .25 .08
❑ 71 George Bell .25 .08
❑ 72 Kirby Puckett 2.00 .75
❑ 73 Lloyd Moseby .15 .05
❑ 74 Bob Kearney .15 .05
❑ 75 Dwight Gooden .75 .30
❑ 76 Gary Matthews .25 .08
❑ 77 Rick Mahler .15 .05
❑ 78 Benny Distefano .15 .05
❑ 79 Jeff Leonard .15 .05
❑ 80 Kevin McReynolds .25 .08
❑ 81 Ron Oester .15 .05
❑ 82 John Russell .15 .05
❑ 83 Tommy Herr .15 .05
❑ 84 Jerry Mumphrey .15 .05
❑ 85 Ron Romanick .15 .05
❑ 86 Daryl Boston .15 .05
❑ 87 Andre Dawson .25 .08
❑ 88 Eddie Murray .75 .30
❑ 89 Dion James .15 .05
❑ 90 Chet Lemon .25 .08
❑ 91 Bob Stanley .15 .05
❑ 92 Willie Randolph .25 .08
❑ 93 Mike Scioscia .25 .08
❑ 94 Tom Waddell .15 .05
❑ 95 Danny Jackson .15 .05
❑ 96 Mike Davis .15 .05
❑ 97 Mike Fitzgerald .15 .05
❑ 98 Gary Ward .15 .05
❑ 99 Pete O'Brien .15 .05
❑ 100 Bret Saberhagen .25 .08
❑ 101 Alfredo Griffin .15 .05
❑ 102 Brett Butler .25 .08
❑ 103 Ron Guidry .25 .08
❑ 104 Jerry Reuss .15 .05
❑ 105 Jack Morris .25 .08
❑ 106 Rick Dempsey .15 .05
❑ 107 Ray Burris .15 .05
❑ 108 Brian Downing .25 .08
❑ 109 Willie McGee .25 .08
❑ 110 Bill Doran .15 .05
❑ 111 Kent Tekulve .15 .05
❑ 112 Tony Gwynn 1.25 .50
❑ 113 Marvell Wynne .15 .05
❑ 114 David Green .15 .05
❑ 115 Jim Gantner .15 .05
❑ 116 George Foster .25 .08
❑ 117 Steve Trout .15 .05
❑ 118 Mark Langston .25 .08
❑ 119 Tony Fernandez .15 .05
❑ 120 John Butcher .15 .05
❑ 121 Ron Robinson .15 .05
❑ 122 Dan Spillner .15 .05
❑ 123 Mike Young .15 .05
❑ 124 Paul Molitor .25 .08
❑ 125 Kirk Gibson .25 .08
❑ 126 Ken Griffey .25 .08
❑ 127 Tony Armas .25 .08
❑ 128 Mariano Duncan RC .50 .20
❑ 129 Pat Tabler .15 .05
❑ 130 Frank White .25 .08
❑ 131 Carney Lansford .25 .08
❑ 132 Vance Law .15 .05
❑ 133 Dick Schofield .15 .05
❑ 134 Wayne Tolleson .15 .05
❑ 135 Greg Walker .15 .05
❑ 136 Denny Walling .15 .05
❑ 137 Ozzie Virgil .15 .05
❑ 138 Ricky Horton .15 .05
❑ 139 LaMarr Hoyt .15 .05
❑ 140 Wayne Krenchicki .15 .05
❑ 141 Glenn Hubbard .15 .05
❑ 142 Cecilio Guante .15 .05
❑ 143 Mike Krukow .15 .05
❑ 144 Lee Smith .25 .08
❑ 145 Edwin Nunez .15 .05
❑ 146 Dave Stieb .25 .08
❑ 147 Mike Smithson .15 .05
❑ 148 Ken Dixon .15 .05
❑ 149 Danny Darwin .15 .05
❑ 150 Chris Pittaro .15 .05
❑ 151 Bill Buckner .25 .08
❑ 152 Mike Pagliarulo .15 .05
❑ 153 Bill Russell .25 .08
❑ 154 Brook Jacoby .15 .05
❑ 155 Pat Sheridan .15 .05
❑ 156 Mike Gallego RC .15 .05
❑ 157 Jim Wohlford .15 .05
❑ 158 Gary Pettis .15 .05
❑ 159 Toby Harrah .25 .08
❑ 160 Richard Dotson .15 .05
❑ 161 Bob Knepper .15 .05
❑ 162 Dave Dravecky .15 .05
❑ 163 Greg Gross .15 .05
❑ 164 Eric Davis .75 .30
❑ 165 Gerald Perry .15 .05
❑ 166 Rick Rhoden .15 .05
❑ 167 Keith Moreland .15 .05
❑ 168 Jack Clark .25 .08
❑ 169 Storm Davis .15 .05
❑ 170 Cecil Cooper .25 .08
❑ 171 Alan Trammell .25 .08
❑ 172 Roger Clemens 5.00 2.00
❑ 173 Don Mattingly 2.50 1.00
❑ 174 Pedro Guerrero .25 .08
❑ 175 Willie Wilson .25 .08
❑ 176 Dwayne Murphy .15 .05
❑ 177 Tim Raines .25 .08
❑ 178 Larry Parrish .15 .05
❑ 179 Mike Witt .15 .05
❑ 180 Harold Baines .25 .08
❑ 181 Vince Coleman UER RC 1.00 .40
❑ 182 Jeff Heathcock .15 .05
❑ 183 Steve Carlton .25 .08

❑	184	Mario Soto	.25	.08
❑	185	Goose Gossage	.25	.08
❑	186	Johnny Ray	.15	.05
❑	187	Dan Gladden	.15	.05
❑	188	Bob Horner	.25	.08
❑	189	Rick Sutcliffe	.25	.08
❑	190	Keith Hernandez	.25	.08
❑	191	Phil Bradley	.15	.05
❑	192	Tom Brunansky	.15	.05
❑	193	Jesse Barfield	.25	.08
❑	194	Frank Viola	.25	.08
❑	195	Willie Upshaw	.15	.05
❑	196	Jim Beattie	.15	.05
❑	197	Darryl Strawberry	.50	.20
❑	198	Ron Cey	.25	.08
❑	199	Steve Bedrosian	.15	.05
❑	200	Steve Kemp	.15	.05
❑	201	Manny Trillo	.15	.05
❑	202	Garry Templeton	.25	.08
❑	203	Dave Parker	.25	.08
❑	204	John Denny	.15	.05
❑	205	Terry Pendleton	.25	.08
❑	206	Terry Puhl	.15	.05
❑	207	Bobby Grich	.25	.08
❑	208	Ozzie Guillen RC	2.00	.75
❑	209	Jeff Reardon	.25	.08
❑	210	Cal Ripken	3.00	1.25
❑	211	Bill Schroeder	.15	.05
❑	212	Dan Petry	.15	.05
❑	213	Jim Rice	.25	.08
❑	214	Dave Righetti	.25	.08
❑	215	Fernando Valenzuela	.25	.08
❑	216	Julio Franco	.25	.08
❑	217	Darryl Motley	.15	.05
❑	218	Dave Collins	.15	.05
❑	219	Tim Wallach	.15	.05
❑	220	George Wright	.15	.05
❑	221	Tommy Dunbar	.15	.05
❑	222	Steve Balboni	.15	.05
❑	223	Jay Howell	.15	.05
❑	224	Joe Carter	.25	.08
❑	225	Ed Whitson	.15	.05
❑	226	Orel Hershiser	.75	.30
❑	227	Willie Hernandez	.15	.05
❑	228	Lee Lacy	.15	.05
❑	229	Rollie Fingers	.25	.08
❑	230	Bob Boone	.25	.08
❑	231	Joaquin Andujar	.25	.08
❑	232	Craig Reynolds	.15	.05
❑	233	Shane Rawley	.15	.05
❑	234	Eric Show	.15	.05
❑	235	Jose DeLeon	.15	.05
❑	236	Jose Uribe	.15	.05
❑	237	Moose Haas	.15	.05
❑	238	Wally Backman	.15	.05
❑	239	Dennis Eckersley	.50	.20
❑	240	Mike Moore	.15	.05
❑	241	Damaso Garcia	.15	.05
❑	242	Tim Teufel	.15	.05
❑	243	Dave Concepcion	.25	.08
❑	244	Floyd Bannister	.15	.05
❑	245	Fred Lynn	.25	.08
❑	246	Charlie Moore	.15	.05
❑	247	Walt Terrell	.15	.05
❑	248	Dave Winfield	.25	.08
❑	249	Dwight Evans	.50	.20
❑	250	Dennis Powell	.15	.05
❑	251	Andre Thornton	.15	.05
❑	252	Onix Concepcion	.15	.05
❑	253	Mike Heath	.15	.05
❑	254A	David Palmer ERR (Position 2B)	.15	.05
❑	254B	David Palmer COR (Position P)	.50	.20
❑	255	Donnie Moore	.15	.05
❑	256	Curtis Wilkerson	.15	.05
❑	257	Julio Cruz	.15	.05
❑	258	Nolan Ryan	4.00	1.50
❑	259	Jeff Stone	.15	.05
❑	260	John Tudor	.25	.08
❑	261	Mark Thurmond	.15	.05
❑	262	Jay Tibbs	.15	.05
❑	263	Rafael Ramirez	.15	.05
❑	264	Larry McWilliams	.15	.05
❑	265	Mark Davis	.15	.05
❑	266	Bob Dernier	.15	.05
❑	267	Matt Young	.15	.05
❑	268	Jim Clancy	.15	.05
❑	269	Mickey Hatcher	.15	.05
❑	270	Sammy Stewart	.15	.05
❑	271	Bob L. Gibson	.15	.05
❑	272	Nelson Simmons	.15	.05
❑	273	Rich Gedman	.15	.05
❑	274	Butch Wynegar	.15	.05
❑	275	Ken Howell	.15	.05
❑	276	Mel Hall	.15	.05
❑	277	Jim Sundberg	.25	.08
❑	278	Chris Codiroli	.15	.05
❑	279	Herm Winningham	.15	.05
❑	280	Rod Carew	.50	.20
❑	281	Don Slaught	.15	.05
❑	282	Scott Fletcher	.15	.05
❑	283	Bill Dawley	.15	.05
❑	284	Andy Hawkins	.15	.05
❑	285	Glenn Wilson	.15	.05
❑	286	Nick Esasky	.15	.05
❑	287	Claudell Washington	.15	.05
❑	288	Lee Mazzilli	.25	.08
❑	289	Jody Davis	.15	.05
❑	290	Darrell Porter	.15	.05
❑	291	Scott McGregor	.15	.05
❑	292	Ted Simmons	.25	.08
❑	293	Aurelio Lopez	.15	.05
❑	294	Marty Barrett	.15	.05
❑	295	Dale Berra	.15	.05
❑	296	Greg Brock	.15	.05
❑	297	Charlie Leibrandt	.15	.05
❑	298	Bill Krueger	.15	.05
❑	299	Bryn Smith	.15	.05
❑	300	Burt Hooton	.15	.05
❑	301	Stu Cliburn	.15	.05
❑	302	Luis Salazar	.15	.05
❑	303	Ken Dayley	.15	.05
❑	304	Frank DiPino	.15	.05
❑	305	Von Hayes	.15	.05
❑	306	Gary Redus	.15	.05
❑	307	Craig Lefferts	.15	.05
❑	308	Sammy Khalifa	.15	.05
❑	309	Scott Garrelts	.15	.05
❑	310	Rick Cerone	.15	.05
❑	311	Shawon Dunston	.25	.08
❑	312	Howard Johnson	.25	.08
❑	313	Jim Presley	.15	.05
❑	314	Gary Gaetti	.25	.08
❑	315	Luis Leal	.15	.05
❑	316	Mark Salas	.15	.05
❑	317	Bill Caudill	.15	.05
❑	318	Dave Henderson	.15	.05
❑	319	Rafael Santana	.15	.05
❑	320	Leon Durham	.15	.05
❑	321	Bruce Sutter	.25	.08
❑	322	Jason Thompson	.15	.05
❑	323	Bob Brenly	.15	.05
❑	324	Carmelo Martinez	.15	.05
❑	325	Eddie Milner	.15	.05
❑	326	Juan Samuel	.15	.05
❑	327	Tom Nieto	.15	.05
❑	328	Dave Smith	.15	.05
❑	329	Urbano Lugo	.15	.05
❑	330	Joel Skinner	.15	.05
❑	331	Bill Gullickson	.15	.05
❑	332	Floyd Rayford	.15	.05
❑	333	Ben Oglivie	.25	.08
❑	334	Lance Parrish	.25	.08
❑	335	Jackie Gutierrez	.15	.05
❑	336	Dennis Rasmussen	.15	.05
❑	337	Terry Whitfield	.15	.05
❑	338	Neal Heaton	.15	.05
❑	339	Jorge Orta	.15	.05
❑	340	Donnie Hill	.15	.05
❑	341	Joe Hesketh	.15	.05
❑	342	Charlie Hough	.25	.08
❑	343	Dave Rozema	.15	.05
❑	344	Greg Pryor	.15	.05
❑	345	Mickey Tettleton RC	.50	.20
❑	346	George Vukovich	.15	.05
❑	347	Don Baylor	.25	.08
❑	348	Carlos Diaz	.15	.05
❑	349	Barbaro Garbey	.15	.05
❑	350	Larry Sheets	.15	.05
❑	351	Teddy Higuera RC*	.50	.20
❑	352	Juan Beniquez	.15	.05
❑	353	Bob Forsch	.15	.05
❑	354	Mark Bailey	.15	.05
❑	355	Larry Andersen	.15	.05
❑	356	Terry Kennedy	.15	.05
❑	357	Don Robinson	.15	.05
❑	358	Jim Gott	.15	.05
❑	359	Earnie Riles	.15	.05
❑	360	John Christensen	.15	.05
❑	361	Ray Fontenot	.15	.05
❑	362	Spike Owen	.15	.05
❑	363	Jim Acker	.15	.05
❑	364	Ron Davis	.15	.05
❑	365	Tom Hume	.15	.05
❑	366	Carlton Fisk	.50	.20
❑	367	Nate Snell	.15	.05
❑	368	Rick Manning	.15	.05
❑	369	Darrell Evans	.25	.08
❑	370	Ron Hassey	.15	.05
❑	371	Wade Boggs	.50	.20
❑	372	Rick Honeycutt	.15	.05
❑	373	Chris Bando	.15	.05
❑	374	Bud Black	.15	.05
❑	375	Steve Henderson	.15	.05
❑	376	Charlie Lea	.15	.05
❑	377	Reggie Jackson	.50	.20
❑	378	Dave Schmidt	.15	.05
❑	379	Bob James	.15	.05
❑	380	Glenn Davis	.15	.05
❑	381	Tim Corcoran	.15	.05
❑	382	Danny Cox	.15	.05
❑	383	Tim Flannery	.15	.05
❑	384	Tom Browning	.15	.05
❑	385	Rick Camp	.15	.05
❑	386	Jim Morrison	.15	.05
❑	387	Dave LaPoint	.15	.05
❑	388	Dave Lopes	.25	.08
❑	389	Al Cowens	.15	.05
❑	390	Doyle Alexander	.15	.05
❑	391	Tim Laudner	.15	.05
❑	392	Don Aase	.15	.05
❑	393	Jaime Cocanower	.15	.05
❑	394	Randy O'Neal	.15	.05
❑	395	Mike Easler	.15	.05
❑	396	Scott Bradley	.15	.05
❑	397	Tom Niedenfuer	.15	.05
❑	398	Jerry Willard	.15	.05
❑	399	Lonnie Smith	.15	.05
❑	400	Bruce Bochte	.15	.05
❑	401	Terry Francona	.25	.08
❑	402	Jim Slaton	.15	.05
❑	403	Bill Stein	.15	.05
❑	404	Tim Hulett	.15	.05
❑	405	Alan Ashby	.15	.05
❑	406	Tim Stoddard	.15	.05
❑	407	Garry Maddox	.15	.05
❑	408	Ted Power	.15	.05
❑	409	Len Barker	.15	.05
❑	410	Denny Gonzalez	.15	.05
❑	411	George Frazier	.15	.05
❑	412	Andy Van Slyke	.50	.20
❑	413	Jim Dwyer	.15	.05
❑	414	Paul Householder	.15	.05
❑	415	Alejandro Sanchez	.15	.05
❑	416	Steve Crawford	.15	.05
❑	417	Dan Pasqua	.15	.05
❑	418	Enos Cabell	.15	.05
❑	419	Mike Jones	.15	.05
❑	420	Steve Kiefer	.15	.05
❑	421	Tim Burke	.15	.05
❑	422	Mike Mason	.15	.05
❑	423	Ruppert Jones	.15	.05
❑	424	Jerry Hairston	.15	.05
❑	425	Tito Landrum	.15	.05
❑	426	Jeff Calhoun	.15	.05
❑	427	Don Carman	.15	.05
❑	428	Tony Perez	.50	.20
❑	429	Jerry Davis	.15	.05
❑	430	Bob Walk	.15	.05
❑	431	Brad Wellman	.15	.05
❑	432	Terry Forster	.25	.08
❑	433	Billy Hatcher	.15	.05
❑	434	Clint Hurdle	.15	.05
❑	435	Ivan Calderon RC*	.50	.20
❑	436	Pete Filson	.15	.05
❑	437	Tom Henke	.25	.08
❑	438	Dave Engle	.15	.05

❑ 439 Tom Filer .15 .05
❑ 440 Gorman Thomas .25 .08
❑ 441 Rick Aguilera RC .50 .20
❑ 442 Scott Sanderson .15 .05
❑ 443 Jeff Dedmon .15 .05
❑ 444 Joe Orsulak RC* .50 .20
❑ 445 Atlee Hammaker .15 .05
❑ 446 Jerry Royster .15 .05
❑ 447 Buddy Bell .25 .08
❑ 448 Dave Rucker .15 .05
❑ 449 Ivan DeJesus .15 .05
❑ 450 Jim Pankovits .15 .05
❑ 451 Jerry Narron .15 .05
❑ 452 Bryan Little .15 .05
❑ 453 Gary Lucas .15 .05
❑ 454 Dennis Martinez .25 .08
❑ 455 Ed Romero .15 .05
❑ 456 Bob Melvin .15 .05
❑ 457 Glenn Hoffman .15 .05
❑ 458 Bob Shirley .15 .05
❑ 459 Bob Welch .25 .08
❑ 460 Carmen Castillo .15 .05
❑ 461 Dave Leeper OF .15 .05
❑ 462 Tim Birtsas .15 .05
❑ 463 Randy St.Claire .15 .05
❑ 464 Chris Welsh .15 .05
❑ 465 Greg Harris .15 .05
❑ 466 Lynn Jones .15 .05
❑ 467 Dusty Baker .25 .08
❑ 468 Roy Smith .15 .05
❑ 469 Andre Robertson .15 .05
❑ 470 Ken Landreaux .15 .05
❑ 471 Dave Bergman .15 .05
❑ 472 Gary Roenicke .15 .05
❑ 473 Pete Vuckovich .15 .05
❑ 474 Kirk McCaskill RC .50 .20
❑ 475 Jeff Lahti .15 .05
❑ 476 Mike Scott .25 .08
❑ 477 Darren Daulton RC 1.00 .40
❑ 478 Graig Nettles .25 .08
❑ 479 Bill Almon .15 .05
❑ 480 Greg Minton .15 .05
❑ 481 Randy Ready .15 .05
❑ 482 Len Dykstra RC 1.50 .60
❑ 483 Thad Bosley .15 .05
❑ 484 Harold Reynolds RC 1.50 .60
❑ 485 Al Oliver .25 .08
❑ 486 Roy Smalley .15 .05
❑ 487 John Franco .25 .08
❑ 488 Juan Agosto .15 .05
❑ 489 Al Pardo .15 .05
❑ 490 Bill Wegman RC .15 .05
❑ 491 Frank Tanana .25 .08
❑ 492 Brian Fisher RC .15 .05
❑ 493 Mark Clear .15 .05
❑ 494 Len Matuszek .15 .05
❑ 495 Ramon Romero .15 .05
❑ 496 John Wathan .15 .05
❑ 497 Rob Picciolo .15 .05
❑ 498 U.L. Washington .15 .05
❑ 499 John Candelaria .15 .05
❑ 500 Duane Walker .15 .05
❑ 501 Gene Nelson .15 .05
❑ 502 John Mizerock .15 .05
❑ 503 Luis Aguayo .15 .05
❑ 504 Kurt Kepshire .15 .05
❑ 505 Ed Wojna .15 .05
❑ 506 Joe Price .15 .05
❑ 507 Milt Thompson RC .50 .20
❑ 508 Junior Ortiz .15 .05
❑ 509 Vida Blue .25 .08
❑ 510 Steve Engel .15 .05
❑ 511 Karl Best .15 .05
❑ 512 Cecil Fielder RC 2.00 .75
❑ 513 Frank Eufemia .15 .05
❑ 514 Tippy Martinez .15 .05
❑ 515 Billy Joe Robidoux .15 .05
❑ 516 Bill Scherrer .15 .05
❑ 517 Bruce Hurst .15 .05
❑ 518 Rich Bordi .15 .05
❑ 519 Steve Yeager .25 .08
❑ 520 Tony Bernazard .15 .05
❑ 521 Hal McRae .25 .08
❑ 522 Jose Rijo .25 .08
❑ 523 Mitch Webster .15 .05
❑ 524 Jack Howell .15 .05
❑ 525 Alan Bannister .15 .05
❑ 526 Ron Kittle .15 .05
❑ 527 Phil Garner .25 .08
❑ 528 Kurt Bevacqua .15 .05
❑ 529 Kevin Gross .15 .05
❑ 530 Bo Diaz .15 .05
❑ 531 Ken Oberkfell .15 .05
❑ 532 Rick Reuschel .25 .08
❑ 533 Ron Meridith .15 .05
❑ 534 Steve Braun .15 .05
❑ 535 Wayne Gross .15 .05
❑ 536 Ray Searage .15 .05
❑ 537 Tom Brookens .15 .05
❑ 538 Al Nipper .15 .05
❑ 539 Billy Sample .15 .05
❑ 540 Steve Sax .15 .05
❑ 541 Dan Quisenberry .15 .05
❑ 542 Tony Phillips .15 .05
❑ 543 Floyd Youmans .15 .05
❑ 544 Steve Buechele RC .50 .20
❑ 545 Craig Gerber .15 .05
❑ 546 Joe DeSa .15 .05
❑ 547 Brian Harper .15 .05
❑ 548 Kevin Bass .15 .05
❑ 549 Tom Foley .15 .05
❑ 550 Dave Van Gorder .15 .05
❑ 551 Bruce Bochy .15 .05
❑ 552 R.J. Reynolds .15 .05
❑ 553 Chris Brown RC .15 .05
❑ 554 Bruce Benedict .15 .05
❑ 555 Warren Brusstar .15 .05
❑ 556 Danny Heep .15 .05
❑ 557 Darnell Coles .15 .05
❑ 558 Greg Gagne .15 .05
❑ 559 Ernie Whitt .15 .05
❑ 560 Ron Washington .15 .05
❑ 561 Jimmy Key .25 .08
❑ 562 Bill Swift .15 .05
❑ 563 Ron Darling .25 .08
❑ 564 Dick Ruthven .15 .05
❑ 565 Zane Smith .15 .05
❑ 566 Sid Bream .15 .05
❑ 567A Joel Youngblood ERR (Position P) .15 .05
❑ 567B Joel Youngblood COR (Position IF) .50 .20
❑ 568 Mario Ramirez .15 .05
❑ 569 Tom Runnells .15 .05
❑ 570 Rick Schu .15 .05
❑ 571 Bill Campbell .15 .05
❑ 572 Dickie Thon .15 .05
❑ 573 Al Holland .15 .05
❑ 574 Reid Nichols .15 .05
❑ 575 Bert Roberge .15 .05
❑ 576 Mike Flanagan .15 .05
❑ 577 Tim Leary .15 .05
❑ 578 Mike Laga .15 .05
❑ 579 Steve Lyons .15 .05
❑ 580 Phil Niekro .25 .08
❑ 581 Gilberto Reyes .15 .05
❑ 582 Jamie Easterly .15 .05
❑ 583 Mark Gubicza .15 .05
❑ 584 Stan Javier RC .50 .20
❑ 585 Bill Laskey .15 .05
❑ 586 Jeff Russell .15 .05
❑ 587 Dickie Noles .15 .05
❑ 588 Steve Farr .15 .05
❑ 589 Steve Ontiveros RC .15 .05
❑ 590 Mike Hargrove .15 .05
❑ 591 Marty Bystrom .15 .05
❑ 592 Franklin Stubbs .15 .05
❑ 593 Larry Herndon .15 .05
❑ 594 Bill Swaggerty .15 .05
❑ 595 Carlos Ponce .15 .05
❑ 596 Pat Perry .15 .05
❑ 597 Ray Knight .25 .08
❑ 598 Steve Lombardozzi .15 .05
❑ 599 Brad Havens .15 .05
❑ 600 Pat Clements .15 .05
❑ 601 Joe Niekro .15 .05
❑ 602 Hank Aaron Puzzle .75 .30
❑ 603 Dwayne Henry .15 .05
❑ 604 Mookie Wilson .25 .08
❑ 605 Buddy Biancalana .15 .05
❑ 606 Rance Mulliniks .15 .05
❑ 607 Alan Wiggins .15 .05
❑ 608 Joe Cowley .15 .05
❑ 609 Tom Seaver .50 .20
❑ 609B Tom Seaver YL 2.00 .75
❑ 610 Neil Allen .15 .05
❑ 611 Don Sutton .25 .08
❑ 612 Fred Toliver .15 .05
❑ 613 Jay Baller .15 .05
❑ 614 Marc Sullivan .15 .05
❑ 615 John Grubb .15 .05
❑ 616 Bruce Kison .15 .05
❑ 617 Bill Madlock .25 .08
❑ 618 Chris Chambliss .25 .08
❑ 619 Dave Stewart .25 .08
❑ 620 Tim Lollar .15 .05
❑ 621 Gary Lavelle .15 .05
❑ 622 Charles Hudson .15 .05
❑ 623 Joel Davis .15 .05
❑ 624 Joe Johnson .15 .05
❑ 625 Sid Fernandez .15 .05
❑ 626 Dennis Lamp .15 .05
❑ 627 Terry Harper .15 .05
❑ 628 Jack Lazorko .15 .05
❑ 629 Roger McDowell RC* .50 .20
❑ 630 Mark Funderburk .15 .05
❑ 631 Ed Lynch .15 .05
❑ 632 Rudy Law .15 .05
❑ 633 Roger Mason RC .15 .05
❑ 634 Mike Felder RC .15 .05
❑ 635 Ken Schrom .15 .05
❑ 636 Bob Ojeda .15 .05
❑ 637 Ed VandeBerg .15 .05
❑ 638 Bobby Meacham .15 .05
❑ 639 Cliff Johnson .15 .05
❑ 640 Garth Iorg .15 .05
❑ 641 Dan Driessen .15 .05
❑ 642 Mike Brown OF .15 .05
❑ 643 John Shelby .15 .05
❑ 644 Pete Rose RB .75 .30
❑ 645 The Knuckle Brothers .25 .08
❑ 646 Jesse Orosco .15 .05
❑ 647 Billy Beane RC 1.00 .40
❑ 648 Cesar Cedeno .25 .08
❑ 649 Bert Blyleven .25 .08
❑ 650 Max Venable .15 .05
❑ 651 Fleet Feet Vince Coleman Willie McGee .15 .05
❑ 652 Calvin Schiraldi .15 .05
❑ 653 Pete Rose KING .75 .30
❑ 654 Diamond Kings CL 1-26 (Unnumbered) .15 .05
❑ 655A CL 1: 27-130 (Unnumbered) (45 Beane ERR) .15 .05
❑ 655B CL 1: 27-130 (Unnumbered) (45 Habyan COR) .15 .05
❑ 656 CL 2: 131-234 (Unnumbered) .15 .05
❑ 657 CL 3: 235-338 (Unnumbered) .15 .05
❑ 658 CL 4: 339-442 (Unnumbered) .15 .05
❑ 659 CL 5: 443-546 (Unnumbered) .15 .05
❑ 660 CL 6: 547-653 (Unnumbered) .15 .05

1986 Donruss Rookies

❑ COMP.FACT.SET (56) 25.00 10.00
❑ 1 Wally Joyner XRC 1.00 .40
❑ 2 Tracy Jones .15 .05
❑ 3 Allan Anderson XRC .15 .05
❑ 4 Ed Correa .15 .05
❑ 5 Reggie Williams .15 .05
❑ 6 Charlie Kerfeld .15 .05
❑ 7 Andres Galarraga 1.50 .60
❑ 8 Bob Tewksbury XRC .50 .20
❑ 9 Al Newman XRC .25 .08
❑ 10 Andres Thomas .15 .05
❑ 11 Barry Bonds XRC 20.00 8.00
❑ 12 Juan Nieves .15 .05
❑ 13 Mark Eichhorn .15 .05
❑ 14 Dan Plesac XRC .50 .20
❑ 15 Cory Snyder .15 .05

❑ 16 Kelly Gruber .15 .05
❑ 17 Kevin Mitchell XRC 1.00 .40
❑ 18 Steve Lombardozzi .15 .05
❑ 19 Mitch Williams XRC .50 .20
❑ 20 John Cerutti .15 .05
❑ 21 Todd Worrell .50 .20
❑ 22 Jose Canseco 4.00 1.50
❑ 23 Pete Incaviglia XRC .50 .20
❑ 24 Jose Guzman .15 .05
❑ 25 Scott Bailes .15 .05
❑ 26 Greg Mathews .15 .05
❑ 27 Eric King .15 .05
❑ 28 Paul Assenmacher .50 .20
❑ 29 Jeff Sellers .15 .05
❑ 30 Bobby Bonilla XRC 1.00 .40
❑ 31 Doug Drabek XRC 1.00 .40
❑ 32 Will Clark XRC 2.00 .75
❑ 33 Bip Roberts XRC .50 .20
❑ 34 Jim Deshaies XRC .15 .05
❑ 35 Mike LaValliere XRC .50 .20
❑ 36 Scott Bankhead .15 .05
❑ 37 Dale Sveum .15 .05
❑ 38 Bo Jackson XRC 5.00 2.00
❑ 39 Robby Thompson XRC .50 .20
❑ 40 Eric Plunk .15 .05
❑ 41 Bill Bathe .15 .05
❑ 42 John Kruk XRC 1.50 .60
❑ 43 Andy Allanson XRC .15 .05
❑ 44 Mark Portugal XRC .50 .20
❑ 45 Danny Tartabull .25 .08
❑ 46 Bob Kipper .15 .05
❑ 47 Gene Walter .15 .05
❑ 48 Rey Quinones UER (Misspelled Quinonez) .15 .05
❑ 49 Bobby Witt XRC .50 .20
❑ 50 Bill Mooneyham .15 .05
❑ 51 John Cangelosi .15 .05
❑ 52 Ruben Sierra XRC 1.50 .60
❑ 53 Rob Woodward .15 .05
❑ 54 Ed Hearn XRC .15 .05
❑ 55 Joel McKeon .15 .05
❑ 56 Checklist 1-56 .15 .05

1987 Donruss

❑ COMPLETE SET (660) 40.00 15.00
❑ COMP.FACT.SET (660) 50.00 20.00
❑ COMP.CLEMENTE PUZZLE 1.50 .60
❑ 1 Wally Joyner DK .40 .15
❑ 2 Roger Clemens DK 2.00 .75
❑ 3 Dale Murphy DK .25 .08
❑ 4 Darryl Strawberry DK .15 .05
❑ 5 Ozzie Smith DK .60 .25
❑ 6 Jose Canseco DK 1.00 .40
❑ 7 Charlie Hough DK .15 .05
❑ 8 Brook Jacoby DK .10 .02
❑ 9 Fred Lynn DK .15 .05
❑ 10 Rick Rhoden DK .10 .02
❑ 11 Chris Brown DK .10 .02
❑ 12 Von Hayes DK .10 .02
❑ 13 Jack Morris DK .15 .05
❑ 14A Kevin McReynolds DK ERR .40 .15
❑ 14B Kevin McReynolds DK COR .10 .02
❑ 15 George Brett DK 1.00 .40
❑ 16 Ted Higuera DK .10 .02
❑ 17 Hubie Brooks DK .10 .02
❑ 18 Mike Scott DK .15 .05
❑ 19 Kirby Puckett DK .75 .30
❑ 20 Dave Winfield DK .15 .05
❑ 21 Lloyd Moseby DK .10 .02
❑ 22A Eric Davis DK ERR .40 .15
❑ 22B Eric Davis DK COR .25 .08
❑ 23 Jim Presley DK .10 .02
❑ 24 Keith Moreland DK .10 .02
❑ 25A Greg Walker DK ERR .40 .15
❑ 25B Greg Walker DK COR .10 .02
❑ 26 Steve Sax DK .10 .02
❑ 27 DK Checklist 1-26 .10 .02
❑ 28 B.J. Surhoff RC .60 .25
❑ 29 Randy Myers RC .60 .25
❑ 30 Ken Gerhart RC .15 .05
❑ 31 Benito Santiago .15 .05
❑ 32 Greg Swindell RC .40 .15
❑ 33 Mike Birkbeck RC .15 .05
❑ 34 Terry Steinbach RC .60 .25
❑ 35 Bo Jackson RC 5.00 2.00
❑ 36 Greg Maddux RC 10.00 4.00
❑ 37 Jim Lindeman RC .15 .05
❑ 38 Devon White RC .60 .25
❑ 39 Eric Bell RC .15 .05
❑ 40 Willie Fraser RC .15 .05
❑ 41 Jerry Browne RC .15 .05
❑ 42 Chris James RC * .15 .05
❑ 43 Rafael Palmeiro RC 5.00 2.00
❑ 44 Pat Dodson RC .15 .05
❑ 45 Duane Ward RC * .40 .15
❑ 46 Mark McGwire 8.00 3.00
❑ 47 Bruce Fields UER RC .15 .05
❑ 48 Eddie Murray .40 .15
❑ 49 Ted Higuera .10 .02
❑ 50 Kirk Gibson .15 .05
❑ 51 Oil Can Boyd .10 .02
❑ 52 Don Mattingly 1.25 .50
❑ 53 Pedro Guerrero .15 .05
❑ 54 George Brett 1.00 .40
❑ 55 Jose Rijo .15 .05
❑ 56 Tim Raines .15 .05
❑ 57 Ed Correa .10 .02
❑ 58 Mike Witt .10 .02
❑ 59 Greg Walker .10 .02
❑ 60 Ozzie Smith .60 .25
❑ 61 Glenn Davis .10 .02
❑ 62 Glenn Wilson .10 .02
❑ 63 Tom Browning .10 .02
❑ 64 Tony Gwynn .60 .25
❑ 65 R.J. Reynolds .10 .02
❑ 66 Will Clark RC 1.50 .60
❑ 67 Ozzie Virgil .10 .02
❑ 68 Rick Sutcliffe .15 .05
❑ 69 Gary Carter .15 .05
❑ 70 Mike Moore .10 .02
❑ 71 Bert Blyleven .15 .05
❑ 72 Tony Fernandez .10 .02
❑ 73 Kent Hrbek .15 .05
❑ 74 Lloyd Moseby .10 .02
❑ 75 Alvin Davis .10 .02
❑ 76 Keith Hernandez .15 .05
❑ 77 Ryne Sandberg .75 .30
❑ 78 Dale Murphy .25 .08
❑ 79 Sid Bream .10 .02
❑ 80 Chris Brown .10 .02
❑ 81 Steve Garvey .15 .05
❑ 82 Mario Soto .15 .05
❑ 83 Shane Rawley .10 .02
❑ 84 Willie McGee .15 .05
❑ 85 Jose Cruz .15 .05
❑ 86 Brian Downing .15 .05
❑ 87 Ozzie Guillen .25 .08
❑ 88 Hubie Brooks .10 .02
❑ 89 Cal Ripken 1.50 .60
❑ 90 Juan Nieves .10 .02
❑ 91 Lance Parrish .15 .05
❑ 92 Jim Rice .15 .05
❑ 93 Ron Guidry .15 .05
❑ 94 Fernando Valenzuela .15 .05
❑ 95 Andy Allanson RC .10 .02
❑ 96 Willie Wilson .15 .05
❑ 97 Jose Canseco 1.00 .40
❑ 98 Jeff Reardon .15 .05
❑ 99 Bobby Witt RC .40 .15
❑ 100 Checklist 28-133 .10 .02
❑ 101 Jose Guzman .10 .02
❑ 102 Steve Balboni .10 .02
❑ 103 Tony Phillips .10 .02
❑ 104 Brook Jacoby .10 .02
❑ 105 Dave Winfield .15 .05
❑ 106 Orel Hershiser .25 .08
❑ 107 Lou Whitaker .15 .05
❑ 108 Fred Lynn .15 .05
❑ 109 Bill Wegman .10 .02
❑ 110 Donnie Moore .10 .02
❑ 111 Jack Clark .15 .05
❑ 112 Bob Knepper .10 .02
❑ 113 Von Hayes .10 .02
❑ 114 Bip Roberts RC .40 .15
❑ 115 Tony Pena .10 .02
❑ 116 Scott Garrelts .10 .02
❑ 117 Paul Molitor .15 .05
❑ 118 Darryl Strawberry .15 .05
❑ 119 Shawon Dunston .10 .02
❑ 120 Jim Presley .10 .02
❑ 121 Jesse Barfield .15 .05
❑ 122 Gary Gaetti .15 .05
❑ 123 Kurt Stillwell .10 .02
❑ 124 Joel Davis .10 .02
❑ 125 Mike Boddicker .10 .02
❑ 126 Robin Yount .60 .25
❑ 127 Alan Trammell .15 .05
❑ 128 Dave Righetti .15 .05
❑ 129 Dwight Evans .25 .08
❑ 130 Mike Scioscia .15 .05
❑ 131 Julio Franco .15 .05
❑ 132 Bret Saberhagen .15 .05
❑ 133 Mike Davis .10 .02
❑ 134 Joe Hesketh .10 .02
❑ 135 Wally Joyner RC .60 .25
❑ 136 Don Slaught .10 .02
❑ 137 Daryl Boston .10 .02
❑ 138 Nolan Ryan 2.00 .75
❑ 139 Mike Schmidt 1.00 .40
❑ 140 Tommy Herr .10 .02
❑ 141 Garry Templeton .15 .05
❑ 142 Kal Daniels .10 .02
❑ 143 Billy Sample .10 .02
❑ 144 Johnny Ray .10 .02
❑ 145 Robby Thompson RC * .40 .15
❑ 146 Bob Dernier .10 .02
❑ 147 Danny Tartabull .10 .02
❑ 148 Ernie Whitt .10 .02
❑ 149 Kirby Puckett .75 .30
❑ 150 Mike Young .10 .02
❑ 151 Ernest Riles .10 .02
❑ 152 Frank Tanana .15 .05
❑ 153 Rich Gedman .10 .02
❑ 154 Willie Randolph .15 .05
❑ 155 Bill Madlock .15 .05
❑ 156 Joe Carter .15 .05
❑ 157 Danny Jackson .10 .02
❑ 158 Carney Lansford .15 .05
❑ 159 Bryn Smith .10 .02
❑ 160 Gary Pettis .10 .02
❑ 161 Oddibe McDowell .10 .02
❑ 162 John Cangelosi .10 .02
❑ 163 Mike Scott .15 .05
❑ 164 Eric Show .10 .02
❑ 165 Juan Samuel .10 .02
❑ 166 Nick Esasky .10 .02
❑ 167 Zane Smith .10 .02
❑ 168 Mike C. Brown OF .10 .02
❑ 169 Keith Moreland .10 .02
❑ 170 John Tudor .15 .05
❑ 171 Ken Dixon .10 .02
❑ 172 Jim Gantner .10 .02

❑ 173 Jack Morris .15 .05
❑ 174 Bruce Hurst .10 .02
❑ 175 Dennis Rasmussen .10 .02
❑ 176 Mike Marshall .10 .02
❑ 177 Dan Quisenberry .10 .02
❑ 178 Eric Plunk .10 .02
❑ 179 Tim Wallach .10 .02
❑ 180 Steve Buechele .10 .02
❑ 181 Don Sutton .15 .05
❑ 182 Dave Schmidt .10 .02
❑ 183 Terry Pendleton .15 .05
❑ 184 Jim Deshaies RC * .15 .05
❑ 185 Steve Bedrosian .10 .02
❑ 186 Pete Rose 1.25 .50
❑ 187 Dave Dravecky .10 .02
❑ 188 Rick Reuschel .15 .05
❑ 189 Dan Gladden .10 .02
❑ 190 Rick Mahler .10 .02
❑ 191 Thad Bosley .10 .02
❑ 192 Ron Darling .15 .05
❑ 193 Matt Young .10 .02
❑ 194 Tom Brunansky .10 .02
❑ 195 Dave Stieb .15 .05
❑ 196 Frank Viola .15 .05
❑ 197 Tom Henke .10 .02
❑ 198 Karl Best .10 .02
❑ 199 Dwight Gooden .25 .08
❑ 200 Checklist 134-239 .10 .02
❑ 201 Steve Trout .10 .02
❑ 202 Rafael Ramirez .10 .02
❑ 203 Bob Walk .10 .02
❑ 204 Roger Mason .10 .02
❑ 205 Terry Kennedy .10 .02
❑ 206 Ron Oester .10 .02
❑ 207 John Russell .10 .02
❑ 208 Greg Mathews .10 .02
❑ 209 Charlie Kerfeld .10 .02
❑ 210 Reggie Jackson .25 .08
❑ 211 Floyd Bannister .10 .02
❑ 212 Vance Law .10 .02
❑ 213 Rich Bordi .10 .02
❑ 214 Dan Plesac .10 .02
❑ 215 Dave Collins .10 .02
❑ 216 Bob Stanley .10 .02
❑ 217 Joe Niekro .10 .02
❑ 218 Tom Niedenfuer .10 .02
❑ 219 Brett Butler .15 .05
❑ 220 Charlie Leibrandt .10 .02
❑ 221 Steve Ontiveros .10 .02
❑ 222 Tim Burke .10 .02
❑ 223 Curtis Wilkerson .10 .02
❑ 224 Pete Incaviglia RC * .40 .15
❑ 225 Lonnie Smith .10 .02
❑ 226 Chris Codiroli .10 .02
❑ 227 Scott Bailes .10 .02
❑ 228 Rickey Henderson .40 .15
❑ 229 Ken Howell .10 .02
❑ 230 Darnell Coles .10 .02
❑ 231 Don Aase .10 .02
❑ 232 Tim Leary .10 .02
❑ 233 Bob Boone .15 .05
❑ 234 Ricky Horton .10 .02
❑ 235 Mark Bailey .10 .02
❑ 236 Kevin Gross .10 .02
❑ 237 Lance McCullers .10 .02
❑ 238 Cecilio Guante .10 .02
❑ 239 Bob Melvin .10 .02
❑ 240 Billy Joe Robidoux .10 .02
❑ 241 Roger McDowell .10 .02
❑ 242 Leon Durham .10 .02
❑ 243 Ed Nunez .10 .02
❑ 244 Jimmy Key .15 .05
❑ 245 Mike Smithson .10 .02
❑ 246 Bo Diaz .10 .02
❑ 247 Carlton Fisk .25 .08
❑ 248 Larry Sheets .10 .02
❑ 249 Juan Castillo RC .15 .05
❑ 250 Eric King .10 .02
❑ 251 Doug Drabek RC .60 .25
❑ 252 Wade Boggs .25 .08
❑ 253 Mariano Duncan .10 .02
❑ 254 Pat Tabler .10 .02
❑ 255 Frank White .15 .05
❑ 256 Alfredo Griffin .10 .02
❑ 257 Floyd Youmans .10 .02
❑ 258 Rob Wilfong .10 .02
❑ 259 Pete O'Brien .10 .02
❑ 260 Tim Hulett .10 .02
❑ 261 Dickie Thon .10 .02
❑ 262 Darren Daulton .15 .05
❑ 263 Vince Coleman .10 .02
❑ 264 Andy Hawkins .10 .02
❑ 265 Eric Davis .25 .08
❑ 266 Andres Thomas .10 .02
❑ 267 Mike Diaz .10 .02
❑ 268 Chili Davis .15 .05
❑ 269 Jody Davis .10 .02
❑ 270 Phil Bradley .10 .02
❑ 271 George Bell .15 .05
❑ 272 Keith Atherton .10 .02
❑ 273 Storm Davis .10 .02
❑ 274 Rob Deer .10 .02
❑ 275 Walt Terrell .10 .02
❑ 276 Roger Clemens 2.00 .75
❑ 277 Mike Easler .10 .02
❑ 278 Steve Sax .10 .02
❑ 279 Andre Thornton .10 .02
❑ 280 Jim Sundberg .15 .05
❑ 281 Bill Bathe .10 .02
❑ 282 Jay Tibbs .10 .02
❑ 283 Dick Schofield .10 .02
❑ 284 Mike Mason .10 .02
❑ 285 Jerry Hairston .10 .02
❑ 286 Bill Doran .10 .02
❑ 287 Tim Flannery .10 .02
❑ 288 Gary Redus .10 .02
❑ 289 John Franco .15 .05
❑ 290 Paul Assenmacher .40 .15
❑ 291 Joe Orsulak .10 .02
❑ 292 Lee Smith .15 .05
❑ 293 Mike Laga .10 .02
❑ 294 Rick Dempsey .10 .02
❑ 295 Mike Felder .10 .02
❑ 296 Tom Brookens .10 .02
❑ 297 Al Nipper .10 .02
❑ 298 Mike Pagliarulo .10 .02
❑ 299 Franklin Stubbs .10 .02
❑ 300 Checklist 240-345 .10 .02
❑ 301 Steve Farr .10 .02
❑ 302 Bill Mooneyham .10 .02
❑ 303 Andres Galarraga .15 .05
❑ 304 Scott Fletcher .10 .02
❑ 305 Jack Howell .10 .02
❑ 306 Russ Morman .10 .02
❑ 307 Todd Worrell .10 .02
❑ 308 Dave Smith .10 .02
❑ 309 Jeff Stone .10 .02
❑ 310 Ron Robinson .10 .02
❑ 311 Bruce Bochy .10 .02
❑ 312 Jim Winn .10 .02
❑ 313 Mark Davis .10 .02
❑ 314 Jeff Dedmon .10 .02
❑ 315 Jamie Moyer RC 1.00 .40
❑ 316 Wally Backman .10 .02
❑ 317 Ken Phelps .10 .02
❑ 318 Steve Lombardozzi .10 .02
❑ 319 Rance Mulliniks .10 .02
❑ 320 Tim Laudner .10 .02
❑ 321 Mark Eichhorn .10 .02
❑ 322 Lee Guetterman .10 .02
❑ 323 Sid Fernandez .10 .02
❑ 324 Jerry Mumphrey .10 .02
❑ 325 David Palmer .10 .02
❑ 326 Bill Almon .10 .02
❑ 327 Candy Maldonado .10 .02
❑ 328 John Kruk RC 1.00 .40
❑ 329 John Denny .10 .02
❑ 330 Milt Thompson .10 .02
❑ 331 Mike LaValliere RC * .40 .15
❑ 332 Alan Ashby .10 .02
❑ 333 Doug Corbett .10 .02
❑ 334 Ron Karkovice RC .40 .15
❑ 335 Mitch Webster .10 .02
❑ 336 Lee Lacy .10 .02
❑ 337 Glenn Braggs RC .15 .05
❑ 338 Dwight Lowry .10 .02
❑ 339 Don Baylor .15 .05
❑ 340 Brian Fisher .10 .02
❑ 341 Reggie Williams .10 .02
❑ 342 Tom Candiotti .10 .02
❑ 343 Rudy Law .10 .02
❑ 344 Curt Young .10 .02
❑ 345 Mike Fitzgerald .10 .02
❑ 346 Ruben Sierra RC 1.00 .40
❑ 347 Mitch Williams RC * .40 .15
❑ 348 Jorge Orta .10 .02
❑ 349 Mickey Tettleton .10 .02
❑ 350 Ernie Camacho .10 .02
❑ 351 Ron Kittle .10 .02
❑ 352 Ken Landreaux .10 .02
❑ 353 Chet Lemon .15 .05
❑ 354 John Shelby .10 .02
❑ 355 Mark Clear .10 .02
❑ 356 Doug DeCinces .10 .02
❑ 357 Ken Dayley .10 .02
❑ 358 Phil Garner .15 .05
❑ 359 Steve Jeltz .10 .02
❑ 360 Ed Whitson .10 .02
❑ 361 Barry Bonds RC 12.00 5.00
❑ 362 Vida Blue .15 .05
❑ 363 Cecil Cooper .15 .05
❑ 364 Bob Ojeda .10 .02
❑ 365 Dennis Eckersley .25 .08
❑ 366 Mike Morgan .10 .02
❑ 367 Willie Upshaw .10 .02
❑ 368 Allan Anderson RC .10 .02
❑ 369 Bill Gullickson .10 .02
❑ 370 Bobby Thigpen RC .40 .15
❑ 371 Juan Beniquez .10 .02
❑ 372 Charlie Moore .10 .02
❑ 373 Dan Petry .10 .02
❑ 374 Rod Scurry .10 .02
❑ 375 Tom Seaver .25 .08
❑ 376 Ed VandeBerg .10 .02
❑ 377 Tony Bernazard .10 .02
❑ 378 Greg Pryor .10 .02
❑ 379 Dwayne Murphy .10 .02
❑ 380 Andy McGaffigan .10 .02
❑ 381 Kirk McCaskill .10 .02
❑ 382 Greg Harris .10 .02
❑ 383 Rich Dotson .10 .02
❑ 384 Craig Reynolds .10 .02
❑ 385 Greg Gross .10 .02
❑ 386 Tito Landrum .10 .02
❑ 387 Craig Lefferts .10 .02
❑ 388 Dave Parker .15 .05
❑ 389 Bob Horner .15 .05
❑ 390 Pat Clements .10 .02
❑ 391 Jeff Leonard .10 .02
❑ 392 Chris Speier .10 .02
❑ 393 John Moses .10 .02
❑ 394 Garth Iorg .10 .02
❑ 395 Greg Gagne .10 .02
❑ 396 Nate Snell .10 .02
❑ 397 Bryan Clutterbuck .10 .02
❑ 398 Darrell Evans .15 .05
❑ 399 Steve Crawford .10 .02
❑ 400 Checklist 346-451 .10 .02
❑ 401 Phil Lombardi .10 .02
❑ 402 Rick Honeycutt .10 .02
❑ 403 Ken Schrom .10 .02
❑ 404 Bud Black .10 .02
❑ 405 Donnie Hill .10 .02
❑ 406 Wayne Krenchicki .10 .02
❑ 407 Chuck Finley RC .60 .25
❑ 408 Toby Harrah .15 .05
❑ 409 Steve Lyons .10 .02
❑ 410 Kevin Bass .10 .02
❑ 411 Marvell Wynne .10 .02
❑ 412 Ron Roenicke .10 .02
❑ 413 Tracy Jones .10 .02
❑ 414 Gene Garber .10 .02
❑ 415 Mike Bielecki .10 .02
❑ 416 Frank DiPino .10 .02
❑ 417 Andy Van Slyke .25 .08
❑ 418 Jim Dwyer .10 .02
❑ 419 Ben Oglivie .15 .05
❑ 420 Dave Bergman .10 .02
❑ 421 Joe Sambito .10 .02
❑ 422 Bob Tewksbury RC * .40 .15
❑ 423 Len Matuszek .10 .02
❑ 424 Mike Kingery RC .15 .05
❑ 425 Dave Kingman .15 .05
❑ 426 Al Newman RC .10 .02
❑ 427 Gary Ward .10 .02
❑ 428 Ruppert Jones .10 .02
❑ 429 Harold Baines .15 .05
❑ 430 Pat Perry .10 .02

❑ 431	Terry Puhl	.10	.02
❑ 432	Don Carman	.10	.02
❑ 433	Eddie Milner	.10	.02
❑ 434	LaMarr Hoyt	.10	.02
❑ 435	Rick Rhoden	.10	.02
❑ 436	Jose Uribe	.10	.02
❑ 437	Ken Oberkfell	.10	.02
❑ 438	Ron Davis	.10	.02
❑ 439	Jesse Orosco	.10	.02
❑ 440	Scott Bradley	.10	.02
❑ 441	Randy Bush	.10	.02
❑ 442	John Cerutti	.10	.02
❑ 443	Roy Smalley	.10	.02
❑ 444	Kelly Gruber	.10	.02
❑ 445	Bob Kearney	.10	.02
❑ 446	Ed Hearn RC	.10	.02
❑ 447	Scott Sanderson	.10	.02
❑ 448	Bruce Benedict	.10	.02
❑ 449	Junior Ortiz	.10	.02
❑ 450	Mike Aldrete	.10	.02
❑ 451	Kevin McReynolds	.10	.02
❑ 452	Rob Murphy	.10	.02
❑ 453	Kent Tekulve	.10	.02
❑ 454	Curt Ford	.10	.02
❑ 455	Dave Lopes	.15	.05
❑ 456	Bob Grich	.15	.05
❑ 457	Jose DeLeon	.10	.02
❑ 458	Andre Dawson	.15	.05
❑ 459	Mike Flanagan	.10	.02
❑ 460	Joey Meyer	.15	.05
❑ 461	Chuck Cary	.10	.02
❑ 462	Bill Buckner	.15	.05
❑ 463	Bob Shirley	.10	.02
❑ 464	Jeff Hamilton	.10	.02
❑ 465	Phil Niekro	.15	.05
❑ 466	Mark Gubicza	.10	.02
❑ 467	Jerry Willard	.10	.02
❑ 468	Bob Sebra	.10	.02
❑ 469	Larry Parrish	.10	.02
❑ 470	Charlie Hough	.15	.05
❑ 471	Hal McRae	.15	.05
❑ 472	Dave Leiper	.10	.02
❑ 473	Mel Hall	.10	.02
❑ 474	Dan Pasqua	.10	.02
❑ 475	Bob Welch	.15	.05
❑ 476	Johnny Grubb	.10	.02
❑ 477	Jim Traber	.10	.02
❑ 478	Chris Bosio RC	.40	.15
❑ 479	Mark McLemore	.15	.05
❑ 480	John Morris	.10	.02
❑ 481	Billy Hatcher	.10	.02
❑ 482	Dan Schatzeder	.10	.02
❑ 483	Rich Gossage	.15	.05
❑ 484	Jim Morrison	.10	.02
❑ 485	Bob Brenly	.10	.02
❑ 486	Bill Schroeder	.10	.02
❑ 487	Mookie Wilson	.15	.05
❑ 488	Dave Martinez RC	.40	.15
❑ 489	Harold Reynolds	.15	.05
❑ 490	Jeff Hearron	.10	.02
❑ 491	Mickey Hatcher	.10	.02
❑ 492	Barry Larkin RC	1.50	.60
❑ 493	Bob James	.10	.02
❑ 494	John Habyan	.10	.02
❑ 495	Jim Adduci	.10	.02
❑ 496	Mike Heath	.10	.02
❑ 497	Tim Stoddard	.10	.02
❑ 498	Tony Armas	.15	.05
❑ 499	Dennis Powell	.10	.02
❑ 500	Checklist 452-557	.10	.02
❑ 501	Chris Bando	.10	.02
❑ 502	David Cone RC	1.00	.40
❑ 503	Jay Howell	.10	.02
❑ 504	Tom Foley	.10	.02
❑ 505	Ray Chadwick	.10	.02
❑ 506	Mike Loynd RC	.15	.05
❑ 507	Neil Allen	.10	.02
❑ 508	Danny Darwin	.10	.02
❑ 509	Rick Schu	.10	.02
❑ 510	Jose Oquendo	.10	.02
❑ 511	Gene Walter	.10	.02
❑ 512	Terry McGriff	.10	.02
❑ 513	Ken Griffey	.15	.05
❑ 514	Benny Distefano	.10	.02
❑ 515	Terry Mulholland RC	.40	.15
❑ 516	Ed Lynch	.10	.02
❑ 517	Bill Swift	.10	.02
❑ 518	Manny Lee	.10	.02
❑ 519	Andre David	.10	.02
❑ 520	Scott McGregor	.10	.02
❑ 521	Rick Manning	.10	.02
❑ 522	Willie Hernandez	.10	.02
❑ 523	Marty Barrett	.10	.02
❑ 524	Wayne Tolleson	.10	.02
❑ 525	Jose Gonzalez RC	.15	.05
❑ 526	Cory Snyder	.10	.02
❑ 527	Buddy Biancalana	.10	.02
❑ 528	Moose Haas	.10	.02
❑ 529	Wilfredo Tejada	.10	.02
❑ 530	Stu Cliburn	.10	.02
❑ 531	Dale Mohorcic	.10	.02
❑ 532	Ron Hassey	.10	.02
❑ 533	Ty Gainey	.10	.02
❑ 534	Jerry Royster	.10	.02
❑ 535	Mike Maddux	.10	.02
❑ 536	Ted Power	.10	.02
❑ 537	Ted Simmons	.15	.05
❑ 538	Rafael Belliard RC	.40	.15
❑ 539	Chico Walker	.10	.02
❑ 540	Bob Forsch	.10	.02
❑ 541	John Stefero	.10	.02
❑ 542	Dale Sveum	.10	.02
❑ 543	Mark Thurmond	.10	.02
❑ 544	Jeff Sellers	.10	.02
❑ 545	Joel Skinner	.10	.02
❑ 546	Alex Trevino	.10	.02
❑ 547	Randy Kutcher	.10	.02
❑ 548	Joaquin Andujar	.15	.05
❑ 549	Casey Candaele	.10	.02
❑ 550	Jeff Russell	.10	.02
❑ 551	John Candelaria	.10	.02
❑ 552	Joe Cowley	.10	.02
❑ 553	Danny Cox	.10	.02
❑ 554	Denny Walling	.10	.02
❑ 555	Bruce Ruffin RC	.15	.05
❑ 556	Buddy Bell	.15	.05
❑ 557	Jimmy Jones RC	.15	.05
❑ 558	Bobby Bonilla RC	.60	.25
❑ 559	Jeff D. Robinson	.10	.02
❑ 560	Ed Olwine	.10	.02
❑ 561	Glenallen Hill RC	.40	.15
❑ 562	Lee Mazzilli	[illegible]	.05
❑ 563	Mike G. Brown P	.10	.02
❑ 564	George Frazier	.10	.02
❑ 565	Mike Sharperson RC	.15	.05
❑ 566	Mark Portugal RC *	.40	.15
❑ 567	Rick Leach	.10	.02
❑ 568	Mark Langston	.10	.02
❑ 569	Rafael Santana	.10	.02
❑ 570	Manny Trillo	.10	.02
❑ 571	Cliff Speck	.10	.02
❑ 572	Bob Kipper	.10	.02
❑ 573	Kelly Downs RC	.15	.05
❑ 574	Randy Asadoor	.10	.02
❑ 575	Dave Magadan RC	.40	.15
❑ 576	Marvin Freeman RC	.15	.05
❑ 577	Jeff Lahti	.10	.02
❑ 578	Jeff Calhoun	.10	.02
❑ 579	Gus Polidor	.10	.02
❑ 580	Gene Nelson	.10	.02
❑ 581	Tim Teufel	.10	.02
❑ 582	Odell Jones	.10	.02
❑ 583	Mark Ryal	.10	.02
❑ 584	Randy O'Neal	.10	.02
❑ 585	Mike Greenwell RC	.40	.15
❑ 586	Ray Knight	.15	.05
❑ 587	Ralph Bryant	.10	.02
❑ 588	Carmen Castillo	.10	.02
❑ 589	Ed Wojna	.10	.02
❑ 590	Stan Javier	.10	.02
❑ 591	Jeff Musselman	.10	.02
❑ 592	Mike Stanley RC	.40	.15
❑ 593	Darrell Porter	.10	.02
❑ 594	Drew Hall	.10	.02
❑ 595	Rob Nelson	.10	.02
❑ 596	Bryan Oelkers	.10	.02
❑ 597	Scott Nielsen	.10	.02
❑ 598	Brian Holton	.10	.02
❑ 599	Kevin Mitchell RC *	.60	.25
❑ 600	Checklist 558-660	.10	.02
❑ 601	Jackie Gutierrez	.10	.02
❑ 602	Barry Jones	.10	.02
❑ 603	Jerry Narron	.10	.02
❑ 604	Steve Lake	.10	.02
❑ 605	Jim Pankovits	.10	.02
❑ 606	Ed Romero	.10	.02
❑ 607	Dave LaPoint	.10	.02
❑ 608	Don Robinson	.10	.02
❑ 609	Mike Krukow	.10	.02
❑ 610	Dave Valle RC **	.15	.05
❑ 611	Len Dykstra	.15	.05
❑ 612	Roberto Clemente PUZ	.50	.20
❑ 613	Mike Trujillo	.10	.02
❑ 614	Damaso Garcia	.10	.02
❑ 615	Neal Heaton	.10	.02
❑ 616	Juan Berenguer	.10	.02
❑ 617	Steve Carlton	.15	.05
❑ 618	Gary Lucas	.10	.02
❑ 619	Geno Petralli	.10	.02
❑ 620	Rick Aguilera	.10	.02
❑ 621	Fred McGriff	.75	.30
❑ 622	Dave Henderson	.10	.02
❑ 623	Dave Clark RC	.15	.05
❑ 624	Angel Salazar	.10	.02
❑ 625	Randy Hunt	.10	.02
❑ 626	John Gibbons	.10	.02
❑ 627	Kevin Brown RC	1.50	.60
❑ 628	Bill Dawley	.10	.02
❑ 629	Aurelio Lopez	.10	.02
❑ 630	Charles Hudson	.10	.02
❑ 631	Ray Soff	.10	.02
❑ 632	Ray Hayward	.10	.02
❑ 633	Spike Owen	.10	.02
❑ 634	Glenn Hubbard	.10	.02
❑ 635	Kevin Elster RC	.40	.15
❑ 636	Mike LaCoss	.10	.02
❑ 637	Dwayne Henry	.10	.02
❑ 638	Rey Quinones	.10	.02
❑ 639	Jim Clancy	.10	.02
❑ 640	Larry Andersen	.10	.02
❑ 641	Calvin Schiraldi	.10	.02
❑ 642	Stan Jefferson	.10	.02
❑ 643	Marc Sullivan	.10	.02
❑ 644	Mark Grant	.10	.02
❑ 645	Cliff Johnson	.10	.02
❑ 646	Howard Johnson	.15	.05
❑ 647	Dave Sax	.10	.02
❑ 648	Dave Stewart	.15	.05
❑ 649	Danny Heep	.10	.02
❑ 650	Joe Johnson	.10	.02
❑ 651	Bob Brower	.10	.02
❑ 652	Rob Woodward	.10	.02
❑ 653	John Mizerock	.10	.02
❑ 654	Tim Pyznarski	.10	.02
❑ 655	Luis Aquino	.10	.02
❑ 656	Mickey Brantley	.10	.02
❑ 657	Doyle Alexander	.10	.02
❑ 658	Sammy Stewart	.10	.02
❑ 659	Jim Acker	.10	.02
❑ 660	Pete Ladd	.10	.02

1987 Donruss Rookies

❑	COMP.FACT.SET (56)	25.00	10.00
❑ 1	Mark McGwire	10.00	4.00
❑ 2	Eric Bell	.15	.05
❑ 3	Mark Williamson	.10	.02
❑ 4	Mike Greenwell	.40	.15
❑ 5	Ellis Burks XRC	.60	.25
❑ 6	DeWayne Buice	.10	.02
❑ 7	Mark McLemore	.25	.08

❑ 8 Devon White .60 .25
❑ 9 Willie Fraser .15 .05
❑ 10 Les Lancaster .10 .02
❑ 11 Ken Williams .10 .02
❑ 12 Matt Nokes XRC .40 .15
❑ 13 Jeff M. Robinson .10 .02
❑ 14 Bo Jackson 5.00 2.00
❑ 15 Kevin Seitzer XRC .40 .15
❑ 16 Bill Ripken XRC .40 .15
❑ 17 B.J. Surhoff .60 .25
❑ 18 Chuck Crim .10 .02
❑ 19 Mike Birkbeck .15 .05
❑ 20 Chris Bosio .40 .15
❑ 21 Les Straker .10 .02
❑ 22 Mark Davidson .10 .02
❑ 23 Gene Larkin XRC .40 .15
❑ 24 Ken Gerhart .10 .02
❑ 25 Luis Polonia XRC .40 .15
❑ 26 Terry Steinbach .60 .25
❑ 27 Mickey Brantley .10 .02
❑ 28 Mike Stanley .40 .15
❑ 29 Jerry Browne .15 .05
❑ 30 Todd Benzinger XRC .40 .15
❑ 31 Fred McGriff 1.50 .60
❑ 32 Mike Henneman XRC .40 .15
❑ 33 Casey Candaele .10 .02
❑ 34 Dave Magadan .40 .15
❑ 35 David Cone 1.00 .40
❑ 36 Mike Jackson XRC .40 .15
❑ 37 John Mitchell XRC .15 .05
❑ 38 Mike Dunne .10 .02
❑ 39 John Smiley XRC .40 .15
❑ 40 Joe Magrane XRC .15 .05
❑ 41 Jim Lindeman .15 .05
❑ 42 Shane Mack .10 .02
❑ 43 Stan Jefferson .10 .02
❑ 44 Benito Santiago .25 .08
❑ 45 Matt Williams XRC 2.50 1.00
❑ 46 Dave Meads .10 .02
❑ 47 Rafael Palmeiro 5.00 2.00
❑ 48 Bill Long .10 .02
❑ 49 Bob Brower .10 .02
❑ 50 James Steels .10 .02
❑ 51 Paul Noce .10 .02
❑ 52 Greg Maddux 8.00 3.00
❑ 53 Jeff Musselman .10 .02
❑ 54 Brian Holton .10 .02
❑ 55 Chuck Jackson .10 .02
❑ 56 Checklist 1-56 .10 .02

1988 Donruss

❑ COMPLETE SET (660) 10.00 4.00
❑ COMP.FACT.SET (660) 15.00 6.00
❑ COMMON CARD (1-660) .05 .01
❑ COMMON SP (648-660) .10 .02
❑ 1 Mark McGwire DK .75 .30
❑ 2 Tim Raines DK .10 .02
❑ 3 Benito Santiago DK .10 .02
❑ 4 Alan Trammell DK .10 .02
❑ 5 Danny Tartabull DK .05 .01
❑ 6 Ron Darling DK .10 .02
❑ 7 Paul Molitor DK .10 .02
❑ 8 Devon White DK .10 .02
❑ 9 Andre Dawson DK .05 .01
❑ 10 Julio Franco DK .10 .02
❑ 11 Scott Fletcher DK .05 .01
❑ 12 Tony Fernandez DK .05 .01
❑ 13 Shane Rawley DK .05 .01
❑ 14 Kal Daniels DK .05 .01
❑ 15 Jack Clark DK .10 .02
❑ 16 Dwight Evans DK .15 .05
❑ 17 Tommy John DK .10 .02
❑ 18 Andy Van Slyke DK .15 .05
❑ 19 Gary Gaetti DK .10 .02
❑ 20 Mark Langston DK .05 .01
❑ 21 Will Clark DK .20 .07
❑ 22 Glenn Hubbard DK .05 .01
❑ 23 Billy Hatcher DK .05 .01
❑ 24 Bob Welch DK .10 .02
❑ 25 Ivan Calderon DK .05 .01
❑ 26 Cal Ripken DK .40 .15
❑ 27 DK Checklist 1-26 .05 .01
❑ 28 Mackey Sasser RC .25 .08
❑ 29 Jeff Treadway RC .25 .08
❑ 30 Mike Campbell RR .05 .01
❑ 31 Lance Johnson RC .25 .08
❑ 32 Nelson Liriano RR .05 .01
❑ 33 Shawn Abner RR .05 .01
❑ 34 Roberto Alomar RC 2.00 .75
❑ 35 Shawn Hillegas RR .05 .01
❑ 36 Joey Meyer RR .05 .01
❑ 37 Kevin Elster RR .05 .01
❑ 38 Jose Lind RC .25 .08
❑ 39 Kirt Manwaring RC .25 .08
❑ 40 Mark Grace RC 2.00 .75
❑ 41 Jody Reed RC .25 .08
❑ 42 John Farrell RR RC .10 .02
❑ 43 Al Leiter RC .75 .30
❑ 44 Gary Thurman RR .05 .01
❑ 45 Vicente Palacios RR .05 .01
❑ 46 Eddie Williams RC .10 .02
❑ 47 Jack McDowell RC .40 .15
❑ 48 Ken Dixon .05 .01
❑ 49 Mike Birkbeck .05 .01
❑ 50 Eric King .05 .01
❑ 51 Roger Clemens 1.00 .40
❑ 52 Pat Clements .05 .01
❑ 53 Fernando Valenzuela .10 .02
❑ 54 Mark Gubicza .05 .01
❑ 55 Jay Howell .05 .01
❑ 56 Floyd Youmans .05 .01
❑ 57 Ed Correa .05 .01
❑ 58 DeWayne Buice .05 .01
❑ 59 Jose DeLeon .05 .01
❑ 60 Danny Cox .05 .01
❑ 61 Nolan Ryan 1.00 .40
❑ 62 Steve Bedrosian .05 .01
❑ 63 Tom Browning .05 .01
❑ 64 Mark Davis .05 .01
❑ 65 R.J. Reynolds .05 .01
❑ 66 Kevin Mitchell .10 .02
❑ 67 Ken Oberkfell .05 .01
❑ 68 Rick Sutcliffe .10 .02
❑ 69 Dwight Gooden .10 .02
❑ 70 Scott Bankhead .05 .01
❑ 71 Bert Blyleven .10 .02
❑ 72 Jimmy Key .10 .02
❑ 73 Les Straker .05 .01
❑ 74 Jim Clancy .05 .01
❑ 75 Mike Moore .05 .01
❑ 76 Ron Darling .10 .02
❑ 77 Ed Lynch .05 .01
❑ 78 Dale Murphy .15 .05
❑ 79 Doug Drabek .05 .01
❑ 80 Scott Garrelts .05 .01
❑ 81 Ed Whitson .05 .01
❑ 82 Rob Murphy .05 .01
❑ 83 Shane Rawley .05 .01
❑ 84 Greg Mathews .05 .01
❑ 85 Jim Deshaies .05 .01
❑ 86 Mike Witt .05 .01
❑ 87 Donnie Hill .05 .01
❑ 88 Jeff Reed .05 .01
❑ 89 Mike Boddicker .05 .01
❑ 90 Ted Higuera .05 .01
❑ 91 Walt Terrell .05 .01
❑ 92 Bob Stanley .05 .01
❑ 93 Dave Righetti .10 .02
❑ 94 Orel Hershiser .10 .02
❑ 95 Chris Bando .05 .01
❑ 96 Bret Saberhagen .10 .02
❑ 97 Curt Young .05 .01
❑ 98 Tim Burke .05 .01
❑ 99 Charlie Hough .10 .02
❑ 100A Checklist 28-137 .05 .01
❑ 100B Checklist 28-133 .05 .01
❑ 101 Bobby Witt .05 .01
❑ 102 George Brett .50 .20
❑ 103 Mickey Tettleton .05 .01
❑ 104 Scott Bailes .05 .01
❑ 105 Mike Pagliarulo .05 .01
❑ 106 Mike Scioscia .10 .02
❑ 107 Tom Brookens .05 .01
❑ 108 Ray Knight .10 .02
❑ 109 Dan Plesac .05 .01
❑ 110 Wally Joyner .10 .02
❑ 111 Bob Forsch .05 .01
❑ 112 Mike Scott .10 .02
❑ 113 Kevin Gross .05 .01
❑ 114 Benito Santiago .10 .02
❑ 115 Bob Kipper .05 .01
❑ 116 Mike Krukow .05 .01
❑ 117 Chris Bosio .05 .01
❑ 118 Sid Fernandez .05 .01
❑ 119 Jody Davis .05 .01
❑ 120 Mike Morgan .05 .01
❑ 121 Mark Eichhorn .05 .01
❑ 122 Jeff Reardon .10 .02
❑ 123 John Franco .10 .02
❑ 124 Richard Dotson .05 .01
❑ 125 Eric Bell .05 .01
❑ 126 Juan Nieves .05 .01
❑ 127 Jack Morris .10 .02
❑ 128 Rick Rhoden .05 .01
❑ 129 Rich Gedman .05 .01
❑ 130 Ken Howell .05 .01
❑ 131 Brook Jacoby .05 .01
❑ 132 Danny Jackson .05 .01
❑ 133 Gene Nelson .05 .01
❑ 134 Neal Heaton .05 .01
❑ 135 Willie Fraser .05 .01
❑ 136 Jose Guzman .05 .01
❑ 137 Ozzie Guillen .10 .02
❑ 138 Bob Knepper .05 .01
❑ 139 Mike Jackson RC* .25 .08
❑ 140 Joe Magrane RC* .25 .08
❑ 141 Jimmy Jones .05 .01
❑ 142 Ted Power .05 .01
❑ 143 Ozzie Virgil .05 .01
❑ 144 Felix Fermin .05 .01
❑ 145 Kelly Downs .05 .01
❑ 146 Shawon Dunston .05 .01
❑ 147 Scott Bradley .05 .01
❑ 148 Dave Stieb .10 .02
❑ 149 Frank Viola .10 .02
❑ 150 Terry Kennedy .05 .01
❑ 151 Bill Wegman .05 .01
❑ 152 Matt Nokes RC* .25 .08
❑ 153 Wade Boggs .15 .05
❑ 154 Wayne Tolleson .05 .01
❑ 155 Mariano Duncan .05 .01
❑ 156 Julio Franco .10 .02
❑ 157 Charlie Leibrandt .05 .01
❑ 158 Terry Steinbach .10 .02
❑ 159 Mike Fitzgerald .05 .01
❑ 160 Jack Lazorko .05 .01
❑ 161 Mitch Williams .05 .01
❑ 162 Greg Walker .05 .01
❑ 163 Alan Ashby .05 .01
❑ 164 Tony Gwynn .30 .10
❑ 165 Bruce Ruffin .05 .01
❑ 166 Ron Robinson .05 .01
❑ 167 Zane Smith .05 .01
❑ 168 Junior Ortiz .05 .01
❑ 169 Jamie Moyer .10 .02
❑ 170 Tony Pena .05 .01
❑ 171 Cal Ripken .75 .30
❑ 172 B.J. Surhoff .10 .02
❑ 173 Lou Whitaker .10 .02
❑ 174 Ellis Burks RC .40 .15
❑ 175 Ron Guidry .10 .02
❑ 176 Steve Sax .05 .01
❑ 177 Danny Tartabull .05 .01
❑ 178 Carney Lansford .10 .02
❑ 179 Casey Candaele .05 .01
❑ 180 Scott Fletcher .05 .01
❑ 181 Mark McLemore .05 .01
❑ 182 Ivan Calderon .05 .01
❑ 183 Jack Clark .10 .02
❑ 184 Glenn Davis .05 .01

❏ 185	Luis Aguayo	.05	.01
❏ 186	Bo Diaz	.05	.01
❏ 187	Stan Jefferson	.05	.01
❏ 188	Sid Bream	.05	.01
❏ 189	Bob Brenly	.05	.01
❏ 190	Dion James	.05	.01
❏ 191	Leon Durham	.05	.01
❏ 192	Jesse Orosco	.05	.01
❏ 193	Alvin Davis	.05	.01
❏ 194	Gary Gaetti	.10	.02
❏ 195	Fred McGriff	.20	.07
❏ 196	Steve Lombardozzi	.05	.01
❏ 197	Rance Mulliniks	.05	.01
❏ 198	Rey Quinones	.05	.01
❏ 199	Gary Carter	.10	.02
❏ 200A	Checklist 138-247	.05	.01
❏ 200B	Checklist 134-239	.05	.01
❏ 201	Keith Moreland	.05	.01
❏ 202	Ken Griffey	.10	.02
❏ 203	Tommy Gregg	.05	.01
❏ 204	Will Clark	.20	.07
❏ 205	John Kruk	.10	.02
❏ 206	Buddy Bell	.10	.02
❏ 207	Von Hayes	.05	.01
❏ 208	Tommy Herr	.05	.01
❏ 209	Craig Reynolds	.05	.01
❏ 210	Gary Pettis	.05	.01
❏ 211	Harold Baines	.10	.02
❏ 212	Vance Law	.05	.01
❏ 213	Ken Gerhart	.05	.01
❏ 214	Jim Gantner	.05	.01
❏ 215	Chet Lemon	.10	.02
❏ 216	Dwight Evans	.15	.05
❏ 217	Don Mattingly	.60	.25
❏ 218	Franklin Stubbs	.05	.01
❏ 219	Pat Tabler	.05	.01
❏ 220	Bo Jackson	.20	.07
❏ 221	Tony Phillips	.05	.01
❏ 222	Tim Wallach	.05	.01
❏ 223	Ruben Sierra	.10	.02
❏ 224	Steve Buechele	.05	.01
❏ 225	Frank White	.10	.02
❏ 226	Alfredo Griffin	.05	.01
❏ 227	Greg Swindell	.05	.01
❏ 228	Willie Randolph	.10	.02
❏ 229	Mike Marshall	.05	.01
❏ 230	Alan Trammell	.10	.02
❏ 231	Eddie Murray	.20	.07
❏ 232	Dale Sveum	.05	.01
❏ 233	Dick Schofield	.05	.01
❏ 234	Jose Oquendo	.05	.01
❏ 235	Bill Doran	.05	.01
❏ 236	Milt Thompson	.05	.01
❏ 237	Marvell Wynne	.05	.01
❏ 238	Bobby Bonilla	.10	.02
❏ 239	Chris Speier	.05	.01
❏ 240	Glenn Braggs	.05	.01
❏ 241	Wally Backman	.05	.01
❏ 242	Ryne Sandberg	.40	.15
❏ 243	Phil Bradley	.05	.01
❏ 244	Kelly Gruber	.05	.01
❏ 245	Tom Brunansky	.05	.01
❏ 246	Ron Oester	.05	.01
❏ 247	Bobby Thigpen	.05	.01
❏ 248	Fred Lynn	.10	.02
❏ 249	Paul Molitor	.10	.02
❏ 250	Darrell Evans	.10	.02
❏ 251	Gary Ward	.05	.01
❏ 252	Bruce Hurst	.05	.01
❏ 253	Bob Welch	.10	.02
❏ 254	Joe Carter	.10	.02
❏ 255	Willie Wilson	.10	.02
❏ 256	Mark McGwire	1.50	.60
❏ 257	Mitch Webster	.05	.01
❏ 258	Brian Downing	.10	.02
❏ 259	Mike Stanley	.05	.01
❏ 260	Carlton Fisk	.15	.05
❏ 261	Billy Hatcher	.05	.01
❏ 262	Glenn Wilson	.05	.01
❏ 263	Ozzie Smith	.30	.10
❏ 264	Randy Ready	.05	.01
❏ 265	Kurt Stillwell	.05	.01
❏ 266	David Palmer	.05	.01
❏ 267	Mike Diaz	.05	.01
❏ 268	Robby Thompson	.05	.01
❏ 269	Andre Dawson	.10	.02
❏ 270	Lee Guetterman	.05	.01
❏ 271	Willie Upshaw	.05	.01
❏ 272	Randy Bush	.05	.01
❏ 273	Larry Sheets	.05	.01
❏ 274	Rob Deer	.05	.01
❏ 275	Kirk Gibson	.20	.07
❏ 276	Marty Barrett	.05	.01
❏ 277	Rickey Henderson	.20	.07
❏ 278	Pedro Guerrero	.10	.02
❏ 279	Brett Butler	.10	.02
❏ 280	Kevin Seitzer	.05	.01
❏ 281	Mike Davis	.05	.01
❏ 282	Andres Galarraga	.10	.02
❏ 283	Devon White	.10	.02
❏ 284	Pete O'Brien	.05	.01
❏ 285	Jerry Hairston	.05	.01
❏ 286	Kevin Bass	.05	.01
❏ 287	Carmelo Martinez	.05	.01
❏ 288	Juan Samuel	.05	.01
❏ 289	Kal Daniels	.05	.01
❏ 290	Albert Hall	.05	.01
❏ 291	Andy Van Slyke	.15	.05
❏ 292	Lee Smith	.10	.02
❏ 293	Vince Coleman	.05	.01
❏ 294	Tom Niedenfuer	.05	.01
❏ 295	Robin Yount	.30	.10
❏ 296	Jeff M. Robinson	.05	.01
❏ 297	Todd Benzinger RC*	.25	.08
❏ 298	Dave Winfield	.10	.02
❏ 299	Mickey Hatcher	.05	.01
❏ 300A	Checklist 248-357	.05	.01
❏ 300B	Checklist 240-345	.05	.01
❏ 301	Bud Black	.05	.01
❏ 302	Jose Canseco	.50	.20
❏ 303	Tom Foley	.05	.01
❏ 304	Pete Incaviglia	.05	.01
❏ 305	Bob Boone	.10	.02
❏ 306	Bill Long	.05	.01
❏ 307	Willie McGee	.10	.02
❏ 308	Ken Caminiti RC	2.00	.75
❏ 309	Darren Daulton	.10	.02
❏ 310	Tracy Jones	.05	.01
❏ 311	Greg Booker	.05	.01
❏ 312	Mike LaValliere	.05	.01
❏ 313	Chili Davis	.10	.02
❏ 314	Glenn Hubbard	.05	.01
❏ 315	Paul Noce	.05	.01
❏ 316	Keith Hernandez	.10	.02
❏ 317	Mark Langston	.05	.01
❏ 318	Keith Atherton	.05	.01
❏ 319	Tony Fernandez	.05	.01
❏ 320	Kent Hrbek	.10	.02
❏ 321	John Cerutti	.05	.01
❏ 322	Mike Kingery	.05	.01
❏ 323	Dave Magadan	.05	.01
❏ 324	Rafael Palmeiro	.40	.15
❏ 325	Jeff Dedmon	.05	.01
❏ 326	Barry Bonds	2.00	.75
❏ 327	Jeffrey Leonard	.05	.01
❏ 328	Tim Flannery	.05	.01
❏ 329	Dave Concepcion	.10	.02
❏ 330	Mike Schmidt	.50	.20
❏ 331	Bill Dawley	.05	.01
❏ 332	Larry Andersen	.05	.01
❏ 333	Jack Howell	.05	.01
❏ 334	Ken Williams	.05	.01
❏ 335	Bryn Smith	.05	.01
❏ 336	Bill Ripken RC*	.25	.08
❏ 337	Greg Brock	.05	.01
❏ 338	Mike Heath	.05	.01
❏ 339	Mike Greenwell	.05	.01
❏ 340	Claudell Washington	.05	.01
❏ 341	Jose Gonzalez	.05	.01
❏ 342	Mel Hall	.05	.01
❏ 343	Jim Eisenreich	.05	.01
❏ 344	Tony Bernazard	.05	.01
❏ 345	Tim Raines	.10	.02
❏ 346	Bob Brower	.05	.01
❏ 347	Larry Parrish	.05	.01
❏ 348	Thad Bosley	.05	.01
❏ 349	Dennis Eckersley	.15	.05
❏ 350	Cory Snyder	.05	.01
❏ 351	Rick Cerone	.05	.01
❏ 352	John Shelby	.05	.01
❏ 353	Larry Herndon	.05	.01
❏ 354	John Habyan	.05	.01
❏ 355	Chuck Crim	.05	.01
❏ 356	Gus Polidor	.05	.01
❏ 357	Ken Dayley	.05	.01
❏ 358	Danny Darwin	.05	.01
❏ 359	Lance Parrish	.10	.02
❏ 360	James Steels	.05	.01
❏ 361	Al Pedrique	.05	.01
❏ 362	Mike Aldrete	.05	.01
❏ 363	Juan Castillo	.05	.01
❏ 364	Len Dykstra	.10	.02
❏ 365	Luis Quinones	.05	.01
❏ 366	Jim Presley	.05	.01
❏ 367	Lloyd Moseby	.05	.01
❏ 368	Kirby Puckett	.20	.07
❏ 369	Eric Davis	.10	.02
❏ 370	Gary Redus	.05	.01
❏ 371	Dave Schmidt	.05	.01
❏ 372	Mark Clear	.05	.01
❏ 373	Dave Bergman	.05	.01
❏ 374	Charles Hudson	.05	.01
❏ 375	Calvin Schiraldi	.05	.01
❏ 376	Alex Trevino	.05	.01
❏ 377	Tom Candiotti	.05	.01
❏ 378	Steve Farr	.05	.01
❏ 379	Mike Gallego	.05	.01
❏ 380	Andy McGaffigan	.05	.01
❏ 381	Kirk McCaskill	.05	.01
❏ 382	Oddibe McDowell	.05	.01
❏ 383	Floyd Bannister	.05	.01
❏ 384	Denny Walling	.05	.01
❏ 385	Don Carman	.05	.01
❏ 386	Todd Worrell	.05	.01
❏ 387	Eric Show	.05	.01
❏ 388	Dave Parker	.10	.02
❏ 389	Rick Mahler	.05	.01
❏ 390	Mike Dunne	.05	.01
❏ 391	Candy Maldonado	.05	.01
❏ 392	Bob Dernier	.05	.01
❏ 393	Dave Valle	.05	.01
❏ 394	Ernie Whitt	.05	.01
❏ 395	Juan Berenguer	.05	.01
❏ 396	Mike Young	.05	.01
❏ 397	Mike Felder	.05	.01
❏ 398	Willie Hernandez	.05	.01
❏ 399	Jim Rice	.10	.02
❏ 400A	Checklist 358-467	.05	.01
❏ 400B	Checklist 346-451	.05	.01
❏ 401	Tommy John	.10	.02
❏ 402	Brian Holton	.05	.01
❏ 403	Carmen Castillo	.05	.01
❏ 404	Jamie Quirk	.05	.01
❏ 405	Dwayne Murphy	.05	.01
❏ 406	Jeff Parrett	.05	.01
❏ 407	Don Sutton	.10	.02
❏ 408	Jerry Browne	.05	.01
❏ 409	Jim Winn	.05	.01
❏ 410	Dave Smith	.05	.01
❏ 411	Shane Mack	.05	.01
❏ 412	Greg Gross	.05	.01
❏ 413	Nick Esasky	.05	.01
❏ 414	Damaso Garcia	.05	.01
❏ 415	Brian Fisher	.05	.01
❏ 416	Brian Dayett	.05	.01
❏ 417	Curt Ford	.05	.01
❏ 418	Mark Williamson	.05	.01
❏ 419	Bill Schroeder	.05	.01
❏ 420	Mike Henneman RC*	.25	.08
❏ 421	John Marzano	.05	.01
❏ 422	Ron Kittle	.05	.01
❏ 423	Matt Young	.05	.01
❏ 424	Steve Balboni	.05	.01
❏ 425	Luis Polonia RC*	.25	.08
❏ 426	Randy St.Claire	.05	.01
❏ 427	Greg Harris	.05	.01
❏ 428	Johnny Ray	.05	.01
❏ 429	Ray Searage	.05	.01
❏ 430	Ricky Horton	.05	.01
❏ 431	Gerald Young	.05	.01
❏ 432	Rick Schu	.05	.01
❏ 433	Paul O'Neill	.15	.05
❏ 434	Rich Gossage	.10	.02
❏ 435	John Cangelosi	.05	.01
❏ 436	Mike LaCoss	.05	.01
❏ 437	Gerald Perry	.05	.01
❏ 438	Dave Martinez	.05	.01
❏ 439	Darryl Strawberry	.10	.02

❑ 440 John Moses .05 .01
❑ 441 Greg Gagne .05 .01
❑ 442 Jesse Barfield .10 .02
❑ 443 George Frazier .05 .01
❑ 444 Garth Iorg .05 .01
❑ 445 Ed Nunez .05 .01
❑ 446 Rick Aguilera .05 .01
❑ 447 Jerry Mumphrey .05 .01
❑ 448 Rafael Ramirez .05 .01
❑ 449 John Smiley RC* .25 .08
❑ 450 Atlee Hammaker .05 .01
❑ 451 Lance McCullers .05 .01
❑ 452 Guy Hoffman .05 .01
❑ 453 Chris James .05 .01
❑ 454 Terry Pendleton .10 .02
❑ 455 Dave Meads .05 .01
❑ 456 Bill Buckner .10 .02
❑ 457 John Pawlowski .05 .01
❑ 458 Bob Sebra .05 .01
❑ 459 Jim Dwyer .05 .01
❑ 460 Jay Aldrich .05 .01
❑ 461 Frank Tanana .10 .02
❑ 462 Oil Can Boyd .05 .01
❑ 463 Dan Pasqua .05 .01
❑ 464 Tim Crews RC .25 .08
❑ 465 Andy Allanson .05 .01
❑ 466 Bill Pecota RC* .10 .02
❑ 467 Steve Ontiveros .05 .01
❑ 468 Hubie Brooks .05 .01
❑ 469 Paul Kilgus .05 .01
❑ 470 Dale Mohorcic .05 .01
❑ 471 Dan Quisenberry .05 .01
❑ 472 Dave Stewart .10 .02
❑ 473 Dave Clark .05 .01
❑ 474 Joel Skinner .05 .01
❑ 475 Dave Anderson .05 .01
❑ 476 Dan Petry .05 .01
❑ 477 Carl Nichols .05 .01
❑ 478 Ernest Riles .05 .01
❑ 479 George Hendrick .10 .02
❑ 480 John Morris .05 .01
❑ 481 Manny Hernandez .05 .01
❑ 482 Jeff Stone .05 .01
❑ 483 Chris Brown .05 .01
❑ 484 Mike Bielecki .05 .01
❑ 485 Dave Dravecky .05 .01
❑ 486 Rick Manning .05 .01
❑ 487 Bill Almon .05 .01
❑ 488 Jim Sundberg .10 .02
❑ 489 Ken Phelps .05 .01
❑ 490 Tom Henke .05 .01
❑ 491 Dan Gladden .05 .01
❑ 492 Barry Larkin .15 .05
❑ 493 Fred Manrique .05 .01
❑ 494 Mike Griffin .05 .01
❑ 495 Mark Knudson .05 .01
❑ 496 Bill Madlock .10 .02
❑ 497 Tim Stoddard .05 .01
❑ 498 Sam Horn RC .10 .02
❑ 499 Tracy Woodson RC .10 .02
❑ 500A Checklist 468-577 .05 .01
❑ 500B Checklist 452-557 .05 .01
❑ 501 Ken Schrom .05 .01
❑ 502 Angel Salazar .05 .01
❑ 503 Eric Plunk .05 .01
❑ 504 Joe Hesketh .05 .01
❑ 505 Greg Minton .05 .01
❑ 506 Geno Petralli .05 .01
❑ 507 Bob James .05 .01
❑ 508 Robbie Wine .05 .01
❑ 509 Jeff Calhoun .05 .01
❑ 510 Steve Lake .05 .01
❑ 511 Mark Grant .05 .01
❑ 512 Frank Williams .05 .01
❑ 513 Jeff Blauser RC .25 .08
❑ 514 Bob Walk .05 .01
❑ 515 Craig Lefferts .05 .01
❑ 516 Manny Trillo .05 .01
❑ 517 Jerry Reed .05 .01
❑ 518 Rick Leach .05 .01
❑ 519 Mark Davidson .05 .01
❑ 520 Jeff Ballard .05 .01
❑ 521 Dave Stapleton .05 .01
❑ 522 Pat Sheridan .05 .01
❑ 523 Al Nipper .05 .01
❑ 524 Steve Trout .05 .01
❑ 525 Jeff Hamilton .05 .01
❑ 526 Tommy Hinzo .05 .01
❑ 527 Lonnie Smith .05 .01
❑ 528 Greg Cadaret .05 .01
❑ 529 Bob McClure UER
(%%Rob~ on front) .05 .01
❑ 530 Chuck Finley .10 .02
❑ 531 Jeff Russell .05 .01
❑ 532 Steve Lyons .05 .01
❑ 533 Terry Puhl .05 .01
❑ 534 Eric Nolte .05 .01
❑ 535 Kent Tekulve .05 .01
❑ 536 Pat Pacillo .05 .01
❑ 537 Charlie Puleo .05 .01
❑ 538 Tom Prince .05 .01
❑ 539 Greg Maddux 1.00 .40
❑ 540 Jim Lindeman .05 .01
❑ 541 Pete Stanicek .05 .01
❑ 542 Steve Kiefer .05 .01
❑ 543A Jim Morrison ERR
(No decimal before
lifetime ave .15 .05
❑ 543B Jim Morrison COR .05 .01
❑ 544 Spike Owen .05 .01
❑ 545 Jay Buhner RC .50 .20
❑ 546 Mike Devereaux RC .25 .08
❑ 547 Jerry Don Gleaton .05 .01
❑ 548 Jose Rijo .10 .02
❑ 549 Dennis Martinez .10 .02
❑ 550 Mike Loynd .05 .01
❑ 551 Darrell Miller .05 .01
❑ 552 Dave LaPoint .05 .01
❑ 553 John Tudor .10 .02
❑ 554 Rocky Childress .05 .01
❑ 555 Wally Ritchie .05 .01
❑ 556 Terry McGriff .05 .01
❑ 557 Dave Leiper .05 .01
❑ 558 Jeff D. Robinson .05 .01
❑ 559 Jose Uribe .05 .01
❑ 560 Ted Simmons .10 .02
❑ 561 Les Lancaster .05 .01
❑ 562 Keith Miller RC .25 .08
❑ 563 Harold Reynolds .10 .02
❑ 564 Gene Larkin RC* .25 .08
❑ 565 Cecil Fielder .10 .02
❑ 566 Roy Smalley .05 .01
❑ 567 Duane Ward .05 .01
❑ 568 Bill Wilkinson .05 .01
❑ 569 Howard Johnson .10 .02
❑ 570 Frank DiPino .05 .01
❑ 571 Pete Smith RC .10 .02
❑ 572 Darnell Coles .05 .01
❑ 573 Don Robinson .05 .01
❑ 574 Rob Nelson UER
(Career 0 RBI,
but 1 RBI in '87) .05 .01
❑ 575 Dennis Rasmussen .05 .01
❑ 576 Steve Jeltz UER
(Photo actually Juan
Samuel; Sam .05 .01
❑ 577 Tom Pagnozzi RC .10 .02
❑ 578 Ty Gainey .05 .01
❑ 579 Gary Lucas .05 .01
❑ 580 Ron Hassey .05 .01
❑ 581 Herm Winningham .05 .01
❑ 582 Rene Gonzales RC .10 .02
❑ 583 Brad Komminsk .05 .01
❑ 584 Doyle Alexander .05 .01
❑ 585 Jeff Sellers .05 .01
❑ 586 Bill Gullickson .05 .01
❑ 587 Tim Belcher .05 .01
❑ 588 Doug Jones RC .25 .08
❑ 589 Melido Perez RC .25 .08
❑ 590 Rick Honeycutt .05 .01
❑ 591 Pascual Perez .05 .01
❑ 592 Curt Wilkerson .05 .01
❑ 593 Steve Howe .05 .01
❑ 594 John Davis .05 .01
❑ 595 Storm Davis .05 .01
❑ 596 Sammy Stewart .05 .01
❑ 597 Neil Allen .05 .01
❑ 598 Alejandro Pena .05 .01
❑ 599 Mark Thurmond .05 .01
❑ 600A Checklist 578-660/BC1-BC26 .05 .01
❑ 600B Checklist 558-660 .05 .01
❑ 601 Jose Mesa RC .25 .08
❑ 602 Don August .05 .01
❑ 603 Terry Leach SP .10 .02
❑ 604 Tom Newell .05 .01
❑ 605 Randall Byers SP .10 .02
❑ 606 Jim Gott .05 .01
❑ 607 Harry Spilman .05 .01
❑ 608 John Candelaria .05 .01
❑ 609 Mike Brumley .05 .01
❑ 610 Mickey Brantley .05 .01
❑ 611 Jose Nunez SP .10 .02
❑ 612 Tom Nieto .05 .01
❑ 613 Rick Reuschel .10 .02
❑ 614 Lee Mazzilli SP .10 .02
❑ 615 Scott Lusader .05 .01
❑ 616 Bobby Meacham .05 .01
❑ 617 Kevin McReynolds SP .10 .02
❑ 618 Gene Garber .05 .01
❑ 619 Barry Lyons SP .10 .02
❑ 620 Randy Myers .10 .02
❑ 621 Donnie Moore .05 .01
❑ 622 Domingo Ramos .05 .01
❑ 623 Ed Romero .05 .01
❑ 624 Greg Myers RC .25 .08
❑ 625 The Ripken Family .40 .15
❑ 626 Pat Perry .05 .01
❑ 627 Andres Thomas SP .10 .02
❑ 628 Matt Williams RC .75 .30
❑ 629 Dave Hengel .05 .01
❑ 630 Jeff Musselman SP .10 .02
❑ 631 Tim Laudner .05 .01
❑ 632 Bob Ojeda SP .10 .02
❑ 633 Rafael Santana .05 .01
❑ 634 Wes Gardner .05 .01
❑ 635 Roberto Kelly SP RC .25 .08
❑ 636 Mike Flanagan SP .10 .02
❑ 637 Jay Bell RC .40 .15
❑ 638 Bob Melvin .05 .01
❑ 639 Damon Berryhill RC .25 .08
❑ 640 David Wells RC 1.00 .40
❑ 641 Stan Musial Puzzle .20 .07
❑ 642 Doug Sisk .05 .01
❑ 643 Keith Hughes .05 .01
❑ 644 Tom Glavine RC 2.50 1.00
❑ 645 Al Newman .05 .01
❑ 646 Scott Sanderson .05 .01
❑ 647 Scott Terry .05 .01
❑ 648 Tim Teufel SP .10 .02
❑ 649 Garry Templeton SP .10 .02
❑ 650 Manny Lee SP .10 .02
❑ 651 Roger McDowell SP .10 .02
❑ 652 Mookie Wilson SP .10 .02
❑ 653 David Cone .10 .02
❑ 654 Ron Gant RC .40 .15
❑ 655 Joe Price SP .10 .02
❑ 656 George Bell SP .10 .02
❑ 657 Gregg Jefferies RC .25 .08
❑ 658 Todd Stottlemyre RC .25 .08
❑ 659 Geronimo Berroa RC .25 .08
❑ 660 Jerry Royster SP .10 .02
❑ XX Kirby Puckett
Blister Pack 1.25 .50

1988 Donruss Rookies

❑ COMP.FACT.SET (56) 10.00 4.00
❑ 1 Mark Grace 2.00 .75
❑ 2 Mike Campbell .15 .05
❑ 3 Todd Frohwirth .15 .05
❑ 4 Dave Stapleton .15 .05

Card		
❑ 5 Shawn Abner	.15	.05
❑ 6 Jose Cecena	.15	.05
❑ 7 Dave Gallagher	.15	.05
❑ 8 Mark Parent	.15	.05
❑ 9 Cecil Espy XRC	.15	.05
❑ 10 Pete Smith	.15	.05
❑ 11 Jay Buhner	1.00	.40
❑ 12 Pat Borders XRC	.50	.20
❑ 13 Doug Jennings	.15	.05
❑ 14 Brady Anderson XRC	.75	.30
❑ 15 Pete Stanicek	.15	.05
❑ 16 Roberto Kelly	.50	.20
❑ 17 Jeff Treadway	.15	.05
❑ 18 Walt Weiss XRC*	.75	.30
❑ 19 Paul Gibson	.15	.05
❑ 20 Tim Crews	.15	.05
❑ 21 Melido Perez	.15	.05
❑ 22 Steve Peters	.15	.05
❑ 23 Craig Worthington	.15	.05
❑ 24 John Trautwein	.15	.05
❑ 25 DeWayne Vaughn	.15	.05
❑ 26 David Wells	1.50	.60
❑ 27 Al Leiter	1.00	.40
❑ 28 Tim Belcher	.15	.05
❑ 29 Johnny Paredes	.15	.05
❑ 30 Chris Sabo XRC	.40	.15
❑ 31 Damon Berryhill	.15	.05
❑ 32 Randy Milligan XRC*	.25	.08
❑ 33 Gary Thurman	.15	.05
❑ 34 Kevin Elster	.15	.05
❑ 35 Roberto Alomar	4.00	1.50
❑ 36 Edgar Martinez XRC	5.00	2.00
❑ 37 Todd Stottlemyre	.15	.05
❑ 38 Joey Meyer	.15	.05
❑ 39 Carl Nichols	.15	.05
❑ 40 Jack McDowell	.75	.30
❑ 41 Jose Bautista XRC	.25	.08
❑ 42 Sil Campusano	.15	.05
❑ 43 John Dopson	.15	.05
❑ 44 Jody Reed	.50	.20
❑ 45 Darrin Jackson XRC*	.25	.08
❑ 46 Mike Capel	.15	.05
❑ 47 Ron Gant	.75	.30
❑ 48 John Davis	.15	.05
❑ 49 Kevin Coffman	.15	.05
❑ 50 Cris Carpenter XRC	.25	.08
❑ 51 Mackey Sasser	.15	.05
❑ 52 Luis Alicea XRC	.50	.20
❑ 53 Bryan Harvey XRC	.30	.10
❑ 54 Steve Ellsworth	.15	.05
❑ 55 Mike Macfarlane XRC	.50	.20
❑ 56 Checklist 1-56	.15	.05

1989 Donruss

Card		
❑ COMPLETE SET (660)	25.00	10.00
❑ COMP.FACT.SET (672)	25.00	10.00
❑ 1 Mike Greenwell DK	.05	.01
❑ 2 Bobby Bonilla DK DP	.10	.02
❑ 3 Pete Incaviglia DK	.05	.01
❑ 4 Chris Sabo DK DP	.10	.02
❑ 5 Robin Yount DK	.40	.15
❑ 6 Tony Gwynn DK DP	.15	.05
❑ 7 Carlton Fisk DK UER	.15	.05
❑ 8 Cory Snyder DK	.05	.01
❑ 9 David Cone DK UER	.10	.02
❑ 10 Kevin Seitzer DK	.05	.01
❑ 11 Rick Reuschel DK	.10	.02
❑ 12 Johnny Ray DK	.05	.01
❑ 13 Dave Schmidt DK	.05	.01
❑ 14 Andres Galarraga DK	.10	.02
❑ 15 Kirk Gibson DK	.10	.02
❑ 16 Fred McGriff DK	.15	.05
❑ 17 Mark Grace DK	.25	.08
❑ 18 Jeff M. Robinson DK	.05	.01
❑ 19 Vince Coleman DK DP	.05	.01
❑ 20 Dave Henderson DK	.05	.01
❑ 21 Harold Reynolds DK	.10	.02
❑ 22 Gerald Perry DK	.05	.01
❑ 23 Frank Viola DK	.10	.02
❑ 24 Steve Bedrosian DK	.05	.01
❑ 25 Glenn Davis DK	.05	.01
❑ 26 Don Mattingly DK	.30	.10
❑ 27 DK Checklist 1-26 DP	.05	.01
❑ 28 Sandy Alomar Jr. RC	.40	.15
❑ 29 Steve Searcy RR	.05	.01
❑ 30 Cameron Drew RR	.05	.01
❑ 31 Gary Sheffield RC	1.50	.60
❑ 32 Erik Hanson RC	.25	.08
❑ 33 Ken Griffey Jr. RC	6.00	2.50
❑ 34 Greg W.Harris RC	.10	.02
❑ 35 Gregg Jefferies	.05	.01
❑ 36 Luis Medina RR	.05	.01
❑ 37 Carlos Quintana RC	.10	.02
❑ 38 Felix Jose RC	.10	.02
❑ 39 Cris Carpenter RC *	.10	.02
❑ 40 Ron Jones RR	.10	.02
❑ 41 Dave West RC	.10	.02
❑ 42 Randy Johnson RC	2.00	.75
❑ 43 Mike Harkey RC	.10	.02
❑ 44 Pete Harnisch RC	.25	.08
❑ 45 Tom Gordon RC	.50	.20
❑ 46 Gregg Olson DP RC	.25	.08
❑ 47 Alex Sanchez RC	.05	.01
❑ 48 Ruben Sierra	.10	.02
❑ 49 Rafael Palmeiro	.25	.08
❑ 50 Ron Gant	.10	.02
❑ 51 Cal Ripken	.75	.30
❑ 52 Wally Joyner	.10	.02
❑ 53 Gary Carter	.10	.02
❑ 54 Andy Van Slyke	.15	.05
❑ 55 Robin Yount	.40	.15
❑ 56 Pete Incaviglia	.05	.01
❑ 57 Greg Brock	.05	.01
❑ 58 Melido Perez	.05	.01
❑ 59 Craig Lefferts	.05	.01
❑ 60 Gary Pettis	.05	.01
❑ 61 Danny Tartabull	.05	.01
❑ 62 Guillermo Hernandez	.05	.01
❑ 63 Ozzie Smith	.40	.15
❑ 64 Gary Gaetti	.10	.02
❑ 65 Mark Davis	.05	.01
❑ 66 Lee Smith	.10	.02
❑ 67 Dennis Eckersley	.15	.05
❑ 68 Wade Boggs	.15	.05
❑ 69 Mike Scott	.10	.02
❑ 70 Fred McGriff	.15	.05
❑ 71 Tom Browning	.05	.01
❑ 72 Claudell Washington	.05	.01
❑ 73 Mel Hall	.05	.01
❑ 74 Don Mattingly	.60	.25
❑ 75 Steve Bedrosian	.05	.01
❑ 76 Juan Samuel	.05	.01
❑ 77 Mike Scioscia	.10	.02
❑ 78 Dave Righetti	.10	.02
❑ 79 Alfredo Griffin	.05	.01
❑ 80 Eric Davis UER (165 games in 1988, should be 135	.10	.02
❑ 81 Juan Berenguer	.05	.01
❑ 82 Todd Worrell	.05	.01
❑ 83 Joe Carter	.10	.02
❑ 84 Steve Sax	.05	.01
❑ 85 Frank White	.10	.02
❑ 86 John Kruk	.10	.02
❑ 87 Rance Mulliniks	.05	.01
❑ 88 Alan Ashby	.05	.01
❑ 89 Charlie Leibrandt	.05	.01
❑ 90 Frank Tanana	.10	.02
❑ 91 Jose Canseco	.25	.08
❑ 92 Barry Bonds	1.50	.60
❑ 93 Harold Reynolds	.10	.02
❑ 94 Mark McLemore	.05	.01
❑ 95 Mark McGwire	1.00	.40
❑ 96 Eddie Murray	.25	.08
❑ 97 Tim Raines	.10	.02
❑ 98 Robby Thompson	.05	.01
❑ 99 Kevin McReynolds	.05	.01
❑ 100 Checklist 28-137	.05	.01
❑ 101 Carlton Fisk	.15	.05
❑ 102 Dave Martinez	.05	.01
❑ 103 Glenn Braggs	.05	.01
❑ 104 Dale Murphy	.15	.05
❑ 105 Ryne Sandberg	.40	.15
❑ 106 Dennis Martinez	.10	.02
❑ 107 Pete O'Brien	.05	.01
❑ 108 Dick Schofield	.05	.01
❑ 109 Henry Cotto	.05	.01
❑ 110 Mike Marshall	.05	.01
❑ 111 Keith Moreland	.05	.01
❑ 112 Tom Brunansky	.05	.01
❑ 113 Kelly Gruber UER (Wrong birthdate)	.05	.01
❑ 114 Brook Jacoby	.05	.01
❑ 115 Keith Brown	.05	.01
❑ 116 Matt Nokes	.05	.01
❑ 117 Keith Hernandez	.10	.02
❑ 118 Bob Forsch	.05	.01
❑ 119 Bert Blyleven UER (... 3000 strikeouts in 1987,	.10	.02
❑ 120 Willie Wilson	.10	.02
❑ 121 Tommy Gregg	.05	.01
❑ 122 Jim Rice	.10	.02
❑ 123 Bob Knepper	.05	.01
❑ 124 Danny Jackson	.05	.01
❑ 125 Eric Plunk	.05	.01
❑ 126 Brian Fisher	.05	.01
❑ 127 Mike Pagliarulo	.05	.01
❑ 128 Tony Gwynn	.30	.10
❑ 129 Lance McCullers	.05	.01
❑ 130 Andres Galarraga	.10	.02
❑ 131 Jose Uribe	.05	.01
❑ 132 Kirk Gibson UER	.10	.02
❑ 133 David Palmer	.05	.01
❑ 134 R.J. Reynolds	.05	.01
❑ 135 Greg Walker	.05	.01
❑ 136 Kirk McCaskill UER (Wrong birthdate)	.05	.01
❑ 137 Shawon Dunston	.05	.01
❑ 138 Andy Allanson	.05	.01
❑ 139 Rob Murphy	.05	.01
❑ 140 Mike Aldrete	.05	.01
❑ 141 Terry Kennedy	.05	.01
❑ 142 Scott Fletcher	.05	.01
❑ 143 Steve Balboni	.05	.01
❑ 144 Bret Saberhagen	.10	.02
❑ 145 Ozzie Virgil	.05	.01
❑ 146 Dale Sveum	.05	.01
❑ 147 Darryl Strawberry	.10	.02
❑ 148 Harold Baines	.10	.02
❑ 149 George Bell	.10	.02
❑ 150 Dave Parker	.10	.02
❑ 151 Bobby Bonilla	.10	.02
❑ 152 Mookie Wilson	.10	.02
❑ 153 Ted Power	.05	.01
❑ 154 Nolan Ryan	1.00	.40
❑ 155 Jeff Reardon	.10	.02
❑ 156 Tim Wallach	.05	.01
❑ 157 Jamie Moyer	.10	.02
❑ 158 Rich Gossage	.10	.02
❑ 159 Dave Winfield	.10	.02
❑ 160 Von Hayes	.05	.01
❑ 161 Willie McGee	.10	.02
❑ 162 Rich Gedman	.05	.01
❑ 163 Tony Pena	.05	.01
❑ 164 Mike Morgan	.05	.01
❑ 165 Charlie Hough	.10	.02
❑ 166 Mike Stanley	.05	.01
❑ 167 Andre Dawson	.10	.02
❑ 168 Joe Boever	.05	.01
❑ 169 Pete Stanicek	.05	.01
❑ 170 Bob Boone	.10	.02
❑ 171 Ron Darling	.10	.02
❑ 172 Bob Walk	.05	.01
❑ 173 Rob Deer	.05	.01
❑ 174 Steve Buechele	.05	.01
❑ 175 Ted Higuera	.05	.01
❑ 176 Ozzie Guillen	.10	.02
❑ 177 Candy Maldonado	.05	.01
❑ 178 Doyle Alexander	.05	.01

❑ 179 Mark Gubicza .05 .01
❑ 180 Alan Trammell .10 .02
❑ 181 Vince Coleman .05 .01
❑ 182 Kirby Puckett .25 .08
❑ 183 Chris Brown .05 .01
❑ 184 Marty Barrett .05 .01
❑ 185 Stan Javier .05 .01
❑ 186 Mike Greenwell .05 .01
❑ 187 Billy Hatcher .05 .01
❑ 188 Jimmy Key .10 .02
❑ 189 Nick Esasky .05 .01
❑ 190 Don Slaught .05 .01
❑ 191 Cory Snyder .05 .01
❑ 192 John Candelaria .05 .01
❑ 193 Mike Schmidt .50 .20
❑ 194 Kevin Gross .05 .01
❑ 195 John Tudor .10 .02
❑ 196 Neil Allen .05 .01
❑ 197 Orel Hershiser .10 .02
❑ 198 Kal Daniels .05 .01
❑ 199 Kent Hrbek .10 .02
❑ 200 Checklist 138-247 .05 .01
❑ 201 Joe Magrane .05 .01
❑ 202 Scott Bailes .05 .01
❑ 203 Tim Belcher .05 .01
❑ 204 George Brett .60 .25
❑ 205 Benito Santiago .10 .02
❑ 206 Tony Fernandez .05 .01
❑ 207 Gerald Young .05 .01
❑ 208 Bo Jackson .25 .08
❑ 209 Chet Lemon .10 .02
❑ 210 Storm Davis .05 .01
❑ 211 Doug Drabek .05 .01
❑ 212 Mickey Brantley UER (Photo actually Nelson Simmo .05 .01
❑ 213 Devon White .10 .02
❑ 214 Dave Stewart .10 .02
❑ 215 Dave Schmidt .05 .01
❑ 216 Bryn Smith .05 .01
❑ 217 Brett Butler .10 .02
❑ 218 Bob Ojeda .05 .01
❑ 219 Steve Rosenberg .05 .01
❑ 220 Hubie Brooks .05 .01
❑ 221 B.J. Surhoff .10 .02
❑ 222 Rick Mahler .05 .01
❑ 223 Rick Sutcliffe .10 .02
❑ 224 Neal Heaton .05 .01
❑ 225 Mitch Williams .05 .01
❑ 226 Chuck Finley .10 .02
❑ 227 Mark Langston .05 .01
❑ 228 Jesse Orosco .05 .01
❑ 229 Ed Whitson .05 .01
❑ 230 Terry Pendleton .10 .02
❑ 231 Lloyd Moseby .05 .01
❑ 232 Greg Swindell .05 .01
❑ 233 John Franco .10 .02
❑ 234 Jack Morris .10 .02
❑ 235 Howard Johnson .10 .02
❑ 236 Glenn Davis .05 .01
❑ 237 Frank Viola .10 .02
❑ 238 Kevin Seitzer .05 .01
❑ 239 Gerald Perry .05 .01
❑ 240 Dwight Evans .15 .05
❑ 241 Jim Deshaies .05 .01
❑ 242 Bo Diaz .05 .01
❑ 243 Carney Lansford .10 .02
❑ 244 Mike LaValliere .05 .01
❑ 245 Rickey Henderson .25 .08
❑ 246 Roberto Alomar .25 .08
❑ 247 Jimmy Jones .05 .01
❑ 248 Pascual Perez .05 .01
❑ 249 Will Clark .15 .05
❑ 250 Fernando Valenzuela .10 .02
❑ 251 Shane Rawley .05 .01
❑ 252 Sid Bream .05 .01
❑ 253 Steve Lyons .05 .01
❑ 254 Brian Downing .10 .02
❑ 255 Mark Grace .25 .08
❑ 256 Tom Candiotti .05 .01
❑ 257 Barry Larkin .15 .05
❑ 258 Mike Krukow .05 .01
❑ 259 Billy Ripken .05 .01
❑ 260 Cecilio Guante .05 .01
❑ 261 Scott Bradley .05 .01
❑ 262 Floyd Bannister .05 .01
❑ 263 Pete Smith .05 .01
❑ 264 Jim Gantner UER (Wrong birthdate) .05 .01
❑ 265 Roger McDowell .05 .01
❑ 266 Bobby Thigpen .05 .01
❑ 267 Jim Clancy .05 .01
❑ 268 Terry Steinbach .10 .02
❑ 269 Mike Dunne .05 .01
❑ 270 Dwight Gooden .10 .02
❑ 271 Mike Heath .05 .01
❑ 272 Dave Smith .05 .01
❑ 273 Keith Atherton .05 .01
❑ 274 Tim Burke .05 .01
❑ 275 Damon Berryhill .05 .01
❑ 276 Vance Law .05 .01
❑ 277 Rich Dotson .05 .01
❑ 278 Lance Parrish .10 .02
❑ 279 Denny Walling .05 .01
❑ 280 Roger Clemens 1.00 .40
❑ 281 Greg Mathews .05 .01
❑ 282 Tom Niedenfuer .05 .01
❑ 283 Paul Kilgus .05 .01
❑ 284 Jose Guzman .05 .01
❑ 285 Calvin Schiraldi .05 .01
❑ 286 Charlie Puleo UER (Career ERA 4.24, should be 4. .05 .01
❑ 287 Joe Orsulak .05 .01
❑ 288 Jack Howell .05 .01
❑ 289 Kevin Elster .05 .01
❑ 290 Jose Lind .05 .01
❑ 291 Paul Molitor .10 .02
❑ 292 Cecil Espy .05 .01
❑ 293 Bill Wegman .05 .01
❑ 294 Dan Pasqua .05 .01
❑ 295 Scott Garrelts UER (Wrong birthdate) .05 .01
❑ 296 Walt Terrell .05 .01
❑ 297 Ed Hearn .05 .01
❑ 298 Lou Whitaker .10 .02
❑ 299 Ken Dayley .05 .01
❑ 300 Checklist 248-357 .05 .01
❑ 301 Tommy Herr .05 .01
❑ 302 Mike Brumley .05 .01
❑ 303 Ellis Burks .10 .02
❑ 304 Curt Young UER (Wrong birthdate) .05 .01
❑ 305 Jody Reed .05 .01
❑ 306 Bill Doran .05 .01
❑ 307 David Wells .10 .02
❑ 308 Ron Robinson .05 .01
❑ 309 Rafael Santana .05 .01
❑ 310 Julio Franco .10 .02
❑ 311 Jack Clark .10 .02
❑ 312 Chris James .05 .01
❑ 313 Milt Thompson .05 .01
❑ 314 John Shelby .05 .01
❑ 315 Al Leiter .25 .08
❑ 316 Mike Davis .05 .01
❑ 317 Chris Sabo RC * .40 .15
❑ 318 Greg Gagne .05 .01
❑ 319 Jose Oquendo .05 .01
❑ 320 John Farrell .05 .01
❑ 321 Franklin Stubbs .05 .01
❑ 322 Kurt Stillwell .05 .01
❑ 323 Shawn Abner .05 .01
❑ 324 Mike Flanagan .05 .01
❑ 325 Kevin Bass .05 .01
❑ 326 Pat Tabler .05 .01
❑ 327 Mike Henneman .05 .01
❑ 328 Rick Honeycutt .05 .01
❑ 329 John Smiley .05 .01
❑ 330 Rey Quinones .05 .01
❑ 331 Johnny Ray .05 .01
❑ 332 Bob Welch .10 .02
❑ 333 Larry Sheets .05 .01
❑ 334 Jeff Parrett .05 .01
❑ 335 Rick Reuschel UER (For Don Robinson, should be J .10 .02
❑ 336 Randy Myers .10 .02
❑ 337 Ken Williams .05 .01
❑ 338 Andy McGaffigan .05 .01
❑ 339 Joey Meyer .05 .01
❑ 340 Dion James .05 .01
❑ 341 Les Lancaster .05 .01
❑ 342 Tom Foley .05 .01
❑ 343 Geno Petralli .05 .01
❑ 344 Dan Petry .05 .01
❑ 345 Alvin Davis .05 .01
❑ 346 Mickey Hatcher .05 .01
❑ 347 Marvell Wynne .05 .01
❑ 348 Danny Cox .05 .01
❑ 349 Dave Stieb .10 .02
❑ 350 Jay Bell .10 .02
❑ 351 Jeff Treadway .05 .01
❑ 352 Luis Salazar .05 .01
❑ 353 Len Dykstra .10 .02
❑ 354 Juan Agosto .05 .01
❑ 355 Gene Larkin .05 .01
❑ 356 Steve Farr .05 .01
❑ 357 Paul Assenmacher .05 .01
❑ 358 Todd Benzinger .05 .01
❑ 359 Larry Andersen .05 .01
❑ 360 Paul O'Neill .15 .05
❑ 361 Ron Hassey .05 .01
❑ 362 Jim Gott .05 .01
❑ 363 Ken Phelps .05 .01
❑ 364 Tim Flannery .05 .01
❑ 365 Randy Ready .05 .01
❑ 366 Nelson Santovenia .05 .01
❑ 367 Kelly Downs .05 .01
❑ 368 Danny Heep .05 .01
❑ 369 Phil Bradley .05 .01
❑ 370 Jeff D. Robinson .05 .01
❑ 371 Ivan Calderon .05 .01
❑ 372 Mike Witt .05 .01
❑ 373 Greg Maddux .50 .20
❑ 374 Carmen Castillo .05 .01
❑ 375 Jose Rijo .10 .02
❑ 376 Joe Price .05 .01
❑ 377 Rene Gonzales .05 .01
❑ 378 Oddibe McDowell .05 .01
❑ 379 Jim Presley .05 .01
❑ 380 Brad Wellman .05 .01
❑ 381 Tom Glavine .25 .08
❑ 382 Dan Plesac .05 .01
❑ 383 Wally Backman .05 .01
❑ 384 Dave Gallagher .05 .01
❑ 385 Tom Henke .05 .01
❑ 386 Luis Polonia .05 .01
❑ 387 Junior Ortiz .05 .01
❑ 388 David Cone .10 .02
❑ 389 Dave Bergman .05 .01
❑ 390 Danny Darwin .05 .01
❑ 391 Dan Gladden .05 .01
❑ 392 John Dopson .05 .01
❑ 393 Frank DiPino .05 .01
❑ 394 Al Nipper .05 .01
❑ 395 Willie Randolph .10 .02
❑ 396 Don Carman .05 .01
❑ 397 Scott Terry .05 .01
❑ 398 Rick Cerone .05 .01
❑ 399 Tom Pagnozzi .05 .01
❑ 400 Checklist 358-467 .05 .01
❑ 401 Mickey Tettleton .05 .01
❑ 402 Curtis Wilkerson .05 .01
❑ 403 Jeff Russell .05 .01
❑ 404 Pat Perry .05 .01
❑ 405 Jose Alvarez RC .10 .02
❑ 406 Rick Schu .05 .01
❑ 407 Sherman Corbett .05 .01
❑ 408 Dave Magadan .05 .01
❑ 409 Bob Kipper .05 .01
❑ 410 Don August .05 .01
❑ 411 Bob Brower .05 .01
❑ 412 Chris Bosio .05 .01
❑ 413 Jerry Reuss .05 .01
❑ 414 Atlee Hammaker .05 .01
❑ 415 Jim Walewander .05 .01
❑ 416 Mike Macfarlane RC * .25 .08
❑ 417 Pat Sheridan .05 .01
❑ 418 Pedro Guerrero .10 .02
❑ 419 Allan Anderson .05 .01
❑ 420 Mark Parent .05 .01
❑ 421 Bob Stanley .05 .01
❑ 422 Mike Gallego .05 .01
❑ 423 Bruce Hurst .05 .01
❑ 424 Dave Meads .05 .01
❑ 425 Jesse Barfield .10 .02
❑ 426 Rob Dibble RC .40 .15
❑ 427 Joel Skinner .05 .01

❑ 428 Ron Kittle .05 .01
❑ 429 Rick Rhoden .05 .01
❑ 430 Bob Dernier .05 .01
❑ 431 Steve Jeltz .05 .01
❑ 432 Rick Dempsey .05 .01
❑ 433 Roberto Kelly .05 .01
❑ 434 Dave Anderson .05 .01
❑ 435 Herm Winningham .05 .01
❑ 436 Al Newman .05 .01
❑ 437 Jose DeLeon .05 .01
❑ 438 Doug Jones .05 .01
❑ 439 Brian Holton .05 .01
❑ 440 Jeff Montgomery .05 .01
❑ 441 Dickie Thon .05 .01
❑ 442 Cecil Fielder .10 .02
❑ 443 John Fishel .05 .01
❑ 444 Jerry Don Gleaton .05 .01
❑ 445 Paul Gibson .05 .01
❑ 446 Walt Weiss .05 .01
❑ 447 Glenn Wilson .05 .01
❑ 448 Mike Moore .05 .01
❑ 449 Chili Davis .10 .02
❑ 450 Dave Henderson .05 .01
❑ 451 Jose Bautista RC .10 .02
❑ 452 Rex Hudler .05 .01
❑ 453 Bob Brenly .05 .01
❑ 454 Mackey Sasser .05 .01
❑ 455 Daryl Boston .05 .01
❑ 456 Mike R. Fitzgerald .05 .01
❑ 457 Jeffrey Leonard .05 .01
❑ 458 Bruce Sutter .10 .02
❑ 459 Mitch Webster .05 .01
❑ 460 Joe Hesketh .05 .01
❑ 461 Bobby Witt .05 .01
❑ 462 Stu Cliburn .05 .01
❑ 463 Scott Bankhead .05 .01
❑ 464 Ramon Martinez RC .25 .08
❑ 465 Dave Leiper .05 .01
❑ 466 Luis Alicea RC * .25 .08
❑ 467 John Cerutti .05 .01
❑ 468 Ron Washington .05 .01
❑ 469 Jeff Reed .05 .01
❑ 470 Jeff M. Robinson .05 .01
❑ 471 Sid Fernandez .05 .01
❑ 472 Terry Puhl .05 .01
❑ 473 Charlie Lea .05 .01
❑ 474 Israel Sanchez .05 .01
❑ 475 Bruce Benedict .05 .01
❑ 476 Oil Can Boyd .05 .01
❑ 477 Craig Reynolds .05 .01
❑ 478 Frank Williams .05 .01
❑ 479 Greg Cadaret .05 .01
❑ 480 Randy Kramer .05 .01
❑ 481 Dave Eiland .05 .01
❑ 482 Eric Show .05 .01
❑ 483 Garry Templeton .10 .02
❑ 484 Wallace Johnson .05 .01
❑ 485 Kevin Mitchell .10 .02
❑ 486 Tim Crews .05 .01
❑ 487 Mike Maddux .05 .01
❑ 488 Dave LaPoint .05 .01
❑ 489 Fred Manrique .05 .01
❑ 490 Greg Minton .05 .01
❑ 491 Doug Dascenzo UER
(Photo actually
Damon Berryhill .05 .01
❑ 492 Willie Upshaw .05 .01
❑ 493 Jack Armstrong RC * .25 .08
❑ 494 Kirt Manwaring .05 .01
❑ 495 Jeff Ballard .05 .01
❑ 496 Jeff Kunkel .05 .01
❑ 497 Mike Campbell .05 .01
❑ 498 Gary Thurman .05 .01
❑ 499 Zane Smith .05 .01
❑ 500 Checklist 468-577 DP .05 .01
❑ 501 Mike Birkbeck .05 .01
❑ 502 Terry Leach .05 .01
❑ 503 Shawn Hillegas .05 .01
❑ 504 Manny Lee .05 .01
❑ 505 Doug Jennings .05 .01
❑ 506 Ken Oberkfell .05 .01
❑ 507 Tim Teufel .05 .01
❑ 508 Tom Brookens .05 .01
❑ 509 Rafael Ramirez .05 .01
❑ 510 Fred Toliver .05 .01
❑ 511 Brian Holman RC * .10 .02
❑ 512 Mike Bielecki .05 .01
❑ 513 Jeff Pico .05 .01
❑ 514 Charles Hudson .05 .01
❑ 515 Bruce Ruffin .05 .01
❑ 516 Larry McWilliams UER
(New Richland, should
be No .05 .01
❑ 517 Jeff Sellers .05 .01
❑ 518 John Costello .05 .01
❑ 519 Brady Anderson RC .40 .15
❑ 520 Craig McMurtry .05 .01
❑ 521 Ray Hayward DP .05 .01
❑ 522 Drew Hall DP .05 .01
❑ 523 Mark Lemke DP RC .40 .15
❑ 524 Oswald Peraza DP .05 .01
❑ 525 Bryan Harvey DP RC * .25 .08
❑ 526 Rick Aguilera DP .05 .01
❑ 527 Tom Prince DP .05 .01
❑ 528 Mark Clear DP .05 .01
❑ 529 Jerry Browne DP .05 .01
❑ 530 Juan Castillo DP .05 .01
❑ 531 Jack McDowell DP .10 .02
❑ 532 Chris Speier DP .05 .01
❑ 533 Darrell Evans DP .10 .02
❑ 534 Luis Aquino DP .05 .01
❑ 535 Eric King DP .05 .01
❑ 536 Ken Hill DP RC .25 .08
❑ 537 Randy Bush DP .05 .01
❑ 538 Shane Mack DP .05 .01
❑ 539 Tom Bolton DP .05 .01
❑ 540 Gene Nelson DP .05 .01
❑ 541 Wes Gardner DP .05 .01
❑ 542 Ken Caminiti DP .15 .05
❑ 543 Duane Ward DP .05 .01
❑ 544 Norm Charlton DP RC .25 .08
❑ 545 Hal Morris DP RC .25 .08
❑ 546 Rich Yett DP .05 .01
❑ 547 Hensley Meulens DP RC .10 .02
❑ 548 Greg A. Harris DP .05 .01
❑ 549 Darren Daulton .10 .02
❑ 550 Jeff Hamilton DP .05 .01
❑ 551 Luis Aguayo DP .05 .01
❑ 552 Tim Leary DP
(Resembles M.Marshall) .05 .01
❑ 553 Ron Oester DP .05 .01
❑ 554 Steve Lombardozzi DP .05 .01
❑ 555 Tim Jones DP .05 .01
❑ 556 Bud Black DP .05 .01
❑ 557 Alejandro Pena DP .05 .01
❑ 558 Jose DeJesus DP .05 .01
❑ 559 Dennis Rasmussen DP .05 .01
❑ 560 Pat Borders DP RC * .25 .08
❑ 561 Craig Biggio RC 3.00 1.25
❑ 562 Luis DeLosSantos DP .05 .01
❑ 563 Fred Lynn DP .10 .02
❑ 564 Todd Burns DP .05 .01
❑ 565 Felix Fermin DP .05 .01
❑ 566 Darnell Coles DP .05 .01
❑ 567 Willie Fraser DP .05 .01
❑ 568 Glenn Hubbard DP .05 .01
❑ 569 Craig Worthington DP .05 .01
❑ 570 Johnny Paredes DP .05 .01
❑ 571 Don Robinson DP .05 .01
❑ 572 Barry Lyons DP .05 .01
❑ 573 Bill Long DP .05 .01
❑ 574 Tracy Jones DP .05 .01
❑ 575 Juan Nieves DP .05 .01
❑ 576 Andres Thomas DP .05 .01
❑ 577 Rolando Roomes DP .05 .01
❑ 578 Luis Rivera UER DP
(Wrong birthdate) .05 .01
❑ 579 Chad Kreuter RC .25 .08
❑ 580 Tony Armas DP .10 .02
❑ 581 Jay Buhner .10 .02
❑ 582 Ricky Horton DP .05 .01
❑ 583 Andy Hawkins DP .05 .01
❑ 584 Sil Campusano .05 .01
❑ 585 Dave Clark .05 .01
❑ 586 Van Snider DP .05 .01
❑ 587 Todd Frohwirth DP .05 .01
❑ 588 Warren Spahn Puzzle DP .15 .05
❑ 589 William Brennan .05 .01
❑ 590 German Gonzalez .05 .01
❑ 591 Ernie Whitt DP .05 .01
❑ 592 Jeff Blauser .05 .01
❑ 593 Spike Owen DP .05 .01
❑ 594 Matt Williams .25 .08
❑ 595 Lloyd McClendon DP .05 .01
❑ 596 Steve Ontiveros .05 .01
❑ 597 Scott Medvin .05 .01
❑ 598 Hipolito Pena DP .05 .01
❑ 599 Jerald Clark DP RC .10 .02
❑ 600A Checklist 578-660 DP .05 .01
❑ 600B Checklist 578-660 DP .05 .01
❑ 600C Checklist 578-660 DP .05 .01
❑ 601 Carmelo Martinez DP .05 .01
❑ 602 Mike LaCoss .05 .01
❑ 603 Mike Devereaux .05 .01
❑ 604 Alex Madrid DP .05 .01
❑ 605 Gary Redus DP .05 .01
❑ 606 Lance Johnson .05 .01
❑ 607 Terry Clark DP .05 .01
❑ 608 Manny Trillo DP .05 .01
❑ 609 Scott Jordan RC .25 .08
❑ 610 Jay Howell DP .05 .01
❑ 611 Francisco Melendez .05 .01
❑ 612 Mike Boddicker .05 .01
❑ 613 Kevin Brown .25 .08
❑ 614 Dave Valle .05 .01
❑ 615 Tim Laudner DP .05 .01
❑ 616 Andy Nezelek UER
(Wrong birthdate) .05 .01
❑ 617 Chuck Crim .05 .01
❑ 618 Jack Savage DP .05 .01
❑ 619 Adam Peterson .05 .01
❑ 620 Todd Stottlemyre .05 .01
❑ 621 Lance Blankenship RC .10 .02
❑ 622 Miguel Garcia DP .05 .01
❑ 623 Keith A. Miller DP .05 .01
❑ 624 Ricky Jordan DP RC * .25 .08
❑ 625 Ernest Riles DP .05 .01
❑ 626 John Moses DP .05 .01
❑ 627 Nelson Liriano DP .05 .01
❑ 628 Mike Smithson DP .05 .01
❑ 629 Scott Sanderson .05 .01
❑ 630 Dale Mohorcic .05 .01
❑ 631 Marvin Freeman DP .05 .01
❑ 632 Mike Young DP .05 .01
❑ 633 Dennis Lamp .05 .01
❑ 634 Dante Bichette RC .40 .15
❑ 635 Curt Schilling RC 4.00 1.50
❑ 636 Scott May DP .05 .01
❑ 637 Mike Schooler .05 .01
❑ 638 Rick Leach .05 .01
❑ 639 Tom Lampkin UER
(Throws Left, should
be Throws R .05 .01
❑ 640 Brian Meyer .05 .01
❑ 641 Brian Harper .05 .01
❑ 642 John Smoltz RC 1.50 .60
❑ 643 Jose Canseco 40/40 .25 .08
❑ 644 Bill Schroeder .05 .01
❑ 645 Edgar Martinez .25 .08
❑ 646 Dennis Cook RC .25 .08
❑ 647 Barry Jones .05 .01
❑ 648 Orel Hershiser
(59 and Counting) .10 .02
❑ 649 Rod Nichols .05 .01
❑ 650 Jody Davis .05 .01
❑ 651 Bob Milacki .05 .01
❑ 652 Mike Jackson .05 .01
❑ 653 Derek Lilliquist RC .10 .02
❑ 654 Paul Mirabella .05 .01
❑ 655 Mike Diaz .05 .01
❑ 656 Jeff Musselman .05 .01
❑ 657 Jerry Reed .05 .01
❑ 658 Kevin Blankenship .05 .01
❑ 659 Wayne Tolleson .05 .01
❑ 660 Eric Hetzel .05 .01
❑ BC Jose Canseco
Blister Pack 2.00 .75

1989 Donruss Rookies

❑ COMP.FACT.SET (56) 15.00 6.00
❑ 1 Gary Sheffield 2.00 .75
❑ 2 Gregg Jefferies .10 .02
❑ 3 Ken Griffey Jr. ! 8.00 3.00
❑ 4 Tom Gordon .25 .10
❑ 5 Billy Spiers RC .25 .08
❑ 6 Deion Sanders RC 1.50 .60
❑ 7 Donn Pall .05 .01

❑ 8 Steve Carter	.05	.01
❑ 9 Francisco Oliveras	.05	.01
❑ 10 Steve Wilson RC	.10	.02
❑ 11 Bob Geren RC	.05	.01
❑ 12 Tony Castillo RC	.10	.02
❑ 13 Kenny Rogers RC	2.50	1.00
❑ 14 Carlos Martinez RC	.10	.02
❑ 15 Edgar Martinez	.25	.08
❑ 16 Jim Abbott RC	1.00	.40
❑ 17 Torey Lovullo RC	.10	.02
❑ 18 Mark Carreon	.05	.01
❑ 19 Geronimo Berroa	.05	.01
❑ 20 Luis Medina	.05	.01
❑ 21 Sandy Alomar Jr.	.15	.05
❑ 22 Bob Milacki	.05	.01
❑ 23 Joe Girardi RC	.40	.15
❑ 24 German Gonzalez	.05	.01
❑ 25 Craig Worthington	.05	.01
❑ 26 Jerome Walton RC	.25	.08
❑ 27 Gary Wayne	.05	.01
❑ 28 Tim Jones	.05	.01
❑ 29 Dante Bichette	.15	.05
❑ 30 Alexis Infante RC	.05	.01
❑ 31 Ken Hill	.25	.08
❑ 32 Dwight Smith RC	.25	.08
❑ 33 Luis de los Santos	.05	.01
❑ 34 Eric Yelding	.05	.01
❑ 35 Gregg Olson	.25	.08
❑ 36 Phil Stephenson	.05	.01
❑ 37 Ken Patterson	.05	.01
❑ 38 Rick Wrona	.05	.01
❑ 39 Mike Brumley	.05	.01
❑ 40 Cris Carpenter	.05	.01
❑ 41 Jeff Brantley RC	.25	.08
❑ 42 Ron Jones	.05	.01
❑ 43 Randy Johnson	2.00	.75
❑ 44 Kevin Brown	.25	.08
❑ 45 Ramon Martinez	.10	.02
❑ 46 Greg W.Harris	.05	.01
❑ 47 Steve Finley RC	.75	.30
❑ 48 Randy Kramer	.05	.01
❑ 49 Erik Hanson	.10	.02
❑ 50 Matt Merullo	.05	.01
❑ 51 Mike Devereaux	.05	.01
❑ 52 Clay Parker	.05	.01
❑ 53 Omar Vizquel RC	1.00	.40
❑ 54 Derek Lilliquist	.05	.01
❑ 55 Junior Felix RC	.10	.02
❑ 56 Checklist 1-56	.05	.01

1990 Donruss

❑ COMPLETE SET (716)	15.00	6.00
❑ COMP.FACT.SET (728)	15.00	6.00
❑ COMP.YAZ PUZZLE	1.00	.40
❑ 1 Bo Jackson DK	.15	.05
❑ 2 Steve Sax DK	.05	.01
❑ 3A Ruben Sierra DK ERR	.10	.02
❑ 3B Ruben Sierra DK COR	.10	.02
❑ 4 Ken Griffey Jr. DK	.40	.15
❑ 5 Mickey Tettleton DK	.05	.01
❑ 6 Dave Stewart DK	.05	.01
❑ 7 Jim Deshaies DK DP	.05	.01
❑ 8 John Smoltz DK	.25	.08
❑ 9 Mike Bielecki DK	.05	.01
❑ 10A Brian Downing DK ERR	.15	.05
❑ 10B Brian Downing DK COR	.05	.01
❑ 11 Kevin Mitchell DK	.05	.01
❑ 12 Kelly Gruber DK	.05	.01
❑ 13 Joe Magrane DK	.05	.01
❑ 14 John Franco DK	.10	.02
❑ 15 Ozzie Guillen DK	.10	.02
❑ 16 Lou Whitaker DK	.05	.01
❑ 17 John Smiley DK	.05	.01
❑ 18 Howard Johnson DK	.05	.01
❑ 19 Willie Randolph DK	.10	.02
❑ 20 Chris Bosio DK	.05	.01
❑ 21 Tommy Herr DK DP	.05	.01
❑ 22 Dan Gladden DK	.05	.01
❑ 23 Ellis Burks DK	.10	.02
❑ 24 Pete O'Brien DK	.05	.01
❑ 25 Bryn Smith DK	.05	.01
❑ 26 Ed Whitson DK DP	.05	.01
❑ 27 DK Checklist 1-27 DP (Comments on Perez-Steele	.05	.01
❑ 28 Robin Ventura	.25	.08
❑ 29 Todd Zeile	.10	.02
❑ 30 Sandy Alomar Jr.	.10	.02
❑ 31 Kent Mercker RC	.25	.08
❑ 32 Ben McDonald RC	.25	.08
❑ 33A Juan Gonzalez RevNg RC	2.00	.75
❑ 33B Juan Gonzalez COR RC	1.00	.40
❑ 34 Eric Anthony RC	.10	.02
❑ 35 Mike Fetters RC	.25	.08
❑ 36 Marquis Grissom RC	.40	.15
❑ 37 Greg Vaughn	.05	.01
❑ 38 Brian DuBois RC	.10	.02
❑ 39 Steve Avery	.05	.01
❑ 40 Mark Gardner RC	.10	.02
❑ 41 Andy Benes	.10	.02
❑ 42 Delino DeShields RC	.25	.08
❑ 43 Scott Coolbaugh RC	.10	.02
❑ 44 Pat Combs DP	.05	.01
❑ 45 Alex Sanchez DP	.05	.01
❑ 46 Kelly Mann DP RC	.10	.02
❑ 47 Julio Machado RC	.10	.02
❑ 48 Pete Incaviglia	.05	.01
❑ 49 Shawon Dunston	.05	.01
❑ 50 Jeff Treadway	.05	.01
❑ 51 Jeff Ballard	.05	.01
❑ 52 Claudell Washington	.05	.01
❑ 53 Juan Samuel	.05	.01
❑ 54 John Smiley	.05	.01
❑ 55 Rob Deer	.05	.01
❑ 56 Geno Petralli	.05	.01
❑ 57 Chris Bosio	.05	.01
❑ 58 Carlton Fisk	.15	.05
❑ 59 Kirt Manwaring	.05	.01
❑ 60 Chet Lemon	.05	.01
❑ 61 Bo Jackson	.25	.08
❑ 62 Doyle Alexander	.05	.01
❑ 63 Pedro Guerrero	.05	.01
❑ 64 Allan Anderson	.05	.01
❑ 65 Greg W. Harris	.05	.01
❑ 66 Mike Greenwell	.05	.01
❑ 67 Walt Weiss	.05	.01
❑ 68 Wade Boggs	.15	.05
❑ 69 Jim Clancy	.05	.01
❑ 70 Junior Felix	.05	.01
❑ 71 Barry Larkin	.15	.05
❑ 72 Dave LaPoint	.05	.01
❑ 73 Joel Skinner	.05	.01
❑ 74 Jesse Barfield	.05	.01
❑ 75 Tommy Herr	.05	.01
❑ 76 Ricky Jordan	.05	.01
❑ 77 Eddie Murray	.25	.08
❑ 78 Steve Sax	.05	.01
❑ 79 Tim Belcher	.05	.01
❑ 80 Danny Jackson	.05	.01
❑ 81 Kent Hrbek	.10	.02
❑ 82 Milt Thompson	.05	.01
❑ 83 Brook Jacoby	.05	.01
❑ 84 Mike Marshall	.05	.01
❑ 85 Kevin Seitzer	.05	.01
❑ 86 Tony Gwynn	.30	.10
❑ 87 Dave Stieb	.10	.02
❑ 88 Dave Smith	.05	.01
❑ 89 Bret Saberhagen	.10	.02
❑ 90 Alan Trammell	.10	.02
❑ 91 Tony Phillips	.05	.01
❑ 92 Doug Drabek	.05	.01
❑ 93 Jeffrey Leonard	.05	.01
❑ 94 Wally Joyner	.10	.02
❑ 95 Carney Lansford	.10	.02
❑ 96 Cal Ripken	.75	.30
❑ 97 Andres Galarraga	.10	.02
❑ 98 Kevin Mitchell	.05	.01
❑ 99 Howard Johnson	.05	.01
❑ 100A Checklist 28-129	.05	.01
❑ 100B Checklist 28-125	.05	.01
❑ 101 Melido Perez	.05	.01
❑ 102 Spike Owen	.05	.01
❑ 103 Paul Molitor	.10	.02
❑ 104 Geronimo Berroa	.05	.01
❑ 105 Ryne Sandberg	.40	.15
❑ 106 Bryn Smith	.05	.01
❑ 107 Steve Buechele	.05	.01
❑ 108 Jim Abbott	.15	.05
❑ 109 Alvin Davis	.05	.01
❑ 110 Lee Smith	.10	.02
❑ 111 Roberto Alomar	.15	.05
❑ 112 Rick Reuschel	.05	.01
❑ 113A Kelly Gruber ERR (Born 2/22)	.05	.01
❑ 113B Kelly Gruber COR (Born 2/26; corrected in factor	.05	.01
❑ 114 Joe Carter	.10	.02
❑ 115 Jose Rijo	.05	.01
❑ 116 Greg Minton	.05	.01
❑ 117 Bob Ojeda	.05	.01
❑ 118 Glenn Davis	.05	.01
❑ 119 Jeff Reardon	.10	.02
❑ 120 Kurt Stillwell	.05	.01
❑ 121 John Smoltz	.25	.08
❑ 122 Dwight Evans	.15	.05
❑ 123 Eric Yelding RC	.05	.01
❑ 124 John Franco	.10	.02
❑ 125 Jose Canseco	.15	.05
❑ 126 Barry Bonds	1.00	.40
❑ 127 Lee Guetterman	.05	.01
❑ 128 Jack Clark	.10	.02
❑ 129 Dave Valle	.05	.01
❑ 130 Hubie Brooks	.05	.01
❑ 131 Ernest Riles	.05	.01
❑ 132 Mike Morgan	.05	.01
❑ 133 Steve Jeltz	.05	.01
❑ 134 Jeff D. Robinson	.05	.01
❑ 135 Ozzie Guillen	.10	.02
❑ 136 Chili Davis	.10	.02
❑ 137 Mitch Webster	.05	.01
❑ 138 Jerry Browne	.05	.01
❑ 139 Bo Diaz	.05	.01
❑ 140 Robby Thompson	.05	.01
❑ 141 Craig Worthington	.05	.01
❑ 142 Julio Franco	.10	.02
❑ 143 Brian Holman	.05	.01
❑ 144 George Brett	.60	.25
❑ 145 Tom Glavine	.15	.05
❑ 146 Robin Yount	.40	.15
❑ 147 Gary Carter	.10	.02
❑ 148 Ron Kittle	.05	.01
❑ 149 Tony Fernandez	.05	.01
❑ 150 Dave Stewart	.10	.02
❑ 151 Gary Gaetti	.10	.02
❑ 152 Kevin Elster	.05	.01
❑ 153 Gerald Perry	.05	.01
❑ 154 Jesse Orosco	.05	.01
❑ 155 Wally Backman	.05	.01
❑ 156 Dennis Martinez	.10	.02
❑ 157 Rick Sutcliffe	.10	.02
❑ 158 Greg Maddux	.40	.15
❑ 159 Andy Hawkins	.05	.01

❑ 160 John Kruk .10 .02
❑ 161 Jose Oquendo .05 .01
❑ 162 John Dopson .05 .01
❑ 163 Joe Magrane .05 .01
❑ 164 Bill Ripken .05 .01
❑ 165 Fred Manrique .05 .01
❑ 166 Nolan Ryan 1.00 .40
❑ 167 Damon Berryhill .05 .01
❑ 168 Dale Murphy .15 .05
❑ 169 Mickey Tettleton .05 .01
❑ 170A Kirk McCaskill ERR (Born 4/19) .05 .01
❑ 170B Kirk McCaskill COR (Born 4/9; corrected in facto .05 .01
❑ 171 Dwight Gooden .10 .02
❑ 172 Jose Lind .05 .01
❑ 173 B.J. Surhoff .10 .02
❑ 174 Ruben Sierra .10 .02
❑ 175 Dan Plesac .05 .01
❑ 176 Dan Pasqua .05 .01
❑ 177 Kelly Downs .05 .01
❑ 178 Matt Nokes .05 .01
❑ 179 Luis Aquino .05 .01
❑ 180 Frank Tanana .05 .01
❑ 181 Tony Pena .05 .01
❑ 182 Dan Gladden .05 .01
❑ 183 Bruce Hurst .05 .01
❑ 184 Roger Clemens 1.00 .40
❑ 185 Mark McGwire 1.00 .40
❑ 186 Rob Murphy .05 .01
❑ 187 Jim Deshaies .05 .01
❑ 188 Fred McGriff .25 .08
❑ 189 Rob Dibble .10 .02
❑ 190 Don Mattingly .60 .25
❑ 191 Felix Fermin .05 .01
❑ 192 Roberto Kelly .05 .01
❑ 193 Dennis Cook .05 .01
❑ 194 Darren Daulton .10 .02
❑ 195 Alfredo Griffin .05 .01
❑ 196 Eric Plunk .05 .01
❑ 197 Orel Hershiser .10 .02
❑ 198 Paul O'Neill .15 .05
❑ 199 Randy Bush .05 .01
❑ 200A Checklist 130-231 .05 .01
❑ 200B Checklist 126-223 .05 .01
❑ 201 Ozzie Smith .40 .15
❑ 202 Pete O'Brien .05 .01
❑ 203 Jay Howell .05 .01
❑ 204 Mark Gubicza .05 .01
❑ 205 Ed Whitson .05 .01
❑ 206 George Bell .05 .01
❑ 207 Mike Scott .05 .01
❑ 208 Charlie Leibrandt .05 .01
❑ 209 Mike Heath .05 .01
❑ 210 Dennis Eckersley .10 .02
❑ 211 Mike LaValliere .05 .01
❑ 212 Darnell Coles .05 .01
❑ 213 Lance Parrish .05 .01
❑ 214 Mike Moore .05 .01
❑ 215 Steve Finley .10 .02
❑ 216 Tim Raines .10 .02
❑ 217A Scott Garrelts ERR (Born 10/20) .05 .01
❑ 217B Scott Garrelts COR (Born 10/30; corrected in fac .05 .01
❑ 218 Kevin McReynolds .05 .01
❑ 219 Dave Gallagher .05 .01
❑ 220 Tim Wallach .05 .01
❑ 221 Chuck Crim .05 .01
❑ 222 Lonnie Smith .05 .01
❑ 223 Andre Dawson .10 .02
❑ 224 Nelson Santovenia .05 .01
❑ 225 Rafael Palmeiro .15 .05
❑ 226 Devon White .10 .02
❑ 227 Harold Reynolds .10 .02
❑ 228 Ellis Burks .15 .05
❑ 229 Mark Parent .05 .01
❑ 230 Will Clark .15 .05
❑ 231 Jimmy Key .10 .02
❑ 232 John Farrell .05 .01
❑ 233 Eric Davis .10 .02
❑ 234 Johnny Ray .05 .01
❑ 235 Darryl Strawberry .10 .02
❑ 236 Bill Doran .05 .01
❑ 237 Greg Gagne .05 .01
❑ 238 Jim Eisenreich .05 .01
❑ 239 Tommy Gregg .05 .01
❑ 240 Marty Barrett .05 .01
❑ 241 Rafael Ramirez .05 .01
❑ 242 Chris Sabo .05 .01
❑ 243 Dave Henderson .05 .01
❑ 244 Andy Van Slyke .15 .05
❑ 245 Alvaro Espinoza .05 .01
❑ 246 Garry Templeton .05 .01
❑ 247 Gene Harris .05 .01
❑ 248 Kevin Gross .05 .01
❑ 249 Brett Butler .10 .02
❑ 250 Willie Randolph .10 .02
❑ 251 Roger McDowell .05 .01
❑ 252 Rafael Belliard .05 .01
❑ 253 Steve Rosenberg .05 .01
❑ 254 Jack Howell .05 .01
❑ 255 Marvell Wynne .05 .01
❑ 256 Tom Candiotti .05 .01
❑ 257 Todd Benzinger .05 .01
❑ 258 Don Robinson .05 .01
❑ 259 Phil Bradley .05 .01
❑ 260 Cecil Espy .05 .01
❑ 261 Scott Bankhead .05 .01
❑ 262 Frank White .10 .02
❑ 263 Andres Thomas .05 .01
❑ 264 Glenn Braggs .05 .01
❑ 265 David Cone .10 .02
❑ 266 Bobby Thigpen .05 .01
❑ 267 Nelson Liriano .05 .01
❑ 268 Terry Steinbach .05 .01
❑ 269 Kirby Puckett .25 .08
❑ 270 Gregg Jefferies .10 .02
❑ 271 Jeff Blauser .05 .01
❑ 272 Cory Snyder .05 .01
❑ 273 Roy Smith .05 .01
❑ 274 Tom Foley .05 .01
❑ 275 Mitch Williams .05 .01
❑ 276 Paul Kilgus .05 .01
❑ 277 Don Slaught .05 .01
❑ 278 Von Hayes .05 .01
❑ 279 Vince Coleman .05 .01
❑ 280 Mike Boddicker .05 .01
❑ 281 Ken Dayley .05 .01
❑ 282 Mike Devereaux .05 .01
❑ 283 Kenny Rogers .10 .02
❑ 284 Jeff Russell .05 .01
❑ 285 Jerome Walton .05 .01
❑ 286 Derek Lilliquist .05 .01
❑ 287 Joe Orsulak .05 .01
❑ 288 Dick Schofield .05 .01
❑ 289 Ron Darling .05 .01
❑ 290 Bobby Bonilla .10 .02
❑ 291 Jim Gantner .05 .01
❑ 292 Bobby Witt .05 .01
❑ 293 Greg Brock .05 .01
❑ 294 Ivan Calderon .05 .01
❑ 295 Steve Bedrosian .05 .01
❑ 296 Mike Henneman .05 .01
❑ 297 Tom Gordon .10 .02
❑ 298 Lou Whitaker .10 .02
❑ 299 Terry Pendleton .10 .02
❑ 300A Checklist 232-333 .05 .01
❑ 300B Checklist 224-321 .05 .01
❑ 301 Juan Berenguer .05 .01
❑ 302 Mark Davis .05 .01
❑ 303 Nick Esasky .05 .01
❑ 304 Rickey Henderson .25 .08
❑ 305 Rick Cerone .05 .01
❑ 306 Craig Biggio .25 .08
❑ 307 Duane Ward .05 .01
❑ 308 Tom Browning .05 .01
❑ 309 Walt Terrell .05 .01
❑ 310 Greg Swindell .05 .01
❑ 311 Dave Righetti .05 .01
❑ 312 Mike Maddux .05 .01
❑ 313 Len Dykstra .10 .02
❑ 314 Jose Gonzalez .05 .01
❑ 315 Steve Balboni .05 .01
❑ 316 Mike Scioscia .05 .01
❑ 317 Ron Oester .05 .01
❑ 318 Gary Wayne .05 .01
❑ 319 Todd Worrell .05 .01
❑ 320 Doug Jones .05 .01
❑ 321 Jeff Hamilton .05 .01
❑ 322 Danny Tartabull .05 .01
❑ 323 Chris James .05 .01
❑ 324 Mike Flanagan .05 .01
❑ 325 Gerald Young .05 .01
❑ 326 Bob Boone .10 .02
❑ 327 Frank Williams .05 .01
❑ 328 Dave Parker .10 .02
❑ 329 Sid Bream .05 .01
❑ 330 Mike Schooler .05 .01
❑ 331 Bert Blyleven .10 .02
❑ 332 Bob Welch .05 .01
❑ 333 Bob Milacki .05 .01
❑ 334 Tim Burke .05 .01
❑ 335 Jose Uribe .05 .01
❑ 336 Randy Myers .10 .02
❑ 337 Eric King .05 .01
❑ 338 Mark Langston .05 .01
❑ 339 Teddy Higuera .05 .01
❑ 340 Oddibe McDowell .05 .01
❑ 341 Lloyd McClendon .05 .01
❑ 342 Pascual Perez .05 .01
❑ 343 Kevin Brown UER (Signed is misspelled as signeed .10 .02
❑ 344 Chuck Finley .10 .02
❑ 345 Erik Hanson .05 .01
❑ 346 Rich Gedman .05 .01
❑ 347 Bip Roberts .05 .01
❑ 348 Matt Williams .10 .02
❑ 349 Tom Henke .05 .01
❑ 350 Brad Komminsk .05 .01
❑ 351 Jeff Reed .05 .01
❑ 352 Brian Downing .05 .01
❑ 353 Frank Viola .05 .01
❑ 354 Terry Puhl .05 .01
❑ 355 Brian Harper .05 .01
❑ 356 Steve Farr .05 .01
❑ 357 Joe Boever .05 .01
❑ 358 Danny Heep .05 .01
❑ 359 Larry Andersen .05 .01
❑ 360 Rolando Roomes .05 .01
❑ 361 Mike Gallego .05 .01
❑ 362 Bob Kipper .05 .01
❑ 363 Clay Parker .05 .01
❑ 364 Mike Pagliarulo .05 .01
❑ 365 Ken Griffey Jr. .75 .30
❑ 366 Rex Hudler .05 .01
❑ 367 Pat Sheridan .05 .01
❑ 368 Kirk Gibson .10 .02
❑ 369 Jeff Parrett .05 .01
❑ 370 Bob Walk .05 .01
❑ 371 Ken Patterson .05 .01
❑ 372 Bryan Harvey .05 .01
❑ 373 Mike Bielecki .05 .01
❑ 374 Tom Magrann RC .05 .01
❑ 375 Rick Mahler .05 .01
❑ 376 Craig Lefferts .05 .01
❑ 377 Gregg Olson .10 .02
❑ 378 Jamie Moyer .10 .02
❑ 379 Randy Johnson .50 .20
❑ 380 Jeff Montgomery .10 .02
❑ 381 Marty Clary .05 .01
❑ 382 Bill Spiers .05 .01
❑ 383 Dave Magadan .05 .01
❑ 384 Greg Hibbard RC .10 .02
❑ 385 Ernie Whitt .05 .01
❑ 386 Rick Honeycutt .05 .01
❑ 387 Dave West .05 .01
❑ 388 Keith Hernandez .10 .02
❑ 389 Jose Alvarez .05 .01
❑ 390 Albert Belle .25 .08
❑ 391 Rick Aguilera .10 .02
❑ 392 Mike Fitzgerald .05 .01
❑ 393 Dwight Smith .05 .01
❑ 394 Steve Wilson .05 .01
❑ 395 Bob Geren .05 .01
❑ 396 Randy Ready .05 .01
❑ 397 Ken Hill .10 .02
❑ 398 Jody Reed .05 .01
❑ 399 Tom Brunansky .05 .01
❑ 400A Checklist 334-435 .05 .01
❑ 400B Checklist 322-419 .05 .01
❑ 401 Rene Gonzales .05 .01
❑ 402 Harold Baines .10 .02
❑ 403 Cecilio Guante .05 .01
❑ 404 Joe Girardi .15 .05

❑ 405A Sergio Valdez ERR RC .05 .01
❑ 405B Sergio Valdez COR RC .05 .01
❑ 406 Mark Williamson .05 .01
❑ 407 Glenn Hoffman .05 .01
❑ 408 Jeff Innis RC .05 .01
❑ 409 Randy Kramer .05 .01
❑ 410 Charlie O'Brien .05 .01
❑ 411 Charlie Hough .10 .02
❑ 412 Gus Polidor .05 .01
❑ 413 Ron Karkovice .05 .01
❑ 414 Trevor Wilson .05 .01
❑ 415 Kevin Ritz RC .05 .01
❑ 416 Gary Thurman .05 .01
❑ 417 Jeff M. Robinson .05 .01
❑ 418 Scott Terry .05 .01
❑ 419 Tim Laudner .05 .01
❑ 420 Dennis Rasmussen .05 .01
❑ 421 Luis Rivera .05 .01
❑ 422 Jim Corsi .05 .01
❑ 423 Dennis Lamp .05 .01
❑ 424 Ken Caminiti .10 .02
❑ 425 David Wells .10 .02
❑ 426 Norm Charlton .05 .01
❑ 427 Deion Sanders .25 .08
❑ 428 Dion James .05 .01
❑ 429 Chuck Cary .05 .01
❑ 430 Ken Howell .05 .01
❑ 431 Steve Lake .05 .01
❑ 432 Kal Daniels .05 .01
❑ 433 Lance McCullers .05 .01
❑ 434 Lenny Harris .05 .01
❑ 435 Scott Scudder .05 .01
❑ 436 Gene Larkin .05 .01
❑ 437 Dan Quisenberry .05 .01
❑ 438 Steve Olin RC .25 .08
❑ 439 Mickey Hatcher .05 .01
❑ 440 Willie Wilson .05 .01
❑ 441 Mark Grant .05 .01
❑ 442 Mookie Wilson .10 .02
❑ 443 Alex Trevino .05 .01
❑ 444 Pat Tabler .05 .01
❑ 445 Dave Bergman .05 .01
❑ 446 Todd Burns .05 .01
❑ 447 R.J. Reynolds .05 .01
❑ 448 Jay Buhner .10 .02
❑ 449 Lee Stevens .10 .02
❑ 450 Ron Hassey .05 .01
❑ 451 Bob Melvin .05 .01
❑ 452 Dave Martinez .05 .01
❑ 453 Greg Litton .05 .01
❑ 454 Mark Carreon .05 .01
❑ 455 Scott Fletcher .05 .01
❑ 456 Otis Nixon .05 .01
❑ 457 Tony Fossas RC .05 .01
❑ 458 John Russell .05 .01
❑ 459 Paul Assenmacher .05 .01
❑ 460 Zane Smith .05 .01
❑ 461 Jack Daugherty RC .05 .01
❑ 462 Rich Monteleone .05 .01
❑ 463 Greg Briley .05 .01
❑ 464 Mike Smithson .05 .01
❑ 465 Benito Santiago .10 .02
❑ 466 Jeff Brantley .05 .01
❑ 467 Jose Nunez .05 .01
❑ 468 Scott Bailes .05 .01
❑ 469 Ken Griffey Sr. .10 .02
❑ 470 Bob McClure .05 .01
❑ 471 Mackey Sasser .05 .01
❑ 472 Glenn Wilson .05 .01
❑ 473 Kevin Tapani RC .25 .08
❑ 474 Bill Buckner .05 .01
❑ 475 Ron Gant .10 .02
❑ 476 Kevin Romine .05 .01
❑ 477 Juan Agosto .05 .01
❑ 478 Herm Winningham .05 .01
❑ 479 Storm Davis .05 .01
❑ 480 Jeff King .05 .01
❑ 481 Kevin Mmahat RC .05 .01
❑ 482 Carmelo Martinez .05 .01
❑ 483 Omar Vizquel .25 .08
❑ 484 Jim Dwyer .05 .01
❑ 485 Bob Knepper .05 .01
❑ 486 Dave Anderson .05 .01
❑ 487 Ron Jones .05 .01
❑ 488 Jay Bell .10 .02
❑ 489 Sammy Sosa RC 2.50 1.00
❑ 490 Kent Anderson .05 .01
❑ 491 Domingo Ramos .05 .01
❑ 492 Dave Clark .05 .01
❑ 493 Tim Birtsas .05 .01
❑ 494 Ken Oberkfell .05 .01
❑ 495 Larry Sheets .05 .01
❑ 496 Jeff Kunkel .05 .01
❑ 497 Jim Presley .05 .01
❑ 498 Mike Macfarlane .05 .01
❑ 499 Pete Smith .05 .01
❑ 500A Checklist 436-537 DP .05 .01
❑ 500B Checklist 420-517 .05 .01
❑ 501 Gary Sheffield .25 .08
❑ 502 Terry Bross RC .05 .01
❑ 503 Jerry Kutzler RC .05 .01
❑ 504 Lloyd Moseby .05 .01
❑ 505 Curt Young .05 .01
❑ 506 Al Newman .05 .01
❑ 507 Keith Miller .05 .01
❑ 508 Mike Stanton RC .25 .08
❑ 509 Rich Yett .05 .01
❑ 510 Tim Drummond RC .05 .01
❑ 511 Joe Hesketh .05 .01
❑ 512 Rick Wrona .05 .01
❑ 513 Luis Salazar .05 .01
❑ 514 Hal Morris .05 .01
❑ 515 Terry Mulholland .05 .01
❑ 516 John Morris .05 .01
❑ 517 Carlos Quintana .05 .01
❑ 518 Frank DiPino .05 .01
❑ 519 Randy Milligan .05 .01
❑ 520 Chad Kreuter .05 .01
❑ 521 Mike Jeffcoat .05 .01
❑ 522 Mike Harkey .05 .01
❑ 523A Andy Nezelek ERR (Wrong birth year) .05 .01
❑ 523B Andy Nezelek COR (Finally corrected in factory s .15 .05
❑ 524 Dave Schmidt .05 .01
❑ 525 Tony Armas .05 .01
❑ 526 Barry Lyons .05 .01
❑ 527 Rick Reed RC .25 .08
❑ 528 Jerry Reuss .05 .01
❑ 529 Dean Palmer RC .25 .08
❑ 530 Jeff Peterek RC .05 .01
❑ 531 Carlos Martinez .05 .01
❑ 532 Atlee Hammaker .05 .01
❑ 533 Mike Brumley .05 .01
❑ 534 Terry Leach .05 .01
❑ 535 Doug Strange RC .05 .01
❑ 536 Jose DeLeon .05 .01
❑ 537 Shane Rawley .05 .01
❑ 538 Joey Cora .10 .02
❑ 539 Eric Hetzel .05 .01
❑ 540 Gene Nelson .05 .01
❑ 541 Wes Gardner .05 .01
❑ 542 Mark Portugal .05 .01
❑ 543 Al Leiter .25 .08
❑ 544 Jack Armstrong .05 .01
❑ 545 Greg Cadaret .05 .01
❑ 546 Rod Nichols .05 .01
❑ 547 Luis Polonia .05 .01
❑ 548 Charlie Hayes .05 .01
❑ 549 Dickie Thon .05 .01
❑ 550 Tim Crews .05 .01
❑ 551 Dave Winfield .10 .02
❑ 552 Mike Davis .05 .01
❑ 553 Ron Robinson .05 .01
❑ 554 Carmen Castillo .05 .01
❑ 555 John Costello .05 .01
❑ 556 Bud Black .05 .01
❑ 557 Rick Dempsey .05 .01
❑ 558 Jim Acker .05 .01
❑ 559 Eric Show .05 .01
❑ 560 Pat Borders .05 .01
❑ 561 Danny Darwin .05 .01
❑ 562 Rick Luecken RC .05 .01
❑ 563 Edwin Nunez .05 .01
❑ 564 Felix Jose .05 .01
❑ 565 John Cangelosi .05 .01
❑ 566 Bill Swift .05 .01
❑ 567 Bill Schroeder .05 .01
❑ 568 Stan Javier .05 .01
❑ 569 Jim Traber .05 .01
❑ 570 Wallace Johnson .05 .01
❑ 571 Donell Nixon .05 .01
❑ 572 Sid Fernandez .05 .01
❑ 573 Lance Johnson .05 .01
❑ 574 Andy McGaffigan .05 .01
❑ 575 Mark Knudson .05 .01
❑ 576 Tommy Greene RC .10 .02
❑ 577 Mark Grace .15 .05
❑ 578 Larry Walker RC 1.00 .40
❑ 579 Mike Stanley .05 .01
❑ 580 Mike Witt DP .05 .01
❑ 581 Scott Bradley .05 .01
❑ 582 Greg A. Harris .05 .01
❑ 583A Kevin Hickey ERR .25 .08
❑ 583B Kevin Hickey COR .05 .01
❑ 584 Lee Mazzilli .05 .01
❑ 585 Jeff Pico .05 .01
❑ 586 Joe Oliver .05 .01
❑ 587 Willie Fraser DP .05 .01
❑ 588 Carl Yastrzemski Puzzle .25 .08
❑ 589 Kevin Bass DP .05 .01
❑ 590 John Moses DP .05 .01
❑ 591 Tom Pagnozzi DP .05 .01
❑ 592 Tony Castillo DP .05 .01
❑ 593 Jerald Clark DP .05 .01
❑ 594 Dan Schatzeder .05 .01
❑ 595 Luis Quinones DP .05 .01
❑ 596 Pete Harnisch DP .05 .01
❑ 597 Gary Redus .05 .01
❑ 598 Mel Hall .05 .01
❑ 599 Rick Schu .05 .01
❑ 600A Checklist 538-639 .05 .01
❑ 600B Checklist 518-617 .05 .01
❑ 601 Mike Kingery DP .05 .01
❑ 602 Terry Kennedy DP .05 .01
❑ 603 Mike Sharperson DP .05 .01
❑ 604 Don Carman DP .05 .01
❑ 605 Jim Gott .05 .01
❑ 606 Donn Pall DP .05 .01
❑ 607 Rance Mulliniks .05 .01
❑ 608 Curt Wilkerson DP .05 .01
❑ 609 Mike Felder DP .05 .01
❑ 610 Guillermo Hernandez DP .05 .01
❑ 611 Candy Maldonado DP .05 .01
❑ 612 Mark Thurmond DP .05 .01
❑ 613 Rick Leach DP RC .05 .01
❑ 614 Jerry Reed DP .05 .01
❑ 615 Franklin Stubbs .05 .01
❑ 616 Billy Hatcher DP .05 .01
❑ 617 Don August DP .05 .01
❑ 618 Tim Teufel .05 .01
❑ 619 Shawn Hillegas DP .05 .01
❑ 620 Manny Lee .05 .01
❑ 621 Gary Ward DP .05 .01
❑ 622 Mark Guthrie DP RC .05 .01
❑ 623 Jeff Musselman DP .05 .01
❑ 624 Mark Lemke DP .05 .01
❑ 625 Fernando Valenzuela .10 .02
❑ 626 Paul Sorrento DP RC .25 .08
❑ 627 Glenallen Hill DP .05 .01
❑ 628 Les Lancaster DP .05 .01
❑ 629 Vance Law DP .05 .01
❑ 630 Randy Velarde DP .05 .01
❑ 631 Todd Frohwirth DP .05 .01
❑ 632 Willie McGee .10 .02
❑ 633 Dennis Boyd DP .05 .01
❑ 634 Cris Carpenter DP .05 .01
❑ 635 Brian Holton .05 .01
❑ 636 Tracy Jones DP .05 .01
❑ 637A Terry Steinbach AS (Recent Major League Performa .05 .01
❑ 637B Terry Steinbach AS (All-Star Game Performance) .05 .01
❑ 638 Brady Anderson .10 .02
❑ 639A Jack Morris ERR (Card front shows black line cro .10 .02
❑ 639B Jack Morris COR .10 .02
❑ 640 Jaime Navarro .05 .01
❑ 641 Darrin Jackson .05 .01
❑ 642 Mike Dyer RC .05 .01
❑ 643 Mike Schmidt .50 .20
❑ 644 Henry Cotto .05 .01
❑ 645 John Cerutti .05 .01
❑ 646 Francisco Cabrera .05 .01

❑ 647 Scott Sanderson .05 .01
❑ 648 Brian Meyer .05 .01
❑ 649 Ray Searage .05 .01
❑ 650A Bo Jackson AS ERR .25 .08
❑ 650B Bo Jackson AS COR .25 .08
❑ 651 Steve Lyons .05 .01
❑ 652 Mike LaCoss .05 .01
❑ 653 Ted Power .05 .01
❑ 654A Howard Johnson AS (Recent Major League Performan .05 .01
❑ 654B Howard Johnson AS (All-Star Game Performance) .05 .01
❑ 655 Mauro Gozzo RC .05 .01
❑ 656 Mike Blowers RC .10 .02
❑ 657 Paul Gibson .05 .01
❑ 658 Neal Heaton .05 .01
❑ 659 Nolan Ryan 5000K .50 .20
❑ 659A Nolan Ryan 5000K ERR 1.50 .60
❑ 660A H.Baines AS ERR/ERR .75 .30
❑ 660B H.Baines AS ERR/COR 1.00 .40
❑ 660C H.Baines AS COR/ERR .25 .08
❑ 660D Harold Baines AS (Black line behind star on fron .05 .01
❑ 661 Gary Pettis .05 .01
❑ 662 Clint Zavaras RC .05 .01
❑ 663A Rick Reuschel AS (Recent Major League Performanc .05 .01
❑ 663B Rick Reuschel AS (All-Star Game Performance) .05 .01
❑ 664 Alejandro Pena .05 .01
❑ 665 Nolan Ryan KING .50 .20
❑ 665A Nolan Ryan KING ERR 1.50 .60
❑ 665C Nolan Ryan KING NNO .75 .30
❑ 666 Ricky Horton .05 .01
❑ 667 Curt Schilling 1.00 .40
❑ 668 Bill Landrum .05 .01
❑ 669 Todd Stottlemyre .10 .02
❑ 670 Tim Leary .05 .01
❑ 671 John Wetteland .25 .08
❑ 672 Calvin Schiraldi .05 .01
❑ 673A Ruben Sierra AS ERR .05 .01
❑ 673B Ruben Sierra AS COR .05 .01
❑ 674A Pedro Guerrero AS (Recent Major League Performan .05 .01
❑ 674B Pedro Guerrero AS (All-Star Game Performance) .05 .01
❑ 675 Ken Phelps .05 .01
❑ 676A Cal Ripken AS .40 .15
❑ 676B Cal Ripken AS ERR .75 .30
❑ 677 Denny Walling .05 .01
❑ 678 Goose Gossage .10 .02
❑ 679 Gary Mielke RC .05 .01
❑ 680 Bill Bathe .05 .01
❑ 681 Tom Lawless .05 .01
❑ 682 Xavier Hernandez RC .05 .01
❑ 683A Kirby Puckett AS ERR .15 .05
❑ 683B Kirby Puckett AS COR .15 .05
❑ 684 Mariano Duncan .05 .01
❑ 685 Ramon Martinez .05 .01
❑ 686 Tim Jones .05 .01
❑ 687 Tom Filer .05 .01
❑ 688 Steve Lombardozzi .05 .01
❑ 689 Bernie Williams RC 1.50 .60
❑ 690 Chip Hale RC .05 .01
❑ 691 Beau Allred RC .05 .01
❑ 692A Ryne Sandberg AS ERR .25 .08
❑ 692B Ryne Sandberg AS COR .25 .08
❑ 693 Jeff Huson RC .10 .02
❑ 694 Curt Ford .05 .01
❑ 695A Eric Davis AS (Recent Major League Performance) .05 .01
❑ 695B Eric Davis AS (All-Star Game Performance) .05 .01
❑ 696 Scott Lusader .05 .01
❑ 697A Mark McGwire AS ERR .50 .20
❑ 697B Mark McGwire AS COR .50 .20
❑ 698 Steve Cummings RC .05 .01
❑ 699 George Canale RC .05 .01
❑ 700A Checklist w/out 716 .25 .08
❑ 700B Checklist with 716 .10 .02
❑ 700C Checklist 618-716 .05 .01
❑ 701A Julio Franco AS (Recent Major League Performance .05 .01
❑ 701B Julio Franco AS (All-Star Game Performance) .05 .01
❑ 702 Dave Wayne Johnson RC .05 .01
❑ 703A Dave Stewart AS ERR .05 .01
❑ 703B Dave Stewart AS COR .05 .01
❑ 704 David Justice RC .50 .20
❑ 705 Tony Gwynn AS .15 .05
❑ 705A Tony Gwynn AS ERR .15 .05
❑ 706 Greg Myers .05 .01
❑ 707A Will Clark AS ERR .15 .05
❑ 707B Will Clark AS COR .15 .05
❑ 708A Benito Santiago AS .05 .01
❑ 708B Benito Santiago AS .05 .01
❑ 709 Larry McWilliams .05 .01
❑ 710A Ozzie Smith AS ML Perf .25 .08
❑ 710B Ozzie Smith AS Perf .25 .08
❑ 711 John Olerud RC .50 .20
❑ 712A Wade Boggs AS ERR .10 .02
❑ 712B Wade Boggs AS COR .10 .02
❑ 713 Gary Eave RC .05 .01
❑ 714 Bob Tewksbury .05 .01
❑ 715A Kevin Mitchell AS (Recent Major League Performan .05 .01
❑ 715B Kevin Mitchell AS (All-Star Game Performance) .05 .01
❑ 716 Bart Giamatti MEM .25 .08

1991 Donruss

❑ COMPLETE SET (770) 8.00 3.00
❑ COMP.FACT.w/LEAF PREV 10.00 4.00
❑ COMP.FACT.w/STUDIO PREV 10.00 4.00
❑ COMP.STARGELL PUZZLE 1.00 .40
❑ 1 Dave Stieb DK .05 .01
❑ 2 Craig Biggio DK .10 .02
❑ 3 Cecil Fielder DK .05 .01
❑ 4 Barry Bonds DK .50 .20
❑ 5 Barry Larkin DK .10 .02
❑ 6 Dave Parker DK .05 .01
❑ 7 Len Dykstra DK .05 .01
❑ 8 Bobby Thigpen DK .05 .01
❑ 9 Roger Clemens DK .40 .15
❑ 10 Ron Gant DK UER .10 .02
❑ 11 Delino DeShields DK .05 .01
❑ 12 Roberto Alomar DK UER .10 .02
❑ 13 Sandy Alomar Jr. DK .05 .01
❑ 14 Ryne Sandberg DK UER .25 .08
❑ 15 Ramon Martinez DK .05 .01
❑ 16 Edgar Martinez DK .15 .05
❑ 17 Dave Magadan DK .05 .01
❑ 18 Matt Williams DK .05 .01
❑ 19 Rafael Palmeiro DK UER .10 .02
❑ 20 Bob Welch DK .05 .01
❑ 21 Dave Righetti DK .05 .01
❑ 22 Brian Harper DK .05 .01
❑ 23 Gregg Olson DK .05 .01
❑ 24 Kurt Stillwell DK .05 .01
❑ 25 Pedro Guerrero DK UER .05 .01
❑ 26 Chuck Finley DK UER .10 .02
❑ 27 DK Checklist 1-27 .05 .01
❑ 28 Tino Martinez RR .25 .08
❑ 29 Mark Lewis RR .05 .01
❑ 30 Bernard Gilkey RR .05 .01
❑ 31 Hensley Meulens RR .05 .01
❑ 32 Derek Bell RR .10 .02
❑ 33 Jose Offerman RR .05 .01
❑ 34 Terry Bross RR .05 .01
❑ 35 Leo Gomez RR .05 .01
❑ 36 Derrick May RR .05 .01
❑ 37 Kevin Morton RR RC .05 .01
❑ 38 Moises Alou RR .10 .02
❑ 39 Julio Valera RR .05 .01
❑ 40 Milt Cuyler RR .05 .01
❑ 41 Phil Plantier RR RC .25 .08
❑ 42 Scott Chiamparino RR .05 .01
❑ 43 Ray Lankford RR .10 .02
❑ 44 Mickey Morandini RR .05 .01
❑ 45 Dave Hansen RR .05 .01
❑ 46 Kevin Belcher RR RC .05 .01
❑ 47 Darrin Fletcher RR .05 .01
❑ 48 Steve Sax AS .05 .01
❑ 49 Ken Griffey Jr. AS .25 .08
❑ 50A Jose Canseco AS ERR .10 .02
❑ 50B Jose Canseco AS COR .15 .05
❑ 51 Sandy Alomar Jr. AS .05 .01
❑ 52 Cal Ripken AS .40 .15
❑ 53 Rickey Henderson AS .15 .05
❑ 54 Bob Welch AS .05 .01
❑ 55 Wade Boggs AS .10 .02
❑ 56 Mark McGwire AS .40 .15
❑ 57A Jack McDowell ERR .25 .08
❑ 57B Jack McDowell COR .50 .20
❑ 58 Jose Lind .05 .01
❑ 59 Alex Fernandez .05 .01
❑ 60 Pat Combs .05 .01
❑ 61 Mike Walker .05 .01
❑ 62 Juan Samuel .05 .01
❑ 63 Mike Blowers UER .05 .01
❑ 64 Mark Guthrie .05 .01
❑ 65 Mark Salas .05 .01
❑ 66 Tim Jones .05 .01
❑ 67 Tim Leary .05 .01
❑ 68 Andres Galarraga .10 .02
❑ 69 Bob Milacki .05 .01
❑ 70 Tim Belcher .05 .01
❑ 71 Todd Zeile .05 .01
❑ 72 Jerome Walton .05 .01
❑ 73 Kevin Seitzer .05 .01
❑ 74 Jerald Clark .05 .01
❑ 75 John Smoltz UER .15 .05
❑ 76 Mike Henneman .05 .01
❑ 77 Ken Griffey Jr. .50 .20
❑ 78 Jim Abbott .15 .05
❑ 79 Gregg Jefferies .05 .01
❑ 80 Kevin Reimer .05 .01
❑ 81 Roger Clemens .75 .30
❑ 82 Mike Fitzgerald .05 .01
❑ 83 Bruce Hurst UER .05 .01
❑ 84 Eric Davis .10 .02
❑ 85 Paul Molitor .10 .02
❑ 86 Will Clark .15 .05
❑ 87 Mike Bielecki .05 .01
❑ 88 Bret Saberhagen .10 .02
❑ 89 Nolan Ryan 1.00 .40
❑ 90 Bobby Thigpen .05 .01
❑ 91 Dickie Thon .05 .01
❑ 92 Duane Ward .05 .01
❑ 93 Luis Polonia .05 .01
❑ 94 Terry Kennedy .05 .01
❑ 95 Kent Hrbek .10 .02
❑ 96 Danny Jackson .05 .01
❑ 97 Sid Fernandez .05 .01
❑ 98 Jimmy Key .10 .02
❑ 99 Franklin Stubbs .05 .01
❑ 100 Checklist 28-103 .05 .01
❑ 101 R.J. Reynolds .05 .01
❑ 102 Dave Stewart .10 .02
❑ 103 Dan Pasqua .05 .01
❑ 104 Dan Plesac .05 .01
❑ 105 Mark McGwire .75 .30
❑ 106 John Farrell .05 .01
❑ 107 Don Mattingly .60 .25
❑ 108 Carlton Fisk .15 .05
❑ 109 Ken Oberkfell .05 .01
❑ 110 Darrel Akerfelds .05 .01

❑ 111 Gregg Olson .05 .01
❑ 112 Mike Scioscia .05 .01
❑ 113 Bryn Smith .05 .01
❑ 114 Bob Geren .05 .01
❑ 115 Tom Candiotti .05 .01
❑ 116 Kevin Tapani .05 .01
❑ 117 Jeff Treadway .05 .01
❑ 118 Alan Trammell .10 .02
❑ 119 Pete O'Brien UER .05 .01
❑ 120 Joel Skinner .05 .01
❑ 121 Mike LaValliere .05 .01
❑ 122 Dwight Evans .15 .05
❑ 123 Jody Reed .05 .01
❑ 124 Lee Guetterman .05 .01
❑ 125 Tim Burke .05 .01
❑ 126 Dave Johnson .05 .01
❑ 127 Fernando Valenzuela UER .10 .02
❑ 128 Jose DeLeon .05 .01
❑ 129 Andre Dawson .10 .02
❑ 130 Gerald Perry .05 .01
❑ 131 Greg W. Harris .05 .01
❑ 132 Tom Glavine .15 .05
❑ 133 Lance McCullers .05 .01
❑ 134 Randy Johnson .30 .10
❑ 135 Lance Parrish UER .10 .02
❑ 136 Mackey Sasser .05 .01
❑ 137 Geno Petralli .05 .01
❑ 138 Dennis Lamp .05 .01
❑ 139 Dennis Martinez .10 .02
❑ 140 Mike Pagliarulo .05 .01
❑ 141 Hal Morris .05 .01
❑ 142 Dave Parker .10 .02
❑ 143 Brett Butler .10 .02
❑ 144 Paul Assenmacher .05 .01
❑ 145 Mark Gubicza .05 .01
❑ 146 Charlie Hough .10 .02
❑ 147 Sammy Sosa .25 .08
❑ 148 Randy Ready .05 .01
❑ 149 Kelly Gruber .05 .01
❑ 150 Devon White .10 .02
❑ 151 Gary Carter .10 .02
❑ 152 Gene Larkin .05 .01
❑ 153 Chris Sabo .05 .01
❑ 154 David Cone .10 .02
❑ 155 Todd Stottlemyre .05 .01
❑ 156 Glenn Wilson .05 .01
❑ 157 Bob Walk .05 .01
❑ 158 Mike Gallego .05 .01
❑ 159 Greg Hibbard .05 .01
❑ 160 Chris Bosio .05 .01
❑ 161 Mike Moore .05 .01
❑ 162 Jerry Browne UER .05 .01
❑ 163 Steve Sax UER .05 .01
❑ 164 Melido Perez .05 .01
❑ 165 Danny Darwin .05 .01
❑ 166 Roger McDowell .05 .01
❑ 167 Bill Ripken .05 .01
❑ 168 Mike Sharperson .05 .01
❑ 169 Lee Smith .10 .02
❑ 170 Matt Nokes .05 .01
❑ 171 Jesse Orosco .05 .01
❑ 172 Rick Aguilera .10 .02
❑ 173 Jim Presley .05 .01
❑ 174 Lou Whitaker .10 .02
❑ 175 Harold Reynolds .10 .02
❑ 176 Brook Jacoby .05 .01
❑ 177 Wally Backman .05 .01
❑ 178 Wade Boggs .15 .05
❑ 179 Chuck Cary UER .05 .01
❑ 180 Tom Foley .05 .01
❑ 181 Pete Harnisch .05 .01
❑ 182 Mike Morgan .05 .01
❑ 183 Bob Tewksbury .05 .01
❑ 184 Joe Girardi .05 .01
❑ 185 Storm Davis .05 .01
❑ 186 Ed Whitson .05 .01
❑ 187 Steve Avery UER .05 .01
❑ 188 Lloyd Moseby .05 .01
❑ 189 Scott Bankhead .05 .01
❑ 190 Mark Langston .05 .01
❑ 191 Kevin McReynolds .05 .01
❑ 192 Julio Franco .10 .02
❑ 193 John Dopson .05 .01
❑ 194 Dennis Boyd .05 .01
❑ 195 Bip Roberts .05 .01
❑ 196 Billy Hatcher .05 .01
❑ 197 Edgar Diaz .05 .01
❑ 198 Greg Litton .05 .01
❑ 199 Mark Grace .15 .05
❑ 200 Checklist 104-179 .05 .01
❑ 201 George Brett .60 .25
❑ 202 Jeff Russell .05 .01
❑ 203 Ivan Calderon .05 .01
❑ 204 Ken Howell .05 .01
❑ 205 Tom Henke .05 .01
❑ 206 Bryan Harvey .05 .01
❑ 207 Steve Bedrosian .05 .01
❑ 208 Al Newman .05 .01
❑ 209 Randy Myers .05 .01
❑ 210 Daryl Boston .05 .01
❑ 211 Manny Lee .05 .01
❑ 212 Dave Smith .05 .01
❑ 213 Don Slaught .05 .01
❑ 214 Walt Weiss .05 .01
❑ 215 Donn Pall .05 .01
❑ 216 Jaime Navarro .05 .01
❑ 217 Willie Randolph .10 .02
❑ 218 Rudy Seanez .05 .01
❑ 219 Jim Leyritz .05 .01
❑ 220 Ron Karkovice .05 .01
❑ 221 Ken Caminiti .10 .02
❑ 222 Von Hayes .05 .01
❑ 223 Cal Ripken .75 .30
❑ 224 Lenny Harris .05 .01
❑ 225 Milt Thompson .05 .01
❑ 226 Alvaro Espinoza .05 .01
❑ 227 Chris James .05 .01
❑ 228 Dan Gladden .05 .01
❑ 229 Jeff Blauser .05 .01
❑ 230 Mike Heath .05 .01
❑ 231 Omar Vizquel .15 .05
❑ 232 Doug Jones .05 .01
❑ 233 Jeff King .05 .01
❑ 234 Luis Rivera .05 .01
❑ 235 Ellis Burks .10 .02
❑ 236 Greg Cadaret .05 .01
❑ 237 Dave Martinez .05 .01
❑ 238 Mark Williamson .05 .01
❑ 239 Stan Javier .05 .01
❑ 240 Ozzie Smith .40 .15
❑ 241 Shawn Boskie .05 .01
❑ 242 Tom Gordon .05 .01
❑ 243 Tony Gwynn .30 .10
❑ 244 Tommy Gregg .05 .01
❑ 245 Jeff M. Robinson .05 .01
❑ 246 Keith Comstock .05 .01
❑ 247 Jack Howell .05 .01
❑ 248 Keith Miller .05 .01
❑ 249 Bobby Witt .05 .01
❑ 250 Rob Murphy UER .05 .01
❑ 251 Spike Owen .05 .01
❑ 252 Garry Templeton .05 .01
❑ 253 Glenn Braggs .05 .01
❑ 254 Ron Robinson .05 .01
❑ 255 Kevin Mitchell .05 .01
❑ 256 Les Lancaster .05 .01
❑ 257 Mel Stottlemyre Jr. .05 .01
❑ 258 Kenny Rogers UER .10 .02
❑ 259 Lance Johnson .05 .01
❑ 260 John Kruk .10 .02
❑ 261 Fred McGriff .15 .05
❑ 262 Dick Schofield .05 .01
❑ 263 Trevor Wilson .05 .01
❑ 264 David West .05 .01
❑ 265 Scott Scudder .05 .01
❑ 266 Dwight Gooden .10 .02
❑ 267 Willie Blair .05 .01
❑ 268 Mark Portugal .05 .01
❑ 269 Doug Drabek .05 .01
❑ 270 Dennis Eckersley .10 .02
❑ 271 Eric King .05 .01
❑ 272 Robin Yount .40 .15
❑ 273 Carney Lansford .10 .02
❑ 274 Carlos Baerga .05 .01
❑ 275 Dave Righetti .10 .02
❑ 276 Scott Fletcher .05 .01
❑ 277 Eric Yelding .05 .01
❑ 278 Charlie Hayes .05 .01
❑ 279 Jeff Ballard .05 .01
❑ 280 Orel Hershiser .10 .02
❑ 281 Jose Oquendo .05 .01
❑ 282 Mike Witt .05 .01
❑ 283 Mitch Webster .05 .01
❑ 284 Greg Gagne .05 .01
❑ 285 Greg Olson .05 .01
❑ 286 Tony Phillips UER .05 .01
❑ 287 Scott Bradley .05 .01
❑ 288 Cory Snyder UER .05 .01
❑ 289 Jay Bell UER .10 .02
❑ 290 Kevin Romine .05 .01
❑ 291 Jeff D. Robinson .05 .01
❑ 292 Steve Frey UER .05 .01
❑ 293 Craig Worthington .05 .01
❑ 294 Tim Crews .05 .01
❑ 295 Joe Magrane .05 .01
❑ 296 Hector Villanueva .05 .01
❑ 297 Terry Shumpert .05 .01
❑ 298 Joe Carter .10 .02
❑ 299 Kent Mercker UER .05 .01
❑ 300 Checklist 180-255 .05 .01
❑ 301 Chet Lemon .05 .01
❑ 302 Mike Schooler .05 .01
❑ 303 Dante Bichette .10 .02
❑ 304 Kevin Elster .05 .01
❑ 305 Jeff Huson .05 .01
❑ 306 Greg A. Harris .05 .01
❑ 307 Marquis Grissom UER .10 .02
❑ 308 Calvin Schiraldi .05 .01
❑ 309 Mariano Duncan .05 .01
❑ 310 Bill Spiers .05 .01
❑ 311 Scott Garrelts .05 .01
❑ 312 Mitch Williams .05 .01
❑ 313 Mike Macfarlane .05 .01
❑ 314 Kevin Brown .10 .02
❑ 315 Robin Ventura .10 .02
❑ 316 Darren Daulton .10 .02
❑ 317 Pat Borders .05 .01
❑ 318 Mark Eichhorn .05 .01
❑ 319 Jeff Brantley .05 .01
❑ 320 Shane Mack .05 .01
❑ 321 Rob Dibble .10 .02
❑ 322 John Franco .10 .02
❑ 323 Junior Felix .05 .01
❑ 324 Casey Candaele .05 .01
❑ 325 Bobby Bonilla .10 .02
❑ 326 Dave Henderson .05 .01
❑ 327 Wayne Edwards .05 .01
❑ 328 Mark Knudson .05 .01
❑ 329 Terry Steinbach .05 .01
❑ 330 Colby Ward UER RC .05 .01
❑ 331 Oscar Azocar .05 .01
❑ 332 Scott Radinsky .05 .01
❑ 333 Eric Anthony .05 .01
❑ 334 Steve Lake .05 .01
❑ 335 Bob Melvin .05 .01
❑ 336 Kal Daniels .05 .01
❑ 337 Tom Pagnozzi .05 .01
❑ 338 Alan Mills .05 .01
❑ 339 Steve Olin .05 .01
❑ 340 Juan Berenguer .05 .01
❑ 341 Francisco Cabrera .05 .01
❑ 342 Dave Bergman .05 .01
❑ 343 Henry Cotto .05 .01
❑ 344 Sergio Valdez .05 .01
❑ 345 Bob Patterson .05 .01
❑ 346 John Marzano .05 .01
❑ 347 Dana Kiecker .05 .01
❑ 348 Dion James .05 .01
❑ 349 Hubie Brooks .05 .01
❑ 350 Bill Landrum .05 .01
❑ 351 Bill Sampen .05 .01
❑ 352 Greg Briley .05 .01
❑ 353 Paul Gibson .05 .01
❑ 354 Dave Eiland .05 .01
❑ 355 Steve Finley .10 .02
❑ 356 Bob Boone .10 .02
❑ 357 Steve Buechele .05 .01
❑ 358 Chris Hoiles FDC .05 .01
❑ 359 Larry Walker .25 .08
❑ 360 Frank DiPino .05 .01
❑ 361 Mark Grant .05 .01
❑ 362 Dave Magadan .05 .01
❑ 363 Robby Thompson .05 .01
❑ 364 Lonnie Smith .05 .01
❑ 365 Steve Farr .05 .01
❑ 366 Dave Valle .05 .01
❑ 367 Tim Naehring .05 .01
❑ 368 Jim Acker .05 .01

❑ 369 Jeff Reardon UER .10 .02
❑ 370 Tim Teufel .05 .01
❑ 371 Juan Gonzalez .25 .08
❑ 372 Luis Salazar .05 .01
❑ 373 Rick Honeycutt .05 .01
❑ 374 Greg Maddux .40 .15
❑ 375 Jose Uribe UER .05 .01
❑ 376 Donnie Hill .05 .01
❑ 377 Don Carman .05 .01
❑ 378 Craig Grebeck .05 .01
❑ 379 Willie Fraser .05 .01
❑ 380 Glenallen Hill .05 .01
❑ 381 Joe Oliver .05 .01
❑ 382 Randy Bush .05 .01
❑ 383 Alex Cole .05 .01
❑ 384 Norm Charlton .05 .01
❑ 385 Gene Nelson .05 .01
❑ 386 Checklist 256-331 .05 .01
❑ 387 Rickey Henderson MVP .15 .05
❑ 388 Lance Parrish MVP .05 .01
❑ 389 Fred McGriff MVP .10 .02
❑ 390 Dave Parker MVP .05 .01
❑ 391 Candy Maldonado MVP .05 .01
❑ 392 Ken Griffey Jr. MVP .25 .08
❑ 393 Gregg Olson MVP .05 .01
❑ 394 Rafael Palmeiro MVP .10 .02
❑ 395 Roger Clemens MVP .40 .15
❑ 396 George Brett MVP .25 .08
❑ 397 Cecil Fielder MVP .05 .01
❑ 398 Brian Harper MVP UER .05 .01
❑ 399 Bobby Thigpen MVP .05 .01
❑ 400 Roberto Kelly MVP UER .05 .01
❑ 401 Danny Darwin MVP .05 .01
❑ 402 David Justice MVP .05 .01
❑ 403 Lee Smith MVP .05 .01
❑ 404 Ryne Sandberg MVP .25 .08
❑ 405 Eddie Murray MVP .15 .05
❑ 406 Tim Wallach MVP .05 .01
❑ 407 Kevin Mitchell MVP .05 .01
❑ 408 Darryl Strawberry MVP .05 .01
❑ 409 Joe Carter MVP .05 .01
❑ 410 Len Dykstra MVP .05 .01
❑ 411 Doug Drabek MVP .05 .01
❑ 412 Chris Sabo MVP .05 .01
❑ 413 Paul Marak RR RC .05 .01
❑ 414 Tim McIntosh RR .05 .01
❑ 415 Brian Barnes RR RC .10 .02
❑ 416 Eric Gunderson RR .05 .01
❑ 417 Mike Gardiner RR RC .05 .01
❑ 418 Steve Carter RR .05 .01
❑ 419 Gerald Alexander RR RC .05 .01
❑ 420 Rich Garces RR RC .10 .02
❑ 421 Chuck Knoblauch .10 .02
❑ 422 Scott Aldred RR .05 .01
❑ 423 Wes Chamberlain RR RC .25 .08
❑ 424 Lance Dickson RR RC .10 .02
❑ 425 Greg Colbrunn RR RC .25 .08
❑ 426 Rich DeLucia RR UER RC .05 .01
❑ 427 Jeff Conine RR RC .40 .15
❑ 428 Steve Decker RR RC .05 .01
❑ 429 Turner Ward RR RC .25 .08
❑ 430 Mo Vaughn .10 .02
❑ 431 Steve Chitren RR RC .05 .01
❑ 432 Mike Benjamin RR .05 .01
❑ 433 Ryne Sandberg AS .25 .08
❑ 434 Len Dykstra AS .05 .01
❑ 435 Andre Dawson AS .05 .01
❑ 436A Mike Scioscia AS White .05 .01
❑ 436B Mike Scioscia AS Yellow .05 .01
❑ 437 Ozzie Smith AS .25 .08
❑ 438 Kevin Mitchell AS .05 .01
❑ 439 Jack Armstrong AS .05 .01
❑ 440 Chris Sabo AS .05 .01
❑ 441 Will Clark AS .10 .02
❑ 442 Mel Hall .05 .01
❑ 443 Mark Gardner .05 .01
❑ 444 Mike Devereaux .05 .01
❑ 445 Kirk Gibson .10 .02
❑ 446 Terry Pendleton .10 .02
❑ 447 Mike Harkey .05 .01
❑ 448 Jim Eisenreich .05 .01
❑ 449 Benito Santiago .10 .02
❑ 450 Oddibe McDowell .05 .01
❑ 451 Cecil Fielder .10 .02
❑ 452 Ken Griffey Sr. .10 .02
❑ 453 Bert Blyleven .10 .02
❑ 454 Howard Johnson .05 .01
❑ 455 Monty Fariss UER .05 .01
❑ 456 Tony Pena .05 .01
❑ 457 Tim Raines .10 .02
❑ 458 Dennis Rasmussen .05 .01
❑ 459 Luis Quinones .05 .01
❑ 460 B.J. Surhoff .10 .02
❑ 461 Ernest Riles .05 .01
❑ 462 Rick Sutcliffe .10 .02
❑ 463 Danny Tartabull .05 .01
❑ 464 Pete Incaviglia .05 .01
❑ 465 Carlos Martinez .05 .01
❑ 466 Ricky Jordan .05 .01
❑ 467 John Cerutti .05 .01
❑ 468 Dave Winfield .10 .02
❑ 469 Francisco Oliveras .05 .01
❑ 470 Roy Smith .05 .01
❑ 471 Barry Larkin .15 .05
❑ 472 Ron Darling .05 .01
❑ 473 David Wells .10 .02
❑ 474 Glenn Davis .05 .01
❑ 475 Neal Heaton .05 .01
❑ 476 Ron Hassey .05 .01
❑ 477 Frank Thomas .25 .08
❑ 478 Greg Vaughn .05 .01
❑ 479 Todd Burns .05 .01
❑ 480 Candy Maldonado .05 .01
❑ 481 Dave LaPoint .05 .01
❑ 482 Alvin Davis .05 .01
❑ 483 Mike Scott .05 .01
❑ 484 Dale Murphy .15 .05
❑ 485 Ben McDonald .05 .01
❑ 486 Jay Howell .05 .01
❑ 487 Vince Coleman .05 .01
❑ 488 Alfredo Griffin .05 .01
❑ 489 Sandy Alomar Jr. .05 .01
❑ 490 Kirby Puckett .25 .08
❑ 491 Andres Thomas .05 .01
❑ 492 Jack Morris .10 .02
❑ 493 Matt Young .05 .01
❑ 494 Greg Myers .05 .01
❑ 495 Barry Bonds 1.00 .40
❑ 496 Scott Cooper UER .05 .01
❑ 497 Dan Schatzeder .05 .01
❑ 498 Jesse Barfield .05 .01
❑ 499 Jerry Goff .05 .01
❑ 500 Checklist 332-408 .05 .01
❑ 501 Anthony Telford RC .05 .01
❑ 502 Eddie Murray .25 .08
❑ 503 Omar Olivares RC .25 .08
❑ 504 Ryne Sandberg .40 .15
❑ 505 Jeff Montgomery .05 .01
❑ 506 Mark Parent .05 .01
❑ 507 Ron Gant .10 .02
❑ 508 Frank Tanana .05 .01
❑ 509 Jay Buhner .10 .02
❑ 510 Max Venable .05 .01
❑ 511 Wally Whitehurst .05 .01
❑ 512 Gary Pettis .05 .01
❑ 513 Tom Brunansky .05 .01
❑ 514 Tim Wallach .05 .01
❑ 515 Craig Lefferts .05 .01
❑ 516 Tim Layana .05 .01
❑ 517 Darryl Hamilton .05 .01
❑ 518 Rick Reuschel .05 .01
❑ 519 Steve Wilson .05 .01
❑ 520 Kurt Stillwell .05 .01
❑ 521 Rafael Palmeiro .15 .05
❑ 522 Ken Patterson .05 .01
❑ 523 Len Dykstra .10 .02
❑ 524 Tony Fernandez .05 .01
❑ 525 Kent Anderson .05 .01
❑ 526 Mark Leonard RC .05 .01
❑ 527 Allan Anderson .05 .01
❑ 528 Tom Browning .05 .01
❑ 529 Frank Viola .10 .02
❑ 530 John Olerud .10 .02
❑ 531 Juan Agosto .05 .01
❑ 532 Zane Smith .05 .01
❑ 533 Scott Sanderson .05 .01
❑ 534 Barry Jones .05 .01
❑ 535 Mike Felder .05 .01
❑ 536 Jose Canseco .15 .05
❑ 537 Felix Fermin .05 .01
❑ 538 Roberto Kelly .05 .01
❑ 539 Brian Holman .05 .01
❑ 540 Mark Davidson .05 .01
❑ 541 Terry Mulholland .05 .01
❑ 542 Randy Milligan .05 .01
❑ 543 Jose Gonzalez .05 .01
❑ 544 Craig Wilson RC .05 .01
❑ 545 Mike Hartley .05 .01
❑ 546 Greg Swindell .05 .01
❑ 547 Gary Gaetti .10 .02
❑ 548 David Justice .10 .02
❑ 549 Steve Searcy .05 .01
❑ 550 Erik Hanson .05 .01
❑ 551 Dave Stieb .05 .01
❑ 552 Andy Van Slyke .15 .05
❑ 553 Mike Greenwell .05 .01
❑ 554 Kevin Maas .05 .01
❑ 555 Delino DeShields .10 .02
❑ 556 Curt Schilling .25 .08
❑ 557 Ramon Martinez .05 .01
❑ 558 Pedro Guerrero .10 .02
❑ 559 Dwight Smith .05 .01
❑ 560 Mark Davis .05 .01
❑ 561 Shawn Abner .05 .01
❑ 562 Charlie Leibrandt .05 .01
❑ 563 John Shelby .05 .01
❑ 564 Bill Swift .05 .01
❑ 565 Mike Fetters .05 .01
❑ 566 Alejandro Pena .05 .01
❑ 567 Ruben Sierra .10 .02
❑ 568 Carlos Quintana .05 .01
❑ 569 Kevin Gross .05 .01
❑ 570 Derek Lilliquist .05 .01
❑ 571 Jack Armstrong .05 .01
❑ 572 Greg Brock .05 .01
❑ 573 Mike Kingery .05 .01
❑ 574 Greg Smith .05 .01
❑ 575 Brian McRae RC .25 .08
❑ 576 Jack Daugherty .05 .01
❑ 577 Ozzie Guillen .10 .02
❑ 578 Joe Boever .05 .01
❑ 579 Luis Sojo .05 .01
❑ 580 Chili Davis .10 .02
❑ 581 Don Robinson .05 .01
❑ 582 Brian Harper .05 .01
❑ 583 Paul O'Neill .15 .05
❑ 584 Bob Ojeda .05 .01
❑ 585 Mookie Wilson .10 .02
❑ 586 Rafael Ramirez .05 .01
❑ 587 Gary Redus .05 .01
❑ 588 Jamie Quirk .05 .01
❑ 589 Shawn Hillegas .05 .01
❑ 590 Tom Edens RC .05 .01
❑ 591 Joe Klink .05 .01
❑ 592 Charles Nagy .05 .01
❑ 593 Eric Plunk .05 .01
❑ 594 Tracy Jones .05 .01
❑ 595 Craig Biggio .15 .05
❑ 596 Jose DeJesus .05 .01
❑ 597 Mickey Tettleton .05 .01
❑ 598 Chris Gwynn .05 .01
❑ 599 Rex Hudler .05 .01
❑ 600 Checklist 409-506 .05 .01
❑ 601 Jim Gott .05 .01
❑ 602 Jeff Manto .05 .01
❑ 603 Nelson Liriano .05 .01
❑ 604 Mark Lemke .05 .01
❑ 605 Clay Parker .05 .01
❑ 606 Edgar Martinez .15 .05
❑ 607 Mark Whiten .05 .01
❑ 608 Ted Power .05 .01
❑ 609 Tom Bolton .05 .01
❑ 610 Tom Herr .05 .01
❑ 611 Andy Hawkins UER .05 .01
❑ 612 Scott Ruskin .05 .01
❑ 613 Ron Kittle .05 .01
❑ 614 John Wetteland .10 .02
❑ 615 Mike Perez RC .10 .02
❑ 616 Dave Clark .05 .01
❑ 617 Brent Mayne .05 .01
❑ 618 Jack Clark .10 .02
❑ 619 Marvin Freeman .05 .01
❑ 620 Edwin Nunez .05 .01
❑ 621 Russ Swan .05 .01
❑ 622 Johnny Ray .05 .01
❑ 623 Charlie O'Brien .05 .01
❑ 624 Joe Bitker RC .05 .01
❑ 625 Mike Marshall .05 .01

❑ 626 Otis Nixon .05 .01
❑ 627 Andy Benes .05 .01
❑ 628 Ron Oester .05 .01
❑ 629 Ted Higuera .05 .01
❑ 630 Kevin Bass .05 .01
❑ 631 Damon Berryhill .05 .01
❑ 632 Bo Jackson .25 .08
❑ 633 Brad Arnsberg .05 .01
❑ 634 Jerry Willard .05 .01
❑ 635 Tommy Greene .05 .01
❑ 636 Bob MacDonald RC .05 .01
❑ 637 Kirk McCaskill .05 .01
❑ 638 John Burkett .05 .01
❑ 639 Paul Abbott RC .05 .01
❑ 640 Todd Benzinger .05 .01
❑ 641 Todd Hundley .05 .01
❑ 642 George Bell .05 .01
❑ 643 Javier Ortiz .05 .01
❑ 644 Sid Bream .05 .01
❑ 645 Bob Welch .05 .01
❑ 646 Phil Bradley .05 .01
❑ 647 Bill Krueger .05 .01
❑ 648 Rickey Henderson .25 .08
❑ 649 Kevin Wickander .05 .01
❑ 650 Steve Balboni .05 .01
❑ 651 Gene Harris .05 .01
❑ 652 Jim Deshaies .05 .01
❑ 653 Jason Grimsley .05 .01
❑ 654 Joe Orsulak .05 .01
❑ 655 Jim Poole .05 .01
❑ 656 Felix Jose .05 .01
❑ 657 Denis Cook .05 .01
❑ 658 Tom Brookens .05 .01
❑ 659 Junior Ortiz .05 .01
❑ 660 Jeff Parrett .05 .01
❑ 661 Jerry Don Gleaton .05 .01
❑ 662 Brent Knackert .05 .01
❑ 663 Rance Mulliniks .05 .01
❑ 664 John Smiley .05 .01
❑ 665 Larry Andersen .05 .01
❑ 666 Willie McGee .10 .02
❑ 667 Chris Nabholz .05 .01
❑ 668 Brady Anderson .10 .02
❑ 669 Darren Holmes UER RC .25 .08
❑ 670 Ken Hill .05 .01
❑ 671 Gary Varsho .05 .01
❑ 672 Bill Pecota .05 .01
❑ 673 Fred Lynn .05 .01
❑ 674 Kevin D. Brown .05 .01
❑ 675 Dan Petry .05 .01
❑ 676 Mike Jackson .05 .01
❑ 677 Wally Joyner .10 .02
❑ 678 Danny Jackson .05 .01
❑ 679 Bill Haselman RC .05 .01
❑ 680 Mike Boddicker .05 .01
❑ 681 Mel Rojas .05 .01
❑ 682 Roberto Alomar .15 .05
❑ 683 David Justice ROY .05 .01
❑ 684 Chuck Crim .05 .01
❑ 685 Matt Williams .10 .02
❑ 686 Shawon Dunston .05 .01
❑ 687 Jeff Schulz RC .05 .01
❑ 688 John Barfield .05 .01
❑ 689 Gerald Young .05 .01
❑ 690 Luis Gonzalez RC .50 .20
❑ 691 Frank Wills .05 .01
❑ 692 Chuck Finley .10 .02
❑ 693 Sandy Alomar Jr. ROY .05 .01
❑ 694 Tim Drummond .05 .01
❑ 695 Herm Winningham .05 .01
❑ 696 Darryl Strawberry .10 .02
❑ 697 Al Leiter .10 .02
❑ 698 Karl Rhodes .05 .01
❑ 699 Stan Belinda .05 .01
❑ 700 Checklist 507-604 .05 .01
❑ 701 Lance Blankenship .05 .01
❑ 702 Willie Stargell PUZ .15 .05
❑ 703 Jim Gantner .05 .01
❑ 704 Reggie Harris .05 .01
❑ 705 Rob Ducey .05 .01
❑ 706 Tim Hulett .05 .01
❑ 707 Atlee Hammaker .05 .01
❑ 708 Xavier Hernandez .05 .01
❑ 709 Chuck McElroy .05 .01
❑ 710 John Mitchell .05 .01
❑ 711 Carlos Hernandez .05 .01
❑ 712 Geronimo Pena .05 .01
❑ 713 Jim Neidlinger RC .05 .01
❑ 714 John Orton .05 .01
❑ 715 Terry Leach .05 .01
❑ 716 Mike Stanton .05 .01
❑ 717 Walt Terrell .05 .01
❑ 718 Luis Aquino .05 .01
❑ 719 Bud Black UER .05 .01
❑ 720 Bob Kipper .05 .01
❑ 721 Jeff Gray RC .05 .01
❑ 722 Jose Rijo .05 .01
❑ 723 Curt Young .05 .01
❑ 724 Jose Vizcaino .05 .01
❑ 725 Randy Tomlin RC .10 .02
❑ 726 Junior Noboa .05 .01
❑ 727 Bob Welch CY .05 .01
❑ 728 Gary Ward .05 .01
❑ 729 Rob Deer UER .05 .01
❑ 730 David Segui .05 .01
❑ 731 Mark Carreon .05 .01
❑ 732 Vicente Palacios .05 .01
❑ 733 Sam Horn .05 .01
❑ 734 Howard Farmer .05 .01
❑ 735 Ken Dayley UER .05 .01
❑ 736 Kelly Mann .05 .01
❑ 737 Joe Grahe RC .10 .02
❑ 738 Kelly Downs .05 .01
❑ 739 Jimmy Kremers .05 .01
❑ 740 Kevin Appier .10 .02
❑ 741 Jeff Reed .05 .01
❑ 742 Jose Rijo WS .05 .01
❑ 743 Dave Rohde .05 .01
❑ 744 L.Dykstra/D.Murphy UER .15 .05
❑ 745 Paul Sorrento .05 .01
❑ 746 Thomas Howard .05 .01
❑ 747 Matt Stark RC .05 .01
❑ 748 Harold Baines .10 .02
❑ 749 Doug Dascenzo .05 .01
❑ 750 Doug Drabek CY .05 .01
❑ 751 Gary Sheffield .10 .02
❑ 752 Terry Lee RC .05 .01
❑ 753 Jim Vatcher RC .05 .01
❑ 754 Lee Stevens .05 .01
❑ 755 Randy Veres .05 .01
❑ 756 Bill Doran .05 .01
❑ 757 Gary Wayne .05 .01
❑ 758 Pedro Munoz RC .10 .02
❑ 759 Chris Hammond FDC .05 .01
❑ 760 Checklist 605-702 .05 .01
❑ 761 Rickey Henderson MVP .15 .05
❑ 762 Barry Bonds MVP .50 .20
❑ 763 Billy Hatcher WS UER .05 .01
❑ 764 Julio Machado .05 .01
❑ 765 Jose Mesa .05 .01
❑ 766 Willie Randolph WS .05 .01
❑ 767 Scott Erickson .05 .01
❑ 768 Travis Fryman .10 .02
❑ 769 Rich Rodriguez RC .05 .01
❑ 770 Checklist 703-770/BC1-BC22 .05 .01

1992 Donruss

❑ COMPLETE SET (784) 10.00 4.00
❑ COMP.HOBBY SET (788) 10.00 4.00
❑ COMP.RETAIL SET (788) 10.00 4.00
❑ COMPLETE SERIES 1 (396) 5.00 2.00
❑ COMPLETE SERIES 2 (388) 5.00 2.00
❑ COMP.CAREW PUZZLE 1.00 .40
❑ 1 Mark Wohlers RR .05 .01
❑ 2 Wil Cordero .05 .01
❑ 3 Kyle Abbott RR .05 .01
❑ 4 Dave Nilsson .05 .01
❑ 5 Kenny Lofton .15 .05
❑ 6 Luis Mercedes RR .05 .01
❑ 7 Roger Salkeld RR .05 .01
❑ 8 Eddie Zosky RR .05 .01
❑ 9 Todd Van Poppel .05 .01
❑ 10 Frank Seminara RR RC .10 .02
❑ 11 Andy Ashby .05 .01
❑ 12 Reggie Jefferson RR .05 .01
❑ 13 Ryan Klesko .10 .02
❑ 14 Carlos Garcia .05 .01
❑ 15 John Ramos RR .05 .01
❑ 16 Eric Karros .10 .02
❑ 17 Patrick Lennon RR .05 .01
❑ 18 Eddie Taubensee RR RC .25 .08
❑ 19 Roberto Hernandez RR .05 .01
❑ 20 D.J. Dozier RR .05 .01
❑ 21 Dave Henderson AS .05 .01
❑ 22 Cal Ripken AS .40 .15
❑ 23 Wade Boggs AS .10 .02
❑ 24 Ken Griffey Jr. AS .25 .08
❑ 25 Jack Morris AS .05 .01
❑ 26 Danny Tartabull AS .05 .01
❑ 27 Cecil Fielder AS .05 .01
❑ 28 Roberto Alomar AS .10 .02
❑ 29 Sandy Alomar Jr. AS .05 .01
❑ 30 Rickey Henderson AS .15 .05
❑ 31 Ken Hill .05 .01
❑ 32 John Habyan .05 .01
❑ 33 Otis Nixon HL .05 .01
❑ 34 Tim Wallach .05 .01
❑ 35 Cal Ripken .75 .30
❑ 36 Gary Carter .10 .02
❑ 37 Juan Agosto .05 .01
❑ 38 Doug Dascenzo .05 .01
❑ 39 Kirk Gibson .10 .02
❑ 40 Benito Santiago .10 .02
❑ 41 Otis Nixon .05 .01
❑ 42 Andy Allanson .05 .01
❑ 43 Brian Holman .05 .01
❑ 44 Dick Schofield .05 .01
❑ 45 Dave Magadan .05 .01
❑ 46 Rafael Palmeiro .15 .05
❑ 47 Jody Reed .05 .01
❑ 48 Ivan Calderon .05 .01
❑ 49 Greg W. Harris .05 .01
❑ 50 Chris Sabo .05 .01
❑ 51 Paul Molitor .10 .02
❑ 52 Robby Thompson .05 .01
❑ 53 Dave Smith .05 .01
❑ 54 Mark Davis .05 .01
❑ 55 Kevin Brown .10 .02
❑ 56 Donn Pall .05 .01
❑ 57 Len Dykstra .10 .02
❑ 58 Roberto Alomar .15 .05
❑ 59 Jeff D. Robinson .05 .01
❑ 60 Willie McGee .10 .02
❑ 61 Jay Buhner .10 .02
❑ 62 Mike Pagliarulo .05 .01
❑ 63 Paul O'Neill .15 .05
❑ 64 Hubie Brooks .05 .01
❑ 65 Kelly Gruber .05 .01
❑ 66 Ken Caminiti .10 .02
❑ 67 Gary Redus .05 .01
❑ 68 Harold Baines .10 .02
❑ 69 Charlie Hough .10 .02
❑ 70 B.J. Surhoff .10 .02
❑ 71 Walt Weiss .05 .01
❑ 72 Shawn Hillegas .05 .01
❑ 73 Roberto Kelly .05 .01
❑ 74 Jeff Ballard .05 .01
❑ 75 Craig Biggio .15 .05
❑ 76 Pat Combs .05 .01
❑ 77 Jeff M. Robinson .05 .01
❑ 78 Tim Belcher .05 .01
❑ 79 Cris Carpenter .05 .01
❑ 80 Checklist 1-79 .05 .01
❑ 81 Steve Avery .05 .01
❑ 82 Chris James .05 .01
❑ 83 Brian Harper .05 .01
❑ 84 Charlie Leibrandt .05 .01
❑ 85 Mickey Tettleton .05 .01
❑ 86 Pete O'Brien .05 .01
❑ 87 Danny Darwin .05 .01

❑ 88 Bob Walk .05 .01
❑ 89 Jeff Reardon .10 .02
❑ 90 Bobby Rose .05 .01
❑ 91 Danny Jackson .05 .01
❑ 92 John Morris .05 .01
❑ 93 Bud Black .05 .01
❑ 94 Tommy Greene HL .05 .01
❑ 95 Rick Aguilera .10 .02
❑ 96 Gary Gaetti .10 .02
❑ 97 David Cone .10 .02
❑ 98 John Olerud .10 .02
❑ 99 Joel Skinner .05 .01
❑ 100 Jay Bell .10 .02
❑ 101 Bob Milacki .05 .01
❑ 102 Norm Charlton .05 .01
❑ 103 Chuck Crim .05 .01
❑ 104 Terry Steinbach .05 .01
❑ 105 Juan Samuel .05 .01
❑ 106 Steve Howe .05 .01
❑ 107 Rafael Belliard .05 .01
❑ 108 Joey Cora .05 .01
❑ 109 Tommy Greene .05 .01
❑ 110 Gregg Olson .05 .01
❑ 111 Frank Tanana .05 .01
❑ 112 Lee Smith .10 .02
❑ 113 Greg A. Harris .05 .01
❑ 114 Dwayne Henry .05 .01
❑ 115 Chili Davis .10 .02
❑ 116 Kent Mercker .05 .01
❑ 117 Brian Barnes .05 .01
❑ 118 Rich DeLucia .05 .01
❑ 119 Andre Dawson .10 .02
❑ 120 Carlos Baerga .05 .01
❑ 121 Mike LaValliere .05 .01
❑ 122 Jeff Gray .05 .01
❑ 123 Bruce Hurst .05 .01
❑ 124 Alvin Davis .05 .01
❑ 125 John Candelaria .05 .01
❑ 126 Matt Nokes .05 .01
❑ 127 George Bell .05 .01
❑ 128 Bret Saberhagen .10 .02
❑ 129 Jeff Russell .05 .01
❑ 130 Jim Abbott .15 .05
❑ 131 Bill Gullickson .05 .01
❑ 132 Todd Zeile .05 .01
❑ 133 Dave Winfield .10 .02
❑ 134 Wally Whitehurst .05 .01
❑ 135 Matt Williams .10 .02
❑ 136 Tom Browning .05 .01
❑ 137 Marquis Grissom .10 .02
❑ 138 Erik Hanson .05 .01
❑ 139 Rob Dibble .10 .02
❑ 140 Don August .05 .01
❑ 141 Tom Henke .05 .01
❑ 142 Dan Pasqua .05 .01
❑ 143 George Brett .60 .25
❑ 144 Jerald Clark .05 .01
❑ 145 Robin Ventura .10 .02
❑ 146 Dale Murphy .15 .05
❑ 147 Dennis Eckersley .10 .02
❑ 148 Eric Yelding .05 .01
❑ 149 Mario Diaz .05 .01
❑ 150 Casey Candaele .05 .01
❑ 151 Steve Olin .05 .01
❑ 152 Luis Salazar .05 .01
❑ 153 Kevin Maas .05 .01
❑ 154 Nolan Ryan HL .50 .20
❑ 155 Barry Jones .05 .01
❑ 156 Chris Hoiles .05 .01
❑ 157 Bob Ojeda .05 .01
❑ 158 Pedro Guerrero .10 .02
❑ 159 Paul Assenmacher .05 .01
❑ 160 Checklist 80-157 .05 .01
❑ 161 Mike Macfarlane .05 .01
❑ 162 Craig Lefferts .05 .01
❑ 163 Brian Hunter .05 .01
❑ 164 Alan Trammell .10 .02
❑ 165 Ken Griffey Jr. .40 .15
❑ 166 Lance Parrish .10 .02
❑ 167 Brian Downing .05 .01
❑ 168 John Barfield .05 .01
❑ 169 Jack Clark .10 .02
❑ 170 Chris Nabholz .05 .01
❑ 171 Tim Teufel .05 .01
❑ 172 Chris Hammond .05 .01
❑ 173 Robin Yount .40 .15
❑ 174 Dave Righetti .10 .02
❑ 175 Joe Girardi .05 .01
❑ 176 Mike Boddicker .05 .01
❑ 177 Dean Palmer .10 .02
❑ 178 Greg Hibbard .05 .01
❑ 179 Randy Ready .05 .01
❑ 180 Devon White .10 .02
❑ 181 Mark Eichhorn .05 .01
❑ 182 Mike Felder .05 .01
❑ 183 Joe Klink .05 .01
❑ 184 Steve Bedrosian .05 .01
❑ 185 Barry Larkin .15 .05
❑ 186 John Franco .10 .02
❑ 187 Ed Sprague .05 .01
❑ 188 Mark Portugal .05 .01
❑ 189 Jose Lind .05 .01
❑ 190 Bob Welch .05 .01
❑ 191 Alex Fernandez .05 .01
❑ 192 Gary Sheffield .10 .02
❑ 193 Rickey Henderson .25 .08
❑ 194 Rod Nichols .05 .01
❑ 195 Scott Kamieniecki .05 .01
❑ 196 Mike Flanagan .05 .01
❑ 197 Steve Finley .10 .02
❑ 198 Darren Daulton .10 .02
❑ 199 Leo Gomez .05 .01
❑ 200 Mike Morgan .05 .01
❑ 201 Bob Tewksbury .05 .01
❑ 202 Sid Bream .05 .01
❑ 203 Sandy Alomar Jr. .05 .01
❑ 204 Greg Gagne .05 .01
❑ 205 Juan Berenguer .05 .01
❑ 206 Cecil Fielder .10 .02
❑ 207 Randy Johnson .25 .08
❑ 208 Tony Pena .05 .01
❑ 209 Doug Drabek .05 .01
❑ 210 Wade Boggs .15 .05
❑ 211 Bryan Harvey .05 .01
❑ 212 Jose Vizcaino .05 .01
❑ 213 Alonzo Powell .05 .01
❑ 214 Will Clark .15 .05
❑ 215 Rickey Henderson HL .15 .05
❑ 216 Jack Morris .10 .02
❑ 217 Junior Felix .05 .01
❑ 218 Vince Coleman .05 .01
❑ 219 Jimmy Key .10 .02
❑ 220 Alex Cole .05 .01
❑ 221 Bill Landrum .05 .01
❑ 222 Randy Milligan .05 .01
❑ 223 Jose Rijo .05 .01
❑ 224 Greg Vaughn .05 .01
❑ 225 Dave Stewart .10 .02
❑ 226 Lenny Harris .05 .01
❑ 227 Scott Sanderson .05 .01
❑ 228 Jeff Blauser .05 .01
❑ 229 Ozzie Guillen .10 .02
❑ 230 John Kruk .10 .02
❑ 231 Bob Melvin .05 .01
❑ 232 Milt Cuyler .05 .01
❑ 233 Felix Jose .05 .01
❑ 234 Ellis Burks .10 .02
❑ 235 Pete Harnisch .05 .01
❑ 236 Kevin Tapani .05 .01
❑ 237 Terry Pendleton .10 .02
❑ 238 Mark Gardner .05 .01
❑ 239 Harold Reynolds .10 .02
❑ 240 Checklist 158-237 .05 .01
❑ 241 Mike Harkey .05 .01
❑ 242 Felix Fermin .05 .01
❑ 243 Barry Bonds 1.00 .40
❑ 244 Roger Clemens .50 .20
❑ 245 Dennis Rasmussen .05 .01
❑ 246 Jose DeLeon .05 .01
❑ 247 Orel Hershiser .10 .02
❑ 248 Mel Hall .05 .01
❑ 249 Rick Wilkins .05 .01
❑ 250 Tom Gordon .05 .01
❑ 251 Kevin Reimer .05 .01
❑ 252 Luis Polonia .05 .01
❑ 253 Mike Henneman .05 .01
❑ 254 Tom Pagnozzi .05 .01
❑ 255 Chuck Finley .10 .02
❑ 256 Mackey Sasser .05 .01
❑ 257 John Burkett .05 .01
❑ 258 Hal Morris .05 .01
❑ 259 Larry Walker .15 .05
❑ 260 Bill Swift .05 .01
❑ 261 Joe Oliver .05 .01
❑ 262 Julio Machado .05 .01
❑ 263 Todd Stottlemyre .05 .01
❑ 264 Matt Merullo .05 .01
❑ 265 Brent Mayne .05 .01
❑ 266 Thomas Howard .05 .01
❑ 267 Lance Johnson .05 .01
❑ 268 Terry Mulholland .05 .01
❑ 269 Rick Honeycutt .05 .01
❑ 270 Luis Gonzalez .10 .02
❑ 271 Jose Guzman .05 .01
❑ 272 Jimmy Jones .05 .01
❑ 273 Mark Lewis .05 .01
❑ 274 Rene Gonzales .05 .01
❑ 275 Jeff Johnson .05 .01
❑ 276 Dennis Martinez HL .05 .01
❑ 277 Delino DeShields .05 .01
❑ 278 Sam Horn .05 .01
❑ 279 Kevin Gross .05 .01
❑ 280 Jose Oquendo .05 .01
❑ 281 Mark Grace .15 .05
❑ 282 Mark Gubicza .05 .01
❑ 283 Fred McGriff .15 .05
❑ 284 Ron Gant .10 .02
❑ 285 Lou Whitaker .10 .02
❑ 286 Edgar Martinez .15 .05
❑ 287 Ron Tingley .05 .01
❑ 288 Kevin McReynolds .05 .01
❑ 289 Ivan Rodriguez .25 .08
❑ 290 Mike Gardiner .05 .01
❑ 291 Chris Haney .05 .01
❑ 292 Darrin Jackson .05 .01
❑ 293 Bill Doran .05 .01
❑ 294 Ted Higuera .05 .01
❑ 295 Jeff Brantley .05 .01
❑ 296 Les Lancaster .05 .01
❑ 297 Jim Eisenreich .05 .01
❑ 298 Ruben Sierra .10 .02
❑ 299 Scott Radinsky .05 .01
❑ 300 Jose DeJesus .05 .01
❑ 301 Mike Timlin .05 .01
❑ 302 Luis Sojo .05 .01
❑ 303 Kelly Downs .05 .01
❑ 304 Scott Bankhead .05 .01
❑ 305 Pedro Munoz .05 .01
❑ 306 Scott Scudder .05 .01
❑ 307 Kevin Elster .05 .01
❑ 308 Duane Ward .05 .01
❑ 309 Darryl Kile .10 .02
❑ 310 Orlando Merced .05 .01
❑ 311 Dave Henderson .05 .01
❑ 312 Tim Raines .10 .02
❑ 313 Mark Lee .05 .01
❑ 314 Mike Gallego .05 .01
❑ 315 Charles Nagy .05 .01
❑ 316 Jesse Barfield .05 .01
❑ 317 Todd Frohwirth .05 .01
❑ 318 Al Osuna .05 .01
❑ 319 Darrin Fletcher .05 .01
❑ 320 Checklist 238-316 .05 .01
❑ 321 David Segui .05 .01
❑ 322 Stan Javier .05 .01
❑ 323 Bryn Smith .05 .01
❑ 324 Jeff Treadway .05 .01
❑ 325 Mark Whiten .05 .01
❑ 326 Kent Hrbek .10 .02
❑ 327 David Justice .10 .02
❑ 328 Tony Phillips .05 .01
❑ 329 Rob Murphy .05 .01
❑ 330 Kevin Morton .05 .01
❑ 331 John Smiley .05 .01
❑ 332 Luis Rivera .05 .01
❑ 333 Wally Joyner .10 .02
❑ 334 Heathcliff Slocumb .05 .01
❑ 335 Rick Cerone .05 .01
❑ 336 Mike Remlinger .05 .01
❑ 337 Mike Moore .05 .01
❑ 338 Lloyd McClendon .05 .01
❑ 339 Al Newman .05 .01
❑ 340 Kirk McCaskill .05 .01
❑ 341 Howard Johnson .05 .01
❑ 342 Greg Myers .05 .01
❑ 343 Kal Daniels .05 .01
❑ 344 Bernie Williams .15 .05
❑ 345 Shane Mack .05 .01

❑ 346 Gary Thurman .05 .01
❑ 347 Dante Bichette .10 .02
❑ 348 Mark McGwire .60 .25
❑ 349 Travis Fryman .10 .02
❑ 350 Ray Lankford .10 .02
❑ 351 Mike Jeffcoat .05 .01
❑ 352 Jack McDowell .05 .01
❑ 353 Mitch Williams .05 .01
❑ 354 Mike Devereaux .05 .01
❑ 355 Andres Galarraga .10 .02
❑ 356 Henry Cotto .05 .01
❑ 357 Scott Bailes .05 .01
❑ 358 Jeff Bagwell .25 .08
❑ 359 Scott Leius .05 .01
❑ 360 Zane Smith .05 .01
❑ 361 Bill Pecota .05 .01
❑ 362 Tony Fernandez .05 .01
❑ 363 Glenn Braggs .05 .01
❑ 364 Bill Spiers .05 .01
❑ 365 Vicente Palacios .05 .01
❑ 366 Tim Burke .05 .01
❑ 367 Randy Tomlin .05 .01
❑ 368 Kenny Rogers .10 .02
❑ 369 Brett Butler .10 .02
❑ 370 Pat Kelly .05 .01
❑ 371 Bip Roberts .05 .01
❑ 372 Gregg Jefferies .05 .01
❑ 373 Kevin Bass .05 .01
❑ 374 Ron Karkovice .05 .01
❑ 375 Paul Gibson .05 .01
❑ 376 Bernard Gilkey .05 .01
❑ 377 Dave Gallagher .05 .01
❑ 378 Bill Wegman .05 .01
❑ 379 Pat Borders .05 .01
❑ 380 Ed Whitson .05 .01
❑ 381 Gilberto Reyes .05 .01
❑ 382 Russ Swan .05 .01
❑ 383 Andy Van Slyke .15 .05
❑ 384 Wes Chamberlain .05 .01
❑ 385 Steve Chitren .05 .01
❑ 386 Greg Olson .05 .01
❑ 387 Brian McRae .05 .01
❑ 388 Rich Rodriguez .05 .01
❑ 389 Steve Decker .05 .01
❑ 390 Chuck Knoblauch .10 .02
❑ 391 Bobby Witt .05 .01
❑ 392 Eddie Murray .25 .08
❑ 393 Juan Gonzalez .15 .05
❑ 394 Scott Ruskin .05 .01
❑ 395 Jay Howell .05 .01
❑ 396 Checklist 317-396 .05 .01
❑ 397 Royce Clayton RR .05 .01
❑ 398 John Jaha RR RC .25 .08
❑ 399 Dan Wilson RR .05 .01
❑ 400 Archie Corbin .05 .01
❑ 401 Barry Manuel RR .05 .01
❑ 402 Kim Batiste RR .05 .01
❑ 403 Pat Mahomes RR RC .25 .08
❑ 404 Dave Fleming .05 .01
❑ 405 Jeff Juden RR .05 .01
❑ 406 Jim Thome .25 .08
❑ 407 Sam Militello RR .05 .01
❑ 408 Jeff Nelson RR RC .40 .15
❑ 409 Anthony Young .05 .01
❑ 410 Tino Martinez RR .15 .05
❑ 411 Jeff Mutis RR .05 .01
❑ 412 Rey Sanchez RR RC .25 .08
❑ 413 Chris Gardner RR .05 .01
❑ 414 John Vander Wal RR .05 .01
❑ 415 Reggie Sanders .10 .02
❑ 416 Brian Williams RR RC .10 .02
❑ 417 Mo Sanford RR .05 .01
❑ 418 David Weathers RR RC .40 .15
❑ 419 Hector Fajardo RR RC .10 .02
❑ 420 Steve Foster RR .05 .01
❑ 421 Lance Dickson RR .05 .01
❑ 422 Andre Dawson AS .05 .01
❑ 423 Ozzie Smith AS .25 .08
❑ 424 Chris Sabo AS .05 .01
❑ 425 Tony Gwynn AS .15 .05
❑ 426 Tom Glavine AS .10 .02
❑ 427 Bobby Bonilla AS .05 .01
❑ 428 Will Clark AS .10 .02
❑ 429 Ryne Sandberg AS .25 .08
❑ 430 Benito Santiago AS .05 .01
❑ 431 Ivan Calderon AS .05 .01
❑ 432 Ozzie Smith .40 .15
❑ 433 Tim Leary .05 .01
❑ 434 Bret Saberhagen HL .05 .01
❑ 435 Mel Rojas .05 .01
❑ 436 Ben McDonald .05 .01
❑ 437 Tim Crews .05 .01
❑ 438 Rex Hudler .05 .01
❑ 439 Chico Walker .05 .01
❑ 440 Kurt Stillwell .05 .01
❑ 441 Tony Gwynn .30 .10
❑ 442 John Smoltz .15 .05
❑ 443 Lloyd Moseby .05 .01
❑ 444 Mike Schooler .05 .01
❑ 445 Joe Grahe .05 .01
❑ 446 Dwight Gooden .10 .02
❑ 447 Oil Can Boyd .05 .01
❑ 448 John Marzano .05 .01
❑ 449 Bret Barberie .05 .01
❑ 450 Mike Maddux .05 .01
❑ 451 Jeff Reed .05 .01
❑ 452 Dale Sveum .05 .01
❑ 453 Jose Uribe .05 .01
❑ 454 Bob Scanlan .05 .01
❑ 455 Kevin Appier .10 .02
❑ 456 Jeff Huson .05 .01
❑ 457 Ken Patterson .05 .01
❑ 458 Ricky Jordan .05 .01
❑ 459 Tom Candiotti .05 .01
❑ 460 Lee Stevens .05 .01
❑ 461 Rod Beck RC .25 .08
❑ 462 Dave Valle .05 .01
❑ 463 Scott Erickson .05 .01
❑ 464 Chris Jones .05 .01
❑ 465 Mark Carreon .05 .01
❑ 466 Rob Ducey .05 .01
❑ 467 Jim Corsi .05 .01
❑ 468 Jeff King .05 .01
❑ 469 Curt Young .05 .01
❑ 470 Bo Jackson .25 .08
❑ 471 Chris Bosio .05 .01
❑ 472 Jamie Quirk .05 .01
❑ 473 Jesse Orosco .05 .01
❑ 474 Alvaro Espinoza .05 .01
❑ 475 Joe Orsulak .05 .01
❑ 476 Checklist 397-477 .05 .01
❑ 477 Gerald Young .05 .01
❑ 478 Wally Backman .05 .01
❑ 479 Juan Bell .05 .01
❑ 480 Mike Scioscia .05 .01
❑ 481 Omar Olivares .05 .01
❑ 482 Francisco Cabrera .05 .01
❑ 483 Greg Swindell UER
(Shown on Indians,
but listed .05 .01
❑ 484 Terry Leach .05 .01
❑ 485 Tommy Gregg .05 .01
❑ 486 Scott Aldred .05 .01
❑ 487 Greg Briley .05 .01
❑ 488 Phil Plantier .05 .01
❑ 489 Curtis Wilkerson .05 .01
❑ 490 Tom Brunansky .05 .01
❑ 491 Mike Fetters .05 .01
❑ 492 Frank Castillo .05 .01
❑ 493 Joe Boever .05 .01
❑ 494 Kirt Manwaring .05 .01
❑ 495 Wilson Alvarez HL .05 .01
❑ 496 Gene Larkin .05 .01
❑ 497 Gary DiSarcina .05 .01
❑ 498 Frank Viola .10 .02
❑ 499 Manuel Lee .05 .01
❑ 500 Albert Belle .10 .02
❑ 501 Stan Belinda .05 .01
❑ 502 Dwight Evans .15 .05
❑ 503 Eric Davis .10 .02
❑ 504 Darren Holmes .05 .01
❑ 505 Mike Bordick .05 .01
❑ 506 Dave Hansen .05 .01
❑ 507 Lee Guetterman .05 .01
❑ 508 Keith Mitchell .05 .01
❑ 509 Melido Perez .05 .01
❑ 510 Dickie Thon .05 .01
❑ 511 Mark Williamson .05 .01
❑ 512 Mark Salas .05 .01
❑ 513 Milt Thompson .05 .01
❑ 514 Mo Vaughn .10 .02
❑ 515 Jim Deshaies .05 .01
❑ 516 Rich Garces .05 .01
❑ 517 Lonnie Smith .05 .01
❑ 518 Spike Owen .05 .01
❑ 519 Tracy Jones .05 .01
❑ 520 Greg Maddux .40 .15
❑ 521 Carlos Martinez .05 .01
❑ 522 Neal Heaton .05 .01
❑ 523 Mike Greenwell .05 .01
❑ 524 Andy Benes .05 .01
❑ 525 Jeff Schaefer UER .05 .01
❑ 526 Mike Sharperson .05 .01
❑ 527 Wade Taylor .05 .01
❑ 528 Jerome Walton .05 .01
❑ 529 Storm Davis .05 .01
❑ 530 Jose Hernandez RC .25 .08
❑ 531 Mark Langston .05 .01
❑ 532 Rob Deer .05 .01
❑ 533 Geronimo Pena .05 .01
❑ 534 Juan Guzman .05 .01
❑ 535 Pete Schourek .05 .01
❑ 536 Todd Benzinger .05 .01
❑ 537 Billy Hatcher .05 .01
❑ 538 Tom Foley .05 .01
❑ 539 Dave Cochrane .05 .01
❑ 540 Mariano Duncan .05 .01
❑ 541 Edwin Nunez .05 .01
❑ 542 Rance Mulliniks .05 .01
❑ 543 Carlton Fisk .15 .05
❑ 544 Luis Aquino .05 .01
❑ 545 Ricky Bones .05 .01
❑ 546 Craig Grebeck .05 .01
❑ 547 Charlie Hayes .05 .01
❑ 548 Jose Canseco .15 .05
❑ 549 Andujar Cedeno .05 .01
❑ 550 Geno Petralli .05 .01
❑ 551 Javier Ortiz .05 .01
❑ 552 Rudy Seanez .05 .01
❑ 553 Rich Gedman .05 .01
❑ 554 Eric Plunk .05 .01
❑ 555 N.Ryan/G.Gossage HL .40 .15
❑ 556 Checklist 478-555 .05 .01
❑ 557 Greg Colbrunn .05 .01
❑ 558 Chito Martinez .05 .01
❑ 559 Darryl Strawberry .10 .02
❑ 560 Luis Alicea .05 .01
❑ 561 Dwight Smith .05 .01
❑ 562 Terry Shumpert .05 .01
❑ 563 Jim Vatcher .05 .01
❑ 564 Deion Sanders .15 .05
❑ 565 Walt Terrell .05 .01
❑ 566 Dave Burba .05 .01
❑ 567 Dave Howard .05 .01
❑ 568 Todd Hundley .05 .01
❑ 569 Jack Daugherty .05 .01
❑ 570 Scott Cooper .05 .01
❑ 571 Bill Sampen .05 .01
❑ 572 Jose Melendez .05 .01
❑ 573 Freddie Benavides .05 .01
❑ 574 Jim Gantner .05 .01
❑ 575 Trevor Wilson .05 .01
❑ 576 Ryne Sandberg .40 .15
❑ 577 Kevin Seitzer .05 .01
❑ 578 Gerald Alexander .05 .01
❑ 579 Mike Huff .05 .01
❑ 580 Von Hayes .05 .01
❑ 581 Derek Bell .10 .02
❑ 582 Mike Stanley .05 .01
❑ 583 Kevin Mitchell .05 .01
❑ 584 Mike Jackson .05 .01
❑ 585 Dan Gladden .05 .01
❑ 586 Ted Power UER
(Wrong year given for
signing with .05 .01
❑ 587 Jeff Innis .05 .01
❑ 588 Bob MacDonald .05 .01
❑ 589 Jose Tolentino .05 .01
❑ 590 Bob Patterson .05 .01
❑ 591 Scott Brosius RC .40 .15
❑ 592 Frank Thomas .25 .08
❑ 593 Darryl Hamilton .05 .01
❑ 594 Kirk Dressendorfer .05 .01
❑ 595 Jeff Shaw .05 .01
❑ 596 Don Mattingly .60 .25
❑ 597 Glenn Davis .05 .01
❑ 598 Andy Mota .05 .01
❑ 599 Jason Grimsley .05 .01

❑ 600 Jim Poole	.05	.01
❑ 601 Jim Gott	.05	.01
❑ 602 Stan Royer	.05	.01
❑ 603 Marvin Freeman	.05	.01
❑ 604 Denis Boucher	.05	.01
❑ 605 Denny Neagle	.10	.02
❑ 606 Mark Lemke	.05	.01
❑ 607 Jerry Don Gleaton	.05	.01
❑ 608 Brent Knackert	.05	.01
❑ 609 Carlos Quintana	.05	.01
❑ 610 Bobby Bonilla	.10	.02
❑ 611 Joe Hesketh	.05	.01
❑ 612 Daryl Boston	.05	.01
❑ 613 Shawon Dunston	.05	.01
❑ 614 Danny Cox	.05	.01
❑ 615 Darren Lewis	.05	.01
❑ 616 Mercker/Pena/Wohlers UER	.05	.01
❑ 617 Kirby Puckett	.25	.08
❑ 618 Franklin Stubbs	.05	.01
❑ 619 Chris Donnels	.05	.01
❑ 620 David Wells UER	.10	.02
❑ 621 Mike Aldrete	.05	.01
❑ 622 Bob Kipper	.05	.01
❑ 623 Anthony Telford	.05	.01
❑ 624 Randy Myers	.05	.01
❑ 625 Willie Randolph	.10	.02
❑ 626 Joe Slusarski	.05	.01
❑ 627 John Wetteland	.10	.02
❑ 628 Greg Cadaret	.05	.01
❑ 629 Tom Glavine	.15	.05
❑ 630 Wilson Alvarez	.05	.01
❑ 631 Wally Ritchie	.05	.01
❑ 632 Mike Mussina	.25	.08
❑ 633 Mark Leiter	.05	.01
❑ 634 Gerald Perry	.05	.01
❑ 635 Matt Young	.05	.01
❑ 636 Checklist 556-635	.05	.01
❑ 637 Scott Hemond	.05	.01
❑ 638 David West	.05	.01
❑ 639 Jim Clancy	.05	.01
❑ 640 Doug Piatt UER (Not born in 1955 as on card; inc	.05	.01
❑ 641 Omar Vizquel	.15	.05
❑ 642 Rick Sutcliffe	.10	.02
❑ 643 Glenallen Hill	.05	.01
❑ 644 Gary Varsho	.05	.01
❑ 645 Tony Fossas	.05	.01
❑ 646 Jack Howell	.05	.01
❑ 647 Jim Campanis	.05	.01
❑ 648 Chris Gwynn	.05	.01
❑ 649 Jim Leyritz	.05	.01
❑ 650 Chuck McElroy	.05	.01
❑ 651 Sean Berry	.05	.01
❑ 652 Donald Harris	.05	.01
❑ 653 Don Slaught	.05	.01
❑ 654 Rusty Meacham	.05	.01
❑ 655 Scott Terry	.05	.01
❑ 656 Ramon Martinez	.05	.01
❑ 657 Keith Miller	.05	.01
❑ 658 Ramon Garcia	.05	.01
❑ 659 Milt Hill	.05	.01
❑ 660 Steve Frey	.05	.01
❑ 661 Bob McClure	.05	.01
❑ 662 Ced Landrum	.05	.01
❑ 663 Doug Henry RC	.10	.02
❑ 664 Candy Maldonado	.05	.01
❑ 665 Carl Willis	.05	.01
❑ 666 Jeff Montgomery	.05	.01
❑ 667 Craig Shipley	.05	.01
❑ 668 Warren Newson	.05	.01
❑ 669 Mickey Morandini	.05	.01
❑ 670 Brook Jacoby	.05	.01
❑ 671 Ryan Bowen	.05	.01
❑ 672 Bill Krueger	.05	.01
❑ 673 Rob Mallicoat	.05	.01
❑ 674 Doug Jones	.05	.01
❑ 675 Scott Livingstone	.05	.01
❑ 676 Danny Tartabull	.05	.01
❑ 677 Joe Carter HL	.05	.01
❑ 678 Cecil Espy	.05	.01
❑ 679 Randy Velarde	.05	.01
❑ 680 Bruce Ruffin	.05	.01
❑ 681 Ted Wood	.05	.01
❑ 682 Dan Plesac	.05	.01
❑ 683 Eric Bullock	.05	.01
❑ 684 Junior Ortiz	.05	.01
❑ 685 Dave Hollins	.05	.01
❑ 686 Dennis Martinez	.10	.02
❑ 687 Larry Andersen	.05	.01
❑ 688 Doug Simons	.05	.01
❑ 689 Tim Spehr	.05	.01
❑ 690 Calvin Jones	.05	.01
❑ 691 Mark Guthrie	.05	.01
❑ 692 Alfredo Griffin	.05	.01
❑ 693 Joe Carter	.10	.02
❑ 694 Terry Mathews	.05	.01
❑ 695 Pascual Perez	.05	.01
❑ 696 Gene Nelson	.05	.01
❑ 697 Gerald Williams	.05	.01
❑ 698 Chris Cron	.05	.01
❑ 699 Steve Buechele	.05	.01
❑ 700 Paul McClellan	.05	.01
❑ 701 Jim Lindeman	.05	.01
❑ 702 Francisco Oliveras	.05	.01
❑ 703 Rob Maurer	.05	.01
❑ 704 Pat Hentgen	.05	.01
❑ 705 Jaime Navarro	.05	.01
❑ 706 Mike Magnante RC	.10	.02
❑ 707 Nolan Ryan	1.00	.40
❑ 708 Bobby Thigpen	.05	.01
❑ 709 John Cerutti	.05	.01
❑ 710 Steve Wilson	.05	.01
❑ 711 Hensley Meulens	.05	.01
❑ 712 Rheal Cormier	.05	.01
❑ 713 Scott Bradley	.05	.01
❑ 714 Mitch Webster	.05	.01
❑ 715 Roger Mason	.05	.01
❑ 716 Checklist 636-716	.05	.01
❑ 717 Jeff Fassero	.05	.01
❑ 718 Cal Eldred	.05	.01
❑ 719 Sid Fernandez	.05	.01
❑ 720 Bob Zupcic RC	.10	.02
❑ 721 Jose Offerman	.05	.01
❑ 722 Cliff Brantley	.05	.01
❑ 723 Ron Darling	.05	.01
❑ 724 Dave Stieb	.05	.01
❑ 725 Hector Villanueva	.05	.01
❑ 726 Mike Hartley	.05	.01
❑ 727 Arthur Rhodes	.05	.01
❑ 728 Randy Bush	.05	.01
❑ 729 Steve Sax	.05	.01
❑ 730 Dave Otto	.05	.01
❑ 731 John Wehner	.05	.01
❑ 732 Dave Martinez	.05	.01
❑ 733 Ruben Amaro	.05	.01
❑ 734 Billy Ripken	.05	.01
❑ 735 Steve Farr	.05	.01
❑ 736 Shawn Abner	.05	.01
❑ 737 Gil Heredia RC	.25	.08
❑ 738 Ron Jones	.05	.01
❑ 739 Tony Castillo	.05	.01
❑ 740 Sammy Sosa	.25	.08
❑ 741 Julio Franco	.10	.02
❑ 742 Tim Naehring	.05	.01
❑ 743 Steve Wapnick	.05	.01
❑ 744 Craig Wilson	.05	.01
❑ 745 Darrin Chapin	.05	.01
❑ 746 Chris George	.05	.01
❑ 747 Mike Simms	.05	.01
❑ 748 Rosario Rodriguez	.05	.01
❑ 749 Skeeter Barnes	.05	.01
❑ 750 Roger McDowell	.05	.01
❑ 751 Dann Howitt	.05	.01
❑ 752 Paul Sorrento	.05	.01
❑ 753 Braulio Castillo	.05	.01
❑ 754 Yorkis Perez	.05	.01
❑ 755 Willie Fraser	.05	.01
❑ 756 Jeremy Hernandez RC	.10	.02
❑ 757 Curt Schilling	.15	.05
❑ 758 Steve Lyons	.05	.01
❑ 759 Dave Anderson	.05	.01
❑ 760 Willie Banks	.05	.01
❑ 761 Mark Leonard	.05	.01
❑ 762 Jack Armstrong (Listed on Indians, but shown on	.05	.01
❑ 763 Scott Servais	.05	.01
❑ 764 Ray Stephens	.05	.01
❑ 765 Junior Noboa	.05	.01
❑ 766 Jim Olander	.05	.01
❑ 767 Joe Magrane	.05	.01
❑ 768 Lance Blankenship	.05	.01
❑ 769 Mike Humphreys	.05	.01
❑ 770 Jarvis Brown	.05	.01
❑ 771 Damon Berryhill	.05	.01
❑ 772 Alejandro Pena	.05	.01
❑ 773 Jose Mesa	.05	.01
❑ 774 Gary Cooper	.05	.01
❑ 775 Carney Lansford	.10	.02
❑ 776 Mike Bielecki (Shown on Cubs, but listed on Brav	.05	.01
❑ 777 Charlie O'Brien	.05	.01
❑ 778 Carlos Hernandez	.05	.01
❑ 779 Howard Farmer	.05	.01
❑ 780 Mike Stanton	.05	.01
❑ 781 Reggie Harris	.05	.01
❑ 782 Xavier Hernandez	.05	.01
❑ 783 Bryan Hickerson RC	.10	.02
❑ 784 Checklist 717-784 and BC1-BC8	.05	.01

1992 Donruss Rookies

❑ COMPLETE SET (132)	10.00	4.00
❑ 1 Kyle Abbott	.05	.01
❑ 2 Troy Afenir	.05	.01
❑ 3 Rich Amaral RC	.10	.02
❑ 4 Ruben Amaro	.05	.01
❑ 5 Billy Ashley RC	.10	.02
❑ 6 Pedro Astacio RC	.25	.08
❑ 7 Jim Austin	.05	.01
❑ 8 Robert Ayrault	.05	.01
❑ 9 Kevin Baez	.05	.01
❑ 10 Esteban Beltre	.05	.01
❑ 11 Brian Bohanon	.05	.01
❑ 12 Kent Bottenfield RC	.25	.08
❑ 13 Jeff Branson	.05	.01
❑ 14 Brad Brink	.05	.01
❑ 15 John Briscoe	.05	.01
❑ 16 Doug Brocail RC	.10	.02
❑ 17 Rico Brogna	.05	.01
❑ 18 J.T. Bruett	.05	.01
❑ 19 Jacob Brumfield	.05	.01
❑ 20 Jim Bullinger	.05	.01
❑ 21 Kevin Campbell	.05	.01
❑ 22 Pedro Castellano RC	.10	.02
❑ 23 Mike Christopher	.05	.01
❑ 24 Archi Cianfrocco RC	.10	.02
❑ 25 Mark Clark RC	.10	.02
❑ 26 Craig Colbert	.05	.01
❑ 27 Victor Cole	.05	.01
❑ 28 Steve Cooke RC	.10	.02
❑ 29 Tim Costo	.05	.01
❑ 30 Chad Curtis RC	.25	.08
❑ 31 Doug Davis	.05	.01
❑ 32 Gary DiSarcina	.05	.01
❑ 33 John Doherty RC	.10	.02
❑ 34 Mike Draper	.05	.01
❑ 35 Monty Fariss	.05	.01
❑ 36 Bien Figueroa	.05	.01
❑ 37 John Flaherty	.05	.01
❑ 38 Tim Fortugno	.05	.01
❑ 39 Eric Fox RC	.10	.02
❑ 40 Jeff Frye RC	.10	.02
❑ 41 Ramon Garcia	.05	.01
❑ 42 Brent Gates RC	.10	.02
❑ 43 Tom Goodwin	.05	.01
❑ 44 Buddy Groom RC	.10	.02
❑ 45 Jeff Grotewold	.05	.01

❑ 46 Juan Guerrero	.05	.01
❑ 47 Johnny Guzman RC	.10	.02
❑ 48 Shawn Hare RC	.10	.02
❑ 49 Ryan Hawblitzel RC	.10	.02
❑ 50 Bert Heffernan	.05	.01
❑ 51 Butch Henry	.05	.01
❑ 52 Cesar Hernandez RC	.10	.02
❑ 53 Vince Horsman	.05	.01
❑ 54 Steve Hosey	.05	.01
❑ 55 Pat Howell	.05	.01
❑ 56 Peter Hoy	.05	.01
❑ 57 Jonathan Hurst RC	.10	.02
❑ 58 Mark Hutton RC	.10	.02
❑ 59 Shawn Jeter RC	.10	.02
❑ 60 Joel Johnston	.05	.01
❑ 61 Jeff Kent RC	2.50	1.00
❑ 62 Kurt Knudsen RC	.10	.02
❑ 63 Kevin Koslofski	.05	.01
❑ 64 Danny Leon	.05	.01
❑ 65 Jesse Levis	.05	.01
❑ 66 Tom Marsh	.05	.01
❑ 67 Ed Martel	.05	.01
❑ 68 Al Martin RC	.25	.08
❑ 69 Pedro Martinez	2.00	.75
❑ 70 Derrick May	.05	.01
❑ 71 Matt Maysey	.05	.01
❑ 72 Russ McGinnis	.05	.01
❑ 73 Tim McIntosh	.05	.01
❑ 74 Jim McNamara	.05	.01
❑ 75 Jeff McNeely	.05	.01
❑ 76 Rusty Meacham	.05	.01
❑ 77 Tony Menendez	.05	.01
❑ 78 Henry Mercedes	.05	.01
❑ 79 Paul Miller	.05	.01
❑ 80 Joe Millette	.05	.01
❑ 81 Blas Minor	.05	.01
❑ 82 Dennis Moeller	.05	.01
❑ 83 Raul Mondesi	.10	.02
❑ 84 Rob Natal	.05	.01
❑ 85 Troy Neel RC	.10	.02
❑ 86 David Nied RC	.10	.02
❑ 87 Jerry Nielson	.05	.01
❑ 88 Donovan Osborne	.05	.01
❑ 89 John Patterson RC	.10	.02
❑ 90 Roger Pavlik RC	.10	.02
❑ 91 Dan Peltier	.05	.01
❑ 92 Jim Pena	.05	.01
❑ 93 William Pennyfeather	.05	.01
❑ 94 Mike Perez	.05	.01
❑ 95 Hipolito Pichardo RC	.10	.02
❑ 96 Greg Pirkl RC	.10	.02
❑ 97 Harvey Pulliam	.05	.01
❑ 98 Manny Ramirez RC	4.00	1.50
❑ 99 Pat Rapp RC	.10	.02
❑ 100 Jeff Reboulet	.05	.01
❑ 101 Darren Reed	.05	.01
❑ 102 Shane Reynolds RC	.25	.08
❑ 103 Bill Risley	.05	.01
❑ 104 Ben Rivera	.05	.01
❑ 105 Henry Rodriguez	.05	.01
❑ 106 Rico Rossy	.05	.01
❑ 107 Johnny Ruffin	.05	.01
❑ 108 Steve Scarsone	.05	.01
❑ 109 Tim Scott	.05	.01
❑ 110 Steve Shifflett	.05	.01
❑ 111 Dave Silvestri	.05	.01
❑ 112 Matt Stairs RC	.25	.08
❑ 113 William Suero	.05	.01
❑ 114 Jeff Tackett	.05	.01
❑ 115 Eddie Taubensee	.10	.02
❑ 116 Rick Trlicek RC	.10	.02
❑ 117 Scooter Tucker	.05	.01
❑ 118 Shane Turner	.05	.01
❑ 119 Julio Valera	.05	.01
❑ 120 Paul Wagner RC	.10	.02
❑ 121 Tim Wakefield RC	3.00	1.25
❑ 122 Mike Walker	.05	.01
❑ 123 Bruce Walton	.05	.01
❑ 124 Lenny Webster	.05	.01
❑ 125 Bob Wickman	.25	.08
❑ 126 Mike Williams RC	.25	.08
❑ 127 Kerry Woodson	.05	.01
❑ 128 Eric Young RC	.25	.08
❑ 129 Kevin Young RC	.25	.08
❑ 130 Pete Young	.05	.01
❑ 131 Checklist 1-66	.05	.01
❑ 132 Checklist 67-132	.05	.01

1993 Donruss

❑ COMPLETE SET (792)	30.00	12.00
❑ COMPLETE SERIES 1 (396)	15.00	6.00
❑ COMPLETE SERIES 2 (396)	15.00	6.00
❑ 1 Craig Lefferts	.10	.02
❑ 2 Kent Mercker	.10	.02
❑ 3 Phil Plantier	.10	.02
❑ 4 Alex Arias	.10	.02
❑ 5 Julio Valera	.10	.02
❑ 6 Dan Wilson	.20	.07
❑ 7 Frank Thomas	.50	.20
❑ 8 Eric Anthony	.10	.02
❑ 9 Derek Lilliquist	.10	.02
❑ 10 Rafael Bournigal	.10	.02
❑ 11 Manny Alexander	.10	.02
❑ 12 Bret Barberie	.10	.02
❑ 13 Mickey Tettleton	.10	.02
❑ 14 Anthony Young	.10	.02
❑ 15 Tim Spehr	.10	.02
❑ 16 Bob Ayrault	.10	.02
❑ 17 Bill Wegman	.10	.02
❑ 18 Jay Bell	.20	.07
❑ 19 Rick Aguilera	.10	.02
❑ 20 Todd Zeile	.10	.02
❑ 21 Steve Farr	.10	.02
❑ 22 Andy Benes	.10	.02
❑ 23 Lance Blankenship	.10	.02
❑ 24 Ted Wood	.10	.02
❑ 25 Omar Vizquel	.30	.10
❑ 26 Steve Avery	.10	.02
❑ 27 Brian Bohanon	.10	.02
❑ 28 Rick Wilkins	.10	.02
❑ 29 Devon White	.20	.07
❑ 30 Bobby Ayala RC	.10	.02
❑ 31 Leo Gomez	.10	.02
❑ 32 Mike Simms	.10	.02
❑ 33 Ellis Burks	.20	.07
❑ 34 Steve Wilson	.10	.02
❑ 35 Jim Abbott	.30	.10
❑ 36 Tim Wallach	.10	.02
❑ 37 Wilson Alvarez	.10	.02
❑ 38 Daryl Boston	.10	.02
❑ 39 Sandy Alomar Jr.	.10	.02
❑ 40 Mitch Williams	.10	.02
❑ 41 Rico Brogna	.10	.02
❑ 42 Gary Varsho	.10	.02
❑ 43 Kevin Appier	.20	.07
❑ 44 Eric Wedge RC	.10	.02
❑ 45 Dante Bichette	.20	.07
❑ 46 Jose Oquendo	.10	.02
❑ 47 Mike Trombley	.10	.02
❑ 48 Dan Walters	.10	.02
❑ 49 Gerald Williams	.10	.02
❑ 50 Bud Black	.10	.02
❑ 51 Bobby Witt	.10	.02
❑ 52 Mark Davis	.10	.02
❑ 53 Shawn Barton RC	.10	.02
❑ 54 Paul Assenmacher	.10	.02
❑ 55 Kevin Reimer	.10	.02
❑ 56 Billy Ashley	.10	.02
❑ 57 Eddie Zosky	.10	.02
❑ 58 Chris Sabo	.10	.02
❑ 59 Billy Ripken	.10	.02
❑ 60 Scooter Tucker	.10	.02
❑ 61 Tim Wakefield	.50	.20
❑ 62 Mitch Webster	.10	.02
❑ 63 Jack Clark	.20	.07
❑ 64 Mark Gardner	.10	.02
❑ 65 Lee Stevens	.10	.02
❑ 66 Todd Hundley	.10	.02
❑ 67 Bobby Thigpen	.10	.02
❑ 68 Dave Hollins	.10	.02
❑ 69 Jack Armstrong	.10	.02
❑ 70 Alex Cole	.10	.02
❑ 71 Mark Carreon	.10	.02
❑ 72 Todd Worrell	.10	.02
❑ 73 Steve Shifflett	.10	.02
❑ 74 Jerald Clark	.10	.02
❑ 75 Paul Molitor	.20	.07
❑ 76 Larry Carter RC	.10	.02
❑ 77 Rich Rowland	.10	.02
❑ 78 Damon Berryhill	.10	.02
❑ 79 Willie Banks	.10	.02
❑ 80 Hector Villanueva	.10	.02
❑ 81 Mike Gallego	.10	.02
❑ 82 Tim Belcher	.10	.02
❑ 83 Mike Bordick	.10	.02
❑ 84 Craig Biggio	.30	.10
❑ 85 Lance Parrish	.20	.07
❑ 86 Brett Butler	.20	.07
❑ 87 Mike Timlin	.10	.02
❑ 88 Brian Barnes	.10	.02
❑ 89 Brady Anderson	.20	.07
❑ 90 D.J. Dozier	.10	.02
❑ 91 Frank Viola	.20	.07
❑ 92 Darren Daulton	.20	.07
❑ 93 Chad Curtis	.10	.02
❑ 94 Zane Smith	.10	.02
❑ 95 George Bell	.10	.02
❑ 96 Rex Hudler	.10	.02
❑ 97 Mark Whiten	.10	.02
❑ 98 Tim Teufel	.10	.02
❑ 99 Kevin Ritz	.10	.02
❑ 100 Jeff Brantley	.10	.02
❑ 101 Jeff Conine	.20	.07
❑ 102 Vinny Castilla	.50	.20
❑ 103 Greg Vaughn	.10	.02
❑ 104 Steve Buechele	.10	.02
❑ 105 Darren Reed	.10	.02
❑ 106 Bip Roberts	.10	.02
❑ 107 John Habyan	.10	.02
❑ 108 Scott Servais	.10	.02
❑ 109 Walt Weiss	.10	.02
❑ 110 J.T.Snow RC	.30	.10
❑ 111 Jay Buhner	.20	.07
❑ 112 Darryl Strawberry	.20	.07
❑ 113 Roger Pavlik	.10	.02
❑ 114 Chris Nabholz	.10	.02
❑ 115 Pat Borders	.10	.02
❑ 116 Pat Howell	.10	.02
❑ 117 Gregg Olson	.10	.02
❑ 118 Curt Schilling	.20	.07
❑ 119 Roger Clemens	1.00	.40
❑ 120 Victor Cole	.10	.02
❑ 121 Gary DiSarcina	.10	.02
❑ 122 Checklist 1-80 Gary Carter and Kirt Manwaring	.10	.02
❑ 123 Steve Sax	.10	.02
❑ 124 Chuck Carr	.10	.02
❑ 125 Mark Lewis	.10	.02
❑ 126 Tony Gwynn	.60	.25
❑ 127 Travis Fryman	.20	.07
❑ 128 Dave Burba	.10	.02
❑ 129 Wally Joyner	.20	.07
❑ 130 John Smoltz	.30	.10
❑ 131 Cal Eldred	.10	.02
❑ 132 Checklist 81-159 (Roberto Alomar and Devon White	.20	.07
❑ 133 Arthur Rhodes	.10	.02
❑ 134 Jeff Blauser	.10	.02
❑ 135 Scott Cooper	.10	.02
❑ 136 Doug Strange	.10	.02
❑ 137 Luis Sojo	.10	.02
❑ 138 Jeff Branson	.10	.02
❑ 139 Alex Fernandez	.10	.02
❑ 140 Ken Caminiti	.20	.07
❑ 141 Charles Nagy	.10	.02
❑ 142 Tom Candiotti	.10	.02
❑ 143 Willie Greene	.10	.02

❑	144	John Vander Wal	.10	.02
❑	145	Kurt Knudsen	.10	.02
❑	146	John Franco	.20	.07
❑	147	Eddie Pierce RC	.10	.02
❑	148	Kim Batiste	.10	.02
❑	149	Darren Holmes	.10	.02
❑	150	Steve Cooke	.10	.02
❑	151	Terry Jorgensen	.10	.02
❑	152	Mark Clark	.10	.02
❑	153	Randy Velarde	.10	.02
❑	154	Greg W. Harris	.10	.02
❑	155	Kevin Campbell	.10	.02
❑	156	John Burkett	.10	.02
❑	157	Kevin Mitchell	.10	.02
❑	158	Deion Sanders	.30	.10
❑	159	Jose Canseco	.30	.10
❑	160	Jeff Hartsock	.10	.02
❑	161	Tom Quinlan RC	.10	.02
❑	162	Tim Pugh RC	.10	.02
❑	163	Glenn Davis	.10	.02
❑	164	Shane Reynolds	.10	.02
❑	165	Jody Reed	.10	.02
❑	166	Mike Sharperson	.10	.02
❑	167	Scott Lewis	.10	.02
❑	168	Dennis Martinez	.20	.07
❑	169	Scott Radinsky	.10	.02
❑	170	Dave Gallagher	.10	.02
❑	171	Jim Thome	.30	.10
❑	172	Terry Mulholland	.10	.02
❑	173	Milt Cuyler	.10	.02
❑	174	Bob Patterson	.10	.02
❑	175	Jeff Montgomery	.10	.02
❑	176	Tim Salmon	.30	.10
❑	177	Franklin Stubbs	.10	.02
❑	178	Donovan Osborne	.10	.02
❑	179	Jeff Reboulet	.10	.02
❑	180	Jeremy Hernandez	.10	.02
❑	181	Charlie Hayes	.10	.02
❑	182	Matt Williams	.20	.07
❑	183	Mike Raczka	.10	.02
❑	184	Francisco Cabrera	.10	.02
❑	185	Rich DeLucia	.10	.02
❑	186	Sammy Sosa	.50	.20
❑	187	Ivan Rodriguez	.30	.10
❑	188	Bret Boone	.20	.07
❑	189	Juan Guzman	.10	.02
❑	190	Tom Browning	.10	.02
❑	191	Randy Milligan	.10	.02
❑	192	Steve Finley	.20	.07
❑	193	John Patterson RR	.10	.02
❑	194	Kip Gross	.10	.02
❑	195	Tony Fossas	.10	.02
❑	196	Ivan Calderon	.10	.02
❑	197	Junior Felix	.10	.02
❑	198	Pete Schourek	.10	.02
❑	199	Craig Grebeck	.10	.02
❑	200	Juan Bell	.10	.02
❑	201	Glenallen Hill	.10	.02
❑	202	Danny Jackson	.10	.02
❑	203	John Kiely	.10	.02
❑	204	Bob Tewksbury	.10	.02
❑	205	Kevin Koslofski	.10	.02
❑	206	Craig Shipley	.10	.02
❑	207	John Jaha	.10	.02
❑	208	Royce Clayton	.10	.02
❑	209	Mike Piazza	3.00	1.25
❑	210	Ron Gant	.20	.07
❑	211	Scott Erickson	.10	.02
❑	212	Doug Dascenzo	.10	.02
❑	213	Andy Stankiewicz	.10	.02
❑	214	Geronimo Berroa	.10	.02
❑	215	Dennis Eckersley	.20	.07
❑	216	Al Osuna	.10	.02
❑	217	Tino Martinez	.30	.10
❑	218	Henry Rodriguez	.10	.02
❑	219	Ed Sprague	.10	.02
❑	220	Ken Hill	.10	.02
❑	221	Chito Martinez	.10	.02
❑	222	Bret Saberhagen	.20	.07
❑	223	Mike Greenwell	.10	.02
❑	224	Mickey Morandini	.10	.02
❑	225	Chuck Finley	.20	.07
❑	226	Denny Neagle	.20	.07
❑	227	Kirk McCaskill	.10	.02
❑	228	Rheal Cormier	.10	.02
❑	229	Paul Sorrento	.10	.02
❑	230	Darrin Jackson	.10	.02
❑	231	Rob Deer	.10	.02
❑	232	Bill Swift	.10	.02
❑	233	Kevin McReynolds	.10	.02
❑	234	Terry Pendleton	.20	.07
❑	235	Dave Nilsson	.10	.02
❑	236	Chuck McElroy	.10	.02
❑	237	Derek Parks	.10	.02
❑	238	Norm Charlton	.10	.02
❑	239	Matt Nokes	.10	.02
❑	240	Juan Guerrero	.10	.02
❑	241	Jeff Parrett	.10	.02
❑	242	Ryan Thompson	.10	.02
❑	243	Dave Fleming	.10	.02
❑	244	Dave Hansen	.10	.02
❑	245	Monty Fariss	.10	.02
❑	246	Archi Cianfrocco	.10	.02
❑	247	Pat Hentgen	.10	.02
❑	248	Bill Pecota	.10	.02
❑	249	Ben McDonald	.10	.02
❑	250	Cliff Brantley	.10	.02
❑	251	John Valentin	.10	.02
❑	252	Jeff King	.10	.02
❑	253	Reggie Williams	.10	.02
❑	254	Checklist 160-238	.10	.02
❑	255	Ozzie Guillen	.20	.07
❑	256	Mike Perez	.10	.02
❑	257	Thomas Howard	.10	.02
❑	258	Kurt Stillwell	.10	.02
❑	259	Mike Henneman	.10	.02
❑	260	Steve Decker	.10	.02
❑	261	Brent Mayne	.10	.02
❑	262	Otis Nixon	.10	.02
❑	263	Mark Kiefer	.10	.02
❑	264	Checklist 239-317 (Don Mattingly and Mike Bordic	.30	.10
❑	265	Richie Lewis RC	.10	.02
❑	266	Pat Gomez RC	.10	.02
❑	267	Scott Taylor	.10	.02
❑	268	Shawon Dunston	.10	.02
❑	269	Greg Myers	.10	.02
❑	270	Tim Costo	.10	.02
❑	271	Greg Hibbard	.10	.02
❑	272	Pete Harnisch	.10	.02
❑	273	Dave Mlicki	.10	.02
❑	274	Orel Hershiser	.20	.07
❑	275	Sean Berry RR	.10	.02
❑	276	Doug Simons	.10	.02
❑	277	John Doherty	.10	.02
❑	278	Eddie Murray	.50	.20
❑	279	Chris Haney	.10	.02
❑	280	Stan Javier	.10	.02
❑	281	Jaime Navarro	.10	.02
❑	282	Orlando Merced	.10	.02
❑	283	Kent Hrbek	.20	.07
❑	284	Bernard Gilkey	.10	.02
❑	285	Russ Springer	.10	.02
❑	286	Mike Maddux	.10	.02
❑	287	Eric Fox	.10	.02
❑	288	Mark Leonard	.10	.02
❑	289	Tim Leary	.10	.02
❑	290	Brian Hunter	.10	.02
❑	291	Donald Harris	.10	.02
❑	292	Bob Scanlan	.10	.02
❑	293	Turner Ward	.10	.02
❑	294	Hal Morris	.10	.02
❑	295	Jimmy Poole	.10	.02
❑	296	Doug Jones	.10	.02
❑	297	Tony Pena	.10	.02
❑	298	Ramon Martinez	.10	.02
❑	299	Tim Fortugno	.10	.02
❑	300	Marquis Grissom	.20	.07
❑	301	Lance Johnson	.10	.02
❑	302	Jeff Kent	.50	.20
❑	303	Reggie Jefferson	.10	.02
❑	304	Wes Chamberlain	.10	.02
❑	305	Shawn Hare	.10	.02
❑	306	Mike LaValliere	.10	.02
❑	307	Gregg Jefferies	.10	.02
❑	308	Troy Neel	.10	.02
❑	309	Pat Listach	.10	.02
❑	310	Geronimo Pena	.10	.02
❑	311	Pedro Munoz	.10	.02
❑	312	Guillermo Velasquez	.10	.02
❑	313	Roberto Kelly	.10	.02
❑	314	Mike Jackson	.10	.02
❑	315	Rickey Henderson	.50	.20
❑	316	Mark Lemke	.10	.02
❑	317	Erik Hanson	.10	.02
❑	318	Derrick May	.10	.02
❑	319	Geno Petralli	.10	.02
❑	320	Melvin Nieves	.10	.02
❑	321	Doug Linton	.10	.02
❑	322	Rob Dibble	.20	.07
❑	323	Chris Hoiles	.10	.02
❑	324	Jimmy Jones	.10	.02
❑	325	Dave Staton	.10	.02
❑	326	Pedro Martinez	1.00	.40
❑	327	Paul Quantrill	.10	.02
❑	328	Greg Colbrunn	.10	.02
❑	329	Hilly Hathaway RC	.10	.02
❑	330	Jeff Innis	.10	.02
❑	331	Ron Karkovice	.10	.02
❑	332	Keith Shepherd RC	.10	.02
❑	333	Alan Embree	.10	.02
❑	334	Paul Wagner	.10	.02
❑	335	Dave Haas	.10	.02
❑	336	Ozzie Canseco	.10	.02
❑	337	Bill Sampen	.10	.02
❑	338	Rich Rodriguez	.10	.02
❑	339	Dean Palmer	.20	.07
❑	340	Greg Litton	.10	.02
❑	341	Jim Tatum RC	.10	.02
❑	342	Todd Haney RC	.10	.02
❑	343	Larry Casian	.10	.02
❑	344	Ryne Sandberg	.75	.30
❑	345	Sterling Hitchcock RC	.20	.07
❑	346	Chris Hammond	.10	.02
❑	347	Vince Horsman	.10	.02
❑	348	Butch Henry	.10	.02
❑	349	Dann Howitt	.10	.02
❑	350	Roger McDowell	.10	.02
❑	351	Jack Morris	.20	.07
❑	352	Bill Krueger	.10	.02
❑	353	Cris Colon	.10	.02
❑	354	Joe Vitko	.10	.02
❑	355	Willie McGee	.20	.07
❑	356	Jay Baller	.10	.02
❑	357	Pat Mahomes	.10	.02
❑	358	Roger Mason	.10	.02
❑	359	Jerry Nielsen	.10	.02
❑	360	Tom Pagnozzi	.10	.02
❑	361	Kevin Baez	.10	.02
❑	362	Tim Scott	.10	.02
❑	363	Domingo Martinez RC	.10	.02
❑	364	Kirt Manwaring	.10	.02
❑	365	Rafael Palmeiro	.30	.10
❑	366	Ray Lankford	.20	.07
❑	367	Tim McIntosh	.10	.02
❑	368	Jessie Hollins	.10	.02
❑	369	Scott Leius	.10	.02
❑	370	Bill Doran	.10	.02
❑	371	Sam Militello	.10	.02
❑	372	Ryan Bowen	.10	.02
❑	373	Dave Henderson	.10	.02
❑	374	Dan Smith	.10	.02
❑	375	Steve Reed RC	.10	.02
❑	376	Jose Offerman	.10	.02
❑	377	Kevin Brown	.20	.07
❑	378	Darrin Fletcher	.10	.02
❑	379	Duane Ward	.10	.02
❑	380	Wayne Kirby	.10	.02
❑	381	Steve Scarsone	.10	.02
❑	382	Mariano Duncan	.10	.02
❑	383	Ken Ryan RC	.10	.02
❑	384	Lloyd McClendon	.10	.02
❑	385	Brian Holman	.10	.02
❑	386	Braulio Castillo	.10	.02
❑	387	Danny Leon	.10	.02
❑	388	Omar Olivares	.10	.02
❑	389	Kevin Wickander	.10	.02
❑	390	Fred McGriff	.30	.10
❑	391	Phil Clark	.10	.02
❑	392	Darren Lewis	.10	.02
❑	393	Phil Hiatt	.10	.02
❑	394	Mike Morgan	.10	.02
❑	395	Shane Mack	.10	.02
❑	396	Checklist 318-396 (Dennis Eckersley and Art Kusn	.20	.07
❑	397	David Segui	.10	.02

❑	398	Rafael Belliard	.10	.02
❑	399	Tim Naehring	.10	.02
❑	400	Frank Castillo	.10	.02
❑	401	Joe Grahe	.10	.02
❑	402	Reggie Sanders	.20	.07
❑	403	Roberto Hernandez	.10	.02
❑	404	Luis Gonzalez	.20	.07
❑	405	Carlos Baerga	.10	.02
❑	406	Carlos Hernandez	.10	.02
❑	407	Pedro Astacio	.10	.02
❑	408	Mel Rojas	.10	.02
❑	409	Scott Livingstone	.10	.02
❑	410	Chico Walker	.10	.02
❑	411	Brian McRae	.10	.02
❑	412	Ben Rivera	.10	.02
❑	413	Ricky Bones	.10	.02
❑	414	Andy Van Slyke	.30	.10
❑	415	Chuck Knoblauch	.20	.07
❑	416	Luis Alicea	.10	.02
❑	417	Bob Wickman	.10	.02
❑	418	Doug Brocail	.10	.02
❑	419	Scott Brosius	.20	.07
❑	420	Rod Beck	.10	.02
❑	421	Edgar Martinez	.30	.10
❑	422	Ryan Klesko	.20	.07
❑	423	Nolan Ryan	2.00	.75
❑	424	Rey Sanchez	.10	.02
❑	425	Roberto Alomar	.30	.10
❑	426	Barry Larkin	.30	.10
❑	427	Mike Mussina	.30	.10
❑	428	Jeff Bagwell	.30	.10
❑	429	Mo Vaughn	.20	.07
❑	430	Eric Karros	.20	.07
❑	431	John Orton	.10	.02
❑	432	Wil Cordero	.10	.02
❑	433	Jack McDowell	.10	.02
❑	434	Howard Johnson	.10	.02
❑	435	Albert Belle	.20	.07
❑	436	John Kruk	.20	.07
❑	437	Skeeter Barnes	.10	.02
❑	438	Don Slaught	.10	.02
❑	439	Rusty Meacham	.10	.02
❑	440	Tim Laker RC	.10	.02
❑	441	Robin Yount	.75	.30
❑	442	Brian Jordan	.20	.07
❑	443	Kevin Tapani	.10	.02
❑	444	Gary Sheffield	.20	.07
❑	445	Rich Monteleone	.10	.02
❑	446	Will Clark	.30	.10
❑	447	Jerry Browne	.10	.02
❑	448	Jeff Treadway	.10	.02
❑	449	Mike Schooler	.10	.02
❑	450	Mike Harkey	.10	.02
❑	451	Julio Franco	.20	.07
❑	452	Kevin Young	.20	.07
❑	453	Kelly Gruber	.10	.02
❑	454	Jose Rijo	.10	.02
❑	455	Mike Devereaux	.10	.02
❑	456	Andujar Cedeno	.10	.02
❑	457	Damion Easley RR	.10	.02
❑	458	Kevin Gross	.10	.02
❑	459	Matt Young	.10	.02
❑	460	Matt Stairs	.10	.02
❑	461	Luis Polonia	.10	.02
❑	462	Dwight Gooden	.20	.07
❑	463	Warren Newson	.10	.02
❑	464	Jose DeLeon	.10	.02
❑	465	Jose Mesa	.10	.02
❑	466	Danny Cox	.10	.02
❑	467	Dan Gladden	.10	.02
❑	468	Gerald Perry	.10	.02
❑	469	Mike Boddicker	.10	.02
❑	470	Jeff Gardner	.10	.02
❑	471	Doug Henry	.10	.02
❑	472	Mike Benjamin	.10	.02
❑	473	Dan Peltier	.10	.02
❑	474	Mike Stanton	.10	.02
❑	475	John Smiley	.10	.02
❑	476	Dwight Smith	.10	.02
❑	477	Jim Leyritz	.10	.02
❑	478	Dwayne Henry	.10	.02
❑	479	Mark McGwire	1.25	.50
❑	480	Pete Incaviglia	.10	.02
❑	481	Dave Cochrane	.10	.02
❑	482	Eric Davis	.20	.07
❑	483	John Olerud	.20	.07
❑	484	Kent Bottenfield	.10	.02
❑	485	Mark McLemore	.10	.02
❑	486	Dave Magadan	.10	.02
❑	487	John Marzano	.10	.02
❑	488	Ruben Amaro	.10	.02
❑	489	Rob Ducey	.10	.02
❑	490	Stan Belinda	.10	.02
❑	491	Dan Pasqua	.10	.02
❑	492	Joe Magrane	.10	.02
❑	493	Brook Jacoby	.10	.02
❑	494	Gene Harris	.10	.02
❑	495	Mark Leiter	.10	.02
❑	496	Bryan Hickerson	.10	.02
❑	497	Tom Gordon	.10	.02
❑	498	Pete Smith	.10	.02
❑	499	Chris Bosio	.10	.02
❑	500	Shawn Boskie	.10	.02
❑	501	Dave West	.10	.02
❑	502	Milt Hill	.10	.02
❑	503	Pat Kelly	.10	.02
❑	504	Joe Boever	.10	.02
❑	505	Terry Steinbach	.10	.02
❑	506	Butch Huskey	.10	.02
❑	507	David Valle	.10	.02
❑	508	Mike Scioscia	.10	.02
❑	509	Kenny Rogers	.20	.07
❑	510	Moises Alou	.20	.07
❑	511	David Wells	.20	.07
❑	512	Mackey Sasser	.10	.02
❑	513	Todd Frohwirth	.10	.02
❑	514	Ricky Jordan	.10	.02
❑	515	Mike Gardiner	.10	.02
❑	516	Gary Redus	.10	.02
❑	517	Gary Gaetti	.20	.07
❑	518	Checklist	.10	.02
❑	519	Carlton Fisk	.30	.10
❑	520	Ozzie Smith	.75	.30
❑	521	Rod Nichols	.10	.02
❑	522	Benito Santiago	.20	.07
❑	523	Bill Gullickson	.10	.02
❑	524	Robby Thompson	.10	.02
❑	525	Mike Macfarlane	.10	.02
❑	526	Sid Bream	.10	.02
❑	527	Darryl Hamilton	.10	.02
❑	528	Checklist	.10	.02
❑	529	Jeff Tackett	.10	.02
❑	530	Greg Olson	.10	.02
❑	531	Bob Zupcic	.10	.02
❑	532	Mark Grace	.30	.10
❑	533	Steve Frey	.10	.02
❑	534	Dave Martinez	.10	.02
❑	535	Robin Ventura	.20	.07
❑	536	Casey Candaele	.10	.02
❑	537	Kenny Lofton	.20	.07
❑	538	Jay Howell	.10	.02
❑	539	Fernando Ramsey RC	.10	.02
❑	540	Larry Walker	.20	.07
❑	541	Cecil Fielder	.20	.07
❑	542	Lee Guetterman	.10	.02
❑	543	Keith Miller	.10	.02
❑	544	Len Dykstra	.20	.07
❑	545	B.J. Surhoff	.20	.07
❑	546	Bob Walk	.10	.02
❑	547	Brian Harper	.10	.02
❑	548	Lee Smith	.20	.07
❑	549	Danny Tartabull	.10	.02
❑	550	Frank Seminara	.10	.02
❑	551	Henry Mercedes	.10	.02
❑	552	Dave Righetti	.20	.07
❑	553	Ken Griffey Jr.	.75	.30
❑	554	Tom Glavine	.30	.10
❑	555	Juan Gonzalez	.20	.07
❑	556	Jim Bullinger	.10	.02
❑	557	Derek Bell	.10	.02
❑	558	Cesar Hernandez	.10	.02
❑	559	Cal Ripken	1.50	.60
❑	560	Eddie Taubensee	.10	.02
❑	561	John Flaherty	.10	.02
❑	562	Todd Benzinger	.10	.02
❑	563	Hubie Brooks	.10	.02
❑	564	Delino DeShields	.10	.02
❑	565	Tim Raines	.20	.07
❑	566	Sid Fernandez	.10	.02
❑	567	Steve Olin	.10	.02
❑	568	Tommy Greene	.10	.02
❑	569	Buddy Groom	.10	.02
❑	570	Randy Tomlin	.10	.02
❑	571	Hipolito Pichardo	.10	.02
❑	572	Rene Arocha RC	.20	.07
❑	573	Mike Fetters	.10	.02
❑	574	Felix Jose	.10	.02
❑	575	Gene Larkin	.10	.02
❑	576	Bruce Hurst	.10	.02
❑	577	Bernie Williams	.30	.10
❑	578	Trevor Wilson	.10	.02
❑	579	Bob Welch	.10	.02
❑	580	David Justice	.20	.07
❑	581	Randy Johnson	.50	.20
❑	582	Jose Vizcaino	.10	.02
❑	583	Jeff Huson	.10	.02
❑	584	Rob Maurer	.10	.02
❑	585	Todd Stottlemyre	.10	.02
❑	586	Joe Oliver	.10	.02
❑	587	Bob Milacki	.10	.02
❑	588	Rob Murphy	.10	.02
❑	589	Greg Pirkl	.10	.02
❑	590	Lenny Harris	.10	.02
❑	591	Luis Rivera	.10	.02
❑	592	John Wetteland	.20	.07
❑	593	Mark Langston	.10	.02
❑	594	Bobby Bonilla	.20	.07
❑	595	Esteban Beltre	.10	.02
❑	596	Mike Hartley	.10	.02
❑	597	Felix Fermin	.10	.02
❑	598	Carlos Garcia	.10	.02
❑	599	Frank Tanana	.10	.02
❑	600	Pedro Guerrero	.20	.07
❑	601	Terry Shumpert	.10	.02
❑	602	Wally Whitehurst	.10	.02
❑	603	Kevin Seitzer	.10	.02
❑	604	Chris James	.10	.02
❑	605	Greg Gohr	.10	.02
❑	606	Mark Wohlers	.10	.02
❑	607	Kirby Puckett	.50	.20
❑	608	Greg Maddux	.75	.30
❑	609	Don Mattingly	1.25	.50
❑	610	Greg Cadaret	.10	.02
❑	611	Dave Stewart	.20	.07
❑	612	Mark Portugal	.10	.02
❑	613	Pete O'Brien	.10	.02
❑	614	Bob Ojeda	.10	.02
❑	615	Joe Carter	.20	.07
❑	616	Pete Young	.10	.02
❑	617	Sam Horn	.10	.02
❑	618	Vince Coleman	.10	.02
❑	619	Wade Boggs	.30	.10
❑	620	Todd Pratt RC	.20	.07
❑	621	Ron Tingley	.10	.02
❑	622	Doug Drabek	.10	.02
❑	623	Scott Hemond	.10	.02
❑	624	Tim Jones	.10	.02
❑	625	Dennis Cook	.10	.02
❑	626	Jose Melendez	.10	.02
❑	627	Mike Munoz	.10	.02
❑	628	Jim Pena	.10	.02
❑	629	Gary Thurman	.10	.02
❑	630	Charlie Leibrandt	.10	.02
❑	631	Scott Fletcher	.10	.02
❑	632	Andre Dawson	.20	.07
❑	633	Greg Gagne	.10	.02
❑	634	Greg Swindell	.10	.02
❑	635	Kevin Maas	.10	.02
❑	636	Xavier Hernandez	.10	.02
❑	637	Ruben Sierra	.20	.07
❑	638	Dmitri Young	.20	.07
❑	639	Harold Reynolds	.20	.07
❑	640	Tom Goodwin	.10	.02
❑	641	Todd Burns	.10	.02
❑	642	Jeff Fassero	.10	.02
❑	643	Dave Winfield	.20	.07
❑	644	Willie Randolph	.20	.07
❑	645	Luis Mercedes	.10	.02
❑	646	Dale Murphy	.30	.10
❑	647	Danny Darwin	.10	.02
❑	648	Dennis Moeller	.10	.02
❑	649	Chuck Crim	.10	.02
❑	650	Checklist	.10	.02
❑	651	Shawn Abner	.10	.02
❑	652	Tracy Woodson	.10	.02
❑	653	Scott Scudder	.10	.02
❑	654	Tom Lampkin	.10	.02
❑	655	Alan Trammell	.20	.07

- ❑ 656 Cory Snyder .10 .02
- ❑ 657 Chris Gwynn .10 .02
- ❑ 658 Lonnie Smith .10 .02
- ❑ 659 Jim Austin .10 .02
- ❑ 660 Rob Picciolo CL .10 .02
- ❑ 661 Tim Hulett .10 .02
- ❑ 662 Marvin Freeman .10 .02
- ❑ 663 Greg A. Harris .10 .02
- ❑ 664 Heathcliff Slocumb .10 .02
- ❑ 665 Mike Butcher .10 .02
- ❑ 666 Steve Foster .10 .02
- ❑ 667 Donn Pall .10 .02
- ❑ 668 Darryl Kile .20 .07
- ❑ 669 Jesse Levis .10 .02
- ❑ 670 Jim Gott .10 .02
- ❑ 671 Mark Hutton .10 .02
- ❑ 672 Brian Drahman .10 .02
- ❑ 673 Chad Kreuter .10 .02
- ❑ 674 Tony Fernandez .10 .02
- ❑ 675 Jose Lind .10 .02
- ❑ 676 Kyle Abbott .10 .02
- ❑ 677 Dan Plesac .10 .02
- ❑ 678 Barry Bonds 1.50 .60
- ❑ 679 Chili Davis .20 .07
- ❑ 680 Stan Royer .10 .02
- ❑ 681 Scott Kamieniecki .10 .02
- ❑ 682 Carlos Martinez .10 .02
- ❑ 683 Mike Moore .10 .02
- ❑ 684 Candy Maldonado .10 .02
- ❑ 685 Jeff Nelson .10 .02
- ❑ 686 Lou Whitaker .20 .07
- ❑ 687 Jose Guzman .10 .02
- ❑ 688 Manuel Lee .10 .02
- ❑ 689 Bob MacDonald .10 .02
- ❑ 690 Scott Bankhead .10 .02
- ❑ 691 Alan Mills .10 .02
- ❑ 692 Brian Williams .10 .02
- ❑ 693 Tom Brunansky .10 .02
- ❑ 694 Lenny Webster .10 .02
- ❑ 695 Greg Briley .10 .02
- ❑ 696 Paul O'Neill .30 .10
- ❑ 697 Joey Cora .10 .02
- ❑ 698 Charlie O'Brien .10 .02
- ❑ 699 Junior Ortiz .10 .02
- ❑ 700 Ron Darling .10 .02
- ❑ 701 Tony Phillips .10 .02
- ❑ 702 William Pennyfeather .10 .02
- ❑ 703 Mark Gubicza .10 .02
- ❑ 704 Steve Hosey .10 .02
- ❑ 705 Henry Cotto .10 .02
- ❑ 706 David Hulse RC .10 .02
- ❑ 707 Mike Pagliarulo .10 .02
- ❑ 708 Dave Stieb .10 .02
- ❑ 709 Melido Perez .10 .02
- ❑ 710 Jimmy Key .20 .07
- ❑ 711 Jeff Russell .10 .02
- ❑ 712 David Cone .20 .07
- ❑ 713 Russ Swan .10 .02
- ❑ 714 Mark Guthrie .10 .02
- ❑ 715 Checklist .10 .02
- ❑ 716 Al Martin .10 .02
- ❑ 717 Randy Knorr .10 .02
- ❑ 718 Mike Stanley .10 .02
- ❑ 719 Rick Sutcliffe .20 .07
- ❑ 720 Terry Leach .10 .02
- ❑ 721 Chipper Jones .50 .20
- ❑ 722 Jim Eisenreich .10 .02
- ❑ 723 Tom Henke .10 .02
- ❑ 724 Jeff Frye .10 .02
- ❑ 725 Harold Baines .20 .07
- ❑ 726 Scott Sanderson .10 .02
- ❑ 727 Tom Foley .10 .02
- ❑ 728 Bryan Harvey .10 .02
- ❑ 729 Tom Edens .10 .02
- ❑ 730 Eric Young .10 .02
- ❑ 731 Dave Weathers .10 .02
- ❑ 732 Spike Owen .10 .02
- ❑ 733 Scott Aldred .10 .02
- ❑ 734 Cris Carpenter .10 .02
- ❑ 735 Dion James .10 .02
- ❑ 736 Joe Girardi .10 .02
- ❑ 737 Nigel Wilson .10 .02
- ❑ 738 Scott Chiamparino .10 .02
- ❑ 739 Jeff Reardon .20 .07
- ❑ 740 Willie Blair .10 .02
- ❑ 741 Jim Corsi .10 .02
- ❑ 742 Ken Patterson .10 .02
- ❑ 743 Andy Ashby .10 .02
- ❑ 744 Rob Natal .10 .02
- ❑ 745 Kevin Bass .10 .02
- ❑ 746 Freddie Benavides .10 .02
- ❑ 747 Chris Donnels .10 .02
- ❑ 748 Kerry Woodson .10 .02
- ❑ 749 Calvin Jones .10 .02
- ❑ 750 Gary Scott .10 .02
- ❑ 751 Joe Orsulak .10 .02
- ❑ 752 Armando Reynoso .10 .02
- ❑ 753 Monty Fariss .10 .02
- ❑ 754 Billy Hatcher .10 .02
- ❑ 755 Denis Boucher .10 .02
- ❑ 756 Walt Weiss .10 .02
- ❑ 757 Mike Fitzgerald .10 .02
- ❑ 758 Rudy Seanez .10 .02
- ❑ 759 Bret Barberie .10 .02
- ❑ 760 Mo Sanford .10 .02
- ❑ 761 Pedro Castellano .10 .02
- ❑ 762 Chuck Carr .10 .02
- ❑ 763 Steve Howe .10 .02
- ❑ 764 Andres Galarraga .20 .07
- ❑ 765 Jeff Conine .20 .07
- ❑ 766 Ted Power .10 .02
- ❑ 767 Butch Henry .10 .02
- ❑ 768 Steve Decker .10 .02
- ❑ 769 Storm Davis .10 .02
- ❑ 770 Vinny Castilla .50 .20
- ❑ 771 Junior Felix .10 .02
- ❑ 772 Walt Terrell .10 .02
- ❑ 773 Brad Ausmus .50 .20
- ❑ 774 Jamie McAndrew .10 .02
- ❑ 775 Milt Thompson .10 .02
- ❑ 776 Charlie Hayes .10 .02
- ❑ 777 Jack Armstrong .10 .02
- ❑ 778 Dennis Rasmussen .10 .02
- ❑ 779 Darren Holmes .10 .02
- ❑ 780 Alex Arias .10 .02
- ❑ 781 Randy Bush .10 .02
- ❑ 782 Javy Lopez .30 .10
- ❑ 783 Dante Bichette .20 .07
- ❑ 784 John Johnstone RC .10 .02
- ❑ 785 Rene Gonzales .10 .02
- ❑ 786 Alex Cole .10 .02
- ❑ 787 Jeromy Burnitz .20 .07
- ❑ 788 Michael Huff .10 .02
- ❑ 789 Anthony Telford .10 .02
- ❑ 790 Jerald Clark .10 .02
- ❑ 791 Joel Johnston .10 .02
- ❑ 792 David Nied .10 .02

1994 Donruss

- ❑ COMPLETE SET (660) 30.00 12.00
- ❑ COMPLETE SERIES 1 (330) 15.00 6.00
- ❑ COMPLETE SERIES 2 (330) 15.00 6.00
- ❑ 1 Nolan Ryan Salute 4.00 1.50
- ❑ 2 Mike Piazza 1.50 .60
- ❑ 3 Moises Alou .30 .10
- ❑ 4 Ken Griffey Jr. 1.25 .50
- ❑ 5 Gary Sheffield .30 .10
- ❑ 6 Roberto Alomar .50 .20
- ❑ 7 John Kruk .30 .10
- ❑ 8 Gregg Olson .15 .05
- ❑ 9 Gregg Jefferies .15 .05
- ❑ 10 Tony Gwynn 1.00 .40
- ❑ 11 Chad Curtis .15 .05
- ❑ 12 Craig Biggio .50 .20
- ❑ 13 John Burkett .15 .05
- ❑ 14 Carlos Baerga .15 .05
- ❑ 15 Robin Yount 1.25 .50
- ❑ 16 Dennis Eckersley .30 .10
- ❑ 17 Dwight Gooden .30 .10
- ❑ 18 Ryne Sandberg 1.25 .50
- ❑ 19 Rickey Henderson .75 .30
- ❑ 20 Jack McDowell .15 .05
- ❑ 21 Jay Bell .30 .10
- ❑ 22 Kevin Brown .30 .10
- ❑ 23 Robin Ventura .30 .10
- ❑ 24 Paul Molitor .30 .10
- ❑ 25 David Justice .30 .10
- ❑ 26 Rafael Palmeiro .50 .20
- ❑ 27 Cecil Fielder .30 .10
- ❑ 28 Chuck Knoblauch .30 .10
- ❑ 29 Dave Hollins .15 .05
- ❑ 30 Jimmy Key .30 .10
- ❑ 31 Mark Langston .15 .05
- ❑ 32 Darryl Kile .30 .10
- ❑ 33 Ruben Sierra .30 .10
- ❑ 34 Ron Gant .30 .10
- ❑ 35 Ozzie Smith 1.25 .50
- ❑ 36 Wade Boggs .50 .20
- ❑ 37 Marquis Grissom .30 .10
- ❑ 38 Will Clark .50 .20
- ❑ 39 Kenny Lofton .30 .10
- ❑ 40 Cal Ripken 2.50 1.00
- ❑ 41 Steve Avery .15 .05
- ❑ 42 Mo Vaughn .30 .10
- ❑ 43 Brian McRae .15 .05
- ❑ 44 Mickey Tettleton .15 .05
- ❑ 45 Barry Larkin .50 .20
- ❑ 46 Charlie Hayes .15 .05
- ❑ 47 Kevin Appier .30 .10
- ❑ 48 Robby Thompson .15 .05
- ❑ 49 Juan Gonzalez .30 .10
- ❑ 50 Paul O'Neill .50 .20
- ❑ 51 Marcos Armas .15 .05
- ❑ 52 Mike Butcher .15 .05
- ❑ 53 Ken Caminiti .30 .10
- ❑ 54 Pat Borders .15 .05
- ❑ 55 Pedro Munoz .15 .05
- ❑ 56 Tim Belcher .15 .05
- ❑ 57 Paul Assenmacher .15 .05
- ❑ 58 Damon Berryhill .15 .05
- ❑ 59 Ricky Bones .15 .05
- ❑ 60 Rene Arocha .15 .05
- ❑ 61 Shawn Boskie .15 .05
- ❑ 62 Pedro Astacio .15 .05
- ❑ 63 Frank Bolick .15 .05
- ❑ 64 Bud Black .15 .05
- ❑ 65 Sandy Alomar Jr. .15 .05
- ❑ 66 Rich Amaral .15 .05
- ❑ 67 Luis Aquino .15 .05
- ❑ 68 Kevin Baez .15 .05
- ❑ 69 Mike Devereaux .15 .05
- ❑ 70 Andy Ashby .15 .05
- ❑ 71 Larry Andersen .15 .05
- ❑ 72 Steve Cooke .15 .05
- ❑ 73 Mario Diaz .15 .05
- ❑ 74 Rob Deer .15 .05
- ❑ 75 Bobby Ayala .15 .05
- ❑ 76 Freddie Benavides .15 .05
- ❑ 77 Stan Belinda .15 .05
- ❑ 78 John Doherty .15 .05
- ❑ 79 Willie Banks .15 .05
- ❑ 80 Spike Owen .15 .05
- ❑ 81 Mike Bordick .15 .05
- ❑ 82 Chili Davis .30 .10
- ❑ 83 Luis Gonzalez .30 .10
- ❑ 84 Ed Sprague .15 .05
- ❑ 85 Jeff Reboulet .15 .05
- ❑ 86 Jason Bere .15 .05
- ❑ 87 Mark Hutton .15 .05
- ❑ 88 Jeff Blauser .15 .05
- ❑ 89 Cal Eldred .15 .05
- ❑ 90 Bernard Gilkey .15 .05
- ❑ 91 Frank Castillo .15 .05
- ❑ 92 Jim Gott .15 .05
- ❑ 93 Greg Colbrunn .15 .05
- ❑ 94 Jeff Brantley .15 .05
- ❑ 95 Jeremy Hernandez .15 .05
- ❑ 96 Norm Charlton .15 .05
- ❑ 97 Alex Arias .15 .05
- ❑ 98 John Franco .30 .10

No.	Player		
99	Chris Hoiles	.15	.05
100	Brad Ausmus	.50	.20
101	Wes Chamberlain	.15	.05
102	Mark Dewey	.15	.05
103	Benji Gil	.15	.05
104	John Dopson	.15	.05
105	John Smiley	.15	.05
106	David Nied	.15	.05
107	George Brett Salute	2.00	.75
108	Kirk Gibson	.30	.10
109	Larry Casian	.15	.05
110	Ryne Sandberg CL	.75	.30
111	Brent Gates	.15	.05
112	Damion Easley	.15	.05
113	Pete Harnisch	.15	.05
114	Danny Cox	.15	.05
115	Kevin Tapani	.15	.05
116	Roberto Hernandez	.15	.05
117	Domingo Jean	.15	.05
118	Sid Bream	.15	.05
119	Doug Henry	.15	.05
120	Omar Olivares	.15	.05
121	Mike Harkey	.15	.05
122	Carlos Hernandez	.15	.05
123	Jeff Fassero	.15	.05
124	Dave Burba	.15	.05
125	Wayne Kirby	.15	.05
126	John Cummings	.15	.05
127	Bret Barberie	.15	.05
128	Todd Hundley	.15	.05
129	Tim Hulett	.15	.05
130	Phil Clark	.15	.05
131	Danny Jackson	.15	.05
132	Tom Foley	.15	.05
133	Donald Harris	.15	.05
134	Scott Fletcher	.15	.05
135	Johnny Ruffin	.15	.05
136	Jerald Clark	.15	.05
137	Billy Brewer	.15	.05
138	Dan Gladden	.15	.05
139	Eddie Guardado	.30	.10
140	Cal Ripken CL	.75	.30
141	Scott Hemond	.15	.05
142	Steve Frey	.15	.05
143	Xavier Hernandez	.15	.05
144	Mark Eichhorn	.15	.05
145	Ellis Burks	.30	.10
146	Jim Leyritz	.15	.05
147	Mark Lemke	.15	.05
148	Pat Listach	.15	.05
149	Donovan Osborne	.15	.05
150	Glenallen Hill	.15	.05
151	Orel Hershiser	.30	.10
152	Darrin Fletcher	.15	.05
153	Royce Clayton	.15	.05
154	Derek Lilliquist	.15	.05
155	Mike Felder	.15	.05
156	Jeff Conine	.30	.10
157	Ryan Thompson	.15	.05
158	Ben McDonald	.15	.05
159	Ricky Gutierrez	.15	.05
160	Terry Mulholland	.15	.05
161	Carlos Garcia	.15	.05
162	Tom Henke	.15	.05
163	Mike Greenwell	.15	.05
164	Thomas Howard	.15	.05
165	Joe Girardi	.15	.05
166	Hubie Brooks	.15	.05
167	Greg Gohr	.15	.05
168	Chip Hale	.15	.05
169	Rick Honeycutt	.15	.05
170	Hilly Hathaway	.15	.05
171	Todd Jones	.15	.05
172	Tony Fernandez	.15	.05
173	Bo Jackson	.75	.30
174	Bobby Munoz	.15	.05
175	Greg McMichael	.15	.05
176	Graeme Lloyd	.15	.05
177	Tom Pagnozzi	.15	.05
178	Derrick May	.15	.05
179	Pedro Martinez	.75	.30
180	Ken Hill	.15	.05
181	Bryan Hickerson	.15	.05
182	Jose Mesa	.15	.05
183	Dave Fleming	.15	.05
184	Henry Cotto	.15	.05
185	Jeff Kent	.50	.20
186	Mark McLemore	.15	.05
187	Trevor Hoffman	.50	.20
188	Todd Pratt	.15	.05
189	Blas Minor	.15	.05
190	Charlie Leibrandt	.15	.05
191	Tony Pena	.15	.05
192	Larry Luebbers RC	.15	.05
193	Greg W. Harris	.15	.05
194	David Cone	.30	.10
195	Bill Gullickson	.15	.05
196	Brian Harper	.15	.05
197	Steve Karsay	.15	.05
198	Greg Myers	.15	.05
199	Mark Portugal	.15	.05
200	Pat Hentgen	.15	.05
201	Mike LaValliere	.15	.05
202	Mike Stanley	.15	.05
203	Kent Mercker	.15	.05
204	Dave Nilsson	.15	.05
205	Erik Pappas	.15	.05
206	Mike Morgan	.15	.05
207	Roger McDowell	.15	.05
208	Mike Lansing	.15	.05
209	Kirt Manwaring	.15	.05
210	Randy Milligan	.15	.05
211	Erik Hanson	.15	.05
212	Orestes Destrade	.15	.05
213	Mike Maddux	.15	.05
214	Alan Mills	.15	.05
215	Tim Mauser	.15	.05
216	Ben Rivera	.15	.05
217	Don Slaught	.15	.05
218	Bob Patterson	.15	.05
219	Carlos Quintana	.15	.05
220	Tim Raines CL	.15	.05
221	Hal Morris	.15	.05
222	Darren Holmes	.15	.05
223	Chris Gwynn	.15	.05
224	Chad Kreuter	.15	.05
225	Mike Hartley	.15	.05
226	Scott Lydy	.15	.05
227	Eduardo Perez	.15	.05
228	Greg Swindell	.15	.05
229	Al Leiter	.30	.10
230	Scott Radinsky	.15	.05
231	Bob Wickman	.15	.05
232	Otis Nixon	.15	.05
233	Kevin Reimer	.15	.05
234	Geronimo Pena	.15	.05
235	Kevin Roberson	.15	.05
236	Jody Reed	.15	.05
237	Kirk Rueter	.15	.05
238	Willie McGee	.30	.10
239	Charles Nagy	.15	.05
240	Tim Leary	.15	.05
241	Carl Everett	.30	.10
242	Charlie O'Brien	.15	.05
243	Mike Pagliarulo	.15	.05
244	Kerry Taylor	.15	.05
245	Kevin Stocker	.15	.05
246	Joel Johnston	.15	.05
247	Geno Petralli	.15	.05
248	Jeff Russell	.15	.05
249	Joe Oliver	.15	.05
250	Roberto Mejia	.15	.05
251	Chris Haney	.15	.05
252	Bill Krueger	.15	.05
253	Shane Mack	.15	.05
254	Terry Steinbach	.15	.05
255	Luis Polonia	.15	.05
256	Eddie Taubensee	.15	.05
257	Dave Stewart	.30	.10
258	Tim Raines	.30	.10
259	Bernie Williams	.50	.20
260	John Smoltz	.50	.20
261	Kevin Seitzer	.15	.05
262	Bob Tewksbury	.15	.05
263	Bob Scanlan	.15	.05
264	Henry Rodriguez	.15	.05
265	Tim Scott	.15	.05
266	Scott Sanderson	.15	.05
267	Eric Plunk	.15	.05
268	Edgar Martinez	.50	.20
269	Charlie Hough	.30	.10
270	Joe Orsulak	.15	.05
271	Harold Reynolds	.30	.10
272	Tim Teufel	.15	.05
273	Bobby Thigpen	.15	.05
274	Randy Tomlin	.15	.05
275	Gary Redus	.15	.05
276	Ken Ryan	.15	.05
277	Tim Pugh	.15	.05
278	Jayhawk Owens	.15	.05
279	Phil Hiatt	.15	.05
280	Alan Trammell	.30	.10
281	David McCarty	.15	.05
282	Bob Welch	.15	.05
283	J.T.Snow	.30	.10
284	Brian Williams	.15	.05
285	Devon White	.30	.10
286	Steve Sax	.15	.05
287	Tony Tarasco	.15	.05
288	Bill Spiers	.15	.05
289	Allen Watson	.15	.05
290	Rickey Henderson CL	.50	.20
291	Jose Vizcaino	.15	.05
292	Darryl Strawberry	.30	.10
293	John Wetteland	.30	.10
294	Bill Swift	.15	.05
295	Jeff Treadway	.15	.05
296	Tino Martinez	.50	.20
297	Richie Lewis	.15	.05
298	Bret Saberhagen	.30	.10
299	Arthur Rhodes	.15	.05
300	Guillermo Velasquez	.15	.05
301	Milt Thompson	.15	.05
302	Doug Strange	.15	.05
303	Aaron Sele	.15	.05
304	Bip Roberts	.15	.05
305	Bruce Ruffin	.15	.05
306	Jose Lind	.15	.05
307	David Wells	.30	.10
308	Bobby Witt	.15	.05
309	Mark Wohlers	.15	.05
310	B.J. Surhoff	.30	.10
311	Mark Whiten	.15	.05
312	Turk Wendell	.15	.05
313	Raul Mondesi	.30	.10
314	Brian Turang RC	.15	.05
315	Chris Hammond	.15	.05
316	Tim Bogar	.15	.05
317	Brad Pennington	.15	.05
318	Tim Worrell	.15	.05
319	Mitch Williams	.15	.05
320	Rondell White	.30	.10
321	Frank Viola	.30	.10
322	Manny Ramirez	.75	.30
323	Gary Wayne	.15	.05
324	Mike Macfarlane	.15	.05
325	Russ Springer	.15	.05
326	Tim Wallach	.15	.05
327	Salomon Torres	.15	.05
328	Omar Vizquel	.50	.20
329	Andy Tomberlin RC	.15	.05
330	Chris Sabo	.15	.05
331	Mike Mussina	.50	.20
332	Andy Benes	.15	.05
333	Darren Daulton	.30	.10
334	Orlando Merced	.15	.05
335	Mark McGwire	2.00	.75
336	Dave Winfield	.30	.10
337	Sammy Sosa	.75	.30
338	Eric Karros	.30	.10
339	Greg Vaughn	.15	.05
340	Don Mattingly	2.00	.75
341	Frank Thomas	.75	.30
342	Fred McGriff	.50	.20
343	Kirby Puckett	.75	.30
344	Roberto Kelly	.15	.05
345	Wally Joyner	.30	.10
346	Andres Galarraga	.30	.10
347	Bobby Bonilla	.30	.10
348	Benito Santiago	.30	.10
349	Barry Bonds	2.00	.75
350	Delino DeShields	.15	.05
351	Albert Belle	.30	.10
352	Randy Johnson	.75	.30
353	Tim Salmon	.50	.20
354	John Olerud	.30	.10
355	Dean Palmer	.30	.10
356	Roger Clemens	1.50	.60

❑	357	Jim Abbott	.50	.20
❑	358	Mark Grace	.50	.20
❑	359	Ozzie Guillen	.30	.10
❑	360	Lou Whitaker	.30	.10
❑	361	Jose Rijo	.15	.05
❑	362	Jeff Montgomery	.15	.05
❑	363	Chuck Finley	.30	.10
❑	364	Tom Glavine	.50	.20
❑	365	Jeff Bagwell	.50	.20
❑	366	Joe Carter	.30	.10
❑	367	Ray Lankford	.30	.10
❑	368	Ramon Martinez	.15	.05
❑	369	Jay Buhner	.30	.10
❑	370	Matt Williams	.30	.10
❑	371	Larry Walker	.30	.10
❑	372	Jose Canseco	.50	.20
❑	373	Lenny Dykstra	.30	.10
❑	374	Bryan Harvey	.15	.05
❑	375	Andy Van Slyke	.50	.20
❑	376	Ivan Rodriguez	.50	.20
❑	377	Kevin Mitchell	.15	.05
❑	378	Travis Fryman	.30	.10
❑	379	Duane Ward	.15	.05
❑	380	Greg Maddux	1.25	.50
❑	381	Scott Servais	.15	.05
❑	382	Greg Olson	.15	.05
❑	383	Rey Sanchez	.15	.05
❑	384	Tom Kramer	.15	.05
❑	385	David Valle	.15	.05
❑	386	Eddie Murray	.75	.30
❑	387	Kevin Higgins	.15	.05
❑	388	Dan Wilson	.15	.05
❑	389	Todd Frohwith	.15	.05
❑	390	Gerald Williams	.15	.05
❑	391	Hipolito Pichardo	.15	.05
❑	392	Pat Meares	.15	.05
❑	393	Luis Lopez	.15	.05
❑	394	Ricky Jordan	.15	.05
❑	395	Bob Walk	.15	.05
❑	396	Sid Fernandez	.15	.05
❑	397	Todd Worrell	.15	.05
❑	398	Darryl Hamilton	.15	.05
❑	399	Randy Myers	.15	.05
❑	400	Rod Brewer	.15	.05
❑	401	Lance Blankenship	.15	.05
❑	402	Steve Finley	.30	.10
❑	403	Phil Leftwich RC	.15	.05
❑	404	Juan Guzman	.15	.05
❑	405	Anthony Young	.15	.05
❑	406	Jeff Gardner	.15	.05
❑	407	Ryan Bowen	.15	.05
❑	408	Fernando Valenzuela	.30	.10
❑	409	David West	.15	.05
❑	410	Kenny Rogers	.30	.10
❑	411	Bob Zupcic	.15	.05
❑	412	Eric Young	.15	.05
❑	413	Bret Boone	.30	.10
❑	414	Danny Tartabull	.15	.05
❑	415	Bob MacDonald	.15	.05
❑	416	Ron Karkovice	.15	.05
❑	417	Scott Cooper	.15	.05
❑	418	Dante Bichette	.30	.10
❑	419	Tripp Cromer	.15	.05
❑	420	Billy Ashley	.15	.05
❑	421	Roger Smithberg	.15	.05
❑	422	Dennis Martinez	.30	.10
❑	423	Mike Blowers	.15	.05
❑	424	Darren Lewis	.15	.05
❑	425	Junior Ortiz	.15	.05
❑	426	Butch Huskey	.15	.05
❑	427	Jimmy Poole	.15	.05
❑	428	Walt Weiss	.15	.05
❑	429	Scott Bankhead	.15	.05
❑	430	Deion Sanders	.50	.20
❑	431	Scott Bullett	.15	.05
❑	432	Jeff Huson	.15	.05
❑	433	Tyler Green	.15	.05
❑	434	Billy Hatcher	.15	.05
❑	435	Bob Hamelin	.15	.05
❑	436	Reggie Sanders	.30	.10
❑	437	Scott Erickson	.15	.05
❑	438	Steve Reed	.15	.05
❑	439	Randy Velarde	.15	.05
❑	440	Tony Gwynn CL	.50	.20
❑	441	Terry Leach	.15	.05
❑	442	Danny Bautista	.15	.05
❑	443	Kent Hrbek	.30	.10
❑	444	Rick Wilkins	.15	.05
❑	445	Tony Phillips	.15	.05
❑	446	Dion James	.15	.05
❑	447	Joey Cora	.15	.05
❑	448	Andre Dawson	.30	.10
❑	449	Pedro Castellano	.15	.05
❑	450	Tom Gordon	.15	.05
❑	451	Rob Dibble	.30	.10
❑	452	Ron Darling	.15	.05
❑	453	Chipper Jones	.75	.30
❑	454	Joe Grahe	.15	.05
❑	455	Domingo Cedeno	.15	.05
❑	456	Tom Edens	.15	.05
❑	457	Mitch Webster	.15	.05
❑	458	Jose Bautista	.15	.05
❑	459	Troy O'Leary	.15	.05
❑	460	Todd Zeile	.15	.05
❑	461	Sean Berry	.15	.05
❑	462	Brad Holman RC	.15	.05
❑	463	Dave Martinez	.15	.05
❑	464	Mark Lewis	.15	.05
❑	465	Paul Carey	.15	.05
❑	466	Jack Armstrong	.15	.05
❑	467	David Telgheder	.15	.05
❑	468	Gene Harris	.15	.05
❑	469	Danny Darwin	.15	.05
❑	470	Kim Batiste	.15	.05
❑	471	Tim Wakefield	.50	.20
❑	472	Craig Lefferts	.15	.05
❑	473	Jacob Brumfield	.15	.05
❑	474	Lance Painter	.15	.05
❑	475	Milt Cuyler	.15	.05
❑	476	Melido Perez	.15	.05
❑	477	Derek Parks	.15	.05
❑	478	Gary DiSarcina	.15	.05
❑	479	Steve Bedrosian	.15	.05
❑	480	Eric Anthony	.15	.05
❑	481	Julio Franco	.30	.10
❑	482	Tommy Greene	.15	.05
❑	483	Pat Kelly	.15	.05
❑	484	Nate Minchey	.15	.05
❑	485	William Pennyfeather	.15	.05
❑	486	Harold Baines	.30	.10
❑	487	Howard Johnson	.15	.05
❑	488	Angel Miranda	.15	.05
❑	489	Scott Sanders	.15	.05
❑	490	Shawon Dunston	.15	.05
❑	491	Mel Rojas	.15	.05
❑	492	Jeff Nelson	.15	.05
❑	493	Archi Cianfrocco	.15	.05
❑	494	Al Martin	.15	.05
❑	495	Mike Gallego	.15	.05
❑	496	Mike Henneman	.15	.05
❑	497	Armando Reynoso	.15	.05
❑	498	Mickey Morandini	.15	.05
❑	499	Rick Renteria	.15	.05
❑	500	Rick Sutcliffe	.30	.10
❑	501	Bobby Jones	.15	.05
❑	502	Gary Gaetti	.30	.10
❑	503	Rick Aguilera	.15	.05
❑	504	Todd Stottlemyre	.15	.05
❑	505	Mike Mohler	.15	.05
❑	506	Mike Stanton	.15	.05
❑	507	Jose Guzman	.15	.05
❑	508	Kevin Rogers	.15	.05
❑	509	Chuck Carr	.15	.05
❑	510	Chris Jones	.15	.05
❑	511	Brent Mayne	.15	.05
❑	512	Greg Harris	.15	.05
❑	513	Dave Henderson	.15	.05
❑	514	Eric Hillman	.15	.05
❑	515	Dan Peltier	.15	.05
❑	516	Craig Shipley	.15	.05
❑	517	John Valentin	.15	.05
❑	518	Wilson Alvarez	.15	.05
❑	519	Andujar Cedeno	.15	.05
❑	520	Troy Neel	.15	.05
❑	521	Tom Candiotti	.15	.05
❑	522	Matt Mieske	.15	.05
❑	523	Jim Thome	.50	.20
❑	524	Lou Frazier	.15	.05
❑	525	Mike Jackson	.15	.05
❑	526	Pedro A.Martinez RC	.15	.05
❑	527	Roger Pavlik	.15	.05
❑	528	Kent Bottenfield	.15	.05
❑	529	Felix Jose	.15	.05
❑	530	Mark Guthrie	.15	.05
❑	531	Steve Farr	.15	.05
❑	532	Craig Paquette	.15	.05
❑	533	Doug Jones	.15	.05
❑	534	Luis Alicea	.15	.05
❑	535	Cory Snyder	.15	.05
❑	536	Paul Sorrento	.15	.05
❑	537	Nigel Wilson	.15	.05
❑	538	Jeff King	.15	.05
❑	539	Willie Greene	.15	.05
❑	540	Kirk McCaskill	.15	.05
❑	541	Al Osuna	.15	.05
❑	542	Greg Hibbard	.15	.05
❑	543	Brett Butler	.30	.10
❑	544	Jose Valentin	.15	.05
❑	545	Wil Cordero	.15	.05
❑	546	Chris Bosio	.15	.05
❑	547	Jamie Moyer	.30	.10
❑	548	Jim Eisenreich	.15	.05
❑	549	Vinny Castilla	.30	.10
❑	550	Dave Winfield CL	.15	.05
❑	551	John Roper	.15	.05
❑	552	Lance Johnson	.15	.05
❑	553	Scott Kamieniecki	.15	.05
❑	554	Mike Moore	.15	.05
❑	555	Steve Buechele	.15	.05
❑	556	Terry Pendleton	.30	.10
❑	557	Todd Van Poppel	.15	.05
❑	558	Rob Butler	.15	.05
❑	559	Zane Smith	.15	.05
❑	560	David Hulse	.15	.05
❑	561	Tim Costo	.15	.05
❑	562	John Habyan	.15	.05
❑	563	Terry Jorgensen	.15	.05
❑	564	Matt Nokes	.15	.05
❑	565	Kevin McReynolds	.15	.05
❑	566	Phil Plantier	.15	.05
❑	567	Chris Turner	.15	.05
❑	568	Carlos Delgado	.50	.20
❑	569	John Jaha	.15	.05
❑	570	Dwight Smith	.15	.05
❑	571	John Vander Wal	.15	.05
❑	572	Trevor Wilson	.15	.05
❑	573	Felix Fermin	.15	.05
❑	574	Marc Newfield	.15	.05
❑	575	Jeromy Burnitz	.30	.10
❑	576	Leo Gomez	.15	.05
❑	577	Curt Schilling	.30	.10
❑	578	Kevin Young	.15	.05
❑	579	Jerry Spradlin RC	.15	.05
❑	580	Curt Leskanic	.15	.05
❑	581	Carl Willis	.15	.05
❑	582	Alex Fernandez	.15	.05
❑	583	Mark Holzemer	.15	.05
❑	584	Domingo Martinez	.15	.05
❑	585	Pete Smith	.15	.05
❑	586	Brian Jordan	.30	.10
❑	587	Kevin Gross	.15	.05
❑	588	J.R. Phillips	.15	.05
❑	589	Chris Nabholz	.15	.05
❑	590	Bill Wertz	.15	.05
❑	591	Derek Bell	.15	.05
❑	592	Brady Anderson	.30	.10
❑	593	Matt Turner	.15	.05
❑	594	Pete Incaviglia	.15	.05
❑	595	Greg Gagne	.15	.05
❑	596	John Flaherty	.15	.05
❑	597	Scott Livingstone	.15	.05
❑	598	Rod Bolton	.15	.05
❑	599	Mike Perez	.15	.05
❑	600	Roger Clemens CL	.75	.30
❑	601	Tony Castillo	.15	.05
❑	602	Henry Mercedes	.15	.05
❑	603	Mike Fetters	.15	.05
❑	604	Rod Beck	.15	.05
❑	605	Damon Buford	.15	.05
❑	606	Matt Whiteside	.15	.05
❑	607	Shawn Green	.75	.30
❑	608	Midre Cummings	.15	.05
❑	609	Jeff McNeely	.15	.05
❑	610	Danny Sheaffer	.15	.05
❑	611	Paul Wagner	.15	.05
❑	612	Torey Lovullo	.15	.05
❑	613	Javier Lopez	.30	.10
❑	614	Mariano Duncan	.15	.05

❑ 615 Doug Brocail .15 .05
❑ 616 Dave Hansen .15 .05
❑ 617 Ryan Klesko .30 .10
❑ 618 Eric Davis .30 .10
❑ 619 Scott Ruffcorn .15 .05
❑ 620 Mike Trombley .15 .05
❑ 621 Jaime Navarro .15 .05
❑ 622 Rheal Cormier .15 .05
❑ 623 Jose Offerman .15 .05
❑ 624 David Segui .15 .05
❑ 625 Robb Nen .30 .10
❑ 626 Dave Gallagher .15 .05
❑ 627 Julian Tavarez RC .30 .10
❑ 628 Chris Gomez .15 .05
❑ 629 Jeffrey Hammonds .15 .05
❑ 630 Scott Brosius .30 .10
❑ 631 Willie Blair .15 .05
❑ 632 Doug Drabek .15 .05
❑ 633 Bill Wegman .15 .05
❑ 634 Jeff McKnight .15 .05
❑ 635 Rich Rodriguez .15 .05
❑ 636 Steve Trachsel .15 .05
❑ 637 Buddy Groom .15 .05
❑ 638 Sterling Hitchcock .15 .05
❑ 639 Chuck McElroy .15 .05
❑ 640 Rene Gonzales .15 .05
❑ 641 Dan Plesac .15 .05
❑ 642 Jeff Branson .15 .05
❑ 643 Darrell Whitmore .15 .05
❑ 644 Paul Quantrill .15 .05
❑ 645 Rich Rowland .15 .05
❑ 646 Curtis Pride RC .30 .10
❑ 647 Erik Plantenberg RC .15 .05
❑ 648 Albie Lopez .15 .05
❑ 649 Rich Batchelor RC .15 .05
❑ 650 Lee Smith .30 .10
❑ 651 Cliff Floyd .30 .10
❑ 652 Pete Schourek .15 .05
❑ 653 Reggie Jefferson .15 .05
❑ 654 Bill Haselman .15 .05
❑ 655 Steve Hosey .15 .05
❑ 656 Mark Clark .15 .05
❑ 657 Mark Davis .15 .05
❑ 658 Dave Magadan .15 .05
❑ 659 Candy Maldonado .15 .05
❑ 660 Mark Langston CL .15 .05

1995 Donruss

❑ COMPLETE SET (550) 30.00 12.00
❑ COMPLETE SERIES 1 (330) 20.00 8.00
❑ COMPLETE SERIES 2 (220) 10.00 4.00
❑ 1 David Justice .30 .10
❑ 2 Rene Arocha .15 .05
❑ 3 Sandy Alomar Jr. .15 .05
❑ 4 Luis Lopez .15 .05
❑ 5 Mike Piazza 1.25 .50
❑ 6 Bobby Jones .15 .05
❑ 7 Damion Easley .15 .05
❑ 8 Barry Bonds 2.00 .75
❑ 9 Mike Mussina .50 .20
❑ 10 Kevin Seitzer .15 .05
❑ 11 John Smiley .15 .05
❑ 12 Wm.VanLandingham .15 .05
❑ 13 Ron Darling .15 .05
❑ 14 Walt Weiss .15 .05
❑ 15 Mike Lansing .15 .05
❑ 16 Allen Watson .15 .05
❑ 17 Aaron Sele .15 .05
❑ 18 Randy Johnson .75 .30
❑ 19 Dean Palmer .30 .10
❑ 20 Jeff Bagwell .50 .20
❑ 21 Curt Schilling .30 .10
❑ 22 Darrell Whitmore .15 .05
❑ 23 Steve Trachsel .15 .05
❑ 24 Dan Wilson .15 .05
❑ 25 Steve Finley .30 .10
❑ 26 Bret Boone .30 .10
❑ 27 Charles Johnson .30 .10
❑ 28 Mike Stanton .15 .05
❑ 29 Ismael Valdes .15 .05
❑ 30 Salomon Torres .15 .05
❑ 31 Eric Anthony .15 .05
❑ 32 Spike Owen .15 .05
❑ 33 Joey Cora .15 .05
❑ 34 Robert Eenhoorn .15 .05
❑ 35 Rick White .15 .05
❑ 36 Omar Vizquel .50 .20
❑ 37 Carlos Delgado .30 .10
❑ 38 Eddie Williams .15 .05
❑ 39 Shawon Dunston .15 .05
❑ 40 Darrin Fletcher .15 .05
❑ 41 Leo Gomez .15 .05
❑ 42 Juan Gonzalez .30 .10
❑ 43 Luis Alicea .15 .05
❑ 44 Ken Ryan .15 .05
❑ 45 Lou Whitaker .30 .10
❑ 46 Mike Blowers .15 .05
❑ 47 Willie Blair .15 .05
❑ 48 Todd Van Poppel .15 .05
❑ 49 Roberto Alomar .50 .20
❑ 50 Ozzie Smith 1.25 .50
❑ 51 Sterling Hitchcock .15 .05
❑ 52 Mo Vaughn .30 .10
❑ 53 Rick Aguilera .15 .05
❑ 54 Kent Mercker .15 .05
❑ 55 Don Mattingly 2.00 .75
❑ 56 Bob Scanlan .15 .05
❑ 57 Wilson Alvarez .15 .05
❑ 58 Jose Mesa .15 .05
❑ 59 Scott Kamieniecki .15 .05
❑ 60 Todd Jones .15 .05
❑ 61 John Kruk .30 .10
❑ 62 Mike Stanley .15 .05
❑ 63 Tino Martinez .50 .20
❑ 64 Eddie Zambrano .15 .05
❑ 65 Todd Hundley .15 .05
❑ 66 Jamie Moyer .30 .10
❑ 67 Rich Amaral .15 .05
❑ 68 Jose Valentin .15 .05
❑ 69 Alex Gonzalez .15 .05
❑ 70 Kurt Abbott .15 .05
❑ 71 Delino DeShields .15 .05
❑ 72 Brian Anderson .15 .05
❑ 73 John Vander Wal .15 .05
❑ 74 Turner Ward .15 .05
❑ 75 Tim Raines .30 .10
❑ 76 Mark Acre .15 .05
❑ 77 Jose Offerman .15 .05
❑ 78 Jimmy Key .30 .10
❑ 79 Mark Whiten .15 .05
❑ 80 Mark Gubicza .15 .05
❑ 81 Darren Hall .15 .05
❑ 82 Travis Fryman .30 .10
❑ 83 Cal Ripken 2.50 1.00
❑ 84 Geronimo Berroa .15 .05
❑ 85 Bret Barberie .15 .05
❑ 86 Andy Ashby .15 .05
❑ 87 Steve Avery .15 .05
❑ 88 Rich Becker .15 .05
❑ 89 John Valentin .15 .05
❑ 90 Glenallen Hill .15 .05
❑ 91 Carlos Garcia .15 .05
❑ 92 Dennis Martinez .30 .10
❑ 93 Pat Kelly .15 .05
❑ 94 Orlando Miller .15 .05
❑ 95 Felix Jose .15 .05
❑ 96 Mike Kingery .15 .05
❑ 97 Jeff Kent .30 .10
❑ 98 Pete Incaviglia .15 .05
❑ 99 Chad Curtis .15 .05
❑ 100 Thomas Howard .15 .05
❑ 101 Hector Carrasco .15 .05
❑ 102 Tom Pagnozzi .15 .05
❑ 103 Danny Tartabull .15 .05
❑ 104 Donnie Elliott .15 .05
❑ 105 Danny Jackson .15 .05
❑ 106 Steve Dunn .15 .05
❑ 107 Roger Salkeld .15 .05
❑ 108 Jeff King .15 .05
❑ 109 Cecil Fielder .30 .10
❑ 110 Paul Molitor CL .15 .05
❑ 111 Denny Neagle .30 .10
❑ 112 Troy Neel .15 .05
❑ 113 Rod Beck .15 .05
❑ 114 Alex Rodriguez 2.00 .75
❑ 115 Joey Eischen .15 .05
❑ 116 Tom Candiotti .15 .05
❑ 117 Ray McDavid .15 .05
❑ 118 Vince Coleman .15 .05
❑ 119 Pete Harnisch .15 .05
❑ 120 David Nied .15 .05
❑ 121 Pat Rapp .15 .05
❑ 122 Sammy Sosa .75 .30
❑ 123 Steve Reed .15 .05
❑ 124 Jose Oliva .15 .05
❑ 125 Ricky Bottalico .15 .05
❑ 126 Jose DeLeon .15 .05
❑ 127 Pat Hentgen .15 .05
❑ 128 Will Clark .50 .20
❑ 129 Mark Dewey .15 .05
❑ 130 Greg Vaughn .15 .05
❑ 131 Darren Dreifort .15 .05
❑ 132 Ed Sprague .15 .05
❑ 133 Lee Smith .30 .10
❑ 134 Charles Nagy .15 .05
❑ 135 Phil Plantier .15 .05
❑ 136 Jason Jacome .15 .05
❑ 137 Jose Lima .15 .05
❑ 138 J.R. Phillips .15 .05
❑ 139 J.T. Snow .30 .10
❑ 140 Michael Huff .15 .05
❑ 141 Billy Brewer .15 .05
❑ 142 Jeromy Burnitz .30 .10
❑ 143 Ricky Bones .15 .05
❑ 144 Carlos Rodriguez .15 .05
❑ 145 Luis Gonzalez .30 .10
❑ 146 Mark Lemke .15 .05
❑ 147 Al Martin .15 .05
❑ 148 Mike Bordick .15 .05
❑ 149 Robb Nen .30 .10
❑ 150 Wil Cordero .15 .05
❑ 151 Edgar Martinez .50 .20
❑ 152 Gerald Williams .15 .05
❑ 153 Esteban Beltre .15 .05
❑ 154 Mike Moore .15 .05
❑ 155 Mark Langston .15 .05
❑ 156 Mark Clark .15 .05
❑ 157 Bobby Ayala .15 .05
❑ 158 Rick Wilkins .15 .05
❑ 159 Bobby Munoz .15 .05
❑ 160 Brett Butler CL .15 .05
❑ 161 Scott Erickson .15 .05
❑ 162 Paul Molitor .30 .10
❑ 163 Jon Lieber .15 .05
❑ 164 Jason Grimsley .15 .05
❑ 165 Norberto Martin .15 .05
❑ 166 Javier Lopez .30 .10
❑ 167 Brian McRae .15 .05
❑ 168 Gary Sheffield .30 .10
❑ 169 Marcus Moore .15 .05
❑ 170 John Hudek .15 .05
❑ 171 Kelly Stinnett .15 .05
❑ 172 Chris Gomez .15 .05
❑ 173 Rey Sanchez .15 .05
❑ 174 Juan Guzman .15 .05
❑ 175 Chan Ho Park .30 .10
❑ 176 Terry Shumpert .15 .05
❑ 177 Steve Ontiveros .15 .05
❑ 178 Brad Ausmus .30 .10
❑ 179 Tim Davis .15 .05
❑ 180 Billy Ashley .15 .05
❑ 181 Vinny Castilla .30 .10
❑ 182 Bill Spiers .15 .05
❑ 183 Randy Knorr .15 .05
❑ 184 Brian L.Hunter .15 .05
❑ 185 Pat Meares .15 .05
❑ 186 Steve Buechele .15 .05
❑ 187 Kirt Manwaring .15 .05
❑ 188 Tim Naehring .15 .05
❑ 189 Matt Mieske .15 .05

❑ 190	Josias Manzanillo	.15	.05
❑ 191	Greg McMichael	.15	.05
❑ 192	Chuck Carr	.15	.05
❑ 193	Midre Cummings	.15	.05
❑ 194	Darryl Strawberry	.30	.10
❑ 195	Greg Gagne	.15	.05
❑ 196	Steve Cooke	.15	.05
❑ 197	Woody Williams	.15	.05
❑ 198	Ron Karkovice	.15	.05
❑ 199	Phil Leftwich	.15	.05
❑ 200	Jim Thome	.50	.20
❑ 201	Brady Anderson	.30	.10
❑ 202	Pedro A.Martinez	.15	.05
❑ 203	Steve Karsay	.15	.05
❑ 204	Reggie Sanders	.30	.10
❑ 205	Bill Risley	.15	.05
❑ 206	Jay Bell	.30	.10
❑ 207	Kevin Brown	.30	.10
❑ 208	Tim Scott	.15	.05
❑ 209	Lenny Dykstra	.30	.10
❑ 210	Willie Greene	.15	.05
❑ 211	Jim Eisenreich	.15	.05
❑ 212	Cliff Floyd	.30	.10
❑ 213	Otis Nixon	.15	.05
❑ 214	Eduardo Perez	.15	.05
❑ 215	Manuel Lee	.15	.05
❑ 216	Armando Benitez	.15	.05
❑ 217	Dave McCarty	.15	.05
❑ 218	Scott Livingstone	.15	.05
❑ 219	Chad Kreuter	.15	.05
❑ 220	Don Mattingly CL	1.00	.40
❑ 221	Brian Jordan	.30	.10
❑ 222	Matt Whiteside	.15	.05
❑ 223	Jim Edmonds	.50	.20
❑ 224	Tony Gwynn	1.00	.40
❑ 225	Jose Lind	.15	.05
❑ 226	Marvin Freeman	.15	.05
❑ 227	Ken Hill	.15	.05
❑ 228	David Hulse	.15	.05
❑ 229	Joe Hesketh	.15	.05
❑ 230	Roberto Petagine	.15	.05
❑ 231	Jeffrey Hammonds	.15	.05
❑ 232	John Jaha	.15	.05
❑ 233	John Burkett	.15	.05
❑ 234	Hal Morris	.15	.05
❑ 235	Tony Castillo	.15	.05
❑ 236	Ryan Bowen	.15	.05
❑ 237	Wayne Kirby	.15	.05
❑ 238	Brent Mayne	.15	.05
❑ 239	Jim Bullinger	.15	.05
❑ 240	Mike Lieberthal	.30	.10
❑ 241	Barry Larkin	.50	.20
❑ 242	David Segui	.15	.05
❑ 243	Jose Bautista	.15	.05
❑ 244	Hector Fajardo	.15	.05
❑ 245	Orel Hershiser	.30	.10
❑ 246	James Mouton	.15	.05
❑ 247	Scott Leius	.15	.05
❑ 248	Tom Glavine	.50	.20
❑ 249	Danny Bautista	.15	.05
❑ 250	Jose Mercedes	.15	.05
❑ 251	Marquis Grissom	.30	.10
❑ 252	Charlie Hayes	.15	.05
❑ 253	Ryan Klesko	.30	.10
❑ 254	Vicente Palacios	.15	.05
❑ 255	Matias Carrillo	.15	.05
❑ 256	Gary DiSarcina	.15	.05
❑ 257	Kirk Gibson	.30	.10
❑ 258	Garey Ingram	.15	.05
❑ 259	Alex Fernandez	.15	.05
❑ 260	John Mabry	.15	.05
❑ 261	Chris Howard	.15	.05
❑ 262	Miguel Jimenez	.15	.05
❑ 263	Heathcliff Slocumb	.15	.05
❑ 264	Albert Belle	.30	.10
❑ 265	Dave Clark	.15	.05
❑ 266	Joe Orsulak	.15	.05
❑ 267	Joey Hamilton	.15	.05
❑ 268	Mark Portugal	.15	.05
❑ 269	Kevin Tapani	.15	.05
❑ 270	Sid Fernandez	.15	.05
❑ 271	Steve Dreyer	.15	.05
❑ 272	Denny Hocking	.15	.05
❑ 273	Troy O'Leary	.15	.05
❑ 274	Milt Cuyler	.15	.05
❑ 275	Frank Thomas	.75	.30
❑ 276	Jorge Fabregas	.15	.05
❑ 277	Mike Gallego	.15	.05
❑ 278	Mickey Morandini	.15	.05
❑ 279	Roberto Hernandez	.15	.05
❑ 280	Henry Rodriguez	.15	.05
❑ 281	Garret Anderson	.30	.10
❑ 282	Bob Wickman	.15	.05
❑ 283	Gar Finnvold	.15	.05
❑ 284	Paul O'Neill	.50	.20
❑ 285	Royce Clayton	.15	.05
❑ 286	Chuck Knoblauch	.30	.10
❑ 287	Johnny Ruffin	.15	.05
❑ 288	Dave Nilsson	.15	.05
❑ 289	David Cone	.30	.10
❑ 290	Chuck McElroy	.15	.05
❑ 291	Kevin Stocker	.15	.05
❑ 292	Jose Rijo	.15	.05
❑ 293	Sean Berry	.15	.05
❑ 294	Ozzie Guillen	.30	.10
❑ 295	Chris Hoiles	.15	.05
❑ 296	Kevin Foster	.15	.05
❑ 297	Jeff Frye	.15	.05
❑ 298	Lance Johnson	.15	.05
❑ 299	Mike Kelly	.15	.05
❑ 300	Ellis Burks	.30	.10
❑ 301	Roberto Kelly	.15	.05
❑ 302	Dante Bichette	.30	.10
❑ 303	Alvaro Espinoza	.15	.05
❑ 304	Alex Cole	.15	.05
❑ 305	Rickey Henderson	.75	.30
❑ 306	Dave Weathers	.15	.05
❑ 307	Shane Reynolds	.15	.05
❑ 308	Bobby Bonilla	.30	.10
❑ 309	Junior Felix	.15	.05
❑ 310	Jeff Fassero	.15	.05
❑ 311	Darren Lewis	.15	.05
❑ 312	John Doherty	.15	.05
❑ 313	Scott Servais	.15	.05
❑ 314	Rick Helling	.15	.05
❑ 315	Pedro Martinez	.50	.20
❑ 316	Wes Chamberlain	.15	.05
❑ 317	Bryan Eversgerd	.15	.05
❑ 318	Trevor Hoffman	.30	.10
❑ 319	John Patterson	.15	.05
❑ 320	Matt Walbeck	.15	.05
❑ 321	Jeff Montgomery	.15	.05
❑ 322	Mel Rojas	.15	.05
❑ 323	Eddie Taubensee	.15	.05
❑ 324	Ray Lankford	.30	.10
❑ 325	Jose Vizcaino	.15	.05
❑ 326	Carlos Baerga	.15	.05
❑ 327	Jack Voigt	.15	.05
❑ 328	Julio Franco	.30	.10
❑ 329	Brent Gates	.15	.05
❑ 330	Kirby Puckett CL	.50	.20
❑ 331	Greg Maddux	1.25	.50
❑ 332	Jason Bere	.15	.05
❑ 333	Bill Wegman	.15	.05
❑ 334	Tuffy Rhodes	.15	.05
❑ 335	Kevin Young	.15	.05
❑ 336	Andy Benes	.15	.05
❑ 337	Pedro Astacio	.15	.05
❑ 338	Reggie Jefferson	.15	.05
❑ 339	Tim Belcher	.15	.05
❑ 340	Ken Griffey Jr.	1.25	.50
❑ 341	Mariano Duncan	.15	.05
❑ 342	Andres Galarraga	.30	.10
❑ 343	Rondell White	.30	.10
❑ 344	Cory Bailey	.15	.05
❑ 345	Bryan Harvey	.15	.05
❑ 346	John Franco	.30	.10
❑ 347	Greg Swindell	.15	.05
❑ 348	David West	.15	.05
❑ 349	Fred McGriff	.50	.20
❑ 350	Jose Canseco	.50	.20
❑ 351	Orlando Merced	.15	.05
❑ 352	Rheal Cormier	.15	.05
❑ 353	Carlos Pulido	.15	.05
❑ 354	Terry Steinbach	.15	.05
❑ 355	Wade Boggs	.50	.20
❑ 356	B.J. Surhoff	.30	.10
❑ 357	Rafael Palmeiro	.50	.20
❑ 358	Anthony Young	.15	.05
❑ 359	Tom Brunansky	.15	.05
❑ 360	Todd Stottlemyre	.15	.05
❑ 361	Chris Turner	.15	.05
❑ 362	Joe Boever	.15	.05
❑ 363	Jeff Blauser	.15	.05
❑ 364	Derek Bell	.15	.05
❑ 365	Matt Williams	.30	.10
❑ 366	Jeremy Hernandez	.15	.05
❑ 367	Joe Girardi	.15	.05
❑ 368	Mike Devereaux	.15	.05
❑ 369	Jim Abbott	.50	.20
❑ 370	Manny Ramirez	.50	.20
❑ 371	Kenny Lofton	.30	.10
❑ 372	Mark Smith	.15	.05
❑ 373	Dave Fleming	.15	.05
❑ 374	Dave Stewart	.30	.10
❑ 375	Roger Pavlik	.15	.05
❑ 376	Hipolito Pichardo	.15	.05
❑ 377	Bill Taylor	.15	.05
❑ 378	Robin Ventura	.30	.10
❑ 379	Bernard Gilkey	.15	.05
❑ 380	Kirby Puckett	.75	.30
❑ 381	Steve Howe	.15	.05
❑ 382	Devon White	.30	.10
❑ 383	Roberto Mejia	.15	.05
❑ 384	Darrin Jackson	.15	.05
❑ 385	Mike Morgan	.15	.05
❑ 386	Rusty Meacham	.15	.05
❑ 387	Bill Swift	.15	.05
❑ 388	Lou Frazier	.15	.05
❑ 389	Andy Van Slyke	.50	.20
❑ 390	Brett Butler	.30	.10
❑ 391	Bobby Witt	.15	.05
❑ 392	Jeff Conine	.30	.10
❑ 393	Tim Hyers	.15	.05
❑ 394	Terry Pendleton	.30	.10
❑ 395	Ricky Jordan	.15	.05
❑ 396	Eric Plunk	.15	.05
❑ 397	Melido Perez	.15	.05
❑ 398	Darryl Kile	.30	.10
❑ 399	Mark McLemore	.15	.05
❑ 400	Greg W.Harris	.15	.05
❑ 401	Jim Leyritz	.15	.05
❑ 402	Doug Strange	.15	.05
❑ 403	Tim Salmon	.50	.20
❑ 404	Terry Mulholland	.15	.05
❑ 405	Robby Thompson	.15	.05
❑ 406	Ruben Sierra	.30	.10
❑ 407	Tony Phillips	.15	.05
❑ 408	Moises Alou	.30	.10
❑ 409	Felix Fermin	.15	.05
❑ 410	Pat Listach	.15	.05
❑ 411	Kevin Bass	.15	.05
❑ 412	Ben McDonald	.15	.05
❑ 413	Scott Cooper	.15	.05
❑ 414	Jody Reed	.15	.05
❑ 415	Deion Sanders	.50	.20
❑ 416	Ricky Gutierrez	.15	.05
❑ 417	Gregg Jefferies	.15	.05
❑ 418	Jack McDowell	.15	.05
❑ 419	Al Leiter	.30	.10
❑ 420	Tony Longmire	.15	.05
❑ 421	Paul Wagner	.15	.05
❑ 422	Geronimo Pena	.15	.05
❑ 423	Ivan Rodriguez	.50	.20
❑ 424	Kevin Gross	.15	.05
❑ 425	Kirk McCaskill	.15	.05
❑ 426	Greg Myers	.15	.05
❑ 427	Roger Clemens	1.50	.60
❑ 428	Chris Hammond	.15	.05
❑ 429	Randy Myers	.15	.05
❑ 430	Roger Mason	.15	.05
❑ 431	Bret Saberhagen	.30	.10
❑ 432	Jeff Reboulet	.15	.05
❑ 433	John Olerud	.30	.10
❑ 434	Bill Gullickson	.15	.05
❑ 435	Eddie Murray	.75	.30
❑ 436	Pedro Munoz	.15	.05
❑ 437	Charlie O'Brien	.15	.05
❑ 438	Jeff Nelson	.15	.05
❑ 439	Mike Macfarlane	.15	.05
❑ 440	Don Mattingly CL	1.00	.40
❑ 441	Derrick May	.15	.05
❑ 442	John Roper	.15	.05
❑ 443	Darryl Hamilton	.15	.05
❑ 444	Dan Miceli	.15	.05
❑ 445	Tony Eusebio	.15	.05
❑ 446	Jerry Browne	.15	.05
❑ 447	Wally Joyner	.30	.10

❑	448 Brian Harper	.15	.05
❑	449 Scott Fletcher	.15	.05
❑	450 Bip Roberts	.15	.05
❑	451 Pete Smith	.15	.05
❑	452 Chili Davis	.30	.10
❑	453 Dave Hollins	.15	.05
❑	454 Tony Pena	.15	.05
❑	455 Butch Henry	.15	.05
❑	456 Craig Biggio	.50	.20
❑	457 Zane Smith	.15	.05
❑	458 Ryan Thompson	.15	.05
❑	459 Mike Jackson	.15	.05
❑	460 Mark McGwire	2.00	.75
❑	461 John Smoltz	.50	.20
❑	462 Steve Scarsone	.15	.05
❑	463 Greg Colbrunn	.15	.05
❑	464 Shawn Green	.30	.10
❑	465 David Wells	.30	.10
❑	466 Jose Hernandez	.15	.05
❑	467 Chip Hale	.15	.05
❑	468 Tony Tarasco	.15	.05
❑	469 Kevin Mitchell	.15	.05
❑	470 Billy Hatcher	.15	.05
❑	471 Jay Buhner	.30	.10
❑	472 Ken Caminiti	.30	.10
❑	473 Tom Henke	.15	.05
❑	474 Todd Worrell	.15	.05
❑	475 Mark Eichhorn	.15	.05
❑	476 Bruce Ruffin	.15	.05
❑	477 Chuck Finley	.30	.10
❑	478 Marc Newfield	.15	.05
❑	479 Paul Shuey	.15	.05
❑	480 Bob Tewksbury	.15	.05
❑	481 Ramon J.Martinez	.15	.05
❑	482 Melvin Nieves	.15	.05
❑	483 Todd Zeile	.15	.05
❑	484 Benito Santiago	.30	.10
❑	485 Stan Javier	.15	.05
❑	486 Kirk Rueter	.15	.05
❑	487 Andre Dawson	.30	.10
❑	488 Eric Karros	.30	.10
❑	489 Dave Magadan	.15	.05
❑	490 Joe Carter CL	.15	.05
❑	491 Randy Velarde	.15	.05
❑	492 Larry Walker	.30	.10
❑	493 Cris Carpenter	.15	.05
❑	494 Tom Gordon	.15	.05
❑	495 Dave Burba	.15	.05
❑	496 Darren Bragg	.15	.05
❑	497 Darren Daulton	.30	.10
❑	498 Don Slaught	.15	.05
❑	499 Pat Borders	.15	.05
❑	500 Lenny Harris	.15	.05
❑	501 Joe Ausanio	.15	.05
❑	502 Alan Trammell	.30	.10
❑	503 Mike Fetters	.15	.05
❑	504 Scott Ruffcorn	.15	.05
❑	505 Rich Rowland	.15	.05
❑	506 Juan Samuel	.15	.05
❑	507 Bo Jackson	.75	.30
❑	508 Jeff Branson	.15	.05
❑	509 Bernie Williams	.50	.20
❑	510 Paul Sorrento	.15	.05
❑	511 Dennis Eckersley	.30	.10
❑	512 Pat Mahomes	.15	.05
❑	513 Rusty Greer	.30	.10
❑	514 Luis Polonia	.15	.05
❑	515 Willie Banks	.15	.05
❑	516 John Wetteland	.30	.10
❑	517 Mike LaValliere	.15	.05
❑	518 Tommy Greene	.15	.05
❑	519 Mark Grace	.50	.20
❑	520 Bob Hamelin	.15	.05
❑	521 Scott Sanderson	.15	.05
❑	522 Joe Carter	.30	.10
❑	523 Jeff Brantley	.15	.05
❑	524 Andrew Lorraine	.15	.05
❑	525 Rico Brogna	.15	.05
❑	526 Shane Mack	.15	.05
❑	527 Mark Wohlers	.15	.05
❑	528 Scott Sanders	.15	.05
❑	529 Chris Bosio	.15	.05
❑	530 Andujar Cedeno	.15	.05
❑	531 Kenny Rogers	.30	.10
❑	532 Doug Drabek	.15	.05
❑	533 Curt Leskanic	.15	.05
❑	534 Craig Shipley	.15	.05
❑	535 Craig Grebeck	.15	.05
❑	536 Cal Eldred	.15	.05
❑	537 Mickey Tettleton	.15	.05
❑	538 Harold Baines	.30	.10
❑	539 Tim Wallach	.15	.05
❑	540 Damon Buford	.15	.05
❑	541 Lenny Webster	.15	.05
❑	542 Kevin Appier	.30	.10
❑	543 Raul Mondesi	.30	.10
❑	544 Eric Young	.15	.05
❑	545 Russ Davis	.15	.05
❑	546 Mike Benjamin	.15	.05
❑	547 Mike Greenwell	.15	.05
❑	548 Scott Brosius	.30	.10
❑	549 Brian Dorsett	.15	.05
❑	550 Chili Davis CL	.15	.05

1996 Donruss

❑	COMPLETE SET (550)	40.00	16.00
❑	COMPLETE SERIES 1 (330)	25.00	10.00
❑	COMPLETE SERIES 2 (220)	15.00	6.00
❑	1 Frank Thomas	.75	.30
❑	2 Jason Bates	.30	.10
❑	3 Steve Sparks	.30	.10
❑	4 Scott Servais	.30	.10
❑	5 Angelo Encarnacion RC	.30	.10
❑	6 Scott Sanders	.30	.10
❑	7 Billy Ashley	.30	.10
❑	8 Alex Rodriguez	1.50	.60
❑	9 Sean Bergman	.30	.10
❑	10 Brad Radke	.30	.10
❑	11 Andy Van Slyke	.50	.20
❑	12 Joe Girardi	.30	.10
❑	13 Mark Grudzielanek	.30	.10
❑	14 Rick Aguilera	.30	.10
❑	15 Randy Veres	.30	.10
❑	16 Tim Bogar	.30	.10
❑	17 Dave Veres	.30	.10
❑	18 Kevin Stocker	.30	.10
❑	19 Marquis Grissom	.30	.10
❑	20 Will Clark	.50	.20
❑	21 Jay Bell	.30	.10
❑	22 Allen Battle	.30	.10
❑	23 Frank Rodriguez	.30	.10
❑	24 Terry Steinbach	.30	.10
❑	25 Gerald Williams	.30	.10
❑	26 Sid Roberson	.30	.10
❑	27 Greg Zaun	.30	.10
❑	28 Ozzie Timmons	.30	.10
❑	29 Vaughn Eshelman	.30	.10
❑	30 Ed Sprague	.30	.10
❑	31 Gary DiSarcina	.30	.10
❑	32 Joe Boever	.30	.10
❑	33 Steve Avery	.30	.10
❑	34 Brad Ausmus	.30	.10
❑	35 Kirt Manwaring	.30	.10
❑	36 Gary Sheffield	.30	.10
❑	37 Jason Bere	.30	.10
❑	38 Jeff Manto	.30	.10
❑	39 David Cone	.30	.10
❑	40 Manny Ramirez	.50	.20
❑	41 Sandy Alomar Jr.	.30	.10
❑	42 Curtis Goodwin	.30	.10
❑	43 Tino Martinez	.50	.20
❑	44 Woody Williams	.30	.10
❑	45 Dean Palmer	.30	.10
❑	46 Hipolito Pichardo	.30	.10
❑	47 Jason Giambi	.30	.10
❑	48 Lance Johnson	.30	.10
❑	49 Bernard Gilkey	.30	.10
❑	50 Kirby Puckett	.75	.30
❑	51 Tony Fernandez	.30	.10
❑	52 Alex Gonzalez	.30	.10
❑	53 Bret Saberhagen	.30	.10
❑	54 Lyle Mouton	.30	.10
❑	55 Brian McRae	.30	.10
❑	56 Mark Gubicza	.30	.10
❑	57 Sergio Valdez	.30	.10
❑	58 Darrin Fletcher	.30	.10
❑	59 Steve Parris	.30	.10
❑	60 Johnny Damon	.50	.20
❑	61 Rickey Henderson	.75	.30
❑	62 Darrell Whitmore	.30	.10
❑	63 Roberto Petagine	.30	.10
❑	64 Trenidad Hubbard	.30	.10
❑	65 Heathcliff Slocumb	.30	.10
❑	66 Steve Finley	.30	.10
❑	67 Mariano Rivera	.75	.30
❑	68 Brian L.Hunter	.30	.10
❑	69 Jamie Moyer	.30	.10
❑	70 Ellis Burks	.30	.10
❑	71 Pat Kelly	.30	.10
❑	72 Mickey Tettleton	.30	.10
❑	73 Garret Anderson	.30	.10
❑	74 Andy Pettitte	.50	.20
❑	75 Glenallen Hill	.30	.10
❑	76 Brent Gates	.30	.10
❑	77 Lou Whitaker	.30	.10
❑	78 David Segui	.30	.10
❑	79 Dan Wilson	.30	.10
❑	80 Pat Listach	.30	.10
❑	81 Jeff Bagwell	.50	.20
❑	82 Ben McDonald	.30	.10
❑	83 John Valentin	.30	.10
❑	84 John Jaha	.30	.10
❑	85 Pete Schourek	.30	.10
❑	86 Bryce Florie	.30	.10
❑	87 Brian Jordan	.30	.10
❑	88 Ron Karkovice	.30	.10
❑	89 Al Leiter	.30	.10
❑	90 Tony Longmire	.30	.10
❑	91 Nelson Liriano	.30	.10
❑	92 David Bell	.30	.10
❑	93 Kevin Gross	.30	.10
❑	94 Tom Candiotti	.30	.10
❑	95 Dave Martinez	.30	.10
❑	96 Greg Myers	.30	.10
❑	97 Rheal Cormier	.30	.10
❑	98 Chris Hammond	.30	.10
❑	99 Randy Myers	.30	.10
❑	100 Bill Pulsipher	.30	.10
❑	101 Jason Isringhausen	.30	.10
❑	102 Dave Stevens	.30	.10
❑	103 Roberto Alomar	.50	.20
❑	104 Bob Higginson	.30	.10
❑	105 Eddie Murray	.75	.30
❑	106 Matt Walbeck	.30	.10
❑	107 Mark Wohlers	.30	.10
❑	108 Jeff Nelson	.30	.10
❑	109 Tom Goodwin	.30	.10
❑	110 Cal Ripken CL	1.25	.50
❑	111 Rey Sanchez	.30	.10
❑	112 Hector Carrasco	.30	.10
❑	113 B.J. Surhoff	.30	.10
❑	114 Dan Miceli	.30	.10
❑	115 Dean Hartgraves	.30	.10
❑	116 John Burkett	.30	.10
❑	117 Gary Gaetti	.30	.10
❑	118 Ricky Bones	.30	.10
❑	119 Mike Macfarlane	.30	.10
❑	120 Bip Roberts	.30	.10
❑	121 Dave Mlicki	.30	.10
❑	122 Chili Davis	.30	.10
❑	123 Mark Whiten	.30	.10
❑	124 Herbert Perry	.30	.10
❑	125 Butch Henry	.30	.10
❑	126 Derek Bell	.30	.10
❑	127 Al Martin	.30	.10
❑	128 John Franco	.30	.10
❑	129 W. VanLandingham	.30	.10
❑	130 Mike Bordick	.30	.10
❑	131 Mike Mordecai	.30	.10
❑	132 Robby Thompson	.30	.10

❑ 133	Greg Colbrunn	.30	.10
❑ 134	Domingo Cedeno	.30	.10
❑ 135	Chad Curtis	.30	.10
❑ 136	Jose Hernandez	.30	.10
❑ 137	Scott Klingenbeck	.30	.10
❑ 138	Ryan Klesko	.30	.10
❑ 139	John Smiley	.30	.10
❑ 140	Charlie Hayes	.30	.10
❑ 141	Jay Buhner	.30	.10
❑ 142	Doug Drabek	.30	.10
❑ 143	Roger Pavlik	.30	.10
❑ 144	Todd Worrell	.30	.10
❑ 145	Cal Ripken	2.50	1.00
❑ 146	Steve Reed	.30	.10
❑ 147	Chuck Finley	.30	.10
❑ 148	Mike Blowers	.30	.10
❑ 149	Orel Hershiser	.30	.10
❑ 150	Allen Watson	.30	.10
❑ 151	Ramon Martinez	.30	.10
❑ 152	Melvin Nieves	.30	.10
❑ 153	Tripp Cromer	.30	.10
❑ 154	Yorkis Perez	.30	.10
❑ 155	Stan Javier	.30	.10
❑ 156	Mel Rojas	.30	.10
❑ 157	Aaron Sele	.30	.10
❑ 158	Eric Karros	.30	.10
❑ 159	Robb Nen	.30	.10
❑ 160	Raul Mondesi	.30	.10
❑ 161	John Wetteland	.30	.10
❑ 162	Tim Scott	.30	.10
❑ 163	Kenny Rogers	.30	.10
❑ 164	Melvin Bunch	.30	.10
❑ 165	Rod Beck	.30	.10
❑ 166	Andy Benes	.30	.10
❑ 167	Lenny Dykstra	.30	.10
❑ 168	Orlando Merced	.30	.10
❑ 169	Tomas Perez	.30	.10
❑ 170	Xavier Hernandez	.30	.10
❑ 171	Ruben Sierra	.30	.10
❑ 172	Alan Trammell	.30	.10
❑ 173	Mike Fetters	.30	.10
❑ 174	Wilson Alvarez	.30	.10
❑ 175	Erik Hanson	.30	.10
❑ 176	Travis Fryman	.30	.10
❑ 177	Jim Abbott	.50	.20
❑ 178	Bret Boone	.30	.10
❑ 179	Sterling Hitchcock	.30	.10
❑ 180	Pat Mahomes	.30	.10
❑ 181	Mark Acre	.30	.10
❑ 182	Charles Nagy	.30	.10
❑ 183	Rusty Greer	.30	.10
❑ 184	Mike Stanley	.30	.10
❑ 185	Jim Bullinger	.30	.10
❑ 186	Shane Andrews	.30	.10
❑ 187	Brian Keyser	.30	.10
❑ 188	Tyler Green	.30	.10
❑ 189	Mark Grace	.50	.20
❑ 190	Bob Hamelin	.30	.10
❑ 191	Luis Ortiz	.30	.10
❑ 192	Joe Carter	.30	.10
❑ 193	Eddie Taubensee	.30	.10
❑ 194	Brian Anderson	.30	.10
❑ 195	Edgardo Alfonzo	.30	.10
❑ 196	Pedro Munoz	.30	.10
❑ 197	David Justice	.30	.10
❑ 198	Trevor Hoffman	.30	.10
❑ 199	Bobby Ayala	.30	.10
❑ 200	Tony Eusebio	.30	.10
❑ 201	Jeff Russell	.30	.10
❑ 202	Mike Hampton	.30	.10
❑ 203	Walt Weiss	.30	.10
❑ 204	Joey Hamilton	.30	.10
❑ 205	Roberto Hernandez	.30	.10
❑ 206	Greg Vaughn	.30	.10
❑ 207	Felipe Lira	.30	.10
❑ 208	Harold Baines	.30	.10
❑ 209	Tim Wallach	.30	.10
❑ 210	Manny Alexander	.30	.10
❑ 211	Tim Laker	.30	.10
❑ 212	Chris Haney	.30	.10
❑ 213	Brian Maxcy	.30	.10
❑ 214	Eric Young	.30	.10
❑ 215	Darryl Strawberry	.30	.10
❑ 216	Barry Bonds	2.00	.75
❑ 217	Tim Naehring	.30	.10
❑ 218	Scott Brosius	.30	.10
❑ 219	Reggie Sanders	.30	.10
❑ 220	Eddie Murray CL	.50	.20
❑ 221	Luis Alicea	.30	.10
❑ 222	Albert Belle	.30	.10
❑ 223	Benji Gil	.30	.10
❑ 224	Dante Bichette	.30	.10
❑ 225	Bobby Bonilla	.30	.10
❑ 226	Todd Stottlemyre	.30	.10
❑ 227	Jim Edmonds	.30	.10
❑ 228	Todd Jones	.30	.10
❑ 229	Shawn Green	.30	.10
❑ 230	Javier Lopez	.30	.10
❑ 231	Ariel Prieto	.30	.10
❑ 232	Tony Phillips	.30	.10
❑ 233	James Mouton	.30	.10
❑ 234	Jose Oquendo	.30	.10
❑ 235	Royce Clayton	.30	.10
❑ 236	Chuck Carr	.30	.10
❑ 237	Doug Jones	.30	.10
❑ 238	Mark McLemore	.30	.10
❑ 239	Bill Swift	.30	.10
❑ 240	Scott Leius	.30	.10
❑ 241	Russ Davis	.30	.10
❑ 242	Ray Durham	.30	.10
❑ 243	Matt Mieske	.30	.10
❑ 244	Brent Mayne	.30	.10
❑ 245	Thomas Howard	.30	.10
❑ 246	Troy O'Leary	.30	.10
❑ 247	Jacob Brumfield	.30	.10
❑ 248	Mickey Morandini	.30	.10
❑ 249	Todd Hundley	.30	.10
❑ 250	Chris Bosio	.30	.10
❑ 251	Omar Vizquel	.50	.20
❑ 252	Mike Lansing	.30	.10
❑ 253	John Mabry	.30	.10
❑ 254	Mike Perez	.30	.10
❑ 255	Delino DeShields	.30	.10
❑ 256	Wil Cordero	.30	.10
❑ 257	Mike James	.30	.10
❑ 258	Todd Van Poppel	.30	.10
❑ 259	Joey Cora	.30	.10
❑ 260	Andre Dawson	.30	.10
❑ 261	Jerry DiPoto	.30	.10
❑ 262	Rick Krivda	.30	.10
❑ 263	Glenn Dishman	.30	.10
❑ 264	Mike Mimbs	.30	.10
❑ 265	John Ericks	.30	.10
❑ 266	Jose Canseco	.50	.20
❑ 267	Jeff Branson	.30	.10
❑ 268	Curt Leskanic	.30	.10
❑ 269	Jon Nunnally	.30	.10
❑ 270	Scott Stahoviak	.30	.10
❑ 271	Jeff Montgomery	.30	.10
❑ 272	Hal Morris	.30	.10
❑ 273	Esteban Loaiza	.30	.10
❑ 274	Rico Brogna	.30	.10
❑ 275	Dave Winfield	.30	.10
❑ 276	J.R. Phillips	.30	.10
❑ 277	Todd Zeile	.30	.10
❑ 278	Tom Pagnozzi	.30	.10
❑ 279	Mark Lemke	.30	.10
❑ 280	Dave Magadan	.30	.10
❑ 281	Greg McMichael	.30	.10
❑ 282	Mike Morgan	.30	.10
❑ 283	Moises Alou	.30	.10
❑ 284	Dennis Martinez	.30	.10
❑ 285	Jeff Kent	.30	.10
❑ 286	Mark Johnson	.30	.10
❑ 287	Darren Lewis	.30	.10
❑ 288	Brad Clontz	.30	.10
❑ 289	Chad Fonville	.30	.10
❑ 290	Paul Sorrento	.30	.10
❑ 291	Lee Smith	.30	.10
❑ 292	Tom Glavine	.50	.20
❑ 293	Antonio Osuna	.30	.10
❑ 294	Kevin Foster	.30	.10
❑ 295	Sandy Martinez	.30	.10
❑ 296	Mark Leiter	.30	.10
❑ 297	Julian Tavarez	.30	.10
❑ 298	Mike Kelly	.30	.10
❑ 299	Joe Oliver	.30	.10
❑ 300	John Flaherty	.30	.10
❑ 301	Don Mattingly	2.00	.75
❑ 302	Pat Meares	.30	.10
❑ 303	John Doherty	.30	.10
❑ 304	Joe Vitiello	.30	.10
❑ 305	Vinny Castilla	.30	.10
❑ 306	Jeff Brantley	.30	.10
❑ 307	Mike Greenwell	.30	.10
❑ 308	Midre Cummings	.30	.10
❑ 309	Curt Schilling	.30	.10
❑ 310	Ken Caminiti	.30	.10
❑ 311	Scott Erickson	.30	.10
❑ 312	Carl Everett	.30	.10
❑ 313	Charles Johnson	.30	.10
❑ 314	Alex Diaz	.30	.10
❑ 315	Jose Mesa	.30	.10
❑ 316	Mark Carreon	.30	.10
❑ 317	Carlos Perez	.30	.10
❑ 318	Ismael Valdes	.30	.10
❑ 319	Frank Castillo	.30	.10
❑ 320	Tom Henke	.30	.10
❑ 321	Spike Owen	.30	.10
❑ 322	Joe Orsulak	.30	.10
❑ 323	Paul Menhart	.30	.10
❑ 324	Pedro Borbon	.30	.10
❑ 325	Paul Molitor CL	.30	.10
❑ 326	Jeff Cirillo	.30	.10
❑ 327	Edwin Hurtado	.30	.10
❑ 328	Orlando Miller	.30	.10
❑ 329	Steve Ontiveros	.30	.10
❑ 330	Kirby Puckett CL	.50	.20
❑ 331	Scott Bullett	.30	.10
❑ 332	Andres Galarraga	.30	.10
❑ 333	Cal Eldred	.30	.10
❑ 334	Sammy Sosa	.75	.30
❑ 335	Don Slaught	.30	.10
❑ 336	Jody Reed	.30	.10
❑ 337	Roger Cedeno	.30	.10
❑ 338	Ken Griffey Jr.	1.25	.50
❑ 339	Todd Hollandsworth	.30	.10
❑ 340	Mike Trombley	.30	.10
❑ 341	Gregg Jefferies	.30	.10
❑ 342	Larry Walker	.30	.10
❑ 343	Pedro Martinez	.50	.20
❑ 344	Dwayne Hosey	.30	.10
❑ 345	Terry Pendleton	.30	.10
❑ 346	Pete Harnisch	.30	.10
❑ 347	Tony Castillo	.30	.10
❑ 348	Paul Quantrill	.30	.10
❑ 349	Fred McGriff	.50	.20
❑ 350	Ivan Rodriguez	.50	.20
❑ 351	Butch Huskey	.30	.10
❑ 352	Ozzie Smith	1.25	.50
❑ 353	Marty Cordova	.30	.10
❑ 354	John Wasdin	.30	.10
❑ 355	Wade Boggs	.50	.20
❑ 356	Dave Nilsson	.30	.10
❑ 357	Rafael Palmeiro	.50	.20
❑ 358	Luis Gonzalez	.30	.10
❑ 359	Reggie Jefferson	.30	.10
❑ 360	Carlos Delgado	.30	.10
❑ 361	Orlando Palmeiro	.30	.10
❑ 362	Chris Gomez	.30	.10
❑ 363	John Smoltz	.50	.20
❑ 364	Marc Newfield	.30	.10
❑ 365	Matt Williams	.30	.10
❑ 366	Jesus Tavarez	.30	.10
❑ 367	Bruce Ruffin	.30	.10
❑ 368	Sean Berry	.30	.10
❑ 369	Randy Velarde	.30	.10
❑ 370	Tony Pena	.30	.10
❑ 371	Jim Thome	.50	.20
❑ 372	Jeffrey Hammonds	.30	.10
❑ 373	Bob Wolcott	.30	.10
❑ 374	Juan Guzman	.30	.10
❑ 375	Juan Gonzalez	.30	.10
❑ 376	Michael Tucker	.30	.10
❑ 377	Doug Johns	.30	.10
❑ 378	Mike Cameron RC	.60	.25
❑ 379	Ray Lankford	.30	.10
❑ 380	Jose Parra	.30	.10
❑ 381	Jimmy Key	.30	.10
❑ 382	John Olerud	.30	.10
❑ 383	Kevin Ritz	.30	.10
❑ 384	Tim Raines	.30	.10
❑ 385	Rich Amaral	.30	.10
❑ 386	Keith Lockhart	.30	.10
❑ 387	Steve Scarsone	.30	.10
❑ 388	Cliff Floyd	.30	.10
❑ 389	Rich Aude	.30	.10
❑ 390	Hideo Nomo	.75	.30

❑ 391 Geronimo Berroa .30 .10
❑ 392 Pat Rapp .30 .10
❑ 393 Dustin Hermanson .30 .10
❑ 394 Greg Maddux 1.25 .50
❑ 395 Darren Daulton .30 .10
❑ 396 Kenny Lofton .30 .10
❑ 397 Ruben Rivera .30 .10
❑ 398 Billy Wagner .30 .10
❑ 399 Kevin Brown .30 .10
❑ 400 Mike Kingery .30 .10
❑ 401 Bernie Williams .50 .20
❑ 402 Otis Nixon .30 .10
❑ 403 Damion Easley .30 .10
❑ 404 Paul O'Neill .50 .20
❑ 405 Deion Sanders .50 .20
❑ 406 Dennis Eckersley .30 .10
❑ 407 Tony Clark .30 .10
❑ 408 Rondell White .30 .10
❑ 409 Luis Sojo .30 .10
❑ 410 David Hulse .30 .10
❑ 411 Shane Reynolds .30 .10
❑ 412 Chris Hoiles .30 .10
❑ 413 Lee Tinsley .30 .10
❑ 414 Scott Karl .30 .10
❑ 415 Ron Gant .30 .10
❑ 416 Brian Johnson .30 .10
❑ 417 Jose Oliva .30 .10
❑ 418 Jack McDowell .30 .10
❑ 419 Paul Molitor .30 .10
❑ 420 Ricky Bottalico .30 .10
❑ 421 Paul Wagner .30 .10
❑ 422 Terry Bradshaw .30 .10
❑ 423 Bob Tewksbury .30 .10
❑ 424 Mike Piazza 1.25 .50
❑ 425 Luis Andujar .30 .10
❑ 426 Mark Langston .30 .10
❑ 427 Stan Belinda .30 .10
❑ 428 Kurt Abbott .30 .10
❑ 429 Shawon Dunston .30 .10
❑ 430 Bobby Jones .30 .10
❑ 431 Jose Vizcaino .30 .10
❑ 432 Matt Lawton RC .40 .15
❑ 433 Pat Hentgen .30 .10
❑ 434 Cecil Fielder .30 .10
❑ 435 Carlos Baerga .30 .10
❑ 436 Rich Becker .30 .10
❑ 437 Chipper Jones .75 .30
❑ 438 Bill Risley .30 .10
❑ 439 Kevin Appier .30 .10
❑ 440 Wade Boggs CL .30 .10
❑ 441 Jaime Navarro .30 .10
❑ 442 Barry Larkin .50 .20
❑ 443 Jose Valentin .30 .10
❑ 444 Bryan Rekar .30 .10
❑ 445 Rick Wilkins .30 .10
❑ 446 Quilvio Veras .30 .10
❑ 447 Greg Gagne .30 .10
❑ 448 Mark Kiefer .30 .10
❑ 449 Bobby Witt .30 .10
❑ 450 Andy Ashby .30 .10
❑ 451 Alex Ochoa .30 .10
❑ 452 Jorge Fabregas .30 .10
❑ 453 Gene Schall .30 .10
❑ 454 Ken Hill .30 .10
❑ 455 Tony Tarasco .30 .10
❑ 456 Donnie Wall .30 .10
❑ 457 Carlos Garcia .30 .10
❑ 458 Ryan Thompson .30 .10
❑ 459 Marvin Benard RC .40 .15
❑ 460 Jose Herrera .30 .10
❑ 461 Jeff Blauser .30 .10
❑ 462 Chris Hook .30 .10
❑ 463 Jeff Conine .30 .10
❑ 464 Devon White .30 .10
❑ 465 Danny Bautista .30 .10
❑ 466 Steve Trachsel .30 .10
❑ 467 C.J. Nitkowski .30 .10
❑ 468 Mike Devereaux .30 .10
❑ 469 David Wells .30 .10
❑ 470 Jim Eisenreich .30 .10
❑ 471 Edgar Martinez .50 .20
❑ 472 Craig Biggio .50 .20
❑ 473 Jeff Frye .30 .10
❑ 474 Karim Garcia .30 .10
❑ 475 Jimmy Haynes .30 .10
❑ 476 Darren Holmes .30 .10
❑ 477 Tim Salmon .50 .20
❑ 478 Randy Johnson .75 .30
❑ 479 Eric Plunk .30 .10
❑ 480 Scott Cooper .30 .10
❑ 481 Chan Ho Park .30 .10
❑ 482 Ray McDavid .30 .10
❑ 483 Mark Petkovsek .30 .10
❑ 484 Greg Swindell .30 .10
❑ 485 George Williams .30 .10
❑ 486 Yamil Benitez .30 .10
❑ 487 Tim Wakefield .30 .10
❑ 488 Kevin Tapani .30 .10
❑ 489 Derrick May .30 .10
❑ 490 Ken Griffey Jr. CL .75 .30
❑ 491 Derek Jeter 2.00 .75
❑ 492 Jeff Fassero .30 .10
❑ 493 Benito Santiago .30 .10
❑ 494 Tom Gordon .30 .10
❑ 495 Jamie Brewington RC .30 .10
❑ 496 Vince Coleman .30 .10
❑ 497 Kevin Jordan .30 .10
❑ 498 Jeff King .30 .10
❑ 499 Mike Simms .30 .10
❑ 500 Jose Rijo .30 .10
❑ 501 Denny Neagle .30 .10
❑ 502 Jose Lima .30 .10
❑ 503 Kevin Seitzer .30 .10
❑ 504 Alex Fernandez .30 .10
❑ 505 Mo Vaughn .30 .10
❑ 506 Phil Nevin .30 .10
❑ 507 J.T. Snow .30 .10
❑ 508 Andujar Cedeno .30 .10
❑ 509 Ozzie Guillen .30 .10
❑ 510 Mark Clark .30 .10
❑ 511 Mark McGwire 2.00 .75
❑ 512 Jeff Reboulet .30 .10
❑ 513 Armando Benitez .30 .10
❑ 514 LaTroy Hawkins .30 .10
❑ 515 Brett Butler .30 .10
❑ 516 Tavo Alvarez .30 .10
❑ 517 Chris Snopek .30 .10
❑ 518 Mike Mussina .50 .20
❑ 519 Darryl Kile .30 .10
❑ 520 Wally Joyner .30 .10
❑ 521 Willie McGee .30 .10
❑ 522 Kent Mercker .30 .10
❑ 523 Mike Jackson .30 .10
❑ 524 Troy Percival .30 .10
❑ 525 Tony Gwynn 1.00 .40
❑ 526 Ron Coomer .30 .10
❑ 527 Darryl Hamilton .30 .10
❑ 528 Phil Plantier .30 .10
❑ 529 Norm Charlton .30 .10
❑ 530 Craig Paquette .30 .10
❑ 531 Dave Burba .30 .10
❑ 532 Mike Henneman .30 .10
❑ 533 Terrell Wade .30 .10
❑ 534 Eddie Williams .30 .10
❑ 535 Robin Ventura .30 .10
❑ 536 Chuck Knoblauch .30 .10
❑ 537 Les Norman .30 .10
❑ 538 Brady Anderson .30 .10
❑ 539 Roger Clemens 1.50 .60
❑ 540 Mark Portugal .30 .10
❑ 541 Mike Matheny .30 .10
❑ 542 Jeff Parrett .30 .10
❑ 543 Roberto Kelly .30 .10
❑ 544 Damon Buford .30 .10
❑ 545 Chad Ogea .30 .10
❑ 546 Jose Offerman .30 .10
❑ 547 Brian Barber .30 .10
❑ 548 Danny Tartabull .30 .10
❑ 549 Duane Singleton .30 .10
❑ 550 Tony Gwynn CL .50 .20

1997 Donruss

❑ COMPLETE SET (450) 50.00 20.00
❑ COMPLETE SERIES 1 (270) 25.00 10.00
❑ COMPLETE UPDATE (180) 25.00 10.00
❑ 1 Juan Gonzalez .30 .10
❑ 2 Jim Edmonds .30 .10
❑ 3 Tony Gwynn 1.00 .40
❑ 4 Andres Galarraga .30 .10
❑ 5 Joe Carter .30 .10
❑ 6 Raul Mondesi .30 .10
❑ 7 Greg Maddux 1.25 .50
❑ 8 Travis Fryman .30 .10
❑ 9 Brian Jordan .30 .10
❑ 10 Henry Rodriguez .30 .10
❑ 11 Manny Ramirez .50 .20
❑ 12 Mark McGwire 2.00 .75
❑ 13 Marc Newfield .30 .10
❑ 14 Craig Biggio .50 .20
❑ 15 Sammy Sosa .75 .30
❑ 16 Brady Anderson .30 .10
❑ 17 Wade Boggs .50 .20
❑ 18 Charles Johnson .30 .10
❑ 19 Matt Williams .30 .10
❑ 20 Denny Neagle .30 .10
❑ 21 Ken Griffey Jr. 1.25 .50
❑ 22 Robin Ventura .30 .10
❑ 23 Barry Larkin .50 .20
❑ 24 Todd Zeile .30 .10
❑ 25 Chuck Knoblauch .30 .10
❑ 26 Todd Hundley .30 .10
❑ 27 Roger Clemens 1.50 .60
❑ 28 Michael Tucker .30 .10
❑ 29 Rondell White .30 .10
❑ 30 Osvaldo Fernandez .30 .10
❑ 31 Ivan Rodriguez .50 .20
❑ 32 Alex Fernandez .30 .10
❑ 33 Jason Isringhausen .30 .10
❑ 34 Chipper Jones .75 .30
❑ 35 Paul O'Neill .50 .20
❑ 36 Hideo Nomo .75 .30
❑ 37 Roberto Alomar .50 .20
❑ 38 Derek Bell .30 .10
❑ 39 Paul Molitor .30 .10
❑ 40 Andy Benes .30 .10
❑ 41 Steve Trachsel .30 .10
❑ 42 J.T. Snow .30 .10
❑ 43 Jason Kendall .30 .10
❑ 44 Alex Rodriguez 1.25 .50
❑ 45 Joey Hamilton .30 .10
❑ 46 Carlos Delgado .30 .10
❑ 47 Jason Giambi .30 .10
❑ 48 Larry Walker .30 .10
❑ 49 Derek Jeter 2.00 .75
❑ 50 Kenny Lofton .30 .10
❑ 51 Devon White .30 .10
❑ 52 Matt Mieske .30 .10
❑ 53 Melvin Nieves .30 .10
❑ 54 Jose Canseco .50 .20
❑ 55 Tino Martinez .50 .20
❑ 56 Rafael Palmeiro .50 .20
❑ 57 Edgardo Alfonzo .30 .10
❑ 58 Jay Buhner .30 .10
❑ 59 Shane Reynolds .30 .10
❑ 60 Steve Finley .30 .10
❑ 61 Bobby Higginson .30 .10
❑ 62 Dean Palmer .30 .10
❑ 63 Terry Pendleton .30 .10
❑ 64 Marquis Grissom .30 .10
❑ 65 Mike Stanley .30 .10
❑ 66 Moises Alou .30 .10
❑ 67 Ray Lankford .30 .10
❑ 68 Marty Cordova .30 .10
❑ 69 John Olerud .30 .10
❑ 70 David Cone .30 .10
❑ 71 Benito Santiago .30 .10
❑ 72 Ryne Sandberg 1.25 .50
❑ 73 Rickey Henderson .75 .30
❑ 74 Roger Cedeno .30 .10
❑ 75 Wilson Alvarez .30 .10

❑	76	Tim Salmon	.50	.20
❑	77	Orlando Merced	.30	.10
❑	78	Vinny Castilla	.30	.10
❑	79	Ismael Valdes	.30	.10
❑	80	Dante Bichette	.30	.10
❑	81	Kevin Brown	.30	.10
❑	82	Andy Pettitte	.50	.20
❑	83	Scott Stahoviak	.30	.10
❑	84	Mickey Tettleton	.30	.10
❑	85	Jack McDowell	.30	.10
❑	86	Tom Glavine	.50	.20
❑	87	Gregg Jefferies	.30	.10
❑	88	Chili Davis	.30	.10
❑	89	Randy Johnson	.75	.30
❑	90	John Mabry	.30	.10
❑	91	Billy Wagner	.30	.10
❑	92	Jeff Cirillo	.30	.10
❑	93	Trevor Hoffman	.30	.10
❑	94	Juan Guzman	.30	.10
❑	95	Geronimo Berroa	.30	.10
❑	96	Bernard Gilkey	.30	.10
❑	97	Danny Tartabull	.30	.10
❑	98	Johnny Damon	.50	.20
❑	99	Charlie Hayes	.30	.10
❑	100	Reggie Sanders	.30	.10
❑	101	Robby Thompson	.30	.10
❑	102	Bobby Bonilla	.30	.10
❑	103	Reggie Jefferson	.30	.10
❑	104	John Smoltz	.50	.20
❑	105	Jim Thome	.50	.20
❑	106	Ruben Rivera	.30	.10
❑	107	Darren Oliver	.30	.10
❑	108	Mo Vaughn	.30	.10
❑	109	Roger Pavlik	.30	.10
❑	110	Terry Steinbach	.30	.10
❑	111	Jermaine Dye	.30	.10
❑	112	Mark Grudzielanek	.30	.10
❑	113	Rick Aguilera	.30	.10
❑	114	Jamey Wright	.30	.10
❑	115	Eddie Murray	.75	.30
❑	116	Brian L. Hunter	.30	.10
❑	117	Hal Morris	.30	.10
❑	118	Tom Pagnozzi	.30	.10
❑	119	Mike Mussina	.50	.20
❑	120	Mark Grace	.50	.20
❑	121	Cal Ripken	2.50	1.00
❑	122	Tom Goodwin	.30	.10
❑	123	Paul Sorrento	.30	.10
❑	124	Jay Bell	.30	.10
❑	125	Todd Hollandsworth	.30	.10
❑	126	Edgar Martinez	.50	.20
❑	127	George Arias	.30	.10
❑	128	Greg Vaughn	.30	.10
❑	129	Roberto Hernandez	.30	.10
❑	130	Delino DeShields	.30	.10
❑	131	Bill Pulsipher	.30	.10
❑	132	Joey Cora	.30	.10
❑	133	Mariano Rivera	.75	.30
❑	134	Mike Piazza	1.25	.50
❑	135	Carlos Baerga	.30	.10
❑	136	Jose Mesa	.30	.10
❑	137	Will Clark	.50	.20
❑	138	Frank Thomas	.75	.30
❑	139	John Wetteland	.30	.10
❑	140	Shawn Estes	.30	.10
❑	141	Garret Anderson	.30	.10
❑	142	Andre Dawson	.30	.10
❑	143	Eddie Taubensee	.30	.10
❑	144	Ryan Klesko	.30	.10
❑	145	Rocky Coppinger	.30	.10
❑	146	Jeff Bagwell	.50	.20
❑	147	Donovan Osborne	.30	.10
❑	148	Greg Myers	.30	.10
❑	149	Brant Brown	.30	.10
❑	150	Kevin Elster	.30	.10
❑	151	Bob Wells	.30	.10
❑	152	Wally Joyner	.30	.10
❑	153	Rico Brogna	.30	.10
❑	154	Dwight Gooden	.30	.10
❑	155	Jermaine Allensworth	.30	.10
❑	156	Ray Durham	.30	.10
❑	157	Cecil Fielder	.30	.10
❑	158	John Burkett	.30	.10
❑	159	Gary Sheffield	.30	.10
❑	160	Albert Belle	.30	.10
❑	161	Tomas Perez	.30	.10
❑	162	David Doster	.30	.10
❑	163	John Valentin	.30	.10
❑	164	Danny Graves	.30	.10
❑	165	Jose Paniagua	.30	.10
❑	166	Brian Giles RC	1.50	.60
❑	167	Barry Bonds	2.00	.75
❑	168	Sterling Hitchcock	.30	.10
❑	169	Bernie Williams	.50	.20
❑	170	Fred McGriff	.50	.20
❑	171	George Williams	.30	.10
❑	172	Amaury Telemaco	.30	.10
❑	173	Ken Caminiti	.30	.10
❑	174	Ron Gant	.30	.10
❑	175	Dave Justice	.30	.10
❑	176	James Baldwin	.30	.10
❑	177	Pat Hentgen	.30	.10
❑	178	Ben McDonald	.30	.10
❑	179	Tim Naehring	.30	.10
❑	180	Jim Eisenreich	.30	.10
❑	181	Ken Hill	.30	.10
❑	182	Paul Wilson	.30	.10
❑	183	Marvin Benard	.30	.10
❑	184	Alan Benes	.30	.10
❑	185	Ellis Burks	.30	.10
❑	186	Scott Servais	.30	.10
❑	187	David Segui	.30	.10
❑	188	Scott Brosius	.30	.10
❑	189	Jose Offerman	.30	.10
❑	190	Eric Davis	.30	.10
❑	191	Brett Butler	.30	.10
❑	192	Curtis Pride	.30	.10
❑	193	Yamil Benitez	.30	.10
❑	194	Chan Ho Park	.30	.10
❑	195	Bret Boone	.30	.10
❑	196	Omar Vizquel	.50	.20
❑	197	Orlando Miller	.30	.10
❑	198	Ramon Martinez	.30	.10
❑	199	Harold Baines	.30	.10
❑	200	Eric Young	.30	.10
❑	201	Fernando Vina	.30	.10
❑	202	Alex Gonzalez	.30	.10
❑	203	Fernando Valenzuela	.30	.10
❑	204	Steve Avery	.30	.10
❑	205	Ernie Young	.30	.10
❑	206	Kevin Appier	.30	.10
❑	207	Randy Myers	.30	.10
❑	208	Jeff Suppan	.30	.10
❑	209	James Mouton	.30	.10
❑	210	Russ Davis	.30	.10
❑	211	Al Martin	.30	.10
❑	212	Troy Percival	.30	.10
❑	213	Al Leiter	.30	.10
❑	214	Dennis Eckersley	.30	.10
❑	215	Mark Johnson	.30	.10
❑	216	Eric Karros	.30	.10
❑	217	Royce Clayton	.30	.10
❑	218	Tony Phillips	.30	.10
❑	219	Tim Wakefield	.30	.10
❑	220	Alan Trammell	.30	.10
❑	221	Eduardo Perez	.30	.10
❑	222	Butch Huskey	.30	.10
❑	223	Tim Belcher	.30	.10
❑	224	Jamie Moyer	.30	.10
❑	225	F.P. Santangelo	.30	.10
❑	226	Rusty Greer	.30	.10
❑	227	Jeff Brantley	.30	.10
❑	228	Mark Langston	.30	.10
❑	229	Ray Montgomery	.30	.10
❑	230	Rich Becker	.30	.10
❑	231	Ozzie Smith	1.25	.50
❑	232	Rey Ordonez	.30	.10
❑	233	Ricky Otero	.30	.10
❑	234	Mike Cameron	.30	.10
❑	235	Mike Sweeney	.30	.10
❑	236	Mark Lewis	.30	.10
❑	237	Luis Gonzalez	.30	.10
❑	238	Marcus Jensen	.30	.10
❑	239	Ed Sprague	.30	.10
❑	240	Jose Valentin	.30	.10
❑	241	Jeff Frye	.30	.10
❑	242	Charles Nagy	.30	.10
❑	243	Carlos Garcia	.30	.10
❑	244	Mike Hampton	.30	.10
❑	245	B.J. Surhoff	.30	.10
❑	246	Wilton Guerrero	.30	.10
❑	247	Frank Rodriguez	.30	.10
❑	248	Gary Gaetti	.30	.10
❑	249	Lance Johnson	.30	.10
❑	250	Darren Bragg	.30	.10
❑	251	Darryl Hamilton	.30	.10
❑	252	John Jaha	.30	.10
❑	253	Craig Paquette	.30	.10
❑	254	Jaime Navarro	.30	.10
❑	255	Shawon Dunston	.30	.10
❑	256	Mark Loretta	.30	.10
❑	257	Tim Belk	.30	.10
❑	258	Jeff Darwin	.30	.10
❑	259	Ruben Sierra	.30	.10
❑	260	Chuck Finley	.30	.10
❑	261	Darryl Strawberry	.30	.10
❑	262	Shannon Stewart	.30	.10
❑	263	Pedro Martinez	.50	.20
❑	264	Neifi Perez	.30	.10
❑	265	Jeff Conine	.30	.10
❑	266	Orel Hershiser	.30	.10
❑	267	Eddie Murray CL	.50	.20
❑	268	Paul Molitor CL	.30	.10
❑	269	Barry Bonds CL	1.00	.40
❑	270	Mark McGwire CL	1.00	.40
❑	271	Matt Williams	.30	.10
❑	272	Todd Zeile	.30	.10
❑	273	Roger Clemens	1.50	.60
❑	274	Michael Tucker	.30	.10
❑	275	J.T. Snow	.30	.10
❑	276	Kenny Lofton	.30	.10
❑	277	Jose Canseco	.50	.20
❑	278	Marquis Grissom	.30	.10
❑	279	Moises Alou	.30	.10
❑	280	Benito Santiago	.30	.10
❑	281	Willie McGee	.30	.10
❑	282	Chili Davis	.30	.10
❑	283	Ron Coomer	.30	.10
❑	284	Orlando Merced	.30	.10
❑	285	Delino DeShields	.30	.10
❑	286	John Wetteland	.30	.10
❑	287	Darren Daulton	.30	.10
❑	288	Lee Stevens	.30	.10
❑	289	Albert Belle	.30	.10
❑	290	Sterling Hitchcock	.30	.10
❑	291	David Justice	.30	.10
❑	292	Eric Davis	.30	.10
❑	293	Brian Hunter	.30	.10
❑	294	Darryl Hamilton	.30	.10
❑	295	Steve Avery	.30	.10
❑	296	Joe Vitiello	.30	.10
❑	297	Jaime Navarro	.30	.10
❑	298	Eddie Murray	.75	.30
❑	299	Randy Myers	.30	.10
❑	300	Francisco Cordova	.30	.10
❑	301	Javier Lopez	.30	.10
❑	302	Geronimo Berroa	.30	.10
❑	303	Jeffrey Hammonds	.30	.10
❑	304	Deion Sanders	.50	.20
❑	305	Jeff Fassero	.30	.10
❑	306	Curt Schilling	.30	.10
❑	307	Robb Nen	.30	.10
❑	308	Mark McLemore	.30	.10
❑	309	Jimmy Key	.30	.10
❑	310	Quilvio Veras	.30	.10
❑	311	Bip Roberts	.30	.10
❑	312	Esteban Loaiza	.30	.10
❑	313	Andy Ashby	.30	.10
❑	314	Sandy Alomar Jr.	.30	.10
❑	315	Shawn Green	.30	.10
❑	316	Luis Castillo	.30	.10
❑	317	Benji Gil	.30	.10
❑	318	Otis Nixon	.30	.10
❑	319	Aaron Sele	.30	.10
❑	320	Brad Ausmus	.30	.10
❑	321	Troy O'Leary	.30	.10
❑	322	Terrell Wade	.30	.10
❑	323	Jeff King	.30	.10
❑	324	Kevin Seitzer	.30	.10
❑	325	Mark Wohlers	.30	.10
❑	326	Edgar Renteria	.30	.10
❑	327	Dan Wilson	.30	.10
❑	328	Brian McRae	.30	.10
❑	329	Rod Beck	.30	.10
❑	330	Julio Franco	.30	.10
❑	331	Dave Nilsson	.30	.10
❑	332	Glenallen Hill	.30	.10
❑	333	Kevin Elster	.30	.10

❑ 334 Joe Girardi .30 .10
❑ 335 David Wells .30 .10
❑ 336 Jeff Blauser .30 .10
❑ 337 Darryl Kile .30 .10
❑ 338 Jeff Kent .30 .10
❑ 339 Jim Leyritz .30 .10
❑ 340 Todd Stottlemyre .30 .10
❑ 341 Tony Clark .30 .10
❑ 342 Chris Hoiles .30 .10
❑ 343 Mike Lieberthal .30 .10
❑ 344 Matt Lawton .30 .10
❑ 345 Alex Ochoa .30 .10
❑ 346 Chris Snopek .30 .10
❑ 347 Rudy Pemberton .30 .10
❑ 348 Eric Owens .30 .10
❑ 349 Joe Randa .30 .10
❑ 350 John Olerud .30 .10
❑ 351 Steve Karsay .30 .10
❑ 352 Mark Whiten .30 .10
❑ 353 Bob Abreu .50 .20
❑ 354 Bartolo Colon .30 .10
❑ 355 Vladimir Guerrero .75 .30
❑ 356 Darin Erstad .30 .10
❑ 357 Scott Rolen .50 .20
❑ 358 Andruw Jones .50 .20
❑ 359 Scott Spiezio .30 .10
❑ 360 Karim Garcia .30 .10
❑ 361 Hideki Irabu RC .40 .15
❑ 362 Nomar Garciaparra 1.25 .50
❑ 363 Dmitri Young .30 .10
❑ 364 Bubba Trammell RC .40 .15
❑ 365 Kevin Orie .30 .10
❑ 366 Jose Rosado .30 .10
❑ 367 Jose Guillen .30 .10
❑ 368 Brooks Kieschnick .30 .10
❑ 369 Pokey Reese .30 .10
❑ 370 Glendon Rusch .30 .10
❑ 371 Jason Dickson .30 .10
❑ 372 Todd Walker .30 .10
❑ 373 Justin Thompson .30 .10
❑ 374 Todd Greene .30 .10
❑ 375 Jeff Suppan .30 .10
❑ 376 Trey Beamon .30 .10
❑ 377 Damon Mashore .30 .10
❑ 378 Wendell Magee .30 .10
❑ 379 Shigetoshi Hasegawa RC .50 .20
❑ 380 Bill Mueller RC 1.25 .50
❑ 381 Chris Widger .30 .10
❑ 382 Tony Graffanino .30 .10
❑ 383 Derrek Lee .50 .20
❑ 384 Brian Moehler RC .40 .15
❑ 385 Quinton McCracken .30 .10
❑ 386 Matt Morris .30 .10
❑ 387 Marvin Benard .30 .10
❑ 388 Deivi Cruz RC .40 .15
❑ 389 Javier Valentin .30 .10
❑ 390 Todd Dunwoody .30 .10
❑ 391 Derrick Gibson .30 .10
❑ 392 Raul Casanova .30 .10
❑ 393 George Arias .30 .10
❑ 394 Tony Womack RC .40 .15
❑ 395 Antone Williamson .30 .10
❑ 396 Jose Cruz Jr. RC .40 .15
❑ 397 Desi Relaford .30 .10
❑ 398 Frank Thomas HIT .50 .20
❑ 399 Ken Griffey Jr. HIT .75 .30
❑ 400 Cal Ripken HIT 1.25 .50
❑ 401 Chipper Jones HIT .50 .20
❑ 402 Mike Piazza HIT .75 .30
❑ 403 Gary Sheffield HIT .30 .10
❑ 404 Alex Rodriguez HIT .75 .30
❑ 405 Wade Boggs HIT .30 .10
❑ 406 Juan Gonzalez HIT .30 .10
❑ 407 Tony Gwynn HIT .50 .20
❑ 408 Edgar Martinez HIT .30 .10
❑ 409 Jeff Bagwell HIT .30 .10
❑ 410 Larry Walker HIT .30 .10
❑ 411 Kenny Lofton HIT .30 .10
❑ 412 Manny Ramirez HIT .30 .10
❑ 413 Mark McGwire HIT 1.00 .40
❑ 414 Roberto Alomar HIT .30 .10
❑ 415 Derek Jeter HIT 1.00 .40
❑ 416 Brady Anderson HIT .30 .10
❑ 417 Paul Molitor HIT .30 .10
❑ 418 Dante Bichette HIT .30 .10
❑ 419 Jim Edmonds HIT .30 .10
❑ 420 Mo Vaughn HIT .30 .10
❑ 421 Barry Bonds HIT 1.00 .40
❑ 422 Rusty Greer HIT .30 .10
❑ 423 Greg Maddux KING .75 .30
❑ 424 Andy Pettitte KING .30 .10
❑ 425 John Smoltz KING .30 .10
❑ 426 Randy Johnson KING .50 .20
❑ 427 Hideo Nomo KING .30 .10
❑ 428 Roger Clemens KING .75 .30
❑ 429 Tom Glavine KING .30 .10
❑ 430 Pat Hentgen KING .30 .10
❑ 431 Kevin Brown KING .30 .10
❑ 432 Mike Mussina KING .30 .10
❑ 433 Alex Fernandez KING .30 .10
❑ 434 Kevin Appier KING .30 .10
❑ 435 David Cone KING .30 .10
❑ 436 Jeff Fassero KING .30 .10
❑ 437 John Wetteland KING .30 .10
❑ 438 B.Bonds/I.Rodriguez IS 1.00 .40
❑ 439 K.Griffey Jr./A.Galarraga IS .75 .30
❑ 440 F.McGriff/R.Palmeiro IS .30 .10
❑ 441 B.Larkin/J.Thome IS .50 .20
❑ 442 S.Sosa/A.Belle IS .50 .20
❑ 443 B.Williams/T.Hundley IS .30 .10
❑ 444 C.Knoblauch/B.Jordan IS .30 .10
❑ 445 M.Vaughn/J.Conine IS .30 .10
❑ 446 K.Caminiti/J.Giambi IS .30 .10
❑ 447 R.Mondesi/T.Salmon IS .30 .10
❑ 448 Cal Ripken CL 1.25 .50
❑ 449 Greg Maddux CL .75 .30
❑ 450 Ken Griffey Jr. CL .75 .30

1998 Donruss

❑ COMPLETE SET (420) 50.00 20.00
❑ COMPLETE SERIES 1 (170) 20.00 8.00
❑ COMPLETE UPDATE (250) 30.00 12.50
❑ 1 Paul Molitor .25 .08
❑ 2 Juan Gonzalez .25 .08
❑ 3 Darryl Kile .25 .08
❑ 4 Randy Johnson .60 .25
❑ 5 Tom Glavine .40 .15
❑ 6 Pat Hentgen .25 .08
❑ 7 David Justice .25 .08
❑ 8 Kevin Brown .40 .15
❑ 9 Mike Mussina .40 .15
❑ 10 Ken Caminiti .25 .08
❑ 11 Todd Hundley .25 .08
❑ 12 Frank Thomas .60 .25
❑ 13 Ray Lankford .25 .08
❑ 14 Justin Thompson .25 .08
❑ 15 Jason Dickson .25 .08
❑ 16 Kenny Lofton .25 .08
❑ 17 Ivan Rodriguez .40 .15
❑ 18 Pedro Martinez .40 .15
❑ 19 Brady Anderson .25 .08
❑ 20 Barry Larkin .40 .15
❑ 21 Chipper Jones .60 .25
❑ 22 Tony Gwynn .75 .30
❑ 23 Roger Clemens 1.25 .50
❑ 24 Sandy Alomar Jr. .25 .08
❑ 25 Tino Martinez .40 .15
❑ 26 Jeff Bagwell .40 .15
❑ 27 Shawn Estes .25 .08
❑ 28 Ken Griffey Jr. 1.00 .40
❑ 29 Javier Lopez .25 .08
❑ 30 Denny Neagle .25 .08
❑ 31 Mike Piazza 1.00 .40
❑ 32 Andres Galarraga .25 .08
❑ 33 Larry Walker .25 .08
❑ 34 Alex Rodriguez 1.00 .40
❑ 35 Greg Maddux 1.00 .40
❑ 36 Albert Belle .25 .08
❑ 37 Barry Bonds 1.50 .60
❑ 38 Mo Vaughn .25 .08
❑ 39 Kevin Appier .25 .08
❑ 40 Wade Boggs .40 .15
❑ 41 Garret Anderson .25 .08
❑ 42 Jeffrey Hammonds .25 .08
❑ 43 Marquis Grissom .25 .08
❑ 44 Jim Edmonds .25 .08
❑ 45 Brian Jordan .25 .08
❑ 46 Raul Mondesi .25 .08
❑ 47 John Valentin .25 .08
❑ 48 Brad Radke .25 .08
❑ 49 Ismael Valdes .25 .08
❑ 50 Matt Stairs .25 .08
❑ 51 Matt Williams .25 .08
❑ 52 Reggie Jefferson .25 .08
❑ 53 Alan Benes .25 .08
❑ 54 Charles Johnson .25 .08
❑ 55 Chuck Knoblauch .25 .08
❑ 56 Edgar Martinez .40 .15
❑ 57 Nomar Garciaparra 1.00 .40
❑ 58 Craig Biggio .40 .15
❑ 59 Bernie Williams .40 .15
❑ 60 David Cone .25 .08
❑ 61 Cal Ripken 2.00 .75
❑ 62 Mark McGwire 1.50 .60
❑ 63 Roberto Alomar .40 .15
❑ 64 Fred McGriff .40 .15
❑ 65 Eric Karros .25 .08
❑ 66 Robin Ventura .25 .08
❑ 67 Darin Erstad .25 .08
❑ 68 Michael Tucker .25 .08
❑ 69 Jim Thome .40 .15
❑ 70 Mark Grace .40 .15
❑ 71 Lou Collier .25 .08
❑ 72 Karim Garcia .25 .08
❑ 73 Alex Fernandez .25 .08
❑ 74 J.T. Snow .25 .08
❑ 75 Reggie Sanders .25 .08
❑ 76 John Smoltz .40 .15
❑ 77 Tim Salmon .40 .15
❑ 78 Paul O'Neill .40 .15
❑ 79 Vinny Castilla .25 .08
❑ 80 Rafael Palmeiro .40 .15
❑ 81 Jaret Wright .25 .08
❑ 82 Jay Buhner .25 .08
❑ 83 Brett Butler .25 .08
❑ 84 Todd Greene .25 .08
❑ 85 Scott Rolen .40 .15
❑ 86 Sammy Sosa .60 .25
❑ 87 Jason Giambi .25 .08
❑ 88 Carlos Delgado .25 .08
❑ 89 Deion Sanders .40 .15
❑ 90 Wilton Guerrero .25 .08
❑ 91 Andy Pettitte .40 .15
❑ 92 Brian Giles .25 .08
❑ 93 Dmitri Young .25 .08
❑ 94 Ron Coomer .25 .08
❑ 95 Mike Cameron .25 .08
❑ 96 Edgardo Alfonzo .25 .08
❑ 97 Jimmy Key .25 .08
❑ 98 Ryan Klesko .25 .08
❑ 99 Andy Benes .25 .08
❑ 100 Derek Jeter 1.50 .60
❑ 101 Jeff Fassero .25 .08
❑ 102 Neifi Perez .25 .08
❑ 103 Hideo Nomo .60 .25
❑ 104 Andruw Jones .40 .15
❑ 105 Todd Helton .40 .15
❑ 106 Livan Hernandez .25 .08
❑ 107 Brett Tomko .25 .08
❑ 108 Shannon Stewart .25 .08
❑ 109 Bartolo Colon .25 .08
❑ 110 Matt Morris .25 .08
❑ 111 Miguel Tejada .60 .25
❑ 112 Pokey Reese .25 .08
❑ 113 Fernando Tatis .25 .08
❑ 114 Todd Dunwoody .25 .08
❑ 115 Jose Cruz Jr. .25 .08
❑ 116 Chan Ho Park .25 .08
❑ 117 Kevin Young .25 .08
❑ 118 Rickey Henderson .60 .25

- ❑ 119 Hideki Irabu .25 .08
- ❑ 120 Francisco Cordova .25 .08
- ❑ 121 Al Martin .25 .08
- ❑ 122 Tony Clark .25 .08
- ❑ 123 Curt Schilling .25 .08
- ❑ 124 Rusty Greer .25 .08
- ❑ 125 Jose Canseco .40 .15
- ❑ 126 Edgar Renteria .25 .08
- ❑ 127 Todd Walker .25 .08
- ❑ 128 Wally Joyner .25 .08
- ❑ 129 Bill Mueller .25 .08
- ❑ 130 Jose Guillen .25 .08
- ❑ 131 Manny Ramirez .40 .15
- ❑ 132 Bobby Higginson .25 .08
- ❑ 133 Kevin Orie .25 .08
- ❑ 134 Will Clark .40 .15
- ❑ 135 Dave Nilsson .25 .08
- ❑ 136 Jason Kendall .25 .08
- ❑ 137 Ivan Cruz .25 .08
- ❑ 138 Gary Sheffield .25 .08
- ❑ 139 Bubba Trammell .25 .08
- ❑ 140 Vladimir Guerrero .60 .25
- ❑ 141 Dennis Reyes .25 .08
- ❑ 142 Bobby Bonilla .25 .08
- ❑ 143 Ruben Rivera .25 .08
- ❑ 144 Ben Grieve .25 .08
- ❑ 145 Moises Alou .25 .08
- ❑ 146 Tony Womack .25 .08
- ❑ 147 Eric Young .25 .08
- ❑ 148 Paul Konerko .25 .08
- ❑ 149 Dante Bichette .25 .08
- ❑ 150 Joe Carter .25 .08
- ❑ 151 Rondell White .25 .08
- ❑ 152 Chris Holt .25 .08
- ❑ 153 Shawn Green .25 .08
- ❑ 154 Mark Grudzielanek .25 .08
- ❑ 155 Jermaine Dye .25 .08
- ❑ 156 Ken Griffey Jr. FC .60 .25
- ❑ 157 Frank Thomas FC .40 .15
- ❑ 158 Chipper Jones FC .40 .15
- ❑ 159 Mike Piazza FC .60 .25
- ❑ 160 Cal Ripken FC 1.00 .40
- ❑ 161 Greg Maddux FC .60 .25
- ❑ 162 Juan Gonzalez FC .25 .08
- ❑ 163 Alex Rodriguez FC .60 .25
- ❑ 164 Mark McGwire FC .75 .30
- ❑ 165 Derek Jeter FC .75 .30
- ❑ 166 Larry Walker CL .25 .08
- ❑ 167 Tony Gwynn CL .40 .15
- ❑ 168 Tino Martinez CL .25 .08
- ❑ 169 Scott Rolen CL .25 .08
- ❑ 170 Nomar Garciaparra CL .60 .25
- ❑ 171 Mike Sweeney .25 .08
- ❑ 172 Dustin Hermanson .25 .08
- ❑ 173 Darren Dreifort .25 .08
- ❑ 174 Ron Gant .25 .08
- ❑ 175 Todd Hollandsworth .25 .08
- ❑ 176 John Jaha .25 .08
- ❑ 177 Kerry Wood .30 .10
- ❑ 178 Chris Stynes .25 .08
- ❑ 179 Kevin Elster .25 .08
- ❑ 180 Derek Bell .25 .08
- ❑ 181 Darryl Strawberry .25 .08
- ❑ 182 Damion Easley .25 .08
- ❑ 183 Jeff Cirillo .25 .08
- ❑ 184 John Thomson .25 .08
- ❑ 185 Dan Wilson .25 .08
- ❑ 186 Jay Bell .25 .08
- ❑ 187 Bernard Gilkey .25 .08
- ❑ 188 Marc Valdes .25 .08
- ❑ 189 Ramon Martinez .25 .08
- ❑ 190 Charles Nagy .25 .08
- ❑ 191 Derek Lowe .25 .08
- ❑ 192 Andy Benes .25 .08
- ❑ 193 Delino DeShields .25 .08
- ❑ 194 Ryan Jackson RC .25 .08
- ❑ 195 Kenny Lofton .25 .08
- ❑ 196 Chuck Knoblauch .25 .08
- ❑ 197 Andres Galarraga .25 .08
- ❑ 198 Jose Canseco .40 .15
- ❑ 199 John Olerud .25 .08
- ❑ 200 Lance Johnson .25 .08
- ❑ 201 Darryl Kile .25 .08
- ❑ 202 Luis Castillo .25 .08
- ❑ 203 Joe Carter .25 .08
- ❑ 204 Dennis Eckersley .25 .08
- ❑ 205 Steve Finley .25 .08
- ❑ 206 Esteban Loaiza .25 .08
- ❑ 207 Ryan Christenson RC .25 .08
- ❑ 208 Deivi Cruz .25 .08
- ❑ 209 Mariano Rivera .60 .25
- ❑ 210 Mike Judd RC .30 .10
- ❑ 211 Billy Wagner .25 .08
- ❑ 212 Scott Spiezio .25 .08
- ❑ 213 Russ Davis .25 .08
- ❑ 214 Jeff Suppan .25 .08
- ❑ 215 Doug Glanville .25 .08
- ❑ 216 Dmitri Young .25 .08
- ❑ 217 Rey Ordonez .25 .08
- ❑ 218 Cecil Fielder .25 .08
- ❑ 219 Masato Yoshii RC .30 .10
- ❑ 220 Raul Casanova .25 .08
- ❑ 221 Rolando Arrojo RC .30 .10
- ❑ 222 Ellis Burks .25 .08
- ❑ 223 Butch Huskey .25 .08
- ❑ 224 Brian Hunter .25 .08
- ❑ 225 Marquis Grissom .25 .08
- ❑ 226 Kevin Brown .40 .15
- ❑ 227 Joe Randa .25 .08
- ❑ 228 Henry Rodriguez .25 .08
- ❑ 229 Omar Vizquel .40 .15
- ❑ 230 Fred McGriff .40 .15
- ❑ 231 Matt Williams .25 .08
- ❑ 232 Moises Alou .25 .08
- ❑ 233 Travis Fryman .25 .08
- ❑ 234 Wade Boggs .40 .15
- ❑ 235 Pedro Martinez .40 .15
- ❑ 236 Rickey Henderson .60 .25
- ❑ 237 Bubba Trammell .25 .08
- ❑ 238 Mike Caruso .25 .08
- ❑ 239 Wilson Alvarez .25 .08
- ❑ 240 Geronimo Berroa .25 .08
- ❑ 241 Eric Milton .25 .08
- ❑ 242 Scott Erickson .25 .08
- ❑ 243 Todd Erdos RC .25 .08
- ❑ 244 Bobby Hughes .25 .08
- ❑ 245 Dave Hollins .25 .08
- ❑ 246 Dean Palmer .25 .08
- ❑ 247 Carlos Baerga .25 .08
- ❑ 248 Jose Silva .25 .08
- ❑ 249 Jose Cabrera RC .25 .08
- ❑ 250 Tom Evans .25 .08
- ❑ 251 Marty Cordova .25 .08
- ❑ 252 Hanley Frias RC .25 .08
- ❑ 253 Javier Valentin .25 .08
- ❑ 254 Mario Valdez .25 .08
- ❑ 255 Joey Cora .25 .08
- ❑ 256 Mike Lansing .25 .08
- ❑ 257 Jeff Kent .25 .08
- ❑ 258 Dave Dellucci RC .50 .20
- ❑ 259 Curtis King RC .25 .08
- ❑ 260 David Segui .25 .08
- ❑ 261 Royce Clayton .25 .08
- ❑ 262 Jeff Blauser .25 .08
- ❑ 263 Manny Aybar RC .25 .08
- ❑ 264 Mike Cather RC .25 .08
- ❑ 265 Todd Zeile .25 .08
- ❑ 266 Richard Hidalgo .25 .08
- ❑ 267 Dante Powell .25 .08
- ❑ 268 Mike DeJean RC .25 .08
- ❑ 269 Ken Cloude .25 .08
- ❑ 270 Danny Klassen .25 .08
- ❑ 271 Sean Casey .25 .08
- ❑ 272 A.J. Hinch .25 .08
- ❑ 273 Rich Butler RC .25 .08
- ❑ 274 Ben Ford RC .25 .08
- ❑ 275 Billy McMillon .25 .08
- ❑ 276 Wilson Delgado .25 .08
- ❑ 277 Orlando Cabrera .25 .08
- ❑ 278 Geoff Jenkins .25 .08
- ❑ 279 Enrique Wilson .25 .08
- ❑ 280 Derrek Lee .40 .15
- ❑ 281 Marc Pisciotta RC .25 .08
- ❑ 282 Abraham Nunez .25 .08
- ❑ 283 Aaron Boone .25 .08
- ❑ 284 Brad Fullmer .25 .08
- ❑ 285 Rob Stanifer RC .25 .08
- ❑ 286 Preston Wilson .25 .08
- ❑ 287 Greg Norton .25 .08
- ❑ 288 Bobby Smith .25 .08
- ❑ 289 Josh Booty .25 .08
- ❑ 290 Russell Branyan .25 .08
- ❑ 291 Jeremi Gonzalez .25 .08
- ❑ 292 Michael Coleman .25 .08
- ❑ 293 Cliff Politte .25 .08
- ❑ 294 Eric Ludwick .25 .08
- ❑ 295 Rafael Medina .25 .08
- ❑ 296 Jason Varitek .60 .25
- ❑ 297 Ron Wright .25 .08
- ❑ 298 Mark Kotsay .25 .08
- ❑ 299 David Ortiz .75 .30
- ❑ 300 Frank Catalanotto RC .50 .20
- ❑ 301 Robinson Checo .25 .08
- ❑ 302 Kevin Millwood RC .75 .30
- ❑ 303 Jacob Cruz .25 .08
- ❑ 304 Javier Vazquez .25 .08
- ❑ 305 Magglio Ordonez RC 2.50 1.00
- ❑ 306 Kevin Witt .25 .08
- ❑ 307 Derrick Gibson .25 .08
- ❑ 308 Shane Monahan .25 .08
- ❑ 309 Brian Rose .25 .08
- ❑ 310 Bobby Estalella .25 .08
- ❑ 311 Felix Heredia .25 .08
- ❑ 312 Desi Relaford .25 .08
- ❑ 313 Esteban Yan RC .30 .10
- ❑ 314 Ricky Ledee .25 .08
- ❑ 315 Steve Woodard .25 .08
- ❑ 316 Pat Watkins .25 .08
- ❑ 317 Damian Moss .25 .08
- ❑ 318 Bob Abreu .25 .08
- ❑ 319 Jeff Abbott .25 .08
- ❑ 320 Miguel Cairo .25 .08
- ❑ 321 Rigo Beltran RC .25 .08
- ❑ 322 Tony Saunders .25 .08
- ❑ 323 Randall Simon .25 .08
- ❑ 324 Hiram Bocachica .25 .08
- ❑ 325 Richie Sexson .25 .08
- ❑ 326 Karim Garcia .25 .08
- ❑ 327 Mike Lowell RC 1.25 .50
- ❑ 328 Pat Cline .25 .08
- ❑ 329 Matt Clement .25 .08
- ❑ 330 Scott Elarton .25 .08
- ❑ 331 Manuel Barrios RC .25 .08
- ❑ 332 Bruce Chen .25 .08
- ❑ 333 Juan Encarnacion .25 .08
- ❑ 334 Travis Lee .25 .08
- ❑ 335 Wes Helms .25 .08
- ❑ 336 Chad Fox RC .25 .08
- ❑ 337 Donnie Sadler .25 .08
- ❑ 338 Carlos Mendoza RC .25 .08
- ❑ 339 Damian Jackson .25 .08
- ❑ 340 Julio Ramirez RC .25 .08
- ❑ 341 John Halama RC .30 .10
- ❑ 342 Edwin Diaz .25 .08
- ❑ 343 Felix Martinez .25 .08
- ❑ 344 Eli Marrero .25 .08
- ❑ 345 Carl Pavano .25 .08
- ❑ 346 Vladimir Guerrero HL .40 .15
- ❑ 347 Barry Bonds HL .75 .30
- ❑ 348 Darin Erstad HL .25 .08
- ❑ 349 Albert Belle HL .25 .08
- ❑ 350 Kenny Lofton HL .25 .08
- ❑ 351 Mo Vaughn HL .25 .08
- ❑ 352 Jose Cruz Jr. HL .25 .08
- ❑ 353 Tony Clark HL .25 .08
- ❑ 354 Roberto Alomar HL .25 .08
- ❑ 355 Manny Ramirez HL .25 .08
- ❑ 356 Paul Molitor HL .25 .08
- ❑ 357 Jim Thome HL .25 .08
- ❑ 358 Tino Martinez HL .25 .08
- ❑ 359 Tim Salmon HL .25 .08
- ❑ 360 David Justice HL .25 .08
- ❑ 361 Raul Mondesi HL .25 .08
- ❑ 362 Mark Grace HL .25 .08
- ❑ 363 Craig Biggio HL .25 .08
- ❑ 364 Larry Walker HL .25 .08
- ❑ 365 Mark McGwire HL .75 .30
- ❑ 366 Juan Gonzalez HL .25 .08
- ❑ 367 Derek Jeter HL .75 .30
- ❑ 368 Chipper Jones HL .40 .15
- ❑ 369 Frank Thomas HL .40 .15
- ❑ 370 Alex Rodriguez HL .60 .25
- ❑ 371 Mike Piazza HL .60 .25
- ❑ 372 Tony Gwynn HL .40 .15
- ❑ 373 Jeff Bagwell HL .25 .08
- ❑ 374 Nomar Garciaparra HL .60 .25
- ❑ 375 Ken Griffey Jr. HL .60 .25
- ❑ 376 Livan Hernandez UN .25 .08

Card		
❑ 377 Chan Ho Park UN	.25	.08
❑ 378 Mike Mussina UN	.25	.08
❑ 379 Andy Pettitte UN	.25	.08
❑ 380 Greg Maddux UN	.60	.25
❑ 381 Hideo Nomo UN	.40	.15
❑ 382 Roger Clemens UN	.60	.25
❑ 383 Randy Johnson UN	.40	.15
❑ 384 Pedro Martinez UN	.40	.15
❑ 385 Jaret Wright UN	.25	.08
❑ 386 Ken Griffey Jr. SG	.60	.25
❑ 387 Todd Helton SG	.25	.08
❑ 388 Paul Konerko SG	.25	.08
❑ 389 Cal Ripken SG	1.00	.40
❑ 390 Larry Walker SG	.25	.08
❑ 391 Ken Caminiti SG	.25	.08
❑ 392 Jose Guillen SG	.25	.08
❑ 393 Jim Edmonds SG	.25	.08
❑ 394 Barry Larkin SG	.25	.08
❑ 395 Bernie Williams SG	.25	.08
❑ 396 Tony Clark SG	.25	.08
❑ 397 Jose Cruz Jr. SG	.25	.08
❑ 398 Ivan Rodriguez SG	.25	.08
❑ 399 Darin Erstad SG	.25	.08
❑ 400 Scott Rolen SG	.25	.08
❑ 401 Mark McGwire SG	.75	.30
❑ 402 Andruw Jones SG	.25	.08
❑ 403 Juan Gonzalez SG	.25	.08
❑ 404 Derek Jeter SG	.75	.30
❑ 405 Chipper Jones SG	.40	.15
❑ 406 Greg Maddux SG	.60	.25
❑ 407 Frank Thomas SG	.40	.15
❑ 408 Alex Rodriguez SG	.60	.25
❑ 409 Mike Piazza SG	.60	.25
❑ 410 Tony Gwynn SG	.40	.15
❑ 411 Jeff Bagwell SG	.25	.08
❑ 412 Nomar Garciaparra SG	.60	.25
❑ 413 Hideo Nomo SG	.40	.15
❑ 414 Barry Bonds SG	.75	.30
❑ 415 Ben Grieve SG	.25	.08
❑ 416 Barry Bonds CL	.75	.30
❑ 417 Mark McGwire CL	.75	.30
❑ 418 Roger Clemens CL	.60	.25
❑ 419 Livan Hernandez CL	.25	.08
❑ 420 Ken Griffey Jr. CL	.60	.25

2001 Donruss

Card		
❑ COMP.SET w/o SP's (150)	25.00	10.00
❑ COMMON CARD (1-150)	.30	.10
❑ COMMON CARD (151-200)	8.00	3.00
❑ COMMON CARD (201-220)	2.50	1.00
❑ 1 Alex Rodriguez	1.25	.50
❑ 2 Barry Bonds	2.00	.75
❑ 3 Cal Ripken	2.50	1.00
❑ 4 Chipper Jones	.75	.30
❑ 5 Derek Jeter	2.00	.75
❑ 6 Troy Glaus	.30	.10
❑ 7 Frank Thomas	.75	.30
❑ 8 Greg Maddux	1.25	.50
❑ 9 Ivan Rodriguez	.50	.20
❑ 10 Jeff Bagwell	.50	.20
❑ 11 Jose Canseco	.50	.20
❑ 12 Todd Helton	.50	.20
❑ 13 Ken Griffey Jr.	1.25	.50
❑ 14 Manny Ramirez Sox	.50	.20
❑ 15 Mark McGwire	2.00	.75
❑ 16 Mike Piazza	1.25	.50
❑ 17 Nomar Garciaparra	1.25	.50
❑ 18 Pedro Martinez	.50	.20
❑ 19 Randy Johnson	.75	.30
❑ 20 Rick Ankiel	.30	.10
❑ 21 Rickey Henderson	.75	.30
❑ 22 Roger Clemens	1.50	.60
❑ 23 Sammy Sosa	.75	.30
❑ 24 Tony Gwynn	1.00	.40
❑ 25 Vladimir Guerrero	.75	.30
❑ 26 Eric Davis	.30	.10
❑ 27 Roberto Alomar	.30	.10
❑ 28 Mark Mulder	.30	.10
❑ 29 Pat Burrell	.30	.10
❑ 30 Harold Baines	.30	.10
❑ 31 Carlos Delgado	.30	.10
❑ 32 J.D. Drew	.30	.10
❑ 33 Jim Edmonds	.30	.10
❑ 34 Darin Erstad	.30	.10
❑ 35 Jason Giambi	.30	.10
❑ 36 Tom Glavine	.50	.20
❑ 37 Juan Gonzalez	.30	.10
❑ 38 Mark Grace	.50	.20
❑ 39 Shawn Green	.30	.10
❑ 40 Tim Hudson	.30	.10
❑ 41 Andruw Jones	.50	.20
❑ 42 David Justice	.30	.10
❑ 43 Jeff Kent	.30	.10
❑ 44 Barry Larkin	.50	.20
❑ 45 Pokey Reese	.30	.10
❑ 46 Mike Mussina	.50	.20
❑ 47 Hideo Nomo	.75	.30
❑ 48 Rafael Palmeiro	.50	.20
❑ 49 Adam Piatt	.30	.10
❑ 50 Scott Rolen	.50	.20
❑ 51 Gary Sheffield	.30	.10
❑ 52 Bernie Williams	.50	.20
❑ 53 Bob Abreu	.30	.10
❑ 54 Edgardo Alfonzo	.30	.10
❑ 55 Jermaine Clark RC	.50	.20
❑ 56 Albert Belle	.30	.10
❑ 57 Craig Biggio	.50	.20
❑ 58 Andres Galarraga	.30	.10
❑ 59 Edgar Martinez	.50	.20
❑ 60 Fred McGriff	.50	.20
❑ 61 Magglio Ordonez	.30	.10
❑ 62 Jim Thome	.50	.20
❑ 63 Matt Williams	.30	.10
❑ 64 Kerry Wood	.30	.10
❑ 65 Moises Alou	.30	.10
❑ 66 Brady Anderson	.30	.10
❑ 67 Garret Anderson	.30	.10
❑ 68 Tony Armas Jr.	.30	.10
❑ 69 Tony Batista	.30	.10
❑ 70 Jose Cruz Jr.	.30	.10
❑ 71 Carlos Beltran	.30	.10
❑ 72 Adrian Beltre	.30	.10
❑ 73 Kris Benson	.30	.10
❑ 74 Lance Berkman	.30	.10
❑ 75 Kevin Brown	.30	.10
❑ 76 Jay Buhner	.30	.10
❑ 77 Jeromy Burnitz	.30	.10
❑ 78 Ken Caminiti	.30	.10
❑ 79 Sean Casey	.30	.10
❑ 80 Luis Castillo	.30	.10
❑ 81 Eric Chavez	.30	.10
❑ 82 Jeff Cirillo	.30	.10
❑ 83 Bartolo Colon	.30	.10
❑ 84 David Cone	.30	.10
❑ 85 Freddy Garcia	.30	.10
❑ 86 Johnny Damon	.50	.20
❑ 87 Ray Durham	.30	.10
❑ 88 Jermaine Dye	.30	.10
❑ 89 Juan Encarnacion	.30	.10
❑ 90 Terrence Long	.30	.10
❑ 91 Carl Everett	.30	.10
❑ 92 Steve Finley	.30	.10
❑ 93 Cliff Floyd	.30	.10
❑ 94 Brad Fullmer	.30	.10
❑ 95 Brian Giles	.30	.10
❑ 96 Luis Gonzalez	.30	.10
❑ 97 Rusty Greer	.30	.10
❑ 98 Jeffrey Hammonds	.30	.10
❑ 99 Mike Hampton	.30	.10
❑ 100 Orlando Hernandez	.30	.10
❑ 101 Richard Hidalgo	.30	.10
❑ 102 Geoff Jenkins	.30	.10
❑ 103 Jacque Jones	.30	.10
❑ 104 Brian Jordan	.30	.10
❑ 105 Gabe Kapler	.30	.10
❑ 106 Eric Karros	.30	.10
❑ 107 Jason Kendall	.30	.10
❑ 108 Adam Kennedy	.30	.10
❑ 109 Byung-Hyun Kim	.30	.10
❑ 110 Ryan Klesko	.30	.10
❑ 111 Chuck Knoblauch	.30	.10
❑ 112 Paul Konerko	.30	.10
❑ 113 Carlos Lee	.30	.10
❑ 114 Kenny Lofton	.30	.10
❑ 115 Javy Lopez	.30	.10
❑ 116 Tino Martinez	.50	.20
❑ 117 Ruben Mateo	.30	.10
❑ 118 Kevin Millwood	.30	.10
❑ 119 Ben Molina	.30	.10
❑ 120 Raul Mondesi	.30	.10
❑ 121 Trot Nixon	.30	.10
❑ 122 John Olerud	.30	.10
❑ 123 Paul O'Neill	.50	.20
❑ 124 Chan Ho Park	.30	.10
❑ 125 Andy Pettitte	.50	.20
❑ 126 Jorge Posada	.50	.20
❑ 127 Mark Quinn	.30	.10
❑ 128 Aramis Ramirez	.30	.10
❑ 129 Mariano Rivera	.75	.30
❑ 130 Tim Salmon	.50	.20
❑ 131 Curt Schilling	.30	.10
❑ 132 Richie Sexson	.30	.10
❑ 133 John Smoltz	.50	.20
❑ 134 J.T. Snow	.30	.10
❑ 135 Jay Payton	.30	.10
❑ 136 Shannon Stewart	.30	.10
❑ 137 B.J. Surhoff	.30	.10
❑ 138 Mike Sweeney	.30	.10
❑ 139 Fernando Tatis	.30	.10
❑ 140 Miguel Tejada	.30	.10
❑ 141 Jason Varitek	.75	.30
❑ 142 Greg Vaughn	.30	.10
❑ 143 Mo Vaughn	.30	.10
❑ 144 Robin Ventura	.30	.10
❑ 145 Jose Vidro	.30	.10
❑ 146 Omar Vizquel	.50	.20
❑ 147 Larry Walker	.30	.10
❑ 148 David Wells	.30	.10
❑ 149 Rondell White	.30	.10
❑ 150 Preston Wilson	.30	.10
❑ 151 Brent Abernathy RR	8.00	3.00
❑ 152 Cory Aldridge RR RC	8.00	3.00
❑ 153 Gene Altman RR RC	8.00	3.00
❑ 154 Josh Beckett RR	10.00	4.00
❑ 155 Wilson Betemit RR RC	10.00	4.00
❑ 156 Albert Pujols RR/500 RC	250.00	125.00
❑ 157 Joe Crede RR	10.00	4.00
❑ 158 Jack Cust RR	8.00	3.00
❑ 159 Ben Sheets RR/500	40.00	15.00
❑ 160 Alex Escobar RR	8.00	3.00
❑ 161 Adrian Hernandez RR RC	8.00	3.00
❑ 162 Pedro Feliz RR	8.00	3.00
❑ 163 Nate Frese RR RC	8.00	3.00
❑ 164 Carlos Garcia RR RC	8.00	3.00
❑ 165 Marcus Giles RR	8.00	3.00
❑ 166 Alexis Gomez RR RC	8.00	3.00
❑ 167 Jason Hart RR	8.00	3.00
❑ 168 Eric Hinske RR RC	10.00	4.00
❑ 169 Cesar Izturis RR	8.00	3.00
❑ 170 Nick Johnson RR	8.00	3.00
❑ 171 Mike Young RR	10.00	4.00
❑ 172 Brian Lawrence RR RC	8.00	3.00
❑ 173 Steve Lomasney RR	8.00	3.00
❑ 174 Nick Maness RR	8.00	3.00
❑ 175 Jose Mieses RR RC	8.00	3.00
❑ 176 Greg Miller RR RC	8.00	3.00
❑ 177 Eric Munson RR	8.00	3.00
❑ 178 Xavier Nady RR	8.00	3.00
❑ 179 Blaine Neal RR RC	8.00	3.00
❑ 180 Abraham Nunez RR	8.00	3.00
❑ 181 Jose Ortiz RR	8.00	3.00
❑ 182 Jeremy Owens RR RC	8.00	3.00
❑ 183 Pablo Ozuna RR	8.00	3.00
❑ 184 Corey Patterson RR	8.00	3.00
❑ 185 Carlos Pena RR	8.00	3.00
❑ 186 Wily Mo Pena RR	8.00	3.00
❑ 187 Timo Perez RR	8.00	3.00
❑ 188 Adam Pettyjohn RR RC	8.00	3.00
❑ 189 Luis Rivas RR	8.00	3.00
❑ 190 Jackson Melian RR RC	8.00	3.00

Card		
❑ 191 Wilken Ruan RR RC	8.00	3.00
❑ 192 Duaner Sanchez RR RC	8.00	3.00
❑ 193 Alfonso Soriano RR	10.00	4.00
❑ 194 Rafael Soriano RR RC	8.00	3.00
❑ 195 Ichiro Suzuki RR RC	60.00	30.00
❑ 196 Billy Sylvester RR RC	8.00	3.00
❑ 197 Juan Uribe RR RC	10.00	4.00
❑ 198 Eric Valent RR	8.00	3.00
❑ 199 Carlos Valderrama RR RC	8.00	3.00
❑ 200 Matt White RR RC	8.00	3.00
❑ 201 Alex Rodriguez FC	6.00	2.50
❑ 202 Barry Bonds FC	10.00	4.00
❑ 203 Cal Ripken FC	12.00	5.00
❑ 204 Chipper Jones FC	4.00	1.50
❑ 205 Derek Jeter FC	10.00	4.00
❑ 206 Troy Glaus FC	2.50	1.00
❑ 207 Frank Thomas FC	4.00	1.50
❑ 208 Greg Maddux FC	6.00	2.50
❑ 209 Ivan Rodriguez FC	2.50	1.00
❑ 210 Jeff Bagwell FC	2.50	1.00
❑ 211 Todd Helton FC	2.50	1.00
❑ 212 Ken Griffey Jr. FC	6.00	2.50
❑ 213 Manny Ramirez Sox FC	2.50	1.00
❑ 214 Mark McGwire FC	10.00	4.00
❑ 215 Mike Piazza FC	6.00	2.50
❑ 216 Pedro Martinez FC	2.50	1.00
❑ 217 Sammy Sosa FC	4.00	1.50
❑ 218 Tony Gwynn FC	5.00	2.00
❑ 219 Vladimir Guerrero FC	4.00	1.50
❑ 220 Nomar Garciaparra FC	6.00	2.50
❑ NNO BB Best Coupon	2.00	.75
❑ NNO The Rookies Coupon	.50	.20

2001 Donruss Rookies

Card		
❑ COMP.FACT.SET (106)	100.00	60.00
❑ COMP.SET w/o SP's (105)	80.00	40.00
❑ R1 Adam Dunn	.75	.30
❑ R2 Ryan Drese RC	.75	.30
❑ R3 Bud Smith RC	.40	.15
❑ R4 Tsuyoshi Shinjo RC	.75	.30
❑ R5 Roy Oswalt	1.00	.40
❑ R6 Wilmy Caceres RC	.50	.20
❑ R7 Willie Harris RC	.50	.20
❑ R8 Andres Torres RC	.40	.15
❑ R9 Brandon Knight RC	.40	.15
❑ R10 Horacio Ramirez RC	.75	.30
❑ R11 Benito Baez RC	.40	.15
❑ R12 Jeremy Affeldt RC	.50	.20
❑ R13 Ryan Jensen RC	.50	.20
❑ R14 Casey Fossum RC	.40	.15
❑ R15 Ramon Vazquez RC	.50	.20
❑ R16 Dustan Mohr RC	.50	.20
❑ R17 Saul Rivera RC	.50	.20
❑ R18 Zach Day RC	.50	.20
❑ R19 Erik Hiljus RC	.40	.15
❑ R20 Cesar Crespo RC	.40	.15
❑ R21 Wilson Guzman RC	.50	.20
❑ R22 Travis Hafner RC	5.00	2.00
❑ R23 Grant Balfour RC	.40	.15
❑ R24 Johnny Estrada RC	.75	.30
❑ R25 Morgan Ensberg RC	2.00	.75
❑ R26 Jack Wilson RC	.75	.30
❑ R27 Aubrey Huff	.50	.20
❑ R28 Endy Chavez RC	.75	.30
❑ R29 Delvin James RC	.40	.15
❑ R30 Michael Cuddyer	.40	.15
❑ R31 Jason Michaels RC	.50	.20
❑ R32 Martin Vargas RC	.50	.20
❑ R33 Donaldo Mendez RC	.40	.15
❑ R34 Jorge Julio RC	.50	.20
❑ R35 Tim Spooneybarger RC	.50	.20
❑ R36 Kurt Ainsworth	.40	.15
❑ R37 Josh Fogg RC	.50	.20
❑ R38 Brian Reith RC	.40	.15
❑ R39 Rick Bauer RC	.40	.15
❑ R40 Tim Redding	.40	.15
❑ R41 Erick Almonte RC	.40	.15
❑ R42 Juan A.Pena RC	.40	.15
❑ R43 Ken Harvey	.40	.15
❑ R44 David Brous RC	.40	.15
❑ R45 Kevin Olsen RC	.50	.20
❑ R46 Henry Mateo RC	.40	.15
❑ R47 Nick Neugebauer	.40	.15
❑ R48 Mike Penney RC	.50	.20
❑ R49 Jay Gibbons RC	.75	.30
❑ R50 Tim Christman RC	.40	.15
❑ R51 Brandon Duckworth RC	.40	.15
❑ R52 Brett Jodie RC	.40	.15
❑ R53 Christian Parker RC	.40	.15
❑ R54 Carlos Hernandez	.40	.15
❑ R55 Brandon Larson RC	.40	.15
❑ R56 Nick Punto RC	.50	.20
❑ R57 Elpidio Guzman RC	.40	.15
❑ R58 Joe Beimel RC	.40	.15
❑ R59 Junior Spivey RC	.75	.30
❑ R60 Will Ohman RC	.50	.20
❑ R61 Brandon Lyon RC	.40	.15
❑ R62 Stubby Clapp RC	.40	.15
❑ R63 Justin Duchscherer RC	.50	.20
❑ R64 Jimmy Rollins	.50	.20
❑ R65 David Williams RC	.40	.15
❑ R66 Craig Monroe RC	2.50	1.00
❑ R67 Jose Acevedo RC	.40	.15
❑ R68 Jason Jennings	.40	.15
❑ R69 Josh Phelps	.40	.15
❑ R70 Brian Roberts RC	2.00	.75
❑ R71 Claudio Vargas RC	.40	.15
❑ R72 Adam Johnson	.40	.15
❑ R73 Bart Miadich RC	.40	.15
❑ R74 Juan Rivera	.40	.15
❑ R75 Brad Voyles RC	.40	.15
❑ R76 Nate Cornejo	.40	.15
❑ R77 Juan Moreno RC	.50	.20
❑ R78 Brian Rogers RC	.40	.15
❑ R79 Ricardo Rodriguez RC	.50	.20
❑ R80 Geronimo Gil RC	.40	.15
❑ R81 Joe Kennedy RC	.75	.30
❑ R82 Kevin Joseph RC	.50	.20
❑ R83 Josue Perez RC	.50	.20
❑ R84 Victor Zambrano RC	.75	.30
❑ R85 Josh Towers RC	.75	.30
❑ R86 Mike Rivera RC	.50	.20
❑ R87 Mark Prior RC	5.00	2.00
❑ R88 Juan Cruz RC	.50	.20
❑ R89 Dewon Brazelton RC	.50	.20
❑ R90 Angel Berroa RC	.75	.30
❑ R91 Mark Teixeira RC	6.00	2.50
❑ R92 Cody Ransom RC	.40	.15
❑ R93 Angel Santos RC	.40	.15
❑ R94 Corky Miller RC	.40	.15
❑ R95 Brandon Berger RC	.40	.15
❑ R96 Corey Patterson UPD	.40	.15
❑ R97 Albert Pujols UPD	60.00	30.00
❑ R98 Josh Beckett UPD	.75	.30
❑ R99 C.C. Sabathia UPD	.50	.20
❑ R100 Alfonso Soriano UPD	.75	.30
❑ R101 Ben Sheets UPD	.75	.30
❑ R102 Rafael Soriano UPD	.50	.20
❑ R103 Wilson Betemit UPD	2.00	.75
❑ R104 Ichiro Suzuki UPD	15.00	6.00
❑ R105 Jose Ortiz UPD	.40	.15

2002 Donruss

Card		
❑ COMPLETE SET (220)	150.00	60.00
❑ COMP.SET w/o SP'S (150)	25.00	10.00
❑ COMMON CARD (1-150)	.30	.10
❑ COMMON CARD (151-200)	3.00	1.25
❑ COMMON CARD (201-220)	1.50	.60
❑ 1 Alex Rodriguez	1.25	.50
❑ 2 Barry Bonds	2.00	.75
❑ 3 Derek Jeter	2.00	.75
❑ 4 Robert Fick	.30	.10
❑ 5 Juan Pierre	.30	.10

Card		
❑ 6 Torii Hunter	.30	.10
❑ 7 Todd Helton	.50	.20
❑ 8 Cal Ripken	2.50	1.00
❑ 9 Manny Ramirez	.50	.20
❑ 10 Johnny Damon	.50	.20
❑ 11 Mike Piazza	1.25	.50
❑ 12 Nomar Garciaparra	1.25	.50
❑ 13 Pedro Martinez	.50	.20
❑ 14 Brian Giles	.30	.10
❑ 15 Albert Pujols	1.50	.60
❑ 16 Roger Clemens	1.50	.60
❑ 17 Sammy Sosa	.75	.30
❑ 18 Vladimir Guerrero	.75	.30
❑ 19 Tony Gwynn	1.00	.40
❑ 20 Pat Burrell	.30	.10
❑ 21 Carlos Delgado	.30	.10
❑ 22 Tino Martinez	.50	.20
❑ 23 Jim Edmonds	.30	.10
❑ 24 Jason Giambi	.30	.10
❑ 25 Tom Glavine	.50	.20
❑ 26 Mark Grace	.50	.20
❑ 27 Tony Armas Jr.	.30	.10
❑ 28 Andruw Jones	.50	.20
❑ 29 Ben Sheets	.30	.10
❑ 30 Jeff Kent	.30	.10
❑ 31 Barry Larkin	.50	.20
❑ 32 Joe Mays	.30	.10
❑ 33 Mike Mussina	.50	.20
❑ 34 Hideo Nomo	.75	.30
❑ 35 Rafael Palmeiro	.50	.20
❑ 36 Scott Brosius	.30	.10
❑ 37 Scott Rolen	.50	.20
❑ 38 Gary Sheffield	.30	.10
❑ 39 Bernie Williams	.50	.20
❑ 40 Bob Abreu	.30	.10
❑ 41 Edgardo Alfonzo	.30	.10
❑ 42 C.C. Sabathia	.30	.10
❑ 43 Jeremy Giambi	.30	.10
❑ 44 Craig Biggio	.50	.20
❑ 45 Andres Galarraga	.30	.10
❑ 46 Edgar Martinez	.50	.20
❑ 47 Fred McGriff	.50	.20
❑ 48 Magglio Ordonez	.30	.10
❑ 49 Jim Thome	.50	.20
❑ 50 Matt Williams	.30	.10
❑ 51 Kerry Wood	.30	.10
❑ 52 Moises Alou	.30	.10
❑ 53 Brady Anderson	.30	.10
❑ 54 Garret Anderson	.30	.10
❑ 55 Juan Gonzalez	.30	.10
❑ 56 Bret Boone	.30	.10
❑ 57 Jose Cruz Jr.	.30	.10
❑ 58 Carlos Beltran	.30	.10
❑ 59 Adrian Beltre	.30	.10
❑ 60 Joe Kennedy	.30	.10
❑ 61 Lance Berkman	.30	.10
❑ 62 Kevin Brown	.30	.10
❑ 63 Tim Hudson	.30	.10
❑ 64 Jeromy Burnitz	.30	.10
❑ 65 Jarrod Washburn	.30	.10
❑ 66 Sean Casey	.30	.10
❑ 67 Eric Chavez	.30	.10
❑ 68 Bartolo Colon	.30	.10
❑ 69 Freddy Garcia	.30	.10
❑ 70 Jermaine Dye	.30	.10
❑ 71 Terrence Long	.30	.10
❑ 72 Cliff Floyd	.30	.10
❑ 73 Luis Gonzalez	.30	.10

❑ 74 Ichiro Suzuki 1.50 .60
❑ 75 Mike Hampton .30 .10
❑ 76 Richard Hidalgo .30 .10
❑ 77 Geoff Jenkins .30 .10
❑ 78 Gabe Kapler .30 .10
❑ 79 Ken Griffey Jr. 1.25 .50
❑ 80 Jason Kendall .30 .10
❑ 81 Josh Towers .30 .10
❑ 82 Ryan Klesko .30 .10
❑ 83 Paul Konerko .30 .10
❑ 84 Carlos Lee .30 .10
❑ 85 Kenny Lofton .30 .10
❑ 86 Josh Beckett .30 .10
❑ 87 Raul Mondesi .30 .10
❑ 88 Trot Nixon .30 .10
❑ 89 John Olerud .30 .10
❑ 90 Paul O'Neill .50 .20
❑ 91 Chan Ho Park .30 .10
❑ 92 Andy Pettitte .50 .20
❑ 93 Jorge Posada .50 .20
❑ 94 Mark Quinn .30 .10
❑ 95 Aramis Ramirez .30 .10
❑ 96 Curt Schilling .30 .10
❑ 97 Richie Sexson .30 .10
❑ 98 John Smoltz .50 .20
❑ 99 Wilson Betemit .30 .10
❑ 100 Shannon Stewart .30 .10
❑ 101 Alfonso Soriano .30 .10
❑ 102 Mike Sweeney .30 .10
❑ 103 Miguel Tejada .30 .10
❑ 104 Greg Vaughn .30 .10
❑ 105 Robin Ventura .30 .10
❑ 106 Jose Vidro .30 .10
❑ 107 Larry Walker .30 .10
❑ 108 Preston Wilson .30 .10
❑ 109 Corey Patterson .30 .10
❑ 110 Mark Mulder .30 .10
❑ 111 Tony Clark .30 .10
❑ 112 Roy Oswalt .30 .10
❑ 113 Jimmy Rollins .30 .10
❑ 114 Kazuhiro Sasaki .30 .10
❑ 115 Barry Zito .30 .10
❑ 116 Javier Vazquez .30 .10
❑ 117 Mike Cameron .30 .10
❑ 118 Phil Nevin .30 .10
❑ 119 Bud Smith .30 .10
❑ 120 Cristian Guzman .30 .10
❑ 121 Al Leiter .30 .10
❑ 122 Brad Radke .30 .10
❑ 123 Bobby Higginson .30 .10
❑ 124 Robert Person .30 .10
❑ 125 Adam Dunn .30 .10
❑ 126 Ben Grieve .30 .10
❑ 127 Rafael Furcal .30 .10
❑ 128 Jay Gibbons .30 .10
❑ 129 Paul LoDuca .30 .10
❑ 130 Wade Miller .30 .10
❑ 131 Tsuyoshi Shinjo .30 .10
❑ 132 Eric Milton .30 .10
❑ 133 Rickey Henderson .75 .30
❑ 134 Roberto Alomar .50 .20
❑ 135 Darin Erstad .30 .10
❑ 136 J.D. Drew .30 .10
❑ 137 Shawn Green .30 .10
❑ 138 Randy Johnson .75 .30
❑ 139 Austin Kearns .30 .10
❑ 140 Jose Canseco .50 .20
❑ 141 Jeff Bagwell .50 .20
❑ 142 Greg Maddux 1.25 .50
❑ 143 Mark Buehrle .30 .10
❑ 144 Ivan Rodriguez .50 .20
❑ 145 Frank Thomas .75 .30
❑ 146 Rich Aurilia .30 .10
❑ 147 Troy Glaus .30 .10
❑ 148 Ryan Dempster .30 .10
❑ 149 Chipper Jones .75 .30
❑ 150 Matt Morris .30 .10
❑ 151 Marlon Byrd RR 3.00 1.25
❑ 152 Ben Howard RR RC 3.00 1.25
❑ 153 Brandon Backe RR RC 3.00 1.25
❑ 154 Jorge De La Rosa RR RC 3.00 1.25
❑ 155 Corky Miller RR 3.00 1.25
❑ 156 Dennis Tankersley RR 3.00 1.25
❑ 157 Kyle Kane RR RC 3.00 1.25
❑ 158 Justin Duchscherer RR 3.00 1.25
❑ 159 Brian Mallette RR RC 3.00 1.25
❑ 160 Chris Baker RR RC 3.00 1.25
❑ 161 Jason Lane RR 3.00 1.25
❑ 162 Hee Seop Choi RR 3.00 1.25
❑ 163 Juan Cruz RR 3.00 1.25
❑ 164 Rodrigo Rosario RR RC 3.00 1.25
❑ 165 Matt Guerrier RR 3.00 1.25
❑ 166 Anderson Machado RR RC 3.00 1.25
❑ 167 Geronimo Gil RR 3.00 1.25
❑ 168 Dewon Brazelton RR 3.00 1.25
❑ 169 Mark Prior RR 4.00 1.50
❑ 170 Bill Hall RR 3.00 1.25
❑ 171 Jorge Padilla RR RC 3.00 1.25
❑ 172 Jose Cueto RR 3.00 1.25
❑ 173 Allan Simpson RR RC 3.00 1.25
❑ 174 Doug Devore RR RC 3.00 1.25
❑ 175 Josh Pearce RR 3.00 1.25
❑ 176 Angel Berroa RR 3.00 1.25
❑ 177 Steve Bechler RR RC 3.00 1.25
❑ 178 Antonio Perez RR 3.00 1.25
❑ 179 Mark Teixeira RR 4.00 1.50
❑ 180 Erick Almonte RR 3.00 1.25
❑ 181 Orlando Hudson RR 3.00 1.25
❑ 182 Michael Rivera RR 3.00 1.25
❑ 183 Raul Chavez RR RC 3.00 1.25
❑ 184 Juan Pena RR 3.00 1.25
❑ 185 Travis Hughes RR RC 3.00 1.25
❑ 186 Ryan Ludwick RR 3.00 1.25
❑ 187 Ed Rogers RR 3.00 1.25
❑ 188 Andy Pratt RR RC 3.00 1.25
❑ 189 Nick Neugebauer RR 3.00 1.25
❑ 190 Tom Shearn RR RC 3.00 1.25
❑ 191 Eric Cyr RR 3.00 1.25
❑ 192 Victor Martinez RR 4.00 1.50
❑ 193 Brandon Berger RR 3.00 1.25
❑ 194 Erik Bedard RR 3.00 1.25
❑ 195 Fernando Rodney RR 3.00 1.25
❑ 196 Joe Thurston RR 3.00 1.25
❑ 197 John Buck RR 3.00 1.25
❑ 198 Jeff Deardorff RR 3.00 1.25
❑ 199 Ryan Jamison RR 3.00 1.25
❑ 200 Alfredo Amezaga RR 3.00 1.25
❑ 201 Luis Gonzalez FC 1.50 .60
❑ 202 Roger Clemens FC 5.00 2.00
❑ 203 Barry Zito FC 1.50 .60
❑ 204 Bud Smith FC 1.50 .60
❑ 205 Magglio Ordonez FC 1.50 .60
❑ 206 Kerry Wood FC 1.50 .60
❑ 207 Freddy Garcia FC 1.50 .60
❑ 208 Adam Dunn FC 1.50 .60
❑ 209 Curt Schilling FC 1.50 .60
❑ 210 Lance Berkman FC 1.50 .60
❑ 211 Rafael Palmeiro FC 1.50 .60
❑ 212 Ichiro Suzuki FC 5.00 2.00
❑ 213 Bob Abreu FC 1.50 .60
❑ 214 Mark Mulder FC 1.50 .60
❑ 215 Roy Oswalt FC 1.50 .60
❑ 216 Mike Sweeney FC 1.50 .60
❑ 217 Paul LoDuca FC 1.50 .60
❑ 218 Aramis Ramirez FC 1.50 .60
❑ 219 Randy Johnson FC 2.50 1.00
❑ 220 Albert Pujols FC 5.00 2.00

2002 Donruss Rookies

❑ COMPLETE SET (110) 25.00 10.00
❑ 1 Kazuhisa Ishii RC .50 .20
❑ 2 P.J. Bevis RC .40 .15
❑ 3 Jason Simontacchi RC .40 .15
❑ 4 John Lackey .25 .08
❑ 5 Travis Driskill RC .40 .15
❑ 6 Carl Sadler RC .40 .15
❑ 7 Tim Kalita RC .40 .15
❑ 8 Nelson Castro RC .40 .15
❑ 9 Francis Beltran RC .40 .15
❑ 10 So Taguchi RC .50 .20
❑ 11 Ryan Bukvich RC .40 .15
❑ 12 Brian Fitzgerald RC .40 .15
❑ 13 Kevin Frederick RC .40 .15
❑ 14 Chone Figgins RC 1.50 .60
❑ 15 Marlon Byrd .25 .08
❑ 16 Ron Calloway RC .40 .15
❑ 17 Jason Lane .40 .15
❑ 18 Satoru Komiyama RC .40 .15
❑ 19 John Ennis RC .40 .15
❑ 20 Juan Brito RC .40 .15
❑ 21 Gustavo Chacin RC .75 .30
❑ 22 Josh Bard RC .40 .15
❑ 23 Brett Myers .40 .15
❑ 24 Mike Smith RC .40 .15
❑ 25 Eric Hinske .25 .08
❑ 26 Jake Peavy .50 .20
❑ 27 Todd Donovan RC .40 .15
❑ 28 Luis Ugueto RC .40 .15
❑ 29 Corey Thurman RC .40 .15
❑ 30 Takahito Nomura RC .40 .15
❑ 31 Andy Shibilo RC .40 .15
❑ 32 Mike Crudale RC .40 .15
❑ 33 Earl Snyder RC .40 .15
❑ 34 Brian Tallet RC .40 .15
❑ 35 Miguel Asencio RC .40 .15
❑ 36 Felix Escalona RC .40 .15
❑ 37 Drew Henson .25 .08
❑ 38 Steve Kent RC .40 .15
❑ 39 Rene Reyes RC .40 .15
❑ 40 Edwin Almonte RC .40 .15
❑ 41 Chris Snelling RC .60 .25
❑ 42 Franklyn German RC .40 .15
❑ 43 Jeriome Robertson RC .40 .15
❑ 44 Colin Young RC .40 .15
❑ 45 Jeremy Lambert RC .40 .15
❑ 46 Kirk Saarloos RC .40 .15
❑ 47 Matt Childers RC .40 .15
❑ 48 Justin Wayne .25 .08
❑ 49 Jose Valverde RC .40 .15
❑ 50 Wily Mo Pena .40 .15
❑ 51 Victor Alvarez RC .40 .15
❑ 52 Julius Matos RC .40 .15
❑ 53 Aaron Cook RC .40 .15
❑ 54 Jeff Austin RC .40 .15
❑ 55 Adrian Burnside RC .40 .15
❑ 56 Brandon Puffer RC .40 .15
❑ 57 Jeremy Hill RC .40 .15
❑ 58 Jaime Cerda RC .40 .15
❑ 59 Aaron Guiel RC .40 .15
❑ 60 Ron Chiavacci .25 .08
❑ 61 Kevin Cash RC .40 .15
❑ 62 Elio Serrano RC .40 .15
❑ 63 Julio Mateo RC .40 .15
❑ 64 Cam Esslinger RC .40 .15
❑ 65 Ken Huckaby RC .40 .15
❑ 66 Will Nieves RC .40 .15
❑ 67 Luis Martinez RC .40 .15
❑ 68 Scotty Layfield RC .40 .15
❑ 69 Jeremy Guthrie RC .50 .20
❑ 70 Hansel Izquierdo RC .40 .15
❑ 71 Shane Nance RC .40 .15
❑ 72 Jeff Baker RC 1.00 .40
❑ 73 Cliff Bartosh RC .40 .15
❑ 74 Mitch Wylie RC .40 .15
❑ 75 Oliver Perez RC .75 .30
❑ 76 Matt Thornton RC .40 .15
❑ 77 John Foster RC .40 .15
❑ 78 Joe Borchard .25 .08
❑ 79 Eric Junge RC .40 .15
❑ 80 Jorge Sosa RC .50 .20
❑ 81 Runelvys Hernandez RC .40 .15
❑ 82 Kevin Mench .25 .08
❑ 83 Ben Kozlowski RC .40 .15
❑ 84 Trey Hodges RC .40 .15
❑ 85 Reed Johnson RC .75 .30
❑ 86 Eric Eckenstahler RC .40 .15
❑ 87 Franklin Nunez RC .40 .15
❑ 88 Victor Martinez .75 .30
❑ 89 Kevin Gryboski RC .40 .15
❑ 90 Jason Jennings .25 .08

❑ 91 Jim Rushford RC	.40	.15
❑ 92 Jeremy Ward RC	.40	.15
❑ 93 Adam Walker RC	.40	.15
❑ 94 Freddy Sanchez RC	2.00	.75
❑ 95 Wilson Valdez RC	.40	.15
❑ 96 Lee Gardner RC	.40	.15
❑ 97 Eric Good RC	.40	.15
❑ 98 Hank Blalock	.50	.20
❑ 99 Mark Corey RC	.40	.15
❑ 100 Jason Davis RC	.40	.15
❑ 101 Mike Gonzalez RC	.40	.15
❑ 102 David Ross RC	.60	.25
❑ 103 Tyler Yates RC	.40	.15
❑ 104 Cliff Lee RC	.75	.30
❑ 105 Mike Moriarty RC	.40	.15
❑ 106 Josh Hancock RC	.50	.20
❑ 107 Jason Beverlin RC	.40	.15
❑ 108 Clay Condrey RC	.40	.15
❑ 109 Shawn Sedlacek RC	.40	.15
❑ 110 Sean Burroughs	.25	.08

2003 Donruss

Card		
❑ COMPLETE SET (400)	50.00	25.00
❑ COMMON CARD (71-400)	.30	.10
❑ COMMON CARD (1-20)	.50	.20
❑ COMMON CARD (21-70)	.50	.20
❑ 1 Vladimir Guerrero DK	.75	.30
❑ 2 Derek Jeter DK	2.00	.75
❑ 3 Adam Dunn DK	.50	.20
❑ 4 Greg Maddux DK	1.25	.50
❑ 5 Lance Berkman DK	.50	.20
❑ 6 Ichiro Suzuki DK	1.50	.60
❑ 7 Mike Piazza DK	1.25	.50
❑ 8 Alex Rodriguez DK	1.25	.50
❑ 9 Tom Glavine DK	.50	.20
❑ 10 Randy Johnson DK	.75	.30
❑ 11 Nomar Garciaparra DK	1.25	.50
❑ 12 Jason Giambi DK	.50	.20
❑ 13 Sammy Sosa DK	.75	.30
❑ 14 Barry Zito DK	.50	.20
❑ 15 Chipper Jones DK	.75	.30
❑ 16 Magglio Ordonez DK	.50	.20
❑ 17 Larry Walker DK	.50	.20
❑ 18 Alfonso Soriano DK	.50	.20
❑ 19 Curt Schilling DK	.50	.20
❑ 20 Barry Bonds DK	2.00	.75
❑ 21 Joe Borchard RR	.50	.20
❑ 22 Chris Snelling RR	.50	.20
❑ 23 Brian Tallet RR	.50	.20
❑ 24 Cliff Lee RR	.50	.20
❑ 25 Freddy Sanchez RR	.50	.20
❑ 26 Chone Figgans RR	.50	.20
❑ 27 Kevin Cash RR	.50	.20
❑ 28 Josh Bard RR	.50	.20
❑ 29 Jeriome Robertson RR	.50	.20
❑ 30 Jeremy Hill RR	.50	.20
❑ 31 Shane Nance RR	.50	.20
❑ 32 Jake Peavy RR	.50	.20
❑ 33 Trey Hodges RR	.50	.20
❑ 34 Eric Eckenstahler RR	.50	.20
❑ 35 Jim Rushford RR	.50	.20
❑ 36 Oliver Perez RR	.50	.20
❑ 37 Kirk Saarloos RR	.50	.20
❑ 38 Hank Blalock RR	.50	.20
❑ 39 Francisco Rodriguez RR	.50	.20
❑ 40 Runelvys Hernandez RR	.50	.20
❑ 41 Aaron Cook RR	.50	.20
❑ 42 Josh Hancock RR	.50	.20
❑ 43 P.J. Bevis RR	.50	.20
❑ 44 Jon Adkins RR	.50	.20
❑ 45 Tim Kalita RR	.50	.20
❑ 46 Nelson Castro RR	.50	.20
❑ 47 Colin Young RR	.50	.20
❑ 48 Adrian Burnside RR	.50	.20
❑ 49 Luis Martinez RR	.50	.20
❑ 50 Pete Zamora RR	.50	.20
❑ 51 Todd Donovan RR	.50	.20
❑ 52 Jeremy Ward RR	.50	.20
❑ 53 Wilson Valdez RR	.50	.20
❑ 54 Eric Good RR	.50	.20
❑ 55 Jeff Baker RR	.50	.20
❑ 56 Mitch Wylie RR	.50	.20
❑ 57 Ron Calloway RR	.50	.20
❑ 58 Jose Valverde RR	.50	.20
❑ 59 Jason Davis RR	.50	.20
❑ 60 Scotty Layfield RR	.50	.20
❑ 61 Matt Thornton RR	.50	.20
❑ 62 Adam Walker RR	.50	.20
❑ 63 Gustavo Chacin RR	.50	.20
❑ 64 Ron Chiavacci RR	.50	.20
❑ 65 Wiki Nieves RR	.50	.20
❑ 66 Cliff Bartosh RR	.50	.20
❑ 67 Mike Gonzalez RR	.50	.20
❑ 68 Justin Wayne RR	.50	.20
❑ 69 Eric Junge RR	.50	.20
❑ 70 Ben Kozlowski RR	.50	.20
❑ 71 Darin Erstad	.30	.10
❑ 72 Garret Anderson	.30	.10
❑ 73 Troy Glaus	.30	.10
❑ 74 David Eckstein	.30	.10
❑ 75 Adam Kennedy	.30	.10
❑ 76 Kevin Appier	.30	.10
❑ 77 Jarrod Washburn	.30	.10
❑ 78 Scott Spiezio	.30	.10
❑ 79 Tim Salmon	.50	.20
❑ 80 Ramon Ortiz	.30	.10
❑ 81 Bengie Molina	.30	.10
❑ 82 Brad Fullmer	.30	.10
❑ 83 Troy Percival	.30	.10
❑ 84 David Segui	.30	.10
❑ 85 Jay Gibbons	.30	.10
❑ 86 Tony Batista	.30	.10
❑ 87 Scott Erickson	.30	.10
❑ 88 Jeff Conine	.30	.10
❑ 89 Melvin Mora	.30	.10
❑ 90 Buddy Groom	.30	.10
❑ 91 Rodrigo Lopez	.30	.10
❑ 92 Marty Cordova	.30	.10
❑ 93 Geronimo Gil	.30	.10
❑ 94 Kenny Lofton	.30	.10
❑ 95 Shea Hillenbrand	.30	.10
❑ 96 Manny Ramirez	.50	.20
❑ 97 Pedro Martinez	.50	.20
❑ 98 Nomar Garciaparra	1.25	.50
❑ 99 Rickey Henderson	.75	.30
❑ 100 Johnny Damon	.50	.20
❑ 101 Trot Nixon	.30	.10
❑ 102 Derek Lowe	.30	.10
❑ 103 Hee Seop Choi	.30	.10
❑ 104 Mark Teixeira	.50	.20
❑ 105 Tim Wakefield	.30	.10
❑ 106 Jason Varitek	.75	.30
❑ 107 Frank Thomas	.75	.30
❑ 108 Joe Crede	.30	.10
❑ 109 Magglio Ordonez	.30	.10
❑ 110 Ray Durham	.30	.10
❑ 111 Mark Buehrle	.30	.10
❑ 112 Paul Konerko	.30	.10
❑ 113 Jose Valentin	.30	.10
❑ 114 Carlos Lee	.30	.10
❑ 115 Royce Clayton	.30	.10
❑ 116 C.C. Sabathia	.30	.10
❑ 117 Ellis Burks	.30	.10
❑ 118 Omar Vizquel	.50	.20
❑ 119 Jim Thome	.50	.20
❑ 120 Matt Lawton	.30	.10
❑ 121 Travis Fryman	.30	.10
❑ 122 Earl Snyder	.30	.10
❑ 123 Ricky Gutierrez	.30	.10
❑ 124 Einar Diaz	.30	.10
❑ 125 Danys Baez	.30	.10
❑ 126 Robert Fick	.30	.10
❑ 127 Bobby Higginson	.30	.10
❑ 128 Steve Sparks	.30	.10
❑ 129 Mike Rivera	.30	.10
❑ 130 Wendell Magee	.30	.10
❑ 131 Randall Simon	.30	.10
❑ 132 Carlos Pena	.30	.10
❑ 133 Mark Redman	.30	.10
❑ 134 Juan Acevedo	.30	.10
❑ 135 Mike Sweeney	.30	.10
❑ 136 Aaron Guiel	.30	.10
❑ 137 Carlos Beltran	.30	.10
❑ 138 Joe Randa	.30	.10
❑ 139 Paul Byrd	.30	.10
❑ 140 Shawn Sedlacek	.30	.10
❑ 141 Raul Ibanez	.30	.10
❑ 142 Michael Tucker	.30	.10
❑ 143 Torii Hunter	.30	.10
❑ 144 Jacque Jones	.30	.10
❑ 145 David Ortiz	.75	.30
❑ 146 Corey Koskie	.30	.10
❑ 147 Brad Radke	.30	.10
❑ 148 Doug Mientkiewicz	.30	.10
❑ 149 A.J. Pierzynski	.30	.10
❑ 150 Dustan Mohr	.30	.10
❑ 151 Michael Cuddyer	.30	.10
❑ 152 Eddie Guardado	.30	.10
❑ 153 Cristian Guzman	.30	.10
❑ 154 Derek Jeter	2.00	.75
❑ 155 Bernie Williams	.50	.20
❑ 156 Roger Clemens	1.50	.60
❑ 157 Mike Mussina	.50	.20
❑ 158 Jorge Posada	.50	.20
❑ 159 Alfonso Soriano	.30	.10
❑ 160 Jason Giambi	.30	.10
❑ 161 Robin Ventura	.30	.10
❑ 162 Andy Pettitte	.50	.20
❑ 163 David Wells	.30	.10
❑ 164 Nick Johnson	.30	.10
❑ 165 Jeff Weaver	.30	.10
❑ 166 Raul Mondesi	.30	.10
❑ 167 Rondell White	.30	.10
❑ 168 Tim Hudson	.30	.10
❑ 169 Barry Zito	.30	.10
❑ 170 Mark Mulder	.30	.10
❑ 171 Miguel Tejada	.30	.10
❑ 172 Eric Chavez	.30	.10
❑ 173 Billy Koch	.30	.10
❑ 174 Jermaine Dye	.30	.10
❑ 175 Scott Hatteberg	.30	.10
❑ 176 Terrence Long	.30	.10
❑ 177 David Justice	.30	.10
❑ 178 Ramon Hernandez	.30	.10
❑ 179 Ted Lilly	.30	.10
❑ 180 Ichiro Suzuki	1.50	.60
❑ 181 Edgar Martinez	.50	.20
❑ 182 Mike Cameron	.30	.10
❑ 183 John Olerud	.30	.10
❑ 184 Bret Boone	.30	.10
❑ 185 Dan Wilson	.30	.10
❑ 186 Freddy Garcia	.30	.10
❑ 187 Jamie Moyer	.30	.10
❑ 188 Carlos Guillen	.30	.10
❑ 189 Ruben Sierra	.30	.10
❑ 190 Kazuhiro Sasaki	.30	.10
❑ 191 Mark McLemore	.30	.10
❑ 192 John Halama	.30	.10
❑ 193 Joel Pineiro	.30	.10
❑ 194 Jeff Cirillo	.30	.10
❑ 195 Rafael Soriano	.30	.10
❑ 196 Ben Grieve	.30	.10
❑ 197 Aubrey Huff	.30	.10
❑ 198 Steve Cox	.30	.10
❑ 199 Toby Hall	.30	.10
❑ 200 Randy Winn	.30	.10
❑ 201 Brent Abernathy	.30	.10
❑ 202 Chris Gomez	.30	.10
❑ 203 John Flaherty	.30	.10
❑ 204 Paul Wilson	.30	.10
❑ 205 Chan Ho Park	.30	.10
❑ 206 Alex Rodriguez	1.25	.50
❑ 207 Juan Gonzalez	.30	.10
❑ 208 Rafael Palmeiro	.50	.20
❑ 209 Ivan Rodriguez	.50	.20
❑ 210 Rusty Greer	.30	.10
❑ 211 Kenny Rogers	.30	.10
❑ 212 Ismael Valdes	.30	.10
❑ 213 Frank Catalanotto	.30	.10
❑ 214 Hank Blalock	.30	.10

215	Michael Young	.50	.20
216	Kevin Mench	.30	.10
217	Herbert Perry	.30	.10
218	Gabe Kapler	.30	.10
219	Carlos Delgado	.30	.10
220	Shannon Stewart	.30	.10
221	Eric Hinske	.30	.10
222	Roy Halladay	.30	.10
223	Felipe Lopez	.30	.10
224	Vernon Wells	.30	.10
225	Josh Phelps	.30	.10
226	Jose Cruz	.30	.10
227	Curt Schilling	.30	.10
228	Randy Johnson	.75	.30
229	Luis Gonzalez	.30	.10
230	Mark Grace	.50	.20
231	Junior Spivey	.30	.10
232	Tony Womack	.30	.10
233	Matt Williams	.30	.10
234	Steve Finley	.30	.10
235	Byung-Hyun Kim	.30	.10
236	Craig Counsell	.30	.10
237	Greg Maddux	1.25	.50
238	Tom Glavine	.50	.20
239	John Smoltz	.50	.20
240	Chipper Jones	.75	.30
241	Gary Sheffield	.30	.10
242	Andruw Jones	.50	.20
243	Vinny Castilla	.30	.10
244	Damian Moss	.30	.10
245	Rafael Furcal	.30	.10
246	Javy Lopez	.30	.10
247	Kevin Millwood	.30	.10
248	Kerry Wood	.30	.10
249	Fred McGriff	.50	.20
250	Sammy Sosa	.75	.30
251	Alex Gonzalez	.30	.10
252	Corey Patterson	.30	.10
253	Moises Alou	.30	.10
254	Juan Cruz	.30	.10
255	Jon Lieber	.30	.10
256	Matt Clement	.30	.10
257	Mark Prior	.50	.20
258	Ken Griffey Jr.	1.25	.50
259	Barry Larkin	.50	.20
260	Adam Dunn	.30	.10
261	Sean Casey	.30	.10
262	Jose Rijo	.30	.10
263	Elmer Dessens	.30	.10
264	Austin Kearns	.30	.10
265	Corky Miller	.30	.10
266	Todd Walker	.30	.10
267	Chris Reitsma	.30	.10
268	Ryan Dempster	.30	.10
269	Aaron Boone	.30	.10
270	Danny Graves	.30	.10
271	Brandon Larson	.30	.10
272	Larry Walker	.30	.10
273	Todd Helton	.50	.20
274	Juan Uribe	.30	.10
275	Juan Pierre	.30	.10
276	Mike Hampton	.30	.10
277	Todd Zeile	.30	.10
278	Todd Hollandsworth	.30	.10
279	Jason Jennings	.30	.10
280	Josh Beckett	.30	.10
281	Mike Lowell	.30	.10
282	Derrek Lee	.50	.20
283	A.J. Burnett	.30	.10
284	Luis Castillo	.30	.10
285	Tim Raines	.30	.10
286	Preston Wilson	.30	.10
287	Juan Encarnacion	.30	.10
288	Charles Johnson	.30	.10
289	Jeff Bagwell	.50	.20
290	Craig Biggio	.50	.20
291	Lance Berkman	.30	.10
292	Daryle Ward	.30	.10
293	Roy Oswalt	.30	.10
294	Richard Hidalgo	.30	.10
295	Octavio Dotel	.30	.10
296	Wade Miller	.30	.10
297	Julio Lugo	.30	.10
298	Billy Wagner	.30	.10
299	Shawn Green	.30	.10
300	Adrian Beltre	.30	.10
301	Paul Lo Duca	.30	.10
302	Eric Karros	.30	.10
303	Kevin Brown	.30	.10
304	Hideo Nomo	.75	.30
305	Odalis Perez	.30	.10
306	Eric Gagne	.30	.10
307	Brian Jordan	.30	.10
308	Cesar Izturis	.30	.10
309	Mark Grudzielanek	.30	.10
310	Kazuhisa Ishii	.30	.10
311	Geoff Jenkins	.30	.10
312	Richie Sexson	.30	.10
313	Jose Hernandez	.30	.10
314	Ben Sheets	.30	.10
315	Ruben Quevedo	.30	.10
316	Jeffrey Hammonds	.30	.10
317	Alex Sanchez	.30	.10
318	Eric Young	.30	.10
319	Takahito Nomura	.30	.10
320	Vladimir Guerrero	.75	.30
321	Jose Vidro	.30	.10
322	Orlando Cabrera	.30	.10
323	Michael Barrett	.30	.10
324	Javier Vazquez	.30	.10
325	Tony Armas Jr.	.30	.10
326	Andres Galarraga	.30	.10
327	Tomo Ohka	.30	.10
328	Bartolo Colon	.30	.10
329	Fernando Tatis	.30	.10
330	Brad Wilkerson	.30	.10
331	Masato Yoshii	.30	.10
332	Mike Piazza	1.25	.50
333	Jeromy Burnitz	.30	.10
334	Roberto Alomar	.50	.20
335	Mo Vaughn	.30	.10
336	Al Leiter	.30	.10
337	Pedro Astacio	.30	.10
338	Edgardo Alfonzo	.30	.10
339	Armando Benitez	.30	.10
340	Timo Perez	.30	.10
341	Jay Payton	.30	.10
342	Roger Cedeno	.30	.10
343	Rey Ordonez	.30	.10
344	Steve Trachsel	.30	.10
345	Satoru Komiyama	.30	.10
346	Scott Rolen	.50	.20
347	Pat Burrell	.30	.10
348	Bobby Abreu	.30	.10
349	Mike Lieberthal	.30	.10
350	Brandon Duckworth	.30	.10
351	Jimmy Rollins	.30	.10
352	Marlon Anderson	.30	.10
353	Travis Lee	.30	.10
354	Vicente Padilla	.30	.10
355	Randy Wolf	.30	.10
356	Jason Kendall	.30	.10
357	Brian Giles	.30	.10
358	Aramis Ramirez	.30	.10
359	Pokey Reese	.30	.10
360	Kip Wells	.30	.10
361	Josh Fogg	.30	.10
362	Mike Williams	.30	.10
363	Jack Wilson	.30	.10
364	Craig Wilson	.30	.10
365	Kevin Young	.30	.10
366	Ryan Klesko	.30	.10
367	Phil Nevin	.30	.10
368	Brian Lawrence	.30	.10
369	Mark Kotsay	.30	.10
370	Brett Tomko	.30	.10
371	Trevor Hoffman	.30	.10
372	Deivi Cruz	.30	.10
373	Bubba Trammell	.30	.10
374	Sean Burroughs	.30	.10
375	Barry Bonds	2.00	.75
376	Jeff Kent	.30	.10
377	Rich Aurilia	.30	.10
378	Tsuyoshi Shinjo	.30	.10
379	Benito Santiago	.30	.10
380	Kirk Rueter	.30	.10
381	Livan Hernandez	.30	.10
382	Russ Ortiz	.30	.10
383	David Bell	.30	.10
384	Jason Schmidt	.30	.10
385	Reggie Sanders	.30	.10
386	J.T. Snow	.30	.10
387	Robb Nen	.30	.10
388	Ryan Jensen	.30	.10
389	Jim Edmonds	.30	.10
390	J.D. Drew	.30	.10
391	Albert Pujols	1.50	.60
392	Fernando Vina	.30	.10
393	Tino Martinez	.50	.20
394	Edgar Renteria	.30	.10
395	Matt Morris	.30	.10
396	Woody Williams	.30	.10
397	Jason Isringhausen	.30	.10
398	Placido Polanco	.30	.10
399	Eli Marrero	.30	.10
400	Jason Simontacchi	.30	.10

2003 Donruss Rookies

	COMPLETE SET (65)	20.00	8.00
	COMMON CARD (1-65)	.20	.07
	COMMON RC	.25	.08
1	Jeremy Bonderman RC	2.00	.75
2	Adam Loewen RC	.50	.20
3	Dan Haren RC	.50	.20
4	Jose Contreras RC	.50	.20
5	Hideki Matsui RC	2.00	.75
6	Arnie Munoz RC	.25	.08
7	Miguel Cabrera	.50	.20
8	Andrew Brown RC	.40	.15
9	Josh Hall RC	.25	.08
10	Josh Stewart RC	.25	.08
11	Clint Barmes RC	.75	.30
12	Luis Ayala RC	.25	.08
13	Brandon Webb RC	1.50	.60
14	Greg Aquino RC	.25	.08
15	Chien-Ming Wang RC	5.00	2.00
16	Rickie Weeks RC	1.50	.60
17	Edgar Gonzalez RC	.25	.08
18	Dontrelle Willis	.50	.20
19	Bo Hart RC	.25	.08
20	Rosman Garcia RC	.25	.08
21	Jeremy Griffiths RC	.25	.08
22	Craig Brazell RC	.25	.08
23	Daniel Cabrera RC	.50	.20
24	Fernando Cabrera RC	.25	.08
25	Terrmel Sledge RC	.25	.08
26	Ramon Nivar RC	.25	.08
27	Rob Hammock RC	.25	.08
28	Francisco Rosario RC	.25	.08
29	Cory Stewart RC	.25	.08
30	Felix Sanchez RC	.25	.08
31	Jorge Cordova RC	.25	.08
32	Rocco Baldelli	.20	.07
33	Beau Kemp RC	.25	.08
34	Mike Nakamura RC	.25	.08
35	Rett Johnson RC	.25	.08
36	Guillermo Quiroz RC	.25	.08
37	Hong-Chih Kuo RC	2.00	.75
38	Ian Ferguson RC	.25	.08
39	Franklin Perez RC	.25	.08
40	Tim Olson RC	.25	.08
41	Jerome Williams	.20	.07
42	Rich Fischer RC	.25	.08
43	Phil Seibel RC	.25	.08
44	Aaron Looper RC	.25	.08
45	Jae Weong Seo	.20	.07
46	Chad Gaudin RC	.25	.08
47	Matt Kata RC	.25	.08
48	Ryan Wagner RC	.25	.08
49	Michel Hernandez RC	.25	.08

❑ 50 Diegomar Markwell RC .25 .08
❑ 51 Doug Waechter RC .40 .15
❑ 52 Mike Nicolas RC .25 .08
❑ 53 Prentice Redman RC .25 .08
❑ 54 Shane Bazzell RC .25 .08
❑ 55 Delmon Young RC 3.00 1.25
❑ 56 Brian Stokes RC .25 .08
❑ 57 Matt Bruback RC .25 .08
❑ 58 Nook Logan RC .40 .15
❑ 59 Oscar Villarreal RC .25 .08
❑ 60 Pete LaForest RC .25 .08
❑ 61 Shea Hillenbrand .20 .07
❑ 62 Aramis Ramirez .20 .07
❑ 63 Aaron Boone .20 .07
❑ 64 Roberto Alomar .30 .10
❑ 65 Rickey Henderson .50 .20

2004 Donruss

❑ COMPLETE SET (400) 150.00 75.00
❑ COMP.SET w/o SP's (300) 25.00 10.00
❑ COMMON CARD (71-370) .30 .10
❑ COMMON CARD (1-25/371-400) 2.00 .75
❑ COMMON CARD (26-70) 2.00 .75
❑ 1-70/370-400 RANDOM INSERTS IN PACKS
❑ 1 Derek Jeter DK 4.00 1.50
❑ 2 Greg Maddux DK 3.00 1.25
❑ 3 Albert Pujols DK 4.00 1.50
❑ 4 Ichiro Suzuki DK 4.00 1.50
❑ 5 Alex Rodriguez DK 3.00 1.25
❑ 6 Roger Clemens DK 4.00 1.50
❑ 7 Andruw Jones DK 2.00 .75
❑ 8 Barry Bonds DK 5.00 2.00
❑ 9 Jeff Bagwell DK 2.00 .75
❑ 10 Randy Johnson DK 2.00 .75
❑ 11 Scott Rolen DK 2.00 .75
❑ 12 Lance Berkman DK 2.00 .75
❑ 13 Barry Zito DK 2.00 .75
❑ 14 Manny Ramirez DK 2.00 .75
❑ 15 Carlos Delgado DK 2.00 .75
❑ 16 Alfonso Soriano DK 2.00 .75
❑ 17 Todd Helton DK 2.00 .75
❑ 18 Mike Mussina DK 2.00 .75
❑ 19 Austin Kearns DK 2.00 .75
❑ 20 Nomar Garciaparra DK 3.00 1.25
❑ 21 Chipper Jones DK 2.00 .75
❑ 22 Mark Prior DK 2.00 .75
❑ 23 Jim Thome DK 2.00 .75
❑ 24 Vladimir Guerrero DK 2.00 .75
❑ 25 Pedro Martinez DK 2.00 .75
❑ 26 Sergio Mitre RR 2.00 .75
❑ 27 Adam Loewen RR 2.00 .75
❑ 28 Alfredo Gonzalez RR 2.00 .75
❑ 29 Miguel Ojeda RR 2.00 .75
❑ 30 Rosman Garcia RR 2.00 .75
❑ 31 Arnie Munoz RR 2.00 .75
❑ 32 Andrew Brown RR 2.00 .75
❑ 33 Josh Hall RR 2.00 .75
❑ 34 Josh Stewart RR 2.00 .75
❑ 35 Clint Barmes RR 3.00 1.25
❑ 36 Brandon Webb RR 2.00 .75
❑ 37 Chien-Ming Wang RR 8.00 3.00
❑ 38 Edgar Gonzalez RR 2.00 .75
❑ 39 Alejandro Machado RR 2.00 .75
❑ 40 Jeremy Griffiths RR 2.00 .75
❑ 41 Craig Brazell RR 2.00 .75
❑ 42 Daniel Cabrera RR 2.00 .75
❑ 43 Fernando Cabrera RR 2.00 .75
❑ 44 Termel Sledge RR 2.00 .75
❑ 45 Rob Hammock RR 2.00 .75
❑ 46 Francisco Rosario RR 2.00 .75
❑ 47 Francisco Cruceta RR 2.00 .75
❑ 48 Rett Johnson RR 2.00 .75
❑ 49 Guillermo Quiroz RR 2.00 .75
❑ 50 Hong-Chih Kuo RR 3.00 1.25
❑ 51 Ian Ferguson RR 2.00 .75
❑ 52 Tim Olson RR 2.00 .75
❑ 53 Todd Wellemeyer RR 2.00 .75
❑ 54 Rich Fischer RR 2.00 .75
❑ 55 Phil Seibel RR 2.00 .75
❑ 56 Joe Valentine RR 2.00 .75
❑ 57 Matt Kata RR 2.00 .75
❑ 58 Michael Hessman RR 2.00 .75
❑ 59 Michel Hernandez RR 2.00 .75
❑ 60 Doug Waechter RR 2.00 .75
❑ 61 Prentice Redman RR 2.00 .75
❑ 62 Nook Logan RR 2.00 .75
❑ 63 Oscar Villarreal RR 2.00 .75
❑ 64 Pete LaForest RR 2.00 .75
❑ 65 Matt Bruback RR 2.00 .75
❑ 66 Dan Haren RR 2.00 .75
❑ 67 Greg Aquino RR 2.00 .75
❑ 68 Lew Ford RR 2.00 .75
❑ 69 Jeff Duncan RR 2.00 .75
❑ 70 Ryan Wagner RR 2.00 .75
❑ 71 Bengie Molina .30 .10
❑ 72 Brad Fullmer .30 .10
❑ 73 Darin Erstad .30 .10
❑ 74 David Eckstein .30 .10
❑ 75 Garret Anderson .30 .10
❑ 76 Jarrod Washburn .30 .10
❑ 77 Kevin Appier .30 .10
❑ 78 Scott Spiezio .30 .10
❑ 79 Tim Salmon .50 .20
❑ 80 Troy Glaus .30 .10
❑ 81 Troy Percival .30 .10
❑ 82 Jason Johnson .30 .10
❑ 83 Jay Gibbons .30 .10
❑ 84 Melvin Mora .30 .10
❑ 85 Sidney Ponson .30 .10
❑ 86 Tony Batista .30 .10
❑ 87 Bill Mueller .30 .10
❑ 88 Byung-Hyun Kim .30 .10
❑ 89 David Ortiz .75 .30
❑ 90 Derek Lowe .30 .10
❑ 91 Johnny Damon .50 .20
❑ 92 Casey Fossum .30 .10
❑ 93 Manny Ramirez .50 .20
❑ 94 Nomar Garciaparra 1.25 .50
❑ 95 Pedro Martinez .50 .20
❑ 96 Todd Walker .30 .10
❑ 97 Trot Nixon .30 .10
❑ 98 Bartolo Colon .30 .10
❑ 99 Carlos Lee .30 .10
❑ 100 D'Angelo Jimenez .30 .10
❑ 101 Esteban Loaiza .30 .10
❑ 102 Frank Thomas .75 .30
❑ 103 Joe Crede .30 .10
❑ 104 Jose Valentin .30 .10
❑ 105 Magglio Ordonez .30 .10
❑ 106 Mark Buehrle .30 .10
❑ 107 Paul Konerko .30 .10
❑ 108 Brandon Phillips .30 .10
❑ 109 C.C Sabathia .30 .10
❑ 110 Ellis Burks .30 .10
❑ 111 Jeremy Guthrie .30 .10
❑ 112 Josh Bard .30 .10
❑ 113 Matt Lawton .30 .10
❑ 114 Milton Bradley .30 .10
❑ 115 Omar Vizquel .50 .20
❑ 116 Travis Hafner .30 .10
❑ 117 Bobby Higginson .30 .10
❑ 118 Carlos Pena .30 .10
❑ 119 Dmitri Young .30 .10
❑ 120 Eric Munson .30 .10
❑ 121 Jeremy Bonderman .30 .10
❑ 122 Nate Cornejo .30 .10
❑ 123 Omar Infante .30 .10
❑ 124 Ramon Santiago .30 .10
❑ 125 Angel Berroa .30 .10
❑ 126 Carlos Beltran .30 .10
❑ 127 Desi Relaford .30 .10
❑ 128 Jeremy Affeldt .30 .10
❑ 129 Joe Randa .30 .10
❑ 130 Ken Harvey .30 .10
❑ 131 Mike MacDougal .30 .10
❑ 132 Michael Tucker .30 .10
❑ 133 Mike Sweeney .30 .10
❑ 134 Raul Ibanez .30 .10
❑ 135 Runelvys Hernandez .30 .10
❑ 136 A.J. Pierzynski .30 .10
❑ 137 Brad Radke .30 .10
❑ 138 Corey Koskie .30 .10
❑ 139 Cristian Guzman .30 .10
❑ 140 Doug Mientkiewicz .30 .10
❑ 141 Dustan Mohr .30 .10
❑ 142 Jacque Jones .30 .10
❑ 143 Kenny Rogers .30 .10
❑ 144 Bobby Kielty .30 .10
❑ 145 Kyle Lohse .30 .10
❑ 146 Luis Rivas .30 .10
❑ 147 Torii Hunter .30 .10
❑ 148 Alfonso Soriano .30 .10
❑ 149 Andy Pettitte .50 .20
❑ 150 Bernie Williams .50 .20
❑ 151 David Wells .30 .10
❑ 152 Derek Jeter 1.50 .60
❑ 153 Hideki Matsui 1.25 .50
❑ 154 Jason Giambi .30 .10
❑ 155 Jorge Posada .50 .20
❑ 156 Jose Contreras .30 .10
❑ 157 Mike Mussina .50 .20
❑ 158 Nick Johnson .30 .10
❑ 159 Robin Ventura .30 .10
❑ 160 Roger Clemens 1.50 .60
❑ 161 Barry Zito .30 .10
❑ 162 Chris Singleton .30 .10
❑ 163 Eric Byrnes .30 .10
❑ 164 Eric Chavez .30 .10
❑ 165 Erubiel Durazo .30 .10
❑ 166 Keith Foulke .30 .10
❑ 167 Mark Ellis .30 .10
❑ 168 Miguel Tejada .30 .10
❑ 169 Mark Mulder .30 .10
❑ 170 Ramon Hernandez .30 .10
❑ 171 Ted Lilly .30 .10
❑ 172 Terrence Long .30 .10
❑ 173 Tim Hudson .30 .10
❑ 174 Bret Boone .30 .10
❑ 175 Carlos Guillen .30 .10
❑ 176 Dan Wilson .30 .10
❑ 177 Edgar Martinez .50 .20
❑ 178 Freddy Garcia .30 .10
❑ 179 Gil Meche .30 .10
❑ 180 Ichiro Suzuki 1.50 .60
❑ 181 Jamie Moyer .30 .10
❑ 182 Joel Pineiro .30 .10
❑ 183 John Olerud .30 .10
❑ 184 Mike Cameron .30 .10
❑ 185 Randy Winn .30 .10
❑ 186 Ryan Franklin .30 .10
❑ 187 Kazuhiro Sasaki .30 .10
❑ 188 Aubrey Huff .30 .10
❑ 189 Carl Crawford .30 .10
❑ 190 Joe Kennedy .30 .10
❑ 191 Marlon Anderson .30 .10
❑ 192 Rey Ordonez .30 .10
❑ 193 Rocco Baldelli .30 .10
❑ 194 Toby Hall .30 .10
❑ 195 Travis Lee .30 .10
❑ 196 Alex Rodriguez 1.25 .50
❑ 197 Carl Everett .30 .10
❑ 198 Chan Ho Park .30 .10
❑ 199 Einar Diaz .30 .10
❑ 200 Hank Blalock .30 .10
❑ 201 Ismael Valdes .30 .10
❑ 202 Juan Gonzalez .30 .10
❑ 203 Mark Teixeira .50 .20
❑ 204 Mike Young .30 .10
❑ 205 Rafael Palmeiro .50 .20
❑ 206 Carlos Delgado .30 .10
❑ 207 Kelvim Escobar .30 .10
❑ 208 Eric Hinske .30 .10
❑ 209 Frank Catalanotto .30 .10
❑ 210 Josh Phelps .30 .10
❑ 211 Orlando Hudson .30 .10
❑ 212 Roy Halladay .30 .10
❑ 213 Shannon Stewart .30 .10
❑ 214 Vernon Wells .30 .10
❑ 215 Carlos Baerga .30 .10
❑ 216 Curt Schilling .30 .10

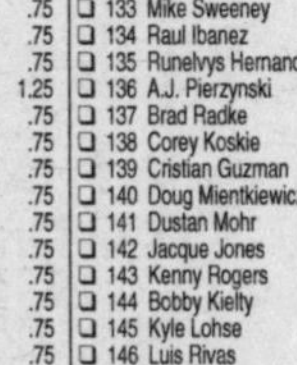

❑ 217 Junior Spivey .30 .10
❑ 218 Luis Gonzalez .30 .10
❑ 219 Lyle Overbay .30 .10
❑ 220 Mark Grace .50 .20
❑ 221 Matt Williams .30 .10
❑ 222 Randy Johnson .75 .30
❑ 223 Shea Hillenbrand .30 .10
❑ 224 Steve Finley .30 .10
❑ 225 Andruw Jones .50 .20
❑ 226 Chipper Jones .75 .30
❑ 227 Gary Sheffield .30 .10
❑ 228 Greg Maddux 1.25 .50
❑ 229 Javy Lopez .30 .10
❑ 230 John Smoltz .50 .20
❑ 231 Marcus Giles .30 .10
❑ 232 Mike Hampton .30 .10
❑ 233 Rafael Furcal .30 .10
❑ 234 Robert Fick .30 .10
❑ 235 Russ Ortiz .30 .10
❑ 236 Alex Gonzalez .30 .10
❑ 237 Carlos Zambrano .30 .10
❑ 238 Corey Patterson .30 .10
❑ 239 Hee Seop Choi .30 .10
❑ 240 Kerry Wood .30 .10
❑ 241 Mark Bellhorn .30 .10
❑ 242 Mark Prior .50 .20
❑ 243 Moises Alou .30 .10
❑ 244 Sammy Sosa .75 .30
❑ 245 Aaron Boone .30 .10
❑ 246 Adam Dunn .30 .10
❑ 247 Austin Kearns .30 .10
❑ 248 Barry Larkin .50 .20
❑ 249 Felipe Lopez .30 .10
❑ 250 Jose Guillen .30 .10
❑ 251 Ken Griffey Jr. 1.25 .50
❑ 252 Jason LaRue .30 .10
❑ 253 Scott Williamson .30 .10
❑ 254 Sean Casey .30 .10
❑ 255 Shawn Chacon .30 .10
❑ 256 Chris Stynes .30 .10
❑ 257 Jason Jennings .30 .10
❑ 258 Jay Payton .30 .10
❑ 259 Jose Hernandez .30 .10
❑ 260 Larry Walker .30 .10
❑ 261 Preston Wilson .30 .10
❑ 262 Ronnie Belliard .30 .10
❑ 263 Todd Helton .50 .20
❑ 264 A.J. Burnett .30 .10
❑ 265 Alex Gonzalez .30 .10
❑ 266 Brad Penny .30 .10
❑ 267 Derrek Lee .50 .20
❑ 268 Ivan Rodriguez .50 .20
❑ 269 Josh Beckett .30 .10
❑ 270 Juan Encarnacion .30 .10
❑ 271 Juan Pierre .30 .10
❑ 272 Luis Castillo .30 .10
❑ 273 Mike Lowell .30 .10
❑ 274 Todd Hollandsworth .30 .10
❑ 275 Billy Wagner .30 .10
❑ 276 Brad Ausmus .30 .10
❑ 277 Craig Biggio .50 .20
❑ 278 Jeff Bagwell .50 .20
❑ 279 Jeff Kent .30 .10
❑ 280 Lance Berkman .30 .10
❑ 281 Richard Hidalgo .30 .10
❑ 282 Roy Oswalt .30 .10
❑ 283 Wade Miller .30 .10
❑ 284 Adrian Beltre .30 .10
❑ 285 Brian Jordan .30 .10
❑ 286 Cesar Izturis .30 .10
❑ 287 Dave Roberts .30 .10
❑ 288 Eric Gagne .30 .10
❑ 289 Fred McGriff .50 .20
❑ 290 Hideo Nomo .75 .30
❑ 291 Kazuhisa Ishii .30 .10
❑ 292 Kevin Brown .30 .10
❑ 293 Paul Lo Duca .30 .10
❑ 294 Shawn Green .30 .10
❑ 295 Ben Sheets .30 .10
❑ 296 Geoff Jenkins .30 .10
❑ 297 Rey Sanchez .30 .10
❑ 298 Richie Sexson .30 .10
❑ 299 Wes Helms .30 .10
❑ 300 Brad Wilkerson .30 .10
❑ 301 Claudio Vargas .30 .10
❑ 302 Endy Chavez .30 .10
❑ 303 Fernando Tatis .30 .10
❑ 304 Javier Vazquez .30 .10
❑ 305 Jose Vidro .30 .10
❑ 306 Michael Barrett .30 .10
❑ 307 Orlando Cabrera .30 .10
❑ 308 Tony Armas Jr. .30 .10
❑ 309 Vladimir Guerrero .75 .30
❑ 310 Zach Day .30 .10
❑ 311 Al Leiter .30 .10
❑ 312 Cliff Floyd .30 .10
❑ 313 Jae Weong Seo .30 .10
❑ 314 Jeromy Burnitz .30 .10
❑ 315 Mike Piazza 1.25 .50
❑ 316 Mo Vaughn .30 .10
❑ 317 Roberto Alomar .50 .20
❑ 318 Roger Cedeno .30 .10
❑ 319 Tom Glavine .50 .20
❑ 320 Jose Reyes .30 .10
❑ 321 Bobby Abreu .30 .10
❑ 322 Brett Myers .30 .10
❑ 323 David Bell .30 .10
❑ 324 Jim Thome .50 .20
❑ 325 Jimmy Rollins .30 .10
❑ 326 Kevin Millwood .30 .10
❑ 327 Marlon Byrd .30 .10
❑ 328 Mike Lieberthal .30 .10
❑ 329 Pat Burrell .30 .10
❑ 330 Randy Wolf .30 .10
❑ 331 Aramis Ramirez .30 .10
❑ 332 Brian Giles .30 .10
❑ 333 Jason Kendall .30 .10
❑ 334 Kenny Lofton .30 .10
❑ 335 Kip Wells .30 .10
❑ 336 Kris Benson .30 .10
❑ 337 Randall Simon .30 .10
❑ 338 Reggie Sanders .30 .10
❑ 339 Albert Pujols 1.50 .60
❑ 340 Edgar Renteria .30 .10
❑ 341 Fernando Vina .30 .10
❑ 342 J.D. Drew .30 .10
❑ 343 Jim Edmonds .30 .10
❑ 344 Matt Morris .30 .10
❑ 345 Mike Matheny .30 .10
❑ 346 Scott Rolen .50 .20
❑ 347 Tino Martinez .50 .20
❑ 348 Woody Williams .30 .10
❑ 349 Brian Lawrence .30 .10
❑ 350 Mark Kotsay .30 .10
❑ 351 Mark Loretta .30 .10
❑ 352 Ramon Vazquez .30 .10
❑ 353 Rondell White .30 .10
❑ 354 Ryan Klesko .30 .10
❑ 355 Sean Burroughs .30 .10
❑ 356 Trevor Hoffman .30 .10
❑ 357 Xavier Nady .30 .10
❑ 358 Andres Galarraga .30 .10
❑ 359 Barry Bonds 2.00 .75
❑ 360 Benito Santiago .30 .10
❑ 361 Deivi Cruz .30 .10
❑ 362 Edgardo Alfonzo .30 .10
❑ 363 J.T. Snow .30 .10
❑ 364 Jason Schmidt .30 .10
❑ 365 Kirk Rueter .30 .10
❑ 366 Kurt Ainsworth .30 .10
❑ 367 Marquis Grissom .30 .10
❑ 368 Ray Durham .30 .10
❑ 369 Rich Aurilia .30 .10
❑ 370 Tim Worrell .30 .10
❑ 371 Troy Glaus TC 2.00 .75
❑ 372 Melvin Mora TC 2.00 .75
❑ 373 Nomar Garciaparra TC 3.00 1.25
❑ 374 Magglio Ordonez TC 2.00 .75
❑ 375 Omar Vizquel TC 2.00 .75
❑ 376 Dmitri Young TC 2.00 .75
❑ 377 Mike Sweeney TC 2.00 .75
❑ 378 Torii Hunter TC 2.00 .75
❑ 379 Derek Jeter TC 4.00 1.50
❑ 380 Barry Zito TC 2.00 .75
❑ 381 Ichiro Suzuki TC 4.00 1.50
❑ 382 Rocco Baldelli TC 2.00 .75
❑ 383 Alex Rodriguez TC 3.00 1.25
❑ 384 Carlos Delgado TC 2.00 .75
❑ 385 Randy Johnson TC 2.00 .75
❑ 386 Greg Maddux TC 3.00 1.25
❑ 387 Sammy Sosa TC 2.00 .75
❑ 388 Ken Griffey Jr. TC 3.00 1.25
❑ 389 Todd Helton TC 2.00 .75
❑ 390 Ivan Rodriguez TC 2.00 .75
❑ 391 Jeff Bagwell TC 2.00 .75
❑ 392 Hideo Nomo TC 2.00 .75
❑ 393 Richie Sexson TC 2.00 .75
❑ 394 Vladimir Guerrero TC 2.00 .75
❑ 395 Mike Piazza TC 3.00 1.25
❑ 396 Jim Thome TC 2.00 .75
❑ 397 Jason Kendall TC 2.00 .75
❑ 398 Albert Pujols TC 4.00 1.50
❑ 399 Ryan Klesko TC 2.00 .75
❑ 400 Barry Bonds TC 5.00 2.00

2005 Donruss

❑ COMPLETE SET (400) 150.00 75.00
❑ COMP.SET w/o SP's (300) 25.00 10.00
❑ COMMON CARD (71-370) .30 .10
❑ COMMON (1-25/371-400) 2.00 .75
❑ COMMON CARD (26-70) 2.00 .75
❑ 1-25 STATED ODDS 1:6
❑ 26-70 STATED ODDS 1:6
❑ 371-400 STATED ODDS 1:6
❑ 1 Garret Anderson DK 2.00 .75
❑ 2 Vladimir Guerrero DK 2.00 .75
❑ 3 Manny Ramirez DK 2.00 .75
❑ 4 Kerry Wood DK 2.00 .75
❑ 5 Sammy Sosa DK 2.00 .75
❑ 6 Magglio Ordonez DK 2.00 .75
❑ 7 Adam Dunn DK 2.00 .75
❑ 8 Todd Helton DK 2.00 .75
❑ 9 Josh Beckett DK 2.00 .75
❑ 10 Miguel Cabrera DK 2.00 .75
❑ 11 Lance Berkman DK 2.00 .75
❑ 12 Carlos Beltran DK 2.00 .75
❑ 13 Shawn Green DK 2.00 .75
❑ 14 Roger Clemens DK 3.00 1.25
❑ 15 Mike Piazza DK 2.00 .75
❑ 16 Alex Rodriguez DK 3.00 1.25
❑ 17 Derek Jeter DK 4.00 1.50
❑ 18 Mark Mulder DK 2.00 .75
❑ 19 Jim Thome DK 2.00 .75
❑ 20 Albert Pujols DK 4.00 1.50
❑ 21 Scott Rolen DK 2.00 .75
❑ 22 Aubrey Huff DK 2.00 .75
❑ 23 Alfonso Soriano DK 2.00 .75
❑ 24 Hank Blalock DK 2.00 .75
❑ 25 Vernon Wells DK 2.00 .75
❑ 26 Kazuo Matsui RR 3.00 1.25
❑ 27 B.J. Upton RR 5.00 2.00
❑ 28 Charles Thomas RR 2.00 .75
❑ 29 Akinori Otsuka RR 3.00 1.25
❑ 30 David Aardsma RR 2.00 .75
❑ 31 Travis Blackley RR 2.00 .75
❑ 32 Brad Halsey RR 2.00 .75
❑ 33 David Wright RR 8.00 3.00
❑ 34 Kazuhito Tadano RR 3.00 1.25
❑ 35 Casey Kotchman RR 3.00 1.25
❑ 36 Khalil Greene RR 5.00 2.00
❑ 37 Adrian Gonzalez RR 2.00 .75
❑ 38 Zack Greinke RR 2.00 .75
❑ 39 Chad Cordero RR 2.00 .75
❑ 40 Scott Kazmir RR 5.00 2.00
❑ 41 Jeremy Guthrie RR 2.00 .75
❑ 42 Noah Lowry RR 3.00 1.25
❑ 43 Chase Utley RR 5.00 2.00
❑ 44 Billy Traber RR 2.00 .75
❑ 45 Aarom Baldiris RR 2.00 .75
❑ 46 Abe Alvarez RR 2.00 .75

❑	47	Angel Chavez RR	2.00	.75
❑	48	Joe Mauer RR	5.00	2.00
❑	49	Joey Gathright RR	3.00	1.25
❑	50	John Gall RR	2.00	.75
❑	51	Ronald Belisario RR	2.00	.75
❑	52	Ryan Wing RR	2.00	.75
❑	53	Scott Proctor RR	2.00	.75
❑	54	Yadier Molina RR	3.00	1.25
❑	55	Carlos Hines RR	2.00	.75
❑	56	Frankie Francisco RR	2.00	.75
❑	57	Graham Koonce RR	2.00	.75
❑	58	Jake Woods RR	2.00	.75
❑	59	Jason Bartlett RR	2.00	.75
❑	60	Mike Rouse RR	2.00	.75
❑	61	Phil Stockman RR	2.00	.75
❑	62	Renyel Pinto RR	2.00	.75
❑	63	Roberto Novoa RR	2.00	.75
❑	64	Ryan Meaux RR	2.00	.75
❑	65	Dave Crouthers RR	2.00	.75
❑	66	Justin Knoedler RR	2.00	.75
❑	67	Justin Leone RR	2.00	.75
❑	68	Nick Regilio RR	2.00	.75
❑	69	Mike Gosling RR	2.00	.75
❑	70	Onil Joseph RR	2.00	.75
❑	71	Bartolo Colon	.30	.10
❑	72	Brad Fullmer	.30	.10
❑	73	Chone Figgins	.30	.10
❑	74	Darin Erstad	.30	.10
❑	75	Francisco Rodriguez	.30	.10
❑	76	Garret Anderson	.30	.10
❑	77	Jarrod Washburn	.30	.10
❑	78	John Lackey	.30	.10
❑	79	Jose Guillen	.30	.10
❑	80	Robb Quinlan	.30	.10
❑	81	Tim Salmon	.50	.20
❑	82	Troy Glaus	.30	.10
❑	83	Troy Percival	.30	.10
❑	84	Vladimir Guerrero	.75	.30
❑	85	Brandon Webb	.30	.10
❑	86	Casey Fossum	.30	.10
❑	87	Luis Gonzalez	.30	.10
❑	88	Randy Johnson	.75	.30
❑	89	Richie Sexson	.30	.10
❑	90	Robby Hammock	.30	.10
❑	91	Roberto Alomar	.50	.20
❑	92	Adam LaRoche	.30	.10
❑	93	Andruw Jones	.50	.20
❑	94	Bubba Nelson	.30	.10
❑	95	Chipper Jones	.75	.30
❑	96	J.D. Drew	.30	.10
❑	97	John Smoltz	.50	.20
❑	98	Johnny Estrada	.30	.10
❑	99	Marcus Giles	.30	.10
❑	100	Mike Hampton	.30	.10
❑	101	Nick Green	.30	.10
❑	102	Rafael Furcal	.30	.10
❑	103	Russ Ortiz	.30	.10
❑	104	Adam Loewen	.30	.10
❑	105	Brian Roberts	.30	.10
❑	106	Javy Lopez	.30	.10
❑	107	Jay Gibbons	.30	.10
❑	108	L.Bigbie UER Roberts	.30	.10
❑	109	Luis Matos	.30	.10
❑	110	Melvin Mora	.30	.10
❑	111	Miguel Tejada	.30	.10
❑	112	Rafael Palmeiro	.50	.20
❑	113	Rodrigo Lopez	.30	.10
❑	114	Sidney Ponson	.30	.10
❑	115	Bill Mueller	.30	.10
❑	116	Byung-Hyun Kim	.30	.10
❑	117	Curt Schilling	.50	.20
❑	118	David Ortiz	.75	.30
❑	119	Derek Lowe	.30	.10
❑	120	Doug Mientkiewicz	.30	.10
❑	121	Jason Varitek	.75	.30
❑	122	Johnny Damon	.50	.20
❑	123	Keith Foulke	.30	.10
❑	124	Kevin Youkilis	.30	.10
❑	125	Manny Ramirez	.50	.20
❑	126	Orlando Cabrera	.30	.10
❑	127	Pedro Martinez	.50	.20
❑	128	Trot Nixon	.30	.10
❑	129	Aramis Ramirez	.30	.10
❑	130	Carlos Zambrano	.30	.10
❑	131	Corey Patterson	.30	.10
❑	132	Derrek Lee	.50	.20
❑	133	Greg Maddux	1.25	.50
❑	134	Kerry Wood	.30	.10
❑	135	Mark Prior	.50	.20
❑	136	Matt Clement	.30	.10
❑	137	Moises Alou	.30	.10
❑	138	Nomar Garciaparra	.75	.30
❑	139	Sammy Sosa	.75	.30
❑	140	Todd Walker	.30	.10
❑	141	Angel Guzman	.30	.10
❑	142	Billy Koch	.30	.10
❑	143	Carlos Lee	.30	.10
❑	144	Frank Thomas	.75	.30
❑	145	Magglio Ordonez	.30	.10
❑	146	Mark Buehrle	.30	.10
❑	147	Paul Konerko	.30	.10
❑	148	Wilson Valdez	.30	.10
❑	149	Adam Dunn	.30	.10
❑	150	Austin Kearns	.30	.10
❑	151	Barry Larkin	.50	.20
❑	152	Benito Santiago	.30	.10
❑	153	Jason LaRue	.30	.10
❑	154	Ken Griffey Jr.	1.25	.50
❑	155	Ryan Wagner	.30	.10
❑	156	Sean Casey	.30	.10
❑	157	Brandon Phillips	.30	.10
❑	158	Brian Tallet	.30	.10
❑	159	C.C. Sabathia	.30	.10
❑	160	Cliff Lee	.30	.10
❑	161	Jeremy Guthrie	.30	.10
❑	162	Jody Gerut	.30	.10
❑	163	Matt Lawton	.30	.10
❑	164	Omar Vizquel	.50	.20
❑	165	Travis Hafner	.30	.10
❑	166	Victor Martinez	.30	.10
❑	167	Charles Johnson	.30	.10
❑	168	Garrett Atkins	.30	.10
❑	169	Jason Jennings	.30	.10
❑	170	Jay Payton	.30	.10
❑	171	Jeromy Burnitz	.30	.10
❑	172	Joe Kennedy	.30	.10
❑	173	Larry Walker	.50	.20
❑	174	Preston Wilson	.30	.10
❑	175	Todd Helton	.50	.20
❑	176	Vinny Castilla	.30	.10
❑	177	Bobby Higginson	.30	.10
❑	178	Brandon Inge	.30	.10
❑	179	Carlos Guillen	.30	.10
❑	180	Carlos Pena	.30	.10
❑	181	Craig Monroe	.30	.10
❑	182	Dmitri Young	.30	.10
❑	183	Eric Munson	.30	.10
❑	184	Fernando Vina	.30	.10
❑	185	Ivan Rodriguez	.50	.20
❑	186	Jeremy Bonderman	.30	.10
❑	187	Rondell White	.30	.10
❑	188	A.J. Burnett	.30	.10
❑	189	Dontrelle Willis	.30	.10
❑	190	Guillermo Mota	.30	.10
❑	191	Hee Seop Choi	.30	.10
❑	192	Jeff Conine	.30	.10
❑	193	Josh Beckett	.30	.10
❑	194	Juan Encarnacion	.30	.10
❑	195	Juan Pierre	.30	.10
❑	196	Luis Castillo	.30	.10
❑	197	Miguel Cabrera	.50	.20
❑	198	Mike Lowell	.30	.10
❑	199	Paul Lo Duca	.30	.10
❑	200	Andy Pettitte	.50	.20
❑	201	Brad Ausmus	.30	.10
❑	202	Carlos Beltran	.30	.10
❑	203	Chris Burke	.30	.10
❑	204	Craig Biggio	.50	.20
❑	205	Jeff Bagwell	.50	.20
❑	206	Jeff Kent	.30	.10
❑	207	Lance Berkman	.30	.10
❑	208	Morgan Ensberg	.30	.10
❑	209	Octavio Dotel	.30	.10
❑	210	Roger Clemens	1.25	.50
❑	211	Roy Oswalt	.30	.10
❑	212	Tim Redding	.30	.10
❑	213	Angel Berroa	.30	.10
❑	214	Juan Gonzalez	.30	.10
❑	215	Ken Harvey	.30	.10
❑	216	Mike Sweeney	.30	.10
❑	217	Adrian Beltre	.30	.10
❑	218	Brad Penny	.30	.10
❑	219	Eric Gagne	.30	.10
❑	220	Hideo Nomo	.75	.30
❑	221	Hong-Chih Kuo	.30	.10
❑	222	Jeff Weaver	.30	.10
❑	223	Kazuhisa Ishii	.30	.10
❑	224	Milton Bradley	.30	.10
❑	225	Shawn Green	.30	.10
❑	226	Steve Finley	.30	.10
❑	227	Danny Kolb	.30	.10
❑	228	Geoff Jenkins	.30	.10
❑	229	Junior Spivey	.30	.10
❑	230	Lyle Overbay	.30	.10
❑	231	Rickie Weeks	.30	.10
❑	232	Scott Podsednik	.30	.10
❑	233	Brad Radke	.30	.10
❑	234	Corey Koskie	.30	.10
❑	235	Cristian Guzman	.30	.10
❑	236	Dustan Mohr	.30	.10
❑	237	Eddie Guardado	.30	.10
❑	238	J.D. Durbin	.30	.10
❑	239	Jacque Jones	.30	.10
❑	240	Joe Nathan	.30	.10
❑	241	Johan Santana	.75	.30
❑	242	Lew Ford	.30	.10
❑	243	Michael Cuddyer	.30	.10
❑	244	Shannon Stewart	.30	.10
❑	245	Torii Hunter	.30	.10
❑	246	Brad Wilkerson	.30	.10
❑	247	Carl Everett	.30	.10
❑	248	Jeff Fassero	.30	.10
❑	249	Jose Vidro	.30	.10
❑	250	Livan Hernandez	.30	.10
❑	251	Michael Barrett	.30	.10
❑	252	Tony Batista	.30	.10
❑	253	Zach Day	.30	.10
❑	254	Al Leiter	.30	.10
❑	255	Cliff Floyd	.30	.10
❑	256	Jae Weong Seo	.30	.10
❑	257	John Olerud	.30	.10
❑	258	Jose Reyes	.30	.10
❑	259	Mike Cameron	.30	.10
❑	260	Mike Piazza	.75	.30
❑	261	Richard Hidalgo	.30	.10
❑	262	Tom Glavine	.50	.20
❑	263	Vance Wilson	.30	.10
❑	264	Alex Rodriguez	1.25	.50
❑	265	Armando Benitez	.30	.10
❑	266	Bernie Williams	.50	.20
❑	267	Bubba Crosby	.30	.10
❑	268	Chien-Ming Wang	1.25	.50
❑	269	Derek Jeter	1.50	.60
❑	270	Esteban Loaiza	.30	.10
❑	271	Gary Sheffield	.30	.10
❑	272	Hideki Matsui	1.25	.50
❑	273	Jason Giambi	.30	.10
❑	274	Javier Vazquez	.30	.10
❑	275	Jorge Posada	.50	.20
❑	276	Jose Contreras	.30	.10
❑	277	Kenny Lofton	.30	.10
❑	278	Kevin Brown	.30	.10
❑	279	Mariano Rivera	.75	.30
❑	280	Mike Mussina	.50	.20
❑	281	Barry Zito	.30	.10
❑	282	Bobby Crosby	.30	.10
❑	283	Eric Byrnes	.30	.10
❑	284	Eric Chavez	.30	.10
❑	285	Erubiel Durazo	.30	.10
❑	286	Jermaine Dye	.30	.10
❑	287	Mark Kotsay	.30	.10
❑	288	Mark Mulder	.30	.10
❑	289	Rich Harden	.30	.10
❑	290	Tim Hudson	.30	.10
❑	291	Billy Wagner	.30	.10
❑	292	Bobby Abreu	.30	.10
❑	293	Brett Myers	.30	.10
❑	294	Eric Milton	.30	.10
❑	295	Jim Thome	.50	.20
❑	296	Jimmy Rollins	.30	.10
❑	297	Kevin Millwood	.30	.10
❑	298	Marlon Byrd	.30	.10
❑	299	Mike Lieberthal	.30	.10
❑	300	Pat Burrell	.30	.10
❑	301	Randy Wolf	.30	.10
❑	302	Craig Wilson	.30	.10
❑	303	Jack Wilson	.30	.10
❑	304	Jacob Cruz	.30	.10

❑ 305 Jason Bay	.30	.10
❑ 306 Jason Kendall	.30	.10
❑ 307 Jose Castillo	.30	.10
❑ 308 Kip Wells	.30	.10
❑ 309 Brian Giles	.30	.10
❑ 310 Brian Lawrence	.30	.10
❑ 311 Chris Oxspring	.30	.10
❑ 312 David Wells	.30	.10
❑ 313 Freddy Guzman	.30	.10
❑ 314 Jake Peavy	.30	.10
❑ 315 Mark Loretta	.30	.10
❑ 316 Ryan Klesko	.30	.10
❑ 317 Sean Burroughs	.30	.10
❑ 318 Trevor Hoffman	.30	.10
❑ 319 Xavier Nady	.30	.10
❑ 320 A.J. Pierzynski	.30	.10
❑ 321 Edgardo Alfonzo	.30	.10
❑ 322 J.T. Snow	.30	.10
❑ 323 Jason Schmidt	.30	.10
❑ 324 Jerome Williams	.30	.10
❑ 325 Kirk Rueter	.30	.10
❑ 326 Bret Boone	.30	.10
❑ 327 Bucky Jacobsen	.30	.10
❑ 328 Edgar Martinez	.50	.20
❑ 329 Freddy Garcia	.30	.10
❑ 330 Ichiro Suzuki	1.50	.60
❑ 331 Jamie Moyer	.30	.10
❑ 332 Joel Pineiro	.30	.10
❑ 333 Scott Spiezio	.30	.10
❑ 334 Shigetoshi Hasegawa	.30	.10
❑ 335 Albert Pujols	1.50	.60
❑ 336 Edgar Renteria	.30	.10
❑ 337 Jason Isringhausen	.30	.10
❑ 338 Jim Edmonds	.30	.10
❑ 339 Matt Morris	.30	.10
❑ 340 Mike Matheny	.30	.10
❑ 341 Reggie Sanders	.30	.10
❑ 342 Scott Rolen	.50	.20
❑ 343 Woody Williams	.30	.10
❑ 344 Jeff Suppan	.30	.10
❑ 345 Aubrey Huff	.30	.10
❑ 346 Carl Crawford	.30	.10
❑ 347 Chad Gaudin	.30	.10
❑ 348 Delmon Young	.50	.20
❑ 349 Dewon Brazelton	.30	.10
❑ 350 Jose Cruz Jr.	.30	.10
❑ 351 Rocco Baldelli	.30	.10
❑ 352 Tino Martinez	.50	.20
❑ 353 Toby Hall	.30	.10
❑ 354 Alfonso Soriano	.30	.10
❑ 355 Brian Jordan	.30	.10
❑ 356 Francisco Cordero	.30	.10
❑ 357 Hank Blalock	.30	.10
❑ 358 Kenny Rogers	.30	.10
❑ 359 Kevin Mench	.30	.10
❑ 360 Laynce Nix	.30	.10
❑ 361 Mark Teixeira	.50	.20
❑ 362 Michael Young	.30	.10
❑ 363 Alex S. Gonzalez	.30	.10
❑ 364 Alexis Rios	.30	.10
❑ 365 Carlos Delgado	.30	.10
❑ 366 Eric Hinske	.30	.10
❑ 367 Frank Catalanotto	.30	.10
❑ 368 Josh Phelps	.30	.10
❑ 369 Roy Halladay	.30	.10
❑ 370 Vernon Wells	.30	.10
❑ 371 Vladimir Guerrero TC	2.00	.75
❑ 372 Randy Johnson TC	2.00	.75
❑ 373 Chipper Jones TC	2.00	.75
❑ 374 Miguel Tejada TC	2.00	.75
❑ 375 Pedro Martinez TC	2.00	.75
❑ 376 Sammy Sosa TC	2.00	.75
❑ 377 Frank Thomas TC	2.00	.75
❑ 378 Ken Griffey Jr. TC	3.00	1.25
❑ 379 Victor Martinez TC	2.00	.75
❑ 380 Todd Helton TC	2.00	.75
❑ 381 Ivan Rodriguez TC	2.00	.75
❑ 382 Miguel Cabrera TC	2.00	.75
❑ 383 Roger Clemens TC	3.00	1.25
❑ 384 Ken Harvey TC	2.00	.75
❑ 385 Eric Gagne TC	2.00	.75
❑ 386 Lyle Overbay TC	2.00	.75
❑ 387 Shannon Stewart TC	2.00	.75
❑ 388 Brad Wilkerson TC	2.00	.75
❑ 389 Mike Piazza TC	2.00	.75
❑ 390 Alex Rodriguez TC	3.00	1.25
❑ 391 Mark Mulder TC	2.00	.75
❑ 392 Jim Thome TC	2.00	.75
❑ 393 Jack Wilson TC	2.00	.75
❑ 394 Khalil Greene TC	2.00	.75
❑ 395 Jason Schmidt TC	2.00	.75
❑ 396 Ichiro Suzuki TC	4.00	1.50
❑ 397 Albert Pujols TC	4.00	1.50
❑ 398 Rocco Baldelli TC	2.00	.75
❑ 399 Alfonso Soriano TC	2.00	.75
❑ 400 Vernon Wells TC	2.00	.75

1993 Finest

❑ COMPLETE SET (199)	150.00	75.00
❑ 1 David Justice	2.50	1.00
❑ 2 Lou Whitaker	2.50	1.00
❑ 3 Bryan Harvey	1.50	.60
❑ 4 Carlos Garcia	1.50	.60
❑ 5 Sid Fernandez	1.50	.60
❑ 6 Brett Butler	2.50	1.00
❑ 7 Scott Cooper	1.50	.60
❑ 8 B.J. Surhoff	2.50	1.00
❑ 9 Steve Finley	2.50	1.00
❑ 10 Curt Schilling	2.50	1.00
❑ 11 Jeff Bagwell	4.00	1.50
❑ 12 Alex Cole	1.50	.60
❑ 13 John Olerud	2.50	1.00
❑ 14 John Smiley	1.50	.60
❑ 15 Bip Roberts	1.50	.60
❑ 16 Albert Belle	2.50	1.00
❑ 17 Duane Ward	1.50	.60
❑ 18 Alan Trammell	2.50	1.00
❑ 19 Andy Benes	1.50	.60
❑ 20 Reggie Sanders	2.50	1.00
❑ 21 Todd Zeile	1.50	.60
❑ 22 Rick Aguilera	1.50	.60
❑ 23 Dave Hollins	1.50	.60
❑ 24 Jose Rijo	1.50	.60
❑ 25 Matt Williams	2.50	1.00
❑ 26 Sandy Alomar Jr.	1.50	.60
❑ 27 Alex Fernandez	1.50	.60
❑ 28 Ozzie Smith	10.00	4.00
❑ 29 Ramon Martinez	1.50	.60
❑ 30 Bernie Williams	4.00	1.50
❑ 31 Gary Sheffield	2.50	1.00
❑ 32 Eric Karros	2.50	1.00
❑ 33 Frank Viola	2.50	1.00
❑ 34 Kevin Young	2.50	1.00
❑ 35 Ken Hill	1.50	.60
❑ 36 Tony Fernandez	1.50	.60
❑ 37 Tim Wakefield	6.00	2.50
❑ 38 John Kruk	2.50	1.00
❑ 39 Chris Sabo	1.50	.60
❑ 40 Marquis Grissom	2.50	1.00
❑ 41 Glenn Davis	1.50	.60
❑ 42 Jeff Montgomery	1.50	.60
❑ 43 Kenny Lofton	2.50	1.00
❑ 44 John Burkett	1.50	.60
❑ 45 Darryl Hamilton	1.50	.60
❑ 46 Jim Abbott	4.00	1.50
❑ 47 Ivan Rodriguez	4.00	1.50
❑ 48 Eric Young	1.50	.60
❑ 49 Mitch Williams	1.50	.60
❑ 50 Harold Reynolds	2.50	1.00
❑ 51 Brian Harper	1.50	.60
❑ 52 Rafael Palmeiro	4.00	1.50
❑ 53 Bret Saberhagen	2.50	1.00
❑ 54 Jeff Conine	2.50	1.00
❑ 55 Ivan Calderon	1.50	.60
❑ 56 Juan Guzman	1.50	.60
❑ 57 Carlos Baerga	1.50	.60
❑ 58 Charles Nagy	1.50	.60
❑ 59 Wally Joyner	2.50	1.00
❑ 60 Charlie Hayes	1.50	.60
❑ 61 Shane Mack	1.50	.60
❑ 62 Pete Harnisch	1.50	.60
❑ 63 George Brett	15.00	6.00
❑ 64 Lance Johnson	1.50	.60
❑ 65 Ben McDonald	1.50	.60
❑ 66 Bobby Bonilla	2.50	1.00
❑ 67 Terry Steinbach	1.50	.60
❑ 68 Ron Gant	2.50	1.00
❑ 69 Doug Jones	1.50	.60
❑ 70 Paul Molitor	2.50	1.00
❑ 71 Brady Anderson	2.50	1.00
❑ 72 Chuck Finley	2.50	1.00
❑ 73 Mark Grace	4.00	1.50
❑ 74 Mike Devereaux	1.50	.60
❑ 75 Tony Phillips	1.50	.60
❑ 76 Chuck Knoblauch	2.50	1.00
❑ 77 Tony Gwynn	8.00	3.00
❑ 78 Kevin Appier	2.50	1.00
❑ 79 Sammy Sosa	6.00	2.50
❑ 80 Mickey Tettleton	1.50	.60
❑ 81 Felix Jose	1.50	.60
❑ 82 Mark Langston	1.50	.60
❑ 83 Gregg Jefferies	1.50	.60
❑ 84 Andre Dawson AS	2.50	1.00
❑ 85 Greg Maddux AS	10.00	4.00
❑ 86 Rickey Henderson AS	6.00	2.50
❑ 87 Tom Glavine AS	4.00	1.50
❑ 88 Roberto Alomar AS	4.00	1.50
❑ 89 Darryl Strawberry AS	2.50	1.00
❑ 90 Wade Boggs AS	4.00	1.50
❑ 91 Bo Jackson AS	6.00	2.50
❑ 92 Mark McGwire AS	15.00	6.00
❑ 93 Robin Ventura AS	2.50	1.00
❑ 94 Joe Carter AS	2.50	1.00
❑ 95 Lee Smith AS	2.50	1.00
❑ 96 Cal Ripken AS	20.00	8.00
❑ 97 Larry Walker AS	2.50	1.00
❑ 98 Don Mattingly AS	15.00	6.00
❑ 99 Jose Canseco AS	4.00	1.50
❑ 100 Dennis Eckersley AS	2.50	1.00
❑ 101 Terry Pendleton AS	2.50	1.00
❑ 102 Frank Thomas AS	6.00	2.50
❑ 103 Barry Bonds AS	15.00	6.00
❑ 104 Roger Clemens AS	12.00	5.00
❑ 105 Ryne Sandberg AS	10.00	4.00
❑ 106 Fred McGriff AS	4.00	1.50
❑ 107 Nolan Ryan AS	25.00	10.00
❑ 108 Will Clark AS	4.00	1.50
❑ 109 Pat Listach AS	1.50	.60
❑ 110 Ken Griffey Jr. AS	10.00	4.00
❑ 111 Cecil Fielder AS	2.50	1.00
❑ 112 Kirby Puckett AS	6.00	2.50
❑ 113 Dwight Gooden AS	2.50	1.00
❑ 114 Barry Larkin AS	4.00	1.50
❑ 115 David Cone AS	2.50	1.00
❑ 116 Juan Gonzalez AS	2.50	1.00
❑ 117 Kent Hrbek	2.50	1.00
❑ 118 Tim Wallach	1.50	.60
❑ 119 Craig Biggio	4.00	1.50
❑ 120 Roberto Kelly	1.50	.60
❑ 121 Gregg Olson	1.50	.60
❑ 122 Eddie Murray	6.00	2.50
❑ 123 Wil Cordero	1.50	.60
❑ 124 Jay Buhner	2.50	1.00
❑ 125 Carlton Fisk	4.00	1.50
❑ 126 Eric Davis	2.50	1.00
❑ 127 Doug Drabek	1.50	.60
❑ 128 Ozzie Guillen	2.50	1.00
❑ 129 John Wetteland	2.50	1.00
❑ 130 Andres Galarraga	2.50	1.00
❑ 131 Ken Caminiti	2.50	1.00
❑ 132 Tom Candiotti	1.50	.60
❑ 133 Pat Borders	1.50	.60
❑ 134 Kevin Brown	2.50	1.00
❑ 135 Travis Fryman	2.50	1.00
❑ 136 Kevin Mitchell	1.50	.60
❑ 137 Greg Swindell	1.50	.60
❑ 138 Benito Santiago	2.50	1.00
❑ 139 Reggie Jefferson	1.50	.60
❑ 140 Chris Bosio	1.50	.60
❑ 141 Deion Sanders	4.00	1.50

❑ 142	Scott Erickson	1.50	.60
❑ 143	Howard Johnson	1.50	.60
❑ 144	Orestes Destrade	1.50	.60
❑ 145	Jose Guzman	1.50	.60
❑ 146	Chad Curtis	1.50	.60
❑ 147	Cal Eldred	1.50	.60
❑ 148	Willie Greene	1.50	.60
❑ 149	Tommy Greene	1.50	.60
❑ 150	Erik Hanson	1.50	.60
❑ 151	Bob Welch	1.50	.60
❑ 152	John Jaha	1.50	.60
❑ 153	Harold Baines	2.50	1.00
❑ 154	Randy Johnson	6.00	2.50
❑ 155	Al Martin	1.50	.60
❑ 156	J.T.Snow RC	4.00	1.50
❑ 157	Mike Mussina	4.00	1.50
❑ 158	Ruben Sierra	2.50	1.00
❑ 159	Dean Palmer	2.50	1.00
❑ 160	Steve Avery	1.50	.60
❑ 161	Julio Franco	2.50	1.00
❑ 162	Dave Winfield	2.50	1.00
❑ 163	Tim Salmon	4.00	1.50
❑ 164	Tom Henke	1.50	.60
❑ 165	Mo Vaughn	2.50	1.00
❑ 166	John Smoltz	4.00	1.50
❑ 167	Danny Tartabull	1.50	.60
❑ 168	Delino DeShields	1.50	.60
❑ 169	Charlie Hough	2.50	1.00
❑ 170	Paul O'Neill	4.00	1.50
❑ 171	Darren Daulton	2.50	1.00
❑ 172	Jack McDowell	1.50	.60
❑ 173	Junior Felix	1.50	.60
❑ 174	Jimmy Key	2.50	1.00
❑ 175	George Bell	1.50	.60
❑ 176	Mike Stanton	1.50	.60
❑ 177	Len Dykstra	2.50	1.00
❑ 178	Norm Charlton	1.50	.60
❑ 179	Eric Anthony	1.50	.60
❑ 180	Rob Dibble	2.50	1.00
❑ 181	Otis Nixon	1.50	.60
❑ 182	Randy Myers	1.50	.60
❑ 183	Tim Raines	2.50	1.00
❑ 184	Orel Hershiser	2.50	1.00
❑ 185	Andy Van Slyke	4.00	1.50
❑ 186	Mike Lansing RC	2.50	1.00
❑ 187	Ray Lankford	2.50	1.00
❑ 188	Mike Morgan	1.50	.60
❑ 189	Moises Alou	2.50	1.00
❑ 190	Edgar Martinez	4.00	1.50
❑ 191	John Franco	2.50	1.00
❑ 192	Robin Yount	10.00	4.00
❑ 193	Bob Tewksbury	1.50	.60
❑ 194	Jay Bell	2.50	1.00
❑ 195	Luis Gonzalez	2.50	1.00
❑ 196	Dave Fleming	1.50	.60
❑ 197	Mike Greenwell	1.50	.60
❑ 198	David Nied	1.50	.60
❑ 199	Mike Piazza	15.00	6.00

1996 Finest

❑	COMP.BRONZE SER.1 (110)	25.00	10.00
❑	COMP.BRONZE SER.2 (110)	25.00	10.00
❑	COMMON BRONZE	.50	.20
❑	COMMON GOLD	5.00	2.00
❑	COMMON G RC	5.00	2.00
❑	COMMON SILVER	2.50	1.00
❑ B5	Roberto Hernandez B	.50	.20
❑ B8	Terry Pendleton B	.50	.20
❑ B12	Ken Caminiti B	.50	.20
❑ B15	Dan Miceli B	.50	.20
❑ B16	Chipper Jones B	1.25	.50
❑ B17	John Wetteland B	.50	.20
❑ B19	Tim Naehring B	.50	.20
❑ B21	Eddie Murray B	1.25	.50
❑ B23	Kevin Appier B	.50	.20
❑ B24	Ken Griffey Jr. B	2.00	.75
❑ B26	Brian McRae B	.50	.20
❑ B27	Pedro Martinez B	.75	.30
❑ B28	Brian Jordan B	.50	.20
❑ B29	Mike Fetters B	.50	.20
❑ B30	Carlos Delgado B	.50	.20
❑ B31	Shane Reynolds B	.50	.20
❑ B32	Terry Steinbach B	.50	.20
❑ B34	Mark Leiter B	.50	.20
❑ B36	David Segui B	.50	.20
❑ B40	Fred McGriff B	.75	.30
❑ B44	Glenallen Hill B	.50	.20
❑ B45	Brady Anderson B	.50	.20
❑ B47	Jim Thome B	.75	.30
❑ B48	Frank Thomas B	1.25	.50
❑ B49	Chuck Knoblauch B	.50	.20
❑ B50	Len Dykstra B	.50	.20
❑ B53	Tom Pagnozzi B	.50	.20
❑ B55	Ricky Bones B	.50	.20
❑ B56	David Justice B	.50	.20
❑ B57	Steve Avery B	.50	.20
❑ B58	Robby Thompson B	.50	.20
❑ B61	Tony Gwynn B	1.50	.60
❑ B63	Denny Neagle B	.50	.20
❑ B67	Robin Ventura B	.50	.20
❑ B70	Kevin Seitzer B	.50	.20
❑ B71	Ramon Martinez B	.50	.20
❑ B75	Brian L.Hunter B	.50	.20
❑ B76	Alan Benes B	.50	.20
❑ B80	Ozzie Guillen B	.50	.20
❑ B82	Benji Gil B	.50	.20
❑ B85	Todd Hundley B	.50	.20
❑ B87	Pat Hentgen B	.50	.20
❑ B89	Chuck Finley B	.50	.20
❑ B92	Derek Jeter B	3.00	1.25
❑ B93	Paul O'Neill B	.75	.30
❑ B94	Darrin Fletcher B	.50	.20
❑ B96	Delino DeShields B	.50	.20
❑ B97	Tim Salmon B	.75	.30
❑ B98	John Olerud B	.50	.20
❑ B101	Tim Wakefield B	.50	.20
❑ B103	Dave Stevens B	.50	.20
❑ B104	Orlando Merced B	.50	.20
❑ B106	Jay Bell B	.50	.20
❑ B107	John Burkett B	.50	.20
❑ B108	Chris Hoiles B	.50	.20
❑ B110	Dave Nilsson B	.50	.20
❑ B111	Rod Beck B	.50	.20
❑ B113	Mike Piazza B	2.00	.75
❑ B114	Mark Langston B	.50	.20
❑ B116	Rico Brogna B	.50	.20
❑ B118	Tom Goodwin B	.50	.20
❑ B119	Bryan Rekar B	.50	.20
❑ B120	David Cone B	.50	.20
❑ B122	Andy Pettitte B	.75	.30
❑ B123	Chili Davis B	.50	.20
❑ B124	John Smoltz B	.75	.30
❑ B125	Heathcliff Slocumb B	.50	.20
❑ B126	Dante Bichette B	.50	.20
❑ B128	Alex Gonzalez B	.50	.20
❑ B129	Jeff Montgomery B	.50	.20
❑ B131	Denny Martinez B	.50	.20
❑ B132	Mel Rojas B	.50	.20
❑ B133	Derek Bell B	.50	.20
❑ B134	Trevor Hoffman B	.50	.20
❑ B136	Darren Daulton B	.50	.20
❑ B137	Pete Schourek B	.50	.20
❑ B138	Phil Nevin B	.50	.20
❑ B139	Andres Galarraga B	.50	.20
❑ B140	Chad Fonville B	.50	.20
❑ B144	J.T. Snow B	.50	.20
❑ B146	Barry Bonds B	3.00	1.25
❑ B147	Orel Hershiser B	.50	.20
❑ B148	Quilvio Veras B	.50	.20
❑ B149	Will Clark B	.75	.30
❑ B150	Jose Rijo B	.50	.20
❑ B152	Travis Fryman B	.50	.20
❑ B154	Alex Fernandez B	.50	.20
❑ B155	Wade Boggs B	.75	.30
❑ B156	Troy Percival B	.50	.20
❑ B157	Moises Alou B	.50	.20
❑ B158	Javy Lopez B	.50	.20
❑ B159	Jason Giambi B	.50	.20
❑ B162	Mark McGwire B	3.00	1.25
❑ B163	Eric Karros B	.50	.20
❑ B166	Mickey Tettleton B	.50	.20
❑ B167	Barry Larkin B	.75	.30
❑ B169	Ruben Sierra B	.50	.20
❑ B170	Bill Swift B	.50	.20
❑ B172	Chad Curtis B	.50	.20
❑ B173	Dean Palmer B	.50	.20
❑ B175	Bobby Bonilla B	.50	.20
❑ B176	Greg Colbrunn B	.50	.20
❑ B177	Jose Mesa B	.50	.20
❑ B178	Mike Greenwell B	.50	.20
❑ B181	Doug Drabek B	.50	.20
❑ B183	Wilson Alvarez B	.50	.20
❑ B184	Marty Cordova B	.50	.20
❑ B185	Hal Morris B	.50	.20
❑ B187	Carlos Garcia B	.50	.20
❑ B190	Marquis Grissom B	.50	.20
❑ B193	Will Clark B	.75	.30
❑ B194	Paul Molitor B	.50	.20
❑ B195	Kenny Rogers B	.50	.20
❑ B196	Reggie Sanders B	.50	.20
❑ B199	Raul Mondesi B	.50	.20
❑ B200	Lance Johnson B	.50	.20
❑ B201	Alvin Morman B	.50	.20
❑ B203	Jack McDowell B	.50	.20
❑ B204	Randy Myers B	.50	.20
❑ B205	Harold Baines B	.50	.20
❑ B206	Marty Cordova B	.50	.20
❑ B207	Rich Hunter B RC	.50	.20
❑ B208	Al Leiter B	.50	.20
❑ B209	Greg Gagne B	.50	.20
❑ B210	Ben McDonald B	.50	.20
❑ B212	Terry Adams B	.50	.20
❑ B213	Paul Sorrento B	.50	.20
❑ B214	Albert Belle B	.50	.20
❑ B215	Mike Blowers B	.50	.20
❑ B216	Jim Edmonds B	.50	.20
❑ B217	Felipe Crespo B	.50	.20
❑ B219	Shawon Dunston B	.50	.20
❑ B220	Jimmy Haynes B	.50	.20
❑ B221	Jose Canseco B	.75	.30
❑ B222	Eric Davis B	.50	.20
❑ B224	Tim Raines B	.50	.20
❑ B225	Tony Phillips B	.50	.20
❑ B226	Charlie Hayes B	.50	.20
❑ B227	Eric Owens B	.50	.20
❑ B228	Roberto Alomar B	.75	.30
❑ B233	Kenny Lofton B	.50	.20
❑ B236	Mark McGwire B	3.00	1.25
❑ B237	Jay Buhner B	.50	.20
❑ B238	Craig Biggio B	.75	.30
❑ B240	Barry Bonds B	3.00	1.25
❑ B244	Ron Gant B	.50	.20
❑ B245	Paul Wilson B	.50	.20
❑ B246	Todd Hollandsworth B	.50	.20
❑ B247	Todd Zeile B	.50	.20
❑ B248	David Justice B	.50	.20
❑ B250	Moises Alou B	.50	.20
❑ B251	Bob Wolcott B	.50	.20
❑ B252	David Wells B	.50	.20
❑ B253	Juan Gonzalez B	.50	.20
❑ B254	Andres Galarraga B	.50	.20
❑ B255	Dave Hollins B	.50	.20
❑ B257	Sammy Sosa B	1.25	.50
❑ B258	Ivan Rodriguez B	.75	.30
❑ B259	Bip Roberts B	.50	.20
❑ B260	Tino Martinez B	.75	.30
❑ B262	Mike Stanley B	.50	.20
❑ B264	Butch Huskey B	.50	.20
❑ B265	Jeff Conine B	.50	.20
❑ B267	Mark Grace B	.75	.30
❑ B268	Jason Schmidt B	.75	.30
❑ B269	Otis Nixon B	.50	.20
❑ B271	Kirby Puckett B	1.25	.50
❑ B273	Andy Benes B	.50	.20
❑ B275	Mike Piazza B	2.00	.75
❑ B276	Rey Ordonez B	.50	.20
❑ B278	Gary Gaetti B	.50	.20
❑ B280	Robin Ventura B	.50	.20
❑ B281	Cal Ripken B	4.00	1.50
❑ B282	Carlos Baerga B	.50	.20

❑ B283 Roger Cedeno B .50 .20
❑ B285 Terrell Wade B .50 .20
❑ B286 Kevin Brown B .50 .20
❑ B287 Rafael Palmeiro B .75 .30
❑ B288 Mo Vaughn B .50 .20
❑ B292 Bob Tewksbury B .50 .20
❑ B297 T.J. Mathews B .50 .20
❑ B298 Manny Ramirez B .75 .30
❑ B299 Jeff Bagwell B .75 .30
❑ B301 Wade Boggs B .75 .30
❑ B303 Steve Gibralter B .50 .20
❑ B304 B.J. Surhoff B .50 .20
❑ B306 Royce Clayton B .50 .20
❑ B307 Sal Fasano B .50 .20
❑ B309 Gary Sheffield B .50 .20
❑ B310 Ken Hill B .50 .20
❑ B311 Joe Girardi B .50 .20
❑ B312 Matt Lawton B RC .50 .20
❑ B314 Julio Franco B .50 .20
❑ B315 Joe Carter B .50 .20
❑ B316 Brooks Kieschnick B .50 .20
❑ B318 Heathcliff Slocumb B .50 .20
❑ B319 Barry Larkin B .75 .30
❑ B320 Tony Gwynn B 1.50 .60
❑ B322 Frank Thomas B 1.25 .50
❑ B323 Edgar Martinez B .75 .30
❑ B325 Henry Rodriguez B .50 .20
❑ B326 Marvin Benard B RC .50 .20
❑ B329 Ugueth Urbina B .50 .20
❑ B331 Roger Salkeld B .50 .20
❑ B332 Edgar Renteria B .50 .20
❑ B333 Ryan Klesko B .50 .20
❑ B334 Ray Lankford B .50 .20
❑ B336 Justin Thompson B .50 .20
❑ B339 Mark Clark B .50 .20
❑ B340 Ruben Rivera B .50 .20
❑ B342 Matt Williams B .50 .20
❑ B343 Francisco Cordova B RC .50 .20
❑ B344 Cecil Fielder B .50 .20
❑ B348 Mark Grudzielanek B .50 .20
❑ B349 Ron Coomer B .50 .20
❑ B351 Rich Aurilia B RC .50 .20
❑ B352 Jose Herrera B .50 .20
❑ B356 Tony Clark B .50 .20
❑ B358 Dan Naulty B .50 .20
❑ B359 Checklist B .50 .20
❑ G4 Marty Cordova G 5.00 2.00
❑ G6 Tony Gwynn G 15.00 6.00
❑ G9 Albert Belle G 5.00 2.00
❑ G18 Kirby Puckett G 12.00 5.00
❑ G20 Karim Garcia G 5.00 2.00
❑ G25 Cal Ripken G 40.00 15.00
❑ G33 Hideo Nomo G 12.00 5.00
❑ G39 Ryne Sandberg G 20.00 8.00
❑ G42 Jeff Bagwell G 4.00 1.50
❑ G51 Jason Isringhausen G 5.00 2.00
❑ G64 Mo Vaughn G 5.00 2.00
❑ G66 Dante Bichette G 5.00 2.00
❑ G74 Mark McGwire G 30.00 12.50
❑ G81 Kenny Lofton G 5.00 2.00
❑ G83 Jim Edmonds G 5.00 2.00
❑ G90 Mike Mussina G 8.00 3.00
❑ G100 Jeff Conine G 5.00 2.00
❑ G102 Johnny Damon G 8.00 3.00
❑ G105 Barry Bonds G 30.00 12.50
❑ G117 Jose Canseco G 8.00 3.00
❑ G135 Ken Griffey Jr. G 20.00 8.00
❑ G141 Chipper Jones G 12.00 5.00
❑ G145 Greg Maddux G 20.00 8.00
❑ G164 Jay Buhner G 5.00 2.00
❑ G186 Frank Thomas G 12.00 5.00
❑ G191 Checklist G 5.00 2.00
❑ G192 Chipper Jones G 12.00 5.00
❑ G197 Roberto Alomar G 8.00 3.00
❑ G198 Dennis Eckersley G 5.00 2.00
❑ G202 George Arias G 5.00 2.00
❑ G232 Hideo Nomo G 12.00 5.00
❑ G243 Chris Snopek G 5.00 2.00
❑ G249 Tim Salmon G 8.00 3.00
❑ G266 Matt Williams G 5.00 2.00
❑ G270 Randy Johnson G 12.00 5.00
❑ G279 Paul Molitor G 5.00 2.00
❑ G290 Cecil Fielder G 5.00 2.00
❑ G294 Livan Hernandez G RC 10.00 4.00
❑ G300 Marty Janzen G RC 5.00 2.00
❑ G308 Ron Gant G 5.00 2.00
❑ G321 Ryan Klesko G 5.00 2.00
❑ G324 Jermaine Dye G 5.00 2.00
❑ G330 Jason Giambi G 5.00 2.00
❑ G335 Edgar Martinez G 8.00 3.00
❑ G338 Rey Ordonez G 5.00 2.00
❑ G347 Sammy Sosa G 12.00 5.00
❑ G354 Juan Gonzalez G 5.00 2.00
❑ G355 Craig Biggio G 8.00 3.00
❑ S1 Greg Maddux S 10.00 4.00
❑ S2 Bernie Williams S 4.00 1.50
❑ S3 Ivan Rodriguez S 4.00 1.50
❑ S7 Barry Larkin S 4.00 1.50
❑ S10 Ray Lankford S 2.50 1.00
❑ S11 Mike Piazza S 10.00 4.00
❑ S13 Larry Walker S 2.50 1.00
❑ S14 Matt Williams S 2.50 1.00
❑ S22 Tim Salmon S 4.00 1.50
❑ S35 Edgar Martinez S 4.00 1.50
❑ S37 Gregg Jefferies S 2.50 1.00
❑ S38 Bill Pulsipher S 2.50 1.00
❑ S41 Shawn Green S 2.50 1.00
❑ S43 Jim Abbott S 4.00 1.50
❑ S46 Roger Clemens S 12.00 5.00
❑ S52 Rondell White S 2.50 1.00
❑ S54 Dennis Eckersley S 2.50 1.00
❑ S59 Hideo Nomo S 6.00 2.50
❑ S60 Gary Sheffield S 2.50 1.00
❑ S62 Will Clark S 4.00 1.50
❑ S65 Bret Boone S 2.50 1.00
❑ S68 Rafael Palmeiro S 4.00 1.50
❑ S69 Carlos Baerga S 2.50 1.00
❑ S72 Tom Glavine S 4.00 1.50
❑ S73 Garret Anderson S 2.50 1.00
❑ S77 Randy Johnson S 6.00 2.50
❑ S78 Jeff King S 2.50 1.00
❑ S79 Kirby Puckett S 6.00 2.50
❑ S84 Cecil Fielder S 2.50 1.00
❑ S86 Reggie Sanders S 2.50 1.00
❑ S88 Ryan Klesko S 2.50 1.00
❑ S91 John Valentin S 2.50 1.00
❑ S95 Manny Ramirez S 4.00 1.50
❑ S99 Vinny Castilla S 2.50 1.00
❑ S109 Carlos Perez S 2.50 1.00
❑ S112 Craig Biggio S 4.00 1.50
❑ S115 Juan Gonzalez S 2.50 1.00
❑ S121 Ray Durham S 2.50 1.00
❑ S127 C.J. Nitkowski S 2.50 1.00
❑ S130 Raul Mondesi S 2.50 1.00
❑ S142 Lee Smith S 2.50 1.00
❑ S143 Joe Carter S 2.50 1.00
❑ S151 Mo Vaughn S 2.50 1.00
❑ S153 Frank Rodriguez S 2.50 1.00
❑ S160 Steve Finley S 2.50 1.00
❑ S161 Jeff Bagwell S 4.00 1.50
❑ S165 Cal Ripken S 20.00 8.00
❑ S168 Lyle Mouton S 2.50 1.00
❑ S171 Sammy Sosa S 6.00 2.50
❑ S174 John Franco S 2.50 1.00
❑ S179 Greg Vaughn S 2.50 1.00
❑ S180 Mark Wohlers S 2.50 1.00
❑ S182 Paul O'Neill S 4.00 1.50
❑ S188 Albert Belle S 2.50 1.00
❑ S189 Mark Grace S 4.00 1.50
❑ S211 Ernie Young S 2.50 1.00
❑ S218 Fred McGriff S 4.00 1.50
❑ S223 Kimera Bartee S 2.50 1.00
❑ S229 Rickey Henderson S 6.00 2.50
❑ S230 Sterling Hitchcock S 2.50 1.00
❑ S231 Bernard Gilkey S 2.50 1.00
❑ S234 Ryne Sandberg S 10.00 4.00
❑ S235 Greg Maddux S 10.00 4.00
❑ S239 Todd Stottlemyre S 2.50 1.00
❑ S241 Jason Kendall S 2.50 1.00
❑ S242 Paul O'Neill S 4.00 1.50
❑ S256 Devon White S 2.50 1.00
❑ S261 Chuck Knoblauch S 2.50 1.00
❑ S263 Wally Joyner S 2.50 1.00
❑ S272 Andy Fox S 2.50 1.00
❑ S274 Sean Berry S 2.50 1.00
❑ S277 Benito Santiago S 2.50 1.00
❑ S284 Chad Mottola S 2.50 1.00
❑ S289 Dante Bichette S 2.50 1.00
❑ S291 Dwight Gooden S 2.50 1.00
❑ S293 Kevin Mitchell S 2.50 1.00
❑ S295 Russ Davis S 2.50 1.00
❑ S296 Chan Ho Park S 2.50 1.00
❑ S302 Larry Walker S 2.50 1.00
❑ S305 Ken Griffey Jr. S 10.00 4.00
❑ S313 Billy Wagner S 2.50 1.00
❑ S317 Mike Grace S RC 2.50 1.00
❑ S327 Kenny Lofton S 2.50 1.00
❑ S328 Derek Bell S 2.50 1.00
❑ S337 Gary Sheffield S 2.50 1.00
❑ S341 Mark Grace S 4.00 1.50
❑ S345 Andres Galarraga S 2.50 1.00
❑ S346 Brady Anderson S 2.50 1.00
❑ S350 Derek Jeter S 12.00 5.00
❑ S353 Jay Buhner S 2.50 1.00
❑ S357 Tino Martinez S 4.00 1.50

1999 Finest

❑ COMPLETE SET (300) 80.00 30.00
❑ COMPLETE SERIES 1 (150) 40.00 15.00
❑ COMPLETE SERIES 2 (150) 40.00 15.00
❑ COMP.SER.1 w/o SP's (100) 15.00 6.00
❑ COMP.SER.2 w/o SP's (100) 15.00 6.00
❑ COMMON (1-100/151-250) .40 .15
❑ COMMON (101-150/251-300) .50 .20
❑ 1 Darin Erstad .40 .15
❑ 2 Javy Lopez .40 .15
❑ 3 Vinny Castilla .40 .15
❑ 4 Jim Thome .60 .25
❑ 5 Tino Martinez .60 .25
❑ 6 Mark Grace .60 .25
❑ 7 Shawn Green .40 .15
❑ 8 Dustin Hermanson .40 .15
❑ 9 Kevin Young .40 .15
❑ 10 Tony Clark .40 .15
❑ 11 Scott Brosius .40 .15
❑ 12 Craig Biggio .60 .25
❑ 13 Brian McRae .40 .15
❑ 14 Chan Ho Park .40 .15
❑ 15 Manny Ramirez .60 .25
❑ 16 Chipper Jones 1.00 .40
❑ 17 Rico Brogna .40 .15
❑ 18 Quinton McCracken .40 .15
❑ 19 J.T. Snow .40 .15
❑ 20 Tony Gwynn 1.25 .50
❑ 21 Juan Guzman .40 .15
❑ 22 John Valentin .40 .15
❑ 23 Rick Helling .40 .15
❑ 24 Sandy Alomar Jr. .40 .15
❑ 25 Frank Thomas 1.00 .40
❑ 26 Jorge Posada .60 .25
❑ 27 Dmitri Young .40 .15
❑ 28 Rick Reed .40 .15
❑ 29 Kevin Tapani .40 .15
❑ 30 Troy Glaus .60 .25
❑ 31 Kenny Rogers .40 .15
❑ 32 Jeromy Burnitz .40 .15
❑ 33 Mark Grudzielanek .40 .15
❑ 34 Mike Mussina .60 .25
❑ 35 Scott Rolen .60 .25
❑ 36 Neifi Perez .40 .15
❑ 37 Brad Radke .40 .15
❑ 38 Darryl Strawberry .40 .15
❑ 39 Robb Nen .40 .15
❑ 40 Moises Alou .40 .15
❑ 41 Eric Young .40 .15
❑ 42 Livan Hernandez .40 .15
❑ 43 John Wetteland .40 .15
❑ 44 Matt Lawton .40 .15
❑ 45 Ben Grieve .40 .15
❑ 46 Fernando Tatis .40 .15

❑ 47 Travis Fryman .40 .15
❑ 48 David Segui .40 .15
❑ 49 Bob Abreu .40 .15
❑ 50 Nomar Garciaparra 1.50 .60
❑ 51 Paul O'Neill .60 .25
❑ 52 Jeff King .40 .15
❑ 53 Francisco Cordova .40 .15
❑ 54 John Olerud .40 .15
❑ 55 Vladimir Guerrero 1.00 .40
❑ 56 Fernando Vina .40 .15
❑ 57 Shane Reynolds .40 .15
❑ 58 Chuck Finley .40 .15
❑ 59 Rondell White .40 .15
❑ 60 Greg Vaughn .40 .15
❑ 61 Ryan Minor .40 .15
❑ 62 Tom Gordon .40 .15
❑ 63 Damion Easley .40 .15
❑ 64 Ray Durham .40 .15
❑ 65 Orlando Hernandez .40 .15
❑ 66 Bartolo Colon .40 .15
❑ 67 Jaret Wright .40 .15
❑ 68 Royce Clayton .40 .15
❑ 69 Tim Salmon .60 .25
❑ 70 Mark McGwire 2.50 1.00
❑ 71 Alex Gonzalez .40 .15
❑ 72 Tom Glavine .60 .25
❑ 73 David Justice .40 .15
❑ 74 Omar Vizquel .60 .25
❑ 75 Juan Gonzalez .40 .15
❑ 76 Bobby Higginson .40 .15
❑ 77 Todd Walker .40 .15
❑ 78 Dante Bichette .40 .15
❑ 79 Kevin Millwood .40 .15
❑ 80 Roger Clemens 2.00 .75
❑ 81 Kerry Wood .40 .15
❑ 82 Cal Ripken 3.00 1.25
❑ 83 Jay Bell .40 .15
❑ 84 Barry Bonds 2.50 1.00
❑ 85 Alex Rodriguez 1.50 .60
❑ 86 Doug Glanville .40 .15
❑ 87 Jason Kendall .40 .15
❑ 88 Sean Casey .40 .15
❑ 89 Aaron Sele .40 .15
❑ 90 Derek Jeter 2.50 1.00
❑ 91 Andy Ashby .40 .15
❑ 92 Rusty Greer .40 .15
❑ 93 Rod Beck .40 .15
❑ 94 Matt Williams .40 .15
❑ 95 Mike Piazza 1.50 .60
❑ 96 Wally Joyner .40 .15
❑ 97 Barry Larkin .60 .25
❑ 98 Eric Milton .40 .15
❑ 99 Gary Sheffield .40 .15
❑ 100 Greg Maddux 1.50 .60
❑ 101 Ken Griffey Jr. GEM 2.50 1.00
❑ 102 Frank Thomas GEM 1.50 .60
❑ 103 Nomar Garciaparra GEM 2.50 1.00
❑ 104 Mark McGwire GEM 4.00 1.50
❑ 105 Alex Rodriguez GEM 2.50 1.00
❑ 106 Tony Gwynn GEM 2.00 .75
❑ 107 Juan Gonzalez GEM .60 .25
❑ 108 Jeff Bagwell GEM 1.00 .40
❑ 109 Sammy Sosa GEM 1.50 .60
❑ 110 Vladimir Guerrero GEM 1.50 .60
❑ 111 Roger Clemens GEM 3.00 1.25
❑ 112 Barry Bonds GEM 4.00 1.50
❑ 113 Darin Erstad GEM .60 .25
❑ 114 Mike Piazza GEM 2.50 1.00
❑ 115 Derek Jeter GEM 4.00 1.50
❑ 116 Chipper Jones GEM 1.50 .60
❑ 117 Larry Walker GEM .60 .25
❑ 118 Scott Rolen GEM 1.00 .40
❑ 119 Cal Ripken GEM 5.00 2.00
❑ 120 Greg Maddux GEM 2.50 1.00
❑ 121 Troy Glaus SENS 1.00 .40
❑ 122 Ben Grieve SENS .50 .20
❑ 123 Ryan Minor SENS .50 .20
❑ 124 Kerry Wood SENS .60 .25
❑ 125 Travis Lee SENS .50 .20
❑ 126 Adrian Beltre SENS .60 .25
❑ 127 Brad Fullmer SENS .50 .20
❑ 128 Aramis Ramirez SENS .60 .25
❑ 129 Eric Chavez SENS .60 .25
❑ 130 Todd Helton SENS 1.00 .40
❑ 131 Pat Burrell RC 3.00 1.25
❑ 132 Ryan Mills RC .50 .20
❑ 133 Austin Kearns RC 3.00 1.25
❑ 134 Josh McKinley RC .50 .20
❑ 135 Adam Everett RC 1.00 .40
❑ 136 Marlon Anderson .50 .20
❑ 137 Bruce Chen .50 .20
❑ 138 Matt Clement .60 .25
❑ 139 Alex Gonzalez .50 .20
❑ 140 Roy Halladay .60 .25
❑ 141 Calvin Pickering .50 .20
❑ 142 Randy Wolf .50 .20
❑ 143 Ryan Anderson .50 .20
❑ 144 Ruben Mateo .50 .20
❑ 145 Alex Escobar RC .60 .25
❑ 146 Jeremy Giambi .50 .20
❑ 147 Lance Berkman .60 .25
❑ 148 Michael Barrett .50 .20
❑ 149 Preston Wilson .60 .25
❑ 150 Gabe Kapler .60 .25
❑ 151 Roger Clemens 2.00 .75
❑ 152 Jay Buhner .40 .15
❑ 153 Brad Fullmer .40 .15
❑ 154 Ray Lankford .40 .15
❑ 155 Jim Edmonds .40 .15
❑ 156 Jason Giambi .40 .15
❑ 157 Bret Boone .40 .15
❑ 158 Jeff Cirillo .40 .15
❑ 159 Rickey Henderson 1.00 .40
❑ 160 Edgar Martinez .60 .25
❑ 161 Ron Gant .40 .15
❑ 162 Mark Kotsay .40 .15
❑ 163 Trevor Hoffman .40 .15
❑ 164 Jason Schmidt .40 .15
❑ 165 Brett Tomko .40 .15
❑ 166 David Ortiz 1.00 .40
❑ 167 Dean Palmer .40 .15
❑ 168 Hideki Irabu .40 .15
❑ 169 Mike Cameron .40 .15
❑ 170 Pedro Martinez .60 .25
❑ 171 Tom Goodwin .40 .15
❑ 172 Brian Hunter .40 .15
❑ 173 Al Leiter .40 .15
❑ 174 Charles Johnson .40 .15
❑ 175 Curt Schilling .40 .15
❑ 176 Robin Ventura .40 .15
❑ 177 Travis Lee .40 .15
❑ 178 Jeff Shaw .40 .15
❑ 179 Ugueth Urbina .40 .15
❑ 180 Roberto Alomar .60 .25
❑ 181 Cliff Floyd .40 .15
❑ 182 Adrian Beltre .40 .15
❑ 183 Tony Womack .40 .15
❑ 184 Brian Jordan .40 .15
❑ 185 Randy Johnson 1.00 .40
❑ 186 Mickey Morandini .40 .15
❑ 187 Todd Hundley .40 .15
❑ 188 Jose Valentin .40 .15
❑ 189 Eric Davis .40 .15
❑ 190 Ken Caminiti .40 .15
❑ 191 David Wells .40 .15
❑ 192 Ryan Klesko .40 .15
❑ 193 Garret Anderson .40 .15
❑ 194 Eric Karros .40 .15
❑ 195 Ivan Rodriguez .60 .25
❑ 196 Aramis Ramirez .40 .15
❑ 197 Mike Lieberthal .40 .15
❑ 198 Will Clark .60 .25
❑ 199 Rey Ordonez .40 .15
❑ 200 Ken Griffey Jr. 1.50 .60
❑ 201 Jose Guillen .40 .15
❑ 202 Scott Erickson .40 .15
❑ 203 Paul Konerko .40 .15
❑ 204 Johnny Damon .60 .25
❑ 205 Larry Walker .40 .15
❑ 206 Denny Neagle .40 .15
❑ 207 Jose Offerman .40 .15
❑ 208 Andy Pettitte .60 .25
❑ 209 Bobby Jones .40 .15
❑ 210 Kevin Brown .60 .25
❑ 211 John Smoltz .60 .25
❑ 212 Henry Rodriguez .40 .15
❑ 213 Tim Belcher .40 .15
❑ 214 Carlos Delgado .40 .15
❑ 215 Andruw Jones .60 .25
❑ 216 Andy Benes .40 .15
❑ 217 Fred McGriff .60 .25
❑ 218 Edgar Renteria .40 .15
❑ 219 Miguel Tejada .40 .15
❑ 220 Bernie Williams .60 .25
❑ 221 Justin Thompson .40 .15
❑ 222 Marty Cordova .40 .15
❑ 223 Delino DeShields .40 .15
❑ 224 Ellis Burks .40 .15
❑ 225 Kenny Lofton .40 .15
❑ 226 Steve Finley .40 .15
❑ 227 Eric Chavez .40 .15
❑ 228 Jose Cruz Jr. .40 .15
❑ 229 Marquis Grissom .40 .15
❑ 230 Jeff Bagwell .60 .25
❑ 231 Jose Canseco .60 .25
❑ 232 Edgardo Alfonzo .40 .15
❑ 233 Richie Sexson .40 .15
❑ 234 Jeff Kent .40 .15
❑ 235 Rafael Palmeiro .60 .25
❑ 236 David Cone .40 .15
❑ 237 Gregg Jefferies .40 .15
❑ 238 Mike Lansing .40 .15
❑ 239 Mariano Rivera 1.00 .40
❑ 240 Albert Belle .40 .15
❑ 241 Chuck Knoblauch .40 .15
❑ 242 Derek Bell .40 .15
❑ 243 Pat Hentgen .40 .15
❑ 244 Andres Galarraga .40 .15
❑ 245 Mo Vaughn .40 .15
❑ 246 Wade Boggs .60 .25
❑ 247 Devon White .40 .15
❑ 248 Todd Helton .60 .25
❑ 249 Raul Mondesi .40 .15
❑ 250 Sammy Sosa 1.00 .40
❑ 251 Nomar Garciaparra ST 2.50 1.00
❑ 252 Mark McGwire ST 4.00 1.50
❑ 253 Alex Rodriguez ST 2.50 1.00
❑ 254 Juan Gonzalez ST .60 .25
❑ 255 Vladimir Guerrero ST 1.50 .60
❑ 256 Ken Griffey Jr. ST 2.50 1.00
❑ 257 Mike Piazza ST 2.50 1.00
❑ 258 Derek Jeter ST 4.00 1.50
❑ 259 Albert Belle ST .60 .25
❑ 260 Greg Vaughn ST .50 .20
❑ 261 Sammy Sosa ST 1.50 .60
❑ 262 Greg Maddux ST 2.50 1.00
❑ 263 Frank Thomas ST 1.50 .60
❑ 264 Mark Grace ST 1.00 .40
❑ 265 Ivan Rodriguez ST 1.00 .40
❑ 266 Roger Clemens GM 3.00 1.25
❑ 267 Mo Vaughn GM .60 .25
❑ 268 Jim Thome GM 1.00 .40
❑ 269 Darin Erstad GM .60 .25
❑ 270 Chipper Jones GM 1.50 .60
❑ 271 Larry Walker GM .60 .25
❑ 272 Cal Ripken GM 5.00 2.00
❑ 273 Scott Rolen GM 1.00 .40
❑ 274 Randy Johnson GM 1.50 .60
❑ 275 Tony Gwynn GM 2.00 .75
❑ 276 Barry Bonds GM 4.00 1.50
❑ 277 Sean Burroughs RC 1.00 .40
❑ 278 J.M. Gold RC .50 .20
❑ 279 Carlos Lee .60 .25
❑ 280 George Lombard .50 .20
❑ 281 Carlos Beltran 1.00 .40
❑ 282 Fernando Seguignol .50 .20
❑ 283 Eric Chavez .60 .25
❑ 284 Carlos Pena RC .75 .30
❑ 285 Corey Patterson RC 1.50 .60
❑ 286 Alfonso Soriano RC 8.00 3.00
❑ 287 Nick Johnson RC 1.50 .60
❑ 288 Jorge Toca RC .60 .25
❑ 289 A.J. Burnett RC 1.50 .60
❑ 290 Andy Brown RC .50 .20
❑ 291 Doug Mientkiewicz RC 1.00 .40
❑ 292 Bobby Seay RC .50 .20
❑ 293 Chip Ambres RC .50 .20
❑ 294 C.C. Sabathia RC 3.00 1.25
❑ 295 Choo Freeman RC .60 .25
❑ 296 Eric Valent RC .60 .25
❑ 297 Matt Belisle RC .50 .20
❑ 298 Jason Tyner RC .50 .20
❑ 299 Masao Kida RC .60 .25
❑ 300 H.Aaron/M.McGwire 3.00 1.25

2000 Finest

Card		
❑ COMP.SERIES 1 w/o SP's (100)	25.00	10.00
❑ COMP.SERIES 2 w/o SP's (100)	25.00	10.00
❑ COMMON (1-100/147-246)	.40	.15
❑ COMMON ROOKIE (101-120)	5.00	2.00
❑ COMMON FEATURES (121-135)	1.50	.60
❑ COMM.GEM (136-145/277-286)	2.00	.75
❑ COMMON ROOKIE (247-266)	5.00	2.00
❑ COMMON COUNTER (267-276)	1.00	.40
❑ 1 Nomar Garciaparra	1.50	.60
❑ 2 Chipper Jones	1.00	.40
❑ 3 Erubiel Durazo	.40	.15
❑ 4 Robin Ventura	.60	.25
❑ 5 Garret Anderson	.40	.15
❑ 6 Dean Palmer	.40	.15
❑ 7 Mariano Rivera	1.00	.40
❑ 8 Rusty Greer	.40	.15
❑ 9 Jim Thome	.60	.25
❑ 10 Jeff Bagwell	.60	.25
❑ 11 Jason Giambi	.40	.15
❑ 12 Jeromy Burnitz	.40	.15
❑ 13 Mark Grace	.60	.25
❑ 14 Russ Ortiz	.40	.15
❑ 15 Kevin Brown	.60	.25
❑ 16 Kevin Millwood	.40	.15
❑ 17 Scott Williamson	.40	.15
❑ 18 Orlando Hernandez	.40	.15
❑ 19 Todd Walker	.40	.15
❑ 20 Carlos Beltran	.40	.15
❑ 21 Ruben Rivera	.40	.15
❑ 22 Curt Schilling	.40	.15
❑ 23 Brian Giles	.40	.15
❑ 24 Eric Karros	.40	.15
❑ 25 Preston Wilson	.40	.15
❑ 26 Al Leiter	.40	.15
❑ 27 Juan Encarnacion	.40	.15
❑ 28 Tim Salmon	.60	.25
❑ 29 B.J. Surhoff	.40	.15
❑ 30 Bernie Williams	.60	.25
❑ 31 Lee Stevens	.40	.15
❑ 32 Pokey Reese	.40	.15
❑ 33 Mike Sweeney	.40	.15
❑ 34 Corey Koskie	.40	.15
❑ 35 Roberto Alomar	.60	.25
❑ 36 Tim Hudson	.40	.15
❑ 37 Tom Glavine	.60	.25
❑ 38 Jeff Kent	.40	.15
❑ 39 Mike Lieberthal	.40	.15
❑ 40 Barry Larkin	.60	.25
❑ 41 Paul O'Neill	.60	.25
❑ 42 Rico Brogna	.40	.15
❑ 43 Brian Daubach	.40	.15
❑ 44 Rich Aurilia	.40	.15
❑ 45 Vladimir Guerrero	1.00	.40
❑ 46 Luis Castillo	.40	.15
❑ 47 Bartolo Colon	.40	.15
❑ 48 Kevin Appier	.40	.15
❑ 49 Mo Vaughn	.40	.15
❑ 50 Alex Rodriguez	1.50	.60
❑ 51 Randy Johnson	1.00	.40
❑ 52 Kris Benson	.40	.15
❑ 53 Tony Clark	.40	.15
❑ 54 Chad Allen	.40	.15
❑ 55 Larry Walker	.40	.15
❑ 56 Freddy Garcia	.40	.15
❑ 57 Paul Konerko	.40	.15
❑ 58 Edgardo Alfonzo	.40	.15
❑ 59 Brady Anderson	.40	.15
❑ 60 Derek Jeter	2.50	1.00
❑ 61 John Smoltz	.60	.25
❑ 62 Doug Glanville	.40	.15
❑ 63 Shannon Stewart	.40	.15
❑ 64 Greg Maddux	1.50	.60
❑ 65 Mark McGwire	2.50	1.00
❑ 66 Gary Sheffield	.40	.15
❑ 67 Kevin Young	.40	.15
❑ 68 Tony Gwynn	1.25	.50
❑ 69 Rey Ordonez	.40	.15
❑ 70 Cal Ripken	3.00	1.25
❑ 71 Todd Helton	.60	.25
❑ 72 Brian Jordan	.40	.15
❑ 73 Jose Canseco	.60	.25
❑ 74 Luis Gonzalez	.40	.15
❑ 75 Barry Bonds	2.50	1.00
❑ 76 Jermaine Dye	.40	.15
❑ 77 Jose Offerman	.40	.15
❑ 78 Magglio Ordonez	.40	.15
❑ 79 Fred Mcgriff	.60	.25
❑ 80 Ivan Rodriguez	.60	.25
❑ 81 Josh Hamilton	1.00	.40
❑ 82 Vernon Wells	.40	.15
❑ 83 Mark Mulder	.40	.15
❑ 84 John Patterson	.40	.15
❑ 85 Nick Johnson	.40	.15
❑ 86 Pablo Ozuna	.40	.15
❑ 87 A.J. Burnett	.40	.15
❑ 88 Jack Cust	.40	.15
❑ 89 Adam Piatt	.40	.15
❑ 90 Rob Ryan	.40	.15
❑ 91 Sean Burroughs	.40	.15
❑ 92 D'Angelo Jimenez	.40	.15
❑ 93 Chad Hermansen	.40	.15
❑ 94 Robert Fick	.40	.15
❑ 95 Ruben Mateo	.40	.15
❑ 96 Alex Escobar	.40	.15
❑ 97 Wily Pena	.40	.15
❑ 98 Corey Patterson	.40	.15
❑ 99 Eric Munson	.40	.15
❑ 100 Pat Burrell	.40	.15
❑ 101 Michael Tejera RC	5.00	2.00
❑ 102 Bobby Bradley RC	5.00	2.00
❑ 103 Larry Bigbie RC	8.00	3.00
❑ 104 B.J. Garbe RC	5.00	2.00
❑ 105 Josh Kalinowski RC	5.00	2.00
❑ 106 Brett Myers RC	8.00	3.00
❑ 107 Chris Mears RC	5.00	2.00
❑ 108 Aaron Rowand RC	10.00	4.00
❑ 109 Corey Myers RC	5.00	2.00
❑ 110 John Sneed RC	5.00	2.00
❑ 111 Ryan Christianson RC	5.00	2.00
❑ 112 Kyle Snyder	5.00	2.00
❑ 113 Mike Paradis	5.00	2.00
❑ 114 Chance Caple RC	5.00	2.00
❑ 115 Ben Christensen RC	5.00	2.00
❑ 116 Brad Baker RC	5.00	2.00
❑ 117 Rob Purvis RC	5.00	2.00
❑ 118 Rick Asadoorian RC	5.00	2.00
❑ 119 Ruben Salazar RC	5.00	2.00
❑ 120 Julio Zuleta RC	5.00	2.00
❑ 121 A.Rodriguez/K.Griffey Jr.	2.50	1.00
❑ 122 N.Garciaparra/D.Jeter	3.00	1.25
❑ 123 M.McGwire/S.Sosa	4.00	1.50
❑ 124 R.Johnson/P.Martinez	2.50	1.00
❑ 125 I.Rodriguez/M.Piazza	2.50	1.00
❑ 126 M.Ramirez/R.Alomar	1.50	.60
❑ 127 C.Jones/A.Jones	2.50	1.00
❑ 128 C.Ripken/T.Gwynn	5.00	2.00
❑ 129 J.Bagwell/C.Biggio	1.50	.60
❑ 130 B.Bonds/V.Guerrero	4.00	1.50
❑ 131 N.Johnson/A.Soriano	2.50	1.00
❑ 132 J.Hamilton/P.Burrell	5.00	2.00
❑ 133 C.Patterson/R.Mateo	1.50	.60
❑ 134 L.Walker/T.Helton	1.50	.60
❑ 135 R.Ordonez/E.Alfonzo	1.50	.60
❑ 136 Derek Jeter GEM	8.00	3.00
❑ 137 Alex Rodriguez GEM	5.00	2.00
❑ 138 Chipper Jones GEM	5.00	2.00
❑ 139 Mike Piazza GEM	5.00	2.00
❑ 140 Mark McGwire GEM	8.00	3.00
❑ 141 Ivan Rodriguez GEM	3.00	1.25
❑ 142 Cal Ripken GEM	10.00	4.00
❑ 143 Vladimir Guerrero GEM	5.00	2.00
❑ 144 Randy Johnson GEM	5.00	2.00
❑ 145 Jeff Bagwell GEM	3.00	1.25
❑ 146 Ken Griffey Jr. ACTION	1.50	.60
❑ 146A Ken Griffey Jr. PORT	1.50	.60
❑ 147 Andruw Jones	.60	.25
❑ 148 Kerry Wood	.40	.15
❑ 149 Jim Edmonds	.40	.15
❑ 150 Pedro Martinez	.60	.25
❑ 151 Warren Morris	.40	.15
❑ 152 Trevor Hoffman	.40	.15
❑ 153 Ryan Klesko	.40	.15
❑ 154 Andy Pettitte	.60	.25
❑ 155 Frank Thomas	1.00	.40
❑ 156 Damion Easley	.40	.15
❑ 157 Cliff Floyd	.40	.15
❑ 158 Ben Davis	.40	.15
❑ 159 John Valentin	.40	.15
❑ 160 Rafael Palmeiro	.60	.25
❑ 161 Andy Ashby	.40	.15
❑ 162 J.D. Drew	.40	.15
❑ 163 Jay Bell	.40	.15
❑ 164 Adam Kennedy	.40	.15
❑ 165 Manny Ramirez	.60	.25
❑ 166 John Halama	.40	.15
❑ 167 Octavio Dotel	.40	.15
❑ 168 Darin Erstad	.40	.15
❑ 169 Jose Lima	.40	.15
❑ 170 Andres Galarraga	.40	.15
❑ 171 Scott Rolen	.60	.25
❑ 172 Delino DeShields	.40	.15
❑ 173 J.T. Snow	.40	.15
❑ 174 Tony Womack	.40	.15
❑ 175 John Olerud	.40	.15
❑ 176 Jason Kendall	.40	.15
❑ 177 Carlos Lee	.40	.15
❑ 178 Eric Milton	.40	.15
❑ 179 Jeff Cirillo	.40	.15
❑ 180 Gabe Kapler	.40	.15
❑ 181 Greg Vaughn	.40	.15
❑ 182 Denny Neagle	.40	.15
❑ 183 Tino Martinez	.60	.25
❑ 184 Doug Mientkiewicz	.40	.15
❑ 185 Juan Gonzalez	.40	.15
❑ 186 Ellis Burks	.40	.15
❑ 187 Mike Hampton	.40	.15
❑ 188 Royce Clayton	.40	.15
❑ 189 Mike Mussina	.60	.25
❑ 190 Carlos Delgado	.40	.15
❑ 191 Ben Grieve	.40	.15
❑ 192 Fernando Tatis	.40	.15
❑ 193 Matt Williams	.40	.15
❑ 194 Rondell White	.40	.15
❑ 195 Shawn Green	.40	.15
❑ 196 Hideki Irabu	.40	.15
❑ 197 Troy Glaus	.40	.15
❑ 198 Roger Cedeno	.40	.15
❑ 199 Ray Lankford	.40	.15
❑ 200 Sammy Sosa	1.00	.40
❑ 201 Kenny Lofton	.40	.15
❑ 202 Edgar Martinez	.60	.25
❑ 203 Mark Kotsay	.40	.15
❑ 204 David Wells	.40	.15
❑ 205 Craig Biggio	.60	.25
❑ 206 Ray Durham	.40	.15
❑ 207 Troy O'Leary	.40	.15
❑ 208 Rickey Henderson	1.00	.40
❑ 209 Bob Abreu	.40	.15
❑ 210 Neifi Perez	.40	.15
❑ 211 Carlos Febles	.40	.15
❑ 212 Chuck Knoblauch	.40	.15
❑ 213 Moises Alou	.40	.15
❑ 214 Omar Vizquel	.60	.25
❑ 215 Vinny Castilla	.40	.15
❑ 216 Javy Lopez	.40	.15
❑ 217 Johnny Damon	.60	.25
❑ 218 Roger Clemens	2.00	.75
❑ 219 Miguel Tejada	.40	.15
❑ 220 Carl Everett	.40	.15
❑ 221 Matt Lawton	.40	.15
❑ 222 Albert Belle	.40	.15
❑ 223 Adrian Beltre	.40	.15
❑ 224 Dante Bichette	.40	.15
❑ 225 Raul Mondesi	.40	.15
❑ 226 Mike Piazza	1.50	.60
❑ 227 Brad Penny	.40	.15
❑ 228 Kip Wells	.40	.15
❑ 229 Adam Everett	.40	.15

❑ 230 Eddie Yarnall .40 .15
❑ 231 Matt LeCroy .40 .15
❑ 232 Jason Tyner .40 .15
❑ 233 Rick Ankiel .40 .15
❑ 234 Lance Berkman .40 .15
❑ 235 Rafael Furcal .40 .15
❑ 236 Dee Brown .40 .15
❑ 237 Gookie Dawkins .40 .15
❑ 238 Eric Valent .40 .15
❑ 239 Peter Bergeron .40 .15
❑ 240 Alfonso Soriano 1.00 .40
❑ 241 Adam Dunn 1.00 .40
❑ 242 Jorge Toca .40 .15
❑ 243 Ryan Anderson .40 .15
❑ 244 Jason Deliaero .40 .15
❑ 245 Jason Grilli .40 .15
❑ 246 Milton Bradley .40 .15
❑ 247 Scott Downs RC 5.00 2.00
❑ 248 Keith Reed RC 5.00 2.00
❑ 249 Edgar Cruz RC 5.00 2.00
❑ 250 Wes Anderson RC 5.00 2.00
❑ 251 Lyle Overbay RC 8.00 3.00
❑ 252 Mike Lamb RC 8.00 3.00
❑ 253 Vince Faison RC 5.00 2.00
❑ 254 Chad Alexander 5.00 2.00
❑ 255 Chris Wakeland RC 5.00 2.00
❑ 256 Aaron McNeal RC 5.00 2.00
❑ 257 Tomo Ohka RC 5.00 2.00
❑ 258 Ty Howington RC 5.00 2.00
❑ 259 Javier Colina RC 5.00 2.00
❑ 260 Jason Jennings 5.00 2.00
❑ 261 Ramon Santiago RC 5.00 2.00
❑ 262 Johan Santana RC 100.00 60.00
❑ 263 Quincy Foster RC 5.00 2.00
❑ 264 Junior Brignac RC 5.00 2.00
❑ 265 Rico Washington RC 5.00 2.00
❑ 266 Scott Sobkowiak RC 5.00 2.00
❑ 267 P.Martinez/R.Ankiel 1.50 .60
❑ 268 M.Ramirez/V.Guerrero 2.50 1.00
❑ 269 A.Burnett/M.Mulder 1.00 .40
❑ 270 M.Piazza/E.Munson 2.50 1.00
❑ 271 J.Hamilton/C.Patterson 1.50 .60
❑ 272 K.Griffey Jr./S.Sosa 2.00 .75
❑ 273 D.Jeter/A.Soriano 4.00 1.50
❑ 274 M.McGwire/P.Burrell 4.00 1.50
❑ 275 C.Jones/C.Ripken 4.00 1.50
❑ 276 N.Garciaparra/A.Rodriguez 2.50 1.00
❑ 277 Pedro Martinez GEM 3.00 1.25
❑ 278 Tony Gwynn GEM 4.00 1.50
❑ 279 Barry Bonds GEM 8.00 3.00
❑ 280 Juan Gonzalez GEM 2.00 .75
❑ 281 Larry Walker GEM 2.00 .75
❑ 282 Nomar Garciaparra GEM 5.00 2.00
❑ 283 Ken Griffey Jr. GEM 5.00 2.00
❑ 284 Manny Ramirez GEM 3.00 1.25
❑ 285 Shawn Green GEM 2.00 .75
❑ 286 Sammy Sosa GEM 5.00 2.00
❑ NNO Graded Gems Ser.1 EXCH/10
❑ NNO Graded Gems Ser.2 EXCH/10

2001 Finest

❑ COMP.SET w/o SP's (100) 25.00 10.00
❑ COMMON CARD (1-110) .40 .15
❑ COMMON SP 10.00 4.00
❑ COMMON PROSPECT (111-140) 10.00 4.00
❑ 1 Mike Piazza SP 20.00 8.00
❑ 2 Andruw Jones .60 .25
❑ 3 Jason Giambi .40 .15
❑ 4 Fred McGriff .60 .25
❑ 5 Vladimir Guerrero SP 10.00 4.00
❑ 6 Adrian Gonzalez .40 .15
❑ 7 Pedro Martinez .60 .25
❑ 8 Mike Lieberthal .40 .15
❑ 9 Warren Morris .40 .15
❑ 10 Juan Gonzalez .40 .15
❑ 11 Jose Canseco .60 .25
❑ 12 Jose Valentin .40 .15
❑ 13 Jeff Cirillo .40 .15
❑ 14 Pokey Reese .40 .15
❑ 15 Scott Rolen .60 .25
❑ 16 Greg Maddux 1.50 .60
❑ 17 Carlos Delgado .40 .15
❑ 18 Rick Ankiel .40 .15
❑ 19 Steve Finley .40 .15
❑ 20 Shawn Green .40 .15
❑ 21 Orlando Cabrera .40 .15
❑ 22 Roberto Alomar .60 .25
❑ 23 John Olerud .40 .15
❑ 24 Albert Belle .40 .15
❑ 25 Edgardo Alfonzo .40 .15
❑ 26 Rafael Palmeiro .60 .25
❑ 27 Mike Sweeney .40 .15
❑ 28 Bernie Williams .60 .25
❑ 29 Larry Walker .40 .15
❑ 30 Barry Bonds SP 25.00 10.00
❑ 31 Orlando Hernandez .40 .15
❑ 32 Randy Johnson 1.00 .40
❑ 33 Shannon Stewart .40 .15
❑ 34 Mark Grace .60 .25
❑ 35 Alex Rodriguez SP 25.00 10.00
❑ 36 Tino Martinez .60 .25
❑ 37 Carlos Febles .40 .15
❑ 38 Al Leiter .40 .15
❑ 39 Omar Vizquel .60 .25
❑ 40 Chuck Knoblauch .40 .15
❑ 41 Tim Salmon .60 .25
❑ 42 Brian Jordan .40 .15
❑ 43 Edgar Renteria .40 .15
❑ 44 Preston Wilson .40 .15
❑ 45 Mariano Rivera 1.00 .40
❑ 46 Gabe Kapler .40 .15
❑ 47 Jason Kendall .40 .15
❑ 48 Rickey Henderson 1.00 .40
❑ 49 Luis Gonzalez .40 .15
❑ 50 Tom Glavine .60 .25
❑ 51 Jeromy Burnitz .40 .15
❑ 52 Garret Anderson .40 .15
❑ 53 Craig Biggio .60 .25
❑ 54 Vinny Castilla .40 .15
❑ 55 Jeff Kent .40 .15
❑ 56 Gary Sheffield .40 .15
❑ 57 Jorge Posada .60 .25
❑ 58 Sean Casey .40 .15
❑ 59 Johnny Damon .60 .25
❑ 60 Dean Palmer .40 .15
❑ 61 Todd Helton .60 .25
❑ 62 Barry Larkin .60 .25
❑ 63 Robin Ventura .40 .15
❑ 64 Kenny Lofton .40 .15
❑ 65 Sammy Sosa SP 10.00 4.00
❑ 66 Rafael Furcal .40 .15
❑ 67 Jay Bell .40 .15
❑ 68 J.T. Snow .40 .15
❑ 69 Jose Vidro .40 .15
❑ 70 Ivan Rodriguez .60 .25
❑ 71 Jermaine Dye .40 .15
❑ 72 Chipper Jones SP 10.00 4.00
❑ 73 Fernando Vina .40 .15
❑ 74 Ben Grieve .40 .15
❑ 75 Mark McGwire SP 25.00 10.00
❑ 76 Matt Williams .40 .15
❑ 77 Mark Grudzielanek .40 .15
❑ 78 Mike Hampton .40 .15
❑ 79 Brian Giles .40 .15
❑ 80 Tony Gwynn 1.25 .50
❑ 81 Carlos Beltran .40 .15
❑ 82 Ray Durham .40 .15
❑ 83 Brad Radke .40 .15
❑ 84 David Justice .40 .15
❑ 85 Frank Thomas 1.00 .40
❑ 86 Todd Zeile .40 .15
❑ 87 Pat Burrell .40 .15
❑ 88 Jim Thome .60 .25
❑ 89 Greg Vaughn .40 .15
❑ 90 Ken Griffey Jr. SP 15.00 6.00
❑ 91 Mike Mussina .60 .25
❑ 92 Magglio Ordonez .40 .15
❑ 93 Bob Abreu .40 .15
❑ 94 Alex Gonzalez .40 .15
❑ 95 Kevin Brown .40 .15
❑ 96 Jay Buhner .40 .15
❑ 97 Roger Clemens 2.00 .75
❑ 98 Nomar Garciaparra SP 15.00 6.00
❑ 99 Derrek Lee .60 .25
❑ 100 Derek Jeter SP 25.00 10.00
❑ 101 Adrian Beltre .40 .15
❑ 102 Geoff Jenkins .40 .15
❑ 103 Javy Lopez .40 .15
❑ 104 Raul Mondesi .40 .15
❑ 105 Troy Glaus .40 .15
❑ 106 Jeff Bagwell .60 .25
❑ 107 Eric Karros .40 .15
❑ 108 Mo Vaughn .40 .15
❑ 109 Cal Ripken 3.00 1.25
❑ 110 Manny Ramirez Sox .60 .25
❑ 111 Scott Heard PROS 10.00 4.00
❑ 112 Luis Montanez PROS RC 10.00 4.00
❑ 113 Ben Diggins PROS 10.00 4.00
❑ 114 Shaun Boyd PROS RC 10.00 4.00
❑ 115 Sean Burnett PROS 10.00 4.00
❑ 116 Carmen Cali PROS RC 10.00 4.00
❑ 117 Derek Thompson PROS 10.00 4.00
❑ 118 David Parrish PROS RC 10.00 4.00
❑ 119 Dominic Rich PROS RC 10.00 4.00
❑ 120 Chad Petty PROS RC 10.00 4.00
❑ 121 Steve Smyth PROS RC 10.00 4.00
❑ 122 John Lackey PROS 10.00 4.00
❑ 123 Matt Galante PROS RC 10.00 4.00
❑ 124 Danny Borrell PROS RC 10.00 4.00
❑ 125 Bob Keppel PROS RC 10.00 4.00
❑ 126 Justin Wayne PROS RC 10.00 4.00
❑ 127 J.R. House PROS 10.00 4.00
❑ 128 Brian Sellier PROS RC 10.00 4.00
❑ 129 Dan Moylan PROS RC 10.00 4.00
❑ 130 Scott Pratt PROS RC 10.00 4.00
❑ 131 Victor Hall PROS RC 10.00 4.00
❑ 132 Joel Pineiro PROS 10.00 4.00
❑ 133 Josh Axelson PROS RC 10.00 4.00
❑ 134 Jose Reyes PROS RC 150.00 90.00
❑ 135 Greg Runser PROS RC 10.00 4.00
❑ 136 Bryan Hebson PROS RC 10.00 4.00
❑ 137 Sammy Serrano PROS RC 10.00 4.00
❑ 138 Kevin Joseph PROS RC 10.00 4.00
❑ 139 Juan Richardson PROS RC 10.00 4.00
❑ 140 Mark Fischer PROS RC 10.00 4.00

2002 Finest

❑ COMP.SET w/o SP's (100) 25.00 10.00
❑ COMMON CARD (1-100) .50 .20
❑ COMMON CARD (101-110) 10.00 4.00
❑ 1 Mike Mussina .75 .30
❑ 2 Steve Sparks .50 .20
❑ 3 Randy Johnson 1.25 .50
❑ 4 Orlando Cabrera .50 .20
❑ 5 Jeff Kent .50 .20
❑ 6 Carlos Delgado .50 .20
❑ 7 Ivan Rodriguez .75 .30
❑ 8 Jose Cruz .50 .20
❑ 9 Jason Giambi .50 .20
❑ 10 Brad Penny .50 .20
❑ 11 Moises Alou .50 .20
❑ 12 Mike Piazza 2.00 .75

Card		
❑ 13 Ben Grieve	.50	.20
❑ 14 Derek Jeter	3.00	1.25
❑ 15 Roy Oswalt	.50	.20
❑ 16 Pat Burrell	.50	.20
❑ 17 Preston Wilson	.50	.20
❑ 18 Kevin Brown	.50	.20
❑ 19 Barry Bonds	3.00	1.25
❑ 20 Phil Nevin	.50	.20
❑ 21 Aramis Ramirez	.50	.20
❑ 22 Carlos Beltran	.50	.20
❑ 23 Chipper Jones	1.25	.50
❑ 24 Curt Schilling	.50	.20
❑ 25 Jorge Posada	.75	.30
❑ 26 Alfonso Soriano	.50	.20
❑ 27 Cliff Floyd	.50	.20
❑ 28 Rafael Palmeiro	.75	.30
❑ 29 Terrence Long	.50	.20
❑ 30 Ken Griffey Jr.	2.00	.75
❑ 31 Jason Kendall	.50	.20
❑ 32 Jose Vidro	.50	.20
❑ 33 Jermaine Dye	.50	.20
❑ 34 Bobby Higginson	.50	.20
❑ 35 Albert Pujols	2.50	1.00
❑ 36 Miguel Tejada	.50	.20
❑ 37 Jim Edmonds	.50	.20
❑ 38 Barry Zito	.50	.20
❑ 39 Jimmy Rollins	.50	.20
❑ 40 Rafael Furcal	.50	.20
❑ 41 Omar Vizquel	.75	.30
❑ 42 Kazuhiro Sasaki	.50	.20
❑ 43 Brian Giles	.50	.20
❑ 44 Darin Erstad	.50	.20
❑ 45 Mariano Rivera	1.25	.50
❑ 46 Troy Percival	.50	.20
❑ 47 Mike Sweeney	.50	.20
❑ 48 Vladimir Guerrero	1.25	.50
❑ 49 Troy Glaus	.50	.20
❑ 50 So Taguchi RC	2.50	1.00
❑ 51 Edgardo Alfonzo	.50	.20
❑ 52 Roger Clemens	2.50	1.00
❑ 53 Eric Chavez	.50	.20
❑ 54 Alex Rodriguez	2.00	.75
❑ 55 Cristian Guzman	.50	.20
❑ 56 Jeff Bagwell	.75	.30
❑ 57 Bernie Williams	.75	.30
❑ 58 Kerry Wood	.50	.20
❑ 59 Ryan Klesko	.50	.20
❑ 60 Ichiro Suzuki	2.50	1.00
❑ 61 Larry Walker	.50	.20
❑ 62 Nomar Garciaparra	2.00	.75
❑ 63 Craig Biggio	.75	.30
❑ 64 J.D. Drew	.50	.20
❑ 65 Juan Pierre	.50	.20
❑ 66 Roberto Alomar	.75	.30
❑ 67 Luis Gonzalez	.50	.20
❑ 68 Bud Smith	.50	.20
❑ 69 Magglio Ordonez	.50	.20
❑ 70 Scott Rolen	.75	.30
❑ 71 Tsuyoshi Shinjo	.50	.20
❑ 72 Paul Konerko	.50	.20
❑ 73 Garret Anderson	.50	.20
❑ 74 Tim Hudson	.50	.20
❑ 75 Adam Dunn	.50	.20
❑ 76 Gary Sheffield	.50	.20
❑ 77 Johnny Damon Sox	.75	.30
❑ 78 Todd Helton	.75	.30
❑ 79 Geoff Jenkins	.50	.20
❑ 80 Shawn Green	.50	.20
❑ 81 C.C. Sabathia	.50	.20
❑ 82 Kazuhisa Ishii RC	2.50	1.00
❑ 83 Rich Aurilia	.50	.20
❑ 84 Mike Hampton	.50	.20
❑ 85 Ben Sheets	.50	.20
❑ 86 Andruw Jones	.75	.30
❑ 87 Richie Sexson	.50	.20
❑ 88 Jim Thome	.75	.30
❑ 89 Sammy Sosa	1.25	.50
❑ 90 Greg Maddux	2.00	.75
❑ 91 Pedro Martinez	.75	.30
❑ 92 Jeromy Burnitz	.50	.20
❑ 93 Raul Mondesi	.50	.20
❑ 94 Bret Boone	.50	.20
❑ 95 Jerry Hairston	.50	.20
❑ 96 Mike Rivera	.50	.20
❑ 97 Juan Cruz	.50	.20
❑ 98 Morgan Ensberg	.50	.20
❑ 99 Nathan Haynes	.50	.20
❑ 100 Xavier Nady	.50	.20
❑ 101 Nic Jackson FY AU RC	10.00	4.00
❑ 102 Mauricio Lara FY AU RC	10.00	4.00
❑ 103 Freddy Sanchez FY AU RC	30.00	12.50
❑ 104 Clint Nageotte FY AU RC	10.00	4.00
❑ 105 Beltran Perez FY AU RC	10.00	4.00
❑ 106 Garrett Gentry FY AU RC	10.00	4.00
❑ 107 Chad Qualls FY AU RC	10.00	4.00
❑ 108 Jason Bay FY AU RC	60.00	30.00
❑ 109 Michael Hill FY AU RC	10.00	4.00
❑ 110 Brian Tallet FY AU RC	10.00	4.00

2003 Finest

Card		
❑ COMP.SET w/o SP's (100)	25.00	10.00
❑ COMMON CARD (1-100)	.50	.20
❑ COMMON CARD (101-110)	15.00	6.00
❑ 1 Sammy Sosa	1.25	.50
❑ 2 Paul Konerko	.50	.20
❑ 3 Todd Helton	.75	.30
❑ 4 Mike Lowell	.50	.20
❑ 5 Lance Berkman	.50	.20
❑ 6 Kazuhisa Ishii	.50	.20
❑ 7 A.J. Pierzynski	.50	.20
❑ 8 Jose Vidro	.50	.20
❑ 9 Roberto Alomar	.75	.30
❑ 10 Derek Jeter	3.00	1.25
❑ 11 Barry Zito	.50	.20
❑ 12 Jimmy Rollins	.50	.20
❑ 13 Brian Giles	.50	.20
❑ 14 Ryan Klesko	.50	.20
❑ 15 Rich Aurilia	.50	.20
❑ 16 Jim Edmonds	.50	.20
❑ 17 Aubrey Huff	.50	.20
❑ 18 Ivan Rodriguez	.75	.30
❑ 19 Eric Hinske	.50	.20
❑ 20 Barry Bonds	3.00	1.25
❑ 21 Darin Erstad	.50	.20
❑ 22 Curt Schilling	.50	.20
❑ 23 Andruw Jones	.75	.30
❑ 24 Jay Gibbons	.50	.20
❑ 25 Nomar Garciaparra	2.00	.75
❑ 26 Kerry Wood	.50	.20
❑ 27 Magglio Ordonez	.50	.20
❑ 28 Austin Kearns	.50	.20
❑ 29 Jason Jennings	.50	.20
❑ 30 Jason Giambi	.50	.20
❑ 31 Tim Hudson	.50	.20
❑ 32 Edgar Martinez	.75	.30
❑ 33 Carl Crawford	.50	.20
❑ 34 Hee Seop Choi	.50	.20
❑ 35 Vladimir Guerrero	1.25	.50
❑ 36 Jeff Kent	.50	.20
❑ 37 John Smoltz	.75	.30
❑ 38 Frank Thomas	1.25	.50
❑ 39 Cliff Floyd	.50	.20
❑ 40 Mike Piazza	2.00	.75
❑ 41 Mark Prior	.75	.30
❑ 42 Tim Salmon	.75	.30
❑ 43 Shawn Green	.50	.20
❑ 44 Bernie Williams	.75	.30
❑ 45 Jim Thome	.75	.30
❑ 46 John Olerud	.50	.20
❑ 47 Orlando Hudson	.50	.20
❑ 48 Mark Teixeira	.75	.30
❑ 49 Gary Sheffield	.50	.20
❑ 50 Ichiro Suzuki	2.50	1.00
❑ 51 Tom Glavine	.75	.30
❑ 52 Torii Hunter	.50	.20
❑ 53 Craig Biggio	.75	.30
❑ 54 Carlos Beltran	.50	.20
❑ 55 Bartolo Colon	.50	.20
❑ 56 Jorge Posada	.75	.30
❑ 57 Pat Burrell	.50	.20
❑ 58 Edgar Renteria	.50	.20
❑ 59 Rafael Palmeiro	.75	.30
❑ 60 Alfonso Soriano	.50	.20
❑ 61 Brandon Phillips	.50	.20
❑ 62 Luis Gonzalez	.50	.20
❑ 63 Manny Ramirez	.75	.30
❑ 64 Garret Anderson	.50	.20
❑ 65 Ken Griffey Jr.	2.00	.75
❑ 66 A.J. Burnett	.50	.20
❑ 67 Mike Sweeney	.50	.20
❑ 68 Doug Mientkiewicz	.50	.20
❑ 69 Eric Chavez	.50	.20
❑ 70 Adam Dunn	.50	.20
❑ 71 Shea Hillenbrand	.50	.20
❑ 72 Troy Glaus	.50	.20
❑ 73 Rodrigo Lopez	.50	.20
❑ 74 Moises Alou	.50	.20
❑ 75 Chipper Jones	1.25	.50
❑ 76 Bobby Abreu	.50	.20
❑ 77 Mark Mulder	.50	.20
❑ 78 Kevin Brown	.50	.20
❑ 79 Josh Beckett	.50	.20
❑ 80 Larry Walker	.50	.20
❑ 81 Randy Johnson	1.25	.50
❑ 82 Greg Maddux	2.00	.75
❑ 83 Johnny Damon	.75	.30
❑ 84 Omar Vizquel	.75	.30
❑ 85 Jeff Bagwell	.75	.30
❑ 86 Carlos Pena	.50	.20
❑ 87 Roy Oswalt	.50	.20
❑ 88 Richie Sexson	.50	.20
❑ 89 Roger Clemens	2.50	1.00
❑ 90 Miguel Tejada	.50	.20
❑ 91 Vicente Padilla	.50	.20
❑ 92 Phil Nevin	.50	.20
❑ 93 Edgardo Alfonzo	.50	.20
❑ 94 Bret Boone	.50	.20
❑ 95 Albert Pujols	2.50	1.00
❑ 96 Carlos Delgado	.50	.20
❑ 97 Jose Contreras RC	2.00	.75
❑ 98 Scott Rolen	.75	.30
❑ 99 Pedro Martinez	.75	.30
❑ 100 Alex Rodriguez	2.00	.75
❑ 101 Adam LaRoche AU	15.00	6.00
❑ 102 Andy Marte AU RC	50.00	25.00
❑ 103 Daryl Clark AU RC	10.00	4.00
❑ 104 J.D. Durbin AU RC	10.00	4.00
❑ 105 Craig Brazell AU RC	10.00	4.00
❑ 106 Brian Burgamy AU RC	10.00	4.00
❑ 107 Tyler Johnson AU RC	10.00	4.00
❑ 108 Joey Gomes AU RC	10.00	4.00
❑ 109 Bryan Bullington AU RC	15.00	6.00
❑ 110 Byron Gettis AU RC	10.00	4.00

2004 Finest

Card		
❑ COMP.SET w/o SP's (100)	25.00	10.00
❑ COMMON CARD (1-100)	.50	.20
❑ COMMON CARD (101-110)	8.00	3.00
❑ 101-110 STATED ODDS 1:7 MINI-BOXES		
❑ COMMON CARD (111-122)	10.00	4.00
❑ 111-122 STATED ODDS 1:3 MINI-BOXES		
❑ EXCHANGE DEADLINE 04/30/06		

❑ CARD 112 EXCH UNABLE TO BE FULFILLED
❑ 04 WS HL B.THOMSON AU SENT INSTEAD
❑ 1 Juan Pierre .50 .20
❑ 2 Derek Jeter 2.50 1.00
❑ 3 Garret Anderson .50 .20
❑ 4 Javy Lopez .50 .20
❑ 5 Corey Patterson .50 .20
❑ 6 Todd Helton .75 .30
❑ 7 Roy Oswalt .50 .20
❑ 8 Shawn Green .50 .20
❑ 9 Vladimir Guerrero 1.25 .50
❑ 10 Jorge Posada .75 .30
❑ 11 Jason Kendall .50 .20
❑ 12 Scott Rolen .75 .30
❑ 13 Randy Johnson 1.25 .50
❑ 14 Bill Mueller .50 .20
❑ 15 Magglio Ordonez .50 .20
❑ 16 Larry Walker .50 .20
❑ 17 Lance Berkman .50 .20
❑ 18 Richie Sexson .50 .20
❑ 19 Orlando Cabrera .50 .20
❑ 20 Alfonso Soriano .50 .20
❑ 21 Kevin Millwood .50 .20
❑ 22 Edgar Martinez .75 .30
❑ 23 Aubrey Huff .50 .20
❑ 24 Carlos Delgado .50 .20
❑ 25 Vernon Wells .50 .20
❑ 26 Mark Teixeira .75 .30
❑ 27 Troy Glaus .50 .20
❑ 28 Jeff Kent .50 .20
❑ 29 Hideo Nomo 1.25 .50
❑ 30 Torii Hunter .50 .20
❑ 31 Hank Blalock .50 .20
❑ 32 Brandon Webb .50 .20
❑ 33 Tony Batista .50 .20
❑ 34 Bret Boone .50 .20
❑ 35 Ryan Klesko .50 .20
❑ 36 Barry Zito .50 .20
❑ 37 Edgar Renteria .50 .20
❑ 38 Geoff Jenkins .50 .20
❑ 39 Jeff Bagwell .75 .30
❑ 40 Dontrelle Willis .75 .30
❑ 41 Adam Dunn .50 .20
❑ 42 Mark Buehrle .50 .20
❑ 43 Esteban Loaiza .50 .20
❑ 44 Angel Berroa .50 .20
❑ 45 Ivan Rodriguez .75 .30
❑ 46 Jose Vidro .50 .20
❑ 47 Mark Mulder .50 .20
❑ 48 Roger Clemens 2.50 1.00
❑ 49 Jim Edmonds .50 .20
❑ 50 Eric Gagne .50 .20
❑ 51 Marcus Giles .50 .20
❑ 52 Curt Schilling .75 .30
❑ 53 Ken Griffey Jr. 2.00 .75
❑ 54 Jason Schmidt .50 .20
❑ 55 Miguel Tejada .50 .20
❑ 56 Dmitri Young .50 .20
❑ 57 Mike Lowell .50 .20
❑ 58 Mike Sweeney .50 .20
❑ 59 Scott Podsednik .50 .20
❑ 60 Miguel Cabrera .75 .30
❑ 61 Johan Santana 1.25 .50
❑ 62 Bernie Williams .75 .30
❑ 63 Eric Chavez .50 .20
❑ 64 Bobby Abreu .50 .20
❑ 65 Brian Giles .50 .20
❑ 66 Michael Young .50 .20
❑ 67 Paul Lo Duca .50 .20
❑ 68 Austin Kearns .50 .20
❑ 69 Jody Gerut .50 .20
❑ 70 Kerry Wood .50 .20
❑ 71 Luis Matos .50 .20
❑ 72 Greg Maddux 2.00 .75
❑ 73 Alex Rodriguez Yanks 2.00 .75
❑ 74 Mike Lieberthal .50 .20
❑ 75 Jim Thome .75 .30
❑ 76 Javier Vazquez .50 .20
❑ 77 Bartolo Colon .50 .20
❑ 78 Manny Ramirez .75 .30
❑ 79 Jacque Jones .50 .20
❑ 80 Johnny Damon .75 .30
❑ 81 Carlos Beltran .50 .20
❑ 82 C.C. Sabathia .50 .20
❑ 83 Preston Wilson .50 .20
❑ 84 Luis Castillo .50 .20
❑ 85 Kevin Brown .50 .20
❑ 86 Shannon Stewart .50 .20
❑ 87 Cliff Floyd .50 .20
❑ 88 Mike Mussina .75 .30
❑ 89 Rafael Furcal .50 .20
❑ 90 Roy Halladay .50 .20
❑ 91 Frank Thomas 1.25 .50
❑ 92 Melvin Mora .50 .20
❑ 93 Andruw Jones .75 .30
❑ 94 Luis Gonzalez .50 .20
❑ 95 David Ortiz 1.25 .50
❑ 96 Gary Sheffield .50 .20
❑ 97 Tim Hudson .50 .20
❑ 98 Phil Nevin .50 .20
❑ 99 Ichiro Suzuki 2.50 1.00
❑ 100 Albert Pujols 2.50 1.00
❑ 101 Nomar Garciaparra SR Jsy 15.00 6.00
❑ 102 Sammy Sosa SR Jsy 10.00 4.00
❑ 103 Josh Beckett SR Jsy 8.00 3.00
❑ 104 Jason Giambi SR Jsy 8.00 3.00
❑ 105 Rocco Baldelli SR Jsy 8.00 3.00
❑ 106 Jose Reyes SR Jsy 8.00 3.00
❑ 107 Chipper Jones SR Jsy 10.00 4.00
❑ 108 Pedro Martinez SR Jsy 10.00 4.00
❑ 109 Mike Piazza SR Jsy 15.00 6.00
❑ 110 Mark Prior SR Jsy 10.00 4.00
❑ 111 Craig Ansman AU RC 10.00 4.00
❑ 113 David Murphy AU RC 10.00 4.00
❑ 114 Jason Hirsh AU RC 25.00 10.00
❑ 115 Matt Moses AU RC 15.00 6.00
❑ 116 Estee Harris AU RC 15.00 6.00
❑ 117 Logan Kensing AU RC 10.00 4.00
❑ 118 L.Milledge AU RC 50.00 20.00
❑ 119 Merkin Valdez AU RC 10.00 4.00
❑ 120 Travis Blackley AU RC 10.00 4.00
❑ 121 Vito Chiaravalloti AU RC 10.00 4.00
❑ 122 Dioner Navarro AU RC 10.00 4.00

2005 Finest

❑ COMP.SET w/o SP's (150) 80.00 40.00
❑ COMMON CARD (1-140) .50 .20
❑ COMMON CARD (157-166) 1.00 .40
❑ AU p/r 970 ODDS 1:3 MINI BOXES
❑ AU p/r 970 PRINT RUN 970 #'d SETS
❑ AU p/r 375 ODDS 1:41 MINI BOXES
❑ AU p/r 375 PRINT RUN 375 #'d SETS
❑ OVERALL PLATE ODDS 1:51 MINI BOX
❑ OVERALL AU PLATE ODDS 1:478 MINI BOX
❑ PLATE PRINT RUN 1 SET PER COLOR
❑ BLACK-CYAN-MAGENTA-YELLOW ISSUED
❑ NO PLATE PRICING DUE TO SCARCITY
❑ 1 Alexis Rios .50 .20
❑ 2 Hank Blalock .50 .20
❑ 3 Bobby Abreu .50 .20
❑ 4 Curt Schilling .75 .30
❑ 5 Albert Pujols 2.50 1.00
❑ 6 Aaron Rowand .50 .20
❑ 7 B.J. Upton .50 .20
❑ 8 Andruw Jones .75 .30
❑ 9 Jeff Francis .50 .20
❑ 10 Sammy Sosa 1.25 .50
❑ 11 Aramis Ramirez .50 .20
❑ 12 Carl Pavano .50 .20
❑ 13 Bartolo Colon .50 .20
❑ 14 Greg Maddux 2.00 .75
❑ 15 Scott Kazmir .50 .20
❑ 16 Melvin Mora .50 .20
❑ 17 Brandon Backe .50 .20
❑ 18 Bobby Crosby .50 .20
❑ 19 Carlos Lee .50 .20
❑ 20 Carl Crawford .50 .20
❑ 21 Brian Giles .50 .20
❑ 22 Jeff Bagwell .75 .30
❑ 23 J.D. Drew .50 .20
❑ 24 C.C. Sabathia .50 .20
❑ 25 Alfonso Soriano .50 .20
❑ 26 Chipper Jones 1.25 .50
❑ 27 Austin Kearns .50 .20
❑ 28 Carlos Delgado .50 .20
❑ 29 Jack Wilson .50 .20
❑ 30 Dmitri Young .50 .20
❑ 31 Carlos Guillen .50 .20
❑ 32 Jim Thome .75 .30
❑ 33 Eric Chavez .50 .20
❑ 34 Jason Schmidt .50 .20
❑ 35 Brad Radke .50 .20
❑ 36 Frank Thomas 1.25 .50
❑ 37 Darin Erstad .50 .20
❑ 38 Javier Vazquez .50 .20
❑ 39 Garret Anderson .50 .20
❑ 40 David Ortiz 1.25 .50
❑ 41 Javy Lopez .50 .20
❑ 42 Geoff Jenkins .50 .20
❑ 43 Jose Vidro .50 .20
❑ 44 Aubrey Huff .50 .20
❑ 45 Bernie Williams .75 .30
❑ 46 Dontrelle Willis .50 .20
❑ 47 Jim Edmonds .50 .20
❑ 48 Ivan Rodriguez .75 .30
❑ 49 Gary Sheffield .50 .20
❑ 50 Alex Rodriguez 2.00 .75
❑ 51 John Buck .50 .20
❑ 52 Andy Pettitte .75 .30
❑ 53 Ichiro Suzuki 2.50 1.00
❑ 54 Johnny Estrada .50 .20
❑ 55 Jake Peavy .50 .20
❑ 56 Carlos Zambrano .50 .20
❑ 57 Jose Reyes .50 .20
❑ 58 Bret Boone .50 .20
❑ 59 Jason Bay .50 .20
❑ 60 David Wright 2.00 .75
❑ 61 Jeromy Burnitz .50 .20
❑ 62 Corey Patterson .50 .20
❑ 63 Juan Pierre .50 .20
❑ 64 Zack Greinke .50 .20
❑ 65 Mike Lowell .50 .20
❑ 66 Ken Griffey Jr. 2.00 .75
❑ 67 Marcus Giles .50 .20
❑ 68 Edgar Renteria .50 .20
❑ 69 Ken Harvey .50 .20
❑ 70 Pedro Martinez .75 .30
❑ 71 Johnny Damon .75 .30
❑ 72 Lyle Overbay .50 .20
❑ 73 Mike Maroth .50 .20
❑ 74 Jorge Posada .75 .30
❑ 75 Carlos Beltran .50 .20
❑ 76 Mark Buehrle .50 .20
❑ 77 Khalil Greene .75 .30
❑ 78 Josh Beckett .50 .20
❑ 79 Mark Loretta .50 .20
❑ 80 Rafael Palmeiro .75 .30
❑ 81 Justin Morneau .50 .20
❑ 82 Rocco Baldelli .50 .20
❑ 83 Ben Sheets .50 .20
❑ 84 Kerry Wood .50 .20
❑ 85 Miguel Tejada .50 .20
❑ 86 Magglio Ordonez .50 .20
❑ 87 Livan Hernandez .50 .20
❑ 88 Kazuo Matsui .50 .20
❑ 89 Manny Ramirez .75 .30
❑ 90 Hideki Matsui 2.00 .75
❑ 91 Jeff Kent .50 .20
❑ 92 Matt Lawton .50 .20
❑ 93 Richie Sexson .50 .20
❑ 94 Mike Mussina .75 .30
❑ 95 Adam Dunn .50 .20
❑ 96 Johan Santana 1.25 .50
❑ 97 Nomar Garciaparra 1.25 .50
❑ 98 Michael Young .50 .20
❑ 99 Victor Martinez .50 .20
❑ 100 Barry Bonds 3.00 1.25
❑ 101 Oliver Perez .50 .20
❑ 102 Randy Johnson 1.25 .50
❑ 103 Mark Mulder .50 .20

❑ 104 Pat Burrell .50 .20
❑ 105 Mike Sweeney .50 .20
❑ 106 Mark Teixeira .75 .30
❑ 107 Paul Lo Duca .50 .20
❑ 108 Jon Lieber .50 .20
❑ 109 Mike Piazza 1.25 .50
❑ 110 Roger Clemens 2.00 .75
❑ 111 Rafael Furcal .50 .20
❑ 112 Troy Glaus .50 .20
❑ 113 Miguel Cabrera .75 .30
❑ 114 Randy Wolf .50 .20
❑ 115 Lance Berkman .50 .20
❑ 116 Mark Prior .75 .30
❑ 117 Rich Harden .50 .20
❑ 118 Preston Wilson .50 .20
❑ 119 Roy Oswalt .50 .20
❑ 120 Luis Gonzalez .50 .20
❑ 121 Ronnie Belliard .50 .20
❑ 122 Sean Casey .50 .20
❑ 123 Barry Zito .50 .20
❑ 124 Larry Walker .75 .30
❑ 125 Derek Jeter 2.50 1.00
❑ 126 Tim Hudson .50 .20
❑ 127 Tom Glavine .75 .30
❑ 128 Scott Rolen .75 .30
❑ 129 Torii Hunter .50 .20
❑ 130 Paul Konerko .50 .20
❑ 131 Shawn Green .50 .20
❑ 132 Travis Hafner .50 .20
❑ 133 Vernon Wells .50 .20
❑ 134 Sidney Ponson .50 .20
❑ 135 Vladimir Guerrero 1.25 .50
❑ 136 Mark Kotsay .50 .20
❑ 137 Todd Helton .75 .30
❑ 138 Adrian Beltre .50 .20
❑ 139 Wily Mo Pena .50 .20
❑ 140 Joe Mauer 1.25 .50
❑ 141 Brian Stavisky AU/970 RC 10.00 4.00
❑ 142 Nate McLouth AU/970 RC 15.00 6.00
❑ 143 Glen Perkins AU/375 RC 20.00 8.00
❑ 144 Chip Cannon AU/970 RC 20.00 8.00
❑ 145 Shane Costa AU/970 RC 10.00 4.00
❑ 146 W.Swackhamer AU/970 RC 10.00 4.00
❑ 147 Kevin Melillo AU/970 RC 15.00 6.00
❑ 148 Billy Butler AU/970 RC 50.00 25.00
❑ 149 Landon Powell AU/970 RC 15.00 6.00
❑ 150 Scott Mathieson AU/970 RC 10.00 4.00
❑ 151 Chris Roberson AU/970 10.00 4.00
❑ 152 Chad Orvella AU/375 RC 15.00 6.00
❑ 153 Eric Nielsen AU/970 RC 10.00 4.00
❑ 154 Matt Campbell AU/970 RC 10.00 4.00
❑ 155 Mike Rogers AU/970 RC 10.00 4.00
❑ 156 Melky Cabrera AU/970 RC 40.00 20.00
❑ 157 Nolan Ryan RET 5.00 2.00
❑ 158 Bo Jackson RET 2.00 .75
❑ 159 Wade Boggs RET 1.50 .60
❑ 160 Andre Dawson RET 1.00 .40
❑ 161 Dave Winfield RET 1.00 .40
❑ 162 Reggie Jackson RET 1.50 .60
❑ 163 David Justice RET 2.00 .75
❑ 164 Dale Murphy RET 1.50 .60
❑ 165 Paul O'Neill RET 1.50 .60
❑ 166 Tom Seaver RET 1.50 .60

2006 Finest

❑ COMPLETE SET (155)
❑ COMP.SET w/o AU's (140) 60.00 30.00
❑ COMMON CARD (1-131) .50 .20
❑ UNLISTED STARS 1-131 1.25 .50
❑ COMMON ROOKIE (132-140) .75 .30
❑ COMMON AUTO (141-155) 10.00 4.00
❑ 141-155 AU ODDS 1:4 MINI BOX
❑ 141-155 AU PRINT RUN 963 SETS
❑ 141-155 AU's NOT SERIAL NUMBERED
❑ PRINT RUN INFO PROVIDED BY TOPPS
❑ 1-140 PLATES RANDOM INSERTS IN PACKS
❑ AU 141-155 PLATE ODDS 1:792 MINI BOX
❑ PLATE PRINT RUN 1 SET PER COLOR
❑ BLACK-CYAN-MAGENTA-YELLOW ISSUED
❑ NO PLATE PRICING DUE TO SCARCITY
❑ 1 Vladimir Guerrero 1.25 .50
❑ 2 Troy Glaus .50 .20
❑ 3 Andruw Jones .75 .30
❑ 4 Miguel Tejada .50 .20
❑ 5 Manny Ramirez .75 .30
❑ 6 Curt Schilling .75 .30
❑ 7 Mark Prior .75 .30
❑ 8 Kerry Wood .50 .20
❑ 9 Tadahito Iguchi .50 .20
❑ 10 Freddy Garcia .50 .20
❑ 11 Ryan Howard 2.00 .75
❑ 12 Mark Buehrle .50 .20
❑ 13 Wily Mo Pena .50 .20
❑ 14 C.C. Sabathia .50 .20
❑ 15 Garret Anderson .50 .20
❑ 16 Shawn Green .50 .20
❑ 17 Rafael Furcal .50 .20
❑ 18 Jeff Francoeur 1.25 .50
❑ 19 Ken Griffey Jr. 2.00 .75
❑ 20 Derrek Lee .50 .20
❑ 21 Paul Konerko .50 .20
❑ 22 Rickie Weeks .50 .20
❑ 23 Magglio Ordonez .50 .20
❑ 24 Juan Pierre .50 .20
❑ 25 Felix Hernandez .75 .30
❑ 26 Roger Clemens 2.50 1.00
❑ 27 Zack Greinke .50 .20
❑ 28 Johan Santana .75 .30
❑ 29 Jose Reyes 1.25 .50
❑ 30 Bobby Crosby .50 .20
❑ 31 Jason Schmidt .50 .20
❑ 32 Khalil Greene .75 .30
❑ 33 Richie Sexson .50 .20
❑ 34 Mark Mulder .50 .20
❑ 35 Mark Teixeira .75 .30
❑ 36 Nick Johnson .50 .20
❑ 37 Vernon Wells .50 .20
❑ 38 Scott Kazmir .75 .30
❑ 39 Jim Edmonds .75 .30
❑ 40 Adrian Beltre .50 .20
❑ 41 Dan Johnson .50 .20
❑ 42 Carlos Lee .50 .20
❑ 43 Lance Berkman .50 .20
❑ 44 Josh Beckett .50 .20
❑ 45 Morgan Ensberg .50 .20
❑ 46 Garrett Atkins .50 .20
❑ 47 Chase Utley 1.25 .50
❑ 48 Joe Mauer .75 .30
❑ 49 Travis Hafner .50 .20
❑ 50 Alex Rodriguez 2.00 .75
❑ 51 Austin Kearns .50 .20
❑ 52 Scott Podsednik .50 .20
❑ 53 Jose Contreras .50 .20
❑ 54 Greg Maddux 2.00 .75
❑ 55 Hideki Matsui 2.00 .75
❑ 56 Matt Clement .50 .20
❑ 57 Javy Lopez .50 .20
❑ 58 Tim Hudson .50 .20
❑ 59 Luis Gonzalez .50 .20
❑ 60 Bartolo Colon .50 .20
❑ 61 Marcus Giles .50 .20
❑ 62 Justin Morneau .50 .20
❑ 63 Nomar Garciaparra 1.25 .50
❑ 64 Robinson Cano .75 .30
❑ 65 Ervin Santana .50 .20
❑ 66 Brady Clark .50 .20
❑ 67 Edgar Renteria .50 .20
❑ 68 Jon Garland .50 .20
❑ 69 Felipe Lopez .50 .20
❑ 70 Ivan Rodriguez .75 .30
❑ 71 Dontrelle Willis .50 .20
❑ 72 Carlos Guillen .50 .20
❑ 73 J.D. Drew .50 .20
❑ 74 Rich Harden .50 .20
❑ 75 Albert Pujols 2.50 1.00
❑ 76 Livan Hernandez .50 .20
❑ 77 Roy Halladay .50 .20
❑ 78 Hank Blalock .50 .20
❑ 79 David Wright 2.00 .75
❑ 80 Jimmy Rollins .50 .20
❑ 81 John Smoltz .75 .30
❑ 82 Miguel Cabrera .75 .30
❑ 83 David DeJesus .50 .20
❑ 83 Zach Duke .50 .20
❑ 84 Torii Hunter .50 .20
❑ 85 Adam Dunn .50 .20
❑ 86 Randy Johnson 1.25 .50
❑ 87 Roy Oswalt .50 .20
❑ 88 Bobby Abreu .50 .20
❑ 89 Rocco Baldelli .50 .20
❑ 90 Ichiro Suzuki 2.00 .75
❑ 91 Jorge Cantu .50 .20
❑ 92 Jack Wilson .50 .20
❑ 93 Jose Vidro .50 .20
❑ 94 Kevin Millwood .50 .20
❑ 95 David Ortiz 1.25 .50
❑ 96 Victor Martinez .50 .20
❑ 97 Jeremy Bonderman .50 .20
❑ 98 Todd Helton .75 .30
❑ 99 Carlos Beltran .50 .20
❑ 100 Barry Bonds 3.00 1.25
❑ 101 Jeff Kent .50 .20
❑ 102 Mike Sweeney .50 .20
❑ 103 Ben Sheets .50 .20
❑ 104 Melvin Mora .50 .20
❑ 105 Gary Sheffield .50 .20
❑ 106 Craig Wilson .50 .20
❑ 107 Chris Carpenter .50 .20
❑ 108 Michael Young .50 .20
❑ 109 Gustavo Chacin .50 .20
❑ 110 Chipper Jones 1.25 .50
❑ 111 Mark Loretta .50 .20
❑ 112 Andy Pettitte .75 .30
❑ 113 Carlos Delgado .50 .20
❑ 114 Pat Burrell .50 .20
❑ 115 Jason Bay .50 .20
❑ 116 Brian Roberts .50 .20
❑ 117 Joe Crede .50 .20
❑ 118 Jake Peavy .50 .20
❑ 119 Aubrey Huff .50 .20
❑ 120 Pedro Martinez .75 .30
❑ 121 Jorge Posada .75 .30
❑ 122 Barry Zito .50 .20
❑ 123 Scott Rolen .75 .30
❑ 124 Brett Myers .50 .20
❑ 125 Derek Jeter 3.00 1.25
❑ 126 Eric Chavez .50 .20
❑ 127 Carl Crawford .50 .20
❑ 128 Jim Thome .75 .30
❑ 129 Johnny Damon .75 .30
❑ 130 Alfonso Soriano .50 .20
❑ 131 Clint Barmes .50 .20
❑ 132 Dustin Nippert (RC) .75 .30
❑ 133 Hanley Ramirez (RC) 2.00 .75
❑ 134 Matt Capps (RC) .75 .30
❑ 135 Miguel Perez (RC) .75 .30
❑ 136 Tom Gorzelanny (RC) .75 .30
❑ 137 Charlton Jimerson (RC) .75 .30
❑ 138 Bryan Bullington (RC) .75 .30
❑ 139 Kenji Johjima RC 4.00 1.50
❑ 140 Craig Hansen RC 3.00 1.25
❑ 141 Craig Breslow AU/963 RC * 10.00 4.00
❑ 142 A.Wainwright AU/963 (RC) * 15.00 6.00
❑ 143 Joey Devine AU/963 RC * 10.00 4.00
❑ 144 H.Kuo AU/963 (RC) * 50.00 20.00
❑ 145 Jason Botts AU/963 (RC) * 10.00 4.00
❑ 146 J.Johnson AU/963 (RC) * 20.00 8.00
❑ 147 J.Bergmann AU/963 RC * 10.00 4.00
❑ 148 Scott Olsen AU/963 (RC) * 15.00 6.00
❑ 149 D.Rasner AU/963 (RC) * 10.00 4.00
❑ 150 Dan Ortmeier AU/963 (RC) * 10.00 4.00
❑ 151 Chuck James AU/963 (RC) * 15.00 6.00
❑ 152 Ryan Garko AU/963 (RC) * 10.00 4.00
❑ 153 Nelson Cruz AU/963 (RC) * 10.00 4.00
❑ 154 A.Lerew AU/963 (RC) * 10.00 4.00
❑ 155 F.Liriano AU/963 (RC) * 50.00 20.00

2007 Finest

Card			
❑ COMP.SET w/o AU's (150)		60.00	30.00
❑ COMMON CARD (1-135)		.40	.15
❑ COMMON ROOKIE (136-150)		1.00	.40
❑ 151-166 AU ODDS 1:3 MINI BOX			
❑ 1-150 PLATE ODDS 1:96 MINI BOX			
❑ AU 151-166 PLATE ODDS 1:909 MINI BOX			
❑ PLATE PRINT RUN 1 SET PER COLOR			
❑ BLACK-CYAN-MAGENTA-YELLOW ISSUED			
❑ NO PLATE PRICING DUE TO SCARCITY			
❑ EXCHANGE DEADLINE 02/28/09			
❑ 1	David Wright	1.50	.60
❑ 2	Jered Weaver	.60	.25
❑ 3	Chipper Jones	1.00	.40
❑ 4	Magglio Ordonez	.40	.15
❑ 5	Ben Sheets	.40	.15
❑ 6	Nick Johnson	.40	.15
❑ 7	Melvin Mora	.40	.15
❑ 8	Chien-Ming Wang	1.50	.60
❑ 9	Andre Ethier	.60	.25
❑ 10	Carlos Beltran	.40	.15
❑ 11	Ryan Zimmerman	1.00	.40
❑ 12	Troy Glaus	.40	.15
❑ 13	Hanley Ramirez	.60	.25
❑ 14	Mark Buehrle	.40	.15
❑ 15	Dan Uggla	.60	.25
❑ 16	Richie Sexson	.40	.15
❑ 17	Scott Kazmir	.60	.25
❑ 18	Garrett Atkins	.40	.15
❑ 19	Matt Cain	.60	.25
❑ 20	Jorge Posada	.60	.25
❑ 21	Brett Myers	.40	.15
❑ 22	Jeff Francoeur	1.00	.40
❑ 23	Scott Rolen	.60	.25
❑ 24	Derrek Lee	.40	.15
❑ 25	Manny Ramirez	.60	.25
❑ 26	Johnny Damon	.60	.25
❑ 27	Mark Teixeira	.60	.25
❑ 28	Mark Prior	.60	.25
❑ 29	Victor Martinez	.40	.15
❑ 30	Greg Maddux	1.50	.60
❑ 31	Prince Fielder	1.00	.40
❑ 32	Jeremy Bonderman	.40	.15
❑ 33	Paul LoDuca	.40	.15
❑ 34	Brandon Webb	.40	.15
❑ 35	Robinson Cano	.60	.25
❑ 36	Josh Beckett	.60	.25
❑ 37	David DeJesus	.40	.15
❑ 38	Kenny Rogers	.40	.15
❑ 39	Jim Thome	.60	.25
❑ 40	Brian McCann	.40	.15
❑ 41	Lance Berkman	.40	.15
❑ 42	Adam Dunn	.40	.15
❑ 43	Rocco Baldelli	.40	.15
❑ 44	Brian Roberts	.40	.15
❑ 45	Vladimir Guerrero	1.00	.40
❑ 46	Dontrelle Willis	.40	.15
❑ 47	Eric Chavez	.40	.15
❑ 48	Carlos Zambrano	.40	.15
❑ 49	Ivan Rodriguez	.60	.25
❑ 50	Alex Rodriguez	1.50	.60
❑ 51	Curt Schilling	.60	.25
❑ 52	Carlos Delgado	.40	.15
❑ 53	Matt Holliday	1.00	.40
❑ 54	Mark Teahen	.40	.15
❑ 55	Frank Thomas	1.00	.40
❑ 56	Grady Sizemore	.60	.25
❑ 57	Aramis Ramirez	.40	.15
❑ 58	Rafael Furcal	.40	.15
❑ 59	David Ortiz	1.00	.40
❑ 60	Paul Konerko	.40	.15
❑ 61	Barry Zito	.40	.15
❑ 62	Travis Hafner	.40	.15
❑ 63	Nick Swisher	.40	.15
❑ 64	Johan Santana	.60	.25
❑ 65	Miguel Tejada	.40	.15
❑ 66	Carl Crawford	.40	.15
❑ 67	Kenji Johjima	1.00	.40
❑ 68	Derek Jeter	2.50	1.00
❑ 69	Francisco Liriano	2.00	.75
❑ 70	Ken Griffey Jr.	1.50	.60
❑ 71	Pat Burrell	.40	.15
❑ 72	Adrian Gonzalez	.40	.15
❑ 73	Miguel Cabrera	.60	.25
❑ 74	Albert Pujols	2.00	.75
❑ 75	Justin Verlander	1.00	.40
❑ 76	Carlos Lee	.40	.15
❑ 77	John Smoltz	.60	.25
❑ 78	Orlando Hudson	.40	.15
❑ 79	Joe Mauer	.60	.25
❑ 80	Freddy Sanchez	.40	.15
❑ 81	Bobby Abreu	.40	.15
❑ 82	Pedro Martinez	.60	.25
❑ 83	Vernon Wells	.40	.15
❑ 84	Justin Morneau	.40	.15
❑ 85	Bill Hall	.40	.15
❑ 86	Jason Schmidt	.40	.15
❑ 87	Michael Young	.40	.15
❑ 88	Tadahito Iguchi	.40	.15
❑ 89	Kevin Millwood	.40	.15
❑ 90	Randy Johnson	1.00	.40
❑ 91	Roy Halladay	.40	.15
❑ 92	Mike Lowell	.40	.15
❑ 93	Jake Peavy	.40	.15
❑ 94	Jason Varitek	1.00	.40
❑ 95	Todd Helton	.60	.25
❑ 96	Mark Loretta	.40	.15
❑ 97	Gary Matthews Jr.	.40	.15
❑ 98	Ryan Howard	1.50	.60
❑ 99	Jose Reyes	.40	.15
❑ 100	Chris Carpenter	.40	.15
❑ 101	Hideki Matsui	1.00	.40
❑ 102	Brian Giles	.40	.15
❑ 103	Torii Hunter	.40	.15
❑ 104	Rich Harden	.40	.15
❑ 105	Ichiro Suzuki	1.50	.60
❑ 106	Chase Utley	1.00	.40
❑ 107	Nick Markakis	.60	.25
❑ 108	Marcus Giles	.40	.15
❑ 109	Gary Sheffield	.40	.15
❑ 110	Jim Edmonds	.60	.25
❑ 111	Brandon Phillips	.40	.15
❑ 112	Roy Oswalt	.40	.15
❑ 113	Jeff Kent	.40	.15
❑ 114	Jason Bay	.40	.15
❑ 115	Raul Ibanez	.40	.15
❑ 116	Stephen Drew	.60	.25
❑ 117	Hank Blalock	.40	.15
❑ 118	Tom Glavine	.60	.25
❑ 119	Andruw Jones	.60	.25
❑ 120	Alfonso Soriano	.40	.15
❑ 121	Mariano Rivera	1.00	.40
❑ 122	Garret Anderson	.40	.15
❑ 123	Erik Bedard UER	.40	.15
❑ 124	Huston Street	.40	.15
❑ 125	Austin Kearns	.40	.15
❑ 126	Jermaine Dye	.40	.15
❑ 127	C.C. Sabathia	.40	.15
❑ 128	Joe Nathan	.40	.15
❑ 129	Craig Monroe	.40	.15
❑ 130	Aubrey Huff	.40	.15
❑ 131	Billy Wagner	.40	.15
❑ 132	Jorge Cantu	.40	.15
❑ 133	Trevor Hoffman	.40	.15
❑ 134	Ronnie Belliard	.40	.15
❑ 135	B.J. Ryan	.40	.15
❑ 136	Adam Lind (RC)	1.00	.40
❑ 137	Hector Gimenez (RC)	1.00	.40
❑ 138	Shawn Riggans UER (RC)	1.00	.40
❑ 139	Joaquin Arias (RC)	1.00	.40
❑ 140	Drew Anderson RC	1.00	.40
❑ 141	Mike Rabelo RC	1.00	.40
❑ 142	Chris Narveson (RC)	1.00	.40
❑ 143	Ryan Feierabend (RC)	1.00	.40
❑ 144	Vinny Rottino (RC)	1.00	.40
❑ 145	Jon Knott (RC)	1.00	.40
❑ 146	Oswaldo Navarro RC	1.00	.40
❑ 147	Brian Stokes (RC)	1.00	.40
❑ 148	Glen Perkins (RC)	1.00	.40
❑ 149	Mitch Maier RC	1.00	.40
❑ 150	Delmon Young (RC)	2.50	1.00
❑ 151	Andrew Miller AU RC	40.00	15.00
❑ 152	T.Tulowitzki AU (RC)	30.00	12.50
❑ 153	Philip Humber AU (RC)	15.00	6.00
❑ 154	K.Kouzmanoff AU (RC)	15.00	6.00
❑ 155	Michael Bourn AU (RC)	10.00	4.00
❑ 156	M.Montero AU (RC) EXCH	10.00	4.00
❑ 157	David Murphy AU (RC)	10.00	4.00
❑ 158	R.Sweeney AU (RC)	10.00	4.00
❑ 159	Jeff Baker AU (RC)	10.00	4.00
❑ 160	Jeff Salazar AU (RC)	10.00	4.00
❑ 161	J.Garcia AU RC EXCH	10.00	4.00
❑ 162	Josh Fields AU (RC)	10.00	4.00
❑ 163	Delwyn Young AU (RC)	10.00	4.00
❑ 164	Fred Lewis AU (RC)	10.00	4.00
❑ 165	Scott Moore AU (RC)	10.00	4.00
❑ 166	Chris Stewart AU RC	10.00	4.00

2006 Flair Showcase

Card			
❑ COMP.SET w/o SP's (100)		40.00	15.00
❑ 101-150 STATED ODDS 1:4 H, 1:8 R			
❑ 151-200 STATED ODDS 1:8 H, 1:16 R			
❑ PLATE ODDS: 1-2 PER HOBBY CASE			
❑ PLATE PRINT RUN 1 SET PER COLOR			
❑ BLACK-CYAN-MAGENTA-YELLOW ISSUED			
❑ NO PLATE PRICING DUE TO SCARCITY			
❑ 1	Jeremy Hermida UD (RC)	1.00	.40
❑ 2	Albert Pujols UD	4.00	1.50
❑ 3	Ryan Shealy UD (RC)	1.00	.40
❑ 4	Mark Prior UD	1.25	.50
❑ 5	Chuck James UD (RC)	1.50	.60
❑ 6	Shawn Green UD	.75	.30
❑ 7	Rickie Weeks UD	.75	.30
❑ 8	Roy Halladay UD	.75	.30
❑ 9	Luis Gonzalez UD	.75	.30
❑ 10	David Ortiz UD	2.00	.75
❑ 11	Josh Beckett UD	.75	.30
❑ 12	Gary Sheffield UD	.75	.30
❑ 13	Jose Reyes UD	2.00	.75
❑ 14	Brandon Watson UD (RC)	1.00	.40
❑ 15	Tadahito Iguchi UD	.75	.30
❑ 16	Rich Harden UD	.75	.30
❑ 17	Skip Schumaker UD (RC)	1.00	.40
❑ 18	Vladimir Guerrero UD	2.00	.75
❑ 19	Chris Carpenter UD	.75	.30
❑ 20	Brian Roberts UD	.75	.30
❑ 21	Roy Oswalt UD	.75	.30
❑ 22	Ben Johnson UD (RC)	1.00	.40
❑ 23	Todd Helton UD	1.25	.50
❑ 24	Wil Nieves UD (RC)	1.00	.40
❑ 25	Michael Young UD	.75	.30
❑ 26	A.J. Burnett UD	.75	.30
❑ 27	J.D. Drew UD	.75	.30
❑ 28	Adrian Beltre UD	.75	.30
❑ 29	Tim Hudson UD	.75	.30
❑ 30	Jake Peavy UD	.75	.30
❑ 31	Magglio Ordonez UD	.75	.30
❑ 32	Brad Wilkerson UD	.75	.30
❑ 33	Ryan Freel UD	.75	.30
❑ 34	Javier Vazquez UD	.75	.30
❑ 35	Tom Glavine UD	1.25	.50

❑ 36 Jason Bergmann UD RC 1.00 .40
❑ 37 Marcus Giles UD .75 .30
❑ 38 Jim Thome UD 1.25 .50
❑ 39 Ichiro Suzuki UD 3.00 1.25
❑ 40 Jeff Harris UD RC .75 .30
❑ 41 Miguel Cabrera UD 1.25 .50
❑ 42 Nomar Garciaparra UD 2.00 .75
❑ 43 Brian Giles UD .75 .30
❑ 44 Jeremy Accardo UD RC 1.00 .40
❑ 45 Taylor Buchholz UD (RC) 1.50 .60
❑ 46 Mike Jacobs UD (RC) 1.00 .40
❑ 47 Chris Denorfia UD (RC) 1.00 .40
❑ 48 Ivan Rodriguez UD 1.25 .50
❑ 49 Mike Piazza UD 2.00 .75
❑ 50 Curt Schilling UD 1.25 .50
❑ 51 Kelly Shoppach UD (RC) 1.00 .40
❑ 52 Jason Kubel UD (RC) 1.00 .40
❑ 53 Craig Biggio UD 1.25 .50
❑ 54 Livan Hernandez UD .75 .30
❑ 55 Joe Mauer UD 1.25 .50
❑ 56 Scott Feldman UD RC 1.00 .40
❑ 57 Garret Anderson UD .75 .30
❑ 58 Steve Stemle UD RC 1.00 .40
❑ 59 Boof Bonser UD (RC) 1.00 .40
❑ 60 Jose Guillen UD .75 .30
❑ 61 Rafael Furcal UD .75 .30
❑ 62 John Van Benschoten UD (RC) 1.00 .40
❑ 63 Dontrelle Willis UD .75 .30
❑ 64 Jose Vidro UD .75 .30
❑ 65 David Wright UD 3.00 1.25
❑ 66 Alfonso Soriano UD .75 .30
❑ 67 Scott Podsednik UD .75 .30
❑ 68 Felix Hernandez UD 1.25 .50
❑ 69 Richie Sexson UD .75 .30
❑ 70 Jeff Francoeur UD 2.00 .75
❑ 71 Conor Jackson UD 1.25 .50
❑ 72 Javy Lopez UD .75 .30
❑ 73 Jonathan Papelbon UD (RC) 5.00 2.00
❑ 74 Frank Thomas UD 2.00 .75
❑ 75 Greg Maddux UD 3.00 1.25
❑ 76 Josh Rupe UD (RC) 1.00 .40
❑ 77 Eric Chavez UD .75 .30
❑ 78 Ben Sheets UD .75 .30
❑ 79 Chase Utley UD 2.00 .75
❑ 80 Derrek Lee UD .75 .30
❑ 81 Manny Ramirez UD 1.25 .50
❑ 82 Pedro Martinez UD 1.25 .50
❑ 83 Hideki Matsui UD 2.00 .75
❑ 84 Jeremy Bonderman UD .75 .30
❑ 85 Ronny Cedeno UD .75 .30
❑ 86 Trevor Hoffman UD .75 .30
❑ 87 Mark Buehrle UD .75 .30
❑ 88 Jason Bay UD .75 .30
❑ 89 Reggie Sanders UD .75 .30
❑ 90 Brian Anderson UD (RC) 1.00 .40
❑ 91 Travis Hafner UD .75 .30
❑ 92 Carlos Beltran UD .75 .30
❑ 93 Cody Ross UD (RC) 1.00 .40
❑ 94 Melvin Mora UD .75 .30
❑ 95 Chris Duffy UD .75 .30
❑ 96 Vernon Wells UD .75 .30
❑ 97 Bartolo Colon UD .75 .30
❑ 98 Aubrey Huff UD .75 .30
❑ 99 Paul Konerko UD .75 .30
❑ 100 Cesar Izturis UD .75 .30
❑ 101 Josh Willingham FB (RC) 2.00 .75
❑ 102 Matt Cain FB (RC) 3.00 1.25
❑ 103 Macay McBride FB (RC) 2.00 .75
❑ 104 Jeff Mathis FB 2.00 .75
❑ 105 Alex Rodriguez FB 8.00 3.00
❑ 106 Justin Morneau FB 2.00 .75
❑ 107 Felipe Lopez FB 2.00 .75
❑ 108 Justin Verlander FB (RC) 8.00 3.00
❑ 109 Ryan Howard FB 8.00 3.00
❑ 110 Mike Sweeney FB 2.00 .75
❑ 111 Scott Rolen FB 3.00 1.25
❑ 112 Hank Blalock FB 2.00 .75
❑ 113 Kerry Wood FB 2.00 .75
❑ 114 B.J. Ryan FB 2.00 .75
❑ 115 Garrett Atkins FB 2.00 .75
❑ 116 Carlos Delgado FB 2.00 .75
❑ 117 Zack Greinke FB 2.00 .75
❑ 118 Chad Cordero FB 2.00 .75
❑ 119 Julio Lugo FB 2.00 .75
❑ 120 Bobby Crosby FB 2.00 .75
❑ 121 Barry Zito FB 2.00 .75
❑ 122 Jhonny Peralta FB 2.00 .75
❑ 123 Miguel Tejada FB 2.00 .75
❑ 124 Grady Sizemore FB 3.00 1.25
❑ 125 Derek Jeter FB 12.00 5.00
❑ 126 Cliff Lee FB 2.00 .75
❑ 127 Khalil Greene FB 3.00 1.25
❑ 128 Lance Berkman FB 2.00 .75
❑ 129 Huston Street FB 2.00 .75
❑ 130 Jermaine Dye FB 2.00 .75
❑ 131 Chone Figgins FB 2.00 .75
❑ 132 Torii Hunter FB 2.00 .75
❑ 133 Jorge Cantu FB 2.00 .75
❑ 134 Jason Giambi FB 2.00 .75
❑ 135 Johan Santana FB 3.00 1.25
❑ 136 Chad Tracy FB 2.00 .75
❑ 137 Troy Glaus FB 2.00 .75
❑ 138 Moises Alou FB 2.00 .75
❑ 139 Jason Schmidt FB 2.00 .75
❑ 140 Ken Griffey Jr. FB 8.00 3.00
❑ 141 Jason Varitek FB 5.00 2.00
❑ 142 John Smoltz FB 3.00 1.25
❑ 143 Andy Pettitte FB 3.00 1.25
❑ 144 Jeff Kent FB 2.00 .75
❑ 145 Coco Crisp FB 2.00 .75
❑ 146 Jonny Gomes FB 2.00 .75
❑ 147 Aaron Rowand FB 2.00 .75
❑ 148 Mike Mussina FB 3.00 1.25
❑ 149 Johnny Damon FB 3.00 1.25
❑ 150 Edgar Renteria FB 2.00 .75
❑ 151 Scott Kazmir SL 5.00 2.00
❑ 152 Lyle Overbay SL 3.00 1.25
❑ 153 Placido Polanco SL 3.00 1.25
❑ 154 Mariano Rivera SL 8.00 3.00
❑ 155 Hanley Ramirez SL (RC) 8.00 3.00
❑ 156 Morgan Ensberg SL 3.00 1.25
❑ 157 Kenny Rogers SL 3.00 1.25
❑ 158 Brad Lidge SL 3.00 1.25
❑ 159 A.J. Pierzynski SL 3.00 1.25
❑ 160 Aramis Ramirez SL 3.00 1.25
❑ 161 Mark Teixeira SL 5.00 2.00
❑ 162 Carl Crawford SL 3.00 1.25
❑ 163 Ryan Zimmerman SL (RC) 12.00 5.00
❑ 164 Adam Dunn SL 3.00 1.25
❑ 165 Joe Nathan SL 3.00 1.25
❑ 166 Juan Pierre SL 3.00 1.25
❑ 167 Pat Burrell SL 3.00 1.25
❑ 168 Carlos Lee SL 3.00 1.25
❑ 169 Billy Wagner SL 3.00 1.25
❑ 170 Prince Fielder SL (RC) 8.00 3.00
❑ 171 Randy Johnson SL 8.00 3.00
❑ 172 Andruw Jones SL 5.00 2.00
❑ 173 Francisco Rodriguez SL 3.00 1.25
❑ 174 Robinson Cano SL 5.00 2.00
❑ 175 Matt Holliday SL 8.00 3.00
❑ 176 Jim Edmonds SL 5.00 2.00
❑ 177 Josh Barfield SL (RC) 3.00 1.25
❑ 178 Chipper Jones SL 8.00 3.00
❑ 179 Bobby Jenks SL 3.00 1.25
❑ 180 Carlos Zambrano SL 3.00 1.25
❑ 181 Bobby Abreu SL 3.00 1.25
❑ 182 Brandon Webb SL 3.00 1.25
❑ 183 Kevin Millwood SL 3.00 1.25
❑ 184 Zach Duke SL 3.00 1.25
❑ 185 Randy Winn SL 3.00 1.25
❑ 186 Eric Gagne SL 3.00 1.25
❑ 187 Kenji Johjima SL RC 10.00 4.00
❑ 188 John Patterson SL 3.00 1.25
❑ 189 Mark Loretta SL 3.00 1.25
❑ 190 Anderson Hernandez SL (RC) 3.00 1.25
❑ 191 Chris Resop SL (RC) 3.00 1.25
❑ 192 Ian Kinsler SL (RC) 5.00 2.00
❑ 193 Francisco Liriano SL (RC) 10.00 4.00
❑ 194 Noah Lowry SL 3.00 1.25
❑ 195 Brett Myers SL 3.00 1.25
❑ 196 Rocco Baldelli SL 3.00 1.25
❑ 197 Cliff Floyd SL 3.00 1.25
❑ 198 Sean Casey SL 3.00 1.25
❑ 199 Geoff Jenkins SL 3.00 1.25
❑ 200 Clint Barmes SL 3.00 1.25

1960 Fleer

❑ COMPLETE SET (79) 600.00 350.00
❑ WRAPPER (5-CENT) 100.00 75.00
❑ 1 Napoleon Lajoie DP 30.00 15.00
❑ 2 Christy Mathewson 15.00 7.50
❑ 3 Babe Ruth 100.00 60.00
❑ 4 Carl Hubbell 8.00 4.00
❑ 5 Grover C. Alexander 8.00 4.00
❑ 6 Walter Johnson DP 10.00 5.00
❑ 7 Chief Bender 4.00 2.00
❑ 8 Roger Bresnahan 4.00 2.00
❑ 9 Mordecai Brown 4.00 2.00
❑ 10 Tris Speaker 8.00 4.00
❑ 11 Arky Vaughan DP 4.00 2.00
❑ 12 Zach Wheat 4.00 2.00
❑ 13 George Sisler 4.00 2.00
❑ 14 Connie Mack 8.00 4.00
❑ 15 Clark Griffith 4.00 2.00
❑ 16 Lou Boudreau DP 8.00 4.00
❑ 17 Ernie Lombardi 4.00 2.00
❑ 18 Heinie Manush 4.00 2.00
❑ 19 Marty Marion 6.00 3.00
❑ 20 Eddie Collins DP 4.00 2.00
❑ 21 Rabbit Maranville DP 4.00 2.00
❑ 22 Joe Medwick 4.00 2.00
❑ 23 Ed Barrow 4.00 2.00
❑ 24 Mickey Cochrane 6.00 3.00
❑ 25 Jimmy Collins 4.00 2.00
❑ 26 Bob Feller DP 15.00 7.50
❑ 27 Luke Appling 6.00 3.00
❑ 28 Lou Gehrig 80.00 50.00
❑ 29 Gabby Hartnett 4.00 2.00
❑ 30 Chuck Klein 4.00 2.00
❑ 31 Tony Lazzeri DP 6.00 3.00
❑ 32 Al Simmons 4.00 2.00
❑ 33 Wilbert Robinson 4.00 2.00
❑ 34 Sam Rice 4.00 2.00
❑ 35 Herb Pennock 4.00 2.00
❑ 36 Mel Ott DP 8.00 4.00
❑ 37 Lefty O'Doul 4.00 2.00
❑ 38 Johnny Mize 8.00 4.00
❑ 39 Edmund (Bing) Miller 4.00 2.00
❑ 40 Joe Tinker 4.00 2.00
❑ 41 Frank Baker DP 4.00 2.00
❑ 42 Ty Cobb 60.00 35.00
❑ 43 Paul Derringer 4.00 2.00
❑ 44 Cap Anson 4.00 2.00
❑ 45 Jim Bottomley 4.00 2.00
❑ 46 Eddie Plank DP 4.00 2.00
❑ 47 Denton (Cy) Young 10.00 5.00
❑ 48 Hack Wilson 6.00 3.00
❑ 49 Ed Walsh UER 4.00 2.00
❑ 50 Frank Chance 4.00 2.00
❑ 51 Dazzy Vance DP 4.00 2.00
❑ 52 Bill Terry 6.00 3.00
❑ 53 Jimmie Foxx 10.00 5.00
❑ 54 Lefty Gomez 8.00 4.00
❑ 55 Branch Rickey 4.00 2.00
❑ 56 Ray Schalk DP 4.00 2.00
❑ 57 Johnny Evers 4.00 2.00
❑ 58 Charley Gehringer 6.00 3.00
❑ 59 Burleigh Grimes 4.00 2.00
❑ 60 Lefty Grove 8.00 4.00
❑ 61 Rube Waddell DP 4.00 2.00
❑ 62 Honus Wagner 15.00 7.50
❑ 63 Red Ruffing 4.00 2.00
❑ 64 Kenesaw M. Landis 4.00 2.00
❑ 65 Harry Heilmann 4.00 2.00
❑ 66 John McGraw DP 4.00 2.00
❑ 67 Hughie Jennings 4.00 2.00
❑ 68 Hal Newhouser 6.00 3.00
❑ 69 Waite Hoyt 4.00 2.00
❑ 70 Bobo Newsom 4.00 2.00

- ❑ 71 Earl Averill DP 4.00 2.00
- ❑ 72 Ted Williams 80.00 50.00
- ❑ 73 Warren Giles 6.00 3.00
- ❑ 74 Ford Frick 6.00 3.00
- ❑ 75 Kiki Cuyler 4.00 2.00
- ❑ 76 Paul Waner DP 6.00 3.00
- ❑ 77 Pie Traynor 4.00 2.00
- ❑ 78 Lloyd Waner 4.00 2.00
- ❑ 79 Ralph Kiner 10.00 5.00
- ❑ 80A P.Martin SP/Eddie Collins 2500.00 1500.00
- ❑ 80B P.Martin SP/Lefty Grove 2000.00 1200.00
- ❑ 80C P.Martin SP/Joe Tinker 2000.00 1200.00

1961 Fleer

- ❑ COMPLETE SET (154) 1200.00 750.00
- ❑ COMMON CARD (1-88) 3.00 1.50
- ❑ COMMON CARD (89-154) 8.00 4.00
- ❑ WRAPPER (5-CENT) 100.00 75.00
- ❑ 1 Baker/Cobb/Wheat 50.00 30.00
- ❑ 2 Grover C. Alexander 6.00 3.00
- ❑ 3 Nick Altrock 3.00 1.50
- ❑ 4 Cap Anson 4.00 2.00
- ❑ 5 Earl Averill 4.00 2.00
- ❑ 6 Frank Baker 4.00 2.00
- ❑ 7 Dave Bancroft 4.00 2.00
- ❑ 8 Chief Bender 4.00 2.00
- ❑ 9 Jim Bottomley 4.00 2.00
- ❑ 10 Roger Bresnahan 4.00 2.00
- ❑ 11 Mordecai Brown 4.00 2.00
- ❑ 12 Max Carey 4.00 2.00
- ❑ 13 Jack Chesbro 4.00 2.00
- ❑ 14 Ty Cobb 50.00 30.00
- ❑ 15 Mickey Cochrane 4.00 2.00
- ❑ 16 Eddie Collins 6.00 3.00
- ❑ 17 Earle Combs 4.00 2.00
- ❑ 18 Charles Comiskey 4.00 2.00
- ❑ 19 Kiki Cuyler 4.00 2.00
- ❑ 20 Paul Derringer 3.00 1.50
- ❑ 21 Howard Ehmke 3.00 1.50
- ❑ 22 Billy Evans UMP 4.00 2.00
- ❑ 23 Johnny Evers 4.00 2.00
- ❑ 24 Urban Faber 4.00 2.00
- ❑ 25 Bob Feller 12.00 6.00
- ❑ 26 Wes Ferrell 3.00 1.50
- ❑ 27 Lew Fonseca 3.00 1.50
- ❑ 28 Jimmie Foxx 6.00 3.00
- ❑ 29 Ford Frick 3.00 1.50
- ❑ 30 Frankie Frisch 4.00 2.00
- ❑ 31 Lou Gehrig 80.00 50.00
- ❑ 32 Charley Gehringer 4.00 2.00
- ❑ 33 Warren Giles 3.00 1.50
- ❑ 34 Lefty Gomez 4.00 2.00
- ❑ 35 Goose Goslin 4.00 2.00
- ❑ 36 Clark Griffith 4.00 2.00
- ❑ 37 Burleigh Grimes 4.00 2.00
- ❑ 38 Lefty Grove 6.00 3.00
- ❑ 39 Chick Hafey 4.00 2.00
- ❑ 40 Jesse Haines 4.00 2.00
- ❑ 41 Gabby Hartnett 4.00 2.00
- ❑ 42 Harry Heilmann 4.00 2.00
- ❑ 43 Rogers Hornsby 6.00 3.00
- ❑ 44 Waite Hoyt 4.00 2.00
- ❑ 45 Carl Hubbell 6.00 3.00
- ❑ 46 Miller Huggins 4.00 2.00
- ❑ 47 Hughie Jennings 4.00 2.00
- ❑ 48 Ban Johnson 4.00 2.00
- ❑ 49 Walter Johnson 12.00 6.00
- ❑ 50 Ralph Kiner 6.00 3.00
- ❑ 51 Chuck Klein 4.00 2.00
- ❑ 52 Johnny Kling 3.00 1.50
- ❑ 53 Kenesaw M. Landis 4.00 2.00
- ❑ 54 Tony Lazzeri 4.00 2.00
- ❑ 55 Ernie Lombardi 4.00 2.00
- ❑ 56 Dolf Luque 3.00 1.50
- ❑ 57 Heinie Manush 4.00 2.00
- ❑ 58 Marty Marion 3.00 1.50
- ❑ 59 Christy Mathewson 12.00 6.00
- ❑ 60 John McGraw 4.00 2.00
- ❑ 61 Joe Medwick 4.00 2.00
- ❑ 62 Edmund (Bing) Miller 3.00 1.50
- ❑ 63 Johnny Mize 4.00 2.00
- ❑ 64 John Mostil 3.00 1.50
- ❑ 65 Art Nehf 3.00 1.50
- ❑ 66 Hal Newhouser 4.00 2.00
- ❑ 67 Bobo Newsom 3.00 1.50
- ❑ 68 Mel Ott 6.00 3.00
- ❑ 69 Allie Reynolds 3.00 1.50
- ❑ 70 Sam Rice 4.00 2.00
- ❑ 71 Eppa Rixey 4.00 2.00
- ❑ 72 Edd Roush 4.00 2.00
- ❑ 73 Schoolboy Rowe 3.00 1.50
- ❑ 74 Red Ruffing 4.00 2.00
- ❑ 75 Babe Ruth 125.00 75.00
- ❑ 76 Joe Sewell 4.00 2.00
- ❑ 77 Al Simmons 4.00 2.00
- ❑ 78 George Sisler 4.00 2.00
- ❑ 79 Tris Speaker 4.00 2.00
- ❑ 80 Fred Toney 3.00 1.50
- ❑ 81 Dazzy Vance 4.00 2.00
- ❑ 82 Hippo Vaughn 3.00 1.50
- ❑ 83 Ed Walsh 4.00 2.00
- ❑ 84 Lloyd Waner 4.00 2.00
- ❑ 85 Paul Waner 4.00 2.00
- ❑ 86 Zack Wheat 4.00 2.00
- ❑ 87 Hack Wilson 4.00 2.00
- ❑ 88 Jimmy Wilson 3.00 1.50
- ❑ 89 G.Sisler/P.Traynor 60.00 35.00
- ❑ 90 Babe Adams 8.00 4.00
- ❑ 91 Dale Alexander 8.00 4.00
- ❑ 92 Jim Bagby 8.00 4.00
- ❑ 93 Ossie Bluege 8.00 4.00
- ❑ 94 Lou Boudreau 10.00 5.00
- ❑ 95 Tommy Bridges 8.00 4.00
- ❑ 96 Donie Bush 8.00 4.00
- ❑ 97 Dolph Camilli 8.00 4.00
- ❑ 98 Frank Chance 10.00 5.00
- ❑ 99 Jimmy Collins 10.00 5.00
- ❑ 100 Stan Coveleskie 10.00 5.00
- ❑ 101 Hugh Critz 8.00 4.00
- ❑ 102 Alvin Crowder 8.00 4.00
- ❑ 103 Joe Dugan 8.00 4.00
- ❑ 104 Bibb Falk 8.00 4.00
- ❑ 105 Rick Ferrell 10.00 5.00
- ❑ 106 Art Fletcher 8.00 4.00
- ❑ 107 Dennis Galehouse 8.00 4.00
- ❑ 108 Chick Galloway 8.00 4.00
- ❑ 109 Mule Haas 8.00 4.00
- ❑ 110 Stan Hack 8.00 4.00
- ❑ 111 Bump Hadley 8.00 4.00
- ❑ 112 Billy Hamilton 10.00 5.00
- ❑ 113 Joe Hauser 8.00 4.00
- ❑ 114 Babe Herman 8.00 4.00
- ❑ 115 Travis Jackson 10.00 5.00
- ❑ 116 Eddie Joost 8.00 4.00
- ❑ 117 Addie Joss 10.00 5.00
- ❑ 118 Joe Judge 8.00 4.00
- ❑ 119 Joe Kuhel 8.00 4.00
- ❑ 120 Napoleon Lajoie 12.00 6.00
- ❑ 121 Dutch Leonard 8.00 4.00
- ❑ 122 Ted Lyons 10.00 5.00
- ❑ 123 Connie Mack 12.00 6.00
- ❑ 124 Rabbit Maranville 10.00 5.00
- ❑ 125 Fred Marberry 8.00 4.00
- ❑ 126 Joe McGinnity 10.00 5.00
- ❑ 127 Oscar Melillo 8.00 4.00
- ❑ 128 Ray Mueller 8.00 4.00
- ❑ 129 Kid Nichols 10.00 5.00
- ❑ 130 Lefty O'Doul 10.00 5.00
- ❑ 131 Bob O'Farrell 8.00 4.00
- ❑ 132 Roger Peckinpaugh 8.00 4.00
- ❑ 133 Herb Pennock 10.00 5.00
- ❑ 134 George Pipgras 8.00 4.00
- ❑ 135 Eddie Plank 10.00 5.00
- ❑ 136 Ray Schalk 10.00 5.00
- ❑ 137 Hal Schumacher 8.00 4.00
- ❑ 138 Luke Sewell 8.00 4.00
- ❑ 139 Bob Shawkey 8.00 4.00
- ❑ 140 Riggs Stephenson 8.00 4.00
- ❑ 141 Billy Sullivan 8.00 4.00
- ❑ 142 Bill Terry 12.00 6.00
- ❑ 143 Joe Tinker 10.00 5.00
- ❑ 144 Pie Traynor 10.00 5.00
- ❑ 145 Hal Trosky 8.00 4.00
- ❑ 146 George Uhle 8.00 4.00
- ❑ 147 Johnny VanderMeer 10.00 5.00
- ❑ 148 Arky Vaughan 10.00 5.00
- ❑ 149 Rube Waddell 10.00 5.00
- ❑ 150 Honus Wagner 50.00 30.00
- ❑ 151 Dixie Walker 8.00 4.00
- ❑ 152 Ted Williams 125.00 75.00
- ❑ 153 Cy Young 40.00 20.00
- ❑ 154 Ross Youngs 40.00 20.00

1963 Fleer

- ❑ COMPLETE SET (67) 1800.00 1200.00
- ❑ WRAPPER (5-CENT) 100.00 75.00
- ❑ 1 Steve Barber 25.00 12.50
- ❑ 2 Ron Hansen 15.00 7.50
- ❑ 3 Milt Pappas 20.00 10.00
- ❑ 4 Brooks Robinson 100.00 60.00
- ❑ 5 Willie Mays 175.00 100.00
- ❑ 6 Lou Clinton 15.00 7.50
- ❑ 7 Bill Monbouquette 15.00 7.50
- ❑ 8 Carl Yastrzemski 100.00 60.00
- ❑ 9 Ray Herbert 15.00 7.50
- ❑ 10 Jim Landis 15.00 7.50
- ❑ 11 Dick Donovan 15.00 7.50
- ❑ 12 Tito Francona 15.00 7.50
- ❑ 13 Jerry Kindall 15.00 7.50
- ❑ 14 Frank Lary 20.00 10.00
- ❑ 15 Dick Howser 20.00 10.00
- ❑ 16 Jerry Lumpe 15.00 7.50
- ❑ 17 Norm Siebern 15.00 7.50
- ❑ 18 Don Lee 15.00 7.50
- ❑ 19 Albie Pearson 20.00 10.00
- ❑ 20 Bob Rodgers 20.00 10.00
- ❑ 21 Leon Wagner 15.00 7.50
- ❑ 22 Jim Kaat 25.00 12.50
- ❑ 23 Vic Power 20.00 10.00
- ❑ 24 Rich Rollins 20.00 10.00
- ❑ 25 Bobby Richardson 25.00 12.50
- ❑ 26 Ralph Terry 20.00 10.00
- ❑ 27 Tom Cheney 15.00 7.50
- ❑ 28 Chuck Cottier 15.00 7.50
- ❑ 29 Jimmy Piersall 20.00 10.00
- ❑ 30 Dave Stenhouse 15.00 7.50
- ❑ 31 Glen Hobbie 15.00 7.50
- ❑ 32 Ron Santo 25.00 12.50
- ❑ 33 Gene Freese 15.00 7.50
- ❑ 34 Vada Pinson 25.00 12.50
- ❑ 35 Bob Purkey 15.00 7.50
- ❑ 36 Joe Amalfitano 15.00 7.50
- ❑ 37 Bob Aspromonte 15.00 7.50
- ❑ 38 Dick Farrell 15.00 7.50
- ❑ 39 Al Spangler 15.00 7.50
- ❑ 40 Tommy Davis 20.00 10.00
- ❑ 41 Don Drysdale 80.00 50.00
- ❑ 42 Sandy Koufax 200.00 125.00
- ❑ 43 Maury Wills RC 100.00 60.00
- ❑ 44 Frank Bolling 15.00 7.50
- ❑ 45 Warren Spahn 80.00 50.00
- ❑ 46 Joe Adcock SP 150.00 90.00

❑ 47 Roger Craig 20.00 10.00
❑ 48 Al Jackson 20.00 10.00
❑ 49 Rod Kanehl 20.00 10.00
❑ 50 Ruben Amaro 15.00 7.50
❑ 51 Johnny Callison 20.00 10.00
❑ 52 Clay Dalrymple 15.00 7.50
❑ 53 Don Demeter 15.00 7.50
❑ 54 Art Mahaffey 15.00 7.50
❑ 55 Smoky Burgess 20.00 10.00
❑ 56 Roberto Clemente 175.00 100.00
❑ 57 Roy Face 20.00 10.00
❑ 58 Vern Law 20.00 10.00
❑ 59 Bill Mazeroski 30.00 15.00
❑ 60 Ken Boyer 25.00 12.50
❑ 61 Bob Gibson 80.00 50.00
❑ 62 Gene Oliver 15.00 7.50
❑ 63 Bill White 20.00 10.00
❑ 64 Orlando Cepeda 30.00 15.00
❑ 65 Jim Davenport 15.00 7.50
❑ 66 Billy O'Dell 25.00 12.50
❑ NNO Checklist SP 500.00 300.00

1981 Fleer

❑ COMPLETE SET (660) 40.00 15.00
❑ 1 Pete Rose 3.00 1.25
❑ 2 Larry Bowa .25 .08
❑ 3 Manny Trillo .10 .02
❑ 4 Bob Boone .25 .08
❑ 5 Mike Schmidt 2.50 1.00
❑ 6 Steve Carlton P1 .50 .20
❑ 6B Steve Carlton P2 1.50 .60
❑ 6C Steve Carlton P3 2.00 .75
❑ 7 Tug McGraw .25 .08
❑ 8 Larry Christenson .10 .02
❑ 9 Bake McBride .25 .08
❑ 10 Greg Luzinski .25 .08
❑ 11 Ron Reed .10 .02
❑ 12 Dickie Noles .10 .02
❑ 13 Keith Moreland RC .10 .02
❑ 14 Bob Walk RC .50 .20
❑ 15 Lonnie Smith .25 .08
❑ 16 Dick Ruthven .10 .02
❑ 17 Sparky Lyle .25 .08
❑ 18 Greg Gross .10 .02
❑ 19 Garry Maddox .10 .02
❑ 20 Nino Espinosa .10 .02
❑ 21 George Vukovich RC .10 .02
❑ 22 John Vukovich .10 .02
❑ 23 Ramon Aviles .10 .02
❑ 24A Kevin Saucier P1 .10 .02
❑ 24B Kevin Saucier P2 .10 .02
❑ 24C Kevin Saucier P3 .50 .20
❑ 25 Randy Lerch .10 .02
❑ 26 Del Unser .10 .02
❑ 27 Tim McCarver .25 .08
❑ 28 George Brett 2.50 1.00
❑ 29 Willie Wilson .25 .08
❑ 30 Paul Splittorff .10 .02
❑ 31 Dan Quisenberry .10 .02
❑ 32A Amos Otis P1 Batting .25 .08
❑ 32B Amos Otis P2 .25 .08
❑ 33 Steve Busby .10 .02
❑ 34 U.L. Washington .10 .02
❑ 35 Dave Chalk .10 .02
❑ 36 Darrell Porter .10 .02
❑ 37 Marty Pattin .10 .02
❑ 38 Larry Gura .10 .02
❑ 39 Renie Martin .10 .02
❑ 40 Rich Gale .10 .02
❑ 41A Hal McRae P1 .50 .20
❑ 41B Hal McRae P2 .25 .08
❑ 42 Dennis Leonard .10 .02
❑ 43 Willie Aikens .10 .02
❑ 44 Frank White .25 .08
❑ 45 Clint Hurdle .10 .02
❑ 46 John Wathan .10 .02
❑ 47 Pete LaCock .10 .02
❑ 48 Rance Mulliniks .10 .02
❑ 49 Jeff Twitty RC .10 .02
❑ 50 Jamie Quirk .10 .02
❑ 51 Art Howe .10 .02
❑ 52 Ken Forsch .10 .02
❑ 53 Vern Ruhle .10 .02
❑ 54 Joe Niekro .10 .02
❑ 55 Frank LaCorte .10 .02
❑ 56 J.R. Richard .25 .08
❑ 57 Nolan Ryan 5.00 2.00
❑ 58 Enos Cabell .10 .02
❑ 59 Cesar Cedeno .25 .08
❑ 60 Jose Cruz .25 .08
❑ 61 Bill Virdon MG .10 .02
❑ 62 Terry Puhl .10 .02
❑ 63 Joaquin Andujar .25 .08
❑ 64 Alan Ashby .10 .02
❑ 65 Joe Sambito .10 .02
❑ 66 Denny Walling .10 .02
❑ 67 Jeff Leonard .25 .08
❑ 68 Luis Pujols .10 .02
❑ 69 Bruce Bochy .10 .02
❑ 70 Rafael Landestoy .10 .02
❑ 71 Dave Smith RC .50 .20
❑ 72 Danny Heep RC .10 .02
❑ 73 Julio Gonzalez .10 .02
❑ 74 Craig Reynolds .10 .02
❑ 75 Gary Woods .10 .02
❑ 76 Dave Bergman .10 .02
❑ 77 Randy Niemann .10 .02
❑ 78 Joe Morgan .50 .20
❑ 79 Reggie Jackson 1.00 .40
❑ 80 Bucky Dent .25 .08
❑ 81 Tommy John .25 .08
❑ 82 Luis Tiant .25 .08
❑ 83 Rick Cerone .10 .02
❑ 84 Dick Howser MG .10 .02
❑ 85 Lou Piniella .25 .08
❑ 86 Ron Davis .10 .02
❑ 87A Craig Nettles P1 5.00 2.00
❑ 87B Graig Nettles COR .25 .08
❑ 88 Ron Guidry .25 .08
❑ 89 Rich Gossage .25 .08
❑ 90 Rudy May .10 .02
❑ 91 Gaylord Perry .25 .08
❑ 92 Eric Soderholm .10 .02
❑ 93 Bob Watson .10 .02
❑ 94 Bobby Murcer .25 .08
❑ 95 Bobby Brown .10 .02
❑ 96 Jim Spencer .10 .02
❑ 97 Tom Underwood .10 .02
❑ 98 Oscar Gamble .10 .02
❑ 99 Johnny Oates .25 .08
❑ 100 Fred Stanley .10 .02
❑ 101 Ruppert Jones .10 .02
❑ 102 Dennis Werth RC .10 .02
❑ 103 Joe Lefebvre RC .10 .02
❑ 104 Brian Doyle .10 .02
❑ 105 Aurelio Rodriguez .10 .02
❑ 106 Doug Bird .10 .02
❑ 107 Mike Griffin RC .15 .05
❑ 108 Tim Lollar RC .10 .02
❑ 109 Willie Randolph .25 .08
❑ 110 Steve Garvey .50 .20
❑ 111 Reggie Smith .25 .08
❑ 112 Don Sutton .25 .08
❑ 113 Burt Hooton .10 .02
❑ 114A Dave Lopes P1 .50 .20
❑ 114B Dave Lopes P2 .25 .08
❑ 115 Dusty Baker .25 .08
❑ 116 Tom Lasorda MG .50 .20
❑ 117 Bill Russell .25 .08
❑ 118 Jerry Reuss UER .10 .02
❑ 119 Terry Forster .25 .08
❑ 120A Bob Welch .25 .08
❑ 120B Bob Welch (Robert) .25 .08
❑ 121 Don Stanhouse .10 .02
❑ 122 Rick Monday .25 .08
❑ 123 Derrel Thomas .10 .02
❑ 124 Joe Ferguson .10 .02
❑ 125 Rick Sutcliffe .25 .08
❑ 126A Ron Cey P1 .25 .08
❑ 126B Ron Cey P2 .25 .08
❑ 127 Dave Goltz .10 .02
❑ 128 Jay Johnstone .10 .02
❑ 129 Steve Yeager .25 .08
❑ 130 Gary Weiss RC .10 .02
❑ 131 Mike Scioscia RC 1.50 .60
❑ 132 Vic Davalillo .10 .02
❑ 133 Doug Rau .10 .02
❑ 134 Pepe Frias .10 .02
❑ 135 Mickey Hatcher .10 .02
❑ 136 Steve Howe RC .50 .20
❑ 137 Robert Castillo RC .10 .02
❑ 138 Gary Thomasson .10 .02
❑ 139 Rudy Law .10 .02
❑ 140 Fernando Valenzuela RC 5.00 2.00
❑ 141 Manny Mota .25 .08
❑ 142 Gary Carter .50 .20
❑ 143 Steve Rogers .25 .08
❑ 144 Warren Cromartie .10 .02
❑ 145 Andre Dawson .50 .20
❑ 146 Larry Parrish .10 .02
❑ 147 Rowland Office .10 .02
❑ 148 Ellis Valentine .10 .02
❑ 149 Dick Williams MG .10 .02
❑ 150 Bill Gullickson RC .50 .20
❑ 151 Elias Sosa .10 .02
❑ 152 John Tamargo .10 .02
❑ 153 Chris Speier .10 .02
❑ 154 Ron LeFlore .25 .08
❑ 155 Rodney Scott .10 .02
❑ 156 Stan Bahnsen .10 .02
❑ 157 Bill Lee .25 .08
❑ 158 Fred Norman .10 .02
❑ 159 Woodie Fryman .10 .02
❑ 160 David Palmer .10 .02
❑ 161 Jerry White .10 .02
❑ 162 Roberto Ramos RC .10 .02
❑ 163 John D'Acquisto .10 .02
❑ 164 Tommy Hutton .10 .02
❑ 165 Charlie Lea RC .10 .02
❑ 166 Scott Sanderson .10 .02
❑ 167 Ken Macha .10 .02
❑ 168 Tony Bernazard .10 .02
❑ 169 Jim Palmer .50 .20
❑ 170 Steve Stone .10 .02
❑ 171 Mike Flanagan .10 .02
❑ 172 Al Bumbry .10 .02
❑ 173 Doug DeCinces .10 .02
❑ 174 Scott McGregor .10 .02
❑ 175 Mark Belanger .10 .02
❑ 176 Tim Stoddard .10 .02
❑ 177A Rick Dempsey P1 .25 .08
❑ 177B Rick Dempsey P2 .10 .02
❑ 178 Earl Weaver MG .25 .08
❑ 179 Tippy Martinez .10 .02
❑ 180 Dennis Martinez .25 .08
❑ 181 Sammy Stewart .10 .02
❑ 182 Rich Dauer .10 .02
❑ 183 Lee May .10 .02
❑ 184 Eddie Murray 1.50 .60
❑ 185 Benny Ayala .10 .02
❑ 186 John Lowenstein .10 .02
❑ 187 Gary Roenicke .10 .02
❑ 188 Ken Singleton .25 .08
❑ 189 Dan Graham .10 .02
❑ 190 Terry Crowley .10 .02
❑ 191 Kiko Garcia .10 .02
❑ 192 Dave Ford RC .10 .02
❑ 193 Mark Corey .10 .02
❑ 194 Lenn Sakata .10 .02
❑ 195 Doug DeCinces .10 .02
❑ 196 Johnny Bench 1.00 .40
❑ 197 Dave Concepcion .25 .08
❑ 198 Ray Knight .25 .08
❑ 199 Ken Griffey .25 .08
❑ 200 Tom Seaver 1.00 .40
❑ 201 Dave Collins .10 .02
❑ 202A George Foster P1 .50 .20
❑ 202B George Foster P2 .50 .20
❑ 203 Junior Kennedy .10 .02
❑ 204 Frank Pastore .10 .02

❑ 205 Dan Driessen	.10	.02
❑ 206 Hector Cruz	.10	.02
❑ 207 Paul Moskau	.10	.02
❑ 208 Charlie Leibrandt RC	.50	.20
❑ 209 Harry Spilman	.10	.02
❑ 210 Joe Price RC	.10	.02
❑ 211 Tom Hume	.10	.02
❑ 212 Joe Nolan RC	.10	.02
❑ 213 Doug Bair	.10	.02
❑ 214 Mario Soto	.25	.08
❑ 215A Bill Bonham P1	.50	.20
❑ 215B Bill Bonham P2	.10	.02
❑ 216 George Foster SLG	.25	.08
❑ 217 Paul Householder RC	.10	.02
❑ 218 Ron Oester	.10	.02
❑ 219 Sam Mejias	.10	.02
❑ 220 Sheldon Burnside RC	.10	.02
❑ 221 Carl Yastrzemski	1.50	.60
❑ 222 Jim Rice	.25	.08
❑ 223 Fred Lynn	.25	.08
❑ 224 Carlton Fisk	.50	.20
❑ 225 Rick Burleson	.10	.02
❑ 226 Dennis Eckersley	.50	.20
❑ 227 Butch Hobson	.10	.02
❑ 228 Tom Burgmeier	.10	.02
❑ 229 Garry Hancock	.10	.02
❑ 230 Don Zimmer MG	.25	.08
❑ 231 Steve Renko	.10	.02
❑ 232 Dwight Evans	.50	.20
❑ 233 Mike Torrez	.10	.02
❑ 234 Bob Stanley	.10	.02
❑ 235 Jim Dwyer	.10	.02
❑ 236 Dave Stapleton RC	.10	.02
❑ 237 Glenn Hoffman RC	.10	.02
❑ 238 Jerry Remy	.10	.02
❑ 239 Dick Drago	.10	.02
❑ 240 Bill Campbell	.10	.02
❑ 241 Tony Perez	.50	.20
❑ 242 Phil Niekro	.25	.08
❑ 243 Dale Murphy	.50	.20
❑ 244 Bob Horner	.25	.08
❑ 245 Jeff Burroughs	.25	.08
❑ 246 Rick Camp	.10	.02
❑ 247 Bobby Cox MG	.25	.08
❑ 248 Bruce Benedict	.10	.02
❑ 249 Gene Garber	.10	.02
❑ 250 Jerry Royster	.10	.02
❑ 251A Gary Matthews P1	.50	.20
❑ 251B Gary Matthews P2	.25	.08
❑ 252 Chris Chambliss	.25	.08
❑ 253 Luis Gomez	.10	.02
❑ 254 Bill Nahorodny	.10	.02
❑ 255 Doyle Alexander	.10	.02
❑ 256 Brian Asselstine	.10	.02
❑ 257 Biff Pocoroba	.10	.02
❑ 258 Mike Lum	.10	.02
❑ 259 Charlie Spikes	.10	.02
❑ 260 Glenn Hubbard	.10	.02
❑ 261 Tommy Boggs	.10	.02
❑ 262 Al Hrabosky	.25	.08
❑ 263 Rick Matula	.10	.02
❑ 264 Preston Hanna	.10	.02
❑ 265 Larry Bradford	.10	.02
❑ 266 Rafael Ramirez RC	.10	.02
❑ 267 Larry McWilliams	.10	.02
❑ 268 Rod Carew	.50	.20
❑ 269 Bobby Grich	.25	.08
❑ 270 Carney Lansford	.25	.08
❑ 271 Don Baylor	.25	.08
❑ 272 Joe Rudi	.25	.08
❑ 273 Dan Ford	.10	.02
❑ 274 Jim Fregosi MG	.10	.02
❑ 275 Dave Frost	.10	.02
❑ 276 Frank Tanana	.25	.08
❑ 277 Dickie Thon	.10	.02
❑ 278 Jason Thompson	.10	.02
❑ 279 Rick Miller	.10	.02
❑ 280 Bert Campaneris	.25	.08
❑ 281 Tom Donohue	.10	.02
❑ 282 Brian Downing	.25	.08
❑ 283 Fred Patek	.10	.02
❑ 284 Bruce Kison	.10	.02
❑ 285 Dave LaRoche	.10	.02
❑ 286 Don Aase	.10	.02
❑ 287 Jim Barr	.10	.02
❑ 288 Alfredo Martinez RC	.10	.02
❑ 289 Larry Harlow	.10	.02
❑ 290 Andy Hassler	.10	.02
❑ 291 Dave Kingman	.25	.08
❑ 292 Bill Buckner	.25	.08
❑ 293 Rick Reuschel	.25	.08
❑ 294 Bruce Sutter	.50	.20
❑ 295 Jerry Martin	.10	.02
❑ 296 Scot Thompson	.10	.02
❑ 297 Ivan DeJesus	.10	.02
❑ 298 Steve Dillard	.10	.02
❑ 299 Dick Tidrow	.10	.02
❑ 300 Randy Martz RC	.10	.02
❑ 301 Lenny Randle	.10	.02
❑ 302 Lynn McGlothen	.10	.02
❑ 303 Cliff Johnson	.10	.02
❑ 304 Tim Blackwell	.10	.02
❑ 305 Dennis Lamp	.10	.02
❑ 306 Bill Caudill	.10	.02
❑ 307 Carlos Lezcano RC	.10	.02
❑ 308 Jim Tracy RC	1.00	.40
❑ 309 Doug Capilla UER	.10	.02
❑ 310 Willie Hernandez	.10	.02
❑ 311 Mike Vail	.10	.02
❑ 312 Mike Krukow RC	.10	.02
❑ 313 Barry Foote	.10	.02
❑ 314 Larry Biittner	.10	.02
❑ 315 Mike Tyson	.10	.02
❑ 316 Lee Mazzilli	.25	.08
❑ 317 John Stearns	.10	.02
❑ 318 Alex Trevino	.10	.02
❑ 319 Craig Swan	.10	.02
❑ 320 Frank Taveras	.10	.02
❑ 321 Steve Henderson	.10	.02
❑ 322 Neil Allen	.10	.02
❑ 323 Mark Bomback RC	.10	.02
❑ 324 Mike Jorgensen	.10	.02
❑ 325 Joe Torre MG	.25	.08
❑ 326 Elliott Maddox	.10	.02
❑ 327 Pete Falcone	.10	.02
❑ 328 Ray Burris	.10	.02
❑ 329 Claudell Washington	.10	.02
❑ 330 Doug Flynn	.10	.02
❑ 331 Joel Youngblood	.10	.02
❑ 332 Bill Almon RC	.10	.02
❑ 333 Tom Hausman	.10	.02
❑ 334 Pat Zachry	.10	.02
❑ 335 Jeff Reardon RC	1.00	.40
❑ 336 Wally Backman RC	.50	.20
❑ 337 Dan Norman	.10	.02
❑ 338 Jerry Morales	.10	.02
❑ 339 Ed Farmer	.10	.02
❑ 340 Bob Molinaro	.10	.02
❑ 341 Todd Cruz	.10	.02
❑ 342A Britt Burns P1	.50	.20
❑ 342B Britt Burns P2 RC	.25	.08
❑ 343 Kevin Bell	.10	.02
❑ 344 Tony LaRussa MG	.25	.08
❑ 345 Steve Trout	.10	.02
❑ 346 Harold Baines RC	2.00	.75
❑ 347 Richard Wortham	.10	.02
❑ 348 Wayne Nordhagen	.10	.02
❑ 349 Mike Squires	.10	.02
❑ 350 Lamar Johnson	.10	.02
❑ 351 Rickey Henderson SB	3.00	1.25
❑ 352 Francisco Barrios	.10	.02
❑ 353 Thad Bosley	.10	.02
❑ 354 Chet Lemon	.25	.08
❑ 355 Bruce Kimm	.10	.02
❑ 356 Richard Dotson RC	.10	.02
❑ 357 Jim Morrison	.10	.02
❑ 358 Mike Proly	.10	.02
❑ 359 Greg Pryor	.10	.02
❑ 360 Dave Parker	.25	.08
❑ 361 Omar Moreno	.10	.02
❑ 362A Kent Tekulve P1	.10	.02
❑ 362B Kent Tekulve P2	.10	.02
❑ 363 Willie Stargell	.50	.20
❑ 364 Phil Garner	.25	.08
❑ 365 Ed Ott	.10	.02
❑ 366 Don Robinson	.10	.02
❑ 367 Chuck Tanner MG	.10	.02
❑ 368 Jim Rooker	.10	.02
❑ 369 Dale Berra	.10	.02
❑ 370 Jim Bibby	.10	.02
❑ 371 Steve Nicosia	.10	.02
❑ 372 Mike Easler	.10	.02
❑ 373 Bill Robinson	.10	.02
❑ 374 Lee Lacy	.10	.02
❑ 375 John Candelaria	.25	.08
❑ 376 Manny Sanguillen	.25	.08
❑ 377 Rick Rhoden	.10	.02
❑ 378 Grant Jackson	.10	.02
❑ 379 Tim Foli	.10	.02
❑ 380 Rod Scurry RC	.10	.02
❑ 381 Bill Madlock	.25	.08
❑ 382A Kurt Bevacqua P1	.25	.08
❑ 382B Kurt Bevacqua P2	.10	.02
❑ 383 Bert Blyleven	.25	.08
❑ 384 Eddie Solomon	.10	.02
❑ 385 Enrique Romo	.10	.02
❑ 386 John Milner	.10	.02
❑ 387 Mike Hargrove	.10	.02
❑ 388 Jorge Orta	.10	.02
❑ 389 Toby Harrah	.25	.08
❑ 390 Tom Veryzer	.10	.02
❑ 391 Miguel Dilone	.10	.02
❑ 392 Dan Spillner	.10	.02
❑ 393 Jack Brohamer	.10	.02
❑ 394 Wayne Garland	.10	.02
❑ 395 Sid Monge	.10	.02
❑ 396 Rick Waits	.10	.02
❑ 397 Joe Charboneau RC	1.00	.40
❑ 398 Gary Alexander	.10	.02
❑ 399 Jerry Dybzinski RC	.10	.02
❑ 400 Mike Stanton RC	.10	.02
❑ 401 Mike Paxton	.10	.02
❑ 402 Gary Gray RC	.10	.02
❑ 403 Rick Manning	.10	.02
❑ 404 Bo Diaz	.10	.02
❑ 405 Ron Hassey	.10	.02
❑ 406 Ross Grimsley	.10	.02
❑ 407 Victor Cruz	.10	.02
❑ 408 Len Barker	.25	.08
❑ 409 Bob Bailor	.10	.02
❑ 410 Otto Velez	.10	.02
❑ 411 Ernie Whitt	.10	.02
❑ 412 Jim Clancy	.10	.02
❑ 413 Barry Bonnell	.10	.02
❑ 414 Dave Stieb	.25	.08
❑ 415 Damaso Garcia RC	.10	.02
❑ 416 John Mayberry	.10	.02
❑ 417 Roy Howell	.10	.02
❑ 418 Danny Ainge RC	3.00	1.25
❑ 419A Jesse Jefferson P1	.10	.02
❑ 419B Jesse Jefferson P2	.10	.02
❑ 419C Jesse Jefferson P3	.50	.20
❑ 420 Joey McLaughlin	.10	.02
❑ 421 Lloyd Moseby RC	.50	.20
❑ 422 Alvis Woods	.10	.02
❑ 423 Garth Iorg	.10	.02
❑ 424 Doug Ault	.10	.02
❑ 425 Ken Schrom RC	.10	.02
❑ 426 Mike Willis	.10	.02
❑ 427 Steve Braun	.10	.02
❑ 428 Bob Davis	.10	.02
❑ 429 Jerry Garvin	.10	.02
❑ 430 Alfredo Griffin	.10	.02
❑ 431 Bob Mattick MG RC	.10	.02
❑ 432 Vida Blue	.25	.08
❑ 433 Jack Clark	.25	.08
❑ 434 Willie McCovey	.50	.20
❑ 435 Mike Ivie	.10	.02
❑ 436A Darrel Evans P1 ERR	.50	.20
❑ 436B Darrell Evans P2 COR	.50	.20
❑ 437 Terry Whitfield	.10	.02
❑ 438 Rennie Stennett	.10	.02
❑ 439 John Montefusco	.10	.02
❑ 440 Jim Wohlford	.10	.02
❑ 441 Bill North	.10	.02
❑ 442 Milt May	.10	.02
❑ 443 Max Venable RC	.10	.02
❑ 444 Ed Whitson	.10	.02
❑ 445 Al Holland RC	.10	.02
❑ 446 Randy Moffitt	.10	.02
❑ 447 Bob Knepper	.10	.02
❑ 448 Gary Lavelle	.10	.02
❑ 449 Greg Minton	.10	.02
❑ 450 Johnnie LeMaster	.10	.02
❑ 451 Larry Herndon	.10	.02
❑ 452 Rich Murray RC	.10	.02
❑ 453 Joe Pettini RC	.10	.02
❑ 454 Allen Ripley	.10	.02

455	Dennis Littlejohn	.10	.02
456	Tom Griffin	.10	.02
457	Alan Hargesheimer RC	.10	.02
458	Joe Strain	.10	.02
459	Steve Kemp	.10	.02
460	Sparky Anderson MG	.25	.08
461	Alan Trammell	.50	.20
462	Mark Fidrych	.25	.08
463	Lou Whitaker	.50	.20
464	Dave Rozema	.10	.02
465	Milt Wilcox	.10	.02
466	Champ Summers	.10	.02
467	Lance Parrish	.25	.08
468	Dan Petry	.10	.02
469	Pat Underwood	.10	.02
470	Rick Peters RC	.10	.02
471	Al Cowens	.10	.02
472	John Wockenfuss	.10	.02
473	Tom Brookens	.10	.02
474	Richie Hebner	.10	.02
475	Jack Morris	.50	.20
476	Jim Lentine RC	.10	.02
477	Bruce Robbins	.10	.02
478	Mark Wagner	.10	.02
479	Tim Corcoran	.10	.02
480A	Stan Papi P1	.25	.08
480B	Stan Papi P2	.10	.02
481	Kirk Gibson RC	5.00	2.00
482	Dan Schatzeder	.10	.02
483A	Amos Otis P1	.25	.08
483B	Amos Otis P2	.25	.08
484	Dave Winfield	.50	.20
485	Rollie Fingers	.25	.08
486	Gene Richards	.10	.02
487	Randy Jones	.10	.02
488	Ozzie Smith	3.00	1.25
489	Gene Tenace	.25	.08
490	Bill Fahey	.10	.02
491	John Curtis	.10	.02
492	Dave Cash	.10	.02
493A	Tim Flannery P1	.25	.08
493B	Tim Flannery P2	.10	.02
494	Jerry Mumphrey	.10	.02
495	Bob Shirley	.10	.02
496	Steve Mura	.10	.02
497	Eric Rasmussen	.10	.02
498	Broderick Perkins	.10	.02
499	Barry Evans RC	.10	.02
500	Chuck Baker	.10	.02
501	Luis Salazar RC	.50	.20
502	Gary Lucas RC	.10	.02
503	Mike Armstrong RC	.10	.02
504	Jerry Turner	.10	.02
505	Dennis Kinney RC	.10	.02
506	Willie Montanez UER	.10	.02
507	Gorman Thomas	.25	.08
508	Ben Oglivie	.25	.08
509	Larry Hisle	.10	.02
510	Sal Bando	.25	.08
511	Robin Yount	1.50	.60
512	Mike Caldwell	.10	.02
513	Sixto Lezcano	.10	.02
514A	Bill Travers P1 ERR	.25	.08
514B	Bill Travers P2 COR	.10	.02
515	Paul Molitor	1.00	.40
516	Moose Haas	.10	.02
517	Bill Castro	.10	.02
518	Jim Slaton	.10	.02
519	Lary Sorensen	.10	.02
520	Bob McClure	.10	.02
521	Charlie Moore	.10	.02
522	Jim Gantner	.10	.02
523	Reggie Cleveland	.10	.02
524	Don Money	.10	.02
525	Bill Travers	.10	.02
526	Buck Martinez	.10	.02
527	Dick Davis	.10	.02
528	Ted Simmons	.25	.08
529	Garry Templeton	.25	.08
530	Ken Reitz	.10	.02
531	Tony Scott	.10	.02
532	Ken Oberkfell	.10	.02
533	Bob Sykes	.10	.02
534	Keith Smith	.10	.02
535	John Littlefield RC	.10	.02
536	Jim Kaat	.25	.08
537	Bob Forsch	.10	.02
538	Mike Phillips	.10	.02
539	Terry Landrum RC	.10	.02
540	Leon Durham RC	.50	.20
541	Terry Kennedy	.10	.02
542	George Hendrick	.25	.08
543	Dane Iorg	.10	.02
544	Mark Littell	.10	.02
545	Keith Hernandez	.25	.08
546	Silvio Martinez	.10	.02
547A	Don Hood P1 ERR	.25	.08
547B	Don Hood P2 COR	.10	.02
548	Bobby Bonds	.25	.08
549	Mike Ramsey RC	.15	.05
550	Tom Herr	.10	.02
551	Roy Smalley	.10	.02
552	Jerry Koosman	.25	.08
553	Ken Landreaux	.10	.02
554	John Castino	.10	.02
555	Doug Corbett RC	.10	.02
556	Bombo Rivera	.10	.02
557	Ron Jackson	.10	.02
558	Butch Wynegar	.10	.02
559	Hosken Powell	.10	.02
560	Pete Redfern	.10	.02
561	Roger Erickson	.10	.02
562	Glenn Adams	.10	.02
563	Rick Sofield	.10	.02
564	Geoff Zahn	.10	.02
565	Pete Mackanin	.10	.02
566	Mike Cubbage	.10	.02
567	Darrell Jackson	.10	.02
568	Dave Edwards	.10	.02
569	Rob Wilfong	.10	.02
570	Sal Butera RC	.10	.02
571	Jose Morales	.10	.02
572	Rick Langford	.10	.02
573	Mike Norris	.10	.02
574	Rickey Henderson	6.00	2.50
575	Tony Armas	.25	.08
576	Dave Revering	.10	.02
577	Jeff Newman	.10	.02
578	Bob Lacey	.10	.02
579	Brian Kingman	.10	.02
580	Mitchell Page	.10	.02
581	Billy Martin MG	.50	.20
582	Rob Picciolo	.10	.02
583	Mike Heath	.10	.02
584	Mickey Klutts	.10	.02
585	Orlando Gonzalez	.10	.02
586	Mike Davis RC	.50	.20
587	Wayne Gross	.10	.02
588	Matt Keough	.10	.02
589	Steve McCatty	.10	.02
590	Dwayne Murphy	.10	.02
591	Mario Guerrero	.10	.02
592	Dave McKay RC	.10	.02
593	Jim Essian	.10	.02
594	Dave Heaverlo	.10	.02
595	Maury Wills MG	.25	.08
596	Juan Beniquez	.10	.02
597	Rodney Craig	.10	.02
598	Jim Anderson	.10	.02
599	Floyd Bannister	.10	.02
600	Bruce Bochte	.10	.02
601	Julio Cruz	.10	.02
602	Ted Cox	.10	.02
603	Dan Meyer	.10	.02
604	Larry Cox	.10	.02
605	Bill Stein	.10	.02
606	Steve Garvey	.50	.20
607	Dave Roberts	.10	.02
608	Leon Roberts	.10	.02
609	Reggie Walton RC	.10	.02
610	Dave Edler RC	.10	.02
611	Larry Milbourne	.10	.02
612	Kim Allen RC	.10	.02
613	Mario Mendoza	.10	.02
614	Tom Paciorek	.10	.02
615	Glenn Abbott	.10	.02
616	Joe Simpson	.10	.02
617	Mickey Rivers	.10	.02
618	Jim Kern	.10	.02
619	Jim Sundberg	.25	.08
620	Richie Zisk	.10	.02
621	Jon Matlack	.10	.02
622	Fergie Jenkins	.25	.08
623	Pat Corrales MG	.10	.02
624	Ed Figueroa	.10	.02
625	Buddy Bell	.25	.08
626	Al Oliver	.25	.08
627	Doc Medich	.10	.02
628	Bump Wills	.10	.02
629	Rusty Staub	.25	.08
630	Pat Putnam	.10	.02
631	John Grubb	.10	.02
632	Danny Darwin	.10	.02
633	Ken Clay	.10	.02
634	Jim Norris	.10	.02
635	John Butcher RC	.10	.02
636	Dave Roberts	.10	.02
637	Billy Sample	.10	.02
638	Carl Yastrzemski	1.50	.60
639	Cecil Cooper	.25	.08
640	M.Schmidt Portrait P1	2.50	1.00
640B	M.Schmidt Portrait P2	2.50	1.00
641A	CL: Phils/Royals P1	.25	.08
641B	CL: Phils/Royals P2	.25	.08
642	CL: Astros/Yankees	.10	.02
643	CL: Expos/Dodgers	.10	.02
644A	CL: Reds/Orioles P1	.25	.08
644B	CL: Reds/Orioles P2	.25	.08
645	Rose/Bowa/Schmidt	1.50	.60
645B	Rose/Bowa/Schmidt	2.50	1.00
646	CL: Braves/Red Sox	.10	.02
647	CL: Cubs/Angels	.10	.02
648	CL: Mets/White Sox	.10	.02
649	CL: Indians/Pirates	.10	.02
650	Reggie Jackson Mr. BB	1.00	.40
650B	R.Jackson Mr. BB P2	.50	.20
651	CL: Giants/Blue Jays	.10	.02
652A	CL: Tigers/Padres P1	.25	.08
652B	CL: Tigers/Padres P2	.25	.08
653A	Willie Wilson Most Hits	.25	.08
653B	W.Wilson Hits P2	.25	.08
654A	CL:Brewers/Cards P1	.25	.08
654B	CL:Brewers/Cards P2	.25	.08
655	George Brett .390 Avg.	2.50	1.00
655B	G.Brett .390 Avg. P2	2.50	1.00
656	CL: Twins/Oakland A's	.25	.08
657A	Tug McGraw Saver	.25	.08
657B	T.McGraw Saver P2	.25	.08
658	CL: Rangers/Mariners	.10	.02
659A	Checklist P1	.10	.02
659B	Checklist P2	.10	.02
660	S.Carlton Gold Arm P1	.50	.20
660B	S.Carlton Golden Arm	2.00	.75

1982 Fleer

	COMPLETE SET (660)	50.00	20.00
1	Dusty Baker	.20	.07
2	Robert Castillo	.10	.02
3	Ron Cey	.20	.07
4	Terry Forster	.20	.07
5	Steve Garvey	.20	.07
6	Dave Goltz	.10	.02
7	Pedro Guerrero	.20	.07
8	Burt Hooton	.10	.02
9	Steve Howe	.10	.02
10	Jay Johnstone	.10	.02
11	Ken Landreaux	.10	.02
12	Dave Lopes	.20	.07
13	Mike A. Marshall RC	.50	.20
14	Bobby Mitchell	.10	.02

	Card		
❑	15 Rick Monday	.20	.07
❑	16 Tom Niedenfuer RC	.50	.20
❑	17 Ted Power RC	.15	.05
❑	18 Jerry Reuss UER (%%Home:~ omitted)	.10	.02
❑	19 Ron Roenicke	.10	.02
❑	20 Bill Russell	.20	.07
❑	21 Steve Sax RC	1.00	.40
❑	22 Mike Scioscia	.20	.07
❑	23 Reggie Smith	.20	.07
❑	24 Dave Stewart RC	1.50	.60
❑	25 Rick Sutcliffe	.20	.07
❑	26 Derrel Thomas	.10	.02
❑	27 Fernando Valenzuela	.75	.30
❑	28 Bob Welch	.20	.07
❑	29 Steve Yeager	.20	.07
❑	30 Bobby Brown	.10	.02
❑	31 Rick Cerone	.10	.02
❑	32 Ron Davis	.10	.02
❑	33 Bucky Dent	.20	.07
❑	34 Barry Foote	.10	.02
❑	35 George Frazier	.10	.02
❑	36 Oscar Gamble	.10	.02
❑	37 Rich Gossage	.20	.07
❑	38 Ron Guidry	.20	.07
❑	39 Reggie Jackson	.40	.15
❑	40 Tommy John	.20	.07
❑	41 Rudy May	.10	.02
❑	42 Larry Milbourne	.10	.02
❑	43 Jerry Mumphrey	.10	.02
❑	44 Bobby Murcer	.20	.07
❑	45 Gene Nelson	.10	.02
❑	46 Graig Nettles	.20	.07
❑	47 Johnny Oates	.20	.07
❑	48 Lou Piniella	.20	.07
❑	49 Willie Randolph	.20	.07
❑	50 Rick Reuschel	.20	.07
❑	51 Dave Revering	.10	.02
❑	52 Dave Righetti RC	1.50	.60
❑	53 Aurelio Rodriguez	.10	.02
❑	54 Bob Watson	.10	.02
❑	55 Dennis Werth	.10	.02
❑	56 Dave Winfield	.20	.07
❑	57 Johnny Bench	.75	.30
❑	58 Bruce Berenyi	.10	.02
❑	59 Larry Biittner	.10	.02
❑	60 Scott Brown	.10	.02
❑	61 Dave Collins	.10	.02
❑	62 Geoff Combe	.10	.02
❑	63 Dave Concepcion	.20	.07
❑	64 Dan Driessen	.10	.02
❑	65 Joe Edelen	.10	.02
❑	66 George Foster	.20	.07
❑	67 Ken Griffey	.20	.07
❑	68 Paul Householder	.10	.02
❑	69 Tom Hume	.10	.02
❑	70 Junior Kennedy	.10	.02
❑	71 Ray Knight	.20	.07
❑	72 Mike LaCoss	.10	.02
❑	73 Rafael Landestoy	.10	.02
❑	74 Charlie Leibrandt	.10	.02
❑	75 Sam Mejias	.10	.02
❑	76 Paul Moskau	.10	.02
❑	77 Joe Nolan	.10	.02
❑	78 Mike O'Berry	.10	.02
❑	79 Ron Oester	.10	.02
❑	80 Frank Pastore	.10	.02
❑	81 Joe Price	.10	.02
❑	82 Tom Seaver	.75	.30
❑	83 Mario Soto	.20	.07
❑	84 Mike Vail	.10	.02
❑	85 Tony Armas	.20	.07
❑	86 Shooty Babitt	.10	.02
❑	87 Dave Beard	.10	.02
❑	88 Rick Bosetti	.10	.02
❑	89 Keith Drumwright	.10	.02
❑	90 Wayne Gross	.10	.02
❑	91 Mike Heath	.10	.02
❑	92 Rickey Henderson	2.50	1.00
❑	93 Cliff Johnson	.10	.02
❑	94 Jeff Jones	.10	.02
❑	95 Matt Keough	.10	.02
❑	96 Brian Kingman	.10	.02
❑	97 Mickey Klutts	.10	.02
❑	98 Rick Langford	.10	.02
❑	99 Steve McCatty	.10	.02
❑	100 Dave McKay	.10	.02
❑	101 Dwayne Murphy	.10	.02
❑	102 Jeff Newman	.10	.02
❑	103 Mike Norris	.10	.02
❑	104 Bob Owchinko	.10	.02
❑	105 Mitchell Page	.10	.02
❑	106 Rob Picciolo	.10	.02
❑	107 Jim Spencer	.10	.02
❑	108 Fred Stanley	.10	.02
❑	109 Tom Underwood	.10	.02
❑	110 Joaquin Andujar	.20	.07
❑	111 Steve Braun	.10	.02
❑	112 Bob Forsch	.10	.02
❑	113 George Hendrick	.20	.07
❑	114 Keith Hernandez	.20	.07
❑	115 Tom Herr	.10	.02
❑	116 Dane Iorg	.10	.02
❑	117 Jim Kaat	.20	.07
❑	118 Tito Landrum	.10	.02
❑	119 Sixto Lezcano	.10	.02
❑	120 Mark Littell	.10	.02
❑	121 John Martin RC	.15	.05
❑	122 Silvio Martinez	.10	.02
❑	123 Ken Oberkfell	.10	.02
❑	124 Darrell Porter	.10	.02
❑	125 Mike Ramsey	.10	.02
❑	126 Orlando Sanchez	.10	.02
❑	127 Bob Shirley	.10	.02
❑	128 Lary Sorensen	.10	.02
❑	129 Bruce Sutter	.40	.15
❑	130 Bob Sykes	.10	.02
❑	131 Garry Templeton	.20	.07
❑	132 Gene Tenace	.20	.07
❑	133 Jerry Augustine	.10	.02
❑	134 Sal Bando	.20	.07
❑	135 Mark Brouhard	.10	.02
❑	136 Mike Caldwell	.10	.02
❑	137 Reggie Cleveland	.10	.02
❑	138 Cecil Cooper	.20	.07
❑	139 Jamie Easterly	.10	.02
❑	140 Marshall Edwards	.10	.02
❑	141 Rollie Fingers	.20	.07
❑	142 Jim Gantner	.10	.02
❑	143 Moose Haas	.10	.02
❑	144 Larry Hisle	.10	.02
❑	145 Roy Howell	.10	.02
❑	146 Rickey Keeton	.10	.02
❑	147 Randy Lerch	.10	.02
❑	148 Paul Molitor	.20	.07
❑	149 Don Money	.10	.02
❑	150 Charlie Moore	.10	.02
❑	151 Ben Oglivie	.20	.07
❑	152 Ted Simmons	.20	.07
❑	153 Jim Slaton	.10	.02
❑	154 Gorman Thomas	.20	.07
❑	155 Robin Yount	1.25	.50
❑	156 Pete Vuckovich (Should precede Yount in the team	.10	.02
❑	157 Benny Ayala	.10	.02
❑	158 Mark Belanger	.10	.02
❑	159 Al Bumbry	.10	.02
❑	160 Terry Crowley	.10	.02
❑	161 Rich Dauer	.10	.02
❑	162 Doug DeCinces	.10	.02
❑	163 Rick Dempsey	.10	.02
❑	164 Jim Dwyer	.10	.02
❑	165 Mike Flanagan	.10	.02
❑	166 Dave Ford	.10	.02
❑	167 Dan Graham	.10	.02
❑	168 Wayne Krenchicki	.10	.02
❑	169 John Lowenstein	.10	.02
❑	170 Dennis Martinez	.20	.07
❑	171 Tippy Martinez	.10	.02
❑	172 Scott McGregor	.10	.02
❑	173 Jose Morales	.10	.02
❑	174 Eddie Murray	.75	.30
❑	175 Jim Palmer	.20	.07
❑	176 Cal Ripken RC	40.00	15.00
❑	177 Gary Roenicke	.10	.02
❑	178 Lenn Sakata	.10	.02
❑	179 Ken Singleton	.20	.07
❑	180 Sammy Stewart	.10	.02
❑	181 Tim Stoddard	.10	.02
❑	182 Steve Stone	.10	.02
❑	183 Stan Bahnsen	.10	.02
❑	184 Ray Burris	.10	.02
❑	185 Gary Carter	.20	.07
❑	186 Warren Cromartie	.10	.02
❑	187 Andre Dawson	.20	.07
❑	188 Terry Francona RC	3.00	1.25
❑	189 Woodie Fryman	.10	.02
❑	190 Bill Gullickson	.10	.02
❑	191 Grant Jackson	.10	.02
❑	192 Wallace Johnson	.10	.02
❑	193 Charlie Lea	.10	.02
❑	194 Bill Lee	.20	.07
❑	195 Jerry Manuel	.10	.02
❑	196 Brad Mills	.10	.02
❑	197 John Milner	.10	.02
❑	198 Rowland Office	.10	.02
❑	199 David Palmer	.10	.02
❑	200 Larry Parrish	.10	.02
❑	201 Mike Phillips	.10	.02
❑	202 Tim Raines	.40	.15
❑	203 Bobby Ramos	.10	.02
❑	204 Jeff Reardon	.20	.07
❑	205 Steve Rogers	.20	.07
❑	206 Scott Sanderson	.10	.02
❑	207 Rodney Scott UER Raines	.40	.15
❑	208 Elias Sosa	.10	.02
❑	209 Chris Speier	.10	.02
❑	210 Tim Wallach RC	1.00	.40
❑	211 Jerry White	.10	.02
❑	212 Alan Ashby	.10	.02
❑	213 Cesar Cedeno	.20	.07
❑	214 Jose Cruz	.20	.07
❑	215 Kiko Garcia	.10	.02
❑	216 Phil Garner	.20	.07
❑	217 Danny Heep	.10	.02
❑	218 Art Howe	.10	.02
❑	219 Bob Knepper	.10	.02
❑	220 Frank LaCorte	.10	.02
❑	221 Joe Niekro	.10	.02
❑	222 Joe Pittman	.10	.02
❑	223 Terry Puhl	.10	.02
❑	224 Luis Pujols	.10	.02
❑	225 Craig Reynolds	.10	.02
❑	226 J.R. Richard	.20	.07
❑	227 Dave Roberts	.10	.02
❑	228 Vern Ruhle	.10	.02
❑	229 Nolan Ryan	4.00	1.50
❑	230 Joe Sambito	.10	.02
❑	231 Tony Scott	.10	.02
❑	232 Dave Smith	.10	.02
❑	233 Harry Spilman	.10	.02
❑	234 Don Sutton	.20	.07
❑	235 Dickie Thon	.10	.02
❑	236 Denny Walling	.10	.02
❑	237 Gary Woods	.10	.02
❑	238 Luis Aguayo	.10	.02
❑	239 Ramon Aviles	.10	.02
❑	240 Bob Boone	.20	.07
❑	241 Larry Bowa	.20	.07
❑	242 Warren Brusstar	.10	.02
❑	243 Steve Carlton	.40	.15
❑	244 Larry Christenson	.10	.02
❑	245 Dick Davis	.10	.02
❑	246 Greg Gross	.10	.02
❑	247 Sparky Lyle	.20	.07
❑	248 Garry Maddox	.10	.02
❑	249 Gary Matthews	.20	.07
❑	250 Bake McBride	.20	.07
❑	251 Tug McGraw	.20	.07
❑	252 Keith Moreland	.10	.02
❑	253 Dickie Noles	.10	.02
❑	254 Mike Proly	.10	.02
❑	255 Ron Reed	.10	.02
❑	256 Pete Rose	2.50	1.00
❑	257 Dick Ruthven	.10	.02
❑	258 Mike Schmidt	2.00	.75
❑	259 Lonnie Smith	.10	.02
❑	260 Manny Trillo	.10	.02
❑	261 Del Unser	.10	.02
❑	262 George Vukovich	.10	.02
❑	263 Tom Brookens	.10	.02
❑	264 George Cappuzzello	.10	.02
❑	265 Marty Castillo	.10	.02
❑	266 Al Cowens	.10	.02
❑	267 Kirk Gibson	.75	.30
❑	268 Richie Hebner	.10	.02
❑	269 Ron Jackson	.10	.02

Card		
❑ 270 Lynn Jones	.10	.02
❑ 271 Steve Kemp	.10	.02
❑ 272 Rick Leach	.10	.02
❑ 273 Aurelio Lopez	.10	.02
❑ 274 Jack Morris	.20	.07
❑ 275 Kevin Saucier	.10	.02
❑ 276 Lance Parrish	.20	.07
❑ 277 Rick Peters	.10	.02
❑ 278 Dan Petry	.10	.02
❑ 279 Dave Rozema	.10	.02
❑ 280 Stan Papi	.10	.02
❑ 281 Dan Schatzeder	.10	.02
❑ 282 Champ Summers	.10	.02
❑ 283 Alan Trammell	.20	.07
❑ 284 Lou Whitaker	.20	.07
❑ 285 Milt Wilcox	.10	.02
❑ 286 John Wockenfuss	.10	.02
❑ 287 Gary Allenson	.10	.02
❑ 288 Tom Burgmeier	.10	.02
❑ 289 Bill Campbell	.10	.02
❑ 290 Mark Clear	.10	.02
❑ 291 Steve Crawford	.10	.02
❑ 292 Dennis Eckersley	.40	.15
❑ 293 Dwight Evans	.40	.15
❑ 294 Rich Gedman	.50	.20
❑ 295 Garry Hancock	.10	.02
❑ 296 Glenn Hoffman	.10	.02
❑ 297 Bruce Hurst	.10	.02
❑ 298 Carney Lansford	.20	.07
❑ 299 Rick Miller	.10	.02
❑ 300 Reid Nichols	.10	.02
❑ 301 Bob Ojeda RC	.50	.20
❑ 302 Tony Perez	.40	.15
❑ 303 Chuck Rainey	.10	.02
❑ 304 Jerry Remy	.10	.02
❑ 305 Jim Rice	.20	.07
❑ 306 Joe Rudi	.20	.07
❑ 307 Bob Stanley	.10	.02
❑ 308 Dave Stapleton	.10	.02
❑ 309 Frank Tanana	.20	.07
❑ 310 Mike Torrez	.10	.02
❑ 311 John Tudor	.20	.07
❑ 312 Carl Yastrzemski	1.25	.50
❑ 313 Buddy Bell	.20	.07
❑ 314 Steve Comer	.10	.02
❑ 315 Danny Darwin	.10	.02
❑ 316 John Ellis	.10	.02
❑ 317 John Grubb	.10	.02
❑ 318 Rick Honeycutt	.10	.02
❑ 319 Charlie Hough	.20	.07
❑ 320 Fergie Jenkins	.20	.07
❑ 321 John Henry Johnson	.10	.02
❑ 322 Jim Kern	.10	.02
❑ 323 Jon Matlack	.10	.02
❑ 324 Doc Medich	.10	.02
❑ 325 Mario Mendoza	.10	.02
❑ 326 Al Oliver	.20	.07
❑ 327 Pat Putnam	.10	.02
❑ 328 Mickey Rivers	.10	.02
❑ 329 Leon Roberts	.10	.02
❑ 330 Billy Sample	.10	.02
❑ 331 Bill Stein	.10	.02
❑ 332 Jim Sundberg	.20	.07
❑ 333 Mark Wagner	.10	.02
❑ 334 Bump Wills	.10	.02
❑ 335 Bill Almon	.10	.02
❑ 336 Harold Baines	.20	.07
❑ 337 Ross Baumgarten	.10	.02
❑ 338 Tony Bernazard	.10	.02
❑ 339 Britt Burns	.10	.02
❑ 340 Richard Dotson	.10	.02
❑ 341 Jim Essian	.10	.02
❑ 342 Ed Farmer	.10	.02
❑ 343 Carlton Fisk	.40	.15
❑ 344 Kevin Hickey RC	.15	.05
❑ 345 LaMarr Hoyt	.10	.02
❑ 346 Lamar Johnson	.10	.02
❑ 347 Jerry Koosman	.20	.07
❑ 348 Rusty Kuntz	.10	.02
❑ 349 Dennis Lamp	.10	.02
❑ 350 Ron LeFlore	.20	.07
❑ 351 Chet Lemon	.20	.07
❑ 352 Greg Luzinski	.20	.07
❑ 353 Bob Molinaro	.10	.02
❑ 354 Jim Morrison	.10	.02
❑ 355 Wayne Nordhagen	.10	.02
❑ 356 Greg Pryor	.10	.02
❑ 357 Mike Squires	.10	.02
❑ 358 Steve Trout	.10	.02
❑ 359 Alan Bannister	.10	.02
❑ 360 Len Barker	.10	.02
❑ 361 Bert Blyleven	.20	.07
❑ 362 Joe Charboneau	.20	.07
❑ 363 John Denny	.10	.02
❑ 364 Bo Diaz	.10	.02
❑ 365 Miguel Dilone	.10	.02
❑ 366 Jerry Dybzinski	.10	.02
❑ 367 Wayne Garland	.10	.02
❑ 368 Mike Hargrove	.10	.02
❑ 369 Toby Harrah	.20	.07
❑ 370 Ron Hassey	.10	.02
❑ 371 Von Hayes RC	.50	.20
❑ 372 Pat Kelly	.10	.02
❑ 373 Duane Kuiper	.10	.02
❑ 374 Rick Manning	.10	.02
❑ 375 Sid Monge	.10	.02
❑ 376 Jorge Orta	.10	.02
❑ 377 Dave Rosello	.10	.02
❑ 378 Dan Spillner	.10	.02
❑ 379 Mike Stanton	.10	.02
❑ 380 Andre Thornton	.10	.02
❑ 381 Tom Veryzer	.10	.02
❑ 382 Rick Waits	.10	.02
❑ 383 Doyle Alexander	.10	.02
❑ 384 Vida Blue	.20	.07
❑ 385 Fred Breining	.10	.02
❑ 386 Enos Cabell	.10	.02
❑ 387 Jack Clark	.20	.07
❑ 388 Darrell Evans	.20	.07
❑ 389 Tom Griffin	.10	.02
❑ 390 Larry Herndon	.10	.02
❑ 391 Al Holland	.10	.02
❑ 392 Gary Lavelle	.10	.02
❑ 393 Johnnie LeMaster	.10	.02
❑ 394 Jerry Martin	.10	.02
❑ 395 Milt May	.10	.02
❑ 396 Greg Minton	.10	.02
❑ 397 Joe Morgan	.20	.07
❑ 398 Joe Pettini	.10	.02
❑ 399 Allen Ripley	.10	.02
❑ 400 Billy Smith	.10	.02
❑ 401 Rennie Stennett	.10	.02
❑ 402 Ed Whitson	.10	.02
❑ 403 Jim Wohlford	.10	.02
❑ 404 Willie Aikens	.10	.02
❑ 405 George Brett	2.00	.75
❑ 406 Ken Brett	.10	.02
❑ 407 Dave Chalk	.10	.02
❑ 408 Rich Gale	.10	.02
❑ 409 Cesar Geronimo	.10	.02
❑ 410 Larry Gura	.10	.02
❑ 411 Clint Hurdle	.10	.02
❑ 412 Mike Jones	.10	.02
❑ 413 Dennis Leonard	.10	.02
❑ 414 Renie Martin	.10	.02
❑ 415 Lee May	.10	.02
❑ 416 Hal McRae	.20	.07
❑ 417 Darryl Motley	.10	.02
❑ 418 Rance Mulliniks	.10	.02
❑ 419 Amos Otis	.20	.07
❑ 420 Ken Phelps	.10	.02
❑ 421 Jamie Quirk	.10	.02
❑ 422 Dan Quisenberry	.10	.02
❑ 423 Paul Splittorff	.10	.02
❑ 424 U.L. Washington	.10	.02
❑ 425 John Wathan	.10	.02
❑ 426 Frank White	.20	.07
❑ 427 Willie Wilson	.20	.07
❑ 428 Brian Asselstine	.10	.02
❑ 429 Bruce Benedict	.10	.02
❑ 430 Tommy Boggs	.10	.02
❑ 431 Larry Bradford	.10	.02
❑ 432 Rick Camp	.10	.02
❑ 433 Chris Chambliss	.20	.07
❑ 434 Gene Garber	.10	.02
❑ 435 Preston Hanna	.10	.02
❑ 436 Bob Horner	.20	.07
❑ 437 Glenn Hubbard	.10	.02
❑ 438A All Hrabosky ERR	8.00	4.00
❑ 438B Al Hrabosky ERR (Height 5'1")	.40	.15
❑ 438C Al Hrabosky (Height 5'10")	.20	.07
❑ 439 Rufino Linares	.10	.02
❑ 440 Rick Mahler	.10	.02
❑ 441 Ed Miller	.10	.02
❑ 442 John Montefusco	.10	.02
❑ 443 Dale Murphy	.40	.15
❑ 444 Phil Niekro	.20	.07
❑ 445 Gaylord Perry	.20	.07
❑ 446 Biff Pocoroba	.10	.02
❑ 447 Rafael Ramirez	.10	.02
❑ 448 Jerry Royster	.10	.02
❑ 449 Claudell Washington	.10	.02
❑ 450 Don Aase	.10	.02
❑ 451 Don Baylor	.20	.07
❑ 452 Juan Beniquez	.10	.02
❑ 453 Rick Burleson	.10	.02
❑ 454 Bert Campaneris	.20	.07
❑ 455 Rod Carew	.40	.15
❑ 456 Bob Clark	.10	.02
❑ 457 Brian Downing	.20	.07
❑ 458 Dan Ford	.10	.02
❑ 459 Ken Forsch	.10	.02
❑ 460A Dave Frost (5 mm space before ERA)	.10	.02
❑ 460B Dave Frost (1 mm space)	.10	.02
❑ 461 Bobby Grich	.20	.07
❑ 462 Larry Harlow	.10	.02
❑ 463 John Harris	.10	.02
❑ 464 Andy Hassler	.10	.02
❑ 465 Butch Hobson	.10	.02
❑ 466 Jesse Jefferson	.10	.02
❑ 467 Bruce Kison	.10	.02
❑ 468 Fred Lynn	.20	.07
❑ 469 Angel Moreno	.10	.02
❑ 470 Ed Ott	.10	.02
❑ 471 Fred Patek	.10	.02
❑ 472 Steve Renko	.10	.02
❑ 473 Mike Witt	.50	.20
❑ 474 Geoff Zahn	.10	.02
❑ 475 Gary Alexander	.10	.02
❑ 476 Dale Berra	.10	.02
❑ 477 Kurt Bevacqua	.10	.02
❑ 478 Jim Bibby	.10	.02
❑ 479 John Candelaria	.10	.02
❑ 480 Victor Cruz	.10	.02
❑ 481 Mike Easler	.10	.02
❑ 482 Tim Foli	.10	.02
❑ 483 Lee Lacy	.10	.02
❑ 484 Vance Law	.10	.02
❑ 485 Bill Madlock	.20	.07
❑ 486 Willie Montanez	.10	.02
❑ 487 Omar Moreno	.10	.02
❑ 488 Steve Nicosia	.10	.02
❑ 489 Dave Parker	.20	.07
❑ 490 Tony Pena	.20	.07
❑ 491 Pascual Perez	.10	.02
❑ 492 Johnny Ray RC	.50	.20
❑ 493 Rick Rhoden	.10	.02
❑ 494 Bill Robinson	.10	.02
❑ 495 Don Robinson	.10	.02
❑ 496 Enrique Romo	.10	.02
❑ 497 Rod Scurry	.10	.02
❑ 498 Eddie Solomon	.10	.02
❑ 499 Willie Stargell	.40	.15
❑ 500 Kent Tekulve	.10	.02
❑ 501 Jason Thompson	.10	.02
❑ 502 Glenn Abbott	.10	.02
❑ 503 Jim Anderson	.10	.02
❑ 504 Floyd Bannister	.10	.02
❑ 505 Bruce Bochte	.10	.02
❑ 506 Jeff Burroughs	.10	.02
❑ 507 Bryan Clark RC	.15	.05
❑ 508 Ken Clay	.10	.02
❑ 509 Julio Cruz	.10	.02
❑ 510 Dick Drago	.10	.02
❑ 511 Gary Gray	.10	.02
❑ 512 Dan Meyer	.10	.02
❑ 513 Jerry Narron	.10	.02
❑ 514 Tom Paciorek	.10	.02
❑ 515 Casey Parsons	.10	.02
❑ 516 Lenny Randle	.10	.02
❑ 517 Shane Rawley	.10	.02
❑ 518 Joe Simpson	.10	.02
❑ 519 Richie Zisk	.10	.02
❑ 520 Neil Allen	.10	.02

❑ 521 Bob Bailor .10 .02
❑ 522 Hubie Brooks .10 .02
❑ 523 Mike Cubbage .10 .02
❑ 524 Pete Falcone .10 .02
❑ 525 Doug Flynn .10 .02
❑ 526 Tom Hausman .10 .02
❑ 527 Ron Hodges .10 .02
❑ 528 Randy Jones .10 .02
❑ 529 Mike Jorgensen .10 .02
❑ 530 Dave Kingman .20 .07
❑ 531 Ed Lynch .10 .02
❑ 532 Mike G. Marshall .10 .02
❑ 533 Lee Mazzilli .20 .07
❑ 534 Dyar Miller .10 .02
❑ 535 Mike Scott .20 .07
❑ 536 Rusty Staub .20 .07
❑ 537 John Stearns .10 .02
❑ 538 Craig Swan .10 .02
❑ 539 Frank Taveras .10 .02
❑ 540 Alex Trevino .10 .02
❑ 541 Ellis Valentine .10 .02
❑ 542 Mookie Wilson .20 .07
❑ 543 Joel Youngblood .10 .02
❑ 544 Pat Zachry .10 .02
❑ 545 Glenn Adams .10 .02
❑ 546 Fernando Arroyo .10 .02
❑ 547 John Verhoeven .10 .02
❑ 548 Sal Butera .10 .02
❑ 549 John Castino .10 .02
❑ 550 Don Cooper .10 .02
❑ 551 Doug Corbett .10 .02
❑ 552 Dave Engle .10 .02
❑ 553 Roger Erickson .10 .02
❑ 554 Danny Goodwin .10 .02
❑ 555A Darrell Jackson
(Black cap) .40 .15
❑ 555B Darrell Jackson
(Red cap with T) .20 .07
❑ 555C Darrell Jackson VAR3 3.00 1.25
❑ 556 Pete Mackanin .10 .02
❑ 557 Jack O'Connor .10 .02
❑ 558 Hosken Powell .10 .02
❑ 559 Pete Redfern .10 .02
❑ 560 Roy Smalley .10 .02
❑ 561 Chuck Baker UER
(Shortshop on front) .10 .02
❑ 562 Gary Ward .10 .02
❑ 563 Rob Wilfong .10 .02
❑ 564 Al Williams .10 .02
❑ 565 Butch Wynegar .10 .02
❑ 566 Randy Bass .50 .20
❑ 567 Juan Bonilla RC .15 .05
❑ 568 Danny Boone .10 .02
❑ 569 John Curtis .10 .02
❑ 570 Juan Eichelberger .10 .02
❑ 571 Barry Evans .10 .02
❑ 572 Tim Flannery .10 .02
❑ 573 Ruppert Jones .10 .02
❑ 574 Terry Kennedy .10 .02
❑ 575 Joe Lefebvre .10 .02
❑ 576A John Littlefield RevNg 100.00 50.00
❑ 576B John Littlefield COR
(Right handed) .20 .07
❑ 577 Gary Lucas .10 .02
❑ 578 Steve Mura .10 .02
❑ 579 Broderick Perkins .10 .02
❑ 580 Gene Richards .10 .02
❑ 581 Luis Salazar .10 .02
❑ 582 Ozzie Smith 1.50 .60
❑ 583 John Urrea .10 .02
❑ 584 Chris Welsh .10 .02
❑ 585 Rick Wise .10 .02
❑ 586 Doug Bird .10 .02
❑ 587 Tim Blackwell .10 .02
❑ 588 Bobby Bonds .20 .07
❑ 589 Bill Buckner .20 .07
❑ 590 Bill Caudill .10 .02
❑ 591 Hector Cruz .10 .02
❑ 592 Jody Davis .10 .02
❑ 593 Ivan DeJesus .10 .02
❑ 594 Steve Dillard .10 .02
❑ 595 Leon Durham .10 .02
❑ 596 Rawly Eastwick .20 .07
❑ 597 Steve Henderson .10 .02
❑ 598 Mike Krukow .10 .02
❑ 599 Mike Lum .10 .02
❑ 600 Randy Martz .10 .02
❑ 601 Jerry Morales .10 .02
❑ 602 Ken Reitz .10 .02
❑ 603 Lee Smith RC 2.00 .75
❑ 603B Lee Smith RC COR 6.00 3.00
❑ 604 Dick Tidrow .10 .02
❑ 605 Jim Tracy .20 .07
❑ 606 Mike Tyson .10 .02
❑ 607 Ty Waller .10 .02
❑ 608 Danny Ainge .20 .07
❑ 609 George Bell RC 1.00 .40
❑ 610 Mark Bomback .10 .02
❑ 611 Barry Bonnell .10 .02
❑ 612 Jim Clancy .10 .02
❑ 613 Damaso Garcia .10 .02
❑ 614 Jerry Garvin .10 .02
❑ 615 Alfredo Griffin .10 .02
❑ 616 Garth Iorg .10 .02
❑ 617 Luis Leal .10 .02
❑ 618 Ken Macha .10 .02
❑ 619 John Mayberry .10 .02
❑ 620 Joey McLaughlin .10 .02
❑ 621 Lloyd Moseby .10 .02
❑ 622 Dave Stieb .20 .07
❑ 623 Jackson Todd .10 .02
❑ 624 Willie Upshaw .50 .20
❑ 625 Otto Velez .10 .02
❑ 626 Ernie Whitt .10 .02
❑ 627 Alvis Woods .10 .02
❑ 628 All Star Game
Cleveland, Ohio .20 .07
❑ 629 All Star Infielders
Frank White
Bucky Dent .20 .07
❑ 630 Big Red Machine
Dan Driessen
Dave Concepcion
Ge .20 .07
❑ 631 Bruce Sutter
Top NL Relief Pitcher .20 .07
❑ 632 Steve Carlton/C.Fisk .20 .07
❑ 633 Yaz 3000th Game .75 .30
❑ 634 J.Bench/T.Seaver .75 .30
❑ 635 West Meets East
Fernando Valenzuela
and Gary Car .10 .02
❑ 636A Fernando Valenzuela IA .40 .15
❑ 636B Fernando Valenzuela:
NL SO King (%%the~ NL) .40 .15
❑ 637 Mike Schmidt IA .75 .30
❑ 638 Gary Carter/D.Parker .10 .02
❑ 639 Perfect Game UER
Len Barker and
Bo Diaz
(Catche .20 .07
❑ 640 Pete and Re-Pete .75 .30
❑ 641 L.Smith/Schmidt/Carlton .75 .30
❑ 642 Red Sox Reunion
Fred Lynn
Dwight Evans .40 .15
❑ 643 Rickey Henderson IA 1.25 .50
❑ 644 R.Fingers Most Saves .20 .07
❑ 645 Tom Seaver Most Wins .20 .07
❑ 646 R.Jackson/D.Winfield .20 .07
❑ 646B Reggie/D.Winfield .20 .07
❑ 647 CL: Yankees/Dodgers .10 .02
❑ 648 CL: A's/Reds .10 .02
❑ 649 CL: Cards/Brewers .10 .02
❑ 650 CL: Expos/Orioles .10 .02
❑ 651 CL: Astros/Phillies .10 .02
❑ 652 CL: Tigers/Red Sox .10 .02
❑ 653 CL: Rangers/White Sox .10 .02
❑ 654 CL: Giants/Indians .10 .02
❑ 655 CL: Royals/Braves .10 .02
❑ 656 CL: Angels/Pirates .10 .02
❑ 657 CL: Mariners/Mets .10 .02
❑ 658 CL: Padres/Twins .10 .02
❑ 659 CL: Blue Jays/Cubs .10 .02
❑ 660 Specials Checklist .10 .02

1983 Fleer

❑ COMPLETE SET (660) 60.00 30.00
❑ 1 Joaquin Andujar .20 .07
❑ 2 Doug Bair .10 .02
❑ 3 Steve Braun .10 .02
❑ 4 Glenn Brummer .10 .02

❑ 5 Bob Forsch .10 .02
❑ 6 David Green RC .50 .20
❑ 7 George Hendrick .20 .07
❑ 8 Keith Hernandez .20 .07
❑ 9 Tom Herr .10 .02
❑ 10 Dane Iorg .10 .02
❑ 11 Jim Kaat .20 .07
❑ 12 Jeff Lahti .10 .02
❑ 13 Tito Landrum .10 .02
❑ 14 Dave LaPoint .10 .02
❑ 15 Willie McGee RC 1.50 .60
❑ 16 Steve Mura .10 .02
❑ 17 Ken Oberkfell .10 .02
❑ 18 Darrell Porter .10 .02
❑ 19 Mike Ramsey .10 .02
❑ 20 Gene Roof .10 .02
❑ 21 Lonnie Smith .10 .02
❑ 22 Ozzie Smith 1.25 .50
❑ 23 John Stuper .10 .02
❑ 24 Bruce Sutter .40 .15
❑ 25 Gene Tenace .20 .07
❑ 26 Jerry Augustine .10 .02
❑ 27 Dwight Bernard .10 .02
❑ 28 Mark Brouhard .10 .02
❑ 29 Mike Caldwell .10 .02
❑ 30 Cecil Cooper .20 .07
❑ 31 Jamie Easterly .10 .02
❑ 32 Marshall Edwards .10 .02
❑ 33 Rollie Fingers .20 .07
❑ 34 Jim Gantner .10 .02
❑ 35 Moose Haas .10 .02
❑ 36 Roy Howell .10 .02
❑ 37 Pete Ladd .10 .02
❑ 38 Bob McClure .10 .02
❑ 39 Doc Medich .10 .02
❑ 40 Paul Molitor .20 .07
❑ 41 Don Money .10 .02
❑ 42 Charlie Moore .10 .02
❑ 43 Ben Oglivie .20 .07
❑ 44 Ed Romero .10 .02
❑ 45 Ted Simmons .20 .07
❑ 46 Jim Slaton .10 .02
❑ 47 Don Sutton .20 .07
❑ 48 Gorman Thomas .20 .07
❑ 49 Pete Vuckovich .10 .02
❑ 50 Ned Yost .10 .02
❑ 51 Robin Yount 1.25 .50
❑ 52 Benny Ayala .10 .02
❑ 53 Bob Bonner .10 .02
❑ 54 Al Bumbry .10 .02
❑ 55 Terry Crowley .10 .02
❑ 56 Storm Davis RC .50 .20
❑ 57 Rich Dauer .10 .02
❑ 58 Rick Dempsey UER .10 .02
❑ 59 Jim Dwyer .10 .02
❑ 60 Mike Flanagan .10 .02
❑ 61 Dan Ford .10 .02
❑ 62 Glenn Gulliver .10 .02
❑ 63 John Lowenstein .10 .02
❑ 64 Dennis Martinez .20 .07
❑ 65 Tippy Martinez .10 .02
❑ 66 Scott McGregor .10 .02
❑ 67 Eddie Murray .75 .30
❑ 68 Joe Nolan .10 .02
❑ 69 Jim Palmer .20 .07
❑ 70 Cal Ripken 6.00 2.50
❑ 71 Gary Roenicke .10 .02
❑ 72 Lenn Sakata .10 .02

❑ 73 Ken Singleton .20 .07
❑ 74 Sammy Stewart .10 .02
❑ 75 Tim Stoddard .10 .02
❑ 76 Don Aase .10 .02
❑ 77 Don Baylor .20 .07
❑ 78 Juan Beniquez .10 .02
❑ 79 Bob Boone .20 .07
❑ 80 Rick Burleson .10 .02
❑ 81 Rod Carew .40 .15
❑ 82 Bobby Clark .10 .02
❑ 83 Doug Corbett .10 .02
❑ 84 John Curtis .10 .02
❑ 85 Doug DeCinces .10 .02
❑ 86 Brian Downing .20 .07
❑ 87 Joe Ferguson .10 .02
❑ 88 Tim Foli .10 .02
❑ 89 Ken Forsch .10 .02
❑ 90 Dave Goltz .10 .02
❑ 91 Bobby Grich .20 .07
❑ 92 Andy Hassler .10 .02
❑ 93 Reggie Jackson .40 .15
❑ 94 Ron Jackson .10 .02
❑ 95 Tommy John .20 .07
❑ 96 Bruce Kison .10 .02
❑ 97 Fred Lynn .20 .07
❑ 98 Ed Ott .10 .02
❑ 99 Steve Renko .10 .02
❑ 100 Luis Sanchez .10 .02
❑ 101 Rob Wilfong .10 .02
❑ 102 Mike Witt .10 .02
❑ 103 Geoff Zahn .10 .02
❑ 104 Willie Aikens .10 .02
❑ 105 Mike Armstrong .10 .02
❑ 106 Vida Blue .20 .07
❑ 107 Bud Black RC .50 .20
❑ 108 George Brett 2.00 .75
❑ 109 Bill Castro .10 .02
❑ 110 Onix Concepcion .10 .02
❑ 111 Dave Frost .10 .02
❑ 112 Cesar Geronimo .10 .02
❑ 113 Larry Gura .10 .02
❑ 114 Steve Hammond .10 .02
❑ 115 Don Hood .10 .02
❑ 116 Dennis Leonard .10 .02
❑ 117 Jerry Martin .10 .02
❑ 118 Lee May .10 .02
❑ 119 Hal McRae .20 .07
❑ 120 Amos Otis .20 .07
❑ 121 Greg Pryor .10 .02
❑ 122 Dan Quisenberry .10 .02
❑ 123 Don Slaught RC .50 .20
❑ 124 Paul Splittorff .10 .02
❑ 125 U.L. Washington .10 .02
❑ 126 John Wathan .10 .02
❑ 127 Frank White .20 .07
❑ 128 Willie Wilson .20 .07
❑ 129 Steve Bedrosian UER
(Height 6'33") .10 .02
❑ 130 Bruce Benedict .10 .02
❑ 131 Tommy Boggs .10 .02
❑ 132 Brett Butler .20 .07
❑ 133 Rick Camp .10 .02
❑ 134 Chris Chambliss .20 .07
❑ 135 Ken Dayley .10 .02
❑ 136 Gene Garber .10 .02
❑ 137 Terry Harper .10 .02
❑ 138 Bob Horner .20 .07
❑ 139 Glenn Hubbard .10 .02
❑ 140 Rufino Linares .10 .02
❑ 141 Rick Mahler .10 .02
❑ 142 Dale Murphy .40 .15
❑ 143 Phil Niekro .20 .07
❑ 144 Pascual Perez .10 .02
❑ 145 Biff Pocoroba .10 .02
❑ 146 Rafael Ramirez .10 .02
❑ 147 Jerry Royster .10 .02
❑ 148 Ken Smith .10 .02
❑ 149 Bob Walk .10 .02
❑ 150 Claudell Washington .10 .02
❑ 151 Bob Watson .10 .02
❑ 152 Larry Whisenton .10 .02
❑ 153 Porfirio Altamirano .10 .02
❑ 154 Marty Bystrom .10 .02
❑ 155 Steve Carlton .40 .15
❑ 156 Larry Christenson .10 .02
❑ 157 Ivan DeJesus .10 .02
❑ 158 John Denny .10 .02
❑ 159 Bob Dernier .10 .02
❑ 160 Bo Diaz .10 .02
❑ 161 Ed Farmer .10 .02
❑ 162 Greg Gross .10 .02
❑ 163 Mike Krukow .10 .02
❑ 164 Garry Maddox .10 .02
❑ 165 Gary Matthews .20 .07
❑ 166 Tug McGraw .20 .07
❑ 167 Bob Molinaro .10 .02
❑ 168 Sid Monge .10 .02
❑ 169 Ron Reed .10 .02
❑ 170 Bill Robinson .10 .02
❑ 171 Pete Rose 2.50 1.00
❑ 172 Dick Ruthven .10 .02
❑ 173 Mike Schmidt 2.00 .75
❑ 174 Manny Trillo .10 .02
❑ 175 Ozzie Virgil .10 .02
❑ 176 George Vukovich .10 .02
❑ 177 Gary Allenson .10 .02
❑ 178 Luis Aponte .10 .02
❑ 179 Wade Boggs RC 10.00 4.00
❑ 180 Tom Burgmeier .10 .02
❑ 181 Mark Clear .10 .02
❑ 182 Dennis Eckersley .40 .15
❑ 183 Dwight Evans .40 .15
❑ 184 Rich Gedman .10 .02
❑ 185 Glenn Hoffman .10 .02
❑ 186 Bruce Hurst .10 .02
❑ 187 Carney Lansford .20 .07
❑ 188 Rick Miller .10 .02
❑ 189 Reid Nichols .10 .02
❑ 190 Bob Ojeda .10 .02
❑ 191 Tony Perez .40 .15
❑ 192 Chuck Rainey .10 .02
❑ 193 Jerry Remy .10 .02
❑ 194 Jim Rice .20 .07
❑ 195 Bob Stanley .10 .02
❑ 196 Dave Stapleton .10 .02
❑ 197 Mike Torrez .10 .02
❑ 198 John Tudor .20 .07
❑ 199 Julio Valdez .10 .02
❑ 200 Carl Yastrzemski 1.25 .50
❑ 201 Dusty Baker .20 .07
❑ 202 Joe Beckwith .10 .02
❑ 203 Greg Brock .10 .02
❑ 204 Ron Cey .20 .07
❑ 205 Terry Forster .20 .07
❑ 206 Steve Garvey .20 .07
❑ 207 Pedro Guerrero .20 .07
❑ 208 Burt Hooton .10 .02
❑ 209 Steve Howe .10 .02
❑ 210 Ken Landreaux .10 .02
❑ 211 Mike Marshall .10 .02
❑ 212 Candy Maldonado RC .50 .20
❑ 213 Rick Monday .20 .07
❑ 214 Tom Niedenfuer .10 .02
❑ 215 Jorge Orta .10 .02
❑ 216 Jerry Reuss UER
(%%Home:- omitted) .10 .02
❑ 217 Ron Roenicke .10 .02
❑ 218 Vicente Romo .10 .02
❑ 219 Bill Russell .20 .07
❑ 220 Steve Sax .20 .07
❑ 221 Mike Scioscia .20 .07
❑ 222 Dave Stewart .20 .07
❑ 223 Derrel Thomas .10 .02
❑ 224 Fernando Valenzuela .20 .07
❑ 225 Bob Welch .20 .07
❑ 226 Ricky Wright .10 .02
❑ 227 Steve Yeager .20 .07
❑ 228 Bill Almon .10 .02
❑ 229 Harold Baines .20 .07
❑ 230 Salome Barojas .10 .02
❑ 231 Tony Bernazard .10 .02
❑ 232 Britt Burns .10 .02
❑ 233 Richard Dotson .10 .02
❑ 234 Ernesto Escarrega .10 .02
❑ 235 Carlton Fisk .40 .15
❑ 236 Jerry Hairston .10 .02
❑ 237 Kevin Hickey .10 .02
❑ 238 LaMarr Hoyt .10 .02
❑ 239 Steve Kemp .10 .02
❑ 240 Jim Kern .10 .02
❑ 241 Ron Kittle RC 1.00 .40
❑ 242 Jerry Koosman .20 .07
❑ 243 Dennis Lamp .10 .02
❑ 244 Rudy Law .10 .02
❑ 245 Vance Law .10 .02
❑ 246 Ron LeFlore .20 .07
❑ 247 Greg Luzinski .20 .07
❑ 248 Tom Paciorek .10 .02
❑ 249 Aurelio Rodriguez .10 .02
❑ 250 Mike Squires .10 .02
❑ 251 Steve Trout .10 .02
❑ 252 Jim Barr .10 .02
❑ 253 Dave Bergman .10 .02
❑ 254 Fred Breining .10 .02
❑ 255 Bob Brenly .10 .02
❑ 256 Jack Clark .20 .07
❑ 257 Chili Davis .20 .07
❑ 258 Darrell Evans .20 .07
❑ 259 Alan Fowlkes .10 .02
❑ 260 Rich Gale .10 .02
❑ 261 Atlee Hammaker .10 .02
❑ 262 Al Holland .10 .02
❑ 263 Duane Kuiper .10 .02
❑ 264 Bill Laskey .10 .02
❑ 265 Gary Lavelle .10 .02
❑ 266 Johnnie LeMaster .10 .02
❑ 267 Renie Martin .10 .02
❑ 268 Milt May .10 .02
❑ 269 Greg Minton .10 .02
❑ 270 Joe Morgan .20 .07
❑ 271 Tom O'Malley .10 .02
❑ 272 Reggie Smith .20 .07
❑ 273 Guy Sularz .10 .02
❑ 274 Champ Summers .10 .02
❑ 275 Max Venable .10 .02
❑ 276 Jim Wohlford .10 .02
❑ 277 Ray Burris .10 .02
❑ 278 Gary Carter .20 .07
❑ 279 Warren Cromartie .10 .02
❑ 280 Andre Dawson .20 .07
❑ 281 Terry Francona .20 .07
❑ 282 Doug Flynn .10 .02
❑ 283 Woodie Fryman .10 .02
❑ 284 Bill Gullickson .10 .02
❑ 285 Wallace Johnson .10 .02
❑ 286 Charlie Lea .10 .02
❑ 287 Randy Lerch .10 .02
❑ 288 Brad Mills .10 .02
❑ 289 Dan Norman .10 .02
❑ 290 Al Oliver .20 .07
❑ 291 David Palmer .10 .02
❑ 292 Tim Raines .20 .07
❑ 293 Jeff Reardon .20 .07
❑ 294 Steve Rogers .20 .07
❑ 295 Scott Sanderson .10 .02
❑ 296 Dan Schatzeder .10 .02
❑ 297 Bryn Smith .10 .02
❑ 298 Chris Speier .10 .02
❑ 299 Tim Wallach .20 .07
❑ 300 Jerry White .10 .02
❑ 301 Joel Youngblood .10 .02
❑ 302 Ross Baumgarten .10 .02
❑ 303 Dale Berra .10 .02
❑ 304 John Candelaria .10 .02
❑ 305 Dick Davis .10 .02
❑ 306 Mike Easler .10 .02
❑ 307 Richie Hebner .10 .02
❑ 308 Lee Lacy .10 .02
❑ 309 Bill Madlock .20 .07
❑ 310 Larry McWilliams .10 .02
❑ 311 John Milner .10 .02
❑ 312 Omar Moreno .10 .02
❑ 313 Jim Morrison .10 .02
❑ 314 Steve Nicosia .10 .02
❑ 315 Dave Parker .20 .07
❑ 316 Tony Pena .10 .02
❑ 317 Johnny Ray .10 .02
❑ 318 Rick Rhoden .10 .02
❑ 319 Don Robinson .10 .02
❑ 320 Enrique Romo .10 .02
❑ 321 Manny Sarmiento .10 .02
❑ 322 Rod Scurry .10 .02
❑ 323 Jimmy Smith .10 .02
❑ 324 Willie Stargell .40 .15
❑ 325 Jason Thompson .10 .02
❑ 326 Kent Tekulve .10 .02
❑ 327A Tom Brookens
(Short .375~ brown box

	shaded in on	.10	.02
❑ 327B	Tom Brookens (Longer 1.25~ brown box shaded in o	.10	.02
❑ 328	Enos Cabell	.10	.02
❑ 329	Kirk Gibson	.20	.07
❑ 330	Larry Herndon	.10	.02
❑ 331	Mike Ivie	.10	.02
❑ 332	Howard Johnson RC	1.00	.40
❑ 333	Lynn Jones	.10	.02
❑ 334	Rick Leach	.10	.02
❑ 335	Chet Lemon	.20	.07
❑ 336	Jack Morris	.20	.07
❑ 337	Lance Parrish	.20	.07
❑ 338	Larry Pashnick	.10	.02
❑ 339	Dan Petry	.10	.02
❑ 340	Dave Rozema	.10	.02
❑ 341	Dave Rucker	.10	.02
❑ 342	Elias Sosa	.10	.02
❑ 343	Dave Tobik	.10	.02
❑ 344	Alan Trammell	.20	.07
❑ 345	Jerry Turner	.10	.02
❑ 346	Jerry Ujdur	.10	.02
❑ 347	Pat Underwood	.10	.02
❑ 348	Lou Whitaker	.20	.07
❑ 349	Milt Wilcox	.10	.02
❑ 350	Glenn Wilson	.50	.20
❑ 351	John Wockenfuss	.10	.02
❑ 352	Kurt Bevacqua	.10	.02
❑ 353	Juan Bonilla	.10	.02
❑ 354	Floyd Chiffer	.10	.02
❑ 355	Luis DeLeon	.10	.02
❑ 356	Dave Dravecky RC	1.00	.40
❑ 357	Dave Edwards	.10	.02
❑ 358	Juan Eichelberger	.10	.02
❑ 359	Tim Flannery	.10	.02
❑ 360	Tony Gwynn RC	15.00	6.00
❑ 361	Ruppert Jones	.10	.02
❑ 362	Terry Kennedy	.10	.02
❑ 363	Joe Lefebvre	.10	.02
❑ 364	Sixto Lezcano	.10	.02
❑ 365	Tim Lollar	.10	.02
❑ 366	Gary Lucas	.10	.02
❑ 367	John Montefusco	.10	.02
❑ 368	Broderick Perkins	.10	.02
❑ 369	Joe Pittman	.10	.02
❑ 370	Gene Richards	.10	.02
❑ 371	Luis Salazar	.10	.02
❑ 372	Eric Show RC	.50	.20
❑ 373	Garry Templeton	.20	.07
❑ 374	Chris Welsh	.10	.02
❑ 375	Alan Wiggins	.10	.02
❑ 376	Rick Cerone	.10	.02
❑ 377	Dave Collins	.10	.02
❑ 378	Roger Erickson	.10	.02
❑ 379	George Frazier	.10	.02
❑ 380	Oscar Gamble	.10	.02
❑ 381	Rich Gossage	.20	.07
❑ 382	Ken Griffey	.20	.07
❑ 383	Ron Guidry	.20	.07
❑ 384	Dave LaRoche	.10	.02
❑ 385	Rudy May	.10	.02
❑ 386	John Mayberry	.10	.02
❑ 387	Lee Mazzilli	.20	.07
❑ 388	Mike Morgan	.10	.02
❑ 389	Jerry Mumphrey	.10	.02
❑ 390	Bobby Murcer	.20	.07
❑ 391	Graig Nettles	.20	.07
❑ 392	Lou Piniella	.20	.07
❑ 393	Willie Randolph	.20	.07
❑ 394	Shane Rawley	.10	.02
❑ 395	Dave Righetti	.20	.07
❑ 396	Andre Robertson	.10	.02
❑ 397	Roy Smalley	.10	.02
❑ 398	Dave Winfield	.20	.07
❑ 399	Butch Wynegar	.10	.02
❑ 400	Chris Bando	.10	.02
❑ 401	Alan Bannister	.10	.02
❑ 402	Len Barker	.10	.02
❑ 403	Tom Brennan	.10	.02
❑ 404	Carmelo Castillo	.10	.02
❑ 405	Miguel Dilone	.10	.02
❑ 406	Jerry Dybzinski	.10	.02
❑ 407	Mike Fischlin	.10	.02
❑ 408	Ed Glynn UER	.10	.02
❑ 409	Mike Hargrove	.10	.02
❑ 410	Toby Harrah	.20	.07
❑ 411	Ron Hassey	.10	.02
❑ 412	Von Hayes	.10	.02
❑ 413	Rick Manning	.10	.02
❑ 414	Bake McBride	.20	.07
❑ 415	Larry Milbourne	.10	.02
❑ 416	Bill Nahorodny	.10	.02
❑ 417	Jack Perconte	.10	.02
❑ 418	Lary Sorensen	.10	.02
❑ 419	Dan Spillner	.10	.02
❑ 420	Rick Sutcliffe	.20	.07
❑ 421	Andre Thornton	.10	.02
❑ 422	Rick Waits	.10	.02
❑ 423	Eddie Whitson	.10	.02
❑ 424	Jesse Barfield	.20	.07
❑ 425	Barry Bonnell	.10	.02
❑ 426	Jim Clancy	.10	.02
❑ 427	Damaso Garcia	.10	.02
❑ 428	Jerry Garvin	.10	.02
❑ 429	Alfredo Griffin	.10	.02
❑ 430	Garth Iorg	.10	.02
❑ 431	Roy Lee Jackson	.10	.02
❑ 432	Luis Leal	.10	.02
❑ 433	Buck Martinez	.10	.02
❑ 434	Joey McLaughlin	.10	.02
❑ 435	Lloyd Moseby	.10	.02
❑ 436	Rance Mulliniks	.10	.02
❑ 437	Dale Murray	.10	.02
❑ 438	Wayne Nordhagen	.10	.02
❑ 439	Geno Petralli	.50	.20
❑ 440	Hosken Powell	.10	.02
❑ 441	Dave Stieb	.20	.07
❑ 442	Willie Upshaw	.10	.02
❑ 443	Ernie Whitt	.10	.02
❑ 444	Alvis Woods	.10	.02
❑ 445	Alan Ashby	.10	.02
❑ 446	Jose Cruz	.20	.07
❑ 447	Kiko Garcia	.10	.02
❑ 448	Phil Garner	.20	.07
❑ 449	Danny Heep	.10	.02
❑ 450	Art Howe	.10	.02
❑ 451	Bob Knepper	.10	.02
❑ 452	Alan Knicely	.10	.02
❑ 453	Ray Knight	.20	.07
❑ 454	Frank LaCorte	.10	.02
❑ 455	Mike LaCoss	.10	.02
❑ 456	Randy Moffitt	.10	.02
❑ 457	Joe Niekro	.10	.02
❑ 458	Terry Puhl	.10	.02
❑ 459	Luis Pujols	.10	.02
❑ 460	Craig Reynolds	.10	.02
❑ 461	Bert Roberge	.10	.02
❑ 462	Vern Ruhle	.10	.02
❑ 463	Nolan Ryan	4.00	1.50
❑ 464	Joe Sambito	.10	.02
❑ 465	Tony Scott	.10	.02
❑ 466	Dave Smith	.10	.02
❑ 467	Harry Spilman	.10	.02
❑ 468	Dickie Thon	.10	.02
❑ 469	Denny Walling	.10	.02
❑ 470	Larry Andersen	.10	.02
❑ 471	Floyd Bannister	.10	.02
❑ 472	Jim Beattie	.10	.02
❑ 473	Bruce Bochte	.10	.02
❑ 474	Manny Castillo	.10	.02
❑ 475	Bill Caudill	.10	.02
❑ 476	Bryan Clark	.10	.02
❑ 477	Al Cowens	.10	.02
❑ 478	Julio Cruz	.10	.02
❑ 479	Todd Cruz	.10	.02
❑ 480	Gary Gray	.10	.02
❑ 481	Dave Henderson	.10	.02
❑ 482	Mike Moore RC	.50	.20
❑ 483	Gaylord Perry	.20	.07
❑ 484	Dave Revering	.10	.02
❑ 485	Joe Simpson	.10	.02
❑ 486	Mike Stanton	.10	.02
❑ 487	Rick Sweet	.10	.02
❑ 488	Ed VandeBerg	.10	.02
❑ 489	Richie Zisk	.10	.02
❑ 490	Doug Bird	.10	.02
❑ 491	Larry Bowa	.20	.07
❑ 492	Bill Buckner	.20	.07
❑ 493	Bill Campbell	.10	.02
❑ 494	Jody Davis	.10	.02
❑ 495	Leon Durham	.10	.02
❑ 496	Steve Henderson	.10	.02
❑ 497	Willie Hernandez	.10	.02
❑ 498	Fergie Jenkins	.20	.07
❑ 499	Jay Johnstone	.10	.02
❑ 500	Junior Kennedy	.10	.02
❑ 501	Randy Martz	.10	.02
❑ 502	Jerry Morales	.10	.02
❑ 503	Keith Moreland	.10	.02
❑ 504	Dickie Noles	.10	.02
❑ 505	Mike Proly	.10	.02
❑ 506	Allen Ripley	.10	.02
❑ 507	Ryne Sandberg RC	10.00	4.00
❑ 508	Lee Smith	.40	.15
❑ 509	Pat Tabler	.10	.02
❑ 510	Dick Tidrow	.10	.02
❑ 511	Bump Wills	.10	.02
❑ 512	Gary Woods	.10	.02
❑ 513	Tony Armas	.20	.07
❑ 514	Dave Beard	.10	.02
❑ 515	Jeff Burroughs	.10	.02
❑ 516	John D'Acquisto	.10	.02
❑ 517	Wayne Gross	.10	.02
❑ 518	Mike Heath	.10	.02
❑ 519	Rickey Henderson	1.50	.60
❑ 520	Cliff Johnson	.10	.02
❑ 521	Matt Keough	.10	.02
❑ 522	Brian Kingman	.10	.02
❑ 523	Rick Langford	.10	.02
❑ 524	Dave Lopes	.20	.07
❑ 525	Steve McCatty	.10	.02
❑ 526	Dave McKay	.10	.02
❑ 527	Dan Meyer	.10	.02
❑ 528	Dwayne Murphy	.10	.02
❑ 529	Jeff Newman	.10	.02
❑ 530	Mike Norris	.10	.02
❑ 531	Bob Owchinko	.10	.02
❑ 532	Joe Rudi	.20	.07
❑ 533	Jimmy Sexton	.10	.02
❑ 534	Fred Stanley	.10	.02
❑ 535	Tom Underwood	.10	.02
❑ 536	Neil Allen	.10	.02
❑ 537	Wally Backman	.10	.02
❑ 538	Bob Bailor	.10	.02
❑ 539	Hubie Brooks	.10	.02
❑ 540	Carlos Diaz RC	.25	.08
❑ 541	Pete Falcone	.10	.02
❑ 542	George Foster	.20	.07
❑ 543	Ron Gardenhire	.10	.02
❑ 544	Brian Giles	.10	.02
❑ 545	Ron Hodges	.10	.02
❑ 546	Randy Jones	.10	.02
❑ 547	Mike Jorgensen	.10	.02
❑ 548	Dave Kingman	.20	.07
❑ 549	Ed Lynch	.10	.02
❑ 550	Jesse Orosco	.10	.02
❑ 551	Rick Ownbey	.10	.02
❑ 552	Charlie Puleo	.10	.02
❑ 553	Gary Rajsich	.10	.02
❑ 554	Mike Scott	.20	.07
❑ 555	Rusty Staub	.20	.07
❑ 556	John Stearns	.10	.02
❑ 557	Craig Swan	.10	.02
❑ 558	Ellis Valentine	.10	.02
❑ 559	Tom Veryzer	.10	.02
❑ 560	Mookie Wilson	.20	.07
❑ 561	Pat Zachry	.10	.02
❑ 562	Buddy Bell	.20	.07
❑ 563	John Butcher	.10	.02
❑ 564	Steve Comer	.10	.02
❑ 565	Danny Darwin	.10	.02
❑ 566	Bucky Dent	.20	.07
❑ 567	John Grubb	.10	.02
❑ 568	Rick Honeycutt	.10	.02
❑ 569	Dave Hostetler	.10	.02
❑ 570	Charlie Hough	.20	.07
❑ 571	Lamar Johnson	.10	.02
❑ 572	Jon Matlack	.10	.02
❑ 573	Paul Mirabella	.10	.02
❑ 574	Larry Parrish	.10	.02
❑ 575	Mike Richardt	.10	.02
❑ 576	Mickey Rivers	.10	.02
❑ 577	Billy Sample	.10	.02
❑ 578	Dave Schmidt	.10	.02
❑ 579	Bill Stein	.10	.02
❑ 580	Jim Sundberg	.20	.07
❑ 581	Frank Tanana	.20	.07

❑ 582	Mark Wagner	.10	.02
❑ 583	George Wright RC	.50	.20
❑ 584	Johnny Bench	.75	.30
❑ 585	Bruce Berenyi	.10	.02
❑ 586	Larry Biittner	.10	.02
❑ 587	Cesar Cedeno	.20	.07
❑ 588	Dave Concepcion	.20	.07
❑ 589	Dan Driessen	.10	.02
❑ 590	Greg Harris	.10	.02
❑ 591	Ben Hayes	.10	.02
❑ 592	Paul Householder	.10	.02
❑ 593	Tom Hume	.10	.02
❑ 594	Wayne Krenchicki	.10	.02
❑ 595	Rafael Landestoy	.10	.02
❑ 596	Charlie Leibrandt	.10	.02
❑ 597	Eddie Milner	.10	.02
❑ 598	Ron Oester	.10	.02
❑ 599	Frank Pastore	.10	.02
❑ 600	Joe Price	.10	.02
❑ 601	Tom Seaver	.75	.30
❑ 602	Bob Shirley	.10	.02
❑ 603	Mario Soto	.20	.07
❑ 604	Alex Trevino	.10	.02
❑ 605	Mike Vail	.10	.02
❑ 606	Duane Walker	.10	.02
❑ 607	Tom Brunansky	.20	.07
❑ 608	Bobby Castillo	.10	.02
❑ 609	John Castino	.10	.02
❑ 610	Ron Davis	.10	.02
❑ 611	Lenny Faedo	.10	.02
❑ 612	Terry Felton	.10	.02
❑ 613	Gary Gaetti RC	1.00	.40
❑ 614	Mickey Hatcher	.10	.02
❑ 615	Brad Havens	.10	.02
❑ 616	Kent Hrbek	.20	.07
❑ 617	Randy Johnson	.10	.02
❑ 618	Tim Laudner	.10	.02
❑ 619	Jeff Little	.10	.02
❑ 620	Bobby Mitchell	.10	.02
❑ 621	Jack O'Connor	.10	.02
❑ 622	John Pacella	.10	.02
❑ 623	Pete Redfern	.10	.02
❑ 624	Jesus Vega	.10	.02
❑ 625	Frank Viola RC	1.50	.60
❑ 626	Ron Washington	.10	.02
❑ 627	Gary Ward	.10	.02
❑ 628	Al Williams	.10	.02
❑ 629	C.Yaz/Eck/M.Clear	.75	.30
❑ 630	G.Perry/T.Bulling	.10	.02
❑ 631	D.Concepcion/M.Trillo	.20	.07
❑ 632	R.Yount/B.Bell	.75	.30
❑ 633	D.Winfield/K.Hrbek	.10	.02
❑ 634	P.Rose/W.Stargell	.75	.30
❑ 635	T.Harrah/A.Thornton	.20	.07
❑ 636	O.Smith/Lo.Smith	.75	.30
❑ 637	B.Diaz/G.Carter	.10	.02
❑ 638	C.Fisk/G.Carter	.20	.07
❑ 639	Rickey Henderson IA	.75	.30
❑ 640	B.Oglivie/R.Jackson	.40	.15
❑ 641	Joel Youngblood	.10	.02
❑ 642	R.Hassey/L.Barker	.20	.07
❑ 643	V.Blue/Black-Blue	.20	.07
❑ 644	B.Black/Black-Blue	.10	.02
❑ 645	Reggie Jackson Power	.20	.07
❑ 646	Rickey Henderson Speed	.75	.30
❑ 647	CL: Cards/Brewers	.10	.02
❑ 648	CL: Orioles/Angels	.10	.02
❑ 649	CL: Royals/Braves	.10	.02
❑ 650	CL: Phillies/Red Sox	.10	.02
❑ 651	CL: Dodgers/White Sox	.10	.02
❑ 652	CL: Giants/Expos	.10	.02
❑ 653	CL: Pirates/Tigers	.10	.02
❑ 654	CL: Padres/Yankees	.10	.02
❑ 655	CL: Indians/Blue Jays	.10	.02
❑ 656	CL: Astros/Mariners	.10	.02
❑ 657	CL: Cubs/A's	.10	.02
❑ 658	CL: Mets/Rangers	.10	.02
❑ 659	CL: Reds/Twins	.10	.02
❑ 660	CL: Specials/Teams	.10	.02

1984 Fleer

❑	COMPLETE SET (660)	50.00	25.00
❑ 1	Mike Boddicker	.15	.05
❑ 2	Al Bumbry	.15	.05
❑ 3	Todd Cruz	.15	.05
❑ 4	Rich Dauer	.15	.05

❑ 5	Storm Davis	.15	.05
❑ 6	Rick Dempsey	.15	.05
❑ 7	Jim Dwyer	.15	.05
❑ 8	Mike Flanagan	.15	.05
❑ 9	Dan Ford	.15	.05
❑ 10	John Lowenstein	.15	.05
❑ 11	Dennis Martinez	.40	.15
❑ 12	Tippy Martinez	.15	.05
❑ 13	Scott McGregor	.15	.05
❑ 14	Eddie Murray	1.50	.60
❑ 15	Joe Nolan	.15	.05
❑ 16	Jim Palmer	.40	.15
❑ 17	Cal Ripken	10.00	4.00
❑ 18	Gary Roenicke	.15	.05
❑ 19	Lenn Sakata	.15	.05
❑ 20	John Shelby	.15	.05
❑ 21	Ken Singleton	.40	.15
❑ 22	Sammy Stewart	.15	.05
❑ 23	Tim Stoddard	.15	.05
❑ 24	Marty Bystrom	.15	.05
❑ 25	Steve Carlton	.75	.30
❑ 26	Ivan DeJesus	.15	.05
❑ 27	John Denny	.15	.05
❑ 28	Bob Dernier	.15	.05
❑ 29	Bo Diaz	.15	.05
❑ 30	Kiko Garcia	.15	.05
❑ 31	Greg Gross	.15	.05
❑ 32	Kevin Gross RC	.50	.20
❑ 33	Von Hayes	.15	.05
❑ 34	Willie Hernandez	.15	.05
❑ 35	Al Holland	.15	.05
❑ 36	Charles Hudson	.15	.05
❑ 37	Joe Lefebvre	.15	.05
❑ 38	Sixto Lezcano	.15	.05
❑ 39	Garry Maddox	.15	.05
❑ 40	Gary Matthews	.40	.15
❑ 41	Len Matuszek	.15	.05
❑ 42	Tug McGraw	.40	.15
❑ 43	Joe Morgan	.40	.15
❑ 44	Tony Perez	.75	.30
❑ 45	Ron Reed	.15	.05
❑ 46	Pete Rose	5.00	2.00
❑ 47	Juan Samuel RC	1.00	.40
❑ 48	Mike Schmidt	4.00	1.50
❑ 49	Ozzie Virgil	.15	.05
❑ 50	Juan Agosto	.15	.05
❑ 51	Harold Baines	.40	.15
❑ 52	Floyd Bannister	.15	.05
❑ 53	Salome Barojas	.15	.05
❑ 54	Britt Burns	.15	.05
❑ 55	Julio Cruz	.15	.05
❑ 56	Richard Dotson	.15	.05
❑ 57	Jerry Dybzinski	.15	.05
❑ 58	Carlton Fisk	.75	.30
❑ 59	Scott Fletcher	.15	.05
❑ 60	Jerry Hairston	.15	.05
❑ 61	Kevin Hickey	.15	.05
❑ 62	Marc Hill	.15	.05
❑ 63	LaMarr Hoyt	.15	.05
❑ 64	Ron Kittle	.15	.05
❑ 65	Jerry Koosman	.40	.15
❑ 66	Dennis Lamp	.15	.05
❑ 67	Rudy Law	.15	.05
❑ 68	Vance Law	.15	.05
❑ 69	Greg Luzinski	.40	.15
❑ 70	Tom Paciorek	.15	.05
❑ 71	Mike Squires	.15	.05
❑ 72	Dick Tidrow	.15	.05
❑ 73	Greg Walker	.50	.20
❑ 74	Glenn Abbott	.15	.05
❑ 75	Howard Bailey	.15	.05
❑ 76	Doug Bair	.15	.05
❑ 77	Juan Berenguer	.15	.05
❑ 78	Tom Brookens	.40	.15
❑ 79	Enos Cabell	.15	.05
❑ 80	Kirk Gibson	1.50	.60
❑ 81	John Grubb	.15	.05
❑ 82	Larry Herndon	.40	.15
❑ 83	Wayne Krenchicki	.15	.05
❑ 84	Rick Leach	.15	.05
❑ 85	Chet Lemon	.40	.15
❑ 86	Aurelio Lopez	.40	.15
❑ 87	Jack Morris	.40	.15
❑ 88	Lance Parrish	.75	.30
❑ 89	Dan Petry	.40	.15
❑ 90	Dave Rozema	.15	.05
❑ 91	Alan Trammell	.40	.15
❑ 92	Lou Whitaker	.40	.15
❑ 93	Milt Wilcox	.15	.05
❑ 94	Glenn Wilson	.40	.15
❑ 95	John Wockenfuss	.15	.05
❑ 96	Dusty Baker	.40	.15
❑ 97	Joe Beckwith	.15	.05
❑ 98	Greg Brock	.15	.05
❑ 99	Jack Fimple	.15	.05
❑ 100	Pedro Guerrero	.40	.15
❑ 101	Rick Honeycutt	.15	.05
❑ 102	Burt Hooton	.15	.05
❑ 103	Steve Howe	.15	.05
❑ 104	Ken Landreaux	.15	.05
❑ 105	Mike Marshall	.15	.05
❑ 106	Rick Monday	.40	.15
❑ 107	Jose Morales	.15	.05
❑ 108	Tom Niedenfuer	.15	.05
❑ 109	Alejandro Pena RC*	1.00	.40
❑ 110	Jerry Reuss UER (%%Home:~ omitted)	.15	.05
❑ 111	Bill Russell	.40	.15
❑ 112	Steve Sax	.15	.05
❑ 113	Mike Scioscia	.40	.15
❑ 114	Derrel Thomas	.15	.05
❑ 115	Fernando Valenzuela	.40	.15
❑ 116	Bob Welch	.40	.15
❑ 117	Steve Yeager	.40	.15
❑ 118	Pat Zachry	.15	.05
❑ 119	Don Baylor	.40	.15
❑ 120	Bert Campaneris	.40	.15
❑ 121	Rick Cerone	.15	.05
❑ 122	Ray Fontenot	.15	.05
❑ 123	George Frazier	.15	.05
❑ 124	Oscar Gamble	.15	.05
❑ 125	Rich Gossage	.40	.15
❑ 126	Ken Griffey	.40	.15
❑ 127	Ron Guidry	.40	.15
❑ 128	Jay Howell	.15	.05
❑ 129	Steve Kemp	.15	.05
❑ 130	Matt Keough	.15	.05
❑ 131	Don Mattingly RC	25.00	10.00
❑ 132	John Montefusco	.15	.05
❑ 133	Omar Moreno	.15	.05
❑ 134	Dale Murray	.15	.05
❑ 135	Graig Nettles	.40	.15
❑ 136	Lou Piniella	.40	.15
❑ 137	Willie Randolph	.40	.15
❑ 138	Shane Rawley	.15	.05
❑ 139	Dave Righetti	.40	.15
❑ 140	Andre Robertson	.15	.05
❑ 141	Bob Shirley	.15	.05
❑ 142	Roy Smalley	.15	.05
❑ 143	Dave Winfield	.40	.15
❑ 144	Butch Wynegar	.15	.05
❑ 145	Jim Acker	.15	.05
❑ 146	Doyle Alexander	.15	.05
❑ 147	Jesse Barfield	.40	.15
❑ 148	George Bell	.40	.15
❑ 149	Barry Bonnell	.15	.05
❑ 150	Jim Clancy	.15	.05
❑ 151	Dave Collins	.15	.05
❑ 152	Tony Fernandez RC	1.00	.40
❑ 153	Damaso Garcia	.15	.05
❑ 154	Dave Geisel	.15	.05
❑ 155	Jim Gott	.15	.05
❑ 156	Alfredo Griffin	.15	.05
❑ 157	Garth Iorg	.15	.05

❑ 158 Roy Lee Jackson .15 .05
❑ 159 Cliff Johnson .15 .05
❑ 160 Luis Leal .15 .05
❑ 161 Buck Martinez .15 .05
❑ 162 Joey McLaughlin .15 .05
❑ 163 Randy Moffitt .15 .05
❑ 164 Lloyd Moseby .15 .05
❑ 165 Rance Mulliniks .15 .05
❑ 166 Jorge Orta .15 .05
❑ 167 Dave Stieb .40 .15
❑ 168 Willie Upshaw .15 .05
❑ 169 Ernie Whitt .15 .05
❑ 170 Len Barker .15 .05
❑ 171 Steve Bedrosian .15 .05
❑ 172 Bruce Benedict .15 .05
❑ 173 Brett Butler .40 .15
❑ 174 Rick Camp .15 .05
❑ 175 Chris Chambliss .40 .15
❑ 176 Ken Dayley .15 .05
❑ 177 Pete Falcone .15 .05
❑ 178 Terry Forster .40 .15
❑ 179 Gene Garber .15 .05
❑ 180 Terry Harper .15 .05
❑ 181 Bob Horner .40 .15
❑ 182 Glenn Hubbard .15 .05
❑ 183 Randy Johnson .15 .05
❑ 184 Craig McMurtry .15 .05
❑ 185 Donnie Moore .15 .05
❑ 186 Dale Murphy .75 .30
❑ 187 Phil Niekro .40 .15
❑ 188 Pascual Perez .15 .05
❑ 189 Biff Pocoroba .15 .05
❑ 190 Rafael Ramirez .15 .05
❑ 191 Jerry Royster .15 .05
❑ 192 Claudell Washington .15 .05
❑ 193 Bob Watson .15 .05
❑ 194 Jerry Augustine .15 .05
❑ 195 Mark Brouhard .15 .05
❑ 196 Mike Caldwell .15 .05
❑ 197 Tom Candiotti RC 1.00 .40
❑ 198 Cecil Cooper .40 .15
❑ 199 Rollie Fingers .40 .15
❑ 200 Jim Gantner .15 .05
❑ 201 Bob L. Gibson RC .25 .08
❑ 202 Moose Haas .15 .05
❑ 203 Roy Howell .15 .05
❑ 204 Pete Ladd .15 .05
❑ 205 Rick Manning .15 .05
❑ 206 Bob McClure .15 .05
❑ 207 Paul Molitor .40 .15
❑ 208 Don Money .15 .05
❑ 209 Charlie Moore .15 .05
❑ 210 Ben Oglivie .40 .15
❑ 211 Chuck Porter .15 .05
❑ 212 Ed Romero .15 .05
❑ 213 Ted Simmons .40 .15
❑ 214 Jim Slaton .15 .05
❑ 215 Don Sutton .40 .15
❑ 216 Tom Tellmann .15 .05
❑ 217 Pete Vuckovich .15 .05
❑ 218 Ned Yost .15 .05
❑ 219 Robin Yount 2.50 1.00
❑ 220 Alan Ashby .15 .05
❑ 221 Kevin Bass .15 .05
❑ 222 Jose Cruz .40 .15
❑ 223 Bill Dawley .15 .05
❑ 224 Frank DiPino .15 .05
❑ 225 Bill Doran RC* .50 .20
❑ 226 Phil Garner .40 .15
❑ 227 Art Howe .15 .05
❑ 228 Bob Knepper .15 .05
❑ 229 Ray Knight .40 .15
❑ 230 Frank LaCorte .15 .05
❑ 231 Mike LaCoss .15 .05
❑ 232 Mike Madden .15 .05
❑ 233 Jerry Mumphrey .15 .05
❑ 234 Joe Niekro .15 .05
❑ 235 Terry Puhl .15 .05
❑ 236 Luis Pujols .15 .05
❑ 237 Craig Reynolds .15 .05
❑ 238 Vern Ruhle .15 .05
❑ 239 Nolan Ryan 8.00 3.00
❑ 240 Mike Scott .40 .15
❑ 241 Tony Scott .15 .05
❑ 242 Dave Smith .15 .05
❑ 243 Dickie Thon .15 .05
❑ 244 Denny Walling .15 .05
❑ 245 Dale Berra .15 .05
❑ 246 Jim Bibby .15 .05
❑ 247 John Candelaria .15 .05
❑ 248 Jose DeLeon RC .50 .20
❑ 249 Mike Easler .15 .05
❑ 250 Cecilio Guante .15 .05
❑ 251 Richie Hebner .15 .05
❑ 252 Lee Lacy .15 .05
❑ 253 Bill Madlock .40 .15
❑ 254 Milt May .15 .05
❑ 255 Lee Mazzilli .40 .15
❑ 256 Larry McWilliams .15 .05
❑ 257 Jim Morrison .15 .05
❑ 258 Dave Parker .40 .15
❑ 259 Tony Pena .15 .05
❑ 260 Johnny Ray .15 .05
❑ 261 Rick Rhoden .15 .05
❑ 262 Don Robinson .15 .05
❑ 263 Manny Sarmiento .15 .05
❑ 264 Rod Scurry .15 .05
❑ 265 Kent Tekulve .15 .05
❑ 266 Gene Tenace .40 .15
❑ 267 Jason Thompson .15 .05
❑ 268 Lee Tunnell .15 .05
❑ 269 Marvell Wynne .50 .20
❑ 270 Ray Burris .15 .05
❑ 271 Gary Carter .40 .15
❑ 272 Warren Cromartie .15 .05
❑ 273 Andre Dawson .40 .15
❑ 274 Doug Flynn .15 .05
❑ 275 Terry Francona .40 .15
❑ 276 Bill Gullickson .15 .05
❑ 277 Bob James .15 .05
❑ 278 Charlie Lea .15 .05
❑ 279 Bryan Little .15 .05
❑ 280 Al Oliver .40 .15
❑ 281 Tim Raines .40 .15
❑ 282 Bobby Ramos .15 .05
❑ 283 Jeff Reardon .40 .15
❑ 284 Steve Rogers .40 .15
❑ 285 Scott Sanderson .15 .05
❑ 286 Dan Schatzeder .15 .05
❑ 287 Bryn Smith .15 .05
❑ 288 Chris Speier .15 .05
❑ 289 Manny Trillo .15 .05
❑ 290 Mike Vail .15 .05
❑ 291 Tim Wallach .15 .05
❑ 292 Chris Welsh .15 .05
❑ 293 Jim Wohlford .15 .05
❑ 294 Kurt Bevacqua .15 .05
❑ 295 Juan Bonilla .15 .05
❑ 296 Bobby Brown .15 .05
❑ 297 Luis DeLeon .15 .05
❑ 298 Dave Dravecky .15 .05
❑ 299 Tim Flannery .15 .05
❑ 300 Steve Garvey .40 .15
❑ 301 Tony Gwynn 6.00 2.50
❑ 302 Andy Hawkins .15 .05
❑ 303 Ruppert Jones .15 .05
❑ 304 Terry Kennedy .15 .05
❑ 305 Tim Lollar .15 .05
❑ 306 Gary Lucas .15 .05
❑ 307 Kevin McReynolds RC 1.00 .40
❑ 308 Sid Monge .15 .05
❑ 309 Mario Ramirez .15 .05
❑ 310 Gene Richards .15 .05
❑ 311 Luis Salazar .15 .05
❑ 312 Eric Show .15 .05
❑ 313 Elias Sosa .15 .05
❑ 314 Garry Templeton .40 .15
❑ 315 Mark Thurmond .15 .05
❑ 316 Ed Whitson .15 .05
❑ 317 Alan Wiggins .15 .05
❑ 318 Neil Allen .15 .05
❑ 319 Joaquin Andujar .40 .15
❑ 320 Steve Braun .15 .05
❑ 321 Glenn Brummer .15 .05
❑ 322 Bob Forsch .15 .05
❑ 323 David Green .15 .05
❑ 324 George Hendrick .40 .15
❑ 325 Tom Herr .15 .05
❑ 326 Dane Iorg .15 .05
❑ 327 Jeff Lahti .15 .05
❑ 328 Dave LaPoint .15 .05
❑ 329 Willie McGee .40 .15
❑ 330 Ken Oberkfell .15 .05
❑ 331 Darrell Porter .15 .05
❑ 332 Jamie Quirk .15 .05
❑ 333 Mike Ramsey .15 .05
❑ 334 Floyd Rayford .15 .05
❑ 335 Lonnie Smith .15 .05
❑ 336 Ozzie Smith 2.50 1.00
❑ 337 John Stuper .15 .05
❑ 338 Bruce Sutter .75 .30
❑ 339 Andy Van Slyke RC 2.50 1.00
❑ 340 Dave Von Ohlen .15 .05
❑ 341 Willie Aikens .15 .05
❑ 342 Mike Armstrong .15 .05
❑ 343 Bud Black .15 .05
❑ 344 George Brett 4.00 1.50
❑ 345 Onix Concepcion .15 .05
❑ 346 Keith Creel .15 .05
❑ 347 Larry Gura .15 .05
❑ 348 Don Hood .15 .05
❑ 349 Dennis Leonard .15 .05
❑ 350 Hal McRae .40 .15
❑ 351 Amos Otis .40 .15
❑ 352 Gaylord Perry .40 .15
❑ 353 Greg Pryor .15 .05
❑ 354 Dan Quisenberry .15 .05
❑ 355 Steve Renko .15 .05
❑ 356 Leon Roberts .15 .05
❑ 357 Pat Sheridan .15 .05
❑ 358 Joe Simpson .15 .05
❑ 359 Don Slaught .40 .15
❑ 360 Paul Splittorff .15 .05
❑ 361 U.L. Washington .15 .05
❑ 362 John Wathan .15 .05
❑ 363 Frank White .40 .15
❑ 364 Willie Wilson .40 .15
❑ 365 Jim Barr .15 .05
❑ 366 Dave Bergman .15 .05
❑ 367 Fred Breining .15 .05
❑ 368 Bob Brenly .15 .05
❑ 369 Jack Clark .40 .15
❑ 370 Chili Davis .40 .15
❑ 371 Mark Davis .15 .05
❑ 372 Darrell Evans .40 .15
❑ 373 Atlee Hammaker .15 .05
❑ 374 Mike Krukow .15 .05
❑ 375 Duane Kuiper .15 .05
❑ 376 Bill Laskey .15 .05
❑ 377 Gary Lavelle .15 .05
❑ 378 Johnnie LeMaster .15 .05
❑ 379 Jeff Leonard .15 .05
❑ 380 Randy Lerch .15 .05
❑ 381 Renie Martin .15 .05
❑ 382 Andy McGaffigan .15 .05
❑ 383 Greg Minton .15 .05
❑ 384 Tom O'Malley .15 .05
❑ 385 Max Venable .15 .05
❑ 386 Brad Wellman .15 .05
❑ 387 Joel Youngblood .15 .05
❑ 388 Gary Allenson .15 .05
❑ 389 Luis Aponte .15 .05
❑ 390 Tony Armas .40 .15
❑ 391 Doug Bird .15 .05
❑ 392 Wade Boggs 4.00 1.50
❑ 393 Dennis Boyd .40 .15
❑ 394 Mike G. Brown UER .25 .08
❑ 395 Mark Clear .15 .05
❑ 396 Dennis Eckersley .75 .30
❑ 397 Dwight Evans .75 .30
❑ 398 Rich Gedman .15 .05
❑ 399 Glenn Hoffman .15 .05
❑ 400 Bruce Hurst .15 .05
❑ 401 John Henry Johnson .15 .05
❑ 402 Ed Jurak .15 .05
❑ 403 Rick Miller .15 .05
❑ 404 Jeff Newman .15 .05
❑ 405 Reid Nichols .15 .05
❑ 406 Bob Ojeda .15 .05
❑ 407 Jerry Remy .15 .05
❑ 408 Jim Rice .40 .15
❑ 409 Bob Stanley .15 .05
❑ 410 Dave Stapleton .15 .05
❑ 411 John Tudor .40 .15
❑ 412 Carl Yastrzemski 1.50 .60
❑ 413 Buddy Bell .40 .15
❑ 414 Larry Biittner .15 .05
❑ 415 John Butcher .15 .05

❑ 416 Danny Darwin .15 .05
❑ 417 Bucky Dent .40 .15
❑ 418 Dave Hostetler .15 .05
❑ 419 Charlie Hough .40 .15
❑ 420 Bobby Johnson .15 .05
❑ 421 Odell Jones .15 .05
❑ 422 Jon Matlack .15 .05
❑ 423 Pete O'Brien RC* .50 .20
❑ 424 Larry Parrish .15 .05
❑ 425 Mickey Rivers .15 .05
❑ 426 Billy Sample .15 .05
❑ 427 Dave Schmidt .15 .05
❑ 428 Mike Smithson .15 .05
❑ 429 Bill Stein .15 .05
❑ 430 Dave Stewart .40 .15
❑ 431 Jim Sundberg .40 .15
❑ 432 Frank Tanana .40 .15
❑ 433 Dave Tobik .15 .05
❑ 434 Wayne Tolleson .15 .05
❑ 435 George Wright .15 .05
❑ 436 Bill Almon .15 .05
❑ 437 Keith Atherton .15 .05
❑ 438 Dave Beard .15 .05
❑ 439 Tom Burgmeier .15 .05
❑ 440 Jeff Burroughs .15 .05
❑ 441 Chris Codiroli .15 .05
❑ 442 Tim Conroy .15 .05
❑ 443 Mike Davis .15 .05
❑ 444 Wayne Gross .15 .05
❑ 445 Garry Hancock .15 .05
❑ 446 Mike Heath .15 .05
❑ 447 Rickey Henderson 2.50 1.00
❑ 448 Donnie Hill .15 .05
❑ 449 Bob Kearney .15 .05
❑ 450 Bill Krueger RC .25 .08
❑ 451 Rick Langford .15 .05
❑ 452 Carney Lansford .40 .15
❑ 453 Dave Lopes .40 .15
❑ 454 Steve McCatty .15 .05
❑ 455 Dan Meyer .15 .05
❑ 456 Dwayne Murphy .15 .05
❑ 457 Mike Norris .15 .05
❑ 458 Ricky Peters .15 .05
❑ 459 Tony Phillips RC 1.00 .40
❑ 460 Tom Underwood .15 .05
❑ 461 Mike Warren .15 .05
❑ 462 Johnny Bench 1.50 .60
❑ 463 Bruce Berenyi .15 .05
❑ 464 Dann Bilardello .15 .05
❑ 465 Cesar Cedeno .40 .15
❑ 466 Dave Concepcion .40 .15
❑ 467 Dan Driessen .15 .05
❑ 468 Nick Esasky .15 .05
❑ 469 Rich Gale .15 .05
❑ 470 Ben Hayes .15 .05
❑ 471 Paul Householder .15 .05
❑ 472 Tom Hume .15 .05
❑ 473 Alan Knicely .15 .05
❑ 474 Eddie Milner .15 .05
❑ 475 Ron Oester .15 .05
❑ 476 Kelly Paris .15 .05
❑ 477 Frank Pastore .15 .05
❑ 478 Ted Power .15 .05
❑ 479 Joe Price .15 .05
❑ 480 Charlie Puleo .15 .05
❑ 481 Gary Redus RC* .50 .20
❑ 482 Bill Scherrer .15 .05
❑ 483 Mario Soto .40 .15
❑ 484 Alex Trevino .15 .05
❑ 485 Duane Walker .15 .05
❑ 486 Larry Bowa .40 .15
❑ 487 Warren Brusstar .15 .05
❑ 488 Bill Buckner .40 .15
❑ 489 Bill Campbell .15 .05
❑ 490 Ron Cey .40 .15
❑ 491 Jody Davis .15 .05
❑ 492 Leon Durham .15 .05
❑ 493 Mel Hall .40 .15
❑ 494 Fergie Jenkins .40 .15
❑ 495 Jay Johnstone .15 .05
❑ 496 Craig Lefferts RC .25 .08
❑ 497 Carmelo Martinez .15 .05
❑ 498 Jerry Morales .15 .05
❑ 499 Keith Moreland .15 .05
❑ 500 Dickie Noles .15 .05
❑ 501 Mike Proly .15 .05
❑ 502 Chuck Rainey .15 .05
❑ 503 Dick Ruthven .15 .05
❑ 504 Ryne Sandberg 6.00 2.50
❑ 505 Lee Smith .40 .15
❑ 506 Steve Trout .15 .05
❑ 507 Gary Woods .15 .05
❑ 508 Juan Beniquez .15 .05
❑ 509 Bob Boone .40 .15
❑ 510 Rick Burleson .15 .05
❑ 511 Rod Carew .75 .30
❑ 512 Bobby Clark .15 .05
❑ 513 John Curtis .15 .05
❑ 514 Doug DeCinces .15 .05
❑ 515 Brian Downing .40 .15
❑ 516 Tim Foli .15 .05
❑ 517 Ken Forsch .15 .05
❑ 518 Bobby Grich .40 .15
❑ 519 Andy Hassler .15 .05
❑ 520 Reggie Jackson .75 .30
❑ 521 Ron Jackson .15 .05
❑ 522 Tommy John .40 .15
❑ 523 Bruce Kison .15 .05
❑ 524 Steve Lubratich .15 .05
❑ 525 Fred Lynn .40 .15
❑ 526 Gary Pettis .15 .05
❑ 527 Luis Sanchez .15 .05
❑ 528 Daryl Sconiers .15 .05
❑ 529 Ellis Valentine .15 .05
❑ 530 Rob Wilfong .15 .05
❑ 531 Mike Witt .15 .05
❑ 532 Geoff Zahn .15 .05
❑ 533 Bud Anderson .15 .05
❑ 534 Chris Bando .15 .05
❑ 535 Alan Bannister .15 .05
❑ 536 Bert Blyleven .40 .15
❑ 537 Tom Brennan .15 .05
❑ 538 Jamie Easterly .15 .05
❑ 539 Juan Eichelberger .15 .05
❑ 540 Jim Essian .15 .05
❑ 541 Mike Fischlin .15 .05
❑ 542 Julio Franco .40 .15
❑ 543 Mike Hargrove .15 .05
❑ 544 Toby Harrah .40 .15
❑ 545 Ron Hassey .15 .05
❑ 546 Neal Heaton .15 .05
❑ 547 Bake McBride .40 .15
❑ 548 Broderick Perkins .15 .05
❑ 549 Lary Sorensen .15 .05
❑ 550 Dan Spillner .15 .05
❑ 551 Rick Sutcliffe .40 .15
❑ 552 Pat Tabler .15 .05
❑ 553 Gorman Thomas .40 .15
❑ 554 Andre Thornton .15 .05
❑ 555 George Vukovich .15 .05
❑ 556 Darrell Brown .15 .05
❑ 557 Tom Brunansky .15 .05
❑ 558 Randy Bush .15 .05
❑ 559 Bobby Castillo .15 .05
❑ 560 John Castino .15 .05
❑ 561 Ron Davis .15 .05
❑ 562 Dave Engle .15 .05
❑ 563 Lenny Faedo .15 .05
❑ 564 Pete Filson .15 .05
❑ 565 Gary Gaetti .75 .30
❑ 566 Mickey Hatcher .15 .05
❑ 567 Kent Hrbek .40 .15
❑ 568 Rusty Kuntz .15 .05
❑ 569 Tim Laudner .15 .05
❑ 570 Rick Lysander .15 .05
❑ 571 Bobby Mitchell .15 .05
❑ 572 Ken Schrom .15 .05
❑ 573 Ray Smith .15 .05
❑ 574 Tim Teufel RC .50 .20
❑ 575 Frank Viola .75 .30
❑ 576 Gary Ward .15 .05
❑ 577 Ron Washington .15 .05
❑ 578 Len Whitehouse .15 .05
❑ 579 Al Williams .15 .05
❑ 580 Bob Bailor .15 .05
❑ 581 Mark Bradley .15 .05
❑ 582 Hubie Brooks .15 .05
❑ 583 Carlos Diaz .15 .05
❑ 584 George Foster .40 .15
❑ 585 Brian Giles .15 .05
❑ 586 Danny Heep .15 .05
❑ 587 Keith Hernandez .40 .15
❑ 588 Ron Hodges .15 .05
❑ 589 Scott Holman .15 .05
❑ 590 Dave Kingman .40 .15
❑ 591 Ed Lynch .15 .05
❑ 592 Jose Oquendo RC .50 .20
❑ 593 Jesse Orosco .15 .05
❑ 594 Junior Ortiz .15 .05
❑ 595 Tom Seaver 1.50 .60
❑ 596 Doug Sisk .15 .05
❑ 597 Rusty Staub .40 .15
❑ 598 John Stearns .15 .05
❑ 599 Darryl Strawberry RC 5.00 2.00
❑ 600 Craig Swan .15 .05
❑ 601 Walt Terrell .15 .05
❑ 602 Mike Torrez .15 .05
❑ 603 Mookie Wilson .40 .15
❑ 604 Jamie Allen .15 .05
❑ 605 Jim Beattie .15 .05
❑ 606 Tony Bernazard .15 .05
❑ 607 Manny Castillo .15 .05
❑ 608 Bill Caudill .15 .05
❑ 609 Bryan Clark .15 .05
❑ 610 Al Cowens .15 .05
❑ 611 Dave Henderson .40 .15
❑ 612 Steve Henderson .15 .05
❑ 613 Orlando Mercado .15 .05
❑ 614 Mike Moore .15 .05
❑ 615 Ricky Nelson UER (Jamie Nelson's stats on back) .15 .05
❑ 616 Spike Owen RC .50 .20
❑ 617 Pat Putnam .15 .05
❑ 618 Ron Roenicke .15 .05
❑ 619 Mike Stanton .15 .05
❑ 620 Bob Stoddard .15 .05
❑ 621 Rick Sweet .15 .05
❑ 622 Roy Thomas .15 .05
❑ 623 Ed VandeBerg .15 .05
❑ 624 Matt Young RC .50 .20
❑ 625 Richie Zisk .15 .05
❑ 626 Fred Lynn 1982 AS Game RB .40 .15
❑ 627 Manny Trillo 1983 AS Game RB .15 .05
❑ 628 Steve Garvey Iron Man .15 .05
❑ 629 Rod Carew AL RunnerUp .40 .15
❑ 630 Wade Boggs AL Champ 1.50 .60
❑ 631 Tim Raines IA .15 .05
❑ 632 Al Oliver Double Trouble .40 .15
❑ 633 Steve Sax AS Second Base .15 .05
❑ 634 Dickie Thon AS Shortstop .15 .05
❑ 635 Ace Firemen Dan Quisenberry and Tippy Martinez .15 .05
❑ 636 J.Morgan/P.Rose/T.Perez 1.50 .60
❑ 637 Backstop Stars Lance Parrish Bob Boone .75 .30
❑ 638 G.Brett/G.Perry 2.00 .75
❑ 639 1983 No Hitters Dave Righetti Mike Warren Bob F .75 .30
❑ 640 J.Bench/C.Yastrzemski 1.50 .60
❑ 641 Gaylord Perry Style .15 .05
❑ 642 Steve Carlton IA .40 .15
❑ 643 Joe Altobelli and Paul Owens World Series Manage .15 .05
❑ 644 Rick Dempsey World Series MVP .15 .05
❑ 645 Mike Boddicker WS Rookie Winner .15 .05
❑ 646 Scott McGregor WS Clincher .15 .05
❑ 647 CL: Orioles/Royals Joe Altobelli MG .15 .05
❑ 648 CL: Phillies/Giants Paul Owens MG .15 .05
❑ 649 CL: White Sox/Red Sox Tony LaRussa MG .75 .30
❑ 650 CL: Tigers/Rangers Sparky Anderson MG .75 .30

❑ 651 CL: Dodgers/A's Tommy Lasorda MG .75 .30
❑ 652 CL: Yankees/Reds Billy Martin MG .75 .30
❑ 653 CL: Blue Jays/Cubs Bobby Cox MG .40 .15
❑ 654 CL: Braves/Angels Joe Torre MG .75 .30
❑ 655 CL: Brewers/Indians Rene Lachemann MG .15 .05
❑ 656 CL: Astros/Twins Bob Lillis MG .15 .05
❑ 657 CL: Pirates/Mets Chuck Tanner MG .15 .05
❑ 658 CL: Expos/Mariners Bill Virdon MG .15 .05
❑ 659 CL: Padres/Specials Dick Williams MG .40 .15
❑ 660 CL: Cardinals/Teams Whitey Herzog MG .75 .30

1984 Fleer Update

❑ COMP.FACT.SET (132) 300.00 175.00
❑ 1 Willie Aikens 1.00 .40
❑ 2 Luis Aponte 1.00 .40
❑ 3 Mark Bailey 1.00 .40
❑ 4 Bob Bailor 1.00 .40
❑ 5 Dusty Baker 1.50 .60
❑ 6 Steve Balboni 1.00 .40
❑ 7 Alan Bannister 1.00 .40
❑ 8 Marty Barrett XRC 2.00 .75
❑ 9 Dave Beard 1.00 .40
❑ 10 Joe Beckwith 1.00 .40
❑ 11 Dave Bergman 1.00 .40
❑ 12 Tony Bernazard 1.00 .40
❑ 13 Bruce Bochte 1.00 .40
❑ 14 Barry Bonnell 1.00 .40
❑ 15 Phil Bradley 2.00 .75
❑ 16 Fred Breining 1.00 .40
❑ 17 Mike C. Brown 1.00 .40
❑ 18 Bill Buckner 1.50 .60
❑ 19 Ray Burris 1.00 .40
❑ 20 John Butcher 1.00 .40
❑ 21 Brett Butler 1.50 .60
❑ 22 Enos Cabell 1.00 .40
❑ 23 Bill Campbell 1.00 .40
❑ 24 Bill Caudill 1.00 .40
❑ 25 Bobby Clark 1.00 .40
❑ 26 Bryan Clark 1.00 .40
❑ 27 Roger Clemens XRC 250.00 150.00
❑ 28 Jaime Cocanower 1.00 .40
❑ 29 Ron Darling XRC 5.00 2.00
❑ 30 Alvin Davis XRC 2.00 .75
❑ 31 Bob Dernier 1.00 .40
❑ 32 Carlos Diaz 1.00 .40
❑ 33 Mike Easler 1.00 .40
❑ 34 Dennis Eckersley 2.50 1.00
❑ 35 Jim Essian 1.00 .40
❑ 36 Darrell Evans 1.50 .60
❑ 37 Mike Fitzgerald 1.00 .40
❑ 38 Tim Foli 1.00 .40
❑ 39 John Franco XRC 5.00 2.00
❑ 40 George Frazier 1.00 .40
❑ 41 Rich Gale 1.00 .40
❑ 42 Barbaro Garbey 1.00 .40
❑ 43 Dwight Gooden XRC 25.00 10.00
❑ 44 Rich Gossage 1.50 .60
❑ 45 Wayne Gross 1.00 .40
❑ 46 Mark Gubicza XRC 2.00 .75
❑ 47 Jackie Gutierrez 1.00 .40
❑ 48 Toby Harrah 1.50 .60
❑ 49 Ron Hassey 1.00 .40
❑ 50 Richie Hebner 1.00 .40
❑ 51 Willie Hernandez 1.00 .40
❑ 52 Ed Hodge 1.00 .40
❑ 53 Ricky Horton 1.00 .40
❑ 54 Art Howe 1.00 .40
❑ 55 Dane Iorg 1.00 .40
❑ 56 Brook Jacoby 2.00 .75
❑ 57 Dion James XRC 1.00 .40
❑ 58 Mike Jeffcoat XRC 1.00 .40
❑ 59 Ruppert Jones 1.00 .40
❑ 60 Bob Kearney 1.00 .40
❑ 61 Jimmy Key XRC 5.00 2.00
❑ 62 Dave Kingman 1.50 .60
❑ 63 Brad Komminsk XRC 1.00 .40
❑ 64 Jerry Koosman 1.50 .60
❑ 65 Wayne Krenchicki 1.00 .40
❑ 66 Rusty Kuntz 1.00 .40
❑ 67 Frank LaCorte 1.00 .40
❑ 68 Dennis Lamp 1.00 .40
❑ 69 Tito Landrum 1.00 .40
❑ 70 Mark Langston XRC 5.00 2.00
❑ 71 Rick Leach 1.00 .40
❑ 72 Craig Lefferts 1.00 .40
❑ 73 Gary Lucas 1.00 .40
❑ 74 Jerry Martin 1.00 .40
❑ 75 Carmelo Martinez 1.00 .40
❑ 76 Mike Mason XRC 1.00 .40
❑ 77 Gary Matthews 1.50 .60
❑ 78 Andy McGaffigan 1.00 .40
❑ 79 Joey McLaughlin 1.00 .40
❑ 80 Joe Morgan 1.50 .60
❑ 81 Darryl Motley 1.00 .40
❑ 82 Graig Nettles 1.50 .60
❑ 83 Phil Niekro 1.50 .60
❑ 84 Ken Oberkfell 1.00 .40
❑ 85 Al Oliver 1.50 .60
❑ 86 Jorge Orta 1.00 .40
❑ 87 Amos Otis 1.50 .60
❑ 88 Bob Owchinko 1.00 .40
❑ 89 Dave Parker 1.50 .60
❑ 90 Jack Perconte 1.00 .40
❑ 91 Tony Perez 2.50 1.00
❑ 92 Gerald Perry 2.00 .75
❑ 93 Kirby Puckett XRC 80.00 40.00
❑ 94 Shane Rawley 1.00 .40
❑ 95 Floyd Rayford 1.00 .40
❑ 96 Ron Reed 1.00 .40
❑ 97 R.J. Reynolds 1.00 .40
❑ 98 Gene Richards 1.00 .40
❑ 99 Jose Rijo XRC 5.00 2.00
❑ 100 Jeff D. Robinson 1.00 .40
❑ 101 Ron Romanick 1.00 .40
❑ 102 Pete Rose 12.00 5.00
❑ 103 Bret Saberhagen XRC 10.00 4.00
❑ 104 Scott Sanderson 1.00 .40
❑ 105 Dick Schofield XRC 2.00 .75
❑ 106 Tom Seaver 4.00 1.50
❑ 107 Jim Slaton 1.00 .40
❑ 108 Mike Smithson 1.00 .40
❑ 109 Lary Sorensen 1.00 .40
❑ 110 Tim Stoddard 1.00 .40
❑ 111 Jeff Stone 1.00 .40
❑ 112 Champ Summers 1.00 .40
❑ 113 Jim Sundberg 1.50 .60
❑ 114 Rick Sutcliffe 1.50 .60
❑ 115 Craig Swan 1.00 .40
❑ 116 Derrel Thomas 1.00 .40
❑ 117 Gorman Thomas 1.50 .60
❑ 118 Alex Trevino 1.00 .40
❑ 119 Manny Trillo 1.00 .40
❑ 120 John Tudor 1.50 .60
❑ 121 Tom Underwood 1.00 .40
❑ 122 Mike Vail 1.00 .40
❑ 123 Tom Waddell 1.00 .40
❑ 124 Gary Ward 1.00 .40
❑ 125 Terry Whitfield 1.00 .40
❑ 126 Curtis Wilkerson 1.00 .40
❑ 127 Frank Williams 1.00 .40
❑ 128 Glenn Wilson 1.50 .60
❑ 129 John Wockenfuss 1.00 .40
❑ 130 Ned Yost 1.00 .40
❑ 131 Mike Young XRC 1.00 .40
❑ 132 Checklist 1-132 1.00 .40

1985 Fleer

❑ COMPLETE SET (660) 60.00 30.00
❑ COMP.FACT.SET (660) 100.00 50.00
❑ 1 Doug Bair .15 .05
❑ 2 Juan Berenguer .15 .05
❑ 3 Dave Bergman .15 .05
❑ 4 Tom Brookens .15 .05
❑ 5 Marty Castillo .15 .05
❑ 6 Darrell Evans .40 .15
❑ 7 Barbaro Garbey .15 .05
❑ 8 Kirk Gibson .40 .15
❑ 9 John Grubb .15 .05
❑ 10 Willie Hernandez .15 .05
❑ 11 Larry Herndon .15 .05
❑ 12 Howard Johnson .40 .15
❑ 13 Ruppert Jones .15 .05
❑ 14 Rusty Kuntz .15 .05
❑ 15 Chet Lemon .40 .15
❑ 16 Aurelio Lopez .15 .05
❑ 17 Sid Monge .15 .05
❑ 18 Jack Morris .40 .15
❑ 19 Lance Parrish .40 .15
❑ 20 Dan Petry .15 .05
❑ 21 Dave Rozema .15 .05
❑ 22 Bill Scherrer .15 .05
❑ 23 Alan Trammell .40 .15
❑ 24 Lou Whitaker .40 .15
❑ 25 Milt Wilcox .15 .05
❑ 26 Kurt Bevacqua .15 .05
❑ 27 Greg Booker .15 .05
❑ 28 Bobby Brown .15 .05
❑ 29 Luis DeLeon .15 .05
❑ 30 Dave Dravecky .15 .05
❑ 31 Tim Flannery .15 .05
❑ 32 Steve Garvey .40 .15
❑ 33 Rich Gossage .40 .15
❑ 34 Tony Gwynn 2.50 1.00
❑ 35 Greg Harris .15 .05
❑ 36 Andy Hawkins .15 .05
❑ 37 Terry Kennedy .15 .05
❑ 38 Craig Lefferts .15 .05
❑ 39 Tim Lollar .15 .05
❑ 40 Carmelo Martinez .15 .05
❑ 41 Kevin McReynolds .40 .15
❑ 42 Graig Nettles .40 .15
❑ 43 Luis Salazar .15 .05
❑ 44 Eric Show .15 .05
❑ 45 Garry Templeton .40 .15
❑ 46 Mark Thurmond .15 .05
❑ 47 Ed Whitson .15 .05
❑ 48 Alan Wiggins .15 .05
❑ 49 Rich Bordi .15 .05
❑ 50 Larry Bowa .40 .15
❑ 51 Warren Brusstar .15 .05
❑ 52 Ron Cey .40 .15
❑ 53 Henry Cotto RC .25 .08
❑ 54 Jody Davis .15 .05
❑ 55 Bob Dernier .15 .05
❑ 56 Leon Durham .15 .05
❑ 57 Dennis Eckersley .75 .30
❑ 58 George Frazier .15 .05
❑ 59 Richie Hebner .15 .05
❑ 60 Dave Lopes .40 .15
❑ 61 Gary Matthews .40 .15
❑ 62 Keith Moreland .15 .05

❑ 63 Rick Reuschel	.40	.15
❑ 64 Dick Ruthven	.15	.05
❑ 65 Ryne Sandberg	2.50	1.00
❑ 66 Scott Sanderson	.15	.05
❑ 67 Lee Smith	.40	.15
❑ 68 Tim Stoddard	.15	.05
❑ 69 Rick Sutcliffe	.40	.15
❑ 70 Steve Trout	.15	.05
❑ 71 Gary Woods	.15	.05
❑ 72 Wally Backman	.15	.05
❑ 73 Bruce Berenyi	.15	.05
❑ 74 Hubie Brooks UER (Kelvin Chapman's stats on card	.15	.05
❑ 75 Kelvin Chapman	.15	.05
❑ 76 Ron Darling	.40	.15
❑ 77 Sid Fernandez	.40	.15
❑ 78 Mike Fitzgerald	.15	.05
❑ 79 George Foster	.40	.15
❑ 80 Brent Gaff	.15	.05
❑ 81 Ron Gardenhire	.15	.05
❑ 82 Dwight Gooden RC	3.00	1.25
❑ 83 Tom Gorman	.15	.05
❑ 84 Danny Heep	.15	.05
❑ 85 Keith Hernandez	.40	.15
❑ 86 Ray Knight	.40	.15
❑ 87 Ed Lynch	.15	.05
❑ 88 Jose Oquendo	.15	.05
❑ 89 Jesse Orosco	.15	.05
❑ 90 Rafael Santana	.15	.05
❑ 91 Doug Sisk	.15	.05
❑ 92 Rusty Staub	.40	.15
❑ 93 Darryl Strawberry	1.25	.50
❑ 94 Walt Terrell	.15	.05
❑ 95 Mookie Wilson	.40	.15
❑ 96 Jim Acker	.15	.05
❑ 97 Willie Aikens	.15	.05
❑ 98 Doyle Alexander	.15	.05
❑ 99 Jesse Barfield	.40	.15
❑ 100 George Bell	.40	.15
❑ 101 Jim Clancy	.15	.05
❑ 102 Dave Collins	.15	.05
❑ 103 Tony Fernandez	.40	.15
❑ 104 Damaso Garcia	.15	.05
❑ 105 Jim Gott	.15	.05
❑ 106 Alfredo Griffin	.15	.05
❑ 107 Garth Iorg	.15	.05
❑ 108 Roy Lee Jackson	.15	.05
❑ 109 Cliff Johnson	.15	.05
❑ 110 Jimmy Key RC	1.00	.40
❑ 111 Dennis Lamp	.15	.05
❑ 112 Rick Leach	.15	.05
❑ 113 Luis Leal	.15	.05
❑ 114 Buck Martinez	.15	.05
❑ 115 Lloyd Moseby	.15	.05
❑ 116 Rance Mulliniks	.15	.05
❑ 117 Dave Stieb	.40	.15
❑ 118 Willie Upshaw	.15	.05
❑ 119 Ernie Whitt	.15	.05
❑ 120 Mike Armstrong	.15	.05
❑ 121 Don Baylor	.40	.15
❑ 122 Marty Bystrom	.15	.05
❑ 123 Rick Cerone	.15	.05
❑ 124 Joe Cowley	.15	.05
❑ 125 Brian Dayett	.15	.05
❑ 126 Tim Foli	.15	.05
❑ 127 Ray Fontenot	.15	.05
❑ 128 Ken Griffey	.40	.15
❑ 129 Ron Guidry	.40	.15
❑ 130 Toby Harrah	.40	.15
❑ 131 Jay Howell	.15	.05
❑ 132 Steve Kemp	.15	.05
❑ 133 Don Mattingly	5.00	2.00
❑ 134 Bobby Meacham	.15	.05
❑ 135 John Montefusco	.15	.05
❑ 136 Omar Moreno	.15	.05
❑ 137 Dale Murray	.15	.05
❑ 138 Phil Niekro	.40	.15
❑ 139 Mike Pagliarulo	.15	.05
❑ 140 Willie Randolph	.40	.15
❑ 141 Dennis Rasmussen	.15	.05
❑ 142 Dave Righetti	.40	.15
❑ 143 Jose Rijo RC	1.00	.40
❑ 144 Andre Robertson	.15	.05
❑ 145 Bob Shirley	.15	.05
❑ 146 Dave Winfield	.40	.15
❑ 147 Butch Wynegar	.15	.05
❑ 148 Gary Allenson	.15	.05
❑ 149 Tony Armas	.40	.15
❑ 150 Marty Barrett	.15	.05
❑ 151 Wade Boggs	1.25	.50
❑ 152 Dennis Boyd	.15	.05
❑ 153 Bill Buckner	.40	.15
❑ 154 Mark Clear	.15	.05
❑ 155 Roger Clemens RC	40.00	15.00
❑ 156 Steve Crawford	.15	.05
❑ 157 Mike Easler	.15	.05
❑ 158 Dwight Evans	.75	.30
❑ 159 Rich Gedman	.15	.05
❑ 160 Jackie Gutierrez w/Boggs	.40	.15
❑ 161 Bruce Hurst	.15	.05
❑ 162 John Henry Johnson	.15	.05
❑ 163 Rick Miller	.15	.05
❑ 164 Reid Nichols	.15	.05
❑ 165 Al Nipper	.15	.05
❑ 166 Bob Ojeda	.15	.05
❑ 167 Jerry Remy	.15	.05
❑ 168 Jim Rice	.40	.15
❑ 169 Bob Stanley	.15	.05
❑ 170 Mike Boddicker	.15	.05
❑ 171 Al Bumbry	.15	.05
❑ 172 Todd Cruz	.15	.05
❑ 173 Rich Dauer	.15	.05
❑ 174 Storm Davis	.15	.05
❑ 175 Rick Dempsey	.15	.05
❑ 176 Jim Dwyer	.15	.05
❑ 177 Mike Flanagan	.15	.05
❑ 178 Dan Ford	.15	.05
❑ 179 Wayne Gross	.15	.05
❑ 180 John Lowenstein	.15	.05
❑ 181 Dennis Martinez	.40	.15
❑ 182 Tippy Martinez	.15	.05
❑ 183 Scott McGregor	.15	.05
❑ 184 Eddie Murray	1.25	.50
❑ 185 Joe Nolan	.15	.05
❑ 186 Floyd Rayford	.15	.05
❑ 187 Cal Ripken	5.00	2.00
❑ 188 Gary Roenicke	.15	.05
❑ 189 Lenn Sakata	.15	.05
❑ 190 John Shelby	.15	.05
❑ 191 Ken Singleton	.40	.15
❑ 192 Sammy Stewart	.15	.05
❑ 193 Bill Swaggerty	.15	.05
❑ 194 Tom Underwood	.15	.05
❑ 195 Mike Young	.15	.05
❑ 196 Steve Balboni	.15	.05
❑ 197 Joe Beckwith	.15	.05
❑ 198 Bud Black	.15	.05
❑ 199 George Brett	3.00	1.25
❑ 200 Onix Concepcion	.15	.05
❑ 201 Mark Gubicza RC*	.50	.20
❑ 202 Larry Gura	.15	.05
❑ 203 Mark Huismann	.15	.05
❑ 204 Dane Iorg	.15	.05
❑ 205 Danny Jackson	.15	.05
❑ 206 Charlie Leibrandt	.15	.05
❑ 207 Hal McRae	.40	.15
❑ 208 Darryl Motley	.15	.05
❑ 209 Jorge Orta	.15	.05
❑ 210 Greg Pryor	.15	.05
❑ 211 Dan Quisenberry	.15	.05
❑ 212 Bret Saberhagen RC	1.50	.60
❑ 213 Pat Sheridan	.15	.05
❑ 214 Don Slaught	.15	.05
❑ 215 U.L. Washington	.15	.05
❑ 216 John Wathan	.15	.05
❑ 217 Frank White	.40	.15
❑ 218 Willie Wilson	.40	.15
❑ 219 Neil Allen	.15	.05
❑ 220 Joaquin Andujar	.40	.15
❑ 221 Steve Braun	.15	.05
❑ 222 Danny Cox	.15	.05
❑ 223 Bob Forsch	.15	.05
❑ 224 David Green	.15	.05
❑ 225 George Hendrick	.40	.15
❑ 226 Tom Herr	.15	.05
❑ 227 Ricky Horton	.15	.05
❑ 228 Art Howe	.15	.05
❑ 229 Mike Jorgensen	.15	.05
❑ 230 Kurt Kepshire	.15	.05
❑ 231 Jeff Lahti	.15	.05
❑ 232 Tito Landrum	.15	.05
❑ 233 Dave LaPoint	.15	.05
❑ 234 Willie McGee	.40	.15
❑ 235 Tom Nieto	.15	.05
❑ 236 Terry Pendleton RC	1.00	.40
❑ 237 Darrell Porter	.15	.05
❑ 238 Dave Rucker	.15	.05
❑ 239 Lonnie Smith	.15	.05
❑ 240 Ozzie Smith	2.00	.75
❑ 241 Bruce Sutter	.40	.15
❑ 242 Andy Van Slyke UER	.75	.30
❑ 243 Dave Von Ohlen	.15	.05
❑ 244 Larry Andersen	.15	.05
❑ 245 Bill Campbell	.15	.05
❑ 246 Steve Carlton	.40	.15
❑ 247 Tim Corcoran	.15	.05
❑ 248 Ivan DeJesus	.15	.05
❑ 249 John Denny	.15	.05
❑ 250 Bo Diaz	.15	.05
❑ 251 Greg Gross	.15	.05
❑ 252 Kevin Gross	.15	.05
❑ 253 Von Hayes	.15	.05
❑ 254 Al Holland	.15	.05
❑ 255 Charles Hudson	.15	.05
❑ 256 Jerry Koosman	.40	.15
❑ 257 Joe Lefebvre	.15	.05
❑ 258 Sixto Lezcano	.15	.05
❑ 259 Garry Maddox	.15	.05
❑ 260 Len Matuszek	.15	.05
❑ 261 Tug McGraw	.40	.15
❑ 262 Al Oliver	.40	.15
❑ 263 Shane Rawley	.15	.05
❑ 264 Juan Samuel	.15	.05
❑ 265 Mike Schmidt	3.00	1.25
❑ 266 Jeff Stone	.15	.05
❑ 267 Ozzie Virgil	.15	.05
❑ 268 Glenn Wilson	.15	.05
❑ 269 John Wockenfuss	.15	.05
❑ 270 Darrell Brown	.15	.05
❑ 271 Tom Brunansky	.15	.05
❑ 272 Randy Bush	.15	.05
❑ 273 John Butcher	.15	.05
❑ 274 Bobby Castillo	.15	.05
❑ 275 Ron Davis	.15	.05
❑ 276 Dave Engle	.15	.05
❑ 277 Pete Filson	.15	.05
❑ 278 Gary Gaetti	.40	.15
❑ 279 Mickey Hatcher	.15	.05
❑ 280 Ed Hodge	.15	.05
❑ 281 Kent Hrbek	.40	.15
❑ 282 Houston Jimenez	.15	.05
❑ 283 Tim Laudner	.15	.05
❑ 284 Rick Lysander	.15	.05
❑ 285 Dave Meier	.15	.05
❑ 286 Kirby Puckett RC	10.00	4.00
❑ 287 Pat Putnam	.15	.05
❑ 288 Ken Schrom	.15	.05
❑ 289 Mike Smithson	.15	.05
❑ 290 Tim Teufel	.15	.05
❑ 291 Frank Viola	.40	.15
❑ 292 Ron Washington	.15	.05
❑ 293 Don Aase	.15	.05
❑ 294 Juan Beniquez	.15	.05
❑ 295 Bob Boone	.40	.15
❑ 296 Mike C. Brown	.15	.05
❑ 297 Rod Carew	.75	.30
❑ 298 Doug Corbett	.15	.05
❑ 299 Doug DeCinces	.15	.05
❑ 300 Brian Downing	.40	.15
❑ 301 Ken Forsch	.15	.05
❑ 302 Bobby Grich	.40	.15
❑ 303 Reggie Jackson	.75	.30
❑ 304 Tommy John	.40	.15
❑ 305 Curt Kaufman	.15	.05
❑ 306 Bruce Kison	.15	.05
❑ 307 Fred Lynn	.40	.15
❑ 308 Gary Pettis	.15	.05
❑ 309 Ron Romanick	.15	.05
❑ 310 Luis Sanchez	.15	.05
❑ 311 Dick Schofield	.15	.05
❑ 312 Daryl Sconiers	.15	.05
❑ 313 Jim Slaton	.15	.05
❑ 314 Derrel Thomas	.15	.05
❑ 315 Rob Wilfong	.15	.05
❑ 316 Mike Witt	.15	.05
❑ 317 Geoff Zahn	.15	.05
❑ 318 Len Barker	.15	.05

- ❑ 319 Steve Bedrosian .15 .05
- ❑ 320 Bruce Benedict .15 .05
- ❑ 321 Rick Camp .15 .05
- ❑ 322 Chris Chambliss .40 .15
- ❑ 323 Jeff Dedmon .15 .05
- ❑ 324 Terry Forster .40 .15
- ❑ 325 Gene Garber .15 .05
- ❑ 326 Albert Hall .15 .05
- ❑ 327 Terry Harper .15 .05
- ❑ 328 Bob Horner .40 .15
- ❑ 329 Glenn Hubbard .15 .05
- ❑ 330 Randy Johnson .15 .05
- ❑ 331 Brad Komminsk .15 .05
- ❑ 332 Rick Mahler .15 .05
- ❑ 333 Craig McMurtry .15 .05
- ❑ 334 Donnie Moore .15 .05
- ❑ 335 Dale Murphy .75 .30
- ❑ 336 Ken Oberkfell .15 .05
- ❑ 337 Pascual Perez .15 .05
- ❑ 338 Gerald Perry .15 .05
- ❑ 339 Rafael Ramirez .15 .05
- ❑ 340 Jerry Royster .15 .05
- ❑ 341 Alex Trevino .15 .05
- ❑ 342 Claudell Washington .15 .05
- ❑ 343 Alan Ashby .15 .05
- ❑ 344 Mark Bailey .15 .05
- ❑ 345 Kevin Bass .15 .05
- ❑ 346 Enos Cabell .15 .05
- ❑ 347 Jose Cruz .40 .15
- ❑ 348 Bill Dawley .15 .05
- ❑ 349 Frank DiPino .15 .05
- ❑ 350 Bill Doran .15 .05
- ❑ 351 Phil Garner .40 .15
- ❑ 352 Bob Knepper .15 .05
- ❑ 353 Mike LaCoss .15 .05
- ❑ 354 Jerry Mumphrey .15 .05
- ❑ 355 Joe Niekro .15 .05
- ❑ 356 Terry Puhl .15 .05
- ❑ 357 Craig Reynolds .15 .05
- ❑ 358 Vern Ruhle .15 .05
- ❑ 359 Nolan Ryan 6.00 2.50
- ❑ 360 Joe Sambito .15 .05
- ❑ 361 Mike Scott .40 .15
- ❑ 362 Dave Smith .15 .05
- ❑ 363 Julio Solano .15 .05
- ❑ 364 Dickie Thon .15 .05
- ❑ 365 Denny Walling .15 .05
- ❑ 366 Dave Anderson .15 .05
- ❑ 367 Bob Bailor .15 .05
- ❑ 368 Greg Brock .15 .05
- ❑ 369 Carlos Diaz .15 .05
- ❑ 370 Pedro Guerrero .40 .15
- ❑ 371 Orel Hershiser RC 3.00 1.25
- ❑ 372 Rick Honeycutt .15 .05
- ❑ 373 Burt Hooton .15 .05
- ❑ 374 Ken Howell .15 .05
- ❑ 375 Ken Landreaux .15 .05
- ❑ 376 Candy Maldonado .15 .05
- ❑ 377 Mike Marshall .15 .05
- ❑ 378 Tom Niedenfuer .15 .05
- ❑ 379 Alejandro Pena .15 .05
- ❑ 380 Jerry Reuss UER (%%Home:~ omitted) .15 .05
- ❑ 381 R.J. Reynolds .15 .05
- ❑ 382 German Rivera .15 .05
- ❑ 383 Bill Russell .40 .15
- ❑ 384 Steve Sax .15 .05
- ❑ 385 Mike Scioscia .40 .15
- ❑ 386 Franklin Stubbs .15 .05
- ❑ 387 Fernando Valenzuela .40 .15
- ❑ 388 Bob Welch .40 .15
- ❑ 389 Terry Whitfield .15 .05
- ❑ 390 Steve Yeager .40 .15
- ❑ 391 Pat Zachry .15 .05
- ❑ 392 Fred Breining .15 .05
- ❑ 393 Gary Carter .40 .15
- ❑ 394 Andre Dawson .40 .15
- ❑ 395 Miguel Dilone .15 .05
- ❑ 396 Dan Driessen .15 .05
- ❑ 397 Doug Flynn .15 .05
- ❑ 398 Terry Francona .40 .15
- ❑ 399 Bill Gullickson .15 .05
- ❑ 400 Bob James .15 .05
- ❑ 401 Charlie Lea .15 .05
- ❑ 402 Bryan Little .15 .05
- ❑ 403 Gary Lucas .15 .05
- ❑ 404 David Palmer .15 .05
- ❑ 405 Tim Raines .40 .15
- ❑ 406 Mike Ramsey .15 .05
- ❑ 407 Jeff Reardon .40 .15
- ❑ 408 Steve Rogers .40 .15
- ❑ 409 Dan Schatzeder .15 .05
- ❑ 410 Bryn Smith .15 .05
- ❑ 411 Mike Stenhouse .15 .05
- ❑ 412 Tim Wallach .15 .05
- ❑ 413 Jim Wohlford .15 .05
- ❑ 414 Bill Almon .15 .05
- ❑ 415 Keith Atherton .15 .05
- ❑ 416 Bruce Bochte .15 .05
- ❑ 417 Tom Burgmeier .15 .05
- ❑ 418 Ray Burris .15 .05
- ❑ 419 Bill Caudill .15 .05
- ❑ 420 Chris Codiroli .15 .05
- ❑ 421 Tim Conroy .15 .05
- ❑ 422 Mike Davis .15 .05
- ❑ 423 Jim Essian .15 .05
- ❑ 424 Mike Heath .15 .05
- ❑ 425 Rickey Henderson 1.50 .60
- ❑ 426 Donnie Hill .15 .05
- ❑ 427 Dave Kingman .40 .15
- ❑ 428 Bill Krueger .15 .05
- ❑ 429 Carney Lansford .40 .15
- ❑ 430 Steve McCatty .15 .05
- ❑ 431 Joe Morgan .40 .15
- ❑ 432 Dwayne Murphy .15 .05
- ❑ 433 Tony Phillips .15 .05
- ❑ 434 Lary Sorensen .15 .05
- ❑ 435 Mike Warren .15 .05
- ❑ 436 Curt Young .15 .05
- ❑ 437 Luis Aponte .15 .05
- ❑ 438 Chris Bando .15 .05
- ❑ 439 Tony Bernazard .15 .05
- ❑ 440 Bert Blyleven .40 .15
- ❑ 441 Brett Butler .40 .15
- ❑ 442 Ernie Camacho .15 .05
- ❑ 443 Joe Carter 1.25 .50
- ❑ 444 Carmelo Castillo .15 .05
- ❑ 445 Jamie Easterly .15 .05
- ❑ 446 Steve Farr RC .50 .20
- ❑ 447 Mike Fischlin .15 .05
- ❑ 448 Julio Franco .40 .15
- ❑ 449 Mel Hall .15 .05
- ❑ 450 Mike Hargrove .15 .05
- ❑ 451 Neal Heaton .15 .05
- ❑ 452 Brook Jacoby .15 .05
- ❑ 453 Mike Jeffcoat .15 .05
- ❑ 454 Don Schulze .15 .05
- ❑ 455 Roy Smith .15 .05
- ❑ 456 Pat Tabler .15 .05
- ❑ 457 Andre Thornton .15 .05
- ❑ 458 George Vukovich .15 .05
- ❑ 459 Tom Waddell .15 .05
- ❑ 460 Jerry Willard .15 .05
- ❑ 461 Dale Berra .15 .05
- ❑ 462 John Candelaria .15 .05
- ❑ 463 Jose DeLeon .15 .05
- ❑ 464 Doug Frobel .15 .05
- ❑ 465 Cecilio Guante .15 .05
- ❑ 466 Brian Harper .15 .05
- ❑ 467 Lee Lacy .15 .05
- ❑ 468 Bill Madlock .40 .15
- ❑ 469 Lee Mazzilli .40 .15
- ❑ 470 Larry McWilliams .15 .05
- ❑ 471 Jim Morrison .15 .05
- ❑ 472 Tony Pena .15 .05
- ❑ 473 Johnny Ray .15 .05
- ❑ 474 Rick Rhoden .15 .05
- ❑ 475 Don Robinson .15 .05
- ❑ 476 Rod Scurry .15 .05
- ❑ 477 Kent Tekulve .15 .05
- ❑ 478 Jason Thompson .15 .05
- ❑ 479 John Tudor .40 .15
- ❑ 480 Lee Tunnell .15 .05
- ❑ 481 Marvell Wynne .15 .05
- ❑ 482 Salome Barojas .15 .05
- ❑ 483 Dave Beard .15 .05
- ❑ 484 Jim Beattie .15 .05
- ❑ 485 Barry Bonnell .15 .05
- ❑ 486 Phil Bradley .50 .20
- ❑ 487 Al Cowens .15 .05
- ❑ 488 Alvin Davis RC* .50 .20
- ❑ 489 Dave Henderson .15 .05
- ❑ 490 Steve Henderson .15 .05
- ❑ 491 Bob Kearney .15 .05
- ❑ 492 Mark Langston RC 1.00 .40
- ❑ 493 Larry Milbourne .15 .05
- ❑ 494 Paul Mirabella .15 .05
- ❑ 495 Mike Moore .15 .05
- ❑ 496 Edwin Nunez .15 .05
- ❑ 497 Spike Owen .15 .05
- ❑ 498 Jack Perconte .15 .05
- ❑ 499 Ken Phelps .15 .05
- ❑ 500 Jim Presley .50 .20
- ❑ 501 Mike Stanton .15 .05
- ❑ 502 Bob Stoddard .15 .05
- ❑ 503 Gorman Thomas .40 .15
- ❑ 504 Ed VandeBerg .15 .05
- ❑ 505 Matt Young .15 .05
- ❑ 506 Juan Agosto .15 .05
- ❑ 507 Harold Baines .40 .15
- ❑ 508 Floyd Bannister .15 .05
- ❑ 509 Britt Burns .15 .05
- ❑ 510 Julio Cruz .15 .05
- ❑ 511 Richard Dotson .15 .05
- ❑ 512 Jerry Dybzinski .15 .05
- ❑ 513 Carlton Fisk .75 .30
- ❑ 514 Scott Fletcher .15 .05
- ❑ 515 Jerry Hairston .15 .05
- ❑ 516 Marc Hill .15 .05
- ❑ 517 LaMarr Hoyt .15 .05
- ❑ 518 Ron Kittle .15 .05
- ❑ 519 Rudy Law .15 .05
- ❑ 520 Vance Law .15 .05
- ❑ 521 Greg Luzinski .40 .15
- ❑ 522 Gene Nelson .15 .05
- ❑ 523 Tom Paciorek .15 .05
- ❑ 524 Ron Reed .15 .05
- ❑ 525 Bert Roberge .15 .05
- ❑ 526 Tom Seaver .75 .30
- ❑ 527 Roy Smalley .15 .05
- ❑ 528 Dan Spillner .15 .05
- ❑ 529 Mike Squires .15 .05
- ❑ 530 Greg Walker .15 .05
- ❑ 531 Cesar Cedeno .40 .15
- ❑ 532 Dave Concepcion .40 .15
- ❑ 533 Eric Davis RC 3.00 1.25
- ❑ 534 Nick Esasky .15 .05
- ❑ 535 Tom Foley .15 .05
- ❑ 536 John Franco UER RC 1.00 .40
- ❑ 537 Brad Gulden .15 .05
- ❑ 538 Tom Hume .15 .05
- ❑ 539 Wayne Krenchicki .15 .05
- ❑ 540 Andy McGaffigan .15 .05
- ❑ 541 Eddie Milner .15 .05
- ❑ 542 Ron Oester .15 .05
- ❑ 543 Bob Owchinko .15 .05
- ❑ 544 Dave Parker .40 .15
- ❑ 545 Frank Pastore .15 .05
- ❑ 546 Tony Perez .75 .30
- ❑ 547 Ted Power .15 .05
- ❑ 548 Joe Price .15 .05
- ❑ 549 Gary Redus .15 .05
- ❑ 550 Pete Rose 4.00 1.50
- ❑ 551 Jeff Russell .15 .05
- ❑ 552 Mario Soto .40 .15
- ❑ 553 Jay Tibbs .15 .05
- ❑ 554 Duane Walker .15 .05
- ❑ 555 Alan Bannister .15 .05
- ❑ 556 Buddy Bell .40 .15
- ❑ 557 Danny Darwin .15 .05
- ❑ 558 Charlie Hough .40 .15
- ❑ 559 Bobby Jones .15 .05
- ❑ 560 Odell Jones .15 .05
- ❑ 561 Jeff Kunkel .15 .05
- ❑ 562 Mike Mason RC .25 .08
- ❑ 563 Pete O'Brien .15 .05
- ❑ 564 Larry Parrish .15 .05
- ❑ 565 Mickey Rivers .15 .05
- ❑ 566 Billy Sample .15 .05
- ❑ 567 Dave Schmidt .15 .05
- ❑ 568 Donnie Scott .15 .05
- ❑ 569 Dave Stewart .40 .15
- ❑ 570 Frank Tanana .40 .15
- ❑ 571 Wayne Tolleson .15 .05
- ❑ 572 Gary Ward .15 .05
- ❑ 573 Curtis Wilkerson .15 .05
- ❑ 574 George Wright .15 .05
- ❑ 575 Ned Yost .15 .05

❑ 576 Mark Brouhard .15 .05
❑ 577 Mike Caldwell .15 .05
❑ 578 Bobby Clark .15 .05
❑ 579 Jaime Cocanower .15 .05
❑ 580 Cecil Cooper .40 .15
❑ 581 Rollie Fingers .40 .15
❑ 582 Jim Gantner .15 .05
❑ 583 Moose Haas .15 .05
❑ 584 Dion James .15 .05
❑ 585 Pete Ladd .15 .05
❑ 586 Rick Manning .15 .05
❑ 587 Bob McClure .15 .05
❑ 588 Paul Molitor .40 .15
❑ 589 Charlie Moore .15 .05
❑ 590 Ben Oglivie .40 .15
❑ 591 Chuck Porter .15 .05
❑ 592 Randy Ready RC* .25 .08
❑ 593 Ed Romero .15 .05
❑ 594 Bill Schroeder .15 .05
❑ 595 Ray Searage .15 .05
❑ 596 Ted Simmons .40 .15
❑ 597 Jim Sundberg .40 .15
❑ 598 Don Sutton .40 .15
❑ 599 Tom Tellmann .15 .05
❑ 600 Rick Waits .15 .05
❑ 601 Robin Yount 2.00 .75
❑ 602 Dusty Baker .40 .15
❑ 603 Bob Brenly .15 .05
❑ 604 Jack Clark .40 .15
❑ 605 Chili Davis .40 .15
❑ 606 Mark Davis .15 .05
❑ 607 Dan Gladden RC .50 .20
❑ 608 Atlee Hammaker .15 .05
❑ 609 Mike Krukow .15 .05
❑ 610 Duane Kuiper .15 .05
❑ 611 Bob Lacey .15 .05
❑ 612 Bill Laskey .15 .05
❑ 613 Gary Lavelle .15 .05
❑ 614 Johnnie LeMaster .15 .05
❑ 615 Jeff Leonard .15 .05
❑ 616 Randy Lerch .15 .05
❑ 617 Greg Minton .15 .05
❑ 618 Steve Nicosia .15 .05
❑ 619 Gene Richards .15 .05
❑ 620 Jeff D. Robinson .15 .05
❑ 621 Scot Thompson .15 .05
❑ 622 Manny Trillo .15 .05
❑ 623 Brad Wellman .15 .05
❑ 624 Frank Williams .15 .05
❑ 625 Joel Youngblood .15 .05
❑ 626 Cal Ripken IA 3.00 1.25
❑ 627 Mike Schmidt IA 1.25 .50
❑ 628 Giving The Signs
Sparky Anderson .40 .15
❑ 629 D.Winfield/R.Henderson .40 .15
❑ 630 M.Schmidt/R.Sandberg 2.00 .75
❑ 631 Straw/Carter/Garvey/Oz 1.25 .50
❑ 632 A-S Winning Battery
Gary Carter
Charlie Lea .15 .05
❑ 633 NL Pennant Clinchers
Steve Garvey
Rich Gossage .40 .15
❑ 634 Dwight Gooden/J.Samuel 1.25 .50
❑ 635 Toronto's Big Guns
Willie Upshaw .15 .05
❑ 636 Toronto's Big Guns
Lloyd Moseby .15 .05
❑ 637 HOLLAND: Al Holland .15 .05
❑ 638 TUNNELL: Lee Tunnell .15 .05
❑ 639 Reggie Jackson IA .40 .15
❑ 640 Pete Rose IA 1.25 .50
❑ 641 Cal Ripken Jr./Sr. 3.00 1.25
❑ 642 Cubs: Division Champs .40 .15
❑ 643 Two Perfect Games
and One No-Hitter:
Mike Witt. .40 .15
❑ 644 W.Lozado RC/V.Mata RC .15 .05
❑ 645 K.Gruber RC/R.O'Neal RC .50 .20
❑ 646 J.Roman RC/J.Skinner .15 .05
❑ 647 S.Kiefer RC/D.Tartabull RC 1.00 .40
❑ 648 R.Deer RC/A.Sanchez RC .50 .20
❑ 649 B.Hatcher RC/S.Dunston RC 1.00 .40
❑ 650 R.Robinson RC/M.Bieliecki RC .15 .05
❑ 651 Z.Smith RC/P.Zuvella RC .50 .20
❑ 652 J.Hesketh RC/G.Davis RC .50 .20
❑ 653 J.Russell RC/S.Jeltz RC .15 .05
❑ 654 CL: Tigers/Padres
and Cubs/Mets .15 .05
❑ 655 CL: Blue Jays/Yankees
and Red Sox/Orioles .15 .05
❑ 656 CL: Royals/Cardinals
and Phillies/Twins .15 .05
❑ 657 CL: Angels/Braves
and Astros/Dodgers .15 .05
❑ 658 CL: Expos/A's
and Indians/Pirates .15 .05
❑ 659 CL: Mariners/White Sox
and Reds/Rangers .15 .05
❑ 660 CL: Brewers/Giants
and Special Cards .15 .05

1985 Fleer Update

❑ COMP.FACT.SET (132) 8.00 3.00
❑ 1 Don Aase .15 .05
❑ 2 Bill Almon .15 .05
❑ 3 Dusty Baker .40 .15
❑ 4 Dale Berra .15 .05
❑ 5 Karl Best .15 .05
❑ 6 Tim Birtsas .15 .05
❑ 7 Vida Blue .40 .15
❑ 8 Rich Bordi .15 .05
❑ 9 Daryl Boston XRC .25 .08
❑ 10 Hubie Brooks .15 .05
❑ 11 Chris Brown XRC .25 .08
❑ 12 Tom Browning XRC .50 .20
❑ 13 Al Bumbry .15 .05
❑ 14 Tim Burke .15 .05
❑ 15 Ray Burris .15 .05
❑ 16 Jeff Burroughs .15 .05
❑ 17 Ivan Calderon XRC .50 .20
❑ 18 Jeff Calhoun .15 .05
❑ 19 Bill Campbell .15 .05
❑ 20 Don Carman .15 .05
❑ 21 Gary Carter .40 .15
❑ 22 Bobby Castillo .15 .05
❑ 23 Bill Caudill .15 .05
❑ 24 Rick Cerone .15 .05
❑ 25 Jack Clark .40 .15
❑ 26 Pat Clements .15 .05
❑ 27 Stu Cliburn .15 .05
❑ 28 Vince Coleman XRC 1.00 .40
❑ 29 Dave Collins .15 .05
❑ 30 Fritz Connally .15 .05
❑ 31 Henry Cotto .25 .08
❑ 32 Danny Darwin .15 .05
❑ 33 Darren Daulton XRC 1.00 .40
❑ 34 Jerry Davis .15 .05
❑ 35 Brian Dayett .15 .05
❑ 36 Ken Dixon .15 .05
❑ 37 Tommy Dunbar .15 .05
❑ 38 Mariano Duncan XRC .50 .20
❑ 39 Bob Fallon .15 .05
❑ 40 Brian Fisher XRC .25 .08
❑ 41 Mike Fitzgerald .15 .05
❑ 42 Ray Fontenot .15 .05
❑ 43 Greg Gagne XRC .50 .20
❑ 44 Oscar Gamble .15 .05
❑ 45 Jim Gott .15 .05
❑ 46 David Green .15 .05
❑ 47 Alfredo Griffin .15 .05
❑ 48 Ozzie Guillen XRC 5.00 2.00
❑ 49 Toby Harrah .40 .15
❑ 50 Ron Hassey .15 .05
❑ 51 Rickey Henderson 2.50 1.00
❑ 52 Steve Henderson .15 .05
❑ 53 George Hendrick .40 .15
❑ 54 Teddy Higuera XRC .50 .20
❑ 55 Al Holland .15 .05
❑ 56 Burt Hooton .15 .05
❑ 57 Jay Howell .15 .05
❑ 58 LaMarr Hoyt .15 .05
❑ 59 Tim Hulett XRC .25 .08
❑ 60 Bob James .15 .05
❑ 61 Cliff Johnson .15 .05
❑ 62 Howard Johnson .40 .15
❑ 63 Ruppert Jones .15 .05
❑ 64 Steve Kemp .15 .05
❑ 65 Bruce Kison .15 .05
❑ 66 Mike LaCoss .15 .05
❑ 67 Lee Lacy .15 .05
❑ 68 Dave LaPoint .15 .05
❑ 69 Gary Lavelle .15 .05
❑ 70 Vance Law .15 .05
❑ 71 Manuel Lee XRC .25 .08
❑ 72 Sixto Lezcano .15 .05
❑ 73 Tim Lollar .15 .05
❑ 74 Urbano Lugo .15 .05
❑ 75 Fred Lynn .40 .15
❑ 76 Steve Lyons XRC .50 .20
❑ 77 Mickey Mahler .15 .05
❑ 78 Ron Mathis .15 .05
❑ 79 Len Matuszek .15 .05
❑ 80 Oddibe McDowell XRC .50 .20
❑ 81 Roger McDowell UER XRC .50 .20
❑ 82 Donnie Moore .15 .05
❑ 83 Ron Musselman .15 .05
❑ 84 Al Oliver .40 .15
❑ 85 Joe Orsulak XRC .50 .20
❑ 86 Dan Pasqua XRC .50 .20
❑ 87 Chris Pittaro .15 .05
❑ 88 Rick Reuschel .40 .15
❑ 89 Earnie Riles .15 .05
❑ 90 Jerry Royster .15 .05
❑ 91 Dave Rozema .15 .05
❑ 92 Dave Rucker .15 .05
❑ 93 Vern Ruhle .15 .05
❑ 94 Mark Salas .15 .05
❑ 95 Luis Salazar .15 .05
❑ 96 Joe Sambito .15 .05
❑ 97 Billy Sample .15 .05
❑ 98 Alejandro Sanchez XRC .25 .08
❑ 99 Calvin Schiraldi XRC .50 .20
❑ 100 Rick Schu .15 .05
❑ 101 Larry Sheets XRC .25 .08
❑ 102 Ron Shephard .15 .05
❑ 103 Nelson Simmons .15 .05
❑ 104 Don Slaught .15 .05
❑ 105 Roy Smalley .15 .05
❑ 106 Lonnie Smith .15 .05
❑ 107 Nate Snell .15 .05
❑ 108 Lary Sorensen .15 .05
❑ 109 Chris Speier .15 .05
❑ 110 Mike Stenhouse .15 .05
❑ 111 Tim Stoddard .15 .05
❑ 112 John Stuper .15 .05
❑ 113 Jim Sundberg .40 .15
❑ 114 Bruce Sutter .40 .15
❑ 115 Don Sutton .40 .15
❑ 116 Bruce Tanner .15 .05
❑ 117 Kent Tekulve .15 .05
❑ 118 Walt Terrell .15 .05
❑ 119 Mickey Tettleton XRC .50 .20
❑ 120 Rich Thompson .15 .05
❑ 121 Louis Thornton .15 .05
❑ 122 Alex Trevino .15 .05
❑ 123 John Tudor .40 .15
❑ 124 Jose Uribe .15 .05
❑ 125 Dave Valle XRC .50 .20
❑ 126 Dave Von Ohlen .15 .05
❑ 127 Curt Wardle .15 .05
❑ 128 U.L. Washington .15 .05
❑ 129 Ed Whitson .15 .05
❑ 130 Herm Winningham .15 .05
❑ 131 Rich Yett .15 .05
❑ 132 Checklist U1-U132 .15 .05

1986 Fleer

Card		
❑ COMPLETE SET (660)	40.00	15.00
❑ COMP.FACT.SET (660)	40.00	15.00
❑ 1 Steve Balboni	.15	.05
❑ 2 Joe Beckwith	.15	.05
❑ 3 Buddy Biancalana	.15	.05
❑ 4 Bud Black	.15	.05
❑ 5 George Brett	2.00	.75
❑ 6 Onix Concepcion	.15	.05
❑ 7 Steve Farr	.15	.05
❑ 8 Mark Gubicza	.15	.05
❑ 9 Dane Iorg	.15	.05
❑ 10 Danny Jackson	.15	.05
❑ 11 Lynn Jones	.15	.05
❑ 12 Mike Jones	.15	.05
❑ 13 Charlie Leibrandt	.15	.05
❑ 14 Hal McRae	.25	.08
❑ 15 Omar Moreno	.15	.05
❑ 16 Darryl Motley	.15	.05
❑ 17 Jorge Orta	.15	.05
❑ 18 Dan Quisenberry	.15	.05
❑ 19 Bret Saberhagen	.25	.08
❑ 20 Pat Sheridan	.15	.05
❑ 21 Lonnie Smith	.15	.05
❑ 22 Jim Sundberg	.25	.08
❑ 23 John Wathan	.15	.05
❑ 24 Frank White	.25	.08
❑ 25 Willie Wilson	.25	.08
❑ 26 Joaquin Andujar	.25	.08
❑ 27 Steve Braun	.15	.05
❑ 28 Bill Campbell	.15	.05
❑ 29 Cesar Cedeno	.25	.08
❑ 30 Jack Clark	.25	.08
❑ 31 Vince Coleman RC	1.00	.40
❑ 32 Danny Cox	.15	.05
❑ 33 Ken Dayley	.15	.05
❑ 34 Ivan DeJesus	.15	.05
❑ 35 Bob Forsch	.15	.05
❑ 36 Brian Harper	.15	.05
❑ 37 Tom Herr	.15	.05
❑ 38 Ricky Horton	.15	.05
❑ 39 Kurt Kepshire	.15	.05
❑ 40 Jeff Lahti	.15	.05
❑ 41 Tito Landrum	.15	.05
❑ 42 Willie McGee	.25	.08
❑ 43 Tom Nieto	.15	.05
❑ 44 Terry Pendleton	.25	.08
❑ 45 Darrell Porter	.15	.05
❑ 46 Ozzie Smith	1.25	.50
❑ 47 John Tudor	.25	.08
❑ 48 Andy Van Slyke	.50	.20
❑ 49 Todd Worrell RC	.50	.20
❑ 50 Jim Acker	.15	.05
❑ 51 Doyle Alexander	.15	.05
❑ 52 Jesse Barfield	.25	.08
❑ 53 George Bell	.25	.08
❑ 54 Jeff Burroughs	.15	.05
❑ 55 Bill Caudill	.15	.05
❑ 56 Jim Clancy	.15	.05
❑ 57 Tony Fernandez	.15	.05
❑ 58 Tom Filer	.15	.05
❑ 59 Damaso Garcia	.15	.05
❑ 60 Tom Henke	.25	.08
❑ 61 Garth Iorg	.15	.05
❑ 62 Cliff Johnson	.15	.05
❑ 63 Jimmy Key	.25	.08
❑ 64 Dennis Lamp	.15	.05
❑ 65 Gary Lavelle	.15	.05
❑ 66 Buck Martinez	.15	.05
❑ 67 Lloyd Moseby	.15	.05
❑ 68 Rance Mulliniks	.15	.05
❑ 69 Al Oliver	.25	.08
❑ 70 Dave Stieb	.25	.08
❑ 71 Louis Thornton	.15	.05
❑ 72 Willie Upshaw	.15	.05
❑ 73 Ernie Whitt	.15	.05
❑ 74 Rick Aguilera RC	.50	.20
❑ 75 Wally Backman	.15	.05
❑ 76 Gary Carter	.25	.08
❑ 77 Ron Darling	.25	.08
❑ 78 Len Dykstra RC	1.50	.60
❑ 79 Sid Fernandez	.15	.05
❑ 80 George Foster	.25	.08
❑ 81 Dwight Gooden	.75	.30
❑ 82 Tom Gorman	.15	.05
❑ 83 Danny Heep	.15	.05
❑ 84 Keith Hernandez	.25	.08
❑ 85 Howard Johnson	.25	.08
❑ 86 Ray Knight	.25	.08
❑ 87 Terry Leach	.15	.05
❑ 88 Ed Lynch	.15	.05
❑ 89 Roger McDowell RC*	.50	.20
❑ 90 Jesse Orosco	.15	.05
❑ 91 Tom Paciorek	.15	.05
❑ 92 Ronn Reynolds	.15	.05
❑ 93 Rafael Santana	.15	.05
❑ 94 Doug Sisk	.15	.05
❑ 95 Rusty Staub	.25	.08
❑ 96 Darryl Strawberry	.50	.20
❑ 97 Mookie Wilson	.25	.08
❑ 98 Neil Allen	.15	.05
❑ 99 Don Baylor	.25	.08
❑ 100 Dale Berra	.15	.05
❑ 101 Rich Bordi	.15	.05
❑ 102 Marty Bystrom	.15	.05
❑ 103 Joe Cowley	.15	.05
❑ 104 Brian Fisher RC	.15	.05
❑ 105 Ken Griffey	.25	.08
❑ 106 Ron Guidry	.25	.08
❑ 107 Ron Hassey	.15	.05
❑ 108 Rickey Henderson	.75	.30
❑ 109 Don Mattingly	2.50	1.00
❑ 110 Bobby Meacham	.15	.05
❑ 111 John Montefusco	.15	.05
❑ 112 Phil Niekro	.25	.08
❑ 113 Mike Pagliarulo	.15	.05
❑ 114 Dan Pasqua	.15	.05
❑ 115 Willie Randolph	.25	.08
❑ 116 Dave Righetti	.25	.08
❑ 117 Andre Robertson	.15	.05
❑ 118 Billy Sample	.15	.05
❑ 119 Bob Shirley	.15	.05
❑ 120 Ed Whitson	.15	.05
❑ 121 Dave Winfield	.25	.08
❑ 122 Butch Wynegar	.15	.05
❑ 123 Dave Anderson	.15	.05
❑ 124 Bob Bailor	.15	.05
❑ 125 Greg Brock	.15	.05
❑ 126 Enos Cabell	.15	.05
❑ 127 Bobby Castillo	.15	.05
❑ 128 Carlos Diaz	.15	.05
❑ 129 Mariano Duncan RC	.50	.20
❑ 130 Pedro Guerrero	.25	.08
❑ 131 Orel Hershiser	.75	.30
❑ 132 Rick Honeycutt	.15	.05
❑ 133 Ken Howell	.15	.05
❑ 134 Ken Landreaux	.15	.05
❑ 135 Bill Madlock	.25	.08
❑ 136 Candy Maldonado	.15	.05
❑ 137 Mike Marshall	.15	.05
❑ 138 Len Matuszek	.15	.05
❑ 139 Tom Niedenfuer	.15	.05
❑ 140 Alejandro Pena	.15	.05
❑ 141 Jerry Reuss	.15	.05
❑ 142 Bill Russell	.25	.08
❑ 143 Steve Sax	.15	.05
❑ 144 Mike Scioscia	.25	.08
❑ 145 Fernando Valenzuela	.25	.08
❑ 146 Bob Welch	.25	.08
❑ 147 Terry Whitfield	.15	.05
❑ 148 Juan Beniquez	.15	.05
❑ 149 Bob Boone	.25	.08
❑ 150 John Candelaria	.15	.05
❑ 151 Rod Carew	.50	.20
❑ 152 Stu Cliburn	.15	.05
❑ 153 Doug DeCinces	.15	.05
❑ 154 Brian Downing	.25	.08
❑ 155 Ken Forsch	.15	.05
❑ 156 Craig Gerber	.15	.05
❑ 157 Bobby Grich	.25	.08
❑ 158 George Hendrick	.25	.08
❑ 159 Al Holland	.15	.05
❑ 160 Reggie Jackson	.50	.20
❑ 161 Ruppert Jones	.15	.05
❑ 162 Urbano Lugo	.15	.05
❑ 163 Kirk McCaskill RC	.50	.20
❑ 164 Donnie Moore	.15	.05
❑ 165 Gary Pettis	.15	.05
❑ 166 Ron Romanick	.15	.05
❑ 167 Dick Schofield	.15	.05
❑ 168 Daryl Sconiers	.15	.05
❑ 169 Jim Slaton	.15	.05
❑ 170 Don Sutton	.25	.08
❑ 171 Mike Witt	.15	.05
❑ 172 Buddy Bell	.25	.08
❑ 173 Tom Browning	.15	.05
❑ 174 Dave Concepcion	.25	.08
❑ 175 Eric Davis	.75	.30
❑ 176 Bo Diaz	.15	.05
❑ 177 Nick Esasky	.15	.05
❑ 178 John Franco	.25	.08
❑ 179 Tom Hume	.15	.05
❑ 180 Wayne Krenchicki	.15	.05
❑ 181 Andy McGaffigan	.15	.05
❑ 182 Eddie Milner	.15	.05
❑ 183 Ron Oester	.15	.05
❑ 184 Dave Parker	.25	.08
❑ 185 Frank Pastore	.15	.05
❑ 186 Tony Perez	.50	.20
❑ 187 Ted Power	.15	.05
❑ 188 Joe Price	.15	.05
❑ 189 Gary Redus	.15	.05
❑ 190 Ron Robinson	.15	.05
❑ 191 Pete Rose	2.50	1.00
❑ 192 Mario Soto	.25	.08
❑ 193 John Stuper	.15	.05
❑ 194 Jay Tibbs	.15	.05
❑ 195 Dave Van Gorder	.15	.05
❑ 196 Max Venable	.15	.05
❑ 197 Juan Agosto	.15	.05
❑ 198 Harold Baines	.25	.08
❑ 199 Floyd Bannister	.15	.05
❑ 200 Britt Burns	.15	.05
❑ 201 Julio Cruz	.15	.05
❑ 202 Joel Davis	.15	.05
❑ 203 Richard Dotson	.15	.05
❑ 204 Carlton Fisk	.50	.20
❑ 205 Scott Fletcher	.15	.05
❑ 206 Ozzie Guillen RC	2.00	.75
❑ 207 Jerry Hairston	.15	.05
❑ 208 Tim Hulett	.15	.05
❑ 209 Bob James	.15	.05
❑ 210 Ron Kittle	.15	.05
❑ 211 Rudy Law	.15	.05
❑ 212 Bryan Little	.15	.05
❑ 213 Gene Nelson	.15	.05
❑ 214 Reid Nichols	.15	.05
❑ 215 Luis Salazar	.15	.05
❑ 216 Tom Seaver	.50	.20
❑ 217 Dan Spillner	.15	.05
❑ 218 Bruce Tanner	.15	.05
❑ 219 Greg Walker	.15	.05
❑ 220 Dave Wehrmeister	.15	.05
❑ 221 Juan Berenguer	.15	.05
❑ 222 Dave Bergman	.15	.05
❑ 223 Tom Brookens	.15	.05
❑ 224 Darrell Evans	.25	.08
❑ 225 Barbaro Garbey	.15	.05
❑ 226 Kirk Gibson	.25	.08
❑ 227 John Grubb	.15	.05
❑ 228 Willie Hernandez	.15	.05
❑ 229 Larry Herndon	.15	.05
❑ 230 Chet Lemon	.25	.08
❑ 231 Aurelio Lopez	.15	.05
❑ 232 Jack Morris	.25	.08
❑ 233 Randy O'Neal	.15	.05
❑ 234 Lance Parrish	.25	.08
❑ 235 Dan Petry	.15	.05
❑ 236 Alejandro Sanchez	.15	.05
❑ 237 Bill Scherrer	.15	.05

❑ 238 Nelson Simmons .15 .05
❑ 239 Frank Tanana .25 .08
❑ 240 Walt Terrell .15 .05
❑ 241 Alan Trammell .25 .08
❑ 242 Lou Whitaker .25 .08
❑ 243 Milt Wilcox .15 .05
❑ 244 Hubie Brooks .15 .05
❑ 245 Tim Burke .15 .05
❑ 246 Andre Dawson .25 .08
❑ 247 Mike Fitzgerald .15 .05
❑ 248 Terry Francona .25 .08
❑ 249 Bill Gullickson .15 .05
❑ 250 Joe Hesketh .15 .05
❑ 251 Bill Laskey .15 .05
❑ 252 Vance Law .15 .05
❑ 253 Charlie Lea .15 .05
❑ 254 Gary Lucas .15 .05
❑ 255 David Palmer .15 .05
❑ 256 Tim Raines .25 .08
❑ 257 Jeff Reardon .25 .08
❑ 258 Bert Roberge .15 .05
❑ 259 Dan Schatzeder .15 .05
❑ 260 Bryn Smith .15 .05
❑ 261 Randy St.Claire .15 .05
❑ 262 Scot Thompson .15 .05
❑ 263 Tim Wallach .15 .05
❑ 264 U.L. Washington .15 .05
❑ 265 Mitch Webster .15 .05
❑ 266 Herm Winningham .15 .05
❑ 267 Floyd Youmans .15 .05
❑ 268 Don Aase .15 .05
❑ 269 Mike Boddicker .15 .05
❑ 270 Rich Dauer .15 .05
❑ 271 Storm Davis .15 .05
❑ 272 Rick Dempsey .15 .05
❑ 273 Ken Dixon .15 .05
❑ 274 Jim Dwyer .15 .05
❑ 275 Mike Flanagan .15 .05
❑ 276 Wayne Gross .15 .05
❑ 277 Lee Lacy .15 .05
❑ 278 Fred Lynn .25 .08
❑ 279 Tippy Martinez .15 .05
❑ 280 Dennis Martinez .25 .08
❑ 281 Scott McGregor .15 .05
❑ 282 Eddie Murray .75 .30
❑ 283 Floyd Rayford .15 .05
❑ 284 Cal Ripken 3.00 1.25
❑ 285 Gary Roenicke .15 .05
❑ 286 Larry Sheets .15 .05
❑ 287 John Shelby .15 .05
❑ 288 Nate Snell .15 .05
❑ 289 Sammy Stewart .15 .05
❑ 290 Alan Wiggins .15 .05
❑ 291 Mike Young .15 .05
❑ 292 Alan Ashby .15 .05
❑ 293 Mark Bailey .15 .05
❑ 294 Kevin Bass .15 .05
❑ 295 Jeff Calhoun .15 .05
❑ 296 Jose Cruz .25 .08
❑ 297 Glenn Davis .15 .05
❑ 298 Bill Dawley .15 .05
❑ 299 Frank DiPino .15 .05
❑ 300 Bill Doran .15 .05
❑ 301 Phil Garner .25 .08
❑ 302 Jeff Heathcock .15 .05
❑ 303 Charlie Kerfeld .15 .05
❑ 304 Bob Knepper .15 .05
❑ 305 Ron Mathis .15 .05
❑ 306 Jerry Mumphrey .15 .05
❑ 307 Jim Pankovits .15 .05
❑ 308 Terry Puhl .15 .05
❑ 309 Craig Reynolds .15 .05
❑ 310 Nolan Ryan 4.00 1.50
❑ 311 Mike Scott .25 .08
❑ 312 Dave Smith .15 .05
❑ 313 Dickie Thon .15 .05
❑ 314 Denny Walling .15 .05
❑ 315 Kurt Bevacqua .15 .05
❑ 316 Al Bumbry .15 .05
❑ 317 Jerry Davis .15 .05
❑ 318 Luis DeLeon .15 .05
❑ 319 Dave Dravecky .15 .05
❑ 320 Tim Flannery .15 .05
❑ 321 Steve Garvey .25 .08
❑ 322 Rich Gossage .25 .08
❑ 323 Tony Gwynn 1.25 .50
❑ 324 Andy Hawkins .15 .05
❑ 325 LaMarr Hoyt .15 .05
❑ 326 Roy Lee Jackson .15 .05
❑ 327 Terry Kennedy .15 .05
❑ 328 Craig Lefferts .15 .05
❑ 329 Carmelo Martinez .15 .05
❑ 330 Lance McCullers .15 .05
❑ 331 Kevin McReynolds .15 .05
❑ 332 Graig Nettles .25 .08
❑ 333 Jerry Royster .15 .05
❑ 334 Eric Show .15 .05
❑ 335 Tim Stoddard .15 .05
❑ 336 Garry Templeton .25 .08
❑ 337 Mark Thurmond .15 .05
❑ 338 Ed Wojna .15 .05
❑ 339 Tony Armas .25 .08
❑ 340 Marty Barrett .15 .05
❑ 341 Wade Boggs .50 .20
❑ 342 Dennis Boyd .15 .05
❑ 343 Bill Buckner .25 .08
❑ 344 Mark Clear .15 .05
❑ 345 Roger Clemens 5.00 2.00
❑ 346 Steve Crawford .15 .05
❑ 347 Mike Easler .15 .05
❑ 348 Dwight Evans .50 .20
❑ 349 Rich Gedman .15 .05
❑ 350 Jackie Gutierrez .15 .05
❑ 351 Glenn Hoffman .15 .05
❑ 352 Bruce Hurst .15 .05
❑ 353 Bruce Kison .15 .05
❑ 354 Tim Lollar .15 .05
❑ 355 Steve Lyons .15 .05
❑ 356 Al Nipper .15 .05
❑ 357 Bob Ojeda .15 .05
❑ 358 Jim Rice .25 .08
❑ 359 Bob Stanley .15 .05
❑ 360 Mike Trujillo .15 .05
❑ 361 Thad Bosley .15 .05
❑ 362 Warren Brusstar .15 .05
❑ 363 Ron Cey .25 .08
❑ 364 Jody Davis .15 .05
❑ 365 Bob Dernier .15 .05
❑ 366 Shawon Dunston .25 .08
❑ 367 Leon Durham .15 .05
❑ 368 Dennis Eckersley .50 .20
❑ 369 Ray Fontenot .15 .05
❑ 370 George Frazier .15 .05
❑ 371 Billy Hatcher .15 .05
❑ 372 Dave Lopes .25 .08
❑ 373 Gary Matthews .25 .08
❑ 374 Ron Meridith .15 .05
❑ 375 Keith Moreland .15 .05
❑ 376 Reggie Patterson .15 .05
❑ 377 Dick Ruthven .15 .05
❑ 378 Ryne Sandberg 1.50 .60
❑ 379 Scott Sanderson .15 .05
❑ 380 Lee Smith .25 .08
❑ 381 Lary Sorensen .15 .05
❑ 382 Chris Speier .15 .05
❑ 383 Rick Sutcliffe .25 .08
❑ 384 Steve Trout .15 .05
❑ 385 Gary Woods .15 .05
❑ 386 Bert Blyleven .25 .08
❑ 387 Tom Brunansky .15 .05
❑ 388 Randy Bush .15 .05
❑ 389 John Butcher .15 .05
❑ 390 Ron Davis .15 .05
❑ 391 Dave Engle .15 .05
❑ 392 Frank Eufemia .15 .05
❑ 393 Pete Filson .15 .05
❑ 394 Gary Gaetti .25 .08
❑ 395 Greg Gagne .15 .05
❑ 396 Mickey Hatcher .15 .05
❑ 397 Kent Hrbek .25 .08
❑ 398 Tim Laudner .15 .05
❑ 399 Rick Lysander .15 .05
❑ 400 Dave Meier .15 .05
❑ 401 Kirby Puckett 2.00 .75
❑ 402 Mark Salas .15 .05
❑ 403 Ken Schrom .15 .05
❑ 404 Roy Smalley .15 .05
❑ 405 Mike Smithson .15 .05
❑ 406 Mike Stenhouse .15 .05
❑ 407 Tim Teufel .15 .05
❑ 408 Frank Viola .25 .08
❑ 409 Ron Washington .15 .05
❑ 410 Keith Atherton .15 .05
❑ 411 Dusty Baker .25 .08
❑ 412 Tim Birtsas .15 .05
❑ 413 Bruce Bochte .15 .05
❑ 414 Chris Codiroli .15 .05
❑ 415 Dave Collins .15 .05
❑ 416 Mike Davis .15 .05
❑ 417 Alfredo Griffin .15 .05
❑ 418 Mike Heath .15 .05
❑ 419 Steve Henderson .15 .05
❑ 420 Donnie Hill .15 .05
❑ 421 Jay Howell .15 .05
❑ 422 Tommy John .25 .08
❑ 423 Dave Kingman .25 .08
❑ 424 Bill Krueger .15 .05
❑ 425 Rick Langford .15 .05
❑ 426 Carney Lansford .25 .08
❑ 427 Steve McCatty .15 .05
❑ 428 Dwayne Murphy .15 .05
❑ 429 Steve Ontiveros RC .15 .05
❑ 430 Tony Phillips .15 .05
❑ 431 Jose Rijo .25 .08
❑ 432 Mickey Tettleton RC .50 .20
❑ 433 Luis Aguayo .15 .05
❑ 434 Larry Andersen .15 .05
❑ 435 Steve Carlton .25 .08
❑ 436 Don Carman .15 .05
❑ 437 Tim Corcoran .15 .05
❑ 438 Darren Daulton RC 1.00 .40
❑ 439 John Denny .15 .05
❑ 440 Tom Foley .15 .05
❑ 441 Greg Gross .15 .05
❑ 442 Kevin Gross .15 .05
❑ 443 Von Hayes .15 .05
❑ 444 Charles Hudson .15 .05
❑ 445 Garry Maddox .15 .05
❑ 446 Shane Rawley .15 .05
❑ 447 Dave Rucker .15 .05
❑ 448 John Russell .15 .05
❑ 449 Juan Samuel .15 .05
❑ 450 Mike Schmidt 2.00 .75
❑ 451 Rick Schu .15 .05
❑ 452 Dave Shipanoff .15 .05
❑ 453 Dave Stewart .25 .08
❑ 454 Jeff Stone .15 .05
❑ 455 Kent Tekulve .15 .05
❑ 456 Ozzie Virgil .15 .05
❑ 457 Glenn Wilson .15 .05
❑ 458 Jim Beattie .15 .05
❑ 459 Karl Best .15 .05
❑ 460 Barry Bonnell .15 .05
❑ 461 Phil Bradley .15 .05
❑ 462 Ivan Calderon RC* .50 .20
❑ 463 Al Cowens .15 .05
❑ 464 Alvin Davis .15 .05
❑ 465 Dave Henderson .15 .05
❑ 466 Bob Kearney .15 .05
❑ 467 Mark Langston .25 .08
❑ 468 Bob Long .15 .05
❑ 469 Mike Moore .15 .05
❑ 470 Edwin Nunez .15 .05
❑ 471 Spike Owen .15 .05
❑ 472 Jack Perconte .15 .05
❑ 473 Jim Presley .15 .05
❑ 474 Donnie Scott .15 .05
❑ 475 Bill Swift .15 .05
❑ 476 Danny Tartabull .25 .08
❑ 477 Gorman Thomas .25 .08
❑ 478 Roy Thomas .15 .05
❑ 479 Ed VandeBerg .15 .05
❑ 480 Frank Wills .15 .05
❑ 481 Matt Young .15 .05
❑ 482 Ray Burris .15 .05
❑ 483 Jaime Cocanower .15 .05
❑ 484 Cecil Cooper .25 .08
❑ 485 Danny Darwin .15 .05
❑ 486 Rollie Fingers .25 .08
❑ 487 Jim Gantner .15 .05
❑ 488 Bob L. Gibson .15 .05
❑ 489 Moose Haas .15 .05
❑ 490 Teddy Higuera RC* .50 .20
❑ 491 Paul Householder .15 .05
❑ 492 Pete Ladd .15 .05
❑ 493 Rick Manning .15 .05
❑ 494 Bob McClure .15 .05
❑ 495 Paul Molitor .25 .08

❑ 496 Charlie Moore .15 .05
❑ 497 Ben Oglivie .25 .08
❑ 498 Randy Ready .15 .05
❑ 499 Earnie Riles .15 .05
❑ 500 Ed Romero .15 .05
❑ 501 Bill Schroeder .15 .05
❑ 502 Ray Searage .15 .05
❑ 503 Ted Simmons .25 .08
❑ 504 Pete Vuckovich .15 .05
❑ 505 Rick Waits .15 .05
❑ 506 Robin Yount 1.25 .50
❑ 507 Len Barker .15 .05
❑ 508 Steve Bedrosian .15 .05
❑ 509 Bruce Benedict .15 .05
❑ 510 Rick Camp .15 .05
❑ 511 Rick Cerone .15 .05
❑ 512 Chris Chambliss .25 .08
❑ 513 Jeff Dedmon .15 .05
❑ 514 Terry Forster .25 .08
❑ 515 Gene Garber .15 .05
❑ 516 Terry Harper .15 .05
❑ 517 Bob Horner .25 .08
❑ 518 Glenn Hubbard .15 .05
❑ 519 Joe Johnson .15 .05
❑ 520 Brad Komminsk .15 .05
❑ 521 Rick Mahler .15 .05
❑ 522 Dale Murphy .50 .20
❑ 523 Ken Oberkfell .15 .05
❑ 524 Pascual Perez .15 .05
❑ 525 Gerald Perry .15 .05
❑ 526 Rafael Ramirez .15 .05
❑ 527 Steve Shields .15 .05
❑ 528 Zane Smith .15 .05
❑ 529 Bruce Sutter .25 .08
❑ 530 Milt Thompson RC .50 .20
❑ 531 Claudell Washington .15 .05
❑ 532 Paul Zuvella .15 .05
❑ 533 Vida Blue .25 .08
❑ 534 Bob Brenly .15 .05
❑ 535 Chris Brown RC .15 .05
❑ 536 Chili Davis .25 .08
❑ 537 Mark Davis .15 .05
❑ 538 Rob Deer .15 .05
❑ 539 Dan Driessen .15 .05
❑ 540 Scott Garrelts .15 .05
❑ 541 Dan Gladden .15 .05
❑ 542 Jim Gott .15 .05
❑ 543 David Green .15 .05
❑ 544 Atlee Hammaker .15 .05
❑ 545 Mike Jeffcoat .15 .05
❑ 546 Mike Krukow .15 .05
❑ 547 Dave LaPoint .15 .05
❑ 548 Jeff Leonard .15 .05
❑ 549 Greg Minton .15 .05
❑ 550 Alex Trevino .15 .05
❑ 551 Manny Trillo .15 .05
❑ 552 Jose Uribe .15 .05
❑ 553 Brad Wellman .15 .05
❑ 554 Frank Williams .15 .05
❑ 555 Joel Youngblood .15 .05
❑ 556 Alan Bannister .15 .05
❑ 557 Glenn Brummer .15 .05
❑ 558 Steve Buechele RC .50 .20
❑ 559 Jose Guzman RC .15 .05
❑ 560 Toby Harrah .25 .08
❑ 561 Greg Harris .15 .05
❑ 562 Dwayne Henry .15 .05
❑ 563 Burt Hooton .15 .05
❑ 564 Charlie Hough .25 .08
❑ 565 Mike Mason .15 .05
❑ 566 Oddibe McDowell .15 .05
❑ 567 Dickie Noles .15 .05
❑ 568 Pete O'Brien .15 .05
❑ 569 Larry Parrish .15 .05
❑ 570 Dave Rozema .15 .05
❑ 571 Dave Schmidt .15 .05
❑ 572 Don Slaught .15 .05
❑ 573 Wayne Tolleson .15 .05
❑ 574 Duane Walker .15 .05
❑ 575 Gary Ward .15 .05
❑ 576 Chris Welsh .15 .05
❑ 577 Curtis Wilkerson .15 .05
❑ 578 George Wright .15 .05
❑ 579 Chris Bando .15 .05
❑ 580 Tony Bernazard .15 .05
❑ 581 Brett Butler .25 .08
❑ 582 Ernie Camacho .15 .05
❑ 583 Joe Carter .25 .08
❑ 584 Carmen Castillo .15 .05
❑ 585 Jamie Easterly .15 .05
❑ 586 Julio Franco .25 .08
❑ 587 Mel Hall .15 .05
❑ 588 Mike Hargrove .15 .05
❑ 589 Neal Heaton .15 .05
❑ 590 Brook Jacoby .15 .05
❑ 591 Otis Nixon RC 1.00 .40
❑ 592 Jerry Reed .15 .05
❑ 593 Vern Ruhle .15 .05
❑ 594 Pat Tabler .15 .05
❑ 595 Rich Thompson .15 .05
❑ 596 Andre Thornton .15 .05
❑ 597 Dave Von Ohlen .15 .05
❑ 598 George Vukovich .15 .05
❑ 599 Tom Waddell .15 .05
❑ 600 Curt Wardle .15 .05
❑ 601 Jerry Willard .15 .05
❑ 602 Bill Almon .15 .05
❑ 603 Mike Bielecki .15 .05
❑ 604 Sid Bream .15 .05
❑ 605 Mike C. Brown .15 .05
❑ 606 Pat Clements .15 .05
❑ 607 Jose DeLeon .15 .05
❑ 608 Denny Gonzalez .15 .05
❑ 609 Cecilio Guante .15 .05
❑ 610 Steve Kemp .15 .05
❑ 611 Sammy Khalifa .15 .05
❑ 612 Lee Mazzilli .25 .08
❑ 613 Larry McWilliams .15 .05
❑ 614 Jim Morrison .15 .05
❑ 615 Joe Orsulak RC* .50 .20
❑ 616 Tony Pena .15 .05
❑ 617 Johnny Ray .15 .05
❑ 618 Rick Reuschel .25 .08
❑ 619 R.J. Reynolds .15 .05
❑ 620 Rick Rhoden .15 .05
❑ 621 Don Robinson .15 .05
❑ 622 Jason Thompson .15 .05
❑ 623 Lee Tunnell .15 .05
❑ 624 Jim Winn .15 .05
❑ 625 Marvell Wynne .15 .05
❑ 626 Dwight Gooden IA .50 .20
❑ 627 Don Mattingly IA 1.25 .50
❑ 628 Pete Rose 4192 .50 .20
❑ 629 Rod Carew 3000 Hits .25 .08
❑ 630 T.Seaver/P.Niekro .25 .08
❑ 631 Don Baylor Ouch .25 .08
❑ 632 Tim Raines/Strawberry .25 .08
❑ 633 C.Ripken/A.Trammell 1.50 .60
❑ 634 Wade Boggs/G.Brett 1.00 .40
❑ 635 B.Horner/D.Murphy .50 .20
❑ 636 W.McGee/V.Coleman .25 .08
❑ 637 Vince Coleman IA .25 .08
❑ 638 Pete Rose/D.Gooden .75 .30
❑ 639 Wade Boggs/D.Mattingly 1.25 .50
❑ 640 Murphy/Garvey/Parker .50 .20
❑ 641 D.Gooden/F.Valenzuela .50 .20
❑ 642 Jimmy Key/D.Stieb .25 .08
❑ 643 C.Fisk/R.Gedman .25 .08
❑ 644 Benito Santiago RC 2.00 .75
❑ 645 M.Woodard/C.Ward RC .15 .05
❑ 646 Paul O'Neill RC 4.00 1.50
❑ 647 Andres Galarraga RC 1.50 .60
❑ 648 B.Kipper/C.Ford RC .15 .05
❑ 649 Jose Canseco RC 8.00 3.00
❑ 650 Mark McLemore RC 1.00 .40
❑ 651 R.Woodward/M.Brantley RC .15 .05
❑ 652 B.Robidoux/M.Funderburk RC .15 .05
❑ 653 Cecil Fielder RC 2.00 .75
❑ 654 CL: Royals/Cardinals Blue Jays/Mets .15 .05
❑ 655 CL: Yankees/Dodgers Angels/Reds UER (168 Darly S .15 .05
❑ 656 CL: White Sox/Tigers Expos/Orioles (279 Dennis,# .15 .05
❑ 657 CL: Astros/Padres Red Sox/Cubs .15 .05
❑ 658 CL: Twins/A's Phillies/Mariners .15 .05
❑ 659 CL: Brewers/Braves Giants/Rangers .15 .05
❑ 660 CL: Indians/Pirates Special Cards .15 .05

1986 Fleer Update

❑ COMP.FACT.SET (132) 30.00 12.00
❑ 1 Mike Aldrete XRC .15 .05
❑ 2 Andy Allanson XRC .15 .05
❑ 3 Neil Allen .15 .05
❑ 4 Joaquin Andujar .25 .08
❑ 5 Paul Assenmacher XRC .50 .20
❑ 6 Scott Bailes XRC .15 .05
❑ 7 Jay Baller XRC .15 .05
❑ 8 Scott Bankhead .15 .05
❑ 9 Bill Bathe XRC .15 .05
❑ 10 Don Baylor .25 .08
❑ 11 Billy Beane XRC 1.00 .40
❑ 12 Steve Bedrosian .15 .05
❑ 13 Juan Beniquez .15 .05
❑ 14 Barry Bonds XRC 25.00 10.00
❑ 15 Bobby Bonilla XRC 1.00 .40
❑ 16 Rich Bordi .15 .05
❑ 17 Bill Campbell .15 .05
❑ 18 Tom Candiotti .15 .05
❑ 19 John Cangelosi XRC .50 .20
❑ 20 Jose Canseco 4.00 1.50
❑ 21 Chuck Cary XRC .15 .05
❑ 22 Juan Castillo XRC .15 .05
❑ 23 Rick Cerone .15 .05
❑ 24 John Cerutti XRC .15 .05
❑ 25 Will Clark XRC 2.00 .75
❑ 26 Mark Clear .15 .05
❑ 27 Darnell Coles .15 .05
❑ 28 Dave Collins .15 .05
❑ 29 Tim Conroy .15 .05
❑ 30 Ed Correa .15 .05
❑ 31 Joe Cowley .15 .05
❑ 32 Bill Dawley .15 .05
❑ 33 Rob Deer .15 .05
❑ 34 John Denny .15 .05
❑ 35 Jim Deshaies XRC .15 .05
❑ 36 Doug Drabek XRC 1.00 .40
❑ 37 Mike Easler .15 .05
❑ 38 Mark Eichhorn .15 .05
❑ 39 Dave Engle .15 .05
❑ 40 Mike Fischlin .15 .05
❑ 41 Scott Fletcher .15 .05
❑ 42 Terry Forster .25 .08
❑ 43 Terry Francona .25 .08
❑ 44 Andres Galarraga 1.50 .60
❑ 45 Lee Guetterman .15 .05
❑ 46 Bill Gullickson .15 .05
❑ 47 Jackie Gutierrez .15 .05
❑ 48 Moose Haas .15 .05
❑ 49 Billy Hatcher .15 .05
❑ 50 Mike Heath .15 .05
❑ 51 Guy Hoffman .15 .05
❑ 52 Tom Hume .15 .05
❑ 53 Pete Incaviglia XRC .50 .20
❑ 54 Dane Iorg .15 .05
❑ 55 Chris James XRC .15 .05
❑ 56 Stan Javier XRC* .50 .20
❑ 57 Tommy John .25 .08
❑ 58 Tracy Jones .15 .05
❑ 59 Wally Joyner XRC 1.00 .40
❑ 60 Wayne Krenchicki .15 .05
❑ 61 John Kruk XRC 1.50 .60
❑ 62 Mike LaCoss .15 .05
❑ 63 Pete Ladd .15 .05

❑ 64 Dave LaPoint .15 .05
❑ 65 Mike LaValliere XRC .50 .20
❑ 66 Rudy Law .15 .05
❑ 67 Dennis Leonard .15 .05
❑ 68 Steve Lombardozzi .15 .05
❑ 69 Aurelio Lopez .15 .05
❑ 70 Mickey Mahler .15 .05
❑ 71 Candy Maldonado .15 .05
❑ 72 Roger Mason XRC* .15 .05
❑ 73 Greg Mathews .15 .05
❑ 74 Andy McGaffigan .15 .05
❑ 75 Joel McKeon .15 .05
❑ 76 Kevin Mitchell XRC 1.00 .40
❑ 77 Bill Mooneyham .15 .05
❑ 78 Omar Moreno .15 .05
❑ 79 Jerry Mumphrey .15 .05
❑ 80 Al Newman XRC .25 .08
❑ 81 Phil Niekro .25 .08
❑ 82 Randy Niemann .15 .05
❑ 83 Juan Nieves .15 .05
❑ 84 Bob Ojeda .15 .05
❑ 85 Rick Ownbey .15 .05
❑ 86 Tom Paciorek .15 .05
❑ 87 David Palmer .15 .05
❑ 88 Jeff Parrett XRC .15 .05
❑ 89 Pat Perry .15 .05
❑ 90 Dan Plesac .15 .05
❑ 91 Darrell Porter .15 .05
❑ 92 Luis Quinones .15 .05
❑ 93 Rey Quinones UER (Misspelled Quinonez) .15 .05
❑ 94 Gary Redus .15 .05
❑ 95 Jeff Reed .15 .05
❑ 96 Bip Roberts XRC .50 .20
❑ 97 Billy Joe Robidoux .15 .05
❑ 98 Gary Roenicke .15 .05
❑ 99 Ron Roenicke .15 .05
❑ 100 Angel Salazar .15 .05
❑ 101 Joe Sambito .15 .05
❑ 102 Billy Sample .15 .05
❑ 103 Dave Schmidt .15 .05
❑ 104 Ken Schrom .15 .05
❑ 105 Ruben Sierra XRC 1.50 .60
❑ 106 Ted Simmons .25 .08
❑ 107 Sammy Stewart .15 .05
❑ 108 Kurt Stillwell .15 .05
❑ 109 Dale Sveum .15 .05
❑ 110 Tim Teufel .15 .05
❑ 111 Bob Tewksbury XRC .50 .20
❑ 112 Andres Thomas .15 .05
❑ 113 Jason Thompson .15 .05
❑ 114 Milt Thompson .50 .20
❑ 115 Robby Thompson XRC .50 .20
❑ 116 Jay Tibbs .15 .05
❑ 117 Fred Toliver .15 .05
❑ 118 Wayne Tolleson .15 .05
❑ 119 Alex Trevino .15 .05
❑ 120 Manny Trillo .15 .05
❑ 121 Ed VandeBerg .15 .05
❑ 122 Ozzie Virgil .15 .05
❑ 123 Tony Walker .15 .05
❑ 124 Gene Walter .15 .05
❑ 125 Duane Ward XRC .50 .20
❑ 126 Jerry Willard .15 .05
❑ 127 Mitch Williams XRC .50 .20
❑ 128 Reggie Williams .15 .05
❑ 129 Bobby Witt XRC .50 .20
❑ 130 Marvell Wynne .15 .05
❑ 131 Steve Yeager .25 .08
❑ 132 Checklist 1-132 .15 .05

1987 Fleer

❑ COMPLETE SET (660) 40.00 20.00
❑ COMP.FACT.SET (672) 50.00 25.00
❑ 1 Rick Aguilera .15 .05
❑ 2 Richard Anderson .15 .05
❑ 3 Wally Backman .15 .05
❑ 4 Gary Carter .25 .08
❑ 5 Ron Darling .25 .08
❑ 6 Len Dykstra .25 .08
❑ 7 Kevin Elster RC .50 .20
❑ 8 Sid Fernandez .15 .05
❑ 9 Dwight Gooden .40 .15
❑ 10 Ed Hearn RC .15 .05
❑ 11 Danny Heep .15 .05
❑ 12 Keith Hernandez .25 .08

❑ 13 Howard Johnson .25 .08
❑ 14 Ray Knight .25 .08
❑ 15 Lee Mazzilli .25 .08
❑ 16 Roger McDowell .15 .05
❑ 17 Kevin Mitchell RC * 1.25 .50
❑ 18 Randy Niemann .15 .05
❑ 19 Bob Ojeda .15 .05
❑ 20 Jesse Orosco .15 .05
❑ 21 Rafael Santana .15 .05
❑ 22 Doug Sisk .15 .05
❑ 23 Darryl Strawberry .25 .08
❑ 24 Tim Teufel .15 .05
❑ 25 Mookie Wilson .25 .08
❑ 26 Tony Armas .25 .08
❑ 27 Marty Barrett .15 .05
❑ 28 Don Baylor .25 .08
❑ 29 Wade Boggs .40 .15
❑ 30 Oil Can Boyd .15 .05
❑ 31 Bill Buckner .25 .08
❑ 32 Roger Clemens 3.00 1.25
❑ 33 Steve Crawford .15 .05
❑ 34 Dwight Evans .40 .15
❑ 35 Rich Gedman .15 .05
❑ 36 Dave Henderson .15 .05
❑ 37 Bruce Hurst .15 .05
❑ 38 Tim Lollar .15 .05
❑ 39 Al Nipper .15 .05
❑ 40 Spike Owen .15 .05
❑ 41 Jim Rice .25 .08
❑ 42 Ed Romero .15 .05
❑ 43 Joe Sambito .15 .05
❑ 44 Calvin Schiraldi .15 .05
❑ 45 Tom Seaver .40 .15
❑ 46 Jeff Sellers .15 .05
❑ 47 Bob Stanley .15 .05
❑ 48 Sammy Stewart .15 .05
❑ 49 Larry Andersen .15 .05
❑ 50 Alan Ashby .15 .05
❑ 51 Kevin Bass .15 .05
❑ 52 Jeff Calhoun .15 .05
❑ 53 Jose Cruz .25 .08
❑ 54 Danny Darwin .15 .05
❑ 55 Glenn Davis .15 .05
❑ 56 Jim Deshaies RC * .25 .08
❑ 57 Bill Doran .15 .05
❑ 58 Phil Garner .25 .08
❑ 59 Billy Hatcher .15 .05
❑ 60 Charlie Kerfeld .15 .05
❑ 61 Bob Knepper .15 .05
❑ 62 Dave Lopes .25 .08
❑ 63 Aurelio Lopez .15 .05
❑ 64 Jim Pankovits .15 .05
❑ 65 Terry Puhl .15 .05
❑ 66 Craig Reynolds .15 .05
❑ 67 Nolan Ryan 3.00 1.25
❑ 68 Mike Scott .25 .08
❑ 69 Dave Smith .15 .05
❑ 70 Dickie Thon .15 .05
❑ 71 Tony Walker .15 .05
❑ 72 Denny Walling .15 .05
❑ 73 Bob Boone .25 .08
❑ 74 Rick Burleson .15 .05
❑ 75 John Candelaria .15 .05
❑ 76 Doug Corbett .15 .05
❑ 77 Doug DeCinces .15 .05
❑ 78 Brian Downing .25 .08
❑ 79 Chuck Finley RC 1.25 .50
❑ 80 Terry Forster .25 .08
❑ 81 Bob Grich .25 .08
❑ 82 George Hendrick .25 .08
❑ 83 Jack Howell .15 .05
❑ 84 Reggie Jackson .40 .15
❑ 85 Ruppert Jones .15 .05
❑ 86 Wally Joyner RC 1.25 .50
❑ 87 Gary Lucas .15 .05
❑ 88 Kirk McCaskill .15 .05
❑ 89 Donnie Moore .15 .05
❑ 90 Gary Pettis .15 .05
❑ 91 Vern Ruhle .15 .05
❑ 92 Dick Schofield .15 .05
❑ 93 Don Sutton .25 .08
❑ 94 Rob Wilfong .15 .05
❑ 95 Mike Witt .15 .05
❑ 96 Doug Drabek RC 1.25 .50
❑ 97 Mike Easler .15 .05
❑ 98 Mike Fischlin .15 .05
❑ 99 Brian Fisher .15 .05
❑ 100 Ron Guidry .25 .08
❑ 101 Rickey Henderson .60 .25
❑ 102 Tommy John .25 .08
❑ 103 Ron Kittle .15 .05
❑ 104 Don Mattingly 2.00 .75
❑ 105 Bobby Meacham .15 .05
❑ 106 Joe Niekro .15 .05
❑ 107 Mike Pagliarulo .15 .05
❑ 108 Dan Pasqua .15 .05
❑ 109 Willie Randolph .25 .08
❑ 110 Dennis Rasmussen .15 .05
❑ 111 Dave Righetti .25 .08
❑ 112 Gary Roenicke .15 .05
❑ 113 Rod Scurry .15 .05
❑ 114 Bob Shirley .15 .05
❑ 115 Joel Skinner .15 .05
❑ 116 Tim Stoddard .15 .05
❑ 117 Bob Tewksbury RC * .50 .20
❑ 118 Wayne Tolleson .15 .05
❑ 119 Claudell Washington .15 .05
❑ 120 Dave Winfield .25 .08
❑ 121 Steve Buechele .15 .05
❑ 122 Ed Correa .15 .05
❑ 123 Scott Fletcher .15 .05
❑ 124 Jose Guzman .15 .05
❑ 125 Toby Harrah .25 .08
❑ 126 Greg Harris .15 .05
❑ 127 Charlie Hough .25 .08
❑ 128 Pete Incaviglia RC * .50 .20
❑ 129 Mike Mason .15 .05
❑ 130 Oddibe McDowell .15 .05
❑ 131 Dale Mohorcic .15 .05
❑ 132 Pete O'Brien .15 .05
❑ 133 Tom Paciorek .15 .05
❑ 134 Larry Parrish .15 .05
❑ 135 Geno Petralli .15 .05
❑ 136 Darrell Porter .15 .05
❑ 137 Jeff Russell .15 .05
❑ 138 Ruben Sierra RC 2.00 .75
❑ 139 Don Slaught .15 .05
❑ 140 Gary Ward .15 .05
❑ 141 Curtis Wilkerson .15 .05
❑ 142 Mitch Williams RC * .50 .20
❑ 143 Bobby Witt RC .50 .20
❑ 144 Dave Bergman .15 .05
❑ 145 Tom Brookens .15 .05
❑ 146 Bill Campbell .15 .05
❑ 147 Chuck Cary .15 .05
❑ 148 Darnell Coles .15 .05
❑ 149 Dave Collins .15 .05
❑ 150 Darrell Evans .25 .08
❑ 151 Kirk Gibson .25 .08
❑ 152 John Grubb .15 .05
❑ 153 Willie Hernandez .15 .05
❑ 154 Larry Herndon .15 .05
❑ 155 Eric King .15 .05
❑ 156 Chet Lemon .25 .08
❑ 157 Dwight Lowry .15 .05
❑ 158 Jack Morris .25 .08
❑ 159 Randy O'Neal .15 .05
❑ 160 Lance Parrish .25 .08
❑ 161 Dan Petry .15 .05
❑ 162 Pat Sheridan .15 .05
❑ 163 Jim Slaton .15 .05
❑ 164 Frank Tanana .25 .08
❑ 165 Walt Terrell .15 .05
❑ 166 Mark Thurmond .15 .05

❑ 167 Alan Trammell .25 .08
❑ 168 Lou Whitaker .25 .08
❑ 169 Luis Aguayo .15 .05
❑ 170 Steve Bedrosian .15 .05
❑ 171 Don Carman .15 .05
❑ 172 Darren Daulton .25 .08
❑ 173 Greg Gross .15 .05
❑ 174 Kevin Gross .15 .05
❑ 175 Von Hayes .15 .05
❑ 176 Charles Hudson .15 .05
❑ 177 Tom Hume .15 .05
❑ 178 Steve Jeltz .15 .05
❑ 179 Mike Maddux .15 .05
❑ 180 Shane Rawley .15 .05
❑ 181 Gary Redus .15 .05
❑ 182 Ron Roenicke .15 .05
❑ 183 Bruce Ruffin RC .25 .08
❑ 184 John Russell .15 .05
❑ 185 Juan Samuel .15 .05
❑ 186 Dan Schatzeder .15 .05
❑ 187 Mike Schmidt 1.50 .60
❑ 188 Rick Schu .15 .05
❑ 189 Jeff Stone .15 .05
❑ 190 Kent Tekulve .15 .05
❑ 191 Milt Thompson .15 .05
❑ 192 Glenn Wilson .15 .05
❑ 193 Buddy Bell .25 .08
❑ 194 Tom Browning .15 .05
❑ 195 Sal Butera .15 .05
❑ 196 Dave Concepcion .25 .08
❑ 197 Kal Daniels .15 .05
❑ 198 Eric Davis .40 .15
❑ 199 John Denny .15 .05
❑ 200 Bo Diaz .15 .05
❑ 201 Nick Esasky .15 .05
❑ 202 John Franco .25 .08
❑ 203 Bill Gullickson .15 .05
❑ 204 Barry Larkin RC 3.00 1.25
❑ 205 Eddie Milner .15 .05
❑ 206 Rob Murphy .15 .05
❑ 207 Ron Oester .15 .05
❑ 208 Dave Parker .25 .08
❑ 209 Tony Perez .40 .15
❑ 210 Ted Power .15 .05
❑ 211 Joe Price .15 .05
❑ 212 Ron Robinson .15 .05
❑ 213 Pete Rose 2.00 .75
❑ 214 Mario Soto .25 .08
❑ 215 Kurt Stillwell .15 .05
❑ 216 Max Venable .15 .05
❑ 217 Chris Welsh .15 .05
❑ 218 Carl Willis RC .25 .08
❑ 219 Jesse Barfield .25 .08
❑ 220 George Bell .25 .08
❑ 221 Bill Caudill .15 .05
❑ 222 John Cerutti .15 .05
❑ 223 Jim Clancy .15 .05
❑ 224 Mark Eichhorn .15 .05
❑ 225 Tony Fernandez .15 .05
❑ 226 Damaso Garcia .15 .05
❑ 227 Kelly Gruber ERR
(Wrong birth year) .15 .05
❑ 228 Tom Henke .15 .05
❑ 229 Garth Iorg .15 .05
❑ 230 Joe Johnson .15 .05
❑ 231 Cliff Johnson .15 .05
❑ 232 Jimmy Key .25 .08
❑ 233 Dennis Lamp .15 .05
❑ 234 Rick Leach .15 .05
❑ 235 Buck Martinez .15 .05
❑ 236 Lloyd Moseby .15 .05
❑ 237 Rance Mulliniks .15 .05
❑ 238 Dave Stieb .25 .08
❑ 239 Willie Upshaw .15 .05
❑ 240 Ernie Whitt .15 .05
❑ 241 Andy Allanson RC .15 .05
❑ 242 Scott Bailes .15 .05
❑ 243 Chris Bando .15 .05
❑ 244 Tony Bernazard .15 .05
❑ 245 John Butcher .15 .05
❑ 246 Brett Butler .25 .08
❑ 247 Ernie Camacho .15 .05
❑ 248 Tom Candiotti .15 .05
❑ 249 Joe Carter .25 .08
❑ 250 Carmen Castillo .15 .05
❑ 251 Julio Franco .25 .08
❑ 252 Mel Hall .15 .05
❑ 253 Brook Jacoby .15 .05
❑ 254 Phil Niekro .25 .08
❑ 255 Otis Nixon .15 .05
❑ 256 Dickie Noles .15 .05
❑ 257 Bryan Oelkers .15 .05
❑ 258 Ken Schrom .15 .05
❑ 259 Don Schulze .15 .05
❑ 260 Cory Snyder .15 .05
❑ 261 Pat Tabler .15 .05
❑ 262 Andre Thornton .15 .05
❑ 263 Rich Yett .15 .05
❑ 264 Mike Aldrete .15 .05
❑ 265 Juan Berenguer .15 .05
❑ 266 Vida Blue .25 .08
❑ 267 Bob Brenly .15 .05
❑ 268 Chris Brown .15 .05
❑ 269 Will Clark RC 3.00 1.25
❑ 270 Chili Davis .25 .08
❑ 271 Mark Davis .15 .05
❑ 272 Kelly Downs RC .25 .08
❑ 273 Scott Garrelts .15 .05
❑ 274 Dan Gladden .15 .05
❑ 275 Mike Krukow .15 .05
❑ 276 Randy Kutcher .15 .05
❑ 277 Mike LaCoss .15 .05
❑ 278 Jeff Leonard .15 .05
❑ 279 Candy Maldonado .15 .05
❑ 280 Roger Mason .15 .05
❑ 281 Bob Melvin .15 .05
❑ 282 Greg Minton .15 .05
❑ 283 Jeff D. Robinson .15 .05
❑ 284 Harry Spilman .15 .05
❑ 285 Robby Thompson RC * .50 .20
❑ 286 Jose Uribe .15 .05
❑ 287 Frank Williams .15 .05
❑ 288 Joel Youngblood .15 .05
❑ 289 Jack Clark .25 .08
❑ 290 Vince Coleman .15 .05
❑ 291 Tim Conroy .15 .05
❑ 292 Danny Cox .15 .05
❑ 293 Ken Dayley .15 .05
❑ 294 Curt Ford .15 .05
❑ 295 Bob Forsch .15 .05
❑ 296 Tom Herr .15 .05
❑ 297 Ricky Horton .15 .05
❑ 298 Clint Hurdle .15 .05
❑ 299 Jeff Lahti .15 .05
❑ 300 Steve Lake .15 .05
❑ 301 Tito Landrum .15 .05
❑ 302 Mike LaValliere RC * .50 .20
❑ 303 Greg Mathews .15 .05
❑ 304 Willie McGee .25 .08
❑ 305 Jose Oquendo .15 .05
❑ 306 Terry Pendleton .25 .08
❑ 307 Pat Perry .15 .05
❑ 308 Ozzie Smith 1.00 .40
❑ 309 Ray Soff .15 .05
❑ 310 John Tudor .25 .08
❑ 311 Andy Van Slyke UER .40 .15
❑ 312 Todd Worrell .15 .05
❑ 313 Dann Bilardello .15 .05
❑ 314 Hubie Brooks .15 .05
❑ 315 Tim Burke .15 .05
❑ 316 Andre Dawson .25 .08
❑ 317 Mike Fitzgerald .15 .05
❑ 318 Tom Foley .15 .05
❑ 319 Andres Galarraga .25 .08
❑ 320 Joe Hesketh .15 .05
❑ 321 Wallace Johnson .15 .05
❑ 322 Wayne Krenchicki .15 .05
❑ 323 Vance Law .15 .05
❑ 324 Dennis Martinez .25 .08
❑ 325 Bob McClure .15 .05
❑ 326 Andy McGaffigan .15 .05
❑ 327 Al Newman RC .15 .05
❑ 328 Tim Raines .25 .08
❑ 329 Jeff Reardon .25 .08
❑ 330 Luis Rivera RC .25 .08
❑ 331 Bob Sebra .15 .05
❑ 332 Bryn Smith .15 .05
❑ 333 Jay Tibbs .15 .05
❑ 334 Tim Wallach .15 .05
❑ 335 Mitch Webster .15 .05
❑ 336 Jim Wohlford .15 .05
❑ 337 Floyd Youmans .15 .05
❑ 338 Chris Bosio RC .50 .20
❑ 339 Glenn Braggs RC .25 .08
❑ 340 Rick Cerone .15 .05
❑ 341 Mark Clear .15 .05
❑ 342 Bryan Clutterbuck .15 .05
❑ 343 Cecil Cooper .25 .08
❑ 344 Rob Deer .15 .05
❑ 345 Jim Gantner .15 .05
❑ 346 Ted Higuera .15 .05
❑ 347 John Henry Johnson .15 .05
❑ 348 Tim Leary .15 .05
❑ 349 Rick Manning .15 .05
❑ 350 Paul Molitor .25 .08
❑ 351 Charlie Moore .15 .05
❑ 352 Juan Nieves .15 .05
❑ 353 Ben Oglivie .25 .08
❑ 354 Dan Plesac .15 .05
❑ 355 Ernest Riles .15 .05
❑ 356 Billy Joe Robidoux .15 .05
❑ 357 Bill Schroeder .15 .05
❑ 358 Dale Sveum .15 .05
❑ 359 Gorman Thomas .25 .08
❑ 360 Bill Wegman .15 .05
❑ 361 Robin Yount 1.00 .40
❑ 362 Steve Balboni .15 .05
❑ 363 Scott Bankhead .15 .05
❑ 364 Buddy Biancalana .15 .05
❑ 365 Bud Black .15 .05
❑ 366 George Brett 1.50 .60
❑ 367 Steve Farr .15 .05
❑ 368 Mark Gubicza .15 .05
❑ 369 Bo Jackson RC 8.00 3.00
❑ 370 Danny Jackson .15 .05
❑ 371 Mike Kingery RC .25 .08
❑ 372 Rudy Law .15 .05
❑ 373 Charlie Leibrandt .15 .05
❑ 374 Dennis Leonard .15 .05
❑ 375 Hal McRae .25 .08
❑ 376 Jorge Orta .15 .05
❑ 377 Jamie Quirk .15 .05
❑ 378 Dan Quisenberry .15 .05
❑ 379 Bret Saberhagen .25 .08
❑ 380 Angel Salazar .15 .05
❑ 381 Lonnie Smith .15 .05
❑ 382 Jim Sundberg .25 .08
❑ 383 Frank White .25 .08
❑ 384 Willie Wilson .25 .08
❑ 385 Joaquin Andujar .25 .08
❑ 386 Doug Bair .15 .05
❑ 387 Dusty Baker .25 .08
❑ 388 Bruce Bochte .15 .05
❑ 389 Jose Canseco 1.50 .60
❑ 390 Chris Codiroli .15 .05
❑ 391 Mike Davis .15 .05
❑ 392 Alfredo Griffin .15 .05
❑ 393 Moose Haas .15 .05
❑ 394 Donnie Hill .15 .05
❑ 395 Jay Howell .15 .05
❑ 396 Dave Kingman .25 .08
❑ 397 Carney Lansford .25 .08
❑ 398 Dave Leiper .15 .05
❑ 399 Bill Mooneyham .15 .05
❑ 400 Dwayne Murphy .15 .05
❑ 401 Steve Ontiveros .15 .05
❑ 402 Tony Phillips .15 .05
❑ 403 Eric Plunk .15 .05
❑ 404 Jose Rijo .25 .08
❑ 405 Terry Steinbach RC 1.25 .50
❑ 406 Dave Stewart .25 .08
❑ 407 Mickey Tettleton .15 .05
❑ 408 Dave Von Ohlen .15 .05
❑ 409 Jerry Willard .15 .05
❑ 410 Curt Young .15 .05
❑ 411 Bruce Bochy .15 .05
❑ 412 Dave Dravecky .15 .05
❑ 413 Tim Flannery .15 .05
❑ 414 Steve Garvey .25 .08
❑ 415 Rich Gossage .25 .08
❑ 416 Tony Gwynn 1.00 .40
❑ 417 Andy Hawkins .15 .05
❑ 418 LaMarr Hoyt .15 .05
❑ 419 Terry Kennedy .15 .05
❑ 420 John Kruk RC 2.00 .75
❑ 421 Dave LaPoint .15 .05
❑ 422 Craig Lefferts .15 .05
❑ 423 Carmelo Martinez .15 .05

❑ 424 Lance McCullers .15 .05
❑ 425 Kevin McReynolds .15 .05
❑ 426 Graig Nettles .25 .08
❑ 427 Bip Roberts RC .50 .20
❑ 428 Jerry Royster .15 .05
❑ 429 Benito Santiago .25 .08
❑ 430 Eric Show .15 .05
❑ 431 Bob Stoddard .15 .05
❑ 432 Garry Templeton .25 .08
❑ 433 Gene Walter .15 .05
❑ 434 Ed Whitson .15 .05
❑ 435 Marvell Wynne .15 .05
❑ 436 Dave Anderson .15 .05
❑ 437 Greg Brock .15 .05
❑ 438 Enos Cabell .15 .05
❑ 439 Mariano Duncan .15 .05
❑ 440 Pedro Guerrero .25 .08
❑ 441 Orel Hershiser .40 .15
❑ 442 Rick Honeycutt .15 .05
❑ 443 Ken Howell .15 .05
❑ 444 Ken Landreaux .15 .05
❑ 445 Bill Madlock .25 .08
❑ 446 Mike Marshall .15 .05
❑ 447 Len Matuszek .15 .05
❑ 448 Tom Niedenfuer .15 .05
❑ 449 Alejandro Pena .15 .05
❑ 450 Dennis Powell .15 .05
❑ 451 Jerry Reuss .15 .05
❑ 452 Bill Russell .25 .08
❑ 453 Steve Sax .15 .05
❑ 454 Mike Scioscia .25 .08
❑ 455 Franklin Stubbs .15 .05
❑ 456 Alex Trevino .15 .05
❑ 457 Fernando Valenzuela .25 .08
❑ 458 Ed VandeBerg .15 .05
❑ 459 Bob Welch .25 .08
❑ 460 Reggie Williams .15 .05
❑ 461 Don Aase .15 .05
❑ 462 Juan Beniquez .15 .05
❑ 463 Mike Boddicker .15 .05
❑ 464 Juan Bonilla .15 .05
❑ 465 Rich Bordi .15 .05
❑ 466 Storm Davis .15 .05
❑ 467 Rick Dempsey .15 .05
❑ 468 Ken Dixon .15 .05
❑ 469 Jim Dwyer .15 .05
❑ 470 Mike Flanagan .15 .05
❑ 471 Jackie Gutierrez .15 .05
❑ 472 Brad Havens .15 .05
❑ 473 Lee Lacy .15 .05
❑ 474 Fred Lynn .25 .08
❑ 475 Scott McGregor .15 .05
❑ 476 Eddie Murray .60 .25
❑ 477 Tom O'Malley .15 .05
❑ 478 Cal Ripken 2.50 1.00
❑ 479 Larry Sheets .15 .05
❑ 480 John Shelby .15 .05
❑ 481 Nate Snell .15 .05
❑ 482 Jim Traber .15 .05
❑ 483 Mike Young .15 .05
❑ 484 Neil Allen .15 .05
❑ 485 Harold Baines .25 .08
❑ 486 Floyd Bannister .15 .05
❑ 487 Daryl Boston .15 .05
❑ 488 Ivan Calderon .15 .05
❑ 489 John Cangelosi .15 .05
❑ 490 Steve Carlton .25 .08
❑ 491 Joe Cowley .15 .05
❑ 492 Julio Cruz .15 .05
❑ 493 Bill Dawley .15 .05
❑ 494 Jose DeLeon .15 .05
❑ 495 Richard Dotson .15 .05
❑ 496 Carlton Fisk .40 .15
❑ 497 Ozzie Guillen .40 .15
❑ 498 Jerry Hairston .15 .05
❑ 499 Ron Hassey .15 .05
❑ 500 Tim Hulett .15 .05
❑ 501 Bob James .15 .05
❑ 502 Steve Lyons .15 .05
❑ 503 Joel McKeon .15 .05
❑ 504 Gene Nelson .15 .05
❑ 505 Dave Schmidt .15 .05
❑ 506 Ray Searage .15 .05
❑ 507 Bobby Thigpen RC .50 .20
❑ 508 Greg Walker .15 .05
❑ 509 Jim Acker .15 .05
❑ 510 Doyle Alexander .15 .05
❑ 511 Paul Assenmacher .50 .20
❑ 512 Bruce Benedict .15 .05
❑ 513 Chris Chambliss .25 .08
❑ 514 Jeff Dedmon .15 .05
❑ 515 Gene Garber .15 .05
❑ 516 Ken Griffey .25 .08
❑ 517 Terry Harper .15 .05
❑ 518 Bob Horner .25 .08
❑ 519 Glenn Hubbard .15 .05
❑ 520 Rick Mahler .15 .05
❑ 521 Omar Moreno .15 .05
❑ 522 Dale Murphy .40 .15
❑ 523 Ken Oberkfell .15 .05
❑ 524 Ed Olwine .15 .05
❑ 525 David Palmer .15 .05
❑ 526 Rafael Ramirez .15 .05
❑ 527 Billy Sample .15 .05
❑ 528 Ted Simmons .25 .08
❑ 529 Zane Smith .15 .05
❑ 530 Bruce Sutter .25 .08
❑ 531 Andres Thomas .15 .05
❑ 532 Ozzie Virgil .15 .05
❑ 533 Allan Anderson RC .15 .05
❑ 534 Keith Atherton .15 .05
❑ 535 Billy Beane .25 .08
❑ 536 Bert Blyleven .25 .08
❑ 537 Tom Brunansky .15 .05
❑ 538 Randy Bush .15 .05
❑ 539 George Frazier .15 .05
❑ 540 Gary Gaetti .25 .08
❑ 541 Greg Gagne .15 .05
❑ 542 Mickey Hatcher .15 .05
❑ 543 Neal Heaton .15 .05
❑ 544 Kent Hrbek .25 .08
❑ 545 Roy Lee Jackson .15 .05
❑ 546 Tim Laudner .15 .05
❑ 547 Steve Lombardozzi .15 .05
❑ 548 Mark Portugal RC * .50 .20
❑ 549 Kirby Puckett 1.00 .40
❑ 550 Jeff Reed .15 .05
❑ 551 Mark Salas .15 .05
❑ 552 Roy Smalley .15 .05
❑ 553 Mike Smithson .15 .05
❑ 554 Frank Viola .25 .08
❑ 555 Thad Bosley .15 .05
❑ 556 Ron Cey .25 .08
❑ 557 Jody Davis .15 .05
❑ 558 Ron Davis .15 .05
❑ 559 Bob Dernier .15 .05
❑ 560 Frank DiPino .15 .05
❑ 561 Shawon Dunston UER
(Wrong birth year
listed on c .15 .05
❑ 562 Leon Durham .15 .05
❑ 563 Dennis Eckersley .40 .15
❑ 564 Terry Francona .25 .08
❑ 565 Dave Gumpert .15 .05
❑ 566 Guy Hoffman .15 .05
❑ 567 Ed Lynch .15 .05
❑ 568 Gary Matthews .25 .08
❑ 569 Keith Moreland .15 .05
❑ 570 Jamie Moyer RC 2.00 .75
❑ 571 Jerry Mumphrey .15 .05
❑ 572 Ryne Sandberg 1.25 .50
❑ 573 Scott Sanderson .15 .05
❑ 574 Lee Smith .25 .08
❑ 575 Chris Speier .15 .05
❑ 576 Rick Sutcliffe .25 .08
❑ 577 Manny Trillo .15 .05
❑ 578 Steve Trout .15 .05
❑ 579 Karl Best .15 .05
❑ 580 Scott Bradley .15 .05
❑ 581 Phil Bradley .15 .05
❑ 582 Mickey Brantley .15 .05
❑ 583 Mike G. Brown P .15 .05
❑ 584 Alvin Davis .15 .05
❑ 585 Lee Guetterman .15 .05
❑ 586 Mark Huismann .15 .05
❑ 587 Bob Kearney .15 .05
❑ 588 Pete Ladd .15 .05
❑ 589 Mark Langston .15 .05
❑ 590 Mike Moore .15 .05
❑ 591 Mike Morgan .15 .05
❑ 592 John Moses .15 .05
❑ 593 Ken Phelps .15 .05
❑ 594 Jim Presley .15 .05
❑ 595 Rey Quinones UER
(Quinonez on front) .15 .05
❑ 596 Harold Reynolds .25 .08
❑ 597 Bill Swift .15 .05
❑ 598 Danny Tartabull .15 .05
❑ 599 Steve Yeager .25 .08
❑ 600 Matt Young .15 .05
❑ 601 Bill Almon .15 .05
❑ 602 Rafael Belliard RC .50 .20
❑ 603 Mike Bielecki .15 .05
❑ 604 Barry Bonds RC 15.00 6.00
❑ 605 Bobby Bonilla RC 1.25 .50
❑ 606 Sid Bream .15 .05
❑ 607 Mike C. Brown .15 .05
❑ 608 Pat Clements .15 .05
❑ 609 Mike Diaz .15 .05
❑ 610 Cecilio Guante .15 .05
❑ 611 Barry Jones .15 .05
❑ 612 Bob Kipper .15 .05
❑ 613 Larry McWilliams .15 .05
❑ 614 Jim Morrison .15 .05
❑ 615 Joe Orsulak .15 .05
❑ 616 Junior Ortiz .15 .05
❑ 617 Tony Pena .15 .05
❑ 618 Johnny Ray .15 .05
❑ 619 Rick Reuschel .25 .08
❑ 620 R.J. Reynolds .15 .05
❑ 621 Rick Rhoden .15 .05
❑ 622 Don Robinson .15 .05
❑ 623 Bob Walk .15 .05
❑ 624 Jim Winn .15 .05
❑ 625 J.Canseco/P.Incaviglia .75 .30
❑ 626 300 Game Winners
Don Sutton
Phil Niekro .25 .08
❑ 627 AL Firemen
Dave Righetti
Don Aase .15 .05
❑ 628 J.Canseco/W.Joyner .75 .30
❑ 629 Magic Mets .40 .15
❑ 630 NL Best Righties
Mike Scott
Mike Krukow .15 .05
❑ 631 Sensational Southpaws
Fernando Valenzuela
John F .15 .05
❑ 632 Count'Em
Bob Horner .15 .05
❑ 633 J.Canseco/Rice/Puckett .75 .30
❑ 634 R.Clemens/G.Carter .60 .25
❑ 635 Steve Carlton 4000 .25 .08
❑ 636 Eddie Murray/G.Davis .60 .25
❑ 637 W.Boggs/K.Hernandez .25 .08
❑ 638 D.Mattingly/Strawberry 1.00 .40
❑ 639 R.Sandberg/D.Parker .60 .25
❑ 640 R.Clemens/D.Gooden .60 .25
❑ 641 AL West Stoppers
Mike Witt
Charlie Hough .15 .05
❑ 642 Doubles and Triples
Juan Samuel
Tim Raines .25 .08
❑ 643 Outfielders with Punch
Harold Baines
Jesse Barfi .25 .08
❑ 644 G.Swindell/D.Clark RC .50 .20
❑ 645 R.Karkovice/R.Morman RC .50 .20
❑ 646 D.White/W.Fraser RC 1.25 .50
❑ 647 M.Stanley/J.Browne RC .50 .20
❑ 648 D.Magadan/P.Lombardi RC .50 .20
❑ 649 J.Gonzalez/R.Bryant RC .25 .08
❑ 650 J.Jones/R.Asadoor RC .25 .08
❑ 651 T.Jones/M.Freeman RC .25 .08
❑ 652 K.Seitzer/J.Stefero RC .50 .20
❑ 653 R.Nelson/S.Fireovid RC .25 .08
❑ 654 CL: Mets/Red Sox
Astros/Angels .15 .05
❑ 655 CL: Yankees/Rangers
Tigers/Phillies .15 .05
❑ 656 CL: Reds/Blue Jays
Indians/Giants
ERR (230/231 w .15 .05
❑ 657 CL: Cardinals/Expos
Brewers/Royals .15 .05
❑ 658 CL: A's/Padres

Dodgers/Orioles .15 .05
❑ 659 CL: White Sox/Braves Twins/Cubs .15 .05
❑ 660 CL: Mariners/Pirates Special Cards ER (580/581 w .15 .05

1987 Fleer Update

❑ COMP.FACT.SET (132) 12.00 5.00
❑ 1 Scott Bankhead .10 .02
❑ 2 Eric Bell .15 .05
❑ 3 Juan Beniquez .10 .02
❑ 4 Juan Berenguer .10 .02
❑ 5 Mike Birkbeck .15 .05
❑ 6 Randy Bockus .10 .02
❑ 7 Rod Booker .10 .02
❑ 8 Thad Bosley .10 .02
❑ 9 Greg Brock .10 .02
❑ 10 Bob Brower .10 .02
❑ 11 Chris Brown .10 .02
❑ 12 Jerry Browne .15 .05
❑ 13 Ralph Bryant .10 .02
❑ 14 DeWayne Buice .10 .02
❑ 15 Ellis Burks XRC .75 .30
❑ 16 Casey Candaele .10 .02
❑ 17 Steve Carlton .15 .05
❑ 18 Juan Castillo .15 .05
❑ 19 Chuck Crim .10 .02
❑ 20 Mark Davidson .10 .02
❑ 21 Mark Davis .10 .02
❑ 22 Storm Davis .10 .02
❑ 23 Bill Dawley .10 .02
❑ 24 Andre Dawson .15 .05
❑ 25 Brian Dayett .10 .02
❑ 26 Rick Dempsey .10 .02
❑ 27 Ken Dowell .10 .02
❑ 28 Dave Dravecky .10 .02
❑ 29 Mike Dunne .10 .02
❑ 30 Dennis Eckersley .25 .08
❑ 31 Cecil Fielder .15 .05
❑ 32 Brian Fisher .10 .02
❑ 33 Willie Fraser .15 .05
❑ 34 Ken Gerhart .10 .02
❑ 35 Jim Gott .10 .02
❑ 36 Dan Gladden .10 .02
❑ 37 Mike Greenwell XRC .30 .10
❑ 38 Cecilio Guante .10 .02
❑ 39 Albert Hall .10 .02
❑ 40 Atlee Hammaker .10 .02
❑ 41 Mickey Hatcher .10 .02
❑ 42 Mike Heath .10 .02
❑ 43 Neal Heaton .10 .02
❑ 44 Mike Henneman XRC .30 .10
❑ 45 Guy Hoffman .10 .02
❑ 46 Charles Hudson .10 .02
❑ 47 Chuck Jackson .10 .02
❑ 48 Mike Jackson XRC .30 .10
❑ 49 Reggie Jackson .25 .08
❑ 50 Chris James .10 .02
❑ 51 Dion James .10 .02
❑ 52 Stan Javier .10 .02
❑ 53 Stan Jefferson .10 .02
❑ 54 Jimmy Jones .15 .05
❑ 55 Tracy Jones .10 .02
❑ 56 Terry Kennedy .10 .02
❑ 57 Mike Kingery .15 .05
❑ 58 Ray Knight .15 .05
❑ 59 Gene Larkin XRC .30 .10
❑ 60 Mike LaValliere .30 .10
❑ 61 Jack Lazorko .10 .02
❑ 62 Terry Leach .10 .02
❑ 63 Rick Leach .10 .02
❑ 64 Craig Lefferts .10 .02
❑ 65 Jim Lindeman .15 .05
❑ 66 Bill Long .10 .02
❑ 67 Mike Loynd XRC .15 .05
❑ 68 Greg Maddux XRC 8.00 3.00
❑ 69 Bill Madlock .15 .05
❑ 70 Dave Magadan .30 .10
❑ 71 Joe Magrane XRC .15 .05
❑ 72 Fred Manrique .10 .02
❑ 73 Mike Mason .10 .02
❑ 74 Lloyd McClendon XRC .30 .10
❑ 75 Fred McGriff 1.00 .40
❑ 76 Mark McGwire 5.00 2.00
❑ 77 Mark McLemore .15 .05
❑ 78 Kevin McReynolds .10 .02
❑ 79 Dave Meads .10 .02
❑ 80 Greg Minton .10 .02
❑ 81 John Mitchell XRC .15 .05
❑ 82 Kevin Mitchell .25 .08
❑ 83 John Morris .10 .02
❑ 84 Jeff Musselman .10 .02
❑ 85 Randy Myers XRC .75 .30
❑ 86 Gene Nelson .10 .02
❑ 87 Joe Niekro .10 .02
❑ 88 Tom Nieto .10 .02
❑ 89 Reid Nichols .10 .02
❑ 90 Matt Nokes XRC .30 .10
❑ 91 Dickie Noles .10 .02
❑ 92 Edwin Nunez .10 .02
❑ 93 Jose Nunez XRC .10 .02
❑ 94 Paul O'Neill .40 .15
❑ 95 Jim Paciorek .10 .02
❑ 96 Lance Parrish .15 .05
❑ 97 Bill Pecota XRC .15 .05
❑ 98 Tony Pena .10 .02
❑ 99 Luis Polonia XRC .30 .10
❑ 100 Randy Ready .10 .02
❑ 101 Jeff Reardon .15 .05
❑ 102 Gary Redus .10 .02
❑ 103 Rick Rhoden .10 .02
❑ 104 Wally Ritchie .10 .02
❑ 105 Jeff M. Robinson UER (Wrong Jeff's stats on back .10 .02
❑ 106 Mark Salas .10 .02
❑ 107 Dave Schmidt .10 .02
❑ 108 Kevin Seitzer UER .30 .10
❑ 109 John Shelby .10 .02
❑ 110 John Smiley XRC .30 .10
❑ 111 Lary Sorensen .10 .02
❑ 112 Chris Speier .10 .02
❑ 113 Randy St.Claire .10 .02
❑ 114 Jim Sundberg .15 .05
❑ 115 B.J. Surhoff XRC .75 .30
❑ 116 Greg Swindell .30 .10
❑ 117 Danny Tartabull .10 .02
❑ 118 Dorn Taylor .10 .02
❑ 119 Lee Tunnell .10 .02
❑ 120 Ed VandeBerg .10 .02
❑ 121 Andy Van Slyke .25 .08
❑ 122 Gary Ward .10 .02
❑ 123 Devon White .75 .30
❑ 124 Alan Wiggins .10 .02
❑ 125 Bill Wilkinson .10 .02
❑ 126 Jim Winn .10 .02
❑ 127 Frank Williams .10 .02
❑ 128 Ken Williams .10 .02
❑ 129 Matt Williams XRC 1.50 .60
❑ 130 Herm Winningham .10 .02
❑ 131 Matt Young .10 .02
❑ 132 Checklist 1-132 .10 .02

1988 Fleer

❑ COMPLETE SET (660) 15.00 6.00
❑ COMP.RETAIL SET (660) 15.00 6.00
❑ COMP.HOBBY SET (672) 15.00 6.00
❑ 1 Keith Atherton .10 .02
❑ 2 Don Baylor .15 .05
❑ 3 Juan Berenguer .10 .02
❑ 4 Bert Blyleven .15 .05
❑ 5 Tom Brunansky .10 .02
❑ 6 Randy Bush .10 .02
❑ 7 Steve Carlton .15 .05

❑ 8 Mark Davidson .10 .02
❑ 9 George Frazier .10 .02
❑ 10 Gary Gaetti .15 .05
❑ 11 Greg Gagne .10 .02
❑ 12 Dan Gladden .10 .02
❑ 13 Kent Hrbek .15 .05
❑ 14 Gene Larkin RC* .40 .15
❑ 15 Tim Laudner .10 .02
❑ 16 Steve Lombardozzi .10 .02
❑ 17 Al Newman .10 .02
❑ 18 Joe Niekro .10 .02
❑ 19 Kirby Puckett .30 .10
❑ 20 Jeff Reardon .15 .05
❑ 21A Dan Schatzeder ERR (Misspelled Schatzader on car .15 .05
❑ 21B Dan Schatzeder COR .10 .02
❑ 22 Roy Smalley .10 .02
❑ 23 Mike Smithson .10 .02
❑ 24 Les Straker .10 .02
❑ 25 Frank Viola .15 .05
❑ 26 Jack Clark .15 .05
❑ 27 Vince Coleman .10 .02
❑ 28 Danny Cox .10 .02
❑ 29 Bill Dawley .10 .02
❑ 30 Ken Dayley .10 .02
❑ 31 Doug DeCinces .10 .02
❑ 32 Curt Ford .10 .02
❑ 33 Bob Forsch .10 .02
❑ 34 David Green .10 .02
❑ 35 Tom Herr .10 .02
❑ 36 Ricky Horton .10 .02
❑ 37 Lance Johnson RC .40 .15
❑ 38 Steve Lake .10 .02
❑ 39 Jim Lindeman .10 .02
❑ 40 Joe Magrane RC* .40 .15
❑ 41 Greg Mathews .10 .02
❑ 42 Willie McGee .15 .05
❑ 43 John Morris .10 .02
❑ 44 Jose Oquendo .10 .02
❑ 45 Tony Pena .10 .02
❑ 46 Terry Pendleton .15 .05
❑ 47 Ozzie Smith .50 .20
❑ 48 John Tudor .15 .05
❑ 49 Lee Tunnell .10 .02
❑ 50 Todd Worrell .10 .02
❑ 51 Doyle Alexander .10 .02
❑ 52 Dave Bergman .10 .02
❑ 53 Tom Brookens .10 .02
❑ 54 Darrell Evans .15 .05
❑ 55 Kirk Gibson .30 .10
❑ 56 Mike Heath .10 .02
❑ 57 Mike Henneman RC* .40 .15
❑ 58 Willie Hernandez .10 .02
❑ 59 Larry Herndon .10 .02
❑ 60 Eric King .10 .02
❑ 61 Chet Lemon .15 .05
❑ 62 Scott Lusader .10 .02
❑ 63 Bill Madlock .15 .05
❑ 64 Jack Morris .15 .05
❑ 65 Jim Morrison .10 .02
❑ 66 Matt Nokes RC* .40 .15
❑ 67 Dan Petry .10 .02
❑ 68A Jeff M. Robinson ERR (Stats for Jeff D. Robinson .20 .07
❑ 68B Jeff M. Robinson COR (Born 12-14-61) .10 .02

❑ 69 Pat Sheridan .10 .02
❑ 70 Nate Snell .10 .02
❑ 71 Frank Tanana .15 .05
❑ 72 Walt Terrell .10 .02
❑ 73 Mark Thurmond .10 .02
❑ 74 Alan Trammell .15 .05
❑ 75 Lou Whitaker .15 .05
❑ 76 Mike Aldrete .10 .02
❑ 77 Bob Brenly .10 .02
❑ 78 Will Clark .30 .10
❑ 79 Chili Davis .15 .05
❑ 80 Kelly Downs .10 .02
❑ 81 Dave Dravecky .10 .02
❑ 82 Scott Garrelts .10 .02
❑ 83 Atlee Hammaker .10 .02
❑ 84 Dave Henderson .10 .02
❑ 85 Mike Krukow .10 .02
❑ 86 Mike LaCoss .10 .02
❑ 87 Craig Lefferts .10 .02
❑ 88 Jeff Leonard .10 .02
❑ 89 Candy Maldonado .10 .02
❑ 90 Eddie Milner .10 .02
❑ 91 Bob Melvin .10 .02
❑ 92 Kevin Mitchell .15 .05
❑ 93 Jon Perlman .10 .02
❑ 94 Rick Reuschel .15 .05
❑ 95 Don Robinson .10 .02
❑ 96 Chris Speier .10 .02
❑ 97 Harry Spilman .10 .02
❑ 98 Robby Thompson .10 .02
❑ 99 Jose Uribe .10 .02
❑ 100 Mark Wasinger .10 .02
❑ 101 Matt Williams RC 1.50 .60
❑ 102 Jesse Barfield .15 .05
❑ 103 George Bell .15 .05
❑ 104 Juan Beniquez .10 .02
❑ 105 John Cerutti .10 .02
❑ 106 Jim Clancy .10 .02
❑ 107 Rob Ducey .10 .02
❑ 108 Mark Eichhorn .10 .02
❑ 109 Tony Fernandez .10 .02
❑ 110 Cecil Fielder .15 .05
❑ 111 Kelly Gruber .10 .02
❑ 112 Tom Henke .10 .02
❑ 113A Garth Iorg ERR (Misspelled Iorq on card front) .20 .07
❑ 113B Garth Iorg COR .10 .02
❑ 114 Jimmy Key .15 .05
❑ 115 Rick Leach .10 .02
❑ 116 Manny Lee .10 .02
❑ 117 Nelson Liriano .10 .02
❑ 118 Fred McGriff .30 .10
❑ 119 Lloyd Moseby .10 .02
❑ 120 Rance Mulliniks .10 .02
❑ 121 Jeff Musselman .10 .02
❑ 122 Jose Nunez .10 .02
❑ 123 Dave Stieb .15 .05
❑ 124 Willie Upshaw .10 .02
❑ 125 Duane Ward .10 .02
❑ 126 Ernie Whitt .10 .02
❑ 127 Rick Aguilera .10 .02
❑ 128 Wally Backman .10 .02
❑ 129 Mark Carreon RC .15 .05
❑ 130 Gary Carter .15 .05
❑ 131 David Cone .15 .05
❑ 132 Ron Darling .15 .05
❑ 133 Len Dykstra .15 .05
❑ 134 Sid Fernandez .10 .02
❑ 135 Dwight Gooden .15 .05
❑ 136 Keith Hernandez .15 .05
❑ 137 Gregg Jefferies RC .40 .15
❑ 138 Howard Johnson .15 .05
❑ 139 Terry Leach .10 .02
❑ 140 Barry Lyons .10 .02
❑ 141 Dave Magadan .10 .02
❑ 142 Roger McDowell .10 .02
❑ 143 Kevin McReynolds .10 .02
❑ 144 Keith Miller RC .40 .15
❑ 145 John Mitchell RC .15 .05
❑ 146 Randy Myers .15 .05
❑ 147 Bob Ojeda .10 .02
❑ 148 Jesse Orosco .10 .02
❑ 149 Rafael Santana .10 .02
❑ 150 Doug Sisk .10 .02
❑ 151 Darryl Strawberry .15 .05
❑ 152 Tim Teufel .10 .02
❑ 153 Gene Walter .10 .02
❑ 154 Mookie Wilson .15 .05
❑ 155 Jay Aldrich .10 .02
❑ 156 Chris Bosio .10 .02
❑ 157 Glenn Braggs .10 .02
❑ 158 Greg Brock .10 .02
❑ 159 Juan Castillo .10 .02
❑ 160 Mark Clear .10 .02
❑ 161 Cecil Cooper .15 .05
❑ 162 Chuck Crim .10 .02
❑ 163 Rob Deer .10 .02
❑ 164 Mike Felder .10 .02
❑ 165 Jim Gantner .10 .02
❑ 166 Ted Higuera .10 .02
❑ 167 Steve Kiefer .10 .02
❑ 168 Rick Manning .10 .02
❑ 169 Paul Molitor .15 .05
❑ 170 Juan Nieves .10 .02
❑ 171 Dan Plesac .10 .02
❑ 172 Earnest Riles .10 .02
❑ 173 Bill Schroeder .10 .02
❑ 174 Steve Stanicek .10 .02
❑ 175 B.J. Surhoff .15 .05
❑ 176 Dale Sveum .10 .02
❑ 177 Bill Wegman .10 .02
❑ 178 Robin Yount .50 .20
❑ 179 Hubie Brooks .10 .02
❑ 180 Tim Burke .10 .02
❑ 181 Casey Candaele .10 .02
❑ 182 Mike Fitzgerald .10 .02
❑ 183 Tom Foley .10 .02
❑ 184 Andres Galarraga .15 .05
❑ 185 Neal Heaton .10 .02
❑ 186 Wallace Johnson .10 .02
❑ 187 Vance Law .10 .02
❑ 188 Dennis Martinez .15 .05
❑ 189 Bob McClure .10 .02
❑ 190 Andy McGaffigan .10 .02
❑ 191 Reid Nichols .10 .02
❑ 192 Pascual Perez .10 .02
❑ 193 Tim Raines .15 .05
❑ 194 Jeff Reed .10 .02
❑ 195 Bob Sebra .10 .02
❑ 196 Bryn Smith .10 .02
❑ 197 Randy St.Claire .10 .02
❑ 198 Tim Wallach .10 .02
❑ 199 Mitch Webster .10 .02
❑ 200 Herm Winningham .10 .02
❑ 201 Floyd Youmans .10 .02
❑ 202 Brad Arnsberg .10 .02
❑ 203 Rick Cerone .10 .02
❑ 204 Pat Clements .10 .02
❑ 205 Henry Cotto .10 .02
❑ 206 Mike Easler .10 .02
❑ 207 Ron Guidry .15 .05
❑ 208 Bill Gullickson .10 .02
❑ 209 Rickey Henderson .30 .10
❑ 210 Charles Hudson .10 .02
❑ 211 Tommy John .15 .05
❑ 212 Roberto Kelly RC .40 .15
❑ 213 Ron Kittle .10 .02
❑ 214 Don Mattingly 1.00 .40
❑ 215 Bobby Meacham .10 .02
❑ 216 Mike Pagliarulo .10 .02
❑ 217 Dan Pasqua .10 .02
❑ 218 Willie Randolph .15 .05
❑ 219 Rick Rhoden .10 .02
❑ 220 Dave Righetti .15 .05
❑ 221 Jerry Royster .10 .02
❑ 222 Tim Stoddard .10 .02
❑ 223 Wayne Tolleson .10 .02
❑ 224 Gary Ward .10 .02
❑ 225 Claudell Washington .10 .02
❑ 226 Dave Winfield .15 .05
❑ 227 Buddy Bell .15 .05
❑ 228 Tom Browning .10 .02
❑ 229 Dave Concepcion .15 .05
❑ 230 Kal Daniels .10 .02
❑ 231 Eric Davis .15 .05
❑ 232 Bo Diaz .10 .02
❑ 233 Nick Esasky (Has a dollar sign before '87 SB tot .10 .02
❑ 234 John Franco .15 .05
❑ 235 Guy Hoffman .10 .02
❑ 236 Tom Hume .10 .02
❑ 237 Tracy Jones .10 .02
❑ 238 Bill Landrum .10 .02
❑ 239 Barry Larkin .20 .07
❑ 240 Terry McGriff .10 .02
❑ 241 Rob Murphy .10 .02
❑ 242 Ron Oester .10 .02
❑ 243 Dave Parker .15 .05
❑ 244 Pat Perry .10 .02
❑ 245 Ted Power .10 .02
❑ 246 Dennis Rasmussen .10 .02
❑ 247 Ron Robinson .10 .02
❑ 248 Kurt Stillwell .10 .02
❑ 249 Jeff Treadway RC .40 .15
❑ 250 Frank Williams .10 .02
❑ 251 Steve Balboni .10 .02
❑ 252 Bud Black .10 .02
❑ 253 Thad Bosley .10 .02
❑ 254 George Brett .75 .30
❑ 255 John Davis .10 .02
❑ 256 Steve Farr .10 .02
❑ 257 Gene Garber .10 .02
❑ 258 Jerry Don Gleaton .10 .02
❑ 259 Mark Gubicza .10 .02
❑ 260 Bo Jackson .30 .10
❑ 261 Danny Jackson .10 .02
❑ 262 Ross Jones .10 .02
❑ 263 Charlie Leibrandt .10 .02
❑ 264 Bill Pecota RC* .15 .05
❑ 265 Melido Perez RC .40 .15
❑ 266 Jamie Quirk .10 .02
❑ 267 Dan Quisenberry .10 .02
❑ 268 Bret Saberhagen .15 .05
❑ 269 Angel Salazar .10 .02
❑ 270 Kevin Seitzer UER (Wrong birth year) .15 .05
❑ 271 Danny Tartabull .10 .02
❑ 272 Gary Thurman .10 .02
❑ 273 Frank White .15 .05
❑ 274 Willie Wilson .15 .05
❑ 275 Tony Bernazard .10 .02
❑ 276 Jose Canseco .75 .30
❑ 277 Mike Davis .10 .02
❑ 278 Storm Davis .10 .02
❑ 279 Dennis Eckersley .20 .07
❑ 280 Alfredo Griffin .10 .02
❑ 281 Rick Honeycutt .10 .02
❑ 282 Jay Howell .10 .02
❑ 283 Reggie Jackson .20 .07
❑ 284 Dennis Lamp .10 .02
❑ 285 Carney Lansford .15 .05
❑ 286 Mark McGwire 2.50 1.00
❑ 287 Dwayne Murphy .10 .02
❑ 288 Gene Nelson .10 .02
❑ 289 Steve Ontiveros .10 .02
❑ 290 Tony Phillips .10 .02
❑ 291 Eric Plunk .10 .02
❑ 292 Luis Polonia RC* .40 .15
❑ 293 Rick Rodriguez .10 .02
❑ 294 Terry Steinbach .15 .05
❑ 295 Dave Stewart .15 .05
❑ 296 Curt Young .10 .02
❑ 297 Luis Aguayo .10 .02
❑ 298 Steve Bedrosian .10 .02
❑ 299 Jeff Calhoun .10 .02
❑ 300 Don Carman .10 .02
❑ 301 Todd Frohwirth .10 .02
❑ 302 Greg Gross .10 .02
❑ 303 Kevin Gross .10 .02
❑ 304 Von Hayes .10 .02
❑ 305 Keith Hughes .10 .02
❑ 306 Mike Jackson RC* .40 .15
❑ 307 Chris James .10 .02
❑ 308 Steve Jeltz .10 .02
❑ 309 Mike Maddux .10 .02
❑ 310 Lance Parrish .15 .05
❑ 311 Shane Rawley .10 .02
❑ 312 Wally Ritchie .10 .02
❑ 313 Bruce Ruffin .10 .02
❑ 314 Juan Samuel .10 .02
❑ 315 Mike Schmidt .75 .30
❑ 316 Rick Schu .10 .02
❑ 317 Jeff Stone .10 .02
❑ 318 Kent Tekulve .10 .02
❑ 319 Milt Thompson .10 .02
❑ 320 Glenn Wilson .10 .02

❑	321	Rafael Belliard	.10	.02
❑	322	Barry Bonds	2.50	1.00
❑	323	Bobby Bonilla	.15	.05
❑	324	Sid Bream	.10	.02
❑	325	John Cangelosi	.10	.02
❑	326	Mike Diaz	.10	.02
❑	327	Doug Drabek	.10	.02
❑	328	Mike Dunne	.10	.02
❑	329	Brian Fisher	.10	.02
❑	330	Brett Gideon	.10	.02
❑	331	Terry Harper	.10	.02
❑	332	Bob Kipper	.10	.02
❑	333	Mike LaValliere	.10	.02
❑	334	Jose Lind RC	.40	.15
❑	335	Junior Ortiz	.10	.02
❑	336	Vicente Palacios	.10	.02
❑	337	Bob Patterson	.10	.02
❑	338	Al Pedrique	.10	.02
❑	339	R.J. Reynolds	.10	.02
❑	340	John Smiley RC*	.40	.15
❑	341	Andy Van Slyke UER (Wrong batting and throwing)	.20	.07
❑	342	Bob Walk	.10	.02
❑	343	Marty Barrett	.10	.02
❑	344	Todd Benzinger RC*	.40	.15
❑	345	Wade Boggs	.20	.07
❑	346	Tom Bolton	.10	.02
❑	347	Oil Can Boyd	.10	.02
❑	348	Ellis Burks RC	.50	.20
❑	349	Roger Clemens	1.50	.60
❑	350	Steve Crawford	.10	.02
❑	351	Dwight Evans	.20	.07
❑	352	Wes Gardner	.10	.02
❑	353	Rich Gedman	.10	.02
❑	354	Mike Greenwell	.10	.02
❑	355	Sam Horn RC	.15	.05
❑	356	Bruce Hurst	.10	.02
❑	357	John Marzano	.10	.02
❑	358	Al Nipper	.10	.02
❑	359	Spike Owen	.10	.02
❑	360	Jody Reed RC	.40	.15
❑	361	Jim Rice	.15	.05
❑	362	Ed Romero	.10	.02
❑	363	Kevin Romine	.10	.02
❑	364	Joe Sambito	.10	.02
❑	365	Calvin Schiraldi	.10	.02
❑	366	Jeff Sellers	.10	.02
❑	367	Bob Stanley	.10	.02
❑	368	Scott Bankhead	.10	.02
❑	369	Phil Bradley	.10	.02
❑	370	Scott Bradley	.10	.02
❑	371	Mickey Brantley	.10	.02
❑	372	Mike Campbell	.10	.02
❑	373	Alvin Davis	.10	.02
❑	374	Lee Guetterman	.10	.02
❑	375	Dave Hengel	.10	.02
❑	376	Mike Kingery	.10	.02
❑	377	Mark Langston	.10	.02
❑	378	Edgar Martinez RC	5.00	2.00
❑	379	Mike Moore	.10	.02
❑	380	Mike Morgan	.10	.02
❑	381	John Moses	.10	.02
❑	382	Donell Nixon	.10	.02
❑	383	Edwin Nunez	.10	.02
❑	384	Ken Phelps	.10	.02
❑	385	Jim Presley	.10	.02
❑	386	Rey Quinones	.10	.02
❑	387	Jerry Reed	.10	.02
❑	388	Harold Reynolds	.15	.05
❑	389	Dave Valle	.10	.02
❑	390	Bill Wilkinson	.10	.02
❑	391	Harold Baines	.15	.05
❑	392	Floyd Bannister	.10	.02
❑	393	Daryl Boston	.10	.02
❑	394	Ivan Calderon	.10	.02
❑	395	Jose DeLeon	.10	.02
❑	396	Richard Dotson	.10	.02
❑	397	Carlton Fisk	.20	.07
❑	398	Ozzie Guillen	.15	.05
❑	399	Ron Hassey	.10	.02
❑	400	Donnie Hill	.10	.02
❑	401	Bob James	.10	.02
❑	402	Dave LaPoint	.10	.02
❑	403	Bill Lindsey	.10	.02
❑	404	Bill Long	.10	.02
❑	405	Steve Lyons	.10	.02
❑	406	Fred Manrique	.10	.02
❑	407	Jack McDowell RC	.50	.20
❑	408	Gary Redus	.10	.02
❑	409	Ray Searage	.10	.02
❑	410	Bobby Thigpen	.10	.02
❑	411	Greg Walker	.10	.02
❑	412	Ken Williams	.10	.02
❑	413	Jim Winn	.10	.02
❑	414	Jody Davis	.10	.02
❑	415	Andre Dawson	.15	.05
❑	416	Brian Dayett	.10	.02
❑	417	Bob Dernier	.10	.02
❑	418	Frank DiPino	.10	.02
❑	419	Shawon Dunston	.10	.02
❑	420	Leon Durham	.10	.02
❑	421	Les Lancaster	.10	.02
❑	422	Ed Lynch	.10	.02
❑	423	Greg Maddux	1.50	.60
❑	424	Dave Martinez	.10	.02
❑	425A	Keith Moreland ERR	1.50	.60
❑	425B	Keith Moreland COR (Bat on shoulder)	.15	.05
❑	426	Jamie Moyer	.15	.05
❑	427	Jerry Mumphrey	.10	.02
❑	428	Paul Noce	.10	.02
❑	429	Rafael Palmeiro	.60	.25
❑	430	Wade Rowdon	.10	.02
❑	431	Ryne Sandberg	.60	.25
❑	432	Scott Sanderson	.10	.02
❑	433	Lee Smith	.15	.05
❑	434	Jim Sundberg	.15	.05
❑	435	Rick Sutcliffe	.15	.05
❑	436	Manny Trillo	.10	.02
❑	437	Juan Agosto	.10	.02
❑	438	Larry Andersen	.10	.02
❑	439	Alan Ashby	.10	.02
❑	440	Kevin Bass	.10	.02
❑	441	Ken Caminiti RC	3.00	1.25
❑	442	Rocky Childress	.10	.02
❑	443	Jose Cruz	.15	.05
❑	444	Danny Darwin	.10	.02
❑	445	Glenn Davis	.10	.02
❑	446	Jim Deshaies	.10	.02
❑	447	Bill Doran	.10	.02
❑	448	Ty Gainey	.10	.02
❑	449	Billy Hatcher	.10	.02
❑	450	Jeff Heathcock	.10	.02
❑	451	Bob Knepper	.10	.02
❑	452	Rob Mallicoat	.10	.02
❑	453	Dave Meads	.10	.02
❑	454	Craig Reynolds	.10	.02
❑	455	Nolan Ryan	1.50	.60
❑	456	Mike Scott	.15	.05
❑	457	Dave Smith	.10	.02
❑	458	Denny Walling	.10	.02
❑	459	Robbie Wine	.10	.02
❑	460	Gerald Young	.10	.02
❑	461	Bob Brower	.10	.02
❑	462A	Jerry Browne ERR	1.50	.60
❑	462B	Jerry Browne COR (Black player)	.15	.05
❑	463	Steve Buechele	.10	.02
❑	464	Edwin Correa	.10	.02
❑	465	Cecil Espy RC	.10	.02
❑	466	Scott Fletcher	.10	.02
❑	467	Jose Guzman	.10	.02
❑	468	Greg Harris	.10	.02
❑	469	Charlie Hough	.15	.05
❑	470	Pete Incaviglia	.10	.02
❑	471	Paul Kilgus	.10	.02
❑	472	Mike Loynd	.10	.02
❑	473	Oddibe McDowell	.10	.02
❑	474	Dale Mohorcic	.10	.02
❑	475	Pete O'Brien	.10	.02
❑	476	Larry Parrish	.10	.02
❑	477	Geno Petralli	.10	.02
❑	478	Jeff Russell	.10	.02
❑	479	Ruben Sierra	.15	.05
❑	480	Mike Stanley	.10	.02
❑	481	Curtis Wilkerson	.10	.02
❑	482	Mitch Williams	.10	.02
❑	483	Bobby Witt	.10	.02
❑	484	Tony Armas	.15	.05
❑	485	Bob Boone	.15	.05
❑	486	Bill Buckner	.15	.05
❑	487	DeWayne Buice	.10	.02
❑	488	Brian Downing	.15	.05
❑	489	Chuck Finley	.15	.05
❑	490	Willie Fraser UER (Wrong bio stats, for George H	.10	.02
❑	491	Jack Howell	.10	.02
❑	492	Ruppert Jones	.10	.02
❑	493	Wally Joyner	.15	.05
❑	494	Jack Lazorko	.10	.02
❑	495	Gary Lucas	.10	.02
❑	496	Kirk McCaskill	.10	.02
❑	497	Mark McLemore	.10	.02
❑	498	Darrell Miller	.10	.02
❑	499	Greg Minton	.10	.02
❑	500	Donnie Moore	.10	.02
❑	501	Gus Polidor	.10	.02
❑	502	Johnny Ray	.10	.02
❑	503	Mark Ryal	.10	.02
❑	504	Dick Schofield	.10	.02
❑	505	Don Sutton	.15	.05
❑	506	Devon White	.15	.05
❑	507	Mike Witt	.10	.02
❑	508	Dave Anderson	.10	.02
❑	509	Tim Belcher	.10	.02
❑	510	Ralph Bryant	.10	.02
❑	511	Tim Crews RC	.40	.15
❑	512	Mike Devereaux RC	.40	.15
❑	513	Mariano Duncan	.10	.02
❑	514	Pedro Guerrero	.15	.05
❑	515	Jeff Hamilton	.10	.02
❑	516	Mickey Hatcher	.10	.02
❑	517	Brad Havens	.10	.02
❑	518	Orel Hershiser	.15	.05
❑	519	Shawn Hillegas	.10	.02
❑	520	Ken Howell	.10	.02
❑	521	Tim Leary	.10	.02
❑	522	Mike Marshall	.10	.02
❑	523	Steve Sax	.10	.02
❑	524	Mike Scioscia	.15	.05
❑	525	Mike Sharperson	.10	.02
❑	526	John Shelby	.10	.02
❑	527	Franklin Stubbs	.10	.02
❑	528	Fernando Valenzuela	.15	.05
❑	529	Bob Welch	.15	.05
❑	530	Matt Young	.10	.02
❑	531	Jim Acker	.10	.02
❑	532	Paul Assenmacher	.10	.02
❑	533	Jeff Blauser RC	.40	.15
❑	534	Joe Boever	.10	.02
❑	535	Martin Clary	.10	.02
❑	536	Kevin Coffman	.10	.02
❑	537	Jeff Dedmon	.10	.02
❑	538	Ron Gant RC	.50	.20
❑	539	Tom Glavine RC	4.00	1.50
❑	540	Ken Griffey	.15	.05
❑	541	Albert Hall	.10	.02
❑	542	Glenn Hubbard	.10	.02
❑	543	Dion James	.10	.02
❑	544	Dale Murphy	.20	.07
❑	545	Ken Oberkfell	.10	.02
❑	546	David Palmer	.10	.02
❑	547	Gerald Perry	.10	.02
❑	548	Charlie Puleo	.10	.02
❑	549	Ted Simmons	.15	.05
❑	550	Zane Smith	.10	.02
❑	551	Andres Thomas	.10	.02
❑	552	Ozzie Virgil	.10	.02
❑	553	Don Aase	.10	.02
❑	554	Jeff Ballard	.10	.02
❑	555	Eric Bell	.10	.02
❑	556	Mike Boddicker	.10	.02
❑	557	Ken Dixon	.10	.02
❑	558	Jim Dwyer	.10	.02
❑	559	Ken Gerhart	.10	.02
❑	560	Rene Gonzales RC	.15	.05
❑	561	Mike Griffin	.10	.02
❑	562	John Habyan UER (Misspelled Hayban on both sides	.10	.02
❑	563	Terry Kennedy	.10	.02
❑	564	Ray Knight	.15	.05
❑	565	Lee Lacy	.10	.02
❑	566	Fred Lynn	.15	.05
❑	567	Eddie Murray	.30	.10
❑	568	Tom Niedenfuer	.10	.02

❑ 569 Bill Ripken RC* .40 .15
❑ 570 Cal Ripken 1.25 .50
❑ 571 Dave Schmidt .10 .02
❑ 572 Larry Sheets .10 .02
❑ 573 Pete Stanicek .10 .02
❑ 574 Mark Williamson .10 .02
❑ 575 Mike Young .10 .02
❑ 576 Shawn Abner .10 .02
❑ 577 Greg Booker .10 .02
❑ 578 Chris Brown .10 .02
❑ 579 Keith Comstock .10 .02
❑ 580 Joey Cora RC .40 .15
❑ 581 Mark Davis .10 .02
❑ 582 Tim Flannery
(With surfboard) .20 .07
❑ 583 Goose Gossage .15 .05
❑ 584 Mark Grant .10 .02
❑ 585 Tony Gwynn .50 .20
❑ 586 Andy Hawkins .10 .02
❑ 587 Stan Jefferson .10 .02
❑ 588 Jimmy Jones .10 .02
❑ 589 John Kruk .15 .05
❑ 590 Shane Mack .10 .02
❑ 591 Carmelo Martinez .10 .02
❑ 592 Lance McCullers UER
(6'11" tall) .10 .02
❑ 593 Eric Nolte .10 .02
❑ 594 Randy Ready .10 .02
❑ 595 Luis Salazar .10 .02
❑ 596 Benito Santiago .15 .05
❑ 597 Eric Show .10 .02
❑ 598 Garry Templeton .15 .05
❑ 599 Ed Whitson .10 .02
❑ 600 Scott Bailes .10 .02
❑ 601 Chris Bando .10 .02
❑ 602 Jay Bell RC .50 .20
❑ 603 Brett Butler .15 .05
❑ 604 Tom Candiotti .10 .02
❑ 605 Joe Carter .15 .05
❑ 606 Carmen Castillo .10 .02
❑ 607 Brian Dorsett .10 .02
❑ 608 John Farrell RC .15 .05
❑ 609 Julio Franco .15 .05
❑ 610 Mel Hall .10 .02
❑ 611 Tommy Hinzo .10 .02
❑ 612 Brook Jacoby .10 .02
❑ 613 Doug Jones RC .40 .15
❑ 614 Ken Schrom .10 .02
❑ 615 Cory Snyder .10 .02
❑ 616 Sammy Stewart .10 .02
❑ 617 Greg Swindell .10 .02
❑ 618 Pat Tabler .10 .02
❑ 619 Ed VandeBerg .10 .02
❑ 620 Eddie Williams RC .15 .05
❑ 621 Rich Yett .10 .02
❑ 622 Slugging Sophomores
Wally Joyner
Cory Snyder .15 .05
❑ 623 Dominican Dynamite
George Bell
Pedro Guerrero .10 .02
❑ 624 M.McGwire/J.Canseco 1.50 .60
❑ 625 Classic Relief
Dave Righetti
Dan Plesac .10 .02
❑ 626 All Star Righties
Bret Saberhagen
Mike Witt
Jac .15 .05
❑ 627 Game Closers
John Franco
Steve Bedrosian .10 .02
❑ 628 O.Smith/R.Sandberg .30 .10
❑ 629 Mark McGwire HL 1.25 .50
❑ 630 Greenwell/Burks/Benz .30 .10
❑ 631 Tony Gwynn/T.Raines .20 .07
❑ 632 Pitching Magic
Mike Scott
Orel Hershiser .15 .05
❑ 633 M.McGwire/P.Tabler 1.25 .50
❑ 634 Tony Gwynn/V.Coleman .20 .07
❑ 635 C.Ripken/Trammell/Fern .50 .20
❑ 636 Mike Schmidt/G.Carter .30 .10
❑ 637 D.Strawberry/E.Davis .15 .05
❑ 638 M.Nokes/K.Puckett .20 .07
❑ 639 NL All-Stars
Keith Hernandez
Dale Murphy .15 .05
❑ 640 Ripken Brothers .75 .30
❑ 641 Mark Grace RC 3.00 1.25
❑ 642 D.Berryhill/J.Montgomery RC .40 .15
❑ 643 F.Fermin/J.Reid RC .15 .05
❑ 644 G.Myers/G.Tabor RC .40 .15
❑ 645 J.Meyer/J.Eppard RC .15 .05
❑ 646 A.Peterson RC/R.Velarde RC .40 .15
❑ 647 P.Smith/C.Gwynn RC .40 .15
❑ 648 T.Newell/G.Jelks RC .15 .05
❑ 649 M.Diaz/C.Parker RC .15 .05
❑ 650 J.Savage/T.Simmons RC .15 .05
❑ 651 John Burkett RC .40 .15
❑ 652 Walt Weiss RC .50 .20
❑ 653 Jeff King RC .40 .15
❑ 654 CL: Twins/Cards
Tigers/Giants UER
(90 Bob Melvin .10 .02
❑ 655 CL: Blue Jays/Mets
Brewers/Expos UER
(Mets liste .10 .02
❑ 656 CL: Yankees/Reds
Royals/A's .10 .02
❑ 657 CL: Phillies/Pirates
Red Sox/Mariners .10 .02
❑ 658 CL: White Sox/Cubs
Astros/Rangers .10 .02
❑ 659 CL: Angels/Dodgers
Braves/Orioles .10 .02
❑ 660 CL: Padres/Indians
Rookies/Specials .10 .02

1988 Fleer Update

❑ COMP.FACT.SET (132) 10.00 4.00
❑ 1 Jose Bautista XRC .25 .08
❑ 2 Joe Orsulak .10 .02
❑ 3 Doug Sisk .10 .02
❑ 4 Craig Worthington .10 .02
❑ 5 Mike Boddicker .10 .02
❑ 6 Rick Cerone .10 .02
❑ 7 Larry Parrish .10 .02
❑ 8 Lee Smith .20 .07
❑ 9 Mike Smithson .10 .02
❑ 10 John Trautwein .10 .02
❑ 11 Sherman Corbett .10 .02
❑ 12 Chili Davis .20 .07
❑ 13 Jim Eppard .10 .02
❑ 14 Bryan Harvey XRC .50 .20
❑ 15 John Davis .10 .02
❑ 16 Dave Gallagher .10 .02
❑ 17 Ricky Horton .10 .02
❑ 18 Dan Pasqua .10 .02
❑ 19 Melido Perez .10 .02
❑ 20 Jose Segura .10 .02
❑ 21 Andy Allanson .10 .02
❑ 22 Jon Perlman .10 .02
❑ 23 Domingo Ramos .10 .02
❑ 24 Rick Rodriguez .10 .02
❑ 25 Willie Upshaw .10 .02
❑ 26 Paul Gibson .10 .02
❑ 27 Don Heinkel .10 .02
❑ 28 Ray Knight .20 .07
❑ 29 Gary Pettis .10 .02
❑ 30 Luis Salazar .10 .02
❑ 31 Mike Macfarlane XRC .50 .20
❑ 32 Jeff Montgomery .50 .20
❑ 33 Ted Power .10 .02
❑ 34 Israel Sanchez .10 .02
❑ 35 Kurt Stillwell .10 .02
❑ 36 Pat Tabler .10 .02
❑ 37 Don August .10 .02
❑ 38 Darryl Hamilton XRC .50 .20
❑ 39 Jeff Leonard .10 .02
❑ 40 Joey Meyer .10 .02
❑ 41 Allan Anderson .10 .02
❑ 42 Brian Harper .10 .02
❑ 43 Tom Herr .10 .02
❑ 44 Charlie Lea .10 .02
❑ 45 John Moses
(Listed as Hohn on
checklist card) .10 .02
❑ 46 John Candelaria .10 .02
❑ 47 Jack Clark .20 .07
❑ 48 Richard Dotson .10 .02
❑ 49 Al Leiter XRC 1.00 .40
❑ 50 Rafael Santana .10 .02
❑ 51 Don Slaught .10 .02
❑ 52 Todd Burns .10 .02
❑ 53 Dave Henderson .10 .02
❑ 54 Doug Jennings .10 .02
❑ 55 Dave Parker .20 .07
❑ 56 Walt Weiss .75 .30
❑ 57 Bob Welch .20 .07
❑ 58 Henry Cotto .10 .02
❑ 59 Mario Diaz UER
(Listed as Marion
on card front) .10 .02
❑ 60 Mike Jackson .20 .07
❑ 61 Bill Swift .10 .02
❑ 62 Jose Cecena .10 .02
❑ 63 Ray Hayward .10 .02
❑ 64 Jim Steels UER
(Listed as Jim Steele
on card bac .10 .02
❑ 65 Pat Borders XRC .50 .20
❑ 66 Sil Campusano .10 .02
❑ 67 Mike Flanagan .10 .02
❑ 68 Todd Stottlemyre XRC .50 .20
❑ 69 David Wells XRC 1.50 .60
❑ 70 Jose Alvarez XRC .25 .08
❑ 71 Paul Runge .10 .02
❑ 72 Cesar Jimenez
(Card was intended
for German Jimi .10 .02
❑ 73 Pete Smith .10 .02
❑ 74 John Smoltz XRC 4.00 1.50
❑ 75 Damon Berryhill .25 .08
❑ 76 Goose Gossage .20 .07
❑ 77 Mark Grace 2.00 .75
❑ 78 Darrin Jackson .25 .08
❑ 79 Vance Law .10 .02
❑ 80 Jeff Pico .10 .02
❑ 81 Gary Varsho .10 .02
❑ 82 Tim Birtsas .10 .02
❑ 83 Rob Dibble XRC .75 .30
❑ 84 Danny Jackson .10 .02
❑ 85 Paul O'Neill .30 .10
❑ 86 Jose Rijo .20 .07
❑ 87 Chris Sabo XRC .75 .30
❑ 88 John Fishel .10 .02
❑ 89 Craig Biggio XRC 5.00 2.00
❑ 90 Terry Puhl .10 .02
❑ 91 Rafael Ramirez .10 .02
❑ 92 Louie Meadows .10 .02
❑ 93 Kirk Gibson .50 .20
❑ 94 Alfredo Griffin .10 .02
❑ 95 Jay Howell .10 .02
❑ 96 Jesse Orosco .10 .02
❑ 97 Alejandro Pena .10 .02
❑ 98 Tracy Woodson XRC* .25 .08
❑ 99 John Dopson .10 .02
❑ 100 Brian Holman XRC .25 .08
❑ 101 Rex Hudler .10 .02
❑ 102 Jeff Parrett .10 .02
❑ 103 Nelson Santovenia .10 .02
❑ 104 Kevin Elster .10 .02
❑ 105 Jeff Innis .10 .02
❑ 106 Mackey Sasser XRC* .50 .20
❑ 107 Phil Bradley .10 .02
❑ 108 Danny Clay .10 .02
❑ 109 Greg Harris .10 .02
❑ 110 Ricky Jordan XRC .50 .20
❑ 111 David Palmer .10 .02

❑ 112 Jim Gott .10 .02
❑ 113 Tommy Gregg UER
(Photo actually
Randy Milligan) .10 .02
❑ 114 Barry Jones .10 .02
❑ 115 Randy Milligan XRC* .25 .08
❑ 116 Luis Alicea XRC .50 .20
❑ 117 Tom Brunansky .10 .02
❑ 118 John Costello .10 .02
❑ 119 Jose DeLeon .10 .02
❑ 120 Bob Horner .20 .07
❑ 121 Scott Terry .10 .02
❑ 122 Roberto Alomar XRC 2.00 .75
❑ 123 Dave Leiper .10 .02
❑ 124 Keith Moreland .10 .02
❑ 125 Mark Parent .10 .02
❑ 126 Dennis Rasmussen .10 .02
❑ 127 Randy Bockus .10 .02
❑ 128 Brett Butler .20 .07
❑ 129 Donell Nixon .10 .02
❑ 130 Earnest Riles .10 .02
❑ 131 Roger Samuels .10 .02
❑ 132 Checklist U1-U132 .10 .02

1989 Fleer

❑ COMPLETE SET (660) 15.00 6.00
❑ COMP.FACT.SET (672) 15.00 6.00
❑ 1 Don Baylor .10 .02
❑ 2 Lance Blankenship RC .10 .02
❑ 3 Todd Burns UER .05 .01
❑ 4 Greg Cadaret UER .05 .01
❑ 5 Jose Canseco .25 .08
❑ 6 Storm Davis .05 .01
❑ 7 Dennis Eckersley .15 .05
❑ 8 Mike Gallego .05 .01
❑ 9 Ron Hassey .05 .01
❑ 10 Dave Henderson .05 .01
❑ 11 Rick Honeycutt .05 .01
❑ 12 Glenn Hubbard .05 .01
❑ 13 Stan Javier .05 .01
❑ 14 Doug Jennings .05 .01
❑ 15 Felix Jose RC .10 .02
❑ 16 Carney Lansford .10 .02
❑ 17 Mark McGwire 1.00 .40
❑ 18 Gene Nelson .05 .01
❑ 19 Dave Parker .10 .02
❑ 20 Eric Plunk .05 .01
❑ 21 Luis Polonia .05 .01
❑ 22 Terry Steinbach .10 .02
❑ 23 Dave Stewart .10 .02
❑ 24 Walt Weiss .05 .01
❑ 25 Bob Welch .10 .02
❑ 26 Curt Young .05 .01
❑ 27 Rick Aguilera .05 .01
❑ 28 Wally Backman .05 .01
❑ 29 Mark Carreon UER .05 .01
❑ 30 Gary Carter .10 .02
❑ 31 David Cone .10 .02
❑ 32 Ron Darling .10 .02
❑ 33 Len Dykstra .10 .02
❑ 34 Kevin Elster .05 .01
❑ 35 Sid Fernandez .05 .01
❑ 36 Dwight Gooden .10 .02
❑ 37 Keith Hernandez .10 .02
❑ 38 Gregg Jefferies .05 .01
❑ 39 Howard Johnson .10 .02
❑ 40 Terry Leach .05 .01
❑ 41 Dave Magadan UER .05 .01
❑ 42 Bob McClure .05 .01
❑ 43 Roger McDowell UER .05 .01
❑ 44 Kevin McReynolds .05 .01
❑ 45 Keith A. Miller .05 .01
❑ 46 Randy Myers .10 .02
❑ 47 Bob Ojeda .05 .01
❑ 48 Mackey Sasser .05 .01
❑ 49 Darryl Strawberry .10 .02
❑ 50 Tim Teufel .05 .01
❑ 51 Dave West RC .10 .02
❑ 52 Mookie Wilson .10 .02
❑ 53 Dave Anderson .05 .01
❑ 54 Tim Belcher .05 .01
❑ 55 Mike Davis .05 .01
❑ 56 Mike Devereaux .05 .01
❑ 57 Kirk Gibson .10 .02
❑ 58 Alfredo Griffin .05 .01
❑ 59 Chris Gwynn .05 .01
❑ 60 Jeff Hamilton .05 .01
❑ 61A Danny Heep ERR .25 .08
❑ 61B Danny Heep COR .05 .01
❑ 62 Orel Hershiser .10 .02
❑ 63 Brian Holton .05 .01
❑ 64 Jay Howell .05 .01
❑ 65 Tim Leary .05 .01
❑ 66 Mike Marshall .05 .01
❑ 67 Ramon Martinez RC .25 .08
❑ 68 Jesse Orosco .05 .01
❑ 69 Alejandro Pena .05 .01
❑ 70 Steve Sax .05 .01
❑ 71 Mike Scioscia .10 .02
❑ 72 Mike Sharperson .05 .01
❑ 73 John Shelby .05 .01
❑ 74 Franklin Stubbs .05 .01
❑ 75 John Tudor .10 .02
❑ 76 Fernando Valenzuela .10 .02
❑ 77 Tracy Woodson .05 .01
❑ 78 Marty Barrett .05 .01
❑ 79 Todd Benzinger .05 .01
❑ 80 Mike Boddicker UER .05 .01
❑ 81 Wade Boggs .15 .05
❑ 82 Oil Can Boyd .05 .01
❑ 83 Ellis Burks .10 .02
❑ 84 Rick Cerone .05 .01
❑ 85 Roger Clemens 1.00 .40
❑ 86 Steve Curry .05 .01
❑ 87 Dwight Evans .15 .05
❑ 88 Wes Gardner .05 .01
❑ 89 Rich Gedman .05 .01
❑ 90 Mike Greenwell .05 .01
❑ 91 Bruce Hurst .05 .01
❑ 92 Dennis Lamp .05 .01
❑ 93 Spike Owen .05 .01
❑ 94 Larry Parrish UER .05 .01
❑ 95 Carlos Quintana RC .10 .02
❑ 96 Jody Reed .05 .01
❑ 97 Jim Rice .10 .02
❑ 98A Kevin Romine ERR .25 .08
❑ 98B Kevin Romine COR .05 .01
❑ 99 Lee Smith .10 .02
❑ 100 Mike Smithson .05 .01
❑ 101 Bob Stanley .05 .01
❑ 102 Allan Anderson .05 .01
❑ 103 Keith Atherton .05 .01
❑ 104 Juan Berenguer .05 .01
❑ 105 Bert Blyleven .10 .02
❑ 106 Eric Bullock UER .05 .01
❑ 107 Randy Bush .05 .01
❑ 108 John Christensen .05 .01
❑ 109 Mark Davidson .05 .01
❑ 110 Gary Gaetti .10 .02
❑ 111 Greg Gagne .05 .01
❑ 112 Dan Gladden .05 .01
❑ 113 German Gonzalez .05 .01
❑ 114 Brian Harper .05 .01
❑ 115 Tom Herr .05 .01
❑ 116 Kent Hrbek .10 .02
❑ 117 Gene Larkin .05 .01
❑ 118 Tim Laudner .05 .01
❑ 119 Charlie Lea .05 .01
❑ 120 Steve Lombardozzi .05 .01
❑ 121A John Moses ERR .25 .08
❑ 121B John Moses COR .05 .01
❑ 122 Al Newman .05 .01
❑ 123 Mark Portugal .05 .01
❑ 124 Kirby Puckett .25 .08
❑ 125 Jeff Reardon .10 .02
❑ 126 Fred Toliver .05 .01
❑ 127 Frank Viola .10 .02
❑ 128 Doyle Alexander .05 .01
❑ 129 Dave Bergman .05 .01
❑ 130A Tom Brookens ERR .75 .30
❑ 130B Tom Brookens COR .05 .01
❑ 131 Paul Gibson .05 .01
❑ 132A Mike Heath ERR .75 .30
❑ 132B Mike Heath COR .05 .01
❑ 133 Don Heinkel .05 .01
❑ 134 Mike Henneman .05 .01
❑ 135 Guillermo Hernandez .05 .01
❑ 136 Eric King .05 .01
❑ 137 Chet Lemon .10 .02
❑ 138 Fred Lynn UER .10 .02
❑ 139 Jack Morris .10 .02
❑ 140 Matt Nokes .05 .01
❑ 141 Gary Pettis .05 .01
❑ 142 Ted Power .05 .01
❑ 143 Jeff M. Robinson .05 .01
❑ 144 Luis Salazar .05 .01
❑ 145 Steve Searcy .05 .01
❑ 146 Pat Sheridan .05 .01
❑ 147 Frank Tanana .10 .02
❑ 148 Alan Trammell .10 .02
❑ 149 Walt Terrell .05 .01
❑ 150 Jim Walewander .05 .01
❑ 151 Lou Whitaker .10 .02
❑ 152 Tim Birtsas .05 .01
❑ 153 Tom Browning .05 .01
❑ 154 Keith Brown .05 .01
❑ 155 Norm Charlton RC .25 .08
❑ 156 Dave Concepcion .10 .02
❑ 157 Kal Daniels .05 .01
❑ 158 Eric Davis .10 .02
❑ 159 Bo Diaz .05 .01
❑ 160 Rob Dibble RC .40 .15
❑ 161 Nick Esasky .05 .01
❑ 162 John Franco .10 .02
❑ 163 Danny Jackson .05 .01
❑ 164 Barry Larkin .15 .05
❑ 165 Rob Murphy .05 .01
❑ 166 Paul O'Neill .15 .05
❑ 167 Jeff Reed .05 .01
❑ 168 Jose Rijo .10 .02
❑ 169 Ron Robinson .05 .01
❑ 170 Chris Sabo RC .40 .15
❑ 171 Candy Sierra .05 .01
❑ 172 Van Snider .05 .01
❑ 173A J.Treadway ERR Target 25.00 10.00
❑ 173B Jeff Treadway No Target .05 .01
❑ 174 Frank Williams UER .05 .01
❑ 175 Herm Winningham .05 .01
❑ 176 Jim Adduci .05 .01
❑ 177 Don August .05 .01
❑ 178 Mike Birkbeck .05 .01
❑ 179 Chris Bosio .05 .01
❑ 180 Glenn Braggs .05 .01
❑ 181 Greg Brock .05 .01
❑ 182 Mark Clear .05 .01
❑ 183 Chuck Crim .05 .01
❑ 184 Rob Deer .05 .01
❑ 185 Tom Filer .05 .01
❑ 186 Jim Gantner .05 .01
❑ 187 Darryl Hamilton RC .25 .08
❑ 188 Ted Higuera .05 .01
❑ 189 Odell Jones .05 .01
❑ 190 Jeffrey Leonard .05 .01
❑ 191 Joey Meyer .05 .01
❑ 192 Paul Mirabella .05 .01
❑ 193 Paul Molitor .10 .02
❑ 194 Charlie O'Brien .05 .01
❑ 195 Dan Plesac .05 .01
❑ 196 Gary Sheffield RC 1.50 .60
❑ 197 B.J. Surhoff .10 .02
❑ 198 Dale Sveum .05 .01
❑ 199 Bill Wegman .05 .01
❑ 200 Robin Yount .40 .15
❑ 201 Rafael Belliard .05 .01
❑ 202 Barry Bonds 1.50 .60
❑ 203 Bobby Bonilla .10 .02
❑ 204 Sid Bream .05 .01
❑ 205 Benny Distefano .05 .01
❑ 206 Doug Drabek .05 .01
❑ 207 Mike Dunne .05 .01

❑	208	Felix Fermin	.05	.01
❑	209	Brian Fisher	.05	.01
❑	210	Jim Gott	.05	.01
❑	211	Bob Kipper	.05	.01
❑	212	Dave LaPoint	.05	.01
❑	213	Mike LaValliere	.05	.01
❑	214	Jose Lind	.05	.01
❑	215	Junior Ortiz	.05	.01
❑	216	Vicente Palacios	.05	.01
❑	217	Tom Prince	.05	.01
❑	218	Gary Redus	.05	.01
❑	219	R.J. Reynolds	.05	.01
❑	220	Jeff D. Robinson	.05	.01
❑	221	John Smiley	.05	.01
❑	222	Andy Van Slyke	.15	.05
❑	223	Bob Walk	.05	.01
❑	224	Glenn Wilson	.05	.01
❑	225	Jesse Barfield	.10	.02
❑	226	George Bell	.10	.02
❑	227	Pat Borders RC	.25	.08
❑	228	John Cerutti	.05	.01
❑	229	Jim Clancy	.05	.01
❑	230	Mark Eichhorn	.05	.01
❑	231	Tony Fernandez	.05	.01
❑	232	Cecil Fielder	.10	.02
❑	233	Mike Flanagan	.05	.01
❑	234	Kelly Gruber	.05	.01
❑	235	Tom Henke	.05	.01
❑	236	Jimmy Key	.10	.02
❑	237	Rick Leach	.05	.01
❑	238	Manny Lee UER	.05	.01
❑	239	Nelson Liriano	.05	.01
❑	240	Fred McGriff	.15	.05
❑	241	Lloyd Moseby	.05	.01
❑	242	Rance Mulliniks	.05	.01
❑	243	Jeff Musselman	.05	.01
❑	244	Dave Stieb	.10	.02
❑	245	Todd Stottlemyre	.05	.01
❑	246	Duane Ward	.05	.01
❑	247	David Wells	.10	.02
❑	248	Ernie Whitt UER	.05	.01
❑	249	Luis Aguayo	.05	.01
❑	250A	Neil Allen ERR	.75	.30
❑	250B	Neil Allen COR	.05	.01
❑	251	John Candelaria	.05	.01
❑	252	Jack Clark	.10	.02
❑	253	Richard Dotson	.05	.01
❑	254	Rickey Henderson	.25	.08
❑	255	Tommy John	.10	.02
❑	256	Roberto Kelly	.05	.01
❑	257	Al Leiter	.25	.08
❑	258	Don Mattingly	.60	.25
❑	259	Dale Mohorcic	.05	.01
❑	260	Hal Morris RC	.25	.08
❑	261	Scott Nielsen	.05	.01
❑	262	Mike Pagliarulo UER	.05	.01
❑	263	Hipolito Pena	.05	.01
❑	264	Ken Phelps	.05	.01
❑	265	Willie Randolph	.10	.02
❑	266	Rick Rhoden	.05	.01
❑	267	Dave Righetti	.10	.02
❑	268	Rafael Santana	.05	.01
❑	269	Steve Shields	.05	.01
❑	270	Joel Skinner	.05	.01
❑	271	Don Slaught	.05	.01
❑	272	Claudell Washington	.05	.01
❑	273	Gary Ward	.05	.01
❑	274	Dave Winfield	.10	.02
❑	275	Luis Aquino	.05	.01
❑	276	Floyd Bannister	.05	.01
❑	277	George Brett	.60	.25
❑	278	Bill Buckner	.10	.02
❑	279	Nick Capra	.05	.01
❑	280	Jose DeJesus	.05	.01
❑	281	Steve Farr	.05	.01
❑	282	Jerry Don Gleaton	.05	.01
❑	283	Mark Gubicza	.05	.01
❑	284	Tom Gordon RC	.50	.20
❑	285	Bo Jackson	.25	.08
❑	286	Charlie Leibrandt	.05	.01
❑	287	Mike Macfarlane RC	.25	.08
❑	288	Jeff Montgomery	.05	.01
❑	289	Bill Pecota UER	.05	.01
❑	290	Jamie Quirk	.05	.01
❑	291	Bret Saberhagen	.10	.02
❑	292	Kevin Seitzer	.05	.01
❑	293	Kurt Stillwell	.05	.01
❑	294	Pat Tabler	.05	.01
❑	295	Danny Tartabull	.05	.01
❑	296	Gary Thurman	.05	.01
❑	297	Frank White	.10	.02
❑	298	Willie Wilson	.10	.02
❑	299	Roberto Alomar	.25	.08
❑	300	Sandy Alomar Jr. RC	.40	.15
❑	301	Chris Brown	.05	.01
❑	302	Mike Brumley UER	.05	.01
❑	303	Mark Davis	.05	.01
❑	304	Mark Grant	.05	.01
❑	305	Tony Gwynn	.30	.10
❑	306	Greg W.Harris RC	.10	.02
❑	307	Andy Hawkins	.05	.01
❑	308	Jimmy Jones	.05	.01
❑	309	John Kruk	.10	.02
❑	310	Dave Leiper	.05	.01
❑	311	Carmelo Martinez	.05	.01
❑	312	Lance McCullers	.05	.01
❑	313	Keith Moreland	.05	.01
❑	314	Dennis Rasmussen	.05	.01
❑	315	Randy Ready UER	.05	.01
❑	316	Benito Santiago	.10	.02
❑	317	Eric Show	.05	.01
❑	318	Todd Simmons	.05	.01
❑	319	Garry Templeton	.10	.02
❑	320	Dickie Thon	.05	.01
❑	321	Ed Whitson	.05	.01
❑	322	Marvell Wynne	.05	.01
❑	323	Mike Aldrete	.05	.01
❑	324	Brett Butler	.10	.02
❑	325	Will Clark	.15	.05
❑	326	Kelly Downs UER	.05	.01
❑	327	Dave Dravecky	.05	.01
❑	328	Scott Garrelts	.05	.01
❑	329	Atlee Hammaker	.05	.01
❑	330	Charlie Hayes RC	.25	.08
❑	331	Mike Krukow	.05	.01
❑	332	Craig Lefferts	.05	.01
❑	333	Candy Maldonado	.05	.01
❑	334	Kirt Manwaring UER	.05	.01
❑	335	Bob Melvin	.05	.01
❑	336	Kevin Mitchell	.10	.02
❑	337	Donell Nixon	.05	.01
❑	338	Tony Perezchica	.05	.01
❑	339	Joe Price	.05	.01
❑	340	Rick Reuschel	.10	.02
❑	341	Earnest Riles	.05	.01
❑	342	Don Robinson	.05	.01
❑	343	Chris Speier	.05	.01
❑	344	Robby Thompson UER	.05	.01
❑	345	Jose Uribe	.05	.01
❑	346	Matt Williams	.25	.08
❑	347	Trevor Wilson RC	.10	.02
❑	348	Juan Agosto	.05	.01
❑	349	Larry Andersen	.05	.01
❑	350A	Alan Ashby ERR	2.00	.75
❑	350B	Alan Ashby COR	.05	.01
❑	351	Kevin Bass	.05	.01
❑	352	Buddy Bell	.10	.02
❑	353	Craig Biggio RC	2.50	1.00
❑	354	Danny Darwin	.05	.01
❑	355	Glenn Davis	.05	.01
❑	356	Jim Deshaies	.05	.01
❑	357	Bill Doran	.05	.01
❑	358	John Fishel	.05	.01
❑	359	Billy Hatcher	.05	.01
❑	360	Bob Knepper	.05	.01
❑	361	Louie Meadows UER	.05	.01
❑	362	Dave Meads	.05	.01
❑	363	Jim Pankovits	.05	.01
❑	364	Terry Puhl	.05	.01
❑	365	Rafael Ramirez	.05	.01
❑	366	Craig Reynolds	.05	.01
❑	367	Mike Scott	.10	.02
❑	368	Nolan Ryan	1.00	.40
❑	369	Dave Smith	.05	.01
❑	370	Gerald Young	.05	.01
❑	371	Hubie Brooks	.05	.01
❑	372	Tim Burke	.05	.01
❑	373	John Dopson	.05	.01
❑	374	Mike R. Fitzgerald	.05	.01
❑	375	Tom Foley	.05	.01
❑	376	Andres Galarraga UER	.10	.02
❑	377	Neal Heaton	.05	.01
❑	378	Joe Hesketh	.05	.01
❑	379	Brian Holman RC	.10	.02
❑	380	Rex Hudler	.05	.01
❑	381	Randy Johnson RC	2.00	.75
❑	381B	R.Johnson Marlboro ERR	25.00	10.00
❑	382	Wallace Johnson	.05	.01
❑	383	Tracy Jones	.05	.01
❑	384	Dave Martinez	.05	.01
❑	385	Dennis Martinez	.10	.02
❑	386	Andy McGaffigan	.05	.01
❑	387	Otis Nixon	.05	.01
❑	388	Johnny Paredes	.05	.01
❑	389	Jeff Parrett	.05	.01
❑	390	Pascual Perez	.05	.01
❑	391	Tim Raines	.10	.02
❑	392	Luis Rivera	.05	.01
❑	393	Nelson Santovenia	.05	.01
❑	394	Bryn Smith	.05	.01
❑	395	Tim Wallach	.05	.01
❑	396	Andy Allanson UER	.05	.01
❑	397	Rod Allen	.05	.01
❑	398	Scott Bailes	.05	.01
❑	399	Tom Candiotti	.05	.01
❑	400	Joe Carter	.10	.02
❑	401	Carmen Castillo UER	.05	.01
❑	402	Dave Clark UER#	.05	.01
❑	403	John Farrell UER	.05	.01
❑	404	Julio Franco	.10	.02
❑	405	Don Gordon	.05	.01
❑	406	Mel Hall	.05	.01
❑	407	Brad Havens	.05	.01
❑	408	Brook Jacoby	.05	.01
❑	409	Doug Jones	.05	.01
❑	410	Jeff Kaiser	.05	.01
❑	411	Luis Medina	.05	.01
❑	412	Cory Snyder	.05	.01
❑	413	Greg Swindell	.05	.01
❑	414	Ron Tingley UER	.05	.01
❑	415	Willie Upshaw	.05	.01
❑	416	Ron Washington	.05	.01
❑	417	Rich Yett	.05	.01
❑	418	Damon Berryhill	.05	.01
❑	419	Mike Bielecki	.05	.01
❑	420	Doug Dascenzo	.05	.01
❑	421	Jody Davis UER	.05	.01
❑	422	Andre Dawson	.10	.02
❑	423	Frank DiPino	.05	.01
❑	424	Shawon Dunston	.05	.01
❑	425	Rich Gossage	.10	.02
❑	426	Mark Grace	.25	.08
❑	427	Mike Harkey RC	.10	.02
❑	428	Darrin Jackson	.10	.02
❑	429	Les Lancaster	.05	.01
❑	430	Vance Law	.05	.01
❑	431	Greg Maddux	.50	.20
❑	432	Jamie Moyer	.10	.02
❑	433	Al Nipper	.05	.01
❑	434	Rafael Palmeiro	.25	.08
❑	435	Pat Perry	.05	.01
❑	436	Jeff Pico	.05	.01
❑	437	Ryne Sandberg	.40	.15
❑	438	Calvin Schiraldi	.05	.01
❑	439	Rick Sutcliffe	.10	.02
❑	440A	Manny Trillo ERR	2.00	.75
❑	440B	Manny Trillo COR	.05	.01
❑	441	Gary Varsho UER	.05	.01
❑	442	Mitch Webster	.05	.01
❑	443	Luis Alicea RC	.25	.08
❑	444	Tom Brunansky	.05	.01
❑	445	Vince Coleman UER	.05	.01
❑	446	John Costello UER	.05	.01
❑	447	Danny Cox	.05	.01
❑	448	Ken Dayley	.05	.01
❑	449	Jose DeLeon	.05	.01
❑	450	Curt Ford	.05	.01
❑	451	Pedro Guerrero	.10	.02
❑	452	Bob Horner	.10	.02
❑	453	Tim Jones	.05	.01
❑	454	Steve Lake	.05	.01
❑	455	Joe Magrane UER	.05	.01
❑	456	Greg Mathews	.05	.01
❑	457	Willie McGee	.10	.02
❑	458	Larry McWilliams	.05	.01
❑	459	Jose Oquendo	.05	.01
❑	460	Tony Pena	.05	.01
❑	461	Terry Pendleton	.10	.02

Card		
❑ 462 Steve Peters UER	.05	.01
❑ 463 Ozzie Smith	.40	.15
❑ 464 Scott Terry	.05	.01
❑ 465 Denny Walling	.05	.01
❑ 466 Todd Worrell	.05	.01
❑ 467 Tony Armas UER	.10	.02
❑ 468 Dante Bichette RC	.40	.15
❑ 469 Bob Boone	.10	.02
❑ 470 Terry Clark	.05	.01
❑ 471 Stu Cliburn	.05	.01
❑ 472 Mike Cook UER	.05	.01
❑ 473 Sherman Corbett	.05	.01
❑ 474 Chili Davis	.10	.02
❑ 475 Brian Downing	.10	.02
❑ 476 Jim Eppard	.05	.01
❑ 477 Chuck Finley	.10	.02
❑ 478 Willie Fraser	.05	.01
❑ 479 Bryan Harvey UER RC	.25	.08
❑ 480 Jack Howell	.05	.01
❑ 481 Wally Joyner UER	.10	.02
❑ 482 Jack Lazorko	.05	.01
❑ 483 Kirk McCaskill	.05	.01
❑ 484 Mark McLemore	.05	.01
❑ 485 Greg Minton	.05	.01
❑ 486 Dan Petry	.05	.01
❑ 487 Johnny Ray	.05	.01
❑ 488 Dick Schofield	.05	.01
❑ 489 Devon White	.10	.02
❑ 490 Mike Witt	.05	.01
❑ 491 Harold Baines	.10	.02
❑ 492 Daryl Boston	.05	.01
❑ 493 Ivan Calderon UER	.05	.01
❑ 494 Mike Diaz	.05	.01
❑ 495 Carlton Fisk	.15	.05
❑ 496 Dave Gallagher	.05	.01
❑ 497 Ozzie Guillen	.10	.02
❑ 498 Shawn Hillegas	.05	.01
❑ 499 Lance Johnson	.05	.01
❑ 500 Barry Jones	.05	.01
❑ 501 Bill Long	.05	.01
❑ 502 Steve Lyons	.05	.01
❑ 503 Fred Manrique	.05	.01
❑ 504 Jack McDowell	.10	.02
❑ 505 Donn Pall	.05	.01
❑ 506 Kelly Paris	.05	.01
❑ 507 Dan Pasqua	.05	.01
❑ 508 Ken Patterson	.05	.01
❑ 509 Melido Perez	.05	.01
❑ 510 Jerry Reuss	.05	.01
❑ 511 Mark Salas	.05	.01
❑ 512 Bobby Thigpen UER	.05	.01
❑ 513 Mike Woodard	.05	.01
❑ 514 Bob Brower	.05	.01
❑ 515 Steve Buechele	.05	.01
❑ 516 Jose Cecena	.05	.01
❑ 517 Cecil Espy	.05	.01
❑ 518 Scott Fletcher	.05	.01
❑ 519 Cecilio Guante	.05	.01
❑ 520 Jose Guzman	.05	.01
❑ 521 Ray Hayward	.05	.01
❑ 522 Charlie Hough	.10	.02
❑ 523 Pete Incaviglia	.05	.01
❑ 524 Mike Jeffcoat	.05	.01
❑ 525 Paul Kilgus	.05	.01
❑ 526 Chad Kreuter RC	.25	.08
❑ 527 Jeff Kunkel	.05	.01
❑ 528 Oddibe McDowell	.05	.01
❑ 529 Pete O'Brien	.05	.01
❑ 530 Geno Petralli	.05	.01
❑ 531 Jeff Russell	.05	.01
❑ 532 Ruben Sierra	.10	.02
❑ 533 Mike Stanley	.05	.01
❑ 534A Ed VandeBerg ERR	2.00	.75
❑ 534B Ed VandeBerg COR	.05	.01
❑ 535 Curtis Wilkerson ERR	.05	.01
❑ 536 Mitch Williams	.05	.01
❑ 537 Bobby Witt UER	.05	.01
❑ 538 Steve Balboni	.05	.01
❑ 539 Scott Bankhead	.05	.01
❑ 540 Scott Bradley	.05	.01
❑ 541 Mickey Brantley	.05	.01
❑ 542 Jay Buhner	.10	.02
❑ 543 Mike Campbell	.05	.01
❑ 544 Darnell Coles	.05	.01
❑ 545 Henry Cotto	.05	.01
❑ 546 Alvin Davis	.05	.01
❑ 547 Mario Diaz	.05	.01
❑ 548 Ken Griffey Jr. RC	6.00	2.50
❑ 549 Erik Hanson RC	.25	.08
❑ 550 Mike Jackson UER	.05	.01
❑ 551 Mark Langston	.05	.01
❑ 552 Edgar Martinez	.25	.08
❑ 553 Bill McGuire	.05	.01
❑ 554 Mike Moore	.05	.01
❑ 555 Jim Presley	.05	.01
❑ 556 Rey Quinones	.05	.01
❑ 557 Jerry Reed	.05	.01
❑ 558 Harold Reynolds	.10	.02
❑ 559 Mike Schooler	.05	.01
❑ 560 Bill Swift	.05	.01
❑ 561 Dave Valle	.05	.01
❑ 562 Steve Bedrosian	.05	.01
❑ 563 Phil Bradley	.05	.01
❑ 564 Don Carman	.05	.01
❑ 565 Bob Dernier	.05	.01
❑ 566 Marvin Freeman	.05	.01
❑ 567 Todd Frohwirth	.05	.01
❑ 568 Greg Gross	.05	.01
❑ 569 Kevin Gross	.05	.01
❑ 570 Greg A. Harris	.05	.01
❑ 571 Von Hayes	.05	.01
❑ 572 Chris James	.05	.01
❑ 573 Steve Jeltz	.05	.01
❑ 574 Ron Jones UER	.10	.02
❑ 575 Ricky Jordan RC	.25	.08
❑ 576 Mike Maddux	.05	.01
❑ 577 David Palmer	.05	.01
❑ 578 Lance Parrish	.10	.02
❑ 579 Shane Rawley	.05	.01
❑ 580 Bruce Ruffin	.05	.01
❑ 581 Juan Samuel	.05	.01
❑ 582 Mike Schmidt	.50	.20
❑ 583 Kent Tekulve	.05	.01
❑ 584 Milt Thompson UER	.05	.01
❑ 585 Jose Alvarez RC	.10	.02
❑ 586 Paul Assenmacher	.05	.01
❑ 587 Bruce Benedict	.05	.01
❑ 588 Jeff Blauser	.05	.01
❑ 589 Terry Blocker	.05	.01
❑ 590 Ron Gant	.10	.02
❑ 591 Tom Glavine	.25	.08
❑ 592 Tommy Gregg	.05	.01
❑ 593 Albert Hall	.05	.01
❑ 594 Dion James	.05	.01
❑ 595 Rick Mahler	.05	.01
❑ 596 Dale Murphy	.15	.05
❑ 597 Gerald Perry	.05	.01
❑ 598 Charlie Puleo	.05	.01
❑ 599 Ted Simmons	.10	.02
❑ 600 Pete Smith	.05	.01
❑ 601 Zane Smith	.05	.01
❑ 602 John Smoltz RC	1.50	.60
❑ 603 Bruce Sutter	.10	.02
❑ 604 Andres Thomas	.05	.01
❑ 605 Ozzie Virgil	.05	.01
❑ 606 Brady Anderson RC	.40	.15
❑ 607 Jeff Ballard	.05	.01
❑ 608 Jose Bautista RC	.10	.02
❑ 609 Ken Gerhart	.05	.01
❑ 610 Terry Kennedy	.05	.01
❑ 611 Eddie Murray	.25	.08
❑ 612 Carl Nichols UER	.05	.01
❑ 613 Tom Niedenfuer	.05	.01
❑ 614 Joe Orsulak	.05	.01
❑ 615 Oswald Peraza UER	.05	.01
❑ 616A Bill Ripken Rick Face	15.00	6.00
❑ 616B Bill Ripken Whiteout	120.00	60.00
❑ 616C Bill Ripken White Scribble	25.00	10.00
❑ 616D Bill Ripken Black Scribble	15.00	6.00
❑ 616E Bill Ripken Black Box	5.00	2.00
❑ 617 Cal Ripken	.75	.30
❑ 618 Dave Schmidt	.05	.01
❑ 619 Rick Schu	.05	.01
❑ 620 Larry Sheets	.05	.01
❑ 621 Doug Sisk	.05	.01
❑ 622 Pete Stanicek	.05	.01
❑ 623 Mickey Tettleton	.05	.01
❑ 624 Jay Tibbs	.05	.01
❑ 625 Jim Traber	.05	.01
❑ 626 Mark Williamson	.05	.01
❑ 627 Craig Worthington	.05	.01
❑ 628 Jose Canseco 40/40	.25	.08
❑ 629 Tom Browning Perfect	.05	.01
❑ 630 R.Alomar/S.Alomar	.25	.08
❑ 631 W.Clark/R.Palmeiro	.15	.05
❑ 632 D.Strawberry/W.Clark	.10	.02
❑ 633 W.Boggs/C.Lansford	.10	.02
❑ 634 McGwire/Cans/Stein	.75	.30
❑ 635 M.Davis/D.Gooden	.05	.01
❑ 636 D.Jackson/D.Cone UER	.05	.01
❑ 637 C.Sabo/B.Bonilla UER	.10	.02
❑ 638 A.Galarraga/G.Perry UER	.05	.01
❑ 639 K.Puckett/E.Davis	.15	.05
❑ 640 S.Wilson/C.Drew	.05	.01
❑ 641 K.Brown/K.Reimer	.25	.08
❑ 642 B.Pounders RC/J.Clark	.10	.02
❑ 643 M.Capel/D.Hall	.05	.01
❑ 644 J.Girardi RC/R.Roomes	.40	.15
❑ 645 L.Harris RC/M.Brown	.25	.08
❑ 646 L.De Los Santos/J.Campbell	.05	.01
❑ 647 R.Kramer/M.Garcia	.05	.01
❑ 648 T.Lovullo RC/R.Palacios	.10	.02
❑ 649 J.Corsi/B.Milacki	.05	.01
❑ 650 G.Hall/M.Rochford	.05	.01
❑ 651 T.Taylor/V.Lovelace RC	.10	.02
❑ 652 K.Hill RC/D.Cook	.25	.08
❑ 653 S.Service/S.Turner	.05	.01
❑ 654 CL: Oakland/Mets Dodgers/Red Sox (10 Henderson;#	.05	.01
❑ 655A CL: Twins/Tigers ERR Reds/Brewers (179 Boslo and	.05	.01
❑ 655B CL: Twins/Tigers COR Reds/Brewers (179 Boslo but	.05	.01
❑ 656 CL: Pirates/Blue Jays Yankees/Royals (225 Jess B	.05	.01
❑ 657 CL: Padres/Giants Astros/Expos (367/368 wrong)	.05	.01
❑ 658 CL: Indians/Cubs Cardinals/Angels (449 Deleon)	.05	.01
❑ 659 CL: White Sox/Rangers Mariners/Phillies	.05	.01
❑ 660 CL: Braves/Orioles Specials/Checklists (632 hyph	.05	.01

1989 Fleer Update

Card		
❑ COMP.FACT.SET (132)	5.00	2.00
❑ 1 Phil Bradley	.05	.01
❑ 2 Mike Devereaux	.05	.01
❑ 3 Steve Finley RC	.75	.30
❑ 4 Kevin Hickey	.05	.01
❑ 5 Brian Holton	.05	.01
❑ 6 Bob Milacki	.05	.01
❑ 7 Randy Milligan	.05	.01
❑ 8 John Dopson	.05	.01
❑ 9 Nick Esasky	.05	.01
❑ 10 Rob Murphy	.05	.01
❑ 11 Jim Abbott RC	1.00	.40
❑ 12 Bert Blyleven	.10	.02
❑ 13 Jeff Manto RC	.10	.02
❑ 14 Bob McClure	.05	.01
❑ 15 Lance Parrish	.10	.02
❑ 16 Lee Stevens RC	.25	.08
❑ 17 Claudell Washington	.05	.01

❑ 18 Mark Davis RC .25 .08
❑ 19 Eric King .05 .01
❑ 20 Ron Kittle .05 .01
❑ 21 Matt Merullo .05 .01
❑ 22 Steve Rosenberg .05 .01
❑ 23 Robin Ventura RC .75 .30
❑ 24 Keith Atherton .05 .01
❑ 25 Albert Belle RC 1.00 .40
❑ 26 Jerry Browne .05 .01
❑ 27 Felix Fermin .05 .01
❑ 28 Brad Komminsk .05 .01
❑ 29 Pete O'Brien .05 .01
❑ 30 Mike Brumley .05 .01
❑ 31 Tracy Jones .05 .01
❑ 32 Mike Schwabe .05 .01
❑ 33 Gary Ward .05 .01
❑ 34 Frank Williams .05 .01
❑ 35 Kevin Appier RC .50 .20
❑ 36 Bob Boone .10 .02
❑ 37 Luis DeLosSantos .05 .01
❑ 38 Jim Eisenreich .05 .01
❑ 39 Jaime Navarro RC .10 .02
❑ 40 Billy Spiers RC .25 .08
❑ 41 Greg Vaughn RC .40 .15
❑ 42 Randy Veres .05 .01
❑ 43 Wally Backman .05 .01
❑ 44 Shane Rawley .05 .01
❑ 45 Steve Balboni .05 .01
❑ 46 Jesse Barfield .10 .02
❑ 47 Alvaro Espinoza .05 .01
❑ 48 Bob Geren RC .05 .01
❑ 49 Mel Hall .05 .01
❑ 50 Andy Hawkins .05 .01
❑ 51 Hensley Meulens RC .10 .02
❑ 52 Steve Sax .05 .01
❑ 53 Deion Sanders RC 1.50 .60
❑ 54 Rickey Henderson .25 .08
❑ 55 Mike Moore .05 .01
❑ 56 Tony Phillips .05 .01
❑ 57 Greg Briley .10 .02
❑ 58 Gene Harris RC .10 .02
❑ 59 Randy Johnson 2.50 1.00
❑ 60 Jeffrey Leonard .05 .01
❑ 61 Dennis Powell .05 .01
❑ 62 Omar Vizquel RC 1.00 .40
❑ 63 Kevin Brown .25 .08
❑ 64 Julio Franco .10 .02
❑ 65 Jamie Moyer .10 .02
❑ 66 Rafael Palmeiro .25 .08
❑ 67 Nolan Ryan 1.50 .60
❑ 68 Francisco Cabrera RC .10 .02
❑ 69 Junior Felix RC .10 .02
❑ 70 Al Leiter .25 .08
❑ 71 Alex Sanchez RC .05 .01
❑ 72 Geronimo Berroa .05 .01
❑ 73 Derek Lilliquist RC .10 .02
❑ 74 Lonnie Smith .05 .01
❑ 75 Jeff Treadway .05 .01
❑ 76 Paul Kilgus .05 .01
❑ 77 Lloyd McClendon .05 .01
❑ 78 Scott Sanderson .05 .01
❑ 79 Dwight Smith RC .25 .08
❑ 80 Jerome Walton RC .25 .08
❑ 81 Mitch Williams .05 .01
❑ 82 Steve Wilson .10 .02
❑ 83 Todd Benzinger .05 .01
❑ 84 Ken Griffey Sr. .10 .02
❑ 85 Rick Mahler .05 .01
❑ 86 Rolando Roomes .05 .01
❑ 87 Scott Scudder RC .10 .02
❑ 88 Jim Clancy .05 .01
❑ 89 Rick Rhoden .05 .01
❑ 90 Dan Schatzeder .05 .01
❑ 91 Mike Morgan .05 .01
❑ 92 Eddie Murray .25 .08
❑ 93 Willie Randolph .10 .02
❑ 94 Ray Searage .05 .01
❑ 95 Mike Aldrete .05 .01
❑ 96 Kevin Gross .05 .01
❑ 97 Mark Langston .05 .01
❑ 98 Spike Owen .05 .01
❑ 99 Zane Smith .05 .01
❑ 100 Don Aase .05 .01
❑ 101 Barry Lyons .05 .01
❑ 102 Juan Samuel .05 .01
❑ 103 Wally Whitehurst RC .10 .02
❑ 104 Dennis Cook .05 .01
❑ 105 Len Dykstra .10 .02
❑ 106 Charlie Hayes .25 .08
❑ 107 Tommy Herr .05 .01
❑ 108 Ken Howell .05 .01
❑ 109 John Kruk .10 .02
❑ 110 Roger McDowell .05 .01
❑ 111 Terry Mulholland .05 .01
❑ 112 Jeff Parrett .05 .01
❑ 113 Neal Heaton .05 .01
❑ 114 Jeff King .05 .01
❑ 115 Randy Kramer .05 .01
❑ 116 Bill Landrum .05 .01
❑ 117 Cris Carpenter RC * .10 .02
❑ 118 Frank DiPino .05 .01
❑ 119 Ken Hill .25 .08
❑ 120 Dan Quisenberry .05 .01
❑ 121 Milt Thompson .05 .01
❑ 122 Todd Zeile RC .40 .15
❑ 123 Jack Clark .10 .02
❑ 124 Bruce Hurst .05 .01
❑ 125 Mark Parent .05 .01
❑ 126 Bip Roberts .05 .01
❑ 127 Jeff Brantley UER RC .25 .08
❑ 128 Terry Kennedy .05 .01
❑ 129 Mike LaCoss .05 .01
❑ 130 Greg Litton .05 .01
❑ 131 Mike Schmidt SPEC .75 .30
❑ 132 Checklist 1-132 .05 .01

1990 Fleer

❑ COMPLETE SET (660) 15.00 6.00
❑ COMP.RETAIL SET (660) 15.00 6.00
❑ COMP.HOBBY SET (672) 15.00 6.00
❑ 1 Lance Blankenship .05 .01
❑ 2 Todd Burns .05 .01
❑ 3 Jose Canseco .15 .05
❑ 4 Jim Corsi .05 .01
❑ 5 Storm Davis .05 .01
❑ 6 Dennis Eckersley .10 .02
❑ 7 Mike Gallego .05 .01
❑ 8 Ron Hassey .05 .01
❑ 9 Dave Henderson .05 .01
❑ 10 Rickey Henderson .25 .08
❑ 11 Rick Honeycutt .05 .01
❑ 12 Stan Javier .05 .01
❑ 13 Felix Jose .05 .01
❑ 14 Carney Lansford .10 .02
❑ 15 Mark McGwire 1.00 .40
❑ 16 Mike Moore .05 .01
❑ 17 Gene Nelson .05 .01
❑ 18 Dave Parker .10 .02
❑ 19 Tony Phillips .05 .01
❑ 20 Terry Steinbach .05 .01
❑ 21 Dave Stewart .10 .02
❑ 22 Walt Weiss .05 .01
❑ 23 Bob Welch .05 .01
❑ 24 Curt Young .05 .01
❑ 25 Paul Assenmacher .05 .01
❑ 26 Damon Berryhill .05 .01
❑ 27 Mike Bielecki .05 .01
❑ 28 Kevin Blankenship .05 .01
❑ 29 Andre Dawson .10 .02
❑ 30 Shawon Dunston .05 .01
❑ 31 Joe Girardi .15 .05
❑ 32 Mark Grace .15 .05
❑ 33 Mike Harkey .05 .01
❑ 34 Paul Kilgus .05 .01
❑ 35 Les Lancaster .05 .01
❑ 36 Vance Law .05 .01
❑ 37 Greg Maddux .40 .15
❑ 38 Lloyd McClendon .05 .01
❑ 39 Jeff Pico .05 .01
❑ 40 Ryne Sandberg .40 .15
❑ 41 Scott Sanderson .05 .01
❑ 42 Dwight Smith .05 .01
❑ 43 Rick Sutcliffe .10 .02
❑ 44 Jerome Walton .05 .01
❑ 45 Mitch Webster .05 .01
❑ 46 Curt Wilkerson .05 .01
❑ 47 Dean Wilkins RC .05 .01
❑ 48 Mitch Williams .05 .01
❑ 49 Steve Wilson .05 .01
❑ 50 Steve Bedrosian .05 .01
❑ 51 Mike Benjamin RC .10 .02
❑ 52 Jeff Brantley .05 .01
❑ 53 Brett Butler .10 .02
❑ 54 Will Clark UER .10 .02
❑ 55 Kelly Downs .05 .01
❑ 56 Scott Garrelts .05 .01
❑ 57 Atlee Hammaker .05 .01
❑ 58 Terry Kennedy .05 .01
❑ 59 Mike LaCoss .05 .01
❑ 60 Craig Lefferts .05 .01
❑ 61 Greg Litton .05 .01
❑ 62 Candy Maldonado .05 .01
❑ 63 Kirt Manwaring UER
(No '88 Phoenix stats
as note .05 .01
❑ 64 Randy McCament RC .05 .01
❑ 65 Kevin Mitchell .05 .01
❑ 66 Donell Nixon .05 .01
❑ 67 Ken Oberkfell .05 .01
❑ 68 Rick Reuschel .05 .01
❑ 69 Ernest Riles .05 .01
❑ 70 Don Robinson .05 .01
❑ 71 Pat Sheridan .05 .01
❑ 72 Chris Speier .05 .01
❑ 73 Robby Thompson .05 .01
❑ 74 Jose Uribe .05 .01
❑ 75 Matt Williams .10 .02
❑ 76 George Bell .05 .01
❑ 77 Pat Borders .05 .01
❑ 78 John Cerutti .05 .01
❑ 79 Junior Felix .05 .01
❑ 80 Tony Fernandez .05 .01
❑ 81 Mike Flanagan .05 .01
❑ 82 Mauro Gozzo RC .05 .01
❑ 83 Kelly Gruber .05 .01
❑ 84 Tom Henke .05 .01
❑ 85 Jimmy Key .10 .02
❑ 86 Manny Lee .05 .01
❑ 87 Nelson Liriano UER
(Should say %%led the
IL~ ins .05 .01
❑ 88 Lee Mazzilli .05 .01
❑ 89 Fred McGriff .25 .08
❑ 90 Lloyd Moseby .05 .01
❑ 91 Rance Mulliniks .05 .01
❑ 92 Alex Sanchez .05 .01
❑ 93 Dave Stieb .10 .02
❑ 94 Todd Stottlemyre .10 .02
❑ 95 Duane Ward UER
(Double line of '87
Syracuse stat .05 .01
❑ 96 David Wells .10 .02
❑ 97 Ernie Whitt .05 .01
❑ 98 Frank Wills .05 .01
❑ 99 Mookie Wilson .10 .02
❑ 100 Kevin Appier .10 .02
❑ 101 Luis Aquino .05 .01
❑ 102 Bob Boone .10 .02
❑ 103 George Brett .60 .25
❑ 104 Jose DeJesus .05 .01
❑ 105 Luis De Los Santos .05 .01
❑ 106 Jim Eisenreich .05 .01
❑ 107 Steve Farr .05 .01
❑ 108 Tom Gordon .10 .02
❑ 109 Mark Gubicza .05 .01
❑ 110 Bo Jackson .25 .08
❑ 111 Terry Leach .05 .01
❑ 112 Charlie Leibrandt .05 .01
❑ 113 Rick Luecken RC .05 .01
❑ 114 Mike Macfarlane .05 .01

❑ 115 Jeff Montgomery .10 .02
❑ 116 Bret Saberhagen .10 .02
❑ 117 Kevin Seitzer .05 .01
❑ 118 Kurt Stillwell .05 .01
❑ 119 Pat Tabler .05 .01
❑ 120 Danny Tartabull .05 .01
❑ 121 Gary Thurman .05 .01
❑ 122 Frank White .10 .02
❑ 123 Willie Wilson .05 .01
❑ 124 Matt Winters RC .05 .01
❑ 125 Jim Abbott .15 .05
❑ 126 Tony Armas .05 .01
❑ 127 Dante Bichette .10 .02
❑ 128 Bert Blyleven .10 .02
❑ 129 Chili Davis .10 .02
❑ 130 Brian Downing .05 .01
❑ 131 Mike Fetters RC .25 .08
❑ 132 Chuck Finley .10 .02
❑ 133 Willie Fraser .05 .01
❑ 134 Bryan Harvey .05 .01
❑ 135 Jack Howell .05 .01
❑ 136 Wally Joyner .10 .02
❑ 137 Jeff Manto .05 .01
❑ 138 Kirk McCaskill .05 .01
❑ 139 Bob McClure .05 .01
❑ 140 Greg Minton .05 .01
❑ 141 Lance Parrish .05 .01
❑ 142 Dan Petry .05 .01
❑ 143 Johnny Ray .05 .01
❑ 144 Dick Schofield .05 .01
❑ 145 Lee Stevens .10 .02
❑ 146 Claudell Washington .05 .01
❑ 147 Devon White .10 .02
❑ 148 Mike Witt .05 .01
❑ 149 Roberto Alomar .15 .05
❑ 150 Sandy Alomar Jr. .10 .02
❑ 151 Andy Benes .10 .02
❑ 152 Jack Clark .10 .02
❑ 153 Pat Clements .05 .01
❑ 154 Joey Cora .10 .02
❑ 155 Mark Davis .05 .01
❑ 156 Mark Grant .05 .01
❑ 157 Tony Gwynn .30 .10
❑ 158 Greg W. Harris .05 .01
❑ 159 Bruce Hurst .05 .01
❑ 160 Darrin Jackson .05 .01
❑ 161 Chris James .05 .01
❑ 162 Carmelo Martinez .05 .01
❑ 163 Mike Pagliarulo .05 .01
❑ 164 Mark Parent .05 .01
❑ 165 Dennis Rasmussen .05 .01
❑ 166 Bip Roberts .05 .01
❑ 167 Benito Santiago .10 .02
❑ 168 Calvin Schiraldi .05 .01
❑ 169 Eric Show .05 .01
❑ 170 Garry Templeton .05 .01
❑ 171 Ed Whitson .05 .01
❑ 172 Brady Anderson .10 .02
❑ 173 Jeff Ballard .05 .01
❑ 174 Phil Bradley .05 .01
❑ 175 Mike Devereaux .05 .01
❑ 176 Steve Finley .10 .02
❑ 177 Pete Harnisch .05 .01
❑ 178 Kevin Hickey .05 .01
❑ 179 Brian Holton .05 .01
❑ 180 Ben McDonald RC .25 .08
❑ 181 Bob Melvin .05 .01
❑ 182 Bob Milacki .05 .01
❑ 183 Randy Milligan UER
(Double line of
'87 stats) .05 .01
❑ 184 Gregg Olson .10 .02
❑ 185 Joe Orsulak .05 .01
❑ 186 Bill Ripken .05 .01
❑ 187 Cal Ripken .75 .30
❑ 188 Dave Schmidt .05 .01
❑ 189 Larry Sheets .05 .01
❑ 190 Mickey Tettleton .05 .01
❑ 191 Mark Thurmond .05 .01
❑ 192 Jay Tibbs .05 .01
❑ 193 Jim Traber .05 .01
❑ 194 Mark Williamson .05 .01
❑ 195 Craig Worthington .05 .01
❑ 196 Don Aase .05 .01
❑ 197 Blaine Beatty RC .05 .01
❑ 198 Mark Carreon .05 .01
❑ 199 Gary Carter .10 .02
❑ 200 David Cone .10 .02
❑ 201 Ron Darling .05 .01
❑ 202 Kevin Elster .05 .01
❑ 203 Sid Fernandez .05 .01
❑ 204 Dwight Gooden .10 .02
❑ 205 Keith Hernandez .10 .02
❑ 206 Jeff Innis RC .05 .01
❑ 207 Gregg Jefferies .10 .02
❑ 208 Howard Johnson .05 .01
❑ 209 Barry Lyons UER
(Double line of
'87 stats) .05 .01
❑ 210 Dave Magadan .05 .01
❑ 211 Kevin McReynolds .05 .01
❑ 212 Jeff Musselman .05 .01
❑ 213 Randy Myers .10 .02
❑ 214 Bob Ojeda .05 .01
❑ 215 Juan Samuel .05 .01
❑ 216 Mackey Sasser .05 .01
❑ 217 Darryl Strawberry .10 .02
❑ 218 Tim Teufel .05 .01
❑ 219 Frank Viola .05 .01
❑ 220 Juan Agosto .05 .01
❑ 221 Larry Andersen .05 .01
❑ 222 Eric Anthony RC .10 .02
❑ 223 Kevin Bass .05 .01
❑ 224 Craig Biggio .25 .08
❑ 225 Ken Caminiti .10 .02
❑ 226 Jim Clancy .05 .01
❑ 227 Danny Darwin .05 .01
❑ 228 Glenn Davis .05 .01
❑ 229 Jim Deshaies .05 .01
❑ 230 Bill Doran .05 .01
❑ 231 Bob Forsch .05 .01
❑ 232 Brian Meyer .05 .01
❑ 233 Terry Puhl .05 .01
❑ 234 Rafael Ramirez .05 .01
❑ 235 Rick Rhoden .05 .01
❑ 236 Dan Schatzeder .05 .01
❑ 237 Mike Scott .05 .01
❑ 238 Dave Smith .05 .01
❑ 239 Alex Trevino .05 .01
❑ 240 Glenn Wilson .05 .01
❑ 241 Gerald Young .05 .01
❑ 242 Tom Brunansky .05 .01
❑ 243 Cris Carpenter .05 .01
❑ 244 Alex Cole RC .10 .02
❑ 245 Vince Coleman .05 .01
❑ 246 John Costello .05 .01
❑ 247 Ken Dayley .05 .01
❑ 248 Jose DeLeon .05 .01
❑ 249 Frank DiPino .05 .01
❑ 250 Pedro Guerrero .05 .01
❑ 251 Ken Hill .10 .02
❑ 252 Joe Magrane .05 .01
❑ 253 Willie McGee UER
(No decimal point
before 353) .10 .02
❑ 254 John Morris .05 .01
❑ 255 Jose Oquendo .05 .01
❑ 256 Tony Pena .05 .01
❑ 257 Terry Pendleton .10 .02
❑ 258 Ted Power .05 .01
❑ 259 Dan Quisenberry .05 .01
❑ 260 Ozzie Smith .40 .15
❑ 261 Scott Terry .05 .01
❑ 262 Milt Thompson .05 .01
❑ 263 Denny Walling .05 .01
❑ 264 Todd Worrell .05 .01
❑ 265 Todd Zeile .10 .02
❑ 266 Marty Barrett .05 .01
❑ 267 Mike Boddicker .05 .01
❑ 268 Wade Boggs .15 .05
❑ 269 Ellis Burks .15 .05
❑ 270 Rick Cerone .05 .01
❑ 271 Roger Clemens 1.00 .40
❑ 272 John Dopson .05 .01
❑ 273 Nick Esasky .05 .01
❑ 274 Dwight Evans .15 .05
❑ 275 Wes Gardner .05 .01
❑ 276 Rich Gedman .05 .01
❑ 277 Mike Greenwell .05 .01
❑ 278 Danny Heep .05 .01
❑ 279 Eric Hetzel .05 .01
❑ 280 Dennis Lamp .05 .01
❑ 281 Rob Murphy UER
('89 stats say Reds,
should say R .05 .01
❑ 282 Joe Price .05 .01
❑ 283 Carlos Quintana .05 .01
❑ 284 Jody Reed .05 .01
❑ 285 Luis Rivera .05 .01
❑ 286 Kevin Romine .05 .01
❑ 287 Lee Smith .10 .02
❑ 288 Mike Smithson .05 .01
❑ 289 Bob Stanley .05 .01
❑ 290 Harold Baines .10 .02
❑ 291 Kevin Brown .10 .02
❑ 292 Steve Buechele .05 .01
❑ 293 Scott Coolbaugh RC .05 .01
❑ 294 Jack Daugherty RC .05 .01
❑ 295 Cecil Espy .05 .01
❑ 296 Julio Franco .10 .02
❑ 297 Juan Gonzalez RC 1.00 .40
❑ 298 Cecilio Guante .05 .01
❑ 299 Drew Hall .05 .01
❑ 300 Charlie Hough .10 .02
❑ 301 Pete Incaviglia .05 .01
❑ 302 Mike Jeffcoat .05 .01
❑ 303 Chad Kreuter .05 .01
❑ 304 Jeff Kunkel .05 .01
❑ 305 Rick Leach .05 .01
❑ 306 Fred Manrique .05 .01
❑ 307 Jamie Moyer .10 .02
❑ 308 Rafael Palmeiro .15 .05
❑ 309 Geno Petralli .05 .01
❑ 310 Kevin Reimer .05 .01
❑ 311 Kenny Rogers .10 .02
❑ 312 Jeff Russell .05 .01
❑ 313 Nolan Ryan 1.00 .40
❑ 314 Ruben Sierra .10 .02
❑ 315 Bobby Witt .05 .01
❑ 316 Chris Bosio .05 .01
❑ 317 Glenn Braggs UER
(Stats say 111 K's,
but bio say .05 .01
❑ 318 Greg Brock .05 .01
❑ 319 Chuck Crim .05 .01
❑ 320 Rob Deer .05 .01
❑ 321 Mike Felder .05 .01
❑ 322 Tom Filer .05 .01
❑ 323 Tony Fossas RC .05 .01
❑ 324 Jim Gantner .05 .01
❑ 325 Darryl Hamilton .05 .01
❑ 326 Teddy Higuera .05 .01
❑ 327 Mark Knudson .05 .01
❑ 328 Bill Krueger UER
('86 stats missing) .05 .01
❑ 329 Tim McIntosh RC .10 .02
❑ 330 Paul Molitor .10 .02
❑ 331 Jaime Navarro .05 .01
❑ 332 Charlie O'Brien .05 .01
❑ 333 Jeff Peterek RC .05 .01
❑ 334 Dan Plesac .05 .01
❑ 335 Jerry Reuss .05 .01
❑ 336 Gary Sheffield .25 .08
❑ 337 Bill Spiers .05 .01
❑ 338 B.J. Surhoff .10 .02
❑ 339 Greg Vaughn .05 .01
❑ 340 Robin Yount .40 .15
❑ 341 Hubie Brooks .05 .01
❑ 342 Tim Burke .05 .01
❑ 343 Mike Fitzgerald .05 .01
❑ 344 Tom Foley .05 .01
❑ 345 Andres Galarraga .10 .02
❑ 346 Damaso Garcia .05 .01
❑ 347 Marquis Grissom RC .40 .15
❑ 348 Kevin Gross .05 .01
❑ 349 Joe Hesketh .05 .01
❑ 350 Jeff Huson RC .05 .01
❑ 351 Wallace Johnson .05 .01
❑ 352 Mark Langston .05 .01
❑ 353A Dave Martinez Yellow 2.00 .75
❑ 353B Dave Martinez Red .05 .01
❑ 354 Dennis Martinez UER
('87 ERA is 616,
should be 6 .10 .02
❑ 355 Andy McGaffigan .05 .01
❑ 356 Otis Nixon .05 .01
❑ 357 Spike Owen .05 .01
❑ 358 Pascual Perez .05 .01

❑ 359 Tim Raines .10 .02
❑ 360 Nelson Santovenia .05 .01
❑ 361 Bryn Smith .05 .01
❑ 362 Zane Smith .05 .01
❑ 363 Larry Walker RC 1.00 .40
❑ 364 Tim Wallach .05 .01
❑ 365 Rick Aguilera .10 .02
❑ 366 Allan Anderson .05 .01
❑ 367 Wally Backman .05 .01
❑ 368 Doug Baker .05 .01
❑ 369 Juan Berenguer .05 .01
❑ 370 Randy Bush .05 .01
❑ 371 Carmelo Castillo .05 .01
❑ 372 Mike Dyer RC .05 .01
❑ 373 Gary Gaetti .10 .02
❑ 374 Greg Gagne .05 .01
❑ 375 Dan Gladden .05 .01
❑ 376 German Gonzalez UER
(Bio says 31 saves in
'88, b .05 .01
❑ 377 Brian Harper .05 .01
❑ 378 Kent Hrbek .10 .02
❑ 379 Gene Larkin .05 .01
❑ 380 Tim Laudner UER
(No decimal point
before '85 BA .05 .01
❑ 381 John Moses .05 .01
❑ 382 Al Newman .05 .01
❑ 383 Kirby Puckett .25 .08
❑ 384 Shane Rawley .05 .01
❑ 385 Jeff Reardon .10 .02
❑ 386 Roy Smith .05 .01
❑ 387 Gary Wayne .05 .01
❑ 388 Dave West .05 .01
❑ 389 Tim Belcher .05 .01
❑ 390 Tim Crews UER
(Stats say 163 IP for
'83, but bio .05 .01
❑ 391 Mike Davis .05 .01
❑ 392 Rick Dempsey .05 .01
❑ 393 Kirk Gibson .10 .02
❑ 394 Jose Gonzalez .05 .01
❑ 395 Alfredo Griffin .05 .01
❑ 396 Jeff Hamilton .05 .01
❑ 397 Lenny Harris .05 .01
❑ 398 Mickey Hatcher .05 .01
❑ 399 Orel Hershiser .10 .02
❑ 400 Jay Howell .05 .01
❑ 401 Mike Marshall .05 .01
❑ 402 Ramon Martinez .05 .01
❑ 403 Mike Morgan .05 .01
❑ 404 Eddie Murray .25 .08
❑ 405 Alejandro Pena .05 .01
❑ 406 Willie Randolph .10 .02
❑ 407 Mike Scioscia .05 .01
❑ 408 Ray Searage .05 .01
❑ 409 Fernando Valenzuela .10 .02
❑ 410 Jose Vizcaino RC .25 .08
❑ 411 John Wetteland .25 .08
❑ 412 Jack Armstrong .05 .01
❑ 413 Todd Benzinger UER
(Bio says .323 at
Pawtucket, .05 .01
❑ 414 Tim Birtsas .05 .01
❑ 415 Tom Browning .05 .01
❑ 416 Norm Charlton .05 .01
❑ 417 Eric Davis .10 .02
❑ 418 Rob Dibble .10 .02
❑ 419 John Franco .10 .02
❑ 420 Ken Griffey Sr. .10 .02
❑ 421 Chris Hammond RC .10 .02
❑ 422 Danny Jackson .05 .01
❑ 423 Barry Larkin .15 .05
❑ 424 Tim Leary .05 .01
❑ 425 Rick Mahler .05 .01
❑ 426 Joe Oliver .05 .01
❑ 427 Paul O'Neill .15 .05
❑ 428 Luis Quinones UER
('86-'88 stats are
omitted fro .05 .01
❑ 429 Jeff Reed .05 .01
❑ 430 Jose Rijo .05 .01
❑ 431 Ron Robinson .05 .01
❑ 432 Rolando Roomes .05 .01
❑ 433 Chris Sabo .05 .01
❑ 434 Scott Scudder .05 .01
❑ 435 Herm Winningham .05 .01
❑ 436 Steve Balboni .05 .01
❑ 437 Jesse Barfield .05 .01
❑ 438 Mike Blowers RC .10 .02
❑ 439 Tom Brookens .05 .01
❑ 440 Greg Cadaret .05 .01
❑ 441 Alvaro Espinoza UER
(Career games say
218, shoul .05 .01
❑ 442 Bob Geren .05 .01
❑ 443 Lee Guetterman .05 .01
❑ 444 Mel Hall .05 .01
❑ 445 Andy Hawkins .05 .01
❑ 446 Roberto Kelly .05 .01
❑ 447 Don Mattingly .60 .25
❑ 448 Lance McCullers .05 .01
❑ 449 Hensley Meulens .05 .01
❑ 450 Dale Mohorcic .05 .01
❑ 451 Clay Parker .05 .01
❑ 452 Eric Plunk .05 .01
❑ 453 Dave Righetti .05 .01
❑ 454 Deion Sanders .25 .08
❑ 455 Steve Sax .05 .01
❑ 456 Don Slaught .05 .01
❑ 457 Walt Terrell .05 .01
❑ 458 Dave Winfield .10 .02
❑ 459 Jay Bell .10 .02
❑ 460 Rafael Belliard .05 .01
❑ 461 Barry Bonds 1.00 .40
❑ 462 Bobby Bonilla .10 .02
❑ 463 Sid Bream .05 .01
❑ 464 Benny Distefano .05 .01
❑ 465 Doug Drabek .05 .01
❑ 466 Jim Gott .05 .01
❑ 467 Billy Hatcher UER
(.1 hits for Cubs
in 1984) .05 .01
❑ 468 Neal Heaton .05 .01
❑ 469 Jeff King .05 .01
❑ 470 Bob Kipper .05 .01
❑ 471 Randy Kramer .05 .01
❑ 472 Bill Landrum .05 .01
❑ 473 Mike LaValliere .05 .01
❑ 474 Jose Lind .05 .01
❑ 475 Junior Ortiz .05 .01
❑ 476 Gary Redus .05 .01
❑ 477 Rick Reed RC .25 .08
❑ 478 R.J. Reynolds .05 .01
❑ 479 Jeff D. Robinson .05 .01
❑ 480 John Smiley .05 .01
❑ 481 Andy Van Slyke .15 .05
❑ 482 Bob Walk .05 .01
❑ 483 Andy Allanson .05 .01
❑ 484 Scott Bailes .05 .01
❑ 485 Albert Belle .25 .08
❑ 486 Bud Black .05 .01
❑ 487 Jerry Browne .05 .01
❑ 488 Tom Candiotti .05 .01
❑ 489 Joe Carter .10 .02
❑ 490 Dave Clark
(No '84 stats) .05 .01
❑ 491 John Farrell .05 .01
❑ 492 Felix Fermin .05 .01
❑ 493 Brook Jacoby .05 .01
❑ 494 Dion James .05 .01
❑ 495 Doug Jones .05 .01
❑ 496 Brad Komminsk .05 .01
❑ 497 Rod Nichols .05 .01
❑ 498 Pete O'Brien .05 .01
❑ 499 Steve Olin RC .10 .02
❑ 500 Jesse Orosco .05 .01
❑ 501 Joel Skinner .05 .01
❑ 502 Cory Snyder .05 .01
❑ 503 Greg Swindell .05 .01
❑ 504 Rich Yett .05 .01
❑ 505 Scott Bankhead .05 .01
❑ 506 Scott Bradley .05 .01
❑ 507 Greg Briley UER
(28 SB's in bio,
but 27 in stats .05 .01
❑ 508 Jay Buhner .10 .02
❑ 509 Darnell Coles .05 .01
❑ 510 Keith Comstock .05 .01
❑ 511 Henry Cotto .05 .01
❑ 512 Alvin Davis .05 .01
❑ 513 Ken Griffey Jr. .75 .30
❑ 514 Erik Hanson .05 .01
❑ 515 Gene Harris .05 .01
❑ 516 Brian Holman .05 .01
❑ 517 Mike Jackson .05 .01
❑ 518 Randy Johnson .50 .20
❑ 519 Jeffrey Leonard .05 .01
❑ 520 Edgar Martinez .15 .05
❑ 521 Dennis Powell .05 .01
❑ 522 Jim Presley .05 .01
❑ 523 Jerry Reed .05 .01
❑ 524 Harold Reynolds .10 .02
❑ 525 Mike Schooler .05 .01
❑ 526 Bill Swift .05 .01
❑ 527 Dave Valle .05 .01
❑ 528 Omar Vizquel .25 .08
❑ 529 Ivan Calderon .05 .01
❑ 530 Carlton Fisk UER .15 .05
❑ 531 Scott Fletcher .05 .01
❑ 532 Dave Gallagher .05 .01
❑ 533 Ozzie Guillen .10 .02
❑ 534 Greg Hibbard RC .10 .02
❑ 535 Shawn Hillegas .05 .01
❑ 536 Lance Johnson .05 .01
❑ 537 Eric King .05 .01
❑ 538 Ron Kittle .05 .01
❑ 539 Steve Lyons .05 .01
❑ 540 Carlos Martinez .05 .01
❑ 541 Tom McCarthy .05 .01
❑ 542 Matt Merullo
(Had 5 ML runs scored
entering '90, .05 .01
❑ 543 Donn Pall UER
(Stats say pro career
began in '85 .05 .01
❑ 544 Dan Pasqua .05 .01
❑ 545 Ken Patterson .05 .01
❑ 546 Melido Perez .05 .01
❑ 547 Steve Rosenberg .05 .01
❑ 548 Sammy Sosa RC 2.50 1.00
❑ 549 Bobby Thigpen .05 .01
❑ 550 Robin Ventura .25 .08
❑ 551 Greg Walker .05 .01
❑ 552 Don Carman .05 .01
❑ 553 Pat Combs
(6 walks for Phillies
in '89 in stats, .05 .01
❑ 554 Dennis Cook .05 .01
❑ 555 Darren Daulton .10 .02
❑ 556 Len Dykstra .10 .02
❑ 557 Curt Ford .05 .01
❑ 558 Charlie Hayes .05 .01
❑ 559 Von Hayes .05 .01
❑ 560 Tommy Herr .05 .01
❑ 561 Ken Howell .05 .01
❑ 562 Steve Jeltz .05 .01
❑ 563 Ron Jones .05 .01
❑ 564 Ricky Jordan UER
(Duplicate line of
statistics o .05 .01
❑ 565 John Kruk .10 .02
❑ 566 Steve Lake .05 .01
❑ 567 Roger McDowell .05 .01
❑ 568 Terry Mulholland UER
(%%Did You Know~ re-
fers t .05 .01
❑ 569 Dwayne Murphy .05 .01
❑ 570 Jeff Parrett .05 .01
❑ 571 Randy Ready .05 .01
❑ 572 Bruce Ruffin .05 .01
❑ 573 Dickie Thon .05 .01
❑ 574 Jose Alvarez UER
('78 and '79 stats
are reversed .05 .01
❑ 575 Geronimo Berroa .05 .01
❑ 576 Jeff Blauser .05 .01
❑ 577 Joe Boever .05 .01
❑ 578 Marty Clary UER
(No comma between
city and state .05 .01
❑ 579 Jody Davis .05 .01
❑ 580 Mark Eichhorn .05 .01
❑ 581 Darrell Evans .10 .02
❑ 582 Ron Gant .10 .02
❑ 583 Tom Glavine .15 .05
❑ 584 Tommy Greene RC .10 .02
❑ 585 Tommy Gregg .05 .01

❑ 586 David Justice RC .50 .20
❑ 587 Mark Lemke .05 .01
❑ 588 Derek Lilliquist .05 .01
❑ 589 Oddibe McDowell .05 .01
❑ 590 Kent Mercker RC .05 .01
❑ 591 Dale Murphy .15 .05
❑ 592 Gerald Perry .05 .01
❑ 593 Lonnie Smith .05 .01
❑ 594 Pete Smith .05 .01
❑ 595 John Smoltz .25 .08
❑ 596 Mike Stanton UER RC .25 .08
❑ 597 Andres Thomas .05 .01
❑ 598 Jeff Treadway .05 .01
❑ 599 Doyle Alexander .05 .01
❑ 600 Dave Bergman .05 .01
❑ 601 Brian DuBois RC .05 .01
❑ 602 Paul Gibson .05 .01
❑ 603 Mike Heath .05 .01
❑ 604 Mike Henneman .05 .01
❑ 605 Guillermo Hernandez .05 .01
❑ 606 Shawn Holman RC .05 .01
❑ 607 Tracy Jones .05 .01
❑ 608 Chet Lemon .05 .01
❑ 609 Fred Lynn .05 .01
❑ 610 Jack Morris .10 .02
❑ 611 Matt Nokes .05 .01
❑ 612 Gary Pettis .05 .01
❑ 613 Kevin Ritz RC .05 .01
❑ 614 Jeff M. Robinson
('88 stats are
not in line) .05 .01
❑ 615 Steve Searcy .05 .01
❑ 616 Frank Tanana .05 .01
❑ 617 Alan Trammell .10 .02
❑ 618 Gary Ward .05 .01
❑ 619 Lou Whitaker .10 .02
❑ 620 Frank Williams .05 .01
❑ 621A George Brett '80 ERR 2.00 .75
❑ 621B George Brett '80 .30 .10
❑ 622 Fern.Valenzuela '81 .05 .01
❑ 623 Dale Murphy '82 .15 .05
❑ 624A Cal Ripkin '83 ERR 5.00 2.00
❑ 624B Cal Ripken '83 COR .40 .15
❑ 625 Ryne Sandberg '84 .25 .08
❑ 626 Don Mattingly '85 .20 .07
❑ 627 Roger Clemens '86 .50 .20
❑ 628 George Bell '87 .05 .01
❑ 629 Jose Canseco '88 UER .10 .02
❑ 630A Will Clark '89 ERR 32 1.00 .40
❑ 630B Will Clark '89 COR 321 .15 .05
❑ 631 M.Davis/M.Williams .05 .01
❑ 632 W.Boggs/M.Greenwell .10 .02
❑ 633 M.Gubicza/J.Russell .05 .01
❑ 634 C.Ripken/T.Fernandez .25 .08
❑ 635 K.Puckett/Bo Jackson .15 .05
❑ 636 N.Ryan/M.Scott .40 .15
❑ 637 W.Clark/K.Mitchell .10 .02
❑ 638 M.McGwire/D.Mattingly .30 .10
❑ 639 R.Sandberg/H.Johnson .25 .08
❑ 640 R.Seanez RC/C.Charland RC .10 .02
❑ 641 G.Canale RC/K.Maas RC .25 .08
❑ 642 Kelly Mann RC/D.Hansen RC .25 .08
❑ 643 G.Smith RC/S.Tate RC .10 .02
❑ 644 T.Drees RC/D.Howitt RC .10 .02
❑ 645 M.Roesler RC/D.May RC .10 .02
❑ 646 S.Hemond RC/M.Gardner RC .10 .02
❑ 647 John Orton RC/S.Leius RC .10 .02
❑ 648 R.Monteleone RC/D.Williams RC .10 .02
❑ 649 M.Huff RC/S.Frey RC .10 .02
❑ 650 C.McElroy RC/M.Alou RC .75 .30
❑ 651 B.Rose RC/M.Hartley RC .25 .08
❑ 652 M.Kinzer RC/W.Edwards RC .10 .02
❑ 653 D.DeShields RC/J.Grimsley RC .25 .08
❑ 654 CL: A's/Cubs
Giants/Blue Jays .05 .01
❑ 655 CL: Royals/Angels
Padres/Orioles .05 .01
❑ 656 CL: Mets/Astros
Cards/Red Sox .05 .01
❑ 657 CL: Rangers/Brewers
Expos/Twins .05 .01
❑ 658 CL: Dodgers/Reds
Yankees/Pirates .05 .01
❑ 659 CL: Indians/Mariners
White Sox/Phillies .05 .01
❑ 660A CL: Braves/Tigers
Specials/Checklists
(Checklist .05 .01
❑ 660B CL: Braves/Tigers
Specials/Checklists
(Checklist .05 .01

1991 Fleer

❑ COMPLETE SET (720) 8.00 3.00
❑ COMP.RETAIL SET (732) 10.00 4.00
❑ COMP.HOBBY SET (732) 10.00 4.00
❑ 1 Troy Afenir RC .05 .01
❑ 2 Harold Baines .10 .02
❑ 3 Lance Blankenship .05 .01
❑ 4 Todd Burns .05 .01
❑ 5 Jose Canseco .15 .05
❑ 6 Dennis Eckersley .10 .02
❑ 7 Mike Gallego .05 .01
❑ 8 Ron Hassey .05 .01
❑ 9 Dave Henderson .05 .01
❑ 10 Rickey Henderson .25 .08
❑ 11 Rick Honeycutt .05 .01
❑ 12 Doug Jennings .05 .01
❑ 13 Joe Klink .05 .01
❑ 14 Carney Lansford .10 .02
❑ 15 Darren Lewis .05 .01
❑ 16 Willie McGee UER .10 .02
❑ 17 Mark McGwire UER .75 .30
❑ 18 Mike Moore .05 .01
❑ 19 Gene Nelson .05 .01
❑ 20 Dave Otto .05 .01
❑ 21 Jamie Quirk .05 .01
❑ 22 Willie Randolph .10 .02
❑ 23 Scott Sanderson .05 .01
❑ 24 Terry Steinbach .05 .01
❑ 25 Dave Stewart .10 .02
❑ 26 Walt Weiss .05 .01
❑ 27 Bob Welch .05 .01
❑ 28 Curt Young .05 .01
❑ 29 Wally Backman .05 .01
❑ 30 Stan Belinda UER .05 .01
❑ 31 Jay Bell .10 .02
❑ 32 Rafael Belliard .05 .01
❑ 33 Barry Bonds 1.00 .40
❑ 34 Bobby Bonilla .10 .02
❑ 35 Sid Bream .05 .01
❑ 36 Doug Drabek .05 .01
❑ 37 Carlos Garcia RC .10 .02
❑ 38 Neal Heaton .05 .01
❑ 39 Jeff King .05 .01
❑ 40 Bob Kipper .05 .01
❑ 41 Bill Landrum .05 .01
❑ 42 Mike LaValliere .05 .01
❑ 43 Jose Lind .05 .01
❑ 44 Carmelo Martinez .05 .01
❑ 45 Bob Patterson .05 .01
❑ 46 Ted Power .05 .01
❑ 47 Gary Redus .05 .01
❑ 48 R.J. Reynolds .05 .01
❑ 49 Don Slaught .05 .01
❑ 50 John Smiley .05 .01
❑ 51 Zane Smith .05 .01
❑ 52 Randy Tomlin RC .10 .02
❑ 53 Andy Van Slyke .15 .05
❑ 54 Bob Walk .05 .01
❑ 55 Jack Armstrong .05 .01
❑ 56 Todd Benzinger .05 .01
❑ 57 Glenn Braggs .05 .01
❑ 58 Keith Brown .05 .01
❑ 59 Tom Browning .05 .01
❑ 60 Norm Charlton .05 .01
❑ 61 Eric Davis .10 .02
❑ 62 Rob Dibble .10 .02
❑ 63 Bill Doran .05 .01
❑ 64 Mariano Duncan .05 .01
❑ 65 Chris Hammond .05 .01
❑ 66 Billy Hatcher .05 .01
❑ 67 Danny Jackson .05 .01
❑ 68 Barry Larkin .15 .05
❑ 69 Tim Layana UER .05 .01
❑ 70 Terry Lee RC .05 .01
❑ 71 Rick Mahler .05 .01
❑ 72 Hal Morris .05 .01
❑ 73 Randy Myers .05 .01
❑ 74 Ron Oester .05 .01
❑ 75 Joe Oliver .05 .01
❑ 76 Paul O'Neill .15 .05
❑ 77 Luis Quinones .05 .01
❑ 78 Jeff Reed .05 .01
❑ 79 Jose Rijo .05 .01
❑ 80 Chris Sabo .05 .01
❑ 81 Scott Scudder .05 .01
❑ 82 Herm Winningham .05 .01
❑ 83 Larry Andersen .05 .01
❑ 84 Marty Barrett .05 .01
❑ 85 Mike Boddicker .05 .01
❑ 86 Wade Boggs .15 .05
❑ 87 Tom Bolton .05 .01
❑ 88 Tom Brunansky .05 .01
❑ 89 Ellis Burks .10 .02
❑ 90 Roger Clemens .75 .30
❑ 91 Scott Cooper .05 .01
❑ 92 John Dopson .05 .01
❑ 93 Dwight Evans .15 .05
❑ 94 Wes Gardner .05 .01
❑ 95 Jeff Gray .05 .01
❑ 96 Mike Greenwell .05 .01
❑ 97 Greg A. Harris .05 .01
❑ 98 Daryl Irvine RC .05 .01
❑ 99 Dana Kiecker .05 .01
❑ 100 Randy Kutcher .05 .01
❑ 101 Dennis Lamp .05 .01
❑ 102 Mike Marshall .05 .01
❑ 103 John Marzano .05 .01
❑ 104 Rob Murphy .05 .01
❑ 105 Tim Naehring .05 .01
❑ 106 Tony Pena .05 .01
❑ 107 Phil Plantier RC .25 .08
❑ 108 Carlos Quintana .05 .01
❑ 109 Jeff Reardon .10 .02
❑ 110 Jerry Reed .05 .01
❑ 111 Jody Reed .05 .01
❑ 112 Luis Rivera UER .05 .01
❑ 113 Kevin Romine .05 .01
❑ 114 Phil Bradley .05 .01
❑ 115 Ivan Calderon .05 .01
❑ 116 Wayne Edwards .05 .01
❑ 117 Alex Fernandez .05 .01
❑ 118 Carlton Fisk .15 .05
❑ 119 Scott Fletcher .05 .01
❑ 120 Craig Grebeck .05 .01
❑ 121 Ozzie Guillen .10 .02
❑ 122 Greg Hibbard .05 .01
❑ 123 Lance Johnson UER .05 .01
❑ 124 Barry Jones .05 .01
❑ 125 Ron Karkovice .05 .01
❑ 126 Eric King .05 .01
❑ 127 Steve Lyons .05 .01
❑ 128 Carlos Martinez .05 .01
❑ 129 Jack McDowell UER .05 .01
❑ 130 Donn Pall .05 .01
❑ 131 Dan Pasqua .05 .01
❑ 132 Ken Patterson .05 .01
❑ 133 Melido Perez .05 .01
❑ 134 Adam Peterson .05 .01
❑ 135 Scott Radinsky .05 .01
❑ 136 Sammy Sosa .25 .08
❑ 137 Bobby Thigpen .05 .01
❑ 138 Frank Thomas .25 .08
❑ 139 Robin Ventura .10 .02
❑ 140 Daryl Boston .05 .01
❑ 141 Chuck Carr .05 .01
❑ 142 Mark Carreon .05 .01
❑ 143 David Cone .10 .02
❑ 144 Ron Darling .05 .01

❑ 145 Kevin Elster .05 .01
❑ 146 Sid Fernandez .05 .01
❑ 147 John Franco .10 .02
❑ 148 Dwight Gooden .10 .02
❑ 149 Tom Herr .05 .01
❑ 150 Todd Hundley .05 .01
❑ 151 Gregg Jefferies .05 .01
❑ 152 Howard Johnson .05 .01
❑ 153 Dave Magadan .05 .01
❑ 154 Kevin McReynolds .05 .01
❑ 155 Keith Miller UER (Text says Rochester in '87, st .05 .01
❑ 156 Bob Ojeda .05 .01
❑ 157 Tom O'Malley .05 .01
❑ 158 Alejandro Pena .05 .01
❑ 159 Darren Reed .05 .01
❑ 160 Mackey Sasser .05 .01
❑ 161 Darryl Strawberry .10 .02
❑ 162 Tim Teufel .05 .01
❑ 163 Kelvin Torve .05 .01
❑ 164 Julio Valera .05 .01
❑ 165 Frank Viola .10 .02
❑ 166 Wally Whitehurst .05 .01
❑ 167 Jim Acker .05 .01
❑ 168 Derek Bell .10 .02
❑ 169 George Bell .05 .01
❑ 170 Willie Blair .05 .01
❑ 171 Pat Borders .05 .01
❑ 172 John Cerutti .05 .01
❑ 173 Junior Felix .05 .01
❑ 174 Tony Fernandez .05 .01
❑ 175 Kelly Gruber UER (Born in Houston, should be Bel .05 .01
❑ 176 Tom Henke .05 .01
❑ 177 Glenallen Hill .05 .01
❑ 178 Jimmy Key .10 .02
❑ 179 Manny Lee .05 .01
❑ 180 Fred McGriff .15 .05
❑ 181 Rance Mulliniks .05 .01
❑ 182 Greg Myers .05 .01
❑ 183 John Olerud .10 .02
❑ 184 Luis Sojo .05 .01
❑ 185 Dave Stieb .05 .01
❑ 186 Todd Stottlemyre .05 .01
❑ 187 Duane Ward .05 .01
❑ 188 David Wells .10 .02
❑ 189 Mark Whiten .05 .01
❑ 190 Ken Williams .05 .01
❑ 191 Frank Wills .05 .01
❑ 192 Mookie Wilson .10 .02
❑ 193 Don Aase .05 .01
❑ 194 Tim Belcher UER (Born Sparta, Ohio, should say M .05 .01
❑ 195 Hubie Brooks .05 .01
❑ 196 Dennis Cook .05 .01
❑ 197 Tim Crews .05 .01
❑ 198 Kal Daniels .05 .01
❑ 199 Kirk Gibson .10 .02
❑ 200 Jim Gott .05 .01
❑ 201 Alfredo Griffin .05 .01
❑ 202 Chris Gwynn .05 .01
❑ 203 Dave Hansen .05 .01
❑ 204 Lenny Harris .05 .01
❑ 205 Mike Hartley .05 .01
❑ 206 Mickey Hatcher .05 .01
❑ 207 Carlos Hernandez .05 .01
❑ 208 Orel Hershiser .10 .02
❑ 209 Jay Howell UER (No 1982 Yankee stats) .05 .01
❑ 210 Mike Huff .05 .01
❑ 211 Stan Javier .05 .01
❑ 212 Ramon Martinez .05 .01
❑ 213 Mike Morgan .05 .01
❑ 214 Eddie Murray .25 .08
❑ 215 Jim Neidlinger RC .05 .01
❑ 216 Jose Offerman .05 .01
❑ 217 Jim Poole .05 .01
❑ 218 Juan Samuel .05 .01
❑ 219 Mike Scioscia .05 .01
❑ 220 Ray Searage .05 .01
❑ 221 Mike Sharperson .05 .01
❑ 222 Fernando Valenzuela .10 .02
❑ 223 Jose Vizcaino .05 .01
❑ 224 Mike Aldrete .05 .01
❑ 225 Scott Anderson RC .05 .01
❑ 226 Dennis Boyd .05 .01
❑ 227 Tim Burke .05 .01
❑ 228 Delino DeShields .10 .02
❑ 229 Mike Fitzgerald .05 .01
❑ 230 Tom Foley .05 .01
❑ 231 Steve Frey .05 .01
❑ 232 Andres Galarraga .10 .02
❑ 233 Mark Gardner .05 .01
❑ 234 Marquis Grissom .10 .02
❑ 235 Kevin Gross (No date given for first Expos win) .05 .01
❑ 236 Drew Hall .05 .01
❑ 237 Dave Martinez .05 .01
❑ 238 Dennis Martinez .10 .02
❑ 239 Dale Mohorcic .05 .01
❑ 240 Chris Nabholz .05 .01
❑ 241 Otis Nixon .05 .01
❑ 242 Junior Noboa .05 .01
❑ 243 Spike Owen .05 .01
❑ 244 Tim Raines .10 .02
❑ 245 Mel Rojas UER (Stats show 3.60 ERA, bio says 3.1 .05 .01
❑ 246 Scott Ruskin .05 .01
❑ 247 Bill Sampen .05 .01
❑ 248 Nelson Santovenia .05 .01
❑ 249 Dave Schmidt .05 .01
❑ 250 Larry Walker .25 .08
❑ 251 Tim Wallach .05 .01
❑ 252 Dave Anderson .05 .01
❑ 253 Kevin Bass .05 .01
❑ 254 Steve Bedrosian .05 .01
❑ 255 Jeff Brantley .05 .01
❑ 256 John Burkett .05 .01
❑ 257 Brett Butler .10 .02
❑ 258 Gary Carter .10 .02
❑ 259 Will Clark .15 .05
❑ 260 Steve Decker RC .10 .02
❑ 261 Kelly Downs .05 .01
❑ 262 Scott Garrelts .05 .01
❑ 263 Terry Kennedy .05 .01
❑ 264 Mike LaCoss .05 .01
❑ 265 Mark Leonard RC .05 .01
❑ 266 Greg Litton .05 .01
❑ 267 Kevin Mitchell .05 .01
❑ 268 Randy O'Neal .05 .01
❑ 269 Rick Parker .05 .01
❑ 270 Rick Reuschel .05 .01
❑ 271 Ernest Riles .05 .01
❑ 272 Don Robinson .05 .01
❑ 273 Robby Thompson .05 .01
❑ 274 Mark Thurmond .05 .01
❑ 275 Jose Uribe .05 .01
❑ 276 Matt Williams .10 .02
❑ 277 Trevor Wilson .05 .01
❑ 278 Gerald Alexander RC .05 .01
❑ 279 Brad Arnsberg .05 .01
❑ 280 Kevin Belcher RC .05 .01
❑ 281 Joe Bitker RC .05 .01
❑ 282 Kevin Brown .10 .02
❑ 283 Steve Buechele .05 .01
❑ 284 Jack Daugherty .05 .01
❑ 285 Julio Franco .10 .02
❑ 286 Juan Gonzalez .25 .08
❑ 287 Bill Haselman RC .05 .01
❑ 288 Charlie Hough .10 .02
❑ 289 Jeff Huson .05 .01
❑ 290 Pete Incaviglia .05 .01
❑ 291 Mike Jeffcoat .05 .01
❑ 292 Jeff Kunkel .05 .01
❑ 293 Gary Mielke .05 .01
❑ 294 Jamie Moyer .10 .02
❑ 295 Rafael Palmeiro .15 .05
❑ 296 Geno Petralli .05 .01
❑ 297 Gary Pettis .05 .01
❑ 298 Kevin Reimer .05 .01
❑ 299 Kenny Rogers .10 .02
❑ 300 Jeff Russell .05 .01
❑ 301 John Russell .05 .01
❑ 302 Nolan Ryan 1.00 .40
❑ 303 Ruben Sierra .10 .02
❑ 304 Bobby Witt .05 .01
❑ 305 Jim Abbott .15 .05
❑ 306 Kent Anderson .05 .01
❑ 307 Dante Bichette .10 .02
❑ 308 Bert Blyleven .10 .02
❑ 309 Chili Davis .10 .02
❑ 310 Brian Downing .05 .01
❑ 311 Mark Eichhorn .05 .01
❑ 312 Mike Fetters .05 .01
❑ 313 Chuck Finley .10 .02
❑ 314 Willie Fraser .05 .01
❑ 315 Bryan Harvey .05 .01
❑ 316 Donnie Hill .05 .01
❑ 317 Wally Joyner .10 .02
❑ 318 Mark Langston .05 .01
❑ 319 Kirk McCaskill .05 .01
❑ 320 John Orton .05 .01
❑ 321 Lance Parrish .10 .02
❑ 322 Luis Polonia UER (1984 Madfison, should be Madis .05 .01
❑ 323 Johnny Ray .05 .01
❑ 324 Bobby Rose .05 .01
❑ 325 Dick Schofield .05 .01
❑ 326 Rick Schu .05 .01
❑ 327 Lee Stevens .05 .01
❑ 328 Devon White .10 .02
❑ 329 Dave Winfield .10 .02
❑ 330 Cliff Young .05 .01
❑ 331 Dave Bergman .05 .01
❑ 332 Phil Clark RC .10 .02
❑ 333 Darnell Coles .05 .01
❑ 334 Milt Cuyler .05 .01
❑ 335 Cecil Fielder .10 .02
❑ 336 Travis Fryman .10 .02
❑ 337 Paul Gibson .05 .01
❑ 338 Jerry Don Gleaton .05 .01
❑ 339 Mike Heath .05 .01
❑ 340 Mike Henneman .05 .01
❑ 341 Chet Lemon .05 .01
❑ 342 Lance McCullers .05 .01
❑ 343 Jack Morris .10 .02
❑ 344 Lloyd Moseby .05 .01
❑ 345 Edwin Nunez .05 .01
❑ 346 Clay Parker .05 .01
❑ 347 Dan Petry .05 .01
❑ 348 Tony Phillips .05 .01
❑ 349 Jeff M. Robinson .05 .01
❑ 350 Mark Salas .05 .01
❑ 351 Mike Schwabe .05 .01
❑ 352 Larry Sheets .05 .01
❑ 353 John Shelby .05 .01
❑ 354 Frank Tanana .05 .01
❑ 355 Alan Trammell .10 .02
❑ 356 Gary Ward .05 .01
❑ 357 Lou Whitaker .10 .02
❑ 358 Beau Allred .05 .01
❑ 359 Sandy Alomar Jr. .05 .01
❑ 360 Carlos Baerga .05 .01
❑ 361 Kevin Bearse .05 .01
❑ 362 Tom Brookens .05 .01
❑ 363 Jerry Browne UER (No dot over i in first text li .05 .01
❑ 364 Tom Candiotti .05 .01
❑ 365 Alex Cole .05 .01
❑ 366 John Farrell UER (Born in Neptune, should be Mon .05 .01
❑ 367 Felix Fermin .05 .01
❑ 368 Keith Hernandez .10 .02
❑ 369 Brook Jacoby .05 .01
❑ 370 Chris James .05 .01
❑ 371 Dion James .05 .01
❑ 372 Doug Jones .05 .01
❑ 373 Candy Maldonado .05 .01
❑ 374 Steve Olin .05 .01
❑ 375 Jesse Orosco .05 .01
❑ 376 Rudy Seanez .05 .01
❑ 377 Joel Skinner .05 .01
❑ 378 Cory Snyder .05 .01
❑ 379 Greg Swindell .05 .01
❑ 380 Sergio Valdez .05 .01
❑ 381 Mike Walker .05 .01
❑ 382 Colby Ward RC .05 .01
❑ 383 Turner Ward RC .25 .08
❑ 384 Mitch Webster .05 .01
❑ 385 Kevin Wickander .05 .01

❑ 386 Darrel Akerfelds .05 .01
❑ 387 Joe Boever .05 .01
❑ 388 Rod Booker .05 .01
❑ 389 Sil Campusano .05 .01
❑ 390 Don Carman .05 .01
❑ 391 Wes Chamberlain RC .25 .08
❑ 392 Pat Combs .05 .01
❑ 393 Darren Daulton .10 .02
❑ 394 Jose DeJesus .05 .01
❑ 395A Len Dykstra .10 .02
❑ 395B Len Dykstra .10 .02
❑ 396 Jason Grimsley .05 .01
❑ 397 Charlie Hayes .05 .01
❑ 398 Von Hayes .05 .01
❑ 399 Dave Hollins UER .05 .01
❑ 400 Ken Howell .05 .01
❑ 401 Ricky Jordan .05 .01
❑ 402 John Kruk .10 .02
❑ 403 Steve Lake .05 .01
❑ 404 Chuck Malone .05 .01
❑ 405 Roger McDowell UER
(Says Phillies is
saves, shou .05 .01
❑ 406 Chuck McElroy .05 .01
❑ 407 Mickey Morandini .05 .01
❑ 408 Terry Mulholland .05 .01
❑ 409 Dale Murphy .15 .05
❑ 410A Randy Ready ERR
(No Brewers stats
listed for 198 .05 .01
❑ 410B Randy Ready COR .05 .01
❑ 411 Bruce Ruffin .05 .01
❑ 412 Dickie Thon .05 .01
❑ 413 Paul Assenmacher .05 .01
❑ 414 Damon Berryhill .05 .01
❑ 415 Mike Bielecki .05 .01
❑ 416 Shawn Boskie .05 .01
❑ 417 Dave Clark .05 .01
❑ 418 Doug Dascenzo .05 .01
❑ 419A Andre Dawson ERR .10 .02
❑ 419B Andre Dawson COR .10 .02
❑ 420 Shawon Dunston .05 .01
❑ 421 Joe Girardi .05 .01
❑ 422 Mark Grace .15 .05
❑ 423 Mike Harkey .05 .01
❑ 424 Les Lancaster .05 .01
❑ 425 Bill Long .05 .01
❑ 426 Greg Maddux .40 .15
❑ 427 Derrick May .05 .01
❑ 428 Jeff Pico .05 .01
❑ 429 Domingo Ramos .05 .01
❑ 430 Luis Salazar .05 .01
❑ 431 Ryne Sandberg .40 .15
❑ 432 Dwight Smith .05 .01
❑ 433 Greg Smith .05 .01
❑ 434 Rick Sutcliffe .10 .02
❑ 435 Gary Varsho .05 .01
❑ 436 Hector Villanueva .05 .01
❑ 437 Jerome Walton .05 .01
❑ 438 Curtis Wilkerson .05 .01
❑ 439 Mitch Williams .05 .01
❑ 440 Steve Wilson .05 .01
❑ 441 Marvell Wynne .05 .01
❑ 442 Scott Bankhead .05 .01
❑ 443 Scott Bradley .05 .01
❑ 444 Greg Briley .05 .01
❑ 445 Mike Brumley UER .05 .01
❑ 446 Jay Buhner .10 .02
❑ 447 Dave Burba RC .25 .08
❑ 448 Henry Cotto .05 .01
❑ 449 Alvin Davis .05 .01
❑ 450 Ken Griffey Jr. .50 .20
❑ 450A Ken Griffey Jr. ERR 1.00 .40
❑ 451 Erik Hanson .05 .01
❑ 452 Gene Harris UER
(63 career runs,
should be 73) .05 .01
❑ 453 Brian Holman .05 .01
❑ 454 Mike Jackson .05 .01
❑ 455 Randy Johnson .30 .10
❑ 456 Jeffrey Leonard .05 .01
❑ 457 Edgar Martinez .15 .05
❑ 458 Tino Martinez .25 .08
❑ 459 Pete O'Brien UER
(1987 BA .266,
should be .286) .05 .01
❑ 460 Harold Reynolds .10 .02
❑ 461 Mike Schooler .05 .01
❑ 462 Bill Swift .05 .01
❑ 463 David Valle .05 .01
❑ 464 Omar Vizquel .15 .05
❑ 465 Matt Young .05 .01
❑ 466 Brady Anderson .10 .02
❑ 467 Jeff Ballard UER
(Missing top of right
parenthes .05 .01
❑ 468 Juan Bell .05 .01
❑ 469A Mike Devereaux
(First line of text
ends with six .10 .02
❑ 469B Mike Devereaux
(First line of text
ends with run .10 .02
❑ 470 Steve Finley .10 .02
❑ 471 Dave Gallagher .05 .01
❑ 472 Leo Gomez .05 .01
❑ 473 Rene Gonzales .05 .01
❑ 474 Pete Harnisch .05 .01
❑ 475 Kevin Hickey .05 .01
❑ 476 Chris Hoiles .05 .01
❑ 477 Sam Horn .05 .01
❑ 478 Tim Hulett
(Photo shows National
Leaguer sliding .05 .01
❑ 479 Dave Johnson .05 .01
❑ 480 Ron Kittle UER
(Edmonton misspelled
as Edmundton .05 .01
❑ 481 Ben McDonald .05 .01
❑ 482 Bob Melvin .05 .01
❑ 483 Bob Milacki .05 .01
❑ 484 Randy Milligan .05 .01
❑ 485 John Mitchell .05 .01
❑ 486 Gregg Olson .05 .01
❑ 487 Joe Orsulak .05 .01
❑ 488 Joe Price .05 .01
❑ 489 Bill Ripken .05 .01
❑ 490 Cal Ripken .75 .30
❑ 491 Curt Schilling .25 .08
❑ 492 David Segui .05 .01
❑ 493 Anthony Telford RC .05 .01
❑ 494 Mickey Tettleton .05 .01
❑ 495 Mark Williamson .05 .01
❑ 496 Craig Worthington .05 .01
❑ 497 Juan Agosto .05 .01
❑ 498 Eric Anthony .05 .01
❑ 499 Craig Biggio .15 .05
❑ 500 Ken Caminiti UER .10 .02
❑ 501 Casey Candaele .05 .01
❑ 502 Andujar Cedeno .05 .01
❑ 503 Danny Darwin .05 .01
❑ 504 Mark Davidson .05 .01
❑ 505 Glenn Davis .05 .01
❑ 506 Jim Deshaies .05 .01
❑ 507 Luis Gonzalez RC .50 .20
❑ 508 Bill Gullickson .05 .01
❑ 509 Xavier Hernandez .05 .01
❑ 510 Brian Meyer .05 .01
❑ 511 Ken Oberkfell .05 .01
❑ 512 Mark Portugal .05 .01
❑ 513 Rafael Ramirez .05 .01
❑ 514 Karl Rhodes .05 .01
❑ 515 Mike Scott .05 .01
❑ 516 Mike Simms RC .05 .01
❑ 517 Dave Smith .05 .01
❑ 518 Franklin Stubbs .05 .01
❑ 519 Glenn Wilson .05 .01
❑ 520 Eric Yelding UER
(Text has 63 steals,
stats have .05 .01
❑ 521 Gerald Young .05 .01
❑ 522 Shawn Abner .05 .01
❑ 523 Roberto Alomar .15 .05
❑ 524 Andy Benes .05 .01
❑ 525 Joe Carter .10 .02
❑ 526 Jack Clark .10 .02
❑ 527 Joey Cora .05 .01
❑ 528 Paul Faries RC .05 .01
❑ 529 Tony Gwynn .30 .10
❑ 530 Atlee Hammaker .05 .01
❑ 531 Greg W. Harris .05 .01
❑ 532 Thomas Howard .05 .01
❑ 533 Bruce Hurst .05 .01
❑ 534 Craig Lefferts .05 .01
❑ 535 Derek Lilliquist .05 .01
❑ 536 Fred Lynn .05 .01
❑ 537 Mike Pagliarulo .05 .01
❑ 538 Mark Parent .05 .01
❑ 539 Dennis Rasmussen .05 .01
❑ 540 Bip Roberts .05 .01
❑ 541 Richard Rodriguez RC .05 .01
❑ 542 Benito Santiago .10 .02
❑ 543 Calvin Schiraldi .05 .01
❑ 544 Eric Show .05 .01
❑ 545 Phil Stephenson .05 .01
❑ 546 Garry Templeton UER
(Born 3/24/57,
should be 3/2 .05 .01
❑ 547 Ed Whitson .05 .01
❑ 548 Eddie Williams .05 .01
❑ 549 Kevin Appier .10 .02
❑ 550 Luis Aquino .05 .01
❑ 551 Bob Boone .10 .02
❑ 552 George Brett .60 .25
❑ 553 Jeff Conine RC .40 .15
❑ 554 Steve Crawford .05 .01
❑ 555 Mark Davis .05 .01
❑ 556 Storm Davis .05 .01
❑ 557 Jim Eisenreich .05 .01
❑ 558 Steve Farr .05 .01
❑ 559 Tom Gordon .05 .01
❑ 560 Mark Gubicza .05 .01
❑ 561 Bo Jackson .25 .08
❑ 562 Mike Macfarlane .05 .01
❑ 563 Brian McRae RC .25 .08
❑ 564 Jeff Montgomery .05 .01
❑ 565 Bill Pecota .05 .01
❑ 566 Gerald Perry .05 .01
❑ 567 Bret Saberhagen .10 .02
❑ 568 Jeff Schulz RC .05 .01
❑ 569 Kevin Seitzer .05 .01
❑ 570 Terry Shumpert .05 .01
❑ 571 Kurt Stillwell .05 .01
❑ 572 Danny Tartabull .05 .01
❑ 573 Gary Thurman .05 .01
❑ 574 Frank White .10 .02
❑ 575 Willie Wilson .05 .01
❑ 576 Chris Bosio .05 .01
❑ 577 Greg Brock .05 .01
❑ 578 George Canale .05 .01
❑ 579 Chuck Crim .05 .01
❑ 580 Rob Deer .05 .01
❑ 581 Edgar Diaz .05 .01
❑ 582 Tom Edens RC .05 .01
❑ 583 Mike Felder .05 .01
❑ 584 Jim Gantner .05 .01
❑ 585 Darryl Hamilton .05 .01
❑ 586 Ted Higuera .05 .01
❑ 587 Mark Knudson .05 .01
❑ 588 Bill Krueger .05 .01
❑ 589 Tim McIntosh .05 .01
❑ 590 Paul Mirabella .05 .01
❑ 591 Paul Molitor .10 .02
❑ 592 Jaime Navarro .05 .01
❑ 593 Dave Parker .10 .02
❑ 594 Dan Plesac .05 .01
❑ 595 Ron Robinson .05 .01
❑ 596 Gary Sheffield .10 .02
❑ 597 Bill Spiers .05 .01
❑ 598 B.J. Surhoff .10 .02
❑ 599 Greg Vaughn .05 .01
❑ 600 Randy Veres .05 .01
❑ 601 Robin Yount .40 .15
❑ 602 Rick Aguilera .10 .02
❑ 603 Allan Anderson .05 .01
❑ 604 Juan Berenguer .05 .01
❑ 605 Randy Bush .05 .01
❑ 606 Carmelo Castillo .05 .01
❑ 607 Tim Drummond .05 .01
❑ 608 Scott Erickson .05 .01
❑ 609 Gary Gaetti .10 .02
❑ 610 Greg Gagne .05 .01
❑ 611 Dan Gladden .05 .01
❑ 612 Mark Guthrie .05 .01
❑ 613 Brian Harper .05 .01
❑ 614 Kent Hrbek .10 .02
❑ 615 Gene Larkin .05 .01
❑ 616 Terry Leach .05 .01

Card		
❑ 617 Nelson Liriano	.05	.01
❑ 618 Shane Mack	.05	.01
❑ 619 John Moses	.05	.01
❑ 620 Pedro Munoz RC	.10	.02
❑ 621 Al Newman	.05	.01
❑ 622 Junior Ortiz	.05	.01
❑ 623 Kirby Puckett	.25	.08
❑ 624 Roy Smith	.05	.01
❑ 625 Kevin Tapani	.05	.01
❑ 626 Gary Wayne	.05	.01
❑ 627 David West	.05	.01
❑ 628 Cris Carpenter	.05	.01
❑ 629 Vince Coleman	.05	.01
❑ 630 Ken Dayley	.05	.01
❑ 631A Jose DeLeon ERR	.05	.01
❑ 631B Jose DeLeon COR	.05	.01
❑ 632 Frank DiPino	.05	.01
❑ 633 Bernard Gilkey	.05	.01
❑ 634A Pedro Guerrero ERR	.10	.02
❑ 634B Pedro Guerrero COR	.10	.02
❑ 635 Ken Hill	.05	.01
❑ 636 Felix Jose	.05	.01
❑ 637 Ray Lankford	.10	.02
❑ 638 Joe Magrane	.05	.01
❑ 639 Tom Niedenfuer	.05	.01
❑ 640 Jose Oquendo	.05	.01
❑ 641 Tom Pagnozzi	.05	.01
❑ 642 Terry Pendleton	.10	.02
❑ 643 Mike Perez RC	.10	.02
❑ 644 Bryn Smith	.05	.01
❑ 645 Lee Smith	.10	.02
❑ 646 Ozzie Smith	.40	.15
❑ 647 Scott Terry	.05	.01
❑ 648 Bob Tewksbury	.05	.01
❑ 649 Milt Thompson	.05	.01
❑ 650 John Tudor	.05	.01
❑ 651 Denny Walling	.05	.01
❑ 652 Craig Wilson RC	.05	.01
❑ 653 Todd Worrell	.05	.01
❑ 654 Todd Zeile	.05	.01
❑ 655 Oscar Azocar	.05	.01
❑ 656 Steve Balboni UER (Born 1/5/57, should be 1/16)	.05	.01
❑ 657 Jesse Barfield	.05	.01
❑ 658 Greg Cadaret	.05	.01
❑ 659 Chuck Cary	.05	.01
❑ 660 Rick Cerone	.05	.01
❑ 661 Dave Eiland	.05	.01
❑ 662 Alvaro Espinoza	.05	.01
❑ 663 Bob Geren	.05	.01
❑ 664 Lee Guetterman	.05	.01
❑ 665 Mel Hall	.05	.01
❑ 666 Andy Hawkins	.05	.01
❑ 667 Jimmy Jones	.05	.01
❑ 668 Roberto Kelly	.05	.01
❑ 669 Dave LaPoint UER (No '81 Brewers stats, totals a	.05	.01
❑ 670 Tim Leary	.05	.01
❑ 671 Jim Leyritz	.05	.01
❑ 672 Kevin Maas	.05	.01
❑ 673 Don Mattingly	.60	.25
❑ 674 Matt Nokes	.05	.01
❑ 675 Pascual Perez	.05	.01
❑ 676 Eric Plunk	.05	.01
❑ 677 Dave Righetti	.10	.02
❑ 678 Jeff D. Robinson	.05	.01
❑ 679 Steve Sax	.05	.01
❑ 680 Mike Witt	.05	.01
❑ 681 Steve Avery UER	.05	.01
❑ 682 Mike Bell RC	.05	.01
❑ 683 Jeff Blauser	.05	.01
❑ 684 Francisco Cabrera UER (Born 10/16, should say 10	.05	.01
❑ 685 Tony Castillo	.05	.01
❑ 686 Marty Clary UER (Shown pitching righty, but bio	.05	.01
❑ 687 Nick Esasky	.05	.01
❑ 688 Ron Gant	.10	.02
❑ 689 Tom Glavine	.15	.05
❑ 690 Mark Grant	.05	.01
❑ 691 Tommy Gregg	.05	.01
❑ 692 Dwayne Henry	.05	.01
❑ 693 David Justice	.10	.02
❑ 694 Jimmy Kremers	.05	.01
❑ 695 Charlie Leibrandt	.05	.01
❑ 696 Mark Lemke	.05	.01
❑ 697 Oddibe McDowell	.05	.01
❑ 698 Greg Olson	.05	.01
❑ 699 Jeff Parrett	.05	.01
❑ 700 Jim Presley	.05	.01
❑ 701 Victor Rosario RC	.05	.01
❑ 702 Lonnie Smith	.05	.01
❑ 703 Pete Smith	.05	.01
❑ 704 John Smoltz	.15	.05
❑ 705 Mike Stanton	.05	.01
❑ 706 Andres Thomas	.05	.01
❑ 707 Jeff Treadway	.05	.01
❑ 708 Jim Vatcher RC	.05	.01
❑ 709 R.Sandberg/C.Fielder	.25	.08
❑ 710 K.Griffey Jr./B.Bonds	1.00	.40
❑ 711 B.Bonilla/B.Larkin	.10	.02
❑ 712 Top Game Savers Bobby Thigpen John Franco	.05	.01
❑ 713 A.Dawson/R.Sandberg UER	.25	.08
❑ 714 CL:A's/Pirates Reds/Red Sox	.05	.01
❑ 715 CL:White Sox/Mets Blue Jays/Dodgers	.05	.01
❑ 716 CL:Expos/Giants Rangers/Angels	.05	.01
❑ 717 CL:Tigers/Indians Phillies/Cubs	.05	.01
❑ 718 CL:Mariners/Orioles Astros/Padres	.05	.01
❑ 719 CL:Royals/Brewers Twins/Cardinals	.05	.01
❑ 720 CL:Yankees/Braves Superstars/Specials	.05	.01

1992 Fleer

Card		
❑ COMPLETE SET (720)	10.00	4.00
❑ COMP.HOBBY SET (732)	20.00	8.00
❑ COMP.RETAIL SET (732)	20.00	8.00
❑ 1 Brady Anderson	.10	.02
❑ 2 Jose Bautista	.10	.02
❑ 3 Juan Bell	.10	.02
❑ 4 Glenn Davis	.10	.02
❑ 5 Mike Devereaux	.10	.02
❑ 6 Dwight Evans	.15	.05
❑ 7 Mike Flanagan	.10	.02
❑ 8 Leo Gomez	.10	.02
❑ 9 Chris Hoiles	.10	.02
❑ 10 Sam Horn	.10	.02
❑ 11 Tim Hulett	.10	.02
❑ 12 Dave Johnson	.10	.02
❑ 13 Chito Martinez	.10	.02
❑ 14 Ben McDonald	.10	.02
❑ 15 Bob Melvin	.10	.02
❑ 16 Luis Mercedes	.10	.02
❑ 17 Jose Mesa	.10	.02
❑ 18 Bob Milacki	.10	.02
❑ 19 Randy Milligan	.10	.02
❑ 20 Mike Mussina	.25	.08
❑ 21 Gregg Olson	.10	.02
❑ 22 Joe Orsulak	.10	.02
❑ 23 Jim Poole	.10	.02
❑ 24 Arthur Rhodes	.10	.02
❑ 25 Billy Ripken	.10	.02
❑ 26 Cal Ripken	.75	.30
❑ 27 David Segui	.10	.02
❑ 28 Roy Smith	.10	.02
❑ 29 Anthony Telford	.10	.02
❑ 30 Mark Williamson	.10	.02
❑ 31 Craig Worthington	.10	.02
❑ 32 Wade Boggs	.15	.05
❑ 33 Tom Bolton	.10	.02
❑ 34 Tom Brunansky	.10	.02
❑ 35 Ellis Burks	.10	.02
❑ 36 Jack Clark	.10	.02
❑ 37 Roger Clemens	.50	.20
❑ 38 Danny Darwin	.10	.02
❑ 39 Mike Greenwell	.10	.02
❑ 40 Joe Hesketh	.10	.02
❑ 41 Daryl Irvine	.10	.02
❑ 42 Dennis Lamp	.10	.02
❑ 43 Tony Pena	.10	.02
❑ 44 Phil Plantier	.10	.02
❑ 45 Carlos Quintana	.10	.02
❑ 46 Jeff Reardon	.10	.02
❑ 47 Jody Reed	.10	.02
❑ 48 Luis Rivera	.10	.02
❑ 49 Mo Vaughn	.10	.02
❑ 50 Jim Abbott	.15	.05
❑ 51 Kyle Abbott	.10	.02
❑ 52 Ruben Amaro	.10	.02
❑ 53 Scott Bailes	.10	.02
❑ 54 Chris Beasley	.10	.02
❑ 55 Mark Eichhorn	.10	.02
❑ 56 Mike Fetters	.10	.02
❑ 57 Chuck Finley	.10	.02
❑ 58 Gary Gaetti	.10	.02
❑ 59 Dave Gallagher	.10	.02
❑ 60 Donnie Hill	.10	.02
❑ 61 Bryan Harvey UER (Lee Smith led the Majors with	.10	.02
❑ 62 Wally Joyner	.10	.02
❑ 63 Mark Langston	.10	.02
❑ 64 Kirk McCaskill	.10	.02
❑ 65 John Orton	.10	.02
❑ 66 Lance Parrish	.10	.02
❑ 67 Luis Polonia	.10	.02
❑ 68 Bobby Rose	.10	.02
❑ 69 Dick Schofield	.10	.02
❑ 70 Luis Sojo	.10	.02
❑ 71 Lee Stevens	.10	.02
❑ 72 Dave Winfield	.10	.02
❑ 73 Cliff Young	.10	.02
❑ 74 Wilson Alvarez	.10	.02
❑ 75 Esteban Beltre	.10	.02
❑ 76 Joey Cora	.10	.02
❑ 77 Brian Drahman	.10	.02
❑ 78 Alex Fernandez	.10	.02
❑ 79 Carlton Fisk	.15	.05
❑ 80 Scott Fletcher	.10	.02
❑ 81 Craig Grebeck	.10	.02
❑ 82 Ozzie Guillen	.10	.02
❑ 83 Greg Hibbard	.10	.02
❑ 84 Charlie Hough	.10	.02
❑ 85 Mike Huff	.10	.02
❑ 86 Bo Jackson	.25	.08
❑ 87 Lance Johnson	.10	.02
❑ 88 Ron Karkovice	.10	.02
❑ 89 Jack McDowell	.10	.02
❑ 90 Matt Merullo	.10	.02
❑ 91 Warren Newson	.10	.02
❑ 92 Donn Pall UER (Called Dunn on card back)	.10	.02
❑ 93 Dan Pasqua	.10	.02
❑ 94 Ken Patterson	.10	.02
❑ 95 Melido Perez	.10	.02
❑ 96 Scott Radinsky	.10	.02
❑ 97 Tim Raines	.10	.02
❑ 98 Sammy Sosa	.25	.08
❑ 99 Bobby Thigpen	.10	.02
❑ 100 Frank Thomas	.25	.08
❑ 101 Robin Ventura	.10	.02
❑ 102 Mike Aldrete	.10	.02
❑ 103 Sandy Alomar Jr.	.10	.02
❑ 104 Carlos Baerga	.10	.02
❑ 105 Albert Belle	.10	.02
❑ 106 Willie Blair	.10	.02
❑ 107 Jerry Browne	.10	.02
❑ 108 Alex Cole	.10	.02

❑ 109 Felix Fermin .10 .02
❑ 110 Glenallen Hill .10 .02
❑ 111 Shawn Hillegas .10 .02
❑ 112 Chris James .10 .02
❑ 113 Reggie Jefferson .10 .02
❑ 114 Doug Jones .10 .02
❑ 115 Eric King .10 .02
❑ 116 Mark Lewis .10 .02
❑ 117 Carlos Martinez .10 .02
❑ 118 Charles Nagy UER (Throws right, but card says le .10 .02
❑ 119 Rod Nichols .10 .02
❑ 120 Steve Olin .10 .02
❑ 121 Jesse Orosco .10 .02
❑ 122 Rudy Seanez .10 .02
❑ 123 Joel Skinner .10 .02
❑ 124 Greg Swindell .10 .02
❑ 125 Jim Thome .25 .08
❑ 126 Mark Whiten .10 .02
❑ 127 Scott Aldred .10 .02
❑ 128 Andy Allanson .10 .02
❑ 129 John Cerutti .10 .02
❑ 130 Milt Cuyler .10 .02
❑ 131 Mike Dalton .10 .02
❑ 132 Rob Deer .10 .02
❑ 133 Cecil Fielder .10 .02
❑ 134 Travis Fryman .10 .02
❑ 135 Dan Gakeler .10 .02
❑ 136 Paul Gibson .10 .02
❑ 137 Bill Gullickson .10 .02
❑ 138 Mike Henneman .10 .02
❑ 139 Pete Incaviglia .10 .02
❑ 140 Mark Leiter .10 .02
❑ 141 Scott Livingstone .10 .02
❑ 142 Lloyd Moseby .10 .02
❑ 143 Tony Phillips .10 .02
❑ 144 Mark Salas .10 .02
❑ 145 Frank Tanana .10 .02
❑ 146 Walt Terrell .10 .02
❑ 147 Mickey Tettleton .10 .02
❑ 148 Alan Trammell .10 .02
❑ 149 Lou Whitaker .10 .02
❑ 150 Kevin Appier .10 .02
❑ 151 Luis Aquino .10 .02
❑ 152 Todd Benzinger .10 .02
❑ 153 Mike Boddicker .10 .02
❑ 154 George Brett .60 .25
❑ 155 Storm Davis .10 .02
❑ 156 Jim Eisenreich .10 .02
❑ 157 Kirk Gibson .10 .02
❑ 158 Tom Gordon .10 .02
❑ 159 Mark Gubicza .10 .02
❑ 160 David Howard .10 .02
❑ 161 Mike Macfarlane .10 .02
❑ 162 Brent Mayne .10 .02
❑ 163 Brian McRae .10 .02
❑ 164 Jeff Montgomery .10 .02
❑ 165 Bill Pecota .10 .02
❑ 166 Harvey Pulliam .10 .02
❑ 167 Bret Saberhagen .10 .02
❑ 168 Kevin Seitzer .10 .02
❑ 169 Terry Shumpert .10 .02
❑ 170 Kurt Stillwell .10 .02
❑ 171 Danny Tartabull .10 .02
❑ 172 Gary Thurman .10 .02
❑ 173 Dante Bichette .10 .02
❑ 174 Kevin D. Brown .10 .02
❑ 175 Chuck Crim .10 .02
❑ 176 Jim Gantner .10 .02
❑ 177 Darryl Hamilton .10 .02
❑ 178 Ted Higuera .10 .02
❑ 179 Darren Holmes .10 .02
❑ 180 Mark Lee .10 .02
❑ 181 Julio Machado .10 .02
❑ 182 Paul Molitor .10 .02
❑ 183 Jaime Navarro .10 .02
❑ 184 Edwin Nunez .10 .02
❑ 185 Dan Plesac .10 .02
❑ 186 Willie Randolph .10 .02
❑ 187 Ron Robinson .10 .02
❑ 188 Gary Sheffield .10 .02
❑ 189 Bill Spiers .10 .02
❑ 190 B.J. Surhoff .10 .02
❑ 191 Dale Sveum .10 .02
❑ 192 Greg Vaughn .10 .02
❑ 193 Bill Wegman .10 .02
❑ 194 Robin Yount .40 .15
❑ 195 Rick Aguilera .10 .02
❑ 196 Allan Anderson .10 .02
❑ 197 Steve Bedrosian .10 .02
❑ 198 Randy Bush .10 .02
❑ 199 Larry Casian .10 .02
❑ 200 Chili Davis .10 .02
❑ 201 Scott Erickson .10 .02
❑ 202 Greg Gagne .10 .02
❑ 203 Dan Gladden .10 .02
❑ 204 Brian Harper .10 .02
❑ 205 Kent Hrbek .10 .02
❑ 206 Chuck Knoblauch UER .10 .02
❑ 207 Gene Larkin .10 .02
❑ 208 Terry Leach .10 .02
❑ 209 Scott Leius .10 .02
❑ 210 Shane Mack .10 .02
❑ 211 Jack Morris .10 .02
❑ 212 Pedro Munoz .10 .02
❑ 213 Denny Neagle .10 .02
❑ 214 Al Newman .10 .02
❑ 215 Junior Ortiz .10 .02
❑ 216 Mike Pagliarulo .10 .02
❑ 217 Kirby Puckett .25 .08
❑ 218 Paul Sorrento .10 .02
❑ 219 Kevin Tapani .10 .02
❑ 220 Lenny Webster .10 .02
❑ 221 Jesse Barfield .10 .02
❑ 222 Greg Cadaret .10 .02
❑ 223 Dave Eiland .10 .02
❑ 224 Alvaro Espinoza .10 .02
❑ 225 Steve Farr .10 .02
❑ 226 Bob Geren .10 .02
❑ 227 Lee Guetterman .10 .02
❑ 228 John Habyan .10 .02
❑ 229 Mel Hall .10 .02
❑ 230 Steve Howe .10 .02
❑ 231 Mike Humphreys .10 .02
❑ 232 Scott Kamieniecki .10 .02
❑ 233 Pat Kelly .10 .02
❑ 234 Roberto Kelly .10 .02
❑ 235 Tim Leary .10 .02
❑ 236 Kevin Maas .10 .02
❑ 237 Don Mattingly .60 .25
❑ 238 Hensley Meulens .10 .02
❑ 239 Matt Nokes .10 .02
❑ 240 Pascual Perez .10 .02
❑ 241 Eric Plunk .10 .02
❑ 242 John Ramos .10 .02
❑ 243 Scott Sanderson .10 .02
❑ 244 Steve Sax .10 .02
❑ 245 Wade Taylor .10 .02
❑ 246 Randy Velarde .10 .02
❑ 247 Bernie Williams .15 .05
❑ 248 Troy Afenir .10 .02
❑ 249 Harold Baines .10 .02
❑ 250 Lance Blankenship .10 .02
❑ 251 Mike Bordick .10 .02
❑ 252 Jose Canseco .15 .05
❑ 253 Steve Chitren .10 .02
❑ 254 Ron Darling .10 .02
❑ 255 Dennis Eckersley .10 .02
❑ 256 Mike Gallego .10 .02
❑ 257 Dave Henderson .10 .02
❑ 258 Rickey Henderson .25 .08
❑ 259 Rick Honeycutt .10 .02
❑ 260 Brook Jacoby .10 .02
❑ 261 Carney Lansford .10 .02
❑ 262 Mark McGwire .60 .25
❑ 263 Mike Moore .10 .02
❑ 264 Gene Nelson .10 .02
❑ 265 Jamie Quirk .10 .02
❑ 266 Joe Slusarski .10 .02
❑ 267 Terry Steinbach .10 .02
❑ 268 Dave Stewart .10 .02
❑ 269 Todd Van Poppel .10 .02
❑ 270 Walt Weiss .10 .02
❑ 271 Bob Welch .10 .02
❑ 272 Curt Young .10 .02
❑ 273 Scott Bradley .10 .02
❑ 274 Greg Briley .10 .02
❑ 275 Jay Buhner .10 .02
❑ 276 Henry Cotto .10 .02
❑ 277 Alvin Davis .10 .02
❑ 278 Rich DeLucia .10 .02
❑ 279 Ken Griffey Jr. .40 .15
❑ 280 Erik Hanson .10 .02
❑ 281 Brian Holman .10 .02
❑ 282 Mike Jackson .10 .02
❑ 283 Randy Johnson .25 .08
❑ 284 Tracy Jones .10 .02
❑ 285 Bill Krueger .10 .02
❑ 286 Edgar Martinez .15 .05
❑ 287 Tino Martinez .15 .05
❑ 288 Rob Murphy .10 .02
❑ 289 Pete O'Brien .10 .02
❑ 290 Alonzo Powell .10 .02
❑ 291 Harold Reynolds .10 .02
❑ 292 Mike Schooler .10 .02
❑ 293 Russ Swan .10 .02
❑ 294 Bill Swift .10 .02
❑ 295 Dave Valle .10 .02
❑ 296 Omar Vizquel .15 .05
❑ 297 Gerald Alexander .10 .02
❑ 298 Brad Arnsberg .10 .02
❑ 299 Kevin Brown .10 .02
❑ 300 Jack Daugherty .10 .02
❑ 301 Mario Diaz .10 .02
❑ 302 Brian Downing .10 .02
❑ 303 Julio Franco .10 .02
❑ 304 Juan Gonzalez .15 .05
❑ 305 Rich Gossage .10 .02
❑ 306 Jose Guzman .10 .02
❑ 307 Jose Hernandez RC .25 .08
❑ 308 Jeff Huson .10 .02
❑ 309 Mike Jeffcoat .10 .02
❑ 310 Terry Mathews .10 .02
❑ 311 Rafael Palmeiro .15 .05
❑ 312 Dean Palmer .10 .02
❑ 313 Geno Petralli .10 .02
❑ 314 Gary Pettis .10 .02
❑ 315 Kevin Reimer .10 .02
❑ 316 Ivan Rodriguez .25 .08
❑ 317 Kenny Rogers .10 .02
❑ 318 Wayne Rosenthal .10 .02
❑ 319 Jeff Russell .10 .02
❑ 320 Nolan Ryan 1.00 .40
❑ 321 Ruben Sierra .10 .02
❑ 322 Jim Acker .10 .02
❑ 323 Roberto Alomar .15 .05
❑ 324 Derek Bell .10 .02
❑ 325 Pat Borders .10 .02
❑ 326 Tom Candiotti .10 .02
❑ 327 Joe Carter .10 .02
❑ 328 Rob Ducey .10 .02
❑ 329 Kelly Gruber .10 .02
❑ 330 Juan Guzman .10 .02
❑ 331 Tom Henke .10 .02
❑ 332 Jimmy Key .10 .02
❑ 333 Manny Lee .10 .02
❑ 334 Al Leiter .10 .02
❑ 335 Bob MacDonald .10 .02
❑ 336 Candy Maldonado .10 .02
❑ 337 Rance Mulliniks .10 .02
❑ 338 Greg Myers .10 .02
❑ 339 John Olerud UER .10 .02
❑ 340 Ed Sprague .10 .02
❑ 341 Dave Stieb .10 .02
❑ 342 Todd Stottlemyre .10 .02
❑ 343 Mike Timlin .10 .02
❑ 344 Duane Ward .10 .02
❑ 345 David Wells .10 .02
❑ 346 Devon White .10 .02
❑ 347 Mookie Wilson .10 .02
❑ 348 Eddie Zosky .10 .02
❑ 349 Steve Avery .10 .02
❑ 350 Mike Bell .10 .02
❑ 351 Rafael Belliard .10 .02
❑ 352 Juan Berenguer .10 .02
❑ 353 Jeff Blauser .10 .02
❑ 354 Sid Bream .10 .02
❑ 355 Francisco Cabrera .10 .02
❑ 356 Marvin Freeman .10 .02
❑ 357 Ron Gant .10 .02
❑ 358 Tom Glavine .15 .05
❑ 359 Brian Hunter .10 .02
❑ 360 David Justice .10 .02
❑ 361 Charlie Leibrandt .10 .02
❑ 362 Mark Lemke .10 .02
❑ 363 Kent Mercker .10 .02
❑ 364 Keith Mitchell .10 .02

❑ 365 Greg Olson .10 .02
❑ 366 Terry Pendleton .10 .02
❑ 367 Armando Reynoso RC .25 .08
❑ 368 Deion Sanders .15 .05
❑ 369 Lonnie Smith .10 .02
❑ 370 Pete Smith .10 .02
❑ 371 John Smoltz .15 .05
❑ 372 Mike Stanton .10 .02
❑ 373 Jeff Treadway .10 .02
❑ 374 Mark Wohlers .10 .02
❑ 375 Paul Assenmacher .10 .02
❑ 376 George Bell .10 .02
❑ 377 Shawn Boskie .10 .02
❑ 378 Frank Castillo .10 .02
❑ 379 Andre Dawson .10 .02
❑ 380 Shawon Dunston .10 .02
❑ 381 Mark Grace .15 .05
❑ 382 Mike Harkey .10 .02
❑ 383 Danny Jackson .10 .02
❑ 384 Les Lancaster .10 .02
❑ 385 Ced Landrum .10 .02
❑ 386 Greg Maddux .40 .15
❑ 387 Derrick May .10 .02
❑ 388 Chuck McElroy .10 .02
❑ 389 Ryne Sandberg .40 .15
❑ 390 Heathcliff Slocumb .10 .02
❑ 391 Dave Smith .10 .02
❑ 392 Dwight Smith .10 .02
❑ 393 Rick Sutcliffe .10 .02
❑ 394 Hector Villanueva .10 .02
❑ 395 Chico Walker .10 .02
❑ 396 Jerome Walton .10 .02
❑ 397 Rick Wilkins .10 .02
❑ 398 Jack Armstrong .10 .02
❑ 399 Freddie Benavides .10 .02
❑ 400 Glenn Braggs .10 .02
❑ 401 Tom Browning .10 .02
❑ 402 Norm Charlton .10 .02
❑ 403 Eric Davis .10 .02
❑ 404 Rob Dibble .10 .02
❑ 405 Bill Doran .10 .02
❑ 406 Mariano Duncan .10 .02
❑ 407 Kip Gross .10 .02
❑ 408 Chris Hammond .10 .02
❑ 409 Billy Hatcher .10 .02
❑ 410 Chris Jones .10 .02
❑ 411 Barry Larkin .15 .05
❑ 412 Hal Morris .10 .02
❑ 413 Randy Myers .10 .02
❑ 414 Joe Oliver .10 .02
❑ 415 Paul O'Neill .15 .05
❑ 416 Ted Power .10 .02
❑ 417 Luis Quinones .10 .02
❑ 418 Jeff Reed .10 .02
❑ 419 Jose Rijo .10 .02
❑ 420 Chris Sabo .10 .02
❑ 421 Reggie Sanders .10 .02
❑ 422 Scott Scudder .10 .02
❑ 423 Glenn Sutko .10 .02
❑ 424 Eric Anthony .10 .02
❑ 425 Jeff Bagwell .25 .08
❑ 426 Craig Biggio .15 .05
❑ 427 Ken Caminiti .10 .02
❑ 428 Casey Candaele .10 .02
❑ 429 Mike Capel .10 .02
❑ 430 Andujar Cedeno .10 .02
❑ 431 Jim Corsi .10 .02
❑ 432 Mark Davidson .10 .02
❑ 433 Steve Finley .10 .02
❑ 434 Luis Gonzalez .10 .02
❑ 435 Pete Harnisch .10 .02
❑ 436 Dwayne Henry .10 .02
❑ 437 Xavier Hernandez .10 .02
❑ 438 Jimmy Jones .10 .02
❑ 439 Darryl Kile .10 .02
❑ 440 Rob Mallicoat .10 .02
❑ 441 Andy Mota .10 .02
❑ 442 Al Osuna .10 .02
❑ 443 Mark Portugal .10 .02
❑ 444 Scott Servais .10 .02
❑ 445 Mike Simms .10 .02
❑ 446 Gerald Young .10 .02
❑ 447 Tim Belcher .10 .02
❑ 448 Brett Butler .10 .02
❑ 449 John Candelaria .10 .02
❑ 450 Gary Carter .10 .02
❑ 451 Dennis Cook .10 .02
❑ 452 Tim Crews .10 .02
❑ 453 Kal Daniels .10 .02
❑ 454 Jim Gott .10 .02
❑ 455 Alfredo Griffin .10 .02
❑ 456 Kevin Gross .10 .02
❑ 457 Chris Gwynn .10 .02
❑ 458 Lenny Harris .10 .02
❑ 459 Orel Hershiser .10 .02
❑ 460 Jay Howell .10 .02
❑ 461 Stan Javier .10 .02
❑ 462 Eric Karros .10 .02
❑ 463 Ramon Martinez UER (Card says bats right, should .10 .02
❑ 464 Roger McDowell UER (Wins add up to 54, totals ha .10 .02
❑ 465 Mike Morgan .10 .02
❑ 466 Eddie Murray .25 .08
❑ 467 Jose Offerman .10 .02
❑ 468 Bob Ojeda .10 .02
❑ 469 Juan Samuel .10 .02
❑ 470 Mike Scioscia .10 .02
❑ 471 Darryl Strawberry .10 .02
❑ 472 Bret Barberie .10 .02
❑ 473 Brian Barnes .10 .02
❑ 474 Eric Bullock .10 .02
❑ 475 Ivan Calderon .10 .02
❑ 476 Delino DeShields .10 .02
❑ 477 Jeff Fassero .10 .02
❑ 478 Mike Fitzgerald .10 .02
❑ 479 Steve Frey .10 .02
❑ 480 Andres Galarraga .10 .02
❑ 481 Mark Gardner .10 .02
❑ 482 Marquis Grissom .10 .02
❑ 483 Chris Haney .10 .02
❑ 484 Barry Jones .10 .02
❑ 485 Dave Martinez .10 .02
❑ 486 Dennis Martinez .10 .02
❑ 487 Chris Nabholz .10 .02
❑ 488 Spike Owen .10 .02
❑ 489 Gilberto Reyes .10 .02
❑ 490 Mel Rojas .10 .02
❑ 491 Scott Ruskin .10 .02
❑ 492 Bill Sampen .10 .02
❑ 493 Larry Walker .15 .05
❑ 494 Tim Wallach .10 .02
❑ 495 Daryl Boston .10 .02
❑ 496 Hubie Brooks .10 .02
❑ 497 Tim Burke .10 .02
❑ 498 Mark Carreon .10 .02
❑ 499 Tony Castillo .10 .02
❑ 500 Vince Coleman .10 .02
❑ 501 David Cone .10 .02
❑ 502 Kevin Elster .10 .02
❑ 503 Sid Fernandez .10 .02
❑ 504 John Franco .10 .02
❑ 505 Dwight Gooden .10 .02
❑ 506 Todd Hundley .10 .02
❑ 507 Jeff Innis .10 .02
❑ 508 Gregg Jefferies .10 .02
❑ 509 Howard Johnson .10 .02
❑ 510 Dave Magadan .10 .02
❑ 511 Terry McDaniel .10 .02
❑ 512 Kevin McReynolds .10 .02
❑ 513 Keith Miller .10 .02
❑ 514 Charlie O'Brien .10 .02
❑ 515 Mackey Sasser .10 .02
❑ 516 Pete Schourek .10 .02
❑ 517 Julio Valera .10 .02
❑ 518 Frank Viola .10 .02
❑ 519 Wally Whitehurst .10 .02
❑ 520 Anthony Young .10 .02
❑ 521 Andy Ashby .10 .02
❑ 522 Kim Batiste .10 .02
❑ 523 Joe Boever .10 .02
❑ 524 Wes Chamberlain .10 .02
❑ 525 Pat Combs .10 .02
❑ 526 Danny Cox .10 .02
❑ 527 Darren Daulton .10 .02
❑ 528 Jose DeJesus .10 .02
❑ 529 Len Dykstra .10 .02
❑ 530 Darrin Fletcher .10 .02
❑ 531 Tommy Greene .10 .02
❑ 532 Jason Grimsley .10 .02
❑ 533 Charlie Hayes .10 .02
❑ 534 Von Hayes .10 .02
❑ 535 Dave Hollins .10 .02
❑ 536 Ricky Jordan .10 .02
❑ 537 John Kruk .10 .02
❑ 538 Jim Lindeman .10 .02
❑ 539 Mickey Morandini .10 .02
❑ 540 Terry Mulholland .10 .02
❑ 541 Dale Murphy .15 .05
❑ 542 Randy Ready .10 .02
❑ 543 Wally Ritchie UER (Letters in data are cut off o .10 .02
❑ 544 Bruce Ruffin .10 .02
❑ 545 Steve Searcy .10 .02
❑ 546 Dickie Thon .10 .02
❑ 547 Mitch Williams .10 .02
❑ 548 Stan Belinda .10 .02
❑ 549 Jay Bell .10 .02
❑ 550 Barry Bonds 1.00 .40
❑ 551 Bobby Bonilla .10 .02
❑ 552 Steve Buechele .10 .02
❑ 553 Doug Drabek .10 .02
❑ 554 Neal Heaton .10 .02
❑ 555 Jeff King .10 .02
❑ 556 Bob Kipper .10 .02
❑ 557 Bill Landrum .10 .02
❑ 558 Mike LaValliere .10 .02
❑ 559 Jose Lind .10 .02
❑ 560 Lloyd McClendon .10 .02
❑ 561 Orlando Merced .10 .02
❑ 562 Bob Patterson .10 .02
❑ 563 Joe Redfield .10 .02
❑ 564 Gary Redus .10 .02
❑ 565 Rosario Rodriguez .10 .02
❑ 566 Don Slaught .10 .02
❑ 567 John Smiley .10 .02
❑ 568 Zane Smith .10 .02
❑ 569 Randy Tomlin .10 .02
❑ 570 Andy Van Slyke .15 .05
❑ 571 Gary Varsho .10 .02
❑ 572 Bob Walk .10 .02
❑ 573 John Wehner UER (Actually played for Carolina in .10 .02
❑ 574 Juan Agosto .10 .02
❑ 575 Cris Carpenter .10 .02
❑ 576 Jose DeLeon .10 .02
❑ 577 Rich Gedman .10 .02
❑ 578 Bernard Gilkey .10 .02
❑ 579 Pedro Guerrero .10 .02
❑ 580 Ken Hill .10 .02
❑ 581 Rex Hudler .10 .02
❑ 582 Felix Jose .10 .02
❑ 583 Ray Lankford .10 .02
❑ 584 Omar Olivares .10 .02
❑ 585 Jose Oquendo .10 .02
❑ 586 Tom Pagnozzi .10 .02
❑ 587 Geronimo Pena .10 .02
❑ 588 Mike Perez .10 .02
❑ 589 Gerald Perry .10 .02
❑ 590 Bryn Smith .10 .02
❑ 591 Lee Smith .10 .02
❑ 592 Ozzie Smith .40 .15
❑ 593 Scott Terry .10 .02
❑ 594 Bob Tewksbury .10 .02
❑ 595 Milt Thompson .10 .02
❑ 596 Todd Zeile .10 .02
❑ 597 Larry Andersen .10 .02
❑ 598 Oscar Azocar .10 .02
❑ 599 Andy Benes .10 .02
❑ 600 Ricky Bones .10 .02
❑ 601 Jerald Clark .10 .02
❑ 602 Pat Clements .10 .02
❑ 603 Paul Faries .10 .02
❑ 604 Tony Fernandez .10 .02
❑ 605 Tony Gwynn .30 .10
❑ 606 Greg W. Harris .10 .02
❑ 607 Thomas Howard .10 .02
❑ 608 Bruce Hurst .10 .02
❑ 609 Darrin Jackson .10 .02
❑ 610 Tom Lampkin .10 .02
❑ 611 Craig Lefferts .10 .02
❑ 612 Jim Lewis RC .10 .02
❑ 613 Mike Maddux .10 .02
❑ 614 Fred McGriff .15 .05

❑ 615 Jose Melendez .10 .02
❑ 616 Jose Mota .10 .02
❑ 617 Dennis Rasmussen .10 .02
❑ 618 Bip Roberts .10 .02
❑ 619 Rich Rodriguez .10 .02
❑ 620 Benito Santiago .10 .02
❑ 621 Craig Shipley .10 .02
❑ 622 Tim Teufel .10 .02
❑ 623 Kevin Ward .10 .02
❑ 624 Ed Whitson .10 .02
❑ 625 Dave Anderson .10 .02
❑ 626 Kevin Bass .10 .02
❑ 627 Rod Beck RC .40 .15
❑ 628 Bud Black .10 .02
❑ 629 Jeff Brantley .10 .02
❑ 630 John Burkett .10 .02
❑ 631 Will Clark .15 .05
❑ 632 Royce Clayton .10 .02
❑ 633 Steve Decker .10 .02
❑ 634 Kelly Downs .10 .02
❑ 635 Mike Felder .10 .02
❑ 636 Scott Garrelts .10 .02
❑ 637 Eric Gunderson .10 .02
❑ 638 Bryan Hickerson RC .10 .02
❑ 639 Darren Lewis .10 .02
❑ 640 Greg Litton .10 .02
❑ 641 Kirt Manwaring .10 .02
❑ 642 Paul McClellan .10 .02
❑ 643 Willie McGee .10 .02
❑ 644 Kevin Mitchell .10 .02
❑ 645 Francisco Oliveras .10 .02
❑ 646 Mike Remlinger .10 .02
❑ 647 Dave Righetti .10 .02
❑ 648 Robby Thompson .10 .02
❑ 649 Jose Uribe .10 .02
❑ 650 Matt Williams .10 .02
❑ 651 Trevor Wilson .10 .02
❑ 652 Tom Goodwin MLP UER .10 .02
❑ 653 Terry Bross MLP .10 .02
❑ 654 Mike Christopher MLP .10 .02
❑ 655 Kenny Lofton .15 .05
❑ 656 Chris Cron MLP .10 .02
❑ 657 Willie Banks MLP .10 .02
❑ 658 Pat Rice MLP .10 .02
❑ 659A Rob Mauer ERR .75 .30
❑ 659B Rob Maurer MLP COR .10 .02
❑ 660 Don Harris MLP .10 .02
❑ 661 Henry Rodriguez MLP .10 .02
❑ 662 Cliff Brantley MLP .10 .02
❑ 663 Mike Linskey MLP UER .10 .02
❑ 664 Gary DiSarcina MLP .10 .02
❑ 665 Gil Heredia RC .25 .08
❑ 666 Vinny Castilla RC 1.00 .40
❑ 667 Paul Abbott MLP .10 .02
❑ 668 Monty Fariss MLP UER (Called Paul on back) .10 .02
❑ 669 Jarvis Brown MLP .10 .02
❑ 670 Wayne Kirby RC .10 .02
❑ 671 Scott Brosius RC .40 .15
❑ 672 Bob Hamelin .10 .02
❑ 673 Joel Johnston MLP .10 .02
❑ 674 Tim Spehr MLP .10 .02
❑ 675A Jeff Gardner ERR P .75 .30
❑ 675B Jeff Gardner MLP COR .10 .02
❑ 676 Rico Rossy MLP .10 .02
❑ 677 Roberto Hernandez MLP .10 .02
❑ 678 Ted Wood MLP .10 .02
❑ 679 Cal Eldred .10 .02
❑ 680 Sean Berry MLP .10 .02
❑ 681 Rickey Henderson RS .15 .05
❑ 682 Nolan Ryan RS .50 .20
❑ 683 Dennis Martinez RS .10 .02
❑ 684 Wilson Alvarez RS .10 .02
❑ 685 Joe Carter RS .10 .02
❑ 686 Dave Winfield RS .10 .02
❑ 687 David Cone RS .10 .02
❑ 688 Jose Canseco LL UER .10 .02
❑ 689 Howard Johnson LL .10 .02
❑ 690 Julio Franco LL .10 .02
❑ 691 Terry Pendleton LL .10 .02
❑ 692 Cecil Fielder LL .10 .02
❑ 693 Scott Erickson LL .10 .02
❑ 694 Tom Glavine LL .10 .02
❑ 695 Dennis Martinez LL .10 .02
❑ 696 Bryan Harvey LL .10 .02
❑ 697 Lee Smith LL .10 .02
❑ 698 Roberto/Sandy Alomar .10 .02
❑ 699 B.Bonilla/W.Clark .10 .02
❑ 700 Wohlers/Mercker/Pena .10 .02
❑ 701 B.Jackson/F.Thomas .15 .05
❑ 702 P.Molitor/Butler .10 .02
❑ 703 C.Ripken/J.Carter .40 .15
❑ 704 B.Larkin/K.Puckett .15 .05
❑ 705 M.Vaughn/C.Fielder .10 .02
❑ 706 R.Martinez/O.Guillen .10 .02
❑ 707 H.Baines/W.Boggs .10 .02
❑ 708 Robin Yount PV .25 .08
❑ 709 Ken Griffey Jr. PV .25 .08
❑ 710 Nolan Ryan PV .50 .20
❑ 711 Cal Ripken PV .40 .15
❑ 712 Frank Thomas PV .15 .05
❑ 713 David Justice PV .10 .02
❑ 714 Checklist 1-101 .10 .02
❑ 715 Checklist 102-194 .10 .02
❑ 716 Checklist 195-296 .10 .02
❑ 717 Checklist 297-397 .10 .02
❑ 718 Checklist 398-494 .10 .02
❑ 719 Checklist 495-596 .10 .02
❑ 720A Checklist 597-720 ERR (659 Rob Mauer) .10 .02
❑ 720B Checklist 597-720 COR (659 Rob Maurer) .10 .02

1993 Fleer

❑ COMPLETE SET (720) 40.00 20.00
❑ COMPLETE SERIES 1 (360) 20.00 10.00
❑ COMPLETE SERIES 2 (360) 20.00 10.00
❑ 1 Steve Avery .10 .02
❑ 2 Sid Bream .10 .02
❑ 3 Ron Gant .20 .07
❑ 4 Tom Glavine .30 .10
❑ 5 Brian Hunter .10 .02
❑ 6 Ryan Klesko .20 .07
❑ 7 Charlie Leibrandt .10 .02
❑ 8 Kent Mercker .10 .02
❑ 9 David Nied .10 .02
❑ 10 Otis Nixon .10 .02
❑ 11 Greg Olson .10 .02
❑ 12 Terry Pendleton .20 .07
❑ 13 Deion Sanders .30 .10
❑ 14 John Smoltz .30 .10
❑ 15 Mike Stanton .10 .02
❑ 16 Mark Wohlers .10 .02
❑ 17 Paul Assenmacher .10 .02
❑ 18 Steve Buechele .10 .02
❑ 19 Shawon Dunston .10 .02
❑ 20 Mark Grace .30 .10
❑ 21 Derrick May .10 .02
❑ 22 Chuck McElroy .10 .02
❑ 23 Mike Morgan .10 .02
❑ 24 Rey Sanchez .10 .02
❑ 25 Ryne Sandberg .75 .30
❑ 26 Bob Scanlan .10 .02
❑ 27 Sammy Sosa .50 .20
❑ 28 Rick Wilkins .10 .02
❑ 29 Bobby Ayala RC .10 .02
❑ 30 Tim Belcher .10 .02
❑ 31 Jeff Branson .10 .02
❑ 32 Norm Charlton .10 .02
❑ 33 Steve Foster .10 .02
❑ 34 Willie Greene .10 .02
❑ 35 Chris Hammond .10 .02
❑ 36 Milt Hill .10 .02
❑ 37 Hal Morris .10 .02
❑ 38 Joe Oliver .10 .02
❑ 39 Paul O'Neill .30 .10
❑ 40 Tim Pugh RC .10 .02
❑ 41 Jose Rijo .10 .02
❑ 42 Bip Roberts .10 .02
❑ 43 Chris Sabo .10 .02
❑ 44 Reggie Sanders .20 .07
❑ 45 Eric Anthony .10 .02
❑ 46 Jeff Bagwell .30 .10
❑ 47 Craig Biggio .30 .10
❑ 48 Joe Boever .10 .02
❑ 49 Casey Candaele .10 .02
❑ 50 Steve Finley .20 .07
❑ 51 Luis Gonzalez .20 .07
❑ 52 Pete Harnisch .10 .02
❑ 53 Xavier Hernandez .10 .02
❑ 54 Doug Jones .10 .02
❑ 55 Eddie Taubensee .10 .02
❑ 56 Brian Williams .10 .02
❑ 57 Pedro Astacio .10 .02
❑ 58 Todd Benzinger .10 .02
❑ 59 Brett Butler .20 .07
❑ 60 Tom Candiotti .10 .02
❑ 61 Lenny Harris .10 .02
❑ 62 Carlos Hernandez .10 .02
❑ 63 Orel Hershiser .20 .07
❑ 64 Eric Karros .20 .07
❑ 65 Ramon Martinez .10 .02
❑ 66 Jose Offerman .10 .02
❑ 67 Mike Scioscia .10 .02
❑ 68 Mike Sharperson .10 .02
❑ 69 Eric Young .10 .02
❑ 70 Moises Alou .20 .07
❑ 71 Ivan Calderon .10 .02
❑ 72 Archi Cianfrocco .10 .02
❑ 73 Wil Cordero .10 .02
❑ 74 Delino DeShields .10 .02
❑ 75 Mark Gardner .10 .02
❑ 76 Ken Hill .10 .02
❑ 77 Tim Laker RC .10 .02
❑ 78 Chris Nabholz .10 .02
❑ 79 Mel Rojas .10 .02
❑ 80 John Vander Wal UER (Misspelled Vander Wall in l .10 .02
❑ 81 Larry Walker .20 .07
❑ 82 Tim Wallach .10 .02
❑ 83 John Wetteland .20 .07
❑ 84 Bobby Bonilla .20 .07
❑ 85 Daryl Boston .10 .02
❑ 86 Sid Fernandez .10 .02
❑ 87 Eric Hillman .10 .02
❑ 88 Todd Hundley .10 .02
❑ 89 Howard Johnson .10 .02
❑ 90 Jeff Kent .50 .20
❑ 91 Eddie Murray .50 .20
❑ 92 Bill Pecota .10 .02
❑ 93 Bret Saberhagen .20 .07
❑ 94 Dick Schofield .10 .02
❑ 95 Pete Schourek .10 .02
❑ 96 Anthony Young .10 .02
❑ 97 Ruben Amaro .10 .02
❑ 98 Juan Bell .10 .02
❑ 99 Wes Chamberlain .10 .02
❑ 100 Darren Daulton .20 .07
❑ 101 Mariano Duncan .10 .02
❑ 102 Mike Hartley .10 .02
❑ 103 Ricky Jordan .10 .02
❑ 104 John Kruk .20 .07
❑ 105 Mickey Morandini .10 .02
❑ 106 Terry Mulholland .10 .02
❑ 107 Ben Rivera .10 .02
❑ 108 Curt Schilling .20 .07
❑ 109 Keith Shepherd RC .10 .02
❑ 110 Stan Belinda .10 .02
❑ 111 Jay Bell .20 .07
❑ 112 Barry Bonds 1.50 .60
❑ 113 Jeff King .10 .02
❑ 114 Mike LaValliere .10 .02
❑ 115 Jose Lind .10 .02
❑ 116 Roger Mason .10 .02
❑ 117 Orlando Merced .10 .02
❑ 118 Bob Patterson .10 .02
❑ 119 Don Slaught .10 .02
❑ 120 Zane Smith .10 .02
❑ 121 Randy Tomlin .10 .02

❑ 122	Andy Van Slyke	.30	.10
❑ 123	Tim Wakefield	.50	.20
❑ 124	Rheal Cormier	.10	.02
❑ 125	Bernard Gilkey	.10	.02
❑ 126	Felix Jose	.10	.02
❑ 127	Ray Lankford	.20	.07
❑ 128	Bob McClure	.10	.02
❑ 129	Donovan Osborne	.10	.02
❑ 130	Tom Pagnozzi	.10	.02
❑ 131	Geronimo Pena	.10	.02
❑ 132	Mike Perez	.10	.02
❑ 133	Lee Smith	.20	.07
❑ 134	Bob Tewksbury	.10	.02
❑ 135	Todd Worrell	.10	.02
❑ 136	Todd Zeile	.10	.02
❑ 137	Jerald Clark	.10	.02
❑ 138	Tony Gwynn	.60	.25
❑ 139	Greg W. Harris	.10	.02
❑ 140	Jeremy Hernandez	.10	.02
❑ 141	Darrin Jackson	.10	.02
❑ 142	Mike Maddux	.10	.02
❑ 143	Fred McGriff	.30	.10
❑ 144	Jose Melendez	.10	.02
❑ 145	Rich Rodriguez	.10	.02
❑ 146	Frank Seminara	.10	.02
❑ 147	Gary Sheffield	.20	.07
❑ 148	Kurt Stillwell	.10	.02
❑ 149	Dan Walters	.10	.02
❑ 150	Rod Beck	.10	.02
❑ 151	Bud Black	.10	.02
❑ 152	Jeff Brantley	.10	.02
❑ 153	John Burkett	.10	.02
❑ 154	Will Clark	.30	.10
❑ 155	Royce Clayton	.10	.02
❑ 156	Mike Jackson	.10	.02
❑ 157	Darren Lewis	.10	.02
❑ 158	Kirt Manwaring	.10	.02
❑ 159	Willie McGee	.20	.07
❑ 160	Cory Snyder	.10	.02
❑ 161	Bill Swift	.10	.02
❑ 162	Trevor Wilson	.10	.02
❑ 163	Brady Anderson	.20	.07
❑ 164	Glenn Davis	.10	.02
❑ 165	Mike Devereaux	.10	.02
❑ 166	Todd Frohwirth	.10	.02
❑ 167	Leo Gomez	.10	.02
❑ 168	Chris Hoiles	.10	.02
❑ 169	Ben McDonald	.10	.02
❑ 170	Randy Milligan	.10	.02
❑ 171	Alan Mills	.10	.02
❑ 172	Mike Mussina	.30	.10
❑ 173	Gregg Olson	.10	.02
❑ 174	Arthur Rhodes	.10	.02
❑ 175	David Segui	.10	.02
❑ 176	Ellis Burks	.20	.07
❑ 177	Roger Clemens	1.00	.40
❑ 178	Scott Cooper	.10	.02
❑ 179	Danny Darwin	.10	.02
❑ 180	Tony Fossas	.10	.02
❑ 181	Paul Quantrill	.10	.02
❑ 182	Jody Reed	.10	.02
❑ 183	John Valentin	.10	.02
❑ 184	Mo Vaughn	.20	.07
❑ 185	Frank Viola	.20	.07
❑ 186	Bob Zupcic	.10	.02
❑ 187	Jim Abbott	.30	.10
❑ 188	Gary DiSarcina	.10	.02
❑ 189	Damion Easley	.10	.02
❑ 190	Junior Felix	.10	.02
❑ 191	Chuck Finley	.20	.07
❑ 192	Joe Grahe	.10	.02
❑ 193	Bryan Harvey	.10	.02
❑ 194	Mark Langston	.10	.02
❑ 195	John Orton	.10	.02
❑ 196	Luis Polonia	.10	.02
❑ 197	Tim Salmon	.30	.10
❑ 198	Luis Sojo	.10	.02
❑ 199	Wilson Alvarez	.10	.02
❑ 200	George Bell	.10	.02
❑ 201	Alex Fernandez	.10	.02
❑ 202	Craig Grebeck	.10	.02
❑ 203	Ozzie Guillen	.20	.07
❑ 204	Lance Johnson	.10	.02
❑ 205	Ron Karkovice	.10	.02
❑ 206	Kirk McCaskill	.10	.02
❑ 207	Jack McDowell	.10	.02
❑ 208	Scott Radinsky	.10	.02
❑ 209	Tim Raines	.20	.07
❑ 210	Frank Thomas	.50	.20
❑ 211	Robin Ventura	.20	.07
❑ 212	Sandy Alomar Jr.	.10	.02
❑ 213	Carlos Baerga	.10	.02
❑ 214	Dennis Cook	.10	.02
❑ 215	Thomas Howard	.10	.02
❑ 216	Mark Lewis	.10	.02
❑ 217	Derek Lilliquist	.10	.02
❑ 218	Kenny Lofton	.20	.07
❑ 219	Charles Nagy	.10	.02
❑ 220	Steve Olin	.10	.02
❑ 221	Paul Sorrento	.10	.02
❑ 222	Jim Thome	.30	.10
❑ 223	Mark Whiten	.10	.02
❑ 224	Milt Cuyler	.10	.02
❑ 225	Rob Deer	.10	.02
❑ 226	John Doherty	.10	.02
❑ 227	Cecil Fielder	.20	.07
❑ 228	Travis Fryman	.20	.07
❑ 229	Mike Henneman	.10	.02
❑ 230	John Kiely UER (Card has batting stats of Pat Ke	.10	.02
❑ 231	Kurt Knudsen	.10	.02
❑ 232	Scott Livingstone	.10	.02
❑ 233	Tony Phillips	.10	.02
❑ 234	Mickey Tettleton	.10	.02
❑ 235	Kevin Appier	.20	.07
❑ 236	George Brett	1.25	.50
❑ 237	Tom Gordon	.10	.02
❑ 238	Gregg Jefferies	.10	.02
❑ 239	Wally Joyner	.20	.07
❑ 240	Kevin Koslofski	.10	.02
❑ 241	Mike Macfarlane	.10	.02
❑ 242	Brian McRae	.10	.02
❑ 243	Rusty Meacham	.10	.02
❑ 244	Keith Miller	.10	.02
❑ 245	Jeff Montgomery	.10	.02
❑ 246	Hipolito Pichardo	.10	.02
❑ 247	Ricky Bones	.10	.02
❑ 248	Cal Eldred	.10	.02
❑ 249	Mike Fetters	.10	.02
❑ 250	Darryl Hamilton	.10	.02
❑ 251	Doug Henry	.10	.02
❑ 252	John Jaha	.10	.02
❑ 253	Pat Listach	.10	.02
❑ 254	Paul Molitor	.20	.07
❑ 255	Jaime Navarro	.10	.02
❑ 256	Kevin Seitzer	.10	.02
❑ 257	B.J. Surhoff	.20	.07
❑ 258	Greg Vaughn	.10	.02
❑ 259	Bill Wegman	.10	.02
❑ 260	Robin Yount	.75	.30
❑ 261	Rick Aguilera	.10	.02
❑ 262	Chili Davis	.20	.07
❑ 263	Scott Erickson	.10	.02
❑ 264	Greg Gagne	.10	.02
❑ 265	Mark Guthrie	.10	.02
❑ 266	Brian Harper	.10	.02
❑ 267	Kent Hrbek	.20	.07
❑ 268	Terry Jorgensen	.10	.02
❑ 269	Gene Larkin	.10	.02
❑ 270	Scott Leius	.10	.02
❑ 271	Pat Mahomes	.10	.02
❑ 272	Pedro Munoz	.10	.02
❑ 273	Kirby Puckett	.50	.20
❑ 274	Kevin Tapani	.10	.02
❑ 275	Carl Willis	.10	.02
❑ 276	Steve Farr	.10	.02
❑ 277	John Habyan	.10	.02
❑ 278	Mel Hall	.10	.02
❑ 279	Charlie Hayes	.10	.02
❑ 280	Pat Kelly	.10	.02
❑ 281	Don Mattingly	1.25	.50
❑ 282	Sam Militello	.10	.02
❑ 283	Matt Nokes	.10	.02
❑ 284	Melido Perez	.10	.02
❑ 285	Andy Stankiewicz	.10	.02
❑ 286	Danny Tartabull	.10	.02
❑ 287	Randy Velarde	.10	.02
❑ 288	Bob Wickman	.10	.02
❑ 289	Bernie Williams	.30	.10
❑ 290	Lance Blankenship	.10	.02
❑ 291	Mike Bordick	.10	.02
❑ 292	Jerry Browne	.10	.02
❑ 293	Dennis Eckersley	.20	.07
❑ 294	Rickey Henderson	.50	.20
❑ 295	Vince Horsman	.10	.02
❑ 296	Mark McGwire	1.25	.50
❑ 297	Jeff Parrett	.10	.02
❑ 298	Ruben Sierra	.20	.07
❑ 299	Terry Steinbach	.10	.02
❑ 300	Walt Weiss	.10	.02
❑ 301	Bob Welch	.10	.02
❑ 302	Willie Wilson	.10	.02
❑ 303	Bobby Witt	.10	.02
❑ 304	Bret Boone	.20	.07
❑ 305	Jay Buhner	.20	.07
❑ 306	Dave Fleming	.10	.02
❑ 307	Ken Griffey Jr.	.75	.30
❑ 308	Erik Hanson	.10	.02
❑ 309	Edgar Martinez	.30	.10
❑ 310	Tino Martinez	.30	.10
❑ 311	Jeff Nelson	.10	.02
❑ 312	Dennis Powell	.10	.02
❑ 313	Mike Schooler	.10	.02
❑ 314	Russ Swan	.10	.02
❑ 315	Dave Valle	.10	.02
❑ 316	Omar Vizquel	.30	.10
❑ 317	Kevin Brown	.20	.07
❑ 318	Todd Burns	.10	.02
❑ 319	Jose Canseco	.30	.10
❑ 320	Julio Franco	.20	.07
❑ 321	Jeff Frye	.10	.02
❑ 322	Juan Gonzalez	.20	.07
❑ 323	Jose Guzman	.10	.02
❑ 324	Jeff Huson	.10	.02
❑ 325	Dean Palmer	.20	.07
❑ 326	Kevin Reimer	.10	.02
❑ 327	Ivan Rodriguez	.30	.10
❑ 328	Kenny Rogers	.20	.07
❑ 329	Dan Smith	.10	.02
❑ 330	Roberto Alomar	.30	.10
❑ 331	Derek Bell	.10	.02
❑ 332	Pat Borders	.10	.02
❑ 333	Joe Carter	.20	.07
❑ 334	Kelly Gruber	.10	.02
❑ 335	Tom Henke	.10	.02
❑ 336	Jimmy Key	.20	.07
❑ 337	Manuel Lee	.10	.02
❑ 338	Candy Maldonado	.10	.02
❑ 339	John Olerud	.20	.07
❑ 340	Todd Stottlemyre	.10	.02
❑ 341	Duane Ward	.10	.02
❑ 342	Devon White	.20	.07
❑ 343	Dave Winfield	.20	.07
❑ 344	Edgar Martinez LL	.20	.07
❑ 345	Cecil Fielder LL	.10	.02
❑ 346	Kenny Lofton LL	.10	.02
❑ 347	Jack Morris LL	.10	.02
❑ 348	Roger Clemens LL	.50	.20
❑ 349	Fred McGriff RT	.20	.07
❑ 350	Barry Bonds RT	.75	.30
❑ 351	Gary Sheffield RT	.10	.02
❑ 352	Darren Daulton RT	.10	.02
❑ 353	Dave Hollins RT	.10	.02
❑ 354	P.Martinez/R.Martinez	.50	.20
❑ 355	K.Puckett/I.Rodriguez	.30	.10
❑ 356	Sandberg/Sheffield	.50	.20
❑ 357	R.Alomar/Knoblauch/Baerg	.20	.07
❑ 358	Checklist 1-120	.10	.02
❑ 359	Checklist 121-240	.10	.02
❑ 360	Checklist 241-360	.10	.02
❑ 361	Rafael Belliard	.10	.02
❑ 362	Damon Berryhill	.10	.02
❑ 363	Mike Bielecki	.10	.02
❑ 364	Jeff Blauser	.10	.02
❑ 365	Francisco Cabrera	.10	.02
❑ 366	Marvin Freeman	.10	.02
❑ 367	David Justice	.20	.07
❑ 368	Mark Lemke	.10	.02
❑ 369	Alejandro Pena	.10	.02
❑ 370	Jeff Reardon	.20	.07
❑ 371	Lonnie Smith	.10	.02
❑ 372	Pete Smith	.10	.02
❑ 373	Shawn Boskie	.10	.02
❑ 374	Jim Bullinger	.10	.02
❑ 375	Frank Castillo	.10	.02
❑ 376	Doug Dascenzo	.10	.02
❑ 377	Andre Dawson	.20	.07

❑	378 Mike Harkey	.10	.02
❑	379 Greg Hibbard	.10	.02
❑	380 Greg Maddux	.75	.30
❑	381 Ken Patterson	.10	.02
❑	382 Jeff D. Robinson	.10	.02
❑	383 Luis Salazar	.10	.02
❑	384 Dwight Smith	.10	.02
❑	385 Jose Vizcaino	.10	.02
❑	386 Scott Bankhead	.10	.02
❑	387 Tom Browning	.10	.02
❑	388 Darnell Coles	.10	.02
❑	389 Rob Dibble	.20	.07
❑	390 Bill Doran	.10	.02
❑	391 Dwayne Henry	.10	.02
❑	392 Cesar Hernandez	.10	.02
❑	393 Roberto Kelly	.10	.02
❑	394 Barry Larkin	.30	.10
❑	395 Dave Martinez	.10	.02
❑	396 Kevin Mitchell	.10	.02
❑	397 Jeff Reed	.10	.02
❑	398 Scott Ruskin	.10	.02
❑	399 Greg Swindell	.10	.02
❑	400 Dan Wilson	.20	.07
❑	401 Andy Ashby	.10	.02
❑	402 Freddie Benavides	.10	.02
❑	403 Dante Bichette	.20	.07
❑	404 Willie Blair	.10	.02
❑	405 Denis Boucher	.10	.02
❑	406 Vinny Castilla	.50	.20
❑	407 Braulio Castillo	.10	.02
❑	408 Alex Cole	.10	.02
❑	409 Andres Galarraga	.20	.07
❑	410 Joe Girardi	.10	.02
❑	411 Butch Henry	.10	.02
❑	412 Darren Holmes	.10	.02
❑	413 Calvin Jones	.10	.02
❑	414 Steve Reed RC	.10	.02
❑	415 Kevin Ritz	.10	.02
❑	416 Jim Tatum RC	.10	.02
❑	417 Jack Armstrong	.10	.02
❑	418 Bret Barberie	.10	.02
❑	419 Ryan Bowen	.10	.02
❑	420 Cris Carpenter	.10	.02
❑	421 Chuck Carr	.10	.02
❑	422 Scott Chiamparino	.10	.02
❑	423 Jeff Conine	.20	.07
❑	424 Jim Corsi	.10	.02
❑	425 Steve Decker	.10	.02
❑	426 Chris Donnels	.10	.02
❑	427 Monty Fariss	.10	.02
❑	428 Bob Natal	.10	.02
❑	429 Pat Rapp	.10	.02
❑	430 Dave Weathers	.10	.02
❑	431 Nigel Wilson	.10	.02
❑	432 Ken Caminiti	.20	.07
❑	433 Andujar Cedeno	.10	.02
❑	434 Tom Edens	.10	.02
❑	435 Juan Guerrero	.10	.02
❑	436 Pete Incaviglia	.10	.02
❑	437 Jimmy Jones	.10	.02
❑	438 Darryl Kile	.20	.07
❑	439 Rob Murphy	.10	.02
❑	440 Al Osuna	.10	.02
❑	441 Mark Portugal	.10	.02
❑	442 Scott Servais	.10	.02
❑	443 John Candelaria	.10	.02
❑	444 Tim Crews	.10	.02
❑	445 Eric Davis	.20	.07
❑	446 Tom Goodwin	.10	.02
❑	447 Jim Gott	.10	.02
❑	448 Kevin Gross	.10	.02
❑	449 Dave Hansen	.10	.02
❑	450 Jay Howell	.10	.02
❑	451 Roger McDowell	.10	.02
❑	452 Bob Ojeda	.10	.02
❑	453 Henry Rodriguez	.10	.02
❑	454 Darryl Strawberry	.20	.07
❑	455 Mitch Webster	.10	.02
❑	456 Steve Wilson	.10	.02
❑	457 Brian Barnes	.10	.02
❑	458 Sean Berry	.10	.02
❑	459 Jeff Fassero	.10	.02
❑	460 Darrin Fletcher	.10	.02
❑	461 Marquis Grissom	.20	.07
❑	462 Dennis Martinez	.20	.07
❑	463 Spike Owen	.10	.02
❑	464 Matt Stairs	.10	.02
❑	465 Sergio Valdez	.10	.02
❑	466 Kevin Bass	.10	.02
❑	467 Vince Coleman	.10	.02
❑	468 Mark Dewey	.10	.02
❑	469 Kevin Elster	.10	.02
❑	470 Tony Fernandez	.10	.02
❑	471 John Franco	.20	.07
❑	472 Dave Gallagher	.10	.02
❑	473 Paul Gibson	.10	.02
❑	474 Dwight Gooden	.20	.07
❑	475 Lee Guetterman	.10	.02
❑	476 Jeff Innis	.10	.02
❑	477 Dave Magadan	.10	.02
❑	478 Charlie O'Brien	.10	.02
❑	479 Willie Randolph	.20	.07
❑	480 Mackey Sasser	.10	.02
❑	481 Ryan Thompson	.10	.02
❑	482 Chico Walker	.10	.02
❑	483 Kyle Abbott	.10	.02
❑	484 Bob Ayrault	.10	.02
❑	485 Kim Batiste	.10	.02
❑	486 Cliff Brantley	.10	.02
❑	487 Jose DeLeon	.10	.02
❑	488 Len Dykstra	.20	.07
❑	489 Tommy Greene	.10	.02
❑	490 Jeff Grotewold	.10	.02
❑	491 Dave Hollins	.10	.02
❑	492 Danny Jackson	.10	.02
❑	493 Stan Javier	.10	.02
❑	494 Tom Marsh	.10	.02
❑	495 Greg Mathews	.10	.02
❑	496 Dale Murphy	.30	.10
❑	497 Todd Pratt RC	.20	.07
❑	498 Mitch Williams	.10	.02
❑	499 Danny Cox	.10	.02
❑	500 Doug Drabek	.10	.02
❑	501 Carlos Garcia	.10	.02
❑	502 Lloyd McClendon	.10	.02
❑	503 Denny Neagle	.20	.07
❑	504 Gary Redus	.10	.02
❑	505 Bob Walk	.10	.02
❑	506 John Wehner	.10	.02
❑	507 Luis Alicea	.10	.02
❑	508 Mark Clark	.10	.02
❑	509 Pedro Guerrero	.20	.07
❑	510 Rex Hudler	.10	.02
❑	511 Brian Jordan	.20	.07
❑	512 Omar Olivares	.10	.02
❑	513 Jose Oquendo	.10	.02
❑	514 Gerald Perry	.10	.02
❑	515 Bryn Smith	.10	.02
❑	516 Craig Wilson	.10	.02
❑	517 Tracy Woodson	.10	.02
❑	518 Larry Andersen	.10	.02
❑	519 Andy Benes	.10	.02
❑	520 Jim Deshaies	.10	.02
❑	521 Bruce Hurst	.10	.02
❑	522 Randy Myers	.10	.02
❑	523 Benito Santiago	.20	.07
❑	524 Tim Scott	.10	.02
❑	525 Tim Teufel	.10	.02
❑	526 Mike Benjamin	.10	.02
❑	527 Dave Burba	.10	.02
❑	528 Craig Colbert	.10	.02
❑	529 Mike Felder	.10	.02
❑	530 Bryan Hickerson	.10	.02
❑	531 Chris James	.10	.02
❑	532 Mark Leonard	.10	.02
❑	533 Greg Litton	.10	.02
❑	534 Francisco Oliveras	.10	.02
❑	535 John Patterson	.10	.02
❑	536 Jim Pena	.10	.02
❑	537 Dave Righetti	.20	.07
❑	538 Robby Thompson	.10	.02
❑	539 Jose Uribe	.10	.02
❑	540 Matt Williams	.20	.07
❑	541 Storm Davis	.10	.02
❑	542 Sam Horn	.10	.02
❑	543 Tim Hulett	.10	.02
❑	544 Craig Lefferts	.10	.02
❑	545 Chito Martinez	.10	.02
❑	546 Mark McLemore	.10	.02
❑	547 Luis Mercedes	.10	.02
❑	548 Bob Milacki	.10	.02
❑	549 Joe Orsulak	.10	.02
❑	550 Billy Ripken	.10	.02
❑	551 Cal Ripken	1.50	.60
❑	552 Rick Sutcliffe	.20	.07
❑	553 Jeff Tackett	.10	.02
❑	554 Wade Boggs	.30	.10
❑	555 Tom Brunansky	.10	.02
❑	556 Jack Clark	.20	.07
❑	557 John Dopson	.10	.02
❑	558 Mike Gardiner	.10	.02
❑	559 Mike Greenwell	.10	.02
❑	560 Greg A. Harris	.10	.02
❑	561 Billy Hatcher	.10	.02
❑	562 Joe Hesketh	.10	.02
❑	563 Tony Pena	.10	.02
❑	564 Phil Plantier	.10	.02
❑	565 Luis Rivera	.10	.02
❑	566 Herm Winningham	.10	.02
❑	567 Matt Young	.10	.02
❑	568 Bert Blyleven	.20	.07
❑	569 Mike Butcher	.10	.02
❑	570 Chuck Crim	.10	.02
❑	571 Chad Curtis	.10	.02
❑	572 Tim Fortugno	.10	.02
❑	573 Steve Frey	.10	.02
❑	574 Gary Gaetti	.20	.07
❑	575 Scott Lewis	.10	.02
❑	576 Lee Stevens	.10	.02
❑	577 Ron Tingley	.10	.02
❑	578 Julio Valera	.10	.02
❑	579 Shawn Abner	.10	.02
❑	580 Joey Cora	.10	.02
❑	581 Chris Cron	.10	.02
❑	582 Carlton Fisk	.30	.10
❑	583 Roberto Hernandez	.10	.02
❑	584 Charlie Hough	.20	.07
❑	585 Terry Leach	.10	.02
❑	586 Donn Pall	.10	.02
❑	587 Dan Pasqua	.10	.02
❑	588 Steve Sax	.10	.02
❑	589 Bobby Thigpen	.10	.02
❑	590 Albert Belle	.20	.07
❑	591 Felix Fermin	.10	.02
❑	592 Glenallen Hill	.10	.02
❑	593 Brook Jacoby	.10	.02
❑	594 Reggie Jefferson	.10	.02
❑	595 Carlos Martinez	.10	.02
❑	596 Jose Mesa	.10	.02
❑	597 Rod Nichols	.10	.02
❑	598 Junior Ortiz	.10	.02
❑	599 Eric Plunk	.10	.02
❑	600 Ted Power	.10	.02
❑	601 Scott Scudder	.10	.02
❑	602 Kevin Wickander	.10	.02
❑	603 Skeeter Barnes	.10	.02
❑	604 Mark Carreon	.10	.02
❑	605 Dan Gladden	.10	.02
❑	606 Bill Gullickson	.10	.02
❑	607 Chad Kreuter	.10	.02
❑	608 Mark Leiter	.10	.02
❑	609 Mike Munoz	.10	.02
❑	610 Rich Rowland	.10	.02
❑	611 Frank Tanana	.10	.02
❑	612 Walt Terrell	.10	.02
❑	613 Alan Trammell	.20	.07
❑	614 Lou Whitaker	.20	.07
❑	615 Luis Aquino	.10	.02
❑	616 Mike Boddicker	.10	.02
❑	617 Jim Eisenreich	.10	.02
❑	618 Mark Gubicza	.10	.02
❑	619 David Howard	.10	.02
❑	620 Mike Magnante	.10	.02
❑	621 Brent Mayne	.10	.02
❑	622 Kevin McReynolds	.10	.02
❑	623 Eddie Pierce RC	.10	.02
❑	624 Bill Sampen	.10	.02
❑	625 Steve Shifflett	.10	.02
❑	626 Gary Thurman	.10	.02
❑	627 Curt Wilkerson	.10	.02
❑	628 Chris Bosio	.10	.02
❑	629 Scott Fletcher	.10	.02
❑	630 Jim Gantner	.10	.02
❑	631 Dave Nilsson	.10	.02
❑	632 Jesse Orosco	.10	.02
❑	633 Dan Plesac	.10	.02
❑	634 Ron Robinson	.10	.02
❑	635 Bill Spiers	.10	.02

❑ 636 Franklin Stubbs .10 .02
❑ 637 Willie Banks .10 .02
❑ 638 Randy Bush .10 .02
❑ 639 Chuck Knoblauch .20 .07
❑ 640 Shane Mack .10 .02
❑ 641 Mike Pagliarulo .10 .02
❑ 642 Jeff Reboulet .10 .02
❑ 643 John Smiley .10 .02
❑ 644 Mike Trombley .10 .02
❑ 645 Gary Wayne .10 .02
❑ 646 Lenny Webster .10 .02
❑ 647 Tim Burke .10 .02
❑ 648 Mike Gallego .10 .02
❑ 649 Dion James .10 .02
❑ 650 Jeff Johnson .10 .02
❑ 651 Scott Kamieniecki .10 .02
❑ 652 Kevin Maas .10 .02
❑ 653 Rich Monteleone .10 .02
❑ 654 Jerry Nielsen .10 .02
❑ 655 Scott Sanderson .10 .02
❑ 656 Mike Stanley .10 .02
❑ 657 Gerald Williams .10 .02
❑ 658 Curt Young .10 .02
❑ 659 Harold Baines .20 .07
❑ 660 Kevin Campbell .10 .02
❑ 661 Ron Darling .10 .02
❑ 662 Kelly Downs .10 .02
❑ 663 Eric Fox .10 .02
❑ 664 Dave Henderson .10 .02
❑ 665 Rick Honeycutt .10 .02
❑ 666 Mike Moore .10 .02
❑ 667 Jamie Quirk .10 .02
❑ 668 Jeff Russell .10 .02
❑ 669 Dave Stewart .20 .07
❑ 670 Greg Briley .10 .02
❑ 671 Dave Cochrane .10 .02
❑ 672 Henry Cotto .10 .02
❑ 673 Rich DeLucia .10 .02
❑ 674 Brian Fisher .10 .02
❑ 675 Mark Grant .10 .02
❑ 676 Randy Johnson .50 .20
❑ 677 Tim Leary .10 .02
❑ 678 Pete O'Brien .10 .02
❑ 679 Lance Parrish .20 .07
❑ 680 Harold Reynolds .20 .07
❑ 681 Shane Turner .10 .02
❑ 682 Jack Daugherty .10 .02
❑ 683 David Hulse RC .10 .02
❑ 684 Terry Mathews .10 .02
❑ 685 Al Newman .10 .02
❑ 686 Edwin Nunez .10 .02
❑ 687 Rafael Palmeiro .30 .10
❑ 688 Roger Pavlik .10 .02
❑ 689 Geno Petralli .10 .02
❑ 690 Nolan Ryan 2.00 .75
❑ 691 David Cone .20 .07
❑ 692 Alfredo Griffin .10 .02
❑ 693 Juan Guzman .10 .02
❑ 694 Pat Hentgen .10 .02
❑ 695 Randy Knorr .10 .02
❑ 696 Bob MacDonald .10 .02
❑ 697 Jack Morris .20 .07
❑ 698 Ed Sprague .10 .02
❑ 699 Dave Stieb .10 .02
❑ 700 Pat Tabler .10 .02
❑ 701 Mike Timlin .10 .02
❑ 702 David Wells .20 .07
❑ 703 Eddie Zosky .10 .02
❑ 704 Gary Sheffield LL .10 .02
❑ 705 Darren Daulton LL .10 .02
❑ 706 Marquis Grissom LL .10 .02
❑ 707 Greg Maddux LL .50 .20
❑ 708 Bill Swift LL .10 .02
❑ 709 Juan Gonzalez RT .10 .02
❑ 710 Mark McGwire RT .60 .25
❑ 711 Cecil Fielder RT .10 .02
❑ 712 Albert Belle RT .20 .07
❑ 713 Joe Carter RT .10 .02
❑ 714 F.Thomas/C.Fielder .30 .10
❑ 715 L.Walker/D.Daulton SS .20 .07
❑ 716 E.Martinez/R.Ventura SS .20 .07
❑ 717 R.Clemens/D.Eckersley .50 .20
❑ 718 Checklist 361-480 .10 .02
❑ 719 Checklist 481-600 .10 .02
❑ 720 Checklist 601-720 .10 .02

1993 Fleer Final Edition

❑ COMP.FACT.SET (310) 10.00 4.00
❑ COMPLETE SET (300) 8.00 3.00
❑ 1 Steve Bedrosian .10 .02
❑ 2 Jay Howell .10 .02
❑ 3 Greg Maddux .75 .30
❑ 4 Greg McMichael RC .15 .05
❑ 5 Tony Tarasco RC .15 .05
❑ 6 Jose Bautista .10 .02
❑ 7 Jose Guzman .10 .02
❑ 8 Greg Hibbard .10 .02
❑ 9 Candy Maldonado .10 .02
❑ 10 Randy Myers .10 .02
❑ 11 Matt Walbeck RC .40 .15
❑ 12 Turk Wendell .10 .02
❑ 13 Willie Wilson .10 .02
❑ 14 Greg Cadaret .10 .02
❑ 15 Roberto Kelly .10 .02
❑ 16 Randy Milligan .10 .02
❑ 17 Kevin Mitchell .10 .02
❑ 18 Jeff Reardon .20 .07
❑ 19 John Roper .10 .02
❑ 20 John Smiley .10 .02
❑ 21 Andy Ashby .10 .02
❑ 22 Dante Bichette .20 .07
❑ 23 Willie Blair .10 .02
❑ 24 Pedro Castellano .10 .02
❑ 25 Vinny Castilla .50 .20
❑ 26 Jerald Clark .10 .02
❑ 27 Alex Cole .10 .02
❑ 28 Scott Fredrickson RC .15 .05
❑ 29 Jay Gainer RC .15 .05
❑ 30 Andres Galarraga .20 .07
❑ 31 Joe Girardi .10 .02
❑ 32 Ryan Hawblitzel .10 .02
❑ 33 Charlie Hayes .10 .02
❑ 34 Darren Holmes .10 .02
❑ 35 Chris Jones .10 .02
❑ 36 David Nied .10 .02
❑ 37 Jayhawk Owens RC .15 .05
❑ 38 Lance Painter RC .40 .15
❑ 39 Jeff Parrett .10 .02
❑ 40 Steve Reed .10 .02
❑ 41 Armando Reynoso .10 .02
❑ 42 Bruce Ruffin .10 .02
❑ 43 Danny Sheaffer RC .15 .05
❑ 44 Keith Shepherd .10 .02
❑ 45 Jim Tatum .10 .02
❑ 46 Gary Wayne .10 .02
❑ 47 Eric Young .10 .02
❑ 48 Luis Aquino .10 .02
❑ 49 Alex Arias .10 .02
❑ 50 Jack Armstrong .10 .02
❑ 51 Bret Barberie .10 .02
❑ 52 Geronimo Berroa .10 .02
❑ 53 Ryan Bowen .10 .02
❑ 54 Greg Briley .10 .02
❑ 55 Cris Carpenter .10 .02
❑ 56 Chuck Carr .10 .02
❑ 57 Jeff Conine .20 .07
❑ 58 Jim Corsi .10 .02
❑ 59 Orestes Destrade .10 .02
❑ 60 Junior Felix .10 .02
❑ 61 Chris Hammond .10 .02
❑ 62 Bryan Harvey .10 .02
❑ 63 Charlie Hough .20 .07
❑ 64 Joe Klink .10 .02
❑ 65 Richie Lewis RC .15 .05
❑ 66 Mitch Lyden RC .15 .05
❑ 67 Bob Natal .10 .02
❑ 68 Scott Pose RC .15 .05
❑ 69 Rich Renteria .10 .02
❑ 70 Benito Santiago .20 .07
❑ 71 Gary Sheffield .20 .07
❑ 72 Matt Turner RC .15 .05
❑ 73 Walt Weiss .10 .02
❑ 74 Darrell Whitmore RC .15 .05
❑ 75 Nigel Wilson .10 .02
❑ 76 Kevin Bass .10 .02
❑ 77 Doug Drabek .10 .02
❑ 78 Tom Edens .10 .02
❑ 79 Chris James .10 .02
❑ 80 Greg Swindell .10 .02
❑ 81 Omar Daal RC .15 .05
❑ 82 Raul Mondesi .20 .07
❑ 83 Jody Reed .10 .02
❑ 84 Cory Snyder .10 .02
❑ 85 Rick Trlicek .10 .02
❑ 86 Tim Wallach .10 .02
❑ 87 Todd Worrell .10 .02
❑ 88 Tavo Alvarez .10 .02
❑ 89 Frank Bolick .10 .02
❑ 90 Kent Bottenfield .10 .02
❑ 91 Greg Colbrunn .10 .02
❑ 92 Cliff Floyd .20 .07
❑ 93 Lou Frazier RC .15 .05
❑ 94 Mike Gardiner .10 .02
❑ 95 Mike Lansing RC .40 .15
❑ 96 Bill Risley .10 .02
❑ 97 Jeff Shaw .10 .02
❑ 98 Kevin Baez .10 .02
❑ 99 Tim Bogar RC .15 .05
❑ 100 Jeromy Burnitz .20 .07
❑ 101 Mike Draper .10 .02
❑ 102 Darrin Jackson .10 .02
❑ 103 Mike Maddux .10 .02
❑ 104 Joe Orsulak .10 .02
❑ 105 Doug Saunders RC .15 .05
❑ 106 Frank Tanana .10 .02
❑ 107 Dave Telgheder RC .15 .05
❑ 108 Larry Andersen .10 .02
❑ 109 Jim Eisenreich .10 .02
❑ 110 Pete Incaviglia .10 .02
❑ 111 Danny Jackson .10 .02
❑ 112 David West .10 .02
❑ 113 Al Martin .10 .02
❑ 114 Blas Minor .10 .02
❑ 115 Dennis Moeller .10 .02
❑ 116 William Pennyfeather .10 .02
❑ 117 Rich Robertson RC .15 .05
❑ 118 Ben Shelton .10 .02
❑ 119 Lonnie Smith .10 .02
❑ 120 Freddie Toliver .10 .02
❑ 121 Paul Wagner .10 .02
❑ 122 Kevin Young .20 .07
❑ 123 Rene Arocha RC .40 .15
❑ 124 Gregg Jefferies .10 .02
❑ 125 Paul Kilgus .10 .02
❑ 126 Les Lancaster .10 .02
❑ 127 Joe Magrane .10 .02
❑ 128 Rob Murphy .10 .02
❑ 129 Erik Pappas .10 .02
❑ 130 Stan Royer .10 .02
❑ 131 Ozzie Smith .75 .30
❑ 132 Tom Urbani RC .15 .05
❑ 133 Mark Whiten .10 .02
❑ 134 Derek Bell .10 .02
❑ 135 Doug Brocail .10 .02
❑ 136 Phil Clark .10 .02
❑ 137 Mark Ettles RC .15 .05
❑ 138 Jeff Gardner .10 .02
❑ 139 Pat Gomez RC .15 .05
❑ 140 Ricky Gutierrez .10 .02
❑ 141 Gene Harris .10 .02
❑ 142 Kevin Higgins .10 .02
❑ 143 Trevor Hoffman .50 .20
❑ 144 Phil Plantier .10 .02
❑ 145 Kerry Taylor RC .15 .05
❑ 146 Guillermo Velasquez .10 .02
❑ 147 Wally Whitehurst .10 .02
❑ 148 Tim Worrell RC .40 .15
❑ 149 Todd Benzinger .10 .02
❑ 150 Barry Bonds 1.50 .60

❑ 151	Greg Brummett RC	.15	.05
❑ 152	Mark Carreon	.10	.02
❑ 153	Dave Martinez	.10	.02
❑ 154	Jeff Reed	.10	.02
❑ 155	Kevin Rogers	.10	.02
❑ 156	Harold Baines	.20	.07
❑ 157	Damon Buford	.10	.02
❑ 158	Paul Carey RC	.15	.05
❑ 159	Jeffrey Hammonds	.10	.02
❑ 160	Jamie Moyer	.20	.07
❑ 161	Sherman Obando RC	.15	.05
❑ 162	John O'Donoghue RC	.15	.05
❑ 163	Brad Pennington	.10	.02
❑ 164	Jim Poole	.10	.02
❑ 165	Harold Reynolds	.20	.07
❑ 166	Fernando Valenzuela	.20	.07
❑ 167	Jack Voigt RC	.15	.05
❑ 168	Mark Williamson	.10	.02
❑ 169	Scott Bankhead	.10	.02
❑ 170	Greg Blosser	.10	.02
❑ 171	Jim Byrd RC	.15	.05
❑ 172	Ivan Calderon	.10	.02
❑ 173	Andre Dawson	.20	.07
❑ 174	Scott Fletcher	.10	.02
❑ 175	Jose Melendez	.10	.02
❑ 176	Carlos Quintana	.10	.02
❑ 177	Jeff Russell	.10	.02
❑ 178	Aaron Sele	.10	.02
❑ 179	Rod Correia RC	.15	.05
❑ 180	Chili Davis	.20	.07
❑ 181	Jim Edmonds RC	3.00	1.25
❑ 182	Rene Gonzales	.10	.02
❑ 183	Hilly Hathaway RC	.15	.05
❑ 184	Torey Lovullo	.10	.02
❑ 185	Greg Myers	.10	.02
❑ 186	Gene Nelson	.10	.02
❑ 187	Troy Percival	.30	.10
❑ 188	Scott Sanderson	.10	.02
❑ 189	Darryl Scott RC	.15	.05
❑ 190	J.T.Snow RC	.60	.25
❑ 191	Russ Springer	.10	.02
❑ 192	Jason Bere	.10	.02
❑ 193	Rodney Bolton	.10	.02
❑ 194	Ellis Burks	.20	.07
❑ 195	Bo Jackson	.50	.20
❑ 196	Mike LaValliere	.10	.02
❑ 197	Scott Ruffcorn	.10	.02
❑ 198	Jeff Schwarz	.10	.02
❑ 199	Jerry DiPoto	.10	.02
❑ 200	Alvaro Espinoza	.10	.02
❑ 201	Wayne Kirby	.10	.02
❑ 202	Tom Kramer RC	.15	.05
❑ 203	Jesse Levis	.10	.02
❑ 204	Manny Ramirez	.75	.30
❑ 205	Jeff Treadway	.10	.02
❑ 206	Bill Wertz RC	.15	.05
❑ 207	Cliff Young	.10	.02
❑ 208	Matt Young	.10	.02
❑ 209	Kirk Gibson	.20	.07
❑ 210	Greg Gohr	.10	.02
❑ 211	Bill Krueger	.10	.02
❑ 212	Bob MacDonald	.10	.02
❑ 213	Mike Moore	.10	.02
❑ 214	David Wells	.20	.07
❑ 215	Billy Brewer	.10	.02
❑ 216	David Cone	.20	.07
❑ 217	Greg Gagne	.10	.02
❑ 218	Mark Gardner	.10	.02
❑ 219	Chris Haney	.10	.02
❑ 220	Phil Hiatt	.10	.02
❑ 221	Jose Lind	.10	.02
❑ 222	Juan Bell	.10	.02
❑ 223	Tom Brunansky	.10	.02
❑ 224	Mike Ignasiak	.10	.02
❑ 225	Joe Kmak	.10	.02
❑ 226	Tom Lampkin	.10	.02
❑ 227	Graeme Lloyd RC	.40	.15
❑ 228	Carlos Maldonado	.10	.02
❑ 229	Matt Mieske	.10	.02
❑ 230	Angel Miranda	.10	.02
❑ 231	Troy O'Leary RC	.40	.15
❑ 232	Kevin Reimer	.10	.02
❑ 233	Larry Casian	.10	.02
❑ 234	Jim Deshaies	.10	.02
❑ 235	Eddie Guardado RC	.60	.25
❑ 236	Chip Hale	.10	.02
❑ 237	Mike Maksudian RC	.15	.05
❑ 238	David McCarty	.10	.02
❑ 239	Pat Meares RC	.40	.15
❑ 240	George Tsamis RC	.15	.05
❑ 241	Dave Winfield	.20	.07
❑ 242	Jim Abbott	.30	.10
❑ 243	Wade Boggs	.30	.10
❑ 244	Andy Cook RC	.15	.05
❑ 245	Russ Davis RC	.15	.05
❑ 246	Mike Humphreys	.10	.02
❑ 247	Jimmy Key	.20	.07
❑ 248	Jim Leyritz	.10	.02
❑ 249	Bobby Munoz	.10	.02
❑ 250	Paul O'Neill	.30	.10
❑ 251	Spike Owen	.10	.02
❑ 252	Dave Silvestri	.10	.02
❑ 253	Marcos Armas RC	.15	.05
❑ 254	Brent Gates	.10	.02
❑ 255	Rich Gossage	.20	.07
❑ 256	Scott Lydy RC	.15	.05
❑ 257	Henry Mercedes	.10	.02
❑ 258	Mike Mohler RC	.40	.15
❑ 259	Troy Neel	.10	.02
❑ 260	Edwin Nunez	.10	.02
❑ 261	Craig Paquette	.10	.02
❑ 262	Kevin Seitzer	.10	.02
❑ 263	Rich Amaral	.10	.02
❑ 264	Mike Blowers	.10	.02
❑ 265	Chris Bosio	.10	.02
❑ 266	Norm Charlton	.10	.02
❑ 267	Jim Converse RC	.15	.05
❑ 268	John Cummings RC	.15	.05
❑ 269	Mike Felder	.10	.02
❑ 270	Mike Hampton	.20	.07
❑ 271	Bill Haselman	.10	.02
❑ 272	Dwayne Henry	.10	.02
❑ 273	Greg Litton	.10	.02
❑ 274	Mackey Sasser	.10	.02
❑ 275	Lee Tinsley	.10	.02
❑ 276	David Wainhouse	.10	.02
❑ 277	Jeff Bronkey	.10	.02
❑ 278	Benji Gil	.10	.02
❑ 279	Tom Henke	.10	.02
❑ 280	Charlie Leibrandt	.10	.02
❑ 281	Robb Nen	.20	.07
❑ 282	Bill Ripken	.10	.02
❑ 283	Jon Shave RC	.15	.05
❑ 284	Doug Strange	.10	.02
❑ 285	Matt Whiteside RC	.15	.05
❑ 286	Scott Brow RC	.15	.05
❑ 287	Willie Canate RC	.15	.05
❑ 288	Tony Castillo	.10	.02
❑ 289	Domingo Cedeno RC	.15	.05
❑ 290	Darnell Coles	.10	.02
❑ 291	Danny Cox	.10	.02
❑ 292	Mark Eichhorn	.10	.02
❑ 293	Tony Fernandez	.10	.02
❑ 294	Al Leiter	.20	.07
❑ 295	Paul Molitor	.20	.07
❑ 296	Dave Stewart	.20	.07
❑ 297	Woody Williams RC	.60	.25
❑ 298	Checklist F1-F100	.10	.02
❑ 299	Checklist F101-F200	.10	.02
❑ 300	Checklist F201-F300	.10	.02

1994 Fleer

❑	COMPLETE SET (720)	50.00	25.00
❑ 1	Brady Anderson	.30	.10
❑ 2	Harold Baines	.30	.10
❑ 3	Mike Devereaux	.15	.05
❑ 4	Todd Frohwirth	.15	.05
❑ 5	Jeffrey Hammonds	.15	.05
❑ 6	Chris Hoiles	.15	.05
❑ 7	Tim Hulett	.15	.05
❑ 8	Ben McDonald	.15	.05
❑ 9	Mark McLemore	.15	.05
❑ 10	Alan Mills	.15	.05
❑ 11	Jamie Moyer	.30	.10
❑ 12	Mike Mussina	.50	.20
❑ 13	Gregg Olson	.15	.05
❑ 14	Mike Pagliarulo	.15	.05
❑ 15	Brad Pennington	.15	.05
❑ 16	Jim Poole	.15	.05
❑ 17	Harold Reynolds	.30	.10
❑ 18	Arthur Rhodes	.15	.05
❑ 19	Cal Ripken	2.50	1.00
❑ 20	David Segui	.15	.05
❑ 21	Rick Sutcliffe	.30	.10
❑ 22	Fernando Valenzuela	.30	.10
❑ 23	Jack Voigt	.15	.05
❑ 24	Mark Williamson	.15	.05
❑ 25	Scott Bankhead	.15	.05
❑ 26	Roger Clemens	1.50	.60
❑ 27	Scott Cooper	.15	.05
❑ 28	Danny Darwin	.15	.05
❑ 29	Andre Dawson	.30	.10
❑ 30	Rob Deer	.15	.05
❑ 31	John Dopson	.15	.05
❑ 32	Scott Fletcher	.15	.05
❑ 33	Mike Greenwell	.15	.05
❑ 34	Greg A. Harris	.15	.05
❑ 35	Billy Hatcher	.15	.05
❑ 36	Bob Melvin	.15	.05
❑ 37	Tony Pena	.15	.05
❑ 38	Paul Quantrill	.15	.05
❑ 39	Carlos Quintana	.15	.05
❑ 40	Ernest Riles	.15	.05
❑ 41	Jeff Russell	.15	.05
❑ 42	Ken Ryan	.15	.05
❑ 43	Aaron Sele	.15	.05
❑ 44	John Valentin	.15	.05
❑ 45	Mo Vaughn	.30	.10
❑ 46	Frank Viola	.30	.10
❑ 47	Bob Zupcic	.15	.05
❑ 48	Mike Butcher	.15	.05
❑ 49	Rod Correia	.15	.05
❑ 50	Chad Curtis	.15	.05
❑ 51	Chili Davis	.30	.10
❑ 52	Gary DiSarcina	.15	.05
❑ 53	Damion Easley	.15	.05
❑ 54	Jim Edmonds	.75	.30
❑ 55	Chuck Finley	.30	.10
❑ 56	Steve Frey	.15	.05
❑ 57	Rene Gonzales	.15	.05
❑ 58	Joe Grahe	.15	.05
❑ 59	Hilly Hathaway	.15	.05
❑ 60	Stan Javier	.15	.05
❑ 61	Mark Langston	.15	.05
❑ 62	Phil Leftwich RC	.15	.05
❑ 63	Torey Lovullo	.15	.05
❑ 64	Joe Magrane	.15	.05
❑ 65	Greg Myers	.15	.05
❑ 66	Ken Patterson	.15	.05
❑ 67	Eduardo Perez	.15	.05
❑ 68	Luis Polonia	.15	.05
❑ 69	Tim Salmon	.50	.20
❑ 70	J.T.Snow	.30	.10
❑ 71	Ron Tingley	.15	.05
❑ 72	Julio Valera	.15	.05
❑ 73	Wilson Alvarez	.15	.05
❑ 74	Tim Belcher	.15	.05
❑ 75	George Bell	.15	.05
❑ 76	Jason Bere	.15	.05
❑ 77	Rod Bolton	.15	.05
❑ 78	Ellis Burks	.30	.10
❑ 79	Joey Cora	.15	.05
❑ 80	Alex Fernandez	.15	.05
❑ 81	Craig Grebeck	.15	.05
❑ 82	Ozzie Guillen	.30	.10
❑ 83	Roberto Hernandez	.15	.05
❑ 84	Bo Jackson	.75	.30
❑ 85	Lance Johnson	.15	.05
❑ 86	Ron Karkovice	.15	.05
❑ 87	Mike LaValliere	.15	.05

❑ 88 Kirk McCaskill .15 .05
❑ 89 Jack McDowell .15 .05
❑ 90 Warren Newson .15 .05
❑ 91 Dan Pasqua .15 .05
❑ 92 Scott Radinsky .15 .05
❑ 93 Tim Raines .30 .10
❑ 94 Steve Sax .15 .05
❑ 95 Jeff Schwarz .15 .05
❑ 96 Frank Thomas .75 .30
❑ 97 Robin Ventura .30 .10
❑ 98 Sandy Alomar Jr. .15 .05
❑ 99 Carlos Baerga .15 .05
❑ 100 Albert Belle .30 .10
❑ 101 Mark Clark .15 .05
❑ 102 Jerry DiPoto .15 .05
❑ 103 Alvaro Espinoza .15 .05
❑ 104 Felix Fermin .15 .05
❑ 105 Jeremy Hernandez .15 .05
❑ 106 Reggie Jefferson .15 .05
❑ 107 Wayne Kirby .15 .05
❑ 108 Tom Kramer .15 .05
❑ 109 Mark Lewis .15 .05
❑ 110 Derek Lilliquist .15 .05
❑ 111 Kenny Lofton .30 .10
❑ 112 Candy Maldonado .15 .05
❑ 113 Jose Mesa .15 .05
❑ 114 Jeff Mutis .15 .05
❑ 115 Charles Nagy .15 .05
❑ 116 Bob Ojeda .15 .05
❑ 117 Junior Ortiz .15 .05
❑ 118 Eric Plunk .15 .05
❑ 119 Manny Ramirez .75 .30
❑ 120 Paul Sorrento .15 .05
❑ 121 Jim Thome .50 .20
❑ 122 Jeff Treadway .15 .05
❑ 123 Bill Wertz .15 .05
❑ 124 Skeeter Barnes .15 .05
❑ 125 Milt Cuyler .15 .05
❑ 126 Eric Davis .30 .10
❑ 127 John Doherty .15 .05
❑ 128 Cecil Fielder .30 .10
❑ 129 Travis Fryman .30 .10
❑ 130 Kirk Gibson .30 .10
❑ 131 Dan Gladden .15 .05
❑ 132 Greg Gohr .15 .05
❑ 133 Chris Gomez .15 .05
❑ 134 Bill Gullickson .15 .05
❑ 135 Mike Henneman .15 .05
❑ 136 Kurt Knudsen .15 .05
❑ 137 Chad Kreuter .15 .05
❑ 138 Bill Krueger .15 .05
❑ 139 Scott Livingstone .15 .05
❑ 140 Bob MacDonald .15 .05
❑ 141 Mike Moore .15 .05
❑ 142 Tony Phillips .15 .05
❑ 143 Mickey Tettleton .15 .05
❑ 144 Alan Trammell .30 .10
❑ 145 David Wells .30 .10
❑ 146 Lou Whitaker .30 .10
❑ 147 Kevin Appier .30 .10
❑ 148 Stan Belinda .15 .05
❑ 149 George Brett 2.00 .75
❑ 150 Billy Brewer .15 .05
❑ 151 Hubie Brooks .15 .05
❑ 152 David Cone .30 .10
❑ 153 Gary Gaetti .30 .10
❑ 154 Greg Gagne .15 .05
❑ 155 Tom Gordon .15 .05
❑ 156 Mark Gubicza .15 .05
❑ 157 Chris Gwynn .15 .05
❑ 158 John Habyan .15 .05
❑ 159 Chris Haney .15 .05
❑ 160 Phil Hiatt .15 .05
❑ 161 Felix Jose .15 .05
❑ 162 Wally Joyner .30 .10
❑ 163 Jose Lind .15 .05
❑ 164 Mike Macfarlane .15 .05
❑ 165 Mike Magnante .15 .05
❑ 166 Brent Mayne .15 .05
❑ 167 Brian McRae .15 .05
❑ 168 Kevin McReynolds .15 .05
❑ 169 Keith Miller .15 .05
❑ 170 Jeff Montgomery .15 .05
❑ 171 Hipolito Pichardo .15 .05
❑ 172 Rico Rossy .15 .05
❑ 173 Juan Bell .15 .05
❑ 174 Ricky Bones .15 .05
❑ 175 Cal Eldred .15 .05
❑ 176 Mike Fetters .15 .05
❑ 177 Darryl Hamilton .15 .05
❑ 178 Doug Henry .15 .05
❑ 179 Mike Ignasiak .15 .05
❑ 180 John Jaha .15 .05
❑ 181 Pat Listach .15 .05
❑ 182 Graeme Lloyd .15 .05
❑ 183 Matt Mieske .15 .05
❑ 184 Angel Miranda .15 .05
❑ 185 Jaime Navarro .15 .05
❑ 186 Dave Nilsson .15 .05
❑ 187 Troy O'Leary .15 .05
❑ 188 Jesse Orosco .15 .05
❑ 189 Kevin Reimer .15 .05
❑ 190 Kevin Seitzer .15 .05
❑ 191 Bill Spiers .15 .05
❑ 192 B.J. Surhoff .30 .10
❑ 193 Dickie Thon .15 .05
❑ 194 Jose Valentin .15 .05
❑ 195 Greg Vaughn .15 .05
❑ 196 Bill Wegman .15 .05
❑ 197 Robin Yount 1.25 .50
❑ 198 Rick Aguilera .15 .05
❑ 199 Willie Banks .15 .05
❑ 200 Bernardo Brito .15 .05
❑ 201 Larry Casian .15 .05
❑ 202 Scott Erickson .15 .05
❑ 203 Eddie Guardado .30 .10
❑ 204 Mark Guthrie .15 .05
❑ 205 Chip Hale .15 .05
❑ 206 Brian Harper .15 .05
❑ 207 Mike Hartley .15 .05
❑ 208 Kent Hrbek .30 .10
❑ 209 Terry Jorgensen .15 .05
❑ 210 Chuck Knoblauch .30 .10
❑ 211 Gene Larkin .15 .05
❑ 212 Shane Mack .15 .05
❑ 213 David McCarty .15 .05
❑ 214 Pat Meares .15 .05
❑ 215 Pedro Munoz .15 .05
❑ 216 Derek Parks .15 .05
❑ 217 Kirby Puckett .75 .30
❑ 218 Jeff Reboulet .15 .05
❑ 219 Kevin Tapani .15 .05
❑ 220 Mike Trombley .15 .05
❑ 221 George Tsamis .15 .05
❑ 222 Carl Willis .15 .05
❑ 223 Dave Winfield .30 .10
❑ 224 Jim Abbott .50 .20
❑ 225 Paul Assenmacher .15 .05
❑ 226 Wade Boggs .50 .20
❑ 227 Russ Davis .15 .05
❑ 228 Steve Farr .15 .05
❑ 229 Mike Gallego .15 .05
❑ 230 Paul Gibson .15 .05
❑ 231 Steve Howe .15 .05
❑ 232 Dion James .15 .05
❑ 233 Domingo Jean .15 .05
❑ 234 Scott Kamieniecki .15 .05
❑ 235 Pat Kelly .15 .05
❑ 236 Jimmy Key .30 .10
❑ 237 Jim Leyritz .15 .05
❑ 238 Kevin Maas .15 .05
❑ 239 Don Mattingly 2.00 .75
❑ 240 Rich Monteleone .15 .05
❑ 241 Bobby Munoz .15 .05
❑ 242 Matt Nokes .15 .05
❑ 243 Paul O'Neill .50 .20
❑ 244 Spike Owen .15 .05
❑ 245 Melido Perez .15 .05
❑ 246 Lee Smith .30 .10
❑ 247 Mike Stanley .15 .05
❑ 248 Danny Tartabull .15 .05
❑ 249 Randy Velarde .15 .05
❑ 250 Bob Wickman .15 .05
❑ 251 Bernie Williams .50 .20
❑ 252 Mike Aldrete .15 .05
❑ 253 Marcos Armas .15 .05
❑ 254 Lance Blankenship .15 .05
❑ 255 Mike Bordick .15 .05
❑ 256 Scott Brosius .30 .10
❑ 257 Jerry Browne .15 .05
❑ 258 Ron Darling .15 .05
❑ 259 Kelly Downs .15 .05
❑ 260 Dennis Eckersley .30 .10
❑ 261 Brent Gates .15 .05
❑ 262 Rich Gossage .30 .10
❑ 263 Scott Hemond .15 .05
❑ 264 Dave Henderson .15 .05
❑ 265 Rick Honeycutt .15 .05
❑ 266 Vince Horsman .15 .05
❑ 267 Scott Lydy .15 .05
❑ 268 Mark McGwire 2.00 .75
❑ 269 Mike Mohler .15 .05
❑ 270 Troy Neel .15 .05
❑ 271 Edwin Nunez .15 .05
❑ 272 Craig Paquette .15 .05
❑ 273 Ruben Sierra .30 .10
❑ 274 Terry Steinbach .15 .05
❑ 275 Todd Van Poppel .15 .05
❑ 276 Bob Welch .15 .05
❑ 277 Bobby Witt .15 .05
❑ 278 Rich Amaral .15 .05
❑ 279 Mike Blowers .15 .05
❑ 280 Bret Boone UER .30 .10
❑ 281 Chris Bosio .15 .05
❑ 282 Jay Buhner .30 .10
❑ 283 Norm Charlton .15 .05
❑ 284 Mike Felder .15 .05
❑ 285 Dave Fleming .15 .05
❑ 286 Ken Griffey Jr. 1.25 .50
❑ 287 Erik Hanson .15 .05
❑ 288 Bill Haselman .15 .05
❑ 289 Brad Holman RC .15 .05
❑ 290 Randy Johnson .75 .30
❑ 291 Tim Leary .15 .05
❑ 292 Greg Litton .15 .05
❑ 293 Dave Magadan .15 .05
❑ 294 Edgar Martinez .50 .20
❑ 295 Tino Martinez .50 .20
❑ 296 Jeff Nelson .15 .05
❑ 297 Erik Plantenberg RC .15 .05
❑ 298 Mackey Sasser .15 .05
❑ 299 Brian Turang RC .15 .05
❑ 300 Dave Valle .15 .05
❑ 301 Omar Vizquel .50 .20
❑ 302 Brian Bohanon .15 .05
❑ 303 Kevin Brown .30 .10
❑ 304 Jose Canseco .50 .20
❑ 305 Mario Diaz .15 .05
❑ 306 Julio Franco .30 .10
❑ 307 Juan Gonzalez .30 .10
❑ 308 Tom Henke .15 .05
❑ 309 David Hulse .15 .05
❑ 310 Manuel Lee .15 .05
❑ 311 Craig Lefferts .15 .05
❑ 312 Charlie Leibrandt .15 .05
❑ 313 Rafael Palmeiro .50 .20
❑ 314 Dean Palmer .30 .10
❑ 315 Roger Pavlik .15 .05
❑ 316 Dan Peltier .15 .05
❑ 317 Gene Petralli .15 .05
❑ 318 Gary Redus .15 .05
❑ 319 Ivan Rodriguez .50 .20
❑ 320 Kenny Rogers .30 .10
❑ 321 Nolan Ryan 3.00 1.25
❑ 322 Doug Strange .15 .05
❑ 323 Matt Whiteside .15 .05
❑ 324 Roberto Alomar .50 .20
❑ 325 Pat Borders .15 .05
❑ 326 Joe Carter .30 .10
❑ 327 Tony Castillo .15 .05
❑ 328 Darnell Coles .15 .05
❑ 329 Danny Cox .15 .05
❑ 330 Mark Eichhorn .15 .05
❑ 331 Tony Fernandez .15 .05
❑ 332 Alfredo Griffin .15 .05
❑ 333 Juan Guzman .15 .05
❑ 334 Rickey Henderson .75 .30
❑ 335 Pat Hentgen .15 .05
❑ 336 Randy Knorr .15 .05
❑ 337 Al Leiter .30 .10
❑ 338 Paul Molitor .30 .10
❑ 339 Jack Morris .30 .10
❑ 340 John Olerud .30 .10
❑ 341 Dick Schofield .15 .05
❑ 342 Ed Sprague .15 .05
❑ 343 Dave Stewart .30 .10
❑ 344 Todd Stottlemyre .15 .05
❑ 345 Mike Timlin .15 .05

❑ 346 Duane Ward .15 .05
❑ 347 Turner Ward .15 .05
❑ 348 Devon White .30 .10
❑ 349 Woody Williams .30 .10
❑ 350 Steve Avery .15 .05
❑ 351 Steve Bedrosian .15 .05
❑ 352 Rafael Belliard .15 .05
❑ 353 Damon Berryhill .15 .05
❑ 354 Jeff Blauser .15 .05
❑ 355 Sid Bream .15 .05
❑ 356 Francisco Cabrera .15 .05
❑ 357 Marvin Freeman .15 .05
❑ 358 Ron Gant .30 .10
❑ 359 Tom Glavine .50 .20
❑ 360 Jay Howell .15 .05
❑ 361 David Justice .30 .10
❑ 362 Ryan Klesko .30 .10
❑ 363 Mark Lemke .15 .05
❑ 364 Javier Lopez .30 .10
❑ 365 Greg Maddux 1.25 .50
❑ 366 Fred McGriff .50 .20
❑ 367 Greg McMichael .15 .05
❑ 368 Kent Mercker .15 .05
❑ 369 Otis Nixon .15 .05
❑ 370 Greg Olson .15 .05
❑ 371 Bill Pecota .15 .05
❑ 372 Terry Pendleton .30 .10
❑ 373 Deion Sanders .50 .20
❑ 374 Pete Smith .15 .05
❑ 375 John Smoltz .50 .20
❑ 376 Mike Stanton .15 .05
❑ 377 Tony Tarasco .15 .05
❑ 378 Mark Wohlers .15 .05
❑ 379 Jose Bautista .15 .05
❑ 380 Shawn Boskie .15 .05
❑ 381 Steve Buechele .15 .05
❑ 382 Frank Castillo .15 .05
❑ 383 Mark Grace .50 .20
❑ 384 Jose Guzman .15 .05
❑ 385 Mike Harkey .15 .05
❑ 386 Greg Hibbard .15 .05
❑ 387 Glenallen Hill .15 .05
❑ 388 Steve Lake .15 .05
❑ 389 Derrick May .15 .05
❑ 390 Chuck McElroy .15 .05
❑ 391 Mike Morgan .15 .05
❑ 392 Randy Myers .15 .05
❑ 393 Dan Plesac .15 .05
❑ 394 Kevin Roberson .15 .05
❑ 395 Rey Sanchez .15 .05
❑ 396 Ryne Sandberg 1.25 .50
❑ 397 Bob Scanlan .15 .05
❑ 398 Dwight Smith .15 .05
❑ 399 Sammy Sosa .75 .30
❑ 400 Jose Vizcaino .15 .05
❑ 401 Rick Wilkins .15 .05
❑ 402 Willie Wilson .15 .05
❑ 403 Eric Yelding .15 .05
❑ 404 Bobby Ayala .15 .05
❑ 405 Jeff Branson .15 .05
❑ 406 Tom Browning .15 .05
❑ 407 Jacob Brumfield .15 .05
❑ 408 Tim Costo .15 .05
❑ 409 Rob Dibble .30 .10
❑ 410 Willie Greene .15 .05
❑ 411 Thomas Howard .15 .05
❑ 412 Roberto Kelly .15 .05
❑ 413 Bill Landrum .15 .05
❑ 414 Barry Larkin .50 .20
❑ 415 Larry Luebbers RC .15 .05
❑ 416 Kevin Mitchell .15 .05
❑ 417 Hal Morris .15 .05
❑ 418 Joe Oliver .15 .05
❑ 419 Tim Pugh .15 .05
❑ 420 Jeff Reardon .30 .10
❑ 421 Jose Rijo .15 .05
❑ 422 Bip Roberts .15 .05
❑ 423 John Roper .15 .05
❑ 424 Johnny Ruffin .15 .05
❑ 425 Chris Sabo .15 .05
❑ 426 Juan Samuel .15 .05
❑ 427 Reggie Sanders .30 .10
❑ 428 Scott Service .15 .05
❑ 429 John Smiley .15 .05
❑ 430 Jerry Spradlin RC .15 .05
❑ 431 Kevin Wickander .15 .05
❑ 432 Freddie Benavides .15 .05
❑ 433 Dante Bichette .30 .10
❑ 434 Willie Blair .15 .05
❑ 435 Daryl Boston .15 .05
❑ 436 Kent Bottenfield .15 .05
❑ 437 Vinny Castilla .30 .10
❑ 438 Jerald Clark .15 .05
❑ 439 Alex Cole .15 .05
❑ 440 Andres Galarraga .30 .10
❑ 441 Joe Girardi .15 .05
❑ 442 Greg W. Harris .15 .05
❑ 443 Charlie Hayes .15 .05
❑ 444 Darren Holmes .15 .05
❑ 445 Chris Jones .15 .05
❑ 446 Roberto Mejia .15 .05
❑ 447 David Nied .15 .05
❑ 448 Jayhawk Owens .15 .05
❑ 449 Jeff Parrett .15 .05
❑ 450 Steve Reed .15 .05
❑ 451 Armando Reynoso .15 .05
❑ 452 Bruce Ruffin .15 .05
❑ 453 Mo Sanford .15 .05
❑ 454 Danny Sheaffer .15 .05
❑ 455 Jim Tatum .15 .05
❑ 456 Gary Wayne .15 .05
❑ 457 Eric Young .15 .05
❑ 458 Luis Aquino .15 .05
❑ 459 Alex Arias .15 .05
❑ 460 Jack Armstrong .15 .05
❑ 461 Bret Barberie .15 .05
❑ 462 Ryan Bowen .15 .05
❑ 463 Chuck Carr .15 .05
❑ 464 Jeff Conine .30 .10
❑ 465 Henry Cotto .15 .05
❑ 466 Orestes Destrade .15 .05
❑ 467 Chris Hammond .15 .05
❑ 468 Bryan Harvey .15 .05
❑ 469 Charlie Hough .30 .10
❑ 470 Joe Klink .15 .05
❑ 471 Richie Lewis .15 .05
❑ 472 Bob Natal .15 .05
❑ 473 Pat Rapp .15 .05
❑ 474 Rich Renteria .15 .05
❑ 475 Rich Rodriguez .15 .05
❑ 476 Benito Santiago .30 .10
❑ 477 Gary Sheffield .30 .10
❑ 478 Matt Turner .15 .05
❑ 479 David Weathers .15 .05
❑ 480 Walt Weiss .15 .05
❑ 481 Darrell Whitmore .15 .05
❑ 482 Eric Anthony .15 .05
❑ 483 Jeff Bagwell .50 .20
❑ 484 Kevin Bass .15 .05
❑ 485 Craig Biggio .50 .20
❑ 486 Ken Caminiti .30 .10
❑ 487 Andujar Cedeno .15 .05
❑ 488 Chris Donnels .15 .05
❑ 489 Doug Drabek .15 .05
❑ 490 Steve Finley .30 .10
❑ 491 Luis Gonzalez .30 .10
❑ 492 Pete Harnisch .15 .05
❑ 493 Xavier Hernandez .15 .05
❑ 494 Doug Jones .15 .05
❑ 495 Todd Jones .15 .05
❑ 496 Darryl Kile .30 .10
❑ 497 Al Osuna .15 .05
❑ 498 Mark Portugal .15 .05
❑ 499 Scott Servais .15 .05
❑ 500 Greg Swindell .15 .05
❑ 501 Eddie Taubensee .15 .05
❑ 502 Jose Uribe .15 .05
❑ 503 Brian Williams .15 .05
❑ 504 Billy Ashley .15 .05
❑ 505 Pedro Astacio .15 .05
❑ 506 Brett Butler .30 .10
❑ 507 Tom Candiotti .15 .05
❑ 508 Omar Daal .15 .05
❑ 509 Jim Gott .15 .05
❑ 510 Kevin Gross .15 .05
❑ 511 Dave Hansen .15 .05
❑ 512 Carlos Hernandez .15 .05
❑ 513 Orel Hershiser .30 .10
❑ 514 Eric Karros .30 .10
❑ 515 Pedro Martinez .75 .30
❑ 516 Ramon Martinez .15 .05
❑ 517 Roger McDowell .15 .05
❑ 518 Raul Mondesi .30 .10
❑ 519 Jose Offerman .15 .05
❑ 520 Mike Piazza 1.50 .60
❑ 521 Jody Reed .15 .05
❑ 522 Henry Rodriguez .15 .05
❑ 523 Mike Sharperson .15 .05
❑ 524 Cory Snyder .15 .05
❑ 525 Darryl Strawberry .30 .10
❑ 526 Rick Trlicek .15 .05
❑ 527 Tim Wallach .15 .05
❑ 528 Mitch Webster .15 .05
❑ 529 Steve Wilson .15 .05
❑ 530 Todd Worrell .15 .05
❑ 531 Moises Alou .30 .10
❑ 532 Brian Barnes .15 .05
❑ 533 Sean Berry .15 .05
❑ 534 Greg Colbrunn .15 .05
❑ 535 Delino DeShields .15 .05
❑ 536 Jeff Fassero .15 .05
❑ 537 Darrin Fletcher .15 .05
❑ 538 Cliff Floyd .30 .10
❑ 539 Lou Frazier .15 .05
❑ 540 Marquis Grissom .30 .10
❑ 541 Butch Henry .15 .05
❑ 542 Ken Hill .15 .05
❑ 543 Mike Lansing .15 .05
❑ 544 Brian Looney RC .15 .05
❑ 545 Dennis Martinez .30 .10
❑ 546 Chris Nabholz .15 .05
❑ 547 Randy Ready .15 .05
❑ 548 Mel Rojas .15 .05
❑ 549 Kirk Rueter .15 .05
❑ 550 Tim Scott .15 .05
❑ 551 Jeff Shaw .15 .05
❑ 552 Tim Spehr .15 .05
❑ 553 John Vander Wal .15 .05
❑ 554 Larry Walker .30 .10
❑ 555 John Wetteland .30 .10
❑ 556 Rondell White .30 .10
❑ 557 Tim Bogar .15 .05
❑ 558 Bobby Bonilla .30 .10
❑ 559 Jeromy Burnitz .30 .10
❑ 560 Sid Fernandez .15 .05
❑ 561 John Franco .30 .10
❑ 562 Dave Gallagher .15 .05
❑ 563 Dwight Gooden .30 .10
❑ 564 Eric Hillman .15 .05
❑ 565 Todd Hundley .15 .05
❑ 566 Jeff Innis .15 .05
❑ 567 Darrin Jackson .15 .05
❑ 568 Howard Johnson .15 .05
❑ 569 Bobby Jones .15 .05
❑ 570 Jeff Kent .50 .20
❑ 571 Mike Maddux .15 .05
❑ 572 Jeff McKnight .15 .05
❑ 573 Eddie Murray .75 .30
❑ 574 Charlie O'Brien .15 .05
❑ 575 Joe Orsulak .15 .05
❑ 576 Bret Saberhagen .30 .10
❑ 577 Pete Schourek .15 .05
❑ 578 Dave Telgheder .15 .05
❑ 579 Ryan Thompson .15 .05
❑ 580 Anthony Young .15 .05
❑ 581 Ruben Amaro .15 .05
❑ 582 Larry Andersen .15 .05
❑ 583 Kim Batiste .15 .05
❑ 584 Wes Chamberlain .15 .05
❑ 585 Darren Daulton .30 .10
❑ 586 Mariano Duncan .15 .05
❑ 587 Lenny Dykstra .30 .10
❑ 588 Jim Eisenreich .15 .05
❑ 589 Tommy Greene .15 .05
❑ 590 Dave Hollins .15 .05
❑ 591 Pete Incaviglia .15 .05
❑ 592 Danny Jackson .15 .05
❑ 593 Ricky Jordan .15 .05
❑ 594 John Kruk .30 .10
❑ 595 Roger Mason .15 .05
❑ 596 Mickey Morandini .15 .05
❑ 597 Terry Mulholland .15 .05
❑ 598 Todd Pratt .15 .05
❑ 599 Ben Rivera .15 .05
❑ 600 Curt Schilling .30 .10
❑ 601 Kevin Stocker .15 .05
❑ 602 Milt Thompson .15 .05
❑ 603 David West .15 .05

- ❑ 604 Mitch Williams .15 .05
- ❑ 605 Jay Bell .30 .10
- ❑ 606 Dave Clark .15 .05
- ❑ 607 Steve Cooke .15 .05
- ❑ 608 Tom Foley .15 .05
- ❑ 609 Carlos Garcia .15 .05
- ❑ 610 Joel Johnston .15 .05
- ❑ 611 Jeff King .15 .05
- ❑ 612 Al Martin .15 .05
- ❑ 613 Lloyd McClendon .15 .05
- ❑ 614 Orlando Merced .15 .05
- ❑ 615 Blas Minor .15 .05
- ❑ 616 Denny Neagle .30 .10
- ❑ 617 Mark Petkovsek RC .15 .05
- ❑ 618 Tom Prince .15 .05
- ❑ 619 Don Slaught .15 .05
- ❑ 620 Zane Smith .15 .05
- ❑ 621 Randy Tomlin .15 .05
- ❑ 622 Andy Van Slyke .50 .20
- ❑ 623 Paul Wagner .15 .05
- ❑ 624 Tim Wakefield .50 .20
- ❑ 625 Bob Walk .15 .05
- ❑ 626 Kevin Young .15 .05
- ❑ 627 Luis Alicea .15 .05
- ❑ 628 Rene Arocha .15 .05
- ❑ 629 Rod Brewer .15 .05
- ❑ 630 Rheal Cormier .15 .05
- ❑ 631 Bernard Gilkey .15 .05
- ❑ 632 Lee Guetterman .15 .05
- ❑ 633 Gregg Jefferies .15 .05
- ❑ 634 Brian Jordan .30 .10
- ❑ 635 Les Lancaster .15 .05
- ❑ 636 Ray Lankford .30 .10
- ❑ 637 Rob Murphy .15 .05
- ❑ 638 Omar Olivares .15 .05
- ❑ 639 Jose Oquendo .15 .05
- ❑ 640 Donovan Osborne .15 .05
- ❑ 641 Tom Pagnozzi .15 .05
- ❑ 642 Erik Pappas .15 .05
- ❑ 643 Geronimo Pena .15 .05
- ❑ 644 Mike Perez .15 .05
- ❑ 645 Gerald Perry .15 .05
- ❑ 646 Ozzie Smith 1.25 .50
- ❑ 647 Bob Tewksbury .15 .05
- ❑ 648 Allen Watson .15 .05
- ❑ 649 Mark Whiten .15 .05
- ❑ 650 Tracy Woodson .15 .05
- ❑ 651 Todd Zeile .15 .05
- ❑ 652 Andy Ashby .15 .05
- ❑ 653 Brad Ausmus .50 .20
- ❑ 654 Billy Bean .15 .05
- ❑ 655 Derek Bell .15 .05
- ❑ 656 Andy Benes .15 .05
- ❑ 657 Doug Brocail .15 .05
- ❑ 658 Jarvis Brown .15 .05
- ❑ 659 Archi Cianfrocco .15 .05
- ❑ 660 Phil Clark .15 .05
- ❑ 661 Mark Davis .15 .05
- ❑ 662 Jeff Gardner .15 .05
- ❑ 663 Pat Gomez .15 .05
- ❑ 664 Ricky Gutierrez .15 .05
- ❑ 665 Tony Gwynn 1.00 .40
- ❑ 666 Gene Harris .15 .05
- ❑ 667 Kevin Higgins .15 .05
- ❑ 668 Trevor Hoffman .50 .20
- ❑ 669 Pedro A.Martinez RC .15 .05
- ❑ 670 Tim Mauser .15 .05
- ❑ 671 Melvin Nieves .15 .05
- ❑ 672 Phil Plantier .15 .05
- ❑ 673 Frank Seminara .15 .05
- ❑ 674 Craig Shipley .15 .05
- ❑ 675 Kerry Taylor .15 .05
- ❑ 676 Tim Teufel .15 .05
- ❑ 677 Guillermo Velasquez .15 .05
- ❑ 678 Wally Whitehurst .15 .05
- ❑ 679 Tim Worrell .15 .05
- ❑ 680 Rod Beck .15 .05
- ❑ 681 Mike Benjamin .15 .05
- ❑ 682 Todd Benzinger .15 .05
- ❑ 683 Bud Black .15 .05
- ❑ 684 Barry Bonds 2.00 .75
- ❑ 685 Jeff Brantley .15 .05
- ❑ 686 Dave Burba .15 .05
- ❑ 687 John Burkett .15 .05
- ❑ 688 Mark Carreon .15 .05
- ❑ 689 Will Clark .50 .20
- ❑ 690 Royce Clayton .15 .05
- ❑ 691 Bryan Hickerson .15 .05
- ❑ 692 Mike Jackson .15 .05
- ❑ 693 Darren Lewis .15 .05
- ❑ 694 Kirt Manwaring .15 .05
- ❑ 695 Dave Martinez .15 .05
- ❑ 696 Willie McGee .30 .10
- ❑ 697 John Patterson .15 .05
- ❑ 698 Jeff Reed .15 .05
- ❑ 699 Kevin Rogers .15 .05
- ❑ 700 Scott Sanderson .15 .05
- ❑ 701 Steve Scarsone .15 .05
- ❑ 702 Billy Swift .15 .05
- ❑ 703 Robby Thompson .15 .05
- ❑ 704 Matt Williams .30 .10
- ❑ 705 Trevor Wilson .15 .05
- ❑ 706 McGriff/Gant/Justice .30 .10
- ❑ 707 J.Olerud/P.Molitor .30 .10
- ❑ 708 M.Mussina/J.McDowell .30 .10
- ❑ 709 L.Whitaker/A.Trammell .30 .10
- ❑ 710 R.Palmeiro/J.Gonzalez .30 .10
- ❑ 711 B.Butler/T.Gwynn .50 .20
- ❑ 712 K.Puckett/C.Knoblauch .50 .20
- ❑ 713 M.Piazza/E.Karros .75 .30
- ❑ 714 Checklist 1 .15 .05
- ❑ 715 Checklist 2 .15 .05
- ❑ 716 Checklist 3 .15 .05
- ❑ 717 Checklist 4 .15 .05
- ❑ 718 Checklist 5 .15 .05
- ❑ 719 Checklist 6 .15 .05
- ❑ 720 Checklist 7 .15 .05
- ❑ P69 Tim Salmon Promo 1.00 .40

1994 Fleer Update

- ❑ COMP.FACT.SET (210) 50.00 25.00
- ❑ 1 Mark Eichhorn .25 .08
- ❑ 2 Sid Fernandez .25 .08
- ❑ 3 Leo Gomez .25 .08
- ❑ 4 Mike Oquist .25 .08
- ❑ 5 Rafael Palmeiro .75 .30
- ❑ 6 Chris Sabo .25 .08
- ❑ 7 Dwight Smith .25 .08
- ❑ 8 Lee Smith .50 .20
- ❑ 9 Damon Berryhill .25 .08
- ❑ 10 Wes Chamberlain .25 .08
- ❑ 11 Gar Finnvold .25 .08
- ❑ 12 Chris Howard .25 .08
- ❑ 13 Tim Naehring .25 .08
- ❑ 14 Otis Nixon .25 .08
- ❑ 15 Brian Anderson RC .50 .20
- ❑ 16 Jorge Fabregas .25 .08
- ❑ 17 Rex Hudler .25 .08
- ❑ 18 Bo Jackson 1.25 .50
- ❑ 19 Mark Leiter .25 .08
- ❑ 20 Spike Owen .25 .08
- ❑ 21 Harold Reynolds .50 .20
- ❑ 22 Chris Turner .25 .08
- ❑ 23 Dennis Cook .25 .08
- ❑ 24 Jose DeLeon .25 .08
- ❑ 25 Julio Franco .50 .20
- ❑ 26 Joe Hall .25 .08
- ❑ 27 Darrin Jackson .25 .08
- ❑ 28 Dane Johnson .25 .08
- ❑ 29 Norberto Martin .25 .08
- ❑ 30 Scott Sanderson .25 .08
- ❑ 31 Jason Grimsley .25 .08
- ❑ 32 Dennis Martinez .50 .20
- ❑ 33 Jack Morris .50 .20
- ❑ 34 Eddie Murray 1.25 .50
- ❑ 35 Chad Ogea .25 .08
- ❑ 36 Tony Pena .25 .08
- ❑ 37 Paul Shuey .25 .08
- ❑ 38 Omar Vizquel .75 .30
- ❑ 39 Danny Bautista .25 .08
- ❑ 40 Tim Belcher .25 .08
- ❑ 41 Joe Boever .25 .08
- ❑ 42 Storm Davis .25 .08
- ❑ 43 Junior Felix .25 .08
- ❑ 44 Mike Gardiner .25 .08
- ❑ 45 Buddy Groom .25 .08
- ❑ 46 Juan Samuel .25 .08
- ❑ 47 Vince Coleman .25 .08
- ❑ 48 Bob Hamelin .25 .08
- ❑ 49 Dave Henderson .25 .08
- ❑ 50 Rusty Meacham .25 .08
- ❑ 51 Terry Shumpert .25 .08
- ❑ 52 Jeff Bronkey .25 .08
- ❑ 53 Alex Diaz .25 .08
- ❑ 54 Brian Harper .25 .08
- ❑ 55 Jose Mercedes .25 .08
- ❑ 56 Jody Reed .25 .08
- ❑ 57 Bob Scanlan .25 .08
- ❑ 58 Turner Ward .25 .08
- ❑ 59 Rich Becker .25 .08
- ❑ 60 Alex Cole .25 .08
- ❑ 61 Denny Hocking .25 .08
- ❑ 62 Scott Leius .25 .08
- ❑ 63 Pat Mahomes .25 .08
- ❑ 64 Carlos Pulido .25 .08
- ❑ 65 Dave Stevens .25 .08
- ❑ 66 Matt Walbeck .25 .08
- ❑ 67 Xavier Hernandez .25 .08
- ❑ 68 Sterling Hitchcock .25 .08
- ❑ 69 Terry Mulholland .25 .08
- ❑ 70 Luis Polonia .25 .08
- ❑ 71 Gerald Williams .25 .08
- ❑ 72 Mark Acre RC .25 .08
- ❑ 73 Geronimo Berroa .25 .08
- ❑ 74 Rickey Henderson 1.25 .50
- ❑ 75 Stan Javier .25 .08
- ❑ 76 Steve Karsay .25 .08
- ❑ 77 Carlos Reyes .25 .08
- ❑ 78 Bill Taylor RC .50 .20
- ❑ 79 Eric Anthony .25 .08
- ❑ 80 Bobby Ayala .25 .08
- ❑ 81 Tim Davis .25 .08
- ❑ 82 Felix Fermin .25 .08
- ❑ 83 Reggie Jefferson .25 .08
- ❑ 84 Keith Mitchell .25 .08
- ❑ 85 Bill Risley .25 .08
- ❑ 86 Alex Rodriguez RC ! 40.00 15.00
- ❑ 87 Roger Salkeld .25 .08
- ❑ 88 Dan Wilson .25 .08
- ❑ 89 Cris Carpenter .25 .08
- ❑ 90 Will Clark .75 .30
- ❑ 91 Jeff Frye .25 .08
- ❑ 92 Rick Helling .25 .08
- ❑ 93 Chris James .25 .08
- ❑ 94 Oddibe McDowell .25 .08
- ❑ 95 Billy Ripken .25 .08
- ❑ 96 Carlos Delgado .75 .30
- ❑ 97 Alex Gonzalez .25 .08
- ❑ 98 Shawn Green 1.25 .50
- ❑ 99 Darren Hall .25 .08
- ❑ 100 Mike Huff .25 .08
- ❑ 101 Mike Kelly .25 .08
- ❑ 102 Roberto Kelly .25 .08
- ❑ 103 Charlie O'Brien .25 .08
- ❑ 104 Jose Oliva .25 .08
- ❑ 105 Gregg Olson .25 .08
- ❑ 106 Willie Banks .25 .08
- ❑ 107 Jim Bullinger .25 .08
- ❑ 108 Chuck Crim .25 .08
- ❑ 109 Shawon Dunston .25 .08
- ❑ 110 Karl Rhodes .25 .08
- ❑ 111 Steve Trachsel .25 .08
- ❑ 112 Anthony Young .25 .08
- ❑ 113 Eddie Zambrano .25 .08
- ❑ 114 Bret Boone .50 .20
- ❑ 115 Jeff Brantley .25 .08
- ❑ 116 Hector Carrasco .25 .08
- ❑ 117 Tony Fernandez .25 .08
- ❑ 118 Tim Fortugno .25 .08
- ❑ 119 Erik Hanson .25 .08

❑ 120 Chuck McElroy	.25	.08
❑ 121 Deion Sanders	.75	.30
❑ 122 Ellis Burks	.50	.20
❑ 123 Marvin Freeman	.25	.08
❑ 124 Mike Harkey	.25	.08
❑ 125 Howard Johnson	.25	.08
❑ 126 Mike Kingery	.25	.08
❑ 127 Nelson Liriano	.25	.08
❑ 128 Marcus Moore	.25	.08
❑ 129 Mike Munoz	.25	.08
❑ 130 Kevin Ritz	.25	.08
❑ 131 Walt Weiss	.25	.08
❑ 132 Kurt Abbott RC	.25	.08
❑ 133 Jerry Browne	.25	.08
❑ 134 Greg Colbrunn	.25	.08
❑ 135 Jeremy Hernandez	.25	.08
❑ 136 Dave Magadan	.25	.08
❑ 137 Kurt Miller	.25	.08
❑ 138 Robb Nen	.50	.20
❑ 139 Jesus Tavarez RC	.25	.08
❑ 140 Sid Bream	.25	.08
❑ 141 Tom Edens	.25	.08
❑ 142 Tony Eusebio	.25	.08
❑ 143 John Hudek RC	.25	.08
❑ 144 Brian L.Hunter	.25	.08
❑ 145 Orlando Miller	.25	.08
❑ 146 James Mouton	.25	.08
❑ 147 Shane Reynolds	.25	.08
❑ 148 Rafael Bournigal	.25	.08
❑ 149 Delino DeShields	.25	.08
❑ 150 Garey Ingram RC	.25	.08
❑ 151 Chan Ho Park RC	.75	.30
❑ 152 Wil Cordero	.25	.08
❑ 153 Pedro Martinez	1.25	.50
❑ 154 Randy Milligan	.25	.08
❑ 155 Lenny Webster	.25	.08
❑ 156 Rico Brogna	.25	.08
❑ 157 Josias Manzanillo	.25	.08
❑ 158 Kevin McReynolds	.25	.08
❑ 159 Mike Remlinger	.25	.08
❑ 160 David Segui	.25	.08
❑ 161 Pete Smith	.25	.08
❑ 162 Kelly Stinnett RC	.50	.20
❑ 163 Jose Vizcaino	.25	.08
❑ 164 Billy Hatcher	.25	.08
❑ 165 Doug Jones	.25	.08
❑ 166 Mike Lieberthal	.50	.20
❑ 167 Tony Longmire	.25	.08
❑ 168 Bobby Munoz	.25	.08
❑ 169 Paul Quantrill	.25	.08
❑ 170 Heathcliff Slocumb	.25	.08
❑ 171 Fernando Valenzuela	.50	.20
❑ 172 Mark Dewey	.25	.08
❑ 173 Brian R. Hunter	.25	.08
❑ 174 Jon Lieber	.50	.20
❑ 175 Ravelo Manzanillo	.25	.08
❑ 176 Dan Miceli	.25	.08
❑ 177 Rick White	.25	.08
❑ 178 Bryan Eversgerd	.25	.08
❑ 179 John Habyan	.25	.08
❑ 180 Terry McGriff	.25	.08
❑ 181 Vicente Palacios	.25	.08
❑ 182 Rich Rodriguez	.25	.08
❑ 183 Rick Sutcliffe	.50	.20
❑ 184 Donnie Elliott	.25	.08
❑ 185 Joey Hamilton	.25	.08
❑ 186 Tim Hyers RC	.25	.08
❑ 187 Luis Lopez	.25	.08
❑ 188 Ray McDavid	.25	.08
❑ 189 Bip Roberts	.25	.08
❑ 190 Scott Sanders	.25	.08
❑ 191 Eddie Williams	.25	.08
❑ 192 Steve Frey	.25	.08
❑ 193 Pat Gomez	.25	.08
❑ 194 Rich Monteleone	.25	.08
❑ 195 Mark Portugal	.25	.08
❑ 196 Darryl Strawberry	.50	.20
❑ 197 Salomon Torres	.25	.08
❑ 198 W.VanLandingham RC	.25	.08
❑ 199 Checklist	.25	.08
❑ 200 Checklist	.25	.08

1995 Fleer

❑ COMPLETE SET (600)	50.00	20.00
❑ 1 Brady Anderson	.30	.10
❑ 2 Harold Baines	.30	.10
❑ 3 Damon Buford	.15	.05
❑ 4 Mike Devereaux	.15	.05
❑ 5 Mark Eichhorn	.15	.05
❑ 6 Sid Fernandez	.15	.05
❑ 7 Leo Gomez	.15	.05
❑ 8 Jeffrey Hammonds	.15	.05
❑ 9 Chris Hoiles	.15	.05
❑ 10 Rick Krivda	.15	.05
❑ 11 Ben McDonald	.15	.05
❑ 12 Mark McLemore	.15	.05
❑ 13 Alan Mills	.15	.05
❑ 14 Jamie Moyer	.30	.10
❑ 15 Mike Mussina	.50	.20
❑ 16 Mike Oquist	.15	.05
❑ 17 Rafael Palmeiro	.50	.20
❑ 18 Arthur Rhodes	.15	.05
❑ 19 Cal Ripken	2.50	1.00
❑ 20 Chris Sabo	.15	.05
❑ 21 Lee Smith	.30	.10
❑ 22 Jack Voigt	.15	.05
❑ 23 Damon Berryhill	.15	.05
❑ 24 Tom Brunansky	.15	.05
❑ 25 Wes Chamberlain	.15	.05
❑ 26 Roger Clemens	1.50	.60
❑ 27 Scott Cooper	.15	.05
❑ 28 Andre Dawson	.30	.10
❑ 29 Gar Finnvold	.16	.05
❑ 30 Tony Fossas	.15	.05
❑ 31 Mike Greenwell	.15	.05
❑ 32 Joe Hesketh	.15	.05
❑ 33 Chris Howard	.15	.05
❑ 34 Chris Nabholz	.15	.05
❑ 35 Tim Naehring	.15	.05
❑ 36 Otis Nixon	.15	.05
❑ 37 Carlos Rodriguez	.15	.05
❑ 38 Rich Rowland	.15	.05
❑ 39 Ken Ryan	.15	.05
❑ 40 Aaron Sele	.15	.05
❑ 41 John Valentin	.15	.05
❑ 42 Mo Vaughn	.30	.10
❑ 43 Frank Viola	.30	.10
❑ 44 Danny Bautista	.15	.05
❑ 45 Joe Boever	.15	.05
❑ 46 Milt Cuyler	.15	.05
❑ 47 Storm Davis	.15	.05
❑ 48 John Doherty	.15	.05
❑ 49 Junior Felix	.15	.05
❑ 50 Cecil Fielder	.30	.10
❑ 51 Travis Fryman	.30	.10
❑ 52 Mike Gardiner	.15	.05
❑ 53 Kirk Gibson	.30	.10
❑ 54 Chris Gomez	.15	.05
❑ 55 Buddy Groom	.15	.05
❑ 56 Mike Henneman	.15	.05
❑ 57 Chad Kreuter	.15	.05
❑ 58 Mike Moore	.15	.05
❑ 59 Tony Phillips	.15	.05
❑ 60 Juan Samuel	.15	.05
❑ 61 Mickey Tettleton	.15	.05
❑ 62 Alan Trammell	.30	.10
❑ 63 David Wells	.30	.10
❑ 64 Lou Whitaker	.30	.10
❑ 65 Jim Abbott	.50	.20
❑ 66 Joe Ausanio	.15	.05
❑ 67 Wade Boggs	.50	.20
❑ 68 Mike Gallego	.15	.05
❑ 69 Xavier Hernandez	.15	.05
❑ 70 Sterling Hitchcock	.15	.05
❑ 71 Steve Howe	.15	.05
❑ 72 Scott Kamieniecki	.15	.05
❑ 73 Pat Kelly	.15	.05
❑ 74 Jimmy Key	.30	.10
❑ 75 Jim Leyritz	.15	.05
❑ 76 Don Mattingly	2.00	.75
❑ 77 Terry Mulholland	.15	.05
❑ 78 Paul O'Neill	.50	.20
❑ 79 Melido Perez	.15	.05
❑ 80 Luis Polonia	.15	.05
❑ 81 Mike Stanley	.15	.05
❑ 82 Danny Tartabull	.15	.05
❑ 83 Randy Velarde	.15	.05
❑ 84 Bob Wickman	.15	.05
❑ 85 Bernie Williams	.50	.20
❑ 86 Gerald Williams	.15	.05
❑ 87 Roberto Alomar	.50	.20
❑ 88 Pat Borders	.15	.05
❑ 89 Joe Carter	.30	.10
❑ 90 Tony Castillo	.15	.05
❑ 91 Brad Cornett RC	.15	.05
❑ 92 Carlos Delgado	.30	.10
❑ 93 Alex Gonzalez	.15	.05
❑ 94 Shawn Green	.30	.10
❑ 95 Juan Guzman	.15	.05
❑ 96 Darren Hall	.15	.05
❑ 97 Pat Hentgen	.15	.05
❑ 98 Mike Huff	.15	.05
❑ 99 Randy Knorr	.15	.05
❑ 100 Al Leiter	.30	.10
❑ 101 Paul Molitor	.30	.10
❑ 102 John Olerud	.30	.10
❑ 103 Dick Schofield	.15	.05
❑ 104 Ed Sprague	.15	.05
❑ 105 Dave Stewart	.30	.10
❑ 106 Todd Stottlemyre	.15	.05
❑ 107 Devon White	.30	.10
❑ 108 Woody Williams	.15	.05
❑ 109 Wilson Alvarez	.15	.05
❑ 110 Paul Assenmacher	.15	.05
❑ 111 Jason Bere	.15	.05
❑ 112 Dennis Cook	.15	.05
❑ 113 Joey Cora	.15	.05
❑ 114 Jose DeLeon	.15	.05
❑ 115 Alex Fernandez	.15	.05
❑ 116 Julio Franco	.30	.10
❑ 117 Craig Grebeck	.15	.05
❑ 118 Ozzie Guillen	.30	.10
❑ 119 Roberto Hernandez	.15	.05
❑ 120 Darrin Jackson	.15	.05
❑ 121 Lance Johnson	.15	.05
❑ 122 Ron Karkovice	.15	.05
❑ 123 Mike LaValliere	.15	.05
❑ 124 Norberto Martin	.15	.05
❑ 125 Kirk McCaskill	.15	.05
❑ 126 Jack McDowell	.15	.05
❑ 127 Tim Raines	.30	.10
❑ 128 Frank Thomas	.75	.30
❑ 129 Robin Ventura	.30	.10
❑ 130 Sandy Alomar Jr.	.15	.05
❑ 131 Carlos Baerga	.15	.05
❑ 132 Albert Belle	.30	.10
❑ 133 Mark Clark	.15	.05
❑ 134 Alvaro Espinoza	.15	.05
❑ 135 Jason Grimsley	.15	.05
❑ 136 Wayne Kirby	.15	.05
❑ 137 Kenny Lofton	.30	.10
❑ 138 Albie Lopez	.15	.05
❑ 139 Dennis Martinez	.30	.10
❑ 140 Jose Mesa	.15	.05
❑ 141 Eddie Murray	.75	.30
❑ 142 Charles Nagy	.15	.05
❑ 143 Tony Pena	.15	.05
❑ 144 Eric Plunk	.15	.05
❑ 145 Manny Ramirez	.50	.20
❑ 146 Jeff Russell	.15	.05
❑ 147 Paul Shuey	.15	.05
❑ 148 Paul Sorrento	.15	.05
❑ 149 Jim Thome	.50	.20
❑ 150 Omar Vizquel	.50	.20
❑ 151 Dave Winfield	.30	.10
❑ 152 Kevin Appier	.30	.10
❑ 153 Billy Brewer	.15	.05
❑ 154 Vince Coleman	.15	.05
❑ 155 David Cone	.30	.10
❑ 156 Gary Gaetti	.30	.10

❑ 157	Greg Gagne	.15	.05
❑ 158	Tom Gordon	.15	.05
❑ 159	Mark Gubicza	.15	.05
❑ 160	Bob Hamelin	.15	.05
❑ 161	Dave Henderson	.15	.05
❑ 162	Felix Jose	.15	.05
❑ 163	Wally Joyner	.30	.10
❑ 164	Jose Lind	.15	.05
❑ 165	Mike Macfarlane	.15	.05
❑ 166	Mike Magnante	.15	.05
❑ 167	Brent Mayne	.15	.05
❑ 168	Brian McRae	.15	.05
❑ 169	Rusty Meacham	.15	.05
❑ 170	Jeff Montgomery	.15	.05
❑ 171	Hipolito Pichardo	.15	.05
❑ 172	Terry Shumpert	.15	.05
❑ 173	Michael Tucker	.15	.05
❑ 174	Ricky Bones	.15	.05
❑ 175	Jeff Cirillo	.15	.05
❑ 176	Alex Diaz	.15	.05
❑ 177	Cal Eldred	.15	.05
❑ 178	Mike Fetters	.15	.05
❑ 179	Darryl Hamilton	.15	.05
❑ 180	Brian Harper	.15	.05
❑ 181	John Jaha	.15	.05
❑ 182	Pat Listach	.15	.05
❑ 183	Graeme Lloyd	.15	.05
❑ 184	Jose Mercedes	.15	.05
❑ 185	Matt Mieske	.15	.05
❑ 186	Dave Nilsson	.15	.05
❑ 187	Jody Reed	.15	.05
❑ 188	Bob Scanlan	.15	.05
❑ 189	Kevin Seitzer	.15	.05
❑ 190	Bill Spiers	.15	.05
❑ 191	B.J. Surhoff	.30	.10
❑ 192	Jose Valentin	.15	.05
❑ 193	Greg Vaughn	.15	.05
❑ 194	Turner Ward	.15	.05
❑ 195	Bill Wegman	.15	.05
❑ 196	Rick Aguilera	.15	.05
❑ 197	Rich Becker	.15	.05
❑ 198	Alex Cole	.15	.05
❑ 199	Marty Cordova	.15	.05
❑ 200	Steve Dunn	.15	.05
❑ 201	Scott Erickson	.15	.05
❑ 202	Mark Guthrie	.15	.05
❑ 203	Chip Hale	.15	.05
❑ 204	LaTroy Hawkins	.15	.05
❑ 205	Denny Hocking	.15	.05
❑ 206	Chuck Knoblauch	.30	.10
❑ 207	Scott Leius	.15	.05
❑ 208	Shane Mack	.15	.05
❑ 209	Pat Mahomes	.15	.05
❑ 210	Pat Meares	.15	.05
❑ 211	Pedro Munoz	.15	.05
❑ 212	Kirby Puckett	.75	.30
❑ 213	Jeff Reboulet	.15	.05
❑ 214	Dave Stevens	.15	.05
❑ 215	Kevin Tapani	.15	.05
❑ 216	Matt Walbeck	.15	.05
❑ 217	Carl Willis	.15	.05
❑ 218	Brian Anderson	.15	.05
❑ 219	Chad Curtis	.15	.05
❑ 220	Chili Davis	.30	.10
❑ 221	Gary DiSarcina	.15	.05
❑ 222	Damion Easley	.15	.05
❑ 223	Jim Edmonds	.50	.20
❑ 224	Chuck Finley	.30	.10
❑ 225	Joe Grahe	.15	.05
❑ 226	Rex Hudler	.15	.05
❑ 227	Bo Jackson	.75	.30
❑ 228	Mark Langston	.15	.05
❑ 229	Phil Leftwich	.15	.05
❑ 230	Mark Leiter	.15	.05
❑ 231	Spike Owen	.15	.05
❑ 232	Bob Patterson	.15	.05
❑ 233	Troy Percival	.30	.10
❑ 234	Eduardo Perez	.15	.05
❑ 235	Tim Salmon	.50	.20
❑ 236	J.T. Snow	.30	.10
❑ 237	Chris Turner	.15	.05
❑ 238	Mark Acre	.15	.05
❑ 239	Geronimo Berroa	.15	.05
❑ 240	Mike Bordick	.15	.05
❑ 241	John Briscoe	.15	.05
❑ 242	Scott Brosius	.30	.10
❑ 243	Ron Darling	.15	.05
❑ 244	Dennis Eckersley	.30	.10
❑ 245	Brent Gates	.15	.05
❑ 246	Rickey Henderson	.75	.30
❑ 247	Stan Javier	.15	.05
❑ 248	Steve Karsay	.15	.05
❑ 249	Mark McGwire	2.00	.75
❑ 250	Troy Neel	.15	.05
❑ 251	Steve Ontiveros	.15	.05
❑ 252	Carlos Reyes	.15	.05
❑ 253	Ruben Sierra	.30	.10
❑ 254	Terry Steinbach	.15	.05
❑ 255	Bill Taylor	.15	.05
❑ 256	Todd Van Poppel	.15	.05
❑ 257	Bobby Witt	.15	.05
❑ 258	Rich Amaral	.15	.05
❑ 259	Eric Anthony	.15	.05
❑ 260	Bobby Ayala	.15	.05
❑ 261	Mike Blowers	.15	.05
❑ 262	Chris Bosio	.15	.05
❑ 263	Jay Buhner	.30	.10
❑ 264	John Cummings	.15	.05
❑ 265	Tim Davis	.15	.05
❑ 266	Felix Fermin	.15	.05
❑ 267	Dave Fleming	.15	.05
❑ 268	Goose Gossage	.30	.10
❑ 269	Ken Griffey Jr.	1.25	.50
❑ 270	Reggie Jefferson	.15	.05
❑ 271	Randy Johnson	.75	.30
❑ 272	Edgar Martinez	.50	.20
❑ 273	Tino Martinez	.50	.20
❑ 274	Greg Pirkl	.15	.05
❑ 275	Bill Risley	.15	.05
❑ 276	Roger Salkeld	.15	.05
❑ 277	Luis Sojo	.15	.05
❑ 278	Mac Suzuki	.15	.05
❑ 279	Dan Wilson	.15	.05
❑ 280	Kevin Brown	.30	.10
❑ 281	Jose Canseco	.50	.20
❑ 282	Cris Carpenter	.15	.05
❑ 283	Will Clark	.50	.20
❑ 284	Jeff Frye	.15	.05
❑ 285	Juan Gonzalez	.30	.10
❑ 286	Rick Helling	.15	.05
❑ 287	Tom Henke	.15	.05
❑ 288	David Hulse	.15	.05
❑ 289	Chris James	.15	.05
❑ 290	Manuel Lee	.15	.05
❑ 291	Oddibe McDowell	.15	.05
❑ 292	Dean Palmer	.30	.10
❑ 293	Roger Pavlik	.15	.05
❑ 294	Bill Ripken	.15	.05
❑ 295	Ivan Rodriguez	.50	.20
❑ 296	Kenny Rogers	.30	.10
❑ 297	Doug Strange	.15	.05
❑ 298	Matt Whiteside	.15	.05
❑ 299	Steve Avery	.15	.05
❑ 300	Steve Bedrosian	.15	.05
❑ 301	Rafael Belliard	.15	.05
❑ 302	Jeff Blauser	.15	.05
❑ 303	Dave Gallagher	.15	.05
❑ 304	Tom Glavine	.50	.20
❑ 305	David Justice	.30	.10
❑ 306	Mike Kelly	.15	.05
❑ 307	Roberto Kelly	.15	.05
❑ 308	Ryan Klesko	.30	.10
❑ 309	Mark Lemke	.15	.05
❑ 310	Javier Lopez	.30	.10
❑ 311	Greg Maddux	1.25	.50
❑ 312	Fred McGriff	.50	.20
❑ 313	Greg McMichael	.15	.05
❑ 314	Kent Mercker	.15	.05
❑ 315	Charlie O'Brien	.15	.05
❑ 316	Jose Oliva	.15	.05
❑ 317	Terry Pendleton	.30	.10
❑ 318	John Smoltz	.50	.20
❑ 319	Mike Stanton	.15	.05
❑ 320	Tony Tarasco	.15	.05
❑ 321	Terrell Wade	.15	.05
❑ 322	Mark Wohlers	.15	.05
❑ 323	Kurt Abbott	.15	.05
❑ 324	Luis Aquino	.15	.05
❑ 325	Bret Barberie	.15	.05
❑ 326	Ryan Bowen	.15	.05
❑ 327	Jerry Browne	.15	.05
❑ 328	Chuck Carr	.15	.05
❑ 329	Matias Carrillo	.15	.05
❑ 330	Greg Colbrunn	.15	.05
❑ 331	Jeff Conine	.30	.10
❑ 332	Mark Gardner	.15	.05
❑ 333	Chris Hammond	.15	.05
❑ 334	Bryan Harvey	.15	.05
❑ 335	Richie Lewis	.15	.05
❑ 336	Dave Magadan	.15	.05
❑ 337	Terry Mathews	.15	.05
❑ 338	Robb Nen	.30	.10
❑ 339	Yorkis Perez	.15	.05
❑ 340	Pat Rapp	.15	.05
❑ 341	Benito Santiago	.30	.10
❑ 342	Gary Sheffield	.30	.10
❑ 343	Dave Weathers	.15	.05
❑ 344	Moises Alou	.30	.10
❑ 345	Sean Berry	.15	.05
❑ 346	Wil Cordero	.15	.05
❑ 347	Joey Eischen	.15	.05
❑ 348	Jeff Fassero	.15	.05
❑ 349	Darrin Fletcher	.15	.05
❑ 350	Cliff Floyd	.30	.10
❑ 351	Marquis Grissom	.30	.10
❑ 352	Butch Henry	.15	.05
❑ 353	Gil Heredia	.15	.05
❑ 354	Ken Hill	.15	.05
❑ 355	Mike Lansing	.15	.05
❑ 356	Pedro Martinez	.50	.20
❑ 357	Mel Rojas	.15	.05
❑ 358	Kirk Rueter	.15	.05
❑ 359	Tim Scott	.15	.05
❑ 360	Jeff Shaw	.15	.05
❑ 361	Larry Walker	.30	.10
❑ 362	Lenny Webster	.15	.05
❑ 363	John Wetteland	.30	.10
❑ 364	Rondell White	.30	.10
❑ 365	Bobby Bonilla	.30	.10
❑ 366	Rico Brogna	.15	.05
❑ 367	Jeromy Burnitz	.30	.10
❑ 368	John Franco	.30	.10
❑ 369	Dwight Gooden	.30	.10
❑ 370	Todd Hundley	.15	.05
❑ 371	Jason Jacome	.15	.05
❑ 372	Bobby Jones	.15	.05
❑ 373	Jeff Kent	.30	.10
❑ 374	Jim Lindeman	.15	.05
❑ 375	Josias Manzanillo	.15	.05
❑ 376	Roger Mason	.15	.05
❑ 377	Kevin McReynolds	.15	.05
❑ 378	Joe Orsulak	.15	.05
❑ 379	Bill Pulsipher	.15	.05
❑ 380	Bret Saberhagen	.30	.10
❑ 381	David Segui	.15	.05
❑ 382	Pete Smith	.15	.05
❑ 383	Kelly Stinnett	.15	.05
❑ 384	Ryan Thompson	.15	.05
❑ 385	Jose Vizcaino	.15	.05
❑ 386	Toby Borland	.15	.05
❑ 387	Ricky Bottalico	.15	.05
❑ 388	Darren Daulton	.30	.10
❑ 389	Mariano Duncan	.15	.05
❑ 390	Lenny Dykstra	.30	.10
❑ 391	Jim Eisenreich	.15	.05
❑ 392	Tommy Greene	.15	.05
❑ 393	Dave Hollins	.15	.05
❑ 394	Pete Incaviglia	.15	.05
❑ 395	Danny Jackson	.15	.05
❑ 396	Doug Jones	.15	.05
❑ 397	Ricky Jordan	.15	.05
❑ 398	John Kruk	.30	.10
❑ 399	Mike Lieberthal	.30	.10
❑ 400	Tony Longmire	.15	.05
❑ 401	Mickey Morandini	.15	.05
❑ 402	Bobby Munoz	.15	.05
❑ 403	Curt Schilling	.30	.10
❑ 404	Heathcliff Slocumb	.15	.05
❑ 405	Kevin Stocker	.15	.05
❑ 406	Fernando Valenzuela	.30	.10
❑ 407	David West	.15	.05
❑ 408	Willie Banks	.15	.05
❑ 409	Jose Bautista	.15	.05
❑ 410	Steve Buechele	.15	.05
❑ 411	Jim Bullinger	.15	.05
❑ 412	Chuck Crim	.15	.05
❑ 413	Shawon Dunston	.15	.05
❑ 414	Kevin Foster	.15	.05

❑ 415 Mark Grace .50 .20
❑ 416 Jose Hernandez .15 .05
❑ 417 Glenallen Hill .15 .05
❑ 418 Brooks Kieschnick .15 .05
❑ 419 Derrick May .15 .05
❑ 420 Randy Myers .15 .05
❑ 421 Dan Plesac .15 .05
❑ 422 Karl Rhodes .15 .05
❑ 423 Rey Sanchez .15 .05
❑ 424 Sammy Sosa .75 .30
❑ 425 Steve Trachsel .15 .05
❑ 426 Rick Wilkins .15 .05
❑ 427 Anthony Young .15 .05
❑ 428 Eddie Zambrano .15 .05
❑ 429 Bret Boone .30 .10
❑ 430 Jeff Branson .15 .05
❑ 431 Jeff Brantley .15 .05
❑ 432 Hector Carrasco .15 .05
❑ 433 Brian Dorsett .15 .05
❑ 434 Tony Fernandez .15 .05
❑ 435 Tim Fortugno .15 .05
❑ 436 Erik Hanson .15 .05
❑ 437 Thomas Howard .15 .05
❑ 438 Kevin Jarvis .15 .05
❑ 439 Barry Larkin .50 .20
❑ 440 Chuck McElroy .15 .05
❑ 441 Kevin Mitchell .15 .05
❑ 442 Hal Morris .15 .05
❑ 443 Jose Rijo .15 .05
❑ 444 John Roper .15 .05
❑ 445 Johnny Ruffin .15 .05
❑ 446 Deion Sanders .50 .20
❑ 447 Reggie Sanders .30 .10
❑ 448 Pete Schourek .15 .05
❑ 449 John Smiley .15 .05
❑ 450 Eddie Taubensee .15 .05
❑ 451 Jeff Bagwell .50 .20
❑ 452 Kevin Bass .15 .05
❑ 453 Craig Biggio .50 .20
❑ 454 Ken Caminiti .30 .10
❑ 455 Andujar Cedeno .15 .05
❑ 456 Doug Drabek .15 .05
❑ 457 Tony Eusebio .15 .05
❑ 458 Mike Felder .15 .05
❑ 459 Steve Finley .30 .10
❑ 460 Luis Gonzalez .30 .10
❑ 461 Mike Hampton .30 .10
❑ 462 Pete Harnisch .15 .05
❑ 463 John Hudek .15 .05
❑ 464 Todd Jones .15 .05
❑ 465 Darryl Kile .30 .10
❑ 466 James Mouton .15 .05
❑ 467 Shane Reynolds .15 .05
❑ 468 Scott Servais .15 .05
❑ 469 Greg Swindell .15 .05
❑ 470 Dave Veres RC .40 .15
❑ 471 Brian Williams .15 .05
❑ 472 Jay Bell .30 .10
❑ 473 Jacob Brumfield .15 .05
❑ 474 Dave Clark .15 .05
❑ 475 Steve Cooke .15 .05
❑ 476 Midre Cummings .15 .05
❑ 477 Mark Dewey .15 .05
❑ 478 Tom Foley .15 .05
❑ 479 Carlos Garcia .15 .05
❑ 480 Jeff King .15 .05
❑ 481 Jon Lieber .15 .05
❑ 482 Ravelo Manzanillo .15 .05
❑ 483 Al Martin .15 .05
❑ 484 Orlando Merced .15 .05
❑ 485 Danny Miceli .15 .05
❑ 486 Denny Neagle .30 .10
❑ 487 Lance Parrish .30 .10
❑ 488 Don Slaught .15 .05
❑ 489 Zane Smith .15 .05
❑ 490 Andy Van Slyke .50 .20
❑ 491 Paul Wagner .15 .05
❑ 492 Rick White .15 .05
❑ 493 Luis Alicea .15 .05
❑ 494 Rene Arocha .15 .05
❑ 495 Rheal Cormier .15 .05
❑ 496 Bryan Eversgerd .15 .05
❑ 497 Bernard Gilkey .15 .05
❑ 498 John Habyan .15 .05
❑ 499 Gregg Jefferies .15 .05
❑ 500 Brian Jordan .30 .10
❑ 501 Ray Lankford .30 .10
❑ 502 John Mabry .15 .05
❑ 503 Terry McGriff .15 .05
❑ 504 Tom Pagnozzi .15 .05
❑ 505 Vicente Palacios .15 .05
❑ 506 Geronimo Pena .15 .05
❑ 507 Gerald Perry .15 .05
❑ 508 Rich Rodriguez .15 .05
❑ 509 Ozzie Smith 1.25 .50
❑ 510 Bob Tewksbury .15 .05
❑ 511 Allen Watson .15 .05
❑ 512 Mark Whiten .15 .05
❑ 513 Todd Zeile .15 .05
❑ 514 Dante Bichette .30 .10
❑ 515 Willie Blair .15 .05
❑ 516 Ellis Burks .30 .10
❑ 517 Marvin Freeman .15 .05
❑ 518 Andres Galarraga .30 .10
❑ 519 Joe Girardi .15 .05
❑ 520 Greg W. Harris .15 .05
❑ 521 Charlie Hayes .15 .05
❑ 522 Mike Kingery .15 .05
❑ 523 Nelson Liriano .15 .05
❑ 524 Mike Munoz .15 .05
❑ 525 David Nied .15 .05
❑ 526 Steve Reed .15 .05
❑ 527 Kevin Ritz .15 .05
❑ 528 Bruce Ruffin .15 .05
❑ 529 John Vander Wal .15 .05
❑ 530 Walt Weiss .15 .05
❑ 531 Eric Young .15 .05
❑ 532 Billy Ashley .15 .05
❑ 533 Pedro Astacio .15 .05
❑ 534 Rafael Bournigal .15 .05
❑ 535 Brett Butler .30 .10
❑ 536 Tom Candiotti .15 .05
❑ 537 Omar Daal .15 .05
❑ 538 Delino DeShields .15 .05
❑ 539 Darren Dreifort .15 .05
❑ 540 Kevin Gross .15 .05
❑ 541 Orel Hershiser .30 .10
❑ 542 Garey Ingram .15 .05
❑ 543 Eric Karros .30 .10
❑ 544 Ramon Martinez .15 .05
❑ 545 Raul Mondesi .30 .10
❑ 546 Chan Ho Park .30 .10
❑ 547 Mike Piazza 1.25 .50
❑ 548 Henry Rodriguez .15 .05
❑ 549 Rudy Seanez .15 .05
❑ 550 Ismael Valdes .15 .05
❑ 551 Tim Wallach .15 .05
❑ 552 Todd Worrell .15 .05
❑ 553 Andy Ashby .15 .05
❑ 554 Brad Ausmus .30 .10
❑ 555 Derek Bell .15 .05
❑ 556 Andy Benes .15 .05
❑ 557 Phil Clark .15 .05
❑ 558 Donnie Elliott .15 .05
❑ 559 Ricky Gutierrez .15 .05
❑ 560 Tony Gwynn 1.00 .40
❑ 561 Joey Hamilton .15 .05
❑ 562 Trevor Hoffman .30 .10
❑ 563 Luis Lopez .15 .05
❑ 564 Pedro A. Martinez .15 .05
❑ 565 Tim Mauser .15 .05
❑ 566 Phil Plantier .15 .05
❑ 567 Bip Roberts .15 .05
❑ 568 Scott Sanders .15 .05
❑ 569 Craig Shipley .15 .05
❑ 570 Jeff Tabaka .15 .05
❑ 571 Eddie Williams .15 .05
❑ 572 Rod Beck .15 .05
❑ 573 Mike Benjamin .15 .05
❑ 574 Barry Bonds 2.00 .75
❑ 575 Dave Burba .15 .05
❑ 576 John Burkett .15 .05
❑ 577 Mark Carreon .15 .05
❑ 578 Royce Clayton .15 .05
❑ 579 Steve Frey .15 .05
❑ 580 Bryan Hickerson .15 .05
❑ 581 Mike Jackson .15 .05
❑ 582 Darren Lewis .15 .05
❑ 583 Kirt Manwaring .15 .05
❑ 584 Rich Monteleone .15 .05
❑ 585 John Patterson .15 .05
❑ 586 J.R. Phillips .15 .05
❑ 587 Mark Portugal .15 .05
❑ 588 Joe Rosselli .15 .05
❑ 589 Darryl Strawberry .30 .10
❑ 590 Bill Swift .15 .05
❑ 591 Robby Thompson .15 .05
❑ 592 William VanLandingham .15 .05
❑ 593 Matt Williams .30 .10
❑ 594 Checklist .15 .05
❑ 595 Checklist .15 .05
❑ 596 Checklist .15 .05
❑ 597 Checklist .15 .05
❑ 598 Checklist .15 .05
❑ 599 Checklist .15 .05
❑ 600 Checklist .15 .05

1996 Fleer

❑ COMPLETE SET (600) 80.00 40.00
❑ 1 Manny Alexander .30 .10
❑ 2 Brady Anderson .30 .10
❑ 3 Harold Baines .30 .10
❑ 4 Armando Benitez .30 .10
❑ 5 Bobby Bonilla .30 .10
❑ 6 Kevin Brown .30 .10
❑ 7 Scott Erickson .30 .10
❑ 8 Curtis Goodwin .30 .10
❑ 9 Jeffrey Hammonds .30 .10
❑ 10 Jimmy Haynes .30 .10
❑ 11 Chris Hoiles .30 .10
❑ 12 Doug Jones .30 .10
❑ 13 Rick Krivda .30 .10
❑ 14 Jeff Manto .30 .10
❑ 15 Ben McDonald .30 .10
❑ 16 Jamie Moyer .30 .10
❑ 17 Mike Mussina .50 .20
❑ 18 Jesse Orosco .30 .10
❑ 19 Rafael Palmeiro .50 .20
❑ 20 Cal Ripken 2.50 1.00
❑ 21 Rick Aguilera .30 .10
❑ 22 Luis Alicea .30 .10
❑ 23 Stan Belinda .30 .10
❑ 24 Jose Canseco .50 .20
❑ 25 Roger Clemens 1.50 .60
❑ 26 Vaughn Eshelman .30 .10
❑ 27 Mike Greenwell .30 .10
❑ 28 Erik Hanson .30 .10
❑ 29 Dwayne Hosey .30 .10
❑ 30 Mike Macfarlane UER .30 .10
❑ 31 Tim Naehring .30 .10
❑ 32 Troy O'Leary .30 .10
❑ 33 Aaron Sele .30 .10
❑ 34 Zane Smith .30 .10
❑ 35 Jeff Suppan .30 .10
❑ 36 Lee Tinsley .30 .10
❑ 37 John Valentin .30 .10
❑ 38 Mo Vaughn .30 .10
❑ 39 Tim Wakefield .30 .10
❑ 40 Jim Abbott .50 .20
❑ 41 Brian Anderson .30 .10
❑ 42 Garret Anderson .30 .10
❑ 43 Chili Davis .30 .10
❑ 44 Gary DiSarcina .30 .10
❑ 45 Damion Easley .30 .10
❑ 46 Jim Edmonds .30 .10
❑ 47 Chuck Finley .30 .10
❑ 48 Todd Greene .30 .10
❑ 49 Mike Harkey .30 .10
❑ 50 Mike James .30 .10
❑ 51 Mark Langston .30 .10

	No.	Player		
❑	52	Greg Myers	.30	.10
❑	53	Orlando Palmeiro	.30	.10
❑	54	Bob Patterson	.30	.10
❑	55	Troy Percival	.30	.10
❑	56	Tony Phillips	.30	.10
❑	57	Tim Salmon	.50	.20
❑	58	Lee Smith	.30	.10
❑	59	J.T. Snow	.30	.10
❑	60	Randy Velarde	.30	.10
❑	61	Wilson Alvarez	.30	.10
❑	62	Luis Andujar	.30	.10
❑	63	Jason Bere	.30	.10
❑	64	Ray Durham	.30	.10
❑	65	Alex Fernandez	.30	.10
❑	66	Ozzie Guillen	.30	.10
❑	67	Roberto Hernandez	.30	.10
❑	68	Lance Johnson	.30	.10
❑	69	Matt Karchner	.30	.10
❑	70	Ron Karkovice	.30	.10
❑	71	Norberto Martin	.30	.10
❑	72	Dave Martinez	.30	.10
❑	73	Kirk McCaskill	.30	.10
❑	74	Lyle Mouton	.30	.10
❑	75	Tim Raines	.30	.10
❑	76	Mike Sirotka RC	.30	.10
❑	77	Frank Thomas	.75	.30
❑	78	Larry Thomas	.30	.10
❑	79	Robin Ventura	.30	.10
❑	80	Sandy Alomar Jr.	.30	.10
❑	81	Paul Assenmacher	.30	.10
❑	82	Carlos Baerga	.30	.10
❑	83	Albert Belle	.30	.10
❑	84	Mark Clark	.30	.10
❑	85	Alan Embree	.30	.10
❑	86	Alvaro Espinoza	.30	.10
❑	87	Orel Hershiser	.30	.10
❑	88	Ken Hill	.30	.10
❑	89	Kenny Lofton	.30	.10
❑	90	Dennis Martinez	.30	.10
❑	91	Jose Mesa	.30	.10
❑	92	Eddie Murray	.75	.30
❑	93	Charles Nagy	.30	.10
❑	94	Chad Ogea	.30	.10
❑	95	Tony Pena	.30	.10
❑	96	Herb Perry	.30	.10
❑	97	Eric Plunk	.30	.10
❑	98	Jim Poole	.30	.10
❑	99	Manny Ramirez	.50	.20
❑	100	Paul Sorrento	.30	.10
❑	101	Julian Tavarez	.30	.10
❑	102	Jim Thome	.50	.20
❑	103	Omar Vizquel	.50	.20
❑	104	Dave Winfield	.30	.10
❑	105	Danny Bautista	.30	.10
❑	106	Joe Boever	.30	.10
❑	107	Chad Curtis	.30	.10
❑	108	John Doherty	.30	.10
❑	109	Cecil Fielder	.30	.10
❑	110	John Flaherty	.30	.10
❑	111	Travis Fryman	.30	.10
❑	112	Chris Gomez	.30	.10
❑	113	Bob Higginson	.30	.10
❑	114	Mark Lewis	.30	.10
❑	115	Jose Lima	.30	.10
❑	116	Felipe Lira	.30	.10
❑	117	Brian Maxcy	.30	.10
❑	118	C.J. Nitkowski	.30	.10
❑	119	Phil Plantier	.30	.10
❑	120	Clint Sodowsky	.30	.10
❑	121	Alan Trammell	.30	.10
❑	122	Lou Whitaker	.30	.10
❑	123	Kevin Appier	.30	.10
❑	124	Johnny Damon	.50	.20
❑	125	Gary Gaetti	.30	.10
❑	126	Tom Goodwin	.30	.10
❑	127	Tom Gordon	.30	.10
❑	128	Mark Gubicza	.30	.10
❑	129	Bob Hamelin	.30	.10
❑	130	David Howard	.30	.10
❑	131	Jason Jacome	.30	.10
❑	132	Wally Joyner	.30	.10
❑	133	Keith Lockhart	.30	.10
❑	134	Brent Mayne	.30	.10
❑	135	Jeff Montgomery	.30	.10
❑	136	Jon Nunnally	.30	.10
❑	137	Juan Samuel	.30	.10
❑	138	Mike Sweeney RC	1.00	.40
❑	139	Michael Tucker	.30	.10
❑	140	Joe Vitiello	.30	.10
❑	141	Ricky Bones	.30	.10
❑	142	Chuck Carr	.30	.10
❑	143	Jeff Cirillo	.30	.10
❑	144	Mike Fetters	.30	.10
❑	145	Darryl Hamilton	.30	.10
❑	146	David Hulse	.30	.10
❑	147	John Jaha	.30	.10
❑	148	Scott Karl	.30	.10
❑	149	Mark Kiefer	.30	.10
❑	150	Pat Listach	.30	.10
❑	151	Mark Loretta	.30	.10
❑	152	Mike Matheny	.30	.10
❑	153	Matt Mieske	.30	.10
❑	154	Dave Nilsson	.30	.10
❑	155	Joe Oliver	.30	.10
❑	156	Al Reyes	.30	.10
❑	157	Kevin Seitzer	.30	.10
❑	158	Steve Sparks	.30	.10
❑	159	B.J. Surhoff	.30	.10
❑	160	Jose Valentin	.30	.10
❑	161	Greg Vaughn	.30	.10
❑	162	Fernando Vina	.30	.10
❑	163	Rich Becker	.30	.10
❑	164	Ron Coomer	.30	.10
❑	165	Marty Cordova	.30	.10
❑	166	Chuck Knoblauch	.30	.10
❑	167	Matt Lawton RC	.50	.20
❑	168	Pat Meares	.30	.10
❑	169	Paul Molitor	.30	.10
❑	170	Pedro Munoz	.30	.10
❑	171	Jose Parra	.30	.10
❑	172	Kirby Puckett	.75	.30
❑	173	Brad Radke	.30	.10
❑	174	Jeff Reboulet	.30	.10
❑	175	Rich Robertson	.30	.10
❑	176	Frank Rodriguez	.30	.10
❑	177	Scott Stahoviak	.30	.10
❑	178	Dave Stevens	.30	.10
❑	179	Matt Walbeck	.30	.10
❑	180	Wade Boggs	.50	.20
❑	181	David Cone	.30	.10
❑	182	Tony Fernandez	.30	.10
❑	183	Joe Girardi	.30	.10
❑	184	Derek Jeter	2.00	.75
❑	185	Scott Kamieniecki	.30	.10
❑	186	Pat Kelly	.30	.10
❑	187	Jim Leyritz	.30	.10
❑	188	Tino Martinez	.50	.20
❑	189	Don Mattingly	2.00	.75
❑	190	Jack McDowell	.30	.10
❑	191	Jeff Nelson	.30	.10
❑	192	Paul O'Neill	.50	.20
❑	193	Melido Perez	.30	.10
❑	194	Andy Pettitte	.50	.20
❑	195	Mariano Rivera	.75	.30
❑	196	Ruben Sierra	.30	.10
❑	197	Mike Stanley	.30	.10
❑	198	Darryl Strawberry	.30	.10
❑	199	John Wetteland	.30	.10
❑	200	Bob Wickman	.30	.10
❑	201	Bernie Williams	.50	.20
❑	202	Mark Acre	.30	.10
❑	203	Geronimo Berroa	.30	.10
❑	204	Mike Bordick	.30	.10
❑	205	Scott Brosius	.30	.10
❑	206	Dennis Eckersley	.30	.10
❑	207	Brent Gates	.30	.10
❑	208	Jason Giambi	.30	.10
❑	209	Rickey Henderson	.75	.30
❑	210	Jose Herrera	.30	.10
❑	211	Stan Javier	.30	.10
❑	212	Doug Johns	.30	.10
❑	213	Mark McGwire	2.00	.75
❑	214	Steve Ontiveros	.30	.10
❑	215	Craig Paquette	.30	.10
❑	216	Ariel Prieto	.30	.10
❑	217	Carlos Reyes	.30	.10
❑	218	Terry Steinbach	.30	.10
❑	219	Todd Stottlemyre	.30	.10
❑	220	Danny Tartabull	.30	.10
❑	221	Todd Van Poppel	.30	.10
❑	222	John Wasdin	.30	.10
❑	223	George Williams	.30	.10
❑	224	Steve Wojciechowski	.30	.10
❑	225	Rich Amaral	.30	.10
❑	226	Bobby Ayala	.30	.10
❑	227	Tim Belcher	.30	.10
❑	228	Andy Benes	.30	.10
❑	229	Chris Bosio	.30	.10
❑	230	Darren Bragg	.30	.10
❑	231	Jay Buhner	.30	.10
❑	232	Norm Charlton	.30	.10
❑	233	Vince Coleman	.30	.10
❑	234	Joey Cora	.30	.10
❑	235	Russ Davis	.30	.10
❑	236	Alex Diaz	.30	.10
❑	237	Felix Fermin	.30	.10
❑	238	Ken Griffey Jr.	1.25	.50
❑	239	Sterling Hitchcock	.30	.10
❑	240	Randy Johnson	.75	.30
❑	241	Edgar Martinez	.50	.20
❑	242	Bill Risley	.30	.10
❑	243	Alex Rodriguez	1.50	.60
❑	244	Luis Sojo	.30	.10
❑	245	Dan Wilson	.30	.10
❑	246	Bob Wolcott	.30	.10
❑	247	Will Clark	.50	.20
❑	248	Jeff Frye	.30	.10
❑	249	Benji Gil	.30	.10
❑	250	Juan Gonzalez	.30	.10
❑	251	Rusty Greer	.30	.10
❑	252	Kevin Gross	.30	.10
❑	253	Roger McDowell	.30	.10
❑	254	Mark McLemore	.30	.10
❑	255	Otis Nixon	.30	.10
❑	256	Luis Ortiz	.30	.10
❑	257	Mike Pagliarulo	.30	.10
❑	258	Dean Palmer	.30	.10
❑	259	Roger Pavlik	.30	.10
❑	260	Ivan Rodriguez	.50	.20
❑	261	Kenny Rogers	.30	.10
❑	262	Jeff Russell	.30	.10
❑	263	Mickey Tettleton	.30	.10
❑	264	Bob Tewksbury	.30	.10
❑	265	Dave Valle	.30	.10
❑	266	Matt Whiteside	.30	.10
❑	267	Roberto Alomar	.50	.20
❑	268	Joe Carter	.30	.10
❑	269	Tony Castillo	.30	.10
❑	270	Domingo Cedeno	.30	.10
❑	271	Tim Crabtree UER	.30	.10
❑	272	Carlos Delgado	.30	.10
❑	273	Alex Gonzalez	.30	.10
❑	274	Shawn Green	.30	.10
❑	275	Juan Guzman	.30	.10
❑	276	Pat Hentgen	.30	.10
❑	277	Al Leiter	.30	.10
❑	278	Sandy Martinez	.30	.10
❑	279	Paul Menhart	.30	.10
❑	280	John Olerud	.30	.10
❑	281	Paul Quantrill	.30	.10
❑	282	Ken Robinson	.30	.10
❑	283	Ed Sprague	.30	.10
❑	284	Mike Timlin	.30	.10
❑	285	Steve Avery	.30	.10
❑	286	Rafael Belliard	.30	.10
❑	287	Jeff Blauser	.30	.10
❑	288	Pedro Borbon	.30	.10
❑	289	Brad Clontz	.30	.10
❑	290	Mike Devereaux	.30	.10
❑	291	Tom Glavine	.50	.20
❑	292	Marquis Grissom	.30	.10
❑	293	Chipper Jones	.75	.30
❑	294	David Justice	.30	.10
❑	295	Mike Kelly	.30	.10
❑	296	Ryan Klesko	.30	.10
❑	297	Mark Lemke	.30	.10
❑	298	Javier Lopez	.30	.10
❑	299	Greg Maddux	1.25	.50
❑	300	Fred McGriff	.50	.20
❑	301	Greg McMichael	.30	.10
❑	302	Kent Mercker	.30	.10
❑	303	Mike Mordecai	.30	.10
❑	304	Charlie O'Brien	.30	.10
❑	305	Eduardo Perez	.30	.10
❑	306	Luis Polonia	.30	.10
❑	307	Jason Schmidt	.50	.20
❑	308	John Smoltz	.50	.20
❑	309	Terrell Wade	.30	.10

❑	310	Mark Wohlers	.30	.10
❑	311	Scott Bullett	.30	.10
❑	312	Jim Bullinger	.30	.10
❑	313	Larry Casian	.30	.10
❑	314	Frank Castillo	.30	.10
❑	315	Shawon Dunston	.30	.10
❑	316	Kevin Foster	.30	.10
❑	317	Matt Franco	.30	.10
❑	318	Luis Gonzalez	.30	.10
❑	319	Mark Grace	.50	.20
❑	320	Jose Hernandez	.30	.10
❑	321	Mike Hubbard	.30	.10
❑	322	Brian McRae	.30	.10
❑	323	Randy Myers	.30	.10
❑	324	Jaime Navarro	.30	.10
❑	325	Mark Parent	.30	.10
❑	326	Mike Perez	.30	.10
❑	327	Rey Sanchez	.30	.10
❑	328	Ryne Sandberg	1.25	.50
❑	329	Scott Servais	.30	.10
❑	330	Sammy Sosa	.75	.30
❑	331	Ozzie Timmons	.30	.10
❑	332	Steve Trachsel	.30	.10
❑	333	Todd Zeile	.30	.10
❑	334	Bret Boone	.30	.10
❑	335	Jeff Branson	.30	.10
❑	336	Jeff Brantley	.30	.10
❑	337	Dave Burba	.30	.10
❑	338	Hector Carrasco	.30	.10
❑	339	Mariano Duncan	.30	.10
❑	340	Ron Gant	.30	.10
❑	341	Lenny Harris	.30	.10
❑	342	Xavier Hernandez	.30	.10
❑	343	Thomas Howard	.30	.10
❑	344	Mike Jackson	.30	.10
❑	345	Barry Larkin	.50	.20
❑	346	Darren Lewis	.30	.10
❑	347	Hal Morris	.30	.10
❑	348	Eric Owens	.30	.10
❑	349	Mark Portugal	.30	.10
❑	350	Jose Rijo	.30	.10
❑	351	Reggie Sanders	.30	.10
❑	352	Benito Santiago	.30	.10
❑	353	Pete Schourek	.30	.10
❑	354	John Smiley	.30	.10
❑	355	Eddie Taubensee	.30	.10
❑	356	Jerome Walton	.30	.10
❑	357	David Wells	.30	.10
❑	358	Roger Bailey	.30	.10
❑	359	Jason Bates	.30	.10
❑	360	Dante Bichette	.30	.10
❑	361	Ellis Burks	.30	.10
❑	362	Vinny Castilla	.30	.10
❑	363	Andres Galarraga	.30	.10
❑	364	Darren Holmes	.30	.10
❑	365	Mike Kingery	.30	.10
❑	366	Curt Leskanic	.30	.10
❑	367	Quinton McCracken	.30	.10
❑	368	Mike Munoz	.30	.10
❑	369	David Nied	.30	.10
❑	370	Steve Reed	.30	.10
❑	371	Bryan Rekar	.30	.10
❑	372	Kevin Ritz	.30	.10
❑	373	Bruce Ruffin	.30	.10
❑	374	Bret Saberhagen	.30	.10
❑	375	Bill Swift	.30	.10
❑	376	John Vander Wal	.30	.10
❑	377	Larry Walker	.30	.10
❑	378	Walt Weiss	.30	.10
❑	379	Eric Young	.30	.10
❑	380	Kurt Abbott	.30	.10
❑	381	Alex Arias	.30	.10
❑	382	Jerry Browne	.30	.10
❑	383	John Burkett	.30	.10
❑	384	Greg Colbrunn	.30	.10
❑	385	Jeff Conine	.30	.10
❑	386	Andre Dawson	.30	.10
❑	387	Chris Hammond	.30	.10
❑	388	Charles Johnson	.30	.10
❑	389	Terry Mathews	.30	.10
❑	390	Robb Nen	.30	.10
❑	391	Joe Orsulak	.30	.10
❑	392	Terry Pendleton	.30	.10
❑	393	Pat Rapp	.30	.10
❑	394	Gary Sheffield	.30	.10
❑	395	Jesus Tavarez	.30	.10
❑	396	Marc Valdes	.30	.10
❑	397	Quilvio Veras	.30	.10
❑	398	Randy Veres	.30	.10
❑	399	Devon White	.30	.10
❑	400	Jeff Bagwell	.50	.20
❑	401	Derek Bell	.30	.10
❑	402	Craig Biggio	.50	.20
❑	403	John Cangelosi	.30	.10
❑	404	Jim Dougherty	.30	.10
❑	405	Doug Drabek	.30	.10
❑	406	Tony Eusebio	.30	.10
❑	407	Ricky Gutierrez	.30	.10
❑	408	Mike Hampton	.30	.10
❑	409	Dean Hartgraves	.30	.10
❑	410	John Hudek	.30	.10
❑	411	Brian Hunter	.30	.10
❑	412	Todd Jones	.30	.10
❑	413	Darryl Kile	.30	.10
❑	414	Dave Magadan	.30	.10
❑	415	Derrick May	.30	.10
❑	416	Orlando Miller	.30	.10
❑	417	James Mouton	.30	.10
❑	418	Shane Reynolds	.30	.10
❑	419	Greg Swindell	.30	.10
❑	420	Jeff Tabaka	.30	.10
❑	421	Dave Veres	.30	.10
❑	422	Billy Wagner	.30	.10
❑	423	Donne Wall	.30	.10
❑	424	Rick Wilkins	.30	.10
❑	425	Billy Ashley	.30	.10
❑	426	Mike Blowers	.30	.10
❑	427	Brett Butler	.30	.10
❑	428	Tom Candiotti	.30	.10
❑	429	Juan Castro	.30	.10
❑	430	John Cummings	.30	.10
❑	431	Delino DeShields	.30	.10
❑	432	Joey Eischen	.30	.10
❑	433	Chad Fonville	.30	.10
❑	434	Greg Gagne	.30	.10
❑	435	Dave Hansen	.30	.10
❑	436	Carlos Hernandez	.30	.10
❑	437	Todd Hollandsworth	.30	.10
❑	438	Eric Karros	.30	.10
❑	439	Roberto Kelly	.30	.10
❑	440	Ramon Martinez	.30	.10
❑	441	Raul Mondesi	.30	.10
❑	442	Hideo Nomo	.75	.30
❑	443	Antonio Osuna	.30	.10
❑	444	Chan Ho Park	.30	.10
❑	445	Mike Piazza	1.25	.50
❑	446	Felix Rodriguez	.30	.10
❑	447	Kevin Tapani	.30	.10
❑	448	Ismael Valdes	.30	.10
❑	449	Todd Worrell	.30	.10
❑	450	Moises Alou	.30	.10
❑	451	Shane Andrews	.30	.10
❑	452	Yamil Benitez	.30	.10
❑	453	Sean Berry	.30	.10
❑	454	Wil Cordero	.30	.10
❑	455	Jeff Fassero	.30	.10
❑	456	Darrin Fletcher	.30	.10
❑	457	Cliff Floyd	.30	.10
❑	458	Mark Grudzielanek	.30	.10
❑	459	Gil Heredia	.30	.10
❑	460	Tim Laker	.30	.10
❑	461	Mike Lansing	.30	.10
❑	462	Pedro Martinez	.50	.20
❑	463	Carlos Perez	.30	.10
❑	464	Curtis Pride	.30	.10
❑	465	Mel Rojas	.30	.10
❑	466	Kirk Rueter	.30	.10
❑	467	F.P. Santangelo	.30	.10
❑	468	Tim Scott	.30	.10
❑	469	David Segui	.30	.10
❑	470	Tony Tarasco	.30	.10
❑	471	Rondell White	.30	.10
❑	472	Edgardo Alfonzo	.30	.10
❑	473	Tim Bogar	.30	.10
❑	474	Rico Brogna	.30	.10
❑	475	Damon Buford	.30	.10
❑	476	Paul Byrd	.30	.10
❑	477	Carl Everett	.30	.10
❑	478	John Franco	.30	.10
❑	479	Todd Hundley	.30	.10
❑	480	Butch Huskey	.30	.10
❑	481	Jason Isringhausen	.30	.10
❑	482	Bobby Jones	.30	.10
❑	483	Chris Jones	.30	.10
❑	484	Jeff Kent	.30	.10
❑	485	Dave Mlicki	.30	.10
❑	486	Robert Person	.30	.10
❑	487	Bill Pulsipher	.30	.10
❑	488	Kelly Stinnett	.30	.10
❑	489	Ryan Thompson	.30	.10
❑	490	Jose Vizcaino	.30	.10
❑	491	Howard Battle	.30	.10
❑	492	Toby Borland	.30	.10
❑	493	Ricky Bottalico	.30	.10
❑	494	Darren Daulton	.30	.10
❑	495	Lenny Dykstra	.30	.10
❑	496	Jim Eisenreich	.30	.10
❑	497	Sid Fernandez	.30	.10
❑	498	Tyler Green	.30	.10
❑	499	Charlie Hayes	.30	.10
❑	500	Gregg Jefferies	.30	.10
❑	501	Kevin Jordan	.30	.10
❑	502	Tony Longmire	.30	.10
❑	503	Tom Marsh	.30	.10
❑	504	Michael Mimbs	.30	.10
❑	505	Mickey Morandini	.30	.10
❑	506	Gene Schall	.30	.10
❑	507	Curt Schilling	.30	.10
❑	508	Heathcliff Slocumb	.30	.10
❑	509	Kevin Stocker	.30	.10
❑	510	Andy Van Slyke	.50	.20
❑	511	Lenny Webster	.30	.10
❑	512	Mark Whiten	.30	.10
❑	513	Mike Williams	.30	.10
❑	514	Jay Bell	.30	.10
❑	515	Jacob Brumfield	.30	.10
❑	516	Jason Christiansen	.30	.10
❑	517	Dave Clark	.30	.10
❑	518	Midre Cummings	.30	.10
❑	519	Angelo Encarnacion	.30	.10
❑	520	John Ericks	.30	.10
❑	521	Carlos Garcia	.30	.10
❑	522	Mark Johnson	.30	.10
❑	523	Jeff King	.30	.10
❑	524	Nelson Liriano	.30	.10
❑	525	Esteban Loaiza	.30	.10
❑	526	Al Martin	.30	.10
❑	527	Orlando Merced	.30	.10
❑	528	Dan Miceli	.30	.10
❑	529	Ramon Morel	.30	.10
❑	530	Denny Neagle	.30	.10
❑	531	Steve Parris	.30	.10
❑	532	Dan Plesac	.30	.10
❑	533	Don Slaught	.30	.10
❑	534	Paul Wagner	.30	.10
❑	535	John Wehner	.30	.10
❑	536	Kevin Young	.30	.10
❑	537	Allen Battle	.30	.10
❑	538	David Bell	.30	.10
❑	539	Alan Benes	.30	.10
❑	540	Scott Cooper	.30	.10
❑	541	Tripp Cromer	.30	.10
❑	542	Tony Fossas	.30	.10
❑	543	Bernard Gilkey	.30	.10
❑	544	Tom Henke	.30	.10
❑	545	Brian Jordan	.30	.10
❑	546	Ray Lankford	.30	.10
❑	547	John Mabry	.30	.10
❑	548	T.J. Mathews	.30	.10
❑	549	Mike Morgan	.30	.10
❑	550	Jose Oliva	.30	.10
❑	551	Jose Oquendo	.30	.10
❑	552	Donovan Osborne	.30	.10
❑	553	Tom Pagnozzi	.30	.10
❑	554	Mark Petkovsek	.30	.10
❑	555	Danny Sheaffer	.30	.10
❑	556	Ozzie Smith	1.25	.50
❑	557	Mark Sweeney	.30	.10
❑	558	Allen Watson	.30	.10
❑	559	Andy Ashby	.30	.10
❑	560	Brad Ausmus	.30	.10
❑	561	Willie Blair	.30	.10
❑	562	Ken Caminiti	.30	.10
❑	563	Andujar Cedeno	.30	.10
❑	564	Glenn Dishman	.30	.10
❑	565	Steve Finley	.30	.10
❑	566	Bryce Florie	.30	.10
❑	567	Tony Gwynn	1.00	.40

❑ 568 Joey Hamilton	.30	.10
❑ 569 Dustin Hermanson UER	.30	.10
❑ 570 Trevor Hoffman	.30	.10
❑ 571 Brian Johnson	.30	.10
❑ 572 Marc Kroon	.30	.10
❑ 573 Scott Livingstone	.30	.10
❑ 574 Marc Newfield	.30	.10
❑ 575 Melvin Nieves	.30	.10
❑ 576 Jody Reed	.30	.10
❑ 577 Bip Roberts	.30	.10
❑ 578 Scott Sanders	.30	.10
❑ 579 Fernando Valenzuela	.30	.10
❑ 580 Eddie Williams	.30	.10
❑ 581 Rod Beck	.30	.10
❑ 582 Marvin Benard RC	.30	.10
❑ 583 Barry Bonds	2.00	.75
❑ 584 Jamie Brewington RC	.30	.10
❑ 585 Mark Carreon	.30	.10
❑ 586 Royce Clayton	.30	.10
❑ 587 Shawn Estes	.30	.10
❑ 588 Glenallen Hill	.30	.10
❑ 589 Mark Leiter	.30	.10
❑ 590 Kirt Manwaring	.30	.10
❑ 591 David McCarty	.30	.10
❑ 592 Terry Mulholland	.30	.10
❑ 593 John Patterson	.30	.10
❑ 594 J.R. Phillips	.30	.10
❑ 595 Deion Sanders	.50	.20
❑ 596 Steve Scarsone	.30	.10
❑ 597 Robby Thompson	.30	.10
❑ 598 Sergio Valdez	.30	.10
❑ 599 William Van Landingham	.30	.10
❑ 600 Matt Williams	.30	.10
❑ P20 Cal Ripken Promo	3.00	1.25

1997 Fleer

❑ COMPLETE SET (761)	140.00	70.00
❑ COMPLETE SERIES 1 (500)	60.00	30.00
❑ COMPLETE SERIES 2 (261)	80.00	40.00
❑ COMMON CARD (1-750)	.30	.10
❑ COMMON CARD (751-761)	.50	.20
❑ 1 Roberto Alomar	.50	.20
❑ 2 Brady Anderson	.30	.10
❑ 3 Bobby Bonilla	.30	.10
❑ 4 Rocky Coppinger	.30	.10
❑ 5 Cesar Devarez	.30	.10
❑ 6 Scott Erickson	.30	.10
❑ 7 Jeffrey Hammonds	.30	.10
❑ 8 Chris Hoiles	.30	.10
❑ 9 Eddie Murray	.75	.30
❑ 10 Mike Mussina	.50	.20
❑ 11 Randy Myers	.30	.10
❑ 12 Rafael Palmeiro	.50	.20
❑ 13 Cal Ripken	2.50	1.00
❑ 14 B.J. Surhoff	.30	.10
❑ 15 David Wells	.30	.10
❑ 16 Todd Zeile	.30	.10
❑ 17 Darren Bragg	.30	.10
❑ 18 Jose Canseco	.50	.20
❑ 19 Roger Clemens	1.50	.60
❑ 20 Wil Cordero	.30	.10
❑ 21 Jeff Frye	.30	.10
❑ 22 Nomar Garciaparra	1.25	.50
❑ 23 Tom Gordon	.30	.10
❑ 24 Mike Greenwell	.30	.10
❑ 25 Reggie Jefferson	.30	.10
❑ 26 Jose Malave	.30	.10
❑ 27 Tim Naehring	.30	.10
❑ 28 Troy O'Leary	.30	.10
❑ 29 Heathcliff Slocumb	.30	.10
❑ 30 Mike Stanley	.30	.10
❑ 31 John Valentin	.30	.10
❑ 32 Mo Vaughn	.30	.10
❑ 33 Tim Wakefield	.30	.10
❑ 34 Garret Anderson	.30	.10
❑ 35 George Arias	.30	.10
❑ 36 Shawn Boskie	.30	.10
❑ 37 Chili Davis	.30	.10
❑ 38 Jason Dickson	.30	.10
❑ 39 Gary DiSarcina	.30	.10
❑ 40 Jim Edmonds	.30	.10
❑ 41 Darin Erstad	.30	.10
❑ 42 Jorge Fabregas	.30	.10
❑ 43 Chuck Finley	.30	.10
❑ 44 Todd Greene	.30	.10
❑ 45 Mike Holtz	.30	.10
❑ 46 Rex Hudler	.30	.10
❑ 47 Mike James	.30	.10
❑ 48 Mark Langston	.30	.10
❑ 49 Troy Percival	.30	.10
❑ 50 Tim Salmon	.50	.20
❑ 51 Jeff Schmidt	.30	.10
❑ 52 J.T. Snow	.30	.10
❑ 53 Randy Velarde	.30	.10
❑ 54 Wilson Alvarez	.30	.10
❑ 55 Harold Baines	.30	.10
❑ 56 James Baldwin	.30	.10
❑ 57 Jason Bere	.30	.10
❑ 58 Mike Cameron	.30	.10
❑ 59 Ray Durham	.30	.10
❑ 60 Alex Fernandez	.30	.10
❑ 61 Ozzie Guillen	.30	.10
❑ 62 Roberto Hernandez	.30	.10
❑ 63 Ron Karkovice	.30	.10
❑ 64 Darren Lewis	.30	.10
❑ 65 Dave Martinez	.30	.10
❑ 66 Lyle Mouton	.30	.10
❑ 67 Greg Norton	.30	.10
❑ 68 Tony Phillips	.30	.10
❑ 69 Chris Snopek	.30	.10
❑ 70 Kevin Tapani	.30	.10
❑ 71 Danny Tartabull	.30	.10
❑ 72 Frank Thomas	.75	.30
❑ 73 Robin Ventura	.30	.10
❑ 74 Sandy Alomar Jr.	.30	.10
❑ 75 Albert Belle	.30	.10
❑ 76 Mark Carreon	.30	.10
❑ 77 Julio Franco	.30	.10
❑ 78 Brian Giles RC	1.50	.60
❑ 79 Orel Hershiser	.30	.10
❑ 80 Kenny Lofton	.30	.10
❑ 81 Dennis Martinez	.30	.10
❑ 82 Jack McDowell	.30	.10
❑ 83 Jose Mesa	.30	.10
❑ 84 Charles Nagy	.30	.10
❑ 85 Chad Ogea	.30	.10
❑ 86 Eric Plunk	.30	.10
❑ 87 Manny Ramirez	.50	.20
❑ 88 Kevin Seitzer	.30	.10
❑ 89 Julian Tavarez	.30	.10
❑ 90 Jim Thome	.50	.20
❑ 91 Jose Vizcaino	.30	.10
❑ 92 Omar Vizquel	.50	.20
❑ 93 Brad Ausmus	.30	.10
❑ 94 Kimera Bartee	.30	.10
❑ 95 Raul Casanova	.30	.10
❑ 96 Tony Clark	.30	.10
❑ 97 John Cummings	.30	.10
❑ 98 Travis Fryman	.30	.10
❑ 99 Bob Higginson	.30	.10
❑ 100 Mark Lewis	.30	.10
❑ 101 Felipe Lira	.30	.10
❑ 102 Phil Nevin	.30	.10
❑ 103 Melvin Nieves	.30	.10
❑ 104 Curtis Pride	.30	.10
❑ 105 A.J. Sager	.30	.10
❑ 106 Ruben Sierra	.30	.10
❑ 107 Justin Thompson	.30	.10
❑ 108 Alan Trammell	.30	.10
❑ 109 Kevin Appier	.30	.10
❑ 110 Tim Belcher	.30	.10
❑ 111 Jaime Bluma	.30	.10
❑ 112 Johnny Damon	.50	.20
❑ 113 Tom Goodwin	.30	.10
❑ 114 Chris Haney	.30	.10
❑ 115 Keith Lockhart	.30	.10
❑ 116 Mike Macfarlane	.30	.10
❑ 117 Jeff Montgomery	.30	.10
❑ 118 Jose Offerman	.30	.10
❑ 119 Craig Paquette	.30	.10
❑ 120 Joe Randa	.30	.10
❑ 121 Bip Roberts	.30	.10
❑ 122 Jose Rosado	.30	.10
❑ 123 Mike Sweeney	.30	.10
❑ 124 Michael Tucker	.30	.10
❑ 125 Jeromy Burnitz	.30	.10
❑ 126 Jeff Cirillo	.30	.10
❑ 127 Jeff D'Amico	.30	.10
❑ 128 Mike Fetters	.30	.10
❑ 129 John Jaha	.30	.10
❑ 130 Scott Karl	.30	.10
❑ 131 Jesse Levis	.30	.10
❑ 132 Mark Loretta	.30	.10
❑ 133 Mike Matheny	.30	.10
❑ 134 Ben McDonald	.30	.10
❑ 135 Matt Mieske	.30	.10
❑ 136 Marc Newfield	.30	.10
❑ 137 Dave Nilsson	.30	.10
❑ 138 Jose Valentin	.30	.10
❑ 139 Fernando Vina	.30	.10
❑ 140 Bob Wickman	.30	.10
❑ 141 Gerald Williams	.30	.10
❑ 142 Rick Aguilera	.30	.10
❑ 143 Rich Becker	.30	.10
❑ 144 Ron Coomer	.30	.10
❑ 145 Marty Cordova	.30	.10
❑ 146 Roberto Kelly	.30	.10
❑ 147 Chuck Knoblauch	.30	.10
❑ 148 Matt Lawton	.30	.10
❑ 149 Pat Meares	.30	.10
❑ 150 Travis Miller	.30	.10
❑ 151 Paul Molitor	.30	.10
❑ 152 Greg Myers	.30	.10
❑ 153 Dan Naulty	.30	.10
❑ 154 Kirby Puckett	.75	.30
❑ 155 Brad Radke	.30	.10
❑ 156 Frank Rodriguez	.30	.10
❑ 157 Scott Stahoviak	.30	.10
❑ 158 Dave Stevens	.30	.10
❑ 159 Matt Walbeck	.30	.10
❑ 160 Todd Walker	.30	.10
❑ 161 Wade Boggs	.50	.20
❑ 162 David Cone	.30	.10
❑ 163 Mariano Duncan	.30	.10
❑ 164 Cecil Fielder	.30	.10
❑ 165 Joe Girardi	.30	.10
❑ 166 Dwight Gooden	.30	.10
❑ 167 Charlie Hayes	.30	.10
❑ 168 Derek Jeter	2.00	.75
❑ 169 Jimmy Key	.30	.10
❑ 170 Jim Leyritz	.30	.10
❑ 171 Tino Martinez	.50	.20
❑ 172 Ramiro Mendoza RC	.30	.10
❑ 173 Jeff Nelson	.30	.10
❑ 174 Paul O'Neill	.50	.20
❑ 175 Andy Pettitte	.50	.20
❑ 176 Mariano Rivera	.75	.30
❑ 177 Ruben Rivera	.30	.10
❑ 178 Kenny Rogers	.30	.10
❑ 179 Darryl Strawberry	.30	.10
❑ 180 John Wetteland	.30	.10
❑ 181 Bernie Williams	.50	.20
❑ 182 Willie Adams	.30	.10
❑ 183 Tony Batista	.30	.10
❑ 184 Geronimo Berroa	.30	.10
❑ 185 Mike Bordick	.30	.10
❑ 186 Scott Brosius	.30	.10
❑ 187 Bobby Chouinard	.30	.10
❑ 188 Jim Corsi	.30	.10
❑ 189 Brent Gates	.30	.10
❑ 190 Jason Giambi	.30	.10
❑ 191 Jose Herrera	.30	.10
❑ 192 Damon Mashore	.30	.10
❑ 193 Mark McGwire	2.00	.75
❑ 194 Mike Mohler	.30	.10
❑ 195 Scott Spiezio	.30	.10
❑ 196 Terry Steinbach	.30	.10
❑ 197 Bill Taylor	.30	.10
❑ 198 John Wasdin	.30	.10

❑ 199 Steve Wojciechowski .30 .10
❑ 200 Ernie Young .30 .10
❑ 201 Rich Amaral .30 .10
❑ 202 Jay Buhner .30 .10
❑ 203 Norm Charlton .30 .10
❑ 204 Joey Cora .30 .10
❑ 205 Russ Davis .30 .10
❑ 206 Ken Griffey Jr. 1.25 .50
❑ 207 Sterling Hitchcock .30 .10
❑ 208 Brian Hunter .30 .10
❑ 209 Raul Ibanez .30 .10
❑ 210 Randy Johnson .75 .30
❑ 211 Edgar Martinez .50 .20
❑ 212 Jamie Moyer .30 .10
❑ 213 Alex Rodriguez 1.25 .50
❑ 214 Paul Sorrento .30 .10
❑ 215 Matt Wagner .30 .10
❑ 216 Bob Wells .30 .10
❑ 217 Dan Wilson .30 .10
❑ 218 Damon Buford .30 .10
❑ 219 Will Clark .50 .20
❑ 220 Kevin Elster .30 .10
❑ 221 Juan Gonzalez .30 .10
❑ 222 Rusty Greer .30 .10
❑ 223 Kevin Gross .30 .10
❑ 224 Darryl Hamilton .30 .10
❑ 225 Mike Henneman .30 .10
❑ 226 Ken Hill .30 .10
❑ 227 Mark McLemore .30 .10
❑ 228 Darren Oliver .30 .10
❑ 229 Dean Palmer .30 .10
❑ 230 Roger Pavlik .30 .10
❑ 231 Ivan Rodriguez .50 .20
❑ 232 Mickey Tettleton .30 .10
❑ 233 Bobby Witt .30 .10
❑ 234 Jacob Brumfield .30 .10
❑ 235 Joe Carter .30 .10
❑ 236 Tim Crabtree .30 .10
❑ 237 Carlos Delgado .30 .10
❑ 238 Huck Flener .30 .10
❑ 239 Alex Gonzalez .30 .10
❑ 240 Shawn Green .30 .10
❑ 241 Juan Guzman .30 .10
❑ 242 Pat Hentgen .30 .10
❑ 243 Marty Janzen .30 .10
❑ 244 Sandy Martinez .30 .10
❑ 245 Otis Nixon .30 .10
❑ 246 Charlie O'Brien .30 .10
❑ 247 John Olerud .30 .10
❑ 248 Robert Perez .30 .10
❑ 249 Ed Sprague .30 .10
❑ 250 Mike Timlin .30 .10
❑ 251 Steve Avery .30 .10
❑ 252 Jeff Blauser .30 .10
❑ 253 Brad Clontz .30 .10
❑ 254 Jermaine Dye .30 .10
❑ 255 Tom Glavine .50 .20
❑ 256 Marquis Grissom .30 .10
❑ 257 Andruw Jones .50 .20
❑ 258 Chipper Jones .75 .30
❑ 259 David Justice .30 .10
❑ 260 Ryan Klesko .30 .10
❑ 261 Mark Lemke .30 .10
❑ 262 Javier Lopez .30 .10
❑ 263 Greg Maddux 1.25 .50
❑ 264 Fred McGriff .50 .20
❑ 265 Greg McMichael .30 .10
❑ 266 Denny Neagle .30 .10
❑ 267 Terry Pendleton .30 .10
❑ 268 Eddie Perez .30 .10
❑ 269 John Smoltz .50 .20
❑ 270 Terrell Wade .30 .10
❑ 271 Mark Wohlers .30 .10
❑ 272 Terry Adams .30 .10
❑ 273 Brant Brown .30 .10
❑ 274 Leo Gomez .30 .10
❑ 275 Luis Gonzalez .30 .10
❑ 276 Mark Grace .50 .20
❑ 277 Tyler Houston .30 .10
❑ 278 Robin Jennings .30 .10
❑ 279 Brooks Kieschnick .30 .10
❑ 280 Brian McRae .30 .10
❑ 281 Jaime Navarro .30 .10
❑ 282 Ryne Sandberg 1.25 .50
❑ 283 Scott Servais .30 .10
❑ 284 Sammy Sosa .75 .30
❑ 285 Dave Swartzbaugh .30 .10
❑ 286 Amaury Telemaco .30 .10
❑ 287 Steve Trachsel .30 .10
❑ 288 Pedro Valdes .30 .10
❑ 289 Turk Wendell .30 .10
❑ 290 Bret Boone .30 .10
❑ 291 Jeff Branson .30 .10
❑ 292 Jeff Brantley .30 .10
❑ 293 Eric Davis .30 .10
❑ 294 Willie Greene .30 .10
❑ 295 Thomas Howard .30 .10
❑ 296 Barry Larkin .50 .20
❑ 297 Kevin Mitchell .30 .10
❑ 298 Hal Morris .30 .10
❑ 299 Chad Mottola .30 .10
❑ 300 Joe Oliver .30 .10
❑ 301 Mark Portugal .30 .10
❑ 302 Roger Salkeld .30 .10
❑ 303 Reggie Sanders .30 .10
❑ 304 Pete Schourek .30 .10
❑ 305 John Smiley .30 .10
❑ 306 Eddie Taubensee .30 .10
❑ 307 Dante Bichette .30 .10
❑ 308 Ellis Burks .30 .10
❑ 309 Vinny Castilla .30 .10
❑ 310 Andres Galarraga .30 .10
❑ 311 Curt Leskanic .30 .10
❑ 312 Quinton McCracken .30 .10
❑ 313 Neifi Perez .30 .10
❑ 314 Jeff Reed .30 .10
❑ 315 Steve Reed .30 .10
❑ 316 Armando Reynoso .30 .10
❑ 317 Kevin Ritz .30 .10
❑ 318 Bruce Ruffin .30 .10
❑ 319 Larry Walker .30 .10
❑ 320 Walt Weiss .30 .10
❑ 321 Jamey Wright .30 .10
❑ 322 Eric Young .30 .10
❑ 323 Kurt Abbott .30 .10
❑ 324 Alex Arias .30 .10
❑ 325 Kevin Brown .30 .10
❑ 326 Luis Castillo .30 .10
❑ 327 Greg Colbrunn .30 .10
❑ 328 Jeff Conine .30 .10
❑ 329 Andre Dawson .30 .10
❑ 330 Charles Johnson .30 .10
❑ 331 Al Leiter .30 .10
❑ 332 Ralph Milliard .30 .10
❑ 333 Robb Nen .30 .10
❑ 334 Pat Rapp .30 .10
❑ 335 Edgar Renteria .30 .10
❑ 336 Gary Sheffield .30 .10
❑ 337 Devon White .30 .10
❑ 338 Bob Abreu .50 .20
❑ 339 Jeff Bagwell .50 .20
❑ 340 Derek Bell .30 .10
❑ 341 Sean Berry .30 .10
❑ 342 Craig Biggio .50 .20
❑ 343 Doug Drabek .30 .10
❑ 344 Tony Eusebio .30 .10
❑ 345 Ricky Gutierrez .30 .10
❑ 346 Mike Hampton .30 .10
❑ 347 Brian Hunter .30 .10
❑ 348 Todd Jones .30 .10
❑ 349 Darryl Kile .30 .10
❑ 350 Derrick May .30 .10
❑ 351 Orlando Miller .30 .10
❑ 352 James Mouton .30 .10
❑ 353 Shane Reynolds .30 .10
❑ 354 Billy Wagner .30 .10
❑ 355 Donne Wall .30 .10
❑ 356 Mike Blowers .30 .10
❑ 357 Brett Butler .30 .10
❑ 358 Roger Cedeno .30 .10
❑ 359 Chad Curtis .30 .10
❑ 360 Delino DeShields .30 .10
❑ 361 Greg Gagne .30 .10
❑ 362 Karim Garcia .30 .10
❑ 363 Wilton Guerrero .30 .10
❑ 364 Todd Hollandsworth .30 .10
❑ 365 Eric Karros .30 .10
❑ 366 Ramon Martinez .30 .10
❑ 367 Raul Mondesi .30 .10
❑ 368 Hideo Nomo .75 .30
❑ 369 Antonio Osuna .30 .10
❑ 370 Chan Ho Park .30 .10
❑ 371 Mike Piazza 1.25 .50
❑ 372 Ismael Valdes .30 .10
❑ 373 Todd Worrell .30 .10
❑ 374 Moises Alou .30 .10
❑ 375 Shane Andrews .30 .10
❑ 376 Yamil Benitez .30 .10
❑ 377 Jeff Fassero .30 .10
❑ 378 Darrin Fletcher .30 .10
❑ 379 Cliff Floyd .30 .10
❑ 380 Mark Grudzielanek .30 .10
❑ 381 Mike Lansing .30 .10
❑ 382 Barry Manuel .30 .10
❑ 383 Pedro Martinez .50 .20
❑ 384 Henry Rodriguez .30 .10
❑ 385 Mel Rojas .30 .10
❑ 386 F.P. Santangelo .30 .10
❑ 387 David Segui .30 .10
❑ 388 Ugueth Urbina .30 .10
❑ 389 Rondell White .30 .10
❑ 390 Edgardo Alfonzo .30 .10
❑ 391 Carlos Baerga .30 .10
❑ 392 Mark Clark .30 .10
❑ 393 Alvaro Espinoza .30 .10
❑ 394 John Franco .30 .10
❑ 395 Bernard Gilkey .30 .10
❑ 396 Pete Harnisch .30 .10
❑ 397 Todd Hundley .30 .10
❑ 398 Butch Huskey .30 .10
❑ 399 Jason Isringhausen .30 .10
❑ 400 Lance Johnson .30 .10
❑ 401 Bobby Jones .30 .10
❑ 402 Alex Ochoa .30 .10
❑ 403 Rey Ordonez .30 .10
❑ 404 Robert Person .30 .10
❑ 405 Paul Wilson .30 .10
❑ 406 Matt Beech .30 .10
❑ 407 Ron Blazier .30 .10
❑ 408 Ricky Bottalico .30 .10
❑ 409 Lenny Dykstra .30 .10
❑ 410 Jim Eisenreich .30 .10
❑ 411 Bobby Estalella .30 .10
❑ 412 Mike Grace .30 .10
❑ 413 Gregg Jefferies .30 .10
❑ 414 Mike Lieberthal .30 .10
❑ 415 Wendell Magee .30 .10
❑ 416 Mickey Morandini .30 .10
❑ 417 Ricky Otero .30 .10
❑ 418 Scott Rolen .50 .20
❑ 419 Ken Ryan .30 .10
❑ 420 Benito Santiago .30 .10
❑ 421 Curt Schilling .30 .10
❑ 422 Kevin Sefcik .30 .10
❑ 423 Jermaine Allensworth .30 .10
❑ 424 Trey Beamon .30 .10
❑ 425 Jay Bell .30 .10
❑ 426 Francisco Cordova .30 .10
❑ 427 Carlos Garcia .30 .10
❑ 428 Mark Johnson .30 .10
❑ 429 Jason Kendall .30 .10
❑ 430 Jeff King .30 .10
❑ 431 Jon Lieber .30 .10
❑ 432 Al Martin .30 .10
❑ 433 Orlando Merced .30 .10
❑ 434 Ramon Morel .30 .10
❑ 435 Matt Ruebel .30 .10
❑ 436 Jason Schmidt .30 .10
❑ 437 Marc Wilkins .30 .10
❑ 438 Alan Benes .30 .10
❑ 439 Andy Benes .30 .10
❑ 440 Royce Clayton .30 .10
❑ 441 Dennis Eckersley .30 .10
❑ 442 Gary Gaetti .30 .10
❑ 443 Ron Gant .30 .10
❑ 444 Aaron Holbert .30 .10
❑ 445 Brian Jordan .30 .10
❑ 446 Ray Lankford .30 .10
❑ 447 John Mabry .30 .10
❑ 448 T.J. Mathews .30 .10
❑ 449 Willie McGee .30 .10
❑ 450 Donovan Osborne .30 .10
❑ 451 Tom Pagnozzi .30 .10
❑ 452 Ozzie Smith 1.25 .50
❑ 453 Todd Stottlemyre .30 .10
❑ 454 Mark Sweeney .30 .10
❑ 455 Dmitri Young .30 .10
❑ 456 Andy Ashby .30 .10

❑ 457	Ken Caminiti	.30	.10
❑ 458	Archi Cianfrocco	.30	.10
❑ 459	Steve Finley	.30	.10
❑ 460	John Flaherty	.30	.10
❑ 461	Chris Gomez	.30	.10
❑ 462	Tony Gwynn	1.00	.40
❑ 463	Joey Hamilton	.30	.10
❑ 464	Rickey Henderson	.75	.30
❑ 465	Trevor Hoffman	.30	.10
❑ 466	Brian Johnson	.30	.10
❑ 467	Wally Joyner	.30	.10
❑ 468	Jody Reed	.30	.10
❑ 469	Scott Sanders	.30	.10
❑ 470	Bob Tewksbury	.30	.10
❑ 471	Fernando Valenzuela	.30	.10
❑ 472	Greg Vaughn	.30	.10
❑ 473	Tim Worrell	.30	.10
❑ 474	Rich Aurilia	.30	.10
❑ 475	Rod Beck	.30	.10
❑ 476	Marvin Benard	.30	.10
❑ 477	Barry Bonds	2.00	.75
❑ 478	Jay Canizaro	.30	.10
❑ 479	Shawon Dunston	.30	.10
❑ 480	Shawn Estes	.30	.10
❑ 481	Mark Gardner	.30	.10
❑ 482	Glenallen Hill	.30	.10
❑ 483	Stan Javier	.30	.10
❑ 484	Marcus Jensen	.30	.10
❑ 485	Bill Mueller RC	1.25	.50
❑ 486	Wm. VanLandingham	.30	.10
❑ 487	Allen Watson	.30	.10
❑ 488	Rick Wilkins	.30	.10
❑ 489	Matt Williams	.30	.10
❑ 490	Desi Wilson	.30	.10
❑ 491	Albert Belle CL	.30	.10
❑ 492	Ken Griffey Jr. CL	.75	.30
❑ 493	Andruw Jones CL	.30	.10
❑ 494	Chipper Jones CL	.50	.20
❑ 495	Mark McGwire CL	1.00	.40
❑ 496	Paul Molitor CL	.30	.10
❑ 497	Mike Piazza CL	.75	.30
❑ 498	Cal Ripken CL	1.25	.50
❑ 499	Alex Rodriguez CL	.75	.30
❑ 500	Frank Thomas CL	.50	.20
❑ 501	Kenny Lofton	.30	.10
❑ 502	Carlos Perez	.30	.10
❑ 503	Tim Raines	.30	.10
❑ 504	Danny Patterson	.30	.10
❑ 505	Derrick May	.30	.10
❑ 506	Dave Hollins	.30	.10
❑ 507	Felipe Crespo	.30	.10
❑ 508	Brian Banks	.30	.10
❑ 509	Jeff Kent	.30	.10
❑ 510	Bubba Trammell RC	.40	.15
❑ 511	Robert Person	.30	.10
❑ 512	David Arias-Ortiz RC	40.00	15.00
❑ 513	Ryan Jones	.30	.10
❑ 514	David Justice	.30	.10
❑ 515	Will Cunnane	.30	.10
❑ 516	Russ Johnson	.30	.10
❑ 517	John Burkett	.30	.10
❑ 518	Robinson Checo RC	.30	.10
❑ 519	Ricardo Rincon RC	.30	.10
❑ 520	Woody Williams	.30	.10
❑ 521	Rick Helling	.30	.10
❑ 522	Jorge Posada	.50	.20
❑ 523	Kevin Orie	.30	.10
❑ 524	Fernando Tatis RC	.30	.10
❑ 525	Jermaine Dye	.30	.10
❑ 526	Brian Hunter	.30	.10
❑ 527	Greg McMichael	.30	.10
❑ 528	Matt Wagner	.30	.10
❑ 529	Richie Sexson	.30	.10
❑ 530	Scott Ruffcorn	.30	.10
❑ 531	Luis Gonzalez	.30	.10
❑ 532	Mike Johnson RC	.30	.10
❑ 533	Mark Petkovsek	.30	.10
❑ 534	Doug Drabek	.30	.10
❑ 535	Jose Canseco	.50	.20
❑ 536	Bobby Bonilla	.30	.10
❑ 537	J.T. Snow	.30	.10
❑ 538	Shawon Dunston	.30	.10
❑ 539	John Ericks	.30	.10
❑ 540	Terry Steinbach	.30	.10
❑ 541	Jay Bell	.30	.10
❑ 542	Joe Borowski RC	.40	.15
❑ 543	David Wells	.30	.10
❑ 544	Justin Towle RC	.30	.10
❑ 545	Mike Blowers	.30	.10
❑ 546	Shannon Stewart	.30	.10
❑ 547	Rudy Pemberton	.30	.10
❑ 548	Bill Swift	.30	.10
❑ 549	Osvaldo Fernandez	.30	.10
❑ 550	Eddie Murray	.75	.30
❑ 551	Don Wengert	.30	.10
❑ 552	Brad Ausmus	.30	.10
❑ 553	Carlos Garcia	.30	.10
❑ 554	Jose Guillen	.30	.10
❑ 555	Rheal Cormier	.30	.10
❑ 556	Doug Brocail	.30	.10
❑ 557	Rex Hudler	.30	.10
❑ 558	Armando Benitez	.30	.10
❑ 559	Eli Marrero	.30	.10
❑ 560	Ricky Ledee RC	.40	.15
❑ 561	Bartolo Colon	.30	.10
❑ 562	Quilvio Veras	.30	.10
❑ 563	Alex Fernandez	.30	.10
❑ 564	Darren Dreifort	.30	.10
❑ 565	Benji Gil	.30	.10
❑ 566	Kent Mercker	.30	.10
❑ 567	Glendon Rusch	.30	.10
❑ 568	Ramon Tatis RC	.30	.10
❑ 569	Roger Clemens	1.50	.60
❑ 570	Mark Lewis	.30	.10
❑ 571	Emil Brown RC	.30	.10
❑ 572	Jaime Navarro	.30	.10
❑ 573	Sherman Obando	.30	.10
❑ 574	John Wasdin	.30	.10
❑ 575	Calvin Maduro	.30	.10
❑ 576	Todd Jones	.30	.10
❑ 577	Orlando Merced	.30	.10
❑ 578	Cal Eldred	.30	.10
❑ 579	Mark Gubicza	.30	.10
❑ 580	Michael Tucker	.30	.10
❑ 581	Tony Saunders RC	.30	.10
❑ 582	Garvin Alston	.30	.10
❑ 583	Joe Roa	.30	.10
❑ 584	Brady Raggio RC	.30	.10
❑ 585	Jimmy Key	.30	.10
❑ 586	Marc Sagmoen RC	.30	.10
❑ 587	Jim Bullinger	.30	.10
❑ 588	Yorkis Perez	.30	.10
❑ 589	Jose Cruz Jr. RC	.40	.15
❑ 590	Mike Stanton	.30	.10
❑ 591	Deivi Cruz RC	.40	.15
❑ 592	Steve Karsay	.30	.10
❑ 593	Mike Trombley	.30	.10
❑ 594	Doug Glanville	.30	.10
❑ 595	Scott Sanders	.30	.10
❑ 596	Thomas Howard	.30	.10
❑ 597	T.J. Staton RC	.30	.10
❑ 598	Garrett Stephenson	.30	.10
❑ 599	Rico Brogna	.30	.10
❑ 600	Albert Belle	.30	.10
❑ 601	Jose Vizcaino	.30	.10
❑ 602	Chili Davis	.30	.10
❑ 603	Shane Mack	.30	.10
❑ 604	Jim Eisenreich	.30	.10
❑ 605	Todd Zeile	.30	.10
❑ 606	Brian Boehringer RC	.30	.10
❑ 607	Paul Shuey	.30	.10
❑ 608	Kevin Tapani	.30	.10
❑ 609	John Wetteland	.30	.10
❑ 610	Jim Leyritz	.30	.10
❑ 611	Ray Montgomery RC	.30	.10
❑ 612	Doug Bochtler	.30	.10
❑ 613	Wady Almonte RC	.30	.10
❑ 614	Danny Tartabull	.30	.10
❑ 615	Orlando Miller	.30	.10
❑ 616	Bobby Ayala	.30	.10
❑ 617	Tony Graffanino	.30	.10
❑ 618	Marc Valdes	.30	.10
❑ 619	Ron Villone	.30	.10
❑ 620	Derrek Lee	.50	.20
❑ 621	Greg Colbrunn	.30	.10
❑ 622	Felix Heredia RC	.40	.15
❑ 623	Carl Everett	.30	.10
❑ 624	Mark Thompson	.30	.10
❑ 625	Jeff Granger	.30	.10
❑ 626	Damian Jackson	.30	.10
❑ 627	Mark Leiter	.30	.10
❑ 628	Chris Holt	.30	.10
❑ 629	Dario Veras RC	.30	.10
❑ 630	Dave Burba	.30	.10
❑ 631	Darryl Hamilton	.30	.10
❑ 632	Mark Acre	.30	.10
❑ 633	Fernando Hernandez RC	.30	.10
❑ 634	Terry Mulholland	.30	.10
❑ 635	Dustin Hermanson	.30	.10
❑ 636	Delino DeShields	.30	.10
❑ 637	Steve Avery	.30	.10
❑ 638	Tony Womack RC	.40	.15
❑ 639	Mark Whiten	.30	.10
❑ 640	Marquis Grissom	.30	.10
❑ 641	Xavier Hernandez	.30	.10
❑ 642	Eric Davis	.30	.10
❑ 643	Bob Tewksbury	.30	.10
❑ 644	Dante Powell	.30	.10
❑ 645	Carlos Castillo RC	.30	.10
❑ 646	Chris Widger	.30	.10
❑ 647	Moises Alou	.30	.10
❑ 648	Pat Listach	.30	.10
❑ 649	Edgar Ramos RC	.30	.10
❑ 650	Deion Sanders	.50	.20
❑ 651	John Olerud	.30	.10
❑ 652	Todd Dunwoody	.30	.10
❑ 653	Randall Simon RC	.40	.15
❑ 654	Dan Carlson	.30	.10
❑ 655	Matt Williams	.30	.10
❑ 656	Jeff King	.30	.10
❑ 657	Luis Alicea	.30	.10
❑ 658	Brian Moehler RC	.40	.15
❑ 659	Ariel Prieto	.30	.10
❑ 660	Kevin Elster	.30	.10
❑ 661	Mark Hutton	.30	.10
❑ 662	Aaron Sele	.30	.10
❑ 663	Graeme Lloyd	.30	.10
❑ 664	John Burke	.30	.10
❑ 665	Mel Rojas	.30	.10
❑ 666	Sid Fernandez	.30	.10
❑ 667	Pedro Astacio	.30	.10
❑ 668	Jeff Abbott	.30	.10
❑ 669	Darren Daulton	.30	.10
❑ 670	Mike Bordick	.30	.10
❑ 671	Sterling Hitchcock	.30	.10
❑ 672	Damion Easley	.30	.10
❑ 673	Armando Reynoso	.30	.10
❑ 674	Pat Cline	.30	.10
❑ 675	Orlando Cabrera RC	.75	.30
❑ 676	Alan Embree	.30	.10
❑ 677	Brian Bevil	.30	.10
❑ 678	David Weathers	.30	.10
❑ 679	Cliff Floyd	.30	.10
❑ 680	Joe Randa	.30	.10
❑ 681	Bill Haselman	.30	.10
❑ 682	Jeff Fassero	.30	.10
❑ 683	Matt Morris	.30	.10
❑ 684	Mark Portugal	.30	.10
❑ 685	Lee Smith	.30	.10
❑ 686	Pokey Reese	.30	.10
❑ 687	Benito Santiago	.30	.10
❑ 688	Brian Johnson	.30	.10
❑ 689	Brent Brede RC	.30	.10
❑ 690	Shigetoshi Hasegawa RC	.50	.20
❑ 691	Julio Santana	.30	.10
❑ 692	Steve Kline	.30	.10
❑ 693	Julian Tavarez	.30	.10
❑ 694	John Hudek	.30	.10
❑ 695	Manny Alexander	.30	.10
❑ 696	Roberto Alomar ENC	.30	.10
❑ 697	Jeff Bagwell ENC	.30	.10
❑ 698	Barry Bonds ENC	1.00	.40
❑ 699	Ken Caminiti ENC	.30	.10
❑ 700	Juan Gonzalez ENC	.30	.10
❑ 701	Ken Griffey Jr. ENC	.75	.30
❑ 702	Tony Gwynn ENC	.50	.20
❑ 703	Derek Jeter ENC	1.00	.40
❑ 704	Andruw Jones ENC	.50	.20
❑ 705	Chipper Jones ENC	.50	.20
❑ 706	Barry Larkin ENC	.30	.10
❑ 707	Greg Maddux ENC	.75	.30
❑ 708	Mark McGwire ENC	1.00	.40
❑ 709	Paul Molitor ENC	.30	.10
❑ 710	Hideo Nomo ENC	.30	.10
❑ 711	Andy Pettitte ENC	.30	.10
❑ 712	Mike Piazza ENC	.75	.30
❑ 713	Manny Ramirez ENC	.50	.20
❑ 714	Cal Ripken ENC	1.25	.50

❑ 715	Alex Rodriguez ENC	.75	.30
❑ 716	Ryne Sandberg ENC	.75	.30
❑ 717	John Smoltz ENC	.30	.10
❑ 718	Frank Thomas ENC	.50	.20
❑ 719	Mo Vaughn ENC	.30	.10
❑ 720	Bernie Williams ENC	.30	.10
❑ 721	Tim Salmon CL	.30	.10
❑ 722	Greg Maddux CL	.75	.30
❑ 723	Cal Ripken CL	1.25	.50
❑ 724	Mo Vaughn CL	.30	.10
❑ 725	Ryne Sandberg CL	.75	.30
❑ 726	Frank Thomas CL	.50	.20
❑ 727	Barry Larkin CL	.30	.10
❑ 728	Manny Ramirez CL	.30	.10
❑ 729	Andres Galarraga CL	.30	.10
❑ 730	Tony Clark CL	.30	.10
❑ 731	Gary Sheffield CL	.30	.10
❑ 732	Jeff Bagwell CL	.30	.10
❑ 733	Kevin Appier CL	.30	.10
❑ 734	Mike Piazza CL	.75	.30
❑ 735	Jeff Cirillo CL	.30	.10
❑ 736	Paul Molitor CL	.30	.10
❑ 737	Henry Rodriguez CL	.30	.10
❑ 738	Todd Hundley CL	.30	.10
❑ 739	Derek Jeter CL	1.00	.40
❑ 740	Mark McGwire CL	1.00	.40
❑ 741	Curt Schilling CL	.30	.10
❑ 742	Jason Kendall CL	.30	.10
❑ 743	Tony Gwynn CL	.50	.20
❑ 744	Barry Bonds CL	1.00	.40
❑ 745	Ken Griffey Jr. CL	.75	.30
❑ 746	Brian Jordan CL	.30	.10
❑ 747	Juan Gonzalez CL	.30	.10
❑ 748	Joe Carter CL	.30	.10
❑ 749	Arizona Diamondbacks CL	.30	.10
❑ 750	Tampa Bay Devil Rays CL	.30	.10
❑ 751	Hideki Irabu RC	.75	.30
❑ 752	Jeremi Gonzalez RC	.50	.20
❑ 753	Mario Valdez RC	.50	.20
❑ 754	Aaron Boone	.75	.30
❑ 755	Brett Tomko	.50	.20
❑ 756	Jaret Wright RC	.75	.30
❑ 757	Ryan McGuire	.50	.20
❑ 758	Jason McDonald	.50	.20
❑ 759	Adrian Brown RC	.50	.20
❑ 760	Keith Foulke RC	2.00	.75
❑ 761	Bonus Checklist (751-761)	.50	.20
❑ P489	Matt Williams Promo	1.00	.40
❑ NNO	A.Jones Circa AU/200	25.00	10.00

2002 Fleer

❑	COMPLETE SET (540)	80.00	30.00
❑	COMMON CARD (1-540)	.25	.08
❑	COMMON CARD (492-531)	.50	.20
❑ 1	Darin Erstad FP	.25	.08
❑ 2	Randy Johnson FP	.60	.25
❑ 3	Chipper Jones FP	.60	.25
❑ 4	Jay Gibbons FP	.25	.08
❑ 5	Nomar Garciaparra FP	1.00	.40
❑ 6	Sammy Sosa FP	.60	.25
❑ 7	Frank Thomas FP	.60	.25
❑ 8	Ken Griffey Jr. FP	1.00	.40
❑ 9	Jim Thome FP	.40	.15
❑ 10	Todd Helton FP	.40	.15
❑ 11	Jeff Weaver FP	.25	.08
❑ 12	Cliff Floyd FP	.25	.08
❑ 13	Jeff Bagwell FP	.40	.15
❑ 14	Mike Sweeney FP	.25	.08
❑ 15	Adrian Beltre FP	.25	.08
❑ 16	Richie Sexson FP	.25	.08
❑ 17	Brad Radke FP	.25	.08
❑ 18	Vladimir Guerrero FP	.60	.25
❑ 19	Mike Piazza FP	1.00	.40
❑ 20	Derek Jeter FP	1.25	.50
❑ 21	Eric Chavez FP	.25	.08
❑ 22	Pat Burrell FP	.25	.08
❑ 23	Brian Giles FP	.25	.08
❑ 24	Trevor Hoffman FP	.25	.08
❑ 25	Barry Bonds FP	1.00	.40
❑ 26	Ichiro Suzuki FP	1.00	.40
❑ 27	Albert Pujols FP	1.00	.40
❑ 28	Ben Grieve FP	.25	.08
❑ 29	Alex Rodriguez FP	1.00	.40
❑ 30	Carlos Delgado FP	.25	.08
❑ 31	Miguel Tejada	.40	.15
❑ 32	Todd Hollandsworth	.25	.08
❑ 33	Marlon Anderson	.25	.08
❑ 34	Kerry Robinson	.25	.08
❑ 35	Chris Richard	.25	.08
❑ 36	Jamey Wright	.25	.08
❑ 37	Ray Lankford	.40	.15
❑ 38	Mike Bordick	.40	.15
❑ 39	Danny Graves	.25	.08
❑ 40	A.J. Pierzynski	.40	.15
❑ 41	Shannon Stewart	.40	.15
❑ 42	Tony Armas Jr.	.25	.08
❑ 43	Brad Ausmus	.40	.15
❑ 44	Alfonso Soriano	.40	.15
❑ 45	Junior Spivey	.25	.08
❑ 46	Brent Mayne	.25	.08
❑ 47	Jim Thome	.60	.25
❑ 48	Dan Wilson	.25	.08
❑ 49	Geoff Jenkins	.25	.08
❑ 50	Kris Benson	.25	.08
❑ 51	Rafael Furcal	.40	.15
❑ 52	Wiki Gonzalez	.25	.08
❑ 53	Jeff Kent	.40	.15
❑ 54	Curt Schilling	.40	.15
❑ 55	Ken Harvey	.25	.08
❑ 56	Roosevelt Brown	.25	.08
❑ 57	David Segui	.25	.08
❑ 58	Mario Valdez	.25	.08
❑ 59	Adam Dunn	.40	.15
❑ 60	Bob Howry	.25	.08
❑ 61	Michael Barrett	.25	.08
❑ 62	Garret Anderson	.40	.15
❑ 63	Kelvim Escobar	.25	.08
❑ 64	Ben Grieve	.25	.08
❑ 65	Randy Johnson	1.00	.40
❑ 66	Jose Offerman	.25	.08
❑ 67	Jason Kendall	.40	.15
❑ 68	Joel Pineiro	.25	.08
❑ 69	Alex Escobar	.25	.08
❑ 70	Chris George	.25	.08
❑ 71	Bobby Higginson	.40	.15
❑ 72	Nomar Garciaparra	1.50	.60
❑ 73	Pat Burrell	.40	.15
❑ 74	Lee Stevens	.25	.08
❑ 75	Felipe Lopez	.25	.08
❑ 76	Al Leiter	.40	.15
❑ 77	Jim Edmonds	.40	.15
❑ 78	Al Levine	.25	.08
❑ 79	Raul Mondesi	.40	.15
❑ 80	Jose Valentin	.25	.08
❑ 81	Matt Clement	.40	.15
❑ 82	Richard Hidalgo	.25	.08
❑ 83	Jamie Moyer	.40	.15
❑ 84	Brian Schneider	.25	.08
❑ 85	John Franco	.40	.15
❑ 86	Brian Buchanan	.25	.08
❑ 87	Roy Oswalt	.40	.15
❑ 88	Johnny Estrada	.25	.08
❑ 89	Marcus Giles	.40	.15
❑ 90	Carlos Valderrama	.25	.08
❑ 91	Mark Mulder	.40	.15
❑ 92	Mark Grace	.60	.25
❑ 93	Andy Ashby	.25	.08
❑ 94	Woody Williams	.25	.08
❑ 95	Ben Petrick	.25	.08
❑ 96	Roy Halladay	.40	.15
❑ 97	Fred McGriff	.60	.25
❑ 98	Shawn Green	.40	.15
❑ 99	Todd Hundley	.25	.08
❑ 100	Carlos Febles	.25	.08
❑ 101	Jason Marquis	.25	.08
❑ 102	Mike Redmond	.25	.08
❑ 103	Shane Halter	.25	.08
❑ 104	Trot Nixon	.40	.15
❑ 105	Jeremy Giambi	.25	.08
❑ 106	Carlos Delgado	.40	.15
❑ 107	Richie Sexson	.40	.15
❑ 108	Russ Ortiz	.25	.08
❑ 109	David Ortiz	1.00	.40
❑ 110	Curtis Leskanic	.25	.08
❑ 111	Jay Payton	.25	.08
❑ 112	Travis Phelps	.25	.08
❑ 113	J.T. Snow	.40	.15
❑ 114	Edgar Renteria	.40	.15
❑ 115	Freddy Garcia	.40	.15
❑ 116	Cliff Floyd	.40	.15
❑ 117	Charles Nagy	.25	.08
❑ 118	Tony Batista	.25	.08
❑ 119	Rafael Palmeiro	.60	.25
❑ 120	Darren Dreifort	.25	.08
❑ 121	Warren Morris	.25	.08
❑ 122	Augie Ojeda	.25	.08
❑ 123	Rusty Greer	.40	.15
❑ 124	Esteban Yan	.25	.08
❑ 125	Corey Patterson	.25	.08
❑ 126	Matt Ginter	.25	.08
❑ 127	Matt Lawton	.25	.08
❑ 128	Miguel Batista	.25	.08
❑ 129	Randy Winn	.25	.08
❑ 130	Eric Milton	.25	.08
❑ 131	Jack Wilson	.25	.08
❑ 132	Sean Casey	.40	.15
❑ 133	Mike Sweeney	.40	.15
❑ 134	Jason Tyner	.25	.08
❑ 135	Carlos Hernandez	.25	.08
❑ 136	Shea Hillenbrand	.40	.15
❑ 137	Shawn Wooten	.25	.08
❑ 138	Peter Bergeron	.25	.08
❑ 139	Travis Lee	.25	.08
❑ 140	Craig Wilson	.25	.08
❑ 141	Carlos Guillen	.40	.15
❑ 142	Chipper Jones	1.00	.40
❑ 143	Gabe Kapler	.40	.15
❑ 144	Raul Ibanez	.25	.08
❑ 145	Eric Chavez	.40	.15
❑ 146	D'Angelo Jimenez	.25	.08
❑ 147	Chad Hermansen	.25	.08
❑ 148	Joe Kennedy	.25	.08
❑ 149	Mariano Rivera	1.00	.40
❑ 150	Jeff Bagwell	.60	.25
❑ 151	Joe McEwing	.25	.08
❑ 152	Ronnie Belliard	.25	.08
❑ 153	Desi Relaford	.25	.08
❑ 154	Vinny Castilla	.40	.15
❑ 155	Tim Hudson	.40	.15
❑ 156	Wilton Guerrero	.25	.08
❑ 157	Raul Casanova	.25	.08
❑ 158	Edgardo Alfonzo	.25	.08
❑ 159	Derrek Lee	.60	.25
❑ 160	Phil Nevin	.40	.15
❑ 161	Roger Clemens	2.00	.75
❑ 162	Jason LaRue	.25	.08
❑ 163	Brian Lawrence	.25	.08
❑ 164	Adrian Beltre	.40	.15
❑ 165	Troy Glaus	.40	.15
❑ 166	Jeff Weaver	.25	.08
❑ 167	B.J. Surhoff	.40	.15
❑ 168	Eric Byrnes	.25	.08
❑ 169	Mike Sirotka	.25	.08
❑ 170	Bill Haselman	.25	.08
❑ 171	Javier Vazquez	.40	.15
❑ 172	Sidney Ponson	.25	.08
❑ 173	Adam Everett	.25	.08
❑ 174	Bubba Trammell	.25	.08
❑ 175	Robb Nen	.40	.15
❑ 176	Barry Larkin	.60	.25
❑ 177	Tony Graffanino	.25	.08
❑ 178	Rich Garces	.25	.08
❑ 179	Juan Uribe	.25	.08
❑ 180	Tom Glavine	.60	.25
❑ 181	Eric Karros	.40	.15
❑ 182	Michael Cuddyer	.25	.08
❑ 183	Wade Miller	.25	.08
❑ 184	Matt Williams	.40	.15
❑ 185	Matt Morris	.40	.15
❑ 186	Rickey Henderson	1.00	.40

187	Trevor Hoffman	.40	.15
188	Wilson Betemit	.25	.08
189	Steve Karsay	.25	.08
190	Frank Catalanotto	.25	.08
191	Jason Schmidt	.40	.15
192	Roger Cedeno	.25	.08
193	Magglio Ordonez	.40	.15
194	Pat Hentgen	.25	.08
195	Mike Lieberthal	.40	.15
196	Andy Pettitte	.60	.25
197	Jay Gibbons	.25	.08
198	Rolando Arrojo	.25	.08
199	Joe Mays	.25	.08
200	Aubrey Huff	.40	.15
201	Nelson Figueroa	.25	.08
202	Paul Konerko	.40	.15
203	Ken Griffey Jr.	1.50	.60
204	Brandon Duckworth	.25	.08
205	Sammy Sosa	1.00	.40
206	Carl Everett	.40	.15
207	Scott Rolen	.60	.25
208	Orlando Hernandez	.40	.15
209	Todd Helton	.60	.25
210	Preston Wilson	.40	.15
211	Gil Meche	.25	.08
212	Bill Mueller	.40	.15
213	Craig Biggio	.60	.25
214	Dean Palmer	.40	.15
215	Randy Wolf	.25	.08
216	Jeff Suppan	.25	.08
217	Jimmy Rollins	.40	.15
218	Alexis Gomez	.25	.08
219	Ellis Burks	.40	.15
220	Ramon E. Martinez	.25	.08
221	Ramiro Mendoza	.25	.08
222	Einar Diaz	.25	.08
223	Brent Abernathy	.25	.08
224	Darin Erstad	.40	.15
225	Reggie Taylor	.25	.08
226	Jason Jennings	.25	.08
227	Ray Durham	.40	.15
228	John Parrish	.25	.08
229	Kevin Young	.25	.08
230	Xavier Nady	.25	.08
231	Juan Cruz	.25	.08
232	Greg Norton	.25	.08
233	Barry Bonds	2.50	1.00
234	Kip Wells	.25	.08
235	Paul LoDuca	.40	.15
236	Javy Lopez	.40	.15
237	Luis Castillo	.25	.08
238	Tom Gordon	.25	.08
239	Mike Mordecai	.25	.08
240	Damian Rolls	.25	.08
241	Julio Lugo	.25	.08
242	Ichiro Suzuki	2.00	.75
243	Tony Womack	.25	.08
244	Matt Anderson	.25	.08
245	Carlos Lee	.40	.15
246	Alex Rodriguez	1.50	.60
247	Bernie Williams	.60	.25
248	Scott Sullivan	.25	.08
249	Mike Hampton	.40	.15
250	Orlando Cabrera	.40	.15
251	Benito Santiago	.40	.15
252	Steve Finley	.40	.15
253	Dave Williams	.25	.08
254	Adam Kennedy	.25	.08
255	Omar Vizquel	.60	.25
256	Garrett Stephenson	.25	.08
257	Fernando Tatis	.25	.08
258	Mike Piazza	1.50	.60
259	Scott Spiezio	.25	.08
260	Jacque Jones	.40	.15
261	Russell Branyan	.25	.08
262	Mark McLemore	.25	.08
263	Mitch Meluskey	.25	.08
264	Marlon Byrd	.25	.08
265	Kyle Farnsworth	.25	.08
266	Billy Sylvester	.25	.08
267	C.C. Sabathia	.40	.15
268	Mark Buehrle	.40	.15
269	Geoff Blum	.25	.08
270	Bret Prinz	.25	.08
271	Placido Polanco	.25	.08
272	John Olerud	.40	.15
273	Pedro Martinez	.60	.25
274	Doug Mientkiewicz	.40	.15
275	Jason Bere	.25	.08
276	Bud Smith	.25	.08
277	Terrence Long	.25	.08
278	Troy Percival	.40	.15
279	Derek Jeter	2.50	1.00
280	Eric Owens	.25	.08
281	Jay Bell	.40	.15
282	Mike Cameron	.25	.08
283	Joe Randa	.40	.15
284	Brian Roberts	.40	.15
285	Ryan Klesko	.40	.15
286	Ryan Dempster	.25	.08
287	Cristian Guzman	.25	.08
288	Tim Salmon	.60	.25
289	Mark Johnson	.25	.08
290	Brian Giles	.40	.15
291	Jon Lieber	.25	.08
292	Fernando Vina	.25	.08
293	Mike Mussina	.60	.25
294	Juan Pierre	.40	.15
295	Carlos Beltran	.40	.15
296	Vladimir Guerrero	1.00	.40
297	Orlando Merced	.25	.08
298	Jose Hernandez	.25	.08
299	Mike Lamb	.25	.08
300	David Eckstein	.40	.15
301	Mark Loretta	.25	.08
302	Greg Vaughn	.25	.08
303	Jose Vidro	.25	.08
304	Jose Ortiz	.25	.08
305	Mark Grudzielanek	.25	.08
306	Rob Bell	.25	.08
307	Elmer Dessens	.25	.08
308	Tomas Perez	.25	.08
309	Jerry Hairston Jr.	.25	.08
310	Mike Stanton	.25	.08
311	Todd Walker	.25	.08
312	Jason Varitek	1.00	.40
313	Masato Yoshii	.25	.08
314	Ben Sheets	.40	.15
315	Roberto Hernandez	.25	.08
316	Eli Marrero	.25	.08
317	Josh Beckett	.40	.15
318	Robert Fick	.25	.08
319	Aramis Ramirez	.40	.15
320	Bartolo Colon	.40	.15
321	Kenny Kelly	.25	.08
322	Luis Gonzalez	.40	.15
323	John Smoltz	.60	.25
324	Homer Bush	.25	.08
325	Kevin Millwood	.40	.15
326	Manny Ramirez	.60	.25
327	Armando Benitez	.25	.08
328	Luis Alicea	.25	.08
329	Mark Kotsay	.40	.15
330	Felix Rodriguez	.25	.08
331	Eddie Taubensee	.25	.08
332	John Burkett	.25	.08
333	Ramon Ortiz	.25	.08
334	Daryle Ward	.25	.08
335	Jarrod Washburn	.25	.08
336	Benji Gil	.25	.08
337	Mike Lowell	.40	.15
338	Larry Walker	.40	.15
339	Andruw Jones	.60	.25
340	Scott Elarton	.25	.08
341	Tony McKnight	.25	.08
342	Frank Thomas	1.00	.40
343	Kevin Brown	.40	.15
344	Jermaine Dye	.40	.15
345	Luis Rivas	.25	.08
346	Jeff Conine	.40	.15
347	Bobby Kielty	.25	.08
348	Jeffrey Hammonds	.25	.08
349	Keith Foulke	.40	.15
350	Dave Martinez	.25	.08
351	Adam Eaton	.25	.08
352	Brandon Inge	.25	.08
353	Tyler Houston	.25	.08
354	Bobby Abreu	.40	.15
355	Ivan Rodriguez	.60	.25
356	Doug Glanville	.25	.08
357	Jorge Julio	.25	.08
358	Kerry Wood	.40	.15
359	Eric Munson	.25	.08
360	Joe Crede	.40	.15
361	Denny Neagle	.25	.08
362	Vance Wilson	.25	.08
363	Neifi Perez	.25	.08
364	Darryl Kile	.40	.15
365	Jose Macias	.25	.08
366	Michael Coleman	.25	.08
367	Erubiel Durazo	.25	.08
368	Darrin Fletcher	.25	.08
369	Matt White	.25	.08
370	Marvin Benard	.25	.08
371	Brad Penny	.25	.08
372	Chuck Finley	.40	.15
373	Delino DeShields	.25	.08
374	Adrian Brown	.25	.08
375	Corey Koskie	.25	.08
376	Kazuhiro Sasaki	.40	.15
377	Brent Butler	.25	.08
378	Paul Wilson	.25	.08
379	Scott Williamson	.25	.08
380	Mike Young	1.00	.40
381	Toby Hall	.25	.08
382	Shane Reynolds	.25	.08
383	Tom Goodwin	.25	.08
384	Seth Etherton	.25	.08
385	Billy Wagner	.40	.15
386	Josh Phelps	.25	.08
387	Kyle Lohse	.25	.08
388	Jeremy Fikac	.25	.08
389	Jorge Posada	.60	.25
390	Bret Boone	.40	.15
391	Angel Berroa	.25	.08
392	Matt Mantei	.25	.08
393	Alex Gonzalez	.25	.08
394	Scott Strickland	.25	.08
395	Charles Johnson	.40	.15
396	Ramon Hernandez	.25	.08
397	Damian Jackson	.25	.08
398	Albert Pujols	2.00	.75
399	Gary Bennett	.25	.08
400	Edgar Martinez	.60	.25
401	Carl Pavano	.40	.15
402	Chris Gomez	.25	.08
403	Jaret Wright	.25	.08
404	Lance Berkman	.40	.15
405	Robert Person	.25	.08
406	Brook Fordyce	.25	.08
407	Adam Pettyjohn	.25	.08
408	Chris Carpenter	.40	.15
409	Rey Ordonez	.25	.08
410	Eric Gagne	.40	.15
411	Damion Easley	.25	.08
412	A.J. Burnett	.40	.15
413	Aaron Boone	.40	.15
414	J.D. Drew	.40	.15
415	Kelly Stinnett	.25	.08
416	Mark Quinn	.25	.08
417	Brad Radke	.40	.15
418	Jose Cruz Jr.	.25	.08
419	Greg Maddux	1.50	.60
420	Steve Cox	.25	.08
421	Torii Hunter	.40	.15
422	Sandy Alomar Jr.	.25	.08
423	Barry Zito	.40	.15
424	Bill Hall	.40	.15
425	Marquis Grissom	.40	.15
426	Rich Aurilia	.25	.08
427	Royce Clayton	.25	.08
428	Travis Fryman	.40	.15
429	Pablo Ozuna	.25	.08
430	David Dellucci	.25	.08
431	Vernon Wells	.40	.15
432	Gregg Zaun CP	.25	.08
433	Alex Gonzalez CP	.25	.08
434	Hideo Nomo CP	1.00	.40
435	Jeromy Burnitz CP	.40	.15
436	Gary Sheffield CP	.40	.15
437	Tino Martinez CP	.60	.25
438	Tsuyoshi Shinjo CP	.40	.15
439	Chan Ho Park CP	.40	.15
440	Tony Clark CP	.25	.08
441	Brad Fullmer CP	.25	.08
442	Jason Giambi CP	.25	.08
443	Billy Koch CP	.25	.08
444	Mo Vaughn CP	.40	.15

❑ 445 Alex Ochoa CP .25 .08
❑ 446 Darren Lewis CP .25 .08
❑ 447 John Rocker CP .40 .15
❑ 448 Scott Hatteberg CP .25 .08
❑ 449 Brady Anderson CP .40 .15
❑ 450 Chuck Knoblauch CP .40 .15
❑ 451 Pokey Reese CP .25 .08
❑ 452 Brian Jordan CP .40 .15
❑ 453 Albie Lopez CP .25 .08
❑ 454 David Bell CP .25 .08
❑ 455 Juan Gonzalez CP .40 .15
❑ 456 Terry Adams CP .25 .08
❑ 457 Kenny Lofton CP .40 .15
❑ 458 Shawn Estes CP .25 .08
❑ 459 Josh Fogg CP .25 .08
❑ 460 Dmitri Young CP .40 .15
❑ 461 Johnny Damon Sox CP .60 .25
❑ 462 Chris Singleton CP .25 .08
❑ 463 Ricky Ledee CP .25 .08
❑ 464 Dustin Hermanson CP .25 .08
❑ 465 Aaron Sele CP .25 .08
❑ 466 Chris Stynes CP .25 .08
❑ 467 Matt Stairs CP .25 .08
❑ 468 Kevin Appier CP .40 .15
❑ 469 Omar Daal CP .25 .08
❑ 470 Moises Alou CP .40 .15
❑ 471 Juan Encarnacion CP .25 .08
❑ 472 Robin Ventura CP .40 .15
❑ 473 Eric Hinske CP .25 .08
❑ 474 Rondell White CP .40 .15
❑ 475 Carlos Pena CP .25 .08
❑ 476 Craig Paquette CP .25 .08
❑ 477 Marty Cordova CP .25 .08
❑ 478 Brett Tomko CP .25 .08
❑ 479 Reggie Sanders CP .25 .08
❑ 480 Roberto Alomar CP .60 .25
❑ 481 Jeff Cirillo CP .25 .08
❑ 482 Todd Zeile CP .40 .15
❑ 483 John Vander Wal CP .25 .08
❑ 484 Rick Helling CP .25 .08
❑ 485 Jeff D'Amico CP .25 .08
❑ 486 David Justice CP .40 .15
❑ 487 Jason Isringhausen CP .40 .15
❑ 488 Shigetoshi Hasegawa CP .40 .15
❑ 489 Eric Young CP .25 .08
❑ 490 David Wells CP .40 .15
❑ 491 Ruben Sierra CP .25 .08
❑ 492 Aaron Cook FF RC .75 .30
❑ 493 Takahito Nomura FF RC .75 .30
❑ 494 Austin Kearns FF .50 .20
❑ 495 Kazuhisa Ishii FF RC 1.25 .50
❑ 496 Mark Teixeira FF 2.00 .75
❑ 497 Rene Reyes FF RC .75 .30
❑ 498 Tim Spooneybarger FF .50 .20
❑ 499 Ben Broussard FF .50 .20
❑ 500 Eric Cyr FF .50 .20
❑ 501 Anastacio Martinez FF RC .75 .30
❑ 502 Morgan Ensberg FF .75 .30
❑ 503 Steve Kent FF RC .75 .30
❑ 504 Franklin Nunez FF RC .75 .30
❑ 505 Adam Walker FF RC .75 .30
❑ 506 Anderson Machado FF RC .75 .30
❑ 507 Ryan Drese FF .50 .20
❑ 508 Luis Ugueto FF RC .75 .30
❑ 509 Jorge Nunez FF RC .75 .30
❑ 510 Colby Lewis FF .50 .20
❑ 511 Ron Calloway FF RC .75 .30
❑ 512 Hansel Izquierdo FF RC .75 .30
❑ 513 Jason Lane FF .75 .30
❑ 514 Rafael Soriano FF .50 .20
❑ 515 Jackson Melian FF .50 .20
❑ 516 Edwin Almonte FF RC .75 .30
❑ 517 Satoru Komiyama FF RC .75 .30
❑ 518 Corey Thurman FF RC .75 .30
❑ 519 Jorge De La Rosa FF RC .75 .30
❑ 520 Victor Martinez FF 2.00 .75
❑ 521 Dewon Brazelton FF .50 .20
❑ 522 Marlon Byrd FF .50 .20
❑ 523 Jae Seo FF .50 .20
❑ 524 Orlando Hudson FF .50 .20
❑ 525 Sean Burroughs FF .50 .20
❑ 526 Ryan Langerhans FF .75 .30
❑ 527 David Kelton FF .50 .20
❑ 528 So Taguchi FF RC 1.25 .50
❑ 529 Tyler Walker FF .50 .20
❑ 530 Hank Blalock FF 1.25 .50
❑ 531 Mark Prior FF 1.25 .50
❑ 532 Yankee Stadium CL .40 .15
❑ 533 Fenway Park CL .40 .15
❑ 534 Wrigley Field CL .40 .15
❑ 535 Dodger Stadium CL .40 .15
❑ 536 Camden Yards CL .40 .15
❑ 537 PacBell Park CL .25 .08
❑ 538 Jacobs Field CL .25 .08
❑ 539 SAFECO Field CL .25 .08
❑ 540 Miller Field CL .25 .08
❑ P279 Derek Jeter Promo

2006 Fleer

❑ Alay Soler RC
❑ COMP.FACT.SET (430) 50.00 20.00
❑ COMPLETE SET (400) 40.00 15.00
❑ COMMON CARD (1-400) .40 .15
❑ COMMON ROOKIE .50 .20
❑ COMMON ROOKIE (401-430) .60 .25
❑ 401-430 AVAIL. IN FLEER FACT.SET
❑ 1 Adam Kennedy .40 .15
❑ 2 Bartolo Colon .40 .15
❑ 3 Bengie Molina .40 .15
❑ 4 Chone Figgins .40 .15
❑ 5 Dallas McPherson .40 .15
❑ 6 Darin Erstad .40 .15
❑ 7 Francisco Rodriguez .40 .15
❑ 8 Garret Anderson .40 .15
❑ 9 Jarrod Washburn .40 .15
❑ 10 John Lackey .40 .15
❑ 11 Orlando Cabrera .40 .15
❑ 12 Ryan Theriot RC .50 .20
❑ 13 Steve Finley .40 .15
❑ 14 Vladimir Guerrero 1.00 .40
❑ 15 Adam Everett .40 .15
❑ 16 Andy Pettitte .60 .25
❑ 17 Charlton Jimerson (RC) .50 .20
❑ 18 Brad Lidge .40 .15
❑ 19 Chris Burke .40 .15
❑ 20 Craig Biggio .60 .25
❑ 21 Jason Lane .40 .15
❑ 22 Jeff Bagwell .60 .25
❑ 23 Lance Berkman .40 .15
❑ 24 Morgan Ensberg .40 .15
❑ 25 Roger Clemens 2.00 .75
❑ 26 Roy Oswalt .40 .15
❑ 27 Willy Taveras .40 .15
❑ 28 Barry Zito .40 .15
❑ 29 Bobby Crosby .40 .15
❑ 30 Bobby Kielty .40 .15
❑ 31 Dan Johnson .40 .15
❑ 32 Danny Haren .40 .15
❑ 33 Eric Chavez .40 .15
❑ 34 Huston Street .40 .15
❑ 35 Jason Kendall .40 .15
❑ 36 Jay Payton .40 .15
❑ 37 Joe Blanton .40 .15
❑ 38 Mark Kotsay .40 .15
❑ 39 Nick Swisher .40 .15
❑ 40 Rich Harden .40 .15
❑ 41 Ron Flores RC .50 .20
❑ 42 Alex Rios .40 .15
❑ 43 John-Ford Griffin (RC) .50 .20
❑ 44 Dave Bush .40 .15
❑ 45 Eric Hinske .40 .15
❑ 46 Frank Catalanotto .40 .15
❑ 47 Gustavo Chacin .40 .15
❑ 48 Josh Towers .40 .15
❑ 49 Miguel Batista .40 .15
❑ 50 Orlando Hudson .40 .15
❑ 51 Roy Halladay .40 .15
❑ 52 Shea Hillenbrand .40 .15
❑ 53 Shaun Marcum (RC) .50 .20
❑ 54 Vernon Wells .40 .15
❑ 55 Adam LaRoche .40 .15
❑ 56 Andruw Jones .60 .25
❑ 57 Chipper Jones 1.00 .40
❑ 58 Anthony Lerew (RC) .50 .20
❑ 59 Jeff Francoeur 1.00 .40
❑ 60 John Smoltz .60 .25
❑ 61 Johnny Estrada .40 .15
❑ 62 Julio Franco .40 .15
❑ 63 Joey Devine RC .50 .20
❑ 64 Marcus Giles .40 .15
❑ 65 Mike Hampton .40 .15
❑ 66 Rafael Furcal .40 .15
❑ 67 Chuck James (RC) .75 .30
❑ 68 Tim Hudson .40 .15
❑ 69 Ben Sheets .40 .15
❑ 70 Bill Hall .40 .15
❑ 71 Brady Clark .40 .15
❑ 72 Carlos Lee .40 .15
❑ 73 Chris Capuano .40 .15
❑ 74 Nelson Cruz (RC) .50 .20
❑ 75 Derrick Turnbow .40 .15
❑ 76 Doug Davis .40 .15
❑ 77 Geoff Jenkins .40 .15
❑ 78 J.J. Hardy .40 .15
❑ 79 Lyle Overbay .40 .15
❑ 80 Prince Fielder 1.50 .60
❑ 81 Rickie Weeks .40 .15
❑ 82 Albert Pujols 2.00 .75
❑ 83 Chris Carpenter .40 .15
❑ 84 David Eckstein .40 .15
❑ 85 Jason Isringhausen .40 .15
❑ 86 Tyler Johnson (RC) .50 .20
❑ 87 Adam Wainwright (RC) .50 .20
❑ 88 Jim Edmonds .60 .25
❑ 89 Chris Duncan (RC) .50 .20
❑ 90 Mark Grudzielanek .40 .15
❑ 91 Mark Mulder .40 .15
❑ 92 Matt Morris .40 .15
❑ 93 Reggie Sanders .40 .15
❑ 94 Scott Rolen .60 .25
❑ 95 Yadier Molina .40 .15
❑ 96 Aramis Ramirez .40 .15
❑ 97 Carlos Zambrano .40 .15
❑ 98 Corey Patterson .40 .15
❑ 99 Derrek Lee .40 .15
❑ 100 Glendon Rusch .40 .15
❑ 101 Greg Maddux 1.50 .60
❑ 102 Jeromy Burnitz .40 .15
❑ 103 Kerry Wood .40 .15
❑ 104 Mark Prior .60 .25
❑ 105 Michael Barrett .40 .15
❑ 106 Geovany Soto (RC) .50 .20
❑ 107 Nomar Garciaparra 1.00 .40
❑ 108 Ryan Dempster .40 .15
❑ 109 Todd Walker .40 .15
❑ 110 Alex S. Gonzalez .40 .15
❑ 111 Aubrey Huff .40 .15
❑ 112 Victor Diaz .40 .15
❑ 113 Carl Crawford .40 .15
❑ 114 Danys Baez .40 .15
❑ 115 Joey Gathright .40 .15
❑ 116 Jonny Gomes .40 .15
❑ 117 Jorge Cantu .40 .15
❑ 118 Julio Lugo .40 .15
❑ 119 Rocco Baldelli .40 .15
❑ 120 Scott Kazmir .60 .25
❑ 121 Toby Hall .40 .15
❑ 122 Tim Corcoran RC .50 .20
❑ 123 Alex Cintron .40 .15
❑ 124 Brandon Webb .40 .15
❑ 125 Chad Tracy .40 .15
❑ 126 Dustin Nippert (RC) .50 .20
❑ 127 Claudio Vargas .40 .15
❑ 128 Craig Counsell .40 .15
❑ 129 Javier Vazquez .40 .15
❑ 130 Jose Valverde .40 .15
❑ 131 Luis Gonzalez .40 .15
❑ 132 Royce Clayton .40 .15
❑ 133 Russ Ortiz .40 .15
❑ 134 Shawn Green .40 .15

❑ 135 Tony Clark .40 .15
❑ 136 Troy Glaus .40 .15
❑ 137 Brad Penny .40 .15
❑ 138 Cesar Izturis .40 .15
❑ 139 Derek Lowe .40 .15
❑ 140 Eric Gagne .40 .15
❑ 141 Hee Seop Choi .40 .15
❑ 142 J.D. Drew .40 .15
❑ 143 Jason Phillips .40 .15
❑ 144 Jayson Werth .40 .15
❑ 145 Jeff Kent .40 .15
❑ 146 Jeff Weaver .40 .15
❑ 147 Milton Bradley .40 .15
❑ 148 Odalis Perez .40 .15
❑ 149 Hong-Chih Kuo (RC) 1.25 .50
❑ 150 Brian Myrow RC .50 .20
❑ 151 Armando Benitez .40 .15
❑ 152 Edgardo Alfonzo .40 .15
❑ 153 J.T. Snow .40 .15
❑ 154 Jason Schmidt .40 .15
❑ 155 Lance Niekro .40 .15
❑ 156 Doug Clark (RC) .50 .20
❑ 157 Dan Ortmeier (RC) .50 .20
❑ 158 Moises Alou .40 .15
❑ 159 Noah Lowry .40 .15
❑ 160 Omar Vizquel .60 .25
❑ 161 Pedro Feliz .40 .15
❑ 162 Randy Winn .40 .15
❑ 163 Jeremy Accardo RC .50 .20
❑ 164 Aaron Boone .40 .15
❑ 165 Ryan Garko (RC) .50 .20
❑ 166 C.C. Sabathia .40 .15
❑ 167 Casey Blake .40 .15
❑ 168 Cliff Lee .40 .15
❑ 169 Coco Crisp .40 .15
❑ 170 Grady Sizemore .60 .25
❑ 171 Jake Westbrook .40 .15
❑ 172 Jhonny Peralta .40 .15
❑ 173 Kevin Millwood .40 .15
❑ 174 Scott Elarton .40 .15
❑ 175 Travis Hafner .40 .15
❑ 176 Victor Martinez .40 .15
❑ 177 Adrian Beltre .40 .15
❑ 178 Eddie Guardado .40 .15
❑ 179 Felix Hernandez .60 .25
❑ 180 Gil Meche .40 .15
❑ 181 Ichiro Suzuki 1.50 .60
❑ 182 Jamie Moyer .40 .15
❑ 183 Jeremy Reed .40 .15
❑ 184 Jaime Bubela (RC) .40 .15
❑ 185 Raul Ibanez .40 .15
❑ 186 Richie Sexson .40 .15
❑ 187 Ryan Franklin .40 .15
❑ 188 Jeff Harris RC .40 .15
❑ 189 A.J. Burnett .40 .15
❑ 190 Josh Wilson (RC) .50 .20
❑ 191 Josh Johnson (RC) .75 .30
❑ 192 Carlos Delgado .40 .15
❑ 193 Dontrelle Willis .40 .15
❑ 194 Bernie Castro (RC) .50 .20
❑ 195 Josh Beckett .40 .15
❑ 196 Juan Encarnacion .40 .15
❑ 197 Juan Pierre .40 .15
❑ 198 Robert Andino RC .50 .20
❑ 199 Miguel Cabrera .60 .25
❑ 200 Ryan Jorgensen RC .50 .20
❑ 201 Paul Lo Duca .40 .15
❑ 202 Todd Jones .40 .15
❑ 203 Braden Looper .40 .15
❑ 204 Carlos Beltran .40 .15
❑ 205 Cliff Floyd .40 .15
❑ 206 David Wright 1.50 .60
❑ 207 Doug Mientkiewicz .40 .15
❑ 208 Jae Seo .40 .15
❑ 209 Jose Reyes 1.00 .40
❑ 210 Anderson Hernandez (RC) .50 .20
❑ 211 Miguel Cairo .40 .15
❑ 212 Mike Cameron .40 .15
❑ 213 Mike Piazza 1.00 .40
❑ 214 Pedro Martinez .60 .25
❑ 215 Tom Glavine .60 .25
❑ 216 Tim Hamulack (RC) .40 .15
❑ 217 Brad Wilkerson .40 .15
❑ 218 Darrell Rasner (RC) .40 .15
❑ 219 Chad Cordero .40 .15
❑ 220 Cristian Guzman .40 .15
❑ 221 Jason Bergmann RC .50 .20
❑ 222 John Patterson .40 .15
❑ 223 Jose Guillen .40 .15
❑ 224 Jose Vidro .40 .15
❑ 225 Livan Hernandez .40 .15
❑ 226 Nick Johnson .40 .15
❑ 227 Preston Wilson .40 .15
❑ 228 Ryan Zimmerman (RC) 3.00 1.25
❑ 229 Vinny Castilla .40 .15
❑ 230 B.J. Ryan .40 .15
❑ 231 B.J. Surhoff .40 .15
❑ 232 Brian Roberts .40 .15
❑ 233 Walter Young (RC) .50 .20
❑ 234 Daniel Cabrera .40 .15
❑ 235 Erik Bedard .40 .15
❑ 236 Javy Lopez .40 .15
❑ 237 Jay Gibbons .40 .15
❑ 238 Luis Matos .40 .15
❑ 239 Melvin Mora .40 .15
❑ 240 Miguel Tejada .40 .15
❑ 241 Rafael Palmeiro .60 .25
❑ 242 Alejandro Freire RC .40 .15
❑ 243 Sammy Sosa 1.00 .40
❑ 244 Adam Eaton .40 .15
❑ 245 Brian Giles .40 .15
❑ 246 Brian Lawrence .40 .15
❑ 247 Dave Roberts .40 .15
❑ 248 Jake Peavy .40 .15
❑ 249 Khalil Greene .60 .25
❑ 250 Mark Loretta .40 .15
❑ 251 Ramon Hernandez .40 .15
❑ 252 Ryan Klesko .40 .15
❑ 253 Trevor Hoffman .40 .15
❑ 254 Woody Williams .40 .15
❑ 255 Craig Breslow RC .50 .20
❑ 256 Billy Wagner .40 .15
❑ 257 Bobby Abreu .40 .15
❑ 258 Brett Myers .40 .15
❑ 259 Chase Utley 1.00 .40
❑ 260 David Bell .40 .15
❑ 261 Jim Thome .60 .25
❑ 262 Jimmy Rollins .40 .15
❑ 263 Jon Lieber .40 .15
❑ 264 Danny Sandoval RC .50 .20
❑ 265 Mike Lieberthal .40 .15
❑ 266 Pat Burrell .40 .15
❑ 267 Randy Wolf .40 .15
❑ 268 Ryan Howard 1.50 .60
❑ 269 J.J. Furmaniak (RC) .50 .20
❑ 270 Ronny Paulino (RC) .50 .20
❑ 271 Craig Wilson .40 .15
❑ 272 Bryan Bullington (RC) .50 .20
❑ 273 Jack Wilson .40 .15
❑ 274 Jason Bay .40 .15
❑ 275 Matt Capps (RC) .50 .20
❑ 276 Oliver Perez .40 .15
❑ 277 Rob Mackowiak .40 .15
❑ 278 Tom Gorzelanny (RC) .50 .20
❑ 279 Zach Duke .40 .15
❑ 280 Alfonso Soriano .40 .15
❑ 281 Chris R. Young .40 .15
❑ 282 David Dellucci .40 .15
❑ 283 Francisco Cordero .40 .15
❑ 284 Jason Botts (RC) UER .50 .20
❑ 285 Hank Blalock .40 .15
❑ 286 Josh Rupe (RC) .50 .20
❑ 287 Kevin Mench .40 .15
❑ 288 Laynce Nix .40 .15
❑ 289 Mark Teixeira .60 .25
❑ 290 Michael Young .40 .15
❑ 291 Richard Hidalgo .40 .15
❑ 292 Scott Feldman RC .50 .20
❑ 293 Bill Mueller .40 .15
❑ 294 Hanley Ramirez (RC) 1.25 .50
❑ 295 Curt Schilling .60 .25
❑ 296 David Ortiz 1.00 .40
❑ 297 Alejandro Machado (RC) .50 .20
❑ 298 Edgar Renteria .40 .15
❑ 299 Jason Varitek 1.00 .40
❑ 300 Johnny Damon .60 .25
❑ 301 Keith Foulke .40 .15
❑ 302 Manny Ramirez .60 .25
❑ 303 Matt Clement .40 .15
❑ 304 Craig Hansen RC 2.00 .75
❑ 305 Tim Wakefield .40 .15
❑ 306 Trot Nixon .40 .15
❑ 307 Aaron Harang .40 .15
❑ 308 Adam Dunn .40 .15
❑ 309 Austin Kearns .40 .15
❑ 310 Brandon Claussen .40 .15
❑ 311 Chris Booker (RC) .50 .20
❑ 312 Edwin Encarnacion .40 .15
❑ 313 Chris Denorfia (RC) .50 .20
❑ 314 Felipe Lopez .40 .15
❑ 315 Miguel Perez (RC) .50 .20
❑ 316 Ken Griffey Jr. 1.50 .60
❑ 317 Ryan Freel .40 .15
❑ 318 Sean Casey .40 .15
❑ 319 Wily Mo Pena .40 .15
❑ 320 Mike Esposito (RC) .50 .20
❑ 321 Aaron Miles .40 .15
❑ 322 Brad Hawpe .40 .15
❑ 323 Brian Fuentes .40 .15
❑ 324 Clint Barmes .40 .15
❑ 325 Cory Sullivan .40 .15
❑ 326 Garrett Atkins .40 .15
❑ 327 J.D. Closser .40 .15
❑ 328 Jeff Francis .40 .15
❑ 329 Luis Gonzalez .40 .15
❑ 330 Matt Holliday 1.00 .40
❑ 331 Todd Helton .60 .25
❑ 332 Angel Berroa .40 .15
❑ 333 David DeJesus .40 .15
❑ 334 Emil Brown .40 .15
❑ 335 Jeremy Affeldt .40 .15
❑ 336 Chris Demaria RC .50 .20
❑ 337 Mark Teahen .40 .15
❑ 338 Matt Stairs .40 .15
❑ 339 Steve Stemle RC .50 .20
❑ 340 Mike Sweeney .40 .15
❑ 341 Runelvys Hernandez .40 .15
❑ 342 Jonah Bayliss RC .50 .20
❑ 343 Zack Greinke .40 .15
❑ 344 Brandon Inge .40 .15
❑ 345 Carlos Guillen .40 .15
❑ 346 Carlos Pena .40 .15
❑ 347 Chris Shelton .40 .15
❑ 348 Craig Monroe .40 .15
❑ 349 Dmitri Young .40 .15
❑ 350 Ivan Rodriguez .60 .25
❑ 351 Jeremy Bonderman .40 .15
❑ 352 Magglio Ordonez .40 .15
❑ 353 Mark Woodyard (RC) .50 .20
❑ 354 Omar Infante .40 .15
❑ 355 Placido Polanco .40 .15
❑ 356 Rondell White .40 .15
❑ 357 Brad Radke .40 .15
❑ 358 Carlos Silva .40 .15
❑ 359 Jacque Jones .40 .15
❑ 360 Joe Mauer .60 .25
❑ 361 Chris Heintz RC .50 .20
❑ 362 Joe Nathan .40 .15
❑ 363 Johan Santana .60 .25
❑ 364 Justin Morneau .40 .15
❑ 365 Francisco Liriano (RC) 2.50 1.00
❑ 366 Travis Bowyer (RC) .50 .20
❑ 367 Michael Cuddyer .40 .15
❑ 368 Scott Baker .40 .15
❑ 369 Shannon Stewart .40 .15
❑ 370 Torii Hunter .40 .15
❑ 371 A.J. Pierzynski .40 .15
❑ 372 Aaron Rowand .40 .15
❑ 373 Carl Everett .40 .15
❑ 374 Dustin Hermanson .40 .15
❑ 375 Frank Thomas 1.00 .40
❑ 376 Freddy Garcia .40 .15
❑ 377 Jermaine Dye .40 .15
❑ 378 Joe Crede .40 .15
❑ 379 Jon Garland .40 .15
❑ 380 Jose Contreras .40 .15
❑ 381 Juan Uribe .40 .15
❑ 382 Mark Buehrle .40 .15
❑ 383 Orlando Hernandez .40 .15
❑ 384 Paul Konerko .40 .15
❑ 385 Scott Podsednik .40 .15
❑ 386 Tadahito Iguchi .40 .15
❑ 387 Alex Rodriguez 1.50 .60
❑ 388 Bernie Williams .60 .25
❑ 389 Chien-Ming Wang 1.50 .60
❑ 390 Derek Jeter 2.50 1.00
❑ 391 Gary Sheffield .40 .15
❑ 392 Hideki Matsui 1.50 .60

❑ 393	Jason Giambi	.40	.15
❑ 394	Jorge Posada	.60	.25
❑ 395	Mike Vento (RC)	.50	.20
❑ 396	Mariano Rivera	1.00	.40
❑ 397	Mike Mussina	.60	.25
❑ 398	Randy Johnson	1.00	.40
❑ 399	Robinson Cano	.60	.25
❑ 400	Tino Martinez	.40	.15
❑ 401	Alay Soler RC	.60	.25
❑ 402	Boof Bonser (RC)	.60	.25
❑ 403	Cole Hamels (RC)	1.50	.60
❑ 404	Ian Kinsler (RC)	1.00	.40
❑ 405	Jason Kubel (RC)	.60	.25
❑ 406	Joel Zumaya (RC)	1.50	.60
❑ 407	Jonathan Papelbon (RC)	3.00	1.25
❑ 408	Jered Weaver (RC)	3.00	1.25
❑ 409	Kendry Morales (RC)	1.50	.60
❑ 410	Lastings Milledge (RC)	1.00	.40
❑ 411	Matt Kemp (RC)	1.00	.40
❑ 412	Taylor Buchholz (RC)	1.00	.40
❑ 413	Andre Ethier (RC)	1.50	.60
❑ 414	Dan Uggla (RC)	1.50	.60
❑ 415	Jeremy Sowers (RC)	.60	.25
❑ 416	Chad Billingsley (RC)	1.00	.40
❑ 417	Josh Barfield (RC)	.60	.25
❑ 418	Matt Cain (RC)	1.00	.40
❑ 419	Fausto Carmona (RC)	.60	.25
❑ 420	Josh Willingham (RC)	.60	.25
❑ 421	Jeremy Hermida (RC)	.60	.25
❑ 422	Conor Jackson (RC)	1.00	.40
❑ 423	Dave Gassner (RC)	.60	.25
❑ 424	Brian Bannister (RC)	.60	.25
❑ 425	Fernando Nieve (RC)	.60	.25
❑ 426	Justin Verlander (RC)	2.50	1.00
❑ 427	Scott Olsen (RC)	.60	.25
❑ 428	Takashi Saito RC	.60	.25
❑ 429	Willie Eyre (RC)	.60	.25
❑ 430	Travis Ishikawa (RC)	.60	.25

2007 Fleer

❑ COMPLETE SET (400)	60.00	30.00
❑ COMP.FACT.SET (430)	60.00	30.00
❑ COMMON CARD (1-430)	.30	.12
❑ COMMON RC	.60	.25
❑ 401-430 ISSUED IN FACT.SET		
❑ OVERALL PRINTING PLATE ODDS 1:720		
❑ PLATE PRINT RUN 1 SET PER COLOR		
❑ BLACK-CYAN-MAGENTA-YELLOW ISSUED		
❑ NO PLATE PRICING DUE TO SCARCITY		

❑ 1	Chad Cordero	.30	.12
❑ 2	Alfonso Soriano	.30	.12
❑ 3	Nick Johnson	.30	.12
❑ 4	Austin Kearns	.30	.12
❑ 5	Ramon Ortiz	.30	.12
❑ 6	Brian Schneider	.30	.12
❑ 7	Ryan Zimmerman	.75	.30
❑ 8	Jose Vidro	.30	.12
❑ 9	Felipe Lopez	.30	.12
❑ 10	Cristian Guzman	.30	.12
❑ 11	B.J. Ryan	.30	.12
❑ 12	Alex Rios	.30	.12
❑ 13	Vernon Wells	.30	.12
❑ 14	Roy Halladay	.30	.12
❑ 15	A.J. Burnett	.30	.12
❑ 16	Lyle Overbay	.30	.12
❑ 17	Troy Glaus	.30	.12
❑ 18	Bengie Molina	.30	.12
❑ 19	Gustavo Chacin	.30	.12
❑ 20	Aaron Hill	.30	.12
❑ 21	Vicente Padilla	.30	.12
❑ 22	Kevin Millwood	.30	.12
❑ 23	Akinori Otsuka	.30	.12
❑ 24	Adam Eaton	.30	.12
❑ 25	Hank Blalock	.30	.12
❑ 26	Mark Teixeira	.50	.20
❑ 27	Michael Young	.30	.12
❑ 28	Mark DeRosa	.30	.12
❑ 29	Gary Matthews	.30	.12
❑ 30	Ian Kinsler	.30	.12
❑ 31	Carlos Lee	.30	.12
❑ 32	James Shields	.30	.12
❑ 33	Scott Kazmir	.50	.20
❑ 34	Carl Crawford	.30	.12
❑ 35	Jonny Gomes	.30	.12
❑ 36	Tim Corcoran	.30	.12
❑ 37	B.J. Upton	.30	.12
❑ 38	Rocco Baldelli	.30	.12
❑ 39	Jae Seo	.30	.12
❑ 40	Jorge Cantu	.30	.12
❑ 41	Ty Wigginton	.30	.12
❑ 42	Chris Carpenter	.30	.12
❑ 43	Albert Pujols	1.50	.60
❑ 44	Scott Rolen	.50	.20
❑ 45	Jim Edmonds	.50	.20
❑ 46	Jason Isringhausen	.30	.12
❑ 47	Yadier Molina	.30	.12
❑ 48	Adam Wainwright	.30	.12
❑ 49	Mark Mulder	.30	.12
❑ 50	Jason Marquis	.30	.12
❑ 51	Juan Encarnacion	.30	.12
❑ 52	Aaron Miles	.30	.12
❑ 53	Ichiro Suzuki	1.25	.50
❑ 54	Felix Hernandez	.50	.20
❑ 55	Kenji Johjima	.75	.30
❑ 56	Richie Sexson	.30	.12
❑ 57	Yuniesky Betancourt	.30	.12
❑ 58	J.J. Putz	.30	.12
❑ 59	Jarrod Washburn	.30	.12
❑ 60	Ben Broussard	.30	.12
❑ 61	Adrian Beltre	.30	.12
❑ 62	Raul Ibanez	.30	.12
❑ 63	Jose Lopez	.30	.12
❑ 64	Matt Cain	.50	.20
❑ 65	Noah Lowry	.30	.12
❑ 66	Jason Schmidt	.30	.12
❑ 67	Pedro Feliz	.30	.12
❑ 68	Matt Morris	.30	.12
❑ 69	Ray Durham	.30	.12
❑ 70	Steve Finley	.30	.12
❑ 71	Randy Winn	.30	.12
❑ 72	Moises Alou	.30	.12
❑ 73	Eliezer Alfonzo	.30	.12
❑ 74	Armando Benitez	.30	.12
❑ 75	Omar Vizquel	.50	.20
❑ 76	Chris R. Young	.30	.12
❑ 77	Adrian Gonzalez	.30	.12
❑ 78	Khalil Greene	.50	.20
❑ 79	Mike Piazza	.75	.30
❑ 80	Josh Barfield	.30	.12
❑ 81	Brian Giles	.30	.12
❑ 82	Jake Peavy	.30	.12
❑ 83	Trevor Hoffman	.30	.12
❑ 84	Mike Cameron	.30	.12
❑ 85	Dave Roberts	.30	.12
❑ 86	David Wells	.30	.12
❑ 87	Zach Duke	.30	.12
❑ 88	Ian Snell	.30	.12
❑ 89	Jason Bay	.30	.12
❑ 90	Freddy Sanchez	.30	.12
❑ 91	Jack Wilson	.30	.12
❑ 92	Tom Gorzelanny	.30	.12
❑ 93	Chris Duffy	.30	.12
❑ 94	Jose Castillo	.30	.12
❑ 95	Matt Capps	.30	.12
❑ 96	Mike Gonzalez	.30	.12
❑ 97	Chase Utley	.75	.30
❑ 98	Jimmy Rollins	.30	.12
❑ 99	Aaron Rowand	.30	.12
❑ 100	Ryan Howard	1.25	.50
❑ 101	Cole Hamels	.50	.20
❑ 102	Pat Burrell	.30	.12
❑ 103	Shane Victorino	.30	.12
❑ 104	Jamie Moyer	.30	.12
❑ 105	Mike Lieberthal	.30	.12
❑ 106	Tom Gordon	.30	.12
❑ 107	Brett Myers	.30	.12
❑ 108	Nick Swisher	.30	.12
❑ 109	Barry Zito	.30	.12
❑ 110	Jason Kendall	.30	.12
❑ 111	Milton Bradley	.30	.12
❑ 112	Bobby Crosby	.30	.12
❑ 113	Huston Street	.30	.12
❑ 114	Eric Chavez	.30	.12
❑ 115	Frank Thomas	.75	.30
❑ 116	Dan Haren	.30	.12
❑ 117	Jay Payton	.30	.12
❑ 118	Randy Johnson	.75	.30
❑ 119	Mike Mussina	.50	.20
❑ 120	Bobby Abreu	.30	.12
❑ 121	Jason Giambi	.30	.12
❑ 122	Derek Jeter	2.00	.75
❑ 123	Alex Rodriguez	1.25	.50
❑ 124	Jorge Posada	.50	.20
❑ 125	Robinson Cano	.50	.20
❑ 126	Mariano Rivera	.75	.30
❑ 127	Chien-Ming Wang	1.25	.50
❑ 128	Hideki Matsui	.75	.30
❑ 129	Gary Sheffield	.30	.12
❑ 130	Lastings Milledge	.50	.20
❑ 131	Tom Glavine	.50	.20
❑ 132	Billy Wagner	.30	.12
❑ 133	Pedro Martinez	.50	.20
❑ 134	Paul LoDuca	.30	.12
❑ 135	Carlos Delgado	.30	.12
❑ 136	Carlos Beltran	.30	.12
❑ 137	David Wright	1.25	.50
❑ 138	Jose Reyes	.30	.12
❑ 139	Julio Franco	.30	.12
❑ 140	Michael Cuddyer	.30	.12
❑ 141	Justin Morneau	.30	.12
❑ 142	Johan Santana	.50	.20
❑ 143	Francisco Liriano	.75	.30
❑ 144	Joe Mauer	.50	.20
❑ 145	Torii Hunter	.30	.12
❑ 146	Luis Castillo	.30	.12
❑ 147	Joe Nathan	.30	.12
❑ 148	Carlos Silva	.30	.12
❑ 149	Boof Bonser	.30	.12
❑ 150	Ben Sheets	.30	.12
❑ 151	Prince Fielder	.75	.30
❑ 152	Bill Hall	.30	.12
❑ 153	Rickie Weeks	.30	.12
❑ 154	Geoff Jenkins	.30	.12
❑ 155	Kevin Mench	.30	.12
❑ 156	Francisco Cordero	.30	.12
❑ 157	Chris Capuano	.30	.12
❑ 158	Brady Clark	.30	.12
❑ 159	Tony Gwynn Jr.	.30	.12
❑ 160	Chad Billingsley	.30	.12
❑ 161	Russell Martin	.30	.12
❑ 162	Wilson Betemit	.30	.12
❑ 163	Nomar Garciaparra	.75	.30
❑ 164	Kenny Lofton	.30	.12
❑ 165	Rafael Furcal	.30	.12
❑ 166	Julio Lugo	.30	.12
❑ 167	Brad Penny	.30	.12
❑ 168	Jeff Kent	.30	.12
❑ 169	Greg Maddux	1.25	.50
❑ 170	Derek Lowe	.30	.12
❑ 171	Andre Ethier	.50	.20
❑ 172	Chone Figgins	.30	.12
❑ 173	Francisco Rodriguez	.30	.12
❑ 174	Garret Anderson	.30	.12
❑ 175	Orlando Cabrera	.30	.12
❑ 176	Adam Kennedy	.30	.12
❑ 177	John Lackey	.30	.12
❑ 178	Vladimir Guerrero	.75	.30
❑ 179	Bartolo Colon	.30	.12
❑ 180	Jered Weaver	.50	.20
❑ 181	Juan Rivera	.30	.12
❑ 182	Howie Kendrick	.30	.12
❑ 183	Ervin Santana	.30	.12
❑ 184	Mark Redman	.30	.12
❑ 185	David DeJesus	.30	.12
❑ 186	Joey Gathright	.30	.12
❑ 187	Mike Sweeney	.30	.12
❑ 188	Mark Teahen	.30	.12
❑ 189	Angel Berroa	.30	.12
❑ 190	Ambiorix Burgos	.30	.12
❑ 191	Luke Hudson	.30	.12

❑ 192	Mark Grudzielanek	.30	.12
❑ 193	Roger Clemens	1.50	.60
❑ 194	Willy Taveras	.30	.12
❑ 195	Craig Biggio	.50	.20
❑ 196	Andy Pettitte	.50	.20
❑ 197	Roy Oswalt	.30	.12
❑ 198	Lance Berkman	.30	.12
❑ 199	Morgan Ensberg	.30	.12
❑ 200	Brad Lidge	.30	.12
❑ 201	Chris Burke	.30	.12
❑ 202	Miguel Cabrera	.50	.20
❑ 203	Dontrelle Willis	.30	.12
❑ 204	Josh Johnson	.30	.12
❑ 205	Ricky Nolasco	.30	.12
❑ 206	Dan Uggla	.50	.20
❑ 207	Jeremy Hermida	.30	.12
❑ 208	Scott Olsen	.30	.12
❑ 209	Josh Willingham	.30	.12
❑ 210	Joe Borowski	.30	.12
❑ 211	Hanley Ramirez	.50	.20
❑ 212	Mike Jacobs	.30	.12
❑ 213	Kenny Rogers	.30	.12
❑ 214	Justin Verlander	.75	.30
❑ 215	Ivan Rodriguez	.50	.20
❑ 216	Magglio Ordonez	.30	.12
❑ 217	Todd Jones	.30	.12
❑ 218	Joel Zumaya	.50	.20
❑ 219	Jeremy Bonderman	.30	.12
❑ 220	Nate Robertson	.30	.12
❑ 221	Brandon Inge	.30	.12
❑ 222	Craig Monroe	.30	.12
❑ 223	Carlos Guillen	.30	.12
❑ 224	Jeff Francis	.30	.12
❑ 225	Brian Fuentes	.30	.12
❑ 226	Todd Helton	.50	.20
❑ 227	Matt Holliday	.75	.30
❑ 228	Garrett Atkins	.30	.12
❑ 229	Clint Barmes	.30	.12
❑ 230	Jason Jennings	.30	.12
❑ 231	Aaron Cook	.30	.12
❑ 232	Brad Hawpe	.30	.12
❑ 233	Cory Sullivan	.30	.12
❑ 234	Aaron Boone	.30	.12
❑ 235	C.C. Sabathia	.30	.12
❑ 236	Grady Sizemore	.50	.20
❑ 237	Travis Hafner	.30	.12
❑ 238	Jhonny Peralta	.30	.12
❑ 239	Jake Westbrook	.30	.12
❑ 240	Jeremy Sowers	.30	.12
❑ 241	Andy Marte	.30	.12
❑ 242	Victor Martinez	.30	.12
❑ 243	Jason Michaels	.30	.12
❑ 244	Cliff Lee	.30	.12
❑ 245	Bronson Arroyo	.30	.12
❑ 246	Aaron Harang	.30	.12
❑ 247	Ken Griffey Jr.	1.25	.50
❑ 248	Adam Dunn	.30	.12
❑ 249	Rich Aurilia	.30	.12
❑ 250	Eric Milton	.30	.12
❑ 251	David Ross	.30	.12
❑ 252	Brandon Phillips	.30	.12
❑ 253	Ryan Freel	.30	.12
❑ 254	Eddie Guardado	.30	.12
❑ 255	Jose Contreras	.30	.12
❑ 256	Freddy Garcia	.30	.12
❑ 257	Jon Garland	.30	.12
❑ 258	Mark Buehrle	.30	.12
❑ 259	Bobby Jenks	.30	.12
❑ 260	Paul Konerko	.30	.12
❑ 261	Jermaine Dye	.30	.12
❑ 262	Joe Crede	.30	.12
❑ 263	Jim Thome	.50	.20
❑ 264	Javier Vazquez	.30	.12
❑ 265	A.J. Pierzynski	.30	.12
❑ 266	Tadahito Iguchi	.30	.12
❑ 267	Carlos Zambrano	.30	.12
❑ 268	Derrek Lee	.30	.12
❑ 269	Aramis Ramirez	.30	.12
❑ 270	Ryan Theriot	.30	.12
❑ 271	Juan Pierre	.30	.12
❑ 272	Rich Hill	.30	.12
❑ 273	Ryan Dempster	.30	.12
❑ 274	Jacque Jones	.30	.12
❑ 275	Mark Prior	.50	.20
❑ 276	Kerry Wood	.30	.12
❑ 277	Josh Beckett	.50	.20
❑ 278	David Ortiz	.75	.30
❑ 279	Kevin Youkilis	.30	.12
❑ 280	Jason Varitek	.75	.30
❑ 281	Manny Ramirez	.50	.20
❑ 282	Curt Schilling	.50	.20
❑ 283	Jon Lester	.50	.20
❑ 284	Jonathan Papelbon	.75	.30
❑ 285	Alex Gonzalez	.30	.12
❑ 286	Mike Lowell	.30	.12
❑ 287	Kyle Snyder	.30	.12
❑ 288	Miguel Tejada	.30	.12
❑ 289	Erik Bedard	.30	.12
❑ 290	Ramon Hernandez	.30	.12
❑ 291	Melvin Mora	.30	.12
❑ 292	Nick Markakis	.50	.20
❑ 293	Brian Roberts	.30	.12
❑ 294	Corey Patterson	.30	.12
❑ 295	Kris Benson	.30	.12
❑ 296	Jay Gibbons	.30	.12
❑ 297	Rodrigo Lopez	.30	.12
❑ 298	Chris Ray	.30	.12
❑ 299	Andruw Jones	.50	.20
❑ 300	Brian McCann	.30	.12
❑ 301	Jeff Francoeur	.75	.30
❑ 302	Chuck James	.30	.12
❑ 303	John Smoltz	.50	.20
❑ 304	Bob Wickman	.30	.12
❑ 305	Edgar Renteria	.30	.12
❑ 306	Adam LaRoche	.30	.12
❑ 307	Marcus Giles	.30	.12
❑ 308	Tim Hudson	.30	.12
❑ 309	Chipper Jones	.75	.30
❑ 310	Miguel Batista	.30	.12
❑ 311	Claudio Vargas	.30	.12
❑ 312	Brandon Webb	.30	.12
❑ 313	Luis Gonzalez	.30	.12
❑ 314	Livan Hernandez	.30	.12
❑ 315	Stephen Drew	.50	.20
❑ 316	Johnny Estrada	.30	.12
❑ 317	Orlando Hudson	.30	.12
❑ 318	Conor Jackson	.30	.12
❑ 319	Chad Tracy	.30	.12
❑ 320	Carlos Quentin	.30	.12
❑ 321	Alvin Colina RC	.60	.25
❑ 322	Miguel Montero (RC)	.60	.25
❑ 323	Jeff Fiorentino (RC)	.60	.25
❑ 324	Jeff Baker (RC)	.60	.25
❑ 325	Brian Burres (RC)	.60	.25
❑ 326	David Murphy (RC)	.60	.25
❑ 327	Francisco Cruceta (RC)	.60	.25
❑ 328	Beltran Perez (RC)	.60	.25
❑ 329	Scott Moore (RC)	.60	.25
❑ 330	Sean Henn (RC)	.60	.25
❑ 331	Ryan Sweeney (RC)	.60	.25
❑ 332	Josh Fields (RC)	.60	.25
❑ 333	Jerry Owens (RC)	.60	.25
❑ 334	Vinny Rottino (RC)	.60	.25
❑ 335	Kevin Kouzmanoff (RC)	.60	.25
❑ 336	Alexi Casilla RC	1.00	.40
❑ 337	Justin Hampson (RC)	.60	.25
❑ 338	Troy Tulowitzki (RC)	1.50	.60
❑ 339	Jose Garcia RC	.60	.25
❑ 340	Andrew Miller RC	4.00	1.50
❑ 341	Glen Perkins (RC)	.60	.25
❑ 342	Ubaldo Jimenez (RC)	.60	.25
❑ 343	Doug Slaten RC	.60	.25
❑ 344	Angel Sanchez RC	.60	.25
❑ 345	Mitch Maier RC	.60	.25
❑ 346	Ryan Braun RC	.60	.25
❑ 347	Joselo Diaz (RC)	.60	.25
❑ 348	Delwyn Young (RC)	.60	.25
❑ 349	Kevin Hooper (RC)	.60	.25
❑ 350	Dennis Sarfate (RC)	.60	.25
❑ 351	Andy Cannizaro RC	.60	.25
❑ 352	Devern Hansack RC	.60	.25
❑ 353	Michael Bourn (RC)	.60	.25
❑ 354	Carlos Maldonado (RC)	.60	.25
❑ 355	Shane Youman RC	.60	.25
❑ 356	Philip Humber (RC)	1.00	.40
❑ 357	Hector Gimenez (RC)	.60	.25
❑ 358	Fred Lewis (RC)	.60	.25
❑ 359	Ryan Feierabend (RC)	.60	.25
❑ 360	Juan Morillo (RC)	.60	.25
❑ 361	Travis Chick (RC)	.60	.25
❑ 362	Oswaldo Navarro RC	.60	.25
❑ 363	Cesar Jimenez RC	.60	.25
❑ 364	Brian Stokes (RC)	.60	.25
❑ 365	Delmon Young (RC)	1.50	.60
❑ 366	Juan Salas (RC)	.60	.25
❑ 367	Shawn Riggans (RC)	.60	.25
❑ 368	Adam Lind (RC)	.60	.25
❑ 369	Joaquin Arias (RC)	.60	.25
❑ 370	Eric Stults RC	.60	.25
❑ 371	Brandon Webb CL	.30	.12
❑ 372	John Smoltz CL	.50	.20
❑ 373	Miguel Tejada CL	.30	.12
❑ 374	David Ortiz CL	.75	.30
❑ 375	Carlos Zambrano CL	.30	.12
❑ 376	Jermaine Dye CL	.30	.12
❑ 377	Ken Griffey Jr. CL	1.25	.50
❑ 378	Victor Martinez CL	.30	.12
❑ 379	Todd Helton CL	.50	.20
❑ 380	Ivan Rodriguez CL	.50	.20
❑ 381	Miguel Cabrera CL	.50	.20
❑ 382	Lance Berkman CL	.30	.12
❑ 383	Mike Sweeney CL	.30	.12
❑ 384	Vladimir Guerrero CL	.75	.30
❑ 385	Derek Lowe CL	.30	.12
❑ 386	Bill Hall CL	.30	.12
❑ 387	Johan Santana CL	.50	.20
❑ 388	Carlos Beltran CL	.30	.12
❑ 389	Derek Jeter CL	2.00	.75
❑ 390	Nick Swisher CL	.30	.12
❑ 391	Ryan Howard CL	1.25	.50
❑ 392	Jason Bay CL	.30	.12
❑ 393	Trevor Hoffman CL	.30	.12
❑ 394	Omar Vizquel CL	.50	.20
❑ 395	Ichiro Suzuki CL	1.25	.50
❑ 396	Albert Pujols CL	1.50	.60
❑ 397	Carl Crawford CL	.30	.12
❑ 398	Mark Teixeira CL	.50	.20
❑ 399	Roy Halladay CL	.30	.12
❑ 400	Ryan Zimmerman CL	.75	.30
❑ 401	Mark Reynolds RC	1.50	.60
❑ 402	Micah Owings (RC)	.60	.25
❑ 403	Jarrod Saltalamacchia (RC)	1.00	.40
❑ 406	Felix Pie (RC)	.60	.25
❑ 407	Mike Fontenot (RC)	.60	.25
❑ 408	John Danks RC	.60	.25
❑ 409	Josh Hamilton (RC)	1.50	.60
❑ 410	Homey Bailey (RC)	1.00	.40
❑ 411	Alejandro De Aza RC	1.00	.40
❑ 412	Matt Lindstrom (RC)	.60	.25
❑ 415	Billy Butler (RC)	1.00	.40
❑ 416	Brandon Wood (RC)	.60	.25
❑ 417	Andy LaRoche (RC)	.60	.25
❑ 419	Joe Smith RC	.60	.25
❑ 420	Carlos Gomez RC	1.00	.40
❑ 421	Tyler Clippard (RC)	1.00	.40
❑ 422	Matt DeSalvo (RC)	.60	.25
❑ 424	Kei Igawa RC	1.50	.60
❑ 425	Chase Wright RC	1.50	.60
❑ 426	Travis Buck (RC)	.60	.25
❑ 427	Zack Segovia (RC)	.60	.25
❑ 429	Elijah Dukes RC	1.00	.40
❑ 430	Akinori Iwamura RC	1.50	.60

1998 Fleer Tradition Update

❑	COMP.FACT.SET (100)	15.00	6.00
❑ U1	Mark McGwire HL	1.25	.50
❑ U2	Sammy Sosa HL	.30	.10
❑ U3	Roger Clemens HL	1.00	.40
❑ U4	Barry Bonds HL	1.50	.60

❑ U5 Kerry Wood HL .25 .08
❑ U6 Paul Molitor HL .20 .07
❑ U7 Ken Griffey Jr. HL .75 .30
❑ U8 Cal Ripken HL 1.50 .60
❑ U9 David Wells HL .20 .07
❑ U10 Alex Rodriguez HL .75 .30
❑ U11 Angel Pena RC .40 .15
❑ U12 Bruce Chen .20 .07
❑ U13 Craig Wilson .20 .07
❑ U14 Orlando Hernandez RC 2.00 .75
❑ U15 Aramis Ramirez .20 .07
❑ U16 Aaron Boone .20 .07
❑ U17 Bob Henley .20 .07
❑ U18 Juan Guzman .20 .07
❑ U19 Darryl Hamilton .20 .07
❑ U20 Jay Payton .20 .07
❑ U21 Jeremy Powell .20 .07
❑ U22 Ben Davis .20 .07
❑ U23 Preston Wilson .20 .07
❑ U24 Jim Parque RC .60 .25
❑ U25 Odalis Perez RC 1.50 .60
❑ U26 Ronnie Belliard .20 .07
❑ U27 Royce Clayton .20 .07
❑ U28 George Lombard .20 .07
❑ U29 Tony Phillips .20 .07
❑ U30 Fernando Seguignol RC .40 .15
❑ U31 Armando Rios RC .60 .25
❑ U32 Jerry Hairston Jr. RC .60 .25
❑ U33 Justin Baughman RC .40 .15
❑ U34 Seth Greisinger .20 .07
❑ U35 Alex Gonzalez .20 .07
❑ U36 Michael Barrett .20 .07
❑ U37 Carlos Beltran 1.00 .40
❑ U38 Ellis Burks .20 .07
❑ U39 Jose Jimenez RC 1.00 .40
❑ U40 Carlos Guillen .20 .07
❑ U41 Marlon Anderson .20 .07
❑ U42 Scott Elarton .20 .07
❑ U43 Glenallen Hill .20 .07
❑ U44 Shane Monahan .20 .07
❑ U45 Dennis Martinez .20 .07
❑ U46 Carlos Febles RC .60 .25
❑ U47 Carlos Perez .20 .07
❑ U48 Wilton Guerrero .20 .07
❑ U49 Randy Johnson .50 .20
❑ U50 Brian Simmons RC .40 .15
❑ U51 Carlton Loewer .20 .07
❑ U52 Mark DeRosa RC 1.00 .40
❑ U53 Tim Young RC .40 .15
❑ U54 Gary Gaetti .20 .07
❑ U55 Eric Chavez .20 .07
❑ U56 Carl Pavano .20 .07
❑ U57 Mike Stanley .20 .07
❑ U58 Todd Stottlemyre .20 .07
❑ U59 Gabe Kapler RC 1.00 .40
❑ U60 Mike Jerzembeck RC .40 .15
❑ U61 Mitch Meluskey RC .60 .25
❑ U62 Bill Pulsipher .20 .07
❑ U63 Derrick Gibson .20 .07
❑ U64 John Rocker RC 1.00 .40
❑ U65 Calvin Pickering .20 .07
❑ U66 Blake Stein .20 .07
❑ U67 Fernando Tatis .20 .07
❑ U68 Gabe Alvarez .20 .07
❑ U69 Jeffrey Hammonds .20 .07
❑ U70 Adrian Beltre .20 .07
❑ U71 Ryan Bradley RC .40 .15
❑ U72 Edgard Clemente .20 .07
❑ U73 Rick Croushore RC .40 .15
❑ U74 Matt Clement .20 .07
❑ U75 Dermal Brown .20 .07
❑ U76 Paul Bako .20 .07
❑ U77 Placido Polanco RC 1.00 .40
❑ U78 Jay Tessmer .20 .07
❑ U79 Jarrod Washburn .20 .07
❑ U80 Kevin Witt .20 .07
❑ U81 Mike Metcalfe .20 .07
❑ U82 Daryle Ward .20 .07
❑ U83 Benj Sampson RC .40 .15
❑ U84 Mike Kinkade RC .40 .15
❑ U85 Randy Winn .20 .07
❑ U86 Jeff Shaw .20 .07
❑ U87 Troy Glaus RC 3.00 1.25
❑ U88 Hideo Nomo .50 .20
❑ U89 Mark Grudzielanek .20 .07
❑ U90 Mike Frank RC .40 .15
❑ U91 Bobby Howry RC .40 .15
❑ U92 Ryan Minor RC .40 .15
❑ U93 Corey Koskie RC 1.00 .40
❑ U94 Matt Anderson RC .40 .15
❑ U95 Joe Carter .20 .07
❑ U96 Paul Konerko .20 .07
❑ U97 Sidney Ponson .20 .07
❑ U98 Jeremy Giambi RC .60 .25
❑ U99 Jeff Kubenka RC .40 .15
❑ U100 J.D. Drew RC 2.50 1.00

1999 Fleer Tradition Update

❑ COMP.FACT.SET (150) 25.00 10.00
❑ U1 Rick Ankiel RC 4.00 1.50
❑ U2 Peter Bergeron RC .25 .08
❑ U3 Pat Burrell RC 2.00 .75
❑ U4 Eric Munson RC .40 .15
❑ U5 Alfonso Soriano RC 5.00 2.00
❑ U6 Tim Hudson RC 2.00 .75
❑ U7 Erubiel Durazo RC .40 .15
❑ U8 Chad Hermansen .20 .07
❑ U9 Jeff Zimmerman RC .25 .08
❑ U10 Jesus Pena RC .25 .08
❑ U11 Ramon Hernandez .25 .08
❑ U12 Trent Durrington RC .25 .08
❑ U13 Tony Armas Jr. .20 .07
❑ U14 Mike Fyhrie RC .25 .08
❑ U15 Danny Kolb RC .75 .30
❑ U16 Mike Porzio RC .25 .08
❑ U17 Will Brunson RC .25 .08
❑ U18 Mike Duvall RC .25 .08
❑ U19 Doug Mientkiewicz RC .75 .30
❑ U20 Gabe Molina RC .25 .08
❑ U21 Luis Vizcaino RC .25 .08
❑ U22 Robinson Cancel RC .25 .08
❑ U23 Brett Laxton RC .25 .08
❑ U24 Joe McEwing RC .25 .08
❑ U25 Justin Speier RC .25 .08
❑ U26 Kip Wells RC .40 .15
❑ U27 Armando Almanza RC .25 .08
❑ U28 Joe Davenport RC .25 .08
❑ U29 Yamid Haad RC .25 .08
❑ U30 John Halama .20 .07
❑ U31 Adam Kennedy .20 .07
❑ U32 Micah Bowie RC .25 .08
❑ U33 Gookie Dawkins RC .40 .15
❑ U34 Ryan Rupe RC .25 .08
❑ U35 B.J. Ryan RC 2.00 .75
❑ U36 Chance Sanford RC .25 .08
❑ U37 Anthony Shumaker RC .25 .08
❑ U38 Ryan Glynn RC .25 .08
❑ U39 Roosevelt Brown RC .25 .08
❑ U40 Ben Molina RC .75 .30
❑ U41 Scott Williamson .20 .07
❑ U42 Eric Gagne RC 4.00 1.50
❑ U43 John McDonald RC .25 .08
❑ U44 Scott Sauerbeck RC .25 .08
❑ U45 Mike Venafro RC .25 .08
❑ U46 Edwards Guzman RC .25 .08
❑ U47 Richard Barker RC .25 .08
❑ U48 Braden Looper .20 .07
❑ U49 Chad Meyers RC .25 .08
❑ U50 Scott Strickland RC .25 .08
❑ U51 Billy Koch .20 .07
❑ U52 David Newhan RC .40 .15
❑ U53 David Riske RC .25 .08
❑ U54 Jose Santiago RC .25 .08
❑ U55 Miguel Del Toro RC .25 .08
❑ U56 Orber Moreno RC .25 .08
❑ U57 Dave Roberts RC .75 .30
❑ U58 Tim Byrdak RC .25 .08
❑ U59 David Lee RC .25 .08
❑ U60 Guillermo Mota RC .25 .08
❑ U61 Wilton Veras RC .25 .08
❑ U62 Joe Mays RC .40 .15
❑ U63 Jose Fernandez RC .25 .08
❑ U64 Ray King RC .25 .08
❑ U65 Chris Petersen RC .25 .08
❑ U66 Vernon Wells .20 .07
❑ U67 Ruben Mateo .20 .07
❑ U68 Ben Petrick .20 .07
❑ U69 Chris Tremie RC .25 .08
❑ U70 Lance Berkman .20 .07
❑ U71 Dan Smith RC .25 .08
❑ U72 Carlos Eduardo Hernandez RC .40 .15
❑ U73 Chad Harville RC .25 .08
❑ U74 Damaso Marte RC .25 .08
❑ U75 Aaron Myette RC .25 .08
❑ U76 Willis Roberts RC .25 .08
❑ U77 Erik Sabel RC .25 .08
❑ U78 Hector Almonte RC .25 .08
❑ U79 Kris Benson .20 .07
❑ U80 Pat Daneker RC .25 .08
❑ U81 Freddy Garcia RC 1.00 .40
❑ U82 Byung-Hyun Kim RC 1.00 .40
❑ U83 Wily Pena RC 3.00 1.25
❑ U84 Dan Wheeler RC .40 .15
❑ U85 Tim Harikkala RC .25 .08
❑ U86 Derrin Ebert RC .25 .08
❑ U87 Horacio Estrada RC .25 .08
❑ U88 Liu Rodriguez RC .25 .08
❑ U89 Jordan Zimmerman RC .25 .08
❑ U90 A.J. Burnett RC 1.00 .40
❑ U91 Doug Davis RC 1.00 .40
❑ U92 Rob Ramsay RC .25 .08
❑ U93 Clay Bellinger RC .25 .08
❑ U94 Charlie Greene RC .25 .08
❑ U95 Bo Porter RC .25 .08
❑ U96 Jorge Toca RC .40 .15
❑ U97 Casey Blake RC 1.25 .50
❑ U98 Amaury Garcia RC .25 .08
❑ U99 Jose Molina RC .40 .15
❑ U100 Melvin Mora RC 2.50 1.00
❑ U101 Joe Nathan RC 1.25 .50
❑ U102 Juan Pena RC .25 .08
❑ U103 Dave Borkowski RC .25 .08
❑ U104 Eddie Gaillard RC .25 .08
❑ U105 Glen Barker RC .25 .08
❑ U106 Brett Hinchliffe RC .25 .08
❑ U107 Carlos Lee .20 .07
❑ U108 Rob Ryan RC .25 .08
❑ U109 Jeff Weaver RC .75 .30
❑ U110 Ed Yarnall .20 .07
❑ U111 Nelson Cruz RC .25 .08
❑ U112 Cleatus Davidson RC .25 .08
❑ U113 Tim Kubinski RC .25 .08
❑ U114 Sean Spencer RC .25 .08
❑ U115 Joe Winkelsas RC .25 .08
❑ U116 Mike Colangelo RC .25 .08
❑ U117 Tom Davey RC .25 .08
❑ U118 Warren Morris .20 .07
❑ U119 Dan Murray RC .25 .08
❑ U120 Jose Nieves RC .25 .08
❑ U121 Mark Quinn RC .25 .08
❑ U122 Josh Beckett RC 15.00 6.00
❑ U123 Chad Allen RC .25 .08
❑ U124 Mike Figga .25 .08
❑ U125 Beiker Graterol RC .25 .08
❑ U126 Aaron Scheffer RC .25 .08
❑ U127 Wiki Gonzalez RC .40 .15
❑ U128 Ramon E.Martinez RC .25 .08
❑ U129 Matt Riley RC .40 .15
❑ U130 Chris Woodward RC .25 .08
❑ U131 Albert Belle .20 .07
❑ U132 Roger Cedeno .20 .07
❑ U133 Roger Clemens 1.00 .40
❑ U134 Brian Giles .20 .07
❑ U135 Rickey Henderson .50 .20
❑ U136 Randy Johnson .50 .20
❑ U137 Brian Jordan .20 .07
❑ U138 Paul Konerko .20 .07
❑ U139 Hideo Nomo .50 .20
❑ U140 Kenny Rogers .20 .07

❑ U141 Wade Boggs HL .30 .10
❑ U142 Jose Canseco HL .20 .07
❑ U143 Roger Clemens HL 1.00 .40
❑ U144 David Cone HL .20 .07
❑ U145 Tony Gwynn HL .60 .25
❑ U146 Mark McGwire HL 1.25 .50
❑ U147 Cal Ripken HL 1.50 .60
❑ U148 Alex Rodriguez HL .75 .30
❑ U149 Fernando Tatis HL .20 .07
❑ U150 Robin Ventura HL .20 .07

2000 Fleer Tradition

❑ COMPLETE SET (450) 50.00 20.00
❑ 1 AL Home Run LL .75 .30
❑ 2 NL Home Run LL .75 .30
❑ 3 AL RBI LL .30 .10
❑ 4 NL RBI LL .75 .30
❑ 5 AL Avg LL .75 .30
❑ 6 NL Avg LL .30 .10
❑ 7 AL Wins LL .30 .10
❑ 8 NL Wins LL .30 .10
❑ 9 AL ERA LL .30 .10
❑ 10 NL ERA LL .50 .20
❑ 11 Matt Mantei .30 .10
❑ 12 John Rocker .30 .10
❑ 13 Kyle Farnsworth .30 .10
❑ 14 Juan Guzman .30 .10
❑ 15 Manny Ramirez .50 .20
❑ 16 M.Riley/C.Pickering .30 .10
❑ 17 Tony Clark .30 .10
❑ 18 Brian Meadows .30 .10
❑ 19 Orber Moreno .30 .10
❑ 20 Eric Karros .30 .10
❑ 21 Steve Woodard .30 .10
❑ 22 Scott Brosius .30 .10
❑ 23 Gary Bennett .30 .10
❑ 24 J.Wood/D.Borkowski .30 .10
❑ 25 Joe McEwing .30 .10
❑ 26 Juan Gonzalez .30 .10
❑ 27 Roy Halladay .30 .10
❑ 28 Trevor Hoffman .30 .10
❑ 29 Arizona Diamondbacks .30 .10
❑ 30 Domingo Guzman RC .30 .10
❑ 31 Bret Boone .30 .10
❑ 32 Nomar Garciaparra 1.25 .50
❑ 33 Bo Porter .30 .10
❑ 34 Eddie Taubensee .30 .10
❑ 35 Pedro Astacio .30 .10
❑ 36 Derek Bell .30 .10
❑ 37 Jacque Jones .30 .10
❑ 38 Ricky Ledee .30 .10
❑ 39 Jeff Kent .30 .10
❑ 40 Matt Williams .30 .10
❑ 41 A.Soriano/D.Jimenez .75 .30
❑ 42 B.J. Surhoff .30 .10
❑ 43 Denny Neagle .30 .10
❑ 44 Omar Vizquel .50 .20
❑ 45 Jeff Bagwell .50 .20
❑ 46 Mark Grudzielanek .30 .10
❑ 47 LaTroy Hawkins .30 .10
❑ 48 Orlando Hernandez .30 .10
❑ 49 Checklist/K.Griffey Jr. .75 .30
❑ 50 Fernando Tatis .30 .10
❑ 51 Quilvio Veras .30 .10
❑ 52 Wayne Gomes .30 .10
❑ 53 Rick Helling .30 .10
❑ 54 Shannon Stewart .30 .10
❑ 55 D.Brown/M.Quinn .30 .10
❑ 56 Randy Johnson .75 .30
❑ 57 Greg Maddux 1.25 .50
❑ 58 Mike Cameron .30 .10
❑ 59 Matt Anderson .30 .10
❑ 60 Milwaukee Brewers .30 .10
❑ 61 Derrek Lee .50 .20
❑ 62 Mike Sweeney .30 .10
❑ 63 Fernando Vina .30 .10
❑ 64 Orlando Cabrera .30 .10
❑ 65 Doug Glanville .30 .10
❑ 66 Stan Spencer .30 .10
❑ 67 Ray Lankford .30 .10
❑ 68 Kelly Dransfeldt .30 .10
❑ 69 Alex Gonzalez .30 .10
❑ 70 R.Branyan/D.Peoples .30 .10
❑ 71 Jim Edmonds .30 .10
❑ 72 Brady Anderson .30 .10
❑ 73 Mike Stanley .30 .10
❑ 74 Travis Fryman .30 .10
❑ 75 Carlos Febles .30 .10
❑ 76 Bobby Higginson .30 .10
❑ 77 Carlos Perez .30 .10
❑ 78 S.Cox/A.Sanchez .30 .10
❑ 79 Dustin Hermanson .30 .10
❑ 80 Kenny Rogers .30 .10
❑ 81 Miguel Tejada .30 .10
❑ 82 Ben Davis .30 .10
❑ 83 Reggie Sanders .30 .10
❑ 84 Eric Davis .30 .10
❑ 85 J.D. Drew .30 .10
❑ 86 Ryan Rupe .30 .10
❑ 87 Bobby Smith .30 .10
❑ 88 Jose Cruz Jr. .30 .10
❑ 89 Carlos Delgado .30 .10
❑ 90 Toronto Blue Jays .30 .10
❑ 91 D.Stark RC/G.Meche .30 .10
❑ 92 Randy Velarde .30 .10
❑ 93 Aaron Boone .30 .10
❑ 94 Javy Lopez .30 .10
❑ 95 Johnny Damon .50 .20
❑ 96 Jon Lieber .30 .10
❑ 97 Montreal Expos .30 .10
❑ 98 Mark Kotsay .30 .10
❑ 99 Luis Gonzalez .30 .10
❑ 100 Larry Walker .30 .10
❑ 101 Adrian Beltre .30 .10
❑ 102 Alex Ochoa .30 .10
❑ 103 Michael Barrett .30 .10
❑ 104 Tampa Bay Devil Rays .30 .10
❑ 105 Rey Ordonez .30 .10
❑ 106 Derek Jeter 1.50 .60
❑ 107 Mike Lieberthal .30 .10
❑ 108 Ellis Burks .30 .10
❑ 109 Steve Finley .30 .10
❑ 110 Ryan Klesko .30 .10
❑ 111 Steve Avery .30 .10
❑ 112 Dave Veres .30 .10
❑ 113 Cliff Floyd .30 .10
❑ 114 Shane Reynolds .30 .10
❑ 115 Kevin Brown .50 .20
❑ 116 Dave Nilsson .30 .10
❑ 117 Mike Trombley .30 .10
❑ 118 Todd Walker .30 .10
❑ 119 John Olerud .30 .10
❑ 120 Chuck Knoblauch .30 .10
❑ 121 Checklist/N.Garciaparra .75 .30
❑ 122 Trot Nixon .30 .10
❑ 123 Erubiel Durazo .30 .10
❑ 124 Edwards Guzman .30 .10
❑ 125 Curt Schilling .30 .10
❑ 126 Brian Jordan .30 .10
❑ 127 Cleveland Indians .30 .10
❑ 128 Benito Santiago .30 .10
❑ 129 Frank Thomas .75 .30
❑ 130 Neifi Perez .30 .10
❑ 131 Alex Fernandez .30 .10
❑ 132 Jose Lima .30 .10
❑ 133 J.Toca/M.Mora .30 .10
❑ 134 Scott Karl .30 .10
❑ 135 Brad Radke .30 .10
❑ 136 Paul O'Neill .50 .20
❑ 137 Kris Benson .30 .10
❑ 138 Colorado Rockies .30 .10
❑ 139 Jason Phillips .30 .10
❑ 140 Robb Nen .30 .10
❑ 141 Ken Hill .30 .10
❑ 142 Charles Johnson .30 .10
❑ 143 Paul Konerko .30 .10
❑ 144 Dmitri Young .30 .10
❑ 145 Justin Thompson .30 .10
❑ 146 Mark Loretta .30 .10
❑ 147 Edgardo Alfonzo .30 .10
❑ 148 Armando Benitez .30 .10
❑ 149 Octavio Dotel .30 .10
❑ 150 Wade Boggs .50 .20
❑ 151 Ramon Hernandez .30 .10
❑ 152 Freddy Garcia .30 .10
❑ 153 Edgar Martinez .50 .20
❑ 154 Ivan Rodriguez .50 .20
❑ 155 Kansas City Royals .30 .10
❑ 156 C.Davidson/C.Guzman .30 .10
❑ 157 Andy Benes .30 .10
❑ 158 Todd Dunwoody .30 .10
❑ 159 Pedro Martinez .50 .20
❑ 160 Mike Caruso .30 .10
❑ 161 Mike Sirotka .30 .10
❑ 162 Houston Astros .30 .10
❑ 163 Darryl Kile .30 .10
❑ 164 Chipper Jones .75 .30
❑ 165 Carl Everett .30 .10
❑ 166 Geoff Jenkins .30 .10
❑ 167 Dan Perkins .30 .10
❑ 168 Andy Pettitte .50 .20
❑ 169 Francisco Cordova .30 .10
❑ 170 Jay Buhner .30 .10
❑ 171 Jay Bell .30 .10
❑ 172 Andruw Jones .50 .20
❑ 173 Bobby Howry .30 .10
❑ 174 Chris Singleton .30 .10
❑ 175 Todd Helton .50 .20
❑ 176 A.J. Burnett .30 .10
❑ 177 Marquis Grissom .30 .10
❑ 178 Eric Milton .30 .10
❑ 179 Los Angeles Dodgers .30 .10
❑ 180 Kevin Appier .30 .10
❑ 181 Brian Giles .30 .10
❑ 182 Tom Davey .30 .10
❑ 183 Mo Vaughn .30 .10
❑ 184 Jose Hernandez .30 .10
❑ 185 Jim Parque .30 .10
❑ 186 Derrick Gibson .30 .10
❑ 187 Bruce Aven .30 .10
❑ 188 Jeff Cirillo .30 .10
❑ 189 Doug Mientkiewicz .30 .10
❑ 190 Eric Chavez .30 .10
❑ 191 Al Martin .30 .10
❑ 192 Tom Glavine .50 .20
❑ 193 Butch Huskey .30 .10
❑ 194 Ray Durham .30 .10
❑ 195 Greg Vaughn .30 .10
❑ 196 Vinny Castilla .30 .10
❑ 197 Ken Caminiti .30 .10
❑ 198 Joe Mays .30 .10
❑ 199 Chicago White Sox .30 .10
❑ 200 Mariano Rivera .75 .30
❑ 201 Checklist/M.McGwire 1.00 .40
❑ 202 Pat Meares .30 .10
❑ 203 Andres Galarraga .30 .10
❑ 204 Tom Gordon .30 .10
❑ 205 Henry Rodriguez .30 .10
❑ 206 Brett Tomko .30 .10
❑ 207 Dante Bichette .30 .10
❑ 208 Craig Biggio .50 .20
❑ 209 Matt Lawton .30 .10
❑ 210 Tino Martinez .50 .20
❑ 211 A.Myette/J.Paul .30 .10
❑ 212 Warren Morris .30 .10
❑ 213 San Diego Padres .30 .10
❑ 214 Ramon E. Martinez .30 .10
❑ 215 Troy Percival .30 .10
❑ 216 Jason Johnson .30 .10
❑ 217 Carlos Lee .30 .10
❑ 218 Scott Williamson .30 .10
❑ 219 Jeff Weaver .30 .10
❑ 220 Ronnie Belliard .30 .10
❑ 221 Jason Giambi .30 .10
❑ 222 Ken Griffey Jr. 1.25 .50
❑ 223 John Halama .30 .10
❑ 224 Brett Hinchliffe .30 .10
❑ 225 Wilson Alvarez .30 .10
❑ 226 Rolando Arrojo .30 .10
❑ 227 Ruben Mateo .30 .10

❑	228	Rafael Palmeiro	.50	.20
❑	229	David Wells	.30	.10
❑	230	E.Gagne RC/J.Williams RC	.75	.30
❑	231	Tim Salmon	.50	.20
❑	232	Mike Mussina	.50	.20
❑	233	Maggio Ordonez	.30	.10
❑	234	Ron Vilone	.30	.10
❑	235	Antonio Alfonseca	.30	.10
❑	236	Jeromy Burnitz	.30	.10
❑	237	Ben Grieve	.30	.10
❑	238	Giomar Guevara	.30	.10
❑	239	Garret Anderson	.30	.10
❑	240	John Smoltz	.50	.20
❑	241	Mark Grace	.50	.20
❑	242	C.Liniak/J.Molina	.30	.10
❑	243	Damion Easley	.30	.10
❑	244	Jeff Montgomery	.30	.10
❑	245	Kenny Lofton	.30	.10
❑	246	Masato Yoshii	.30	.10
❑	247	Philadelphia Phillies	.30	.10
❑	248	Raul Mondesi	.30	.10
❑	249	Marlon Anderson	.30	.10
❑	250	Shawn Green	.30	.10
❑	251	Sterling Hitchcock	.30	.10
❑	252	R.Wolf/A.Shumaker	.30	.10
❑	253	Jeff Fassero	.30	.10
❑	254	Eli Marrero	.30	.10
❑	255	Cincinnati Reds	.30	.10
❑	256	Rick Ankiel	.30	.10
❑	257	Darin Erstad	.30	.10
❑	258	Albert Belle	.30	.10
❑	259	Bartolo Colon	.30	.10
❑	260	Bret Saberhagen	.30	.10
❑	261	Carlos Beltran	.30	.10
❑	262	Glenallen Hill	.30	.10
❑	263	Gregg Jefferies	.30	.10
❑	264	Matt Clement	.30	.10
❑	265	Miguel Del Toro	.30	.10
❑	266	R.Cancel/K.Barker	.30	.10
❑	267	San Francisco Giants	.30	.10
❑	268	Kent Bottenfield	.30	.10
❑	269	Fred McGriff	.50	.20
❑	270	Chris Carpenter	.30	.10
❑	271	Atlanta Braves	.30	.10
❑	272	Tomo Ohka RC	.40	.15
❑	273	Will Clark	.50	.20
❑	274	Troy O'Leary	.30	.10
❑	275	Checklist/S.Sosa	.50	.20
❑	276	Travis Lee	.30	.10
❑	277	Sean Casey	.30	.10
❑	278	Ron Gant	.30	.10
❑	279	Roger Clemens	1.50	.60
❑	280	Phil Nevin	.30	.10
❑	281	Mike Piazza	1.25	.50
❑	282	Mike Lowell	.30	.10
❑	283	Kevin Millwood	.30	.10
❑	284	Joe Randa	.30	.10
❑	285	Jeff Shaw	.30	.10
❑	286	Jason Varitek	.75	.30
❑	287	Harold Baines	.30	.10
❑	288	Gabe Kapler	.30	.10
❑	289	Chuck Finley	.30	.10
❑	290	Carl Pavano	.30	.10
❑	291	Brad Ausmus	.30	.10
❑	292	Brad Fullmer	.30	.10
❑	293	Boston Red Sox	.30	.10
❑	294	Bob Wickman	.30	.10
❑	295	Billy Wagner	.30	.10
❑	296	Shawn Estes	.30	.10
❑	297	Gary Sheffield	.30	.10
❑	298	Fernando Seguignol	.30	.10
❑	299	Omar Olivares	.30	.10
❑	300	Baltimore Orioles	.30	.10
❑	301	Matt Stairs	.30	.10
❑	302	Andy Ashby	.30	.10
❑	303	Todd Greene	.30	.10
❑	304	Jesse Garcia	.30	.10
❑	305	Kerry Wood	.30	.10
❑	306	Roberto Alomar	.50	.20
❑	307	New York Mets	.30	.10
❑	308	Dean Palmer	.30	.10
❑	309	Mike Hampton	.30	.10
❑	310	Devon White	.30	.10
❑	311	Mike Garcia RC	.30	.10
❑	312	Tim Hudson	.30	.10
❑	313	John Franco	.30	.10
❑	314	Jason Schmidt	.30	.10
❑	315	J.T. Snow	.30	.10
❑	316	Ed Sprague	.30	.10
❑	317	Chris Widger	.30	.10
❑	318	Luther Hackman RC	.30	.10
❑	319	Jose Mesa	.30	.10
❑	320	Jose Canseco	.50	.20
❑	321	John Wetteland	.30	.10
❑	322	Minnesota Twins	.30	.10
❑	323	Jeff DaVanon RC	.40	.15
❑	324	Tony Womack	.30	.10
❑	325	Rod Beck	.30	.10
❑	326	Mickey Morandini	.30	.10
❑	327	Pokey Reese	.30	.10
❑	328	Jaret Wright	.30	.10
❑	329	Glen Barker	.30	.10
❑	330	Darren Dreifort	.30	.10
❑	331	Torii Hunter	.30	.10
❑	332	T.Armas/P.Bergeron	.30	.10
❑	333	Hideki Irabu	.30	.10
❑	334	Desi Relaford	.30	.10
❑	335	Barry Bonds	2.00	.75
❑	336	Gary DiSarcina	.30	.10
❑	337	Gerald Williams	.30	.10
❑	338	John Valentin	.30	.10
❑	339	David Justice	.30	.10
❑	340	Juan Encarnacion	.30	.10
❑	341	Jeremy Giambi	.30	.10
❑	342	Chan Ho Park	.30	.10
❑	343	Vladimir Guerrero	.75	.30
❑	344	Robin Ventura	.50	.20
❑	345	Bob Abreu	.30	.10
❑	346	Tony Gwynn	1.00	.40
❑	347	Jose Jimenez	.30	.10
❑	348	Royce Clayton	.30	.10
❑	349	Kelvim Escobar	.30	.10
❑	350	Chicago Cubs	.30	.10
❑	351	T.Dawkins/J.LaRue	.30	.10
❑	352	Barry Larkin	.50	.20
❑	353	Cal Ripken	2.50	1.00
❑	354	Checklist/A.Rodriguez	.75	.30
❑	355	Todd Stottlemyre	.30	.10
❑	356	Terry Adams	.30	.10
❑	357	Pittsburgh Pirates	.30	.10
❑	358	Jim Thome	.50	.20
❑	359	C.Lee/D.Davis	.30	.10
❑	360	Moises Alou	.30	.10
❑	361	Todd Hollandsworth	.30	.10
❑	362	Marty Cordova	.30	.10
❑	363	David Cone	.30	.10
❑	364	J.Nathan/W.Delgado	.30	.10
❑	365	Paul Byrd	.30	.10
❑	366	Edgar Renteria	.30	.10
❑	367	Rusty Greer	.30	.10
❑	368	David Segui	.30	.10
❑	369	New York Yankees	.50	.20
❑	370	D.Ward/C.Hernandez	.30	.10
❑	371	Troy Glaus	.30	.10
❑	372	Delion DeShields	.30	.10
❑	373	Jose Offerman	.30	.10
❑	374	Sammy Sosa	.75	.30
❑	375	Sandy Alomar Jr.	.30	.10
❑	376	Masao Kida	.30	.10
❑	377	Richard Hidalgo	.30	.10
❑	378	Ismael Valdes	.30	.10
❑	379	Ugueth Urbina	.30	.10
❑	380	Darryl Hamilton	.30	.10
❑	381	John Jaha	.30	.10
❑	382	St. Louis Cardinals	.30	.10
❑	383	Scott Sauerbeck	.30	.10
❑	384	Russ Ortiz	.30	.10
❑	385	Jamie Moyer	.30	.10
❑	386	Dave Martinez	.30	.10
❑	387	Todd Zeile	.30	.10
❑	388	Anaheim Angels	.30	.10
❑	389	R.Ryan/N.Bierbrodt	.30	.10
❑	390	Rickey Henderson	.75	.30
❑	391	Alex Rodriguez	1.25	.50
❑	392	Texas Rangers	.30	.10
❑	393	Roberto Hernandez	.30	.10
❑	394	Tony Batista	.30	.10
❑	395	Oakland Athletics	.30	.10
❑	396	Dave Cortes RC	.30	.10
❑	397	Gregg Olson	.30	.10
❑	398	Sidney Ponson	.30	.10
❑	399	Micah Bowie	.30	.10
❑	400	Mark McGwire	2.00	.75
❑	401	Florida Marlins	.30	.10
❑	402	Chad Allen	.30	.10
❑	403	C.Blake/V.Wells	.30	.10
❑	404	Pete Harnisch	.30	.10
❑	405	Preston Wilson	.30	.10
❑	406	Richie Sexson	.30	.10
❑	407	Rico Brogna	.30	.10
❑	408	Todd Hundley	.30	.10
❑	409	Wally Joyner	.30	.10
❑	410	Tom Goodwin	.30	.10
❑	411	Joey Hamilton	.30	.10
❑	412	Detroit Tigers	.30	.10
❑	413	Michael Tejera RC	.30	.10
❑	414	Alex Gonzalez	.30	.10
❑	415	Jermaine Dye	.30	.10
❑	416	Jose Rosada	.30	.10
❑	417	Wilton Guerrero	.30	.10
❑	418	Rondell White	.30	.10
❑	419	Al Leiter	.30	.10
❑	420	Bernie Williams	.50	.20
❑	421	A.J. Hinch	.30	.10
❑	422	Pat Burrell	.30	.10
❑	423	Scott Rolen	.50	.20
❑	424	Jason Kendall	.30	.10
❑	425	Kevin Young	.30	.10
❑	426	Eric Owens	.30	.10
❑	427	Checklist/D.Jeter	.75	.30
❑	428	Livan Hernandez	.30	.10
❑	429	Russ Davis	.30	.10
❑	430	Dan Wilson	.30	.10
❑	431	Quinton McCracken	.30	.10
❑	432	Homer Bush	.30	.10
❑	433	Seattle Mariners	.30	.10
❑	434	C.Harville/L.Vizcaino	.30	.10
❑	435	Carlos Beltran AW	.30	.10
❑	436	Scott Williamson AW	.30	.10
❑	437	Pedro Martinez AW	.50	.20
❑	438	Randy Johnson AW	.50	.20
❑	439	Ivan Rodriguez AW	.30	.10
❑	440	Chipper Jones AW	.50	.20
❑	441	Bernie Williams DIV	.30	.10
❑	442	Pedro Martinez DIV	.50	.20
❑	443	Derek Jeter DIV	1.00	.40
❑	444	Brian Jordan DIV	.30	.10
❑	445	Todd Pratt DIV	.30	.10
❑	446	Kevin Millwood DIV	.30	.10
❑	447	Orlando Hernandez WS	.30	.10
❑	448	Derek Jeter WS	1.00	.40
❑	449	Chad Curtis WS	.30	.10
❑	450	Roger Clemens WS	.75	.30
❑	P353	Cal Ripken Promo	3.00	1.25

2000 Fleer Tradition Update

❑		COMP.FACT.SET (149)	20.00	8.00
❑	1	Ken Griffey Jr. SH	.75	.30
❑	2	Cal Ripken SH	1.00	.40
❑	3	Randy Velarde SH	.30	.10
❑	4	Fred McGriff SH	.30	.10
❑	5	Derek Jeter SH	.75	.30
❑	6	Tom Glavine SH	.30	.10
❑	7	Brent Mayne SH	.30	.10
❑	8	Alex Ochoa SH	.30	.10
❑	9	Scott Sheldon SH	.30	.10
❑	10	Randy Johnson SH	.50	.20
❑	11	Daniel Garibay RC	.30	.10
❑	12	Brad Fullmer	.30	.10

❑	13 Kazuhiro Sasaki RC	.60	.25
❑	14 Andy Tracy RC	.30	.10
❑	15 Bret Boone	.30	.10
❑	16 Chad Durbin RC	.40	.15
❑	17 Mark Buehrle RC	2.50	1.00
❑	18 Julio Zuleta RC	.30	.10
❑	19 Jeremy Giambi	.30	.10
❑	20 Gene Stechschulte RC	.30	.10
❑	21 L.Pote/B.Molina	.30	.10
❑	22 Darrell Einertson RC	.30	.10
❑	23 Ken Griffey Jr.	1.25	.50
❑	24 J.Sparks RC/D.Wheeler	.30	.10
❑	25 Aaron Fultz RC	.30	.10
❑	26 Derek Bell	.30	.10
❑	27 R.Bell/D.Cromer	.30	.10
❑	28 Robert Fick	.30	.10
❑	29 Darryl Kile	.30	.10
❑	30 C.Andrews/J.Bale RC	.30	.10
❑	31 Dave Veres	.30	.10
❑	32 Hector Mercado RC	.30	.10
❑	33 Willie Morales RC	.30	.10
❑	34 K.Wunsch/K.Wells	.30	.10
❑	35 Hideki Irabu	.30	.10
❑	36 Sean DePaula RC	.30	.10
❑	37 D.Wise/C.Woodward	.30	.10
❑	38 Curt Schilling	.30	.10
❑	39 Mark Johnson	.30	.10
❑	40 Mike Cameron	.30	.10
❑	41 S.Sheldon/T.Evans	.30	.10
❑	42 Brett Tomko	.30	.10
❑	43 Johan Santana RC	15.00	6.00
❑	44 Andy Benes	.30	.10
❑	45 M.LeCroy/M.Redman	.30	.10
❑	46 Ryan Klesko	.30	.10
❑	47 Andy Ashby	.30	.10
❑	48 Octavio Dotel	.30	.10
❑	49 Eric Byrnes RC	.40	.15
❑	50 Does Not Exist		
❑	51 Kenny Rogers	.30	.10
❑	52 Ben Weber RC	.30	.10
❑	53 M.Blank/S.Strickland	.30	.10
❑	54 Tom Goodwin	.30	.10
❑	55 Jim Edmonds Cards	.30	.10
❑	56 Derrick Turnbow RC	1.50	.60
❑	57 Mark Mulder	.30	.10
❑	58 T.Brock/R.Quevedo	.30	.10
❑	59 Danny Young RC	.30	.10
❑	60 Fernando Vina	.30	.10
❑	61 Justin Brunette RC	.30	.10
❑	62 Jimmy Anderson	.30	.10
❑	63 Reggie Sanders	.30	.10
❑	64 Adam Kennedy	.30	.10
❑	65 J.Garcia/B.Ryan	.30	.10
❑	66 Al Martin	.30	.10
❑	67 Kevin Walker RC	.30	.10
❑	68 Brad Penny	.30	.10
❑	69 B.J. Surhoff	.30	.10
❑	70 G.Blum/T.Coquillette RC	.30	.10
❑	71 Jose Jimenez	.30	.10
❑	72 Chuck Finley	.30	.10
❑	73 V.De Los Santos/E.Stull	.30	.10
❑	74 Terry Adams	.30	.10
❑	75 Rafael Furcal	.30	.10
❑	76 J.Roskos/M.Darr	.30	.10
❑	77 Quilvio Veras	.30	.10
❑	78 A.Almanza/N.Rolison	.30	.10
❑	79 Greg Vaughn	.30	.10
❑	80 Keith McDonald RC	.30	.10
❑	81 Eric Cammack RC	.30	.10
❑	82 H.Estrada/R.King	.30	.10
❑	83 Kory DeHaan	.30	.10
❑	84 Kevin Hodges RC	.30	.10
❑	85 Mike Lamb RC	.60	.25
❑	86 Shawn Green	.30	.10
❑	87 D.Reichert/J.Rakers	.30	.10
❑	88 Adam Piatt	.30	.10
❑	89 Mike Garcia	.30	.10
❑	90 Rodrigo Lopez RC	.60	.25
❑	91 John Olerud	.30	.10
❑	92 B.Zito RC/T.Long	4.00	1.50
❑	93 Jimmy Rollins	.30	.10
❑	94 Denny Neagle	.30	.10
❑	95 Rickey Henderson	.75	.30
❑	96 A.Eaton/B.Carlyle	.30	.10
❑	97 Brian O'Connor RC	.30	.10
❑	98 Andy Thompson RC	.30	.10
❑	99 Jason Boyd RC	.30	.10
❑	100 J.Pineiro RC/C.Guillen	1.00	.40
❑	101 Raul Gonzalez RC	.30	.10
❑	102 Brandon Kolb RC	.30	.10
❑	103 J.Maxwell/M.Lincoln	.30	.10
❑	104 Luis Matos RC	.40	.15
❑	105 Morgan Burkhart RC	.30	.10
❑	106 I.Villegas/S.Sisco RC	.30	.10
❑	107 David Justice Yankees	.30	.10
❑	108 Pablo Ozuna	.30	.10
❑	109 Jose Canseco Yankees	.50	.20
❑	110 A.Cora/S.Gilbert	.30	.10
❑	111 Will Clark Cardinals	.50	.20
❑	112 K.Luuloa/E.Weaver	.30	.10
❑	113 Bruce Chen	.30	.10
❑	114 Adam Hyzdu	.30	.10
❑	115 S.Forster/Y.Lara RC	.30	.10
❑	116 A.McDill RC/J.Macias	.30	.10
❑	117 Kevin Nicholson	.30	.10
❑	118 I.Alcantara/T.Young	.30	.10
❑	119 Juan Alvarez RC	.30	.10
❑	120 J.Lugo/M.Meluskey	.30	.10
❑	121 B.J. Waszgis RC	.30	.10
❑	122 J.D'Amico RC/B.Laxton	.30	.10
❑	123 Ricky Ledee	.30	.10
❑	124 M.DeRosa/J.Marquis	.30	.10
❑	125 Alex Cabrera RC	.40	.15
❑	126 A.Ojeda RC/G.Matthews Jr.	.30	.10
❑	127 Richie Sexson	.30	.10
❑	128 S.Perez/H.Ramirez RC	.30	.10
❑	129 Rondell White	.30	.10
❑	130 Craig House RC	.30	.10
❑	131 K.Beirne/J.Garland	.30	.10
❑	132 Wayne Franklin RC	.30	.10
❑	133 Henry Rodriguez	.30	.10
❑	134 J.Payton/J.Mann	.30	.10
❑	135 Ron Gant	.30	.10
❑	136 P.Crawford/S.Lee RC	.30	.10
❑	137 Kent Bottenfield	.30	.10
❑	138 Rocky Biddle RC	.30	.10
❑	139 Travis Lee	.30	.10
❑	140 Ryan Vogelsong RC	.30	.10
❑	141 J.Conti/G.Guzman RC	.30	.10
❑	142 M.Watson RC/T.Drew	.30	.10
❑	143 J.Parrish/C.Richard RC	.30	.10
❑	144 J.Cardona/B.Villafuerte RC	.30	.10
❑	145 T.Redman/S.Sparks RC	.60	.25
❑	146 B.Schneider/M.Skrmetta RC	.30	.10
❑	147 Pasqual Coco RC	.30	.10
❑	148 L.Barcelo RC/J.Crede	1.00	.40
❑	149 Jace Brewer RC	.30	.10
❑	150 T.De La Rosa RC/M.Bradley	.40	.15
❑	MP1 Mickey Mantle Pants	175.00	100.00

2001 Fleer Tradition

❑	COMP.FACT.SET (485)	100.00	50.00
❑	COMPLETE SET (450)	50.00	20.00
❑	COMMON CARD (1-450)	.30	.10
❑	COMMON CARD (451-485)	.50	.20
❑	1 Andres Galarraga	.30	.10
❑	2 Armando Rios	.30	.10
❑	3 Julio Lugo	.30	.10
❑	4 Darryl Hamilton	.30	.10
❑	5 Dave Veres	.30	.10
❑	6 Edgardo Alfonzo	.30	.10
❑	7 Brook Fordyce	.30	.10
❑	8 Eric Karros	.30	.10
❑	9 Neifi Perez	.30	.10
❑	10 Jim Edmonds	.30	.10
❑	11 Barry Larkin	.50	.20
❑	12 Trot Nixon	.30	.10
❑	13 Andy Pettitte	.50	.20
❑	14 Jose Guillen	.30	.10
❑	15 David Wells	.30	.10
❑	16 Magglio Ordonez	.30	.10
❑	17 David Segui	.30	.10
❑	17A David Segui ERR Card has no number on the back	.30	.10
❑	18 Juan Encarnacion	.30	.10
❑	19 Robert Person	.30	.10
❑	20 Quilvio Veras	.30	.10
❑	21 Mo Vaughn	.30	.10
❑	22 B.J. Surhoff	.30	.10
❑	23 Ken Caminiti	.30	.10
❑	24 Frank Catalanotto	.30	.10
❑	25 Luis Gonzalez	.30	.10
❑	26 Pete Harnisch	.30	.10
❑	27 Alex Gonzalez	.30	.10
❑	28 Mark Quinn	.30	.10
❑	29 Luis Castillo	.30	.10
❑	30 Rick Helling	.30	.10
❑	31 Barry Bonds	2.00	.75
❑	32 Warren Morris	.30	.10
❑	33 Aaron Boone	.30	.10
❑	34 Ricky Gutierrez	.30	.10
❑	35 Preston Wilson	.30	.10
❑	36 Erubiel Durazo	.30	.10
❑	37 Jermaine Dye	.30	.10
❑	38 John Rocker	.30	.10
❑	39 Mark Grudzielanek	.30	.10
❑	40 Pedro Martinez	.50	.20
❑	41 Phil Nevin	.30	.10
❑	42 Luis Matos	.30	.10
❑	43 Orlando Hernandez	.30	.10
❑	44 Steve Cox	.30	.10
❑	45 James Baldwin	.30	.10
❑	46 Rafael Furcal	.30	.10
❑	47 Todd Zeile	.30	.10
❑	48 Elmer Dessens	.30	.10
❑	49 Russell Branyan	.30	.10
❑	50 Juan Gonzalez	.30	.10
❑	51 Mac Suzuki	.30	.10
❑	52 Adam Kennedy	.30	.10
❑	53 Randy Velarde	.30	.10
❑	54 David Bell	.30	.10
❑	55 Royce Clayton	.30	.10
❑	56 Greg Colbrunn	.30	.10
❑	57 Rey Ordonez	.30	.10
❑	58 Kevin Millwood	.30	.10
❑	59 Fernando Vina	.30	.10
❑	60 Eddie Taubensee	.30	.10
❑	61 Enrique Wilson	.30	.10
❑	62 Jay Bell	.30	.10
❑	63 Brian Moehler	.30	.10
❑	64 Brad Fullmer	.30	.10
❑	65 Ben Petrick	.30	.10
❑	66 Orlando Cabrera	.30	.10
❑	67 Shane Reynolds	.30	.10
❑	68 Mitch Meluskey	.30	.10
❑	69 Jeff Shaw	.30	.10
❑	70 Chipper Jones	.75	.30
❑	71 Tomo Ohka	.30	.10
❑	72 Ruben Rivera	.30	.10
❑	73 Mike Sirotka	.30	.10
❑	74 Scott Rolen	.50	.20
❑	75 Glendon Rusch	.30	.10
❑	76 Miguel Tejada	.30	.10
❑	77 Brady Anderson	.30	.10
❑	78 Bartolo Colon	.30	.10
❑	79 Ron Coomer	.30	.10
❑	80 Gary DiSarcina	.30	.10
❑	81 Geoff Jenkins	.30	.10
❑	82 Billy Koch	.30	.10
❑	83 Mike Lamb	.30	.10
❑	84 Alex Rodriguez	1.25	.50
❑	85 Denny Neagle	.30	.10
❑	86 Michael Tucker	.30	.10
❑	87 Edgar Renteria	.30	.10
❑	88 Brian Anderson	.30	.10
❑	89 Glenallen Hill	.30	.10
❑	90 Aramis Ramirez	.30	.10
❑	91 Rondell White	.30	.10
❑	92 Tony Womack	.30	.10
❑	93 Jeffrey Hammonds	.30	.10

❑ 94	Freddy Garcia	.30	.10
❑ 95	Bill Mueller	.30	.10
❑ 96	Mike Lieberthal	.30	.10
❑ 97	Michael Barrett	.30	.10
❑ 98	Derrek Lee	.50	.20
❑ 99	Bill Spiers	.30	.10
❑ 100	Derek Lowe	.30	.10
❑ 101	Javy Lopez	.30	.10
❑ 102	Adrian Beltre	.30	.10
❑ 103	Jim Parque	.30	.10
❑ 104	Marquis Grissom	.30	.10
❑ 105	Eric Chavez	.30	.10
❑ 106	Todd Jones	.30	.10
❑ 107	Eric Owens	.30	.10
❑ 108	Roger Clemens	1.50	.60
❑ 109	Denny Hocking	.30	.10
❑ 110	Roberto Hernandez	.30	.10
❑ 111	Albert Belle	.30	.10
❑ 112	Troy Glaus	.30	.10
❑ 113	Ivan Rodriguez	.50	.20
❑ 114	Carlos Guillen	.30	.10
❑ 115	Chuck Finley	.30	.10
❑ 116	Dmitri Young	.30	.10
❑ 117	Paul Konerko	.30	.10
❑ 118	Damon Buford	.30	.10
❑ 119	Fernando Tatis	.30	.10
❑ 120	Larry Walker	.30	.10
❑ 121	Jason Kendall	.30	.10
❑ 122	Matt Williams	.30	.10
❑ 123	Henry Rodriguez	.30	.10
❑ 124	Placido Polanco	.30	.10
❑ 125	Bobby Estalella	.30	.10
❑ 126	Pat Burrell	.30	.10
❑ 127	Mark Loretta	.30	.10
❑ 128	Moises Alou	.30	.10
❑ 129	Tino Martinez	.50	.20
❑ 130	Milton Bradley	.30	.10
❑ 131	Todd Hundley	.30	.10
❑ 132	Keith Foulke	.30	.10
❑ 133	Robert Fick	.30	.10
❑ 134	Cristian Guzman	.30	.10
❑ 135	Rusty Greer	.30	.10
❑ 136	John Olerud	.30	.10
❑ 137	Mariano Rivera	.75	.30
❑ 138	Jeromy Burnitz	.30	.10
❑ 139	Dave Burba	.30	.10
❑ 140	Ken Griffey Jr.	1.25	.50
❑ 141	Tony Gwynn	1.00	.40
❑ 142	Carlos Delgado	.30	.10
❑ 143	Edgar Martinez	.50	.20
❑ 144	Ramon Hernandez	.30	.10
❑ 145	Pedro Astacio	.30	.10
❑ 146	Ray Lankford	.30	.10
❑ 147	Mike Mussina	.50	.20
❑ 148	Ray Durham	.30	.10
❑ 149	Lee Stevens	.30	.10
❑ 150	Jay Canizaro	.30	.10
❑ 151	Adrian Brown	.30	.10
❑ 152	Mike Piazza	1.25	.50
❑ 153	Cliff Floyd	.30	.10
❑ 154	Jose Vidro	.30	.10
❑ 155	Jason Giambi	.30	.10
❑ 156	Andruw Jones	.50	.20
❑ 157	Robin Ventura	.30	.10
❑ 158	Gary Sheffield	.30	.10
❑ 159	Jeff D'Amico	.30	.10
❑ 160	Chuck Knoblauch	.30	.10
❑ 161	Roger Cedeno	.30	.10
❑ 162	Jim Thome	.50	.20
❑ 163	Peter Bergeron	.30	.10
❑ 164	Kerry Wood	.30	.10
❑ 165	Gabe Kapler	.30	.10
❑ 166	Corey Koskie	.30	.10
❑ 167	Doug Glanville	.30	.10
❑ 168	Brent Mayne	.30	.10
❑ 169	Scott Spiezio	.30	.10
❑ 170	Steve Karsay	.30	.10
❑ 171	Al Martin	.30	.10
❑ 172	Fred McGriff	.50	.20
❑ 173	Gabe White	.30	.10
❑ 174	Alex Gonzalez	.30	.10
❑ 175	Mike Darr	.30	.10
❑ 176	Bengie Molina	.30	.10
❑ 177	Ben Grieve	.30	.10
❑ 178	Marlon Anderson	.30	.10
❑ 179	Brian Giles	.30	.10
❑ 180	Jose Valentin	.30	.10
❑ 181	Brian Jordan	.30	.10
❑ 182	Randy Johnson	.75	.30
❑ 183	Ricky Ledee	.30	.10
❑ 184	Russ Ortiz	.30	.10
❑ 185	Mike Lowell	.30	.10
❑ 186	Curtis Leskanic	.30	.10
❑ 187	Bob Abreu	.30	.10
❑ 188	Derek Jeter	2.00	.75
❑ 189	Lance Berkman	.30	.10
❑ 190	Roberto Alomar	.50	.20
❑ 191	Darin Erstad	.30	.10
❑ 192	Richie Sexson	.30	.10
❑ 193	Alex Ochoa	.30	.10
❑ 194	Carlos Febles	.30	.10
❑ 195	David Ortiz	.75	.30
❑ 196	Shawn Green	.30	.10
❑ 197	Mike Sweeney	.30	.10
❑ 198	Vladimir Guerrero	.75	.30
❑ 199	Jose Jimenez	.30	.10
❑ 200	Travis Lee	.30	.10
❑ 201	Rickey Henderson	.75	.30
❑ 202	Bob Wickman	.30	.10
❑ 203	Miguel Cairo	.30	.10
❑ 204	Steve Finley	.30	.10
❑ 205	Tony Batista	.30	.10
❑ 206	Jamey Wright	.30	.10
❑ 207	Terrence Long	.30	.10
❑ 208	Trevor Hoffman	.30	.10
❑ 209	John VanderWal	.30	.10
❑ 210	Greg Maddux	1.25	.50
❑ 211	Tim Salmon	.50	.20
❑ 212	Herbert Perry	.30	.10
❑ 213	Marvin Benard	.30	.10
❑ 214	Jose Offerman	.30	.10
❑ 215	Jay Payton	.30	.10
❑ 216	Jon Lieber	.30	.10
❑ 217	Mark Kotsay	.30	.10
❑ 218	Scott Brosius	.30	.10
❑ 219	Scott Williamson	.30	.10
❑ 220	Omar Vizquel	.50	.20
❑ 221	Mike Hampton	.30	.10
❑ 222	Richard Hidalgo	.30	.10
❑ 223	Rey Sanchez	.30	.10
❑ 224	Matt Lawton	.30	.10
❑ 225	Bruce Chen	.30	.10
❑ 226	Ryan Klesko	.30	.10
❑ 227	Garret Anderson	.30	.10
❑ 228	Kevin Brown	.30	.10
❑ 229	Mike Cameron	.30	.10
❑ 230	Tony Clark	.30	.10
❑ 231	Curt Schilling	.30	.10
❑ 232	Vinny Castilla	.30	.10
❑ 233	Carl Pavano	.30	.10
❑ 234	Eric Davis	.30	.10
❑ 235	Darrin Fletcher	.30	.10
❑ 236	Matt Stairs	.30	.10
❑ 237	Octavio Dotel	.30	.10
❑ 238	Mark Grace	.50	.20
❑ 239	John Smoltz	.50	.20
❑ 240	Matt Clement	.30	.10
❑ 241	Ellis Burks	.30	.10
❑ 242	Charles Johnson	.30	.10
❑ 243	Jeff Bagwell	.50	.20
❑ 244	Derek Bell	.30	.10
❑ 245	Nomar Garciaparra	1.25	.50
❑ 246	Jorge Posada	.50	.20
❑ 247	Ryan Dempster	.30	.10
❑ 248	J.T. Snow	.30	.10
❑ 249	Eric Young	.30	.10
❑ 250	Daryle Ward	.30	.10
❑ 251	Joe Randa	.30	.10
❑ 252	Travis Fryman	.30	.10
❑ 253	Mike Williams	.30	.10
❑ 254	Jacque Jones	.30	.10
❑ 255	Scott Elarton	.30	.10
❑ 256	Mark McGwire	2.00	.75
❑ 257	Jay Buhner	.30	.10
❑ 258	Randy Wolf	.30	.10
❑ 259	Sammy Sosa	.75	.30
❑ 260	Chan Ho Park	.30	.10
❑ 261	Damion Easley	.30	.10
❑ 262	Rick Ankiel	.30	.10
❑ 263	Frank Thomas	.75	.30
❑ 264	Kris Benson	.30	.10
❑ 265	Luis Alicea	.30	.10
❑ 266	Jeromy Burnitz	.30	.10
❑ 267	Geoff Blum	.30	.10
❑ 268	Joe Girardi	.30	.10
❑ 269	Livan Hernandez	.30	.10
❑ 270	Jeff Conine	.30	.10
❑ 271	Danny Graves	.30	.10
❑ 272	Craig Biggio	.50	.20
❑ 273	Jose Canseco	.50	.20
❑ 274	Tom Glavine	.50	.20
❑ 275	Ruben Mateo	.30	.10
❑ 276	Jeff Kent	.30	.10
❑ 277	Kevin Young	.30	.10
❑ 278	A.J. Burnett	.30	.10
❑ 279	Dante Bichette	.30	.10
❑ 280	Sandy Alomar Jr.	.30	.10
❑ 281	John Wetteland	.30	.10
❑ 282	Torii Hunter	.30	.10
❑ 283	Jarrod Washburn	.30	.10
❑ 284	Rich Aurilia	.30	.10
❑ 285	Jeff Cirillo	.30	.10
❑ 286	Fernando Seguignol	.30	.10
❑ 287	Darren Dreifort	.30	.10
❑ 288	Deivi Cruz	.30	.10
❑ 289	Pokey Reese	.30	.10
❑ 290	Garrett Stephenson	.30	.10
❑ 291	Bret Boone	.30	.10
❑ 292	Tim Hudson	.30	.10
❑ 293	John Flaherty	.30	.10
❑ 294	Shannon Stewart	.30	.10
❑ 295	Shawn Estes	.30	.10
❑ 296	Wilton Guerrero	.30	.10
❑ 297	Delino DeShields	.30	.10
❑ 298	David Justice	.30	.10
❑ 299	Harold Baines	.30	.10
❑ 300	Al Leiter	.30	.10
❑ 301	Wil Cordero	.30	.10
❑ 302	Antonio Alfonseca	.30	.10
❑ 303	Sean Casey	.30	.10
❑ 304	Carlos Beltran	.30	.10
❑ 305	Brad Radke	.30	.10
❑ 306	Jason Varitek	.75	.30
❑ 307	Shigetoshi Hasegawa	.30	.10
❑ 308	Todd Stottlemyre	.30	.10
❑ 309	Raul Mondesi	.30	.10
❑ 310	Mike Bordick	.30	.10
❑ 311	Darryl Kile	.30	.10
❑ 312	Dean Palmer	.30	.10
❑ 313	Johnny Damon	.50	.20
❑ 314	Todd Helton	.50	.20
❑ 315	Chad Hermansen	.30	.10
❑ 316	Kevin Appier	.30	.10
❑ 317	Greg Vaughn	.30	.10
❑ 318	Robb Nen	.30	.10
❑ 319	Jose Cruz Jr.	.30	.10
❑ 320	Ron Belliard	.30	.10
❑ 321	Bernie Williams	.50	.20
❑ 322	Melvin Mora	.30	.10
❑ 323	Kenny Lofton	.30	.10
❑ 324	Armando Benitez	.30	.10
❑ 325	Carlos Lee	.30	.10
❑ 326	Damian Jackson	.30	.10
❑ 327	Eric Milton	.30	.10
❑ 328	J.D. Drew	.30	.10
❑ 329	Byung-Hyun Kim	.30	.10
❑ 330	Chris Stynes	.30	.10
❑ 331	Kazuhiro Sasaki	.30	.10
❑ 332	Troy O'Leary	.30	.10
❑ 333	Pat Hentgen	.30	.10
❑ 334	Brad Ausmus	.30	.10
❑ 335	Todd Walker	.30	.10
❑ 336	Jason Isringhausen	.30	.10
❑ 337	Gerald Williams	.30	.10
❑ 338	Aaron Sele	.30	.10
❑ 339	Paul O'Neill	.50	.20
❑ 340	Cal Ripken	2.50	1.00
❑ 341	Manny Ramirez	.50	.20
❑ 342	Will Clark	.50	.20
❑ 343	Mark Redman	.30	.10
❑ 344	Bubba Trammell	.30	.10
❑ 345	Troy Percival	.30	.10
❑ 346	Chris Singleton	.30	.10
❑ 347	Rafael Palmeiro	.50	.20
❑ 348	Carl Everett	.30	.10
❑ 349	Andy Benes	.30	.10
❑ 350	Bobby Higginson	.30	.10
❑ 351	Alex Cabrera	.30	.10

❑ 352	Barry Zito	.50	.20
❑ 353	Jace Brewer	.30	.10
❑ 354	Paxton Crawford	.30	.10
❑ 355	Oswaldo Mairena	.30	.10
❑ 356	Joe Crede	.75	.30
❑ 357	A.J. Pierzynski	.30	.10
❑ 358	Daniel Garibay	.30	.10
❑ 359	Jason Tyner	.30	.10
❑ 360	Nate Rolison	.30	.10
❑ 361	Scott Downs	.30	.10
❑ 362	Keith Ginter	.30	.10
❑ 363	Juan Pierre	.30	.10
❑ 364	Adam Bernero	.30	.10
❑ 365	Chris Richard	.30	.10
❑ 366	Joey Nation	.30	.10
❑ 367	Aubrey Huff	.30	.10
❑ 368	Adam Eaton	.30	.10
❑ 369	Jose Ortiz	.30	.10
❑ 370	Eric Munson	.30	.10
❑ 371	Matt Kinney	.30	.10
❑ 372	Eric Byrnes	.30	.10
❑ 373	Keith McDonald	.30	.10
❑ 374	Matt Wise	.30	.10
❑ 375	Timo Perez	.30	.10
❑ 376	Julio Zuleta	.30	.10
❑ 377	Jimmy Rollins	.30	.10
❑ 378	Xavier Nady	.30	.10
❑ 379	Ryan Kohlmeier	.30	.10
❑ 380	Corey Patterson	.30	.10
❑ 381	Todd Helton LL	.30	.10
❑ 382	Moises Alou LL	.30	.10
❑ 383	Vladimir Guerrero LL	.50	.20
❑ 384	Luis Castillo LL	.30	.10
❑ 385	Jeffrey Hammonds LL	.30	.10
❑ 386	Nomar Garciaparra LL	.75	.30
❑ 387	Carlos Delgado LL	.30	.10
❑ 388	Darin Erstad LL	.30	.10
❑ 389	Manny Ramirez LL	.30	.10
❑ 390	Mike Sweeney LL	.30	.10
❑ 391	Sammy Sosa LL	.50	.20
❑ 392	Barry Bonds LL	1.00	.40
❑ 393	Jeff Bagwell LL	.30	.10
❑ 394	Richard Hidalgo LL	.30	.10
❑ 395	Vladimir Guerrero LL	.50	.20
❑ 396	Troy Glaus LL	.30	.10
❑ 397	Frank Thomas LL	.50	.20
❑ 398	Carlos Delgado LL	.30	.10
❑ 399	David Justice LL	.30	.10
❑ 400	Jason Giambi LL	.30	.10
❑ 401	Randy Johnson LL	.50	.20
❑ 402	Kevin Brown LL	.30	.10
❑ 403	Greg Maddux LL	.75	.30
❑ 404	Al Leiter LL	.30	.10
❑ 405	Mike Hampton LL	.30	.10
❑ 406	Pedro Martinez LL	.50	.20
❑ 407	Roger Clemens LL	.75	.30
❑ 408	Mike Sirotka LL	.30	.10
❑ 409	Mike Mussina LL	.30	.10
❑ 410	Bartolo Colon LL	.30	.10
❑ 411	Subway Series WS	.50	.20
❑ 412	Jose Vizcaino WS	.50	.20
❑ 413	Jose Vizcaino WS	.50	.20
❑ 414	Roger Clemens WS	.75	.30
❑ 415	Benitez/Alfonzo/Perez WS	.30	.10
❑ 416	Al Leiter WS	.50	.20
❑ 417	Luis Sojo WS	.50	.20
❑ 418	Yankees 3-Peat WS	.75	.30
❑ 419	Derek Jeter WS	1.00	.40
❑ 420	Toast of the Town WS	.50	.20
❑ 421	Atlanta Braves CL	.30	.10
❑ 422	New York Mets CL	.75	.30
❑ 423	Florida Marlins CL	.30	.10
❑ 424	Philadelphia Phillies CL	.30	.10
❑ 425	Montreal Expos CL	.30	.10
❑ 426	St. Louis Cardinals CL	.30	.10
❑ 427	Cincinnati Reds CL	.30	.10
❑ 428	Chicago Cubs CL	.50	.20
❑ 429	Milwaukee Brewers CL	.30	.10
❑ 430	Houston Astros CL	.30	.10
❑ 431	Pittsburgh Pirates CL	.50	.20
❑ 432	San Francisco Giants CL	.30	.10
❑ 433	Arizona Diamondbacks CL	.30	.10
❑ 434	Los Angeles Dodgers CL UER	.30	.10
❑ 435	Colorado Rockies CL UER	.30	.10
❑ 436	San Diego Padres CL	.30	.10
❑ 437	New York Yankees CL	.75	.30
❑ 438	Boston Red Sox CL	.50	.20
❑ 439	Baltimore Orioles CL	.30	.10
❑ 440	Toronto Blue Jays CL	.30	.10
❑ 441	Tampa Bay Devil Rays CL	.30	.10
❑ 442	Chicago White Sox CL	.50	.20
❑ 443	Cleveland Indians CL	.30	.10
❑ 444	Detoit Tigers CL	.30	.10
❑ 445	Kansas City Royals CL	.30	.10
❑ 446	Minnesota Twins CL	.30	.10
❑ 447	Seattle Mariners CL	.30	.10
❑ 448	Oakland Athletics CL	.30	.10
❑ 449	Anaheim Angels CL	.30	.10
❑ 450	Texas Rangers CL	.30	.10
❑ 451	Albert Pujols RC	70.00	40.00
❑ 452	Ichiro Suzuki RC	15.00	6.00
❑ 453	Tsuyoshi Shinjo RC	.75	.30
❑ 454	Johnny Estrada RC	.75	.30
❑ 455	Elpidio Guzman RC	.50	.20
❑ 456	Adrian Hernandez RC	.50	.20
❑ 457	Rafael Soriano RC	.50	.20
❑ 458	Drew Henson RC	.75	.30
❑ 459	Juan Uribe RC	.75	.30
❑ 460	Matt White RC	.50	.20
❑ 461	Endy Chavez RC	.50	.20
❑ 462	Bud Smith RC	.50	.20
❑ 463	Morgan Ensberg RC	2.50	1.00
❑ 464	Jay Gibbons RC	.75	.30
❑ 465	Jackson Melian RC	.50	.20
❑ 466	Junior Spivey RC	.75	.30
❑ 467	Juan Cruz RC	.50	.20
❑ 468	Wilson Betemit RC	2.50	1.00
❑ 469	Alexis Gomez RC	.50	.20
❑ 470	Mark Teixeira RC	10.00	4.00
❑ 471	Erick Almonte RC	.50	.20
❑ 472	Travis Hafner RC	8.00	3.00
❑ 473	Carlos Valderrama RC	.50	.20
❑ 474	Brandon Duckworth RC	.50	.20
❑ 475	Ryan Freel RC	1.50	.60
❑ 476	Wilkin Ruan RC	.50	.20
❑ 477	Andres Torres RC	.50	.20
❑ 478	Josh Towers RC	.75	.30
❑ 479	Kyle Lohse RC	.75	.30
❑ 480	Jason Michaels RC	.50	.20
❑ 481	Alfonso Soriano	.75	.30
❑ 482	C.C. Sabathia	.50	.20
❑ 483	Roy Oswalt	1.25	.50
❑ 484	Ben Sheets	.75	.30
❑ 485	Adam Dunn	.75	.30
❑ NNO	Uncut Sheet EXCH/100	2.00	.75

2003 Fleer Tradition Update

❑	COMP.SET w/o SP's (285)	40.00	15.00
❑	COMMON CARD (1-285)	.30	.10
❑	COMMON CARD (286-299)	1.00	.40
❑	COMMON RC (286-299)	1.00	.40
❑	286-299 STATED ODDS 1:4 HOB/RET		
❑	COMMON CARD (300-398)	1.00	.40
❑	COMMON RC (300-398)	1.00	.40
❑	300-398 ISSUED IN MINI-BOXES		
❑	ONE MINI-BOX PER UPDATE BOX		
❑	25 CARDS PER MINI-BOX		
❑ 1	Aaron Boone	.30	.10
❑ 2	Carl Everett	.30	.10
❑ 3	Eduardo Perez	.30	.10
❑ 4	Jason Michaels	.30	.10
❑ 5	Karim Garcia	.30	.10
❑ 6	Rainer Olmedo	.30	.10
❑ 7	Scott Williamson	.30	.10
❑ 8	Adam Kennedy	.30	.10
❑ 9	Carl Pavano	.30	.10
❑ 10	Eli Marrero	.30	.10
❑ 11	Jason Simontacchi	.30	.10
❑ 12	Keith Foulke	.30	.10
❑ 13	Preston Wilson	.30	.10
❑ 14	Scott Hatteberg	.30	.10
❑ 15	Adam Dunn	.30	.10
❑ 16	Carlos Baerga	.30	.10
❑ 17	Elmer Dessens	.30	.10
❑ 18	Javier Vazquez	.30	.10
❑ 19	Kenny Rogers	.30	.10
❑ 20	Quinton McCracken	.30	.10
❑ 21	Shane Reynolds	.30	.10
❑ 22	Adam Eaton	.30	.10
❑ 23	Carlos Zambrano	.30	.10
❑ 24	Enrique Wilson	.30	.10
❑ 25	Jeff DaVanon	.30	.10
❑ 26	Kenny Lofton	.30	.10
❑ 27	Ramon Castro	.30	.10
❑ 28	Shannon Stewart	.30	.10
❑ 29	Al Martin	.30	.10
❑ 30	Carlos Guillen	.30	.10
❑ 31	Eric Karros	.30	.10
❑ 32	Tim Worrell	.30	.10
❑ 33	Kevin Millwood	.30	.10
❑ 34	Randall Simon	.30	.10
❑ 35	Shawn Chacon	.30	.10
❑ 36	Alex Rodriguez	1.25	.50
❑ 37	Casey Blake	.30	.10
❑ 38	Eric Munson	.30	.10
❑ 39	Jeff Kent	.30	.10
❑ 40	Kris Benson	.30	.10
❑ 41	Randy Winn	.30	.10
❑ 42	Shea Hillenbrand	.30	.10
❑ 43	Alfonso Soriano	.30	.10
❑ 44	Chris George	.30	.10
❑ 45	Eric Bruntlett	.30	.10
❑ 46	Jeromy Burnitz	.30	.10
❑ 47	Kyle Farnsworth	.30	.10
❑ 48	Torii Hunter	.30	.10
❑ 49	Sidney Ponson	.30	.10
❑ 50	Andres Galarraga	.30	.10
❑ 51	Chris Singleton	.30	.10
❑ 52	Eric Gagne	.30	.10
❑ 53	Jesse Foppert	.30	.10
❑ 54	Lance Carter	.30	.10
❑ 55	Ray Durham	.30	.10
❑ 56	Tanyon Sturtze	.30	.10
❑ 57	Andy Ashby	.30	.10
❑ 58	Cliff Floyd	.30	.10
❑ 59	Eric Young	.30	.10
❑ 60	Jhonny Peralta	1.25	.50
❑ 61	Livan Hernandez	.30	.10
❑ 62	Reggie Sanders	.30	.10
❑ 63	Tim Spooneybarger	.30	.10
❑ 64	Angel Berroa	.30	.10
❑ 65	Coco Crisp	.50	.20
❑ 66	Eric Hinske	.30	.10
❑ 67	Jim Edmonds	.30	.10
❑ 68	Luis Matos	.30	.10
❑ 69	Rickey Henderson	.75	.30
❑ 70	Todd Walker	.30	.10
❑ 71	Antonio Alfonseca	.30	.10
❑ 72	Corey Koskie	.30	.10
❑ 73	Erubiel Durazo	.30	.10
❑ 74	Jim Thome	.50	.20
❑ 75	Lyle Overbay	.30	.10
❑ 76	Robert Fick	.30	.10
❑ 77	Todd Hollandsworth	.30	.10
❑ 78	Aramis Ramirez	.30	.10
❑ 79	Cristian Guzman	.30	.10
❑ 80	Esteban Loaiza	.30	.10
❑ 81	Jody Gerut	.30	.10
❑ 82	Mark Grudzielanek	.30	.10
❑ 83	Roberto Alomar	.50	.20
❑ 84	Todd Hundley	.30	.10
❑ 85	Mike Hampton	.30	.10
❑ 86	Curt Schilling	.30	.10
❑ 87	Francisco Rodriguez	.30	.10
❑ 88	John Lackey	.30	.10
❑ 89	Mark Redman	.30	.10
❑ 90	Robin Ventura	.30	.10
❑ 91	Todd Zeile	.30	.10
❑ 92	B.J. Surhoff	.30	.10

❑ 93 Raul Mondesi .30 .10
❑ 94 Frank Catalanotto .30 .10
❑ 95 John Smoltz .50 .20
❑ 96 Mark Ellis .30 .10
❑ 97 Rocco Baldelli .30 .10
❑ 98 Todd Pratt .30 .10
❑ 99 Barry Bonds 2.00 .75
❑ 100 Danny Graves .30 .10
❑ 101 Fred McGriff .50 .20
❑ 102 John Burkett .30 .10
❑ 103 Marquis Grissom .30 .10
❑ 104 Rocky Biddle .30 .10
❑ 105 Tom Glavine .50 .20
❑ 106 Bartolo Colon .30 .10
❑ 107 Darren Bragg .30 .10
❑ 108 Gabe Kapler .30 .10
❑ 109 John Franco .30 .10
❑ 110 Matt Mantei .30 .10
❑ 111 Rod Beck .30 .10
❑ 112 Tomo Ohka .30 .10
❑ 113 Ben Petrick .30 .10
❑ 114 Darren Dreifort .30 .10
❑ 115 Garret Anderson .30 .10
❑ 116 John Vander Wal .30 .10
❑ 117 Melvin Mora .30 .10
❑ 118 Rodrigo Lopez .30 .10
❑ 119 Raul Ibanez .30 .10
❑ 120 Benito Santiago .30 .10
❑ 121 David Ortiz Sox .75 .30
❑ 122 Gary Bennett .30 .10
❑ 123 Jon Garland .30 .10
❑ 124 Michael Young .50 .20
❑ 125 Rodrigo Rosario .30 .10
❑ 126 Travis Lee .30 .10
❑ 127 Bill Mueller .30 .10
❑ 128 Derek Lowe .30 .10
❑ 129 Gil Meche .30 .10
❑ 130 Jose Guillen .30 .10
❑ 131 Miguel Cabrera .75 .30
❑ 132 Ron Calloway .30 .10
❑ 133 Troy Percival .30 .10
❑ 134 Billy Koch .30 .10
❑ 135 Dmitri Young .30 .10
❑ 136 Glendon Rusch .30 .10
❑ 137 Jose Jimenez .30 .10
❑ 138 Miguel Tejada .30 .10
❑ 139 John Thomson .30 .10
❑ 140 Troy O'Leary .30 .10
❑ 141 Bobby Kielty .30 .10
❑ 142 Dontrelle Willis .75 .30
❑ 143 Greg Myers .30 .10
❑ 144 Jose Vizcaino .30 .10
❑ 145 Mike MacDougal .30 .10
❑ 146 Ronnie Belliard .30 .10
❑ 147 Tyler Houston .30 .10
❑ 148 Brady Clark .30 .10
❑ 149 Edgardo Alfonzo .30 .10
❑ 150 Guillermo Mota .30 .10
❑ 151 Jose Lima .30 .10
❑ 152 Mike Williams .30 .10
❑ 153 Roy Oswalt .30 .10
❑ 154 Scott Podsednik 5.00 2.00
❑ 155 Brandon Lyon .30 .10
❑ 156 Henry Mateo .30 .10
❑ 157 Jose Macias .30 .10
❑ 158 Mike Bordick .30 .10
❑ 159 Royce Clayton .30 .10
❑ 160 Vance Wilson .30 .10
❑ 161 Brent Abernathy .30 .10
❑ 162 Horacio Ramirez .30 .10
❑ 163 Jose Reyes .30 .10
❑ 164 Nick Punto .30 .10
❑ 165 Ruben Sierra .30 .10
❑ 166 Victor Zambrano .30 .10
❑ 167 Brett Tomko .30 .10
❑ 168 Ivan Rodriguez .50 .20
❑ 169 Jose Mesa .30 .10
❑ 170 Octavio Dotel .30 .10
❑ 171 Russ Ortiz .30 .10
❑ 172 Vladimir Guerrero .75 .30
❑ 173 Brian Lawrence .30 .10
❑ 174 Jae Weong Seo .30 .10
❑ 175 Jose Cruz Jr. .30 .10
❑ 176 Pat Burrell .30 .10
❑ 177 Russell Branyan .30 .10
❑ 178 Warren Morris .30 .10
❑ 179 Brian Boehringer .30 .10
❑ 180 Jason Johnson .30 .10
❑ 181 Josh Phelps .30 .10
❑ 182 Paul Konerko .30 .10
❑ 183 Ryan Franklin .30 .10
❑ 184 Wes Helms .30 .10
❑ 185 Brooks Kieschnick .30 .10
❑ 186 Jason Davis .30 .10
❑ 187 Juan Pierre .30 .10
❑ 188 Paul Wilson .30 .10
❑ 189 Sammy Sosa .75 .30
❑ 190 Wil Cordero .30 .10
❑ 191 Byung-Hyun Kim .30 .10
❑ 192 Juan Encarnacion .30 .10
❑ 193 Placido Polanco .30 .10
❑ 194 Sandy Alomar Jr. .30 .10
❑ 195 Julio Lugo .30 .10
❑ 196 Junior Spivey .30 .10
❑ 197 Woody Williams .30 .10
❑ 198 Xavier Nady .30 .10
❑ 199 Mark Loretta .30 .10
❑ 200 Deivi Cruz .30 .10
❑ 201 Jorge Posada AS .30 .10
❑ 202 Carlos Delgado AS .30 .10
❑ 203 Alfonso Soriano AS .30 .10
❑ 204 Alex Rodriguez AS .75 .30
❑ 205 Troy Glaus AS .30 .10
❑ 206 Garret Anderson AS .30 .10
❑ 207 Hideki Matsui AS 2.00 .75
❑ 208 Ichiro Suzuki AS .75 .30
❑ 209 Esteban Loaiza AS .30 .10
❑ 210 Manny Ramirez AS .50 .20
❑ 211 Roger Clemens AS .75 .30
❑ 212 Roy Halladay AS .30 .10
❑ 213 Jason Giambi AS .30 .10
❑ 214 Edgar Martinez AS .30 .10
❑ 215 Bret Boone AS .30 .10
❑ 216 Hank Blalock AS .30 .10
❑ 217 Nomar Garciaparra AS .75 .30
❑ 218 Vernon Wells AS .30 .10
❑ 219 Melvin Mora AS .30 .10
❑ 220 Magglio Ordonez AS .30 .10
❑ 221 Mike Sweeney AS .30 .10
❑ 222 Barry Zito AS .30 .10
❑ 223 Carl Everett AS .30 .10
❑ 224 Shigetoshi Hasegawa AS .30 .10
❑ 225 Jamie Moyer AS .30 .10
❑ 226 Mark Mulder AS .30 .10
❑ 227 Eddie Guardado AS .30 .10
❑ 228 Ramon Hernandez AS .30 .10
❑ 229 Keith Foulke AS .30 .10
❑ 230 Javy Lopez AS .30 .10
❑ 231 Todd Helton AS .30 .10
❑ 232 Marcus Giles AS .30 .10
❑ 233 Edgar Renteria AS .30 .10
❑ 234 Scott Rolen AS .30 .10
❑ 235 Barry Bonds AS 1.00 .40
❑ 236 Albert Pujols AS .75 .30
❑ 237 Gary Sheffield AS .30 .10
❑ 238 Jim Edmonds AS .30 .10
❑ 239 Jason Schmidt AS .30 .10
❑ 240 Mark Prior AS .30 .10
❑ 241 Dontrelle Willis AS .50 .20
❑ 242 Kerry Wood AS .30 .10
❑ 243 Kevin Brown AS .30 .10
❑ 244 Woody Williams AS .30 .10
❑ 245 Paul Lo Duca AS .30 .10
❑ 246 Richie Sexson AS .30 .10
❑ 247 Jose Vidro AS .30 .10
❑ 248 Luis Castillo AS .30 .10
❑ 249 Aaron Boone AS .30 .10
❑ 250 Mike Lowell AS .30 .10
❑ 251 Rafael Furcal AS .30 .10
❑ 252 Andruw Jones AS .30 .10
❑ 253 Preston Wilson AS .30 .10
❑ 254 John Smoltz AS .30 .10
❑ 255 Eric Gagne AS .30 .10
❑ 256 Randy Wolf AS .30 .10
❑ 257 Billy Wagner AS .30 .10
❑ 258 Luis Gonzalez AS .30 .10
❑ 259 Russ Ortiz AS .30 .10
❑ 260 J.Thome/P.Martinez IL .50 .20
❑ 261 A.Soriano/J.Bagwell IL .50 .20
❑ 262 D.Willis/R.Baldelli IL .50 .20
❑ 263 C.Delgado/V.Guerrero IL .50 .20
❑ 264 S.Sosa/M.Ordonez IL .75 .30
❑ 265 J.Giambi/A.Dunn IL .30 .10
❑ 266 M.Sweeney/A.Pujols IL .75 .30
❑ 267 B.Bonds/T.Hunter IL 1.00 .40
❑ 268 I.Suzuki/A.Jones IL .75 .30
❑ 269 C.Jones/H.Blalock IL .50 .20
❑ 270 M.Prior/V.Wells IL .30 .10
❑ 271 N.Garciaparra/S.Rolen IL .75 .30
❑ 272 A.Rodriguez/L.Berkman IL .75 .30
❑ 273 R.Clemens/K.Wood IL .75 .30
❑ 274 D.Jeter/J.Reyes IL 1.00 .40
❑ 275 G.Maddux/B.Zito IL .75 .30
❑ 276 Carlos Delgado TT .30 .10
❑ 277 J.D. Drew TT .30 .10
❑ 278 Barry Bonds TT 1.00 .40
❑ 279 Albert Pujols TT .75 .30
❑ 280 Jim Thome TT .30 .10
❑ 281 Sammy Sosa TT .50 .20
❑ 282 Alfonso Soriano TT .30 .10
❑ 283 Hideki Matsui TT 2.00 .75
❑ 284 Mike Piazza TT .75 .30
❑ 285 Vladimir Guerrero TT .50 .20
❑ 286 Rich Harden ROO 1.50 .60
❑ 287 Chin-Hui Tsao ROO 1.00 .40
❑ 288 Edwin Jackson ROO RC 1.50 .60
❑ 289 Chien-Ming Wang ROO RC 10.00 4.00
❑ 290 Josh Willingham ROO RC 2.50 1.00
❑ 291 Matt Kata ROO RC 1.00 .40
❑ 292 Jose Contreras ROO RC 2.00 .75
❑ 293 Chris Bootcheck ROO 1.00 .40
❑ 294 Javier A. Lopez ROO RC 1.00 .40
❑ 295 Delmon Young ROO RC 8.00 3.00
❑ 296 Pedro Liriano ROO 1.00 .40
❑ 297 Noah Lowry ROO 1.50 .60
❑ 298 Khalil Greene ROO 2.50 1.00
❑ 299 Rob Bowen ROO 1.00 .40
❑ 300 Bo Hart ROO RC 1.00 .40
❑ 301 Beau Kemp ROO RC 1.00 .40
❑ 302 Gerald Laird ROO 1.00 .40
❑ 303 Miguel Ojeda ROO RC 1.00 .40
❑ 304 Todd Wellemeyer ROO RC 1.00 .40
❑ 305 Ryan Wagner ROO RC 1.00 .40
❑ 306 Jeff Duncan ROO RC 1.00 .40
❑ 307 Wilfredo Ledezma ROO RC 1.00 .40
❑ 308 Wes Obermueller ROO 1.00 .40
❑ 309 Bernie Castro ROO RC 1.00 .40
❑ 310 Tim Olson ROO RC 1.00 .40
❑ 311 Colin Porter ROO RC 1.00 .40
❑ 312 Francisco Cruceta ROO RC 1.00 .40
❑ 313 Guillermo Quiroz ROO RC 1.00 .40
❑ 314 Brian Stokes ROO RC 1.00 .40
❑ 315 Robby Hammock ROO RC 1.00 .40
❑ 316 Lew Ford ROO RC 1.50 .60
❑ 317 Todd Linden ROO 1.00 .40
❑ 318 Mike Gallo ROO RC 1.00 .40
❑ 319 Francisco Rosario ROO RC 1.00 .40
❑ 320 Rosman Garcia ROO RC 1.00 .40
❑ 321 Felix Sanchez ROO RC 1.00 .40
❑ 322 Chad Gaudin ROO RC 1.00 .40
❑ 323 Phil Seibel ROO RC 1.00 .40
❑ 324 Jason Gilfillan ROO RC 1.00 .40
❑ 325 Termel Sledge ROO RC 1.00 .40
❑ 326 Alfredo Gonzalez ROO RC 1.00 .40
❑ 327 Josh Stewart ROO RC 1.00 .40
❑ 328 Jeremy Griffiths ROO RC 1.00 .40
❑ 329 Cory Stewart ROO RC 1.00 .40
❑ 330 Josh Hall ROO RC 1.00 .40
❑ 331 Arnie Munoz ROO RC 1.00 .40
❑ 332 Garrett Atkins ROO 1.00 .40
❑ 333 Neal Cotts ROO 1.00 .40
❑ 334 Dan Haren ROO RC 2.00 .75
❑ 335 Shane Victorino ROO RC 2.00 .75
❑ 336 David Sanders ROO RC 1.00 .40
❑ 337 Oscar Villarreal ROO RC 1.00 .40
❑ 338 Michael Hessman ROO RC 1.00 .40
❑ 339 Andrew Brown ROO RC 1.50 .60
❑ 340 Kevin Hooper ROO 1.00 .40
❑ 341 Prentice Redman ROO RC 1.00 .40
❑ 342 Brandon Webb ROO RC 5.00 2.00
❑ 343 Jimmy Gobble ROO 1.00 .40
❑ 344 Pete LaForest ROO RC 1.00 .40
❑ 345 Chris Waters ROO RC 1.00 .40
❑ 346 Hideki Matsui ROO RC 8.00 3.00
❑ 347 Chris Capuano ROO RC 2.00 .75
❑ 348 Jon Leicester ROO RC 1.00 .40
❑ 349 Mike Nicolas ROO RC 1.00 .40
❑ 350 Nook Logan ROO RC 1.50 .60

❑ 351 Craig Brazell ROO RC 1.00 .40
❑ 352 Aaron Looper ROO RC 1.00 .40
❑ 353 D.J. Carrasco ROO RC 1.00 .40
❑ 354 Clint Barmes ROO RC 2.00 .75
❑ 355 Doug Waechter ROO RC 1.50 .60
❑ 356 Julio Manon ROO RC 1.00 .40
❑ 357 Jeremy Bonderman ROO RC 6.00 2.50
❑ 358 Diegomar Markwell ROO RC 1.00 .40
❑ 359 Dave Matranga ROO RC 1.00 .40
❑ 360 Luis Ayala ROO RC 1.00 .40
❑ 361 Jason Stanford ROO 1.00 .40
❑ 362 Roger Deago ROO RC 1.00 .40
❑ 363 Geoff Geary ROO RC 1.00 .40
❑ 364 Edgar Gonzalez ROO RC 1.00 .40
❑ 365 Michel Hernandez ROO RC 1.00 .40
❑ 366 Aquilino Lopez ROO RC 1.00 .40
❑ 367 David Manning ROO 1.00 .40
❑ 368 Carlos Mendez ROO RC 1.00 .40
❑ 369 Matt Miller ROO RC 1.00 .40
❑ 370 Michael Nakamura ROO RC 1.00 .40
❑ 371 Mike Neu ROO RC 1.00 .40
❑ 372 Ramon Nivar ROO RC 1.00 .40
❑ 373 Kevin Ohme ROO RC 1.00 .40
❑ 374 Alex Prieto ROO RC 1.00 .40
❑ 375 Stephen Randolph ROO RC 1.00 .40
❑ 376 Brian Sweeney ROO RC 1.00 .40
❑ 377 Matt Diaz ROO RC 2.00 .75
❑ 378 Mike Gonzalez ROO 1.00 .40
❑ 379 Daniel Cabrera ROO RC 2.00 .75
❑ 380 Fernando Cabrera ROO RC 1.00 .40
❑ 381 David DeJesus ROO RC 2.00 .75
❑ 382 Mike Ryan ROO RC 1.00 .40
❑ 383 Rick Roberts ROO RC 1.00 .40
❑ 384 Seung Song ROO 1.00 .40
❑ 385 Rickie Weeks ROO RC 5.00 2.00
❑ 386 Humberto Quintero ROO RC 1.00 .40
❑ 387 Alexis Rios ROO 1.00 .40
❑ 388 Aaron Miles ROO RC 1.50 .60
❑ 389 Tom Gregorio ROO RC 1.00 .40
❑ 390 Anthony Ferrari ROO RC 1.00 .40
❑ 391 Kevin Correia ROO RC 1.00 .40
❑ 392 Rafael Betancourt ROO RC 1.50 .60
❑ 393 Rett Johnson ROO RC 1.00 .40
❑ 394 Richard Fischer ROO RC 1.00 .40
❑ 395 Greg Aquino ROO RC 1.00 .40
❑ 396 Daniel Garcia ROO RC 1.00 .40
❑ 397 Sergio Mitre ROO RC 1.50 .60
❑ 398 Edwin Almonte ROO 1.00 .40

2004 Fleer Tradition

❑ COMPLETE SET (500) 150.00 75.00
❑ COMP.SET w/o SP's (400) 40.00 15.00
❑ COMMON CARD (1-400) .30 .10
❑ COMMON CARD (401-470) 1.00 .40
❑ COMMON CARD (471-500) 1.00 .40
❑ 401-445 STATED ODDS 1:2
❑ 446-461 STATED ODDS 1:6
❑ 462-470 STATED ODDS 1:9
❑ 471-500 STATED ODDS 1:3
❑ 1 Juan Pierre WS .30 .10
❑ 2 Josh Beckett WS .30 .10
❑ 3 Ivan Rodriguez WS .50 .20
❑ 4 Miguel Cabrera WS .50 .20
❑ 5 Dontrelle Willis WS .50 .20
❑ 6 Derek Jeter WS 1.50 .60
❑ 7 Jason Giambi WS .30 .10
❑ 8 Bernie Williams WS .50 .20
❑ 9 Alfonso Soriano WS .30 .10
❑ 10 Hideki Matsui WS 1.25 .50
❑ 11 Anderson/Ortiz/Lackey TL .30 .10
❑ 12 Gonzalez/Webb/Schilling TL .30 .10
❑ 13 Lopez/Sheffield/Ortiz TL .30 .10
❑ 14 Batista/Gibb/Ponson/John TL .30 .10
❑ 15 Manny/Nomar/Lowe/Pedro TL .50 .20
❑ 16 Sosa/Prior/Wood TL .50 .20
❑ 17 Thomas/Lee/Loaiza TL .50 .20
❑ 18 Dunn/Casey/Reit/Wilson TL .30 .10
❑ 19 Gerut/Sabathia TL .30 .10
❑ 20 Wilson/Oliver/Jennings TL .30 .10
❑ 21 Young/Maroth/Bonderman TL .30 .10
❑ 22 Lowell/Willis/Beckett TL .50 .20
❑ 23 Bagwell/Robertson/Miller TL .30 .10
❑ 24 Beltran/May TL .30 .10
❑ 25 Beltre/Green/Nomo/Brown TL .30 .10
❑ 26 Sexson/Sheets TL .30 .10
❑ 27 Hunter/Radke/Santana TL .50 .20
❑ 28 Vlad/Cabrera/Livan/Vazq TL .50 .20
❑ 29 Floyd/Wigg/Trach/Leiter TL .30 .10
❑ 30 Giambi/Pettitte/Mussina TL .50 .20
❑ 31 Chavez/Tejada/Hudson TL .30 .10
❑ 32 Thome/Wolf TL .30 .10
❑ 33 Sanders/Fogg/Wells TL .30 .10
❑ 34 Klesko/Loretta/Peavy TL .30 .10
❑ 35 Cruz Jr./Alfonzo/Schmidt TL .30 .10
❑ 36 Boone/Moyer/Pineiro TL .30 .10
❑ 37 Pujols/Williams TL .75 .30
❑ 38 Huff/Zambrano TL .30 .10
❑ 39 A.Rodriguez/Thomson TL .75 .30
❑ 40 Delgado/Halladay TL .30 .10
❑ 41 Greg Maddux 1.25 .50
❑ 42 Ben Grieve .30 .10
❑ 43 Darin Erstad .30 .10
❑ 44 Ruben Sierra .30 .10
❑ 45 Byung-Hyung Kim .30 .10
❑ 46 Freddy Garcia .30 .10
❑ 47 Richard Hidalgo .30 .10
❑ 48 Tike Redman .30 .10
❑ 49 Kevin Millwood .30 .10
❑ 50 Marquis Grissom .30 .10
❑ 51 Jae Weong Seo .30 .10
❑ 52 Wil Cordero .30 .10
❑ 53 LaTroy Hawkins .30 .10
❑ 54 Jolbert Cabrera .30 .10
❑ 55 Kevin Appier .30 .10
❑ 56 John Lackey .30 .10
❑ 57 Garret Anderson .30 .10
❑ 58 R.A. Dickey .30 .10
❑ 59 David Segui .30 .10
❑ 60 Erubiel Durazo .30 .10
❑ 61 Bobby Abreu .30 .10
❑ 62 Travis Hafner .30 .10
❑ 63 Victor Zambrano .30 .10
❑ 64 Randy Johnson .75 .30
❑ 65 Bernie Williams .50 .20
❑ 66 J.T. Snow .30 .10
❑ 67 Sammy Sosa .75 .30
❑ 68 Al Leiter .30 .10
❑ 69 Jason Jennings .30 .10
❑ 70 Matt Morris .30 .10
❑ 71 Mike Hampton .30 .10
❑ 72 Juan Encarnacion .30 .10
❑ 73 Alex Gonzalez .30 .10
❑ 74 Bartolo Colon .30 .10
❑ 75 Brett Myers .30 .10
❑ 76 Michael Young .30 .10
❑ 77 Ichiro Suzuki 1.50 .60
❑ 78 Jason Johnson .30 .10
❑ 79 Brad Ausmus .30 .10
❑ 80 Ted Lilly .30 .10
❑ 81 Ken Griffey Jr. 1.25 .50
❑ 82 Chone Figgins .30 .10
❑ 83 Edgar Martinez .50 .20
❑ 84 Adam Eaton .30 .10
❑ 85 Ken Harvey .30 .10
❑ 86 Francisco Rodriguez .30 .10
❑ 87 Bill Mueller .30 .10
❑ 88 Mike Maroth .30 .10
❑ 89 Charles Johnson .30 .10
❑ 90 Jhonny Peralta .30 .10
❑ 91 Kip Wells .30 .10
❑ 92 Cesar Izturis .30 .10
❑ 93 Matt Clement .30 .10
❑ 94 Lyle Overbay .30 .10
❑ 95 Kirk Rueter .30 .10
❑ 96 Cristian Guzman .30 .10
❑ 97 Garrett Stephenson .30 .10
❑ 98 Lance Berkman .30 .10
❑ 99 Brett Tomko .30 .10
❑ 100 Chris Stynes .30 .10
❑ 101 Nate Cornejo .30 .10
❑ 102 Aaron Rowand .30 .10
❑ 103 Javier Vazquez .30 .10
❑ 104 Jason Kendall .30 .10
❑ 105 Mark Redman .30 .10
❑ 106 Benito Santiago .30 .10
❑ 107 C.C. Sabathia .30 .10
❑ 108 David Wells .30 .10
❑ 109 Mark Ellis .30 .10
❑ 110 Casey Blake .30 .10
❑ 111 Sean Burroughs .30 .10
❑ 112 Carlos Beltran .30 .10
❑ 113 Ramon Hernandez .30 .10
❑ 114 Eric Hinske .30 .10
❑ 115 Luis Gonzalez .30 .10
❑ 116 Jarrod Washburn .30 .10
❑ 117 Ronnie Belliard .30 .10
❑ 118 Troy Percival .30 .10
❑ 119 Jose Valentin .30 .10
❑ 120 Chase Utley .50 .20
❑ 121 Odalis Perez .30 .10
❑ 122 Steve Finley .30 .10
❑ 123 Bret Boone .30 .10
❑ 124 Jeff Conine .30 .10
❑ 125 Josh Fogg .30 .10
❑ 126 Neifi Perez .30 .10
❑ 127 Ben Sheets .30 .10
❑ 128 Randy Winn .30 .10
❑ 129 Matt Stairs .30 .10
❑ 130 Carlos Delgado .30 .10
❑ 131 Morgan Ensberg .30 .10
❑ 132 Vinny Castilla .30 .10
❑ 133 Matt Mantei .30 .10
❑ 134 Alex Rodriguez 1.25 .50
❑ 135 Matthew LeCroy .30 .10
❑ 136 Woody Williams .30 .10
❑ 137 Frank Catalanotto .30 .10
❑ 138 Rondell White .30 .10
❑ 139 Scott Rolen .50 .20
❑ 140 Cliff Floyd .30 .10
❑ 141 Chipper Jones .75 .30
❑ 142 Robin Ventura .30 .10
❑ 143 Mariano Rivera .75 .30
❑ 144 Brady Clark .30 .10
❑ 145 Ramon Ortiz .30 .10
❑ 146 Omar Infante .30 .10
❑ 147 Mike Matheny .30 .10
❑ 148 Pedro Martinez .50 .20
❑ 149 Carlos Baerga .30 .10
❑ 150 Shannon Stewart .30 .10
❑ 151 Travis Lee .30 .10
❑ 152 Eric Byrnes .30 .10
❑ 153 Rafael Furcal .30 .10
❑ 154 B.J. Surhoff .30 .10
❑ 155 Zach Day .30 .10
❑ 156 Marlon Anderson .30 .10
❑ 157 Mark Hendrickson .30 .10
❑ 158 Mike Mussina .50 .20
❑ 159 Randall Simon .30 .10
❑ 160 Jeff DaVanon .30 .10
❑ 161 Joel Pineiro .30 .10
❑ 162 Vernon Wells .30 .10
❑ 163 Adam Kennedy .30 .10
❑ 164 Trot Nixon .30 .10
❑ 165 Rodrigo Lopez .30 .10
❑ 166 Curt Schilling .30 .10
❑ 167 Horacio Ramirez .30 .10
❑ 168 Jason Marquis .30 .10
❑ 169 Magglio Ordonez .30 .10
❑ 170 Scott Schoeneweis .30 .10
❑ 171 Andruw Jones .50 .20
❑ 172 Tino Martinez .50 .20
❑ 173 Moises Alou .30 .10
❑ 174 Kelvim Escobar .30 .10
❑ 175 Xavier Nady .30 .10
❑ 176 Ramon Martinez .30 .10
❑ 177 Pat Hentgen .30 .10
❑ 178 Austin Kearns .30 .10
❑ 179 D'Angelo Jimenez .30 .10
❑ 180 Deivi Cruz .30 .10
❑ 181 John Smoltz .50 .20

❑ 182 Toby Hall .30 .10
❑ 183 Mark Buehrle .30 .10
❑ 184 Howie Clark .30 .10
❑ 185 David Ortiz .75 .30
❑ 186 Raul Mondesi .30 .10
❑ 187 Milton Bradley .30 .10
❑ 188 Jorge Julio .30 .10
❑ 189 Victor Martinez .30 .10
❑ 190 Gabe Kapler .30 .10
❑ 191 Julio Franco .30 .10
❑ 192 Ryan Freel .30 .10
❑ 193 Brad Fullmer .30 .10
❑ 194 Joe Borowski .30 .10
❑ 195 Darren Oliver .30 .10
❑ 196 Jason Varitek .75 .30
❑ 197 Greg Myers .30 .10
❑ 198 Eric Munson .30 .10
❑ 199 Tim Wakefield .30 .10
❑ 200 Kyle Farnsworth .30 .10
❑ 201 Johnny Vander Wal .30 .10
❑ 202 Alex Escobar .30 .10
❑ 203 Sean Casey .30 .10
❑ 204 John Thomson .30 .10
❑ 205 Carlos Zambrano .30 .10
❑ 206 Kenny Lofton .30 .10
❑ 207 Marcus Giles .30 .10
❑ 208 Wade Miller .30 .10
❑ 209 Geoff Blum .30 .10
❑ 210 Jason LaRue .30 .10
❑ 211 Omar Vizquel .50 .20
❑ 212 Carlos Pena .30 .10
❑ 213 Adam Dunn .30 .10
❑ 214 Oscar Villarreal .30 .10
❑ 215 Paul Konerko .30 .10
❑ 216 Hideo Nomo .75 .30
❑ 217 Mike Sweeney .30 .10
❑ 218 Coco Crisp .30 .10
❑ 219 Shawn Chacon .30 .10
❑ 220 Brook Fordyce .30 .10
❑ 221 Josh Beckett .30 .10
❑ 222 Paul Wilson .30 .10
❑ 223 Josh Towers .30 .10
❑ 224 Geoff Jenkins .30 .10
❑ 225 Shawn Green .30 .10
❑ 226 Derrek Lee .50 .20
❑ 227 Karim Garcia .30 .10
❑ 228 Preston Wilson .30 .10
❑ 229 Dane Sardinha .30 .10
❑ 230 Aramis Ramirez .30 .10
❑ 231 Doug Mientkiewicz .30 .10
❑ 232 Jay Gibbons .30 .10
❑ 233 Adam Everett .30 .10
❑ 234 Brooks Kieschnick .30 .10
❑ 235 Dmitri Young .30 .10
❑ 236 Brad Penny .30 .10
❑ 237 Todd Zeile .30 .10
❑ 238 Eric Gagne .30 .10
❑ 239 Esteban Loaiza .30 .10
❑ 240 Billy Wagner .30 .10
❑ 241 Nomar Garciaparra 1.25 .50
❑ 242 Desi Relaford .30 .10
❑ 243 Luis Rivas .30 .10
❑ 244 Andy Pettitte .50 .20
❑ 245 Ty Wigginton .30 .10
❑ 246 Edgar Gonzalez .30 .10
❑ 247 Brian Anderson .30 .10
❑ 248 Richie Sexson .30 .10
❑ 249 Russell Branyan .30 .10
❑ 250 Jose Guillen .30 .10
❑ 251 Chin-Hui Tsao .30 .10
❑ 252 Jose Hernandez .30 .10
❑ 253 Kevin Brown .30 .10
❑ 254 Pete LaForest .30 .10
❑ 255 Adrian Beltre .30 .10
❑ 256 Jacque Jones .30 .10
❑ 257 Jimmy Rollins .30 .10
❑ 258 Brandon Phillips .30 .10
❑ 259 Derek Jeter 1.50 .60
❑ 260 Carl Everett .30 .10
❑ 261 Wes Helms .30 .10
❑ 262 Kyle Lohse .30 .10
❑ 263 Jason Phillips .30 .10
❑ 264 Jake Peavy .30 .10
❑ 265 Orlando Hernandez .30 .10
❑ 266 Keith Foulke .30 .10
❑ 267 Brad Wilkerson .30 .10
❑ 268 Corey Koskie .30 .10
❑ 269 Josh Hall .30 .10
❑ 270 Bobby Higginson .30 .10
❑ 271 Andres Galarraga .30 .10
❑ 272 Alfonso Soriano .30 .10
❑ 273 Carlos Rivera .30 .10
❑ 274 Steve Trachsel .30 .10
❑ 275 David Bell .30 .10
❑ 276 Endy Chavez .30 .10
❑ 277 Jay Payton .30 .10
❑ 278 Mark Mulder .30 .10
❑ 279 Terrence Long .30 .10
❑ 280 A.J. Burnett .30 .10
❑ 281 Pokey Reese .30 .10
❑ 282 Phil Nevin .30 .10
❑ 283 Jose Contreras .30 .10
❑ 284 Jim Thome .50 .20
❑ 285 Pat Burrell .30 .10
❑ 286 Luis Castillo .30 .10
❑ 287 Juan Uribe .30 .10
❑ 288 Raul Ibanez .30 .10
❑ 289 Sidney Ponson .30 .10
❑ 290 Scott Hatteberg .30 .10
❑ 291 Jack Wilson .30 .10
❑ 292 Reggie Sanders .30 .10
❑ 293 Brian Giles .30 .10
❑ 294 Craig Biggio .50 .20
❑ 295 Kazuhisa Ishii .30 .10
❑ 296 Jim Edmonds .30 .10
❑ 297 Trevor Hoffman .30 .10
❑ 298 Ray Durham .30 .10
❑ 299 Mike Lieberthal .30 .10
❑ 300 Tim Worrell .30 .10
❑ 301 Chris George .30 .10
❑ 302 Jamie Moyer .30 .10
❑ 303 Mike Cameron .30 .10
❑ 304 Matt Kinney .30 .10
❑ 305 Aubrey Huff .30 .10
❑ 306 Brian Lawrence .30 .10
❑ 307 Carlos Guillen .30 .10
❑ 308 J.D. Drew .30 .10
❑ 309 Paul Lo Duca .30 .10
❑ 310 Tim Salmon .50 .20
❑ 311 Jason Schmidt .30 .10
❑ 312 A.J. Pierzynski .30 .10
❑ 313 Lance Carter .30 .10
❑ 314 Julio Lugo .30 .10
❑ 315 Johan Santana .75 .30
❑ 316 Laynce Nix .30 .10
❑ 317 John Olerud .30 .10
❑ 318 Robb Quinlan .30 .10
❑ 319 Scott Spiezio .30 .10
❑ 320 Tony Clark .30 .10
❑ 321 Jose Vidro .30 .10
❑ 322 Shea Hillenbrand .30 .10
❑ 323 Doug Glanville .30 .10
❑ 324 Orlando Palmeiro .30 .10
❑ 325 Juan Gonzalez .30 .10
❑ 326 Jason Giambi .30 .10
❑ 327 Junior Spivey .30 .10
❑ 328 Tom Glavine .50 .20
❑ 329 Reed Johnson .30 .10
❑ 330 David Eckstein .30 .10
❑ 331 Damian Jackson .30 .10
❑ 332 Orlando Hudson .30 .10
❑ 333 Barry Zito .30 .10
❑ 334 Robert Fick .30 .10
❑ 335 Aaron Boone .30 .10
❑ 336 Rafael Palmeiro .50 .20
❑ 337 Bobby Kielty .30 .10
❑ 338 Tony Batista .30 .10
❑ 339 Ryan Dempster .30 .10
❑ 340 Derek Lowe .30 .10
❑ 341 Alex Cintron .30 .10
❑ 342 Jermaine Dye .30 .10
❑ 343 John Burkett .30 .10
❑ 344 Javy Lopez .30 .10
❑ 345 Eric Karros .30 .10
❑ 346 Corey Patterson .30 .10
❑ 347 Josh Phelps .30 .10
❑ 348 Ryan Klesko .30 .10
❑ 349 Craig Wilson .30 .10
❑ 350 Brian Roberts .30 .10
❑ 351 Roberto Alomar .50 .20
❑ 352 Frank Thomas .75 .30
❑ 353 Gary Sheffield .30 .10
❑ 354 Alex Gonzalez .30 .10
❑ 355 Jose Cruz Jr. .30 .10
❑ 356 Jerome Williams .30 .10
❑ 357 Mark Kotsay .30 .10
❑ 358 Chris Reitsma .30 .10
❑ 359 Carlos Lee .30 .10
❑ 360 Todd Helton .50 .20
❑ 361 Gil Meche .30 .10
❑ 362 Ryan Franklin .30 .10
❑ 363 Josh Bard .30 .10
❑ 364 Juan Pierre .30 .10
❑ 365 Barry Larkin .50 .20
❑ 366 Edgar Renteria .30 .10
❑ 367 Alex Sanchez .30 .10
❑ 368 Jeff Bagwell .50 .20
❑ 369 Ben Broussard .30 .10
❑ 370 Chan-Ho Park .30 .10
❑ 371 Darrell May .30 .10
❑ 372 Roy Oswalt .30 .10
❑ 373 Craig Monroe .30 .10
❑ 374 Fred McGriff .50 .20
❑ 375 Bengie Molina .30 .10
❑ 376 Aaron Guiel .30 .10
❑ 377 Jeriome Robertson .30 .10
❑ 378 Kenny Rogers .30 .10
❑ 379 Colby Lewis .30 .10
❑ 380 Jeromy Burnitz .30 .10
❑ 381 Orlando Cabrera .30 .10
❑ 382 Joe Randa .30 .10
❑ 383 Miguel Batista .30 .10
❑ 384 Brad Radke .30 .10
❑ 385 Jeremy Giambi .30 .10
❑ 386 Vladimir Guerrero .75 .30
❑ 387 Melvin Mora .30 .10
❑ 388 Royce Clayton .30 .10
❑ 389 Danny Garcia .30 .10
❑ 390 Manny Ramirez .50 .20
❑ 391 Dave McCarty .30 .10
❑ 392 Mark Grudzielanek .30 .10
❑ 393 Mike Piazza 1.25 .50
❑ 394 Jorge Posada .50 .20
❑ 395 Tim Hudson .30 .10
❑ 396 Placido Polanco .30 .10
❑ 397 Mark Loretta .30 .10
❑ 398 Jesse Foppert .30 .10
❑ 399 Albert Pujols 1.50 .60
❑ 400 Jeremi Gonzalez .30 .10
❑ 401 Paul Bako SP 1.00 .40
❑ 402 Luis Matos SP 1.00 .40
❑ 403 Johnny Damon SP 1.50 .60
❑ 404 Kerry Wood SP 1.00 .40
❑ 405 Joe Crede SP 1.00 .40
❑ 406 Jason Davis SP 1.00 .40
❑ 407 Larry Walker SP 1.00 .40
❑ 408 Ivan Rodriguez SP 1.50 .60
❑ 409 Nick Johnson SP 1.00 .40
❑ 410 Jose Lima SP 1.00 .40
❑ 411 Brian Jordan SP 1.00 .40
❑ 412 Eddie Guardado SP 1.00 .40
❑ 413 Ron Calloway SP 1.00 .40
❑ 414 Aaron Heilman SP 1.00 .40
❑ 415 Eric Chavez SP 1.00 .40
❑ 416 Randy Wolf SP 1.00 .40
❑ 417 Jason Bay SP 1.00 .40
❑ 418 Edgardo Alfonzo SP 1.00 .40
❑ 419 Kazuhiro Sasaki SP 1.00 .40
❑ 420 Eduardo Perez SP 1.00 .40
❑ 421 Carl Crawford SP 1.00 .40
❑ 422 Troy Glaus SP 1.00 .40
❑ 423 Joaquin Benoit SP 1.00 .40
❑ 424 Russ Ortiz SP 1.00 .40
❑ 425 Larry Bigbie SP 1.00 .40
❑ 426 Todd Walker SP 1.00 .40
❑ 427 Kris Benson SP 1.00 .40
❑ 428 Sandy Alomar Jr. SP 1.00 .40
❑ 429 Jody Gerut SP 1.00 .40
❑ 430 Rene Reyes SP 1.00 .40
❑ 431 Mike Lowell SP 1.00 .40
❑ 432 Jeff Kent SP 1.00 .40
❑ 433 Mike MacDougal SP 1.00 .40
❑ 434 Dave Roberts SP 1.00 .40
❑ 435 Torii Hunter SP 1.00 .40
❑ 436 Tomo Ohka SP 1.00 .40
❑ 437 Jeremy Griffiths SP 1.00 .40
❑ 438 Miguel Tejada SP 1.00 .40
❑ 439 Vicente Padilla SP 1.00 .40

Card		
❑ 440 Bobby Hill SP	1.00	.40
❑ 441 Rich Aurilia SP	1.00	.40
❑ 442 Shigetoshi Hasegawa SP	1.00	.40
❑ 443 So Taguchi SP	1.00	.40
❑ 444 Damian Rolls SP	1.00	.40
❑ 445 Roy Halladay SP	1.00	.40
❑ 446 Rocco Baldelli SO SP	1.00	.40
❑ 447 Dontrelle Willis SO SP	1.50	.60
❑ 448 Mark Prior SO SP	1.50	.60
❑ 449 Jason Lane SO SP	1.00	.40
❑ 450 Angel Berroa SO SP	1.00	.40
❑ 451 Jose Reyes SO SP	1.00	.40
❑ 452 Ryan Wagner SO SP	1.00	.40
❑ 453 Marlon Byrd SO SP	1.00	.40
❑ 454 Hee Seop Choi SO SP	1.00	.40
❑ 455 Brandon Webb SO SP	1.00	.40
❑ 456 Bo Hart SO SP	1.00	.40
❑ 457 Hank Blalock SO SP	1.00	.40
❑ 458 Mark Teixeira SO SP	1.50	.60
❑ 459 Hideki Matsui SO SP	4.00	1.50
❑ 460 Scott Podsednik SO SP	1.00	.40
❑ 461 Miguel Cabrera SO SP	1.50	.60
❑ 462 Josh Beckett AW SP	1.00	.40
❑ 463 Mariano Rivera AW SP	2.50	1.00
❑ 464 Ivan Rodriguez AW SP	1.50	.60
❑ 465 Alex Rodriguez AW SP	4.00	1.50
❑ 466 Albert Pujols AW SP	5.00	2.00
❑ 467 Roy Halladay AW SP	1.00	.40
❑ 468 Eric Gagne AW SP	1.00	.40
❑ 469 Angel Berroa AW SP	1.00	.40
❑ 470 Dontrelle Willis AW SP	1.50	.60
❑ 471 Boot/Gregorio/Fischer SP	1.00	.40
❑ 472 Kata/Olson/Hammock SP	1.00	.40
❑ 473 Hessman/Waters/Aquino SP	1.00	.40
❑ 474 Mendez/Cabrera/Guthrie SP	1.00	.40
❑ 475 Almonte/Seibel/Sanchez SP	1.00	.40
❑ 476 Wellemeyer/Leicester/Mitre SP	1.00	.40
❑ 477 Stewart/Cotts/Miles SP	1.00	.40
❑ 478 Sledge/Hall/Claussen SP	1.00	.40
❑ 479 Cruceta/Stanford/Betan SP	1.00	.40
❑ 480 Lopez/Atkins/Barmes SP	1.50	.60
❑ 481 Ledez/Logan/Bonderman SP	1.50	.60
❑ 482 Willingham/Hoop/Roberts SP	1.00	.40
❑ 483 Porter/Gallo/Matranga SP	1.00	.40
❑ 484 DeJesus/Gilfillan/Gobble SP	1.00	.40
❑ 485 Hill/Gonzalez/Brown SP	1.00	.40
❑ 486 Weeks/Liriano/Oberm SP	1.50	.60
❑ 487 Prieto/Ryan/Ford SP	1.00	.40
❑ 488 Manon/Ayala/Song SP	1.00	.40
❑ 489 Duncan/Redman/Brazell SP	1.50	.60
❑ 490 Wang/M.Hern/M.Gonz SP	5.00	2.00
❑ 491 Harden/Neu/Geary SP	1.50	.60
❑ 492 Markwell/Gaudin/Sanders SP	1.00	.40
❑ 493 Kemp/Nakamura/Carrasco SP	1.00	.40
❑ 494 Greene/Ojeda/Castro SP	2.50	1.00
❑ 495 Lowry/Linden/Correia SP	1.50	.60
❑ 496 Looper/Sweeney/R.John SP	1.00	.40
❑ 497 J.Gall RC/Haren/Ohme SP	2.50	1.00
❑ 498 Young/Waechter/Diaz SP	2.50	1.00
❑ 499 Laird/Garcia/Nivar SP	1.00	.40
❑ 500 Rios/Quiroz/Rosario SP	1.50	.60

2005 Fleer Tradition

Card		
❑ COMPLETE SET (350)	150.00	75.00
❑ COMP.SET w/o SP's (300)	40.00	15.00
❑ COMMON CARD (1-300)	.30	.10
❑ COMMON CARD (301-330)	5.00	2.00
❑ COMMON CARD (331-350)	1.00	.40
❑ 301-350 STATED ODDS 1:2 H, 1:4 R		
❑ 1 Johan/Schil/Westbrook SL	.50	.20
❑ 2 Sheets/Peavy/Randy SL	.50	.20
❑ 3 Johan/Colon/Schilling SL	.30	.10
❑ 4 Pavanvo/Oswalt/Clemens SL	.75	.30
❑ 5 Johan/Pedro/Schilling SL	.30	.10
❑ 6 Schmidt/Randy/Sheets SL	.50	.20
❑ 7 Mora/Guerrero/Ichiro SL	.75	.30
❑ 8 Beltre/Helton/Loretta SL	.30	.10
❑ 9 Manny/Konerko/Ortiz SL	.50	.20
❑ 10 Pujols/Beltre/Dunn SL	.75	.30
❑ 11 Ortiz/Manny/Tejada SL	.50	.20
❑ 12 Pujols/Castilla/Rolen SL	.50	.20
❑ 13 Jason Bay	.30	.10
❑ 14 Greg Maddux	1.25	.50
❑ 15 Melvin Mora	.30	.10
❑ 16 Matt Stairs	.30	.10
❑ 17 Scott Podsednik	.30	.10
❑ 18 Bartolo Colon	.30	.10
❑ 19 Roger Clemens	1.25	.50
❑ 20 Eric Hinske	.30	.10
❑ 21 Johnny Estrada	.30	.10
❑ 22 Brett Tomko	.30	.10
❑ 23 John Buck	.30	.10
❑ 24 Nomar Garciaparra	.75	.30
❑ 25 Milton Bradley	.30	.10
❑ 26 Craig Biggio	.50	.20
❑ 27 Kyle Denney	.30	.10
❑ 28 Brad Penny	.30	.10
❑ 29 Todd Helton	.50	.20
❑ 30 Luis Gonzalez	.30	.10
❑ 31 Bill Hall	.30	.10
❑ 32 Ruben Sierra	.30	.10
❑ 33 Zack Greinke	.30	.10
❑ 34 Sandy Alomar Jr.	.30	.10
❑ 35 Jason Giambi	.30	.10
❑ 36 Ben Sheets	.30	.10
❑ 37 Edgardo Alfonzo	.30	.10
❑ 38 Kenny Rogers	.30	.10
❑ 39 Coco Crisp	.30	.10
❑ 40 Randy Choate	.30	.10
❑ 41 Braden Looper	.30	.10
❑ 42 Adam Dunn	.30	.10
❑ 43 Adam Eaton	.30	.10
❑ 44 Luis Castillo	.30	.10
❑ 45 Casey Fossum	.30	.10
❑ 46 Mike Piazza	.75	.30
❑ 47 Juan Pierre	.30	.10
❑ 48 Doug Davis	.30	.10
❑ 49 Manny Ramirez	.50	.20
❑ 50 Travis Hafner	.30	.10
❑ 51 Jack Wilson	.30	.10
❑ 52 Mike Maroth	.30	.10
❑ 53 Ken Harvey	.30	.10
❑ 54 Brooks Kieschnick	.30	.10
❑ 55 Brad Fullmer	.30	.10
❑ 56 Octavio Dotel	.30	.10
❑ 57 Mike Matheny	.30	.10
❑ 58 Andruw Jones	.50	.20
❑ 59 Alfonso Soriano	.30	.10
❑ 60 Royce Clayton	.30	.10
❑ 61 Jon Garland	.30	.10
❑ 62 John Mabry	.30	.10
❑ 63 Rafael Palmeiro	.50	.20
❑ 64 Garett Atkins	.30	.10
❑ 65 Brian Meadows	.30	.10
❑ 66 Tony Armas Jr.	.30	.10
❑ 67 Toby Hall	.30	.10
❑ 68 Carlos Baerga	.30	.10
❑ 69 Barry Larkin	.50	.20
❑ 70 Jody Gerut	.30	.10
❑ 71 Brent Mayne	.30	.10
❑ 72 Shigetoshi Hasegawa	.30	.10
❑ 73 Jose Cruz Jr.	.30	.10
❑ 74 Dan Wilson	.30	.10
❑ 75 Sidney Ponson	.30	.10
❑ 76 Jason Jennings	.30	.10
❑ 77 A.J. Burnett	.30	.10
❑ 78 Tony Batista	.30	.10
❑ 79 Kris Benson	.30	.10
❑ 80 Sean Burroughs	.30	.10
❑ 81 Eric Young	.30	.10
❑ 82 Casey Kotchman	.30	.10
❑ 83 Derrek Lee	.50	.20
❑ 84 Mariano Rivera	.75	.30
❑ 85 Julio Franco	.30	.10
❑ 86 Corey Patterson	.30	.10
❑ 87 Carlos Beltran	.30	.10
❑ 88 Trevor Hoffman	.30	.10
❑ 89 Danny Garcia	.30	.10
❑ 90 Marcos Scutaro	.30	.10
❑ 91 Marquis Grissom	.30	.10
❑ 92 Aubrey Huff	.30	.10
❑ 93 Tony Womack	.30	.10
❑ 94 Placido Polanco	.30	.10
❑ 95 Bengie Molina	.30	.10
❑ 96 Roger Cedeno	.30	.10
❑ 97 Geoff Jenkins	.30	.10
❑ 98 Kip Wells	.30	.10
❑ 99 Derek Jeter	1.50	.60
❑ 100 Omar Infante	.30	.10
❑ 101 Phil Nevin	.30	.10
❑ 102 Edgar Renteria	.30	.10
❑ 103 B.J. Surhoff	.30	.10
❑ 104 David DeJesus	.30	.10
❑ 105 Raul Ibanez	.30	.10
❑ 106 Hank Blalock	.30	.10
❑ 107 Shawn Estes	.30	.10
❑ 108 Wily Mo Pena	.30	.10
❑ 109 Shawn Green	.30	.10
❑ 110 David Wright	2.00	.75
❑ 111 Kenny Lofton	.30	.10
❑ 112 Matt Clement	.30	.10
❑ 113 Cesar Izturis	.30	.10
❑ 114 John Lackey	.30	.10
❑ 115 Torii Hunter	.30	.10
❑ 116 Charles Johnson	.30	.10
❑ 117 Ray Durham	.30	.10
❑ 118 Luke Hudson	.30	.10
❑ 119 Jeremy Bonderman	.30	.10
❑ 120 Sean Casey	.30	.10
❑ 121 Johnny Damon	.50	.20
❑ 122 Eric Milton	.30	.10
❑ 123 Shea Hillenbrand	.30	.10
❑ 124 Johan Santana	.75	.30
❑ 125 Jim Edmonds	.30	.10
❑ 126 Javier Vazquez	.30	.10
❑ 127 Jon Adkins	.30	.10
❑ 128 Mike Lowell	.30	.10
❑ 129 Khalil Greene	.50	.20
❑ 130 Quinton McCracken	.30	.10
❑ 131 Edgar Martinez	.50	.20
❑ 132 Matt Lawton	.30	.10
❑ 133 Jeff Weaver	.30	.10
❑ 134 Marlon Byrd	.30	.10
❑ 135 John Smoltz	.50	.20
❑ 136 Grady Sizemore	.50	.20
❑ 137 Brian Roberts	.30	.10
❑ 138 Dee Brown	.30	.10
❑ 139 Joel Pineiro	.30	.10
❑ 140 David Dellucci	.30	.10
❑ 141 Bobby Higginson	.30	.10
❑ 142 Ryan Madson	.30	.10
❑ 143 Scott Hatteberg	.30	.10
❑ 144 Greg Zaun	.30	.10
❑ 145 Brian Jordan	.30	.10
❑ 146 Jason Isringhausen	.30	.10
❑ 147 Vinnie Chulk	.30	.10
❑ 148 Al Leiter	.30	.10
❑ 149 Pedro Martinez	.50	.20
❑ 150 Carlos Guillen	.30	.10
❑ 151 Randy Wolf	.30	.10
❑ 152 Vernon Wells	.30	.10
❑ 153 Barry Zito	.30	.10
❑ 154 Pedro Feliz	.30	.10
❑ 155 Omar Vizquel	.50	.20
❑ 156 Chone Figgins	.30	.10
❑ 157 David Ortiz	.50	.20
❑ 158 Sunny Kim	.30	.10
❑ 159 Adam Kennedy	.30	.10
❑ 160 Carlos Lee	.30	.10
❑ 161 Rick Ankiel	.30	.10
❑ 162 Roy Oswalt	.30	.10
❑ 163 Armando Benitez	.30	.10
❑ 164 Erubiel Durazo	.30	.10
❑ 165 Adam Hyzdu	.30	.10
❑ 166 Esteban Yan	.30	.10
❑ 167 Victor Santos	.30	.10
❑ 168 Kevin Millwood	.30	.10
❑ 169 Andy Pettitte	.50	.20
❑ 170 Mike Cameron	.30	.10
❑ 171 Scott Rolen	.50	.20

❑ 172	Trot Nixon	.30	.10
❑ 173	Eric Munson	.30	.10
❑ 174	Roy Halladay	.30	.10
❑ 175	Juan Encarnacion	.30	.10
❑ 176	Eric Chavez	.30	.10
❑ 177	Terrmel Sledge	.30	.10
❑ 178	Jason Schmidt	.30	.10
❑ 179	Endy Chavez	.30	.10
❑ 180	Carlos Zambrano	.30	.10
❑ 181	Carlos Delgado	.30	.10
❑ 182	Dewon Brazelton	.30	.10
❑ 183	J.D. Drew	.30	.10
❑ 184	Orlando Cabrera	.30	.10
❑ 185	Craig Wilson	.30	.10
❑ 186	Chin-Hui Tsao	.30	.10
❑ 187	Jolbert Cabrera	.30	.10
❑ 188	Rod Barajas	.30	.10
❑ 189	Craig Monroe	.30	.10
❑ 190	Dave Berg	.30	.10
❑ 191	Carlos Silva	.30	.10
❑ 192	Eric Gagne	.30	.10
❑ 193	Marcus Giles	.30	.10
❑ 194	Nick Johnson	.30	.10
❑ 195	Kelvim Escobar	.30	.10
❑ 196	Wade Miller	.30	.10
❑ 197	David Bell	.30	.10
❑ 198	Rondell White	.30	.10
❑ 199	Brian Giles	.30	.10
❑ 200	Jeromy Burnitz	.30	.10
❑ 201	Carl Pavano	.30	.10
❑ 202	Alex Rios	.30	.10
❑ 203	Ryan Freel	.30	.10
❑ 204	R.A. Dickey	.30	.10
❑ 205	Miguel Cairo	.30	.10
❑ 206	Kerry Wood	.30	.10
❑ 207	C.C. Sabathia	.30	.10
❑ 208	Jaime Cerda	.30	.10
❑ 209	Jerome Williams	.30	.10
❑ 210	Ryan Wagner	.30	.10
❑ 211	Javy Lopez	.30	.10
❑ 212	Tike Redman	.30	.10
❑ 213	Richie Sexson	.30	.10
❑ 214	Shannon Stewart	.30	.10
❑ 215	Ben Davis	.30	.10
❑ 216	Jeff Bagwell	.50	.20
❑ 217	David Wells	.30	.10
❑ 218	Justin Leone	.30	.10
❑ 219	Brad Radke	.30	.10
❑ 220	Ramon Santiago	.30	.10
❑ 221	Richard Hidalgo	.30	.10
❑ 222	Aaron Miles	.30	.10
❑ 223	Mark Loretta	.30	.10
❑ 224	Aaron Boone	.30	.10
❑ 225	Steve Trachsel	.30	.10
❑ 226	Geoff Blum	.30	.10
❑ 227	Shingo Takatsu	.30	.10
❑ 228	Kevin Youkilis	.30	.10
❑ 229	Laynce Nix	.30	.10
❑ 230	Daniel Cabrera	.30	.10
❑ 231	Kyle Lohse	.30	.10
❑ 232	Todd Pratt	.30	.10
❑ 233	Reed Johnson	.30	.10
❑ 234	Lance Berkman	.30	.10
❑ 235	Hideki Matsui	1.25	.50
❑ 236	Randy Winn	.30	.10
❑ 237	Joe Randa	.30	.10
❑ 238	Bob Howry	.30	.10
❑ 239	Jason LaRue	.30	.10
❑ 240	Jose Valentin	.30	.10
❑ 241	Livan Hernandez	.30	.10
❑ 242	Jamie Moyer	.30	.10
❑ 243	Garret Anderson	.30	.10
❑ 244	Brad Ausmus	.30	.10
❑ 245	Russell Branyan	.30	.10
❑ 246	Paul Wilson	.30	.10
❑ 247	Tim Wakefield	.30	.10
❑ 248	Roberto Alomar	.50	.20
❑ 249	Kazuhisa Ishii	.30	.10
❑ 250	Tino Martinez	.50	.20
❑ 251	Tomo Ohka	.30	.10
❑ 252	Mark Redman	.30	.10
❑ 253	Paul Byrd	.30	.10
❑ 254	Greg Aquino	.30	.10
❑ 255	Adrian Beltre	.30	.10
❑ 256	Ricky Ledee	.30	.10
❑ 257	Josh Fogg	.30	.10
❑ 258	Derek Lowe	.30	.10
❑ 259	Lew Ford	.30	.10
❑ 260	Bobby Crosby	.30	.10
❑ 261	Jim Thome	.50	.20
❑ 262	Jaret Wright	.30	.10
❑ 263	Chin-Feng Chen	.30	.10
❑ 264	Troy Glaus	.30	.10
❑ 265	Jorge Sosa	.30	.10
❑ 266	Mike Lamb	.30	.10
❑ 267	Russ Ortiz	.30	.10
❑ 268	Reggie Sanders	.30	.10
❑ 269	Orlando Hudson	.30	.10
❑ 270	Rodrigo Lopez	.30	.10
❑ 271	Jose Vidro	.30	.10
❑ 272	Akinori Otsuka	.30	.10
❑ 273	Victor Martinez	.30	.10
❑ 274	Carl Crawford	.30	.10
❑ 275	Roberto Novoa	.30	.10
❑ 276	Brian Lawrence	.30	.10
❑ 277	Angel Berroa	.30	.10
❑ 278	Josh Beckett	.30	.10
❑ 279	Lyle Overbay	.30	.10
❑ 280	Dustin Hermanson	.30	.10
❑ 281	Jeff Conine	.30	.10
❑ 282	Mark Prior	.50	.20
❑ 283	Kevin Brown	.30	.10
❑ 284	Magglio Ordonez	.30	.10
❑ 285	Dontrelle Willis	.30	.10
❑ 286	Dallas McPherson	.30	.10
❑ 287	Rafael Furcal	.30	.10
❑ 288	Ty Wigginton	.30	.10
❑ 289	Moises Alou	.30	.10
❑ 290	A.J. Pierzynski	.30	.10
❑ 291	Todd Walker	.30	.10
❑ 292	Hideo Nomo	.75	.30
❑ 293	Larry Walker	.50	.20
❑ 294	Choo Freeman	.30	.10
❑ 295	Eduardo Perez	.30	.10
❑ 296	Miguel Tejada	.30	.10
❑ 297	Corey Koskie	.30	.10
❑ 298	Jermaine Dye	.30	.10
❑ 299	John Riedling	.30	.10
❑ 300	John Olerud	.30	.10
❑ 301	Bittner/Woods/Jenks TP	5.00	2.00
❑ 302	Kroeger/Daigle/Medders TP	5.00	2.00
❑ 303	K.Johnson/Thom/Meyer TP	5.00	2.00
❑ 304	E.Rod/Hannam/Maine TP	5.00	2.00
❑ 305	A.Mart/Gamble/Dinardo TP	5.00	2.00
❑ 306	Cedeno/Vasquez/Pinto TP	5.00	2.00
❑ 307	Munoz/Wing/Diaz TP	5.00	2.00
❑ 308	Bergolla/Olmedo/E.Enc TP	5.00	2.00
❑ 309	Gomez/Ochoa/Tadano TP	5.00	2.00
❑ 310	Miller/Baker/Holliday TP	6.00	2.50
❑ 311	Larris/Grander/Raburn TP	5.00	2.00
❑ 312	Wilson/Kensing/Cave TP	5.00	2.00
❑ 313	H.Gim/Taveras/Buch TP	5.00	2.00
❑ 314	Gotay/Bass/Blanco TP	5.00	2.00
❑ 315	Hanrahan/Aybar/Braz TP	5.00	2.00
❑ 316	Krynzel/Hendr/Hart TP	5.00	2.00
❑ 317	Miller/Kubel/Durbin TP	5.00	2.00
❑ 318	Izturis/Cordero/Watson TP	5.00	2.00
❑ 319	Diaz/Baldiris/Lydon TP	5.00	2.00
❑ 320	Sierra/Navarro/Henn TP	5.00	2.00
❑ 321	Swish/Blant/D.Johnson TP	5.00	2.00
❑ 322	Howard/Floyd/Bucktrot TP	5.00	2.00
❑ 323	Doumit/Burnett/Bradley TP	5.00	2.00
❑ 324	Germ/Tucker/Guzman TP	5.00	2.00
❑ 325	Aardsma/Knoedler/Simon TP	5.00	2.00
❑ 326	Lopez/Rivera/Baek TP	5.00	2.00
❑ 327	Molina/Rust/Wainwright TP	5.00	2.00
❑ 328	Cantu/Kazmir/Upton TP	5.00	2.00
❑ 329	Gonzalez/Nivar/Bourg TP	5.00	2.00
❑ 330	Adams/McGow/Chacin TP	5.00	2.00
❑ 331	Alfonso Soriano AW	1.00	.40
❑ 332	Albert Pujols AW	3.00	1.25
❑ 333	David Ortiz AW	1.50	.60
❑ 334	Manny Ramirez AW	1.50	.60
❑ 335	Jason Bay AW	1.00	.40
❑ 336	Bobby Crosby AW	1.00	.40
❑ 337	Roger Clemens AW	2.50	1.00
❑ 338	Johan Santana AW	1.50	.60
❑ 339	Jim Thome AW	1.50	.60
❑ 340	Vladimir Guerrero AW	1.50	.60
❑ 341	David Ortiz PS	1.50	.60
❑ 342	Alex Rodriguez PS	2.50	1.00
❑ 343	Albert Pujols PS	3.00	1.25
❑ 344	Carlos Beltran PS	1.00	.40
❑ 345	Johnny Damon PS	1.50	.60
❑ 346	Scott Rolen PS	1.50	.60
❑ 347	Larry Walker PS	1.50	.60
❑ 348	Curt Schilling PS	1.50	.60
❑ 349	Pedro Martinez PS	1.50	.60
❑ 350	David Ortiz PS	1.50	.60

2006 Fleer Tradition

❑	COMPLETE SET (200)	30.00	12.50
❑	COMMON CARD (1-200)	.30	.12
❑	COMMON RC (1-200)	.50	.20
❑	OVERALL PLATE ODDS 1:288 HOBBY		
❑	PLATE PRINT RUN 1 SET PER COLOR		
❑	BLACK-CYAN-MAGENTA-YELLOW ISSUED		
❑	NO PLATE PRICING DUE TO SCARCITY		
❑	EXQUISITE EXCH ODDS 1:864 HOBBY		
❑	EXQUISITE EXCH DEADLINE 07/27/07		
❑ 1	Andruw Jones	.50	.20
❑ 2	Chipper Jones	.75	.30
❑ 3	John Smoltz	.50	.20
❑ 4	Tim Hudson	.30	.12
❑ 5	Joey Devine RC	.50	.20
❑ 6	Chuck James (RC)	.75	.30
❑ 7	Alay Soler RC	.50	.20
❑ 8	Conor Jackson (RC)	.75	.30
❑ 9	Luis Gonzalez	.30	.12
❑ 10	Brandon Webb	.30	.12
❑ 11	Chad Tracy	.30	.12
❑ 12	Orlando Hudson	.30	.12
❑ 13	Shawn Green	.30	.12
❑ 14	Vladimir Guerrero	.75	.30
❑ 15	Bartolo Colon	.30	.12
❑ 16	Chone Figgins	.30	.12
❑ 17	Garret Anderson	.30	.12
❑ 18	Francisco Rodriguez	.30	.12
❑ 19	Casey Kotchman	.30	.12
❑ 20	Lance Berkman	.30	.12
❑ 21	Craig Biggio	.50	.20
❑ 22	Andy Pettitte	.50	.20
❑ 23	Morgan Ensberg	.30	.12
❑ 24	Brad Lidge	.30	.12
❑ 25	Jered Weaver (RC)	2.50	1.00
❑ 26	Roy Oswalt	.30	.12
❑ 27	Eric Chavez	.30	.12
❑ 28	Rich Harden	.30	.12
❑ 29	Cole Hamels (RC)	1.25	.50
❑ 30	Huston Street	.30	.12
❑ 31	Bobby Crosby	.30	.12
❑ 32	Nick Swisher	.30	.12
❑ 33	Vernon Wells	.30	.12
❑ 34	Roy Halladay	.30	.12
❑ 35	A.J. Burnett	.30	.12
❑ 36	Troy Glaus	.30	.12
❑ 37	B.J. Ryan	.30	.12
❑ 38	Bengie Molina	.30	.12
❑ 39	Alex Rios	.30	.12
❑ 40	Prince Fielder (RC)	2.00	.75
❑ 41	Jose Capellan (RC)	.50	.20
❑ 42	Rickie Weeks	.30	.12
❑ 43	Ben Sheets	.30	.12
❑ 44	Carlos Lee	.30	.12
❑ 45	J.J. Hardy	.30	.12
❑ 46	Albert Pujols	1.50	.60
❑ 47	Skip Schumaker (RC)	.50	.20
❑ 48	Adam Wainwright (RC)	.50	.20
❑ 49	Jim Edmonds	.50	.20
❑ 50	Scott Rolen	.50	.20

❑ 51 Chris Carpenter .30 .12
❑ 52 David Eckstein .30 .12
❑ 53 Derrek Lee .30 .12
❑ 54 Jon Lester RC 1.50 .60
❑ 55 Mark Prior .50 .20
❑ 56 Aramis Ramirez .30 .12
❑ 57 Juan Pierre .30 .12
❑ 58 Greg Maddux 1.25 .50
❑ 59 Michael Barrett .30 .12
❑ 60 Carl Crawford .30 .12
❑ 61 Scott Kazmir .50 .20
❑ 62 Jorge Cantu .30 .12
❑ 63 Jonny Gomes .30 .12
❑ 64 Julio Lugo .30 .12
❑ 65 Aubrey Huff .30 .12
❑ 66 Jeff Kent .30 .12
❑ 67 Nomar Garciaparra .75 .30
❑ 68 Rafael Furcal .30 .12
❑ 69 Tim Hamulack (RC) .50 .20
❑ 70 Chad Billingsley (RC) .75 .30
❑ 71 Hong-Chih Kuo (RC) 1.25 .50
❑ 72 J.D. Drew .30 .12
❑ 73 Moises Alou .30 .12
❑ 74 Randy Winn .30 .12
❑ 75 Jason Schmidt .30 .12
❑ 76 Jeremy Accardo RC .50 .20
❑ 77 Matt Cain (RC) .75 .30
❑ 78 Joel Zumaya (RC) 1.25 .50
❑ 79 Travis Hafner .30 .12
❑ 80 Victor Martinez .30 .12
❑ 81 Grady Sizemore .50 .20
❑ 82 C.C. Sabathia .30 .12
❑ 83 Jhonny Peralta .30 .12
❑ 84 Jason Michaels .30 .12
❑ 85 Jeremy Sowers (RC) .50 .20
❑ 86 Ichiro Suzuki 1.25 .50
❑ 87 Richie Sexson .30 .12
❑ 88 Adrian Beltre .30 .12
❑ 89 Felix Hernandez .50 .20
❑ 90 Kenji Johjima RC 2.50 1.00
❑ 91 Jeff Harris RC .50 .20
❑ 92 Taylor Buchholz (RC) .75 .30
❑ 93 Miguel Cabrera .50 .20
❑ 94 Dontrelle Willis .30 .12
❑ 95 Jeremy Hermida (RC) .50 .20
❑ 96 Mike Jacobs (RC) .50 .20
❑ 97 Josh Johnson (RC) .75 .30
❑ 98 Hanley Ramirez (RC) 1.25 .50
❑ 99 Josh Willingham (RC) .50 .20
❑ 100 Dan Uggla (RC) 1.25 .50
❑ 101 David Wright 1.25 .50
❑ 102 Jose Reyes .75 .30
❑ 103 Pedro Martinez .50 .20
❑ 104 Carlos Beltran .30 .12
❑ 105 Carlos Delgado .30 .12
❑ 106 Billy Wagner .30 .12
❑ 107 Lastings Milledge (RC) .75 .30
❑ 108 Alfonso Soriano .30 .12
❑ 109 Jose Vidro .30 .12
❑ 110 Livan Hernandez .30 .12
❑ 111 Matt Kemp (RC) .75 .30
❑ 112 Brandon Watson (RC) .50 .20
❑ 113 Ryan Zimmerman (RC) 3.00 1.25
❑ 114 Miguel Tejada .30 .12
❑ 115 Ramon Hernandez .30 .12
❑ 116 Brian Roberts .30 .12
❑ 117 Melvin Mora .30 .12
❑ 118 Erik Bedard .30 .12
❑ 119 Jay Gibbons .30 .12
❑ 120 Aaron Rakers (RC) .50 .20
❑ 121 Jake Peavy .30 .12
❑ 122 Brian Giles .30 .12
❑ 123 Khalil Greene .50 .20
❑ 124 Trevor Hoffman .30 .12
❑ 125 Josh Barfield (RC) .50 .20
❑ 126 Ben Johnson (RC) .50 .20
❑ 127 Ryan Howard 1.25 .50
❑ 128 Bobby Abreu .30 .12
❑ 129 Chase Utley .75 .30
❑ 130 Pat Burrell .30 .12
❑ 131 Jimmy Rollins .30 .12
❑ 132 Brett Myers .30 .12
❑ 133 Mike Thompson RC .50 .20
❑ 134 Jason Bay .30 .12
❑ 135 Oliver Perez .30 .12
❑ 136 Matt Capps (RC) .50 .20
❑ 137 Paul Maholm (RC) .50 .20
❑ 138 Nate McLouth (RC) .50 .20
❑ 139 John Van Benschoten (RC) .50 .20
❑ 140 Mark Teixeira .50 .20
❑ 141 Michael Young .30 .12
❑ 142 Hank Blalock .30 .12
❑ 143 Kevin Millwood .30 .12
❑ 144 Laynce Nix .30 .12
❑ 145 Francisco Cordero .30 .12
❑ 146 Ian Kinsler (RC) .75 .30
❑ 147 David Ortiz .75 .30
❑ 148 Manny Ramirez .50 .20
❑ 149 Jason Varitek .75 .30
❑ 150 Curt Schilling .50 .20
❑ 151 Josh Beckett .30 .12
❑ 152 Coco Crisp .30 .12
❑ 153 Jonathan Papelbon (RC) 2.50 1.00
❑ 154 Ken Griffey Jr. 1.25 .50
❑ 155 Adam Dunn .30 .12
❑ 156 Felipe Lopez .30 .12
❑ 157 Bronson Arroyo .30 .12
❑ 158 Ryan Freel .30 .12
❑ 159 Chris Denorfia (RC) .50 .20
❑ 160 Todd Helton .50 .20
❑ 161 Garrett Atkins .30 .12
❑ 162 Matt Holliday .75 .30
❑ 163 Clint Barmes .30 .12
❑ 164 Kendry Morales (RC) 1.25 .50
❑ 165 Ryan Shealy (RC) .50 .20
❑ 166 Josh Wilson (RC) .50 .20
❑ 167 Reggie Sanders .30 .12
❑ 168 Angel Berroa .30 .12
❑ 169 Mike Sweeney .30 .12
❑ 170 Mark Grudzielanek .30 .12
❑ 171 Jeremy Affeldt .30 .12
❑ 172 Steve Stemle RC .50 .20
❑ 173 Justin Verlander (RC) 2.00 .75
❑ 174 Ivan Rodriguez .50 .20
❑ 175 Chris Shelton .30 .12
❑ 176 Jeremy Bonderman .30 .12
❑ 177 Magglio Ordonez .30 .12
❑ 178 Carlos Guillen .30 .12
❑ 179 Placido Polanco .30 .12
❑ 180 Johan Santana .50 .20
❑ 181 Torii Hunter .30 .12
❑ 182 Joe Nathan .30 .12
❑ 183 Joe Mauer .50 .20
❑ 184 Dave Gassner (RC) .50 .20
❑ 185 Jason Kubel (RC) .50 .20
❑ 186 Francisco Liriano (RC) 2.50 1.00
❑ 187 Jim Thome .50 .20
❑ 188 Paul Konerko .30 .12
❑ 189 Scott Podsednik .30 .12
❑ 190 Tadahito Iguchi .30 .12
❑ 191 A.J. Pierzynski .30 .12
❑ 192 Jose Contreras .30 .12
❑ 193 Brian Anderson (RC) .50 .20
❑ 194 Hideki Matsui .75 .30
❑ 195 Wil Nieves (RC) .50 .20
❑ 196 Alex Rodriguez 1.25 .50
❑ 197 Gary Sheffield .30 .12
❑ 198 Randy Johnson .75 .30
❑ 199 Johnny Damon .50 .20
❑ 200 Derek Jeter 2.00 .75
❑ NNO Exquisite Redemption 200.00 125.00

1933 Goudey

❑ COMPLETE SET (239) 40000.00 25000.00
❑ COMMON CARD (1-52) 75.00 45.00
❑ COMMON (41/43/53-240) 60.00 35.00
❑ WRAPPER (1-CENT, BAT.) 100.00 75.00
❑ WRAPPER (1-CENT, AD) 175.00 150.00
❑ 1 Benny Bengough RC 1500.00 900.00
❑ 2 Dazzy Vance RC 200.00 125.00
❑ 3 Hugh Critz BAT RC 75.00 40.00
❑ 4 Heinie Schuble RC 75.00 45.00
❑ 5 Babe Herman RC 75.00 40.00
❑ 6 Jimmy Dykes RC 75.00 40.00
❑ 7 Ted Lyons RC 150.00 90.00
❑ 8 Roy Johnson RC 75.00 45.00
❑ 9 Dave Harris RC 75.00 45.00
❑ 10 Glenn Myatt RC 75.00 45.00
❑ 11 Billy Rogell RC 75.00 45.00
❑ 12 George Pipgras RC 75.00 45.00
❑ 13 Fresco Thompson RC 75.00 45.00
❑ 14 Henry Johnson RC 75.00 45.00
❑ 15 Victor Sorrell RC 75.00 45.00
❑ 16 George Blaeholder RC 75.00 45.00
❑ 17 Watson Clark RC 75.00 45.00
❑ 18 Muddy Ruel RC 75.00 45.00
❑ 19 Bill Dickey RC 350.00 200.00
❑ 20 Bill Terry THROW RC 250.00 150.00
❑ 21 Phil Collins RC 75.00 45.00
❑ 22 Pie Traynor RC 250.00 150.00
❑ 23 Kiki Cuyler RC 200.00 125.00
❑ 24 Horace Ford RC 75.00 45.00
❑ 25 Paul Waner RC 200.00 125.00
❑ 26 Bill Cissell RC 75.00 45.00
❑ 27 George Connally RC 75.00 45.00
❑ 28 Dick Bartell RC 75.00 40.00
❑ 29 Jimmie Foxx RC 600.00 350.00
❑ 30 Frank Hogan RC 75.00 45.00
❑ 31 Tony Lazzeri RC 400.00 250.00
❑ 32 Bud Clancy RC 75.00 40.00
❑ 33 Ralph Kress RC 75.00 45.00
❑ 34 Bob O'Farrell RC 75.00 45.00
❑ 35 Al Simmons RC 350.00 200.00
❑ 36 Tommy Thevenow RC 75.00 45.00
❑ 37 Jimmy Wilson RC 75.00 45.00
❑ 38 Fred Brickell RC 75.00 45.00
❑ 39 Mark Koenig RC 75.00 40.00
❑ 40 Taylor Douthit RC 75.00 45.00
❑ 41 Gus Mancuso CATCH 60.00 35.00
❑ 42 Eddie Collins RC 150.00 90.00
❑ 43 Lew Fonseca RC 60.00 35.00
❑ 44 Jim Bottomley RC 150.00 90.00
❑ 45 Larry Benton RC 75.00 45.00
❑ 46 Ethan Allen RC 75.00 40.00
❑ 47 Heinie Manush BAT RC 175.00 100.00
❑ 48 Marty McManus RC 75.00 45.00
❑ 49 Frankie Frisch RC 300.00 175.00
❑ 50 Ed Brandt RC 75.00 45.00
❑ 51 Charlie Grimm RC 75.00 40.00
❑ 52 Andy Cohen RC 75.00 45.00
❑ 53 Babe Ruth RC 8000.00 5000.00
❑ 54 Ray Kremer RC 60.00 35.00
❑ 55 Pat Malone RC 60.00 35.00
❑ 56 Red Ruffing RC 175.00 100.00
❑ 57 Earl Clark RC 60.00 35.00
❑ 58 Lefty O'Doul RC 125.00 75.00
❑ 59 Bing Miller RC 60.00 35.00
❑ 60 Waite Hoyt RC 125.00 75.00
❑ 61 Max Bishop RC 60.00 35.00
❑ 62 Pepper Martin RC 125.00 75.00
❑ 63 Joe Cronin BAT RC 150.00 90.00
❑ 64 Burleigh Grimes RC 250.00 150.00
❑ 65 Milt Gaston RC 60.00 35.00
❑ 66 George Grantham RC 60.00 35.00
❑ 67 Guy Bush RC 60.00 35.00
❑ 68 Horace Lisenbee RC 60.00 35.00
❑ 69 Randy Moore RC 60.00 35.00
❑ 70 Floyd (Pete) Scott RC 60.00 35.00
❑ 71 Robert J. Burke RC 60.00 35.00
❑ 72 Owen Carroll RC 60.00 35.00
❑ 73 Jesse Haines RC 125.00 75.00
❑ 74 Eppa Rixey RC 150.00 90.00
❑ 75 Willie Kamm RC 60.00 35.00
❑ 76 Mickey Cochrane RC 500.00 300.00
❑ 77 Adam Comorosky RC 60.00 35.00
❑ 78 Jack Quinn RC 60.00 35.00
❑ 79 Red Faber RC 125.00 75.00
❑ 80 Clyde Manion RC 60.00 35.00
❑ 81 Sam Jones RC 60.00 35.00
❑ 82 Dib Williams RC 60.00 35.00
❑ 83 Pete Jablonowski RC 60.00 35.00
❑ 84 Glenn Spencer RC 60.00 35.00

❑ 85 Heinie Sand RC 60.00 35.00
❑ 86 Phil Todt RC 60.00 35.00
❑ 87 Frank O'Rourke RC 60.00 35.00
❑ 88 Russell Rollings RC 60.00 35.00
❑ 89 Tris Speaker RET 300.00 175.00
❑ 90 Jess Petty RC 60.00 35.00
❑ 91 Tom Zachary RC 60.00 35.00
❑ 92 Lou Gehrig RC 2500.001500.00
❑ 93 John Welch RC 60.00 35.00
❑ 94 Bill Walker RC 60.00 35.00
❑ 95 Alvin Crowder RC 60.00 35.00
❑ 96 Willis Hudlin RC 60.00 35.00
❑ 97 Joe Morrissey RC 60.00 35.00
❑ 98 Wally Berger RC 75.00 45.00
❑ 99 Tony Cuccinello RC 75.00 45.00
❑ 100 George Uhle RC 60.00 35.00
❑ 101 Richard Coffman RC 60.00 35.00
❑ 102 Travis Jackson RC 150.00 90.00
❑ 103 Earle Combs RC 125.00 75.00
❑ 104 Fred Marberry RC 60.00 35.00
❑ 105 Bernie Friberg RC 60.00 35.00
❑ 106 Napoleon Lajoie SP 25000.00 15000.00
❑ 107 Heinie Manush RC 125.00 75.00
❑ 108 Joe Kuhel RC 60.00 35.00
❑ 109 Joe Cronin RC 300.00 175.00
❑ 110 Goose Goslin RC 250.00 150.00
❑ 111 Monte Weaver RC 60.00 35.00
❑ 112 Fred Schulte RC 60.00 35.00
❑ 113 Oswald Bluege POR RC 60.00 35.00
❑ 114 Luke Sewell FIELD RC 75.00 45.00
❑ 115 Cliff Heathcote RC 60.00 35.00
❑ 116 Eddie Morgan RC 60.00 35.00
❑ 117 Rabbit Maranville RC 125.00 75.00
❑ 118 Val Picinich RC 60.00 35.00
❑ 119 Rogers Hornsby Field RC 600.00 350.00
❑ 120 Carl Reynolds RC 60.00 35.00
❑ 121 Walter Stewart RC 60.00 35.00
❑ 122 Alvin Crowder RC 60.00 35.00
❑ 123 Jack Russell RC 60.00 35.00
❑ 124 Earl Whitehill RC 60.00 35.00
❑ 125 Bill Terry RC 250.00 150.00
❑ 126 Joe Moore BAT RC 60.00 35.00
❑ 127 Mel Ott RC 400.00 250.00
❑ 128 Chuck Klein RC 175.00 100.00
❑ 129 Hal Schumacher PIT RC 60.00 35.00
❑ 130 Fred Fitzsimmons POR RC 60.0035.00
❑ 131 Fred Frankhouse RC 60.00 35.00
❑ 132 Jim Elliott RC 60.00 35.00
❑ 133 Fred Lindstrom RC 125.00 75.00
❑ 134 Sam Rice RC 200.00 125.00
❑ 135 Woody English RC 60.00 35.00
❑ 136 Flint Rhem RC 60.00 35.00
❑ 137 Red Lucas RC 60.00 35.00
❑ 138 Herb Pennock RC 175.00 100.00
❑ 139 Ben Cantwell RC 60.00 35.00
❑ 140 Bump Hadley RC 60.00 35.00
❑ 141 Ray Benge RC 60.00 35.00
❑ 142 Paul Richards RC 75.00 45.00
❑ 143 Glenn Wright RC 60.00 35.00
❑ 144 Babe Ruth Bat DP RC 4000.002500.00
❑ 145 Rube Walberg RC 60.00 35.00
❑ 146 Walter Stewart PIT RC 60.00 35.00
❑ 147 Leo Durocher RC 200.00 125.00
❑ 148 Eddie Farrell RC 60.00 35.00
❑ 149 Babe Ruth RC 5000.003000.00
❑ 150 Ray Kolp RC 60.00 35.00
❑ 151 Jake Flowers RC 60.00 35.00
❑ 152 Zack Taylor RC 60.00 35.00
❑ 153 Buddy Myer RC 60.00 35.00
❑ 154 Jimmie Foxx RC 600.00 350.00
❑ 155 Joe Judge RC 60.00 35.00
❑ 156 Danny MacFayden RC 60.00 35.00
❑ 157 Sam Byrd RC 60.00 35.00
❑ 158 Moe Berg RC 400.00 250.00
❑ 159 Oswald Bluege FIELD RC 60.00 35.00
❑ 160 Lou Gehrig RC 3000.001800.00
❑ 161 Al Spohrer RC 60.00 35.00
❑ 162 Leo Mangum RC 60.00 35.00
❑ 163 Luke Sewell POR RC 75.00 45.00
❑ 164 Lloyd Waner RC 250.00 150.00
❑ 165 Joe Sewell RC 125.00 75.00
❑ 166 Sam West RC 60.00 35.00
❑ 167 Jack Russell RC 60.00 35.00
❑ 168 Goose Goslin RC 200.00 125.00
❑ 169 Al Thomas RC 60.00 35.00
❑ 170 Harry McCurdy RC 60.00 35.00
❑ 171 Charlie Jamieson RC 60.00 35.00
❑ 172 Billy Hargrave RC 60.00 35.00
❑ 173 Roscoe Holm RC 60.00 35.00
❑ 174 Warren (Curly) Ogden RC 60.00 35.00
❑ 175 Dan Howley MG RC 60.00 35.00
❑ 176 John Ogden RC 60.00 35.00
❑ 177 Walter French RC 60.00 35.00
❑ 178 Jackie Warner RC 60.00 35.00
❑ 179 Fred Leach RC 60.00 35.00
❑ 180 Eddie Moore RC 60.00 35.00
❑ 181 Babe Ruth RC 5000.003500.00
❑ 182 Andy High RC 60.00 35.00
❑ 183 Rube Walberg RC 60.00 35.00
❑ 184 Charley Berry RC 60.00 35.00
❑ 185 Bob Smith RC 60.00 35.00
❑ 186 John Schulte RC 60.00 35.00
❑ 187 Heinie Manush RC 150.00 90.00
❑ 188 Rogers Hornsby RC 600.00 350.00
❑ 189 Joe Cronin RC 200.00 125.00
❑ 190 Fred Schulte RC 60.00 35.00
❑ 191 Ben Chapman RC 75.00 45.00
❑ 192 Walter Brown RC 60.00 35.00
❑ 193 Lynford Lary RC 60.00 35.00
❑ 194 Earl Averill RC 200.00 125.00
❑ 195 Evar Swanson RC 60.00 35.00
❑ 196 Leroy Mahaffey RC 60.00 35.00
❑ 197 Rick Ferrell RC 125.00 75.00
❑ 198 Jack Burns RC 60.00 35.00
❑ 199 Tom Bridges RC 60.00 35.00
❑ 200 Bill Hallahan RC 60.00 35.00
❑ 201 Ernie Orsatti RC 60.00 35.00
❑ 202 Gabby Hartnett RC 250.00 150.00
❑ 203 Lon Warneke RC 60.00 35.00
❑ 204 Riggs Stephenson RC 60.00 35.00
❑ 205 Heinie Meine RC 60.00 35.00
❑ 206 Gus Suhr RC 60.00 35.00
❑ 207 Mel Ott Bat RC 400.00 250.00
❑ 208 Bernie James RC 60.00 35.00
❑ 209 Adolfo Luque RC 75.00 45.00
❑ 210 Spud Davis RC 60.00 35.00
❑ 211 Hack Wilson RC 400.00 250.00
❑ 212 Billy Urbanski RC 60.00 35.00
❑ 213 Earl Adams RC 60.00 35.00
❑ 214 John Kerr RC 60.00 35.00
❑ 215 Russ Van Atta RC 60.00 35.00
❑ 216 Lefty Gomez RC 300.00 175.00
❑ 217 Frank Crosetti RC 150.00 90.00
❑ 218 Wes Ferrell RC 75.00 45.00
❑ 219 Mule Haas UER RC 60.00 35.00
❑ 220 Lefty Grove RC 500.00 300.00
❑ 221 Dale Alexander RC 60.00 35.00
❑ 222 Charley Gehringer RC 400.00 250.00
❑ 223 Dizzy Dean RC 800.00 500.00
❑ 224 Frank Demaree RC 60.00 35.00
❑ 225 Bill Jurges RC 60.00 35.00
❑ 226 Charley Root RC 60.00 35.00
❑ 227 Billy Herman RC 150.00 90.00
❑ 228 Tony Piet RC 60.00 35.00
❑ 229 Arky Vaughan RC 150.00 90.00
❑ 230 Carl Hubbell PIT RC 400.00 250.00
❑ 231 Joe Moore FIELD RC 60.00 35.00
❑ 232 Lefty O'Doul RC 125.00 75.00
❑ 233 Johnny Vergez RC 60.00 35.00
❑ 234 Carl Hubbell RC 400.00 250.00
❑ 235 Fred Fitzsimmons PIT RC 60.00 35.00
❑ 236 George Davis RC 60.00 35.00
❑ 237 Gus Mancuso FIELD RC 60.00 35.00
❑ 238 Hugh Critz FIELD RC 60.00 35.00
❑ 239 Leroy Parmelee RC 60.00 35.00
❑ 240 Hal Schumacher RC 125.00 75.00

1934 Goudey

❑ COMPLETE SET (96) 16000.009000.00
❑ COMMON CARD (1-48) 50.00 30.00
❑ COMMON CARD (49-72) 75.00 40.00
❑ COMMON CARD (73-96) 175.00 100.00
❑ WRAPPER (1-CENT, WHT.) 100.00 75.00
❑ WRAPPER (1-CENT, CLR.) 100.00 75.00
❑ 1 Jimmie Foxx 750.00 450.00
❑ 2 Mickey Cochrane 175.00 100.00
❑ 3 Charlie Grimm 60.00 35.00
❑ 4 Woody English 50.00 30.00
❑ 5 Ed Brandt 50.00 30.00
❑ 6 Dizzy Dean 700.00 400.00
❑ 7 Leo Durocher 175.00 100.00
❑ 8 Tony Piet 50.00 30.00
❑ 9 Ben Chapman 60.00 35.00
❑ 10 Chuck Klein 150.00 90.00
❑ 11 Paul Waner 150.00 90.00
❑ 12 Carl Hubbell 175.00 100.00
❑ 13 Frankie Frisch 175.00 100.00
❑ 14 Willie Kamm 50.00 30.00
❑ 15 Alvin Crowder 50.00 30.00
❑ 16 Joe Kuhel 50.00 30.00
❑ 17 Hugh Critz 50.00 30.00
❑ 18 Heinie Manush 125.00 75.00
❑ 19 Lefty Grove 300.00 175.00
❑ 20 Frank Hogan 50.00 30.00
❑ 21 Bill Terry 200.00 125.00
❑ 22 Arky Vaughan 125.00 75.00
❑ 23 Charley Gehringer 200.00 125.00
❑ 24 Ray Benge 50.00 30.00
❑ 25 Roger Cramer RC 60.00 35.00
❑ 26 Gerald Walker RC 50.00 30.00
❑ 27 Luke Appling RC 150.00 90.00
❑ 28 Ed Coleman RC 50.00 30.00
❑ 29 Larry French RC 50.00 30.00
❑ 30 Julius Solters RC 50.00 30.00
❑ 31 Buck Jordan RC 50.00 30.00
❑ 32 Blondy Ryan RC 50.00 30.00
❑ 33 Don Hurst RC 50.00 30.00
❑ 34 Chick Hafey RC 125.00 75.00
❑ 35 Ernie Lombardi RC 150.00 90.00
❑ 36 Walter Betts RC 50.00 30.00
❑ 37 Lou Gehrig 3000.002000.00
❑ 38 Oral Hildebrand RC 50.00 30.00
❑ 39 Fred Walker RC 50.00 30.00
❑ 40 John Stone 50.00 30.00
❑ 41 George Earnshaw RC 50.00 30.00
❑ 42 John Allen RC 50.00 30.00
❑ 43 Dick Porter RC 50.00 30.00
❑ 44 Tom Bridges 60.00 35.00
❑ 45 Oscar Melillo RC 50.00 30.00
❑ 46 Joe Stripp RC 50.00 30.00
❑ 47 John Frederick RC 50.00 30.00
❑ 48 Tex Carleton RC 50.00 30.00
❑ 49 Sam Leslie RC 75.00 40.00
❑ 50 Walter Beck RC 75.00 40.00
❑ 51 Rip Collins RC 75.00 40.00
❑ 52 Herman Bell RC 75.00 40.00
❑ 53 George Watkins RC 75.00 40.00
❑ 54 Wesley Schulmerich RC 75.00 40.00
❑ 55 Ed Holley RC 75.00 40.00
❑ 56 Mark Koenig 100.00 60.00
❑ 57 Bill Swift RC 75.00 40.00
❑ 58 Earl Grace RC 75.00 40.00
❑ 59 Joe Mowry RC 75.00 40.00
❑ 60 Lynn Nelson RC 75.00 40.00
❑ 61 Lou Gehrig 3000.002000.00
❑ 62 Hank Greenberg RC 700.00 400.00
❑ 63 Minter Hayes RC 75.00 40.00
❑ 64 Frank Grube RC 75.00 40.00
❑ 65 Cliff Bolton RC 75.00 40.00
❑ 66 Mel Harder RC 100.00 60.00
❑ 67 Bob Weiland RC 75.00 40.00
❑ 68 Bob Johnson RC 100.00 60.00
❑ 69 John Marcum RC 75.00 40.00
❑ 70 Pete Fox RC 75.00 40.00
❑ 71 Lyle Tinning RC 75.00 40.00
❑ 72 Arndt Jorgens RC 75.00 40.00
❑ 73 Ed Wells RC 175.00 100.00
❑ 74 Bob Boken RC 175.00 100.00
❑ 75 Bill Werber RC 175.00 100.00
❑ 76 Hal Trosky RC 200.00 125.00
❑ 77 Joe Vosmik RC 175.00 100.00
❑ 78 Pinky Higgins RC 200.00 125.00
❑ 79 Eddie Durham RC 175.00 100.00

❑ 80 Marty McManus CK 175.00 100.00
❑ 81 Bob Brown CK RC 175.00 100.00
❑ 82 Bill Hallahan CK 175.00 100.00
❑ 83 Jim Mooney CK RC 175.00 100.00
❑ 84 Paul Derringer CK RC 225.00 125.00
❑ 85 Adam Comorosky CK 175.00 100.00
❑ 86 Lloyd Johnson CK RC 175.00 100.00
❑ 87 George Darrow CK RC 175.00 100.00
❑ 88 Homer Peel CK RC 175.00 100.00
❑ 89 Linus Frey CK RC 175.00 100.00
❑ 90 KiKi Cuyler CK 350.00 200.00
❑ 91 Dolph Camilli CK RC 200.00 125.00
❑ 92 Steve Larkin RC 175.00 100.00
❑ 93 Fred Ostermueller RC 175.00 100.00
❑ 94 Red Rolfe RC 200.00 125.00
❑ 95 Myril Hoag RC 175.00 100.00
❑ 96 James DeShong RC 500.00 300.00

2006 Greats of the Game

❑ COMPLETE SET (100) 50.00 20.00
❑ COMMON CARD (1-100) .75 .30
❑ ONE PLATE PER FOIL PLATE PACK
❑ PLATE PACKS ISSUED TO DEALERS
❑ PLATE PRINT RUN 1 SET PER COLOR
❑ BLACK-CYAN-MAGENTA-YELLOW ISSUED
❑ NO PLATE PRICING DUE TO SCARCITY
❑ 1 Al Kaline 2.00 .75
❑ 2 Alan Trammell .75 .30
❑ 3 Andre Dawson .75 .30
❑ 4 Barry Larkin 1.25 .50
❑ 5 Bill Buckner .75 .30
❑ 6 Bill Freehan .75 .30
❑ 7 Bill Madlock .75 .30
❑ 8 Bill Mazeroski 1.25 .50
❑ 9 Billy Williams .75 .30
❑ 10 Bo Jackson 2.00 .75
❑ 11 Bob Feller .75 .30
❑ 12 Bob Gibson 1.25 .50
❑ 13 Bobby Doerr .75 .30
❑ 14 Bobby Murcer .75 .30
❑ 15 Boog Powell .75 .30
❑ 16 Brooks Robinson 1.25 .50
❑ 17 Bruce Sutter .75 .30
❑ 18 Bucky Dent .75 .30
❑ 19 Cal Ripken 8.00 3.00
❑ 20 Rico Petrocelli .75 .30
❑ 21 Carlton Fisk 1.25 .50
❑ 22 Chris Chambliss .75 .30
❑ 23 Dave Concepcion .75 .30
❑ 24 Dave Parker .75 .30
❑ 25 Dave Winfield .75 .30
❑ 26 David Cone .75 .30
❑ 27 Denny McLain .75 .30
❑ 28 Don Mattingly 4.00 1.50
❑ 29 Don Newcombe .75 .30
❑ 30 Don Sutton .75 .30
❑ 31 Dusty Baker .75 .30
❑ 32 Dwight Evans .75 .30
❑ 33 Eric Davis .75 .30
❑ 34 Ernie Banks 2.00 .75
❑ 35 Fergie Jenkins .75 .30
❑ 36 Frank Robinson .75 .30
❑ 37 Fred Lynn .75 .30
❑ 38 Fred McGriff 1.25 .50
❑ 39 Andre Thornton .75 .30
❑ 40 Garry Maddox .75 .30
❑ 41 Gary Matthews .75 .30
❑ 42 Gaylord Perry .75 .30
❑ 43 George Foster .75 .30
❑ 44 George Kell .75 .30
❑ 45 Graig Nettles .75 .30
❑ 46 Greg Luzinski .75 .30
❑ 47 Harmon Killebrew 2.00 .75
❑ 48 Jack Clark .75 .30
❑ 49 Jack Morris .75 .30
❑ 50 Jim Palmer .75 .30
❑ 51 Jim Rice .75 .30
❑ 52 Joe Morgan .75 .30
❑ 53 John Kruk .75 .30
❑ 54 Johnny Bench 2.00 .75
❑ 55 Jose Canseco 1.25 .50
❑ 56 Kirby Puckett 2.00 .75
❑ 57 Kirk Gibson .75 .30
❑ 58 Lee Mazzilli .75 .30
❑ 59 Lou Brock 1.25 .50
❑ 60 Lou Piniella .75 .30
❑ 61 Luis Aparicio .75 .30
❑ 62 Luis Tiant .75 .30
❑ 63 Mark Fidrych .75 .30
❑ 64 Mark Grace 1.25 .50
❑ 65 Maury Wills .75 .30
❑ 66 Mike Schmidt 3.00 1.25
❑ 67 Nolan Ryan 5.00 2.00
❑ 68 Ozzie Smith 3.00 1.25
❑ 69 Paul Molitor .75 .30
❑ 70 Paul O'Neill 1.25 .50
❑ 71 Phil Niekro .75 .30
❑ 72 Ralph Kiner 1.25 .50
❑ 73 Randy Hundley .75 .30
❑ 74 Red Schoendienst .75 .30
❑ 75 Reggie Jackson 1.25 .50
❑ 76 Robin Yount 2.00 .75
❑ 77 Rod Carew 1.25 .50
❑ 78 Rollie Fingers .75 .30
❑ 79 Ron Cey .75 .30
❑ 80 Ron Guidry .75 .30
❑ 81 Ron Santo 1.25 .50
❑ 82 Rusty Staub .75 .30
❑ 83 Ryne Sandberg 4.00 1.50
❑ 84 Sparky Lyle .75 .30
❑ 85 Stan Musial 3.00 1.25
❑ 86 Steve Carlton .75 .30
❑ 87 Steve Garvey .75 .30
❑ 88 Steve Sax .75 .30
❑ 89 Tommy Herr .75 .30
❑ 90 Tim McCarver .75 .30
❑ 91 Tim Raines .75 .30
❑ 92 Tom Seaver 1.25 .50
❑ 93 Tony Gwynn 2.00 .75
❑ 94 Tony Perez .75 .30
❑ 95 Wade Boggs 1.25 .50
❑ 96 Whitey Ford 1.25 .50
❑ 97 Will Clark 1.25 .50
❑ 98 Willie Horton .75 .30
❑ 99 Willie McCovey 1.25 .50
❑ 100 Yogi Berra 2.00 .75

1949 Leaf

❑ COMPLETE SET (98) 4000.00 2500.00
❑ COMMON CARD (1-168) 25.00 15.00
❑ COMMON SP's 300.00 200.00
❑ WRAPPER (1-CENT) 160.00 120.00
❑ 1 Joe DiMaggio 3000.001800.00
❑ 3 Babe Ruth 2500.001500.00
❑ 4 Stan Musial 1000.00 600.00
❑ 5 Virgil Trucks SP RC 400.00 250.00
❑ 8 S.Paige SP RC 15000.009000.00
❑ 10 Dizzy Trout 40.00 25.00
❑ 11 Phil Rizzuto 350.00 200.00
❑ 13 Cass Michaels SP RC 300.00 200.00
❑ 14 Billy Johnson 40.00 25.00
❑ 17 Frank Overmire RC 25.00 15.00
❑ 19 Johnny Wyrostek SP 300.00 200.00
❑ 20 Hank Sauer SP 400.00 250.00
❑ 22 Al Evans RC 25.00 15.00
❑ 26 Sam Chapman 40.00 25.00
❑ 27 Mickey Harris RC 25.00 15.00
❑ 28 Jim Hegan RC 40.00 25.00
❑ 29 Elmer Valo RC 40.00 25.00
❑ 30 Billy Goodman SP RC 400.00 250.00
❑ 31 Lou Brissie RC 25.00 15.00
❑ 32 Warren Spahn 350.00 200.00
❑ 33 Peanuts Lowrey SP RC 300.00 200.00
❑ 36 Al Zarilla SP 300.00 200.00
❑ 38 Ted Kluszewski RC 200.00 125.00
❑ 39 Ewell Blackwell 60.00 35.00
❑ 42A Kent Peterson RC 25.00 15.00
❑ 42B Kent Peterson Red Cap
❑ 43 Ed Stevens SP RC 300.00 200.00
❑ 45 Ken Keltner SP RC 300.00 200.00
❑ 46 Johnny Mize 100.00 60.00
❑ 47 George Vico RC 25.00 15.00
❑ 48 Johnny Schmitz SP RC 300.00 200.00
❑ 49 Del Ennis RC 60.00 35.00
❑ 50 Dick Wakefield RC 25.00 15.00
❑ 51 Alvin Dark SP RC 500.00 300.00
❑ 53 Johnny VanderMeer 100.00 60.00
❑ 54 Bobby Adams SP RC 300.00 200.00
❑ 55 Tommy Henrich SP 500.00 300.00
❑ 56 Larry Jansen 40.00 25.00
❑ 57 Bob McCall RC 25.00 15.00
❑ 59 Luke Appling 100.00 60.00
❑ 61 Jake Early RC 25.00 15.00
❑ 62 Eddie Joost SP 300.00 200.00
❑ 63 Barney McCosky SP 300.00 200.00
❑ 65 Bob Elliott UER 100.00 60.00
❑ 66 Orval Grove SP RC 300.00 200.00
❑ 68 Eddie Miller SP 300.00 200.00
❑ 70 Honus Wagner 350.00 200.00
❑ 72 Hank Edwards RC 25.00 15.00
❑ 73 Pat Seerey RC 25.00 15.00
❑ 75 Dom DiMaggio SP 600.00 350.00
❑ 76 Ted Williams 1200.00 700.00
❑ 77 Roy Smalley RC 25.00 15.00
❑ 78 Hoot Evers SP RC 300.00 200.00
❑ 79 Jackie Robinson RC 2000.001200.00
❑ 81 Whitey Kurowski SP RC 300.00 200.00
❑ 82 Johnny Lindell 40.00 25.00
❑ 83 Bobby Doerr 100.00 60.00
❑ 84 Sid Hudson 25.00 15.00
❑ 85 Dave Philley SP RC 400.00 250.00
❑ 86 Ralph Weigel RC 25.00 15.00
❑ 88 Frank Gustine SP RC 300.00 200.00
❑ 91 Ralph Kiner 200.00 125.00
❑ 93 Bob Feller SP 2000.001400.00
❑ 95 Snuffy Stirnweiss 40.00 25.00
❑ 97 Marty Marion 60.00 35.00
❑ 98 Hal Newhouser SP RC 600.00 350.00
❑ 102A G.Hermansk ERR 250.00 150.00
❑ 102B Gene Hermanski COR RC 40.0025.00
❑ 104 Eddie Stewart SP RC 300.00 200.00
❑ 106 Lou Boudreau MG RC 100.00 60.00
❑ 108 Matt Batts SP RC 300.00 200.00
❑ 111 Jerry Priddy RC 25.00 15.00
❑ 113 Dutch Leonard SP 300.00 200.00
❑ 117 Joe Gordon RC 40.00 25.00
❑ 120 George Kell SP RC 600.00 350.00
❑ 121 Johnny Pesky SP RC 400.00 250.00
❑ 123 Cliff Fannin SP RC 300.00 200.00
❑ 125 Andy Pafko RC 25.00 15.00
❑ 127 Enos Slaughter SP 800.00 500.00
❑ 128 Buddy Rosar 25.00 15.00
❑ 129 Kirby Higbe SP 300.00 200.00
❑ 131 Sid Gordon SP 300.00 200.00
❑ 133 Tommy Holmes SP RC 500.00 300.00
❑ 136A C.Aberson Full Slv RC 25.00 15.00
❑ 136B C.Aberson Short Slv 250.00 150.00
❑ 137 Harry Walker SP RC 400.00 250.00
❑ 138 Larry Doby SP RC 700.00 400.00
❑ 139 Johnny Hopp RC 25.00 15.00
❑ 142 D.Murtaugh SP RC 400.00 250.00
❑ 143 Dick Sisler SP RC 300.00 200.00
❑ 144 Bob Dillinger SP RC 300.00 200.00
❑ 146 Pete Reiser SP 500.00 300.00
❑ 149 Hank Majeski SP RC 300.00 200.00

❑ 153 Floyd Baker SP RC	300.00	200.00
❑ 158 H.Brecheen SP RC	400.00	250.00
❑ 159 Mizell Platt RC	25.00	15.00
❑ 160 Bob Scheffing SP RC	300.00	200.00
❑ 161 V.Stephens SP RC	400.00	250.00
❑ 163 F.Hutchinson SP RC	400.00	250.00
❑ 165 Dale Mitchell SP RC	400.00	250.00
❑ 168 Phil Cavarretta SP RC	500.00	300.00
❑ NNO Album		

1990 Leaf

❑ COMPLETE SET (528)	60.00	30.00
❑ COMPLETE SERIES 1 (264)	40.00	20.00
❑ COMPLETE SERIES 2 (264)	20.00	10.00
❑ COMP. BERRA PUZZLE	1.00	.40
❑ 1 Introductory Card	.40	.15
❑ 2 Mike Henneman	.40	.15
❑ 3 Steve Bedrosian	.40	.15
❑ 4 Mike Scott	.40	.15
❑ 5 Allan Anderson	.40	.15
❑ 6 Rick Sutcliffe	.60	.25
❑ 7 Gregg Olson	.60	.25
❑ 8 Kevin Elster	.40	.15
❑ 9 Pete O'Brien	.40	.15
❑ 10 Carlton Fisk	1.00	.40
❑ 11 Joe Magrane	.40	.15
❑ 12 Roger Clemens	4.00	1.50
❑ 13 Tom Glavine	1.00	.40
❑ 14 Tom Gordon	.60	.25
❑ 15 Todd Benzinger	.40	.15
❑ 16 Hubie Brooks	.40	.15
❑ 17 Roberto Kelly	.40	.15
❑ 18 Barry Larkin	1.00	.40
❑ 19 Mike Boddicker	.40	.15
❑ 20 Roger McDowell	.40	.15
❑ 21 Nolan Ryan	5.00	2.00
❑ 22 John Farrell	.40	.15
❑ 23 Bruce Hurst	.40	.15
❑ 24 Wally Joyner	.60	.25
❑ 25 Greg Maddux	5.00	2.00
❑ 26 Chris Bosio	.40	.15
❑ 27 John Cerutti	.40	.15
❑ 28 Tim Burke	.40	.15
❑ 29 Dennis Eckersley	.60	.25
❑ 30 Glenn Davis	.40	.15
❑ 31 Jim Abbott	1.00	.40
❑ 32 Mike LaValliere	.40	.15
❑ 33 Andres Thomas	.40	.15
❑ 34 Lou Whitaker	.60	.25
❑ 35 Alvin Davis	.40	.15
❑ 36 Melido Perez	.40	.15
❑ 37 Craig Biggio	1.50	.60
❑ 38 Rick Aguilera	.60	.25
❑ 39 Pete Harnisch	.40	.15
❑ 40 David Cone	.60	.25
❑ 41 Scott Garrelts	.40	.15
❑ 42 Jay Howell	.40	.15
❑ 43 Eric King	.40	.15
❑ 44 Pedro Guerrero	.40	.15
❑ 45 Mike Bielecki	.40	.15
❑ 46 Bob Boone	.60	.25
❑ 47 Kevin Brown	.60	.25
❑ 48 Jerry Browne	.40	.15
❑ 49 Mike Scioscia	.40	.15
❑ 50 Chuck Cary	.40	.15
❑ 51 Wade Boggs	1.00	.40
❑ 52 Von Hayes	.40	.15
❑ 53 Tony Fernandez	.40	.15
❑ 54 Dennis Martinez	.60	.25
❑ 55 Tom Candiotti	.40	.15
❑ 56 Andy Benes	.60	.25
❑ 57 Rob Dibble	.60	.25
❑ 58 Chuck Crim	.40	.15
❑ 59 John Smoltz	1.50	.60
❑ 60 Mike Heath	.40	.15
❑ 61 Kevin Gross	.40	.15
❑ 62 Mark McGwire	4.00	1.50
❑ 63 Bert Blyleven	.60	.25
❑ 64 Bob Walk	.40	.15
❑ 65 Mickey Tettleton	.40	.15
❑ 66 Sid Fernandez	.40	.15
❑ 67 Terry Kennedy	.40	.15
❑ 68 Fernando Valenzuela	.60	.25
❑ 69 Don Mattingly	4.00	1.50
❑ 70 Paul O'Neill	1.00	.40
❑ 71 Robin Yount	2.50	1.00
❑ 72 Bret Saberhagen	.60	.25
❑ 73 Geno Petralli	.40	.15
❑ 74 Brook Jacoby	.40	.15
❑ 75 Roberto Alomar	1.00	.40
❑ 76 Devon White	.60	.25
❑ 77 Jose Lind	.40	.15
❑ 78 Pat Combs	.40	.15
❑ 79 Dave Stieb	.60	.25
❑ 80 Tim Wallach	.40	.15
❑ 81 Dave Stewart	.60	.25
❑ 82 Eric Anthony RC	.40	.15
❑ 83 Randy Bush	.40	.15
❑ 84 Rickey Henderson CL	.60	.25
❑ 85 Jaime Navarro	.40	.15
❑ 86 Tommy Gregg	.40	.15
❑ 87 Frank Tanana	.40	.15
❑ 88 Omar Vizquel	1.50	.60
❑ 89 Ivan Calderon	.40	.15
❑ 90 Vince Coleman	.40	.15
❑ 91 Barry Bonds	5.00	2.00
❑ 92 Randy Milligan	.40	.15
❑ 93 Frank Viola	.40	.15
❑ 94 Matt Williams	.60	.25
❑ 95 Alfredo Griffin	.40	.15
❑ 96 Steve Sax	.40	.15
❑ 97 Gary Gaetti	.60	.25
❑ 98 Ryne Sandberg	3.00	1.25
❑ 99 Danny Tartabull	.40	.15
❑ 100 Rafael Palmeiro	1.00	.40
❑ 101 Jesse Orosco	.40	.15
❑ 102 Garry Templeton	.40	.15
❑ 103 Frank DiPino	.40	.15
❑ 104 Tony Pena	.40	.15
❑ 105 Dickie Thon	.40	.15
❑ 106 Kelly Gruber	.40	.15
❑ 107 Marquis Grissom RC	2.00	.75
❑ 108 Jose Canseco	1.00	.40
❑ 109 Mike Blowers RC	.40	.15
❑ 110 Tom Browning	.40	.15
❑ 111 Greg Vaughn	.40	.15
❑ 112 Oddibe McDowell	.40	.15
❑ 113 Gary Ward	.40	.15
❑ 114 Jay Buhner	.60	.25
❑ 115 Eric Show	.40	.15
❑ 116 Bryan Harvey	.40	.15
❑ 117 Andy Van Slyke	1.00	.40
❑ 118 Jeff Ballard	.40	.15
❑ 119 Barry Lyons	.40	.15
❑ 120 Kevin Mitchell	.40	.15
❑ 121 Mike Gallego	.40	.15
❑ 122 Dave Smith	.40	.15
❑ 123 Kirby Puckett	1.50	.60
❑ 124 Jerome Walton	.40	.15
❑ 125 Bo Jackson	1.50	.60
❑ 126 Harold Baines	.60	.25
❑ 127 Scott Bankhead	.40	.15
❑ 128 Ozzie Guillen	.60	.25
❑ 129 Jose Oquendo UER (League misspelled as Legue)	.40	.15
❑ 130 John Dopson	.40	.15
❑ 131 Charlie Hayes	.40	.15
❑ 132 Fred McGriff	1.50	.60
❑ 133 Chet Lemon	.40	.15
❑ 134 Gary Carter	.60	.25
❑ 135 Rafael Ramirez	.40	.15
❑ 136 Shane Mack	.40	.15
❑ 137 Mark Grace	1.00	.40
❑ 138 Phil Bradley	.40	.15
❑ 139 Dwight Gooden	.60	.25
❑ 140 Harold Reynolds	.60	.25
❑ 141 Scott Fletcher	.40	.15
❑ 142 Ozzie Smith	2.50	1.00
❑ 143 Mike Greenwell	.40	.15
❑ 144 Pete Smith	.40	.15
❑ 145 Mark Gubicza	.40	.15
❑ 146 Chris Sabo	.40	.15
❑ 147 Ramon Martinez	.40	.15
❑ 148 Tim Leary	.40	.15
❑ 149 Randy Myers	.60	.25
❑ 150 Jody Reed	.40	.15
❑ 151 Bruce Ruffin	.40	.15
❑ 152 Jeff Russell	.40	.15
❑ 153 Doug Jones	.40	.15
❑ 154 Tony Gwynn	2.00	.75
❑ 155 Mark Langston	.40	.15
❑ 156 Mitch Williams	.40	.15
❑ 157 Gary Sheffield	1.50	.60
❑ 158 Tom Henke	.40	.15
❑ 159 Oil Can Boyd	.40	.15
❑ 160 Rickey Henderson	1.50	.60
❑ 161 Bill Doran	.40	.15
❑ 162 Chuck Finley	.60	.25
❑ 163 Jeff King	.40	.15
❑ 164 Nick Esasky	.40	.15
❑ 165 Cecil Fielder	.60	.25
❑ 166 Dave Valle	.40	.15
❑ 167 Robin Ventura	1.50	.60
❑ 168 Jim Deshaies	.40	.15
❑ 169 Juan Berenguer	.40	.15
❑ 170 Craig Worthington	.40	.15
❑ 171 Gregg Jefferies	.60	.25
❑ 172 Will Clark	1.00	.40
❑ 173 Kirk Gibson	.60	.25
❑ 174 Checklist 89-176 (Carlton Fisk)	.60	.25
❑ 175 Bobby Thigpen	.40	.15
❑ 176 John Tudor	.40	.15
❑ 177 Andre Dawson	.60	.25
❑ 178 George Brett	4.00	1.50
❑ 179 Steve Buechele	.40	.15
❑ 180 Albert Belle	1.50	.60
❑ 181 Eddie Murray	1.50	.60
❑ 182 Bob Geren	.40	.15
❑ 183 Rob Murphy	.40	.15
❑ 184 Tom Herr	.40	.15
❑ 185 George Bell	.40	.15
❑ 186 Spike Owen	.40	.15
❑ 187 Cory Snyder	.40	.15
❑ 188 Fred Lynn	.40	.15
❑ 189 Eric Davis	.60	.25
❑ 190 Dave Parker	.60	.25
❑ 191 Jeff Blauser	.40	.15
❑ 192 Matt Nokes	.40	.15
❑ 193 Delino DeShields RC	1.00	.40
❑ 194 Scott Sanderson	.40	.15
❑ 195 Lance Parrish	.40	.15
❑ 196 Bobby Bonilla	.60	.25
❑ 197 Cal Ripken	5.00	2.00
❑ 198 Kevin McReynolds	.40	.15
❑ 199 Robby Thompson	.40	.15
❑ 200 Tim Belcher	.40	.15
❑ 201 Jesse Barfield	.40	.15
❑ 202 Mariano Duncan	.40	.15
❑ 203 Bill Spiers	.40	.15
❑ 204 Frank White	.60	.25
❑ 205 Julio Franco	.60	.25
❑ 206 Greg Swindell	.40	.15
❑ 207 Benito Santiago	.60	.25
❑ 208 Johnny Ray	.40	.15
❑ 209 Gary Redus	.40	.15
❑ 210 Jeff Parrett	.40	.15
❑ 211 Jimmy Key	.60	.25
❑ 212 Tim Raines	.60	.25
❑ 213 Carney Lansford	.60	.25
❑ 214 Gerald Young	.40	.15
❑ 215 Gene Larkin	.40	.15
❑ 216 Dan Plesac	.40	.15
❑ 217 Lonnie Smith	.40	.15
❑ 218 Alan Trammell	.60	.25
❑ 219 Jeffrey Leonard	.40	.15
❑ 220 Sammy Sosa RC	15.00	6.00
❑ 221 Todd Zeile	.60	.25
❑ 222 Bill Landrum	.40	.15

❑ 223 Mike Devereaux .40 .15
❑ 224 Mike Marshall .40 .15
❑ 225 Jose Uribe .40 .15
❑ 226 Juan Samuel .40 .15
❑ 227 Mel Hall .40 .15
❑ 228 Kent Hrbek .60 .25
❑ 229 Shawon Dunston .40 .15
❑ 230 Kevin Seitzer .40 .15
❑ 231 Pete Incaviglia .40 .15
❑ 232 Sandy Alomar Jr. .60 .25
❑ 233 Bip Roberts .40 .15
❑ 234 Scott Terry .40 .15
❑ 235 Dwight Evans 1.00 .40
❑ 236 Ricky Jordan .40 .15
❑ 237 John Olerud RC 3.00 1.25
❑ 238 Zane Smith .40 .15
❑ 239 Walt Weiss .40 .15
❑ 240 Alvaro Espinoza .40 .15
❑ 241 Billy Hatcher .40 .15
❑ 242 Paul Molitor .60 .25
❑ 243 Dale Murphy 1.00 .40
❑ 244 Dave Bergman .40 .15
❑ 245 Ken Griffey Jr. 5.00 2.00
❑ 246 Ed Whitson .40 .15
❑ 247 Kirk McCaskill .40 .15
❑ 248 Jay Bell .60 .25
❑ 249 Ben McDonald RC 1.00 .40
❑ 250 Darryl Strawberry .60 .25
❑ 251 Brett Butler .60 .25
❑ 252 Terry Steinbach .40 .15
❑ 253 Ken Caminiti .60 .25
❑ 254 Dan Gladden .40 .15
❑ 255 Dwight Smith .40 .15
❑ 256 Kurt Stillwell .40 .15
❑ 257 Ruben Sierra .60 .25
❑ 258 Mike Schooler .40 .15
❑ 259 Lance Johnson .40 .15
❑ 260 Terry Pendleton .60 .25
❑ 261 Ellis Burks 1.00 .40
❑ 262 Len Dykstra .60 .25
❑ 263 Mookie Wilson .60 .25
❑ 264 Nolan Ryan CL UER 1.50 .60
❑ 265 Nolan Ryan SPEC 2.50 1.00
❑ 266 Brian DuBois RC .40 .15
❑ 267 Don Robinson .40 .15
❑ 268 Glenn Wilson .40 .15
❑ 269 Kevin Tapani RC 1.00 .40
❑ 270 Marvell Wynne .40 .15
❑ 271 Bill Ripken .40 .15
❑ 272 Howard Johnson .40 .15
❑ 273 Brian Holman .40 .15
❑ 274 Dan Pasqua .40 .15
❑ 275 Ken Dayley .40 .15
❑ 276 Jeff Reardon .60 .25
❑ 277 Jim Presley .40 .15
❑ 278 Jim Eisenreich .40 .15
❑ 279 Danny Jackson .40 .15
❑ 280 Orel Hershiser .60 .25
❑ 281 Andy Hawkins .40 .15
❑ 282 Jose Rijo .40 .15
❑ 283 Luis Rivera .40 .15
❑ 284 John Kruk .60 .25
❑ 285 Jeff Huson RC .40 .15
❑ 286 Joel Skinner .40 .15
❑ 287 Jack Clark .60 .25
❑ 288 Chili Davis .60 .25
❑ 289 Joe Girardi 1.00 .40
❑ 290 B.J. Surhoff .60 .25
❑ 291 Luis Sojo RC .40 .15
❑ 292 Tom Foley .40 .15
❑ 293 Mike Moore .40 .15
❑ 294 Ken Oberkfell .40 .15
❑ 295 Luis Polonia .40 .15
❑ 296 Doug Drabek .40 .15
❑ 297 David Justice RC 3.00 1.25
❑ 298 Paul Gibson .40 .15
❑ 299 Edgar Martinez 1.00 .40
❑ 300 Frank Thomas RC 15.00 6.00
❑ 301 Eric Yelding RC .40 .15
❑ 302 Greg Gagne .40 .15
❑ 303 Brad Komminsk .40 .15
❑ 304 Ron Darling .40 .15
❑ 305 Kevin Bass .40 .15
❑ 306 Jeff Hamilton .40 .15
❑ 307 Ron Karkovice .40 .15
❑ 308 M.Thompson UER Lankford 1.00 .40
❑ 309 Mike Harkey .40 .15
❑ 310 Mel Stottlemyre Jr. .40 .15
❑ 311 Kenny Rogers .60 .25
❑ 312 Mitch Webster .40 .15
❑ 313 Kal Daniels .40 .15
❑ 314 Matt Nokes .40 .15
❑ 315 Dennis Lamp .40 .15
❑ 316 Ken Howell .40 .15
❑ 317 Glenallen Hill .40 .15
❑ 318 Dave Martinez .40 .15
❑ 319 Chris James .40 .15
❑ 320 Mike Pagliarulo .40 .15
❑ 321 Hal Morris .40 .15
❑ 322 Rob Deer .40 .15
❑ 323 Greg Olson (C) RC .40 .15
❑ 324 Tony Phillips .40 .15
❑ 325 Larry Walker RC 8.00 3.00
❑ 326 Ron Hassey .40 .15
❑ 327 Jack Howell .40 .15
❑ 328 John Smiley .40 .15
❑ 329 Steve Finley .60 .25
❑ 330 Dave Magadan .40 .15
❑ 331 Greg Litton .40 .15
❑ 332 Mickey Hatcher .40 .15
❑ 333 Lee Guetterman .40 .15
❑ 334 Norm Charlton .40 .15
❑ 335 Edgar Diaz RC .40 .15
❑ 336 Willie Wilson .40 .15
❑ 337 Bobby Witt .40 .15
❑ 338 Candy Maldonado .40 .15
❑ 339 Craig Lefferts .40 .15
❑ 340 Dante Bichette .60 .25
❑ 341 Wally Backman .40 .15
❑ 342 Dennis Cook .40 .15
❑ 343 Pat Borders .40 .15
❑ 344 Wallace Johnson .40 .15
❑ 345 Willie Randolph .60 .25
❑ 346 Danny Darwin .40 .15
❑ 347 Al Newman .40 .15
❑ 348 Mark Knudson .40 .15
❑ 349 Joe Boever .40 .15
❑ 350 Larry Sheets .40 .15
❑ 351 Mike Jackson .40 .15
❑ 352 Wayne Edwards RC .40 .15
❑ 353 Bernard Gilkey RC 1.00 .40
❑ 354 Don Slaught .40 .15
❑ 355 Joe Orsulak .40 .15
❑ 356 John Franco .60 .25
❑ 357 Jeff Brantley .40 .15
❑ 358 Mike Morgan .40 .15
❑ 359 Deion Sanders 1.50 .60
❑ 360 Terry Leach .40 .15
❑ 361 Les Lancaster .40 .15
❑ 362 Storm Davis .40 .15
❑ 363 Scott Coolbaugh RC .40 .15
❑ 364 Checklist 265-352
(Ozzie Smith) 1.00 .40
❑ 365 Cecilio Guante .40 .15
❑ 366 Joey Cora .60 .25
❑ 367 Willie McGee .60 .25
❑ 368 Jerry Reed .40 .15
❑ 369 Darren Daulton .60 .25
❑ 370 Manny Lee .40 .15
❑ 371 Mark Gardner RC .40 .15
❑ 372 Rick Honeycutt .40 .15
❑ 373 Steve Balboni .40 .15
❑ 374 Jack Armstrong .40 .15
❑ 375 Charlie O'Brien .40 .15
❑ 376 Ron Gant .60 .25
❑ 377 Lloyd Moseby .40 .15
❑ 378 Gene Harris .40 .15
❑ 379 Joe Carter .60 .25
❑ 380 Scott Bailes .40 .15
❑ 381 R.J. Reynolds .40 .15
❑ 382 Bob Melvin .40 .15
❑ 383 Tim Teufel .40 .15
❑ 384 John Burkett .40 .15
❑ 385 Felix Jose .40 .15
❑ 386 Larry Andersen .40 .15
❑ 387 David West .40 .15
❑ 388 Luis Salazar .40 .15
❑ 389 Mike Macfarlane .40 .15
❑ 390 Charlie Hough .60 .25
❑ 391 Greg Briley .40 .15
❑ 392 Donn Pall .40 .15
❑ 393 Bryn Smith .40 .15
❑ 394 Carlos Quintana .40 .15
❑ 395 Steve Lake .40 .15
❑ 396 Mark Whiten RC 1.00 .40
❑ 397 Edwin Nunez .40 .15
❑ 398 Rick Parker RC .40 .15
❑ 399 Mark Portugal .40 .15
❑ 400 Roy Smith .40 .15
❑ 401 Hector Villanueva RC .40 .15
❑ 402 Bob Milacki .40 .15
❑ 403 Alejandro Pena .40 .15
❑ 404 Scott Bradley .40 .15
❑ 405 Ron Kittle .40 .15
❑ 406 Bob Tewksbury .40 .15
❑ 407 Wes Gardner .40 .15
❑ 408 Ernie Whitt .40 .15
❑ 409 Terry Shumpert RC .40 .15
❑ 410 Tim Layana RC .40 .15
❑ 411 Chris Gwynn .40 .15
❑ 412 Jeff D. Robinson .40 .15
❑ 413 Scott Scudder .40 .15
❑ 414 Kevin Romine .40 .15
❑ 415 Jose DeJesus .40 .15
❑ 416 Mike Jeffcoat .40 .15
❑ 417 Rudy Seanez RC .40 .15
❑ 418 Mike Dunne .40 .15
❑ 419 Dick Schofield .40 .15
❑ 420 Steve Wilson .40 .15
❑ 421 Bill Krueger .40 .15
❑ 422 Junior Felix .40 .15
❑ 423 Drew Hall .40 .15
❑ 424 Curt Young .40 .15
❑ 425 Franklin Stubbs .40 .15
❑ 426 Dave Winfield .60 .25
❑ 427 Rick Reed RC 1.00 .40
❑ 428 Charlie Leibrandt .40 .15
❑ 429 Jeff M. Robinson .40 .15
❑ 430 Erik Hanson .40 .15
❑ 431 Barry Jones .40 .15
❑ 432 Alex Trevino .40 .15
❑ 433 John Moses .40 .15
❑ 434 Dave Wayne Johnson RC .40 .15
❑ 435 Mackey Sasser .40 .15
❑ 436 Rick Leach .40 .15
❑ 437 Lenny Harris .40 .15
❑ 438 Carlos Martinez .40 .15
❑ 439 Rex Hudler .40 .15
❑ 440 Domingo Ramos .40 .15
❑ 441 Gerald Perry .40 .15
❑ 442 Jeff Russell .40 .15
❑ 443 Carlos Baerga RC 1.00 .40
❑ 444 Will Clark CL .60 .25
❑ 445 Stan Javier .40 .15
❑ 446 Kevin Maas RC 1.00 .40
❑ 447 Tom Brunansky .40 .15
❑ 448 Carmelo Martinez .40 .15
❑ 449 Willie Blair RC .40 .15
❑ 450 Andres Galarraga .60 .25
❑ 451 Bud Black .40 .15
❑ 452 Greg W. Harris .40 .15
❑ 453 Joe Oliver .40 .15
❑ 454 Greg Brock .40 .15
❑ 455 Jeff Treadway .40 .15
❑ 456 Lance McCullers .40 .15
❑ 457 Dave Schmidt .40 .15
❑ 458 Todd Burns .40 .15
❑ 459 Max Venable .40 .15
❑ 460 Neal Heaton .40 .15
❑ 461 Mark Williamson .40 .15
❑ 462 Keith Miller .40 .15
❑ 463 Mike LaCoss .40 .15
❑ 464 Jose Offerman RC 1.00 .40
❑ 465 Jim Leyritz RC 2.00 .75
❑ 466 Glenn Braggs .40 .15
❑ 467 Ron Robinson .40 .15
❑ 468 Mark Davis .40 .15
❑ 469 Gary Pettis .40 .15
❑ 470 Keith Hernandez .60 .25
❑ 471 Dennis Rasmussen .40 .15
❑ 472 Mark Eichhorn .40 .15
❑ 473 Ted Power .40 .15
❑ 474 Terry Mulholland .40 .15
❑ 475 Todd Stottlemyre .60 .25
❑ 476 Jerry Goff RC .40 .15
❑ 477 Gene Nelson .40 .15
❑ 478 Rich Gedman .40 .15
❑ 479 Brian Harper .40 .15

❑ 480	Mike Felder	.40	.15
❑ 481	Steve Avery	.40	.15
❑ 482	Jack Morris	.60	.25
❑ 483	Randy Johnson	3.00	1.25
❑ 484	Scott Radinsky RC	.40	.15
❑ 485	Jose DeLeon	.40	.15
❑ 486	Stan Belinda RC	.40	.15
❑ 487	Brian Holton	.40	.15
❑ 488	Mark Carreon	.40	.15
❑ 489	Trevor Wilson	.40	.15
❑ 490	Mike Sharperson	.40	.15
❑ 491	Alan Mills RC	.40	.15
❑ 492	John Candelaria	.40	.15
❑ 493	Paul Assenmacher	.40	.15
❑ 494	Steve Crawford	.40	.15
❑ 495	Brad Arnsberg	.40	.15
❑ 496	Sergio Valdez RC	.40	.15
❑ 497	Mark Parent	.40	.15
❑ 498	Tom Pagnozzi	.40	.15
❑ 499	Greg A. Harris	.40	.15
❑ 500	Randy Ready	.40	.15
❑ 501	Duane Ward	.40	.15
❑ 502	Nelson Santovenia	.40	.15
❑ 503	Joe Klink RC	.40	.15
❑ 504	Eric Plunk	.40	.15
❑ 505	Jeff Reed	.40	.15
❑ 506	Ted Higuera	.40	.15
❑ 507	Joe Hesketh	.40	.15
❑ 508	Dan Petry	.40	.15
❑ 509	Matt Young	.40	.15
❑ 510	Jerald Clark	.40	.15
❑ 511	John Orton RC	.40	.15
❑ 512	Scott Ruskin RC	.40	.15
❑ 513	Chris Hoiles RC	1.00	.40
❑ 514	Daryl Boston	.40	.15
❑ 515	Francisco Oliveras	.40	.15
❑ 516	Ozzie Canseco	.40	.15
❑ 517	Xavier Hernandez RC	.40	.15
❑ 518	Fred Manrique	.40	.15
❑ 519	Shawn Boskie RC	.40	.15
❑ 520	Jeff Montgomery	.60	.25
❑ 521	Jack Daugherty RC	.40	.15
❑ 522	Keith Comstock	.40	.15
❑ 523	Greg Hibbard RC	.40	.15
❑ 524	Lee Smith	.60	.25
❑ 525	Dana Kiecker RC	.40	.15
❑ 526	Darrel Akerfelds	.40	.15
❑ 527	Greg Myers	.40	.15
❑ 528	Ryne Sandberg CL	1.50	.60

1998 Leaf Rookies and Stars

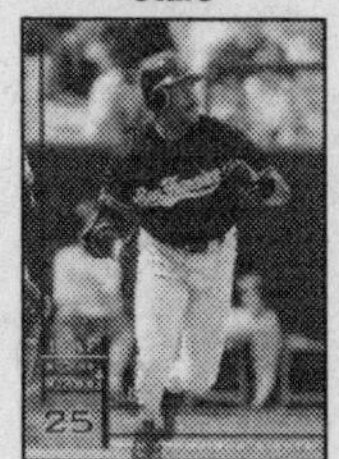

❑	COMPLETE SET (339)	250.00	125.00
❑	COMP.SET w/o SP's (200)	25.00	10.00
❑	COMMON (1-130/231-300)	.30	.10
❑	COMMON CARD (131-190)	1.00	.40
❑	COMMON CARD (191-230)	2.00	.75
❑	COMMON RC (191-230)	2.00	.75
❑	COMMON CARD (301-339)	2.50	1.00
❑	COMMON RC (301-339)	2.50	1.00
❑ 1	Andy Pettitte	.50	.20
❑ 2	Roberto Alomar	.50	.20
❑ 3	Randy Johnson	.75	.30
❑ 4	Manny Ramirez	.50	.20
❑ 5	Paul Molitor	.30	.10
❑ 6	Mike Mussina	.50	.20
❑ 7	Jim Thome	.50	.20
❑ 8	Tino Martinez	.50	.20
❑ 9	Gary Sheffield	.30	.10
❑ 10	Chuck Knoblauch	.30	.10
❑ 11	Bernie Williams	.50	.20
❑ 12	Tim Salmon	.50	.20
❑ 13	Sammy Sosa	.75	.30
❑ 14	Wade Boggs	.50	.20
❑ 15	Andres Galarraga	.30	.10
❑ 16	Pedro Martinez	.50	.20
❑ 17	David Justice	.30	.10
❑ 18	Chan Ho Park	.30	.10
❑ 19	Jay Buhner	.30	.10
❑ 20	Ryan Klesko	.30	.10
❑ 21	Barry Larkin	.50	.20
❑ 22	Will Clark	.50	.20
❑ 23	Raul Mondesi	.30	.10
❑ 24	Rickey Henderson	.75	.30
❑ 25	Jim Edmonds	.30	.10
❑ 26	Ken Griffey Jr.	1.25	.50
❑ 27	Frank Thomas	.75	.30
❑ 28	Cal Ripken	2.50	1.00
❑ 29	Alex Rodriguez	1.25	.50
❑ 30	Mike Piazza	1.25	.50
❑ 31	Greg Maddux	1.25	.50
❑ 32	Chipper Jones	.75	.30
❑ 33	Tony Gwynn	1.00	.40
❑ 34	Derek Jeter	2.00	.75
❑ 35	Jeff Bagwell	.50	.20
❑ 36	Juan Gonzalez	.30	.10
❑ 37	Nomar Garciaparra	1.25	.50
❑ 38	Andruw Jones	.50	.20
❑ 39	Hideo Nomo	.75	.30
❑ 40	Roger Clemens	1.50	.60
❑ 41	Mark McGwire	2.00	.75
❑ 42	Scott Rolen	.50	.20
❑ 43	Vladimir Guerrero	.75	.30
❑ 44	Barry Bonds	2.00	.75
❑ 45	Darin Erstad	.30	.10
❑ 46	Albert Belle	.30	.10
❑ 47	Kenny Lofton	.30	.10
❑ 48	Mo Vaughn	.30	.10
❑ 49	Ivan Rodriguez	.50	.20
❑ 50	Jose Cruz Jr.	.30	.10
❑ 51	Tony Clark	.30	.10
❑ 52	Larry Walker	.30	.10
❑ 53	Mark Grace	.50	.20
❑ 54	Edgar Martinez	.50	.20
❑ 55	Fred McGriff	.50	.20
❑ 56	Rafael Palmeiro	.50	.20
❑ 57	Matt Williams	.30	.10
❑ 58	Craig Biggio	.50	.20
❑ 59	Ken Caminiti	.30	.10
❑ 60	Jose Canseco	.50	.20
❑ 61	Brady Anderson	.30	.10
❑ 62	Moises Alou	.30	.10
❑ 63	Justin Thompson	.30	.10
❑ 64	John Smoltz	.50	.20
❑ 65	Carlos Delgado	.30	.10
❑ 66	J.T. Snow	.30	.10
❑ 67	Jason Giambi	.30	.10
❑ 68	Garret Anderson	.30	.10
❑ 69	Rondell White	.30	.10
❑ 70	Eric Karros	.30	.10
❑ 71	Javier Lopez	.30	.10
❑ 72	Pat Hentgen	.30	.10
❑ 73	Dante Bichette	.30	.10
❑ 74	Charles Johnson	.30	.10
❑ 75	Tom Glavine	.50	.20
❑ 76	Rusty Greer	.30	.10
❑ 77	Travis Fryman	.30	.10
❑ 78	Todd Hundley	.30	.10
❑ 79	Ray Lankford	.30	.10
❑ 80	Denny Neagle	.30	.10
❑ 81	Henry Rodriguez	.30	.10
❑ 82	Sandy Alomar Jr.	.30	.10
❑ 83	Robin Ventura	.30	.10
❑ 84	John Olerud	.30	.10
❑ 85	Omar Vizquel	.50	.20
❑ 86	Darren Dreifort	.30	.10
❑ 87	Kevin Brown	.30	.10
❑ 88	Curt Schilling	.30	.10
❑ 89	Francisco Cordova	.30	.10
❑ 90	Brad Radke	.30	.10
❑ 91	David Cone	.30	.10
❑ 92	Paul O'Neill	.50	.20
❑ 93	Vinny Castilla	.30	.10
❑ 94	Marquis Grissom	.30	.10
❑ 95	Brian L.Hunter	.30	.10
❑ 96	Kevin Appier	.30	.10
❑ 97	Bobby Bonilla	.30	.10
❑ 98	Eric Young	.30	.10
❑ 99	Jason Kendall	.30	.10
❑ 100	Shawn Green	.30	.10
❑ 101	Edgardo Alfonzo	.30	.10
❑ 102	Alan Benes	.30	.10
❑ 103	Bobby Higginson	.30	.10
❑ 104	Todd Greene	.30	.10
❑ 105	Jose Guillen	.30	.10
❑ 106	Neifi Perez	.30	.10
❑ 107	Edgar Renteria	.30	.10
❑ 108	Chris Stynes	.30	.10
❑ 109	Todd Walker	.30	.10
❑ 110	Brian Jordan	.30	.10
❑ 111	Joe Carter	.30	.10
❑ 112	Ellis Burks	.30	.10
❑ 113	Brett Tomko	.30	.10
❑ 114	Mike Cameron	.30	.10
❑ 115	Shannon Stewart	.30	.10
❑ 116	Kevin Orie	.30	.10
❑ 117	Brian Giles	.30	.10
❑ 118	Hideki Irabu	.30	.10
❑ 119	Delino DeShields	.30	.10
❑ 120	David Segui	.30	.10
❑ 121	Dustin Hermanson	.30	.10
❑ 122	Kevin Young	.30	.10
❑ 123	Jay Bell	.30	.10
❑ 124	Doug Glanville	.30	.10
❑ 125	John Roskos RC	.30	.10
❑ 126	Damon Hollins	.30	.10
❑ 127	Matt Stairs	.30	.10
❑ 128	Cliff Floyd	.30	.10
❑ 129	Derek Bell	.30	.10
❑ 130	Darryl Strawberry	.30	.10
❑ 131	Ken Griffey Jr. PT SP	4.00	1.50
❑ 132	Tim Salmon PT SP	1.50	.60
❑ 133	Manny Ramirez PT SP	1.50	.60
❑ 134	Paul Konerko PT SP	1.00	.40
❑ 135	Frank Thomas PT SP	2.50	1.00
❑ 136	Todd Helton PT SP	1.50	.60
❑ 137	Larry Walker PT SP	1.00	.40
❑ 138	Mo Vaughn PT SP	1.00	.40
❑ 139	Travis Lee PT SP	1.00	.40
❑ 140	Ivan Rodriguez PT SP	1.50	.60
❑ 141	Ben Grieve PT SP	1.00	.40
❑ 142	Brad Fullmer PT SP	1.00	.40
❑ 143	Alex Rodriguez PT SP	4.00	1.50
❑ 144	Mike Piazza PT SP	4.00	1.50
❑ 145	Greg Maddux PT SP	4.00	1.50
❑ 146	Chipper Jones PT SP	2.50	1.00
❑ 147	Kenny Lofton PT SP	1.00	.40
❑ 148	Albert Belle PT SP	1.00	.40
❑ 149	Barry Bonds PT SP	6.00	2.50
❑ 150	Vladimir Guerrero PT SP	2.50	1.00
❑ 151	Tony Gwynn PT SP	3.00	1.25
❑ 152	Derek Jeter PT SP	6.00	2.50
❑ 153	Jeff Bagwell PT SP	1.50	.60
❑ 154	Juan Gonzalez PT SP	1.00	.40
❑ 155	N.Garciaparra PT SP	4.00	1.50
❑ 156	Andruw Jones PT SP	1.50	.60
❑ 157	Hideo Nomo PT SP	2.50	1.00
❑ 158	Roger Clemens PT SP	5.00	2.00
❑ 159	Mark McGwire PT SP	6.00	2.50
❑ 160	Scott Rolen PT SP	1.50	.60
❑ 161	Travis Lee TLU SP	1.00	.40
❑ 162	Ben Grieve TLU SP	1.00	.40
❑ 163	Jose Guillen TLU SP	1.00	.40
❑ 164	Mike Piazza TLU SP	4.00	1.50
❑ 165	Kevin Appier TLU SP	1.00	.40
❑ 166	Marquis Grissom TLU SP	1.00	.40
❑ 167	Rusty Greer TLU SP	1.00	.40
❑ 168	Ken Caminiti TLU SP	1.00	.40
❑ 169	Craig Biggio TLU SP	1.50	.60
❑ 170	Ken Griffey Jr. TLU SP	4.00	1.50
❑ 171	Larry Walker TLU SP	1.00	.40
❑ 172	Barry Larkin TLU SP	1.50	.60
❑ 173	A.Galarraga TLU SP	1.00	.40
❑ 174	Wade Boggs TLU SP	1.50	.60
❑ 175	Sammy Sosa TLU SP	2.50	1.00
❑ 176	Todd Dunwoody TLU SP	1.00	.40
❑ 177	Jim Thome TLU SP	1.50	.60
❑ 178	Paul Molitor TLU SP	1.00	.40
❑ 179	Tony Clark TLU SP	1.00	.40
❑ 180	Jose Cruz Jr. TLU SP	1.00	.40

- ❑ 181 Darin Erstad TLU SP 1.00 .40
- ❑ 182 Barry Bonds TLU SP 6.00 2.50
- ❑ 183 Vlad.Guerrero TLU SP 2.50 1.00
- ❑ 184 Scott Rolen TLU SP 1.50 .60
- ❑ 185 Mark McGwire TLU SP 6.00 2.50
- ❑ 186 N.Garciaparra TLU SP 4.00 1.50
- ❑ 187 Gary Sheffield TLU SP 1.00 .40
- ❑ 188 Cal Ripken TLU SP 8.00 3.00
- ❑ 189 Frank Thomas TLU SP 2.50 1.00
- ❑ 190 Andy Pettitte TLU SP 1.50 .60
- ❑ 191 Paul Konerko SP 2.00 .75
- ❑ 192 Todd Helton SP 3.00 1.25
- ❑ 193 Mark Kotsay SP 2.00 .75
- ❑ 194 Brad Fullmer SP 2.00 .75
- ❑ 195 Kevin Millwood SP RC 8.00 3.00
- ❑ 196 David Ortiz SP 12.00 5.00
- ❑ 197 Kerry Wood SP 2.50 1.00
- ❑ 198 Miguel Tejada SP 5.00 2.00
- ❑ 199 Fernando Tatis SP 2.00 .75
- ❑ 200 Jaret Wright SP 2.00 .75
- ❑ 201 Ben Grieve SP 2.00 .75
- ❑ 202 Travis Lee SP 2.00 .75
- ❑ 203 Wes Helms SP 2.00 .75
- ❑ 204 Geoff Jenkins SP 10.00 4.00
- ❑ 205 Russell Branyan SP 2.00 .75
- ❑ 206 Esteban Yan SP RC 3.00 1.25
- ❑ 207 Ben Ford SP RC 2.00 .75
- ❑ 208 Rich Butler SP RC 2.00 .75
- ❑ 209 Ryan Jackson SP RC 2.00 .75
- ❑ 210 A.J. Hinch SP 2.00 .75
- ❑ 211 Magglio Ordonez RC 25.00 10.00
- ❑ 212 Dave Dellucci SP RC 5.00 2.00
- ❑ 213 Billy McMillon SP 2.00 .75
- ❑ 214 Mike Lowell SP RC 10.00 4.00
- ❑ 215 Todd Erdos SP RC 2.00 .75
- ❑ 216 Carlos Mendoza SP RC 2.00 .75
- ❑ 217 Frank Catalanotto SP RC 5.00 2.00
- ❑ 218 Julio Ramirez SP RC 3.00 1.25
- ❑ 219 John Halama SP RC 3.00 1.25
- ❑ 220 Wilson Delgado SP 2.00 .75
- ❑ 221 Mike Judd SP RC 3.00 1.25
- ❑ 222 Rolando Arrojo SP RC 3.00 1.25
- ❑ 223 Jason LaRue SP RC 3.00 1.25
- ❑ 224 Manny Aybar SP RC 3.00 1.25
- ❑ 225 Jorge Velandia SP 2.00 .75
- ❑ 226 Mike Kinkade SP RC 3.00 1.25
- ❑ 227 Carlos Lee SP RC 15.00 6.00
- ❑ 228 Bobby Hughes SP 2.00 .75
- ❑ 229 Ryan Christenson SP RC 2.00 .75
- ❑ 230 Masato Yoshii SP RC 3.00 1.25
- ❑ 231 Richard Hidalgo .30 .10
- ❑ 232 Rafael Medina .30 .10
- ❑ 233 Damian Jackson .30 .10
- ❑ 234 Derek Lowe .30 .10
- ❑ 235 Mario Valdez .30 .10
- ❑ 236 Eli Marrero .30 .10
- ❑ 237 Juan Encarnacion .30 .10
- ❑ 238 Livan Hernandez .30 .10
- ❑ 239 Bruce Chen .30 .10
- ❑ 240 Eric Milton .30 .10
- ❑ 241 Jason Varitek .75 .30
- ❑ 242 Scott Elarton .30 .10
- ❑ 243 Manuel Barrios RC .30 .10
- ❑ 244 Mike Caruso .30 .10
- ❑ 245 Tom Evans .30 .10
- ❑ 246 Pat Cline .30 .10
- ❑ 247 Matt Clement .30 .10
- ❑ 248 Karim Garcia .30 .10
- ❑ 249 Richie Sexson .30 .10
- ❑ 250 Sidney Ponson .30 .10
- ❑ 251 Randall Simon .30 .10
- ❑ 252 Tony Saunders .30 .10
- ❑ 253 Javier Valentin .30 .10
- ❑ 254 Danny Clyburn .30 .10
- ❑ 255 Michael Coleman .30 .10
- ❑ 256 Hanley Frias RC .30 .10
- ❑ 257 Miguel Cairo .30 .10
- ❑ 258 Rob Stanifer RC .30 .10
- ❑ 259 Lou Collier .30 .10
- ❑ 260 Abraham Nunez .30 .10
- ❑ 261 Ricky Ledee .30 .10
- ❑ 262 Carl Pavano .30 .10
- ❑ 263 Derrek Lee .50 .20
- ❑ 264 Jeff Abbott .30 .10
- ❑ 265 Bob Abreu .30 .10
- ❑ 266 Bartolo Colon .30 .10
- ❑ 267 Mike Drumright .30 .10
- ❑ 268 Daryle Ward .30 .10
- ❑ 269 Gabe Alvarez .30 .10
- ❑ 270 Josh Booty .30 .10
- ❑ 271 Damian Moss .30 .10
- ❑ 272 Brian Rose .30 .10
- ❑ 273 Jarrod Washburn .30 .10
- ❑ 274 Bobby Estalella .30 .10
- ❑ 275 Enrique Wilson .30 .10
- ❑ 276 Derrick Gibson .30 .10
- ❑ 277 Ken Cloude .30 .10
- ❑ 278 Kevin Witt .30 .10
- ❑ 279 Donnie Sadler .30 .10
- ❑ 280 Sean Casey .30 .10
- ❑ 281 Jacob Cruz .30 .10
- ❑ 282 Ron Wright .30 .10
- ❑ 283 Jeremi Gonzalez .30 .10
- ❑ 284 Desi Relaford .30 .10
- ❑ 285 Bobby Smith .30 .10
- ❑ 286 Javier Vazquez .30 .10
- ❑ 287 Steve Woodard .30 .10
- ❑ 288 Greg Norton .30 .10
- ❑ 289 Cliff Politte .30 .10
- ❑ 290 Felix Heredia .30 .10
- ❑ 291 Braden Looper .30 .10
- ❑ 292 Felix Martinez .30 .10
- ❑ 293 Brian Meadows .30 .10
- ❑ 294 Edwin Diaz .30 .10
- ❑ 295 Pat Watkins .30 .10
- ❑ 296 Marc Pisciotta RC .30 .10
- ❑ 297 Rick Gorecki .30 .10
- ❑ 298 DaRond Stovall .30 .10
- ❑ 299 Andy Larkin .30 .10
- ❑ 300 Felix Rodriguez .30 .10
- ❑ 301 Blake Stein SP 2.50 1.00
- ❑ 302 John Rocker SP RC 6.00 2.50
- ❑ 303 Justin Baughman SP RC 2.50 1.00
- ❑ 304 Jesus Sanchez SP RC 4.00 1.50
- ❑ 305 Randy Winn SP 2.50 1.00
- ❑ 306 Lou Merloni SP 2.50 1.00
- ❑ 307 Jim Parque SP RC 4.00 1.50
- ❑ 308 Dennis Reyes SP 2.50 1.00
- ❑ 309 Orlando Hernandez SP RC 10.00 4.00
- ❑ 310 Jason Johnson SP 2.50 1.00
- ❑ 311 Torii Hunter SP 2.50 1.00
- ❑ 312 Mike Piazza Marlins SP 10.00 4.00
- ❑ 313 Mike Frank SP RC 2.50 1.00
- ❑ 314 Troy Glaus SP RC 60.00 30.00
- ❑ 315 Jin Ho Cho SP RC 4.00 1.50
- ❑ 316 Ruben Mateo SP RC 2.50 1.00
- ❑ 317 Ryan Minor SP RC 4.00 1.50
- ❑ 318 Aramis Ramirez SP 2.50 1.00
- ❑ 319 Adrian Beltre SP 2.50 1.00
- ❑ 320 Matt Anderson SP RC 2.50 1.00
- ❑ 321 Gabe Kapler SP RC 6.00 2.50
- ❑ 322 Jeremy Giambi SP RC 4.00 1.50
- ❑ 323 Carlos Beltran SP 8.00 3.00
- ❑ 324 Dermal Brown SP 2.50 1.00
- ❑ 325 Ben Davis SP 2.50 1.00
- ❑ 326 Eric Chavez SP 2.50 1.00
- ❑ 327 Bobby Howry SP RC 2.50 1.00
- ❑ 328 Roy Halladay SP 2.50 1.00
- ❑ 329 George Lombard SP 2.50 1.00
- ❑ 330 Michael Barrett SP 2.50 1.00
- ❑ 331 Fernando Seguignol SP RC 2.50 1.00
- ❑ 332 J.D. Drew SP RC 12.00 5.00
- ❑ 333 Odalis Perez SP RC 10.00 4.00
- ❑ 334 Alex Cora SP RC 4.00 1.50
- ❑ 335 Placido Polanco SP RC 5.00 2.00
- ❑ 336 Armando Rios SP RC 4.00 1.50
- ❑ 337 Sammy Sosa HR SP 6.00 2.50
- ❑ 338 Mark McGwire HR SP 15.00 6.00
- ❑ 339 S.Sosa/M.McGwire CL SP 10.00 4.00

2001 Leaf Rookies and Stars

- ❑ COMP.SET w/o SP'S (100) 20.00 8.00
- ❑ COMMON CARD (1-100) .30 .10
- ❑ COMMON CARD (101-200) 3.00 1.25
- ❑ COMMON CARD (201-300) 5.00 2.00
- ❑ 1 Alex Rodriguez 1.25 .50
- ❑ 2 Derek Jeter 2.00 .75
- ❑ 3 Aramis Ramirez .30 .10
- ❑ 4 Cliff Floyd .30 .10
- ❑ 5 Nomar Garciaparra 1.25 .50
- ❑ 6 Craig Biggio .50 .20
- ❑ 7 Ivan Rodriguez .50 .20
- ❑ 8 Cal Ripken 2.50 1.00
- ❑ 9 Fred McGriff .50 .20
- ❑ 10 Chipper Jones .75 .30
- ❑ 11 Roberto Alomar .50 .20
- ❑ 12 Moises Alou .30 .10
- ❑ 13 Freddy Garcia .30 .10
- ❑ 14 Bobby Abreu .30 .10
- ❑ 15 Shawn Green .30 .10
- ❑ 16 Jason Giambi .30 .10
- ❑ 17 Todd Helton .50 .20
- ❑ 18 Robert Fick .30 .10
- ❑ 19 Tony Gwynn 1.00 .40
- ❑ 20 Luis Gonzalez .30 .10
- ❑ 21 Sean Casey .30 .10
- ❑ 22 Roger Clemens 1.50 .60
- ❑ 23 Brian Giles .30 .10
- ❑ 24 Manny Ramirez Sox .50 .20
- ❑ 25 Barry Bonds 2.00 .75
- ❑ 26 Richard Hidalgo .30 .10
- ❑ 27 Vladimir Guerrero .75 .30
- ❑ 28 Kevin Brown .30 .10
- ❑ 29 Mike Sweeney .30 .10
- ❑ 30 Ken Griffey Jr. 1.25 .50
- ❑ 31 Mike Piazza 1.25 .50
- ❑ 32 Richie Sexson .30 .10
- ❑ 33 Matt Morris .30 .10
- ❑ 34 Jorge Posada .50 .20
- ❑ 35 Eric Chavez .30 .10
- ❑ 36 Mark Buehrle .50 .20
- ❑ 37 Jeff Bagwell .50 .20
- ❑ 38 Curt Schilling .30 .10
- ❑ 39 Bartolo Colon .30 .10
- ❑ 40 Mark Quinn .30 .10
- ❑ 41 Tony Clark .30 .10
- ❑ 42 Brad Radke .30 .10
- ❑ 43 Gary Sheffield .30 .10
- ❑ 44 Doug Mientkiewicz .30 .10
- ❑ 45 Pedro Martinez .50 .20
- ❑ 46 Carlos Lee .30 .10
- ❑ 47 Troy Glaus .30 .10
- ❑ 48 Preston Wilson .30 .10
- ❑ 49 Phil Nevin .30 .10
- ❑ 50 Chan Ho Park .30 .10
- ❑ 51 Randy Johnson .75 .30
- ❑ 52 Jermaine Dye .30 .10
- ❑ 53 Terrence Long .30 .10
- ❑ 54 Joe Mays .30 .10
- ❑ 55 Scott Rolen .50 .20
- ❑ 56 Miguel Tejada .30 .10
- ❑ 57 Jim Thome .50 .20
- ❑ 58 Jose Vidro .30 .10
- ❑ 59 Gabe Kapler .30 .10
- ❑ 60 Darin Erstad .30 .10
- ❑ 61 Jim Edmonds .30 .10
- ❑ 62 Jarrod Washburn .30 .10
- ❑ 63 Tom Glavine .50 .20
- ❑ 64 Adrian Beltre .30 .10
- ❑ 65 Sammy Sosa .75 .30
- ❑ 66 Juan Gonzalez .30 .10
- ❑ 67 Rafael Furcal .30 .10
- ❑ 68 Mike Mussina .50 .20
- ❑ 69 Mark McGwire 2.00 .75
- ❑ 70 Ryan Klesko .30 .10
- ❑ 71 Raul Mondesi .30 .10
- ❑ 72 Trot Nixon .30 .10
- ❑ 73 Barry Larkin .50 .20

❑	74	Rafael Palmeiro	.50	.20
❑	75	Mark Mulder	.30	.10
❑	76	Carlos Delgado	.30	.10
❑	77	Mike Hampton	.30	.10
❑	78	Carl Everett	.30	.10
❑	79	Paul Konerko	.30	.10
❑	80	Larry Walker	.30	.10
❑	81	Kerry Wood	.30	.10
❑	82	Frank Thomas	.75	.30
❑	83	Andruw Jones	.50	.20
❑	84	Eric Milton	.30	.10
❑	85	Ben Grieve	.30	.10
❑	86	Carlos Beltran	.30	.10
❑	87	Tim Hudson	.30	.10
❑	88	Hideo Nomo	.75	.30
❑	89	Greg Maddux	1.25	.50
❑	90	Edgar Martinez	.50	.20
❑	91	Lance Berkman	.30	.10
❑	92	Pat Burrell	.30	.10
❑	93	Jeff Kent	.30	.10
❑	94	Magglio Ordonez	.30	.10
❑	95	Cristian Guzman	.30	.10
❑	96	Jose Canseco	.50	.20
❑	97	J.D. Drew	.30	.10
❑	98	Bernie Williams	.50	.20
❑	99	Kazuhiro Sasaki	.30	.10
❑	100	Rickey Henderson	.75	.30
❑	101	Wilson Guzman RC	3.00	1.25
❑	102	Nick Neugebauer	3.00	1.25
❑	103	Lance Davis RC	3.00	1.25
❑	104	Felipe Lopez	3.00	1.25
❑	105	Toby Hall	3.00	1.25
❑	106	Jack Cust	3.00	1.25
❑	107	Jason Karnuth RC	3.00	1.25
❑	108	Bart Miadich RC	3.00	1.25
❑	109	Brian Roberts RC	8.00	3.00
❑	110	Brandon Larson RC	3.00	1.25
❑	111	Sean Douglass RC	3.00	1.25
❑	112	Joe Crede	5.00	2.00
❑	113	Tim Redding	3.00	1.25
❑	114	Adam Johnson	3.00	1.25
❑	115	Marcus Giles	3.00	1.25
❑	116	Jose Ortiz	3.00	1.25
❑	117	Jose Mieses RC	3.00	1.25
❑	118	Nick Maness RC	3.00	1.25
❑	119	Les Walrond RC	3.00	1.25
❑	120	Travis Phelps RC	3.00	1.25
❑	121	Troy Mattes RC	3.00	1.25
❑	122	Carlos Garcia RC	3.00	1.25
❑	123	Bill Ortega RC	3.00	1.25
❑	124	Gene Altman RC	3.00	1.25
❑	125	Nate Frese RC	3.00	1.25
❑	126	Alfonso Soriano	5.00	2.00
❑	127	Jose Nunez RC	3.00	1.25
❑	128	Bob File RC	3.00	1.25
❑	129	Dan Wright	3.00	1.25
❑	130	Nick Johnson	3.00	1.25
❑	131	Brent Abernathy	3.00	1.25
❑	132	Steve Green RC	3.00	1.25
❑	133	Billy Sylvester RC	3.00	1.25
❑	134	Scott MacRae RC	3.00	1.25
❑	135	Kris Keller RC	3.00	1.25
❑	136	Scott Stewart RC	3.00	1.25
❑	137	Henry Mateo RC	3.00	1.25
❑	138	Timo Perez	3.00	1.25
❑	139	Nate Teut RC	3.00	1.25
❑	140	Jason Michaels RC	3.00	1.25
❑	141	Junior Spivey RC	5.00	2.00
❑	142	Carlos Pena	3.00	1.25
❑	143	Wilmy Caceres RC	3.00	1.25
❑	144	David Lundquist	3.00	1.25
❑	145	Jack Wilson RC	5.00	2.00
❑	146	Jeremy Fikac RC	3.00	1.25
❑	147	Alex Escobar	3.00	1.25
❑	148	Abraham Nunez	3.00	1.25
❑	149	Xavier Nady	3.00	1.25
❑	150	Michael Cuddyer	3.00	1.25
❑	151	Greg Miller RC	3.00	1.25
❑	152	Eric Munson	3.00	1.25
❑	153	Aubrey Huff	3.00	1.25
❑	154	Tim Christman RC	3.00	1.25
❑	155	Erick Almonte RC	3.00	1.25
❑	156	Mike Penney RC	3.00	1.25
❑	157	Delvin James RC	3.00	1.25
❑	158	Ben Sheets	5.00	2.00
❑	159	Jason Hart	3.00	1.25
❑	160	Jose Acevedo RC	3.00	1.25
❑	161	Will Ohman RC	3.00	1.25
❑	162	Erik Hiljus RC	3.00	1.25
❑	163	Juan Moreno RC	3.00	1.25
❑	164	Mike Koplove RC	3.00	1.25
❑	165	Pedro Santana RC	3.00	1.25
❑	166	Jimmy Rollins	3.00	1.25
❑	167	Matt White RC	3.00	1.25
❑	168	Cesar Crespo RC	3.00	1.25
❑	169	Carlos Hernandez	3.00	1.25
❑	170	Chris George	3.00	1.25
❑	171	Brad Voyles RC	3.00	1.25
❑	172	Luis Pineda RC	3.00	1.25
❑	173	Carlos Zambrano	5.00	2.00
❑	174	Nate Cornejo	3.00	1.25
❑	175	Jason Smith RC	3.00	1.25
❑	176	Craig Monroe RC	8.00	3.00
❑	177	Cody Ransom RC	3.00	1.25
❑	178	John Grabow RC	3.00	1.25
❑	179	Pedro Feliz	3.00	1.25
❑	180	Jeremy Owens RC	3.00	1.25
❑	181	Kurt Ainsworth	3.00	1.25
❑	182	Luis Lopez	3.00	1.25
❑	183	Stubby Clapp RC	3.00	1.25
❑	184	Ryan Freel RC	8.00	3.00
❑	185	Duaner Sanchez RC	3.00	1.25
❑	186	Jason Jennings	3.00	1.25
❑	187	Kyle Lohse RC	5.00	2.00
❑	188	Jerrod Riggan RC	3.00	1.25
❑	189	Joe Beimel RC	3.00	1.25
❑	190	Nick Punto RC	3.00	1.25
❑	191	Willie Harris RC	3.00	1.25
❑	192	Ryan Jensen RC	3.00	1.25
❑	193	Adam Pettyjohn RC	3.00	1.25
❑	194	Donaldo Mendez RC	3.00	1.25
❑	195	Bret Prinz RC	3.00	1.25
❑	196	Paul Phillips RC	3.00	1.25
❑	197	Brian Lawrence RC	3.00	1.25
❑	198	Cesar Izturis	3.00	1.25
❑	199	Blaine Neal RC	3.00	1.25
❑	200	Josh Fogg RC	5.00	2.00
❑	201	Josh Towers RC	8.00	3.00
❑	202	Tim Spooneybarger RC	5.00	2.00
❑	203	Michael Rivera RC	5.00	2.00
❑	204	Juan Cruz RC	5.00	2.00
❑	205	Albert Pujols RC	200.00	125.00
❑	206	Josh Beckett	8.00	3.00
❑	207	Roy Oswalt	8.00	3.00
❑	208	Elpidio Guzman RC	5.00	2.00
❑	209	Horacio Ramirez RC	8.00	3.00
❑	210	Corey Patterson	5.00	2.00
❑	211	Geronimo Gil RC	5.00	2.00
❑	212	Jay Gibbons RC	8.00	3.00
❑	213	Orlando Woodards RC	5.00	2.00
❑	214	David Espinosa	5.00	2.00
❑	215	Angel Berroa RC	8.00	3.00
❑	216	Brandon Duckworth RC	5.00	2.00
❑	217	Brian Reith RC	5.00	2.00
❑	218	David Brous RC	5.00	2.00
❑	219	Bud Smith RC	5.00	2.00
❑	220	Ramon Vazquez RC	5.00	2.00
❑	221	Mark Teixeira RC	30.00	12.50
❑	222	Justin Atchley RC	5.00	2.00
❑	223	Tony Cogan RC	5.00	2.00
❑	224	Grant Balfour RC	5.00	2.00
❑	225	Ricardo Rodriguez RC	5.00	2.00
❑	226	Brian Rogers RC	5.00	2.00
❑	227	Adam Dunn	8.00	3.00
❑	228	Wilson Betemit RC	8.00	3.00
❑	229	Juan Diaz RC	5.00	2.00
❑	230	Jackson Melian RC	5.00	2.00
❑	231	Claudio Vargas RC	5.00	2.00
❑	232	Wilkin Ruan RC	5.00	2.00
❑	233	Justin Duchscherer RC	5.00	2.00
❑	234	Kevin Olsen RC	5.00	2.00
❑	235	Tony Fiore RC	5.00	2.00
❑	236	Jeremy Affeldt RC	5.00	2.00
❑	237	Mike Maroth RC	5.00	2.00
❑	238	C.C. Sabathia	5.00	2.00
❑	239	Cory Aldridge RC	5.00	2.00
❑	240	Zach Day RC	5.00	2.00
❑	241	Brett Jodie RC	5.00	2.00
❑	242	Winston Abreu RC	5.00	2.00
❑	243	Travis Hafner RC	25.00	10.00
❑	244	Joe Kennedy RC	8.00	3.00
❑	245	Rick Bauer RC	5.00	2.00
❑	246	Mike Young	8.00	3.00
❑	247	Ken Vining RC	5.00	2.00
❑	248	Doug Nickle RC	5.00	2.00
❑	249	Pablo Ozuna	5.00	2.00
❑	250	Dustan Mohr RC	5.00	2.00
❑	251	Ichiro Suzuki RC	50.00	20.00
❑	252	Ryan Drese RC	8.00	3.00
❑	253	Morgan Ensberg RC	8.00	3.00
❑	254	George Perez RC	5.00	2.00
❑	255	Roy Smith RC	5.00	2.00
❑	256	Juan Uribe RC	8.00	3.00
❑	257	Dewon Brazelton RC	5.00	2.00
❑	258	Endy Chavez RC	5.00	2.00
❑	259	Kris Foster RC	5.00	2.00
❑	260	Eric Knott RC	5.00	2.00
❑	261	Corky Miller RC	5.00	2.00
❑	262	Larry Bigbie	5.00	2.00
❑	263	Andres Torres RC	5.00	2.00
❑	264	Adrian Hernandez RC	5.00	2.00
❑	265	Johnny Estrada RC	8.00	3.00
❑	266	David Williams RC	5.00	2.00
❑	267	Steve Lomasney	5.00	2.00
❑	268	Victor Zambrano RC	8.00	3.00
❑	269	Keith Ginter	5.00	2.00
❑	270	Casey Fossum RC	5.00	2.00
❑	271	Josue Perez RC	5.00	2.00
❑	272	Josh Phelps	5.00	2.00
❑	273	Mark Prior RC	25.00	10.00
❑	274	Brandon Berger RC	5.00	2.00
❑	275	Scott Podsednik RC	12.00	5.00
❑	276	Jorge Julio RC	5.00	2.00
❑	277	Esix Snead RC	5.00	2.00
❑	278	Brandon Knight RC	5.00	2.00
❑	279	Saul Rivera RC	5.00	2.00
❑	280	Benito Baez RC	5.00	2.00
❑	281	Rob MacKowiak RC	8.00	3.00
❑	282	Eric Hinske RC	8.00	3.00
❑	283	Juan Rivera	5.00	2.00
❑	284	Kevin Joseph RC	5.00	2.00
❑	285	Juan A. Pena RC	5.00	2.00
❑	286	Brandon Lyon RC	5.00	2.00
❑	287	Adam Everett	5.00	2.00
❑	288	Eric Valent	5.00	2.00
❑	289	Ken Harvey	5.00	2.00
❑	290	Bert Snow RC	5.00	2.00
❑	291	Wily Mo Pena	5.00	2.00
❑	292	Rafael Soriano RC	5.00	2.00
❑	293	Carlos Valderrama RC	5.00	2.00
❑	294	Christian Parker RC	5.00	2.00
❑	295	Tsuyoshi Shinjo RC	8.00	3.00
❑	296	Martin Vargas RC	5.00	2.00
❑	297	Luke Hudson RC	5.00	2.00
❑	298	Dee Brown	5.00	2.00
❑	299	Alexis Gomez RC	5.00	2.00
❑	300	Angel Santos RC	5.00	2.00

1939 Play Ball

❑		COMPLETE SET (161)	10000.00	6000.00
❑		COMMON CARD (1-115)	20.00	12.00
❑		COMMON CARD (116-162)	75.00	40.00
❑		WRAPPER (1-CENT)	200.00	150.00
❑	1	Jake Powell RC	60.00	30.00
❑	2	Lee Grissom RC	20.00	12.00
❑	3	Red Ruffing	75.00	40.00
❑	4	Eldon Auker RC	20.00	12.00
❑	5	Luke Sewell	25.00	15.00
❑	6	Leo Durocher	100.00	60.00
❑	7	Bobby Doerr RC	75.00	40.00
❑	8	Henry Pippen RC	20.00	12.00
❑	9	James Tobin RC	20.00	12.00

❑ 10 James DeShong 20.00 12.00
❑ 11 Johnny Rizzo RC 20.00 12.00
❑ 12 Hershel Martin RC 20.00 12.00
❑ 13 Luke Hamlin RC 20.00 12.00
❑ 14 Jim Tabor RC 20.00 12.00
❑ 15 Paul Derringer 30.00 18.00
❑ 16 John Peacock RC 20.00 12.00
❑ 17 Emerson Dickman RC 20.00 12.00
❑ 18 Harry Danning RC 20.00 12.00
❑ 19 Paul Dean RC 40.00 25.00
❑ 20 Joe Heving RC 20.00 12.00
❑ 21 Dutch Leonard RC 30.00 18.00
❑ 22 Bucky Walters RC 30.00 18.00
❑ 23 Burgess Whitehead RC 20.00 12.00
❑ 24 Richard Coffman 20.00 12.00
❑ 25 George Selkirk RC 40.00 25.00
❑ 26 Joe DiMaggio RC 1400.00 900.00
❑ 27 Fred Ostermueller 20.00 12.00
❑ 28 Sylvester Johnson RC 20.00 12.00
❑ 29 John(Jack) Wilson RC 20.00 12.00
❑ 30 Bill Dickey 125.00 75.00
❑ 31 Sam West 20.00 12.00
❑ 32 Bob Seeds RC 20.00 12.00
❑ 33 Del Young RC 20.00 12.00
❑ 34 Frank Demaree 20.00 12.00
❑ 35 Bill Jurges 20.00 12.00
❑ 36 Frank McCormick RC 20.00 12.00
❑ 37 Virgil Davis 20.00 12.00
❑ 38 Billy Myers RC 20.00 12.00
❑ 39 Rick Ferrell 75.00 40.00
❑ 40 James Bagby Jr. RC 20.00 12.00
❑ 41 Lon Warneke 25.00 15.00
❑ 42 Arndt Jorgens 20.00 12.00
❑ 43 Melo Almada RC 25.00 15.00
❑ 44 Don Heffner RC 20.00 12.00
❑ 45 Merrill May RC 20.00 12.00
❑ 46 Morris Arnovich RC 20.00 12.00
❑ 47 Buddy Lewis RC 20.00 12.00
❑ 48 Lefty Gomez 125.00 75.00
❑ 49 Eddie Miller RC 20.00 12.00
❑ 50 Charley Gehringer 125.00 75.00
❑ 51 Mel Ott 125.00 75.00
❑ 52 Tommy Henrich RC 40.00 25.00
❑ 53 Carl Hubbell 125.00 75.00
❑ 54 Harry Gumpert RC 20.00 12.00
❑ 55 Arky Vaughan 75.00 40.00
❑ 56 Hank Greenberg 200.00 125.00
❑ 57 Buddy Hassett RC 20.00 12.00
❑ 58 Lou Chiozza RC 20.00 12.00
❑ 59 Ken Chase RC 20.00 12.00
❑ 60 Schoolboy Rowe RC 40.00 25.00
❑ 61 Tony Cuccinello 25.00 15.00
❑ 62 Tom Carey RC 20.00 12.00
❑ 63 Emmett Mueller RC 20.00 12.00
❑ 64 Wally Moses RC 25.00 15.00
❑ 65 Harry Craft RC 25.00 15.00
❑ 66 Jimmy Ripple RC 20.00 12.00
❑ 67 Ed Joost RC 25.00 15.00
❑ 68 Fred Sington RC 20.00 12.00
❑ 69 Elbie Fletcher RC 20.00 12.00
❑ 70 Fred Frankhouse 20.00 12.00
❑ 71 Monte Pearson RC 30.00 18.00
❑ 72 Debs Garms RC 20.00 12.00
❑ 73 Hal Schumacher 25.00 15.00
❑ 74 Cookie Lavagetto RC 25.00 15.00
❑ 75 Stan Bordagaray RC 20.00 12.00
❑ 76 Goody Rosen RC 20.00 12.00
❑ 77 Lew Riggs RC 20.00 12.00
❑ 78 Julius Solters 20.00 12.00
❑ 79 Jo Jo Moore 20.00 12.00
❑ 80 Pete Fox 20.00 12.00
❑ 81 Babe Dahlgren RC 30.00 18.00
❑ 82 Chuck Klein 100.00 60.00
❑ 83 Gus Suhr 20.00 12.00
❑ 84 Skeeter Newsom RC 20.00 12.00
❑ 85 Johnny Cooney RC 20.00 12.00
❑ 86 Dolph Camilli 25.00 15.00
❑ 87 Milburn Shoffner RC 20.00 12.00
❑ 88 Charlie Keller RC 40.00 25.00
❑ 89 Lloyd Waner 75.00 40.00
❑ 90 Robert Klinger RC 20.00 12.00
❑ 91 John Knott RC 20.00 12.00
❑ 92 Ted Williams RC 1800.00 1000.00
❑ 93 Charles Gelbert RC 20.00 12.00
❑ 94 Heinie Manush 75.00 40.00
❑ 95 Whit Wyatt RC 25.00 15.00
❑ 96 Babe Phelps RC 20.00 12.00
❑ 97 Bob Johnson 30.00 18.00
❑ 98 Pinky Whitney RC 20.00 12.00
❑ 99 Wally Berger 30.00 18.00
❑ 100 Buddy Myer 25.00 15.00
❑ 101 Roger Cramer 25.00 15.00
❑ 102 Lem (Pep) Young RC 20.00 12.00
❑ 103 Moe Berg 125.00 75.00
❑ 104 Tom Bridges 25.00 15.00
❑ 105 Rabbit McNair RC 20.00 12.00
❑ 106 Dolly Stark UMP 30.00 18.00
❑ 107 Joe Vosmik 20.00 12.00
❑ 108 Frank Hayes 20.00 12.00
❑ 109 Myril Hoag 20.00 12.00
❑ 110 Fred Fitzsimmons 25.00 15.00
❑ 111 Van Lingle Mungo RC 30.00 18.00
❑ 112 Paul Waner 100.00 60.00
❑ 113 Al Schacht 30.00 18.00
❑ 114 Cecil Travis RC 25.00 15.00
❑ 115 Ralph Kress 20.00 12.00
❑ 116 Gene Desautels RC 75.00 40.00
❑ 117 Wayne Ambler RC 75.00 40.00
❑ 118 Lynn Nelson 75.00 40.00
❑ 119 Will Hershberger RC 100.00 50.00
❑ 120 Rabbit Warstler RC 75.00 40.00
❑ 121 Bill Posedel RC 75.00 40.00
❑ 122 George McQuinn RC 75.00 40.00
❑ 123 Ray T. Davis RC 75.00 40.00
❑ 124 Walter Brown 75.00 40.00
❑ 125 Cliff Melton RC 75.00 40.00
❑ 126 Not issued
❑ 127 Gil Brack RC 75.00 40.00
❑ 128 Joe Bowman RC 75.00 40.00
❑ 129 Bill Swift 75.00 40.00
❑ 130 Bill Brubaker RC 75.00 40.00
❑ 131 Mort Cooper RC 100.00 50.00
❑ 132 Jim Brown RC 75.00 40.00
❑ 133 Lynn Myers RC 75.00 40.00
❑ 134 Tot Presnell RC 75.00 40.00
❑ 135 Mickey Owen RC 100.00 50.00
❑ 136 Roy Bell RC 75.00 40.00
❑ 137 Pete Appleton 75.00 40.00
❑ 138 George Case RC 100.00 50.00
❑ 139 Vito Tamulis RC 75.00 40.00
❑ 140 Ray Hayworth RC 75.00 40.00
❑ 141 Pete Coscarart RC 75.00 40.00
❑ 142 Ira Hutchinson RC 75.00 40.00
❑ 143 Earl Averill 175.00 100.00
❑ 144 Zeke Bonura RC 100.00 50.00
❑ 145 Hugh Mulcahy RC 75.00 40.00
❑ 146 Tom Sunkel RC 75.00 40.00
❑ 147 George Coffman RC 75.00 40.00
❑ 148 Bill Trotter RC 75.00 40.00
❑ 149 Max West RC 75.00 40.00
❑ 150 James Walkup RC 75.00 40.00
❑ 151 Hugh Casey RC 100.00 50.00
❑ 152 Roy Weatherly RC 75.00 40.00
❑ 153 Dizzy Trout RC 100.00 50.00
❑ 154 Johnny Hudson RC 75.00 40.00
❑ 155 Jimmy Outlaw RC 75.00 40.00
❑ 156 Ray Berres RC 75.00 40.00
❑ 157 Don Padgett RC 75.00 40.00
❑ 158 Bud Thomas RC 75.00 40.00
❑ 159 Red Evans RC 75.00 40.00
❑ 160 Gene Moore RC 75.00 40.00
❑ 161 Lonnie Frey 75.00 40.00
❑ 162 Whitey Moore RC 100.00 50.00

1940 Play Ball

❑ COMPLETE SET (240) 15000.00 10000.00
❑ COMMON CARD (1-120) 20.00 12.00
❑ COMMON CARD (121-180) 20.00 12.00
❑ COMMON CARD (181-240) 70.00 35.00
❑ WRAP.(1-CENT, DIFF. COL.) 800.00 700.00
❑ 1 Joe DiMaggio 2500.00 1500.00
❑ 2 Art Jorgens 25.00 15.00
❑ 3 Babe Dahlgren 25.00 15.00
❑ 4 Tommy Henrich 50.00 25.00
❑ 5 Monte Pearson 25.00 15.00
❑ 6 Lefty Gomez 150.00 90.00
❑ 7 Bill Dickey 175.00 100.00
❑ 8 George Selkirk 25.00 15.00
❑ 9 Charlie Keller 50.00 25.00
❑ 10 Red Ruffing 90.00 50.00
❑ 11 Jake Powell 25.00 15.00

❑ 12 Johnny Schulte 20.00 12.00
❑ 13 Jack Knott 20.00 12.00
❑ 14 Rabbit McNair 20.00 12.00
❑ 15 George Case 25.00 15.00
❑ 16 Cecil Travis 25.00 15.00
❑ 17 Buddy Myer 25.00 15.00
❑ 18 Charlie Gelbert 20.00 12.00
❑ 19 Ken Chase 20.00 12.00
❑ 20 Buddy Lewis 20.00 12.00
❑ 21 Rick Ferrell 80.00 45.00
❑ 22 Sammy West 20.00 12.00
❑ 23 Dutch Leonard 25.00 15.00
❑ 24 Frank Hayes 20.00 12.00
❑ 25 Bob Johnson 25.00 15.00
❑ 26 Wally Moses 25.00 15.00
❑ 27 Ted Williams 1200.00 800.00
❑ 28 Gene Desautels 20.00 12.00
❑ 29 Doc Cramer 25.00 15.00
❑ 30 Moe Berg 150.00 90.00
❑ 31 Jack Wilson 20.00 12.00
❑ 32 Jim Bagby 20.00 12.00
❑ 33 Fritz Ostermueller 20.00 12.00
❑ 34 John Peacock 20.00 12.00
❑ 35 Joe Heving 20.00 12.00
❑ 36 Jim Tabor 20.00 12.00
❑ 37 Emerson Dickman 20.00 12.00
❑ 38 Bobby Doerr 90.00 50.00
❑ 39 Tom Carey 20.00 12.00
❑ 40 Hank Greenberg 200.00 100.00
❑ 41 Charley Gehringer 150.00 90.00
❑ 42 Bud Thomas 20.00 12.00
❑ 43 Pete Fox 20.00 12.00
❑ 44 Dizzy Trout 25.00 15.00
❑ 45 Red Kress 20.00 12.00
❑ 46 Earl Averill 90.00 50.00
❑ 47 Oscar Vitt RC 20.00 12.00
❑ 48 Luke Sewell 25.00 15.00
❑ 49 Stormy Weatherly 20.00 12.00
❑ 50 Hal Trosky 25.00 15.00
❑ 51 Don Heffner 20.00 12.00
❑ 52 Myril Hoag 20.00 12.00
❑ 53 George McQuinn 25.00 15.00
❑ 54 Bill Trotter 20.00 12.00
❑ 55 Slick Coffman 20.00 12.00
❑ 56 Eddie Miller RC 25.00 15.00
❑ 57 Max West 20.00 12.00
❑ 58 Bill Posedel 20.00 12.00
❑ 59 Rabbit Warstler 20.00 12.00
❑ 60 John Cooney 20.00 12.00
❑ 61 Tony Cuccinello 25.00 15.00
❑ 62 Buddy Hassett 20.00 12.00
❑ 63 Pete Coscarart 20.00 12.00
❑ 64 Van Lingle Mungo 25.00 15.00
❑ 65 Fred Fitzsimmons 25.00 15.00
❑ 66 Babe Phelps 20.00 12.00
❑ 67 Whit Wyatt 25.00 15.00
❑ 68 Dolph Camilli 25.00 15.00
❑ 69 Cookie Lavagetto 25.00 15.00
❑ 70 Luke Hamlin (Hot Potato) 20.00 12.00
❑ 71 Mel Almada 20.00 12.00
❑ 72 Chuck Dressen RC 25.00 15.00
❑ 73 Bucky Walters 25.00 15.00
❑ 74 Paul(Duke) Derringer 25.00 15.00
❑ 75 Frank (Buck) McCormick 25.00 15.00
❑ 76 Lonny Frey 20.00 12.00
❑ 77 Willard Hershberger 25.00 15.00
❑ 78 Lew Riggs 20.00 12.00
❑ 79 Harry Craft 25.00 15.00
❑ 80 Billy Myers 20.00 12.00

❑ 81 Wally Berger	25.00	15.00
❑ 82 Hank Gowdy CO	25.00	15.00
❑ 83 Cliff Melton	20.00	12.00
❑ 84 Jo Jo Moore	20.00	12.00
❑ 85 Hal Schumacher	25.00	15.00
❑ 86 Harry Gumbert	20.00	12.00
❑ 87 Carl Hubbell	125.00	75.00
❑ 88 Mel Ott	175.00	100.00
❑ 89 Bill Jurges	20.00	12.00
❑ 90 Frank Demaree	20.00	12.00
❑ 91 Bob Seeds	20.00	12.00
❑ 92 Whitey Whitehead	20.00	12.00
❑ 93 Harry Danning	20.00	12.00
❑ 94 Gus Suhr	20.00	12.00
❑ 95 Hugh Mulcahy	20.00	12.00
❑ 96 Heinie Mueller	20.00	12.00
❑ 97 Morry Arnovich	20.00	12.00
❑ 98 Pinky May	20.00	12.00
❑ 99 Syl Johnson	20.00	12.00
❑ 100 Hersh Martin	20.00	12.00
❑ 101 Del Young	20.00	12.00
❑ 102 Chuck Klein	100.00	60.00
❑ 103 Elbie Fletcher	20.00	12.00
❑ 104 Paul Waner	90.00	50.00
❑ 105 Lloyd Waner	80.00	45.00
❑ 106 Pep Young	20.00	12.00
❑ 107 Arky Vaughan	80.00	45.00
❑ 108 Johnny Rizzo	20.00	12.00
❑ 109 Don Padgett	20.00	12.00
❑ 110 Tom Sunkel	20.00	12.00
❑ 111 Mickey Owen	25.00	15.00
❑ 112 Jimmy Brown	20.00	12.00
❑ 113 Mort Cooper	25.00	15.00
❑ 114 Lon Warneke	25.00	15.00
❑ 115 Mike Gonzalez CO	25.00	15.00
❑ 116 Al Schacht	25.00	15.00
❑ 117 Dolly Stark UMP	25.00	15.00
❑ 118 Waite Hoyt	90.00	50.00
❑ 119 Grover C. Alexander	175.00	100.00
❑ 120 Walter Johnson	200.00	100.00
❑ 121 Atley Donald RC	25.00	15.00
❑ 122 Sandy Sundra RC	25.00	15.00
❑ 123 Hildy Hildebrand	25.00	15.00
❑ 124 Earle Combs	100.00	60.00
❑ 125 Art Fletcher RC	25.00	15.00
❑ 126 Jake Solters	20.00	12.00
❑ 127 Muddy Ruel	20.00	12.00
❑ 128 Pete Appleton	20.00	12.00
❑ 129 Bucky Harris MG RC	80.00	45.00
❑ 130 Clyde Milan RC	25.00	15.00
❑ 131 Zeke Bonura	25.00	15.00
❑ 132 Connie Mack MG RC	150.00	75.00
❑ 133 Jimmie Foxx	200.00	100.00
❑ 134 Joe Cronin	100.00	60.00
❑ 135 Line Drive Nelson	20.00	12.00
❑ 136 Cotton Pippen	20.00	12.00
❑ 137 Bing Miller	20.00	12.00
❑ 138 Beau Bell	20.00	12.00
❑ 139 Elden Auker	20.00	12.00
❑ 140 Dick Coffman	20.00	12.00
❑ 141 Casey Stengel MG RC	175.00	100.00
❑ 142 George Kelly RC	90.00	50.00
❑ 143 Gene Moore	20.00	12.00
❑ 144 Joe Vosmik	20.00	12.00
❑ 145 Vito Tamulis	20.00	12.00
❑ 146 Tot Pressnell	20.00	12.00
❑ 147 Johnny Hudson	20.00	12.00
❑ 148 Hugh Casey	25.00	15.00
❑ 149 Pinky Shoffner	20.00	12.00
❑ 150 Whitey Moore	20.00	12.00
❑ 151 Edwin Joost	25.00	15.00
❑ 152 Jimmy Wilson	20.00	12.00
❑ 153 Bill McKechnie MG RC	80.00	45.00
❑ 154 Jumbo Brown	20.00	12.00
❑ 155 Ray Hayworth	20.00	12.00
❑ 156 Daffy Dean	50.00	25.00
❑ 157 Lou Chiozza	20.00	12.00
❑ 158 Travis Jackson	90.00	50.00
❑ 159 Pancho Snyder RC	20.00	12.00
❑ 160 Hans Lobert CO	20.00	12.00
❑ 161 Debs Garms	20.00	12.00
❑ 162 Joe Bowman	20.00	12.00
❑ 163 Spud Davis	20.00	12.00
❑ 164 Ray Berres	20.00	12.00
❑ 165 Bob Klinger	20.00	12.00
❑ 166 Bill Brubaker	20.00	12.00
❑ 167 Frankie Frisch MG	90.00	50.00
❑ 168 Honus Wagner CO	200.00	100.00
❑ 169 Gabby Street	20.00	12.00
❑ 170 Tris Speaker	175.00	100.00
❑ 171 Harry Heilmann	80.00	45.00
❑ 172 Chief Bender	80.00	45.00
❑ 173 Napoleon Lajoie	175.00	100.00
❑ 174 Johnny Evers	90.00	50.00
❑ 175 Christy Mathewson	250.00	150.00
❑ 176 Heinie Manush	90.00	50.00
❑ 177 Frank Baker	100.00	60.00
❑ 178 Max Carey	90.00	50.00
❑ 179 George Sisler	125.00	75.00
❑ 180 Mickey Cochrane	150.00	90.00
❑ 181 Spud Chandler RC	80.00	45.00
❑ 182 Knick Knickerbocker RC	70.00	35.00
❑ 183 Marvin Breuer RC	70.00	35.00
❑ 184 Mule Haas	70.00	35.00
❑ 185 Joe Kuhel	70.00	35.00
❑ 186 Taft Wright RC	70.00	35.00
❑ 187 Jimmy Dykes MG	80.00	45.00
❑ 188 Joe Krakauskas RC	70.00	35.00
❑ 189 Jim Bloodworth RC	70.00	35.00
❑ 190 Charley Berry	70.00	35.00
❑ 191 John Babich RC	70.00	35.00
❑ 192 Dick Siebert RC	70.00	35.00
❑ 193 Chubby Dean RC	70.00	35.00
❑ 194 Sam Chapman RC	70.00	35.00
❑ 195 Dee Miles RC	70.00	35.00
❑ 196 Red (Nonny) Nonnenkamp RC	70.00	35.00
❑ 197 Lou Finney RC	70.00	35.00
❑ 198 Denny Galehouse RC	70.00	35.00
❑ 199 Pinky Higgins	70.00	35.00
❑ 200 Soup Campbell RC	70.00	35.00
❑ 201 Barney McCosky RC	70.00	35.00
❑ 202 Al Milnar RC	70.00	35.00
❑ 203 Bad News Hale RC	70.00	35.00
❑ 204 Harry Eisenstat RC	70.00	35.00
❑ 205 Rollie Hemsley RC	70.00	35.00
❑ 206 Chet Laabs RC	70.00	35.00
❑ 207 Gus Mancuso	70.00	35.00
❑ 208 Lee Gamble RC	70.00	35.00
❑ 209 Hy Vandenberg RC	70.00	35.00
❑ 210 Bill Lohrman RC	70.00	35.00
❑ 211 Pop Joiner RC	70.00	35.00
❑ 212 Babe Young RC	70.00	35.00
❑ 213 John Rucker RC	70.00	35.00
❑ 214 Ken O'Dea RC	70.00	35.00
❑ 215 Johnnie McCarthy RC	70.00	35.00
❑ 216 Joe Marty RC	70.00	35.00
❑ 217 Walter Beck	70.00	35.00
❑ 218 Wally Millies RC	70.00	35.00
❑ 219 Russ Bauers RC	70.00	35.00
❑ 220 Mace Brown RC	70.00	35.00
❑ 221 Lee Handley RC	70.00	35.00
❑ 222 Max Butcher RC	70.00	35.00
❑ 223 Hughie Jennings	150.00	90.00
❑ 224 Pie Traynor	175.00	100.00
❑ 225 Joe Jackson	2500.00	1500.00
❑ 226 Harry Hooper	150.00	90.00
❑ 227 Jesse Haines	150.00	90.00
❑ 228 Charlie Grimm	80.00	45.00
❑ 229 Buck Herzog	70.00	35.00
❑ 230 Red Faber	175.00	100.00
❑ 231 Dolf Luque	100.00	60.00
❑ 232 Goose Goslin	150.00	90.00
❑ 233 George Earnshaw	80.00	45.00
❑ 234 Frank Chance	150.00	90.00
❑ 235 John McGraw	175.00	100.00
❑ 236 Jim Bottomley	150.00	90.00
❑ 237 Willie Keeler	175.00	100.00
❑ 238 Tony Lazzeri	175.00	100.00
❑ 239 George Uhle	70.00	35.00
❑ 240 Bill Atwood RC	100.00	60.00

1941 Play Ball

❑ COMPLETE SET (72)	10000.00	6000.00
❑ COMMON CARD (1-48)	40.00	20.00
❑ COMMON CARD (49-72)	60.00	30.00
❑ WRAPPER (1-CENT)	800.00	700.00
❑ 1 Eddie Miller	125.00	75.00
❑ 2 Max West	40.00	20.00
❑ 3 Bucky Walters	45.00	25.00
❑ 4 Paul Derringer	50.00	30.00
❑ 5 Frank (Buck) McCormick	45.00	25.00
❑ 6 Carl Hubbell	175.00	100.00
❑ 7 Harry Danning	40.00	20.00
❑ 8 Mel Ott	225.00	125.00
❑ 9 Pinky May	40.00	20.00
❑ 10 Arky Vaughan	100.00	60.00
❑ 11 Debs Garms	40.00	20.00
❑ 12 Jimmy Brown	40.00	20.00
❑ 13 Jimmie Foxx	300.00	175.00
❑ 14 Ted Williams	1500.00	900.00
❑ 15 Joe Cronin	125.00	75.00
❑ 16 Hal Trosky	45.00	25.00
❑ 17 Roy Weatherly	40.00	20.00
❑ 18 Hank Greenberg	300.00	175.00
❑ 19 Charley Gehringer	200.00	125.00
❑ 20 Red Ruffing	125.00	75.00
❑ 21 Charlie Keller	60.00	35.00
❑ 22 Bob Johnson	50.00	30.00
❑ 23 George McQuinn	40.00	20.00
❑ 24 Dutch Leonard	45.00	25.00
❑ 25 Gene Moore	40.00	20.00
❑ 26 Harry Gumpert	40.00	20.00
❑ 27 Babe Young	40.00	20.00
❑ 28 Joe Marty	40.00	20.00
❑ 29 Jack Wilson	40.00	20.00
❑ 30 Lou Finney	40.00	20.00
❑ 31 Joe Kuhel	40.00	20.00
❑ 32 Taft Wright	40.00	20.00
❑ 33 Al Milnar	40.00	20.00
❑ 34 Rollie Hemsley	40.00	20.00
❑ 35 Pinky Higgins	45.00	25.00
❑ 36 Barney McCosky	40.00	20.00
❑ 37 Bruce Campbell RC	40.00	20.00
❑ 38 Atley Donald	50.00	30.00
❑ 39 Tommy Henrich	60.00	35.00
❑ 40 John Babich	40.00	20.00
❑ 41 Frank (Blimp) Hayes	40.00	20.00
❑ 42 Wally Moses	45.00	25.00
❑ 43 Al Brancato RC	40.00	20.00
❑ 44 Sam Chapman	40.00	20.00
❑ 45 Eldon Auker	40.00	20.00
❑ 46 Sid Hudson RC	40.00	20.00
❑ 47 Buddy Lewis	40.00	20.00
❑ 48 Cecil Travis	45.00	25.00
❑ 49 Babe Dahlgren	65.00	35.00
❑ 50 Johnny Cooney	60.00	30.00
❑ 51 Dolph Camilli	65.00	35.00
❑ 52 Kirby Higbe RC	60.00	30.00
❑ 53 Luke Hamlin	60.00	30.00
❑ 54 Pee Wee Reese RC	600.00	350.00
❑ 55 Whit Wyatt	65.00	35.00
❑ 56 Johnny VanderMeer RC	100.00	60.00
❑ 57 Moe Arnovich	60.00	30.00
❑ 58 Frank Demaree	60.00	30.00
❑ 59 Bill Jurges	60.00	30.00
❑ 60 Chuck Klein	150.00	90.00
❑ 61 Vince DiMaggio RC	225.00	125.00
❑ 62 Elbie Fletcher	60.00	30.00
❑ 63 Dom DiMaggio RC	250.00	150.00
❑ 64 Bobby Doerr	175.00	100.00
❑ 65 Tommy Bridges	65.00	35.00
❑ 66 Harland Clift RC	60.00	30.00
❑ 67 Walt Judnich RC	60.00	30.00
❑ 68 John Knott	60.00	30.00
❑ 69 George Case	65.00	35.00
❑ 70 Bill Dickey	400.00	250.00
❑ 71 Joe DiMaggio	2500.00	1500.00
❑ 72 Lefty Gomez	475.00	275.00

1988 Score

Card		
❑ COMPLETE SET (660)	10.00	5.00
❑ COMP.FACT.SET (660)	15.00	7.50
❑ 1 Don Mattingly	.60	.25
❑ 2 Wade Boggs	.15	.05
❑ 3 Tim Raines	.10	.02
❑ 4 Andre Dawson	.10	.02
❑ 5 Mark McGwire	1.50	.60
❑ 6 Kevin Seitzer	.05	.01
❑ 7 Wally Joyner	.10	.02
❑ 8 Jesse Barfield	.10	.02
❑ 9 Pedro Guerrero	.10	.02
❑ 10 Eric Davis	.10	.02
❑ 11 George Brett	.50	.20
❑ 12 Ozzie Smith	.30	.10
❑ 13 Rickey Henderson	.20	.07
❑ 14 Jim Rice	.10	.02
❑ 15 Matt Nokes RC*	.25	.08
❑ 16 Mike Schmidt	.50	.20
❑ 17 Dave Parker	.10	.02
❑ 18 Eddie Murray	.20	.07
❑ 19 Andres Galarraga	.10	.02
❑ 20 Tony Fernandez	.05	.01
❑ 21 Kevin McReynolds	.05	.01
❑ 22 B.J. Surhoff	.10	.02
❑ 23 Pat Tabler	.05	.01
❑ 24 Kirby Puckett	.20	.07
❑ 25 Benito Santiago	.10	.02
❑ 26 Ryne Sandberg	.40	.15
❑ 27 Kelly Downs	.05	.01
❑ 28 Jose Cruz	.10	.02
❑ 29 Pete O'Brien	.05	.01
❑ 30 Mark Langston	.05	.01
❑ 31 Lee Smith	.10	.02
❑ 32 Juan Samuel	.05	.01
❑ 33 Kevin Bass	.05	.01
❑ 34 R.J. Reynolds	.05	.01
❑ 35 Steve Sax	.05	.01
❑ 36 John Kruk	.10	.02
❑ 37 Alan Trammell	.10	.02
❑ 38 Chris Bosio	.05	.01
❑ 39 Brook Jacoby	.05	.01
❑ 40 Willie McGee UER		
(Excited misspelled		
as excitd)	.10	.02
❑ 41 Dave Magadan	.05	.01
❑ 42 Fred Lynn	.10	.02
❑ 43 Kent Hrbek	.10	.02
❑ 44 Brian Downing	.10	.02
❑ 45 Jose Canseco	.50	.20
❑ 46 Jim Presley	.05	.01
❑ 47 Mike Stanley	.05	.01
❑ 48 Tony Pena	.05	.01
❑ 49 David Cone	.10	.02
❑ 50 Rick Sutcliffe	.10	.02
❑ 51 Doug Drabek	.05	.01
❑ 52 Bill Doran	.05	.01
❑ 53 Mike Scioscia	.10	.02
❑ 54 Candy Maldonado	.05	.01
❑ 55 Dave Winfield	.10	.02
❑ 56 Lou Whitaker	.10	.02
❑ 57 Tom Henke	.05	.01
❑ 58 Ken Gerhart	.05	.01
❑ 59 Glenn Braggs	.05	.01
❑ 60 Julio Franco	.10	.02
❑ 61 Charlie Leibrandt	.05	.01
❑ 62 Gary Gaetti	.10	.02
❑ 63 Bob Boone	.10	.02
❑ 64 Luis Polonia RC*	.25	.08
❑ 65 Dwight Evans	.15	.05
❑ 66 Phil Bradley	.05	.01
❑ 67 Mike Boddicker	.05	.01
❑ 68 Vince Coleman	.05	.01
❑ 69 Howard Johnson	.10	.02
❑ 70 Tim Wallach	.05	.01
❑ 71 Keith Moreland	.05	.01
❑ 72 Barry Larkin	.15	.05
❑ 73 Alan Ashby	.05	.01
❑ 74 Rick Rhoden	.05	.01
❑ 75 Darrell Evans	.10	.02
❑ 76 Dave Stieb	.10	.02
❑ 77 Dan Plesac	.05	.01
❑ 78 Will Clark	.20	.07
❑ 79 Frank White	.10	.02
❑ 80 Joe Carter	.10	.02
❑ 81 Mike Witt	.05	.01
❑ 82 Terry Steinbach	.10	.02
❑ 83 Alvin Davis	.05	.01
❑ 84 Tommy Herr	.10	.02
❑ 85 Vance Law	.05	.01
❑ 86 Kal Daniels	.05	.01
❑ 87 Rick Honeycutt UER		
(Wrong years for		
stats on bac	.05	.01
❑ 88 Alfredo Griffin	.05	.01
❑ 89 Bret Saberhagen	.10	.02
❑ 90 Bert Blyleven	.10	.02
❑ 91 Jeff Reardon	.10	.02
❑ 92 Cory Snyder	.05	.01
❑ 93A Greg Walker ERR	2.00	.75
❑ 93B Greg Walker COR		
(93 of 660)	.05	.01
❑ 94 Joe Magrane RC*	.25	.08
❑ 95 Rob Deer	.05	.01
❑ 96 Ray Knight	.10	.02
❑ 97 Casey Candaele	.05	.01
❑ 98 John Cerutti	.05	.01
❑ 99 Buddy Bell	.10	.02
❑ 100 Jack Clark	.10	.02
❑ 101 Eric Bell	.05	.01
❑ 102 Willie Wilson	.10	.02
❑ 103 Dave Schmidt	.05	.01
❑ 104 Dennis Eckersley UER	.15	.05
❑ 105 Don Sutton	.10	.02
❑ 106 Danny Tartabull	.05	.01
❑ 107 Fred McGriff	.20	.07
❑ 108 Les Straker	.05	.01
❑ 109 Lloyd Moseby	.05	.01
❑ 110 Roger Clemens	1.00	.40
❑ 111 Glenn Hubbard	.05	.01
❑ 112 Ken Williams	.05	.01
❑ 113 Ruben Sierra	.10	.02
❑ 114 Stan Jefferson	.05	.01
❑ 115 Milt Thompson	.05	.01
❑ 116 Bobby Bonilla	.10	.02
❑ 117 Wayne Tolleson	.05	.01
❑ 118 Matt Williams RC	.75	.30
❑ 119 Chet Lemon	.10	.02
❑ 120 Dale Sveum	.05	.01
❑ 121 Dennis Boyd	.05	.01
❑ 122 Brett Butler	.10	.02
❑ 123 Terry Kennedy	.05	.01
❑ 124 Jack Howell	.05	.01
❑ 125 Curt Young	.05	.01
❑ 126A Dave Valle ERR		
(Misspelled Dale		
on card front)	.10	.02
❑ 126B Dave Valle COR	.05	.01
❑ 127 Curt Wilkerson	.05	.01
❑ 128 Tim Teufel	.05	.01
❑ 129 Ozzie Virgil	.05	.01
❑ 130 Brian Fisher	.05	.01
❑ 131 Lance Parrish	.10	.02
❑ 132 Tom Browning	.05	.01
❑ 133A Larry Andersen ERR		
(Misspelled Anderson		
on card	.10	.02
❑ 133B Larry Andersen COR	.05	.01
❑ 134A Bob Brenly ERR		
(Misspelled Brenley		
on card front	.10	.02
❑ 134B Bob Brenly COR	.05	.01
❑ 135 Mike Marshall	.05	.01
❑ 136 Gerald Perry	.05	.01
❑ 137 Bobby Meacham	.05	.01
❑ 138 Larry Herndon	.05	.01
❑ 139 Fred Manrique	.05	.01
❑ 140 Charlie Hough	.10	.02
❑ 141 Ron Darling	.10	.02
❑ 142 Herm Winningham	.05	.01
❑ 143 Mike Diaz	.05	.01
❑ 144 Mike Jackson RC*	.25	.08
❑ 145 Denny Walling	.05	.01
❑ 146 Robby Thompson	.05	.01
❑ 147 Franklin Stubbs	.05	.01
❑ 148 Albert Hall	.05	.01
❑ 149 Bobby Witt	.05	.01
❑ 150 Lance McCullers	.05	.01
❑ 151 Scott Bradley	.05	.01
❑ 152 Mark McLemore	.05	.01
❑ 153 Tim Laudner	.05	.01
❑ 154 Greg Swindell	.05	.01
❑ 155 Marty Barrett	.05	.01
❑ 156 Mike Heath	.05	.01
❑ 157 Gary Ward	.05	.01
❑ 158A Lee Mazzilli ERR		
(Misspelled Mazili		
on card fro	.10	.02
❑ 158B Lee Mazzilli COR	.10	.02
❑ 159 Tom Foley	.05	.01
❑ 160 Robin Yount	.30	.10
❑ 161 Steve Bedrosian	.05	.01
❑ 162 Bob Walk	.05	.01
❑ 163 Nick Esasky	.05	.01
❑ 164 Ken Caminiti RC	2.00	.75
❑ 165 Jose Uribe	.05	.01
❑ 166 Dave Anderson	.05	.01
❑ 167 Ed Whitson	.05	.01
❑ 168 Ernie Whitt	.05	.01
❑ 169 Cecil Cooper	.10	.02
❑ 170 Mike Pagliarulo	.05	.01
❑ 171 Pat Sheridan	.05	.01
❑ 172 Chris Bando	.05	.01
❑ 173 Lee Lacy	.05	.01
❑ 174 Steve Lombardozzi	.05	.01
❑ 175 Mike Greenwell	.05	.01
❑ 176 Greg Minton	.05	.01
❑ 177 Moose Haas	.05	.01
❑ 178 Mike Kingery	.05	.01
❑ 179 Greg A. Harris	.05	.01
❑ 180 Bo Jackson	.20	.07
❑ 181 Carmelo Martinez	.05	.01
❑ 182 Alex Trevino	.05	.01
❑ 183 Ron Oester	.05	.01
❑ 184 Danny Darwin	.05	.01
❑ 185 Mike Krukow	.05	.01
❑ 186 Rafael Palmeiro	.40	.15
❑ 187 Tim Burke	.05	.01
❑ 188 Roger McDowell	.05	.01
❑ 189 Garry Templeton	.10	.02
❑ 190 Terry Pendleton	.10	.02
❑ 191 Larry Parrish	.05	.01
❑ 192 Rey Quinones	.05	.01
❑ 193 Joaquin Andujar	.10	.02
❑ 194 Tom Brunansky	.05	.01
❑ 195 Donnie Moore	.05	.01
❑ 196 Dan Pasqua	.05	.01
❑ 197 Jim Gantner	.05	.01
❑ 198 Mark Eichhorn	.05	.01
❑ 199 John Grubb	.05	.01
❑ 200 Bill Ripken RC*	.25	.08
❑ 201 Sam Horn RC	.10	.02
❑ 202 Todd Worrell	.05	.01
❑ 203 Terry Leach	.05	.01
❑ 204 Garth Iorg	.05	.01
❑ 205 Brian Dayett	.05	.01
❑ 206 Bo Diaz	.05	.01
❑ 207 Craig Reynolds	.05	.01
❑ 208 Brian Holton	.05	.01
❑ 209 Marvell Wynne UER		
(Misspelled Marvelle		
on card f	.05	.01
❑ 210 Dave Concepcion	.10	.02
❑ 211 Mike Davis	.05	.01
❑ 212 Devon White	.10	.02
❑ 213 Mickey Brantley	.05	.01
❑ 214 Greg Gagne	.05	.01
❑ 215 Oddibe McDowell	.05	.01
❑ 216 Jimmy Key	.10	.02
❑ 217 Dave Bergman	.05	.01

❑ 218 Calvin Schiraldi .05 .01
❑ 219 Larry Sheets .05 .01
❑ 220 Mike Easler .05 .01
❑ 221 Kurt Stillwell .05 .01
❑ 222 Chuck Jackson .05 .01
❑ 223 Dave Martinez .05 .01
❑ 224 Tim Leary .05 .01
❑ 225 Steve Garvey .10 .02
❑ 226 Greg Mathews .05 .01
❑ 227 Doug Sisk .05 .01
❑ 228 Dave Henderson (Wearing Red Sox uniform; Red Sox .05 .01
❑ 229 Jimmy Dwyer .05 .01
❑ 230 Larry Owen .05 .01
❑ 231 Andre Thornton .05 .01
❑ 232 Mark Salas .05 .01
❑ 233 Tom Brookens .05 .01
❑ 234 Greg Brock .05 .01
❑ 235 Rance Mulliniks .05 .01
❑ 236 Bob Brower .05 .01
❑ 237 Joe Niekro .05 .01
❑ 238 Scott Bankhead .05 .01
❑ 239 Doug DeCinces .05 .01
❑ 240 Tommy John .10 .02
❑ 241 Rich Gedman .05 .01
❑ 242 Ted Power .05 .01
❑ 243 Dave Meads .05 .01
❑ 244 Jim Sundberg .10 .02
❑ 245 Ken Oberkfell .05 .01
❑ 246 Jimmy Jones .05 .01
❑ 247 Ken Landreaux .05 .01
❑ 248 Jose Oquendo .05 .01
❑ 249 John Mitchell RC .10 .02
❑ 250 Don Baylor .10 .02
❑ 251 Scott Fletcher .05 .01
❑ 252 Al Newman .05 .01
❑ 253 Carney Lansford .10 .02
❑ 254 Johnny Ray .05 .01
❑ 255 Gary Pettis .05 .01
❑ 256 Ken Phelps .05 .01
❑ 257 Rick Leach .05 .01
❑ 258 Tim Stoddard .05 .01
❑ 259 Ed Romero .05 .01
❑ 260 Sid Bream .05 .01
❑ 261A Tom Niedenfuer ERR (Misspelled Neidenfuer on car .10 .02
❑ 261B Tom Niedenfuer COR .05 .01
❑ 262 Rick Dempsey .05 .01
❑ 263 Lonnie Smith .05 .01
❑ 264 Bob Forsch .05 .01
❑ 265 Barry Bonds 2.00 .75
❑ 266 Willie Randolph .10 .02
❑ 267 Mike Ramsey .05 .01
❑ 268 Don Slaught .05 .01
❑ 269 Mickey Tettleton .05 .01
❑ 270 Jerry Reuss .05 .01
❑ 271 Marc Sullivan .05 .01
❑ 272 Jim Morrison .05 .01
❑ 273 Steve Balboni .05 .01
❑ 274 Dick Schofield .05 .01
❑ 275 John Tudor .10 .02
❑ 276 Gene Larkin RC* .25 .08
❑ 277 Harold Reynolds .10 .02
❑ 278 Jerry Browne .05 .01
❑ 279 Willie Upshaw .05 .01
❑ 280 Ted Higuera .05 .01
❑ 281 Terry McGriff .05 .01
❑ 282 Terry Puhl .05 .01
❑ 283 Mark Wasinger .05 .01
❑ 284 Luis Salazar .05 .01
❑ 285 Ted Simmons .10 .02
❑ 286 John Shelby .05 .01
❑ 287 John Smiley RC* .25 .08
❑ 288 Curt Ford .05 .01
❑ 289 Steve Crawford .05 .01
❑ 290 Dan Quisenberry .05 .01
❑ 291 Alan Wiggins .05 .01
❑ 292 Randy Bush .05 .01
❑ 293 John Candelaria .05 .01
❑ 294 Tony Phillips .05 .01
❑ 295 Mike Morgan .05 .01
❑ 296 Bill Wegman .05 .01
❑ 297A Terry Francona ERR (Misspelled Franconia on card .10 .02
❑ 297B Terry Francona COR .10 .02
❑ 298 Mickey Hatcher .05 .01
❑ 299 Andres Thomas .05 .01
❑ 300 Bob Stanley .05 .01
❑ 301 Al Pedrique .05 .01
❑ 302 Jim Lindeman .05 .01
❑ 303 Wally Backman .05 .01
❑ 304 Paul O'Neill .15 .05
❑ 305 Hubie Brooks .05 .01
❑ 306 Steve Buechele .05 .01
❑ 307 Bobby Thigpen .05 .01
❑ 308 George Hendrick .10 .02
❑ 309 John Moses .05 .01
❑ 310 Ron Guidry .10 .02
❑ 311 Bill Schroeder .05 .01
❑ 312 Jose Nunez .05 .01
❑ 313 Bud Black .05 .01
❑ 314 Joe Sambito .05 .01
❑ 315 Scott McGregor .05 .01
❑ 316 Rafael Santana .05 .01
❑ 317 Frank Williams .05 .01
❑ 318 Mike Fitzgerald .05 .01
❑ 319 Rick Mahler .05 .01
❑ 320 Jim Gott .05 .01
❑ 321 Mariano Duncan .05 .01
❑ 322 Jose Guzman .05 .01
❑ 323 Lee Guetterman .05 .01
❑ 324 Dan Gladden .05 .01
❑ 325 Gary Carter .10 .02
❑ 326 Tracy Jones .05 .01
❑ 327 Floyd Youmans .05 .01
❑ 328 Bill Dawley .05 .01
❑ 329 Paul Noce .05 .01
❑ 330 Angel Salazar .05 .01
❑ 331 Goose Gossage .10 .02
❑ 332 George Frazier .05 .01
❑ 333 Ruppert Jones .05 .01
❑ 334 Billy Joe Robidoux .05 .01
❑ 335 Mike Scott .10 .02
❑ 336 Randy Myers .10 .02
❑ 337 Bob Sebra .05 .01
❑ 338 Eric Show .05 .01
❑ 339 Mitch Williams .05 .01
❑ 340 Paul Molitor .10 .02
❑ 341 Gus Polidor .05 .01
❑ 342 Steve Trout .05 .01
❑ 343 Jerry Don Gleaton .05 .01
❑ 344 Bob Knepper .05 .01
❑ 345 Mitch Webster .05 .01
❑ 346 John Morris .05 .01
❑ 347 Andy Hawkins .05 .01
❑ 348 Dave Leiper .05 .01
❑ 349 Ernest Riles .05 .01
❑ 350 Dwight Gooden .10 .02
❑ 351 Dave Righetti .10 .02
❑ 352 Pat Dodson .05 .01
❑ 353 John Habyan .05 .01
❑ 354 Jim Deshaies .05 .01
❑ 355 Butch Wynegar .05 .01
❑ 356 Bryn Smith .05 .01
❑ 357 Matt Young .05 .01
❑ 358 Tom Pagnozzi RC .10 .02
❑ 359 Floyd Rayford .05 .01
❑ 360 Darryl Strawberry .10 .02
❑ 361 Sal Butera .05 .01
❑ 362 Domingo Ramos .05 .01
❑ 363 Chris Brown .05 .01
❑ 364 Jose Gonzalez .05 .01
❑ 365 Dave Smith .05 .01
❑ 366 Andy McGaffigan .05 .01
❑ 367 Stan Javier .05 .01
❑ 368 Henry Cotto .05 .01
❑ 369 Mike Birkbeck .05 .01
❑ 370 Len Dykstra .10 .02
❑ 371 Dave Collins .05 .01
❑ 372 Spike Owen .05 .01
❑ 373 Geno Petralli .05 .01
❑ 374 Ron Karkovice .05 .01
❑ 375 Shane Rawley .05 .01
❑ 376 DeWayne Buice .05 .01
❑ 377 Bill Pecota RC* .10 .02
❑ 378 Leon Durham .05 .01
❑ 379 Ed Olwine .05 .01
❑ 380 Bruce Hurst .05 .01
❑ 381 Bob McClure .05 .01
❑ 382 Mark Thurmond .05 .01
❑ 383 Buddy Biancalana .05 .01
❑ 384 Tim Conroy .05 .01
❑ 385 Tony Gwynn .30 .10
❑ 386 Greg Gross .05 .01
❑ 387 Barry Lyons .05 .01
❑ 388 Mike Felder .05 .01
❑ 389 Pat Clements .05 .01
❑ 390 Ken Griffey .10 .02
❑ 391 Mark Davis .05 .01
❑ 392 Jose Rijo .10 .02
❑ 393 Mike Young .05 .01
❑ 394 Willie Fraser .05 .01
❑ 395 Dion James .05 .01
❑ 396 Steve Shields .05 .01
❑ 397 Randy St.Claire .05 .01
❑ 398 Danny Jackson .05 .01
❑ 399 Cecil Fielder .10 .02
❑ 400 Keith Hernandez .10 .02
❑ 401 Don Carman .05 .01
❑ 402 Chuck Crim .05 .01
❑ 403 Rob Woodward .05 .01
❑ 404 Junior Ortiz .05 .01
❑ 405 Glenn Wilson .05 .01
❑ 406 Ken Howell .05 .01
❑ 407 Jeff Kunkel .05 .01
❑ 408 Jeff Reed .05 .01
❑ 409 Chris James .05 .01
❑ 410 Zane Smith .05 .01
❑ 411 Ken Dixon .05 .01
❑ 412 Ricky Horton .05 .01
❑ 413 Frank DiPino .05 .01
❑ 414 Shane Mack .05 .01
❑ 415 Danny Cox .05 .01
❑ 416 Andy Van Slyke .15 .05
❑ 417 Danny Heep .05 .01
❑ 418 John Cangelosi .05 .01
❑ 419A John Christensen ERR (Christiansen on card front .10 .02
❑ 419B John Christensen COR .05 .01
❑ 420 Joey Cora RC .25 .08
❑ 421 Mike LaValliere .05 .01
❑ 422 Kelly Gruber .05 .01
❑ 423 Bruce Benedict .05 .01
❑ 424 Len Matuszek .05 .01
❑ 425 Kent Tekulve .05 .01
❑ 426 Rafael Ramirez .05 .01
❑ 427 Mike Flanagan .05 .01
❑ 428 Mike Gallego .05 .01
❑ 429 Juan Castillo .05 .01
❑ 430 Neal Heaton .05 .01
❑ 431 Phil Garner .10 .02
❑ 432 Mike Dunne .05 .01
❑ 433 Wallace Johnson .05 .01
❑ 434 Jack O'Connor .05 .01
❑ 435 Steve Jeltz .05 .01
❑ 436 Donell Nixon .05 .01
❑ 437 Jack Lazorko .05 .01
❑ 438 Keith Comstock .05 .01
❑ 439 Jeff D. Robinson .05 .01
❑ 440 Graig Nettles .10 .02
❑ 441 Mel Hall .05 .01
❑ 442 Gerald Young .05 .01
❑ 443 Gary Redus .05 .01
❑ 444 Charlie Moore .05 .01
❑ 445 Bill Madlock .10 .02
❑ 446 Mark Clear .05 .01
❑ 447 Greg Booker .05 .01
❑ 448 Rick Schu .05 .01
❑ 449 Ron Kittle .05 .01
❑ 450 Dale Murphy .15 .05
❑ 451 Bob Dernier .05 .01
❑ 452 Dale Mohorcic .05 .01
❑ 453 Rafael Belliard .05 .01
❑ 454 Charlie Puleo .05 .01
❑ 455 Dwayne Murphy .05 .01
❑ 456 Jim Eisenreich .05 .01
❑ 457 David Palmer .05 .01
❑ 458 Dave Stewart .10 .02
❑ 459 Pascual Perez .05 .01
❑ 460 Glenn Davis .05 .01
❑ 461 Dan Petry .05 .01
❑ 462 Jim Winn .05 .01
❑ 463 Darrell Miller .05 .01
❑ 464 Mike Moore .05 .01

Card		
❑ 465 Mike LaCoss	.05	.01
❑ 466 Steve Farr	.05	.01
❑ 467 Jerry Mumphrey	.05	.01
❑ 468 Kevin Gross	.05	.01
❑ 469 Bruce Bochy	.05	.01
❑ 470 Orel Hershiser	.10	.02
❑ 471 Eric King	.05	.01
❑ 472 Ellis Burks RC	.40	.15
❑ 473 Darren Daulton	.10	.02
❑ 474 Mookie Wilson	.10	.02
❑ 475 Frank Viola	.10	.02
❑ 476 Ron Robinson	.05	.01
❑ 477 Bob Melvin	.05	.01
❑ 478 Jeff Musselman	.05	.01
❑ 479 Charlie Kerfeld	.05	.01
❑ 480 Richard Dotson	.05	.01
❑ 481 Kevin Mitchell	.10	.02
❑ 482 Gary Roenicke	.05	.01
❑ 483 Tim Flannery	.05	.01
❑ 484 Rich Yett	.05	.01
❑ 485 Pete Incaviglia	.05	.01
❑ 486 Rick Cerone	.05	.01
❑ 487 Tony Armas	.10	.02
❑ 488 Jerry Reed	.05	.01
❑ 489 Dave Lopes	.10	.02
❑ 490 Frank Tanana	.10	.02
❑ 491 Mike Loynd	.05	.01
❑ 492 Bruce Ruffin	.05	.01
❑ 493 Chris Speier	.05	.01
❑ 494 Tom Hume	.05	.01
❑ 495 Jesse Orosco	.05	.01
❑ 496 Robbie Wine UER (Misspelled Robby on card front)	.05	.01
❑ 497 Jeff Montgomery RC	.25	.08
❑ 498 Jeff Dedmon	.05	.01
❑ 499 Luis Aguayo	.05	.01
❑ 500 Reggie Jackson A's	.15	.05
❑ 501 Reggie Jackson O's	.15	.05
❑ 502 Reggie Jackson Yankees	.15	.05
❑ 503 Reggie Jackson Angels	.15	.05
❑ 504 Reggie Jackson A's	.15	.05
❑ 505 Billy Hatcher	.05	.01
❑ 506 Ed Lynch	.05	.01
❑ 507 Willie Hernandez	.05	.01
❑ 508 Jose DeLeon	.05	.01
❑ 509 Joel Youngblood	.05	.01
❑ 510 Bob Welch	.10	.02
❑ 511 Steve Ontiveros	.05	.01
❑ 512 Randy Ready	.05	.01
❑ 513 Juan Nieves	.05	.01
❑ 514 Jeff Russell	.05	.01
❑ 515 Von Hayes	.05	.01
❑ 516 Mark Gubicza	.05	.01
❑ 517 Ken Dayley	.05	.01
❑ 518 Don Aase	.05	.01
❑ 519 Rick Reuschel	.10	.02
❑ 520 Mike Henneman RC*	.25	.08
❑ 521 Rick Aguilera	.05	.01
❑ 522 Jay Howell	.05	.01
❑ 523 Ed Correa	.05	.01
❑ 524 Manny Trillo	.05	.01
❑ 525 Kirk Gibson	.20	.07
❑ 526 Wally Ritchie	.05	.01
❑ 527 Al Nipper	.05	.01
❑ 528 Atlee Hammaker	.05	.01
❑ 529 Shawon Dunston	.05	.01
❑ 530 Jim Clancy	.05	.01
❑ 531 Tom Paciorek	.05	.01
❑ 532 Joel Skinner	.05	.01
❑ 533 Scott Garrelts	.05	.01
❑ 534 Tom O'Malley	.05	.01
❑ 535 John Franco	.10	.02
❑ 536 Paul Kilgus	.05	.01
❑ 537 Darrell Porter	.05	.01
❑ 538 Walt Terrell	.05	.01
❑ 539 Bill Long	.05	.01
❑ 540 George Bell	.10	.02
❑ 541 Jeff Sellers	.05	.01
❑ 542 Joe Boever	.05	.01
❑ 543 Steve Howe	.05	.01
❑ 544 Scott Sanderson	.05	.01
❑ 545 Jack Morris	.10	.02
❑ 546 Todd Benzinger RC*	.25	.08
❑ 547 Steve Henderson	.05	.01
❑ 548 Eddie Milner	.05	.01
❑ 549 Jeff M. Robinson	.05	.01
❑ 550 Cal Ripken	.75	.30
❑ 551 Jody Davis	.05	.01
❑ 552 Kirk McCaskill	.05	.01
❑ 553 Craig Lefferts	.05	.01
❑ 554 Darnell Coles	.05	.01
❑ 555 Phil Niekro	.10	.02
❑ 556 Mike Aldrete	.05	.01
❑ 557 Pat Perry	.05	.01
❑ 558 Juan Agosto	.05	.01
❑ 559 Rob Murphy	.05	.01
❑ 560 Dennis Rasmussen	.05	.01
❑ 561 Manny Lee	.05	.01
❑ 562 Jeff Blauser RC	.25	.08
❑ 563 Bob Ojeda	.05	.01
❑ 564 Dave Dravecky	.05	.01
❑ 565 Gene Garber	.05	.01
❑ 566 Ron Roenicke	.05	.01
❑ 567 Tommy Hinzo	.05	.01
❑ 568 Eric Nolte	.05	.01
❑ 569 Ed Hearn	.05	.01
❑ 570 Mark Davidson	.05	.01
❑ 571 Jim Walewander	.05	.01
❑ 572 Donnie Hill UER (84 Stolen Base total listed as	.05	.01
❑ 573 Jamie Moyer	.10	.02
❑ 574 Ken Schrom	.05	.01
❑ 575 Nolan Ryan	1.00	.40
❑ 576 Jim Acker	.05	.01
❑ 577 Jamie Quirk	.05	.01
❑ 578 Jay Aldrich	.05	.01
❑ 579 Claudell Washington	.05	.01
❑ 580 Jeff Leonard	.05	.01
❑ 581 Carmen Castillo	.05	.01
❑ 582 Daryl Boston	.05	.01
❑ 583 Jeff DeWillis	.05	.01
❑ 584 John Marzano	.05	.01
❑ 585 Bill Gullickson	.05	.01
❑ 586 Andy Allanson	.05	.01
❑ 587 Lee Tunnell UER (1987 stat line reads .4.84 ERA)	.05	.01
❑ 588 Gene Nelson	.05	.01
❑ 589 Dave LaPoint	.05	.01
❑ 590 Harold Baines	.10	.02
❑ 591 Bill Buckner	.10	.02
❑ 592 Carlton Fisk	.15	.05
❑ 593 Rick Manning	.05	.01
❑ 594 Doug Jones RC	.25	.08
❑ 595 Tom Candiotti	.05	.01
❑ 596 Steve Lake	.05	.01
❑ 597 Jose Lind RC	.25	.08
❑ 598 Ross Jones	.05	.01
❑ 599 Gary Matthews	.10	.02
❑ 600 Fernando Valenzuela	.10	.02
❑ 601 Dennis Martinez	.10	.02
❑ 602 Les Lancaster	.05	.01
❑ 603 Ozzie Guillen	.10	.02
❑ 604 Tony Bernazard	.05	.01
❑ 605 Chili Davis	.10	.02
❑ 606 Roy Smalley	.05	.01
❑ 607 Ivan Calderon	.05	.01
❑ 608 Jay Tibbs	.05	.01
❑ 609 Guy Hoffman	.05	.01
❑ 610 Doyle Alexander	.05	.01
❑ 611 Mike Bielecki	.05	.01
❑ 612 Shawn Hillegas	.05	.01
❑ 613 Keith Atherton	.05	.01
❑ 614 Eric Plunk	.05	.01
❑ 615 Sid Fernandez	.05	.01
❑ 616 Dennis Lamp	.05	.01
❑ 617 Dave Engle	.05	.01
❑ 618 Harry Spilman	.05	.01
❑ 619 Don Robinson	.05	.01
❑ 620 John Farrell RC	.10	.02
❑ 621 Nelson Liriano	.05	.01
❑ 622 Floyd Bannister	.05	.01
❑ 623 Randy Milligan RC	.10	.02
❑ 624 Kevin Elster	.05	.01
❑ 625 Jody Reed RC	.25	.08
❑ 626 Shawn Abner	.05	.01
❑ 627 Kirt Manwaring RC	.25	.08
❑ 628 Pete Stanicek	.05	.01
❑ 629 Rob Ducey	.05	.01
❑ 630 Steve Kiefer	.05	.01
❑ 631 Gary Thurman	.05	.01
❑ 632 Darrel Akerfelds	.05	.01
❑ 633 Dave Clark	.05	.01
❑ 634 Roberto Kelly RC	.25	.08
❑ 635 Keith Hughes	.05	.01
❑ 636 John Davis	.05	.01
❑ 637 Mike Devereaux RC	.25	.08
❑ 638 Tom Glavine RC	2.50	1.00
❑ 639 Keith Miller RC	.25	.08
❑ 640 Chris Gwynn UER RC	.25	.08
❑ 641 Tim Crews RC	.25	.08
❑ 642 Mackey Sasser RC	.25	.08
❑ 643 Vicente Palacios	.05	.01
❑ 644 Kevin Romine	.05	.01
❑ 645 Gregg Jefferies RC	.25	.08
❑ 646 Jeff Treadway RC	.25	.08
❑ 647 Ron Gant RC	.40	.15
❑ 648 M.McGwire/M.Nokes	.75	.30
❑ 649 Eric Davis and Tim Raines (Speed and Power)	.10	.02
❑ 650 Don Mattingly/J.Clark	.30	.10
❑ 651 C.Ripken/Trammell/Fern	.25	.08
❑ 652 Vince Coleman HL 100 Stolen Bases	.05	.01
❑ 653 Kirby Puckett HL	.15	.05
❑ 654 Benito Santiago HL	.05	.01
❑ 655 Juan Nieves HL No Hitter	.05	.01
❑ 656 Steve Bedrosian HL Saves Record	.05	.01
❑ 657 Mike Schmidt HL	.20	.07
❑ 658 Don Mattingly HL	.30	.10
❑ 659 Mark McGwire HL	.75	.30
❑ 660 Paul Molitor HL	.05	.01

1988 Score Rookie/Traded

Card		
❑ COMP.FACT.SET (110)	40.00	15.00
❑ 1T Jack Clark	.75	.30
❑ 2T Danny Jackson	.25	.08
❑ 3T Brett Butler	.75	.30
❑ 4T Kurt Stillwell	.25	.08
❑ 5T Tom Brunansky	.25	.08
❑ 6T Dennis Lamp	.25	.08
❑ 7T Jose DeLeon	.25	.08
❑ 8T Tom Herr	.25	.08
❑ 9T Keith Moreland	.25	.08
❑ 10T Kirk Gibson	2.00	.75
❑ 11T Bud Black	.25	.08
❑ 12T Rafael Ramirez	.25	.08
❑ 13T Luis Salazar	.25	.08
❑ 14T Goose Gossage	.75	.30
❑ 15T Bob Welch	.75	.30
❑ 16T Vance Law	.25	.08
❑ 17T Ray Knight	.75	.30
❑ 18T Dan Quisenberry	.25	.08
❑ 19T Don Slaught	.25	.08
❑ 20T Lee Smith	.75	.30
❑ 21T Rick Cerone	.25	.08
❑ 22T Pat Tabler	.25	.08
❑ 23T Larry McWilliams	.25	.08
❑ 24T Ricky Horton	.25	.08
❑ 25T Graig Nettles	.75	.30
❑ 26T Dan Petry	.25	.08
❑ 27T Jose Rijo	.75	.30
❑ 28T Chili Davis	.75	.30
❑ 29T Dickie Thon	.25	.08

❑ 30T	Mackey Sasser	.25	.08
❑ 31T	Mickey Tettleton	.25	.08
❑ 32T	Rick Dempsey	.25	.08
❑ 33T	Ron Hassey	.25	.08
❑ 34T	Phil Bradley	.25	.08
❑ 35T	Jay Howell	.25	.08
❑ 36T	Bill Buckner	.75	.30
❑ 37T	Alfredo Griffin	.25	.08
❑ 38T	Gary Pettis	.25	.08
❑ 39T	Calvin Schiraldi	.25	.08
❑ 40T	John Candelaria	.25	.08
❑ 41T	Joe Orsulak	.25	.08
❑ 42T	Willie Upshaw	.25	.08
❑ 43T	Herm Winningham	.25	.08
❑ 44T	Ron Kittle	.25	.08
❑ 45T	Bob Dernier	.25	.08
❑ 46T	Steve Balboni	.25	.08
❑ 47T	Steve Shields	.25	.08
❑ 48T	Henry Cotto	.25	.08
❑ 49T	Dave Henderson	.25	.08
❑ 50T	Dave Parker	.75	.30
❑ 51T	Mike Young	.25	.08
❑ 52T	Mark Salas	.25	.08
❑ 53T	Mike Davis	.25	.08
❑ 54T	Rafael Santana	.25	.08
❑ 55T	Don Baylor	.75	.30
❑ 56T	Dan Pasqua	.25	.08
❑ 57T	Ernest Riles	.25	.08
❑ 58T	Glenn Hubbard	.25	.08
❑ 59T	Mike Smithson	.25	.08
❑ 60T	Richard Dotson	.25	.08
❑ 61T	Jerry Reuss	.25	.08
❑ 62T	Mike Jackson	.75	.30
❑ 63T	Floyd Bannister	.25	.08
❑ 64T	Jesse Orosco	.25	.08
❑ 65T	Larry Parrish	.25	.08
❑ 66T	Jeff Bittiger	.25	.08
❑ 67T	Ray Hayward	.25	.08
❑ 68T	Ricky Jordan XRC	.75	.30
❑ 69T	Tommy Gregg	.25	.08
❑ 70T	Brady Anderson XRC	1.25	.50
❑ 71T	Jeff Montgomery	.75	.30
❑ 72T	Darryl Hamilton XRC	.75	.30
❑ 73T	Cecil Espy XRC	.25	.08
❑ 74T	Greg Briley XRC	.25	.08
❑ 75T	Joey Meyer	.25	.08
❑ 76T	Mike Macfarlane XRC	.75	.30
❑ 77T	Oswald Peraza	.25	.08
❑ 78T	Jack Armstrong XRC	.25	.08
❑ 79T	Don Heinkel	.25	.08
❑ 80T	Mark Grace XRC	8.00	3.00
❑ 81T	Steve Curry	.25	.08
❑ 82T	Damon Berryhill XRC*	.75	.30
❑ 83T	Steve Ellsworth	.25	.08
❑ 84T	Pete Smith XRC*	.25	.08
❑ 85T	Jack McDowell XRC	1.25	.50
❑ 86T	Rob Dibble XRC	1.25	.50
❑ 87T	Bryan Harvey XRC	.75	.30
❑ 88T	John Dopson	.25	.08
❑ 89T	Dave Gallagher	.25	.08
❑ 90T	Todd Stottlemyre XRC	.75	.30
❑ 91T	Mike Schooler	.25	.08
❑ 92T	Don Gordon	.25	.08
❑ 93T	Sil Campusano	.25	.08
❑ 94T	Jeff Pico	.25	.08
❑ 95T	Jay Buhner XRC	2.00	.75
❑ 96T	Nelson Santovenia	.25	.08
❑ 97T	Al Leiter XRC	3.00	1.25
❑ 98T	Luis Alicea XRC	.75	.30
❑ 99T	Pat Borders XRC	.75	.30
❑ 100T	Chris Sabo XRC	1.25	.50
❑ 101T	Tim Belcher	.25	.08
❑ 102T	Walt Weiss XRC*	1.25	.50
❑ 103T	Craig Biggio XRC	15.00	6.00
❑ 104T	Don August	.25	.08
❑ 105T	Roberto Alomar XRC	10.00	4.00
❑ 106T	Todd Burns	.25	.08
❑ 107T	John Costello	.25	.08
❑ 108T	Melido Perez XRC*	.75	.30
❑ 109T	Darrin Jackson XRC*	.25	.08
❑ 110T	Orestes Destrade XRC	.25	.08

1989 Score Rookie/Traded

❑	COMP.FACT.SET (110)	15.00	6.00
❑ 1T	Rafael Palmeiro	.25	.08
❑ 2T	Nolan Ryan	1.50	.60
❑ 3T	Jack Clark	.10	.02
❑ 4T	Dave LaPoint	.05	.01
❑ 5T	Mike Moore	.05	.01
❑ 6T	Pete O'Brien	.05	.01
❑ 7T	Jeffrey Leonard	.05	.01
❑ 8T	Rob Murphy	.05	.01
❑ 9T	Tom Herr	.05	.01
❑ 10T	Claudell Washington	.05	.01
❑ 11T	Mike Pagliarulo	.05	.01
❑ 12T	Steve Lake	.05	.01
❑ 13T	Spike Owen	.05	.01
❑ 14T	Andy Hawkins	.05	.01
❑ 15T	Todd Benzinger	.05	.01
❑ 16T	Mookie Wilson	.10	.02
❑ 17T	Bert Blyleven	.10	.02
❑ 18T	Jeff Treadway	.05	.01
❑ 19T	Bruce Hurst	.05	.01
❑ 20T	Steve Sax	.05	.01
❑ 21T	Juan Samuel	.05	.01
❑ 22T	Jesse Barfield	.10	.02
❑ 23T	Carmen Castillo	.05	.01
❑ 24T	Terry Leach	.05	.01
❑ 25T	Mark Langston	.05	.01
❑ 26T	Eric King	.05	.01
❑ 27T	Steve Balboni	.05	.01
❑ 28T	Len Dykstra	.10	.02
❑ 29T	Keith Moreland	.05	.01
❑ 30T	Terry Kennedy	.05	.01
❑ 31T	Eddie Murray	.25	.08
❑ 32T	Mitch Williams	.05	.01
❑ 33T	Jeff Parrett	.05	.01
❑ 34T	Wally Backman	.05	.01
❑ 35T	Julio Franco	.10	.02
❑ 36T	Lance Parrish	.10	.02
❑ 37T	Nick Esasky	.05	.01
❑ 38T	Luis Polonia	.05	.01
❑ 39T	Kevin Gross	.05	.01
❑ 40T	John Dopson	.05	.01
❑ 41T	Willie Randolph	.10	.02
❑ 42T	Jim Clancy	.05	.01
❑ 43T	Tracy Jones	.05	.01
❑ 44T	Phil Bradley	.05	.01
❑ 45T	Milt Thompson	.05	.01
❑ 46T	Chris James	.05	.01
❑ 47T	Scott Fletcher	.05	.01
❑ 48T	Kal Daniels	.05	.01
❑ 49T	Steve Bedrosian	.05	.01
❑ 50T	Rickey Henderson	.25	.08
❑ 51T	Dion James	.05	.01
❑ 52T	Tim Leary	.05	.01
❑ 53T	Roger McDowell	.05	.01
❑ 54T	Mel Hall	.05	.01
❑ 55T	Dickie Thon	.05	.01
❑ 56T	Zane Smith	.05	.01
❑ 57T	Danny Heep	.05	.01
❑ 58T	Bob McClure	.05	.01
❑ 59T	Brian Holton	.05	.01
❑ 60T	Randy Ready	.05	.01
❑ 61T	Bob Melvin	.05	.01
❑ 62T	Harold Baines	.10	.02
❑ 63T	Lance McCullers	.05	.01
❑ 64T	Jody Davis	.05	.01
❑ 65T	Darrell Evans	.10	.02
❑ 66T	Joel Youngblood	.05	.01
❑ 67T	Frank Viola	.10	.02
❑ 68T	Mike Aldrete	.05	.01
❑ 69T	Greg Cadaret	.05	.01
❑ 70T	John Kruk	.10	.02
❑ 71T	Pat Sheridan	.05	.01
❑ 72T	Oddibe McDowell	.05	.01
❑ 73T	Tom Brookens	.05	.01
❑ 74T	Bob Boone	.10	.02
❑ 75T	Walt Terrell	.05	.01
❑ 76T	Joel Skinner	.05	.01
❑ 77T	Randy Johnson	1.50	.60
❑ 78T	Felix Fermin	.05	.01
❑ 79T	Rick Mahler	.05	.01
❑ 80T	Richard Dotson	.05	.01
❑ 81T	Cris Carpenter RC *	.10	.02
❑ 82T	Billy Spiers RC	.25	.08
❑ 83T	Junior Felix RC	.10	.02
❑ 84T	Joe Girardi RC	.40	.15
❑ 85T	Jerome Walton RC	.25	.08
❑ 86T	Greg Litton	.05	.01
❑ 87T	Greg W.Harris RC	.10	.02
❑ 88T	Jim Abbott RC	1.00	.40
❑ 89T	Kevin Brown	.25	.08
❑ 90T	John Wetteland RC	.40	.15
❑ 91T	Gary Wayne	.05	.01
❑ 92T	Rich Monteleone	.05	.01
❑ 93T	Bob Geren RC	.05	.01
❑ 94T	Clay Parker	.05	.01
❑ 95T	Steve Finley RC	.75	.30
❑ 96T	Gregg Olson RC	.25	.08
❑ 97T	Ken Patterson	.05	.01
❑ 98T	Ken Hill RC	.25	.08
❑ 99T	Scott Scudder RC	.10	.02
❑ 100T	Ken Griffey Jr. RC	6.00	2.50
❑ 101T	Jeff Brantley RC	.25	.08
❑ 102T	Donn Pall	.05	.01
❑ 103T	Carlos Martinez RC	.10	.02
❑ 104T	Joe Oliver RC	.25	.08
❑ 105T	Omar Vizquel RC	1.00	.40
❑ 106T	Albert Belle RC	1.00	.40
❑ 107T	Kenny Rogers RC	2.00	.75
❑ 108T	Mark Carreon	.05	.01
❑ 109T	Rolando Roomes	.05	.01
❑ 110T	Pete Harnisch RC	.25	.08

1990 Score

❑	COMPLETE SET (704)	15.00	6.00
❑	COMP.RETAIL SET (704)	15.00	6.00
❑	COMP.HOBBY SET (714)	15.00	6.00
❑ 1	Don Mattingly	.60	.25
❑ 2	Cal Ripken	.75	.30
❑ 3	Dwight Evans	.15	.05
❑ 4	Barry Bonds	1.00	.40
❑ 5	Kevin McReynolds	.05	.01
❑ 6	Ozzie Guillen	.10	.02
❑ 7	Terry Kennedy	.05	.01
❑ 8	Bryan Harvey	.05	.01
❑ 9	Alan Trammell	.10	.02
❑ 10	Cory Snyder	.05	.01
❑ 11	Jody Reed	.05	.01
❑ 12	Roberto Alomar	.15	.05
❑ 13	Pedro Guerrero	.05	.01
❑ 14	Gary Redus	.05	.01
❑ 15	Marty Barrett	.05	.01
❑ 16	Ricky Jordan	.05	.01
❑ 17	Joe Magrane	.05	.01

Card	Nrmt	Vg-E
❑ 18 Sid Fernandez	.05	.01
❑ 19 Richard Dotson	.05	.01
❑ 20 Jack Clark	.10	.02
❑ 21 Bob Walk	.05	.01
❑ 22 Ron Karkovice	.05	.01
❑ 23 Lenny Harris	.05	.01
❑ 24 Phil Bradley	.05	.01
❑ 25 Andres Galarraga	.10	.02
❑ 26 Brian Downing	.05	.01
❑ 27 Dave Martinez	.05	.01
❑ 28 Eric King	.05	.01
❑ 29 Barry Lyons	.05	.01
❑ 30 Dave Schmidt	.05	.01
❑ 31 Mike Boddicker	.05	.01
❑ 32 Tom Foley	.05	.01
❑ 33 Brady Anderson	.10	.02
❑ 34 Jim Presley	.05	.01
❑ 35 Lance Parrish	.05	.01
❑ 36 Von Hayes	.05	.01
❑ 37 Lee Smith	.10	.02
❑ 38 Herm Winningham	.05	.01
❑ 39 Alejandro Pena	.05	.01
❑ 40 Mike Scott	.05	.01
❑ 41 Joe Orsulak	.05	.01
❑ 42 Rafael Ramirez	.05	.01
❑ 43 Gerald Young	.05	.01
❑ 44 Dick Schofield	.05	.01
❑ 45 Dave Smith	.05	.01
❑ 46 Dave Magadan	.05	.01
❑ 47 Dennis Martinez	.10	.02
❑ 48 Greg Minton	.05	.01
❑ 49 Milt Thompson	.05	.01
❑ 50 Orel Hershiser	.10	.02
❑ 51 Bip Roberts	.05	.01
❑ 52 Jerry Browne	.05	.01
❑ 53 Bob Ojeda	.05	.01
❑ 54 Fernando Valenzuela	.10	.02
❑ 55 Matt Nokes	.05	.01
❑ 56 Brook Jacoby	.05	.01
❑ 57 Frank Tanana	.05	.01
❑ 58 Scott Fletcher	.05	.01
❑ 59 Ron Oester	.05	.01
❑ 60 Bob Boone	.10	.02
❑ 61 Dan Gladden	.05	.01
❑ 62 Darnell Coles	.05	.01
❑ 63 Gregg Olson	.10	.02
❑ 64 Todd Burns	.05	.01
❑ 65 Todd Benzinger	.05	.01
❑ 66 Dale Murphy	.15	.05
❑ 67 Mike Flanagan	.05	.01
❑ 68 Jose Oquendo	.05	.01
❑ 69 Cecil Espy	.05	.01
❑ 70 Chris Sabo	.05	.01
❑ 71 Shane Rawley	.05	.01
❑ 72 Tom Brunansky	.05	.01
❑ 73 Vance Law	.05	.01
❑ 74 B.J. Surhoff	.10	.02
❑ 75 Lou Whitaker	.10	.02
❑ 76 Ken Caminiti UER	.10	.02
❑ 77 Nelson Liriano	.05	.01
❑ 78 Tommy Gregg	.05	.01
❑ 79 Don Slaught	.05	.01
❑ 80 Eddie Murray	.25	.08
❑ 81 Joe Boever	.05	.01
❑ 82 Charlie Leibrandt	.05	.01
❑ 83 Jose Lind	.05	.01
❑ 84 Tony Phillips	.05	.01
❑ 85 Mitch Webster	.05	.01
❑ 86 Dan Plesac	.05	.01
❑ 87 Rick Mahler	.05	.01
❑ 88 Steve Lyons	.05	.01
❑ 89 Tony Fernandez	.05	.01
❑ 90 Ryne Sandberg	.40	.15
❑ 91 Nick Esasky	.05	.01
❑ 92 Luis Salazar	.05	.01
❑ 93 Pete Incaviglia	.05	.01
❑ 94 Ivan Calderon	.05	.01
❑ 95 Jeff Treadway	.05	.01
❑ 96 Kurt Stillwell	.05	.01
❑ 97 Gary Sheffield	.25	.08
❑ 98 Jeffrey Leonard	.05	.01
❑ 99 Andres Thomas	.05	.01
❑ 100 Roberto Kelly	.05	.01
❑ 101 Alvaro Espinoza	.05	.01
❑ 102 Greg Gagne	.05	.01
❑ 103 John Farrell	.05	.01
❑ 104 Willie Wilson	.05	.01
❑ 105 Glenn Braggs	.05	.01
❑ 106 Chet Lemon	.05	.01
❑ 107A Jamie Moyer ERR	.10	.02
❑ 107B Jamie Moyer COR	.50	.20
❑ 108 Chuck Crim	.05	.01
❑ 109 Dave Valle	.05	.01
❑ 110 Walt Weiss	.05	.01
❑ 111 Larry Sheets	.05	.01
❑ 112 Don Robinson	.05	.01
❑ 113 Danny Heep	.05	.01
❑ 114 Carmelo Martinez	.05	.01
❑ 115 Dave Gallagher	.05	.01
❑ 116 Mike LaValliere	.05	.01
❑ 117 Bob McClure	.05	.01
❑ 118 Rene Gonzales	.05	.01
❑ 119 Mark Parent	.05	.01
❑ 120 Wally Joyner	.10	.02
❑ 121 Mark Gubicza	.05	.01
❑ 122 Tony Pena	.05	.01
❑ 123 Carmelo Castillo	.05	.01
❑ 124 Howard Johnson	.05	.01
❑ 125 Steve Sax	.05	.01
❑ 126 Tim Belcher	.05	.01
❑ 127 Tim Burke	.05	.01
❑ 128 Al Newman	.05	.01
❑ 129 Dennis Rasmussen	.05	.01
❑ 130 Doug Jones	.05	.01
❑ 131 Fred Lynn	.05	.01
❑ 132 Jeff Hamilton	.05	.01
❑ 133 German Gonzalez	.05	.01
❑ 134 John Morris	.05	.01
❑ 135 Dave Parker	.10	.02
❑ 136 Gary Pettis	.05	.01
❑ 137 Dennis Boyd	.05	.01
❑ 138 Candy Maldonado	.05	.01
❑ 139 Rick Cerone	.05	.01
❑ 140 George Brett	.60	.25
❑ 141 Dave Clark	.05	.01
❑ 142 Dickie Thon	.05	.01
❑ 143 Junior Ortiz	.05	.01
❑ 144 Don August	.05	.01
❑ 145 Gary Gaetti	.10	.02
❑ 146 Kirt Manwaring	.05	.01
❑ 147 Jeff Reed	.05	.01
❑ 148 Jose Alvarez	.05	.01
❑ 149 Mike Schooler	.05	.01
❑ 150 Mark Grace	.15	.05
❑ 151 Geronimo Berroa	.05	.01
❑ 152 Barry Jones	.05	.01
❑ 153 Geno Petralli	.05	.01
❑ 154 Jim Deshaies	.05	.01
❑ 155 Barry Larkin	.15	.05
❑ 156 Alfredo Griffin	.05	.01
❑ 157 Tom Henke	.05	.01
❑ 158 Mike Jeffcoat	.05	.01
❑ 159 Bob Welch	.05	.01
❑ 160 Julio Franco	.10	.02
❑ 161 Henry Cotto	.05	.01
❑ 162 Terry Steinbach	.05	.01
❑ 163 Damon Berryhill	.05	.01
❑ 164 Tim Crews	.05	.01
❑ 165 Tom Browning	.05	.01
❑ 166 Fred Manrique	.05	.01
❑ 167 Harold Reynolds	.10	.02
❑ 168A Ron Hassey ERR (27 on back)	.05	.01
❑ 168B Ron Hassey COR	.50	.20
❑ 169 Shawon Dunston	.05	.01
❑ 170 Bobby Bonilla	.10	.02
❑ 171 Tommy Herr	.05	.01
❑ 172 Mike Heath	.05	.01
❑ 173 Rich Gedman	.05	.01
❑ 174 Bill Ripken	.05	.01
❑ 175 Pete O'Brien	.05	.01
❑ 176A Lloyd McClendon ERR (Uniform number on back list	.05	.01
❑ 176B Lloyd McClendon COR (Uniform number on back list	.50	.20
❑ 177 Brian Holton	.05	.01
❑ 178 Jeff Blauser	.05	.01
❑ 179 Jim Eisenreich	.05	.01
❑ 180 Bert Blyleven	.10	.02
❑ 181 Rob Murphy	.05	.01
❑ 182 Bill Doran	.05	.01
❑ 183 Curt Ford	.05	.01
❑ 184 Mike Henneman	.05	.01
❑ 185 Eric Davis	.10	.02
❑ 186 Lance McCullers	.05	.01
❑ 187 Steve Davis RC	.05	.01
❑ 188 Bill Wegman	.05	.01
❑ 189 Brian Harper	.05	.01
❑ 190 Mike Moore	.05	.01
❑ 191 Dale Mohorcic	.05	.01
❑ 192 Tim Wallach	.05	.01
❑ 193 Keith Hernandez	.10	.02
❑ 194 Dave Righetti	.05	.01
❑ 195A Bret Saberhagen ERR (Joke)	.10	.02
❑ 195B Bret Saberhagen COR (Joker)	.50	.20
❑ 196 Paul Kilgus	.05	.01
❑ 197 Bud Black	.05	.01
❑ 198 Juan Samuel	.05	.01
❑ 199 Kevin Seitzer	.05	.01
❑ 200 Darryl Strawberry	.10	.02
❑ 201 Dave Stieb	.10	.02
❑ 202 Charlie Hough	.10	.02
❑ 203 Jack Morris	.10	.02
❑ 204 Rance Mulliniks	.05	.01
❑ 205 Alvin Davis	.05	.01
❑ 206 Jack Howell	.05	.01
❑ 207 Ken Patterson	.05	.01
❑ 208 Terry Pendleton	.10	.02
❑ 209 Craig Lefferts	.05	.01
❑ 210 Kevin Brown UER (First mention of '89 Rangers sh	.10	.02
❑ 211 Dan Petry	.05	.01
❑ 212 Dave Leiper	.05	.01
❑ 213 Daryl Boston	.05	.01
❑ 214 Kevin Hickey	.05	.01
❑ 215 Mike Krukow	.05	.01
❑ 216 Terry Francona	.10	.02
❑ 217 Kirk McCaskill	.05	.01
❑ 218 Scott Bailes	.05	.01
❑ 219 Bob Forsch	.05	.01
❑ 220A Mike Aldrete ERR (25 on back)	.05	.01
❑ 220B Mike Aldrete COR (24 on back)	.50	.20
❑ 221 Steve Buechele	.05	.01
❑ 222 Jesse Barfield	.05	.01
❑ 223 Juan Berenguer	.05	.01
❑ 224 Andy McGaffigan	.05	.01
❑ 225 Pete Smith	.05	.01
❑ 226 Mike Witt	.05	.01
❑ 227 Jay Howell	.05	.01
❑ 228 Scott Bradley	.05	.01
❑ 229 Jerome Walton	.05	.01
❑ 230 Greg Swindell	.05	.01
❑ 231 Atlee Hammaker	.05	.01
❑ 232A Mike Devereaux ERR (RF on front)	.05	.01
❑ 232B Mike Devereaux COR	.50	.20
❑ 233 Ken Hill	.10	.02
❑ 234 Craig Worthington	.05	.01
❑ 235 Scott Terry	.05	.01
❑ 236 Brett Butler	.10	.02
❑ 237 Doyle Alexander	.05	.01
❑ 238 Dave Anderson	.05	.01
❑ 239 Bob Milacki	.05	.01
❑ 240 Dwight Smith	.05	.01
❑ 241 Otis Nixon	.05	.01
❑ 242 Pat Tabler	.05	.01
❑ 243 Derek Lilliquist	.05	.01
❑ 244 Danny Tartabull	.05	.01
❑ 245 Wade Boggs	.15	.05
❑ 246 Scott Garrelts (Should say Relief Pitcher on fro	.05	.01
❑ 247 Spike Owen	.05	.01
❑ 248 Norm Charlton	.05	.01
❑ 249 Gerald Perry	.05	.01
❑ 250 Nolan Ryan	1.00	.40
❑ 251 Kevin Gross	.05	.01
❑ 252 Randy Milligan	.05	.01
❑ 253 Mike LaCoss	.05	.01
❑ 254 Dave Bergman	.05	.01
❑ 255 Tony Gwynn	.30	.10

❑ 256	Felix Fermin	.05	.01
❑ 257	Greg W. Harris	.05	.01
❑ 258	Junior Felix	.05	.01
❑ 259	Mark Davis	.05	.01
❑ 260	Vince Coleman	.05	.01
❑ 261	Paul Gibson	.05	.01
❑ 262	Mitch Williams	.05	.01
❑ 263	Jeff Russell	.05	.01
❑ 264	Omar Vizquel	.25	.08
❑ 265	Andre Dawson	.10	.02
❑ 266	Storm Davis	.05	.01
❑ 267	Guillermo Hernandez	.05	.01
❑ 268	Mike Felder	.05	.01
❑ 269	Tom Candiotti	.05	.01
❑ 270	Bruce Hurst	.05	.01
❑ 271	Fred McGriff	.25	.08
❑ 272	Glenn Davis	.05	.01
❑ 273	John Franco	.10	.02
❑ 274	Rich Yett	.05	.01
❑ 275	Craig Biggio	.25	.08
❑ 276	Gene Larkin	.05	.01
❑ 277	Rob Dibble	.10	.02
❑ 278	Randy Bush	.05	.01
❑ 279	Kevin Bass	.05	.01
❑ 280A	Bo Jackson ERR Watham	.25	.08
❑ 280B	Bo Jackson COR Wathan	.75	.30
❑ 281	Wally Backman	.05	.01
❑ 282	Larry Andersen	.05	.01
❑ 283	Chris Bosio	.05	.01
❑ 284	Juan Agosto	.05	.01
❑ 285	Ozzie Smith	.40	.15
❑ 286	George Bell	.05	.01
❑ 287	Rex Hudler	.05	.01
❑ 288	Pat Borders	.05	.01
❑ 289	Danny Jackson	.05	.01
❑ 290	Carlton Fisk	.15	.05
❑ 291	Tracy Jones	.05	.01
❑ 292	Allan Anderson	.05	.01
❑ 293	Johnny Ray	.05	.01
❑ 294	Lee Guetterman	.05	.01
❑ 295	Paul O'Neill	.15	.05
❑ 296	Carney Lansford	.10	.02
❑ 297	Tom Brookens	.05	.01
❑ 298	Claudell Washington	.05	.01
❑ 299	Hubie Brooks	.05	.01
❑ 300	Will Clark	.15	.05
❑ 301	Kenny Rogers	.10	.02
❑ 302	Darrell Evans	.10	.02
❑ 303	Greg Briley	.05	.01
❑ 304	Donn Pall	.05	.01
❑ 305	Teddy Higuera	.05	.01
❑ 306	Dan Pasqua	.05	.01
❑ 307	Dave Winfield	.10	.02
❑ 308	Dennis Powell	.05	.01
❑ 309	Jose DeLeon	.05	.01
❑ 310	Roger Clemens	1.00	.40
❑ 311	Melido Perez	.05	.01
❑ 312	Devon White	.10	.02
❑ 313	Dwight Gooden	.10	.02
❑ 314	Carlos Martinez	.05	.01
❑ 315	Dennis Eckersley	.10	.02
❑ 316	Clay Parker UER (Height 6'11")	.05	.01
❑ 317	Rick Honeycutt	.05	.01
❑ 318	Tim Laudner	.05	.01
❑ 319	Joe Carter	.10	.02
❑ 320	Robin Yount	.40	.15
❑ 321	Felix Jose	.05	.01
❑ 322	Mickey Tettleton	.05	.01
❑ 323	Mike Gallego	.05	.01
❑ 324	Edgar Martinez	.15	.05
❑ 325	Dave Henderson	.05	.01
❑ 326	Chili Davis	.10	.02
❑ 327	Steve Balboni	.05	.01
❑ 328	Jody Davis	.05	.01
❑ 329	Shawn Hillegas	.05	.01
❑ 330	Jim Abbott	.15	.05
❑ 331	John Dopson	.05	.01
❑ 332	Mark Williamson	.05	.01
❑ 333	Jeff D. Robinson	.05	.01
❑ 334	John Smiley	.05	.01
❑ 335	Bobby Thigpen	.05	.01
❑ 336	Garry Templeton	.05	.01
❑ 337	Marvell Wynne	.05	.01
❑ 338A	Ken Griffey Sr. ERR (Uniform number on back list	.10	.02
❑ 338B	Ken Griffey Sr. COR	.50	.20
❑ 339	Steve Finley	.10	.02
❑ 340	Ellis Burks	.15	.05
❑ 341	Frank Williams	.05	.01
❑ 342	Mike Morgan	.05	.01
❑ 343	Kevin Mitchell	.05	.01
❑ 344	Joel Youngblood	.05	.01
❑ 345	Mike Greenwell	.05	.01
❑ 346	Glenn Wilson	.05	.01
❑ 347	John Costello	.05	.01
❑ 348	Wes Gardner	.05	.01
❑ 349	Jeff Ballard	.05	.01
❑ 350	Mark Thurmond UER (ERA is 192, should be 1.92)	.05	.01
❑ 351	Randy Myers	.10	.02
❑ 352	Shawn Abner	.05	.01
❑ 353	Jesse Orosco	.05	.01
❑ 354	Greg Walker	.05	.01
❑ 355	Pete Harnisch	.05	.01
❑ 356	Steve Farr	.05	.01
❑ 357	Dave LaPoint	.05	.01
❑ 358	Willie Fraser	.05	.01
❑ 359	Mickey Hatcher	.05	.01
❑ 360	Rickey Henderson	.25	.08
❑ 361	Mike Fitzgerald	.05	.01
❑ 362	Bill Schroeder	.05	.01
❑ 363	Mark Carreon	.05	.01
❑ 364	Ron Jones	.05	.01
❑ 365	Jeff Montgomery	.10	.02
❑ 366	Bill Krueger	.05	.01
❑ 367	John Cangelosi	.05	.01
❑ 368	Jose Gonzalez	.05	.01
❑ 369	Greg Hibbard RC	.10	.02
❑ 370	John Smoltz	.25	.08
❑ 371	Jeff Brantley	.05	.01
❑ 372	Frank White	.10	.02
❑ 373	Ed Whitson	.05	.01
❑ 374	Willie McGee	.10	.02
❑ 375	Jose Canseco	.15	.05
❑ 376	Randy Ready	.05	.01
❑ 377	Don Aase	.05	.01
❑ 378	Tony Armas	.05	.01
❑ 379	Steve Bedrosian	.05	.01
❑ 380	Chuck Finley	.10	.02
❑ 381	Kent Hrbek	.10	.02
❑ 382	Jim Gantner	.05	.01
❑ 383	Mel Hall	.05	.01
❑ 384	Mike Marshall	.05	.01
❑ 385	Mark McGwire	1.00	.40
❑ 386	Wayne Tolleson	.05	.01
❑ 387	Brian Holman	.05	.01
❑ 388	John Wetteland	.25	.08
❑ 389	Darren Daulton	.10	.02
❑ 390	Rob Deer	.05	.01
❑ 391	John Moses	.05	.01
❑ 392	Todd Worrell	.05	.01
❑ 393	Chuck Cary	.05	.01
❑ 394	Stan Javier	.05	.01
❑ 395	Willie Randolph	.10	.02
❑ 396	Bill Buckner	.05	.01
❑ 397	Robby Thompson	.05	.01
❑ 398	Mike Scioscia	.05	.01
❑ 399	Lonnie Smith	.05	.01
❑ 400	Kirby Puckett	.25	.08
❑ 401	Mark Langston	.05	.01
❑ 402	Danny Darwin	.05	.01
❑ 403	Greg Maddux	.40	.15
❑ 404	Lloyd Moseby	.05	.01
❑ 405	Rafael Palmeiro	.15	.05
❑ 406	Chad Kreuter	.05	.01
❑ 407	Jimmy Key	.10	.02
❑ 408	Tim Birtsas	.05	.01
❑ 409	Tim Raines	.10	.02
❑ 410	Dave Stewart	.10	.02
❑ 411	Eric Yelding RC	.05	.01
❑ 412	Kent Anderson	.05	.01
❑ 413	Les Lancaster	.05	.01
❑ 414	Rick Dempsey	.05	.01
❑ 415	Randy Johnson	.50	.20
❑ 416	Gary Carter	.10	.02
❑ 417	Rolando Roomes	.05	.01
❑ 418	Dan Schatzeder	.05	.01
❑ 419	Bryn Smith	.05	.01
❑ 420	Ruben Sierra	.10	.02
❑ 421	Steve Jeltz	.05	.01
❑ 422	Ken Oberkfell	.05	.01
❑ 423	Sid Bream	.05	.01
❑ 424	Jim Clancy	.05	.01
❑ 425	Kelly Gruber	.05	.01
❑ 426	Rick Leach	.05	.01
❑ 427	Len Dykstra	.10	.02
❑ 428	Jeff Pico	.05	.01
❑ 429	John Cerutti	.05	.01
❑ 430	David Cone	.10	.02
❑ 431	Jeff Kunkel	.05	.01
❑ 432	Luis Aquino	.05	.01
❑ 433	Ernie Whitt	.05	.01
❑ 434	Bo Diaz	.05	.01
❑ 435	Steve Lake	.05	.01
❑ 436	Pat Perry	.05	.01
❑ 437	Mike Davis	.05	.01
❑ 438	Cecilio Guante	.05	.01
❑ 439	Duane Ward	.05	.01
❑ 440	Andy Van Slyke	.15	.05
❑ 441	Gene Nelson	.05	.01
❑ 442	Luis Polonia	.05	.01
❑ 443	Kevin Elster	.05	.01
❑ 444	Keith Moreland	.05	.01
❑ 445	Roger McDowell	.05	.01
❑ 446	Ron Darling	.05	.01
❑ 447	Ernest Riles	.05	.01
❑ 448	Mookie Wilson	.10	.02
❑ 449A	Billy Spiers ERR (No birth year)	.05	.01
❑ 449B	Billy Spiers COR (Born in 1966)	.50	.20
❑ 450	Rick Sutcliffe	.10	.02
❑ 451	Nelson Santovenia	.05	.01
❑ 452	Andy Allanson	.05	.01
❑ 453	Bob Melvin	.05	.01
❑ 454	Benito Santiago	.10	.02
❑ 455	Jose Uribe	.05	.01
❑ 456	Bill Landrum	.05	.01
❑ 457	Bobby Witt	.05	.01
❑ 458	Kevin Romine	.05	.01
❑ 459	Lee Mazzilli	.05	.01
❑ 460	Paul Molitor	.10	.02
❑ 461	Ramon Martinez	.05	.01
❑ 462	Frank DiPino	.05	.01
❑ 463	Walt Terrell	.05	.01
❑ 464	Bob Geren	.05	.01
❑ 465	Rick Reuschel	.05	.01
❑ 466	Mark Grant	.05	.01
❑ 467	John Kruk	.10	.02
❑ 468	Gregg Jefferies	.10	.02
❑ 469	R.J. Reynolds	.05	.01
❑ 470	Harold Baines	.10	.02
❑ 471	Dennis Lamp	.05	.01
❑ 472	Tom Gordon	.10	.02
❑ 473	Terry Puhl	.05	.01
❑ 474	Curt Wilkerson	.05	.01
❑ 475	Dan Quisenberry	.05	.01
❑ 476	Oddibe McDowell	.05	.01
❑ 477A	Zane Smith ERR	.05	.01
❑ 477B	Zane Smith COR	.50	.20
❑ 478	Franklin Stubbs	.05	.01
❑ 479	Wallace Johnson	.05	.01
❑ 480	Jay Tibbs	.05	.01
❑ 481	Tom Glavine	.15	.05
❑ 482	Manny Lee	.05	.01
❑ 483	Joe Hesketh UER (Says Rookiess on back, should s	.05	.01
❑ 484	Mike Bielecki	.05	.01
❑ 485	Greg Brock	.05	.01
❑ 486	Pascual Perez	.05	.01
❑ 487	Kirk Gibson	.10	.02
❑ 488	Scott Sanderson	.05	.01
❑ 489	Domingo Ramos	.05	.01
❑ 490	Kal Daniels	.05	.01
❑ 491A	David Wells ERR	.10	.02
❑ 491B	David Wells COR	.50	.20
❑ 492	Jerry Reed	.05	.01
❑ 493	Eric Show	.05	.01
❑ 494	Mike Pagliarulo	.05	.01
❑ 495	Ron Robinson	.05	.01
❑ 496	Brad Komminsk	.05	.01
❑ 497	Greg Litton	.05	.01
❑ 498	Chris James	.05	.01
❑ 499	Luis Quinones	.05	.01

❑ 500 Frank Viola .05 .01
❑ 501 Tim Teufel UER
(Twins '85, the s is
lower case, .05 .01
❑ 502 Terry Leach .05 .01
❑ 503 Matt Williams .10 .02
❑ 504 Tim Leary .05 .01
❑ 505 Doug Drabek .05 .01
❑ 506 Mariano Duncan .05 .01
❑ 507 Charlie Hayes .05 .01
❑ 508 Albert Belle .25 .08
❑ 509 Pat Sheridan .05 .01
❑ 510 Mackey Sasser .05 .01
❑ 511 Jose Rijo .05 .01
❑ 512 Mike Smithson .05 .01
❑ 513 Gary Ward .05 .01
❑ 514 Dion James .05 .01
❑ 515 Jim Gott .05 .01
❑ 516 Drew Hall .05 .01
❑ 517 Doug Bair .05 .01
❑ 518 Scott Scudder .05 .01
❑ 519 Rick Aguilera .10 .02
❑ 520 Rafael Belliard .05 .01
❑ 521 Jay Buhner .10 .02
❑ 522 Jeff Reardon .10 .02
❑ 523 Steve Rosenberg .05 .01
❑ 524 Randy Velarde .05 .01
❑ 525 Jeff Musselman .05 .01
❑ 526 Bill Long .05 .01
❑ 527 Gary Wayne .05 .01
❑ 528 Dave Wayne Johnson RC .05 .01
❑ 529 Ron Kittle .05 .01
❑ 530 Erik Hanson UER
(5th line on back
says seson, sh .05 .01
❑ 531 Steve Wilson .05 .01
❑ 532 Joey Meyer .05 .01
❑ 533 Curt Young .05 .01
❑ 534 Kelly Downs .05 .01
❑ 535 Joe Girardi .15 .05
❑ 536 Lance Blankenship .05 .01
❑ 537 Greg Mathews .05 .01
❑ 538 Donell Nixon .05 .01
❑ 539 Mark Knudson .05 .01
❑ 540 Jeff Wetherby RC .05 .01
❑ 541 Darrin Jackson .05 .01
❑ 542 Terry Mulholland .05 .01
❑ 543 Eric Hetzel .05 .01
❑ 544 Rick Reed RC .25 .08
❑ 545 Dennis Cook .05 .01
❑ 546 Mike Jackson .05 .01
❑ 547 Brian Fisher .05 .01
❑ 548 Gene Harris .05 .01
❑ 549 Jeff King .05 .01
❑ 550 Dave Dravecky .25 .08
❑ 551 Randy Kutcher .05 .01
❑ 552 Mark Portugal .05 .01
❑ 553 Jim Corsi .05 .01
❑ 554 Todd Stottlemyre .10 .02
❑ 555 Scott Bankhead .05 .01
❑ 556 Ken Dayley .05 .01
❑ 557 Rick Wrona .05 .01
❑ 558 Sammy Sosa RC 2.50 1.00
❑ 559 Keith Miller .05 .01
❑ 560 Ken Griffey Jr. .75 .30
❑ 561A R.Sandberg HL ERR 3B 8.00 3.00
❑ 561B R.Sandberg HL COR .25 .08
❑ 562 Billy Hatcher .05 .01
❑ 563 Jay Bell .10 .02
❑ 564 Jack Daugherty RC .05 .01
❑ 565 Rich Monteleone .05 .01
❑ 566 Bo Jackson AS-MVP .10 .02
❑ 567 Tony Fossas RC .05 .01
❑ 568 Roy Smith .05 .01
❑ 569 Jaime Navarro .05 .01
❑ 570 Lance Johnson .05 .01
❑ 571 Mike Dyer RC .05 .01
❑ 572 Kevin Ritz RC .05 .01
❑ 573 Dave West .05 .01
❑ 574 Gary Mielke RC .05 .01
❑ 575 Scott Lusader .05 .01
❑ 576 Joe Oliver .05 .01
❑ 577 Sandy Alomar Jr. .10 .02
❑ 578 Andy Benes UER .10 .02
❑ 579 Tim Jones .05 .01
❑ 580 Randy McCament RC .05 .01
❑ 581 Curt Schilling 1.00 .40
❑ 582 John Orton RC .10 .02
❑ 583A Milt Cuyler ERR RC .10 .02
❑ 583B Milt Cuyler COR .50 .20
❑ 584 Eric Anthony RC .10 .02
❑ 585 Greg Vaughn .05 .01
❑ 586 Deion Sanders .25 .08
❑ 587 Jose DeJesus .05 .01
❑ 588 Chip Hale RC .05 .01
❑ 589 John Olerud RC .50 .20
❑ 590 Steve Olin RC .25 .08
❑ 591 Marquis Grissom RC .40 .15
❑ 592 Moises Alou RC .75 .30
❑ 593 Mark Lemke .05 .01
❑ 594 Dean Palmer RC .25 .08
❑ 595 Robin Ventura .25 .08
❑ 596 Tino Martinez .50 .20
❑ 597 Mike Huff RC .05 .01
❑ 598 Scott Hemond RC .10 .02
❑ 599 Wally Whitehurst .05 .01
❑ 600 Todd Zeile .10 .02
❑ 601 Glenallen Hill .05 .01
❑ 602 Hal Morris .05 .01
❑ 603 Juan Bell .05 .01
❑ 604 Bobby Rose .05 .01
❑ 605 Matt Merullo .05 .01
❑ 606 Kevin Maas RC .25 .08
❑ 607 Randy Nosek RC .05 .01
❑ 608A Billy Bates RC .05 .01
❑ 608B Billy Bates
(Text has no mention
of triples) .05 .01
❑ 609 Mike Stanton RC .25 .08
❑ 610 Mauro Gozzo RC .05 .01
❑ 611 Charles Nagy .05 .01
❑ 612 Scott Coolbaugh RC .05 .01
❑ 613 Jose Vizcaino RC .25 .08
❑ 614 Greg Smith RC .05 .01
❑ 615 Jeff Huson RC .10 .02
❑ 616 Mickey Weston RC .05 .01
❑ 617 John Pawlowski .05 .01
❑ 618A Joe Skalski ERR
(27 on back) .05 .01
❑ 618B Joe Skalski COR .50 .20
❑ 619 Bernie Williams RC 1.50 .60
❑ 620 Shawn Holman RC .05 .01
❑ 621 Gary Eave RC .05 .01
❑ 622 Darrin Fletcher UER RC .10 .02
❑ 623 Pat Combs .05 .01
❑ 624 Mike Blowers RC .10 .02
❑ 625 Kevin Appier .10 .02
❑ 626 Pat Austin .05 .01
❑ 627 Kelly Mann RC .05 .01
❑ 628 Matt Kinzer RC .05 .01
❑ 629 Chris Hammond RC .10 .02
❑ 630 Dean Wilkins RC .05 .01
❑ 631 Larry Walker RC 1.00 .40
❑ 632 Blaine Beatty RC .05 .01
❑ 633A Tommy Barrett ERR .05 .01
❑ 633B Tommy Barrett COR .50 .20
❑ 634 Stan Belinda RC .10 .02
❑ 635 Mike (Texas) Smith RC .05 .01
❑ 636 Hensley Meulens .05 .01
❑ 637 Juan Gonzalez RC 1.00 .40
❑ 638 Lenny Webster RC .10 .02
❑ 639 Mark Gardner RC .10 .02
❑ 640 Tommy Greene RC .10 .02
❑ 641 Mike Hartley RC .05 .01
❑ 642 Phil Stephenson .05 .01
❑ 643 Kevin Mmahat RC .05 .01
❑ 644 Ed Whited RC .05 .01
❑ 645 Delino DeShields RC .25 .08
❑ 646 Kevin Blankenship .05 .01
❑ 647 Paul Sorrento RC .25 .08
❑ 648 Mike Roesler RC .05 .01
❑ 649 Jason Grimsley RC .10 .02
❑ 650 David Justice RC .50 .20
❑ 651 Scott Cooper RC .10 .02
❑ 652 Dave Eiland .05 .01
❑ 653 Mike Munoz RC .05 .01
❑ 654 Jeff Fischer RC .05 .01
❑ 655 Terry Jorgensen RC .05 .01
❑ 656 George Canale RC .05 .01
❑ 657 Brian DuBois UER RC .05 .01
❑ 658 Carlos Quintana .05 .01
❑ 659 Luis de los Santos .05 .01
❑ 660 Jerald Clark .05 .01
❑ 661 Donald Harris RC .05 .01
❑ 662 Paul Coleman RC .10 .02
❑ 663 Frank Thomas RC 2.00 .75
❑ 664 Brent Mayne RC .25 .08
❑ 665 Eddie Zosky RC .10 .02
❑ 666 Steve Hosey RC .10 .02
❑ 667 Scott Bryant RC .10 .02
❑ 668 Tom Goodwin RC .25 .08
❑ 669 Cal Eldred RC .25 .08
❑ 670 Earl Cunningham RC .10 .02
❑ 671 Alan Zinter RC .10 .02
❑ 672 Chuck Knoblauch RC .40 .15
❑ 673 Kyle Abbott RC .05 .01
❑ 674 Roger Salkeld RC .05 .01
❑ 675 Mo Vaughn RC .50 .20
❑ 676 Keith (Kiki) Jones RC .05 .01
❑ 677 Tyler Houston RC .25 .08
❑ 678 Jeff Jackson RC .10 .02
❑ 679 Greg Gohr RC .10 .02
❑ 680 Ben McDonald RC .25 .08
❑ 681 Greg Blosser RC .10 .02
❑ 682 Willie Greene RC .25 .08
❑ 683A Wade Boggs DT ERR .10 .02
❑ 683B Wade Boggs DT COR .50 .20
❑ 684 Will Clark DT .10 .02
❑ 685 Tony Gwynn DT .15 .05
❑ 686 Rickey Henderson DT .15 .05
❑ 687 Bo Jackson DT .10 .02
❑ 688 Mark Langston DT .05 .01
❑ 689 Barry Larkin DT .10 .02
❑ 690 Kirby Puckett DT .15 .05
❑ 691 Ryne Sandberg DT .25 .08
❑ 692 Mike Scott DT .05 .01
❑ 693A Terry Steinbach DT
ERR (cathers) .05 .01
❑ 693B Terry Steinbach DT
COR (catchers) .05 .01
❑ 694 Bobby Thigpen DT .05 .01
❑ 695 Mitch Williams DT .05 .01
❑ 696 Nolan Ryan HL .40 .15
❑ 697 Bo Jackson FB/BB .50 .20
❑ 698 Rickey Henderson ALCS .15 .05
❑ 699 Will Clark NLCS .10 .02
❑ 700 WS Games 1/2
(Dave Stewart
Mike Moore) .10 .02
❑ 701 Candlestick/Earthquake .25 .08
❑ 702 WS Game 3 .15 .05
❑ 703 WS Game 4/Wrap-up
A's Sweep Battle of
of the Bay .05 .01
❑ 704 Wade Boggs HL .10 .02

1991 Score

❑ COMPLETE SET (893) 20.00 8.00
❑ COMP.FACT.SET (900) 25.00 10.00
❑ 1 Jose Canseco .15 .05
❑ 2 Ken Griffey Jr. .50 .20
❑ 3 Ryne Sandberg .40 .15
❑ 4 Nolan Ryan 1.00 .40
❑ 5 Bo Jackson .25 .08
❑ 6 Bret Saberhagen UER
(In bio, missed
misspelled a .05 .01
❑ 7 Will Clark .15 .05
❑ 8 Ellis Burks .10 .02
❑ 9 Joe Carter .10 .02

- ❑ 10 Rickey Henderson .25 .08
- ❑ 11 Ozzie Guillen .10 .02
- ❑ 12 Wade Boggs .15 .05
- ❑ 13 Jerome Walton .05 .01
- ❑ 14 John Franco .10 .02
- ❑ 15 Ricky Jordan UER (League misspelled as legue) .05 .01
- ❑ 16 Wally Backman .05 .01
- ❑ 17 Rob Dibble .10 .02
- ❑ 18 Glenn Braggs .05 .01
- ❑ 19 Cory Snyder .05 .01
- ❑ 20 Kal Daniels .05 .01
- ❑ 21 Mark Langston .05 .01
- ❑ 22 Kevin Gross .05 .01
- ❑ 23 Don Mattingly .60 .25
- ❑ 24 Dave Righetti .10 .02
- ❑ 25 Roberto Alomar .15 .05
- ❑ 26 Robby Thompson .05 .01
- ❑ 27 Jack McDowell .05 .01
- ❑ 28 Bip Roberts UER (Bio reads playd) .05 .01
- ❑ 29 Jay Howell .05 .01
- ❑ 30 Dave Stieb UER (17 wins in bio, 18 in stats) .05 .01
- ❑ 31 Johnny Ray .05 .01
- ❑ 32 Steve Sax .05 .01
- ❑ 33 Terry Mulholland .05 .01
- ❑ 34 Lee Guetterman .05 .01
- ❑ 35 Tim Raines .10 .02
- ❑ 36 Scott Fletcher .05 .01
- ❑ 37 Lance Parrish .10 .02
- ❑ 38 Tony Phillips UER (Born 4/15, should be 4/25) .05 .01
- ❑ 39 Todd Stottlemyre .05 .01
- ❑ 40 Alan Trammell .10 .02
- ❑ 41 Todd Burns .05 .01
- ❑ 42 Mookie Wilson .10 .02
- ❑ 43 Chris Bosio .05 .01
- ❑ 44 Jeffrey Leonard .05 .01
- ❑ 45 Doug Jones .05 .01
- ❑ 46 Mike Scott UER .05 .01
- ❑ 47 Andy Hawkins .05 .01
- ❑ 48 Harold Reynolds .10 .02
- ❑ 49 Paul Molitor .10 .02
- ❑ 50 John Farrell .05 .01
- ❑ 51 Danny Darwin .05 .01
- ❑ 52 Jeff Blauser .05 .01
- ❑ 53 John Tudor UER (41 wins in '81) .05 .01
- ❑ 54 Milt Thompson .05 .01
- ❑ 55 David Justice .10 .02
- ❑ 56 Greg Olson .05 .01
- ❑ 57 Willie Blair .05 .01
- ❑ 58 Rick Parker .05 .01
- ❑ 59 Shawn Boskie .05 .01
- ❑ 60 Kevin Tapani .05 .01
- ❑ 61 Dave Hollins .05 .01
- ❑ 62 Scott Radinsky .05 .01
- ❑ 63 Francisco Cabrera .05 .01
- ❑ 64 Tim Layana .05 .01
- ❑ 65 Jim Leyritz .05 .01
- ❑ 66 Wayne Edwards .05 .01
- ❑ 67 Lee Stevens .05 .01
- ❑ 68 Bill Sampen UER (Fourth line, long is spelled al .05 .01
- ❑ 69 Craig Grebeck UER (Born in Cerritos, not Johnsto .05 .01
- ❑ 70 John Burkett .05 .01
- ❑ 71 Hector Villanueva .05 .01
- ❑ 72 Oscar Azocar .05 .01
- ❑ 73 Alan Mills .05 .01
- ❑ 74 Carlos Baerga .05 .01
- ❑ 75 Charles Nagy .05 .01
- ❑ 76 Tim Drummond .05 .01
- ❑ 77 Dana Kiecker .05 .01
- ❑ 78 Tom Edens RC .05 .01
- ❑ 79 Kent Mercker .05 .01
- ❑ 80 Steve Avery .05 .01
- ❑ 81 Lee Smith .10 .02
- ❑ 82 Dave Martinez .05 .01
- ❑ 83 Dave Winfield .10 .02
- ❑ 84 Bill Spiers .05 .01
- ❑ 85 Dan Pasqua .05 .01
- ❑ 86 Randy Milligan .05 .01
- ❑ 87 Tracy Jones .05 .01
- ❑ 88 Greg Myers .05 .01
- ❑ 89 Keith Hernandez .10 .02
- ❑ 90 Todd Benzinger .05 .01
- ❑ 91 Mike Jackson .05 .01
- ❑ 92 Mike Stanley .05 .01
- ❑ 93 Candy Maldonado .05 .01
- ❑ 94 John Kruk UER .10 .02
- ❑ 95 Cal Ripken .75 .30
- ❑ 96 Willie Fraser .05 .01
- ❑ 97 Mike Felder .05 .01
- ❑ 98 Bill Landrum .05 .01
- ❑ 99 Chuck Crim .05 .01
- ❑ 100 Chuck Finley .10 .02
- ❑ 101 Kirt Manwaring .05 .01
- ❑ 102 Jaime Navarro .05 .01
- ❑ 103 Dickie Thon .05 .01
- ❑ 104 Brian Downing .05 .01
- ❑ 105 Jim Abbott .15 .05
- ❑ 106 Tom Brookens .05 .01
- ❑ 107 Darryl Hamilton UER (Bio info is for Jeff Hamilt .05 .01
- ❑ 108 Bryan Harvey .05 .01
- ❑ 109 Greg A. Harris UER (Shown pitching lefty, bio sa .05 .01
- ❑ 110 Greg Swindell .05 .01
- ❑ 111 Juan Berenguer .05 .01
- ❑ 112 Mike Heath .05 .01
- ❑ 113 Scott Bradley .05 .01
- ❑ 114 Jack Morris .10 .02
- ❑ 115 Barry Jones .05 .01
- ❑ 116 Kevin Romine .05 .01
- ❑ 117 Garry Templeton .05 .01
- ❑ 118 Scott Sanderson .05 .01
- ❑ 119 Roberto Kelly .05 .01
- ❑ 120 George Brett .60 .25
- ❑ 121 Oddibe McDowell .05 .01
- ❑ 122 Jim Acker .05 .01
- ❑ 123 Bill Swift UER (Born 12/27/61, should be 10/27) .05 .01
- ❑ 124 Eric King .05 .01
- ❑ 125 Jay Buhner .10 .02
- ❑ 126 Matt Young .05 .01
- ❑ 127 Alvaro Espinoza .05 .01
- ❑ 128 Greg Hibbard .05 .01
- ❑ 129 Jeff M. Robinson .05 .01
- ❑ 130 Mike Greenwell .05 .01
- ❑ 131 Dion James .05 .01
- ❑ 132 Donn Pall UER (1988 ERA in stats 0.00) .05 .01
- ❑ 133 Lloyd Moseby .05 .01
- ❑ 134 Randy Velarde .05 .01
- ❑ 135 Allan Anderson .05 .01
- ❑ 136 Mark Davis .05 .01
- ❑ 137 Eric Davis .10 .02
- ❑ 138 Phil Stephenson .05 .01
- ❑ 139 Felix Fermin .05 .01
- ❑ 140 Pedro Guerrero .10 .02
- ❑ 141 Charlie Hough .10 .02
- ❑ 142 Mike Henneman .05 .01
- ❑ 143 Jeff Montgomery .05 .01
- ❑ 144 Lenny Harris .05 .01
- ❑ 145 Bruce Hurst .05 .01
- ❑ 146 Eric Anthony .05 .01
- ❑ 147 Paul Assenmacher .05 .01
- ❑ 148 Jesse Barfield .05 .01
- ❑ 149 Carlos Quintana .05 .01
- ❑ 150 Dave Stewart .10 .02
- ❑ 151 Roy Smith .05 .01
- ❑ 152 Paul Gibson .05 .01
- ❑ 153 Mickey Hatcher .05 .01
- ❑ 154 Jim Eisenreich .05 .01
- ❑ 155 Kenny Rogers .10 .02
- ❑ 156 Dave Schmidt .05 .01
- ❑ 157 Lance Johnson .05 .01
- ❑ 158 Dave West .05 .01
- ❑ 159 Steve Balboni .05 .01
- ❑ 160 Jeff Brantley .05 .01
- ❑ 161 Craig Biggio .15 .05
- ❑ 162 Brook Jacoby .05 .01
- ❑ 163 Dan Gladden .05 .01
- ❑ 164 Jeff Reardon UER .10 .02
- ❑ 165 Mark Carreon .05 .01
- ❑ 166 Mel Hall .05 .01
- ❑ 167 Gary Mielke .05 .01
- ❑ 168 Cecil Fielder .10 .02
- ❑ 169 Darrin Jackson .05 .01
- ❑ 170 Rick Aguilera .10 .02
- ❑ 171 Walt Weiss .05 .01
- ❑ 172 Steve Farr .05 .01
- ❑ 173 Jody Reed .05 .01
- ❑ 174 Mike Jeffcoat .05 .01
- ❑ 175 Mark Grace .15 .05
- ❑ 176 Larry Sheets .05 .01
- ❑ 177 Bill Gullickson .05 .01
- ❑ 178 Chris Gwynn .05 .01
- ❑ 179 Melido Perez .05 .01
- ❑ 180 Sid Fernandez UER (779 runs in 1990) .05 .01
- ❑ 181 Tim Burke .05 .01
- ❑ 182 Gary Pettis .05 .01
- ❑ 183 Rob Murphy .05 .01
- ❑ 184 Craig Lefferts .05 .01
- ❑ 185 Howard Johnson .05 .01
- ❑ 186 Ken Caminiti .10 .02
- ❑ 187 Tim Belcher .05 .01
- ❑ 188 Greg Cadaret .05 .01
- ❑ 189 Matt Williams .10 .02
- ❑ 190 Dave Magadan .05 .01
- ❑ 191 Geno Petralli .05 .01
- ❑ 192 Jeff D. Robinson .05 .01
- ❑ 193 Jim Deshaies .05 .01
- ❑ 194 Willie Randolph .10 .02
- ❑ 195 George Bell .05 .01
- ❑ 196 Hubie Brooks .05 .01
- ❑ 197 Tom Gordon .05 .01
- ❑ 198 Mike Fitzgerald .05 .01
- ❑ 199 Mike Pagliarulo .05 .01
- ❑ 200 Kirby Puckett .25 .08
- ❑ 201 Shawon Dunston .05 .01
- ❑ 202 Dennis Boyd .05 .01
- ❑ 203 Junior Felix UER (Text has him in NL) .05 .01
- ❑ 204 Alejandro Pena .05 .01
- ❑ 205 Pete Smith .05 .01
- ❑ 206 Tom Glavine .15 .05
- ❑ 207 Luis Salazar .05 .01
- ❑ 208 John Smoltz .15 .05
- ❑ 209 Doug Dascenzo .05 .01
- ❑ 210 Tim Wallach .05 .01
- ❑ 211 Greg Gagne .05 .01
- ❑ 212 Mark Gubicza .05 .01
- ❑ 213 Mark Parent .05 .01
- ❑ 214 Ken Oberkfell .05 .01
- ❑ 215 Gary Carter .10 .02
- ❑ 216 Rafael Palmeiro .15 .05
- ❑ 217 Tom Niedenfuer .05 .01
- ❑ 218 Dave LaPoint .05 .01
- ❑ 219 Jeff Treadway .05 .01
- ❑ 220 Mitch Williams UER ('89 ERA shown as 2.76, shoul .05 .01
- ❑ 221 Jose DeLeon .05 .01
- ❑ 222 Mike LaValliere .05 .01
- ❑ 223 Darrel Akerfelds .05 .01
- ❑ 224A Kent Anderson ERR (First line, flachy should rea .10 .02
- ❑ 224B Kent Anderson COR (Corrected in factory sets) .10 .02
- ❑ 225 Dwight Evans .15 .05
- ❑ 226 Gary Redus .05 .01
- ❑ 227 Paul O'Neill .15 .05
- ❑ 228 Marty Barrett .05 .01
- ❑ 229 Tom Browning .05 .01
- ❑ 230 Terry Pendleton .10 .02
- ❑ 231 Jack Armstrong .05 .01
- ❑ 232 Mike Boddicker .05 .01
- ❑ 233 Neal Heaton .05 .01
- ❑ 234 Marquis Grissom .10 .02
- ❑ 235 Bert Blyleven .10 .02
- ❑ 236 Curt Young .05 .01
- ❑ 237 Don Carman .05 .01
- ❑ 238 Charlie Hayes .05 .01
- ❑ 239 Mark Knudson .05 .01

❑ 240 Todd Zeile .05 .01
❑ 241 Larry Walker .25 .08
❑ 242 Jerald Clark .05 .01
❑ 243 Jeff Ballard .05 .01
❑ 244 Jeff King .05 .01
❑ 245 Tom Brunansky .05 .01
❑ 246 Darren Daulton .10 .02
❑ 247 Scott Terry .05 .01
❑ 248 Rob Deer .05 .01
❑ 249 Brady Anderson UER .10 .02
❑ 250 Len Dykstra .10 .02
❑ 251 Greg W. Harris .05 .01
❑ 252 Mike Hartley .05 .01
❑ 253 Joey Cora .05 .01
❑ 254 Ivan Calderon .05 .01
❑ 255 Ted Power .05 .01
❑ 256 Sammy Sosa .25 .08
❑ 257 Steve Buechele .05 .01
❑ 258 Mike Devereaux UER
(No comma between
city and st .05 .01
❑ 259 Brad Komminsk UER
(Last text line,
Ba should be .05 .01
❑ 260 Ted Higuera .05 .01
❑ 261 Shawn Abner .05 .01
❑ 262 Dave Valle .05 .01
❑ 263 Jeff Huson .05 .01
❑ 264 Edgar Martinez .15 .05
❑ 265 Carlton Fisk .15 .05
❑ 266 Steve Finley .10 .02
❑ 267 John Wetteland .10 .02
❑ 268 Kevin Appier .10 .02
❑ 269 Steve Lyons .05 .01
❑ 270 Mickey Tettleton .05 .01
❑ 271 Luis Rivera .05 .01
❑ 272 Steve Jeltz .05 .01
❑ 273 R.J. Reynolds .05 .01
❑ 274 Carlos Martinez .05 .01
❑ 275 Dan Plesac .05 .01
❑ 276 Mike Morgan UER
(Total IP shown as
1149.1, shoul .05 .01
❑ 277 Jeff Russell .05 .01
❑ 278 Pete Incaviglia .05 .01
❑ 279 Kevin Seitzer UER
(Bio has 200 hits twice
and .3 .05 .01
❑ 280 Bobby Thigpen .05 .01
❑ 281 Stan Javier UER
(Born 1/9,
should say 9/1) .05 .01
❑ 282 Henry Cotto .05 .01
❑ 283 Gary Wayne .05 .01
❑ 284 Shane Mack .05 .01
❑ 285 Brian Holman .05 .01
❑ 286 Gerald Perry .05 .01
❑ 287 Steve Crawford .05 .01
❑ 288 Nelson Liriano .05 .01
❑ 289 Don Aase .05 .01
❑ 290 Randy Johnson .30 .10
❑ 291 Harold Baines .10 .02
❑ 292 Kent Hrbek .10 .02
❑ 293A Les Lancaster ERR
(No comma between
Dallas and T .05 .01
❑ 293B Les Lancaster COR
(Corrected in
factory sets) .05 .01
❑ 294 Jeff Musselman .05 .01
❑ 295 Kurt Stillwell .05 .01
❑ 296 Stan Belinda .05 .01
❑ 297 Lou Whitaker .10 .02
❑ 298 Glenn Wilson .05 .01
❑ 299 Omar Vizquel UER .15 .05
❑ 300 Ramon Martinez .05 .01
❑ 301 Dwight Smith .05 .01
❑ 302 Tim Crews .05 .01
❑ 303 Lance Blankenship .05 .01
❑ 304 Sid Bream .05 .01
❑ 305 Rafael Ramirez .05 .01
❑ 306 Steve Wilson .05 .01
❑ 307 Mackey Sasser .05 .01
❑ 308 Franklin Stubbs .05 .01
❑ 309 Jack Daugherty UER
(Born 6/3/60,
should say July .05 .01
❑ 310 Eddie Murray .25 .08
❑ 311 Bob Welch .05 .01
❑ 312 Brian Harper .05 .01
❑ 313 Lance McCullers .05 .01
❑ 314 Dave Smith .05 .01
❑ 315 Bobby Bonilla .10 .02
❑ 316 Jerry Don Gleaton .05 .01
❑ 317 Greg Maddux .40 .15
❑ 318 Keith Miller .05 .01
❑ 319 Mark Portugal .05 .01
❑ 320 Robin Ventura .10 .02
❑ 321 Bob Ojeda .05 .01
❑ 322 Mike Harkey .05 .01
❑ 323 Jay Bell .10 .02
❑ 324 Mark McGwire .75 .30
❑ 325 Gary Gaetti .10 .02
❑ 326 Jeff Pico .05 .01
❑ 327 Kevin McReynolds .05 .01
❑ 328 Frank Tanana .05 .01
❑ 329 Eric Yelding UER
(Listed as 6'3"
should be 5'11 .05 .01
❑ 330 Barry Bonds 1.00 .40
❑ 331 Brian McRae RC .25 .08
❑ 332 Pedro Munoz RC .10 .02
❑ 333 Daryl Irvine RC .05 .01
❑ 334 Chris Hoiles .05 .01
❑ 335 Thomas Howard .05 .01
❑ 336 Jeff Schulz RC .05 .01
❑ 337 Jeff Manto .05 .01
❑ 338 Beau Allred .05 .01
❑ 339 Mike Bordick RC .40 .15
❑ 340 Todd Hundley .05 .01
❑ 341 Jim Vatcher UER RC .05 .01
❑ 342 Luis Sojo .05 .01
❑ 343 Jose Offerman UER .05 .01
❑ 344 Pete Coachman RC .05 .01
❑ 345 Mike Benjamin .05 .01
❑ 346 Ozzie Canseco .05 .01
❑ 347 Tim McIntosh .05 .01
❑ 348 Phil Plantier RC .10 .02
❑ 349 Terry Shumpert .05 .01
❑ 350 Darren Lewis FSC .05 .01
❑ 351 David Walsh RC .05 .01
❑ 352A Scott Chiamparino
ERR (Bats left,
should be righ .10 .02
❑ 352B Scott Chiamparino
COR (corrected in
factory sets .10 .02
❑ 353 Julio Valera
UER (Progressed mis-
spelled as pro .05 .01
❑ 354 Anthony Telford RC .05 .01
❑ 355 Kevin Wickander .05 .01
❑ 356 Tim Naehring .05 .01
❑ 357 Jim Poole .05 .01
❑ 358 Mark Whiten FSC UER .05 .01
❑ 359 Terry Wells RC .05 .01
❑ 360 Rafael Valdez .05 .01
❑ 361 Mel Stottlemyre Jr. .05 .01
❑ 362 David Segui .05 .01
❑ 363 Paul Abbott RC .05 .01
❑ 364 Steve Howard .05 .01
❑ 365 Karl Rhodes .05 .01
❑ 366 Rafael Novoa RC .05 .01
❑ 367 Joe Grahe RC .05 .01
❑ 368 Darren Reed .05 .01
❑ 369 Jeff McKnight .05 .01
❑ 370 Scott Leius .05 .01
❑ 371 Mark Dewey RC .05 .01
❑ 372 Mark Lee UER RC .10 .02
❑ 373 Rosario Rodriguez UER RC .05 .01
❑ 374 Chuck McElroy .05 .01
❑ 375 Mike Bell RC .05 .01
❑ 376 Mickey Morandini .05 .01
❑ 377 Bill Haselman RC .05 .01
❑ 378 Dave Pavlas RC .05 .01
❑ 379 Derrick May .05 .01
❑ 380 Jeromy Burnitz RC .40 .15
❑ 381 Donald Peters RC .05 .01
❑ 382 Alex Fernandez .05 .01
❑ 383 Mike Mussina RC 2.00 .75
❑ 384 Dan Smith RC .10 .02
❑ 385 Lance Dickson RC .10 .02
❑ 386 Carl Everett RC .50 .20
❑ 387 Tom Nevers RC .10 .02
❑ 388 Adam Hyzdu RC .25 .08
❑ 389 Todd Van Poppel RC .25 .08
❑ 390 Rondell White RC .40 .15
❑ 391 Marc Newfield RC .10 .02
❑ 392 Julio Franco AS .05 .01
❑ 393 Wade Boggs AS .10 .02
❑ 394 Ozzie Guillen AS .05 .01
❑ 395 Cecil Fielder AS .05 .01
❑ 396 Ken Griffey Jr. AS .25 .08
❑ 397 Rickey Henderson AS .15 .05
❑ 398 Jose Canseco AS .10 .02
❑ 399 Roger Clemens AS .40 .15
❑ 400 Sandy Alomar Jr. AS .05 .01
❑ 401 Bobby Thigpen AS .05 .01
❑ 402 Bobby Bonilla MB .05 .01
❑ 403 Eric Davis MB .05 .01
❑ 404 Fred McGriff MB .10 .02
❑ 405 Glenn Davis MB .05 .01
❑ 406 Kevin Mitchell MB .05 .01
❑ 407 Rob Dibble KM .05 .01
❑ 408 Ramon Martinez KM .05 .01
❑ 409 David Cone KM .05 .01
❑ 410 Bobby Witt KM .05 .01
❑ 411 Mark Langston KM .05 .01
❑ 412 Bo Jackson RIF .10 .02
❑ 413 Shawon Dunston RIF
UER (In the baseball,
should .05 .01
❑ 414 Jesse Barfield RIF .05 .01
❑ 415 Ken Caminiti RIF .05 .01
❑ 416 Benito Santiago RIF .05 .01
❑ 417 Nolan Ryan HL .50 .20
❑ 418 Bobby Thigpen HL UER
(Back refers to Hal
McRae J .05 .01
❑ 419 Ramon Martinez HL .05 .01
❑ 420 Bo Jackson HL .10 .02
❑ 421 Carlton Fisk HL .10 .02
❑ 422 Jimmy Key .10 .02
❑ 423 Junior Noboa .05 .01
❑ 424 Al Newman .05 .01
❑ 425 Pat Borders .05 .01
❑ 426 Von Hayes .05 .01
❑ 427 Tim Teufel .05 .01
❑ 428 Eric Plunk UER
(Text says Eric's had,
no apostro .05 .01
❑ 429 John Moses .05 .01
❑ 430 Mike Witt .05 .01
❑ 431 Otis Nixon .05 .01
❑ 432 Tony Fernandez .05 .01
❑ 433 Rance Mulliniks .05 .01
❑ 434 Dan Petry .05 .01
❑ 435 Bob Geren .05 .01
❑ 436 Steve Frey .05 .01
❑ 437 Jamie Moyer .10 .02
❑ 438 Junior Ortiz .05 .01
❑ 439 Tom O'Malley .05 .01
❑ 440 Pat Combs .05 .01
❑ 441 Jose Canseco DT .15 .05
❑ 442 Alfredo Griffin .05 .01
❑ 443 Andres Galarraga .10 .02
❑ 444 Bryn Smith .05 .01
❑ 445 Andre Dawson .10 .02
❑ 446 Juan Samuel .05 .01
❑ 447 Mike Aldrete .05 .01
❑ 448 Ron Gant .10 .02
❑ 449 Fernando Valenzuela .10 .02
❑ 450 Vince Coleman UER
(Should say topped
majors in s .05 .01
❑ 451 Kevin Mitchell .05 .01
❑ 452 Spike Owen .05 .01
❑ 453 Mike Bielecki .05 .01
❑ 454 Dennis Martinez .10 .02
❑ 455 Brett Butler .10 .02
❑ 456 Ron Darling .05 .01
❑ 457 Dennis Rasmussen .05 .01
❑ 458 Ken Howell .05 .01
❑ 459 Steve Bedrosian .05 .01
❑ 460 Frank Viola .10 .02
❑ 461 Jose Lind .05 .01
❑ 462 Chris Sabo .05 .01
❑ 463 Dante Bichette .10 .02

❑	464	Rick Mahler	.05	.01
❑	465	John Smiley	.05	.01
❑	466	Devon White	.10	.02
❑	467	John Orton	.05	.01
❑	468	Mike Stanton	.05	.01
❑	469	Billy Hatcher	.05	.01
❑	470	Wally Joyner	.10	.02
❑	471	Gene Larkin	.05	.01
❑	472	Doug Drabek	.05	.01
❑	473	Gary Sheffield	.10	.02
❑	474	David Wells	.10	.02
❑	475	Andy Van Slyke	.15	.05
❑	476	Mike Gallego	.05	.01
❑	477	B.J. Surhoff	.10	.02
❑	478	Gene Nelson	.05	.01
❑	479	Mariano Duncan	.05	.01
❑	480	Fred McGriff	.15	.05
❑	481	Jerry Browne	.05	.01
❑	482	Alvin Davis	.05	.01
❑	483	Bill Wegman	.05	.01
❑	484	Dave Parker	.10	.02
❑	485	Dennis Eckersley	.10	.02
❑	486	Erik Hanson UER (Basketball misspelled as baseke	.05	.01
❑	487	Bill Ripken	.05	.01
❑	488	Tom Candiotti	.05	.01
❑	489	Mike Schooler	.05	.01
❑	490	Gregg Olson	.05	.01
❑	491	Chris James	.05	.01
❑	492	Pete Harnisch	.05	.01
❑	493	Julio Franco	.10	.02
❑	494	Greg Briley	.05	.01
❑	495	Ruben Sierra	.10	.02
❑	496	Steve Olin	.05	.01
❑	497	Mike Fetters	.05	.01
❑	498	Mark Williamson	.05	.01
❑	499	Bob Tewksbury	.05	.01
❑	500	Tony Gwynn	.30	.10
❑	501	Randy Myers	.05	.01
❑	502	Keith Comstock	.05	.01
❑	503	Craig Worthington UER (DeCinces misspelled DiCin	.05	.01
❑	504	Mark Eichhorn UER (Stats incomplete, doesn't hav	.05	.01
❑	505	Barry Larkin	.15	.05
❑	506	Dave Johnson	.05	.01
❑	507	Bobby Witt	.05	.01
❑	508	Joe Orsulak	.05	.01
❑	509	Pete O'Brien	.05	.01
❑	510	Brad Arnsberg	.05	.01
❑	511	Storm Davis	.05	.01
❑	512	Bob Milacki	.05	.01
❑	513	Bill Pecota	.05	.01
❑	514	Glenallen Hill	.05	.01
❑	515	Danny Tartabull	.05	.01
❑	516	Mike Moore	.05	.01
❑	517	Ron Robinson UER (577 K's in 1990)	.05	.01
❑	518	Mark Gardner	.05	.01
❑	519	Rick Wrona	.05	.01
❑	520	Mike Scioscia	.05	.01
❑	521	Frank Wills	.05	.01
❑	522	Greg Brock	.05	.01
❑	523	Jack Clark	.10	.02
❑	524	Bruce Ruffin	.05	.01
❑	525	Robin Yount	.40	.15
❑	526	Tom Foley	.05	.01
❑	527	Pat Perry	.05	.01
❑	528	Greg Vaughn	.05	.01
❑	529	Wally Whitehurst	.05	.01
❑	530	Norm Charlton	.05	.01
❑	531	Marvell Wynne	.05	.01
❑	532	Jim Gantner	.05	.01
❑	533	Greg Litton	.05	.01
❑	534	Manny Lee	.05	.01
❑	535	Scott Bailes	.05	.01
❑	536	Charlie Leibrandt	.05	.01
❑	537	Roger McDowell	.05	.01
❑	538	Andy Benes	.05	.01
❑	539	Rick Honeycutt	.05	.01
❑	540	Dwight Gooden	.10	.02
❑	541	Scott Garrelts	.05	.01
❑	542	Dave Clark	.05	.01
❑	543	Lonnie Smith	.05	.01
❑	544	Rick Reuschel	.05	.01
❑	545	Delino DeShields	.10	.02
❑	546	Mike Sharperson	.05	.01
❑	547	Mike Kingery	.05	.01
❑	548	Terry Kennedy	.05	.01
❑	549	David Cone	.10	.02
❑	550	Orel Hershiser	.10	.02
❑	551	Matt Nokes	.05	.01
❑	552	Eddie Williams	.05	.01
❑	553	Frank DiPino	.05	.01
❑	554	Fred Lynn	.05	.01
❑	555	Alex Cole	.05	.01
❑	556	Terry Leach	.05	.01
❑	557	Chet Lemon	.05	.01
❑	558	Paul Mirabella	.05	.01
❑	559	Bill Long	.05	.01
❑	560	Phil Bradley	.05	.01
❑	561	Duane Ward	.05	.01
❑	562	Dave Bergman	.05	.01
❑	563	Eric Show	.05	.01
❑	564	Xavier Hernandez	.05	.01
❑	565	Jeff Parrett	.05	.01
❑	566	Chuck Cary	.05	.01
❑	567	Ken Hill	.05	.01
❑	568	Bob Welch Hand (Complement should be compliment)	.05	.01
❑	569	John Mitchell	.05	.01
❑	570	Travis Fryman	.10	.02
❑	571	Derek Lilliquist	.05	.01
❑	572	Steve Lake	.05	.01
❑	573	John Barfield	.05	.01
❑	574	Randy Bush	.05	.01
❑	575	Joe Magrane	.05	.01
❑	576	Eddie Diaz	.05	.01
❑	577	Casey Candaele	.05	.01
❑	578	Jesse Orosco	.05	.01
❑	579	Tom Henke	.05	.01
❑	580	Rick Cerone UER (Actually his third go-round wit	.05	.01
❑	581	Drew Hall	.05	.01
❑	582	Tony Castillo	.05	.01
❑	583	Jimmy Jones	.05	.01
❑	584	Rick Reed	.05	.01
❑	585	Joe Girardi	.05	.01
❑	586	Jeff Gray RC	.05	.01
❑	587	Luis Polonia	.05	.01
❑	588	Joe Klink	.05	.01
❑	589	Rex Hudler	.05	.01
❑	590	Kirk McCaskill	.05	.01
❑	591	Juan Agosto	.05	.01
❑	592	Wes Gardner	.05	.01
❑	593	Rich Rodriguez RC	.05	.01
❑	594	Mitch Webster	.05	.01
❑	595	Kelly Gruber	.05	.01
❑	596	Dale Mohorcic	.05	.01
❑	597	Willie McGee	.10	.02
❑	598	Bill Krueger	.05	.01
❑	599	Bob Walk UER (Cards says he's 33, but actually h	.05	.01
❑	600	Kevin Maas	.05	.01
❑	601	Danny Jackson	.05	.01
❑	602	Craig McMurtry UER (Anonymously misspelled anoni	.05	.01
❑	603	Curtis Wilkerson	.05	.01
❑	604	Adam Peterson	.05	.01
❑	605	Sam Horn	.05	.01
❑	606	Tommy Gregg	.05	.01
❑	607	Ken Dayley	.05	.01
❑	608	Carmelo Castillo	.05	.01
❑	609	John Shelby	.05	.01
❑	610	Don Slaught	.05	.01
❑	611	Calvin Schiraldi	.05	.01
❑	612	Dennis Lamp	.05	.01
❑	613	Andres Thomas	.05	.01
❑	614	Jose Gonzalez	.05	.01
❑	615	Randy Ready	.05	.01
❑	616	Kevin Bass	.05	.01
❑	617	Mike Marshall	.05	.01
❑	618	Daryl Boston	.05	.01
❑	619	Andy McGaffigan	.05	.01
❑	620	Joe Oliver	.05	.01
❑	621	Jim Gott	.05	.01
❑	622	Jose Oquendo	.05	.01
❑	623	Jose DeJesus	.05	.01
❑	624	Mike Brumley	.05	.01
❑	625	John Olerud	.10	.02
❑	626	Ernest Riles	.05	.01
❑	627	Gene Harris	.05	.01
❑	628	Jose Uribe	.05	.01
❑	629	Darnell Coles	.05	.01
❑	630	Carney Lansford	.10	.02
❑	631	Tim Leary	.05	.01
❑	632	Tim Hulett	.05	.01
❑	633	Kevin Elster	.05	.01
❑	634	Tony Fossas	.05	.01
❑	635	Francisco Oliveras	.05	.01
❑	636	Bob Patterson	.05	.01
❑	637	Gary Ward	.05	.01
❑	638	Rene Gonzales	.05	.01
❑	639	Don Robinson	.05	.01
❑	640	Darryl Strawberry	.10	.02
❑	641	Dave Anderson	.05	.01
❑	642	Scott Scudder	.05	.01
❑	643	Reggie Harris UER (Hepatitis misspelled as hepit	.05	.01
❑	644	Dave Henderson	.05	.01
❑	645	Ben McDonald	.05	.01
❑	646	Bob Kipper	.05	.01
❑	647	Hal Morris UER (It's should be its)	.05	.01
❑	648	Tim Birtsas	.05	.01
❑	649	Steve Searcy	.05	.01
❑	650	Dale Murphy	.15	.05
❑	651	Ron Oester	.05	.01
❑	652	Mike LaCoss	.05	.01
❑	653	Ron Jones	.05	.01
❑	654	Kelly Downs	.05	.01
❑	655	Roger Clemens	.75	.30
❑	656	Herm Winningham	.05	.01
❑	657	Trevor Wilson	.05	.01
❑	658	Jose Rijo	.05	.01
❑	659	Dann Bilardello UER (Bio has 13 games, 1 hit, an	.05	.01
❑	660	Gregg Jefferies	.05	.01
❑	661	Doug Drabek AS UER (Through is mis-spelled thou	.05	.01
❑	662	Randy Myers AS	.05	.01
❑	663	Benny Santiago AS	.05	.01
❑	664	Will Clark AS	.10	.02
❑	665	Ryne Sandberg AS	.25	.08
❑	666	Barry Larkin AS UER (Line 13, coolly misspelled	.10	.02
❑	667	Matt Williams AS	.05	.01
❑	668	Barry Bonds AS	.50	.20
❑	669	Eric Davis AS	.05	.01
❑	670	Bobby Bonilla AS	.05	.01
❑	671	Chipper Jones RC	4.00	1.50
❑	672	Eric Christopherson RC	.10	.02
❑	673	Robbie Beckett RC	.10	.02
❑	674	Shane Andrews RC	.25	.08
❑	675	Steve Karsay RC	.25	.08
❑	676	Aaron Holbert RC	.10	.02
❑	677	Donovan Osborne RC	.10	.02
❑	678	Todd Ritchie RC	.25	.08
❑	679	Ronnie Walden RC	.10	.02
❑	680	Tim Costo RC	.10	.02
❑	681	Dan Wilson RC	.25	.08
❑	682	Kurt Miller RC	.10	.02
❑	683	Mike Lieberthal RC	.40	.15
❑	684	Roger Clemens KM	.40	.15
❑	685	Dwight Gooden KM	.05	.01
❑	686	Nolan Ryan KM	.50	.20
❑	687	Frank Viola KM	.05	.01
❑	688	Erik Hanson KM	.05	.01
❑	689	Matt Williams MB	.05	.01
❑	690	Jose Canseco MB	.10	.02
❑	691	Darryl Strawberry MB	.05	.01
❑	692	Bo Jackson MB	.10	.02
❑	693	Cecil Fielder MB	.05	.01
❑	694	Sandy Alomar Jr. RF	.05	.01
❑	695	Cory Snyder RF	.05	.01
❑	696	Eric Davis RF	.05	.01
❑	697	Ken Griffey Jr. RF	.25	.08

❑ 698 Andy Van Slyke RF UER .10 .02
❑ 699 Langston/Witt NH
Mark Langston
Mike Witt .05 .01
❑ 700 Randy Johnson NH .15 .05
❑ 701 Nolan Ryan NH .50 .20
❑ 702 Dave Stewart NH .05 .01
❑ 703 Fernando Valenzuela NH .05 .01
❑ 704 Andy Hawkins NH .05 .01
❑ 705 Melido Perez NH .05 .01
❑ 706 Terry Mulholland NH .05 .01
❑ 707 Dave Stieb NH .05 .01
❑ 708 Brian Barnes RC .05 .01
❑ 709 Bernard Gilkey .05 .01
❑ 710 Steve Decker RC .05 .01
❑ 711 Paul Faries RC .05 .01
❑ 712 Paul Marak RC .05 .01
❑ 713 Wes Chamberlain RC .10 .02
❑ 714 Kevin Belcher RC .05 .01
❑ 715 Dan Boone UER
(IP adds up to 101,
but card has 1 .05 .01
❑ 716 Steve Adkins RC .05 .01
❑ 717 Geronimo Pena .05 .01
❑ 718 Howard Farmer .05 .01
❑ 719 Mark Leonard RC .05 .01
❑ 720 Tom Lampkin .05 .01
❑ 721 Mike Gardiner RC .05 .01
❑ 722 Jeff Conine RC .40 .15
❑ 723 Efrain Valdez RC .05 .01
❑ 724 Chuck Malone .05 .01
❑ 725 Leo Gomez .05 .01
❑ 726 Paul McClellan RC .05 .01
❑ 727 Mark Leiter RC .10 .02
❑ 728 Rich DeLucia UER RC .05 .01
❑ 729 Mel Rojas .05 .01
❑ 730 Hector Wagner RC .05 .01
❑ 731 Ray Lankford .10 .02
❑ 732 Turner Ward RC .10 .02
❑ 733 Gerald Alexander RC .05 .01
❑ 734 Scott Anderson RC .05 .01
❑ 735 Tony Perezchica .05 .01
❑ 736 Jimmy Kremers .05 .01
❑ 737 American Flag/Peace .25 .08
❑ 738 Mike York RC .05 .01
❑ 739 Mike Rochford .05 .01
❑ 740 Scott Aldred .05 .01
❑ 741 Rico Brogna .05 .01
❑ 742 Dave Burba RC .25 .08
❑ 743 Ray Stephens RC .05 .01
❑ 744 Eric Gunderson .05 .01
❑ 745 Troy Afenir RC .05 .01
❑ 746 Jeff Shaw .05 .01
❑ 747 Orlando Merced RC .10 .02
❑ 748 Omar Olivares UER RC .10 .02
❑ 749 Jerry Kutzler .05 .01
❑ 750 Mo Vaughn .10 .02
❑ 751 Matt Stark RC .05 .01
❑ 752 Randy Hennis RC .05 .01
❑ 753 Andujar Cedeno .05 .01
❑ 754 Kelvin Torve .05 .01
❑ 755 Joe Kraemer .05 .01
❑ 756 Phil Clark RC .10 .02
❑ 757 Ed Vosberg RC .05 .01
❑ 758 Mike Perez RC .10 .02
❑ 759 Scott Lewis RC .05 .01
❑ 760 Steve Chitren RC .05 .01
❑ 761 Ray Young RC .05 .01
❑ 762 Andres Santana .05 .01
❑ 763 Rodney McCray RC .05 .01
❑ 764 Sean Berry UER RC .10 .02
❑ 765 Brent Mayne .05 .01
❑ 766 Mike Simms RC .05 .01
❑ 767 Glenn Sutko RC .05 .01
❑ 768 Gary DiSarcina .05 .01
❑ 769 George Brett HL .25 .08
❑ 770 Cecil Fielder HL .05 .01
❑ 771 Jim Presley .05 .01
❑ 772 John Dopson .05 .01
❑ 773 Bo Jackson Breaker .10 .02
❑ 774 Brent Knackert UER
(Born in 1954, shown
throwing .05 .01
❑ 775 Bill Doran UER
(Reds in NL East) .05 .01
❑ 776 Dick Schofield .05 .01
❑ 777 Nelson Santovenia .05 .01
❑ 778 Mark Guthrie .05 .01
❑ 779 Mark Lemke .05 .01
❑ 780 Terry Steinbach .05 .01
❑ 781 Tom Bolton .05 .01
❑ 782 Randy Tomlin RC .10 .02
❑ 783 Jeff Kunkel .05 .01
❑ 784 Felix Jose .05 .01
❑ 785 Rick Sutcliffe .10 .02
❑ 786 John Cerutti .05 .01
❑ 787 Jose Vizcaino UER .05 .01
❑ 788 Curt Schilling .25 .08
❑ 789 Ed Whitson .05 .01
❑ 790 Tony Pena .05 .01
❑ 791 John Candelaria .05 .01
❑ 792 Carmelo Martinez .05 .01
❑ 793 Sandy Alomar Jr. UER .05 .01
❑ 794 Jim Neidlinger RC .05 .01
❑ 795 Barry Larkin WS
and Chris Sabo .10 .02
❑ 796 Paul Sorrento .05 .01
❑ 797 Tom Pagnozzi .05 .01
❑ 798 Tino Martinez .25 .08
❑ 799 Scott Ruskin UER
(Text says first three
seasons .05 .01
❑ 800 Kirk Gibson .10 .02
❑ 801 Walt Terrell .05 .01
❑ 802 John Russell .05 .01
❑ 803 Chili Davis .10 .02
❑ 804 Chris Nabholz .05 .01
❑ 805 Juan Gonzalez .25 .08
❑ 806 Ron Hassey .05 .01
❑ 807 Todd Worrell .05 .01
❑ 808 Tommy Greene .05 .01
❑ 809 Joel Skinner UER
(Joel, not Bob, was
drafted in .05 .01
❑ 810 Benito Santiago .10 .02
❑ 811 Pat Tabler UER
(Line 3, always
misspelled alway) .05 .01
❑ 812 Scott Erickson UER RC .05 .01
❑ 813 Moises Alou .10 .02
❑ 814 Dale Sveum .05 .01
❑ 815 Ryne Sandberg MANYR .25 .08
❑ 816 Rick Dempsey .05 .01
❑ 817 Scott Bankhead .05 .01
❑ 818 Jason Grimsley .05 .01
❑ 819 Doug Jennings .05 .01
❑ 820 Tom Herr .05 .01
❑ 821 Rob Ducey .05 .01
❑ 822 Luis Quinones .05 .01
❑ 823 Greg Minton .05 .01
❑ 824 Mark Grant .05 .01
❑ 825 Ozzie Smith .40 .15
❑ 826 Dave Eiland .05 .01
❑ 827 Danny Heep .05 .01
❑ 828 Hensley Meulens .05 .01
❑ 829 Charlie O'Brien .05 .01
❑ 830 Glenn Davis .05 .01
❑ 831 John Marzano UER
(International mis-
spelled Int .05 .01
❑ 832 Steve Ontiveros .05 .01
❑ 833 Ron Karkovice .05 .01
❑ 834 Jerry Goff .05 .01
❑ 835 Ken Griffey Sr. .10 .02
❑ 836 Kevin Reimer .05 .01
❑ 837 Randy Kutcher UER
(Infectious mis-
spelled infec .05 .01
❑ 838 Mike Blowers .05 .01
❑ 839 Mike Macfarlane .05 .01
❑ 840 Frank Thomas .25 .08
❑ 841 K.Griffey Jr./K.Griffey Sr. .40 .15
❑ 842 Jack Howell .05 .01
❑ 843 Goose Gozzo .05 .01
❑ 844 Gerald Young .05 .01
❑ 845 Zane Smith .05 .01
❑ 846 Kevin Brown .10 .02
❑ 847 Sil Campusano .05 .01
❑ 848 Larry Andersen .05 .01
❑ 849 Cal Ripken FRAN .40 .15
❑ 850 Roger Clemens FRAN .40 .15
❑ 851 Sandy Alomar Jr. FRAN .05 .01
❑ 852 Alan Trammell FRAN .10 .02
❑ 853 George Brett FRAN .25 .08
❑ 854 Robin Yount FRAN .25 .08
❑ 855 Kirby Puckett FRAN .15 .05
❑ 856 Don Mattingly FRAN .30 .10
❑ 857 Rickey Henderson FRAN .15 .05
❑ 858 Ken Griffey Jr. FRAN .25 .08
❑ 859 Ruben Sierra FRAN .05 .01
❑ 860 John Olerud FRAN .05 .01
❑ 861 David Justice FRAN .05 .01
❑ 862 Ryne Sandberg FRAN .25 .08
❑ 863 Eric Davis FRAN .05 .01
❑ 864 Darryl Strawberry FRAN .05 .01
❑ 865 Tim Wallach FRAN .05 .01
❑ 866 Dwight Gooden FRAN .05 .01
❑ 867 Len Dykstra FRAN .05 .01
❑ 868 Barry Bonds FRAN .50 .20
❑ 869 Todd Zeile FRAN .05 .01
❑ 870 Benito Santiago FRAN .05 .01
❑ 871 Will Clark FRAN .10 .02
❑ 872 Craig Biggio FRAN .10 .02
❑ 873 Wally Joyner FRAN .05 .01
❑ 874 Frank Thomas FRAN .15 .05
❑ 875 Rickey Henderson MVP .15 .05
❑ 876 Barry Bonds MVP .50 .20
❑ 877 Bob Welch CY .05 .01
❑ 878 Doug Drabek CY .05 .01
❑ 879 Sandy Alomar Jr. ROY .05 .01
❑ 880 David Justice ROY .05 .01
❑ 881 Damon Berryhill .05 .01
❑ 882 Frank Viola DT .05 .01
❑ 883 Dave Stewart DT .05 .01
❑ 884 Doug Jones DT .05 .01
❑ 885 Randy Myers DT .05 .01
❑ 886 Will Clark DT .10 .02
❑ 887 Roberto Alomar DT .10 .02
❑ 888 Barry Larkin DT .10 .02
❑ 889 Wade Boggs DT .15 .05
❑ 890 Rickey Henderson DT .25 .08
❑ 891 Kirby Puckett DT .15 .05
❑ 892 Ken Griffey Jr. DT .50 .20
❑ 893 Benny Santiago DT .10 .02

1992 Score

❑ COMPLETE SET (893) 15.00 6.00
❑ COMP.FACT.SET (910) 20.00 8.00
❑ COMPLETE SERIES 1 (442) 8.00 3.00
❑ COMPLETE SERIES 2 (451) 8.00 3.00
❑ 1 Ken Griffey Jr. .40 .15
❑ 2 Nolan Ryan 1.00 .40
❑ 3 Will Clark .15 .05
❑ 4 David Justice .10 .02
❑ 5 Dave Henderson .05 .01
❑ 6 Bret Saberhagen .10 .02
❑ 7 Fred McGriff .15 .05
❑ 8 Erik Hanson .05 .01
❑ 9 Darryl Strawberry .10 .02
❑ 10 Dwight Gooden .10 .02
❑ 11 Juan Gonzalez .15 .05
❑ 12 Mark Langston .05 .01
❑ 13 Lonnie Smith .05 .01
❑ 14 Jeff Montgomery .05 .01
❑ 15 Roberto Alomar .15 .05
❑ 16 Delino DeShields .05 .01
❑ 17 Steve Bedrosian .05 .01
❑ 18 Terry Pendleton .10 .02
❑ 19 Mark Carreon .05 .01
❑ 20 Mark McGwire .60 .25

❑ 21 Roger Clemens .50 .20
❑ 22 Chuck Crim .05 .01
❑ 23 Don Mattingly .60 .25
❑ 24 Dickie Thon .05 .01
❑ 25 Ron Gant .10 .02
❑ 26 Milt Cuyler .05 .01
❑ 27 Mike Macfarlane .05 .01
❑ 28 Dan Gladden .05 .01
❑ 29 Melido Perez .05 .01
❑ 30 Willie Randolph .10 .02
❑ 31 Albert Belle .10 .02
❑ 32 Dave Winfield .10 .02
❑ 33 Jimmy Jones .05 .01
❑ 34 Kevin Gross .05 .01
❑ 35 Andres Galarraga .10 .02
❑ 36 Mike Devereaux .05 .01
❑ 37 Chris Bosio .05 .01
❑ 38 Mike LaValliere .05 .01
❑ 39 Gary Gaetti .10 .02
❑ 40 Felix Jose .05 .01
❑ 41 Alvaro Espinoza .05 .01
❑ 42 Rick Aguilera .10 .02
❑ 43 Mike Gallego .05 .01
❑ 44 Eric Davis .10 .02
❑ 45 George Bell .05 .01
❑ 46 Tom Brunansky .05 .01
❑ 47 Steve Farr .05 .01
❑ 48 Duane Ward .05 .01
❑ 49 David Wells .10 .02
❑ 50 Cecil Fielder .10 .02
❑ 51 Walt Weiss .05 .01
❑ 52 Todd Zeile .05 .01
❑ 53 Doug Jones .05 .01
❑ 54 Bob Walk .05 .01
❑ 55 Rafael Palmeiro .15 .05
❑ 56 Rob Deer .05 .01
❑ 57 Paul O'Neill .15 .05
❑ 58 Jeff Reardon .10 .02
❑ 59 Randy Ready .05 .01
❑ 60 Scott Erickson .05 .01
❑ 61 Paul Molitor .10 .02
❑ 62 Jack McDowell .05 .01
❑ 63 Jim Acker .05 .01
❑ 64 Jay Buhner .10 .02
❑ 65 Travis Fryman .10 .02
❑ 66 Marquis Grissom .10 .02
❑ 67 Mike Harkey .05 .01
❑ 68 Luis Polonia .05 .01
❑ 69 Ken Caminiti .10 .02
❑ 70 Chris Sabo .05 .01
❑ 71 Gregg Olson .05 .01
❑ 72 Carlton Fisk .15 .05
❑ 73 Juan Samuel .05 .01
❑ 74 Todd Stottlemyre .05 .01
❑ 75 Andre Dawson .10 .02
❑ 76 Alvin Davis .05 .01
❑ 77 Bill Doran .05 .01
❑ 78 B.J. Surhoff .10 .02
❑ 79 Kirk McCaskill .05 .01
❑ 80 Dale Murphy .15 .05
❑ 81 Jose DeLeon .05 .01
❑ 82 Alex Fernandez .05 .01
❑ 83 Ivan Calderon .05 .01
❑ 84 Brent Mayne .05 .01
❑ 85 Jody Reed .05 .01
❑ 86 Randy Tomlin .05 .01
❑ 87 Randy Milligan .05 .01
❑ 88 Pascual Perez .05 .01
❑ 89 Hensley Meulens .05 .01
❑ 90 Joe Carter .10 .02
❑ 91 Mike Moore .05 .01
❑ 92 Ozzie Guillen .10 .02
❑ 93 Shawn Hillegas .05 .01
❑ 94 Chili Davis .10 .02
❑ 95 Vince Coleman .05 .01
❑ 96 Jimmy Key .10 .02
❑ 97 Billy Ripken .05 .01
❑ 98 Dave Smith .05 .01
❑ 99 Tom Bolton .05 .01
❑ 100 Barry Larkin .15 .05
❑ 101 Kenny Rogers .10 .02
❑ 102 Mike Boddicker .05 .01
❑ 103 Kevin Elster .05 .01
❑ 104 Ken Hill .05 .01
❑ 105 Charlie Leibrandt .05 .01
❑ 106 Pat Combs .05 .01
❑ 107 Hubie Brooks .05 .01
❑ 108 Julio Franco .10 .02
❑ 109 Vicente Palacios .05 .01
❑ 110 Kal Daniels .05 .01
❑ 111 Bruce Hurst .05 .01
❑ 112 Willie McGee .10 .02
❑ 113 Ted Power .05 .01
❑ 114 Milt Thompson .05 .01
❑ 115 Doug Drabek .05 .01
❑ 116 Rafael Belliard .05 .01
❑ 117 Scott Garrelts .05 .01
❑ 118 Terry Mulholland .05 .01
❑ 119 Jay Howell .05 .01
❑ 120 Danny Jackson .05 .01
❑ 121 Scott Ruskin .05 .01
❑ 122 Robin Ventura .10 .02
❑ 123 Bip Roberts .05 .01
❑ 124 Jeff Russell .05 .01
❑ 125 Hal Morris .05 .01
❑ 126 Teddy Higuera .05 .01
❑ 127 Luis Sojo .05 .01
❑ 128 Carlos Baerga .05 .01
❑ 129 Jeff Ballard .05 .01
❑ 130 Tom Gordon .05 .01
❑ 131 Sid Bream .05 .01
❑ 132 Rance Mulliniks .05 .01
❑ 133 Andy Benes .05 .01
❑ 134 Mickey Tettleton .05 .01
❑ 135 Rich DeLucia .05 .01
❑ 136 Tom Pagnozzi .05 .01
❑ 137 Harold Baines .10 .02
❑ 138 Danny Darwin .05 .01
❑ 139 Kevin Bass .05 .01
❑ 140 Chris Nabholz .05 .01
❑ 141 Pete O'Brien .05 .01
❑ 142 Jeff Treadway .05 .01
❑ 143 Mickey Morandini .05 .01
❑ 144 Eric King .05 .01
❑ 145 Danny Tartabull .05 .01
❑ 146 Lance Johnson .05 .01
❑ 147 Casey Candaele .05 .01
❑ 148 Felix Fermin .05 .01
❑ 149 Rich Rodriguez .05 .01
❑ 150 Dwight Evans .15 .05
❑ 151 Joe Klink .05 .01
❑ 152 Kevin Reimer .05 .01
❑ 153 Orlando Merced .05 .01
❑ 154 Mel Hall .05 .01
❑ 155 Randy Myers .05 .01
❑ 156 Greg A. Harris .05 .01
❑ 157 Jeff Brantley .05 .01
❑ 158 Jim Eisenreich .05 .01
❑ 159 Luis Rivera .05 .01
❑ 160 Cris Carpenter .05 .01
❑ 161 Bruce Ruffin .05 .01
❑ 162 Omar Vizquel .15 .05
❑ 163 Gerald Alexander .05 .01
❑ 164 Mark Guthrie .05 .01
❑ 165 Scott Lewis .05 .01
❑ 166 Bill Sampen .05 .01
❑ 167 Dave Anderson .05 .01
❑ 168 Kevin McReynolds .05 .01
❑ 169 Jose Vizcaino .05 .01
❑ 170 Bob Geren .05 .01
❑ 171 Mike Morgan .05 .01
❑ 172 Jim Gott .05 .01
❑ 173 Mike Pagliarulo .05 .01
❑ 174 Mike Jeffcoat .05 .01
❑ 175 Craig Lefferts .05 .01
❑ 176 Steve Finley .10 .02
❑ 177 Wally Backman .05 .01
❑ 178 Kent Mercker .05 .01
❑ 179 John Cerutti .05 .01
❑ 180 Jay Bell .10 .02
❑ 181 Dale Sveum .05 .01
❑ 182 Greg Gagne .05 .01
❑ 183 Donnie Hill .05 .01
❑ 184 Rex Hudler .05 .01
❑ 185 Pat Kelly .05 .01
❑ 186 Jeff D. Robinson .05 .01
❑ 187 Jeff Gray .05 .01
❑ 188 Jerry Willard .05 .01
❑ 189 Carlos Quintana .05 .01
❑ 190 Dennis Eckersley .10 .02
❑ 191 Kelly Downs .05 .01
❑ 192 Gregg Jefferies .05 .01
❑ 193 Darrin Fletcher .05 .01
❑ 194 Mike Jackson .05 .01
❑ 195 Eddie Murray .25 .08
❑ 196 Bill Landrum .05 .01
❑ 197 Eric Yelding .05 .01
❑ 198 Devon White .10 .02
❑ 199 Larry Walker .15 .05
❑ 200 Ryne Sandberg .40 .15
❑ 201 Dave Magadan .05 .01
❑ 202 Steve Chitren .05 .01
❑ 203 Scott Fletcher .05 .01
❑ 204 Dwayne Henry .05 .01
❑ 205 Scott Coolbaugh .05 .01
❑ 206 Tracy Jones .05 .01
❑ 207 Von Hayes .05 .01
❑ 208 Bob Melvin .05 .01
❑ 209 Scott Scudder .05 .01
❑ 210 Luis Gonzalez .10 .02
❑ 211 Scott Sanderson .05 .01
❑ 212 Chris Donnels .05 .01
❑ 213 Heathcliff Slocumb .05 .01
❑ 214 Mike Timlin .05 .01
❑ 215 Brian Harper .05 .01
❑ 216 Juan Berenguer UER (Decimal point missing in IP .05 .01
❑ 217 Mike Henneman .05 .01
❑ 218 Bill Spiers .05 .01
❑ 219 Scott Terry .05 .01
❑ 220 Frank Viola .10 .02
❑ 221 Mark Eichhorn .05 .01
❑ 222 Ernest Riles .05 .01
❑ 223 Ray Lankford .10 .02
❑ 224 Pete Harnisch .05 .01
❑ 225 Bobby Bonilla .10 .02
❑ 226 Mike Scioscia .05 .01
❑ 227 Joel Skinner .05 .01
❑ 228 Brian Holman .05 .01
❑ 229 Gilberto Reyes .05 .01
❑ 230 Matt Williams .10 .02
❑ 231 Jaime Navarro .05 .01
❑ 232 Jose Rijo .05 .01
❑ 233 Atlee Hammaker .05 .01
❑ 234 Tim Teufel .05 .01
❑ 235 John Kruk .10 .02
❑ 236 Kurt Stillwell .05 .01
❑ 237 Dan Pasqua .05 .01
❑ 238 Tim Crews .05 .01
❑ 239 Dave Gallagher .05 .01
❑ 240 Leo Gomez .05 .01
❑ 241 Steve Avery .05 .01
❑ 242 Bill Gullickson .05 .01
❑ 243 Mark Portugal .05 .01
❑ 244 Lee Guetterman .05 .01
❑ 245 Benito Santiago .10 .02
❑ 246 Jim Gantner .05 .01
❑ 247 Robby Thompson .05 .01
❑ 248 Terry Shumpert .05 .01
❑ 249 Mike Bell .05 .01
❑ 250 Harold Reynolds .10 .02
❑ 251 Mike Felder .05 .01
❑ 252 Bill Pecota .05 .01
❑ 253 Bill Krueger .05 .01
❑ 254 Alfredo Griffin .05 .01
❑ 255 Lou Whitaker .10 .02
❑ 256 Roy Smith .05 .01
❑ 257 Jerald Clark .05 .01
❑ 258 Sammy Sosa .25 .08
❑ 259 Tim Naehring .05 .01
❑ 260 Dave Righetti .10 .02
❑ 261 Paul Gibson .05 .01
❑ 262 Chris James .05 .01
❑ 263 Larry Andersen .05 .01
❑ 264 Storm Davis .05 .01
❑ 265 Jose Lind .05 .01
❑ 266 Greg Hibbard .05 .01
❑ 267 Norm Charlton .05 .01
❑ 268 Paul Kilgus .05 .01
❑ 269 Greg Maddux .40 .15
❑ 270 Ellis Burks .10 .02
❑ 271 Frank Tanana .05 .01
❑ 272 Gene Larkin .05 .01
❑ 273 Ron Hassey .05 .01
❑ 274 Jeff M. Robinson .05 .01
❑ 275 Steve Howe .05 .01
❑ 276 Daryl Boston .05 .01

❑ 277 Mark Lee .05 .01
❑ 278 Jose Segura .05 .01
❑ 279 Lance Blankenship .05 .01
❑ 280 Don Slaught .05 .01
❑ 281 Russ Swan .05 .01
❑ 282 Bob Tewksbury .05 .01
❑ 283 Geno Petralli .05 .01
❑ 284 Shane Mack .05 .01
❑ 285 Bob Scanlan .05 .01
❑ 286 Tim Leary .05 .01
❑ 287 John Smoltz .15 .05
❑ 288 Pat Borders .05 .01
❑ 289 Mark Davidson .05 .01
❑ 290 Sam Horn .05 .01
❑ 291 Lenny Harris .05 .01
❑ 292 Franklin Stubbs .05 .01
❑ 293 Thomas Howard .05 .01
❑ 294 Steve Lyons .05 .01
❑ 295 Francisco Oliveras .05 .01
❑ 296 Terry Leach .05 .01
❑ 297 Barry Jones .05 .01
❑ 298 Lance Parrish .10 .02
❑ 299 Wally Whitehurst .05 .01
❑ 300 Bob Welch .05 .01
❑ 301 Charlie Hayes .05 .01
❑ 302 Charlie Hough .10 .02
❑ 303 Gary Redus .05 .01
❑ 304 Scott Bradley .05 .01
❑ 305 Jose Oquendo .05 .01
❑ 306 Pete Incaviglia .05 .01
❑ 307 Marvin Freeman .05 .01
❑ 308 Gary Pettis .05 .01
❑ 309 Joe Slusarski .05 .01
❑ 310 Kevin Seitzer .05 .01
❑ 311 Jeff Reed .05 .01
❑ 312 Pat Tabler .05 .01
❑ 313 Mike Maddux .05 .01
❑ 314 Bob Milacki .05 .01
❑ 315 Eric Anthony .05 .01
❑ 316 Dante Bichette .10 .02
❑ 317 Steve Decker .05 .01
❑ 318 Jack Clark .10 .02
❑ 319 Doug Dascenzo .05 .01
❑ 320 Scott Leius .05 .01
❑ 321 Jim Lindeman .05 .01
❑ 322 Bryan Harvey .05 .01
❑ 323 Spike Owen .05 .01
❑ 324 Roberto Kelly .05 .01
❑ 325 Stan Belinda .05 .01
❑ 326 Joey Cora .05 .01
❑ 327 Jeff Innis .05 .01
❑ 328 Willie Wilson .05 .01
❑ 329 Juan Agosto .05 .01
❑ 330 Charles Nagy .05 .01
❑ 331 Scott Bailes .05 .01
❑ 332 Pete Schourek .05 .01
❑ 333 Mike Flanagan .05 .01
❑ 334 Omar Olivares .05 .01
❑ 335 Dennis Lamp .05 .01
❑ 336 Tommy Greene .05 .01
❑ 337 Randy Velarde .05 .01
❑ 338 Tom Lampkin .05 .01
❑ 339 John Russell .05 .01
❑ 340 Bob Kipper .05 .01
❑ 341 Todd Burns .05 .01
❑ 342 Ron Jones .05 .01
❑ 343 Dave Valle .05 .01
❑ 344 Mike Heath .05 .01
❑ 345 John Olerud .10 .02
❑ 346 Gerald Young .05 .01
❑ 347 Ken Patterson .05 .01
❑ 348 Les Lancaster .05 .01
❑ 349 Steve Crawford .05 .01
❑ 350 John Candelaria .05 .01
❑ 351 Mike Aldrete .05 .01
❑ 352 Mariano Duncan .05 .01
❑ 353 Julio Machado .05 .01
❑ 354 Ken Williams .05 .01
❑ 355 Walt Terrell .05 .01
❑ 356 Mitch Williams .05 .01
❑ 357 Al Newman .05 .01
❑ 358 Bud Black .05 .01
❑ 359 Joe Hesketh .05 .01
❑ 360 Paul Assenmacher .05 .01
❑ 361 Bo Jackson .25 .08
❑ 362 Jeff Blauser .05 .01
❑ 363 Mike Brumley .05 .01
❑ 364 Jim Deshaies .05 .01
❑ 365 Brady Anderson .10 .02
❑ 366 Chuck McElroy .05 .01
❑ 367 Matt Merullo .05 .01
❑ 368 Tim Belcher .05 .01
❑ 369 Luis Aquino .05 .01
❑ 370 Joe Oliver .05 .01
❑ 371 Greg Swindell .05 .01
❑ 372 Lee Stevens .05 .01
❑ 373 Mark Knudson .05 .01
❑ 374 Bill Wegman .05 .01
❑ 375 Jerry Don Gleaton .05 .01
❑ 376 Pedro Guerrero .10 .02
❑ 377 Randy Bush .05 .01
❑ 378 Greg W. Harris .05 .01
❑ 379 Eric Plunk .05 .01
❑ 380 Jose DeJesus .05 .01
❑ 381 Bobby Witt .05 .01
❑ 382 Curtis Wilkerson .05 .01
❑ 383 Gene Nelson .05 .01
❑ 384 Wes Chamberlain .05 .01
❑ 385 Tom Henke .05 .01
❑ 386 Mark Lemke .05 .01
❑ 387 Greg Briley .05 .01
❑ 388 Rafael Ramirez .05 .01
❑ 389 Tony Fossas .05 .01
❑ 390 Henry Cotto .05 .01
❑ 391 Tim Hulett .05 .01
❑ 392 Dean Palmer .10 .02
❑ 393 Glenn Braggs .05 .01
❑ 394 Mark Salas .05 .01
❑ 395 Rusty Meacham .05 .01
❑ 396 Andy Ashby .05 .01
❑ 397 Jose Melendez .05 .01
❑ 398 Warren Newson .05 .01
❑ 399 Frank Castillo .05 .01
❑ 400 Chito Martinez .05 .01
❑ 401 Bernie Williams .15 .05
❑ 402 Derek Bell .10 .02
❑ 403 Javier Ortiz .05 .01
❑ 404 Tim Sherrill .05 .01
❑ 405 Rob MacDonald .05 .01
❑ 406 Phil Plantier .05 .01
❑ 407 Troy Afenir .05 .01
❑ 408 Gino Minutelli .05 .01
❑ 409 Reggie Jefferson .05 .01
❑ 410 Mike Remlinger .05 .01
❑ 411 Carlos Rodriguez .05 .01
❑ 412 Joe Redfield .05 .01
❑ 413 Alonzo Powell .05 .01
❑ 414 Scott Livingstone UER (Travis Fryman, not Woody, .05 .01
❑ 415 Scott Kamieniecki .05 .01
❑ 416 Tim Spehr .05 .01
❑ 417 Brian Hunter .05 .01
❑ 418 Ced Landrum .05 .01
❑ 419 Bret Barberie .05 .01
❑ 420 Kevin Morton .05 .01
❑ 421 Doug Henry RC .10 .02
❑ 422 Doug Piatt .05 .01
❑ 423 Pat Rice .05 .01
❑ 424 Juan Guzman .05 .01
❑ 425 Nolan Ryan SPEC .50 .20
❑ 426 Tommy Greene NH .05 .01
❑ 427 Bob Milacki and Mike Flanagan NH (Mark Williamso .05 .01
❑ 428 Wilson Alvarez NH .05 .01
❑ 429 Otis Nixon HL .05 .01
❑ 430 Rickey Henderson HL .15 .05
❑ 431 Cecil Fielder AS .05 .01
❑ 432 Julio Franco AS .05 .01
❑ 433 Cal Ripken AS .40 .15
❑ 434 Wade Boggs AS .10 .02
❑ 435 Joe Carter AS .05 .01
❑ 436 Ken Griffey Jr. AS .25 .08
❑ 437 Ruben Sierra AS .05 .01
❑ 438 Scott Erickson AS .05 .01
❑ 439 Tom Henke AS .05 .01
❑ 440 Terry Steinbach AS .05 .01
❑ 441 Rickey Henderson DT .25 .08
❑ 442 Ryne Sandberg DT .40 .15
❑ 443 Otis Nixon .05 .01
❑ 444 Scott Radinsky .05 .01
❑ 445 Mark Grace .15 .05
❑ 446 Tony Pena .05 .01
❑ 447 Billy Hatcher .05 .01
❑ 448 Glenallen Hill .05 .01
❑ 449 Chris Gwynn .05 .01
❑ 450 Tom Glavine .15 .05
❑ 451 John Habyan .05 .01
❑ 452 Al Osuna .05 .01
❑ 453 Tony Phillips .05 .01
❑ 454 Greg Cadaret .05 .01
❑ 455 Rob Dibble .10 .02
❑ 456 Rick Honeycutt .05 .01
❑ 457 Jerome Walton .05 .01
❑ 458 Mookie Wilson .10 .02
❑ 459 Mark Gubicza .05 .01
❑ 460 Craig Biggio .15 .05
❑ 461 Dave Cochrane .05 .01
❑ 462 Keith Miller .05 .01
❑ 463 Alex Cole .05 .01
❑ 464 Pete Smith .05 .01
❑ 465 Brett Butler .10 .02
❑ 466 Jeff Huson .05 .01
❑ 467 Steve Lake .05 .01
❑ 468 Lloyd Moseby .05 .01
❑ 469 Tim McIntosh .05 .01
❑ 470 Dennis Martinez .10 .02
❑ 471 Greg Myers .05 .01
❑ 472 Mackey Sasser .05 .01
❑ 473 Junior Ortiz .05 .01
❑ 474 Greg Olson .05 .01
❑ 475 Steve Sax .05 .01
❑ 476 Ricky Jordan .05 .01
❑ 477 Max Venable .05 .01
❑ 478 Brian McRae .05 .01
❑ 479 Doug Simons .05 .01
❑ 480 Rickey Henderson .25 .08
❑ 481 Gary Varsho .05 .01
❑ 482 Carl Willis .05 .01
❑ 483 Rick Wilkins .05 .01
❑ 484 Donn Pall .05 .01
❑ 485 Edgar Martinez .15 .05
❑ 486 Tom Foley .05 .01
❑ 487 Mark Williamson .05 .01
❑ 488 Jack Armstrong .05 .01
❑ 489 Gary Carter .10 .02
❑ 490 Ruben Sierra .10 .02
❑ 491 Gerald Perry .05 .01
❑ 492 Rob Murphy .05 .01
❑ 493 Zane Smith .05 .01
❑ 494 Darryl Kile .10 .02
❑ 495 Kelly Gruber .05 .01
❑ 496 Jerry Browne .05 .01
❑ 497 Darryl Hamilton .05 .01
❑ 498 Mike Stanton .05 .01
❑ 499 Mark Leonard .05 .01
❑ 500 Jose Canseco .15 .05
❑ 501 Dave Martinez .05 .01
❑ 502 Jose Guzman .05 .01
❑ 503 Terry Kennedy .05 .01
❑ 504 Ed Sprague .05 .01
❑ 505 Frank Thomas .25 .08
❑ 506 Darren Daulton .10 .02
❑ 507 Kevin Tapani .05 .01
❑ 508 Luis Salazar .05 .01
❑ 509 Paul Faries .05 .01
❑ 510 Sandy Alomar Jr. .05 .01
❑ 511 Jeff King .05 .01
❑ 512 Gary Thurman .05 .01
❑ 513 Chris Hammond .05 .01
❑ 514 Pedro Munoz .05 .01
❑ 515 Alan Trammell .10 .02
❑ 516 Geronimo Pena .05 .01
❑ 517 Rodney McCray UER (Stole 6 bases in 1990, not 5; .05 .01
❑ 518 Manny Lee .05 .01
❑ 519 Junior Felix .05 .01
❑ 520 Kirk Gibson .10 .02
❑ 521 Darrin Jackson .05 .01
❑ 522 John Burkett .05 .01
❑ 523 Jeff Johnson .05 .01
❑ 524 Jim Corsi .05 .01
❑ 525 Robin Yount .40 .15
❑ 526 Jamie Quirk .05 .01
❑ 527 Bob Ojeda .05 .01
❑ 528 Mark Lewis .05 .01

❑ 529	Bryn Smith	.05	.01
❑ 530	Kent Hrbek	.10	.02
❑ 531	Dennis Boyd	.05	.01
❑ 532	Ron Karkovice	.05	.01
❑ 533	Don August	.05	.01
❑ 534	Todd Frohwirth	.05	.01
❑ 535	Wally Joyner	.10	.02
❑ 536	Dennis Rasmussen	.05	.01
❑ 537	Andy Allanson	.05	.01
❑ 538	Rich Gossage	.10	.02
❑ 539	John Marzano	.05	.01
❑ 540	Cal Ripken	.75	.30
❑ 541	Bill Swift UER (Brewers logo on front)	.05	.01
❑ 542	Kevin Appier	.10	.02
❑ 543	Dave Bergman	.05	.01
❑ 544	Bernard Gilkey	.05	.01
❑ 545	Mike Greenwell	.05	.01
❑ 546	Jose Uribe	.05	.01
❑ 547	Jesse Orosco	.05	.01
❑ 548	Bob Patterson	.05	.01
❑ 549	Mike Stanley	.05	.01
❑ 550	Howard Johnson	.05	.01
❑ 551	Joe Orsulak	.05	.01
❑ 552	Dick Schofield	.05	.01
❑ 553	Dave Hollins	.05	.01
❑ 554	David Segui	.05	.01
❑ 555	Barry Bonds	1.00	.40
❑ 556	Mo Vaughn	.10	.02
❑ 557	Craig Wilson	.05	.01
❑ 558	Bobby Rose	.05	.01
❑ 559	Rod Nichols	.05	.01
❑ 560	Len Dykstra	.10	.02
❑ 561	Craig Grebeck	.05	.01
❑ 562	Darren Lewis	.05	.01
❑ 563	Todd Benzinger	.05	.01
❑ 564	Ed Whitson	.05	.01
❑ 565	Jesse Barfield	.05	.01
❑ 566	Lloyd McClendon	.05	.01
❑ 567	Dan Plesac	.05	.01
❑ 568	Danny Cox	.05	.01
❑ 569	Skeeter Barnes	.05	.01
❑ 570	Bobby Thigpen	.05	.01
❑ 571	Deion Sanders	.15	.05
❑ 572	Chuck Knoblauch	.10	.02
❑ 573	Matt Nokes	.05	.01
❑ 574	Herm Winningham	.05	.01
❑ 575	Tom Candiotti	.05	.01
❑ 576	Jeff Bagwell	.25	.08
❑ 577	Brook Jacoby	.05	.01
❑ 578	Chico Walker	.05	.01
❑ 579	Brian Downing	.05	.01
❑ 580	Dave Stewart	.10	.02
❑ 581	Francisco Cabrera	.05	.01
❑ 582	Rene Gonzales	.05	.01
❑ 583	Stan Javier	.05	.01
❑ 584	Randy Johnson	.25	.08
❑ 585	Chuck Finley	.10	.02
❑ 586	Mark Gardner	.05	.01
❑ 587	Mark Whiten	.05	.01
❑ 588	Garry Templeton	.05	.01
❑ 589	Gary Sheffield	.10	.02
❑ 590	Ozzie Smith	.40	.15
❑ 591	Candy Maldonado	.05	.01
❑ 592	Mike Sharperson	.05	.01
❑ 593	Carlos Martinez	.05	.01
❑ 594	Scott Bankhead	.05	.01
❑ 595	Tim Wallach	.05	.01
❑ 596	Tino Martinez	.15	.05
❑ 597	Roger McDowell	.05	.01
❑ 598	Cory Snyder	.05	.01
❑ 599	Andujar Cedeno	.05	.01
❑ 600	Kirby Puckett	.25	.08
❑ 601	Rick Parker	.05	.01
❑ 602	Todd Hundley	.05	.01
❑ 603	Greg Litton	.05	.01
❑ 604	Dave Johnson	.05	.01
❑ 605	John Franco	.10	.02
❑ 606	Mike Fetters	.05	.01
❑ 607	Luis Alicea	.05	.01
❑ 608	Trevor Wilson	.05	.01
❑ 609	Rob Ducey	.05	.01
❑ 610	Ramon Martinez	.05	.01
❑ 611	Dave Burba	.05	.01
❑ 612	Dwight Smith	.05	.01
❑ 613	Kevin Maas	.05	.01
❑ 614	John Costello	.05	.01
❑ 615	Glenn Davis	.05	.01
❑ 616	Shawn Abner	.05	.01
❑ 617	Scott Hemond	.05	.01
❑ 618	Tom Prince	.05	.01
❑ 619	Wally Ritchie	.05	.01
❑ 620	Jim Abbott	.15	.05
❑ 621	Charlie O'Brien	.05	.01
❑ 622	Jack Daugherty	.05	.01
❑ 623	Tommy Gregg	.05	.01
❑ 624	Jeff Shaw	.05	.01
❑ 625	Tony Gwynn	.30	.10
❑ 626	Mark Leiter	.05	.01
❑ 627	Jim Clancy	.05	.01
❑ 628	Tim Layana	.05	.01
❑ 629	Jeff Schaefer	.05	.01
❑ 630	Lee Smith	.10	.02
❑ 631	Wade Taylor	.05	.01
❑ 632	Mike Simms	.05	.01
❑ 633	Terry Steinbach	.05	.01
❑ 634	Shawon Dunston	.05	.01
❑ 635	Tim Raines	.10	.02
❑ 636	Kirt Manwaring	.05	.01
❑ 637	Warren Cromartie	.05	.01
❑ 638	Luis Quinones	.05	.01
❑ 639	Greg Vaughn	.05	.01
❑ 640	Kevin Mitchell	.05	.01
❑ 641	Chris Hoiles	.05	.01
❑ 642	Tom Browning	.05	.01
❑ 643	Mitch Webster	.05	.01
❑ 644	Steve Olin	.05	.01
❑ 645	Tony Fernandez	.05	.01
❑ 646	Juan Bell	.05	.01
❑ 647	Joe Boever	.05	.01
❑ 648	Carney Lansford	.10	.02
❑ 649	Mike Benjamin	.05	.01
❑ 650	George Brett	.60	.25
❑ 651	Tim Burke	.05	.01
❑ 652	Jack Morris	.10	.02
❑ 653	Orel Hershiser	.10	.02
❑ 654	Mike Schooler	.05	.01
❑ 655	Andy Van Slyke	.15	.05
❑ 656	Dave Stieb	.05	.01
❑ 657	Dave Clark	.05	.01
❑ 658	Ben McDonald	.05	.01
❑ 659	John Smiley	.05	.01
❑ 660	Wade Boggs	.15	.05
❑ 661	Eric Bullock	.05	.01
❑ 662	Eric Show	.05	.01
❑ 663	Lenny Webster	.05	.01
❑ 664	Mike Huff	.05	.01
❑ 665	Rick Sutcliffe	.10	.02
❑ 666	Jeff Manto	.05	.01
❑ 667	Mike Fitzgerald	.05	.01
❑ 668	Matt Young	.05	.01
❑ 669	Dave West	.05	.01
❑ 670	Mike Hartley	.05	.01
❑ 671	Curt Schilling	.15	.05
❑ 672	Brian Bohanon	.05	.01
❑ 673	Cecil Espy	.05	.01
❑ 674	Joe Grahe	.05	.01
❑ 675	Sid Fernandez	.05	.01
❑ 676	Edwin Nunez	.05	.01
❑ 677	Hector Villanueva	.05	.01
❑ 678	Sean Berry	.05	.01
❑ 679	Dave Eiland	.05	.01
❑ 680	David Cone	.10	.02
❑ 681	Mike Bordick	.05	.01
❑ 682	Tony Castillo	.05	.01
❑ 683	John Barfield	.05	.01
❑ 684	Jeff Hamilton	.05	.01
❑ 685	Ken Dayley	.05	.01
❑ 686	Carmelo Martinez	.05	.01
❑ 687	Mike Capel	.05	.01
❑ 688	Scott Chiamparino	.05	.01
❑ 689	Rich Gedman	.05	.01
❑ 690	Rich Monteleone	.05	.01
❑ 691	Alejandro Pena	.05	.01
❑ 692	Oscar Azocar	.05	.01
❑ 693	Jim Poole	.05	.01
❑ 694	Mike Gardiner	.05	.01
❑ 695	Steve Buechele	.05	.01
❑ 696	Rudy Seanez	.05	.01
❑ 697	Paul Abbott	.05	.01
❑ 698	Steve Searcy	.05	.01
❑ 699	Jose Offerman	.05	.01
❑ 700	Ivan Rodriguez	.25	.08
❑ 701	Joe Girardi	.05	.01
❑ 702	Tony Perezchica	.05	.01
❑ 703	Paul McClellan	.05	.01
❑ 704	David Howard	.05	.01
❑ 705	Dan Petry	.05	.01
❑ 706	Jack Howell	.05	.01
❑ 707	Jose Mesa	.05	.01
❑ 708	Randy St. Claire	.05	.01
❑ 709	Kevin Brown	.10	.02
❑ 710	Ron Darling	.05	.01
❑ 711	Jason Grimsley	.05	.01
❑ 712	John Orton	.05	.01
❑ 713	Shawn Boskie	.05	.01
❑ 714	Pat Clements	.05	.01
❑ 715	Brian Barnes	.05	.01
❑ 716	Luis Lopez	.05	.01
❑ 717	Bob McClure	.05	.01
❑ 718	Mark Davis	.05	.01
❑ 719	Dann Bilardello	.05	.01
❑ 720	Tom Edens	.05	.01
❑ 721	Willie Fraser	.05	.01
❑ 722	Curt Young	.05	.01
❑ 723	Neal Heaton	.05	.01
❑ 724	Craig Worthington	.05	.01
❑ 725	Mel Rojas	.05	.01
❑ 726	Daryl Irvine	.05	.01
❑ 727	Roger Mason	.05	.01
❑ 728	Kirk Dressendorfer	.05	.01
❑ 729	Scott Aldred	.05	.01
❑ 730	Willie Blair	.05	.01
❑ 731	Allan Anderson	.05	.01
❑ 732	Dana Kiecker	.05	.01
❑ 733	Jose Gonzalez	.05	.01
❑ 734	Brian Drahman	.05	.01
❑ 735	Brad Komminsk	.05	.01
❑ 736	Arthur Rhodes	.05	.01
❑ 737	Terry Mathews	.05	.01
❑ 738	Jeff Fassero	.05	.01
❑ 739	Mike Magnante RC	.10	.02
❑ 740	Kip Gross	.05	.01
❑ 741	Jim Hunter	.05	.01
❑ 742	Jose Mota	.05	.01
❑ 743	Joe Bitker	.05	.01
❑ 744	Tim Mauser	.05	.01
❑ 745	Ramon Garcia	.05	.01
❑ 746	Rod Beck RC	.25	.08
❑ 747	Jim Austin RC	.05	.01
❑ 748	Keith Mitchell	.05	.01
❑ 749	Wayne Rosenthal	.05	.01
❑ 750	Bryan Hickerson RC	.10	.02
❑ 751	Bruce Egloff	.05	.01
❑ 752	John Wehner	.05	.01
❑ 753	Darren Holmes	.05	.01
❑ 754	Dave Hansen	.05	.01
❑ 755	Mike Mussina	.25	.08
❑ 756	Anthony Young	.05	.01
❑ 757	Ron Tingley	.05	.01
❑ 758	Ricky Bones	.05	.01
❑ 759	Mark Wohlers	.05	.01
❑ 760	Wilson Alvarez	.05	.01
❑ 761	Harvey Pulliam	.05	.01
❑ 762	Ryan Bowen	.05	.01
❑ 763	Terry Bross	.05	.01
❑ 764	Joel Johnston	.05	.01
❑ 765	Terry McDaniel	.05	.01
❑ 766	Esteban Beltre	.05	.01
❑ 767	Rob Maurer	.05	.01
❑ 768	Ted Wood	.05	.01
❑ 769	Mo Sanford	.05	.01
❑ 770	Jeff Carter	.05	.01
❑ 771	Gil Heredia RC	.25	.08
❑ 772	Monty Fariss	.05	.01
❑ 773	Will Clark AS	.10	.02
❑ 774	Ryne Sandberg AS	.25	.08
❑ 775	Barry Larkin AS	.10	.02
❑ 776	Howard Johnson AS	.05	.01
❑ 777	Barry Bonds AS	.50	.20
❑ 778	Brett Butler AS	.05	.01
❑ 779	Tony Gwynn AS	.15	.05
❑ 780	Ramon Martinez AS	.05	.01
❑ 781	Lee Smith AS	.05	.01
❑ 782	Mike Scioscia AS	.05	.01
❑ 783	Dennis Martinez HL UER	.05	.01
❑ 784	Dennis Martinez NH	.05	.01
❑ 785	Mark Gardner NH	.05	.01

❑ 786 Bret Saberhagen NH	.05	.01
❑ 787 Kent Mercker NH Mark Wohlers Alejandro Pena	.05	.01
❑ 788 Cal Ripken MVP	.40	.15
❑ 789 Terry Pendleton MVP	.05	.01
❑ 790 Roger Clemens CY	.25	.08
❑ 791 Tom Glavine CY	.10	.02
❑ 792 Chuck Knoblauch ROY	.05	.01
❑ 793 Jeff Bagwell ROY	.15	.05
❑ 794 Cal Ripken MOY	.40	.15
❑ 795 David Cone HL	.05	.01
❑ 796 Kirby Puckett HL	.15	.05
❑ 797 Steve Avery HL	.05	.01
❑ 798 Jack Morris HL	.05	.01
❑ 799 Allen Watson RC	.10	.02
❑ 800 Manny Ramirez RC	4.00	1.50
❑ 801 Cliff Floyd RC	.75	.30
❑ 802 Al Shirley RC	.10	.02
❑ 803 Brian Barber RC	.10	.02
❑ 804 Jon Farrell RC	.10	.02
❑ 805 Brent Gates RC	.10	.02
❑ 806 Scott Ruffcorn RC	.10	.02
❑ 807 Tyrone Hill RC	.10	.02
❑ 808 Benji Gil RC	.25	.08
❑ 809 Aaron Sele RC	.25	.08
❑ 810 Tyler Green RC	.10	.02
❑ 811 Chris Jones	.05	.01
❑ 812 Steve Wilson	.05	.01
❑ 813 Freddie Benavides	.05	.01
❑ 814 Don Wakamatsu	.05	.01
❑ 815 Mike Humphreys	.05	.01
❑ 816 Scott Servais	.05	.01
❑ 817 Rico Rossy	.05	.01
❑ 818 John Ramos	.05	.01
❑ 819 Rob Mallicoat	.05	.01
❑ 820 Milt Hill	.05	.01
❑ 821 Carlos Garcia	.05	.01
❑ 822 Stan Royer	.05	.01
❑ 823 Jeff Plympton	.05	.01
❑ 824 Braulio Castillo	.05	.01
❑ 825 David Haas	.05	.01
❑ 826 Luis Mercedes	.05	.01
❑ 827 Eric Karros	.10	.02
❑ 828 Shawn Hare RC	.10	.02
❑ 829 Reggie Sanders	.10	.02
❑ 830 Tom Goodwin	.05	.01
❑ 831 Dan Gakeler	.05	.01
❑ 832 Stacy Jones	.05	.01
❑ 833 Kim Batiste	.05	.01
❑ 834 Cal Eldred	.05	.01
❑ 835 Chris George	.05	.01
❑ 836 Wayne Housie	.05	.01
❑ 837 Mike Ignasiak	.05	.01
❑ 838 Josias Manzanillo RC	.10	.02
❑ 839 Jim Olander	.05	.01
❑ 840 Gary Cooper	.05	.01
❑ 841 Royce Clayton	.05	.01
❑ 842 Hector Fajardo RC	.10	.02
❑ 843 Blaine Beatty	.05	.01
❑ 844 Jorge Pedre	.05	.01
❑ 845 Kenny Lofton	.15	.05
❑ 846 Scott Brosius RC	.50	.20
❑ 847 Chris Cron	.05	.01
❑ 848 Denis Boucher	.05	.01
❑ 849 Kyle Abbott	.05	.01
❑ 850 Bob Zupcic RC	.10	.02
❑ 851 Rheal Cormier	.05	.01
❑ 852 Jimmy Lewis RC	.05	.01
❑ 853 Anthony Telford	.05	.01
❑ 854 Cliff Brantley	.05	.01
❑ 855 Kevin Campbell	.05	.01
❑ 856 Craig Shipley	.05	.01
❑ 857 Chuck Carr	.05	.01
❑ 858 Tony Eusebio	.10	.02
❑ 859 Jim Thome	.25	.08
❑ 860 Vinny Castilla RC	1.00	.40
❑ 861 Dann Howitt	.05	.01
❑ 862 Kevin Ward	.05	.01
❑ 863 Steve Wapnick	.05	.01
❑ 864 Rod Brewer RC	.10	.02
❑ 865 Todd Van Poppel	.05	.01
❑ 866 Jose Hernandez RC	.25	.08
❑ 867 Amalio Carreno	.05	.01
❑ 868 Calvin Jones	.05	.01
❑ 869 Jeff Gardner	.05	.01
❑ 870 Jarvis Brown	.05	.01
❑ 871 Eddie Taubensee RC	.25	.08
❑ 872 Andy Mota	.05	.01
❑ 873 Chris Haney	.05	.01
❑ 874 Roberto Hernandez	.05	.01
❑ 875 Laddie Renfroe	.05	.01
❑ 876 Scott Cooper	.05	.01
❑ 877 Armando Reynoso RC	.25	.08
❑ 878 Ty Cobb MEMO	.25	.08
❑ 879 Babe Ruth MEMO	.50	.20
❑ 880 Honus Wagner MEMO	.25	.08
❑ 881 Lou Gehrig MEMO	.40	.15
❑ 882 Satchel Paige MEMO	.25	.08
❑ 883 Will Clark DT	.10	.02
❑ 884 Cal Ripken DT	2.00	.75
❑ 885 Wade Boggs DT	.10	.02
❑ 886 Kirby Puckett DT	.15	.05
❑ 887 Tony Gwynn DT	.15	.05
❑ 888 Craig Biggio DT	.10	.02
❑ 889 Scott Erickson DT	.05	.01
❑ 890 Tom Glavine DT	.10	.02
❑ 891 Rob Dibble DT	.10	.02
❑ 892 Mitch Williams DT	.05	.01
❑ 893 Frank Thomas DT	.15	.05
❑ X672 C.Knob 90S AU/3000	25.00	10.00

1992 Score Rookie/Traded

❑ COMP.FACT.SET (110)	8.00	3.00
❑ 1T Gary Sheffield	.30	.10
❑ 2T Kevin Seitzer	.20	.07
❑ 3T Danny Tartabull	.20	.07
❑ 4T Steve Sax	.20	.07
❑ 5T Bobby Bonilla	.30	.10
❑ 6T Frank Viola	.30	.10
❑ 7T Dave Winfield	.30	.10
❑ 8T Rick Sutcliffe	.30	.10
❑ 9T Jose Canseco	.50	.20
❑ 10T Greg Swindell	.20	.07
❑ 11T Eddie Murray	.75	.30
❑ 12T Randy Myers	.20	.07
❑ 13T Wally Joyner	.30	.10
❑ 14T Kenny Lofton	.50	.20
❑ 15T Jack Morris	.30	.10
❑ 16T Charlie Hayes	.20	.07
❑ 17T Pete Incaviglia	.20	.07
❑ 18T Kevin Mitchell	.20	.07
❑ 19T Kurt Stillwell	.20	.07
❑ 20T Bret Saberhagen	.30	.10
❑ 21T Steve Buechele	.20	.07
❑ 22T John Smiley	.20	.07
❑ 23T Sammy Sosa Cubs	.75	.30
❑ 24T George Bell	.20	.07
❑ 25T Curt Schilling	.50	.20
❑ 26T Dick Schofield	.20	.07
❑ 27T David Cone	.30	.10
❑ 28T Dan Gladden	.20	.07
❑ 29T Kirk McCaskill	.20	.07
❑ 30T Mike Gallego	.20	.07
❑ 31T Kevin McReynolds	.20	.07
❑ 32T Bill Swift	.20	.07
❑ 33T Dave Martinez	.20	.07
❑ 34T Storm Davis	.20	.07
❑ 35T Willie Randolph	.30	.10
❑ 36T Melido Perez	.20	.07
❑ 37T Mark Carreon	.20	.07
❑ 38T Doug Jones	.20	.07
❑ 39T Gregg Jefferies	.20	.07
❑ 40T Mike Jackson	.20	.07
❑ 41T Dickie Thon	.20	.07
❑ 42T Eric King	.20	.07
❑ 43T Herm Winningham	.20	.07
❑ 44T Derek Lilliquist	.20	.07
❑ 45T Dave Anderson	.20	.07
❑ 46T Jeff Reardon	.30	.10
❑ 47T Scott Bankhead	.20	.07
❑ 48T Cory Snyder	.20	.07
❑ 49T Al Newman	.20	.07
❑ 50T Keith Miller	.20	.07
❑ 51T Dave Burba	.20	.07
❑ 52T Bill Pecota	.20	.07
❑ 53T Chuck Crim	.20	.07
❑ 54T Mariano Duncan	.20	.07
❑ 55T Dave Gallagher	.20	.07
❑ 56T Chris Gwynn	.20	.07
❑ 57T Scott Ruskin	.20	.07
❑ 58T Jack Armstrong	.20	.07
❑ 59T Gary Carter	.30	.10
❑ 60T Andres Galarraga	.30	.10
❑ 61T Ken Hill	.20	.07
❑ 62T Eric Davis	.30	.10
❑ 63T Ruben Sierra	.30	.10
❑ 64T Darrin Fletcher	.20	.07
❑ 65T Tim Belcher	.20	.07
❑ 66T Mike Morgan	.20	.07
❑ 67T Scott Scudder	.20	.07
❑ 68T Tom Candiotti	.20	.07
❑ 69T Hubie Brooks	.20	.07
❑ 70T Kal Daniels	.20	.07
❑ 71T Bruce Ruffin	.20	.07
❑ 72T Billy Hatcher	.20	.07
❑ 73T Bob Melvin	.20	.07
❑ 74T Lee Guetterman	.20	.07
❑ 75T Rene Gonzales	.20	.07
❑ 76T Kevin Bass	.20	.07
❑ 77T Tom Bolton	.20	.07
❑ 78T John Wetteland	.30	.10
❑ 79T Bip Roberts	.20	.07
❑ 80T Pat Listach RC	.40	.15
❑ 81T John Doherty RC	.20	.07
❑ 82T Sam Militello	.20	.07
❑ 83T Brian Jordan RC	.60	.25
❑ 84T Jeff Kent RC	3.00	1.25
❑ 85T Dave Fleming	.20	.07
❑ 86T Jeff Tackett	.20	.07
❑ 87T Chad Curtis RC	.40	.15
❑ 88T Eric Fox RC	.20	.07
❑ 89T Denny Neagle	.30	.10
❑ 90T Donovan Osborne	.20	.07
❑ 91T Carlos Hernandez	.20	.07
❑ 92T Tim Wakefield RC	3.00	1.20
❑ 93T Tim Salmon	.50	.20
❑ 94T Dave Nilsson	.20	.07
❑ 95T Mike Perez	.20	.07
❑ 96T Pat Hentgen	.20	.07
❑ 97T Frank Seminara RC	.20	.07
❑ 98T Ruben Amaro	.20	.07
❑ 99T Archi Cianfrocco RC	.20	.07
❑ 100T Andy Stankiewicz	.20	.07
❑ 101T Jim Bullinger	.20	.07
❑ 102T Pat Mahomes RC	.40	.15
❑ 103T Hipolito Pichardo RC	.20	.07
❑ 104T Bret Boone	.50	.20
❑ 105T John Vander Wal	.20	.07
❑ 106T Vince Horsman	.20	.07
❑ 107T Jim Austin	.20	.07
❑ 108T Brian Williams RC	.20	.07
❑ 109T Dan Walters	.20	.07
❑ 110T Wil Cordero	.20	.07

1993 Score

❑ COMPLETE SET (660)	40.00	15.00
❑ 1 Ken Griffey Jr.	.75	.30
❑ 2 Gary Sheffield	.20	.07
❑ 3 Frank Thomas	.50	.20
❑ 4 Ryne Sandberg	.75	.30
❑ 5 Larry Walker	.20	.07
❑ 6 Cal Ripken	1.50	.60
❑ 7 Roger Clemens	1.00	.40
❑ 8 Bobby Bonilla	.20	.07
❑ 9 Carlos Baerga	.10	.02
❑ 10 Darren Daulton	.20	.07
❑ 11 Travis Fryman	.20	.07
❑ 12 Andy Van Slyke	.30	.10

❑	13	Jose Canseco	.30	.10
❑	14	Roberto Alomar	.30	.10
❑	15	Tom Glavine	.30	.10
❑	16	Barry Larkin	.30	.10
❑	17	Gregg Jefferies	.10	.02
❑	18	Craig Biggio	.30	.10
❑	19	Shane Mack	.10	.02
❑	20	Brett Butler	.20	.07
❑	21	Dennis Eckersley	.20	.07
❑	22	Will Clark	.30	.10
❑	23	Don Mattingly	1.25	.50
❑	24	Tony Gwynn	.60	.25
❑	25	Ivan Rodriguez	.30	.10
❑	26	Shawon Dunston	.10	.02
❑	27	Mike Mussina	.30	.10
❑	28	Marquis Grissom	.20	.07
❑	29	Charles Nagy	.10	.02
❑	30	Len Dykstra	.20	.07
❑	31	Cecil Fielder	.20	.07
❑	32	Jay Bell	.20	.07
❑	33	B.J. Surhoff	.20	.07
❑	34	Bob Tewksbury	.10	.02
❑	35	Danny Tartabull	.10	.02
❑	36	Terry Pendleton	.20	.07
❑	37	Jack Morris	.20	.07
❑	38	Hal Morris	.10	.02
❑	39	Luis Polonia	.10	.02
❑	40	Ken Caminiti	.20	.07
❑	41	Robin Ventura	.20	.07
❑	42	Darryl Strawberry	.20	.07
❑	43	Wally Joyner	.20	.07
❑	44	Fred McGriff	.30	.10
❑	45	Kevin Tapani	.10	.02
❑	46	Matt Williams	.20	.07
❑	47	Robin Yount	.75	.30
❑	48	Ken Hill	.10	.02
❑	49	Edgar Martinez	.30	.10
❑	50	Mark Grace	.30	.10
❑	51	Juan Gonzalez	.20	.07
❑	52	Curt Schilling	.20	.07
❑	53	Dwight Gooden	.20	.07
❑	54	Chris Hoiles	.10	.02
❑	55	Frank Viola	.20	.07
❑	56	Ray Lankford	.20	.07
❑	57	George Brett	1.25	.50
❑	58	Kenny Lofton	.20	.07
❑	59	Nolan Ryan	2.00	.75
❑	60	Mickey Tettleton	.10	.02
❑	61	John Smoltz	.30	.10
❑	62	Howard Johnson	.10	.02
❑	63	Eric Karros	.20	.07
❑	64	Rick Aguilera	.10	.02
❑	65	Steve Finley	.20	.07
❑	66	Mark Langston	.10	.02
❑	67	Bill Swift	.10	.02
❑	68	John Olerud	.20	.07
❑	69	Kevin McReynolds	.10	.02
❑	70	Jack McDowell	.10	.02
❑	71	Rickey Henderson	.50	.20
❑	72	Brian Harper	.10	.02
❑	73	Mike Morgan	.10	.02
❑	74	Rafael Palmeiro	.30	.10
❑	75	Dennis Martinez	.20	.07
❑	76	Tino Martinez	.30	.10
❑	77	Eddie Murray	.50	.20
❑	78	Ellis Burks	.20	.07
❑	79	John Kruk	.20	.07
❑	80	Gregg Olson	.10	.02
❑	81	Bernard Gilkey	.10	.02
❑	82	Milt Cuyler	.10	.02
❑	83	Mike LaValliere	.10	.02
❑	84	Albert Belle	.20	.07
❑	85	Bip Roberts	.10	.02
❑	86	Melido Perez	.10	.02
❑	87	Otis Nixon	.10	.02
❑	88	Bill Spiers	.10	.02
❑	89	Jeff Bagwell	.30	.10
❑	90	Orel Hershiser	.20	.07
❑	91	Andy Benes	.10	.02
❑	92	Devon White	.20	.07
❑	93	Willie McGee	.20	.07
❑	94	Ozzie Guillen	.20	.07
❑	95	Ivan Calderon	.10	.02
❑	96	Keith Miller	.10	.02
❑	97	Steve Buechele	.10	.02
❑	98	Kent Hrbek	.20	.07
❑	99	Dave Hollins	.10	.02
❑	100	Mike Bordick	.10	.02
❑	101	Randy Tomlin	.10	.02
❑	102	Omar Vizquel	.30	.10
❑	103	Lee Smith	.20	.07
❑	104	Leo Gomez	.10	.02
❑	105	Jose Rijo	.10	.02
❑	106	Mark Whiten	.10	.02
❑	107	David Justice	.20	.07
❑	108	Eddie Taubensee	.10	.02
❑	109	Lance Johnson	.10	.02
❑	110	Felix Jose	.10	.02
❑	111	Mike Harkey	.10	.02
❑	112	Randy Milligan	.10	.02
❑	113	Anthony Young	.10	.02
❑	114	Rico Brogna	.10	.02
❑	115	Bret Saberhagen	.20	.07
❑	116	Sandy Alomar Jr.	.10	.02
❑	117	Terry Mulholland	.10	.02
❑	118	Darryl Hamilton	.10	.02
❑	119	Todd Zeile	.10	.02
❑	120	Bernie Williams	.30	.10
❑	121	Zane Smith	.10	.02
❑	122	Derek Bell	.10	.02
❑	123	Deion Sanders	.30	.10
❑	124	Luis Sojo	.10	.02
❑	125	Joe Oliver	.10	.02
❑	126	Craig Grebeck	.10	.02
❑	127	Andujar Cedeno	.10	.02
❑	128	Brian McRae	.10	.02
❑	129	Jose Offerman	.10	.02
❑	130	Pedro Munoz	.10	.02
❑	131	Bud Black	.10	.02
❑	132	Mo Vaughn	.20	.07
❑	133	Bruce Hurst	.10	.02
❑	134	Dave Henderson	.10	.02
❑	135	Tom Pagnozzi	.10	.02
❑	136	Erik Hanson	.10	.02
❑	137	Orlando Merced	.10	.02
❑	138	Dean Palmer	.20	.07
❑	139	John Franco	.20	.07
❑	140	Brady Anderson	.20	.07
❑	141	Ricky Jordan	.10	.02
❑	142	Jeff Blauser	.10	.02
❑	143	Sammy Sosa	.50	.20
❑	144	Bob Walk	.10	.02
❑	145	Delino DeShields	.10	.02
❑	146	Kevin Brown	.20	.07
❑	147	Mark Lemke	.10	.02
❑	148	Chuck Knoblauch	.20	.07
❑	149	Chris Sabo	.10	.02
❑	150	Bobby Witt	.10	.02
❑	151	Luis Gonzalez	.20	.07
❑	152	Ron Karkovice	.10	.02
❑	153	Jeff Brantley	.10	.02
❑	154	Kevin Appier	.20	.07
❑	155	Darrin Jackson	.10	.02
❑	156	Kelly Gruber	.10	.02
❑	157	Royce Clayton	.10	.02
❑	158	Chuck Finley	.20	.07
❑	159	Jeff King	.10	.02
❑	160	Greg Vaughn	.10	.02
❑	161	Geronimo Pena	.10	.02
❑	162	Steve Farr	.10	.02
❑	163	Jose Oquendo	.10	.02
❑	164	Mark Lewis	.10	.02
❑	165	John Wetteland	.20	.07
❑	166	Mike Henneman	.10	.02
❑	167	Todd Hundley	.10	.02
❑	168	Wes Chamberlain	.10	.02
❑	169	Steve Avery	.10	.02
❑	170	Mike Devereaux	.10	.02
❑	171	Reggie Sanders	.20	.07
❑	172	Jay Buhner	.20	.07
❑	173	Eric Anthony	.10	.02
❑	174	John Burkett	.10	.02
❑	175	Tom Candiotti	.10	.02
❑	176	Phil Plantier	.10	.02
❑	177	Doug Henry	.10	.02
❑	178	Scott Leius	.10	.02
❑	179	Kirt Manwaring	.10	.02
❑	180	Jeff Parrett	.10	.02
❑	181	Don Slaught	.10	.02
❑	182	Scott Radinsky	.10	.02
❑	183	Luis Alicea	.10	.02
❑	184	Tom Gordon	.10	.02
❑	185	Rick Wilkins	.10	.02
❑	186	Todd Stottlemyre	.10	.02
❑	187	Moises Alou	.20	.07
❑	188	Joe Grahe	.10	.02
❑	189	Jeff Kent	.50	.20
❑	190	Bill Wegman	.10	.02
❑	191	Kim Batiste	.10	.02
❑	192	Matt Nokes	.10	.02
❑	193	Mark Wohlers	.10	.02
❑	194	Paul Sorrento	.10	.02
❑	195	Chris Hammond	.10	.02
❑	196	Scott Livingstone	.10	.02
❑	197	Doug Jones	.10	.02
❑	198	Scott Cooper	.10	.02
❑	199	Ramon Martinez	.10	.02
❑	200	Dave Valle	.10	.02
❑	201	Mariano Duncan	.10	.02
❑	202	Ben McDonald	.10	.02
❑	203	Darren Lewis	.10	.02
❑	204	Kenny Rogers	.20	.07
❑	205	Manuel Lee	.10	.02
❑	206	Scott Erickson	.10	.02
❑	207	Dan Gladden	.10	.02
❑	208	Bob Welch	.10	.02
❑	209	Greg Olson	.10	.02
❑	210	Dan Pasqua	.10	.02
❑	211	Tim Wallach	.10	.02
❑	212	Jeff Montgomery	.10	.02
❑	213	Derrick May	.10	.02
❑	214	Ed Sprague	.10	.02
❑	215	David Haas	.10	.02
❑	216	Darrin Fletcher	.10	.02
❑	217	Brian Jordan	.20	.07
❑	218	Jaime Navarro	.10	.02
❑	219	Randy Velarde	.10	.02
❑	220	Ron Gant	.20	.07
❑	221	Paul Quantrill	.10	.02
❑	222	Damion Easley	.10	.02
❑	223	Charlie Hough	.20	.07
❑	224	Brad Brink	.10	.02
❑	225	Barry Manuel	.10	.02
❑	226	Kevin Koslofski	.10	.02
❑	227	Ryan Thompson	.10	.02
❑	228	Mike Munoz	.10	.02
❑	229	Dan Wilson	.20	.07
❑	230	Peter Hoy	.10	.02
❑	231	Pedro Astacio	.10	.02
❑	232	Matt Stairs	.10	.02
❑	233	Jeff Reboulet	.10	.02
❑	234	Manny Alexander	.10	.02
❑	235	Willie Banks	.10	.02
❑	236	John Jaha	.10	.02
❑	237	Scooter Tucker	.10	.02
❑	238	Russ Springer	.10	.02
❑	239	Paul Miller	.10	.02
❑	240	Dan Peltier	.10	.02
❑	241	Ozzie Canseco	.10	.02
❑	242	Ben Rivera	.10	.02
❑	243	John Valentin	.10	.02
❑	244	Henry Rodriguez	.10	.02
❑	245	Derek Parks	.10	.02
❑	246	Carlos Garcia	.10	.02
❑	247	Tim Pugh RC	.10	.02
❑	248	Melvin Nieves	.10	.02
❑	249	Rich Amaral	.10	.02
❑	250	Willie Greene	.10	.02
❑	251	Tim Scott	.10	.02
❑	252	Dave Silvestri	.10	.02

❑ 253 Rob Mallicoat .10 .02
❑ 254 Donald Harris .10 .02
❑ 255 Craig Colbert .10 .02
❑ 256 Jose Guzman .10 .02
❑ 257 Domingo Martinez RC .10 .02
❑ 258 William Suero .10 .02
❑ 259 Juan Guerrero .10 .02
❑ 260 J.T.Snow RC .50 .20
❑ 261 Tony Pena .10 .02
❑ 262 Tim Fortugno .10 .02
❑ 263 Tom Marsh .10 .02
❑ 264 Kurt Knudsen .10 .02
❑ 265 Tim Costo .10 .02
❑ 266 Steve Shifflett .10 .02
❑ 267 Billy Ashley .10 .02
❑ 268 Jerry Nielsen .10 .02
❑ 269 Pete Young .10 .02
❑ 270 Johnny Guzman .10 .02
❑ 271 Greg Colbrunn .10 .02
❑ 272 Jeff Nelson .10 .02
❑ 273 Kevin Young .20 .07
❑ 274 Jeff Frye .10 .02
❑ 275 J.T. Bruett .10 .02
❑ 276 Todd Pratt RC .25 .08
❑ 277 Mike Butcher .10 .02
❑ 278 John Flaherty .10 .02
❑ 279 John Patterson .10 .02
❑ 280 Eric Hillman .10 .02
❑ 281 Bien Figueroa .10 .02
❑ 282 Shane Reynolds .10 .02
❑ 283 Rich Rowland .10 .02
❑ 284 Steve Foster .10 .02
❑ 285 Dave Mlicki .10 .02
❑ 286 Mike Piazza 3.00 1.25
❑ 287 Mike Trombley .10 .02
❑ 288 Jim Pena .10 .02
❑ 289 Bob Ayrault .10 .02
❑ 290 Henry Mercedes .10 .02
❑ 291 Bob Wickman .10 .02
❑ 292 Jacob Brumfield .10 .02
❑ 293 David Hulse RC .10 .02
❑ 294 Ryan Klesko .20 .07
❑ 295 Doug Linton .10 .02
❑ 296 Steve Cooke .10 .02
❑ 297 Eddie Zosky .10 .02
❑ 298 Gerald Williams .10 .02
❑ 299 Jonathan Hurst .10 .02
❑ 300 Larry Carter RC .10 .02
❑ 301 William Pennyfeather .10 .02
❑ 302 Cesar Hernandez .10 .02
❑ 303 Steve Hosey .10 .02
❑ 304 Blas Minor .10 .02
❑ 305 Jeff Grotewald .10 .02
❑ 306 Bernardo Brito .10 .02
❑ 307 Rafael Bournigal .10 .02
❑ 308 Jeff Branson .10 .02
❑ 309 Tom Quinlan RC .10 .02
❑ 310 Pat Gomez RC .10 .02
❑ 311 Sterling Hitchcock RC .25 .08
❑ 312 Kent Bottenfield .10 .02
❑ 313 Alan Trammell .20 .07
❑ 314 Cris Colon .10 .02
❑ 315 Paul Wagner .10 .02
❑ 316 Matt Maysey .10 .02
❑ 317 Mike Stanton .10 .02
❑ 318 Rick Trlicek .10 .02
❑ 319 Kevin Rogers .10 .02
❑ 320 Mark Clark .10 .02
❑ 321 Pedro Martinez 1.00 .40
❑ 322 Al Martin .10 .02
❑ 323 Mike Macfarlane .10 .02
❑ 324 Rey Sanchez .10 .02
❑ 325 Roger Pavlik .10 .02
❑ 326 Troy Neel .10 .02
❑ 327 Kerry Woodson .10 .02
❑ 328 Wayne Kirby .10 .02
❑ 329 Ken Ryan RC .25 .08
❑ 330 Jesse Levis .10 .02
❑ 331 Jim Austin .10 .02
❑ 332 Dan Walters .10 .02
❑ 333 Brian Williams .10 .02
❑ 334 Wil Cordero .10 .02
❑ 335 Bret Boone .20 .07
❑ 336 Hipolito Pichardo .10 .02
❑ 337 Pat Mahomes .10 .02
❑ 338 Andy Stankiewicz .10 .02
❑ 339 Jim Bullinger .10 .02
❑ 340 Archi Cianfrocco .10 .02
❑ 341 Ruben Amaro .10 .02
❑ 342 Frank Seminara .10 .02
❑ 343 Pat Hentgen .10 .02
❑ 344 Dave Nilsson .10 .02
❑ 345 Mike Perez .10 .02
❑ 346 Tim Salmon .30 .10
❑ 347 Tim Wakefield .50 .20
❑ 348 Carlos Hernandez .10 .02
❑ 349 Donovan Osborne .10 .02
❑ 350 Denny Neagle .20 .07
❑ 351 Sam Militello .10 .02
❑ 352 Eric Fox .10 .02
❑ 353 John Doherty .10 .02
❑ 354 Chad Curtis .10 .02
❑ 355 Jeff Tackett .10 .02
❑ 356 Dave Fleming .10 .02
❑ 357 Pat Listach .10 .02
❑ 358 Kevin Wickander .10 .02
❑ 359 John Vander Wal .10 .02
❑ 360 Arthur Rhodes .10 .02
❑ 361 Bob Scanlan .10 .02
❑ 362 Bob Zupcic .10 .02
❑ 363 Mel Rojas .10 .02
❑ 364 Jim Thome .30 .10
❑ 365 Bill Pecota .10 .02
❑ 366 Mark Carreon .10 .02
❑ 367 Mitch Williams .10 .02
❑ 368 Cal Eldred .10 .02
❑ 369 Stan Belinda .10 .02
❑ 370 Pat Kelly .10 .02
❑ 371 Rheal Cormier .10 .02
❑ 372 Juan Guzman .10 .02
❑ 373 Damon Berryhill .10 .02
❑ 374 Gary DiSarcina .10 .02
❑ 375 Norm Charlton .10 .02
❑ 376 Roberto Hernandez .10 .02
❑ 377 Scott Kamieniecki .10 .02
❑ 378 Rusty Meacham .10 .02
❑ 379 Kurt Stillwell .10 .02
❑ 380 Lloyd McClendon .10 .02
❑ 381 Mark Leonard .10 .02
❑ 382 Jerry Browne .10 .02
❑ 383 Glenn Davis .10 .02
❑ 384 Randy Johnson .50 .20
❑ 385 Mike Greenwell .10 .02
❑ 386 Scott Chiamparino .10 .02
❑ 387 George Bell .10 .02
❑ 388 Steve Olin .10 .02
❑ 389 Chuck McElroy .10 .02
❑ 390 Mark Gardner .10 .02
❑ 391 Rod Beck .10 .02
❑ 392 Dennis Rasmussen .10 .02
❑ 393 Charlie Leibrandt .10 .02
❑ 394 Julio Franco .20 .07
❑ 395 Pete Harnisch .10 .02
❑ 396 Sid Bream .10 .02
❑ 397 Milt Thompson .10 .02
❑ 398 Glenallen Hill .10 .02
❑ 399 Chico Walker .10 .02
❑ 400 Alex Cole .10 .02
❑ 401 Trevor Wilson .10 .02
❑ 402 Jeff Conine .20 .07
❑ 403 Kyle Abbott .10 .02
❑ 404 Tom Browning .10 .02
❑ 405 Jerald Clark .10 .02
❑ 406 Vince Horsman .10 .02
❑ 407 Kevin Mitchell .10 .02
❑ 408 Pete Smith .10 .02
❑ 409 Jeff Innis .10 .02
❑ 410 Mike Timlin .10 .02
❑ 411 Charlie Hayes .10 .02
❑ 412 Alex Fernandez .10 .02
❑ 413 Jeff Russell .10 .02
❑ 414 Jody Reed .10 .02
❑ 415 Mickey Morandini .10 .02
❑ 416 Darnell Coles .10 .02
❑ 417 Xavier Hernandez .10 .02
❑ 418 Steve Sax .10 .02
❑ 419 Joe Girardi .10 .02
❑ 420 Mike Fetters .10 .02
❑ 421 Danny Jackson .10 .02
❑ 422 Jim Gott .10 .02
❑ 423 Tim Belcher .10 .02
❑ 424 Jose Mesa .10 .02
❑ 425 Junior Felix .10 .02
❑ 426 Thomas Howard .10 .02
❑ 427 Julio Valera .10 .02
❑ 428 Dante Bichette .20 .07
❑ 429 Mike Sharperson .10 .02
❑ 430 Darryl Kile .20 .07
❑ 431 Lonnie Smith .10 .02
❑ 432 Monty Fariss .10 .02
❑ 433 Reggie Jefferson .10 .02
❑ 434 Bob McClure .10 .02
❑ 435 Craig Lefferts .10 .02
❑ 436 Duane Ward .10 .02
❑ 437 Shawn Abner .10 .02
❑ 438 Roberto Kelly .10 .02
❑ 439 Paul O'Neill .30 .10
❑ 440 Alan Mills .10 .02
❑ 441 Roger Mason .10 .02
❑ 442 Gary Pettis .10 .02
❑ 443 Steve Lake .10 .02
❑ 444 Gene Larkin .10 .02
❑ 445 Larry Andersen .10 .02
❑ 446 Doug Dascenzo .10 .02
❑ 447 Daryl Boston .10 .02
❑ 448 John Candelaria .10 .02
❑ 449 Storm Davis .10 .02
❑ 450 Tom Edens .10 .02
❑ 451 Mike Maddux .10 .02
❑ 452 Tim Naehring .10 .02
❑ 453 John Orton .10 .02
❑ 454 Joey Cora .10 .02
❑ 455 Chuck Crim .10 .02
❑ 456 Dan Plesac .10 .02
❑ 457 Mike Bielecki .10 .02
❑ 458 Terry Jorgensen .10 .02
❑ 459 John Habyan .10 .02
❑ 460 Pete O'Brien .10 .02
❑ 461 Jeff Treadway .10 .02
❑ 462 Frank Castillo .10 .02
❑ 463 Jimmy Jones .10 .02
❑ 464 Tommy Greene .10 .02
❑ 465 Tracy Woodson .10 .02
❑ 466 Rich Rodriguez .10 .02
❑ 467 Joe Hesketh .10 .02
❑ 468 Greg Myers .10 .02
❑ 469 Kirk McCaskill .10 .02
❑ 470 Ricky Bones .10 .02
❑ 471 Lenny Webster .10 .02
❑ 472 Francisco Cabrera .10 .02
❑ 473 Turner Ward .10 .02
❑ 474 Dwayne Henry .10 .02
❑ 475 Al Osuna .10 .02
❑ 476 Craig Wilson .10 .02
❑ 477 Chris Nabholz .10 .02
❑ 478 Rafael Belliard .10 .02
❑ 479 Terry Leach .10 .02
❑ 480 Tim Teufel .10 .02
❑ 481 Dennis Eckersley AW .20 .07
❑ 482 Barry Bonds MVP .75 .30
❑ 483 Dennis Eckersley AW .20 .07
❑ 484 Greg Maddux CY .50 .20
❑ 485 Pat Listach AW .10 .02
❑ 486 Eric Karros AW .10 .02
❑ 487 Jamie Arnold RC .10 .02
❑ 488 B.J.Wallace .10 .02
❑ 489 Derek Jeter RC 12.00 5.00
❑ 490 Jason Kendall RC 1.00 .40
❑ 491 Rick Helling .10 .02
❑ 492 Derek Wallace RC .10 .02
❑ 493 Sean Lowe RC .10 .02
❑ 494 Shannon Stewart RC .75 .30
❑ 495 Benji Grigsby RC .10 .02
❑ 496 Todd Steverson RC .10 .02
❑ 497 Dan Serafini RC .10 .02
❑ 498 Michael Tucker .10 .02
❑ 499 Chris Roberts .10 .02
❑ 500 Pete Janicki RC .10 .02
❑ 501 Jeff Schmidt RC .10 .02
❑ 502 Edgar Martinez AS .20 .07
❑ 503 Omar Vizquel AS .20 .07
❑ 504 Ken Griffey Jr. AS .50 .20
❑ 505 Kirby Puckett AS .30 .10
❑ 506 Joe Carter AS .10 .02
❑ 507 Ivan Rodriguez AS .20 .07
❑ 508 Jack Morris AS .10 .02
❑ 509 Dennis Eckersley AS .20 .07
❑ 510 Frank Thomas AS .30 .10

- ❑ 511 Roberto Alomar AS .20 .07
- ❑ 512 Mickey Morandini AS .10 .02
- ❑ 513 Dennis Eckersley HL .20 .07
- ❑ 514 Jeff Reardon HL .10 .02
- ❑ 515 Danny Tartabull HL .10 .02
- ❑ 516 Bip Roberts HL .10 .02
- ❑ 517 George Brett HL .60 .25
- ❑ 518 Robin Yount HL .50 .20
- ❑ 519 Kevin Gross HL .10 .02
- ❑ 520 Ed Sprague WS .10 .02
- ❑ 521 Dave Winfield WS .10 .02
- ❑ 522 Ozzie Smith AS .50 .20
- ❑ 523 Barry Bonds AS .75 .30
- ❑ 524 Andy Van Slyke AS .20 .07
- ❑ 525 Tony Gwynn AS .30 .10
- ❑ 526 Darren Daulton AS .10 .02
- ❑ 527 Greg Maddux AS .50 .20
- ❑ 528 Fred McGriff AS .30 .10
- ❑ 529 Lee Smith AS .10 .02
- ❑ 530 Ryne Sandberg AS .50 .20
- ❑ 531 Gary Sheffield AS .10 .02
- ❑ 532 Ozzie Smith DT .50 .20
- ❑ 533 Kirby Puckett DT .30 .10
- ❑ 534 Gary Sheffield DT .10 .02
- ❑ 535 Andy Van Slyke DT .20 .07
- ❑ 536 Ken Griffey Jr. DT .50 .20
- ❑ 537 Ivan Rodriguez DT .20 .07
- ❑ 538 Charles Nagy DT .10 .02
- ❑ 539 Tom Glavine DT .20 .07
- ❑ 540 Dennis Eckersley DT .20 .07
- ❑ 541 Frank Thomas DT .30 .10
- ❑ 542 Roberto Alomar DT .20 .07
- ❑ 543 Sean Berry .10 .02
- ❑ 544 Mike Schooler .10 .02
- ❑ 545 Chuck Carr .10 .02
- ❑ 546 Lenny Harris .10 .02
- ❑ 547 Gary Scott .10 .02
- ❑ 548 Derek Lilliquist .10 .02
- ❑ 549 Brian Hunter .10 .02
- ❑ 550 Kirby Puckett MOY .30 .10
- ❑ 551 Jim Eisenreich .10 .02
- ❑ 552 Andre Dawson .20 .07
- ❑ 553 David Nied .10 .02
- ❑ 554 Spike Owen .10 .02
- ❑ 555 Greg Gagne .10 .02
- ❑ 556 Sid Fernandez .10 .02
- ❑ 557 Mark McGwire 1.25 .50
- ❑ 558 Bryan Harvey .10 .02
- ❑ 559 Harold Reynolds .20 .07
- ❑ 560 Barry Bonds 1.50 .60
- ❑ 561 Eric Wedge RC .25 .08
- ❑ 562 Ozzie Smith .75 .30
- ❑ 563 Rick Sutcliffe .20 .07
- ❑ 564 Jeff Reardon .20 .07
- ❑ 565 Alex Arias .10 .02
- ❑ 566 Greg Swindell .10 .02
- ❑ 567 Brook Jacoby .10 .02
- ❑ 568 Pete Incaviglia .10 .02
- ❑ 569 Butch Henry .10 .02
- ❑ 570 Eric Davis .20 .07
- ❑ 571 Kevin Seitzer .10 .02
- ❑ 572 Tony Fernandez .10 .02
- ❑ 573 Steve Reed RC .10 .02
- ❑ 574 Cory Snyder .10 .02
- ❑ 575 Joe Carter .20 .07
- ❑ 576 Greg Maddux .75 .30
- ❑ 577 Bert Blyleven UER (Should say 3701 career strike .20 .07
- ❑ 578 Kevin Bass .10 .02
- ❑ 579 Carlton Fisk .30 .10
- ❑ 580 Doug Drabek .10 .02
- ❑ 581 Mark Gubicza .10 .02
- ❑ 582 Bobby Thigpen .10 .02
- ❑ 583 Chili Davis .20 .07
- ❑ 584 Scott Bankhead .10 .02
- ❑ 585 Harold Baines .20 .07
- ❑ 586 Eric Young .10 .02
- ❑ 587 Lance Parrish .20 .07
- ❑ 588 Juan Bell .10 .02
- ❑ 589 Bob Ojeda .10 .02
- ❑ 590 Joe Orsulak .10 .02
- ❑ 591 Benito Santiago .20 .07
- ❑ 592 Wade Boggs .30 .10
- ❑ 593 Robby Thompson .10 .02
- ❑ 594 Eric Plunk .10 .02
- ❑ 595 Hensley Meulens .10 .02
- ❑ 596 Lou Whitaker .20 .07
- ❑ 597 Dale Murphy .30 .10
- ❑ 598 Paul Molitor .20 .07
- ❑ 599 Greg W. Harris .10 .02
- ❑ 600 Darren Holmes .10 .02
- ❑ 601 Dave Martinez .10 .02
- ❑ 602 Tom Henke .10 .02
- ❑ 603 Mike Benjamin .10 .02
- ❑ 604 Rene Gonzales .10 .02
- ❑ 605 Roger McDowell .10 .02
- ❑ 606 Kirby Puckett .50 .20
- ❑ 607 Randy Myers .10 .02
- ❑ 608 Ruben Sierra .20 .07
- ❑ 609 Wilson Alvarez .10 .02
- ❑ 610 David Segui .10 .02
- ❑ 611 Juan Samuel .10 .02
- ❑ 612 Tom Brunansky .10 .02
- ❑ 613 Willie Randolph .20 .07
- ❑ 614 Tony Phillips .10 .02
- ❑ 615 Candy Maldonado .10 .02
- ❑ 616 Chris Bosio .10 .02
- ❑ 617 Bret Barberie .10 .02
- ❑ 618 Scott Sanderson .10 .02
- ❑ 619 Ron Darling .10 .02
- ❑ 620 Dave Winfield .20 .07
- ❑ 621 Mike Felder .10 .02
- ❑ 622 Greg Hibbard .10 .02
- ❑ 623 Mike Scioscia .10 .02
- ❑ 624 John Smiley .10 .02
- ❑ 625 Alejandro Pena .10 .02
- ❑ 626 Terry Steinbach .10 .02
- ❑ 627 Freddie Benavides .10 .02
- ❑ 628 Kevin Reimer .10 .02
- ❑ 629 Braulio Castillo .10 .02
- ❑ 630 Dave Stieb .10 .02
- ❑ 631 Dave Magadan .10 .02
- ❑ 632 Scott Fletcher .10 .02
- ❑ 633 Cris Carpenter .10 .02
- ❑ 634 Kevin Maas .10 .02
- ❑ 635 Todd Worrell .10 .02
- ❑ 636 Rob Deer .10 .02
- ❑ 637 Dwight Smith .10 .02
- ❑ 638 Chito Martinez .10 .02
- ❑ 639 Jimmy Key .20 .07
- ❑ 640 Greg A. Harris .10 .02
- ❑ 641 Mike Moore .10 .02
- ❑ 642 Pat Borders .10 .02
- ❑ 643 Bill Gullickson .10 .02
- ❑ 644 Gary Gaetti .20 .07
- ❑ 645 David Howard .10 .02
- ❑ 646 Jim Abbott .30 .10
- ❑ 647 Willie Wilson .10 .02
- ❑ 648 David Wells .20 .07
- ❑ 649 Andres Galarraga .20 .07
- ❑ 650 Vince Coleman .10 .02
- ❑ 651 Rob Dibble .20 .07
- ❑ 652 Frank Tanana .10 .02
- ❑ 653 Steve Decker .10 .02
- ❑ 654 David Cone .20 .07
- ❑ 655 Jack Armstrong .10 .02
- ❑ 656 Dave Stewart .20 .07
- ❑ 657 Billy Hatcher .10 .02
- ❑ 658 Tim Raines .20 .07
- ❑ 659 Walt Weiss .10 .02
- ❑ 660 Jose Lind .10 .02

1994 Score

- ❑ COMPLETE SET (660) 24.00 10.00
- ❑ COMPLETE SERIES 1 (330) 12.00 5.00
- ❑ COMPLETE SERIES 2 (330) 12.00 5.00
- ❑ 1 Barry Bonds 1.50 .60
- ❑ 2 John Olerud .20 .07
- ❑ 3 Ken Griffey Jr. .75 .30
- ❑ 4 Jeff Bagwell .30 .10
- ❑ 5 John Burkett .10 .02
- ❑ 6 Jack McDowell .10 .02
- ❑ 7 Albert Belle .20 .07
- ❑ 8 Andres Galarraga .20 .07
- ❑ 9 Mike Mussina .30 .10
- ❑ 10 Will Clark .30 .10
- ❑ 11 Travis Fryman .20 .07
- ❑ 12 Tony Gwynn .60 .25
- ❑ 13 Robin Yount .75 .30
- ❑ 14 Dave Magadan .10 .02
- ❑ 15 Paul O'Neill .30 .10
- ❑ 16 Ray Lankford .20 .07
- ❑ 17 Damion Easley .10 .02
- ❑ 18 Andy Van Slyke .30 .10
- ❑ 19 Brian McRae .10 .02
- ❑ 20 Ryne Sandberg .75 .30
- ❑ 21 Kirby Puckett .50 .20
- ❑ 22 Dwight Gooden .20 .07
- ❑ 23 Don Mattingly 1.25 .50
- ❑ 24 Kevin Mitchell .10 .02
- ❑ 25 Roger Clemens 1.00 .40
- ❑ 26 Eric Karros .20 .07
- ❑ 27 Juan Gonzalez .20 .07
- ❑ 28 John Kruk .20 .07
- ❑ 29 Gregg Jefferies .10 .02
- ❑ 30 Tom Glavine .30 .10
- ❑ 31 Ivan Rodriguez .30 .10
- ❑ 32 Jay Bell .20 .07
- ❑ 33 Randy Johnson .50 .20
- ❑ 34 Darren Daulton .20 .07
- ❑ 35 Rickey Henderson .50 .20
- ❑ 36 Eddie Murray .50 .20
- ❑ 37 Brian Harper .10 .02
- ❑ 38 Delino DeShields .10 .02
- ❑ 39 Jose Lind .10 .02
- ❑ 40 Benito Santiago .20 .07
- ❑ 41 Frank Thomas .50 .20
- ❑ 42 Mark Grace .30 .10
- ❑ 43 Roberto Alomar .30 .10
- ❑ 44 Andy Benes .10 .02
- ❑ 45 Luis Polonia .10 .02
- ❑ 46 Brett Butler .20 .07
- ❑ 47 Terry Steinbach .10 .02
- ❑ 48 Craig Biggio .30 .10
- ❑ 49 Greg Vaughn .10 .02
- ❑ 50 Charlie Hayes .10 .02
- ❑ 51 Mickey Tettleton .10 .02
- ❑ 52 Jose Rijo .10 .02
- ❑ 53 Carlos Baerga .10 .02
- ❑ 54 Jeff Blauser .10 .02
- ❑ 55 Leo Gomez .10 .02
- ❑ 56 Bob Tewksbury .10 .02
- ❑ 57 Mo Vaughn .20 .07
- ❑ 58 Orlando Merced .10 .02
- ❑ 59 Tino Martinez .30 .10
- ❑ 60 Lenny Dykstra .20 .07
- ❑ 61 Jose Canseco .30 .10
- ❑ 62 Tony Fernandez .10 .02
- ❑ 63 Donovan Osborne .10 .02
- ❑ 64 Ken Hill .10 .02
- ❑ 65 Kent Hrbek .20 .07
- ❑ 66 Bryan Harvey .10 .02
- ❑ 67 Wally Joyner .20 .07
- ❑ 68 Derrick May .10 .02
- ❑ 69 Lance Johnson .10 .02
- ❑ 70 Willie McGee .20 .07
- ❑ 71 Mark Langston .10 .02
- ❑ 72 Terry Pendleton .20 .07
- ❑ 73 Joe Carter .20 .07
- ❑ 74 Barry Larkin .30 .10
- ❑ 75 Jimmy Key .20 .07
- ❑ 76 Joe Girardi .10 .02
- ❑ 77 B.J. Surhoff .20 .07
- ❑ 78 Pete Harnisch .10 .02
- ❑ 79 Lou Whitaker UER .20 .07
- ❑ 80 Cory Snyder .10 .02
- ❑ 81 Kenny Lofton .20 .07
- ❑ 82 Fred McGriff .30 .10
- ❑ 83 Mike Greenwell .10 .02

❑ 84 Mike Perez .10 .02
❑ 85 Cal Ripken 1.50 .60
❑ 86 Don Slaught .10 .02
❑ 87 Omar Vizquel .30 .10
❑ 88 Curt Schilling .20 .07
❑ 89 Chuck Knoblauch .20 .07
❑ 90 Moises Alou .20 .07
❑ 91 Greg Gagne .10 .02
❑ 92 Bret Saberhagen .20 .07
❑ 93 Ozzie Guillen .20 .07
❑ 94 Matt Williams .20 .07
❑ 95 Chad Curtis .10 .02
❑ 96 Mike Harkey .10 .02
❑ 97 Devon White .20 .07
❑ 98 Walt Weiss .10 .02
❑ 99 Kevin Brown .20 .07
❑ 100 Gary Sheffield .20 .07
❑ 101 Wade Boggs .30 .10
❑ 102 Orel Hershiser .20 .07
❑ 103 Tony Phillips .10 .02
❑ 104 Andujar Cedeno .10 .02
❑ 105 Bill Spiers .10 .02
❑ 106 Otis Nixon .10 .02
❑ 107 Felix Fermin .10 .02
❑ 108 Bip Roberts .10 .02
❑ 109 Dennis Eckersley .20 .07
❑ 110 Dante Bichette .20 .07
❑ 111 Ben McDonald .10 .02
❑ 112 Jim Poole .10 .02
❑ 113 John Dopson .10 .02
❑ 114 Rob Dibble .20 .07
❑ 115 Jeff Treadway .10 .02
❑ 116 Ricky Jordan .10 .02
❑ 117 Mike Henneman .10 .02
❑ 118 Willie Blair .10 .02
❑ 119 Doug Henry .10 .02
❑ 120 Gerald Perry .10 .02
❑ 121 Greg Myers .10 .02
❑ 122 John Franco .20 .07
❑ 123 Roger Mason .10 .02
❑ 124 Chris Hammond .10 .02
❑ 125 Hubie Brooks .10 .02
❑ 126 Kent Mercker .10 .02
❑ 127 Jim Abbott .30 .10
❑ 128 Kevin Bass .10 .02
❑ 129 Rick Aguilera .10 .02
❑ 130 Mitch Webster .10 .02
❑ 131 Eric Plunk .10 .02
❑ 132 Mark Carreon .10 .02
❑ 133 Dave Stewart .20 .07
❑ 134 Willie Wilson .10 .02
❑ 135 Dave Fleming .10 .02
❑ 136 Jeff Tackett .10 .02
❑ 137 Geno Petralli .10 .02
❑ 138 Gene Harris .10 .02
❑ 139 Scott Bankhead .10 .02
❑ 140 Trevor Wilson .10 .02
❑ 141 Alvaro Espinoza .10 .02
❑ 142 Ryan Bowen .10 .02
❑ 143 Mike Moore .10 .02
❑ 144 Bill Pecota .10 .02
❑ 145 Jaime Navarro .10 .02
❑ 146 Jack Daugherty .10 .02
❑ 147 Bob Wickman .10 .02
❑ 148 Chris Jones .10 .02
❑ 149 Todd Stottlemyre .10 .02
❑ 150 Brian Williams .10 .02
❑ 151 Chuck Finley .20 .07
❑ 152 Lenny Harris .10 .02
❑ 153 Alex Fernandez .10 .02
❑ 154 Candy Maldonado .10 .02
❑ 155 Jeff Montgomery .10 .02
❑ 156 David West .10 .02
❑ 157 Mark Williamson .10 .02
❑ 158 Milt Thompson .10 .02
❑ 159 Ron Darling .10 .02
❑ 160 Stan Belinda .10 .02
❑ 161 Henry Cotto .10 .02
❑ 162 Mel Rojas .10 .02
❑ 163 Doug Strange .10 .02
❑ 164 Rene Arocha .10 .02
❑ 165 Tim Hulett .10 .02
❑ 166 Steve Avery .10 .02
❑ 167 Jim Thome .30 .10
❑ 168 Tom Browning .10 .02
❑ 169 Mario Diaz .10 .02
❑ 170 Steve Reed .10 .02
❑ 171 Scott Livingstone .10 .02
❑ 172 Chris Donnels .10 .02
❑ 173 John Jaha .10 .02
❑ 174 Carlos Hernandez .10 .02
❑ 175 Dion James .10 .02
❑ 176 Bud Black .10 .02
❑ 177 Tony Castillo .10 .02
❑ 178 Jose Guzman .10 .02
❑ 179 Torey Lovullo .10 .02
❑ 180 John Vander Wal .10 .02
❑ 181 Mike LaValliere .10 .02
❑ 182 Sid Fernandez .10 .02
❑ 183 Brent Mayne .10 .02
❑ 184 Terry Mulholland .10 .02
❑ 185 Willie Banks .10 .02
❑ 186 Steve Cooke .10 .02
❑ 187 Brent Gates .10 .02
❑ 188 Erik Pappas .10 .02
❑ 189 Bill Haselman .10 .02
❑ 190 Fernando Valenzuela .20 .07
❑ 191 Gary Redus .10 .02
❑ 192 Danny Darwin .10 .02
❑ 193 Mark Portugal .10 .02
❑ 194 Derek Lilliquist .10 .02
❑ 195 Charlie O'Brien .10 .02
❑ 196 Matt Nokes .10 .02
❑ 197 Danny Sheaffer .10 .02
❑ 198 Bill Gullickson .10 .02
❑ 199 Alex Arias .10 .02
❑ 200 Mike Fetters .10 .02
❑ 201 Brian Jordan .20 .07
❑ 202 Joe Grahe .10 .02
❑ 203 Tom Candiotti .10 .02
❑ 204 Jeremy Hernandez .10 .02
❑ 205 Mike Stanton .10 .02
❑ 206 David Howard .10 .02
❑ 207 Darren Holmes .10 .02
❑ 208 Rick Honeycutt .10 .02
❑ 209 Danny Jackson .10 .02
❑ 210 Rich Amaral .10 .02
❑ 211 Blas Minor .10 .02
❑ 212 Kenny Rogers .20 .07
❑ 213 Jim Leyritz .10 .02
❑ 214 Mike Morgan .10 .02
❑ 215 Dan Gladden .10 .02
❑ 216 Randy Velarde .10 .02
❑ 217 Mitch Williams .10 .02
❑ 218 Hipolito Pichardo .10 .02
❑ 219 Dave Burba .10 .02
❑ 220 Wilson Alvarez .10 .02
❑ 221 Bob Zupcic .10 .02
❑ 222 Francisco Cabrera .10 .02
❑ 223 Julio Valera .10 .02
❑ 224 Paul Assenmacher .10 .02
❑ 225 Jeff Branson .10 .02
❑ 226 Todd Frohwirth .10 .02
❑ 227 Armando Reynoso .10 .02
❑ 228 Rich Rowland .10 .02
❑ 229 Freddie Benavides .10 .02
❑ 230 Wayne Kirby .10 .02
❑ 231 Darryl Kile .20 .07
❑ 232 Skeeter Barnes .10 .02
❑ 233 Ramon Martinez .10 .02
❑ 234 Tom Gordon .10 .02
❑ 235 Dave Gallagher .10 .02
❑ 236 Ricky Bones .10 .02
❑ 237 Larry Andersen .10 .02
❑ 238 Pat Meares .10 .02
❑ 239 Zane Smith .10 .02
❑ 240 Tim Leary .10 .02
❑ 241 Phil Clark .10 .02
❑ 242 Danny Cox .10 .02
❑ 243 Mike Jackson .10 .02
❑ 244 Mike Gallego .10 .02
❑ 245 Lee Smith .20 .07
❑ 246 Todd Jones .10 .02
❑ 247 Steve Bedrosian .10 .02
❑ 248 Troy Neel .10 .02
❑ 249 Jose Bautista .10 .02
❑ 250 Steve Frey .10 .02
❑ 251 Jeff Reardon .20 .07
❑ 252 Stan Javier .10 .02
❑ 253 Mo Sanford .10 .02
❑ 254 Steve Sax .10 .02
❑ 255 Luis Aquino .10 .02
❑ 256 Domingo Jean .10 .02
❑ 257 Scott Servais .10 .02
❑ 258 Brad Pennington .10 .02
❑ 259 Dave Hansen .10 .02
❑ 260 Rich Gossage .20 .07
❑ 261 Jeff Fassero .10 .02
❑ 262 Junior Ortiz .10 .02
❑ 263 Anthony Young .10 .02
❑ 264 Chris Bosio .10 .02
❑ 265 Ruben Amaro .10 .02
❑ 266 Mark Eichhorn .10 .02
❑ 267 Dave Clark .10 .02
❑ 268 Gary Thurman .10 .02
❑ 269 Les Lancaster .10 .02
❑ 270 Jamie Moyer .20 .07
❑ 271 Ricky Gutierrez .10 .02
❑ 272 Greg A. Harris .10 .02
❑ 273 Mike Benjamin .10 .02
❑ 274 Gene Nelson .10 .02
❑ 275 Damon Berryhill .10 .02
❑ 276 Scott Radinsky .10 .02
❑ 277 Mike Aldrete .10 .02
❑ 278 Jerry DiPoto .10 .02
❑ 279 Chris Haney .10 .02
❑ 280 Richie Lewis .10 .02
❑ 281 Jarvis Brown .10 .02
❑ 282 Juan Bell .10 .02
❑ 283 Joe Klink .10 .02
❑ 284 Graeme Lloyd .10 .02
❑ 285 Casey Candaele .10 .02
❑ 286 Bob MacDonald .10 .02
❑ 287 Mike Sharperson .10 .02
❑ 288 Gene Larkin .10 .02
❑ 289 Brian Barnes .10 .02
❑ 290 David McCarty .10 .02
❑ 291 Jeff Innis .10 .02
❑ 292 Bob Patterson .10 .02
❑ 293 Ben Rivera .10 .02
❑ 294 John Habyan .10 .02
❑ 295 Rich Rodriguez .10 .02
❑ 296 Edwin Nunez .10 .02
❑ 297 Rod Brewer .10 .02
❑ 298 Mike Timlin .10 .02
❑ 299 Jesse Orosco .10 .02
❑ 300 Gary Gaetti .20 .07
❑ 301 Todd Benzinger .10 .02
❑ 302 Jeff Nelson .10 .02
❑ 303 Rafael Belliard .10 .02
❑ 304 Matt Whiteside .10 .02
❑ 305 Vinny Castilla .20 .07
❑ 306 Matt Turner .10 .02
❑ 307 Eduardo Perez .10 .02
❑ 308 Joel Johnston .10 .02
❑ 309 Chris Gomez .10 .02
❑ 310 Pat Rapp .10 .02
❑ 311 Jim Tatum .10 .02
❑ 312 Kirk Rueter .10 .02
❑ 313 John Flaherty .10 .02
❑ 314 Tom Kramer .10 .02
❑ 315 Mark Whiten .10 .02
❑ 316 Chris Bosio .10 .02
❑ 317 Baltimore Orioles CL .10 .02
❑ 318 Boston Red Sox CL UER
(Viola listed as 316; shoul .10 .02
❑ 319 California Angels CL .10 .02
❑ 320 Chicago White Sox CL .10 .02
❑ 321 Cleveland Indians CL .10 .02
❑ 322 Detroit Tigers CL .10 .02
❑ 323 Kansas City Royals CL .10 .02
❑ 324 Milwaukee Brewers CL .10 .02
❑ 325 Minnesota Twins CL .10 .02
❑ 326 New York Yankees CL .10 .02
❑ 327 Oakland Athletics CL .10 .02
❑ 328 Seattle Mariners CL .10 .02
❑ 329 Texas Rangers CL .10 .02
❑ 330 Toronto Blue Jays CL .10 .02
❑ 331 Frank Viola .20 .07
❑ 332 Ron Gant .20 .07
❑ 333 Charles Nagy .10 .02
❑ 334 Roberto Kelly .10 .02
❑ 335 Brady Anderson .20 .07
❑ 336 Alex Cole .10 .02
❑ 337 Alan Trammell .20 .07
❑ 338 Derek Bell .10 .02
❑ 339 Bernie Williams .30 .10
❑ 340 Jose Offerman .10 .02

❑ 341 Bill Wegman .10 .02
❑ 342 Ken Caminiti .20 .07
❑ 343 Pat Borders .10 .02
❑ 344 Kirt Manwaring .10 .02
❑ 345 Chili Davis .20 .07
❑ 346 Steve Buechele .10 .02
❑ 347 Robin Ventura .20 .07
❑ 348 Teddy Higuera .10 .02
❑ 349 Jerry Browne .10 .02
❑ 350 Scott Kamieniecki .10 .02
❑ 351 Kevin Tapani .10 .02
❑ 352 Marquis Grissom .20 .07
❑ 353 Jay Buhner .20 .07
❑ 354 Dave Hollins .10 .02
❑ 355 Dan Wilson .10 .02
❑ 356 Bob Walk .10 .02
❑ 357 Chris Hoiles .10 .02
❑ 358 Todd Zeile .10 .02
❑ 359 Kevin Appier .20 .07
❑ 360 Chris Sabo .10 .02
❑ 361 David Segui .10 .02
❑ 362 Jerald Clark .10 .02
❑ 363 Tony Pena .10 .02
❑ 364 Steve Finley .20 .07
❑ 365 Roger Pavlik .10 .02
❑ 366 John Smoltz .30 .10
❑ 367 Scott Fletcher .10 .02
❑ 368 Jody Reed .10 .02
❑ 369 David Wells .20 .07
❑ 370 Jose Vizcaino .10 .02
❑ 371 Pat Listach .10 .02
❑ 372 Orestes Destrade .10 .02
❑ 373 Danny Tartabull .10 .02
❑ 374 Greg W. Harris .10 .02
❑ 375 Juan Guzman .10 .02
❑ 376 Larry Walker .20 .07
❑ 377 Gary DiSarcina .10 .02
❑ 378 Bobby Bonilla .20 .07
❑ 379 Tim Raines .20 .07
❑ 380 Tommy Greene .10 .02
❑ 381 Chris Gwynn .10 .02
❑ 382 Jeff King .10 .02
❑ 383 Shane Mack .10 .02
❑ 384 Ozzie Smith .75 .30
❑ 385 Eddie Zambrano RC .10 .02
❑ 386 Mike Devereaux .10 .02
❑ 387 Erik Hanson .10 .02
❑ 388 Scott Cooper .10 .02
❑ 389 Dean Palmer .20 .07
❑ 390 John Wetteland .20 .07
❑ 391 Reggie Jefferson .10 .02
❑ 392 Mark Lemke .10 .02
❑ 393 Cecil Fielder .20 .07
❑ 394 Reggie Sanders .20 .07
❑ 395 Darryl Hamilton .10 .02
❑ 396 Daryl Boston .10 .02
❑ 397 Pat Kelly .10 .02
❑ 398 Joe Orsulak .10 .02
❑ 399 Ed Sprague .10 .02
❑ 400 Eric Anthony .10 .02
❑ 401 Scott Sanderson .10 .02
❑ 402 Jim Gott .10 .02
❑ 403 Ron Karkovice .10 .02
❑ 404 Phil Plantier .10 .02
❑ 405 David Cone .20 .07
❑ 406 Robby Thompson .10 .02
❑ 407 Dave Winfield .20 .07
❑ 408 Dwight Smith .10 .02
❑ 409 Ruben Sierra .20 .07
❑ 410 Jack Armstrong .10 .02
❑ 411 Mike Felder .10 .02
❑ 412 Wil Cordero .10 .02
❑ 413 Julio Franco .20 .07
❑ 414 Howard Johnson .10 .02
❑ 415 Mark McLemore .10 .02
❑ 416 Pete Incaviglia .10 .02
❑ 417 John Valentin .10 .02
❑ 418 Tim Wakefield .30 .10
❑ 419 Jose Mesa .10 .02
❑ 420 Bernard Gilkey .10 .02
❑ 421 Kirk Gibson .20 .07
❑ 422 David Justice .20 .07
❑ 423 Tom Brunansky .10 .02
❑ 424 John Smiley .10 .02
❑ 425 Kevin Maas .10 .02
❑ 426 Doug Drabek .10 .02
❑ 427 Paul Molitor .20 .07
❑ 428 Darryl Strawberry .20 .07
❑ 429 Tim Naehring .10 .02
❑ 430 Bill Swift .10 .02
❑ 431 Ellis Burks .20 .07
❑ 432 Greg Hibbard .10 .02
❑ 433 Felix Jose .10 .02
❑ 434 Bret Barberie .10 .02
❑ 435 Pedro Munoz .10 .02
❑ 436 Darrin Fletcher .10 .02
❑ 437 Bobby Witt .10 .02
❑ 438 Wes Chamberlain .10 .02
❑ 439 Mackey Sasser .10 .02
❑ 440 Mark Whiten .10 .02
❑ 441 Harold Reynolds .20 .07
❑ 442 Greg Olson .10 .02
❑ 443 Billy Hatcher .10 .02
❑ 444 Joe Oliver .10 .02
❑ 445 Sandy Alomar Jr. .10 .02
❑ 446 Tim Wallach .10 .02
❑ 447 Karl Rhodes .10 .02
❑ 448 Royce Clayton .10 .02
❑ 449 Cal Eldred .10 .02
❑ 450 Rick Wilkins .10 .02
❑ 451 Mike Stanley .10 .02
❑ 452 Charlie Hough .20 .07
❑ 453 Jack Morris .20 .07
❑ 454 Jon Ratliff RC .10 .02
❑ 455 Rene Gonzales .10 .02
❑ 456 Eddie Taubensee .10 .02
❑ 457 Roberto Hernandez .10 .02
❑ 458 Todd Hundley .10 .02
❑ 459 Mike Macfarlane .10 .02
❑ 460 Mickey Morandini .10 .02
❑ 461 Scott Erickson .10 .02
❑ 462 Lonnie Smith .10 .02
❑ 463 Dave Henderson .10 .02
❑ 464 Ryan Klesko .20 .07
❑ 465 Edgar Martinez .30 .10
❑ 466 Tom Pagnozzi .10 .02
❑ 467 Charlie Leibrandt .10 .02
❑ 468 Brian Anderson RC .25 .08
❑ 469 Harold Baines .20 .07
❑ 470 Tim Belcher .10 .02
❑ 471 Andre Dawson .20 .07
❑ 472 Eric Young .10 .02
❑ 473 Paul Sorrento .10 .02
❑ 474 Luis Gonzalez .20 .07
❑ 475 Rob Deer .10 .02
❑ 476 Mike Piazza 1.00 .40
❑ 477 Kevin Reimer .10 .02
❑ 478 Jeff Gardner .10 .02
❑ 479 Melido Perez .10 .02
❑ 480 Darren Lewis .10 .02
❑ 481 Duane Ward .10 .02
❑ 482 Rey Sanchez .10 .02
❑ 483 Mark Lewis .10 .02
❑ 484 Jeff Conine .20 .07
❑ 485 Joey Cora .10 .02
❑ 486 Trot Nixon RC 1.00 .40
❑ 487 Kevin McReynolds .10 .02
❑ 488 Mike Lansing .10 .02
❑ 489 Mike Pagliarulo .10 .02
❑ 490 Mariano Duncan .10 .02
❑ 491 Mike Bordick .10 .02
❑ 492 Kevin Young .10 .02
❑ 493 Dave Valle .10 .02
❑ 494 Wayne Gomes RC .10 .02
❑ 495 Rafael Palmeiro .30 .10
❑ 496 Deion Sanders .30 .10
❑ 497 Rick Sutcliffe .20 .07
❑ 498 Randy Milligan .10 .02
❑ 499 Carlos Quintana .10 .02
❑ 500 Chris Turner .10 .02
❑ 501 Thomas Howard .10 .02
❑ 502 Greg Swindell .10 .02
❑ 503 Chad Kreuter .10 .02
❑ 504 Eric Davis .20 .07
❑ 505 Dickie Thon .10 .02
❑ 506 Matt Drews RC .10 .02
❑ 507 Spike Owen .10 .02
❑ 508 Rod Beck .10 .02
❑ 509 Pat Hentgen .10 .02
❑ 510 Sammy Sosa .50 .20
❑ 511 J.T. Snow .20 .07
❑ 512 Chuck Carr .10 .02
❑ 513 Bo Jackson .50 .20
❑ 514 Dennis Martinez .20 .07
❑ 515 Phil Hiatt .10 .02
❑ 516 Jeff Kent .30 .10
❑ 517 Brooks Kieschnick RC .10 .02
❑ 518 Kirk Presley RC .10 .02
❑ 519 Kevin Seitzer .10 .02
❑ 520 Carlos Garcia .10 .02
❑ 521 Mike Blowers .10 .02
❑ 522 Luis Alicea .10 .02
❑ 523 David Hulse .10 .02
❑ 524 Greg Maddux .75 .30
❑ 525 Gregg Olson .10 .02
❑ 526 Hal Morris .10 .02
❑ 527 Daron Kirkreit .10 .02
❑ 528 David Nied .10 .02
❑ 529 Jeff Russell .10 .02
❑ 530 Kevin Gross .10 .02
❑ 531 John Doherty .10 .02
❑ 532 Matt Brunson RC .10 .02
❑ 533 Dave Nilsson .10 .02
❑ 534 Randy Myers .10 .02
❑ 535 Steve Farr .10 .02
❑ 536 Billy Wagner RC 1.25 .50
❑ 537 Darnell Coles .10 .02
❑ 538 Frank Tanana .10 .02
❑ 539 Tim Salmon .30 .10
❑ 540 Kim Batiste .10 .02
❑ 541 George Bell .10 .02
❑ 542 Tom Henke .10 .02
❑ 543 Sam Horn .10 .02
❑ 544 Doug Jones .10 .02
❑ 545 Scott Leius .10 .02
❑ 546 Al Martin .10 .02
❑ 547 Bob Welch .10 .02
❑ 548 Scott Christman RC .10 .02
❑ 549 Norm Charlton .10 .02
❑ 550 Mark McGwire 1.25 .50
❑ 551 Greg McMichael .10 .02
❑ 552 Tim Costo .10 .02
❑ 553 Rodney Bolton .10 .02
❑ 554 Pedro Martinez .50 .20
❑ 555 Marc Valdes .10 .02
❑ 556 Darrell Whitmore .10 .02
❑ 557 Tim Bogar .10 .02
❑ 558 Steve Karsay .10 .02
❑ 559 Danny Bautista .10 .02
❑ 560 Jeffrey Hammonds .10 .02
❑ 561 Aaron Sele .10 .02
❑ 562 Russ Springer .10 .02
❑ 563 Jason Bere .10 .02
❑ 564 Billy Brewer .10 .02
❑ 565 Sterling Hitchcock .10 .02
❑ 566 Bobby Munoz .10 .02
❑ 567 Craig Paquette .10 .02
❑ 568 Bret Boone .20 .07
❑ 569 Dan Peltier .10 .02
❑ 570 Jeromy Burnitz .20 .07
❑ 571 John Wasdin RC .10 .02
❑ 572 Chipper Jones .50 .20
❑ 573 Jamey Wright RC .10 .02
❑ 574 Jeff Granger .10 .02
❑ 575 Jay Powell RC .10 .02
❑ 576 Ryan Thompson .10 .02
❑ 577 Lou Frazier .10 .02
❑ 578 Paul Wagner .10 .02
❑ 579 Brad Ausmus .30 .10
❑ 580 Jack Voigt .10 .02
❑ 581 Kevin Rogers .10 .02
❑ 582 Damon Buford .10 .02
❑ 583 Paul Quantrill .10 .02
❑ 584 Marc Newfield .10 .02
❑ 585 Derrek Lee RC 1.50 .60
❑ 586 Shane Reynolds .10 .02
❑ 587 Cliff Floyd .20 .07
❑ 588 Jeff Schwarz .10 .02
❑ 589 Ross Powell RC .10 .02
❑ 590 Gerald Williams .10 .02
❑ 591 Mike Trombley .10 .02
❑ 592 Ken Ryan .10 .02
❑ 593 John O'Donoghue .10 .02
❑ 594 Rod Correia .10 .02
❑ 595 Darrell Sherman .10 .02
❑ 596 Steve Scarsone .10 .02
❑ 597 Sherman Obando .10 .02
❑ 598 Kurt Abbott RC .10 .02

❑	599 Dave Telgheder	.10	.02
❑	600 Rick Trlicek	.10	.02
❑	601 Carl Everett	.20	.07
❑	602 Luis Ortiz	.10	.02
❑	603 Larry Luebbers	.10	.02
❑	604 Kevin Roberson	.10	.02
❑	605 Butch Huskey	.10	.02
❑	606 Benji Gil	.10	.02
❑	607 Todd Van Poppel	.10	.02
❑	608 Mark Hutton	.10	.02
❑	609 Chip Hale	.10	.02
❑	610 Matt Maysey	.10	.02
❑	611 Scott Ruffcorn	.10	.02
❑	612 Hilly Hathaway	.10	.02
❑	613 Allen Watson	.10	.02
❑	614 Carlos Delgado	.30	.10
❑	615 Roberto Mejia	.10	.02
❑	616 Turk Wendell	.10	.02
❑	617 Tony Tarasco	.10	.02
❑	618 Raul Mondesi	.20	.07
❑	619 Kevin Stocker	.10	.02
❑	620 Javier Lopez	.20	.07
❑	621 Keith Kessinger	.10	.02
❑	622 Bob Hamelin	.10	.02
❑	623 John Roper	.10	.02
❑	624 Lenny Dykstra WS	.10	.02
❑	625 Joe Carter WS	.10	.02
❑	626 Jim Abbott HL	.20	.07
❑	627 Lee Smith HL	.10	.02
❑	628 Ken Griffey Jr. HL	.50	.20
❑	629 Dave Winfield HL	.10	.02
❑	630 Darryl Kile HL	.10	.02
❑	631 Frank Thomas MVP	.30	.10
❑	632 Barry Bonds MVP	.75	.30
❑	633 Jack McDowell AL CY	.10	.02
❑	634 Greg Maddux CY	.50	.20
❑	635 Tim Salmon ROY	.20	.07
❑	636 Mike Piazza ROY	.50	.20
❑	637 Brian Turang RC	.10	.02
❑	638 Rondell White	.20	.07
❑	639 Nigel Wilson	.10	.02
❑	640 Torii Hunter RC	1.00	.40
❑	641 Salomon Torres	.10	.02
❑	642 Kevin Higgins	.10	.02
❑	643 Eric Wedge	.10	.02
❑	644 Roger Salkeld	.10	.02
❑	645 Manny Ramirez	.50	.20
❑	646 Jeff McNeely	.10	.02
❑	647 Checklist Atlanta Braves	.10	.02
❑	648 Checklist Chicago Cubs	.10	.02
❑	649 Checklist Cincinnati Reds	.10	.02
❑	650 Checklist Colorado Rockies	.10	.02
❑	651 Checklist Florida Marlins	.10	.02
❑	652 Checklist Houston Astros	.10	.02
❑	653 Checklist Los Angeles Dodgers	.10	.02
❑	654 Checklist Montreal Expos	.10	.02
❑	655 Checklist New York Mets	.10	.02
❑	656 Checklist Philadelphia Phillies	.10	.02
❑	657 Checklist Pittsburgh Pirates	.10	.02
❑	658 Checklist St. Louis Cardinals	.10	.02
❑	659 Checklist San Diego Padres	.10	.02
❑	660 Checklist San Francisco Giants	.10	.02

1994 Score Rookie/Traded

❑	COMPLETE SET (165)	15.00	6.00
❑	ACTUAL CARD REDEEMED IN 1995		
❑	RT1 Will Clark	.50	.20
❑	RT2 Lee Smith	.30	.10
❑	RT3 Bo Jackson	.75	.30
❑	RT4 Ellis Burks	.30	.10
❑	RT5 Eddie Murray	.75	.30
❑	RT6 Delino DeShields	.15	.05
❑	RT7 Erik Hanson	.15	.05
❑	RT8 Rafael Palmeiro	.50	.20
❑	RT9 Luis Polonia	.15	.05
❑	RT10 Omar Vizquel	.50	.20
❑	RT11 Kurt Abbott	.15	.05
❑	RT12 Vince Coleman	.15	.05
❑	RT13 Rickey Henderson	.75	.30
❑	RT14 Terry Mulholland	.15	.05
❑	RT15 Greg Hibbard	.15	.05
❑	RT16 Walt Weiss	.15	.05
❑	RT17 Chris Sabo	.15	.05
❑	RT18 Dave Henderson	.15	.05
❑	RT19 Rick Sutcliffe	.30	.10
❑	RT20 Harold Reynolds	.30	.10
❑	RT21 Jack Morris	.30	.10
❑	RT22 Dan Wilson	.15	.05
❑	RT23 Dave Magadan	.15	.05
❑	RT24 Dennis Martinez	.30	.10
❑	RT25 Wes Chamberlain	.15	.05
❑	RT26 Otis Nixon	.15	.05
❑	RT27 Eric Anthony	.15	.05
❑	RT28 Randy Milligan	.15	.05
❑	RT29 Julio Franco	.30	.10
❑	RT30 Kevin McReynolds	.15	.05
❑	RT31 Anthony Young	.15	.05
❑	RT32 Brian Harper	.15	.05
❑	RT33 Gene Harris	.15	.05
❑	RT34 Eddie Taubensee	.15	.05
❑	RT35 David Segui	.15	.05
❑	RT36 Stan Javier	.15	.05
❑	RT37 Felix Fermin	.15	.05
❑	RT38 Darrin Jackson	.15	.05
❑	RT39 Tony Fernandez	.15	.05
❑	RT40 Jose Vizcaino	.15	.05
❑	RT41 Willie Banks	.15	.05
❑	RT42 Brian Hunter	.15	.05
❑	RT43 Reggie Jefferson	.15	.05
❑	RT44 Junior Felix	.15	.05
❑	RT45 Jack Armstrong	.15	.05
❑	RT46 Bip Roberts	.15	.05
❑	RT47 Jerry Browne	.15	.05
❑	RT48 Marvin Freeman	.15	.05
❑	RT49 Jody Reed	.15	.05
❑	RT50 Alex Cole	.15	.05
❑	RT51 Sid Fernandez	.15	.05
❑	RT52 Pete Smith	.15	.05
❑	RT53 Xavier Hernandez	.15	.05
❑	RT54 Scott Sanderson	.15	.05
❑	RT55 Turner Ward	.15	.05
❑	RT56 Rex Hudler	.15	.05
❑	RT57 Deion Sanders	.50	.20
❑	RT58 Sid Bream	.15	.05
❑	RT59 Tony Pena	.15	.05
❑	RT60 Bret Boone	.30	.10
❑	RT61 Bobby Ayala	.15	.05
❑	RT62 Pedro Martinez	.75	.30
❑	RT63 Howard Johnson	.15	.05
❑	RT64 Mark Portugal	.15	.05
❑	RT65 Roberto Kelly	.15	.05
❑	RT66 Spike Owen	.15	.05
❑	RT67 Jeff Treadway	.15	.05
❑	RT68 Mike Harkey	.15	.05
❑	RT69 Doug Jones	.15	.05
❑	RT70 Steve Farr	.15	.05
❑	RT71 Billy Taylor RC	.15	.05
❑	RT72 Manny Ramirez	.75	.30
❑	RT73 Bob Hamelin	.15	.05
❑	RT74 Steve Karsay	.15	.05
❑	RT75 Ryan Klesko	.30	.10
❑	RT76 Cliff Floyd	.30	.10
❑	RT77 Jeffrey Hammonds	.15	.05
❑	RT78 Javier Lopez	.30	.10
❑	RT79 Roger Salkeld	.15	.05
❑	RT80 Hector Carrasco	.15	.05
❑	RT81 Gerald Williams	.15	.05
❑	RT82 Raul Mondesi	.30	.10
❑	RT83 Sterling Hitchcock	.15	.05
❑	RT84 Danny Bautista	.15	.05
❑	RT85 Chris Turner	.15	.05
❑	RT86 Shane Reynolds	.15	.05
❑	RT87 Rondell White	.30	.10
❑	RT88 Salomon Torres	.15	.05
❑	RT89 Turk Wendell	.15	.05
❑	RT90 Tony Tarasco	.15	.05
❑	RT91 Shawn Green	.75	.30
❑	RT92 Greg Colbrunn	.15	.05
❑	RT93 Eddie Zambrano	.15	.05
❑	RT94 Rich Becker	.15	.05
❑	RT95 Chris Gomez	.15	.05
❑	RT96 John Patterson	.15	.05
❑	RT97 Derek Parks	.15	.05
❑	RT98 Rich Rowland	.15	.05
❑	RT99 James Mouton	.15	.05
❑	RT100 Tim Hyers RC	.15	.05
❑	RT101 Jose Valentin	.15	.05
❑	RT102 Carlos Delgado	.50	.20
❑	RT103 Robert Eenhoorn	.15	.05
❑	RT104 John Hudek RC	.15	.05
❑	RT105 Domingo Cedeno	.15	.05
❑	RT106 Denny Hocking	.15	.05
❑	RT107 Greg Pirkl	.15	.05
❑	RT108 Mark Smith	.15	.05
❑	RT109 Paul Shuey	.15	.05
❑	RT110 Jorge Fabregas	.15	.05
❑	RT111 Rikkert Faneyte RC	.15	.05
❑	RT112 Rob Butler	.15	.05
❑	RT113 Darren Oliver RC	.30	.10
❑	RT114 Troy O'Leary	.15	.05
❑	RT115 Scott Brow	.15	.05
❑	RT116 Tony Eusebio	.15	.05
❑	RT117 Carlos Reyes	.15	.05
❑	RT118 J.R. Phillips	.15	.05
❑	RT119 Alex Diaz	.15	.05
❑	RT120 Charles Johnson	.30	.10
❑	RT121 Nate Minchey	.15	.05
❑	RT122 Scott Sanders	.15	.05
❑	RT123 Daryl Boston	.15	.05
❑	RT124 Joey Hamilton	.15	.05
❑	RT125 Brian Anderson	.30	.10
❑	RT126 Dan Miceli	.15	.05
❑	RT127 Tom Brunansky	.15	.05
❑	RT128 Dave Staton	.15	.05
❑	RT129 Mike Oquist	.15	.05
❑	RT130 John Mabry RC	.30	.10
❑	RT131 Norberto Martin	.15	.05
❑	RT132 Hector Fajardo	.15	.05
❑	RT133 Mark Hutton	.15	.05
❑	RT134 Fernando Vina	.15	.05
❑	RT135 Lee Tinsley	.15	.05
❑	RT136 Chan Ho Park RC	.50	.20
❑	RT137 Paul Spoljaric	.15	.05
❑	RT138 Matias Carrillo	.15	.05
❑	RT139 Mark Kiefer	.15	.05
❑	RT140 Stan Royer	.15	.05
❑	RT141 Bryan Eversgerd	.15	.05
❑	RT142 Brian L. Hunter	.15	.05
❑	RT143 Joe Hall	.15	.05
❑	RT144 Johnny Ruffin	.15	.05
❑	RT145 Alex Gonzalez	.15	.05
❑	RT146 Keith Lockhart RC	.30	.10
❑	RT147 Tom Marsh	.15	.05
❑	RT148 Tony Longmire	.15	.05
❑	RT149 Keith Mitchell	.15	.05
❑	RT150 Melvin Nieves	.15	.05
❑	RT151 Kelly Stinnett RC	.15	.05
❑	RT152 Miguel Jimenez	.15	.05
❑	RT153 Jeff Juden	.15	.05
❑	RT154 Matt Walbeck	.15	.05
❑	RT155 Marc Newfield	.15	.05
❑	RT156 Matt Mieske	.15	.05
❑	RT157 Marcus Moore	.15	.05
❑	RT158 Jose Lima RC SP	5.00	2.00

❑ RT159 Mike Kelly .15 .05
❑ RT160 Jim Edmonds .75 .30
❑ RT161 Steve Trachsel .15 .05
❑ RT162 Greg Blosser .15 .05
❑ RT163 Mark Acre RC .15 .05
❑ RT164 AL Checklist .15 .05
❑ RT165 NL Checklist .15 .05
❑ HC1 Alex Rodriguez CU 800.00 600.00
❑ NNO September Call-Up Trade EXP 2.00 .75

1993 SP

❑ COMPLETE SET (290) 80.00 40.00
❑ COMMON CARD (1-270) .50 .20
❑ FOIL PROSPECTS (271-290) 1.00 .40
❑ 1 Roberto Alomar AS 1.25 .50
❑ 2 Wade Boggs AS 1.25 .50
❑ 3 Joe Carter AS .50 .20
❑ 4 Ken Griffey Jr. AS 3.00 1.25
❑ 5 Mark Langston AS .50 .20
❑ 6 John Olerud AS .75 .30
❑ 7 Kirby Puckett AS 2.00 .75
❑ 8 Cal Ripken AS 6.00 2.50
❑ 9 Ivan Rodriguez AS 1.25 .50
❑ 10 Barry Bonds AS 5.00 2.00
❑ 11 Darren Daulton AS .75 .30
❑ 12 Marquis Grissom AS .75 .30
❑ 13 David Justice AS .75 .30
❑ 14 John Kruk AS .75 .30
❑ 15 Barry Larkin AS 1.25 .50
❑ 16 Terry Mulholland AS .50 .20
❑ 17 Ryne Sandberg AS 3.00 1.25
❑ 18 Gary Sheffield AS .75 .30
❑ 19 Chad Curtis .50 .20
❑ 20 Chili Davis .75 .30
❑ 21 Gary DiSarcina .50 .20
❑ 22 Damion Easley .50 .20
❑ 23 Chuck Finley .75 .30
❑ 24 Luis Polonia .50 .20
❑ 25 Tim Salmon 1.25 .50
❑ 26 J.T.Snow RC 1.25 .50
❑ 27 Russ Springer .50 .20
❑ 28 Jeff Bagwell 1.25 .50
❑ 29 Craig Biggio 1.25 .50
❑ 30 Ken Caminiti .75 .30
❑ 31 Andujar Cedeno .50 .20
❑ 32 Doug Drabek .50 .20
❑ 33 Steve Finley .75 .30
❑ 34 Luis Gonzalez .75 .30
❑ 35 Pete Harnisch .50 .20
❑ 36 Darryl Kile .75 .30
❑ 37 Mike Bordick .50 .20
❑ 38 Dennis Eckersley .75 .30
❑ 39 Brent Gates .50 .20
❑ 40 Rickey Henderson 2.00 .75
❑ 41 Mark McGwire 5.00 2.00
❑ 42 Craig Paquette .50 .20
❑ 43 Ruben Sierra .75 .30
❑ 44 Terry Steinbach .50 .20
❑ 45 Todd Van Poppel .50 .20
❑ 46 Pat Borders .50 .20
❑ 47 Tony Fernandez .50 .20
❑ 48 Juan Guzman .50 .20
❑ 49 Pat Hentgen .50 .20
❑ 50 Paul Molitor .75 .30
❑ 51 Jack Morris .75 .30
❑ 52 Ed Sprague .50 .20
❑ 53 Duane Ward .50 .20
❑ 54 Devon White .75 .30
❑ 55 Steve Avery .50 .20
❑ 56 Jeff Blauser .50 .20
❑ 57 Ron Gant .75 .30
❑ 58 Tom Glavine 1.25 .50
❑ 59 Greg Maddux 3.00 1.25
❑ 60 Fred McGriff 1.25 .50
❑ 61 Terry Pendleton .75 .30
❑ 62 Deion Sanders 1.25 .50
❑ 63 John Smoltz 1.25 .50
❑ 64 Cal Eldred .50 .20
❑ 65 Darryl Hamilton .50 .20
❑ 66 John Jaha .50 .20
❑ 67 Pat Listach .50 .20
❑ 68 Jaime Navarro .50 .20
❑ 69 Kevin Reimer .50 .20
❑ 70 B.J. Surhoff .75 .30
❑ 71 Greg Vaughn .50 .20
❑ 72 Robin Yount 3.00 1.25
❑ 73 Rene Arocha RC .75 .30
❑ 74 Bernard Gilkey .50 .20
❑ 75 Gregg Jefferies .50 .20
❑ 76 Ray Lankford .75 .30
❑ 77 Tom Pagnozzi .50 .20
❑ 78 Lee Smith .75 .30
❑ 79 Ozzie Smith 3.00 1.25
❑ 80 Bob Tewksbury .50 .20
❑ 81 Mark Whiten .50 .20
❑ 82 Steve Buechele .50 .20
❑ 83 Mark Grace 1.25 .50
❑ 84 Jose Guzman .50 .20
❑ 85 Derrick May .50 .20
❑ 86 Mike Morgan .50 .20
❑ 87 Randy Myers .50 .20
❑ 88 Kevin Roberson RC .50 .20
❑ 89 Sammy Sosa 2.00 .75
❑ 90 Rick Wilkins .50 .20
❑ 91 Brett Butler .75 .30
❑ 92 Eric Davis .75 .30
❑ 93 Orel Hershiser .75 .30
❑ 94 Eric Karros .75 .30
❑ 95 Ramon Martinez .50 .20
❑ 96 Raul Mondesi .75 .30
❑ 97 Jose Offerman .50 .20
❑ 98 Mike Piazza 5.00 2.00
❑ 99 Darryl Strawberry .75 .30
❑ 100 Moises Alou .75 .30
❑ 101 Wil Cordero .50 .20
❑ 102 Delino DeShields .50 .20
❑ 103 Darrin Fletcher .50 .20
❑ 104 Ken Hill .50 .20
❑ 105 Mike Lansing RC .75 .30
❑ 106 Dennis Martinez .75 .30
❑ 107 Larry Walker .75 .30
❑ 108 John Wetteland .75 .30
❑ 109 Rod Beck .50 .20
❑ 110 John Burkett .50 .20
❑ 111 Will Clark 1.25 .50
❑ 112 Royce Clayton .50 .20
❑ 113 Darren Lewis .50 .20
❑ 114 Willie McGee .75 .30
❑ 115 Bill Swift .50 .20
❑ 116 Robby Thompson .50 .20
❑ 117 Matt Williams .75 .30
❑ 118 Sandy Alomar Jr. .50 .20
❑ 119 Carlos Baerga .50 .20
❑ 120 Albert Belle .75 .30
❑ 121 Reggie Jefferson .50 .20
❑ 122 Wayne Kirby .50 .20
❑ 123 Kenny Lofton .75 .30
❑ 124 Carlos Martinez .50 .20
❑ 125 Charles Nagy .50 .20
❑ 126 Paul Sorrento .50 .20
❑ 127 Rich Amaral .50 .20
❑ 128 Jay Buhner .75 .30
❑ 129 Norm Charlton .50 .20
❑ 130 Dave Fleming .50 .20
❑ 131 Erik Hanson .50 .20
❑ 132 Randy Johnson 2.00 .75
❑ 133 Edgar Martinez 1.25 .50
❑ 134 Tino Martinez 1.25 .50
❑ 135 Omar Vizquel 1.25 .50
❑ 136 Bret Barberie .50 .20
❑ 137 Chuck Carr .50 .20
❑ 138 Jeff Conine .75 .30
❑ 139 Orestes Destrade .50 .20
❑ 140 Chris Hammond .50 .20
❑ 141 Bryan Harvey .50 .20
❑ 142 Benito Santiago .75 .30
❑ 143 Walt Weiss .50 .20
❑ 144 Darrell Whitmore RC .50 .20
❑ 145 Tim Bogar RC .50 .20
❑ 146 Bobby Bonilla .75 .30
❑ 147 Jeromy Burnitz .75 .30
❑ 148 Vince Coleman .50 .20
❑ 149 Dwight Gooden .75 .30
❑ 150 Todd Hundley .50 .20
❑ 151 Howard Johnson .50 .20
❑ 152 Eddie Murray 2.00 .75
❑ 153 Bret Saberhagen .75 .30
❑ 154 Brady Anderson .75 .30
❑ 155 Mike Devereaux .50 .20
❑ 156 Jeffrey Hammonds .50 .20
❑ 157 Chris Hoiles .50 .20
❑ 158 Ben McDonald .50 .20
❑ 159 Mark McLemore .50 .20
❑ 160 Mike Mussina 1.25 .50
❑ 161 Gregg Olson .50 .20
❑ 162 David Segui .50 .20
❑ 163 Derek Bell .50 .20
❑ 164 Andy Benes .50 .20
❑ 165 Archi Cianfrocco .50 .20
❑ 166 Ricky Gutierrez .50 .20
❑ 167 Tony Gwynn 2.50 1.00
❑ 168 Gene Harris .50 .20
❑ 169 Trevor Hoffman 2.00 .75
❑ 170 Ray McDavid RC .50 .20
❑ 171 Phil Plantier .50 .20
❑ 172 Mariano Duncan .50 .20
❑ 173 Len Dykstra .75 .30
❑ 174 Tommy Greene .50 .20
❑ 175 Dave Hollins .50 .20
❑ 176 Pete Incaviglia .50 .20
❑ 177 Mickey Morandini .50 .20
❑ 178 Curt Schilling .75 .30
❑ 179 Kevin Stocker .50 .20
❑ 180 Mitch Williams .50 .20
❑ 181 Stan Belinda .50 .20
❑ 182 Jay Bell .75 .30
❑ 183 Steve Cooke .50 .20
❑ 184 Carlos Garcia .50 .20
❑ 185 Jeff King .50 .20
❑ 186 Orlando Merced .50 .20
❑ 187 Don Slaught .50 .20
❑ 188 Andy Van Slyke 1.25 .50
❑ 189 Kevin Young .75 .30
❑ 190 Kevin Brown .75 .30
❑ 191 Jose Canseco 1.25 .50
❑ 192 Julio Franco .75 .30
❑ 193 Benji Gil .50 .20
❑ 194 Juan Gonzalez .75 .30
❑ 195 Tom Henke .50 .20
❑ 196 Rafael Palmeiro 1.25 .50
❑ 197 Dean Palmer .75 .30
❑ 198 Nolan Ryan 8.00 3.00
❑ 199 Roger Clemens 4.00 1.50
❑ 200 Scott Cooper .50 .20
❑ 201 Andre Dawson .75 .30
❑ 202 Mike Greenwell .50 .20
❑ 203 Carlos Quintana .50 .20
❑ 204 Jeff Russell .50 .20
❑ 205 Aaron Sele .50 .20
❑ 206 Mo Vaughn .75 .30
❑ 207 Frank Viola .75 .30
❑ 208 Rob Dibble .75 .30
❑ 209 Roberto Kelly .50 .20
❑ 210 Kevin Mitchell .50 .20
❑ 211 Hal Morris .50 .28
❑ 212 Joe Oliver .50 .20
❑ 213 Jose Rijo .50 .20
❑ 214 Bip Roberts .50 .20
❑ 215 Chris Sabo .50 .20
❑ 216 Reggie Sanders .75 .30
❑ 217 Dante Bichette .75 .30
❑ 218 Jerald Clark .50 .20
❑ 219 Alex Cole .50 .20
❑ 220 Andres Galarraga .75 .30
❑ 221 Joe Girardi .50 .20
❑ 222 Charlie Hayes .50 .20
❑ 223 Roberto Mejia RC .50 .20
❑ 224 Armando Reynoso .50 .20
❑ 225 Eric Young .50 .20
❑ 226 Kevin Appier .75 .30

❑ 227 George Brett 5.00 2.00
❑ 228 David Cone .75 .30
❑ 229 Phil Hiatt .50 .20
❑ 230 Felix Jose .50 .20
❑ 231 Wally Joyner .75 .30
❑ 232 Mike Macfarlane .50 .20
❑ 233 Brian McRae .50 .20
❑ 234 Jeff Montgomery .50 .20
❑ 235 Rob Deer .50 .20
❑ 236 Cecil Fielder .75 .30
❑ 237 Travis Fryman .75 .30
❑ 238 Mike Henneman .50 .20
❑ 239 Tony Phillips .50 .20
❑ 240 Mickey Tettleton .50 .20
❑ 241 Alan Trammell .75 .30
❑ 242 David Wells .75 .30
❑ 243 Lou Whitaker .75 .30
❑ 244 Rick Aguilera .50 .20
❑ 245 Scott Erickson .50 .20
❑ 246 Brian Harper .50 .20
❑ 247 Kent Hrbek .75 .30
❑ 248 Chuck Knoblauch .75 .30
❑ 249 Shane Mack .50 .20
❑ 250 David McCarty .50 .20
❑ 251 Pedro Munoz .50 .20
❑ 252 Dave Winfield .75 .30
❑ 253 Alex Fernandez .50 .20
❑ 254 Ozzie Guillen .75 .30
❑ 255 Bo Jackson 2.00 .75
❑ 256 Lance Johnson .50 .20
❑ 257 Ron Karkovice .50 .20
❑ 258 Jack McDowell .50 .20
❑ 259 Tim Raines .75 .30
❑ 260 Frank Thomas 2.00 .75
❑ 261 Robin Ventura .75 .30
❑ 262 Jim Abbott 1.25 .50
❑ 263 Steve Farr .50 .20
❑ 264 Jimmy Key .75 .30
❑ 265 Don Mattingly 5.00 2.00
❑ 266 Paul O'Neill 1.25 .50
❑ 267 Mike Stanley .50 .20
❑ 268 Danny Tartabull .50 .20
❑ 269 Bob Wickman .50 .20
❑ 270 Bernie Williams 1.25 .50
❑ 271 Jason Bere FOIL 1.00 .40
❑ 272 Roger Cedeno FOIL RC 1.50 .60
❑ 273 Johnny Damon FOIL RC 12.00 5.00
❑ 274 Russ Davis FOIL RC 1.50 .60
❑ 275 Carlos Delgado FOIL 4.00 1.50
❑ 276 Carl Everett FOIL 1.50 .60
❑ 277 Cliff Floyd FOIL .75 .30
❑ 278 Alex Gonzalez FOIL 1.00 .40
❑ 279 Derek Jeter FOIL RC ! 80.00 40.00
❑ 280 Chipper Jones FOIL 4.00 1.50
❑ 281 Javier Lopez FOIL 1.25 .50
❑ 282 Chad Mottola FOIL RC 1.00 .40
❑ 283 Marc Newfield FOIL 1.00 .40
❑ 284 Eduardo Perez FOIL 1.00 .40
❑ 285 Manny Ramirez FOIL 5.00 2.00
❑ 286 Todd Steverson FOIL RC 1.00 .40
❑ 287 Michael Tucker FOIL 1.00 .40
❑ 288 Allen Watson FOIL 1.00 .40
❑ 289 Rondell White FOIL 1.50 .60
❑ 290 Dmitri Young FOIL 1.50 .60

1994 SP

❑ COMPLETE SET (200) 150.00 75.00
❑ COMMON CARD (21-200) .20 .07
❑ COMMON FOIL (1-20) .50 .20
❑ 1 Mike Bell FOIL RC .50 .20
❑ 2 D.J. Boston FOIL RC .50 .20
❑ 3 Johnny Damon FOIL 2.00 .75
❑ 4 Brad Fullmer FOIL RC 1.00 .40
❑ 5 Joey Hamilton FOIL .50 .20
❑ 6 Todd Hollandsworth FOIL .50 .20
❑ 7 Brian L.Hunter FOIL .50 .20
❑ 8 LaTroy Hawkins FOIL RC 1.00 .40
❑ 9 Brooks Kieschnick FOIL RC .50 .20
❑ 10 Derrek Lee FOIL RC 10.00 4.00
❑ 11 Trot Nixon FOIL RC 4.00 1.50
❑ 12 Alex Ochoa FOIL .50 .20
❑ 13 Chan Ho Park FOIL RC 2.00 .75
❑ 14 Kirk Presley FOIL RC .50 .20
❑ 15 Alex Rodriguez FOIL RC 150.00 75.00
❑ 16 Jose Silva FOIL RC .50 .20
❑ 17 Terrell Wade FOIL RC .50 .20
❑ 18 Billy Wagner FOIL RC 4.00 1.50
❑ 19 Glenn Williams FOIL RC .50 .20
❑ 20 Preston Wilson FOIL 1.00 .40
❑ 21 Brian Anderson RC .40 .15
❑ 22 Chad Curtis .20 .07
❑ 23 Chili Davis .40 .15
❑ 24 Bo Jackson 1.00 .40
❑ 25 Mark Langston .20 .07
❑ 26 Tim Salmon .60 .25
❑ 27 Jeff Bagwell .60 .25
❑ 28 Craig Biggio .60 .25
❑ 29 Ken Caminiti .40 .15
❑ 30 Doug Drabek .20 .07
❑ 31 John Hudek RC .20 .07
❑ 32 Greg Swindell .20 .07
❑ 33 Brent Gates .20 .07
❑ 34 Rickey Henderson 1.00 .40
❑ 35 Steve Karsay .20 .07
❑ 36 Mark McGwire 2.50 1.00
❑ 37 Ruben Sierra .40 .15
❑ 38 Terry Steinbach .20 .07
❑ 39 Roberto Alomar .60 .25
❑ 40 Joe Carter .40 .15
❑ 41 Carlos Delgado .60 .25
❑ 42 Alex Gonzalez .20 .07
❑ 43 Juan Guzman .20 .07
❑ 44 Paul Molitor .40 .15
❑ 45 John Olerud .40 .15
❑ 46 Devon White .40 .15
❑ 47 Steve Avery .20 .07
❑ 48 Jeff Blauser .20 .07
❑ 49 Tom Glavine .60 .25
❑ 50 David Justice .40 .15
❑ 51 Roberto Kelly .20 .07
❑ 52 Ryan Klesko .40 .15
❑ 53 Javier Lopez .40 .15
❑ 54 Greg Maddux 1.50 .60
❑ 55 Fred McGriff .60 .25
❑ 56 Ricky Bones .20 .07
❑ 57 Cal Eldred .20 .07
❑ 58 Brian Harper .20 .07
❑ 59 Pat Listach .20 .07
❑ 60 B.J. Surhoff .40 .15
❑ 61 Greg Vaughn .20 .07
❑ 62 Bernard Gilkey .20 .07
❑ 63 Gregg Jefferies .20 .07
❑ 64 Ray Lankford .40 .15
❑ 65 Ozzie Smith 1.50 .60
❑ 66 Bob Tewksbury .20 .07
❑ 67 Mark Whiten .20 .07
❑ 68 Todd Zeile .20 .07
❑ 69 Mark Grace .60 .25
❑ 70 Randy Myers .20 .07
❑ 71 Ryne Sandberg 1.50 .60
❑ 72 Sammy Sosa 1.00 .40
❑ 73 Steve Trachsel .20 .07
❑ 74 Rick Wilkins .20 .07
❑ 75 Brett Butler .40 .15
❑ 76 Delino DeShields .20 .07
❑ 77 Orel Hershiser .40 .15
❑ 78 Eric Karros .40 .15
❑ 79 Raul Mondesi .40 .15
❑ 80 Mike Piazza 2.00 .75
❑ 81 Tim Wallach .20 .07
❑ 82 Moises Alou .40 .15
❑ 83 Cliff Floyd .40 .15
❑ 84 Marquis Grissom .40 .15
❑ 85 Pedro Martinez 1.00 .40
❑ 86 Larry Walker .40 .15
❑ 87 John Wetteland .40 .15
❑ 88 Rondell White .40 .15
❑ 89 Rod Beck .20 .07
❑ 90 Barry Bonds 2.50 1.00
❑ 91 John Burkett .20 .07
❑ 92 Royce Clayton .20 .07
❑ 93 Billy Swift .20 .07
❑ 94 Robby Thompson .20 .07
❑ 95 Matt Williams .40 .15
❑ 96 Carlos Baerga .20 .07
❑ 97 Albert Belle .40 .15
❑ 98 Kenny Lofton .40 .15
❑ 99 Dennis Martinez .40 .15
❑ 100 Eddie Murray 1.00 .40
❑ 101 Manny Ramirez 1.00 .40
❑ 102 Eric Anthony .20 .07
❑ 103 Chris Bosio .20 .07
❑ 104 Jay Buhner .40 .15
❑ 105 Ken Griffey Jr. 1.50 .60
❑ 106 Randy Johnson 1.00 .40
❑ 107 Edgar Martinez .60 .25
❑ 108 Chuck Carr .20 .07
❑ 109 Jeff Conine .40 .15
❑ 110 Carl Everett .40 .15
❑ 111 Chris Hammond .20 .07
❑ 112 Bryan Harvey .20 .07
❑ 113 Charles Johnson .40 .15
❑ 114 Gary Sheffield .40 .15
❑ 115 Bobby Bonilla .40 .15
❑ 116 Dwight Gooden .40 .15
❑ 117 Todd Hundley .20 .07
❑ 118 Bobby Jones .20 .07
❑ 119 Jeff Kent .60 .25
❑ 120 Bret Saberhagen .40 .15
❑ 121 Jeffrey Hammonds .20 .07
❑ 122 Chris Hoiles .20 .07
❑ 123 Ben McDonald .20 .07
❑ 124 Mike Mussina .60 .25
❑ 125 Rafael Palmeiro .60 .25
❑ 126 Cal Ripken 3.00 1.25
❑ 127 Lee Smith .40 .15
❑ 128 Derek Bell .20 .07
❑ 129 Andy Benes .20 .07
❑ 130 Tony Gwynn 1.25 .50
❑ 131 Trevor Hoffman .60 .25
❑ 132 Phil Plantier .20 .07
❑ 133 Bip Roberts .20 .07
❑ 134 Darren Daulton .40 .15
❑ 135 Lenny Dykstra .40 .15
❑ 136 Dave Hollins .20 .07
❑ 137 Danny Jackson .20 .07
❑ 138 John Kruk .40 .15
❑ 139 Kevin Stocker .20 .07
❑ 140 Jay Bell .40 .15
❑ 141 Carlos Garcia .20 .07
❑ 142 Jeff King .20 .07
❑ 143 Orlando Merced .20 .07
❑ 144 Andy Van Slyke .60 .25
❑ 145 Rick White .20 .07
❑ 146 Jose Canseco .60 .25
❑ 147 Will Clark .60 .25
❑ 148 Juan Gonzalez .40 .15
❑ 149 Rick Helling .20 .07
❑ 150 Dean Palmer .40 .15
❑ 151 Ivan Rodriguez .60 .25
❑ 152 Roger Clemens 2.00 .75
❑ 153 Scott Cooper .20 .07
❑ 154 Andre Dawson .40 .15
❑ 155 Mike Greenwell .20 .07
❑ 156 Aaron Sele .20 .07
❑ 157 Mo Vaughn .40 .15
❑ 158 Bret Boone .40 .15
❑ 159 Barry Larkin .60 .25
❑ 160 Kevin Mitchell .20 .07
❑ 161 Jose Rijo .20 .07
❑ 162 Deion Sanders .60 .25
❑ 163 Reggie Sanders .40 .15
❑ 164 Dante Bichette .40 .15
❑ 165 Ellis Burks .40 .15
❑ 166 Andres Galarraga .40 .15
❑ 167 Charlie Hayes .20 .07
❑ 168 David Nied .20 .07
❑ 169 Walt Weiss .20 .07
❑ 170 Kevin Appier .40 .15
❑ 171 David Cone .40 .15

❑ 172 Jeff Granger .20 .07
❑ 173 Felix Jose .20 .07
❑ 174 Wally Joyner .40 .15
❑ 175 Brian McRae .20 .07
❑ 176 Cecil Fielder .40 .15
❑ 177 Travis Fryman .40 .15
❑ 178 Mike Henneman .20 .07
❑ 179 Tony Phillips .20 .07
❑ 180 Mickey Tettleton .20 .07
❑ 181 Alan Trammell .40 .15
❑ 182 Rick Aguilera .20 .07
❑ 183 Rich Becker .20 .07
❑ 184 Scott Erickson .20 .07
❑ 185 Chuck Knoblauch .40 .15
❑ 186 Kirby Puckett 1.00 .40
❑ 187 Dave Winfield .40 .15
❑ 188 Wilson Alvarez .20 .07
❑ 189 Jason Bere .20 .07
❑ 190 Alex Fernandez .20 .07
❑ 191 Julio Franco .40 .15
❑ 192 Jack McDowell .20 .07
❑ 193 Frank Thomas 1.00 .40
❑ 194 Robin Ventura .40 .15
❑ 195 Jim Abbott .60 .25
❑ 196 Wade Boggs .60 .25
❑ 197 Jimmy Key .40 .15
❑ 198 Don Mattingly 2.50 1.00
❑ 199 Paul O'Neill .60 .25
❑ 200 Danny Tartabull .20 .07
❑ P24 Ken Griffey Jr. Promo 2.00 .75

2000 SP Authentic

❑ COMP.BASIC w/o SP's (90) 25.00 10.00
❑ COMP.UPDATE w/o SP'S (30) 10.00 4.00
❑ COMMON CARD (1-90) .40 .15
❑ COMMON SUP (91-105) 3.00 1.25
❑ COMMON FW (106-135) 5.00 2.00
❑ COMMON FW (136-164) 5.00 2.00
❑ COMMON CARD (166-195) .60 .25
❑ 1 Mo Vaughn .40 .15
❑ 2 Troy Glaus .40 .15
❑ 3 Jason Giambi .40 .15
❑ 4 Tim Hudson .40 .15
❑ 5 Eric Chavez .40 .15
❑ 6 Shannon Stewart .40 .15
❑ 7 Raul Mondesi .40 .15
❑ 8 Carlos Delgado .40 .15
❑ 9 Jose Canseco .60 .25
❑ 10 Vinny Castilla .40 .15
❑ 11 Greg Vaughn .40 .15
❑ 12 Manny Ramirez .60 .25
❑ 13 Roberto Alomar .60 .25
❑ 14 Jim Thome .60 .25
❑ 15 Richie Sexson .40 .15
❑ 16 Alex Rodriguez 1.50 .60
❑ 17 Freddy Garcia .40 .15
❑ 18 John Olerud .40 .15
❑ 19 Albert Belle .40 .15
❑ 20 Cal Ripken 3.00 1.25
❑ 21 Mike Mussina .60 .25
❑ 22 Ivan Rodriguez .60 .25
❑ 23 Gabe Kapler .40 .15
❑ 24 Rafael Palmeiro .60 .25
❑ 25 Nomar Garciaparra 1.50 .60
❑ 26 Pedro Martinez .60 .25
❑ 27 Carl Everett .40 .15
❑ 28 Carlos Beltran .40 .15
❑ 29 Jermaine Dye .40 .15
❑ 30 Juan Gonzalez .40 .15
❑ 31 Dean Palmer .40 .15
❑ 32 Corey Koskie .40 .15
❑ 33 Jacque Jones .40 .15
❑ 34 Frank Thomas 1.00 .40
❑ 35 Paul Konerko .40 .15
❑ 36 Magglio Ordonez .40 .15
❑ 37 Bernie Williams .60 .25
❑ 38 Derek Jeter 2.50 1.00
❑ 39 Roger Clemens 2.00 .75
❑ 40 Mariano Rivera 1.00 .40
❑ 41 Jeff Bagwell .60 .25
❑ 42 Craig Biggio .60 .25
❑ 43 Jose Lima .40 .15
❑ 44 Moises Alou .40 .15
❑ 45 Chipper Jones 1.00 .40
❑ 46 Greg Maddux 1.50 .60
❑ 47 Andruw Jones .60 .25
❑ 48 Andres Galarraga .40 .15
❑ 49 Jeromy Burnitz .40 .15
❑ 50 Geoff Jenkins .40 .15
❑ 51 Mark McGwire 2.50 1.00
❑ 52 Fernando Tatis .40 .15
❑ 53 J.D. Drew .40 .15
❑ 54 Sammy Sosa 1.00 .40
❑ 55 Kerry Wood .40 .15
❑ 56 Mark Grace .60 .25
❑ 57 Matt Williams .40 .15
❑ 58 Randy Johnson 1.00 .40
❑ 59 Erubiel Durazo .40 .15
❑ 60 Gary Sheffield .40 .15
❑ 61 Kevin Brown .60 .25
❑ 62 Shawn Green .40 .15
❑ 63 Vladimir Guerrero 1.00 .40
❑ 64 Michael Barrett .40 .15
❑ 65 Barry Bonds 2.50 1.00
❑ 66 Jeff Kent .40 .15
❑ 67 Russ Ortiz .40 .15
❑ 68 Preston Wilson .40 .15
❑ 69 Mike Lowell .40 .15
❑ 70 Mike Piazza 1.50 .60
❑ 71 Mike Hampton .40 .15
❑ 72 Robin Ventura .40 .15
❑ 73 Edgardo Alfonzo .40 .15
❑ 74 Tony Gwynn 1.25 .50
❑ 75 Ryan Klesko .40 .15
❑ 76 Trevor Hoffman .40 .15
❑ 77 Scott Rolen .60 .25
❑ 78 Bob Abreu .40 .15
❑ 79 Mike Lieberthal .40 .15
❑ 80 Curt Schilling .40 .15
❑ 81 Jason Kendall .40 .15
❑ 82 Brian Giles .40 .15
❑ 83 Kris Benson .40 .15
❑ 84 Ken Griffey Jr. 1.50 .60
❑ 85 Sean Casey .40 .15
❑ 86 Pokey Reese .40 .15
❑ 87 Barry Larkin .60 .25
❑ 88 Larry Walker .40 .15
❑ 89 Todd Helton .60 .25
❑ 90 Jeff Cirillo .40 .15
❑ 91 Ken Griffey Jr. SUP 8.00 3.00
❑ 92 Mark McGwire SUP 12.00 5.00
❑ 93 Chipper Jones SUP 5.00 2.00
❑ 94 Derek Jeter SUP 12.00 5.00
❑ 95 Shawn Green SUP 3.00 1.25
❑ 96 Pedro Martinez SUP 3.00 1.25
❑ 97 Mike Piazza SUP 8.00 3.00
❑ 98 Alex Rodriguez SUP 8.00 3.00
❑ 99 Jeff Bagwell SUP 3.00 1.25
❑ 100 Cal Ripken SUP 15.00 6.00
❑ 101 Sammy Sosa SUP 5.00 2.00
❑ 102 Barry Bonds SUP 12.00 5.00
❑ 103 Jose Canseco SUP 3.00 1.25
❑ 104 Nomar Garciaparra SUP 8.00 3.00
❑ 105 Ivan Rodriguez SUP 3.00 1.25
❑ 106 Rick Ankiel FW 8.00 3.00
❑ 107 Pat Burrell FW 3.00 1.25
❑ 108 Vernon Wells FW 5.00 2.00
❑ 109 Nick Johnson FW 5.00 2.00
❑ 110 Kip Wells FW 5.00 2.00
❑ 111 Matt Riley FW 5.00 2.00
❑ 112 Alfonso Soriano FW 8.00 3.00
❑ 113 Josh Beckett FW 8.00 3.00
❑ 114 Danys Baez FW RC 5.00 2.00
❑ 115 Travis Dawkins FW 5.00 2.00
❑ 116 Eric Gagne FW 8.00 3.00
❑ 117 Mike Lamb FW RC 8.00 3.00
❑ 118 Eric Munson FW 5.00 2.00
❑ 119 Wilfredo Rodriguez FW RC 5.00 2.00
❑ 120 Kazuhiro Sasaki FW RC 8.00 3.00
❑ 121 Chad Hutchinson FW 5.00 2.00
❑ 122 Peter Bergeron FW 5.00 2.00
❑ 123 Wascar Serrano FW RC 5.00 2.00
❑ 124 Tony Armas Jr. FW 5.00 2.00
❑ 125 Ramon Ortiz FW 5.00 2.00
❑ 126 Adam Kennedy FW 5.00 2.00
❑ 127 Joe Crede FW 10.00 4.00
❑ 128 Roosevelt Brown FW 5.00 2.00
❑ 129 Mark Mulder FW 5.00 2.00
❑ 130 Brad Penny FW 5.00 2.00
❑ 131 Terrence Long FW 5.00 2.00
❑ 132 Ruben Mateo FW 5.00 2.00
❑ 133 Wily Mo Pena FW 5.00 2.00
❑ 134 Rafael Furcal FW 5.00 2.00
❑ 135 Mario Encarnacion FW 5.00 2.00
❑ 136 Barry Zito FW RC 20.00 8.00
❑ 137 Aaron McNeal FW RC 5.00 2.00
❑ 138 Timo Perez FW RC 5.00 2.00
❑ 139 Sun Woo Kim FW RC 5.00 2.00
❑ 140 Xavier Nady FW RC 10.00 4.00
❑ 141 Matt Wheatland FW RC 5.00 2.00
❑ 142 Brent Abernathy FW RC 5.00 2.00
❑ 143 Cory Vance FW RC 5.00 2.00
❑ 144 Scott Heard FW RC 5.00 2.00
❑ 145 Mike Meyers FW RC 5.00 2.00
❑ 146 Ben Diggins FW RC 5.00 2.00
❑ 147 Luis Matos FW RC 5.00 2.00
❑ 148 Ben Sheets FW RC 12.00 5.00
❑ 149 Kurt Ainsworth FW RC 5.00 2.00
❑ 150 Dave Krynzel FW RC 5.00 2.00
❑ 151 Alex Cabrera FW RC 5.00 2.00
❑ 152 Mike Tonis FW RC 5.00 2.00
❑ 153 Dane Sardinha FW RC 5.00 2.00
❑ 154 Keith Ginter FW RC 5.00 2.00
❑ 155 David Espinosa FW RC 5.00 2.00
❑ 156 Joe Torres FW RC 5.00 2.00
❑ 157 Daylan Holt FW RC 5.00 2.00
❑ 158 Koyie Hill FW RC 5.00 2.00
❑ 159 Brad Wilkerson FW RC 8.00 3.00
❑ 160 Juan Pierre FW RC 8.00 3.00
❑ 161 Matt Ginter FW RC 5.00 2.00
❑ 162 Dane Artman FW RC 5.00 2.00
❑ 163 Jon Rauch FW RC 5.00 2.00
❑ 164 Sean Burnett FW RC 5.00 2.00
❑ 165 Does Not Exist
❑ 166 Darin Erstad .60 .25
❑ 167 Ben Grieve .60 .25
❑ 168 David Wells .60 .25
❑ 169 Fred McGriff 1.00 .40
❑ 170 Bob Wickman .60 .25
❑ 171 Al Martin .60 .25
❑ 172 Melvin Mora .60 .25
❑ 173 Ricky Ledee .60 .25
❑ 174 Dante Bichette .60 .25
❑ 175 Mike Sweeney .60 .25
❑ 176 Bobby Higginson .60 .25
❑ 177 Matt Lawton .60 .25
❑ 178 Charles Johnson .60 .25
❑ 179 David Justice .60 .25
❑ 180 Richard Hidalgo .60 .25
❑ 181 B.J. Surhoff .60 .25
❑ 182 Richie Sexson .60 .25
❑ 183 Jim Edmonds .60 .25
❑ 184 Rondell White .60 .25
❑ 185 Curt Schilling .60 .25
❑ 186 Tom Goodwin .60 .25
❑ 187 Jose Vidro .60 .25
❑ 188 Ellis Burks .60 .25
❑ 189 Henry Rodriguez .60 .25
❑ 190 Mike Bordick .60 .25
❑ 191 Eric Owens .60 .25
❑ 192 Travis Lee .60 .25
❑ 193 Kevin Young .60 .25
❑ 194 Aaron Boone .60 .25
❑ 195 Todd Hollandsworth .60 .25
❑ SPA Ken Griffey Jr. Sample 2.00 .75

2001 SP Authentic

❑ COMP.BASIC w/o SP's (90) 25.00 10.00
❑ COMP.UPDATE w/o SP's (30) 10.00 4.00
❑ COMMON CARD (1-90) .40 .15
❑ COMMON FW (91-135) 8.00 3.00

Card		
❑ COMMON SS (136-180)	5.00	2.00
❑ COMMON CARD (181-210)	.60	.25
❑ COMMON CARD (211-240)	6.00	2.50
❑ 1 Troy Glaus	.40	.15
❑ 2 Darin Erstad	.40	.15
❑ 3 Jason Giambi	.40	.15
❑ 4 Tim Hudson	.40	.15
❑ 5 Eric Chavez	.40	.15
❑ 6 Miguel Tejada	.40	.15
❑ 7 Jose Ortiz	.40	.15
❑ 8 Carlos Delgado	.40	.15
❑ 9 Tony Batista	.40	.15
❑ 10 Raul Mondesi	.40	.15
❑ 11 Aubrey Huff	.40	.15
❑ 12 Greg Vaughn	.40	.15
❑ 13 Roberto Alomar	.60	.25
❑ 14 Juan Gonzalez	.40	.15
❑ 15 Jim Thome	.60	.25
❑ 16 Omar Vizquel	.60	.25
❑ 17 Edgar Martinez	.60	.25
❑ 18 Freddy Garcia	.40	.15
❑ 19 Cal Ripken	3.00	1.25
❑ 20 Ivan Rodriguez	.60	.25
❑ 21 Rafael Palmeiro	.60	.25
❑ 22 Alex Rodriguez	1.50	.60
❑ 23 Manny Ramirez Sox	.60	.25
❑ 24 Pedro Martinez	.60	.25
❑ 25 Nomar Garciaparra	1.50	.60
❑ 26 Mike Sweeney	.40	.15
❑ 27 Jermaine Dye	.40	.15
❑ 28 Bobby Higginson	.40	.15
❑ 29 Dean Palmer	.40	.15
❑ 30 Matt Lawton	.40	.15
❑ 31 Eric Milton	.40	.15
❑ 32 Frank Thomas	1.00	.40
❑ 33 Magglio Ordonez	.40	.15
❑ 34 David Wells	.40	.15
❑ 35 Paul Konerko	.40	.15
❑ 36 Derek Jeter	2.50	1.00
❑ 37 Bernie Williams	.60	.25
❑ 38 Roger Clemens	2.00	.75
❑ 39 Mike Mussina	.60	.25
❑ 40 Jorge Posada	.60	.25
❑ 41 Jeff Bagwell	.60	.25
❑ 42 Richard Hidalgo	.40	.15
❑ 43 Craig Biggio	.60	.25
❑ 44 Greg Maddux	1.50	.60
❑ 45 Chipper Jones	1.00	.40
❑ 46 Andruw Jones	.60	.25
❑ 47 Rafael Furcal	.40	.15
❑ 48 Tom Glavine	.60	.25
❑ 49 Jeromy Burnitz	.40	.15
❑ 50 Jeffrey Hammonds	.40	.15
❑ 51 Mark McGwire	2.50	1.00
❑ 52 Jim Edmonds	.40	.15
❑ 53 Rick Ankiel	.40	.15
❑ 54 J.D. Drew	.40	.15
❑ 55 Sammy Sosa	1.00	.40
❑ 56 Corey Patterson	.40	.15
❑ 57 Kerry Wood	.40	.15
❑ 58 Randy Johnson	1.00	.40
❑ 59 Luis Gonzalez	.40	.15
❑ 60 Curt Schilling	.40	.15
❑ 61 Gary Sheffield	.40	.15
❑ 62 Shawn Green	.40	.15
❑ 63 Kevin Brown	.40	.15
❑ 64 Vladimir Guerrero	1.00	.40
❑ 65 Jose Vidro	.40	.15
❑ 66 Barry Bonds	2.50	1.00
❑ 67 Jeff Kent	.40	.15
❑ 68 Livan Hernandez	.40	.15
❑ 69 Preston Wilson	.40	.15
❑ 70 Charles Johnson	.40	.15
❑ 71 Ryan Dempster	.40	.15
❑ 72 Mike Piazza	1.50	.60
❑ 73 Al Leiter	.40	.15
❑ 74 Edgardo Alfonzo	.40	.15
❑ 75 Robin Ventura	.40	.15
❑ 76 Tony Gwynn	1.25	.50
❑ 77 Phil Nevin	.40	.15
❑ 78 Trevor Hoffman	.40	.15
❑ 79 Scott Rolen	.60	.25
❑ 80 Pat Burrell	.40	.15
❑ 81 Bob Abreu	.40	.15
❑ 82 Jason Kendall	.40	.15
❑ 83 Brian Giles	.40	.15
❑ 84 Kris Benson	.40	.15
❑ 85 Ken Griffey Jr.	1.50	.60
❑ 86 Barry Larkin	.60	.25
❑ 87 Sean Casey	.40	.15
❑ 88 Todd Helton	.60	.25
❑ 89 Mike Hampton	.40	.15
❑ 90 Larry Walker	.40	.15
❑ 91 Ichiro Suzuki FW RC	150.00	90.00
❑ 92 Wilson Betemit FW RC	15.00	6.00
❑ 93 Adrian Hernandez FW RC	8.00	3.00
❑ 94 Juan Uribe FW RC	10.00	4.00
❑ 95 Travis Hafner FW RC	60.00	30.00
❑ 96 Morgan Ensberg FW RC	15.00	6.00
❑ 97 Sean Douglass FW RC	8.00	3.00
❑ 98 Juan Diaz FW RC	8.00	3.00
❑ 99 Erick Almonte FW RC	8.00	3.00
❑ 100 Ryan Freel FW RC	8.00	3.00
❑ 101 Elpidio Guzman FW RC	8.00	3.00
❑ 102 Christian Parker FW RC	8.00	3.00
❑ 103 Josh Fogg FW RC	8.00	3.00
❑ 104 Bert Snow FW RC	8.00	3.00
❑ 105 Horacio Ramirez FW RC	10.00	4.00
❑ 106 Ricardo Rodriguez FW RC	8.00	3.00
❑ 107 Tyler Walker FW RC	8.00	3.00
❑ 108 Jose Mieses FW RC	8.00	3.00
❑ 109 Billy Sylvester FW RC	8.00	3.00
❑ 110 Martin Vargas FW RC	8.00	3.00
❑ 111 Andres Torres FW RC	8.00	3.00
❑ 112 Greg Miller FW RC	8.00	3.00
❑ 113 Alexis Gomez FW RC	8.00	3.00
❑ 114 Grant Balfour FW RC	8.00	3.00
❑ 115 Henry Mateo FW RC	8.00	3.00
❑ 116 Esix Snead FW RC	8.00	3.00
❑ 117 Jackson Melian FW RC	8.00	3.00
❑ 118 Nate Teut FW RC	8.00	3.00
❑ 119 Tsuyoshi Shinjo FW RC	10.00	4.00
❑ 120 Carlos Valderrama FW RC	8.00	3.00
❑ 121 Johnny Estrada FW RC	10.00	4.00
❑ 122 Jason Michaels FW RC	8.00	3.00
❑ 123 William Ortega FW RC	8.00	3.00
❑ 124 Jason Smith FW RC	8.00	3.00
❑ 125 Brian Lawrence FW RC	8.00	3.00
❑ 126 Albert Pujols FW RC	400.00	250.00
❑ 127 Wilkin Ruan FW RC	8.00	3.00
❑ 128 Josh Towers FW RC	10.00	4.00
❑ 129 Kris Keller FW RC	8.00	3.00
❑ 130 Nick Maness FW RC	8.00	3.00
❑ 131 Jack Wilson FW RC	10.00	4.00
❑ 132 Brandon Duckworth FW RC	8.00	3.00
❑ 133 Mike Penney FW RC	8.00	3.00
❑ 134 Jay Gibbons FW RC	10.00	4.00
❑ 135 Cesar Crespo FW RC	8.00	3.00
❑ 136 Ken Griffey Jr. SS	10.00	4.00
❑ 137 Mark McGwire SS	15.00	6.00
❑ 138 Derek Jeter SS	15.00	6.00
❑ 139 Alex Rodriguez SS	10.00	4.00
❑ 140 Sammy Sosa SS	6.00	2.50
❑ 141 Carlos Delgado SS	5.00	2.00
❑ 142 Cal Ripken SS	20.00	8.00
❑ 143 Pedro Martinez SS	5.00	2.00
❑ 144 Frank Thomas SS	6.00	2.50
❑ 145 Juan Gonzalez SS	5.00	2.00
❑ 146 Troy Glaus SS	5.00	2.00
❑ 147 Jason Giambi SS	5.00	2.00
❑ 148 Ivan Rodriguez SS	5.00	2.00
❑ 149 Chipper Jones SS	6.00	2.50
❑ 150 Vladimir Guerrero SS	6.00	2.50
❑ 151 Mike Piazza SS	10.00	4.00
❑ 152 Jeff Bagwell SS	5.00	2.00
❑ 153 Randy Johnson SS	6.00	2.50
❑ 154 Todd Helton SS	5.00	2.00
❑ 155 Gary Sheffield SS	5.00	2.00
❑ 156 Tony Gwynn SS	8.00	3.00
❑ 157 Barry Bonds SS	15.00	6.00
❑ 158 Nomar Garciaparra SS	10.00	4.00
❑ 159 Bernie Williams SS	5.00	2.00
❑ 160 Greg Vaughn SS	5.00	2.00
❑ 161 David Wells SS	5.00	2.00
❑ 162 Roberto Alomar SS	5.00	2.00
❑ 163 Jermaine Dye SS	5.00	2.00
❑ 164 Rafael Palmeiro SS	5.00	2.00
❑ 165 Andruw Jones SS	5.00	2.00
❑ 166 Preston Wilson SS	5.00	2.00
❑ 167 Edgardo Alfonzo SS	5.00	2.00
❑ 168 Pat Burrell SS	5.00	2.00
❑ 169 Jim Edmonds SS	5.00	2.00
❑ 170 Mike Hampton SS	5.00	2.00
❑ 171 Jeff Kent SS	5.00	2.00
❑ 172 Kevin Brown SS	5.00	2.00
❑ 173 Manny Ramirez Sox SS	5.00	2.00
❑ 174 Magglio Ordonez SS	5.00	2.00
❑ 175 Roger Clemens SS	12.00	5.00
❑ 176 Jim Thome SS	5.00	2.00
❑ 177 Barry Zito SS	5.00	2.00
❑ 178 Brian Giles SS	5.00	2.00
❑ 179 Rick Ankiel SS	5.00	2.00
❑ 180 Corey Patterson SS	5.00	2.00
❑ 181 Garret Anderson	.60	.25
❑ 182 Jermaine Dye	.60	.25
❑ 183 Shannon Stewart	.60	.25
❑ 184 Ben Grieve	.60	.25
❑ 185 Ellis Burks	.60	.25
❑ 186 John Olerud	.60	.25
❑ 187 Tony Batista	.60	.25
❑ 188 Ruben Sierra	.60	.25
❑ 189 Carl Everett	.60	.25
❑ 190 Neifi Perez	.60	.25
❑ 191 Tony Clark	.60	.25
❑ 192 Doug Mientkiewicz	.60	.25
❑ 193 Carlos Lee	.60	.25
❑ 194 Jorge Posada	1.00	.40
❑ 195 Lance Berkman	5.00	2.00
❑ 196 Ken Caminiti	.60	.25
❑ 197 Ben Sheets	1.00	.40
❑ 198 Matt Morris	.60	.25
❑ 199 Fred McGriff	1.00	.40
❑ 200 Mark Grace	1.00	.40
❑ 201 Paul LoDuca	.60	.25
❑ 202 Tony Armas Jr.	.60	.25
❑ 203 Andres Galarraga	.60	.25
❑ 204 Cliff Floyd	.60	.25
❑ 205 Matt Lawton	.60	.25
❑ 206 Ryan Klesko	.60	.25
❑ 207 Jimmy Rollins	.60	.25
❑ 208 Aramis Ramirez	.60	.25
❑ 209 Aaron Boone	.60	.25
❑ 210 Jose Ortiz	.60	.25
❑ 211 Mark Prior FW RC	40.00	15.00
❑ 212 Mark Teixeira FW RC	80.00	40.00
❑ 213 Bud Smith FW RC	6.00	2.50
❑ 214 Wilmy Caceres FW RC	6.00	2.50
❑ 215 Dave Williams FW RC	6.00	2.50
❑ 216 Delvin James FW RC	6.00	2.50
❑ 217 Endy Chavez FW RC	6.00	2.50
❑ 218 Doug Nickle FW RC	6.00	2.50
❑ 219 Bret Prinz FW RC	6.00	2.50
❑ 220 Troy Mattes FW RC	6.00	2.50
❑ 221 Duaner Sanchez FW RC	6.00	2.50
❑ 222 Dewon Brazelton FW RC	6.00	2.50
❑ 223 Brian Bowles FW RC	6.00	2.50
❑ 224 Donaldo Mendez FW RC	6.00	2.50
❑ 225 Jorge Julio FW RC	6.00	2.50
❑ 226 Matt White FW RC	6.00	2.50
❑ 227 Casey Fossum FW RC	6.00	2.50
❑ 228 Mike Rivera FW RC	6.00	2.50
❑ 229 Joe Kennedy FW RC	8.00	3.00
❑ 230 Kyle Lohse FW RC	8.00	3.00
❑ 231 Juan Cruz FW RC	6.00	2.50
❑ 232 Jeremy Affeldt FW RC	6.00	2.50
❑ 233 Brandon Lyon FW RC	6.00	2.50
❑ 234 Brian Roberts FW RC	20.00	8.00
❑ 235 Willie Harris FW RC	6.00	2.50
❑ 236 Pedro Santana FW RC	6.00	2.50
❑ 237 Rafael Soriano FW RC	6.00	2.50
❑ 238 Steve Green FW RC	6.00	2.50

- ❑ 239 Junior Spivey FW RC 8.00 3.00
- ❑ 240 Rob Mackowiak FW RC 8.00 3.00
- ❑ NNO Ken Griffey Jr. Promo 2.00 .75

2002 SP Authentic

- ❑ COMP.LOW w/o SP's (90) 15.00 6.00
- ❑ COMP.UPDATE w/o SP's (30) 10.00 4.00
- ❑ COMMON CARD (1-90) .40 .15
- ❑ COMMON (91-135/201-230) 5.00 2.00
- ❑ COMMON CARD (136-170) 10.00 4.00
- ❑ COMMON CARD (171-200) .60 .25
- ❑ 1 Troy Glaus .40 .15
- ❑ 2 Darin Erstad .40 .15
- ❑ 3 Barry Zito .40 .15
- ❑ 4 Eric Chavez .40 .15
- ❑ 5 Tim Hudson .40 .15
- ❑ 6 Miguel Tejada .40 .15
- ❑ 7 Carlos Delgado .40 .15
- ❑ 8 Shannon Stewart .40 .15
- ❑ 9 Ben Grieve .40 .15
- ❑ 10 Jim Thome .60 .25
- ❑ 11 C.C. Sabathia .40 .15
- ❑ 12 Ichiro Suzuki 2.00 .75
- ❑ 13 Freddy Garcia .40 .15
- ❑ 14 Edgar Martinez .60 .25
- ❑ 15 Bret Boone .40 .15
- ❑ 16 Jeff Conine .40 .15
- ❑ 17 Alex Rodriguez 1.50 .60
- ❑ 18 Juan Gonzalez .40 .15
- ❑ 19 Ivan Rodriguez .60 .25
- ❑ 20 Rafael Palmeiro .60 .25
- ❑ 21 Hank Blalock .60 .25
- ❑ 22 Pedro Martinez .60 .25
- ❑ 23 Manny Ramirez .60 .25
- ❑ 24 Nomar Garciaparra 1.50 .60
- ❑ 25 Carlos Beltran .40 .15
- ❑ 26 Mike Sweeney .40 .15
- ❑ 27 Randall Simon .40 .15
- ❑ 28 Dmitri Young .40 .15
- ❑ 29 Bobby Higginson .40 .15
- ❑ 30 Corey Koskie .40 .15
- ❑ 31 Eric Milton .40 .15
- ❑ 32 Torii Hunter .40 .15
- ❑ 33 Joe Mays .40 .15
- ❑ 34 Frank Thomas 1.00 .40
- ❑ 35 Mark Buehrle .40 .15
- ❑ 36 Magglio Ordonez .40 .15
- ❑ 37 Kenny Lofton .40 .15
- ❑ 38 Roger Clemens 2.00 .75
- ❑ 39 Derek Jeter 2.50 1.00
- ❑ 40 Jason Giambi .40 .15
- ❑ 41 Bernie Williams .60 .25
- ❑ 42 Alfonso Soriano .40 .15
- ❑ 43 Lance Berkman .40 .15
- ❑ 44 Roy Oswalt .40 .15
- ❑ 45 Jeff Bagwell .60 .25
- ❑ 46 Craig Biggio .60 .25
- ❑ 47 Chipper Jones 1.00 .40
- ❑ 48 Greg Maddux 1.50 .60
- ❑ 49 Gary Sheffield .40 .15
- ❑ 50 Andruw Jones .60 .25
- ❑ 51 Ben Sheets .40 .15
- ❑ 52 Richie Sexson .40 .15
- ❑ 53 Albert Pujols 2.00 .75
- ❑ 54 Matt Morris .40 .15
- ❑ 55 J.D. Drew .40 .15
- ❑ 56 Sammy Sosa 1.00 .40
- ❑ 57 Kerry Wood .40 .15
- ❑ 58 Corey Patterson .40 .15
- ❑ 59 Mark Prior .60 .25
- ❑ 60 Randy Johnson 1.00 .40
- ❑ 61 Luis Gonzalez .40 .15
- ❑ 62 Curt Schilling .40 .15
- ❑ 63 Shawn Green .40 .15
- ❑ 64 Kevin Brown .40 .15
- ❑ 65 Hideo Nomo 1.00 .40
- ❑ 66 Vladimir Guerrero 1.00 .40
- ❑ 67 Jose Vidro .40 .15
- ❑ 68 Barry Bonds 2.50 1.00
- ❑ 69 Jeff Kent .40 .15
- ❑ 70 Rich Aurilia .40 .15
- ❑ 71 Preston Wilson .40 .15
- ❑ 72 Josh Beckett .40 .15
- ❑ 73 Mike Lowell .40 .15
- ❑ 74 Roberto Alomar .60 .25
- ❑ 75 Mo Vaughn .40 .15
- ❑ 76 Jeromy Burnitz .40 .15
- ❑ 77 Mike Piazza 1.50 .60
- ❑ 78 Sean Burroughs .40 .15
- ❑ 79 Phil Nevin .40 .15
- ❑ 80 Bobby Abreu .40 .15
- ❑ 81 Pat Burrell .40 .15
- ❑ 82 Scott Rolen .60 .25
- ❑ 83 Jason Kendall .40 .15
- ❑ 84 Brian Giles .40 .15
- ❑ 85 Ken Griffey Jr. 1.50 .60
- ❑ 86 Adam Dunn .40 .15
- ❑ 87 Sean Casey .40 .15
- ❑ 88 Todd Helton .60 .25
- ❑ 89 Larry Walker .40 .15
- ❑ 90 Mike Hampton .40 .15
- ❑ 91 Brandon Puffer FW RC 5.00 2.00
- ❑ 92 Tom Shearn FW RC 5.00 2.00
- ❑ 93 Chris Baker FW RC 5.00 2.00
- ❑ 94 Gustavo Chacin FW RC 8.00 3.00
- ❑ 95 Joe Orloski FW RC 5.00 2.00
- ❑ 96 Mike Smith FW RC 5.00 2.00
- ❑ 97 John Ennis FW RC 5.00 2.00
- ❑ 98 John Foster FW RC 5.00 2.00
- ❑ 99 Kevin Gryboski FW RC 5.00 2.00
- ❑ 100 Brian Mallette FW RC 5.00 2.00
- ❑ 101 Takahito Nomura FW RC 5.00 2.00
- ❑ 102 So Taguchi FW RC 8.00 3.00
- ❑ 103 Jeremy Lambert FW RC 5.00 2.00
- ❑ 104 Jason Simontacchi FW RC 5.00 2.00
- ❑ 105 Jorge Sosa FW RC 8.00 3.00
- ❑ 106 Brandon Backe FW RC 8.00 3.00
- ❑ 107 P.J. Bevis FW RC 5.00 2.00
- ❑ 108 Jeremy Ward FW RC 5.00 2.00
- ❑ 109 Doug Devore FW RC 5.00 2.00
- ❑ 110 Ron Chiavacci FW 5.00 2.00
- ❑ 111 Ron Calloway FW RC 5.00 2.00
- ❑ 112 Nelson Castro FW RC 5.00 2.00
- ❑ 113 Deivis Santos FW 5.00 2.00
- ❑ 114 Earl Snyder FW RC 5.00 2.00
- ❑ 115 Julio Mateo FW RC 5.00 2.00
- ❑ 116 J.J. Putz FW RC 5.00 2.00
- ❑ 117 Allan Simpson FW RC 5.00 2.00
- ❑ 118 Satoru Komiyama FW RC 5.00 2.00
- ❑ 119 Adam Walker FW RC 5.00 2.00
- ❑ 120 Oliver Perez FW RC 8.00 3.00
- ❑ 121 Cliff Bartosh FW RC 5.00 2.00
- ❑ 122 Todd Donovan FW RC 5.00 2.00
- ❑ 123 Elio Serrano FW RC 5.00 2.00
- ❑ 124 Pete Zamora FW RC 5.00 2.00
- ❑ 125 Mike Gonzalez FW RC 5.00 2.00
- ❑ 126 Travis Hughes FW RC 5.00 2.00
- ❑ 127 Jorge De La Rosa FW RC 5.00 2.00
- ❑ 128 Anastacio Martinez FW RC 5.00 2.00
- ❑ 129 Colin Young FW RC 5.00 2.00
- ❑ 130 Nate Field FW RC 5.00 2.00
- ❑ 131 Tim Kalita FW RC 5.00 2.00
- ❑ 132 Julius Matos FW RC 5.00 2.00
- ❑ 133 Terry Pearson FW RC 5.00 2.00
- ❑ 134 Kyle Kane FW RC 5.00 2.00
- ❑ 135 Mitch Wylie FW RC 5.00 2.00
- ❑ 136 Rodrigo Rosario AU RC 10.00 4.00
- ❑ 137 Franklyn German AU RC 10.00 4.00
- ❑ 138 Reed Johnson AU RC 20.00 8.00
- ❑ 139 Luis Martinez AU RC 10.00 4.00
- ❑ 140 Michael Crudale AU RC 10.00 4.00
- ❑ 141 Francis Beltran AU RC 10.00 4.00
- ❑ 142 Steve Kent AU RC 10.00 4.00
- ❑ 143 Felix Escalona AU RC 10.00 4.00
- ❑ 144 Jose Valverde AU RC 10.00 4.00
- ❑ 145 Victor Alvarez AU RC 10.00 4.00
- ❑ 146 Kazuhisa Ishii AU/249 RC 40.00 15.00
- ❑ 147 Jorge Nunez AU RC 10.00 4.00
- ❑ 148 Eric Good AU RC 10.00 4.00
- ❑ 149 Luis Ugueto AU RC 10.00 4.00
- ❑ 150 Matt Thornton AU RC 10.00 4.00
- ❑ 151 Wilson Valdez AU RC 10.00 4.00
- ❑ 152 Han Izquierdo AU/249 RC 40.00 15.00
- ❑ 153 Jaime Cerda AU RC 10.00 4.00
- ❑ 154 Mark Corey AU RC 10.00 4.00
- ❑ 155 Tyler Yates AU RC 10.00 4.00
- ❑ 156 Steve Bechler AU RC 10.00 4.00
- ❑ 157 Ben Howard AU/249 RC 40.00 15.00
- ❑ 158 Anderson Machado AU RC 10.00 4.00
- ❑ 159 Jorge Padilla AU RC 10.00 4.00
- ❑ 160 Eric Junge AU RC 10.00 4.00
- ❑ 161 Adrian Burnside AU RC 10.00 4.00
- ❑ 162 Josh Hancock AU RC 20.00 8.00
- ❑ 163 Chris Booker AU RC 10.00 4.00
- ❑ 164 Cam Esslinger AU RC 10.00 4.00
- ❑ 165 Rene Reyes AU RC 10.00 4.00
- ❑ 166 Aaron Cook AU RC 10.00 4.00
- ❑ 167 Juan Brito AU RC 10.00 4.00
- ❑ 168 Miguel Ascencio AU RC 10.00 4.00
- ❑ 169 Kevin Frederick AU RC 10.00 4.00
- ❑ 170 Edwin Almonte AU RC 10.00 4.00
- ❑ 171 Erubiel Durazo .60 .25
- ❑ 172 Junior Spivey .60 .25
- ❑ 173 Geronimo Gil .60 .25
- ❑ 174 Cliff Floyd .60 .25
- ❑ 175 Brandon Larson .60 .25
- ❑ 176 Aaron Boone .60 .25
- ❑ 177 Shawn Estes .60 .25
- ❑ 178 Austin Kearns .60 .25
- ❑ 179 Joe Borchard .60 .25
- ❑ 180 Russell Branyan .60 .25
- ❑ 181 Jay Payton .60 .25
- ❑ 182 Andres Torres .60 .25
- ❑ 183 Andy Van Hekken .60 .25
- ❑ 184 Alex Sanchez .60 .25
- ❑ 185 Endy Chavez .60 .25
- ❑ 186 Bartolo Colon .60 .25
- ❑ 187 Raul Mondesi .60 .25
- ❑ 188 Robin Ventura .60 .25
- ❑ 189 Mike Mussina 1.00 .40
- ❑ 190 Jorge Posada 1.00 .40
- ❑ 191 Ted Lilly .60 .25
- ❑ 192 Ray Durham .60 .25
- ❑ 193 Brett Myers .60 .25
- ❑ 194 Marlon Byrd .60 .25
- ❑ 195 Vicente Padilla .60 .25
- ❑ 196 Josh Fogg .60 .25
- ❑ 197 Kenny Lofton .60 .25
- ❑ 198 Scott Rolen 1.00 .40
- ❑ 199 Jason Lane .60 .25
- ❑ 200 Josh Phelps .60 .25
- ❑ 201 Travis Driskill FW RC 5.00 2.00
- ❑ 202 Howie Clark FW RC 5.00 2.00
- ❑ 203 Mike Mahoney FW 5.00 2.00
- ❑ 204 Brian Tallet FW RC 5.00 2.00
- ❑ 205 Kirk Saarloos FW RC 5.00 2.00
- ❑ 206 Barry Wesson FW RC 5.00 2.00
- ❑ 207 Aaron Guiel FW RC 5.00 2.00
- ❑ 208 Shawn Sedlacek FW RC 5.00 2.00
- ❑ 209 Jose Diaz FW RC 5.00 2.00
- ❑ 210 Jorge Nunez FW 5.00 2.00
- ❑ 211 Danny Mota FW RC 5.00 2.00
- ❑ 212 David Ross FW RC 8.00 3.00
- ❑ 213 Jayson Durocher FW RC 5.00 2.00
- ❑ 214 Shane Nance FW RC 5.00 2.00
- ❑ 215 Wil Nieves FW RC 5.00 2.00
- ❑ 216 Freddy Sanchez FW RC 10.00 4.00
- ❑ 217 Alex Pelaez FW RC 5.00 2.00
- ❑ 218 Jamey Carroll FW RC 8.00 3.00
- ❑ 219 J.J. Trujillo FW RC 5.00 2.00
- ❑ 220 Kevin Pickford FW RC 5.00 2.00
- ❑ 221 Clay Condrey FW RC 5.00 2.00
- ❑ 222 Chris Snelling FW RC 6.00 2.50
- ❑ 223 Cliff Lee FW RC 8.00 3.00
- ❑ 224 Jeremy Hill FW RC 5.00 2.00
- ❑ 225 Jose Rodriguez FW RC 5.00 2.00
- ❑ 226 Lance Carter FW RC 5.00 2.00
- ❑ 227 Ken Huckaby FW RC 5.00 2.00
- ❑ 228 Scott Wiggins FW RC 5.00 2.00
- ❑ 229 Corey Thurman FW RC 5.00 2.00

❑ 230 Kevin Cash FW RC 5.00 2.00
❑ RJ-D Joe DiMaggio AU Poster 200.00 125.00

2003 SP Authentic

❑ COMP.LO SET w/o SP's (90) 15.00 6.00
❑ COMMON CARD (1-90) .40 .15
❑ COMMON CARD (91-123) 3.00 1.25
❑ COMMON CARD (124-150) 3.00 1.25
❑ COMMON CARD (151-180) 5.00 2.00
❑ COMMON CARD (181-189) 15.00 6.00
❑ 91-189 RANDOM INSERTS IN PACKS
❑ COMMON CARD (190-239) 5.00 2.00
❑ 190-239 RANDOM IN 03 UD FINITE PACKS
❑ 190-239 PRINT RUN 699 SERIAL #'d SETS
❑ 1 Darin Erstad .40 .15
❑ 2 Garret Anderson .40 .15
❑ 3 Troy Glaus .40 .15
❑ 4 Eric Chavez .40 .15
❑ 5 Barry Zito .40 .15
❑ 6 Miguel Tejada .40 .15
❑ 7 Eric Hinske .40 .15
❑ 8 Carlos Delgado .40 .15
❑ 9 Josh Phelps .40 .15
❑ 10 Ben Grieve .40 .15
❑ 11 Carl Crawford .40 .15
❑ 12 Omar Vizquel .60 .25
❑ 13 Matt Lawton .40 .15
❑ 14 C.C. Sabathia .40 .15
❑ 15 Ichiro Suzuki 2.00 .75
❑ 16 John Olerud .40 .15
❑ 17 Freddy Garcia .40 .15
❑ 18 Jay Gibbons .40 .15
❑ 19 Tony Batista .40 .15
❑ 20 Melvin Mora .40 .15
❑ 21 Alex Rodriguez 1.50 .60
❑ 22 Rafael Palmeiro .60 .25
❑ 23 Hank Blalock .40 .15
❑ 24 Nomar Garciaparra 1.50 .60
❑ 25 Pedro Martinez .60 .25
❑ 26 Johnny Damon .60 .25
❑ 27 Mike Sweeney .40 .15
❑ 28 Carlos Febles .40 .15
❑ 29 Carlos Beltran .40 .15
❑ 30 Carlos Pena .40 .15
❑ 31 Eric Munson .40 .15
❑ 32 Bobby Higginson .40 .15
❑ 33 Torii Hunter .40 .15
❑ 34 Doug Mientkiewicz .40 .15
❑ 35 Jacque Jones .40 .15
❑ 36 Paul Konerko .40 .15
❑ 37 Bartolo Colon .40 .15
❑ 38 Magglio Ordonez .40 .15
❑ 39 Derek Jeter 2.50 1.00
❑ 40 Bernie Williams .60 .25
❑ 41 Jason Giambi .40 .15
❑ 42 Alfonso Soriano .40 .15
❑ 43 Roger Clemens 2.00 .75
❑ 44 Jeff Bagwell .60 .25
❑ 45 Jeff Kent .40 .15
❑ 46 Lance Berkman .40 .15
❑ 47 Chipper Jones 1.00 .40
❑ 48 Andruw Jones .60 .25
❑ 49 Gary Sheffield .40 .15
❑ 50 Ben Sheets .40 .15
❑ 51 Richie Sexson .40 .15
❑ 52 Geoff Jenkins .40 .15
❑ 53 Jim Edmonds .40 .15
❑ 54 Albert Pujols 2.00 .75
❑ 55 Scott Rolen .60 .25
❑ 56 Sammy Sosa 1.00 .40
❑ 57 Kerry Wood .40 .15
❑ 58 Eric Karros .40 .15
❑ 59 Luis Gonzalez .40 .15
❑ 60 Randy Johnson 1.00 .40
❑ 61 Curt Schilling .40 .15
❑ 62 Fred McGriff .60 .25
❑ 63 Shawn Green .40 .15
❑ 64 Paul Lo Duca .40 .15
❑ 65 Vladimir Guerrero 1.00 .40
❑ 66 Jose Vidro .40 .15
❑ 67 Barry Bonds 2.50 1.00
❑ 68 Rich Aurilia .40 .15
❑ 69 Edgardo Alfonzo .40 .15
❑ 70 Ivan Rodriguez .60 .25
❑ 71 Mike Lowell .40 .15
❑ 72 Derrek Lee .60 .25
❑ 73 Tom Glavine .60 .25
❑ 74 Mike Piazza 1.50 .60
❑ 75 Roberto Alomar .60 .25
❑ 76 Ryan Klesko .40 .15
❑ 77 Phil Nevin .40 .15
❑ 78 Mark Kotsay .40 .15
❑ 79 Jim Thome .60 .25
❑ 80 Pat Burrell .40 .15
❑ 81 Bobby Abreu .40 .15
❑ 82 Jason Kendall .40 .15
❑ 83 Brian Giles .40 .15
❑ 84 Aramis Ramirez .40 .15
❑ 85 Austin Kearns .40 .15
❑ 86 Ken Griffey Jr. 1.50 .60
❑ 87 Adam Dunn .40 .15
❑ 88 Larry Walker .40 .15
❑ 89 Todd Helton .60 .25
❑ 90 Preston Wilson .40 .15
❑ 91 Derek Jeter RA 8.00 3.00
❑ 92 Johnny Damon RA 3.00 1.25
❑ 93 Chipper Jones RA 3.00 1.25
❑ 94 Manny Ramirez RA 3.00 1.25
❑ 95 Trot Nixon RA 3.00 1.25
❑ 96 Alex Rodriguez RA 5.00 2.00
❑ 97 Chan Ho Park RA 3.00 1.25
❑ 98 Brad Fullmer RA 3.00 1.25
❑ 99 Billy Wagner RA 3.00 1.25
❑ 100 Hideo Nomo RA 3.00 1.25
❑ 101 Freddy Garcia RA 3.00 1.25
❑ 102 Darin Erstad RA 3.00 1.25
❑ 103 Jose Cruz Jr. RA 3.00 1.25
❑ 104 Nomar Garciaparra RA 5.00 2.00
❑ 105 Magglio Ordonez RA 3.00 1.25
❑ 106 Kerry Wood RA 3.00 1.25
❑ 107 Troy Glaus RA 3.00 1.25
❑ 108 J.D. Drew RA 3.00 1.25
❑ 109 Alfonso Soriano RA 3.00 1.25
❑ 110 Danys Baez RA 3.00 1.25
❑ 111 Kazuhiro Sasaki RA 3.00 1.25
❑ 112 Barry Zito RA 3.00 1.25
❑ 113 Brent Abernathy RA 3.00 1.25
❑ 114 Ben Diggins RA 3.00 1.25
❑ 115 Ben Sheets RA 3.00 1.25
❑ 116 Brad Wilkerson RA 3.00 1.25
❑ 117 Juan Pierre RA 3.00 1.25
❑ 118 Jon Rauch RA 3.00 1.25
❑ 119 Ichiro Suzuki RA 6.00 2.50
❑ 120 Albert Pujols RA 6.00 2.50
❑ 121 Mark Prior RA 3.00 1.25
❑ 122 Mark Teixeira RA 3.00 1.25
❑ 123 Kazuhisa Ishii RA 3.00 1.25
❑ 124 Troy Glaus B93 3.00 1.25
❑ 125 Randy Johnson B93 3.00 1.25
❑ 126 Curt Schilling B93 3.00 1.25
❑ 127 Chipper Jones B93 3.00 1.25
❑ 128 Greg Maddux B93 5.00 2.00
❑ 129 Nomar Garciaparra B93 5.00 2.00
❑ 130 Pedro Martinez B93 3.00 1.25
❑ 131 Sammy Sosa B93 3.00 1.25
❑ 132 Mark Prior B93 3.00 1.25
❑ 133 Ken Griffey Jr. B93 5.00 2.00
❑ 134 Adam Dunn B93 3.00 1.25
❑ 135 Jeff Bagwell B93 3.00 1.25
❑ 136 Vladimir Guerrero B93 3.00 1.25
❑ 137 Mike Piazza B93 5.00 2.00
❑ 138 Tom Glavine B93 3.00 1.25
❑ 139 Derek Jeter B93 8.00 3.00
❑ 140 Roger Clemens B93 6.00 2.50
❑ 141 Jason Giambi B93 3.00 1.25
❑ 142 Alfonso Soriano B93 3.00 1.25
❑ 143 Miguel Tejada B93 3.00 1.25
❑ 144 Barry Zito B93 3.00 1.25
❑ 145 Jim Thome B93 3.00 1.25
❑ 146 Barry Bonds B93 8.00 3.00
❑ 147 Ichiro Suzuki B93 6.00 2.50
❑ 148 Albert Pujols B93 6.00 2.50
❑ 149 Alex Rodriguez B93 5.00 2.00
❑ 150 Carlos Delgado B93 3.00 1.25
❑ 151 Rich Fischer FW RC 5.00 2.00
❑ 152 Brandon Webb FW RC 12.00 5.00
❑ 153 Rob Hammock FW RC 5.00 2.00
❑ 154 Matt Kata FW RC 5.00 2.00
❑ 155 Tim Olson FW RC 5.00 2.00
❑ 156 Oscar Villarreal FW RC 5.00 2.00
❑ 157 Michael Hessman FW RC 5.00 2.00
❑ 158 Daniel Cabrera FW RC 8.00 3.00
❑ 159 Jon Leicester FW RC 5.00 2.00
❑ 160 Todd Wellemeyer FW RC 5.00 2.00
❑ 161 Felix Sanchez FW RC 5.00 2.00
❑ 162 David Sanders FW RC 5.00 2.00
❑ 163 Josh Stewart FW RC 5.00 2.00
❑ 164 Arnie Munoz FW RC 5.00 2.00
❑ 165 Ryan Cameron FW RC 5.00 2.00
❑ 166 Clint Barmes FW RC 5.00 2.00
❑ 167 Josh Willingham FW RC 10.00 4.00
❑ 169 Willie Eyre FW RC 5.00 2.00
❑ 170 Brent Hoard FW RC 5.00 2.00
❑ 171 Termel Sledge FW RC 5.00 2.00
❑ 172 Phil Seibel FW RC 5.00 2.00
❑ 173 Craig Brazell FW RC 5.00 2.00
❑ 174 Jeff Duncan FW RC 5.00 2.00
❑ 176 Bernie Castro FW RC 5.00 2.00
❑ 177 Mike Nicolas FW RC 5.00 2.00
❑ 178 Rett Johnson FW RC 5.00 2.00
❑ 179 Bobby Madritsch FW RC 5.00 2.00
❑ 180 Chris Capuano FW RC 25.00 10.00
❑ 181 Hid Matsui FW AU RC 300.00 175.00
❑ 182 Jose Contreras FW AU RC 30.0012.50
❑ 183 Lew Ford FW AU RC 25.00 10.00
❑ 184 Jeremy Griffiths FW AU RC 15.00 6.00
❑ 185 G.Quiroz FW AU RC 15.00 6.00
❑ 186 Alej Machado FW AU RC 15.00 6.00
❑ 187 Fran Cruceta FW AU RC 15.00 6.00
❑ 188 Prentice Redman FW AU RC 15.006.00
❑ 189 Shane Bazzell FW AU RC 15.00 6.00
❑ 190 Aaron Looper FW RC 5.00 2.00
❑ 191 Alex Prieto FW RC 5.00 2.00
❑ 192 Alfredo Gonzalez FW RC 5.00 2.00
❑ 193 Andrew Brown FW RC 8.00 3.00
❑ 194 Anthony Ferrari FW RC 5.00 2.00
❑ 195 Aquilino Lopez FW RC 5.00 2.00
❑ 196 Beau Kemp FW RC 5.00 2.00
❑ 197 Bo Hart FW RC 5.00 2.00
❑ 198 Chad Gaudin FW RC 5.00 2.00
❑ 199 Colin Porter FW RC 5.00 2.00
❑ 200 D.J. Carrasco FW RC 5.00 2.00
❑ 201 Dan Haren FW RC 8.00 3.00
❑ 202 Danny Garcia FW RC 5.00 2.00
❑ 203 Jon Switzer FW 5.00 2.00
❑ 204 Edwin Jackson FW RC 8.00 3.00
❑ 205 Fernando Cabrera FW RC 5.00 2.00
❑ 206 Garrett Atkins FW 5.00 2.00
❑ 207 Gerald Laird FW 5.00 2.00
❑ 208 Greg Jones FW RC 5.00 2.00
❑ 209 Ian Ferguson FW RC 5.00 2.00
❑ 210 Jason Roach FW RC 5.00 2.00
❑ 211 Jason Shiell FW RC 5.00 2.00
❑ 212 Jeremy Bonderman FW RC 25.0010.00
❑ 213 Jeremy Wedel FW RC 5.00 2.00
❑ 214 Jhonny Peralta FW 8.00 3.00
❑ 215 Delmon Young FW RC 50.00 25.00
❑ 216 Jorge DePaula FW 5.00 2.00
❑ 217 Josh Hall FW RC 5.00 2.00
❑ 218 Julio Manon FW RC 5.00 2.00
❑ 219 Kevin Correia FW RC 5.00 2.00
❑ 220 Kevin Ohme FW RC 5.00 2.00
❑ 221 Kevin Tolar FW RC 5.00 2.00
❑ 222 Luis Ayala FW RC 5.00 2.00
❑ 223 Luis De Los Santos FW 5.00 2.00
❑ 224 Chad Cordero FW RC 10.00 4.00
❑ 225 Mark Malaska FW RC 5.00 2.00
❑ 226 Khalil Greene FW 8.00 3.00
❑ 227 Michael Nakamura FW RC 5.00 2.00
❑ 228 Michel Hernandez FW RC 5.00 2.00

❑ 229 Miguel Ojeda FW RC 5.00 2.00
❑ 230 Mike Neu FW RC 5.00 2.00
❑ 231 Nate Bland FW RC 5.00 2.00
❑ 232 Pete LaForest FW RC 5.00 2.00
❑ 233 Rickie Weeks FW RC 20.00 8.00
❑ 234 Rosman Garcia FW RC 5.00 2.00
❑ 235 Ryan Wagner FW RC 5.00 2.00
❑ 236 Lance Niekro FW 5.00 2.00
❑ 237 Tom Gregorio FW RC 5.00 2.00
❑ 238 Tommy Phelps FW 5.00 2.00
❑ 239 Wilfredo Ledezma FW RC 5.00 2.00

2004 SP Authentic

❑ COMP.SET w/o SP's (90) 15.00 6.00
❑ COMMON CARD (1-90) .40 .15
❑ COMMON (91-132/178-191) 5.00 2.00
❑ 91-132/178-191 OVERALL FW ODDS 1:24
❑ 91-132/178-179/181-191 PRINT 704 #'d SETS
❑ 91-132/178-179/181-191 #'d FROM 296-999
❑ CARD 180 PRINT RUN 999 #'d COPIES
❑ CARD 180 #'d FROM 1-999
❑ COMMON CARD (133-177) 3.00 1.25
❑ 133-177 STATED ODDS 1:24
❑ 133-177 PRINT RUN 999 SERIAL #'d SETS
❑ 1 Bret Boone .40 .15
❑ 2 Gary Sheffield .40 .15
❑ 3 Rafael Palmeiro .60 .25
❑ 4 Jorge Posada .60 .25
❑ 5 Derek Jeter 2.00 .75
❑ 6 Garret Anderson .40 .15
❑ 7 Bartolo Colon .40 .15
❑ 8 Kevin Brown .40 .15
❑ 9 Shea Hillenbrand .40 .15
❑ 10 Ryan Klesko .40 .15
❑ 11 Bobby Abreu .40 .15
❑ 12 Scott Rolen .60 .25
❑ 13 Alfonso Soriano .40 .15
❑ 14 Jason Giambi .40 .15
❑ 15 Tom Glavine .60 .25
❑ 16 Hideo Nomo 1.00 .40
❑ 17 Johan Santana 1.00 .40
❑ 18 Sammy Sosa 1.00 .40
❑ 19 Rickie Weeks .40 .15
❑ 20 Barry Zito .40 .15
❑ 21 Kerry Wood .40 .15
❑ 22 Austin Kearns .40 .15
❑ 23 Shawn Green .40 .15
❑ 24 Miguel Cabrera .60 .25
❑ 25 Richard Hidalgo .40 .15
❑ 26 Andruw Jones .60 .25
❑ 27 Randy Wolf .40 .15
❑ 28 David Ortiz 1.00 .40
❑ 29 Roy Oswalt .40 .15
❑ 30 Vernon Wells .40 .15
❑ 31 Ben Sheets .40 .15
❑ 32 Mike Lowell .40 .15
❑ 33 Todd Helton .60 .25
❑ 34 Jacque Jones .40 .15
❑ 35 Mike Sweeney .40 .15
❑ 36 Hank Blalock .40 .15
❑ 37 Jason Schmidt .40 .15
❑ 38 Jeff Kent .40 .15
❑ 39 Josh Beckett .40 .15
❑ 40 Manny Ramirez .60 .25
❑ 41 Torii Hunter .40 .15
❑ 42 Brian Giles .40 .15
❑ 43 Javier Vazquez .40 .15
❑ 44 Jim Edmonds .40 .15
❑ 45 Dmitri Young .40 .15
❑ 46 Preston Wilson .40 .15
❑ 47 Jeff Bagwell .60 .25
❑ 48 Pedro Martinez .60 .25
❑ 49 Eric Chavez .40 .15
❑ 50 Ken Griffey Jr. 1.50 .60
❑ 51 Shannon Stewart .40 .15
❑ 52 Rafael Furcal .40 .15
❑ 53 Brandon Webb .40 .15
❑ 54 Juan Pierre .40 .15
❑ 55 Roger Clemens 2.00 .75
❑ 56 Geoff Jenkins .40 .15
❑ 57 Lance Berkman .40 .15
❑ 58 Albert Pujols 2.00 .75
❑ 59 Frank Thomas 1.00 .40
❑ 60 Edgar Martinez .60 .25
❑ 61 Tim Hudson .40 .15
❑ 62 Eric Gagne .40 .15
❑ 63 Richie Sexson .40 .15
❑ 64 Corey Patterson .40 .15
❑ 65 Nomar Garciaparra 1.50 .60
❑ 66 Hideki Matsui 1.50 .60
❑ 67 Mark Teixeira .60 .25
❑ 68 Troy Glaus .40 .15
❑ 69 Carlos Lee .40 .15
❑ 70 Mike Mussina .60 .25
❑ 71 Maggio Ordonez .40 .15
❑ 72 Roy Halladay .40 .15
❑ 73 Ichiro Suzuki 2.00 .75
❑ 74 Randy Johnson 1.00 .40
❑ 75 Luis Gonzalez .40 .15
❑ 76 Mark Prior .60 .25
❑ 77 Carlos Beltran .40 .15
❑ 78 Ivan Rodriguez .60 .25
❑ 79 Alex Rodriguez 1.50 .60
❑ 80 Dontrelle Willis .60 .25
❑ 81 Mike Piazza 1.50 .60
❑ 82 Curt Schilling .60 .25
❑ 83 Vladimir Guerrero 1.00 .40
❑ 84 Greg Maddux 1.50 .60
❑ 85 Jim Thome .60 .25
❑ 86 Miguel Tejada .40 .15
❑ 87 Carlos Delgado .40 .15
❑ 88 Jose Reyes .40 .15
❑ 89 Matt Morris .40 .15
❑ 90 Mark Mulder .40 .15
❑ 91 Angel Chavez FW RC 5.00 2.00
❑ 92 Brandon Medders FW RC 5.00 2.00
❑ 93 Carlos Vasquez FW RC 5.00 2.00
❑ 94 Chris Aguila FW RC 5.00 2.00
❑ 95 Colby Miller FW RC 5.00 2.00
❑ 96 Dave Crouthers FW RC 5.00 2.00
❑ 97 Dennis Sarfate FW RC 5.00 2.00
❑ 98 Donnie Kelly FW RC 5.00 2.00
❑ 99 Merkin Valdez FW RC 5.00 2.00
❑ 100 Eddy Rodriguez FW RC 5.00 2.00
❑ 101 Edwin Moreno FW RC 5.00 2.00
❑ 102 Enemencio Pacheco FW RC 5.00 2.00
❑ 103 Roberto Novoa FW RC 5.00 2.00
❑ 104 Greg Dobbs FW RC 5.00 2.00
❑ 105 Hector Gimenez FW RC 5.00 2.00
❑ 106 Ian Snell FW RC 8.00 3.00
❑ 107 Jake Woods FW RC 5.00 2.00
❑ 108 Jamie Brown FW RC 5.00 2.00
❑ 109 Jason Frasor FW RC 5.00 2.00
❑ 110 Jerome Gamble FW RC 5.00 2.00
❑ 111 Jerry Gil FW RC 5.00 2.00
❑ 112 Jesse Harper FW RC 5.00 2.00
❑ 113 Jorge Vasquez FW RC 5.00 2.00
❑ 114 Jose Capellan FW RC 5.00 2.00
❑ 115 Josh Labandeira FW RC 5.00 2.00
❑ 116 Justin Hampson FW RC 5.00 2.00
❑ 117 Justin Huisman FW RC 5.00 2.00
❑ 118 Justin Leone FW RC 5.00 2.00
❑ 119 Lincoln Holdzkom FW RC 5.00 2.00
❑ 120 Lino Urdaneta FW RC 5.00 2.00
❑ 121 Mike Gosling FW RC 5.00 2.00
❑ 122 Mike Johnston FW RC 5.00 2.00
❑ 123 Mike Rouse FW RC 5.00 2.00
❑ 124 Scott Proctor FW RC 5.00 2.00
❑ 125 Roman Colon FW RC 5.00 2.00
❑ 126 Ronny Cedeno FW RC 8.00 3.00
❑ 127 Ryan Meaux FW RC 5.00 2.00
❑ 128 Scott Dohmann FW RC 5.00 2.00
❑ 129 Sean Henn FW RC 5.00 2.00
❑ 130 Tim Bausher FW RC 5.00 2.00
❑ 131 Tim Bittner FW RC 5.00 2.00
❑ 132 William Bergolla FW RC 5.00 2.00
❑ 133 Rick Ferrell ASM 3.00 1.25
❑ 134 Joe DiMaggio ASM 5.00 2.00
❑ 135 Bob Feller ASM 3.00 1.25
❑ 136 Ted Williams ASM 8.00 3.00
❑ 137 Stan Musial ASM 5.00 2.00
❑ 138 Larry Doby ASM 3.00 1.25
❑ 139 Red Schoendienst ASM 3.00 1.25
❑ 140 Enos Slaughter ASM 3.00 1.25
❑ 141 Stan Musial ASM 5.00 2.00
❑ 142 Mickey Mantle ASM 10.00 4.00
❑ 143 Ted Williams ASM 8.00 3.00
❑ 144 Mickey Mantle ASM 10.00 4.00
❑ 145 Stan Musial ASM 5.00 2.00
❑ 146 Tom Seaver ASM 4.00 1.50
❑ 147 Willie McCovey ASM 4.00 1.50
❑ 148 Bob Gibson ASM 4.00 1.50
❑ 149 Frank Robinson ASM 3.00 1.25
❑ 150 Joe Morgan ASM 3.00 1.25
❑ 151 Billy Williams ASM 3.00 1.25
❑ 152 Catfish Hunter ASM 4.00 1.50
❑ 153 Joe Morgan ASM 3.00 1.25
❑ 154 Joe Morgan ASM 3.00 1.25
❑ 155 Mike Schmidt ASM 8.00 3.00
❑ 156 Tommy Lasorda ASM 3.00 1.25
❑ 157 Robin Yount ASM 4.00 1.50
❑ 158 Nolan Ryan ASM 10.00 4.00
❑ 159 John Franco ASM 3.00 1.25
❑ 160 Nolan Ryan ASM 10.00 4.00
❑ 161 Ken Griffey Jr. ASM 5.00 2.00
❑ 162 Cal Ripken ASM 10.00 4.00
❑ 163 Ken Griffey Jr. ASM 5.00 2.00
❑ 164 Gary Sheffield ASM 3.00 1.25
❑ 165 Fred McGriff ASM 4.00 1.50
❑ 166 Hideo Nomo ASM 4.00 1.50
❑ 167 Mike Piazza ASM 5.00 2.00
❑ 168 Sandy Alomar Jr. ASM 3.00 1.25
❑ 169 Roberto Alomar ASM 4.00 1.50
❑ 170 Ted Williams ASM 8.00 3.00
❑ 171 Pedro Martinez ASM 4.00 1.50
❑ 172 Derek Jeter ASM 6.00 2.50
❑ 173 Cal Ripken ASM 10.00 4.00
❑ 174 Torii Hunter ASM 3.00 1.25
❑ 175 Alfonso Soriano ASM 3.00 1.25
❑ 176 Hank Blalock ASM 3.00 1.25
❑ 177 Ichiro Suzuki ASM 6.00 2.50
❑ 178 Orlando Rodriguez FW RC 5.00 2.00
❑ 179 Ramon Ramirez FW RC 5.00 2.00
❑ 180 Kazuo Matsui FW RC 5.00 2.00
❑ 181 Kevin Cave FW RC 5.00 2.00
❑ 182 John Gall FW RC 5.00 2.00
❑ 183 Freddy Guzman FW RC 5.00 2.00
❑ 184 Chris Oxspring FW RC 5.00 2.00
❑ 185 Rusty Tucker FW RC 5.00 2.00
❑ 186 Jorge Sequea FW RC 5.00 2.00
❑ 187 Carlos Hines FW RC 5.00 2.00
❑ 188 Michael Vento FW RC 5.00 2.00
❑ 189 Ryan Wing FW RC 5.00 2.00
❑ 190 Jeff Bennett FW RC 5.00 2.00
❑ 191 Luis A. Gonzalez FW RC 5.00 2.00

2005 SP Authentic

❑ COMP.BASIC SET (100) 25.00 10.00
❑ COMMON CARD (1-100) .40 .15
❑ COMMON RETIRED 1-100 .40 .15
❑ 1-100 ISSUED IN 05 SP COLLECTION PACKS
❑ COMMON AUTO (101-186) 10.00 4.00

❑ 101-186 ODDS APPX 1:8 '05 UD UPDATE
❑ 101-186 PRINT RUN 185 SERIAL #'d SETS
❑ 105, 115, 118-119, 142, 154 DO NOT EXIST
❑ 161, 180, 183, 186 DO NOT EXIST
❑ 1 A.J. Burnett .40 .15
❑ 2 Aaron Rowand .40 .15
❑ 3 Adam Dunn .40 .15
❑ 4 Adrian Beltre .40 .15
❑ 5 Adrian Gonzalez .40 .15
❑ 6 Akinori Otsuka .40 .15
❑ 7 Albert Pujols 2.00 .75
❑ 8 Andre Dawson .40 .15
❑ 9 Andruw Jones .60 .25
❑ 10 Aramis Ramirez .40 .15
❑ 11 Barry Larkin .60 .25
❑ 12 Ben Sheets .40 .15
❑ 13 Bo Jackson 1.00 .40
❑ 14 Bobby Abreu .40 .15
❑ 15 Bobby Crosby .40 .15
❑ 16 Bronson Arroyo .40 .15
❑ 17 Cal Ripken 3.00 1.25
❑ 18 Carl Crawford .40 .15
❑ 19 Carlos Zambrano .40 .15
❑ 20 Casey Kotchman .40 .15
❑ 21 Cesar Izturis .40 .15
❑ 22 Chone Figgins .40 .15
❑ 23 Corey Patterson .40 .15
❑ 24 Craig Biggio .60 .25
❑ 25 Dale Murphy .60 .25
❑ 26 Dallas McPherson .40 .15
❑ 27 Danny Haren .40 .15
❑ 28 Darryl Strawberry .40 .15
❑ 29 David Ortiz .60 .25
❑ 30 David Wright 1.50 .60
❑ 31 Derek Jeter 2.00 .75
❑ 32 Derrek Lee .60 .25
❑ 33 Don Mattingly 2.00 .75
❑ 34 Dwight Gooden .40 .15
❑ 35 Edgar Renteria .40 .15
❑ 36 Eric Chavez .40 .15
❑ 37 Eric Gagne .40 .15
❑ 38 Gary Sheffield .40 .15
❑ 39 Gavin Floyd .40 .15
❑ 40 Pedro Martinez .60 .25
❑ 41 Greg Maddux 1.50 .60
❑ 42 Hank Blalock .40 .15
❑ 43 Huston Street .60 .25
❑ 44 J.D. Drew .40 .15
❑ 45 Jake Peavy .40 .15
❑ 46 Jake Westbrook .40 .15
❑ 47 Jason Bay .40 .15
❑ 48 Austin Kearns .40 .15
❑ 49 Jeremy Reed .40 .15
❑ 50 Jim Rice .40 .15
❑ 51 Jimmy Rollins .40 .15
❑ 52 Joe Blanton .40 .15
❑ 53 Joe Mauer 1.00 .40
❑ 54 Johan Santana 1.00 .40
❑ 55 John Smoltz .60 .25
❑ 56 Johnny Estrada .40 .15
❑ 57 Jose Reyes .40 .15
❑ 58 Ken Griffey Jr. 1.50 .60
❑ 59 Kerry Wood .40 .15
❑ 60 Khalil Greene .60 .25
❑ 61 Marcus Giles .40 .15
❑ 62 Melvin Mora .40 .15
❑ 63 Mark Grace .60 .25
❑ 64 Mark Mulder .40 .15
❑ 65 Mark Prior .60 .25
❑ 66 Mark Teixeria .60 .25
❑ 67 Matt Clement .40 .15
❑ 68 Michael Young .40 .15
❑ 69 Miguel Cabrera .60 .25
❑ 70 Miguel Tejada .40 .15
❑ 71 Mike Piazza 1.00 .40
❑ 72 Mike Schmidt 2.00 .75
❑ 73 Nolan Ryan 2.50 1.00
❑ 74 Oliver Perez .40 .15
❑ 75 Nick Johnson .40 .15
❑ 76 Paul Molitor .40 .15
❑ 77 Rafael Palmeiro .60 .25
❑ 78 Randy Johnson 1.00 .40
❑ 79 Reggie Jackson .60 .25
❑ 80 Rich Harden .40 .15
❑ 81 Rickie Weeks .40 .15
❑ 82 Robin Yount 1.00 .40
❑ 83 Roger Clemens 1.50 .60
❑ 84 Roy Oswalt .40 .15
❑ 85 Ryan Howard 2.50 1.00
❑ 86 Ryne Sandberg 2.00 .75
❑ 87 Scott Kazmir .40 .15
❑ 88 Scott Rolen .60 .25
❑ 89 Sean Burroughs .40 .15
❑ 90 Sean Casey .40 .15
❑ 91 Shingo Takatsu .40 .15
❑ 92 Tim Hudson .40 .15
❑ 93 Tony Gwynn 1.25 .50
❑ 94 Torii Hunter .40 .15
❑ 95 Travis Hafner .40 .15
❑ 96 Victor Martinez .40 .15
❑ 97 Vladimir Guerrero 1.00 .40
❑ 98 Wade Boggs .60 .25
❑ 99 Will Clark .60 .25
❑ 100 Yadier Molina .40 .15
❑ 101 Adam Shabala AU RC 10.00 4.00
❑ 102 Ambiorix Burgos AU RC 10.00 4.00
❑ 103 Ambiorix Concepcion AU RC 10.004.00
❑ 104 Anibal Sanchez AU RC 80.00 40.00
❑ 106 Brandon McCarthy AU RC 40.00 15.00
❑ 107 Brian Burres AU RC 10.00 4.00
❑ 108 Carlos Ruiz AU RC 25.00 10.00
❑ 109 Casey Rogowski AU RC 15.00 6.00
❑ 110 Chad Orvella AU RC 10.00 4.00
❑ 111 Chris Resop AU RC 15.00 6.00
❑ 112 Chris Roberson AU RC 10.00 4.00
❑ 113 Chris Seddon AU RC 10.00 4.00
❑ 114 Colter Bean AU RC 15.00 6.00
❑ 116 Dave Gassner AU RC 10.00 4.00
❑ 117 Brian Anderson AU RC 40.00 15.00
❑ 120 Devon Lowery AU RC 10.00 4.00
❑ 121 Enrique Gonzalez AU RC 15.00 6.00
❑ 122 Eude Brito AU RC 10.00 4.00
❑ 123 Francisco Butto AU RC 10.00 4.00
❑ 124 Franquelis Osoria AU RC 10.00 4.00
❑ 125 Garrett Jones AU RC 10.00 4.00
❑ 126 Geovany Soto AU RC 80.00 40.00
❑ 127 Hayden Penn AU RC 25.00 10.00
❑ 128 Ismael Ramirez AU RC 10.00 4.00
❑ 129 Jared Gothreaux AU RC 10.00 4.00
❑ 130 Jason Hammel AU RC 10.00 4.00
❑ 131 Jeff Miller AU RC 10.00 4.00
❑ 132 Jeff Niemann AU RC 30.00 12.50
❑ 133 Joel Peralta AU RC 10.00 4.00
❑ 134 John Hattig AU RC 10.00 4.00
❑ 135 Jorge Campillo AU RC 10.00 4.00
❑ 136 Juan Morillo AU RC 10.00 4.00
❑ 137 Justin Verlander AU RC 150.00 90.00
❑ 138 Ryan Garko AU RC 50.00 25.00
❑ 139 Keiichi Yabu AU RC 15.00 6.00
❑ 140 Kendry Morales AU RC 60.00 30.00
❑ 141 Luis Hernandez AU RC 10.00 4.00
❑ 143 Luis O.Rodriguez AU RC 10.00 4.00
❑ 144 Luke Scott AU RC 60.00 30.00
❑ 145 Marcos Carvajal AU RC 10.00 4.00
❑ 146 Mark Woodyard AU RC 10.00 4.00
❑ 147 Matt A.Smith AU RC 10.00 4.00
❑ 148 Matthew Lindstrom AU RC 10.00 4.00
❑ 149 Miguel Negron AU RC 15.00 6.00
❑ 150 Mike Morse AU RC 15.00 6.00
❑ 151 Nate McLouth AU RC 15.00 6.00
❑ 152 Nelson Cruz AU RC 50.00 25.00
❑ 153 Nick Masset AU RC 10.00 4.00
❑ 155 Paulino Reynoso AU RC 10.00 4.00
❑ 156 Pedro Lopez AU RC 10.00 4.00
❑ 157 Pete Orr AU RC 10.00 4.00
❑ 158 Philip Humber AU RC 30.00 12.50
❑ 159 Prince Fielder AU RC 300.00 225.00
❑ 160 Randy Messenger AU RC 10.00 4.00
❑ 162 Raul Tablado AU RC 10.00 4.00
❑ 163 Ronny Paulino AU RC 25.00 10.00
❑ 164 Russ Rohlicek AU RC 10.00 4.00
❑ 165 Russell Martin AU RC 120.00 60.00
❑ 166 Scott Baker AU RC 15.00 6.00
❑ 167 Scott Munter AU RC 10.00 4.00
❑ 168 Sean Thompson AU RC 10.00 4.00
❑ 169 Sean Tracey AU RC 10.00 4.00
❑ 170 Shane Costa AU RC 10.00 4.00
❑ 171 Stephen Drew AU RC 60.00 30.00
❑ 172 Steve Schmoll AU RC 10.00 4.00
❑ 173 Tadahito Iguchi AU RC 50.00 20.00
❑ 174 Tony Giarratano AU RC 10.00 4.00
❑ 175 Tony Pena AU RC 10.00 4.00
❑ 176 Travis Bowyer AU RC 10.00 4.00
❑ 177 Ubaldo Jimenez AU RC 40.00 15.00
❑ 178 Wladimir Balentien AU RC 100.0050.00
❑ 179 Yorman Bazardo AU RC 10.00 4.00
❑ 181 Ryan Zimmerman AU RC 225.00150.00
❑ 182 Chris Denorfia AU RC 25.00 10.00
❑ 184 Jermaine Van Buren AU 10.00 4.00
❑ 185 Mark McLemore AU RC 10.00 4.00

2006 SP Authentic

❑ COMP.SET w/o SP's (100) 15.00 6.00
❑ 1 Erik Bedard .40 .15
❑ 2 Corey Patterson .40 .15
❑ 3 Ramon Hernandez .40 .15
❑ 4 Kris Benson .40 .15
❑ 5 Miguel Batista .40 .15
❑ 6 Orlando Hudson .40 .15
❑ 7 Shawn Green .40 .15
❑ 8 Jeff Francoeur 1.00 .40
❑ 9 Marcus Giles .40 .15
❑ 10 Edgar Renteria .40 .15
❑ 11 Tim Hudson .40 .15
❑ 12 Tim Wakefield .40 .15
❑ 13 Mark Loretta .40 .15
❑ 14 Kevin Youkilis .40 .15
❑ 15 Mike Lowell .40 .15
❑ 16 Coco Crisp .40 .15
❑ 17 Tadahito Iguchi .40 .15
❑ 18 Scott Podsednik .40 .15
❑ 19 Jermaine Dye .40 .15
❑ 20 Jose Contreras .40 .15
❑ 21 Carlos Zambrano .40 .15
❑ 22 Aramis Ramirez .40 .15
❑ 23 Jacque Jones .40 .15
❑ 24 Austin Kearns .40 .15
❑ 25 Felipe Lopez .40 .15
❑ 26 Brandon Phillips .40 .15
❑ 27 Aaron Harang .40 .15
❑ 28 Cliff Lee .40 .15
❑ 29 Jhonny Peralta .40 .15
❑ 30 Jason Michaels .40 .15
❑ 31 Clint Barmes .40 .15
❑ 32 Brad Hawpe .40 .15
❑ 33 Aaron Cook .40 .15
❑ 34 Kenny Rogers .40 .15
❑ 35 Carlos Guillen .40 .15
❑ 36 Brian Moehler .40 .15
❑ 37 Andy Pettitte .60 .25
❑ 38 Wandy Rodriguez .40 .15
❑ 39 Morgan Ensberg .40 .15
❑ 40 Preston Wilson .40 .15
❑ 41 Mark Grudzielanek .40 .15
❑ 42 Angel Berroa .40 .15
❑ 43 Jeremy Affeldt .40 .15
❑ 44 Zack Greinke .40 .15
❑ 45 Orlando Cabrera .40 .15
❑ 46 Garret Anderson .40 .15
❑ 47 Ervin Santana .40 .15
❑ 48 Derek Lowe .40 .15
❑ 49 Nomar Garciaparra 1.00 .40
❑ 50 J.D. Drew .40 .15
❑ 51 Rafael Furcal .40 .15
❑ 52 Rickie Weeks .40 .15
❑ 53 Geoff Jenkins .40 .15
❑ 54 Bill Hall .40 .15
❑ 55 Chris Capuano .40 .15
❑ 56 Derrick Turnbow .40 .15
❑ 57 Justin Morneau .40 .15

❑ 58 Michael Cuddyer .40 .15
❑ 59 Luis Castillo .40 .15
❑ 60 Hideki Matsui 1.00 .40
❑ 61 Jason Giambi .40 .15
❑ 62 Jorge Posada .60 .25
❑ 63 Mariano Rivera 1.00 .40
❑ 64 Billy Wagner .40 .15
❑ 65 Carlos Delgado .40 .15
❑ 66 Jose Reyes 1.00 .40
❑ 67 Nick Swisher .40 .15
❑ 68 Bobby Crosby .40 .15
❑ 69 Frank Thomas 1.00 .40
❑ 70 Ryan Howard 1.50 .60
❑ 71 Pat Burrell .40 .15
❑ 72 Jimmy Rollins .40 .15
❑ 73 Craig Wilson .40 .15
❑ 74 Freddy Sanchez .40 .15
❑ 75 Sean Casey .40 .15
❑ 76 Mike Piazza 1.00 .40
❑ 77 Dave Roberts .40 .15
❑ 78 Chris Young .40 .15
❑ 79 Noah Lowry .40 .15
❑ 80 Armando Benitez .40 .15
❑ 81 Pedro Feliz .40 .15
❑ 82 Jose Lopez .40 .15
❑ 83 Adrian Beltre .40 .15
❑ 84 Jamie Moyer .40 .15
❑ 85 Jason Isringhausen .40 .15
❑ 86 Jason Marquis .40 .15
❑ 87 David Eckstein .40 .15
❑ 88 Juan Encarnacion .40 .15
❑ 89 Julio Lugo .40 .15
❑ 90 Ty Wigginton .40 .15
❑ 91 Jorge Cantu .40 .15
❑ 92 Akinori Otsuka .40 .15
❑ 93 Hank Blalock .40 .15
❑ 94 Kevin Mench .40 .15
❑ 95 Lyle Overbay .40 .15
❑ 96 Shea Hillenbrand .40 .15
❑ 97 B.J. Ryan .40 .15
❑ 98 Tony Armas .40 .15
❑ 99 Chad Cordero .40 .15
❑ 100 Jose Guillen .40 .15
❑ 101 Miguel Tejada 4.00 1.50
❑ 102 Brian Roberts 4.00 1.50
❑ 103 Melvin Mora 4.00 1.50
❑ 104 Brandon Webb 4.00 1.50
❑ 105 Chad Tracy 4.00 1.50
❑ 106 Luis Gonzalez 4.00 1.50
❑ 107 Andruw Jones 5.00 2.00
❑ 108 Chipper Jones 5.00 2.00
❑ 109 John Smoltz 5.00 2.00
❑ 110 Curt Schilling 5.00 2.00
❑ 111 Josh Beckett 4.00 1.50
❑ 112 David Ortiz 5.00 2.00
❑ 113 Manny Ramirez 5.00 2.00
❑ 114 Jason Varitek 5.00 2.00
❑ 115 Jim Thome 5.00 2.00
❑ 116 Paul Konerko 4.00 1.50
❑ 117 Javier Vazquez 4.00 1.50
❑ 118 Mark Prior 4.00 1.50
❑ 119 Derrek Lee 4.00 1.50
❑ 120 Greg Maddux 8.00 3.00
❑ 121 Ken Griffey Jr. 8.00 3.00
❑ 122 Adam Dunn 4.00 1.50
❑ 123 Bronson Arroyo 5.00 2.00
❑ 124 Travis Hafner 4.00 1.50
❑ 125 Victor Martinez 4.00 1.50
❑ 126 Grady Sizemore 5.00 2.00
❑ 127 C.C. Sabathia 4.00 1.50
❑ 128 Todd Helton 5.00 2.00
❑ 129 Matt Holliday 5.00 2.00
❑ 130 Garrett Atkins 4.00 1.50
❑ 131 Jeff Francis 4.00 1.50
❑ 132 Jeremy Bonderman 4.00 1.50
❑ 133 Ivan Rodriguez 5.00 2.00
❑ 134 Chris Shelton 4.00 1.50
❑ 135 Magglio Ordonez 4.00 1.50
❑ 136 Dontrelle Willis 4.00 1.50
❑ 137 Miguel Cabrera 5.00 2.00
❑ 138 Roger Clemens 8.00 3.00
❑ 139 Roy Oswalt 4.00 1.50
❑ 140 Lance Berkman 4.00 1.50
❑ 141 Reggie Sanders 4.00 1.50
❑ 142 Vladimir Guerrero 5.00 2.00
❑ 143 Bartolo Colon 4.00 1.50
❑ 144 Chone Figgins 4.00 1.50
❑ 145 Francisco Rodriguez 4.00 1.50
❑ 146 Brad Penny 4.00 1.50
❑ 147 Jeff Kent 4.00 1.50
❑ 148 Eric Gagne 4.00 1.50
❑ 149 Carlos Lee 4.00 1.50
❑ 150 Ben Sheets 4.00 1.50
❑ 151 Johan Santana 5.00 2.00
❑ 152 Torii Hunter 4.00 1.50
❑ 153 Joe Nathan 4.00 1.50
❑ 154 Alex Rodriguez 8.00 3.00
❑ 155 Derek Jeter 10.00 4.00
❑ 156 Randy Johnson 5.00 2.00
❑ 157 Johnny Damon 5.00 2.00
❑ 158 Mike Mussina 5.00 2.00
❑ 159 Pedro Martinez 5.00 2.00
❑ 160 Tom Glavine 5.00 2.00
❑ 161 David Wright 8.00 3.00
❑ 162 Carlos Beltran 4.00 1.50
❑ 163 Rich Harden 4.00 1.50
❑ 164 Barry Zito 4.00 1.50
❑ 165 Eric Chavez 4.00 1.50
❑ 166 Huston Street 4.00 1.50
❑ 167 Bobby Abreu 4.00 1.50
❑ 168 Chase Utley 5.00 2.00
❑ 169 Brett Myers 4.00 1.50
❑ 170 Jason Bay 4.00 1.50
❑ 171 Zach Duke 4.00 1.50
❑ 172 Jake Peavy 4.00 1.50
❑ 173 Brian Giles 4.00 1.50
❑ 174 Khalil Greene 5.00 2.00
❑ 175 Trevor Hoffman 4.00 1.50
❑ 176 Jason Schmidt 4.00 1.50
❑ 177 Randy Winn 4.00 1.50
❑ 178 Omar Vizquel 5.00 2.00
❑ 179 Kenji Johjima 8.00 3.00
❑ 180 Ichiro Suzuki 8.00 3.00
❑ 181 Richie Sexson 4.00 1.50
❑ 182 Felix Hernandez 5.00 2.00
❑ 183 Albert Pujols 10.00 4.00
❑ 184 Chris Carpenter 5.00 2.00
❑ 185 Jim Edmonds 5.00 2.00
❑ 186 Scott Rolen 5.00 2.00
❑ 187 Carl Crawford 4.00 1.50
❑ 188 Scott Kazmir 4.00 1.50
❑ 189 Jonny Gomes 4.00 1.50
❑ 190 Mark Teixeira 5.00 2.00
❑ 191 Michael Young 4.00 1.50
❑ 192 Kevin Millwood 4.00 1.50
❑ 193 Vernon Wells 4.00 1.50
❑ 194 Troy Glaus 4.00 1.50
❑ 195 Roy Halladay 4.00 1.50
❑ 196 Alex Rios 4.00 1.50
❑ 197 Nick Johnson 4.00 1.50
❑ 198 Livan Hernandez 4.00 1.50
❑ 199 Alfonso Soriano 4.00 1.50
❑ 200 Jose Vidro 4.00 1.50
❑ 201 A.Rakers AU/399 (RC) 8.00 3.00
❑ 202 A.Pagan AU/399 (RC) 15.00 6.00
❑ 203 B.Hendrick AU/399 (RC) 8.00 3.00
❑ 204 B.Livingston AU/399 (RC) 8.00 3.00
❑ 205 D.Rasner AU/399 (RC) 8.00 3.00
❑ 206 B.Bannister AU/399 (RC) 15.00 6.00
❑ 207 B.Wilson AU/899 RC 8.00 3.00
❑ 208 B.Keppel AU/199 (RC) 15.00 6.00
❑ 209 C.Freeman AU/399 (RC) 8.00 3.00
❑ 210 C.Booker AU/899 (RC) 8.00 3.00
❑ 211 C.Britton AU/399 (RC) 10.00 4.00
❑ 212 C.Demaria AU/329 RC 10.00 4.00
❑ 213 C.Resop AU/899 (RC) 8.00 3.00
❑ 214 T.Gwynn Jr. AU/399 (RC) 60.00 30.00
❑ 215 E.Reed AU/399 (RC) 8.00 3.00
❑ 216 F.Castro AU/399 RC 20.00 8.00
❑ 217 F.Nieve AU/299 (RC) 10.00 4.00
❑ 218 F.Bynum AU/899 (RC) 8.00 3.00
❑ 219 G.Quiroz AU/399 (RC) 8.00 3.00
❑ 220 H.Kuo AU/899 (RC) 60.00 30.00
❑ 221 R.Theriot AU/399 RC 60.00 30.00
❑ 222 J.Taschner AU/899 (RC) 8.00 3.00
❑ 223 J.Bergmann AU/899 (RC) 8.00 3.00
❑ 224 J.Hammel AU/899 (RC) 8.00 3.00
❑ 225 J.Harris AU/399 RC 8.00 3.00
❑ 226 J.Accardo AU/399 RC 10.00 4.00
❑ 227 T.Taubenheim AU/399 RC 30.00 12.50
❑ 228 J.Zumaya AU/399 (RC) 40.00 15.00
❑ 229 J.Koronka AU/399 (RC) 8.00 3.00
❑ 230 E.Aybar AU/399 (RC) 8.00 3.00
❑ 231 J.Tata AU/399 RC 15.00 6.00
❑ 232 R.Martin AU/399 (RC) 40.00 15.00
❑ 233 J.Rupe AU/399 (RC) 8.00 3.00
❑ 234 K.Frandsen AU/399 (RC) 15.00 6.00
❑ 235 M.Prado AU/399 (RC) 15.00 6.00
❑ 236 M.Capps AU/399 (RC) 8.00 3.00
❑ 237 A.Montero AU/199 (RC) 10.00 4.00
❑ 238 M.Thompson AU/399 RC 8.00 3.00
❑ 239 N.McLouth AU/399 (RC) 8.00 3.00
❑ 240 P.Moylan AU/399 RC 8.00 3.00
❑ 241 R.Abercrom AU/399 (RC) 8.00 3.00
❑ 242 C.Quentin AU/399 (RC) 15.00 6.00
❑ 243 R.Flores AU/399 RC 8.00 3.00
❑ 244 R.Shealy AU/399 (RC) 20.00 8.00
❑ 245 M.Rouse AU/399 (RC) 8.00 3.00
❑ 246 S.Ramirez AU/399 (RC) 8.00 3.00
❑ 247 C.Hensley AU/899 (RC) 8.00 3.00
❑ 248 S.Schumaker AU/399 (RC) 10.00 4.00
❑ 249 E.Alfonzo AU/899 RC 8.00 3.00
❑ 250 S.Stemle AU/399 RC 8.00 3.00
❑ 251 T.Hamulack AU/399 (RC) 8.00 3.00
❑ 252 T.Pena Jr. AU/299 (RC) 10.00 4.00
❑ 253 E.Fruto AU/899 RC 8.00 3.00
❑ 254 W.Nieves AU/399 (RC) 10.00 4.00
❑ 255 J.Devine AU/399 RC 10.00 4.00
❑ 256 A.Wainwright AU/399 (RC) 25.00 10.00
❑ 257 A.Ethier AU/399 (RC) 25.00 10.00
❑ 258 B.Johnson AU/399 (RC) 8.00 3.00
❑ 259 B.Logan AU/399 RC 15.00 6.00
❑ 260 C.Denorfia AU/899 (RC) 10.00 4.00
❑ 261 A.Soler AU/299 RC 15.00 6.00
❑ 262 C.Ross AU/899 (RC) 8.00 3.00
❑ 263 D.Gassner AU/399 (RC) 8.00 3.00
❑ 264 F.Carmona AU/399 (RC) 40.00 15.00
❑ 265 J.Sowers AU/299 (RC) 25.00 10.00
❑ 266 J.Kubel AU/399 (RC) 10.00 4.00
❑ 267 J.VanBenSch AU/399 (RC) 8.00 3.00
❑ 268 J.Capellan AU/399 (RC) 8.00 3.00
❑ 269 J.Wilson AU/399 (RC) 8.00 3.00
❑ 270 K.Shoppach AU/399 (RC) 8.00 3.00
❑ 271 M.McBride AU/399 (RC) 10.00 4.00
❑ 272 M.Cain AU/399 (RC) 25.00 10.00
❑ 273 M.Jacobs AU/399 (RC) 15.00 6.00
❑ 274 P.Maholm AU/399 (RC) 10.00 4.00
❑ 275 C.Billingsley AU/399 (RC) 25.00 10.00
❑ 276 R.Lugo AU/399 (RC) 8.00 3.00
❑ 277 J.Lester AU/399 RC 40.00 15.00
❑ 278 S.Marshall AU/383 (RC) 25.00 10.00
❑ 279 Me.Cabrera AU/399 (RC) 40.00 15.00
❑ 280 Y.Petit AU/399 (RC) 10.00 4.00
❑ 281 A.Hernandez AU/299 (RC) 10.00 4.00
❑ 282 B.Anderson AU/699 (RC) 10.00 4.00
❑ 283 C.Hamels AU/299 (RC) 50.00 20.00
❑ 284 B.Bonser AU/299 (RC) 15.00 6.00
❑ 285 D.Uggla AU/199 (RC) 30.00 12.50
❑ 286 F.Liriano AU/299 (RC) 40.00 15.00
❑ 287 H.Ramirez AU/199 (RC) 25.00 10.00
❑ 288 I.Kinsler AU/299 (RC) 40.00 15.00
❑ 289 J.Hermida AU/299 (RC) 15.00 6.00
❑ 290 J.Papelbon AU/199 (RC) 60.00 30.00
❑ 291 J.Weaver AU/199 (RC) 40.00 15.00
❑ 292 J.Johnson AU/299 (RC) 15.00 6.00
❑ 293 J.Willingham AU/199 (RC) 15.00 6.00
❑ 294 J.Verlander AU/199 (RC) 80.00 40.00
❑ 295 S.Drew AU/299 (RC) 30.00 12.50
❑ 296 P.Fielder AU/125 (RC) 120.00 60.00
❑ 297 R.Zimmer AU/199 (RC) 70.00 40.00
❑ 298 T.Saito AU/283 RC 40.00 15.00
❑ 299 T.Buchholz AU/299 (RC) 10.00 4.00
❑ 300 Co.Jackson AU/299 (RC) 15.00 6.00

2007 SP Authentic

❑ COMP.SET w/o RCs (100) 15.00 6.00
❑ COMMON CARD (1-100) .40 .15
❑ COMMON AU RC (101-158) 12.00 5.00
❑ OVERALL BY THE LETTER AUTOS 1:12
❑ AU RC PRINT RUN B/WN 20-120 COPIES PER
❑ EXCHANGE DEADLINE 11/08/2008
❑ 1 Chipper Jones 1.00 .40
❑ 2 Andruw Jones .60 .25
❑ 3 John Smoltz .60 .25
❑ 4 Carlos Quentin .40 .15
❑ 5 Randy Johnson 1.00 .40
❑ 6 Brandon Webb .40 .15
❑ 7 Alfonso Soriano .40 .15

❑ 8 Derrek Lee .40 .15
❑ 9 Aramis Ramirez .40 .15
❑ 10 Carlos Zambrano .40 .15
❑ 11 Ken Griffey Jr. 1.50 .60
❑ 12 Adam Dunn .40 .15
❑ 13 Josh Hamilton 1.00 .40
❑ 14 Todd Helton .60 .25
❑ 15 Jeff Francis .40 .15
❑ 16 Matt Holliday 1.00 .40
❑ 17 Hanley Ramirez .60 .25
❑ 18 Dontrelle Willis .40 .15
❑ 19 Miguel Cabrera .60 .25
❑ 20 Lance Berkman .40 .15
❑ 21 Roy Oswalt .40 .15
❑ 22 Carlos Lee .40 .15
❑ 23 Nomar Garciaparra 1.00 .40
❑ 24 Derek Lowe .40 .15
❑ 25 Juan Pierre .40 .15
❑ 26 Rafael Furcal .40 .15
❑ 27 Rickie Weeks .40 .15
❑ 28 Prince Fielder 1.00 .40
❑ 29 Ben Sheets .40 .15
❑ 30 David Wright 1.50 .60
❑ 31 Jose Reyes 1.00 .40
❑ 32 Tom Glavine .60 .25
❑ 33 Carlos Beltran .40 .15
❑ 34 Cole Hamels .60 .25
❑ 35 Jimmy Rollins .40 .15
❑ 36 Ryan Howard 1.50 .60
❑ 37 Jason Bay .40 .15
❑ 38 Freddy Sanchez .40 .15
❑ 39 Ian Snell .40 .15
❑ 40 Jake Peavy .40 .15
❑ 41 Greg Maddux 1.50 .60
❑ 42 Trevor Hoffman .40 .15
❑ 43 Matt Cain .60 .25
❑ 44 Barry Zito .40 .15
❑ 45 Ray Durham .40 .15
❑ 46 Albert Pujols 2.00 .75
❑ 47 Chris Carpenter .40 .15
❑ 48 Jim Edmonds .60 .25
❑ 49 Scott Rolen .60 .25
❑ 50 Ryan Zimmerman 1.00 .40
❑ 51 Felipe Lopez .40 .15
❑ 52 Austin Kearns .40 .15
❑ 53 Miguel Tejada .40 .15
❑ 54 Erik Bedard .40 .15
❑ 55 Daniel Cabrera .40 .15
❑ 56 David Ortiz 1.00 .40
❑ 57 Curt Schilling .60 .25
❑ 58 Manny Ramirez .60 .25
❑ 59 Jonathan Papelbon 1.00 .40
❑ 60 Jim Thome .60 .25
❑ 61 Paul Konerko .40 .15
❑ 62 Bobby Jenks .40 .15
❑ 63 Grady Sizemore .60 .25
❑ 64 Victor Martinez .40 .15
❑ 65 Travis Hafner .40 .15
❑ 66 Ivan Rodriguez .60 .25
❑ 67 Justin Verlander 1.00 .40
❑ 68 Joel Zumaya .60 .25
❑ 69 Jeremy Bonderman .40 .15
❑ 70 Gil Meche .40 .15
❑ 71 Mike Sweeney .40 .15
❑ 72 Mark Teahen .40 .15
❑ 73 Vladimir Guerrero 1.00 .40
❑ 74 Howie Kendrick .40 .15
❑ 75 Francisco Rodriguez .40 .15
❑ 76 Johan Santana .60 .25
❑ 77 Justin Morneau .40 .15
❑ 78 Joe Mauer .60 .25
❑ 79 Joe Nathan .40 .15
❑ 80a Alex Rodriguez 1.50 .60
❑ 80b A.Rodriguez Angels
❑ 80c A.Rodriguez Cubs
❑ 80d A.Rodriguez Dodgers
❑ 80e A.Rodriguez Mets
❑ 80f A.Rodriguez Red Sox
❑ 81 Derek Jeter 2.50 1.00
❑ 82 Johnny Damon .60 .25
❑ 83 Chien-Ming Wang 1.50 .60
❑ 84 Rich Harden .40 .15
❑ 85 Mike Piazza 1.00 .40
❑ 86 Dan Haren .40 .15
❑ 87 Ichiro Suzuki 1.50 .60
❑ 88 Felix Hernandez .60 .25
❑ 89 Kenji Johjima 1.00 .40
❑ 90 Adrian Beltre .40 .15
❑ 91 Carl Crawford .40 .15
❑ 92 Scott Kazmir .60 .25
❑ 93 Delmon Young .60 .25
❑ 94 Michael Young .40 .15
❑ 95 Mark Teixeira .60 .25
❑ 96 Eric Gagne .40 .15
❑ 97 Hank Blalock .40 .15
❑ 98 Vernon Wells .40 .15
❑ 99 Roy Halladay .40 .15
❑ 100 Frank Thomas 1.00 .40
❑ 101 Joaquin Arias AU/75 (RC) 12.00 5.00
❑ 102 Jeff Baker AU (RC) EXCH 12.00 5.00
❑ 103 M.Bourn AU/75 (RC) 15.00 6.00
❑ 104 Brian Burres AU/75 (RC) 15.00 6.00
❑ 105 Jared Burton AU/75 RC 15.00 6.00
❑ 106 Ryan Braun AU/50 (RC) 150.00 60.00
❑ 109 Alex Gordon AU/50 RC 80.00 40.00
❑ 112 Sean Henn AU/75 (RC) 25.00 10.00
❑ 113 P.Hughes AU (RC) EXCH 80.00 40.00
❑ 114 Kei Igawa AU/25 RC 60.00 30.00
❑ 115 A.Iwamura AU/20 RC 80.00 40.00
❑ 119 Adam Lind AU/75 (RC) 25.00 10.00
❑ 123 Brad Salmon AU/75 RC 12.00 5.00
❑ 127 Cesar Jimenez AU RC EXCH 12.00 5.00
❑ 129 T.Tulowit AU (RC) EXCH 60.00 30.00
❑ 130 Chase Wright AU/75 RC 30.00 12.50
❑ 131 Delmon Young AU/20 (RC) 50.0020.00
❑ 133 Brian Barden AU/75 RC 12.00 5.00
❑ 137 Billy Butler AU/75 (RC) 50.00 20.00
❑ 139 Kory Casto AU/75 (RC) 15.00 6.00
❑ 140 Matt Chico AU/75 (RC) 15.00 6.00
❑ 141 John Danks AU/75 RC 25.00 10.00
❑ 142 Andrew Miller AU/50 RC 50.00 20.00
❑ 145 D.Hansack AU RC EXCH 15.00 6.00
❑ 146 Mike Rabelo AU/75 RC 20.00 8.00
❑ 150 D.Matsuzaka AU RC EXCH 350.00 300.00
❑ 152 Micah Owings AU/75 (RC) 50.00 20.00
❑ 153 Hunter Pence AU/75 (RC) 80.00 40.00
❑ 156 Danny Putnam AU/75 (RC) 15.00 6.00
❑ 159 Doug Slaten AU/75 RC 15.00 6.00
❑ 160 Joe Smith AU/75 RC 20.00 8.00
❑ 161 Justin Upton AU/120 RC 100.00 50.00
❑ 162 J.Chamberlain AU/60 RC 250.00150.00
❑ 107a Y.Gallardo AU/75 (RC) 50.00 20.00
❑ 107b Y.Gallardo AU/35 (RC) 60.00 30.00
❑ 108a H.Gimenez AU/75 (RC) 15.00 6.00
❑ 108b H.Gimenez AU/50 (RC) 15.00 6.00
❑ 110a J.Hamilton AU/50 (RC) 30.00 12.50
❑ 110b J.Hamilton AU/35 (RC) 40.00 15.00
❑ 111a Justin Hampson AU/75 (RC) 12.00 5.00
❑ 111b Justin Hampson AU/50 (RC) 12.00 5.00
❑ 116a M.Reynolds AU/75 RC 30.00 12.50
❑ 116b M.Reynolds AU/35 (RC) 40.00 15.00
❑ 117a Homer Bailey AU/75 (RC) 40.0015.00
❑ 117b Homer Bailey AU/50 (RC) 40.0015.00
❑ 118a K.Kouzmanoff AU/75 (RC) 20.00 8.00
❑ 118b K.Kouzmanoff AU/40 (RC) 20.00 8.00
❑ 120a Carlos Gomez AU/75 RC 50.00 20.00
❑ 120b Carlos Gomez AU/50 (RC) 50.0020.00
❑ 121a Glen Perkins AU/75 (RC) 15.00 6.00
❑ 121b Glen Perkins AU/50 (RC) 15.00 6.00
❑ 122a R.Vanden Hurk AU/75 RC 25.0010.00
❑ 122b R.Vanden Hurk AU/35 (RC) 30.00 12.50
❑ 124a Zack Segovia AU/75 (RC) 12.00 5.00
❑ 124b Zack Segovia AU/50 (RC) 12.00 5.00
❑ 125a Kurt Suzuki AU/75 (RC) 30.00 12.50
❑ 125b Kurt Suzuki AU/50 (RC) 30.00 12.50
❑ 126a Chris Stewart AU/75 RC 12.00 5.00
❑ 126b Chris Stewart AU/50 (RC) 12.00 5.00
❑ 128a Ryan Sweeney AU/50 (RC) 15.006.00
❑ 128b Ryan Sweeney AU/40 (RC) 15.006.00
❑ 132a Tony Abreu AU/75 RC 25.00 10.00
❑ 132b Tony Abreu AU/57 (RC) 25.00 10.00
❑ 132c Tony Abreu AU/50 (RC) 25.00 10.00
❑ 134a C.Thigpen AU/75 (RC) 25.00 10.00
❑ 134b C.Thigpen AU/40 (RC) 25.00 10.00
❑ 135a Jon Coutlangus AU/75 (RC) 12.005.00
❑ 135b Jon Coutlangus AU/55 (RC) 12.005.00
❑ 136a Kevin Cameron AU/75 RC 12.00 5.00
❑ 136b Kevin Cameron AU/50 (RC) 12.005.00
❑ 138a A.Casilla AU/75 RC 15.00 6.00
❑ 138b A.Casilla AU/50 (RC) 15.00 6.00
❑ 143a B.Francisco AU/75 (RC) 15.00 6.00
❑ 143b B.Francisco AU/40 (RC) 15.00 6.00
❑ 144a Andy Gonzalez AU/75 RC 12.00 5.00
❑ 144b Andy Gonzalez AU/50 RC 12.00 5.00
❑ 147a Tim Lincecum AU/50 RC 150.0060.00
❑ 147b Tim Lincecum AU/25 (RC) 200.00 75.00
❑ 148a M.Lindstrom AU/75 (RC) 15.00 6.00
❑ 148b M.Lindstrom AU/40 (RC) 15.00 6.00
❑ 149a Jay Marshall AU/75 RC 12.00 5.00
❑ 149b Jay Marshall AU/50 (RC) 12.00 5.00
❑ 151a M.Montero AU/75 (RC) 15.00 6.00
❑ 151b M.Montero AU/60 (RC) 15.00 6.00
❑ 154a Brandon Wood AU/75 (RC) 25.00 10.00
❑ 155a Felix Pie AU/75 (RC) 30.00 12.50
❑ 155b Felix Pie AU/70 (RC) 30.00 12.50
❑ 157a Andy LaRoche AU/50 (RC) 25.00 10.00
❑ 157b Andy LaRoche AU/40 (RC) 25.00 10.00
❑ 158a J.Saltalamac AU/75 (RC) 25.00 10.00
❑ 158b J.Saltalamac AU/25 (RC) 30.00 12.50

2004 SP Legendary Cuts

❑ COMPLETE SET (126) 40.00 15.00
❑ 1 Al Kaline 1.50 .60
❑ 2 Al Lopez .60 .25
❑ 3 Alan Trammell .60 .25
❑ 4 Andre Dawson .60 .25
❑ 5 Babe Ruth 5.00 2.00
❑ 6 Bert Campaneris .40 .15
❑ 7 Bill Mazeroski 1.00 .40
❑ 8 Bill Russell .40 .15
❑ 9 Billy Williams .60 .25
❑ 10 Bob Feller 1.00 .40
❑ 11 Bob Gibson 1.00 .40
❑ 12 Bob Lemon .60 .25
❑ 13 Bobby Doerr .60 .25
❑ 14 Brooks Robinson 1.00 .40
❑ 15 Cal Ripken 5.00 2.00
❑ 16 Carl Yastrzemski 2.50 1.00
❑ 17 Carlton Fisk 1.00 .40
❑ 18 Catfish Hunter .60 .25
❑ 19 Dale Murphy 1.00 .40
❑ 20 Darryl Strawberry .60 .25
❑ 21 Dave Concepcion .60 .25
❑ 22 Dave Winfield .60 .25
❑ 23 Dennis Eckersley .60 .25
❑ 24 Denny McLain .60 .25
❑ 25 Don Drysdale 1.00 .40
❑ 26 Don Larsen .60 .25
❑ 27 Don Mattingly 3.00 1.25
❑ 28 Don Sutton .60 .25
❑ 29 Duke Snider 1.00 .40
❑ 30 Dusty Baker .60 .25

❑	31 Dwight Gooden	.60	.25
❑	32 Earl Weaver	.40	.15
❑	33 Early Wynn	.60	.25
❑	34 Eddie Mathews	1.50	.60
❑	35 Eddie Murray	1.50	.60
❑	36 Enos Slaughter	.60	.25
❑	37 Ernie Banks	1.50	.60
❑	38 Fergie Jenkins	.60	.25
❑	39 Frank Robinson	.60	.25
❑	40 Fred Lynn	.40	.15
❑	41 Gary Carter	.60	.25
❑	42 Gaylord Perry	.60	.25
❑	43 George Brett	3.00	1.25
❑	44 George Foster	.40	.15
❑	45 George Kell	.60	.25
❑	46 Greg Luzinski	.60	.25
❑	47 Hal Newhouser	.60	.25
❑	48 Hank Greenberg	1.50	.60
❑	49 Harmon Killebrew	1.50	.60
❑	50 Honus Wagner	1.50	.60
❑	51 Hoyt Wilhelm	.60	.25
❑	52 Jackie Robinson	1.50	.60
❑	53 Jim Bunning	1.00	.40
❑	54 Jim Palmer	.60	.25
❑	55 Jimmie Foxx	1.50	.60
❑	56 Joe Carter	.60	.25
❑	57 Joe DiMaggio	2.50	1.00
❑	58 Joe Morgan	.60	.25
❑	59 Joe Torre	1.00	.40
❑	60 Johnny Bench	1.50	.60
❑	61 Johnny Podres	.60	.25
❑	62 Johnny Roseboro	.40	.15
❑	63 Johnny Sain	.60	.25
❑	64 Juan Marichal	.60	.25
❑	65 Keith Hernandez	.60	.25
❑	66 Kirby Puckett	1.50	.60
❑	67 Kirk Gibson	.60	.25
❑	68 Will Clark	1.00	.40
❑	69 Jim Rice	.60	.25
❑	70 Larry Doby	.60	.25
❑	71 Lou Boudreau	.60	.25
❑	72 Lou Brock	1.00	.40
❑	73 Lou Gehrig	2.50	1.00
❑	74 Lou Piniella	.60	.25
❑	75 Luis Aparicio	.60	.25
❑	76 Mark Grace	1.00	.40
❑	77 Mel Ott	1.50	.60
❑	78 Mickey Lolich	.60	.25
❑	79 Mickey Mantle	8.00	3.00
❑	80 Mike Greenwell	.40	.15
❑	81 Mike Schmidt	3.00	1.25
❑	82 Monte Irvin	.60	.25
❑	83 Nellie Fox	1.00	.40
❑	84 Nolan Ryan	4.00	1.50
❑	85 Orlando Cepeda	.60	.25
❑	86 Ozzie Smith	2.50	1.00
❑	87 Paul Molitor	.60	.25
❑	88 Pee Wee Reese	1.00	.40
❑	89 Phil Niekro	.60	.25
❑	90 Phil Rizzuto	1.00	.40
❑	91 Ralph Kiner	1.00	.40
❑	92 Red Rolfe	.40	.15
❑	93 Red Schoendienst	.60	.25
❑	94 Reggie Smith	.40	.15
❑	95 Rich Gossage	.60	.25
❑	96 Richie Ashburn	1.00	.40
❑	97 Rick Ferrell	.60	.25
❑	98 Elston Howard	.60	.25
❑	99 Roberto Clemente	4.00	1.50
❑	100 Robin Roberts	.60	.25
❑	101 Robin Yount	1.50	.60
❑	102 Roger Maris	1.50	.60
❑	103 Rollie Fingers	.60	.25
❑	104 Ron Santo	1.00	.40
❑	105 Roy Campanella	1.50	.60
❑	106 Ryne Sandberg	3.00	1.25
❑	107 Sparky Anderson	.60	.25
❑	108 Sparky Lyle	.40	.15
❑	109 Stan Musial	2.50	1.00
❑	110 Steve Carlton	.60	.25
❑	111 Steve Garvey	.60	.25
❑	112 Ted Williams	3.00	1.25
❑	113 Thurman Munson	1.50	.60
❑	114 Tom Seaver	1.00	.40
❑	115 Tommy Henrich	.60	.25
❑	116 Tommy Lasorda	.60	.25
❑	117 Tony Gwynn	2.00	.75
❑	118 Tony Perez	.60	.25
❑	119 Ty Cobb	2.00	.75
❑	120 Wade Boggs	1.00	.40
❑	121 Warren Spahn	1.00	.40
❑	122 Whitey Ford	1.00	.40
❑	123 Willie McCovey	1.00	.40
❑	124 Willie Randolph	.60	.25
❑	125 Willie Stargell	1.00	.40
❑	126 Yogi Berra	1.50	.60

2005 SP Legendary Cuts

❑	COMPLETE SET (90)	25.00	10.00
❑	COMMON CARD (1-90)	.40	.15
❑	1 Al Kaline	1.50	.60
❑	2 Babe Ruth	5.00	2.00
❑	3 Bill Mazeroski	1.00	.40
❑	4 Billy Williams	.60	.25
❑	5 Bob Feller	1.00	.40
❑	6 Bob Gibson	1.00	.40
❑	7 Bob Lemon	.60	.25
❑	8 Bobby Doerr	.60	.25
❑	9 Brooks Robinson	1.00	.40
❑	10 Carl Yastrzemski	2.50	1.00
❑	11 Carlton Fisk	1.00	.40
❑	12 Casey Stengel	1.00	.40
❑	13 Catfish Hunter	.60	.25
❑	14 Christy Mathewson	1.50	.60
❑	15 Cy Young	1.50	.60
❑	16 Dennis Eckersley	.60	.25
❑	17 Dizzy Dean	1.00	.40
❑	18 Don Drysdale	1.00	.40
❑	19 Don Sutton	.60	.25
❑	20 Duke Snider	1.00	.40
❑	21 Early Wynn	.60	.25
❑	22 Eddie Mathews	1.50	.60
❑	23 Eddie Murray	1.50	.60
❑	24 Enos Slaughter	.60	.25
❑	25 Ernie Banks	1.50	.60
❑	26 Fergie Jenkins	.60	.25
❑	27 Frank Robinson	.60	.25
❑	28 Gary Carter	.60	.25
❑	29 Gaylord Perry	.60	.25
❑	30 Reggie Jackson	1.00	.40
❑	31 George Kell	.60	.25
❑	32 George Sisler	.60	.25
❑	33 Hal Newhouser	.60	.25
❑	34 Harmon Killebrew	1.50	.60
❑	35 Honus Wagner	1.50	.60
❑	36 Jackie Robinson	1.50	.60
❑	37 Jim Bunning	1.00	.40
❑	38 Jim Palmer	.60	.25
❑	39 Jimmie Foxx	1.50	.60
❑	40 Joe DiMaggio	2.50	1.00
❑	41 Joe Morgan	.60	.25
❑	42 Johnny Bench	1.50	.60
❑	43 Johnny Mize	.60	.25
❑	44 Juan Marichal	.60	.25
❑	45 Kirby Puckett	1.50	.60
❑	46 Larry Doby	.60	.25
❑	47 Lefty Grove	1.00	.40
❑	48 Lou Boudreau	.60	.25
❑	49 Lou Brock	1.00	.40
❑	50 Lou Gehrig	2.50	1.00
❑	51 Luis Aparicio	.60	.25
❑	52 Mel Ott	1.50	.60
❑	53 Mickey Cochrane	.60	.25
❑	54 Mickey Mantle	8.00	3.00
❑	55 Mike Schmidt	3.00	1.25
❑	56 Monte Irvin	.60	.25
❑	57 Nolan Ryan	4.00	1.50
❑	58 Orlando Cepeda	.60	.25
❑	59 Ozzie Smith	2.50	1.00
❑	60 Paul Molitor	.60	.25
❑	61 Pee Wee Reese	1.00	.40
❑	62 Phil Niekro	.60	.25
❑	63 Phil Rizzuto	1.00	.40
❑	64 Ralph Kiner	1.00	.40
❑	65 Red Schoendienst	.60	.25
❑	66 Richie Ashburn	1.00	.40
❑	67 Rick Ferrell	.60	.25
❑	68 Robin Roberts	.60	.25
❑	69 Robin Yount	1.50	.60
❑	70 Rod Carew	1.00	.40
❑	71 Rogers Hornsby	1.00	.40
❑	72 Rollie Fingers	.60	.25
❑	73 Roy Campanella	1.50	.60
❑	74 Ryne Sandberg	3.00	1.25
❑	75 Satchel Paige	1.50	.60
❑	76 Stan Musial	2.50	1.00
❑	77 Steve Carlton	.60	.25
❑	78 Ted Williams	3.00	1.25
❑	79 Thurman Munson	1.50	.60
❑	80 Tom Seaver	1.00	.40
❑	81 Tony Gwynn	2.00	.75
❑	82 Tony Perez	.60	.25
❑	83 Ty Cobb	2.00	.75
❑	84 Wade Boggs	1.00	.40
❑	85 Walter Johnson	1.50	.60
❑	86 Warren Spahn	1.00	.40
❑	87 Whitey Ford	1.00	.40
❑	88 Willie McCovey	1.00	.40
❑	89 Willie Stargell	1.00	.40
❑	90 Yogi Berra	1.50	.60

2006 SP Legendary Cuts

❑	COMP.SET w/o SP's (100)	25.00	10.00
❑	COMMON CARD (1-100)	.60	.25
❑	COMMON CARD (101-200)	5.00	2.00
❑	101-200: ONE BASIC OR BRONZE PER BOX		
❑	101-200 PRINT RUN 550 SERIAL #'d SETS		
❑	EXQUISITE EXCH ODDS 1:60		
❑	EXQUISITE EXCH DEADLINE 07/27/07		
❑	1 Juan Marichal	.60	.25
❑	2 Monte Irvin	.60	.25
❑	3 Will Clark	1.00	.40
❑	4 Willie McCovey	1.00	.40
❑	5 Eddie Gaedel	.60	.25
❑	6 Ken Williams	.60	.25
❑	7 Earl Battey	.60	.25
❑	8 Rick Ferrell	.60	.25
❑	9 Bob Gibson	1.00	.40
❑	10 Elmer Flick	.60	.25
❑	11 Joe Medwick	.60	.25
❑	12 Lou Brock	1.00	.40
❑	13 Ozzie Smith	2.50	1.00
❑	14 Red Schoendienst	.60	.25
❑	15 Stan Musial	2.50	1.00
❑	16 Tony Oliva	.60	.25
❑	17 Phil Niekro	.60	.25
❑	18 Boog Powell	.60	.25
❑	19 Brooks Robinson	1.00	.40
❑	20 Cal Ripken	6.00	2.50
❑	21 Eddie Murray	1.50	.60
❑	22 Frank Robinson	.60	.25
❑	23 Jim Palmer	.60	.25

❑ 24	Jocko Conlon	.60	.25
❑ 25	Carlton Fisk	1.00	.40
❑ 26	Dwight Evans	.60	.25
❑ 27	Fred Lynn	.60	.25
❑ 28	Jim Rice	.60	.25
❑ 29	Ted Williams	4.00	1.50
❑ 30	Wade Boggs	1.00	.40
❑ 31	Hugh Duffy	.60	.25
❑ 32	Kid Nichols	.60	.25
❑ 33	Johnny Vander Meer	.60	.25
❑ 34	Dolph Camilli	.60	.25
❑ 35	Carl Yastrzemski	2.50	1.00
❑ 36	Chick Hafey	.60	.25
❑ 37	Kirby Higbe	.60	.25
❑ 38	Pee Wee Reese	1.00	.40
❑ 39	Pete Reiser	.60	.25
❑ 40	Don Sutton	.60	.25
❑ 41	Rod Carew	1.00	.40
❑ 42	Andre Dawson	.60	.25
❑ 43	Billy Herman	.60	.25
❑ 44	Billy Williams	.60	.25
❑ 45	Charley Root	.60	.25
❑ 46	Hack Wilson	1.00	.40
❑ 47	Ernie Banks	1.50	.60
❑ 48	Fergie Jenkins	.60	.25
❑ 49	Gabby Hartnett	.60	.25
❑ 50	Ken Hubbs	.60	.25
❑ 51	Kiki Cuyler	.60	.25
❑ 52	Mark Grace	1.00	.40
❑ 53	Ryne Sandberg	3.00	1.25
❑ 54	Harold Newhouser	.60	.25
❑ 55	Charlie Robertson	.60	.25
❑ 56	Harold Baines	.60	.25
❑ 57	Luis Aparicio	.60	.25
❑ 58	Luke Appling	.60	.25
❑ 59	Nellie Fox	1.00	.40
❑ 60	Ray Schalk	.60	.25
❑ 61	Red Faber	.60	.25
❑ 62	Sloppy Thurston	.60	.25
❑ 63	Freddie Lindstrom	.60	.25
❑ 64	Vern Kennedy	.60	.25
❑ 65	Barry Larkin	1.00	.40
❑ 66	Bucky Walters	.60	.25
❑ 67	Dolf Luque	.60	.25
❑ 68	Al Campanis	.60	.25
❑ 69	Ernie Lombardi	.60	.25
❑ 70	George Foster	.60	.25
❑ 71	Joe Morgan	.60	.25
❑ 72	Johnny Bench	1.50	.60
❑ 73	Ken Griffey Sr.	.60	.25
❑ 74	Ted Kluszewski	1.00	.40
❑ 75	Tony Perez	.60	.25
❑ 76	Wally Post	.60	.25
❑ 77	Bob Feller	.60	.25
❑ 78	Bob Lemon	.60	.25
❑ 79	Earl Averill	.60	.25
❑ 80	Joe Sewell	.60	.25
❑ 81	Johnny Hodapp	.60	.25
❑ 82	Larry Doby	.60	.25
❑ 83	Lou Boudreau	.60	.25
❑ 84	Rocky Colavito	1.00	.40
❑ 85	Stan Coveleski	.60	.25
❑ 86	Nap Lajoie	1.00	.40
❑ 87	Al Kaline	1.50	.60
❑ 88	Alan Trammell	.60	.25
❑ 89	Charlie Gehringer	.60	.25
❑ 90	Denny McLain	.60	.25
❑ 91	Hank Greenberg	1.50	.60
❑ 92	Jack Morris	.60	.25
❑ 93	Mark Fidrych	.60	.25
❑ 94	Ray Boone	.60	.25
❑ 95	Rudy York	.60	.25
❑ 96	Buck Leonard	.60	.25
❑ 97	Bo Jackson	1.50	.60
❑ 98	Zoilo Versalles	.60	.25
❑ 99	John Kruk	.60	.25
❑ 100	Don Drysdale	1.00	.40
❑ 101	Cecil Cooper	5.00	2.00
❑ 102	Vic Wertz	5.00	2.00
❑ 103	Kirk Gibson	5.00	2.00
❑ 104	Maury Wills	5.00	2.00
❑ 105	Steve Garvey	5.00	2.00
❑ 106	Warren Spahn	8.00	3.00
❑ 107	Paul Molitor	5.00	2.00
❑ 108	Robin Yount	8.00	3.00
❑ 109	Rollie Fingers	5.00	2.00
❑ 110	Bob Allison	5.00	2.00
❑ 111	Kirby Puckett	8.00	3.00
❑ 112	Tim Raines	5.00	2.00
❑ 113	George Pipgras	5.00	2.00
❑ 114	Eddie Grant	5.00	2.00
❑ 115	Hoyt Wilhelm	5.00	2.00
❑ 116	Sal Maglie	5.00	2.00
❑ 117	Ron Santo	8.00	3.00
❑ 118	Wally Joyner	5.00	2.00
❑ 119	Tom Seaver	8.00	3.00
❑ 120	Tommie Agee	5.00	2.00
❑ 121	Harmon Killebrew	8.00	3.00
❑ 122	Bill Dickey	5.00	2.00
❑ 123	Early Wynn	5.00	2.00
❑ 124	Bobby Murcer	8.00	3.00
❑ 125	Bucky Dent	5.00	2.00
❑ 126	Dave Winfield	5.00	2.00
❑ 127	Don Larsen	5.00	2.00
❑ 128	Don Mattingly	10.00	4.00
❑ 129	Earle Combs	5.00	2.00
❑ 130	Ed Lopat	5.00	2.00
❑ 131	Elston Howard	5.00	2.00
❑ 132	Everett Scott	5.00	2.00
❑ 133	Goose Gossage	5.00	2.00
❑ 134	Graig Nettles	5.00	2.00
❑ 135	Joe DiMaggio	10.00	4.00
❑ 136	Lou Piniella	5.00	2.00
❑ 137	Bill Skowron	5.00	2.00
❑ 138	Phil Rizzuto	8.00	3.00
❑ 139	Red Ruffing	5.00	2.00
❑ 140	Reggie Jackson	8.00	3.00
❑ 141	Roger Maris	8.00	3.00
❑ 142	Ron Guidry	5.00	2.00
❑ 143	Tiny Bonham	5.00	2.00
❑ 144	Bruce Sutter	5.00	2.00
❑ 145	Tony Lazzeri	5.00	2.00
❑ 146	Waite Hoyt	5.00	2.00
❑ 147	Whitey Ford	8.00	3.00
❑ 148	Steve Sax	5.00	2.00
❑ 149	Yogi Berra	8.00	3.00
❑ 150	Enos Slaughter	5.00	2.00
❑ 151	Catfish Hunter	5.00	2.00
❑ 152	Dennis Eckersley	5.00	2.00
❑ 153	Jose Canseco	8.00	3.00
❑ 154	Al Rosen	5.00	2.00
❑ 155	Al Simmons	5.00	2.00
❑ 156	Chief Bender	5.00	2.00
❑ 157	Cy Williams	5.00	2.00
❑ 158	Mike Schmidt	10.00	4.00
❑ 159	Richie Ashburn	8.00	3.00
❑ 160	Robin Roberts	5.00	2.00
❑ 161	Steve Carlton	5.00	2.00
❑ 162	Judy Johnson	5.00	2.00
❑ 163	Al Oliver	5.00	2.00
❑ 164	Bill Mazeroski	8.00	3.00
❑ 165	Dave Parker	5.00	2.00
❑ 166	Max Carey	5.00	2.00
❑ 167	Pie Traynor	5.00	2.00
❑ 168	Ralph Kiner	5.00	2.00
❑ 169	Roberto Clemente	15.00	6.00
❑ 170	Willie Stargell	5.00	2.00
❑ 171	Gaylord Perry	5.00	2.00
❑ 172	Tony Gwynn	8.00	3.00
❑ 173	Nolan Ryan	10.00	4.00
❑ 174	Joe Carter	5.00	2.00
❑ 175	Frank Howard	5.00	2.00
❑ 176	George Kell	5.00	2.00
❑ 177	Heinie Manush	5.00	2.00
❑ 178	Sam Rice	5.00	2.00
❑ 179	Babe Ruth	15.00	6.00
❑ 180	Casey Stengel	8.00	3.00
❑ 181	Christy Mathewson	8.00	3.00
❑ 182	Cy Young	8.00	3.00
❑ 183	Dizzy Dean	8.00	3.00
❑ 184	Eddie Mathews	8.00	3.00
❑ 185	George Sisler	5.00	2.00
❑ 186	Honus Wagner	8.00	3.00
❑ 187	Jackie Robinson	8.00	3.00
❑ 188	Jimmie Foxx	8.00	3.00
❑ 189	Johnny Mize	5.00	2.00
❑ 190	Lefty Gomez	5.00	2.00
❑ 191	Lou Gehrig	10.00	4.00
❑ 192	Mel Ott	8.00	3.00
❑ 193	Mickey Cochrane	5.00	2.00
❑ 194	Rogers Hornsby	8.00	3.00
❑ 195	Roy Campanella	8.00	3.00
❑ 196	Satchel Paige	8.00	3.00
❑ 197	Thurman Munson	8.00	3.00
❑ 198	Ty Cobb	10.00	4.00
❑ 199	Walter Johnson	8.00	3.00
❑ 200	Lefty Grove	5.00	2.00
❑ NNO	Exquisite Redemption	200.00	125.00

2007 SP Legendary Cuts

❑	COMP.SET w/o SP's (100)	25.00	10.00
❑	COMMON CARD (1-100)	.60	.25
❑	COMMON CARD (101-200)	5.00	2.00
❑	101-200 RANDOMLY INSERTED		
❑	101-200 PRINT RUN 550 SERIAL #'d SETS		
❑ 1	Phil Niekro	.60	.25
❑ 2	Brooks Robinson	1.00	.40
❑ 3	Frank Robinson	.60	.25
❑ 4	Jim Palmer	.60	.25
❑ 5	Cal Ripken Jr.	6.00	2.50
❑ 6	Warren Spahn	1.00	.40
❑ 7	Cy Young	1.50	.60
❑ 8	Carl Yastrzemski	2.50	1.00
❑ 9	Wade Boggs	1.00	.40
❑ 10	Carlton Fisk	1.00	.40
❑ 11	Joe Cronin	.60	.25
❑ 12	Bobby Doerr	.60	.25
❑ 13	Roy Campanella	1.50	.60
❑ 14	Pee Wee Reese	1.00	.40
❑ 15	Rod Carew	1.00	.40
❑ 16	Ernie Banks	1.50	.60
❑ 17	Fergie Jenkins	.60	.25
❑ 18	Billy Williams	.60	.25
❑ 19	Gabby Hartnett	.60	.25
❑ 20	Luis Aparicio	.60	.25
❑ 21	Nellie Fox	1.00	.40
❑ 22	Luke Appling	.60	.25
❑ 23	Joe Morgan	.60	.25
❑ 24	Johnny Bench	1.50	.60
❑ 25	Tony Perez	.60	.25
❑ 26	George Foster	.60	.25
❑ 27	Johnny Vander Meer	.60	.25
❑ 28	Bob Feller	.60	.25
❑ 29	Bob Lemon	.60	.25
❑ 30	Lou Boudreau	.60	.25
❑ 31	Early Wynn	.60	.25
❑ 32	Charlie Gehringer	.60	.25
❑ 33	George Kell	.60	.25
❑ 34	Hal Newhouser	.60	.25
❑ 35	Al Kaline	1.50	.60
❑ 36	Ted Kluszewski	1.00	.40
❑ 37	Harvey Kuenn	.60	.25
❑ 38	Maury Wills	.60	.25
❑ 39	Don Drysdale	1.00	.40
❑ 40	Don Sutton	.60	.25
❑ 41	Eddie Mathews	1.50	.60
❑ 42	Joe Adcock	.60	.25
❑ 43	Paul Molitor	.60	.25
❑ 44	Kirby Puckett	1.50	.60
❑ 45	Harmon Killebrew	1.50	.60
❑ 46	Monte Irvin	.60	.25
❑ 47	Ralph Kiner	1.00	.40
❑ 48	Christy Mathewson	1.50	.60
❑ 49	Hoyt Wilhelm	.60	.25
❑ 50	Tom Seaver	1.00	.40
❑ 51	Allie Reynolds	.60	.25
❑ 52	Joe DiMaggio	3.00	1.25
❑ 53	Lou Gehrig	3.00	1.25
❑ 54	Babe Ruth	4.00	1.50
❑ 55	Casey Stengel	.60	.25

❑ 56 Phil Rizzuto 1.00 .40
❑ 57 Thurman Munson 1.50 .60
❑ 58 Johnny Mize .60 .25
❑ 59 Yogi Berra 1.50 .60
❑ 60 Rube Marquard .60 .25
❑ 61 Don Mattingly 3.00 1.25
❑ 62 Ray Dandridge .60 .25
❑ 63 Rollie Fingers .60 .25
❑ 64 Roberto Clemente 5.00 2.00
❑ 65 Reggie Jackson 1.00 .40
❑ 66 Dennis Eckersley .60 .25
❑ 67 Robin Yount 1.50 .60
❑ 68 Jimmie Foxx 1.50 .60
❑ 69 Lefty Grove .60 .25
❑ 70 Richie Ashburn 1.00 .40
❑ 71 Jim Bunning .60 .25
❑ 72 Steve Carlton .60 .25
❑ 73 Robin Roberts .60 .25
❑ 74 Mike Schmidt 2.50 1.00
❑ 75 Willie Stargell 1.00 .40
❑ 76 Ozzie Smith 2.50 1.00
❑ 77 Bill Mazeroski 1.00 .40
❑ 78 Honus Wagner 1.50 .60
❑ 79 Pie Traynor .60 .25
❑ 80 Tony Gwynn 1.50 .60
❑ 81 Willie McCovey 1.00 .40
❑ 82 Gaylord Perry .60 .25
❑ 83 Juan Marichal .60 .25
❑ 84 Orlando Cepeda .60 .25
❑ 85 Satchel Paige 1.50 .60
❑ 86 George Sisler .60 .25
❑ 87 Ken Boyer .60 .25
❑ 88 Joe Medwick .60 .25
❑ 89 Travis Jackson .60 .25
❑ 90 Stan Musial 2.50 1.00
❑ 91 Dizzy Dean 1.00 .40
❑ 92 Bob Gibson 1.00 .40
❑ 93 Red Schoendienst .60 .25
❑ 94 Lou Brock 1.00 .40
❑ 95 Enos Slaughter .60 .25
❑ 96 Nolan Ryan 4.00 1.50
❑ 97 Smokey Burgess .60 .25
❑ 98 Mickey Vernon .60 .25
❑ 99 Vern Stephens .60 .25
❑ 100 Rick Ferrell .60 .25
❑ 101 Phil Niekro LL 5.00 2.00
❑ 102 Brooks Robinson LL 8.00 3.00
❑ 103 Frank Robinson LL 5.00 2.00
❑ 104 Jim Palmer LL 5.00 2.00
❑ 105 Cal Ripken Jr. LL 12.00 5.00
❑ 106 Warren Spahn LL 8.00 3.00
❑ 107 Cy Young LL 8.00 3.00
❑ 108 Nellie Fox LL 8.00 3.00
❑ 109 Carl Yastrzemski LL 8.00 3.00
❑ 110 Joe Sewell LL 5.00 2.00
❑ 111 Wade Boggs LL 8.00 3.00
❑ 112 Carlton Fisk LL 8.00 3.00
❑ 113 Jackie Robinson LL 8.00 3.00
❑ 114 Roy Campanella LL 8.00 3.00
❑ 115 Pee Wee Reese LL 8.00 3.00
❑ 116 Earl Averill LL 5.00 2.00
❑ 117 Rod Carew LL 8.00 3.00
❑ 118 Ernie Banks LL 8.00 3.00
❑ 119 Fergie Jenkins LL 5.00 2.00
❑ 120 Billy Williams LL 5.00 2.00
❑ 121 Al Lopez LL 5.00 2.00
❑ 122 Luis Aparicio LL 5.00 2.00
❑ 123 Luke Appling LL 5.00 2.00
❑ 124 Joe Morgan LL 5.00 2.00
❑ 125 Johnny Bench LL 8.00 3.00
❑ 126 Tony Perez LL 5.00 2.00
❑ 127 George Foster LL 5.00 2.00
❑ 128 Bob Feller LL 5.00 2.00
❑ 129 Bob Lemon LL 5.00 2.00
❑ 130 Larry Doby LL 5.00 2.00
❑ 131 Lou Boudreau LL 5.00 2.00
❑ 132 George Kell LL 5.00 2.00
❑ 133 Hal Newhouser LL 5.00 2.00
❑ 134 Al Kaline LL 8.00 3.00
❑ 135 Ty Cobb LL 10.00 4.00
❑ 136 Charlie Keller LL 5.00 2.00
❑ 137 Buck Leonard LL 5.00 2.00
❑ 138 Maury Wills LL 5.00 2.00
❑ 139 Don Drysdale LL 8.00 3.00
❑ 140 Don Sutton LL 5.00 2.00
❑ 141 Eddie Mathews LL 8.00 3.00
❑ 142 Paul Molitor LL 5.00 2.00
❑ 143 Kirby Puckett LL 10.00 4.00
❑ 144 Harmon Killebrew LL 8.00 3.00
❑ 145 Monte Irvin LL 5.00 2.00
❑ 146 Mel Ott LL 5.00 2.00
❑ 147 Charlie Gehringer LL 5.00 2.00
❑ 148 Hoyt Wilhelm LL 5.00 2.00
❑ 149 Tom Seaver LL 8.00 3.00
❑ 150 Ted Kluszewski LL 8.00 3.00
❑ 151 Joe DiMaggio LL 10.00 4.00
❑ 152 Lou Gehrig LL 10.00 4.00
❑ 153 Babe Ruth LL 12.00 5.00
❑ 154 Casey Stengel LL 5.00 2.00
❑ 155 Phil Rizzuto LL 8.00 3.00
❑ 156 Thurman Munson LL 8.00 3.00
❑ 157 Johnny Mize LL 5.00 2.00
❑ 158 Yogi Berra LL 8.00 3.00
❑ 159 Roger Maris LL 8.00 3.00
❑ 160 Early Wynn LL 5.00 2.00
❑ 161 Bobby Doerr LL 5.00 2.00
❑ 162 Joe Cronin LL 5.00 2.00
❑ 163 Don Mattingly LL 10.00 4.00
❑ 164 Ray Dandridge LL 5.00 2.00
❑ 165 Rollie Fingers LL 5.00 2.00
❑ 166 Christy Mathewson LL 8.00 3.00
❑ 167 Reggie Jackson LL 8.00 3.00
❑ 168 Dennis Eckersley LL 5.00 2.00
❑ 169 Mickey Cochrane LL 5.00 2.00
❑ 170 Jimmie Foxx LL 8.00 3.00
❑ 171 Lefty Gomez LL 5.00 2.00
❑ 172 Jim Bunning LL 5.00 2.00
❑ 173 Steve Carlton LL 5.00 2.00
❑ 174 Robin Roberts LL 5.00 2.00
❑ 175 Richie Ashburn LL 8.00 3.00
❑ 176 Mike Schmidt LL 8.00 3.00
❑ 177 Ralph Kiner LL 8.00 3.00
❑ 178 Willie Stargell LL 8.00 3.00
❑ 179 Roberto Clemente LL 15.00 6.00
❑ 180 Bill Mazeroski LL 8.00 3.00
❑ 181 Honus Wagner LL 8.00 3.00
❑ 182 Pie Traynor LL 5.00 2.00
❑ 183 Tony Gwynn LL 8.00 3.00
❑ 184 Willie McCovey LL 8.00 3.00
❑ 185 Gaylord Perry LL 5.00 2.00
❑ 186 Juan Marichal LL 5.00 2.00
❑ 187 Orlando Cepeda LL 5.00 2.00
❑ 188 Satchel Paige LL 8.00 3.00
❑ 189 George Sisler LL 5.00 2.00
❑ 190 Rogers Hornsby LL 8.00 3.00
❑ 191 Stan Musial LL 8.00 3.00
❑ 192 Dizzy Dean LL 8.00 3.00
❑ 193 Bob Gibson LL 8.00 3.00
❑ 194 Red Schoendienst LL 5.00 2.00
❑ 195 Lou Brock LL 8.00 3.00
❑ 196 Enos Slaughter LL 5.00 2.00
❑ 197 Nolan Ryan LL 12.00 5.00
❑ 198 Mickey Vernon LL 5.00 2.00
❑ 199 Walter Johnson LL 8.00 3.00
❑ 200 Rick Ferrell LL 5.00 2.00

2004 SP Prospects

❑ COMP.ROOKIES SET (198) 50.00 20.00
❑ COMMON CARD (1-90) 1.00 .40
❑ 1-90 APPX. 2X TOUGHER THAN 91-290
❑ COMMON CARD (91-190 1.00 .40
❑ 91-190 ODDS TWO PER PACK
❑ COMMON CARD (191-290) 1.00 .40
❑ 191-290 APPX.TWO PER PACK
❑ OVERALL AU ODDS 1:5
❑ AU PRINT RUNS B/WN 400-600 PER
❑ 233/237/345/438-443/445 DO NOT EXIST
❑ 1 Roger Clemens 5.00 2.00
❑ 2 Melvin Mora 1.00 .40
❑ 3 Dontrelle Willis 1.50 .60
❑ 4 Jose Vidro 1.00 .40
❑ 5 Oliver Perez 1.00 .40
❑ 6 Carlos Zambrano 1.00 .40
❑ 7 Chipper Jones 2.50 1.00
❑ 8 Greg Maddux 4.00 1.50
❑ 9 Curt Schilling 1.50 .60
❑ 10 Jose Reyes 1.00 .40
❑ 11 David Ortiz 2.50 1.00
❑ 12 Mike Piazza 4.00 1.50
❑ 13 Jason Schmidt 1.00 .40
❑ 14 Randy Johnson 2.50 1.00
❑ 15 Magglio Ordonez 1.00 .40
❑ 16 Mike Mussina 1.50 .60
❑ 17 Jake Peavy 1.00 .40
❑ 18 Jim Edmonds 1.00 .40
❑ 19 Ken Griffey Jr. 4.00 1.50
❑ 20 Jason Giambi 1.00 .40
❑ 21 Mike Sweeney 1.00 .40
❑ 22 Carlos Lee 1.00 .40
❑ 23 Craig Wilson 1.00 .40
❑ 24 Pedro Martinez 1.50 .60
❑ 25 Bobby Abreu 1.00 .40
❑ 26 Mike Lowell 1.00 .40
❑ 27 Miguel Cabrera 1.50 .60
❑ 28 Hank Blalock 1.00 .40
❑ 29 Frank Thomas 2.50 1.00
❑ 30 Manny Ramirez 1.50 .60
❑ 31 Mark Mulder 1.00 .40
❑ 32 Scott Podsednik 1.00 .40
❑ 33 Albert Pujols 5.00 2.00
❑ 34 Preston Wilson 1.00 .40
❑ 35 Todd Helton 1.50 .60
❑ 36 Victor Martinez 1.00 .40
❑ 37 Kerry Wood 1.00 .40
❑ 38 Carlos Beltran 1.00 .40
❑ 39 Vernon Wells 1.00 .40
❑ 40 Sammy Sosa 2.50 1.00
❑ 41 Pat Burrell 1.00 .40
❑ 42 Tim Hudson 1.00 .40
❑ 43 Eric Gagne 1.00 .40
❑ 44 Jim Thome 1.50 .60
❑ 45 Vladimir Guerrero 2.50 1.00
❑ 46 Travis Hafner 1.00 .40
❑ 47 Rickie Weeks 1.00 .40
❑ 48 Miguel Tejada 1.00 .40
❑ 49 Ivan Rodriguez 1.50 .60
❑ 50 J.D. Drew 1.00 .40
❑ 51 Ben Sheets 1.00 .40
❑ 52 Garret Anderson 1.00 .40
❑ 53 Aubrey Huff 1.00 .40
❑ 54 Nomar Garciaparra 4.00 1.50
❑ 55 Luis Gonzalez 1.00 .40
❑ 56 Lance Berkman 1.00 .40
❑ 57 Ichiro Suzuki 5.00 2.00
❑ 58 Torii Hunter 1.00 .40
❑ 59 Adam Dunn 1.00 .40
❑ 60 Mark Teixeira 1.50 .60
❑ 61 Bret Boone 1.00 .40
❑ 62 Roy Oswalt 1.00 .40
❑ 63 Joe Mauer 1.25 .50
❑ 64 Scott Rolen 1.50 .60
❑ 65 Hideki Matsui 4.00 1.50
❑ 66 Richie Sexson 1.00 .40
❑ 67 Jeff Kent 1.00 .40
❑ 68 Barry Zito 1.00 .40
❑ 69 C.C. Sabathia 1.00 .40
❑ 70 Carlos Delgado 1.00 .40
❑ 71 Gary Sheffield 1.00 .40
❑ 72 Shawn Green 1.00 .40
❑ 73 Jason Bay 1.00 .40
❑ 74 Andruw Jones 1.50 .60
❑ 75 Jeff Bagwell 1.50 .60
❑ 76 Rafael Palmeiro 1.50 .60
❑ 77 Alex Rodriguez 4.00 1.50
❑ 78 Adrian Beltre 1.00 .40
❑ 79 Troy Glaus 1.00 .40
❑ 80 Tom Glavine 1.50 .60
❑ 81 Paul Konerko 1.00 .40
❑ 82 Alfonso Soriano 1.00 .40
❑ 83 Roy Halladay 1.00 .40

❑ 84 Derek Jeter 5.00 2.00
❑ 85 Josh Beckett 1.00 .40
❑ 86 Delmon Young 1.50 .60
❑ 87 Brian Giles 1.00 .40
❑ 88 Eric Chavez 1.00 .40
❑ 89 Lyle Overbay 1.00 .40
❑ 90 Mark Prior 1.50 .60
❑ 91 Shawn Camp RC 1.00 .40
❑ 92 Travis Smith 1.00 .40
❑ 93 Juan Padilla RC 1.00 .40
❑ 94 Brad Halsey RC 1.50 .60
❑ 95 Scott Kazmir RC 6.00 2.50
❑ 96 Sam Narron RC 1.00 .40
❑ 97 Frank Francisco RC 1.00 .40
❑ 98 Mike Johnston RC 1.00 .40
❑ 99 Sam McConnell RC 1.00 .40
❑ 100 Josh Labandeira RC 1.00 .40
❑ 101 Kazuhito Tadano RC 1.50 .60
❑ 102 Hector Gimenez RC 1.00 .40
❑ 103 David Aardsma RC 1.50 .60
❑ 104 Charles Thomas RC 1.00 .40
❑ 105 Ian Snell RC 2.00 .75
❑ 106 Jeff Keppinger RC 1.00 .40
❑ 107 Michael Vento RC 1.50 .60
❑ 108 Jerry Gil RC 1.00 .40
❑ 109 Marty McLeary RC 1.00 .40
❑ 110 Donnie Kelly RC 1.00 .40
❑ 111 Roman Colon RC 1.00 .40
❑ 112 Travis Blackley RC 1.00 .40
❑ 113 Edwardo Sierra RC 1.50 .60
❑ 114 Chris Shelton RC 2.00 .75
❑ 115 Bartolome Fortunato RC 1.00 .40
❑ 116 Brandon Medders RC 1.00 .40
❑ 117 Merkin Valdez RC 1.50 .60
❑ 118 Carlos Vasquez RC 1.50 .60
❑ 119 Shingo Takatsu RC 1.50 .60
❑ 120 Aarom Baldiris RC 1.50 .60
❑ 121 Chris Aguila RC 1.00 .40
❑ 122 Jimmy Serrano RC 1.00 .40
❑ 123 Mike Gosling RC 1.00 .40
❑ 124 Brian Dallimore RC 1.00 .40
❑ 125 Ronald Belisario RC 1.00 .40
❑ 126 George Sherrill RC 1.00 .40
❑ 127 Fernando Nieve RC 1.50 .60
❑ 128 Abe Alvarez RC 1.50 .60
❑ 129 Jeff Bennett RC 1.00 .40
❑ 130 Ryan Meaux RC 1.00 .40
❑ 131 Edwin Moreno RC 1.50 .60
❑ 132 Jesse Crain RC 1.50 .60
❑ 133 Scott Dohmann RC 1.00 .40
❑ 134 Ronny Cedeno RC 2.00 .75
❑ 135 Orlando Rodriguez RC 1.00 .40
❑ 136 Michael Wuertz RC 1.50 .60
❑ 137 Justin Hampson RC 1.00 .40
❑ 138 Matt Treanor RC 1.00 .40
❑ 139 Andy Green RC 1.00 .40
❑ 140 Yadier Molina RC 2.50 1.00
❑ 141 Joe Nelson RC 1.00 .40
❑ 142 Justin Lehr RC 1.00 .40
❑ 143 Ryan Wing RC 1.00 .40
❑ 144 Kevin Cave RC 1.00 .40
❑ 145 Evan Rust RC 1.00 .40
❑ 146 Mike Rouse RC 1.00 .40
❑ 147 Lance Cormier RC 1.00 .40
❑ 148 Eduardo Villacis RC 1.00 .40
❑ 149 Justin Knoedler RC 1.00 .40
❑ 150 Freddy Guzman RC 1.00 .40
❑ 151 Casey Daigle RC 1.00 .40
❑ 152 Joey Gathright RC 2.00 .75
❑ 153 Tim Bittner RC 1.00 .40
❑ 154 Scott Atchison RC 1.00 .40
❑ 155 Ivan Ochoa RC 1.00 .40
❑ 156 Lincoln Holdzkom RC 1.00 .40
❑ 157 Onil Joseph RC 1.00 .40
❑ 158 Jason Bartlett RC 1.50 .60
❑ 159 Jon Knott RC 1.00 .40
❑ 160 Jake Woods RC 1.00 .40
❑ 161 Jerome Gamble RC 1.00 .40
❑ 162 Sean Henn RC 1.00 .40
❑ 163 Kazuo Matsui RC 1.50 .60
❑ 164 Roberto Novoa RC 1.50 .60
❑ 165 Eddy Rodriguez RC 1.50 .60
❑ 166 Ramon Ramirez RC 1.00 .40
❑ 167 Enemencio Pacheco RC 1.00 .40
❑ 168 Chad Bentz RC 1.00 .40
❑ 169 Chris Oxspring RC 1.00 .40
❑ 170 Justin Leone RC 1.50 .60
❑ 171 Joe Horgan RC 1.00 .40
❑ 172 Jose Capellan RC 1.50 .60
❑ 173 Greg Dobbs RC 1.00 .40
❑ 174 Jason Frasor RC 1.00 .40
❑ 175 Shawn Hill RC 1.00 .40
❑ 176 Carlos Hines RC 1.00 .40
❑ 177 John Gall RC 1.50 .60
❑ 178 Steve Andrade RC 1.00 .40
❑ 179 Scott Proctor RC 1.50 .60
❑ 180 Rusty Tucker RC 1.50 .60
❑ 181 Dave Crouthers RC 1.00 .40
❑ 182 Franklyn Gracesqui RC 1.00 .40
❑ 183 Justin Germano RC 1.00 .40
❑ 184 Alfredo Simon RC 1.00 .40
❑ 185 Jorge Sequea RC 1.00 .40
❑ 186 Nick Regilio RC 1.00 .40
❑ 187 Justin Huisman RC 1.00 .40
❑ 188 Akinori Otsuka RC 1.00 .40
❑ 189 Luis Gonzalez RC 1.00 .40
❑ 190 Renyel Pinto RC 1.50 .60
❑ 191 Joshua Leblanc RC 1.50 .60
❑ 192 Devin Ivany RC 2.00 .75
❑ 193 Chad Blackwell RC 1.50 .60
❑ 194 Brandon Burgess RC 1.50 .60
❑ 195 Cory Patton RC 1.50 .60
❑ 196 Daniel Batz RC 1.50 .60
❑ 197 Adam Russell RC 1.50 .60
❑ 198 Jarrett Hoffpauir RC 2.00 .75
❑ 199 Patrick Bryant RC 1.50 .60
❑ 200 Sean Gamble RC 2.00 .75
❑ 201 Jermaine Brock RC 2.00 .75
❑ 202 Ben Zobrist RC 2.00 .75
❑ 203 Clay Meredith RC 2.00 .75
❑ 204 Derek Tharpe RC 1.50 .60
❑ 205 Bradley McCann RC 2.50 1.00
❑ 206 Justin Hedrick RC 1.50 .60
❑ 207 Clint Sammons RC 2.00 .75
❑ 208 Richard Steik RC 1.50 .60
❑ 209 Fernando Perez RC 2.00 .75
❑ 210 Mark Jecmen RC 1.50 .60
❑ 211 Benjamin Harrison RC 1.50 .60
❑ 212 Jason Quarles RC 1.50 .60
❑ 213 William Layman RC 1.50 .60
❑ 214 Koley Kolberg RC 1.50 .60
❑ 215 Randy Dicken RC 1.00 .40
❑ 216 Barry Richmond RC 1.50 .60
❑ 217 Timothy Murphey RC 1.50 .60
❑ 218 John Hardy RC 1.50 .60
❑ 219 Sebastien Boucher RC 2.00 .75
❑ 220 Andrew Alvarado RC 1.50 .60
❑ 221 Patrick Perry RC 2.00 .75
❑ 222 Jarod McAuliff RC 1.50 .60
❑ 223 Jared Gaston RC 1.50 .60
❑ 224 William Thompson RC 1.50 .60
❑ 225 Lucas French RC 1.50 .60
❑ 226 Brandon Parillo RC 2.00 .75
❑ 227 Gregory Goetz RC 1.50 .60
❑ 228 David Haehnel RC 2.00 .75
❑ 229 James Miller RC 1.50 .60
❑ 230 Mark Roberts RC 1.50 .60
❑ 231 Eric Ridener RC 1.50 .60
❑ 232 Freddy Sandoval RC 1.50 .60
❑ 234 Carlos Medero-Stullz RC 1.50 .60
❑ 235 Matthew Shepherd RC 1.50 .60
❑ 236 Thomas Hubbard RC 1.50 .60
❑ 238 Kyle Bono RC 2.00 .75
❑ 239 Craig Moldrem RC 1.00 .40
❑ 240 Brandon Timm RC 2.00 .75
❑ 241 Mike Carp RC 2.50 1.00
❑ 242 Joseph Muro RC 1.50 .60
❑ 243 Derek Decarlo RC 1.50 .60
❑ 244 Christopher Niesel RC 2.00 .75
❑ 245 Trevor Lawhorn RC 2.00 .75
❑ 246 Joey Howell RC 2.00 .75
❑ 247 Dustin Hahn RC 1.50 .60
❑ 248 James Fasano RC 2.00 .75
❑ 249 Hainley Statia RC 2.00 .75
❑ 250 Brandon Conway RC 1.50 .60
❑ 251 Christopher McConnell RC 2.50 1.00
❑ 252 Austin Shappi RC 2.00 .75
❑ 253 Joseph Metropoulos RC 2.00 .75
❑ 254 David Nicholson RC 2.00 .75
❑ 255 Ryan McCarthy RC 2.00 .75
❑ 256 Michael Parisi RC 1.50 .60
❑ 257 Andrew Macfarlane RC 1.50 .60
❑ 258 Jeffrey Dominguez RC 2.00 .75
❑ 259 Troy Patton RC 5.00 2.00
❑ 260 Ryan Norwood RC 2.50 1.00
❑ 261 Chad Boyd RC 1.50 .60
❑ 262 Grant Plumley RC 1.50 .60
❑ 263 Jeffrey Katz RC 2.00 .75
❑ 264 Cory Middleton RC 1.50 .60
❑ 265 Andrew Moffitt RC 1.00 .40
❑ 266 Jarrett Grube RC 1.50 .60
❑ 267 Derek Hankins RC 1.50 .60
❑ 268 Douglas Reinhardt RC 1.50 .60
❑ 269 Duron Legrande RC 1.50 .60
❑ 270 Steven Jackson RC 1.50 .60
❑ 271 Brian Hall RC 2.00 .75
❑ 272 Cory Wade RC 2.00 .75
❑ 273 John Grogan RC 1.50 .60
❑ 274 Robert Asanovich RC 2.00 .75
❑ 275 Kevin Hart RC 2.00 .75
❑ 276 Matthew Guillory RC 1.50 .60
❑ 277 Clifton Remole RC 1.50 .60
❑ 278 David Trahan RC 1.50 .60
❑ 279 Kristian Bell RC 1.00 .40
❑ 280 Christopher Westervelt RC 1.50 .60
❑ 281 Garry Bakker RC 1.50 .60
❑ 282 Jonathan Ash RC 2.00 .75
❑ 283 Ryan Phillips RC 1.50 .60
❑ 284 Wesley Letson RC 1.50 .60
❑ 285 Jeffrey Landing RC 1.50 .60
❑ 286 Mark Worrell RC 1.50 .60
❑ 287 Sean Gallagher RC 5.00 2.00
❑ 288 Nicholas Blasi RC 1.50 .60
❑ 289 Kevin Frandsen RC 3.00 1.25
❑ 290 Richard Mercado RC 1.50 .60
❑ 291 Matt Bush AU 400/RC 30.00 15.00
❑ 292 Mark Rogers AU 400/RC 25.00 10.00
❑ 293 Homer Bailey AU 400/RC 150.00 100.00
❑ 294 Chris Nelson AU 400/RC 60.00 30.00
❑ 295 T.Diamond AU 400/RC 30.00 12.50
❑ 296 Neil Walker AU 400/RC 80.00 40.00
❑ 297 Bill Bray AU 400/RC 10.00 4.00
❑ 298 David Purcey AU 400/RC 15.00 6.00
❑ 299 Scott Elbert AU 400/RC 60.00 30.00
❑ 300 Josh Fields AU 400/RC 100.00 50.00
❑ 301 Chris Lambert AU 400/RC 25.00 10.00
❑ 302 Trevor Plouffe AU 400/RC 30.00 12.50
❑ 303 Greg Golson AU 400/RC 30.00 12.50
❑ 304 Philip Hughes AU 400/RC 250.00 150.00
❑ 305 Kyle Waldrop AU 400/RC 25.00 10.00
❑ 306 Richie Robnett AU 350/RC 40.0015.00
❑ 307 T.Tankersley AU 400/RC 15.00 6.00
❑ 308 Blake Dewitt AU 400/RC 40.00 20.00
❑ 309 Eric Hurley AU 400/RC 60.00 30.00
❑ 310 J.Howell AU 400/RC EX * 25.00 10.00
❑ 311 Zachary Jackson AU 400/RC 15.006.00
❑ 312 Justin Orenduff AU 400/RC 25.0010.00
❑ 313 Tyler Lumsden AU 400/RC 15.00 6.00
❑ 314 Matthew Fox AU 600/RC 8.00 3.00
❑ 315 Danny Putnam AU 450/RC 15.00 6.00
❑ 316 Jon Poterson AU 400/RC 15.00 6.00
❑ 317 Gio Gonzalez AU 400/RC 80.00 40.00
❑ 318 Jay Rainville AU 475/RC 25.00 10.00
❑ 319 Huston Street AU 400/RC 50.00 20.00
❑ 320 Jeff Marquez AU 400/RC 50.00 20.00
❑ 321 Eric Beattie AU 500/RC 15.00 6.00
❑ 322 Reid Brignac AU 325/RC 175.00100.00
❑ 323 Y.Gallardo AU 400/RC 150.00 75.00
❑ 324 Justin Hoyman AU 400/RC 15.00 6.00
❑ 325 B.J. Szymanski AU 400/RC 20.00 8.00
❑ 326 Seth Smith AU 600/RC 30.00 12.50
❑ 327 Karl Herren AU 600/RC 15.00 6.00
❑ 328 Brian Bixler AU 600/RC 15.00 6.00
❑ 329 Wesley Whisler AU 600/RC 8.00 3.00
❑ 330 E.San Pedro AU 400/RC 15.00 6.00
❑ 331 Billy Buckner AU 400/RC 15.00 6.00
❑ 332 Jon Zeringue AU 400/RC 25.00 10.00
❑ 333 Curtis Thigpen AU 400/RC 25.00 10.00
❑ 334 Blake Johnson AU 400/RC 15.00 6.00
❑ 335 Donald Lucy AU 400/RC 10.00 4.00
❑ 336 Michael Ferris AU 600/RC 12.00 5.00
❑ 337 A.Swarzak AU 600/RC 25.00 10.00
❑ 338 Jason Jaramillo AU 400/RC 20.00 8.00
❑ 339 Hunter Pence AU 600/RC 250.00 190.00
❑ 340 Dustin Pedroia AU 400/RC 120.00 60.00
❑ 341 Grant Johnson AU 400/RC 15.00 6.00
❑ 342 Kurt Suzuki AU 400/RC 40.00 15.00
❑ 343 Jason Vargas AU 600/RC 25.00 10.00

344 Raymond Liotta AU 400/RC	30.00	15.00
346 Eric Campbell AU 400/RC	60.00	30.00
347 Jeffrey Frazier AU 400/RC	20.00	8.00
348 G.Hernandez AU 400/RC	25.00	10.00
349 Wade Davis AU 600/RC	80.00	40.00
350 J.Wahpepah AU 400/RC	10.00	4.00
351 Scott Lewis AU 400/RC	30.00	12.50
352 Jeff Fiorentino AU 400/RC	20.00	8.00
353 S.Register AU 600/RC	8.00	3.00
354 Michael Schlact AU 400/RC	10.00	4.00
355 Eddie Prasch AU 400/RC	15.00	6.00
356 Adam Lind AU 400/RC	150.00	75.00
357 Ian Desmond AU 400/RC	25.00	10.00
358 Josh Johnson AU 575/RC	12.00	5.00
359 Garrett Mock AU 600/RC	8.00	3.00
360 Danny Hill AU 600/RC	8.00	3.00
361 Cory Dunlap AU 600/RC	25.00	10.00
362 Grant Hansen AU 600/RC	8.00	3.00
363 Eric Haberer AU 400/RC	10.00	4.00
364 E.Morlan AU 400/RC	25.00	10.00
365 James Happ AU 600/RC	25.00	10.00
366 M.Tuiasosopo AU 600/RC	50.00	20.00
367 Jordan Parraz AU 400/RC	20.00	8.00
368 Andrew Dobies AU 400/RC	20.00	8.00
369 Mark Reed AU 400/RC	25.00	10.00
370 Jason Windsor AU 400/RC	20.00	8.00
371 Gregory Burns AU 600/RC	15.00	6.00
372 Christian Garcia AU 600/RC	20.00	8.00
373 John Bowker AU 575/RC	25.00	10.00
374 J.C. Holt AU 550/RC	12.00	5.00
375 Daryl Jones AU 400/RC	25.00	10.00
376 Collin Mahoney AU 400/RC	15.00	6.00
377 A.Hathaway AU 400/RC	15.00	6.00
378 Matthew Spring AU 400/RC	10.00	4.00
379 Joshua Baker AU 400/RC	10.00	4.00
380 Charles Lofgren AU 400/RC	50.00	20.00
381 Raf Gonzalez AU 400/RC	25.00	10.00
382 Brad Bergesen AU 575/RC	15.00	6.00
383 Brandon Boggs AU 400/RC	15.00	6.00
384 J.Bauserman AU 400/RC	10.00	4.00
385 Collin Balester AU 500/RC	40.00	15.00
386 James Moore AU 400/RC	10.00	4.00
387 Robert Janssen AU 400/RC	25.00	10.00
388 Luis Guerra AU 400/RC	15.00	6.00
389 Lucas Harrell AU 550/RC	15.00	6.00
390 Donnie Smith AU 500/RC	12.00	5.00
391 Mark Robinson AU 525/RC	12.00	5.00
392 Louis Marson AU 550/RC	15.00	6.00
393 Rob Johnson AU 600/RC	12.00	5.00
394 L.Santangelo AU 600/RC	12.00	5.00
395 T.Hottovy AU 400/RC	15.00	6.00
396 Ryan Webb AU 400/RC	15.00	6.00
397 Jamar Walton AU 400/RC	15.00	6.00
398 Jason Jones AU 400/RC	25.00	10.00
399 Clay Timpner AU 600/RC	12.00	5.00
400 James Parr AU 400/RC	15.00	6.00
401 Sean Kazmar AU 400/RC	10.00	4.00
402 Andrew Kown AU 400/RC	15.00	6.00
403 Jacob McGee AU 600/RC	80.00	40.00
404 Michael Butia AU 600/RC	8.00	3.00
405 Paul Janish AU 500/RC	15.00	6.00
406 Matthew Macri AU 400/RC	25.00	10.00
407 Mike Nickeas AU 500/RC	12.00	5.00
408 Kyle Bloom AU 550/RC	10.00	4.00
409 Luis Rivera AU 500/RC	12.00	5.00
410 William Bunn AU 600/RC	25.00	10.00
411 Enrique Barrera AU 400/RC	25.00	10.00
412 R.Klosterman AU 400/RC	10.00	4.00
413 John Raglani AU 515/RC	20.00	8.00
414 Brandon Allen AU 500/RC	20.00	8.00
415 A.Baldwin AU 600/RC	8.00	3.00
416 Mark Lowe AU 400/RC	50.00	20.00
417 Mitch Einertson AU 400/RC	50.00	20.00
418 Ryan Schroyer AU 600/RC	12.00	5.00
419 Bradley Davis AU 400/RC	10.00	4.00
420 Jesse Hoover AU 500/RC	12.00	5.00
421 G.Broshuis AU 400/RC	20.00	8.00
422 Peter Pope AU 400/RC	20.00	8.00
423 Brent Dlugach AU 400/RC	15.00	6.00
424 Ryan Coultas AU 400/RC	15.00	6.00
425 Ryan Royster AU 400/RC	80.00	40.00
426 S.Chapman AU 400/RC	15.00	6.00
427 B.Chamberlin AU 400/RC	20.00	8.00
428 J.Koshansky AU 550/RC	60.00	30.00
429 William Susdorf AU 400/RC	10.00	4.00
430 A.J. Johnson AU 400/RC	20.00	8.00
431 Jeremy Sowers AU 400/RC	60.00	30.00
432 Justin Pekarek AU 400/RC	15.00	6.00
433 Brett Smith AU 400/RC	30.00	12.50
434 Matt Durkin AU 400/RC	15.00	6.00
435 Daniel Barone AU 400/RC	10.00	4.00
436 Scott Hyde AU 400/RC	15.00	6.00
437 T.Everidge AU 400/RC	50.00	20.00
444 Mark Trumbo AU 400/RC	40.00	15.00
446 Eric Patterson AU 400/RC	25.00	10.00
447 Michael Rozier AU 400/RC	15.00	6.00

1996 SPx

COMPLETE SET (60)	50.00	20.00
1 Greg Maddux	3.00	1.25
2 Chipper Jones	2.00	.75
3 Fred McGriff	1.25	.50
4 Tom Glavine	1.25	.50
5 Cal Ripken	6.00	2.50
6 Roberto Alomar	1.25	.50
7 Rafael Palmeiro	1.25	.50
8 Jose Canseco	1.25	.50
9 Roger Clemens	4.00	1.50
10 Mo Vaughn	.75	.30
11 Jim Edmonds	.75	.30
12 Tim Salmon	1.25	.50
13 Sammy Sosa	2.00	.75
14 Ryne Sandberg	3.00	1.25
15 Mark Grace	1.25	.50
16 Frank Thomas	2.00	.75
17 Barry Larkin	1.25	.50
18 Kenny Lofton	.75	.30
19 Albert Belle	.75	.30
20 Eddie Murray	2.00	.75
21 Manny Ramirez	1.25	.50
22 Dante Bichette	.75	.30
23 Larry Walker	.75	.30
24 Vinny Castilla	.75	.30
25 Andres Galarraga	.75	.30
26 Cecil Fielder	.75	.30
27 Gary Sheffield	.75	.30
28 Craig Biggio	1.25	.50
29 Jeff Bagwell	1.25	.50
30 Derek Bell	.75	.30
31 Johnny Damon	1.25	.50
32 Eric Karros	.75	.30
33 Mike Piazza	3.00	1.25
34 Raul Mondesi	.75	.30
35 Hideo Nomo	2.00	.75
36 Kirby Puckett	2.00	.75
37 Paul Molitor	.75	.30
38 Marty Cordova	.75	.30
39 Rondell White	.75	.30
40 Jason Isringhausen	.75	.30
41 Paul Wilson	.75	.30
42 Rey Ordonez	.75	.30
43 Derek Jeter	5.00	2.00
44 Wade Boggs	1.25	.50
45 Mark McGwire	5.00	2.00
46 Jason Kendall	.75	.30
47 Ron Gant	.75	.30
48 Ozzie Smith	3.00	1.25
49 Tony Gwynn	2.50	1.00
50 Ken Caminiti	.75	.30
51 Barry Bonds	5.00	2.00
52 Matt Williams	.75	.30
53 Osvaldo Fernandez	.75	.30
54 Jay Buhner	.75	.30
55 Ken Griffey Jr.	3.00	1.25
56 Randy Johnson	2.00	.75
57 Alex Rodriguez	4.00	1.50
58 Juan Gonzalez	.75	.30
59 Joe Carter	.75	.30
60 Carlos Delgado	.75	.30
KG1 Ken Griffey Jr. Comm.	5.00	2.00
MP1 Mike Piazza Trib.	5.00	2.00
KGA1 Ken Griffey Jr. Auto.	175.00	90.00
MPA1 Mike Piazza Auto.	200.00	125.00

1998 SPx Finite

COMP.YM SER.1 (30)	40.00	15.00
COMMON YM (1-30)	1.50	.60
COMP.PE SER.1 (20)	120.00	50.00
COMMON PE (31-50)	2.50	1.00
COMP.BASIC SER.1 (90)	80.00	30.00
COMMON CARD (51-140)	1.00	.40
COMP.SF SER.1 (30)	100.00	40.00
COMMON SF (141-170)	1.25	.50
COMP.HG SER.1 (10)	150.00	60.00
COMMON HG (171-180)	4.00	1.50
COMP.YM SER.2 (30)	60.00	25.00
COMMON YM (181-210)	1.50	.60
COMP.PP SER.2 (30)	80.00	30.00
COMMON PP (211-240)	1.25	.50
COMP.BASIC SER.2 (90)	50.00	20.00
COMMON CARD (241-330)	1.00	.40
COMP.TW SER.2 (20)	30.00	12.50
COMMON TW (331-350)	2.50	1.00
COMP.CG SER.2 (10)	150.00	60.00
COMMON CG (351-360)	4.00	1.50
1 Nomar Garciaparra YM	6.00	2.50
2 Miguel Tejada YM	4.00	1.50
3 Mike Cameron YM	1.50	.60
4 Ken Cloude YM	1.50	.60
5 Jaret Wright YM	1.50	.60
6 Mark Kotsay YM	1.50	.60
7 Craig Counsell YM	1.50	.60
8 Jose Guillen YM	1.50	.60
9 Neifi Perez YM	1.50	.60
10 Jose Cruz Jr. YM	1.50	.60
11 Brett Tomko YM	1.50	.60
12 Matt Morris YM	1.50	.60
13 Justin Thompson YM	1.50	.60
14 Jeremi Gonzalez YM	1.50	.60
15 Scott Rolen YM	2.50	1.00
16 Vladimir Guerrero YM	4.00	1.50
17 Brad Fullmer YM	1.50	.60
18 Brian Giles YM	1.50	.60
19 Todd Dunwoody YM	1.50	.60
20 Ben Grieve YM	1.50	.60
21 Juan Encarnacion YM	1.50	.60
22 Aaron Boone YM	1.50	.60
23 Richie Sexson YM	1.50	.60
24 Richard Hidalgo YM	1.50	.60
25 Andruw Jones YM	2.50	1.00
26 Todd Helton YM	2.50	1.00
27 Paul Konerko YM	1.50	.60
28 Dante Powell YM	1.50	.60
29 Eli Marrero YM	1.50	.60
30 Derek Jeter YM	10.00	4.00
31 Mike Piazza PE	10.00	4.00
32 Tony Clark PE	2.50	1.00
33 Larry Walker PE	2.50	1.00
34 Jim Thome PE	4.00	1.50
35 Juan Gonzalez PE	5.00	2.00
36 Jeff Bagwell PE	4.00	1.50
37 Jay Buhner PE	2.50	1.00

❑ 38 Tim Salmon PE 4.00 1.50
❑ 39 Albert Belle PE 2.50 1.00
❑ 40 Mark McGwire PE 15.00 6.00
❑ 41 Sammy Sosa PE 6.00 2.50
❑ 42 Mo Vaughn PE 2.50 1.00
❑ 43 Manny Ramirez PE 4.00 1.50
❑ 44 Tino Martinez PE 4.00 1.50
❑ 45 Frank Thomas PE 6.00 2.50
❑ 46 Nomar Garciaparra PE 10.00 4.00
❑ 47 Alex Rodriguez PE 10.00 4.00
❑ 48 Chipper Jones PE 6.00 2.50
❑ 49 Barry Bonds PE 15.00 6.00
❑ 50 Ken Griffey Jr. PE 10.00 4.00
❑ 51 Jason Dickson 1.00 .40
❑ 52 Jim Edmonds 1.00 .40
❑ 53 Darin Erstad 1.00 .40
❑ 54 Tim Salmon 1.50 .60
❑ 55 Chipper Jones 2.50 1.00
❑ 56 Ryan Klesko 1.00 .40
❑ 57 Tom Glavine 1.50 .60
❑ 58 Denny Neagle 1.00 .40
❑ 59 John Smoltz 1.50 .60
❑ 60 Javy Lopez 1.00 .40
❑ 61 Roberto Alomar 1.50 .60
❑ 62 Rafael Palmeiro 1.50 .60
❑ 63 Mike Mussina 1.50 .60
❑ 64 Cal Ripken 8.00 3.00
❑ 65 Mo Vaughn 1.00 .40
❑ 66 Tim Naehring 1.00 .40
❑ 67 John Valentin 1.00 .40
❑ 68 Mark Grace 1.50 .60
❑ 69 Kevin Orie 1.00 .40
❑ 70 Sammy Sosa 2.50 1.00
❑ 71 Albert Belle 1.00 .40
❑ 72 Frank Thomas 2.50 1.00
❑ 73 Robin Ventura 1.00 .40
❑ 74 David Justice 1.00 .40
❑ 75 Kenny Lofton 1.00 .40
❑ 76 Omar Vizquel 1.50 .60
❑ 77 Manny Ramirez 1.50 .60
❑ 78 Jim Thome 1.50 .60
❑ 79 Dante Bichette 1.00 .40
❑ 80 Larry Walker 1.00 .40
❑ 81 Vinny Castilla 1.00 .40
❑ 82 Ellis Burks 1.00 .40
❑ 83 Bobby Higginson 1.00 .40
❑ 84 Brian Hunter 1.00 .40
❑ 85 Tony Clark 1.00 .40
❑ 86 Mike Hampton 1.00 .40
❑ 87 Jeff Bagwell 1.50 .60
❑ 88 Craig Biggio 1.50 .60
❑ 89 Derek Bell 1.00 .40
❑ 90 Mike Piazza 4.00 1.50
❑ 91 Ramon Martinez 1.00 .40
❑ 92 Raul Mondesi 1.00 .40
❑ 93 Hideo Nomo 2.50 1.00
❑ 94 Eric Karros 1.00 .40
❑ 95 Paul Molitor 1.00 .40
❑ 96 Marty Cordova 1.00 .40
❑ 97 Brad Radke 1.00 .40
❑ 98 Mark Grudzielanek 1.00 .40
❑ 99 Carlos Perez 1.00 .40
❑ 100 Rondell White 1.00 .40
❑ 101 Todd Hundley 1.00 .40
❑ 102 Edgardo Alfonzo 1.00 .40
❑ 103 John Franco 1.00 .40
❑ 104 John Olerud 1.00 .40
❑ 105 Tino Martinez 1.50 .60
❑ 106 David Cone 1.00 .40
❑ 107 Paul O'Neill 1.50 .60
❑ 108 Andy Pettitte 1.50 .60
❑ 109 Bernie Williams 1.50 .60
❑ 110 Rickey Henderson 4.00 1.50
❑ 111 Jason Giambi 1.00 .40
❑ 112 Matt Stairs 1.00 .40
❑ 113 Gregg Jefferies 1.00 .40
❑ 114 Rico Brogna 1.00 .40
❑ 115 Curt Schilling 1.00 .40
❑ 116 Jason Schmidt 1.00 .40
❑ 117 Jose Guillen 1.00 .40
❑ 118 Kevin Young 1.00 .40
❑ 119 Ray Lankford 1.00 .40
❑ 120 Mark McGwire 6.00 2.50
❑ 121 Delino DeShields 1.00 .40
❑ 122 Ken Caminiti 1.00 .40
❑ 123 Tony Gwynn 3.00 1.25
❑ 124 Trevor Hoffman 1.00 .40
❑ 125 Barry Bonds 6.00 2.50
❑ 126 Jeff Kent 1.00 .40
❑ 127 Shawn Estes 1.00 .40
❑ 128 J.T. Snow 1.00 .40
❑ 129 Jay Buhner 1.00 .40
❑ 130 Ken Griffey Jr. 4.00 1.50
❑ 131 Dan Wilson 1.00 .40
❑ 132 Edgar Martinez 1.50 .60
❑ 133 Alex Rodriguez 4.00 1.50
❑ 134 Rusty Greer 1.00 .40
❑ 135 Juan Gonzalez 1.00 .40
❑ 136 Fernando Tatis 1.00 .40
❑ 137 Ivan Rodriguez 1.50 .60
❑ 138 Carlos Delgado 1.00 .40
❑ 139 Pat Hentgen 1.00 .40
❑ 140 Roger Clemens 5.00 2.00
❑ 141 Chipper Jones SF 3.00 1.25
❑ 142 Greg Maddux SF 5.00 2.00
❑ 143 Rafael Palmeiro SF 2.00 .75
❑ 144 Mike Mussina SF 2.00 .75
❑ 145 Cal Ripken SF 10.00 4.00
❑ 146 Nomar Garciaparra SF 5.00 2.00
❑ 147 Mo Vaughn SF 1.25 .50
❑ 148 Sammy Sosa SF 3.00 1.25
❑ 149 Albert Belle SF 1.25 .50
❑ 150 Frank Thomas SF 3.00 1.25
❑ 151 Jim Thome SF 2.00 .75
❑ 152 Kenny Lofton SF 1.25 .50
❑ 153 Manny Ramirez SF 2.00 .75
❑ 154 Larry Walker SF 1.25 .50
❑ 155 Jeff Bagwell SF 2.00 .75
❑ 156 Craig Biggio SF 2.00 .75
❑ 157 Mike Piazza SF 5.00 2.00
❑ 158 Paul Molitor SF 1.25 .50
❑ 159 Derek Jeter SF 8.00 3.00
❑ 160 Tino Martinez SF 2.00 .75
❑ 161 Curt Schilling SF 1.25 .50
❑ 162 Mark McGwire SF 8.00 3.00
❑ 163 Tony Gwynn SF 4.00 1.50
❑ 164 Barry Bonds SF 8.00 3.00
❑ 165 Ken Griffey Jr. SF 5.00 2.00
❑ 166 Randy Johnson SF 3.00 1.25
❑ 167 Alex Rodriguez SF 5.00 2.00
❑ 168 Juan Gonzalez SF 1.25 .50
❑ 169 Ivan Rodriguez SF 2.00 .75
❑ 170 Roger Clemens SF 6.00 2.50
❑ 171 Greg Maddux HG 15.00 6.00
❑ 172 Cal Ripken HG 30.00 12.50
❑ 173 Frank Thomas HG 10.00 4.00
❑ 174 Jeff Bagwell HG 6.00 2.50
❑ 175 Mike Piazza HG 15.00 6.00
❑ 176 Mark McGwire HG 25.00 10.00
❑ 177 Barry Bonds HG 25.00 10.00
❑ 178 Ken Griffey Jr. HG 15.00 6.00
❑ 179 Alex Rodriguez HG 15.00 6.00
❑ 180 Roger Clemens HG 20.00 8.00
❑ 181 Mike Caruso YM 1.50 .60
❑ 182 David Ortiz YM 5.00 2.00
❑ 183 Gabe Alvarez YM 1.50 .60
❑ 184 Gary Matthews Jr. YM RC 2.50 1.00
❑ 185 Kerry Wood YM 2.00 .75
❑ 186 Carl Pavano YM 1.50 .60
❑ 187 Alex Gonzalez YM 1.50 .60
❑ 188 Masato Yoshii YM RC 1.50 .60
❑ 189 Larry Sutton YM 1.50 .60
❑ 190 Russell Branyan YM 1.50 .60
❑ 191 Bruce Chen YM 1.50 .60
❑ 192 Rolando Arrojo YM RC 1.50 .60
❑ 193 Ryan Christenson YM RC 1.50 .60
❑ 194 Cliff Politte YM 1.50 .60
❑ 195 A.J. Hinch YM 1.50 .60
❑ 196 Kevin Witt YM 1.50 .60
❑ 197 Daryle Ward YM 1.50 .60
❑ 198 Corey Koskie YM RC 2.50 1.00
❑ 199 Mike Lowell YM RC 10.00 4.00
❑ 200 Travis Lee YM 1.50 .60
❑ 201 Kevin Millwood YM RC 5.00 2.00
❑ 202 Robert Smith YM 1.50 .60
❑ 203 Magglio Ordonez YM RC 15.00 6.00
❑ 204 Eric Milton YM 1.50 .60
❑ 205 Geoff Jenkins YM 1.50 .60
❑ 206 Rich Butler YM RC 1.50 .60
❑ 207 Mike Kinkade YM RC 1.50 .60
❑ 208 Braden Looper YM 1.50 .60
❑ 209 Matt Clement YM 1.50 .60
❑ 210 Derrek Lee YM 2.50 1.00
❑ 211 Randy Johnson PP 3.00 1.25
❑ 212 John Smoltz PP 2.00 .75
❑ 213 Roger Clemens PP 6.00 2.50
❑ 214 Curt Schilling PP 1.25 .50
❑ 215 Pedro Martinez PP 2.00 .75
❑ 216 Vinny Castilla PP 1.25 .50
❑ 217 Jose Cruz Jr. PP 1.25 .50
❑ 218 Jim Thome PP 2.00 .75
❑ 219 Alex Rodriguez PP 5.00 2.00
❑ 220 Frank Thomas PP 3.00 1.25
❑ 221 Tim Salmon PP 2.00 .75
❑ 222 Larry Walker PP 1.25 .50
❑ 223 Albert Belle PP 1.25 .50
❑ 224 Manny Ramirez PP 2.00 .75
❑ 225 Mark McGwire PP 8.00 3.00
❑ 226 Mo Vaughn PP 1.25 .50
❑ 227 Andres Galarraga PP 1.25 .50
❑ 228 Scott Rolen PP 2.00 .75
❑ 229 Travis Lee PP 1.25 .50
❑ 230 Mike Piazza PP 5.00 2.00
❑ 231 Nomar Garciaparra PP 5.00 2.00
❑ 232 Andruw Jones PP 2.00 .75
❑ 233 Barry Bonds PP 8.00 3.00
❑ 234 Jeff Bagwell PP 2.00 .75
❑ 235 Juan Gonzalez PP 1.25 .50
❑ 236 Tino Martinez PP 2.00 .75
❑ 237 Vladimir Guerrero PP 3.00 1.25
❑ 238 Rafael Palmeiro PP 2.00 .75
❑ 239 Russell Branyan PP 1.25 .50
❑ 240 Ken Griffey Jr. PP 5.00 2.00
❑ 241 Cecil Fielder 1.00 .40
❑ 242 Chuck Finley 1.00 .40
❑ 243 Jay Bell 1.00 .40
❑ 244 Andy Benes 1.00 .40
❑ 245 Matt Williams 1.00 .40
❑ 246 Brian Anderson 1.00 .40
❑ 247 Dave Dellucci RC 1.50 .60
❑ 248 Andres Galarraga 1.00 .40
❑ 249 Andruw Jones 1.50 .60
❑ 250 Greg Maddux 4.00 1.50
❑ 251 Brady Anderson 1.00 .40
❑ 252 Joe Carter 1.00 .40
❑ 253 Eric Davis 1.00 .40
❑ 254 Pedro Martinez 1.50 .60
❑ 255 Nomar Garciaparra 4.00 1.50
❑ 256 Dennis Eckersley 1.00 .40
❑ 257 Henry Rodriguez 1.00 .40
❑ 258 Jeff Blauser 1.00 .40
❑ 259 Jaime Navarro 1.00 .40
❑ 260 Ray Durham 1.00 .40
❑ 261 Chris Stynes 1.00 .40
❑ 262 Willie Greene 1.00 .40
❑ 263 Reggie Sanders 1.00 .40
❑ 264 Bret Boone 1.00 .40
❑ 265 Barry Larkin 1.50 .60
❑ 266 Travis Fryman 1.00 .40
❑ 267 Charles Nagy 1.00 .40
❑ 268 Sandy Alomar Jr. 1.00 .40
❑ 269 Darryl Kile 1.00 .40
❑ 270 Mike Lansing 1.00 .40
❑ 271 Pedro Astacio 1.00 .40
❑ 272 Damion Easley 1.00 .40
❑ 273 Joe Randa 1.00 .40
❑ 274 Luis Gonzalez 1.00 .40
❑ 275 Mike Piazza 4.00 1.50
❑ 276 Todd Zeile 1.00 .40
❑ 277 Edgar Renteria 1.00 .40
❑ 278 Livan Hernandez 1.00 .40
❑ 279 Cliff Floyd 1.00 .40
❑ 280 Moises Alou 1.00 .40
❑ 281 Billy Wagner 1.00 .40
❑ 282 Jeff King 1.00 .40
❑ 283 Hal Morris 1.00 .40
❑ 284 Johnny Damon 1.50 .60
❑ 285 Dean Palmer 1.00 .40
❑ 286 Tim Belcher 1.00 .40
❑ 287 Eric Young 1.00 .40
❑ 288 Bobby Bonilla 1.00 .40
❑ 289 Gary Sheffield 1.00 .40
❑ 290 Chan Ho Park 1.00 .40
❑ 291 Charles Johnson 1.00 .40
❑ 292 Jeff Cirillo 1.00 .40
❑ 293 Jeromy Burnitz 1.00 .40
❑ 294 Jose Valentin 1.00 .40
❑ 295 Marquis Grissom 1.00 .40

❑ 296 Todd Walker	1.00	.40
❑ 297 Terry Steinbach	1.00	.40
❑ 298 Rick Aguilera	1.00	.40
❑ 299 Vladimir Guerrero	2.50	1.00
❑ 300 Rey Ordonez	1.00	.40
❑ 301 Butch Huskey	1.00	.40
❑ 302 Bernard Gilkey	1.00	.40
❑ 303 Mariano Rivera	2.50	1.00
❑ 304 Chuck Knoblauch	1.00	.40
❑ 305 Derek Jeter	6.00	2.50
❑ 306 Ricky Bottalico	1.00	.40
❑ 307 Bob Abreu	1.00	.40
❑ 308 Scott Rolen	1.50	.60
❑ 309 Al Martin	1.00	.40
❑ 310 Jason Kendall	1.00	.40
❑ 311 Brian Jordan	1.00	.40
❑ 312 Ron Gant	1.00	.40
❑ 313 Todd Stottlemyre	1.00	.40
❑ 314 Greg Vaughn	1.00	.40
❑ 315 Kevin Brown	1.50	.60
❑ 316 Wally Joyner	1.00	.40
❑ 317 Robb Nen	1.00	.40
❑ 318 Orel Hershiser	1.00	.40
❑ 319 Russ Davis	1.00	.40
❑ 320 Randy Johnson	2.50	1.00
❑ 321 Quinton McCracken	1.00	.40
❑ 322 Tony Saunders	1.00	.40
❑ 323 Wilson Alvarez	1.00	.40
❑ 324 Wade Boggs	1.50	.60
❑ 325 Fred McGriff	1.50	.60
❑ 326 Lee Stevens	1.00	.40
❑ 327 John Wetteland	1.00	.40
❑ 328 Jose Canseco	1.50	.60
❑ 329 Randy Myers	1.00	.40
❑ 330 Jose Cruz Jr.	1.00	.40
❑ 331 Matt Williams TW	2.50	1.00
❑ 332 Andres Galarraga TW	2.50	1.00
❑ 333 Walt Weiss TW	2.50	1.00
❑ 334 Joe Carter TW	2.50	1.00
❑ 335 Pedro Martinez TW	4.00	1.50
❑ 336 Henry Rodriguez TW	2.50	1.00
❑ 337 Travis Fryman TW	2.50	1.00
❑ 338 Darryl Kile TW	2.50	1.00
❑ 339 Mike Lansing TW	2.50	1.00
❑ 340 Mike Piazza TW	10.00	4.00
❑ 341 Moises Alou TW	2.50	1.00
❑ 342 Charles Johnson TW	2.50	1.00
❑ 343 Chuck Knoblauch TW	2.50	1.00
❑ 344 Rickey Henderson TW	6.00	2.50
❑ 345 Kevin Brown TW	4.00	1.50
❑ 346 Orel Hershiser TW	2.50	1.00
❑ 347 Wade Boggs TW	4.00	1.50
❑ 348 Fred McGriff TW	4.00	1.50
❑ 349 Jose Canseco TW	4.00	1.50
❑ 350 Gary Sheffield TW	2.50	1.00
❑ 351 Travis Lee CG	4.00	1.50
❑ 352 Nomar Garciaparra CG	15.00	6.00
❑ 353 Frank Thomas CG	10.00	4.00
❑ 354 Cal Ripken CG	30.00	12.50
❑ 355 Mark McGwire CG	25.00	10.00
❑ 356 Mike Piazza CG	15.00	6.00
❑ 357 Alex Rodriguez CG	15.00	6.00
❑ 358 Barry Bonds CG	25.00	10.00
❑ 359 Tony Gwynn CG	12.00	5.00
❑ 360 Ken Griffey Jr. CG	15.00	6.00

1999 SPx

❑ COMP.SET w/o SP's (80)	25.00	10.00
❑ COMMON MCGWIRE (1-10)	1.50	.60
❑ COMMON CARD (11-80)	.50	.20
❑ COMMON SP (81-120)	10.00	4.00
❑ 1 Mark McGwire 61	3.00	1.25
❑ 2 Mark McGwire 62	3.00	1.25
❑ 3 Mark McGwire 63	1.50	.60
❑ 4 Mark McGwire 64	1.50	.60
❑ 5 Mark McGwire 65	1.50	.60
❑ 6 Mark McGwire 66	1.50	.60
❑ 7 Mark McGwire 67	1.50	.60
❑ 8 Mark McGwire 68	1.50	.60
❑ 9 Mark McGwire 69	1.50	.60
❑ 10 Mark McGwire 70	4.00	1.50
❑ 11 Mo Vaughn	.50	.20
❑ 12 Darin Erstad	.50	.20
❑ 13 Travis Lee	.50	.20
❑ 14 Randy Johnson	1.25	.50
❑ 15 Matt Williams	.50	.20
❑ 16 Chipper Jones	1.25	.50
❑ 17 Greg Maddux	2.00	.75
❑ 18 Andruw Jones	.75	.30
❑ 19 Andres Galarraga	.50	.20
❑ 20 Cal Ripken	4.00	1.50
❑ 21 Albert Belle	.50	.20
❑ 22 Mike Mussina	.75	.30
❑ 23 Nomar Garciaparra	2.00	.75
❑ 24 Pedro Martinez	.75	.30
❑ 25 John Valentin	.50	.20
❑ 26 Kerry Wood	.50	.20
❑ 27 Sammy Sosa	1.25	.50
❑ 28 Mark Grace	.75	.30
❑ 29 Frank Thomas	1.25	.50
❑ 30 Mike Caruso	.50	.20
❑ 31 Barry Larkin	.75	.30
❑ 32 Sean Casey	.50	.20
❑ 33 Jim Thome	.75	.30
❑ 34 Kenny Lofton	.50	.20
❑ 35 Manny Ramirez	.75	.30
❑ 36 Larry Walker	.50	.20
❑ 37 Todd Helton	.75	.30
❑ 38 Vinny Castilla	.50	.20
❑ 39 Tony Clark	.50	.20
❑ 40 Derrek Lee	.75	.30
❑ 41 Mark Kotsay	.50	.20
❑ 42 Jeff Bagwell	.75	.30
❑ 43 Craig Biggio	.75	.30
❑ 44 Moises Alou	.50	.20
❑ 45 Larry Sutton	.50	.20
❑ 46 Johnny Damon	.75	.30
❑ 47 Gary Sheffield	.50	.20
❑ 48 Raul Mondesi	.50	.20
❑ 49 Jeromy Burnitz	.50	.20
❑ 50 Todd Walker	.50	.20
❑ 51 David Ortiz	1.25	.50
❑ 52 Vladimir Guerrero	1.25	.50
❑ 53 Rondell White	.50	.20
❑ 54 Mike Piazza	2.00	.75
❑ 55 Derek Jeter	3.00	1.25
❑ 56 Tino Martinez	.75	.30
❑ 57 Roger Clemens	2.50	1.00
❑ 58 Ben Grieve	.50	.20
❑ 59 A.J. Hinch	.50	.20
❑ 60 Scott Rolen	.75	.30
❑ 61 Doug Glanville	.50	.20
❑ 62 Aramis Ramirez	.50	.20
❑ 63 Jose Guillen	.50	.20
❑ 64 Tony Gwynn	1.50	.60
❑ 65 Greg Vaughn	.50	.20
❑ 66 Ruben Rivera	.50	.20
❑ 67 Barry Bonds	3.00	1.25
❑ 68 J.T. Snow	.50	.20
❑ 69 Alex Rodriguez	2.00	.75
❑ 70 Ken Griffey Jr.	2.00	.75
❑ 71 Jay Buhner	.50	.20
❑ 72 Mark McGwire	3.00	1.25
❑ 73 Fernando Tatis	.50	.20
❑ 74 Quinton McCracken	.50	.20
❑ 75 Wade Boggs	.75	.30
❑ 76 Ivan Rodriguez	.75	.30
❑ 77 Juan Gonzalez	.50	.20
❑ 78 Rafael Palmeiro	.75	.30
❑ 79 Jose Cruz Jr.	.50	.20
❑ 80 Carlos Delgado	.50	.20
❑ 81 Troy Glaus SP	15.00	6.00
❑ 82 Vladimir Nunez SP	10.00	4.00
❑ 83 George Lombard SP	10.00	4.00
❑ 84 Bruce Chen SP	10.00	4.00
❑ 85 Ryan Minor SP	10.00	4.00
❑ 86 Calvin Pickering SP	10.00	4.00
❑ 87 Jin Ho Cho SP	10.00	4.00
❑ 88 Russ Branyan SP	10.00	4.00
❑ 89 Derrick Gibson SP	10.00	4.00
❑ 90 Gabe Kapler SP AU	15.00	6.00
❑ 91 Matt Anderson SP	10.00	4.00
❑ 92 Robert Fick SP	10.00	4.00
❑ 93 Juan Encarnacion SP	10.00	4.00
❑ 94 Preston Wilson SP	10.00	4.00
❑ 95 Alex Gonzalez SP	10.00	4.00
❑ 96 Carlos Beltran SP	15.00	6.00
❑ 97 Jeremy Giambi SP	10.00	4.00
❑ 98 Dee Brown SP	10.00	4.00
❑ 99 Adrian Beltre SP	10.00	4.00
❑ 100 Alex Cora SP	10.00	4.00
❑ 101 Angel Pena SP	10.00	4.00
❑ 102 Geoff Jenkins SP	10.00	4.00
❑ 103 Ronnie Belliard SP	10.00	4.00
❑ 104 Corey Koskie SP	10.00	4.00
❑ 105 A.J. Pierzynski SP	10.00	4.00
❑ 106 Michael Barrett SP	10.00	4.00
❑ 107 Fernando Seguignol SP	10.00	4.00
❑ 108 Mike Kinkade SP	10.00	4.00
❑ 109 Mike Lowell SP	10.00	4.00
❑ 110 Ricky Ledee SP	10.00	4.00
❑ 111 Eric Chavez SP	10.00	4.00
❑ 112 Abraham Nunez SP	10.00	4.00
❑ 113 Matt Clement SP	10.00	4.00
❑ 114 Ben Davis SP	10.00	4.00
❑ 115 Mike Darr SP	10.00	4.00
❑ 116 Ramon E.Martinez SP RC	10.00	4.00
❑ 117 Carlos Guillen SP	10.00	4.00
❑ 118 Shane Monahan SP	10.00	4.00
❑ 119 J.D. Drew SP AU	15.00	6.00
❑ 120 Kevin Witt SP	10.00	4.00
❑ 24EAST Ken Griffey Jr. Sample	2.00	.75

2000 SPx

❑ COMP.BASIC w/o SP's (90)	25.00	10.00
❑ COMP.UPDATE w/o SP's (30)	10.00	4.00
❑ COMMON CARD (1-90)	.50	.20
❑ COMMON AU/1500 (91-120)	10.00	4.00
❑ COMMON (121-135/182-196)	8.00	3.00
❑ COMMON CARD (136-151)	10.00	4.00
❑ COMMON CARD (152-181)	.75	.30
❑ 1 Troy Glaus	.50	.20
❑ 2 Mo Vaughn	.50	.20
❑ 3 Ramon Ortiz	.50	.20
❑ 4 Jeff Bagwell	.75	.30
❑ 5 Moises Alou	.50	.20
❑ 6 Craig Biggio	.75	.30
❑ 7 Jose Lima	.50	.20
❑ 8 Jason Giambi	.50	.20
❑ 9 John Jaha	.50	.20
❑ 10 Matt Stairs	.50	.20
❑ 11 Chipper Jones	1.25	.50
❑ 12 Greg Maddux	2.00	.75
❑ 13 Andres Galarraga	.50	.20
❑ 14 Andruw Jones	.75	.30
❑ 15 Jeromy Burnitz	.50	.20
❑ 16 Ron Belliard	.50	.20
❑ 17 Carlos Delgado	.50	.20
❑ 18 David Wells	.50	.20
❑ 19 Tony Batista	.50	.20
❑ 20 Shannon Stewart	.50	.20

	Card		
❑	21 Sammy Sosa	1.25	.50
❑	22 Mark Grace	.75	.30
❑	23 Henry Rodriguez	.50	.20
❑	24 Mark McGwire	3.00	1.25
❑	25 J.D. Drew	.50	.20
❑	26 Luis Gonzalez	.50	.20
❑	27 Randy Johnson	1.25	.50
❑	28 Matt Williams	.50	.20
❑	29 Steve Finley	.50	.20
❑	30 Shawn Green	.50	.20
❑	31 Kevin Brown	.75	.30
❑	32 Gary Sheffield	.50	.20
❑	33 Jose Canseco	.75	.30
❑	34 Greg Vaughn	.50	.20
❑	35 Vladimir Guerrero	1.25	.50
❑	36 Michael Barrett	.50	.20
❑	37 Russ Ortiz	.50	.20
❑	38 Barry Bonds	3.00	1.25
❑	39 Jeff Kent	.50	.20
❑	40 Richie Sexson	.50	.20
❑	41 Manny Ramirez	.75	.30
❑	42 Jim Thome	.75	.30
❑	43 Roberto Alomar	.75	.30
❑	44 Edgar Martinez	.75	.30
❑	45 Alex Rodriguez	2.00	.75
❑	46 John Olerud	.50	.20
❑	47 Alex Gonzalez	.50	.20
❑	48 Cliff Floyd	.50	.20
❑	49 Mike Piazza	2.00	.75
❑	50 Al Leiter	.50	.20
❑	51 Robin Ventura	.75	.30
❑	52 Edgardo Alfonzo	.50	.20
❑	53 Albert Belle	.50	.20
❑	54 Cal Ripken	4.00	1.50
❑	55 B.J. Surhoff	.50	.20
❑	56 Tony Gwynn	1.50	.60
❑	57 Trevor Hoffman	.50	.20
❑	58 Brian Giles	.50	.20
❑	59 Jason Kendall	.50	.20
❑	60 Kris Benson	.50	.20
❑	61 Bob Abreu	.50	.20
❑	62 Scott Rolen	.75	.30
❑	63 Curt Schilling	.50	.20
❑	64 Mike Lieberthal	.50	.20
❑	65 Sean Casey	.50	.20
❑	66 Dante Bichette	.50	.20
❑	67 Ken Griffey Jr.	2.00	.75
❑	68 Pokey Reese	.50	.20
❑	69 Mike Sweeney	.50	.20
❑	70 Carlos Febles	.50	.20
❑	71 Ivan Rodriguez	.75	.30
❑	72 Ruben Mateo	.50	.20
❑	73 Rafael Palmeiro	.75	.30
❑	74 Larry Walker	.50	.20
❑	75 Todd Helton	.75	.30
❑	76 Nomar Garciaparra	2.00	.75
❑	77 Pedro Martinez	.75	.30
❑	78 Troy O'Leary	.50	.20
❑	79 Jacque Jones	.50	.20
❑	80 Corey Koskie	.50	.20
❑	81 Juan Gonzalez	.50	.20
❑	82 Dean Palmer	.50	.20
❑	83 Juan Encarnacion	.50	.20
❑	84 Frank Thomas	1.25	.50
❑	85 Magglio Ordonez	.50	.20
❑	86 Paul Konerko	.50	.20
❑	87 Bernie Williams	.75	.30
❑	88 Derek Jeter	3.00	1.25
❑	89 Roger Clemens	2.50	1.00
❑	90 Orlando Hernandez	.50	.20
❑	91 Vernon Wells AU/1500	25.00	10.00
❑	93 Eric Chavez AU/1500	25.00	10.00
❑	94 Alfonso Soriano AU/1500	60.00	30.00
❑	95 Eric Gagne AU/1500	60.00	30.00
❑	96 Rob Bell AU/1500	10.00	4.00
❑	97 Matt Riley AU/1500	10.00	4.00
❑	98 Josh Beckett AU/1500	100.00	50.00
❑	99 Ben Petrick AU/1500	10.00	4.00
❑	100 Rob Ramsay AU/1500	10.00	4.00
❑	101 Scott Williamson AU/1500	10.00	4.00
❑	102 Doug Davis AU/1500	15.00	6.00
❑	103 Eric Munson AU/1500	10.00	4.00
❑	104 Pat Burrell AU/500	80.00	40.00
❑	105 Jim Morris AU/1500	25.00	10.00
❑	106 Gabe Kapler AU/500	40.00	15.00
❑	107 Lance Berkman/1000	8.00	3.00
❑	108 Erubiel Durazo AU/1500	10.00	4.00
❑	109 Tim Hudson AU/1500	40.00	15.00
❑	110 Ben Davis AU/1500	10.00	4.00
❑	111 Nick Johnson AU/1500	15.00	6.00
❑	112 Octavio Dotel AU/1500	10.00	4.00
❑	113 Jerry Hairston/1000	8.00	3.00
❑	114 Ruben Mateo/1000	8.00	3.00
❑	115 Chris Singleton/1000	8.00	3.00
❑	116 Bruce Chen AU/1500	10.00	4.00
❑	117 Derrick Gibson/1000	8.00	3.00
❑	118 Carlos Beltran AU/500	125.00	75.00
❑	119 Freddy Garcia AU/1500	15.00	6.00
❑	120 Preston Wilson AU/1500	15.00	6.00
❑	121 Brad Wilkerson/1600 RC	10.00	4.00
❑	122 Roy Oswalt/1600 RC	150.00	75.00
❑	123 Wascar Serrano/1600 RC	8.00	3.00
❑	124 Sean Burnett/1600 RC	8.00	3.00
❑	125 Alex Cabrera/1600 RC	8.00	3.00
❑	126 Timo Perez/1600 RC	8.00	3.00
❑	127 Juan Pierre/1600 RC	10.00	4.00
❑	128 Daylan Holt/1600 RC	8.00	3.00
❑	129 Tomokazu Ohka/1600 RC	8.00	3.00
❑	130 Kazuhiro Sasaki/1600 RC	10.00	4.00
❑	131 Kurt Ainsworth/1600 RC	8.00	3.00
❑	132 Brent Abernathy/1600 RC	8.00	3.00
❑	133 Danys Baez/1600 RC	8.00	3.00
❑	134 Brad Cresse/1600 RC	8.00	3.00
❑	135 Ryan Franklin/1600 RC	8.00	3.00
❑	136 Mike Lamb AU/1500 RC	15.00	6.00
❑	137 David Espinosa AU/1500 RC	10.00	4.00
❑	138 Matt Wheatland AU/1500 RC	10.00	4.00
❑	139 Xavier Nady AU/1500 RC	40.00	15.00
❑	140 Scott Heard AU/1500 RC	10.00	4.00
❑	141 P.Coco AU/1500 UER54 RC	10.00	4.00
❑	142 Justin Miller AU/1500 RC	10.00	4.00
❑	143 Dave Krynzel AU/1500 RC	10.00	4.00
❑	144 Dane Sardinha AU/1500 RC	10.00	4.00
❑	145 Ben Sheets AU/1500 RC	50.00	20.00
❑	146 Leo Estrella AU/1500 RC	10.00	4.00
❑	147 Ben Diggins AU/1500 RC	10.00	4.00
❑	148 Barry Zito AU/1500 RC	80.00	40.00
❑	149 Joe Torres AU/1500 RC	10.00	4.00
❑	150 Mike Meyers AU/1500 RC	10.00	4.00
❑	151 Kris Wilson AU/1500 RC	10.00	4.00
❑	152 Darin Erstad	.75	.30
❑	153 Richard Hidalgo	.75	.30
❑	154 Eric Chavez	.75	.30
❑	155 B.J. Surhoff	.75	.30
❑	156 Richie Sexson	.75	.30
❑	157 Raul Mondesi	.75	.30
❑	158 Rondell White	.75	.30
❑	159 Jim Edmonds	.75	.30
❑	160 Curt Schilling	.75	.30
❑	161 Tom Goodwin	.75	.30
❑	162 Fred McGriff	1.25	.50
❑	163 Jose Vidro	.75	.30
❑	164 Ellis Burks	.75	.30
❑	165 David Segui	.75	.30
❑	166 Aaron Sele	.75	.30
❑	167 Henry Rodriguez	.75	.30
❑	168 Mike Bordick	.75	.30
❑	169 Mike Mussina	1.25	.50
❑	170 Ryan Klesko	.75	.30
❑	171 Kevin Young	.75	.30
❑	172 Travis Lee	.75	.30
❑	173 Aaron Boone	.75	.30
❑	174 Jermaine Dye	.75	.30
❑	175 Ricky Ledee	.75	.30
❑	176 Jeffrey Hammonds	.75	.30
❑	177 Carl Everett	.75	.30
❑	178 Matt Lawton	.75	.30
❑	179 Bobby Higginson	.75	.30
❑	180 Charles Johnson	.75	.30
❑	181 David Justice	.75	.30
❑	182 Joey Nation/1600 RC	8.00	3.00
❑	183 Rico Washington/1600 RC	8.00	3.00
❑	184 Luis Matos/1600 RC	8.00	3.00
❑	185 Chris Wakeland/1600 RC	8.00	3.00
❑	186 Sun Woo Kim/1600 RC	8.00	3.00
❑	187 Keith Ginter/1600 RC	8.00	3.00
❑	188 Geraldo Guzman/1600 RC	8.00	3.00
❑	189 Jay Spurgeon/1600 RC	8.00	3.00
❑	190 Jace Brewer/1600 RC	8.00	3.00
❑	191 Juan Guzman/1600 RC	8.00	3.00
❑	192 Ross Gload/1600 RC	8.00	3.00
❑	193 Paxton Crawford/1600 RC	8.00	3.00
❑	194 Ryan Kohlmeier/1600 RC	8.00	3.00
❑	195 Julio Zuleta/1600 RC	8.00	3.00
❑	196 Matt Ginter/1600 RC	8.00	3.00

2001 SPx

	Card		
❑	COMP.BASIC w/o SP's (90)	25.00	10.00
❑	COMP.UPDATE w/o SP's (30)	10.00	4.00
❑	COMMON CARD (1-90)	.50	.20
❑	COMMON YS (91-120)	5.00	2.00
❑	COMMON JSY (121-135)	8.00	3.00
❑	COMMON JSY AU (136-150)	15.00	6.00
❑	COMMON CARD (151-180)	.75	.30
❑	COMMON CARD (181-205)	5.00	2.00
❑	1 Darin Erstad	.50	.20
❑	2 Troy Glaus	.50	.20
❑	3 Mo Vaughn	.50	.20
❑	4 Johnny Damon	.75	.30
❑	5 Jason Giambi	.50	.20
❑	6 Tim Hudson	.50	.20
❑	7 Miguel Tejada	.50	.20
❑	8 Carlos Delgado	.50	.20
❑	9 Raul Mondesi	.50	.20
❑	10 Tony Batista	.50	.20
❑	11 Ben Grieve	.50	.20
❑	12 Greg Vaughn	.50	.20
❑	13 Juan Gonzalez	.50	.20
❑	14 Jim Thome	.75	.30
❑	15 Roberto Alomar	.75	.30
❑	16 John Olerud	.50	.20
❑	17 Edgar Martinez	.75	.30
❑	18 Albert Belle	.50	.20
❑	19 Cal Ripken	4.00	1.50
❑	20 Ivan Rodriguez	.75	.30
❑	21 Rafael Palmeiro	.75	.30
❑	22 Alex Rodriguez	2.00	.75
❑	23 Nomar Garciaparra	2.00	.75
❑	24 Pedro Martinez	.75	.30
❑	25 Manny Ramirez Sox	.75	.30
❑	26 Jermaine Dye	.50	.20
❑	27 Mark Quinn	.50	.20
❑	28 Carlos Beltran	.50	.20
❑	29 Tony Clark	.50	.20
❑	30 Bobby Higginson	.50	.20
❑	31 Eric Milton	.50	.20
❑	32 Matt Lawton	.50	.20
❑	33 Frank Thomas	1.25	.50
❑	34 Magglio Ordonez	.50	.20
❑	35 Ray Durham	.50	.20
❑	36 David Wells	.50	.20
❑	37 Derek Jeter	3.00	1.25
❑	38 Bernie Williams	.75	.30
❑	39 Roger Clemens	2.50	1.00
❑	40 David Justice	.50	.20
❑	41 Jeff Bagwell	.75	.30
❑	42 Richard Hidalgo	.50	.20
❑	43 Moises Alou	.50	.20
❑	44 Chipper Jones	1.25	.50
❑	45 Andruw Jones	.75	.30
❑	46 Greg Maddux	2.00	.75
❑	47 Rafael Furcal	.50	.20
❑	48 Jeromy Burnitz	.50	.20
❑	49 Geoff Jenkins	.50	.20
❑	50 Mark McGwire	3.00	1.25
❑	51 Jim Edmonds	.50	.20
❑	52 Rick Ankiel	.50	.20
❑	53 Edgar Renteria	.50	.20
❑	54 Sammy Sosa	1.25	.50
❑	55 Kerry Wood	.50	.20

❑ 56 Rondell White .50 .20
❑ 57 Randy Johnson 1.25 .50
❑ 58 Steve Finley .50 .20
❑ 59 Matt Williams .50 .20
❑ 60 Luis Gonzalez .50 .20
❑ 61 Kevin Brown .50 .20
❑ 62 Gary Sheffield .50 .20
❑ 63 Shawn Green .50 .20
❑ 64 Vladimir Guerrero 1.25 .50
❑ 65 Jose Vidro .50 .20
❑ 66 Barry Bonds 3.00 1.25
❑ 67 Jeff Kent .50 .20
❑ 68 Livan Hernandez .50 .20
❑ 69 Preston Wilson .50 .20
❑ 70 Charles Johnson .50 .20
❑ 71 Cliff Floyd .50 .20
❑ 72 Mike Piazza 2.00 .75
❑ 73 Edgardo Alfonzo .50 .20
❑ 74 Jay Payton .50 .20
❑ 75 Robin Ventura .50 .20
❑ 76 Tony Gwynn 1.50 .60
❑ 77 Phil Nevin .50 .20
❑ 78 Ryan Klesko .50 .20
❑ 79 Scott Rolen .75 .30
❑ 80 Pat Burrell .50 .20
❑ 81 Bob Abreu .50 .20
❑ 82 Brian Giles .50 .20
❑ 83 Kris Benson .50 .20
❑ 84 Jason Kendall .50 .20
❑ 85 Ken Griffey Jr. 2.00 .75
❑ 86 Barry Larkin .75 .30
❑ 87 Sean Casey .50 .20
❑ 88 Todd Helton .75 .30
❑ 89 Larry Walker .50 .20
❑ 90 Mike Hampton .50 .20
❑ 91 Billy Sylvester YS RC 5.00 2.00
❑ 92 Josh Towers YS RC 8.00 3.00
❑ 93 Zach Day YS RC 5.00 2.00
❑ 94 Martin Vargas YS RC 5.00 2.00
❑ 95 Adam Pettyjohn YS RC 5.00 2.00
❑ 96 Andres Torres YS RC 5.00 2.00
❑ 97 Kris Keller YS RC 5.00 2.00
❑ 98 Blaine Neal YS RC 5.00 2.00
❑ 99 Kyle Kessel YS RC 5.00 2.00
❑ 100 Greg Miller YS RC 5.00 2.00
❑ 101 Shawn Sonnier YS 5.00 2.00
❑ 102 Alexis Gomez YS RC 5.00 2.00
❑ 103 Grant Balfour YS RC 5.00 2.00
❑ 104 Henry Mateo YS RC 5.00 2.00
❑ 105 Wilken Ruan YS RC 5.00 2.00
❑ 106 Nick Maness YS RC 5.00 2.00
❑ 107 Jason Michaels YS RC 5.00 2.00
❑ 108 Esix Snead YS RC 5.00 2.00
❑ 109 William Ortega YS RC 5.00 2.00
❑ 110 David Elder YS RC 5.00 2.00
❑ 111 Jackson Melian YS RC 5.00 2.00
❑ 112 Nate Teut YS RC 5.00 2.00
❑ 113 Jason Smith YS RC 5.00 2.00
❑ 114 Mike Penney YS RC 5.00 2.00
❑ 115 Jose Mieses YS RC 5.00 2.00
❑ 116 Juan Pena YS 5.00 2.00
❑ 117 Brian Lawrence YS RC 5.00 2.00
❑ 118 Jeremy Owens YS RC 5.00 2.00
❑ 119 Carlos Valderrama YS RC 5.00 2.00
❑ 120 Rafael Soriano YS RC 5.00 2.00
❑ 121 Horacio Ramirez JSY RC 10.00 4.00
❑ 122 Ricardo Rodriguez JSY RC 8.00 3.00
❑ 123 Juan Diaz JSY RC 8.00 3.00
❑ 124 Donnie Bridges JSY 8.00 3.00
❑ 125 Tyler Walker JSY RC 8.00 3.00
❑ 126 Erick Almonte JSY RC 8.00 3.00
❑ 127 Jesus Colome JSY 8.00 3.00
❑ 128 Ryan Freel JSY RC 10.00 4.00
❑ 129 Elpidio Guzman JSY RC 8.00 3.00
❑ 130 Jack Cust JSY 8.00 3.00
❑ 131 Eric Hinske JSY RC 10.00 4.00
❑ 132 Josh Fogg JSY RC 8.00 3.00
❑ 133 Juan Uribe JSY RC 10.00 4.00
❑ 134 Bert Snow JSY RC 8.00 3.00
❑ 135 Pedro Feliz JSY 8.00 3.00
❑ 136 Wilson Betemit JSY AU RC 40.0015.00
❑ 137 Sean Douglass JSY AU RC 15.00 6.00
❑ 138 Demell Stenson JSY AU 15.00 6.00
❑ 139 Brandon Inge JSY AU 15.00 6.00
❑ 140 Mor.Ensberg JSY AU RC 40.00 15.00
❑ 141 Brian Cole JSY AU 15.00 6.00
❑ 142 A.Hernandez JSY AU RC 15.00 6.00
❑ 143 B.Duckworth JSY AU RC 15.00 6.00
❑ 144 Jack Wilson JSY AU RC 25.00 10.00
❑ 145 Travis Hafner JSY AU RC 80.00 40.00
❑ 146 Carlos Pena JSY AU 15.00 6.00
❑ 147 Corey Patterson JSY AU 15.00 6.00
❑ 148 Xavier Nady JSY AU 25.00 10.00
❑ 149 Jason Hart JSY AU 15.00 6.00
❑ 150 I.Suzuki JSY AU RC 800.00 600.00
❑ 151 Garret Anderson .75 .30
❑ 152 Jermaine Dye .75 .30
❑ 153 Shannon Stewart .75 .30
❑ 154 Toby Hall .75 .30
❑ 155 C.C. Sabathia .75 .30
❑ 156 Bret Boone .75 .30
❑ 157 Tony Batista .75 .30
❑ 158 Gabe Kapler .75 .30
❑ 159 Carl Everett .75 .30
❑ 160 Mike Sweeney .75 .30
❑ 161 Dean Palmer .75 .30
❑ 162 Doug Mientkiewicz .75 .30
❑ 163 Carlos Lee .75 .30
❑ 164 Mike Mussina 1.25 .50
❑ 165 Lance Berkman .75 .30
❑ 166 Ken Caminiti .75 .30
❑ 167 Ben Sheets 1.25 .50
❑ 168 Matt Morris .75 .30
❑ 169 Fred McGriff 1.25 .50
❑ 170 Curt Schilling .75 .30
❑ 171 Paul LoDuca .75 .30
❑ 172 Javier Vazquez .75 .30
❑ 173 Rich Aurilia .75 .30
❑ 174 A.J. Burnett .75 .30
❑ 175 Al Leiter .75 .30
❑ 176 Mark Kotsay .75 .30
❑ 177 Jimmy Rollins .75 .30
❑ 178 Aramis Ramirez .75 .30
❑ 179 Aaron Boone .75 .30
❑ 180 Jeff Cirillo .75 .30
❑ 181 Johnny Estrada YS RC 8.00 3.00
❑ 182 Dave Williams YS RC 5.00 2.00
❑ 183 Donaldo Mendez YS RC 5.00 2.00
❑ 184 Junior Spivey YS RC 8.00 3.00
❑ 185 Jay Gibbons YS RC 8.00 3.00
❑ 186 Kyle Lohse YS RC 8.00 3.00
❑ 187 Willie Harris YS RC 5.00 2.00
❑ 188 Juan Cruz YS RC 5.00 2.00
❑ 189 Joe Kennedy YS RC 8.00 3.00
❑ 190 Duaner Sanchez YS RC 5.00 2.00
❑ 191 Jorge Julio YS RC 5.00 2.00
❑ 192 Cesar Crespo YS RC 5.00 2.00
❑ 193 Casey Fossum YS RC 5.00 2.00
❑ 194 Brian Roberts YS RC 15.00 6.00
❑ 195 Troy Mattes YS RC 5.00 2.00
❑ 196 Rob Mackowiak YS RC 8.00 3.00
❑ 197 Tsuyoshi Shinjo YS RC 8.00 3.00
❑ 198 Nick Punto YS RC 5.00 2.00
❑ 199 Wilmy Caceres YS RC 5.00 2.00
❑ 200 Jeremy Affeldt YS RC 5.00 2.00
❑ 201 Bret Prinz YS RC 5.00 2.00
❑ 202 Delvin James YS RC 5.00 2.00
❑ 203 Luis Pineda YS RC 5.00 2.00
❑ 204 Matt White YS RC 5.00 2.00
❑ 205 Brandon Knight YS RC 5.00 2.00
❑ 206 Albert Pujols YS AU RC 800.00 450.00
❑ 207 Mark Teixeira YS AU RC 150.00 90.00
❑ 208 Mark Prior YS AU RC 60.00 30.00
❑ 209 Dewon Brazelton YS AU RC 15.006.00
❑ 210 Bud Smith YS AU RC 15.00 6.00

2002 SPx

❑ COMP.LOW w/o SP's (90) 25.00 10.00
❑ COMP.UPDATE w/o SP's (30) 10.00 4.00
❑ COMMON CARD (1-90) .50 .20
❑ COMMON CARD (91-120) 8.00 3.00
❑ COMMON CARD (121-150) 15.00 6.00
❑ COMMON CARD (151-190) 8.00 3.00
❑ COMMON CARD (191-220) .75 .30
❑ COMMON CARD (221-250) 10.00 4.00
❑ 1 Troy Glaus .50 .20
❑ 2 Darin Erstad .50 .20
❑ 3 David Justice .50 .20
❑ 4 Tim Hudson .50 .20
❑ 5 Miguel Tejada .50 .20
❑ 6 Barry Zito .50 .20
❑ 7 Carlos Delgado .50 .20
❑ 8 Shannon Stewart .50 .20
❑ 9 Greg Vaughn .50 .20
❑ 10 Toby Hall .50 .20
❑ 11 Jim Thome .75 .30
❑ 12 C.C. Sabathia .50 .20
❑ 13 Ichiro Suzuki 2.50 1.00
❑ 14 Edgar Martinez .75 .30
❑ 15 Freddy Garcia .50 .20
❑ 16 Mike Cameron .50 .20
❑ 17 Jeff Conine .50 .20
❑ 18 Tony Batista .50 .20
❑ 19 Alex Rodriguez 2.00 .75
❑ 20 Rafael Palmeiro .75 .30
❑ 21 Ivan Rodriguez .75 .30
❑ 22 Carl Everett .50 .20
❑ 23 Pedro Martinez .75 .30
❑ 24 Manny Ramirez .75 .30
❑ 25 Nomar Garciaparra 2.00 .75
❑ 26 Johnny Damon Sox .75 .30
❑ 27 Mike Sweeney .50 .20
❑ 28 Carlos Beltran .50 .20
❑ 29 Dmitri Young .50 .20
❑ 30 Joe Mays .50 .20
❑ 31 Doug Mientkiewicz .50 .20
❑ 32 Cristian Guzman .50 .20
❑ 33 Corey Koskie .50 .20
❑ 34 Frank Thomas 1.25 .50
❑ 35 Magglio Ordonez .50 .20
❑ 36 Mark Buehrle .50 .20
❑ 37 Bernie Williams .75 .30
❑ 38 Roger Clemens 2.50 1.00
❑ 39 Derek Jeter 3.00 1.25
❑ 40 Jason Giambi .50 .20
❑ 41 Mike Mussina .75 .30
❑ 42 Lance Berkman .50 .20
❑ 43 Jeff Bagwell .75 .30
❑ 44 Roy Oswalt .50 .20
❑ 45 Greg Maddux 2.00 .75
❑ 46 Chipper Jones 1.25 .50
❑ 47 Andruw Jones .75 .30
❑ 48 Gary Sheffield .50 .20
❑ 49 Geoff Jenkins .50 .20
❑ 50 Richie Sexson .50 .20
❑ 51 Ben Sheets .50 .20
❑ 52 Albert Pujols 2.50 1.00
❑ 53 J.D. Drew .50 .20
❑ 54 Jim Edmonds .50 .20
❑ 55 Sammy Sosa 1.25 .50
❑ 56 Moises Alou .50 .20
❑ 57 Kerry Wood .50 .20
❑ 58 Jon Lieber .50 .20
❑ 59 Fred McGriff .75 .30
❑ 60 Randy Johnson 1.25 .50
❑ 61 Luis Gonzalez .50 .20
❑ 62 Curt Schilling .50 .20
❑ 63 Kevin Brown .50 .20
❑ 64 Hideo Nomo 1.25 .50
❑ 65 Shawn Green .50 .20
❑ 66 Vladimir Guerrero 1.25 .50
❑ 67 Jose Vidro .50 .20
❑ 68 Barry Bonds 3.00 1.25
❑ 69 Jeff Kent .50 .20
❑ 70 Rich Aurilia .50 .20
❑ 71 Cliff Floyd .50 .20
❑ 72 Josh Beckett .50 .20
❑ 73 Preston Wilson .50 .20
❑ 74 Mike Piazza 2.00 .75
❑ 75 Mo Vaughn .50 .20

❑ 76 Jeromy Burnitz	.50	.20
❑ 77 Roberto Alomar	.75	.30
❑ 78 Phil Nevin	.50	.20
❑ 79 Ryan Klesko	.50	.20
❑ 80 Scott Rolen	.75	.30
❑ 81 Bobby Abreu	.50	.20
❑ 82 Jimmy Rollins	.50	.20
❑ 83 Brian Giles	.50	.20
❑ 84 Aramis Ramirez	.50	.20
❑ 85 Ken Griffey Jr.	2.00	.75
❑ 86 Sean Casey	.50	.20
❑ 87 Barry Larkin	.75	.30
❑ 88 Mike Hampton	.50	.20
❑ 89 Larry Walker	.50	.20
❑ 90 Todd Helton	.75	.30
❑ 91A Ron Calloway YS RC	8.00	3.00
❑ 91P Ron Calloway YS RC	8.00	3.00
❑ 92A Joe Orloski YS RC	8.00	3.00
❑ 92P Joe Orloski YS RC	8.00	3.00
❑ 93A Anderson Machado YS RC	8.00	3.00
❑ 93P Anderson Machado YS RC	8.00	3.00
❑ 94A Eric Good YS RC	8.00	3.00
❑ 94P Eric Good YS RC	8.00	3.00
❑ 95A Reed Johnson YS RC	10.00	4.00
❑ 95P Reed Johnson YS RC	10.00	4.00
❑ 96A Brendan Donnelly YS RC	8.00	3.00
❑ 96P Brendan Donnelly YS RC	8.00	3.00
❑ 97A Chris Baker YS RC	8.00	3.00
❑ 97P Chris Baker YS RC	8.00	3.00
❑ 98A Wilson Valdez YS RC	8.00	3.00
❑ 98P Wilson Valdez YS RC	8.00	3.00
❑ 99A Scotty Layfield YS RC	8.00	3.00
❑ 99P Scotty Layfield YS RC	8.00	3.00
❑ 100A P.J. Bevis YS RC	8.00	3.00
❑ 100P P.J. Bevis YS RC	8.00	3.00
❑ 101A Edwin Almonte YS RC	8.00	3.00
❑ 101P Edwin Almonte YS RC	8.00	3.00
❑ 102A Francis Beltran YS RC	8.00	3.00
❑ 102P Francis Beltran YS RC	8.00	3.00
❑ 103A Val Pascucci YS	8.00	3.00
❑ 103P Val Pascucci YS	8.00	3.00
❑ 104A Nelson Castro YS RC	8.00	3.00
❑ 104P Nelson Castro YS RC	8.00	3.00
❑ 105A Michael Crudale YS RC	8.00	3.00
❑ 105P Michael Crudale YS RC	8.00	3.00
❑ 106A Colin Young YS RC	8.00	3.00
❑ 106P Colin Young YS RC	8.00	3.00
❑ 107A Todd Donovan YS RC	8.00	3.00
❑ 107P Todd Donovan YS RC	8.00	3.00
❑ 108A Felix Escalona YS RC	8.00	3.00
❑ 108P Felix Escalona YS RC	8.00	3.00
❑ 109A Brandon Backe YS RC	10.00	4.00
❑ 109P Brandon Backe YS RC	10.00	4.00
❑ 110A Corey Thurman YS RC	8.00	3.00
❑ 110P Corey Thurman YS RC	8.00	3.00
❑ 111A Kyle Kane YS RC	8.00	3.00
❑ 111P Kyle Kane YS RC	8.00	3.00
❑ 112A Allan Simpson YS RC	8.00	3.00
❑ 112P Allan Simpson YS RC	8.00	3.00
❑ 113A Jose Valverde YS RC	8.00	3.00
❑ 113P Jose Valverde YS RC	8.00	3.00
❑ 114A Chris Booker YS RC	8.00	3.00
❑ 114P Chris Booker YS RC	8.00	3.00
❑ 115A Brandon Puffer YS RC	8.00	3.00
❑ 115P Brandon Puffer YS RC	8.00	3.00
❑ 116A John Foster YS RC	8.00	3.00
❑ 116P John Foster YS RC	8.00	3.00
❑ 117A Cliff Bartosh YS RC	8.00	3.00
❑ 117P Cliff Bartosh YS RC	8.00	3.00
❑ 118A Gustavo Chacin YS RC	10.00	4.00
❑ 118P Gustavo Chacin YS RC	10.00	4.00
❑ 119A Steve Kent YS RC	8.00	3.00
❑ 119P Steve Kent YS RC	8.00	3.00
❑ 120A Nate Field YS RC	8.00	3.00
❑ 120P Nate Field YS RC	8.00	3.00
❑ 121 Victor Alvarez AU RC	10.00	4.00
❑ 122 Steve Bechler AU RC	10.00	4.00
❑ 123 Adrian Burnside AU RC	10.00	4.00
❑ 124 Marlon Byrd AU	15.00	6.00
❑ 125 Jaime Cerda AU RC	10.00	4.00
❑ 126 Brandon Claussen AU	15.00	6.00
❑ 127 Mark Corey AU RC	10.00	4.00
❑ 128 Doug Devore AU RC	10.00	4.00
❑ 129 Kazuhisa Ishii AU SP RC	60.00	30.00
❑ 130 John Ennis AU RC	10.00	4.00
❑ 131 Kevin Frederick AU RC	10.00	4.00
❑ 132 Josh Hancock AU RC	20.00	8.00
❑ 133 Ben Howard AU RC	10.00	4.00
❑ 134 Orlando Hudson AU	15.00	6.00
❑ 135 Hansel Izquierdo AU RC	10.00	4.00
❑ 136 Eric Junge AU RC	10.00	4.00
❑ 137 Austin Kearns AU	15.00	6.00
❑ 138 Victor Martinez AU	25.00	10.00
❑ 139 Luis Martinez AU RC	10.00	4.00
❑ 140 Danny Mota AU RC	10.00	4.00
❑ 141 Jorge Padilla AU RC	10.00	4.00
❑ 142 Andy Pratt AU RC	10.00	4.00
❑ 143 Rene Reyes AU RC	10.00	4.00
❑ 144 Rodrigo Rosario AU RC	10.00	4.00
❑ 145 Tom Shearn AU RC	10.00	4.00
❑ 146 So Taguchi AU SP RC	25.00	10.00
❑ 147 Dennis Tankersley AU	15.00	6.00
❑ 148 Matt Thornton AU RC	10.00	4.00
❑ 149 Jeremy Ward AU RC	10.00	4.00
❑ 150 Mitch Wylie AU RC	10.00	4.00
❑ 151 Pedro Martinez JSY/800	10.00	4.00
❑ 152 Cal Ripken JSY/800	25.00	10.00
❑ 153 Roger Clemens JSY/800	15.00	6.00
❑ 154 Bernie Williams JSY/800	10.00	4.00
❑ 155 Jason Giambi JSY/700	8.00	3.00
❑ 156 Robin Ventura JSY/800	8.00	3.00
❑ 157 Carlos Delgado JSY/800	8.00	3.00
❑ 158 Frank Thomas JSY/800	10.00	4.00
❑ 159 Magglio Ordonez JSY/800	8.00	3.00
❑ 160 Jim Thome JSY/800	10.00	4.00
❑ 161 Darin Erstad JSY/800	8.00	3.00
❑ 162 Tim Salmon JSY/800	10.00	4.00
❑ 163 Tim Hudson JSY/800	8.00	3.00
❑ 164 Barry Zito JSY/800	8.00	3.00
❑ 165 Ichiro Suzuki JSY/800	25.00	10.00
❑ 166 Edgar Martinez JSY/800	10.00	4.00
❑ 167 Alex Rodriguez JSY/800	15.00	6.00
❑ 168 Ivan Rodriguez JSY/800	10.00	4.00
❑ 169 Juan Gonzalez JSY/800	8.00	3.00
❑ 170 Greg Maddux JSY/800	15.00	6.00
❑ 171 Chipper Jones JSY/800	10.00	4.00
❑ 172 Andruw Jones JSY/800	10.00	4.00
❑ 173 Tom Glavine JSY/800	10.00	4.00
❑ 174 Mike Piazza JSY/800	15.00	4.00
❑ 175 Roberto Alomar JSY/800	10.00	4.00
❑ 176 Scott Rolen JSY/800	10.00	4.00
❑ 177 Sammy Sosa JSY/800	10.00	4.00
❑ 178 Moises Alou JSY/800	8.00	3.00
❑ 179 Ken Griffey Jr. JSY/700	20.00	8.00
❑ 180 Jeff Bagwell JSY/800	10.00	4.00
❑ 181 Jim Edmonds JSY/800	8.00	3.00
❑ 182 J.D. Drew JSY/800	8.00	3.00
❑ 183 Brian Giles JSY/800	8.00	3.00
❑ 184 Randy Johnson JSY/800	10.00	4.00
❑ 185 Curt Schilling JSY/800	8.00	3.00
❑ 186 Luis Gonzalez JSY/800	8.00	3.00
❑ 187 Todd Helton JSY/800	10.00	4.00
❑ 188 Shawn Green JSY/800	8.00	3.00
❑ 189 David Wells JSY/800	8.00	3.00
❑ 190 Jeff Kent JSY/800	8.00	3.00
❑ 191 Tom Glavine	1.25	.50
❑ 192 Cliff Floyd	.75	.30
❑ 193 Mark Prior	1.25	.50
❑ 194 Corey Patterson	.75	.30
❑ 195 Paul Konerko	.75	.30
❑ 196 Adam Dunn	.75	.30
❑ 197 Joe Borchard	.75	.30
❑ 198 Carlos Pena	.75	.30
❑ 199 Juan Encarnacion	.75	.30
❑ 200 Luis Castillo	.75	.30
❑ 201 Torii Hunter	.75	.30
❑ 202 Hee Seop Choi	.75	.30
❑ 203 Bartolo Colon	.75	.30
❑ 204 Raul Mondesi	.75	.30
❑ 205 Jeff Weaver	.75	.30
❑ 206 Eric Munson	.75	.30
❑ 207 Alfonso Soriano	.75	.30
❑ 208 Ray Durham	.75	.30
❑ 209 Eric Chavez	.75	.30
❑ 210 Brett Myers	.75	.30
❑ 211 Jeremy Giambi	.75	.30
❑ 212 Vicente Padilla	.75	.30
❑ 213 Felipe Lopez	.75	.30
❑ 214 Sean Burroughs	.75	.30
❑ 215 Kenny Lofton	.75	.30
❑ 216 Scott Rolen	1.25	.50
❑ 217 Carl Crawford	.75	.30
❑ 218 Juan Gonzalez	.75	.30
❑ 219 Orlando Hudson	.75	.30
❑ 220 Eric Hinske	.75	.30
❑ 221 Adam Walker AU RC	10.00	4.00
❑ 222 Aaron Cook AU RC	10.00	4.00
❑ 223 Cam Esslinger AU RC	10.00	4.00
❑ 224 Kirk Saarloos AU RC	10.00	4.00
❑ 225 Jose Diaz AU RC	10.00	4.00
❑ 226 David Ross AU RC	25.00	10.00
❑ 227 Jayson Durocher AU RC	10.00	4.00
❑ 228 Brian Mallette AU RC	10.00	4.00
❑ 229 Aaron Guiel AU RC	10.00	4.00
❑ 230 Jorge Nunez AU RC	10.00	4.00
❑ 231 Satoru Komiyama AU RC	25.00	10.00
❑ 232 Tyler Yates AU RC	10.00	4.00
❑ 233 Pete Zamora AU RC	10.00	4.00
❑ 234 Mike Gonzalez AU RC	10.00	4.00
❑ 235 Oliver Perez AU RC	30.00	15.00
❑ 236 Julius Matos AU RC	10.00	4.00
❑ 237 Andy Shibilo AU RC	10.00	4.00
❑ 238 Jason Simontacchi AU RC	10.00	4.00
❑ 239 Ron Chiavacci AU	10.00	4.00
❑ 240 Deivis Santos AU	10.00	4.00
❑ 241 Travis Driskill AU RC	10.00	4.00
❑ 242 Jorge De La Rosa AU RC	10.00	4.00
❑ 243 Anastacio Martinez AU RC	10.00	4.00
❑ 244 Earl Snyder AU RC	10.00	4.00
❑ 245 Freddy Sanchez AU RC	30.00	15.00
❑ 246 Miguel Asencio AU RC	10.00	4.00
❑ 247 Juan Brito AU RC	10.00	4.00
❑ 248 Franklyn German AU RC	10.00	4.00
❑ 249 Chris Snelling AU RC	15.00	6.00
❑ 250 Ken Huckaby AU RC	10.00	4.00

2003 SPx

❑ COMP.LO SET w/o SP's (100)	25.00	10.00
❑ COMP.LO SET w/ SP's (125)	100.00	50.00
❑ COMMON CARD (1-125)	.50	.20
❑ COMMON SP (1-125)	4.00	1.50
❑ COMMON CARD (126-160)	8.00	3.00
❑ COMMON CARD (161-178)	15.00	6.00
❑ 163-178 PRINT RUN 1224 SERIAL #'d SETS		
❑ 126-178 RANDOM INSERTS IN SPx PACKS		
❑ COMMON CARD (179-193)	15.00	6.00
❑ COMMON CARD (381-387)	15.00	6.00
❑ 1 Darin Erstad	.50	.20
❑ 2 Garret Anderson	.50	.20
❑ 3 Tim Salmon	.75	.30
❑ 4 Troy Glaus SP	4.00	1.50
❑ 5 Luis Gonzalez	.50	.20
❑ 6 Randy Johnson	1.25	.50
❑ 7 Curt Schilling	.50	.20
❑ 8 Lyle Overbay	.50	.20
❑ 9 Andruw Jones SP	4.00	1.50
❑ 10 Gary Sheffield	.50	.20
❑ 11 Rafael Furcal	.50	.20
❑ 12 Greg Maddux	2.00	.75
❑ 13 Chipper Jones SP	5.00	2.00
❑ 14 Tony Batista	.50	.20
❑ 15 Rodrigo Lopez	.50	.20
❑ 16 Jay Gibbons	.50	.20
❑ 17 Byung-Hyun Kim	.50	.20
❑ 18 Johnny Damon	.75	.30
❑ 19 Derek Lowe	.50	.20
❑ 20 Nomar Garciaparra SP	8.00	3.00
❑ 21 Pedro Martinez	.75	.30
❑ 22 Manny Ramirez SP	4.00	1.50
❑ 23 Mark Prior	.75	.30

❑ 73 Jason Repko .40 .15
❑ 74 Kevin Youkilis .40 .15
❑ 75 Koyie Hill .40 .15
❑ 76 Laynce Nix .40 .15
❑ 77 Luke Scott RC 2.00 .75
❑ 78 Juan Rivera .40 .15
❑ 79 Justin Duchscherer .40 .15
❑ 80 Mark Teahen .40 .15
❑ 81 Lance Niekro .40 .15
❑ 82 Michael Cuddyer .40 .15
❑ 83 Nick Swisher .40 .15
❑ 84 Noah Lowry .40 .15
❑ 85 Matt Holliday .50 .20
❑ 86 Reed Johnson .40 .15
❑ 87 Rich Harden .40 .15
❑ 88 Robb Quinlan .40 .15
❑ 89 Nick Johnson .40 .15
❑ 90 Ryan Howard 2.50 1.00
❑ 91 Nook Logan .40 .15
❑ 92 Steve Schmoll RC .60 .25
❑ 93 Tadahito Iguchi RC 4.00 1.50
❑ 94 Willy Taveras .40 .15
❑ 95 Wily Mo Pena .40 .15
❑ 96 Xavier Nady .40 .15
❑ 97 Yadier Molina .40 .15
❑ 98 Yhency Brazoban .40 .15
❑ 99 Ryan Freel .40 .15
❑ 100 Zack Greinke .40 .15
❑ 101 Adam Shabala AU RC 10.00 4.00
❑ 102 Ambiorix Burgos AU RC 10.00 4.00
❑ 103 Ambiorix Concepcion AU RC 10.00 4.00
❑ 104 Anibal Sanchez AU RC 60.00 30.00
❑ 106 Brandon McCarthy AU RC 30.00 12.50
❑ 107 Brian Burres AU RC 10.00 4.00
❑ 108 Carlos Ruiz AU RC 15.00 6.00
❑ 109 Casey Rogowski AU RC 15.00 6.00
❑ 110 Chad Orvella AU RC 10.00 4.00
❑ 111 Chris Resop AU RC 15.00 6.00
❑ 112 Chris Roberson AU RC 10.00 4.00
❑ 113 Chris Seddon AU RC 10.00 4.00
❑ 114 Colter Bean AU RC 15.00 6.00
❑ 115 Dave Gassner AU RC 10.00 4.00
❑ 116 Brian Anderson AU RC 40.00 15.00
❑ 118 Devon Lowery AU RC 10.00 4.00
❑ 119 Enrique Gonzalez AU RC 15.00 6.00
❑ 120 Eude Brito AU RC 10.00 4.00
❑ 121 Francisco Butto AU RC 10.00 4.00
❑ 122 Franquelis Osoria AU RC 10.00 4.00
❑ 123 Garrett Jones AU RC 10.00 4.00
❑ 124 Geovany Soto AU RC 80.00 40.00
❑ 125 Hayden Penn AU RC 20.00 8.00
❑ 126 Ismael Ramirez AU RC 10.00 4.00
❑ 127 Jared Gothreaux AU RC 10.00 4.00
❑ 128 Jason Hammel AU RC 10.00 4.00
❑ 129 Jeff Miller AU RC 10.00 4.00
❑ 130 Jeff Niemann AU RC 30.00 12.50
❑ 131 Joel Peralta AU RC 10.00 4.00
❑ 132 John Hattig AU RC 10.00 4.00
❑ 133 Jorge Campillo AU RC 10.00 4.00
❑ 134 Juan Morillo AU RC 10.00 4.00
❑ 135 Justin Verlander AU RC 200.00 125.00
❑ 136 Ryan Garko AU RC 40.00 15.00
❑ 137 Kendry Morales AU RC 60.00 30.00
❑ 138 Luis Hernandez AU RC 10.00 4.00
❑ 140 Luis O.Rodriguez AU RC 10.00 4.00
❑ 141 Mark Woodyard AU RC 10.00 4.00
❑ 142 Matt A.Smith AU RC 10.00 4.00
❑ 143 Matthew Lindstrom AU RC 10.00 4.00
❑ 144 Miguel Negron AU RC 15.00 6.00
❑ 145 Mike Morse AU RC 15.00 6.00
❑ 146 Nate McLouth AU RC 15.00 6.00
❑ 147 Nelson Cruz AU RC 40.00 15.00
❑ 148 Nick Masset AU RC 10.00 4.00
❑ 150 Paulino Reynoso AU RC 10.00 4.00
❑ 151 Pedro Lopez AU RC 10.00 4.00
❑ 152 Philip Humber AU RC 30.00 12.50
❑ 153 Prince Fielder AU RC 200.00 125.00
❑ 154 Randy Messenger AU RC 10.00 4.00
❑ 156 Raul Tablado AU RC 10.00 4.00
❑ 157 Ronny Paulino AU RC 15.00 6.00
❑ 158 Russ Rohlicek AU RC 10.00 4.00
❑ 159 Russell Martin AU RC 60.00 30.00
❑ 160 Scott Baker AU RC 15.00 6.00
❑ 161 Scott Munter AU RC 10.00 4.00
❑ 162 Sean Thompson AU RC 10.00 4.00
❑ 163 Sean Tracey AU RC 10.00 4.00
❑ 164 Shane Costa AU RC 10.00 4.00
❑ 165 Stephen Drew AU RC 60.00 30.00
❑ 166 Tony Giarratano AU RC 10.00 4.00
❑ 167 Tony Pena AU RC 10.00 4.00
❑ 168 Travis Bowyer AU RC 10.00 4.00
❑ 169 Ubaldo Jimenez AU RC 40.00 15.00
❑ 170 Wladimir Balentien AU RC 80.00 40.00
❑ 171 Yorman Bazardo AU RC 10.00 4.00
❑ 173 Ryan Zimmerman AU RC 150.00 75.00
❑ 174 Chris Denorfia AU RC 15.00 6.00
❑ 176 Jermaine Van Buren AU 10.00 4.00
❑ 177 Mark McLemore AU RC 10.00 4.00
❑ 179 Ryan Speier AU RC 10.00 4.00

2006 SPx

❑ COMP.BASIC SET (100) 25.00 10.00
❑ COMMON CARD (1-100) .40 .15
❑ COMMON AU p/r 659-999 10.00 4.00
❑ COMMON AU p/r 350-500 10.00 4.00
❑ OVERALL 101-161 AU ODDS 1:9
❑ 101-161 AU EXCH DEADLINE 09/07/08
❑ 101-161 AU PRINT RUN B/WN 190-999 PER
❑ 101-161 PRINTING PLATE ODDS 1:224
❑ 101-161 PLATES PRINT RUN 1 SET PER CLR
❑ 101-161 PLATES FEATURE AUTOS
❑ BLACK-CYAN-MAGENTA-YELLOW ISSUED
❑ NO PLATE PRICING DUE TO SCARCITY
❑ EXQUISITE EXCH ODDS 1:36
❑ EXQUISITE EXCH DEADLINE 07/27/07
❑ 1 Luis Gonzalez .40 .15
❑ 2 Chad Tracy .40 .15
❑ 3 Brandon Webb .40 .15
❑ 4 Andruw Jones .60 .25
❑ 5 Chipper Jones 1.00 .40
❑ 6 John Smoltz .60 .25
❑ 7 Tim Hudson .40 .15
❑ 8 Miguel Tejada .40 .15
❑ 9 Brian Roberts .40 .15
❑ 10 Ramon Hernandez .40 .15
❑ 11 Curt Schilling .60 .25
❑ 12 David Ortiz 1.00 .40
❑ 13 Manny Ramirez .60 .25
❑ 14 Jason Varitek 1.00 .40
❑ 15 Josh Beckett .40 .15
❑ 16 Greg Maddux 1.50 .60
❑ 17 Derrek Lee .40 .15
❑ 18 Mark Prior .60 .25
❑ 19 Aramis Ramirez .40 .15
❑ 20 Jim Thome .60 .25
❑ 21 Paul Konerko .40 .15
❑ 22 Scott Podsednik .40 .15
❑ 23 Jose Contreras .40 .15
❑ 24 Ken Griffey Jr. 1.50 .60
❑ 25 Adam Dunn .40 .15
❑ 26 Felipe Lopez .40 .15
❑ 27 Travis Hafner .40 .15
❑ 28 Victor Martinez .40 .15
❑ 29 Grady Sizemore .60 .25
❑ 30 Jhonny Peralta .40 .15
❑ 31 Todd Helton .60 .25
❑ 32 Garrett Atkins .40 .15
❑ 33 Clint Barmes .40 .15
❑ 34 Ivan Rodriguez .60 .25
❑ 35 Chris Shelton .40 .15
❑ 36 Jeremy Bonderman .40 .15
❑ 37 Miguel Cabrera .60 .25
❑ 38 Dontrelle Willis .40 .15
❑ 39 Lance Berkman .40 .15
❑ 40 Morgan Ensberg .40 .15
❑ 41 Roy Oswalt .40 .15
❑ 42 Reggie Sanders .40 .15
❑ 43 Mike Sweeney .40 .15
❑ 44 Vladimir Guerrero 1.00 .40
❑ 45 Bartolo Colon .40 .15
❑ 46 Chone Figgins .40 .15
❑ 47 Nomar Garciaparra 1.00 .40
❑ 48 Jeff Kent .40 .15
❑ 49 J.D. Drew .40 .15
❑ 50 Carlos Lee .40 .15
❑ 51 Ben Sheets .40 .15
❑ 52 Rickie Weeks .40 .15
❑ 53 Johan Santana .60 .25
❑ 54 Torii Hunter .40 .15
❑ 55 Joe Mauer .60 .25
❑ 56 Pedro Martinez .60 .25
❑ 57 David Wright 1.50 .60
❑ 58 Carlos Beltran .40 .15
❑ 59 Carlos Delgado .40 .15
❑ 60 Jose Reyes 1.00 .40
❑ 61 Derek Jeter 2.50 1.00
❑ 62 Alex Rodriguez 1.50 .60
❑ 63 Randy Johnson 1.00 .40
❑ 64 Hideki Matsui 1.00 .40
❑ 65 Gary Sheffield .40 .15
❑ 66 Rich Harden .40 .15
❑ 67 Eric Chavez .40 .15
❑ 68 Huston Street .40 .15
❑ 69 Bobby Crosby .40 .15
❑ 70 Bobby Abreu .40 .15
❑ 71 Ryan Howard 1.50 .60
❑ 72 Chase Utley 1.00 .40
❑ 73 Pat Burrell .40 .15
❑ 74 Jason Bay .40 .15
❑ 75 Sean Casey .40 .15
❑ 76 Mike Piazza 1.00 .40
❑ 77 Jake Peavy .40 .15
❑ 78 Brian Giles .40 .15
❑ 79 Milton Bradley .40 .15
❑ 80 Omar Vizquel .60 .25
❑ 81 Jason Schmidt .40 .15
❑ 82 Ichiro Suzuki 1.50 .60
❑ 83 Felix Hernandez .60 .25
❑ 84 Richie Sexson .40 .15
❑ 85 Albert Pujols 2.00 .75
❑ 86 Chris Carpenter .40 .15
❑ 87 Scott Rolen .60 .25
❑ 88 Jim Edmonds .60 .25
❑ 89 Carl Crawford .40 .15
❑ 90 Jonny Gomes .40 .15
❑ 91 Scott Kazmir .60 .25
❑ 92 Mark Teixeira .60 .25
❑ 93 Michael Young .40 .15
❑ 94 Phil Nevin .40 .15
❑ 95 Vernon Wells .40 .15
❑ 96 Roy Halladay .40 .15
❑ 97 Troy Glaus .40 .15
❑ 98 Alfonso Soriano .40 .15
❑ 99 Nick Johnson .40 .15
❑ 100 Jose Vidro .40 .15
❑ 101 Conor Jackson AU/999 (RC) 15.00 6.00
❑ 102 J.Weaver AU/299 (RC) EXCH 40.00 15.00
❑ 103 Macay McBride AU/999 (RC) 10.00 4.00
❑ 104 Aaron Rakers AU/499 (RC) 10.00 4.00
❑ 105 J.Papelbon AU/499 (RC) 50.00 20.00
❑ 106 J.Bergmann AU/999 RC 10.00 4.00
❑ 107 S.Drew AU/350 (RC) 30.00 12.50
❑ 108 Chris Denorfia AU/999 (RC) 10.00 4.00
❑ 109 Kelly Shoppach AU/999 (RC) 10.00 4.00
❑ 110 Ryan Shealy AU/999 (RC) 10.00 4.00
❑ 111 Josh Wilson AU/999 (RC) 10.00 4.00
❑ 112 Brian Anderson AU/999 (RC) 10.00 4.00
❑ 113 J.Verlander AU/749 (RC) 50.00 20.00
❑ 114 J.Hermida AU/999 (RC) 15.00 6.00
❑ 115 Mike Jacobs AU/999 (RC) 10.00 4.00
❑ 116 Josh Johnson AU/999 (RC) 15.00 6.00
❑ 117 Hanley Ramirez AU/659 (RC) 20.00 8.00
❑ 118 Chris Resop AU/999 (RC) 10.00 4.00
❑ 119 J.Willingham AU/999 (RC) 10.00 4.00
❑ 120 Cole Hamels AU/499 (RC) 50.00 20.00
❑ 121 Matt Cain AU/999 (RC) 20.00 8.00
❑ 122 Steve Stemle AU/999 RC 10.00 4.00
❑ 123 Tim Hamulack AU/999 (RC) 10.00 4.00
❑ 124 Choo Freeman AU/999 (RC) 10.00 4.00
❑ 125 H.Kuo AU/999 (RC) 50.00 20.00

❑ 126 Cody Ross AU/999 (RC) 10.00 4.00
❑ 127 Jose Capellan AU/999 (RC) 10.00 4.00
❑ 128 Prince Fielder AU/190 (RC) 120.00 60.00
❑ 129 David Gassner AU/999 (RC) 10.00 4.00
❑ 130 Jason Kubel AU/999 (RC) 10.00 4.00
❑ 131 F.Liriano AU/299 (RC) 50.00 20.00
❑ 132 A.Hernandez AU/999 (RC) 15.00 6.00
❑ 133 Joey Devine AU/499 RC 10.00 4.00
❑ 134 Chris Booker AU/999 (RC) 10.00 4.00
❑ 135 Matt Capps AU/999 (RC) 10.00 4.00
❑ 136 Paul Maholm AU/999 (RC) 10.00 4.00
❑ 137 Nate McLouth AU/999 (RC) 10.00 4.00
❑ 138 J.Van Benschoten AU/999 (RC) 10.00 4.00
❑ 139 Jeff Harris AU/999 RC 10.00 4.00
❑ 140 Ben Johnson AU/999 (RC) 10.00 4.00
❑ 141 Wil Nieves AU/999 (RC) 10.00 4.00
❑ 142 G.Quiroz AU/999 (RC) 10.00 4.00
❑ 143 Josh Rupe AU/500 (RC) 10.00 4.00
❑ 144 Skip Schumaker AU/999 (RC) 10.00 4.00
❑ 145 Jack Taschner AU/999 (RC) 10.00 4.00
❑ 146 A.Wainwright AU/999 (RC) 25.00 10.00
❑ 147 Alay Soler AU/499 RC 25.00 10.00
❑ 148 Kendry Morales AU/999 (RC) 15.00 6.00
❑ 149 Ian Kinsler AU/999 (RC) 25.00 10.00
❑ 150 Jason Hammel AU/999 (RC) 10.00 4.00
❑ 151 C.Billingsley AU/499 (RC) 25.00 10.00
❑ 152 Boof Bonser AU/999 (RC) 15.00 6.00
❑ 153 Peter Moylan AU/999 RC 10.00 4.00
❑ 154 Chris Britton AU/999 RC 10.00 4.00
❑ 155 Takashi Saito AU/999 RC 30.00 12.50
❑ 156 Scott Dunn AU/999 (RC) 10.00 4.00
❑ 157 J.Zumaya AU/299 (RC) EXCH 30.00 12.50
❑ 158 Dan Uggla AU/999 (RC) 30.00 12.50
❑ 159 Taylor Buchholz AU/999 (RC) 10.00 4.00
❑ 160 M.Cabrera AU/499 (RC) EXCH 40.00 15.00
❑ NNO Exquisite Redemption 200.00 125.00

2007 SPx

❑ COMMON CARD (1-100) .75 .30
❑ COMMON AU RC (101-150) 8.00 3.00
❑ OVERALL 101-150 AU RC ODDS 1:3
❑ 101-150 AU RC EXCH DEADLINE 05/10/2010
❑ ASTERISK EQUALS PARTIAL EXCH
❑ APPX.PRINTING PLATE ODDS 2 PER CASE
❑ PLATES PRINT RUN 1 SET PER COLOR
❑ BLACK-CYAN-MAGENTA-YELLOW ISSUED
❑ NO PLATE PRICING DUE TO SCARCITY
❑ 1 Miguel Tejada .75 .30
❑ 2 Brian Roberts .75 .30
❑ 3 Melvin Mora .75 .30
❑ 4 David Ortiz 2.00 .75
❑ 5 Manny Ramirez 1.25 .50
❑ 6 Jason Varitek 2.00 .75
❑ 7 Curt Schilling 1.25 .50
❑ 8 Jim Thome 1.25 .50
❑ 9 Paul Konerko .75 .30
❑ 10 Jermaine Dye .75 .30
❑ 11 Travis Hafner .75 .30
❑ 12 Victor Martinez .75 .30
❑ 13 Grady Sizemore 1.25 .50
❑ 14 C.C. Sabathia .75 .30
❑ 15 Ivan Rodriguez 1.25 .50
❑ 16 Magglio Ordonez .75 .30
❑ 17 Carlos Guillen .75 .30
❑ 18 Justin Verlander 2.00 .75
❑ 19 Shane Costa .75 .30
❑ 20 Emil Brown .75 .30
❑ 21 Mark Teahen .75 .30
❑ 22 Vladimir Guerrero 2.00 .75
❑ 23 Jered Weaver 1.25 .50
❑ 24 Juan Rivera .75 .30
❑ 25 Justin Morneau .75 .30
❑ 26 Joe Mauer 1.25 .50
❑ 27 Torii Hunter .75 .30
❑ 28 Johan Santana 1.25 .50
❑ 29 Derek Jeter 5.00 2.00
❑ 30 Alex Rodriguez 3.00 1.25
❑ 31 Johnny Damon 1.25 .50
❑ 32 Jason Giambi .75 .30
❑ 33 Bobby Crosby .75 .30
❑ 34 Nick Swisher .75 .30
❑ 35 Eric Chavez .75 .30
❑ 36 Ichiro Suzuki 3.00 1.25
❑ 37 Raul Ibanez .75 .30
❑ 38 Richie Sexson .75 .30
❑ 39 Carl Crawford .75 .30
❑ 40 Rocco Baldelli .75 .30
❑ 41 Scott Kazmir 1.25 .50
❑ 42 Michael Young .75 .30
❑ 43 Mark Teixeira 1.25 .50
❑ 44 Ian Kinsler .75 .30
❑ 45 Troy Glaus .75 .30
❑ 46 Vernon Wells .75 .30
❑ 47 Roy Halladay .75 .30
❑ 48 Lyle Overbay .75 .30
❑ 49 Brandon Webb .75 .30
❑ 50 Conor Jackson .75 .30
❑ 51 Stephen Drew 1.25 .50
❑ 52 Chipper Jones 2.00 .75
❑ 53 Andruw Jones 1.25 .50
❑ 54 Adam LaRoche .75 .30
❑ 55 John Smoltz 1.25 .50
❑ 56 Derrek Lee .75 .30
❑ 57 Aramis Ramirez .75 .30
❑ 58 Carlos Zambrano .75 .30
❑ 59 Ken Griffey Jr. 3.00 1.25
❑ 60 Adam Dunn .75 .30
❑ 61 Aaron Harang .75 .30
❑ 62 Todd Helton 1.25 .50
❑ 63 Matt Holliday 1.00 .40
❑ 64 Garrett Atkins .75 .30
❑ 65 Miguel Cabrera 1.25 .50
❑ 66 Hanley Ramirez 1.25 .50
❑ 67 Dontrelle Willis .75 .30
❑ 68 Lance Berkman .75 .30
❑ 69 Roy Oswalt .75 .30
❑ 70 Craig Biggio 1.25 .50
❑ 71 J.D. Drew .75 .30
❑ 72 Nomar Garciaparra 2.00 .75
❑ 73 Rafael Furcal .75 .30
❑ 74 Jeff Kent .75 .30
❑ 75 Prince Fielder 2.00 .75
❑ 76 Bill Hall .75 .30
❑ 77 Rickie Weeks .75 .30
❑ 78 Jose Reyes .75 .30
❑ 79 David Wright 3.00 1.25
❑ 80 Carlos Delgado .75 .30
❑ 81 Carlos Beltran .75 .30
❑ 82 Ryan Howard 3.00 1.25
❑ 83 Chase Utley 2.00 .75
❑ 84 Jimmy Rollins .75 .30
❑ 85 Jason Bay .75 .30
❑ 86 Freddy Sanchez .75 .30
❑ 87 Zach Duke .75 .30
❑ 88 Trevor Hoffman .75 .30
❑ 89 Adrian Gonzalez .75 .30
❑ 90 Chris Young .75 .30
❑ 91 Ray Durham .75 .30
❑ 92 Omar Vizquel 1.25 .50
❑ 93 Jason Schmidt .75 .30
❑ 94 Albert Pujols 4.00 1.50
❑ 95 Scott Rolen 1.25 .50
❑ 96 Jim Edmonds 1.25 .50
❑ 97 Chris Carpenter .75 .30
❑ 98 Alfonso Soriano .75 .30
❑ 99 Ryan Zimmerman 2.00 .75
❑ 100 Nick Johnson .75 .30
❑ 101 Delmon Young AU (RC) 25.00 10.00
❑ 102 A.Miller AU RC EXCH * 25.00 10.00
❑ 103 Troy Tulowitzki AU (RC) 30.00 12.50
❑ 104 Jeff Fiorentino AU (RC) 8.00 3.00
❑ 105 David Murphy AU (RC) 8.00 3.00
❑ 106 T.Lincecum AU RC EXCH 150.00 100.00
❑ 107 P.Hughes AU (RC) EXCH 100.00 50.00
❑ 108 K.Kouzmanoff AU (RC) EXCH 15.00 6.00
❑ 109 A.Lind AU (RC) EXCH * 15.00 6.00
❑ 110 M.Reynolds AU RC EXCH 50.00 20.00
❑ 111 Kevin Hooper AU (RC) 8.00 3.00
❑ 112 Mitch Maier AU RC 8.00 3.00
❑ 113 Homey Bailey AU (RC) EXCH 50.00 20.00
❑ 114 Dennis Sarfate AU (RC) 8.00 3.00
❑ 115 Drew Anderson AU RC 8.00 3.00
❑ 116 Miguel Montero AU (RC) 8.00 3.00
❑ 117 G.Perkins AU (RC) EXCH 8.00 3.00
❑ 118 Kevin Slowey AU (RC) EXCH 25.00 10.00
❑ 119 Tim Gradoville AU RC 8.00 3.00
❑ 120 Ryan Braun AU (RC) EXCH 150.00 100.00
❑ 121 Chris Narveson AU (RC) 8.00 3.00
❑ 122 P.Misch AU (RC) EXCH * 8.00 3.00
❑ 123 Juan Salas AU (RC) 8.00 3.00
❑ 124 Beltran Perez AU (RC) 8.00 3.00
❑ 125 Joaquin Arias AU (RC) 8.00 3.00
❑ 126 Philip Humber AU (RC) 15.00 6.00
❑ 127 Kei Igawa AU RC 60.00 30.00
❑ 128 Daisuke Matsuzaka RC 300.00 250.00
❑ 129 Andy Cannizaro AU RC 15.00 6.00
❑ 130 Ubaldo Jimenez AU (RC) 15.00 6.00
❑ 131 Fred Lewis AU (RC) 15.00 6.00
❑ 132 Ryan Sweeney AU (RC) 8.00 3.00
❑ 133 Jeff Baker AU (RC) 8.00 3.00
❑ 134 Michael Bourn AU (RC) 8.00 3.00
❑ 135 Akinori Iwamura AU RC 25.00 10.00
❑ 136 Oswaldo Navarro AU RC 8.00 3.00
❑ 137 Hunter Pence AU (RC) 60.00 30.00
❑ 138 Jon Knott AU (RC) 8.00 3.00
❑ 139 J.Hampson AU (RC) EXCH 8.00 3.00
❑ 140 J.Salazar AU (RC) EXCH 8.00 3.00
❑ 141 Juan Morillo AU (RC) 8.00 3.00
❑ 142 Delwyn Young AU (RC) 8.00 3.00
❑ 143 Brian Burres AU (RC) 12.00 5.00
❑ 144 Chris Stewart AU RC 8.00 3.00
❑ 145 Eric Stults AU RC 8.00 3.00
❑ 146 Carlos Maldonado AU (RC) 8.00 3.00
❑ 147 Angel Sanchez AU RC 8.00 3.00
❑ 148 Cesar Jimenez AU RC 8.00 3.00
❑ 149 Shawn Riggans AU (RC) 8.00 3.00
❑ 150 John Nelson AU (RC) 8.00 3.00

2001 Sweet Spot

❑ COMP.BASIC w/o SP's (60) 20.00 8.00
❑ COMP.UPDATE w/o SP's (30) 10.00 4.00
❑ COMMON CARD (1-60) .40 .15
❑ COMMON CARD (61-90) 10.00 4.00
❑ COMMON CARD (91-120) .60 .25
❑ COMMON CARD (121-150) 5.00 2.00
❑ 1 Troy Glaus .40 .15
❑ 2 Darin Erstad .40 .15
❑ 3 Jason Giambi .40 .15
❑ 4 Tim Hudson .40 .15
❑ 5 Ben Grieve .40 .15
❑ 6 Carlos Delgado .40 .15
❑ 7 David Wells .40 .15
❑ 8 Greg Vaughn .40 .15
❑ 9 Roberto Alomar .60 .25
❑ 10 Jim Thome .60 .25
❑ 11 John Olerud .40 .15
❑ 12 Edgar Martinez .60 .25
❑ 13 Cal Ripken 3.00 1.25
❑ 14 Albert Belle .40 .15
❑ 15 Ivan Rodriguez .60 .25
❑ 16 Alex Rodriguez Rangers 3.00 1.25
❑ 17 Pedro Martinez .60 .25
❑ 18 Nomar Garciaparra 1.50 .60
❑ 19 Manny Ramirez .60 .25

❑ 20 Jermaine Dye .40 .15
❑ 21 Juan Gonzalez .40 .15
❑ 22 Dean Palmer .40 .15
❑ 23 Matt Lawton .40 .15
❑ 24 Eric Milton .40 .15
❑ 25 Frank Thomas 1.00 .40
❑ 26 Magglio Ordonez .40 .15
❑ 27 Derek Jeter 2.50 1.00
❑ 28 Bernie Williams .60 .25
❑ 29 Roger Clemens 2.00 .75
❑ 30 Jeff Bagwell .60 .25
❑ 31 Richard Hidalgo .40 .15
❑ 32 Chipper Jones 1.00 .40
❑ 33 Greg Maddux 1.50 .60
❑ 34 Richie Sexson .40 .15
❑ 35 Jeromy Burnitz .40 .15
❑ 36 Mark McGwire 2.50 1.00
❑ 37 Jim Edmonds .40 .15
❑ 38 Sammy Sosa 1.00 .40
❑ 39 Randy Johnson 1.00 .40
❑ 40 Steve Finley .40 .15
❑ 41 Gary Sheffield .40 .15
❑ 42 Shawn Green .40 .15
❑ 43 Vladimir Guerrero 1.00 .40
❑ 44 Jose Vidro .40 .15
❑ 45 Barry Bonds 2.50 1.00
❑ 46 Jeff Kent .40 .15
❑ 47 Preston Wilson .40 .15
❑ 48 Luis Castillo .40 .15
❑ 49 Mike Piazza 1.50 .60
❑ 50 Edgardo Alfonzo .40 .15
❑ 51 Tony Gwynn 1.25 .50
❑ 52 Ryan Klesko .40 .15
❑ 53 Scott Rolen .60 .25
❑ 54 Bob Abreu .40 .15
❑ 55 Jason Kendall .40 .15
❑ 56 Brian Giles .40 .15
❑ 57 Ken Griffey Jr. 1.50 .60
❑ 58 Barry Larkin .60 .25
❑ 59 Todd Helton .60 .25
❑ 60 Mike Hampton UER .40 .15
❑ 61 Corey Patterson SB 10.00 4.00
❑ 62 Ichiro Suzuki SB RC 200.00 125.00
❑ 63 Jason Grilli SB 10.00 4.00
❑ 64 Brian Cole SB 10.00 4.00
❑ 65 Juan Pierre SB 10.00 4.00
❑ 66 Matt Ginter SB 10.00 4.00
❑ 67 Jimmy Rollins SB 10.00 4.00
❑ 68 Jason Smith SB RC 10.00 4.00
❑ 69 Israel Alcantara SB 10.00 4.00
❑ 70 Adam Pettyjohn SB RC 10.00 4.00
❑ 71 Luke Prokopec SB 10.00 4.00
❑ 72 Barry Zito SB 12.00 5.00
❑ 73 Keith Ginter SB 10.00 4.00
❑ 74 Sun Woo Kim SB 10.00 4.00
❑ 75 Ross Gload SB 10.00 4.00
❑ 76 Matt Wise SB 10.00 4.00
❑ 77 Aubrey Huff SB 10.00 4.00
❑ 78 Ryan Franklin SB 10.00 4.00
❑ 79 Brandon Inge SB 10.00 4.00
❑ 80 Wes Helms SB 10.00 4.00
❑ 81 Junior Spivey SB RC 12.00 5.00
❑ 82 Ryan Vogelsong SB 10.00 4.00
❑ 83 John Parrish SB 10.00 4.00
❑ 84 Joe Crede SB 12.00 5.00
❑ 85 Damian Rolls SB 10.00 4.00
❑ 86 Esix Snead SB RC 10.00 4.00
❑ 87 Rocky Biddle SB 10.00 4.00
❑ 88 Brady Clark SB 10.00 4.00
❑ 89 Timo Perez SB 10.00 4.00
❑ 90 Jay Spurgeon SB 10.00 4.00
❑ 91 Garret Anderson .60 .25
❑ 92 Jermaine Dye .60 .25
❑ 93 Shannon Stewart .60 .25
❑ 94 Ben Grieve .60 .25
❑ 95 Juan Gonzalez .60 .25
❑ 96 Brett Boone .60 .25
❑ 97 Tony Batista .60 .25
❑ 98 Rafael Palmeiro 1.00 .40
❑ 99 Carl Everett .60 .25
❑ 100 Mike Sweeney .60 .25
❑ 101 Tony Clark .60 .25
❑ 102 Doug Mientkiewicz .60 .25
❑ 103 Jose Canseco 1.00 .40
❑ 104 Mike Mussina 1.00 .40
❑ 105 Lance Berkman .60 .25
❑ 106 Andruw Jones 1.00 .40
❑ 107 Geoff Jenkins .60 .25
❑ 108 Matt Morris .60 .25
❑ 109 Fred McGriff 1.00 .40
❑ 110 Luis Gonzalez .60 .25
❑ 111 Kevin Brown .60 .25
❑ 112 Tony Armas Jr. .60 .25
❑ 113 John Vander Wal .60 .25
❑ 114 Cliff Floyd .60 .25
❑ 115 Matt Lawton .60 .25
❑ 116 Phil Nevin .60 .25
❑ 117 Pat Burrell .60 .25
❑ 118 Aramis Ramirez .60 .25
❑ 119 Sean Casey .60 .25
❑ 120 Larry Walker .60 .25
❑ 121 Albert Pujols SB RC 250.00 150.00
❑ 122 Johnny Estrada SB RC 5.00 2.00
❑ 123 Wilson Betemit SB RC 8.00 3.00
❑ 124 Adrian Hernandez SB RC 5.00 2.00
❑ 125 Morgan Ensberg SB RC 8.00 3.00
❑ 126 Horacio Ramirez SB RC 5.00 2.00
❑ 127 Josh Towers SB RC 5.00 2.00
❑ 128 Juan Uribe SB RC 5.00 2.00
❑ 129 Wilken Ruan SB RC 5.00 2.00
❑ 130 Andres Torres SB RC 5.00 2.00
❑ 131 Brian Lawrence SB RC 5.00 2.00
❑ 132 Ryan Freel SB RC 5.00 2.00
❑ 133 Brandon Duckworth SB RC 5.00 2.00
❑ 134 Juan Diaz SB RC 5.00 2.00
❑ 135 Rafael Soriano SB RC 5.00 2.00
❑ 136 Ricardo Rodriguez SB RC 5.00 2.00
❑ 137 Bud Smith SB RC 5.00 2.00
❑ 138 Mark Teixeira SB RC 30.00 12.50
❑ 139 Mark Prior SB RC 15.00 6.00
❑ 140 Jackson Melian SB RC 5.00 2.00
❑ 141 Dewon Brazelton SB RC 5.00 2.00
❑ 142 Greg Miller SB RC 5.00 2.00
❑ 143 Billy Sylvester SB RC 5.00 2.00
❑ 144 Elpidio Guzman SB RC 5.00 2.00
❑ 145 Jack Wilson SB RC 5.00 2.00
❑ 146 Jose Mieses SB RC 5.00 2.00
❑ 147 Brandon Lyon SB RC 5.00 2.00
❑ 148 Tsuyoshi Shinjo SB RC 5.00 2.00
❑ 149 Juan Cruz SB RC 5.00 2.00
❑ 150 Jay Gibbons SB RC 5.00 2.00

2002 Sweet Spot

❑ COMP.SET w/o SP's (90) 20.00 8.00
❑ COMMON CARD (1-90) .40 .15
❑ COMMON CARD (91-130) 4.00 1.50
❑ COMMON TIER 1 AU (131-145) 15.00 6.00
❑ COMMON TIER 2 AU (131-145) 25.0010.00
❑ COMMON CARD (146-175) 10.00 4.00
❑ MCGWIRE AU EXCH.RANDOM IN PACKS
❑ 1 Troy Glaus .40 .15
❑ 2 Darin Erstad .40 .15
❑ 3 Tim Hudson .40 .15
❑ 4 Eric Chavez .40 .15
❑ 5 Barry Zito .40 .15
❑ 6 Miguel Tejada .40 .15
❑ 7 Carlos Delgado .40 .15
❑ 8 Eric Hinske .40 .15
❑ 9 Ben Grieve .40 .15
❑ 10 Jim Thome .60 .25
❑ 11 C.C. Sabathia .40 .15
❑ 12 Omar Vizquel .60 .25
❑ 13 Ichiro Suzuki 2.00 .75
❑ 14 Edgar Martinez .60 .25
❑ 15 Bret Boone .40 .15
❑ 16 Freddy Garcia .40 .15
❑ 17 Tony Batista .40 .15
❑ 18 Geronimo Gil .40 .15
❑ 19 Alex Rodriguez 1.50 .60
❑ 20 Rafael Palmeiro .60 .25
❑ 21 Ivan Rodriguez .60 .25
❑ 22 Hank Blalock .60 .25
❑ 23 Juan Gonzalez .40 .15
❑ 24 Nomar Garciaparra 1.50 .60
❑ 25 Pedro Martinez .60 .25
❑ 26 Manny Ramirez .60 .25
❑ 27 Mike Sweeney .40 .15
❑ 28 Carlos Beltran .40 .15
❑ 29 Dmitri Young .40 .15
❑ 30 Torii Hunter .40 .15
❑ 31 Eric Milton .40 .15
❑ 32 Corey Koskie .40 .15
❑ 33 Frank Thomas 1.00 .40
❑ 34 Mark Buehrle .40 .15
❑ 35 Magglio Ordonez .40 .15
❑ 36 Roger Clemens 2.00 .75
❑ 37 Derek Jeter 2.50 1.00
❑ 38 Jason Giambi .40 .15
❑ 39 Alfonso Soriano .40 .15
❑ 40 Bernie Williams .60 .25
❑ 41 Jeff Bagwell .60 .25
❑ 42 Roy Oswalt .40 .15
❑ 43 Lance Berkman .40 .15
❑ 44 Greg Maddux 1.50 .60
❑ 45 Chipper Jones 1.00 .40
❑ 46 Gary Sheffield .40 .15
❑ 47 Andruw Jones .60 .25
❑ 48 Richie Sexson .40 .15
❑ 49 Ben Sheets .40 .15
❑ 50 Albert Pujols 2.00 .75
❑ 51 Matt Morris .40 .15
❑ 52 J.D. Drew .40 .15
❑ 53 Sammy Sosa 1.00 .40
❑ 54 Kerry Wood .40 .15
❑ 55 Mark Prior .60 25.00
❑ 56 Moises Alou .40 .15
❑ 57 Corey Patterson .40 .15
❑ 58 Randy Johnson 1.00 .40
❑ 59 Luis Gonzalez .40 .15
❑ 60 Curt Schilling .40 .15
❑ 61 Shawn Green .40 .15
❑ 62 Kevin Brown .40 .15
❑ 63 Paul Lo Duca .40 .15
❑ 64 Adrian Beltre .40 .15
❑ 65 Vladimir Guerrero 1.00 .40
❑ 66 Jose Vidro .40 .15
❑ 67 Javier Vazquez .40 .15
❑ 68 Barry Bonds 2.50 1.00
❑ 69 Jeff Kent .40 .15
❑ 70 Rich Aurilia .40 .15
❑ 71 Mike Lowell .40 .15
❑ 72 Josh Beckett .40 .15
❑ 73 Brad Penny .40 .15
❑ 74 Roberto Alomar .60 .25
❑ 75 Mike Piazza 1.50 .60
❑ 76 Jeromy Burnitz .40 .15
❑ 77 Mo Vaughn .40 .15
❑ 78 Phil Nevin .40 .15
❑ 79 Sean Burroughs .40 .15
❑ 80 Jeremy Giambi .40 .15
❑ 81 Bobby Abreu .40 .15
❑ 82 Jimmy Rollins .40 .15
❑ 83 Pat Burrell .40 .15
❑ 84 Brian Giles .40 .15
❑ 85 Aramis Ramirez .40 .15
❑ 86 Ken Griffey Jr. 1.50 .60
❑ 87 Adam Dunn .40 .15
❑ 88 Austin Kearns .40 .15
❑ 89 Todd Helton .60 .25
❑ 90 Larry Walker .40 .15
❑ 91 Earl Snyder SB RC 4.00 1.50
❑ 92 Jorge Padilla SB RC 4.00 1.50
❑ 93 Felix Escalona SB RC 4.00 1.50
❑ 94 John Foster SB RC 4.00 1.50
❑ 95 Brandon Puffer SB RC 4.00 1.50
❑ 96 Steve Bechler SB RC 4.00 1.50
❑ 97 Hansel Izquierdo SB RC 4.00 1.50
❑ 98 Chris Baker SB RC 4.00 1.50
❑ 99 Jeremy Ward SB RC 4.00 1.50
❑ 100 Kevin Frederick SB RC 4.00 1.50

❑ 101 Josh Hancock SB RC 5.00 2.00
❑ 102 Allan Simpson SB RC 4.00 1.50
❑ 103 Mitch Wylie SB RC 4.00 1.50
❑ 104 Mark Corey SB RC 4.00 1.50
❑ 105 Victor Alvarez SB RC 4.00 1.50
❑ 106 Todd Donovan SB RC 4.00 1.50
❑ 107 Nelson Castro SB RC 4.00 1.50
❑ 108 Chris Booker SB RC 4.00 1.50
❑ 109 Corey Thurman SB RC 4.00 1.50
❑ 110 Kirk Saarloos SB RC 4.00 1.50
❑ 111 Michael Crudale SB RC 4.00 1.50
❑ 112 Jason Simontacchi SB RC 4.00 1.50
❑ 113 Ron Calloway SB RC 4.00 1.50
❑ 114 Brandon Backe SB RC 5.00 2.00
❑ 115 Tom Shearn SB RC 4.00 1.50
❑ 116 Oliver Perez SB RC 5.00 2.00
❑ 117 Kyle Kane SB RC 4.00 1.50
❑ 118 Francis Beltran SB RC 4.00 1.50
❑ 119 So Taguchi SB RC 5.00 2.00
❑ 120 Doug Devore SB RC 4.00 1.50
❑ 121 Juan Brito SB RC 4.00 1.50
❑ 122 Cliff Bartosh SB RC 4.00 1.50
❑ 123 Eric Junge SB RC 4.00 1.50
❑ 124 Joe Orloski SB RC 4.00 1.50
❑ 125 Scotty Layfield SB RC 4.00 1.50
❑ 126 Jorge Sosa SB RC 5.00 2.00
❑ 127 Satoru Komiyama SB RC 4.00 1.50
❑ 128 Edwin Almonte SB RC 4.00 1.50
❑ 129 Takahito Nomura SB RC 4.00 1.50
❑ 130 John Ennis SB RC 4.00 1.50
❑ 131 Kazuhisa Ishii T2 AU RC 80.00 40.00
❑ 132 Ben Howard T2 AU RC 25.00 10.00
❑ 133 Aaron Cook T1 AU RC 15.00 6.00
❑ 134 Andy Machado T1 AU RC 15.00 6.00
❑ 135 Luis Ugueto T1 AU RC 15.00 6.00
❑ 136 Tyler Yates T1 AU RC 15.00 6.00
❑ 137 Rodrigo Rosario T1 AU RC 15.00 6.00
❑ 138 Jaime Cerda T1 AU RC 15.00 6.00
❑ 139 Luis Martinez T1 AU RC 15.00 6.00
❑ 140 Rene Reyes T1 AU RC 15.00 6.00
❑ 141 Eric Good T1 AU RC 15.00 6.00
❑ 142 Matt Thornton T2 AU RC 25.00 10.00
❑ 143 Steve Kent T1 AU RC 15.00 6.00
❑ 144 Jose Valverde T1 AU RC 15.00 6.00
❑ 145 Adrian Burnside T1 AU RC 15.00 6.00
❑ 146 Barry Bonds GF 25.00 10.00
❑ 147 Ken Griffey Jr. GF 15.00 6.00
❑ 148 Alex Rodriguez GF 15.00 6.00
❑ 149 Jason Giambi GF 4.00 1.50
❑ 150 Chipper Jones GF 10.00 4.00
❑ 151 Nomar Garciaparra GF 15.00 6.00
❑ 152 Mike Piazza GF 15.00 6.00
❑ 153 Sammy Sosa GF 10.00 4.00
❑ 154 Derek Jeter GF 25.00 10.00
❑ 155 Jeff Bagwell GF 10.00 4.00
❑ 156 Albert Pujols GF 15.00 6.00
❑ 157 Ichiro Suzuki GF 15.00 6.00
❑ 158 Randy Johnson GF 10.00 4.00
❑ 159 Frank Thomas GF 10.00 4.00
❑ 160 Greg Maddux GF 15.00 6.00
❑ 161 Jim Thome GF 10.00 4.00
❑ 162 Scott Rolen GF 10.00 4.00
❑ 163 Shawn Green GF 10.00 4.00
❑ 164 Vladimir Guerrero GF 10.00 4.00
❑ 165 Troy Glaus GF 10.00 4.00
❑ 166 Carlos Delgado GF 10.00 4.00
❑ 167 Luis Gonzalez GF 10.00 4.00
❑ 168 Roger Clemens GF 20.00 8.00
❑ 169 Todd Helton GF 10.00 4.00
❑ 170 Eric Chavez GF 10.00 4.00
❑ 171 Rafael Palmeiro GF 10.00 4.00
❑ 172 Pedro Martinez GF 10.00 4.00
❑ 173 Lance Berkman GF 10.00 4.00
❑ 174 Josh Beckett GF 10.00 4.00
❑ 175 Sean Burroughs GF 10.00 4.00
❑ MM Mark McGwire AU EXCH/100

2003 Sweet Spot

❑ COMP.SET w/o SP's (100) 20.00 8.00
❑ COMP.SET w/SP's (130) 120.00 60.00
❑ COMMON CARD (1-130) .50 .20
❑ COMMON SP (1-130) 3.00 1.25
❑ COMMON CARD (131-190) 3.00 1.25
❑ 131-190 PRINT RUN 2003 SERIAL #'d SETS
❑ COMMON P1 (191-232) 4.00 1.50
❑ P1 191-232 PRINT RUN 500 SERIAL #'d SETS
❑ COMMON P2-P3 (191-232) 3.00 1.25
❑ P2 191-232 PRINT RUN 1200 SERIAL #'d SETS
❑ P3 191-232 PRINT RUN 1430 SERIAL #'d SETS
❑ 1 Darin Erstad .50 .20
❑ 2 Garret Anderson .50 .20
❑ 3 Tim Salmon .75 .30
❑ 4 Troy Glaus .50 .20
❑ 5 Luis Gonzalez .50 .20
❑ 6 Randy Johnson 1.25 .50
❑ 7 Curt Schilling .50 .20
❑ 8 Lyle Overbay .50 .20
❑ 9 Andruw Jones SP 4.00 1.50
❑ 10 Gary Sheffield SP 3.00 1.25
❑ 11 Rafael Furcal SP 3.00 1.25
❑ 12 Greg Maddux SP 6.00 2.50
❑ 13 Chipper Jones SP 4.00 1.50
❑ 14 Tony Batista .50 .20
❑ 15 Rodrigo Lopez .50 .20
❑ 16 Jay Gibbons .50 .20
❑ 17 Jason Johnson .50 .20
❑ 18 Byung-Hyun Kim SP 3.00 1.25
❑ 19 Johnny Damon SP 4.00 1.50
❑ 20 Derek Lowe SP 3.00 1.25
❑ 21 Nomar Garciaparra SP 6.00 2.50
❑ 22 Pedro Martinez SP 4.00 1.50
❑ 23 Manny Ramirez SP 4.00 1.50
❑ 24 Mark Prior .75 .30
❑ 25 Kerry Wood .50 .20
❑ 26 Corey Patterson .50 .20
❑ 27 Sammy Sosa 1.25 .50
❑ 28 Moises Alou .50 .20
❑ 29 Magglio Ordonez .50 .20
❑ 30 Frank Thomas 1.25 .50
❑ 31 Paul Konerko .50 .20
❑ 32 Roberto Alomar .75 .30
❑ 33 Adam Dunn .50 .20
❑ 34 Austin Kearns .50 .20
❑ 35 Ryan Wagner RC .50 .20
❑ 36 Ken Griffey Jr. 2.00 .75
❑ 37 Sean Casey .50 .20
❑ 38 Omar Vizquel .75 .30
❑ 39 C.C. Sabathia .50 .20
❑ 40 Jason Davis .50 .20
❑ 41 Travis Hafner .50 .20
❑ 42 Brandon Phillips .50 .20
❑ 43 Larry Walker .50 .20
❑ 44 Preston Wilson .50 .20
❑ 45 Jay Payton .50 .20
❑ 46 Todd Helton .75 .30
❑ 47 Carlos Pena .50 .20
❑ 48 Eric Munson .50 .20
❑ 49 Ivan Rodriguez .75 .30
❑ 50 Josh Beckett .50 .20
❑ 51 Alex Gonzalez .50 .20
❑ 52 Roy Oswalt .50 .20
❑ 53 Craig Biggio .75 .30
❑ 54 Jeff Bagwell .75 .30
❑ 55 Lance Berkman .50 .20
❑ 56 Mike Sweeney .50 .20
❑ 57 Carlos Beltran .50 .20
❑ 58 Brent Mayne .50 .20
❑ 59 Mike MacDougal .50 .20
❑ 60 Hideo Nomo 1.25 .50
❑ 61 Dave Roberts .50 .20
❑ 62 Adrian Beltre .50 .20
❑ 63 Shawn Green .50 .20
❑ 64 Kazuhisa Ishii .50 .20
❑ 65 Rickey Henderson 1.25 .50
❑ 66 Richie Sexson .50 .20
❑ 67 Torii Hunter .50 .20
❑ 68 Jacque Jones .50 .20
❑ 69 Joe Mays .50 .20
❑ 70 Corey Koskie .50 .20
❑ 71 A.J. Pierzynski .50 .20
❑ 72 Jose Vidro .50 .20
❑ 73 Vladimir Guerrero 1.25 .50
❑ 74 Tom Glavine .75 .30
❑ 75 Mike Piazza 2.00 .75
❑ 76 Jose Reyes .50 .20
❑ 77 Jae Weong Seo .50 .20
❑ 78 Jorge Posada SP 4.00 1.50
❑ 79 Mike Mussina SP 4.00 1.50
❑ 80 Robin Ventura SP 3.00 1.25
❑ 81 Mariano Rivera SP 4.00 1.50
❑ 82 Roger Clemens SP 8.00 3.00
❑ 83 Jason Giambi SP 3.00 1.25
❑ 84 Bernie Williams SP 4.00 1.50
❑ 85 Alfonso Soriano SP 3.00 1.25
❑ 86 Derek Jeter 3.00 1.25
❑ 87 Miguel Tejada .50 .20
❑ 88 Eric Chavez .50 .20
❑ 89 Tim Hudson .50 .20
❑ 90 Barry Zito .50 .20
❑ 91 Mark Mulder .50 .20
❑ 92 Erubiel Durazo .50 .20
❑ 93 Pat Burrell .50 .20
❑ 94 Jim Thome .75 .30
❑ 95 Bobby Abreu .50 .20
❑ 96 Brian Giles .50 .20
❑ 97 Reggie Sanders .50 .20
❑ 98 Jose Hernandez .50 .20
❑ 99 Ryan Klesko .50 .20
❑ 100 Sean Burroughs .50 .20
❑ 101 Edgardo Alfonzo SP 3.00 1.25
❑ 102 Rich Aurilia SP 3.00 1.25
❑ 103 Jose Cruz Jr. SP 3.00 1.25
❑ 104 Barry Bonds SP 10.00 4.00
❑ 105 Andres Galarraga SP 3.00 1.25
❑ 106 Mike Cameron .50 .20
❑ 107 Kazuhiro Sasaki .50 .20
❑ 108 Bret Boone .50 .20
❑ 109 Ichiro Suzuki 2.50 1.00
❑ 110 John Olerud .50 .20
❑ 111 J.D. Drew SP 3.00 1.25
❑ 112 Jim Edmonds SP 3.00 1.25
❑ 113 Scott Rolen SP 4.00 1.50
❑ 114 Matt Morris SP 3.00 1.25
❑ 115 Tino Martinez SP 4.00 1.50
❑ 116 Albert Pujols SP 8.00 3.00
❑ 117 Jared Sandberg .50 .20
❑ 118 Carl Crawford .50 .20
❑ 119 Rafael Palmeiro .75 .30
❑ 120 Hank Blalock .50 .20
❑ 121 Alex Rodriguez SP 6.00 2.50
❑ 122 Kevin Mench .50 .20
❑ 123 Juan Gonzalez .50 .20
❑ 124 Mark Teixeira .75 .30
❑ 125 Shannon Stewart .50 .20
❑ 126 Vernon Wells .50 .20
❑ 127 Josh Phelps .50 .20
❑ 128 Eric Hinske .50 .20
❑ 129 Orlando Hudson .50 .20
❑ 130 Carlos Delgado .50 .20
❑ 131 Jason Shiell SB RC 3.00 1.25
❑ 132 Kevin Tolar SB RC 3.00 1.25
❑ 133 Nathan Bland SB RC 3.00 1.25
❑ 134 Brent Hoard SB RC 3.00 1.25
❑ 135 Jon Pridie SB RC 3.00 1.25
❑ 136 Mike Ryan SB RC 3.00 1.25
❑ 137 Francisco Rosario SB RC 3.00 1.25
❑ 138 Runelvys Hernandez SB 3.00 1.25
❑ 139 Guillermo Quiroz SB RC 3.00 1.25
❑ 140 Chin-Hui Tsao SB 3.00 1.25
❑ 141 Rett Johnson SB RC 3.00 1.25
❑ 142 Colin Porter SB RC 3.00 1.25
❑ 143 Jose Castillo SB 3.00 1.25
❑ 144 Chris Waters SB RC 3.00 1.25
❑ 145 Jeremy Guthrie SB 3.00 1.25
❑ 146 Pedro Liriano SB 3.00 1.25
❑ 147 Joe Borowski SB 3.00 1.25
❑ 148 Felix Sanchez SB RC 3.00 1.25
❑ 149 Todd Wellemeyer SB RC 3.00 1.25
❑ 150 Gerald Laird SB 3.00 1.25
❑ 151 Brandon Webb SB RC 8.00 3.00

❑ 152 Tommy Whiteman SB 3.00 1.25
❑ 153 Carlos Rivera SB 3.00 1.25
❑ 154 Rick Roberts SB RC 3.00 1.25
❑ 155 Termel Sledge SB RC 3.00 1.25
❑ 156 Jeff Duncan SB RC 3.00 1.25
❑ 157 Craig Brazell SB RC 3.00 1.25
❑ 158 Bernie Castro SB RC 3.00 1.25
❑ 159 Cory Stewart SB RC 3.00 1.25
❑ 160 Brandon Villafuerte SB 3.00 1.25
❑ 161 Tommy Phelps SB 3.00 1.25
❑ 162 Josh Hall SB RC 3.00 1.25
❑ 163 Ryan Cameron SB RC 3.00 1.25
❑ 164 Garret Atkins SB 3.00 1.25
❑ 165 Brian Stokes SB RC 3.00 1.25
❑ 166 Rafael Betancourt SB RC 4.00 1.50
❑ 167 Jaime Cerda SB 3.00 1.25
❑ 168 D.J. Carrasco SB RC 3.00 1.25
❑ 169 Ian Ferguson SB RC 3.00 1.25
❑ 170 Jorge Cordova SB RC 3.00 1.25
❑ 171 Eric Munson SB 3.00 1.25
❑ 172 Nook Logan SB RC 4.00 1.50
❑ 173 Jeremy Bonderman SB RC 12.00 5.00
❑ 174 Kyle Snyder SB 3.00 1.25
❑ 175 Rich Harden SB 4.00 1.50
❑ 176 Kevin Ohme SB RC 3.00 1.25
❑ 177 Roger Deago SB RC 3.00 1.25
❑ 178 Marlon Byrd SB 3.00 1.25
❑ 179 Dontrelle Willis SB 4.00 1.50
❑ 180 Bobby Hill SB 3.00 1.25
❑ 181 Jesse Foppert SB 3.00 1.25
❑ 182 Andrew Good SB 3.00 1.25
❑ 183 Chase Utley SB 4.00 1.50
❑ 184 Bo Hart SB RC 3.00 1.25
❑ 185 Dan Haren SB RC 4.00 1.50
❑ 186 Tim Olson SB RC 3.00 1.25
❑ 187 Joe Thurston SB 3.00 1.25
❑ 188 Jason Anderson SB 3.00 1.25
❑ 189 Jason Gilfillan SB RC 3.00 1.25
❑ 190 Rickie Weeks SB RC 8.00 3.00
❑ 191 Hideki Matsui SB P1 RC 25.00 10.00
❑ 192 Jose Contreras SB P3 RC 4.00 1.50
❑ 193 Willie Eyre SB P3 RC 3.00 1.25
❑ 194 Matt Bruback SB P3 RC 3.00 1.25
❑ 195 Heath Bell SB P3 RC 3.00 1.25
❑ 196 Lew Ford SB P3 RC 4.00 1.50
❑ 197 Jeremy Griffiths SB P3 RC 3.00 1.25
❑ 198 Oscar Villarreal SB P1 RC 4.00 1.50
❑ 199 Francisco Cruceta SB P3 RC 3.00 1.25
❑ 200 Fern Cabrera SB P3 RC 3.00 1.25
❑ 201 Jhonny Peralta SB P3 4.00 1.50
❑ 202 Shane Bazzell SB P3 RC 3.00 1.25
❑ 203 Bobby Madritsch SB P1 RC 4.00 1.50
❑ 204 Phil Seibel SB P3 RC 3.00 1.25
❑ 205 Josh Willingham SB P3 RC 5.00 2.00
❑ 206 Rob Hammock SB P1 RC 4.00 1.50
❑ 207 Alejandro Machado SB P3 RC 3.00 1.25
❑ 208 David Sanders SB P3 RC 3.00 1.25
❑ 209 Mike Neu SB P1 RC 4.00 1.50
❑ 210 Andrew Brown SB P3 RC 4.00 1.50
❑ 211 Nate Robertson SB P3 RC 5.00 2.00
❑ 212 Miguel Ojeda SB P3 RC 3.00 1.25
❑ 213 Beau Kemp SB P3 RC 3.00 1.25
❑ 214 Aaron Looper SB P3 RC 3.00 1.25
❑ 215 Alfredo Gonzalez SB P3 RC 3.00 1.25
❑ 216 Rich Fischer SB P1 RC 4.00 1.50
❑ 218 Jeremy Wedel SB P3 RC 3.00 1.25
❑ 219 Prentice Redman SB P3 RC 3.00 1.25
❑ 220 Michel Hernandez SB P3 RC 3.00 1.25
❑ 221 Rocco Baldelli SB P1 4.00 1.50
❑ 222 Luis Ayala SB P3 RC 3.00 1.25
❑ 223 Arnaldo Munoz SB P3 RC 3.00 1.25
❑ 224 Wilfredo Ledezma SB P3 RC 3.00 1.25
❑ 225 Chris Capuano SB P3 RC 4.00 1.50
❑ 226 Aquilino Lopez SB P3 RC 3.00 1.25
❑ 227 Joe Valentine SB P1 RC 4.00 1.50
❑ 228 Matt Kata SB P2 RC 3.00 1.25
❑ 229 Diegomar Markwell SB P2 RC 3.00 1.25
❑ 230 Clint Barmes SB P2 RC 3.00 1.25
❑ 231 Mike Nicolas SB P1 RC 4.00 1.50
❑ 232 Jon Leicester SB P2 RC 3.00 1.25

2004 Sweet Spot

❑ COMP.SET w/o SP's (90) 20.00 8.00
❑ COMMON CARD (1-90) .50 .20
❑ COMMON (91-170/261-262) 4.00 1.50
❑ 91-170/261-262 STATED ODDS 1:12
❑ 91-170/261-262 PRINT RUN 799 #'d SETS
❑ COMMON CARD (171-230) 4.00 1.50
❑ 171-230 PRINT RUN 399 SERIAL #'d SETS
❑ COMMON CARD (231-250) 4.00 1.50
❑ 231-250 PRINT RUN 299 SERIAL #'d SETS
❑ COMMON CARD (251-260) 6.00 2.50
❑ 251-260 PRINT RUN 199 SERIAL #'d SETS
❑ 171-260/Ltd 10/W99 OVERALL ODDS 1:12
❑ OVERALL PLATES ODDS 1:360 HOBBY
❑ PLATES PRINT RUN 1 SET PER COLOR
❑ BLACK-CYAN-MAGENTA-YELLOW ISSUED
❑ NO PLATES PRICING DUE TO SACRCITY
❑ 1 Albert Pujols 2.50 1.00
❑ 2 Alex Rodriguez 2.00 .75
❑ 3 Alfonso Soriano .50 .20
❑ 4 Andruw Jones .75 .30
❑ 5 Andy Pettitte .75 .30
❑ 6 Aubrey Huff .50 .20
❑ 7 Austin Kearns .50 .20
❑ 8 Barry Zito .50 .20
❑ 9 Bobby Abreu .50 .20
❑ 10 Brandon Webb .50 .20
❑ 11 Bret Boone .50 .20
❑ 12 Brian Giles .50 .20
❑ 13 C.C. Sabathia .50 .20
❑ 14 Carlos Beltran .50 .20
❑ 15 Carlos Delgado .50 .20
❑ 16 Chipper Jones 1.25 .50
❑ 17 Cliff Floyd .50 .20
❑ 18 Curt Schilling .75 .30
❑ 19 Delmon Young .75 .30
❑ 20 Derek Jeter 2.50 1.00
❑ 21 Dontrelle Willis .75 .30
❑ 22 Edgar Martinez .75 .30
❑ 23 Edgar Renteria .50 .20
❑ 24 Eric Chavez .50 .20
❑ 25 Eric Gagne .50 .20
❑ 26 Frank Thomas 1.25 .50
❑ 27 Garret Anderson .50 .20
❑ 28 Gary Sheffield .50 .20
❑ 29 Geoff Jenkins .50 .20
❑ 30 Greg Maddux 2.00 .75
❑ 31 Hank Blalock .50 .20
❑ 32 Hideo Nomo 1.25 .50
❑ 33 Ichiro Suzuki 2.50 1.00
❑ 34 Ivan Rodriguez .75 .30
❑ 35 Jacque Jones .50 .20
❑ 36 Jason Giambi .50 .20
❑ 37 Jason Schmidt .50 .20
❑ 38 Javier Vazquez .50 .20
❑ 39 Javy Lopez .50 .20
❑ 40 Jeff Bagwell .75 .30
❑ 41 Jim Edmonds .50 .20
❑ 42 Jim Thome .75 .30
❑ 43 Joe Mauer 1.25 .50
❑ 44 John Smoltz .50 .20
❑ 45 Jose Cruz Jr. .50 .20
❑ 46 Jose Reyes .50 .20
❑ 47 Jose Vidro .50 .20
❑ 48 Josh Beckett .50 .20
❑ 49 Ken Griffey Jr. 2.00 .75
❑ 50 Kerry Wood .50 .20
❑ 51 Kevin Brown .50 .20
❑ 52 Larry Walker .50 .20
❑ 53 Magglio Ordonez .50 .20
❑ 54 Manny Ramirez .75 .30
❑ 55 Mark Mulder .50 .20
❑ 56 Mark Prior .75 .30
❑ 57 Mark Teixeira .75 .30
❑ 58 Miguel Cabrera .75 .30
❑ 59 Miguel Tejada .50 .20
❑ 60 Mike Lowell .50 .20
❑ 61 Mike Mussina .75 .30
❑ 62 Mike Piazza 2.00 .75
❑ 63 Nomar Garciaparra 2.00 .75
❑ 64 Orlando Cabrera .50 .20
❑ 65 Pat Burrell .50 .20
❑ 66 Pedro Martinez .75 .30
❑ 67 Phil Nevin .50 .20
❑ 68 Preston Wilson .50 .20
❑ 69 Rafael Furcal .50 .20
❑ 70 Rafael Palmeiro .75 .30
❑ 71 Randy Johnson 1.25 .50
❑ 72 Craig Wilson .50 .20
❑ 73 Rich Harden .50 .20
❑ 74 Richie Sexson .50 .20
❑ 75 Rickie Weeks .50 .20
❑ 76 Rocco Baldelli .50 .20
❑ 77 Roger Clemens 2.50 1.00
❑ 78 Roy Halladay .50 .20
❑ 79 Roy Oswalt .50 .20
❑ 80 Ryan Klesko .50 .20
❑ 81 Sammy Sosa 1.25 .50
❑ 82 Scott Podsednik .50 .20
❑ 83 Scott Rolen .75 .30
❑ 84 Shawn Green .50 .20
❑ 85 Tim Hudson .50 .20
❑ 86 Todd Helton .75 .30
❑ 87 Torii Hunter .50 .20
❑ 88 Troy Glaus .50 .20
❑ 89 Vernon Wells .50 .20
❑ 90 Vladimir Guerrero 1.25 .50
❑ 91 Aarom Baldiris SB RC 5.00 2.00
❑ 92 Akinori Otsuka SB RC 4.00 1.50
❑ 93 Andres Blanco SB RC 4.00 1.50
❑ 94 Angel Chavez SB RC 4.00 1.50
❑ 95 Brian Dallimore SB RC 4.00 1.50
❑ 96 Carlos Hines SB RC 4.00 1.50
❑ 97 Carlos Vasquez SB RC 5.00 2.00
❑ 98 Casey Daigle SB RC 4.00 1.50
❑ 99 Chad Bentz SB RC 4.00 1.50
❑ 100 Chris Aguila SB RC 4.00 1.50
❑ 101 Chris Oxspring SB RC 4.00 1.50
❑ 102 Chris Saenz SB RC 4.00 1.50
❑ 103 Chris Shelton SB RC 5.00 2.00
❑ 104 Colby Miller SB RC 4.00 1.50
❑ 105 Dave Crouthers SB RC 4.00 1.50
❑ 106 David Aardsma SB RC 5.00 2.00
❑ 107 Dennis Sarfate SB RC 4.00 1.50
❑ 108 Donnie Kelly SB RC 4.00 1.50
❑ 109 Eddy Rodriguez SB RC 5.00 2.00
❑ 110 Eduardo Villacis SB RC 4.00 1.50
❑ 111 Edwin Moreno SB RC 5.00 2.00
❑ 112 Enemencio Pacheco SB RC 4.00 1.50
❑ 113 Fernando Nieve SB RC 5.00 2.00
❑ 114 Franklyn Gracesqui SB RC 4.00 1.50
❑ 115 Freddy Guzman SB RC 4.00 1.50
❑ 116 Greg Dobbs SB RC 4.00 1.50
❑ 117 Hector Gimenez SB RC 4.00 1.50
❑ 118 Ian Snell SB RC 5.00 2.00
❑ 119 Ivan Ochoa SB RC 4.00 1.50
❑ 120 Jake Woods SB RC 4.00 1.50
❑ 121 Jamie Brown SB RC 4.00 1.50
❑ 122 Jason Bartlett SB RC 5.00 2.00
❑ 123 Jason Frasor SB RC 4.00 1.50
❑ 124 Jeff Bennett SB RC 4.00 1.50
❑ 125 Jerome Gamble SB RC 4.00 1.50
❑ 126 Jerry Gil SB RC 4.00 1.50
❑ 127 Brandon Medders SB RC 4.00 1.50
❑ 128 Ryan Meaux SB RC 4.00 1.50
❑ 129 John Gall SB RC 5.00 2.00
❑ 130 Jorge Sequea SB RC 4.00 1.50
❑ 131 Jorge Vasquez SB RC 4.00 1.50
❑ 132 Jose Capellan SB RC 5.00 2.00
❑ 133 Josh Labandeira SB RC 4.00 1.50
❑ 134 Justin Germano SB RC 4.00 1.50
❑ 135 Justin Hampson SB RC 4.00 1.50
❑ 136 Justin Huisman SB RC 4.00 1.50
❑ 137 Justin Knoedler SB RC 4.00 1.50
❑ 138 Justin Leone SB RC 5.00 2.00
❑ 139 Kazuhito Tadano SB RC 5.00 2.00
❑ 140 Kazuo Matsui SB RC 5.00 2.00
❑ 141 Kevin Cave SB RC 4.00 1.50
❑ 142 Lincoln Holdzkom SB RC 4.00 1.50

- ❑ 143 Lino Urdaneta SB RC 4.00 1.50
- ❑ 144 Luis A. Gonzalez SB RC 4.00 1.50
- ❑ 145 Mariano Gomez SB RC 4.00 1.50
- ❑ 146 Merkin Valdez SB RC 5.00 2.00
- ❑ 147 Michael Vento SB RC 5.00 2.00
- ❑ 148 Michael Wuertz SB RC 5.00 2.00
- ❑ 149 Mike Gosling SB RC 4.00 1.50
- ❑ 150 Mike Johnston SB RC 4.00 1.50
- ❑ 151 Mike Rouse SB RC 4.00 1.50
- ❑ 152 Nick Regilio SB RC 4.00 1.50
- ❑ 153 Onil Joseph SB RC 4.00 1.50
- ❑ 154 Orlando Rodriguez SB RC 4.00 1.50
- ❑ 155 Ramon Ramirez SB RC 4.00 1.50
- ❑ 156 Renyel Pinto SB RC 5.00 2.00
- ❑ 157 Roberto Novoa SB RC 5.00 2.00
- ❑ 158 Roman Colon SB RC 4.00 1.50
- ❑ 159 Ronald Belisario SB RC 4.00 1.50
- ❑ 160 Ronny Cedeno SB RC 5.00 2.00
- ❑ 161 Rusty Tucker SB RC 5.00 2.00
- ❑ 162 Ryan Wing SB RC 4.00 1.50
- ❑ 163 Scott Dohmann SB RC 4.00 1.50
- ❑ 164 Scott Proctor SB RC 5.00 2.00
- ❑ 165 Sean Henn SB RC 4.00 1.50
- ❑ 166 Shawn Camp SB RC 4.00 1.50
- ❑ 167 Shawn Hill SB RC 4.00 1.50
- ❑ 168 Shingo Takatsu SB RC 5.00 2.00
- ❑ 169 Tim Hamulack SB RC 4.00 1.50
- ❑ 170 William Bergolla SB RC 4.00 1.50
- ❑ 171 Adam Dunn SF 4.00 1.50
- ❑ 172 Albert Pujols SF 10.00 4.00
- ❑ 173 Alex Rodriguez SF 8.00 3.00
- ❑ 174 Alfonso Soriano SF 4.00 1.50
- ❑ 175 Andruw Jones SF 5.00 2.00
- ❑ 176 Bret Boone SF 4.00 1.50
- ❑ 177 Brian Giles SF 4.00 1.50
- ❑ 178 Carlos Delgado SF 4.00 1.50
- ❑ 179 Derrek Lee SF 5.00 2.00
- ❑ 180 Eric Chavez SF 4.00 1.50
- ❑ 181 Frank Thomas SF 5.00 2.00
- ❑ 182 Garret Anderson SF 4.00 1.50
- ❑ 183 Gary Sheffield SF 4.00 1.50
- ❑ 184 Hank Blalock SF 4.00 1.50
- ❑ 185 Jason Giambi SF 4.00 1.50
- ❑ 186 Javy Lopez SF 4.00 1.50
- ❑ 187 Jeff Bagwell SF 5.00 2.00
- ❑ 188 Jim Edmonds SF 4.00 1.50
- ❑ 189 Jim Thome SF 5.00 2.00
- ❑ 190 Ken Griffey Jr. SF 8.00 3.00
- ❑ 191 Lance Berkman SF 4.00 1.50
- ❑ 192 Magglio Ordonez SF 4.00 1.50
- ❑ 193 Manny Ramirez SF 5.00 2.00
- ❑ 194 Mike Lowell SF 4.00 1.50
- ❑ 195 Mike Piazza SF 8.00 3.00
- ❑ 196 Preston Wilson SF 4.00 1.50
- ❑ 197 Rafael Palmeiro SF 5.00 2.00
- ❑ 198 Richie Sexson SF 4.00 1.50
- ❑ 199 Sammy Sosa SF 5.00 2.00
- ❑ 200 Scott Rolen SF 5.00 2.00
- ❑ 201 Shawn Green SF 4.00 1.50
- ❑ 202 Todd Helton SF 5.00 2.00
- ❑ 203 Troy Glaus SF 4.00 1.50
- ❑ 204 Vernon Wells SF 4.00 1.50
- ❑ 205 Vladimir Guerrero SF 5.00 2.00
- ❑ 206 G.Anderson/V.Guerrero SL 5.00 2.00
- ❑ 207 L.Gonzalez/R.Sexson SL 4.00 1.50
- ❑ 208 A.Jones/C.Jones SL 5.00 2.00
- ❑ 209 J.Lopez/M.Tejada SL 4.00 1.50
- ❑ 210 M.Ramirez/D.Ortiz SL 5.00 2.00
- ❑ 211 D.Lee/S.Sosa SL 5.00 2.00
- ❑ 212 F.Thomas/M.Ordonez SL 5.00 2.00
- ❑ 213 A.Kearns/K.Griffey Jr. SL 8.00 3.00
- ❑ 214 P.Wilson/T.Helton SL 5.00 2.00
- ❑ 215 D.Young/I.Rodriguez SL 5.00 2.00
- ❑ 216 M.Cabrera/M.Lowell SL 5.00 2.00
- ❑ 217 J.Bagwell/L.Berkman SL 5.00 2.00
- ❑ 218 L.Overbay/G.Jenkins SL 4.00 1.50
- ❑ 219 A.Beltre/S.Green SL 4.00 1.50
- ❑ 220 J.Jones/T.Hunter SL 4.00 1.50
- ❑ 221 J.Vidro/N.Johnson SL 4.00 1.50
- ❑ 222 K.Matsui/M.Piazza SL 8.00 3.00
- ❑ 223 A.Rodriguez/J.Giambi SL 8.00 3.00
- ❑ 224 E.Chavez/J.Dye SL 4.00 1.50
- ❑ 225 J.Thome/P.Burrell SL 5.00 2.00
- ❑ 226 B.Giles/P.Nevin SL 4.00 1.50
- ❑ 227 B.Boone/I.Suzuki SL 10.00 4.00
- ❑ 228 A.Pujols/S.Rolen SL 10.00 4.00
- ❑ 229 H.Blalock/M.Teixeira SL 5.00 2.00
- ❑ 230 C.Delgado/V.Wells SL 4.00 1.50
- ❑ 231 Albert Pujols PD 10.00 4.00
- ❑ 232 Alex Rodriguez PD 8.00 3.00
- ❑ 233 Chipper Jones PD 5.00 2.00
- ❑ 234 Craig Biggio PD 5.00 2.00
- ❑ 235 Curt Schilling PD 5.00 2.00
- ❑ 236 Derek Jeter PD 10.00 4.00
- ❑ 237 Ivan Rodriguez PD 5.00 2.00
- ❑ 238 Jeff Bagwell PD 5.00 2.00
- ❑ 239 Jim Edmonds PD 4.00 1.50
- ❑ 240 Jim Thome PD 5.00 2.00
- ❑ 241 Josh Beckett PD 4.00 1.50
- ❑ 242 Kerry Wood PD 4.00 1.50
- ❑ 243 Kevin Brown PD 4.00 1.50
- ❑ 244 Mark Prior PD 5.00 2.00
- ❑ 245 Miguel Tejada PD 4.00 1.50
- ❑ 246 Mike Mussina PD 5.00 2.00
- ❑ 247 Nomar Garciaparra PD 8.00 3.00
- ❑ 248 Pedro Martinez PD 5.00 2.00
- ❑ 249 Randy Johnson PD 5.00 2.00
- ❑ 250 Roger Clemens PD 10.00 4.00
- ❑ 251 A.Rodriguez/D.Jeter DD 15.00 6.00
- ❑ 252 A.Soriano/H.Blalock DD 6.00 2.50
- ❑ 253 B.Abreu/P.Burrell DD 6.00 2.50
- ❑ 254 E.Renteria/S.Rolen DD 8.00 3.00
- ❑ 255 G.Anderson/V.Guerrero DD 8.00 3.00
- ❑ 256 J.Bagwell/J.Kent DD 8.00 3.00
- ❑ 257 J.Reyes/K.Matsui DD 8.00 3.00
- ❑ 258 K.Greene/S.Burroughs DD 8.00 3.00
- ❑ 259 M.Giles/R.Furcal DD 6.00 2.50
- ❑ 260 M.Ramirez/J.Damon DD 8.00 3.00
- ❑ 261 Tim Bausher SB RC 4.00 1.50
- ❑ 262 Tim Bittner SB RC 4.00 1.50

2005 Sweet Spot

- ❑ COMP.BASIC SET (90) 20.00 8.00
- ❑ COMP.UPDATE SET (84) 25.00 10.00
- ❑ COMMON CARD (1-90) .50 .20
- ❑ COMMON CARD (91-174) 1.00 .40
- ❑ 91-174 ONE PER '05 UD UPDATE PACK
- ❑ 1 Magglio Ordonez .50 .20
- ❑ 2 Craig Biggio .75 .30
- ❑ 3 Hank Blalock .50 .20
- ❑ 4 Nomar Garciaparra 1.25 .50
- ❑ 5 Ken Griffey Jr. 2.00 .75
- ❑ 6 Khalil Greene .75 .30
- ❑ 7 Andruw Jones .75 .30
- ❑ 8 Ichiro Suzuki 2.50 1.00
- ❑ 9 Philip Humber RC 1.25 .50
- ❑ 10 Vladimir Guerrero 1.25 .50
- ❑ 11 Carlos Delgado .50 .20
- ❑ 12 Jeff Niemann RC 1.25 .50
- ❑ 13 Chipper Jones 1.25 .50
- ❑ 14 Jose Vidro .50 .20
- ❑ 15 Miguel Cabrera .75 .30
- ❑ 16 Albert Pujols 2.50 1.00
- ❑ 17 Tadahito Iguchi RC 2.00 .75
- ❑ 18 Norihiro Nakamura RC 1.50 .60
- ❑ 19 Jeff Bagwell .75 .30
- ❑ 20 Troy Glaus .50 .20
- ❑ 21 Scott Rolen .75 .30
- ❑ 22 Derek Lowe .50 .20
- ❑ 23 Mark Prior .75 .30
- ❑ 24 Bobby Abreu .50 .20
- ❑ 25 David Wright 2.00 .75
- ❑ 26 Barry Zito .50 .20
- ❑ 27 Livan Hernandez .50 .20
- ❑ 28 Mark Teixeira .75 .30
- ❑ 29 Manny Ramirez .75 .30
- ❑ 30 Paul Konerko .50 .20
- ❑ 31 Victor Martinez .50 .20
- ❑ 32 Greg Maddux 2.00 .75
- ❑ 33 Jim Thome .75 .30
- ❑ 34 Miguel Tejada .50 .20
- ❑ 35 Ivan Rodriguez .75 .30
- ❑ 36 Carlos Beltran .50 .20
- ❑ 37 Steve Finley .50 .20
- ❑ 38 Torii Hunter .50 .20
- ❑ 39 Bobby Crosby .50 .20
- ❑ 40 Jorge Posada .75 .30
- ❑ 41 Ben Sheets .50 .20
- ❑ 42 Mike Piazza 1.25 .50
- ❑ 43 Luis Gonzalez .50 .20
- ❑ 44 Joe Mauer 1.25 .50
- ❑ 45 Shawn Green .50 .20
- ❑ 46 Eric Gagne .50 .20
- ❑ 47 Kerry Wood .50 .20
- ❑ 48 Derek Jeter 3.00 1.25
- ❑ 49 Josh Beckett .50 .20
- ❑ 50 Alex Rodriguez 2.00 .75
- ❑ 51 Aubrey Huff .50 .20
- ❑ 52 Eric Chavez .50 .20
- ❑ 53 Sammy Sosa 1.25 .50
- ❑ 54 Roger Clemens 2.00 .75
- ❑ 55 Mike Mussina .75 .30
- ❑ 56 Mike Sweeney .50 .20
- ❑ 57 Oliver Perez .50 .20
- ❑ 58 Tim Hudson .50 .20
- ❑ 59 Justin Verlander RC 4.00 1.50
- ❑ 60 Johan Santana 1.25 .50
- ❑ 61 Hideki Matsui 2.00 .75
- ❑ 62 Mark Mulder .50 .20
- ❑ 63 Jake Peavy .50 .20
- ❑ 64 Adam Dunn .50 .20
- ❑ 65 Dallas McPherson .50 .20
- ❑ 66 Jeff Kent .50 .20
- ❑ 67 Pedro Martinez .75 .30
- ❑ 68 J.D. Drew .50 .20
- ❑ 69 Frank Thomas 1.25 .50
- ❑ 70 Kazuo Matsui .50 .20
- ❑ 71 Travis Hafner .50 .20
- ❑ 72 John Smoltz .75 .30
- ❑ 73 Jason Schmidt .50 .20
- ❑ 74 Carlos Lee .50 .20
- ❑ 75 Todd Helton .75 .30
- ❑ 76 David Ortiz 1.25 .50
- ❑ 77 Roy Oswalt .50 .20
- ❑ 78 Brian Giles .50 .20
- ❑ 79 Gary Sheffield .50 .20
- ❑ 80 Jason Bay .50 .20
- ❑ 81 Alfonso Soriano .50 .20
- ❑ 82 Randy Johnson 1.25 .50
- ❑ 83 Tom Glavine .75 .30
- ❑ 84 Richie Sexson .50 .20
- ❑ 85 Curt Schilling .75 .30
- ❑ 86 Adrian Beltre .50 .20
- ❑ 87 Jim Edmonds .50 .20
- ❑ 88 Roy Halladay .50 .20
- ❑ 89 Johnny Damon .75 .30
- ❑ 90 Lance Berkman .50 .20
- ❑ 91 Adam Shabala SB RC 1.00 .40
- ❑ 92 Ambiorix Burgos SB RC 1.00 .40
- ❑ 93 Ambiorix Concepcion SB RC 1.00 .40
- ❑ 94 Anibal Sanchez SB RC 3.00 1.25
- ❑ 95 Bill McCarthy SB RC 1.00 .40
- ❑ 96 Brandon McCarthy SB RC 1.50 .60
- ❑ 97 Brian Burres SB RC 1.00 .40
- ❑ 98 Carlos Ruiz SB RC 1.00 .40
- ❑ 99 Casey Rogowski SB RC 1.25 .50
- ❑ 100 Chad Orvella SB RC 1.00 .40
- ❑ 101 Chris Resop SB RC 1.00 .40
- ❑ 102 Chris Roberson SB RC 1.00 .40
- ❑ 103 Chris Seddon SB RC 1.00 .40
- ❑ 104 Colter Bean SB RC 1.00 .40
- ❑ 105 Dae-Sung Koo SB RC 1.00 .40
- ❑ 106 Ryan Zimmerman SB RC 8.00 3.00
- ❑ 107 Dave Gassner SB RC 1.00 .40
- ❑ 108 Brian Anderson SB RC 1.50 .60
- ❑ 109 D.J. Houlton SB RC 1.00 .40
- ❑ 110 Derek Wathan SB RC 1.00 .40
- ❑ 111 Devon Lowery SB RC 1.00 .40
- ❑ 112 Enrique Gonzalez SB RC 1.00 .40
- ❑ 113 Chris Denorfia SB RC 1.25 .50

Card		
❑ 114 Eude Brito SB RC	1.00	.40
❑ 115 Francisco Butto SB RC	1.00	.40
❑ 116 Franquelis Osoria SB RC	1.00	.40
❑ 117 Garrett Jones SB RC	1.00	.40
❑ 118 Geovany Soto SB RC	1.00	.40
❑ 119 Hayden Penn SB RC	1.25	.50
❑ 120 Ismael Ramirez SB RC	1.00	.40
❑ 121 Jared Gothreaux SB RC	1.00	.40
❑ 122 Jason Hammel SB RC	1.00	.40
❑ 123 Dana Eveland SB RC	1.00	.40
❑ 124 Jeff Miller SB RC	1.00	.40
❑ 125 Jermaine Van Buren SB	1.00	.40
❑ 126 Joel Peralta SB RC	1.00	.40
❑ 127 John Hattig SB RC	1.00	.40
❑ 128 Jorge Campillo SB RC	1.00	.40
❑ 129 Juan Morillo SB RC	1.00	.40
❑ 130 Ryan Garko SB RC	2.00	.75
❑ 131 Keiichi Yabu SB RC	1.00	.40
❑ 132 Kendry Morales SB RC	2.50	1.00
❑ 133 Luis Hernandez SB RC	1.00	.40
❑ 134 Mark McLemore SB RC	1.00	.40
❑ 135 Luis Pena SB RC	1.00	.40
❑ 136 Luis O.Rodriguez SB RC	1.00	.40
❑ 137 Luke Scott SB RC	2.00	.75
❑ 138 Marcos Carvajal SB RC	1.00	.40
❑ 139 Mark Woodyard SB RC	1.00	.40
❑ 140 Matt A.Smith SB RC	1.00	.40
❑ 141 Matthew Lindstrom SB RC	1.00	.40
❑ 142 Miguel Negron SB RC	1.25	.50
❑ 143 Mike Morse SB RC	1.00	.40
❑ 144 Nate McLouth SB RC	1.25	.50
❑ 145 Nelson Cruz SB RC	2.00	.75
❑ 146 Nick Masset SB RC	1.00	.40
❑ 147 Ryan Spilborghs SB RC	1.25	.50
❑ 148 Oscar Robles SB RC	1.00	.40
❑ 149 Paulino Reynoso SB RC	1.00	.40
❑ 150 Pedro Lopez SB RC	1.00	.40
❑ 151 Pete Orr SB RC	1.00	.40
❑ 152 Prince Fielder SB RC	4.00	1.50
❑ 153 Randy Messenger SB RC	1.00	.40
❑ 154 Randy Williams SB RC	1.00	.40
❑ 155 Raul Tablado SB RC	1.00	.40
❑ 156 Ronny Paulino SB RC	1.25	.50
❑ 157 Russ Rohlicek SB RC	1.00	.40
❑ 158 Russell Martin SB RC	2.00	.75
❑ 159 Scott Baker SB RC	1.25	.50
❑ 160 Scott Munter SB RC	1.00	.40
❑ 161 Sean Thompson SB RC	1.00	.40
❑ 162 Sean Tracey SB RC	1.00	.40
❑ 163 Shane Costa SB RC	1.00	.40
❑ 164 Stephen Drew SB RC	5.00	2.00
❑ 165 Steve Schmoll SB RC	1.00	.40
❑ 166 Ryan Speier SB RC	1.00	.40
❑ 167 Tadahito Iguchi SB	2.00	.75
❑ 168 Tony Giarratano SB RC	1.00	.40
❑ 169 Tony Pena SB RC	1.00	.40
❑ 170 Travis Bowyer SB RC	1.00	.40
❑ 171 Ubaldo Jimenez SB RC	2.00	.75
❑ 172 Wladimir Balentien SB RC	1.25	.50
❑ 173 Yorman Bazardo SB RC	1.00	.40
❑ 174 Yuniesky Betancourt SB RC	2.00	.75

2006 Sweet Spot

Card		
❑ COMP.SET w/o AU's (100)	25.00	10.00
❑ COMMON CARD (1-100)	.50	.20
❑ OVERALL AU ODDS 1:12		
❑ AU PRINT RUNS B/WN 45-275 PER		
❑ EXCHANGE DEADLINE 05/25/08		
❑ ASTERISK = PARTIAL EXCHANGE		
❑ 1 Bartolo Colon	.50	.20
❑ 2 Garret Anderson	.50	.20
❑ 3 Francisco Rodriguez	.50	.20
❑ 4 Dallas McPherson	.50	.20
❑ 5 Andy Pettitte	.75	.30
❑ 6 Lance Berkman	.50	.20
❑ 7 Willy Taveras	.50	.20
❑ 8 Bobby Crosby	.50	.20
❑ 9 Dan Haren	.50	.20
❑ 10 Nick Swisher	.50	.20
❑ 11 Vernon Wells	.50	.20
❑ 12 Orlando Hudson	.50	.20
❑ 13 Roy Halladay	.50	.20
❑ 14 Andruw Jones	.75	.30
❑ 15 Chipper Jones	1.25	.50
❑ 16 Jeff Francoeur	1.25	.50
❑ 17 John Smoltz	.75	.30
❑ 18 Carlos Lee	.50	.20
❑ 19 Rickie Weeks	.50	.20
❑ 20 Bill Hall	.50	.20
❑ 21 Jim Edmonds	.75	.30
❑ 22 David Eckstein	.50	.20
❑ 23 Mark Mulder	.50	.20
❑ 24 Aramis Ramirez	.50	.20
❑ 25 Greg Maddux	2.00	.75
❑ 26 Nomar Garciaparra	1.25	.50
❑ 27 Carlos Zambrano	.50	.20
❑ 28 Scott Kazmir	.75	.30
❑ 29 Jorge Cantu	.50	.20
❑ 30 Carl Crawford	.50	.20
❑ 31 Luis Gonzalez	.50	.20
❑ 32 Troy Glaus	.50	.20
❑ 33 Shawn Green	.50	.20
❑ 34 Jeff Kent	.50	.20
❑ 35 Milton Bradley	.50	.20
❑ 36 Cesar Izturis	.50	.20
❑ 37 Omar Vizquel	.75	.30
❑ 38 Moises Alou	.50	.20
❑ 39 Randy Winn	.50	.20
❑ 40 Jason Schmidt	.50	.20
❑ 41 Coco Crisp	.50	.20
❑ 42 C.C. Sabathia	.50	.20
❑ 43 Cliff Lee	.50	.20
❑ 44 Ichiro Suzuki	2.00	.75
❑ 45 Richie Sexson	.50	.20
❑ 46 Jeremy Reed	.50	.20
❑ 47 Carlos Delgado	.50	.20
❑ 48 Miguel Cabrera	.75	.30
❑ 49 Luis Castillo	.50	.20
❑ 50 Carlos Beltran	.50	.20
❑ 51 Tom Glavine	.75	.30
❑ 52 David Wright	2.00	.75
❑ 53 Cliff Floyd	.50	.20
❑ 54 Chad Cordero	.50	.20
❑ 55 Jose Vidro	.50	.20
❑ 56 Jose Guillen	.50	.20
❑ 57 Nick Johnson	.50	.20
❑ 58 Miguel Tejada	.50	.20
❑ 59 Melvin Mora	.50	.20
❑ 60 Javy Lopez	.50	.20
❑ 61 Khalil Greene	.75	.30
❑ 62 Brian Giles	.50	.20
❑ 63 Trevor Hoffman	.50	.20
❑ 64 Bobby Abreu	.50	.20
❑ 65 Jimmy Rollins	.50	.20
❑ 66 Pat Burrell	.50	.20
❑ 67 Billy Wagner	.50	.20
❑ 68 Jack Wilson	.50	.20
❑ 69 Zach Duke	.50	.20
❑ 70 Craig Wilson	.50	.20
❑ 71 Mark Teixeira	.75	.30
❑ 72 Hank Blalock	.50	.20
❑ 73 David Dellucci	.50	.20
❑ 74 Manny Ramirez	.75	.30
❑ 75 Johnny Damon	.75	.30
❑ 76 Jason Varitek	1.25	.50
❑ 77 Trot Nixon	.50	.20
❑ 78 Adam Dunn	.50	.20
❑ 79 Felipe Lopez	.50	.20
❑ 80 Brandon Claussen	.50	.20
❑ 81 Sean Casey	.50	.20
❑ 82 Todd Helton	.75	.30
❑ 83 Clint Barmes	.50	.20
❑ 84 Matt Holliday	1.25	.50
❑ 85 Mike Sweeney	.50	.20
❑ 86 Zack Greinke	.50	.20
❑ 87 David DeJesus	.50	.20
❑ 88 Ivan Rodriguez	.75	.30
❑ 89 Jeremy Bonderman	.50	.20
❑ 90 Magglio Ordonez	.50	.20
❑ 91 Torii Hunter	.50	.20
❑ 92 Joe Nathan	.50	.20
❑ 93 Michael Cuddyer	.50	.20
❑ 94 Paul Konerko	.50	.20
❑ 95 Jermaine Dye	.50	.20
❑ 96 Jon Garland	.50	.20
❑ 97 Alex Rodriguez	2.00	.75
❑ 98 Hideki Matsui	1.25	.50
❑ 99 Jason Giambi	.50	.20
❑ 100 Mariano Rivera	1.25	.50
❑ 101 Adrian Beltre AU/99	40.00	15.00
❑ 102 Matt Cain AU/275 (RC)	40.00	15.00
❑ 103 Craig Biggio AU/99	60.00	30.00
❑ 104 Eric Chavez AU/99	30.00	12.50
❑ 105 J.D. Drew AU/99	30.00	12.50
❑ 106 Eric Gagne AU/99	50.00	20.00
❑ 107 Tim Hudson AU/99	40.00	15.00
❑ 108 Tom Glavine AU/275	50.00	20.00
❑ 109 David Ortiz AU/99	80.00	40.00
❑ 110 Scott Rolen AU/275	40.00	15.00
❑ 111 Johan Santana AU/99	50.00	20.00
❑ 112 Curt Schilling AU/96	80.00	40.00
❑ 113 John Smoltz AU/99	60.00	30.00
❑ 114 Alfonso Soriano AU/99	60.00	30.00
❑ 115 Kerry Wood AU/99	30.00	12.50
❑ 116 Edwin Jackson AU/99	20.00	8.00
❑ 117 Felix Hernandez AU/125	50.00	20.00
❑ 118 Prince Fielder AU/99 (RC)	120.00	60.00
❑ 119 Vladimir Guerrero AU/86	60.00	30.00
❑ 120 Roger Clemens AU/99	150.00	75.00
❑ 121 Albert Pujols AU/45	300.00	175.00
❑ 122 Chris Carpenter AU/99	50.00	20.00
❑ 123 Derrek Lee AU/99	40.00	15.00
❑ 124 Dontrelle Willis AU/99	30.00	12.50
❑ 125 Roy Oswalt AU/99	40.00	15.00
❑ 126 Ryan Garko AU/275 (RC)	25.00	10.00
❑ 127 Tadahito Iguchi AU/275	50.00	20.00
❑ 128 Mark Loretta AU/275	25.00	10.00
❑ 129 Joe Mauer AU/275	50.00	20.00
❑ 130 Victor Martinez AU/275	25.00	10.00
❑ 131 Wily Mo Pena AU/275	25.00	10.00
❑ 132 Oliver Perez AU/274	15.00	6.00
❑ 133 C.Patterson AU/275 EXCH	25.00	10.00
❑ 134 Ben Sheets AU/275	25.00	10.00
❑ 135 Michael Young AU/275	25.00	10.00
❑ 136 Jonny Gomes AU/275	15.00	6.00
❑ 137 Derek Jeter AU/99	200.00	125.00
❑ 138 K.Griffey Jr. AU/275 EXCH *	80.00	40.00
❑ 139 R.Zimmerman AU/275 (RC)	60.00	30.00
❑ 140 Scott Baker AU/275 (RC)	15.00	6.00
❑ 141 Huston Street AU/275	25.00	10.00
❑ 142 Jason Bay AU/275 EXCH	25.00	10.00
❑ 143 Ryan Howard AU/275	80.00	40.00
❑ 145 Travis Hafner AU/275	25.00	10.00
❑ 146 Brian Myrow AU/275 RC	15.00	6.00
❑ 147 Scott Podsednik AU/275	25.00	10.00
❑ 148 Brian Roberts AU/275	25.00	10.00
❑ 149 Grady Sizemore AU/135	40.00	15.00
❑ 150 Chris Demaria AU/275 RC	15.00	6.00
❑ 151 Jonah Bayliss AU/275 RC	15.00	6.00
❑ 152 Geovany Soto AU/275 (RC)	20.00	8.00
❑ 153 Lyle Overbay AU/275	15.00	6.00
❑ 154 Joey Devine AU/275 RC	15.00	6.00
❑ 155 A.Freire AU/275 RC	15.00	6.00
❑ 156 Conor Jackson AU/275 (RC)	25.00	10.00
❑ 157 Danny Sandoval AU/275 RC	15.00	6.00
❑ 158 Chase Utley AU/275	50.00	20.00
❑ 159 Jeff Harris AU/275 RC	15.00	6.00
❑ 160 Ron Flores AU/275 RC	15.00	6.00
❑ 161 Scott Feldman AU/275 RC	15.00	6.00
❑ 162 Yadier Molina AU/275	25.00	10.00
❑ 163 Tim Corcoran AU/275 RC	15.00	6.00
❑ 164 Craig Hansen AU/275 RC	40.00	15.00
❑ 165 Jason Bergmann AU/275 RC	15.00	6.00
❑ 166 Craig Breslow AU/275 RC	15.00	6.00
❑ 167 Jhonny Peralta AU/275	15.00	6.00
❑ 168 J.Hermida AU/275 (RC)	25.00	10.00
❑ 169 Scott Kazmir AU/275	25.00	10.00
❑ 170 Bobby Crosby AU/99	30.00	12.50
❑ 171 Rich Harden AU/275	15.00	6.00
❑ 172 Casey Kotchman AU/275	15.00	6.00

- ❑ 173 Tim Hamulack AU/275 (RC) 15.00 6.00
- ❑ 174 Justin Morneau AU/275 25.00 10.00
- ❑ 175 Jake Peavy AU/275 25.00 10.00
- ❑ 176 Y.Betancourt AU/275 25.00 10.00
- ❑ 177 Jeremy Accardo AU/275 RC 15.00 6.00
- ❑ 178 Jorge Cantu AU/200 25.00 10.00
- ❑ 179 Marlon Byrd AU/275 15.00 6.00
- ❑ 180 R.Jorgensen AU/275 RC 15.00 6.00
- ❑ 181 C.Denorfia AU/275 (RC) 15.00 6.00
- ❑ 182 Steve Stemle AU/275 RC 15.00 6.00
- ❑ 183 Robert Andino AU/275 RC 15.00 6.00
- ❑ 184 Chris Heintz AU/275 RC 15.00 6.00

2004 Sweet Spot Classic

- ❑ COMP.SET w/o SP'S (90) 40.00 15.00
- ❑ COMMON CARD (1-90) .75 .30
- ❑ COMMON CARD (91-161) 5.00 2.00
- ❑ 91-161 STATED ODDS 1:3
- ❑ 1 Al Kaline 2.00 .75
- ❑ 2 Andre Dawson .75 .30
- ❑ 3 Bert Blyleven .75 .30
- ❑ 4 Bill Dickey 1.25 .50
- ❑ 5 Bill Mazeroski 1.25 .50
- ❑ 6 Billy Martin 1.25 .50
- ❑ 7 Bob Feller .75 .30
- ❑ 8 Bob Gibson 1.25 .50
- ❑ 9 Bob Lemon .75 .30
- ❑ 10 George Kell .75 .30
- ❑ 11 Bobby Doerr .75 .30
- ❑ 12 Brooks Robinson 1.25 .50
- ❑ 13 Cal Ripken 6.00 2.50
- ❑ 14 Carl Hubbell 1.25 .50
- ❑ 15 Carl Yastrzemski 3.00 1.25
- ❑ 16 Charlie Keller .75 .30
- ❑ 17 Chuck Dressen .75 .30
- ❑ 18 Cy Young 2.00 .75
- ❑ 19 Dave Winfield .75 .30
- ❑ 20 Dizzy Dean 1.25 .50
- ❑ 21 Don Drysdale 1.25 .50
- ❑ 22 Don Larsen .75 .30
- ❑ 23 Don Mattingly 4.00 1.50
- ❑ 24 Don Newcombe .75 .30
- ❑ 25 Duke Snider 1.25 .50
- ❑ 26 Early Wynn .75 .30
- ❑ 27 Eddie Mathews 2.00 .75
- ❑ 28 Elston Howard .75 .30
- ❑ 29 Frank Robinson .75 .30
- ❑ 30 Gary Carter .75 .30
- ❑ 31 Gil Hodges 1.25 .50
- ❑ 32 Gil McDougald 1.25 .50
- ❑ 33 Hank Greenberg 2.00 .75
- ❑ 34 Harmon Killebrew 2.00 .75
- ❑ 35 Harry Caray .75 .30
- ❑ 36 Honus Wagner 2.00 .75
- ❑ 37 Hoyt Wilhelm .75 .30
- ❑ 38 Jackie Robinson 2.00 .75
- ❑ 39 Jim Bunning .75 .30
- ❑ 40 Jim Palmer .75 .30
- ❑ 41 Jimmie Foxx 2.00 .75
- ❑ 42 Jimmy Wynn .75 .30
- ❑ 43 Joe DiMaggio 4.00 1.50
- ❑ 44 Joe Torre 1.25 .50
- ❑ 45 Johnny Mize .75 .30
- ❑ 46 Juan Marichal .75 .30
- ❑ 47 Larry Doby .75 .30
- ❑ 48 Lefty Gomez 1.25 .50
- ❑ 49 Lefty Grove 1.25 .50
- ❑ 50 Leo Durocher .75 .30
- ❑ 51 Lou Boudreau .75 .30
- ❑ 52 Lou Brock 1.25 .50
- ❑ 53 Lou Gehrig 4.00 1.50
- ❑ 54 Luis Aparicio .75 .30
- ❑ 55 Maury Wills .75 .30
- ❑ 56 Mel Allen .75 .30
- ❑ 57 Mel Ott 2.00 .75
- ❑ 58 Mickey Cochrane .75 .30
- ❑ 59 Mickey Mantle 8.00 3.00
- ❑ 60 Mike Schmidt 4.00 1.50
- ❑ 61 Monte Irvin .75 .30
- ❑ 62 Nolan Ryan 5.00 2.00
- ❑ 63 Pee Wee Reese 1.25 .50
- ❑ 64 Phil Rizzuto 1.25 .50
- ❑ 65 Ralph Kiner .75 .30
- ❑ 66 Richie Ashburn 1.25 .50
- ❑ 67 Rick Ferrell .75 .30
- ❑ 68 Roberto Clemente 5.00 2.00
- ❑ 69 Robin Roberts .75 .30
- ❑ 70 Robin Yount 2.00 .75
- ❑ 71 Rogers Hornsby 2.00 .75
- ❑ 72 Rollie Fingers .75 .30
- ❑ 73 Roy Campanella 2.00 .75
- ❑ 74 Ryne Sandberg 4.00 1.50
- ❑ 75 Tony Gwynn 2.50 1.00
- ❑ 76 Satchel Paige 2.00 .75
- ❑ 77 Shoeless Joe Jackson 3.00 1.25
- ❑ 78 Stan Musial 3.00 1.25
- ❑ 79 Ted Williams 4.00 1.50
- ❑ 80 Thurman Munson 2.00 .75
- ❑ 81 Tom Seaver 1.25 .50
- ❑ 82 Tommy Henrich .75 .30
- ❑ 83 Tony Perez .75 .30
- ❑ 84 Tris Speaker 1.25 .50
- ❑ 85 Vida Blue .75 .30
- ❑ 86 Wade Boggs 1.25 .50
- ❑ 87 Walter Johnson 2.00 .75
- ❑ 88 Warren Spahn 1.25 .50
- ❑ 89 Whitey Ford 1.25 .50
- ❑ 90 Willie McCovey .75 .30
- ❑ 91 Andre Dawson FF/1987 5.00 2.00
- ❑ 92 Andre Dawson FF/1990 5.00 2.00
- ❑ 93 Ernie Banks FF/1958 8.00 3.00
- ❑ 94 Bob Lemon FF/1948 5.00 2.00
- ❑ 95 Cal Ripken FF/1982 15.00 6.00
- ❑ 96 Cal Ripken FF/1995 15.00 6.00
- ❑ 97 Carl Yastrzemski FF/1979 8.00 3.00
- ❑ 98 Carlton Fisk FF/1972 8.00 3.00
- ❑ 99 Cy Young FF/1910 8.00 3.00
- ❑ 100 Don Larsen FF/1956 5.00 2.00
- ❑ 101 Don Newcombe FF/1949 5.00 2.00
- ❑ 102 Don Newcombe FF/1956 5.00 2.00
- ❑ 103 Dwight Evans FF/1986 8.00 3.00
- ❑ 104 Elston Howard FF/1955 5.00 2.00
- ❑ 105 Frank Robinson FF/1956 5.00 2.00
- ❑ 106 Frank Robinson FF/1966 5.00 2.00
- ❑ 107 Frank Robinson FF/1973 5.00 2.00
- ❑ 108 Gil McDougald FF/1951 8.00 3.00
- ❑ 109 Hank Greenberg FF/1941 8.00 3.00
- ❑ 110 Harmon Killebrew FF/1964 8.00 3.00
- ❑ 111 Hoyt Wilhelm FF/1952 5.00 2.00
- ❑ 112 Hoyt Wilhelm FF/1958 5.00 2.00
- ❑ 113 Jackie Robinson FF/1946 8.00 3.00
- ❑ 114 J.Robinson FF Black/1947 8.00 3.00
- ❑ 115 J.Robinson FF ROY/1947 8.00 3.00
- ❑ 116 Jackie Robinson FF/1997 8.00 3.00
- ❑ 117 Jim Bunning FF/1964 5.00 2.00
- ❑ 118 J.DiMaggio FF Bench/1950 10.00 4.00
- ❑ 119 Joe Morgan FF/1976 5.00 2.00
- ❑ 120 Johnny Mize FF/1939 5.00 2.00
- ❑ 121 Johnny Mize FF/1947 5.00 2.00
- ❑ 122 Juan Marichal FF/1968 5.00 2.00
- ❑ 123 Ken Griffey Sr. FF/1990 5.00 2.00
- ❑ 124 Larry Doby FF/1947 5.00 2.00
- ❑ 125 Lefty Gomez FF/1933 8.00 3.00
- ❑ 126 Lou Boudreau FF/1946 5.00 2.00
- ❑ 127 Lou Gehrig FF Lineup/1939 10.00 4.00
- ❑ 128 Lou Gehrig FF Number/1939 10.00 4.00
- ❑ 129 Mark McGwire FF/1989 12.00 5.00
- ❑ 130 Mark McGwire FF/1998 12.00 5.00
- ❑ 131 Maury Wills FF/1962 5.00 2.00
- ❑ 132 Mel Ott FF/1946 8.00 3.00
- ❑ 133 Mike Schmidt FF/1980 10.00 4.00
- ❑ 134 Nolan Ryan FF/1973 12.00 5.00
- ❑ 135 Nolan Ryan FF/1989 12.00 5.00
- ❑ 136 Pee Wee Reese FF/1955 8.00 3.00
- ❑ 137 Nolan Ryan FF/1979 12.00 5.00
- ❑ 138 Richie Ashburn FF/1962 8.00 3.00
- ❑ 139 Roberto Clemente FF/1971 12.00 5.00
- ❑ 140 Roberto Clemente FF/1973 12.00 5.00
- ❑ 141 Robin Roberts FF/1956 5.00 2.00
- ❑ 142 Robin Yount FF/1982 8.00 3.00
- ❑ 144 Rollie Fingers FF/1975 5.00 2.00
- ❑ 145 Rollie Fingers FF/1981 5.00 2.00
- ❑ 146 Roy Campanella FF/1953 8.00 3.00
- ❑ 147 Ryne Sandberg FF/1990 10.00 4.00
- ❑ 149 Satchel Paige FF/1948 8.00 3.00
- ❑ 150 Stan Musial FF/1952 8.00 3.00
- ❑ 151 Stan Musial FF/1954 8.00 3.00
- ❑ 152 Stan Musial FF/1963 8.00 3.00
- ❑ 153 Ted Williams FF/1947 10.00 4.00
- ❑ 154 Ted Williams FF/1957 10.00 4.00
- ❑ 155 Tom Seaver FF/1970 8.00 3.00
- ❑ 156 Tom Seaver FF/1975 8.00 3.00
- ❑ 157 Wade Boggs FF/1999 8.00 3.00
- ❑ 158 Warren Spahn FF/1957 8.00 3.00
- ❑ 159 Warren Spahn FF/1958 8.00 3.00
- ❑ 160 Joe DiMaggio FF AS/1950 10.00 4.00
- ❑ 161 Yogi Berra FF/1947 8.00 3.00

2005 Sweet Spot Classic

- ❑ COMPLETE SET (100) 40.00 15.00
- ❑ 1 Al Kaline 2.00 .75
- ❑ 2 Al Rosen .75 .30
- ❑ 3 Babe Ruth 6.00 2.50
- ❑ 4 Bill Mazeroski 1.25 .50
- ❑ 5 Billy Williams .75 .30
- ❑ 6 Bob Feller 1.25 .50
- ❑ 7 Bob Gibson 1.25 .50
- ❑ 8 Bobby Doerr .75 .30
- ❑ 9 Brooks Robinson 1.25 .50
- ❑ 10 Cal Ripken 6.00 2.50
- ❑ 11 Carl Yastrzemski 3.00 1.25
- ❑ 12 Carlton Fisk 1.25 .50
- ❑ 13 Casey Stengel 1.25 .50
- ❑ 14 Christy Mathewson 2.00 .75
- ❑ 15 Cy Young 2.00 .75
- ❑ 16 Dale Murphy 1.25 .50
- ❑ 17 Dave Winfield .75 .30
- ❑ 18 Dennis Eckersley .75 .30
- ❑ 19 Dizzy Dean 1.25 .50
- ❑ 20 Don Drysdale 1.25 .50
- ❑ 21 Don Mattingly 4.00 1.50
- ❑ 22 Don Newcombe .75 .30
- ❑ 23 Don Sutton .75 .30
- ❑ 24 Duke Snider 1.25 .50
- ❑ 25 Dwight Evans 1.25 .50
- ❑ 26 Eddie Mathews 2.00 .75
- ❑ 27 Eddie Murray 2.00 .75
- ❑ 28 Enos Slaughter .75 .30
- ❑ 29 Ernie Banks 2.00 .75
- ❑ 30 Frank Howard .75 .30
- ❑ 31 Frank Robinson .75 .30
- ❑ 32 Gary Carter .75 .30
- ❑ 33 Gaylord Perry .75 .30
- ❑ 34 George Brett 4.00 1.50
- ❑ 35 George Kell .75 .30
- ❑ 36 George Sisler .75 .30
- ❑ 37 Larry Doby .75 .30
- ❑ 38 Harmon Killebrew 2.00 .75
- ❑ 39 Honus Wagner 2.00 .75
- ❑ 40 Jackie Robinson 2.00 .75
- ❑ 41 Jim Bunning .75 .30
- ❑ 42 Jim Palmer .75 .30

❑ 43	Jim Rice	.75	.30
❑ 44	Jimmie Foxx	2.00	.75
❑ 45	Joe DiMaggio	4.00	1.50
❑ 46	Joe Morgan	.75	.30
❑ 47	Johnny Bench	2.00	.75
❑ 48	Johnny Mize	.75	.30
❑ 49	Johnny Podres	.75	.30
❑ 50	Juan Marichal	.75	.30
❑ 51	Keith Hernandez	.75	.30
❑ 52	Kirby Puckett	2.00	.75
❑ 53	Lefty Grove	.75	.30
❑ 54	Lou Brock	1.25	.50
❑ 55	Lou Gehrig	4.00	1.50
❑ 56	Luis Aparicio	.75	.30
❑ 57	Fergie Jenkins	.75	.30
❑ 58	Maury Wills	.75	.30
❑ 59	Mel Ott	2.00	.75
❑ 60	Mickey Cochrane	.75	.30
❑ 61	Mickey Mantle	8.00	3.00
❑ 62	Mike Schmidt	4.00	1.50
❑ 63	Monte Irvin	.75	.30
❑ 64	Nolan Ryan	5.00	2.00
❑ 65	Orlando Cepeda	.75	.30
❑ 66	Ozzie Smith	3.00	1.25
❑ 67	Paul Molitor	.75	.30
❑ 68	Pee Wee Reese	1.25	.50
❑ 69	Phil Niekro	.75	.30
❑ 70	Phil Rizzuto	1.25	.50
❑ 71	Ralph Kiner	1.25	.50
❑ 72	Richie Ashburn	1.25	.50
❑ 73	Roberto Clemente	5.00	2.00
❑ 74	Robin Roberts	.75	.30
❑ 75	Robin Yount	2.00	.75
❑ 76	Rocky Colavito	1.25	.50
❑ 77	Rod Carew	1.25	.50
❑ 78	Rogers Hornsby	2.00	.75
❑ 79	Rollie Fingers	.75	.30
❑ 80	Roy Campanella	2.00	.75
❑ 81	Bob Lemon	.75	.30
❑ 82	Red Schoendienst	.75	.30
❑ 83	Satchel Paige	2.00	.75
❑ 84	Stan Musial	3.00	1.25
❑ 85	Steve Carlton	.75	.30
❑ 86	Ted Williams	4.00	1.50
❑ 87	Thurman Munson	2.00	.75
❑ 88	Tom Seaver	1.25	.50
❑ 89	Tony Gwynn	2.50	1.00
❑ 90	Tony Perez	1.25	.50
❑ 91	Ty Cobb	3.00	1.25
❑ 92	Wade Boggs	1.25	.50
❑ 93	Walter Johnson	2.00	.75
❑ 94	Warren Spahn	1.25	.50
❑ 95	Whitey Ford	1.25	.50
❑ 96	Will Clark	1.25	.50
❑ 97	Catfish Hunter	1.25	.50
❑ 98	Willie McCovey	1.25	.50
❑ 99	Willie Stargell	1.25	.50
❑ 100	Yogi Berra	2.00	.75

2007 Sweet Spot Classic

❑	COMMON CARD	1.50	.60
❑	STATED PRINT RUN 575 SER.#'d SETS		
❑ 1	Phil Niekro	1.50	.60
❑ 2	Fred McGriff	2.50	1.00
❑ 3	Bob Horner	1.50	.60
❑ 4	Earl Weaver	1.50	.60
❑ 5	Boog Powell	1.50	.60
❑ 6	Eddie Murray	4.00	1.50
❑ 7	Fred Lynn	1.50	.60
❑ 8	Dwight Evans	1.50	.60
❑ 9	Jim Rice	1.50	.60
❑ 10	Carlton Fisk	2.50	1.00
❑ 11	Luis Tiant	1.50	.60
❑ 12	Robin Yount	4.00	1.50
❑ 13	Bobby Doerr	1.50	.60
❑ 14	Ryne Sandberg	8.00	3.00
❑ 15	Billy Williams	1.50	.60
❑ 16	Andre Dawson	1.50	.60
❑ 17	Mark Grace	2.50	1.00
❑ 18	Ron Santo	2.50	1.00
❑ 19	Shawon Dunston	1.50	.60
❑ 20	Harold Baines	1.50	.60
❑ 21	Carlton Fisk	2.50	1.00
❑ 22	Sparky Anderson	1.50	.60
❑ 23	George Foster	1.50	.60
❑ 24	Dave Parker	1.50	.60
❑ 25	Ken Griffey Sr.	1.50	.60
❑ 26	Dave Concepcion	1.50	.60
❑ 27	Rafael Palmeiro	2.50	1.00
❑ 28	Al Rosen	1.50	.60
❑ 29	Kirk Gibson	1.50	.60
❑ 30	Alan Trammell	1.50	.60
❑ 31	Jack Morris	1.50	.60
❑ 32	Willie Horton	1.50	.60
❑ 33	JR Richard	1.50	.60
❑ 34	Jose Cruz	1.50	.60
❑ 36	Willie Wilson	1.50	.60
❑ 37	Bo Jackson	4.00	1.50
❑ 38	Nolan Ryan	10.00	4.00
❑ 39	Don Baylor	1.50	.60
❑ 40	Maury Wills	1.50	.60
❑ 41	Tommy John	1.50	.60
❑ 42	Ron Cey	1.50	.60
❑ 43	Davey Lopes	1.50	.60
❑ 44	Tommy Lasorda	1.50	.60
❑ 45	Burt Hooton	1.50	.60
❑ 46	Reggie Smith	1.50	.60
❑ 47	Rollie Fingers	1.50	.60
❑ 48	Cecil Cooper	1.50	.60
❑ 49	Paul Molitor	1.50	.60
❑ 50	Vern Stephens	1.50	.60
❑ 51	Tony Oliva	1.50	.60
❑ 52	Andres Galarraga	1.50	.60
❑ 53	Tim Raines	1.50	.60
❑ 54	Dennis Martinez	1.50	.60
❑ 55	Lee Mazzilli	1.50	.60
❑ 56	Rusty Staub	1.50	.60
❑ 57	David Cone	1.50	.60
❑ 58	Reggie Jackson	2.50	1.00
❑ 59	Ron Guidry	1.50	.60
❑ 60	Tino Martinez	1.50	.60
❑ 61	Don Mattingly	8.00	3.00
❑ 62	Chris Chambliss	1.50	.60
❑ 63	Sparky Lyle	1.50	.60
❑ 64	Goose Gossage	1.50	.60
❑ 65	Dave Righetti	1.50	.60
❑ 66	Phil Garner	1.50	.60
❑ 67	Bill Madlock	1.50	.60
❑ 68	Kent Hrbek	1.50	.60
❑ 69	Al Oliver	1.50	.60
❑ 70	John Kruk	1.50	.60
❑ 71	Greg Luzinski	1.50	.60
❑ 72	Dick Allen	1.50	.60
❑ 73	Richie Ashburn	2.50	1.00
❑ 74	Gary Matthews	1.50	.60
❑ 76	Mike Schmidt	6.00	2.50
❑ 77	Waite Hoyt	1.50	.60
❑ 78	Bruce Sutter	1.50	.60
❑ 79	Roger Maris	4.00	1.50
❑ 80	Joe Torre	2.50	1.00
❑ 81	Kevin Mitchell	1.50	.60
❑ 82	John Montefusco	1.50	.60
❑ 83	Rick Reuschel	1.50	.60
❑ 84	Will Clark	2.50	1.00
❑ 85	Jack Clark	1.50	.60
❑ 86	Matt Williams	1.50	.60
❑ 87	Steve Garvey	1.50	.60
❑ 88	Dave Winfield	1.50	.60
❑ 89	Jay Buhner	1.50	.60
❑ 90	Edgar Martinez	2.50	1.00
❑ 91	Carney Lansford	1.50	.60
❑ 92	Sal Bando	1.50	.60
❑ 93	Dave Stewart	1.50	.60
❑ 94	Dennis Eckersley	1.50	.60
❑ 95	Jose Canseco	2.50	1.00
❑ 96	Dennis Eckersley	1.50	.60
❑ 97	Roberto Alomar	2.50	1.00
❑ 98	George Bell	1.50	.60
❑ 99	Joe Carter	1.50	.60
❑ 100	Frank Howard	1.50	.60
❑ 101	Brooks Robinson	2.50	1.00
❑ 102	Frank Robinson	1.50	.60
❑ 103	Jim Palmer	1.50	.60
❑ 104	Cal Ripken Jr.	15.00	6.00
❑ 105	Warren Spahn	2.50	1.00
❑ 106	Cy Young	4.00	1.50
❑ 107	Waite Hoyt	1.50	.60
❑ 108	Carl Yastrzemski	6.00	2.50
❑ 109	Johnny Pesky	1.50	.60
❑ 110	Wade Boggs	2.50	1.00
❑ 111	Jackie Robinson	4.00	1.50
❑ 112	Roy Campanella	4.00	1.50
❑ 113	Pee Wee Reese	2.50	1.00
❑ 114	Don Newcombe	1.50	.60
❑ 115	Rod Carew	2.50	1.00
❑ 116	Ernie Banks	4.00	1.50
❑ 117	Fergie Jenkins	1.50	.60
❑ 118	Al Lopez	1.50	.60
❑ 119	Luis Aparicio	1.50	.60
❑ 120	Toby Harrah	1.50	.60
❑ 121	Joe Morgan	1.50	.60
❑ 122	Johnny Bench	4.00	1.50
❑ 123	Tony Perez	1.50	.60
❑ 124	Ted Kluszewski	2.50	1.00
❑ 125	Bob Feller	1.50	.60
❑ 126	Bob Lemon	1.50	.60
❑ 127	Larry Doby	1.50	.60
❑ 128	Lou Boudreau	1.50	.60
❑ 129	George Kell	1.50	.60
❑ 130	Hal Newhouser	1.50	.60
❑ 131	Al Kaline	4.00	1.50
❑ 132	Ty Cobb	6.00	2.50
❑ 133	Denny McLain	1.50	.60
❑ 134	Buck Leonard	1.50	.60
❑ 135	Dean Chance	1.50	.60
❑ 136	Don Drysdale	2.50	1.00
❑ 137	Don Sutton	1.50	.60
❑ 138	Eddie Mathews	4.00	1.50
❑ 139	Paul Molitor	1.50	.60
❑ 140	Kirby Puckett	4.00	1.50
❑ 141	Rod Carew	2.50	1.00
❑ 142	Harmon Killebrew	4.00	1.50
❑ 143	Monte Irvin	1.50	.60
❑ 144	Mel Ott	1.50	.60
❑ 145	Christy Mathewson	4.00	1.50
❑ 146	Hoyt Wilhelm	1.50	.60
❑ 147	Tom Seaver	2.50	1.00
❑ 148	Joe McCarthy	1.50	.60
❑ 149	Joe DiMaggio	8.00	3.00
❑ 150	Lou Gehrig	8.00	3.00
❑ 151	Babe Ruth	10.00	4.00
❑ 152	Casey Stengel	1.50	.60
❑ 153	Phil Rizzuto	2.50	1.00
❑ 154	Thurman Munson	4.00	1.50
❑ 155	Johnny Mize	1.50	.60
❑ 156	Yogi Berra	4.00	1.50
❑ 157	Roger Maris	4.00	1.50
❑ 158	Don Larsen	1.50	.60
❑ 159	Bill Skowron	1.50	.60
❑ 160	Lou Piniella	1.50	.60
❑ 161	Joe Pepitone	1.50	.60
❑ 162	Ray Dandridge	1.50	.60
❑ 163	Rollie Fingers	1.50	.60
❑ 165	Reggie Jackson	2.50	1.00
❑ 166	Mickey Cochrane	1.50	.60
❑ 167	Jimmie Foxx	4.00	1.50
❑ 168	Lefty Grove	1.50	.60
❑ 169	Gus Zernial	1.50	.60
❑ 170	Jim Bunning	1.50	.60
❑ 171	Steve Carlton	1.50	.60
❑ 172	Robin Roberts	1.50	.60
❑ 173	Ralph Kiner	2.50	1.00
❑ 174	Willie Stargell	2.50	1.00
❑ 175	Roberto Clemente	12.00	5.00
❑ 176	Bill Mazeroski	2.50	1.00
❑ 177	Honus Wagner	4.00	1.50
❑ 178	Pie Traynor	1.50	.60
❑ 179	Elroy Face	1.50	.60
❑ 180	Dick Groat	1.50	.60
❑ 181	Tony Gwynn	4.00	1.50

Card		
❑ 182 Willie McCovey	2.50	1.00
❑ 183 Gaylord Perry	1.50	.60
❑ 184 Juan Marichal	1.50	.60
❑ 185 Orlando Cepeda	1.50	.60
❑ 186 Satchel Paige	4.00	1.50
❑ 187 George Sisler	1.50	.60
❑ 188 Rogers Hornsby	2.50	1.00
❑ 189 Stan Musial	6.00	2.50
❑ 190 Dizzy Dean	2.50	1.00
❑ 191 Bob Gibson	2.50	1.00
❑ 192 Red Schoendienst	1.50	.60
❑ 193 Lou Brock	2.50	1.00
❑ 194 Enos Slaughter	1.50	.60
❑ 195 Nolan Ryan	10.00	4.00
❑ 196 Mickey Vernon	1.50	.60
❑ 197 Walter Johnson	4.00	1.50
❑ 198 Rick Ferrell	1.50	.60
❑ 199 Roy Sievers	1.50	.60
❑ 200 Judy Johnson	1.50	.60

2006 Sweet Spot Update

Card		
❑ COMP.SET w/o AU's (100)	25.00	10.00
❑ COMMON CARD (1-100)	.50	.20
❑ COMMON AU p/r 399-499	8.00	3.00
❑ COMMON AU p/r 150-240	10.00	4.00
❑ COMMON AU p/r 98-125	10.00	4.00
❑ OVERALL AU ODDS 1:6		
❑ AU PRINT RUNS B/WN 98-499 PER		
❑ EXCHANGE DEADLINE 12/19/09		
❑ 1 Luis Gonzalez	.50	.20
❑ 2 Chad Tracy	.50	.20
❑ 3 Brandon Webb	.50	.20
❑ 4 Andruw Jones	.75	.30
❑ 5 Chipper Jones	1.25	.50
❑ 6 John Smoltz	.75	.30
❑ 7 Tim Hudson	.50	.20
❑ 8 Miguel Tejada	.50	.20
❑ 9 Brian Roberts	.50	.20
❑ 10 Ramon Hernandez	.50	.20
❑ 11 Curt Schilling	.75	.30
❑ 12 David Ortiz	1.25	.50
❑ 13 Manny Ramirez	.75	.30
❑ 14 Jason Varitek	1.25	.50
❑ 15 Josh Beckett	.50	.20
❑ 16 Greg Maddux	2.00	.75
❑ 17 Derrek Lee	.50	.20
❑ 18 Mark Prior	.75	.30
❑ 19 Aramis Ramirez	.50	.20
❑ 20 Jim Thome	.75	.30
❑ 21 Paul Konerko	.50	.20
❑ 22 Scott Podsednik	.50	.20
❑ 23 Jose Contreras	.50	.20
❑ 24 Ken Griffey Jr.	2.00	.75
❑ 25 Adam Dunn	.50	.20
❑ 26 Felipe Lopez	.50	.20
❑ 27 Travis Hafner	.50	.20
❑ 28 Victor Martinez	.50	.20
❑ 29 Grady Sizemore	.75	.30
❑ 30 Jhonny Peralta	.50	.20
❑ 31 Todd Helton	.75	.30
❑ 32 Garrett Atkins	.50	.20
❑ 33 Clint Barmes	.50	.20
❑ 34 Ivan Rodriguez	.75	.30
❑ 35 Chris Shelton	.50	.20
❑ 36 Jeremy Bonderman	.50	.20
❑ 37 Miguel Cabrera	.75	.30
❑ 38 Dontrelle Willis	.50	.20
❑ 39 Lance Berkman	.50	.20
❑ 40 Morgan Ensberg	.50	.20
❑ 41 Roy Oswalt	.50	.20
❑ 42 Reggie Sanders	.50	.20
❑ 43 Mike Sweeney	.50	.20
❑ 44 Vladimir Guerrero	1.25	.50
❑ 45 Bartolo Colon	.50	.20
❑ 46 Chone Figgins	.50	.20
❑ 47 Nomar Garciaparra	1.25	.50
❑ 48 Jeff Kent	.50	.20
❑ 49 J.D. Drew	.50	.20
❑ 50 Carlos Lee	.50	.20
❑ 51 Ben Sheets	.50	.20
❑ 52 Rickie Weeks	.50	.20
❑ 53 Johan Santana	.75	.30
❑ 54 Torii Hunter	.50	.20
❑ 55 Joe Mauer	.75	.30
❑ 56 Pedro Martinez	.75	.30
❑ 57 David Wright	2.00	.75
❑ 58 Carlos Beltran	.50	.20
❑ 59 Carlos Delgado	.50	.20
❑ 60 Jose Reyes	1.25	.50
❑ 61 Derek Jeter	3.00	1.25
❑ 62 Alex Rodriguez	2.00	.75
❑ 63 Randy Johnson	1.25	.50
❑ 64 Hideki Matsui	1.25	.50
❑ 65 Gary Sheffield	.50	.20
❑ 66 Rich Harden	.50	.20
❑ 67 Eric Chavez	.50	.20
❑ 68 Huston Street	.50	.20
❑ 69 Bobby Crosby	.50	.20
❑ 70 Bobby Abreu	.50	.20
❑ 71 Ryan Howard	2.00	.75
❑ 72 Chase Utley	1.25	• .50
❑ 73 Pat Burrell	.50	.20
❑ 74 Jason Bay	.50	.20
❑ 75 Sean Casey	.50	.20
❑ 76 Mike Piazza	1.25	.50
❑ 77 Jake Peavy	.50	.20
❑ 78 Brian Giles	.50	.20
❑ 79 Milton Bradley	.50	.20
❑ 80 Omar Vizquel	.75	.30
❑ 81 Jason Schmidt	.50	.20
❑ 82 Ichiro Suzuki	2.00	.75
❑ 83 Felix Hernandez	.75	.30
❑ 84 Kenji Johjima RC	2.50	1.00
❑ 85 Albert Pujols	2.50	1.00
❑ 86 Chris Carpenter	.50	.20
❑ 87 Scott Rolen	.75	.30
❑ 88 Jim Edmonds	.75	.30
❑ 89 Carl Crawford	.50	.20
❑ 90 Jonny Gomes	.50	.20
❑ 91 Scott Kazmir	.75	.30
❑ 92 Mark Teixeira	.75	.30
❑ 93 Michael Young	.50	.20
❑ 94 Phil Nevin	.50	.20
❑ 95 Vernon Wells	.50	.20
❑ 96 Roy Halladay	.50	.20
❑ 97 Troy Glaus	.50	.20
❑ 98 Alfonso Soriano	.50	.20
❑ 99 Nick Johnson	.50	.20
❑ 100 Jose Vidro	.50	.20
❑ 101 A.Wainwright AU/100 (RC)	40.00	15.00
❑ 102 A.Hernandez AU/100 (RC) EXCH	15.00	6.00
❑ 103 A.Ethier AU/150 (RC)	30.00	12.50
❑ 104 J.Botts AU/100 (RC) EXCH	15.00	6.00
❑ 105 B.Johnson AU/400 (RC)	8.00	3.00
❑ 106 B.Bonser AU/100 (RC)	15.00	6.00
❑ 107 B.Logan AU/200 RC	10.00	4.00
❑ 108 B.Anderson AU/200 (RC)	10.00	4.00
❑ 109 B.Bannister AU/100 (RC)	20.00	8.00
❑ 110 C.Denorfia AU/100 (RC)	10.00	4.00
❑ 111 A.Montero AU/100 (RC)	15.00	6.00
❑ 112 C.Ross AU/100 (RC)	10.00	4.00
❑ 113 C.Hamels AU/399 (RC)	40.00	15.00
❑ 114 C.Jackson AU/400 (RC)	10.00	4.00
❑ 115 D.Uggla AU/125 (RC)	25.00	10.00
❑ 116 D.Gassner AU/100 (RC)	10.00	4.00
❑ 117 C.Wilson AU/150 (RC)	10.00	4.00
❑ 118 E.Reed AU/150 (RC)	10.00	4.00
❑ 119 F.Carmona AU/99 (RC)	25.00	10.00
❑ 120 F.Nieve AU/100 (RC)	10.00	4.00
❑ 121 F.Liriano AU/499 (RC)	25.00	10.00
❑ 122 F.Bynum AU/100 (RC)	10.00	4.00
❑ 123 H.Ramirez AU/100 (RC)	30.00	12.50
❑ 124 H.Kuo AU/100 (RC)	150.00	75.00
❑ 125 I.Kinsler AU/100 (RC)	30.00	12.50
❑ 126 C.Marmol AU/100 RC	15.00	6.00
❑ 127 B.Keppel AU/200 (RC)	10.00	4.00
❑ 128 J.Kubel AU/100 (RC)	15.00	6.00
❑ 129 J.Harris AU/100 RC	10.00	4.00
❑ 130 A.Soler AU/100 RC	15.00	6.00
❑ 131 J.Weaver AU/100 (RC) EXCH	25.00	10.00
❑ 132 C.Quentin AU/100 (RC)	25.00	10.00
❑ 133 J.Hermida AU/100 (RC)	15.00	6.00
❑ 134 J.Zumaya AU/100 (RC)	50.00	20.00
❑ 135 J.Devine AU/100 RC	15.00	6.00
❑ 136 J.Koronka AU/98 (RC)	10.00	4.00
❑ 137 J.Papelbon AU/399 (RC)	40.00	15.00
❑ 138 J.Capellan AU/240 (RC)	10.00	4.00
❑ 139 J.Johnson AU/100 (RC)	15.00	6.00
❑ 140 J.Rupe AU/100 (RC) EXCH	10.00	4.00
❑ 141 J.Willingham AU/100 (RC)	10.00	4.00
❑ 143 J.Verlander AU/100 (RC)	40.00	15.00
❑ 144 K.Shoppach AU/100 (RC)	15.00	6.00
❑ 145 K.Morales AU/100 (RC) EXCH	10.00	4.00
❑ 146 K.Thompson AU/100 (RC)	10.00	4.00
❑ 147 M.McBride AU/100 (RC)	10.00	4.00
❑ 148 M.Prado AU/100 (RC) EXCH	10.00	4.00
❑ 149 M.Cain AU/150 (RC) EXCH	15.00	6.00
❑ 150 C.Hensley AU/100 (RC)	10.00	4.00
❑ 151 T.Taubenheim AU/100 RC	25.00	10.00
❑ 152 M.Jacobs AU/200 (RC)	10.00	4.00
❑ 153 S.Rivera AU/100 (RC)	10.00	4.00
❑ 154 M.Thompson AU/100 RC	10.00	4.00
❑ 155 N.McLouth AU/100 (RC)	10.00	4.00
❑ 156 M.Vento AU/100 (RC)	10.00	4.00
❑ 157 P.Maholm AU/200 (RC)	10.00	4.00
❑ 159 R.Abercrombie AU/100 (RC)	10.00	4.00
❑ 160 M.Rouse AU/100 (RC)	10.00	4.00
❑ 161 K.Ray AU/100 (RC)	10.00	4.00
❑ 162 R.Flores AU/100 RC	10.00	4.00
❑ 163 R.Zimmerman AU/100 (RC)	60.00	30.00
❑ 164 E.Aybar AU/100 (RC)	15.00	6.00
❑ 165 S.Marshall AU/150 (RC)	20.00	8.00
❑ 166 T.Saito AU/100 RC EXCH		
❑ 167 T.Buchholz AU/100 (RC)	10.00	4.00
❑ 168 M.Murton AU/100 (RC)	30.00	12.50
❑ 169 L.Figueroa AU/100 RC EXCH	15.00	6.00
❑ 170 W.Nieves AU/100 (RC)	15.00	6.00
❑ 171 J.Shields AU/100 RC	15.00	6.00
❑ 172 J.Lester AU/399 RC	30.00	12.50
❑ 173 C.Hansen AU/100 RC EXCH	30.00	12.50
❑ 174 A.Rakers AU/100 (RC)	10.00	4.00
❑ 175 B.Livingston AU/100 (RC)	15.00	6.00
❑ 176 B.Harris AU/100 (RC)	10.00	4.00
❑ 177 Z.Jackson AU/100 (RC)	15.00	6.00
❑ 178 C.Britton AU/100 RC	10.00	4.00
❑ 179 H.Kendrick AU/399 (RC)	25.00	10.00
❑ 180 Z.Miner AU/100 (RC)	15.00	6.00
❑ 181 K.Frandsen AU/100 (RC)	10.00	4.00
❑ 182 M.Capps AU/100 (RC)	10.00	4.00
❑ 183 P.Moylan AU/100 RC	10.00	4.00
❑ 184 M.Cabrera AU/100 (RC) EXCH	50.00	20.00

1911 T205 Gold Border

Card		
❑ COMPLETE SET (218)	50000.00	25000.00
❑ COMMON MAJOR (1-186)	150.00	90.00
❑ COM. MINOR (187-198)	300.00	150.00
❑ 1 Ed Abbaticchio	150.00	90.00
❑ 2 Merle (Doc) Adkins	250.00	150.00
❑ 3 Red Ames	150.00	90.00
❑ 4 Jimmy Archer	150.00	90.00
❑ 5 Jimmy Austin	150.00	90.00
❑ 6 Bill Bailey	150.00	90.00
❑ 7 Frank Baker	500.00	300.00

❑ 8 Neal Ball 150.00 90.00
❑ 9 Cy Barger Full B 150.00 90.00
❑ 10 Cy Barger Part B 400.00 250.00
❑ 11 Jack Barry 150.00 90.00
❑ 12 Emil Batch 250.00 150.00
❑ 13 Johnny Bates 150.00 90.00
❑ 14 Fred Beck 150.00 90.00
❑ 15 Beals Becker 150.00 90.00
❑ 16 George Bell 150.00 90.00
❑ 17 Chief Bender 250.00 150.00
❑ 18 Bill Bergen 150.00 90.00
❑ 19 Bob Bescher 150.00 90.00
❑ 20 Joe Birmingham 150.00 90.00
❑ 21 Russ Blackburne 150.00 90.00
❑ 22 Kitty Bransfield 150.00 90.00
❑ 23 R.Bresnahan Closed 250.00 150.00
❑ 24 R.Bresnahan Open 500.00 300.00
❑ 25 Al Bridwell 150.00 90.00
❑ 26 Mordecai Brown 500.00 300.00
❑ 27 Bobby Byrne 150.00 90.00
❑ 28 Hick Cady 250.00 150.00
❑ 29 Howie Camnitz 150.00 90.00
❑ 30 Bill Carrigan 150.00 90.00
❑ 31 Frank Chance 400.00 250.00
❑ 32A Hal Chase Both Ears at Shoulders 200.00 120.00
❑ 32B Hal Chase Both Ears Below Shoulders 200.00 120.00
❑ 33 Hal Chase Left Ear 400.00 250.00
❑ 34 Eddie Cicotte 250.00 150.00
❑ 35 Fred Clarke 500.00 300.00
❑ 36 Ty Cobb 6000.00 3500.00
❑ 37 E.Collins Mouth Closed 400.00 250.00
❑ 38 E.Collins Mouth Open 600.00 350.00
❑ 39 Jimmy Collins 600.00 350.00
❑ 40 Frank Corridon 150.00 90.00
❑ 41A Otis Crandall (Otis) 150.00 90.00
❑ 41B Otis Crandall (Olis) 150.00 90.00
❑ 42 Lou Criger 150.00 90.00
❑ 43 Bill Dahlen 200.00 120.00
❑ 44 Jake Daubert 200.00 120.00
❑ 45 Jim Delahanty 150.00 90.00
❑ 46 Art Devlin 150.00 90.00
❑ 47 Josh Devore 150.00 90.00
❑ 48 Walt Dickson 150.00 90.00
❑ 49 Jiggs Donohue 200.00 120.00
❑ 50 Red Dooin 150.00 90.00
❑ 51 Mickey Doolan 150.00 90.00
❑ 52A Patsy Dougherty Red 150.00 90.00
❑ 52B Patsy Dougherty White 200.00 120.00
❑ 53 Tom Downey 150.00 90.00
❑ 54 Larry Doyle 150.00 90.00
❑ 55 Hugh Duffy 400.00 250.00
❑ 56 Jack Dunn 250.00 150.00
❑ 57 Jimmy Dygert 150.00 90.00
❑ 58 Dick Egan 150.00 90.00
❑ 59 Kid Elberfeld 150.00 90.00
❑ 60 Clyde Engle 150.00 90.00
❑ 61 Steve Evans 150.00 90.00
❑ 62 Johnny Evers 250.00 150.00
❑ 63 Bob Ewing 150.00 90.00
❑ 64 George Ferguson 150.00 90.00
❑ 65 Ray Fisher 200.00 120.00
❑ 66 Art Fletcher 150.00 90.00
❑ 67 John Flynn 150.00 90.00
❑ 68 Russ Ford Dark Cap 150.00 90.00
❑ 69 Russ Ford Light Cap 200.00 120.00
❑ 70 Bill Foxen 150.00 90.00
❑ 71 James Frick 250.00 150.00
❑ 72 Art Fromme 150.00 90.00
❑ 73 Earl Gardner 150.00 90.00
❑ 74 Harry Gaspar 150.00 90.00
❑ 75 George Gibson 150.00 90.00
❑ 76 Wilbur Good 150.00 90.00
❑ 77 P.Graham Cubs 500.00 300.00
❑ 78 P.Graham Rustlers 150.00 90.00
❑ 79 Eddie Grant 200.00 120.00
❑ 80A Dolly Gray w/o Stats 150.00 90.00
❑ 80B Dolly Gray w/Stats 500.00 300.00
❑ 81 Clark Griffith 400.00 250.00
❑ 82 Bob Groom 150.00 90.00
❑ 83 Charles Hanford 250.00 150.00
❑ 84 Bob Harmon Both Ears 150.00 90.00
❑ 85 Bob Harmon Left Ear 400.00 250.00
❑ 86 Topsy Hartsel 150.00 90.00
❑ 87 Arnold Hauser 150.00 90.00
❑ 88 Charlie Hemphill 150.00 90.00
❑ 89 Buck Herzog 150.00 90.00
❑ 90A D.Hoblitzell No Stats 12000.00 7000.00
❑ 90B D.Hoblitzell w/CIN 200.00 120.00
❑ 90C D.Hoblitzell (Hoblitzel) 150.00 90.00
❑ 90D D.Hoblitzell w/o CIN 150.00 90.00
❑ 91 Danny Hoffman 150.00 90.00
❑ 92 Miller Huggins 500.00 300.00
❑ 93 John Hummell 150.00 90.00
❑ 94 Fred Jacklitsch 150.00 90.00
❑ 95 Hughie Jennings 400.00 250.00
❑ 96 Walter Johnson 2500.00 1500.00
❑ 97 Davy Jones 150.00 90.00
❑ 98 Tom Jones 150.00 90.00
❑ 99 Addie Joss 1000.00 600.00
❑ 100 Ed Karger 200.00 120.00
❑ 101 Ed Killian 150.00 90.00
❑ 102 Red Kleinow 200.00 120.00
❑ 103 John Kling 150.00 90.00
❑ 104 John Knight 150.00 90.00
❑ 105 Ed Konetchy 150.00 90.00
❑ 106 Harry Krause 150.00 90.00
❑ 107 Rube Kroh 150.00 90.00
❑ 108 Frank Lang 150.00 90.00
❑ 109 Frank LaPorte 150.00 90.00
❑ 110A Arlie Latham (A.) 150.00 90.00
❑ 110B Arlie Latham (W.A.) 150.00 90.00
❑ 111 Tommy Leach 150.00 90.00
❑ 112 Wyatt Lee 250.00 150.00
❑ 113 Sam Leever 150.00 90.00
❑ 114A Lefty Leifield (A.) 150.00 90.00
❑ 114B Lefty Leifield (A.P.) 150.00 90.00
❑ 115 Ed Lennox 150.00 90.00
❑ 116 Paddy Livingston 150.00 90.00
❑ 117 Hans Lobert 150.00 90.00
❑ 118 Bris Lord 150.00 90.00
❑ 119 Harry Lord 150.00 90.00
❑ 120 John Lush 150.00 90.00
❑ 121 Nick Maddox 150.00 90.00
❑ 122 Sherry Magee 150.00 90.00
❑ 123 Rube Marquard 500.00 300.00
❑ 124 Christy Mathewson 2500.00 1500.00
❑ 125 Al Mattern 150.00 90.00
❑ 126 Lewis McAllister 250.00 150.00
❑ 127 George McBride 150.00 90.00
❑ 128 Amby McConnell 150.00 90.00
❑ 129 Pryor McElveen 150.00 90.00
❑ 130 John McGraw MG 500.00 300.00
❑ 131 Harry McIntire 150.00 90.00
❑ 132 Matty McIntyre 150.00 90.00
❑ 133 Larry McLean 150.00 90.00
❑ 134 Fred Merkle 150.00 90.00
❑ 135 George Merritt 250.00 150.00
❑ 136 Chief Meyers 150.00 90.00
❑ 137 Clyde Milan 150.00 90.00
❑ 138 Dots Miller 150.00 90.00
❑ 139 Mike Mitchell 150.00 90.00
❑ 140A Pat Moran Extra Stat 400.00 250.00
❑ 140B Pat Moran 150.00 90.00
❑ 141 George Moriarty 150.00 90.00
❑ 142 George Mullin 150.00 90.00
❑ 143 Danny Murphy 150.00 90.00
❑ 144 Red Murray 150.00 90.00
❑ 145 John Nee 250.00 150.00
❑ 146 Tom Needham 150.00 90.00
❑ 147 Rebel Oakes 150.00 90.00
❑ 148 Rube Oldring 150.00 90.00
❑ 149 Charley O'Leary 150.00 90.00
❑ 150 Fred Olmstead 150.00 90.00
❑ 151 Orval Overall 150.00 90.00
❑ 152 Freddy Parent 150.00 90.00
❑ 153 Dode Paskert 150.00 90.00
❑ 154 Fred Payne 150.00 90.00
❑ 155 Barney Pelty 150.00 90.00
❑ 156 Jack Pfiester 150.00 90.00
❑ 157 James Phelan 250.00 150.00
❑ 158 Ed Phelps 150.00 90.00
❑ 159 Decon Phillippe 150.00 90.00
❑ 160 Jack Quinn 150.00 90.00
❑ 161 Bugs Raymond 200.00 120.00
❑ 162 Ed Reulbach 150.00 90.00
❑ 163 Lewis Richie 150.00 90.00
❑ 164 Jack Rowan 200.00 120.00
❑ 165 Nap Rucker 150.00 90.00
❑ 166 Doc Scanlan 200.00 120.00
❑ 167 Germany Schaefer 150.00 90.00
❑ 168 Admiral Schlei 150.00 90.00
❑ 169 Boss Schmidt 150.00 90.00
❑ 170 Wildfire Schulte 150.00 90.00
❑ 171 Jim Scott 150.00 90.00
❑ 172 Bayard Sharpe 150.00 90.00
❑ 173 David Shean Cubs 500.00 300.00
❑ 174 David Shean Rustlers 150.00 90.00
❑ 175 Jimmy Sheckard 150.00 90.00
❑ 176 Hack Simmons 150.00 90.00
❑ 177 Tony Smith 150.00 90.00
❑ 178 Fred Snodgrass 150.00 90.00
❑ 179 Tris Speaker 1200.00 700.00
❑ 180 Jake Stahl 150.00 90.00
❑ 181 Oscar Stanage 150.00 90.00
❑ 182 Harry Steinfeldt 150.00 90.00
❑ 183 George Stone 150.00 90.00
❑ 184 George Stovall 150.00 90.00
❑ 185 Gabby Street 150.00 90.00
❑ 186 George Suggs 200.00 120.00
❑ 187 Ed Summers 150.00 90.00
❑ 188 Jeff Sweeney 200.00 120.00
❑ 189 Lee Tannehill 150.00 90.00
❑ 190 Ira Thomas 150.00 90.00
❑ 191 Joe Tinker 800.00 500.00
❑ 192 John Titus 150.00 90.00
❑ 193 Terry Turner 400.00 250.00
❑ 194 Hippo Vaughn 200.00 120.00
❑ 195 Heinie Wagner 200.00 120.00
❑ 196 B.Wallace w/cap 250.00 150.00
❑ 197A B.Wallace w/o Cap 1 Line 600.00 350.00
❑ 197B B.Wallace w/o Cap 2 Lines 400.00 250.00
❑ 198 Ed Walsh 600.00 350.00
❑ 199 Zach Wheat 400.00 250.00
❑ 200 Doc White 150.00 90.00
❑ 201 Kirby White 200.00 120.00
❑ 202A Irvin K. Wilhelm 200.00 120.00
❑ 202B Irvin K. Wilhelm Missing Letter 200.00 120.00
❑ 203 Ed Willett 150.00 90.00
❑ 204 Owen Wilson 150.00 90.00
❑ 205 H.Wiltse Both Ears 150.00 90.00
❑ 206 H.Wiltse Right Ear 400.00 250.00
❑ 207 Harry Wolter 150.00 90.00
❑ 208 Cy Young 2500.00 1500.00

1909-11 T206

❑ COMPLETE SET (520) 55000.00 30000.00
❑ COMMON MAJOR (1-389) 100.00 50.00
❑ COMMON MINOR (390-475) 100.00 50.00
❑ COM. SO. LEA. (476-523) 250.00 125.00
❑ 1 Ed Abbaticchio Follow Through 120.00 60.00
❑ 2 Ed Abbaticchio Waiting 150.00 75.00
❑ 3 Fred Abbott 100.00 50.00
❑ 4 Bill Abstein 120.00 60.00
❑ 5 Merle (Doc) Adkins 100.00 50.00
❑ 6 Whitey Alperman 150.00 75.00
❑ 7 Red Ames Hands over Chest 150.00 75.00
❑ 8 Red Ames Hands over Head 120.00 60.00
❑ 9 Red Ames Portrait 150.00 75.00
❑ 10 John Anderson 100.00 50.00
❑ 11 Frank Arellanes 120.00 60.00
❑ 12 Herman Armbruster 100.00 50.00
❑ 13 Harry Arndt 100.00 50.00
❑ 14 Jake Atz 120.00 60.00
❑ 15 Frank Baker 800.00 400.00
❑ 16 Neal Ball Cleveland 120.00 60.00
❑ 17 Neal Ball New York 150.00 75.00
❑ 18 Jap Barbeau 120.00 60.00
❑ 19 Cy Barger 120.00 60.00

❑ 20 Jack Barry 120.00 60.00
❑ 21 John Barry 100.00 50.00
❑ 22 Jack Bastian 250.00 125.00
❑ 23 Emil H. Batch 100.00 50.00
❑ 24 Johnny Bates 150.00 75.00
❑ 25 Harry Bay 250.00 125.00
❑ 26 Ginger Beaumont 150.00 75.00
❑ 27 Fred Beck 120.00 60.00
❑ 28 Beals Becker 120.00 60.00
❑ 29 Jake Beckley 500.00 250.00
❑ 30 George Bell Pitching 120.00 60.00
❑ 31 George Bell Hands over Head 150.00 75.00
❑ 32 Chief Bender w/o Trees 800.00 400.00
❑ 33 Chief Bender w/Trees 1000.00 500.00
❑ 34 Chief Bender Portrait 1000.00 500.00
❑ 35 Bill Bergen Batting 150.00 75.00
❑ 36 Bill Bergen Catching 120.00 60.00
❑ 37 Heinie Berger 120.00 60.00
❑ 38 Wm. Bernhard 250.00 125.00
❑ 39 Bob Bescher Fly Ball 120.00 60.00
❑ 40 Bob Bescher Portrait 120.00 60.00
❑ 41 Joe Birmingham 150.00 75.00
❑ 42 Lena Blackburne 150.00 75.00
❑ 43 Jack Bliss 120.00 60.00
❑ 44 Frank Bowerman 150.00 75.00
❑ 45 Bill Bradley Batting 120.00 60.00
❑ 46 Bill Bradley Portrait 150.00 75.00
❑ 47 David Brain 100.00 50.00
❑ 48 Kitty Bransfield 150.00 75.00
❑ 49 Roy Brashear 100.00 50.00
❑ 50 Ted Breitenstein 250.00 125.00
❑ 51 Roger Bresnahan Portrait 600.00300.00
❑ 52 Roger Bresnahan Batting 600.00 300.00
❑ 53 Al Bridwell Portrait 150.00 75.00
❑ 54 Al Bridwell Sweater 120.00 60.00
❑ 55 George Brown Chicago 250.00 125.00
❑ 56 George Brown Wash 800.00 400.00
❑ 57 Mord.Brown Chi Shirt 1000.00 500.00
❑ 58 Mord.Brown Cubs Shirt 1000.00 500.00
❑ 59 Mord.Brown Portrait 1000.00 500.00
❑ 60 Al Burch Batting 250.00 125.00
❑ 61 Al Burch Fielding 120.00 60.00
❑ 62 Fred Burchell 100.00 50.00
❑ 63 Jimmy Burke 100.00 50.00
❑ 64 Bill Burns 120.00 60.00
❑ 65 Donie Bush 150.00 75.00
❑ 66 John Butler 100.00 50.00
❑ 67 Bobby Byrne 120.00 60.00
❑ 68 Howie Camnitz Arm at Side 120.00 60.00
❑ 69 Howie Camnitz Arms Folded 150.00 75.00
❑ 70 Howie Camnitz Hands above Head 120.00 60.00
❑ 71 Billy Campbell 120.00 60.00
❑ 72 George Carey 250.00 125.00
❑ 73 Charles Carr 100.00 50.00
❑ 74 Bill Carrigan 120.00 60.00
❑ 75 Doc Casey 100.00 50.00
❑ 76 Peter Cassidy 100.00 50.00
❑ 77 Frank Chance Batting 800.00 400.00
❑ 78 F.Chance Red Portrait 1000.00 500.00
❑ 79 F.Chance Yellow Portrait 1000.00500.00
❑ 80 William Chappelle 120.00 60.00
❑ 81 Chappy Charles 120.00 60.00
❑ 82 Hal Chase Dark Cap 250.00 125.00
❑ 83 Hal Chase Holding Trophy 250.00125.00
❑ 84 Hal Chase Portrait Blue 250.00 125.00
❑ 85 Hal Chase Portrait Pink 400.00 200.00
❑ 86 Hal Chase White Cap 300.00 150.00
❑ 87 Jack Chesbro 500.00 250.00
❑ 88 Ed Cicotte 400.00 200.00
❑ 89 William Clancy 100.00 50.00
❑ 90 Fred Clarke w/Bat 400.00 200.00
❑ 91 Fred Clarke Portrait 400.00 200.00
❑ 92 Joshua Clarke 100.00 50.00
❑ 93 Nig Clarke 150.00 75.00
❑ 94 William Clymer 100.00 50.00
❑ 95 Ty Cobb Bat off Shoulder 3000.00 1500.00
❑ 96 Ty Cobb Bat on Shoulder 3000.00 1500.00
❑ 97 Ty Cobb Portrait Green 6000.00 3500.00
❑ 98 Ty Cobb Portrait Red 3000.00 1500.00
❑ 99 Cad Coles 250.00 125.00
❑ 100 Eddie Collins 800.00 400.00
❑ 101 Jimmy Collins 800.00 400.00
❑ 102 Bunk Congalton 100.00 50.00
❑ 103 Wid Conroy Fielding 150.00 75.00
❑ 104 Wid Conroy with Bat 120.00 60.00
❑ 105 Harry Covaleski 150.00 75.00
❑ 106 Doc Crandall w/o Cap 120.00 60.00
❑ 107 Doc Crandall w/Cap 120.00 60.00
❑ 108 William Cranston 250.00 125.00
❑ 109 Gavvy Cravath 250.00 125.00
❑ 110 Sam Crawford Throwing 1000.00 500.00
❑ 111 Sam Crawford with Bat 1000.00 500.00
❑ 112 Birdie Cree 120.00 60.00
❑ 113 Lou Criger 150.00 75.00
❑ 114 Dode Criss 150.00 75.00
❑ 115 Monte Cross 120.00 60.00
❑ 116 Bill Dahlen Boston 250.00 125.00
❑ 117 Bill Dahlen Brooklyn 400.00 200.00
❑ 118 Paul Davidson 100.00 50.00
❑ 119 George Davis 400.00 200.00
❑ 120 Harry Davis (Davis on Front) 120.00 60.00
❑ 121 Harry Davis (H.Davis on Front) 150.00 75.00
❑ 122 Frank Delehanty 150.00 75.00
❑ 123 Jim Delehanty 150.00 75.00
❑ 124 Ray Demmitt New York 150.00 75.00
❑ 125 Ray Demmitt St. Louis 6000.00 3000.00
❑ 126 Rube Dessau 100.00 50.00
❑ 127 Art Devlin 150.00 75.00
❑ 128 Josh Devore 120.00 60.00
❑ 129 Bill Dineen 120.00 60.00
❑ 130 Mike Donlin Fielding 250.00 125.00
❑ 131 Mike Donlin Sitting 250.00 125.00
❑ 132 Mike Donlin Batting 150.00 75.00
❑ 133 Jiggs Donohue 150.00 75.00
❑ 134 Bill Donovan Portrait 150.00 75.00
❑ 135 Bill Donovan Throwing 120.00 60.00
❑ 136 Red Dooin 150.00 75.00
❑ 137 Mickey Doolan Batting 120.00 60.00
❑ 138 Mickey Doolan Fielding 120.00 60.00
❑ 139 Mickey Doolan (Doolin) 150.00 75.00
❑ 140 Gus Dorner 100.00 50.00
❑ 141 Patsy Dougherty Fielding 120.00 60.00
❑ 142 Patsy Dougherty Portrait 150.00 75.00
❑ 143 Tom Downey Batting 120.00 60.00
❑ 144 Tom Downey Fielding 120.00 60.00
❑ 145 Jerome Downs 100.00 50.00
❑ 146 Joe Doyle 250.00 125.00
❑ 147 Joe Doyle Nat'l 80000.00 40000.00
❑ 148 Larry Doyle Sweater 150.00 75.00
❑ 149 Larry Doyle Throwing 250.00 125.00
❑ 150 Larry Doyle Bat on Shldr 150.00 75.00
❑ 151 Jean Dubuc 120.00 60.00
❑ 152 Hugh Duffy 800.00 400.00
❑ 153 Jack Dunn 150.00 75.00
❑ 154 Joe Dunn 120.00 60.00
❑ 155 Bull Durham 150.00 75.00
❑ 156 Jimmy Dygert 120.00 60.00
❑ 157 Ted Easterly 120.00 60.00
❑ 158 Dick Egan 120.00 60.00
❑ 159 Kid Elberfeld Fielding 120.00 60.00
❑ 160 Kid Elberfeld NY Port 150.00 75.00
❑ 161 Kid Elberfeld Wash Port 1500.00 750.00
❑ 162 Roy Ellam 250.00 125.00
❑ 163 Clyde Engle 120.00 60.00
❑ 164 Steve Evans 120.00 60.00
❑ 165 J.Evers Portrait 1200.00 600.00
❑ 166 J.Evers Chi Shirt 1000.00 500.00
❑ 167 J.Evers Cubs Shirt 1000.00 500.00
❑ 168 Bob Ewing 150.00 75.00
❑ 169 George Ferguson 120.00 60.00
❑ 170 Hobe Ferris 150.00 75.00
❑ 171 Lou Fiene Portrait 120.00 60.00
❑ 172 Lou Fiene Throwing 120.00 60.00
❑ 173 James Flanagan 100.00 50.00
❑ 174 Art Fletcher 120.00 60.00
❑ 175 Elmer Flick 600.00 300.00
❑ 176 Russ Ford 120.00 60.00
❑ 177 Edward Foster 250.00 125.00
❑ 178 James Freeman 100.00 50.00
❑ 179 John Frill 120.00 60.00
❑ 180 Charles Fritz 250.00 125.00
❑ 181 Art Fromme 120.00 60.00
❑ 182 Chick Gandil 500.00 250.00
❑ 183 Bob Ganley 150.00 75.00
❑ 184 John Ganzel 100.00 50.00
❑ 185 Harry Gasper 120.00 60.00
❑ 186 Rube Geyer 120.00 60.00
❑ 187 George Gibson 150.00 75.00
❑ 188 Billy Gilbert 150.00 75.00
❑ 189 Wilbur Goode 150.00 75.00
❑ 190 Bill Graham 120.00 60.00
❑ 191 Peaches Graham 120.00 60.00
❑ 192 Dolly Gray 150.00 75.00
❑ 193 Ed Greminger 250.00 125.00
❑ 194 Clark Griffith Batting 500.00 250.00
❑ 195 Clark Griffith Portrait 500.00 250.00
❑ 196 Myron Grimshaw 100.00 50.00
❑ 197 Bob Groom 120.00 60.00
❑ 198 Tom Guiheen 250.00 125.00
❑ 199 Ed Hahn 150.00 75.00
❑ 200 Robert Hall 100.00 50.00
❑ 201 William Hallman 120.00 60.00
❑ 202 John Hannifan 100.00 50.00
❑ 203 William F. Hart 250.00 125.00
❑ 204 James Henry Hart 250.00 125.00
❑ 205 Topsy Hartsel 120.00 60.00
❑ 206 Jack Hayden 100.00 50.00
❑ 207 J.R. Helm 250.00 125.00
❑ 208 Charlie Hemphill 150.00 75.00
❑ 209 Buck Herzog Boston 120.00 60.00
❑ 210 Buck Herzog New York 150.00 75.00
❑ 211 Gordon Hickman 250.00 125.00
❑ 212 Bill Hinchman 150.00 75.00
❑ 213 Harry Hinchman 100.00 50.00
❑ 214 Doc Hoblitzell 120.00 60.00
❑ 215 Danny Hoffman 120.00 60.00
❑ 216 Harry C. Hoffman 100.00 50.00
❑ 217 Solly Hofman 120.00 60.00
❑ 218 Buck Hooker 250.00 125.00
❑ 219 Del Howard 120.00 60.00
❑ 220 Ernie Howard 250.00 125.00
❑ 221 Harry Howell Hand on Hip 120.0060.00
❑ 222 Harry Howell Portrait 120.00 60.00
❑ 223 M.Huggins Mouth 800.00 400.00
❑ 224 M.Huggins Portrait 800.00 400.00
❑ 225 Rudy Hulswitt 120.00 60.00
❑ 226 John Hummel 120.00 60.00
❑ 227 George Hunter 120.00 60.00
❑ 228 Frank Isbell 150.00 75.00
❑ 229 Fred Jacklitsch 150.00 75.00
❑ 230 James B. Jackson 120.00 60.00
❑ 231 H.Jennings Both 800.00 400.00
❑ 232 H.Jennings One 800.00 400.00
❑ 233 H.Jennings Port 800.00 400.00
❑ 234 Walter Johnson Hands 2000.00 1000.00
❑ 235 Walter Johnson Port 3000.00 2000.00
❑ 236 Davy Jones 120.00 60.00
❑ 237 Fielder Jones Hands on Hips 150.00 75.00
❑ 238 Fielder Jones Portrait 150.00 75.00
❑ 239 Tom Jones 150.00 75.00
❑ 240 Adolph Jordan 250.00 125.00
❑ 241 Tim Jordan Batting 120.00 60.00
❑ 242 Tim Jordan Portrait 150.00 75.00
❑ 243 Addie Joss Pitching 1000.00 500.00
❑ 244 Addie Joss Portrait 1200.00 600.00
❑ 245 Ed Karger 150.00 75.00
❑ 246 Willie Keeler Portrait 1200.00 600.00
❑ 247 Willie Keeler Batting 1000.00 500.00
❑ 248 Joe Kelley 500.00 250.00
❑ 249 J.F. Kiernan 250.00 125.00
❑ 250 Ed Killian Pitching 120.00 60.00
❑ 251 Ed Killian Portrait 150.00 75.00
❑ 252 Frank King 250.00 125.00
❑ 253 Rube Kissinger 120.00 60.00
❑ 254 Red Kleinow Catch Bos 1500.00750.00
❑ 255 Red Kleinow Catch NY 120.00 60.00
❑ 256 Red Kleinow Batting 150.00 75.00
❑ 257 Johnny Kling 150.00 75.00
❑ 258 Otto Knabe 120.00 60.00
❑ 259 John Knight Portrait 120.00 60.00
❑ 260 John Knight Batting 120.00 60.00
❑ 261 Ed Konetchy Awaiting Ball 120.00 60.00
❑ 262 Ed Konetchy Glove over Head 150.00 75.00
❑ 263 Harry Krause Pitching 120.00 60.00
❑ 264 Harry Krause Portrait 120.00 60.00
❑ 265 Rube Kroh 120.00 60.00
❑ 266 Otto Krueger 100.00 50.00
❑ 267 James LaFitte 250.00 125.00
❑ 268 Nap Lajoie Portrait 1500.00 750.00
❑ 269 Nap Lajoie Throwing 1200.00 600.00
❑ 270 Nap Lajoie Batting 1500.00 900.00
❑ 271 Joe Lake NY 150.00 75.00
❑ 272 Joe Lake Stl Throwing 120.00 60.00
❑ 273 Joe Lake Stl Hands over Head 120.00 60.00
❑ 274 Frank LaPorte 120.00 30.00
❑ 275 Arlie Latham 150.00 75.00
❑ 276 William Lattimore 100.00 50.00

❑ 277 James Lavender 100.00 50.00
❑ 278 Tommy Leach Fielding 120.00 60.00
❑ 279 Tommy Leach Portrait 150.00 75.00
❑ 280 Lefty Leifield Batting 120.00 60.00
❑ 281 Lefty Leifield Hands behind Head 150.00 75.00
❑ 282 Ed Lennox 120.00 60.00
❑ 283 Harry Lentz 250.00 125.00
❑ 284 Glenn Liebhardt 150.00 75.00
❑ 285 Vive Lindaman 250.00 125.00
❑ 286 Perry Lipe 250.00 125.00
❑ 287 Paddy Livingstone 120.00 60.00
❑ 288 Hans Lobert 150.00 75.00
❑ 289 Harry Lord 120.00 60.00
❑ 290 Harry Lumley 150.00 75.00
❑ 291 Carl Lundgren 600.00 300.00
❑ 292 Carl Lundgren 100.00 50.00
❑ 293 Nick Maddox 120.00 60.00
❑ 294 Sherry Magee with Bat 120.00 60.00
❑ 295 Sherry Magee Portrait 250.00 125.00
❑ 296 Sherry Magie Portrait ERR 20000.00 10000.00
❑ 297 William Malarkey 120.00 60.00
❑ 298 Bill Maloney 100.00 50.00
❑ 299 George Manion 250.00 125.00
❑ 300 Rube Manning Batting 150.00 75.00
❑ 301 Rube Manning Hands over Head 120.00 60.00
❑ 302 R.Marquard Pitching 800.00 400.00
❑ 303 R.Marquard Standing 800.00 400.00
❑ 304 R.Marquard Portrait 1000.00 500.00
❑ 305 Doc Marshall 120.00 60.00
❑ 306 C.Mathewson Drk Cap 2000.00 1000.00
❑ 307 C.Mathewson Portrait 2500.00 1250.00
❑ 308 C.Mathewson Wht Cap 2000.00 1000.00
❑ 309 Al Mattern 120.00 60.00
❑ 310 Jack McAleese 120.00 60.00
❑ 311 George McBride 120.00 60.00
❑ 312 McCauley 250.00 125.00
❑ 313 Moose McCormick 120.00 60.00
❑ 314 Pryor McElveen 120.00 60.00
❑ 315 Dennis McGann 100.00 50.00
❑ 316 James McGinley 100.00 50.00
❑ 317 Joe McGinnity 500.00 250.00
❑ 318 Ulysses McGlynn 100.00 50.00
❑ 319 J.McGraw Finger 1000.00 500.00
❑ 320 J.McGraw Glove-Hip 1000.00 500.00
❑ 321 J.McGraw w/o Cap 1000.00 500.00
❑ 322 J.McGraw w/Cap 1000.00 500.00
❑ 323 Harry McIntyre Brooklyn 150.00 75.00
❑ 324 Harry McIntyre Brooklyn-Chicago 120.00 60.00
❑ 325 Matty McIntyre 120.00 60.00
❑ 326 Larry McLean 120.00 60.00
❑ 327 George McQuillan Ball in Hand 150.00 75.00
❑ 328 George McQuillan with Bat 120.00 60.00
❑ 329 Fred Merkle Portrait 250.00 125.00
❑ 330 Fred Merkle Throwing 250.00 125.00
❑ 331 George Merritt 100.00 50.00
❑ 332 Chief Meyers 120.00 60.00
❑ 333 Chief Meyers Batting 150.00 75.00
❑ 334 Chief Meyers Fielding 120.00 60.00
❑ 335 Clyde Milan 120.00 60.00
❑ 336 Charles B. Miller 250.00 125.00
❑ 337 Dots Miller 120.00 60.00
❑ 338 Wm. Milligan 100.00 50.00
❑ 339 Fred Mitchell. 100.00 50.00
❑ 340 Mike Mitchell 120.00 60.00
❑ 341 Dan Moeller 100.00 50.00
❑ 342 Carlton Molesworth 250.00 125.00
❑ 343 Joseph H. Moran 100.00 50.00
❑ 344 Pat Moran 120.00 60.00
❑ 345 George Moriarty 120.00 60.00
❑ 346 Mike Mowrey 120.00 60.00
❑ 347 Dominic Mullaney 250.00 125.00
❑ 348 George Mullen 120.00 60.00
❑ 349 George Mullin with Bat 120.00 60.00
❑ 350 George Mullin Throwing 150.00 75.00
❑ 351 Danny Murphy Bat on Shoulder 120.00 60.00
❑ 352 Danny Murphy Throwing 150.00 75.00
❑ 353 Red Murray Bat on Shoulder 120.00 60.00
❑ 354 Red Murray Sweater 120.00 60.00
❑ 355 William Nattress 100.00 50.00
❑ 356 Tom Needham 120.00 60.00
❑ 357 Simon Nicholls 150.00 75.00
❑ 358 Simon Nichols 120.00 60.00
❑ 359 Harry Niles 150.00 75.00
❑ 360 Rebel Oakes 120.00 60.00
❑ 361 Frank Oberlin 100.00 50.00
❑ 362 Peter O'Brien 100.00 50.00
❑ 363 Bill O'Hara NY 120.00 60.00
❑ 364 Bill O'Hara Stl 6000.00 3000.00
❑ 365 Rube Oldring Bat on Shoulder 150.00 75.00
❑ 366 Rube Oldring Fielding 150.00 75.00
❑ 367 Charley O'Leary Hands on Knees 120.00 60.00
❑ 368 Charley O'Leary Portrait 150.00 75.00
❑ 369 William O'Neil 100.00 50.00
❑ 370 Albert Orth 250.00 125.00
❑ 371 William Otey 250.00 125.00
❑ 372 Orval Overall Hand at Face 120.00 60.00
❑ 373 Orval Overall Hands at Waist 120.00 60.00
❑ 374 Orval Overall Portrait 150.00 75.00
❑ 375 Frank Owen 150.00 75.00
❑ 376 George Paige 250.00 125.00
❑ 377 Freddy Parent 150.00 75.00
❑ 378 Dode Paskert 120.00 60.00
❑ 379 Jim Pastorius 150.00 75.00
❑ 380 Harry Pattee 300.00 150.00
❑ 381 Fred Payne 120.00 60.00
❑ 382 Barney Pelty Horizontal 250.00 125.00
❑ 383 Barney Pelty Vertical 120.00 60.00
❑ 384 Hub Perdue 300.00 150.00
❑ 385 George Perring 120.00 60.00
❑ 386 Archie Persons 250.00 125.00
❑ 387 Big Jeff Pfeffer 120.00 60.00
❑ 388 Jake Pfeister Seated 120.00 60.00
❑ 389 Jake Pfeister Throwing 120.00 60.00
❑ 390 James Phelan 100.00 50.00
❑ 391 Ed Phelps 120.00 60.00
❑ 392 Deacon Phillippe 250.00 125.00
❑ 393 Oliver Pickering 100.00 50.00
❑ 394 Eddie Plank 40000.00 20000.00
❑ 395 Philip Poland 100.00 50.00
❑ 396 Jack Powell 150.00 75.00
❑ 397 Mike Powers 250.00 125.00
❑ 398 Billy Purtell 120.00 60.00
❑ 399 Ambrose Puttman 100.00 50.00
❑ 400 Lee Quillen 100.00 50.00
❑ 401 Jack Quinn 120.00 60.00
❑ 402 Newton Randall 100.00 50.00
❑ 403 Bugs Raymond 150.00 75.00
❑ 404 Edward Reagan 250.00 125.00
❑ 405 Ed Reulbach Hands at Side 250.00 125.00
❑ 406 Ed Reulbach Pitching 250.00 125.00
❑ 407 R.H. Revelle 250.00 125.00
❑ 408 Bob Rhoades Ready to Pitch 120.00 60.00
❑ 409 Bob Rhoades Hand in Air 120.00 60.00
❑ 410 Charlie Rhodes 120.00 60.00
❑ 411 Claude Ritchey 150.00 75.00
❑ 412 Louis Ritter 100.00 50.00
❑ 413 Isaac Rockenfeld 250.00 125.00
❑ 414 Claude Rossman 120.00 60.00
❑ 415 Nap Rucker Portrait 250.00 125.00
❑ 416 Nap Rucker Pitching 150.00 75.00
❑ 417 Dick Rudolph 100.00 50.00
❑ 418 Ray Ryan 250.00 125.00
❑ 419 Germany Schaefer Det 150.00 75.00
❑ 420 Germany Schaefer Wash 150.00 75.00
❑ 421 George Schirm 100.00 50.00
❑ 422 Larry Schlafly 100.00 50.00
❑ 423 Admiral Schlei Batting 120.00 60.00
❑ 424 Admiral Schlei Fielding 150.00 75.00
❑ 425 Admiral Schlei Sweater 120.00 60.00
❑ 426 Boss Schmidt Portrait 120.00 60.00
❑ 427 Boss Schmidt Throwing 150.00 75.00
❑ 428 Ossie Schreckengost 120.00 60.00
❑ 429 Frank Schulte Back Turned 120.00 60.00
❑ 430 Frank Schulte Front Pose 150.00 75.00
❑ 431 Jim Scott 120.00 60.00
❑ 432 Charles Seitz 250.00 125.00
❑ 433 Cy Seymour Batting 150.00 75.00
❑ 434 Cy Seymour Portrait 120.00 60.00
❑ 435 Cy Seymour Throwing 120.00 60.00
❑ 436 William Shannon 100.00 50.00
❑ 437 Bayard Sharpe 100.00 50.00
❑ 437B Bayard Shappe UER 1000.00 500.00
❑ 438 Frank Shaughnessy 300.00 150.00
❑ 439 Al Shaw 150.00 75.00
❑ 440 Royal Shaw 100.00 50.00
❑ 441 Jimmy Sheckard Throwing 120.00 60.00
❑ 442 Jimmy Sheckard Side View 150.00 75.00
❑ 443 Bill Shipke 150.00 75.00
❑ 444 James Slagle 100.00 50.00
❑ 445 Carlos Smith 250.00 125.00
❑ 446 Frank Smith Chi-Bos 800.00 400.00
❑ 447 Frank Smith Listed-F.Smith 150.00 75.00
❑ 448 Frank Smith Listed-Smith 120.00 60.00
❑ 449 Heinie Smith ML 100.00 50.00
❑ 450 Happy Smith 120.00 60.00
❑ 451 Sid Smith 250.00 125.00
❑ 452 F.Snodgrass Bat 150.00 75.00
❑ 452B F.Snodgrass Bat UER 4000.00 2500.00
❑ 453 F.Snodgrass Catching 150.00 75.00
❑ 454 Bob Spade 150.00 75.00
❑ 455 Tris Speaker 2000.00 1200.00
❑ 456 Tubby Spencer 150.00 75.00
❑ 457 Jake Stahl Fly Ball 150.00 75.00
❑ 458 Jake Stahl Arms Down 150.00 75.00
❑ 459 Oscar Stanage 120.00 60.00
❑ 460 Dolly Stark 300.00 150.00
❑ 461 Charlie Starr 120.00 60.00
❑ 462 Harry Steinfeldt Batting 150.00 75.00
❑ 463 Harry Steinfeldt Portrait 250.00 125.00
❑ 464 Jim Stephens 120.00 60.00
❑ 465 George Stone 150.00 75.00
❑ 466 George Stovall Batting 120.00 60.00
❑ 467 George Stovall Portrait 150.00 75.00
❑ 468 Samuel Strang 100.00 50.00
❑ 469 Gabby Street Catching 120.00 60.00
❑ 470 Gabby Street Portrait 150.00 75.00
❑ 471 Billy Sullivan 150.00 75.00
❑ 472 Ed Summers 120.00 60.00
❑ 473 Bill Sweeney 120.00 60.00
❑ 474 Jeff Sweeney 120.00 60.00
❑ 475 Jesse Tannehill 120.00 60.00
❑ 476 Lee Tannehill Listed-L.Tannehill 150.00 75.00
❑ 477 Lee Tannehill Listed-Tannehill 120.00 60.00
❑ 478 Luther (Dummy) Taylor 250.00 125.00
❑ 479 Fred Tenney 150.00 75.00
❑ 480 Tony Thebo 250.00 125.00
❑ 481 John Thielman 100.00 50.00
❑ 482 Ira Thomas 120.00 60.00
❑ 483 Woodie Thornton 250.00 125.00
❑ 484 J.Tinker Bat off Shldr 1200.00 600.00
❑ 485 J.Tinker Bat on Shldr 1200.00 600.00
❑ 486 J.Tinker Hand-Knee 1200.00 600.00
❑ 487 J.Tinker Portrait 1500.00 750.00
❑ 488 John Titus 120.00 60.00
❑ 489 Terry Turner 150.00 75.00
❑ 490 Bob Unglaub 120.00 60.00
❑ 491 Juan Violat 250.00 125.00
❑ 492 R.Waddell Portrait 1200.00 600.00
❑ 493 R.Waddell Pitching 1000.00 500.00
❑ 494 Heinie Wagner Left Shldr 250.00 125.00
❑ 495 Heinie Wagner Right Shldr 150.00 75.00
❑ 496 Honus Wagner 600000.00 300000.00
❑ 497 Bobby Wallace 800.00 400.00
❑ 498 Ed Walsh 1200.00 600.00
❑ 499 Jack Warhop 120.00 60.00
❑ 500 Jake Weimer 150.00 75.00
❑ 501 James Westlake 250.00 125.00
❑ 502 Zach Wheat 800.00 400.00
❑ 503 Doc White Pitching 120.00 60.00
❑ 504 Doc White Portrait 150.00 75.00
❑ 505 Foley White 250.00 125.00
❑ 506 John F. White 100.00 50.00
❑ 507 Kaiser Wilhelm Hands to Chest 150.00 75.00
❑ 508 Kaiser Wilhelm Batting 120.00 60.00
❑ 509 Ed Willett Batting 120.00 60.00
❑ 510 Ed Willett Pitching 120.00 60.00
❑ 511 Jimmy Williams 150.00 75.00
❑ 512 Vic Willis Pitt 500.00 250.00
❑ 513 Vic Willis Stl Pitch 400.00 200.00
❑ 514 Vic Willis Stl Bat 400.00 200.00
❑ 515 Chief Wilson 120.00 60.00
❑ 516 Hooks Wiltse Pirching 120.00 60.00
❑ 517 Hooks Wiltse Portrait 150.00 75.00
❑ 518 Hooks Wiltse Sweater 120.00 60.00
❑ 519 William Wright 100.00 50.00
❑ 520 Cy Young Bare Hand 2000.00 1000.00
❑ 521 Cy Young w/Glove 2500.00 1500.00
❑ 522 Cy Young Portrait 2500.00 1500.00
❑ 523 Irving M. Young 120.00 60.00
❑ 524 Heinie Zimmerman 120.00 60.00

1952 Topps

❑ COMP.MASTER SET (487) 80000.00 40000.00
❑ COMPLETE SET (407) 65000.00 40000.00
❑ COMMON CARD (1-80) 60.00 35.00

❑ COMMON CARD (81-250) 40.00 20.00
❑ COMMON CARD (251-310) 50.00 30.00
❑ COMMON CARD (311-407) 250.00 150.00
❑ WRAPPER (1-CENT) 250.00 200.00
❑ WRAPPER (5-CENT) 100.00 75.00
❑ 1 Andy Pafko 5000.00 3000.00
❑ 1A Andy Pafko Black 3000.00 1800.00
❑ 2 Pete Runnels RC 250.00 150.00
❑ 2A Pete Runnels Black 250.00 150.00
❑ 3 Hank Thompson 70.00 40.00
❑ 3A Hank Thompson Black 70.00 40.00
❑ 4 Don Lenhardt 60.00 35.00
❑ 4A Don Lenhardt Black 60.00 35.00
❑ 5 Larry Jansen 70.00 40.00
❑ 5A Larry Jansen Black 70.00 40.00
❑ 6 Grady Hatton 60.00 35.00
❑ 6A Grady Hatton Black 60.00 35.00
❑ 7 Wayne Terwilliger 60.00 35.00
❑ 7A Wayne Terwilliger Black 60.00 35.00
❑ 8 Fred Marsh RC 60.00 35.00
❑ 8A Fred Marsh Black 60.00 35.00
❑ 9 Robert Hogue RC 60.00 35.00
❑ 9A Robert Hogue Black 60.00 35.00
❑ 10 Al Rosen 70.00 40.00
❑ 10A Al Rosen Black 70.00 40.00
❑ 11 Phil Rizzuto 400.00 250.00
❑ 11A Phil Rizzuto Black 350.00 200.00
❑ 12 Monty Basgall RC 60.00 35.00
❑ 12A Monty Basgall Black 60.00 35.00
❑ 13 Johnny Wyrostek 60.00 35.00
❑ 13A Johnny Wyrostek Black 60.00 35.00
❑ 14 Bob Elliott 70.00 40.00
❑ 14A Bob Elliott Black 70.00 40.00
❑ 15 Johnny Pesky 70.00 40.00
❑ 15A Johnny Pesky Black 70.00 40.00
❑ 16 Gene Hermanski 60.00 35.00
❑ 16A Gene Hermanski Black 60.00 35.00
❑ 17 Jim Hegan 70.00 40.00
❑ 17A Jim Hegan Black 70.00 40.00
❑ 18 Merrill Combs RC 60.00 35.00
❑ 18A Merrill Combs Black 60.00 35.00
❑ 19 Johnny Bucha RC 60.00 35.00
❑ 19A Johnny Bucha Black 60.00 35.00
❑ 20 Billy Loes SP RC 150.00 90.00
❑ 20A Billy Loes Black 150.00 90.00
❑ 21 Ferris Fain 70.00 40.00
❑ 21A Ferris Fain Black 70.00 40.00
❑ 22 Dom DiMaggio 125.00 75.00
❑ 22A Dom DiMaggio Black 100.00 60.00
❑ 23 Billy Goodman 70.00 40.00
❑ 23A Billy Goodman Black 70.00 40.00
❑ 24 Luke Easter 80.00 50.00
❑ 24A Luke Easter Black 80.00 50.00
❑ 25 Johnny Groth 60.00 35.00
❑ 25A Johnny Groth Black 60.00 35.00
❑ 26 Monte Irvin 150.00 90.00
❑ 26A Monte Irvin Black 150.00 90.00
❑ 27 Sam Jethroe 70.00 40.00
❑ 27A Sam Jethroe Black 70.00 40.00
❑ 28 Jerry Priddy 60.00 35.00
❑ 28A Jerry Priddy Black 60.00 35.00
❑ 29 Ted Kluszewski 125.00 75.00
❑ 29A Ted Kluszewski Black 125.00 75.00
❑ 30 Mel Parnell 70.00 40.00
❑ 30A Mel Parnell Black 70.00 40.00
❑ 31 Gus Zernial Baseballs 80.00 50.00
❑ 31A Gus Zernial Black 80.00 50.00
❑ 32 Eddie Robinson 60.00 35.00
❑ 32A Eddie Robinson Black 60.00 35.00
❑ 33 Warren Spahn 300.00 175.00
❑ 33A Warren Spahn Black 300.00 175.00
❑ 34 Elmer Valo 60.00 35.00
❑ 34A Elmer Valo Black 60.00 35.00
❑ 35 Hank Sauer 70.00 40.00
❑ 35A Hank Sauer Black 70.00 40.00
❑ 36 Gil Hodges 300.00 175.00
❑ 36A Gil Hodges Black 300.00 175.00
❑ 37 Duke Snider 500.00 300.00
❑ 37A Duke Snider Black 500.00 300.00
❑ 38 Wally Westlake 60.00 35.00
❑ 38A Wally Westlake Black 60.00 35.00
❑ 39 Dizzy Trout 70.00 40.00
❑ 39A Dizzy Trout Black 70.00 40.00
❑ 40 Irv Noren 70.00 40.00
❑ 40A Irv Noren Black 70.00 40.00
❑ 41 Bob Wellman RC 60.00 35.00
❑ 41A Bob Wellman Black 60.00 35.00
❑ 42 Lou Kretlow RC 60.00 35.00
❑ 42A Lou Kretlow Black 60.00 35.00
❑ 43 Ray Scarborough 60.00 35.00
❑ 43A Ray Scarborough Black 60.00 35.00
❑ 44 Con Dempsey RC 60.00 35.00
❑ 44A Con Dempsey Black 60.00 35.00
❑ 45 Eddie Joost 60.00 35.00
❑ 45A Eddie Joost Black 60.00 35.00
❑ 46 Gordon Goldsberry RC 60.00 35.00
❑ 46A Gordon Goldsberry Black 60.00 35.00
❑ 47 Willie Jones 70.00 40.00
❑ 47A Willie Jones Black 70.00 40.00
❑ 48A Joe Page ERR BLA 400.00 250.00
❑ 48B Joe Page COR BLA 125.00 75.00
❑ 48C Joe Page COR Red 125.00 75.00
❑ 49A John Sain ERR BLA 400.00 250.00
❑ 49B John Sain COR BLA 125.00 75.00
❑ 49C Joe Page COR Red 125.00 75.00
❑ 50 Marv Rickert RC 60.00 35.00
❑ 50A Marv Rickert Black 60.00 35.00
❑ 51 Jim Russell 60.00 35.00
❑ 51A Jim Russell Black 60.00 35.00
❑ 52 Don Mueller 70.00 40.00
❑ 52A Don Mueller Black 70.00 40.00
❑ 53 Chris Van Cuyk RC 60.00 35.00
❑ 53A Chris Van Cuyk Black 60.00 35.00
❑ 54 Leo Kiely RC 60.00 35.00
❑ 54A Leo Kiely Black 60.00 35.00
❑ 55 Ray Boone 80.00 50.00
❑ 55A Ray Boone Black 80.00 50.00
❑ 56 Tommy Glaviano 60.00 35.00
❑ 56A Tommy Glaviano Black 60.00 35.00
❑ 57 Ed Lopat 100.00 60.00
❑ 57A Ed Lopat Black 100.00 60.00
❑ 58 Bob Mahoney RC 60.00 35.00
❑ 58A Bob Mahoney Black 60.00 35.00
❑ 59 Robin Roberts 175.00 100.00
❑ 59A Robin Roberts Black 175.00 100.00
❑ 60 Sid Hudson 60.00 35.00
❑ 60A Sid Hudson Black 60.00 35.00
❑ 61 Tookie Gilbert 60.00 35.00
❑ 61A Tookie Gilbert Black 60.00 35.00
❑ 62 Chuck Stobbs RC 60.00 35.00
❑ 62A Chuck Stobbs Black 60.00 35.00
❑ 63 Howie Pollet 60.00 35.00
❑ 63A Howie Pollet Black 60.00 35.00
❑ 64 Roy Sievers 70.00 40.00
❑ 64A Roy Sievers Black 70.00 40.00
❑ 65 Enos Slaughter 175.00 100.00
❑ 65A Enos Slaughter Black 175.00 100.00
❑ 66 Preacher Roe 100.00 60.00
❑ 66A Preacher Roe Black 100.00 60.00
❑ 67 Allie Reynolds 125.00 75.00
❑ 67A Allie Reynolds Black 125.00 75.00
❑ 68 Cliff Chambers 60.00 35.00
❑ 68A Cliff Chambers Black 60.00 35.00
❑ 69 Virgil Stallcup 60.00 35.00
❑ 69A Virgil Stallcup Black 60.00 35.00
❑ 70 Al Zarilla 60.00 35.00
❑ 70A Al Zarilla Black 60.00 35.00
❑ 71 Tom Upton RC 60.00 35.00
❑ 71A Tom Upton Black 60.00 35.00
❑ 72 Karl Olson RC 60.00 35.00
❑ 72A Karl Olson Black 60.00 35.00
❑ 73 Bill Werle 60.00 35.00
❑ 73A Bill Werle Black 60.00 35.00
❑ 74 Andy Hansen RC 60.00 35.00
❑ 74A Andy Hansen Black 60.00 35.00
❑ 75 Wes Westrum 70.00 40.00
❑ 75A Wes Westrum Black 70.00 40.00
❑ 76 Eddie Stanky 70.00 40.00
❑ 76A Eddie Stanky Black 70.00 40.00
❑ 77 Bob Kennedy 70.00 40.00
❑ 77A Bob Kennedy Black 70.00 40.00
❑ 78 Ellis Kinder 60.00 35.00
❑ 78A Ellis Kinder Black 60.00 35.00
❑ 79 Gerry Staley 60.00 35.00
❑ 79A Gerry Staley Black 60.00 35.00
❑ 80 Herman Wehmeier 80.00 50.00
❑ 80A Herman Wehmeier Black 80.00 50.00
❑ 81 Vern Law 80.00 50.00
❑ 82 Duane Pillette 40.00 20.00
❑ 83 Billy Johnson 40.00 20.00
❑ 84 Vern Stephens 50.00 30.00
❑ 85 Bob Kuzava 50.00 30.00
❑ 86 Ted Gray 40.00 20.00
❑ 87 Dale Coogan 40.00 20.00
❑ 88 Bob Feller 250.00 150.00
❑ 89 Johnny Lipon 40.00 20.00
❑ 90 Mickey Grasso 40.00 20.00
❑ 91 Red Schoendienst 150.00 90.00
❑ 92 Dale Mitchell 50.00 30.00
❑ 93 Al Sima RC 40.00 20.00
❑ 94 Sam Mele 40.00 20.00
❑ 95 Ken Holcombe 40.00 20.00
❑ 96 Willard Marshall 40.00 20.00
❑ 97 Earl Torgeson 40.00 20.00
❑ 98 Billy Pierce 50.00 30.00
❑ 99 Gene Woodling 60.00 35.00
❑ 100 Del Rice 40.00 20.00
❑ 101 Max Lanier 40.00 20.00
❑ 102 Bill Kennedy 40.00 20.00
❑ 103 Cliff Mapes 40.00 20.00
❑ 104 Don Kolloway 40.00 20.00
❑ 105 Johnny Pramesa 40.00 20.00
❑ 106 Mickey Vernon 60.00 35.00
❑ 107 Connie Ryan 40.00 20.00
❑ 108 Jim Konstanty 60.00 35.00
❑ 109 Ted Wilks 40.00 20.00
❑ 110 Dutch Leonard 40.00 20.00
❑ 111 Peanuts Lowrey 40.00 20.00
❑ 112 Hank Majeski 40.00 20.00
❑ 113 Dick Sisler 50.00 30.00
❑ 114 Willard Ramsdell 40.00 20.00
❑ 115 George Munger 40.00 20.00
❑ 116 Carl Scheib 40.00 20.00
❑ 117 Sherm Lollar 50.00 30.00
❑ 118 Ken Raffensberger 40.00 20.00
❑ 119 Mickey McDermott 40.00 20.00
❑ 120 Bob Chakales RC 40.00 20.00
❑ 121 Gus Niarhos 40.00 20.00
❑ 122 Jackie Jensen 80.00 50.00
❑ 123 Eddie Yost 50.00 30.00
❑ 124 Monte Kennedy 40.00 20.00
❑ 125 Bill Rigney 40.00 20.00
❑ 126 Fred Hutchinson 50.00 30.00
❑ 127 Paul Minner RC 40.00 20.00
❑ 128 Don Bollweg RC 40.00 20.00
❑ 129 Johnny Mize 150.00 90.00
❑ 130 Sheldon Jones 40.00 20.00
❑ 131 Morrie Martin RC 40.00 20.00
❑ 132 Clyde Kluttz RC 40.00 20.00
❑ 133 Al Widmar 40.00 20.00
❑ 134 Joe Tipton 40.00 20.00
❑ 135 Dixie Howell 40.00 20.00
❑ 136 Johnny Schmitz 40.00 20.00
❑ 137 Roy McMillan RC 50.00 30.00
❑ 138 Bill MacDonald 40.00 20.00
❑ 139 Ken Wood 40.00 20.00
❑ 140 Johnny Antonelli 60.00 35.00
❑ 141 Clint Hartung 40.00 20.00
❑ 142 Harry Perkowski RC 40.00 20.00
❑ 143 Les Moss 40.00 20.00
❑ 144 Ed Blake RC 40.00 20.00
❑ 145 Joe Haynes 40.00 20.00
❑ 146 Frank House RC 40.00 20.00
❑ 147 Bob Young RC 40.00 20.00
❑ 148 Johnny Klippstein 40.00 20.00
❑ 149 Dick Kryhoski 40.00 20.00
❑ 150 Ted Beard 40.00 20.00
❑ 151 Wally Post RC 50.00 30.00
❑ 152 Al Evans 40.00 20.00
❑ 153 Bob Rush 40.00 20.00

❑ 154 Joe Muir RC 40.00 20.00
❑ 155 Frank Overmire 40.00 20.00
❑ 156 Frank Hiller RC 40.00 20.00
❑ 157 Bob Usher 40.00 20.00
❑ 158 Eddie Waitkus 40.00 20.00
❑ 159 Saul Rogovin RC 40.00 20.00
❑ 160 Owen Friend 40.00 20.00
❑ 161 Bud Byerly RC 40.00 20.00
❑ 162 Del Crandall 50.00 30.00
❑ 163 Stan Rojek 40.00 20.00
❑ 164 Walt Dubiel 40.00 20.00
❑ 165 Eddie Kazak 40.00 20.00
❑ 166 Paul LaPalme RC 40.00 20.00
❑ 167 Bill Howerton 40.00 20.00
❑ 168 Charlie Silvera RC 60.00 35.00
❑ 169 Howie Judson 40.00 20.00
❑ 170 Gus Bell 50.00 30.00
❑ 171 Ed Erautt RC 40.00 20.00
❑ 172 Eddie Miksis 40.00 20.00
❑ 173 Roy Smalley 40.00 20.00
❑ 174 Clarence Marshall RC 60.00 35.00
❑ 175 Billy Martin RC 500.00 300.00
❑ 176 Hank Edwards 40.00 20.00
❑ 177 Bill Wight 40.00 20.00
❑ 178 Cass Michaels 40.00 20.00
❑ 179 Frank Smith RC 40.00 20.00
❑ 180 Charlie Maxwell RC 50.00 30.00
❑ 181 Bob Swift 40.00 20.00
❑ 182 Billy Hitchcock 40.00 20.00
❑ 183 Erv Dusak 40.00 20.00
❑ 184 Bob Ramazzotti 40.00 20.00
❑ 185 Bill Nicholson 50.00 30.00
❑ 186 Walt Masterson 40.00 20.00
❑ 187 Bob Miller 40.00 20.00
❑ 188 Clarence Podbielan RC 40.00 20.00
❑ 189 Pete Reiser 60.00 35.00
❑ 190 Don Johnson RC 40.00 20.00
❑ 191 Yogi Berra 800.00 500.00
❑ 192 Myron Ginsberg RC 40.00 20.00
❑ 193 Harry Simpson RC 50.00 30.00
❑ 194 Joe Hatton 40.00 20.00
❑ 195 Minnie Minoso RC 150.00 90.00
❑ 196 Solly Hemus RC 60.00 35.00
❑ 197 George Strickland RC 40.00 20.00
❑ 198 Phil Haugstad RC 40.00 20.00
❑ 199 George Zuverink RC 40.00 20.00
❑ 200 Ralph Houk RC 80.00 50.00
❑ 201 Alex Kellner 40.00 20.00
❑ 202 Joe Collins RC 60.00 35.00
❑ 203 Curt Simmons 60.00 35.00
❑ 204 Ron Northey 40.00 20.00
❑ 205 Clyde King 60.00 35.00
❑ 206 Joe Ostrowski RC 40.00 20.00
❑ 207 Mickey Harris 40.00 20.00
❑ 208 Marlin Stuart RC 40.00 20.00
❑ 209 Howie Fox 40.00 20.00
❑ 210 Dick Fowler 40.00 20.00
❑ 211 Ray Coleman 40.00 20.00
❑ 212 Ned Garver 40.00 20.00
❑ 213 Nippy Jones 40.00 20.00
❑ 214 Johnny Hopp 50.00 30.00
❑ 215 Hank Bauer 100.00 60.00
❑ 216 Richie Ashburn 250.00 150.00
❑ 217 Snuffy Stirnweiss 50.00 30.00
❑ 218 Clyde McCullough 40.00 20.00
❑ 219 Bobby Shantz 60.00 35.00
❑ 220 Joe Presko RC 40.00 20.00
❑ 221 Granny Hamner 40.00 20.00
❑ 222 Hoot Evers 40.00 20.00
❑ 223 Del Ennis 50.00 30.00
❑ 224 Bruce Edwards 40.00 20.00
❑ 225 Frank Baumholtz 40.00 20.00
❑ 226 Dave Philley 40.00 20.00
❑ 227 Joe Garagiola 80.00 50.00
❑ 228 Al Brazle 40.00 20.00
❑ 229 Gene Bearden UER 40.00 20.00
❑ 230 Matt Batts 40.00 20.00
❑ 231 Sam Zoldak 40.00 20.00
❑ 232 Billy Cox 50.00 30.00
❑ 233 Bob Friend RC 80.00 50.00
❑ 234 Steve Souchock RC 40.00 20.00
❑ 235 Walt Dropo 40.00 20.00
❑ 236 Ed Fitzgerald 40.00 20.00
❑ 237 Jerry Coleman 60.00 35.00
❑ 238 Art Houtteman 40.00 20.00
❑ 239 Rocky Bridges RC 50.00 30.00
❑ 240 Jack Phillips RC 40.00 20.00
❑ 241 Tommy Byrne 40.00 20.00
❑ 242 Tom Poholsky RC 40.00 20.00
❑ 243 Larry Doby 80.00 50.00
❑ 244 Vic Wertz 40.00 20.00
❑ 245 Sherry Robertson 40.00 20.00
❑ 246 George Kell 80.00 50.00
❑ 247 Randy Gumpert 40.00 20.00
❑ 248 Frank Shea 40.00 20.00
❑ 249 Bobby Adams 40.00 20.00
❑ 250 Carl Erskine 100.00 60.00
❑ 251 Chico Carrasquel 50.00 30.00
❑ 252 Vern Bickford 50.00 30.00
❑ 253 John Berardino 100.00 60.00
❑ 254 Joe Dobson 50.00 30.00
❑ 255 Clyde Vollmer 50.00 30.00
❑ 256 Pete Suder 50.00 30.00
❑ 257 Bobby Avila 60.00 35.00
❑ 258 Steve Gromek 60.00 35.00
❑ 259 Bob Addis RC 50.00 30.00
❑ 260 Pete Castiglione 50.00 30.00
❑ 261 Willie Mays 3000.00 2000.00
❑ 262 Virgil Trucks 60.00 35.00
❑ 263 Harry Brecheen 60.00 35.00
❑ 264 Roy Hartsfield 50.00 30.00
❑ 265 Chuck Diering 50.00 30.00
❑ 266 Murry Dickson 50.00 30.00
❑ 267 Sid Gordon 60.00 35.00
❑ 268 Bob Lemon 150.00 90.00
❑ 269 Willard Nixon 50.00 30.00
❑ 270 Lou Brissie 50.00 30.00
❑ 271 Jim Delsing 60.00 35.00
❑ 272 Mike Garcia 80.00 50.00
❑ 273 Erv Palica 50.00 30.00
❑ 274 Ralph Branca 125.00 75.00
❑ 275 Pat Mullin 50.00 30.00
❑ 276 Jim Wilson RC 50.00 30.00
❑ 277 Early Wynn 175.00 100.00
❑ 278 Allie Clark 50.00 30.00
❑ 279 Eddie Stewart 50.00 30.00
❑ 280 Cloyd Boyer 80.00 50.00
❑ 281 Tommy Brown SP 80.00 50.00
❑ 282 Birdie Tebbetts SP 80.00 50.00
❑ 283 Phil Masi SP 60.00 35.00
❑ 284 Hank Arft SP 60.00 35.00
❑ 285 Cliff Fannin SP 60.00 35.00
❑ 286 Joe DeMaestri SP RC 60.00 35.00
❑ 287 Steve Bilko SP 60.00 35.00
❑ 288 Chet Nichols SP RC 80.00 50.00
❑ 289 Tommy Holmes MG 100.00 60.00
❑ 290 Joe Astroth SP 60.00 35.00
❑ 291 Gil Coan SP 60.00 35.00
❑ 292 Floyd Baker SP 60.00 35.00
❑ 293 Sibby Sisti SP 60.00 35.00
❑ 294 Walker Cooper SP 60.00 35.00
❑ 295 Phil Cavarretta 80.00 50.00
❑ 296 Red Rolfe MG 60.00 35.00
❑ 297 Andy Seminick SP 60.00 35.00
❑ 298 Bob Ross SP RC 60.00 35.00
❑ 299 Ray Murray SP RC 80.00 50.00
❑ 300 Barney McCosky SP 80.00 50.00
❑ 301 Bob Porterfield 50.00 30.00
❑ 302 Max Surkont RC 50.00 30.00
❑ 303 Harry Dorish 50.00 30.00
❑ 304 Sam Dente 50.00 30.00
❑ 305 Paul Richards MG 60.00 35.00
❑ 306 Lou Sleater RC 50.00 30.00
❑ 307 Frank Campos RC 50.00 30.00
❑ 307A Frank Campos Star
❑ 308 Luis Aloma 50.00 30.00
❑ 309 Jim Busby 60.00 35.00
❑ 310 George Metkovich 100.00 60.00
❑ 311 Mickey Mantle DP 30000.00 18000.00
❑ 311A Mickey Mantle Stitch
❑ 312 Jackie Robinson DP 2500.00 1500.00
❑ 312A Jackie Robinson Stitch
❑ 313 Bobby Thomson DP 350.00 200.00
❑ 313A Bobby Thomson Stitch
❑ 314 Roy Campanella 2500.00 1500.00
❑ 315 Leo Durocher MG 600.00 350.00
❑ 316 Dave Williams RC 300.00 175.00
❑ 317 Conrado Marrero 300.00 175.00
❑ 318 Harold Gregg RC 300.00 175.00
❑ 319 Rube Walker RC 250.00 150.00
❑ 320 John Rutherford RC 300.00 175.00
❑ 321 Joe Black RC 500.00 350.00
❑ 322 Randy Jackson RC 300.00 175.00
❑ 323 Bubba Church 250.00 150.00
❑ 324 Warren Hacker 250.00 150.00
❑ 325 Bill Serena 300.00 175.00
❑ 326 George Shuba RC 500.00 350.00
❑ 327 Al Wilson RC 250.00 150.00
❑ 328 Bob Borkowski RC 300.00 175.00
❑ 329 Ike Delock RC 300.00 175.00
❑ 330 Turk Lown RC 300.00 175.00
❑ 331 Tom Morgan RC 300.00 175.00
❑ 332 Tony Bartirome RC 300.00 175.00
❑ 333 Pee Wee Reese 1800.00 1000.00
❑ 334 Wilmer Mizell RC 300.00 175.00
❑ 335 Ted Lepcio RC 250.00 150.00
❑ 336 Dave Koslo 250.00 150.00
❑ 337 Jim Hearn 300.00 175.00
❑ 338 Sal Yvars RC 300.00 175.00
❑ 339 Russ Meyer 300.00 175.00
❑ 340 Bob Hooper 300.00 175.00
❑ 341 Hal Jeffcoat 300.00 175.00
❑ 342 Clem Labine RC 500.00 350.00
❑ 343 Dick Gernert RC 250.00 150.00
❑ 344 Ewell Blackwell 300.00 175.00
❑ 345 Sammy White RC 250.00 150.00
❑ 346 George Spencer RC 250.00 150.00
❑ 347 Joe Adcock 400.00 250.00
❑ 348 Robert Kelly RC 250.00 150.00
❑ 349 Bob Cain 300.00 175.00
❑ 350 Cal Abrams 300.00 175.00
❑ 351 Alvin Dark 300.00 175.00
❑ 352 Karl Drews 300.00 175.00
❑ 353 Bobby Del Greco RC 300.00 175.00
❑ 354 Fred Hatfield RC 300.00 175.00
❑ 355 Bobby Morgan 300.00 175.00
❑ 356 Toby Atwell RC 300.00 175.00
❑ 357 Smoky Burgess 300.00 175.00
❑ 358 John Kucab RC 300.00 175.00
❑ 359 Dee Fondy RC 250.00 150.00
❑ 360 George Crowe RC 300.00 175.00
❑ 361 Bill Posedel CO 250.00 150.00
❑ 362 Ken Heintzelman 300.00 175.00
❑ 363 Dick Rozek RC 300.00 175.00
❑ 364 Clyde Sukeforth CO RC 300.00 175.00
❑ 365 Cookie Lavagetto CO 400.00 250.00
❑ 366 Dave Madison RC 250.00 150.00
❑ 367 Ben Thorpe RC 300.00 175.00
❑ 368 Ed Wright RC 300.00 175.00
❑ 369 Dick Groat RC 500.00 350.00
❑ 370 Billy Hoeft RC 300.00 175.00
❑ 371 Bobby Hofman 250.00 150.00
❑ 372 Gil McDougald RC 500.00 300.00
❑ 373 Jim Turner CO RC 400.00 250.00
❑ 374 Al Benton RC 250.00 150.00
❑ 375 John Merson RC 250.00 150.00
❑ 376 Faye Throneberry RC 250.00 150.00
❑ 377 Chuck Dressen MG 400.00 250.00
❑ 378 Leroy Fusselman RC 300.00 175.00
❑ 379 Joe Rossi RC 250.00 150.00
❑ 380 Clem Koshorek RC 250.00 150.00
❑ 381 Milton Stock CO RC 300.00 175.00
❑ 382 Sam Jones RC 350.00 200.00
❑ 383 Del Wilber RC 250.00 150.00
❑ 384 Frank Crosetti CO 500.00 300.00
❑ 385 Herman Franks CO RC 250.00 150.00
❑ 386 Ed Yuhas RC 300.00 175.00
❑ 387 Billy Meyer MG 250.00 150.00
❑ 388 Bob Chipman 250.00 150.00
❑ 389 Ben Wade RC 300.00 175.00
❑ 390 Rocky Nelson RC 300.00 175.00
❑ 391 Ben Chapman CO UER 250.00 150.00
❑ 392 Hoyt Wilhelm RC 1000.00 600.00
❑ 393 Ebba St.Claire RC 300.00 175.00
❑ 394 Billy Herman CO 600.00 350.00
❑ 395 Jake Pitler CO 300.00 175.00
❑ 396 Dick Williams RC 500.00 300.00
❑ 397 Forrest Main RC 250.00 150.00
❑ 398 Hal Rice 250.00 150.00
❑ 399 Jim Fridley RC 250.00 150.00
❑ 400 Bill Dickey CO 1800.00 1000.00
❑ 401 Bob Schultz RC 300.00 175.00
❑ 402 Earl Harrist RC 300.00 175.00
❑ 403 Bill Miller RC 300.00 175.00
❑ 404 Dick Brodowski RC 300.00 175.00
❑ 405 Eddie Pellagrini 300.00 175.00
❑ 406 Joe Nuxhall RC 400.00 250.00
❑ 407 Eddie Mathews RC 10000.00 6000.00

1953 Topps

❑ COMPLETE SET (274)	15000.00	9000.00
❑ COMMON CARD (1-165)	30.00	15.00
❑ COMMON DP (1-165)	15.00	7.50
❑ COMMON CARD (166-220)	25.00	12.50
❑ COMMON CARD (221-280)	100.00	50.00
❑ NOT ISSUED (253/261/267)		
❑ NOT ISSUED (268/271/275)		
❑ WRAP.(1-CENT, DATED)	200.00	150.00
❑ WRAP.(1-CENT,NO DATE)	300.00	250.00
❑ WRAP.(5-CENT, DATED)	400.00	300.00
❑ WRAP.(5-CENT,NO DATE)	350.00	275.00
❑ 1 Jackie Robinson DP	800.00	500.00
❑ 2 Luke Easter DP	20.00	10.00
❑ 3 George Crowe	40.00	25.00
❑ 4 Ben Wade	30.00	15.00
❑ 5 Joe Dobson	30.00	15.00
❑ 6 Sam Jones	40.00	25.00
❑ 7 Bob Borkowski DP	15.00	7.50
❑ 8 Clem Koshorek DP	15.00	7.50
❑ 9 Joe Collins	60.00	35.00
❑ 10 Smoky Burgess SP	80.00	50.00
❑ 11 Sal Yvars	30.00	15.00
❑ 12 Howie Judson DP	15.00	7.50
❑ 13 Conrado Marrero DP	15.00	7.50
❑ 14 Clem Labine DP	20.00	10.00
❑ 15 Bobo Newsom DP RC	20.00	10.00
❑ 16 Peanuts Lowrey DP	15.00	7.50
❑ 17 Billy Hitchcock	30.00	15.00
❑ 18 Ted Lepcio DP	15.00	7.50
❑ 19 Mel Parnell DP	20.00	10.00
❑ 20 Hank Thompson	40.00	25.00
❑ 21 Billy Johnson	30.00	15.00
❑ 22 Howie Fox	30.00	15.00
❑ 23 Toby Atwell DP	15.00	7.50
❑ 24 Ferris Fain	40.00	25.00
❑ 25 Ray Boone	40.00	25.00
❑ 26 Dale Mitchell DP	20.00	10.00
❑ 27 Roy Campanella DP	300.00	175.00
❑ 28 Eddie Pellagrini	30.00	15.00
❑ 29 Hal Jeffcoat	30.00	15.00
❑ 30 Willard Nixon	30.00	15.00
❑ 31 Ewell Blackwell	60.00	35.00
❑ 32 Clyde Vollmer	30.00	15.00
❑ 33 Bob Kennedy DP	15.00	7.50
❑ 34 George Shuba	40.00	25.00
❑ 35 Irv Noren DP	15.00	7.50
❑ 36 Johnny Groth DP	15.00	7.50
❑ 37 Eddie Mathews DP	250.00	150.00
❑ 38 Jim Hearn DP	15.00	7.50
❑ 39 Eddie Miksis	30.00	15.00
❑ 40 John Lipon	30.00	15.00
❑ 41 Enos Slaughter	80.00	50.00
❑ 42 Gus Zernial DP	20.00	10.00
❑ 43 Gil McDougald	60.00	35.00
❑ 44 Ellis Kinder SP	60.00	35.00
❑ 45 Grady Hatton DP	15.00	7.50
❑ 46 Johnny Klippstein DP	15.00	7.50
❑ 47 Bubba Church DP	15.00	7.50
❑ 48 Bob Del Greco DP	15.00	7.50
❑ 49 Faye Throneberry DP	15.00	7.50
❑ 50 Chuck Dressen DP	20.00	10.00
❑ 51 Frank Campos DP	15.00	7.50
❑ 52 Ted Gray DP	15.00	7.50
❑ 53 Sherm Lollar DP	20.00	10.00
❑ 54 Bob Feller DP	150.00	90.00
❑ 55 Maurice McDermott DP	15.00	7.50
❑ 56 Gerry Staley DP	15.00	7.50
❑ 57 Carl Scheib	30.00	15.00
❑ 58 George Metkovich	30.00	15.00
❑ 59 Karl Drews DP	15.00	7.50
❑ 60 Cloyd Boyer DP	15.00	7.50
❑ 61 Early Wynn SP	125.00	75.00
❑ 62 Monte Irvin DP	40.00	25.00
❑ 63 Gus Niarhos DP	15.00	7.50
❑ 64 Dave Philley	30.00	15.00
❑ 65 Earl Harrist	30.00	15.00
❑ 66 Minnie Minoso	60.00	35.00
❑ 67 Roy Sievers DP	20.00	10.00
❑ 68 Del Rice	30.00	15.00
❑ 69 Dick Brodowski	30.00	15.00
❑ 70 Ed Yuhas	30.00	15.00
❑ 71 Tony Bartirome	30.00	15.00
❑ 72 Fred Hutchinson SP	60.00	35.00
❑ 73 Eddie Robinson	30.00	15.00
❑ 74 Joe Rossi	30.00	15.00
❑ 75 Mike Garcia	40.00	25.00
❑ 76 Pee Wee Reese	175.00	100.00
❑ 77 Johnny Mize DP	80.00	50.00
❑ 78 Red Schoendienst	80.00	50.00
❑ 79 Johnny Wyrostek	30.00	15.00
❑ 80 Jim Hegan	40.00	25.00
❑ 81 Joe Black SP	80.00	50.00
❑ 82 Mickey Mantle	3000.00	2000.00
❑ 83 Howie Pollet	30.00	15.00
❑ 84 Bob Hooper DP	15.00	7.50
❑ 85 Bobby Morgan DP	15.00	7.50
❑ 86 Billy Martin	125.00	75.00
❑ 87 Ed Lopat	60.00	35.00
❑ 88 Willie Jones DP	15.00	7.50
❑ 89 Chuck Stobbs DP	15.00	7.50
❑ 90 Hank Edwards DP	15.00	7.50
❑ 91 Ebba St.Claire DP	15.00	7.50
❑ 92 Paul Minner DP	15.00	7.50
❑ 93 Hal Rice DP	15.00	7.50
❑ 94 Bill Kennedy DP	15.00	7.50
❑ 95 Willard Marshall DP	15.00	7.50
❑ 96 Virgil Trucks	40.00	25.00
❑ 97 Don Kolloway DP	15.00	7.50
❑ 98 Cal Abrams DP	15.00	7.50
❑ 99 Dave Madison	30.00	15.00
❑ 100 Bill Miller	30.00	15.00
❑ 101 Ted Wilks	30.00	15.00
❑ 102 Connie Ryan DP	15.00	7.50
❑ 103 Joe Astroth DP	15.00	7.50
❑ 104 Yogi Berra	400.00	250.00
❑ 105 Joe Nuxhall DP	20.00	10.00
❑ 106 Johnny Antonelli	40.00	25.00
❑ 107 Danny O'Connell DP	15.00	7.50
❑ 108 Bob Porterfield DP	15.00	7.50
❑ 109 Alvin Dark	60.00	35.00
❑ 110 Herman Wehmeier DP	15.00	7.50
❑ 111 Hank Sauer DP	15.00	7.50
❑ 112 Ned Garver DP	15.00	7.50
❑ 113 Jerry Priddy	30.00	15.00
❑ 114 Phil Rizzuto	250.00	150.00
❑ 115 George Spencer	30.00	15.00
❑ 116 Frank Smith DP	15.00	7.50
❑ 117 Sid Gordon DP	15.00	7.50
❑ 118 Gus Bell DP	20.00	10.00
❑ 119 Johnny Sain SP	60.00	35.00
❑ 120 Davey Williams	40.00	25.00
❑ 121 Walt Dropo	40.00	25.00
❑ 122 Elmer Valo	30.00	15.00
❑ 123 Tommy Byrne DP	15.00	7.50
❑ 124 Sibby Sisti DP	15.00	7.50
❑ 125 Dick Williams DP	20.00	10.00
❑ 126 Bill Connelly DP RC	15.00	7.50
❑ 127 Clint Courtney DP RC	15.00	7.50
❑ 128 Wilmer Mizell DP	20.00	10.00
❑ 129 Keith Thomas RC	30.00	15.00
❑ 130 Turk Lown DP	15.00	7.50
❑ 131 Harry Byrd DP RC	15.00	7.50
❑ 132 Tom Morgan	30.00	15.00
❑ 133 Gil Coan	30.00	15.00
❑ 134 Rube Walker	40.00	25.00
❑ 135 Al Rosen DP	20.00	10.00
❑ 136 Ken Heintzelman DP	15.00	7.50
❑ 137 John Rutherford DP	15.00	7.50
❑ 138 George Kell	80.00	50.00
❑ 139 Sammy White	30.00	15.00
❑ 140 Tommy Glaviano	30.00	15.00
❑ 141 Allie Reynolds DP	15.00	7.50
❑ 142 Vic Wertz	40.00	25.00
❑ 143 Billy Pierce	60.00	35.00
❑ 144 Bob Schultz DP	15.00	7.50
❑ 145 Harry Dorish DP	15.00	7.50
❑ 146 Granny Hamner	30.00	15.00
❑ 147 Warren Spahn	175.00	100.00
❑ 148 Mickey Grasso	30.00	15.00
❑ 149 Dom DiMaggio DP	15.00	7.50
❑ 150 Harry Simpson DP	15.00	7.50
❑ 151 Hoyt Wilhelm	100.00	60.00
❑ 152 Bob Adams DP	15.00	7.50
❑ 153 Andy Seminick DP	15.00	7.50
❑ 154 Dick Groat	40.00	25.00
❑ 155 Dutch Leonard	30.00	15.00
❑ 156 Jim Rivera DP RC	20.00	10.00
❑ 157 Bob Addis DP	15.00	7.50
❑ 158 Johnny Logan RC	40.00	25.00
❑ 159 Wayne Terwilliger DP	15.00	7.50
❑ 160 Bob Young	30.00	15.00
❑ 161 Vern Bickford DP	15.00	7.50
❑ 162 Ted Kluszewski	60.00	35.00
❑ 163 Fred Hatfield DP	15.00	7.50
❑ 164 Frank Shea DP	15.00	7.50
❑ 165 Billy Hoeft	30.00	15.00
❑ 166 Billy Hunter RC	25.00	12.50
❑ 167 Art Schult RC	25.00	12.50
❑ 168 Willard Schmidt RC	25.00	12.50
❑ 169 Dizzy Trout	30.00	15.00
❑ 170 Bill Werle	25.00	12.50
❑ 171 Bill Glynn RC	25.00	12.50
❑ 172 Rip Repulski RC	25.00	12.50
❑ 173 Preston Ward	25.00	12.50
❑ 174 Billy Loes	30.00	15.00
❑ 175 Ron Kline RC	25.00	12.50
❑ 176 Don Hoak RC	40.00	25.00
❑ 177 Jim Dyck RC	25.00	12.50
❑ 178 Jim Waugh RC	25.00	12.50
❑ 179 Gene Hermanski	25.00	12.50
❑ 180 Virgil Stallcup	25.00	12.50
❑ 181 Al Zarilla	25.00	12.50
❑ 182 Bobby Hofman	25.00	12.50
❑ 183 Stu Miller RC	40.00	25.00
❑ 184 Hal Brown RC	25.00	12.50
❑ 185 Jim Pendleton RC	25.00	12.50
❑ 186 Charlie Bishop RC	25.00	12.50
❑ 187 Jim Fridley	25.00	12.50
❑ 188 Andy Carey RC	40.00	25.00
❑ 189 Ray Jablonski RC	25.00	12.50
❑ 190 Dixie Walker CO	30.00	15.00
❑ 191 Ralph Kiner	80.00	50.00
❑ 192 Wally Westlake	25.00	12.50
❑ 193 Mike Clark RC	25.00	12.50
❑ 194 Eddie Kazak	25.00	12.50
❑ 195 Ed McGhee RC	25.00	12.50
❑ 196 Bob Keegan RC	25.00	12.50
❑ 197 Del Crandall	40.00	25.00
❑ 198 Forrest Main	25.00	12.50
❑ 199 Marion Fricano RC	25.00	12.50
❑ 200 Gordon Goldsberry	25.00	12.50
❑ 201 Paul LaPalme	25.00	12.50
❑ 202 Carl Sawatski RC	25.00	12.50
❑ 203 Cliff Fannin	25.00	12.50
❑ 204 Dick Bokelman RC	25.00	12.50
❑ 205 Vern Benson RC	25.00	12.50
❑ 206 Ed Bailey RC	30.00	15.00
❑ 207 Whitey Ford	300.00	175.00
❑ 208 Jim Wilson	25.00	12.50
❑ 209 Jim Greengrass RC	25.00	12.50
❑ 210 Bob Cerv RC	40.00	25.00
❑ 211 J.W. Porter RC	25.00	12.50
❑ 212 Jack Dittmer RC	25.00	12.50
❑ 213 Ray Scarborough	25.00	12.50
❑ 214 Bill Bruton RC	40.00	25.00
❑ 215 Gene Conley RC	30.00	15.00
❑ 216 Jim Hughes RC	25.00	12.50
❑ 217 Murray Wall RC	25.00	12.50
❑ 218 Les Fusselman	25.00	12.50
❑ 219 Pete Runnels UER (Photo actually Don Johnson)	30.00	15.00
❑ 220 Satchel Paige UER	600.00	350.00
❑ 221 Bob Milliken RC	100.00	50.00
❑ 222 Vic Janowicz DP RC	50.00	25.00
❑ 223 Johnny O'Brien DP RC	50.00	25.00
❑ 224 Lou Sleater DP	50.00	25.00
❑ 225 Bobby Shantz	125.00	75.00

❑ 226 Ed Erautt 100.00 50.00
❑ 227 Morrie Martin 100.00 50.00
❑ 228 Hal Newhouser 150.00 90.00
❑ 229 Rocky Krsnich RC 100.00 50.00
❑ 230 Johnny Lindell DP 50.00 25.00
❑ 231 Solly Hemus DP 50.00 25.00
❑ 232 Dick Kokos 100.00 50.00
❑ 233 Al Aber RC 100.00 50.00
❑ 234 Ray Murray DP 50.00 25.00
❑ 235 John Hetki DP RC 50.00 25.00
❑ 236 Harry Perkowski DP 50.00 25.00
❑ 237 Bud Podbielan DP 50.00 25.00
❑ 238 Cal Hogue DP RC 50.00 25.00
❑ 239 Jim Delsing 100.00 50.00
❑ 240 Fred Marsh 100.00 50.00
❑ 241 Al Sima DP 50.00 25.00
❑ 242 Charlie Silvera 125.00 75.00
❑ 243 Carlos Bernier DP RC 50.00 25.00
❑ 244 Willie Mays 2500.00 1500.00
❑ 245 Bill Norman CO 100.00 50.00
❑ 246 Roy Face RC DP RC 80.00 50.00
❑ 247 Mike Sandlock DP RC 50.00 25.00
❑ 248 Gene Stephens DP RC 50.00 25.00
❑ 249 Eddie O'Brien RC 100.00 50.00
❑ 250 Bob Wilson RC 100.00 50.00
❑ 251 Sid Hudson 100.00 50.00
❑ 252 Hank Foiles RC 100.00 50.00
❑ 253 Does not exist
❑ 254 Preacher Roe DP 80.00 50.00
❑ 255 Dixie Howell 100.00 50.00
❑ 256 Les Peden RC 100.00 50.00
❑ 257 Bob Boyd RC 100.00 50.00
❑ 258 Jim Gilliam RC 400.00 250.00
❑ 259 Roy McMillan DP 50.00 25.00
❑ 260 Sam Calderone RC 100.00 50.00
❑ 261 Does not exist
❑ 262 Bob Oldis RC 100.00 50.00
❑ 263 Johnny Podres RC 300.00 175.00
❑ 264 Gene Woodling DP 60.00 30.00
❑ 265 Jackie Jensen 125.00 75.00
❑ 266 Bob Cain 100.00 50.00
❑ 267 Does not exist
❑ 268 Does not exist
❑ 269 Duane Pillette 100.00 50.00
❑ 270 Vern Stephens 125.00 75.00
❑ 271 Does not exist
❑ 272 Bill Antonello RC 100.00 50.00
❑ 273 Harvey Haddix RC 150.00 90.00
❑ 274 John Riddle CO 100.00 50.00
❑ 275 Does not exist
❑ 276 Ken Raffensberger 100.00 50.00
❑ 277 Don Lund RC 100.00 50.00
❑ 278 Willie Miranda RC 100.00 50.00
❑ 279 Joe Coleman DP 50.00 25.00
❑ 280 Milt Bolling RC 350.00 200.00

1954 Topps

❑ COMPLETE SET (250) 8000.00 5000.00
❑ COMMON (1-50/76-250) 15.00 7.50
❑ COMMON CARD (51-75) 25.00 12.50
❑ WRAP.(1-CENT, DATED) 200.00 150.00
❑ WRAP.(1-CENT, UNDAT) 150.00 100.00
❑ WRAP.(5-CENT, DATED) 300.00 250.00
❑ WRAP.(5-CENT, UNDAT) 250.00 200.00
❑ 1 Ted Williams 800.00 500.00
❑ 2 Gus Zernial 25.00 12.50
❑ 3 Monte Irvin 50.00 25.00
❑ 4 Hank Sauer 25.00 12.50
❑ 5 Ed Lopat 25.00 12.50
❑ 6 Pete Runnels 25.00 12.50
❑ 7 Ted Kluszewski 50.00 25.00
❑ 8 Bob Young 15.00 7.50
❑ 9 Harvey Haddix 25.00 12.50
❑ 10 Jackie Robinson 400.00 250.00
❑ 11 Paul Leslie Smith RC 15.00 7.50
❑ 12 Del Crandall 25.00 12.50
❑ 13 Billy Martin 100.00 60.00
❑ 14 Preacher Roe UER 25.00 12.50
❑ 15 Al Rosen 25.00 12.50
❑ 16 Vic Janowicz 25.00 12.50
❑ 17 Phil Rizzuto 125.00 75.00
❑ 18 Walt Dropo 25.00 12.50
❑ 19 Johnny Lipon 15.00 7.50
❑ 20 Warren Spahn 125.00 75.00
❑ 21 Bobby Shantz 25.00 12.50
❑ 22 Jim Greengrass 15.00 7.50
❑ 23 Luke Easter 25.00 12.50
❑ 24 Granny Hamner 15.00 7.50
❑ 25 Harvey Kuenn RC 40.00 20.00
❑ 26 Ray Jablonski 15.00 7.50
❑ 27 Ferris Fain 25.00 12.50
❑ 28 Paul Minner 15.00 7.50
❑ 29 Jim Hegan 25.00 12.50
❑ 30 Eddie Mathews 100.00 60.00
❑ 31 Johnny Klippstein 15.00 7.50
❑ 32 Duke Snider 200.00 125.00
❑ 33 Johnny Schmitz 15.00 7.50
❑ 34 Jim Rivera 15.00 7.50
❑ 35 Junior Gilliam 50.00 25.00
❑ 36 Hoyt Wilhelm 50.00 25.00
❑ 37 Whitey Ford 200.00 125.00
❑ 38 Eddie Stanky MG 25.00 12.50
❑ 39 Sherm Lollar 25.00 12.50
❑ 40 Mel Parnell 25.00 12.50
❑ 41 Willie Jones 15.00 7.50
❑ 42 Don Mueller 25.00 12.50
❑ 43 Dick Groat 25.00 12.50
❑ 44 Ned Garver 15.00 7.50
❑ 45 Richie Ashburn 80.00 50.00
❑ 46 Ken Raffensberger 15.00 7.50
❑ 47 Ellis Kinder 15.00 7.50
❑ 48 Billy Hunter 25.00 12.50
❑ 49 Ray Murray 15.00 7.50
❑ 50 Yogi Berra 300.00 175.00
❑ 51 Johnny Lindell 25.00 12.50
❑ 52 Vic Power RC 30.00 15.00
❑ 53 Jack Dittmer 25.00 12.50
❑ 54 Vern Stephens 30.00 15.00
❑ 55 Phil Cavarretta MG 30.00 15.00
❑ 56 Willie Miranda 25.00 12.50
❑ 57 Luis Aloma 25.00 12.50
❑ 58 Bob Wilson 25.00 12.50
❑ 59 Gene Conley 30.00 15.00
❑ 60 Frank Baumholtz 25.00 12.50
❑ 61 Bob Cain 25.00 12.50
❑ 62 Eddie Robinson 25.00 12.50
❑ 63 Johnny Pesky 30.00 15.00
❑ 64 Hank Thompson 25.00 12.50
❑ 65 Bob Swift CO 25.00 12.50
❑ 66 Ted Lepcio 25.00 12.50
❑ 67 Jim Willis RC 25.00 12.50
❑ 68 Sam Calderone 25.00 12.50
❑ 69 Bud Podbielan 25.00 12.50
❑ 70 Larry Doby 60.00 30.00
❑ 71 Frank Smith 25.00 12.50
❑ 72 Preston Ward 25.00 12.50
❑ 73 Wayne Terwilliger 25.00 12.50
❑ 74 Bill Taylor RC 25.00 12.50
❑ 75 Fred Haney MG RC 25.00 12.50
❑ 76 Bob Scheffing CO 15.00 7.50
❑ 77 Ray Boone 25.00 12.50
❑ 78 Ted Kazanski RC 15.00 7.50
❑ 79 Andy Pafko 25.00 12.50
❑ 80 Jackie Jensen 25.00 12.50
❑ 81 Dave Hoskins RC 15.00 7.50
❑ 82 Milt Bolling 15.00 7.50
❑ 83 Joe Collins 25.00 12.50
❑ 84 Dick Cole RC 15.00 7.50
❑ 85 Bob Turley RC 40.00 20.00
❑ 86 Billy Herman CO 25.00 12.50
❑ 87 Roy Face 25.00 12.50
❑ 88 Matt Batts 15.00 7.50
❑ 89 Howie Pollet 15.00 7.50
❑ 90 Willie Mays 800.00 500.00
❑ 91 Bob Oldis 15.00 7.50
❑ 92 Wally Westlake 15.00 7.50
❑ 93 Sid Hudson 15.00 7.50
❑ 94 Ernie Banks RC 1500.00 900.00
❑ 95 Hal Rice 15.00 7.50
❑ 96 Charlie Silvera 25.00 12.50
❑ 97 Jerald Hal Lane RC 15.00 7.50
❑ 98 Joe Black 40.00 20.00
❑ 99 Bobby Hofman 15.00 7.50
❑ 100 Bob Keegan 15.00 7.50
❑ 101 Gene Woodling 25.00 12.50
❑ 102 Gil Hodges 80.00 50.00
❑ 103 Jim Lemon RC 15.00 7.50
❑ 104 Mike Sandlock 15.00 7.50
❑ 105 Andy Carey 25.00 12.50
❑ 106 Dick Kokos 15.00 7.50
❑ 107 Duane Pillette 15.00 7.50
❑ 108 Thornton Kipper RC 15.00 7.50
❑ 109 Bill Bruton 25.00 12.50
❑ 110 Harry Dorish 15.00 7.50
❑ 111 Jim Delsing 15.00 7.50
❑ 112 Bill Renna RC 15.00 7.50
❑ 113 Bob Boyd 15.00 7.50
❑ 114 Dean Stone RC 15.00 7.50
❑ 115 Rip Repulski 15.00 7.50
❑ 116 Steve Bilko 15.00 7.50
❑ 117 Solly Hemus 15.00 7.50
❑ 118 Carl Scheib 15.00 7.50
❑ 119 Johnny Antonelli 25.00 12.50
❑ 120 Roy McMillan 25.00 12.50
❑ 121 Clem Labine 25.00 12.50
❑ 122 Johnny Logan 25.00 12.50
❑ 123 Bobby Adams 15.00 7.50
❑ 124 Marion Fricano 15.00 7.50
❑ 125 Harry Perkowski 15.00 7.50
❑ 126 Ben Wade 15.00 7.50
❑ 127 Steve O'Neill MG 15.00 7.50
❑ 128 Hank Aaron RC 1800.00 1000.00
❑ 129 Forrest Jacobs RC 15.00 7.50
❑ 130 Hank Bauer 25.00 12.50
❑ 131 Reno Bertoia RC 25.00 12.50
❑ 132 Tommy Lasorda RC 250.00 150.00
❑ 133 Del Baker CO 15.00 7.50
❑ 134 Cal Hogue 15.00 7.50
❑ 135 Joe Presko 15.00 7.50
❑ 136 Connie Ryan 15.00 7.50
❑ 137 Wally Moon RC 40.00 20.00
❑ 138 Bob Borkowski 15.00 7.50
❑ 139 J.O'Brien/E.O'Brien 50.00 25.00
❑ 140 Tom Wright 15.00 7.50
❑ 141 Joey Jay RC 25.00 12.50
❑ 142 Tom Poholsky 15.00 7.50
❑ 143 Rollie Hemsley CO 15.00 7.50
❑ 144 Bill Werle 15.00 7.50
❑ 145 Elmer Valo 15.00 7.50
❑ 146 Don Johnson 15.00 7.50
❑ 147 Johnny Riddle CO 15.00 7.50
❑ 148 Bob Trice RC 15.00 7.50
❑ 149 Al Robertson 15.00 7.50
❑ 150 Dick Kryhoski 15.00 7.50
❑ 151 Alex Grammas RC 15.00 7.50
❑ 152 Michael Blyzka RC 15.00 7.50
❑ 153 Al Walker 25.00 12.50
❑ 154 Mike Fornieles RC 15.00 7.50
❑ 155 Bob Kennedy 25.00 12.50
❑ 156 Joe Coleman 25.00 12.50
❑ 157 Don Lenhardt 25.00 12.50
❑ 158 Peanuts Lowrey 15.00 7.50
❑ 159 Dave Philley 15.00 7.50
❑ 160 Ralph Kress CO 15.00 7.50
❑ 161 John Hetki 15.00 7.50
❑ 162 Herman Wehmeier 15.00 7.50
❑ 163 Frank House 15.00 7.50
❑ 164 Stu Miller 25.00 12.50
❑ 165 Jim Pendleton 15.00 7.50
❑ 166 Johnny Podres 40.00 20.00
❑ 167 Don Lund 15.00 7.50
❑ 168 Morrie Martin 25.00 12.50
❑ 169 Jim Hughes 40.00 20.00
❑ 170 Dusty Rhodes RC 25.00 12.50
❑ 171 Leo Kiely 15.00 7.50
❑ 172 Harold Brown RC 15.00 7.50
❑ 173 Jack Harshman RC 15.00 7.50
❑ 174 Tom Qualters RC 15.00 7.50
❑ 175 Frank Leja RC 25.00 12.50
❑ 176 Robert Keely CO 15.00 7.50

❑ 177 Bob Milliken 15.00 7.50
❑ 178 Bill Glynn UER 15.00 7.50
❑ 179 Gair Allie RC 15.00 7.50
❑ 180 Wes Westrum 25.00 12.50
❑ 181 Mel Roach RC 15.00 7.50
❑ 182 Chuck Harmon RC 15.00 7.50
❑ 183 Earle Combs CO 25.00 12.50
❑ 184 Ed Bailey 15.00 7.50
❑ 185 Chuck Stobbs 15.00 7.50
❑ 186 Karl Olson 15.00 7.50
❑ 187 Heinie Manush CO 25.00 12.50
❑ 188 Dave Jolly RC 15.00 7.50
❑ 189 Bob Ross 15.00 7.50
❑ 190 Ray Herbert RC 15.00 7.50
❑ 191 Dick Schofield RC 25.00 12.50
❑ 192 Ellis Deal CO 15.00 7.50
❑ 193 Johnny Hopp CO 25.00 12.50
❑ 194 Bill Sarni RC 15.00 7.50
❑ 195 Billy Consolo RC 15.00 7.50
❑ 196 Stan Jok RC 15.00 7.50
❑ 197 Lynwood Rowe CO 25.00 12.50
❑ 198 Carl Sawatski 15.00 7.50
❑ 199 Glenn (Rocky) Nelson 15.00 7.50
❑ 200 Larry Jansen 25.00 12.50
❑ 201 Al Kaline RC 700.00 400.00
❑ 202 Bob Purkey RC 25.00 12.50
❑ 203 Harry Brecheen CO 25.00 12.50
❑ 204 Angel Scull RC 15.00 7.50
❑ 205 Johnny Sain 40.00 20.00
❑ 206 Ray Crone RC 15.00 7.50
❑ 207 Tom Oliver CO RC 15.00 7.50
❑ 208 Grady Hatton 15.00 7.50
❑ 209 Chuck Thompson RC 15.00 7.50
❑ 210 Bob Buhl RC 25.00 12.50
❑ 211 Don Hoak 25.00 12.50
❑ 212 Bob Micelotta RC 15.00 7.50
❑ 213 Johnny Fitzpatrick CO RC 15.00 7.50
❑ 214 Arnie Portocarrero RC 15.00 7.50
❑ 215 Ed McGhee 25.00 12.50
❑ 216 Al Sima 15.00 7.50
❑ 217 Paul Schreiber CO RC 15.00 7.50
❑ 218 Fred Marsh 15.00 7.50
❑ 219 Chuck Kress RC 15.00 7.50
❑ 220 Ruben Gomez RC 25.00 12.50
❑ 221 Dick Brodowski 15.00 7.50
❑ 222 Bill Wilson RC 15.00 7.50
❑ 223 Joe Haynes CO 15.00 7.50
❑ 224 Dick Weik RC 15.00 7.50
❑ 225 Don Liddle RC 15.00 7.50
❑ 226 Jehosie Heard RC 25.00 12.50
❑ 227 Buster Mills CO RC 15.00 7.50
❑ 228 Gene Hermanski 15.00 7.50
❑ 229 Bob Talbot RC 15.00 7.50
❑ 230 Bob Kuzava 25.00 12.50
❑ 231 Roy Smalley 15.00 7.50
❑ 232 Lou Limmer RC 15.00 7.50
❑ 233 Augie Galan CO 15.00 7.50
❑ 234 Jerry Lynch RC 15.00 7.50
❑ 235 Vern Law 25.00 12.50
❑ 236 Paul Penson RC 15.00 7.50
❑ 237 Mike Ryba CO RC 15.00 7.50
❑ 238 Al Aber 15.00 7.50
❑ 239 Bill Skowron RC 100.00 60.00
❑ 240 Sam Mele 25.00 12.50
❑ 241 Robert Miller RC 15.00 7.50
❑ 242 Curt Roberts RC 15.00 7.50
❑ 243 Ray Blades CO RC 15.00 7.50
❑ 244 Leroy Wheat RC 15.00 7.50
❑ 245 Roy Sievers 25.00 12.50
❑ 246 Howie Fox 15.00 7.50
❑ 247 Ed Mayo CO 15.00 7.50
❑ 248 Al Smith RC 25.00 12.50
❑ 249 Wilmer Mizell 25.00 12.50
❑ 250 Ted Williams 1000.00 500.00

1955 Topps

❑ COMPLETE SET (206) 8000.00 5000.00
❑ COMMON CARD (1-150) 12.00 6.00
❑ COMMON CARD (151-160) 20.00 10.00
❑ COMMON CARD (161-210) 30.00 15.00
❑ NOT ISSUED (175/186/203/209)
❑ WRAP.(1-CENT, DATED) 150.00 100.00
❑ WRAP.(1-CENT, UNDAT) 50.00 40.00
❑ WRAP.(5-CENT, DATED) 150.00 100.00
❑ WRAP.(5-CENT, UNDAT) 100.00 75.00
❑ 1 Dusty Rhodes 125.00 75.00

❑ 2 Ted Williams 700.00 400.00
❑ 3 Art Fowler RC 15.00 7.50
❑ 4 Al Kaline 150.00 90.00
❑ 5 Jim Gilliam 40.00 20.00
❑ 6 Stan Hack MG RC 25.00 12.50
❑ 7 Jim Hegan 15.00 7.50
❑ 8 Harold Smith RC 12.00 6.00
❑ 9 Robert Miller 12.00 6.00
❑ 10 Bob Keegan 12.00 6.00
❑ 11 Ferris Fain 15.00 7.50
❑ 12 Vernon (Jake) Thies RC 12.00 6.00
❑ 13 Fred Marsh 12.00 6.00
❑ 14 Jim Finigan RC 12.00 6.00
❑ 15 Jim Pendleton 12.00 6.00
❑ 16 Roy Sievers 15.00 7.50
❑ 17 Bobby Hofman 12.00 6.00
❑ 18 Russ Kemmerer RC 12.00 6.00
❑ 19 Billy Herman CO 15.00 7.50
❑ 20 Andy Carey 15.00 7.50
❑ 21 Alex Grammas 12.00 6.00
❑ 22 Bill Skowron 40.00 20.00
❑ 23 Jack Parks RC 12.00 6.00
❑ 24 Hal Newhouser 40.00 20.00
❑ 25 Johnny Podres 25.00 12.50
❑ 26 Dick Groat 15.00 7.50
❑ 27 Billy Gardner RC 15.00 7.50
❑ 28 Ernie Banks 200.00 125.00
❑ 29 Herman Wehmeier 12.00 6.00
❑ 30 Vic Power 15.00 7.50
❑ 31 Warren Spahn 100.00 60.00
❑ 32 Warren McGhee RC 12.00 6.00
❑ 33 Tom Qualters 12.00 6.00
❑ 34 Wayne Terwilliger 12.00 6.00
❑ 35 Dave Jolly 12.00 6.00
❑ 36 Leo Kiely 12.00 6.00
❑ 37 Joe Cunningham RC 15.00 7.50
❑ 38 Bob Turley 15.00 7.50
❑ 39 Bill Glynn 12.00 6.00
❑ 40 Don Hoak 15.00 7.50
❑ 41 Chuck Stobbs 12.00 6.00
❑ 42 John (Windy) McCall RC 12.00 6.00
❑ 43 Harvey Haddix 15.00 7.50
❑ 44 Harold Valentine RC 12.00 6.00
❑ 45 Hank Sauer 15.00 7.50
❑ 46 Ted Kazanski 12.00 6.00
❑ 47 Hank Aaron 400.00 250.00
❑ 48 Bob Kennedy 15.00 7.50
❑ 49 J.W. Porter 12.00 6.00
❑ 50 Jackie Robinson 500.00 300.00
❑ 51 Jim Hughes 15.00 7.50
❑ 52 Bill Tremel RC 12.00 6.00
❑ 53 Bill Taylor 12.00 6.00
❑ 54 Lou Limmer 12.00 6.00
❑ 55 Rip Repulski 12.00 6.00
❑ 56 Ray Jablonski 12.00 6.00
❑ 57 Billy O'Dell RC 12.00 6.00
❑ 58 Jim Rivera 12.00 6.00
❑ 59 Gair Allie 12.00 6.00
❑ 60 Dean Stone 12.00 6.00
❑ 61 Forrest Jacobs 12.00 6.00
❑ 62 Thornton Kipper 12.00 6.00
❑ 63 Joe Collins 15.00 7.50
❑ 64 Gus Triandos RC 15.00 7.50
❑ 65 Ray Boone 15.00 7.50
❑ 66 Ron Jackson RC 12.00 6.00
❑ 67 Wally Moon 15.00 7.50
❑ 68 Jim Davis RC 12.00 6.00
❑ 69 Ed Bailey 15.00 7.50

❑ 70 Al Rosen 15.00 7.50
❑ 71 Ruben Gomez 12.00 6.00
❑ 72 Karl Olson 12.00 6.00
❑ 73 Jack Shepard RC 12.00 6.00
❑ 74 Bob Borkowski 12.00 6.00
❑ 75 Sandy Amoros RC 40.00 20.00
❑ 76 Howie Pollet 12.00 6.00
❑ 77 Arnie Portocarrero 12.00 6.00
❑ 78 Gordon Jones RC 12.00 6.00
❑ 79 Clyde (Danny) Schell RC 12.00 6.00
❑ 80 Bob Grim RC 15.00 7.50
❑ 81 Gene Conley 15.00 7.50
❑ 82 Chuck Harmon 12.00 6.00
❑ 83 Tom Brewer RC 12.00 6.00
❑ 84 Camilo Pascual RC 15.00 7.50
❑ 85 Don Mossi RC 25.00 12.50
❑ 86 Bill Wilson 12.00 6.00
❑ 87 Frank House 12.00 6.00
❑ 88 Bob Skinner RC 15.00 7.50
❑ 89 Joe Frazier RC 15.00 7.50
❑ 90 Karl Spooner RC 15.00 7.50
❑ 91 Milt Bolling 12.00 6.00
❑ 92 Don Zimmer RC 25.00 12.50
❑ 93 Steve Bilko 12.00 6.00
❑ 94 Reno Bertoia 12.00 6.00
❑ 95 Preston Ward 12.00 6.00
❑ 96 Chuck Bishop 12.00 6.00
❑ 97 Carlos Paula RC 12.00 6.00
❑ 98 John Riddle CO 12.00 6.00
❑ 99 Frank Leja 12.00 6.00
❑ 100 Monte Irvin 40.00 20.00
❑ 101 Johnny Gray RC 12.00 6.00
❑ 102 Wally Westlake 12.00 6.00
❑ 103 Chuck White RC 12.00 6.00
❑ 104 Jack Harshman 12.00 6.00
❑ 105 Chuck Diering 12.00 6.00
❑ 106 Frank Sullivan RC 12.00 6.00
❑ 107 Curt Roberts 12.00 6.00
❑ 108 Rube Walker 15.00 7.50
❑ 109 Ed Lopat 15.00 7.50
❑ 110 Gus Zernial 15.00 7.50
❑ 111 Bob Milliken 15.00 7.50
❑ 112 Nelson King RC 12.00 6.00
❑ 113 Harry Brecheen CO 15.00 7.50
❑ 114 Louis Ortiz RC 12.00 6.00
❑ 115 Ellis Kinder 12.00 6.00
❑ 116 Tom Hurd RC 12.00 6.00
❑ 117 Mel Roach 12.00 6.00
❑ 118 Bob Purkey 12.00 6.00
❑ 119 Bob Lennon RC 12.00 6.00
❑ 120 Ted Kluszewski 80.00 50.00
❑ 121 Bill Renna 12.00 6.00
❑ 122 Carl Sawatski 12.00 6.00
❑ 123 Sandy Koufax RC 1200.00 700.00
❑ 124 Harmon Killebrew RC 250.00 150.00
❑ 125 Ken Boyer RC 80.00 50.00
❑ 126 Dick Hall RC 12.00 6.00
❑ 127 Dale Long RC 15.00 7.50
❑ 128 Ted Lepcio 12.00 6.00
❑ 129 Elvin Tappe 15.00 7.50
❑ 130 Mayo Smith MG RC 12.00 6.00
❑ 131 Grady Hatton 12.00 6.00
❑ 132 Bob Trice 12.00 6.00
❑ 133 Dave Hoskins 12.00 6.00
❑ 134 Joey Jay 15.00 7.50
❑ 135 Johnny O'Brien 15.00 7.50
❑ 136 Veston (Bunky) Stewart RC 12.00 6.00
❑ 137 Harry Elliott RC 12.00 6.00
❑ 138 Ray Herbert 12.00 6.00
❑ 139 Steve Kraly RC 12.00 6.00
❑ 140 Mel Parnell 15.00 7.50
❑ 141 Tom Wright 12.00 6.00
❑ 142 Jerry Lynch 15.00 7.50
❑ 143 John Schofield 15.00 7.50
❑ 144 Joe Amalfitano RC 12.00 6.00
❑ 145 Elmer Valo 12.00 6.00
❑ 146 Dick Donovan RC 12.00 6.00
❑ 147 Hugh Pepper RC 12.00 6.00
❑ 148 Hector Brown 12.00 6.00
❑ 149 Ray Crone 12.00 6.00
❑ 150 Mike Higgins MG 12.00 6.00
❑ 151 Ralph Kress CO 20.00 10.00
❑ 152 Harry Agganis RC 100.00 60.00
❑ 153 Bud Podbielan 25.00 12.50
❑ 154 Willie Miranda 20.00 10.00
❑ 155 Eddie Mathews 200.00 125.00

Card		
❑ 156 Joe Black	50.00	30.00
❑ 157 Robert Miller	20.00	10.00
❑ 158 Tommy Carroll RC	25.00	12.50
❑ 159 Johnny Schmitz	20.00	10.00
❑ 160 Ray Narleski RC	20.00	10.00
❑ 161 Chuck Tanner RC	40.00	20.00
❑ 162 Joe Coleman	30.00	15.00
❑ 163 Faye Throneberry	30.00	15.00
❑ 164 Roberto Clemente RC	2200.00	1400.00
❑ 165 Don Johnson	30.00	15.00
❑ 166 Hank Bauer	80.00	50.00
❑ 167 Tom Casagrande RC	30.00	15.00
❑ 168 Duane Pillette	30.00	15.00
❑ 169 Bob Oldis	40.00	20.00
❑ 170 Jim Pearce DP RC	15.00	7.50
❑ 171 Dick Brodowski	30.00	15.00
❑ 172 Frank Baumholtz DP	15.00	7.50
❑ 173 Bob Kline RC	30.00	15.00
❑ 174 Rudy Minarcin RC	30.00	15.00
❑ 175 Does not exist		
❑ 176 Norm Zauchin RC	30.00	15.00
❑ 177 Al Robertson	30.00	15.00
❑ 178 Bobby Adams	30.00	15.00
❑ 179 Jim Bolger RC	30.00	15.00
❑ 180 Clem Labine	60.00	30.00
❑ 181 Roy McMillan	40.00	20.00
❑ 182 Humberto Robinson RC	30.00	15.00
❑ 183 Anthony Jacobs RC	30.00	15.00
❑ 184 Harry Perkowski DP	15.00	7.50
❑ 185 Don Ferrarese RC	30.00	15.00
❑ 186 Does not exist		
❑ 187 Gil Hodges	175.00	100.00
❑ 188 Charlie Silvera DP	15.00	7.50
❑ 189 Phil Rizzuto	175.00	100.00
❑ 190 Gene Woodling	40.00	20.00
❑ 191 Eddie Stanky MG	40.00	20.00
❑ 192 Jim Delsing	40.00	20.00
❑ 193 Johnny Sain	60.00	30.00
❑ 194 Willie Mays	600.00	350.00
❑ 195 Ed Roebuck RC	60.00	30.00
❑ 196 Gale Wade RC	30.00	15.00
❑ 197 Al Smith	60.00	30.00
❑ 198 Yogi Berra	300.00	175.00
❑ 199 Bert Hamric RC	40.00	20.00
❑ 200 Jackie Jensen	60.00	30.00
❑ 201 Sherman Lollar	40.00	20.00
❑ 202 Jim Owens RC	30.00	15.00
❑ 203 Does not exist		
❑ 204 Frank Smith	30.00	15.00
❑ 205 Gene Freese RC	40.00	20.00
❑ 206 Pete Daley RC	30.00	15.00
❑ 207 Billy Consolo	30.00	15.00
❑ 208 Ray Moore RC	40.00	20.00
❑ 209 Does not exist		
❑ 210 Duke Snider	600.00	350.00

1956 Topps

Card		
❑ COMPLETE SET (340)	8000.00	5000.00
❑ COMMON CARD (1-100)	10.00	5.00
❑ COMMON CARD (101-180)	12.00	6.00
❑ COMMON CARD (261-340)	12.00	6.00
❑ COMMON CARD (181-260)	15.00	7.50
❑ WRAP.(1-CENT)	250.00	200.00
❑ WRAP.(1-CENT, REPEAT)	100.00	75.00
❑ WRAPPER (5-CENT)	200.00	150.00
❑ 1 Will Harridge PRES	125.00	75.00
❑ 2 Warren Giles PRES DP	50.00	30.00
❑ 3 Elmer Valo	15.00	7.50
❑ 4 Carlos Paula	15.00	7.50
❑ 5 Ted Williams	500.00	300.00
❑ 6 Ray Boone	25.00	15.00
❑ 7 Ron Negray RC	10.00	5.00
❑ 8 Walter Alston MG RC	40.00	25.00
❑ 9 Ruben Gomez DP	10.00	5.00
❑ 10 Warren Spahn	120.00	70.00
❑ 11A Chicago Cubs TC Center	30.00	15.00
❑ 11B Chicago Cubs TC D'55	80.00	50.00
❑ 11C Chicago Cubs TC Left	30.00	15.00
❑ 12 Andy Carey	15.00	7.50
❑ 13 Roy Face	15.00	7.50
❑ 14 Ken Boyer DP	15.00	7.50
❑ 15 Ernie Banks DP	100.00	60.00
❑ 16 Hector Lopez RC	15.00	7.50
❑ 17 Gene Conley	15.00	7.50
❑ 18 Dick Donovan	10.00	5.00
❑ 19 Chuck Diering DP	10.00	5.00
❑ 20 Al Kaline	125.00	75.00
❑ 21 Joe Collins DP	15.00	7.50
❑ 22 Jim Finigan	10.00	5.00
❑ 23 Fred Marsh	10.00	5.00
❑ 24 Dick Groat	15.00	7.50
❑ 25 Ted Kluszewski	80.00	50.00
❑ 25A Ted Kluszewski GB		
❑ 26 Grady Hatton	10.00	5.00
❑ 27 Nelson Burbrink DP RC	10.00	5.00
❑ 28 Bobby Hofman	10.00	5.00
❑ 29 Jack Harshman	10.00	5.00
❑ 30 Jackie Robinson DP	250.00	150.00
❑ 31 Hank Aaron UER DP	350.00	200.00
❑ 32 Frank House	10.00	5.00
❑ 33 Roberto Clemente	400.00	250.00
❑ 34 Tom Brewer DP	10.00	5.00
❑ 35 Al Rosen	15.00	7.50
❑ 36 Rudy Minarcin	15.00	7.50
❑ 37 Alex Grammas	10.00	5.00
❑ 38 Bob Kennedy	15.00	7.50
❑ 39 Don Mossi	15.00	7.50
❑ 40 Bob Turley	15.00	7.50
❑ 41 Hank Sauer	15.00	7.50
❑ 42 Sandy Amoros	25.00	15.00
❑ 43 Ray Moore	10.00	5.00
❑ 44 Windy McCall	10.00	5.00
❑ 45 Gus Zernial	15.00	7.50
❑ 46 Gene Freese DP	10.00	5.00
❑ 47 Art Fowler	10.00	5.00
❑ 48 Jim Hegan	15.00	7.50
❑ 49 Pedro Ramos RC	10.00	5.00
❑ 50 Dusty Rhodes DP	15.00	7.50
❑ 51 Ernie Oravetz RC	10.00	5.00
❑ 52 Bob Grim DP	15.00	7.50
❑ 53 Arnie Portocarrero	10.00	5.00
❑ 54 Bob Keegan	10.00	5.00
❑ 55 Wally Moon	15.00	7.50
❑ 56 Dale Long	15.00	7.50
❑ 57 Duke Maas RC	10.00	5.00
❑ 58 Ed Roebuck	25.00	15.00
❑ 59 Jose Santiago RC	10.00	5.00
❑ 60 Mayo Smith MG DP	10.00	5.00
❑ 61 Bill Skowron	25.00	15.00
❑ 62 Hal Smith	15.00	7.50
❑ 63 Roger Craig RC	40.00	25.00
❑ 64 Luis Arroyo RC	10.00	5.00
❑ 65 Johnny O'Brien	15.00	7.50
❑ 66 Bob Speake DP RC	10.00	5.00
❑ 67 Vic Power	15.00	7.50
❑ 68 Chuck Stobbs	10.00	5.00
❑ 69 Chuck Tanner	15.00	7.50
❑ 70 Jim Rivera	10.00	5.00
❑ 71 Frank Sullivan	10.00	5.00
❑ 72A Philadelphia Phillies TC Center	30.00	15.00
❑ 72B Philadelphia Phillies TC D'55	80.00	50.00
❑ 72C Philadelphia Phillies TC Left DP	30.00	15.00
❑ 73 Wayne Terwilliger	10.00	5.00
❑ 74 Jim King RC	10.00	5.00
❑ 75 Roy Sievers DP	15.00	7.50
❑ 76 Ray Crone	10.00	5.00
❑ 77 Harvey Haddix	15.00	7.50
❑ 78 Herman Wehmeier	10.00	5.00
❑ 79 Sandy Koufax	350.00	200.00
❑ 80 Gus Triandos DP	10.00	5.00
❑ 81 Wally Westlake	10.00	5.00
❑ 82 Bill Renna DP	10.00	5.00
❑ 83 Karl Spooner	15.00	7.50
❑ 84 Babe Birrer RC	10.00	5.00
❑ 85A Cleveland Indians TC Center	30.00	15.00
❑ 85B Cleveland Indians TC D'55	80.00	50.00
❑ 85C Cleveland Indians TC Left	30.00	15.00
❑ 86 Ray Jablonski DP	10.00	5.00
❑ 87 Dean Stone	10.00	5.00
❑ 88 Johnny Kucks RC	15.00	7.50
❑ 89 Norm Zauchin	10.00	5.00
❑ 90A Cincinnati Redlegs TC Center	30.00	15.00
❑ 90B Cincinnati Reds TC D'55	80.00	50.00
❑ 90C Cincinnati Reds TC Left	30.00	15.00
❑ 91 Gail Harris RC	10.00	5.00
❑ 92 Bob (Red) Wilson	10.00	5.00
❑ 93 George Susce	10.00	5.00
❑ 94 Ron Kline	10.00	5.00
❑ 95A Milwaukee Braves TC Center	40.00	20.00
❑ 95B Milwaukee Braves TC D'55	80.00	50.00
❑ 95C Milwaukee Braves TC Left	40.00	20.00
❑ 96 Bill Tremel	10.00	5.00
❑ 97 Jerry Lynch	15.00	7.50
❑ 98 Camilo Pascual	15.00	7.50
❑ 99 Don Zimmer	25.00	15.00
❑ 100A Baltimore Orioles TC Center	40.00	20.00
❑ 100B Baltimore Orioles TC D'55	80.00	50.00
❑ 100C Baltimore Orioles TC Left	40.00	20.00
❑ 101 Roy Campanella	150.00	90.00
❑ 102 Jim Davis	12.00	6.00
❑ 103 Willie Miranda	12.00	6.00
❑ 104 Bob Lennon	12.00	6.00
❑ 105 Al Smith	12.00	6.00
❑ 106 Joe Astroth	12.00	6.00
❑ 107 Eddie Mathews	100.00	60.00
❑ 108 Laurin Pepper	12.00	6.00
❑ 109 Enos Slaughter	40.00	25.00
❑ 110 Yogi Berra	175.00	100.00
❑ 111 Boston Red Sox TC	40.00	20.00
❑ 112 Dee Fondy	12.00	6.00
❑ 113 Phil Rizzuto	150.00	90.00
❑ 114 Jim Owens	15.00	7.50
❑ 115 Jackie Jensen	15.00	7.50
❑ 116 Eddie O'Brien	12.00	6.00
❑ 117 Virgil Trucks	15.00	7.50
❑ 118 Nellie Fox	80.00	50.00
❑ 119 Larry Jackson RC	15.00	7.50
❑ 120 Richie Ashburn	60.00	35.00
❑ 121 Pittsburgh Pirates TC	40.00	20.00
❑ 122 Willard Nixon	12.00	6.00
❑ 123 Roy McMillan	15.00	7.50
❑ 124 Don Kaiser	12.00	6.00
❑ 125 Minnie Minoso	40.00	25.00
❑ 126 Jim Brady RC	12.00	6.00
❑ 127 Willie Jones	15.00	7.50
❑ 128 Eddie Yost	15.00	7.50
❑ 129 Jake Martin RC	12.00	6.00
❑ 130 Willie Mays	300.00	175.00
❑ 131 Bob Roselli RC	12.00	6.00
❑ 132 Bobby Avila	12.00	6.00
❑ 133 Ray Narleski	12.00	6.00
❑ 134 St. Louis Cardinals TC	40.00	20.00
❑ 135 Mickey Mantle	1500.00	900.00
❑ 136 Johnny Logan	15.00	7.50
❑ 137 Al Silvera RC	12.00	6.00
❑ 138 Johnny Antonelli	15.00	7.50
❑ 139 Tommy Carroll	15.00	7.50
❑ 140 Herb Score RC	60.00	35.00
❑ 141 Joe Frazier	12.00	6.00
❑ 142 Gene Baker	12.00	6.00
❑ 143 Jim Piersall	15.00	7.50
❑ 144 Leroy Powell RC	12.00	6.00
❑ 145 Gil Hodges	60.00	35.00
❑ 146 Washington Nationals TC	40.00	20.00
❑ 147 Earl Torgeson	12.00	6.00
❑ 148 Alvin Dark	15.00	7.50
❑ 149 Dixie Howell	12.00	6.00
❑ 150 Duke Snider	125.00	75.00
❑ 151 Spook Jacobs	15.00	7.50
❑ 152 Billy Hoeft	15.00	7.50
❑ 153 Frank Thomas	15.00	7.50
❑ 154 Dave Pope	12.00	6.00
❑ 155 Harvey Kuenn	15.00	7.50
❑ 156 Wes Westrum	15.00	7.50
❑ 157 Dick Brodowski	12.00	6.00
❑ 158 Wally Post	15.00	7.50
❑ 159 Clint Courtney	12.00	6.00
❑ 160 Billy Pierce	15.00	7.50
❑ 161 Joe DeMaestri	12.00	6.00
❑ 162 Dave (Gus) Bell	15.00	7.50
❑ 163 Gene Woodling	15.00	7.50

	Card		
❑	164 Harmon Killebrew	100.00	60.00
❑	165 Red Schoendienst	40.00	25.00
❑	166 Brooklyn Dodgers TC	200.00	125.00
❑	167 Harry Dorish	12.00	6.00
❑	168 Sammy White	12.00	6.00
❑	169 Bob Nelson RC	12.00	6.00
❑	170 Bill Virdon	15.00	7.50
❑	171 Jim Wilson	12.00	6.00
❑	172 Frank Torre RC	15.00	7.50
❑	173 Johnny Podres	25.00	15.00
❑	174 Glen Gorbous RC	12.00	6.00
❑	175 Del Crandall	15.00	7.50
❑	176 Alex Kellner	12.00	6.00
❑	177 Hank Bauer	25.00	15.00
❑	178 Joe Black	15.00	7.50
❑	179 Harry Chiti	12.00	6.00
❑	180 Robin Roberts	50.00	30.00
❑	181 Billy Martin	125.00	75.00
❑	182 Paul Minner	15.00	7.50
❑	183 Stan Lopata	20.00	10.00
❑	184 Don Bessent RC	20.00	10.00
❑	185 Bill Bruton	20.00	10.00
❑	186 Ron Jackson	15.00	7.50
❑	187 Early Wynn	50.00	30.00
❑	188 Chicago White Sox TC	50.00	30.00
❑	189 Ned Garver	15.00	7.50
❑	190 Carl Furillo	30.00	18.00
❑	191 Frank Lary	20.00	10.00
❑	192 Smoky Burgess	20.00	10.00
❑	193 Wilmer Mizell	20.00	10.00
❑	194 Monte Irvin	30.00	18.00
❑	195 George Kell	30.00	18.00
❑	196 Tom Poholsky	15.00	7.50
❑	197 Granny Hamner	15.00	7.50
❑	198 Ed Fitzgerald	15.00	7.50
❑	199 Hank Thompson	20.00	10.00
❑	200 Bob Feller	125.00	75.00
❑	201 Rip Repulski	15.00	7.50
❑	202 Jim Hearn	15.00	7.50
❑	203 Bill Tuttle	15.00	7.50
❑	204 Art Swanson RC	15.00	7.50
❑	205 Whitey Lockman	20.00	10.00
❑	206 Erv Palica	15.00	7.50
❑	207 Jim Small RC	15.00	7.50
❑	208 Elston Howard	60.00	35.00
❑	209 Max Surkont	15.00	7.50
❑	210 Mike Garcia	20.00	10.00
❑	211 Murry Dickson	15.00	7.50
❑	212 Johnny Temple	15.00	7.50
❑	213 Detroit Tigers TC	60.00	35.00
❑	214 Bob Rush	15.00	7.50
❑	215 Tommy Byrne	20.00	10.00
❑	216 Jerry Schoonmaker RC	15.00	7.50
❑	217 Billy Klaus	15.00	7.50
❑	218 Joe Nuxhall UER	20.00	10.00
❑	219 Lew Burdette	20.00	10.00
❑	220 Del Ennis	20.00	10.00
❑	221 Bob Friend	20.00	10.00
❑	222 Dave Philley	15.00	7.50
❑	223 Randy Jackson	15.00	7.50
❑	224 Bud Podbielan	15.00	7.50
❑	225 Gil McDougald	50.00	30.00
❑	226 New York Giants TC	80.00	50.00
❑	227 Russ Meyer	15.00	7.50
❑	228 Mickey Vernon	20.00	10.00
❑	229 Harry Brecheen CO	20.00	10.00
❑	230 Chico Carrasquel	15.00	7.50
❑	231 Bob Hale RC	15.00	7.50
❑	232 Toby Atwell	15.00	7.50
❑	233 Carl Erskine	30.00	18.00
❑	234 Pete Runnels	15.00	7.50
❑	235 Don Newcombe	50.00	30.00
❑	236 Kansas City Athletics TC	40.00	20.00
❑	237 Jose Valdivielso RC	15.00	7.50
❑	238 Walt Dropo	20.00	10.00
❑	239 Harry Simpson	15.00	7.50
❑	240 Whitey Ford	125.00	75.00
❑	241 Don Mueller UER	20.00	10.00
❑	242 Hershell Freeman	15.00	7.50
❑	243 Sherm Lollar	20.00	10.00
❑	244 Bob Buhl	30.00	18.00
❑	245 Billy Goodman	20.00	10.00
❑	246 Tom Gorman	15.00	7.50
❑	247 Bill Sarni	15.00	7.50
❑	248 Bob Porterfield	15.00	7.50
❑	249 Johnny Klippstein	15.00	7.50
❑	250 Larry Doby	30.00	18.00
❑	251 New York Yankees TC UER	250.00	150.00
❑	252 Vern Law	20.00	10.00
❑	253 Irv Noren	30.00	18.00
❑	254 George Crowe	15.00	7.50
❑	255 Bob Lemon	50.00	30.00
❑	256 Tom Hurd	15.00	7.50
❑	257 Bobby Thomson	30.00	18.00
❑	258 Art Ditmar	15.00	7.50
❑	259 Sam Jones	20.00	10.00
❑	260 Pee Wee Reese	150.00	90.00
❑	261 Bobby Shantz	15.00	7.50
❑	262 Howie Pollet	12.00	6.00
❑	263 Bob Miller	12.00	6.00
❑	264 Ray Monzant RC	12.00	6.00
❑	265 Sandy Consuegra	12.00	6.00
❑	266 Don Ferrarese	12.00	6.00
❑	267 Bob Nieman	12.00	6.00
❑	268 Dale Mitchell	15.00	7.50
❑	269 Jack Meyer RC	12.00	6.00
❑	270 Billy Loes	15.00	7.50
❑	271 Foster Castleman RC	12.00	6.00
❑	272 Danny O'Connell	12.00	6.00
❑	273 Walker Cooper	12.00	6.00
❑	274 Frank Baumholtz	12.00	6.00
❑	275 Jim Greengrass	12.00	6.00
❑	276 George Zuverink	12.00	6.00
❑	277 Daryl Spencer	12.00	6.00
❑	278 Chet Nichols	12.00	6.00
❑	279 Johnny Groth	12.00	6.00
❑	280 Jim Gilliam	40.00	25.00
❑	281 Art Houtteman	12.00	6.00
❑	282 Warren Hacker	12.00	6.00
❑	283 Hal R.Smith RC	15.00	7.50
❑	284 Ike Delock	12.00	6.00
❑	285 Eddie Miksis	12.00	6.00
❑	286 Bill Wight	12.00	6.00
❑	287 Bobby Adams	12.00	6.00
❑	288 Bob Cerv	40.00	25.00
❑	289 Hal Jeffcoat	12.00	6.00
❑	290 Curt Simmons	15.00	7.50
❑	291 Frank Kellert RC	12.00	6.00
❑	292 Luis Aparicio RC	150.00	90.00
❑	293 Stu Miller	25.00	15.00
❑	294 Ernie Johnson	15.00	7.50
❑	295 Clem Labine	15.00	7.50
❑	296 Andy Seminick	12.00	6.00
❑	297 Bob Skinner	15.00	7.50
❑	298 Johnny Schmitz	12.00	6.00
❑	299 Charlie Neal	40.00	25.00
❑	300 Vic Wertz	15.00	7.50
❑	301 Marv Grissom	12.00	6.00
❑	302 Eddie Robinson	12.00	6.00
❑	303 Jim Dyck	12.00	6.00
❑	304 Frank Malzone	15.00	7.50
❑	305 Brooks Lawrence	12.00	6.00
❑	306 Curt Roberts	12.00	6.00
❑	307 Hoyt Wilhelm	40.00	25.00
❑	308 Chuck Harmon	12.00	6.00
❑	309 Don Blasingame RC	15.00	7.50
❑	310 Steve Gromek	12.00	6.00
❑	311 Hal Naragon	12.00	6.00
❑	312 Andy Pafko	15.00	7.50
❑	313 Gene Stephens	12.00	6.00
❑	314 Hobie Landrith	12.00	6.00
❑	315 Milt Bolling	12.00	6.00
❑	316 Jerry Coleman	15.00	7.50
❑	317 Al Aber	12.00	6.00
❑	318 Fred Hatfield	12.00	6.00
❑	319 Jack Crimian RC	12.00	6.00
❑	320 Joe Adcock	15.00	7.50
❑	321 Jim Konstanty	15.00	7.50
❑	322 Karl Olson	12.00	6.00
❑	323 Willard Schmidt	12.00	6.00
❑	324 Rocky Bridges	15.00	7.50
❑	325 Don Liddle	12.00	6.00
❑	326 Connie Johnson RC	12.00	6.00
❑	327 Bob Wiesler RC	12.00	6.00
❑	328 Preston Ward	12.00	6.00
❑	329 Lou Berberet RC	12.00	6.00
❑	330 Jim Busby	15.00	7.50
❑	331 Dick Hall	12.00	6.00
❑	332 Don Larsen	60.00	35.00
❑	333 Rube Walker	12.00	6.00
❑	334 Bob Miller	15.00	7.50
❑	335 Don Hoak	15.00	7.50
❑	336 Ellis Kinder	12.00	6.00
❑	337 Bobby Morgan	12.00	6.00
❑	338 Jim Delsing	12.00	6.00
❑	339 Rance Pless RC	12.00	6.00
❑	340 Mickey McDermott	60.00	35.00
❑	CL1 Checklist 1/3	300.00	175.00
❑	CL2 Checklist 2/4	300.00	175.00

1957 Topps

	Card		
❑	COMPLETE SET (407)	10000.00	7000.00
❑	COMMON CARD (1-88)	10.00	5.00
❑	COMMON CARD (89-176)	8.00	4.00
❑	COMMON CARD (177-264)	8.00	4.00
❑	COMMON CARD (265-352)	20.00	10.00
❑	COMMON CARD (353-407)	8.00	4.00
❑	COMMON DP (265-352)	12.00	6.00
❑	WRAPPER (1-CENT)	300.00	250.00
❑	WRAPPER (5-CENT)	200.00	150.00
❑	1 Ted Williams	600.00	350.00
❑	2 Yogi Berra	200.00	125.00
❑	3 Dale Long	20.00	10.00
❑	4 Johnny Logan	20.00	10.00
❑	5 Sal Maglie	20.00	10.00
❑	6 Hector Lopez	15.00	7.50
❑	7 Luis Aparicio	30.00	15.00
❑	8 Don Mossi	15.00	7.50
❑	9 Johnny Temple	15.00	7.50
❑	10 Willie Mays	400.00	250.00
❑	11 George Zuverink	10.00	5.00
❑	12 Dick Groat	20.00	10.00
❑	13 Wally Burnette RC	10.00	5.00
❑	14 Bob Nieman	10.00	5.00
❑	15 Robin Roberts	30.00	15.00
❑	16 Walt Moryn	10.00	5.00
❑	17 Billy Gardner	10.00	5.00
❑	18 Don Drysdale RC	250.00	150.00
❑	19 Bob Wilson	10.00	5.00
❑	20 Hank Aaron UER	300.00	175.00
❑	21 Frank Sullivan	10.00	5.00
❑	22 Jerry Snyder UER	10.00	5.00
❑	23 Sherm Lollar	15.00	7.50
❑	24 Bill Mazeroski RC	80.00	50.00
❑	25 Whitey Ford	175.00	100.00
❑	26 Bob Boyd	10.00	5.00
❑	27 Ted Kazanski	10.00	5.00
❑	28 Gene Conley	15.00	7.50
❑	29 Whitey Herzog RC	30.00	15.00
❑	30 Pee Wee Reese	80.00	50.00
❑	31 Ron Northey	10.00	5.00
❑	32 Hershell Freeman	10.00	5.00
❑	33 Jim Small	10.00	5.00
❑	34 Tom Sturdivant RC	15.00	7.50
❑	35 Frank Robinson RC	300.00	175.00
❑	36 Bob Grim	10.00	5.00
❑	37 Frank Torre	15.00	7.50
❑	38 Nellie Fox	50.00	30.00
❑	39 Al Worthington RC	10.00	5.00
❑	40 Early Wynn	30.00	15.00
❑	41 Hal W. Smith	10.00	5.00
❑	42 Dee Fondy	10.00	5.00
❑	43 Connie Johnson	10.00	5.00
❑	44 Joe DeMaestri	10.00	5.00
❑	45 Carl Furillo	30.00	15.00
❑	46 Robert J. Miller	10.00	5.00
❑	47 Don Blasingame	10.00	5.00
❑	48 Bill Bruton	15.00	7.50
❑	49 Daryl Spencer	10.00	5.00
❑	50 Herb Score	30.00	15.00

❑ 51 Clint Courtney 10.00 5.00
❑ 52 Lee Walls 10.00 5.00
❑ 53 Clem Labine 20.00 10.00
❑ 54 Elmer Valo 10.00 5.00
❑ 55 Ernie Banks 125.00 75.00
❑ 56 Dave Sisler RC 10.00 5.00
❑ 57 Jim Lemon 15.00 7.50
❑ 58 Ruben Gomez 10.00 5.00
❑ 59 Dick Williams 15.00 7.50
❑ 60 Billy Hoeft 15.00 7.50
❑ 61 Dusty Rhodes 15.00 7.50
❑ 62 Billy Martin 60.00 35.00
❑ 63 Ike Delock 10.00 5.00
❑ 64 Pete Runnels 15.00 7.50
❑ 65 Wally Moon 15.00 7.50
❑ 66 Brooks Lawrence 10.00 5.00
❑ 67 Chico Carrasquel 10.00 5.00
❑ 68 Ray Crone 10.00 5.00
❑ 69 Roy McMillan 15.00 7.50
❑ 70 Richie Ashburn 50.00 30.00
❑ 71 Murry Dickson 10.00 5.00
❑ 72 Bill Tuttle 10.00 5.00
❑ 73 George Crowe 10.00 5.00
❑ 74 Vito Valentinetti RC 10.00 5.00
❑ 75 Jimmy Piersall 15.00 7.50
❑ 76 Roberto Clemente 300.00 175.00
❑ 77 Paul Foytack RC 10.00 5.00
❑ 78 Vic Wertz 15.00 7.50
❑ 79 Lindy McDaniel RC 15.00 7.50
❑ 80 Gil Hodges 50.00 30.00
❑ 81 Herman Wehmeier 10.00 5.00
❑ 82 Elston Howard 30.00 15.00
❑ 83 Lou Skizas RC 10.00 5.00
❑ 84 Moe Drabowsky RC 15.00 7.50
❑ 85 Larry Doby 30.00 15.00
❑ 86 Bill Sarni 10.00 5.00
❑ 87 Tom Gorman 10.00 5.00
❑ 88 Harvey Kuenn 15.00 7.50
❑ 89 Roy Sievers 15.00 7.50
❑ 90 Warren Spahn 80.00 50.00
❑ 91 Mack Burk RC 8.00 4.00
❑ 92 Mickey Vernon 15.00 7.50
❑ 93 Hal Jeffcoat 8.00 4.00
❑ 94 Bobby Del Greco 8.00 4.00
❑ 95 Mickey Mantle 1200.00 700.00
❑ 96 Hank Aguirre RC 8.00 4.00
❑ 97 New York Yankees TC 100.00 60.00
❑ 98 Alvin Dark 15.00 7.50
❑ 99 Bob Keegan 8.00 4.00
❑ 100 W.Giles/W.Harridge 15.00 7.50
❑ 101 Chuck Stobbs 8.00 4.00
❑ 102 Ray Boone 15.00 7.50
❑ 103 Joe Nuxhall 15.00 7.50
❑ 104 Hank Foiles 8.00 4.00
❑ 105 Johnny Antonelli 15.00 7.50
❑ 106 Ray Moore 8.00 4.00
❑ 107 Jim Rivera 8.00 4.00
❑ 108 Tommy Byrne 15.00 7.50
❑ 109 Hank Thompson 8.00 4.00
❑ 110 Bill Virdon 15.00 7.50
❑ 111 Hal R. Smith 8.00 4.00
❑ 112 Tom Brewer 8.00 4.00
❑ 113 Wilmer Mizell 15.00 7.50
❑ 114 Milwaukee Braves TC 20.00 10.00
❑ 115 Jim Gilliam 15.00 7.50
❑ 116 Mike Fornieles 8.00 4.00
❑ 117 Joe Adcock 20.00 10.00
❑ 118 Bob Porterfield 8.00 4.00
❑ 119 Stan Lopata 8.00 4.00
❑ 120 Bob Lemon 30.00 15.00
❑ 121 Clete Boyer RC 30.00 15.00
❑ 122 Ken Boyer 20.00 10.00
❑ 123 Steve Ridzik 8.00 4.00
❑ 124 Dave Philley 8.00 4.00
❑ 125 Al Kaline 100.00 60.00
❑ 126 Bob Wiesler 8.00 4.00
❑ 127 Bob Buhl 15.00 7.50
❑ 128 Ed Bailey 15.00 7.50
❑ 129 Saul Rogovin 8.00 4.00
❑ 130 Don Newcombe 20.00 10.00
❑ 131 Milt Bolling 8.00 4.00
❑ 132 Art Ditmar 15.00 7.50
❑ 133 Del Crandall 15.00 7.50
❑ 134 Don Kaiser 8.00 4.00
❑ 135 Bill Skowron 20.00 10.00
❑ 136 Jim Hegan 15.00 7.50
❑ 137 Bob Rush 8.00 4.00
❑ 138 Minnie Minoso 20.00 10.00
❑ 139 Lou Kretlow 8.00 4.00
❑ 140 Frank Thomas 15.00 7.50
❑ 141 Al Aber 8.00 4.00
❑ 142 Charley Thompson 8.00 4.00
❑ 143 Andy Pafko 15.00 7.50
❑ 144 Ray Narleski 8.00 4.00
❑ 145 Al Smith 8.00 4.00
❑ 146 Don Ferrarese 8.00 4.00
❑ 147 Al Walker 8.00 4.00
❑ 148 Don Mueller 15.00 7.50
❑ 149 Bob Kennedy 15.00 7.50
❑ 150 Bob Friend 15.00 7.50
❑ 151 Willie Miranda 8.00 4.00
❑ 152 Jack Harshman 8.00 4.00
❑ 153 Karl Olson 8.00 4.00
❑ 154 Red Schoendienst 30.00 15.00
❑ 155 Jim Brosnan 15.00 7.50
❑ 156 Gus Triandos 15.00 7.50
❑ 157 Wally Post 15.00 7.50
❑ 158 Curt Simmons 15.00 7.50
❑ 159 Solly Drake RC 8.00 4.00
❑ 160 Billy Pierce 15.00 7.50
❑ 161 Pittsburgh Pirates TC 15.00 7.50
❑ 162 Jack Meyer 8.00 4.00
❑ 163 Sammy White 8.00 4.00
❑ 164 Tommy Carroll 8.00 4.00
❑ 165 Ted Kluszewski 100.00 60.00
❑ 166 Roy Face 15.00 7.50
❑ 167 Vic Power 15.00 7.50
❑ 168 Frank Lary 15.00 7.50
❑ 169 Herb Plews RC 8.00 4.00
❑ 170 Duke Snider 125.00 75.00
❑ 171 Boston Red Sox TC 15.00 7.50
❑ 172 Gene Woodling 15.00 7.50
❑ 173 Roger Craig 15.00 7.50
❑ 174 Willie Jones 8.00 4.00
❑ 175 Don Larsen 30.00 15.00
❑ 176A Gene Bakep ERR 350.00 200.00
❑ 176B Gene Baker COR 15.00 7.50
❑ 177 Eddie Yost 15.00 7.50
❑ 178 Don Bessent 8.00 4.00
❑ 179 Ernie Oravetz 8.00 4.00
❑ 180 Gus Bell 15.00 7.50
❑ 181 Dick Donovan 8.00 4.00
❑ 182 Hobie Landrith 8.00 4.00
❑ 183 Chicago Cubs TC 15.00 7.50
❑ 184 Tito Francona RC 8.00 4.00
❑ 185 Johnny Kucks 15.00 7.50
❑ 186 Jim King 15.00 7.50
❑ 187 Virgil Trucks 15.00 7.50
❑ 188 Felix Mantilla RC 15.00 7.50
❑ 189 Willard Nixon 8.00 4.00
❑ 190 Randy Jackson 8.00 4.00
❑ 191 Joe Margoneri RC 8.00 4.00
❑ 192 Jerry Coleman 15.00 7.50
❑ 193 Del Rice 8.00 4.00
❑ 194 Hal Brown 8.00 4.00
❑ 195 Bobby Avila 8.00 4.00
❑ 196 Larry Jackson 15.00 7.50
❑ 197 Hank Sauer 15.00 7.50
❑ 198 Detroit Tigers TC 15.00 7.50
❑ 199 Vern Law 15.00 7.50
❑ 200 Gil McDougald 15.00 7.50
❑ 201 Sandy Amoros 15.00 7.50
❑ 202 Dick Gernert 8.00 4.00
❑ 203 Hoyt Wilhelm 30.00 15.00
❑ 204 Kansas City Athletics TC 15.00 7.50
❑ 205 Charlie Maxwell 15.00 7.50
❑ 206 Willard Schmidt 8.00 4.00
❑ 207 Gordon (Billy) Hunter 8.00 4.00
❑ 208 Lew Burdette 15.00 7.50
❑ 209 Bob Skinner 15.00 7.50
❑ 210 Roy Campanella 150.00 90.00
❑ 211 Camilo Pascual 15.00 7.50
❑ 212 Rocky Colavito RC 125.00 75.00
❑ 213 Les Moss 8.00 4.00
❑ 214 Philadelphia Phillies TC 15.00 7.50
❑ 215 Enos Slaughter 30.00 15.00
❑ 216 Marv Grissom 8.00 4.00
❑ 217 Gene Stephens 8.00 4.00
❑ 218 Ray Jablonski 8.00 4.00
❑ 219 Tom Acker RC 8.00 4.00
❑ 220 Jackie Jensen 20.00 10.00
❑ 221 Dixie Howell 8.00 4.00
❑ 222 Alex Grammas 8.00 4.00
❑ 223 Frank House 8.00 4.00
❑ 224 Marv Blaylock 8.00 4.00
❑ 225 Harry Simpson 8.00 4.00
❑ 226 Preston Ward 8.00 4.00
❑ 227 Gerry Staley 8.00 4.00
❑ 228 Smoky Burgess UER 15.00 7.50
❑ 229 George Susce 8.00 4.00
❑ 230 George Kell 30.00 15.00
❑ 231 Solly Hemus 8.00 4.00
❑ 232 Whitey Lockman 15.00 7.50
❑ 233 Art Fowler 8.00 4.00
❑ 234 Dick Cole 8.00 4.00
❑ 235 Tom Poholsky 8.00 4.00
❑ 236 Joe Ginsberg 8.00 4.00
❑ 237 Foster Castleman 8.00 4.00
❑ 238 Eddie Robinson 8.00 4.00
❑ 239 Tom Morgan 8.00 4.00
❑ 240 Hank Bauer 15.00 7.50
❑ 241 Joe Lonnett RC 8.00 4.00
❑ 242 Charlie Neal 15.00 7.50
❑ 243 St. Louis Cardinals TC 15.00 7.50
❑ 244 Billy Loes 15.00 7.50
❑ 245 Rip Repulski 8.00 4.00
❑ 246 Jose Valdivielso 8.00 4.00
❑ 247 Turk Lown 8.00 4.00
❑ 248 Jim Finigan 8.00 4.00
❑ 249 Dave Pope 8.00 4.00
❑ 250 Eddie Mathews 50.00 30.00
❑ 251 Baltimore Orioles TC 15.00 7.50
❑ 252 Carl Erskine 15.00 7.50
❑ 253 Gus Zernial 15.00 7.50
❑ 254 Ron Negray 8.00 4.00
❑ 255 Charlie Silvera 15.00 7.50
❑ 256 Ron Kline 8.00 4.00
❑ 257 Walt Dropo 8.00 4.00
❑ 258 Steve Gromek 8.00 4.00
❑ 259 Eddie O'Brien 8.00 4.00
❑ 260 Del Ennis 15.00 7.50
❑ 261 Bob Chakales 8.00 4.00
❑ 262 Bobby Thomson 15.00 7.50
❑ 263 George Strickland 8.00 4.00
❑ 264 Bob Turley 15.00 7.50
❑ 265 Harvey Haddix DP 12.00 6.00
❑ 266 Ken Kuhn DP RC 12.00 6.00
❑ 267 Danny Kravitz RC 20.00 10.00
❑ 268 Jack Collum 20.00 10.00
❑ 269 Bob Cerv 30.00 15.00
❑ 270 Washington Senators TC 60.00 35.00
❑ 271 Danny O'Connell DP 12.00 6.00
❑ 272 Bobby Shantz 30.00 15.00
❑ 273 Jim Davis 20.00 10.00
❑ 274 Don Hoak 15.00 7.50
❑ 275 Cleveland Indians TC UER 60.0035.00
❑ 276 Jim Pyburn RC 20.00 10.00
❑ 277 Johnny Podres DP 40.00 20.00
❑ 278 Fred Hatfield DP 12.00 6.00
❑ 279 Bob Thurman RC 20.00 10.00
❑ 280 Alex Kellner 20.00 10.00
❑ 281 Gail Harris 20.00 10.00
❑ 282 Jack Dittmer DP 12.00 6.00
❑ 283 Wes Covington DP RC 12.00 6.00
❑ 284 Don Zimmer 40.00 20.00
❑ 285 Ned Garver 20.00 10.00
❑ 286 Bobby Richardson RC 125.00 75.00
❑ 287 Sam Jones 20.00 10.00
❑ 288 Ted Lepcio 20.00 10.00
❑ 289 Jim Bolger DP 12.00 6.00
❑ 290 Andy Carey DP 40.00 20.00
❑ 291 Windy McCall 20.00 10.00
❑ 292 Billy Klaus 20.00 10.00
❑ 293 Ted Abernathy RC 20.00 10.00
❑ 294 Rocky Bridges DP 12.00 6.00
❑ 295 Joe Collins DP 40.00 20.00
❑ 296 Johnny Klippstein 20.00 10.00
❑ 297 Jack Crimian 20.00 10.00
❑ 298 Irv Noren DP 12.00 6.00
❑ 299 Chuck Harmon 20.00 10.00
❑ 300 Mike Garcia 30.00 15.00
❑ 301 Sammy Esposito DP RC 20.00 10.00
❑ 302 Sandy Koufax DP 350.00 200.00
❑ 303 Billy Goodman 30.00 15.00
❑ 304 Joe Cunningham 30.00 15.00
❑ 305 Chico Fernandez 20.00 10.00
❑ 306 Darrell Johnson DP RC 12.00 6.00
❑ 307 Jack D. Phillips DP 12.00 6.00

Card		
❑ 308 Dick Hall	20.00	10.00
❑ 309 Jim Busby DP	12.00	6.00
❑ 310 Max Surkont DP	12.00	6.00
❑ 311 Al Pilarcik DP RC	12.00	6.00
❑ 312 Tony Kubek DP RC	100.00	60.00
❑ 313 Mel Parnell	15.00	7.50
❑ 314 Ed Bouchee DP RC	12.00	6.00
❑ 315 Lou Berberet DP	12.00	6.00
❑ 316 Billy O'Dell	20.00	10.00
❑ 317 New York Giants TC	80.00	50.00
❑ 318 Mickey McDermott	20.00	10.00
❑ 319 Gino Cimoli RC	20.00	10.00
❑ 320 Neil Chrisley RC	20.00	10.00
❑ 321 John (Red) Murff RC	20.00	10.00
❑ 322 Cincinnati Reds TC	80.00	50.00
❑ 323 Wes Westrum	30.00	15.00
❑ 324 Brooklyn Dodgers TC	150.00	90.00
❑ 325 Frank Bolling	20.00	10.00
❑ 326 Pedro Ramos	20.00	10.00
❑ 327 Jim Pendleton	20.00	10.00
❑ 328 Brooks Robinson RC	400.00	250.00
❑ 329 Chicago White Sox TC	60.00	35.00
❑ 330 Jim Wilson	20.00	10.00
❑ 331 Ray Katt	20.00	10.00
❑ 332 Bob Bowman RC	20.00	10.00
❑ 333 Ernie Johnson	20.00	10.00
❑ 334 Jerry Schoonmaker	20.00	10.00
❑ 335 Granny Hamner	20.00	10.00
❑ 336 Haywood Sullivan RC	40.00	20.00
❑ 337 Rene Valdes RC	20.00	10.00
❑ 338 Jim Bunning RC	150.00	90.00
❑ 339 Bob Speake	20.00	10.00
❑ 340 Bill Wight	20.00	10.00
❑ 341 Don Gross RC	20.00	10.00
❑ 342 Gene Mauch	30.00	15.00
❑ 343 Taylor Phillips RC	15.00	7.50
❑ 344 Paul LaPalme	20.00	10.00
❑ 345 Paul Smith	20.00	10.00
❑ 346 Dick Littlefield	20.00	10.00
❑ 347 Hal Naragon	20.00	10.00
❑ 348 Jim Hearn	20.00	10.00
❑ 349 Nellie King	20.00	10.00
❑ 350 Eddie Miksis	20.00	10.00
❑ 351 Dave Hillman RC	20.00	10.00
❑ 352 Ellis Kinder	20.00	10.00
❑ 353 Cal Neeman RC	8.00	4.00
❑ 354 Rip Coleman RC	8.00	4.00
❑ 355 Frank Malzone	15.00	7.50
❑ 356 Faye Throneberry	8.00	4.00
❑ 357 Earl Torgeson	8.00	4.00
❑ 358 Jerry Lynch	15.00	7.50
❑ 359 Tom Cheney RC	8.00	4.00
❑ 360 Johnny Groth	8.00	4.00
❑ 361 Curt Barclay RC	8.00	4.00
❑ 362 Roman Mejias RC	15.00	7.50
❑ 363 Eddie Kasko RC	8.00	4.00
❑ 364 Cal McLish RC	15.00	7.50
❑ 365 Ozzie Virgil RC	8.00	4.00
❑ 366 Ken Lehman	8.00	4.00
❑ 367 Ed Fitzgerald	8.00	4.00
❑ 368 Bob Purkey	8.00	4.00
❑ 369 Milt Graff RC	8.00	4.00
❑ 370 Warren Hacker	8.00	4.00
❑ 371 Bob Lennon	8.00	4.00
❑ 372 Norm Zauchin	8.00	4.00
❑ 373 Pete Whisenant RC	8.00	4.00
❑ 374 Don Cardwell RC	8.00	4.00
❑ 375 Jim Landis RC	15.00	7.50
❑ 376 Don Elston RC	8.00	4.00
❑ 377 Andre Rodgers RC	8.00	4.00
❑ 378 Elmer Singleton	8.00	4.00
❑ 379 Don Lee RC	8.00	4.00
❑ 380 Walker Cooper	8.00	4.00
❑ 381 Dean Stone	8.00	4.00
❑ 382 Jim Brideweser	8.00	4.00
❑ 383 Juan Pizarro RC	8.00	4.00
❑ 384 Bobby G. Smith RC	8.00	4.00
❑ 385 Art Houtteman	8.00	4.00
❑ 386 Lyle Luttrell RC	8.00	4.00
❑ 387 Jack Sanford RC	15.00	7.50
❑ 388 Pete Daley	8.00	4.00
❑ 389 Dave Jolly	8.00	4.00
❑ 390 Reno Bertoia	8.00	4.00
❑ 391 Ralph Terry RC	15.00	7.50
❑ 392 Chuck Tanner	15.00	7.50
❑ 393 Raul Sanchez RC	8.00	4.00
❑ 394 Luis Arroyo	15.00	7.50
❑ 395 Bubba Phillips	8.00	4.00
❑ 396 Casey Wise RC	8.00	4.00
❑ 397 Roy Smalley	8.00	4.00
❑ 398 Al Cicotte RC	15.00	7.50
❑ 399 Billy Consolo	8.00	4.00
❑ 400 Fur/Hodges/Campy/Snider	250.00	150.00
❑ 401 Earl Battey RC	15.00	7.50
❑ 402 Jim Pisoni RC	8.00	4.00
❑ 403 Dick Hyde RC	8.00	4.00
❑ 404 Harry Anderson RC	8.00	4.00
❑ 405 Duke Maas	8.00	4.00
❑ 406 Bob Hale	8.00	4.00
❑ 407 Y.Berra/M.Mantle	600.00	350.00
❑ CC1 Contest May 4	100.00	60.00
❑ CC2 Contest May 25	100.00	60.00
❑ CC3 Contest June 22	125.00	75.00
❑ CC4 Contest July 19	125.00	75.00
❑ NNO Checklist 1/2 Bazooka	250.00	150.00
❑ NNO Checklist 1/2 Blony	250.00	150.00
❑ NNO Checklist 2/3 Bazooka	400.00	250.00
❑ NNO Checklist 2/3 Blony	400.00	250.00
❑ NNO Checklist 3/4 Bazooka	800.00	500.00
❑ NNO Checklist 3/4 Blony	600.00	350.00
❑ NNO Checklist 4/5 Bazooka	1000.00	600.00
❑ NNO Checklist 4/5 Blony	800.00	500.00
❑ NNO Lucky Penny Card	100.00	60.00

1958 Topps

Card		
❑ COMP. MASTER SET (534)	12000.00	8000.00
❑ COMPLETE SET (494)	6000.00	4000.00
❑ COMMON CARD (1-110)	12.00	6.00
❑ COMMON CARD (111-495)	8.00	4.00
❑ WRAPPER (1-CENT)	100.00	75.00
❑ WRAPPER (5-CENT)	125.00	100.00
❑ 1 Ted Williams	600.00	350.00
❑ 2A Bob Lemon	30.00	15.00
❑ 2B Bob Lemon YT	60.00	35.00
❑ 3 Alex Kellner	12.00	6.00
❑ 4 Hank Foiles	12.00	6.00
❑ 5 Willie Mays	300.00	175.00
❑ 6 George Zuverink	12.00	6.00
❑ 7 Dale Long	15.00	7.50
❑ 8A Eddie Kasko	12.00	6.00
❑ 8B Eddie Kasko YN	40.00	20.00
❑ 9 Hank Bauer	20.00	10.00
❑ 10 Lew Burdette	20.00	10.00
❑ 11A Jim Rivera	12.00	6.00
❑ 11B Jim Rivera YT	40.00	20.00
❑ 12 George Crowe	12.00	6.00
❑ 13A Billy Hoeft	12.00	6.00
❑ 13B Billy Hoeft YN	40.00	20.00
❑ 14 Rip Repulski	12.00	6.00
❑ 15 Jim Lemon	15.00	7.50
❑ 16 Charlie Neal	15.00	7.50
❑ 17 Felix Mantilla	12.00	6.00
❑ 18 Frank Sullivan	12.00	6.00
❑ 19 San Francisco Giants TC	40.00	20.00
❑ 20A Gil McDougald	20.00	10.00
❑ 20B Gil McDougald YN	60.00	35.00
❑ 21 Curt Barclay	12.00	6.00
❑ 22 Hal Naragon	12.00	6.00
❑ 23A Bill Tuttle	12.00	6.00
❑ 23B Bill Tuttle YN	40.00	20.00
❑ 24A Hobie Landrith	12.00	6.00
❑ 24B Hobie Landrith YN	40.00	20.00
❑ 25 Don Drysdale	100.00	60.00
❑ 26 Ron Jackson	12.00	6.00
❑ 27 Bud Freeman	12.00	6.00
❑ 28 Jim Busby	12.00	6.00
❑ 29 Ted Lepcio	12.00	6.00
❑ 30A Hank Aaron	200.00	125.00
❑ 30B Hank Aaron YN	600.00	350.00
❑ 31 Tex Clevenger RC	12.00	6.00
❑ 32A J.W. Porter	12.00	6.00
❑ 32B J.W. Porter YN	40.00	20.00
❑ 33A Cal Neeman	12.00	6.00
❑ 33B Cal Neeman YT	40.00	20.00
❑ 34 Bob Thurman	12.00	6.00
❑ 35A Don Mossi	15.00	7.50
❑ 35B Don Mossi YT	40.00	20.00
❑ 36 Ted Kazanski	12.00	6.00
❑ 37 Mike McCormick UER RC	15.00	7.50
❑ 38 Dick Gernert	12.00	6.00
❑ 39 Bob Martyn RC	12.00	6.00
❑ 40 George Kell	30.00	15.00
❑ 41 Dave Hillman	12.00	6.00
❑ 42 John Roseboro RC	30.00	15.00
❑ 43 Sal Maglie	15.00	7.50
❑ 44 Washington Senators TC	20.00	10.00
❑ 45 Dick Groat	15.00	7.50
❑ 46A Lou Sleater	12.00	6.00
❑ 46B Lou Sleater YN	40.00	20.00
❑ 47 Roger Maris RC	500.00	300.00
❑ 48 Chuck Harmon	12.00	6.00
❑ 49 Smoky Burgess	15.00	7.50
❑ 50A Billy Pierce	15.00	7.50
❑ 50B Billy Pierce YT	40.00	20.00
❑ 51 Del Rice	12.00	6.00
❑ 52A Roberto Clemente	300.00	175.00
❑ 52B Roberto Clemente YT	500.00	300.00
❑ 53A Morrie Martin	12.00	6.00
❑ 53B Morrie Martin YN	40.00	20.00
❑ 54 Norm Siebern RC	20.00	10.00
❑ 55 Chico Carrasquel	12.00	6.00
❑ 56 Bill Fischer RC	12.00	6.00
❑ 57A Tim Thompson	12.00	6.00
❑ 57B Tim Thompson YN	40.00	20.00
❑ 58A Art Schult	12.00	6.00
❑ 58B Art Schult YT	40.00	20.00
❑ 59 Dave Sisler	12.00	6.00
❑ 60A Del Ennis	15.00	7.50
❑ 60B Del Ennis YN	40.00	20.00
❑ 61A Darrell Johnson	12.00	6.00
❑ 61B Darrell Johnson YN	40.00	20.00
❑ 62 Joe DeMaestri	12.00	6.00
❑ 63 Joe Nuxhall	15.00	7.50
❑ 64 Joe Lonnett	12.00	6.00
❑ 65A Von McDaniel RC	12.00	6.00
❑ 65B Von McDaniel YN	40.00	20.00
❑ 66 Lee Walls	12.00	6.00
❑ 67 Joe Ginsberg	12.00	6.00
❑ 68 Daryl Spencer	12.00	6.00
❑ 69 Wally Burnette	12.00	6.00
❑ 70A Al Kaline	100.00	60.00
❑ 70B Al Kaline YN	250.00	150.00
❑ 71 Los Angeles Dodgers TC	60.00	35.00
❑ 72 Bud Byerly UER	12.00	6.00
❑ 73 Pete Daley	12.00	6.00
❑ 74 Roy Face	15.00	7.50
❑ 75 Gus Bell	15.00	7.50
❑ 76A Dick Farrell RC	12.00	6.00
❑ 76B Dick Farrell YT	40.00	20.00
❑ 77A Don Zimmer	15.00	7.50
❑ 77B Don Zimmer YT	40.00	20.00
❑ 78A Ernie Johnson	15.00	7.50
❑ 78B Ernie Johnson YN	40.00	20.00
❑ 79A Dick Williams	15.00	7.50
❑ 79B Dick Williams YT	40.00	20.00
❑ 80 Dick Drott RC	12.00	6.00
❑ 81A Steve Boros RC	12.00	6.00
❑ 81B Steve Boros YT	40.00	20.00
❑ 82 Ron Kline	12.00	6.00
❑ 83 Bob Hazle RC	12.00	6.00
❑ 84 Billy O'Dell	12.00	6.00
❑ 85A Luis Aparicio	30.00	15.00
❑ 85B Luis Aparicio YT	80.00	50.00
❑ 86 Valmy Thomas RC	12.00	6.00
❑ 87 Johnny Kucks	12.00	6.00
❑ 88 Duke Snider	80.00	50.00
❑ 89 Billy Klaus	12.00	6.00
❑ 90 Robin Roberts	30.00	15.00
❑ 91 Chuck Tanner	15.00	7.50
❑ 92A Clint Courtney	12.00	6.00
❑ 92B Clint Courtney YN	40.00	20.00

Card		
❑ 93 Sandy Amoros	15.00	7.50
❑ 94 Bob Skinner	15.00	7.50
❑ 95 Frank Bolling	12.00	6.00
❑ 96 Joe Durham RC	12.00	6.00
❑ 97A Larry Jackson	12.00	6.00
❑ 97B Larry Jackson YN	40.00	20.00
❑ 98A Billy Hunter	12.00	6.00
❑ 98B Billy Hunter YN	40.00	20.00
❑ 99 Bobby Adams	12.00	6.00
❑ 100A Early Wynn	30.00	15.00
❑ 100B Early Wynn YT	80.00	50.00
❑ 101A Bobby Richardson	30.00	15.00
❑ 101B B.Richardson YN	60.00	35.00
❑ 102 George Strickland	12.00	6.00
❑ 103 Jerry Lynch	15.00	7.50
❑ 104 Jim Pendleton	12.00	6.00
❑ 105 Billy Gardner	12.00	6.00
❑ 106 Dick Schofield	15.00	7.50
❑ 107 Ossie Virgil	12.00	6.00
❑ 108A Jim Landis	12.00	6.00
❑ 108B Jim Landis YT	40.00	20.00
❑ 109 Herb Plews	12.00	6.00
❑ 110 Johnny Logan	15.00	7.50
❑ 111 Stu Miller	10.00	5.00
❑ 112 Gus Zernial	10.00	5.00
❑ 113 Jerry Walker RC	8.00	4.00
❑ 114 Irv Noren	10.00	5.00
❑ 115 Jim Bunning	30.00	15.00
❑ 116 Dave Philley	8.00	4.00
❑ 117 Frank Torre	10.00	5.00
❑ 118 Harvey Haddix	10.00	5.00
❑ 119 Harry Chiti	8.00	4.00
❑ 120 Johnny Podres	10.00	5.00
❑ 121 Eddie Miksis	8.00	4.00
❑ 122 Walt Moryn	8.00	4.00
❑ 123 Dick Tomanek RC	8.00	4.00
❑ 124 Bobby Usher	8.00	4.00
❑ 125 Alvin Dark	10.00	5.00
❑ 126 Stan Palys RC	8.00	4.00
❑ 127 Tom Sturdivant	10.00	5.00
❑ 128 Willie Kirkland RC	8.00	4.00
❑ 129 Jim Derrington RC	8.00	4.00
❑ 130 Jackie Jensen	10.00	5.00
❑ 131 Bob Henrich RC	8.00	4.00
❑ 132 Vern Law	10.00	5.00
❑ 133 Russ Nixon RC	8.00	4.00
❑ 134 Philadelphia Phillies TC	15.00	7.50
❑ 135 Mike (Moe)Drabowsky	10.00	5.00
❑ 136 Jim Finigan	8.00	4.00
❑ 137 Russ Kemmerer	8.00	4.00
❑ 138 Earl Torgeson	8.00	4.00
❑ 139 George Brunet RC	8.00	4.00
❑ 140 Wes Covington	10.00	5.00
❑ 141 Ken Lehman	8.00	4.00
❑ 142 Enos Slaughter	25.00	12.50
❑ 143 Billy Muffett RC	8.00	4.00
❑ 144 Bobby Morgan	8.00	4.00
❑ 145 Never issued		
❑ 146 Dick Gray RC	8.00	4.00
❑ 147 Don McMahon RC	8.00	4.00
❑ 148 Billy Consolo	8.00	4.00
❑ 149 Tom Acker	8.00	4.00
❑ 150 Mickey Mantle	1000.00	600.00
❑ 151 Buddy Pritchard RC	8.00	4.00
❑ 152 Johnny Antonelli	10.00	5.00
❑ 153 Les Moss	8.00	4.00
❑ 154 Harry Byrd	8.00	4.00
❑ 155 Hector Lopez	10.00	5.00
❑ 156 Dick Hyde	8.00	4.00
❑ 157 Dee Fondy	8.00	4.00
❑ 158 Cleveland Indians TC	15.00	7.50
❑ 159 Taylor Phillips	8.00	4.00
❑ 160 Don Hoak	10.00	5.00
❑ 161 Don Larsen	15.00	7.50
❑ 162 Gil Hodges	40.00	20.00
❑ 163 Jim Wilson	8.00	4.00
❑ 164 Bob Taylor RC	8.00	4.00
❑ 165 Bob Nieman	8.00	4.00
❑ 166 Danny O'Connell	8.00	4.00
❑ 167 Frank Baumann RC	8.00	4.00
❑ 168 Joe Cunningham	8.00	4.00
❑ 169 Ralph Terry	10.00	5.00
❑ 170 Vic Wertz	10.00	5.00
❑ 171 Harry Anderson	8.00	4.00
❑ 172 Don Gross	8.00	4.00
❑ 173 Eddie Yost	8.00	4.00
❑ 174 Kansas City Athletics TC	15.00	7.50
❑ 175 Marv Throneberry RC	15.00	7.50
❑ 176 Bob Buhl	10.00	5.00
❑ 177 Al Smith	8.00	4.00
❑ 178 Ted Kluszewski	25.00	12.50
❑ 179 Willie Miranda	8.00	4.00
❑ 180 Lindy McDaniel	10.00	5.00
❑ 181 Willie Jones	8.00	4.00
❑ 182 Joe Caffie RC	8.00	4.00
❑ 183 Dave Jolly	8.00	4.00
❑ 184 Elvin Tappe	8.00	4.00
❑ 185 Ray Boone	10.00	5.00
❑ 186 Jack Meyer	8.00	4.00
❑ 187 Sandy Koufax	250.00	150.00
❑ 188 Milt Bolling UER	8.00	4.00
❑ 189 George Susce	8.00	4.00
❑ 190 Red Schoendienst	25.00	12.50
❑ 191 Art Ceccarelli RC	8.00	4.00
❑ 192 Milt Graff	8.00	4.00
❑ 193 Jerry Lumpe RC	8.00	4.00
❑ 194 Roger Craig	10.00	5.00
❑ 195 Whitey Lockman	10.00	5.00
❑ 196 Mike Garcia	10.00	5.00
❑ 197 Haywood Sullivan	10.00	5.00
❑ 198 Bill Virdon	10.00	5.00
❑ 199 Don Blasingame	8.00	4.00
❑ 200 Bob Keegan	8.00	4.00
❑ 201 Jim Bolger	8.00	4.00
❑ 202 Woody Held RC	8.00	4.00
❑ 203 Al Walker	8.00	4.00
❑ 204 Leo Kiely	8.00	4.00
❑ 205 Johnny Temple	10.00	5.00
❑ 206 Bob Shaw RC	8.00	4.00
❑ 207 Solly Hemus	8.00	4.00
❑ 208 Cal McLish	8.00	4.00
❑ 209 Bob Anderson RC	8.00	4.00
❑ 210 Wally Moon	10.00	5.00
❑ 211 Pete Burnside RC	8.00	4.00
❑ 212 Bubba Phillips	8.00	4.00
❑ 213 Red Wilson	8.00	4.00
❑ 214 Willard Schmidt	8.00	4.00
❑ 215 Jim Gilliam	15.00	7.50
❑ 216 St. Louis Cardinals TC	15.00	7.50
❑ 217 Jack Harshman	8.00	4.00
❑ 218 Dick Rand RC	8.00	4.00
❑ 219 Camilo Pascual	10.00	5.00
❑ 220 Tom Brewer	8.00	4.00
❑ 221 Jerry Kindall RC	8.00	4.00
❑ 222 Bud Daley RC	8.00	4.00
❑ 223 Andy Pafko	10.00	5.00
❑ 224 Bob Grim	10.00	5.00
❑ 225 Billy Goodman	10.00	5.00
❑ 226 Bob Smith RC	8.00	4.00
❑ 227 Gene Stephens	8.00	4.00
❑ 228 Duke Maas	8.00	4.00
❑ 229 Frank Zupo RC	8.00	4.00
❑ 230 Richie Ashburn	40.00	20.00
❑ 231 Lloyd Merritt RC	8.00	4.00
❑ 232 Reno Bertoia	8.00	4.00
❑ 233 Mickey Vernon	10.00	5.00
❑ 234 Carl Sawatski	8.00	4.00
❑ 235 Tom Gorman	8.00	4.00
❑ 236 Ed Fitzgerald	8.00	4.00
❑ 237 Bill Wight	8.00	4.00
❑ 238 Bill Mazeroski	30.00	15.00
❑ 239 Chuck Stobbs	8.00	4.00
❑ 240 Bill Skowron	25.00	12.50
❑ 241 Dick Littlefield	8.00	4.00
❑ 242 Johnny Klippstein	8.00	4.00
❑ 243 Larry Raines RC	8.00	4.00
❑ 244 Don Demeter RC	8.00	4.00
❑ 245 Frank Lary	10.00	5.00
❑ 246 New York Yankees TC	100.00	60.00
❑ 247 Casey Wise	8.00	4.00
❑ 248 Herman Wehmeier	8.00	4.00
❑ 249 Ray Moore	8.00	4.00
❑ 250 Roy Sievers	10.00	5.00
❑ 251 Warren Hacker	8.00	4.00
❑ 252 Bob Trowbridge RC	8.00	4.00
❑ 253 Don Mueller	10.00	5.00
❑ 254 Alex Grammas	8.00	4.00
❑ 255 Bob Turley	10.00	5.00
❑ 256 Chicago White Sox TC	15.00	7.50
❑ 257 Hal Smith	8.00	4.00
❑ 258 Carl Erskine	15.00	7.50
❑ 259 Al Pilarcik	8.00	4.00
❑ 260 Frank Malzone	10.00	5.00
❑ 261 Turk Lown	8.00	4.00
❑ 262 Johnny Groth	8.00	4.00
❑ 263 Eddie Bressoud RC	10.00	5.00
❑ 264 Jack Sanford	10.00	5.00
❑ 265 Pete Runnels	10.00	5.00
❑ 266 Connie Johnson	8.00	4.00
❑ 267 Sherm Lollar	10.00	5.00
❑ 268 Granny Hamner	8.00	4.00
❑ 269 Paul Smith	8.00	4.00
❑ 270 Warren Spahn	60.00	35.00
❑ 271 Billy Martin	40.00	20.00
❑ 272 Ray Crone	8.00	4.00
❑ 273 Hal Smith	8.00	4.00
❑ 274 Rocky Bridges	8.00	4.00
❑ 275 Elston Howard	15.00	7.50
❑ 276 Bobby Avila	8.00	4.00
❑ 277 Virgil Trucks	10.00	5.00
❑ 278 Mack Burk	8.00	4.00
❑ 279 Bob Boyd	8.00	4.00
❑ 280 Jim Piersall	10.00	5.00
❑ 281 Sammy Taylor RC	8.00	4.00
❑ 282 Paul Foytack	8.00	4.00
❑ 283 Ray Shearer RC	8.00	4.00
❑ 284 Ray Katt	8.00	4.00
❑ 285 Frank Robinson	100.00	60.00
❑ 286 Gino Cimoli	8.00	4.00
❑ 287 Sam Jones	10.00	5.00
❑ 288 Harmon Killebrew	100.00	60.00
❑ 289 B.Shantz/L.Burdette	10.00	5.00
❑ 290 Dick Donovan	8.00	4.00
❑ 291 Don Landrum RC	8.00	4.00
❑ 292 Ned Garver	8.00	4.00
❑ 293 Gene Freese	8.00	4.00
❑ 294 Hal Jeffcoat	8.00	4.00
❑ 295 Minnie Minoso	25.00	12.50
❑ 296 Ryne Duren RC	15.00	7.50
❑ 297 Don Buddin RC	8.00	4.00
❑ 298 Jim Hearn	8.00	4.00
❑ 299 Harry Simpson	8.00	4.00
❑ 300 W.Harridge/W.Giles	15.00	7.50
❑ 301 Randy Jackson	8.00	4.00
❑ 302 Mike Baxes RC	8.00	4.00
❑ 303 Neil Chrisley	8.00	4.00
❑ 304 H.Kuenn/A.Kaline	25.00	12.50
❑ 305 Clem Labine	10.00	5.00
❑ 306 Whammy Douglas RC	8.00	4.00
❑ 307 Brooks Robinson	100.00	60.00
❑ 308 Paul Giel	10.00	5.00
❑ 309 Gail Harris	8.00	4.00
❑ 310 Ernie Banks	100.00	60.00
❑ 311 Bob Purkey	8.00	4.00
❑ 312 Boston Red Sox TC	15.00	7.50
❑ 313 Bob Rush	8.00	4.00
❑ 314 D.Snider/W.Alston	50.00	30.00
❑ 315 Bob Friend	10.00	5.00
❑ 316 Tito Francona	10.00	5.00
❑ 317 Albie Pearson RC	10.00	5.00
❑ 318 Frank House	8.00	4.00
❑ 319 Lou Skizas	8.00	4.00
❑ 320 Whitey Ford	60.00	35.00
❑ 321 T.Kluszewski/T.Williams	100.00	60.00
❑ 322 Harding Peterson RC	10.00	5.00
❑ 323 Elmer Valo	8.00	4.00
❑ 324 Hoyt Wilhelm	25.00	12.50
❑ 325 Joe Adcock	10.00	5.00
❑ 326 Bob Miller	8.00	4.00
❑ 327 Chicago Cubs TC	15.00	7.50
❑ 328 Ike Delock	8.00	4.00
❑ 329 Bob Cerv	10.00	5.00
❑ 330 Ed Bailey	10.00	5.00
❑ 331 Pedro Ramos	8.00	4.00
❑ 332 Jim King	8.00	4.00
❑ 333 Andy Carey	10.00	5.00
❑ 334 B.Friend/B.Pierce	10.00	5.00
❑ 335 Ruben Gomez	8.00	4.00
❑ 336 Bert Hamric	8.00	4.00
❑ 337 Hank Aguirre	8.00	4.00
❑ 338 Walt Dropo	10.00	5.00
❑ 339 Fred Hatfield	8.00	4.00
❑ 340 Don Newcombe	15.00	7.50
❑ 341 Pittsburgh Pirates TC	15.00	7.50
❑ 342 Jim Brosnan	10.00	5.00
❑ 343 Orlando Cepeda RC	100.00	60.00
❑ 344 Bob Porterfield	8.00	4.00
❑ 345 Jim Hegan	10.00	5.00

❑ 346 Steve Bilko 8.00 4.00
❑ 347 Don Rudolph RC 8.00 4.00
❑ 348 Chico Fernandez 8.00 4.00
❑ 349 Murry Dickson 8.00 4.00
❑ 350 Ken Boyer 25.00 12.50
❑ 351 Cran/Math/Aaron/Adcock 40.00 20.00
❑ 352 Herb Score 15.00 7.50
❑ 353 Stan Lopata 8.00 4.00
❑ 354 Art Ditmar 10.00 5.00
❑ 355 Bill Bruton 10.00 5.00
❑ 356 Bob Malkmus RC 8.00 4.00
❑ 357 Danny McDevitt RC 8.00 4.00
❑ 358 Gene Baker 8.00 4.00
❑ 359 Billy Loes 10.00 5.00
❑ 360 Roy McMillan 10.00 5.00
❑ 361 Mike Fornieles 8.00 4.00
❑ 362 Ray Jablonski 8.00 4.00
❑ 363 Don Elston 8.00 4.00
❑ 364 Earl Battey 8.00 4.00
❑ 365 Tom Morgan 8.00 4.00
❑ 366 Gene Green RC 8.00 4.00
❑ 367 Jack Urban RC 8.00 4.00
❑ 368 Rocky Colavito 50.00 30.00
❑ 369 Ralph Lumenti RC 8.00 4.00
❑ 370 Yogi Berra 100.00 60.00
❑ 371 Marty Keough RC 8.00 4.00
❑ 372 Don Cardwell 8.00 4.00
❑ 373 Joe Pignatano RC 8.00 4.00
❑ 374 Brooks Lawrence 8.00 4.00
❑ 375 Pee Wee Reese 80.00 50.00
❑ 376 Charley Rabe RC 8.00 4.00
❑ 377A Milwaukee Braves TC Alpha 15.00 7.50
❑ 377B Milwaukee Braves TC Num 100.00 60.00
❑ 378 Hank Sauer 10.00 5.00
❑ 379 Ray Herbert 8.00 4.00
❑ 380 Charlie Maxwell 10.00 5.00
❑ 381 Hal Brown 8.00 4.00
❑ 382 Al Cicotte 8.00 4.00
❑ 383 Lou Berberet 8.00 4.00
❑ 384 John Goryl RC 8.00 4.00
❑ 385 Wilmer Mizell 10.00 5.00
❑ 386 Bailey/Tebbets/F.Rob 15.00 7.50
❑ 387 Wally Post 10.00 5.00
❑ 388 Billy Moran RC 8.00 4.00
❑ 389 Bill Taylor 8.00 4.00
❑ 390 Del Crandall 10.00 5.00
❑ 391 Dave Melton RC 8.00 4.00
❑ 392 Bennie Daniels RC 8.00 4.00
❑ 393 Tony Kubek 30.00 15.00
❑ 394 Jim Grant RC 8.00 4.00
❑ 395 Willard Nixon 8.00 4.00
❑ 396 Dutch Dotterer RC 8.00 4.00
❑ 397A Detroit Tigers TC Alpha 15.00 7.50
❑ 397B Detroit Tigers TC Num 100.00 60.00
❑ 398 Gene Woodling 10.00 5.00
❑ 399 Marv Grissom 8.00 4.00
❑ 400 Nellie Fox 40.00 20.00
❑ 401 Don Bessent 8.00 4.00
❑ 402 Bobby Gene Smith 8.00 4.00
❑ 403 Steve Korcheck RC 8.00 4.00
❑ 404 Curt Simmons 10.00 5.00
❑ 405 Ken Aspromonte RC 8.00 4.00
❑ 406 Vic Power 10.00 5.00
❑ 407 Carlton Willey RC 10.00 5.00
❑ 408A Baltimore Orioles TC Alpha 15.00 7.50
❑ 408B Baltimore Orioles TC Num 100.00 60.00
❑ 409 Frank Thomas 10.00 5.00
❑ 410 Murray Wall 8.00 4.00
❑ 411 Tony Taylor RC 10.00 5.00
❑ 412 Gerry Staley 8.00 4.00
❑ 413 Jim Davenport RC 8.00 4.00
❑ 414 Sammy White 8.00 4.00
❑ 415 Bob Bowman 8.00 4.00
❑ 416 Foster Castleman 8.00 4.00
❑ 417 Carl Furillo 15.00 7.50
❑ 418 M.Mantle/H.Aaron 400.00 250.00
❑ 419 Bobby Shantz 10.00 5.00
❑ 420 Vada Pinson RC 40.00 20.00
❑ 421 Dixie Howell 8.00 4.00
❑ 422 Norm Zauchin 8.00 4.00
❑ 423 Phil Clark RC 8.00 4.00
❑ 424 Larry Doby 25.00 12.50
❑ 425 Sammy Esposito 8.00 4.00
❑ 426 Johnny O'Brien 10.00 5.00
❑ 427 Al Worthington 8.00 4.00
❑ 428A Cincinnati Reds TC Alpha 15.00 7.50
❑ 428B Cincinnati Reds TC Num 100.0060.00
❑ 429 Gus Triandos 10.00 5.00
❑ 430 Bobby Thomson 10.00 5.00
❑ 431 Gene Conley 10.00 5.00
❑ 432 John Powers RC 8.00 4.00
❑ 433A Pancho Herrer ERR 600.00 350.00
❑ 433B Pancho Herrera COR RC 10.00 5.00
❑ 434 Harvey Kuenn 10.00 5.00
❑ 435 Ed Roebuck 10.00 5.00
❑ 436 W.Mays/D.Snider 100.00 60.00
❑ 437 Bob Speake 8.00 4.00
❑ 438 Whitey Herzog 10.00 5.00
❑ 439 Ray Narleski 8.00 4.00
❑ 440 Eddie Mathews 80.00 50.00
❑ 441 Jim Marshall RC 10.00 5.00
❑ 442 Phil Paine RC 8.00 4.00
❑ 443 Billy Harrell SP RC 20.00 10.00
❑ 444 Danny Kravitz 8.00 4.00
❑ 445 Bob Smith RC 8.00 4.00
❑ 446 Carroll Hardy SP RC 20.00 10.00
❑ 447 Ray Monzant 8.00 4.00
❑ 448 Charley Lau RC 10.00 5.00
❑ 449 Gene Fodge RC 8.00 4.00
❑ 450 Preston Ward SP 20.00 10.00
❑ 451 Joe Taylor RC 8.00 4.00
❑ 452 Roman Mejias 8.00 4.00
❑ 453 Tom Qualters 8.00 4.00
❑ 454 Harry Hanebrink RC 8.00 4.00
❑ 455 Hal Griggs RC 8.00 4.00
❑ 456 Dick Brown RC 8.00 4.00
❑ 457 Milt Pappas RC 10.00 5.00
❑ 458 Julio Becquer RC 8.00 4.00
❑ 459 Ron Blackburn RC 8.00 4.00
❑ 460 Chuck Essegian RC 8.00 4.00
❑ 461 Ed Mayer RC 8.00 4.00
❑ 462 Gary Geiger SP RC 20.00 10.00
❑ 463 Vito Valentinetti 8.00 4.00
❑ 464 Curt Flood RC 30.00 15.00
❑ 465 Arnie Portocarrero 8.00 4.00
❑ 466 Pete Whisenant 8.00 4.00
❑ 467 Glen Hobbie RC 8.00 4.00
❑ 468 Bob Schmidt RC 8.00 4.00
❑ 469 Don Ferrarese 8.00 4.00
❑ 470 R.C. Stevens RC 8.00 4.00
❑ 471 Lenny Green RC 8.00 4.00
❑ 472 Joey Jay 10.00 5.00
❑ 473 Bill Renna 8.00 4.00
❑ 474 Roman Semproch RC 8.00 4.00
❑ 475 F.Haney/C.Stengel AS 25.00 12.50
❑ 476 Stan Musial AS TP 50.00 30.00
❑ 477 Bill Skowron AS 10.00 5.00
❑ 478 Johnny Temple AS UER 8.00 4.00
❑ 479 Nellie Fox AS 15.00 7.50
❑ 480 Eddie Mathews AS 30.00 15.00
❑ 481 Frank Malzone AS 8.00 4.00
❑ 482 Ernie Banks AS 40.00 20.00
❑ 483 Luis Aparicio AS 15.00 7.50
❑ 484 Frank Robinson AS 40.00 20.00
❑ 485 Ted Williams AS 150.00 90.00
❑ 486 Willie Mays AS 60.00 35.00
❑ 487 Mickey Mantle AS TP 200.00 125.00
❑ 488 Hank Aaron AS 60.00 35.00
❑ 489 Jackie Jensen AS 10.00 5.00
❑ 490 Ed Bailey AS 8.00 4.00
❑ 491 Sherm Lollar AS 8.00 4.00
❑ 492 Bob Friend AS 8.00 4.00
❑ 493 Bob Turley AS 10.00 5.00
❑ 494 Warren Spahn AS 25.00 12.50
❑ 495 Herb Score AS 15.00 7.50
❑ NNO Contest Cards 40.00 20.00
❑ NNO Felt Emblem Insert

1959 Topps

❑ COMPLETE SET (572) 8000.005000.00
❑ COMMON CARD (1-110) 6.00 3.00
❑ COMMON CARD (111-506) 4.00 2.00
❑ COMMON CARD (507-572) 15.00 7.50
❑ WRAPPER (1-CENT) 125.00 100.00
❑ WRAPPER (5-CENT) 100.00 75.00
❑ 1 Ford Frick COMM 60.00 35.00
❑ 2 Eddie Yost 8.00 4.00
❑ 3 Don McMahon 8.00 4.00
❑ 4 Albie Pearson 8.00 4.00
❑ 5 Dick Donovan 8.00 4.00
❑ 6 Alex Grammas 6.00 3.00
❑ 7 Al Pilarcik 6.00 3.00
❑ 8 Philadelphia Phillies CL 80.00 50.00
❑ 9 Paul Giel 8.00 4.00
❑ 10 Mickey Mantle 1000.00 600.00
❑ 11 Billy Hunter 8.00 4.00
❑ 12 Vern Law 8.00 4.00
❑ 13 Dick Gernert 6.00 3.00
❑ 14 Pete Whisenant 6.00 3.00
❑ 15 Dick Drott 6.00 3.00
❑ 16 Joe Pignatano 6.00 3.00
❑ 17 Thomas/Murtaugh/Klusz 8.00 4.00
❑ 18 Jack Urban 6.00 3.00
❑ 19 Eddie Bressoud 6.00 3.00
❑ 20 Duke Snider 60.00 35.00
❑ 21 Connie Johnson 6.00 3.00
❑ 22 Al Smith 8.00 4.00
❑ 23 Murry Dickson 8.00 4.00
❑ 24 Red Wilson 6.00 3.00
❑ 25 Don Hoak 8.00 4.00
❑ 26 Chuck Stobbs 6.00 3.00
❑ 27 Andy Pafko 8.00 4.00
❑ 28 Al Worthington 6.00 3.00
❑ 29 Jim Bolger 6.00 3.00
❑ 30 Nellie Fox 30.00 15.00
❑ 31 Ken Lehman 6.00 3.00
❑ 32 Don Buddin 6.00 3.00
❑ 33 Ed Fitzgerald 6.00 3.00
❑ 34 Al Kaline/C.Maxwell 20.00 10.00
❑ 35 Ted Kluszewski 12.00 6.00
❑ 36 Hank Aguirre 6.00 3.00
❑ 37 Gene Green 6.00 3.00
❑ 38 Morrie Martin 6.00 3.00
❑ 39 Ed Bouchee 6.00 3.00
❑ 40A Warren Spahn ERR 80.00 50.00
❑ 40B Warren Spahn ERR 100.00 60.00
❑ 40C Warren Spahn COR 60.00 35.00
❑ 41 Bob Martyn 6.00 3.00
❑ 42 Murray Wall 6.00 3.00
❑ 43 Steve Bilko 6.00 3.00
❑ 44 Vito Valentinetti 6.00 3.00
❑ 45 Andy Carey 8.00 4.00
❑ 46 Bill R. Henry 6.00 3.00
❑ 47 Jim Finigan 6.00 3.00
❑ 48 Baltimore Orioles CL 25.00 12.50
❑ 49 Bill Hall RC 6.00 3.00
❑ 50 Willie Mays 175.00 100.00
❑ 51 Rip Coleman 6.00 3.00
❑ 52 Coot Veal RC 6.00 3.00
❑ 53 Stan Williams RC 8.00 4.00
❑ 54 Mel Roach 6.00 3.00
❑ 55 Tom Brewer 6.00 3.00
❑ 56 Carl Sawatski 6.00 3.00
❑ 57 Al Cicotte 6.00 3.00
❑ 58 Eddie Miksis 6.00 3.00
❑ 59 Irv Noren 8.00 4.00
❑ 60 Bob Turley 8.00 4.00
❑ 61 Dick Brown 6.00 3.00
❑ 62 Tony Taylor 8.00 4.00
❑ 63 Jim Hearn 6.00 3.00
❑ 64 Joe DeMaestri 6.00 3.00
❑ 65 Frank Torre 8.00 4.00
❑ 66 Joe Ginsberg 6.00 3.00
❑ 67 Brooks Lawrence 6.00 3.00
❑ 68 Dick Schofield 8.00 4.00
❑ 69 San Francisco Giants CL 25.00 12.50
❑ 70 Harvey Kuenn 8.00 4.00
❑ 71 Don Bessent 6.00 3.00
❑ 72 Bill Renna 6.00 3.00
❑ 73 Ron Jackson 8.00 4.00

❑	74 Lemon/Lavagetto/Sievers	8.00	4.00
❑	75 Sam Jones	8.00	4.00
❑	76 Bobby Richardson	20.00	10.00
❑	77 John Goryl	6.00	3.00
❑	78 Pedro Ramos	6.00	3.00
❑	79 Harry Chiti	6.00	3.00
❑	80 Minnie Minoso	12.00	6.00
❑	81 Hal Jeffcoat	6.00	3.00
❑	82 Bob Boyd	6.00	3.00
❑	83 Bob Smith	6.00	3.00
❑	84 Reno Bertoia	6.00	3.00
❑	85 Harry Anderson	6.00	3.00
❑	86 Bob Keegan	8.00	4.00
❑	87 Danny O'Connell	6.00	3.00
❑	88 Herb Score	12.00	6.00
❑	89 Billy Gardner	6.00	3.00
❑	90 Bill Skowron	12.00	6.00
❑	91 Herb Moford RC	6.00	3.00
❑	92 Dave Philley	6.00	3.00
❑	93 Julio Becquer	6.00	3.00
❑	94 Chicago White Sox CL	40.00	20.00
❑	95 Carl Willey	6.00	3.00
❑	96 Lou Berberet	6.00	3.00
❑	97 Jerry Lynch	8.00	4.00
❑	98 Arnie Portocarrero	6.00	3.00
❑	99 Ted Kazanski	6.00	3.00
❑	100 Bob Cerv	8.00	4.00
❑	101 Alex Kellner	6.00	3.00
❑	102 Felipe Alou RC	30.00	15.00
❑	103 Billy Goodman	8.00	4.00
❑	104 Del Rice	8.00	4.00
❑	105 Lee Walls	6.00	3.00
❑	106 Hal Woodeshick RC	6.00	3.00
❑	107 Norm Larker RC	8.00	4.00
❑	108 Zack Monroe RC	8.00	4.00
❑	109 Bob Schmidt	6.00	3.00
❑	110 George Witt RC	8.00	4.00
❑	111 Cincinnati Redlegs CL	15.00	7.50
❑	112 Billy Consolo	4.00	2.00
❑	113 Taylor Phillips	4.00	2.00
❑	114 Earl Battey	8.00	4.00
❑	115 Mickey Vernon	8.00	4.00
❑	116 Bob Allison RS RC	12.00	6.00
❑	117 John Blanchard RS RC	12.00	6.00
❑	118 John Buzhardt RS RC	5.00	2.50
❑	119 Johnny Callison RS RC	12.00	6.00
❑	120 Chuck Coles RS RC	5.00	2.50
❑	121 Bob Conley RS RC	5.00	2.50
❑	122 Bennie Daniels RS	5.00	2.50
❑	123 Don Dillard RS RC	5.00	2.50
❑	124 Dan Dobbek RS RC	5.00	2.50
❑	125 Ron Fairly RS RC	12.00	6.00
❑	126 Eddie Haas RS RC	5.00	2.50
❑	127 Kent Hadley RS RC	5.00	2.50
❑	128 Bob Hartman RS RC	5.00	2.50
❑	129 Frank Herrera RS	5.00	2.50
❑	130 Lou Jackson RS RC	5.00	2.50
❑	131 Deron Johnson RS RC	12.00	6.00
❑	132 Don Lee RS	5.00	2.50
❑	133 Bob Lillis RS RC	5.00	2.50
❑	134 Jim McDaniel RS RC	5.00	2.50
❑	135 Gene Oliver RS RC	5.00	2.50
❑	136 Jim O'Toole RS RC	5.00	2.50
❑	137 Dick Ricketts RS RC	5.00	2.50
❑	138 John Romano RS RC	5.00	2.50
❑	139 Ed Sadowski RS RC	5.00	2.50
❑	140 Charlie Secrest RS RC	5.00	2.50
❑	141 Joe Shipley RS RC	5.00	2.50
❑	142 Dick Stigman RS RC	5.00	2.50
❑	143 Willie Tasby RS RC	5.00	2.50
❑	144 Jerry Walker RS	5.00	2.50
❑	145 Dom Zanni RS RC	5.00	2.50
❑	146 Jerry Zimmerman RS RC	5.00	2.50
❑	147 Long/Banks/Moryn	30.00	15.00
❑	148 Mike McCormick	8.00	4.00
❑	149 Jim Bunning	20.00	10.00
❑	150 Stan Musial	120.00	60.00
❑	151 Bob Malkmus	4.00	2.00
❑	152 Johnny Klippstein	4.00	2.00
❑	153 Jim Marshall	4.00	2.00
❑	154 Ray Herbert	4.00	2.00
❑	155 Enos Slaughter	20.00	10.00
❑	156 B.Pierce/R.Roberts	12.00	6.00
❑	157 Felix Mantilla	4.00	2.00
❑	158 Walt Dropo	4.00	2.00
❑	159 Bob Shaw	8.00	4.00
❑	160 Dick Groat	8.00	4.00
❑	161 Frank Baumann	4.00	2.00
❑	162 Bobby G. Smith	4.00	2.00
❑	163 Sandy Koufax	150.00	90.00
❑	164 Johnny Groth	4.00	2.00
❑	165 Bill Bruton	4.00	2.00
❑	166 Minoso/Colavito/Doby	30.00	15.00
❑	167 Duke Maas	4.00	2.00
❑	168 Carroll Hardy	4.00	2.00
❑	169 Ted Abernathy	4.00	2.00
❑	170 Gene Woodling	8.00	4.00
❑	171 Willard Schmidt	4.00	2.00
❑	172 Kansas City Athletics CL	15.00	7.50
❑	173 Bill Monbouquette RC	8.00	4.00
❑	174 Jim Pendleton	4.00	2.00
❑	175 Dick Farrell	8.00	4.00
❑	176 Preston Ward	4.00	2.00
❑	177 John Briggs RC	4.00	2.00
❑	178 Ruben Amaro RC	12.00	6.00
❑	179 Don Rudolph	4.00	2.00
❑	180 Yogi Berra	80.00	50.00
❑	181 Bob Porterfield	4.00	2.00
❑	182 Milt Graff	4.00	2.00
❑	183 Stu Miller	8.00	4.00
❑	184 Harvey Haddix	8.00	4.00
❑	185 Jim Busby	4.00	2.00
❑	186 Mudcat Grant	8.00	4.00
❑	187 Bubba Phillips	8.00	4.00
❑	188 Juan Pizarro	4.00	2.00
❑	189 Neil Chrisley	4.00	2.00
❑	190 Bill Virdon	8.00	4.00
❑	191 Russ Kemmerer	4.00	2.00
❑	192 Charlie Beamon RC	4.00	2.00
❑	193 Sammy Taylor	4.00	2.00
❑	194 Jim Brosnan	8.00	4.00
❑	195 Rip Repulski	4.00	2.00
❑	196 Billy Moran	4.00	2.00
❑	197 Ray Semproch	4.00	2.00
❑	198 Jim Davenport	8.00	4.00
❑	199 Leo Kiely	4.00	2.00
❑	200 W.Giles NL PRES	8.00	4.00
❑	201 Tom Acker	4.00	2.00
❑	202 Roger Maris	125.00	75.00
❑	203 Ossie Virgil	4.00	2.00
❑	204 Casey Wise	4.00	2.00
❑	205 Don Larsen	8.00	4.00
❑	206 Carl Furillo	12.00	6.00
❑	207 George Strickland	4.00	2.00
❑	208 Willie Jones	4.00	2.00
❑	209 Lenny Green	4.00	2.00
❑	210 Ed Bailey	4.00	2.00
❑	211 Bob Blaylock RC	4.00	2.00
❑	212 H.Aaron/E.Mathews	80.00	50.00
❑	213 Jim Rivera	8.00	4.00
❑	214 Marcelino Solis RC	4.00	2.00
❑	215 Jim Lemon	8.00	4.00
❑	216 Andre Rodgers	4.00	2.00
❑	217 Carl Erskine	12.00	6.00
❑	218 Roman Mejias	4.00	2.00
❑	219 George Zuverink	4.00	2.00
❑	220 Frank Malzone	8.00	4.00
❑	221 Bob Bowman	4.00	2.00
❑	222 Bobby Shantz	8.00	4.00
❑	223 St. Louis Cardinals CL	15.00	7.50
❑	224 Claude Osteen RC	8.00	4.00
❑	225 Johnny Logan	8.00	4.00
❑	226 Art Ceccarelli	4.00	2.00
❑	227 Hal W. Smith	4.00	2.00
❑	228 Don Gross	4.00	2.00
❑	229 Vic Power	8.00	4.00
❑	230 Bill Fischer	4.00	2.00
❑	231 Ellis Burton RC	4.00	2.00
❑	232 Eddie Kasko	4.00	2.00
❑	233 Paul Foytack	4.00	2.00
❑	234 Chuck Tanner	8.00	4.00
❑	235 Valmy Thomas	4.00	2.00
❑	236 Ted Bowsfield RC	4.00	2.00
❑	237 McDougald/Turley/B.Rich	12.00	6.00
❑	238 Gene Baker	4.00	2.00
❑	239 Bob Trowbridge	4.00	2.00
❑	240 Hank Bauer	12.00	6.00
❑	241 Billy Muffett	4.00	2.00
❑	242 Ron Samford RC	4.00	2.00
❑	243 Marv Grissom	4.00	2.00
❑	244 Ted Gray	4.00	2.00
❑	245 Ned Garver	4.00	2.00
❑	246 J.W. Porter	4.00	2.00
❑	247 Don Ferrarese	4.00	2.00
❑	248 Boston Red Sox CL	15.00	7.50
❑	249 Bobby Adams	4.00	2.00
❑	250 Billy O'Dell	4.00	2.00
❑	251 Clete Boyer	12.00	6.00
❑	252 Ray Boone	8.00	4.00
❑	253 Seth Morehead RC	4.00	2.00
❑	254 Zeke Bella RC	4.00	2.00
❑	255 Del Ennis	8.00	4.00
❑	256 Jerry Davie RC	4.00	2.00
❑	257 Leon Wagner RC	8.00	4.00
❑	258 Fred Kipp RC	4.00	2.00
❑	259 Jim Pisoni	4.00	2.00
❑	260 Early Wynn UER	20.00	10.00
❑	261 Gene Stephens	4.00	2.00
❑	262 Podres/Labine/Drysdale	12.00	6.00
❑	263 Bud Daley	4.00	2.00
❑	264 Chico Carrasquel	4.00	2.00
❑	265 Ron Kline	4.00	2.00
❑	266 Woody Held	4.00	2.00
❑	267 John Romonosky RC	4.00	2.00
❑	268 Tito Francona	8.00	4.00
❑	269 Jack Meyer	4.00	2.00
❑	270 Gil Hodges	30.00	15.00
❑	271 Orlando Pena RC	4.00	2.00
❑	272 Jerry Lumpe	4.00	2.00
❑	273 Joey Jay	8.00	4.00
❑	274 Jerry Kindall	8.00	4.00
❑	275 Jack Sanford	8.00	4.00
❑	276 Pete Daley	4.00	2.00
❑	277 Turk Lown	8.00	4.00
❑	278 Chuck Essegian	4.00	2.00
❑	279 Ernie Johnson	4.00	2.00
❑	280 Frank Bolling	4.00	2.00
❑	281 Walt Craddock RC	4.00	2.00
❑	282 R.C. Stevens	4.00	2.00
❑	283 Russ Heman RC	4.00	2.00
❑	284 Steve Korcheck	4.00	2.00
❑	285 Joe Cunningham	4.00	2.00
❑	286 Dean Stone	4.00	2.00
❑	287 Don Zimmer	12.00	6.00
❑	288 Dutch Dotterer	4.00	2.00
❑	289 Johnny Kucks	8.00	4.00
❑	290 Wes Covington	4.00	2.00
❑	291 P.Ramos/C.Pascual	4.00	2.00
❑	292 Dick Williams	8.00	4.00
❑	293 Ray Moore	4.00	2.00
❑	294 Hank Foiles	4.00	2.00
❑	295 Billy Martin	30.00	15.00
❑	296 Ernie Broglio RC	4.00	2.00
❑	297 Jackie Brandt RC	4.00	2.00
❑	298 Tex Clevenger	4.00	2.00
❑	299 Billy Klaus	4.00	2.00
❑	300 Richie Ashburn	30.00	15.00
❑	301 Earl Averill Jr. RC	4.00	2.00
❑	302 Don Mossi	8.00	4.00
❑	303 Marty Keough	4.00	2.00
❑	304 Chicago Cubs CL	15.00	7.50
❑	305 Curt Raydon RC	4.00	2.00
❑	306 Jim Gilliam	8.00	4.00
❑	307 Curt Barclay	4.00	2.00
❑	308 Norm Siebern	4.00	2.00
❑	309 Sal Maglie	8.00	4.00
❑	310 Luis Aparicio	20.00	10.00
❑	311 Norm Zauchin	4.00	2.00
❑	312 Don Newcombe	8.00	4.00
❑	313 Frank House	4.00	2.00
❑	314 Don Cardwell	4.00	2.00
❑	315 Joe Adcock	8.00	4.00
❑	316A Ralph Lumenti UER	4.00	2.00
❑	316B Ralph Lumenti UER	80.00	50.00
❑	317 R.Ashburn/W.Mays	80.00	50.00
❑	318 Rocky Bridges	4.00	2.00
❑	319 Dave Hillman	4.00	2.00
❑	320 Bob Skinner	8.00	4.00
❑	321A Bob Giallombardo RC	8.00	4.00
❑	321B Bob Giallombardo ERR	80.00	50.00
❑	322A Harry Hanebrink TR	8.00	4.00
❑	322B H.Hanebrink ERR	80.00	50.00
❑	323 Frank Sullivan	4.00	2.00
❑	324 Don Demeter	4.00	2.00
❑	325 Ken Boyer	12.00	6.00
❑	326 Marv Throneberry	8.00	4.00
❑	327 Gary Bell RC	4.00	2.00
❑	328 Lou Skizas	4.00	2.00

❑ 329 Detroit Tigers CL 15.00 7.50
❑ 330 Gus Triandos 8.00 4.00
❑ 331 Steve Boros 4.00 2.00
❑ 332 Ray Monzant 4.00 2.00
❑ 333 Harry Simpson 4.00 2.00
❑ 334 Glen Hobbie 4.00 2.00
❑ 335 Johnny Temple 8.00 4.00
❑ 336A Billy Loes TR 8.00 4.00
❑ 336B Billy Loes ERR 80.00 50.00
❑ 337 George Crowe 4.00 2.00
❑ 338 Sparky Anderson RC 60.00 35.00
❑ 339 Roy Face 8.00 4.00
❑ 340 Roy Sievers 8.00 4.00
❑ 341 Tom Qualters 4.00 2.00
❑ 342 Ray Jablonski 4.00 2.00
❑ 343 Billy Hoeft 4.00 2.00
❑ 344 Russ Nixon 4.00 2.00
❑ 345 Gil McDougald 12.00 6.00
❑ 346 D.Sisler/T.Brewer 4.00 2.00
❑ 347 Bob Buhl 4.00 2.00
❑ 348 Ted Lepcio 4.00 2.00
❑ 349 Hoyt Wilhelm 20.00 10.00
❑ 350 Ernie Banks 80.00 50.00
❑ 351 Earl Torgeson 4.00 2.00
❑ 352 Robin Roberts 20.00 10.00
❑ 353 Curt Flood 8.00 4.00
❑ 354 Pete Burnside 4.00 2.00
❑ 355 Jimmy Piersall 8.00 4.00
❑ 356 Bob Mabe RC 4.00 2.00
❑ 357 Dick Stuart RC 8.00 4.00
❑ 358 Ralph Terry 8.00 4.00
❑ 359 Bill White RC 20.00 10.00
❑ 360 Al Kaline 60.00 35.00
❑ 361 Willard Nixon 4.00 2.00
❑ 362A Dolan Nichols RC 4.00 2.00
❑ 362B Dolan Nichols ERR 80.00 50.00
❑ 363 Bobby Avila 4.00 2.00
❑ 364 Danny McDevitt 4.00 2.00
❑ 365 Gus Bell 8.00 4.00
❑ 366 Humberto Robinson 4.00 2.00
❑ 367 Cal Neeman 4.00 2.00
❑ 368 Don Mueller 8.00 4.00
❑ 369 Dick Tomanek 4.00 2.00
❑ 370 Pete Runnels 8.00 4.00
❑ 371 Dick Brodowski 4.00 2.00
❑ 372 Jim Hegan 8.00 4.00
❑ 373 Herb Plews 4.00 2.00
❑ 374 Art Ditmar 8.00 4.00
❑ 375 Bob Nieman 4.00 2.00
❑ 376 Hal Naragon 4.00 2.00
❑ 377 John Antonelli 8.00 4.00
❑ 378 Gail Harris 4.00 2.00
❑ 379 Bob Miller 4.00 2.00
❑ 380 Hank Aaron 150.00 90.00
❑ 381 Mike Baxes 4.00 2.00
❑ 382 Curt Simmons 8.00 4.00
❑ 383 D.Larsen/C.Stengel 12.00 6.00
❑ 384 Dave Sisler 4.00 2.00
❑ 385 Sherm Lollar 8.00 4.00
❑ 386 Jim Delsing 4.00 2.00
❑ 387 Don Drysdale 50.00 30.00
❑ 388 Bob Will RC 4.00 2.00
❑ 389 Joe Nuxhall 8.00 4.00
❑ 390 Orlando Cepeda 20.00 10.00
❑ 391 Milt Pappas 8.00 4.00
❑ 392 Whitey Herzog 8.00 4.00
❑ 393 Frank Lary 8.00 4.00
❑ 394 Randy Jackson 4.00 2.00
❑ 395 Elston Howard 12.00 6.00
❑ 396 Bob Rush 4.00 2.00
❑ 397 Washington Senators CL 15.00 7.50
❑ 398 Wally Post 8.00 4.00
❑ 399 Larry Jackson 4.00 2.00
❑ 400 Jackie Jensen 8.00 4.00
❑ 401 Ron Blackburn 4.00 2.00
❑ 402 Hector Lopez 8.00 4.00
❑ 403 Clem Labine 8.00 4.00
❑ 404 Hank Sauer 8.00 4.00
❑ 405 Roy McMillan 8.00 4.00
❑ 406 Solly Drake 4.00 2.00
❑ 407 Moe Drabowsky 8.00 4.00
❑ 408 N.Fox/L.Aparicio 40.00 20.00
❑ 409 Gus Zernial 8.00 4.00
❑ 410 Billy Pierce 8.00 4.00
❑ 411 Whitey Lockman 8.00 4.00
❑ 412 Stan Lopata 4.00 2.00
❑ 413 Camilo Pascual UER 8.00 4.00
❑ 414 Dale Long 8.00 4.00
❑ 415 Bill Mazeroski 12.00 6.00
❑ 416 Haywood Sullivan 8.00 4.00
❑ 417 Virgil Trucks 8.00 4.00
❑ 418 Gino Cimoli 4.00 2.00
❑ 419 Milwaukee Braves CL 15.00 7.50
❑ 420 Rocky Colavito 30.00 15.00
❑ 421 Herman Wehmeier 4.00 2.00
❑ 422 Hobie Landrith 4.00 2.00
❑ 423 Bob Grim 8.00 4.00
❑ 424 Ken Aspromonte 4.00 2.00
❑ 425 Del Crandall 8.00 4.00
❑ 426 Gerry Staley 8.00 4.00
❑ 427 Charlie Neal 8.00 4.00
❑ 428 Kline/Friend/Law/Face 4.00 2.00
❑ 429 Bobby Thomson 8.00 4.00
❑ 430 Whitey Ford 60.00 35.00
❑ 431 Whammy Douglas 4.00 2.00
❑ 432 Smoky Burgess 8.00 4.00
❑ 433 Billy Harrell 4.00 2.00
❑ 434 Hal Griggs 4.00 2.00
❑ 435 Frank Robinson 50.00 30.00
❑ 436 Granny Hamner 4.00 2.00
❑ 437 Ike Delock 4.00 2.00
❑ 438 Sammy Esposito 4.00 2.00
❑ 439 Brooks Robinson 50.00 30.00
❑ 440 Lew Burdette UER 8.00 4.00
❑ 441 John Roseboro 8.00 4.00
❑ 442 Ray Narleski 4.00 2.00
❑ 443 Daryl Spencer 4.00 2.00
❑ 444 Ron Hansen RC 8.00 4.00
❑ 445 Cal McLish 4.00 2.00
❑ 446 Rocky Nelson 4.00 2.00
❑ 447 Bob Anderson 4.00 2.00
❑ 448 Vada Pinson UER 12.00 6.00
❑ 449 Tom Gorman 4.00 2.00
❑ 450 Eddie Mathews 40.00 20.00
❑ 451 Jimmy Constable RC 4.00 2.00
❑ 452 Chico Fernandez 4.00 2.00
❑ 453 Les Moss 4.00 2.00
❑ 454 Phil Clark 4.00 2.00
❑ 455 Larry Doby 12.00 6.00
❑ 456 Jerry Casale RC 4.00 2.00
❑ 457 Los Angeles Dodgers CL 30.00 15.00
❑ 458 Gordon Jones 4.00 2.00
❑ 459 Bill Tuttle 4.00 2.00
❑ 460 Bob Friend 8.00 4.00
❑ 461 Mickey Mantle BT 125.00 75.00
❑ 462 Rocky Colavito BT 12.00 6.00
❑ 463 Al Kaline BT 30.00 15.00
❑ 464 Willie Mays BT 40.00 20.00
❑ 465 Roy Sievers BT 8.00 4.00
❑ 466 Billy Pierce BT 8.00 4.00
❑ 467 Hank Aaron BT 40.00 20.00
❑ 468 Duke Snider BT 20.00 10.00
❑ 469 Ernie Banks BT 20.00 10.00
❑ 470 Stan Musial BT 30.00 15.00
❑ 471 Tom Sturdivant 4.00 2.00
❑ 472 Gene Freese 4.00 2.00
❑ 473 Mike Fornieles 4.00 2.00
❑ 474 Moe Thacker RC 4.00 2.00
❑ 475 Jack Harshman 4.00 2.00
❑ 476 Cleveland Indians CL 15.00 7.50
❑ 477 Barry Latman RC 4.00 2.00
❑ 478 Roberto Clemente 175.00 100.00
❑ 479 Lindy McDaniel 8.00 4.00
❑ 480 Red Schoendienst 12.00 6.00
❑ 481 Charlie Maxwell 8.00 4.00
❑ 482 Russ Meyer 4.00 2.00
❑ 483 Clint Courtney 4.00 2.00
❑ 484 Willie Kirkland 4.00 2.00
❑ 485 Ryne Duren 8.00 4.00
❑ 486 Sammy White 4.00 2.00
❑ 487 Hal Brown 4.00 2.00
❑ 488 Walt Moryn 4.00 2.00
❑ 489 John Powers 4.00 2.00
❑ 490 Frank Thomas 8.00 4.00
❑ 491 Don Blasingame 4.00 2.00
❑ 492 Gene Conley 8.00 4.00
❑ 493 Jim Landis 8.00 4.00
❑ 494 Don Pavletich RC 4.00 2.00
❑ 495 Johnny Podres 12.00 6.00
❑ 496 Wayne Terwilliger UER 4.00 2.00
❑ 497 Hal R. Smith 4.00 2.00
❑ 498 Dick Hyde 4.00 2.00
❑ 499 Johnny O'Brien 8.00 4.00
❑ 500 Vic Wertz 8.00 4.00
❑ 501 Bob Tiefenauer RC 4.00 2.00
❑ 502 Alvin Dark 8.00 4.00
❑ 503 Jim Owens 4.00 2.00
❑ 504 Ossie Alvarez RC 4.00 2.00
❑ 505 Tony Kubek 12.00 6.00
❑ 506 Bob Purkey 4.00 2.00
❑ 507 Bob Hale 15.00 7.50
❑ 508 Art Fowler 15.00 7.50
❑ 509 Norm Cash RC 80.00 50.00
❑ 510 New York Yankees CL 125.00 75.00
❑ 511 George Susce 15.00 7.50
❑ 512 George Altman RC 15.00 7.50
❑ 513 Tommy Carroll 15.00 7.50
❑ 514 Bob Gibson RC 300.00 175.00
❑ 515 Harmon Killebrew 125.00 75.00
❑ 516 Mike Garcia 20.00 10.00
❑ 517 Joe Koppe RC 15.00 7.50
❑ 518 Mike Cuellar UER RC 30.00 18.00
❑ 519 Runnels/Gernert/Malzone 20.00 10.00
❑ 520 Don Elston 15.00 7.50
❑ 521 Gary Geiger 15.00 7.50
❑ 522 Gene Snyder RC 15.00 7.50
❑ 523 Harry Bright RC 15.00 7.50
❑ 524 Larry Osborne RC 15.00 7.50
❑ 525 Jim Coates RC 20.00 10.00
❑ 526 Bob Speake 15.00 7.50
❑ 527 Solly Hemus 15.00 7.50
❑ 528 Pittsburgh Pirates CL 80.00 50.00
❑ 529 George Bamberger RC 20.00 10.00
❑ 530 Wally Moon 20.00 10.00
❑ 531 Ray Webster RC 15.00 7.50
❑ 532 Mark Freeman RC 15.00 7.50
❑ 533 Darrell Johnson 20.00 10.00
❑ 534 Faye Throneberry 15.00 7.50
❑ 535 Ruben Gomez 15.00 7.50
❑ 536 Danny Kravitz 15.00 7.50
❑ 537 Rudolph Arias RC 15.00 7.50
❑ 538 Chick King 15.00 7.50
❑ 539 Gary Blaylock RC 15.00 7.50
❑ 540 Willie Miranda 15.00 7.50
❑ 541 Bob Thurman 15.00 7.50
❑ 542 Jim Perry RC 30.00 18.00
❑ 543 Skinner/Virdon/Clemente 125.00 75.00
❑ 544 Lee Tate RC 15.00 7.50
❑ 545 Tom Morgan 15.00 7.50
❑ 546 Al Schroll 15.00 7.50
❑ 547 Jim Baxes RC 15.00 7.50
❑ 548 Elmer Singleton 15.00 7.50
❑ 549 Howie Nunn RC 15.00 7.50
❑ 550 R.Campanella Courage 150.00 90.00
❑ 551 Fred Haney AS MG 15.00 7.50
❑ 552 Casey Stengel AS 30.00 18.00
❑ 553 Orlando Cepeda AS 30.00 18.00
❑ 554 Bill Skowron AS 20.00 10.00
❑ 555 Bill Mazeroski AS 30.00 18.00
❑ 556 Nellie Fox AS 40.00 20.00
❑ 557 Ken Boyer AS 30.00 18.00
❑ 558 Frank Malzone AS 15.00 7.50
❑ 559 Ernie Banks AS 60.00 35.00
❑ 560 Luis Aparicio AS 40.00 25.00
❑ 561 Hank Aaron AS 125.00 75.00
❑ 562 Al Kaline AS 60.00 35.00
❑ 563 Willie Mays AS 125.00 75.00
❑ 564 Mickey Mantle AS 300.00 175.00
❑ 565 Wes Covington AS 20.00 10.00
❑ 566 Roy Sievers AS 15.00 7.50
❑ 567 Del Crandall AS 15.00 7.50
❑ 568 Gus Triandos AS 15.00 7.50
❑ 569 Bob Friend AS 15.00 7.50
❑ 570 Bob Turley AS 15.00 7.50
❑ 571 Warren Spahn AS 50.00 30.00
❑ 572 Billy Pierce AS 40.00 25.00

1960 Topps

❑ COMPLETE SET (572) 5000.00 3000.00
❑ COMMON CARD (1-440) 4.00 2.00
❑ COMMON CARD (441-506) 8.00 4.00
❑ COMMON CARD (507-572) 15.00 7.50
❑ WRAPPER (1-CENT) 900.00 750.00
❑ WRAP. (1-CENT REPEAT) 500.00 400.00
❑ WRAPPER (5-CENT) 40.00 30.00
❑ 1 Early Wynn 40.00 20.00
❑ 2 Roman Mejias 4.00 2.00
❑ 3 Joe Adcock 6.00 3.00

❑ 4	Bob Purkey	4.00	2.00
❑ 5	Wally Moon	6.00	3.00
❑ 6	Lou Berberet	4.00	2.00
❑ 7	W.Mays/B.Rigney	25.00	12.50
❑ 8	Bud Daley	4.00	2.00
❑ 9	Faye Throneberry	4.00	2.00
❑ 10	Ernie Banks	50.00	30.00
❑ 11	Norm Siebern	4.00	2.00
❑ 12	Milt Pappas	6.00	3.00
❑ 13	Wally Post	6.00	3.00
❑ 14	Jim Grant	6.00	3.00
❑ 15	Pete Runnels	6.00	3.00
❑ 16	Ernie Broglio	6.00	3.00
❑ 17	Johnny Callison	6.00	3.00
❑ 18	Los Angeles Dodgers CL	50.00	30.00
❑ 19	Felix Mantilla	4.00	2.00
❑ 20	Roy Face	6.00	3.00
❑ 21	Dutch Dotterer	4.00	2.00
❑ 22	Rocky Bridges	4.00	2.00
❑ 23	Eddie Fisher RC	4.00	2.00
❑ 24	Dick Gray	4.00	2.00
❑ 25	Roy Sievers	6.00	3.00
❑ 26	Wayne Terwilliger	4.00	2.00
❑ 27	Dick Drott	4.00	2.00
❑ 28	Brooks Robinson	50.00	30.00
❑ 29	Clem Labine	6.00	3.00
❑ 30	Tito Francona	4.00	2.00
❑ 31	Sammy Esposito	4.00	2.00
❑ 32	J.O'Toole/V.Pinson	4.00	2.00
❑ 33	Tom Morgan	4.00	2.00
❑ 34	Sparky Anderson	15.00	7.50
❑ 35	Whitey Ford	50.00	30.00
❑ 36	Russ Nixon	4.00	2.00
❑ 37	Bill Bruton	4.00	2.00
❑ 38	Jerry Casale	4.00	2.00
❑ 39	Earl Averill Jr.	4.00	2.00
❑ 40	Joe Cunningham	4.00	2.00
❑ 41	Barry Latman	4.00	2.00
❑ 42	Hobie Landrith	4.00	2.00
❑ 43	Washington Senators CL	10.00	5.00
❑ 44	Bobby Locke RC	4.00	2.00
❑ 45	Roy McMillan	6.00	3.00
❑ 46	Jack Fisher RC	4.00	2.00
❑ 47	Don Zimmer	6.00	3.00
❑ 48	Hal W. Smith	4.00	2.00
❑ 49	Curt Raydon	4.00	2.00
❑ 50	Al Kaline	50.00	30.00
❑ 51	Jim Coates	6.00	3.00
❑ 52	Dave Philley	4.00	2.00
❑ 53	Jackie Brandt	4.00	2.00
❑ 54	Mike Fornieles	4.00	2.00
❑ 55	Bill Mazeroski	15.00	7.50
❑ 56	Steve Korcheck	4.00	2.00
❑ 57	T.Lown/G.Staley	4.00	2.00
❑ 58	Gino Cimoli	4.00	2.00
❑ 58A	Gino Cimoli Cards		
❑ 59	Juan Pizarro	4.00	2.00
❑ 60	Gus Triandos	6.00	3.00
❑ 61	Eddie Kasko	4.00	2.00
❑ 62	Roger Craig	6.00	3.00
❑ 63	George Strickland	4.00	2.00
❑ 64	Jack Meyer	4.00	2.00
❑ 65	Elston Howard	6.00	3.00
❑ 66	Bob Trowbridge	4.00	2.00
❑ 67	Jose Pagan RC	4.00	2.00
❑ 68	Dave Hillman	4.00	2.00
❑ 69	Billy Goodman	6.00	3.00
❑ 70	Lew Burdette UER	6.00	3.00
❑ 71	Marty Keough	4.00	2.00
❑ 72	Detroit Tigers CL	25.00	12.50
❑ 73	Bob Gibson	50.00	30.00
❑ 74	Walt Moryn	4.00	2.00
❑ 75	Vic Power	6.00	3.00
❑ 76	Bill Fischer	4.00	2.00
❑ 77	Hank Foiles	4.00	2.00
❑ 78	Bob Grim	4.00	2.00
❑ 79	Walt Dropo	4.00	2.00
❑ 80	Johnny Antonelli	6.00	3.00
❑ 81	Russ Snyder RC	4.00	2.00
❑ 82	Ruben Gomez	4.00	2.00
❑ 83	Tony Kubek	15.00	7.50
❑ 84	Hal R. Smith	4.00	2.00
❑ 85	Frank Lary	6.00	3.00
❑ 86	Dick Gernert	4.00	2.00
❑ 87	John Romonosky	4.00	2.00
❑ 88	John Roseboro	6.00	3.00
❑ 89	Hal Brown	4.00	2.00
❑ 90	Bobby Avila	4.00	2.00
❑ 91	Bennie Daniels	4.00	2.00
❑ 92	Whitey Herzog	6.00	3.00
❑ 93	Art Schult	4.00	2.00
❑ 94	Leo Kiely	4.00	2.00
❑ 95	Frank Thomas	6.00	3.00
❑ 96	Ralph Terry	6.00	3.00
❑ 97	Ted Lepcio	4.00	2.00
❑ 98	Gordon Jones	4.00	2.00
❑ 99	Lenny Green	4.00	2.00
❑ 100	Nellie Fox	20.00	10.00
❑ 101	Bob Miller RC	4.00	2.00
❑ 102	Kent Hadley	4.00	2.00
❑ 102A	Kent Hadley A's		
❑ 103	Dick Farrell	6.00	3.00
❑ 104	Dick Schofield	6.00	3.00
❑ 105	Larry Sherry RC	6.00	3.00
❑ 106	Billy Gardner	4.00	2.00
❑ 107	Carlton Willey	4.00	2.00
❑ 108	Pete Daley	4.00	2.00
❑ 109	Clete Boyer	15.00	7.50
❑ 110	Cal McLish	4.00	2.00
❑ 111	Vic Wertz	6.00	3.00
❑ 112	Jack Harshman	4.00	2.00
❑ 113	Bob Skinner	4.00	2.00
❑ 114	Ken Aspromonte	4.00	2.00
❑ 115	R.Face/H.Wilhelm	6.00	3.00
❑ 116	Jim Rivera	4.00	2.00
❑ 117	Tom Borland RS	4.00	2.00
❑ 118	Bob Bruce RS RC	4.00	2.00
❑ 119	Chico Cardenas RS RC	6.00	3.00
❑ 120	Duke Carmel RS RC	4.00	2.00
❑ 121	Camilo Carreon RS RC	4.00	2.00
❑ 122	Don Dillard RS	4.00	2.00
❑ 123	Dan Dobbek RS	4.00	2.00
❑ 124	Jim Donohue RS RC	4.00	2.00
❑ 125	Dick Ellsworth RS RC	6.00	3.00
❑ 126	Chuck Estrada RS RC	4.00	2.00
❑ 127	Ron Hansen RS	6.00	3.00
❑ 128	Bill Harris RS RC	4.00	2.00
❑ 129	Bob Hartman RS	4.00	2.00
❑ 130	Frank Herrera RS	4.00	2.00
❑ 131	Ed Hobaugh RS RC	4.00	2.00
❑ 132	Frank Howard RS RC	25.00	12.50
❑ 133	Julian Javier RS RC	6.00	3.00
❑ 134	Deron Johnson RS	6.00	3.00
❑ 135	Ken Johnson RS RC	4.00	2.00
❑ 136	Jim Kaat RS RC	40.00	20.00
❑ 137	Lou Klimchock RS RC	4.00	2.00
❑ 138	Art Mahaffey RS RC	6.00	3.00
❑ 139	Carl Mathias RS RC	4.00	2.00
❑ 140	Julio Navarro RS RC	4.00	2.00
❑ 141	Jim Proctor RS RC	4.00	2.00
❑ 142	Bill Short RS RC	4.00	2.00
❑ 143	Al Spangler RS RC	4.00	2.00
❑ 144	Al Stieglitz RS RC	4.00	2.00
❑ 145	Jim Umbricht RS RC	4.00	2.00
❑ 146	Ted Wieand RS RC	4.00	2.00
❑ 147	Bob Will RS	4.00	2.00
❑ 148	C.Yastrzemski RS RC	200.00	125.00
❑ 149	Bob Nieman	4.00	2.00
❑ 150	Billy Pierce	6.00	3.00
❑ 151	San Francisco Giants CL	10.00	5.00
❑ 152	Gail Harris	4.00	2.00
❑ 153	Bobby Thomson	6.00	3.00
❑ 154	Jim Davenport	6.00	3.00
❑ 155	Charlie Neal	6.00	3.00
❑ 156	Art Ceccarelli	4.00	2.00
❑ 157	Rocky Nelson	6.00	3.00
❑ 158	Wes Covington	6.00	3.00
❑ 159	Jim Piersall	6.00	3.00
❑ 160	M.Mantle/K.Boyer	125.00	75.00
❑ 161	Ray Narleski	4.00	2.00
❑ 162	Sammy Taylor	4.00	2.00
❑ 163	Hector Lopez	6.00	3.00
❑ 164	Cincinnati Reds CL	10.00	5.00
❑ 165	Jack Sanford	6.00	3.00
❑ 166	Chuck Essegian	4.00	2.00
❑ 167	Valmy Thomas	4.00	2.00
❑ 168	Alex Grammas	4.00	2.00
❑ 169	Jake Striker RC	4.00	2.00
❑ 170	Del Crandall	6.00	3.00
❑ 171	Johnny Groth	4.00	2.00
❑ 172	Willie Kirkland	4.00	2.00
❑ 173	Billy Martin	20.00	10.00
❑ 174	Cleveland Indians CL	10.00	5.00
❑ 175	Pedro Ramos	4.00	2.00
❑ 176	Vada Pinson	6.00	3.00
❑ 177	Johnny Kucks	4.00	2.00
❑ 178	Woody Held	4.00	2.00
❑ 179	Rip Coleman	4.00	2.00
❑ 180	Harry Simpson	4.00	2.00
❑ 181	Billy Loes	6.00	3.00
❑ 182	Glen Hobbie	4.00	2.00
❑ 183	Eli Grba RC	4.00	2.00
❑ 184	Gary Geiger	4.00	2.00
❑ 185	Jim Owens	4.00	2.00
❑ 186	Dave Sisler	4.00	2.00
❑ 187	Jay Hook RC	4.00	2.00
❑ 188	Dick Williams	6.00	3.00
❑ 189	Don McMahon	4.00	2.00
❑ 190	Gene Woodling	6.00	3.00
❑ 191	Johnny Klippstein	4.00	2.00
❑ 192	Danny O'Connell	4.00	2.00
❑ 193	Dick Hyde	4.00	2.00
❑ 194	Bobby Gene Smith	4.00	2.00
❑ 195	Lindy McDaniel	6.00	3.00
❑ 196	Andy Carey	6.00	3.00
❑ 197	Ron Kline	4.00	2.00
❑ 198	Jerry Lynch	6.00	3.00
❑ 199	Dick Donovan	6.00	3.00
❑ 200	Willie Mays	125.00	75.00
❑ 201	Larry Osborne	4.00	2.00
❑ 202	Fred Kipp	4.00	2.00
❑ 203	Sammy White	4.00	2.00
❑ 204	Ryne Duren	6.00	3.00
❑ 205	Johnny Logan	6.00	3.00
❑ 206	Claude Osteen	6.00	3.00
❑ 207	Bob Boyd	4.00	2.00
❑ 208	Chicago White Sox CL	10.00	5.00
❑ 209	Ron Blackburn	4.00	2.00
❑ 210	Harmon Killebrew	40.00	20.00
❑ 211	Taylor Phillips	4.00	2.00
❑ 212	Walter Alston MG	10.00	5.00
❑ 213	Chuck Dressen MG	6.00	3.00
❑ 214	Jimmy Dykes MG	6.00	3.00
❑ 215	Bob Elliott MG	6.00	3.00
❑ 216	Joe Gordon MG	6.00	3.00
❑ 217	Charlie Grimm MG	6.00	3.00
❑ 218	Solly Hemus MG	4.00	2.00
❑ 219	Fred Hutchinson MG	6.00	3.00
❑ 220	Billy Jurges MG	4.00	2.00
❑ 221	Cookie Lavagetto MG	4.00	2.00
❑ 222	Al Lopez MG	10.00	5.00
❑ 223	Danny Murtaugh MG	6.00	3.00
❑ 224	Paul Richards MG	6.00	3.00
❑ 225	Bill Rigney MG	4.00	2.00
❑ 226	Eddie Sawyer MG	4.00	2.00
❑ 227	Casey Stengel MG	15.00	7.50
❑ 228	Ernie Johnson	6.00	3.00
❑ 229	Joe M. Morgan RC	4.00	2.00
❑ 230	Burdette/Spahn/Buhl	10.00	5.00
❑ 231	Hal Naragon	4.00	2.00
❑ 232	Jim Busby	4.00	2.00
❑ 233	Don Elston	4.00	2.00
❑ 234	Don Demeter	4.00	2.00
❑ 235	Gus Bell	6.00	3.00
❑ 236	Dick Ricketts	4.00	2.00
❑ 237	Elmer Valo	4.00	2.00
❑ 238	Danny Kravitz	4.00	2.00
❑ 239	Joe Shipley	4.00	2.00
❑ 240	Luis Aparicio	15.00	7.50
❑ 241	Albie Pearson	6.00	3.00

❑ 242 St. Louis Cardinals CL 10.00 5.00
❑ 243 Bubba Phillips 4.00 2.00
❑ 244 Hal Griggs 4.00 2.00
❑ 245 Eddie Yost 6.00 3.00
❑ 246 Lee Maye RC 6.00 3.00
❑ 247 Gil McDougald 10.00 5.00
❑ 248 Del Rice 4.00 2.00
❑ 249 Earl Wilson RC 6.00 3.00
❑ 250 Stan Musial 100.00 60.00
❑ 251 Bob Malkmus 4.00 2.00
❑ 252 Ray Herbert 4.00 2.00
❑ 253 Eddie Bressoud 4.00 2.00
❑ 254 Arnie Portocarrero 4.00 2.00
❑ 255 Jim Gilliam 6.00 3.00
❑ 256 Dick Brown 4.00 2.00
❑ 257 Gordy Coleman RC 4.00 2.00
❑ 258 Dick Groat 6.00 3.00
❑ 259 George Altman 4.00 2.00
❑ 260 R.Colavito/T.Francona 15.00 7.50
❑ 261 Pete Burnside 4.00 2.00
❑ 262 Hank Bauer 6.00 3.00
❑ 263 Darrell Johnson 4.00 2.00
❑ 264 Robin Roberts 15.00 7.50
❑ 265 Rip Repulski 4.00 2.00
❑ 266 Joey Jay 6.00 3.00
❑ 267 Jim Marshall 4.00 2.00
❑ 268 Al Worthington 4.00 2.00
❑ 269 Gene Green 4.00 2.00
❑ 270 Bob Turley 6.00 3.00
❑ 271 Julio Becquer 4.00 2.00
❑ 272 Fred Green RC 6.00 3.00
❑ 273 Neil Chrisley 4.00 2.00
❑ 274 Tom Acker 4.00 2.00
❑ 275 Curt Flood 6.00 3.00
❑ 276 Ken McBride RC 4.00 2.00
❑ 277 Harry Bright 4.00 2.00
❑ 278 Stan Williams 6.00 3.00
❑ 279 Chuck Tanner 6.00 3.00
❑ 280 Frank Sullivan 4.00 2.00
❑ 281 Ray Boone 6.00 3.00
❑ 282 Joe Nuxhall 6.00 3.00
❑ 283 Johnny Blanchard 6.00 3.00
❑ 284 Don Gross 4.00 2.00
❑ 285 Harry Anderson 4.00 2.00
❑ 286 Ray Semproch 4.00 2.00
❑ 287 Felipe Alou 6.00 3.00
❑ 288 Bob Mabe 4.00 2.00
❑ 289 Willie Jones 4.00 2.00
❑ 290 Jerry Lumpe 4.00 2.00
❑ 291 Bob Keegan 4.00 2.00
❑ 292 J.Pignatano/J.Roseboro 6.00 3.00
❑ 293 Gene Conley 6.00 3.00
❑ 294 Tony Taylor 6.00 3.00
❑ 295 Gil Hodges 25.00 12.50
❑ 296 Nelson Chittum RC 4.00 2.00
❑ 297 Reno Bertoia 4.00 2.00
❑ 298 George Witt 4.00 2.00
❑ 299 Earl Torgeson 4.00 2.00
❑ 300 Hank Aaron 125.00 75.00
❑ 301 Jerry Davie 4.00 2.00
❑ 302 Philadelphia Phillies CL 10.00 5.00
❑ 303 Billy O'Dell 4.00 2.00
❑ 304 Joe Ginsberg 4.00 2.00
❑ 305 Richie Ashburn 20.00 10.00
❑ 306 Frank Baumann 4.00 2.00
❑ 307 Gene Oliver 4.00 2.00
❑ 308 Dick Hall 4.00 2.00
❑ 309 Bob Hale 4.00 2.00
❑ 310 Frank Malzone 6.00 3.00
❑ 311 Raul Sanchez 4.00 2.00
❑ 312 Charley Lau 6.00 3.00
❑ 313 Turk Lown 4.00 2.00
❑ 314 Chico Fernandez 4.00 2.00
❑ 315 Bobby Shantz 10.00 5.00
❑ 316 W.McCovey ASR RC 125.00 75.00
❑ 317 Pumpsie Green ASR RC 6.00 3.00
❑ 318 Jim Baxes ASR 6.00 3.00
❑ 319 Joe Koppe ASR 6.00 3.00
❑ 320 Bob Allison ASR 6.00 3.00
❑ 321 Ron Fairly ASR 6.00 3.00
❑ 322 Willie Tasby ASR 6.00 3.00
❑ 323 John Romano ASR 6.00 3.00
❑ 324 Jim Perry ASR 6.00 3.00
❑ 325 Jim O'Toole ASR 6.00 3.00
❑ 326 Roberto Clemente 175.00 100.00
❑ 327 Ray Sadecki RC 4.00 2.00
❑ 328 Earl Battey 4.00 2.00
❑ 329 Zack Monroe 4.00 2.00
❑ 330 Harvey Kuenn 6.00 3.00
❑ 331 Henry Mason RC 4.00 2.00
❑ 332 New York Yankees CL 80.00 50.00
❑ 333 Danny McDevitt 4.00 2.00
❑ 334 Ted Abernathy 4.00 2.00
❑ 335 Red Schoendienst 15.00 7.50
❑ 336 Ike Delock 4.00 2.00
❑ 337 Cal Neeman 4.00 2.00
❑ 338 Ray Monzant 4.00 2.00
❑ 339 Harry Chiti 4.00 2.00
❑ 340 Harvey Haddix 6.00 3.00
❑ 341 Carroll Hardy 4.00 2.00
❑ 342 Casey Wise 4.00 2.00
❑ 343 Sandy Koufax 125.00 75.00
❑ 344 Clint Courtney 4.00 2.00
❑ 345 Don Newcombe 6.00 3.00
❑ 346 J.C. Martin UER RC 6.00 3.00
❑ 347 Ed Bouchee 4.00 2.00
❑ 348 Barry Shetrone RC 4.00 2.00
❑ 349 Moe Drabowsky 6.00 3.00
❑ 350 Mickey Mantle 600.00 350.00
❑ 351 Don Nottebart RC 4.00 2.00
❑ 352 Bell/F.Robinson/Lynch 10.00 5.00
❑ 353 Don Larsen 6.00 3.00
❑ 354 Bob Lillis 4.00 2.00
❑ 355 Bill White 6.00 3.00
❑ 356 Joe Amalfitano 4.00 2.00
❑ 357 Al Schroll 4.00 2.00
❑ 358 Joe DeMaestri 4.00 2.00
❑ 359 Buddy Gilbert RC 4.00 2.00
❑ 360 Herb Score 6.00 3.00
❑ 361 Bob Oldis 6.00 3.00
❑ 362 Russ Kemmerer 4.00 2.00
❑ 363 Gene Stephens 4.00 2.00
❑ 364 Paul Foytack 4.00 2.00
❑ 365 Minnie Minoso 10.00 5.00
❑ 366 Dallas Green RC 10.00 5.00
❑ 367 Bill Tuttle 4.00 2.00
❑ 368 Daryl Spencer 4.00 2.00
❑ 369 Billy Hoeft 4.00 2.00
❑ 370 Bill Skowron 10.00 5.00
❑ 371 Bud Byerly 4.00 2.00
❑ 372 Frank House 4.00 2.00
❑ 373 Don Hoak 6.00 3.00
❑ 374 Bob Buhl 6.00 3.00
❑ 375 Dale Long 10.00 5.00
❑ 376 John Briggs 4.00 2.00
❑ 377 Roger Maris 100.00 60.00
❑ 378 Stu Miller 6.00 3.00
❑ 379 Red Wilson 4.00 2.00
❑ 380 Bob Shaw 4.00 2.00
❑ 381 Milwaukee Braves CL 10.00 5.00
❑ 382 Ted Bowsfield 4.00 2.00
❑ 383 Leon Wagner 4.00 2.00
❑ 384 Don Cardwell 4.00 2.00
❑ 385 Charlie Neal WS1 8.00 4.00
❑ 386 Charlie Neal WS2 8.00 4.00
❑ 387 Carl Furillo WS3 8.00 4.00
❑ 388 Gil Hodges WS4 10.00 5.00
❑ 389 L.Aparicio WS5 w/M.Wills 10.00 5.00
❑ 390 Scrambling After Ball WS6 8.00 4.00
❑ 391 Champs Celebrate WS 8.00 4.00
❑ 392 Tex Clevenger 4.00 2.00
❑ 393 Smoky Burgess 6.00 3.00
❑ 394 Norm Larker 6.00 3.00
❑ 395 Hoyt Wilhelm 15.00 7.50
❑ 396 Steve Bilko 4.00 2.00
❑ 397 Don Blasingame 4.00 2.00
❑ 398 Mike Cuellar 6.00 3.00
❑ 399 Pappas/Fisher/Walker 6.00 3.00
❑ 400 Rocky Colavito 20.00 10.00
❑ 401 Bob Duliba RC 4.00 2.00
❑ 402 Dick Stuart 15.00 7.50
❑ 403 Ed Sadowski 4.00 2.00
❑ 404 Bob Rush 4.00 2.00
❑ 405 Bobby Richardson 15.00 7.50
❑ 406 Billy Klaus 4.00 2.00
❑ 407 Gary Peters UER RC 6.00 3.00
❑ 408 Carl Furillo 10.00 5.00
❑ 409 Ron Samford 4.00 2.00
❑ 410 Sam Jones 6.00 3.00
❑ 411 Ed Bailey 4.00 2.00
❑ 412 Bob Anderson 4.00 2.00
❑ 413 Kansas City Athletics CL 10.00 5.00
❑ 414 Don Williams RC 4.00 2.00
❑ 415 Bob Cerv 4.00 2.00
❑ 416 Humberto Robinson 4.00 2.00
❑ 417 Chuck Cottier RC 4.00 2.00
❑ 418 Don Mossi 6.00 3.00
❑ 419 George Crowe 4.00 2.00
❑ 420 Eddie Mathews 40.00 20.00
❑ 421 Duke Maas 4.00 2.00
❑ 422 John Powers 4.00 2.00
❑ 423 Ed Fitzgerald 4.00 2.00
❑ 424 Pete Whisenant 4.00 2.00
❑ 425 Johnny Podres 6.00 3.00
❑ 426 Ron Jackson 4.00 2.00
❑ 427 Al Grunwald RC 4.00 2.00
❑ 428 Al Smith 4.00 2.00
❑ 429 Nellie Fox/H.Kuenn 10.00 5.00
❑ 430 Art Ditmar 4.00 2.00
❑ 431 Andre Rodgers 4.00 2.00
❑ 432 Chuck Stobbs 4.00 2.00
❑ 433 Irv Noren 4.00 2.00
❑ 434 Brooks Lawrence 6.00 3.00
❑ 435 Gene Freese 4.00 2.00
❑ 436 Marv Throneberry 6.00 3.00
❑ 437 Bob Friend 6.00 3.00
❑ 438 Jim Coker RC 4.00 2.00
❑ 439 Tom Brewer 4.00 2.00
❑ 440 Jim Lemon 6.00 3.00
❑ 441 Gary Bell 10.00 5.00
❑ 442 Joe Pignatano 8.00 4.00
❑ 443 Charlie Maxwell 8.00 4.00
❑ 444 Jerry Kindall 8.00 4.00
❑ 445 Warren Spahn 50.00 30.00
❑ 446 Ellis Burton 8.00 4.00
❑ 447 Ray Moore 8.00 4.00
❑ 448 Jim Gentile RC 15.00 7.50
❑ 449 Jim Brosnan 8.00 4.00
❑ 450 Orlando Cepeda 25.00 12.50
❑ 451 Curt Simmons 8.00 4.00
❑ 452 Ray Webster 8.00 4.00
❑ 453 Vern Law 25.00 12.50
❑ 454 Hal Woodeshick 8.00 4.00
❑ 455 Baltimore Coaches 8.00 4.00
❑ 456 Red Sox Coaches 10.00 5.00
❑ 457 Cubs Coaches 8.00 4.00
❑ 458 White Sox Coaches 8.00 4.00
❑ 459 Reds Coaches 8.00 4.00
❑ 460 Indians Coaches 15.00 7.50
❑ 461 Tigers Coaches 10.00 5.00
❑ 462 Athletics Coaches 8.00 4.00
❑ 463 Dodgers Coaches 8.00 4.00
❑ 464 Braves Coaches 8.00 4.00
❑ 465 Yankees Coaches 25.00 12.50
❑ 466 Phillies Coaches 8.00 4.00
❑ 467 Pirates Coaches 8.00 4.00
❑ 468 Cardinals Coaches 8.00 4.00
❑ 469 Giants Coaches 8.00 4.00
❑ 470 Senators Coaches 8.00 4.00
❑ 471 Ned Garver 8.00 4.00
❑ 472 Alvin Dark 8.00 4.00
❑ 473 Al Cicotte 8.00 4.00
❑ 474 Haywood Sullivan 8.00 4.00
❑ 475 Don Drysdale 40.00 20.00
❑ 476 Lou Johnson RC 8.00 4.00
❑ 477 Don Ferrarese 8.00 4.00
❑ 478 Frank Torre 8.00 4.00
❑ 479 Georges Maranda RC 8.00 4.00
❑ 480 Yogi Berra 80.00 50.00
❑ 481 Wes Stock RC 8.00 4.00
❑ 482 Frank Bolling 8.00 4.00
❑ 483 Camilo Pascual 8.00 4.00
❑ 484 Pittsburgh Pirates CL 40.00 20.00
❑ 485 Ken Boyer 15.00 7.50
❑ 486 Bobby Del Greco 8.00 4.00
❑ 487 Tom Sturdivant 8.00 4.00
❑ 488 Norm Cash 25.00 12.50
❑ 489 Steve Ridzik 8.00 4.00
❑ 490 Frank Robinson 50.00 30.00
❑ 491 Mel Roach 8.00 4.00
❑ 492 Larry Jackson 8.00 4.00
❑ 493 Duke Snider 50.00 30.00
❑ 494 Baltimore Orioles CL 25.00 12.50
❑ 495 Sherm Lollar 8.00 4.00
❑ 496 Bill Virdon 10.00 5.00
❑ 497 John Tsitouris 8.00 4.00
❑ 498 Al Pilarcik 8.00 4.00
❑ 499 Johnny James RC 10.00 5.00

❑ 500 Johnny Temple 8.00 4.00
❑ 501 Bob Schmidt 8.00 4.00
❑ 502 Jim Bunning 25.00 12.50
❑ 503 Don Lee 8.00 4.00
❑ 504 Seth Morehead 8.00 4.00
❑ 505 Ted Kluszewski 25.00 12.50
❑ 506 Lee Walls 8.00 4.00
❑ 507 Dick Stigman 15.00 7.50
❑ 508 Billy Consolo 15.00 7.50
❑ 509 Tommy Davis RC 25.00 12.50
❑ 510 Gerry Staley 15.00 7.50
❑ 511 Ken Walters RC 15.00 7.50
❑ 512 Joe Gibbon RC 15.00 7.50
❑ 513 Chicago Cubs CL 30.00 15.00
❑ 514 Steve Barber RC 15.00 7.50
❑ 515 Stan Lopata 15.00 7.50
❑ 516 Marty Kutyna RC 15.00 7.50
❑ 517 Charlie James RC 25.00 12.50
❑ 518 Tony Gonzalez RC 15.00 7.50
❑ 519 Ed Roebuck 15.00 7.50
❑ 520 Don Buddin 15.00 7.50
❑ 521 Mike Lee RC 15.00 7.50
❑ 522 Ken Hunt RC 30.00 15.00
❑ 523 Clay Dalrymple RC 15.00 7.50
❑ 524 Bill Henry 15.00 7.50
❑ 525 Marv Breeding RC 15.00 7.50
❑ 526 Paul Giel 25.00 12.50
❑ 527 Jose Valdivielso 25.00 12.50
❑ 528 Ben Johnson RC 15.00 7.50
❑ 529 Norm Sherry RC 20.00 10.00
❑ 530 Mike McCormick 15.00 7.50
❑ 531 Sandy Amoros 20.00 10.00
❑ 532 Mike Garcia 20.00 10.00
❑ 533 Lu Clinton RC 15.00 7.50
❑ 534 Ken MacKenzie RC 15.00 7.50
❑ 535 Whitey Lockman 15.00 7.50
❑ 536 Wynn Hawkins RC 15.00 7.50
❑ 537 Boston Red Sox CL 30.00 15.00
❑ 538 Frank Barnes RC 15.00 7.50
❑ 539 Gene Baker 15.00 7.50
❑ 540 Jerry Walker 15.00 7.50
❑ 541 Tony Curry RC 15.00 7.50
❑ 542 Ken Hamlin RC 15.00 7.50
❑ 543 Elio Chacon RC 15.00 7.50
❑ 544 Bill Monbouquette 20.00 10.00
❑ 545 Carl Sawatski 15.00 7.50
❑ 546 Hank Aguirre 15.00 7.50
❑ 547 Bob Aspromonte RC 20.00 10.00
❑ 548 Don Mincher RC 15.00 7.50
❑ 549 John Buzhardt 15.00 7.50
❑ 550 Jim Landis 15.00 7.50
❑ 551 Ed Rakow RC 15.00 7.50
❑ 552 Walt Bond RC 15.00 7.50
❑ 553 Bill Skowron AS 20.00 10.00
❑ 554 Willie McCovey AS 40.00 20.00
❑ 555 Nellie Fox AS 30.00 15.00
❑ 556 Charlie Neal AS 15.00 7.50
❑ 557 Frank Malzone AS 15.00 7.50
❑ 558 Eddie Mathews AS 40.00 20.00
❑ 559 Luis Aparicio AS 30.00 15.00
❑ 560 Ernie Banks AS 60.00 35.00
❑ 561 Al Kaline AS 60.00 35.00
❑ 562 Joe Cunningham AS 15.00 7.50
❑ 563 Mickey Mantle AS 250.00 150.00
❑ 564 Willie Mays AS 100.00 60.00
❑ 565 Roger Maris AS 100.00 60.00
❑ 566 Hank Aaron AS 100.00 60.00
❑ 567 Sherm Lollar AS 15.00 7.50
❑ 568 Del Crandall AS 15.00 7.50
❑ 569 Camilo Pascual AS 15.00 7.50
❑ 570 Don Drysdale AS 40.00 20.00
❑ 571 Billy Pierce AS 15.00 7.50
❑ 572 Johnny Antonelli AS 30.00 15.00
❑ NNO Iron-on team transfer 5.00 2.00

1961 Topps

❑ COMPLETE SET (587) 7000.00 4500.00
❑ COMMON CARD (1-370) 3.00 1.50
❑ COMMON CARD (371-446) 4.00 2.00
❑ COMMON CARD (447-522) 8.00 4.00
❑ COMMON CARD (523-589) 30.00 15.00
❑ NOT ISSUED (587/588)
❑ WRAPPER (1-CENT) 200.00 150.00
❑ WRAP.(1-CENT, REPEAT) 100.00 75.00
❑ WRAPPER (5-CENT) 40.00 30.00
❑ 1 Dick Groat 30.00 15.00

❑ 2 Roger Maris 250.00 150.00
❑ 3 John Buzhardt 3.00 1.50
❑ 4 Lenny Green 3.00 1.50
❑ 5 John Romano 3.00 1.50
❑ 6 Ed Roebuck 3.00 1.50
❑ 7 Chicago White Sox TC 8.00 4.00
❑ 8 Dick Williams 6.00 3.00
❑ 9 Bob Purkey 3.00 1.50
❑ 10 Brooks Robinson 50.00 30.00
❑ 11 Curt Simmons 6.00 3.00
❑ 12 Moe Thacker 3.00 1.50
❑ 13 Chuck Cottier 3.00 1.50
❑ 14 Don Mossi 6.00 3.00
❑ 15 Willie Kirkland 3.00 1.50
❑ 16 Billy Muffett 3.00 1.50
❑ 17 Checklist 1 10.00 5.00
❑ 18 Jim Grant 6.00 3.00
❑ 19 Clete Boyer 8.00 4.00
❑ 20 Robin Roberts 15.00 7.50
❑ 21 Zoilo Versalles UER RC 8.00 4.00
❑ 22 Clem Labine 6.00 3.00
❑ 23 Don Demeter 3.00 1.50
❑ 24 Ken Johnson 6.00 3.00
❑ 25 Pinson/Bell/F.Robinson 8.00 4.00
❑ 26 Wes Stock 3.00 1.50
❑ 27 Jerry Kindall 3.00 1.50
❑ 28 Hector Lopez 6.00 3.00
❑ 29 Don Nottebart 3.00 1.50
❑ 30 Nellie Fox 15.00 7.50
❑ 31 Bob Schmidt 3.00 1.50
❑ 32 Ray Sadecki 3.00 1.50
❑ 33 Gary Geiger 3.00 1.50
❑ 34 Wynn Hawkins 3.00 1.50
❑ 35 Ron Santo RC 40.00 20.00
❑ 36 Jack Kralick RC 3.00 1.50
❑ 37 Charley Maxwell 6.00 3.00
❑ 38 Bob Lillis 3.00 1.50
❑ 39 Leo Posada RC 3.00 1.50
❑ 40 Bob Turley 6.00 3.00
❑ 41 Groat/Mays/Clemente LL 40.00 20.00
❑ 42 Runnels/Minoso/Skow LL 8.00 4.00
❑ 43 Banks/Aaron/Mathews LL 30.00 15.00
❑ 44 Mante/Maris/Colavito LL 80.00 50.00
❑ 45 McCormick/Drysdale LL 8.00 4.00
❑ 46 Baumann/Bunning/Dit LL 8.00 4.00
❑ 47 Broglio/Spahn/Burdette LL 8.00 4.00
❑ 48 Estrada/Perry/Daley LL 8.00 4.00
❑ 49 Drysdale/Koufax LL 20.00 10.00
❑ 50 Bunning/Ramos/Wynn LL 8.00 4.00
❑ 51 Detroit Tigers TC 8.00 4.00
❑ 52 George Crowe 3.00 1.50
❑ 53 Russ Nixon 3.00 1.50
❑ 54 Earl Francis RC 3.00 1.50
❑ 55 Jim Davenport 6.00 3.00
❑ 56 Russ Kemmerer 3.00 1.50
❑ 57 Marv Throneberry 6.00 3.00
❑ 58 Joe Schaffernoth RC 3.00 1.50
❑ 59 Jim Woods 3.00 1.50
❑ 60 Woody Held 3.00 1.50
❑ 61 Ron Piche RC 3.00 1.50
❑ 62 Al Pilarcik 3.00 1.50
❑ 63 Jim Kaat 8.00 4.00
❑ 64 Alex Grammas 3.00 1.50
❑ 65 Ted Kluszewski 8.00 4.00
❑ 66 Bill Henry 3.00 1.50
❑ 67 Ossie Virgil 3.00 1.50
❑ 68 Deron Johnson 6.00 3.00
❑ 69 Earl Wilson 6.00 3.00
❑ 70 Bill Virdon 6.00 3.00
❑ 71 Jerry Adair 3.00 1.50
❑ 72 Stu Miller 6.00 3.00
❑ 73 Al Spangler 3.00 1.50
❑ 74 Joe Pignatano 3.00 1.50
❑ 75 L.McDaniel/L.Jackson 6.00 3.00
❑ 76 Harry Anderson 3.00 1.50
❑ 77 Dick Stigman 3.00 1.50
❑ 78 Lee Walls 6.00 3.00
❑ 79 Joe Ginsberg 3.00 1.50
❑ 80 Harmon Killebrew 20.00 10.00
❑ 81 Tracy Stallard RC 3.00 1.50
❑ 82 Joe Christopher RC 3.00 1.50
❑ 83 Bob Bruce 3.00 1.50
❑ 84 Lee Maye 3.00 1.50
❑ 85 Jerry Walker 3.00 1.50
❑ 86 Los Angeles Dodgers TC 8.00 4.00
❑ 87 Joe Amalfitano 3.00 1.50
❑ 88 Richie Ashburn 15.00 7.50
❑ 89 Billy Martin 15.00 7.50
❑ 90 Gerry Staley 3.00 1.50
❑ 91 Walt Moryn 3.00 1.50
❑ 92 Hal Naragon 3.00 1.50
❑ 93 Tony Gonzalez 3.00 1.50
❑ 94 Johnny Kucks 3.00 1.50
❑ 95 Norm Cash 8.00 4.00
❑ 96 Billy O'Dell 3.00 1.50
❑ 97 Jerry Lynch 6.00 3.00
❑ 98A Checklist 2 Red 10.00 5.00
❑ 98B Checklist 2 Yellow B/W 10.00 5.00
❑ 98C Checklist 2 Yellow W/B 10.00 5.00
❑ 99 Don Buddin UER 3.00 1.50
❑ 100 Harvey Haddix 6.00 3.00
❑ 101 Bubba Phillips 3.00 1.50
❑ 102 Gene Stephens 3.00 1.50
❑ 103 Ruben Amaro 3.00 1.50
❑ 104 John Blanchard 8.00 4.00
❑ 105 Carl Willey 3.00 1.50
❑ 106 Whitey Herzog 3.00 1.50
❑ 107 Seth Morehead 3.00 1.50
❑ 108 Dan Dobbek 3.00 1.50
❑ 109 Johnny Podres 8.00 4.00
❑ 110 Vada Pinson 8.00 4.00
❑ 111 Jack Meyer 3.00 1.50
❑ 112 Chico Fernandez 3.00 1.50
❑ 113 Mike Fornieles 3.00 1.50
❑ 114 Hobie Landrith 3.00 1.50
❑ 115 Johnny Antonelli 6.00 3.00
❑ 116 Joe DeMaestri 3.00 1.50
❑ 117 Dale Long 6.00 3.00
❑ 118 Chris Cannizzaro RC 3.00 1.50
❑ 119 Siebern/Bauer/Lumpe 6.00 3.00
❑ 120 Eddie Mathews 30.00 15.00
❑ 121 Eli Grba 6.00 3.00
❑ 122 Chicago Cubs TC 8.00 4.00
❑ 123 Billy Gardner 3.00 1.50
❑ 124 J.C. Martin 3.00 1.50
❑ 125 Steve Barber 3.00 1.50
❑ 126 Dick Stuart 6.00 3.00
❑ 127 Ron Kline 3.00 1.50
❑ 128 Rip Repulski 3.00 1.50
❑ 129 Ed Hobaugh 3.00 1.50
❑ 130 Norm Larker 3.00 1.50
❑ 131 Paul Richards MG 6.00 3.00
❑ 132 Al Lopez MG 8.00 4.00
❑ 133 Ralph Houk MG 6.00 3.00
❑ 134 Mickey Vernon MG 6.00 3.00
❑ 135 Fred Hutchinson MG 6.00 3.00
❑ 136 Walter Alston MG 8.00 4.00
❑ 137 Chuck Dressen MG 6.00 3.00
❑ 138 Danny Murtaugh MG 6.00 3.00
❑ 139 Solly Hemus MG 6.00 3.00
❑ 140 Gus Triandos 6.00 3.00
❑ 141 Billy Williams RC 60.00 35.00
❑ 142 Luis Arroyo 6.00 3.00
❑ 143 Russ Snyder 3.00 1.50
❑ 144 Jim Coker 3.00 1.50
❑ 145 Bob Buhl 6.00 3.00
❑ 146 Marty Keough 3.00 1.50
❑ 147 Ed Rakow 3.00 1.50
❑ 148 Julian Javier 6.00 3.00
❑ 149 Bob Oldis 3.00 1.50
❑ 150 Willie Mays 100.00 60.00
❑ 151 Jim Donohue 3.00 1.50
❑ 152 Earl Torgeson 3.00 1.50
❑ 153 Don Lee 3.00 1.50

#	Card		
❑ 154	Bobby Del Greco	3.00	1.50
❑ 155	Johnny Temple	6.00	3.00
❑ 156	Ken Hunt	6.00	3.00
❑ 157	Cal McLish	3.00	1.50
❑ 158	Pete Daley	3.00	1.50
❑ 159	Baltimore Orioles TC	8.00	4.00
❑ 160	Whitey Ford UER	50.00	30.00
❑ 161	Sherman Jones UER RC	3.00	1.50
❑ 162	Jay Hook	3.00	1.50
❑ 163	Ed Sadowski	3.00	1.50
❑ 164	Felix Mantilla	3.00	1.50
❑ 165	Gino Cimoli	3.00	1.50
❑ 166	Danny Kravitz	3.00	1.50
❑ 167	San Francisco Giants TC	8.00	4.00
❑ 168	Tommy Davis	8.00	4.00
❑ 169	Don Elston	3.00	1.50
❑ 170	Al Smith	3.00	1.50
❑ 171	Paul Foytack	3.00	1.50
❑ 172	Don Dillard	3.00	1.50
❑ 173	Malzone/Wertz/Jensen	6.00	3.00
❑ 174	Ray Semproch	3.00	1.50
❑ 175	Gene Freese	3.00	1.50
❑ 176	Ken Aspromonte	3.00	1.50
❑ 177	Don Larsen	6.00	3.00
❑ 178	Bob Nieman	3.00	1.50
❑ 179	Joe Koppe	3.00	1.50
❑ 180	Bobby Richardson	12.00	6.00
❑ 181	Fred Green	3.00	1.50
❑ 182	Dave Nicholson RC	3.00	1.50
❑ 183	Andre Rodgers	3.00	1.50
❑ 184	Steve Bilko	6.00	3.00
❑ 185	Herb Score	6.00	3.00
❑ 186	Elmer Valo	6.00	3.00
❑ 187	Billy Klaus	3.00	1.50
❑ 188	Jim Marshall	3.00	1.50
❑ 189A	Checklist 3 Copyright 263	10.00	5.00
❑ 189B	Checklist 3 Copyright 264	10.00	5.00
❑ 190	Stan Williams	6.00	3.00
❑ 191	Mike de la Hoz RC	3.00	1.50
❑ 192	Dick Brown	3.00	1.50
❑ 193	Gene Conley	6.00	3.00
❑ 194	Gordy Coleman	6.00	3.00
❑ 195	Jerry Casale	3.00	1.50
❑ 196	Ed Bouchee	3.00	1.50
❑ 197	Dick Hall	3.00	1.50
❑ 198	Carl Sawatski	3.00	1.50
❑ 199	Bob Boyd	3.00	1.50
❑ 200	Warren Spahn	40.00	20.00
❑ 201	Pete Whisenant	3.00	1.50
❑ 202	Al Neiger RC	3.00	1.50
❑ 203	Eddie Bressoud	3.00	1.50
❑ 204	Bob Skinner	6.00	3.00
❑ 205	Billy Pierce	6.00	3.00
❑ 206	Gene Green	3.00	1.50
❑ 207	S.Koufax/J.Podres	30.00	15.00
❑ 208	Larry Osborne	3.00	1.50
❑ 209	Ken McBride	3.00	1.50
❑ 210	Pete Runnels	6.00	3.00
❑ 211	Bob Gibson	40.00	20.00
❑ 212	Haywood Sullivan	6.00	3.00
❑ 213	Bill Stafford RC	3.00	1.50
❑ 214	Danny Murphy RC	6.00	3.00
❑ 215	Gus Bell	6.00	3.00
❑ 216	Ted Bowsfield	3.00	1.50
❑ 217	Mel Roach	3.00	1.50
❑ 218	Hal Brown	3.00	1.50
❑ 219	Gene Mauch MG	6.00	3.00
❑ 220	Alvin Dark MG	6.00	3.00
❑ 221	Mike Higgins MG	3.00	1.50
❑ 222	Jimmy Dykes MG	6.00	3.00
❑ 223	Bob Scheffing MG	3.00	1.50
❑ 224	Joe Gordon MG	6.00	3.00
❑ 225	Bill Rigney MG	6.00	3.00
❑ 226	Cookie Lavagetto MG	6.00	3.00
❑ 227	Juan Pizarro	3.00	1.50
❑ 228	New York Yankees TC	60.00	35.00
❑ 229	Rudy Hernandez RC	3.00	1.50
❑ 230	Don Hoak	6.00	3.00
❑ 231	Dick Drott	3.00	1.50
❑ 232	Bill White	6.00	3.00
❑ 233	Joey Jay	6.00	3.00
❑ 234	Ted Lepcio	3.00	1.50
❑ 235	Camilo Pascual	6.00	3.00
❑ 236	Don Gile RC	3.00	1.50
❑ 237	Billy Loes	6.00	3.00
❑ 238	Jim Gilliam	6.00	3.00
❑ 239	Dave Sisler	3.00	1.50
❑ 240	Ron Hansen	3.00	1.50
❑ 241	Al Cicotte	3.00	1.50
❑ 242	Hal Smith	3.00	1.50
❑ 243	Frank Lary	6.00	3.00
❑ 244	Chico Cardenas	6.00	3.00
❑ 245	Joe Adcock	6.00	3.00
❑ 246	Bob Davis RC	3.00	1.50
❑ 247	Billy Goodman	6.00	3.00
❑ 248	Ed Keegan RC	3.00	1.50
❑ 249	Cincinnati Reds TC	8.00	4.00
❑ 250	V.Law/R.Face	6.00	3.00
❑ 251	Bill Bruton	3.00	1.50
❑ 252	Bill Short	3.00	1.50
❑ 253	Sammy Taylor	3.00	1.50
❑ 254	Ted Sadowski RC	6.00	3.00
❑ 255	Vic Power	6.00	3.00
❑ 256	Billy Hoeft	3.00	1.50
❑ 257	Carroll Hardy	3.00	1.50
❑ 258	Jack Sanford	6.00	3.00
❑ 259	John Schaive RC	3.00	1.50
❑ 260	Don Drysdale	30.00	15.00
❑ 261	Charlie Lau	6.00	3.00
❑ 262	Tony Curry	3.00	1.50
❑ 263	Ken Hamlin	3.00	1.50
❑ 264	Glen Hobbie	3.00	1.50
❑ 265	Tony Kubek	12.00	6.00
❑ 266	Lindy McDaniel	6.00	3.00
❑ 267	Norm Siebern	3.00	1.50
❑ 268	Ike Delock	3.00	1.50
❑ 269	Harry Chiti	3.00	1.50
❑ 270	Bob Friend	6.00	3.00
❑ 271	Jim Landis	3.00	1.50
❑ 272	Tom Morgan	3.00	1.50
❑ 273A	Checklist 4 Copyright 336	15.00	7.50
❑ 273B	Checklist 4 Copyright 339	10.00	5.00
❑ 274	Gary Bell	3.00	1.50
❑ 275	Gene Woodling	6.00	3.00
❑ 276	Ray Rippelmeyer RC	3.00	1.50
❑ 277	Hank Foiles	3.00	1.50
❑ 278	Don McMahon	3.00	1.50
❑ 279	Jose Pagan	3.00	1.50
❑ 280	Frank Howard	8.00	4.00
❑ 281	Frank Sullivan	3.00	1.50
❑ 282	Faye Throneberry	3.00	1.50
❑ 283	Bob Anderson	3.00	1.50
❑ 284	Dick Gernert	3.00	1.50
❑ 285	Sherm Lollar	6.00	3.00
❑ 286	George Witt	3.00	1.50
❑ 287	Carl Yastrzemski	50.00	30.00
❑ 288	Albie Pearson	6.00	3.00
❑ 289	Ray Moore	3.00	1.50
❑ 290	Stan Musial	100.00	60.00
❑ 291	Tex Clevenger	3.00	1.50
❑ 292	Jim Baumer RC	3.00	1.50
❑ 293	Tom Sturdivant	3.00	1.50
❑ 294	Don Blasingame	3.00	1.50
❑ 295	Milt Pappas	6.00	3.00
❑ 296	Wes Covington	6.00	3.00
❑ 297	Kansas City Athletics TC	8.00	4.00
❑ 298	Jim Golden RC	3.00	1.50
❑ 299	Clay Dalrymple	3.00	1.50
❑ 300	Mickey Mantle	600.00	350.00
❑ 301	Chet Nichols	3.00	1.50
❑ 302	Al Heist RC	3.00	1.50
❑ 303	Gary Peters	6.00	3.00
❑ 304	Rocky Nelson	3.00	1.50
❑ 305	Mike McCormick	6.00	3.00
❑ 306	Bill Virdon WS1	10.00	5.00
❑ 307	Mickey Mantle WS2	80.00	50.00
❑ 308	Bobby Richardson WS3	12.00	6.00
❑ 309	Gino Cimoli WS4	10.00	5.00
❑ 310	Roy Face WS5	10.00	5.00
❑ 311	Whitey Ford WS6	15.00	7.50
❑ 312	Bill Mazeroski WS7	20.00	10.00
❑ 313	Pirates Celebrate WS	15.00	7.50
❑ 314	Bob Miller	3.00	1.50
❑ 315	Earl Battey	6.00	3.00
❑ 316	Bobby Gene Smith	3.00	1.50
❑ 317	Jim Brewer RC	3.00	1.50
❑ 318	Danny O'Connell	3.00	1.50
❑ 319	Valmy Thomas	3.00	1.50
❑ 320	Lou Burdette	6.00	3.00
❑ 321	Marv Breeding	3.00	1.50
❑ 322	Bill Kunkel RC	6.00	3.00
❑ 323	Sammy Esposito	3.00	1.50
❑ 324	Hank Aguirre	3.00	1.50
❑ 325	Wally Moon	6.00	3.00
❑ 326	Dave Hillman	3.00	1.50
❑ 327	Matty Alou RC	12.00	6.00
❑ 328	Jim O'Toole	6.00	3.00
❑ 329	Julio Becquer	3.00	1.50
❑ 330	Rocky Colavito	20.00	10.00
❑ 331	Ned Garver	3.00	1.50
❑ 332	Dutch Dotterer UER	3.00	1.50
❑ 333	Fritz Brickell	3.00	1.50
❑ 334	Walt Bond	3.00	1.50
❑ 335	Frank Bolling	3.00	1.50
❑ 336	Don Mincher	6.00	3.00
❑ 337	Wynn/Lopez/Score	8.00	4.00
❑ 338	Don Landrum	3.00	1.50
❑ 339	Gene Baker	3.00	1.50
❑ 340	Vic Wertz	6.00	3.00
❑ 341	Jim Owens	3.00	1.50
❑ 342	Clint Courtney	3.00	1.50
❑ 343	Earl Robinson RC	3.00	1.50
❑ 344	Sandy Koufax	100.00	60.00
❑ 345	Jimmy Piersall	8.00	4.00
❑ 346	Howie Nunn	3.00	1.50
❑ 347	St. Louis Cardinals TC	8.00	4.00
❑ 348	Steve Boros	3.00	1.50
❑ 349	Danny McDevitt	3.00	1.50
❑ 350	Ernie Banks	40.00	20.00
❑ 351	Jim King	3.00	1.50
❑ 352	Bob Shaw	3.00	1.50
❑ 353	Howie Bedell RC	3.00	1.50
❑ 354	Billy Harrell	6.00	3.00
❑ 355	Bob Allison	8.00	4.00
❑ 356	Ryne Duren	3.00	1.50
❑ 357	Daryl Spencer	3.00	1.50
❑ 358	Earl Averill Jr.	6.00	3.00
❑ 359	Dallas Green	3.00	1.50
❑ 360	Frank Robinson	40.00	20.00
❑ 361A	Checklist 5 No Ad on Back	15.00	7.50
❑ 361B	Checklist 5 Ad on Back	15.00	7.50
❑ 362	Frank Funk RC	3.00	1.50
❑ 363	John Roseboro	6.00	3.00
❑ 364	Moe Drabowsky	6.00	3.00
❑ 365	Jerry Lumpe	3.00	1.50
❑ 366	Eddie Fisher	3.00	1.50
❑ 367	Jim Rivera	3.00	1.50
❑ 368	Bennie Daniels	3.00	1.50
❑ 369	Dave Philley	3.00	1.50
❑ 370	Roy Face	6.00	3.00
❑ 371	Bill Skowron SP	50.00	30.00
❑ 372	Bob Hendley RC	4.00	2.00
❑ 373	Boston Red Sox TC	8.00	4.00
❑ 374	Paul Giel	4.00	2.00
❑ 375	Ken Boyer	12.00	6.00
❑ 376	Mike Roarke RC	6.00	3.00
❑ 377	Ruben Gomez	4.00	2.00
❑ 378	Wally Post	6.00	3.00
❑ 379	Bobby Shantz	4.00	2.00
❑ 380	Minnie Minoso	8.00	4.00
❑ 381	Dave Wickersham RC	4.00	2.00
❑ 382	Frank Thomas	6.00	3.00
❑ 383	McCormick/Sanford/O'Dell	6.00	3.00
❑ 384	Chuck Essegian	4.00	2.00
❑ 385	Jim Perry	6.00	3.00
❑ 386	Joe Hicks	4.00	2.00
❑ 387	Duke Maas	4.00	2.00
❑ 388	Roberto Clemente	125.00	75.00
❑ 389	Ralph Terry	6.00	3.00
❑ 390	Del Crandall	8.00	4.00
❑ 391	Winston Brown RC	4.00	2.00
❑ 392	Reno Bertoia	4.00	2.00
❑ 393	D.Cardwell/G.Hobbie	4.00	2.00
❑ 394	Ken Walters	4.00	2.00
❑ 395	Chuck Estrada	6.00	3.00
❑ 396	Bob Aspromonte	4.00	2.00
❑ 397	Hal Woodeshick	4.00	2.00
❑ 398	Hank Bauer	6.00	3.00
❑ 399	Cliff Cook RC	4.00	2.00
❑ 400	Vern Law	6.00	3.00
❑ 401	Babe Ruth 60th HR	60.00	35.00
❑ 402	Don Larsen Perfect SP	25.00	12.50
❑ 403	26 Inning Tie/Oeschger/Cadore	8.00	4.00
❑ 404	Rogers Hornsby .424	12.00	6.00
❑ 405	Lou Gehrig Streak	80.00	50.00
❑ 406	Mickey Mantle 565 HR	100.00	60.00
❑ 407	Jack Chesbro Wins 41	8.00	4.00
❑ 408	Christy Mathewson K's SP	20.00	10.00

❑ 409 Walter Johnson Shutout 12.00 6.00
❑ 410 Harvey Haddix 12 Perfect 8.00 4.00
❑ 411 Tony Taylor 6.00 3.00
❑ 412 Larry Sherry 6.00 3.00
❑ 413 Eddie Yost 6.00 3.00
❑ 414 Dick Donovan 6.00 3.00
❑ 415 Hank Aaron 125.00 75.00
❑ 416 Dick Howser RC 8.00 4.00
❑ 417 Juan Marichal SP RC 100.00 60.00
❑ 418 Ed Bailey 6.00 3.00
❑ 419 Tom Borland 4.00 2.00
❑ 420 Ernie Broglio 6.00 3.00
❑ 421 Ty Cline SP RC 20.00 10.00
❑ 422 Bud Daley 4.00 2.00
❑ 423 Charlie Neal SP 20.00 10.00
❑ 424 Turk Lown 4.00 2.00
❑ 425 Yogi Berra 80.00 50.00
❑ 426 Milwaukee Braves TC UER 12.00 6.00
❑ 427 Dick Ellsworth 6.00 3.00
❑ 428 Ray Barker SP RC 20.00 10.00
❑ 429 Al Kaline 50.00 30.00
❑ 430 Bill Mazeroski SP 50.00 30.00
❑ 431 Chuck Stobbs 4.00 2.00
❑ 432 Coot Veal 6.00 3.00
❑ 433 Art Mahaffey 4.00 2.00
❑ 434 Tom Brewer 4.00 2.00
❑ 435 Orlando Cepeda UER 12.00 6.00
❑ 436 Jim Maloney SP RC 20.00 10.00
❑ 437A Checklist 6 440 Louis 15.00 7.50
❑ 437B Checklist 6 440 Luis 15.00 7.50
❑ 438 Curt Flood 8.00 4.00
❑ 439 Phil Regan RC 6.00 3.00
❑ 440 Luis Aparicio 12.00 6.00
❑ 441 Dick Bertell RC 4.00 2.00
❑ 442 Gordon Jones 4.00 2.00
❑ 443 Duke Snider 50.00 30.00
❑ 444 Joe Nuxhall 6.00 3.00
❑ 445 Frank Malzone 6.00 3.00
❑ 446 Bob Taylor 4.00 2.00
❑ 447 Harry Bright 8.00 4.00
❑ 448 Del Rice 15.00 7.50
❑ 449 Bob Bolin RC 8.00 4.00
❑ 450 Jim Lemon 8.00 4.00
❑ 451 Spencer/White/Broglio 8.00 4.00
❑ 452 Bob Allen RC 8.00 4.00
❑ 453 Dick Schofield 8.00 4.00
❑ 454 Pumpsie Green 8.00 4.00
❑ 455 Early Wynn 15.00 7.50
❑ 456 Hal Bevan 8.00 4.00
❑ 457 Johnny James 8.00 4.00
❑ 458 Willie Tasby 8.00 4.00
❑ 459 Terry Fox RC 10.00 5.00
❑ 460 Gil Hodges 25.00 12.50
❑ 461 Smoky Burgess 15.00 7.50
❑ 462 Lou Klimchock 8.00 4.00
❑ 463 Jack Fisher See 426 8.00 4.00
❑ 464 Lee Thomas RC 10.00 5.00
❑ 465 Roy McMillan 15.00 7.50
❑ 466 Ron Moeller RC 8.00 4.00
❑ 467 Cleveland Indians TC 12.00 6.00
❑ 468 John Callison 10.00 5.00
❑ 469 Ralph Lumenti 8.00 4.00
❑ 470 Roy Sievers 10.00 5.00
❑ 471 Phil Rizzuto MVP 25.00 12.50
❑ 472 Yogi Berra MVP SP 50.00 30.00
❑ 473 Bob Shantz MVP 8.00 4.00
❑ 474 Al Rosen MVP 10.00 5.00
❑ 475 Mickey Mantle MVP 200.00 125.00
❑ 476 Jackie Jensen MVP 10.00 5.00
❑ 477 Nellie Fox MVP 15.00 7.50
❑ 478 Roger Maris MVP 60.00 35.00
❑ 479 Jim Konstanty MVP 8.00 4.00
❑ 480 Roy Campanella MVP 40.00 20.00
❑ 481 Hank Sauer MVP 8.00 4.00
❑ 482 Willie Mays MVP 50.00 30.00
❑ 483 Don Newcombe MVP 10.00 5.00
❑ 484 Hank Aaron MVP 50.00 30.00
❑ 485 Ernie Banks MVP 40.00 20.00
❑ 486 Dick Groat MVP 10.00 5.00
❑ 487 Gene Oliver 8.00 4.00
❑ 488 Joe McClain RC 10.00 5.00
❑ 489 Walt Dropo 8.00 4.00
❑ 490 Jim Bunning 25.00 12.50
❑ 491 Philadelphia Phillies TC 12.00 6.00
❑ 492 Ron Fairly 10.00 5.00
❑ 493 Don Zimmer UER 10.00 5.00
❑ 494 Tom Cheney 15.00 7.50
❑ 495 Elston Howard 10.00 5.00
❑ 496 Ken MacKenzie 8.00 4.00
❑ 497 Willie Jones 8.00 4.00
❑ 498 Ray Herbert 8.00 4.00
❑ 499 Chuck Schilling RC 8.00 4.00
❑ 500 Harvey Kuenn 10.00 5.00
❑ 501 John DeMerit RC 8.00 4.00
❑ 502 Choo Choo Coleman RC 10.00 5.00
❑ 503 Tito Francona 8.00 4.00
❑ 504 Billy Consolo 8.00 4.00
❑ 505 Red Schoendienst 15.00 7.50
❑ 506 Willie Davis RC 15.00 7.50
❑ 507 Pete Burnside 8.00 4.00
❑ 508 Rocky Bridges 8.00 4.00
❑ 509 Camilo Carreon 8.00 4.00
❑ 510 Art Ditmar 8.00 4.00
❑ 511 Joe M. Morgan 8.00 4.00
❑ 512 Bob Will 8.00 4.00
❑ 513 Jim Brosnan 8.00 4.00
❑ 514 Jake Wood RC 8.00 4.00
❑ 515 Jackie Brandt 8.00 4.00
❑ 516 Checklist 7 15.00 7.50
❑ 517 Willie McCovey 40.00 20.00
❑ 518 Andy Carey 8.00 4.00
❑ 519 Jim Pagliaroni RC 8.00 4.00
❑ 520 Joe Cunningham 8.00 4.00
❑ 521 N.Sherry/L.Sherry 8.00 4.00
❑ 522 Dick Farrell UER 15.00 7.50
❑ 523 Joe Gibbon 30.00 15.00
❑ 524 Johnny Logan 30.00 15.00
❑ 525 Ron Perranoski RC 60.00 35.00
❑ 526 R.C. Stevens 30.00 15.00
❑ 527 Gene Leek RC 30.00 15.00
❑ 528 Pedro Ramos 30.00 15.00
❑ 529 Bob Roselli 30.00 15.00
❑ 530 Bob Malkmus 30.00 15.00
❑ 531 Jim Coates 50.00 25.00
❑ 532 Bob Hale 30.00 15.00
❑ 533 Jack Curtis RC 30.00 15.00
❑ 534 Eddie Kasko 40.00 20.00
❑ 535 Larry Jackson 30.00 15.00
❑ 536 Bill Tuttle 30.00 15.00
❑ 537 Bobby Locke 30.00 15.00
❑ 538 Chuck Hiller RC 30.00 15.00
❑ 539 Johnny Klippstein 30.00 15.00
❑ 540 Jackie Jensen 40.00 20.00
❑ 541 Rollie Sheldon RC 50.00 25.00
❑ 542 Minnesota Twins TC 60.00 35.00
❑ 543 Roger Craig 40.00 20.00
❑ 544 George Thomas RC 50.00 25.00
❑ 545 Hoyt Wilhelm 60.00 35.00
❑ 546 Marty Kutyna 30.00 15.00
❑ 547 Leon Wagner 30.00 15.00
❑ 548 Ted Wills 30.00 15.00
❑ 549 Hal R. Smith 30.00 15.00
❑ 550 Frank Baumann 30.00 15.00
❑ 551 George Altman 40.00 20.00
❑ 552 Jim Archer RC 30.00 15.00
❑ 553 Bill Fischer 30.00 15.00
❑ 554 Pittsburgh Pirates TC 80.00 50.00
❑ 555 Sam Jones 30.00 15.00
❑ 556 Ken R. Hunt RC 30.00 15.00
❑ 557 Jose Valdivielso 30.00 15.00
❑ 558 Don Ferrarese 30.00 15.00
❑ 559 Jim Gentile 60.00 35.00
❑ 560 Barry Latman 40.00 20.00
❑ 561 Charley James 30.00 15.00
❑ 562 Bill Monbouquette 30.00 15.00
❑ 563 Bob Cerv 60.00 35.00
❑ 564 Don Cardwell 30.00 15.00
❑ 565 Felipe Alou 50.00 25.00
❑ 566 Paul Richards AS MG 30.00 15.00
❑ 567 Danny Murtaugh AS MG 30.00 15.00
❑ 568 Bill Skowron AS 50.00 25.00
❑ 569 Frank Herrera AS 40.00 20.00
❑ 570 Nellie Fox AS 60.00 35.00
❑ 571 Bill Mazeroski AS 60.00 35.00
❑ 572 Brooks Robinson AS 80.00 50.00
❑ 573 Ken Boyer AS 50.00 25.00
❑ 574 Luis Aparicio AS 60.00 35.00
❑ 575 Ernie Banks AS 80.00 50.00
❑ 576 Roger Maris AS 175.00 100.00
❑ 577 Hank Aaron AS 150.00 90.00
❑ 578 Mickey Mantle AS 500.00 300.00
❑ 579 Willie Mays AS 150.00 90.00
❑ 580 Al Kaline AS 80.00 50.00
❑ 581 Frank Robinson AS 80.00 50.00
❑ 582 Earl Battey AS 30.00 15.00
❑ 583 Del Crandall AS 30.00 15.00
❑ 584 Jim Perry AS 30.00 15.00
❑ 585 Bob Friend AS 30.00 15.00
❑ 586 Whitey Ford AS 100.00 60.00
❑ 589 Warren Spahn AS 100.00 60.00

1962 Topps

❑ COMP. MASTER SET (689) 10000.00 6000.00
❑ COMPLETE SET (598) 8000.00 5000.00
❑ COMMON CARD (1-370) 5.00 2.50
❑ COMMON CARD (371-446) 6.00 3.00
❑ COMMON CARD (447-522) 12.00 6.00
❑ COMMON CARD (523-598) 20.00 10.00
❑ WRAPPER (1-CENT) 100.00 75.00
❑ WRAPPER (5-CENT) 30.00 20.00
❑ 1 Roger Maris 500.00 300.00
❑ 2 Jim Brosnan 5.00 2.50
❑ 3 Pete Runnels 5.00 2.50
❑ 4 John DeMerit 8.00 4.00
❑ 5 Sandy Koufax UER 150.00 90.00
❑ 6 Marv Breeding 5.00 2.50
❑ 7 Frank Thomas 10.00 5.00
❑ 8 Ray Herbert 5.00 2.50
❑ 9 Jim Davenport 8.00 4.00
❑ 10 Roberto Clemente 200.00 125.00
❑ 11 Tom Morgan 5.00 2.50
❑ 12 Harry Craft MG 8.00 4.00
❑ 13 Dick Howser 8.00 4.00
❑ 14 Bill White 8.00 4.00
❑ 15 Dick Donovan 5.00 2.50
❑ 16 Darrell Johnson 5.00 2.50
❑ 17 Johnny Callison 8.00 4.00
❑ 18 M.Mantle/W.Mays 175.00 100.00
❑ 19 Ray Washburn RC 5.00 2.50
❑ 20 Rocky Colavito 15.00 7.50
❑ 21 Jim Kaat 8.00 4.00
❑ 22A Checklist 1 ERR 12.00 6.00
❑ 22B Checklist 1 COR 12.00 6.00
❑ 23 Norm Larker 5.00 2.50
❑ 24 Detroit Tigers TC 10.00 5.00
❑ 25 Ernie Banks 50.00 30.00
❑ 26 Chris Cannizzaro 8.00 4.00
❑ 27 Chuck Cottier 5.00 2.50
❑ 28 Minnie Minoso 10.00 5.00
❑ 29 Casey Stengel MG 20.00 10.00
❑ 30 Eddie Mathews 40.00 20.00
❑ 31 Tom Tresh RC 15.00 7.50
❑ 32 John Roseboro 8.00 4.00
❑ 33 Don Larsen 8.00 4.00
❑ 34 Johnny Temple 8.00 4.00
❑ 35 Don Schwall RC 10.00 5.00
❑ 36 Don Leppert RC 5.00 2.50
❑ 37 Latman/Stigman/Perry 5.00 2.50
❑ 38 Gene Stephens 5.00 2.50
❑ 39 Joe Koppe 5.00 2.50
❑ 40 Orlando Cepeda 15.00 7.50
❑ 41 Cliff Cook 5.00 2.50
❑ 42 Jim King 5.00 2.50
❑ 43 Los Angeles Dodgers TC 10.00 5.00
❑ 44 Don Taussig RC 5.00 2.50
❑ 45 Brooks Robinson 50.00 30.00
❑ 46 Jack Baldschun RC 5.00 2.50
❑ 47 Bob Will 5.00 2.50
❑ 48 Ralph Terry 8.00 4.00

❑ 49	Hal Jones RC	5.00	2.50
❑ 50	Stan Musial	100.00	60.00
❑ 51	Cash/Kaline/Howard LL	8.00	4.00
❑ 52	Clemente/Pins/Boyer LL	20.00	10.00
❑ 53	Maris/Mantle/Kill LL	100.00	60.00
❑ 54	Cepeda/Mays/F.Rob LL	20.00	10.00
❑ 55	Donovan/Staff/Mossi LL	8.00	4.00
❑ 56	Spahn/O'Toole/Simm LL	8.00	4.00
❑ 57	Ford/Lary/Bunning LL	8.00	4.00
❑ 58	Spahn/Jay/O'Toole LL	8.00	4.00
❑ 59	Pascual/Ford/Bunning LL	8.00	4.00
❑ 60	Koufax/Will/Drysdale LL	20.00	10.00
❑ 61	St. Louis Cardinals TC	10.00	5.00
❑ 62	Steve Boros	5.00	2.50
❑ 63	Tony Cloninger RC	8.00	4.00
❑ 64	Russ Snyder	5.00	2.50
❑ 65	Bobby Richardson	10.00	5.00
❑ 66	Cuno Barragan RC	5.00	2.50
❑ 67	Harvey Haddix	8.00	4.00
❑ 68	Ken Hunt	5.00	2.50
❑ 69	Phil Ortega RC	5.00	2.50
❑ 70	Harmon Killebrew	25.00	12.50
❑ 71	Dick LeMay RC	5.00	2.50
❑ 72	Boros/Scheffing/Wood	5.00	2.50
❑ 73	Nellie Fox	20.00	10.00
❑ 74	Bob Lillis	8.00	4.00
❑ 75	Milt Pappas	8.00	4.00
❑ 76	Howie Bedell	5.00	2.50
❑ 77	Tony Taylor	8.00	4.00
❑ 78	Gene Green	5.00	2.50
❑ 79	Ed Hobaugh	5.00	2.50
❑ 80	Vada Pinson	8.00	4.00
❑ 81	Jim Pagliaroni	5.00	2.50
❑ 82	Deron Johnson	8.00	4.00
❑ 83	Larry Jackson	5.00	2.50
❑ 84	Lenny Green	5.00	2.50
❑ 85	Gil Hodges	20.00	10.00
❑ 86	Donn Clendenon RC	8.00	4.00
❑ 87	Mike Roarke	5.00	2.50
❑ 88	Ralph Houk MG	8.00	4.00
❑ 89	Barney Schultz RC	5.00	2.50
❑ 90	Jimmy Piersall	8.00	4.00
❑ 91	J.C. Martin	5.00	2.50
❑ 92	Sam Jones	5.00	2.50
❑ 93	John Blanchard	8.00	4.00
❑ 94	Jay Hook	8.00	4.00
❑ 95	Don Hoak	8.00	4.00
❑ 96	Eli Grba	5.00	2.50
❑ 97	Tito Francona	5.00	2.50
❑ 98	Checklist 2	12.00	6.00
❑ 99	Boog Powell RC	30.00	15.00
❑ 100	Warren Spahn	40.00	20.00
❑ 101	Carroll Hardy	5.00	2.50
❑ 102	Al Schroll	5.00	2.50
❑ 103	Don Blasingame	5.00	2.50
❑ 104	Ted Savage RC	5.00	2.50
❑ 105	Don Mossi	8.00	4.00
❑ 106	Carl Sawatski	5.00	2.50
❑ 107	Mike McCormick	8.00	4.00
❑ 108	Willie Davis	8.00	4.00
❑ 109	Bob Shaw	5.00	2.50
❑ 110	Bill Skowron	8.00	4.00
❑ 110A	Bill Skowron Green Tint	8.00	4.00
❑ 111	Dallas Green	8.00	4.00
❑ 111A	Dallas Green Green Tint	8.00	4.00
❑ 112	Hank Foiles	5.00	2.50
❑ 112A	Hank Foiles Green Tint	5.00	2.50
❑ 113	Chicago White Sox TC	10.00	5.00
❑ 113A	Chicago White Sox TC Green Tint	10.00	5.00
❑ 114	Howie Koplitz RC	5.00	2.50
❑ 114A	Howie Koplitz Green Tint	5.00	2.50
❑ 115	Bob Skinner	8.00	4.00
❑ 115A	Bob Skinner Green Tint	8.00	4.00
❑ 116	Herb Score	8.00	4.00
❑ 116A	Herb Score Green Tint	8.00	4.00
❑ 117	Gary Geiger	8.00	4.00
❑ 117A	Gary Geiger Green Tint	8.00	4.00
❑ 118	Julian Javier	8.00	4.00
❑ 118A	Julian Javier Green Tint	8.00	4.00
❑ 119	Danny Murphy	5.00	2.50
❑ 119A	Danny Murphy Green Tint	5.00	2.50
❑ 120	Bob Purkey	5.00	2.50
❑ 120A	Bob Purkey Green Tint	5.00	2.50
❑ 121	Billy Hitchcock MG	5.00	2.50
❑ 121A	Billy Hitchcock Green Tint	5.00	2.50
❑ 122	Norm Bass RC	5.00	2.50
❑ 122A	Norm Bass Green Tint	5.00	2.50
❑ 123	Mike de la Hoz	5.00	2.50
❑ 123A	Mike de la Hoz Green Tint	5.00	2.50
❑ 124	Bill Pleis RC	5.00	2.50
❑ 124A	Bill Pleis Green Tint	5.00	2.50
❑ 125	Gene Woodling	8.00	4.00
❑ 125A	Gene Woodling Green Tint	8.00	4.00
❑ 126	Al Cicotte	5.00	2.50
❑ 126A	Al Cicotte Green Tint	5.00	2.50
❑ 127	Siebern/Bauer/Lumpe	5.00	2.50
❑ 127A	Siebern/Bauer/Lumpe Green Tint	5.00	2.50
❑ 128	Art Fowler	5.00	2.50
❑ 128A	Art Fowler Green Tint	5.00	2.50
❑ 129A	Lee Walls Facing Right	5.00	2.50
❑ 129B	Lee Walls Facing Left	30.00	15.00
❑ 130	Frank Bolling	5.00	2.50
❑ 130A	Frank Bolling Green Tint	5.00	2.50
❑ 131	Pete Richert RC	5.00	2.50
❑ 131A	Pete Richert Green Tint	5.00	2.50
❑ 132A	Los Angeles Angels TC w/o Photo	10.00	5.00
❑ 132B	Los Angeles Angels TC w/Photo	30.00	15.00
❑ 133	Felipe Alou	8.00	4.00
❑ 133A	Felipe Alou Green Tint	8.00	4.00
❑ 134A	Billy Hoeft	5.00	2.50
❑ 134B	Billy Hoeft Green Tint	30.00	15.00
❑ 135	Babe Ruth Boy	20.00	10.00
❑ 135A	Babe Ruth Boy Green	20.00	10.00
❑ 136	B.Ruth/J.Ruppert	20.00	10.00
❑ 136A	B.Ruth/J.Ruppert Green	20.00	10.00
❑ 137	B.Ruth/M.Huggins	20.00	10.00
❑ 137A	B.Ruth/M.Huggins Green	20.00	10.00
❑ 138	Babe Ruth Slugger	20.00	10.00
❑ 138A	Babe Ruth Slugger Green	20.00	10.00
❑ 139A	Babe Ruth Story	30.00	15.00
❑ 139B	Hal Reniff Portrait	15.00	7.50
❑ 139C	Hal Reniff Pitching	60.00	35.00
❑ 140	B.Ruth/L.Gehrig	60.00	35.00
❑ 140A	B.Ruth/L.Gehrig Green	60.00	35.00
❑ 141	Babe Ruth Twilight	20.00	10.00
❑ 141A	Babe Ruth Twilight Green	20.00	10.00
❑ 142	Babe Ruth Coaching	20.00	10.00
❑ 142A	Babe Ruth Coaching Green	20.00	10.00
❑ 143	Babe Ruth Sports Hero	20.00	10.00
❑ 143A	Babe Ruth Sports Hero Green	20.00	10.00
❑ 144	Babe Ruth Farewell Speech	20.00	10.00
❑ 144A	B.Ruth Farewell Speech Green	20.00	10.00
❑ 145	Barry Latman	5.00	2.50
❑ 145A	Barry Latman Green Tint	5.00	2.50
❑ 146	Don Demeter	5.00	2.50
❑ 146A	Don Demeter Green Tint	5.00	2.50
❑ 147A	Bill Kunkel Portrait	5.00	2.50
❑ 147B	Bill Kunkel Pitching	30.00	15.00
❑ 148	Wally Post	5.00	2.50
❑ 148A	Wally Post Green Tint	5.00	2.50
❑ 149	Bob Duliba	5.00	2.50
❑ 149A	Bob Duliba Green Tint	5.00	2.50
❑ 150	Al Kaline	50.00	30.00
❑ 150A	Al Kaline Green Tint	50.00	30.00
❑ 151	Johnny Klippstein	5.00	2.50
❑ 151A	Johnny Klippstei Green Tint	5.00	2.50
❑ 152	Mickey Vernon MG	8.00	4.00
❑ 152A	Mickey Vernon MG Green Tint	8.00	4.00
❑ 153	Pumpsie Green	6.00	3.00
❑ 153A	Pumpsie Green Green Tint	6.00	3.00
❑ 154	Lee Thomas	6.00	3.00
❑ 154A	Lee Thomas Green Tint	6.00	3.00
❑ 155	Stu Miller	6.00	3.00
❑ 155A	Stu Miller Green Tint	6.00	3.00
❑ 156	Merritt Ranew RC	5.00	2.50
❑ 156A	Merritt Ranew Green Tint	5.00	2.50
❑ 157	Wes Covington	8.00	4.00
❑ 157A	Wes Covington Green Tint	8.00	4.00
❑ 158	Milwaukee Braves TC	10.00	5.00
❑ 158A	Milwaukee Braves TC Green Tint	15.00	7.50
❑ 159	Hal Reniff RC	8.00	4.00
❑ 160	Dick Stuart	8.00	4.00
❑ 160A	Dick Stuart Green Tint	8.00	4.00
❑ 161	Frank Baumann	5.00	2.50
❑ 161A	Frank Baumann Green Tint	5.00	2.50
❑ 162	Sammy Drake RC	5.00	2.50
❑ 162A	Sammy Drake Green Tint	5.00	2.50
❑ 163	B.Gardner/C.Boyer	8.00	4.00
❑ 163A	B.Gardner/C.Boyer Green Tint	8.00	4.00
❑ 164	Hal Naragon	5.00	2.50
❑ 164A	Hal Naragon Green Tint	5.00	2.50
❑ 165	Jackie Brandt	5.00	2.50
❑ 165A	Jackie Brandt Green Tint	5.00	2.50
❑ 166	Don Lee	5.00	2.50
❑ 166A	Don Lee Green Tint	5.00	2.50
❑ 167	Tim McCarver RC	30.00	15.00
❑ 167A	Tim McCarver Green Tint	30.00	15.00
❑ 168	Leo Posada	5.00	2.50
❑ 168A	Leo Posada Green Tint	5.00	2.50
❑ 169	Bob Cerv	10.00	5.00
❑ 169A	Bob Cerv Green Tint	10.00	5.00
❑ 170	Ron Santo	15.00	7.50
❑ 170A	Ron Santo Green Tint	15.00	7.50
❑ 171	Dave Sisler	5.00	2.50
❑ 171A	Dave Sisler Green Tint	5.00	2.50
❑ 172	Fred Hutchinson MG	8.00	4.00
❑ 172A	Fred Hutchinson MG Green Tint	8.00	4.00
❑ 173	Chico Fernandez	5.00	2.50
❑ 173A	Chico Fernandez Green Tint	5.00	2.50
❑ 174A	Carl Willey w/o Cap	5.00	2.50
❑ 174B	Carl Willey w/Cap	30.00	15.00
❑ 175	Frank Howard	10.00	5.00
❑ 175A	Frank Howard Green Tint	10.00	5.00
❑ 176A	Eddie Yost Portrait	5.00	2.50
❑ 176B	Eddie Yost Batting	30.00	15.00
❑ 177	Bobby Shantz	8.00	4.00
❑ 177A	Bobby Shantz Green Tint	8.00	4.00
❑ 178	Camilo Carreon	5.00	2.50
❑ 178A	Camilo Carreon Green Tint	5.00	2.50
❑ 179	Tom Sturdivant	5.00	2.50
❑ 179A	Tom Sturdivant Green Tint	5.00	2.50
❑ 180	Bob Allison	10.00	5.00
❑ 180A	Bob Allison Green Tint	10.00	5.00
❑ 181	Paul Brown RC	5.00	2.50
❑ 181A	Paul Brown Green Tint	5.00	2.50
❑ 182	Bob Nieman	5.00	2.50
❑ 182A	Bob Nieman Green Tint	5.00	2.50
❑ 183	Roger Craig	8.00	4.00
❑ 183A	Roger Craig Green Tint	8.00	4.00
❑ 184	Haywood Sullivan	8.00	4.00
❑ 184A	Haywood Sullivan Green Tint	8.00	4.00
❑ 185	Roland Sheldon	10.00	5.00
❑ 185A	Roland Sheldon Green Tint	10.00	5.00
❑ 186	Mack Jones RC	5.00	2.50
❑ 186A	Mack Jones Green Tint	5.00	2.50
❑ 187	Gene Conley	5.00	2.50
❑ 187A	Gene Conley Green Tint	5.00	2.50
❑ 188	Chuck Hiller	5.00	2.50
❑ 188A	Chuck Hiller Green Tint	5.00	2.50
❑ 189	Dick Hall	5.00	2.50
❑ 189A	Dick Hall Green Tint	5.00	2.50
❑ 190A	Wally Moon Portrait	8.00	4.00
❑ 190B	Wally Moon Batting	30.00	15.00
❑ 191	Jim Brewer	5.00	2.50
❑ 191A	Jim Brewer Green Tint	5.00	2.50
❑ 192A	Checklist 3 w/o Comma	12.00	6.00
❑ 192B	Checklist 3 w/Comma	15.00	7.50
❑ 193	Eddie Kasko	5.00	2.50
❑ 193A	Eddie Kasko Green Tint	5.00	2.50
❑ 194	Dean Chance RC	8.00	4.00
❑ 194A	Dean Chance Green Tint	8.00	4.00
❑ 195	Joe Cunningham	5.00	2.50
❑ 195A	Joe Cunningham Green Tint	5.00	2.50
❑ 196	Terry Fox	5.00	2.50
❑ 196A	Terry Fox Green Tint	5.00	2.50
❑ 197	Daryl Spencer	5.00	2.50
❑ 198	Johnny Keane MG	5.00	2.50
❑ 199	Gaylord Perry RC	80.00	50.00
❑ 200	Mickey Mantle	600.00	350.00
❑ 201	Ike Delock	5.00	2.50
❑ 202	Carl Warwick RC	5.00	2.50
❑ 203	Jack Fisher	5.00	2.50
❑ 204	Johnny Weekly RC	5.00	2.50
❑ 205	Gene Freese	5.00	2.50
❑ 206	Washington Senators TC	10.00	5.00
❑ 207	Pete Burnside	5.00	2.50
❑ 208	Billy Martin	20.00	10.00
❑ 209	Jim Fregosi RC	15.00	7.50
❑ 210	Roy Face	8.00	4.00
❑ 211	F.Bolling/R.McMillan	5.00	2.50
❑ 212	Jim Owens	5.00	2.50
❑ 213	Richie Ashburn	20.00	10.00
❑ 214	Dom Zanni	5.00	2.50
❑ 215	Woody Held	5.00	2.50
❑ 216	Ron Kline	5.00	2.50
❑ 217	Walter Alston MG	10.00	5.00
❑ 218	Joe Torre RC	40.00	20.00

	Card	Player		
❑	219	Al Downing RC	8.00	4.00
❑	220	Roy Sievers	8.00	4.00
❑	221	Bill Short	5.00	2.50
❑	222	Jerry Zimmerman	5.00	2.50
❑	223	Alex Grammas	5.00	2.50
❑	224	Don Rudolph	5.00	2.50
❑	225	Frank Malzone	8.00	4.00
❑	226	San Francisco Giants TC	10.00	5.00
❑	227	Bob Tiefenauer	5.00	2.50
❑	228	Dale Long	10.00	5.00
❑	229	Jesus McFarlane RC	5.00	2.50
❑	230	Camilo Pascual	8.00	4.00
❑	231	Ernie Bowman RC	5.00	2.50
❑	232	Yanks Win Opener WS1	10.00	5.00
❑	233	Joey Jay WS2	10.00	5.00
❑	234	Roger Maris WS3	25.00	12.50
❑	235	Whitey Ford WS4	15.00	7.50
❑	236	Yanks Crush Reds WS5	10.00	5.00
❑	237	Yanks Celebrate WS	10.00	5.00
❑	238	Norm Sherry	5.00	2.50
❑	239	Cecil Butler RC	5.00	2.50
❑	240	George Altman	5.00	2.50
❑	241	Johnny Kucks	5.00	2.50
❑	242	Mel McGaha MG RC	5.00	2.50
❑	243	Robin Roberts	15.00	7.50
❑	244	Don Gile	5.00	2.50
❑	245	Ron Hansen	5.00	2.50
❑	246	Art Ditmar	5.00	2.50
❑	247	Joe Pignatano	5.00	2.50
❑	248	Bob Aspromonte	8.00	4.00
❑	249	Ed Keegan	5.00	2.50
❑	250	Norm Cash	10.00	5.00
❑	251	New York Yankees TC	50.00	30.00
❑	252	Earl Francis	5.00	2.50
❑	253	Harry Chiti CO	5.00	2.50
❑	254	Gordon Windhorn RC	5.00	2.50
❑	255	Juan Pizarro	5.00	2.50
❑	256	Elio Chacon	8.00	4.00
❑	257	Jack Spring RC	5.00	2.50
❑	258	Marty Keough	5.00	2.50
❑	259	Lou Klimchock	5.00	2.50
❑	260	Billy Pierce	8.00	4.00
❑	261	George Alusik RC	5.00	2.50
❑	262	Bob Schmidt	5.00	2.50
❑	263	Purkey/Turner/Jay	5.00	2.50
❑	264	Dick Ellsworth	8.00	4.00
❑	265	Joe Adcock	8.00	4.00
❑	266	John Anderson RC	5.00	2.50
❑	267	Dan Dobbek	5.00	2.50
❑	268	Ken McBride	5.00	2.50
❑	269	Bob Oldis	5.00	2.50
❑	270	Dick Groat	8.00	4.00
❑	271	Ray Rippelmeyer	5.00	2.50
❑	272	Earl Robinson	5.00	2.50
❑	273	Gary Bell	5.00	2.50
❑	274	Sammy Taylor	5.00	2.50
❑	275	Norm Siebern	5.00	2.50
❑	276	Hal Kolstad RC	5.00	2.50
❑	277	Checklist 4	15.00	7.50
❑	278	Ken Johnson	8.00	4.00
❑	279	Hobie Landrith UER	8.00	4.00
❑	280	Johnny Podres	8.00	4.00
❑	281	Jake Gibbs RC	10.00	5.00
❑	282	Dave Hillman	5.00	2.50
❑	283	Charlie Smith RC	5.00	2.50
❑	284	Ruben Amaro	5.00	2.50
❑	285	Curt Simmons	8.00	4.00
❑	286	Al Lopez MG	10.00	5.00
❑	287	George Witt	5.00	2.50
❑	288	Billy Williams	30.00	15.00
❑	289	Mike Krsnich RC	5.00	2.50
❑	290	Jim Gentile	8.00	4.00
❑	291	Hal Stowe RC	5.00	2.50
❑	292	Jerry Kindall	5.00	2.50
❑	293	Bob Miller	8.00	4.00
❑	294	Philadelphia Phillies TC	10.00	5.00
❑	295	Vern Law	8.00	4.00
❑	296	Ken Hamlin	5.00	2.50
❑	297	Ron Perranoski	8.00	4.00
❑	298	Bill Tuttle	5.00	2.50
❑	299	Don Wert RC	5.00	2.50
❑	300	Willie Mays	250.00	150.00
❑	301	Galen Cisco RC	5.00	2.50
❑	302	Johnny Edwards RC	5.00	2.50
❑	303	Frank Torre	8.00	4.00
❑	304	Dick Farrell	8.00	4.00
❑	305	Jerry Lumpe	5.00	2.50
❑	306	L.McDaniel/L.Jackson	5.00	2.50
❑	307	Jim Grant	8.00	4.00
❑	308	Neil Chrisley	8.00	4.00
❑	309	Moe Morhardt RC	5.00	2.50
❑	310	Whitey Ford	50.00	30.00
❑	311	Tony Kubek IA	8.00	4.00
❑	312	Warren Spahn IA	15.00	7.50
❑	313	Roger Maris IA	80.00	50.00
❑	314	Rocky Colavito IA	8.00	4.00
❑	315	Whitey Ford IA	15.00	7.50
❑	316	Harmon Killebrew IA	15.00	7.50
❑	317	Stan Musial IA	20.00	10.00
❑	318	Mickey Mantle IA	150.00	90.00
❑	319	Mike McCormick IA	5.00	2.50
❑	320	Hank Aaron	150.00	90.00
❑	321	Lee Stange RC	5.00	2.50
❑	322	Alvin Dark MG	8.00	4.00
❑	323	Don Landrum	5.00	2.50
❑	324	Joe McClain	5.00	2.50
❑	325	Luis Aparicio	15.00	7.50
❑	326	Tom Parsons RC	5.00	2.50
❑	327	Ozzie Virgil	5.00	2.50
❑	328	Ken Walters	5.00	2.50
❑	329	Bob Bolin	5.00	2.50
❑	330	John Romano	5.00	2.50
❑	331	Moe Drabowsky	8.00	4.00
❑	332	Don Buddin	5.00	2.50
❑	333	Frank Cipriani RC	5.00	2.50
❑	334	Boston Red Sox TC	10.00	5.00
❑	335	Bill Bruton	5.00	2.50
❑	336	Billy Muffett	5.00	2.50
❑	337	Jim Marshall	8.00	4.00
❑	338	Billy Gardner	5.00	2.50
❑	339	Jose Valdivielso	5.00	2.50
❑	340	Don Drysdale	50.00	30.00
❑	341	Mike Hershberger RC	5.00	2.50
❑	342	Ed Rakow	5.00	2.50
❑	343	Albie Pearson	8.00	4.00
❑	344	Ed Bauta RC	5.00	2.50
❑	345	Chuck Schilling	5.00	2.50
❑	346	Jack Kralick	5.00	2.50
❑	347	Chuck Hinton RC	5.00	2.50
❑	348	Larry Burright RC	8.00	4.00
❑	349	Paul Foytack	5.00	2.50
❑	350	Frank Robinson	50.00	30.00
❑	351	J.Torre/D.Crandall	8.00	4.00
❑	352	Frank Sullivan	5.00	2.50
❑	353	Bill Mazeroski	15.00	7.50
❑	354	Roman Mejias	8.00	4.00
❑	355	Steve Barber	5.00	2.50
❑	356	Tom Haller RC	5.00	2.50
❑	357	Jerry Walker	5.00	2.50
❑	358	Tommy Davis	8.00	4.00
❑	359	Bobby Locke	5.00	2.50
❑	360	Yogi Berra	80.00	50.00
❑	361	Bob Hendley	5.00	2.50
❑	362	Ty Cline	5.00	2.50
❑	363	Bob Roselli	5.00	2.50
❑	364	Ken Hunt	5.00	2.50
❑	365	Charlie Neal	8.00	4.00
❑	366	Phil Regan	8.00	4.00
❑	367	Checklist 5	15.00	7.50
❑	368	Bob Tillman RC	5.00	2.50
❑	369	Ted Bowsfield	5.00	2.50
❑	370	Ken Boyer	10.00	5.00
❑	371	Earl Battey	6.00	3.00
❑	372	Jack Curtis	6.00	3.00
❑	373	Al Heist	6.00	3.00
❑	374	Gene Mauch MG	10.00	5.00
❑	375	Ron Fairly	10.00	5.00
❑	376	Bud Daley	8.00	4.00
❑	377	John Orsino RC	6.00	3.00
❑	378	Bennie Daniels	6.00	3.00
❑	379	Chuck Essegian	6.00	3.00
❑	380	Lew Burdette	10.00	5.00
❑	381	Chico Cardenas	10.00	5.00
❑	382	Dick Williams	8.00	4.00
❑	383	Ray Sadecki	6.00	3.00
❑	384	Kansas City Athletics TC	10.00	5.00
❑	385	Early Wynn	15.00	7.50
❑	386	Don Mincher	8.00	4.00
❑	387	Lou Brock RC	125.00	75.00
❑	388	Ryne Duren	8.00	4.00
❑	389	Smoky Burgess	10.00	5.00
❑	390	Orlando Cepeda AS	10.00	5.00
❑	391	Bill Mazeroski AS	10.00	5.00
❑	392	Ken Boyer AS UER	8.00	4.00
❑	393	Roy McMillan AS	6.00	3.00
❑	394	Hank Aaron AS	50.00	30.00
❑	395	Willie Mays AS	50.00	30.00
❑	396	Frank Robinson AS	15.00	7.50
❑	397	John Roseboro AS	6.00	3.00
❑	398	Don Drysdale AS	15.00	7.50
❑	399	Warren Spahn AS	15.00	7.50
❑	400	Elston Howard	10.00	5.00
❑	401	O.Cepeda/R.Maris	60.00	35.00
❑	402	Gino Cimoli	6.00	3.00
❑	403	Chet Nichols	6.00	3.00
❑	404	Tim Harkness RC	8.00	4.00
❑	405	Jim Perry	8.00	4.00
❑	406	Bob Taylor	6.00	3.00
❑	407	Hank Aguirre	6.00	3.00
❑	408	Gus Bell	8.00	4.00
❑	409	Pittsburgh Pirates TC	10.00	5.00
❑	410	Al Smith	6.00	3.00
❑	411	Danny O'Connell	6.00	3.00
❑	412	Charlie James	6.00	3.00
❑	413	Matty Alou	10.00	5.00
❑	414	Joe Gaines RC	6.00	3.00
❑	415	Bill Virdon	10.00	5.00
❑	416	Bob Scheffing MG	6.00	3.00
❑	417	Joe Azcue RC	6.00	3.00
❑	418	Andy Carey	6.00	3.00
❑	419	Bob Bruce	8.00	4.00
❑	420	Gus Triandos	8.00	4.00
❑	421	Ken MacKenzie	8.00	4.00
❑	422	Steve Bilko	6.00	3.00
❑	423	R.Face/H.Wilhelm	10.00	5.00
❑	424	Al McBean RC	6.00	3.00
❑	425	Carl Yastrzemski	125.00	75.00
❑	426	Bob Farley RC	6.00	3.00
❑	427	Jake Wood	6.00	3.00
❑	428	Joe Hicks	6.00	3.00
❑	429	Billy O'Dell	6.00	3.00
❑	430	Tony Kubek	15.00	7.50
❑	431	Bob (Buck) Rodgers RC	8.00	4.00
❑	432	Jim Pendleton	6.00	3.00
❑	433	Jim Archer	6.00	3.00
❑	434	Clay Dalrymple	6.00	3.00
❑	435	Larry Sherry	8.00	4.00
❑	436	Felix Mantilla	8.00	4.00
❑	437	Ray Moore	6.00	3.00
❑	438	Dick Brown	6.00	3.00
❑	439	Jerry Buchek RC	6.00	3.00
❑	440	Joey Jay	6.00	3.00
❑	441	Checklist 6	15.00	7.50
❑	442	Wes Stock	6.00	3.00
❑	443	Del Crandall	8.00	4.00
❑	444	Ted Wills	6.00	3.00
❑	445	Vic Power	8.00	4.00
❑	446	Don Elston	6.00	3.00
❑	447	Willie Kirkland	12.00	6.00
❑	448	Joe Gibbon	12.00	6.00
❑	449	Jerry Adair	12.00	6.00
❑	450	Jim O'Toole	15.00	7.50
❑	451	Jose Tartabull RC	15.00	7.50
❑	452	Earl Averill Jr.	12.00	6.00
❑	453	Cal McLish	12.00	6.00
❑	454	Floyd Robinson RC	12.00	6.00
❑	455	Luis Arroyo	15.00	7.50
❑	456	Joe Amalfitano	15.00	7.50
❑	457	Lou Clinton	12.00	6.00
❑	458A	Bob Buhl Emblem	15.00	7.50
❑	458B	Bob Buhl No Emblem	50.00	30.00
❑	459	Ed Bailey	12.00	6.00
❑	460	Jim Bunning	20.00	10.00
❑	461	Ken Hubbs RC	30.00	15.00
❑	462A	Willie Tasby Emblem	12.00	6.00
❑	462B	Willie Tasby No Emblem	50.00	30.00
❑	463	Hank Bauer MG	15.00	7.50
❑	464	Al Jackson RC	12.00	6.00
❑	465	Cincinnati Reds TC	20.00	10.00
❑	466	Norm Cash AS	15.00	7.50
❑	467	Chuck Schilling AS	12.00	6.00
❑	468	Brooks Robinson AS	25.00	12.50
❑	469	Luis Aparicio AS	15.00	7.50
❑	470	Al Kaline AS	25.00	12.50
❑	471	Mickey Mantle AS	200.00	125.00
❑	472	Rocky Colavito AS	15.00	7.50
❑	473	Elston Howard AS	15.00	7.50
❑	474	Frank Lary AS	12.00	6.00

❑ 475	Whitey Ford AS	20.00	10.00
❑ 476	Baltimore Orioles TC	20.00	10.00
❑ 477	Andre Rodgers	12.00	6.00
❑ 478	Don Zimmer	20.00	10.00
❑ 479	Joel Horlen RC	12.00	6.00
❑ 480	Harvey Kuenn	15.00	7.50
❑ 481	Vic Wertz	15.00	7.50
❑ 482	Sam Mele MG	12.00	6.00
❑ 483	Don McMahon	12.00	6.00
❑ 484	Dick Schofield	12.00	6.00
❑ 485	Pedro Ramos	12.00	6.00
❑ 486	Jim Gilliam	15.00	7.50
❑ 487	Jerry Lynch	12.00	6.00
❑ 488	Hal Brown	12.00	6.00
❑ 489	Julio Gotay RC	12.00	6.00
❑ 490	Clete Boyer UER	15.00	7.50
❑ 491	Leon Wagner	12.00	6.00
❑ 492	Hal W. Smith	15.00	7.50
❑ 493	Danny McDevitt	12.00	6.00
❑ 494	Sammy White	12.00	6.00
❑ 495	Don Cardwell	12.00	6.00
❑ 496	Wayne Causey RC	12.00	6.00
❑ 497	Ed Bouchee	15.00	7.50
❑ 498	Jim Donohue	12.00	6.00
❑ 499	Zoilo Versalles	15.00	7.50
❑ 500	Duke Snider	60.00	35.00
❑ 501	Claude Osteen	15.00	7.50
❑ 502	Hector Lopez	15.00	7.50
❑ 503	Danny Murtaugh MG	15.00	7.50
❑ 504	Eddie Bressoud	12.00	6.00
❑ 505	Juan Marichal	40.00	20.00
❑ 506	Charlie Maxwell	15.00	7.50
❑ 507	Ernie Broglio	15.00	7.50
❑ 508	Gordy Coleman	15.00	7.50
❑ 509	Dave Giusti RC	15.00	7.50
❑ 510	Jim Lemon	12.00	6.00
❑ 511	Bubba Phillips	12.00	6.00
❑ 512	Mike Fornieles	12.00	6.00
❑ 513	Whitey Herzog	15.00	7.50
❑ 514	Sherm Lollar	15.00	7.50
❑ 515	Stan Williams	15.00	7.50
❑ 516A	Checklist 7 White	15.00	7.50
❑ 516B	Checklist 7 Yellow	15.00	7.50
❑ 517	Dave Wickersham	12.00	6.00
❑ 518	Lee Maye	12.00	6.00
❑ 519	Bob Johnson RC	12.00	6.00
❑ 520	Bob Friend	15.00	7.50
❑ 521	Jacke Davis UER RC	12.00	6.00
❑ 522	Lindy McDaniel	15.00	7.50
❑ 523	Russ Nixon SP	30.00	18.00
❑ 524	Howie Nunn SP	30.00	18.00
❑ 525	George Thomas	20.00	10.00
❑ 526	Hal Woodeshick SP	30.00	18.00
❑ 527	Dick McAuliffe RC	30.00	18.00
❑ 528	Turk Lown	20.00	10.00
❑ 529	John Schaive SP	30.00	18.00
❑ 530	Bob Gibson SP	125.00	75.00
❑ 531	Bobby G. Smith	20.00	10.00
❑ 532	Dick Stigman	20.00	10.00
❑ 533	Charley Lau SP	30.00	18.00
❑ 534	Tony Gonzalez SP	30.00	18.00
❑ 535	Ed Roebuck	20.00	10.00
❑ 536	Dick Gernert	20.00	10.00
❑ 537	Cleveland Indians TC	50.00	30.00
❑ 538	Jack Sanford	20.00	10.00
❑ 539	Billy Moran	20.00	10.00
❑ 540	Jim Landis SP	30.00	18.00
❑ 541	Don Nottebart SP	30.00	18.00
❑ 542	Dave Philley	20.00	10.00
❑ 543	Bob Allen SP	30.00	18.00
❑ 544	Willie McCovey SP	125.00	75.00
❑ 545	Hoyt Wilhelm SP	50.00	30.00
❑ 546	Moe Thacker SP	30.00	18.00
❑ 547	Don Ferrarese	20.00	10.00
❑ 548	Bobby Del Greco	20.00	10.00
❑ 549	Bill Rigney MG SP	30.00	18.00
❑ 550	Art Mahaffey SP	30.00	18.00
❑ 551	Harry Bright	20.00	10.00
❑ 552	Chicago Cubs TC SP	50.00	30.00
❑ 553	Jim Coates	30.00	18.00
❑ 554	Bubba Morton SP RC	30.00	18.00
❑ 555	John Buzhardt SP	30.00	18.00
❑ 556	Al Spangler	20.00	10.00
❑ 557	Bob Anderson SP	30.00	18.00
❑ 558	John Goryl	20.00	10.00
❑ 559	Mike Higgins MG	20.00	10.00
❑ 560	Chuck Estrada SP	30.00	18.00
❑ 561	Gene Oliver SP	30.00	18.00
❑ 562	Bill Henry	20.00	10.00
❑ 563	Ken Aspromonte	20.00	10.00
❑ 564	Bob Grim	20.00	10.00
❑ 565	Jose Pagan	20.00	10.00
❑ 566	Marty Kutyna SP	30.00	18.00
❑ 567	Tracy Stallard SP	30.00	18.00
❑ 568	Jim Golden	20.00	10.00
❑ 569	Ed Sadowski SP	30.00	18.00
❑ 570	Bill Stafford SP	30.00	18.00
❑ 571	Billy Klaus SP	30.00	18.00
❑ 572	Bob G.Miller SP	30.00	18.00
❑ 573	Johnny Logan	20.00	10.00
❑ 574	Dean Stone	20.00	10.00
❑ 575	Red Schoendienst SP	50.00	30.00
❑ 576	Russ Kemmerer SP	30.00	18.00
❑ 577	Dave Nicholson SP	30.00	18.00
❑ 578	Jim Duffalo RC	20.00	10.00
❑ 579	Jim Schaffer SP RC	30.00	18.00
❑ 580	Bill Monbouquette	20.00	10.00
❑ 581	Mel Roach	20.00	10.00
❑ 582	Ron Piche	20.00	10.00
❑ 583	Larry Osborne	20.00	10.00
❑ 584	Minnesota Twins TC SP	60.00	35.00
❑ 585	Glen Hobbie SP	30.00	18.00
❑ 586	Sammy Esposito SP	30.00	18.00
❑ 587	Frank Funk SP	30.00	18.00
❑ 588	Birdie Tebbetts MG	20.00	10.00
❑ 589	Bob Turley	30.00	18.00
❑ 590	Curt Flood	30.00	18.00
❑ 591	Sam McDowell SP RC	80.00	50.00
❑ 592	Jim Bouton SP RC	80.00	50.00
❑ 593	Rookie Pitchers SP	50.00	30.00
❑ 594	Bob Uecker SP RC	80.00	50.00
❑ 595	Rookie Infielders SP	50.00	30.00
❑ 596	Joe Pepitone SP RC	80.00	50.00
❑ 597	Rookie Infield SP	50.00	30.00
❑ 598	Rookie Outfielders SP	80.00	50.00

1963 Topps

❑	COMPLETE SET (576)	6000.00	3500.00
❑	COMMON CARD (1-196)	4.00	2.00
❑	COMMON CARD (197-283)	5.00	2.50
❑	COMMON CARD (284-370)	5.00	2.50
❑	COMMON CARD (371-446)	5.00	2.50
❑	COMMON CARD (447-522)	25.00	12.50
❑	COMMON CARD (523-576)	15.00	7.50
❑	WRAPPER (1-CENT)	40.00	30.00
❑	WRAPPER (5-CENT)	30.00	20.00
❑ 1	F.Rob/Musial/Aaron LL	40.00	20.00
❑ 2	Runnels/Mantle/Rob LL	50.00	30.00
❑ 3	Mays/Aaron/Rob/Cep/Banks LL	40.00	20.00
❑ 4	Kill/Cash/Colav/Maris LL	20.00	10.00
❑ 5	Koufax/Gibson/Drysdale LL	25.00	12.50
❑ 6	Aguirre/Roberts/Ford LL	10.00	5.00
❑ 7	Drysdale/Sanf/Purk LL	10.00	5.00
❑ 8	Terry/Donovan/Bunning LL	8.00	4.00
❑ 9	Drysdale/Koufax/Gibson LL	30.00	15.00
❑ 10	Pascual/Bunning/Kaat LL	8.00	4.00
❑ 11	Lee Walls	4.00	2.00
❑ 12	Steve Barber	4.00	2.00
❑ 13	Philadelphia Phillies TC	8.00	4.00
❑ 14	Pedro Ramos	4.00	2.00
❑ 15	Ken Hubbs UER NPO	10.00	5.00
❑ 16	Al Smith	4.00	2.00
❑ 17	Ryne Duren	8.00	4.00
❑ 18	Burg/Stu/Clemente/Skin	80.00	50.00
❑ 19	Pete Burnside	4.00	2.00
❑ 20	Tony Kubek	10.00	5.00
❑ 21	Marty Keough	4.00	2.00
❑ 22	Curt Simmons	8.00	4.00
❑ 23	Ed Lopat MG	8.00	4.00
❑ 24	Bob Bruce	4.00	2.00
❑ 25	Al Kaline	50.00	30.00
❑ 26	Ray Moore	4.00	2.00
❑ 27	Choo Choo Coleman	8.00	4.00
❑ 28	Mike Fornieles	4.00	2.00
❑ 29A	Rookie Stars 1962	10.00	5.00
❑ 29B	Rookie Stars 1963	4.00	2.00
❑ 30	Harvey Kuenn	8.00	4.00
❑ 31	Cal Koonce RC	4.00	2.00
❑ 32	Tony Gonzalez	4.00	2.00
❑ 33	Bo Belinsky	8.00	4.00
❑ 34	Dick Schofield	4.00	2.00
❑ 35	John Buzhardt	4.00	2.00
❑ 36	Jerry Kindall	4.00	2.00
❑ 37	Jerry Lynch	4.00	2.00
❑ 38	Bud Daley	8.00	4.00
❑ 39	Los Angeles Angels TC	8.00	4.00
❑ 40	Vic Power	8.00	4.00
❑ 41	Charley Lau	8.00	4.00
❑ 42	Stan Williams	8.00	4.00
❑ 43	C.Stengel/G.Woodling	8.00	4.00
❑ 44	Terry Fox	4.00	2.00
❑ 45	Bob Aspromonte	4.00	2.00
❑ 46	Tommie Aaron RC	8.00	4.00
❑ 47	Don Lock RC	4.00	2.00
❑ 48	Birdie Tebbetts MG	8.00	4.00
❑ 49	Dal Maxvill RC	8.00	4.00
❑ 50	Billy Pierce	8.00	4.00
❑ 51	George Alusik	4.00	2.00
❑ 52	Chuck Schilling	4.00	2.00
❑ 53	Joe Moeller RC	8.00	4.00
❑ 54A	Dave DeBusschere 62	15.00	7.50
❑ 54B	Dave DeBusschere 63 RC	8.00	4.00
❑ 55	Bill Virdon	8.00	4.00
❑ 56	Dennis Bennett RC	4.00	2.00
❑ 57	Billy Moran	4.00	2.00
❑ 58	Bob Will	4.00	2.00
❑ 59	Craig Anderson	4.00	2.00
❑ 60	Elston Howard	8.00	4.00
❑ 61	Ernie Bowman	4.00	2.00
❑ 62	Bob Hendley	4.00	2.00
❑ 63	Cincinnati Reds TC	8.00	4.00
❑ 64	Dick McAuliffe	8.00	4.00
❑ 65	Jackie Brandt	4.00	2.00
❑ 66	Mike Joyce RC	4.00	2.00
❑ 67	Ed Charles	4.00	2.00
❑ 68	G.Hodges/D.Snider	25.00	12.50
❑ 69	Bud Zipfel RC	4.00	2.00
❑ 70	Jim O'Toole	8.00	4.00
❑ 71	Bobby Wine RC	8.00	4.00
❑ 72	Johnny Romano	4.00	2.00
❑ 73	Bobby Bragan MG RC	8.00	4.00
❑ 74	Denny Lemaster RC	4.00	2.00
❑ 75	Bob Allison	8.00	4.00
❑ 76	Earl Wilson	8.00	4.00
❑ 77	Al Spangler	4.00	2.00
❑ 78	Marv Throneberry	8.00	4.00
❑ 79	Checklist 1	12.00	6.00
❑ 80	Jim Gilliam	8.00	4.00
❑ 81	Jim Schaffer	4.00	2.00
❑ 82	Ed Rakow	4.00	2.00
❑ 83	Charley James	4.00	2.00
❑ 84	Ron Kline	4.00	2.00
❑ 85	Tom Haller	8.00	4.00
❑ 86	Charley Maxwell	8.00	4.00
❑ 87	Bob Veale	8.00	4.00
❑ 88	Ron Hansen	4.00	2.00
❑ 89	Dick Stigman	4.00	2.00
❑ 90	Gordy Coleman	8.00	4.00
❑ 91	Dallas Green	8.00	4.00
❑ 92	Hector Lopez	8.00	4.00
❑ 93	Galen Cisco	4.00	2.00
❑ 94	Bob Schmidt	4.00	2.00
❑ 95	Larry Jackson	4.00	2.00
❑ 96	Lou Clinton	4.00	2.00
❑ 97	Bob Duliba	4.00	2.00
❑ 98	George Thomas	4.00	2.00
❑ 99	Jim Umbricht	4.00	2.00
❑ 100	Joe Cunningham	4.00	2.00
❑ 101	Joe Gibbon	4.00	2.00
❑ 102A	Checklist 2 Red/Yellow	12.00	6.00

❑ 102B Checklist 2 White/Red 12.00 6.00
❑ 103 Chuck Essegian 4.00 2.00
❑ 104 Lew Krausse RC 4.00 2.00
❑ 105 Ron Fairly 8.00 4.00
❑ 106 Bobby Bolin 4.00 2.00
❑ 107 Jim Hickman 8.00 4.00
❑ 108 Hoyt Wilhelm 10.00 5.00
❑ 109 Lee Maye 4.00 2.00
❑ 110 Rich Rollins 8.00 4.00
❑ 111 Al Jackson 4.00 2.00
❑ 112 Dick Brown 4.00 2.00
❑ 113 Don Landrum UER 4.00 2.00
❑ 114 Dan Osinski RC 4.00 2.00
❑ 115 Carl Yastrzemski 40.00 20.00
❑ 116 Jim Brosnan 8.00 4.00
❑ 117 Jacke Davis 4.00 2.00
❑ 118 Sherm Lollar 4.00 2.00
❑ 119 Bob Lillis 4.00 2.00
❑ 120 Roger Maris 80.00 50.00
❑ 121 Jim Hannan RC 4.00 2.00
❑ 122 Julio Gotay 4.00 2.00
❑ 123 Frank Howard 8.00 4.00
❑ 124 Dick Howser 8.00 4.00
❑ 125 Robin Roberts 15.00 7.50
❑ 126 Bob Uecker 15.00 7.50
❑ 127 Bill Tuttle 4.00 2.00
❑ 128 Matty Alou 8.00 4.00
❑ 129 Gary Bell 4.00 2.00
❑ 130 Dick Groat 8.00 4.00
❑ 131 Washington Senators TC 8.00 4.00
❑ 132 Jack Hamilton 4.00 2.00
❑ 133 Gene Freese 4.00 2.00
❑ 134 Bob Scheffing MG 4.00 2.00
❑ 135 Richie Ashburn 20.00 10.00
❑ 136 Ike Delock 4.00 2.00
❑ 137 Mack Jones 4.00 2.00
❑ 138 W.Mays/S.Musial 80.00 50.00
❑ 139 Earl Averill Jr. 4.00 2.00
❑ 140 Frank Lary 8.00 4.00
❑ 141 Manny Mota RC 8.00 4.00
❑ 142 Whitey Ford WS1 10.00 5.00
❑ 143 Jack Sanford WS2 8.00 4.00
❑ 144 Roger Maris WS3 15.00 7.50
❑ 145 Chuck Hiller WS4 8.00 4.00
❑ 146 Tom Tresh WS5 8.00 4.00
❑ 147 Billy Pierce WS6 8.00 4.00
❑ 148 Ralph Terry WS7 8.00 4.00
❑ 149 Marv Breeding 4.00 2.00
❑ 150 Johnny Podres 8.00 4.00
❑ 151 Pittsburgh Pirates TC 8.00 4.00
❑ 152 Ron Nischwitz 4.00 2.00
❑ 153 Hal Smith 4.00 2.00
❑ 154 Walter Alston MG 8.00 4.00
❑ 155 Bill Stafford 4.00 2.00
❑ 156 Roy McMillan 8.00 4.00
❑ 157 Diego Segui RC 8.00 4.00
❑ 158 Tommy Harper RC 8.00 4.00
❑ 159 Jim Pagliaroni 4.00 2.00
❑ 160 Juan Pizarro 4.00 2.00
❑ 161 Frank Torre 8.00 4.00
❑ 162 Minnesota Twins TC 8.00 4.00
❑ 163 Don Larsen 8.00 4.00
❑ 164 Bubba Morton 4.00 2.00
❑ 165 Jim Kaat 8.00 4.00
❑ 166 Johnny Keane MG 4.00 2.00
❑ 167 Jim Fregosi 8.00 4.00
❑ 168 Russ Nixon 4.00 2.00
❑ 169 Gaylord Perry 25.00 12.50
❑ 170 Joe Adcock 8.00 4.00
❑ 171 Steve Hamilton RC 4.00 2.00
❑ 172 Gene Oliver 4.00 2.00
❑ 173 Tresh/Mantle/Richardson 150.00 90.00
❑ 174 Larry Burright 4.00 2.00
❑ 175 Bob Buhl 8.00 4.00
❑ 176 Jim King 4.00 2.00
❑ 177 Bubba Phillips 4.00 2.00
❑ 178 Johnny Edwards 4.00 2.00
❑ 179 Ron Piche 4.00 2.00
❑ 180 Bill Skowron 8.00 4.00
❑ 181 Sammy Esposito 4.00 2.00
❑ 182 Albie Pearson 8.00 4.00
❑ 183 Joe Pepitone 8.00 4.00
❑ 184 Vern Law 8.00 4.00
❑ 185 Chuck Hiller 4.00 2.00
❑ 186 Jerry Zimmerman 4.00 2.00
❑ 187 Willie Kirkland 4.00 2.00
❑ 188 Eddie Bressoud 4.00 2.00
❑ 189 Dave Giusti 8.00 4.00
❑ 190 Minnie Minoso 8.00 4.00
❑ 191 Checklist 3 12.00 6.00
❑ 192 Clay Dalrymple 4.00 2.00
❑ 193 Andre Rodgers 4.00 2.00
❑ 194 Joe Nuxhall 8.00 4.00
❑ 195 Manny Jimenez 4.00 2.00
❑ 196 Doug Camilli 4.00 2.00
❑ 197 Roger Craig 8.00 4.00
❑ 198 Lenny Green 5.00 2.50
❑ 199 Joe Amalfitano 5.00 2.50
❑ 200 Mickey Mantle 600.00 350.00
❑ 201 Cecil Butler 5.00 2.50
❑ 202 Boston Red Sox TC 8.00 4.00
❑ 203 Chico Cardenas 8.00 4.00
❑ 204 Don Nottebart 5.00 2.50
❑ 205 Luis Aparicio 15.00 7.50
❑ 206 Ray Washburn 5.00 2.50
❑ 207 Ken Hunt 5.00 2.50
❑ 208 Rookie Stars 5.00 2.50
❑ 209 Hobie Landrith 5.00 2.50
❑ 210 Sandy Koufax 150.00 90.00
❑ 211 Fred Whitfield RC 5.00 2.50
❑ 212 Glen Hobbie 5.00 2.50
❑ 213 Billy Hitchcock MG 5.00 2.50
❑ 214 Orlando Pena 5.00 2.50
❑ 215 Bob Skinner 8.00 4.00
❑ 216 Gene Conley 8.00 4.00
❑ 217 Joe Christopher 5.00 2.50
❑ 218 Lary/Mossi/Bunning 8.00 4.00
❑ 219 Chuck Cottier 5.00 2.50
❑ 220 Camilo Pascual 8.00 4.00
❑ 221 Cookie Rojas RC 8.00 4.00
❑ 222 Chicago Cubs TC 8.00 4.00
❑ 223 Eddie Fisher 5.00 2.50
❑ 224 Mike Roarke 5.00 2.50
❑ 225 Joey Jay 5.00 2.50
❑ 226 Julian Javier 8.00 4.00
❑ 227 Jim Grant 8.00 4.00
❑ 228 Tony Oliva RC 50.00 30.00
❑ 229 Willie Davis 8.00 4.00
❑ 230 Pete Runnels 8.00 4.00
❑ 231 Eli Grba UER 5.00 2.50
❑ 232 Frank Malzone 8.00 4.00
❑ 233 Casey Stengel MG 20.00 10.00
❑ 234 Dave Nicholson 5.00 2.50
❑ 235 Billy O'Dell 5.00 2.50
❑ 236 Bill Bryan RC 5.00 2.50
❑ 237 Jim Coates 8.00 4.00
❑ 238 Lou Johnson 5.00 2.50
❑ 239 Harvey Haddix 8.00 4.00
❑ 240 Rocky Colavito 15.00 7.50
❑ 241 Billy Smith RC 5.00 2.50
❑ 242 E.Banks/H.Aaron 60.00 35.00
❑ 243 Don Leppert 5.00 2.50
❑ 244 John Tsitouris 5.00 2.50
❑ 245 Gil Hodges 20.00 10.00
❑ 246 Lee Stange 5.00 2.50
❑ 247 New York Yankees TC 50.00 30.00
❑ 248 Tito Francona 5.00 2.50
❑ 249 Leo Burke RC 5.00 2.50
❑ 250 Stan Musial 100.00 60.00
❑ 251 Jack Lamabe 5.00 2.50
❑ 252 Ron Santo 10.00 5.00
❑ 253 Rookie Stars 5.00 2.50
❑ 254 Mike Hershberger 5.00 2.50
❑ 255 Bob Shaw 5.00 2.50
❑ 256 Jerry Lumpe 5.00 2.50
❑ 257 Hank Aguirre 5.00 2.50
❑ 258 Alvin Dark MG 8.00 4.00
❑ 259 Johnny Logan 8.00 4.00
❑ 260 Jim Gentile 8.00 4.00
❑ 261 Bob Miller 5.00 2.50
❑ 262 Ellis Burton 5.00 2.50
❑ 263 Dave Stenhouse 5.00 2.50
❑ 264 Phil Linz 5.00 2.50
❑ 265 Vada Pinson 8.00 4.00
❑ 266 Bob Allen 5.00 2.50
❑ 267 Carl Sawatski 5.00 2.50
❑ 268 Don Demeter 5.00 2.50
❑ 269 Don Mincher 5.00 2.50
❑ 270 Felipe Alou 8.00 4.00
❑ 271 Dean Stone 5.00 2.50
❑ 272 Danny Murphy 5.00 2.50
❑ 273 Sammy Taylor 5.00 2.50
❑ 274 Checklist 4 12.00 6.00
❑ 275 Eddie Mathews 30.00 15.00
❑ 276 Barry Shetrone 5.00 2.50
❑ 277 Dick Farrell 5.00 2.50
❑ 278 Chico Fernandez 5.00 2.50
❑ 279 Wally Moon 8.00 4.00
❑ 280 Bob (Buck) Rodgers 5.00 2.50
❑ 281 Tom Sturdivant 5.00 2.50
❑ 282 Bobby Del Greco 5.00 2.50
❑ 283 Roy Sievers 8.00 4.00
❑ 284 Dave Sisler 5.00 2.50
❑ 285 Dick Stuart 8.00 4.00
❑ 286 Stu Miller 8.00 4.00
❑ 287 Dick Bertell 5.00 2.50
❑ 288 Chicago White Sox TC 10.00 5.00
❑ 289 Hal Brown 5.00 2.50
❑ 290 Bill White 8.00 4.00
❑ 291 Don Rudolph 5.00 2.50
❑ 292 Pumpsie Green 8.00 4.00
❑ 293 Bill Pleis 5.00 2.50
❑ 294 Bill Rigney MG 5.00 2.50
❑ 295 Ed Roebuck 5.00 2.50
❑ 296 Doc Edwards 5.00 2.50
❑ 297 Jim Golden 5.00 2.50
❑ 298 Don Dillard 5.00 2.50
❑ 299 Rookie Stars 8.00 4.00
❑ 300 Willie Mays 150.00 90.00
❑ 301 Bill Fischer 5.00 2.50
❑ 302 Whitey Herzog 8.00 4.00
❑ 303 Earl Francis 5.00 2.50
❑ 304 Harry Bright 5.00 2.50
❑ 305 Don Hoak 5.00 2.50
❑ 306 E.Battey/E.Howard 10.00 5.00
❑ 307 Chet Nichols 5.00 2.50
❑ 308 Camilo Carreon 5.00 2.50
❑ 309 Jim Brewer 5.00 2.50
❑ 310 Tommy Davis 8.00 4.00
❑ 311 Joe McClain 5.00 2.50
❑ 312 Houston Colts TC 25.00 12.50
❑ 313 Ernie Broglio 5.00 2.50
❑ 314 John Goryl 5.00 2.50
❑ 315 Ralph Terry 8.00 4.00
❑ 316 Norm Sherry 8.00 4.00
❑ 317 Sam McDowell 8.00 4.00
❑ 318 Gene Mauch MG 8.00 4.00
❑ 319 Joe Gaines 5.00 2.50
❑ 320 Warren Spahn 60.00 35.00
❑ 321 Gino Cimoli 5.00 2.50
❑ 322 Bob Turley 8.00 4.00
❑ 323 Bill Mazeroski 15.00 7.50
❑ 324 Vic Davalillo RC 8.00 4.00
❑ 325 Jack Sanford 5.00 2.50
❑ 326 Hank Foiles 5.00 2.50
❑ 327 Paul Foytack 5.00 2.50
❑ 328 Dick Williams 8.00 4.00
❑ 329 Lindy McDaniel 8.00 4.00
❑ 330 Chuck Hinton 5.00 2.50
❑ 331 Stafford/Pierce 8.00 4.00
❑ 332 Joel Horlen 8.00 4.00
❑ 333 Carl Warwick 5.00 2.50
❑ 334 Wynn Hawkins 5.00 2.50
❑ 335 Leon Wagner 5.00 2.50
❑ 336 Ed Bauta 5.00 2.50
❑ 337 Los Angeles Dodgers TC 25.00 12.50
❑ 338 Russ Kemmerer 5.00 2.50
❑ 339 Ted Bowsfield 5.00 2.50
❑ 340 Yogi Berra P/CO 100.00 60.00
❑ 341 Jack Baldschun 5.00 2.50
❑ 342 Gene Woodling 8.00 4.00
❑ 343 Johnny Pesky MG 8.00 4.00
❑ 344 Don Schwall 5.00 2.50
❑ 345 Brooks Robinson 60.00 35.00
❑ 346 Billy Hoeft 5.00 2.50
❑ 347 Joe Torre 15.00 7.50
❑ 348 Vic Wertz 8.00 4.00
❑ 349 Zoilo Versalles 8.00 4.00
❑ 350 Bob Purkey 5.00 2.50
❑ 351 Al Luplow 5.00 2.50
❑ 352 Ken Johnson 5.00 2.50
❑ 353 Billy Williams 30.00 15.00
❑ 354 Dom Zanni 5.00 2.50
❑ 355 Dean Chance 8.00 4.00
❑ 356 John Schaive 5.00 2.50
❑ 357 George Altman 5.00 2.50
❑ 358 Milt Pappas 8.00 4.00
❑ 359 Haywood Sullivan 8.00 4.00

360	Don Drysdale	60.00	35.00
361	Clete Boyer	10.00	5.00
362	Checklist 5	12.00	6.00
363	Dick Radatz	8.00	4.00
364	Howie Goss	5.00	2.50
365	Jim Bunning	20.00	10.00
366	Tony Taylor	8.00	4.00
367	Tony Cloninger	5.00	2.50
368	Ed Bailey	5.00	2.50
369	Jim Lemon	5.00	2.50
370	Dick Donovan	5.00	2.50
371	Rod Kanehl	8.00	4.00
372	Don Lee	5.00	2.50
373	Jim Campbell RC	5.00	2.50
374	Claude Osteen	8.00	4.00
375	Ken Boyer	15.00	7.50
376	John Wyatt RC	5.00	2.50
377	Baltimore Orioles TC	10.00	5.00
378	Bill Henry	5.00	2.50
379	Bob Anderson	5.00	2.50
380	Ernie Banks UER	100.00	60.00
381	Frank Baumann	5.00	2.50
382	Ralph Houk MG	10.00	5.00
383	Pete Richert	5.00	2.50
384	Bob Tillman	5.00	2.50
385	Art Mahaffey	5.00	2.50
386	Rookie Stars	5.00	2.50
387	Al McBean	5.00	2.50
388	Jim Davenport	8.00	4.00
389	Frank Sullivan	5.00	2.50
390	Hank Aaron	175.00	100.00
391	Bill Dailey RC	5.00	2.50
392	Romano/Francona	5.00	2.50
393	Ken MacKenzie	8.00	4.00
394	Tim McCarver	15.00	7.50
395	Don McMahon	5.00	2.50
396	Joe Koppe	5.00	2.50
397	Kansas City Athletics TC	10.00	5.00
398	Boog Powell	25.00	12.50
399	Dick Ellsworth	5.00	2.50
400	Frank Robinson	60.00	35.00
401	Jim Bouton	15.00	7.50
402	Mickey Vernon MG	8.00	4.00
403	Ron Perranoski	8.00	4.00
404	Bob Oldis	5.00	2.50
405	Floyd Robinson	5.00	2.50
406	Howie Koplitz	5.00	2.50
407	Rookie Stars	8.00	4.00
408	Billy Gardner	5.00	2.50
409	Roy Face	8.00	4.00
410	Earl Battey	5.00	2.50
411	Jim Constable	5.00	2.50
412	Podres/Drysdale/Koufax	50.00	30.00
413	Jerry Walker	5.00	2.50
414	Ty Cline	5.00	2.50
415	Bob Gibson	60.00	35.00
416	Alex Grammas	5.00	2.50
417	San Francisco Giants TC	10.00	5.00
418	John Orsino	5.00	2.50
419	Tracy Stallard	5.00	2.50
420	Bobby Richardson	15.00	7.50
421	Tom Morgan	5.00	2.50
422	Fred Hutchinson MG	8.00	4.00
423	Ed Hobaugh	5.00	2.50
424	Charlie Smith	5.00	2.50
425	Smoky Burgess	8.00	4.00
426	Barry Latman	5.00	2.50
427	Bernie Allen	5.00	2.50
428	Carl Boles RC	5.00	2.50
429	Lew Burdette	8.00	4.00
430	Norm Siebern	5.00	2.50
431A	Checklist 6 White/Red	12.00	6.00
431B	Checklist 6 Black/Orange	30.00	15.00
432	Roman Mejias	5.00	2.50
433	Denis Menke	5.00	2.50
434	John Callison	8.00	4.00
435	Woody Held	5.00	2.50
436	Tim Harkness	8.00	4.00
437	Bill Bruton	5.00	2.50
438	Wes Stock	5.00	2.50
439	Don Zimmer	8.00	4.00
440	Juan Marichal	30.00	15.00
441	Lee Thomas	8.00	4.00
442	J.C. Hartman RC	5.00	2.50
443	Jimmy Piersall	8.00	4.00
444	Jim Maloney	8.00	4.00
445	Norm Cash	10.00	5.00
446	Whitey Ford	60.00	35.00
447	Felix Mantilla	25.00	12.50
448	Jack Kralick	25.00	12.50
449	Jose Tartabull	25.00	12.50
450	Bob Friend	30.00	15.00
451	Cleveland Indians TC	40.00	20.00
452	Barney Schultz	25.00	12.50
453	Jake Wood	25.00	12.50
454A	Art Fowler White	25.00	12.50
454B	Art Fowler Orange	30.00	15.00
455	Ruben Amaro	25.00	12.50
456	Jim Coker	25.00	12.50
457	Tex Clevenger	25.00	12.50
458	Al Lopez MG	30.00	15.00
459	Dick LeMay	25.0z0	12.50
460	Del Crandall	30.00	15.00
461	Norm Bass	25.00	12.50
462	Wally Post	25.00	12.50
463	Joe Schaffernoth	25.00	12.50
464	Ken Aspromonte	25.00	12.50
465	Chuck Estrada	25.00	12.50
466	Bill Freehan SP RC	60.00	35.00
467	Phil Ortega	25.00	12.50
468	Carroll Hardy	30.00	15.00
469	Jay Hook	30.00	15.00
470	Tom Tresh SP	60.00	35.00
471	Ken Retzer	25.00	12.50
472	Lou Brock	80.00	50.00
473	New York Mets TC	100.00	60.00
474	Jack Fisher	25.00	12.50
475	Gus Triandos	30.00	15.00
476	Frank Funk	25.00	12.50
477	Donn Clendenon	30.00	15.00
478	Paul Brown	25.00	12.50
479	Ed Brinkman RC	25.00	12.50
480	Bill Monbouquette	25.00	12.50
481	Bob Taylor	25.00	12.50
482	Felix Torres	25.00	12.50
483	Jim Owens UER	25.00	12.50
484	Dale Long SP	30.00	15.00
485	Jim Landis	25.00	12.50
486	Ray Sadecki	25.00	12.50
487	John Roseboro	30.00	15.00
488	Jerry Adair	25.00	12.50
489	Paul Toth RC	25.00	12.50
490	Willie McCovey	100.00	60.00
491	Harry Craft MG	25.00	12.50
492	Dave Wickersham	25.00	12.50
493	Walt Bond	25.00	12.50
494	Phil Regan	25.00	12.50
495	Frank Thomas SP	30.00	15.00
496	Rookie Stars	30.00	15.00
497	Bennie Daniels	25.00	12.50
498	Eddie Kasko	25.00	12.50
499	J.C. Martin	25.00	12.50
500	Harmon Killebrew SP	150.00	90.00
501	Joe Azcue	25.00	12.50
502	Daryl Spencer	25.00	12.50
503	Milwaukee Braves TC	40.00	20.00
504	Bob Johnson	25.00	12.50
505	Curt Flood	40.00	20.00
506	Gene Green	25.00	12.50
507	Roland Sheldon	30.00	15.00
508	Ted Savage	25.00	12.50
509A	Checklist 7 Centered	30.00	15.00
509B	Checklist 7 Right	30.00	15.00
510	Ken McBride	25.00	12.50
511	Charlie Neal	30.00	15.00
512	Cal McLish	25.00	12.50
513	Gary Geiger	25.00	12.50
514	Larry Osborne	25.00	12.50
515	Don Elston	25.00	12.50
516	Purnell Goldy RC	25.00	12.50
517	Hal Woodeshick	25.00	12.50
518	Don Blasingame	25.00	12.50
519	Claude Raymond RC	25.00	12.50
520	Orlando Cepeda	40.00	20.00
521	Dan Pfister	25.00	12.50
522	Rookie Stars	30.00	15.00
523	Bill Kunkel	15.00	7.50
524	St. Louis Cardinals TC	30.00	15.00
525	Nellie Fox	50.00	30.00
526	Dick Hall	15.00	7.50
527	Ed Sadowski	15.00	7.50
528	Carl Willey	15.00	7.50
529	Wes Covington	15.00	7.50
530	Don Mossi	20.00	10.00
531	Sam Mele MG	15.00	7.50
532	Steve Boros	15.00	7.50
533	Bobby Shantz	20.00	10.00
534	Ken Walters	15.00	7.50
535	Jim Perry	20.00	10.00
536	Norm Larker	15.00	7.50
537	Pete Rose RC	1000.00	600.00
538	George Brunet	15.00	7.50
539	Wayne Causey	15.00	7.50
540	Roberto Clemente	250.00	150.00
541	Ron Moeller	15.00	7.50
542	Lou Klimchock	15.00	7.50
543	Russ Snyder	15.00	7.50
544	Rusty Staub RC	50.00	30.00
545	Jose Pagan	15.00	7.50
546	Hal Reniff	20.00	10.00
547	Gus Bell	15.00	7.50
548	Tom Satriano RC	15.00	7.50
549	Rookie Stars	15.00	7.50
550	Duke Snider	80.00	50.00
551	Billy Klaus	15.00	7.50
552	Detroit Tigers TC	50.00	30.00
553	Willie Stargell RC	125.00	75.00
554	Hank Fischer RC	15.00	7.50
555	John Blanchard	20.00	10.00
556	Al Worthington	15.00	7.50
557	Cuno Barragan	15.00	7.50
558	Ron Hunt RC	20.00	10.00
559	Danny Murtaugh MG	15.00	7.50
560	Ray Herbert	15.00	7.50
561	Mike De La Hoz	15.00	7.50
562	Dave McNally RC	30.00	15.00
563	Mike McCormick	15.00	7.50
564	George Banks RC	15.00	7.50
565	Larry Sherry	15.00	7.50
566	Cliff Cook	15.00	7.50
567	Jim Duffalo	15.00	7.50
568	Bob Sadowski	15.00	7.50
569	Luis Arroyo	20.00	10.00
570	Frank Bolling	15.00	7.50
571	Johnny Klippstein	15.00	7.50
572	Jack Spring	15.00	7.50
573	Coot Veal	15.00	7.50
574	Hal Kolstad	15.00	7.50
575	Don Cardwell	15.00	7.50
576	Johnny Temple	30.00	15.00

1964 Topps

	COMPLETE SET (587)	3500.00	2500.00
	COMMON CARD (1-196)	3.00	1.50
	COMMON CARD (197-370)	4.00	2.00
	COMMON CARD (371-522)	8.00	4.00
	COMMON CARD (523-587)	15.00	7.50
	WRAPPER (1-CENT)	100.00	75.00
	WRAP.(1-CENT, REPEAT)	125.00	100.00
	WRAPPER (5-CENT)	30.00	20.00
	WRAPPER (5-CENT, COIN)	40.00	30.00
1	Koufax/Ellis/Friend LL	30.00	15.00
2	Peters/Pizarro/Pascual LL	8.00	4.00
3	Koufax/Marichal/Spahn LL	20.00	10.00
4	Ford/Pascual/Bouton LL	8.00	4.00
5	Koufax/Malon/Drysdale LL	15.00	7.50
6	Pascual/Bunning/Stigman LL	8.00	4.00
7	Clemente/Groat/Aaron LL	20.00	10.00
8	Yaz/Kaline/Rollins LL	15.00	7.50
9	Aaron/McCov/Mays/Cep LL	30.00	15.00

❑ 10 Killebrew/Stuart/Allison LL 8.00 4.00
❑ 11 Aaron/Boyer/White LL 15.00 7.50
❑ 12 Stuart/Kaline/Killebrew LL 8.00 4.00
❑ 13 Hoyt Wilhelm 12.00 6.00
❑ 14 D.Nen RC/N.Willhite RC 3.00 1.50
❑ 15 Zoilo Versalles 6.00 3.00
❑ 16 John Boozer 3.00 1.50
❑ 17 Willie Kirkland 3.00 1.50
❑ 18 Billy O'Dell 3.00 1.50
❑ 19 Don Wert 3.00 1.50
❑ 20 Bob Friend 6.00 3.00
❑ 21 Yogi Berra MG 40.00 20.00
❑ 22 Jerry Adair 3.00 1.50
❑ 23 Chris Zachary RC 3.00 1.50
❑ 24 Carl Sawatski 3.00 1.50
❑ 25 Bill Monbouquette 3.00 1.50
❑ 26 Gino Cimoli 3.00 1.50
❑ 27 New York Mets TC 8.00 4.00
❑ 28 Claude Osteen 6.00 3.00
❑ 29 Lou Brock 40.00 20.00
❑ 30 Ron Perranoski 6.00 3.00
❑ 31 Dave Nicholson 3.00 1.50
❑ 32 Dean Chance 6.00 3.00
❑ 33 S.Ellis/M.Queen 6.00 3.00
❑ 34 Jim Perry 6.00 3.00
❑ 35 Eddie Mathews 20.00 10.00
❑ 36 Hal Reniff 3.00 1.50
❑ 37 Smoky Burgess 6.00 3.00
❑ 38 Jim Wynn RC 8.00 4.00
❑ 39 Hank Aguirre 3.00 1.50
❑ 40 Dick Groat 6.00 3.00
❑ 41 W.McCovey/L.Wagner 8.00 4.00
❑ 42 Moe Drabowsky 6.00 3.00
❑ 43 Roy Sievers 6.00 3.00
❑ 44 Duke Carmel 3.00 1.50
❑ 45 Milt Pappas 6.00 3.00
❑ 46 Ed Brinkman 3.00 1.50
❑ 47 J.Alou RC/R.Herbel 6.00 3.00
❑ 48 Bob Perry RC 3.00 1.50
❑ 49 Bill Henry 3.00 1.50
❑ 50 Mickey Mantle 500.00 300.00
❑ 51 Pete Richert 3.00 1.50
❑ 52 Chuck Hinton 3.00 1.50
❑ 53 Denis Menke 3.00 1.50
❑ 54 Sam Mele MG 3.00 1.50
❑ 55 Ernie Banks 40.00 20.00
❑ 56 Hal Brown 3.00 1.50
❑ 57 Tim Harkness 6.00 3.00
❑ 58 Don Demeter 6.00 3.00
❑ 59 Ernie Broglio 3.00 1.50
❑ 60 Frank Malzone 6.00 3.00
❑ 61 B.Rodgers/E.Sadowski 6.00 3.00
❑ 62 Ted Savage 3.00 1.50
❑ 63 John Orsino 3.00 1.50
❑ 64 Ted Abernathy 3.00 1.50
❑ 65 Felipe Alou 6.00 3.00
❑ 66 Eddie Fisher 3.00 1.50
❑ 67 Detroit Tigers TC 6.00 3.00
❑ 68 Willie Davis 6.00 3.00
❑ 69 Clete Boyer 6.00 3.00
❑ 70 Joe Torre 8.00 4.00
❑ 71 Jack Spring 3.00 1.50
❑ 72 Chico Cardenas 6.00 3.00
❑ 73 Jimmie Hall RC 8.00 4.00
❑ 74 B.Priddy RC/T.Butters 3.00 1.50
❑ 75 Wayne Causey 3.00 1.50
❑ 76 Checklist 1 10.00 5.00
❑ 77 Jerry Walker 3.00 1.50
❑ 78 Merritt Ranew 3.00 1.50
❑ 79 Bob Heffner RC 3.00 1.50
❑ 80 Vada Pinson 8.00 4.00
❑ 81 N.Fox/H.Killebrew 12.00 6.00
❑ 82 Jim Davenport 6.00 3.00
❑ 83 Gus Triandos 6.00 3.00
❑ 84 Carl Willey 3.00 1.50
❑ 85 Pete Ward 3.00 1.50
❑ 86 Al Downing 6.00 3.00
❑ 87 St. Louis Cardinals TC 6.00 3.00
❑ 88 John Roseboro 6.00 3.00
❑ 89 Boog Powell 6.00 3.00
❑ 90 Earl Battey 3.00 1.50
❑ 91 Bob Bailey 6.00 3.00
❑ 92 Steve Ridzik 3.00 1.50
❑ 93 Gary Geiger 3.00 1.50
❑ 94 J.Britton RC/L.Maxie RC 3.00 1.50
❑ 95 George Altman 3.00 1.50
❑ 96 Bob Buhl 6.00 3.00
❑ 97 Jim Fregosi 6.00 3.00
❑ 98 Bill Bruton 3.00 1.50
❑ 99 Al Stanek RC 3.00 1.50
❑ 100 Elston Howard 6.00 3.00
❑ 101 Walt Alston MG 8.00 4.00
❑ 102 Checklist 2 10.00 5.00
❑ 103 Curt Flood 6.00 3.00
❑ 104 Art Mahaffey 6.00 3.00
❑ 105 Woody Held 3.00 1.50
❑ 106 Joe Nuxhall 6.00 3.00
❑ 107 B.Howard RC/F.Kruetzer RC 3.00 1.50
❑ 108 John Wyatt 3.00 1.50
❑ 109 Rusty Staub 6.00 3.00
❑ 110 Albie Pearson 6.00 3.00
❑ 111 Don Elston 3.00 1.50
❑ 112 Bob Tillman 3.00 1.50
❑ 113 Grover Powell RC 6.00 3.00
❑ 114 Don Lock 3.00 1.50
❑ 115 Frank Bolling 3.00 1.50
❑ 116 J.Ward RC/T.Oliva 12.00 6.00
❑ 117 Earl Francis 3.00 1.50
❑ 118 John Blanchard 6.00 3.00
❑ 119 Gary Kolb RC 3.00 1.50
❑ 120 Don Drysdale 20.00 10.00
❑ 121 Pete Runnels 6.00 3.00
❑ 122 Don McMahon 3.00 1.50
❑ 123 Jose Pagan 3.00 1.50
❑ 124 Orlando Pena 3.00 1.50
❑ 125 Pete Rose UER 250.00 150.00
❑ 126 Russ Snyder 3.00 1.50
❑ 127 A.Gatewood RC/D.Simpson 3.00 1.50
❑ 128 Mickey Lolich RC 20.00 10.00
❑ 129 Amado Samuel 3.00 1.50
❑ 130 Gary Peters 6.00 3.00
❑ 131 Steve Boros 3.00 1.50
❑ 132 Milwaukee Braves TC 6.00 3.00
❑ 133 Jim Grant 6.00 3.00
❑ 134 Don Zimmer 6.00 3.00
❑ 135 Johnny Callison 6.00 3.00
❑ 136 Sandy Koufax WS1 20.00 10.00
❑ 137 Willie Davis WS2 8.00 4.00
❑ 138 Ron Fairly WS3 8.00 4.00
❑ 139 Frank Howard WS4 8.00 4.00
❑ 140 Dodgers Celebrate WS 8.00 4.00
❑ 141 Danny Murtaugh MG 6.00 3.00
❑ 142 John Bateman 3.00 1.50
❑ 143 Bubba Phillips 3.00 1.50
❑ 144 Al Worthington 3.00 1.50
❑ 145 Norm Siebern 3.00 1.50
❑ 146 T.John RC/B.Chance RC 30.00 15.00
❑ 147 Ray Sadecki 3.00 1.50
❑ 148 J.C. Martin 3.00 1.50
❑ 149 Paul Foytack 3.00 1.50
❑ 150 Willie Mays 125.00 75.00
❑ 151 Kansas City Athletics TC 6.00 3.00
❑ 152 Denny Lemaster 3.00 1.50
❑ 153 Dick Williams 6.00 3.00
❑ 154 Dick Tracewski RC 6.00 3.00
❑ 155 Duke Snider 30.00 15.00
❑ 156 Bill Dailey 3.00 1.50
❑ 157 Gene Mauch MG 6.00 3.00
❑ 158 Ken Johnson 3.00 1.50
❑ 159 Charlie Dees RC 3.00 1.50
❑ 160 Ken Boyer 6.00 3.00
❑ 161 Dave McNally 6.00 3.00
❑ 162 D.Sisler/V.Pinson 6.00 3.00
❑ 163 Donn Clendenon 6.00 3.00
❑ 164 Bud Daley 3.00 1.50
❑ 165 Jerry Lumpe 3.00 1.50
❑ 166 Marty Keough 3.00 1.50
❑ 167 M.Brumley RC/L.Piniella RC 30.00 15.00
❑ 168 Al Weis 3.00 1.50
❑ 169 Del Crandall 6.00 3.00
❑ 170 Dick Radatz 6.00 3.00
❑ 171 Ty Cline 3.00 1.50
❑ 172 Cleveland Indians TC 6.00 3.00
❑ 173 Ryne Duren 6.00 3.00
❑ 174 Doc Edwards 3.00 1.50
❑ 175 Billy Williams 12.00 6.00
❑ 176 Tracy Stallard 3.00 1.50
❑ 177 Harmon Killebrew 20.00 10.00
❑ 178 Hank Bauer MG 6.00 3.00
❑ 179 Carl Warwick 3.00 1.50
❑ 180 Tommy Davis 6.00 3.00
❑ 181 Dave Wickersham 3.00 1.50
❑ 182 C.Yastrzemski/C.Schilling 15.00 7.50
❑ 183 Ron Taylor 3.00 1.50
❑ 184 Al Luplow 3.00 1.50
❑ 185 Jim O'Toole 6.00 3.00
❑ 186 Roman Mejias 3.00 1.50
❑ 187 Ed Roebuck 3.00 1.50
❑ 188 Checklist 3 10.00 5.00
❑ 189 Bob Hendley 3.00 1.50
❑ 190 Bobby Richardson 8.00 4.00
❑ 191 Clay Dalrymple 6.00 3.00
❑ 192 J.Boccabella RC/B.Cowan RC 3.00 1.50
❑ 193 Jerry Lynch 3.00 1.50
❑ 194 John Goryl 3.00 1.50
❑ 195 Floyd Robinson 3.00 1.50
❑ 196 Jim Gentile 3.00 1.50
❑ 197 Frank Lary 6.00 3.00
❑ 198 Len Gabrielson 4.00 2.00
❑ 199 Joe Azcue 4.00 2.00
❑ 200 Sandy Koufax 120.00 70.00
❑ 201 S.Bowens RC/W.Bunker RC 6.00 3.00
❑ 202 Galen Cisco 6.00 3.00
❑ 203 John Kennedy RC 6.00 3.00
❑ 204 Matty Alou 6.00 3.00
❑ 205 Nellie Fox 12.00 6.00
❑ 206 Steve Hamilton 6.00 3.00
❑ 207 Fred Hutchinson MG 6.00 3.00
❑ 208 Wes Covington 6.00 3.00
❑ 209 Bob Allen 4.00 2.00
❑ 210 Carl Yastrzemski 40.00 20.00
❑ 211 Jim Coker 4.00 2.00
❑ 212 Pete Lovrich 4.00 2.00
❑ 213 Los Angeles Angels TC 6.00 3.00
❑ 214 Ken McMullen 6.00 3.00
❑ 215 Ray Herbert 4.00 2.00
❑ 216 Mike de la Hoz 4.00 2.00
❑ 217 Jim King 4.00 2.00
❑ 218 Hank Fischer 4.00 2.00
❑ 219 A.Downing/J.Bouton 6.00 3.00
❑ 220 Dick Ellsworth 6.00 3.00
❑ 221 Bob Saverine 4.00 2.00
❑ 222 Billy Pierce 6.00 3.00
❑ 223 George Banks 4.00 2.00
❑ 224 Tommie Sisk 4.00 2.00
❑ 225 Roger Maris 60.00 35.00
❑ 226 J.Grote RC/L.Yellen RC 6.00 3.00
❑ 227 Barry Latman 4.00 2.00
❑ 228 Felix Mantilla 4.00 2.00
❑ 229 Charley Lau 6.00 3.00
❑ 230 Brooks Robinson 40.00 20.00
❑ 231 Dick Calmus RC 4.00 2.00
❑ 232 Al Lopez MG 8.00 4.00
❑ 233 Hal Smith 4.00 2.00
❑ 234 Gary Bell 4.00 2.00
❑ 235 Ron Hunt 4.00 2.00
❑ 236 Bill Faul 4.00 2.00
❑ 237 Chicago Cubs TC 6.00 3.00
❑ 238 Roy McMillan 6.00 3.00
❑ 239 Herm Starrette RC 4.00 2.00
❑ 240 Bill White 6.00 3.00
❑ 241 Jim Owens 4.00 2.00
❑ 242 Harvey Kuenn 6.00 3.00
❑ 243 R.Allen RC/J.Hernstein 30.00 15.00
❑ 244 Tony LaRussa RC 30.00 15.00
❑ 245 Dick Stigman 4.00 2.00
❑ 246 Manny Mota 6.00 3.00
❑ 247 Dave DeBusschere 6.00 3.00
❑ 248 Johnny Pesky MG 6.00 3.00
❑ 249 Doug Camilli 4.00 2.00
❑ 250 Al Kaline 40.00 20.00
❑ 251 Choo Choo Coleman 6.00 3.00
❑ 252 Ken Aspromonte 4.00 2.00
❑ 253 Wally Post 6.00 3.00
❑ 254 Don Hoak 6.00 3.00
❑ 255 Lee Thomas 6.00 3.00
❑ 256 Johnny Weekly 4.00 2.00
❑ 257 San Francisco Giants TC 6.00 3.00
❑ 258 Garry Roggenburk 4.00 2.00
❑ 259 Harry Bright 4.00 2.00
❑ 260 Frank Robinson 40.00 20.00
❑ 261 Jim Hannan 4.00 2.00
❑ 262 M.Shannon RC/H.Fanok 8.00 4.00
❑ 263 Chuck Estrada 4.00 2.00
❑ 264 Jim Landis 4.00 2.00
❑ 265 Jim Bunning 12.00 6.00
❑ 266 Gene Freese 4.00 2.00
❑ 267 Wilbur Wood RC 6.00 3.00

❑ 268 D.Murtaugh/B.Virdon 6.00 3.00
❑ 269 Ellis Burton 4.00 2.00
❑ 270 Rich Rollins 6.00 3.00
❑ 271 Bob Sadowski 4.00 2.00
❑ 272 Jake Wood 4.00 2.00
❑ 273 Mel Nelson 4.00 2.00
❑ 274 Checklist 4 10.00 5.00
❑ 275 John Tsitouris 4.00 2.00
❑ 276 Jose Tartabull 6.00 3.00
❑ 277 Ken Retzer 4.00 2.00
❑ 278 Bobby Shantz 6.00 3.00
❑ 279 Joe Koppe 4.00 2.00
❑ 280 Juan Marichal 15.00 7.50
❑ 281 J.,Gibbs/T.Metclaf RC 6.00 3.00
❑ 282 Bob Bruce 4.00 2.00
❑ 283 Tom McCraw RC 4.00 2.00
❑ 284 Dick Schofield 4.00 2.00
❑ 285 Robin Roberts 15.00 7.50
❑ 286 Don Landrum 4.00 2.00
❑ 287 T.Conig.RC/B.Spans.RC 50.00 30.00
❑ 288 Al Moran 4.00 2.00
❑ 289 Frank Funk 4.00 2.00
❑ 290 Bob Allison 6.00 3.00
❑ 291 Phil Ortega 4.00 2.00
❑ 292 Mike Roarke 4.00 2.00
❑ 293 Philadelphia Phillies TC 6.00 3.00
❑ 294 Ken L. Hunt 4.00 2.00
❑ 295 Roger Craig 6.00 3.00
❑ 296 Ed Kirkpatrick 4.00 2.00
❑ 297 Ken MacKenzie 4.00 2.00
❑ 298 Harry Craft MG 4.00 2.00
❑ 299 Bill Stafford 4.00 2.00
❑ 300 Hank Aaron 100.00 60.00
❑ 301 Larry Brown RC 4.00 2.00
❑ 302 Dan Pfister 4.00 2.00
❑ 303 Jim Campbell 4.00 2.00
❑ 304 Bob Johnson 4.00 2.00
❑ 305 Jack Lamabe 4.00 2.00
❑ 306 Willie Mays/O.Cepeda 40.00 20.00
❑ 307 Joe Gibbon 4.00 2.00
❑ 308 Gene Stephens 4.00 2.00
❑ 309 Paul Toth 4.00 2.00
❑ 310 Jim Gilliam 6.00 3.00
❑ 311 Tom W. Brown RC 6.00 3.00
❑ 312 F.Fisher RC/F.Gladding RC 4.00 2.00
❑ 313 Chuck Hiller 4.00 2.00
❑ 314 Jerry Buchek 4.00 2.00
❑ 315 Bo Belinsky 6.00 3.00
❑ 316 Gene Oliver 4.00 2.00
❑ 317 Al Smith 4.00 2.00
❑ 318 Minnesota Twins TC 6.00 3.00
❑ 319 Paul Brown 4.00 2.00
❑ 320 Rocky Colavito 12.00 6.00
❑ 321 Bob Lillis 4.00 2.00
❑ 322 George Brunet 4.00 2.00
❑ 323 John Buzhardt 4.00 2.00
❑ 324 Casey Stengel MG 15.00 7.50
❑ 325 Hector Lopez 6.00 3.00
❑ 326 Ron Brand RC 4.00 2.00
❑ 327 Don Blasingame 4.00 2.00
❑ 328 Bob Shaw 4.00 2.00
❑ 329 Russ Nixon 4.00 2.00
❑ 330 Tommy Harper 6.00 3.00
❑ 331 Maris/Cash/Mantle/Kaline 150.0090.00
❑ 332 Ray Washburn 4.00 2.00
❑ 333 Billy Moran 4.00 2.00
❑ 334 Lew Krausse 4.00 2.00
❑ 335 Don Mossi 6.00 3.00
❑ 336 Andre Rodgers 4.00 2.00
❑ 337 A.Ferrara RC/J.Torborg RC 6.00 3.00
❑ 338 Jack Kralick 4.00 2.00
❑ 339 Walt Bond 4.00 2.00
❑ 340 Joe Cunningham 4.00 2.00
❑ 341 Jim Roland 4.00 2.00
❑ 342 Willie Stargell 30.00 15.00
❑ 343 Washington Senators TC 6.00 3.00
❑ 344 Phil Linz 6.00 3.00
❑ 345 Frank Thomas 8.00 4.00
❑ 346 Joey Jay 4.00 2.00
❑ 347 Bobby Wine 6.00 3.00
❑ 348 Ed Lopat MG 6.00 3.00
❑ 349 Art Fowler 4.00 2.00
❑ 350 Willie McCovey 25.00 12.50
❑ 351 Dan Schneider 4.00 2.00
❑ 352 Eddie Bressoud 4.00 2.00
❑ 353 Wally Moon 6.00 3.00
❑ 354 Dave Giusti 4.00 2.00
❑ 355 Vic Power 6.00 3.00
❑ 356 B.McCool RC/C.Ruiz 6.00 3.00
❑ 357 Charley James 4.00 2.00
❑ 358 Ron Kline 4.00 2.00
❑ 359 Jim Schaffer 4.00 2.00
❑ 360 Joe Pepitone 12.00 6.00
❑ 361 Jay Hook 4.00 2.00
❑ 362 Checklist 5 10.00 5.00
❑ 363 Dick McAuliffe 6.00 3.00
❑ 364 Joe Gaines 4.00 2.00
❑ 365 Cal McLish 6.00 3.00
❑ 366 Nelson Mathews 4.00 2.00
❑ 367 Fred Whitfield 4.00 2.00
❑ 368 F.Ackley RC/D.Buford RC 6.00 3.00
❑ 369 Jerry Zimmerman 4.00 2.00
❑ 370 Hal Woodeshick 4.00 2.00
❑ 371 Frank Howard 8.00 4.00
❑ 372 Howie Koplitz 8.00 4.00
❑ 373 Pittsburgh Pirates TC 12.00 6.00
❑ 374 Bobby Bolin 8.00 4.00
❑ 375 Ron Santo 10.00 5.00
❑ 376 Dave Morehead 8.00 4.00
❑ 377 Bob Skinner 8.00 4.00
❑ 378 W.Woodward RC/J.Smith 10.00 5.00
❑ 379 Tony Gonzalez 8.00 4.00
❑ 380 Whitey Ford 40.00 20.00
❑ 381 Bob Taylor 8.00 4.00
❑ 382 Wes Stock 8.00 4.00
❑ 383 Bill Rigney MG 8.00 4.00
❑ 384 Ron Hansen 8.00 4.00
❑ 385 Curt Simmons 10.00 5.00
❑ 386 Lenny Green 8.00 4.00
❑ 387 Terry Fox 8.00 4.00
❑ 388 J.O'Donoghue RC/G.Williams 10.00 5.00
❑ 389 Jim Umbricht 10.00 5.00
❑ 390 Orlando Cepeda 25.00 12.50
❑ 391 Sam McDowell 10.00 5.00
❑ 392 Jim Pagliaroni 8.00 4.00
❑ 393 C.Stengel/E.Kranepool 15.00 7.50
❑ 394 Bob Miller 8.00 4.00
❑ 395 Tom Tresh 10.00 5.00
❑ 396 Dennis Bennett 8.00 4.00
❑ 397 Chuck Cottier 8.00 4.00
❑ 398 B.Haas/D.Smith 10.00 5.00
❑ 399 Jackie Brandt 8.00 4.00
❑ 400 Warren Spahn 40.00 20.00
❑ 401 Charlie Maxwell 8.00 4.00
❑ 402 Tom Sturdivant 8.00 4.00
❑ 403 Cincinnati Reds TC 12.00 6.00
❑ 404 Tony Martinez 8.00 4.00
❑ 405 Ken McBride 8.00 4.00
❑ 406 Al Spangler 8.00 4.00
❑ 407 Bill Freehan 10.00 5.00
❑ 408 J.Stewart RC/F.Burdette RC 8.00 4.00
❑ 409 Bill Fischer 8.00 4.00
❑ 410 Dick Stuart 10.00 5.00
❑ 411 Lee Walls 8.00 4.00
❑ 412 Ray Culp 10.00 5.00
❑ 413 Johnny Keane MG 8.00 4.00
❑ 414 Jack Sanford 8.00 4.00
❑ 415 Tony Kubek 15.00 7.50
❑ 416 Lee Maye 8.00 4.00
❑ 417 Don Cardwell 8.00 4.00
❑ 418 D.Knowles RC/B.Narum RC 10.005.00
❑ 419 Ken Harrelson RC 15.00 7.50
❑ 420 Jim Maloney 10.00 5.00
❑ 421 Camilo Carreon 8.00 4.00
❑ 422 Jack Fisher 8.00 4.00
❑ 423 H.Aaron/W.Mays 125.00 75.00
❑ 424 Dick Bertell 8.00 4.00
❑ 425 Norm Cash 10.00 5.00
❑ 426 Bob Rodgers 8.00 4.00
❑ 427 Don Rudolph 8.00 4.00
❑ 428 A.Skeen RC/P.Smith RC 8.00 4.00
❑ 429 Tim McCarver 10.00 5.00
❑ 430 Juan Pizarro 8.00 4.00
❑ 431 George Alusik 8.00 4.00
❑ 432 Ruben Amaro 10.00 5.00
❑ 433 New York Yankees TC 40.00 20.00
❑ 434 Don Nottebart 8.00 4.00
❑ 435 Vic Davalillo 8.00 4.00
❑ 436 Charlie Neal 10.00 5.00
❑ 437 Ed Bailey 8.00 4.00
❑ 438 Checklist 6 15.00 7.50
❑ 439 Harvey Haddix 10.00 5.00
❑ 440 Roberto Clemente UER 200.00 125.00
❑ 441 Bob Duliba 8.00 4.00
❑ 442 Pumpsie Green 10.00 5.00
❑ 443 Chuck Dressen MG 10.00 5.00
❑ 444 Larry Jackson 8.00 4.00
❑ 445 Bill Skowron 10.00 5.00
❑ 446 Julian Javier 15.00 7.50
❑ 447 Ted Bowsfield 8.00 4.00
❑ 448 Cookie Rojas 10.00 5.00
❑ 449 Deron Johnson 10.00 5.00
❑ 450 Steve Barber 8.00 4.00
❑ 451 Joe Amalfitano 8.00 4.00
❑ 452 G.Garrido RC/J.Hart RC 10.00 5.00
❑ 453 Frank Baumann 8.00 4.00
❑ 454 Tommie Aaron 10.00 5.00
❑ 455 Bernie Allen 8.00 4.00
❑ 456 W.Parker RC/J.Werhas RC 10.00 5.00
❑ 457 Jesse Gonder 8.00 4.00
❑ 458 Ralph Terry 10.00 5.00
❑ 459 P.Charton RC/D.Jones RC 8.00 4.00
❑ 460 Bob Gibson 40.00 20.00
❑ 461 George Thomas 8.00 4.00
❑ 462 Birdie Tebbetts MG 8.00 4.00
❑ 463 Don Leppert 8.00 4.00
❑ 464 Dallas Green 15.00 7.50
❑ 465 Mike Hershberger 8.00 4.00
❑ 466 D.Green RC/A.Monteagudo RC 10.00 5.00
❑ 467 Bob Aspromonte 8.00 4.00
❑ 468 Gaylord Perry 40.00 20.00
❑ 469 F.Norman RC/S.Slaughter RC 10.00 5.00
❑ 470 Jim Bouton 10.00 5.00
❑ 471 Gates Brown RC 10.00 5.00
❑ 472 Vern Law 10.00 5.00
❑ 473 Baltimore Orioles TC 12.00 6.00
❑ 474 Larry Sherry 10.00 5.00
❑ 475 Ed Charles 8.00 4.00
❑ 476 R.Carty RC/D.Kelley RC 15.00 7.50
❑ 477 Mike Joyce 8.00 4.00
❑ 478 Dick Howser 10.00 5.00
❑ 479 D.Bakenhaster RC/J.Lewis RC 8.00 4.00
❑ 480 Bob Purkey 8.00 4.00
❑ 481 Chuck Schilling 8.00 4.00
❑ 482 J.Briggs RC/D.Cater RC 10.00 5.00
❑ 483 Fred Valentine RC 8.00 4.00
❑ 484 Bill Pleis 8.00 4.00
❑ 485 Tom Haller 8.00 4.00
❑ 486 Bob Kennedy MG 8.00 4.00
❑ 487 Mike McCormick 10.00 5.00
❑ 488 P.Mikkelsen RC/B.Meyer RC 15.007.50
❑ 489 Julio Navarro 8.00 4.00
❑ 490 Ron Fairly 10.00 5.00
❑ 491 Ed Rakow 8.00 4.00
❑ 492 J.Beauchamp RC/M.White RC 8.004.00
❑ 493 Don Lee 8.00 4.00
❑ 494 Al Jackson 8.00 4.00
❑ 495 Bill Virdon 10.00 5.00
❑ 496 Chicago White Sox TC 12.00 6.00
❑ 497 Jeoff Long RC 8.00 4.00
❑ 498 Dave Stenhouse 8.00 4.00
❑ 499 C.Slamon RC/G.Seyfried RC 8.00 4.00
❑ 500 Camilo Pascual 10.00 5.00
❑ 501 Bob Veale 10.00 5.00
❑ 502 B.Knoop RC/B.Lee RC 8.00 4.00
❑ 503 Earl Wilson 8.00 4.00
❑ 504 Claude Raymond 8.00 4.00
❑ 505 Stan Williams 8.00 4.00
❑ 506 Bobby Bragan MG 8.00 4.00
❑ 507 Johnny Edwards 8.00 4.00
❑ 508 Diego Segui 8.00 4.00
❑ 509 G.Alley RC/O.McFarlane RC 10.00 5.00
❑ 510 Lindy McDaniel 10.00 5.00
❑ 511 Lou Jackson 10.00 5.00
❑ 512 W.Horton RC/J.Sparma RC 15.00 7.50
❑ 513 Don Larsen 10.00 5.00
❑ 514 Jim Hickman 10.00 5.00
❑ 515 Johnny Romano 8.00 4.00
❑ 516 J.Arrigo RC/D.Siebler RC 8.00 4.00
❑ 517A Checklist 7 ERR 25.00 12.50
❑ 517B Checklist 7 COR 15.00 7.50
❑ 518 Carl Bouldin 8.00 4.00
❑ 519 Charlie Smith 8.00 4.00
❑ 520 Jack Baldschun 10.00 5.00
❑ 521 Tom Satriano 8.00 4.00
❑ 522 Bob Tiefenauer 8.00 4.00
❑ 523 Lou Burdette UER 20.00 10.00
❑ 524 J.Dickson RC/B.Klaus RC 15.00 7.50

❑ 525 Al McBean 15.00 7.50
❑ 526 Lou Clinton 15.00 7.50
❑ 527 Larry Bearnarth 15.00 7.50
❑ 528 D.Duncan RC/T.Reynolds RC 20.00 10.00
❑ 529 Alvin Dark MG 20.00 10.00
❑ 530 Leon Wagner 15.00 7.50
❑ 531 Los Angeles Dodgers TC 25.00 12.50
❑ 532 B.Bloomfield RC/J.Nossek RC 15.00 7.50
❑ 533 Johnny Klippstein 15.00 7.50
❑ 534 Gus Bell 15.00 7.50
❑ 535 Phil Regan 15.00 7.50
❑ 536 L.Elliot/J.Stephenson RC 15.00 7.50
❑ 537 Dan Osinski 15.00 7.50
❑ 538 Minnie Minoso 20.00 10.00
❑ 539 Roy Face 20.00 10.00
❑ 540 Luis Aparicio 40.00 20.00
❑ 541 P.Roof/P.Niekro RC 80.00 50.00
❑ 542 Don Mincher 15.00 7.50
❑ 543 Bob Uecker 40.00 20.00
❑ 544 S.Hertz RC/J.Hoerner RC 15.00 7.50
❑ 545 Max Alvis 15.00 7.50
❑ 546 Joe Christopher 15.00 7.50
❑ 547 Gil Hodges MG 30.00 15.00
❑ 548 W.Schurr RC/P.Speckenbach RC 20.00 10.00
❑ 549 Joe Moeller 15.00 7.50
❑ 550 Ken Hubbs MEM 40.00 20.00
❑ 551 Billy Hoeft 15.00 7.50
❑ 552 T.Kelley RC/S.Siebert RC 15.00 7.50
❑ 553 Jim Brewer 15.00 7.50
❑ 554 Hank Foiles 15.00 7.50
❑ 555 Lee Stange 15.00 7.50
❑ 556 S.Dillon RC/R.Locke RC 15.00 7.50
❑ 557 Leo Burke 15.00 7.50
❑ 558 Don Schwall 15.00 7.50
❑ 559 Dick Phillips 15.00 7.50
❑ 560 Dick Farrell 15.00 7.50
❑ 561 D.Bennett RC/R.Wise RC 20.00 10.00
❑ 562 Pedro Ramos 15.00 7.50
❑ 563 Dal Maxvill 20.00 10.00
❑ 564 J.McCabe RC/J.McNertney RC 20.00 10.00
❑ 565 Stu Miller 15.00 7.50
❑ 566 Ed Kranepool 20.00 10.00
❑ 567 Jim Kaat 20.00 10.00
❑ 568 P.Gagliano RC/C.Peterson RC 15.00 7.50
❑ 569 Fred Newman 15.00 7.50
❑ 570 Bill Mazeroski 40.00 20.00
❑ 571 Gene Conley 15.00 7.50
❑ 572 D.Gray RC/D.Egan 15.00 7.50
❑ 573 Jim Duffalo 15.00 7.50
❑ 574 Manny Jimenez 15.00 7.50
❑ 575 Tony Cloninger 15.00 7.50
❑ 576 J.Hinsley RC/B.Wakefield RC 15.00 7.50
❑ 577 Gordy Coleman 15.00 7.50
❑ 578 Glen Hobbie 15.00 7.50
❑ 579 Boston Red Sox TC 25.00 12.50
❑ 580 Johnny Podres 20.00 10.00
❑ 581 P.Gonzalez/A.Moore RC 20.00 10.00
❑ 582 Rod Kanehl 20.00 10.00
❑ 583 Tito Francona 15.00 7.50
❑ 584 Joel Horlen 15.00 7.50
❑ 585 Tony Taylor 20.00 10.00
❑ 586 Jimmy Piersall 20.00 10.00
❑ 587 Bennie Daniels 20.00 10.00

1965 Topps

❑ COMPLETE SET (598) 5000.00 3000.00
❑ COMMON CARD (1-196) 2.00 1.00
❑ COMMON CARD (197-283) 2.50 1.25
❑ COMMON CARD (284-370) 4.00 2.00
❑ COMMON CARD (371-598) 8.00 4.00
❑ WRAPPER (1-CENT) 125.00 100.00
❑ WRAPPER (5-CENT) 100.00 75.00
❑ 1 Oliva/Howard/Brooks LL 20.00 10.00
❑ 2 Clemente/Aaron/Carty LL 25.00 12.50
❑ 3 Killebrew/Mantle/Powell LL 50.00 30.00
❑ 4 Mays/B.Will/Cepeda LL 15.00 7.50
❑ 5 Brooks/Kill/Mantle LL 40.00 20.00
❑ 6 Boyer/Mays Santo LL 12.00 6.00
❑ 7 D.Chance/J.Horlen LL 5.00 2.50
❑ 8 S.Koufax/D.Drysdale LL 20.00 10.00
❑ 9 Chance/Peters/Wick LL 5.00 2.50
❑ 10 Jackson/Sad/Marichal LL 5.00 2.50
❑ 11 Downing/Chance/Pascual LL 5.00 2.50
❑ 12 Veale/Drysdale/Gibson LL 10.00 5.00
❑ 13 Pedro Ramos 4.00 2.00
❑ 14 Len Gabrielson 2.00 1.00
❑ 15 Robin Roberts 10.00 5.00
❑ 16 Joe Morgan RC DP 60.00 35.00
❑ 17 Johnny Romano 2.00 1.00
❑ 18 Bill McCool 2.00 1.00
❑ 19 Gates Brown 4.00 2.00
❑ 20 Jim Bunning 10.00 5.00
❑ 21 Don Blasingame 2.00 1.00
❑ 22 Charlie Smith 2.00 1.00
❑ 23 Bob Tiefenauer 2.00 1.00
❑ 24 Minnesota Twins TC 6.00 3.00
❑ 25 Al McBean 2.00 1.00
❑ 26 Bobby Knoop 2.00 1.00
❑ 27 Dick Bertell 2.00 1.00
❑ 28 Barney Schultz 2.00 1.00
❑ 29 Felix Mantilla 2.00 1.00
❑ 30 Jim Bouton 6.00 3.00
❑ 31 Mike White 2.00 1.00
❑ 32 Herman Franks MG 2.00 1.00
❑ 33 Jackie Brandt 2.00 1.00
❑ 34 Cal Koonce 2.00 1.00
❑ 35 Ed Charles 2.00 1.00
❑ 36 Bobby Wine 2.00 1.00
❑ 37 Fred Gladding 2.00 1.00
❑ 38 Jim King 2.00 1.00
❑ 39 Gerry Arrigo 2.00 1.00
❑ 40 Frank Howard 6.00 3.00
❑ 41 B.Howard/M.Staehle RC 2.00 1.00
❑ 42 Earl Wilson 4.00 2.00
❑ 43 Mike Shannon 4.00 2.00
❑ 44 Wade Blasingame RC 2.00 1.00
❑ 45 Roy McMillan 4.00 2.00
❑ 46 Bob Lee 2.00 1.00
❑ 47 Tommy Harper 4.00 2.00
❑ 48 Claude Raymond 4.00 2.00
❑ 49 C.Blefary RC/J.Miller 4.00 2.00
❑ 50 Juan Marichal 10.00 5.00
❑ 51 Bill Bryan 2.00 1.00
❑ 52 Ed Roebuck 2.00 1.00
❑ 53 Dick McAuliffe 4.00 2.00
❑ 54 Joe Gibbon 2.00 1.00
❑ 55 Tony Conigliaro 15.00 7.50
❑ 56 Ron Kline 2.00 1.00
❑ 57 St. Louis Cardinals TC 6.00 3.00
❑ 58 Fred Talbot RC 2.00 1.00
❑ 59 Nate Oliver 2.00 1.00
❑ 60 Jim O'Toole 4.00 2.00
❑ 61 Chris Cannizzaro 2.00 1.00
❑ 62 Jim Kaat UER DP 6.00 3.00
❑ 63 Ty Cline 2.00 1.00
❑ 64 Lou Burdette 4.00 2.00
❑ 65 Tony Kubek 10.00 5.00
❑ 66 Bill Rigney MG 2.00 1.00
❑ 67 Harvey Haddix 4.00 2.00
❑ 68 Del Crandall 4.00 2.00
❑ 69 Bill Virdon 4.00 2.00
❑ 70 Bill Skowron 6.00 3.00
❑ 71 John O'Donoghue 2.00 1.00
❑ 72 Tony Gonzalez 2.00 1.00
❑ 73 Dennis Ribant RC 2.00 1.00
❑ 74 R.Petrocelli RC/J.Steph RC 10.00 5.00
❑ 75 Deron Johnson 4.00 2.00
❑ 76 Sam McDowell 6.00 3.00
❑ 77 Doug Camilli 2.00 1.00
❑ 78 Dal Maxvill 2.00 1.00
❑ 79A Checklist 1 Cannizzaro 10.00 5.00
❑ 79B Checklist 1 C.Cannizzaro 10.00 5.00
❑ 80 Turk Farrell 2.00 1.00
❑ 81 Don Buford 4.00 2.00
❑ 82 S.Alomar RC/J.Braun RC 6.00 3.00
❑ 83 George Thomas 2.00 1.00
❑ 84 Ron Herbel 2.00 1.00
❑ 85 Willie Smith RC 2.00 1.00
❑ 86 Buster Narum 2.00 1.00
❑ 87 Nelson Mathews 2.00 1.00
❑ 88 Jack Lamabe 2.00 1.00
❑ 89 Mike Hershberger 2.00 1.00
❑ 90 Rich Rollins 4.00 2.00
❑ 91 Chicago Cubs TC 6.00 3.00
❑ 92 Dick Howser 4.00 2.00
❑ 93 Jack Fisher 2.00 1.00
❑ 94 Charlie Lau 4.00 2.00
❑ 95 Bill Mazeroski DP 6.00 3.00
❑ 96 Sonny Siebert 4.00 2.00
❑ 97 Pedro Gonzalez 2.00 1.00
❑ 98 Bob Miller 2.00 1.00
❑ 99 Gil Hodges MG 6.00 3.00
❑ 100 Ken Boyer 10.00 5.00
❑ 101 Fred Newman 2.00 1.00
❑ 102 Steve Boros 2.00 1.00
❑ 103 Harvey Kuenn 4.00 2.00
❑ 104 Checklist 2 10.00 5.00
❑ 105 Chico Salmon 2.00 1.00
❑ 106 Gene Oliver 2.00 1.00
❑ 107 P.Corrales RC/C.Shockley RC 4.00 2.00
❑ 108 Don Mincher 2.00 1.00
❑ 109 Walt Bond 2.00 1.00
❑ 110 Ron Santo 6.00 3.00
❑ 111 Lee Thomas 4.00 2.00
❑ 112 Derrell Griffith RC 2.00 1.00
❑ 113 Steve Barber 2.00 1.00
❑ 114 Jim Hickman 4.00 2.00
❑ 115 Bobby Richardson 10.00 5.00
❑ 116 D.Dowling RC/B.Tolan RC 4.00 2.00
❑ 117 Wes Stock 2.00 1.00
❑ 118 Hal Lanier RC 4.00 2.00
❑ 119 John Kennedy 2.00 1.00
❑ 120 Frank Robinson 40.00 20.00
❑ 121 Gene Alley 4.00 2.00
❑ 122 Bill Pleis 2.00 1.00
❑ 123 Frank Thomas 4.00 2.00
❑ 124 Tom Satriano 2.00 1.00
❑ 125 Juan Pizarro 2.00 1.00
❑ 126 Los Angeles Dodgers TC 6.00 3.00
❑ 127 Frank Lary 2.00 1.00
❑ 128 Vic Davalillo 2.00 1.00
❑ 129 Bennie Daniels 2.00 1.00
❑ 130 Al Kaline 40.00 20.00
❑ 131 Johnny Keane MG 2.00 1.00
❑ 132 Cards Take Opener WS1 10.00 5.00
❑ 133 Mel Stottlemyre WS2 6.00 3.00
❑ 134 Mickey Mantle WS3 80.00 50.00
❑ 135 Ken Boyer WS4 10.00 5.00
❑ 136 Tim McCarver WS5 6.00 3.00
❑ 137 Jim Bouton WS6 6.00 3.00
❑ 138 Bob Gibson WS7 12.00 6.00
❑ 139 Cards Celebrate WS 6.00 3.00
❑ 140 Dean Chance 4.00 2.00
❑ 141 Charlie James 2.00 1.00
❑ 142 Bill Monbouquette 2.00 1.00
❑ 143 J.Gelnar RC/J.May RC 2.00 1.00
❑ 144 Ed Kranepool 4.00 2.00
❑ 145 Luis Tiant RC 10.00 5.00
❑ 146 Ron Hansen 2.00 1.00
❑ 147 Dennis Bennett 2.00 1.00
❑ 148 Willie Kirkland 2.00 1.00
❑ 149 Wayne Schurr 2.00 1.00
❑ 150 Brooks Robinson 40.00 20.00
❑ 151 Kansas City Athletics TC 6.00 3.00
❑ 152 Phil Ortega 2.00 1.00
❑ 153 Norm Cash 6.00 3.00
❑ 154 Bob Humphreys RC 2.00 1.00
❑ 155 Roger Maris 60.00 35.00
❑ 156 Bob Sadowski 2.00 1.00
❑ 157 Zoilo Versalles 4.00 2.00
❑ 158 Dick Sisler 2.00 1.00
❑ 159 Jim Duffalo 2.00 1.00
❑ 160 Roberto Clemente UER 175.00 100.00
❑ 161 Frank Baumann 2.00 1.00
❑ 162 Russ Nixon 2.00 1.00
❑ 163 Johnny Briggs 2.00 1.00
❑ 164 Al Spangler 2.00 1.00
❑ 165 Dick Ellsworth 2.00 1.00
❑ 166 G.Culver RC/T.Agee RC 4.00 2.00
❑ 167 Bill Wakefield 2.00 1.00

❑ 168 Dick Green 2.00 1.00
❑ 169 Dave Vineyard RC 2.00 1.00
❑ 170 Hank Aaron 150.00 90.00
❑ 171 Jim Roland 2.00 1.00
❑ 172 Jimmy Piersall 6.00 3.00
❑ 173 Detroit Tigers TC 6.00 3.00
❑ 174 Joey Jay 2.00 1.00
❑ 175 Bob Aspromonte 2.00 1.00
❑ 176 Willie McCovey 20.00 10.00
❑ 177 Pete Mikkelsen 2.00 1.00
❑ 178 Dalton Jones 2.00 1.00
❑ 179 Hal Woodeshick 2.00 1.00
❑ 180 Bob Allison 4.00 2.00
❑ 181 D.Loun RC/J.McCabe 2.00 1.00
❑ 182 Mike de la Hoz 2.00 1.00
❑ 183 Dave Nicholson 2.00 1.00
❑ 184 John Boozer 2.00 1.00
❑ 185 Max Alvis 2.00 1.00
❑ 186 Billy Cowan 2.00 1.00
❑ 187 Casey Stengel MG 15.00 7.50
❑ 188 Sam Bowens 2.00 1.00
❑ 189 Checklist 3 10.00 5.00
❑ 190 Bill White 6.00 3.00
❑ 191 Phil Regan 4.00 2.00
❑ 192 Jim Coker 2.00 1.00
❑ 193 Gaylord Perry 15.00 7.50
❑ 194 B.Kelso RC/R.Reichardt RC 2.00 1.00
❑ 195 Bob Veale 4.00 2.00
❑ 196 Ron Fairly 4.00 2.00
❑ 197 Diego Segui 2.50 1.25
❑ 198 Smoky Burgess 4.00 2.00
❑ 199 Bob Heffner 2.50 1.25
❑ 200 Joe Torre 6.00 3.00
❑ 201 S.Valdespino RC/C.Tovar RC 4.002.00
❑ 202 Leo Burke 2.50 1.25
❑ 203 Dallas Green 4.00 2.00
❑ 204 Russ Snyder 2.50 1.25
❑ 205 Warren Spahn 30.00 15.00
❑ 206 Willie Horton 4.00 2.00
❑ 207 Pete Rose 175.00 100.00
❑ 208 Tommy John 6.00 3.00
❑ 209 Pittsburgh Pirates TC 6.00 3.00
❑ 210 Jim Fregosi 4.00 2.00
❑ 211 Steve Ridzik 2.50 1.25
❑ 212 Ron Brand 2.50 1.25
❑ 213 Jim Davenport 2.50 1.25
❑ 214 Bob Purkey 2.50 1.25
❑ 215 Pete Ward 2.50 1.25
❑ 216 Al Worthington 2.50 1.25
❑ 217 Walter Alston MG 6.00 3.00
❑ 218 Dick Schofield 2.50 1.25
❑ 219 Bob Meyer 2.50 1.25
❑ 220 Billy Williams 10.00 5.00
❑ 221 John Tsitouris 2.50 1.25
❑ 222 Bob Tillman 2.50 1.25
❑ 223 Dan Osinski 2.50 1.25
❑ 224 Bob Chance 2.50 1.25
❑ 225 Bo Belinsky 4.00 2.00
❑ 226 E.Jimenez RC/J.Gibbs 6.00 3.00
❑ 227 Bobby Klaus 2.50 1.25
❑ 228 Jack Sanford 2.50 1.25
❑ 229 Lou Clinton 2.50 1.25
❑ 230 Ray Sadecki 2.50 1.25
❑ 231 Jerry Adair 2.50 1.25
❑ 232 Steve Blass RC 4.00 2.00
❑ 233 Don Zimmer 4.00 2.00
❑ 234 Chicago White Sox TC 6.00 3.00
❑ 235 Chuck Hinton 2.50 1.25
❑ 236 Denny McLain RC 25.00 12.50
❑ 237 Bernie Allen 2.50 1.25
❑ 238 Joe Moeller 2.50 1.25
❑ 239 Doc Edwards 2.50 1.25
❑ 240 Bob Bruce 2.50 1.25
❑ 241 Mack Jones 2.50 1.25
❑ 242 George Brunet 2.50 1.25
❑ 243 T.Davidson RC/T.Helms RC 4.00 2.00
❑ 244 Lindy McDaniel 4.00 2.00
❑ 245 Joe Pepitone 6.00 3.00
❑ 246 Tom Butters 4.00 2.00
❑ 247 Wally Moon 4.00 2.00
❑ 248 Gus Triandos 4.00 2.00
❑ 249 Dave McNally 4.00 2.00
❑ 250 Willie Mays 150.00 90.00
❑ 251 Billy Herman MG 4.00 2.00
❑ 252 Pete Richert 2.50 1.25
❑ 253 Danny Cater 2.50 1.25
❑ 254 Roland Sheldon 2.50 1.25
❑ 255 Camilo Pascual 4.00 2.00
❑ 256 Tito Francona 2.50 1.25
❑ 257 Jim Wynn 4.00 2.00
❑ 258 Larry Bearnarth 2.50 1.25
❑ 259 J.Northrup RC/R.Oyler RC 6.00 3.00
❑ 260 Don Drysdale 20.00 10.00
❑ 261 Duke Carmel 2.50 1.25
❑ 262 Bud Daley 2.50 1.25
❑ 263 Marty Keough 2.50 1.25
❑ 264 Bob Buhl 4.00 2.00
❑ 265 Jim Pagliaroni 2.50 1.25
❑ 266 Bert Campaneris RC 10.00 5.00
❑ 267 Washington Senators TC 6.00 3.00
❑ 268 Ken McBride 2.50 1.25
❑ 269 Frank Bolling 2.50 1.25
❑ 270 Milt Pappas 4.00 2.00
❑ 271 Don Wert 4.00 2.00
❑ 272 Chuck Schilling 2.50 1.25
❑ 273 Checklist 4 10.00 5.00
❑ 274 Lum Harris MG RC 2.50 1.25
❑ 275 Dick Groat 6.00 3.00
❑ 276 Hoyt Wilhelm 10.00 5.00
❑ 277 Johnny Lewis 2.50 1.25
❑ 278 Ken Retzer 2.50 1.25
❑ 279 Dick Tracewski 2.50 1.25
❑ 280 Dick Stuart 4.00 2.00
❑ 281 Bill Stafford 2.50 1.25
❑ 282 D.Est RC/M.Murakami RC 40.00 20.00
❑ 283 Fred Whitfield 2.50 1.25
❑ 284 Nick Willhite 4.00 2.00
❑ 285 Ron Hunt 4.00 2.00
❑ 286 J.Dickson/A.Monteagudo 4.00 2.00
❑ 287 Gary Kolb 4.00 2.00
❑ 288 Jack Hamilton 4.00 2.00
❑ 289 Gordy Coleman 6.00 3.00
❑ 290 Wally Bunker 6.00 3.00
❑ 291 Jerry Lynch 4.00 2.00
❑ 292 Larry Yellen 4.00 2.00
❑ 293 Los Angeles Angels TC 6.00 3.00
❑ 294 Tim McCarver 10.00 5.00
❑ 295 Dick Radatz 6.00 3.00
❑ 296 Tony Taylor 6.00 3.00
❑ 297 Dave DeBusschere 10.00 5.00
❑ 298 Jim Stewart 4.00 2.00
❑ 299 Jerry Zimmerman 4.00 2.00
❑ 300 Sandy Koufax 100.00 60.00
❑ 301 Birdie Tebbetts MG 6.00 3.00
❑ 302 Al Stanek 4.00 2.00
❑ 303 John Orsino 4.00 2.00
❑ 304 Dave Stenhouse 4.00 2.00
❑ 305 Rico Carty 6.00 3.00
❑ 306 Bubba Phillips 4.00 2.00
❑ 307 Barry Latman 4.00 2.00
❑ 308 C.Jones RC/T.Parsons 6.00 3.00
❑ 309 Steve Hamilton 6.00 3.00
❑ 310 Johnny Callison 6.00 3.00
❑ 311 Orlando Pena 4.00 2.00
❑ 312 Joe Nuxhall 4.00 2.00
❑ 313 Jim Schaffer 4.00 2.00
❑ 314 Sterling Slaughter 4.00 2.00
❑ 315 Frank Malzone 6.00 3.00
❑ 316 Cincinnati Reds TC 6.00 3.00
❑ 317 Don McMahon 4.00 2.00
❑ 318 Matty Alou 6.00 3.00
❑ 319 Ken McMullen 4.00 2.00
❑ 320 Bob Gibson 50.00 30.00
❑ 321 Rusty Staub 10.00 5.00
❑ 322 Rick Wise 6.00 3.00
❑ 323 Hank Bauer MG 6.00 3.00
❑ 324 Bobby Locke 4.00 2.00
❑ 325 Donn Clendenon 6.00 3.00
❑ 326 Dwight Siebler 4.00 2.00
❑ 327 Denis Menke 4.00 2.00
❑ 328 Eddie Fisher 4.00 2.00
❑ 329 Hawk Taylor RC 4.00 2.00
❑ 330 Whitey Ford 40.00 20.00
❑ 331 A.Ferrara/J.Purdin RC 6.00 3.00
❑ 332 Ted Abernathy 4.00 2.00
❑ 333 Tom Reynolds 4.00 2.00
❑ 334 Vic Roznovsky RC 4.00 2.00
❑ 335 Mickey Lolich 6.00 3.00
❑ 336 Woody Held 4.00 2.00
❑ 337 Mike Cuellar 6.00 3.00
❑ 338 Philadelphia Phillies TC 6.00 3.00
❑ 339 Ryne Duren 6.00 3.00
❑ 340 Tony Oliva 20.00 10.00
❑ 341 Bob Bolin 4.00 2.00
❑ 342 Bob Rodgers 6.00 3.00
❑ 343 Mike McCormick 6.00 3.00
❑ 344 Wes Parker 6.00 3.00
❑ 345 Floyd Robinson 4.00 2.00
❑ 346 Bobby Bragan MG 4.00 2.00
❑ 347 Roy Face 6.00 3.00
❑ 348 George Banks 4.00 2.00
❑ 349 Larry Miller RC 4.00 2.00
❑ 350 Mickey Mantle 600.00 350.00
❑ 351 Jim Perry 6.00 3.00
❑ 352 Alex Johnson RC 6.00 3.00
❑ 353 Jerry Lumpe 4.00 2.00
❑ 354 B.Ott RC/J.Warner RC 4.00 2.00
❑ 355 Vada Pinson 10.00 5.00
❑ 356 Bill Spanswick 4.00 2.00
❑ 357 Carl Warwick 4.00 2.00
❑ 358 Albie Pearson 6.00 3.00
❑ 359 Ken Johnson 4.00 2.00
❑ 360 Orlando Cepeda 15.00 7.50
❑ 361 Checklist 5 12.00 6.00
❑ 362 Don Schwall 4.00 2.00
❑ 363 Bob Johnson 4.00 2.00
❑ 364 Galen Cisco 4.00 2.00
❑ 365 Jim Gentile 6.00 3.00
❑ 366 Dan Schneider 4.00 2.00
❑ 367 Leon Wagner 4.00 2.00
❑ 368 K.Berry RC/J.Gibson RC 6.00 3.00
❑ 369 Phil Linz 6.00 3.00
❑ 370 Tommy Davis 6.00 3.00
❑ 371 Frank Kreutzer 8.00 4.00
❑ 372 Clay Dalrymple 8.00 4.00
❑ 373 Curt Simmons 8.00 4.00
❑ 374 J.Cardenal RC/D.Simpson 8.00 4.00
❑ 375 Dave Wickersham 8.00 4.00
❑ 376 Jim Landis 8.00 4.00
❑ 377 Willie Stargell 25.00 12.50
❑ 378 Chuck Estrada 8.00 4.00
❑ 379 San Francisco Giants TC 8.00 4.00
❑ 380 Rocky Colavito 25.00 12.50
❑ 381 Al Jackson 8.00 4.00
❑ 382 J.C. Martin 8.00 4.00
❑ 383 Felipe Alou 15.00 7.50
❑ 384 Johnny Klippstein 8.00 4.00
❑ 385 Carl Yastrzemski 60.00 35.00
❑ 386 P.Jaeckel RC/F.Norman 8.00 4.00
❑ 387 Johnny Podres 15.00 7.50
❑ 388 John Blanchard 15.00 7.50
❑ 389 Don Larsen 15.00 7.50
❑ 390 Bill Freehan 15.00 7.50
❑ 391 Mel McGaha MG 8.00 4.00
❑ 392 Bob Friend 15.00 7.50
❑ 393 Ed Kirkpatrick 8.00 4.00
❑ 394 Jim Hannan 8.00 4.00
❑ 395 Jim Ray Hart 8.00 4.00
❑ 396 Frank Bertaina RC 8.00 4.00
❑ 397 Jerry Buchek 8.00 4.00
❑ 398 D.Neville RC/A.Shamsky RC 15.007.50
❑ 399 Ray Herbert 8.00 4.00
❑ 400 Harmon Killebrew 50.00 30.00
❑ 401 Carl Willey 8.00 4.00
❑ 402 Joe Amalfitano 8.00 4.00
❑ 403 Boston Red Sox TC 8.00 4.00
❑ 404 Stan Williams 8.00 4.00
❑ 405 John Roseboro 20.00 10.00
❑ 406 Ralph Terry 15.00 7.50
❑ 407 Lee Maye 8.00 4.00
❑ 408 Larry Sherry 8.00 4.00
❑ 409 J.Beauchamp RC/L.Dierker RC 15.00 7.50
❑ 410 Luis Aparicio 25.00 12.50
❑ 411 Roger Craig 15.00 7.50
❑ 412 Bob Bailey 8.00 4.00
❑ 413 Hal Reniff 8.00 4.00
❑ 414 Al Lopez MG 15.00 7.50
❑ 415 Curt Flood 15.00 7.50
❑ 416 Jim Brewer 8.00 4.00
❑ 417 Ed Brinkman 8.00 4.00
❑ 418 Johnny Edwards 8.00 4.00
❑ 419 Ruben Amaro 8.00 4.00
❑ 420 Larry Jackson 8.00 4.00
❑ 421 G.Dotter RC/J.Ward 8.00 4.00
❑ 422 Aubrey Gatewood 8.00 4.00
❑ 423 Jesse Gonder 8.00 4.00
❑ 424 Gary Bell 8.00 4.00
❑ 425 Wayne Causey 8.00 4.00

❑ 426 Milwaukee Braves TC	8.00	4.00
❑ 427 Bob Saverine	8.00	4.00
❑ 428 Bob Shaw	8.00	4.00
❑ 429 Don Demeter	8.00	4.00
❑ 430 Gary Peters	8.00	4.00
❑ 431 N.Briles RC/W.Spiezio RC	15.00	7.50
❑ 432 Jim Grant	15.00	7.50
❑ 433 John Bateman	8.00	4.00
❑ 434 Dave Morehead	8.00	4.00
❑ 435 Willie Davis	15.00	7.50
❑ 436 Don Elston	8.00	4.00
❑ 437 Chico Cardenas	15.00	7.50
❑ 438 Harry Walker MG	8.00	4.00
❑ 439 Moe Drabowsky	15.00	7.50
❑ 440 Tom Tresh	15.00	7.50
❑ 441 Denny Lemaster	8.00	4.00
❑ 442 Vic Power	8.00	4.00
❑ 443 Checklist 6	12.00	6.00
❑ 444 Bob Hendley	8.00	4.00
❑ 445 Don Lock	8.00	4.00
❑ 446 Art Mahaffey	8.00	4.00
❑ 447 Julian Javier	15.00	7.50
❑ 448 Lee Stange	8.00	4.00
❑ 449 J.Hinsley/G.Kroll RC	15.00	7.50
❑ 450 Elston Howard	15.00	7.50
❑ 451 Jim Owens	8.00	4.00
❑ 452 Gary Geiger	8.00	4.00
❑ 453 W.Crawford RC/J.Werhas	15.00	7.50
❑ 454 Ed Rakow	8.00	4.00
❑ 455 Norm Siebern	8.00	4.00
❑ 456 Bill Henry	8.00	4.00
❑ 457 Bob Kennedy MG	15.00	7.50
❑ 458 John Buzhardt	8.00	4.00
❑ 459 Frank Kostro	8.00	4.00
❑ 460 Richie Allen	40.00	20.00
❑ 461 C.Carroll RC/P.Niekro	50.00	30.00
❑ 462 Lew Krausse UER	8.00	4.00
❑ 463 Manny Mota	15.00	7.50
❑ 464 Ron Piche	8.00	4.00
❑ 465 Tom Haller	15.00	7.50
❑ 466 P.Craig RC/D.Nen	8.00	4.00
❑ 467 Ray Washburn	8.00	4.00
❑ 468 Larry Brown	8.00	4.00
❑ 469 Don Nottebart	8.00	4.00
❑ 470 Yogi Berra P/CO	50.00	30.00
❑ 471 Billy Hoeft	8.00	4.00
❑ 472 Don Pavletich	8.00	4.00
❑ 473 P.Blair RC/D.Johnson RC	15.00	7.50
❑ 474 Cookie Rojas	15.00	7.50
❑ 475 Clete Boyer	15.00	7.50
❑ 476 Billy O'Dell	8.00	4.00
❑ 477 Steve Carlton RC	175.00	100.00
❑ 478 Wilbur Wood	15.00	7.50
❑ 479 Ken Harrelson	15.00	7.50
❑ 480 Joel Horlen	8.00	4.00
❑ 481 Cleveland Indians TC	10.00	6.00
❑ 482 Bob Priddy	8.00	4.00
❑ 483 George Smith RC	8.00	4.00
❑ 484 Ron Perranoski	20.00	10.00
❑ 485 Nellie Fox	25.00	12.50
❑ 486 T.Egan/P.Rogan RC	8.00	4.00
❑ 487 Woody Woodward	15.00	7.50
❑ 488 Ted Wills	8.00	4.00
❑ 489 Gene Mauch MG	15.00	7.50
❑ 490 Earl Battey	8.00	4.00
❑ 491 Tracy Stallard	8.00	4.00
❑ 492 Gene Freese	8.00	4.00
❑ 493 B.Roman RC/B.Brubaker RC	8.00	4.00
❑ 494 Jay Ritchie RC	8.00	4.00
❑ 495 Joe Christopher	8.00	4.00
❑ 496 Joe Cunningham	8.00	4.00
❑ 497 K.Henderson RC/J.Hiatt RC	15.00	7.50
❑ 498 Gene Stephens	8.00	4.00
❑ 499 Stu Miller	15.00	7.50
❑ 500 Eddie Mathews	40.00	20.00
❑ 501 R.Gagliano RC/J.Rittwage RC	8.00	4.00
❑ 502 Don Cardwell	8.00	4.00
❑ 503 Phil Gagliano	8.00	4.00
❑ 504 Jerry Grote	15.00	7.50
❑ 505 Ray Culp	8.00	4.00
❑ 506 Sam Mele MG	8.00	4.00
❑ 507 Sammy Ellis	8.00	4.00
❑ 508 Checklist 7	12.00	6.00
❑ 509 B.Guindon RC/G.Vezendy RC	8.00	4.00
❑ 510 Ernie Banks	80.00	50.00
❑ 511 Ron Locke	8.00	4.00

❑ 512 Cap Peterson	8.00	4.00
❑ 513 New York Yankees TC	40.00	20.00
❑ 514 Joe Azcue	8.00	4.00
❑ 515 Vern Law	15.00	7.50
❑ 516 Al Weis	8.00	4.00
❑ 517 P.Schaal RC/J.Warner	15.00	7.50
❑ 518 Ken Rowe	8.00	4.00
❑ 519 Bob Uecker UER	30.00	15.00
❑ 520 Tony Cloninger	8.00	4.00
❑ 521 D.Bennett/M.Stevens RC	8.00	4.00
❑ 522 Hank Aguirre	8.00	4.00
❑ 523 Mike Brumley SP	12.00	6.00
❑ 524 Dave Giusti SP	12.00	6.00
❑ 525 Eddie Bressoud	8.00	4.00
❑ 526 J.Odom/J.Hunter SP RC	80.00	50.00
❑ 527 Jeff Torborg SP	12.00	6.00
❑ 528 George Altman	8.00	4.00
❑ 529 Jerry Fosnow SP RC	12.00	6.00
❑ 530 Jim Maloney	15.00	7.50
❑ 531 Chuck Hiller	8.00	4.00
❑ 532 Hector Lopez	15.00	7.50
❑ 533 R.Swob/T.McGraw SP RC	25.00	12.50
❑ 534 John Herrnstein	8.00	4.00
❑ 535 Jack Kralick SP	12.00	6.00
❑ 536 Andre Rodgers SP	12.00	6.00
❑ 537 Lopez/Roof/May RC	8.00	4.00
❑ 538 Chuck Dressen MG SP	12.00	6.00
❑ 539 Herm Starrette	8.00	4.00
❑ 540 Lou Brock SP	50.00	30.00
❑ 541 G.Bollo RC/B.Locker RC	8.00	4.00
❑ 542 Lou Klimchock	8.00	4.00
❑ 543 Ed Connolly SP RC	12.00	6.00
❑ 544 Howie Reed RC	8.00	4.00
❑ 545 Jesus Alou SP	15.00	7.50
❑ 546 Davis/Hed/Bark/Weav RC	8.00	4.00
❑ 547 Jake Wood SP	12.00	6.00
❑ 548 Dick Stigman	8.00	4.00
❑ 549 R.Pena RC/G.Beckert RC	20.00	10.00
❑ 550 Mel Stottlemyre SP RC	30.00	15.00
❑ 551 New York Mets TC SP	30.00	15.00
❑ 552 Julio Gotay	8.00	4.00
❑ 553 Coombs/Ratliff/McClure RC	8.00	4.00
❑ 554 Chico Ruiz SP	12.00	6.00
❑ 555 Jack Baldschun SP	12.00	6.00
❑ 556 R.Schoendienst SP	25.00	12.50
❑ 557 Jose Santiago RC	8.00	4.00
❑ 558 Tommie Sisk	8.00	4.00
❑ 559 Ed Bailey SP	12.00	6.00
❑ 560 Boog Powell SP	25.00	12.50
❑ 561 Dab/Kek/Valle/Lefebvre RC	15.00	7.50
❑ 562 Billy Moran	8.00	4.00
❑ 563 Julio Navarro	8.00	4.00
❑ 564 Mel Nelson	8.00	4.00
❑ 565 Ernie Broglio SP	12.00	6.00
❑ 566 Blanco/Moschitto/Lopez RC	12.00	6.00
❑ 567 Tommie Aaron	8.00	4.00
❑ 568 Ron Taylor SP	12.00	6.00
❑ 569 Gino Cimoli SP	12.00	6.00
❑ 570 Claude Osteen SP	15.00	7.50
❑ 571 Ossie Virgil SP	12.00	6.00
❑ 572 Baltimore Orioles TC SP	25.00	12.50
❑ 573 Jim Lonborg SP RC	25.00	12.50
❑ 574 Roy Sievers	15.00	7.50
❑ 575 Jose Pagan	8.00	4.00
❑ 576 Terry Fox SP	12.00	6.00
❑ 577 Knowles/Busch/Schein RC	12.00	6.00
❑ 578 Camilo Carreon SP	12.00	6.00
❑ 579 Dick Smith SP	12.00	6.00
❑ 580 Jimmie Hall SP	12.00	6.00
❑ 581 Tony Perez SP RC	80.00	50.00
❑ 582 Bob Schmidt SP	12.00	6.00
❑ 583 Wes Covington SP	12.00	6.00
❑ 584 Harry Bright	15.00	7.50
❑ 585 Hank Fischer	8.00	4.00
❑ 586 Tom McCraw SP	12.00	6.00
❑ 587 Joe Sparma	8.00	4.00
❑ 588 Lenny Green	8.00	4.00
❑ 589 F.Linzy RC/B.Schroder RC	12.00	6.00
❑ 590 John Wyatt	8.00	4.00
❑ 591 Bob Skinner SP	12.00	6.00
❑ 592 Frank Bork SP RC	12.00	6.00
❑ 593 J.Sullivan RC/J.Moore RC SP	12.00	6.00
❑ 594 Joe Gaines	8.00	4.00
❑ 595 Don Lee	8.00	4.00
❑ 596 Don Landrum SP	12.00	6.00

❑ 597 Nossek/Sevcik/Reese RC	8.00	4.00
❑ 598 Al Downing SP	25.00	12.50

1966 Topps

❑ COMPLETE SET (598)	4000.00	2500.00
❑ COMMON CARD (1-109)	1.50	.75
❑ COMMON CARD (110-283)	2.00	1.00
❑ COMMON CARD (284-370)	3.00	1.50
❑ COMMON CARD (371-446)	5.00	2.50
❑ COMMON CARD (447-522)	10.00	5.00
❑ COMMON CARD (523-598)	15.00	7.50
❑ COMMON SP (523-598)	30.00	15.00
❑ WRAPPER (5-CENT)	25.00	20.00
❑ 1 Willie Mays	250.00	150.00
❑ 2 Ted Abernathy	1.50	.75
❑ 3 Sam Mele MG	1.50	.75
❑ 4 Ray Culp	1.50	.75
❑ 5 Jim Fregosi	2.00	1.00
❑ 6 Chuck Schilling	1.50	.75
❑ 7 Tracy Stallard	1.50	.75
❑ 8 Floyd Robinson	1.50	.75
❑ 9 Clete Boyer	2.00	1.00
❑ 10 Tony Cloninger	1.50	.75
❑ 11 B.Alyea RC/P.Craig	1.50	.75
❑ 12 John Tsitouris	1.50	.75
❑ 13 Lou Johnson	2.00	1.00
❑ 14 Norm Siebern	1.50	.75
❑ 15 Vern Law	2.00	1.00
❑ 16 Larry Brown	1.50	.75
❑ 17 John Stephenson	1.50	.75
❑ 18 Roland Sheldon	1.50	.75
❑ 19 San Francisco Giants TC	5.00	2.50
❑ 20 Willie Horton	2.00	1.00
❑ 21 Don Nottebart	1.50	.75
❑ 22 Joe Nossek	1.50	.75
❑ 23 Jack Sanford	1.50	.75
❑ 24 Don Kessinger RC	4.00	2.00
❑ 25 Pete Ward	1.50	.75
❑ 26 Ray Sadecki	1.50	.75
❑ 27 D.Knowles/A.Etchebarren RC	1.50	.75
❑ 28 Phil Niekro	20.00	10.00
❑ 29 Mike Brumley	1.50	.75
❑ 30 Pete Rose UER DP	100.00	60.00
❑ 31 Jack Cullen	2.00	1.00
❑ 32 Adolfo Phillips RC	1.50	.75
❑ 33 Jim Pagliaroni	1.50	.75
❑ 34 Checklist 1	8.00	4.00
❑ 35 Ron Swoboda	4.00	2.00
❑ 36 Jim Hunter UER DP	20.00	10.00
❑ 37 Billy Herman MG	2.00	1.00
❑ 38 Ron Nischwitz	1.50	.75
❑ 39 Ken Henderson	1.50	.75
❑ 40 Jim Grant	1.50	.75
❑ 41 Don LeJohn RC	1.50	.75
❑ 42 Aubrey Gatewood	1.50	.75
❑ 43A D.Landrum Dark Button	2.00	1.00
❑ 43B D.Landrum Airbrush Button	20.00	10.00
❑ 43C D.Landrum No Button	2.00	1.00
❑ 44 B.Davis/T.Kelley	1.50	.75
❑ 45 Jim Gentile	2.00	1.00
❑ 46 Howie Koplitz	1.50	.75
❑ 47 J.C. Martin	1.50	.75
❑ 48 Paul Blair	2.00	1.00
❑ 49 Woody Woodward	2.00	1.00
❑ 50 Mickey Mantle DP	350.00	200.00
❑ 51 Gordon Richardson RC	1.50	.75
❑ 52 W.Covington/J.Callison	4.00	2.00
❑ 53 Bob Duliba	1.50	.75

❑ 54 Jose Pagan 1.50 .75
❑ 55 Ken Harrelson 2.00 1.00
❑ 56 Sandy Valdespino 1.50 .75
❑ 57 Jim Lefebvre 2.00 1.00
❑ 58 Dave Wickersham 1.50 .75
❑ 59 Cincinnati Reds TC 5.00 2.50
❑ 60 Curt Flood 4.00 2.00
❑ 61 Bob Bolin 1.50 .75
❑ 62A Merritt Ranew Sold Line 2.00 1.00
❑ 62B Merritt Ranew NTR 30.00 15.00
❑ 63 Jim Stewart 1.50 .75
❑ 64 Bob Bruce 1.50 .75
❑ 65 Leon Wagner 1.50 .75
❑ 66 Al Weis 1.50 .75
❑ 67 C.Jones/D.Selma RC 4.00 2.00
❑ 68 Hal Reniff 1.50 .75
❑ 69 Ken Hamlin 1.50 .75
❑ 70 Carl Yastrzemski 30.00 15.00
❑ 71 Frank Carpin RC 1.50 .75
❑ 72 Tony Perez 25.00 12.50
❑ 73 Jerry Zimmerman 1.50 .75
❑ 74 Don Mossi 2.00 1.00
❑ 75 Tommy Davis 2.00 1.00
❑ 76 Red Schoendienst MG 4.00 2.00
❑ 77 John Orsino 1.50 .75
❑ 78 Frank Linzy 1.50 .75
❑ 79 Joe Pepitone 4.00 2.00
❑ 80 Richie Allen 6.00 3.00
❑ 81 Ray Oyler 1.50 .75
❑ 82 Bob Hendley 1.50 .75
❑ 83 Albie Pearson 2.00 1.00
❑ 84 J.Beauchamp/D.Kelley 1.50 .75
❑ 85 Eddie Fisher 1.50 .75
❑ 86 John Bateman 1.50 .75
❑ 87 Dan Napoleon 1.50 .75
❑ 88 Fred Whitfield 1.50 .75
❑ 89 Ted Davidson 1.50 .75
❑ 90 Luis Aparicio DP 8.00 4.00
❑ 91A Bob Uecker TR 10.00 5.00
❑ 91B Bob Uecker NTR 40.00 20.00
❑ 92 New York Yankees TC 15.00 7.50
❑ 93 Jim Lonborg DP 2.00 1.00
❑ 94 Matty Alou 2.00 1.00
❑ 95 Pete Richert 1.50 .75
❑ 96 Felipe Alou 4.00 2.00
❑ 97 Jim Merritt RC 1.50 .75
❑ 98 Don Demeter 1.50 .75
❑ 99 W.Stargell/D.Clendenon 6.00 3.00
❑ 100 Sandy Koufax DP 100.00 60.00
❑ 101A Checklist 2 Spahn ERR 15.00 7.50
❑ 101B Cheklist 2 Henry COR 10.00 5.00
❑ 102 Ed Kirkpatrick 1.50 .75
❑ 103A Dick Groat TR 2.00 1.00
❑ 103B Dick Groat NTR 40.00 20.00
❑ 104A Alex Johnson TR 2.00 1.00
❑ 104B Alex Johnson NTR 30.00 15.00
❑ 105 Milt Pappas 2.00 1.00
❑ 106 Rusty Staub 4.00 2.00
❑ 107 L.Stahl RC/R.Tompkins RC 1.50 .75
❑ 108 Bobby Klaus 1.50 .75
❑ 109 Ralph Terry 2.00 1.00
❑ 110 Ernie Banks 30.00 15.00
❑ 111 Gary Peters 2.00 1.00
❑ 112 Manny Mota 4.00 2.00
❑ 113 Hank Aguirre 2.00 1.00
❑ 114 Jim Gosger 2.00 1.00
❑ 115 Bill Henry 2.00 1.00
❑ 116 Walter Alston MG 6.00 3.00
❑ 117 Jake Gibbs 2.00 1.00
❑ 118 Mike McCormick 2.00 1.00
❑ 119 Art Shamsky 2.00 1.00
❑ 120 Harmon Killebrew 15.00 7.50
❑ 121 Ray Herbert 2.00 1.00
❑ 122 Joe Gaines 2.00 1.00
❑ 123 F.Bork/J.May 2.00 1.00
❑ 124 Tug McGraw 4.00 2.00
❑ 125 Lou Brock 20.00 10.00
❑ 126 Jim Palmer UER RC 100.00 60.00
❑ 127 Ken Berry 2.00 1.00
❑ 128 Jim Landis 2.00 1.00
❑ 129 Jack Kralick 2.00 1.00
❑ 130 Joe Torre 6.00 3.00
❑ 131 California Angels TC 5.00 2.50
❑ 132 Orlando Cepeda 8.00 4.00
❑ 133 Don McMahon 2.00 1.00
❑ 134 Wes Parker 4.00 2.00
❑ 135 Dave Morehead 2.00 1.00
❑ 136 Woody Held 2.00 1.00
❑ 137 Pat Corrales 2.00 1.00
❑ 138 Roger Repoz RC 2.00 1.00
❑ 139 B.Browne RC/D.Young RC 2.00 1.00
❑ 140 Jim Maloney 4.00 2.00
❑ 141 Tom McCraw 2.00 1.00
❑ 142 Don Dennis RC 2.00 1.00
❑ 143 Jose Tartabull 4.00 2.00
❑ 144 Don Schwall 2.00 1.00
❑ 145 Bill Freehan 4.00 2.00
❑ 146 George Altman 2.00 1.00
❑ 147 Lum Harris MG 2.00 1.00
❑ 148 Bob Johnson 2.00 1.00
❑ 149 Dick Nen 2.00 1.00
❑ 150 Rocky Colavito 8.00 4.00
❑ 151 Gary Wagner RC 2.00 1.00
❑ 152 Frank Malzone 4.00 2.00
❑ 153 Rico Carty 4.00 2.00
❑ 154 Chuck Hiller 2.00 1.00
❑ 155 Marcelino Lopez 2.00 1.00
❑ 156 D.Schofield/H.Lanier 2.00 1.00
❑ 157 Rene Lachemann 2.00 1.00
❑ 158 Jim Brewer 2.00 1.00
❑ 159 Chico Ruiz 2.00 1.00
❑ 160 Whitey Ford 30.00 15.00
❑ 161 Jerry Lumpe 2.00 1.00
❑ 162 Lee Maye 2.00 1.00
❑ 163 Tito Francona 2.00 1.00
❑ 164 T.Agee/M.Staehle 4.00 2.00
❑ 165 Don Lock 2.00 1.00
❑ 166 Chris Krug RC 2.00 1.00
❑ 167 Boog Powell 6.00 3.00
❑ 168 Dan Osinski 2.00 1.00
❑ 169 Duke Sims RC 2.00 1.00
❑ 170 Cookie Rojas 4.00 2.00
❑ 171 Nick Willhite 2.00 1.00
❑ 172 New York Mets TC 5.00 2.50
❑ 173 Al Spangler 2.00 1.00
❑ 174 Ron Taylor 2.00 1.00
❑ 175 Bert Campaneris 4.00 2.00
❑ 176 Jim Davenport 2.00 1.00
❑ 177 Hector Lopez 2.00 1.00
❑ 178 Bob Tillman 2.00 1.00
❑ 179 D.Aust RC/B.Tolan 4.00 2.00
❑ 180 Vada Pinson 4.00 2.00
❑ 181 Al Worthington 2.00 1.00
❑ 182 Jerry Lynch 2.00 1.00
❑ 183A Checklist 3 Large Print 8.00 4.00
❑ 183B Checklist 3 Small Print 8.00 4.00
❑ 184 Denis Menke 2.00 1.00
❑ 185 Bob Buhl 4.00 2.00
❑ 186 Ruben Amaro 2.00 1.00
❑ 187 Chuck Dressen MG 4.00 2.00
❑ 188 Al Luplow 2.00 1.00
❑ 189 John Roseboro 4.00 2.00
❑ 190 Jimmie Hall 2.00 1.00
❑ 191 Darrell Sutherland RC 2.00 1.00
❑ 192 Vic Power 4.00 2.00
❑ 193 Dave McNally 4.00 2.00
❑ 194 Washington Senators TC 5.00 2.50
❑ 195 Joe Morgan 15.00 7.50
❑ 196 Don Pavletich 2.00 1.00
❑ 197 Sonny Siebert 2.00 1.00
❑ 198 Mickey Stanley RC 6.00 3.00
❑ 199 Skowron/Romano/Robinson 4.00 2.00
❑ 200 Eddie Mathews 15.00 7.50
❑ 201 Jim Dickson 2.00 1.00
❑ 202 Clay Dalrymple 2.00 1.00
❑ 203 Jose Santiago 2.00 1.00
❑ 204 Chicago Cubs TC 5.00 2.50
❑ 205 Tom Tresh 4.00 2.00
❑ 206 Al Jackson 2.00 1.00
❑ 207 Frank Quilici RC 2.00 1.00
❑ 208 Bob Miller 2.00 1.00
❑ 209 F.Fisher/J.Hiller RC 4.00 2.00
❑ 210 Bill Mazeroski 8.00 4.00
❑ 211 Frank Kreutzer 2.00 1.00
❑ 212 Ed Kranepool 4.00 2.00
❑ 213 Fred Newman 2.00 1.00
❑ 214 Tommy Harper 4.00 2.00
❑ 215 Clemente/Aaron/Mays LL 50.00 30.00
❑ 216 Oliva/Yaz/Davalillo LL 5.00 2.50
❑ 217 Mays/McCovey/B.Will LL 20.00 10.00
❑ 218 Conigliaro/Cash/Horton LL 5.00 2.50
❑ 219 Johnson/F.Rob/Mays LL 12.00 6.00
❑ 220 Colavito/Horton/Oliva LL 5.00 2.50
❑ 221 Koufax/Marichal/Law LL 12.00 6.00
❑ 222 McDowell/Fisher/Siebert LL 5.00 2.50
❑ 223 Koufax/Clon/Drysdale LL 12.00 6.00
❑ 224 Grant/Stottlemyre/Kaat LL 5.00 2.50
❑ 225 Koufax/Veale/Gibson LL 12.00 6.00
❑ 226 McDowell/Lolich/McLain LL 5.00 2.50
❑ 227 Russ Nixon 2.00 1.00
❑ 228 Larry Dierker 4.00 2.00
❑ 229 Hank Bauer MG 4.00 2.00
❑ 230 Johnny Callison 4.00 2.00
❑ 231 Floyd Weaver 2.00 1.00
❑ 232 Glenn Beckert 4.00 2.00
❑ 233 Dom Zanni 2.00 1.00
❑ 234 R.Beck RC/R.White RC 8.00 4.00
❑ 235 Don Cardwell 2.00 1.00
❑ 236 Mike Hershberger 2.00 1.00
❑ 237 Billy O'Dell 2.00 1.00
❑ 238 Los Angeles Dodgers TC 5.00 2.50
❑ 239 Orlando Pena 2.00 1.00
❑ 240 Earl Battey 2.00 1.00
❑ 241 Dennis Ribant 2.00 1.00
❑ 242 Jesus Alou 2.00 1.00
❑ 243 Nelson Briles 4.00 2.00
❑ 244 C.Harrison RC//S.Jackson 2.00 1.00
❑ 245 John Buzhardt 2.00 1.00
❑ 246 Ed Bailey 2.00 1.00
❑ 247 Carl Warwick 2.00 1.00
❑ 248 Pete Mikkelsen 2.00 1.00
❑ 249 Bill Rigney MG 2.00 1.00
❑ 250 Sammy Ellis 2.00 1.00
❑ 251 Ed Brinkman 2.00 1.00
❑ 252 Denny Lemaster 2.00 1.00
❑ 253 Don Wert 2.00 1.00
❑ 254 Fergie Jenkins RC 60.00 35.00
❑ 255 Willie Stargell 20.00 10.00
❑ 256 Lew Krausse 2.00 1.00
❑ 257 Jeff Torborg 4.00 2.00
❑ 258 Dave Giusti 2.00 1.00
❑ 259 Boston Red Sox TC 5.00 2.50
❑ 260 Bob Shaw 2.00 1.00
❑ 261 Ron Hansen 2.00 1.00
❑ 262 Jack Hamilton 2.00 1.00
❑ 263 Tom Egan 2.00 1.00
❑ 264 A.Kosco RC/T.Uhlaender RC 2.00 1.00
❑ 265 Stu Miller 4.00 2.00
❑ 266 Pedro Gonzalez UER 2.00 1.00
❑ 267 Joe Sparma 2.00 1.00
❑ 268 John Blanchard 2.00 1.00
❑ 269 Don Heffner MG 2.00 1.00
❑ 270 Claude Osteen 4.00 2.00
❑ 271 Hal Lanier 2.00 1.00
❑ 272 Jack Baldschun 2.00 1.00
❑ 273 B.Aspromonte/R.Staub 4.00 2.00
❑ 274 Buster Narum 2.00 1.00
❑ 275 Tim McCarver 4.00 2.00
❑ 276 Jim Bouton 4.00 2.00
❑ 277 George Thomas 2.00 1.00
❑ 278 Cal Koonce 2.00 1.00
❑ 279A Checklist 4 Black Cap 8.00 4.00
❑ 279B Checklist 4 Red Cap 8.00 4.00
❑ 280 Bobby Knoop 2.00 1.00
❑ 281 Bruce Howard 2.00 1.00
❑ 282 Johnny Lewis 2.00 1.00
❑ 283 Jim Perry 4.00 2.00
❑ 284 Bobby Wine 3.00 1.50
❑ 285 Luis Tiant 5.00 2.50
❑ 286 Gary Geiger 3.00 1.50
❑ 287 Jack Aker RC 3.00 1.50
❑ 288 D.Sutton RC/B.Singer RC 60.00 35.00
❑ 289 Larry Sherry 3.00 1.50
❑ 290 Ron Santo 5.00 2.50
❑ 291 Moe Drabowsky 5.00 2.50
❑ 292 Jim Coker 3.00 1.50
❑ 293 Mike Shannon 5.00 2.50
❑ 294 Steve Ridzik 3.00 1.50
❑ 295 Jim Ray Hart 5.00 2.50
❑ 296 Johnny Keane MG 5.00 2.50
❑ 297 Jim Owens 3.00 1.50
❑ 298 Rico Petrocelli 5.00 2.50
❑ 299 Lou Burdette 5.00 2.50
❑ 300 Roberto Clemente 150.00 90.00
❑ 301 Greg Bollo 3.00 1.50
❑ 302 Ernie Bowman 3.00 1.50
❑ 303 Cleveland Indians TC 5.00 2.50
❑ 304 John Herrnstein 3.00 1.50

❑ 305 Camilo Pascual 5.00 2.50
❑ 306 Ty Cline 3.00 1.50
❑ 307 Clay Carroll 5.00 2.50
❑ 308 Tom Haller 5.00 2.50
❑ 309 Diego Segui 3.00 1.50
❑ 310 Frank Robinson 40.00 20.00
❑ 311 T.Helms/D.Simpson 5.00 2.50
❑ 312 Bob Saverine 3.00 1.50
❑ 313 Chris Zachary 3.00 1.50
❑ 314 Hector Valle 3.00 1.50
❑ 315 Norm Cash 5.00 2.50
❑ 316 Jack Fisher 3.00 1.50
❑ 317 Dalton Jones 3.00 1.50
❑ 318 Harry Walker MG 3.00 1.50
❑ 319 Gene Freese 3.00 1.50
❑ 320 Bob Gibson 25.00 12.50
❑ 321 Rick Reichardt 3.00 1.50
❑ 322 Bill Faul 3.00 1.50
❑ 323 Ray Barker 3.00 1.50
❑ 324 John Boozer 3.00 1.50
❑ 325 Vic Davalillo 3.00 1.50
❑ 326 Atlanta Braves TC 5.00 2.50
❑ 327 Bernie Allen 3.00 1.50
❑ 328 Jerry Grote 5.00 2.50
❑ 329 Pete Charton 3.00 1.50
❑ 330 Ron Fairly 5.00 2.50
❑ 331 Ron Herbel 3.00 1.50
❑ 332 Bill Bryan 3.00 1.50
❑ 333 J.Coleman RC/J.French RC 3.00 1.50
❑ 334 Marty Keough 3.00 1.50
❑ 335 Juan Pizarro 3.00 1.50
❑ 336 Gene Alley 5.00 2.50
❑ 337 Fred Gladding 3.00 1.50
❑ 338 Dal Maxvill 3.00 1.50
❑ 339 Del Crandall 5.00 2.50
❑ 340 Dean Chance 5.00 2.50
❑ 341 Wes Westrum MG 5.00 2.50
❑ 342 Bob Humphreys 3.00 1.50
❑ 343 Joe Christopher 3.00 1.50
❑ 344 Steve Blass 5.00 2.50
❑ 345 Bob Allison 5.00 2.50
❑ 346 Mike de la Hoz 3.00 1.50
❑ 347 Phil Regan 5.00 2.50
❑ 348 Baltimore Orioles TC 8.00 4.00
❑ 349 Cap Peterson 3.00 1.50
❑ 350 Mel Stottlemyre 8.00 4.00
❑ 351 Fred Valentine 3.00 1.50
❑ 352 Bob Aspromonte 3.00 1.50
❑ 353 Al McBean 3.00 1.50
❑ 354 Smoky Burgess 5.00 2.50
❑ 355 Wade Blasingame 3.00 1.50
❑ 356 O.Johnson RC/K.Sanders RC 3.00 1.50
❑ 357 Gerry Arrigo 3.00 1.50
❑ 358 Charlie Smith 3.00 1.50
❑ 359 Johnny Briggs 3.00 1.50
❑ 360 Ron Hunt 3.00 1.50
❑ 361 Tom Satriano 3.00 1.50
❑ 362 Gates Brown 5.00 2.50
❑ 363 Checklist 5 10.00 5.00
❑ 364 Nate Oliver 3.00 1.50
❑ 365 Roger Maris UER 50.00 30.00
❑ 366 Wayne Causey 3.00 1.50
❑ 367 Mel Nelson 3.00 1.50
❑ 368 Charlie Lau 5.00 2.50
❑ 369 Jim King 3.00 1.50
❑ 370 Chico Cardenas 3.00 1.50
❑ 371 Lee Stange 5.00 2.50
❑ 372 Harvey Kuenn 8.00 4.00
❑ 373 J.Hiatt/D.Estelle 8.00 4.00
❑ 374 Bob Locker 5.00 2.50
❑ 375 Donn Clendenon 8.00 4.00
❑ 376 Paul Schaal 5.00 2.50
❑ 377 Turk Farrell 5.00 2.50
❑ 378 Dick Tracewski 5.00 2.50
❑ 379 St. Louis Cardinals TC 10.00 5.00
❑ 380 Tony Conigliaro 10.00 5.00
❑ 381 Hank Fischer 5.00 2.50
❑ 382 Phil Roof 5.00 2.50
❑ 383 Jackie Brandt 5.00 2.50
❑ 384 Al Downing 8.00 4.00
❑ 385 Ken Boyer 10.00 5.00
❑ 386 Gil Hodges MG 8.00 4.00
❑ 387 Howie Reed 5.00 2.50
❑ 388 Don Mincher 5.00 2.50
❑ 389 Jim O'Toole 8.00 4.00
❑ 390 Brooks Robinson 50.00 30.00
❑ 391 Chuck Hinton 5.00 2.50
❑ 392 B.Hands RC/R.Hundley RC 8.00 4.00
❑ 393 George Brunet 5.00 2.50
❑ 394 Ron Brand 5.00 2.50
❑ 395 Len Gabrielson 5.00 2.50
❑ 396 Jerry Stephenson 5:00 2.50
❑ 397 Bill White 8.00 4.00
❑ 398 Danny Cater 5.00 2.50
❑ 399 Ray Washburn 5.00 2.50
❑ 400 Zoilo Versalles 8.00 4.00
❑ 401 Ken McMullen 5.00 2.50
❑ 402 Jim Hickman 5.00 2.50
❑ 403 Fred Talbot 5.00 2.50
❑ 404 Pittsburgh Pirates TC 10.00 5.00
❑ 405 Elston Howard 8.00 4.00
❑ 406 Joey Jay 5.00 2.50
❑ 407 John Kennedy 5.00 2.50
❑ 408 Lee Thomas 8.00 4.00
❑ 409 Billy Hoeft 5.00 2.50
❑ 410 Al Kaline 40.00 20.00
❑ 411 Gene Mauch MG 5.00 2.50
❑ 412 Sam Bowens 5.00 2.50
❑ 413 Johnny Romano 5.00 2.50
❑ 414 Dan Coombs 5.00 2.50
❑ 415 Max Alvis 5.00 2.50
❑ 416 Phil Ortega 5.00 2.50
❑ 417 J.McGlothlin RC/E.Sukla RC 5.00 2.50
❑ 418 Phil Gagliano 5.00 2.50
❑ 419 Mike Ryan 5.00 2.50
❑ 420 Juan Marichal 15.00 7.50
❑ 421 Roy McMillan 8.00 4.00
❑ 422 Ed Charles 5.00 2.50
❑ 423 Ernie Broglio 5.00 2.50
❑ 424 L.May RC/D.Osteen RC 10.00 5.00
❑ 425 Bob Veale 8.00 4.00
❑ 426 Chicago White Sox TC 10.00 5.00
❑ 427 John Miller 5.00 2.50
❑ 428 Sandy Alomar 5.00 2.50
❑ 429 Bill Monbouquette 5.00 2.50
❑ 430 Don Drysdale 20.00 10.00
❑ 431 Walt Bond 5.00 2.50
❑ 432 Bob Heffner 5.00 2.50
❑ 433 Alvin Dark MG 8.00 4.00
❑ 434 Willie Kirkland 5.00 2.50
❑ 435 Jim Bunning 15.00 7.50
❑ 436 Julian Javier 8.00 4.00
❑ 437 Al Stanek 5.00 2.50
❑ 438 Willie Smith 5.00 2.50
❑ 439 Pedro Ramos 5.00 2.50
❑ 440 Deron Johnson 8.00 4.00
❑ 441 Tommie Sisk 5.00 2.50
❑ 442 E.Barnowski RC/E.Watt RC 5.00 2.50
❑ 443 Bill Wakefield 3.00 1.50
❑ 444 Checklist 6 10.00 5.00
❑ 445 Jim Kaat 10.00 5.00
❑ 446 Mack Jones 5.00 2.50
❑ 447 D.Ellsw UER Hubbs 15.00 7.50
❑ 448 Eddie Stanky MG 10.00 5.00
❑ 449 Joe Moeller 10.00 5.00
❑ 450 Tony Oliva 15.00 7.50
❑ 451 Barry Latman 10.00 5.00
❑ 452 Joe Azcue 10.00 5.00
❑ 453 Ron Kline 10.00 5.00
❑ 454 Jerry Buchek 10.00 5.00
❑ 455 Mickey Lolich 15.00 7.50
❑ 456 D.Brandon RC/J.Foy RC 10.00 5.00
❑ 457 Joe Gibbon 10.00 5.00
❑ 458 Manny Jiminez 10.00 5.00
❑ 459 Bill McCool 10.00 5.00
❑ 460 Curt Blefary 10.00 5.00
❑ 461 Roy Face 15.00 7.50
❑ 462 Bob Rodgers 10.00 5.00
❑ 463 Philadelphia Phillies TC 15.00 7.50
❑ 464 Larry Bearnarth 10.00 5.00
❑ 465 Don Buford 10.00 5.00
❑ 466 Ken Johnson 10.00 5.00
❑ 467 Vic Roznovsky 10.00 5.00
❑ 468 Johnny Podres 15.00 7.50
❑ 469 B.Murcer RC/D.Womack RC 30.00 15.00
❑ 470 Sam McDowell 15.00 7.50
❑ 471 Bob Skinner 10.00 5.00
❑ 472 Terry Fox 10.00 5.00
❑ 473 Rich Rollins 10.00 5.00
❑ 474 Dick Schofield 10.00 5.00
❑ 475 Dick Radatz 10.00 5.00
❑ 476 Bobby Bragan MG 10.00 5.00
❑ 477 Steve Barber 10.00 5.00
❑ 478 Tony Gonzalez 10.00 5.00
❑ 479 Jim Hannan 10.00 5.00
❑ 480 Dick Stuart 10.00 5.00
❑ 481 Bob Lee 10.00 5.00
❑ 482 J.Boccabella/D.Dowling 10.00 5.00
❑ 483 Joe Nuxhall 10.00 5.00
❑ 484 Wes Covington 10.00 5.00
❑ 485 Bob Bailey 10.00 5.00
❑ 486 Tommy John 15.00 7.50
❑ 487 Al Ferrara 10.00 5.00
❑ 488 George Banks 10.00 5.00
❑ 489 Curt Simmons 10.00 5.00
❑ 490 Bobby Richardson 25.00 12.50
❑ 491 Dennis Bennett 10.00 5.00
❑ 492 Kansas City Athletics TC 15.00 7.50
❑ 493 Johnny Klippstein 10.00 5.00
❑ 494 Gordy Coleman 10.00 5.00
❑ 495 Dick McAuliffe 15.00 7.50
❑ 496 Lindy McDaniel 10.00 5.00
❑ 497 Chris Cannizzaro 10.00 5.00
❑ 498 L.Walker RC/W.Fryman RC 10.00 5.00
❑ 499 Wally Bunker 10.00 5.00
❑ 500 Hank Aaron 125.00 75.00
❑ 501 John O'Donoghue 10.00 5.00
❑ 502 Lenny Green UER 10.00 5.00
❑ 503 Steve Hamilton 15.00 7.50
❑ 504 Grady Hatton MG 10.00 5.00
❑ 505 Jose Cardenal 10.00 5.00
❑ 506 Bo Belinsky 15.00 7.50
❑ 507 Johnny Edwards 10.00 5.00
❑ 508 Steve Hargan RC 15.00 7.50
❑ 509 Jake Wood 10.00 5.00
❑ 510 Hoyt Wilhelm 25.00 12.50
❑ 511 B.Barton RC/T.Fuentes RC 10.00 5.00
❑ 512 Dick Stigman 10.00 5.00
❑ 513 Camilo Carreon 10.00 5.00
❑ 514 Hal Woodeshick 10.00 5.00
❑ 515 Frank Howard 15.00 7.50
❑ 516 Eddie Bressoud 10.00 5.00
❑ 517A Checklist 7 White Sox 15.00 7.50
❑ 517B Checklist 7 W.Sox 15.00 7.50
❑ 518 H.Hippauf RC/A.Umbach RC 10.00 5.00
❑ 519 Bob Friend 15.00 7.50
❑ 520 Jim Wynn 15.00 7.50
❑ 521 John Wyatt 10.00 5.00
❑ 522 Phil Linz 10.00 5.00
❑ 523 Bob Sadowski 10.00 5.00
❑ 524 O.Brown RC/D.Mason RC SP 30.00 15.00
❑ 525 Gary Bell SP 30.00 15.00
❑ 526 Minnesota Twins TC SP 100.00 60.00
❑ 527 Julio Navarro 15.00 7.50
❑ 528 Jesse Gonder SP 30.00 15.00
❑ 529 Elia/Higgins/Voss RC 15.00 7.50
❑ 530 Robin Roberts 50.00 30.00
❑ 531 Joe Cunningham 15.00 7.50
❑ 532 A.Monteagudo SP 30.00 15.00
❑ 533 Jerry Adair SP 30.00 15.00
❑ 534 D.Eilers RC/R.Gardner RC 15.00 7.50
❑ 535 Willie Davis SP 40.00 20.00
❑ 536 Dick Egan 15.00 7.50
❑ 537 Herman Franks MG 15.00 7.50
❑ 538 Bob Allen SP 30.00 15.00
❑ 539 B.Heath RC/C.Sembera RC 25.0012.50
❑ 540 Denny McLain SP 60.00 35.00
❑ 541 Gene Oliver SP 30.00 15.00
❑ 542 George Smith 15.00 7.50
❑ 543 Roger Craig SP 30.00 15.00
❑ 544 Hoerner/Kernek/Williams RC SP 30.00 15.00
❑ 545 Dick Green SP 30.00 15.00
❑ 546 Dwight Siebler 25.00 12.50
❑ 547 Horace Clarke SP RC 40.00 20.00
❑ 548 Gary Kroll SP 30.00 15.00
❑ 549 A.Closter RC/C.Cox RC 15.00 7.50
❑ 550 Willie McCovey SP 100.00 60.00
❑ 551 Bob Purkey SP 30.00 15.00
❑ 552 B.Tebbetts MG SP 30.00 15.00
❑ 553 P.Garrett RC/J.Warner 15.00 7.50
❑ 554 Jim Northrup SP 30.00 15.00
❑ 555 Ron Perranoski SP 30.00 15.00
❑ 556 Mel Queen SP 30.00 15.00
❑ 557 Felix Mantilla SP 30.00 15.00
❑ 558 Grilli/Magrini/Scott RC 20.00 10.00
❑ 559 Roberto Pena SP 30.00 15.00
❑ 560 Joel Horlen 15.00 7.50
❑ 561 Choo Choo Coleman SP 30.00 15.00

❑ 562 Russ Snyder 25.00 12.50
❑ 563 P.Cimino RC/C.Tovar RC 15.00 7.50
❑ 564 Bob Chance SP 30.00 15.00
❑ 565 Jimmy Piersall SP 40.00 20.00
❑ 566 Mike Cuellar SP 30.00 15.00
❑ 567 Dick Howser SP 40.00 20.00
❑ 568 P.Lindblad RC/R.Stone RC 15.00 7.50
❑ 569 Orlando McFarlane SP 30.00 15.00
❑ 570 Art Mahaffey SP 30.00 15.00
❑ 571 Dave Roberts SP 30.00 15.00
❑ 572 Bob Priddy 15.00 7.50
❑ 573 Derrell Griffith 15.00 7.50
❑ 574 B.Hepler RC/B.Murphy RC 15.00 7.50
❑ 575 Earl Wilson 15.00 7.50
❑ 576 Dave Nicholson SP 30.00 15.00
❑ 577 Jack Lamabe SP 30.00 15.00
❑ 578 Chi Chi Olivo SP RC 30.00 15.00
❑ 579 Bertaina/Brabender/Johnson RC 20.00 10.00
❑ 580 Billy Williams SP 60.00 35.00
❑ 581 Tony Martinez 15.00 7.50
❑ 582 Garry Roggenburk 15.00 7.50
❑ 583 Detroit Tigers TC SP 125.00 75.00
❑ 584 F.Fernandez RC/F.Peterson RC 15.00 7.50
❑ 585 Tony Taylor 25.00 12.50
❑ 586 Claude Raymond SP 30.00 15.00
❑ 587 Dick Bertell 15.00 7.50
❑ 588 C.Dobson RC/K.Suarez RC 15.00 7.50
❑ 589 Lou Klimchock SP 30.00 15.00
❑ 590 Bill Skowron SP 40.00 20.00
❑ 591 B.Shirley RC/G.Jackson RC SP 40.00 20.00
❑ 592 Andre Rodgers 15.00 7.50
❑ 593 Doug Camilli SP 30.00 15.00
❑ 594 Chico Salmon 15.00 7.50
❑ 595 Larry Jackson 15.00 7.50
❑ 596 N.Colbert RC/G.Sims RC SP 30.00 15.00
❑ 597 John Sullivan 15.00 7.50
❑ 598 Gaylord Perry SP 175.00 100.00

1967 Topps

❑ COMPLETE SET (609) 5000.00 3000.00
❑ COMMON CARD (1-109) 1.50 .75
❑ COMMON CARD (110-283) 2.00 1.00
❑ COMMON CARD (284-370) 2.50 1.25
❑ COMMON CARD (371-457) 4.00 2.00
❑ COMMON CARD (458-533) 6.00 3.00
❑ COMMON CARD (534-609) 15.00 7.50
❑ COMMON DP (534-609) 8.00 4.00
❑ WRAPPER (5-CENT) 25.00 20.00
❑ 1 Robinson/Bauer/Robinson DP 25.00 12.50
❑ 2 Jack Hamilton 1.50 .75
❑ 3 Duke Sims 1.50 .75
❑ 4 Hal Lanier 1.50 .75
❑ 5 Whitey Ford UER 20.00 10.00
❑ 6 Dick Simpson 1.50 .75
❑ 7 Don McMahon 1.50 .75
❑ 8 Chuck Harrison 1.50 .75
❑ 9 Ron Hansen 1.50 .75
❑ 10 Matty Alou 4.00 2.00
❑ 11 Barry Moore RC 1.50 .75
❑ 12 J.Campanis RC/B.Singer 4.00 2.00
❑ 13 Joe Sparma 1.50 .75
❑ 14 Phil Linz 4.00 2.00
❑ 15 Earl Battey 1.50 .75
❑ 16 Bill Hands 1.50 .75
❑ 17 Jim Gosger 1.50 .75
❑ 18 Gene Oliver 1.50 .75
❑ 19 Jim McGlothlin 1.50 .75
❑ 20 Orlando Cepeda 8.00 4.00
❑ 21 Dave Bristol MG RC 1.50 .75
❑ 22 Gene Brabender 1.50 .75
❑ 23 Larry Elliot 1.50 .75
❑ 24 Bob Allen 1.50 .75
❑ 25 Elston Howard 4.00 2.00
❑ 26A Bob Priddy NTR 30.00 15.00
❑ 26B Bob Priddy TR 4.00 2.00
❑ 27 Bob Saverine 1.50 .75
❑ 28 Barry Latman 1.50 .75
❑ 29 Tom McCraw 1.50 .75
❑ 30 Al Kaline DP 20.00 10.00
❑ 31 Jim Brewer 1.50 .75
❑ 32 Bob Bailey 4.00 2.00
❑ 33 S.Bando RC/R.Schwartz RC 6.00 3.00
❑ 34 Pete Cimino 1.50 .75
❑ 35 Rico Carty 4.00 2.00
❑ 36 Bob Tillman 1.50 .75
❑ 37 Rick Wise 4.00 2.00
❑ 38 Bob Johnson 1.50 .75
❑ 39 Curt Simmons 4.00 2.00
❑ 40 Rick Reichardt 1.50 .75
❑ 41 Joe Hoerner 1.50 .75
❑ 42 New York Mets TC 10.00 5.00
❑ 43 Chico Salmon 1.50 .75
❑ 44 Joe Nuxhall 4.00 2.00
❑ 45 Roger Maris 50.00 30.00
❑ 45A R.Maris Yanks/Blank Back 1000.00 600.00
❑ 46 Lindy McDaniel 4.00 2.00
❑ 47 Ken McMullen 1.50 .75
❑ 48 Bill Freehan 4.00 2.00
❑ 49 Roy Face 4.00 2.00
❑ 50 Tony Oliva 6.00 3.00
❑ 51 D.Adlesh RC/W.Bales RC 1.50 .75
❑ 52 Dennis Higgins 1.50 .75
❑ 53 Clay Dalrymple 1.50 .75
❑ 54 Dick Green 1.50 .75
❑ 55 Don Drysdale 15.00 7.50
❑ 56 Jose Tartabull 4.00 2.00
❑ 57 Pat Jarvis RC 4.00 2.00
❑ 58A Paul Schaal Green Bat 20.00 10.00
❑ 58B P.Schaal Normal Bat 1.50 .75
❑ 59 Ralph Terry 4.00 2.00
❑ 60 Luis Aparicio 8.00 4.00
❑ 61 Gordy Coleman 1.50 .75
❑ 62 Frank Robinson CL1 8.00 4.00
❑ 63 L.Brock/C.Flood 8.00 4.00
❑ 64 Fred Valentine 1.50 .75
❑ 65 Tom Haller 4.00 2.00
❑ 66 Manny Mota 4.00 2.00
❑ 67 Ken Berry 1.50 .75
❑ 68 Bob Buhl 4.00 2.00
❑ 69 Vic Davalillo 1.50 .75
❑ 70 Ron Santo 6.00 3.00
❑ 71 Camilo Pascual 4.00 2.00
❑ 72 G.Korince ERR RC/T.Matchick RC 1.50 .75
❑ 73 Rusty Staub 6.00 3.00
❑ 74 Wes Stock 1.50 .75
❑ 75 George Scott 4.00 2.00
❑ 76 Jim Barbieri RC 1.50 .75
❑ 77 Dooley Womack 4.00 2.00
❑ 78 Pat Corrales 1.50 .75
❑ 79 Bubba Morton 1.50 .75
❑ 80 Jim Maloney 4.00 2.00
❑ 81 Eddie Stanky MG 4.00 2.00
❑ 82 Steve Barber 1.50 .75
❑ 83 Ollie Brown 1.50 .75
❑ 84 Tommie Sisk 1.50 .75
❑ 85 Johnny Callison 4.00 2.00
❑ 86A Mike McCormick NTR 30.00 15.00
❑ 86B Mike McCormick TR 4.00 2.00
❑ 87 George Altman 1.50 .75
❑ 88 Mickey Lolich 4.00 2.00
❑ 89 Felix Millan RC 4.00 2.00
❑ 90 Jim Nash RC 1.50 .75
❑ 91 Johnny Lewis 1.50 .75
❑ 92 Ray Washburn 1.50 .75
❑ 93 S.Bahnsen RC/B.Murcer 4.00 2.00
❑ 94 Ron Fairly 4.00 2.00
❑ 95 Sonny Siebert 1.50 .75
❑ 96 Art Shamsky 1.50 .75
❑ 97 Mike Cuellar 4.00 2.00
❑ 98 Rich Rollins 1.50 .75
❑ 99 Lee Stange 1.50 .75
❑ 100 Frank Robinson DP 15.00 7.50
❑ 101 Ken Johnson 1.50 .75
❑ 102 Philadelphia Phillies TC 4.00 2.00
❑ 103 Mickey Mantle CL2 DP 20.00 10.00
❑ 104 Minnie Rojas RC 1.50 .75
❑ 105 Ken Boyer 6.00 3.00
❑ 106 Randy Hundley 4.00 2.00
❑ 107 Joel Horlen 1.50 .75
❑ 108 Alex Johnson 4.00 2.00
❑ 109 R.Colavito/L.Wagner 6.00 3.00
❑ 110 Jack Aker 4.00 2.00
❑ 111 John Kennedy 2.00 1.00
❑ 112 Dave Wickersham 2.00 1.00
❑ 113 Dave Nicholson 2.00 1.00
❑ 114 Jack Baldschun 2.00 1.00
❑ 115 Paul Casanova RC 2.00 1.00
❑ 116 Herman Franks MG 2.00 1.00
❑ 117 Darrell Brandon 2.00 1.00
❑ 118 Bernie Allen 2.00 1.00
❑ 119 Wade Blasingame 2.00 1.00
❑ 120 Floyd Robinson 2.00 1.00
❑ 121 Eddie Bressoud 2.00 1.00
❑ 122 George Brunet 2.00 1.00
❑ 123 J.Price RC/L.Walker 4.00 2.00
❑ 124 Jim Stewart 2.00 1.00
❑ 125 Moe Drabowsky 4.00 2.00
❑ 126 Tony Taylor 2.00 1.00
❑ 127 John O'Donoghue 2.00 1.00
❑ 128 Ed Spiezio RC 2.00 1.00
❑ 129 Phil Roof 2.00 1.00
❑ 130 Phil Regan 4.00 2.00
❑ 131 New York Yankees TC 10.00 5.00
❑ 132 Ozzie Virgil 2.00 1.00
❑ 133 Ron Kline 2.00 1.00
❑ 134 Gates Brown 6.00 3.00
❑ 135 Deron Johnson 4.00 2.00
❑ 136 Carroll Sembera 2.00 1.00
❑ 137 R.Clark RC/J.Ollum 2.00 1.00
❑ 138 Dick Kelley 2.00 1.00
❑ 139 Dalton Jones 4.00 2.00
❑ 140 Willie Stargell 20.00 10.00
❑ 141 John Miller 2.00 1.00
❑ 142 Jackie Brandt 2.00 1.00
❑ 143 P.Ward/D.Buford 2.00 1.00
❑ 144 Bill Hepler 2.00 1.00
❑ 145 Larry Brown 2.00 1.00
❑ 146 Steve Carlton 50.00 30.00
❑ 147 Tom Egan 2.00 1.00
❑ 148 Adolfo Phillips 2.00 1.00
❑ 149 Joe Moeller 2.00 1.00
❑ 150 Mickey Mantle 350.00 200.00
❑ 151 Moe Drabowsky WS1 5.00 2.50
❑ 152 Jim Palmer WS2 8.00 4.00
❑ 153 Paul Blair WS3 5.00 2.50
❑ 154 Robinson/McNally WS4 5.00 2.50
❑ 155 Orioles Celebrate WS 5.00 2.50
❑ 156 Ron Herbel 2.00 1.00
❑ 157 Danny Cater 2.00 1.00
❑ 158 Jimmie Coker 2.00 1.00
❑ 159 Bruce Howard 2.00 1.00
❑ 160 Willie Davis 4.00 2.00
❑ 161 Dick Williams MG 4.00 2.00
❑ 162 Billy O'Dell 2.00 1.00
❑ 163 Vic Roznovsky 2.00 1.00
❑ 164 Dwight Siebler UER 2.00 1.00
❑ 165 Cleon Jones 4.00 2.00
❑ 166 Eddie Mathews 15.00 7.50
❑ 167 J.Coleman RC/T.Cullen RC 2.00 1.00
❑ 168 Ray Culp 2.00 1.00
❑ 169 Horace Clarke 4.00 2.00
❑ 170 Dick McAuliffe 4.00 2.00
❑ 171 Cal Koonce 2.00 1.00
❑ 172 Bill Heath 2.00 1.00
❑ 173 St. Louis Cardinals TC 4.00 2.00
❑ 174 Dick Radatz 4.00 2.00
❑ 175 Bobby Knoop 2.00 1.00
❑ 176 Sammy Ellis 2.00 1.00
❑ 177 Tito Fuentes 1.50 .75
❑ 178 John Buzhardt 2.00 1.00
❑ 179 C.Vaughan RC/C.Epshaw RC 4.00 2.00
❑ 180 Curt Blefary 2.00 1.00
❑ 181 Terry Fox 2.00 1.00
❑ 182 Ed Charles 2.00 1.00
❑ 183 Jim Pagliaroni 2.00 1.00
❑ 184 George Thomas 2.00 1.00
❑ 185 Ken Holtzman RC 4.00 2.00
❑ 186 E.Kranepool/R.Swoboda 4.00 2.00
❑ 187 Pedro Ramos 2.00 1.00
❑ 188 Ken Harrelson 4.00 2.00

❑ 189 Chuck Hinton 2.00 1.00
❑ 190 Turk Farrell 2.00 1.00
❑ 191A W.Mays CL3 214 Tom 10.00 5.00
❑ 191B W.Mays CL3 214 Dick 12.00 6.00
❑ 192 Fred Gladding 2.00 1.00
❑ 193 Jose Cardenal 4.00 2.00
❑ 194 Bob Allison 4.00 2.00
❑ 195 Al Jackson 2.00 1.00
❑ 196 Johnny Romano 2.00 1.00
❑ 197 Ron Perranoski 4.00 2.00
❑ 198 Chuck Hiller 2.00 1.00
❑ 199 Billy Hitchcock MG 2.00 1.00
❑ 200 Willie Mays UER 100.00 60.00
❑ 201 Hal Reniff 4.00 2.00
❑ 202 Johnny Edwards 2.00 1.00
❑ 203 Al McBean 2.00 1.00
❑ 204 M.Epstein RC/T.Phoebus RC 6.00 3.00
❑ 205 Dick Groat 4.00 2.00
❑ 206 Dennis Bennett 2.00 1.00
❑ 207 John Orsino 2.00 1.00
❑ 208 Jack Lamabe 2.00 1.00
❑ 209 Joe Nossek 2.00 1.00
❑ 210 Bob Gibson 20.00 10.00
❑ 211 Minnesota Twins TC 4.00 2.00
❑ 212 Chris Zachary 2.00 1.00
❑ 213 Jay Johnstone RC 4.00 2.00
❑ 214 Dick Kelley 2.00 1.00
❑ 215 Ernie Banks 20.00 10.00
❑ 216 A.Kaline/N.Cash 8.00 4.00
❑ 217 Rob Gardner 2.00 1.00
❑ 218 Wes Parker 4.00 2.00
❑ 219 Clay Carroll 4.00 2.00
❑ 220 Jim Ray Hart 4.00 2.00
❑ 221 Woody Fryman 4.00 2.00
❑ 222 D.Osteen/L.May 4.00 2.00
❑ 223 Mike Ryan 4.00 2.00
❑ 224 Walt Bond 2.00 1.00
❑ 225 Mel Stottlemyre 6.00 3.00
❑ 226 Julian Javier 4.00 2.00
❑ 227 Paul Lindblad 2.00 1.00
❑ 228 Gil Hodges MG 6.00 3.00
❑ 229 Larry Jackson 2.00 1.00
❑ 230 Boog Powell 6.00 3.00
❑ 231 John Bateman 2.00 1.00
❑ 232 Don Buford 2.00 1.00
❑ 233 Peters/Horlen/Hargan LL 4.00 2.00
❑ 234 Koufax/Cuellar/Marichal LL 15.00 7.50
❑ 235 Kaat/McLain/Wilson LL 6.00 3.00
❑ 236 Koufax/Mari/Gibs/Perry LL 25.00 12.50
❑ 237 McDowell/Kaat/Wilson LL 6.00 3.00
❑ 238 Koufax/Bunning/Veale LL 12.00 6.00
❑ 239 F.Rob/Oliva/Kaline LL 10.00 5.00
❑ 240 Alou/Alou/Carty LL 6.00 3.00
❑ 241 F.Rob/Killebrew/Powell LL 10.00 5.00
❑ 242 Aaron/Clemente/Allen LL 25.00 12.50
❑ 243 F.Rob/Killebrew/Powell LL 10.00 5.00
❑ 244 Aaron/Allen/Mays LL 20.00 10.00
❑ 245 Curt Flood 6.00 3.00
❑ 246 Jim Perry 4.00 2.00
❑ 247 Jerry Lumpe 2.00 1.00
❑ 248 Gene Mauch MG 4.00 2.00
❑ 249 Nick Willhite 2.00 1.00
❑ 250 Hank Aaron UER 80.00 50.00
❑ 251 Woody Held 2.00 1.00
❑ 252 Bob Bolin 2.00 1.00
❑ 253 B.Davis/G.Gil RC 2.00 1.00
❑ 254 Milt Pappas 4.00 2.00
❑ 255 Frank Howard 4.00 2.00
❑ 256 Bob Hendley 2.00 1.00
❑ 257 Charlie Smith 2.00 1.00
❑ 258 Lee Maye 2.00 1.00
❑ 259 Don Dennis 2.00 1.00
❑ 260 Jim Lefebvre 4.00 2.00
❑ 261 John Wyatt 2.00 1.00
❑ 262 Kansas City Athletics TC 4.00 2.00
❑ 263 Hank Aguirre 2.00 1.00
❑ 264 Ron Swoboda 4.00 2.00
❑ 265 Lou Burdette 4.00 2.00
❑ 266 W.Stargell/D.Clendenon 4.00 2.00
❑ 267 Don Schwall 2.00 1.00
❑ 268 Johnny Briggs 2.00 1.00
❑ 269 Don Nottebart 2.00 1.00
❑ 270 Zoilo Versalles 2.00 1.00
❑ 271 Eddie Watt 2.00 1.00
❑ 272 B.Connors RC/D.Dowling 4.00 2.00
❑ 273 Dick Lines RC 2.00 1.00
❑ 274 Bob Aspromonte 2.00 1.00
❑ 275 Fred Whitfield 2.00 1.00
❑ 276 Bruce Brubaker 2.00 1.00
❑ 277 Steve Whitaker RC 6.00 3.00
❑ 278 Jim Kaat CL4 8.00 4.00
❑ 279 Frank Linzy 2.00 1.00
❑ 280 Tony Conigliaro 8.00 4.00
❑ 281 Bob Rodgers 2.00 1.00
❑ 282 John Odom 2.00 1.00
❑ 283 Gene Alley 4.00 2.00
❑ 284 Johnny Podres 4.00 2.00
❑ 285 Lou Brock 20.00 10.00
❑ 286 Wayne Causey 2.50 1.25
❑ 287 G.Goosen RC/B.Shirley 2.50 1.25
❑ 288 Denny Lemaster 2.50 1.25
❑ 289 Tom Tresh 5.00 2.50
❑ 290 Bill White 5.00 2.50
❑ 291 Jim Hannan 2.50 1.25
❑ 292 Don Pavletich 2.50 1.25
❑ 293 Ed Kirkpatrick 2.50 1.25
❑ 294 Walter Alston MG 8.00 4.00
❑ 295 Sam McDowell 5.00 2.50
❑ 296 Glenn Beckert 5.00 2.50
❑ 297 Dave Morehead 5.00 2.50
❑ 298 Ron Davis RC 2.50 1.25
❑ 299 Norm Siebern 2.50 1.25
❑ 300 Jim Kaat 5.00 2.50
❑ 301 Jesse Gonder 2.50 1.25
❑ 302 Baltimore Orioles TC 8.00 4.00
❑ 303 Gil Blanco 2.50 1.25
❑ 304 Phil Gagliano 2.50 1.25
❑ 305 Earl Wilson 5.00 2.50
❑ 306 Bud Harrelson RC 5.00 2.50
❑ 307 Jim Beauchamp 2.50 1.25
❑ 308 Al Downing 5.00 2.50
❑ 309 J.Callison/R.Allen 5.00 2.50
❑ 310 Gary Peters 2.50 1.25
❑ 311 Ed Brinkman 2.50 1.25
❑ 312 Don Mincher 2.50 1.25
❑ 313 Bob Lee 2.50 1.25
❑ 314 M.Andrews RC/R.Smith RC 8.00 4.00
❑ 315 Billy Williams 15.00 7.50
❑ 316 Jack Kralick 2.50 1.25
❑ 317 Cesar Tovar 2.50 1.25
❑ 318 Dave Giusti 2.50 1.25
❑ 319 Paul Blair 5.00 2.50
❑ 320 Gaylord Perry 15.00 7.50
❑ 321 Mayo Smith MG 2.50 1.25
❑ 322 Jose Pagan 2.50 1.25
❑ 323 Mike Hershberger 2.50 1.25
❑ 324 Hal Woodeshick 2.50 1.25
❑ 325 Chico Cardenas 5.00 2.50
❑ 326 Bob Uecker 10.00 5.00
❑ 327 California Angels TC 8.00 4.00
❑ 328 Clete Boyer UER 5.00 2.50
❑ 329 Charlie Lau 5.00 2.50
❑ 330 Claude Osteen 5.00 2.50
❑ 331 Joe Foy 5.00 2.50
❑ 332 Jesus Alou 2.50 1.25
❑ 333 Fergie Jenkins 20.00 10.00
❑ 334 H.Killebrew/B.Allison 10.00 5.00
❑ 335 Bob Veale 5.00 2.50
❑ 336 Joe Azcue 2.50 1.25
❑ 337 Joe Morgan 15.00 7.50
❑ 338 Bob Locker 2.50 1.25
❑ 339 Chico Ruiz 2.50 1.25
❑ 340 Joe Pepitone 8.00 4.00
❑ 341 D.Dietz RC/B.Sorrell 2.50 1.25
❑ 342 Hank Fischer 2.50 1.25
❑ 343 Tom Satriano 2.50 1.25
❑ 344 Ossie Chavarria RC 2.50 1.25
❑ 345 Stu Miller 5.00 2.50
❑ 346 Jim Hickman 2.50 1.25
❑ 347 Grady Hatton MG 2.50 1.25
❑ 348 Tug McGraw 5.00 2.50
❑ 349 Bob Chance 2.50 1.25
❑ 350 Joe Torre 8.00 4.00
❑ 351 Vern Law 5.00 2.50
❑ 352 Ray Oyler 2.50 1.25
❑ 353 Bill McCool 2.50 1.25
❑ 354 Chicago Cubs TC 8.00 4.00
❑ 355 Carl Yastrzemski 60.00 35.00
❑ 356 Larry Jaster RC 2.50 1.25
❑ 357 Bill Skowron 5.00 2.50
❑ 358 Ruben Amaro 2.50 1.25
❑ 359 Dick Ellsworth 2.50 1.25
❑ 360 Leon Wagner 2.50 1.25
❑ 361 Roberto Clemente CL5 15.00 7.50
❑ 362 Darold Knowles 2.50 1.25
❑ 363 Davey Johnson 5.00 2.50
❑ 364 Claude Raymond 2.50 1.25
❑ 365 John Roseboro 5.00 2.50
❑ 366 Andy Kosco 2.50 1.25
❑ 367 B.Kelso/D.Wallace RC 2.50 1.25
❑ 368 Jack Hiatt 2.50 1.25
❑ 369 Jim Hunter 15.00 7.50
❑ 370 Tommy Davis 5.00 2.50
❑ 371 Jim Lonborg 8.00 4.00
❑ 372 Mike de la Hoz 4.00 2.00
❑ 373 D.Josephson RC/F.Klages RC DP 4.00 2.00
❑ 374A Mel Queen ERR 20.00 10.00
❑ 374B Mel Queen COR DP 4.00 2.00
❑ 375 Jake Gibbs 8.00 4.00
❑ 376 Don Lock DP 4.00 2.00
❑ 377 Luis Tiant 8.00 4.00
❑ 378 Detroit Tigers TC UER 8.00 4.00
❑ 379 Jerry May DP 4.00 2.00
❑ 380 Dean Chance DP 4.00 2.00
❑ 381 Dick Schofield DP 4.00 2.00
❑ 382 Dave McNally 8.00 4.00
❑ 383 Ken Henderson DP 4.00 2.00
❑ 384 J.Cosman RC/D.Hughes RC 4.00 2.00
❑ 385 Jim Fregosi 8.00 4.00
❑ 386 Dick Selma DP 4.00 2.00
❑ 387 Cap Peterson DP 4.00 2.00
❑ 388 Arnold Earley DP 4.00 2.00
❑ 389 Alvin Dark MG DP 8.00 4.00
❑ 390 Jim Wynn DP 8.00 4.00
❑ 391 Wilbur Wood DP 8.00 4.00
❑ 392 Tommy Harper DP 8.00 4.00
❑ 393 Jim Bouton DP 8.00 4.00
❑ 394 Jake Wood DP 4.00 2.00
❑ 395 Chris Short RC 8.00 4.00
❑ 396 D.Menke/T.Cloninger 4.00 2.00
❑ 397 Willie Smith DP 4.00 2.00
❑ 398 Jeff Torborg 8.00 4.00
❑ 399 Al Worthington DP 4.00 2.00
❑ 400 Roberto Clemente DP 120.00 70.00
❑ 401 Jim Coates 4.00 2.00
❑ 402A G.Jackson/B.Wilson Stat Line 20.00 10.00
❑ 402B G.Jackson/B.Wilson RC DP 8.00 4.00
❑ 403 Dick Nen 4.00 2.00
❑ 404 Nelson Briles 8.00 4.00
❑ 405 Russ Snyder 4.00 2.00
❑ 406 Lee Elia DP 4.00 2.00
❑ 407 Cincinnati Reds TC 8.00 4.00
❑ 408 Jim Northrup DP 8.00 4.00
❑ 409 Ray Sadecki 4.00 2.00
❑ 410 Lou Johnson DP 4.00 2.00
❑ 411 Dick Howser DP 4.00 2.00
❑ 412 N.Miller RC/D.Rader RC 8.00 4.00
❑ 413 Jerry Grote 4.00 2.00
❑ 414 Casey Cox 4.00 2.00
❑ 415 Sonny Jackson 4.00 2.00
❑ 416 Roger Repoz 4.00 2.00
❑ 417A Bob Bruce ERR 30.00 15.00
❑ 417B Bob Bruce COR DP 4.00 2.00
❑ 418 Sam Mele MG 4.00 2.00
❑ 419 Don Kessinger DP 8.00 4.00
❑ 420 Denny McLain 12.00 6.00
❑ 421 Dal Maxvill DP 4.00 2.00
❑ 422 Hoyt Wilhelm 15.00 7.50
❑ 423 W.Mays/W.McCovey DP 25.00 12.50
❑ 424 Pedro Gonzalez 4.00 2.00
❑ 425 Pete Mikkelsen 4.00 2.00
❑ 426 Lou Clinton 4.00 2.00
❑ 427A Ruben Gomez ERR 20.00 10.00
❑ 427B Ruben Gomez COR DP 4.00 2.00
❑ 428 T.Hutton RC/G.Michael RC DP 8.00 4.00
❑ 429 Garry Roggenburk DP 4.00 2.00
❑ 430 Pete Rose 100.00 60.00
❑ 431 Ted Uhlaender 4.00 2.00
❑ 432 Jimmie Hall DP 4.00 2.00
❑ 433 Al Luplow DP 4.00 2.00
❑ 434 Eddie Fisher DP 4.00 2.00
❑ 435 Mack Jones DP 4.00 2.00
❑ 436 Pete Ward 4.00 2.00
❑ 437 Washington Senators TC 8.00 4.00
❑ 438 Chuck Dobson 4.00 2.00
❑ 439 Byron Browne 4.00 2.00
❑ 440 Steve Hargan 4.00 2.00
❑ 441 Jim Davenport 4.00 2.00

❑ 442 B.Robinson RC/J.Verbanic RC DP 8.00 4.00
❑ 443 Tito Francona DP 4.00 2.00
❑ 444 George Smith 4.00 2.00
❑ 445 Don Sutton 25.00 12.50
❑ 446 Russ Nixon DP 4.00 2.00
❑ 447A Bo Belinsky ERR DP 4.00 2.00
❑ 447B Bo Belinsky COR 8.00 4.00
❑ 448 Harry Walker MG DP 4.00 2.00
❑ 449 Orlando Pena 4.00 2.00
❑ 450 Richie Allen 8.00 4.00
❑ 451 Fred Newman DP 4.00 2.00
❑ 452 Ed Kranepool 8.00 4.00
❑ 453 Aurelio Monteagudo DP 4.00 2.00
❑ 454A J.Marichal CL6 No Ear DP 12.00 6.00
❑ 454B Juan Marichal CL6 w/Ear DP 12.00 6.00
❑ 455 Tommie Agee 8.00 4.00
❑ 456 Phil Niekro 15.00 7.50
❑ 457 Andy Etchebarren DP 8.00 4.00
❑ 458 Lee Thomas 6.00 3.00
❑ 459 D.Bosman RC/P.Craig 6.00 3.00
❑ 460 Harmon Killebrew 60.00 35.00
❑ 461 Bob Miller 12.00 6.00
❑ 462 Bob Barton 6.00 3.00
❑ 463 S.McDowell/S.Siebert 12.00 6.00
❑ 464 Dan Coombs 6.00 3.00
❑ 465 Willie Horton 12.00 6.00
❑ 466 Bobby Wine 6.00 3.00
❑ 467 Jim O'Toole 6.00 3.00
❑ 468 Ralph Houk MG 6.00 3.00
❑ 469 Len Gabrielson 6.00 3.00
❑ 470 Bob Shaw 6.00 3.00
❑ 471 Rene Lachemann 6.00 3.00
❑ 472 J.Gelnar/G.Spriggs RC 6.00 3.00
❑ 473 Jose Santiago 6.00 3.00
❑ 474 Bob Tolan 6.00 3.00
❑ 475 Jim Palmer 80.00 50.00
❑ 476 Tony Perez SP 60.00 35.00
❑ 477 Atlanta Braves TC 15.00 7.50
❑ 478 Bob Humphreys 6.00 3.00
❑ 479 Gary Bell 6.00 3.00
❑ 480 Willie McCovey 40.00 20.00
❑ 481 Leo Durocher MG 20.00 10.00
❑ 482 Bill Monbouquette 6.00 3.00
❑ 483 Jim Landis 6.00 3.00
❑ 484 Jerry Adair 6.00 3.00
❑ 485 Tim McCarver 25.00 12.50
❑ 486 R.Reese RC/B.Whitby RC 6.00 3.00
❑ 487 Tommie Reynolds 6.00 3.00
❑ 488 Gerry Arrigo 6.00 3.00
❑ 489 Doug Clemens RC 6.00 3.00
❑ 490 Tony Cloninger 6.00 3.00
❑ 491 Sam Bowens 6.00 3.00
❑ 492 Pittsburgh Pirates TC 15.00 7.50
❑ 493 Phil Ortega 6.00 3.00
❑ 494 Bill Rigney MG 6.00 3.00
❑ 495 Fritz Peterson 6.00 3.00
❑ 496 Orlando McFarlane 6.00 3.00
❑ 497 Ron Campbell RC 6.00 3.00
❑ 498 Larry Dierker 12.00 6.00
❑ 499 G.Culver/J.Vidal RC 6.00 3.00
❑ 500 Juan Marichal 25.00 12.50
❑ 501 Jerry Zimmerman 6.00 3.00
❑ 502 Derrell Griffith 6.00 3.00
❑ 503 Los Angeles Dodgers TC 20.00 10.00
❑ 504 Orlando Martinez RC 6.00 3.00
❑ 505 Tommy Helms 12.00 6.00
❑ 506 Smoky Burgess 6.00 3.00
❑ 507 E.Barnowski/L.Haney RC 6.00 3.00
❑ 508 Dick Hall 6.00 3.00
❑ 509 Jim King 6.00 3.00
❑ 510 Bill Mazeroski 25.00 12.50
❑ 511 Don Wert 6.00 3.00
❑ 512 Red Schoendienst MG 25.00 12.50
❑ 513 Marcelino Lopez 6.00 3.00
❑ 514 John Werhas 6.00 3.00
❑ 515 Bert Campaneris 12.00 6.00
❑ 516 San Francisco Giants TC 15.00 7.50
❑ 517 Fred Talbot 12.00 6.00
❑ 518 Denis Menke 6.00 3.00
❑ 519 Ted Davidson 6.00 3.00
❑ 520 Max Alvis 6.00 3.00
❑ 521 B.Powell/C.Blefary 12.00 6.00
❑ 522 John Stephenson 6.00 3.00
❑ 523 Jim Merritt 6.00 3.00
❑ 524 Felix Mantilla 6.00 3.00
❑ 525 Ron Hunt 6.00 3.00
❑ 526 P.Dobson RC/G.Korince RC 6.00 3.00
❑ 527 Dennis Ribant 6.00 3.00
❑ 528 Rico Petrocelli 20.00 10.00
❑ 529 Gary Wagner 6.00 3.00
❑ 530 Felipe Alou 12.00 6.00
❑ 531 B.Robinson CL7 DP 15.00 7.50
❑ 532 Jim Hicks RC 6.00 3.00
❑ 533 Jack Fisher 6.00 3.00
❑ 534 Hank Bauer MG DP 8.00 4.00
❑ 535 Donn Clendenon 25.00 12.50
❑ 536 J.Niekro RC/P.Popovich RC 50.00 30.00
❑ 537 Chuck Estrada DP 8.00 4.00
❑ 538 J.C. Martin 15.00 7.50
❑ 539 Dick Egan DP 8.00 4.00
❑ 540 Norm Cash 50.00 30.00
❑ 541 Joe Gibbon 15.00 7.50
❑ 542 R.Monday RC/T.Pierce RC DP 15.00 7.50
❑ 543 Dan Schneider 15.00 7.50
❑ 544 Cleveland Indians TC 30.00 15.00
❑ 545 Jim Grant 25.00 12.50
❑ 546 Woody Woodward 25.00 12.50
❑ 547 R.Gibson RC/B.Rohr RC DP 8.00 4.00
❑ 548 Tony Gonzalez DP 8.00 4.00
❑ 549 Jack Sanford 15.00 7.50
❑ 550 Vada Pinson DP 10.00 5.00
❑ 551 Doug Camilli DP 8.00 4.00
❑ 552 Ted Savage 25.00 12.50
❑ 553 M.Hegan RC/T.Tillotson 40.00 20.00
❑ 554 Andre Rodgers DP 8.00 4.00
❑ 555 Don Cardwell 25.00 12.50
❑ 556 Al Weis DP 8.00 4.00
❑ 557 Al Ferrara 25.00 12.50
❑ 558 M.Belanger RC/B.Dillman RC 50.00 30.00
❑ 559 Dick Tracewski DP 8.00 4.00
❑ 560 Jim Bunning 60.00 35.00
❑ 561 Sandy Alomar 40.00 20.00
❑ 562 Steve Blass DP 8.00 4.00
❑ 563 Joe Adcock MG 40.00 20.00
❑ 564 A.Harris RC/A.Pointer RC DP 8.00 4.00
❑ 565 Lew Krausse 25.00 12.50
❑ 566 Gary Geiger DP 8.00 4.00
❑ 567 Steve Hamilton 40.00 20.00
❑ 568 John Sullivan 40.00 20.00
❑ 569 Rod Carew RC DP 300.00 175.00
❑ 570 Maury Wills 80.00 50.00
❑ 571 Larry Sherry 25.00 12.50
❑ 572 Don Demeter 25.00 12.50
❑ 573 Chicago White Sox TC 30.00 15.00
❑ 574 Jerry Buchek 25.00 12.50
❑ 575 Dave Boswell RC 15.00 7.50
❑ 576 R.Hernandez RC/N.Gigon RC 40.00 20.00
❑ 577 Bill Short 15.00 7.50
❑ 578 John Boccabella 15.00 7.50
❑ 579 Bill Henry 15.00 7.50
❑ 580 Rocky Colavito 150.00 90.00
❑ 581 Tom Seaver RC 600.00 350.00
❑ 582 Jim Owens DP 8.00 4.00
❑ 583 Ray Barker 40.00 20.00
❑ 584 Jimmy Piersall 40.00 20.00
❑ 585 Wally Bunker 25.00 12.50
❑ 586 Manny Jimenez 15.00 7.50
❑ 587 D.Shaw RC/G.Sutherland RC 40.00 20.00
❑ 588 Johnny Klippstein DP 8.00 4.00
❑ 589 Dave Ricketts DP 8.00 4.00
❑ 590 Pete Richert 15.00 7.50
❑ 591 Ty Cline 25.00 12.50
❑ 592 J.Shellenback RC/R.Willis RC 25.00 12.50
❑ 593 Wes Westrum MG 50.00 30.00
❑ 594 Dan Osinski 40.00 20.00
❑ 595 Cookie Rojas 25.00 12.50
❑ 596 Galen Cisco DP 8.00 4.00
❑ 597 Ted Abernathy 15.00 7.50
❑ 598 W.Williams RC/E.Stroud RC 25.00 12.50
❑ 599 Bob Duliba DP 8.00 4.00
❑ 600 Brooks Robinson 250.00 150.00
❑ 601 Bill Bryan DP 8.00 4.00
❑ 602 Juan Pizarro 40.00 20.00
❑ 603 T.Talton RC/R.Webster RC 25.00 12.50
❑ 604 Boston Red Sox TC 125.00 75.00
❑ 605 Mike Shannon 50.00 30.00
❑ 606 Ron Taylor 25.00 12.50
❑ 607 Mickey Stanley 50.00 30.00
❑ 608 R.Nye RC/J.Upham RC DP 8.00 4.00
❑ 609 Tommy John 80.00 50.00

1968 Topps

❑ COMPLETE SET (598) 3000.00 1800.00
❑ COMMON CARD (1-457) 2.00 .75
❑ COMMON CARD (458-598) 4.00 1.50
❑ WRAPPER (5-CENT) 25.00 20.00
❑ 1 Clemente/Gonz/Alou LL 30.00 15.00
❑ 2 Yaz/F.Rob/Kaline LL 15.00 7.50
❑ 3 Cep/Clemente/Aaron LL 20.00 10.00
❑ 4 Yaz/Killebrew/F.Rob LL 15.00 7.50
❑ 5 Aaron/Santo/McCovey LL 8.00 4.00
❑ 6 Yaz/Killebrew/Howard LL 8.00 4.00
❑ 7 Niekro/Bunning/Short LL 4.00 1.50
❑ 8 Horlen/Peters/Siebert LL 4.00 1.50
❑ 9 McCor/Jenkins/Bunning LL 4.00 1.50
❑ 10A Lonb/Wils/Chance LL ERR 4.00 1.50
❑ 10B Lonb/Wils/Chance LL COR 4.00 1.50
❑ 11 Bunning/jenkins/Perry LL 6.00 3.00
❑ 12 Lonborg/McDow/Chance LL 4.00 1.50
❑ 13 Chuck Hartenstein RC 2.00 .75
❑ 14 Jerry McNertney 2.00 .75
❑ 15 Ron Hunt 2.00 .75
❑ 16 L.Piniella/R.Scheinblum 6.00 3.00
❑ 17 Dick Hall 2.00 .75
❑ 18 Mike Hershberger 2.00 .75
❑ 19 Juan Pizarro 2.00 .75
❑ 20 Brooks Robinson 25.00 12.50
❑ 21 Ron Davis 2.00 .75
❑ 22 Pat Dobson 4.00 1.50
❑ 23 Chico Cardenas 4.00 1.50
❑ 24 Bobby Locke 2.00 .75
❑ 25 Julian Javier 4.00 1.50
❑ 26 Darrell Brandon 2.00 .75
❑ 27 Gil Hodges MG 8.00 4.00
❑ 28 Ted Uhlaender 2.00 .75
❑ 29 Joe Verbanic 2.00 .75
❑ 30 Joe Torre 6.00 3.00
❑ 31 Ed Stroud 2.00 .75
❑ 32 Joe Gibbon 2.00 .75
❑ 33 Pete Ward 2.00 .75
❑ 34 Al Ferrara 2.00 .75
❑ 35 Steve Hargan 2.00 .75
❑ 36 B.Moose RC/B.Robertson RC 4.00 1.50
❑ 37 Billy Williams 8.00 4.00
❑ 38 Tony Pierce 2.00 .75
❑ 39 Cookie Rojas 2.00 .75
❑ 40 Denny McLain 8.00 4.00
❑ 41 Julio Gotay 2.00 .75
❑ 42 Larry Haney 2.00 .75
❑ 43 Gary Bell 2.00 .75
❑ 44 Frank Kostro 2.00 .75
❑ 45 Tom Seaver DP 50.00 30.00
❑ 46 Dave Ricketts 2.00 .75
❑ 47 Ralph Houk MG 4.00 1.50
❑ 48 Ted Davidson 2.00 .75
❑ 49A E.Brinkman White 2.00 .75
❑ 49B E.Brinkman Yellow Tm 50.00 30.00
❑ 50 Willie Mays 60.00 35.00
❑ 51 Bob Locker 2.00 .75
❑ 52 Hawk Taylor 2.00 .75
❑ 53 Gene Alley 4.00 1.50
❑ 54 Stan Williams 2.00 .75
❑ 55 Felipe Alou 4.00 1.50
❑ 56 D.Leonhard RC/D.May RC 2.00 .75
❑ 57 Dan Schneider 2.00 .75
❑ 58 Eddie Mathews 15.00 7.50
❑ 59 Don Lock 2.00 .75
❑ 60 Ken Holtzman 4.00 1.50

❑ 61 Reggie Smith 4.00 1.50
❑ 62 Chuck Dobson 2.00 .75
❑ 63 Dick Kenworthy RC 2.00 .75
❑ 64 Jim Merritt 2.00 .75
❑ 65 John Roseboro 4.00 1.50
❑ 66A Casey Cox White 2.00 .75
❑ 66B C.Cox Yellow Tm 100.00 60.00
❑ 67 Checklist 1/Kaat 6.00 3.00
❑ 68 Ron Willis 2.00 .75
❑ 69 Tom Tresh 4.00 1.50
❑ 70 Bob Veale 4.00 1.50
❑ 71 Vern Fuller RC 2.00 .75
❑ 72 Tommy John 6.00 3.00
❑ 73 Jim Ray Hart 4.00 1.50
❑ 74 Milt Pappas 4.00 1.50
❑ 75 Don Mincher 2.00 .75
❑ 76 J.Britton/R.Reed RC 4.00 1.50
❑ 77 Don Wilson RC 4.00 1.50
❑ 78 Jim Northrup 6.00 3.00
❑ 79 Ted Kubiak RC 2.00 .75
❑ 80 Rod Carew 50.00 30.00
❑ 81 Larry Jackson 2.00 .75
❑ 82 Sam Bowens 2.00 .75
❑ 83 John Stephenson 2.00 .75
❑ 84 Bob Tolan 2.00 .75
❑ 85 Gaylord Perry 8.00 4.00
❑ 86 Willie Stargell 8.00 4.00
❑ 87 Dick Williams MG 4.00 1.50
❑ 88 Phil Regan 4.00 1.50
❑ 89 Jake Gibbs 4.00 1.50
❑ 90 Vada Pinson 4.00 1.50
❑ 91 Jim Ollom RC 2.00 .75
❑ 92 Ed Kranepool 4.00 1.50
❑ 93 Tony Cloninger 2.00 .75
❑ 94 Lee Maye 2.00 .75
❑ 95 Bob Aspromonte 2.00 .75
❑ 96 F.Coggins RC/D.Nold 2.00 .75
❑ 97 Tom Phoebus 2.00 .75
❑ 98 Gary Sutherland 2.00 .75
❑ 99 Rocky Colavito 8.00 4.00
❑ 100 Bob Gibson 25.00 12.50
❑ 101 Glenn Beckert 4.00 1.50
❑ 102 Jose Cardenal 4.00 1.50
❑ 103 Don Sutton 8.00 4.00
❑ 104 Dick Dietz 2.00 .75
❑ 105 Al Downing 4.00 1.50
❑ 106 Dalton Jones 2.00 .75
❑ 107A Checklist 2/Marichal Wide 6.00 3.00
❑ 107B Checklist 2/J.Marichal Fine 6.00 3.00
❑ 108 Don Pavletich 2.00 .75
❑ 109 Bert Campaneris 4.00 1.50
❑ 110 Hank Aaron 60.00 35.00
❑ 111 Rich Reese 2.00 .75
❑ 112 Woody Fryman 2.00 .75
❑ 113 T.Matchick/D.Patterson RC 4.00 1.50
❑ 114 Ron Swoboda 4.00 1.50
❑ 115 Sam McDowell 4.00 1.50
❑ 116 Ken McMullen 2.00 .75
❑ 117 Larry Jaster 2.00 .75
❑ 118 Mark Belanger 4.00 1.50
❑ 119 Ted Savage 2.00 .75
❑ 120 Mel Stottlemyre 4.00 1.50
❑ 121 Jimmie Hall 2.00 .75
❑ 122 Gene Mauch MG 4.00 1.50
❑ 123 Jose Santiago 2.00 .75
❑ 124 Nate Oliver 2.00 .75
❑ 125 Joel Horlen 2.00 .75
❑ 126 Bobby Etheridge RC 2.00 .75
❑ 127 Paul Lindblad 2.00 .75
❑ 128 T.Dukes RC/A.Harris 2.00 .75
❑ 129 Mickey Stanley 6.00 3.00
❑ 130 Tony Perez 8.00 4.00
❑ 131 Frank Bertaina 2.00 .75
❑ 132 Bud Harrelson 4.00 1.50
❑ 133 Fred Whitfield 2.00 .75
❑ 134 Pat Jarvis 2.00 .75
❑ 135 Paul Blair 4.00 1.50
❑ 136 Randy Hundley 4.00 1.50
❑ 137 Minnesota Twins TC 4.00 1.50
❑ 138 Ruben Amaro 2.00 .75
❑ 139 Chris Short 2.00 .75
❑ 140 Tony Conigliaro 8.00 4.00
❑ 141 Dal Maxvill 2.00 .75
❑ 142 B.Bradford RC/B.Voss 2.00 .75
❑ 143 Pete Cimino 2.00 .75
❑ 144 Joe Morgan 12.00 6.00
❑ 145 Don Drysdale 12.00 6.00
❑ 146 Sal Bando 4.00 1.50
❑ 147 Frank Linzy 2.00 .75
❑ 148 Dave Bristol MG 2.00 .75
❑ 149 Bob Saverine 2.00 .75
❑ 150 Roberto Clemente 80.00 50.00
❑ 151 Lou Brock WS1 10.00 5.00
❑ 152 Carl Yastrzemski WS2 10.00 5.00
❑ 153 Nelson Briles WS3 5.00 2.00
❑ 154 Bob Gibson WS4 10.00 5.00
❑ 155 Jim Lonborg WS5 5.00 2.00
❑ 156 Rico Petrocelli WS6 5.00 2.00
❑ 157 St. Louis Wins It WS7 5.00 2.00
❑ 158 Cardinals Celebrate WS 5.00 2.00
❑ 159 Don Kessinger 4.00 1.50
❑ 160 Earl Wilson 4.00 1.50
❑ 161 Norm Miller 2.00 .75
❑ 162 H.Gilson RC/M.Torrez RC 4.00 1.50
❑ 163 Gene Brabender 2.00 .75
❑ 164 Ramon Webster 2.00 .75
❑ 165 Tony Oliva 6.00 3.00
❑ 166 Claude Raymond 2.00 .75
❑ 167 Elston Howard 6.00 3.00
❑ 168 Los Angeles Dodgers TC 4.00 1.50
❑ 169 Bob Bolin 2.00 .75
❑ 170 Jim Fregosi 4.00 1.50
❑ 171 Don Nottebart 2.00 .75
❑ 172 Walt Williams 2.00 .75
❑ 173 John Boozer 2.00 .75
❑ 174 Bob Tillman 2.00 .75
❑ 175 Maury Wills 6.00 3.00
❑ 176 Bob Allen 2.00 .75
❑ 177 N.Ryan RC/J.Koosman RC 500.00 300.00
❑ 178 Don Wert 4.00 1.50
❑ 179 Bill Stoneman RC 2.00 .75
❑ 180 Curt Flood 6.00 3.00
❑ 181 Jerry Zimmerman 2.00 .75
❑ 182 Dave Giusti 2.00 .75
❑ 183 Bob Kennedy MG 4.00 1.50
❑ 184 Lou Johnson 2.00 .75
❑ 185 Tom Haller 2.00 .75
❑ 186 Eddie Watt 2.00 .75
❑ 187 Sonny Jackson 2.00 .75
❑ 188 Cap Peterson 2.00 .75
❑ 189 Bill Landis RC 2.00 .75
❑ 190 Bill White 4.00 1.50
❑ 191 Dan Frisella RC 2.00 .75
❑ 192A Checklist 3/Yaz Ball 8.00 4.00
❑ 192B Checklist 3/Yaz Game 8.00 4.00
❑ 193 Jack Hamilton 2.00 .75
❑ 194 Don Buford 2.00 .75
❑ 195 Joe Pepitone 4.00 1.50
❑ 196 Gary Nolan RC 4.00 1.50
❑ 197 Larry Brown 2.00 .75
❑ 198 Roy Face 4.00 1.50
❑ 199 R.Rodriguez RC/D.Osteen 2.00 .75
❑ 200 Orlando Cepeda 8.00 4.00
❑ 201 Mike Marshall RC 4.00 1.50
❑ 202 Adolfo Phillips 2.00 .75
❑ 203 Dick Kelley 2.00 .75
❑ 204 Andy Etchebarren 2.00 .75
❑ 205 Juan Marichal 8.00 4.00
❑ 206 Cal Ermer MG RC 2.00 .75
❑ 207 Carroll Sembera 2.00 .75
❑ 208 Willie Davis 4.00 1.50
❑ 209 Tim Cullen 2.00 .75
❑ 210 Gary Peters 2.00 .75
❑ 211 J.C. Martin 2.00 .75
❑ 212 Dave Morehead 2.00 .75
❑ 213 Chico Ruiz 2.00 .75
❑ 214 S.Bahnsen/F.Fernandez 4.00 1.50
❑ 215 Jim Bunning 8.00 4.00
❑ 216 Bubba Morton 2.00 .75
❑ 217 Dick Farrell 2.00 .75
❑ 218 Ken Suarez 2.00 .75
❑ 219 Rob Gardner 2.00 .75
❑ 220 Harmon Killebrew 15.00 7.50
❑ 221 Atlanta Braves TC 4.00 1.50
❑ 222 Jim Hardin RC 2.00 .75
❑ 223 Ollie Brown 2.00 .75
❑ 224 Jack Aker 2.00 .75
❑ 225 Richie Allen 6.00 3.00
❑ 226 Jimmie Price 2.00 .75
❑ 227 Joe Hoerner 2.00 .75
❑ 228 J.Billingham RC/J.Fairey RC 4.00 1.50
❑ 229 Fred Klages 2.00 .75
❑ 230 Pete Rose 60.00 35.00
❑ 231 Dave Baldwin RC 2.00 .75
❑ 232 Denis Menke 2.00 .75
❑ 233 George Scott 4.00 1.50
❑ 234 Bill Monbouquette 2.00 .75
❑ 235 Ron Santo 8.00 4.00
❑ 236 Tug McGraw 6.00 3.00
❑ 237 Alvin Dark MG 4.00 1.50
❑ 238 Tom Satriano 2.00 .75
❑ 239 Bill Henry 2.00 .75
❑ 240 Al Kaline 40.00 20.00
❑ 241 Felix Millan 2.00 .75
❑ 242 Moe Drabowsky 4.00 1.50
❑ 243 Rich Rollins 2.00 .75
❑ 244 John Donaldson RC 2.00 .75
❑ 245 Tony Gonzalez 2.00 .75
❑ 246 Fritz Peterson 4.00 1.50
❑ 247 Johnny Bench RC 125.00 75.00
❑ 248 Fred Valentine 2.00 .75
❑ 249 Bill Singer 2.00 .75
❑ 250 Carl Yastrzemski 30.00 15.00
❑ 251 Manny Sanguillen RC 6.00 3.00
❑ 252 California Angels TC 4.00 1.50
❑ 253 Dick Hughes 2.00 .75
❑ 254 Cleon Jones 4.00 1.50
❑ 255 Dean Chance 4.00 1.50
❑ 256 Norm Cash 6.00 3.00
❑ 257 Phil Niekro 8.00 4.00
❑ 258 J.Arcia RC/B.Schlesinger 2.00 .75
❑ 259 Ken Boyer 6.00 3.00
❑ 260 Jim Wynn 4.00 1.50
❑ 261 Dave Duncan 4.00 1.50
❑ 262 Rick Wise 4.00 1.50
❑ 263 Horace Clarke 4.00 1.50
❑ 264 Ted Abernathy 2.00 .75
❑ 265 Tommy Davis 4.00 1.50
❑ 266 Paul Popovich 2.00 .75
❑ 267 Herman Franks MG 2.00 .75
❑ 268 Bob Humphreys 2.00 .75
❑ 269 Bob Tiefenauer 2.00 .75
❑ 270 Matty Alou 4.00 1.50
❑ 271 Bobby Knoop 2.00 .75
❑ 272 Ray Culp 2.00 .75
❑ 273 Dave Johnson 4.00 1.50
❑ 274 Mike Cuellar 4.00 1.50
❑ 275 Tim McCarver 6.00 3.00
❑ 276 Jim Roland 2.00 .75
❑ 277 Jerry Buchek 2.00 .75
❑ 278 Checklist 4/Cepeda 6.00 3.00
❑ 279 Bill Hands 2.00 .75
❑ 280 Mickey Mantle 350.00 200.00
❑ 281 Jim Campanis 2.00 .75
❑ 282 Rick Monday 4.00 1.50
❑ 283 Mel Queen 2.00 .75
❑ 284 Johnny Briggs 2.00 .75
❑ 285 Dick McAuliffe 6.00 3.00
❑ 286 Cecil Upshaw 2.00 .75
❑ 287 M.Abarbanel RC/C.Carlos RC 2.00 .75
❑ 288 Dave Wickersham 2.00 .75
❑ 289 Woody Held 2.00 .75
❑ 290 Willie McCovey 12.00 6.00
❑ 291 Dick Lines 2.00 .75
❑ 292 Art Shamsky 2.00 .75
❑ 293 Bruce Howard 2.00 .75
❑ 294 Red Schoendienst MG 6.00 3.00
❑ 295 Sonny Siebert 2.00 .75
❑ 296 Byron Browne 2.00 .75
❑ 297 Russ Gibson 2.00 .75
❑ 298 Jim Brewer 2.00 .75
❑ 299 Gene Michael 4.00 1.50
❑ 300 Rusty Staub 4.00 1.50
❑ 301 G.Mitterwald RC/R.Renick RC 2.00 .75
❑ 302 Gerry Arrigo 2.00 .75
❑ 303 Dick Green 4.00 1.50
❑ 304 Sandy Valdespino 2.00 .75
❑ 305 Minnie Rojas 2.00 .75
❑ 306 Mike Ryan 2.00 .75
❑ 307 John Hiller 4.00 1.50
❑ 308 Pittsburgh Pirates TC 4.00 1.50
❑ 309 Ken Henderson 2.00 .75
❑ 310 Luis Aparicio 8.00 4.00
❑ 311 Jack Lamabe 2.00 .75
❑ 312 Curt Blefary 2.00 .75
❑ 313 Al Weis 2.00 .75
❑ 314 B.Rohr/G.Spriggs 2.00 .75

315	Zoilo Versalles	2.00	.75
316	Steve Barber	2.00	.75
317	Ron Brand	2.00	.75
318	Chico Salmon	2.00	.75
319	George Culver	2.00	.75
320	Frank Howard	4.00	1.50
321	Leo Durocher MG	6.00	3.00
322	Dave Boswell	2.00	.75
323	Deron Johnson	4.00	1.50
324	Jim Nash	2.00	.75
325	Manny Mota	4.00	1.50
326	Dennis Ribant	2.00	.75
327	Tony Taylor	4.00	1.50
328	C.Vinson RC/J.Weaver RC	2.00	.75
329	Duane Josephson	2.00	.75
330	Roger Maris	50.00	30.00
331	Dan Osinski	2.00	.75
332	Doug Rader	4.00	1.50
333	Ron Herbel	2.00	.75
334	Baltimore Orioles TC	4.00	1.50
335	Bob Allison	4.00	1.50
336	John Purdin	2.00	.75
337	Bill Robinson	4.00	1.50
338	Bob Johnson	2.00	.75
339	Rich Nye	2.00	.75
340	Max Alvis	2.00	.75
341	Jim Lemon MG	2.00	.75
342	Ken Johnson	2.00	.75
343	Jim Gosger	2.00	.75
344	Donn Clendenon	4.00	1.50
345	Bob Hendley	2.00	.75
346	Jerry Adair	2.00	.75
347	George Brunet	2.00	.75
348	L.Colton RC/D.Thoenen RC	2.00	.75
349	Ed Spiezio	4.00	1.50
350	Hoyt Wilhelm	8.00	4.00
351	Bob Barton	2.00	.75
352	Jackie Hernandez RC	2.00	.75
353	Mack Jones	2.00	.75
354	Pete Richert	2.00	.75
355	Ernie Banks	25.00	12.50
356A	Checklist 5/Holtzman Center	6.00	3.00
356B	Checklist 5/Holtzman Right	6.00	3.00
357	Len Gabrielson	2.00	.75
358	Mike Epstein	2.00	.75
359	Joe Moeller	2.00	.75
360	Willie Horton	6.00	3.00
361	Harmon Killebrew AS	8.00	4.00
362	Orlando Cepeda AS	6.00	3.00
363	Rod Carew AS	8.00	4.00
364	Joe Morgan AS	8.00	4.00
365	Brooks Robinson AS	8.00	4.00
366	Ron Santo AS	6.00	3.00
367	Jim Fregosi AS	4.00	1.50
368	Gene Alley AS	4.00	1.50
369	Carl Yastrzemski AS	10.00	5.00
370	Hank Aaron AS	20.00	10.00
371	Tony Oliva AS	6.00	3.00
372	Lou Brock AS	8.00	4.00
373	Frank Robinson AS	8.00	4.00
374	Roberto Clemente AS	30.00	15.00
375	Bill Freehan AS	4.00	1.50
376	Tim McCarver AS	4.00	1.50
377	Joel Horlen AS	4.00	1.50
378	Bob Gibson AS	8.00	4.00
379	Gary Peters AS	4.00	1.50
380	Ken Holtzman AS	4.00	1.50
381	Boog Powell	4.00	1.50
382	Ramon Hernandez	2.00	.75
383	Steve Whitaker	2.00	.75
384	B.Henry/H.McRae RC	6.00	3.00
385	Jim Hunter	10.00	5.00
386	Greg Goossen	2.00	.75
387	Joe Foy	2.00	.75
388	Ray Washburn	2.00	.75
389	Jay Johnstone	4.00	1.50
390	Bill Mazeroski	8.00	4.00
391	Bob Priddy	2.00	.75
392	Grady Hatton MG	2.00	.75
393	Jim Perry	4.00	1.50
394	Tommie Aaron	6.00	3.00
395	Camilo Pascual	4.00	1.50
396	Bobby Wine	2.00	.75
397	Vic Davalillo	2.00	.75
398	Jim Grant	2.00	.75
399	Ray Oyler	4.00	1.50
400A	Mike McCormick YT	4.00	1.50
400B	M.McCormick White Tm	150.00	90.00
401	Mets Team	4.00	1.50
402	Mike Hegan	4.00	1.50
403	John Buzhardt	2.00	.75
404	Floyd Robinson	2.00	.75
405	Tommy Helms	4.00	1.50
406	Dick Ellsworth	2.00	.75
407	Gary Kolb	2.00	.75
408	Steve Carlton	30.00	15.00
409	F.Peters RC/R.Stone	2.00	.75
410	Ferguson Jenkins	10.00	5.00
411	Ron Hansen	2.00	.75
412	Clay Carroll	4.00	1.50
413	Tom McCraw	2.00	.75
414	Mickey Lolich	8.00	4.00
415	Johnny Callison	4.00	1.50
416	Bill Rigney MG	2.00	.75
417	Willie Crawford	2.00	.75
418	Eddie Fisher	2.00	.75
419	Jack Hiatt	2.00	.75
420	Cesar Tovar	2.00	.75
421	Ron Taylor	2.00	.75
422	Rene Lachemann	2.00	.75
423	Fred Gladding	2.00	.75
424	Chicago White Sox TC	4.00	1.50
425	Jim Maloney	4.00	1.50
426	Hank Allen	2.00	.75
427	Dick Calmus	2.00	.75
428	Vic Roznovsky	2.00	.75
429	Tommie Sisk	2.00	.75
430	Rico Petrocelli	4.00	1.50
431	Dooley Womack	2.00	.75
432	B.Davis/J.Vidal	2.00	.75
433	Bob Rodgers	2.00	.75
434	Ricardo Joseph RC	2.00	.75
435	Ron Perranoski	4.00	1.50
436	Hal Lanier	2.00	.75
437	Don Cardwell	2.00	.75
438	Lee Thomas	4.00	1.50
439	Lum Harris MG	2.00	.75
440	Claude Osteen	4.00	1.50
441	Alex Johnson	4.00	1.50
442	Dick Bosman	2.00	.75
443	Joe Azcue	2.00	.75
444	Jack Fisher	2.00	.75
445	Mike Shannon	4.00	1.50
446	Ron Kline	2.00	.75
447	G.Korince/F.Lasher RC	4.00	1.50
448	Gary Wagner	2.00	.75
449	Gene Oliver	2.00	.75
450	Jim Kaat	6.00	3.00
451	Al Spangler	2.00	.75
452	Jesus Alou	2.00	.75
453	Sammy Ellis	2.00	.75
454A	Checklist 6/F.Rob Complete	8.00	4.00
454B	Checklist 6/F.Rob Partial	8.00	4.00
455	Rico Carty	4.00	1.50
456	John O'Donoghue	2.00	.75
457	Jim Lefebvre	4.00	1.50
458	Lew Krausse	6.00	3.00
459	Dick Simpson	4.00	1.50
460	Jim Lonborg	6.00	3.00
461	Chuck Hiller	4.00	1.50
462	Barry Moore	4.00	1.50
463	Jim Schaffer	4.00	1.50
464	Don McMahon	4.00	1.50
465	Tommie Agee	10.00	5.00
466	Bill Dillman	4.00	1.50
467	Dick Howser	10.00	5.00
468	Larry Sherry	4.00	1.50
469	Ty Cline	4.00	1.50
470	Bill Freehan	10.00	5.00
471	Orlando Pena	4.00	1.50
472	Walter Alston MG	6.00	3.00
473	Al Worthington	4.00	1.50
474	Paul Schaal	4.00	1.50
475	Joe Niekro	6.00	3.00
476	Woody Woodward	4.00	1.50
477	Philadelphia Phillies TC	8.00	4.00
478	Dave McNally	6.00	3.00
479	Phil Gagliano	6.00	3.00
480	Oliva/Chico/Clemente	80.00	50.00
481	John Wyatt	4.00	1.50
482	Jose Pagan	4.00	1.50
483	Darold Knowles	4.00	1.50
484	Phil Roof	4.00	1.50
485	Ken Berry	6.00	3.00
486	Cal Koonce	4.00	1.50
487	Lee May	10.00	5.00
488	Dick Tracewski	6.00	3.00
489	Wally Bunker	4.00	1.50
490	Kill/Mays/Mantle	150.00	90.00
491	Denny Lemaster	4.00	1.50
492	Jeff Torborg	6.00	3.00
493	Jim McGlothlin	4.00	1.50
494	Ray Sadecki	4.00	1.50
495	Leon Wagner	4.00	1.50
496	Steve Hamilton	6.00	3.00
497	St. Louis Cardinals TC	8.00	4.00
498	Bill Bryan	6.00	3.00
499	Steve Blass	6.00	3.00
500	Frank Robinson	30.00	15.00
501	John Odom	6.00	3.00
502	Mike Andrews	4.00	1.50
503	Al Jackson	6.00	3.00
504	Russ Snyder	4.00	1.50
505	Joe Sparma	10.00	5.00
506	Clarence Jones RC	4.00	1.50
507	Wade Blasingame	4.00	1.50
508	Duke Sims	4.00	1.50
509	Dennis Higgins	4.00	1.50
510	Ron Fairly	10.00	5.00
511	Bill Kelso	4.00	1.50
512	Grant Jackson	4.00	1.50
513	Hank Bauer MG	6.00	3.00
514	Al McBean	4.00	1.50
515	Russ Nixon	4.00	1.50
516	Pete Mikkelsen	4.00	1.50
517	Diego Segui	6.00	3.00
518A	Checklist 7/Boyer ERR	12.00	6.00
518B	Checklist 7/Boyer COR	12.00	6.00
519	Jerry Stephenson	4.00	1.50
520	Lou Brock	25.00	12.50
521	Don Shaw	4.00	1.50
522	Wayne Causey	4.00	1.50
523	John Tsitouris	4.00	1.50
524	Andy Kosco	6.00	3.00
525	Jim Davenport	4.00	1.50
526	Bill Denehy	4.00	1.50
527	Tito Francona	4.00	1.50
528	Detroit Tigers TC	60.00	35.00
529	Bruce Von Hoff RC	4.00	1.50
530	B.Robinson/F.Robinson	40.00	20.00
531	Chuck Hinton	4.00	1.50
532	Luis Tiant	6.00	3.00
533	Wes Parker	6.00	3.00
534	Bob Miller	6.00	3.00
535	Danny Cater	6.00	3.00
536	Bill Short	4.00	1.50
537	Norm Siebern	6.00	3.00
538	Manny Jimenez	6.00	3.00
539	J.Ray RC/M.Ferraro RC	4.00	1.50
540	Nelson Briles	6.00	3.00
541	Sandy Alomar	6.00	3.00
542	John Boccabella	4.00	1.50
543	Bob Lee	4.00	1.50
544	Mayo Smith MG	12.00	6.00
545	Lindy McDaniel	6.00	3.00
546	Roy White	6.00	3.00
547	Dan Coombs	4.00	1.50
548	Bernie Allen	4.00	1.50
549	C.Motton RC/R.Nelson RC	4.00	1.50
550	Clete Boyer	6.00	3.00
551	Darrell Sutherland	4.00	1.50
552	Ed Kirkpatrick	4.00	1.50
553	Hank Aguirre	4.00	1.50
554	Oakland Athletics TC	10.00	5.00
555	Jose Tartabull	6.00	3.00
556	Dick Selma	4.00	1.50
557	Frank Quilici	6.00	3.00
558	Johnny Edwards	4.00	1.50
559	C.Taylor RC/L.Walker	4.00	1.50
560	Paul Casanova	4.00	1.50
561	Lee Elia	4.00	1.50
562	Jim Bouton	6.00	3.00
563	Ed Charles	4.00	1.50
564	Eddie Stanky MG	6.00	3.00
565	Larry Dierker	6.00	3.00
566	Ken Harrelson	6.00	3.00
567	Clay Dalrymple	4.00	1.50
568	Willie Smith	4.00	1.50

❑ 569 I.Murrell RC/L.Rohr RC 4.00 1.50
❑ 570 Rick Reichardt 4.00 1.50
❑ 571 Tony LaRussa 12.00 6.00
❑ 572 Don Bosch RC 4.00 1.50
❑ 573 Joe Coleman 4.00 1.50
❑ 574 Cincinnati Reds TC 10.00 5.00
❑ 575 Jim Palmer 40.00 20.00
❑ 576 Dave Adlesh 4.00 1.50
❑ 577 Fred Talbot 4.00 1.50
❑ 578 Orlando Martinez 4.00 1.50
❑ 579 L.Hisle RC/M.Lum RC 10.00 5.00
❑ 580 Bob Bailey 4.00 1.50
❑ 581 Garry Roggenburk 4.00 1.50
❑ 582 Jerry Grote 10.00 5.00
❑ 583 Gates Brown 10.00 5.00
❑ 584 Larry Shepard MG RC 4.00 1.50
❑ 585 Wilbur Wood 6.00 3.00
❑ 586 Jim Pagliaroni 6.00 3.00
❑ 587 Roger Repoz 4.00 1.50
❑ 588 Dick Schofield 4.00 1.50
❑ 589 R.Clark/M.Ogier RC 4.00 1.50
❑ 590 Tommy Harper 6.00 3.00
❑ 591 Dick Nen 4.00 1.50
❑ 592 John Bateman 4.00 1.50
❑ 593 Lee Stange 4.00 1.50
❑ 594 Phil Linz 6.00 3.00
❑ 595 Phil Ortega 4.00 1.50
❑ 596 Charlie Smith 4.00 1.50
❑ 597 Bill McCool 4.00 1.50
❑ 598 Jerry May 6.00 3.00

1969 Topps

❑ COMP. MASTER SET (695) 5000.00 2500.00
❑ COMPLETE SET (664) 2800.00 1700.00
❑ COMMON (1-218/328-512) 1.50 .60
❑ COMMON CARD (219-327) 2.50 1.00
❑ COMMON CARD (513-588) 2.00 .75
❑ COMMON CARD (589-664) 3.00 1.25
❑ WRAPPER (5-CENT) 20.00 15.00
❑ 1 Yaz/Cater/Oliva LL 15.00 7.50
❑ 2 Rose/Alou/Alou LL 8.00 4.00
❑ 3 Harrelson/Howard/North LL 4.00 1.50
❑ 4 McCovey/Santo/B.Will LL 6.00 3.00
❑ 5 Howard/Horton/Harrelson LL 4.00 1.50
❑ 6 McCovey/Allen/Banks LL 6.00 3.00
❑ 7 Tiant/McDow/McNally LL 4.00 1.50
❑ 8 Gibson/Bolin/Veale LL 6.00 3.00
❑ 9 McLain/McNal/Tiant/Stott LL 4.00 1.50
❑ 10 Marichal/Gibson/Jenkins LL 8.00 4.00
❑ 11 McDowell/McLain/Tiant LL 4.00 1.50
❑ 12 Gibson/Jenkins/Singer LL 4.00 1.50
❑ 13 Mickey Stanley 2.50 1.00
❑ 14 Al McBean 1.50 .60
❑ 15 Boog Powell 4.00 1.50
❑ 16 C.Gutierrez RC/R.Robertson RC 1.50 .60
❑ 17 Mike Marshall 2.50 1.00
❑ 18 Dick Schofield 1.50 .60
❑ 19 Ken Suarez 1.50 .60
❑ 20 Ernie Banks 20.00 10.00
❑ 21 Jose Santiago 1.50 .60
❑ 22 Jesus Alou 2.50 1.00
❑ 23 Lew Krausse 1.50 .60
❑ 24 Walt Alston MG 4.00 1.50
❑ 25 Roy White 2.50 1.00
❑ 26 Clay Carroll 2.50 1.00
❑ 27 Bernie Allen 1.50 .60
❑ 28 Mike Ryan 1.50 .60
❑ 29 Dave Morehead 1.50 .60
❑ 30 Bob Allison 2.50 1.00
❑ 31 G.Gentry RC/A.Otis RC 2.50 1.00
❑ 32 Sammy Ellis 1.50 .60
❑ 33 Wayne Causey 1.50 .60
❑ 34 Gary Peters 1.50 .60
❑ 35 Joe Morgan 10.00 5.00
❑ 36 Luke Walker 1.50 .60
❑ 37 Curt Motton 1.50 .60
❑ 38 Zoilo Versalles 2.50 1.00
❑ 39 Dick Hughes 1.50 .60
❑ 40 Mayo Smith MG 1.50 .60
❑ 41 Bob Barton 1.50 .60
❑ 42 Tommy Harper 2.50 1.00
❑ 43 Joe Niekro 2.50 1.00
❑ 44 Danny Cater 1.50 .60
❑ 45 Maury Wills 2.50 1.00
❑ 46 Fritz Peterson 2.50 1.00
❑ 47A P.Popovich Thick Airbrush 2.50 1.00
❑ 47B P.Popovich Light Airbrush 2.50 1.00
❑ 47C P.Popovich C on Helmet 25.00 12.50
❑ 48 Brant Alyea 1.50 .60
❑ 49A S.Jones/E.Rodriguez ERR 25.00 12.50
❑ 49B S.Jones RC/E.Rodriguez RC 1.50 .60
❑ 50 Roberto Clemente UER 60.00 35.00
❑ 51 Woody Fryman 2.50 1.00
❑ 52 Mike Andrews 1.50 .60
❑ 53 Sonny Jackson 1.50 .60
❑ 54 Cisco Carlos 1.50 .60
❑ 55 Jerry Grote 2.50 1.00
❑ 56 Rich Reese 1.50 .60
❑ 57 Checklist 1/McLain 6.00 3.00
❑ 58 Fred Gladding 1.50 .60
❑ 59 Jay Johnstone 2.50 1.00
❑ 60 Nelson Briles 2.50 1.00
❑ 61 Jimmie Hall 1.50 .60
❑ 62 Chico Salmon 1.50 .60
❑ 63 Jim Hickman 2.50 1.00
❑ 64 Bill Monbouquette 1.50 .60
❑ 65 Willie Davis 2.50 1.00
❑ 66 M.Adamson RC/M.Rettenmund RC 1.50 .60
❑ 67 Bill Stoneman 2.50 1.00
❑ 68 Dave Duncan 2.50 1.00
❑ 69 Steve Hamilton 2.50 1.00
❑ 70 Tommy Helms 2.50 1.00
❑ 71 Steve Whitaker 2.50 1.00
❑ 72 Ron Taylor 1.50 .60
❑ 73 Johnny Briggs 1.50 .60
❑ 74 Preston Gomez MG 2.50 1.00
❑ 75 Luis Aparicio 6.00 3.00
❑ 76 Norm Miller 1.50 .60
❑ 77A R.Perranoski No LA 2.50 1.00
❑ 77B R.Perranoski LA Cap 25.00 12.50
❑ 78 Tom Satriano 1.50 .60
❑ 79 Milt Pappas 2.50 1.00
❑ 80 Norm Cash 2.50 1.00
❑ 81 Mel Queen 1.50 .60
❑ 82 R.Hebner RC/A.Oliver RC 8.00 4.00
❑ 83 Mike Ferraro 2.50 1.00
❑ 84 Bob Humphreys 1.50 .60
❑ 85 Lou Brock 20.00 10.00
❑ 86 Pete Richert 1.50 .60
❑ 87 Horace Clarke 2.50 1.00
❑ 88 Rich Nye 1.50 .60
❑ 89 Russ Gibson 1.50 .60
❑ 90 Jerry Koosman 2.50 1.00
❑ 91 Alvin Dark MG 2.50 1.00
❑ 92 Jack Billingham 2.50 1.00
❑ 93 Joe Foy 2.50 1.00
❑ 94 Hank Aguirre 1.50 .60
❑ 95 Johnny Bench 50.00 30.00
❑ 96 Denny Lemaster 1.50 .60
❑ 97 Buddy Bradford 1.50 .60
❑ 98 Dave Giusti 1.50 .60
❑ 99A D.Morris RC/G.Nettles RC 15.00 7.50
❑ 99B D.Morris/G.Nettles ERR 15.00 7.50
❑ 100 Hank Aaron 50.00 30.00
❑ 101 Daryl Patterson 1.50 .60
❑ 102 Jim Davenport 1.50 .60
❑ 103 Roger Repoz 1.50 .60
❑ 104 Steve Blass 1.50 .60
❑ 105 Rick Monday 2.50 1.00
❑ 106 Jim Hannan 1.50 .60
❑ 107A Checklist 2/Gibson ERR 6.00 3.00
❑ 107B Checklist 2/Gibson COR 8.00 4.00
❑ 108 Tony Taylor 2.50 1.00
❑ 109 Jim Lonborg 2.50 1.00
❑ 110 Mike Shannon 2.50 1.00
❑ 111 John Morris RC 1.50 .60
❑ 112 J.C. Martin 2.50 1.00
❑ 113 Dave May 1.50 .60
❑ 114 A.Closter/J.Cumberland RC 2.50 1.00
❑ 115 Bill Hands 1.50 .60
❑ 116 Chuck Harrison 1.50 .60
❑ 117 Jim Fairey 2.50 1.00
❑ 118 Stan Williams 1.50 .60
❑ 119 Doug Rader 2.50 1.00
❑ 120 Pete Rose 50.00 30.00
❑ 121 Joe Grzenda RC 1.50 .60
❑ 122 Ron Fairly 2.50 1.00
❑ 123 Wilbur Wood 2.50 1.00
❑ 124 Hank Bauer MG 2.50 1.00
❑ 125 Ray Sadecki 1.50 .60
❑ 126 Dick Tracewski 1.50 .60
❑ 127 Kevin Collins 2.50 1.00
❑ 128 Tommie Aaron 2.50 1.00
❑ 129 Bill McCool 1.50 .60
❑ 130 Carl Yastrzemski 20.00 10.00
❑ 131 Chris Cannizzaro 1.50 .60
❑ 132 Dave Baldwin 1.50 .60
❑ 133 Johnny Callison 2.50 1.00
❑ 134 Jim Weaver 1.50 .60
❑ 135 Tommy Davis 2.50 1.00
❑ 136 S.Huntz RC/M.Torrez 1.50 .60
❑ 137 Wally Bunker 1.50 .60
❑ 138 John Bateman 1.50 .60
❑ 139 Andy Kosco 1.50 .60
❑ 140 Jim Lefebvre 2.50 1.00
❑ 141 Bill Dillman 1.50 .60
❑ 142 Woody Woodward 1.50 .60
❑ 143 Joe Nossek 1.50 .60
❑ 144 Bob Hendley 2.50 1.00
❑ 145 Max Alvis 1.50 .60
❑ 146 Jim Perry 2.50 1.00
❑ 147 Leo Durocher MG 4.00 1.50
❑ 148 Lee Stange 1.50 .60
❑ 149 Ollie Brown 2.50 1.00
❑ 150 Denny McLain 4.00 1.50
❑ 151A C.Dalrymple Portrait 1.50 .60
❑ 151B C.Dalrymple Catch 15.00 7.50
❑ 152 Tommie Sisk 1.50 .60
❑ 153 Ed Brinkman 1.50 .60
❑ 154 Jim Britton 1.50 .60
❑ 155 Pete Ward 1.50 .60
❑ 156 H.Gilson/L.McFadden RC 1.50 .60
❑ 157 Bob Rodgers 2.50 1.00
❑ 158 Joe Gibbon 1.50 .60
❑ 159 Jerry Adair 1.50 .60
❑ 160 Vada Pinson 2.50 1.00
❑ 161 John Purdin 1.50 .60
❑ 162 Bob Gibson WS1 8.00 4.00
❑ 163 Willie Horton WS2 6.00 3.00
❑ 164 T.McCarv w/Maris WS3 12.00 6.00
❑ 165 Lou Brock WS4 8.00 4.00
❑ 166 Al Kaline WS5 8.00 4.00
❑ 167 Jim Northrup WS6 6.00 3.00
❑ 168 M.Lolich/B.Gibson WS7 8.00 4.00
❑ 169 Tigers Celebrate WS 6.00 3.00
❑ 170 Frank Howard 2.50 1.00
❑ 171 Glenn Beckert 2.50 1.00
❑ 172 Jerry Stephenson 1.50 .60
❑ 173 B.Christian RC/G.Nyman RC 1.50 .60
❑ 174 Grant Jackson 1.50 .60
❑ 175 Jim Bunning 6.00 3.00
❑ 176 Joe Azcue 1.50 .60
❑ 177 Ron Reed 1.50 .60
❑ 178 Ray Oyler 2.50 1.00
❑ 179 Don Pavletich 1.50 .60
❑ 180 Willie Horton 2.50 1.00
❑ 181 Mel Nelson 1.50 .60
❑ 182 Bill Rigney MG 1.50 .60
❑ 183 Don Shaw 2.50 1.00
❑ 184 Roberto Pena 1.50 .60
❑ 185 Tom Phoebus 1.50 .60
❑ 186 Johnny Edwards 1.50 .60
❑ 187 Leon Wagner 1.50 .60
❑ 188 Rick Wise 2.50 1.00
❑ 189 J.Lahoud RC/J.Thibodeau RC 1.50 .60
❑ 190 Willie Mays 80.00 50.00
❑ 191 Lindy McDaniel 2.50 1.00
❑ 192 Jose Pagan 1.50 .60
❑ 193 Don Cardwell 2.50 1.00
❑ 194 Ted Uhlaender 1.50 .60

❑	195	John Odom	1.50	.60
❑	196	Lum Harris MG	1.50	.60
❑	197	Dick Selma	1.50	.60
❑	198	Willie Smith	1.50	.60
❑	199	Jim French	1.50	.60
❑	200	Bob Gibson	12.00	6.00
❑	201	Russ Snyder	1.50	.60
❑	202	Don Wilson	2.50	1.00
❑	203	Dave Johnson	2.50	1.00
❑	204	Jack Hiatt	1.50	.60
❑	205	Rick Reichardt	1.50	.60
❑	206	L.Hisle/B.Lersch RC	2.50	1.00
❑	207	Roy Face	2.50	1.00
❑	208A	D.Clendenon Houston	2.50	1.00
❑	208B	D.Clendenon Expos	15.00	7.50
❑	209	Larry Haney UER	1.50	.60
❑	210	Felix Millan	1.50	.60
❑	211	Galen Cisco	1.50	.60
❑	212	Tom Tresh	2.50	1.00
❑	213	Gerry Arrigo	1.50	.60
❑	214	Checklist 3	6.00	3.00
❑	215	Rico Petrocelli	2.50	1.00
❑	216	Don Sutton DP	6.00	3.00
❑	217	John Donaldson	1.50	.60
❑	218	John Roseboro	2.50	1.00
❑	219	Fred Patek RC	4.00	1.50
❑	220	Sam McDowell	4.00	1.50
❑	221	Art Shamsky	4.00	1.50
❑	222	Duane Josephson	2.50	1.00
❑	223	Tom Dukes	4.00	1.50
❑	224	B.Harrelson RC/S.Kealey RC	2.50	1.00
❑	225	Don Kessinger	4.00	1.50
❑	226	Bruce Howard	2.50	1.00
❑	227	Frank Johnson RC	2.50	1.00
❑	228	Dave Leonhard	2.50	1.00
❑	229	Don Lock	2.50	1.00
❑	230	Rusty Staub UER	4.00	1.50
❑	231	Pat Dobson	4.00	1.50
❑	232	Dave Ricketts	2.50	1.00
❑	233	Steve Barber	4.00	1.50
❑	234	Dave Bristol MG	2.50	1.00
❑	235	Jim Hunter	10.00	5.00
❑	236	Manny Mota	4.00	1.50
❑	237	Bobby Cox RC	10.00	5.00
❑	238	Ken Johnson	2.50	1.00
❑	239	Bob Taylor	4.00	1.50
❑	240	Ken Harrelson	4.00	1.50
❑	241	Jim Brewer	2.50	1.00
❑	242	Frank Kostro	2.50	1.00
❑	243	Ron Kline	2.50	1.00
❑	244	R.Fosse RC/G.Woodson RC	4.00	1.50
❑	245	Ed Charles	4.00	1.50
❑	246	Joe Coleman	2.50	1.00
❑	247	Gene Oliver	2.50	1.00
❑	248	Bob Priddy	2.50	1.00
❑	249	Ed Spiezio	4.00	1.50
❑	250	Frank Robinson	20.00	10.00
❑	251	Ron Herbel	2.50	1.00
❑	252	Chuck Cottier	2.50	1.00
❑	253	Jerry Johnson RC	2.50	1.00
❑	254	Joe Schultz MG RC	4.00	1.50
❑	255	Steve Carlton	30.00	15.00
❑	256	Gates Brown	4.00	1.50
❑	257	Jim Ray	2.50	1.00
❑	258	Jackie Hernandez	4.00	1.50
❑	259	Bill Short	2.50	1.00
❑	260	Reggie Jackson RC	300.00	175.00
❑	261	Bob Johnson	2.50	1.00
❑	262	Mike Kekich	4.00	1.50
❑	263	Jerry May	2.50	1.00
❑	264	Bill Landis	2.50	1.00
❑	265	Chico Cardenas	4.00	1.50
❑	266	T.Hutton/A.Foster RC	4.00	1.50
❑	267	Vicente Romo RC	2.50	1.00
❑	268	Al Spangler	2.50	1.00
❑	269	Al Weis	4.00	1.50
❑	270	Mickey Lolich	4.00	1.50
❑	271	Larry Stahl	4.00	1.50
❑	272	Ed Stroud	2.50	1.00
❑	273	Ron Willis	2.50	1.00
❑	274	Clyde King MG	2.50	1.00
❑	275	Vic Davalillo	2.50	1.00
❑	276	Gary Wagner	2.50	1.00
❑	277	Elrod Hendricks RC	2.50	1.00
❑	278	Gary Geiger UER	2.50	1.00
❑	279	Roger Nelson	4.00	1.50
❑	280	Alex Johnson	4.00	1.50
❑	281	Ted Kubiak	2.50	1.00
❑	282	Pat Jarvis	2.50	1.00
❑	283	Sandy Alomar	4.00	1.50
❑	284	J.Robertson RC/M.Wegener RC	4.00	1.50
❑	285	Don Mincher	4.00	1.50
❑	286	Dock Ellis RC	4.00	1.50
❑	287	Jose Tartabull	4.00	1.50
❑	288	Ken Holtzman	4.00	1.50
❑	289	Bart Shirley	2.50	1.00
❑	290	Jim Kaat	4.00	1.50
❑	291	Vern Fuller	2.50	1.00
❑	292	Al Downing	4.00	1.50
❑	293	Dick Dietz	2.50	1.00
❑	294	Jim Lemon MG	2.50	1.00
❑	295	Tony Perez	12.00	6.00
❑	296	Andy Messersmith RC	4.00	1.50
❑	297	Deron Johnson	2.50	1.00
❑	298	Dave Nicholson	4.00	1.50
❑	299	Mark Belanger	4.00	1.50
❑	300	Felipe Alou	4.00	1.50
❑	301	Darrell Brandon	4.00	1.50
❑	302	Jim Pagliaroni	2.50	1.00
❑	303	Cal Koonce	4.00	1.50
❑	304	B.Davis/C.Gaston RC	6.00	3.00
❑	305	Dick McAuliffe	4.00	1.50
❑	306	Jim Grant	4.00	1.50
❑	307	Gary Kolb	2.50	1.00
❑	308	Wade Blasingame	2.50	1.00
❑	309	Walt Williams	2.50	1.00
❑	310	Tom Haller	2.50	1.00
❑	311	Sparky Lyle RC	10.00	5.00
❑	312	Lee Elia	2.50	1.00
❑	313	Bill Robinson	4.00	1.50
❑	314	Checklist 4/Drysdale	6.00	3.00
❑	315	Eddie Fisher	2.50	1.00
❑	316	Hal Lanier	2.50	1.00
❑	317	Bruce Look RC	2.50	1.00
❑	318	Jack Fisher	2.50	1.00
❑	319	Ken McMullen UER	2.50	1.00
❑	320	Dal Maxvill	2.50	1.00
❑	321	Jim McAndrew RC	4.00	1.50
❑	322	Jose Vidal	4.00	1.50
❑	323	Larry Miller	2.50	1.00
❑	324	L.Cain RC/D.Campbell RC	4.00	1.50
❑	325	Jose Cardenal	4.00	1.50
❑	326	Gary Sutherland	4.00	1.50
❑	327	Willie Crawford	2.50	1.00
❑	328	Joel Horlen	1.50	.60
❑	329	Rick Joseph	1.50	.60
❑	330	Tony Conigliaro	4.00	1.50
❑	331	G.Garrido/T.House RC	2.50	1.00
❑	332	Fred Talbot	1.50	.60
❑	333	Ivan Murrell	1.50	.60
❑	334	Phil Roof	1.50	.60
❑	335	Bill Mazeroski	6.00	3.00
❑	336	Jim Roland	1.50	.60
❑	337	Marty Martinez RC	1.50	.60
❑	338	Del Unser RC	1.50	.60
❑	339	S.Mingori RC/J.Pena RC	1.50	.60
❑	340	Dave McNally	2.50	1.00
❑	341	Dave Adlesh	1.50	.60
❑	342	Bubba Morton	1.50	.60
❑	343	Dan Frisella	1.50	.60
❑	344	Tom Matchick	1.50	.60
❑	345	Frank Linzy	1.50	.60
❑	346	Wayne Comer RC	1.50	.60
❑	347	Randy Hundley	2.50	1.00
❑	348	Steve Hargan	1.50	.60
❑	349	Dick Williams MG	2.50	1.00
❑	350	Richie Allen	4.00	1.50
❑	351	Carroll Sembera	1.50	.60
❑	352	Paul Schaal	2.50	1.00
❑	353	Jeff Torborg	2.50	1.00
❑	354	Nate Oliver	1.50	.60
❑	355	Phil Niekro	6.00	3.00
❑	356	Frank Quilici	1.50	.60
❑	357	Carl Taylor	1.50	.60
❑	358	G.Lauzerique RC/R.Rodriguez	1.50	.60
❑	359	Dick Kelley	1.50	.60
❑	360	Jim Wynn	2.50	1.00
❑	361	Gary Holman RC	1.50	.60
❑	362	Jim Maloney	2.50	1.00
❑	363	Russ Nixon	1.50	.60
❑	364	Tommie Agee	4.00	1.50
❑	365	Jim Fregosi	2.50	1.00
❑	366	Bo Belinsky	2.50	1.00
❑	367	Lou Johnson	2.50	1.00
❑	368	Vic Roznovsky	1.50	.60
❑	369	Bob Skinner MG	2.50	1.00
❑	370	Juan Marichal	8.00	4.00
❑	371	Sal Bando	2.50	1.00
❑	372	Adolfo Phillips	1.50	.60
❑	373	Fred Lasher	1.50	.60
❑	374	Bob Tillman	1.50	.60
❑	375	Harmon Killebrew	15.00	7.50
❑	376	M.Fiore RC/J.Rooker RC	1.50	.60
❑	377	Gary Bell	2.50	1.00
❑	378	Jose Herrera RC	1.50	.60
❑	379	Ken Boyer	2.50	1.00
❑	380	Stan Bahnsen	2.50	1.00
❑	381	Ed Kranepool	2.50	1.00
❑	382	Pat Corrales	2.50	1.00
❑	383	Casey Cox	1.50	.60
❑	384	Larry Shepard MG	1.50	.60
❑	385	Orlando Cepeda	6.00	3.00
❑	386	Jim McGlothlin	1.50	.60
❑	387	Bobby Klaus	1.50	.60
❑	388	Tom McCraw	1.50	.60
❑	389	Dan Coombs	1.50	.60
❑	390	Bill Freehan	2.50	1.00
❑	391	Ray Culp	1.50	.60
❑	392	Bob Burda RC	1.50	.60
❑	393	Gene Brabender	2.50	1.00
❑	394	L.Piniella/M.Staehle	6.00	3.00
❑	395	Chris Short	1.50	.60
❑	396	Jim Campanis	1.50	.60
❑	397	Chuck Dobson	1.50	.60
❑	398	Tito Francona	1.50	.60
❑	399	Bob Bailey	2.50	1.00
❑	400	Don Drysdale	15.00	7.50
❑	401	Jake Gibbs	2.50	1.00
❑	402	Ken Boswell RC	2.50	1.00
❑	403	Bob Miller	1.50	.60
❑	404	V.LaRose RC/G.Ross RC	2.50	1.00
❑	405	Lee May	2.50	1.00
❑	406	Phil Ortega	1.50	.60
❑	407	Tom Egan	1.50	.60
❑	408	Nate Colbert	1.50	.60
❑	409	Bob Moose	1.50	.60
❑	410	Al Kaline	25.00	12.50
❑	411	Larry Dierker	2.50	1.00
❑	412	Checklist 5/Mantle DP	15.00	7.50
❑	413	Roland Sheldon	2.50	1.00
❑	414	Duke Sims	1.50	.60
❑	415	Ray Washburn	1.50	.60
❑	416	Willie McCovey AS	8.00	4.00
❑	417	Ken Harrelson AS	3.00	1.25
❑	418	Tommy Helms AS	3.00	1.25
❑	419	Rod Carew AS	10.00	5.00
❑	420	Ron Santo AS	4.00	1.50
❑	421	Brooks Robinson AS	8.00	4.00
❑	422	Don Kessinger AS	3.00	1.25
❑	423	Bert Campaneris AS	4.00	1.50
❑	424	Pete Rose AS	15.00	7.50
❑	425	Carl Yastrzemski AS	10.00	5.00
❑	426	Curt Flood AS	4.00	1.50
❑	427	Tony Oliva AS	4.00	1.50
❑	428	Lou Brock AS	6.00	3.00
❑	429	Willie Horton AS	3.00	1.25
❑	430	Johnny Bench AS	10.00	5.00
❑	431	Bill Freehan AS	4.00	1.50
❑	432	Bob Gibson AS	6.00	3.00
❑	433	Denny McLain AS	3.00	1.25
❑	434	Jerry Koosman AS	3.00	1.25
❑	435	Sam McDowell AS	2.50	1.00
❑	436	Gene Alley	2.50	1.00
❑	437	Luis Alcaraz RC	1.50	.60
❑	438	Gary Waslewski RC	1.50	.60
❑	439	E.Herrmann RC/D.Lazar RC	1.50	.60
❑	440A	Willie McCovey	15.00	7.50
❑	440B	Willie McCovey WL	100.00	60.00
❑	441A	Dennis Higgins	1.50	.60
❑	441B	Dennis Higgins WL		
❑	442	Ty Cline	1.50	.60
❑	443	Don Wert	1.50	.60
❑	444A	Joe Moeller	1.50	.60
❑	444B	Joe Moeller WL		
❑	445	Bobby Knoop	1.50	.60
❑	446	Claude Raymond	1.50	.60
❑	447A	Ralph Houk MG	2.50	1.00
❑	447B	Ralph Houk MG WL		

❑ 448 Bob Tolan 2.50 1.00
❑ 449 Paul Lindblad 1.50 .60
❑ 450 Billy Williams 8.00 4.00
❑ 451A Rich Rollins 2.50 1.00
❑ 451B Rich Rollins WL
❑ 452A Al Ferrara 1.50 .60
❑ 452B Al Ferrara WL
❑ 453 Mike Cuellar 2.50 1.00
❑ 454A L.Colton/D.Money RC 2.50 1.00
❑ 454B L.Colton/D.Money WL
❑ 455 Sonny Siebert 1.50 .60
❑ 456 Bud Harrelson 2.50 1.00
❑ 457 Dalton Jones 1.50 .60
❑ 458 Curt Blefary 1.50 .60
❑ 459 Dave Boswell 1.50 .60
❑ 460 Joe Torre 4.00 1.50
❑ 461A Mike Epstein 1.50 .60
❑ 461B Mike Epstein WL
❑ 462 R.Schoendienst MG 2.50 1.00
❑ 463 Dennis Ribant 1.50 .60
❑ 464A Dave Marshall RC 1.50 .60
❑ 464B Dave Marshall WL
❑ 465 Tommy John 4.00 1.50
❑ 466 John Boccabella 2.50 1.00
❑ 467 Tommie Reynolds 1.50 .60
❑ 468A B.Dal Canton RC/B.Robertson 1.50 .60
❑ 468B B.Dal Canton/B.Robertson WL
❑ 469 Chico Ruiz 1.50 .60
❑ 470A Mel Stottlemyre 2.50 1.00
❑ 470B Mel Stottlemyre WL 30.00 15.00
❑ 471A Ted Savage 1.50 .60
❑ 471B Ted Savage WL
❑ 472 Jim Price 1.50 .60
❑ 473A Jose Arcia 1.50 .60
❑ 473B Jose Arcia WL
❑ 474 Tom Murphy RC 1.50 .60
❑ 475 Tim McCarver 4.00 1.50
❑ 476A K.Brett RC/G.Moses 2.50 1.00
❑ 476B K.Brett/G.Moses WL 30.00 15.00
❑ 477 Jeff James RC 1.50 .60
❑ 478 Don Buford 1.50 .60
❑ 479 Richie Scheinblum 1.50 .60
❑ 480 Tom Seaver 80.00 50.00
❑ 481 Bill Melton RC 2.50 1.00
❑ 482A Jim Gosger 1.50 .60
❑ 482B Jim Gosger WL
❑ 483 Ted Abernathy 1.50 .60
❑ 484 Joe Gordon MG 2.50 1.00
❑ 485A Gaylord Perry 10.00 5.00
❑ 485B Gaylord Perry WL 80.00 50.00
❑ 486A Paul Casanova 1.50 .60
❑ 486B Paul Casanova WL
❑ 487 Denis Menke 1.50 .60
❑ 488 Joe Sparma 1.50 .60
❑ 489 Clete Boyer 2.50 1.00
❑ 490 Matty Alou 2.50 1.00
❑ 491A J.Crider RC/G.Mitterwald 1.50 .60
❑ 491B J.Crider/G.Mitterwald WL
❑ 492 Tony Cloninger 1.50 .60
❑ 493A Wes Parker 2.50 1.00
❑ 493B Wes Parker WL
❑ 494 Ken Berry 1.50 .60
❑ 495 Bert Campaneris 2.50 1.00
❑ 496 Larry Jaster 1.50 .60
❑ 497 Julian Javier 2.50 1.00
❑ 498 Juan Pizarro 2.50 1.00
❑ 499 D.Bryant RC/S.Shea RC 1.50 .60
❑ 500A Mickey Mantle UER 350.00 200.00
❑ 500B Mickey Mantle UER WL 2000.00 1200.00
❑ 501A Tony Gonzalez 2.50 1.00
❑ 501B Tony Gonzalez WL
❑ 502 Minnie Rojas 1.50 .60
❑ 503 Larry Brown 1.50 .60
❑ 504 Checklist 6/B.Robinson 8.00 4.00
❑ 505A Bobby Bolin 1.50 .60
❑ 505B Bobby Bolin WL
❑ 506 Paul Blair 2.50 1.00
❑ 507 Cookie Rojas 2.50 1.00
❑ 508 Moe Drabowsky 2.50 1.00
❑ 509 Manny Sanguillen 2.50 1.00
❑ 510 Rod Carew 40.00 20.00
❑ 511A Diego Segui 2.50 1.00
❑ 511B Diego Segui WL
❑ 512 Cleon Jones 2.50 1.00
❑ 513 Camilo Pascual 3.00 1.25
❑ 514 Mike Lum 2.00 .75
❑ 515 Dick Green 2.00 .75
❑ 516 Earl Weaver MG RC 20.00 10.00
❑ 517 Mike McCormick 3.00 1.25
❑ 518 Fred Whitfield 2.00 .75
❑ 519 J.Kenney RC/L.Boehmer RC 2.00 .75
❑ 520 Bob Veale 3.00 1.25
❑ 521 George Thomas 2.00 .75
❑ 522 Joe Hoerner 2.00 .75
❑ 523 Bob Chance 2.00 .75
❑ 524 J.Laboy RC/F.Wicker RC 3.00 1.25
❑ 525 Earl Wilson 3.00 1.25
❑ 526 Hector Torres RC 2.00 .75
❑ 527 Al Lopez MG 5.00 2.00
❑ 528 Claude Osteen 3.00 1.25
❑ 529 Ed Kirkpatrick 3.00 1.25
❑ 530 Cesar Tovar 2.00 .75
❑ 531 Dick Farrell 2.00 .75
❑ 532 Phoeb/Hard/McNally/Cuellar 3.00 1.25
❑ 533 Nolan Ryan 200.00 125.00
❑ 534 Jerry McNertney 3.00 1.25
❑ 535 Phil Regan 3.00 1.25
❑ 536 D.Breeden RC/D.Roberts RC 2.00 .75
❑ 537 Mike Paul RC 2.00 .75
❑ 538 Charlie Smith 2.00 .75
❑ 539 T.Williams/M.Epstein 12.00 6.00
❑ 540 Curt Flood 3.00 1.25
❑ 541 Joe Verbanic 2.00 .75
❑ 542 Bob Aspromonte 2.00 .75
❑ 543 Fred Newman 2.00 .75
❑ 544 M.Kilkenny RC/R.Woods RC 2.00 .75
❑ 545 Willie Stargell 12.00 6.00
❑ 546 Jim Nash 2.00 .75
❑ 547 Billy Martin MG 5.00 2.00
❑ 548 Bob Locker 2.00 .75
❑ 549 Ron Brand 2.00 .75
❑ 550 Brooks Robinson 30.00 15.00
❑ 551 Wayne Granger RC 2.00 .75
❑ 552 T.Sizemore RC/B.Sudakis RC 3.001.25
❑ 553 Ron Davis 2.00 .75
❑ 554 Frank Bertaina 2.00 .75
❑ 555 Jim Ray Hart 3.00 1.25
❑ 556 Bando/Campaneris/Cater 3.00 1.25
❑ 557 Frank Fernandez 2.00 .75
❑ 558 Tom Burgmeier RC 3.00 1.25
❑ 559 J.Hague RC/J.Hicks 2.00 .75
❑ 560 Luis Tiant 3.00 1.25
❑ 561 Ron Clark 2.00 .75
❑ 562 Bob Watson RC 8.00 4.00
❑ 563 Marty Pattin RC 3.00 1.25
❑ 564 Gil Hodges MG 10.00 5.00
❑ 565 Hoyt Wilhelm 8.00 4.00
❑ 566 Ron Hansen 2.00 .75
❑ 567 E.Jimenez/J.Shellenback 2.00 .75
❑ 568 Cecil Upshaw 2.00 .75
❑ 569 Billy Harris 1.50 .60
❑ 570 Ron Santo 8.00 4.00
❑ 571 Cap Peterson 2.00 .75
❑ 572 W.McCovey/J.Marichal 15.00 7.50
❑ 573 Jim Palmer 30.00 15.00
❑ 574 George Scott 3.00 1.25
❑ 575 Bill Singer 3.00 1.25
❑ 576 R.Stone/B.Wilson 2.00 .75
❑ 577 Mike Hegan 3.00 1.25
❑ 578 Don Bosch 2.00 .75
❑ 579 Dave Nelson RC 2.00 .75
❑ 580 Jim Northrup 3.00 1.25
❑ 581 Gary Nolan 3.00 1.25
❑ 582A Checklist 7/Oliva White 6.00 3.00
❑ 582B Checklist 7/Oliva Red 8.00 4.00
❑ 583 Clyde Wright RC 2.00 .75
❑ 584 Don Mason 2.00 .75
❑ 585 Ron Swoboda 3.00 1.25
❑ 586 Tim Cullen 2.00 .75
❑ 587 Joe Rudi RC 8.00 4.00
❑ 588 Bill White 3.00 1.25
❑ 589 Joe Pepitone 5.00 2.00
❑ 590 Rico Carty 5.00 2.00
❑ 591 Mike Hedlund 3.00 1.25
❑ 592 R.Robles RC/A.Santorini RC 5.00 2.00
❑ 593 Don Nottebart 3.00 1.25
❑ 594 Dooley Womack 3.00 1.25
❑ 595 Lee Maye 3.00 1.25
❑ 596 Chuck Hartenstein 3.00 1.25
❑ 597 Rollie Fingers RC 40.00 20.00
❑ 598 Ruben Amaro 3.00 1.25
❑ 599 John Boozer 3.00 1.25
❑ 600 Tony Oliva 8.00 4.00
❑ 601 Tug McGraw SP 8.00 4.00
❑ 602 Distaso/Young/Qualls RC 5.00 2.00
❑ 603 Joe Keough RC 3.00 1.25
❑ 604 Bobby Etheridge 3.00 1.25
❑ 605 Dick Ellsworth 3.00 1.25
❑ 606 Gene Mauch MG 5.00 2.00
❑ 607 Dick Bosman 3.00 1.25
❑ 608 Dick Simpson 3.00 1.25
❑ 609 Phil Gagliano 3.00 1.25
❑ 610 Jim Hardin 3.00 1.25
❑ 611 Didier/Hriniak/Niebauer RC 5.00 2.00
❑ 612 Jack Aker 5.00 2.00
❑ 613 Jim Beauchamp 3.00 1.25
❑ 614 T.Griffin RC/S.Guinn RC 3.00 1.25
❑ 615 Len Gabrielson 3.00 1.25
❑ 616 Don McMahon 3.00 1.25
❑ 617 Jesse Gonder 3.00 1.25
❑ 618 Ramon Webster 3.00 1.25
❑ 619 Butler/Kelly/Rios RC 5.00 2.00
❑ 620 Dean Chance 5.00 2.00
❑ 621 Bill Voss 3.00 1.25
❑ 622 Dan Osinski 3.00 1.25
❑ 623 Hank Allen 3.00 1.25
❑ 624 Chaney/Dyer/Harmon RC 5.00 2.00
❑ 625 Mack Jones UER 5.00 2.00
❑ 626 Gene Michael 5.00 2.00
❑ 627 George Stone RC 3.00 1.25
❑ 628 Conigliaro/O'Brien/Wenz RC 5.00 2.00
❑ 629 Jack Hamilton 3.00 1.25
❑ 630 Bobby Bonds RC 30.00 15.00
❑ 631 John Kennedy 5.00 2.00
❑ 632 Jon Warden RC 3.00 1.25
❑ 633 Harry Walker MG 3.00 1.25
❑ 634 Andy Etchebarren 3.00 1.25
❑ 635 George Culver 3.00 1.25
❑ 636 Woody Held 3.00 1.25
❑ 637 DaVanon/Reberger/Kirby RC 5.00 2.00
❑ 638 Ed Sprague RC 3.00 1.25
❑ 639 Barry Moore 3.00 1.25
❑ 640 Ferguson Jenkins 20.00 10.00
❑ 641 Darwin/Miller/Dean RC 5.00 2.00
❑ 642 John Hiller 3.00 1.25
❑ 643 Billy Cowan 3.00 1.25
❑ 644 Chuck Hinton 3.00 1.25
❑ 645 George Brunet 3.00 1.25
❑ 646 D.McGinn RC/C.Morton RC 5.00 2.00
❑ 647 Dave Wickersham 3.00 1.25
❑ 648 Bobby Wine 5.00 2.00
❑ 649 Al Jackson 3.00 1.25
❑ 650 Ted Williams MG 20.00 10.00
❑ 651 Gus Gil 5.00 2.00
❑ 652 Eddie Watt 3.00 1.25
❑ 653 Aurelio Rodriguez UER RC 5.00 2.00
❑ 654 May/Secrist/Morales RC 5.00 2.00
❑ 655 Mike Hershberger 3.00 1.25
❑ 656 Dan Schneider 3.00 1.25
❑ 657 Bobby Murcer 8.00 4.00
❑ 658 Hall/Burbach/Miles RC 3.00 1.25
❑ 659 Johnny Podres 5.00 2.00
❑ 660 Reggie Smith 5.00 2.00
❑ 661 Jim Merritt 3.00 1.25
❑ 662 Drago/Spriggs/Oliver RC 5.00 2.00
❑ 663 Dick Radatz 5.00 2.00
❑ 664 Ron Hunt 5.00 2.00

1970 Topps

❑ COMPLETE SET (720)	2000.00	1200.00
❑ COMMON CARD (1-132)	.75	.30
❑ COMMON CARD (133-372)	1.00	.40
❑ COMMON CARD (373-459)	1.50	.60
❑ COMMON CARD (460-546)	2.00	.75
❑ COMMON CARD (547-633)	4.00	1.50
❑ COMMON CARD (634-720)	10.00	5.00
❑ WRAPPER (10-CENT)	20.00	15.00
❑ 1 New York Mets TC	30.00	15.00
❑ 2 Diego Segui	1.00	.40
❑ 3 Darrel Chaney	.75	.30
❑ 4 Tom Egan	.75	.30
❑ 5 Wes Parker	1.00	.40
❑ 6 Grant Jackson	.75	.30
❑ 7 G.Boyd RC/R.Nagelson RC	.75	.30
❑ 8 Jose Martinez RC	.75	.30
❑ 9 Checklist 1	12.00	6.00
❑ 10 Carl Yastrzemski	20.00	10.00
❑ 11 Nate Colbert	.75	.30
❑ 12 John Hiller	.75	.30
❑ 13 Jack Hiatt	.75	.30
❑ 14 Hank Allen	.75	.30
❑ 15 Larry Dierker	.75	.30
❑ 16 Charlie Metro MG RC	.75	.30
❑ 17 Hoyt Wilhelm	4.00	1.50
❑ 18 Carlos May	1.00	.40
❑ 19 John Boccabella	.75	.30
❑ 20 Dave McNally	1.00	.40
❑ 21 V.Blue RC/G.Tenace RC	4.00	1.50
❑ 22 Ray Washburn	.75	.30
❑ 23 Bill Robinson	1.00	.40
❑ 24 Dick Selma	.75	.30
❑ 25 Cesar Tovar	.75	.30
❑ 26 Tug McGraw	2.00	.75
❑ 27 Chuck Hinton	.75	.30
❑ 28 Billy Wilson	.75	.30
❑ 29 Sandy Alomar	1.00	.40
❑ 30 Matty Alou	1.00	.40
❑ 31 Marty Pattin	1.00	.40
❑ 32 Harry Walker MG	.75	.30
❑ 33 Don Wert	.75	.30
❑ 34 Willie Crawford	.75	.30
❑ 35 Joel Horlen	.75	.30
❑ 36 D.Breeden/B.Carbo RC	1.00	.40
❑ 37 Dick Drago	.75	.30
❑ 38 Mack Jones	.75	.30
❑ 39 Mike Nagy RC	.75	.30
❑ 40 Richie Allen	2.00	.75
❑ 41 George Lauzerique	.75	.30
❑ 42 Tito Fuentes	.75	.30
❑ 43 Jack Aker	.75	.30
❑ 44 Roberto Pena	.75	.30
❑ 45 Dave Johnson	1.00	.40
❑ 46 Ken Rudolph RC	.75	.30
❑ 47 Bob Miller	.75	.30
❑ 48 Gil Garrido	.75	.30
❑ 49 Tim Cullen	.75	.30
❑ 50 Tommie Agee	1.00	.40
❑ 51 Bob Christian	.75	.30
❑ 52 Bruce Dal Canton	.75	.30
❑ 53 John Kennedy	.75	.30
❑ 54 Jeff Torborg	1.00	.40
❑ 55 John Odom	.75	.30
❑ 56 J.Lis RC/S.Reid RC	.75	.30
❑ 57 Pat Kelly	.75	.30
❑ 58 Dave Marshall	.75	.30
❑ 59 Dick Ellsworth	.75	.30
❑ 60 Jim Wynn	1.00	.40
❑ 61 Rose/Clemente/Jones LL	12.00	6.00
❑ 62 Carew/Smith/Oliva LL	2.00	.75
❑ 63 McCovey/Santo/Perez LL	2.00	.75
❑ 64 Kill/Powell/Jackson LL	4.00	1.50
❑ 65 McCovey/Aaron/May LL	4.00	1.50
❑ 66 Kill/Howard/Jackson LL	4.00	1.50
❑ 67 Marichal/Carlton/Gibson LL	4.00	1.50
❑ 68 Bosman/Palmer/Cuellar LL	1.00	.40
❑ 69 Seav/Niek/Jenk/Mari LL	4.00	1.50
❑ 70 McLain/Cuellar/Boswell LL	1.00	.40
❑ 71 Jenkins/Gibson/Singer LL	2.00	.75
❑ 72 McDowell/Lolich/Mess LL	1.00	.40
❑ 73 Wayne Granger	.75	.30
❑ 74 G.Washburn RC/W.Wolf	.75	.30
❑ 75 Jim Kaat	1.00	.40
❑ 76 Carl Taylor	.75	.30
❑ 77 Frank Linzy	.75	.30
❑ 78 Joe Lahoud	.75	.30
❑ 79 Clay Kirby	.75	.30
❑ 80 Don Kessinger	1.00	.40
❑ 81 Dave May	.75	.30
❑ 82 Frank Fernandez	.75	.30
❑ 83 Don Cardwell	.75	.30
❑ 84 Paul Casanova	.75	.30
❑ 85 Max Alvis	.75	.30
❑ 86 Lum Harris MG	.75	.30
❑ 87 Steve Renko RC	.75	.30
❑ 88 M.Fuentes RC/D.Baney RC	1.00	.40
❑ 89 Juan Rios	.75	.30
❑ 90 Tim McCarver	1.00	.40
❑ 91 Rich Morales	.75	.30
❑ 92 George Culver	.75	.30
❑ 93 Rick Renick	.75	.30
❑ 94 Freddie Patek	1.00	.40
❑ 95 Earl Wilson	1.00	.40
❑ 96 L.Lee RC/J.Reuss RC	1.00	.40
❑ 97 Joe Moeller	.75	.30
❑ 98 Gates Brown	1.00	.40
❑ 99 Bobby Pfeil RC	.75	.30
❑ 100 Mel Stottlemyre	1.00	.40
❑ 101 Bobby Floyd	.75	.30
❑ 102 Joe Rudi	1.00	.40
❑ 103 Frank Reberger	.75	.30
❑ 104 Gerry Moses	.75	.30
❑ 105 Tony Gonzalez	.75	.30
❑ 106 Darold Knowles	.75	.30
❑ 107 Bobby Etheridge	.75	.30
❑ 108 Tom Burgmeier	.75	.30
❑ 109 G.Jestadt RC/C.Morton	.75	.30
❑ 110 Bob Moose	.75	.30
❑ 111 Mike Hegan	1.00	.40
❑ 112 Dave Nelson	.75	.30
❑ 113 Jim Ray	.75	.30
❑ 114 Gene Michael	1.00	.40
❑ 115 Alex Johnson	1.00	.40
❑ 116 Sparky Lyle	1.00	.40
❑ 117 Don Young	.75	.30
❑ 118 George Mitterwald	.75	.30
❑ 119 Chuck Taylor RC	.75	.30
❑ 120 Sal Bando	1.00	.40
❑ 121 F.Beene RC/T.Crowley RC	.75	.30
❑ 122 George Stone	.75	.30
❑ 123 Don Gutteridge MG RC	.75	.30
❑ 124 Larry Jaster	.75	.30
❑ 125 Deron Johnson	.75	.30
❑ 126 Marty Martinez	.75	.30
❑ 127 Joe Coleman	.75	.30
❑ 128A Checklist 2 R Perranoski	6.00	3.00
❑ 128B Checklist 2 R. Perranoski	6.00	3.00
❑ 129 Jimmie Price	.75	.30
❑ 130 Ollie Brown	.75	.30
❑ 131 R.Lamb RC/B.Stinson RC	.75	.30
❑ 132 Jim McGlothlin	.75	.30
❑ 133 Clay Carroll	1.00	.40
❑ 134 Danny Walton RC	1.00	.40
❑ 135 Dick Dietz	1.00	.40
❑ 136 Steve Hargan	1.00	.40
❑ 137 Art Shamsky	1.00	.40
❑ 138 Joe Foy	1.00	.40
❑ 139 Rich Nye	1.00	.40
❑ 140 Reggie Jackson	50.00	30.00
❑ 141 D.Cash RC/J.Jeter RC	1.50	.60
❑ 142 Fritz Peterson	1.00	.40
❑ 143 Phil Gagliano	1.00	.40
❑ 144 Ray Culp	1.00	.40
❑ 145 Rico Carty	1.50	.60
❑ 146 Danny Murphy	1.00	.40
❑ 147 Angel Hermoso RC	1.00	.40
❑ 148 Earl Weaver MG	3.00	1.25
❑ 149 Billy Champion RC	1.00	.40
❑ 150 Harmon Killebrew	8.00	4.00
❑ 151 Dave Roberts	1.00	.40
❑ 152 Ike Brown RC	1.00	.40
❑ 153 Gary Gentry	1.00	.40
❑ 154 J.Miles/J.Dukes RC	1.00	.40
❑ 155 Denis Menke	1.00	.40
❑ 156 Eddie Fisher	1.00	.40
❑ 157 Manny Mota	1.50	.60
❑ 158 Jerry McNertney	1.50	.60
❑ 159 Tommy Helms	1.50	.60
❑ 160 Phil Niekro	5.00	2.00
❑ 161 Richie Scheinblum	1.00	.40
❑ 162 Jerry Johnson	1.00	.40
❑ 163 Syd O'Brien	1.00	.40
❑ 164 Ty Cline	1.00	.40
❑ 165 Ed Kirkpatrick	1.00	.40
❑ 166 Al Oliver	3.00	1.25
❑ 167 Bill Burbach	1.00	.40
❑ 168 Dave Watkins RC	1.00	.40
❑ 169 Tom Hall	1.00	.40
❑ 170 Billy Williams	5.00	2.00
❑ 171 Jim Nash	1.00	.40
❑ 172 G.Hill RC/R.Garr RC	1.50	.60
❑ 173 Jim Hicks	1.00	.40
❑ 174 Ted Sizemore	1.50	.60
❑ 175 Dick Bosman	1.00	.40
❑ 176 Jim Ray Hart	1.50	.60
❑ 177 Jim Northrup	1.50	.60
❑ 178 Denny Lemaster	1.00	.40
❑ 179 Ivan Murrell	1.00	.40
❑ 180 Tommy John	1.50	.60
❑ 181 Sparky Anderson MG	5.00	2.00
❑ 182 Dick Hall	1.00	.40
❑ 183 Jerry Grote	1.50	.60
❑ 184 Ray Fosse	1.00	.40
❑ 185 Don Mincher	1.50	.60
❑ 186 Rick Joseph	1.00	.40
❑ 187 Mike Hedlund	1.00	.40
❑ 188 Manny Sanguillen	1.50	.60
❑ 189 Thurman Munson RC	100.00	60.00
❑ 190 Joe Torre	3.00	1.25
❑ 191 Vicente Romo	1.00	.40
❑ 192 Jim Qualls	1.00	.40
❑ 193 Mike Wegener	1.00	.40
❑ 194 Chuck Manuel RC	1.00	.40
❑ 195 Tom Seaver NLCS1	15.00	7.50
❑ 196 Ken Boswell NLCS2	2.00	.75
❑ 197 Nolan Ryan NLCS3	30.00	15.00
❑ 198 Mets Celebrate/w/Ryan	15.00	7.50
❑ 199 Mike Cuellar ALCS1	2.00	.75
❑ 200 Boog Powell ALCS2	3.00	1.25
❑ 201 B.Powell/A.Etch ALCS3	2.00	.75
❑ 202 Orioles Celebrate ALCS	2.00	.75
❑ 203 Rudy May	1.00	.40
❑ 204 Len Gabrielson	1.00	.40
❑ 205 Bert Campaneris	1.50	.60
❑ 206 Clete Boyer	1.50	.60
❑ 207 N.McRae RC/B.Reed RC	1.00	.40
❑ 208 Fred Gladding	1.00	.40
❑ 209 Ken Suarez	1.00	.40
❑ 210 Juan Marichal	5.00	2.00
❑ 211 Ted Williams MG UER	15.00	7.50
❑ 212 Al Santorini	1.00	.40
❑ 213 Andy Etchebarren	1.00	.40
❑ 214 Ken Boswell	1.00	.40
❑ 215 Reggie Smith	1.50	.60
❑ 216 Chuck Hartenstein	1.00	.40
❑ 217 Ron Hansen	1.00	.40
❑ 218 Ron Stone	1.00	.40
❑ 219 Jerry Kenney	1.00	.40
❑ 220 Steve Carlton	15.00	7.50
❑ 221 Ron Brand	1.00	.40
❑ 222 Jim Rooker	1.00	.40
❑ 223 Nate Oliver	1.00	.40
❑ 224 Steve Barber	1.50	.60
❑ 225 Lee May	1.50	.60
❑ 226 Ron Perranoski	1.00	.40
❑ 227 J.Mayberry RC/B.Watkins RC	1.50	.60
❑ 228 Aurelio Rodriguez	1.00	.40
❑ 229 Rich Robertson	1.00	.40
❑ 230 Brooks Robinson	15.00	7.50
❑ 231 Luis Tiant	1.50	.60
❑ 232 Bob Didier	1.00	.40
❑ 233 Lew Krausse	1.00	.40
❑ 234 Tommy Dean	1.00	.40
❑ 235 Mike Epstein	1.00	.40
❑ 236 Bob Veale	1.00	.40
❑ 237 Russ Gibson	1.00	.40
❑ 238 Jose Laboy	1.00	.40
❑ 239 Ken Berry	1.00	.40
❑ 240 Ferguson Jenkins	5.00	2.00
❑ 241 A.Fitzmorris RC/S.Northey RC	1.00	.40
❑ 242 Walt Alston MG	3.00	1.25
❑ 243 Joe Sparma	1.00	.40
❑ 244A Checklist 3 Red Bat	6.00	3.00
❑ 244B Checklist 3 Brown Bat	6.00	3.00
❑ 245 Leo Cardenas	1.00	.40
❑ 246 Jim McAndrew	1.00	.40
❑ 247 Lou Klimchock	1.00	.40
❑ 248 Jesus Alou	1.00	.40

❑ 249 Bob Locker 1.00 .40
❑ 250 Willie McCovey UER 10.00 5.00
❑ 251 Dick Schofield 1.00 .40
❑ 252 Lowell Palmer RC 1.00 .40
❑ 253 Ron Woods 1.00 .40
❑ 254 Camilo Pascual 1.00 .40
❑ 255 Jim Spencer RC 1.00 .40
❑ 256 Vic Davalillo 1.00 .40
❑ 257 Dennis Higgins 1.00 .40
❑ 258 Paul Popovich 1.00 .40
❑ 259 Tommie Reynolds 1.00 .40
❑ 260 Claude Osteen 1.00 .40
❑ 261 Curt Motton 1.00 .40
❑ 262 J.Morales RC/J.Williams RC 1.00 .40
❑ 263 Duane Josephson 1.00 .40
❑ 264 Rich Hebner 1.00 .40
❑ 265 Randy Hundley 1.00 .40
❑ 266 Wally Bunker 1.00 .40
❑ 267 H.Hill RC/P.Ratliff 1.00 .40
❑ 268 Claude Raymond 1.00 .40
❑ 269 Cesar Gutierrez 1.00 .40
❑ 270 Chris Short 1.00 .40
❑ 271 Greg Goossen 1.50 .60
❑ 272 Hector Torres 1.00 .40
❑ 273 Ralph Houk MG 1.50 .60
❑ 274 Gerry Arrigo 1.00 .40
❑ 275 Duke Sims 1.00 .40
❑ 276 Ron Hunt 1.00 .40
❑ 277 Paul Doyle RC 1.00 .40
❑ 278 Tommie Aaron 1.00 .40
❑ 279 Bill Lee RC 1.50 .60
❑ 280 Donn Clendenon 1.50 .60
❑ 281 Casey Cox 1.00 .40
❑ 282 Steve Huntz 1.00 .40
❑ 283 Angel Bravo RC 1.00 .40
❑ 284 Jack Baldschun 1.00 .40
❑ 285 Paul Blair 1.50 .60
❑ 286 J.Jenkins RC/B.Buckner RC 5.00 2.00
❑ 287 Fred Talbot 1.00 .40
❑ 288 Larry Hisle 1.50 .60
❑ 289 Gene Brabender 1.00 .40
❑ 290 Rod Carew 15.00 7.50
❑ 291 Leo Durocher MG 3.00 1.25
❑ 292 Eddie Leon RC 1.00 .40
❑ 293 Bob Bailey 1.50 .60
❑ 294 Jose Azcue 1.00 .40
❑ 295 Cecil Upshaw 1.00 .40
❑ 296 Woody Woodward 1.00 .40
❑ 297 Curt Blefary 1.00 .40
❑ 298 Ken Henderson 1.00 .40
❑ 299 Buddy Bradford 1.00 .40
❑ 300 Tom Seaver 30.00 15.00
❑ 301 Chico Salmon 1.00 .40
❑ 302 Jeff James 1.00 .40
❑ 303 Brant Alyea 1.00 .40
❑ 304 Bill Russell RC 5.00 2.00
❑ 305 Don Buford WS1 4.00 1.50
❑ 306 Donn Clendenon WS2 4.00 1.50
❑ 307 Tommie Agee WS3 4.00 1.50
❑ 308 J.C. Martin WS4 4.00 1.50
❑ 309 Jerry Koosman WS5 4.00 1.50
❑ 310 Mets Celebrate WS 5.00 2.00
❑ 311 Dick Green 1.00 .40
❑ 312 Mike Torrez 1.00 .40
❑ 313 Mayo Smith MG 1.00 .40
❑ 314 Bill McCool 1.00 .40
❑ 315 Luis Aparicio 5.00 2.00
❑ 316 Skip Guinn 1.00 .40
❑ 317 B.Conigliaro/L.Alvarado RC 1.50 .60
❑ 318 Willie Smith 1.00 .40
❑ 319 Clay Dalrymple 1.00 .40
❑ 320 Jim Maloney 1.50 .60
❑ 321 Lou Piniella 1.50 .60
❑ 322 Luke Walker 1.00 .40
❑ 323 Wayne Comer 1.00 .40
❑ 324 Tony Taylor 1.50 .60
❑ 325 Dave Boswell 1.00 .40
❑ 326 Bill Voss 1.00 .40
❑ 327 Hal King RC 1.00 .40
❑ 328 George Brunet 1.00 .40
❑ 329 Chris Cannizzaro 1.00 .40
❑ 330 Lou Brock 10.00 5.00
❑ 331 Chuck Dobson 1.00 .40
❑ 332 Bobby Wine 1.00 .40
❑ 333 Bobby Murcer 1.50 .60
❑ 334 Phil Regan 1.00 .40
❑ 335 Bill Freehan 1.50 .60
❑ 336 Del Unser 1.00 .40
❑ 337 Mike McCormick 1.50 .60
❑ 338 Paul Schaal 1.00 .40
❑ 339 Johnny Edwards 1.00 .40
❑ 340 Tony Conigliaro 3.00 1.25
❑ 341 Bill Sudakis 1.00 .40
❑ 342 Wilbur Wood 1.50 .60
❑ 343A Checklist 4 Red Bat 6.00 3.00
❑ 343B Checklist 4 Brown Bat 6.00 3.00
❑ 344 Marcelino Lopez 1.00 .40
❑ 345 Al Ferrara 1.00 .40
❑ 346 Red Schoendienst MG 1.50 .60
❑ 347 Russ Snyder 1.00 .40
❑ 348 M.Jorgensen RC/J.Hudson RC 1.50 .60
❑ 349 Steve Hamilton 1.00 .40
❑ 350 Roberto Clemente 60.00 35.00
❑ 351 Tom Murphy 1.00 .40
❑ 352 Bob Barton 1.00 .40
❑ 353 Stan Williams 1.00 .40
❑ 354 Amos Otis 1.50 .60
❑ 355 Doug Rader 1.00 .40
❑ 356 Fred Lasher 1.00 .40
❑ 357 Bob Burda 1.00 .40
❑ 358 Pedro Borbon RC 1.50 .60
❑ 359 Phil Roof 1.00 .40
❑ 360 Curt Flood 1.50 .60
❑ 361 Ray Jarvis 1.00 .40
❑ 362 Joe Hague 1.00 .40
❑ 363 Tom Shopay RC 1.00 .40
❑ 364 Dan McGinn 1.00 .40
❑ 365 Zoilo Versalles 1.00 .40
❑ 366 Barry Moore 1.00 .40
❑ 367 Mike Lum 1.00 .40
❑ 368 Ed Herrmann 1.00 .40
❑ 369 Alan Foster 1.00 .40
❑ 370 Tommy Harper 1.50 .60
❑ 371 Rod Gaspar RC 1.00 .40
❑ 372 Dave Giusti 1.00 .40
❑ 373 Roy White 2.00 .75
❑ 374 Tommie Sisk 1.50 .60
❑ 375 Johnny Callison 2.00 .75
❑ 376 Lefty Phillips MG RC 1.50 .60
❑ 377 Bill Butler 1.50 .60
❑ 378 Jim Davenport 1.50 .60
❑ 379 Tom Tischinski RC 1.50 .60
❑ 380 Tony Perez 6.00 3.00
❑ 381 B.Brooks RC/M.Olivo RC 1.50 .60
❑ 382 Jack DiLauro RC 1.50 .60
❑ 383 Mickey Stanley 2.00 .75
❑ 384 Gary Neibauer 1.50 .60
❑ 385 George Scott 2.00 .75
❑ 386 Bill Dillman 1.50 .60
❑ 387 Baltimore Orioles TC 3.00 1.25
❑ 388 Byron Browne 1.50 .60
❑ 389 Jim Shellenback 1.50 .60
❑ 390 Willie Davis 2.00 .75
❑ 391 Larry Brown 1.50 .60
❑ 392 Walt Hriniak 2.00 .75
❑ 393 John Gelnar 1.50 .60
❑ 394 Gil Hodges MG 4.00 1.50
❑ 395 Walt Williams 1.50 .60
❑ 396 Steve Blass 2.00 .75
❑ 397 Roger Repoz 1.50 .60
❑ 398 Bill Stoneman 1.50 .60
❑ 399 New York Yankees TC 3.00 1.25
❑ 400 Denny McLain 4.00 1.50
❑ 401 J.Harrell RC/B.Williams RC 1.50 .60
❑ 402 Ellie Rodriguez 1.50 .60
❑ 403 Jim Bunning 6.00 3.00
❑ 404 Rich Reese 1.50 .60
❑ 405 Bill Hands 1.50 .60
❑ 406 Mike Andrews 1.50 .60
❑ 407 Bob Watson 2.00 .75
❑ 408 Paul Lindblad 1.50 .60
❑ 409 Bob Tolan 1.50 .60
❑ 410 Boog Powell 4.00 1.50
❑ 411 Los Angeles Dodgers TC 3.00 1.25
❑ 412 Larry Burchart 1.50 .60
❑ 413 Sonny Jackson 1.50 .60
❑ 414 Paul Edmondson RC 1.50 .60
❑ 415 Julian Javier 2.00 .75
❑ 416 Joe Verbanic 1.50 .60
❑ 417 John Bateman 1.50 .60
❑ 418 John Donaldson 1.50 .60
❑ 419 Ron Taylor 1.50 .60
❑ 420 Ken McMullen 2.00 .75
❑ 421 Pat Dobson 2.00 .75
❑ 422 Kansas City Royals TC 3.00 1.25
❑ 423 Jerry May 1.50 .60
❑ 424 Mike Kilkenny 1.50 .60
❑ 425 Bobby Bonds 6.00 3.00
❑ 426 Bill Rigney MG 1.50 .60
❑ 427 Fred Norman 1.50 .60
❑ 428 Don Buford 1.50 .60
❑ 429 R.Bobb RC/J.Cosman 1.50 .60
❑ 430 Andy Messersmith 2.00 .75
❑ 431 Ron Swoboda 2.00 .75
❑ 432A Checklist 5 Yellow Ltr 6.00 3.00
❑ 432B Checklist 5 White Ltr 6.00 3.00
❑ 433 Ron Bryant RC 1.50 .60
❑ 434 Felipe Alou 2.00 .75
❑ 435 Nelson Briles 2.00 .75
❑ 436 Philadelphia Phillies TC 3.00 1.25
❑ 437 Danny Cater 1.50 .60
❑ 438 Pat Jarvis 1.50 .60
❑ 439 Lee Maye 1.50 .60
❑ 440 Bill Mazeroski 6.00 3.00
❑ 441 John O'Donoghue 1.50 .60
❑ 442 Gene Mauch MG 2.00 .75
❑ 443 Al Jackson 1.50 .60
❑ 444 B.Farmer RC/J.Matias RC 1.50 .60
❑ 445 Vada Pinson 2.00 .75
❑ 446 Billy Grabarkewitz RC 1.50 .60
❑ 447 Lee Stange 1.50 .60
❑ 448 Houston Astros TC 3.00 1.25
❑ 449 Jim Palmer 12.00 6.00
❑ 450 Willie McCovey AS 6.00 3.00
❑ 451 Boog Powell AS 4.00 1.50
❑ 452 Felix Millan AS 2.00 .75
❑ 453 Rod Carew AS 6.00 3.00
❑ 454 Ron Santo AS 4.00 1.50
❑ 455 Brooks Robinson AS 6.00 3.00
❑ 456 Don Kessinger AS 2.00 .75
❑ 457 Rico Petrocelli AS 4.00 1.50
❑ 458 Pete Rose AS 15.00 7.50
❑ 459 Reggie Jackson AS 12.00 6.00
❑ 460 Matty Alou AS 3.00 1.25
❑ 461 Carl Yastrzemski AS 10.00 5.00
❑ 462 Hank Aaron AS 15.00 7.50
❑ 463 Frank Robinson AS 8.00 4.00
❑ 464 Johnny Bench AS 15.00 7.50
❑ 465 Bill Freehan AS 3.00 1.25
❑ 466 Juan Marichal AS 5.00 2.00
❑ 467 Denny McLain AS 3.00 1.25
❑ 468 Jerry Koosman AS 3.00 1.25
❑ 469 Sam McDowell AS 3.00 1.25
❑ 470 Willie Stargell 10.00 5.00
❑ 471 Chris Zachary 2.00 .75
❑ 472 Atlanta Braves TC 4.00 1.50
❑ 473 Don Bryant 2.00 .75
❑ 474 Dick Kelley 2.00 .75
❑ 475 Dick McAuliffe 3.00 1.25
❑ 476 Don Shaw 2.00 .75
❑ 477 A.Severinsen RC/R.Freed RC 2.00 .75
❑ 478 Bobby Heise RC 2.00 .75
❑ 479 Dick Woodson RC 2.00 .75
❑ 480 Glenn Beckert 3.00 1.25
❑ 481 Jose Tartabull 2.00 .75
❑ 482 Tom Hilgendorf RC 2.00 .75
❑ 483 Gail Hopkins RC 2.00 .75
❑ 484 Gary Nolan 3.00 1.25
❑ 485 Jay Johnstone 3.00 1.25
❑ 486 Terry Harmon 2.00 .75
❑ 487 Cisco Carlos 2.00 .75
❑ 488 J.C. Martin 2.00 .75
❑ 489 Eddie Kasko MG 2.00 .75
❑ 490 Bill Singer 3.00 1.25
❑ 491 Graig Nettles 5.00 2.00
❑ 492 K.Lampard RC/S.Spinks RC 2.00 .75
❑ 493 Lindy McDaniel 3.00 1.25
❑ 494 Larry Stahl 2.00 .75
❑ 495 Dave Morehead 2.00 .75
❑ 496 Steve Whitaker 2.00 .75
❑ 497 Eddie Watt 2.00 .75
❑ 498 Al Weis 2.00 .75
❑ 499 Skip Lockwood 3.00 1.25
❑ 500 Hank Aaron 50.00 30.00
❑ 501 Chicago White Sox TC 4.00 1.50
❑ 502 Rollie Fingers 10.00 5.00
❑ 503 Dal Maxvill 2.00 .75
❑ 504 Don Pavletich 2.00 .75

❑ 505	Ken Holtzman	3.00	1.25
❑ 506	Ed Stroud	2.00	.75
❑ 507	Pat Corrales	2.00	.75
❑ 508	Joe Niekro	3.00	1.25
❑ 509	Montreal Expos TC	4.00	1.50
❑ 510	Tony Oliva	5.00	2.00
❑ 511	Joe Hoerner	2.00	.75
❑ 512	Billy Harris	2.00	.75
❑ 513	Preston Gomez MG	2.00	.75
❑ 514	Steve Hovley RC	2.00	.75
❑ 515	Don Wilson	3.00	1.25
❑ 516	J.Ellis RC/J.Lyttle RC	2.00	.75
❑ 517	Joe Gibbon	2.00	.75
❑ 518	Bill Melton	2.00	.75
❑ 519	Don McMahon	2.00	.75
❑ 520	Willie Horton	3.00	1.25
❑ 521	Cal Koonce	2.00	.75
❑ 522	California Angels TC	4.00	1.50
❑ 523	Jose Pena	2.00	.75
❑ 524	Alvin Dark MG	3.00	1.25
❑ 525	Jerry Adair	2.00	.75
❑ 526	Ron Herbel	2.00	.75
❑ 527	Don Bosch	2.00	.75
❑ 528	Elrod Hendricks	2.00	.75
❑ 529	Bob Aspromonte	2.00	.75
❑ 530	Bob Gibson	15.00	7.50
❑ 531	Ron Clark	2.00	.75
❑ 532	Danny Murtaugh MG	3.00	1.25
❑ 533	Buzz Stephen RC	2.00	.75
❑ 534	Minnesota Twins TC	4.00	1.50
❑ 535	Andy Kosco	2.00	.75
❑ 536	Mike Kekich	2.00	.75
❑ 537	Joe Morgan	10.00	5.00
❑ 538	Bob Humphreys	2.00	.75
❑ 539	D.Doyle RC/L.Bowa RC	8.00	4.00
❑ 540	Gary Peters	2.00	.75
❑ 541	Bill Heath	2.00	.75
❑ 542	Checklist 6	6.00	3.00
❑ 543	Clyde Wright	2.00	.75
❑ 544	Cincinnati Reds TC	4.00	1.50
❑ 545	Ken Harrelson	3.00	1.25
❑ 546	Ron Reed	2.00	.75
❑ 547	Rick Monday	6.00	3.00
❑ 548	Howie Reed	4.00	1.50
❑ 549	St. Louis Cardinals TC	6.00	3.00
❑ 550	Frank Howard	6.00	3.00
❑ 551	Dock Ellis	6.00	3.00
❑ 552	O'Riley/Paepke/Rico RC	4.00	1.50
❑ 553	Jim Lefebvre	6.00	3.00
❑ 554	Tom Timmermann RC	4.00	1.50
❑ 555	Orlando Cepeda	12.00	6.00
❑ 556	Dave Bristol MG	6.00	3.00
❑ 557	Ed Kranepool	6.00	3.00
❑ 558	Vern Fuller	4.00	1.50
❑ 559	Tommy Davis	6.00	3.00
❑ 560	Gaylord Perry	12.00	6.00
❑ 561	Tom McCraw	4.00	1.50
❑ 562	Ted Abernathy	4.00	1.50
❑ 563	Boston Red Sox TC	6.00	3.00
❑ 564	Johnny Briggs	4.00	1.50
❑ 565	Jim Hunter	12.00	6.00
❑ 566	Gene Alley	6.00	3.00
❑ 567	Bob Oliver	4.00	1.50
❑ 568	Stan Bahnsen	6.00	3.00
❑ 569	Cookie Rojas	6.00	3.00
❑ 570	Jim Fregosi	6.00	3.00
❑ 571	Jim Brewer	4.00	1.50
❑ 572	Frank Quilici	4.00	1.50
❑ 573	Corkins/Robles/Slocum RC	4.00	1.50
❑ 574	Bobby Bolin	6.00	3.00
❑ 575	Cleon Jones	6.00	3.00
❑ 576	Milt Pappas	6.00	3.00
❑ 577	Bernie Allen	4.00	1.50
❑ 578	Tom Griffin	4.00	1.50
❑ 579	Detroit Tigers TC	6.00	3.00
❑ 580	Pete Rose	60.00	35.00
❑ 581	Tom Satriano	4.00	1.50
❑ 582	Mike Paul	4.00	1.50
❑ 583	Hal Lanier	4.00	1.50
❑ 584	Al Downing	6.00	3.00
❑ 585	Rusty Staub	8.00	4.00
❑ 586	Rickey Clark RC	4.00	1.50
❑ 587	Jose Arcia	4.00	1.50
❑ 588A	Checklist 7 Adolfo	8.00	4.00
❑ 588B	Checklist 7 Adolpho	6.00	3.00
❑ 589	Joe Keough	4.00	1.50
❑ 590	Mike Cuellar	6.00	3.00
❑ 591	Mike Ryan UER	4.00	1.50
❑ 592	Daryl Patterson	4.00	1.50
❑ 593	Chicago Cubs TC	8.00	4.00
❑ 594	Jake Gibbs	4.00	1.50
❑ 595	Maury Wills	8.00	4.00
❑ 596	Mike Hershberger	6.00	3.00
❑ 597	Sonny Siebert	4.00	1.50
❑ 598	Joe Pepitone	6.00	3.00
❑ 599	Stelmaszek/Martin/Such RC	4.00	1.50
❑ 600	Willie Mays	80.00	50.00
❑ 601	Pete Richert	4.00	1.50
❑ 602	Ted Savage	4.00	1.50
❑ 603	Ray Oyler	4.00	1.50
❑ 604	Cito Gaston	6.00	3.00
❑ 605	Rick Wise	6.00	3.00
❑ 606	Chico Ruiz	4.00	1.50
❑ 607	Gary Waslewski	4.00	1.50
❑ 608	Pittsburgh Pirates TC	6.00	3.00
❑ 609	Buck Martinez RC	6.00	3.00
❑ 610	Jerry Koosman	8.00	4.00
❑ 611	Norm Cash	6.00	3.00
❑ 612	Jim Hickman	6.00	3.00
❑ 613	Dave Baldwin	6.00	3.00
❑ 614	Mike Shannon	6.00	3.00
❑ 615	Mark Belanger	6.00	3.00
❑ 616	Jim Merritt	4.00	1.50
❑ 617	Jim French	4.00	1.50
❑ 618	Billy Wynne RC	4.00	1.50
❑ 619	Norm Miller	4.00	1.50
❑ 620	Jim Perry	6.00	3.00
❑ 621	McQueen/Evans/Kester RC	12.00	6.00
❑ 622	Don Sutton	12.00	6.00
❑ 623	Horace Clarke	6.00	3.00
❑ 624	Clyde King MG	4.00	1.50
❑ 625	Dean Chance	4.00	1.50
❑ 626	Dave Ricketts	4.00	1.50
❑ 627	Gary Wagner	4.00	1.50
❑ 628	Wayne Garrett RC	4.00	1.50
❑ 629	Merv Rettenmund	4.00	1.50
❑ 630	Ernie Banks	50.00	30.00
❑ 631	Oakland Athletics TC	6.00	3.00
❑ 632	Gary Sutherland	4.00	1.50
❑ 633	Roger Nelson	4.00	1.50
❑ 634	Bud Harrelson	15.00	7.50
❑ 635	Bob Allison	15.00	7.50
❑ 636	Jim Stewart	10.00	5.00
❑ 637	Cleveland Indians TC	12.00	6.00
❑ 638	Frank Bertaina	10.00	5.00
❑ 639	Dave Campbell	15.00	7.50
❑ 640	Al Kaline	50.00	30.00
❑ 641	Al McBean	10.00	5.00
❑ 642	Garrett/Lund/Tatum RC	10.00	5.00
❑ 643	Jose Pagan	10.00	5.00
❑ 644	Gerry Nyman	10.00	5.00
❑ 645	Don Money	15.00	7.50
❑ 646	Jim Britton	10.00	5.00
❑ 647	Tom Matchick	10.00	5.00
❑ 648	Larry Haney	10.00	5.00
❑ 649	Jimmie Hall	10.00	5.00
❑ 650	Sam McDowell	15.00	7.50
❑ 651	Jim Gosger	10.00	5.00
❑ 652	Rich Rollins	15.00	7.50
❑ 653	Moe Drabowsky	10.00	5.00
❑ 654	Gamble/Day/Mangual RC	15.00	7.50
❑ 655	John Roseboro	15.00	7.50
❑ 656	Jim Hardin	10.00	5.00
❑ 657	San Diego Padres TC	12.00	6.00
❑ 658	Ken Tatum RC	10.00	5.00
❑ 659	Pete Ward	10.00	5.00
❑ 660	Johnny Bench	80.00	50.00
❑ 661	Jerry Robertson	10.00	5.00
❑ 662	Frank Lucchesi MG RC	10.00	5.00
❑ 663	Tito Francona	10.00	5.00
❑ 664	Bob Robertson	10.00	5.00
❑ 665	Jim Lonborg	15.00	7.50
❑ 666	Adolpho Phillips	10.00	5.00
❑ 667	Bob Meyer	15.00	7.50
❑ 668	Bob Tillman	10.00	5.00
❑ 669	Johnson/Lazar/Scott RC	10.00	5.00
❑ 670	Ron Santo	15.00	7.50
❑ 671	Jim Campanis	10.00	5.00
❑ 672	Leon McFadden	10.00	5.00
❑ 673	Ted Uhlaender	10.00	5.00
❑ 674	Dave Leonhard	10.00	5.00
❑ 675	Jose Cardenal	15.00	7.50
❑ 676	Washington Senators TC	12.00	6.00
❑ 677	Woodie Fryman	10.00	5.00
❑ 678	Dave Duncan	15.00	7.50
❑ 679	Ray Sadecki	10.00	5.00
❑ 680	Rico Petrocelli	15.00	7.50
❑ 681	Bob Garibaldi RC	10.00	5.00
❑ 682	Dalton Jones	10.00	5.00
❑ 683	Geishart/McRae/Simpson RC	15.00	7.50
❑ 684	Jack Fisher	10.00	5.00
❑ 685	Tom Haller	10.00	5.00
❑ 686	Jackie Hernandez	10.00	5.00
❑ 687	Bob Priddy	10.00	5.00
❑ 688	Ted Kubiak	15.00	7.50
❑ 689	Frank Tepedino RC	15.00	7.50
❑ 690	Ron Fairly	15.00	7.50
❑ 691	Joe Grzenda	10.00	5.00
❑ 692	Duffy Dyer	10.00	5.00
❑ 693	Bob Johnson	10.00	5.00
❑ 694	Gary Ross	10.00	5.00
❑ 695	Bobby Knoop	10.00	5.00
❑ 696	San Francisco Giants TC	12.00	6.00
❑ 697	Jim Hannan	10.00	5.00
❑ 698	Tom Tresh	15.00	7.50
❑ 699	Hank Aguirre	10.00	5.00
❑ 700	Frank Robinson	50.00	30.00
❑ 701	Jack Billingham	10.00	5.00
❑ 702	Johnson/Klimkowski/Zepp RC	10.00	5.00
❑ 703	Lou Marone RC	10.00	5.00
❑ 704	Frank Baker RC	10.00	5.00
❑ 705	Tony Cloninger UER	10.00	5.00
❑ 706	John McNamara MG RC	10.00	5.00
❑ 707	Kevin Collins	10.00	5.00
❑ 708	Jose Santiago	10.00	5.00
❑ 709	Mike Fiore	10.00	5.00
❑ 710	Felix Millan	10.00	5.00
❑ 711	Ed Brinkman	10.00	5.00
❑ 712	Nolan Ryan	200.00	125.00
❑ 713	Seattle Pilots TC	25.00	12.50
❑ 714	Al Spangler	10.00	5.00
❑ 715	Mickey Lolich	15.00	7.50
❑ 716	Campisi/Cleveland/Guzman RC	15.00	7.50
❑ 717	Tom Phoebus	10.00	5.00
❑ 718	Ed Spiezio	10.00	5.00
❑ 719	Jim Roland	10.00	5.00
❑ 720	Rick Reichardt	15.00	7.50

1971 Topps

❑	COMPLETE SET (752)	2500.00	1500.00
❑	COMMON CARD (1-393)	1.50	.60
❑	COMMON CARD (394-523)	2.50	1.00
❑	COMMON CARD (524-643)	4.00	1.50
❑	COMMON CARD (644-752)	8.00	4.00
❑	COMMON SP (644-752)	12.00	6.00
❑	WRAPPER (10-CENT)	15.00	10.00
❑ 1	Baltimore Orioles TC	20.00	10.00
❑ 2	Dock Ellis	1.50	.60
❑ 3	Dick McAuliffe	2.00	.75
❑ 4	Vic Davalillo	1.50	.60
❑ 5	Thurman Munson	120.00	70.00
❑ 6	Ed Spiezio	1.50	.60
❑ 7	Jim Holt RC	1.50	.60
❑ 8	Mike McQueen	1.50	.60
❑ 9	George Scott	2.00	.75
❑ 10	Claude Osteen	2.00	.75
❑ 11	Elliott Maddox RC	1.50	.60
❑ 12	Johnny Callison	2.00	.75
❑ 13	C.Brinkman RC/D.Moloney RC	1.50	.60
❑ 14	Dave Concepcion RC	15.00	7.50

Card	Player		
❑ 15	Andy Messersmith	2.00	.75
❑ 16	Ken Singleton RC	4.00	1.50
❑ 17	Billy Sorrell	1.50	.60
❑ 18	Norm Miller	1.50	.60
❑ 19	Skip Pitlock RC	1.50	.60
❑ 20	Reggie Jackson	50.00	30.00
❑ 21	Dan McGinn	1.50	.60
❑ 22	Phil Roof	1.50	.60
❑ 23	Oscar Gamble	1.50	.60
❑ 24	Rich Hand RC	1.50	.60
❑ 25	Cito Gaston	2.00	.75
❑ 26	Bert Blyleven RC	20.00	10.00
❑ 27	F.Cambria RC/G.Clines RC	1.50	.60
❑ 28	Ron Klimkowski	1.50	.60
❑ 29	Don Buford	1.50	.60
❑ 30	Phil Niekro	6.00	3.00
❑ 31	Eddie Kasko MG	1.50	.60
❑ 32	Jerry DaVanon	1.50	.60
❑ 33	Del Unser	1.50	.60
❑ 34	Sandy Vance RC	1.50	.60
❑ 35	Lou Piniella	2.00	.75
❑ 36	Dean Chance	2.00	.75
❑ 37	Rich McKinney RC	1.50	.60
❑ 38	Jim Colborn RC	1.50	.60
❑ 39	L.LaGrow RC/G.Lamont RC	2.00	.75
❑ 40	Lee May	2.00	.75
❑ 41	Rick Austin RC	1.50	.60
❑ 42	Boots Day	1.50	.60
❑ 43	Steve Kealey	1.50	.60
❑ 44	Johnny Edwards	1.50	.60
❑ 45	Jim Hunter	6.00	3.00
❑ 46	Dave Campbell	2.00	.75
❑ 47	Johnny Jeter	1.50	.60
❑ 48	Dave Baldwin	1.50	.60
❑ 49	Don Money	1.50	.60
❑ 50	Willie McCovey	10.00	5.00
❑ 51	Steve Kline RC	1.50	.60
❑ 52	O.Brown RC/E.Williams RC	1.50	.60
❑ 53	Paul Blair	2.00	.75
❑ 54	Checklist 1	10.00	5.00
❑ 55	Steve Carlton	20.00	10.00
❑ 56	Duane Josephson	1.50	.60
❑ 57	Von Joshua RC	1.50	.60
❑ 58	Bill Lee	2.00	.75
❑ 59	Gene Mauch MG	2.00	.75
❑ 60	Dick Bosman	1.50	.60
❑ 61	Johnson/Yaz/Oliva LL	4.00	1.50
❑ 62	Carty/Torre/Sang LL	2.00	.75
❑ 63	Howard/Conig/Powell LL	4.00	1.50
❑ 64	Bench/Perez/B.Will LL	6.00	3.00
❑ 65	Howard/Killebrew/Yaz LL	4.00	1.50
❑ 66	Bench/B.Will/Perez LL	6.00	3.00
❑ 67	Segui/Palmer/Wright LL	4.00	1.50
❑ 68	Seaver/Simp/Walk LL	4.00	1.50
❑ 69	Cuellar/McNally/Perry LL	2.00	.75
❑ 70	Gibson/Perry/Jenkins LL	6.00	3.00
❑ 71	McDowell/Lolich/John LL	2.00	.75
❑ 72	Seaver/Gibson/Jenkins LL	6.00	3.00
❑ 73	George Brunet	1.50	.60
❑ 74	P.Hamm RC/J.Nettles RC	1.50	.60
❑ 75	Gary Nolan	2.00	.75
❑ 76	Ted Savage	1.50	.60
❑ 77	Mike Compton RC	1.50	.60
❑ 78	Jim Spencer	1.50	.60
❑ 79	Wade Blasingame	1.50	.60
❑ 80	Bill Melton	1.50	.60
❑ 81	Felix Millan	1.50	.60
❑ 82	Casey Cox	1.50	.60
❑ 83	T.Foli RC/R.Bobb	2.00	.75
❑ 84	Marcel Lachemann RC	1.50	.60
❑ 85	Billy Grabarkewitz	1.50	.60
❑ 86	Mike Kilkenny	1.50	.60
❑ 87	Jack Heidemann RC	1.50	.60
❑ 88	Hal King	1.50	.60
❑ 89	Ken Brett	1.50	.60
❑ 90	Joe Pepitone	2.00	.75
❑ 91	Bob Lemon MG	2.00	.75
❑ 92	Fred Wenz	1.50	.60
❑ 93	N.McRae/D.Riddleberger	1.50	.60
❑ 94	Don Hahn RC	1.50	.60
❑ 95	Luis Tiant	2.00	.75
❑ 96	Joe Hague	1.50	.60
❑ 97	Floyd Wicker	1.50	.60
❑ 98	Joe Decker RC	1.50	.60
❑ 99	Mark Belanger	2.00	.75
❑ 100	Pete Rose	80.00	50.00
❑ 101	Les Cain	1.50	.60
❑ 102	K.Forsch RC/L.Howard RC	2.00	.75
❑ 103	Rich Severson RC	1.50	.60
❑ 104	Dan Frisella	1.50	.60
❑ 105	Tony Conigliaro	2.00	.75
❑ 106	Tom Dukes	1.50	.60
❑ 107	Roy Foster RC	1.50	.60
❑ 108	John Cumberland	1.50	.60
❑ 109	Steve Hovley	1.50	.60
❑ 110	Bill Mazeroski	6.00	3.00
❑ 111	L.Colson RC/B.Mitchell RC	1.50	.60
❑ 112	Manny Mota	2.00	.75
❑ 113	Jerry Crider	1.50	.60
❑ 114	Billy Conigliaro	2.00	.75
❑ 115	Donn Clendenon	2.00	.75
❑ 116	Ken Sanders	1.50	.60
❑ 117	Ted Simmons RC	8.00	4.00
❑ 118	Cookie Rojas	2.00	.75
❑ 119	Frank Lucchesi MG	1.50	.60
❑ 120	Willie Horton	2.00	.75
❑ 121	J.Dunegan/R.Skidmore RC	1.50	.60
❑ 122	Eddie Watt	1.50	.60
❑ 123A	Checklist 2 Right	10.00	5.00
❑ 123B	Checklist 2 Centered	10.00	5.00
❑ 124	Don Gullett RC	2.00	.75
❑ 125	Ray Fosse	1.50	.60
❑ 126	Danny Coombs	1.50	.60
❑ 127	Danny Thompson RC	2.00	.75
❑ 128	Frank Johnson	1.50	.60
❑ 129	Aurelio Monteagudo	1.50	.60
❑ 130	Denis Menke	1.50	.60
❑ 131	Curt Blefary	1.50	.60
❑ 132	Jose Laboy	1.50	.60
❑ 133	Mickey Lolich	2.00	.75
❑ 134	Jose Arcia	1.50	.60
❑ 135	Rick Monday	2.00	.75
❑ 136	Duffy Dyer	1.50	.60
❑ 137	Marcelino Lopez	1.50	.60
❑ 138	J.Lis/W.Montanez RC	2.00	.75
❑ 139	Paul Casanova	1.50	.60
❑ 140	Gaylord Perry	6.00	3.00
❑ 141	Frank Quilici	1.50	.60
❑ 142	Mack Jones	1.50	.60
❑ 143	Steve Blass	2.00	.75
❑ 144	Jackie Hernandez	1.50	.60
❑ 145	Bill Singer	2.00	.75
❑ 146	Ralph Houk MG	2.00	.75
❑ 147	Bob Priddy	1.50	.60
❑ 148	John Mayberry	2.00	.75
❑ 149	Mike Hershberger	1.50	.60
❑ 150	Sam McDowell	2.00	.75
❑ 151	Tommy Davis	2.00	.75
❑ 152	L.Allen RC/W.Llenas RC	1.50	.60
❑ 153	Gary Ross	1.50	.60
❑ 154	Cesar Gutierrez	1.50	.60
❑ 155	Ken Henderson	1.50	.60
❑ 156	Bart Johnson	1.50	.60
❑ 157	Bob Bailey	2.00	.75
❑ 158	Jerry Reuss	2.00	.75
❑ 159	Jarvis Tatum	1.50	.60
❑ 160	Tom Seaver	30.00	15.00
❑ 161	Coin Checklist	10.00	5.00
❑ 162	Jack Billingham	1.50	.60
❑ 163	Buck Martinez	2.00	.75
❑ 164	F.Duffy RC/M.Wilcox RC	2.00	.75
❑ 165	Cesar Tovar	1.50	.60
❑ 166	Joe Hoerner	1.50	.60
❑ 167	Tom Grieve RC	2.00	.75
❑ 168	Bruce Dal Canton	1.50	.60
❑ 169	Ed Herrmann	1.50	.60
❑ 170	Mike Cuellar	2.00	.75
❑ 171	Bobby Wine	1.50	.60
❑ 172	Duke Sims	1.50	.60
❑ 173	Gil Garrido	1.50	.60
❑ 174	Dave LaRoche RC	1.50	.60
❑ 175	Jim Hickman	1.50	.60
❑ 176	B.Montgomery RC/D.Griffin RC	2.00	.75
❑ 177	Hal McRae	2.00	.75
❑ 178	Dave Duncan	2.00	.75
❑ 179	Mike Corkins	1.50	.60
❑ 180	Al Kaline UER	20.00	10.00
❑ 181	Hal Lanier	1.50	.60
❑ 182	Al Downing	2.00	.75
❑ 183	Gil Hodges MG	4.00	1.50
❑ 184	Stan Bahnsen	1.50	.60
❑ 185	Julian Javier	1.50	.60
❑ 186	Bob Spence RC	1.50	.60
❑ 187	Ted Abernathy	1.50	.60
❑ 188	B.Valentine RC/M.Strahler RC	6.00	3.00
❑ 189	George Mitterwald	1.50	.60
❑ 190	Bob Tolan	1.50	.60
❑ 191	Mike Andrews	1.50	.60
❑ 192	Billy Wilson	1.50	.60
❑ 193	Bob Grich RC	4.00	1.50
❑ 194	Mike Lum	1.50	.60
❑ 195	Boog Powell ALCS	2.00	.75
❑ 196	Dave McNally ALCS	2.00	.75
❑ 197	Jim Palmer ALCS	4.00	1.50
❑ 198	Orioles Celebrate ALCS	2.00	.75
❑ 199	Ty Cline NLCS	2.00	.75
❑ 200	Bobby Tolan NLCS	2.00	.75
❑ 201	Ty Cline NLCS	2.00	.75
❑ 202	Reds Celebrate NLCS	2.00	.75
❑ 203	Larry Gura RC	2.00	.75
❑ 204	B.Smith RC/G.Kopacz RC	1.50	.60
❑ 205	Gerry Moses	1.50	.60
❑ 206	Checklist 3	10.00	5.00
❑ 207	Alan Foster	1.50	.60
❑ 208	Billy Martin MG	4.00	1.50
❑ 209	Steve Renko	1.50	.60
❑ 210	Rod Carew	15.00	7.50
❑ 211	Phil Hennigan RC	1.50	.60
❑ 212	Rich Hebner	2.00	.75
❑ 213	Frank Baker RC	1.50	.60
❑ 214	Al Ferrara	1.50	.60
❑ 215	Diego Segui	1.50	.60
❑ 216	R.Cleveland/L.Melendez RC	1.50	.60
❑ 217	Ed Stroud	1.50	.60
❑ 218	Tony Cloninger	1.50	.60
❑ 219	Elrod Hendricks	1.50	.60
❑ 220	Ron Santo	4.00	1.50
❑ 221	Dave Morehead	1.50	.60
❑ 222	Bob Watson	2.00	.75
❑ 223	Cecil Upshaw	1.50	.60
❑ 224	Alan Gallagher RC	1.50	.60
❑ 225	Gary Peters	1.50	.60
❑ 226	Bill Russell	2.00	.75
❑ 227	Floyd Weaver	1.50	.60
❑ 228	Wayne Garrett	1.50	.60
❑ 229	Jim Hannan	1.50	.60
❑ 230	Willie Stargell	15.00	7.50
❑ 231	V.Colbert RC/J.Lowenstein RC	2.00	.75
❑ 232	John Strohmayer RC	1.50	.60
❑ 233	Larry Bowa	2.00	.75
❑ 234	Jim Lyttle	1.50	.60
❑ 235	Nate Colbert	1.50	.60
❑ 236	Bob Humphreys	1.50	.60
❑ 237	Cesar Cedeno RC	2.00	.75
❑ 238	Chuck Dobson	1.50	.60
❑ 239	Red Schoendienst MG	2.00	.75
❑ 240	Clyde Wright	1.50	.60
❑ 241	Dave Nelson	1.50	.60
❑ 242	Jim Ray	1.50	.60
❑ 243	Carlos May	1.50	.60
❑ 244	Bob Tillman	1.50	.60
❑ 245	Jim Kaat	2.00	.75
❑ 246	Tony Taylor	1.50	.60
❑ 247	J.Cram RC/P.Splittorff RC	2.00	.75
❑ 248	Hoyt Wilhelm	6.00	3.00
❑ 249	Chico Salmon	1.50	.60
❑ 250	Johnny Bench	50.00	30.00
❑ 251	Frank Reberger	1.50	.60
❑ 252	Eddie Leon	1.50	.60
❑ 253	Bill Sudakis	1.50	.60
❑ 254	Cal Koonce	1.50	.60
❑ 255	Bob Robertson	2.00	.75
❑ 256	Tony Gonzalez	1.50	.60
❑ 257	Nelson Briles	2.00	.75
❑ 258	Dick Green	1.50	.60
❑ 259	Dave Marshall	1.50	.60
❑ 260	Tommy Harper	2.00	.75
❑ 261	Darold Knowles	1.50	.60
❑ 262	J.Williams/D.Robinson RC	1.50	.60
❑ 263	John Ellis	1.50	.60
❑ 264	Joe Morgan	8.00	4.00
❑ 265	Jim Northrup	2.00	.75
❑ 266	Bill Stoneman	1.50	.60
❑ 267	Rich Morales	1.50	.60
❑ 268	Philadelphia Phillies TC	4.00	1.50
❑ 269	Gail Hopkins	1.50	.60
❑ 270	Rico Carty	2.00	.75
❑ 271	Bill Zepp	1.50	.60

❑ 272 Tommy Helms 2.00 .75
❑ 273 Pete Richert 1.50 .60
❑ 274 Ron Slocum 1.50 .60
❑ 275 Vada Pinson 2.00 .75
❑ 276 M.Davison RC/G.Foster RC 8.00 4.00
❑ 277 Gary Waslewski 1.50 .60
❑ 278 Jerry Grote 2.00 .75
❑ 279 Lefty Phillips MG 1.50 .60
❑ 280 Ferguson Jenkins 6.00 3.00
❑ 281 Danny Walton 1.50 .60
❑ 282 Jose Pagan 1.50 .60
❑ 283 Dick Such 1.50 .60
❑ 284 Jim Gosger 1.50 .60
❑ 285 Sal Bando 2.00 .75
❑ 286 Jerry McNertney 1.50 .60
❑ 287 Mike Fiore 1.50 .60
❑ 288 Joe Moeller 1.50 .60
❑ 289 Chicago White Sox TC 4.00 1.50
❑ 290 Tony Oliva 4.00 1.50
❑ 291 George Culver 1.50 .60
❑ 292 Jay Johnstone 2.00 .75
❑ 293 Pat Corrales 2.00 .75
❑ 294 Steve Dunning RC 1.50 .60
❑ 295 Bobby Bonds 4.00 1.50
❑ 296 Tom Timmermann 1.50 .60
❑ 297 Johnny Briggs 1.50 .60
❑ 298 Jim Nelson RC 1.50 .60
❑ 299 Ed Kirkpatrick 1.50 .60
❑ 300 Brooks Robinson 20.00 10.00
❑ 301 Earl Wilson 1.50 .60
❑ 302 Phil Gagliano 1.50 .60
❑ 303 Lindy McDaniel 2.00 .75
❑ 304 Ron Brand 1.50 .60
❑ 305 Reggie Smith 2.00 .75
❑ 306 Jim Nash 1.50 .60
❑ 307 Don Wert 1.50 .60
❑ 308 St. Louis Cardinals TC 4.00 1.50
❑ 309 Dick Ellsworth 1.50 .60
❑ 310 Tommie Agee 2.00 .75
❑ 311 Lee Stange 1.50 .60
❑ 312 Harry Walker MG 1.50 .60
❑ 313 Tom Hall 1.50 .60
❑ 314 Jeff Torborg 2.00 .75
❑ 315 Ron Fairly 2.00 .75
❑ 316 Fred Scherman RC 1.50 .60
❑ 317 J.Driscoll RC/A.Mangual 1.50 .60
❑ 318 Rudy May 1.50 .60
❑ 319 Ty Cline 1.50 .60
❑ 320 Dave McNally 2.00 .75
❑ 321 Tom Matchick 1.50 .60
❑ 322 Jim Beauchamp 1.50 .60
❑ 323 Billy Champion 1.50 .60
❑ 324 Graig Nettles 2.00 .75
❑ 325 Juan Marichal 8.00 4.00
❑ 326 Richie Scheinblum 1.50 .60
❑ 327 Boog Powell WS 2.00 .75
❑ 328 Don Buford WS 2.00 .75
❑ 329 Frank Robinson WS 4.00 1.50
❑ 330 Reds Stay Alive WS 2.00 .75
❑ 331 Brooks Robinson WS 6.00 3.00
❑ 332 Orioles Celebrate WS 2.00 .75
❑ 333 Clay Kirby 1.50 .60
❑ 334 Roberto Pena 1.50 .60
❑ 335 Jerry Koosman 2.00 .75
❑ 336 Detroit Tigers TC 4.00 1.50
❑ 337 Jesus Alou 1.50 .60
❑ 338 Gene Tenace 2.00 .75
❑ 339 Wayne Simpson 1.50 .60
❑ 340 Rico Petrocelli 2.00 .75
❑ 341 Steve Garvey RC 40.00 20.00
❑ 342 Frank Tepedino 2.00 .75
❑ 343 E.Acosta RC/M.May RC 2.00 .75
❑ 344 Ellie Rodriguez 1.50 .60
❑ 345 Joel Horlen 1.50 .60
❑ 346 Lum Harris MG 1.50 .60
❑ 347 Ted Uhlaender 1.50 .60
❑ 348 Fred Norman 1.50 .60
❑ 349 Rich Reese 1.50 .60
❑ 350 Billy Williams 6.00 3.00
❑ 351 Jim Shellenback 1.50 .60
❑ 352 Denny Doyle 1.50 .60
❑ 353 Carl Taylor 1.50 .60
❑ 354 Don McMahon 1.50 .60
❑ 355 Bud Harrelson w/Ryan 4.00 1.50
❑ 356 Bob Locker 1.50 .60
❑ 357 Cincinnati Reds TC 4.00 1.50
❑ 358 Danny Cater 1.50 .60
❑ 359 Ron Reed 1.50 .60
❑ 360 Jim Fregosi 2.00 .75
❑ 361 Don Sutton 6.00 3.00
❑ 362 M.Adamson/R.Freed 1.50 .60
❑ 363 Mike Nagy 1.50 .60
❑ 364 Tommy Dean 1.50 .60
❑ 365 Bob Johnson 1.50 .60
❑ 366 Ron Stone 1.50 .60
❑ 367 Dalton Jones 1.50 .60
❑ 368 Bob Veale 2.00 .75
❑ 369 Checklist 4 10.00 5.00
❑ 370 Joe Torre 4.00 1.50
❑ 371 Jack Hiatt 1.50 .60
❑ 372 Lew Krausse 1.50 .60
❑ 373 Tom McCraw 1.50 .60
❑ 374 Clete Boyer 2.00 .75
❑ 375 Steve Hargan 1.50 .60
❑ 376 C.Mashore RC/E.McAnally RC 1.50 .60
❑ 377 Greg Garrett 1.50 .60
❑ 378 Tito Fuentes 1.50 .60
❑ 379 Wayne Granger 1.50 .60
❑ 380 Ted Williams MG 12.00 6.00
❑ 381 Fred Gladding 1.50 .60
❑ 382 Jake Gibbs 1.50 .60
❑ 383 Rod Gaspar 1.50 .60
❑ 384 Rollie Fingers 6.00 3.00
❑ 385 Maury Wills 4.00 1.50
❑ 386 Boston Red Sox TC 2.00 .75
❑ 387 Ron Herbel 1.50 .60
❑ 388 Al Oliver 4.00 1.50
❑ 389 Ed Brinkman 1.50 .60
❑ 390 Glenn Beckert 2.00 .75
❑ 391 S.Brye RC/C.Nash RC 2.00 .75
❑ 392 Grant Jackson 1.50 .60
❑ 393 Merv Rettenmund 2.00 .75
❑ 394 Clay Carroll 2.50 1.00
❑ 395 Roy White 4.00 1.50
❑ 396 Dick Schofield 2.50 1.00
❑ 397 Alvin Dark MG 4.00 1.50
❑ 398 Howie Reed 2.50 1.00
❑ 399 Jim French 2.50 1.00
❑ 400 Hank Aaron 60.00 35.00
❑ 401 Tom Murphy 2.50 1.00
❑ 402 Los Angeles Dodgers TC 6.00 3.00
❑ 403 Joe Coleman 2.50 1.00
❑ 404 B.Harris RC/R.Metzger RC 2.50 1.00
❑ 405 Leo Cardenas 2.50 1.00
❑ 406 Ray Sadecki 2.50 1.00
❑ 407 Joe Rudi 4.00 1.50
❑ 408 Rafael Robles 2.50 1.00
❑ 409 Don Pavletich 2.50 1.00
❑ 410 Ken Holtzman 4.00 1.50
❑ 411 George Spriggs 2.50 1.00
❑ 412 Jerry Johnson 2.50 1.00
❑ 413 Pat Kelly 2.50 1.00
❑ 414 Woodie Fryman 2.50 1.00
❑ 415 Mike Hegan 2.50 1.00
❑ 416 Gene Alley 2.50 1.00
❑ 417 Dick Hall 2.50 1.00
❑ 418 Adolfo Phillips 2.50 1.00
❑ 419 Ron Hansen 2.50 1.00
❑ 420 Jim Merritt 2.50 1.00
❑ 421 John Stephenson 2.50 1.00
❑ 422 Frank Bertaina 2.50 1.00
❑ 423 D.Saunders/T.Marting RC 2.50 1.00
❑ 424 Roberto Rodriquez 2.50 1.00
❑ 425 Doug Rader 4.00 1.50
❑ 426 Chris Cannizzaro 2.50 1.00
❑ 427 Bernie Allen 2.50 1.00
❑ 428 Jim McAndrew 2.50 1.00
❑ 429 Chuck Hinton 2.50 1.00
❑ 430 Wes Parker 4.00 1.50
❑ 431 Tom Burgmeier 2.50 1.00
❑ 432 Bob Didier 2.50 1.00
❑ 433 Skip Lockwood 2.50 1.00
❑ 434 Gary Sutherland 2.50 1.00
❑ 435 Jose Cardenal 4.00 1.50
❑ 436 Wilbur Wood 4.00 1.50
❑ 437 Danny Murtaugh MG 4.00 1.50
❑ 438 Mike McCormick 4.00 1.50
❑ 439 G.Luzinski RC/S.Reid 6.00 3.00
❑ 440 Bert Campaneris 4.00 1.50
❑ 441 Milt Pappas 4.00 1.50
❑ 442 California Angels TC 4.00 1.50
❑ 443 Rich Robertson 2.50 1.00
❑ 444 Jimmie Price 2.50 1.00
❑ 445 Art Shamsky 2.50 1.00
❑ 446 Bobby Bolin 2.50 1.00
❑ 447 Cesar Geronimo RC 4.00 1.50
❑ 448 Dave Roberts 2.50 1.00
❑ 449 Brant Alyea 2.50 1.00
❑ 450 Bob Gibson 15.00 7.50
❑ 451 Joe Keough 2.50 1.00
❑ 452 John Boccabella 2.50 1.00
❑ 453 Terry Crowley 2.50 1.00
❑ 454 Mike Paul 2.50 1.00
❑ 455 Don Kessinger 4.00 1.50
❑ 456 Bob Meyer 2.50 1.00
❑ 457 Willie Smith 2.50 1.00
❑ 458 R.Lolich RC/D.Lemonds RC 2.50 1.00
❑ 459 Jim Lefebvre 2.50 1.00
❑ 460 Fritz Peterson 2.50 1.00
❑ 461 Jim Ray Hart 2.50 1.00
❑ 462 Washington Senators TC 6.00 3.00
❑ 463 Tom Kelley 2.50 1.00
❑ 464 Aurelio Rodriguez 2.50 1.00
❑ 465 Tim McCarver 6.00 3.00
❑ 466 Ken Berry 2.50 1.00
❑ 467 Al Santorini 2.50 1.00
❑ 468 Frank Fernandez 2.50 1.00
❑ 469 Bob Aspromonte 2.50 1.00
❑ 470 Bob Oliver 2.50 1.00
❑ 471 Tom Griffin 2.50 1.00
❑ 472 Ken Rudolph 2.50 1.00
❑ 473 Gary Wagner 2.50 1.00
❑ 474 Jim Fairey 2.50 1.00
❑ 475 Ron Perranoski 2.50 1.00
❑ 476 Dal Maxvill 2.50 1.00
❑ 477 Earl Weaver MG 6.00 3.00
❑ 478 Bernie Carbo 2.50 1.00
❑ 479 Dennis Higgins 2.50 1.00
❑ 480 Manny Sanguillen 4.00 1.50
❑ 481 Daryl Patterson 2.50 1.00
❑ 482 San Diego Padres TC 6.00 3.00
❑ 483 Gene Michael 2.50 1.00
❑ 484 Don Wilson 2.50 1.00
❑ 485 Ken McMullen 2.50 1.00
❑ 486 Steve Huntz 2.50 1.00
❑ 487 Paul Schaal 2.50 1.00
❑ 488 Jerry Stephenson 2.50 1.00
❑ 489 Luis Alvarado 2.50 1.00
❑ 490 Deron Johnson 2.50 1.00
❑ 491 Jim Hardin 2.50 1.00
❑ 492 Ken Boswell 2.50 1.00
❑ 493 Dave May 2.50 1.00
❑ 494 R.Garr/R.Kester 4.00 1.50
❑ 495 Felipe Alou 4.00 1.50
❑ 496 Woody Woodward 2.50 1.00
❑ 497 Horacio Pina RC 2.50 1.00
❑ 498 John Kennedy 2.50 1.00
❑ 499 Checklist 5 10.00 5.00
❑ 500 Jim Perry 4.00 1.50
❑ 501 Andy Etchebarren 2.50 1.00
❑ 502 Chicago Cubs TC 6.00 3.00
❑ 503 Gates Brown 4.00 1.50
❑ 504 Ken Wright RC 2.50 1.00
❑ 505 Ollie Brown 2.50 1.00
❑ 506 Bobby Knoop 2.50 1.00
❑ 507 George Stone 2.50 1.00
❑ 508 Roger Repoz 2.50 1.00
❑ 509 Jim Grant 2.50 1.00
❑ 510 Ken Harrelson 4.00 1.50
❑ 511 Chris Short w/Rose 4.00 1.50
❑ 512 D.Mills RC/M.Garman RC 2.50 1.00
❑ 513 Nolan Ryan 150.00 90.00
❑ 514 Ron Woods 2.50 1.00
❑ 515 Carl Morton 2.50 1.00
❑ 516 Ted Kubiak 2.50 1.00
❑ 517 Charlie Fox MG RC 2.50 1.00
❑ 518 Joe Grzenda 2.50 1.00
❑ 519 Willie Crawford 2.50 1.00
❑ 520 Tommy John 6.00 3.00
❑ 521 Leron Lee 2.50 1.00
❑ 522 Minnesota Twins TC 6.00 3.00
❑ 523 John Odom 2.50 1.00
❑ 524 Mickey Stanley 6.00 3.00
❑ 525 Ernie Banks 50.00 30.00
❑ 526 Ray Jarvis 4.00 1.50
❑ 527 Cleon Jones 6.00 3.00
❑ 528 Wally Bunker 4.00 1.50
❑ 529 Hernandez/Bucker/Perez RC 6.00 3.00

❑	530 Carl Yastrzemski	30.00	15.00
❑	531 Mike Torrez	4.00	1.50
❑	532 Bill Rigney MG	4.00	1.50
❑	533 Mike Ryan	4.00	1.50
❑	534 Luke Walker	4.00	1.50
❑	535 Curt Flood	6.00	3.00
❑	536 Claude Raymond	4.00	1.50
❑	537 Tom Egan	4.00	1.50
❑	538 Angel Bravo	4.00	1.50
❑	539 Larry Brown	4.00	1.50
❑	540 Larry Dierker	6.00	3.00
❑	541 Bob Burda	4.00	1.50
❑	542 Bob Miller	4.00	1.50
❑	543 New York Yankees TC	10.00	5.00
❑	544 Vida Blue	6.00	3.00
❑	545 Dick Dietz	4.00	1.50
❑	546 John Matias	4.00	1.50
❑	547 Pat Dobson	6.00	3.00
❑	548 Don Mason	4.00	1.50
❑	549 Jim Brewer	6.00	3.00
❑	550 Harmon Killebrew	25.00	12.50
❑	551 Frank Linzy	4.00	1.50
❑	552 Buddy Bradford	4.00	1.50
❑	553 Kevin Collins	4.00	1.50
❑	554 Lowell Palmer	4.00	1.50
❑	555 Walt Williams	4.00	1.50
❑	556 Jim McGlothlin	4.00	1.50
❑	557 Tom Satriano	4.00	1.50
❑	558 Hector Torres	4.00	1.50
❑	559 Cox/Gogolewsk/Jones RC	4.00	1.50
❑	560 Rusty Staub	6.00	3.00
❑	561 Syd O'Brien	4.00	1.50
❑	562 Dave Giusti	4.00	1.50
❑	563 San Francisco Giants TC	8.00	4.00
❑	564 Al Fitzmorris	4.00	1.50
❑	565 Jim Wynn	6.00	3.00
❑	566 Tim Cullen	4.00	1.50
❑	567 Walt Alston MG	8.00	4.00
❑	568 Sal Campisi	4.00	1.50
❑	569 Ivan Murrell	4.00	1.50
❑	570 Jim Palmer	30.00	15.00
❑	571 Ted Sizemore	4.00	1.50
❑	572 Jerry Kenney	4.00	1.50
❑	573 Ed Kranepool	6.00	3.00
❑	574 Jim Bunning	8.00	4.00
❑	575 Bill Freehan	6.00	3.00
❑	576 Garrett/Davis/Jestadt RC	4.00	1.50
❑	577 Jim Lonborg	6.00	3.00
❑	578 Ron Hunt	4.00	1.50
❑	579 Marty Pattin	4.00	1.50
❑	580 Tony Perez	20.00	10.00
❑	581 Roger Nelson	4.00	1.50
❑	582 Dave Cash	6.00	3.00
❑	583 Ron Cook RC	4.00	1.50
❑	584 Cleveland Indians TC	8.00	4.00
❑	585 Willie Davis	6.00	3.00
❑	586 Dick Woodson	4.00	1.50
❑	587 Sonny Jackson	4.00	1.50
❑	588 Tom Bradley RC	4.00	1.50
❑	589 Bob Barton	4.00	1.50
❑	590 Alex Johnson	6.00	3.00
❑	591 Jackie Brown RC	4.00	1.50
❑	592 Randy Hundley	6.00	3.00
❑	593 Jack Aker	4.00	1.50
❑	594 Chlupsa/Stinson/Hrabosky RC	6.00	3.00
❑	595 Dave Johnson	6.00	3.00
❑	596 Mike Jorgensen	4.00	1.50
❑	597 Ken Suarez	4.00	1.50
❑	598 Rick Wise	6.00	3.00
❑	599 Norm Cash	6.00	3.00
❑	600 Willie Mays	100.00	60.00
❑	601 Ken Tatum	4.00	1.50
❑	602 Marty Martinez	4.00	1.50
❑	603 Pittsburgh Pirates TC	8.00	4.00
❑	604 John Gelnar	4.00	1.50
❑	605 Orlando Cepeda	8.00	4.00
❑	606 Chuck Taylor	4.00	1.50
❑	607 Paul Ratliff	4.00	1.50
❑	608 Mike Wegener	4.00	1.50
❑	609 Leo Durocher MG	8.00	4.00
❑	610 Amos Otis	6.00	3.00
❑	611 Tom Phoebus	4.00	1.50
❑	612 Camilli/Ford/Mingori RC	4.00	1.50
❑	613 Pedro Borbon	4.00	1.50
❑	614 Billy Cowan	4.00	1.50
❑	615 Mel Stottlemyre	6.00	3.00
❑	616 Larry Hisle	6.00	3.00
❑	617 Clay Dalrymple	4.00	1.50
❑	618 Tug McGraw	6.00	3.00
❑	619A Checklist 6 ERR w/o Copy	10.00	5.00
❑	619B Checklist 6 COR w/Copy	6.00	3.00
❑	620 Frank Howard	6.00	3.00
❑	621 Ron Bryant	4.00	1.50
❑	622 Joe Lahoud	4.00	1.50
❑	623 Pat Jarvis	4.00	1.50
❑	624 Oakland Athletics TC	8.00	4.00
❑	625 Lou Brock	30.00	15.00
❑	626 Freddie Patek	6.00	3.00
❑	627 Steve Hamilton	4.00	1.50
❑	628 John Bateman	4.00	1.50
❑	629 John Hiller	6.00	3.00
❑	630 Roberto Clemente	150.00	90.00
❑	631 Eddie Fisher	4.00	1.50
❑	632 Darrel Chaney	4.00	1.50
❑	633 Brooks/Koegel/Northey RC	4.00	1.50
❑	634 Phil Regan	4.00	1.50
❑	635 Bobby Murcer	6.00	3.00
❑	636 Denny Lemaster	4.00	1.50
❑	637 Dave Bristol MG	4.00	1.50
❑	638 Stan Williams	4.00	1.50
❑	639 Tom Haller	4.00	1.50
❑	640 Frank Robinson	40.00	20.00
❑	641 New York Mets TC	15.00	7.50
❑	642 Jim Roland	4.00	1.50
❑	643 Rick Reichardt	4.00	1.50
❑	644 Jim Stewart SP	12.00	6.00
❑	645 Jim Maloney SP	15.00	7.50
❑	646 Bobby Floyd SP	12.00	6.00
❑	647 Juan Pizarro	8.00	4.00
❑	648 Folkers/Martinez/Matlack SP RC	25.00	12.50
❑	649 Sparky Lyle SP	15.00	7.50
❑	650 Richie Allen SP	30.00	15.00
❑	651 Jerry Robertson SP	12.00	6.00
❑	652 Atlanta Braves TC	12.00	6.00
❑	653 Russ Snyder SP	12.00	6.00
❑	654 Don Shaw SP	12.00	6.00
❑	655 Mike Epstein SP	12.00	6.00
❑	656 Gerry Nyman SP	12.00	6.00
❑	657 Jose Azcue	8.00	4.00
❑	658 Paul Lindblad SP	12.00	6.00
❑	659 Byron Browne SP	12.00	6.00
❑	660 Ray Culp	8.00	4.00
❑	661 Chuck Tanner MG SP	15.00	7.50
❑	662 Mike Hedlund SP	12.00	6.00
❑	663 Marv Staehle	8.00	4.00
❑	664 Reynolds/Reynolds/Reynolds SP RC	12.00	6.00
❑	665 Ron Swoboda SP	15.00	7.50
❑	666 Gene Brabender SP	12.00	6.00
❑	667 Pete Ward	8.00	4.00
❑	668 Gary Neibauer	8.00	4.00
❑	669 Ike Brown SP	12.00	6.00
❑	670 Bill Hands	8.00	4.00
❑	671 Bill Voss SP	12.00	6.00
❑	672 Ed Crosby SP RC	12.00	6.00
❑	673 Gerry Janeski SP RC	12.00	6.00
❑	674 Montreal Expos TC	12.00	6.00
❑	675 Dave Boswell	8.00	4.00
❑	676 Tommie Reynolds	8.00	4.00
❑	677 Jack DiLauro SP	12.00	6.00
❑	678 George Thomas	8.00	4.00
❑	679 Don O'Riley	8.00	4.00
❑	680 Don Mincher SP	12.00	6.00
❑	681 Bill Butler	8.00	4.00
❑	682 Terry Harmon	8.00	4.00
❑	683 Bill Burbach SP	12.00	6.00
❑	684 Curt Motton	8.00	4.00
❑	685 Moe Drabowsky	8.00	4.00
❑	686 Chico Ruiz SP	12.00	6.00
❑	687 Ron Taylor SP	12.00	6.00
❑	688 S.Anderson MG SP	30.00	15.00
❑	689 Frank Baker	8.00	4.00
❑	690 Bob Moose	8.00	4.00
❑	691 Bobby Heise	8.00	4.00
❑	692 Haydel/Moret/Twitchell SP RC	12.00	6.00
❑	693 Jose Pena SP	12.00	6.00
❑	694 Rick Renick SP	12.00	6.00
❑	695 Joe Niekro	12.00	6.00
❑	696 Jerry Morales	8.00	4.00
❑	697 Rickey Clark SP	12.00	6.00
❑	698 Milwaukee Brewers TC SP	20.00	10.00
❑	699 Jim Britton	8.00	4.00
❑	700 Boog Powell SP	25.00	12.50
❑	701 Bob Garibaldi	8.00	4.00
❑	702 Milt Ramirez RC	8.00	4.00
❑	703 Mike Kekich	8.00	4.00
❑	704 J.C. Martin SP	12.00	6.00
❑	705 Dick Selma SP	12.00	6.00
❑	706 Joe Foy SP	12.00	6.00
❑	707 Fred Lasher	8.00	4.00
❑	708 Russ Nagelson SP	12.00	6.00
❑	709 Baker/Baylor/Pac SP RC	80.00	50.00
❑	710 Sonny Siebert	8.00	4.00
❑	711 Larry Stahl SP	12.00	6.00
❑	712 Jose Martinez	8.00	4.00
❑	713 Mike Marshall SP	15.00	7.50
❑	714 Dick Williams MG SP	15.00	7.50
❑	715 Horace Clarke SP	15.00	7.50
❑	716 Dave Leonhard	8.00	4.00
❑	717 Tommie Aaron SP	12.00	6.00
❑	718 Billy Wynne	8.00	4.00
❑	719 Jerry May SP	12.00	6.00
❑	720 Matty Alou	12.00	6.00
❑	721 John Morris	8.00	4.00
❑	722 Houston Astros TC SP	20.00	10.00
❑	723 Vicente Romo SP	12.00	6.00
❑	724 Tom Tischinski SP	12.00	6.00
❑	725 Gary Gentry SP	12.00	6.00
❑	726 Paul Popovich	8.00	4.00
❑	727 Ray Lamb SP	12.00	6.00
❑	728 Redmond/Lampard/Williams RC	8.00	4.00
❑	729 Dick Billings RC	8.00	4.00
❑	730 Jim Rooker	8.00	4.00
❑	731 Jim Qualls SP	12.00	6.00
❑	732 Bob Reed	8.00	4.00
❑	733 Lee Maye SP	12.00	6.00
❑	734 Rob Gardner SP	12.00	6.00
❑	735 Mike Shannon SP	15.00	7.50
❑	736 Mel Queen SP	12.00	6.00
❑	737 Preston Gomez MG SP	12.00	6.00
❑	738 Russ Gibson SP	12.00	6.00
❑	739 Barry Lersch SP	12.00	6.00
❑	740 Luis Aparicio SP	30.00	15.00
❑	741 Skip Guinn	8.00	4.00
❑	742 Kansas City Royals TC	12.00	6.00
❑	743 John O'Donoghue SP	12.00	6.00
❑	744 Chuck Manuel SP	12.00	6.00
❑	745 Sandy Alomar SP	12.00	6.00
❑	746 Andy Kosco	8.00	4.00
❑	747 Severinsen/Spinks/Moore RC	8.00	4.00
❑	748 John Purdin SP	12.00	6.00
❑	749 Ken Szotkiewicz RC	8.00	4.00
❑	750 Denny McLain SP	25.00	12.50
❑	751 Al Weis SP	15.00	7.50
❑	752 Dick Drago	12.00	6.00

1972 Topps

❑	COMPLETE SET (787)	1500.00	1000.00
❑	COMMON CARD (1-132)	.60	.25
❑	COMMON CARD (133-263)	1.00	.40
❑	COMMON CARD (264-394)	1.25	.50
❑	COMMON CARD (395-525)	1.50	.60
❑	COMMON CARD (526-656)	4.00	1.50
❑	COMMON CARD (657-787)	12.00	6.00
❑	WRAPPER (10-CENT)	15.00	10.00
❑	1 Pittsburgh Pirates TC	8.00	4.00
❑	2 Ray Culp	.60	.25
❑	3 Bob Tolan	.60	.25
❑	4 Checklist 1-132	6.00	3.00
❑	5 John Bateman	.60	.25
❑	6 Fred Scherman	.60	.25

❑ 7 Enzo Hernandez .60 .25
❑ 8 Ron Swoboda 1.25 .50
❑ 9 Stan Williams .60 .25
❑ 10 Amos Otis 1.25 .50
❑ 11 Bobby Valentine 1.25 .50
❑ 12 Jose Cardenal .60 .25
❑ 13 Joe Grzenda .60 .25
❑ 14 Koegel/Anderson/Twitchell RC .60 .25
❑ 15 Walt Williams .60 .25
❑ 16 Mike Jorgensen .60 .25
❑ 17 Dave Duncan 1.25 .50
❑ 18A Juan Pizarro Yellow .60 .25
❑ 18B Juan Pizarro Green 5.00 2.00
❑ 19 Billy Cowan .60 .25
❑ 20 Don Wilson .60 .25
❑ 21 Atlanta Braves TC 1.50 .60
❑ 22 Rob Gardner .60 .25
❑ 23 Ted Kubiak .60 .25
❑ 24 Ted Ford .60 .25
❑ 25 Bill Singer .60 .25
❑ 26 Andy Etchebarren .60 .25
❑ 27 Bob Johnson .60 .25
❑ 28 Gebhard/Brye Haydel RC .60 .25
❑ 29A Bill Bonham Yellow RC .60 .25
❑ 29B Bill Bonham Green 5.00 2.00
❑ 30 Rico Petrocelli 1.25 .50
❑ 31 Cleon Jones 1.25 .50
❑ 32 Cleon Jones IA .60 .25
❑ 33 Billy Martin MG 4.00 1.50
❑ 34 Billy Martin IA 2.50 1.00
❑ 35 Jerry Johnson .60 .25
❑ 36 Jerry Johnson IA .60 .25
❑ 37 Carl Yastrzemski 10.00 5.00
❑ 38 Carl Yastrzemski IA 8.00 4.00
❑ 39 Bob Barton .60 .25
❑ 40 Bob Barton IA .60 .25
❑ 41 Tommy Davis 1.25 .50
❑ 42 Tommy Davis IA .60 .25
❑ 43 Rick Wise 1.25 .50
❑ 44 Rick Wise IA .60 .25
❑ 45A Glenn Beckert Yellow 1.25 .50
❑ 45B Glenn Beckert Green 5.00 2.00
❑ 46 Glenn Beckert IA .60 .25
❑ 47 John Ellis .60 .25
❑ 48 John Ellis IA .60 .25
❑ 49 Willie Mays 40.00 20.00
❑ 50 Willie Mays IA 20.00 10.00
❑ 51 Harmon Killebrew 8.00 4.00
❑ 52 Harmon Killebrew IA 4.00 1.50
❑ 53 Bud Harrelson 1.25 .50
❑ 54 Bud Harrelson IA .60 .25
❑ 55 Clyde Wright .60 .25
❑ 56 Rich Chiles RC .60 .25
❑ 57 Bob Oliver .60 .25
❑ 58 Ernie McAnally .60 .25
❑ 59 Fred Stanley RC .60 .25
❑ 60 Manny Sanguillen 1.25 .50
❑ 61 Hooten/Hisler/Stephenson RC 1.25 .50
❑ 62 Angel Mangual .60 .25
❑ 63 Duke Sims .60 .25
❑ 64 Pete Broberg RC .60 .25
❑ 65 Cesar Cedeno 1.25 .50
❑ 66 Ray Corbin RC .60 .25
❑ 67 Red Schoendienst MG 2.50 1.00
❑ 68 Jim York RC .60 .25
❑ 69 Roger Freed .60 .25
❑ 70 Mike Cuellar 1.25 .50
❑ 71 California Angels TC 1.50 .60
❑ 72 Bruce Kison RC .60 .25
❑ 73 Steve Huntz .60 .25
❑ 74 Cecil Upshaw .60 .25
❑ 75 Bert Campaneris 1.25 .50
❑ 76 Don Carrithers RC .60 .25
❑ 77 Ron Theobald RC .60 .25
❑ 78 Steve Arlin RC .60 .25
❑ 79 C.Fisk RC/C.Cooper RC 50.00 30.00
❑ 80 Tony Perez 4.00 1.50
❑ 81 Mike Hedlund .60 .25
❑ 82 Ron Woods .60 .25
❑ 83 Dalton Jones .60 .25
❑ 84 Vince Colbert .60 .25
❑ 85 Torre/Garr/Beckert LL 2.50 1.00
❑ 86 Oliva/Murcer/Rett LL 2.50 1.00
❑ 87 Torre/Stargell/Aaron LL 4.00 1.50
❑ 88 Kill/F.Rob/Smith LL 4.00 1.50
❑ 89 Stargell/Aaron/May LL 2.50 1.00
❑ 90 Melton/Cash/Jackson LL 2.50 1.00
❑ 91 Seaver/Roberts/Wilson LL 2.50 1.00
❑ 92 Blue/Wood/Palmer LL 2.50 1.00
❑ 93 Jenkins/Carlton/Seaver LL 4.00 1.50
❑ 94 Lolich/Blue/Wood LL 2.50 1.00
❑ 95 Seaver/Jenkins/Stone LL 4.00 1.50
❑ 96 Lolich/Blue/Coleman LL 2.50 1.00
❑ 97 Tom Kelley .60 .25
❑ 98 Chuck Tanner MG 1.25 .50
❑ 99 Ross Grimsley RC .60 .25
❑ 100 Frank Robinson 8.00 4.00
❑ 101 Grief/Richard/Busse RC 2.50 1.00
❑ 102 Lloyd Allen .60 .25
❑ 103 Checklist 133-263 6.00 3.00
❑ 104 Toby Harrah RC 1.25 .50
❑ 105 Gary Gentry .60 .25
❑ 106 Milwaukee Brewers TC 1.50 .60
❑ 107 Jose Cruz RC 1.25 .50
❑ 108 Gary Waslewski .60 .25
❑ 109 Jerry May .60 .25
❑ 110 Ron Hunt .60 .25
❑ 111 Jim Grant .60 .25
❑ 112 Greg Luzinski 1.25 .50
❑ 113 Rogelio Moret .60 .25
❑ 114 Bill Buckner 1.25 .50
❑ 115 Jim Fregosi 1.25 .50
❑ 116 Ed Farmer RC .60 .25
❑ 117A Cleo James Yellow RC .60 .25
❑ 117B Cleo James Green 5.00 2.00
❑ 118 Skip Lockwood .60 .25
❑ 119 Marty Perez .60 .25
❑ 120 Bill Freehan 1.25 .50
❑ 121 Ed Sprague .60 .25
❑ 122 Larry Biittner RC .60 .25
❑ 123 Ed Acosta .60 .25
❑ 124 Closter/Torres/Hambright RC .60 .25
❑ 125 Dave Cash 1.25 .50
❑ 126 Bart Johnson .60 .25
❑ 127 Duffy Dyer .60 .25
❑ 128 Eddie Watt .60 .25
❑ 129 Charlie Fox MG .60 .25
❑ 130 Bob Gibson 8.00 4.00
❑ 131 Jim Nettles .60 .25
❑ 132 Joe Morgan 6.00 3.00
❑ 133 Joe Keough 1.00 .40
❑ 134 Carl Morton 1.00 .40
❑ 135 Vada Pinson 2.00 .75
❑ 136 Darrel Chaney 1.00 .40
❑ 137 Dick Williams MG 2.00 .75
❑ 138 Mike Kekich 1.00 .40
❑ 139 Tim McCarver 2.00 .75
❑ 140 Pat Dobson 2.00 .75
❑ 141 Capra/Stanton/Matlack RC 2.00 .75
❑ 142 Chris Chambliss RC 4.00 1.50
❑ 143 Garry Jestadt 1.00 .40
❑ 144 Marty Pattin 1.00 .40
❑ 145 Don Kessinger 2.00 .75
❑ 146 Steve Kealey 1.00 .40
❑ 147 Dave Kingman RC 6.00 3.00
❑ 148 Dick Billings 1.00 .40
❑ 149 Gary Neibauer 1.00 .40
❑ 150 Norm Cash 2.00 .75
❑ 151 Jim Brewer 1.00 .40
❑ 152 Gene Clines 1.00 .40
❑ 153 Rick Auerbach RC 1.00 .40
❑ 154 Ted Simmons 4.00 1.50
❑ 155 Larry Dierker 1.00 .40
❑ 156 Minnesota Twins TC 2.00 .75
❑ 157 Don Gullett 1.00 .40
❑ 158 Jerry Kenney 1.00 .40
❑ 159 John Boccabella 1.00 .40
❑ 160 Andy Messersmith 2.00 .75
❑ 161 Brock Davis 1.00 .40
❑ 162 Bell/Porter/Reynolds RC 2.00 .75
❑ 163 Tug McGraw 4.00 1.50
❑ 164 Tug McGraw IA 2.00 .75
❑ 165 Chris Speier RC 2.00 .75
❑ 166 Chris Speier IA 1.00 .40
❑ 167 Deron Johnson 1.00 .40
❑ 168 Deron Johnson IA 1.00 .40
❑ 169 Vida Blue 4.00 1.50
❑ 170 Vida Blue IA 2.00 .75
❑ 171 Darrell Evans 4.00 1.50
❑ 172 Darrell Evans IA 2.00 .75
❑ 173 Clay Kirby 1.00 .40
❑ 174 Clay Kirby IA 1.00 .40
❑ 175 Tom Haller 1.00 .40
❑ 176 Tom Haller IA 1.00 .40
❑ 177 Paul Schaal 1.00 .40
❑ 178 Paul Schaal IA 1.00 .40
❑ 179 Dock Ellis 1.00 .40
❑ 180 Dock Ellis IA 1.00 .40
❑ 181 Ed Kranepool 2.00 .75
❑ 182 Ed Kranepool IA 1.00 .40
❑ 183 Bill Melton 1.00 .40
❑ 184 Bill Melton IA 1.00 .40
❑ 185 Ron Bryant 1.00 .40
❑ 186 Ron Bryant IA 1.00 .40
❑ 187 Gates Brown 1.00 .40
❑ 188 Frank Lucchesi MG 1.00 .40
❑ 189 Gene Tenace 2.00 .75
❑ 190 Dave Giusti 1.00 .40
❑ 191 Jeff Burroughs RC 4.00 1.50
❑ 192 Chicago Cubs TC 2.00 .75
❑ 193 Kurt Bevacqua RC 1.00 .40
❑ 194 Fred Norman 1.00 .40
❑ 195 Orlando Cepeda 6.00 3.00
❑ 196 Mel Queen 1.00 .40
❑ 197 Johnny Briggs 1.00 .40
❑ 198 Hough/O'Brien/Strahler RC 6.00 3.00
❑ 199 Mike Fiore 1.00 .40
❑ 200 Lou Brock 8.00 4.00
❑ 201 Phil Roof 1.00 .40
❑ 202 Scipio Spinks 1.00 .40
❑ 203 Ron Blomberg RC 1.00 .40
❑ 204 Tommy Helms 1.00 .40
❑ 205 Dick Drago 1.00 .40
❑ 206 Dal Maxvill 1.00 .40
❑ 207 Tom Egan 1.00 .40
❑ 208 Milt Pappas 2.00 .75
❑ 209 Joe Rudi 2.00 .75
❑ 210 Denny McLain 2.00 .75
❑ 211 Gary Sutherland 1.00 .40
❑ 212 Grant Jackson 1.00 .40
❑ 213 Parker/Kusnyer/Silverio RC 1.00 .40
❑ 214 Mike McQueen 1.00 .40
❑ 215 Alex Johnson 2.00 .75
❑ 216 Joe Niekro 2.00 .75
❑ 217 Roger Metzger 1.00 .40
❑ 218 Eddie Kasko MG 1.00 .40
❑ 219 Rennie Stennett RC 2.00 .75
❑ 220 Jim Perry 2.00 .75
❑ 221 NL Playoffs Bucs 2.00 .75
❑ 222 AL Playoffs B.Robinson 4.00 1.50
❑ 223 Dave McNally WS 2.00 .75
❑ 224 D.Johnson/M.Belanger WS 2.00 .75
❑ 225 Manny Sanguillen WS 2.00 .75
❑ 226 Roberto Clemente WS 8.00 4.00
❑ 227 Nellie Briles WS 2.00 .75
❑ 228 F.Robinson/M.Sanguillen WS 2.00 .75
❑ 229 Steve Blass WS 2.00 .75
❑ 230 Pirates Celebrate WS 2.00 .75
❑ 231 Casey Cox 1.00 .40
❑ 232 Arnold/Barr/Rader RC 1.00 .40
❑ 233 Jay Johnstone 2.00 .75
❑ 234 Ron Taylor 1.00 .40
❑ 235 Merv Rettenmund 1.00 .40
❑ 236 Jim McGlothlin 1.00 .40
❑ 237 New York Yankees TC 2.00 .75
❑ 238 Leron Lee 1.00 .40
❑ 239 Tom Timmermann 1.00 .40
❑ 240 Richie Allen 2.00 .75
❑ 241 Rollie Fingers 6.00 3.00
❑ 242 Don Mincher 1.00 .40
❑ 243 Frank Linzy 1.00 .40
❑ 244 Steve Braun RC 1.00 .40
❑ 245 Tommie Agee 2.00 .75
❑ 246 Tom Burgmeier 1.00 .40
❑ 247 Milt May 1.00 .40
❑ 248 Tom Bradley 1.00 .40
❑ 249 Harry Walker MG 1.00 .40
❑ 250 Boog Powell 2.00 .75
❑ 251 Checklist 264-394 6.00 3.00
❑ 252 Ken Reynolds 1.00 .40
❑ 253 Sandy Alomar 2.00 .75
❑ 254 Boots Day 1.00 .40
❑ 255 Jim Lonborg 2.00 .75
❑ 256 George Foster 2.00 .75
❑ 257 Foor/Hosley/Jata RC 1.00 .40
❑ 258 Randy Hundley 1.00 .40
❑ 259 Sparky Lyle 2.00 .75
❑ 260 Ralph Garr 2.00 .75

❑	261	Steve Mingori	1.00	.40
❑	262	San Diego Padres TC	2.00	.75
❑	263	Felipe Alou	2.00	.75
❑	264	Tommy John	2.00	.75
❑	265	Wes Parker	2.00	.75
❑	266	Bobby Bolin	1.25	.50
❑	267	Dave Concepcion	4.00	1.50
❑	268	D.Anderson RC/C.Floethe RC	1.25	.50
❑	269	Don Hahn	1.25	.50
❑	270	Jim Palmer	8.00	4.00
❑	271	Ken Rudolph	1.25	.50
❑	272	Mickey Rivers RC	2.00	.75
❑	273	Bobby Floyd	1.25	.50
❑	274	Al Severinsen	1.25	.50
❑	275	Cesar Tovar	1.25	.50
❑	276	Gene Mauch MG	2.00	.75
❑	277	Elliott Maddox	1.25	.50
❑	278	Dennis Higgins	1.25	.50
❑	279	Larry Brown	1.25	.50
❑	280	Willie McCovey	6.00	3.00
❑	281	Bill Parsons RC	1.25	.50
❑	282	Houston Astros TC	2.00	.75
❑	283	Darrell Brandon	1.25	.50
❑	284	Ike Brown	1.25	.50
❑	285	Gaylord Perry	6.00	3.00
❑	286	Gene Alley	1.25	.50
❑	287	Jim Hardin	1.25	.50
❑	288	Johnny Jeter	1.25	.50
❑	289	Syd O'Brien	1.25	.50
❑	290	Sonny Siebert	1.25	.50
❑	291	Hal McRae	2.00	.75
❑	292	Hal McRae IA	1.25	.50
❑	293	Dan Frisella	1.25	.50
❑	294	Dan Frisella IA	1.25	.50
❑	295	Dick Dietz	1.25	.50
❑	296	Dick Dietz IA	1.25	.50
❑	297	Claude Osteen	2.00	.75
❑	298	Claude Osteen IA	1.25	.50
❑	299	Hank Aaron	40.00	20.00
❑	300	Hank Aaron IA	20.00	10.00
❑	301	George Mitterwald	1.25	.50
❑	302	George Mitterwald IA	1.25	.50
❑	303	Joe Pepitone	2.00	.75
❑	304	Joe Pepitone IA	1.25	.50
❑	305	Ken Boswell	1.25	.50
❑	306	Ken Boswell IA	1.25	.50
❑	307	Steve Renko	1.25	.50
❑	308	Steve Renko IA	1.25	.50
❑	309	Roberto Clemente	50.00	30.00
❑	310	Roberto Clemente IA	25.00	12.50
❑	311	Clay Carroll	1.25	.50
❑	312	Clay Carroll IA	1.25	.50
❑	313	Luis Aparicio	6.00	3.00
❑	314	Luis Aparicio IA	2.00	.75
❑	315	Paul Splittorff	1.25	.50
❑	316	Bibby/Roque/Guzman RC	2.00	.75
❑	317	Rich Hand	1.25	.50
❑	318	Sonny Jackson	1.25	.50
❑	319	Aurelio Rodriguez	1.25	.50
❑	320	Steve Blass	2.00	.75
❑	321	Joe Lahoud	1.25	.50
❑	322	Jose Pena	1.25	.50
❑	323	Earl Weaver MG	4.00	1.50
❑	324	Mike Ryan	1.25	.50
❑	325	Mel Stottlemyre	2.00	.75
❑	326	Pat Kelly	1.25	.50
❑	327	Steve Stone RC	2.00	.75
❑	328	Boston Red Sox TC	2.00	.75
❑	329	Roy Foster	1.25	.50
❑	330	Jim Hunter	6.00	3.00
❑	331	Stan Swanson RC	1.25	.50
❑	332	Buck Martinez	1.25	.50
❑	333	Steve Barber	1.25	.50
❑	334	Fahey/Mason Ragland RC	1.25	.50
❑	335	Bill Hands	1.25	.50
❑	336	Marty Martinez	1.25	.50
❑	337	Mike Kilkenny	1.25	.50
❑	338	Bob Grich	2.00	.75
❑	339	Ron Cook	1.25	.50
❑	340	Roy White	2.00	.75
❑	341	Joe Torre KP	1.25	.50
❑	342	Wilbur Wood KP	1.25	.50
❑	343	Willie Stargell KP	2.00	.75
❑	344	Dave McNally KP	1.25	.50
❑	345	Rick Wise KP	1.25	.50
❑	346	Jim Fregosi KP	1.25	.50
❑	347	Tom Seaver KP	4.00	1.50
❑	348	Sal Bando KP	1.25	.50
❑	349	Al Fitzmorris	1.25	.50
❑	350	Frank Howard	2.00	.75
❑	351	House/Kester/Britton	2.00	.75
❑	352	Dave LaRoche	1.25	.50
❑	353	Art Shamsky	1.25	.50
❑	354	Tom Murphy	1.25	.50
❑	355	Bob Watson	2.00	.75
❑	356	Gerry Moses	1.25	.50
❑	357	Woody Fryman	1.25	.50
❑	358	Sparky Anderson MG	4.00	1.50
❑	359	Don Pavletich	1.25	.50
❑	360	Dave Roberts	1.25	.50
❑	361	Mike Andrews	1.25	.50
❑	362	New York Mets TC	2.00	.75
❑	363	Ron Klimkowski	1.25	.50
❑	364	Johnny Callison	2.00	.75
❑	365	Dick Bosman	2.00	.75
❑	366	Jimmy Rosario RC	1.25	.50
❑	367	Ron Perranoski	1.25	.50
❑	368	Danny Thompson	1.25	.50
❑	369	Jim Lefebvre	2.00	.75
❑	370	Don Buford	1.25	.50
❑	371	Denny Lemaster	1.25	.50
❑	372	L.Clemons RC/M.Montgomery RC	1.25	.50
❑	373	John Mayberry	2.00	.75
❑	374	Jack Heidemann	1.25	.50
❑	375	Reggie Cleveland	1.25	.50
❑	376	Andy Kosco	1.25	.50
❑	377	Terry Harmon	1.25	.50
❑	378	Checklist 395-525	6.00	3.00
❑	379	Ken Berry	1.25	.50
❑	380	Earl Williams	1.25	.50
❑	381	Chicago White Sox TC	2.00	.75
❑	382	Joe Gibbon	1.25	.50
❑	383	Brant Alyea	1.25	.50
❑	384	Dave Campbell	2.00	.75
❑	385	Mickey Stanley	2.00	.75
❑	386	Jim Colborn	1.25	.50
❑	387	Horace Clarke	2.00	.75
❑	388	Charlie Williams RC	1.25	.50
❑	389	Bill Rigney MG	1.25	.50
❑	390	Willie Davis	2.00	.75
❑	391	Ken Sanders	1.25	.50
❑	392	F.Cambria/R.Zisk RC	2.00	.75
❑	393	Curt Motton	1.25	.50
❑	394	Ken Forsch	2.00	.75
❑	395	Matty Alou	2.00	.75
❑	396	Paul Lindblad	1.50	.60
❑	397	Philadelphia Phillies TC	2.00	.75
❑	398	Larry Hisle	2.00	.75
❑	399	Milt Wilcox	2.00	.75
❑	400	Tony Oliva	4.00	1.50
❑	401	Jim Nash	1.50	.60
❑	402	Bobby Heise	1.50	.60
❑	403	John Cumberland	1.50	.60
❑	404	Jeff Torborg	2.00	.75
❑	405	Ron Fairly	2.00	.75
❑	406	George Hendrick RC	2.00	.75
❑	407	Chuck Taylor	1.50	.60
❑	408	Jim Northrup	2.00	.75
❑	409	Frank Baker	1.50	.60
❑	410	Ferguson Jenkins	6.00	3.00
❑	411	Bob Montgomery	1.50	.60
❑	412	Dick Kelley	1.50	.60
❑	413	D.Eddy RC/D.Lemonds	1.50	.60
❑	414	Bob Miller	1.50	.60
❑	415	Cookie Rojas	2.00	.75
❑	416	Johnny Edwards	1.50	.60
❑	417	Tom Hall	1.50	.60
❑	418	Tom Shopay	1.50	.60
❑	419	Jim Spencer	1.50	.60
❑	420	Steve Carlton	20.00	10.00
❑	421	Ellie Rodriguez	1.50	.60
❑	422	Ray Lamb	1.50	.60
❑	423	Oscar Gamble	2.00	.75
❑	424	Bill Gogolewski	1.50	.60
❑	425	Ken Singleton	2.00	.75
❑	426	Ken Singleton IA	1.50	.60
❑	427	Tito Fuentes	1.50	.60
❑	428	Tito Fuentes IA	1.50	.60
❑	429	Bob Robertson	1.50	.60
❑	430	Bob Robertson IA	1.50	.60
❑	431	Cito Gaston	2.00	.75
❑	432	Cito Gaston IA	2.00	.75
❑	433	Johnny Bench	25.00	12.50
❑	434	Johnny Bench IA	15.00	7.50
❑	435	Reggie Jackson	30.00	15.00
❑	436	Reggie Jackson IA	12.00	6.00
❑	437	Maury Wills	2.00	.75
❑	438	Maury Wills IA	2.00	.75
❑	439	Billy Williams	6.00	3.00
❑	440	Billy Williams IA	4.00	1.50
❑	441	Thurman Munson	15.00	7.50
❑	442	Thurman Munson IA	8.00	4.00
❑	443	Ken Henderson	1.50	.60
❑	444	Ken Henderson IA	1.50	.60
❑	445	Tom Seaver	30.00	15.00
❑	446	Tom Seaver IA	15.00	7.50
❑	447	Willie Stargell	8.00	4.00
❑	448	Willie Stargell IA	4.00	1.50
❑	449	Bob Lemon MG	2.00	.75
❑	450	Mickey Lolich	2.00	.75
❑	451	Tony LaRussa	4.00	1.50
❑	452	Ed Herrmann	1.50	.60
❑	453	Barry Lersch	1.50	.60
❑	454	Oakland Athletics TC	2.00	.75
❑	455	Tommy Harper	2.00	.75
❑	456	Mark Belanger	2.00	.75
❑	457	Fast/Thomas/Ivie RC	1.50	.60
❑	458	Aurelio Monteagudo	1.50	.60
❑	459	Rick Renick	1.50	.60
❑	460	Al Downing	1.50	.60
❑	461	Tim Cullen	1.50	.60
❑	462	Rickey Clark	1.50	.60
❑	463	Bernie Carbo	1.50	.60
❑	464	Jim Roland	1.50	.60
❑	465	Gil Hodges MG	4.00	1.50
❑	466	Norm Miller	1.50	.60
❑	467	Steve Kline	1.50	.60
❑	468	Richie Scheinblum	1.50	.60
❑	469	Ron Herbel	1.50	.60
❑	470	Ray Fosse	1.50	.60
❑	471	Luke Walker	1.50	.60
❑	472	Phil Gagliano	1.50	.60
❑	473	Dan McGinn	1.50	.60
❑	474	Baylor/Harrison/Oates RC	15.00	7.50
❑	475	Gary Nolan	2.00	.75
❑	476	Lee Richard RC	1.50	.60
❑	477	Tom Phoebus	1.50	.60
❑	478	Checklist 526-656	6.00	3.00
❑	479	Don Shaw	1.50	.60
❑	480	Lee May	2.00	.75
❑	481	Billy Conigliaro	2.00	.75
❑	482	Joe Hoerner	1.50	.60
❑	483	Ken Suarez	1.50	.60
❑	484	Lum Harris MG	1.50	.60
❑	485	Phil Regan	2.00	.75
❑	486	John Lowenstein	1.50	.60
❑	487	Detroit Tigers TC	2.00	.75
❑	488	Mike Nagy	1.50	.60
❑	489	T.Humphrey RC/K.Lampard	1.50	.60
❑	490	Dave McNally	2.00	.75
❑	491	Lou Piniella KP	2.00	.75
❑	492	Mel Stottlemyre KP	2.00	.75
❑	493	Bob Bailey KP	2.00	.75
❑	494	Willie Horton KP	2.00	.75
❑	495	Bill Melton KP	2.00	.75
❑	496	Bud Harrelson KP	2.00	.75
❑	497	Jim Perry KP	2.00	.75
❑	498	Brooks Robinson KP	4.00	1.50
❑	499	Vicente Romo	1.50	.60
❑	500	Joe Torre	4.00	1.50
❑	501	Pete Hamm	1.50	.60
❑	502	Jackie Hernandez	1.50	.60
❑	503	Gary Peters	1.50	.60
❑	504	Ed Spiezio	1.50	.60
❑	505	Mike Marshall	2.00	.75
❑	506	Ley/Moyer/Tidrow RC	1.50	.60
❑	507	Fred Gladding	1.50	.60
❑	508	Elrod Hendricks	1.50	.60
❑	509	Don McMahon	1.50	.60
❑	510	Ted Williams MG	12.00	6.00
❑	511	Tony Taylor	2.00	.75
❑	512	Paul Popovich	1.50	.60
❑	513	Lindy McDaniel	2.00	.75
❑	514	Ted Sizemore	1.50	.60
❑	515	Bert Blyleven	4.00	1.50
❑	516	Oscar Brown	1.50	.60
❑	517	Ken Brett	1.50	.60
❑	518	Wayne Garrett	1.50	.60

❑ 519	Ted Abernathy	1.50	.60
❑ 520	Larry Bowa	2.00	.75
❑ 521	Alan Foster	1.50	.60
❑ 522	Los Angeles Dodgers TC	2.00	.75
❑ 523	Chuck Dobson	1.50	.60
❑ 524	E.Armbrister RC/M.Behney RC	1.50	.60
❑ 525	Carlos May	2.00	.75
❑ 526	Bob Bailey	6.00	3.00
❑ 527	Dave Leonhard	4.00	1.50
❑ 528	Ron Stone	4.00	1.50
❑ 529	Dave Nelson	6.00	3.00
❑ 530	Don Sutton	12.00	6.00
❑ 531	Freddie Patek	6.00	3.00
❑ 532	Fred Kendall RC	4.00	1.50
❑ 533	Ralph Houk MG	6.00	3.00
❑ 534	Jim Hickman	6.00	3.00
❑ 535	Ed Brinkman	4.00	1.50
❑ 536	Doug Rader	6.00	3.00
❑ 537	Bob Locker	4.00	1.50
❑ 538	Charlie Sands RC	4.00	1.50
❑ 539	Terry Forster RC	6.00	3.00
❑ 540	Felix Millan	4.00	1.50
❑ 541	Roger Repoz	4.00	1.50
❑ 542	Jack Billingham	4.00	1.50
❑ 543	Duane Josephson	4.00	1.50
❑ 544	Ted Martinez	4.00	1.50
❑ 545	Wayne Granger	4.00	1.50
❑ 546	Joe Hague	4.00	1.50
❑ 547	Cleveland Indians TC	8.00	4.00
❑ 548	Frank Reberger	4.00	1.50
❑ 549	Dave May	4.00	1.50
❑ 550	Brooks Robinson	25.00	12.50
❑ 551	Ollie Brown	4.00	1.50
❑ 552	Ollie Brown IA	4.00	1.50
❑ 553	Wilbur Wood	6.00	3.00
❑ 554	Wilbur Wood IA	4.00	1.50
❑ 555	Ron Santo	8.00	4.00
❑ 556	Ron Santo IA	6.00	3.00
❑ 557	John Odom	4.00	1.50
❑ 558	John Odom IA	4.00	1.50
❑ 559	Pete Rose	50.00	30.00
❑ 560	Pete Rose IA	25.00	12.50
❑ 561	Leo Cardenas	4.00	1.50
❑ 562	Leo Cardenas IA	4.00	1.50
❑ 563	Ray Sadecki	4.00	1.50
❑ 564	Ray Sadecki IA	4.00	1.50
❑ 565	Reggie Smith	6.00	3.00
❑ 566	Reggie Smith IA	4.00	1.50
❑ 567	Juan Marichal	12.00	6.00
❑ 568	Juan Marichal IA	6.00	3.00
❑ 569	Ed Kirkpatrick	4.00	1.50
❑ 570	Ed Kirkpatrick IA	4.00	1.50
❑ 571	Nate Colbert	4.00	1.50
❑ 572	Nate Colbert IA	4.00	1.50
❑ 573	Fritz Peterson	4.00	1.50
❑ 574	Fritz Peterson IA	4.00	1.50
❑ 575	Al Oliver	8.00	4.00
❑ 576	Leo Durocher MG	6.00	3.00
❑ 577	Mike Paul	6.00	3.00
❑ 578	Billy Grabarkewitz	4.00	1.50
❑ 579	Doyle Alexander RC	6.00	3.00
❑ 580	Lou Piniella	6.00	3.00
❑ 581	Wade Blasingame	4.00	1.50
❑ 582	Montreal Expos TC	8.00	4.00
❑ 583	Darold Knowles	4.00	1.50
❑ 584	Jerry McNertney	4.00	1.50
❑ 585	George Scott	6.00	3.00
❑ 586	Denis Menke	4.00	1.50
❑ 587	Billy Wilson	4.00	1.50
❑ 588	Jim Holt	4.00	1.50
❑ 589	Hal Lanier	4.00	1.50
❑ 590	Graig Nettles	8.00	4.00
❑ 591	Paul Casanova	4.00	1.50
❑ 592	Lew Krausse	4.00	1.50
❑ 593	Rich Morales	4.00	1.50
❑ 594	Jim Beauchamp	4.00	1.50
❑ 595	Nolan Ryan	100.00	60.00
❑ 596	Manny Mota	6.00	3.00
❑ 597	Jim Magnuson RC	4.00	1.50
❑ 598	Hal King	6.00	3.00
❑ 599	Billy Champion	4.00	1.50
❑ 600	Al Kaline	25.00	12.50
❑ 601	George Stone	4.00	1.50
❑ 602	Dave Bristol MG	4.00	1.50
❑ 603	Jim Ray	4.00	1.50
❑ 604A	Checklist 657-787 Right Copy	12.00	6.00
❑ 604B	Checklist 657-787 Left Copy	12.00	6.00
❑ 605	Nelson Briles	6.00	3.00
❑ 606	Luis Melendez	4.00	1.50
❑ 607	Frank Duffy	4.00	1.50
❑ 608	Mike Corkins	4.00	1.50
❑ 609	Tom Grieve	6.00	3.00
❑ 610	Bill Stoneman	6.00	3.00
❑ 611	Rich Reese	4.00	1.50
❑ 612	Joe Decker	4.00	1.50
❑ 613	Mike Ferraro	4.00	1.50
❑ 614	Ted Uhlaender	4.00	1.50
❑ 615	Steve Hargan	4.00	1.50
❑ 616	Joe Ferguson RC	6.00	3.00
❑ 617	Kansas City Royals TC	8.00	4.00
❑ 618	Rich Robertson	4.00	1.50
❑ 619	Rich McKinney	4.00	1.50
❑ 620	Phil Niekro	12.00	6.00
❑ 621	Commish Award	8.00	4.00
❑ 622	MVP Award	8.00	4.00
❑ 623	Cy Young Award	8.00	4.00
❑ 624	Minor Lg POY Award	8.00	4.00
❑ 625	Rookie of the Year	8.00	4.00
❑ 626	Babe Ruth Award	8.00	4.00
❑ 627	Moe Drabowsky	4.00	1.50
❑ 628	Terry Crowley	4.00	1.50
❑ 629	Paul Doyle	4.00	1.50
❑ 630	Rich Hebner	6.00	3.00
❑ 631	John Strohmayer	4.00	1.50
❑ 632	Mike Hegan	4.00	1.50
❑ 633	Jack Hiatt	4.00	1.50
❑ 634	Dick Woodson	4.00	1.50
❑ 635	Don Money	6.00	3.00
❑ 636	Bill Lee	6.00	3.00
❑ 637	Preston Gomez MG	4.00	1.50
❑ 638	Ken Wright	4.00	1.50
❑ 639	J.C. Martin	4.00	1.50
❑ 640	Joe Coleman	4.00	1.50
❑ 641	Mike Lum	4.00	1.50
❑ 642	Dennis Riddleberger RC	4.00	1.50
❑ 643	Russ Gibson	4.00	1.50
❑ 644	Bernie Allen	4.00	1.50
❑ 645	Jim Maloney	6.00	3.00
❑ 646	Chico Salmon	4.00	1.50
❑ 647	Bob Moose	4.00	1.50
❑ 648	Jim Lyttle	4.00	1.50
❑ 649	Pete Richert	4.00	1.50
❑ 650	Sal Bando	6.00	3.00
❑ 651	Cincinnati Reds TC	8.00	4.00
❑ 652	Marcelino Lopez	4.00	1.50
❑ 653	Jim Fairey	4.00	1.50
❑ 654	Horacio Pina	6.00	3.00
❑ 655	Jerry Grote	4.00	1.50
❑ 656	Rudy May	4.00	1.50
❑ 657	Bobby Wine	12.00	6.00
❑ 658	Steve Dunning	12.00	6.00
❑ 659	Bob Aspromonte	12.00	6.00
❑ 660	Paul Blair	15.00	7.50
❑ 661	Bill Virdon MG	12.00	6.00
❑ 662	Stan Bahnsen	12.00	6.00
❑ 663	Fran Healy RC	15.00	7.50
❑ 664	Bobby Knoop	12.00	6.00
❑ 665	Chris Short	12.00	6.00
❑ 666	Hector Torres	12.00	6.00
❑ 667	Ray Newman RC	12.00	6.00
❑ 668	Texas Rangers TC	30.00	15.00
❑ 669	Willie Crawford	12.00	6.00
❑ 670	Ken Holtzman	15.00	7.50
❑ 671	Donn Clendenon	15.00	7.50
❑ 672	Archie Reynolds	12.00	6.00
❑ 673	Dave Marshall	12.00	6.00
❑ 674	John Kennedy	12.00	6.00
❑ 675	Pat Jarvis	12.00	6.00
❑ 676	Danny Cater	12.00	6.00
❑ 677	Ivan Murrell	12.00	6.00
❑ 678	Steve Luebber RC	12.00	6.00
❑ 679	B.Fenwick RC/B.Stinson	12.00	6.00
❑ 680	Dave Johnson	15.00	7.50
❑ 681	Bobby Pfeil	12.00	6.00
❑ 682	Mike McCormick	15.00	7.50
❑ 683	Steve Hovley	12.00	6.00
❑ 684	Hal Breeden RC	12.00	6.00
❑ 685	Joel Horlen	12.00	6.00
❑ 686	Steve Garvey	40.00	20.00
❑ 687	Del Unser	12.00	6.00
❑ 688	St. Louis Cardinals TC	20.00	10.00
❑ 689	Eddie Fisher	12.00	6.00
❑ 690	Willie Montanez	15.00	7.50
❑ 691	Curt Blefary	12.00	6.00
❑ 692	Curt Blefary IA	12.00	6.00
❑ 693	Alan Gallagher	12.00	6.00
❑ 694	Alan Gallagher IA	12.00	6.00
❑ 695	Rod Carew	50.00	30.00
❑ 696	Rod Carew IA	30.00	15.00
❑ 697	Jerry Koosman	15.00	7.50
❑ 698	Jerry Koosman IA	15.00	7.50
❑ 699	Bobby Murcer	15.00	7.50
❑ 700	Bobby Murcer IA	15.00	7.50
❑ 701	Jose Pagan	12.00	6.00
❑ 702	Jose Pagan IA	12.00	6.00
❑ 703	Doug Griffin	12.00	6.00
❑ 704	Doug Griffin IA	12.00	6.00
❑ 705	Pat Corrales	15.00	7.50
❑ 706	Pat Corrales IA	12.00	6.00
❑ 707	Tim Foli	12.00	6.00
❑ 708	Tim Foli IA	12.00	6.00
❑ 709	Jim Kaat	15.00	7.50
❑ 710	Jim Kaat IA	15.00	7.50
❑ 711	Bobby Bonds	20.00	10.00
❑ 712	Bobby Bonds IA	15.00	7.50
❑ 713	Gene Michael	20.00	10.00
❑ 714	Gene Michael IA	15.00	7.50
❑ 715	Mike Epstein	12.00	6.00
❑ 716	Jesus Alou	12.00	6.00
❑ 717	Bruce Dal Canton	12.00	6.00
❑ 718	Del Rice MG	12.00	6.00
❑ 719	Cesar Geronimo	12.00	6.00
❑ 720	Sam McDowell	15.00	7.50
❑ 721	Eddie Leon	12.00	6.00
❑ 722	Bill Sudakis	12.00	6.00
❑ 723	Al Santorini	12.00	6.00
❑ 724	Curtis/Hinton/Scott RC	12.00	6.00
❑ 725	Dick McAuliffe	15.00	7.50
❑ 726	Dick Selma	12.00	6.00
❑ 727	Jose Laboy	12.00	6.00
❑ 728	Gail Hopkins	12.00	6.00
❑ 729	Bob Veale	15.00	7.50
❑ 730	Rick Monday	15.00	7.50
❑ 731	Baltimore Orioles TC	20.00	10.00
❑ 732	George Culver	12.00	6.00
❑ 733	Jim Ray Hart	15.00	7.50
❑ 734	Bob Burda	12.00	6.00
❑ 735	Diego Segui	12.00	6.00
❑ 736	Bill Russell	15.00	7.50
❑ 737	Len Randle RC	15.00	7.50
❑ 738	Jim Merritt	12.00	6.00
❑ 739	Don Mason	12.00	6.00
❑ 740	Rico Carty	15.00	7.50
❑ 741	Hutton/Milner/Miller RC	15.00	7.50
❑ 742	Jim Rooker	12.00	6.00
❑ 743	Cesar Gutierrez	12.00	6.00
❑ 744	Jim Slaton RC	12.00	6.00
❑ 745	Julian Javier	15.00	7.50
❑ 746	Lowell Palmer	12.00	6.00
❑ 747	Jim Stewart	12.00	6.00
❑ 748	Phil Hennigan	12.00	6.00
❑ 749	Walt Alston MG	20.00	10.00
❑ 750	Willie Horton	15.00	7.50
❑ 751	Steve Carlton TR	40.00	20.00
❑ 752	Joe Morgan TR	40.00	20.00
❑ 753	Denny McLain TR	20.00	10.00
❑ 754	Frank Robinson TR	40.00	20.00
❑ 755	Jim Fregosi TR	15.00	7.50
❑ 756	Rick Wise TR	15.00	7.50
❑ 757	Jose Cardenal TR	15.00	7.50
❑ 758	Gil Garrido	12.00	6.00
❑ 759	Chris Cannizzaro	12.00	6.00
❑ 760	Bill Mazeroski	25.00	12.50
❑ 761	Oglivie/Cey/Williams RC	25.00	12.50
❑ 762	Wayne Simpson	12.00	6.00
❑ 763	Ron Hansen	12.00	6.00
❑ 764	Dusty Baker	20.00	10.00
❑ 765	Ken McMullen	12.00	6.00
❑ 766	Steve Hamilton	12.00	6.00
❑ 767	Tom McCraw	15.00	7.50
❑ 768	Denny Doyle	12.00	6.00
❑ 769	Jack Aker	12.00	6.00
❑ 770	Jim Wynn	15.00	7.50
❑ 771	San Francisco Giants TC	20.00	10.00
❑ 772	Ken Tatum	12.00	6.00
❑ 773	Ron Brand	12.00	6.00
❑ 774	Luis Alvarado	12.00	6.00
❑ 775	Jerry Reuss	15.00	7.50

- ❑ 776 Bill Voss 12.00 6.00
- ❑ 777 Hoyt Wilhelm 25.00 12.50
- ❑ 778 Albury/Dempsey/Strickland RC 20.00 10.00
- ❑ 779 Tony Cloninger 12.00 6.00
- ❑ 780 Dick Green 12.00 6.00
- ❑ 781 Jim McAndrew 12.00 6.00
- ❑ 782 Larry Stahl 12.00 6.00
- ❑ 783 Les Cain 12.00 6.00
- ❑ 784 Ken Aspromonte 12.00 6.00
- ❑ 785 Vic Davalillo 12.00 6.00
- ❑ 786 Chuck Brinkman 12.00 6.00
- ❑ 787 Ron Reed 15.00 7.50

1973 Topps

- ❑ COMPLETE SET (660) 700.00 400.00
- ❑ COMMON CARD (1-264) .50 .20
- ❑ COMMON CARD (265-396) .75 .30
- ❑ COMMON CARD (397-528) 1.25 .50
- ❑ COMMON CARD (529-660) 3.00 1.25
- ❑ WRAPPER (10-CENT, BAT) 15.00 10.00
- ❑ WRAPPER (10-CENT) 15.00 10.00
- ❑ 1 Ruth/Aaron/Mays HR 40.00 20.00
- ❑ 2 Rich Hebner 1.50 .60
- ❑ 3 Jim Lonborg 1.50 .60
- ❑ 4 John Milner .50 .20
- ❑ 5 Ed Brinkman .50 .20
- ❑ 6 Mac Scarce RC .50 .20
- ❑ 7 Texas Rangers TC 2.00 .75
- ❑ 8 Tom Hall .50 .20
- ❑ 9 Johnny Oates 1.50 .60
- ❑ 10 Don Sutton 4.00 1.50
- ❑ 11 Chris Chambliss UER 1.50 .60
- ❑ 12A Don Zimmer MG w/o Ear 3.00 1.25
- ❑ 12B Don Zimmer MG w/Ear .75 .30
- ❑ 13 George Hendrick 1.50 .60
- ❑ 14 Sonny Siebert .50 .20
- ❑ 15 Ralph Garr 1.50 .60
- ❑ 16 Steve Braun .50 .20
- ❑ 17 Fred Gladding .50 .20
- ❑ 18 Leroy Stanton .50 .20
- ❑ 19 Tim Foli .50 .20
- ❑ 20 Stan Bahnsen .50 .20
- ❑ 21 Randy Hundley 1.50 .60
- ❑ 22 Ted Abernathy .50 .20
- ❑ 23 Dave Kingman 1.50 .60
- ❑ 24 Al Santorini .50 .20
- ❑ 25 Roy White 1.50 .60
- ❑ 26 Pittsburgh Pirates TC 2.00 .75
- ❑ 27 Bill Gogolewski .50 .20
- ❑ 28 Hal McRae 1.50 .60
- ❑ 29 Tony Taylor 1.50 .60
- ❑ 30 Tug McGraw 1.50 .60
- ❑ 31 Buddy Bell RC 2.50 1.00
- ❑ 32 Fred Norman .50 .20
- ❑ 33 Jim Breazeale RC .50 .20
- ❑ 34 Pat Dobson .50 .20
- ❑ 35 Willie Davis 1.50 .60
- ❑ 36 Steve Barber .50 .20
- ❑ 37 Bill Robinson 1.50 .60
- ❑ 38 Mike Epstein .50 .20
- ❑ 39 Dave Roberts .50 .20
- ❑ 40 Reggie Smith 1.50 .60
- ❑ 41 Tom Walker RC .50 .20
- ❑ 42 Mike Andrews .50 .20
- ❑ 43 Randy Moffitt RC .50 .20
- ❑ 44 Rick Monday 1.50 .60
- ❑ 45 Ellie Rodriguez UER .50 .20
- ❑ 46 Lindy McDaniel 1.50 .60
- ❑ 47 Luis Melendez .50 .20
- ❑ 48 Paul Splittorff .50 .20
- ❑ 49A Frank Quilici MG Solid 3.00 1.25
- ❑ 49B Frank Quilici MG Natural .75 .30
- ❑ 50 Roberto Clemente 40.00 20.00
- ❑ 51 Chuck Seelbach RC .50 .20
- ❑ 52 Denis Menke .50 .20
- ❑ 53 Steve Dunning .50 .20
- ❑ 54 Checklist 1-132 3.00 1.25
- ❑ 55 Jon Matlack 1.50 .60
- ❑ 56 Merv Rettenmund .50 .20
- ❑ 57 Derrel Thomas .50 .20
- ❑ 58 Mike Paul .50 .20
- ❑ 59 Steve Yeager RC 1.50 .60
- ❑ 60 Ken Holtzman 1.50 .60
- ❑ 61 B.Williams/R.Carew LL 2.50 1.00
- ❑ 62 J.Bench/D.Allen LL 2.50 1.00
- ❑ 63 J.Bench/D.Allen LL 2.50 1.00
- ❑ 64 L.Brock/Campaneris LL 1.50 .60
- ❑ 65 S.Carlton/L.Tiant LL 1.50 .60
- ❑ 66 Carlton/Perry/Wood LL 1.50 .60
- ❑ 67 S.Carlton/N.Ryan LL 25.00 12.50
- ❑ 68 C.Carroll/S.Lyle LL 1.50 .60
- ❑ 69 Phil Gagliano .50 .20
- ❑ 70 Milt Pappas 1.50 .60
- ❑ 71 Johnny Briggs .50 .20
- ❑ 72 Ron Reed .50 .20
- ❑ 73 Ed Herrmann .50 .20
- ❑ 74 Billy Champion .50 .20
- ❑ 75 Vada Pinson 1.50 .60
- ❑ 76 Doug Rader .50 .20
- ❑ 77 Mike Torrez 1.50 .60
- ❑ 78 Richie Scheinblum .50 .20
- ❑ 79 Jim Willoughby RC .50 .20
- ❑ 80 Tony Oliva UER 2.50 1.00
- ❑ 81A W.Lockman MG w/Banks Solid 1.50 .60
- ❑ 81B W.Lockman MG w/Banks Natural 1.50 .60
- ❑ 82 Fritz Peterson .50 .20
- ❑ 83 Leron Lee .50 .20
- ❑ 84 Rollie Fingers 4.00 1.50
- ❑ 85 Ted Simmons 1.50 .60
- ❑ 86 Tom McCraw .50 .20
- ❑ 87 Ken Boswell .50 .20
- ❑ 88 Mickey Stanley 1.50 .60
- ❑ 89 Jack Billingham .50 .20
- ❑ 90 Brooks Robinson 8.00 4.00
- ❑ 91 Los Angeles Dodgers TC 2.00 .75
- ❑ 92 Jerry Bell .50 .20
- ❑ 93 Jesus Alou .50 .20
- ❑ 94 Dick Billings .50 .20
- ❑ 95 Steve Blass 1.50 .60
- ❑ 96 Doug Griffin .50 .20
- ❑ 97 Willie Montanez 1.50 .60
- ❑ 98 Dick Woodson .50 .20
- ❑ 99 Carl Taylor .50 .20
- ❑ 100 Hank Aaron 40.00 20.00
- ❑ 101 Ken Henderson .50 .20
- ❑ 102 Rudy May .50 .20
- ❑ 103 Celerino Sanchez RC .50 .20
- ❑ 104 Reggie Cleveland .50 .20
- ❑ 105 Carlos May .50 .20
- ❑ 106 Terry Humphrey .50 .20
- ❑ 107 Phil Hennigan .50 .20
- ❑ 108 Bill Russell 1.50 .60
- ❑ 109 Doyle Alexander 1.50 .60
- ❑ 110 Bob Watson 1.50 .60
- ❑ 111 Dave Nelson .50 .20
- ❑ 112 Gary Ross .50 .20
- ❑ 113 Jerry Grote 1.50 .60
- ❑ 114 Lynn McGlothen RC .50 .20
- ❑ 115 Ron Santo 1.50 .60
- ❑ 116A Ralph Houk MG Solid 3.00 1.25
- ❑ 116B Ralph Houk MG Natural .75 .30
- ❑ 117 Ramon Hernandez .50 .20
- ❑ 118 John Mayberry 1.50 .60
- ❑ 119 Larry Bowa 1.50 .60
- ❑ 120 Joe Coleman .50 .20
- ❑ 121 Dave Rader .50 .20
- ❑ 122 Jim Strickland .50 .20
- ❑ 123 Sandy Alomar 1.50 .60
- ❑ 124 Jim Hardin .50 .20
- ❑ 125 Ron Fairly 1.50 .60
- ❑ 126 Jim Brewer .50 .20
- ❑ 127 Milwaukee Brewers TC 2.00 .75
- ❑ 128 Ted Sizemore .50 .20
- ❑ 129 Terry Forster 1.50 .60
- ❑ 130 Pete Rose 30.00 15.00
- ❑ 131A Eddie Kasko MG w/oEar 3.00 1.25
- ❑ 131B Eddie Kasko MG w/Ear 1.50 .60
- ❑ 132 Matty Alou 1.50 .60
- ❑ 133 Dave Roberts RC .50 .20
- ❑ 134 Milt Wilcox .50 .20
- ❑ 135 Lee May UER 1.50 .60
- ❑ 136A Earl Weaver MG Orange 1.50 .60
- ❑ 136B Earl Weaver MG Pale 3.00 1.25
- ❑ 137 Jim Beauchamp .50 .20
- ❑ 138 Horacio Pina .50 .20
- ❑ 139 Carmen Fanzone RC .50 .20
- ❑ 140 Lou Piniella 2.50 1.00
- ❑ 141 Bruce Kison .50 .20
- ❑ 142 Thurman Munson 8.00 4.00
- ❑ 143 John Curtis .50 .20
- ❑ 144 Marty Perez .50 .20
- ❑ 145 Bobby Bonds 2.50 1.00
- ❑ 146 Woodie Fryman .50 .20
- ❑ 147 Mike Anderson .50 .20
- ❑ 148 Dave Goltz RC .50 .20
- ❑ 149 Ron Hunt .50 .20
- ❑ 150 Wilbur Wood 1.50 .60
- ❑ 151 Wes Parker 1.50 .60
- ❑ 152 Dave May .50 .20
- ❑ 153 Al Hrabosky 1.50 .60
- ❑ 154 Jeff Torborg 1.50 .60
- ❑ 155 Sal Bando 1.50 .60
- ❑ 156 Cesar Geronimo .50 .20
- ❑ 157 Denny Riddleberger .50 .20
- ❑ 158 Houston Astros TC 2.00 .75
- ❑ 159 Cito Gaston 1.50 .60
- ❑ 160 Jim Palmer 6.00 3.00
- ❑ 161 Ted Martinez .50 .20
- ❑ 162 Pete Broberg .50 .20
- ❑ 163 Vic Davalillo .50 .20
- ❑ 164 Monty Montgomery .50 .20
- ❑ 165 Luis Aparicio 4.00 1.50
- ❑ 166 Terry Harmon .50 .20
- ❑ 167 Steve Stone 1.50 .60
- ❑ 168 Jim Northrup 1.50 .60
- ❑ 169 Ron Schueler RC 1.50 .60
- ❑ 170 Harmon Killebrew 5.00 2.00
- ❑ 171 Bernie Carbo .50 .20
- ❑ 172 Steve Kline .50 .20
- ❑ 173 Hal Breeden .50 .20
- ❑ 174 Goose Gossage RC 6.00 3.00
- ❑ 175 Frank Robinson 6.00 3.00
- ❑ 176 Chuck Taylor .50 .20
- ❑ 177 Bill Plummer RC .50 .20
- ❑ 178 Don Rose RC .50 .20
- ❑ 179A Dick Williams w/Ear 4.00 1.50
- ❑ 179B Dick Williams w/o Ear 1.50 .60
- ❑ 180 Ferguson Jenkins 4.00 1.50
- ❑ 181 Jack Brohamer RC .50 .20
- ❑ 182 Mike Caldwell RC 1.50 .60
- ❑ 183 Don Buford .50 .20
- ❑ 184 Jerry Koosman 1.50 .60
- ❑ 185 Jim Wynn 1.50 .60
- ❑ 186 Bill Fahey .50 .20
- ❑ 187 Luke Walker .50 .20
- ❑ 188 Cookie Rojas 1.50 .60
- ❑ 189 Greg Luzinski 2.50 1.00
- ❑ 190 Bob Gibson 8.00 4.00
- ❑ 191 Detroit Tigers TC 2.50 1.00
- ❑ 192 Pat Jarvis .50 .20
- ❑ 193 Carlton Fisk 10.00 5.00
- ❑ 194 Jorge Orta RC .50 .20
- ❑ 195 Clay Carroll .50 .20
- ❑ 196 Ken McMullen .50 .20
- ❑ 197 Ed Goodson RC .50 .20
- ❑ 198 Horace Clarke .50 .20
- ❑ 199 Bert Blyleven 2.50 1.00
- ❑ 200 Billy Williams 4.00 1.50
- ❑ 201 George Hendrick ALCS 1.50 .60
- ❑ 202 George Foster NLCS 1.50 .60
- ❑ 203 Gene Tenace WS 1.50 .60
- ❑ 204 A's Two Straight WS 1.50 .60
- ❑ 205 Tony Perez WS 2.50 1.00
- ❑ 206 Gene Tenace WS 1.50 .60
- ❑ 207 Blue Moon Odom WS 1.50 .60
- ❑ 208 Johnny Bench WS 5.00 2.00
- ❑ 209 Bert Campaneris WS 1.50 .60
- ❑ 210 A's Win WS .50 .20
- ❑ 211 Balor Moore .50 .20
- ❑ 212 Joe Lahoud .50 .20

❑ 213 Steve Garvey 5.00 2.00
❑ 214 Dave Hamilton RC .50 .20
❑ 215 Dusty Baker 2.50 1.00
❑ 216 Toby Harrah 1.50 .60
❑ 217 Don Wilson .50 .20
❑ 218 Aurelio Rodriguez .50 .20
❑ 219 St. Louis Cardinals TC 2.50 1.00
❑ 220 Nolan Ryan 50.00 30.00
❑ 221 Fred Kendall .50 .20
❑ 222 Rob Gardner .50 .20
❑ 223 Bud Harrelson 1.50 .60
❑ 224 Bill Lee 1.50 .60
❑ 225 Al Oliver 1.50 .60
❑ 226 Ray Fosse .50 .20
❑ 227 Wayne Twitchell .50 .20
❑ 228 Bobby Darwin .50 .20
❑ 229 Roric Harrison .50 .20
❑ 230 Joe Morgan 6.00 3.00
❑ 231 Bill Parsons .50 .20
❑ 232 Ken Singleton 1.50 .60
❑ 233 Ed Kirkpatrick .50 .20
❑ 234 Bill North RC .50 .20
❑ 235 Jim Hunter 4.00 1.50
❑ 236 Tito Fuentes .50 .20
❑ 237A Eddie Mathews MG w/Ear 1.50 .60
❑ 237B Eddie Mathews MG w/o Ear 3.00 1.25
❑ 238 Tony Muser RC .50 .20
❑ 239 Pete Richert .50 .20
❑ 240 Bobby Murcer 1.50 .60
❑ 241 Dwain Anderson .50 .20
❑ 242 George Culver .50 .20
❑ 243 California Angels TC 2.50 1.00
❑ 244 Ed Acosta .50 .20
❑ 245 Carl Yastrzemski 10.00 5.00
❑ 246 Ken Sanders .50 .20
❑ 247 Del Unser .50 .20
❑ 248 Jerry Johnson .50 .20
❑ 249 Larry Biittner .50 .20
❑ 250 Manny Sanguillen 1.50 .60
❑ 251 Roger Nelson .50 .20
❑ 252A Charlie Fox MG Orange 4.00 1.50
❑ 252B Charlie Fox MG Pale 1.50 .60
❑ 253 Mark Belanger 1.50 .60
❑ 254 Bill Stoneman .50 .20
❑ 255 Reggie Jackson 15.00 7.50
❑ 256 Chris Zachary .50 .20
❑ 257A Yogi Berra MG Orange 3.00 1.25
❑ 257B Yogi Berra MG Pale 5.00 2.00
❑ 258 Tommy John 1.50 .60
❑ 259 Jim Holt .50 .20
❑ 260 Gary Nolan 1.50 .60
❑ 261 Pat Kelly .50 .20
❑ 262 Jack Aker .50 .20
❑ 263 George Scott 1.50 .60
❑ 264 Checklist 133-264 3.00 1.25
❑ 265 Gene Michael 1.50 .60
❑ 266 Mike Lum .75 .30
❑ 267 Lloyd Allen .75 .30
❑ 268 Jerry Morales .75 .30
❑ 269 Tim McCarver 1.50 .60
❑ 270 Luis Tiant 1.50 .60
❑ 271 Tom Hutton .75 .30
❑ 272 Ed Farmer .75 .30
❑ 273 Chris Speier .75 .30
❑ 274 Darold Knowles .75 .30
❑ 275 Tony Perez 4.00 1.50
❑ 276 Joe Lovitto RC .75 .30
❑ 277 Bob Miller .75 .30
❑ 278 Baltimore Orioles TC 1.50 .60
❑ 279 Mike Strahler .75 .30
❑ 280 Al Kaline 8.00 4.00
❑ 281 Mike Jorgensen .75 .30
❑ 282 Steve Hovley .75 .30
❑ 283 Ray Sadecki .75 .30
❑ 284 Glenn Borgmann RC .75 .30
❑ 285 Don Kessinger 1.50 .60
❑ 286 Frank Linzy .75 .30
❑ 287 Eddie Leon .75 .30
❑ 288 Gary Gentry .75 .30
❑ 289 Bob Oliver .75 .30
❑ 290 Cesar Cedeno 1.50 .60
❑ 291 Rogelio Moret .75 .30
❑ 292 Jose Cruz 1.50 .60
❑ 293 Bernie Allen .75 .30
❑ 294 Steve Arlin .75 .30
❑ 295 Bert Campaneris 1.50 .60
❑ 296 Sparky Anderson MG 2.50 1.00
❑ 297 Walt Williams .75 .30
❑ 298 Ron Bryant .75 .30
❑ 299 Ted Ford .75 .30
❑ 300 Steve Carlton 10.00 5.00
❑ 301 Billy Grabarkewitz .75 .30
❑ 302 Terry Crowley .75 .30
❑ 303 Nelson Briles .75 .30
❑ 304 Duke Sims .75 .30
❑ 305 Willie Mays 40.00 20.00
❑ 306 Tom Burgmeier .75 .30
❑ 307 Boots Day .75 .30
❑ 308 Skip Lockwood .75 .30
❑ 309 Paul Popovich .75 .30
❑ 310 Dick Allen 1.50 .60
❑ 311 Joe Decker .75 .30
❑ 312 Oscar Brown .75 .30
❑ 313 Jim Ray .75 .30
❑ 314 Ron Swoboda 1.50 .60
❑ 315 John Odom .75 .30
❑ 316 San Diego Padres TC 1.50 .60
❑ 317 Danny Cater .75 .30
❑ 318 Jim McGlothlin .75 .30
❑ 319 Jim Spencer .75 .30
❑ 320 Lou Brock 8.00 4.00
❑ 321 Rich Hinton .75 .30
❑ 322 Garry Maddox RC 1.50 .60
❑ 323 Billy Martin MG 1.50 .60
❑ 324 Al Downing .75 .30
❑ 325 Boog Powell 1.50 .60
❑ 326 Darrell Brandon .75 .30
❑ 327 John Lowenstein .75 .30
❑ 328 Bill Bonham .75 .30
❑ 329 Ed Kranepool 1.50 .60
❑ 330 Rod Carew 8.00 4.00
❑ 331 Carl Morton .75 .30
❑ 332 John Felske RC .75 .30
❑ 333 Gene Clines .75 .30
❑ 334 Freddie Patek .75 .30
❑ 335 Bob Tolan .75 .30
❑ 336 Tom Bradley .75 .30
❑ 337 Dave Duncan 1.50 .60
❑ 338 Checklist 265-396 3.00 1.25
❑ 339 Dick Tidrow .75 .30
❑ 340 Nate Colbert .75 .30
❑ 341 Jim Palmer KP 2.50 1.00
❑ 342 Sam McDowell KP .75 .30
❑ 343 Bobby Murcer KP .75 .30
❑ 344 Jim Hunter KP 2.50 1.00
❑ 345 Chris Speier KP .75 .30
❑ 346 Gaylord Perry KP 1.50 .60
❑ 347 Kansas City Royals TC 1.50 .60
❑ 348 Rennie Stennett .75 .30
❑ 349 Dick McAuliffe .75 .30
❑ 350 Tom Seaver 12.00 6.00
❑ 351 Jimmy Stewart .75 .30
❑ 352 Don Stanhouse RC .75 .30
❑ 353 Steve Brye .75 .30
❑ 354 Billy Parker .75 .30
❑ 355 Mike Marshall 1.50 .60
❑ 356 Chuck Tanner MG 4.00 1.50
❑ 357 Ross Grimsley .75 .30
❑ 358 Jim Nettles .75 .30
❑ 359 Cecil Upshaw .75 .30
❑ 360 Joe Rudi UER 1.50 .60
❑ 361 Fran Healy .75 .30
❑ 362 Eddie Watt .75 .30
❑ 363 Jackie Hernandez .75 .30
❑ 364 Rick Wise .75 .30
❑ 365 Rico Petrocelli 1.50 .60
❑ 366 Brock Davis .75 .30
❑ 367 Burt Hooton 1.50 .60
❑ 368 Bill Buckner 1.50 .60
❑ 369 Lerrin LaGrow .75 .30
❑ 370 Willie Stargell 5.00 2.00
❑ 371 Mike Kekich .75 .30
❑ 372 Oscar Gamble .75 .30
❑ 373 Clyde Wright .75 .30
❑ 374 Darrell Evans 1.50 .60
❑ 375 Larry Dierker 1.50 .60
❑ 376 Frank Duffy .75 .30
❑ 377 Gene Mauch MG 4.00 1.50
❑ 378 Len Randle .75 .30
❑ 379 Cy Acosta RC .75 .30
❑ 380 Johnny Bench 12.00 6.00
❑ 381 Vicente Romo .75 .30
❑ 382 Mike Hegan .75 .30
❑ 383 Diego Segui .75 .30
❑ 384 Don Baylor 4.00 1.50
❑ 385 Jim Perry 1.50 .60
❑ 386 Don Money .75 .30
❑ 387 Jim Barr .75 .30
❑ 388 Ben Oglivie 1.50 .60
❑ 389 New York Mets TC 4.00 1.50
❑ 390 Mickey Lolich 1.50 .60
❑ 391 Lee Lacy RC 1.50 .60
❑ 392 Dick Drago .75 .30
❑ 393 Jose Cardenal .75 .30
❑ 394 Sparky Lyle 1.50 .60
❑ 395 Roger Metzger .75 .30
❑ 396 Grant Jackson .75 .30
❑ 397 Dave Cash 1.25 .50
❑ 398 Rich Hand 1.25 .50
❑ 399 George Foster 2.00 .75
❑ 400 Gaylord Perry 5.00 2.00
❑ 401 Clyde Mashore 1.25 .50
❑ 402 Jack Hiatt 1.25 .50
❑ 403 Sonny Jackson 1.25 .50
❑ 404 Chuck Brinkman 1.25 .50
❑ 405 Cesar Tovar 1.25 .50
❑ 406 Paul Lindblad 1.25 .50
❑ 407 Felix Millan 1.25 .50
❑ 408 Jim Colborn 1.25 .50
❑ 409 Ivan Murrell 1.25 .50
❑ 410 Willie McCovey 6.00 3.00
❑ 411 Ray Corbin 1.25 .50
❑ 412 Manny Mota 2.00 .75
❑ 413 Tom Timmermann 1.25 .50
❑ 414 Ken Rudolph 1.25 .50
❑ 415 Marty Pattin 1.25 .50
❑ 416 Paul Schaal 1.25 .50
❑ 417 Scipio Spinks 1.25 .50
❑ 418 Bob Grich 2.00 .75
❑ 419 Casey Cox 1.25 .50
❑ 420 Tommie Agee 1.25 .50
❑ 421A B.Winkles MG RC Orange 1.50 .60
❑ 421B Bobby Winkles MG Pale 3.00 1.25
❑ 422 Bob Robertson 1.25 .50
❑ 423 Johnny Jeter 1.25 .50
❑ 424 Denny Doyle 1.25 .50
❑ 425 Alex Johnson 1.25 .50
❑ 426 Dave LaRoche 1.25 .50
❑ 427 Rick Auerbach 1.25 .50
❑ 428 Wayne Simpson 1.25 .50
❑ 429 Jim Fairey 1.25 .50
❑ 430 Vida Blue 2.00 .75
❑ 431 Gerry Moses 1.25 .50
❑ 432 Dan Frisella 1.25 .50
❑ 433 Willie Horton 2.00 .75
❑ 434 San Francisco Giants TC 3.00 1.25
❑ 435 Rico Carty 2.00 .75
❑ 436 Jim McAndrew 1.25 .50
❑ 437 John Kennedy 1.25 .50
❑ 438 Enzo Hernandez 1.25 .50
❑ 439 Eddie Fisher 1.25 .50
❑ 440 Glenn Beckert 1.25 .50
❑ 441 Gail Hopkins 1.25 .50
❑ 442 Dick Dietz 1.25 .50
❑ 443 Danny Thompson 1.25 .50
❑ 444 Ken Brett 1.25 .50
❑ 445 Ken Berry 1.25 .50
❑ 446 Jerry Reuss 2.00 .75
❑ 447 Joe Hague 1.25 .50
❑ 448 John Hiller 1.25 .50
❑ 449A K.Aspro MG w/Spahn Point 4.00 1.50
❑ 449B K.Aspro MG w/Spahn Round 4.00 1.50
❑ 450 Joe Torre 3.00 1.25
❑ 451 John Vukovich RC 1.25 .50
❑ 452 Paul Casanova 1.25 .50
❑ 453 Checklist 397-528 3.00 1.25
❑ 454 Tom Haller 1.25 .50
❑ 455 Bill Melton 1.25 .50
❑ 456 Dick Green 1.25 .50
❑ 457 John Strohmayer 1.25 .50
❑ 458 Jim Mason 1.25 .50
❑ 459 Jimmy Howarth RC 1.25 .50
❑ 460 Bill Freehan 2.00 .75
❑ 461 Mike Corkins 1.25 .50
❑ 462 Ron Blomberg 1.25 .50
❑ 463 Ken Tatum 1.25 .50
❑ 464 Chicago Cubs TC 3.00 1.25
❑ 465 Dave Giusti 1.25 .50

Card		
❑ 466 Jose Arcia	1.25	.50
❑ 467 Mike Ryan	1.25	.50
❑ 468 Tom Griffin	1.25	.50
❑ 469 Dan Monzon RC	1.25	.50
❑ 470 Mike Cuellar	2.00	.75
❑ 471 Ty Cobb LDR	10.00	5.00
❑ 472 Lou Gehrig LDR	15.00	7.50
❑ 473 Hank Aaron LDR	10.00	5.00
❑ 474 Babe Ruth LDR	20.00	10.00
❑ 475 Ty Cobb LDR	8.00	4.00
❑ 476 Walter Johnson LDR	3.00	1.25
❑ 477 Cy Young LDR	3.00	1.25
❑ 478 Walter Johnson LDR	3.00	1.25
❑ 479 Hal Lanier	1.25	.50
❑ 480 Juan Marichal	5.00	2.00
❑ 481 Chicago White Sox TC	3.00	1.25
❑ 482 Rick Reuschel RC	3.00	1.25
❑ 483 Dal Maxvill	1.25	.50
❑ 484 Ernie McAnally	1.25	.50
❑ 485 Norm Cash	2.00	.75
❑ 486A D.Ozark MG RC Orange	1.50	.60
❑ 486B Danny Ozark MG Pale	3.00	1.25
❑ 487 Bruce Dal Canton	1.25	.50
❑ 488 Dave Campbell	2.00	.75
❑ 489 Jeff Burroughs	2.00	.75
❑ 490 Claude Osteen	2.00	.75
❑ 491 Bob Montgomery	1.25	.50
❑ 492 Pedro Borbon	1.25	.50
❑ 493 Duffy Dyer	1.25	.50
❑ 494 Rich Morales	1.25	.50
❑ 495 Tommy Helms	1.25	.50
❑ 496 Ray Lamb	1.25	.50
❑ 497A R.Schoen MG Orange	2.00	.75
❑ 497B R.Schoen MG Pale	3.00	1.25
❑ 498 Graig Nettles	3.00	1.25
❑ 499 Bob Moose	1.25	.50
❑ 500 Oakland Athletics TC	3.00	1.25
❑ 501 Larry Gura	1.25	.50
❑ 502 Bobby Valentine	3.00	1.25
❑ 503 Phil Niekro	5.00	2.00
❑ 504 Earl Williams	1.25	.50
❑ 505 Bob Bailey	1.25	.50
❑ 506 Bart Johnson	1.25	.50
❑ 507 Darrel Chaney	1.25	.50
❑ 508 Gates Brown	1.25	.50
❑ 509 Jim Nash	1.25	.50
❑ 510 Amos Otis	2.00	.75
❑ 511 Sam McDowell	2.00	.75
❑ 512 Dalton Jones	1.25	.50
❑ 513 Dave Marshall	1.25	.50
❑ 514 Jerry Kenney	1.25	.50
❑ 515 Andy Messersmith	2.00	.75
❑ 516 Danny Walton	1.25	.50
❑ 517A Bill Virdon MG w/o Ear	1.50	.60
❑ 517B Bill Virdon MG w/Ear	3.00	1.25
❑ 518 Bob Veale	1.25	.50
❑ 519 Johnny Edwards	1.25	.50
❑ 520 Mel Stottlemyre	2.00	.75
❑ 521 Atlanta Braves TC	3.00	1.25
❑ 522 Leo Cardenas	1.25	.50
❑ 523 Wayne Granger	1.25	.50
❑ 524 Gene Tenace	2.00	.75
❑ 525 Jim Fregosi	2.00	.75
❑ 526 Ollie Brown	1.25	.50
❑ 527 Dan McGinn	1.25	.50
❑ 528 Paul Blair	1.25	.50
❑ 529 Milt May	3.00	1.25
❑ 530 Jim Kaat	5.00	2.00
❑ 531 Ron Woods	3.00	1.25
❑ 532 Steve Mingori	3.00	1.25
❑ 533 Larry Stahl	3.00	1.25
❑ 534 Dave Lemonds	3.00	1.25
❑ 535 Johnny Callison	5.00	2.00
❑ 536 Philadelphia Phillies TC	6.00	3.00
❑ 537 Bill Slayback RC	3.00	1.25
❑ 538 Jim Ray Hart	5.00	2.00
❑ 539 Tom Murphy	3.00	1.25
❑ 540 Cleon Jones	5.00	2.00
❑ 541 Bob Bolin	3.00	1.25
❑ 542 Pat Corrales	5.00	2.00
❑ 543 Alan Foster	3.00	1.25
❑ 544 Von Joshua	3.00	1.25
❑ 545 Orlando Cepeda	8.00	4.00
❑ 546 Jim York	3.00	1.25
❑ 547 Bobby Heise	3.00	1.25
❑ 548 Don Durham RC	3.00	1.25

Card		
❑ 549 Whitey Herzog MG	5.00	2.00
❑ 550 Dave Johnson	5.00	2.00
❑ 551 Mike Kilkenny	3.00	1.25
❑ 552 J.C. Martin	3.00	1.25
❑ 553 Mickey Scott	3.00	1.25
❑ 554 Dave Concepcion	5.00	2.00
❑ 555 Bill Hands	3.00	1.25
❑ 556 New York Yankees TC	8.00	4.00
❑ 557 Bernie Williams	3.00	1.25
❑ 558 Jerry May	3.00	1.25
❑ 559 Barry Lersch	3.00	1.25
❑ 560 Frank Howard	5.00	2.00
❑ 561 Jim Geddes RC	3.00	1.25
❑ 562 Wayne Garrett	3.00	1.25
❑ 563 Larry Haney	3.00	1.25
❑ 564 Mike Thompson RC	3.00	1.25
❑ 565 Jim Hickman	3.00	1.25
❑ 566 Lew Krausse	3.00	1.25
❑ 567 Bob Fenwick	3.00	1.25
❑ 568 Ray Newman	3.00	1.25
❑ 569 Walt Alston MG	8.00	4.00
❑ 570 Bill Singer	5.00	2.00
❑ 571 Rusty Torres	3.00	1.25
❑ 572 Gary Sutherland	3.00	1.25
❑ 573 Fred Beene	3.00	1.25
❑ 574 Bob Didier	3.00	1.25
❑ 575 Dock Ellis	3.00	1.25
❑ 576 Montreal Expos TC	6.00	3.00
❑ 577 Eric Soderholm RC	3.00	1.25
❑ 578 Ken Wright	3.00	1.25
❑ 579 Tom Grieve	5.00	2.00
❑ 580 Joe Pepitone	5.00	2.00
❑ 581 Steve Kealey	3.00	1.25
❑ 582 Darrell Porter	5.00	2.00
❑ 583 Bill Greif	3.00	1.25
❑ 584 Chris Arnold	3.00	1.25
❑ 585 Joe Niekro	5.00	2.00
❑ 586 Bill Sudakis	3.00	1.25
❑ 587 Rich McKinney	3.00	1.25
❑ 588 Checklist 529-660	20.00	10.00
❑ 589 Ken Forsch	3.00	1.25
❑ 590 Deron Johnson	3.00	1.25
❑ 591 Mike Hedlund	3.00	1.25
❑ 592 John Boccabella	3.00	1.25
❑ 593 Jack McKeon MG RC	4.00	1.50
❑ 594 Vic Harris RC	3.00	1.25
❑ 595 Don Gullett	5.00	2.00
❑ 596 Boston Red Sox TC	6.00	3.00
❑ 597 Mickey Rivers	5.00	2.00
❑ 598 Phil Roof	3.00	1.25
❑ 599 Ed Crosby	3.00	1.25
❑ 600 Dave McNally	5.00	2.00
❑ 601 Robles/Pena/Stelmaszek RC	5.00	2.00
❑ 602 Behney/Garcia/Rau RC	5.00	2.00
❑ 603 Hughes/McNulty/Reitz RC	5.00	2.00
❑ 604 Jefferson/O'Toole/Stampe RC	5.00	2.00
❑ 605 Cabell/Bourque/Marquez RC	5.00	2.00
❑ 606 Matthews/Pac/Roque RC	5.00	2.00
❑ 607 Frias/Busse/Guerrero RC	5.00	2.00
❑ 608 Busby/Colpaert/Medich RC	5.00	2.00
❑ 609 Blanks/Garcia/Lopes RC	5.00	2.00
❑ 610 Freeman/Hough/Webb RC	5.00	2.00
❑ 611 Coggins/Wohlford/Zisk RC	5.00	2.00
❑ 612 Lawson/Reynolds/Strom RC	5.00	2.00
❑ 613 Boone/Jutze/Ivie RC	15.00	7.50
❑ 614 Bumbry/Evans/Spikes RC	20.00	10.00
❑ 615 Mike Schmidt RC	150.00	90.00
❑ 616 Angelini/Blateric/Garman RC	5.00	2.00
❑ 617 Rich Chiles	3.00	1.25
❑ 618 Andy Etchebarren	3.00	1.25
❑ 619 Billy Wilson	3.00	1.25
❑ 620 Tommy Harper	5.00	2.00
❑ 621 Joe Ferguson	5.00	2.00
❑ 622 Larry Hisle	5.00	2.00
❑ 623 Steve Renko	3.00	1.25
❑ 624 Leo Durocher MG	5.00	2.00
❑ 625 Angel Mangual	3.00	1.25
❑ 626 Bob Barton	3.00	1.25
❑ 627 Luis Alvarado	3.00	1.25
❑ 628 Jim Slaton	3.00	1.25
❑ 629 Cleveland Indians TC	6.00	3.00
❑ 630 Denny McLain	8.00	4.00
❑ 631 Tom Matchick	3.00	1.25
❑ 632 Dick Selma	3.00	1.25
❑ 633 Ike Brown	3.00	1.25
❑ 634 Alan Closter	3.00	1.25

Card		
❑ 635 Gene Alley	5.00	2.00
❑ 636 Rickey Clark	3.00	1.25
❑ 637 Norm Miller	3.00	1.25
❑ 638 Ken Reynolds	3.00	1.25
❑ 639 Willie Crawford	3.00	1.25
❑ 640 Dick Bosman	3.00	1.25
❑ 641 Cincinnati Reds TC	6.00	3.00
❑ 642 Jose Laboy	3.00	1.25
❑ 643 Al Fitzmorris	3.00	1.25
❑ 644 Jack Heidemann	3.00	1.25
❑ 645 Bob Locker	3.00	1.25
❑ 646 Del Crandall MG	4.00	1.50
❑ 647 George Stone	3.00	1.25
❑ 648 Tom Egan	3.00	1.25
❑ 649 Rich Folkers	3.00	1.25
❑ 650 Felipe Alou	5.00	2.00
❑ 651 Don Carrithers	3.00	1.25
❑ 652 Ted Kubiak	3.00	1.25
❑ 653 Joe Hoerner	3.00	1.25
❑ 654 Minnesota Twins TC	6.00	3.00
❑ 655 Clay Kirby	3.00	1.25
❑ 656 John Ellis	3.00	1.25
❑ 657 Bob Johnson	3.00	1.25
❑ 658 Elliott Maddox	3.00	1.25
❑ 659 Jose Pagan	3.00	1.25
❑ 660 Fred Scherman	5.00	2.00

1974 Topps

Card		
❑ COMPLETE SET (660)	400.00	250.00
❑ COMP.FACT.SET (660)	600.00	350.00
❑ WRAPPERS (10-CENTS)	10.00	5.00
❑ 1 Hank Aaron 715	50.00	25.00
❑ 2 Aaron Special 54-57	8.00	4.00
❑ 3 Aaron Special 58-61	8.00	4.00
❑ 4 Aaron Special 62-65	8.00	4.00
❑ 5 Aaron Special 66-69	8.00	4.00
❑ 6 Aaron Special 70-73	8.00	4.00
❑ 7 Jim Hunter	4.00	1.50
❑ 8 George Theodore RC	.50	.20
❑ 9 Mickey Lolich	1.00	.40
❑ 10 Johnny Bench	15.00	6.00
❑ 11 Jim Bibby	.50	.20
❑ 12 Dave May	.50	.20
❑ 13 Tom Hilgendorf	.50	.20
❑ 14 Paul Popovich	.50	.20
❑ 15 Joe Torre	2.00	.75
❑ 16 Baltimore Orioles TC	1.00	.40
❑ 17 Doug Bird RC	.50	.20
❑ 18 Gary Thomasson RC	.50	.20
❑ 19 Gerry Moses	.50	.20
❑ 20 Nolan Ryan	40.00	20.00
❑ 21 Bob Gallagher RC	.50	.20
❑ 22 Cy Acosta	.50	.20
❑ 23 Craig Robinson RC	.50	.20
❑ 24 John Hiller	1.00	.40
❑ 25 Ken Singleton	1.00	.40
❑ 26 Bill Campbell RC	.50	.20
❑ 27 George Scott	1.00	.40
❑ 28 Manny Sanguillen	1.00	.40
❑ 29 Phil Niekro	3.00	1.25
❑ 30 Bobby Bonds	2.00	.75
❑ 31 Preston Gomez MG	1.00	.40
❑ 32A Johnny Grubb SD RC	1.00	.40
❑ 32B Johnny Grubb WASH	4.00	1.50
❑ 33 Don Newhauser RC	.50	.20
❑ 34 Andy Kosco	.50	.20
❑ 35 Gaylord Perry	3.00	1.25
❑ 36 St. Louis Cardinals TC	1.00	.40
❑ 37 Dave Sells RC	.50	.20

Card		
❑ 38 Don Kessinger	1.00	.40
❑ 39 Ken Suarez	.50	.20
❑ 40 Jim Palmer	8.00	3.00
❑ 41 Bobby Floyd	.50	.20
❑ 42 Claude Osteen	1.00	.40
❑ 43 Jim Wynn	1.00	.40
❑ 44 Mel Stottlemyre	1.00	.40
❑ 45 Dave Johnson	1.00	.40
❑ 46 Pat Kelly	.50	.20
❑ 47 Dick Ruthven RC	.50	.20
❑ 48 Dick Sharon RC	.50	.20
❑ 49 Steve Renko	.50	.20
❑ 50 Rod Carew	8.00	3.00
❑ 51 Bobby Heise	.50	.20
❑ 52 Al Oliver	1.00	.40
❑ 53A Fred Kendall SD	1.00	.40
❑ 53B Fred Kendall WASH	4.00	1.50
❑ 54 Elias Sosa RC	.50	.20
❑ 55 Frank Robinson	8.00	3.00
❑ 56 New York Mets TC	1.00	.40
❑ 57 Darold Knowles	.50	.20
❑ 58 Charlie Spikes	.50	.20
❑ 59 Ross Grimsley	.50	.20
❑ 60 Lou Brock	6.00	2.50
❑ 61 Luis Aparicio	3.00	1.25
❑ 62 Bob Locker	.50	.20
❑ 63 Bill Sudakis	.50	.20
❑ 64 Doug Rau	.50	.20
❑ 65 Amos Otis	1.00	.40
❑ 66 Sparky Lyle	1.00	.40
❑ 67 Tommy Helms	.50	.20
❑ 68 Grant Jackson	.50	.20
❑ 69 Del Unser	.50	.20
❑ 70 Dick Allen	2.00	.75
❑ 71 Dan Frisella	.50	.20
❑ 72 Aurelio Rodriguez	.50	.20
❑ 73 Mike Marshall	2.00	.75
❑ 74 Minnesota Twins TC	1.00	.40
❑ 75 Jim Colborn	.50	.20
❑ 76 Mickey Rivers	1.00	.40
❑ 77A Rich Troedson SD	1.00	.40
❑ 77B Rich Troedson WASH	4.00	1.50
❑ 78 Charlie Fox MG	1.00	.40
❑ 79 Gene Tenace	1.00	.40
❑ 80 Tom Seaver	12.00	5.00
❑ 81 Frank Duffy	.50	.20
❑ 82 Dave Giusti	.50	.20
❑ 83 Orlando Cepeda	3.00	1.25
❑ 84 Rick Wise	.50	.20
❑ 85 Joe Morgan	8.00	3.00
❑ 86 Joe Ferguson	1.00	.40
❑ 87 Fergie Jenkins	3.00	1.25
❑ 88 Freddie Patek	1.00	.40
❑ 89 Jackie Brown	.50	.20
❑ 90 Bobby Murcer	1.00	.40
❑ 91 Ken Forsch	.50	.20
❑ 92 Paul Blair	1.00	.40
❑ 93 Rod Gilbreath RC	.50	.20
❑ 94 Detroit Tigers TC	1.00	.40
❑ 95 Steve Carlton	8.00	3.00
❑ 96 Jerry Hairston RC	.50	.20
❑ 97 Bob Bailey	.50	.20
❑ 98 Bert Blyleven	2.00	.75
❑ 99 Del Crandall MG	1.00	.40
❑ 100 Willie Stargell	6.00	2.50
❑ 101 Bobby Valentine	1.00	.40
❑ 102A Bill Greif SD	1.00	.40
❑ 102B Bill Greif WASH	4.00	1.50
❑ 103 Sal Bando	1.00	.40
❑ 104 Ron Bryant	.50	.20
❑ 105 Carlton Fisk	12.00	5.00
❑ 106 Harry Parker RC	.50	.20
❑ 107 Alex Johnson	.50	.20
❑ 108 Al Hrabosky	1.00	.40
❑ 109 Bob Grich	1.00	.40
❑ 110 Billy Williams	3.00	1.25
❑ 111 Clay Carroll	.50	.20
❑ 112 Davey Lopes	2.00	.75
❑ 113 Dick Drago	.50	.20
❑ 114 California Angels TC	1.00	.40
❑ 115 Willie Horton	1.00	.40
❑ 116 Jerry Reuss	1.00	.40
❑ 117 Ron Blomberg	.50	.20
❑ 118 Bill Lee	1.00	.40
❑ 119 Danny Ozark MG	1.00	.40
❑ 120 Wilbur Wood	.50	.20
❑ 121 Larry Lintz RC	.50	.20
❑ 122 Jim Holt	.50	.20
❑ 123 Nelson Briles	1.00	.40
❑ 124 Bobby Coluccio RC	.50	.20
❑ 125A Nate Colbert SD	1.00	.40
❑ 125B Nate Colbert WASH	4.00	1.50
❑ 126 Checklist 1-132	3.00	1.25
❑ 127 Tom Paciorek	1.00	.40
❑ 128 John Ellis	.50	.20
❑ 129 Chris Speier	.50	.20
❑ 130 Reggie Jackson	15.00	6.00
❑ 131 Bob Boone	2.00	.75
❑ 132 Felix Millan	.50	.20
❑ 133 David Clyde RC	1.00	.40
❑ 134 Denis Menke	.50	.20
❑ 135 Roy White	1.00	.40
❑ 136 Rick Reuschel	1.00	.40
❑ 137 Al Bumbry	1.00	.40
❑ 138 Eddie Brinkman	.50	.20
❑ 139 Aurelio Monteagudo	.50	.20
❑ 140 Darrell Evans	2.00	.75
❑ 141 Pat Bourque	.50	.20
❑ 142 Pedro Garcia	.50	.20
❑ 143 Dick Woodson	.50	.20
❑ 144 Walter Alston MG	3.00	1.25
❑ 145 Dock Ellis	.50	.20
❑ 146 Ron Fairly	1.00	.40
❑ 147 Bart Johnson	.50	.20
❑ 148A Dave Hilton SD	1.00	.40
❑ 148B Dave Hilton WASH	4.00	1.50
❑ 149 Mac Scarce	.50	.20
❑ 150 John Mayberry	1.00	.40
❑ 151 Diego Segui	.50	.20
❑ 152 Oscar Gamble	1.00	.40
❑ 153 Jon Matlack	1.00	.40
❑ 154 Houston Astros TC	1.00	.40
❑ 155 Bert Campaneris	1.00	.40
❑ 156 Randy Moffitt	.50	.20
❑ 157 Vic Harris	.50	.20
❑ 158 Jack Billingham	.50	.20
❑ 159 Jim Ray Hart	.50	.20
❑ 160 Brooks Robinson	8.00	3.00
❑ 161 Ray Burris UER RC	1.00	.40
❑ 162 Bill Freehan	1.00	.40
❑ 163 Ken Berry	.50	.20
❑ 164 Tom House	.50	.20
❑ 165 Willie Davis	1.00	.40
❑ 166 Jack McKeon MG	1.00	.40
❑ 167 Luis Tiant	2.00	.75
❑ 168 Danny Thompson	.50	.20
❑ 169 Steve Rogers RC	2.00	.75
❑ 170 Bill Melton	.50	.20
❑ 171 Eduardo Rodriguez RC	.50	.20
❑ 172 Gene Clines	.50	.20
❑ 173A Randy Jones SD RC	2.00	.75
❑ 173B Randy Jones WASH	5.00	2.00
❑ 174 Bill Robinson	1.00	.40
❑ 175 Reggie Cleveland	.50	.20
❑ 176 John Lowenstein	.50	.20
❑ 177 Dave Roberts	.50	.20
❑ 178 Garry Maddox	1.00	.40
❑ 179 Yogi Berra MG	5.00	2.00
❑ 180 Ken Holtzman	1.00	.40
❑ 181 Cesar Geronimo	.50	.20
❑ 182 Lindy McDaniel	1.00	.40
❑ 183 Johnny Oates	1.00	.40
❑ 184 Texas Rangers TC	1.00	.40
❑ 185 Jose Cardenal	.50	.20
❑ 186 Fred Scherman	.50	.20
❑ 187 Don Baylor	2.00	.75
❑ 188 Rudy Meoli RC	.50	.20
❑ 189 Jim Brewer	.50	.20
❑ 190 Tony Oliva	2.00	.75
❑ 191 Al Fitzmorris	.50	.20
❑ 192 Mario Guerrero	.50	.20
❑ 193 Tom Walker	.50	.20
❑ 194 Darrell Porter	1.00	.40
❑ 195 Carlos May	.50	.20
❑ 196 Jim Fregosi	1.00	.40
❑ 197A Vicente Romo SD	1.00	.40
❑ 197B Vicente Romo WASH	4.00	1.50
❑ 198 Dave Cash	.50	.20
❑ 199 Mike Kekich	.50	.20
❑ 200 Cesar Cedeno	1.00	.40
❑ 201 R.Carew/P.Rose LL	6.00	2.50
❑ 202 R.Jackson/W.Stargell LL	5.00	2.00
❑ 203 R.Jackson/W.Stargell LL	5.00	2.00
❑ 204 T.Harper/L.Brock LL	2.00	.75
❑ 205 W.Wood/R.Bryant LL	1.00	.40
❑ 206 J.Palmer/T.Seaver LL	5.00	2.00
❑ 207 N.Ryan/T.Seaver LL	12.00	5.00
❑ 208 J.Hiller/M.Marshall LL	1.00	.40
❑ 209 Ted Sizemore	.50	.20
❑ 210 Bill Singer	.50	.20
❑ 211 Chicago Cubs TC	1.00	.40
❑ 212 Rollie Fingers	3.00	1.25
❑ 213 Dave Rader	.50	.20
❑ 214 Billy Grabarkewitz	.50	.20
❑ 215 Al Kaline UER	10.00	4.00
❑ 216 Ray Sadecki	.50	.20
❑ 217 Tim Foli	.50	.20
❑ 218 Johnny Briggs	.50	.20
❑ 219 Doug Griffin	.50	.20
❑ 220 Don Sutton	3.00	1.25
❑ 221 Chuck Tanner MG	1.00	.40
❑ 222 Ramon Hernandez	.50	.20
❑ 223 Jeff Burroughs	2.00	.75
❑ 224 Roger Metzger	.50	.20
❑ 225 Paul Splittorff	.50	.20
❑ 226A San Diego Padres TC SD	2.00	.75
❑ 226B San Diego Padres TC WASH	8.00	3.00
❑ 227 Mike Lum	.50	.20
❑ 228 Ted Kubiak	.50	.20
❑ 229 Fritz Peterson	.50	.20
❑ 230 Tony Perez	4.00	1.50
❑ 231 Dick Tidrow	.50	.20
❑ 232 Steve Brye	.50	.20
❑ 233 Jim Barr	.50	.20
❑ 234 John Milner	.50	.20
❑ 235 Dave McNally	1.00	.40
❑ 236 Red Schoendienst MG	3.00	1.25
❑ 237 Ken Brett	.50	.20
❑ 238 F.Healy w/Munson	.50	.20
❑ 239 Bill Russell	1.00	.40
❑ 240 Joe Coleman	.50	.20
❑ 241A Glenn Beckert SD	1.00	.40
❑ 241B Glenn Beckert WASH	4.00	1.50
❑ 242 Bill Gogolewski	.50	.20
❑ 243 Bob Oliver	.50	.20
❑ 244 Carl Morton	.50	.20
❑ 245 Cleon Jones	.50	.20
❑ 246 Oakland Athletics TC	2.00	.75
❑ 247 Rick Miller	.50	.20
❑ 248 Tom Hall	.50	.20
❑ 249 George Mitterwald	.50	.20
❑ 250A Willie McCovey SD	8.00	3.00
❑ 250B Willie McCovey WASH	25.00	10.00
❑ 251 Graig Nettles	2.00	.75
❑ 252 Dave Parker RC	10.00	4.00
❑ 253 John Boccabella	.50	.20
❑ 254 Stan Bahnsen	.50	.20
❑ 255 Larry Bowa	1.00	.40
❑ 256 Tom Griffin	.50	.20
❑ 257 Buddy Bell	2.00	.75
❑ 258 Jerry Morales	.50	.20
❑ 259 Bob Reynolds	.50	.20
❑ 260 Ted Simmons	2.00	.75
❑ 261 Jerry Bell	.50	.20
❑ 262 Ed Kirkpatrick	.50	.20
❑ 263 Checklist 133-264	3.00	1.25
❑ 264 Joe Rudi	1.00	.40
❑ 265 Tug McGraw	2.00	.75
❑ 266 Jim Northrup	1.00	.40
❑ 267 Andy Messersmith	1.00	.40
❑ 268 Tom Grieve	1.00	.40
❑ 269 Bob Johnson	.50	.20
❑ 270 Ron Santo	2.00	.75
❑ 271 Bill Hands	.50	.20
❑ 272 Paul Casanova	.50	.20
❑ 273 Checklist 265-396	3.00	1.25
❑ 274 Fred Beene	.50	.20
❑ 275 Ron Hunt	.50	.20
❑ 276 Bobby Winkles MG	1.00	.40
❑ 277 Gary Nolan	1.00	.40
❑ 278 Cookie Rojas	1.00	.40
❑ 279 Jim Crawford RC	.50	.20
❑ 280 Carl Yastrzemski	12.00	5.00
❑ 281 San Francisco Giants TC	1.00	.40
❑ 282 Doyle Alexander	1.00	.40
❑ 283 Mike Schmidt	20.00	8.00
❑ 284 Dave Duncan	1.00	.40
❑ 285 Reggie Smith	1.00	.40

❑ 286	Tony Muser	.50	.20
❑ 287	Clay Kirby	.50	.20
❑ 288	Gorman Thomas RC	2.00	.75
❑ 289	Rick Auerbach	.50	.20
❑ 290	Vida Blue	1.00	.40
❑ 291	Don Hahn	.50	.20
❑ 292	Chuck Seelbach	.50	.20
❑ 293	Milt May	.50	.20
❑ 294	Steve Foucault RC	.50	.20
❑ 295	Rick Monday	1.00	.40
❑ 296	Ray Corbin	.50	.20
❑ 297	Hal Breeden	.50	.20
❑ 298	Roric Harrison	.50	.20
❑ 299	Gene Michael	.50	.20
❑ 300	Pete Rose	25.00	10.00
❑ 301	Bob Montgomery	.50	.20
❑ 302	Rudy May	.50	.20
❑ 303	George Hendrick	1.00	.40
❑ 304	Don Wilson	.50	.20
❑ 305	Tito Fuentes	.50	.20
❑ 306	Earl Weaver MG	3.00	1.25
❑ 307	Luis Melendez	.50	.20
❑ 308	Bruce Dal Canton	.50	.20
❑ 309A	Dave Roberts SD	1.00	.40
❑ 309B	Dave Roberts WASH	6.00	2.50
❑ 310	Terry Forster	1.00	.40
❑ 311	Jerry Grote	1.00	.40
❑ 312	Deron Johnson	.50	.20
❑ 313	Barry Lersch	.50	.20
❑ 314	Milwaukee Brewers TC	1.00	.40
❑ 315	Ron Cey	2.00	.75
❑ 316	Jim Perry	1.00	.40
❑ 317	Richie Zisk	1.00	.40
❑ 318	Jim Merritt	.50	.20
❑ 319	Randy Hundley	.50	.20
❑ 320	Dusty Baker	2.00	.75
❑ 321	Steve Braun	.50	.20
❑ 322	Ernie McAnally	.50	.20
❑ 323	Richie Scheinblum	.50	.20
❑ 324	Steve Kline	.50	.20
❑ 325	Tommy Harper	1.00	.40
❑ 326	Sparky Anderson MG	3.00	1.25
❑ 327	Tom Timmermann	.50	.20
❑ 328	Skip Jutze	.50	.20
❑ 329	Mark Belanger	1.00	.40
❑ 330	Juan Marichal	5.00	2.00
❑ 331	C.Fisk/J.Bench AS	5.00	2.00
❑ 332	D.Allen/H.Aaron AS	8.00	3.00
❑ 333	R.Carew/J.Morgan AS	4.00	1.50
❑ 334	B.Robinson/R.Santo AS	2.00	.75
❑ 335	B.Campaneris/C.Speier AS	1.00	.40
❑ 336	B.Murcer/P.Rose AS	5.00	2.00
❑ 337	A.Otis/C.Cedeno AS	1.00	.40
❑ 338	R.Jackson/B.Williams AS	5.00	2.00
❑ 339	J.Hunter/R.Wise AS	3.00	1.25
❑ 340	Thurman Munson	8.00	3.00
❑ 341	Dan Driessen RC	1.00	.40
❑ 342	Jim Lonborg	1.00	.40
❑ 343	Kansas City Royals TC	1.00	.40
❑ 344	Mike Caldwell	.50	.20
❑ 345	Bill North	.50	.20
❑ 346	Ron Reed	.50	.20
❑ 347	Sandy Alomar	1.00	.40
❑ 348	Pete Richert	.50	.20
❑ 349	John Vukovich	.50	.20
❑ 350	Bob Gibson	8.00	3.00
❑ 351	Dwight Evans	3.00	1.25
❑ 352	Bill Stoneman	.50	.20
❑ 353	Rich Coggins	.50	.20
❑ 354	Whitey Lockman MG	1.00	.40
❑ 355	Dave Nelson	.50	.20
❑ 356	Jerry Koosman	1.00	.40
❑ 357	Buddy Bradford	.50	.20
❑ 358	Dal Maxvill	.50	.20
❑ 359	Brent Strom	.50	.20
❑ 360	Greg Luzinski	2.00	.75
❑ 361	Don Carrithers	.50	.20
❑ 362	Hal King	.50	.20
❑ 363	New York Yankees TC	2.00	.75
❑ 364A	Cito Gaston SD	2.00	.75
❑ 364B	Cito Gaston WASH	8.00	3.00
❑ 365	Steve Busby	1.00	.40
❑ 366	Larry Hisle	1.00	.40
❑ 367	Norm Cash	2.00	.75
❑ 368	Manny Mota	1.00	.40
❑ 369	Paul Lindblad	.50	.20
❑ 370	Bob Watson	1.00	.40
❑ 371	Jim Slaton	.50	.20
❑ 372	Ken Reitz	.50	.20
❑ 373	John Curtis	.50	.20
❑ 374	Marty Perez	.50	.20
❑ 375	Earl Williams	.50	.20
❑ 376	Jorge Orta	.50	.20
❑ 377	Ron Woods	.50	.20
❑ 378	Burt Hooton	1.00	.40
❑ 379	Billy Martin MG	2.00	.75
❑ 380	Bud Harrelson	1.00	.40
❑ 381	Charlie Sands	.50	.20
❑ 382	Bob Moose	.50	.20
❑ 383	Philadelphia Phillies TC	1.00	.40
❑ 384	Chris Chambliss	1.00	.40
❑ 385	Don Gullett	1.00	.40
❑ 386	Gary Matthews	2.00	.75
❑ 387A	Rich Morales SD	1.00	.40
❑ 387B	Rich Morales WASH	6.00	2.50
❑ 388	Phil Roof	.50	.20
❑ 389	Gates Brown	.50	.20
❑ 390	Lou Piniella	2.00	.75
❑ 391	Billy Champion	.50	.20
❑ 392	Dick Green	.50	.20
❑ 393	Orlando Pena	.50	.20
❑ 394	Ken Henderson	.50	.20
❑ 395	Doug Rader	.50	.20
❑ 396	Tommy Davis	1.00	.40
❑ 397	George Stone	.50	.20
❑ 398	Duke Sims	.50	.20
❑ 399	Mike Paul	.50	.20
❑ 400	Harmon Killebrew	6.00	2.50
❑ 401	Elliott Maddox	.50	.20
❑ 402	Jim Rooker	.50	.20
❑ 403	Darrell Johnson MG	1.00	.40
❑ 404	Jim Howarth	.50	.20
❑ 405	Ellie Rodriguez	.50	.20
❑ 406	Steve Arlin	.50	.20
❑ 407	Jim Wohlford	.50	.20
❑ 408	Charlie Hough	1.00	.40
❑ 409	Ike Brown	.50	.20
❑ 410	Pedro Borbon	.50	.20
❑ 411	Frank Baker	.50	.20
❑ 412	Chuck Taylor	.50	.20
❑ 413	Don Money	1.00	.40
❑ 414	Checklist 397-528	3.00	1.25
❑ 415	Gary Gentry	.50	.20
❑ 416	Chicago White Sox TC	1.00	.40
❑ 417	Rich Folkers	.50	.20
❑ 418	Walt Williams	.50	.20
❑ 419	Wayne Twitchell	.50	.20
❑ 420	Ray Fosse	.50	.20
❑ 421	Dan Fife RC	.50	.20
❑ 422	Gonzalo Marquez	.50	.20
❑ 423	Fred Stanley	.50	.20
❑ 424	Jim Beauchamp	.50	.20
❑ 425	Pete Broberg	.50	.20
❑ 426	Rennie Stennett	.50	.20
❑ 427	Bobby Bolin	.50	.20
❑ 428	Gary Sutherland	.50	.20
❑ 429	Dick Lange RC	.50	.20
❑ 430	Matty Alou	1.00	.40
❑ 431	Gene Garber RC	1.00	.40
❑ 432	Chris Arnold	.50	.20
❑ 433	Lerrin LaGrow	.50	.20
❑ 434	Ken McMullen	.50	.20
❑ 435	Dave Concepcion	2.00	.75
❑ 436	Don Hood RC	.50	.20
❑ 437	Jim Lyttle	.50	.20
❑ 438	Ed Herrmann	.50	.20
❑ 439	Norm Miller	.50	.20
❑ 440	Jim Kaat	2.00	.75
❑ 441	Tom Ragland	.50	.20
❑ 442	Alan Foster	.50	.20
❑ 443	Tom Hutton	.50	.20
❑ 444	Vic Davalillo	.50	.20
❑ 445	George Medich	.50	.20
❑ 446	Len Randle	.50	.20
❑ 447	Frank Quilici MG	1.00	.40
❑ 448	Ron Hodges RC	.50	.20
❑ 449	Tom McCraw	.50	.20
❑ 450	Rich Hebner	1.00	.40
❑ 451	Tommy John	2.00	.75
❑ 452	Gene Hiser	.50	.20
❑ 453	Balor Moore	.50	.20
❑ 454	Kurt Bevacqua	.50	.20
❑ 455	Tom Bradley	.50	.20
❑ 456	Dave Winfield RC	50.00	25.00
❑ 457	Chuck Goggin RC	.50	.20
❑ 458	Jim Ray	.50	.20
❑ 459	Cincinnati Reds TC	2.00	.75
❑ 460	Boog Powell	2.00	.75
❑ 461	John Odom	.50	.20
❑ 462	Luis Alvarado	.50	.20
❑ 463	Pat Dobson	.50	.20
❑ 464	Jose Cruz	2.00	.75
❑ 465	Dick Bosman	.50	.20
❑ 466	Dick Billings	.50	.20
❑ 467	Winston Llenas	.50	.20
❑ 468	Pepe Frias	.50	.20
❑ 469	Joe Decker	.50	.20
❑ 470	Reggie Jackson ALCS	5.00	2.00
❑ 471	Jon Matlack NLCS	1.00	.40
❑ 472	Darold Knowles WS1	1.00	.40
❑ 473	Willie Mays WS	8.00	3.00
❑ 474	Bert Campaneris WS3	1.00	.40
❑ 475	Rusty Staub WS4	1.00	.40
❑ 476	Cleon Jones WS5	1.00	.40
❑ 477	Reggie Jackson WS	5.00	2.00
❑ 478	Bert Campaneris WS7	1.00	.40
❑ 479	A's Celebrate WS	1.00	.40
❑ 480	Willie Crawford	.50	.20
❑ 481	Jerry Terrell RC	.50	.20
❑ 482	Bob Didier	.50	.20
❑ 483	Atlanta Braves TC	1.00	.40
❑ 484	Carmen Fanzone	.50	.20
❑ 485	Felipe Alou	2.00	.75
❑ 486	Steve Stone	1.00	.40
❑ 487	Ted Martinez	.50	.20
❑ 488	Andy Etchebarren	.50	.20
❑ 489	Danny Murtaugh MG	1.00	.40
❑ 490	Vada Pinson	2.00	.75
❑ 491	Roger Nelson	.50	.20
❑ 492	Mike Rogodzinski RC	.50	.20
❑ 493	Joe Hoerner	.50	.20
❑ 494	Ed Goodson	.50	.20
❑ 495	Dick McAuliffe	1.00	.40
❑ 496	Tom Murphy	.50	.20
❑ 497	Bobby Mitchell	.50	.20
❑ 498	Pat Corrales	.50	.20
❑ 499	Rusty Torres	.50	.20
❑ 500	Lee May	1.00	.40
❑ 501	Eddie Leon	.50	.20
❑ 502	Dave LaRoche	.50	.20
❑ 503	Eric Soderholm	.50	.20
❑ 504	Joe Niekro	1.00	.40
❑ 505	Bill Buckner	1.00	.40
❑ 506	Ed Farmer	.50	.20
❑ 507	Larry Stahl	.50	.20
❑ 508	Montreal Expos TC	1.00	.40
❑ 509	Jesse Jefferson	.50	.20
❑ 510	Wayne Garrett	.50	.20
❑ 511	Toby Harrah	1.00	.40
❑ 512	Joe Lahoud	.50	.20
❑ 513	Jim Campanis	.50	.20
❑ 514	Paul Schaal	.50	.20
❑ 515	Willie Montanez	.50	.20
❑ 516	Horacio Pina	.50	.20
❑ 517	Mike Hegan	.50	.20
❑ 518	Derrel Thomas	.50	.20
❑ 519	Bill Sharp RC	.50	.20
❑ 520	Tim McCarver	2.00	.75
❑ 521	Ken Aspromonte MG	1.00	.40
❑ 522	J.R. Richard	2.00	.75
❑ 523	Cecil Cooper	2.00	.75
❑ 524	Bill Plummer	.50	.20
❑ 525	Clyde Wright	.50	.20
❑ 526	Frank Tepedino	1.00	.40
❑ 527	Bobby Darwin	.50	.20
❑ 528	Bill Bonham	.50	.20
❑ 529	Horace Clarke	1.00	.40
❑ 530	Mickey Stanley	1.00	.40
❑ 531	Gene Mauch MG	1.00	.40
❑ 532	Skip Lockwood	.50	.20
❑ 533	Mike Phillips RC	.50	.20
❑ 534	Eddie Watt	.50	.20
❑ 535	Bob Tolan	.50	.20
❑ 536	Duffy Dyer	.50	.20
❑ 537	Steve Mingori	.50	.20
❑ 538	Cesar Tovar	.50	.20
❑ 539	Lloyd Allen	.50	.20
❑ 540	Bob Robertson	.50	.20

❑ 541 Cleveland Indians TC 1.00 .40
❑ 542 Goose Gossage 2.00 .75
❑ 543 Danny Cater .50 .20
❑ 544 Ron Schueler .50 .20
❑ 545 Billy Conigliaro 1.00 .40
❑ 546 Mike Corkins .50 .20
❑ 547 Glenn Borgmann .50 .20
❑ 548 Sonny Siebert .50 .20
❑ 549 Mike Jorgensen .50 .20
❑ 550 Sam McDowell 1.00 .40
❑ 551 Von Joshua .50 .20
❑ 552 Denny Doyle .50 .20
❑ 553 Jim Willoughby .50 .20
❑ 554 Tim Johnson RC .50 .20
❑ 555 Woodie Fryman .50 .20
❑ 556 Dave Campbell 1.00 .40
❑ 557 Jim McGlothlin .50 .20
❑ 558 Bill Fahey .50 .20
❑ 559 Darrel Chaney .50 .20
❑ 560 Mike Cuellar 1.00 .40
❑ 561 Ed Kranepool 1.00 .40
❑ 562 Jack Aker .50 .20
❑ 563 Hal McRae 1.00 .40
❑ 564 Mike Ryan .50 .20
❑ 565 Milt Wilcox .50 .20
❑ 566 Jackie Hernandez .50 .20
❑ 567 Boston Red Sox TC 1.00 .40
❑ 568 Mike Torrez 1.00 .40
❑ 569 Rick Dempsey 1.00 .40
❑ 570 Ralph Garr 1.00 .40
❑ 571 Rich Hand .50 .20
❑ 572 Enzo Hernandez .50 .20
❑ 573 Mike Adams RC .50 .20
❑ 574 Bill Parsons .50 .20
❑ 575 Steve Garvey 3.00 1.25
❑ 576 Scipio Spinks .50 .20
❑ 577 Mike Sadek RC .50 .20
❑ 578 Ralph Houk MG 1.00 .40
❑ 579 Cecil Upshaw .50 .20
❑ 580 Jim Spencer .50 .20
❑ 581 Fred Norman .50 .20
❑ 582 Bucky Dent RC 5.00 2.00
❑ 583 Marty Pattin .50 .20
❑ 584 Ken Rudolph .50 .20
❑ 585 Merv Rettenmund .50 .20
❑ 586 Jack Brohamer .50 .20
❑ 587 Larry Christenson RC .50 .20
❑ 588 Hal Lanier .50 .20
❑ 589 Boots Day .50 .20
❑ 590 Roger Moret .50 .20
❑ 591 Sonny Jackson .50 .20
❑ 592 Ed Bane RC .50 .20
❑ 593 Steve Yeager 1.00 .40
❑ 594 Leroy Stanton .50 .20
❑ 595 Steve Blass 1.00 .40
❑ 596 Gar/Hold/Lit/Pole RC .50 .20
❑ 597 Chalk/Gam/Mac/Trillo RC 1.00 .40
❑ 598 Ken Griffey RC 12.00 5.00
❑ 599A Dior/Freis/Ric/Shan Wash 2.00 .75
❑ 599B Dior/Freis/Ric/Shan Lg 15.00 7.50
❑ 599C Dior/Freis/Ric/Shan Sm 6.00 2.50
❑ 600 Cash/Cox/Madlock/Sand RC 5.00 2.00
❑ 601 Arm/Bladt/Downing/McBride RC 3.00 1.25
❑ 602 Abb/Henn/Swan/Voss RC 1.00 .40
❑ 603 Foote/Lund/Moore/Robles RC 1.00 .40
❑ 604 Hugh/Knox/Thornton/White RC 5.00 2.00
❑ 605 Alb/Frail/Kob/Tanana RC 4.00 1.50
❑ 606 Fuller/Howard/Smith/Velez RC 1.00 .40
❑ 607 Fost/Hein/Ros/Taveras RC 1.00 .40
❑ 608A Apod/Ban/D'Acq/Wall ERR 2.00 .75
❑ 608B Apod/Ban/D'Acq/Wall RC 1.00 .40
❑ 609 Rico Petrocelli 1.00 .40
❑ 610 Dave Kingman 2.00 .75
❑ 611 Rich Stelmaszek .50 .20
❑ 612 Luke Walker .50 .20
❑ 613 Dan Monzon .50 .20
❑ 614 Adrian Devine RC .50 .20
❑ 615 Johnny Jeter UER .50 .20
❑ 616 Larry Gura .50 .20
❑ 617 Ted Ford .50 .20
❑ 618 Jim Mason .50 .20
❑ 619 Mike Anderson .50 .20
❑ 620 Al Downing .50 .20
❑ 621 Bernie Carbo .50 .20
❑ 622 Phil Gagliano .50 .20
❑ 623 Celerino Sanchez .50 .20
❑ 624 Bob Miller .50 .20
❑ 625 Ollie Brown .50 .20
❑ 626 Pittsburgh Pirates TC 1.00 .40
❑ 627 Carl Taylor .50 .20
❑ 628 Ivan Murrell .50 .20
❑ 629 Rusty Staub 2.00 .75
❑ 630 Tommie Agee 1.00 .40
❑ 631 Steve Barber .50 .20
❑ 632 George Culver .50 .20
❑ 633 Dave Hamilton .50 .20
❑ 634 Eddie Mathews MG 3.00 1.25
❑ 635 Johnny Edwards .50 .20
❑ 636 Dave Goltz .50 .20
❑ 637 Checklist 529-660 3.00 1.25
❑ 638 Ken Sanders .50 .20
❑ 639 Joe Lovitto .50 .20
❑ 640 Milt Pappas 1.00 .40
❑ 641 Chuck Brinkman .50 .20
❑ 642 Terry Harmon .50 .20
❑ 643 Los Angeles Dodgers TC 1.00 .40
❑ 644 Wayne Granger .50 .20
❑ 645 Ken Boswell .50 .20
❑ 646 George Foster 2.00 .75
❑ 647 Juan Beniquez RC .50 .20
❑ 648 Terry Crowley .50 .20
❑ 649 Fernando Gonzalez RC .50 .20
❑ 650 Mike Epstein .50 .20
❑ 651 Leron Lee .50 .20
❑ 652 Gail Hopkins .50 .20
❑ 653 Bob Stinson .50 .20
❑ 654A Jesus Alou NPOF 4.00 1.50
❑ 654B Jesus Alou COR 1.00 .40
❑ 655 Mike Tyson RC .50 .20
❑ 656 Adrian Garrett .50 .20
❑ 657 Jim Shellenback .50 .20
❑ 658 Lee Lacy .50 .20
❑ 659 Joe Lis .50 .20
❑ 660 Larry Dierker 2.00 .75

1975 Topps

❑ COMPLETE SET (660) 600.00 300.00
❑ WRAPPER (15-CENT) 8.00 4.00
❑ 1 Hank Aaron HL 30.00 12.50
❑ 2 Lou Brock HL 3.00 1.25
❑ 3 Bob Gibson HL 3.00 1.25
❑ 4 Al Kaline HL 6.00 2.50
❑ 5 Nolan Ryan HL 15.00 6.00
❑ 6 Mike Marshall HL 1.00 .40
❑ 7 Ryan/Busby/Bosman HL 8.00 3.00
❑ 8 Rogelio Moret .50 .20
❑ 9 Frank Tepedino 1.00 .40
❑ 10 Willie Davis 1.00 .40
❑ 11 Bill Melton .50 .20
❑ 12 David Clyde .50 .20
❑ 13 Gene Locklear RC 1.00 .40
❑ 14 Milt Wilcox .50 .20
❑ 15 Jose Cardenal 1.00 .40
❑ 16 Frank Tanana 2.00 .75
❑ 17 Dave Concepcion 2.00 .75
❑ 18 Detroit Tigers CL/Houk 2.00 .75
❑ 19 Jerry Koosman 1.00 .40
❑ 20 Thurman Munson 8.00 3.00
❑ 21 Rollie Fingers 3.00 1.25
❑ 22 Dave Cash .50 .20
❑ 23 Bill Russell 1.00 .40
❑ 24 Al Fitzmorris .50 .20
❑ 25 Lee May 1.00 .40
❑ 26 Dave McNally 1.00 .40
❑ 27 Ken Reitz .50 .20
❑ 28 Tom Murphy .50 .20
❑ 29 Dave Parker 3.00 1.25
❑ 30 Bert Blyleven 2.00 .75
❑ 31 Dave Rader .50 .20
❑ 32 Reggie Cleveland .50 .20
❑ 33 Dusty Baker 2.00 .75
❑ 34 Steve Renko .50 .20
❑ 35 Ron Santo 1.00 .40
❑ 36 Joe Lovitto .50 .20
❑ 37 Dave Freisleben .50 .20
❑ 38 Buddy Bell 2.00 .75
❑ 39 Andre Thornton 1.00 .40
❑ 40 Bill Singer .50 .20
❑ 41 Cesar Geronimo 1.00 .40
❑ 42 Joe Coleman .50 .20
❑ 43 Cleon Jones 1.00 .40
❑ 44 Pat Dobson .50 .20
❑ 45 Joe Rudi 1.00 .40
❑ 46 Philadelphia Phillies CL/Ozark 2.00 .75
❑ 47 Tommy John 2.00 .75
❑ 48 Freddie Patek 1.00 .40
❑ 49 Larry Dierker 1.00 .40
❑ 50 Brooks Robinson 8.00 3.00
❑ 51 Bob Forsch RC 1.00 .40
❑ 52 Darrell Porter 1.00 .40
❑ 53 Dave Giusti .50 .20
❑ 54 Eric Soderholm .50 .20
❑ 55 Bobby Bonds 2.00 .75
❑ 56 Rick Wise 1.00 .40
❑ 57 Dave Johnson 1.00 .40
❑ 58 Chuck Taylor .50 .20
❑ 59 Ken Henderson .50 .20
❑ 60 Fergie Jenkins 3.00 1.25
❑ 61 Dave Winfield 15.00 6.00
❑ 62 Fritz Peterson .50 .20
❑ 63 Steve Swisher RC .50 .20
❑ 64 Dave Chalk .50 .20
❑ 65 Don Gullett 1.00 .40
❑ 66 Willie Horton 1.00 .40
❑ 67 Tug McGraw 1.00 .40
❑ 68 Ron Blomberg .50 .20
❑ 69 John Odom .50 .20
❑ 70 Mike Schmidt 20.00 8.00
❑ 71 Charlie Hough 1.00 .40
❑ 72 Kansas City Royals CL/McKeon 2.00 .75
❑ 73 J.R. Richard 1.00 .40
❑ 74 Mark Belanger 1.00 .40
❑ 75 Ted Simmons 2.00 .75
❑ 76 Ed Sprague .50 .20
❑ 77 Richie Zisk 1.00 .40
❑ 78 Ray Corbin .50 .20
❑ 79 Gary Matthews 1.00 .40
❑ 80 Carlton Fisk 8.00 3.00
❑ 81 Ron Reed .50 .20
❑ 82 Pat Kelly .50 .20
❑ 83 Jim Merritt .50 .20
❑ 84 Enzo Hernandez .50 .20
❑ 85 Bill Bonham .50 .20
❑ 86 Joe Lis .50 .20
❑ 87 George Foster 2.00 .75
❑ 88 Tom Egan .50 .20
❑ 89 Jim Ray .50 .20
❑ 90 Rusty Staub 2.00 .75
❑ 91 Dick Green .50 .20
❑ 92 Cecil Upshaw .50 .20
❑ 93 Davey Lopes 2.00 .75
❑ 94 Jim Lonborg 1.00 .40
❑ 95 John Mayberry 1.00 .40
❑ 96 Mike Cosgrove RC .50 .20
❑ 97 Earl Williams .50 .20
❑ 98 Rich Folkers .50 .20
❑ 99 Mike Hegan .50 .20
❑ 100 Willie Stargell 4.00 1.50
❑ 101 Montreal Expos CL/Mauch 2.00 .75
❑ 102 Joe Decker .50 .20
❑ 103 Rick Miller .50 .20
❑ 104 Bill Madlock 2.00 .75
❑ 105 Buzz Capra .50 .20
❑ 106 Mike Hargrove UER RC 3.00 1.25
❑ 107 Jim Barr .50 .20
❑ 108 Tom Hall .50 .20
❑ 109 George Hendrick 1.00 .40
❑ 110 Wilbur Wood .50 .20
❑ 111 Wayne Garrett .50 .20

❑ 112 Larry Hardy RC .50 .20
❑ 113 Elliott Maddox .50 .20
❑ 114 Dick Lange .50 .20
❑ 115 Joe Ferguson .50 .20
❑ 116 Lerrin LaGrow .50 .20
❑ 117 Baltimore Orioles CL/Weaver 3.00 1.25
❑ 118 Mike Anderson .50 .20
❑ 119 Tommy Helms .50 .20
❑ 120 Steve Busby UER 1.00 .40
❑ 121 Bill North .50 .20
❑ 122 Al Hrabosky 1.00 .40
❑ 123 Johnny Briggs .50 .20
❑ 124 Jerry Reuss 1.00 .40
❑ 125 Ken Singleton 1.00 .40
❑ 126 Checklist 1-132 3.00 1.25
❑ 127 Glenn Borgmann .50 .20
❑ 128 Bill Lee 1.00 .40
❑ 129 Rick Monday 1.00 .40
❑ 130 Phil Niekro 3.00 1.25
❑ 131 Toby Harrah 1.00 .40
❑ 132 Randy Moffitt .50 .20
❑ 133 Dan Driessen 1.00 .40
❑ 134 Ron Hodges .50 .20
❑ 135 Charlie Spikes .50 .20
❑ 136 Jim Mason .50 .20
❑ 137 Terry Forster 1.00 .40
❑ 138 Del Unser .50 .20
❑ 139 Horacio Pina .50 .20
❑ 140 Steve Garvey 3.00 1.25
❑ 141 Mickey Stanley 1.00 .40
❑ 142 Bob Reynolds .50 .20
❑ 143 Cliff Johnson RC 1.00 .40
❑ 144 Jim Wohlford .50 .20
❑ 145 Ken Holtzman 1.00 .40
❑ 146 San Diego Padres CL/McNamara 2.00 .75
❑ 147 Pedro Garcia .50 .20
❑ 148 Jim Rooker .50 .20
❑ 149 Tim Foli .50 .20
❑ 150 Bob Gibson 6.00 2.50
❑ 151 Steve Brye .50 .20
❑ 152 Mario Guerrero .50 .20
❑ 153 Rick Reuschel 1.00 .40
❑ 154 Mike Lum .50 .20
❑ 155 Jim Bibby .50 .20
❑ 156 Dave Kingman 2.00 .75
❑ 157 Pedro Borbon 1.00 .40
❑ 158 Jerry Grote .50 .20
❑ 159 Steve Arlin .50 .20
❑ 160 Graig Nettles 2.00 .75
❑ 161 Stan Bahnsen .50 .20
❑ 162 Willie Montanez .50 .20
❑ 163 Jim Brewer .50 .20
❑ 164 Mickey Rivers 1.00 .40
❑ 165 Doug Rader 1.00 .40
❑ 166 Woodie Fryman .50 .20
❑ 167 Rich Coggins .50 .20
❑ 168 Bill Greif .50 .20
❑ 169 Cookie Rojas .50 .20
❑ 170 Bert Campaneris 1.00 .40
❑ 171 Ed Kirkpatrick .50 .20
❑ 172 Boston Red Sox CL/Johnson 3.00 1.25
❑ 173 Steve Rogers 1.00 .40
❑ 174 Bake McBride 1.00 .40
❑ 175 Don Money 1.00 .40
❑ 176 Burt Hooton 1.00 .40
❑ 177 Vic Correll RC .50 .20
❑ 178 Cesar Tovar .50 .20
❑ 179 Tom Bradley .50 .20
❑ 180 Joe Morgan 6.00 2.50
❑ 181 Fred Beene .50 .20
❑ 182 Don Hahn .50 .20
❑ 183 Mel Stottlemyre 1.00 .40
❑ 184 Jorge Orta .50 .20
❑ 185 Steve Carlton 8.00 3.00
❑ 186 Willie Crawford .50 .20
❑ 187 Denny Doyle .50 .20
❑ 188 Tom Griffin .50 .20
❑ 189 Y.Berra/Campanella MVP 4.00 1.50
❑ 190 B.Shantz/H.Sauer MVP 2.00 .75
❑ 191 Al Rosen/Campanella MVP 2.00 .75
❑ 192 Y.Berra/W.Mays MVP 4.00 1.50
❑ 193 Y.Berra/Campanella MVP 3.00 1.25
❑ 194 M.Mantle/D.Newcombe MVP 10.00 4.00
❑ 195 M.Mantle/H.Aaron MVP 12.00 5.00
❑ 196 J.Jensen/E.Banks MVP 3.00 1.25
❑ 197 N.Fox/E.Banks MVP 2.00 .75
❑ 198 R.Maris/D.Groat MVP 2.00 .75
❑ 199 R.Maris/F.Robinson MVP 3.00 1.25
❑ 200 M.Mantle/M.Wills MVP 10.00 4.00
❑ 201 E.Howard/S.Koufax MVP 2.00 .75
❑ 202 B.Robinson/K.Boyer MVP 1.00 .40
❑ 203 Z.Versailes/W.Mays MVP 2.00 .75
❑ 204 F.Robinson/B.Clemente MVP 6.00 2.50
❑ 205 C.Yastrzemski/O.Cepeda MVP 2.00 .75
❑ 206 D.McLain/B.Gibson MVP 2.00 .75
❑ 207 H.Killebrew/W.McCovey MVP 1.00 .40
❑ 208 B.Powell/J.Bench MVP 2.00 .75
❑ 209 V.Blue/J.Torre MVP 2.00 .75
❑ 210 R.Allen/J.Bench MVP 2.00 .75
❑ 211 R.Jackson/P.Rose MVP 5.00 2.00
❑ 212 J.Burroughs/S.Garvey MVP 2.00 .75
❑ 213 Oscar Gamble 1.00 .40
❑ 214 Harry Parker .50 .20
❑ 215 Bobby Valentine 1.00 .40
❑ 216 San Francisco Giants CL/Westrum 2.00 .75
❑ 217 Lou Piniella 2.00 .75
❑ 218 Jerry Johnson .50 .20
❑ 219 Ed Herrmann .50 .20
❑ 220 Don Sutton 3.00 1.25
❑ 221 Aurelio Rodriguez .50 .20
❑ 222 Dan Spillner RC .50 .20
❑ 223 Robin Yount RC 50.00 25.00
❑ 224 Ramon Hernandez .50 .20
❑ 225 Bob Grich 1.00 .40
❑ 226 Bill Campbell .50 .20
❑ 227 Bob Watson 1.00 .40
❑ 228 George Brett RC 80.00 40.00
❑ 229 Barry Foote .50 .20
❑ 230 Jim Hunter 4.00 1.50
❑ 231 Mike Tyson .50 .20
❑ 232 Diego Segui .50 .20
❑ 233 Billy Grabarkewitz .50 .20
❑ 234 Tom Grieve 1.00 .40
❑ 235 Jack Billingham 1.00 .40
❑ 236 California Angels CL/Williams 2.00 .75
❑ 237 Carl Morton 1.00 .40
❑ 238 Dave Duncan 1.00 .40
❑ 239 George Stone .50 .20
❑ 240 Garry Maddox 1.00 .40
❑ 241 Dick Tidrow .50 .20
❑ 242 Jay Johnstone 1.00 .40
❑ 243 Jim Kaat 2.00 .75
❑ 244 Bill Buckner 1.00 .40
❑ 245 Mickey Lolich 2.00 .75
❑ 246 St. Louis Cardinals CL/Schoen 2.00 .75
❑ 247 Enos Cabell .50 .20
❑ 248 Randy Jones 2.00 .75
❑ 249 Danny Thompson .50 .20
❑ 250 Ken Brett .50 .20
❑ 251 Fran Healy .50 .20
❑ 252 Fred Scherman .50 .20
❑ 253 Jesus Alou .50 .20
❑ 254 Mike Torrez 1.00 .40
❑ 255 Dwight Evans 2.00 .75
❑ 256 Billy Champion .50 .20
❑ 257 Checklist: 133-264 3.00 1.25
❑ 258 Dave LaRoche .50 .20
❑ 259 Len Randle .50 .20
❑ 260 Johnny Bench 15.00 6.00
❑ 261 Andy Hassler RC .50 .20
❑ 262 Rowland Office RC .50 .20
❑ 263 Jim Perry 1.00 .40
❑ 264 John Milner .50 .20
❑ 265 Ron Bryant .50 .20
❑ 266 Sandy Alomar 1.00 .40
❑ 267 Dick Ruthven .50 .20
❑ 268 Hal McRae 1.00 .40
❑ 269 Doug Rau .50 .20
❑ 270 Ron Fairly 1.00 .40
❑ 271 Gerry Moses .50 .20
❑ 272 Lynn McGlothen .50 .20
❑ 273 Steve Braun .50 .20
❑ 274 Vicente Romo .50 .20
❑ 275 Paul Blair 1.00 .40
❑ 276 Chicago White Sox CL/Tanner 2.00 .75
❑ 277 Frank Taveras .50 .20
❑ 278 Paul Lindblad .50 .20
❑ 279 Milt May .50 .20
❑ 280 Carl Yastrzemski 12.00 5.00
❑ 281 Jim Slaton .50 .20
❑ 282 Jerry Morales .50 .20
❑ 283 Steve Foucault .50 .20
❑ 284 Ken Griffey Sr. 4.00 1.50
❑ 285 Ellie Rodriguez .50 .20
❑ 286 Mike Jorgensen .50 .20
❑ 287 Roric Harrison .50 .20
❑ 288 Bruce Ellingsen RC .50 .20
❑ 289 Ken Rudolph .50 .20
❑ 290 Jon Matlack .50 .20
❑ 291 Bill Sudakis .50 .20
❑ 292 Ron Schueler .50 .20
❑ 293 Dick Sharon .50 .20
❑ 294 Geoff Zahn RC .50 .20
❑ 295 Vada Pinson 2.00 .75
❑ 296 Alan Foster .50 .20
❑ 297 Craig Kusick RC .50 .20
❑ 298 Johnny Grubb .50 .20
❑ 299 Bucky Dent 2.00 .75
❑ 300 Reggie Jackson 15.00 6.00
❑ 301 Dave Roberts .50 .20
❑ 302 Rick Burleson RC 1.00 .40
❑ 303 Grant Jackson .50 .20
❑ 304 Pittsburgh Pirates CL/Murtaugh 2.00 .75
❑ 305 Jim Colborn .50 .20
❑ 306 R.Carew/R.Garr LL 2.00 .75
❑ 307 D.Allen/M.Schmidt LL 4.00 1.50
❑ 308 J.Burroughs/J.Bench LL 2.00 .75
❑ 309 B.North/L.Brock LL 2.00 .75
❑ 310 Hunter/Jenk/Mess/Niek LL 2.00 .75
❑ 311 J.Hunter/B.Capra LL 2.00 .75
❑ 312 N.Ryan/S.Carlton LL 12.00 5.00
❑ 313 T.Forster/M.Marshall LL 1.00 .40
❑ 314 Buck Martinez .50 .20
❑ 315 Don Kessinger 1.00 .40
❑ 316 Jackie Brown .50 .20
❑ 317 Joe Lahoud .50 .20
❑ 318 Ernie McAnally .50 .20
❑ 319 Johnny Oates 1.00 .40
❑ 320 Pete Rose 30.00 12.50
❑ 321 Rudy May .50 .20
❑ 322 Ed Goodson .50 .20
❑ 323 Fred Holdsworth .50 .20
❑ 324 Ed Kranepool 1.00 .40
❑ 325 Tony Oliva 2.00 .75
❑ 326 Wayne Twitchell .50 .20
❑ 327 Jerry Hairston .50 .20
❑ 328 Sonny Siebert .50 .20
❑ 329 Ted Kubiak .50 .20
❑ 330 Mike Marshall 1.00 .40
❑ 331 Cleveland Indians CL/Robinson 2.00 .75
❑ 332 Fred Kendall .50 .20
❑ 333 Dick Drago .50 .20
❑ 334 Greg Gross RC .50 .20
❑ 335 Jim Palmer 6.00 2.50
❑ 336 Rennie Stennett .50 .20
❑ 337 Kevin Kobel .50 .20
❑ 338 Rich Stelmaszek .50 .20
❑ 339 Jim Fregosi 1.00 .40
❑ 340 Paul Splittorff .50 .20
❑ 341 Hal Breeden .50 .20
❑ 342 Leroy Stanton .50 .20
❑ 343 Danny Frisella .50 .20
❑ 344 Ben Oglivie 1.00 .40
❑ 345 Clay Carroll 1.00 .40
❑ 346 Bobby Darwin .50 .20
❑ 347 Mike Caldwell .50 .20
❑ 348 Tony Muser .50 .20
❑ 349 Ray Sadecki .50 .20
❑ 350 Bobby Murcer 1.00 .40
❑ 351 Bob Boone 2.00 .75
❑ 352 Darold Knowles .50 .20
❑ 353 Luis Melendez .50 .20
❑ 354 Dick Bosman .50 .20
❑ 355 Chris Cannizzaro .50 .20
❑ 356 Rico Petrocelli 1.00 .40
❑ 357 Ken Forsch UER .50 .20
❑ 358 Al Bumbry 1.00 .40
❑ 359 Paul Popovich .50 .20
❑ 360 George Scott 1.00 .40
❑ 361 Los Angeles Dodgers CL/Alston 2.00 .75
❑ 362 Steve Hargan .50 .20
❑ 363 Carmen Fanzone .50 .20
❑ 364 Doug Bird .50 .20
❑ 365 Bob Bailey .50 .20
❑ 366 Ken Sanders .50 .20
❑ 367 Craig Robinson .50 .20
❑ 368 Vic Albury .50 .20
❑ 369 Merv Rettenmund .50 .20

❑ 370 Tom Seaver 12.00 5.00
❑ 371 Gates Brown .50 .20
❑ 372 John D'Acquisto .50 .20
❑ 373 Bill Sharp .50 .20
❑ 374 Eddie Watt .50 .20
❑ 375 Roy White 1.00 .40
❑ 376 Steve Yeager 1.00 .40
❑ 377 Tom Hilgendorf .50 .20
❑ 378 Derrel Thomas .50 .20
❑ 379 Bernie Carbo .50 .20
❑ 380 Sal Bando 1.00 .40
❑ 381 John Curtis .50 .20
❑ 382 Don Baylor 2.00 .75
❑ 383 Jim York .50 .20
❑ 384 Milwaukee Brewers CL/Crandall 2.00 .75
❑ 385 Dock Ellis .50 .20
❑ 386 Checklist: 265-396 UER 3.00 1.25
❑ 387 Jim Spencer .50 .20
❑ 388 Steve Stone 1.00 .40
❑ 389 Tony Solaita RC .50 .20
❑ 390 Ron Cey 2.00 .75
❑ 391 Don DeMola RC .50 .20
❑ 392 Bruce Bochte RC 1.00 .40
❑ 393 Gary Gentry .50 .20
❑ 394 Larvell Blanks .50 .20
❑ 395 Bud Harrelson 1.00 .40
❑ 396 Fred Norman 1.00 .40
❑ 397 Bill Freehan 1.00 .40
❑ 398 Elias Sosa .50 .20
❑ 399 Terry Harmon .50 .20
❑ 400 Dick Allen 2.00 .75
❑ 401 Mike Wallace .50 .20
❑ 402 Bob Tolan .50 .20
❑ 403 Tom Buskey RC .50 .20
❑ 404 Ted Sizemore .50 .20
❑ 405 John Montague RC .50 .20
❑ 406 Bob Gallagher .50 .20
❑ 407 Herb Washington RC 2.00 .75
❑ 408 Clyde Wright UER .50 .20
❑ 409 Bob Robertson .50 .20
❑ 410 Mike Cuellar UER 1.00 .40
❑ 411 George Mitterwald .50 .20
❑ 412 Bill Hands .50 .20
❑ 413 Marty Pattin .50 .20
❑ 414 Manny Mota 1.00 .40
❑ 415 John Hiller 1.00 .40
❑ 416 Larry Lintz .50 .20
❑ 417 Skip Lockwood .50 .20
❑ 418 Leo Foster .50 .20
❑ 419 Dave Goltz .50 .20
❑ 420 Larry Bowa 2.00 .75
❑ 421 New York Mets CL/Berra 3.00 1.25
❑ 422 Brian Downing 1.00 .40
❑ 423 Clay Kirby .50 .20
❑ 424 John Lowenstein .50 .20
❑ 425 Tito Fuentes .50 .20
❑ 426 George Medich .50 .20
❑ 427 Clarence Gaston 1.00 .40
❑ 428 Dave Hamilton .50 .20
❑ 429 Jim Dwyer RC .50 .20
❑ 430 Luis Tiant 2.00 .75
❑ 431 Rod Gilbreath .50 .20
❑ 432 Ken Berry .50 .20
❑ 433 Larry Demery RC .50 .20
❑ 434 Bob Locker .50 .20
❑ 435 Dave Nelson .50 .20
❑ 436 Ken Frailing .50 .20
❑ 437 Al Cowens RC 1.00 .40
❑ 438 Don Carrithers .50 .20
❑ 439 Ed Brinkman .50 .20
❑ 440 Andy Messersmith 1.00 .40
❑ 441 Bobby Heise .50 .20
❑ 442 Maximino Leon RC .50 .20
❑ 443 Minnesota Twins CL/Quilici 2.00 .75
❑ 444 Gene Garber 1.00 .40
❑ 445 Felix Millan .50 .20
❑ 446 Bart Johnson .50 .20
❑ 447 Terry Crowley .50 .20
❑ 448 Frank Duffy .50 .20
❑ 449 Charlie Williams .50 .20
❑ 450 Willie McCovey 6.00 2.50
❑ 451 Rick Dempsey 1.00 .40
❑ 452 Angel Mangual .50 .20
❑ 453 Claude Osteen 1.00 .40
❑ 454 Doug Griffin .50 .20
❑ 455 Don Wilson .50 .20
❑ 456 Bob Coluccio .50 .20
❑ 457 Mario Mendoza RC .50 .20
❑ 458 Ross Grimsley .50 .20
❑ 459 1974 AL Championships 1.00 .40
❑ 460 1974 NL Championships 2.00 .75
❑ 461 Reggie Jackson WS1 5.00 2.00
❑ 462 W.Alston/J.Ferguson WS2 1.00 .40
❑ 463 Rollie Fingers WS3 2.00 .75
❑ 464 A's Batter WS4 1.00 .40
❑ 465 Joe Rudi WS5 1.00 .40
❑ 466 A's Do it Again WS 2.00 .75
❑ 467 Ed Halicki RC .50 .20
❑ 468 Bobby Mitchell .50 .20
❑ 469 Tom Dettore RC .50 .20
❑ 470 Jeff Burroughs 1.00 .40
❑ 471 Bob Stinson .50 .20
❑ 472 Bruce Dal Canton .50 .20
❑ 473 Ken McMullen .50 .20
❑ 474 Luke Walker .50 .20
❑ 475 Darrell Evans 1.00 .40
❑ 476 Ed Figueroa RC .50 .20
❑ 477 Tom Hutton .50 .20
❑ 478 Tom Burgmeier .50 .20
❑ 479 Ken Boswell .50 .20
❑ 480 Carlos May .50 .20
❑ 481 Will McEnaney RC 1.00 .40
❑ 482 Tom McCraw .50 .20
❑ 483 Steve Ontiveros .50 .20
❑ 484 Glenn Beckert 1.00 .40
❑ 485 Sparky Lyle 1.00 .40
❑ 486 Ray Fosse .50 .20
❑ 487 Houston Astros CL/Gomez 2.00 .75
❑ 488 Bill Travers RC .50 .20
❑ 489 Cecil Cooper 2.00 .75
❑ 490 Reggie Smith 1.00 .40
❑ 491 Doyle Alexander 1.00 .40
❑ 492 Rich Hebner 1.00 .40
❑ 493 Don Stanhouse .50 .20
❑ 494 Pete LaCock RC .50 .20
❑ 495 Nelson Briles 1.00 .40
❑ 496 Pepe Frias .50 .20
❑ 497 Jim Nettles .50 .20
❑ 498 Al Downing .50 .20
❑ 499 Marty Perez .50 .20
❑ 500 Nolan Ryan 50.00 25.00
❑ 501 Bill Robinson 1.00 .40
❑ 502 Pat Bourque .50 .20
❑ 503 Fred Stanley .50 .20
❑ 504 Buddy Bradford .50 .20
❑ 505 Chris Speier .50 .20
❑ 506 Leron Lee .50 .20
❑ 507 Tom Carroll RC .50 .20
❑ 508 Bob Hansen RC .50 .20
❑ 509 Dave Hilton .50 .20
❑ 510 Vida Blue 1.00 .40
❑ 511 Texas Rangers CL/Martin 2.00 .75
❑ 512 Larry Milbourne RC .50 .20
❑ 513 Dick Pole .50 .20
❑ 514 Jose Cruz 2.00 .75
❑ 515 Manny Sanguillen 1.00 .40
❑ 516 Don Hood .50 .20
❑ 517 Checklist: 397-528 3.00 1.25
❑ 518 Leo Cardenas .50 .20
❑ 519 Jim Todd RC .50 .20
❑ 520 Amos Otis 1.00 .40
❑ 521 Dennis Blair RC .50 .20
❑ 522 Gary Sutherland .50 .20
❑ 523 Tom Paciorek 1.00 .40
❑ 524 John Doherty RC .50 .20
❑ 525 Tom House .50 .20
❑ 526 Larry Hisle 1.00 .40
❑ 527 Mac Scarce .50 .20
❑ 528 Eddie Leon .50 .20
❑ 529 Gary Thomasson .50 .20
❑ 530 Gaylord Perry 3.00 1.25
❑ 531 Cincinnati Reds CL/Anderson 5.002.00
❑ 532 Gorman Thomas 1.00 .40
❑ 533 Rudy Meoli .50 .20
❑ 534 Alex Johnson .50 .20
❑ 535 Gene Tenace 1.00 .40
❑ 536 Bob Moose .50 .20
❑ 537 Tommy Harper 1.00 .40
❑ 538 Duffy Dyer .50 .20
❑ 539 Jesse Jefferson .50 .20
❑ 540 Lou Brock 6.00 2.50
❑ 541 Roger Metzger .50 .20
❑ 542 Pete Broberg .50 .20
❑ 543 Larry Biittner .50 .20
❑ 544 Steve Mingori .50 .20
❑ 545 Billy Williams 3.00 1.25
❑ 546 John Knox .50 .20
❑ 547 Von Joshua .50 .20
❑ 548 Charlie Sands .50 .20
❑ 549 Bill Butler .50 .20
❑ 550 Ralph Garr 1.00 .40
❑ 551 Larry Christenson .50 .20
❑ 552 Jack Brohamer .50 .20
❑ 553 John Boccabella .50 .20
❑ 554 Goose Gossage 2.00 .75
❑ 555 Al Oliver 1.00 .40
❑ 556 Tim Johnson .50 .20
❑ 557 Larry Gura .50 .20
❑ 558 Dave Roberts .50 .20
❑ 559 Bob Montgomery .50 .20
❑ 560 Tony Perez 4.00 1.50
❑ 561 Oakland Athletics CL/Dark 2.00 .75
❑ 562 Gary Nolan 1.00 .40
❑ 563 Wilbur Howard .50 .20
❑ 564 Tommy Davis 1.00 .40
❑ 565 Joe Torre 2.00 .75
❑ 566 Ray Burris .50 .20
❑ 567 Jim Sundberg RC 2.00 .75
❑ 568 Dale Murray RC .50 .20
❑ 569 Frank White 1.00 .40
❑ 570 Jim Wynn 1.00 .40
❑ 571 Dave Lemanczyk RC .50 .20
❑ 572 Roger Nelson .50 .20
❑ 573 Orlando Pena .50 .20
❑ 574 Tony Taylor .50 .20
❑ 575 Gene Clines .50 .20
❑ 576 Phil Roof .50 .20
❑ 577 John Morris .50 .20
❑ 578 Dave Tomlin RC .50 .20
❑ 579 Skip Pitlock .50 .20
❑ 580 Frank Robinson 6.00 2.50
❑ 581 Darrel Chaney .50 .20
❑ 582 Eduardo Rodriguez .50 .20
❑ 583 Andy Etchebarren .50 .20
❑ 584 Mike Garman .50 .20
❑ 585 Chris Chambliss 1.00 .40
❑ 586 Tim McCarver 2.00 .75
❑ 587 Chris Ward RC .50 .20
❑ 588 Rick Auerbach .50 .20
❑ 589 Atlanta Braves CL/King 2.00 .75
❑ 590 Cesar Cedeno 1.00 .40
❑ 591 Glenn Abbott .50 .20
❑ 592 Balor Moore .50 .20
❑ 593 Gene Lamont .50 .20
❑ 594 Jim Fuller .50 .20
❑ 595 Joe Niekro 1.00 .40
❑ 596 Ollie Brown .50 .20
❑ 597 Winston Llenas .50 .20
❑ 598 Bruce Kison .50 .20
❑ 599 Nate Colbert .50 .20
❑ 600 Rod Carew 8.00 3.00
❑ 601 Juan Beniquez .50 .20
❑ 602 John Vukovich .50 .20
❑ 603 Lew Krausse .50 .20
❑ 604 Oscar Zamora RC .50 .20
❑ 605 John Ellis .50 .20
❑ 606 Bruce Miller RC .50 .20
❑ 607 Jim Holt .50 .20
❑ 608 Gene Michael .50 .20
❑ 609 Elrod Hendricks .50 .20
❑ 610 Ron Hunt .50 .20
❑ 611 New York Yankees CL/Virdon 2.00 .75
❑ 612 Terry Hughes .50 .20
❑ 613 Bill Parsons .50 .20
❑ 614 Kuc/Mill/Ruhle/Sieb RC 1.00 .40
❑ 615 Darcy/Leonard/Und/Webb RC 2.00 .75
❑ 616 Jim Rice RC 15.00 6.00
❑ 617 Cubb/DeCinces/Sand/Trillo RC 2.00 .75
❑ 618 East/John/McGregor/Rhoden RC 1.00 .40
❑ 619 Ayala/Nyman/Smith Turner RC 1.00 .40
❑ 620 Gary Carter RC 15.00 6.00
❑ 621 Denny/Eastwick/Kern/Vein RC 2.00 .75
❑ 622 Fred Lynn RC 8.00 3.00
❑ 623 K.Hern RC/P.Garner RC 10.00 4.00
❑ 624 Kon/Lavelle/Otten/Sol RC 1.00 .40
❑ 625 Boog Powell 2.00 .75
❑ 626 Larry Haney UER .50 .20
❑ 627 Tom Walker .50 .20

628	Ron LeFlore RC	1.00	.40
629	Joe Hoerner	.50	.20
630	Greg Luzinski	2.00	.75
631	Lee Lacy	.50	.20
632	Morris Nettles RC	.50	.20
633	Paul Casanova	.50	.20
634	Cy Acosta	.50	.20
635	Chuck Dobson	.50	.20
636	Charlie Moore	.50	.20
637	Ted Martinez	.50	.20
638	Chicago Cubs CL/Marshall	2.00	.75
639	Steve Kline	.50	.20
640	Harmon Killebrew	6.00	2.50
641	Jim Northrup	1.00	.40
642	Mike Phillips	.50	.20
643	Brent Strom	.50	.20
644	Bill Fahey	.50	.20
645	Danny Cater	.50	.20
646	Checklist: 529-660	3.00	1.25
647	Claudell Washington RC	2.00	.75
648	Dave Pagan RC	.50	.20
649	Jack Heidemann	.50	.20
650	Dave May	.50	.20
651	John Morlan RC	.50	.20
652	Lindy McDaniel	1.00	.40
653	Lee Richard UER	.50	.20
654	Jerry Terrell	.50	.20
655	Rico Carty	1.00	.40
656	Bill Plummer	.50	.20
657	Bob Oliver	.50	.20
658	Vic Harris	.50	.20
659	Bob Apodaca	.50	.20
660	Hank Aaron	30.00	12.50

1976 Topps

	COMPLETE SET (660)	250.00	150.00
1	Hank Aaron RB	15.00	6.00
2	Bobby Bonds RB	1.50	.60
3	Mickey Lolich RB	.75	.30
4	Dave Lopes RB	.75	.30
5	Tom Seaver RB	5.00	2.00
6	Rennie Stennett RB	.75	.30
7	Jim Umbarger RC	.40	.15
8	Tito Fuentes	.40	.15
9	Paul Lindblad	.40	.15
10	Lou Brock	5.00	2.00
11	Jim Hughes	.40	.15
12	Richie Zisk	.75	.30
13	John Wockenfuss RC	.40	.15
14	Gene Garber	.75	.30
15	George Scott	.75	.30
16	Bob Apodaca	.40	.15
17	New York Yankees CL/Martin	1.50	.60
18	Dale Murray	.40	.15
19	George Brett	30.00	12.50
20	Bob Watson	.75	.30
21	Dave LaRoche	.40	.15
22	Bill Russell	.75	.30
23	Brian Downing	.40	.15
24	Cesar Geronimo	.75	.30
25	Mike Torrez	.75	.30
26	Andre Thornton	.75	.30
27	Ed Figueroa	.40	.15
28	Dusty Baker	1.50	.60
29	Rick Burleson	.75	.30
30	John Montefusco RC	.75	.30
31	Len Randle	.40	.15
32	Danny Frisella	.40	.15
33	Bill North	.40	.15
34	Mike Garman	.40	.15
35	Tony Oliva	1.50	.60
36	Frank Taveras	.40	.15
37	John Hiller	.75	.30
38	Garry Maddox	.75	.30
39	Pete Broberg	.40	.15
40	Dave Kingman	1.50	.60
41	Tippy Martinez RC	.75	.30
42	Barry Foote	.40	.15
43	Paul Splittorff	.40	.15
44	Doug Rader	.75	.30
45	Boog Powell	1.50	.60
46	Los Angeles Dodgers CL/Alston	1.50	.60
47	Jesse Jefferson	.40	.15
48	Dave Concepcion	1.50	.60
49	Dave Duncan	.75	.30
50	Fred Lynn	1.50	.60
51	Ray Burris	.40	.15
52	Dave Chalk	.40	.15
53	Mike Beard RC	.40	.15
54	Dave Rader	.40	.15
55	Gaylord Perry	2.50	1.00
56	Bob Tolan	.40	.15
57	Phil Garner	.75	.30
58	Ron Reed	.40	.15
59	Larry Hisle	.75	.30
60	Jerry Reuss	.75	.30
61	Ron LeFlore	.75	.30
62	Johnny Oates	.75	.30
63	Bobby Darwin	.40	.15
64	Jerry Koosman	.75	.30
65	Chris Chambliss	.75	.30
66	Gus/Buddy Bell FS	.75	.30
67	Bob/Ray Boone FS	.75	.30
68	Joe/Joe Jr. Coleman FS	.40	.15
69	Jim/Mike Hegan FS	.40	.15
70	Roy/Roy Jr. Smalley FS	.75	.30
71	Steve Rogers	.75	.30
72	Hal McRae	.75	.30
73	Baltimore Orioles CL/Weaver	1.50	.60
74	Oscar Gamble	.75	.30
75	Larry Dierker	.75	.30
76	Willie Crawford	.40	.15
77	Pedro Borbon	.75	.30
78	Cecil Cooper	.75	.30
79	Jerry Morales	.40	.15
80	Jim Kaat	1.50	.60
81	Darrell Evans	.75	.30
82	Von Joshua	.40	.15
83	Jim Spencer	.40	.15
84	Brent Strom	.40	.15
85	Mickey Rivers	.75	.30
86	Mike Tyson	.40	.15
87	Tom Burgmeier	.40	.15
88	Duffy Dyer	.40	.15
89	Vern Ruhle	.40	.15
90	Sal Bando	.75	.30
91	Tom Hutton	.40	.15
92	Eduardo Rodriguez	.40	.15
93	Mike Phillips	.40	.15
94	Jim Dwyer	.40	.15
95	Brooks Robinson	6.00	2.50
96	Doug Bird	.40	.15
97	Wilbur Howard	.40	.15
98	Dennis Eckersley RC	30.00	12.50
99	Lee Lacy	.40	.15
100	Jim Hunter	3.00	1.25
101	Pete LaCock	.40	.15
102	Jim Willoughby	.40	.15
103	Biff Pocoroba RC	.40	.15
104	Cincinnati Reds CL/Anderson	2.50	1.00
105	Gary Lavelle	.40	.15
106	Tom Grieve	.75	.30
107	Dave Roberts	.40	.15
108	Don Kirkwood RC	.40	.15
109	Larry Lintz	.40	.15
110	Carlos May	.40	.15
111	Danny Thompson	.40	.15
112	Kent Tekulve RC	1.50	.60
113	Gary Sutherland	.40	.15
114	Jay Johnstone	.75	.30
115	Ken Holtzman	.75	.30
116	Charlie Moore	.40	.15
117	Mike Jorgensen	.40	.15
118	Boston Red Sox CL/Johnson	1.50	.60
119	Checklist 1-132	1.50	.60
120	Rusty Staub	.75	.30
121	Tony Solaita	.40	.15
122	Mike Cosgrove	.40	.15
123	Walt Williams	.40	.15
124	Doug Rau	.40	.15
125	Don Baylor	1.50	.60
126	Tom Dettore	.40	.15
127	Larvell Blanks	.40	.15
128	Ken Griffey Sr.	2.50	1.00
129	Andy Etchebarren	.40	.15
130	Luis Tiant	1.50	.60
131	Bill Stein RC	.40	.15
132	Don Hood	.40	.15
133	Gary Matthews	.75	.30
134	Mike Ivie	.40	.15
135	Bake McBride	.75	.30
136	Dave Goltz	.40	.15
137	Bill Robinson	.75	.30
138	Lerrin LaGrow	.40	.15
139	Gorman Thomas	.75	.30
140	Vida Blue	.75	.30
141	Larry Parrish RC	1.50	.60
142	Dick Drago	.40	.15
143	Jerry Grote	.40	.15
144	Al Fitzmorris	.40	.15
145	Larry Bowa	.75	.30
146	George Medich	.40	.15
147	Houston Astros CL/Virdon	1.50	.60
148	Stan Thomas RC	.40	.15
149	Tommy Davis	.75	.30
150	Steve Garvey	2.50	1.00
151	Bill Bonham	.40	.15
152	Leroy Stanton	.40	.15
153	Buzz Capra	.40	.15
154	Bucky Dent	.75	.30
155	Jack Billingham	.75	.30
156	Rico Carty	.75	.30
157	Mike Caldwell	.40	.15
158	Ken Reitz	.40	.15
159	Jerry Terrell	.40	.15
160	Dave Winfield	10.00	4.00
161	Bruce Kison	.40	.15
162	Jack Pierce RC	.40	.15
163	Jim Slaton	.40	.15
164	Pepe Mangual	.40	.15
165	Gene Tenace	.75	.30
166	Skip Lockwood	.40	.15
167	Freddie Patek	.75	.30
168	Tom Hilgendorf	.40	.15
169	Graig Nettles	1.50	.60
170	Rick Wise	.40	.15
171	Greg Gross	.40	.15
172	Texas Rangers CL/Lucchesi	1.50	.60
173	Steve Swisher	.40	.15
174	Charlie Hough	.75	.30
175	Ken Singleton	.75	.30
176	Dick Lange	.40	.15
177	Marty Perez	.40	.15
178	Tom Buskey	.40	.15
179	George Foster	1.50	.60
180	Goose Gossage	1.50	.60
181	Willie Montanez	.40	.15
182	Harry Rasmussen	.40	.15
183	Steve Braun	.40	.15
184	Bill Greif	.40	.15
185	Dave Parker	1.50	.60
186	Tom Walker	.40	.15
187	Pedro Garcia	.40	.15
188	Fred Scherman	.40	.15
189	Claudell Washington	.75	.30
190	Jon Matlack	.40	.15
191	Madlock/Simm/Mang LL	.75	.30
192	Carew/Lynn/Munson LL	2.50	1.00
193	Schmidt/King/Luz LL	3.00	1.25
194	Reggie/Scott/Mayb LL	3.00	1.25
195	Luz/Bench/Perez LL	1.50	.60
196	Scott/Mayb/Lynn LL	.75	.30
197	Lopes/Morgan/Brock LL	1.50	.60
198	Rivers/Wash/Otis LL	.75	.30
199	Seaver/Jones/Mess LL	2.50	1.00
200	Hunter/Palmer/Blue LL	1.50	.60
201	Jones/Mess/Seaver LL	1.50	.60
202	Palmer/Hunter/Eck LL	3.00	1.25
203	Seaver/Mont/Mess LL	2.50	1.00
204	Tanana/Blyleven/Perry LL	.75	.30

	Card		
❑	205 A.Hrabosky/G.Gossage LL	.75	.30
❑	206 Manny Trillo	.40	.15
❑	207 Andy Hassler	.40	.15
❑	208 Mike Lum	.40	.15
❑	209 Alan Ashby RC	.40	.15
❑	210 Lee May	.75	.30
❑	211 Clay Carroll	.75	.30
❑	212 Pat Kelly	.40	.15
❑	213 Dave Heaverlo RC	.40	.15
❑	214 Eric Soderholm	.40	.15
❑	215 Reggie Smith	.75	.30
❑	216 Montreal Expos CL/Kuehl	1.50	.60
❑	217 Dave Freisleben	.40	.15
❑	218 John Knox	.40	.15
❑	219 Tom Murphy	.40	.15
❑	220 Manny Sanguillen	.75	.30
❑	221 Jim Todd	.40	.15
❑	222 Wayne Garrett	.40	.15
❑	223 Ollie Brown	.40	.15
❑	224 Jim York	.40	.15
❑	225 Roy White	.75	.30
❑	226 Jim Sundberg	.75	.30
❑	227 Oscar Zamora	.40	.15
❑	228 John Hale RC	.40	.15
❑	229 Jerry Remy RC	.40	.15
❑	230 Carl Yastrzemski	10.00	4.00
❑	231 Tom House	.40	.15
❑	232 Frank Duffy	.40	.15
❑	233 Grant Jackson	.40	.15
❑	234 Mike Sadek	.40	.15
❑	235 Bert Blyleven	1.50	.60
❑	236 Kansas City Royals CL/Herzog	1.50	.60
❑	237 Dave Hamilton	.40	.15
❑	238 Larry Biittner	.40	.15
❑	239 John Curtis	.40	.15
❑	240 Pete Rose	25.00	10.00
❑	241 Hector Torres	.40	.15
❑	242 Dan Meyer	.40	.15
❑	243 Jim Rooker	.40	.15
❑	244 Bill Sharp	.40	.15
❑	245 Felix Millan	.40	.15
❑	246 Cesar Tovar	.40	.15
❑	247 Terry Harmon	.40	.15
❑	248 Dick Tidrow	.40	.15
❑	249 Cliff Johnson	.75	.30
❑	250 Fergie Jenkins	2.50	1.00
❑	251 Rick Monday	.75	.30
❑	252 Tim Nordbrook RC	.40	.15
❑	253 Bill Buckner	.75	.30
❑	254 Rudy Meoli	.40	.15
❑	255 Fritz Peterson	.40	.15
❑	256 Rowland Office	.40	.15
❑	257 Ross Grimsley	.40	.15
❑	258 Nyls Nyman	.40	.15
❑	259 Darrel Chaney	.40	.15
❑	260 Steve Busby	.40	.15
❑	261 Gary Thomasson	.40	.15
❑	262 Checklist 133-264	1.50	.60
❑	263 Lyman Bostock RC	1.50	.60
❑	264 Steve Renko	.40	.15
❑	265 Willie Davis	.75	.30
❑	266 Alan Foster	.40	.15
❑	267 Aurelio Rodriguez	.40	.15
❑	268 Del Unser	.40	.15
❑	269 Rick Austin	.40	.15
❑	270 Willie Stargell	3.00	1.25
❑	271 Jim Lonborg	.75	.30
❑	272 Rick Dempsey	.75	.30
❑	273 Joe Niekro	.75	.30
❑	274 Tommy Harper	.75	.30
❑	275 Rick Manning RC	.40	.15
❑	276 Mickey Scott	.40	.15
❑	277 Chicago Cubs CL/Marshall	1.50	.60
❑	278 Bernie Carbo	.40	.15
❑	279 Roy Howell RC	.40	.15
❑	280 Burt Hooton	.75	.30
❑	281 Dave May	.40	.15
❑	282 Dan Osborn RC	.40	.15
❑	283 Merv Rettenmund	.40	.15
❑	284 Steve Ontiveros	.40	.15
❑	285 Mike Cuellar	.75	.30
❑	286 Jim Wohlford	.40	.15
❑	287 Pete Mackanin	.40	.15
❑	288 Bill Campbell	.40	.15
❑	289 Enzo Hernandez	.40	.15
❑	290 Ted Simmons	.75	.30
❑	291 Ken Sanders	.40	.15
❑	292 Leon Roberts	.40	.15
❑	293 Bill Castro RC	.40	.15
❑	294 Ed Kirkpatrick	.40	.15
❑	295 Dave Cash	.40	.15
❑	296 Pat Dobson	.40	.15
❑	297 Roger Metzger	.40	.15
❑	298 Dick Bosman	.40	.15
❑	299 Champ Summers RC	.40	.15
❑	300 Johnny Bench	12.00	5.00
❑	301 Jackie Brown	.40	.15
❑	302 Rick Miller	.40	.15
❑	303 Steve Foucault	.40	.15
❑	304 California Angels CL/Williams	1.50	.60
❑	305 Andy Messersmith	.75	.30
❑	306 Rod Gilbreath	.40	.15
❑	307 Al Bumbry	.75	.30
❑	308 Jim Barr	.40	.15
❑	309 Bill Melton	.40	.15
❑	310 Randy Jones	.75	.30
❑	311 Cookie Rojas	.40	.15
❑	312 Don Carrithers	.40	.15
❑	313 Dan Ford RC	.40	.15
❑	314 Ed Kranepool	.40	.15
❑	315 Al Hrabosky	.75	.30
❑	316 Robin Yount	15.00	6.00
❑	317 John Candelaria RC	1.50	.60
❑	318 Bob Boone	1.50	.60
❑	319 Larry Gura	.40	.15
❑	320 Willie Horton	.75	.30
❑	321 Jose Cruz	1.50	.60
❑	322 Glenn Abbott	.40	.15
❑	323 Rob Sperring RC	.40	.15
❑	324 Jim Bibby	.40	.15
❑	325 Tony Perez	3.00	1.25
❑	326 Dick Pole	.40	.15
❑	327 Dave Moates RC	.40	.15
❑	328 Carl Morton	.40	.15
❑	329 Joe Ferguson	.40	.15
❑	330 Nolan Ryan	25.00	10.00
❑	331 San Diego Padres CL/McNamara	1.50	.60
❑	332 Charlie Williams	.40	.15
❑	333 Bob Coluccio	.40	.15
❑	334 Dennis Leonard	.75	.30
❑	335 Bob Grich	.75	.30
❑	336 Vic Albury	.40	.15
❑	337 Bud Harrelson	.75	.30
❑	338 Bob Bailey	.40	.15
❑	339 John Denny	.75	.30
❑	340 Jim Rice	4.00	1.50
❑	341 Lou Gehrig ATG	12.00	5.00
❑	342 Rogers Hornsby ATG	3.00	1.25
❑	343 Pie Traynor ATG	1.50	.60
❑	344 Honus Wagner ATG	5.00	2.00
❑	345 Babe Ruth ATG	15.00	6.00
❑	346 Ty Cobb ATG	12.00	5.00
❑	347 Ted Williams ATG	12.00	5.00
❑	348 Mickey Cochrane ATG	1.50	.60
❑	349 Walter Johnson ATG	5.00	2.00
❑	350 Lefty Grove ATG	1.50	.60
❑	351 Randy Hundley	.75	.30
❑	352 Dave Giusti	.40	.15
❑	353 Sixto Lezcano RC	.75	.30
❑	354 Ron Blomberg	.40	.15
❑	355 Steve Carlton	6.00	2.50
❑	356 Ted Martinez	.40	.15
❑	357 Ken Forsch	.40	.15
❑	358 Buddy Bell	.75	.30
❑	359 Rick Reuschel	.75	.30
❑	360 Jeff Burroughs	.75	.30
❑	361 Detroit Tigers CL/Houk	1.50	.60
❑	362 Will McEnaney	.75	.30
❑	363 Dave Collins RC	.75	.30
❑	364 Elias Sosa	.40	.15
❑	365 Carlton Fisk	6.00	2.50
❑	366 Bobby Valentine	.75	.30
❑	367 Bruce Miller	.40	.15
❑	368 Wilbur Wood	.40	.15
❑	369 Frank White	.75	.30
❑	370 Ron Cey	.75	.30
❑	371 Elrod Hendricks	.40	.15
❑	372 Rick Baldwin RC	.40	.15
❑	373 Johnny Briggs	.40	.15
❑	374 Dan Warthen RC	.40	.15
❑	375 Ron Fairly	.75	.30
❑	376 Rich Hebner	.75	.30
❑	377 Mike Hegan	.40	.15
❑	378 Steve Stone	.75	.30
❑	379 Ken Boswell	.40	.15
❑	380 Bobby Bonds	1.50	.60
❑	381 Denny Doyle	.40	.15
❑	382 Matt Alexander RC	.40	.15
❑	383 John Ellis	.40	.15
❑	384 Philadelphia Phillies CL/Ozark	1.50	.60
❑	385 Mickey Lolich	.75	.30
❑	386 Ed Goodson	.40	.15
❑	387 Mike Miley RC	.40	.15
❑	388 Stan Perzanowski RC	.40	.15
❑	389 Glenn Adams RC	.40	.15
❑	390 Don Gullett	.75	.30
❑	391 Jerry Hairston	.40	.15
❑	392 Checklist 265-396	1.50	.60
❑	393 Paul Mitchell RC	.40	.15
❑	394 Fran Healy	.40	.15
❑	395 Jim Wynn	.75	.30
❑	396 Bill Lee	.40	.15
❑	397 Tim Foli	.40	.15
❑	398 Dave Tomlin	.40	.15
❑	399 Luis Melendez	.40	.15
❑	400 Rod Carew	6.00	2.50
❑	401 Ken Brett	.40	.15
❑	402 Don Money	.75	.30
❑	403 Geoff Zahn	.40	.15
❑	404 Enos Cabell	.40	.15
❑	405 Rollie Fingers	2.50	1.00
❑	406 Ed Herrmann	.40	.15
❑	407 Tom Underwood	.40	.15
❑	408 Charlie Spikes	.40	.15
❑	409 Dave Lemanczyk	.40	.15
❑	410 Ralph Garr	.75	.30
❑	411 Bill Singer	.40	.15
❑	412 Toby Harrah	.75	.30
❑	413 Pete Varney RC	.40	.15
❑	414 Wayne Garland	.40	.15
❑	415 Vada Pinson	1.50	.60
❑	416 Tommy John	1.50	.60
❑	417 Gene Clines	.40	.15
❑	418 Jose Morales RC	.40	.15
❑	419 Reggie Cleveland	.40	.15
❑	420 Joe Morgan	5.00	2.00
❑	421 Oakland Athletics CL	1.50	.60
❑	422 Johnny Grubb	.40	.15
❑	423 Ed Halicki	.40	.15
❑	424 Phil Roof	.40	.15
❑	425 Rennie Stennett	.40	.15
❑	426 Bob Forsch	.40	.15
❑	427 Kurt Bevacqua	.40	.15
❑	428 Jim Crawford	.40	.15
❑	429 Fred Stanley	.40	.15
❑	430 Jose Cardenal	.75	.30
❑	431 Dick Ruthven	.40	.15
❑	432 Tom Veryzer	.40	.15
❑	433 Rick Waits RC	.40	.15
❑	434 Morris Nettles	.40	.15
❑	435 Phil Niekro	2.50	1.00
❑	436 Bill Fahey	.40	.15
❑	437 Terry Forster	.40	.15
❑	438 Doug DeCinces	.75	.30
❑	439 Rick Rhoden	.75	.30
❑	440 John Mayberry	.75	.30
❑	441 Gary Carter	4.00	1.50
❑	442 Hank Webb	.40	.15
❑	443 San Francisco Giants CL	1.50	.60
❑	444 Gary Nolan	.75	.30
❑	445 Rico Petrocelli	.75	.30
❑	446 Larry Haney	.40	.15
❑	447 Gene Locklear	.75	.30
❑	448 Tom Johnson	.40	.15
❑	449 Bob Robertson	.40	.15
❑	450 Jim Palmer	5.00	2.00
❑	451 Buddy Bradford	.40	.15
❑	452 Tom Hausman RC	.40	.15
❑	453 Lou Piniella	1.50	.60
❑	454 Tom Griffin	.40	.15
❑	455 Dick Allen	1.50	.60
❑	456 Joe Coleman	.40	.15
❑	457 Ed Crosby	.40	.15
❑	458 Earl Williams	.40	.15
❑	459 Jim Brewer	.40	.15
❑	460 Cesar Cedeno	.75	.30
❑	461 NL/AL Champs	.75	.30
❑	462 1975 WS/Reds Champs	.75	.30

463	Steve Hargan	.40	.15
464	Ken Henderson	.40	.15
465	Mike Marshall	.75	.30
466	Bob Stinson	.40	.15
467	Woodie Fryman	.40	.15
468	Jesus Alou	.40	.15
469	Rawly Eastwick	.75	.30
470	Bobby Murcer	.75	.30
471	Jim Burton	.40	.15
472	Bob Davis RC	.40	.15
473	Paul Blair	.75	.30
474	Ray Corbin	.40	.15
475	Joe Rudi	.75	.30
476	Bob Moose	.40	.15
477	Cleveland Indians CL/Robinson	1.50	.60
478	Lynn McGlothen	.40	.15
479	Bobby Mitchell	.40	.15
480	Mike Schmidt	15.00	6.00
481	Rudy May	.40	.15
482	Tim Hosley	.40	.15
483	Mickey Stanley	.40	.15
484	Eric Raich RC	.40	.15
485	Mike Hargrove	.75	.30
486	Bruce Dal Canton	.40	.15
487	Leron Lee	.40	.15
488	Claude Osteen	.75	.30
489	Skip Jutze	.40	.15
490	Frank Tanana	.75	.30
491	Terry Crowley	.40	.15
492	Marty Pattin	.40	.15
493	Derrel Thomas	.40	.15
494	Craig Swan	.75	.30
495	Nate Colbert	.40	.15
496	Juan Beniquez	.40	.15
497	Joe McIntosh RC	.40	.15
498	Glenn Borgmann	.40	.15
499	Mario Guerrero	.40	.15
500	Reggie Jackson	12.00	5.00
501	Billy Champion	.40	.15
502	Tim McCarver	1.50	.60
503	Elliott Maddox	.40	.15
504	Pittsburgh Pirates CL/Murtaugh	1.50	.60
505	Mark Belanger	.75	.30
506	George Mitterwald	.40	.15
507	Ray Bare RC	.40	.15
508	Duane Kuiper RC	.40	.15
509	Bill Hands	.40	.15
510	Amos Otis	.75	.30
511	Jamie Easterley	.40	.15
512	Ellie Rodriguez	.40	.15
513	Bart Johnson	.40	.15
514	Dan Driessen	.75	.30
515	Steve Yeager	.75	.30
516	Wayne Granger	.40	.15
517	John Milner	.40	.15
518	Doug Flynn RC	.40	.15
519	Steve Brye	.40	.15
520	Willie McCovey	5.00	2.00
521	Jim Colborn	.40	.15
522	Ted Sizemore	.40	.15
523	Bob Montgomery	.40	.15
524	Pete Falcone RC	.40	.15
525	Billy Williams	2.50	1.00
526	Checklist 397-528	1.50	.60
527	Mike Anderson	.40	.15
528	Dock Ellis	.40	.15
529	Deron Johnson	.40	.15
530	Don Sutton	2.50	1.00
531	New York Mets CL/Frazier	1.50	.60
532	Milt May	.40	.15
533	Lee Richard	.40	.15
534	Stan Bahnsen	.40	.15
535	Dave Nelson	.40	.15
536	Mike Thompson	.40	.15
537	Tony Muser	.40	.15
538	Pat Darcy	.40	.15
539	John Balaz RC	.40	.15
540	Bill Freehan	.75	.30
541	Steve Mingori	.40	.15
542	Keith Hernandez	.75	.30
543	Wayne Twitchell	.40	.15
544	Pepe Frias	.40	.15
545	Sparky Lyle	.75	.30
546	Dave Rosello	.40	.15
547	Roric Harrison	.40	.15
548	Manny Mota	.75	.30
549	Randy Tate RC	.40	.15
550	Hank Aaron	25.00	10.00
551	Jerry DaVanon	.40	.15
552	Terry Humphrey	.40	.15
553	Randy Moffitt	.40	.15
554	Ray Fosse	.40	.15
555	Dyar Miller	.40	.15
556	Minnesota Twins CL/Mauch	1.50	.60
557	Dan Spillner	.40	.15
558	Clarence Gaston	.75	.30
559	Clyde Wright	.40	.15
560	Jorge Orta	.40	.15
561	Tom Carroll	.40	.15
562	Adrian Garrett	.40	.15
563	Larry Demery	.40	.15
564	Kurt Bevacqua GUM	1.50	.60
565	Tug McGraw	.75	.30
566	Ken McMullen	.40	.15
567	George Stone	.40	.15
568	Rob Andrews RC	.40	.15
569	Nelson Briles	.75	.30
570	George Hendrick	.75	.30
571	Don DeMola	.40	.15
572	Rich Coggins	.40	.15
573	Bill Travers	.40	.15
574	Don Kessinger	.75	.30
575	Dwight Evans	1.50	.60
576	Maximino Leon	.40	.15
577	Marc Hill	.40	.15
578	Ted Kubiak	.40	.15
579	Clay Kirby	.40	.15
580	Bert Campaneris	.75	.30
581	St. Louis Cardinals CL/Schoendienst	1.50	.60
582	Mike Kekich	.40	.15
583	Tommy Helms	.40	.15
584	Stan Wall RC	.40	.15
585	Joe Torre	1.50	.60
586	Ron Schueler	.40	.15
587	Leo Cardenas	.40	.15
588	Kevin Kobel	.40	.15
589	Alc/Flanagan/Pac/Torr RC	1.50	.60
590	Cruz/Lemon/Valen/Whit RC	.75	.30
591	Grilli/Mitch/Sosa/Throop RC	.75	.30
592	Randolph/McK/Roy/Sta RC	5.00	2.00
593	And/Crosby/Litell/Metzger RC	.75	.30
594	Mer/Ott/Still/White RC	.75	.30
595	DeFil/Lerch/Monge/Barr RC	.75	.30
596	Rey/John/LeMas/Manuel RC	.75	.30
597	Aase/Kucek/LaCorte/Pazik RC	.75	.30
598	Cruz/Quirk/Turner/Wallis RC	.75	.30
599	Dres/Guidry/McCl/Zach RC	8.00	3.00
600	Tom Seaver	10.00	4.00
601	Ken Rudolph	.40	.15
602	Doug Konieczny	.40	.15
603	Jim Holt	.40	.15
604	Joe Lovitto	.40	.15
605	Al Downing	.40	.15
606	Milwaukee Brewers CL/Grammas	1.50	.60
607	Rich Hinton	.40	.15
608	Vic Correll	.40	.15
609	Fred Norman	.40	.15
610	Greg Luzinski	1.50	.60
611	Rich Folkers	.40	.15
612	Joe Lahoud	.40	.15
613	Tim Johnson	.40	.15
614	Fernando Arroyo RC	.40	.15
615	Mike Cubbage	.40	.15
616	Buck Martinez	.40	.15
617	Darold Knowles	.40	.15
618	Jack Brohamer	.40	.15
619	Bill Butler	.40	.15
620	Al Oliver	.75	.30
621	Tom Hall	.40	.15
622	Rick Auerbach	.40	.15
623	Bob Allietta RC	.40	.15
624	Tony Taylor	.40	.15
625	J.R. Richard	.75	.30
626	Bob Sheldon	.40	.15
627	Bill Plummer	.40	.15
628	John D'Acquisto	.40	.15
629	Sandy Alomar	.75	.30
630	Chris Speier	.40	.15
631	Atlanta Braves CL/Bristol	1.50	.60
632	Rogelio Moret	.40	.15
633	John Stearns RC	.75	.30
634	Larry Christenson	.40	.15
635	Jim Fregosi	.75	.30
636	Joe Decker	.40	.15
637	Bruce Bochte	.40	.15
638	Doyle Alexander	.75	.30
639	Fred Kendall	.40	.15
640	Bill Madlock	1.50	.60
641	Tom Paciorek	.75	.30
642	Dennis Blair	.40	.15
643	Checklist 529-660	1.50	.60
644	Tom Bradley	.40	.15
645	Darrell Porter	.75	.30
646	John Lowenstein	.40	.15
647	Ramon Hernandez	.40	.15
648	Al Cowens	.75	.30
649	Dave Roberts	.40	.15
650	Thurman Munson	6.00	2.50
651	John Odom	.40	.15
652	Ed Armbrister	.40	.15
653	Mike Norris RC	.75	.30
654	Doug Griffin	.40	.15
655	Mike Vail RC	.40	.15
656	Chicago White Sox CL/Tanner	1.50	.60
657	Roy Smalley RC	.75	.30
658	Jerry Johnson	.40	.15
659	Ben Oglivie	.75	.30
660	Davey Lopes	1.50	.60

1977 Topps

	COMPLETE SET (660)	225.00	125.00
1	G.Brett/B.Madlock LL	8.00	3.00
2	G.Nettles/M.Schmidt LL	2.50	1.00
3	L.May/G.Foster LL	1.50	.60
4	B.North/D.Lopes LL	.75	.30
5	J.Palmer/R.Jones LL	1.50	.60
6	N.Ryan/T.Seaver LL	15.00	6.00
7	M.Fidrych/J.Denny LL	.75	.30
8	B.Campbell/R.Eastwick LL	.75	.30
9	Doug Rader	.30	.10
10	Reggie Jackson	10.00	4.00
11	Rob Dressler	.30	.10
12	Larry Haney	.30	.10
13	Luis Gomez RC	.30	.10
14	Tommy Smith	.30	.10
15	Don Gullett	.75	.30
16	Bob Jones RC	.30	.10
17	Steve Stone	.75	.30
18	Cleveland Indians CL/Robinson	1.50	.60
19	John D'Acquisto	.30	.10
20	Graig Nettles	1.50	.60
21	Ken Forsch	.30	.10
22	Bill Freehan	.75	.30
23	Dan Driessen	.30	.10
24	Carl Morton	.30	.10
25	Dwight Evans	1.50	.60
26	Ray Sadecki	.30	.10
27	Bill Buckner	.75	.30
28	Woodie Fryman	.30	.10
29	Bucky Dent	.75	.30
30	Greg Luzinski	1.50	.60
31	Jim Todd	.30	.10
32	Checklist 1-132	1.50	.60
33	Wayne Garland	.30	.10
34	California Angels CL/Sherry	1.50	.60
35	Rennie Stennett	.30	.10
36	John Ellis	.30	.10
37	Steve Hargan	.30	.10
38	Craig Kusick	.30	.10
39	Tom Griffin	.30	.10

- ❑ 40 Bobby Murcer .75 .30
- ❑ 41 Jim Kern .30 .10
- ❑ 42 Jose Cruz .75 .30
- ❑ 43 Ray Bare .30 .10
- ❑ 44 Bud Harrelson .75 .30
- ❑ 45 Rawly Eastwick .30 .10
- ❑ 46 Buck Martinez .30 .10
- ❑ 47 Lynn McGlothen .30 .10
- ❑ 48 Tom Paciorek .75 .30
- ❑ 49 Grant Jackson .30 .10
- ❑ 50 Ron Cey .75 .30
- ❑ 51 Milwaukee Brewers CL/Grammas 1.50 .60
- ❑ 52 Ellis Valentine .30 .10
- ❑ 53 Paul Mitchell .30 .10
- ❑ 54 Sandy Alomar .75 .30
- ❑ 55 Jeff Burroughs .75 .30
- ❑ 56 Rudy May .30 .10
- ❑ 57 Marc Hill .30 .10
- ❑ 58 Chet Lemon .75 .30
- ❑ 59 Larry Christenson .30 .10
- ❑ 60 Jim Rice 2.50 1.00
- ❑ 61 Manny Sanguillen .75 .30
- ❑ 62 Eric Raich .30 .10
- ❑ 63 Tito Fuentes .30 .10
- ❑ 64 Larry Biittner .30 .10
- ❑ 65 Skip Lockwood .30 .10
- ❑ 66 Roy Smalley .75 .30
- ❑ 67 Joaquin Andujar RC .75 .30
- ❑ 68 Bruce Bochte .30 .10
- ❑ 69 Jim Crawford .30 .10
- ❑ 70 Johnny Bench 10.00 4.00
- ❑ 71 Dock Ellis .30 .10
- ❑ 72 Mike Anderson .30 .10
- ❑ 73 Charlie Williams .30 .10
- ❑ 74 Oakland Athletics CL/McKeon 1.50 .60
- ❑ 75 Dennis Leonard .75 .30
- ❑ 76 Tim Foli .30 .10
- ❑ 77 Dyar Miller .30 .10
- ❑ 78 Bob Davis .30 .10
- ❑ 79 Don Money .75 .30
- ❑ 80 Andy Messersmith .75 .30
- ❑ 81 Juan Beniquez .30 .10
- ❑ 82 Jim Rooker .30 .10
- ❑ 83 Kevin Bell RC .30 .10
- ❑ 84 Ollie Brown .30 .10
- ❑ 85 Duane Kuiper .30 .10
- ❑ 86 Pat Zachry .30 .10
- ❑ 87 Glenn Borgmann .30 .10
- ❑ 88 Stan Wall .30 .10
- ❑ 89 Butch Hobson RC .75 .30
- ❑ 90 Cesar Cedeno .75 .30
- ❑ 91 John Verhoeven RC .30 .10
- ❑ 92 Dave Rosello .30 .10
- ❑ 93 Tom Poquette .30 .10
- ❑ 94 Craig Swan .30 .10
- ❑ 95 Keith Hernandez .75 .30
- ❑ 96 Lou Piniella .75 .30
- ❑ 97 Dave Heaverlo .30 .10
- ❑ 98 Milt May .30 .10
- ❑ 99 Tom Hausman .30 .10
- ❑ 100 Joe Morgan 4.00 1.50
- ❑ 101 Dick Bosman .30 .10
- ❑ 102 Jose Morales .30 .10
- ❑ 103 Mike Bacsik RC .30 .10
- ❑ 104 Omar Moreno RC .75 .30
- ❑ 105 Steve Yeager .75 .30
- ❑ 106 Mike Flanagan .75 .30
- ❑ 107 Bill Melton .30 .10
- ❑ 108 Alan Foster .30 .10
- ❑ 109 Jorge Orta .30 .10
- ❑ 110 Steve Carlton 5.00 2.00
- ❑ 111 Rico Petrocelli .75 .30
- ❑ 112 Bill Greif .30 .10
- ❑ 113 Toronto Blue Jays CL/Hartsfield 1.50 .60
- ❑ 114 Bruce Dal Canton .30 .10
- ❑ 115 Rick Manning .30 .10
- ❑ 116 Joe Niekro .75 .30
- ❑ 117 Frank White .75 .30
- ❑ 118 Rick Jones RC .30 .10
- ❑ 119 John Stearns .30 .10
- ❑ 120 Rod Carew 5.00 2.00
- ❑ 121 Gary Nolan .30 .10
- ❑ 122 Ben Oglivie .75 .30
- ❑ 123 Fred Stanley .30 .10
- ❑ 124 George Mitterwald .30 .10
- ❑ 125 Bill Travers .30 .10
- ❑ 126 Rod Gilbreath .30 .10
- ❑ 127 Ron Fairly .75 .30
- ❑ 128 Tommy John 1.50 .60
- ❑ 129 Mike Sadek .30 .10
- ❑ 130 Al Oliver .75 .30
- ❑ 131 Orlando Ramirez RC .30 .10
- ❑ 132 Chip Lang RC .30 .10
- ❑ 133 Ralph Garr .75 .30
- ❑ 134 San Diego Padres CL/McNamara 1.50 .60
- ❑ 135 Mark Belanger .75 .30
- ❑ 136 Jerry Mumphrey RC .75 .30
- ❑ 137 Jeff Terpko RC .30 .10
- ❑ 138 Bob Stinson .30 .10
- ❑ 139 Fred Norman .30 .10
- ❑ 140 Mike Schmidt 12.00 5.00
- ❑ 141 Mark Littell .30 .10
- ❑ 142 Steve Dillard RC .30 .10
- ❑ 143 Ed Herrmann .30 .10
- ❑ 144 Bruce Sutter RC 15.00 6.00
- ❑ 145 Tom Veryzer .30 .10
- ❑ 146 Dusty Baker 1.50 .60
- ❑ 147 Jackie Brown .30 .10
- ❑ 148 Fran Healy .30 .10
- ❑ 149 Mike Cubbage .30 .10
- ❑ 150 Tom Seaver 8.00 3.00
- ❑ 151 Johnny LeMaster .30 .10
- ❑ 152 Gaylord Perry 2.50 1.00
- ❑ 153 Ron Jackson RC .30 .10
- ❑ 154 Dave Giusti .30 .10
- ❑ 155 Joe Rudi .75 .30
- ❑ 156 Pete Mackanin .30 .10
- ❑ 157 Ken Brett .30 .10
- ❑ 158 Ted Kubiak .30 .10
- ❑ 159 Bernie Carbo .30 .10
- ❑ 160 Will McEnaney .30 .10
- ❑ 161 Garry Templeton RC 1.50 .60
- ❑ 162 Mike Cuellar .75 .30
- ❑ 163 Dave Hilton .30 .10
- ❑ 164 Tug McGraw .75 .30
- ❑ 165 Jim Wynn .75 .30
- ❑ 166 Bill Campbell .30 .10
- ❑ 167 Rich Hebner .75 .30
- ❑ 168 Charlie Spikes .30 .10
- ❑ 169 Darold Knowles .30 .10
- ❑ 170 Thurman Munson 5.00 2.00
- ❑ 171 Ken Sanders .30 .10
- ❑ 172 John Milner .30 .10
- ❑ 173 Chuck Scrivener RC .30 .10
- ❑ 174 Nelson Briles .75 .30
- ❑ 175 Butch Wynegar RC .75 .30
- ❑ 176 Bob Robertson .30 .10
- ❑ 177 Bart Johnson .30 .10
- ❑ 178 Bombo Rivera RC .30 .10
- ❑ 179 Paul Hartzell RC .30 .10
- ❑ 180 Dave Lopes .75 .30
- ❑ 181 Ken McMullen .30 .10
- ❑ 182 Dan Spillner .30 .10
- ❑ 183 St.Louis Cardinals CL/V.Rapp 1.50 .60
- ❑ 184 Bo McLaughlin RC .30 .10
- ❑ 185 Sixto Lezcano .30 .10
- ❑ 186 Doug Flynn .30 .10
- ❑ 187 Dick Pole .30 .10
- ❑ 188 Bob Tolan .30 .10
- ❑ 189 Rick Dempsey .75 .30
- ❑ 190 Ray Burris .30 .10
- ❑ 191 Doug Griffin .30 .10
- ❑ 192 Clarence Gaston .75 .30
- ❑ 193 Larry Gura .30 .10
- ❑ 194 Gary Matthews .75 .30
- ❑ 195 Ed Figueroa .30 .10
- ❑ 196 Len Randle .30 .10
- ❑ 197 Ed Ott .30 .10
- ❑ 198 Wilbur Wood .30 .10
- ❑ 199 Pepe Frias .30 .10
- ❑ 200 Frank Tanana .75 .30
- ❑ 201 Ed Kranepool .30 .10
- ❑ 202 Tom Johnson .30 .10
- ❑ 203 Ed Armbrister .30 .10
- ❑ 204 Jeff Newman RC .30 .10
- ❑ 205 Pete Falcone .30 .10
- ❑ 206 Boog Powell 1.50 .60
- ❑ 207 Glenn Abbott .30 .10
- ❑ 208 Checklist 133-264 1.50 .60
- ❑ 209 Rob Andrews .30 .10
- ❑ 210 Fred Lynn .75 .30
- ❑ 211 San Francisco Giants CL/Altobelli 1.50 .60
- ❑ 212 Jim Mason .30 .10
- ❑ 213 Maximino Leon .30 .10
- ❑ 214 Darrell Porter .75 .30
- ❑ 215 Butch Metzger .30 .10
- ❑ 216 Doug DeCinces .75 .30
- ❑ 217 Tom Underwood .30 .10
- ❑ 218 John Wathan RC .75 .30
- ❑ 219 Joe Coleman .30 .10
- ❑ 220 Chris Chambliss .75 .30
- ❑ 221 Bob Bailey .30 .10
- ❑ 222 Francisco Barrios RC .30 .10
- ❑ 223 Earl Williams .30 .10
- ❑ 224 Rusty Torres .30 .10
- ❑ 225 Bob Apodaca .30 .10
- ❑ 226 Leroy Stanton .75 .30
- ❑ 227 Joe Sambito RC .30 .10
- ❑ 228 Minnesota Twins CL/Mauch 1.50 .60
- ❑ 229 Don Kessinger .75 .30
- ❑ 230 Vida Blue .75 .30
- ❑ 231 George Brett RB 8.00 3.00
- ❑ 232 Minnie Minoso RB .75 .30
- ❑ 233 Jose Morales RB .30 .10
- ❑ 234 Nolan Ryan RB 15.00 6.00
- ❑ 235 Cecil Cooper .75 .30
- ❑ 236 Tom Buskey .30 .10
- ❑ 237 Gene Clines .30 .10
- ❑ 238 Tippy Martinez .30 .10
- ❑ 239 Bill Plummer .30 .10
- ❑ 240 Ron LeFlore .75 .30
- ❑ 241 Dave Tomlin .30 .10
- ❑ 242 Ken Henderson .30 .10
- ❑ 243 Ron Reed .30 .10
- ❑ 244 John Mayberry .75 .30
- ❑ 245 Rick Rhoden .75 .30
- ❑ 246 Mike Vail .30 .10
- ❑ 247 Chris Knapp RC .30 .10
- ❑ 248 Wilbur Howard .30 .10
- ❑ 249 Pete Redfern RC .30 .10
- ❑ 250 Bill Madlock .75 .30
- ❑ 251 Tony Muser .30 .10
- ❑ 252 Dale Murray .30 .10
- ❑ 253 John Hale .30 .10
- ❑ 254 Doyle Alexander .30 .10
- ❑ 255 George Scott .75 .30
- ❑ 256 Joe Hoerner .30 .10
- ❑ 257 Mike Miley .30 .10
- ❑ 258 Luis Tiant .75 .30
- ❑ 259 New York Mets CL/Frazier 1.50 .60
- ❑ 260 J.R. Richard .75 .30
- ❑ 261 Phil Garner .75 .30
- ❑ 262 Al Cowens .75 .30
- ❑ 263 Mike Marshall .75 .30
- ❑ 264 Tom Hutton .30 .10
- ❑ 265 Mark Fidrych RC 3.00 1.25
- ❑ 266 Derrel Thomas .30 .10
- ❑ 267 Ray Fosse .30 .10
- ❑ 268 Rick Sawyer RC .30 .10
- ❑ 269 Joe Lis .30 .10
- ❑ 270 Dave Parker 1.50 .60
- ❑ 271 Terry Forster .30 .10
- ❑ 272 Lee Lacy .30 .10
- ❑ 273 Eric Soderholm .30 .10
- ❑ 274 Don Stanhouse .30 .10
- ❑ 275 Mike Hargrove .75 .30
- ❑ 276 Chris Chambliss ALCS 1.50 .60
- ❑ 277 Pete Rose NLCS 5.00 2.00
- ❑ 278 Danny Frisella .30 .10
- ❑ 279 Joe Wallis .30 .10
- ❑ 280 Jim Hunter 2.50 1.00
- ❑ 281 Roy Staiger .30 .10
- ❑ 282 Sid Monge .30 .10
- ❑ 283 Jerry DaVanon .30 .10
- ❑ 284 Mike Norris .30 .10
- ❑ 285 Brooks Robinson 5.00 2.00
- ❑ 286 Johnny Grubb .30 .10
- ❑ 287 Cincinnati Reds CL/Anderson 1.50 .60
- ❑ 288 Bob Montgomery .30 .10
- ❑ 289 Gene Garber .75 .30
- ❑ 290 Amos Otis .75 .30
- ❑ 291 Jason Thompson RC .75 .30
- ❑ 292 Rogelio Moret .30 .10
- ❑ 293 Jack Brohamer .30 .10
- ❑ 294 George Medich .30 .10
- ❑ 295 Gary Carter 2.50 1.00
- ❑ 296 Don Hood .30 .10
- ❑ 297 Ken Reitz .30 .10

❑ 298 Charlie Hough .75 .30
❑ 299 Otto Velez .75 .30
❑ 300 Jerry Koosman .75 .30
❑ 301 Toby Harrah .75 .30
❑ 302 Mike Garman .30 .10
❑ 303 Gene Tenace .75 .30
❑ 304 Jim Hughes .30 .10
❑ 305 Mickey Rivers .75 .30
❑ 306 Rick Waits .30 .10
❑ 307 Gary Sutherland .30 .10
❑ 308 Gene Pentz RC .30 .10
❑ 309 Boston Red Sox CL/Zimmer 1.50 .60
❑ 310 Larry Bowa .75 .30
❑ 311 Vern Ruhle .30 .10
❑ 312 Rob Belloir RC .30 .10
❑ 313 Paul Blair .75 .30
❑ 314 Steve Mingori .30 .10
❑ 315 Dave Chalk .30 .10
❑ 316 Steve Rogers .30 .10
❑ 317 Kurt Bevacqua .30 .10
❑ 318 Duffy Dyer .30 .10
❑ 319 Goose Gossage 1.50 .60
❑ 320 Ken Griffey Sr. 1.50 .60
❑ 321 Dave Goltz .30 .10
❑ 322 Bill Russell .75 .30
❑ 323 Larry Lintz .30 .10
❑ 324 John Curtis .30 .10
❑ 325 Mike Ivie .30 .10
❑ 326 Jesse Jefferson .30 .10
❑ 327 Houston Astros CL/Virdon 1.50 .60
❑ 328 Tommy Boggs RC .30 .10
❑ 329 Ron Hodges .30 .10
❑ 330 George Hendrick .75 .30
❑ 331 Jim Colborn .30 .10
❑ 332 Elliott Maddox .30 .10
❑ 333 Paul Reuschel RC .30 .10
❑ 334 Bill Stein .30 .10
❑ 335 Bill Robinson .75 .30
❑ 336 Denny Doyle .30 .10
❑ 337 Ron Schueler .30 .10
❑ 338 Dave Duncan .75 .30
❑ 339 Adrian Devine .30 .10
❑ 340 Hal McRae .75 .30
❑ 341 Joe Kerrigan RC .30 .10
❑ 342 Jerry Remy .30 .10
❑ 343 Ed Halicki .30 .10
❑ 344 Brian Downing .75 .30
❑ 345 Reggie Smith .75 .30
❑ 346 Bill Singer .30 .10
❑ 347 George Foster 1.50 .60
❑ 348 Brent Strom .30 .10
❑ 349 Jim Holt .30 .10
❑ 350 Larry Dierker .75 .30
❑ 351 Jim Sundberg .75 .30
❑ 352 Mike Phillips .30 .10
❑ 353 Stan Thomas .30 .10
❑ 354 Pittsburgh Pirates CL/Tanner 1.50 .60
❑ 355 Lou Brock 4.00 1.50
❑ 356 Checklist 265-396 1.50 .60
❑ 357 Tim McCarver 1.50 .60
❑ 358 Tom House .30 .10
❑ 359 Willie Randolph 1.50 .60
❑ 360 Rick Monday .75 .30
❑ 361 Eduardo Rodriguez .30 .10
❑ 362 Tommy Davis .75 .30
❑ 363 Dave Roberts .30 .10
❑ 364 Vic Correll .30 .10
❑ 365 Mike Torrez .75 .30
❑ 366 Ted Sizemore .30 .10
❑ 367 Dave Hamilton .30 .10
❑ 368 Mike Jorgensen .30 .10
❑ 369 Terry Humphrey .30 .10
❑ 370 John Montefusco .30 .10
❑ 371 Kansas City Royals CL/Herzog 1.50 .60
❑ 372 Rich Folkers .30 .10
❑ 373 Bert Campaneris .75 .30
❑ 374 Kent Tekulve .75 .30
❑ 375 Larry Hisle .75 .30
❑ 376 Nino Espinosa RC .30 .10
❑ 377 Dave McKay .30 .10
❑ 378 Jim Umbarger .30 .10
❑ 379 Larry Cox RC .30 .10
❑ 380 Lee May .75 .30
❑ 381 Bob Forsch .30 .10
❑ 382 Charlie Moore .30 .10
❑ 383 Stan Bahnsen .30 .10
❑ 384 Darrel Chaney .30 .10
❑ 385 Dave LaRoche .30 .10
❑ 386 Manny Mota .75 .30
❑ 387 New York Yankees CL/Martin 2.50 1.00
❑ 388 Terry Harmon .30 .10
❑ 389 Ken Kravec RC .30 .10
❑ 390 Dave Winfield 6.00 2.50
❑ 391 Dan Warthen .30 .10
❑ 392 Phil Roof .30 .10
❑ 393 John Lowenstein .30 .10
❑ 394 Bill Laxton RC .30 .10
❑ 395 Manny Trillo .30 .10
❑ 396 Tom Murphy .30 .10
❑ 397 Larry Herndon RC .75 .30
❑ 398 Tom Burgmeier .30 .10
❑ 399 Bruce Boisclair RC .30 .10
❑ 400 Steve Garvey 2.50 1.00
❑ 401 Mickey Scott .30 .10
❑ 402 Tommy Helms .30 .10
❑ 403 Tom Grieve .75 .30
❑ 404 Eric Rasmussen RC .30 .10
❑ 405 Claudell Washington .75 .30
❑ 406 Tim Johnson .30 .10
❑ 407 Dave Freisleben .30 .10
❑ 408 Cesar Tovar .30 .10
❑ 409 Pete Broberg .30 .10
❑ 410 Willie Montanez .30 .10
❑ 411 J.Morgan/J.Bench WS 2.50 1.00
❑ 412 Johnny Bench WS 2.50 1.00
❑ 413 Cincy Wins WS .75 .30
❑ 414 Tommy Harper .75 .30
❑ 415 Jay Johnstone .75 .30
❑ 416 Chuck Hartenstein .30 .10
❑ 417 Wayne Garrett .30 .10
❑ 418 Chicago White Sox CL/Lemon 1.50 .60
❑ 419 Steve Swisher .30 .10
❑ 420 Rusty Staub 1.50 .60
❑ 421 Doug Rau .30 .10
❑ 422 Freddie Patek .75 .30
❑ 423 Gary Lavelle .30 .10
❑ 424 Steve Brye .30 .10
❑ 425 Joe Torre 1.50 .60
❑ 426 Dick Drago .30 .10
❑ 427 Dave Rader .30 .10
❑ 428 Texas Rangers CL/Lucchesi 1.50 .60
❑ 429 Ken Boswell .30 .10
❑ 430 Fergie Jenkins 2.50 1.00
❑ 431 Dave Collins UER .75 .30
❑ 432 Buzz Capra .30 .10
❑ 433 Nate Colbert TBC .30 .10
❑ 434 Carl Yastrzemski TBC 1.50 .60
❑ 435 Maury Wills TBC .75 .30
❑ 436 Bob Keegan TBC .30 .10
❑ 437 Ralph Kiner TBC 1.50 .60
❑ 438 Marty Perez .30 .10
❑ 439 Gorman Thomas .75 .30
❑ 440 Jon Matlack .30 .10
❑ 441 Larvell Blanks .30 .10
❑ 442 Atlanta Braves CL/Bristol 1.50 .60
❑ 443 Lamar Johnson .30 .10
❑ 444 Wayne Twitchell .30 .10
❑ 445 Ken Singleton .75 .30
❑ 446 Bill Bonham .30 .10
❑ 447 Jerry Turner .30 .10
❑ 448 Ellie Rodriguez .30 .10
❑ 449 Al Fitzmorris .30 .10
❑ 450 Pete Rose 20.00 8.00
❑ 451 Checklist 397-528 1.50 .60
❑ 452 Mike Caldwell .30 .10
❑ 453 Pedro Garcia .30 .10
❑ 454 Andy Etchebarren .30 .10
❑ 455 Rick Wise .30 .10
❑ 456 Leon Roberts .30 .10
❑ 457 Steve Luebber .30 .10
❑ 458 Leo Foster .30 .10
❑ 459 Steve Foucault .30 .10
❑ 460 Willie Stargell 2.50 1.00
❑ 461 Dick Tidrow .30 .10
❑ 462 Don Baylor 1.50 .60
❑ 463 Jamie Quirk .30 .10
❑ 464 Randy Moffitt .30 .10
❑ 465 Rico Carty .75 .30
❑ 466 Fred Holdsworth .30 .10
❑ 467 Philadelphia Phillies CL/Ozark 1.50 .60
❑ 468 Ramon Hernandez .30 .10
❑ 469 Pat Kelly .30 .10
❑ 470 Ted Simmons .75 .30
❑ 471 Del Unser .30 .10
❑ 472 Aase/McCl/Patt/Wehr RC .30 .10
❑ 473 Andre Dawson RC 20.00 8.00
❑ 474 Bailor/Gar/Reyn/Tav RC .75 .30
❑ 475 Batt/Camp/McGr/Sarm RC .75 .30
❑ 476 Dale Murphy RC 15.00 6.00
❑ 477 Ault/Dauer/Gonz/Mank RC .75 .30
❑ 478 Gid/Hoot/John/Lemong RC .75 .30
❑ 479 Assel/Gross/Mej/Woods RC .75 .30
❑ 480 Carl Yastrzemski 8.00 3.00
❑ 481 Roger Metzger .30 .10
❑ 482 Tony Solaita .30 .10
❑ 483 Richie Zisk .30 .10
❑ 484 Burt Hooton .75 .30
❑ 485 Roy White .75 .30
❑ 486 Ed Bane .30 .10
❑ 487 And/Glynn/Hend/Terl RC .75 .30
❑ 488 Clark/Jon/Mazzilli/Tho RC 3.00 1.25
❑ 489 Barker/Ler/Mint/Overy RC .75 .30
❑ 490 Almon/Klutts/McM/Wag RC .75 .30
❑ 491 Dup/Martinez/Mitch/Sykes RC 3.00 1.25
❑ 492 Armas/Kemp/Lop/Woods RC .75 .30
❑ 493 Krukow/Ott/Wheel/Will RC .75 .30
❑ 494 Bern/Cha/Gantner/Wills RC 1.50 .60
❑ 495 Al Hrabosky .75 .30
❑ 496 Gary Thomasson .30 .10
❑ 497 Clay Carroll .30 .10
❑ 498 Sal Bando .75 .30
❑ 499 Pablo Torrealba .30 .10
❑ 500 Dave Kingman 1.50 .60
❑ 501 Jim Bibby .30 .10
❑ 502 Randy Hundley .30 .10
❑ 503 Bill Lee .30 .10
❑ 504 Los Angeles Dodgers CL/Lasorda 1.50 .60
❑ 505 Oscar Gamble .75 .30
❑ 506 Steve Grilli .30 .10
❑ 507 Mike Hegan .30 .10
❑ 508 Dave Pagan .30 .10
❑ 509 Cookie Rojas .75 .30
❑ 510 John Candelaria .30 .10
❑ 511 Bill Fahey .30 .10
❑ 512 Jack Billingham .30 .10
❑ 513 Jerry Terrell .30 .10
❑ 514 Cliff Johnson .30 .10
❑ 515 Chris Speier .30 .10
❑ 516 Bake McBride .75 .30
❑ 517 Pete Vuckovich RC .75 .30
❑ 518 Chicago Cubs CL/Franks 1.50 .60
❑ 519 Don Kirkwood .30 .10
❑ 520 Garry Maddox .30 .10
❑ 521 Bob Grich .75 .30
❑ 522 Enzo Hernandez .30 .10
❑ 523 Rollie Fingers 2.50 1.00
❑ 524 Rowland Office .30 .10
❑ 525 Dennis Eckersley 5.00 2.50
❑ 526 Larry Parrish .75 .30
❑ 527 Dan Meyer .75 .30
❑ 528 Bill Castro .30 .10
❑ 529 Jim Essian RC .30 .10
❑ 530 Rick Reuschel .75 .30
❑ 531 Lyman Bostock .75 .30
❑ 532 Jim Willoughby .30 .10
❑ 533 Mickey Stanley .30 .10
❑ 534 Paul Splittorff .30 .10
❑ 535 Cesar Geronimo .30 .10
❑ 536 Vic Albury .30 .10
❑ 537 Dave Roberts .30 .10
❑ 538 Frank Taveras .30 .10
❑ 539 Mike Wallace .30 .10
❑ 540 Bob Watson .75 .30
❑ 541 John Denny .75 .30
❑ 542 Frank Duffy .30 .10
❑ 543 Ron Blomberg .30 .10
❑ 544 Gary Ross .30 .10
❑ 545 Bob Boone .75 .30
❑ 546 Baltimore Orioles CL/Weaver 1.50 .60
❑ 547 Willie McCovey 4.00 1.50
❑ 548 Joel Youngblood RC .30 .10
❑ 549 Jerry Royster .30 .10
❑ 550 Randy Jones .30 .10
❑ 551 Bill North .30 .10
❑ 552 Pepe Mangual .30 .10
❑ 553 Jack Heidemann .30 .10
❑ 554 Bruce Kimm RC .30 .10
❑ 555 Dan Ford .30 .10

❑ 556 Doug Bird .30 .10
❑ 557 Jerry White .30 .10
❑ 558 Elias Sosa .30 .10
❑ 559 Alan Bannister RC .30 .10
❑ 560 Dave Concepcion 1.50 .60
❑ 561 Pete LaCock .30 .10
❑ 562 Checklist 529-660 1.50 .60
❑ 563 Bruce Kison .30 .10
❑ 564 Alan Ashby .30 .10
❑ 565 Mickey Lolich .75 .30
❑ 566 Rick Miller .30 .10
❑ 567 Enos Cabell .30 .10
❑ 568 Carlos May .30 .10
❑ 569 Jim Lonborg .75 .30
❑ 570 Bobby Bonds 1.50 .60
❑ 571 Darrell Evans .75 .30
❑ 572 Ross Grimsley .30 .10
❑ 573 Joe Ferguson .30 .10
❑ 574 Aurelio Rodriguez .30 .10
❑ 575 Dick Ruthven .30 .10
❑ 576 Fred Kendall .30 .10
❑ 577 Jerry Augustine RC .30 .10
❑ 578 Bob Randall RC .30 .10
❑ 579 Don Carrithers .30 .10
❑ 580 George Brett 15.00 6.00
❑ 581 Pedro Borbon .30 .10
❑ 582 Ed Kirkpatrick .30 .10
❑ 583 Paul Lindblad .30 .10
❑ 584 Ed Goodson .30 .10
❑ 585 Rick Burleson .75 .30
❑ 586 Steve Renko .30 .10
❑ 587 Rick Baldwin .30 .10
❑ 588 Dave Moates .30 .10
❑ 589 Mike Cosgrove .30 .10
❑ 590 Buddy Bell .75 .30
❑ 591 Chris Arnold .30 .10
❑ 592 Dan Briggs RC .30 .10
❑ 593 Dennis Blair .30 .10
❑ 594 Biff Pocoroba .30 .10
❑ 595 John Hiller .30 .10
❑ 596 Jerry Martin RC .30 .10
❑ 597 Seattle Mariners CL/Johnson 1.50 .60
❑ 598 Sparky Lyle .75 .30
❑ 599 Mike Tyson .30 .10
❑ 600 Jim Palmer 4.00 1.50
❑ 601 Mike Lum .30 .10
❑ 602 Andy Hassler .30 .10
❑ 603 Willie Davis .75 .30
❑ 604 Jim Slaton .30 .10
❑ 605 Felix Millan .30 .10
❑ 606 Steve Braun .30 .10
❑ 607 Larry Demery .30 .10
❑ 608 Roy Howell .30 .10
❑ 609 Jim Barr .30 .10
❑ 610 Jose Cardenal .75 .30
❑ 611 Dave Lemanczyk .30 .10
❑ 612 Barry Foote .30 .10
❑ 613 Reggie Cleveland .30 .10
❑ 614 Greg Gross .30 .10
❑ 615 Phil Niekro 2.50 1.00
❑ 616 Tommy Sandt RC .30 .10
❑ 617 Bobby Darwin .30 .10
❑ 618 Pat Dobson .30 .10
❑ 619 Johnny Oates .75 .30
❑ 620 Don Sutton 2.50 1.00
❑ 621 Detroit Tigers CL/Houk 1.50 .60
❑ 622 Jim Wohlford .30 .10
❑ 623 Jack Kucek .30 .10
❑ 624 Hector Cruz .30 .10
❑ 625 Ken Holtzman .75 .30
❑ 626 Al Bumbry .75 .30
❑ 627 Bob Myrick RC .30 .10
❑ 628 Mario Guerrero .30 .10
❑ 629 Bobby Valentine .75 .30
❑ 630 Bert Blyleven 1.50 .60
❑ 631 Brett Brothers 6.00 2.50
❑ 632 Forsch Brothers .75 .30
❑ 633 May Brothers .75 .30
❑ 634 Reuschel Brothers UER .75 .30
❑ 635 Robin Yount 8.00 3.00
❑ 636 Santo Alcala .30 .10
❑ 637 Alex Johnson .30 .10
❑ 638 Jim Kaat 1.50 .60
❑ 639 Jerry Morales .30 .10
❑ 640 Carlton Fisk 5.00 2.00
❑ 641 Dan Larson RC .30 .10
❑ 642 Willie Crawford .30 .10
❑ 643 Mike Pazik .30 .10
❑ 644 Matt Alexander .30 .10
❑ 645 Jerry Reuss .75 .30
❑ 646 Andres Mora RC .30 .10
❑ 647 Montreal Expos CL/Williams 1.50 .60
❑ 648 Jim Spencer .30 .10
❑ 649 Dave Cash .30 .10
❑ 650 Nolan Ryan 30.00 12.50
❑ 651 Von Joshua .30 .10
❑ 652 Tom Walker .30 .10
❑ 653 Diego Segui .75 .30
❑ 654 Ron Pruitt RC .30 .10
❑ 655 Tony Perez 2.50 1.00
❑ 656 Ron Guidry 1.50 .60
❑ 657 Mick Kelleher RC .30 .10
❑ 658 Marty Pattin .30 .10
❑ 659 Merv Rettenmund .30 .10
❑ 660 Willie Horton 1.50 .60

1978 Topps

❑ COMPLETE SET (726) 200.00 125.00
❑ COMMON CARD (1-726) .25 .08
❑ COMMON CARD DP .15 .05
❑ 1 Lou Brock RB 3.00 1.25
❑ 2 Sparky Lyle RB .60 .25
❑ 3 Willie McCovey RB 2.50 1.00
❑ 4 Brooks Robinson RB 1.25 .50
❑ 5 Pete Rose RB 8.00 3.00
❑ 6 Nolan Ryan RB 15.00 6.00
❑ 7 Reggie Jackson RB 4.00 1.50
❑ 8 Mike Sadek .25 .08
❑ 9 Doug DeCinces .60 .25
❑ 10 Phil Niekro 2.50 1.00
❑ 11 Rick Manning .25 .08
❑ 12 Don Aase .25 .08
❑ 13 Art Howe RC .60 .25
❑ 14 Lerrin LaGrow .25 .08
❑ 15 Tony Perez DP 1.25 .50
❑ 16 Roy White .60 .25
❑ 17 Mike Krukow .25 .08
❑ 18 Bob Grich .60 .25
❑ 19 Darrell Porter .60 .25
❑ 20 Pete Rose DP 12.00 5.00
❑ 21 Steve Kemp .25 .08
❑ 22 Charlie Hough .60 .25
❑ 23 Bump Wills .25 .08
❑ 24 Don Money DP .15 .05
❑ 25 Jon Matlack .25 .08
❑ 26 Rich Hebner .60 .25
❑ 27 Geoff Zahn .25 .08
❑ 28 Ed Ott .25 .08
❑ 29 Bob Lacey RC .25 .08
❑ 30 George Hendrick .60 .25
❑ 31 Glenn Abbott .25 .08
❑ 32 Garry Templeton .60 .25
❑ 33 Dave Lemanczyk .25 .08
❑ 34 Willie McCovey 3.00 1.25
❑ 35 Sparky Lyle .60 .25
❑ 36 Eddie Murray RC 50.00 20.00
❑ 37 Rick Waits .25 .08
❑ 38 Willie Montanez .25 .08
❑ 39 Floyd Bannister RC .25 .08
❑ 40 Carl Yastrzemski 6.00 2.50
❑ 41 Burt Hooton .60 .25
❑ 42 Jorge Orta .25 .08
❑ 43 Bill Atkinson RC .25 .08
❑ 44 Toby Harrah .60 .25
❑ 45 Mark Fidrych 2.50 1.00
❑ 46 Al Cowens .60 .25
❑ 47 Jack Billingham .25 .08
❑ 48 Don Baylor 1.25 .50
❑ 49 Ed Kranepool .60 .25
❑ 50 Rick Reuschel .60 .25
❑ 51 Charlie Moore DP .15 .05
❑ 52 Jim Lonborg .60 .25
❑ 53 Phil Garner DP .25 .08
❑ 54 Tom Johnson .25 .08
❑ 55 Mitchell Page RC .25 .08
❑ 56 Randy Jones .25 .08
❑ 57 Dan Meyer .25 .08
❑ 58 Bob Forsch .25 .08
❑ 59 Otto Velez .25 .08
❑ 60 Thurman Munson 4.00 1.50
❑ 61 Larvell Blanks .25 .08
❑ 62 Jim Barr .25 .08
❑ 63 Don Zimmer MG .60 .25
❑ 64 Gene Pentz .25 .08
❑ 65 Ken Singleton .60 .25
❑ 66 Chicago White Sox CL 1.25 .50
❑ 67 Claudell Washington .60 .25
❑ 68 Steve Foucault DP .15 .05
❑ 69 Mike Vail .25 .08
❑ 70 Goose Gossage 1.25 .50
❑ 71 Terry Humphrey .25 .08
❑ 72 Andre Dawson 4.00 1.50
❑ 73 Andy Hassler .25 .08
❑ 74 Checklist 1-121 1.25 .50
❑ 75 Dick Ruthven .25 .08
❑ 76 Steve Ontiveros .25 .08
❑ 77 Ed Kirkpatrick .25 .08
❑ 78 Pablo Torrealba .25 .08
❑ 79 Darrell Johnson MG DP .15 .05
❑ 80 Ken Griffey Sr. 1.25 .50
❑ 81 Pete Redfern .25 .08
❑ 82 San Francisco Giants CL 1.25 .50
❑ 83 Bob Montgomery .25 .08
❑ 84 Kent Tekulve .60 .25
❑ 85 Ron Fairly .60 .25
❑ 86 Dave Tomlin .25 .08
❑ 87 John Lowenstein .25 .08
❑ 88 Mike Phillips .25 .08
❑ 89 Ken Clay RC .25 .08
❑ 90 Larry Bowa 1.25 .50
❑ 91 Oscar Zamora .25 .08
❑ 92 Adrian Devine .25 .08
❑ 93 Bobby Cox DP .15 .05
❑ 94 Chuck Scrivener .25 .08
❑ 95 Jamie Quirk .25 .08
❑ 96 Baltimore Orioles CL 1.25 .50
❑ 97 Stan Bahnsen .25 .08
❑ 98 Jim Essian .60 .25
❑ 99 Willie Hernandez RC 1.25 .50
❑ 100 George Brett 15.00 6.00
❑ 101 Sid Monge .25 .08
❑ 102 Matt Alexander .25 .08
❑ 103 Tom Murphy .25 .08
❑ 104 Lee Lacy .25 .08
❑ 105 Reggie Cleveland .25 .08
❑ 106 Bill Plummer .25 .08
❑ 107 Ed Halicki .25 .08
❑ 108 Von Joshua .25 .08
❑ 109 Joe Torre MG .60 .25
❑ 110 Richie Zisk .25 .08
❑ 111 Mike Tyson .25 .08
❑ 112 Houston Astros CL 1.25 .50
❑ 113 Don Carrithers .25 .08
❑ 114 Paul Blair .60 .25
❑ 115 Gary Nolan .25 .08
❑ 116 Tucker Ashford RC .25 .08
❑ 117 John Montague .25 .08
❑ 118 Terry Harmon .25 .08
❑ 119 Dennis Martinez 2.50 1.00
❑ 120 Gary Carter 2.50 1.00
❑ 121 Alvis Woods .25 .08
❑ 122 Dennis Eckersley 3.00 1.25
❑ 123 Manny Trillo .25 .08
❑ 124 Dave Rozema RC .25 .08
❑ 125 George Scott .60 .25
❑ 126 Paul Moskau RC .25 .08
❑ 127 Chet Lemon .60 .25
❑ 128 Bill Russell .60 .25
❑ 129 Jim Colborn .25 .08
❑ 130 Jeff Burroughs .60 .25
❑ 131 Bert Blyleven 1.25 .50

❑ 132	Enos Cabell	.25	.08
❑ 133	Jerry Augustine	.25	.08
❑ 134	Steve Henderson RC	.25	.08
❑ 135	Ron Guidry DP	1.25	.50
❑ 136	Ted Sizemore	.25	.08
❑ 137	Craig Kusick	.25	.08
❑ 138	Larry Demery	.25	.08
❑ 139	Wayne Gross	.25	.08
❑ 140	Rollie Fingers	2.50	1.00
❑ 141	Ruppert Jones	.25	.08
❑ 142	John Montefusco	.25	.08
❑ 143	Keith Hernandez	.60	.25
❑ 144	Jesse Jefferson	.25	.08
❑ 145	Rick Monday	.60	.25
❑ 146	Doyle Alexander	.60	.25
❑ 147	Lee Mazzilli	.25	.08
❑ 148	Andre Thornton	.60	.25
❑ 149	Dale Murray	.25	.08
❑ 150	Bobby Bonds	1.25	.50
❑ 151	Milt Wilcox	.25	.08
❑ 152	Ivan DeJesus RC	.25	.08
❑ 153	Steve Stone	.60	.25
❑ 154	Cecil Cooper DP	.25	.08
❑ 155	Butch Hobson	.25	.08
❑ 156	Andy Messersmith	.60	.25
❑ 157	Pete LaCock DP	.15	.05
❑ 158	Joaquin Andujar	.60	.25
❑ 159	Lou Piniella	.60	.25
❑ 160	Jim Palmer	3.00	1.25
❑ 161	Bob Boone	1.25	.50
❑ 162	Paul Thormodsgard RC	.25	.08
❑ 163	Bill North	.25	.08
❑ 164	Bob Owchinko RC	.25	.08
❑ 165	Rennie Stennett	.25	.08
❑ 166	Carlos Lopez	.25	.08
❑ 167	Tim Foli	.25	.08
❑ 168	Reggie Smith	.60	.25
❑ 169	Jerry Johnson	.25	.08
❑ 170	Lou Brock	3.00	1.25
❑ 171	Pat Zachry	.25	.08
❑ 172	Mike Hargrove	.60	.25
❑ 173	Robin Yount UER	5.00	2.00
❑ 174	Wayne Garland	.25	.08
❑ 175	Jerry Morales	.25	.08
❑ 176	Milt May	.25	.08
❑ 177	Gene Garber DP	.25	.08
❑ 178	Dave Chalk	.25	.08
❑ 179	Dick Tidrow	.25	.08
❑ 180	Dave Concepcion	1.25	.50
❑ 181	Ken Forsch	.25	.08
❑ 182	Jim Spencer	.25	.08
❑ 183	Doug Bird	.25	.08
❑ 184	Checklist 122-242	1.25	.50
❑ 185	Ellis Valentine	.25	.08
❑ 186	Bob Stanley DP RC	.15	.05
❑ 187	Jerry Royster DP	.15	.05
❑ 188	Al Bumbry	.60	.25
❑ 189	Tom Lasorda MG DP	2.50	1.00
❑ 190	John Candelaria	.60	.25
❑ 191	Rodney Scott RC	.25	.08
❑ 192	San Diego Padres CL	1.25	.50
❑ 193	Rich Chiles	.25	.08
❑ 194	Derrel Thomas	.25	.08
❑ 195	Larry Dierker	.60	.25
❑ 196	Bob Bailor	.25	.08
❑ 197	Nino Espinosa	.25	.08
❑ 198	Ron Pruitt	.25	.08
❑ 199	Craig Reynolds	.25	.08
❑ 200	Reggie Jackson	8.00	3.00
❑ 201	D.Parker/R.Carew LL	1.25	.50
❑ 202	G.Foster/J.Rice LL DP	.60	.25
❑ 203	G.Foster/L.Hisle LL	.60	.25
❑ 204	F.Taveras/F.Patek LL DP	.25	.08
❑ 205	Carlton/Gol/Leon/Palm LL	2.50	1.00
❑ 206	P.Niekro/N.Ryan LL DP	6.00	2.50
❑ 207	J.Cand/F.Tanana LL DP	.60	.25
❑ 208	R.Fingers/B.Campbell LL	1.25	.50
❑ 209	Dock Ellis	.25	.08
❑ 210	Jose Cardenal	.25	.08
❑ 211	Earl Weaver MG DP	1.25	.50
❑ 212	Mike Caldwell	.25	.08
❑ 213	Alan Bannister	.25	.08
❑ 214	California Angels CL	1.25	.50
❑ 215	Darrell Evans	.60	.25
❑ 216	Mike Paxton RC	.25	.08
❑ 217	Rod Gilbreath	.25	.08
❑ 218	Marty Pattin	.25	.08
❑ 219	Mike Cubbage	.25	.08
❑ 220	Pedro Borbon	.25	.08
❑ 221	Chris Speier	.25	.08
❑ 222	Jerry Martin	.25	.08
❑ 223	Bruce Kison	.25	.08
❑ 224	Jerry Tabb RC	.25	.08
❑ 225	Don Gullett DP	.25	.08
❑ 226	Joe Ferguson	.25	.08
❑ 227	Al Fitzmorris	.25	.08
❑ 228	Manny Mota DP	.25	.08
❑ 229	Leo Foster	.25	.08
❑ 230	Al Hrabosky	.60	.25
❑ 231	Wayne Nordhagen RC	.25	.08
❑ 232	Mickey Stanley	.25	.08
❑ 233	Dick Pole	.25	.08
❑ 234	Herman Franks MG	.25	.08
❑ 235	Tim McCarver	.60	.25
❑ 236	Terry Whitfield	.25	.08
❑ 237	Rich Dauer	.25	.08
❑ 238	Juan Beniquez	.25	.08
❑ 239	Dyar Miller	.25	.08
❑ 240	Gene Tenace	.60	.25
❑ 241	Pete Vuckovich	.60	.25
❑ 242	Barry Bonnell DP RC	.15	.05
❑ 243	Bob McClure	.25	.08
❑ 244	Montreal Expos CL DP	.60	.25
❑ 245	Rick Burleson	.60	.25
❑ 246	Dan Driessen	.25	.08
❑ 247	Larry Christenson	.25	.08
❑ 248	Frank White DP	.60	.25
❑ 249	Dave Goltz DP	.15	.05
❑ 250	Graig Nettles DP	.60	.25
❑ 251	Don Kirkwood	.25	.08
❑ 252	Steve Swisher DP	.15	.05
❑ 253	Jim Kern	.25	.08
❑ 254	Dave Collins	.60	.25
❑ 255	Jerry Reuss	.60	.25
❑ 256	Joe Altobelli MG RC	.25	.08
❑ 257	Hector Cruz	.25	.08
❑ 258	John Hiller	.25	.08
❑ 259	Los Angeles Dodgers CL	1.25	.50
❑ 260	Bert Campaneris	.60	.25
❑ 261	Tim Hosley	.25	.08
❑ 262	Rudy May	.25	.08
❑ 263	Danny Walton	.25	.08
❑ 264	Jamie Easterly	.25	.08
❑ 265	Sal Bando DP	.60	.25
❑ 266	Bob Shirley RC	.25	.08
❑ 267	Doug Ault	.25	.08
❑ 268	Gil Flores RC	.25	.08
❑ 269	Wayne Twitchell	.25	.08
❑ 270	Carlton Fisk	4.00	1.50
❑ 271	Randy Lerch DP	.15	.05
❑ 272	Royle Stillman	.25	.08
❑ 273	Fred Norman	.25	.08
❑ 274	Freddie Patek	.60	.25
❑ 275	Dan Ford	.25	.08
❑ 276	Bill Bonham DP	.15	.05
❑ 277	Bruce Boisclair	.25	.08
❑ 278	Enrique Romo RC	.25	.08
❑ 279	Bill Virdon MG	.25	.08
❑ 280	Buddy Bell	.60	.25
❑ 281	Eric Rasmussen DP	.15	.05
❑ 282	New York Yankees CL	2.50	1.00
❑ 283	Omar Moreno	.25	.08
❑ 284	Randy Moffitt	.25	.08
❑ 285	Steve Yeager DP	.60	.25
❑ 286	Ben Oglivie	.60	.25
❑ 287	Kiko Garcia	.25	.08
❑ 288	Dave Hamilton	.25	.08
❑ 289	Checklist 243-363	1.25	.50
❑ 290	Willie Horton	.60	.25
❑ 291	Gary Ross	.25	.08
❑ 292	Gene Richards	.25	.08
❑ 293	Mike Willis	.25	.08
❑ 294	Larry Parrish	.60	.25
❑ 295	Bill Lee	.25	.08
❑ 296	Biff Pocoroba	.25	.08
❑ 297	Warren Brusstar DP RC	.15	.05
❑ 298	Tony Armas	.60	.25
❑ 299	Whitey Herzog MG	.60	.25
❑ 300	Joe Morgan	3.00	1.25
❑ 301	Buddy Schultz RC	.25	.08
❑ 302	Chicago Cubs CL	1.25	.50
❑ 303	Sam Hinds RC	.25	.08
❑ 304	John Milner	.25	.08
❑ 305	Rico Carty	.60	.25
❑ 306	Joe Niekro	.60	.25
❑ 307	Glenn Borgmann	.25	.08
❑ 308	Jim Rooker	.25	.08
❑ 309	Cliff Johnson	.25	.08
❑ 310	Don Sutton	2.50	1.00
❑ 311	Jose Baez DP RC	.15	.05
❑ 312	Greg Minton	.25	.08
❑ 313	Andy Etchebarren	.25	.08
❑ 314	Paul Lindblad	.25	.08
❑ 315	Mark Belanger	.60	.25
❑ 316	Henry Cruz DP	.15	.05
❑ 317	Dave Johnson	.25	.08
❑ 318	Tom Griffin	.25	.08
❑ 319	Alan Ashby	.25	.08
❑ 320	Fred Lynn	.60	.25
❑ 321	Santo Alcala	.25	.08
❑ 322	Tom Paciorek	.60	.25
❑ 323	Jim Fregosi DP	.25	.08
❑ 324	Vern Rapp MG RC	.25	.08
❑ 325	Bruce Sutter	3.00	1.25
❑ 326	Mike Lum DP	.15	.05
❑ 327	Rick Langford DP RC	.15	.05
❑ 328	Milwaukee Brewers CL	1.25	.50
❑ 329	John Verhoeven	.25	.08
❑ 330	Bob Watson	.60	.25
❑ 331	Mark Littell	.25	.08
❑ 332	Duane Kuiper	.25	.08
❑ 333	Jim Todd	.25	.08
❑ 334	John Stearns	.25	.08
❑ 335	Bucky Dent	.60	.25
❑ 336	Steve Busby	.25	.08
❑ 337	Tom Grieve	.60	.25
❑ 338	Dave Heaverlo	.25	.08
❑ 339	Mario Guerrero	.25	.08
❑ 340	Bake McBride	.60	.25
❑ 341	Mike Flanagan	.60	.25
❑ 342	Aurelio Rodriguez	.25	.08
❑ 343	John Wathan DP	.15	.05
❑ 344	Sam Ewing RC	.25	.08
❑ 345	Luis Tiant	.60	.25
❑ 346	Larry Biittner	.25	.08
❑ 347	Terry Forster	.25	.08
❑ 348	Del Unser	.25	.08
❑ 349	Rick Camp DP	.15	.05
❑ 350	Steve Garvey	2.50	1.00
❑ 351	Jeff Torborg	.60	.25
❑ 352	Tony Scott RC	.25	.08
❑ 353	Doug Bair RC	.25	.08
❑ 354	Cesar Geronimo	.25	.08
❑ 355	Bill Travers	.25	.08
❑ 356	New York Mets CL	1.25	.50
❑ 357	Tom Poquette	.25	.08
❑ 358	Mark Lemongello	.25	.08
❑ 359	Marc Hill	.25	.08
❑ 360	Mike Schmidt	10.00	4.00
❑ 361	Chris Knapp	.25	.08
❑ 362	Dave May	.25	.08
❑ 363	Bob Randall	.25	.08
❑ 364	Jerry Turner	.25	.08
❑ 365	Ed Figueroa	.25	.08
❑ 366	Larry Milbourne DP	.15	.05
❑ 367	Rick Dempsey	.60	.25
❑ 368	Balor Moore	.25	.08
❑ 369	Tim Nordbrook	.25	.08
❑ 370	Rusty Staub	1.25	.50
❑ 371	Ray Burris	.25	.08
❑ 372	Brian Asselstine	.25	.08
❑ 373	Jim Willoughby	.25	.08
❑ 374	Jose Morales	.25	.08
❑ 375	Tommy John	1.25	.50
❑ 376	Jim Wohlford	.25	.08
❑ 377	Manny Sarmiento	.25	.08
❑ 378	Bobby Winkles MG	.25	.08
❑ 379	Skip Lockwood	.25	.08
❑ 380	Ted Simmons	.60	.25
❑ 381	Philadelphia Phillies CL	1.25	.50
❑ 382	Joe Lahoud	.25	.08
❑ 383	Mario Mendoza	.25	.08
❑ 384	Jack Clark	1.25	.50
❑ 385	Tito Fuentes	.25	.08
❑ 386	Bob Gorinski RC	.25	.08
❑ 387	Ken Holtzman	.60	.25
❑ 388	Bill Fahey DP	.15	.05
❑ 389	Julio Gonzalez RC	.25	.08

❑ 390 Oscar Gamble .60 .25
❑ 391 Larry Haney .25 .08
❑ 392 Billy Almon .25 .08
❑ 393 Tippy Martinez .60 .25
❑ 394 Roy Howell DP .15 .05
❑ 395 Jim Hughes .25 .08
❑ 396 Bob Stinson DP .15 .05
❑ 397 Greg Gross .25 .08
❑ 398 Don Hood .25 .08
❑ 399 Pete Mackanin .25 .08
❑ 400 Nolan Ryan 25.00 10.00
❑ 401 Sparky Anderson MG .60 .25
❑ 402 Dave Campbell .25 .08
❑ 403 Bud Harrelson .60 .25
❑ 404 Detroit Tigers CL 1.25 .50
❑ 405 Rawly Eastwick .25 .08
❑ 406 Mike Jorgensen .25 .08
❑ 407 Odell Jones RC .25 .08
❑ 408 Joe Zdeb RC .25 .08
❑ 409 Ron Schueler .25 .08
❑ 410 Bill Madlock .60 .25
❑ 411 Mickey Rivers ALCS .60 .25
❑ 412 Davey Lopes NLCS .60 .25
❑ 413 Reggie Jackson WS 4.00 1.50
❑ 414 Darold Knowles DP .15 .05
❑ 415 Ray Fosse .25 .08
❑ 416 Jack Brohamer .25 .08
❑ 417 Mike Garman DP .15 .05
❑ 418 Tony Muser .25 .08
❑ 419 Jerry Garvin RC .25 .08
❑ 420 Greg Luzinski 1.25 .50
❑ 421 Junior Moore RC .25 .08
❑ 422 Steve Braun .25 .08
❑ 423 Dave Rosello .25 .08
❑ 424 Boston Red Sox CL 1.25 .50
❑ 425 Steve Rogers DP .25 .08
❑ 426 Fred Kendall .25 .08
❑ 427 Mario Soto RC .60 .25
❑ 428 Joel Youngblood .25 .08
❑ 429 Mike Barlow RC .25 .08
❑ 430 Al Oliver .60 .25
❑ 431 Butch Metzger .25 .08
❑ 432 Terry Bulling RC .25 .08
❑ 433 Fernando Gonzalez .25 .08
❑ 434 Mike Norris .25 .08
❑ 435 Checklist 364-484 1.25 .50
❑ 436 Vic Harris DP .15 .05
❑ 437 Bo McLaughlin .25 .08
❑ 438 John Ellis .25 .08
❑ 439 Ken Kravec .25 .08
❑ 440 Dave Lopes .60 .25
❑ 441 Larry Gura .25 .08
❑ 442 Elliott Maddox .25 .08
❑ 443 Darrel Chaney .25 .08
❑ 444 Roy Hartsfield MG .25 .08
❑ 445 Mike Ivie .25 .08
❑ 446 Tug McGraw .60 .25
❑ 447 Leroy Stanton .25 .08
❑ 448 Bill Castro .25 .08
❑ 449 Tim Blackwell DP RC .15 .05
❑ 450 Tom Seaver 6.00 2.50
❑ 451 Minnesota Twins CL 1.25 .50
❑ 452 Jerry Mumphrey .25 .08
❑ 453 Doug Flynn .25 .08
❑ 454 Dave LaRoche .25 .08
❑ 455 Bill Robinson .60 .25
❑ 456 Vern Ruhle .25 .08
❑ 457 Bob Bailey .25 .08
❑ 458 Jeff Newman .25 .08
❑ 459 Charlie Spikes .25 .08
❑ 460 Jim Hunter 2.50 1.00
❑ 461 Rob Andrews DP .15 .05
❑ 462 Rogelio Moret .25 .08
❑ 463 Kevin Bell .25 .08
❑ 464 Jerry Grote .25 .08
❑ 465 Hal McRae .60 .25
❑ 466 Dennis Blair .25 .08
❑ 467 Alvin Dark MG .60 .25
❑ 468 Warren Cromartie RC .60 .25
❑ 469 Rick Cerone .60 .25
❑ 470 J.R. Richard .60 .25
❑ 471 Roy Smalley .60 .25
❑ 472 Ron Reed .25 .08
❑ 473 Bill Buckner .60 .25
❑ 474 Jim Slaton .25 .08
❑ 475 Gary Matthews .60 .25
❑ 476 Bill Stein .25 .08
❑ 477 Doug Capilla RC .25 .08
❑ 478 Jerry Remy .25 .08
❑ 479 St. Louis Cardinals CL 1.25 .50
❑ 480 Ron LeFlore .60 .25
❑ 481 Jackson Todd RC .25 .08
❑ 482 Rick Miller .25 .08
❑ 483 Ken Macha RC .25 .08
❑ 484 Jim Norris RC .25 .08
❑ 485 Chris Chambliss .60 .25
❑ 486 John Curtis .25 .08
❑ 487 Jim Tyrone .25 .08
❑ 488 Dan Spillner .25 .08
❑ 489 Rudy Meoli .25 .08
❑ 490 Amos Otis .60 .25
❑ 491 Scott McGregor .60 .25
❑ 492 Jim Sundberg .60 .25
❑ 493 Steve Renko .25 .08
❑ 494 Chuck Tanner MG .60 .25
❑ 495 Dave Cash .25 .08
❑ 496 Jim Clancy DP RC .15 .05
❑ 497 Glenn Adams .25 .08
❑ 498 Joe Sambito .25 .08
❑ 499 Seattle Mariners CL 1.25 .50
❑ 500 George Foster 1.25 .50
❑ 501 Dave Roberts .25 .08
❑ 502 Pat Rockett RC .25 .08
❑ 503 Ike Hampton RC .25 .08
❑ 504 Roger Freed .25 .08
❑ 505 Felix Millan .25 .08
❑ 506 Ron Blomberg .25 .08
❑ 507 Willie Crawford .25 .08
❑ 508 Johnny Oates .60 .25
❑ 509 Brent Strom .25 .08
❑ 510 Willie Stargell 2.50 1.00
❑ 511 Frank Duffy .25 .08
❑ 512 Larry Herndon .25 .08
❑ 513 Barry Foote .25 .08
❑ 514 Rob Sperring .25 .08
❑ 515 Tim Corcoran RC .25 .08
❑ 516 Gary Beare RC .25 .08
❑ 517 Andres Mora .25 .08
❑ 518 Tommy Boggs DP .15 .05
❑ 519 Brian Downing .60 .25
❑ 520 Larry Hisle .25 .08
❑ 521 Steve Staggs RC .25 .08
❑ 522 Dick Williams MG .60 .25
❑ 523 Donnie Moore RC .25 .08
❑ 524 Bernie Carbo .25 .08
❑ 525 Jerry Terrell .25 .08
❑ 526 Cincinnati Reds CL 1.25 .50
❑ 527 Vic Correll .25 .08
❑ 528 Rob Picciolo RC .25 .08
❑ 529 Paul Hartzell .25 .08
❑ 530 Dave Winfield 4.00 1.50
❑ 531 Tom Underwood .25 .08
❑ 532 Skip Jutze .25 .08
❑ 533 Sandy Alomar .60 .25
❑ 534 Wilbur Howard .25 .08
❑ 535 Checklist 485-605 1.25 .50
❑ 536 Roric Harrison .25 .08
❑ 537 Bruce Bochte .25 .08
❑ 538 Johnny LeMaster .25 .08
❑ 539 Vic Davalillo DP .15 .05
❑ 540 Steve Carlton 4.00 1.50
❑ 541 Larry Cox .25 .08
❑ 542 Tim Johnson .25 .08
❑ 543 Larry Harlow DP RC .15 .05
❑ 544 Len Randle DP .15 .05
❑ 545 Bill Campbell .25 .08
❑ 546 Ted Martinez .25 .08
❑ 547 John Scott .25 .08
❑ 548 Billy Hunter MG DP .15 .05
❑ 549 Joe Kerrigan .25 .08
❑ 550 John Mayberry .60 .25
❑ 551 Atlanta Braves CL 1.25 .50
❑ 552 Francisco Barrios .25 .08
❑ 553 Terry Puhl RC .60 .25
❑ 554 Joe Coleman .25 .08
❑ 555 Butch Wynegar .25 .08
❑ 556 Ed Armbrister .25 .08
❑ 557 Tony Solaita .25 .08
❑ 558 Paul Mitchell .25 .08
❑ 559 Phil Mankowski .25 .08
❑ 560 Dave Parker 1.25 .50
❑ 561 Charlie Williams .25 .08
❑ 562 Glenn Burke RC .25 .08
❑ 563 Dave Rader .25 .08
❑ 564 Mick Kelleher .25 .08
❑ 565 Jerry Koosman .60 .25
❑ 566 Merv Rettenmund .25 .08
❑ 567 Dick Drago .25 .08
❑ 568 Tom Hutton .25 .08
❑ 569 Lary Sorensen RC .25 .08
❑ 570 Dave Kingman 1.25 .50
❑ 571 Buck Martinez .25 .08
❑ 572 Rick Wise .25 .08
❑ 573 Luis Gomez .25 .08
❑ 574 Bob Lemon MG 1.25 .50
❑ 575 Pat Dobson .25 .08
❑ 576 Sam Mejias .25 .08
❑ 577 Oakland Athletics CL 1.25 .50
❑ 578 Buzz Capra .25 .08
❑ 579 Rance Mulliniks RC .25 .08
❑ 580 Rod Carew 4.00 1.50
❑ 581 Lynn McGlothen .25 .08
❑ 582 Fran Healy .25 .08
❑ 583 George Medich .25 .08
❑ 584 John Hale .25 .08
❑ 585 Woodie Fryman DP .15 .05
❑ 586 Ed Goodson .25 .08
❑ 587 John Urrea RC .25 .08
❑ 588 Jim Mason .25 .08
❑ 589 Bob Knepper RC .25 .08
❑ 590 Bobby Murcer .60 .25
❑ 591 George Zeber RC .25 .08
❑ 592 Bob Apodaca .25 .08
❑ 593 Dave Skaggs RC .25 .08
❑ 594 Dave Freisleben .25 .08
❑ 595 Sixto Lezcano .25 .08
❑ 596 Gary Wheelock .25 .08
❑ 597 Steve Dillard .25 .08
❑ 598 Eddie Solomon .25 .08
❑ 599 Gary Woods .25 .08
❑ 600 Frank Tanana .60 .25
❑ 601 Gene Mauch MG .60 .25
❑ 602 Eric Soderholm .25 .08
❑ 603 Will McEnaney .25 .08
❑ 604 Earl Williams .25 .08
❑ 605 Rick Rhoden .60 .25
❑ 606 Pittsburgh Pirates CL 1.25 .50
❑ 607 Fernando Arroyo .25 .08
❑ 608 Johnny Grubb .25 .08
❑ 609 John Denny .25 .08
❑ 610 Garry Maddox .60 .25
❑ 611 Pat Scanlon RC .25 .08
❑ 612 Ken Henderson .25 .08
❑ 613 Marty Perez .25 .08
❑ 614 Joe Wallis .25 .08
❑ 615 Clay Carroll .25 .08
❑ 616 Pat Kelly .25 .08
❑ 617 Joe Nolan RC .25 .08
❑ 618 Tommy Helms .25 .08
❑ 619 Thad Bosley DP RC .15 .05
❑ 620 Willie Randolph 1.25 .50
❑ 621 Craig Swan DP .15 .05
❑ 622 Champ Summers .25 .08
❑ 623 Eduardo Rodriguez .25 .08
❑ 624 Gary Alexander DP .15 .05
❑ 625 Jose Cruz .60 .25
❑ 626 Toronto Blue Jays CL DP 1.25 .50
❑ 627 David Johnson .25 .08
❑ 628 Ralph Garr .60 .25
❑ 629 Don Stanhouse .25 .08
❑ 630 Ron Cey 1.25 .50
❑ 631 Danny Ozark MG .25 .08
❑ 632 Rowland Office .25 .08
❑ 633 Tom Veryzer .25 .08
❑ 634 Len Barker .25 .08
❑ 635 Joe Rudi .60 .25
❑ 636 Jim Bibby .25 .08
❑ 637 Duffy Dyer .25 .08
❑ 638 Paul Splittorff .25 .08
❑ 639 Gene Clines .25 .08
❑ 640 Lee May DP .25 .08
❑ 641 Doug Rau .25 .08
❑ 642 Denny Doyle .25 .08
❑ 643 Tom House .25 .08
❑ 644 Jim Dwyer .25 .08
❑ 645 Mike Torrez .60 .25
❑ 646 Rick Auerbach DP .15 .05
❑ 647 Steve Dunning .25 .08

❑ 648 Gary Thomasson .25 .08
❑ 649 Moose Haas RC .25 .08
❑ 650 Cesar Cedeno .60 .25
❑ 651 Doug Rader .25 .08
❑ 652 Checklist 606-726 1.25 .50
❑ 653 Ron Hodges DP .15 .05
❑ 654 Pepe Frias .25 .08
❑ 655 Lyman Bostock .60 .25
❑ 656 Dave Garcia MG RC .25 .08
❑ 657 Bombo Rivera .25 .08
❑ 658 Manny Sanguillen .60 .25
❑ 659 Texas Rangers CL 1.25 .50
❑ 660 Jason Thompson .60 .25
❑ 661 Grant Jackson .25 .08
❑ 662 Paul Dade RC .25 .08
❑ 663 Paul Reuschel .25 .08
❑ 664 Fred Stanley .25 .08
❑ 665 Dennis Leonard .60 .25
❑ 666 Billy Smith RC .25 .08
❑ 667 Jeff Byrd RC .25 .08
❑ 668 Dusty Baker 1.25 .50
❑ 669 Pete Falcone .25 .08
❑ 670 Jim Rice 1.25 .50
❑ 671 Gary Lavelle .25 .08
❑ 672 Don Kessinger .60 .25
❑ 673 Steve Brye .25 .08
❑ 674 Ray Knight RC 2.50 1.00
❑ 675 Jay Johnstone .60 .25
❑ 676 Bob Myrick .25 .08
❑ 677 Ed Herrmann .25 .08
❑ 678 Tom Burgmeier .25 .08
❑ 679 Wayne Garrett .25 .08
❑ 680 Vida Blue .60 .25
❑ 681 Rob Belloir .25 .08
❑ 682 Ken Brett .25 .08
❑ 683 Mike Champion .25 .08
❑ 684 Ralph Houk MG .60 .25
❑ 685 Frank Taveras .25 .08
❑ 686 Gaylord Perry 2.50 1.00
❑ 687 Julio Cruz RC .25 .08
❑ 688 George Mitterwald .25 .08
❑ 689 Cleveland Indians CL 1.25 .50
❑ 690 Mickey Rivers .60 .25
❑ 691 Ross Grimsley .25 .08
❑ 692 Ken Reitz .25 .08
❑ 693 Lamar Johnson .25 .08
❑ 694 Elias Sosa .25 .08
❑ 695 Dwight Evans 1.25 .50
❑ 696 Steve Mingori .25 .08
❑ 697 Roger Metzger .25 .08
❑ 698 Juan Bernhardt .25 .08
❑ 699 Jackie Brown .25 .08
❑ 700 Johnny Bench 8.00 3.00
❑ 701 Hume/Land/McC/Tay RC .60 .25
❑ 702 Nah/Pas/Sweet/Wer RC .60 .25
❑ 703 Jack Morris DP RC 5.00 2.00
❑ 704 Lou Whitaker RC 8.00 3.00
❑ 705 Berg/Milone/Hurdle/Nor RC 1.25 .50
❑ 706 Cage/Cox/Put/Rev RC .60 .25
❑ 707 P.Molitor RC/A.Trammell RC 50.00 20.00
❑ 708 Diaz/Murphy/Parrish/Whitt RC 4.00 1.50
❑ 709 Burke/Keough/Rau/Schat RC .60 .25
❑ 710 Alston/Bos/Easler/Smith RC 1.25 .50
❑ 711 Camp/Lamp/Mit/Tho DP RC .25 .08
❑ 712 Bobby Valentine .60 .25
❑ 713 Bob Davis .25 .08
❑ 714 Mike Anderson .25 .08
❑ 715 Jim Kaat 1.25 .50
❑ 716 Clarence Gaston .60 .25
❑ 717 Nelson Briles .25 .08
❑ 718 Ron Jackson .25 .08
❑ 719 Randy Elliott RC .25 .08
❑ 720 Fergie Jenkins 2.50 1.00
❑ 721 Billy Martin MG 1.25 .50
❑ 722 Pete Broberg .25 .08
❑ 723 John Wockenfuss .25 .08
❑ 724 Kansas City Royals CL 1.25 .50
❑ 725 Kurt Bevacqua .25 .08
❑ 726 Wilbur Wood 1.25 .50

1979 Topps

❑ COMPLETE SET (726) 175.00 100.00
❑ COMMON CARD (1-726) .25 .08
❑ COMMON CARD DP .15 .05
❑ 1 R.Carew/D.Parker LL 2.50 1.00
❑ 2 J.Rice/G.Foster LL 1.50 .60

❑ 3 J.Rice/G.Foster LL 1.50 .60
❑ 4 R.LeFlore/O.Moreno LL .75 .30
❑ 5 R.Guidry/G.Perry LL .75 .30
❑ 6 N.Ryan/J.Richard LL 5.00 2.00
❑ 7 R.Guidry/C.Swan LL .75 .30
❑ 8 R.Gossage/R.Fingers LL 1.50 .60
❑ 9 Dave Campbell .25 .08
❑ 10 Lee May .75 .30
❑ 11 Marc Hill .25 .08
❑ 12 Dick Drago .25 .08
❑ 13 Paul Dade .25 .08
❑ 14 Rafael Landestoy RC .25 .08
❑ 15 Ross Grimsley .25 .08
❑ 16 Fred Stanley .25 .08
❑ 17 Donnie Moore .25 .08
❑ 18 Tony Solaita .25 .08
❑ 19 Larry Gura DP .15 .05
❑ 20 Joe Morgan DP 2.50 1.00
❑ 21 Kevin Kobel .25 .08
❑ 22 Mike Jorgensen .25 .08
❑ 23 Terry Forster .25 .08
❑ 24 Paul Molitor 10.00 4.00
❑ 25 Steve Carlton 3.00 1.25
❑ 26 Jamie Quirk .25 .08
❑ 27 Dave Goltz .25 .08
❑ 28 Steve Brye .25 .08
❑ 29 Rick Langford .25 .08
❑ 30 Dave Winfield 4.00 1.50
❑ 31 Tom House DP .15 .05
❑ 32 Jerry Mumphrey .25 .08
❑ 33 Dave Rozema .25 .08
❑ 34 Rob Andrews .25 .08
❑ 35 Ed Figueroa .25 .08
❑ 36 Alan Ashby .25 .08
❑ 37 Joe Kerrigan DP .15 .05
❑ 38 Bernie Carbo .25 .08
❑ 39 Dale Murphy 3.00 1.25
❑ 40 Dennis Eckersley 2.50 1.00
❑ 41 Minnesota Twins CL/Mauch 1.50 .60
❑ 42 Ron Blomberg .25 .08
❑ 43 Wayne Twitchell .25 .08
❑ 44 Kurt Bevacqua .25 .08
❑ 45 Al Hrabosky .75 .30
❑ 46 Ron Hodges .25 .08
❑ 47 Fred Norman .25 .08
❑ 48 Merv Rettenmund .25 .08
❑ 49 Vern Ruhle .25 .08
❑ 50 Steve Garvey DP 1.50 .60
❑ 51 Ray Fosse DP .15 .05
❑ 52 Randy Lerch .25 .08
❑ 53 Mick Kelleher .25 .08
❑ 54 Dell Alston DP .15 .05
❑ 55 Willie Stargell 2.50 1.00
❑ 56 John Hale .25 .08
❑ 57 Eric Rasmussen .25 .08
❑ 58 Bob Randall DP .15 .05
❑ 59 John Denny DP .25 .08
❑ 60 Mickey Rivers .75 .30
❑ 61 Bo Diaz .25 .08
❑ 62 Randy Moffitt .25 .08
❑ 63 Jack Brohamer .25 .08
❑ 64 Tom Underwood .25 .08
❑ 65 Mark Belanger .75 .30
❑ 66 Detroit Tigers CL/Moss 1.50 .60
❑ 67 Jim Mason DP .15 .05
❑ 68 Joe Niekro DP .25 .08
❑ 69 Elliott Maddox .25 .08
❑ 70 John Candelaria .75 .30
❑ 71 Brian Downing .75 .30
❑ 72 Steve Mingori .25 .08
❑ 73 Ken Henderson .25 .08
❑ 74 Shane Rawley RC .25 .08
❑ 75 Steve Yeager .75 .30
❑ 76 Warren Cromartie .75 .30
❑ 77 Dan Briggs DP .15 .05
❑ 78 Elias Sosa .25 .08
❑ 79 Ted Cox .25 .08
❑ 80 Jason Thompson .75 .30
❑ 81 Roger Erickson RC .25 .08
❑ 82 New York Mets CL/Torre 1.50 .60
❑ 83 Fred Kendall .25 .08
❑ 84 Greg Minton .25 .08
❑ 85 Gary Matthews .75 .30
❑ 86 Rodney Scott .25 .08
❑ 87 Pete Falcone .25 .08
❑ 88 Bob Molinaro RC .25 .08
❑ 89 Dick Tidrow .25 .08
❑ 90 Bob Boone 1.50 .60
❑ 91 Terry Crowley .25 .08
❑ 92 Jim Bibby .25 .08
❑ 93 Phil Mankowski .25 .08
❑ 94 Len Barker .25 .08
❑ 95 Robin Yount 5.00 2.00
❑ 96 Cleveland Indians CL/Torborg 1.50 .60
❑ 97 Sam Mejias .25 .08
❑ 98 Ray Burris .25 .08
❑ 99 John Wathan .75 .30
❑ 100 Tom Seaver DP 4.00 1.50
❑ 101 Roy Howell .25 .08
❑ 102 Mike Anderson .25 .08
❑ 103 Jim Todd .25 .08
❑ 104 Johnny Oates DP .25 .08
❑ 105 Rick Camp DP .15 .05
❑ 106 Frank Duffy .25 .08
❑ 107 Jesus Alou DP .15 .05
❑ 108 Eduardo Rodriguez .25 .08
❑ 109 Joel Youngblood .25 .08
❑ 110 Vida Blue .75 .30
❑ 111 Roger Freed .25 .08
❑ 112 Philadelphia Phillies CL/Ozark 1.50 .60
❑ 113 Pete Redfern .25 .08
❑ 114 Cliff Johnson .25 .08
❑ 115 Nolan Ryan 20.00 8.00
❑ 116 Ozzie Smith RC 60.00 30.00
❑ 117 Grant Jackson .25 .08
❑ 118 Bud Harrelson .75 .30
❑ 119 Don Stanhouse .25 .08
❑ 120 Jim Sundberg .75 .30
❑ 121 Checklist 1-121 DP .75 .30
❑ 122 Mike Paxton .25 .08
❑ 123 Lou Whitaker 2.50 1.00
❑ 124 Dan Schatzeder .25 .08
❑ 125 Rick Burleson .25 .08
❑ 126 Doug Bair .25 .08
❑ 127 Thad Bosley .25 .08
❑ 128 Ted Martinez .25 .08
❑ 129 Marty Pattin DP .15 .05
❑ 130 Bob Watson DP .25 .08
❑ 131 Jim Clancy .25 .08
❑ 132 Rowland Office .25 .08
❑ 133 Bill Castro .25 .08
❑ 134 Alan Bannister .25 .08
❑ 135 Bobby Murcer .75 .30
❑ 136 Jim Kaat .75 .30
❑ 137 Larry Wolfe DP RC .15 .05
❑ 138 Mark Lee RC .25 .08
❑ 139 Luis Pujols RC .25 .08
❑ 140 Don Gullett .75 .30
❑ 141 Tom Paciorek .75 .30
❑ 142 Charlie Williams .25 .08
❑ 143 Tony Scott .25 .08
❑ 144 Sandy Alomar .25 .08
❑ 145 Rick Rhoden .25 .08
❑ 146 Duane Kuiper .25 .08
❑ 147 Dave Hamilton .25 .08
❑ 148 Bruce Boisclair .25 .08
❑ 149 Manny Sarmiento .25 .08
❑ 150 Wayne Cage .25 .08
❑ 151 John Hiller .25 .08
❑ 152 Rick Cerone .25 .08
❑ 153 Dennis Lamp .25 .08
❑ 154 Jim Gantner DP .25 .08
❑ 155 Dwight Evans 1.50 .60
❑ 156 Buddy Solomon RC .25 .08
❑ 157 U.L. Washington UER .25 .08

❑ 158 Joe Sambito .25 .08
❑ 159 Roy White .75 .30
❑ 160 Mike Flanagan 1.50 .60
❑ 161 Barry Foote .25 .08
❑ 162 Tom Johnson .25 .08
❑ 163 Glenn Burke .25 .08
❑ 164 Mickey Lolich .75 .30
❑ 165 Frank Taveras .25 .08
❑ 166 Leon Roberts .25 .08
❑ 167 Roger Metzger DP .15 .05
❑ 168 Dave Freisleben .25 .08
❑ 169 Bill Nahorodny .25 .08
❑ 170 Don Sutton 2.50 1.00
❑ 171 Gene Clines .25 .08
❑ 172 Mike Bruhert RC .25 .08
❑ 173 John Lowenstein .25 .08
❑ 174 Rick Auerbach .25 .08
❑ 175 George Hendrick 1.50 .60
❑ 176 Aurelio Rodriguez .25 .08
❑ 177 Ron Reed .25 .08
❑ 178 Alvis Woods .25 .08
❑ 179 Jim Beattie DP RC .15 .05
❑ 180 Larry Hisle .25 .08
❑ 181 Mike Garman .25 .08
❑ 182 Tim Johnson .25 .08
❑ 183 Paul Splittorff .25 .08
❑ 184 Darrel Chaney .25 .08
❑ 185 Mike Torrez .75 .30
❑ 186 Eric Soderholm .25 .08
❑ 187 Mark Lemongello .25 .08
❑ 188 Pat Kelly .25 .08
❑ 189 Ed Whitson RC .25 .08
❑ 190 Ron Cey .75 .30
❑ 191 Mike Norris .25 .08
❑ 192 St. Louis Cardinals CL/Boyer 1.50 .60
❑ 193 Glenn Adams .25 .08
❑ 194 Randy Jones .25 .08
❑ 195 Bill Madlock .75 .30
❑ 196 Steve Kemp DP .25 .08
❑ 197 Bob Apodaca .25 .08
❑ 198 Johnny Grubb .25 .08
❑ 199 Larry Milbourne .25 .08
❑ 200 Johnny Bench DP 5.00 2.00
❑ 201 Mike Edwards RB .25 .08
❑ 202 Ron Guidry RB .75 .30
❑ 203 J.R. Richard RB .25 .08
❑ 204 Pete Rose RB 5.00 2.00
❑ 205 John Stearns RB .25 .08
❑ 206 Sammy Stewart RB .25 .08
❑ 207 Dave Lemanczyk .25 .08
❑ 208 Clarence Gaston .25 .08
❑ 209 Reggie Cleveland .25 .08
❑ 210 Larry Bowa .75 .30
❑ 211 Dennis Martinez 2.50 1.00
❑ 212 Carney Lansford RC 1.50 .60
❑ 213 Bill Travers .25 .08
❑ 214 Boston Red Sox CL/Zimmer 1.50 .60
❑ 215 Willie McCovey 2.50 1.00
❑ 216 Wilbur Wood .25 .08
❑ 217 Steve Dillard .25 .08
❑ 218 Dennis Leonard .75 .30
❑ 219 Roy Smalley .75 .30
❑ 220 Cesar Geronimo .25 .08
❑ 221 Jesse Jefferson .25 .08
❑ 222 Bob Beall RC .25 .08
❑ 223 Kent Tekulve .75 .30
❑ 224 Dave Revering .25 .08
❑ 225 Goose Gossage 1.50 .60
❑ 226 Ron Pruitt .25 .08
❑ 227 Steve Stone .75 .30
❑ 228 Vic Davalillo .25 .08
❑ 229 Doug Flynn .25 .08
❑ 230 Bob Forsch .25 .08
❑ 231 John Wockenfuss .25 .08
❑ 232 Jimmy Sexton RC .25 .08
❑ 233 Paul Mitchell .25 .08
❑ 234 Toby Harrah .75 .30
❑ 235 Steve Rogers .25 .08
❑ 236 Jim Dwyer .25 .08
❑ 237 Billy Smith .25 .08
❑ 238 Balor Moore .25 .08
❑ 239 Willie Horton .75 .30
❑ 240 Rick Reuschel .75 .30
❑ 241 Checklist 122-242 DP .75 .30
❑ 242 Pablo Torrealba .25 .08
❑ 243 Buck Martinez DP .15 .05
❑ 244 Pittsburgh Pirates CL/Tanner 1.50 .60
❑ 245 Jeff Burroughs .75 .30
❑ 246 Darrell Jackson RC .25 .08
❑ 247 Tucker Ashford DP .15 .05
❑ 248 Pete LaCock .25 .08
❑ 249 Paul Thormodsgard .25 .08
❑ 250 Willie Randolph .75 .30
❑ 251 Jack Morris 2.50 1.00
❑ 252 Bob Stinson .25 .08
❑ 253 Rick Wise .25 .08
❑ 254 Luis Gomez .25 .08
❑ 255 Tommy John 1.50 .60
❑ 256 Mike Sadek .25 .08
❑ 257 Adrian Devine .25 .08
❑ 258 Mike Phillips .25 .08
❑ 259 Cincinnati Reds CL/Anderson 1.50 .60
❑ 260 Richie Zisk .25 .08
❑ 261 Mario Guerrero .25 .08
❑ 262 Nelson Briles .25 .08
❑ 263 Oscar Gamble .75 .30
❑ 264 Don Robinson RC .25 .08
❑ 265 Don Money .25 .08
❑ 266 Jim Willoughby .25 .08
❑ 267 Joe Rudi .75 .30
❑ 268 Julio Gonzalez .25 .08
❑ 269 Woodie Fryman .25 .08
❑ 270 Butch Hobson .75 .30
❑ 271 Rawly Eastwick .25 .08
❑ 272 Tim Corcoran .25 .08
❑ 273 Jerry Terrell .25 .08
❑ 274 Willie Norwood .25 .08
❑ 275 Junior Moore .25 .08
❑ 276 Jim Colborn .25 .08
❑ 277 Tom Grieve .75 .30
❑ 278 Andy Messersmith .75 .30
❑ 279 Jerry Grote DP .15 .05
❑ 280 Andre Thornton .75 .30
❑ 281 Vic Correll DP .15 .05
❑ 282 Toronto Blue Jays CL/Hartsfield .75 .30
❑ 283 Ken Kravec .25 .08
❑ 284 Johnnie LeMaster .25 .08
❑ 285 Bobby Bonds 1.50 .60
❑ 286 Duffy Dyer .25 .08
❑ 287 Andres Mora .25 .08
❑ 288 Milt Wilcox .25 .08
❑ 289 Jose Cruz 1.50 .60
❑ 290 Dave Lopes .75 .30
❑ 291 Tom Griffin .25 .08
❑ 292 Don Reynolds RC .25 .08
❑ 293 Jerry Garvin .25 .08
❑ 294 Pepe Frias .25 .08
❑ 295 Mitchell Page .25 .08
❑ 296 Preston Hanna RC .25 .08
❑ 297 Ted Sizemore .25 .08
❑ 298 Rich Gale RC .25 .08
❑ 299 Steve Ontiveros .25 .08
❑ 300 Rod Carew 3.00 1.25
❑ 301 Tom Hume .25 .08
❑ 302 Atlanta Braves CL/Cox 1.50 .60
❑ 303 Lary Sorensen DP .15 .05
❑ 304 Steve Swisher .25 .08
❑ 305 Willie Montanez .25 .08
❑ 306 Floyd Bannister .25 .08
❑ 307 Larvell Blanks .25 .08
❑ 308 Bert Blyleven 1.50 .60
❑ 309 Ralph Garr .75 .30
❑ 310 Thurman Munson 3.00 1.25
❑ 311 Gary Lavelle .25 .08
❑ 312 Bob Robertson .25 .08
❑ 313 Dyar Miller .25 .08
❑ 314 Larry Harlow .25 .08
❑ 315 Jon Matlack .25 .08
❑ 316 Milt May .25 .08
❑ 317 Jose Cardenal .75 .30
❑ 318 Bob Welch RC 2.50 1.00
❑ 319 Wayne Garrett .25 .08
❑ 320 Carl Yastrzemski 5.00 2.00
❑ 321 Gaylord Perry 2.50 1.00
❑ 322 Danny Goodwin RC .25 .08
❑ 323 Lynn McGlothen .25 .08
❑ 324 Mike Tyson .25 .08
❑ 325 Cecil Cooper .75 .30
❑ 326 Pedro Borbon .25 .08
❑ 327 Art Howe DP .25 .08
❑ 328 Oakland Athletics CL/McKeon 1.50 .60
❑ 329 Joe Coleman .25 .08
❑ 330 George Brett 10.00 4.00
❑ 331 Mickey Mahler .25 .08
❑ 332 Gary Alexander .25 .08
❑ 333 Chet Lemon .75 .30
❑ 334 Craig Swan .25 .08
❑ 335 Chris Chambliss .75 .30
❑ 336 Bobby Thompson RC .25 .08
❑ 337 John Montague .25 .08
❑ 338 Vic Harris .25 .08
❑ 339 Ron Jackson .25 .08
❑ 340 Jim Palmer 2.50 1.00
❑ 341 Willie Upshaw RC .75 .30
❑ 342 Dave Roberts .25 .08
❑ 343 Ed Glynn .25 .08
❑ 344 Jerry Royster .25 .08
❑ 345 Tug McGraw .75 .30
❑ 346 Bill Buckner .75 .30
❑ 347 Doug Rau .25 .08
❑ 348 Andre Dawson 3.00 1.25
❑ 349 Jim Wright RC .25 .08
❑ 350 Garry Templeton .75 .30
❑ 351 Wayne Nordhagen DP .15 .05
❑ 352 Steve Renko .25 .08
❑ 353 Checklist 243-363 1.50 .60
❑ 354 Bill Bonham .25 .08
❑ 355 Lee Mazzilli .25 .08
❑ 356 San Francisco Giants CL/Altobelli 1.50 .60
❑ 357 Jerry Augustine .25 .08
❑ 358 Alan Trammell 3.00 1.25
❑ 359 Dan Spillner DP .15 .05
❑ 360 Amos Otis .75 .30
❑ 361 Tom Dixon RC .25 .08
❑ 362 Mike Cubbage .25 .08
❑ 363 Craig Skok RC .25 .08
❑ 364 Gene Richards .25 .08
❑ 365 Sparky Lyle .75 .30
❑ 366 Juan Bernhardt .25 .08
❑ 367 Dave Skaggs .25 .08
❑ 368 Don Aase .25 .08
❑ 369A Bump Wills ERR 3.00 1.25
❑ 369B Bump Wills COR 3.00 1.25
❑ 370 Dave Kingman 1.50 .60
❑ 371 Jeff Holly RC .25 .08
❑ 372 Lamar Johnson .25 .08
❑ 373 Lance Rautzhan .25 .08
❑ 374 Ed Herrmann .25 .08
❑ 375 Bill Campbell .25 .08
❑ 376 Gorman Thomas .75 .30
❑ 377 Paul Moskau .25 .08
❑ 378 Rob Picciolo DP .15 .05
❑ 379 Dale Murray .25 .08
❑ 380 John Mayberry .75 .30
❑ 381 Houston Astros CL/Virdon 1.50 .60
❑ 382 Jerry Martin .25 .08
❑ 383 Phil Garner .75 .30
❑ 384 Tommy Boggs .25 .08
❑ 385 Dan Ford .25 .08
❑ 386 Francisco Barrios .25 .08
❑ 387 Gary Thomasson .25 .08
❑ 388 Jack Billingham .25 .08
❑ 389 Joe Zdeb .25 .08
❑ 390 Rollie Fingers 2.50 1.00
❑ 391 Al Oliver .75 .30
❑ 392 Doug Ault .25 .08
❑ 393 Scott McGregor .75 .30
❑ 394 Randy Stein RC .25 .08
❑ 395 Dave Cash .25 .08
❑ 396 Bill Plummer .25 .08
❑ 397 Sergio Ferrer RC .25 .08
❑ 398 Ivan DeJesus .25 .08
❑ 399 David Clyde .25 .08
❑ 400 Jim Rice 1.50 .60
❑ 401 Ray Knight .75 .30
❑ 402 Paul Hartzell .25 .08
❑ 403 Tim Foli .25 .08
❑ 404 Chicago White Sox CL/Kessinger 1.50 .60
❑ 405 Butch Wynegar DP .15 .05
❑ 406 Joe Wallis DP .15 .05
❑ 407 Pete Vuckovich .75 .30
❑ 408 Charlie Moore DP .15 .05
❑ 409 Willie Wilson RC 1.50 .60
❑ 410 Darrell Evans 1.50 .60
❑ 411 G.Sisler/T.Cobb ATL 2.50 1.00
❑ 412 H.Wilson/H.Aaron ATL 2.50 1.00
❑ 413 R.Maris/H.Aaron ATL 4.00 1.50
❑ 414 R.Hornsby/T.Cobb ATL 2.50 1.00

❑ 415 L.Brock/L.Brock ATL 1.50 .60
❑ 416 J.Chesbro/C.Young ATL .75 .30
❑ 417 N.Ryan/W.Johnson ATL DP 5.00 2.00
❑ 418 D.Leonard/W.Johnson ATL DP .25 .08
❑ 419 Dick Ruthven .25 .08
❑ 420 Ken Griffey Sr. .75 .30
❑ 421 Doug DeCinces .75 .30
❑ 422 Ruppert Jones .25 .08
❑ 423 Bob Montgomery .25 .08
❑ 424 California Angels CL/Fregosi 1.50 .60
❑ 425 Rick Manning .25 .08
❑ 426 Chris Speier .25 .08
❑ 427 Andy Replogle RC .25 .08
❑ 428 Bobby Valentine .75 .30
❑ 429 John Urrea DP .15 .05
❑ 430 Dave Parker .75 .30
❑ 431 Glenn Borgmann .25 .08
❑ 432 Dave Heaverlo .25 .08
❑ 433 Larry Biittner .25 .08
❑ 434 Ken Clay .25 .08
❑ 435 Gene Tenace .75 .30
❑ 436 Hector Cruz .25 .08
❑ 437 Rick Williams RC .25 .08
❑ 438 Horace Speed RC .25 .08
❑ 439 Frank White .75 .30
❑ 440 Rusty Staub 1.50 .60
❑ 441 Lee Lacy .25 .08
❑ 442 Doyle Alexander .25 .08
❑ 443 Bruce Bochte .25 .08
❑ 444 Aurelio Lopez RC .25 .08
❑ 445 Steve Henderson .25 .08
❑ 446 Jim Lonborg .75 .30
❑ 447 Manny Sanguillen .75 .30
❑ 448 Moose Haas .25 .08
❑ 449 Bombo Rivera .25 .08
❑ 450 Dave Concepcion 1.50 .60
❑ 451 Kansas City Royals CL/Herzog 1.50 .60
❑ 452 Jerry Morales .25 .08
❑ 453 Chris Knapp .25 .08
❑ 454 Len Randle .25 .08
❑ 455 Bill Lee DP .15 .05
❑ 456 Chuck Baker RC .25 .08
❑ 457 Bruce Sutter 2.50 1.00
❑ 458 Jim Essian .25 .08
❑ 459 Sid Monge .25 .08
❑ 460 Graig Nettles 1.50 .60
❑ 461 Jim Barr DP .15 .05
❑ 462 Otto Velez .25 .08
❑ 463 Steve Comer RC .25 .08
❑ 464 Joe Nolan .25 .08
❑ 465 Reggie Smith .75 .30
❑ 466 Mark Littell .25 .08
❑ 467 Don Kessinger DP .25 .08
❑ 468 Stan Bahnsen DP .15 .05
❑ 469 Lance Parrish 1.50 .60
❑ 470 Garry Maddox DP .25 .08
❑ 471 Joaquin Andujar .75 .30
❑ 472 Craig Kusick .25 .08
❑ 473 Dave Roberts .25 .08
❑ 474 Dick Davis RC .25 .08
❑ 475 Dan Driessen .25 .08
❑ 476 Tom Poquette .25 .08
❑ 477 Bob Grich .75 .30
❑ 478 Juan Beniquez .25 .08
❑ 479 San Diego Padres CL/Craig 1.50 .60
❑ 480 Fred Lynn .75 .30
❑ 481 Skip Lockwood .25 .08
❑ 482 Craig Reynolds .25 .08
❑ 483 Checklist 364-484 DP .75 .30
❑ 484 Rick Waits .25 .08
❑ 485 Bucky Dent .75 .30
❑ 486 Bob Knepper .25 .08
❑ 487 Miguel Dilone .25 .08
❑ 488 Bob Owchinko .25 .08
❑ 489 Larry Cox UER .25 .08
❑ 490 Al Cowens .75 .30
❑ 491 Tippy Martinez .25 .08
❑ 492 Bob Bailor .25 .08
❑ 493 Larry Christenson .25 .08
❑ 494 Jerry White .25 .08
❑ 495 Tony Perez 2.50 1.00
❑ 496 Barry Bonnell DP .15 .05
❑ 497 Glenn Abbott .25 .08
❑ 498 Rich Chiles .25 .08
❑ 499 Texas Rangers CL/Corrrales 1.50 .60
❑ 500 Ron Guidry .75 .30
❑ 501 Junior Kennedy RC .25 .08
❑ 502 Steve Braun .25 .08
❑ 503 Terry Humphrey .25 .08
❑ 504 Larry McWilliams RC .25 .08
❑ 505 Ed Kranepool .25 .08
❑ 506 John D'Acquisto .25 .08
❑ 507 Tony Armas .75 .30
❑ 508 Charlie Hough .75 .30
❑ 509 Mario Mendoza UER .25 .08
❑ 510 Ted Simmons 1.50 .60
❑ 511 Paul Reuschel DP .15 .05
❑ 512 Jack Clark .75 .30
❑ 513 Dave Johnson .75 .30
❑ 514 Mike Proly RC .25 .08
❑ 515 Enos Cabell .25 .08
❑ 516 Champ Summers DP .15 .05
❑ 517 Al Bumbry .75 .30
❑ 518 Jim Umbarger .25 .08
❑ 519 Ben Oglivie .75 .30
❑ 520 Gary Carter 1.50 .60
❑ 521 Sam Ewing .25 .08
❑ 522 Ken Holtzman .75 .30
❑ 523 John Milner .25 .08
❑ 524 Tom Burgmeier .25 .08
❑ 525 Freddie Patek .25 .08
❑ 526 Los Angeles Dodgers CL/Lasorda 1.50 .60
❑ 527 Lerrin LaGrow .25 .08
❑ 528 Wayne Gross DP .15 .05
❑ 529 Brian Asselstine .25 .08
❑ 530 Frank Tanana .75 .30
❑ 531 Fernando Gonzalez .25 .08
❑ 532 Buddy Schultz .25 .08
❑ 533 Leroy Stanton .25 .08
❑ 534 Ken Forsch .25 .08
❑ 535 Ellis Valentine .25 .08
❑ 536 Jerry Reuss .75 .30
❑ 537 Tom Veryzer .25 .08
❑ 538 Mike Ivie DP .15 .05
❑ 539 John Ellis .25 .08
❑ 540 Greg Luzinski .75 .30
❑ 541 Jim Slaton .25 .08
❑ 542 Rick Bosetti .25 .08
❑ 543 Kiko Garcia .25 .08
❑ 544 Fergie Jenkins 2.50 1.00
❑ 545 John Stearns .25 .08
❑ 546 Bill Russell .75 .30
❑ 547 Clint Hurdle .25 .08
❑ 548 Enrique Romo .25 .08
❑ 549 Bob Bailey .25 .08
❑ 550 Sal Bando .75 .30
❑ 551 Chicago Cubs CL/Franks 1.50 .60
❑ 552 Jose Morales .25 .08
❑ 553 Denny Walling .25 .08
❑ 554 Matt Keough .25 .08
❑ 555 Biff Pocoroba .25 .08
❑ 556 Mike Lum .25 .08
❑ 557 Ken Brett .25 .08
❑ 558 Jay Johnstone .75 .30
❑ 559 Greg Pryor RC .25 .08
❑ 560 John Montefusco .25 .08
❑ 561 Ed Ott .25 .08
❑ 562 Dusty Baker 1.50 .60
❑ 563 Roy Thomas .25 .08
❑ 564 Jerry Turner .25 .08
❑ 565 Rico Carty .75 .30
❑ 566 Nino Espinosa .25 .08
❑ 567 Richie Hebner .75 .30
❑ 568 Carlos Lopez .25 .08
❑ 569 Bob Sykes .25 .08
❑ 570 Cesar Cedeno .75 .30
❑ 571 Darrell Porter .75 .30
❑ 572 Rod Gilbreath .25 .08
❑ 573 Jim Kern .25 .08
❑ 574 Claudell Washington .75 .30
❑ 575 Luis Tiant .75 .30
❑ 576 Mike Parrott RC .25 .08
❑ 577 Milwaukee Brewers CL/Bamberger 1.50 .60
❑ 578 Pete Broberg .25 .08
❑ 579 Greg Gross .25 .08
❑ 580 Ron Fairly .75 .30
❑ 581 Darold Knowles .25 .08
❑ 582 Paul Blair .75 .30
❑ 583 Julio Cruz .25 .08
❑ 584 Jim Rooker .25 .08
❑ 585 Hal McRae 1.50 .60
❑ 586 Bob Horner RC 1.50 .60
❑ 587 Ken Reitz .25 .08
❑ 588 Tom Murphy .25 .08
❑ 589 Terry Whitfield .25 .08
❑ 590 J.R. Richard .75 .30
❑ 591 Mike Hargrove .75 .30
❑ 592 Mike Krukow .25 .08
❑ 593 Rick Dempsey .75 .30
❑ 594 Bob Shirley .25 .08
❑ 595 Phil Niekro 2.50 1.00
❑ 596 Jim Wohlford .25 .08
❑ 597 Bob Stanley .25 .08
❑ 598 Mark Wagner .25 .08
❑ 599 Jim Spencer .25 .08
❑ 600 George Foster .75 .30
❑ 601 Dave LaRoche .25 .08
❑ 602 Checklist 485-605 1.50 .60
❑ 603 Rudy May .25 .08
❑ 604 Jeff Newman .25 .08
❑ 605 Rick Monday DP .25 .08
❑ 606 Montreal Expos CL/Williams 1.50 .60
❑ 607 Omar Moreno .25 .08
❑ 608 Dave McKay .25 .08
❑ 609 Silvio Martinez RC .25 .08
❑ 610 Mike Schmidt 8.00 3.00
❑ 611 Jim Norris .25 .08
❑ 612 Rick Honeycutt RC .75 .30
❑ 613 Mike Edwards RC .25 .08
❑ 614 Willie Hernandez .75 .30
❑ 615 Ken Singleton .75 .30
❑ 616 Billy Almon .25 .08
❑ 617 Terry Puhl .25 .08
❑ 618 Jerry Remy .25 .08
❑ 619 Ken Landreaux RC .75 .30
❑ 620 Bert Campaneris .75 .30
❑ 621 Pat Zachry .25 .08
❑ 622 Dave Collins .75 .30
❑ 623 Bob McClure .25 .08
❑ 624 Larry Herndon .25 .08
❑ 625 Mark Fidrych 2.50 1.00
❑ 626 New York Yankees CL/Lemon 1.50 .60
❑ 627 Gary Serum RC .25 .08
❑ 628 Del Unser .25 .08
❑ 629 Gene Garber .75 .30
❑ 630 Bake McBride .75 .30
❑ 631 Jorge Orta .25 .08
❑ 632 Don Kirkwood .25 .08
❑ 633 Rob Wilfong DP RC .15 .05
❑ 634 Paul Lindblad .25 .08
❑ 635 Don Baylor 1.50 .60
❑ 636 Wayne Garland .25 .08
❑ 637 Bill Robinson .75 .30
❑ 638 Al Fitzmorris .25 .08
❑ 639 Manny Trillo .25 .08
❑ 640 Eddie Murray 12.00 5.00
❑ 641 Bobby Castillo RC .25 .08
❑ 642 Wilbur Howard DP .15 .05
❑ 643 Tom Hausman .25 .08
❑ 644 Manny Mota .75 .30
❑ 645 George Scott DP .25 .08
❑ 646 Rick Sweet .25 .08
❑ 647 Bob Lacey .25 .08
❑ 648 Lou Piniella .75 .30
❑ 649 John Curtis .25 .08
❑ 650 Pete Rose 12.00 5.00
❑ 651 Mike Caldwell .25 .08
❑ 652 Stan Papi RC .25 .08
❑ 653 Warren Brusstar DP .15 .05
❑ 654 Rick Miller .25 .08
❑ 655 Jerry Koosman .75 .30
❑ 656 Hosken Powell RC .25 .08
❑ 657 George Medich .25 .08
❑ 658 Taylor Duncan RC .25 .08
❑ 659 Seattle Mariners CL/Johnson 1.50 .60
❑ 660 Ron LeFlore DP .25 .08
❑ 661 Bruce Kison .25 .08
❑ 662 Kevin Bell .25 .08
❑ 663 Mike Vail .25 .08
❑ 664 Doug Bird .25 .08
❑ 665 Lou Brock 2.50 1.00
❑ 666 Rich Dauer .25 .08
❑ 667 Don Hood .25 .08
❑ 668 Bill North .25 .08
❑ 669 Checklist 606-726 1.50 .60
❑ 670 Jim Hunter DP 1.50 .60
❑ 671 Joe Ferguson DP .15 .05
❑ 672 Ed Halicki .25 .08

❑ 673 Tom Hutton .25 .08
❑ 674 Dave Tomlin .25 .08
❑ 675 Tim McCarver 1.50 .60
❑ 676 Johnny Sutton RC .25 .08
❑ 677 Larry Parrish .75 .30
❑ 678 Geoff Zahn .25 .08
❑ 679 Derrel Thomas .25 .08
❑ 680 Carlton Fisk 3.00 1.25
❑ 681 John Henry Johnson RC .25 .08
❑ 682 Dave Chalk .25 .08
❑ 683 Dan Meyer DP .15 .05
❑ 684 Jamie Easterly DP .15 .05
❑ 685 Sixto Lezcano .25 .08
❑ 686 Ron Schueler DP .15 .05
❑ 687 Rennie Stennett .25 .08
❑ 688 Mike Willis .25 .08
❑ 689 Baltimore Orioles CL/Weaver 1.50 .60
❑ 690 Buddy Bell DP .25 .08
❑ 691 Dock Ellis DP .15 .05
❑ 692 Mickey Stanley .25 .08
❑ 693 Dave Rader .25 .08
❑ 694 Burt Hooton .75 .30
❑ 695 Keith Hernandez .75 .30
❑ 696 Andy Hassler .25 .08
❑ 697 Dave Bergman .25 .08
❑ 698 Bill Stein .25 .08
❑ 699 Hal Dues RC .25 .08
❑ 700 Reggie Jackson DP 5.00 2.00
❑ 701 Corey/Flinn/Stewart RC .75 .30
❑ 702 Finch/Hancock/Ripley RC .75 .30
❑ 703 Anderson/Frost/Slater RC .75 .30
❑ 704 Baumgarten/Colbern/Squires RC .75 .30
❑ 705 Griffin/Norrid/Oliver RC 1.50 .60
❑ 706 Stegman/Tobik/Young RC .75 .30
❑ 707 Bass/Gaudet/McGilberry RC 1.50 .60
❑ 708 Bass/Romero/Yost RC 1.50 .60
❑ 709 Perlozzo/Sofield/Stanfield RC .75 .30
❑ 710 Doyle/Heath/Rajisch RC .75 .30
❑ 711 Murphy/Robinson/Wirth RC 1.50 .60
❑ 712 Anderson/Biercevicz/McLaughlin RC .75 .30
❑ 713 Darwin/Putnam/Sample RC 1.50 .60
❑ 714 Cruz/Kelly/Whitt RC .75 .30
❑ 715 Benedict/Hubbard/Whisenton RC 1.50 .60
❑ 716 Geisel/Pagel/Thompson RC .75 .30
❑ 717 LaCoss/Oester/Spilman RC .75 .30
❑ 718 Bochy/Fischlin/Pisker RC .75 .30
❑ 719 Guerrero/Law/Simpson RC 1.50 .60
❑ 720 Fry/Pirtle/Sanderson RC 1.50 .60
❑ 721 Berenguer/Bernard/Norman RC .75 .30
❑ 722 Morrison/Smith/Wright RC 1.50 .60
❑ 723 Berra/Cotes/Wiltbank RC .75 .30
❑ 724 Bruno/Frazier/Kennedy RC 1.50 .60
❑ 725 Beswick/Mura/Perkins RC .75 .30
❑ 726 Johnston/Strain/Tamargo RC .75 .30

1980 Topps

❑ COMPLETE SET (726) 120.00 70.00
❑ COMMON CARD (1-726) .25 .08
❑ COMMON DP .25 .08
❑ 1 L.Brock/C.Yastrzemski HL 2.50 1.00
❑ 2 Willie McCovey HL .75 .30
❑ 3 Manny Mota HL .25 .08
❑ 4 Pete Rose HL 3.00 1.25
❑ 5 Garry Templeton HL .25 .08
❑ 6 Del Unser HL .25 .08
❑ 7 Mike Lum .25 .08
❑ 8 Craig Swan .25 .08
❑ 9 Steve Braun .25 .08
❑ 10 Dennis Martinez .75 .30
❑ 11 Jimmy Sexton .25 .08
❑ 12 John Curtis DP .25 .08
❑ 13 Ron Pruitt .25 .08
❑ 14 Dave Cash .75 .30
❑ 15 Bill Campbell .25 .08
❑ 16 Jerry Narron RC .25 .08
❑ 17 Bruce Sutter 1.50 .60
❑ 18 Ron Jackson .25 .08
❑ 19 Balor Moore .25 .08
❑ 20 Dan Ford .25 .08
❑ 21 Manny Sarmiento .25 .08
❑ 22 Pat Putnam .25 .08
❑ 23 Derrel Thomas .25 .08
❑ 24 Jim Slaton .25 .08
❑ 25 Lee Mazzilli .75 .30
❑ 26 Marty Pattin .25 .08
❑ 27 Del Unser .25 .08
❑ 28 Bruce Kison .25 .08
❑ 29 Mark Wagner .25 .08
❑ 30 Vida Blue .75 .30
❑ 31 Jay Johnstone .25 .08
❑ 32 Julio Cruz DP .25 .08
❑ 33 Tony Scott .25 .08
❑ 34 Jeff Newman DP .25 .08
❑ 35 Luis Tiant .75 .30
❑ 36 Rusty Torres .25 .08
❑ 37 Kiko Garcia .25 .08
❑ 38 Dan Spillner DP .25 .08
❑ 39 Rowland Office .25 .08
❑ 40 Carlton Fisk 2.50 1.00
❑ 41 Texas Rangers CL/Corrrales .75 .30
❑ 42 David Palmer RC .25 .08
❑ 43 Bombo Rivera .25 .08
❑ 44 Bill Fahey .25 .08
❑ 45 Frank White .75 .30
❑ 46 Rico Carty .75 .30
❑ 47 Bill Bonham DP .25 .08
❑ 48 Rick Miller .25 .08
❑ 49 Mario Guerrero .25 .08
❑ 50 J.R. Richard .75 .30
❑ 51 Joe Ferguson DP .25 .08
❑ 52 Warren Brusstar .25 .08
❑ 53 Ben Oglivie .75 .30
❑ 54 Dennis Lamp .25 .08
❑ 55 Bill Madlock .75 .30
❑ 56 Bobby Valentine .75 .30
❑ 57 Pete Vuckovich .25 .08
❑ 58 Doug Flynn .25 .08
❑ 59 Eddy Putman RC .25 .08
❑ 60 Bucky Dent .75 .30
❑ 61 Gary Serum .25 .08
❑ 62 Mike Ivie .25 .08
❑ 63 Bob Stanley .25 .08
❑ 64 Joe Nolan .25 .08
❑ 65 Al Bumbry .75 .30
❑ 66 Kansas City Royals CL/Frey .75 .30
❑ 67 Doyle Alexander .25 .08
❑ 68 Larry Harlow .25 .08
❑ 69 Rick Williams .25 .08
❑ 70 Gary Carter 1.50 .60
❑ 71 John Milner DP .25 .08
❑ 72 Fred Howard DP RC .25 .08
❑ 73 Dave Collins .25 .08
❑ 74 Sid Monge .25 .08
❑ 75 Bill Russell .75 .30
❑ 76 John Stearns .25 .08
❑ 77 Dave Stieb RC 1.50 .60
❑ 78 Ruppert Jones .25 .08
❑ 79 Bob Owchinko .25 .08
❑ 80 Ron LeFlore .75 .30
❑ 81 Ted Sizemore .25 .08
❑ 82 Houston Astros CL/Virdon .75 .30
❑ 83 Steve Trout RC .25 .08
❑ 84 Gary Lavelle .25 .08
❑ 85 Ted Simmons .75 .30
❑ 86 Dave Hamilton .25 .08
❑ 87 Pepe Frias .25 .08
❑ 88 Ken Landreaux .25 .08
❑ 89 Don Hood .25 .08
❑ 90 Manny Trillo .75 .30
❑ 91 Rick Dempsey .75 .30
❑ 92 Rick Rhoden .25 .08
❑ 93 Dave Roberts DP .25 .08
❑ 94 Neil Allen RC .25 .08
❑ 95 Cecil Cooper .75 .30
❑ 96 Oakland Athletics CL/Marshall .75 .30
❑ 97 Bill Lee .75 .30
❑ 98 Jerry Terrell .25 .08
❑ 99 Victor Cruz .25 .08
❑ 100 Johnny Bench 3.00 1.25
❑ 101 Aurelio Lopez .25 .08
❑ 102 Rich Dauer .25 .08
❑ 103 Bill Caudill RC .25 .08
❑ 104 Manny Mota .75 .30
❑ 105 Frank Tanana .75 .30
❑ 106 Jeff Leonard RC 1.50 .60
❑ 107 Francisco Barrios .25 .08
❑ 108 Bob Horner .75 .30
❑ 109 Bill Travers .25 .08
❑ 110 Fred Lynn DP .50 .20
❑ 111 Bob Knepper .25 .08
❑ 112 Chicago White Sox CL/LaRussa .75 .30
❑ 113 Geoff Zahn .25 .08
❑ 114 Juan Beniquez .25 .08
❑ 115 Sparky Lyle .75 .30
❑ 116 Larry Cox .25 .08
❑ 117 Dock Ellis .75 .30
❑ 118 Phil Garner .75 .30
❑ 119 Sammy Stewart .25 .08
❑ 120 Greg Luzinski .75 .30
❑ 121 Checklist 1-121 .75 .30
❑ 122 Dave Rosello DP .25 .08
❑ 123 Lynn Jones RC .25 .08
❑ 124 Dave Lemanczyk .25 .08
❑ 125 Tony Perez .75 .30
❑ 126 Dave Tomlin .25 .08
❑ 127 Gary Thomasson .25 .08
❑ 128 Tom Burgmeier .25 .08
❑ 129 Craig Reynolds .25 .08
❑ 130 Amos Otis .75 .30
❑ 131 Paul Mitchell .25 .08
❑ 132 Biff Pocoroba .25 .08
❑ 133 Jerry Turner .25 .08
❑ 134 Matt Keough .25 .08
❑ 135 Bill Buckner .75 .30
❑ 136 Dick Ruthven .25 .08
❑ 137 John Castino RC .25 .08
❑ 138 Ross Baumgarten .25 .08
❑ 139 Dane Iorg RC .25 .08
❑ 140 Rich Gossage .75 .30
❑ 141 Gary Alexander .25 .08
❑ 142 Phil Huffman RC .25 .08
❑ 143 Bruce Bochte DP .25 .08
❑ 144 Steve Comer .25 .08
❑ 145 Darrell Evans .75 .30
❑ 146 Bob Welch .75 .30
❑ 147 Terry Puhl .25 .08
❑ 148 Manny Sanguillen .75 .30
❑ 149 Tom Hume .25 .08
❑ 150 Jason Thompson .25 .08
❑ 151 Tom Hausman DP .25 .08
❑ 152 John Fulgham RC .25 .08
❑ 153 Tim Blackwell .25 .08
❑ 154 Lary Sorensen .25 .08
❑ 155 Jerry Remy .25 .08
❑ 156 Tony Brizzolara RC .25 .08
❑ 157 Willie Wilson DP .50 .20
❑ 158 Rob Picciolo DP .25 .08
❑ 159 Ken Clay .25 .08
❑ 160 Eddie Murray 5.00 2.00
❑ 161 Larry Christenson .25 .08
❑ 162 Bob Randall .25 .08
❑ 163 Steve Swisher .25 .08
❑ 164 Greg Pryor .25 .08
❑ 165 Omar Moreno .25 .08
❑ 166 Glenn Abbott .25 .08
❑ 167 Jack Clark .75 .30
❑ 168 Rick Waits .25 .08
❑ 169 Luis Gomez .25 .08
❑ 170 Burt Hooton .75 .30
❑ 171 Fernando Gonzalez .25 .08
❑ 172 Ron Hodges .25 .08
❑ 173 John Henry Johnson .25 .08
❑ 174 Ray Knight .75 .30
❑ 175 Rick Reuschel .75 .30
❑ 176 Champ Summers .25 .08
❑ 177 Dave Heaverlo .25 .08
❑ 178 Tim McCarver .75 .30
❑ 179 Ron Davis RC .25 .08
❑ 180 Warren Cromartie .25 .08
❑ 181 Moose Haas .25 .08

❑ 182 Ken Reitz .25 .08
❑ 183 Jim Anderson DP .25 .08
❑ 184 Steve Renko DP .25 .08
❑ 185 Hal McRae .75 .30
❑ 186 Junior Moore .25 .08
❑ 187 Alan Ashby .25 .08
❑ 188 Terry Crowley .25 .08
❑ 189 Kevin Kobel .25 .08
❑ 190 Buddy Bell .75 .30
❑ 191 Ted Martinez .25 .08
❑ 192 Atlanta Braves CL/Cox .75 .30
❑ 193 Dave Goltz .25 .08
❑ 194 Mike Easler .25 .08
❑ 195 John Montefusco .75 .30
❑ 196 Lance Parrish .75 .30
❑ 197 Byron McLaughlin .25 .08
❑ 198 Dell Alston DP .25 .08
❑ 199 Mike LaCoss .25 .08
❑ 200 Jim Rice .75 .30
❑ 201 K.Hernandez/F.Lynn LL .75 .30
❑ 202 D.Kingman/G.Thomas LL 1.50 .60
❑ 203 D.Winfield/D.Baylor LL 1.50 .60
❑ 204 O.Moreno/W.Wilson LL .75 .30
❑ 205 Niekro/Niekro/Flan LL .75 .30
❑ 206 J.Richard/N.Ryan LL 5.00 2.00
❑ 207 J.Richard/R.Guidry LL .75 .30
❑ 208 Wayne Cage .25 .08
❑ 209 Von Joshua .25 .08
❑ 210 Steve Carlton 1.50 .60
❑ 211 Dave Skaggs DP .25 .08
❑ 212 Dave Roberts .25 .08
❑ 213 Mike Jorgensen DP .25 .08
❑ 214 California Angels CL/Fregosi .75 .30
❑ 215 Sixto Lezcano .25 .08
❑ 216 Phil Mankowski .25 .08
❑ 217 Ed Halicki .25 .08
❑ 218 Jose Morales .25 .08
❑ 219 Steve Mingori .25 .08
❑ 220 Dave Concepcion .75 .30
❑ 221 Joe Cannon RC .25 .08
❑ 222 Ron Hassey RC .25 .08
❑ 223 Bob Sykes .25 .08
❑ 224 Willie Montanez .25 .08
❑ 225 Lou Piniella .75 .30
❑ 226 Bill Stein .25 .08
❑ 227 Len Barker .75 .30
❑ 228 Johnny Oates .75 .30
❑ 229 Jim Bibby .25 .08
❑ 230 Dave Winfield 1.50 .60
❑ 231 Steve McCatty .25 .08
❑ 232 Alan Trammell 1.50 .60
❑ 233 LaRue Washington RC .25 .08
❑ 234 Vern Ruhle .25 .08
❑ 235 Andre Dawson 1.50 .60
❑ 236 Marc Hill .25 .08
❑ 237 Scott McGregor .75 .30
❑ 238 Rob Wilfong .25 .08
❑ 239 Don Aase .25 .08
❑ 240 Dave Kingman .75 .30
❑ 241 Checklist 122-242 .75 .30
❑ 242 Lamar Johnson .25 .08
❑ 243 Jerry Augustine .25 .08
❑ 244 St. Louis Cardinals CL/Boyer .75 .30
❑ 245 Phil Niekro .75 .30
❑ 246 Tim Foli DP .25 .08
❑ 247 Frank Riccelli .25 .08
❑ 248 Jamie Quirk .25 .08
❑ 249 Jim Clancy .25 .08
❑ 250 Jim Kaat .75 .30
❑ 251 Kip Young .25 .08
❑ 252 Ted Cox .25 .08
❑ 253 John Montague .25 .08
❑ 254 Paul Dade DP .25 .08
❑ 255 Dusty Baker DP .50 .20
❑ 256 Roger Erickson .25 .08
❑ 257 Larry Herndon .25 .08
❑ 258 Paul Moskau .25 .08
❑ 259 New York Mets CL/Torre 1.50 .60
❑ 260 Al Oliver .75 .30
❑ 261 Dave Chalk .25 .08
❑ 262 Benny Ayala .25 .08
❑ 263 Dave LaRoche DP .25 .08
❑ 264 Bill Robinson .25 .08
❑ 265 Robin Yount 3.00 1.25
❑ 266 Bernie Carbo .25 .08
❑ 267 Dan Schatzeder .25 .08
❑ 268 Rafael Landestoy .25 .08
❑ 269 Dave Tobik .25 .08
❑ 270 Mike Schmidt DP 3.00 1.25
❑ 271 Dick Drago DP .25 .08
❑ 272 Ralph Garr .75 .30
❑ 273 Eduardo Rodriguez .25 .08
❑ 274 Dale Murphy 2.50 1.00
❑ 275 Jerry Koosman .75 .30
❑ 276 Tom Veryzer .25 .08
❑ 277 Rick Bosetti .25 .08
❑ 278 Jim Spencer .25 .08
❑ 279 Rob Andrews .25 .08
❑ 280 Gaylord Perry .75 .30
❑ 281 Paul Blair .75 .30
❑ 282 Seattle Mariners CL/Johnson .75 .30
❑ 283 John Ellis .25 .08
❑ 284 Larry Murray DP RC .25 .08
❑ 285 Don Baylor .75 .30
❑ 286 Darold Knowles DP .25 .08
❑ 287 John Lowenstein .25 .08
❑ 288 Dave Rozema .25 .08
❑ 289 Bruce Bochy .25 .08
❑ 290 Steve Garvey 1.50 .60
❑ 291 Randy Scarberry RC .25 .08
❑ 292 Dale Berra .25 .08
❑ 293 Elias Sosa .25 .08
❑ 294 Charlie Spikes .25 .08
❑ 295 Larry Gura .25 .08
❑ 296 Dave Rader .25 .08
❑ 297 Tim Johnson .25 .08
❑ 298 Ken Holtzman .75 .30
❑ 299 Steve Henderson .25 .08
❑ 300 Ron Guidry .75 .30
❑ 301 Mike Edwards .25 .08
❑ 302 Los Angeles Dodgers CL/Lasorda 1.50 .60
❑ 303 Bill Castro .25 .08
❑ 304 Butch Wynegar .25 .08
❑ 305 Randy Jones .75 .30
❑ 306 Denny Walling .25 .08
❑ 307 Rick Honeycutt .25 .08
❑ 308 Mike Hargrove .75 .30
❑ 309 Larry McWilliams .25 .08
❑ 310 Dave Parker .75 .30
❑ 311 Roger Metzger .25 .08
❑ 312 Mike Barlow .25 .08
❑ 313 Johnny Grubb .25 .08
❑ 314 Tim Stoddard RC .25 .08
❑ 315 Steve Kemp .75 .30
❑ 316 Bob Lacey .25 .08
❑ 317 Mike Anderson DP .25 .08
❑ 318 Jerry Reuss .75 .30
❑ 319 Chris Speier .25 .08
❑ 320 Dennis Eckersley 1.50 .60
❑ 321 Keith Hernandez .75 .30
❑ 322 Claudell Washington .25 .08
❑ 323 Mick Kelleher .25 .08
❑ 324 Tom Underwood .25 .08
❑ 325 Dan Driessen .25 .08
❑ 326 Bo McLaughlin .25 .08
❑ 327 Ray Fosse DP .50 .20
❑ 328 Minnesota Twins CL/Mauch .75 .30
❑ 329 Bert Roberge RC .25 .08
❑ 330 Al Cowens .75 .30
❑ 331 Richie Hebner .25 .08
❑ 332 Enrique Romo .25 .08
❑ 333 Jim Norris DP .25 .08
❑ 334 Jim Beattie .25 .08
❑ 335 Willie McCovey 1.50 .60
❑ 336 George Medich .25 .08
❑ 337 Carney Lansford .75 .30
❑ 338 John Wockenfuss .25 .08
❑ 339 John D'Acquisto .25 .08
❑ 340 Ken Singleton .75 .30
❑ 341 Jim Essian .25 .08
❑ 342 Odell Jones .25 .08
❑ 343 Mike Vail .25 .08
❑ 344 Randy Lerch .25 .08
❑ 345 Larry Parrish .75 .30
❑ 346 Buddy Solomon .25 .08
❑ 347 Harry Chappas RC .25 .08
❑ 348 Checklist 243-363 .75 .30
❑ 349 Jack Brohamer .25 .08
❑ 350 George Hendrick .75 .30
❑ 351 Bob Davis .25 .08
❑ 352 Dan Briggs .25 .08
❑ 353 Andy Hassler .25 .08
❑ 354 Rick Auerbach .25 .08
❑ 355 Gary Matthews .75 .30
❑ 356 San Diego Padres CL/Coleman .75 .30
❑ 357 Bob McClure .25 .08
❑ 358 Lou Whitaker .75 .30
❑ 359 Randy Moffitt .25 .08
❑ 360 Darrell Porter DP .50 .20
❑ 361 Wayne Garland .25 .08
❑ 362 Danny Goodwin .25 .08
❑ 363 Wayne Gross .25 .08
❑ 364 Ray Burris .25 .08
❑ 365 Bobby Murcer .75 .30
❑ 366 Rob Dressler .25 .08
❑ 367 Billy Smith .25 .08
❑ 368 Willie Aikens RC .25 .08
❑ 369 Jim Kern .25 .08
❑ 370 Cesar Cedeno .75 .30
❑ 371 Jack Morris .75 .30
❑ 372 Joel Youngblood .25 .08
❑ 373 Dan Petry DP RC .75 .30
❑ 374 Jim Gantner .75 .30
❑ 375 Ross Grimsley .25 .08
❑ 376 Gary Allenson RC .25 .08
❑ 377 Junior Kennedy .25 .08
❑ 378 Jerry Mumphrey .25 .08
❑ 379 Kevin Bell .25 .08
❑ 380 Garry Maddox .75 .30
❑ 381 Chicago Cubs CL/Gomez .75 .30
❑ 382 Dave Freisleben .25 .08
❑ 383 Ed Ott .25 .08
❑ 384 Joey McLaughlin RC .25 .08
❑ 385 Enos Cabell .25 .08
❑ 386 Darrell Jackson .25 .08
❑ 387A F.Stanley Yellow 2.00 .75
❑ 387B F.Stanley Red Name .25 .08
❑ 388 Mike Paxton .25 .08
❑ 389 Pete LaCock .25 .08
❑ 390 Fergie Jenkins .75 .30
❑ 391 Tony Armas DP .50 .20
❑ 392 Milt Wilcox .25 .08
❑ 393 Ozzie Smith 10.00 4.00
❑ 394 Reggie Cleveland .25 .08
❑ 395 Ellis Valentine .25 .08
❑ 396 Dan Meyer .25 .08
❑ 397 Roy Thomas DP .25 .08
❑ 398 Barry Foote .25 .08
❑ 399 Mike Proly DP .25 .08
❑ 400 George Foster .75 .30
❑ 401 Pete Falcone .25 .08
❑ 402 Merv Rettenmund .25 .08
❑ 403 Pete Redfern DP .25 .08
❑ 404 Baltimore Orioles CL/Weaver .75 .30
❑ 405 Dwight Evans 1.50 .60
❑ 406 Paul Molitor 4.00 1.50
❑ 407 Tony Solaita .25 .08
❑ 408 Bill North .25 .08
❑ 409 Paul Splittorff .25 .08
❑ 410 Bobby Bonds .75 .30
❑ 411 Frank LaCorte .25 .08
❑ 412 Thad Bosley .25 .08
❑ 413 Allen Ripley .25 .08
❑ 414 George Scott .75 .30
❑ 415 Bill Atkinson .25 .08
❑ 416 Tom Brookens RC .25 .08
❑ 417 Craig Chamberlain DP RC .25 .08
❑ 418 Roger Freed DP .25 .08
❑ 419 Vic Correll .25 .08
❑ 420 Butch Hobson .25 .08
❑ 421 Doug Bird .25 .08
❑ 422 Larry Milbourne .25 .08
❑ 423 Dave Frost .25 .08
❑ 424 New York Yankees CL/Howser .75 .30
❑ 424A New York Yankees CL/Martin
❑ 425 Mark Belanger .75 .30
❑ 426 Grant Jackson .25 .08
❑ 427 Tom Hutton DP .25 .08
❑ 428 Pat Zachry .25 .08
❑ 429 Duane Kuiper .25 .08
❑ 430 Larry Hisle DP .25 .08
❑ 431 Mike Krukow .25 .08
❑ 432 Willie Norwood .25 .08
❑ 433 Rich Gale .25 .08
❑ 434 Johnnie LeMaster .25 .08
❑ 435 Don Gullett .75 .30
❑ 436 Billy Almon .25 .08
❑ 437 Joe Niekro .75 .30

- ❑ 438 Dave Revering .25 .08
- ❑ 439 Mike Phillips .25 .08
- ❑ 440 Don Sutton .75 .30
- ❑ 441 Eric Soderholm .25 .08
- ❑ 442 Jorge Orta .25 .08
- ❑ 443 Mike Parrott .25 .08
- ❑ 444 Alvis Woods .25 .08
- ❑ 445 Mark Fidrych .75 .30
- ❑ 446 Duffy Dyer .25 .08
- ❑ 447 Nino Espinosa .25 .08
- ❑ 448 Jim Wohlford .25 .08
- ❑ 449 Doug Bair .25 .08
- ❑ 450 George Brett 8.00 3.00
- ❑ 451 Cleveland Indians CL/Garcia .75 .30
- ❑ 452 Steve Dillard .25 .08
- ❑ 453 Mike Bacsik .25 .08
- ❑ 454 Tom Donohue RC .25 .08
- ❑ 455 Mike Torrez .75 .30
- ❑ 456 Frank Taveras .25 .08
- ❑ 457 Bert Blyleven .75 .30
- ❑ 458 Billy Sample .25 .08
- ❑ 459 Mickey Lolich DP .50 .20
- ❑ 460 Willie Randolph .75 .30
- ❑ 461 Dwayne Murphy .25 .08
- ❑ 462 Mike Sadek DP .25 .08
- ❑ 463 Jerry Royster .25 .08
- ❑ 464 John Denny .75 .30
- ❑ 465 Rick Monday .75 .30
- ❑ 466 Mike Squires .25 .08
- ❑ 467 Jesse Jefferson .25 .08
- ❑ 468 Aurelio Rodriguez .25 .08
- ❑ 469 Randy Niemann DP RC .25 .08
- ❑ 470 Bob Boone .75 .30
- ❑ 471 Hosken Powell DP .25 .08
- ❑ 472 Willie Hernandez .75 .30
- ❑ 473 Bump Wills .25 .08
- ❑ 474 Steve Busby .25 .08
- ❑ 475 Cesar Geronimo .75 .30
- ❑ 476 Bob Shirley .25 .08
- ❑ 477 Buck Martinez .25 .08
- ❑ 478 Gil Flores .25 .08
- ❑ 479 Montreal Expos CL/Williams .75 .30
- ❑ 480 Bob Watson .75 .30
- ❑ 481 Tom Paciorek .75 .30
- ❑ 482 Rickey Henderson RC 50.00 20.00
- ❑ 483 Bo Diaz .25 .08
- ❑ 484 Checklist 364-484 .75 .30
- ❑ 485 Mickey Rivers .75 .30
- ❑ 486 Mike Tyson DP .25 .08
- ❑ 487 Wayne Nordhagen .25 .08
- ❑ 488 Roy Howell .25 .08
- ❑ 489 Preston Hanna DP .25 .08
- ❑ 490 Lee May .75 .30
- ❑ 491 Steve Mura DP .25 .08
- ❑ 492 Todd Cruz RC .25 .08
- ❑ 493 Jerry Martin .25 .08
- ❑ 494 Craig Minetto RC .25 .08
- ❑ 495 Bake McBride .75 .30
- ❑ 496 Silvio Martinez .25 .08
- ❑ 497 Jim Mason .25 .08
- ❑ 498 Danny Darwin .25 .08
- ❑ 499 San Francisco Giants CL/Bristol .75 .30
- ❑ 500 Tom Seaver 3.00 1.25
- ❑ 501 Rennie Stennett .25 .08
- ❑ 502 Rich Wortham DP RC .25 .08
- ❑ 503 Mike Cubbage .25 .08
- ❑ 504 Gene Garber .25 .08
- ❑ 505 Bert Campaneris .75 .30
- ❑ 506 Tom Buskey .25 .08
- ❑ 507 Leon Roberts .25 .08
- ❑ 508 U.L. Washington .25 .08
- ❑ 509 Ed Glynn .25 .08
- ❑ 510 Ron Cey .75 .30
- ❑ 511 Eric Wilkins RC .25 .08
- ❑ 512 Jose Cardenal .25 .08
- ❑ 513 Tom Dixon DP .25 .08
- ❑ 514 Steve Ontiveros .25 .08
- ❑ 515 Mike Caldwell UER .25 .08
- ❑ 516 Hector Cruz .25 .08
- ❑ 517 Don Stanhouse .25 .08
- ❑ 518 Nelson Norman RC .25 .08
- ❑ 519 Steve Nicosia RC .25 .08
- ❑ 520 Steve Rogers .75 .30
- ❑ 521 Ken Brett .25 .08
- ❑ 522 Jim Morrison .25 .08
- ❑ 523 Ken Henderson .25 .08
- ❑ 524 Jim Wright DP .25 .08
- ❑ 525 Clint Hurdle .25 .08
- ❑ 526 Philadelphia Phillies CL/Green .75 .30
- ❑ 527 Doug Rau DP .25 .08
- ❑ 528 Adrian Devine .25 .08
- ❑ 529 Jim Barr .25 .08
- ❑ 530 Jim Sundberg DP .50 .20
- ❑ 531 Eric Rasmussen .25 .08
- ❑ 532 Willie Horton .75 .30
- ❑ 533 Checklist 485-605 .75 .30
- ❑ 534 Andre Thornton .75 .30
- ❑ 535 Bob Forsch .25 .08
- ❑ 536 Lee Lacy .25 .08
- ❑ 537 Alex Trevino RC .25 .08
- ❑ 538 Joe Strain .25 .08
- ❑ 539 Rudy May .25 .08
- ❑ 540 Pete Rose 8.00 3.00
- ❑ 541 Miguel Dilone .25 .08
- ❑ 542 Joe Coleman .25 .08
- ❑ 543 Pat Kelly .25 .08
- ❑ 544 Rick Sutcliffe RC 1.50 .60
- ❑ 545 Jeff Burroughs .75 .30
- ❑ 546 Rick Langford .25 .08
- ❑ 547 John Wathan .25 .08
- ❑ 548 Dave Rajsich .25 .08
- ❑ 549 Larry Wolfe .25 .08
- ❑ 550 Ken Griffey Sr. .75 .30
- ❑ 551 Pittsburgh Pirates CL/Tanner .75 .30
- ❑ 552 Bill Nahorodny .25 .08
- ❑ 553 Dick Davis .25 .08
- ❑ 554 Art Howe .75 .30
- ❑ 555 Ed Figueroa .25 .08
- ❑ 556 Joe Rudi .75 .30
- ❑ 557 Mark Lee .25 .08
- ❑ 558 Alfredo Griffin .25 .08
- ❑ 559 Dale Murray .25 .08
- ❑ 560 Dave Lopes .75 .30
- ❑ 561 Eddie Whitson .25 .08
- ❑ 562 Joe Wallis .25 .08
- ❑ 563 Will McEnaney .25 .08
- ❑ 564 Rick Manning .25 .08
- ❑ 565 Dennis Leonard .25 .08
- ❑ 566 Bud Harrelson .75 .30
- ❑ 567 Skip Lockwood .25 .08
- ❑ 568 Gary Roenicke RC .25 .08
- ❑ 569 Terry Kennedy .25 .08
- ❑ 570 Roy Smalley .75 .30
- ❑ 571 Joe Sambito .25 .08
- ❑ 572 Jerry Morales DP .25 .08
- ❑ 573 Kent Tekulve .75 .30
- ❑ 574 Scot Thompson .25 .08
- ❑ 575 Ken Kravec .25 .08
- ❑ 576 Jim Dwyer .25 .08
- ❑ 577 Toronto Blue Jays CL/Matlick .75 .30
- ❑ 578 Scott Sanderson .25 .08
- ❑ 579 Charlie Moore .25 .08
- ❑ 580 Nolan Ryan 15.00 6.00
- ❑ 581 Bob Bailor .25 .08
- ❑ 582 Brian Doyle .25 .08
- ❑ 583 Bob Stinson .25 .08
- ❑ 584 Kurt Bevacqua .25 .08
- ❑ 585 Al Hrabosky .75 .30
- ❑ 586 Mitchell Page .25 .08
- ❑ 587 Garry Templeton .75 .30
- ❑ 588 Greg Minton .25 .08
- ❑ 589 Chet Lemon .75 .30
- ❑ 590 Jim Palmer 1.50 .60
- ❑ 591 Rick Cerone .25 .08
- ❑ 592 Jon Matlack .75 .30
- ❑ 593 Jesus Alou .25 .08
- ❑ 594 Dick Tidrow .25 .08
- ❑ 595 Don Money .25 .08
- ❑ 596 Rick Matula RC .25 .08
- ❑ 597 Tom Poquette .25 .08
- ❑ 598 Fred Kendall DP .25 .08
- ❑ 599 Mike Norris .25 .08
- ❑ 600 Reggie Jackson 3.00 1.25
- ❑ 601 Buddy Schultz .25 .08
- ❑ 602 Brian Downing .75 .30
- ❑ 603 Jack Billingham DP .25 .08
- ❑ 604 Glenn Adams .25 .08
- ❑ 605 Terry Forster .75 .30
- ❑ 606 Cincinnati Reds CL/McNamara .75 .30
- ❑ 607 Woodie Fryman .25 .08
- ❑ 608 Alan Bannister .25 .08
- ❑ 609 Ron Reed .25 .08
- ❑ 610 Willie Stargell 1.50 .60
- ❑ 611 Jerry Garvin DP .25 .08
- ❑ 612 Cliff Johnson .25 .08
- ❑ 613 Randy Stein .25 .08
- ❑ 614 John Hiller .25 .08
- ❑ 615 Doug DeCinces .75 .30
- ❑ 616 Gene Richards .25 .08
- ❑ 617 Joaquin Andujar .75 .30
- ❑ 618 Bob Montgomery DP .25 .08
- ❑ 619 Sergio Ferrer .25 .08
- ❑ 620 Richie Zisk .75 .30
- ❑ 621 Bob Grich .75 .30
- ❑ 622 Mario Soto .75 .30
- ❑ 623 Gorman Thomas .75 .30
- ❑ 624 Lerrin LaGrow .25 .08
- ❑ 625 Chris Chambliss .75 .30
- ❑ 626 Detroit Tigers CL/Anderson .75 .30
- ❑ 627 Pedro Borbon .25 .08
- ❑ 628 Doug Capilla .25 .08
- ❑ 629 Jim Todd .25 .08
- ❑ 630 Larry Bowa .75 .30
- ❑ 631 Mark Littell .25 .08
- ❑ 632 Barry Bonnell .25 .08
- ❑ 633 Bob Apodaca .25 .08
- ❑ 634 Glenn Borgmann DP .25 .08
- ❑ 635 John Candelaria .75 .30
- ❑ 636 Toby Harrah .75 .30
- ❑ 637 Joe Simpson .25 .08
- ❑ 638 Mark Clear RC .25 .08
- ❑ 639 Larry Biittner .25 .08
- ❑ 640 Mike Flanagan .75 .30
- ❑ 641 Ed Kranepool .75 .30
- ❑ 642 Ken Forsch DP .25 .08
- ❑ 643 John Mayberry .75 .30
- ❑ 644 Charlie Hough .75 .30
- ❑ 645 Rick Burleson .75 .30
- ❑ 646 Checklist 606-726 .75 .30
- ❑ 647 Milt May .25 .08
- ❑ 648 Roy White .75 .30
- ❑ 649 Tom Griffin .25 .08
- ❑ 650 Joe Morgan 1.50 .60
- ❑ 651 Rollie Fingers .75 .30
- ❑ 652 Mario Mendoza .25 .08
- ❑ 653 Stan Bahnsen .25 .08
- ❑ 654 Bruce Boisclair DP .25 .08
- ❑ 655 Tug McGraw .75 .30
- ❑ 656 Larvell Blanks .25 .08
- ❑ 657 Dave Edwards RC .25 .08
- ❑ 658 Chris Knapp .25 .08
- ❑ 659 Milwaukee Brewers CL/Bamberger .75 .30
- ❑ 660 Rusty Staub .75 .30
- ❑ 661 Corey/Ford/Krenchiki RC .25 .08
- ❑ 662 Finch/O'Berry/Rainey RC .25 .08
- ❑ 663 Botting/Clark/Thon RC .75 .30
- ❑ 664 Colbern/Hoffman/Robinson RC .25 .08
- ❑ 665 Andersen/Cuellar/Wihtol RC .25 .08
- ❑ 666 Chris/Greene/Robbins RC .25 .08
- ❑ 667 Mart/Pasch/Quisenberry RC .75 .30
- ❑ 668 Boitano/Mueller/Sakata RC .25 .08
- ❑ 669 Graham/Sofield/Ward RC .75 .30
- ❑ 670 Brown/Gulden/Jones RC .25 .08
- ❑ 671 Bryant/Kingman/Morgan RC .75 .30
- ❑ 672 Beamon/Craig/Vasquez RC .25 .08
- ❑ 673 Allard/Gleaton/Mahlberg RC .25 .08
- ❑ 674 Edge/Kelly/Wilborn RC .25 .08
- ❑ 675 Benedict/Bradford/Miller RC .25 .08
- ❑ 676 Geisel/Macko/Pagel RC .25 .08
- ❑ 677 DeFreites/Pastore/Spilman RC .25 .08
- ❑ 678 Baldwin/Knicely/Ladd RC .25 .08
- ❑ 679 Beckwith/Hatcher/Patterson RC .75 .30
- ❑ 680 Bernazard/Miller/Tamargo RC .25 .08
- ❑ 681 Norman/Orosco/Scott RC 1.50 .60
- ❑ 682 Aviles/Noles/Saucier RC .25 .08
- ❑ 683 Boyland/Lois/Saferight RC .25 .08
- ❑ 684 Frazier/Herr/O'Brien RC .75 .30
- ❑ 685 Flannery/Greer/Wilhelm RC .25 .08
- ❑ 686 Johnston/Littlejohn/Nastu RC .25 .08
- ❑ 687 Mike Heath DP .25 .08
- ❑ 688 Steve Stone .75 .30
- ❑ 689 Boston Red Sox CL/Zimmer .75 .30
- ❑ 690 Tommy John .75 .30
- ❑ 691 Ivan DeJesus .25 .08
- ❑ 692 Rawly Eastwick DP .50 .20
- ❑ 693 Craig Kusick .25 .08
- ❑ 694 Jim Rooker .25 .08
- ❑ 695 Reggie Smith .75 .30

❑ 696 Julio Gonzalez .25 .08
❑ 697 David Clyde .25 .08
❑ 698 Oscar Gamble .75 .30
❑ 699 Floyd Bannister .25 .08
❑ 700 Rod Carew DP .75 .30
❑ 701 Ken Oberkfell RC .25 .08
❑ 702 Ed Farmer .25 .08
❑ 703 Otto Velez .25 .08
❑ 704 Gene Tenace .75 .30
❑ 705 Freddie Patek .75 .30
❑ 706 Tippy Martinez .25 .08
❑ 707 Elliott Maddox .25 .08
❑ 708 Bob Tolan .25 .08
❑ 709 Pat Underwood RC .25 .08
❑ 710 Graig Nettles .75 .30
❑ 711 Bob Galasso RC .25 .08
❑ 712 Rodney Scott .25 .08
❑ 713 Terry Whitfield .25 .08
❑ 714 Fred Norman .25 .08
❑ 715 Sal Bando .75 .30
❑ 716 Lynn McGlothen .25 .08
❑ 717 Mickey Klutts DP .25 .08
❑ 718 Greg Gross .25 .08
❑ 719 Don Robinson .75 .30
❑ 720 Carl Yastrzemski DP 2.00 .75
❑ 721 Paul Hartzell .25 .08
❑ 722 Jose Cruz .75 .30
❑ 723 Shane Rawley .25 .08
❑ 724 Jerry White .25 .08
❑ 725 Rick Wise .25 .08
❑ 726 Steve Yeager .75 .30

1981 Topps

❑ COMPLETE SET (726) 60.00 30.00
❑ COMMON CARD (1-726) .15 .05
❑ COMMON CARD DP .15 .05
❑ 1 G.Brett/B.Buckner LL 3.00 1.25
❑ 2 Reggie/Ogliv/Schmidt LL 1.50 .60
❑ 3 C.Cooper/M.Schmidt LL 1.50 .60
❑ 4 R.Henderson/LeFlore LL 3.00 1.25
❑ 5 S.Stone/S.Carlton LL .40 .15
❑ 6 Len Barker/S.Carlton LL .40 .15
❑ 7 R.May/D.Sutton LL .40 .15
❑ 8 Quis/Fingers/Hume LL .40 .15
❑ 9 Pete LaCock DP .15 .05
❑ 10 Mike Flanagan .15 .05
❑ 11 Jim Wohlford DP .15 .05
❑ 12 Mark Clear .15 .05
❑ 13 Joe Charboneau RC 1.50 .60
❑ 14 John Tudor RC 1.50 .60
❑ 15 Larry Parrish .15 .05
❑ 16 Ron Davis .15 .05
❑ 17 Cliff Johnson .15 .05
❑ 18 Glenn Adams .15 .05
❑ 19 Jim Clancy .15 .05
❑ 20 Jeff Burroughs .40 .15
❑ 21 Ron Oester .15 .05
❑ 22 Danny Darwin .15 .05
❑ 23 Alex Trevino .15 .05
❑ 24 Don Stanhouse .15 .05
❑ 25 Sixto Lezcano .15 .05
❑ 26 U.L. Washington .15 .05
❑ 27 Champ Summers DP .15 .05
❑ 28 Enrique Romo .15 .05
❑ 29 Gene Tenace .40 .15
❑ 30 Jack Clark .40 .15
❑ 31 Checklist 1-121 DP .25 .08
❑ 32 Ken Oberkfell .15 .05
❑ 33 Rick Honeycutt .15 .05
❑ 34 Aurelio Rodriguez .15 .05
❑ 35 Mitchell Page .15 .05
❑ 36 Ed Farmer .15 .05
❑ 37 Gary Roenicke .15 .05
❑ 38 Win Remmerswaal RC .15 .05
❑ 39 Tom Veryzer .15 .05
❑ 40 Tug McGraw .40 .15
❑ 41 Babcock/Butcher/Gleaton RC .25 .08
❑ 42 Jerry White DP .15 .05
❑ 43 Jose Morales .15 .05
❑ 44 Larry McWilliams .15 .05
❑ 45 Enos Cabell .15 .05
❑ 46 Rick Bosetti .15 .05
❑ 47 Ken Brett .15 .05
❑ 48 Dave Skaggs .15 .05
❑ 49 Bob Shirley .15 .05
❑ 50 Dave Lopes .40 .15
❑ 51 Bill Robinson DP .15 .05
❑ 52 Hector Cruz .15 .05
❑ 53 Kevin Saucier .15 .05
❑ 54 Ivan DeJesus .15 .05
❑ 55 Mike Norris .15 .05
❑ 56 Buck Martinez .15 .05
❑ 57 Dave Roberts .15 .05
❑ 58 Joel Youngblood .15 .05
❑ 59 Dan Petry .15 .05
❑ 60 Willie Randolph .40 .15
❑ 61 Butch Wynegar .15 .05
❑ 62 Joe Pettini RC .15 .05
❑ 63 Steve Renko DP .15 .05
❑ 64 Brian Asselstine .15 .05
❑ 65 Scott McGregor .15 .05
❑ 66 Castillo/Ireland/M.Jones RC .25 .08
❑ 67 Ken Kravec .15 .05
❑ 68 Matt Alexander DP .15 .05
❑ 69 Ed Halicki .15 .05
❑ 70 Al Oliver DP .25 .08
❑ 71 Hal Dues .15 .05
❑ 72 Barry Evans DP RC .15 .05
❑ 73 Doug Bair .15 .05
❑ 74 Mike Hargrove .15 .05
❑ 75 Reggie Smith .40 .15
❑ 76 Mario Mendoza .15 .05
❑ 77 Mike Barlow .15 .05
❑ 78 Steve Dillard .15 .05
❑ 79 Bruce Robbins .15 .05
❑ 80 Rusty Staub .40 .15
❑ 81 Dave Stapleton RC .15 .05
❑ 82 Heep/Knicely/Sprowl RC .25 .08
❑ 83 Mike Proly .15 .05
❑ 84 Johnnie LeMaster .15 .05
❑ 85 Mike Caldwell .15 .05
❑ 86 Wayne Gross .15 .05
❑ 87 Rick Camp .15 .05
❑ 88 Joe Lefebvre RC .15 .05
❑ 89 Darrell Jackson .15 .05
❑ 90 Bake McBride .40 .15
❑ 91 Tim Stoddard DP .15 .05
❑ 92 Mike Easler .15 .05
❑ 93 Ed Glynn DP .15 .05
❑ 94 Harry Spilman DP .15 .05
❑ 95 Jim Sundberg .40 .15
❑ 96 Beard/Camacho/Dempsey RC .25 .08
❑ 97 Chris Speier .15 .05
❑ 98 Clint Hurdle .15 .05
❑ 99 Eric Wilkins .15 .05
❑ 100 Rod Carew .75 .30
❑ 101 Benny Ayala .15 .05
❑ 102 Dave Tobik .15 .05
❑ 103 Jerry Martin .15 .05
❑ 104 Terry Forster .40 .15
❑ 105 Jose Cruz .40 .15
❑ 106 Don Money .15 .05
❑ 107 Rich Wortham .15 .05
❑ 108 Bruce Benedict .15 .05
❑ 109 Mike Scott .40 .15
❑ 110 Carl Yastrzemski 2.50 1.00
❑ 111 Greg Minton .15 .05
❑ 112 Kuntz/Mullins/Sutherland RC .25 .08
❑ 113 Mike Phillips .15 .05
❑ 114 Tom Underwood .15 .05
❑ 115 Roy Smalley .40 .15
❑ 116 Joe Simpson .15 .05
❑ 117 Pete Falcone .15 .05
❑ 118 Kurt Bevacqua .15 .05
❑ 119 Tippy Martinez .15 .05
❑ 120 Larry Bowa .40 .15
❑ 121 Larry Harlow .15 .05
❑ 122 John Denny .15 .05
❑ 123 Al Cowens .15 .05
❑ 124 Jerry Garvin .15 .05
❑ 125 Andre Dawson .75 .30
❑ 126 Charlie Leibrandt RC .75 .30
❑ 127 Rudy Law .15 .05
❑ 128 Gary Allenson DP .15 .05
❑ 129 Art Howe .15 .05
❑ 130 Larry Gura .15 .05
❑ 131 Keith Moreland RC .15 .05
❑ 132 Tommy Boggs .15 .05
❑ 133 Jeff Cox RC .15 .05
❑ 134 Steve Mura .15 .05
❑ 135 Gorman Thomas .40 .15
❑ 136 Doug Capilla .15 .05
❑ 137 Hosken Powell .15 .05
❑ 138 Rich Dotson DP RC .15 .05
❑ 139 Oscar Gamble .15 .05
❑ 140 Bob Forsch .15 .05
❑ 141 Miguel Dilone .15 .05
❑ 142 Jackson Todd .15 .05
❑ 143 Dan Meyer .15 .05
❑ 144 Allen Ripley .15 .05
❑ 145 Mickey Rivers .15 .05
❑ 146 Bobby Castillo .15 .05
❑ 147 Dale Berra .15 .05
❑ 148 Randy Niemann .15 .05
❑ 149 Joe Nolan RC .15 .05
❑ 150 Mark Fidrych .40 .15
❑ 151 Claudell Washington .15 .05
❑ 152 John Urrea .15 .05
❑ 153 Tom Poquette .15 .05
❑ 154 Rick Langford .15 .05
❑ 155 Chris Chambliss .40 .15
❑ 156 Bob McClure .15 .05
❑ 157 John Wathan .15 .05
❑ 158 Fergie Jenkins .40 .15
❑ 159 Brian Doyle .15 .05
❑ 160 Garry Maddox .15 .05
❑ 161 Dan Graham .15 .05
❑ 162 Doug Corbett RC .15 .05
❑ 163 Bill Almon RC .15 .05
❑ 164 LaMarr Hoyt RC .75 .30
❑ 165 Tony Scott .15 .05
❑ 166 Floyd Bannister .15 .05
❑ 167 Terry Whitfield .15 .05
❑ 168 Don Robinson DP .15 .05
❑ 169 John Mayberry .15 .05
❑ 170 Ross Grimsley .15 .05
❑ 171 Gene Richards .15 .05
❑ 172 Gary Woods .15 .05
❑ 173 Bump Wills .15 .05
❑ 174 Doug Rau .15 .05
❑ 175 Dave Collins .15 .05
❑ 176 Mike Krukow RC .15 .05
❑ 177 Rick Peters RC .15 .05
❑ 178 Jim Essian DP .15 .05
❑ 179 Rudy May .15 .05
❑ 180 Pete Rose 5.00 2.00
❑ 181 Elias Sosa .15 .05
❑ 182 Bob Grich .40 .15
❑ 183 Dick Davis DP .15 .05
❑ 184 Jim Dwyer .15 .05
❑ 185 Dennis Leonard .15 .05
❑ 186 Wayne Nordhagen .15 .05
❑ 187 Mike Parrott .15 .05
❑ 188 Doug DeCinces .15 .05
❑ 189 Craig Swan .15 .05
❑ 190 Cesar Cedeno .40 .15
❑ 191 Rick Sutcliffe .40 .15
❑ 192 Harper/Miller/Ramirez RC .25 .08
❑ 193 Pete Vuckovich .15 .05
❑ 194 Rod Scurry RC .15 .05
❑ 195 Rich Murray RC .15 .05
❑ 196 Duffy Dyer .15 .05
❑ 197 Jim Kern .15 .05
❑ 198 Jerry Dybzinski RC .15 .05
❑ 199 Chuck Rainey .15 .05
❑ 200 George Foster .40 .15
❑ 201 Johnny Bench RB .75 .30
❑ 202 Steve Carlton RB .40 .15
❑ 203 Bill Gullickson RB .15 .05
❑ 204 R.LeFlore/R.Scott RB .40 .15

	No.	Player		
❑	205	Pete Rose RB	1.50	.60
❑	206	Mike Schmidt RB	1.50	.60
❑	207	Ozzie Smith RB	2.00	.75
❑	208	Willie Wilson RB	.15	.05
❑	209	Dickie Thon DP	.15	.05
❑	210	Jim Palmer	.75	.30
❑	211	Derrel Thomas	.15	.05
❑	212	Steve Nicosia	.15	.05
❑	213	Al Holland RC	.15	.05
❑	214	Botting/Dorsey/J.Harris RC	.25	.08
❑	215	Larry Hisle	.15	.05
❑	216	John Henry Johnson	.15	.05
❑	217	Rich Hebner	.15	.05
❑	218	Paul Splittorff	.15	.05
❑	219	Ken Landreaux	.15	.05
❑	220	Tom Seaver	1.50	.60
❑	221	Bob Davis	.15	.05
❑	222	Jorge Orta	.15	.05
❑	223	Roy Lee Jackson RC	.15	.05
❑	224	Pat Zachry	.15	.05
❑	225	Ruppert Jones	.15	.05
❑	226	Manny Sanguillen DP	.25	.08
❑	227	Fred Martinez RC	.15	.05
❑	228	Tom Paciorek	.15	.05
❑	229	Rollie Fingers	.40	.15
❑	230	George Hendrick	.40	.15
❑	231	Joe Beckwith	.15	.05
❑	232	Mickey Klutts	.15	.05
❑	233	Skip Lockwood	.15	.05
❑	234	Lou Whitaker	.75	.30
❑	235	Scott Sanderson	.15	.05
❑	236	Mike Ivie	.15	.05
❑	237	Charlie Moore	.15	.05
❑	238	Willie Hernandez	.15	.05
❑	239	Rick Miller DP	.15	.05
❑	240	Nolan Ryan	8.00	3.00
❑	241	Checklist 122-242 DP	.25	.08
❑	242	Chet Lemon	.40	.15
❑	243	Sal Butera RC	.15	.05
❑	244	Landrum/Olmsted/Rincon RC	.25	.08
❑	245	Ed Figueroa	.15	.05
❑	246	Ed Ott DP	.15	.05
❑	247	Glenn Hubbard DP	.15	.05
❑	248	Joey McLaughlin	.15	.05
❑	249	Larry Cox	.15	.05
❑	250	Ron Guidry	.40	.15
❑	251	Tom Brookens	.15	.05
❑	252	Victor Cruz	.15	.05
❑	253	Dave Bergman	.15	.05
❑	254	Ozzie Smith	5.00	2.00
❑	255	Mark Littell	.15	.05
❑	256	Bombo Rivera	.15	.05
❑	257	Rennie Stennett	.15	.05
❑	258	Joe Price RC	.15	.05
❑	259	M.Wilson/H.Brooks RC	5.00	2.00
❑	260	Ron Cey	.40	.15
❑	261	Rickey Henderson	10.00	4.00
❑	262	Sammy Stewart	.15	.05
❑	263	Brian Downing	.40	.15
❑	264	Jim Norris	.15	.05
❑	265	John Candelaria	.40	.15
❑	266	Tom Herr	.15	.05
❑	267	Stan Bahnsen	.15	.05
❑	268	Jerry Royster	.15	.05
❑	269	Ken Forsch	.15	.05
❑	270	Greg Luzinski	.40	.15
❑	271	Bill Castro	.15	.05
❑	272	Bruce Kimm	.15	.05
❑	273	Stan Papi	.15	.05
❑	274	Craig Chamberlain	.15	.05
❑	275	Dwight Evans	.75	.30
❑	276	Dan Spillner	.15	.05
❑	277	Alfredo Griffin	.15	.05
❑	278	Rick Sofield	.15	.05
❑	279	Bob Knepper	.15	.05
❑	280	Ken Griffey	.40	.15
❑	281	Fred Stanley	.15	.05
❑	282	Anderson/Biercevicz/Craig RC	.25	.08
❑	283	Billy Sample	.15	.05
❑	284	Brian Kingman	.15	.05
❑	285	Jerry Turner	.15	.05
❑	286	Dave Frost	.15	.05
❑	287	Lenn Sakata	.15	.05
❑	288	Bob Clark	.15	.05
❑	289	Mickey Hatcher	.15	.05
❑	290	Bob Boone DP	.25	.08
❑	291	Aurelio Lopez	.15	.05
❑	292	Mike Squires	.15	.05
❑	293	Charlie Lea RC	.15	.05
❑	294	Mike Tyson DP	.15	.05
❑	295	Hal McRae	.40	.15
❑	296	Bill Nahorodny DP	.15	.05
❑	297	Bob Bailor	.15	.05
❑	298	Buddy Solomon	.15	.05
❑	299	Elliott Maddox	.15	.05
❑	300	Paul Molitor	1.50	.60
❑	301	Matt Keough	.15	.05
❑	302	F.Valenzuela/M.Scioscia RC	8.00	3.00
❑	303	Johnny Oates	.40	.15
❑	304	John Castino	.15	.05
❑	305	Ken Clay	.15	.05
❑	306	Juan Beniquez DP	.15	.05
❑	307	Gene Garber	.15	.05
❑	308	Rick Manning	.15	.05
❑	309	Luis Salazar RC	.75	.30
❑	310	Vida Blue DP	.25	.08
❑	311	Freddie Patek	.15	.05
❑	312	Rick Rhoden	.15	.05
❑	313	Luis Pujols	.15	.05
❑	314	Rich Dauer	.15	.05
❑	315	Kirk Gibson RC	8.00	3.00
❑	316	Craig Minetto	.15	.05
❑	317	Lonnie Smith	.40	.15
❑	318	Steve Yeager	.40	.15
❑	319	Rowland Office	.15	.05
❑	320	Tom Burgmeier	.15	.05
❑	321	Leon Durham RC	.75	.30
❑	322	Neil Allen	.15	.05
❑	323	Jim Morrison DP	.15	.05
❑	324	Mike Willis	.15	.05
❑	325	Ray Knight	.40	.15
❑	326	Biff Pocoroba	.15	.05
❑	327	Moose Haas	.15	.05
❑	328	Engle/Johnston/G.Ward	.25	.08
❑	329	Joaquin Andujar	.40	.15
❑	330	Frank White	.40	.15
❑	331	Dennis Lamp	.15	.05
❑	332	Lee Lacy DP	.15	.05
❑	333	Sid Monge	.15	.05
❑	334	Dane Iorg	.15	.05
❑	335	Rick Cerone	.15	.05
❑	336	Eddie Whitson	.15	.05
❑	337	Lynn Jones	.15	.05
❑	338	Checklist 243-363	.40	.15
❑	339	John Ellis	.15	.05
❑	340	Bruce Kison	.15	.05
❑	341	Dwayne Murphy	.15	.05
❑	342	Eric Rasmussen DP	.15	.05
❑	343	Frank Taveras	.15	.05
❑	344	Byron McLaughlin	.15	.05
❑	345	Warren Cromartie	.15	.05
❑	346	Larry Christenson DP	.15	.05
❑	347	Harold Baines RC	3.00	1.25
❑	348	Bob Sykes	.15	.05
❑	349	Glenn Hoffman RC	.15	.05
❑	350	J.R. Richard	.40	.15
❑	351	Otto Velez	.15	.05
❑	352	Dick Tidrow DP	.15	.05
❑	353	Terry Kennedy	.15	.05
❑	354	Mario Soto	.40	.15
❑	355	Bob Horner	.40	.15
❑	356	Stablein/Stimac/Tellmann RC	.25	.08
❑	357	Jim Slaton	.15	.05
❑	358	Mark Wagner	.15	.05
❑	359	Tom Hausman	.15	.05
❑	360	Willie Wilson	.40	.15
❑	361	Joe Strain	.15	.05
❑	362	Bo Diaz	.15	.05
❑	363	Geoff Zahn	.15	.05
❑	364	Mike Davis RC	.25	.08
❑	365	Graig Nettles DP	.25	.08
❑	366	Mike Ramsey RC	.25	.08
❑	367	Dennis Martinez	.40	.15
❑	368	Leon Roberts	.15	.05
❑	369	Frank Tanana	.40	.15
❑	370	Dave Winfield	.75	.30
❑	371	Charlie Hough	.40	.15
❑	372	Jay Johnstone	.15	.05
❑	373	Pat Underwood	.15	.05
❑	374	Tommy Hutton	.15	.05
❑	375	Dave Concepcion	.40	.15
❑	376	Ron Reed	.15	.05
❑	377	Jerry Morales	.15	.05
❑	378	Dave Rader	.15	.05
❑	379	Lary Sorensen	.15	.05
❑	380	Willie Stargell	.75	.30
❑	381	Lezcano/Macko/Martz RC	.25	.08
❑	382	Paul Mirabella RC	.15	.05
❑	383	Eric Soderholm DP	.15	.05
❑	384	Mike Sadek	.15	.05
❑	385	Joe Sambito	.15	.05
❑	386	Dave Edwards	.15	.05
❑	387	Phil Niekro	.40	.15
❑	388	Andre Thornton	.40	.15
❑	389	Marty Pattin	.15	.05
❑	390	Cesar Geronimo	.15	.05
❑	391	Dave Lemanczyk DP	.15	.05
❑	392	Lance Parrish	.40	.15
❑	393	Broderick Perkins	.15	.05
❑	394	Woodie Fryman	.15	.05
❑	395	Scot Thompson	.15	.05
❑	396	Bill Campbell	.15	.05
❑	397	Julio Cruz	.15	.05
❑	398	Ross Baumgarten	.15	.05
❑	399	Boddicker/Corey/Rayford RC	.75	.30
❑	400	Reggie Jackson	1.50	.60
❑	401	George Brett ALCS	2.50	1.00
❑	402	NL Champs	.75	.30
❑	403	Larry Bowa WS	.75	.30
❑	404	Tug McGraw WS	.75	.30
❑	405	Nino Espinosa	.15	.05
❑	406	Dickie Noles	.15	.05
❑	407	Ernie Whitt	.15	.05
❑	408	Fernando Arroyo	.15	.05
❑	409	Larry Herndon	.15	.05
❑	410	Bert Campaneris	.40	.15
❑	411	Terry Puhl	.15	.05
❑	412	Britt Burns RC	.15	.05
❑	413	Tony Bernazard	.15	.05
❑	414	John Pacella DP RC	.15	.05
❑	415	Ben Oglivie	.40	.15
❑	416	Gary Alexander	.15	.05
❑	417	Dan Schatzeder	.15	.05
❑	418	Bobby Brown	.15	.05
❑	419	Tom Hume	.15	.05
❑	420	Keith Hernandez	.40	.15
❑	421	Bob Stanley	.15	.05
❑	422	Dan Ford	.15	.05
❑	423	Shane Rawley	.15	.05
❑	424	Lollar/Robinson/Werth RC	.25	.08
❑	425	Al Bumbry	.15	.05
❑	426	Warren Brusstar	.15	.05
❑	427	John D'Acquisto	.15	.05
❑	428	John Stearns	.15	.05
❑	429	Mick Kelleher	.15	.05
❑	430	Jim Bibby	.15	.05
❑	431	Dave Roberts	.15	.05
❑	432	Len Barker	.40	.15
❑	433	Rance Mulliniks	.15	.05
❑	434	Roger Erickson	.15	.05
❑	435	Jim Spencer	.15	.05
❑	436	Gary Lucas RC	.15	.05
❑	437	Mike Heath DP	.15	.05
❑	438	John Montefusco	.15	.05
❑	439	Denny Walling	.15	.05
❑	440	Jerry Reuss	.15	.05
❑	441	Ken Reitz	.15	.05
❑	442	Ron Pruitt	.15	.05
❑	443	Jim Beattie DP	.15	.05
❑	444	Garth Iorg	.15	.05
❑	445	Ellis Valentine	.15	.05
❑	446	Checklist 364-484	.40	.15
❑	447	Junior Kennedy DP	.15	.05
❑	448	Tim Corcoran	.15	.05
❑	449	Paul Mitchell	.15	.05
❑	450	Dave Kingman DP	.25	.08
❑	451	Bando/Brennan/Wihtol RC	.25	.08
❑	452	Renie Martin	.15	.05
❑	453	Rob Wilfong DP	.15	.05
❑	454	Andy Hassler	.15	.05
❑	455	Rick Burleson	.15	.05
❑	456	Jeff Reardon RC	1.50	.60
❑	457	Mike Lum	.15	.05
❑	458	Randy Jones	.40	.15
❑	459	Greg Gross	.15	.05
❑	460	Rich Gossage	.40	.15
❑	461	Dave McKay RC	.15	.05
❑	462	Jack Brohamer	.15	.05

❑ 463 Milt May .15 .05
❑ 464 Adrian Devine .15 .05
❑ 465 Bill Russell .40 .15
❑ 466 Bob Molinaro .15 .05
❑ 467 Dave Stieb .40 .15
❑ 468 John Wockenfuss .15 .05
❑ 469 Jeff Leonard .40 .15
❑ 470 Manny Trillo .15 .05
❑ 471 Mike Vail .15 .05
❑ 472 Dyar Miller DP .15 .05
❑ 473 Jose Cardenal .15 .05
❑ 474 Mike LaCoss .15 .05
❑ 475 Buddy Bell .40 .15
❑ 476 Jerry Koosman .40 .15
❑ 477 Luis Gomez .15 .05
❑ 478 Juan Eichelberger RC .15 .05
❑ 479 Tim Raines RC 4.00 1.50
❑ 480 Carlton Fisk .75 .30
❑ 481 Bob Lacey DP .15 .05
❑ 482 Jim Gantner .15 .05
❑ 483 Mike Griffin RC .25 .08
❑ 484 Max Venable DP RC .15 .05
❑ 485 Garry Templeton .40 .15
❑ 486 Marc Hill .15 .05
❑ 487 Dewey Robinson .15 .05
❑ 488 Damaso Garcia RC .15 .05
❑ 489 John Littlefield RC .15 .05
❑ 490 Eddie Murray 2.50 1.00
❑ 491 Gordy Pladson RC .15 .05
❑ 492 Barry Foote .15 .05
❑ 493 Dan Quisenberry .15 .05
❑ 494 Bob Walk RC .75 .30
❑ 495 Dusty Baker .40 .15
❑ 496 Paul Dade .15 .05
❑ 497 Fred Norman .15 .05
❑ 498 Pat Putnam .15 .05
❑ 499 Frank Pastore .15 .05
❑ 500 Jim Rice .40 .15
❑ 501 Tim Foli DP .15 .05
❑ 502 Bourjos/Hargesheimer/Rowland RC .25 .08
❑ 503 Steve McCatty .15 .05
❑ 504 Dale Murphy .75 .30
❑ 505 Jason Thompson .15 .05
❑ 506 Phil Huffman .15 .05
❑ 507 Jamie Quirk .15 .05
❑ 508 Rob Dressler .15 .05
❑ 509 Pete Mackanin .15 .05
❑ 510 Lee Mazzilli .40 .15
❑ 511 Wayne Garland .15 .05
❑ 512 Gary Thomasson .15 .05
❑ 513 Frank LaCorte .15 .05
❑ 514 George Riley RC .15 .05
❑ 515 Robin Yount 2.50 1.00
❑ 516 Doug Bird .15 .05
❑ 517 Richie Zisk .15 .05
❑ 518 Grant Jackson .15 .05
❑ 519 John Tamargo DP .15 .05
❑ 520 Steve Stone .15 .05
❑ 521 Sam Mejias .15 .05
❑ 522 Mike Colbern .15 .05
❑ 523 John Fulgham .15 .05
❑ 524 Willie Aikens .15 .05
❑ 525 Mike Torrez .15 .05
❑ 526 Bystrom/Loviglio/Wright RC .25 .08
❑ 527 Danny Goodwin .15 .05
❑ 528 Gary Matthews .40 .15
❑ 529 Dave LaRoche .15 .05
❑ 530 Steve Garvey .75 .30
❑ 531 John Curtis .15 .05
❑ 532 Bill Stein .15 .05
❑ 533 Jesus Figueroa RC .15 .05
❑ 534 Dave Smith RC .75 .30
❑ 535 Omar Moreno .15 .05
❑ 536 Bob Owchinko DP .15 .05
❑ 537 Ron Hodges .15 .05
❑ 538 Tom Griffin .15 .05
❑ 539 Rodney Scott .15 .05
❑ 540 Mike Schmidt DP 2.00 .75
❑ 541 Steve Swisher .15 .05
❑ 542 Larry Bradford DP .15 .05
❑ 543 Terry Crowley .15 .05
❑ 544 Rich Gale .15 .05
❑ 545 Johnny Grubb .15 .05
❑ 546 Paul Moskau .15 .05
❑ 547 Mario Guerrero .15 .05
❑ 548 Dave Goltz .15 .05
❑ 549 Jerry Remy .15 .05
❑ 550 Tommy John .40 .15
❑ 551 Law/Pena/Perez RC .75 .30
❑ 552 Steve Trout .15 .05
❑ 553 Tim Blackwell .15 .05
❑ 554 Bert Blyleven .40 .15
❑ 555 Cecil Cooper .40 .15
❑ 556 Jerry Mumphrey .15 .05
❑ 557 Chris Knapp .15 .05
❑ 558 Barry Bonnell .15 .05
❑ 559 Willie Montanez .15 .05
❑ 560 Joe Morgan .75 .30
❑ 561 Dennis Littlejohn .15 .05
❑ 562 Checklist 485-605 .40 .15
❑ 563 Jim Kaat .40 .15
❑ 564 Ron Hassey DP .15 .05
❑ 565 Burt Hooton .15 .05
❑ 566 Del Unser .15 .05
❑ 567 Mark Bomback RC .15 .05
❑ 568 Dave Revering .15 .05
❑ 569 Al Williams DP RC .15 .05
❑ 570 Ken Singleton .40 .15
❑ 571 Todd Cruz .15 .05
❑ 572 Jack Morris .75 .30
❑ 573 Phil Garner .40 .15
❑ 574 Bill Caudill .15 .05
❑ 575 Tony Perez .75 .30
❑ 576 Reggie Cleveland .15 .05
❑ 577 Leal/Milner/Schrom RC .25 .08
❑ 578 Bill Gullickson RC .75 .30
❑ 579 Tim Flannery .15 .05
❑ 580 Don Baylor .40 .15
❑ 581 Roy Howell .15 .05
❑ 582 Gaylord Perry .40 .15
❑ 583 Larry Milbourne .15 .05
❑ 584 Randy Lerch .15 .05
❑ 585 Amos Otis .40 .15
❑ 586 Silvio Martinez .15 .05
❑ 587 Jeff Newman .15 .05
❑ 588 Gary Lavelle .15 .05
❑ 589 Lamar Johnson .15 .05
❑ 590 Bruce Sutter .75 .30
❑ 591 John Lowenstein .15 .05
❑ 592 Steve Comer .15 .05
❑ 593 Steve Kemp .15 .05
❑ 594 Preston Hanna DP .15 .05
❑ 595 Butch Hobson .15 .05
❑ 596 Jerry Augustine .15 .05
❑ 597 Rafael Landestoy .15 .05
❑ 598 George Vukovich DP RC .15 .05
❑ 599 Dennis Kinney RC .15 .05
❑ 600 Johnny Bench 1.50 .60
❑ 601 Don Aase .15 .05
❑ 602 Bobby Murcer .40 .15
❑ 603 John Verhoeven .15 .05
❑ 604 Rob Picciolo .15 .05
❑ 605 Don Sutton .40 .15
❑ 606 Bereny/Combe/Householder DP RC .25 .08
❑ 607 David Palmer .15 .05
❑ 608 Greg Pryor .15 .05
❑ 609 Lynn McGlothen .15 .05
❑ 610 Darrell Porter .15 .05
❑ 611 Rick Matula DP .15 .05
❑ 612 Duane Kuiper .15 .05
❑ 613 Jim Anderson .15 .05
❑ 614 Dave Rozema .15 .05
❑ 615 Rick Dempsey .15 .05
❑ 616 Rick Wise .15 .05
❑ 617 Craig Reynolds .15 .05
❑ 618 John Milner .15 .05
❑ 619 Steve Henderson .15 .05
❑ 620 Dennis Eckersley .75 .30
❑ 621 Tom Donohue .15 .05
❑ 622 Randy Moffitt .15 .05
❑ 623 Sal Bando .40 .15
❑ 624 Bob Welch .40 .15
❑ 625 Bill Buckner .40 .15
❑ 626 Steffen/Ujdur/Weaver RC .25 .08
❑ 627 Luis Tiant .40 .15
❑ 628 Vic Correll .15 .05
❑ 629 Tony Armas .40 .15
❑ 630 Steve Carlton .75 .30
❑ 631 Ron Jackson .15 .05
❑ 632 Alan Bannister .15 .05
❑ 633 Bill Lee .40 .15
❑ 634 Doug Flynn .15 .05
❑ 635 Bobby Bonds .40 .15
❑ 636 Al Hrabosky .40 .15
❑ 637 Jerry Narron .15 .05
❑ 638 Checklist 606-726 .40 .15
❑ 639 Carney Lansford .40 .15
❑ 640 Dave Parker .40 .15
❑ 641 Mark Belanger .15 .05
❑ 642 Vern Ruhle .15 .05
❑ 643 Lloyd Moseby RC .75 .30
❑ 644 Ramon Aviles DP .15 .05
❑ 645 Rick Reuschel .40 .15
❑ 646 Marvis Foley RC .15 .05
❑ 647 Dick Drago .15 .05
❑ 648 Darrell Evans .40 .15
❑ 649 Manny Sarmiento .15 .05
❑ 650 Bucky Dent .40 .15
❑ 651 Pedro Guerrero .40 .15
❑ 652 John Montague .15 .05
❑ 653 Bill Fahey .15 .05
❑ 654 Ray Burris .15 .05
❑ 655 Dan Driessen .15 .05
❑ 656 Jon Matlack .15 .05
❑ 657 Mike Cubbage DP .15 .05
❑ 658 Milt Wilcox .15 .05
❑ 659 Flinn/Romero/Yost .75 .30
❑ 660 Gary Carter .75 .30
❑ 661 Orioles Team CL Earl Weaver MG .40 .15
❑ 662 Red Sox Team CL Ralph Houk MG .40 .15
❑ 663 Angels Team CL Jim Fregosi MG .40 .15
❑ 664 White Sox Team/Mgr. Tony LaRussa (Checklist back .40 .15
❑ 665 Indians Team CL Dave Garcia MG .40 .15
❑ 666 Tigers Team/Mgr. Sparky Anderson (Checklist back .40 .15
❑ 667 Royals Team CL Jim Frey MG .40 .15
❑ 668 Brewers Team CL Bob Rodgers MG .40 .15
❑ 669 Twins Team CL John Goryl MG .40 .15
❑ 670 Yankees Team CL Gene Michael MG .40 .15
❑ 671 A's Team CL Billy Martin MG .75 .30
❑ 672 Mariners Team CL Maury Wills MG .40 .15
❑ 673 Rangers Team CL Don Zimmer MG .40 .15
❑ 674 Blue Jays Team/Mgr. Bobby Mattick (Checklist bac .40 .15
❑ 675 Braves Team CL Bobby Cox MG .40 .15
❑ 676 Cubs Team CL Joe Amalfitano MG .40 .15
❑ 677 Reds Team CL John McNamara MG .40 .15
❑ 678 Astros Team CL Bill Virdon MG .40 .15
❑ 679 Dodgers Team CL Tom Lasorda MG .75 .30
❑ 680 Expos Team CL Dick Williams MG .40 .15
❑ 681 Mets Team CL Joe Torre MG .75 .30
❑ 682 Phillies Team CL Dallas Green MG .40 .15
❑ 683 Pirates Team CL Chuck Tanner MG .40 .15
❑ 684 Cardinals Team/Mgr. Whitey Herzog (Checklist bac .40 .15
❑ 685 Padres Team CL Frank Howard MG .40 .15
❑ 686 Giants Team CL Dave Bristol MG .40 .15
❑ 687 Jeff Jones RC .15 .05
❑ 688 Kiko Garcia .15 .05
❑ 689 Bruce Hurst RC .75 .30
❑ 690 Bob Watson .15 .05

❑ 691 Dick Ruthven .15 .05
❑ 692 Lenny Randle .15 .05
❑ 693 Steve Howe RC .25 .08
❑ 694 Bud Harrelson DP .25 .08
❑ 695 Kent Tekulve .15 .05
❑ 696 Alan Ashby .15 .05
❑ 697 Rick Waits .15 .05
❑ 698 Mike Jorgensen .15 .05
❑ 699 Glenn Abbott .15 .05
❑ 700 George Brett 4.00 1.50
❑ 701 Joe Rudi .40 .15
❑ 702 George Medich .15 .05
❑ 703 Alvis Woods .15 .05
❑ 704 Bill Travers DP .15 .05
❑ 705 Ted Simmons .40 .15
❑ 706 Dave Ford RC .15 .05
❑ 707 Dave Cash .15 .05
❑ 708 Doyle Alexander .15 .05
❑ 709 Alan Trammell DP .50 .20
❑ 710 Ron LeFlore DP .25 .08
❑ 711 Joe Ferguson .15 .05
❑ 712 Bill Bonham .15 .05
❑ 713 Bill North .15 .05
❑ 714 Pete Redfern .15 .05
❑ 715 Bill Madlock .40 .15
❑ 716 Glenn Borgmann .15 .05
❑ 717 Jim Barr DP .15 .05
❑ 718 Larry Biittner .15 .05
❑ 719 Sparky Lyle .40 .15
❑ 720 Fred Lynn .40 .15
❑ 721 Toby Harrah .40 .15
❑ 722 Joe Niekro .15 .05
❑ 723 Bruce Bochte .15 .05
❑ 724 Lou Piniella .40 .15
❑ 725 Steve Rogers .40 .15
❑ 726 Rick Monday .40 .15

1981 Topps Traded

❑ COMP.FACT.SET (132) 25.00 10.00
❑ 727 Danny Ainge XRC 5.00 2.00
❑ 728 Doyle Alexander .25 .08
❑ 729 Gary Alexander .25 .08
❑ 730 Bill Almon .25 .08
❑ 731 Joaquin Andujar 1.00 .40
❑ 732 Bob Bailor .25 .08
❑ 733 Juan Beniquez .25 .08
❑ 734 Dave Bergman .25 .08
❑ 735 Tony Bernazard .25 .08
❑ 736 Larry Biittner .25 .08
❑ 737 Doug Bird .25 .08
❑ 738 Bert Blyleven 1.00 .40
❑ 739 Mark Bomback .25 .08
❑ 740 Bobby Bonds 1.00 .40
❑ 741 Rick Bosetti .25 .08
❑ 742 Hubie Brooks 2.00 .75
❑ 743 Rick Burleson .25 .08
❑ 744 Ray Burris .25 .08
❑ 745 Jeff Burroughs 1.00 .40
❑ 746 Enos Cabell .25 .08
❑ 747 Ken Clay .25 .08
❑ 748 Mark Clear .25 .08
❑ 749 Larry Cox .25 .08
❑ 750 Hector Cruz .25 .08
❑ 751 Victor Cruz .25 .08
❑ 752 Mike Cubbage .25 .08
❑ 753 Dick Davis .25 .08
❑ 754 Brian Doyle .25 .08
❑ 755 Dick Drago .25 .08
❑ 756 Leon Durham 1.00 .40
❑ 757 Jim Dwyer .25 .08
❑ 758 Dave Edwards .25 .08
❑ 759 Jim Essian .25 .08
❑ 760 Bill Fahey .25 .08
❑ 761 Rollie Fingers 1.00 .40
❑ 762 Carlton Fisk 2.00 .75
❑ 763 Barry Foote .25 .08
❑ 764 Ken Forsch .25 .08
❑ 765 Kiko Garcia .25 .08
❑ 766 Cesar Geronimo .25 .08
❑ 767 Gary Gray XRC .25 .08
❑ 768 Mickey Hatcher .25 .08
❑ 769 Steve Henderson .25 .08
❑ 770 Marc Hill .25 .08
❑ 771 Butch Hobson .25 .08
❑ 772 Rick Honeycutt .25 .08
❑ 773 Roy Howell .25 .08
❑ 774 Mike Ivie .25 .08
❑ 775 Roy Lee Jackson .25 .08
❑ 776 Cliff Johnson .25 .08
❑ 777 Randy Jones 1.00 .40
❑ 778 Ruppert Jones .25 .08
❑ 779 Mick Kelleher .25 .08
❑ 780 Terry Kennedy .25 .08
❑ 781 Dave Kingman 1.00 .40
❑ 782 Bob Knepper .25 .08
❑ 783 Ken Kravec .25 .08
❑ 784 Bob Lacey .25 .08
❑ 785 Dennis Lamp .25 .08
❑ 786 Rafael Landestoy .25 .08
❑ 787 Ken Landreaux .25 .08
❑ 788 Carney Lansford 1.00 .40
❑ 789 Dave LaRoche .25 .08
❑ 790 Joe Lefebvre .25 .08
❑ 791 Ron LeFlore 1.00 .40
❑ 792 Randy Lerch .25 .08
❑ 793 Sixto Lezcano .25 .08
❑ 794 John Littlefield .25 .08
❑ 795 Mike Lum .25 .08
❑ 796 Greg Luzinski 1.00 .40
❑ 797 Fred Lynn 1.00 .40
❑ 798 Jerry Martin .25 .08
❑ 799 Buck Martinez .25 .08
❑ 800 Gary Matthews 1.00 .40
❑ 801 Mario Mendoza .25 .08
❑ 802 Larry Milbourne .25 .08
❑ 803 Rick Miller .25 .08
❑ 804 John Montefusco .25 .08
❑ 805 Jerry Morales .25 .08
❑ 806 Jose Morales .25 .08
❑ 807 Joe Morgan 2.00 .75
❑ 808 Jerry Mumphrey .25 .08
❑ 809 Gene Nelson XRC .25 .08
❑ 810 Ed Ott .25 .08
❑ 811 Bob Owchinko .25 .08
❑ 812 Gaylord Perry 1.00 .40
❑ 813 Mike Phillips .25 .08
❑ 814 Darrell Porter .25 .08
❑ 815 Mike Proly .25 .08
❑ 816 Tim Raines 5.00 2.00
❑ 817 Lenny Randle .25 .08
❑ 818 Doug Rau .25 .08
❑ 819 Jeff Reardon 2.00 .75
❑ 820 Ken Reitz .25 .08
❑ 821 Steve Renko .25 .08
❑ 822 Rick Reuschel 1.00 .40
❑ 823 Dave Revering .25 .08
❑ 824 Dave Roberts .25 .08
❑ 825 Leon Roberts .25 .08
❑ 826 Joe Rudi 1.00 .40
❑ 827 Kevin Saucier .25 .08
❑ 828 Tony Scott .25 .08
❑ 829 Bob Shirley .25 .08
❑ 830 Ted Simmons 1.00 .40
❑ 831 Lary Sorensen .25 .08
❑ 832 Jim Spencer .25 .08
❑ 833 Harry Spilman .25 .08
❑ 834 Fred Stanley .25 .08
❑ 835 Rusty Staub 1.00 .40
❑ 836 Bill Stein .25 .08
❑ 837 Joe Strain .25 .08
❑ 838 Bruce Sutter 2.00 .75
❑ 839 Don Sutton 1.00 .40
❑ 840 Steve Swisher .25 .08
❑ 841 Frank Tanana 1.00 .40
❑ 842 Gene Tenace 1.00 .40
❑ 843 Jason Thompson .25 .08
❑ 844 Dickie Thon .25 .08
❑ 845 Bill Travers .25 .08
❑ 846 Tom Underwood .25 .08
❑ 847 John Urrea .25 .08
❑ 848 Mike Vail .25 .08
❑ 849 Ellis Valentine .25 .08
❑ 850 Fernando Valenzuela 10.00 4.00
❑ 851 Pete Vuckovich .25 .08
❑ 852 Mark Wagner .25 .08
❑ 853 Bob Walk 1.00 .40
❑ 854 Claudell Washington .25 .08
❑ 855 Dave Winfield 2.00 .75
❑ 856 Geoff Zahn .25 .08
❑ 857 Richie Zisk .25 .08
❑ 858 Checklist 727-858 .25 .08

1982 Topps

❑ COMPLETE SET (792) 80.00 40.00
❑ 1 Steve Carlton HL .30 .10
❑ 2 Ron Davis HL
Fans 8 straight
in relief .15 .05
❑ 3 Tim Raines HL .30 .10
❑ 4 Pete Rose HL .60 .25
❑ 5 Nolan Ryan HL 3.00 1.25
❑ 6 Fernando Valenzuela HL
8 shutouts as rookie .60 .25
❑ 7 Scott Sanderson .15 .05
❑ 8 Rich Dauer .15 .05
❑ 9 Ron Guidry .30 .10
❑ 10 Ron Guidry SA .15 .05
❑ 11 Gary Alexander .15 .05
❑ 12 Moose Haas .15 .05
❑ 13 Lamar Johnson .15 .05
❑ 14 Steve Howe .15 .05
❑ 15 Ellis Valentine .15 .05
❑ 16 Steve Comer .15 .05
❑ 17 Darrell Evans .30 .10
❑ 18 Fernando Arroyo .15 .05
❑ 19 Ernie Whitt .15 .05
❑ 20 Garry Maddox .15 .05
❑ 21 Cal Ripken RC 50.00 20.00
❑ 22 Jim Beattie .15 .05
❑ 23 Willie Hernandez .15 .05
❑ 24 Dave Frost .15 .05
❑ 25 Jerry Remy .15 .05
❑ 26 Jorge Orta .15 .05
❑ 27 Tom Herr .15 .05
❑ 28 John Urrea .15 .05
❑ 29 Dwayne Murphy .15 .05
❑ 30 Tom Seaver 1.25 .50
❑ 31 Tom Seaver SA .30 .10
❑ 32 Gene Garber .15 .05
❑ 33 Jerry Morales .15 .05
❑ 34 Joe Sambito .15 .05
❑ 35 Willie Aikens .15 .05
❑ 36 Rangers TL
BA: Al Oliver
Pitching: Doc Medich .60 .25
❑ 37 Dan Graham .15 .05
❑ 38 Charlie Lea .15 .05
❑ 39 Lou Whitaker .30 .10
❑ 40 Dave Parker .30 .10
❑ 41 Dave Parker SA .15 .05
❑ 42 Rick Sofield .15 .05
❑ 43 Mike Cubbage .15 .05

❑ 44 Britt Burns .15 .05
❑ 45 Rick Cerone .15 .05
❑ 46 Jerry Augustine .15 .05
❑ 47 Jeff Leonard .15 .05
❑ 48 Bobby Castillo .15 .05
❑ 49 Alvis Woods .15 .05
❑ 50 Buddy Bell .30 .10
❑ 51 Howell/Lezcano/Waller RC .75 .30
❑ 52 Larry Andersen .15 .05
❑ 53 Greg Gross .15 .05
❑ 54 Ron Hassey .15 .05
❑ 55 Rick Burleson .15 .05
❑ 56 Mark Littell .15 .05
❑ 57 Craig Reynolds .15 .05
❑ 58 John D'Acquisto .15 .05
❑ 59 Rich Gedman .75 .30
❑ 60 Tony Armas .30 .10
❑ 61 Tommy Boggs .15 .05
❑ 62 Mike Tyson .15 .05
❑ 63 Mario Soto .30 .10
❑ 64 Lynn Jones .15 .05
❑ 65 Terry Kennedy .15 .05
❑ 66 Astros TL/Nolan Ryan 2.00 .75
❑ 67 Rich Gale .15 .05
❑ 68 Roy Howell .15 .05
❑ 69 Al Williams .15 .05
❑ 70 Tim Raines .60 .25
❑ 71 Roy Lee Jackson .15 .05
❑ 72 Rick Auerbach .15 .05
❑ 73 Buddy Solomon .15 .05
❑ 74 Bob Clark .15 .05
❑ 75 Tommy John .30 .10
❑ 76 Greg Pryor .15 .05
❑ 77 Miguel Dilone .15 .05
❑ 78 George Medich .15 .05
❑ 79 Bob Bailor .15 .05
❑ 80 Jim Palmer .30 .10
❑ 81 Jim Palmer SA .15 .05
❑ 82 Bob Welch .30 .10
❑ 83 Balboni/McGaf/Rob RC .75 .30
❑ 84 Rennie Stennett .15 .05
❑ 85 Lynn McGlothen .15 .05
❑ 86 Dane Iorg .15 .05
❑ 87 Matt Keough .15 .05
❑ 88 Biff Pocoroba .15 .05
❑ 89 Steve Henderson .15 .05
❑ 90 Nolan Ryan 6.00 2.50
❑ 91 Carney Lansford .30 .10
❑ 92 Brad Havens .15 .05
❑ 93 Larry Hisle .15 .05
❑ 94 Andy Hassler .15 .05
❑ 95 Ozzie Smith 2.50 1.00
❑ 96 Royals TL/George Brett 1.25 .50
❑ 97 Paul Moskau .15 .05
❑ 98 Terry Bulling .15 .05
❑ 99 Barry Bonnell .15 .05
❑ 100 Mike Schmidt 3.00 1.25
❑ 101 Mike Schmidt SA 1.25 .50
❑ 102 Dan Briggs .15 .05
❑ 103 Bob Lacey .15 .05
❑ 104 Rance Mulliniks .15 .05
❑ 105 Kirk Gibson 1.25 .50
❑ 106 Enrique Romo .15 .05
❑ 107 Wayne Krenchicki .15 .05
❑ 108 Bob Sykes .15 .05
❑ 109 Dave Revering .15 .05
❑ 110 Carlton Fisk .60 .25
❑ 111 Carlton Fisk SA .30 .10
❑ 112 Billy Sample .15 .05
❑ 113 Steve McCatty .15 .05
❑ 114 Ken Landreaux .15 .05
❑ 115 Gaylord Perry .30 .10
❑ 116 Jim Wohlford .15 .05
❑ 117 Rawly Eastwick .30 .10
❑ 118 Francona/Mills/Smith RC 5.00 2.00
❑ 119 Joe Pittman .15 .05
❑ 120 Gary Lucas .15 .05
❑ 121 Ed Lynch .15 .05
❑ 122 Jamie Easterly UER
(Photo actually
Reggie Clevel .15 .05
❑ 123 Danny Goodwin .15 .05
❑ 124 Reid Nichols .15 .05
❑ 125 Danny Ainge .30 .10
❑ 126 Braves TL
BA: Claudell Washington
Pitching: Rick .60 .25
❑ 127 Lonnie Smith .15 .05
❑ 128 Frank Pastore .15 .05
❑ 129 Checklist 1-132 .30 .10
❑ 130 Julio Cruz .15 .05
❑ 131 Stan Bahnsen .15 .05
❑ 132 Lee May .15 .05
❑ 133 Pat Underwood .15 .05
❑ 134 Dan Ford .15 .05
❑ 135 Andy Rincon .15 .05
❑ 136 Lenn Sakata .15 .05
❑ 137 George Cappuzzello .15 .05
❑ 138 Tony Pena .30 .10
❑ 139 Jeff Jones .15 .05
❑ 140 Ron LeFlore .30 .10
❑ 141 Bando/Brennan/Hayes RC .75 .30
❑ 142 Dave LaRoche .15 .05
❑ 143 Mookie Wilson .30 .10
❑ 144 Fred Breining .15 .05
❑ 145 Bob Horner .30 .10
❑ 146 Mike Griffin .15 .05
❑ 147 Denny Walling .15 .05
❑ 148 Mickey Klutts .15 .05
❑ 149 Pat Putnam .15 .05
❑ 150 Ted Simmons .30 .10
❑ 151 Dave Edwards .15 .05
❑ 152 Ramon Aviles .15 .05
❑ 153 Roger Erickson .15 .05
❑ 154 Dennis Werth .15 .05
❑ 155 Otto Velez .15 .05
❑ 156 A's TL/Rickey Henderson 1.25 .50
❑ 157 Steve Crawford .15 .05
❑ 158 Brian Downing .30 .10
❑ 159 Larry Biittner .15 .05
❑ 160 Luis Tiant .30 .10
❑ 161 Bill Madlock
Carney Lansford LL .30 .10
❑ 162 Schmidt/Armas/Murray LL 1.25 .50
❑ 163 Mike Schmidt/E.Murray LL 1.25 .50
❑ 164 T.Raines/R.Henderson LL 1.25 .50
❑ 165 Seav/Martinez/Morris LL .30 .10
❑ 166 Strikeout Leaders
Fernando Valenzuela
Len Barker .30 .10
❑ 167 N.Ryan/S.McCatty LL 2.00 .75
❑ 168 B.Sutter/R.Fingers LL .30 .10
❑ 169 Charlie Leibrandt .15 .05
❑ 170 Jim Bibby .15 .05
❑ 171 Brenly/Davis/Tufts RC 1.50 .60
❑ 172 Bill Gullickson .15 .05
❑ 173 Jamie Quirk .15 .05
❑ 174 Dave Ford .15 .05
❑ 175 Jerry Mumphrey .15 .05
❑ 176 Dewey Robinson .15 .05
❑ 177 John Ellis .15 .05
❑ 178 Dyar Miller .15 .05
❑ 179 Steve Garvey .30 .10
❑ 180 Steve Garvey SA .15 .05
❑ 181 Silvio Martinez .15 .05
❑ 182 Larry Herndon .15 .05
❑ 183 Mike Proly .15 .05
❑ 184 Mick Kelleher .15 .05
❑ 185 Phil Niekro .30 .10
❑ 186 Cardinals TL
BA: Keith Hernandez
Pitching: Bob F .30 .10
❑ 187 Jeff Newman .15 .05
❑ 188 Randy Martz .15 .05
❑ 189 Glenn Hoffman .15 .05
❑ 190 J.R. Richard .30 .10
❑ 191 Tim Wallach RC 1.50 .60
❑ 192 Broderick Perkins .15 .05
❑ 193 Darrell Jackson .15 .05
❑ 194 Mike Vail .15 .05
❑ 195 Paul Molitor .30 .10
❑ 196 Willie Upshaw .75 .30
❑ 197 Shane Rawley .15 .05
❑ 198 Chris Speier .15 .05
❑ 199 Don Aase .15 .05
❑ 200 George Brett 3.00 1.25
❑ 201 George Brett SA 1.50 .60
❑ 202 Rick Manning .15 .05
❑ 203 Barfield/Miln/Wells RC 1.50 .60
❑ 204 Gary Roenicke .15 .05
❑ 205 Neil Allen .15 .05
❑ 206 Tony Bernazard .15 .05
❑ 207 Rod Scurry .15 .05
❑ 208 Bobby Murcer .30 .10
❑ 209 Gary Lavelle .15 .05
❑ 210 Keith Hernandez .30 .10
❑ 211 Dan Petry .15 .05
❑ 212 Mario Mendoza .15 .05
❑ 213 Dave Stewart RC 2.50 1.00
❑ 214 Brian Asselstine .15 .05
❑ 215 Mike Krukow .15 .05
❑ 216 White Sox TL
BA: Chet Lemon
Pitching: Dennis Lam .60 .25
❑ 217 Bo McLaughlin .15 .05
❑ 218 Dave Roberts .15 .05
❑ 219 John Curtis .15 .05
❑ 220 Manny Trillo .15 .05
❑ 221 Jim Slaton .15 .05
❑ 222 Butch Wynegar .15 .05
❑ 223 Lloyd Moseby .15 .05
❑ 224 Bruce Bochte .15 .05
❑ 225 Mike Torrez .15 .05
❑ 226 Checklist 133-264 .60 .25
❑ 227 Ray Burris .15 .05
❑ 228 Sam Mejias .15 .05
❑ 229 Geoff Zahn .15 .05
❑ 230 Willie Wilson .30 .10
❑ 231 Davis/Dernier/Virgil RC .75 .30
❑ 232 Terry Crowley .15 .05
❑ 233 Duane Kuiper .15 .05
❑ 234 Ron Hodges .15 .05
❑ 235 Mike Easler .15 .05
❑ 236 John Martin RC .25 .08
❑ 237 Rusty Kuntz .15 .05
❑ 238 Kevin Saucier .15 .05
❑ 239 Jon Matlack .15 .05
❑ 240 Bucky Dent .30 .10
❑ 241 Bucky Dent SA .15 .05
❑ 242 Milt May .15 .05
❑ 243 Bob Owchinko .15 .05
❑ 244 Rufino Linares .15 .05
❑ 245 Ken Reitz .15 .05
❑ 246 New York Mets TL
BA: Hubie Brooks
Pitching: Mike .60 .25
❑ 247 Pedro Guerrero .30 .10
❑ 248 Frank LaCorte .15 .05
❑ 249 Tim Flannery .15 .05
❑ 250 Tug McGraw .30 .10
❑ 251 Fred Lynn .30 .10
❑ 252 Fred Lynn SA .15 .05
❑ 253 Chuck Baker .15 .05
❑ 254 George Bell RC 1.50 .60
❑ 255 Tony Perez .60 .25
❑ 256 Tony Perez SA .30 .10
❑ 257 Larry Harlow .15 .05
❑ 258 Bo Diaz .15 .05
❑ 259 Rodney Scott .15 .05
❑ 260 Bruce Sutter .60 .25
❑ 261 Bailey/Castillo/Rucker RC .15 .05
❑ 262 Doug Bair .15 .05
❑ 263 Victor Cruz .15 .05
❑ 264 Dan Quisenberry .15 .05
❑ 265 Al Bumbry .15 .05
❑ 266 Rick Leach .15 .05
❑ 267 Kurt Bevacqua .15 .05
❑ 268 Rickey Keeton .15 .05
❑ 269 Jim Essian .15 .05
❑ 270 Rusty Staub .30 .10
❑ 271 Larry Bradford .15 .05
❑ 272 Bump Wills .15 .05
❑ 273 Doug Bird .15 .05
❑ 274 Bob Ojeda RC .75 .30
❑ 275 Bob Watson .15 .05
❑ 276 Angels TL/Rod Carew .60 .25
❑ 277 Terry Puhl .15 .05
❑ 278 John Littlefield .15 .05
❑ 279 Bill Russell .30 .10
❑ 280 Ben Oglivie .30 .10
❑ 281 John Verhoeven .15 .05
❑ 282 Ken Macha .15 .05
❑ 283 Brian Allard .15 .05
❑ 284 Bob Grich .30 .10
❑ 285 Sparky Lyle .30 .10
❑ 286 Bill Fahey .15 .05
❑ 287 Alan Bannister .15 .05
❑ 288 Garry Templeton .30 .10

❑ 289 Bob Stanley .15 .05
❑ 290 Ken Singleton .30 .10
❑ 291 Law/Long/Ray RC .30 .10
❑ 292 David Palmer .15 .05
❑ 293 Rob Picciolo .15 .05
❑ 294 Mike LaCoss .15 .05
❑ 295 Jason Thompson .15 .05
❑ 296 Bob Walk .15 .05
❑ 297 Clint Hurdle .15 .05
❑ 298 Danny Darwin .15 .05
❑ 299 Steve Trout .15 .05
❑ 300 Reggie Jackson .60 .25
❑ 301 Reggie Jackson SA .30 .10
❑ 302 Doug Flynn .15 .05
❑ 303 Bill Caudill .15 .05
❑ 304 Johnnie LeMaster .15 .05
❑ 305 Don Sutton .30 .10
❑ 306 Don Sutton SA .15 .05
❑ 307 Randy Bass .75 .30
❑ 308 Charlie Moore .15 .05
❑ 309 Pete Redfern .15 .05
❑ 310 Mike Hargrove .15 .05
❑ 311 Dusty Baker
Burt Hooton TL .30 .10
❑ 312 Lenny Randle .15 .05
❑ 313 John Harris .15 .05
❑ 314 Buck Martinez .15 .05
❑ 315 Burt Hooton .15 .05
❑ 316 Steve Braun .15 .05
❑ 317 Dick Ruthven .15 .05
❑ 318 Mike Heath .15 .05
❑ 319 Dave Rozema .15 .05
❑ 320 Chris Chambliss .30 .10
❑ 321 Chris Chambliss SA .15 .05
❑ 322 Garry Hancock .15 .05
❑ 323 Bill Lee .30 .10
❑ 324 Steve Dillard .15 .05
❑ 325 Jose Cruz .30 .10
❑ 326 Pete Falcone .15 .05
❑ 327 Joe Nolan .15 .05
❑ 328 Ed Farmer .15 .05
❑ 329 U.L. Washington .15 .05
❑ 330 Rick Wise .15 .05
❑ 331 Benny Ayala .15 .05
❑ 332 Don Robinson .15 .05
❑ 333 DiPino/Edwards/Porter RC .15 .05
❑ 334 Aurelio Rodriguez .15 .05
❑ 335 Jim Sundberg .30 .10
❑ 336 Mariners TL
BA: Tom Paciorek
Pitching: Glenn Abb .60 .25
❑ 337 Pete Rose AS .60 .25
❑ 338 Dave Lopes AS .15 .05
❑ 339 Mike Schmidt AS 1.25 .50
❑ 340 Dave Concepcion AS .15 .05
❑ 341 Andre Dawson AS .15 .05
❑ 342A George Foster AS
(With autograph) .30 .10
❑ 342B G.Foster AS ERR NO AU 1.25 .50
❑ 343 Dave Parker AS .15 .05
❑ 344 Gary Carter AS .15 .05
❑ 345 Fernando Valenzuela AS .60 .25
❑ 346 Tom Seaver AS .30 .10
❑ 346B Tom Seaver AS COR .30 .10
❑ 347 Bruce Sutter AS .30 .10
❑ 348 Derrel Thomas .15 .05
❑ 349 George Frazier .15 .05
❑ 350 Thad Bosley .15 .05
❑ 351 Brown/Comb/House RC .15 .05
❑ 352 Dick Davis .15 .05
❑ 353 Jack O'Connor .15 .05
❑ 354 Roberto Ramos .15 .05
❑ 355 Dwight Evans .60 .25
❑ 356 Denny Lewallyn .15 .05
❑ 357 Butch Hobson .15 .05
❑ 358 Mike Parrott .15 .05
❑ 359 Jim Dwyer .15 .05
❑ 360 Len Barker .15 .05
❑ 361 Rafael Landestoy .15 .05
❑ 362 Jim Wright UER
(Wrong Jim Wright
pictured) .15 .05
❑ 363 Bob Molinaro .15 .05
❑ 364 Doyle Alexander .15 .05
❑ 365 Bill Madlock .30 .10
❑ 366 Padres TL
BA: Luis Salazar
Pitching: Juan
Eiche .60 .25
❑ 367 Jim Kaat .30 .10
❑ 368 Alex Trevino .15 .05
❑ 369 Champ Summers .15 .05
❑ 370 Mike Norris .15 .05
❑ 371 Jerry Don Gleaton .15 .05
❑ 372 Luis Gomez .15 .05
❑ 373 Gene Nelson .15 .05
❑ 374 Tim Blackwell .15 .05
❑ 375 Dusty Baker .30 .10
❑ 376 Chris Welsh .15 .05
❑ 377 Kiko Garcia .15 .05
❑ 378 Mike Caldwell .15 .05
❑ 379 Rob Wilfong .15 .05
❑ 380 Dave Stieb .30 .10
❑ 381 Bruce Hurst
Dave Schmidt RC
Julio Valdez RC .15 .05
❑ 382 Joe Simpson .15 .05
❑ 383A Pascual Perez ERR NPO 40.00 15.00
❑ 383B Pascual Perez COR .30 .10
❑ 384 Keith Moreland .15 .05
❑ 385 Ken Forsch .15 .05
❑ 386 Jerry White .15 .05
❑ 387 Tom Veryzer .15 .05
❑ 388 Joe Rudi .30 .10
❑ 389 George Vukovich .15 .05
❑ 390 Eddie Murray 1.25 .50
❑ 391 Dave Tobik .15 .05
❑ 392 Rick Bosetti .15 .05
❑ 393 Al Hrabosky .15 .05
❑ 394 Checklist 265-396 .60 .25
❑ 395 Omar Moreno .15 .05
❑ 396 Twins TL
BA: John Castino
Pitching: Fernando
Ar .60 .25
❑ 397 Ken Brett .15 .05
❑ 398 Mike Squires .15 .05
❑ 399 Pat Zachry .15 .05
❑ 400 Johnny Bench 1.25 .50
❑ 401 Johnny Bench SA .60 .25
❑ 402 Bill Stein .15 .05
❑ 403 Jim Tracy .30 .10
❑ 404 Dickie Thon .15 .05
❑ 405 Rick Reuschel .30 .10
❑ 406 Al Holland .15 .05
❑ 407 Danny Boone .15 .05
❑ 408 Ed Romero .15 .05
❑ 409 Don Cooper .15 .05
❑ 410 Ron Cey .30 .10
❑ 411 Ron Cey SA .15 .05
❑ 412 Luis Leal .15 .05
❑ 413 Dan Meyer .15 .05
❑ 414 Elias Sosa .15 .05
❑ 415 Don Baylor .30 .10
❑ 416 Marty Bystrom .15 .05
❑ 417 Pat Kelly .15 .05
❑ 418 Butcher/John/Schmidt RC .15 .05
❑ 419 Steve Stone .15 .05
❑ 420 George Hendrick .30 .10
❑ 421 Mark Clear .15 .05
❑ 422 Cliff Johnson .15 .05
❑ 423 Stan Papi .15 .05
❑ 424 Bruce Benedict .15 .05
❑ 425 John Candelaria .15 .05
❑ 426 Orioles TL/Eddie Murray .60 .25
❑ 427 Ron Oester .15 .05
❑ 428 LaMarr Hoyt .15 .05
❑ 429 John Wathan .15 .05
❑ 430 Vida Blue .30 .10
❑ 431 Vida Blue SA .15 .05
❑ 432 Mike Scott .30 .10
❑ 433 Alan Ashby .15 .05
❑ 434 Joe Lefebvre .15 .05
❑ 435 Robin Yount 2.00 .75
❑ 436 Joe Strain .15 .05
❑ 437 Juan Berenguer .15 .05
❑ 438 Pete Mackanin .15 .05
❑ 439 Dave Righetti RC 2.50 1.00
❑ 440 Jeff Burroughs .15 .05
❑ 441 Heep/Smith/Sprowl RC .15 .05
❑ 442 Bruce Kison .15 .05
❑ 443 Mark Wagner .15 .05
❑ 444 Terry Forster .30 .10
❑ 445 Larry Parrish .15 .05
❑ 446 Wayne Garland .15 .05
❑ 447 Darrell Porter .15 .05
❑ 448 Darrell Porter SA .15 .05
❑ 449 Luis Aguayo .15 .05
❑ 450 Jack Morris .30 .10
❑ 451 Ed Miller .15 .05
❑ 452 Lee Smith RC 3.00 1.25
❑ 453 Art Howe .15 .05
❑ 454 Rick Langford .15 .05
❑ 455 Tom Burgmeier .15 .05
❑ 456 Chicago Cubs TL
BA: Bill Buckner
Pitching: Randy .30 .10
❑ 457 Tim Stoddard .15 .05
❑ 458 Willie Montanez .15 .05
❑ 459 Bruce Berenyi .15 .05
❑ 460 Jack Clark .30 .10
❑ 461 Rich Dotson .15 .05
❑ 462 Dave Chalk .15 .05
❑ 463 Jim Kern .15 .05
❑ 464 Juan Bonilla RC .25 .08
❑ 465 Lee Mazzilli .30 .10
❑ 466 Randy Lerch .15 .05
❑ 467 Mickey Hatcher .15 .05
❑ 468 Floyd Bannister .15 .05
❑ 469 Ed Ott .15 .05
❑ 470 John Mayberry .15 .05
❑ 471 Hammaker/Jones/Motley RC .15 .05
❑ 472 Oscar Gamble .15 .05
❑ 473 Mike Stanton .15 .05
❑ 474 Ken Oberkfell .15 .05
❑ 475 Alan Trammell .30 .10
❑ 476 Brian Kingman .15 .05
❑ 477 Steve Yeager .30 .10
❑ 478 Ray Searage .15 .05
❑ 479 Rowland Office .15 .05
❑ 480 Steve Carlton .60 .25
❑ 481 Steve Carlton SA .30 .10
❑ 482 Glenn Hubbard .15 .05
❑ 483 Gary Woods .15 .05
❑ 484 Ivan DeJesus .15 .05
❑ 485 Kent Tekulve .15 .05
❑ 486 Yankees TL
BA: Jerry Mumphrey
Pitching: Tommy Jo .30 .10
❑ 487 Bob McClure .15 .05
❑ 488 Ron Jackson .15 .05
❑ 489 Rick Dempsey .15 .05
❑ 490 Dennis Eckersley .60 .25
❑ 491 Checklist 397-528 .60 .25
❑ 492 Joe Price .15 .05
❑ 493 Chet Lemon .30 .10
❑ 494 Hubie Brooks .15 .05
❑ 495 Dennis Leonard .15 .05
❑ 496 Johnny Grubb .15 .05
❑ 497 Jim Anderson .15 .05
❑ 498 Dave Bergman .15 .05
❑ 499 Paul Mirabella .15 .05
❑ 500 Rod Carew .60 .25
❑ 501 Rod Carew SA .30 .10
❑ 502 Brett Butler RC 1.50 .60
❑ 503 Julio Gonzalez .15 .05
❑ 504 Rick Peters .15 .05
❑ 505 Graig Nettles .30 .10
❑ 506 Graig Nettles SA .15 .05
❑ 507 Terry Harper .15 .05
❑ 508 Jody Davis .15 .05
❑ 509 Harry Spilman .15 .05
❑ 510 Fernando Valenzuela 1.25 .50
❑ 511 Ruppert Jones .15 .05
❑ 512 Jerry Dybzinski .15 .05
❑ 513 Rick Rhoden .15 .05
❑ 514 Joe Ferguson .15 .05
❑ 515 Larry Bowa .30 .10
❑ 516 Larry Bowa SA .15 .05
❑ 517 Mark Brouhard .15 .05
❑ 518 Garth Iorg .15 .05
❑ 519 Glenn Adams .15 .05
❑ 520 Mike Flanagan .15 .05
❑ 521 Bill Almon .15 .05
❑ 522 Chuck Rainey .15 .05
❑ 523 Gary Gray .15 .05
❑ 524 Tom Hausman .15 .05
❑ 525 Ray Knight .30 .10

Card	Player		
❑ 526	Expos TL BA: Warren Cromartie Pitching: Bill Gul	.60	.25
❑ 527	John Henry Johnson	.15	.05
❑ 528	Matt Alexander	.15	.05
❑ 529	Allen Ripley	.15	.05
❑ 530	Dickie Noles	.15	.05
❑ 531	Bordi/Budaska/Moore RC	.15	.05
❑ 532	Toby Harrah	.30	.10
❑ 533	Joaquin Andujar	.30	.10
❑ 534	Dave McKay	.15	.05
❑ 535	Lance Parrish	.30	.10
❑ 536	Rafael Ramirez	.15	.05
❑ 537	Doug Capilla	.15	.05
❑ 538	Lou Piniella	.30	.10
❑ 539	Vern Ruhle	.15	.05
❑ 540	Andre Dawson	.30	.10
❑ 541	Barry Evans	.15	.05
❑ 542	Ned Yost	.15	.05
❑ 543	Bill Robinson	.15	.05
❑ 544	Larry Christenson	.15	.05
❑ 545	Reggie Smith	.30	.10
❑ 546	Reggie Smith SA	.15	.05
❑ 547	Rod Carew AS	.30	.10
❑ 548	Willie Randolph AS	.15	.05
❑ 549	George Brett AS	1.50	.60
❑ 550	Bucky Dent AS	.15	.05
❑ 551	Reggie Jackson AS	.30	.10
❑ 552	Ken Singleton AS	.15	.05
❑ 553	Dave Winfield AS	.15	.05
❑ 554	Carlton Fisk AS	.30	.10
❑ 555	Scott McGregor AS	.15	.05
❑ 556	Jack Morris AS	.15	.05
❑ 557	Rich Gossage AS	.15	.05
❑ 558	John Tudor	.30	.10
❑ 559	Indians TL BA: Mike Hargrove Pitching: Bert Blyl	.30	.10
❑ 560	Doug Corbett	.15	.05
❑ 561	Brum/DeLeon/Roof RC	.15	.05
❑ 562	Mike O'Berry	.15	.05
❑ 563	Ross Baumgarten	.15	.05
❑ 564	Doug DeCinces	.15	.05
❑ 565	Jackson Todd	.15	.05
❑ 566	Mike Jorgensen	.15	.05
❑ 567	Bob Babcock	.15	.05
❑ 568	Joe Pettini	.15	.05
❑ 569	Willie Randolph	.30	.10
❑ 570	Willie Randolph SA	.15	.05
❑ 571	Glenn Abbott	.15	.05
❑ 572	Juan Beniquez	.15	.05
❑ 573	Rick Waits	.15	.05
❑ 574	Mike Ramsey	.15	.05
❑ 575	Al Cowens	.15	.05
❑ 576	Giants TL BA: Milt May Pitching: Vida Blue (Che	.60	.25
❑ 577	Rick Monday	.30	.10
❑ 578	Shooty Babitt	.15	.05
❑ 579	Rick Mahler	.15	.05
❑ 580	Bobby Bonds	.30	.10
❑ 581	Ron Reed	.15	.05
❑ 582	Luis Pujols	.15	.05
❑ 583	Tippy Martinez	.15	.05
❑ 584	Hosken Powell	.15	.05
❑ 585	Rollie Fingers	.30	.10
❑ 586	Rollie Fingers SA	.15	.05
❑ 587	Tim Lollar	.15	.05
❑ 588	Dale Berra	.15	.05
❑ 589	Dave Stapleton	.15	.05
❑ 590	Al Oliver	.30	.10
❑ 591	Al Oliver SA	.15	.05
❑ 592	Craig Swan	.15	.05
❑ 593	Billy Smith	.15	.05
❑ 594	Renie Martin	.15	.05
❑ 595	Dave Collins	.15	.05
❑ 596	Damaso Garcia	.15	.05
❑ 597	Wayne Nordhagen	.15	.05
❑ 598	Bob Galasso	.15	.05
❑ 599	Lovig/Patt/Suth RC	.15	.05
❑ 600	Dave Winfield	.30	.10
❑ 601	Sid Monge	.15	.05
❑ 602	Freddie Patek	.15	.05
❑ 603	Rich Hebner	.15	.05
❑ 604	Orlando Sanchez	.15	.05
❑ 605	Steve Rogers	.30	.10
❑ 606	Blue Jays TL BA: John Mayberry Pitching: Dave St	.30	.10
❑ 607	Leon Durham	.15	.05
❑ 608	Jerry Royster	.15	.05
❑ 609	Rick Sutcliffe	.30	.10
❑ 610	Rickey Henderson	4.00	1.50
❑ 611	Joe Niekro	.15	.05
❑ 612	Gary Ward	.15	.05
❑ 613	Jim Gantner	.15	.05
❑ 614	Juan Eichelberger	.15	.05
❑ 615	Bob Boone	.30	.10
❑ 616	Bob Boone SA	.15	.05
❑ 617	Scott McGregor	.15	.05
❑ 618	Tim Foli	.15	.05
❑ 619	Bill Campbell	.15	.05
❑ 620	Ken Griffey	.30	.10
❑ 621	Ken Griffey SA	.15	.05
❑ 622	Dennis Lamp	.15	.05
❑ 623	Gardenhire/Leach/Leary RC	.75	.30
❑ 624	Fergie Jenkins	.30	.10
❑ 625	Hal McRae	.30	.10
❑ 626	Randy Jones	.15	.05
❑ 627	Enos Cabell	.15	.05
❑ 628	Bill Travers	.15	.05
❑ 629	John Wockenfuss	.15	.05
❑ 630	Joe Charboneau	.30	.10
❑ 631	Gene Tenace	.30	.10
❑ 632	Bryan Clark RC	.25	.08
❑ 633	Mitchell Page	.15	.05
❑ 634	Checklist 529-660	.60	.25
❑ 635	Ron Davis	.15	.05
❑ 636	Phillies TL/Rose/Carlton	1.25	.50
❑ 637	Rick Camp	.15	.05
❑ 638	John Milner	.15	.05
❑ 639	Ken Kravec	.15	.05
❑ 640	Cesar Cedeno	.30	.10
❑ 641	Steve Mura	.15	.05
❑ 642	Mike Scioscia	.30	.10
❑ 643	Pete Vuckovich	.15	.05
❑ 644	John Castino	.15	.05
❑ 645	Frank White	.30	.10
❑ 646	Frank White SA	.15	.05
❑ 647	Warren Brusstar	.15	.05
❑ 648	Jose Morales	.15	.05
❑ 649	Ken Clay	.15	.05
❑ 650	Carl Yastrzemski	2.00	.75
❑ 651	Carl Yastrzemski SA	1.25	.50
❑ 652	Steve Nicosia	.15	.05
❑ 653	Brunansky/Sanch/Scon RC	1.50	.60
❑ 654	Jim Morrison	.15	.05
❑ 655	Joel Youngblood	.15	.05
❑ 656	Eddie Whitson	.15	.05
❑ 657	Tom Poquette	.15	.05
❑ 658	Tito Landrum	.15	.05
❑ 659	Fred Martinez	.15	.05
❑ 660	Dave Concepcion	.30	.10
❑ 661	Dave Concepcion SA	.15	.05
❑ 662	Luis Salazar	.15	.05
❑ 663	Hector Cruz	.15	.05
❑ 664	Dan Spillner	.15	.05
❑ 665	Jim Clancy	.15	.05
❑ 666	Tigers TL BA: Steve Kemp Pitching: Dan Petry C	.60	.25
❑ 667	Jeff Reardon	.30	.10
❑ 668	Dale Murphy	.60	.25
❑ 669	Larry Milbourne	.15	.05
❑ 670	Steve Kemp	.15	.05
❑ 671	Mike Davis	.15	.05
❑ 672	Bob Knepper	.15	.05
❑ 673	Keith Drumwright	.15	.05
❑ 674	Dave Goltz	.15	.05
❑ 675	Cecil Cooper	.30	.10
❑ 676	Sal Butera	.15	.05
❑ 677	Alfredo Griffin	.15	.05
❑ 678	Tom Paciorek	.15	.05
❑ 679	Sammy Stewart	.15	.05
❑ 680	Gary Matthews	.30	.10
❑ 681	Marshall/Roen/Sax RC	1.50	.60
❑ 682	Jesse Jefferson	.15	.05
❑ 683	Phil Garner	.30	.10
❑ 684	Harold Baines	.30	.10
❑ 685	Bert Blyleven	.30	.10
❑ 686	Gary Allenson	.15	.05
❑ 687	Greg Minton	.15	.05
❑ 688	Leon Roberts	.15	.05
❑ 689	Lary Sorensen	.15	.05
❑ 690	Dave Kingman	.30	.10
❑ 691	Dan Schatzeder	.15	.05
❑ 692	Wayne Gross	.15	.05
❑ 693	Cesar Geronimo	.15	.05
❑ 694	Dave Wehrmeister	.15	.05
❑ 695	Warren Cromartie	.15	.05
❑ 696	Pirates TL BA: Bill Madlock Pitching: Eddie Solo	.60	.25
❑ 697	John Montefusco	.15	.05
❑ 698	Tony Scott	.15	.05
❑ 699	Dick Tidrow	.15	.05
❑ 700	George Foster	.30	.10
❑ 701	George Foster SA	.15	.05
❑ 702	Steve Renko	.15	.05
❑ 703	Brewers TL BA: Cecil Cooper Pitching: Pete Vucko	.60	.25
❑ 704	Mickey Rivers	.15	.05
❑ 705	Mickey Rivers SA	.15	.05
❑ 706	Barry Foote	.15	.05
❑ 707	Mark Bomback	.15	.05
❑ 708	Gene Richards	.15	.05
❑ 709	Don Money	.15	.05
❑ 710	Jerry Reuss	.15	.05
❑ 711	Edler/Henderson/Walton RC	.75	.30
❑ 712	Dennis Martinez	.30	.10
❑ 713	Del Unser	.15	.05
❑ 714	Jerry Koosman	.30	.10
❑ 715	Willie Stargell	.60	.25
❑ 716	Willie Stargell SA	.30	.10
❑ 717	Rick Miller	.15	.05
❑ 718	Charlie Hough	.30	.10
❑ 719	Jerry Narron	.15	.05
❑ 720	Greg Luzinski	.30	.10
❑ 721	Greg Luzinski SA	.15	.05
❑ 722	Jerry Martin	.15	.05
❑ 723	Junior Kennedy	.15	.05
❑ 724	Dave Rosello	.15	.05
❑ 725	Amos Otis	.30	.10
❑ 726	Amos Otis SA	.15	.05
❑ 727	Sixto Lezcano	.15	.05
❑ 728	Aurelio Lopez	.15	.05
❑ 729	Jim Spencer	.15	.05
❑ 730	Gary Carter	.30	.10
❑ 731	Armstrong/Gwosdz/Kuhaulua RC	.15	.05
❑ 732	Mike Lum	.15	.05
❑ 733	Larry McWilliams	.15	.05
❑ 734	Mike Ivie	.15	.05
❑ 735	Rudy May	.15	.05
❑ 736	Jerry Turner	.15	.05
❑ 737	Reggie Cleveland	.15	.05
❑ 738	Dave Engle	.15	.05
❑ 739	Joey McLaughlin	.15	.05
❑ 740	Dave Lopes	.30	.10
❑ 741	Dave Lopes SA	.15	.05
❑ 742	Dick Drago	.15	.05
❑ 743	John Stearns	.15	.05
❑ 744	Mike Witt	.75	.30
❑ 745	Bake McBride	.30	.10
❑ 746	Andre Thornton	.15	.05
❑ 747	John Lowenstein	.15	.05
❑ 748	Marc Hill	.15	.05
❑ 749	Bob Shirley	.15	.05
❑ 750	Jim Rice	.30	.10
❑ 751	Rick Honeycutt	.15	.05
❑ 752	Lee Lacy	.15	.05
❑ 753	Tom Brookens	.15	.05
❑ 754	Joe Morgan	.30	.10
❑ 755	Joe Morgan SA	.15	.05
❑ 756	Reds TL/Griffey/Seaver	.30	.10
❑ 757	Tom Underwood	.15	.05
❑ 758	Claudell Washington	.15	.05
❑ 759	Paul Splittorff	.15	.05
❑ 760	Bill Buckner	.30	.10
❑ 761	Dave Smith	.15	.05
❑ 762	Mike Phillips	.15	.05
❑ 763	Tom Hume	.15	.05
❑ 764	Steve Swisher	.15	.05
❑ 765	Gorman Thomas	.30	.10
❑ 766	Faedo/Hrbek/Laudner RC	1.50	.60
❑ 767	Roy Smalley	.15	.05
❑ 768	Jerry Garvin	.15	.05

❑	769 Richie Zisk	.15	.05
❑	770 Rich Gossage	.30	.10
❑	771 Rich Gossage SA	.15	.05
❑	772 Bert Campaneris	.30	.10
❑	773 John Denny	.15	.05
❑	774 Jay Johnstone	.15	.05
❑	775 Bob Forsch	.15	.05
❑	776 Mark Belanger	.15	.05
❑	777 Tom Griffin	.15	.05
❑	778 Kevin Hickey RC	.25	.08
❑	779 Grant Jackson	.15	.05
❑	780 Pete Rose	4.00	1.50
❑	781 Pete Rose SA	1.25	.50
❑	782 Frank Taveras	.15	.05
❑	783 Greg Harris RC	.25	.08
❑	784 Milt Wilcox	.15	.05
❑	785 Dan Driessen	.15	.05
❑	786 Red Sox TL BA: Carney Lansford Pitching: Mike To	.60	.25
❑	787 Fred Stanley	.15	.05
❑	788 Woodie Fryman	.15	.05
❑	789 Checklist 661-792	.60	.25
❑	790 Larry Gura	.15	.05
❑	791 Bobby Brown	.15	.05
❑	792 Frank Tanana	.30	.10

1982 Topps Traded

❑	COMP.FACT.SET (132)	175.00	100.00
❑	1T Doyle Alexander	.50	.20
❑	2T Jesse Barfield	3.00	1.25
❑	3T Ross Baumgarten	.50	.20
❑	4T Steve Bedrosian	1.50	.60
❑	5T Mark Belanger	.50	.20
❑	6T Kurt Bevacqua	.50	.20
❑	7T Tim Blackwell	.50	.20
❑	8T Vida Blue	1.00	.40
❑	9T Bob Boone	1.00	.40
❑	10T Larry Bowa	1.00	.40
❑	11T Dan Briggs	.50	.20
❑	12T Bobby Brown	.50	.20
❑	13T Tom Brunansky	3.00	1.25
❑	14T Jeff Burroughs	.50	.20
❑	15T Enos Cabell	.50	.20
❑	16T Bill Campbell	.50	.20
❑	17T Bobby Castillo	.50	.20
❑	18T Bill Caudill	.50	.20
❑	19T Cesar Cedeno	1.00	.40
❑	20T Dave Collins	.50	.20
❑	21T Doug Corbett	.50	.20
❑	22T Al Cowens	.50	.20
❑	23T Chili Davis	3.00	1.25
❑	24T Dick Davis	.50	.20
❑	25T Ron Davis	.50	.20
❑	26T Doug DeCinces	.50	.20
❑	27T Ivan DeJesus	.50	.20
❑	28T Bob Dernier	.50	.20
❑	29T Bo Diaz	.50	.20
❑	30T Roger Erickson	.50	.20
❑	31T Jim Essian	.50	.20
❑	32T Ed Farmer	.50	.20
❑	33T Doug Flynn	.50	.20
❑	34T Tim Foli	.50	.20
❑	35T Dan Ford	.50	.20
❑	36T George Foster	1.00	.40
❑	37T Dave Frost	.50	.20
❑	38T Rich Gale	.50	.20
❑	39T Ron Gardenhire	1.50	.60
❑	40T Ken Griffey	1.00	.40
❑	41T Greg Harris	.50	.20
❑	42T Von Hayes	1.50	.60
❑	43T Larry Herndon	.50	.20
❑	44T Kent Hrbek	3.00	1.25
❑	45T Mike Ivie	.50	.20
❑	46T Grant Jackson	.50	.20
❑	47T Reggie Jackson	2.00	.75
❑	48T Ron Jackson	.50	.20
❑	49T Fergie Jenkins	1.00	.40
❑	50T Lamar Johnson	.50	.20
❑	51T Randy Johnson	.50	.20
❑	52T Jay Johnstone	.50	.20
❑	53T Mick Kelleher	.50	.20
❑	54T Steve Kemp	.50	.20
❑	55T Junior Kennedy	.50	.20
❑	56T Jim Kern	.50	.20
❑	57T Ray Knight	1.00	.40
❑	58T Wayne Krenchicki	.50	.20
❑	59T Mike Krukow	.50	.20
❑	60T Duane Kuiper	.50	.20
❑	61T Mike LaCoss	.50	.20
❑	62T Chet Lemon	1.00	.40
❑	63T Sixto Lezcano	.50	.20
❑	64T Dave Lopes	1.00	.40
❑	65T Jerry Martin	.50	.20
❑	66T Renie Martin	.50	.20
❑	67T John Mayberry	.50	.20
❑	68T Lee Mazzilli	1.00	.40
❑	69T Bake McBride	1.00	.40
❑	70T Dan Meyer	.50	.20
❑	71T Larry Milbourne	.50	.20
❑	72T Eddie Milner	.50	.20
❑	73T Sid Monge	.50	.20
❑	74T John Montefusco	.50	.20
❑	75T Jose Morales	.50	.20
❑	76T Keith Moreland	.50	.20
❑	77T Jim Morrison	.50	.20
❑	78T Rance Mulliniks	.50	.20
❑	79T Steve Mura	.50	.20
❑	80T Gene Nelson	.50	.20
❑	81T Joe Nolan	.50	.20
❑	82T Dickie Noles	.50	.20
❑	83T Al Oliver	1.00	.40
❑	84T Jorge Orta	.50	.20
❑	85T Tom Paciorek	.50	.20
❑	86T Larry Parrish	.50	.20
❑	87T Jack Perconte	.50	.20
❑	88T Gaylord Perry	1.00	.40
❑	89T Rob Picciolo	.50	.20
❑	90T Joe Pittman	.50	.20
❑	91T Hosken Powell	.50	.20
❑	92T Mike Proly	.50	.20
❑	93T Greg Pryor	.50	.20
❑	94T Charlie Puleo	.50	.20
❑	95T Shane Rawley	.50	.20
❑	96T Johnny Ray	1.50	.60
❑	97T Dave Revering	.50	.20
❑	98T Cal Ripken	150.00	90.00
❑	99T Allen Ripley	.50	.20
❑	100T Bill Robinson	.50	.20
❑	101T Aurelio Rodriguez	.50	.20
❑	102T Joe Rudi	1.00	.40
❑	103T Steve Sax	3.00	1.25
❑	104T Dan Schatzeder	.50	.20
❑	105T Bob Shirley	.50	.20
❑	106T Eric Show XRC	1.50	.60
❑	107T Roy Smalley	.50	.20
❑	108T Lonnie Smith	.50	.20
❑	109T Ozzie Smith	15.00	6.00
❑	110T Reggie Smith	1.00	.40
❑	111T Lary Sorensen	.50	.20
❑	112T Elias Sosa	.50	.20
❑	113T Mike Stanton	.50	.20
❑	114T Steve Stroughter	.50	.20
❑	115T Champ Summers	.50	.20
❑	116T Rick Sutcliffe	1.00	.40
❑	117T Frank Tanana	1.00	.40
❑	118T Frank Taveras	.50	.20
❑	119T Garry Templeton	1.00	.40
❑	120T Alex Trevino	.50	.20
❑	121T Jerry Turner	.50	.20
❑	122T Ed VandeBerg	.50	.20
❑	123T Tom Veryzer	.50	.20
❑	124T Ron Washington	.50	.20
❑	125T Bob Watson	.50	.20
❑	126T Dennis Werth	.50	.20
❑	127T Eddie Whitson	.50	.20
❑	128T Rob Wilfong	.50	.20
❑	129T Bump Wills	.50	.20
❑	130T Gary Woods	.50	.20
❑	131T Butch Wynegar	.50	.20
❑	132T Checklist: 1-132	.50	.20

1983 Topps

❑	COMPLETE SET (792)	80.00	40.00
❑	1 Tony Armas RB	.30	.10
❑	2 Rickey Henderson RB	1.25	.50
❑	3 Greg Minton RB	.15	.05
❑	4 Lance Parrish RB	.15	.05
❑	5 Manny Trillo RB	.15	.05
❑	6 John Wathan RB	.15	.05
❑	7 Gene Richards	.15	.05
❑	8 Steve Balboni	.15	.05
❑	9 Joey McLaughlin	.15	.05
❑	10 Gorman Thomas	.30	.10
❑	11 Billy Gardner MG	.15	.05
❑	12 Paul Mirabella	.15	.05
❑	13 Larry Herndon	.15	.05
❑	14 Frank LaCorte	.15	.05
❑	15 Ron Cey	.30	.10
❑	16 George Vukovich	.15	.05
❑	17 Kent Tekulve	.15	.05
❑	18 Kent Tekulve SV	.15	.05
❑	19 Oscar Gamble	.15	.05
❑	20 Carlton Fisk	.60	.25
❑	21 Orioles TL/Murray/Palmer	.60	.25
❑	22 Randy Martz	.15	.05
❑	23 Mike Heath	.15	.05
❑	24 Steve Mura	.15	.05
❑	25 Hal McRae	.30	.10
❑	26 Jerry Royster	.15	.05
❑	27 Doug Corbett	.15	.05
❑	28 Bruce Bochte	.15	.05
❑	29 Randy Jones	.15	.05
❑	30 Jim Rice	.30	.10
❑	31 Bill Gullickson	.15	.05
❑	32 Dave Bergman	.15	.05
❑	33 Jack O'Connor	.15	.05
❑	34 Paul Householder	.15	.05
❑	35 Rollie Fingers	.30	.10
❑	36 Rollie Fingers SV	.15	.05
❑	37 Darrell Johnson MG	.15	.05
❑	38 Tim Flannery	.15	.05
❑	39 Terry Puhl	.15	.05
❑	40 Fernando Valenzuela	.30	.10
❑	41 Jerry Turner	.15	.05
❑	42 Dale Murray	.15	.05
❑	43 Bob Dernier	.15	.05
❑	44 Don Robinson	.15	.05
❑	45 John Mayberry	.15	.05
❑	46 Richard Dotson	.15	.05
❑	47 Dave McKay	.15	.05
❑	48 Lary Sorensen	.15	.05
❑	49 Willie McGee RC	2.50	1.00
❑	50 Bob Horner UER	.30	.10
❑	51 Cubs TL/F.Jenkins	.15	.05
❑	52 Onix Concepcion	.15	.05
❑	53 Mike Witt	.15	.05
❑	54 Jim Maler	.15	.05
❑	55 Mookie Wilson	.30	.10
❑	56 Chuck Rainey	.15	.05
❑	57 Tim Blackwell	.15	.05
❑	58 Al Holland	.15	.05

59	Benny Ayala	.15	.05
60	Johnny Bench	1.25	.50
61	Johnny Bench SV	.60	.25
62	Bob McClure	.15	.05
63	Rick Monday	.30	.10
64	Bill Stein	.15	.05
65	Jack Morris	.30	.10
66	Bob Lillis MG	.15	.05
67	Sal Butera	.15	.05
68	Eric Show RC	.75	.30
69	Lee Lacy	.15	.05
70	Steve Carlton	.60	.25
71	Steve Carlton SV	.30	.10
72	Tom Paciorek	.15	.05
73	Allen Ripley	.15	.05
74	Julio Gonzalez	.15	.05
75	Amos Otis	.30	.10
76	Rick Mahler	.15	.05
77	Hosken Powell	.15	.05
78	Bill Caudill	.15	.05
79	Mick Kelleher	.15	.05
80	George Foster	.30	.10
81	J.Mumphrey/D.Righetti TL	.30	.10
82	Bruce Hurst	.15	.05
83	Ryne Sandberg RC	15.00	6.00
84	Milt May	.15	.05
85	Ken Singleton	.30	.10
86	Tom Hume	.15	.05
87	Joe Rudi	.30	.10
88	Jim Gantner	.15	.05
89	Leon Roberts	.15	.05
90	Jerry Reuss	.15	.05
91	Larry Milbourne	.15	.05
92	Mike LaCoss	.15	.05
93	John Castino	.15	.05
94	Dave Edwards	.15	.05
95	Alan Trammell	.30	.10
96	Dick Howser MG	.15	.05
97	Ross Baumgarten	.15	.05
98	Vance Law	.15	.05
99	Dickie Noles	.15	.05
100	Pete Rose	4.00	1.50
101	Pete Rose SV	1.25	.50
102	Dave Beard	.15	.05
103	Darrell Porter	.15	.05
104	Bob Walk	.15	.05
105	Don Baylor	.30	.10
106	Gene Nelson	.15	.05
107	Mike Jorgensen	.15	.05
108	Glenn Hoffman	.15	.05
109	Luis Leal	.15	.05
110	Ken Griffey	.30	.10
111	Montreal Expos TL		
	BA: Al Oliver		
	ERA: Steve Roger	.30	.10
112	Bob Shirley	.15	.05
113	Ron Roenicke	.15	.05
114	Jim Slaton	.15	.05
115	Chili Davis	.30	.10
116	Dave Schmidt	.15	.05
117	Alan Knicely	.15	.05
118	Chris Welsh	.15	.05
119	Tom Brookens	.15	.05
120	Len Barker	.15	.05
121	Mickey Hatcher	.15	.05
122	Jimmy Smith	.15	.05
123	George Frazier	.15	.05
124	Marc Hill	.15	.05
125	Leon Durham	.15	.05
126	Joe Torre MG	.30	.10
127	Preston Hanna	.15	.05
128	Mike Ramsey	.15	.05
129	Checklist: 1-132	.30	.10
130	Dave Stieb	.30	.10
131	Ed Ott	.15	.05
132	Todd Cruz	.15	.05
133	Jim Barr	.15	.05
134	Hubie Brooks	.15	.05
135	Dwight Evans	.60	.25
136	Willie Aikens	.15	.05
137	Woodie Fryman	.15	.05
138	Rick Dempsey	.15	.05
139	Bruce Berenyi	.15	.05
140	Willie Randolph	.30	.10
141	Indians TL		
	BA: Toby Harrah		
	ERA: Rick Sutcliffe	.30	.10
142	Mike Caldwell	.15	.05
143	Joe Pettini	.15	.05
144	Mark Wagner	.15	.05
145	Don Sutton	.30	.10
146	Don Sutton SV	.15	.05
147	Rick Leach	.15	.05
148	Dave Roberts	.15	.05
149	Johnny Ray	.15	.05
150	Bruce Sutter	.60	.25
151	Bruce Sutter SV	.30	.10
152	Jay Johnstone	.15	.05
153	Jerry Koosman	.30	.10
154	Johnnie LeMaster	.15	.05
155	Dan Quisenberry	.15	.05
156	Billy Martin MG	.60	.25
157	Steve Bedrosian	.15	.05
158	Rob Wilfong	.15	.05
159	Mike Stanton	.15	.05
160	Dave Kingman	.30	.10
161	Dave Kingman SV	.15	.05
162	Mark Clear	.15	.05
163	Cal Ripken	10.00	4.00
164	David Palmer	.15	.05
165	Dan Driessen	.15	.05
166	John Pacella	.15	.05
167	Mark Brouhard	.15	.05
168	Juan Eichelberger	.15	.05
169	Doug Flynn	.15	.05
170	Steve Howe	.15	.05
171	Giants TL/Joe Morgan	.30	.10
172	Vern Ruhle	.15	.05
173	Jim Morrison	.15	.05
174	Jerry Ujdur	.15	.05
175	Bo Diaz	.15	.05
176	Dave Righetti	.30	.10
177	Harold Baines	.30	.10
178	Luis Tiant	.30	.10
179	Luis Tiant SV	.15	.05
180	Rickey Henderson	2.50	1.00
181	Terry Felton	.15	.05
182	Mike Fischlin	.15	.05
183	Ed VandeBerg	.15	.05
184	Bob Clark	.15	.05
185	Tim Lollar	.15	.05
186	Whitey Herzog MG	.30	.10
187	Terry Leach	.15	.05
188	Rick Miller	.15	.05
189	Dan Schatzeder	.15	.05
190	Cecil Cooper	.30	.10
191	Joe Price	.15	.05
192	Floyd Rayford	.15	.05
193	Harry Spilman	.15	.05
194	Cesar Geronimo	.15	.05
195	Bob Stoddard	.15	.05
196	Bill Fahey	.15	.05
197	Jim Eisenreich RC	.75	.30
198	Kiko Garcia	.15	.05
199	Marty Bystrom	.15	.05
200	Rod Carew	.60	.25
201	Rod Carew SV	.30	.10
202	Blue Jays TL		
	BA: Damaso Garcia		
	ERA: Dave Stieb	.30	.10
203	Mike Morgan	.15	.05
204	Junior Kennedy	.15	.05
205	Dave Parker	.30	.10
206	Ken Oberkfell	.15	.05
207	Rick Camp	.15	.05
208	Dan Meyer	.15	.05
209	Mike Moore RC	.75	.30
210	Jack Clark	.30	.10
211	John Denny	.15	.05
212	John Stearns	.15	.05
213	Tom Burgmeier	.15	.05
214	Jerry White	.15	.05
215	Mario Soto	.30	.10
216	Tony LaRussa MG	.30	.10
217	Tim Stoddard	.15	.05
218	Roy Howell	.15	.05
219	Mike Armstrong	.15	.05
220	Dusty Baker	.30	.10
221	Joe Niekro	.15	.05
222	Damaso Garcia	.15	.05
223	John Montefusco	.15	.05
224	Mickey Rivers	.15	.05
225	Enos Cabell	.15	.05
226	Enrique Romo	.15	.05
227	Chris Bando	.15	.05
228	Joaquin Andujar	.30	.10
229	Phillies TL/S.Carlton	.15	.05
230	Fergie Jenkins	.30	.10
231	Fergie Jenkins SV	.15	.05
232	Tom Brunansky	.30	.10
233	Wayne Gross	.15	.05
234	Larry Andersen	.15	.05
235	Claudell Washington	.15	.05
236	Steve Renko	.15	.05
237	Dan Norman	.15	.05
238	Bud Black RC	.75	.30
239	Dave Stapleton	.15	.05
240	Rich Gossage	.30	.10
241	Rich Gossage SV	.15	.05
242	Joe Nolan	.15	.05
243	Duane Walker	.15	.05
244	Dwight Bernard	.15	.05
245	Steve Sax	.30	.10
246	George Bamberger MG	.15	.05
247	Dave Smith	.15	.05
248	Bake McBride	.30	.10
249	Checklist: 133-264	.30	.10
250	Bill Buckner	.30	.10
251	Alan Wiggins	.15	.05
252	Luis Aguayo	.15	.05
253	Larry McWilliams	.15	.05
254	Rick Cerone	.15	.05
255	Gene Garber	.15	.05
256	Gene Garber SV	.15	.05
257	Jesse Barfield	.30	.10
258	Manny Castillo	.15	.05
259	Jeff Jones	.15	.05
260	Steve Kemp	.15	.05
261	Tigers TL		
	BA: Larry Herndon		
	ERA: Dan Petry		
	(Che	.30	.10
262	Ron Jackson	.15	.05
263	Renie Martin	.15	.05
264	Jamie Quirk	.15	.05
265	Joel Youngblood	.15	.05
266	Paul Boris	.15	.05
267	Terry Francona	.30	.10
268	Storm Davis RC	.75	.30
269	Ron Oester	.15	.05
270	Dennis Eckersley	.60	.25
271	Ed Romero	.15	.05
272	Frank Tanana	.30	.10
273	Mark Belanger	.15	.05
274	Terry Kennedy	.15	.05
275	Ray Knight	.30	.10
276	Gene Mauch MG	.15	.05
277	Rance Mulliniks	.15	.05
278	Kevin Hickey	.15	.05
279	Greg Gross	.15	.05
280	Bert Blyleven	.30	.10
281	Andre Robertson	.15	.05
282	R.Smith w/Sandberg	1.25	.50
283	Reggie Smith SV	.15	.05
284	Jeff Lahti	.15	.05
285	Lance Parrish	.30	.10
286	Rick Langford	.15	.05
287	Bobby Brown	.15	.05
288	Joe Cowley	.15	.05
289	Jerry Dybzinski	.15	.05
290	Jeff Reardon	.30	.10
291	Bill Madlock		
	John Candelaria TL	.30	.10
292	Craig Swan	.15	.05
293	Glenn Gulliver	.15	.05
294	Dave Engle	.15	.05
295	Jerry Remy	.15	.05
296	Greg Harris	.15	.05
297	Ned Yost	.15	.05
298	Floyd Chiffer	.15	.05
299	George Wright RC	.75	.30
300	Mike Schmidt	3.00	1.25
301	Mike Schmidt SV	1.25	.50
302	Ernie Whitt	.15	.05
303	Miguel Dilone	.15	.05
304	Dave Rucker	.15	.05
305	Larry Bowa	.30	.10
306	Tom Lasorda MG	.60	.25

❑ 307 Lou Piniella .30 .10
❑ 308 Jesus Vega .15 .05
❑ 309 Jeff Leonard .15 .05
❑ 310 Greg Luzinski .30 .10
❑ 311 Glenn Brummer .15 .05
❑ 312 Brian Kingman .15 .05
❑ 313 Gary Gray .15 .05
❑ 314 Ken Dayley .15 .05
❑ 315 Rick Burleson .15 .05
❑ 316 Paul Splittorff .15 .05
❑ 317 Gary Rajsich .15 .05
❑ 318 John Tudor .30 .10
❑ 319 Lenn Sakata .15 .05
❑ 320 Steve Rogers .30 .10
❑ 321 Brewers TL/Robin Yount 1.25 .50
❑ 322 Dave Van Gorder .15 .05
❑ 323 Luis DeLeon .15 .05
❑ 324 Mike Marshall .15 .05
❑ 325 Von Hayes .15 .05
❑ 326 Garth Iorg .15 .05
❑ 327 Bobby Castillo .15 .05
❑ 328 Craig Reynolds .15 .05
❑ 329 Randy Niemann .15 .05
❑ 330 Buddy Bell .30 .10
❑ 331 Mike Krukow .15 .05
❑ 332 Glenn Wilson .75 .30
❑ 333 Dave LaRoche .15 .05
❑ 334 Dave LaRoche SV .15 .05
❑ 335 Steve Henderson .15 .05
❑ 336 Rene Lachemann MG .15 .05
❑ 337 Tito Landrum .15 .05
❑ 338 Bob Owchinko .15 .05
❑ 339 Terry Harper .15 .05
❑ 340 Larry Gura .15 .05
❑ 341 Doug DeCinces .15 .05
❑ 342 Atlee Hammaker .15 .05
❑ 343 Bob Bailor .15 .05
❑ 344 Roger LaFrancois .15 .05
❑ 345 Jim Clancy .15 .05
❑ 346 Joe Pittman .15 .05
❑ 347 Sammy Stewart .15 .05
❑ 348 Alan Bannister .15 .05
❑ 349 Checklist: 265-396 .30 .10
❑ 350 Robin Yount 2.00 .75
❑ 351 Reds TL
BA: Cesar Cedeno
ERA: Mario Soto
(Check .30 .10
❑ 352 Mike Scioscia .30 .10
❑ 353 Steve Comer .15 .05
❑ 354 Randy Johnson .15 .05
❑ 355 Jim Bibby .15 .05
❑ 356 Gary Woods .15 .05
❑ 357 Len Matuszek .15 .05
❑ 358 Jerry Garvin .15 .05
❑ 359 Dave Collins .15 .05
❑ 360 Nolan Ryan 6.00 2.50
❑ 361 Nolan Ryan SV 3.00 1.25
❑ 362 Bill Almon .15 .05
❑ 363 John Stuper .15 .05
❑ 364 Brett Butler .30 .10
❑ 365 Dave Lopes .30 .10
❑ 366 Dick Williams MG .15 .05
❑ 367 Bud Anderson .15 .05
❑ 368 Richie Zisk .15 .05
❑ 369 Jesse Orosco .15 .05
❑ 370 Gary Carter .30 .10
❑ 371 Mike Richardt .15 .05
❑ 372 Terry Crowley .15 .05
❑ 373 Kevin Saucier .15 .05
❑ 374 Wayne Krenchicki .15 .05
❑ 375 Pete Vuckovich .15 .05
❑ 376 Ken Landreaux .15 .05
❑ 377 Lee May .15 .05
❑ 378 Lee May SV .15 .05
❑ 379 Guy Sularz .15 .05
❑ 380 Ron Davis .15 .05
❑ 381 Red Sox TL
BA: Jim Rice
ERA: Bob Stanley
(Check .30 .10
❑ 382 Bob Knepper .15 .05
❑ 383 Ozzie Virgil .15 .05
❑ 384 Dave Dravecky RC 1.50 .60
❑ 385 Mike Easler .15 .05
❑ 386 Rod Carew AS .30 .10
❑ 387 Bob Grich AS .15 .05
❑ 388 George Brett AS 1.50 .60
❑ 389 Robin Yount AS 1.25 .50
❑ 390 Reggie Jackson AS .30 .10
❑ 391 Rickey Henderson AS 1.25 .50
❑ 392 Fred Lynn AS .15 .05
❑ 393 Carlton Fisk AS .30 .10
❑ 394 Pete Vuckovich AS .15 .05
❑ 395 Larry Gura AS .15 .05
❑ 396 Dan Quisenberry AS .15 .05
❑ 397 Pete Rose AS .60 .25
❑ 398 Manny Trillo AS .15 .05
❑ 399 Mike Schmidt AS 1.25 .50
❑ 400 Dave Concepcion AS .15 .05
❑ 401 Dale Murphy AS .30 .10
❑ 402 Andre Dawson AS .15 .05
❑ 403 Tim Raines AS .15 .05
❑ 404 Gary Carter AS .15 .05
❑ 405 Steve Rogers AS .15 .05
❑ 406 Steve Carlton AS .30 .10
❑ 407 Bruce Sutter AS .30 .10
❑ 408 Rudy May .15 .05
❑ 409 Marvis Foley .15 .05
❑ 410 Phil Niekro .30 .10
❑ 411 Phil Niekro SV .15 .05
❑ 412 Rangers TL
BA: Buddy Bell
ERA: Charlie Hough
(C .30 .10
❑ 413 Matt Keough .15 .05
❑ 414 Julio Cruz .15 .05
❑ 415 Bob Forsch .15 .05
❑ 416 Joe Ferguson .15 .05
❑ 417 Tom Hausman .15 .05
❑ 418 Greg Pryor .15 .05
❑ 419 Steve Crawford .15 .05
❑ 420 Al Oliver .30 .10
❑ 421 Al Oliver SV .15 .05
❑ 422 George Cappuzzello .15 .05
❑ 423 Tom Lawless .15 .05
❑ 424 Jerry Augustine .15 .05
❑ 425 Pedro Guerrero .30 .10
❑ 426 Earl Weaver MG .30 .10
❑ 427 Roy Lee Jackson .15 .05
❑ 428 Champ Summers .15 .05
❑ 429 Eddie Whitson .15 .05
❑ 430 Kirk Gibson .30 .10
❑ 431 Gary Gaetti RC 1.50 .60
❑ 432 Porfirio Altamirano .15 .05
❑ 433 Dale Berra .15 .05
❑ 434 Dennis Lamp .15 .05
❑ 435 Tony Armas .30 .10
❑ 436 Bill Campbell .15 .05
❑ 437 Rick Sweet .15 .05
❑ 438 Dave LaPoint .15 .05
❑ 439 Rafael Ramirez .15 .05
❑ 440 Ron Guidry .30 .10
❑ 441 Astros TL
BA: Ray Knight
ERA: Joe Niekro
(Check .30 .10
❑ 442 Brian Downing .30 .10
❑ 443 Don Hood .15 .05
❑ 444 Wally Backman .15 .05
❑ 445 Mike Flanagan .15 .05
❑ 446 Reid Nichols .15 .05
❑ 447 Bryn Smith .15 .05
❑ 448 Darrell Evans .30 .10
❑ 449 Eddie Milner .15 .05
❑ 450 Ted Simmons .30 .10
❑ 451 Ted Simmons SV .15 .05
❑ 452 Lloyd Moseby .15 .05
❑ 453 Lamar Johnson .15 .05
❑ 454 Bob Welch .30 .10
❑ 455 Sixto Lezcano .15 .05
❑ 456 Lee Elia MG .15 .05
❑ 457 Milt Wilcox .15 .05
❑ 458 Ron Washington .15 .05
❑ 459 Ed Farmer .15 .05
❑ 460 Roy Smalley .15 .05
❑ 461 Steve Trout .15 .05
❑ 462 Steve Nicosia .15 .05
❑ 463 Gaylord Perry .30 .10
❑ 464 Gaylord Perry SV .15 .05
❑ 465 Lonnie Smith .15 .05
❑ 466 Tom Underwood .15 .05
❑ 467 Rufino Linares .15 .05
❑ 468 Dave Goltz .15 .05
❑ 469 Ron Gardenhire .15 .05
❑ 470 Greg Minton .15 .05
❑ 471 Kansas City Royals TL
BA: Willie Wilson
ERA: Vid .30 .10
❑ 472 Gary Allenson .15 .05
❑ 473 John Lowenstein .15 .05
❑ 474 Ray Burris .15 .05
❑ 475 Cesar Cedeno .30 .10
❑ 476 Rob Picciolo .15 .05
❑ 477 Tom Niedenfuer .15 .05
❑ 478 Phil Garner .30 .10
❑ 479 Charlie Hough .30 .10
❑ 480 Toby Harrah .30 .10
❑ 481 Scot Thompson .15 .05
❑ 482 Tony Gwynn RC 25.00 10.00
❑ 483 Lynn Jones .15 .05
❑ 484 Dick Ruthven .15 .05
❑ 485 Omar Moreno .15 .05
❑ 486 Clyde King MG .15 .05
❑ 487 Jerry Hairston .15 .05
❑ 488 Alfredo Griffin .15 .05
❑ 489 Tom Herr .15 .05
❑ 490 Jim Palmer .30 .10
❑ 491 Jim Palmer SV .15 .05
❑ 492 Paul Serna .15 .05
❑ 493 Steve McCatty .15 .05
❑ 494 Bob Brenly .15 .05
❑ 495 Warren Cromartie .15 .05
❑ 496 Tom Veryzer .15 .05
❑ 497 Rick Sutcliffe .30 .10
❑ 498 Wade Boggs RC 15.00 6.00
❑ 499 Jeff Little .15 .05
❑ 500 Reggie Jackson .60 .25
❑ 501 Reggie Jackson SV .30 .10
❑ 502 Braves TL/Murphy/Niekro .60 .25
❑ 503 Moose Haas .15 .05
❑ 504 Don Werner .15 .05
❑ 505 Garry Templeton .30 .10
❑ 506 Jim Gott RC .75 .30
❑ 507 Tony Scott .15 .05
❑ 508 Tom Filer .15 .05
❑ 509 Lou Whitaker .30 .10
❑ 510 Tug McGraw .30 .10
❑ 511 Tug McGraw SV .15 .05
❑ 512 Doyle Alexander .15 .05
❑ 513 Fred Stanley .15 .05
❑ 514 Rudy Law .15 .05
❑ 515 Gene Tenace .30 .10
❑ 516 Bill Virdon MG .15 .05
❑ 517 Gary Ward .15 .05
❑ 518 Bill Laskey .15 .05
❑ 519 Terry Bulling .15 .05
❑ 520 Fred Lynn .30 .10
❑ 521 Bruce Benedict .15 .05
❑ 522 Pat Zachry .15 .05
❑ 523 Carney Lansford .30 .10
❑ 524 Tom Brennan .15 .05
❑ 525 Frank White .30 .10
❑ 526 Checklist: 397-528 .30 .10
❑ 527 Larry Biittner .15 .05
❑ 528 Jamie Easterly .15 .05
❑ 529 Tim Laudner .15 .05
❑ 530 Eddie Murray 1.25 .50
❑ 531 A's TL/Rickey Henderson 1.25 .50
❑ 532 Dave Stewart .30 .10
❑ 533 Luis Salazar .15 .05
❑ 534 John Butcher .15 .05
❑ 535 Manny Trillo .15 .05
❑ 536 John Wockenfuss .15 .05
❑ 537 Rod Scurry .15 .05
❑ 538 Danny Heep .15 .05
❑ 539 Roger Erickson .15 .05
❑ 540 Ozzie Smith 2.00 .75
❑ 541 Britt Burns .15 .05
❑ 542 Jody Davis .15 .05
❑ 543 Alan Fowlkes .15 .05
❑ 544 Larry Whisenton .15 .05
❑ 545 Floyd Bannister .15 .05
❑ 546 Dave Garcia MG .15 .05
❑ 547 Geoff Zahn .15 .05
❑ 548 Brian Giles .15 .05
❑ 549 Charlie Puleo .15 .05
❑ 550 Carl Yastrzemski 2.00 .75

❑ 551 Carl Yastrzemski SV 1.25 .50
❑ 552 Tim Wallach .30 .10
❑ 553 Dennis Martinez .30 .10
❑ 554 Mike Vail .15 .05
❑ 555 Steve Yeager .30 .10
❑ 556 Willie Upshaw .15 .05
❑ 557 Rick Honeycutt .15 .05
❑ 558 Dickie Thon .15 .05
❑ 559 Pete Redfern .15 .05
❑ 560 Ron LeFlore .30 .10
❑ 561 Cardinals TL
BA: Lonnie Smith
ERA: Joaquin Anduj .30 .10
❑ 562 Dave Rozema .15 .05
❑ 563 Juan Bonilla .15 .05
❑ 564 Sid Monge .15 .05
❑ 565 Bucky Dent .30 .10
❑ 566 Manny Sarmiento .15 .05
❑ 567 Joe Simpson .15 .05
❑ 568 Willie Hernandez .15 .05
❑ 569 Jack Perconte .15 .05
❑ 570 Vida Blue .30 .10
❑ 571 Mickey Klutts .15 .05
❑ 572 Bob Watson .15 .05
❑ 573 Andy Hassler .15 .05
❑ 574 Glenn Adams .15 .05
❑ 575 Neil Allen .15 .05
❑ 576 Frank Robinson MG .60 .25
❑ 577 Luis Aponte .15 .05
❑ 578 David Green RC .75 .30
❑ 579 Rich Dauer .15 .05
❑ 580 Tom Seaver 1.25 .50
❑ 581 Tom Seaver SV .30 .10
❑ 582 Marshall Edwards .15 .05
❑ 583 Terry Forster .30 .10
❑ 584 Dave Hostetler .15 .05
❑ 585 Jose Cruz .30 .10
❑ 586 Frank Viola RC 2.50 1.00
❑ 587 Ivan DeJesus .15 .05
❑ 588 Pat Underwood .15 .05
❑ 589 Alvis Woods .15 .05
❑ 590 Tony Pena .15 .05
❑ 591 White Sox TL
BA: Greg Luzinski
ERA: LaMarr Hoyt# .30 .10
❑ 592 Shane Rawley .15 .05
❑ 593 Broderick Perkins .15 .05
❑ 594 Eric Rasmussen .15 .05
❑ 595 Tim Raines .30 .10
❑ 596 Randy Johnson .15 .05
❑ 597 Mike Proly .15 .05
❑ 598 Dwayne Murphy .15 .05
❑ 599 Don Aase .15 .05
❑ 600 George Brett 3.00 1.25
❑ 601 Ed Lynch .15 .05
❑ 602 Rich Gedman .15 .05
❑ 603 Joe Morgan .30 .10
❑ 604 Joe Morgan SV .15 .05
❑ 605 Gary Roenicke .15 .05
❑ 606 Bobby Cox MG .30 .10
❑ 607 Charlie Leibrandt .15 .05
❑ 608 Don Money .15 .05
❑ 609 Danny Darwin .15 .05
❑ 610 Steve Garvey .30 .10
❑ 611 Bert Roberge .15 .05
❑ 612 Steve Swisher .15 .05
❑ 613 Mike Ivie .15 .05
❑ 614 Ed Glynn .15 .05
❑ 615 Garry Maddox .15 .05
❑ 616 Bill Nahorodny .15 .05
❑ 617 Butch Wynegar .15 .05
❑ 618 LaMarr Hoyt .15 .05
❑ 619 Keith Moreland .15 .05
❑ 620 Mike Norris .15 .05
❑ 621 New York Mets TL
BA: Mookie Wilson
ERA: Craig Sw .30 .10
❑ 622 Dave Edler .15 .05
❑ 623 Luis Sanchez .15 .05
❑ 624 Glenn Hubbard .15 .05
❑ 625 Ken Forsch .15 .05
❑ 626 Jerry Martin .15 .05
❑ 627 Doug Bair .15 .05
❑ 628 Julio Valdez .15 .05
❑ 629 Charlie Lea .15 .05
❑ 630 Paul Molitor .30 .10

❑ 631 Tippy Martinez .15 .05
❑ 632 Alex Trevino .15 .05
❑ 633 Vicente Romo .15 .05
❑ 634 Max Venable .15 .05
❑ 635 Graig Nettles .30 .10
❑ 636 Graig Nettles SV .15 .05
❑ 637 Pat Corrales MG .15 .05
❑ 638 Dan Petry .15 .05
❑ 639 Art Howe .15 .05
❑ 640 Andre Thornton .15 .05
❑ 641 Billy Sample .15 .05
❑ 642 Checklist: 529-660 .30 .10
❑ 643 Bump Wills .15 .05
❑ 644 Joe Lefebvre .15 .05
❑ 645 Bill Madlock .30 .10
❑ 646 Jim Essian .15 .05
❑ 647 Bobby Mitchell .15 .05
❑ 648 Jeff Burroughs .15 .05
❑ 649 Tommy Boggs .15 .05
❑ 650 George Hendrick .30 .10
❑ 651 Angels TL/Rod Carew .30 .10
❑ 652 Butch Hobson .15 .05
❑ 653 Ellis Valentine .15 .05
❑ 654 Bob Ojeda .15 .05
❑ 655 Al Bumbry .15 .05
❑ 656 Dave Frost .15 .05
❑ 657 Mike Gates .15 .05
❑ 658 Frank Pastore .15 .05
❑ 659 Charlie Moore .15 .05
❑ 660 Mike Hargrove .15 .05
❑ 661 Bill Russell .30 .10
❑ 662 Joe Sambito .15 .05
❑ 663 Tom O'Malley .15 .05
❑ 664 Bob Molinaro .15 .05
❑ 665 Jim Sundberg .30 .10
❑ 666 Sparky Anderson MG .30 .10
❑ 667 Dick Davis .15 .05
❑ 668 Larry Christenson .15 .05
❑ 669 Mike Squires .15 .05
❑ 670 Jerry Mumphrey .15 .05
❑ 671 Lenny Faedo .15 .05
❑ 672 Jim Kaat .30 .10
❑ 673 Jim Kaat SV .15 .05
❑ 674 Kurt Bevacqua .15 .05
❑ 675 Jim Beattie .15 .05
❑ 676 Biff Pocoroba .15 .05
❑ 677 Dave Revering .15 .05
❑ 678 Juan Beniquez .15 .05
❑ 679 Mike Scott .30 .10
❑ 680 Andre Dawson .30 .10
❑ 681 Dodgers Leaders
BA: Pedro Guerrero
ERA: Fernando .30 .10
❑ 682 Bob Stanley .15 .05
❑ 683 Dan Ford .15 .05
❑ 684 Rafael Landestoy .15 .05
❑ 685 Lee Mazzilli .30 .10
❑ 686 Randy Lerch .15 .05
❑ 687 U.L. Washington .15 .05
❑ 688 Jim Wohlford .15 .05
❑ 689 Ron Hassey .15 .05
❑ 690 Kent Hrbek .30 .10
❑ 691 Dave Tobik .15 .05
❑ 692 Denny Walling .15 .05
❑ 693 Sparky Lyle .30 .10
❑ 694 Sparky Lyle SV .15 .05
❑ 695 Ruppert Jones .15 .05
❑ 696 Chuck Tanner MG .15 .05
❑ 697 Barry Foote .15 .05
❑ 698 Tony Bernazard .15 .05
❑ 699 Lee Smith .60 .25
❑ 700 Keith Hernandez .30 .10
❑ 701 Willie Wilson
Al Oliver LL .30 .10
❑ 702 Reggie/Thomas/Kingman LL .30 .10
❑ 703 RBI Leaders
AL: Hal McRae
NL: Dale Murphy
NL: A .60 .25
❑ 704 R.Henderson/T.Raines LL 1.25 .50
❑ 705 L.Hoyt/S.Carlton LL .30 .10
❑ 706 F.Bannister/Carlton LL .30 .10
❑ 707 Rick Sutcliffe
Steve Rogers LL .30 .10
❑ 708 Leading Firemen
AL: Dan Quisenberry
NL: Bruce Su .30 .10
❑ 709 Jimmy Sexton .15 .05
❑ 710 Willie Wilson .30 .10
❑ 711 Mariners TL
BA: Bruce Bochte
ERA: Jim Beattie .30 .10
❑ 712 Bruce Kison .15 .05
❑ 713 Ron Hodges .15 .05
❑ 714 Wayne Nordhagen .15 .05
❑ 715 Tony Perez .60 .25
❑ 716 Tony Perez SV .30 .10
❑ 717 Scott Sanderson .15 .05
❑ 718 Jim Dwyer .15 .05
❑ 719 Rich Gale .15 .05
❑ 720 Dave Concepcion .30 .10
❑ 721 John Martin .15 .05
❑ 722 Jorge Orta .15 .05
❑ 723 Randy Moffitt .15 .05
❑ 724 Johnny Grubb .15 .05
❑ 725 Dan Spillner .15 .05
❑ 726 Harvey Kuenn MG .15 .05
❑ 727 Chet Lemon .30 .10
❑ 728 Ron Reed .15 .05
❑ 729 Jerry Morales .15 .05
❑ 730 Jason Thompson .15 .05
❑ 731 Al Williams .15 .05
❑ 732 Dave Henderson .15 .05
❑ 733 Buck Martinez .15 .05
❑ 734 Steve Braun .15 .05
❑ 735 Tommy John .30 .10
❑ 736 Tommy John SV .15 .05
❑ 737 Mitchell Page .15 .05
❑ 738 Tim Foli .15 .05
❑ 739 Rick Ownbey .15 .05
❑ 740 Rusty Staub .30 .10
❑ 741 Rusty Staub SV .15 .05
❑ 742 Padres TL
BA: Terry Kennedy
ERA: Tim Lollar
(Ch .30 .10
❑ 743 Mike Torrez .15 .05
❑ 744 Brad Mills .15 .05
❑ 745 Scott McGregor .15 .05
❑ 746 John Wathan .15 .05
❑ 747 Fred Breining .15 .05
❑ 748 Derrel Thomas .15 .05
❑ 749 Jon Matlack .15 .05
❑ 750 Ben Oglivie .30 .10
❑ 751 Brad Havens .15 .05
❑ 752 Luis Pujols .15 .05
❑ 753 Elias Sosa .15 .05
❑ 754 Bill Robinson .15 .05
❑ 755 John Candelaria .15 .05
❑ 756 Russ Nixon MG .15 .05
❑ 757 Rick Manning .15 .05
❑ 758 Aurelio Rodriguez .15 .05
❑ 759 Doug Bird .15 .05
❑ 760 Dale Murphy .60 .25
❑ 761 Gary Lucas .15 .05
❑ 762 Cliff Johnson .15 .05
❑ 763 Al Cowens .15 .05
❑ 764 Pete Falcone .15 .05
❑ 765 Bob Boone .30 .10
❑ 766 Barry Bonnell .15 .05
❑ 767 Duane Kuiper .15 .05
❑ 768 Chris Speier .15 .05
❑ 769 Checklist: 661-792 .30 .10
❑ 770 Dave Winfield .30 .10
❑ 771 Twins TL
BA: Kent Hrbek
ERA: Bobby Castillo
(Ch .30 .10
❑ 772 Jim Kern .15 .05
❑ 773 Larry Hisle .15 .05
❑ 774 Alan Ashby .15 .05
❑ 775 Burt Hooton .15 .05
❑ 776 Larry Parrish .15 .05
❑ 777 John Curtis .15 .05
❑ 778 Rich Hebner .15 .05
❑ 779 Rick Waits .15 .05
❑ 780 Gary Matthews .30 .10
❑ 781 Rick Rhoden .15 .05
❑ 782 Bobby Murcer .30 .10
❑ 783 Bobby Murcer SV .15 .05
❑ 784 Jeff Newman .15 .05
❑ 785 Dennis Leonard .15 .05

❑ 786 Ralph Houk MG .15 .05
❑ 787 Dick Tidrow .15 .05
❑ 788 Dane Iorg .15 .05
❑ 789 Bryan Clark .15 .05
❑ 790 Bob Grich .30 .10
❑ 791 Gary Lavelle .15 .05
❑ 792 Chris Chambliss .30 .10
❑ XX Game Insert Card .10 .05

1983 Topps Traded

❑ COMP.FACT.SET (132) 40.00 15.00
❑ 1T Neil Allen .25 .08
❑ 2T Bill Almon .25 .08
❑ 3T Joe Altobelli MG .25 .08
❑ 4T Tony Armas 1.00 .40
❑ 5T Doug Bair .25 .08
❑ 6T Steve Baker .25 .08
❑ 7T Floyd Bannister .25 .08
❑ 8T Don Baylor 1.00 .40
❑ 9T Tony Bernazard .25 .08
❑ 10T Larry Biittner .25 .08
❑ 11T Dann Bilardello .25 .08
❑ 12T Doug Bird .25 .08
❑ 13T Steve Boros MG .25 .08
❑ 14T Greg Brock .25 .08
❑ 15T Mike C. Brown .25 .08
❑ 16T Tom Burgmeier .25 .08
❑ 17T Randy Bush .25 .08
❑ 18T Bert Campaneris 1.00 .40
❑ 19T Ron Cey 1.00 .40
❑ 20T Chris Codiroli .25 .08
❑ 21T Dave Collins .25 .08
❑ 22T Terry Crowley .25 .08
❑ 23T Julio Cruz .25 .08
❑ 24T Mike Davis .25 .08
❑ 25T Frank DiPino .25 .08
❑ 26T Bill Doran XRC 1.00 .40
❑ 27T Jerry Dybzinski .25 .08
❑ 28T Jamie Easterly .25 .08
❑ 29T Juan Eichelberger .25 .08
❑ 30T Jim Essian .25 .08
❑ 31T Pete Falcone .25 .08
❑ 32T Mike Ferraro MG .25 .08
❑ 33T Terry Forster 1.00 .40
❑ 34T Julio Franco XRC 8.00 3.00
❑ 35T Rich Gale .25 .08
❑ 36T Kiko Garcia .25 .08
❑ 37T Steve Garvey 1.00 .40
❑ 38T Johnny Grubb .25 .08
❑ 39T Mel Hall XRC 1.00 .40
❑ 40T Von Hayes .25 .08
❑ 41T Danny Heep .25 .08
❑ 42T Steve Henderson .25 .08
❑ 43T Keith Hernandez 1.00 .40
❑ 44T Leo Hernandez .25 .08
❑ 45T Willie Hernandez .25 .08
❑ 46T Al Holland .25 .08
❑ 47T Frank Howard MG 1.00 .40
❑ 48T Bobby Johnson .25 .08
❑ 49T Cliff Johnson .25 .08
❑ 50T Odell Jones .25 .08
❑ 51T Mike Jorgensen .25 .08
❑ 52T Bob Kearney .25 .08
❑ 53T Steve Kemp .25 .08
❑ 54T Matt Keough .25 .08
❑ 55T Ron Kittle XRC 2.00 .75
❑ 56T Mickey Klutts .25 .08
❑ 57T Alan Knicely .25 .08
❑ 58T Mike Krukow .25 .08
❑ 59T Rafael Landestoy .25 .08
❑ 60T Carney Lansford 1.00 .40
❑ 61T Joe Lefebvre .25 .08
❑ 62T Bryan Little .25 .08
❑ 63T Aurelio Lopez .25 .08
❑ 64T Mike Madden .25 .08
❑ 65T Rick Manning .25 .08
❑ 66T Billy Martin MG 2.00 .75
❑ 67T Lee Mazzilli 1.00 .40
❑ 68T Andy McGaffigan .25 .08
❑ 69T Craig McMurtry .25 .08
❑ 70T John McNamara MG .25 .08
❑ 71T Orlando Mercado .25 .08
❑ 72T Larry Milbourne .25 .08
❑ 73T Randy Moffitt .25 .08
❑ 74T Sid Monge .25 .08
❑ 75T Jose Morales .25 .08
❑ 76T Omar Moreno .25 .08
❑ 77T Joe Morgan 1.00 .40
❑ 78T Mike Morgan .25 .08
❑ 79T Dale Murray .25 .08
❑ 80T Jeff Newman .25 .08
❑ 81T Pete O'Brien XRC 1.00 .40
❑ 82T Jorge Orta .25 .08
❑ 83T Alejandro Pena XRC 2.00 .75
❑ 84T Pascual Perez .25 .08
❑ 85T Tony Perez 2.00 .75
❑ 86T Broderick Perkins .25 .08
❑ 87T Tony Phillips XRC 2.00 .75
❑ 88T Charlie Puleo .25 .08
❑ 89T Pat Putnam .25 .08
❑ 90T Jamie Quirk .25 .08
❑ 91T Doug Rader MG .25 .08
❑ 92T Chuck Rainey .25 .08
❑ 93T Bobby Ramos .25 .08
❑ 94T Gary Redus XRC 1.00 .40
❑ 95T Steve Renko .25 .08
❑ 96T Leon Roberts .25 .08
❑ 97T Aurelio Rodriguez .25 .08
❑ 98T Dick Ruthven .25 .08
❑ 99T Daryl Sconiers .25 .08
❑ 100T Mike Scott 1.00 .40
❑ 101T Tom Seaver 2.00 .75
❑ 102T John Shelby .25 .08
❑ 103T Bob Shirley .25 .08
❑ 104T Joe Simpson .25 .08
❑ 105T Doug Sisk .25 .08
❑ 106T Mike Smithson .25 .08
❑ 107T Elias Sosa .25 .08
❑ 108T Darryl Strawberry XRC 20.00 8.00
❑ 109T Tom Tellmann .25 .08
❑ 110T Gene Tenace 1.00 .40
❑ 111T Gorman Thomas 1.00 .40
❑ 112T Dick Tidrow .25 .08
❑ 113T Dave Tobik .25 .08
❑ 114T Wayne Tolleson .25 .08
❑ 115T Mike Torrez .25 .08
❑ 116T Manny Trillo .25 .08
❑ 117T Steve Trout .25 .08
❑ 118T Lee Tunnell .25 .08
❑ 119T Mike Vail .25 .08
❑ 120T Ellis Valentine .25 .08
❑ 121T Tom Veryzer .25 .08
❑ 122T George Vukovich .25 .08
❑ 123T Rick Waits .25 .08
❑ 124T Greg Walker 1.00 .40
❑ 125T Chris Welsh .25 .08
❑ 126T Len Whitehouse .25 .08
❑ 127T Eddie Whitson .25 .08
❑ 128T Jim Wohlford .25 .08
❑ 129T Matt Young XRC 1.00 .40
❑ 130T Joel Youngblood .25 .08
❑ 131T Pat Zachry .25 .08
❑ 132T Checklist 1T-132T .25 .08

1984 Topps

❑ COMPLETE SET (792) 50.00 20.00
❑ 1 Steve Carlton HL .25 .08
❑ 2 Rickey Henderson HL .60 .25
❑ 3 Dan Quisenberry HL
Sets save record .15 .05
❑ 4 N.Ryan/Carlton/Perry HL 1.00 .40
❑ 5 Dave Righetti,
Bob Forsch,
and Mike Warren HL. .25 .08
❑ 6 J.Bench/G.Perry/C.Yaz HL .40 .15
❑ 7 Gary Lucas .15 .05
❑ 8 Don Mattingly RC 15.00 6.00
❑ 9 Jim Gott .15 .05
❑ 10 Robin Yount 1.00 .40
❑ 11 Minnesota Twins TL
Kent Hrbek
Ken Schrom
(Check .25 .08
❑ 12 Billy Sample .15 .05
❑ 13 Scott Holman .15 .05
❑ 14 Tom Brookens .25 .08
❑ 15 Burt Hooton .15 .05
❑ 16 Omar Moreno .15 .05
❑ 17 John Denny .15 .05
❑ 18 Dale Berra .15 .05
❑ 19 Ray Fontenot .15 .05
❑ 20 Greg Luzinski .25 .08
❑ 21 Joe Altobelli MG .15 .05
❑ 22 Bryan Clark .15 .05
❑ 23 Keith Moreland .15 .05
❑ 24 John Martin .15 .05
❑ 25 Glenn Hubbard .15 .05
❑ 26 Bud Black .15 .05
❑ 27 Daryl Sconiers .15 .05
❑ 28 Frank Viola .40 .15
❑ 29 Danny Heep .15 .05
❑ 30 Wade Boggs 1.50 .60
❑ 31 Andy McGaffigan .15 .05
❑ 32 Bobby Ramos .15 .05
❑ 33 Tom Burgmeier .15 .05
❑ 34 Eddie Milner .15 .05
❑ 35 Don Sutton .25 .08
❑ 36 Denny Walling .15 .05
❑ 37 Texas Rangers TL
Buddy Bell
Rick Honeycutt
(Che .25 .08
❑ 38 Luis DeLeon .15 .05
❑ 39 Garth Iorg .15 .05
❑ 40 Dusty Baker .25 .08
❑ 41 Tony Bernazard .15 .05
❑ 42 Johnny Grubb .15 .05
❑ 43 Ron Reed .15 .05
❑ 44 Jim Morrison .15 .05
❑ 45 Jerry Mumphrey .15 .05
❑ 46 Ray Smith .15 .05
❑ 47 Rudy Law .15 .05
❑ 48 Julio Franco .25 .08
❑ 49 John Stuper .15 .05
❑ 50 Chris Chambliss .25 .08
❑ 51 Jim Frey MG .15 .05
❑ 52 Paul Splittorff .15 .05
❑ 53 Juan Beniquez .15 .05
❑ 54 Jesse Orosco .15 .05
❑ 55 Dave Concepcion .25 .08
❑ 56 Gary Allenson .15 .05
❑ 57 Dan Schatzeder .15 .05
❑ 58 Max Venable .15 .05
❑ 59 Sammy Stewart .15 .05
❑ 60 Paul Molitor .25 .08
❑ 61 Chris Codiroli .15 .05
❑ 62 Dave Hostetler .15 .05
❑ 63 Ed VandeBerg .15 .05
❑ 64 Mike Scioscia .25 .08
❑ 65 Kirk Gibson .60 .25
❑ 66 Astros TL/Nolan Ryan 1.00 .40
❑ 67 Gary Ward .15 .05
❑ 68 Luis Salazar .15 .05

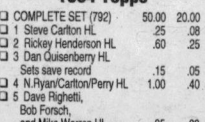

❑	69	Rod Scurry	.15	.05
❑	70	Gary Matthews	.25	.08
❑	71	Leo Hernandez	.15	.05
❑	72	Mike Squires	.15	.05
❑	73	Jody Davis	.15	.05
❑	74	Jerry Martin	.15	.05
❑	75	Bob Forsch	.15	.05
❑	76	Alfredo Griffin	.15	.05
❑	77	Brett Butler	.25	.08
❑	78	Mike Torrez	.15	.05
❑	79	Rob Wilfong	.15	.05
❑	80	Steve Rogers	.25	.08
❑	81	Billy Martin MG	.40	.15
❑	82	Doug Bird	.15	.05
❑	83	Richie Zisk	.15	.05
❑	84	Lenny Faedo	.15	.05
❑	85	Atlee Hammaker	.15	.05
❑	86	John Shelby	.15	.05
❑	87	Frank Pastore	.15	.05
❑	88	Rob Picciolo	.15	.05
❑	89	Mike Smithson	.15	.05
❑	90	Pedro Guerrero	.25	.08
❑	91	Dan Spillner	.15	.05
❑	92	Lloyd Moseby	.15	.05
❑	93	Bob Knepper	.15	.05
❑	94	Mario Ramirez	.15	.05
❑	95	Aurelio Lopez	.25	.08
❑	96	Kansas City Royals TL Hal McRae Larry Gura (Che	.25	.08
❑	97	LaMarr Hoyt	.15	.05
❑	98	Steve Nicosia	.15	.05
❑	99	Craig Lefferts RC	.15	.05
❑	100	Reggie Jackson	.40	.15
❑	101	Porfirio Altamirano	.15	.05
❑	102	Ken Oberkfell	.15	.05
❑	103	Dwayne Murphy	.15	.05
❑	104	Ken Dayley	.15	.05
❑	105	Tony Armas	.25	.08
❑	106	Tim Stoddard	.15	.05
❑	107	Ned Yost	.15	.05
❑	108	Randy Moffitt	.15	.05
❑	109	Brad Wellman	.15	.05
❑	110	Ron Guidry	.25	.08
❑	111	Bill Virdon MG	.15	.05
❑	112	Tom Niedenfuer	.15	.05
❑	113	Kelly Paris	.15	.05
❑	114	Checklist 1-132	.25	.08
❑	115	Andre Thornton	.15	.05
❑	116	George Bjorkman	.15	.05
❑	117	Tom Veryzer	.15	.05
❑	118	Charlie Hough	.25	.08
❑	119	John Wockenfuss	.15	.05
❑	120	Keith Hernandez	.25	.08
❑	121	Pat Sheridan	.15	.05
❑	122	Cecilio Guante	.15	.05
❑	123	Butch Wynegar	.15	.05
❑	124	Damaso Garcia	.15	.05
❑	125	Britt Burns	.15	.05
❑	126	Braves TL/Dale Murphy	.40	.15
❑	127	Mike Madden	.15	.05
❑	128	Rick Manning	.15	.05
❑	129	Bill Laskey	.15	.05
❑	130	Ozzie Smith	1.00	.40
❑	131	W.Boggs/B.Madlock LL	.60	.25
❑	132	Mike Schmidt/J.Rice LL	.60	.25
❑	133	D.Murphy/Coop/Rice LL	.40	.15
❑	134	T.Raines/R.Henderson LL	.60	.25
❑	135	John Denny LaMarr Hoyt LL	.60	.25
❑	136	S.Carlton/J.Morris LL	.25	.08
❑	137	A.Hammaker/R.Honeycutt LL	.25	.08
❑	138	Al Holland Dan Quisenberry LL	.25	.08
❑	139	Bert Campaneris	.25	.08
❑	140	Storm Davis	.15	.05
❑	141	Pat Corrales MG	.15	.05
❑	142	Rich Gale	.15	.05
❑	143	Jose Morales	.15	.05
❑	144	Brian Harper RC	.40	.15
❑	145	Gary Lavelle	.15	.05
❑	146	Ed Romero	.15	.05
❑	147	Dan Petry	.25	.08
❑	148	Joe Lefebvre	.15	.05
❑	149	Jon Matlack	.15	.05
❑	150	Dale Murphy	.40	.15
❑	151	Steve Trout	.15	.05
❑	152	Glenn Brummer	.15	.05
❑	153	Dick Tidrow	.15	.05
❑	154	Dave Henderson	.25	.08
❑	155	Frank White	.25	.08
❑	156	A's TL/Rickey Henderson	.60	.25
❑	157	Gary Gaetti	.40	.15
❑	158	John Curtis	.15	.05
❑	159	Darryl Cias	.15	.05
❑	160	Mario Soto	.25	.08
❑	161	Junior Ortiz	.15	.05
❑	162	Bob Ojeda	.15	.05
❑	163	Lorenzo Gray	.15	.05
❑	164	Scott Sanderson	.15	.05
❑	165	Ken Singleton	.25	.08
❑	166	Jamie Nelson	.15	.05
❑	167	Marshall Edwards	.15	.05
❑	168	Juan Bonilla	.15	.05
❑	169	Larry Parrish	.15	.05
❑	170	Jerry Reuss	.15	.05
❑	171	Frank Robinson MG	.40	.15
❑	172	Frank DiPino	.15	.05
❑	173	Marvell Wynne	.40	.15
❑	174	Juan Berenguer	.15	.05
❑	175	Graig Nettles	.25	.08
❑	176	Lee Smith	.25	.08
❑	177	Jerry Hairston	.15	.05
❑	178	Bill Krueger RC	.15	.05
❑	179	Buck Martinez	.15	.05
❑	180	Manny Trillo	.15	.05
❑	181	Roy Thomas	.15	.05
❑	182	Darryl Strawberry RC	3.00	1.25
❑	183	Al Williams	.15	.05
❑	184	Mike O'Berry	.15	.05
❑	185	Sixto Lezcano	.15	.05
❑	186	Cardinal TL Lonnie Smith John Stuper (Checklist	.25	.08
❑	187	Luis Aponte	.15	.05
❑	188	Bryan Little	.15	.05
❑	189	Tim Conroy	.15	.05
❑	190	Ben Oglivie	.25	.08
❑	191	Mike Boddicker	.15	.05
❑	192	Nick Esasky	.15	.05
❑	193	Darrell Brown	.15	.05
❑	194	Domingo Ramos	.15	.05
❑	195	Jack Morris	.25	.08
❑	196	Don Slaught	.25	.08
❑	197	Garry Hancock	.15	.05
❑	198	Bill Doran RC*	.40	.15
❑	199	Willie Hernandez	.15	.05
❑	200	Andre Dawson	.25	.08
❑	201	Bruce Kison	.15	.05
❑	202	Bobby Cox MG	.25	.08
❑	203	Matt Keough	.15	.05
❑	204	Bobby Meacham	.15	.05
❑	205	Greg Minton	.15	.05
❑	206	Andy Van Slyke RC	1.50	.60
❑	207	Donnie Moore	.15	.05
❑	208	Jose Oquendo RC	.40	.15
❑	209	Manny Sarmiento	.15	.05
❑	210	Joe Morgan	.25	.08
❑	211	Rick Sweet	.15	.05
❑	212	Broderick Perkins	.15	.05
❑	213	Bruce Hurst	.15	.05
❑	214	Paul Householder	.15	.05
❑	215	Tippy Martinez	.15	.05
❑	216	White Sox TL/C.Fisk	.25	.08
❑	217	Alan Ashby	.15	.05
❑	218	Rick Waits	.15	.05
❑	219	Joe Simpson	.15	.05
❑	220	Fernando Valenzuela	.25	.08
❑	221	Cliff Johnson	.15	.05
❑	222	Rick Honeycutt	.15	.05
❑	223	Wayne Krenchicki	.15	.05
❑	224	Sid Monge	.15	.05
❑	225	Lee Mazzilli	.25	.08
❑	226	Juan Eichelberger	.15	.05
❑	227	Steve Braun	.15	.05
❑	228	John Rabb	.15	.05
❑	229	Paul Owens MG	.15	.05
❑	230	Rickey Henderson	1.00	.40
❑	231	Gary Woods	.15	.05
❑	232	Tim Wallach	.15	.05
❑	233	Checklist 133-264	.25	.08
❑	234	Rafael Ramirez	.15	.05
❑	235	Matt Young RC	.40	.15
❑	236	Ellis Valentine	.15	.05
❑	237	John Castino	.15	.05
❑	238	Reid Nichols	.15	.05
❑	239	Jay Howell	.15	.05
❑	240	Eddie Murray	.60	.25
❑	241	Bill Almon	.15	.05
❑	242	Alex Trevino	.15	.05
❑	243	Pete Ladd	.15	.05
❑	244	Candy Maldonado	.15	.05
❑	245	Rick Sutcliffe	.25	.08
❑	246	Mets TL/Tom Seaver	.25	.08
❑	247	Onix Concepcion	.15	.05
❑	248	Bill Dawley	.15	.05
❑	249	Jay Johnstone	.15	.05
❑	250	Bill Madlock	.25	.08
❑	251	Tony Gwynn	2.50	1.00
❑	252	Larry Christenson	.15	.05
❑	253	Jim Wohlford	.15	.05
❑	254	Shane Rawley	.15	.05
❑	255	Bruce Benedict	.15	.05
❑	256	Dave Geisel	.15	.05
❑	257	Julio Cruz	.15	.05
❑	258	Luis Sanchez	.15	.05
❑	259	Sparky Anderson MG	.25	.08
❑	260	Scott McGregor	.15	.05
❑	261	Bobby Brown	.15	.05
❑	262	Tom Candiotti RC	.75	.30
❑	263	Jack Fimple	.15	.05
❑	264	Doug Frobel RC	.15	.05
❑	265	Donnie Hill	.15	.05
❑	266	Steve Lubratich	.15	.05
❑	267	Carmelo Martinez	.15	.05
❑	268	Jack O'Connor	.15	.05
❑	269	Aurelio Rodriguez	.15	.05
❑	270	Jeff Russell RC	.40	.15
❑	271	Moose Haas	.15	.05
❑	272	Rick Dempsey	.15	.05
❑	273	Charlie Puleo	.15	.05
❑	274	Rick Monday	.25	.08
❑	275	Len Matuszek	.15	.05
❑	276	Angels TL/Rod Carew	.25	.08
❑	277	Eddie Whitson	.15	.05
❑	278	George Bell	.25	.08
❑	279	Ivan DeJesus	.15	.05
❑	280	Floyd Bannister	.15	.05
❑	281	Larry Milbourne	.15	.05
❑	282	Jim Barr	.15	.05
❑	283	Larry Biittner	.15	.05
❑	284	Howard Bailey	.15	.05
❑	285	Darrell Porter	.15	.05
❑	286	Lary Sorensen	.15	.05
❑	287	Warren Cromartie	.15	.05
❑	288	Jim Beattie	.15	.05
❑	289	Randy Johnson	.15	.05
❑	290	Dave Dravecky	.15	.05
❑	291	Chuck Tanner MG	.15	.05
❑	292	Tony Scott	.15	.05
❑	293	Ed Lynch	.15	.05
❑	294	U.L. Washington	.15	.05
❑	295	Mike Flanagan	.15	.05
❑	296	Jeff Newman	.15	.05
❑	297	Bruce Berenyi	.15	.05
❑	298	Jim Gantner	.15	.05
❑	299	John Butcher	.15	.05
❑	300	Pete Rose	2.00	.75
❑	301	Frank LaCorte	.15	.05
❑	302	Barry Bonnell	.15	.05
❑	303	Marty Castillo	.15	.05
❑	304	Warren Brusstar	.15	.05
❑	305	Roy Smalley	.15	.05
❑	306	Dodgers TL Pedro Guerrero Bob Welch (Checklist	.25	.08
❑	307	Bobby Mitchell	.15	.05
❑	308	Ron Hassey	.15	.05
❑	309	Tony Phillips RC	.75	.30
❑	310	Willie McGee	.25	.08
❑	311	Jerry Koosman	.25	.08
❑	312	Jorge Orta	.15	.05
❑	313	Mike Jorgensen	.15	.05
❑	314	Orlando Mercado	.15	.05
❑	315	Bob Grich	.25	.08

316	Mark Bradley	.15	.05
317	Greg Pryor	.15	.05
318	Bill Gullickson	.15	.05
319	Al Bumbry	.15	.05
320	Bob Stanley	.15	.05
321	Harvey Kuenn MG	.15	.05
322	Ken Schrom	.15	.05
323	Alan Knicely	.15	.05
324	Alejandro Pena RC*	.75	.30
325	Darrell Evans	.25	.08
326	Bob Kearney	.15	.05
327	Ruppert Jones	.15	.05
328	Vern Ruhle	.15	.05
329	Pat Tabler	.15	.05
330	John Candelaria	.15	.05
331	Bucky Dent	.25	.08
332	Kevin Gross RC	.40	.15
333	Larry Herndon	.25	.08
334	Chuck Rainey	.15	.05
335	Don Baylor	.25	.08
336	Seattle Mariners TL Pat Putnam Matt Young (Chec	.25	.08
337	Kevin Hagen	.15	.05
338	Mike Warren	.15	.05
339	Roy Lee Jackson	.15	.05
340	Hal McRae	.25	.08
341	Dave Tobik	.15	.05
342	Tim Foli	.15	.05
343	Mark Davis	.15	.05
344	Rick Miller	.15	.05
345	Kent Hrbek	.25	.08
346	Kurt Bevacqua	.15	.05
347	Allan Ramirez	.15	.05
348	Toby Harrah	.25	.08
349	Bob L. Gibson RC	.15	.05
350	George Foster	.25	.08
351	Russ Nixon MG	.15	.05
352	Dave Stewart	.25	.08
353	Jim Anderson	.15	.05
354	Jeff Burroughs	.15	.05
355	Jason Thompson	.15	.05
356	Glenn Abbott	.15	.05
357	Ron Cey	.25	.08
358	Bob Dernier	.15	.05
359	Jim Acker	.15	.05
360	Willie Randolph	.25	.08
361	Dave Smith	.15	.05
362	David Green	.15	.05
363	Tim Laudner	.15	.05
364	Scott Fletcher	.15	.05
365	Steve Bedrosian	.15	.05
366	Padres TL Terry Kennedy Dave Dravecky (Checklis	.25	.08
367	Jamie Easterly	.15	.05
368	Hubie Brooks	.15	.05
369	Steve McCatty	.15	.05
370	Tim Raines	.25	.08
371	Dave Gumpert	.15	.05
372	Gary Roenicke	.15	.05
373	Bill Scherrer	.15	.05
374	Don Money	.15	.05
375	Dennis Leonard	.15	.05
376	Dave Anderson RC	.15	.05
377	Danny Darwin	.15	.05
378	Bob Brenly	.15	.05
379	Checklist 265-396	.25	.08
380	Steve Garvey	.25	.08
381	Ralph Houk MG	.15	.05
382	Chris Nyman	.15	.05
383	Terry Puhl	.15	.05
384	Lee Tunnell	.15	.05
385	Tony Perez	.40	.15
386	George Hendrick AS	.15	.05
387	Johnny Ray AS	.15	.05
388	Mike Schmidt AS	.60	.25
389	Ozzie Smith AS	.60	.25
390	Tim Raines AS	.15	.05
391	Dale Murphy AS	.25	.08
392	Andre Dawson AS	.15	.05
393	Gary Carter AS	.15	.05
394	Steve Rogers AS	.15	.05
395	Steve Carlton AS	.25	.08
396	Jesse Orosco AS	.15	.05
397	Eddie Murray AS	.40	.15
398	Lou Whitaker AS	.15	.05
399	George Brett AS	.60	.25
400	Cal Ripken AS	2.00	.75
401	Jim Rice AS	.15	.05
402	Dave Winfield AS	.15	.05
403	Lloyd Moseby AS	.15	.05
404	Ted Simmons AS	.15	.05
405	LaMarr Hoyt AS	.15	.05
406	Ron Guidry AS	.15	.05
407	Dan Quisenberry AS	.15	.05
408	Lou Piniella	.25	.08
409	Juan Agosto	.15	.05
410	Claudell Washington	.15	.05
411	Houston Jimenez	.15	.05
412	Doug Rader MG	.15	.05
413	Spike Owen RC	.40	.15
414	Mitchell Page	.15	.05
415	Tommy John	.25	.08
416	Dane Iorg	.15	.05
417	Mike Armstrong	.15	.05
418	Ron Hodges	.15	.05
419	John Henry Johnson	.15	.05
420	Cecil Cooper	.25	.08
421	Charlie Lea	.15	.05
422	Jose Cruz	.25	.08
423	Mike Morgan	.15	.05
424	Dann Bilardello	.15	.05
425	Steve Howe	.15	.05
426	Orioles TL/Cal Ripken	1.50	.60
427	Rick Leach	.15	.05
428	Fred Breining	.15	.05
429	Randy Bush	.15	.05
430	Rusty Staub	.25	.08
431	Chris Bando	.15	.05
432	Charles Hudson	.15	.05
433	Rich Hebner	.15	.05
434	Harold Baines	.25	.08
435	Neil Allen	.15	.05
436	Rick Peters	.15	.05
437	Mike Proly	.15	.05
438	Biff Pocoroba	.15	.05
439	Bob Stoddard	.15	.05
440	Steve Kemp	.15	.05
441	Bob Lillis MG	.15	.05
442	Byron McLaughlin	.15	.05
443	Benny Ayala	.15	.05
444	Steve Renko	.15	.05
445	Jerry Remy	.15	.05
446	Luis Pujols	.15	.05
447	Tom Brunansky	.15	.05
448	Ben Hayes	.15	.05
449	Joe Pettini	.15	.05
450	Gary Carter	.25	.08
451	Bob Jones	.15	.05
452	Chuck Porter	.15	.05
453	Willie Upshaw	.15	.05
454	Joe Beckwith	.15	.05
455	Terry Kennedy	.15	.05
456	Cubs TL/F.Jenkins	.15	.05
457	Dave Rozema	.15	.05
458	Kiko Garcia	.15	.05
459	Kevin Hickey	.15	.05
460	Dave Winfield	.25	.08
461	Jim Maler	.15	.05
462	Lee Lacy	.15	.05
463	Dave Engle	.15	.05
464	Jeff A. Jones	.15	.05
465	Mookie Wilson	.25	.08
466	Gene Garber	.15	.05
467	Mike Ramsey	.15	.05
468	Geoff Zahn	.15	.05
469	Tom O'Malley	.15	.05
470	Nolan Ryan	3.00	1.25
471	Dick Howser MG	.15	.05
472	Mike G. Brown RC	.15	.05
473	Jim Dwyer	.15	.05
474	Greg Bargar	.15	.05
475	Gary Redus RC*	.40	.15
476	Tom Tellmann	.15	.05
477	Rafael Landestoy	.15	.05
478	Alan Bannister	.15	.05
479	Frank Tanana	.25	.08
480	Ron Kittle	.15	.05
481	Mark Thurmond	.15	.05
482	Enos Cabell	.15	.05
483	Fergie Jenkins	.25	.08
484	Ozzie Virgil	.15	.05
485	Rick Rhoden	.15	.05
486	D.Baylor/R.Guidry TL	.25	.08
487	Ricky Adams	.15	.05
488	Jesse Barfield	.25	.08
489	Dave Von Ohlen	.15	.05
490	Cal Ripken	4.00	1.50
491	Bobby Castillo	.15	.05
492	Tucker Ashford	.15	.05
493	Mike Norris	.15	.05
494	Chili Davis	.25	.08
495	Rollie Fingers	.25	.08
496	Terry Francona	.25	.08
497	Bud Anderson	.15	.05
498	Rich Gedman	.15	.05
499	Mike Witt	.15	.05
500	George Brett	1.50	.60
501	Steve Henderson	.15	.05
502	Joe Torre MG	.25	.08
503	Elias Sosa	.15	.05
504	Mickey Rivers	.15	.05
505	Pete Vuckovich	.15	.05
506	Ernie Whitt	.15	.05
507	Mike LaCoss	.15	.05
508	Mel Hall	.25	.08
509	Brad Havens	.15	.05
510	Alan Trammell	.25	.08
511	Marty Bystrom	.15	.05
512	Oscar Gamble	.15	.05
513	Dave Beard	.15	.05
514	Floyd Rayford	.15	.05
515	Gorman Thomas	.25	.08
516	Montreal Expos TL Al Oliver Charlie Lea (Checkl	.25	.08
517	John Moses	.15	.05
518	Greg Walker	.40	.15
519	Ron Davis	.15	.05
520	Bob Boone	.25	.08
521	Pete Falcone	.15	.05
522	Dave Bergman	.15	.05
523	Glenn Hoffman	.15	.05
524	Carlos Diaz	.15	.05
525	Willie Wilson	.25	.08
526	Ron Oester	.15	.05
527	Checklist 397-528	.25	.08
528	Mark Brouhard	.15	.05
529	Keith Atherton	.15	.05
530	Dan Ford	.15	.05
531	Steve Boros MG	.15	.05
532	Eric Show	.15	.05
533	Ken Landreaux	.15	.05
534	Pete O'Brien RC*	.40	.15
535	Bo Diaz	.15	.05
536	Doug Bair	.15	.05
537	Johnny Ray	.15	.05
538	Kevin Bass	.15	.05
539	George Frazier	.15	.05
540	George Hendrick	.25	.08
541	Dennis Lamp	.15	.05
542	Duane Kuiper	.15	.05
543	Craig McMurtry	.15	.05
544	Cesar Geronimo	.15	.05
545	Bill Buckner	.25	.08
546	Indians TL Mike Hargrove Lary Sorensen (Checkli	.25	.08
547	Mike Moore	.15	.05
548	Ron Jackson	.15	.05
549	Walt Terrell	.15	.05
550	Jim Rice	.25	.08
551	Scott Ullger	.15	.05
552	Ray Burris	.15	.05
553	Joe Nolan	.15	.05
554	Ted Power	.15	.05
555	Greg Brock	.15	.05
556	Joey McLaughlin	.15	.05
557	Wayne Tolleson	.15	.05
558	Mike Davis	.15	.05
559	Mike Scott	.25	.08
560	Carlton Fisk	.40	.15
561	Whitey Herzog MG	.25	.08

❑ 562 Manny Castillo .15 .05
❑ 563 Glenn Wilson .25 .08
❑ 564 Al Holland .15 .05
❑ 565 Leon Durham .15 .05
❑ 566 Jim Bibby .15 .05
❑ 567 Mike Heath .15 .05
❑ 568 Pete Filson .15 .05
❑ 569 Bake McBride .25 .08
❑ 570 Dan Quisenberry .15 .05
❑ 571 Bruce Bochy .15 .05
❑ 572 Jerry Royster .15 .05
❑ 573 Dave Kingman .25 .08
❑ 574 Brian Downing .25 .08
❑ 575 Jim Clancy .15 .05
❑ 576 Giants TL
Jeff Leonard
Atlee Hammaker
(Checklis .25 .08
❑ 577 Mark Clear .15 .05
❑ 578 Lenn Sakata .15 .05
❑ 579 Bob James .15 .05
❑ 580 Lonnie Smith .15 .05
❑ 581 Jose DeLeon RC .40 .15
❑ 582 Bob McClure .15 .05
❑ 583 Derrel Thomas .15 .05
❑ 584 Dave Schmidt .15 .05
❑ 585 Dan Driessen .15 .05
❑ 586 Joe Niekro .15 .05
❑ 587 Von Hayes .15 .05
❑ 588 Milt Wilcox .15 .05
❑ 589 Mike Easler .15 .05
❑ 590 Dave Stieb .25 .08
❑ 591 Tony LaRussa MG .25 .08
❑ 592 Andre Robertson .15 .05
❑ 593 Jeff Lahti .15 .05
❑ 594 Gene Richards .15 .05
❑ 595 Jeff Reardon .25 .08
❑ 596 Ryne Sandberg 2.50 1.00
❑ 597 Rick Camp .15 .05
❑ 598 Rusty Kuntz .15 .05
❑ 599 Doug Sisk .15 .05
❑ 600 Rod Carew .40 .15
❑ 601 John Tudor .25 .08
❑ 602 John Wathan .15 .05
❑ 603 Renie Martin .15 .05
❑ 604 John Lowenstein .15 .05
❑ 605 Mike Caldwell .15 .05
❑ 606 Blue Jays TL
Lloyd Moseby
Dave Stieb
(Checklist .25 .08
❑ 607 Tom Hume .15 .05
❑ 608 Bobby Johnson .15 .05
❑ 609 Dan Meyer .15 .05
❑ 610 Steve Sax .15 .05
❑ 611 Chet Lemon .25 .08
❑ 612 Harry Spilman .15 .05
❑ 613 Greg Gross .15 .05
❑ 614 Len Barker .15 .05
❑ 615 Garry Templeton .25 .08
❑ 616 Don Robinson .15 .05
❑ 617 Rick Cerone .15 .05
❑ 618 Dickie Noles .15 .05
❑ 619 Jerry Dybzinski .15 .05
❑ 620 Al Oliver .25 .08
❑ 621 Frank Howard MG .25 .08
❑ 622 Al Cowens .15 .05
❑ 623 Ron Washington .15 .05
❑ 624 Terry Harper .15 .05
❑ 625 Larry Gura .15 .05
❑ 626 Bob Clark .15 .05
❑ 627 Dave LaPoint .15 .05
❑ 628 Ed Jurak .15 .05
❑ 629 Rick Langford .15 .05
❑ 630 Ted Simmons .25 .08
❑ 631 Dennis Martinez .25 .08
❑ 632 Tom Foley .15 .05
❑ 633 Mike Krukow .15 .05
❑ 634 Mike Marshall .15 .05
❑ 635 Dave Righetti .25 .08
❑ 636 Pat Putnam .15 .05
❑ 637 Phillies TL
Gary Matthews
John Denny
(Checklist .25 .08
❑ 638 George Vukovich .15 .05
❑ 639 Rick Lysander .15 .05
❑ 640 Lance Parrish .40 .15
❑ 641 Mike Richardt .15 .05
❑ 642 Tom Underwood .15 .05
❑ 643 Mike C. Brown .15 .05
❑ 644 Tim Lollar .15 .05
❑ 645 Tony Pena .15 .05
❑ 646 Checklist 529-660 .25 .08
❑ 647 Ron Roenicke .15 .05
❑ 648 Len Whitehouse .15 .05
❑ 649 Tom Herr .15 .05
❑ 650 Phil Niekro .25 .08
❑ 651 John McNamara MG .15 .05
❑ 652 Rudy May .15 .05
❑ 653 Dave Stapleton .15 .05
❑ 654 Bob Bailor .15 .05
❑ 655 Amos Otis .25 .08
❑ 656 Bryn Smith .15 .05
❑ 657 Thad Bosley .15 .05
❑ 658 Jerry Augustine .15 .05
❑ 659 Duane Walker .15 .05
❑ 660 Ray Knight .25 .08
❑ 661 Steve Yeager .25 .08
❑ 662 Tom Brennan .15 .05
❑ 663 Johnnie LeMaster .15 .05
❑ 664 Dave Stegman .15 .05
❑ 665 Buddy Bell .25 .08
❑ 666 Tigers TL/Morris/Whitak .25 .08
❑ 667 Vance Law .15 .05
❑ 668 Larry McWilliams .15 .05
❑ 669 Dave Lopes .25 .08
❑ 670 Rich Gossage .25 .08
❑ 671 Jamie Quirk .15 .05
❑ 672 Ricky Nelson .15 .05
❑ 673 Mike Walters .15 .05
❑ 674 Tim Flannery .15 .05
❑ 675 Pascual Perez .15 .05
❑ 676 Brian Giles .15 .05
❑ 677 Doyle Alexander .15 .05
❑ 678 Chris Speier .15 .05
❑ 679 Art Howe .15 .05
❑ 680 Fred Lynn .25 .08
❑ 681 Tom Lasorda MG .40 .15
❑ 682 Dan Morogiello .15 .05
❑ 683 Marty Barrett RC .40 .15
❑ 684 Bob Shirley .15 .05
❑ 685 Willie Aikens .15 .05
❑ 686 Joe Price .15 .05
❑ 687 Roy Howell .15 .05
❑ 688 George Wright .15 .05
❑ 689 Mike Fischlin .15 .05
❑ 690 Jack Clark .25 .08
❑ 691 Steve Lake .15 .05
❑ 692 Dickie Thon .15 .05
❑ 693 Alan Wiggins .15 .05
❑ 694 Mike Stanton .15 .05
❑ 695 Lou Whitaker .25 .08
❑ 696 Pirates TL
Bill Madlock
Rick Rhoden
(Checklist .25 .08
❑ 697 Dale Murray .15 .05
❑ 698 Marc Hill .15 .05
❑ 699 Dave Rucker .15 .05
❑ 700 Mike Schmidt 1.50 .60
❑ 701 Madlock/Rose/Parker LL .60 .25
❑ 702 Rose/Staub/Perez LL .60 .25
❑ 703 Schmidt/Perez/Kingm LL .60 .25
❑ 704 Tony Perez
Rusty Staub
Al Oliver LL .25 .08
❑ 705 Morgan/Cedeno/Bowa LL .40 .15
❑ 706 S.Carlton/Jenk/Seaver LL .25 .08
❑ 707 N.Ryan/Seaver/Carlton LL 1.50 .60
❑ 708 Seaver/Carlton/Rog LL .25 .08
❑ 709 NL Active Save
Bruce Sutter
Tug McGraw
Gene Gar .25 .08
❑ 710 Carew/Brett/Cooper LL .40 .15
❑ 711 Carew/Camp/Reggie LL .25 .08
❑ 712 Reggie/Nettles/Luz LL .25 .08
❑ 713 Reggie/Simmons/Nett LL .25 .08
❑ 714 AL Active Steals
Bert Campaneris
Dave Lopes
Oma .25 .08
❑ 715 Palmer/Sutton/John LL .25 .08
❑ 716 AL Active Strikeout
Don Sutton
Bert Blyleven
Je .40 .15
❑ 717 Jim Palmer/Fingers LL .25 .08
❑ 718 Fingers/Goose/Quis LL .25 .08
❑ 719 Andy Hassler .15 .05
❑ 720 Dwight Evans .40 .15
❑ 721 Del Crandall MG .15 .05
❑ 722 Bob Welch .25 .08
❑ 723 Rich Dauer .15 .05
❑ 724 Eric Rasmussen .15 .05
❑ 725 Cesar Cedeno .25 .08
❑ 726 Brewers TL
Ted Simmons
Moose Haas
(Checklist on .25 .08
❑ 727 Joel Youngblood .15 .05
❑ 728 Tug McGraw .25 .08
❑ 729 Gene Tenace .25 .08
❑ 730 Bruce Sutter .40 .15
❑ 731 Lynn Jones .15 .05
❑ 732 Terry Crowley .15 .05
❑ 733 Dave Collins .15 .05
❑ 734 Odell Jones .15 .05
❑ 735 Rick Burleson .15 .05
❑ 736 Dick Ruthven .15 .05
❑ 737 Jim Essian .15 .05
❑ 738 Bill Schroeder .15 .05
❑ 739 Bob Watson .15 .05
❑ 740 Tom Seaver .60 .25
❑ 741 Wayne Gross .15 .05
❑ 742 Dick Williams MG .15 .05
❑ 743 Don Hood .15 .05
❑ 744 Jamie Allen .15 .05
❑ 745 Dennis Eckersley .40 .15
❑ 746 Mickey Hatcher .15 .05
❑ 747 Pat Zachry .15 .05
❑ 748 Jeff Leonard .15 .05
❑ 749 Doug Flynn .15 .05
❑ 750 Jim Palmer .25 .08
❑ 751 Charlie Moore .15 .05
❑ 752 Phil Garner .25 .08
❑ 753 Doug Gwosdz .15 .05
❑ 754 Kent Tekulve .15 .05
❑ 755 Garry Maddox .15 .05
❑ 756 Reds TL
Ron Oester
Mario Soto
(Checklist on bac .25 .08
❑ 757 Larry Bowa .25 .08
❑ 758 Bill Stein .15 .05
❑ 759 Richard Dotson .15 .05
❑ 760 Bob Horner .25 .08
❑ 761 John Montefusco .15 .05
❑ 762 Rance Mulliniks .15 .05
❑ 763 Craig Swan .15 .05
❑ 764 Mike Hargrove .15 .05
❑ 765 Ken Forsch .15 .05
❑ 766 Mike Vail .15 .05
❑ 767 Carney Lansford .25 .08
❑ 768 Champ Summers .15 .05
❑ 769 Bill Caudill .15 .05
❑ 770 Ken Griffey .25 .08
❑ 771 Billy Gardner MG .15 .05
❑ 772 Jim Slaton .15 .05
❑ 773 Todd Cruz .15 .05
❑ 774 Tom Gorman .15 .05
❑ 775 Dave Parker .25 .08
❑ 776 Craig Reynolds .15 .05
❑ 777 Tom Paciorek .15 .05
❑ 778 Andy Hawkins .15 .05
❑ 779 Jim Sundberg .25 .08
❑ 780 Steve Carlton .40 .15
❑ 781 Checklist 661-792 .25 .08
❑ 782 Steve Balboni .15 .05
❑ 783 Luis Leal .15 .05
❑ 784 Leon Roberts .15 .05
❑ 785 Joaquin Andujar .25 .08
❑ 786 Red Sox TL/Boggs/Ojeda .40 .15
❑ 787 Bill Campbell .15 .05
❑ 788 Milt May .15 .05
❑ 789 Bert Blyleven .25 .08
❑ 790 Doug DeCinces .15 .05

❑ 791	Terry Forster	.25	.08
❑ 792	Bill Russell	.25	.08

1984 Topps Traded

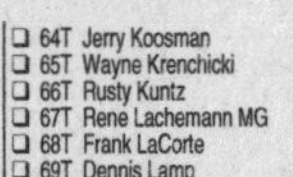

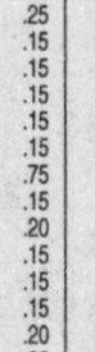

❑	COMP.FACT.SET (132)	30.00	15.00
❑ 1T	Willie Aikens	.40	.15
❑ 2T	Luis Aponte	.40	.15
❑ 3T	Mike Armstrong	.40	.15
❑ 4T	Bob Bailor	.40	.15
❑ 5T	Dusty Baker	.60	.25
❑ 6T	Steve Balboni	.40	.15
❑ 7T	Alan Bannister	.40	.15
❑ 8T	Dave Beard	.40	.15
❑ 9T	Joe Beckwith	.40	.15
❑ 10T	Bruce Berenyi	.40	.15
❑ 11T	Dave Bergman	.40	.15
❑ 12T	Tony Bernazard	.40	.15
❑ 13T	Yogi Berra MG	1.50	.60
❑ 14T	Barry Bonnell	.40	.15
❑ 15T	Phil Bradley	1.00	.40
❑ 16T	Fred Breining	.40	.15
❑ 17T	Bill Buckner	.60	.25
❑ 18T	Ray Burris	.40	.15
❑ 19T	John Butcher	.40	.15
❑ 20T	Brett Butler	.60	.25
❑ 21T	Enos Cabell	.40	.15
❑ 22T	Bill Campbell	.40	.15
❑ 23T	Bill Caudill	.40	.15
❑ 24T	Bob Clark	.40	.15
❑ 25T	Bryan Clark	.40	.15
❑ 26T	Jaime Cocanower	.40	.15
❑ 27T	Ron Darling XRC*	2.00	.75
❑ 28T	Alvin Davis XRC	1.00	.40
❑ 29T	Ken Dayley	.40	.15
❑ 30T	Jeff Dedmon	.40	.15
❑ 31T	Bob Dernier	.40	.15
❑ 32T	Carlos Diaz	.40	.15
❑ 33T	Mike Easler	.40	.15
❑ 34T	Dennis Eckersley	1.00	.40
❑ 35T	Jim Essian	.40	.15
❑ 36T	Darrell Evans	.60	.25
❑ 37T	Mike Fitzgerald	.40	.15
❑ 38T	Tim Foli	.40	.15
❑ 39T	George Frazier	.40	.15
❑ 40T	Rich Gale	.40	.15
❑ 41T	Barbaro Garbey	.40	.15
❑ 42T	Dwight Gooden XRC	10.00	4.00
❑ 43T	Rich Gossage	.60	.25
❑ 44T	Wayne Gross	.40	.15
❑ 45T	Mark Gubicza XRC	1.00	.40
❑ 46T	Jackie Gutierrez	.40	.15
❑ 47T	Mel Hall	.60	.25
❑ 48T	Toby Harrah	.60	.25
❑ 49T	Ron Hassey	.40	.15
❑ 50T	Rich Hebner	.40	.15
❑ 51T	Willie Hernandez	.40	.15
❑ 52T	Ricky Horton	.40	.15
❑ 53T	Art Howe	.40	.15
❑ 54T	Dane Iorg	.40	.15
❑ 55T	Brook Jacoby	1.00	.40
❑ 56T	Mike Jeffcoat XRC	.50	.20
❑ 57T	Dave Johnson MG	.40	.15
❑ 58T	Lynn Jones	.40	.15
❑ 59T	Ruppert Jones	.40	.15
❑ 60T	Mike Jorgensen	.40	.15
❑ 61T	Bob Kearney	.40	.15
❑ 62T	Jimmy Key XRC	2.00	.75
❑ 63T	Dave Kingman	.60	.25
❑ 64T	Jerry Koosman	.60	.25
❑ 65T	Wayne Krenchicki	.40	.15
❑ 66T	Rusty Kuntz	.40	.15
❑ 67T	Rene Lachemann MG	.40	.15
❑ 68T	Frank LaCorte	.40	.15
❑ 69T	Dennis Lamp	.40	.15
❑ 70T	Mark Langston XRC	2.00	.75
❑ 71T	Rick Leach	.40	.15
❑ 72T	Craig Lefferts	.50	.20
❑ 73T	Gary Lucas	.40	.15
❑ 74T	Jerry Martin	.40	.15
❑ 75T	Carmelo Martinez	.40	.15
❑ 76T	Mike Mason XRC	.50	.20
❑ 77T	Gary Matthews	.60	.25
❑ 78T	Andy McGaffigan	.40	.15
❑ 79T	Larry Milbourne	.40	.15
❑ 80T	Sid Monge	.40	.15
❑ 81T	Jackie Moore MG	.40	.15
❑ 82T	Joe Morgan	.60	.25
❑ 83T	Graig Nettles	.60	.25
❑ 84T	Phil Niekro	.60	.25
❑ 85T	Ken Oberkfell	.40	.15
❑ 86T	Mike O'Berry	.40	.15
❑ 87T	Al Oliver	.60	.25
❑ 88T	Jorge Orta	.40	.15
❑ 89T	Amos Otis	.60	.25
❑ 90T	Dave Parker	.60	.25
❑ 91T	Tony Perez	1.00	.40
❑ 92T	Gerald Perry	1.00	.40
❑ 93T	Gary Pettis	.40	.15
❑ 94T	Rob Picciolo	.40	.15
❑ 95T	Vern Rapp MG	.40	.15
❑ 96T	Floyd Rayford	.40	.15
❑ 97T	Randy Ready XRC	1.00	.40
❑ 98T	Ron Reed	.40	.15
❑ 99T	Gene Richards	.40	.15
❑ 100T	Jose Rijo XRC	2.00	.75
❑ 101T	Jeff D. Robinson	.40	.15
❑ 102T	Ron Romanick	.40	.15
❑ 103T	Pete Rose	5.00	2.00
❑ 104T	Bret Saberhagen XRC	4.00	1.50
❑ 105T	Juan Samuel XRC*	2.00	.75
❑ 106T	Scott Sanderson	.40	.15
❑ 107T	Dick Schofield XRC*	1.00	.40
❑ 108T	Tom Seaver	1.50	.60
❑ 109T	Jim Slaton	.40	.15
❑ 110T	Mike Smithson	.40	.15
❑ 111T	Lary Sorensen	.40	.15
❑ 112T	Tim Stoddard	.40	.15
❑ 113T	Champ Summers	.40	.15
❑ 114T	Jim Sundberg	.60	.25
❑ 115T	Rick Sutcliffe	.60	.25
❑ 116T	Craig Swan	.40	.15
❑ 117T	Tim Teufel XRC*	1.00	.40
❑ 118T	Derrel Thomas	.40	.15
❑ 119T	Gorman Thomas	.60	.25
❑ 120T	Alex Trevino	.40	.15
❑ 121T	Manny Trillo	.40	.15
❑ 122T	John Tudor	.60	.25
❑ 123T	Tom Underwood	.40	.15
❑ 124T	Mike Vail	.40	.15
❑ 125T	Tom Waddell	.40	.15
❑ 126T	Gary Ward	.40	.15
❑ 127T	Curt Wilkerson	.40	.15
❑ 128T	Frank Williams	.40	.15
❑ 129T	Glenn Wilson	.60	.25
❑ 130T	John Wockenfuss	.40	.15
❑ 131T	Ned Yost	.40	.15
❑ 132T	Checklist 1T-132T	.40	.15

1985 Topps

❑	COMPLETE SET (792)	80.00	40.00
❑	COMP.FACT.SET (792)	175.00	100.00
❑ 1	Carlton Fisk RB	.25	.08
❑ 2	Steve Garvey RB	.15	.05
❑ 3	Dwight Gooden RB	.60	.25
❑ 4	Cliff Johnson RB	.15	.05
❑ 5	Joe Morgan RB	.15	.05
❑ 6	Pete Rose RB	.40	.15
❑ 7	Nolan Ryan RB	1.50	.60
❑ 8	Juan Samuel RB	.15	.05
❑ 9	Bruce Sutter RB	.15	.05
❑ 10	Don Sutton RB	.15	.05
❑ 11	Ralph Houk MG	.15	.05
❑ 12	Dave Lopes	.25	.08
❑ 13	Tim Lollar	.15	.05
❑ 14	Chris Bando	.15	.05
❑ 15	Jerry Koosman	.25	.08
❑ 16	Bobby Meacham	.15	.05
❑ 17	Mike Scott	.25	.08
❑ 18	Mickey Hatcher	.15	.05
❑ 19	George Frazier	.15	.05
❑ 20	Chet Lemon	.25	.08
❑ 21	Lee Tunnell	.15	.05
❑ 22	Duane Kuiper	.15	.05
❑ 23	Bret Saberhagen RC	1.00	.40
❑ 24	Jesse Barfield	.25	.08
❑ 25	Steve Bedrosian	.15	.05
❑ 26	Roy Smalley	.15	.05
❑ 27	Bruce Berenyi	.15	.05
❑ 28	Dann Bilardello	.15	.05
❑ 29	Odell Jones	.15	.05
❑ 30	Cal Ripken	2.50	1.00
❑ 31	Terry Whitfield	.15	.05
❑ 32	Chuck Porter	.15	.05
❑ 33	Tito Landrum	.15	.05
❑ 34	Ed Nunez	.15	.05
❑ 35	Graig Nettles	.25	.08
❑ 36	Fred Breining	.15	.05
❑ 37	Reid Nichols	.15	.05
❑ 38	Jackie Moore MG	.15	.05
❑ 39	John Wockenfuss	.15	.05
❑ 40	Phil Niekro	.25	.08
❑ 41	Mike Fischlin	.15	.05
❑ 42	Luis Sanchez	.15	.05
❑ 43	Andre David	.15	.05
❑ 44	Dickie Thon	.15	.05
❑ 45	Greg Minton	.15	.05
❑ 46	Gary Woods	.15	.05
❑ 47	Dave Rozema	.15	.05
❑ 48	Tony Fernandez	.25	.08
❑ 49	Butch Davis	.15	.05
❑ 50	John Candelaria	.15	.05
❑ 51	Bob Watson	.15	.05
❑ 52	Jerry Dybzinski	.15	.05
❑ 53	Tom Gorman	.15	.05
❑ 54	Cesar Cedeno	.25	.08
❑ 55	Frank Tanana	.25	.08
❑ 56	Jim Dwyer	.15	.05
❑ 57	Pat Zachry	.15	.05
❑ 58	Orlando Mercado	.15	.05
❑ 59	Rick Waits	.15	.05
❑ 60	George Hendrick	.25	.08
❑ 61	Curt Kaufman	.15	.05
❑ 62	Mike Ramsey	.15	.05
❑ 63	Steve McCatty	.15	.05
❑ 64	Mark Bailey	.15	.05
❑ 65	Bill Buckner	.25	.08
❑ 66	Dick Williams MG	.15	.05
❑ 67	Rafael Santana	.15	.05
❑ 68	Von Hayes	.15	.05
❑ 69	Jim Winn	.15	.05
❑ 70	Don Baylor	.25	.08
❑ 71	Tim Laudner	.15	.05
❑ 72	Rick Sutcliffe	.25	.08
❑ 73	Rusty Kuntz	.15	.05
❑ 74	Mike Krukow	.15	.05
❑ 75	Willie Upshaw	.15	.05
❑ 76	Alan Bannister	.15	.05
❑ 77	Joe Beckwith	.15	.05
❑ 78	Scott Fletcher	.15	.05
❑ 79	Rick Mahler	.15	.05
❑ 80	Keith Hernandez	.25	.08
❑ 81	Lenn Sakata	.15	.05
❑ 82	Joe Price	.15	.05

❑	83	Charlie Moore	.15	.05
❑	84	Spike Owen	.15	.05
❑	85	Mike Marshall	.15	.05
❑	86	Don Aase	.15	.05
❑	87	David Green	.15	.05
❑	88	Bryn Smith	.15	.05
❑	89	Jackie Gutierrez	.15	.05
❑	90	Rich Gossage	.25	.08
❑	91	Jeff Burroughs	.15	.05
❑	92	Paul Owens MG	.15	.05
❑	93	Don Schulze	.15	.05
❑	94	Toby Harrah	.25	.08
❑	95	Jose Cruz	.25	.08
❑	96	Johnny Ray	.15	.05
❑	97	Pete Filson	.15	.05
❑	98	Steve Lake	.15	.05
❑	99	Milt Wilcox	.15	.05
❑	100	George Brett	1.50	.60
❑	101	Jim Acker	.15	.05
❑	102	Tommy Dunbar	.15	.05
❑	103	Randy Lerch	.15	.05
❑	104	Mike Fitzgerald	.15	.05
❑	105	Ron Kittle	.15	.05
❑	106	Pascual Perez	.15	.05
❑	107	Tom Foley	.15	.05
❑	108	Darnell Coles	.15	.05
❑	109	Gary Roenicke	.15	.05
❑	110	Alejandro Pena	.15	.05
❑	111	Doug DeCinces	.15	.05
❑	112	Tom Tellmann	.15	.05
❑	113	Tom Herr	.15	.05
❑	114	Bob James	.15	.05
❑	115	Rickey Henderson	.75	.30
❑	116	Dennis Boyd	.15	.05
❑	117	Greg Gross	.15	.05
❑	118	Eric Show	.15	.05
❑	119	Pat Corrales MG	.15	.05
❑	120	Steve Kemp	.15	.05
❑	121	Checklist: 1-132	.15	.05
❑	122	Tom Brunansky	.15	.05
❑	123	Dave Smith	.15	.05
❑	124	Rich Hebner	.15	.05
❑	125	Kent Tekulve	.15	.05
❑	126	Ruppert Jones	.15	.05
❑	127	Mark Gubicza RC*	.40	.15
❑	128	Ernie Whitt	.15	.05
❑	129	Gene Garber	.15	.05
❑	130	Al Oliver	.25	.08
❑	131	Buddy/Gus Bell FS	.25	.08
❑	132	Yogi/Dale Berra FS	.60	.25
❑	133	Bob/Ray Boone FS	.15	.05
❑	134	Terry/Tito Francona FS	.25	.08
❑	135	Terry/Bob Kennedy FS	.15	.05
❑	136	Jeff/Bill Kunkel FS	.15	.05
❑	137	Vance/Vern Law FS	.25	.08
❑	138	Dick/Dick Schofield FS	.15	.05
❑	139	Joel/Bob Skinner FS	.15	.05
❑	140	Roy/Roy Smalley FS	.15	.05
❑	141	Mike/Dave Stenhouse FS	.15	.05
❑	142	Steve/Dizzy Trout FS	.15	.05
❑	143	Ozzie/Ossie Virgil FS	.15	.05
❑	144	Ron Gardenhire	.15	.05
❑	145	Alvin Davis RC*	.40	.15
❑	146	Gary Redus	.15	.05
❑	147	Bill Swaggerty	.15	.05
❑	148	Steve Yeager	.25	.08
❑	149	Dickie Noles	.15	.05
❑	150	Jim Rice	.25	.08
❑	151	Moose Haas	.15	.05
❑	152	Steve Braun	.15	.05
❑	153	Frank LaCorte	.15	.05
❑	154	Angel Salazar	.15	.05
❑	155	Yogi Berra MG/TC	.60	.25
❑	156	Craig Reynolds	.15	.05
❑	157	Tug McGraw	.25	.08
❑	158	Pat Tabler	.15	.05
❑	159	Carlos Diaz	.15	.05
❑	160	Lance Parrish	.25	.08
❑	161	Ken Schrom	.15	.05
❑	162	Benny Distefano	.15	.05
❑	163	Dennis Eckersley	.40	.15
❑	164	Jorge Orta	.15	.05
❑	165	Dusty Baker	.25	.08
❑	166	Keith Atherton	.15	.05
❑	167	Rufino Linares	.15	.05
❑	168	Garth Iorg	.15	.05
❑	169	Dan Spillner	.15	.05
❑	170	George Foster	.25	.08
❑	171	Bill Stein	.15	.05
❑	172	Jack Perconte	.15	.05
❑	173	Mike Young	.15	.05
❑	174	Rick Honeycutt	.15	.05
❑	175	Dave Parker	.25	.08
❑	176	Bill Schroeder	.15	.05
❑	177	Dave Von Ohlen	.15	.05
❑	178	Miguel Dilone	.15	.05
❑	179	Tommy John	.25	.08
❑	180	Dave Winfield	.25	.08
❑	181	Roger Clemens RC	25.00	10.00
❑	182	Tim Flannery	.15	.05
❑	183	Larry McWilliams	.15	.05
❑	184	Carmen Castillo	.15	.05
❑	185	Al Holland	.15	.05
❑	186	Bob Lillis MG	.15	.05
❑	187	Mike Walters	.15	.05
❑	188	Greg Pryor	.15	.05
❑	189	Warren Brusstar	.15	.05
❑	190	Rusty Staub	.25	.08
❑	191	Steve Nicosia	.15	.05
❑	192	Howard Johnson	.25	.08
❑	193	Jimmy Key RC	.75	.30
❑	194	Dave Stegman	.15	.05
❑	195	Glenn Hubbard	.15	.05
❑	196	Pete O'Brien	.15	.05
❑	197	Mike Warren	.15	.05
❑	198	Eddie Milner	.15	.05
❑	199	Dennis Martinez	.25	.08
❑	200	Reggie Jackson	.40	.15
❑	201	Burt Hooton	.15	.05
❑	202	Gorman Thomas	.25	.08
❑	203	Bob McClure	.15	.05
❑	204	Art Howe	.15	.05
❑	205	Steve Rogers	.25	.08
❑	206	Phil Garner	.25	.08
❑	207	Mark Clear	.15	.05
❑	208	Champ Summers	.15	.05
❑	209	Bill Campbell	.15	.05
❑	210	Gary Matthews	.25	.08
❑	211	Clay Christiansen	.15	.05
❑	212	George Vukovich	.15	.05
❑	213	Billy Gardner MG	.15	.05
❑	214	John Tudor	.25	.08
❑	215	Bob Brenly	.15	.05
❑	216	Jerry Don Gleaton	.15	.05
❑	217	Leon Roberts	.15	.05
❑	218	Doyle Alexander	.15	.05
❑	219	Gerald Perry	.15	.05
❑	220	Fred Lynn	.25	.08
❑	221	Ron Reed	.15	.05
❑	222	Hubie Brooks	.15	.05
❑	223	Tom Hume	.15	.05
❑	224	Al Cowens	.15	.05
❑	225	Mike Boddicker	.15	.05
❑	226	Juan Beniquez	.15	.05
❑	227	Danny Darwin	.15	.05
❑	228	Dion James	.15	.05
❑	229	Dave LaPoint	.15	.05
❑	230	Gary Carter	.25	.08
❑	231	Dwayne Murphy	.15	.05
❑	232	Dave Beard	.15	.05
❑	233	Ed Jurak	.15	.05
❑	234	Jerry Narron	.15	.05
❑	235	Garry Maddox	.15	.05
❑	236	Mark Thurmond	.15	.05
❑	237	Julio Franco	.25	.08
❑	238	Jose Rijo RC	.75	.30
❑	239	Tim Teufel	.15	.05
❑	240	Dave Stieb	.25	.08
❑	241	Jim Frey MG	.15	.05
❑	242	Greg Harris	.15	.05
❑	243	Barbaro Garbey	.15	.05
❑	244	Mike Jones	.15	.05
❑	245	Chili Davis	.25	.08
❑	246	Mike Norris	.15	.05
❑	247	Wayne Tolleson	.15	.05
❑	248	Terry Forster	.25	.08
❑	249	Harold Baines	.25	.08
❑	250	Jesse Orosco	.15	.05
❑	251	Brad Gulden	.15	.05
❑	252	Dan Ford	.15	.05
❑	253	Sid Bream RC	.40	.15
❑	254	Pete Vuckovich	.15	.05
❑	255	Lonnie Smith	.15	.05
❑	256	Mike Stanton	.15	.05
❑	257	Bryan Little	.15	.05
❑	258	Mike C. Brown	.15	.05
❑	259	Gary Allenson	.15	.05
❑	260	Dave Righetti	.25	.08
❑	261	Checklist: 133-264	.15	.05
❑	262	Greg Booker	.15	.05
❑	263	Mel Hall	.15	.05
❑	264	Joe Sambito	.15	.05
❑	265	Juan Samuel	.15	.05
❑	266	Frank Viola	.25	.08
❑	267	Henry Cotto RC	.15	.05
❑	268	Chuck Tanner MG	.15	.05
❑	269	Doug Baker	.15	.05
❑	270	Dan Quisenberry	.15	.05
❑	271	Tim Foli FDP	.15	.05
❑	272	Jeff Burroughs FDP	.15	.05
❑	273	Bill Almon FDP	.15	.05
❑	274	Floyd Bannister FDP	.15	.05
❑	275	Harold Baines FDP	.15	.05
❑	276	Bob Horner FDP	.15	.05
❑	277	Al Chambers FDP	.15	.05
❑	278	Darryl Strawberry FDP	.40	.15
❑	279	Mike Moore FDP	.15	.05
❑	280	Shawon Dunston FDP RC	.75	.30
❑	281	Tim Belcher FDP RC	.40	.15
❑	282	Shawn Abner FDP RC	.15	.05
❑	283	Fran Mullins	.15	.05
❑	284	Marty Bystrom	.15	.05
❑	285	Dan Driessen	.15	.05
❑	286	Rudy Law	.15	.05
❑	287	Walt Terrell	.15	.05
❑	288	Jeff Kunkel	.15	.05
❑	289	Tom Underwood	.15	.05
❑	290	Cecil Cooper	.25	.08
❑	291	Bob Welch	.25	.08
❑	292	Brad Komminsk	.15	.05
❑	293	Curt Young	.15	.05
❑	294	Tom Nieto	.15	.05
❑	295	Joe Niekro	.15	.05
❑	296	Ricky Nelson	.15	.05
❑	297	Gary Lucas	.15	.05
❑	298	Marty Barrett	.15	.05
❑	299	Andy Hawkins	.15	.05
❑	300	Rod Carew	.40	.15
❑	301	John Montefusco	.15	.05
❑	302	Tim Corcoran	.15	.05
❑	303	Mike Jeffcoat	.15	.05
❑	304	Gary Gaetti	.25	.08
❑	305	Dale Berra	.15	.05
❑	306	Rick Reuschel	.25	.08
❑	307	Sparky Anderson MG	.25	.08
❑	308	John Wathan	.15	.05
❑	309	Mike Witt	.15	.05
❑	310	Manny Trillo	.15	.05
❑	311	Jim Gott	.15	.05
❑	312	Marc Hill	.15	.05
❑	313	Dave Schmidt	.15	.05
❑	314	Ron Oester	.15	.05
❑	315	Doug Sisk	.15	.05
❑	316	John Lowenstein	.15	.05
❑	317	Jack Lazorko	.15	.05
❑	318	Ted Simmons	.25	.08
❑	319	Jeff Jones	.15	.05
❑	320	Dale Murphy	.40	.15
❑	321	Ricky Horton	.15	.05
❑	322	Dave Stapleton	.15	.05
❑	323	Andy McGaffigan	.15	.05
❑	324	Bruce Bochy	.15	.05
❑	325	John Denny	.15	.05
❑	326	Kevin Bass	.15	.05
❑	327	Brook Jacoby	.15	.05
❑	328	Bob Shirley	.15	.05
❑	329	Ron Washington	.15	.05
❑	330	Leon Durham	.15	.05
❑	331	Bill Laskey	.15	.05
❑	332	Brian Harper	.15	.05
❑	333	Willie Hernandez	.15	.05
❑	334	Dick Howser MG	.15	.05
❑	335	Bruce Benedict	.15	.05
❑	336	Rance Mulliniks	.15	.05
❑	337	Billy Sample	.15	.05
❑	338	Britt Burns	.15	.05
❑	339	Danny Heep	.15	.05
❑	340	Robin Yount	1.00	.40

❑ 341 Floyd Rayford	.15	.05
❑ 342 Ted Power	.15	.05
❑ 343 Bill Russell	.25	.08
❑ 344 Dave Henderson	.15	.05
❑ 345 Charlie Lea	.15	.05
❑ 346 Terry Pendleton RC	.75	.30
❑ 347 Rick Langford	.15	.05
❑ 348 Bob Boone	.25	.08
❑ 349 Domingo Ramos	.15	.05
❑ 350 Wade Boggs	.60	.25
❑ 351 Juan Agosto	.15	.05
❑ 352 Joe Morgan	.25	.08
❑ 353 Julio Solano	.15	.05
❑ 354 Andre Robertson	.15	.05
❑ 355 Bert Blyleven	.25	.08
❑ 356 Dave Meier	.15	.05
❑ 357 Rich Bordi	.15	.05
❑ 358 Tony Pena	.15	.05
❑ 359 Pat Sheridan	.15	.05
❑ 360 Steve Carlton	.25	.08
❑ 361 Alfredo Griffin	.15	.05
❑ 362 Craig McMurtry	.15	.05
❑ 363 Ron Hodges	.15	.05
❑ 364 Richard Dotson	.15	.05
❑ 365 Danny Ozark MG	.15	.05
❑ 366 Todd Cruz	.15	.05
❑ 367 Keefe Cato	.15	.05
❑ 368 Dave Bergman	.15	.05
❑ 369 R.J. Reynolds	.15	.05
❑ 370 Bruce Sutter	.25	.08
❑ 371 Mickey Rivers	.15	.05
❑ 372 Roy Howell	.15	.05
❑ 373 Mike Moore	.15	.05
❑ 374 Brian Downing	.25	.08
❑ 375 Jeff Reardon	.25	.08
❑ 376 Jeff Newman	.15	.05
❑ 377 Checklist: 265-396	.15	.05
❑ 378 Alan Wiggins	.15	.05
❑ 379 Charles Hudson	.15	.05
❑ 380 Ken Griffey	.25	.08
❑ 381 Roy Smith	.15	.05
❑ 382 Denny Walling	.15	.05
❑ 383 Rick Lysander	.15	.05
❑ 384 Jody Davis	.15	.05
❑ 385 Jose DeLeon	.15	.05
❑ 386 Dan Gladden RC	.40	.15
❑ 387 Buddy Biancalana	.15	.05
❑ 388 Bert Roberge	.15	.05
❑ 389 Rod Dedeaux OLY CO RC	.25	.08
❑ 390 Sid Akins OLY RC	.15	.05
❑ 391 Flavio Alfaro OLY RC	.15	.05
❑ 392 Don August OLY RC	.15	.05
❑ 393 Scott Bankhead OLY RC	.15	.05
❑ 394 Bob Caffrey OLY RC	.15	.05
❑ 395 Mike Dunne OLY RC	.15	.05
❑ 396 Gary Green OLY RC	.15	.05
❑ 397 John Hoover OLY RC	.15	.05
❑ 398 Shane Mack OLY RC	.40	.15
❑ 399 John Marzano OLY RC	.15	.05
❑ 400 Oddibe McDowell OLY RC	.40	.15
❑ 401 Mark McGwire OLY RC	30.00	12.50
❑ 402 Pat Pacillo OLY RC	.15	.05
❑ 403 Cory Snyder OLY RC	.75	.30
❑ 404 Bill Swift OLY RC	.40	.15
❑ 405 Tom Veryzer	.15	.05
❑ 406 Len Whitehouse	.15	.05
❑ 407 Bobby Ramos	.15	.05
❑ 408 Sid Monge	.15	.05
❑ 409 Brad Wellman	.15	.05
❑ 410 Bob Horner	.25	.08
❑ 411 Bobby Cox MG	.25	.08
❑ 412 Bud Black	.15	.05
❑ 413 Vance Law	.15	.05
❑ 414 Gary Ward	.15	.05
❑ 415 Ron Darling UER	.25	.08
❑ 416 Wayne Gross	.15	.05
❑ 417 John Franco RC	.75	.30
❑ 418 Ken Landreaux	.15	.05
❑ 419 Mike Caldwell	.15	.05
❑ 420 Andre Dawson	.25	.08
❑ 421 Dave Rucker	.15	.05
❑ 422 Carney Lansford	.25	.08
❑ 423 Barry Bonnell	.15	.05
❑ 424 Al Nipper	.15	.05
❑ 425 Mike Hargrove	.15	.05
❑ 426 Vern Ruhle	.15	.05
❑ 427 Mario Ramirez	.15	.05
❑ 428 Larry Andersen	.15	.05
❑ 429 Rick Cerone	.15	.05
❑ 430 Ron Davis	.15	.05
❑ 431 U.L. Washington	.15	.05
❑ 432 Thad Bosley	.15	.05
❑ 433 Jim Morrison	.15	.05
❑ 434 Gene Richards	.15	.05
❑ 435 Dan Petry	.15	.05
❑ 436 Willie Aikens	.15	.05
❑ 437 Al Jones	.15	.05
❑ 438 Joe Torre MG	.25	.08
❑ 439 Junior Ortiz	.15	.05
❑ 440 Fernando Valenzuela	.25	.08
❑ 441 Duane Walker	.15	.05
❑ 442 Ken Forsch	.15	.05
❑ 443 George Wright	.15	.05
❑ 444 Tony Phillips	.15	.05
❑ 445 Tippy Martinez	.15	.05
❑ 446 Jim Sundberg	.25	.08
❑ 447 Jeff Lahti	.15	.05
❑ 448 Derrel Thomas	.15	.05
❑ 449 Phil Bradley	.40	.15
❑ 450 Steve Garvey	.25	.08
❑ 451 Bruce Hurst	.15	.05
❑ 452 John Castino	.15	.05
❑ 453 Tom Waddell	.15	.05
❑ 454 Glenn Wilson	.15	.05
❑ 455 Bob Knepper	.15	.05
❑ 456 Tim Foli	.15	.05
❑ 457 Cecilio Guante	.15	.05
❑ 458 Randy Johnson	.15	.05
❑ 459 Charlie Leibrandt	.15	.05
❑ 460 Ryne Sandberg	1.25	.50
❑ 461 Marty Castillo	.15	.05
❑ 462 Gary Lavelle	.15	.05
❑ 463 Dave Collins	.15	.05
❑ 464 Mike Mason RC	.15	.05
❑ 465 Bob Grich	.25	.08
❑ 466 Tony LaRussa MG	.25	.08
❑ 467 Ed Lynch	.15	.05
❑ 468 Wayne Krenchicki	.15	.05
❑ 469 Sammy Stewart	.15	.05
❑ 470 Steve Sax	.15	.05
❑ 471 Pete Ladd	.15	.05
❑ 472 Jim Essian	.15	.05
❑ 473 Tim Wallach	.15	.05
❑ 474 Kurt Kepshire	.15	.05
❑ 475 Andre Thornton	.15	.05
❑ 476 Jeff Stone	.15	.05
❑ 477 Bob Ojeda	.15	.05
❑ 478 Kurt Bevacqua	.15	.05
❑ 479 Mike Madden	.15	.05
❑ 480 Lou Whitaker	.25	.08
❑ 481 Dale Murray	.15	.05
❑ 482 Harry Spilman	.15	.05
❑ 483 Mike Smithson	.15	.05
❑ 484 Larry Bowa	.25	.08
❑ 485 Matt Young	.15	.05
❑ 486 Steve Balboni	.15	.05
❑ 487 Frank Williams	.15	.05
❑ 488 Joel Skinner	.15	.05
❑ 489 Bryan Clark	.15	.05
❑ 490 Jason Thompson	.15	.05
❑ 491 Rick Camp	.15	.05
❑ 492 Dave Johnson MG	.15	.05
❑ 493 Orel Hershiser RC	2.00	.75
❑ 494 Rich Dauer	.15	.05
❑ 495 Mario Soto	.25	.08
❑ 496 Donnie Scott	.15	.05
❑ 497 Gary Pettis UER	.15	.05
❑ 498 Ed Romero	.15	.05
❑ 499 Danny Cox	.15	.05
❑ 500 Mike Schmidt	1.50	.60
❑ 501 Dan Schatzeder	.15	.05
❑ 502 Rick Miller	.15	.05
❑ 503 Tim Conroy	.15	.05
❑ 504 Jerry Willard	.15	.05
❑ 505 Jim Beattie	.15	.05
❑ 506 Franklin Stubbs	.15	.05
❑ 507 Ray Fontenot	.15	.05
❑ 508 John Shelby	.15	.05
❑ 509 Milt May	.15	.05
❑ 510 Kent Hrbek	.25	.08
❑ 511 Lee Smith	.25	.08
❑ 512 Tom Brookens	.15	.05
❑ 513 Lynn Jones	.15	.05
❑ 514 Jeff Cornell	.15	.05
❑ 515 Dave Concepcion	.25	.08
❑ 516 Roy Lee Jackson	.15	.05
❑ 517 Jerry Martin	.15	.05
❑ 518 Chris Chambliss	.25	.08
❑ 519 Doug Rader MG	.15	.05
❑ 520 LaMarr Hoyt	.15	.05
❑ 521 Rick Dempsey	.15	.05
❑ 522 Paul Molitor	.25	.08
❑ 523 Candy Maldonado	.15	.05
❑ 524 Rob Wilfong	.15	.05
❑ 525 Darrell Porter	.15	.05
❑ 526 David Palmer	.15	.05
❑ 527 Checklist: 397-528	.15	.05
❑ 528 Bill Krueger	.15	.05
❑ 529 Rich Gedman	.15	.05
❑ 530 Dave Dravecky	.15	.05
❑ 531 Joe Lefebvre	.15	.05
❑ 532 Frank DiPino	.15	.05
❑ 533 Tony Bernazard	.15	.05
❑ 534 Brian Dayett	.15	.05
❑ 535 Pat Putnam	.15	.05
❑ 536 Kirby Puckett RC	10.00	4.00
❑ 537 Don Robinson	.15	.05
❑ 538 Keith Moreland	.15	.05
❑ 539 Aurelio Lopez	.15	.05
❑ 540 Claudell Washington	.15	.05
❑ 541 Mark Davis	.15	.05
❑ 542 Don Slaught	.15	.05
❑ 543 Mike Squires	.15	.05
❑ 544 Bruce Kison	.15	.05
❑ 545 Lloyd Moseby	.15	.05
❑ 546 Brent Gaff	.15	.05
❑ 547 Pete Rose MG/TC	.40	.15
❑ 548 Larry Parrish	.15	.05
❑ 549 Mike Scioscia	.25	.08
❑ 550 Scott McGregor	.15	.05
❑ 551 Andy Van Slyke	.40	.15
❑ 552 Chris Codiroli	.15	.05
❑ 553 Bob Clark	.15	.05
❑ 554 Doug Flynn	.15	.05
❑ 555 Bob Stanley	.15	.05
❑ 556 Sixto Lezcano	.15	.05
❑ 557 Len Barker	.15	.05
❑ 558 Carmelo Martinez	.15	.05
❑ 559 Jay Howell	.15	.05
❑ 560 Bill Madlock	.25	.08
❑ 561 Darryl Motley	.15	.05
❑ 562 Houston Jimenez	.15	.05
❑ 563 Dick Ruthven	.15	.05
❑ 564 Alan Ashby	.15	.05
❑ 565 Kirk Gibson	.25	.08
❑ 566 Ed VandeBerg	.15	.05
❑ 567 Joel Youngblood	.15	.05
❑ 568 Cliff Johnson	.15	.05
❑ 569 Ken Oberkfell	.15	.05
❑ 570 Darryl Strawberry	.60	.25
❑ 571 Charlie Hough	.25	.08
❑ 572 Tom Paciorek	.15	.05
❑ 573 Jay Tibbs	.15	.05
❑ 574 Joe Altobelli MG	.15	.05
❑ 575 Pedro Guerrero	.25	.08
❑ 576 Jaime Cocanower	.15	.05
❑ 577 Chris Speier	.15	.05
❑ 578 Terry Francona	.25	.08
❑ 579 Ron Romanick	.15	.05
❑ 580 Dwight Evans	.40	.15
❑ 581 Mark Wagner	.15	.05
❑ 582 Ken Phelps	.15	.05
❑ 583 Bobby Brown	.15	.05
❑ 584 Kevin Gross	.15	.05
❑ 585 Butch Wynegar	.15	.05
❑ 586 Bill Scherrer	.15	.05
❑ 587 Doug Frobel	.15	.05
❑ 588 Bobby Castillo	.15	.05
❑ 589 Bob Dernier	.15	.05
❑ 590 Ray Knight	.25	.08
❑ 591 Larry Herndon	.15	.05
❑ 592 Jeff D. Robinson	.15	.05
❑ 593 Rick Leach	.15	.05
❑ 594 Curt Wilkerson	.15	.05
❑ 595 Larry Gura	.15	.05
❑ 596 Jerry Hairston	.15	.05
❑ 597 Brad Lesley	.15	.05
❑ 598 Jose Oquendo	.15	.05

❑ 599 Storm Davis .15 .05
❑ 600 Pete Rose 1.50 .60
❑ 601 Tom Lasorda MG .40 .15
❑ 602 Jeff Dedmon .15 .05
❑ 603 Rick Manning .15 .05
❑ 604 Daryl Sconiers .15 .05
❑ 605 Ozzie Smith 1.00 .40
❑ 606 Rich Gale .15 .05
❑ 607 Bill Almon .15 .05
❑ 608 Craig Lefferts .15 .05
❑ 609 Broderick Perkins .15 .05
❑ 610 Jack Morris .25 .08
❑ 611 Ozzie Virgil .15 .05
❑ 612 Mike Armstrong .15 .05
❑ 613 Terry Puhl .15 .05
❑ 614 Al Williams .15 .05
❑ 615 Marvell Wynne .15 .05
❑ 616 Scott Sanderson .15 .05
❑ 617 Willie Wilson .25 .08
❑ 618 Pete Falcone .15 .05
❑ 619 Jeff Leonard .15 .05
❑ 620 Dwight Gooden RC 2.00 .75
❑ 621 Marvis Foley .15 .05
❑ 622 Luis Leal .15 .05
❑ 623 Greg Walker .15 .05
❑ 624 Benny Ayala .15 .05
❑ 625 Mark Langston RC .75 .30
❑ 626 German Rivera .15 .05
❑ 627 Eric Davis RC 2.00 .75
❑ 628 Rene Lachemann MG .15 .05
❑ 629 Dick Schofield .15 .05
❑ 630 Tim Raines .25 .08
❑ 631 Bob Forsch .15 .05
❑ 632 Bruce Bochte .15 .05
❑ 633 Glenn Hoffman .15 .05
❑ 634 Bill Dawley .15 .05
❑ 635 Terry Kennedy .15 .05
❑ 636 Shane Rawley .15 .05
❑ 637 Brett Butler .25 .08
❑ 638 Mike Pagliarulo .15 .05
❑ 639 Ed Hodge .15 .05
❑ 640 Steve Henderson .15 .05
❑ 641 Rod Scurry .15 .05
❑ 642 Dave Owen .15 .05
❑ 643 Johnny Grubb .15 .05
❑ 644 Mark Huismann .15 .05
❑ 645 Damaso Garcia .15 .05
❑ 646 Scot Thompson .15 .05
❑ 647 Rafael Ramirez .15 .05
❑ 648 Bob Jones .15 .05
❑ 649 Sid Fernandez .25 .08
❑ 650 Greg Luzinski .25 .08
❑ 651 Jeff Russell .15 .05
❑ 652 Joe Nolan .15 .05
❑ 653 Mark Brouhard .15 .05
❑ 654 Dave Anderson .15 .05
❑ 655 Joaquin Andujar .25 .08
❑ 656 Chuck Cottier MG .15 .05
❑ 657 Jim Slaton .15 .05
❑ 658 Mike Stenhouse .15 .05
❑ 659 Checklist: 529-660 .15 .05
❑ 660 Tony Gwynn 1.25 .50
❑ 661 Steve Crawford .15 .05
❑ 662 Mike Heath .15 .05
❑ 663 Luis Aguayo .15 .05
❑ 664 Steve Farr RC .40 .15
❑ 665 Don Mattingly 2.50 1.00
❑ 666 Mike LaCoss .15 .05
❑ 667 Dave Engle .15 .05
❑ 668 Steve Trout .15 .05
❑ 669 Lee Lacy .15 .05
❑ 670 Tom Seaver .40 .15
❑ 671 Dane Iorg .15 .05
❑ 672 Juan Berenguer .15 .05
❑ 673 Buck Martinez .15 .05
❑ 674 Atlee Hammaker .15 .05
❑ 675 Tony Perez .40 .15
❑ 676 Albert Hall .15 .05
❑ 677 Wally Backman .15 .05
❑ 678 Joey McLaughlin .15 .05
❑ 679 Bob Kearney .15 .05
❑ 680 Jerry Reuss .15 .05
❑ 681 Ben Oglivie .25 .08
❑ 682 Doug Corbett .15 .05
❑ 683 Whitey Herzog MG .25 .08
❑ 684 Bill Doran .15 .05
❑ 685 Bill Caudill .15 .05
❑ 686 Mike Easler .15 .05
❑ 687 Bill Gullickson .15 .05
❑ 688 Len Matuszek .15 .05
❑ 689 Luis DeLeon .15 .05
❑ 690 Alan Trammell .25 .08
❑ 691 Dennis Rasmussen .15 .05
❑ 692 Randy Bush .15 .05
❑ 693 Tim Stoddard .15 .05
❑ 694 Joe Carter .60 .25
❑ 695 Rick Rhoden .15 .05
❑ 696 John Rabb .15 .05
❑ 697 Onix Concepcion .15 .05
❑ 698 George Bell .25 .08
❑ 699 Donnie Moore .15 .05
❑ 700 Eddie Murray .60 .25
❑ 701 Eddie Murray AS .40 .15
❑ 702 Damaso Garcia AS .15 .05
❑ 703 George Brett AS .60 .25
❑ 704 Cal Ripken AS 1.50 .60
❑ 705 Dave Winfield AS .15 .05
❑ 706 Rickey Henderson AS .40 .15
❑ 707 Tony Armas AS .15 .05
❑ 708 Lance Parrish AS .15 .05
❑ 709 Mike Boddicker AS .15 .05
❑ 710 Frank Viola AS .15 .05
❑ 711 Dan Quisenberry AS .15 .05
❑ 712 Keith Hernandez AS .15 .05
❑ 713 Ryne Sandberg AS .60 .25
❑ 714 Mike Schmidt AS .60 .25
❑ 715 Ozzie Smith AS .60 .25
❑ 716 Dale Murphy AS .25 .08
❑ 717 Tony Gwynn AS 1.00 .40
❑ 718 Jeff Leonard AS .15 .05
❑ 719 Gary Carter AS .15 .05
❑ 720 Rick Sutcliffe AS .15 .05
❑ 721 Bob Knepper AS .15 .05
❑ 722 Bruce Sutter AS .15 .05
❑ 723 Dave Stewart .25 .08
❑ 724 Oscar Gamble .15 .05
❑ 725 Floyd Bannister .15 .05
❑ 726 Al Bumbry .15 .05
❑ 727 Frank Pastore .15 .05
❑ 728 Bob Bailor .15 .05
❑ 729 Don Sutton .25 .08
❑ 730 Dave Kingman .25 .08
❑ 731 Neil Allen .15 .05
❑ 732 John McNamara MG .15 .05
❑ 733 Tony Scott .15 .05
❑ 734 John Henry Johnson .15 .05
❑ 735 Garry Templeton .25 .08
❑ 736 Jerry Mumphrey .15 .05
❑ 737 Bo Diaz .15 .05
❑ 738 Omar Moreno .15 .05
❑ 739 Ernie Camacho .15 .05
❑ 740 Jack Clark .25 .08
❑ 741 John Butcher .15 .05
❑ 742 Ron Hassey .15 .05
❑ 743 Frank White .25 .08
❑ 744 Doug Bair .15 .05
❑ 745 Buddy Bell .25 .08
❑ 746 Jim Clancy .15 .05
❑ 747 Alex Trevino .15 .05
❑ 748 Lee Mazzilli .25 .08
❑ 749 Julio Cruz .15 .05
❑ 750 Rollie Fingers .25 .08
❑ 751 Kelvin Chapman .15 .05
❑ 752 Bob Owchinko .15 .05
❑ 753 Greg Brock .15 .05
❑ 754 Larry Milbourne .15 .05
❑ 755 Ken Singleton .25 .08
❑ 756 Rob Picciolo .15 .05
❑ 757 Willie McGee .25 .08
❑ 758 Ray Burris .15 .05
❑ 759 Jim Fanning MG .15 .05
❑ 760 Nolan Ryan 3.00 1.25
❑ 761 Jerry Remy .15 .05
❑ 762 Eddie Whitson .15 .05
❑ 763 Kiko Garcia .15 .05
❑ 764 Jamie Easterly .15 .05
❑ 765 Willie Randolph .25 .08
❑ 766 Paul Mirabella .15 .05
❑ 767 Darrell Brown .15 .05
❑ 768 Ron Cey .25 .08
❑ 769 Joe Cowley .15 .05
❑ 770 Carlton Fisk .40 .15
❑ 771 Geoff Zahn .15 .05
❑ 772 Johnnie LeMaster .15 .05
❑ 773 Hal McRae .25 .08
❑ 774 Dennis Lamp .15 .05
❑ 775 Mookie Wilson .25 .08
❑ 776 Jerry Royster .15 .05
❑ 777 Ned Yost .15 .05
❑ 778 Mike Davis .15 .05
❑ 779 Nick Esasky .15 .05
❑ 780 Mike Flanagan .15 .05
❑ 781 Jim Gantner .15 .05
❑ 782 Tom Niedenfuer .15 .05
❑ 783 Mike Jorgensen .15 .05
❑ 784 Checklist: 661-792 .15 .05
❑ 785 Tony Armas .25 .08
❑ 786 Enos Cabell .15 .05
❑ 787 Jim Wohlford .15 .05
❑ 788 Steve Comer .15 .05
❑ 789 Luis Salazar .15 .05
❑ 790 Ron Guidry .25 .08
❑ 791 Ivan DeJesus .15 .05
❑ 792 Darrell Evans .25 .08

1985 Topps Traded

❑ COMP.FACT.SET (132) 8.00 3.00
❑ 1T Don Aase .15 .05
❑ 2T Bill Almon .15 .05
❑ 3T Benny Ayala .15 .05
❑ 4T Dusty Baker .40 .15
❑ 5T George Bamberger MG .15 .05
❑ 6T Dale Berra .15 .05
❑ 7T Rich Bordi .15 .05
❑ 8T Daryl Boston XRC* .25 .08
❑ 9T Hubie Brooks .15 .05
❑ 10T Chris Brown XRC .25 .08
❑ 11T Tom Browning XRC* .50 .20
❑ 12T Al Bumbry .15 .05
❑ 13T Ray Burris .15 .05
❑ 14T Jeff Burroughs .15 .05
❑ 15T Bill Campbell .15 .05
❑ 16T Don Carman .15 .05
❑ 17T Gary Carter .40 .15
❑ 18T Bobby Castillo .15 .05
❑ 19T Bill Caudill .15 .05
❑ 20T Rick Cerone .15 .05
❑ 21T Bryan Clark .15 .05
❑ 22T Jack Clark .40 .15
❑ 23T Pat Clements .15 .05
❑ 24T Vince Coleman XRC 1.00 .40
❑ 25T Dave Collins .15 .05
❑ 26T Danny Darwin .15 .05
❑ 27T Jim Davenport MG .15 .05
❑ 28T Jerry Davis .15 .05
❑ 29T Brian Dayett .15 .05
❑ 30T Ivan DeJesus .15 .05
❑ 31T Ken Dixon .15 .05
❑ 32T Mariano Duncan XRC .50 .20
❑ 33T John Felske MG .15 .05
❑ 34T Mike Fitzgerald .15 .05
❑ 35T Ray Fontenot .15 .05
❑ 36T Greg Gagne XRC* .50 .20
❑ 37T Oscar Gamble .15 .05
❑ 38T Scott Garrelts .15 .05
❑ 39T Bob L. Gibson .15 .05
❑ 40T Jim Gott .15 .05
❑ 41T David Green .15 .05
❑ 42T Alfredo Griffin .15 .05
❑ 43T Ozzie Guillen XRC 5.00 2.00

❑	44T Eddie Haas MG	.15	.05
❑	45T Terry Harper	.15	.05
❑	46T Toby Harrah	.40	.15
❑	47T Greg Harris	.15	.05
❑	48T Ron Hassey	.15	.05
❑	49T Rickey Henderson	2.50	1.00
❑	50T Steve Henderson	.15	.05
❑	51T George Hendrick	.40	.15
❑	52T Joe Hesketh	.15	.05
❑	53T Teddy Higuera XRC	.50	.20
❑	54T Donnie Hill	.15	.05
❑	55T Al Holland	.15	.05
❑	56T Burt Hooton	.15	.05
❑	57T Jay Howell	.15	.05
❑	58T Ken Howell	.15	.05
❑	59T LaMarr Hoyt	.15	.05
❑	60T Tim Hulett XRC*	.25	.08
❑	61T Bob James	.15	.05
❑	62T Steve Jeltz XRC	.25	.08
❑	63T Cliff Johnson	.15	.05
❑	64T Howard Johnson	.40	.15
❑	65T Ruppert Jones	.15	.05
❑	66T Steve Kemp	.15	.05
❑	67T Bruce Kison	.15	.05
❑	68T Alan Knicely	.15	.05
❑	69T Mike LaCoss	.15	.05
❑	70T Lee Lacy	.15	.05
❑	71T Dave LaPoint	.15	.05
❑	72T Gary Lavelle	.15	.05
❑	73T Vance Law	.15	.05
❑	74T Johnnie LeMaster	.15	.05
❑	75T Sixto Lezcano	.15	.05
❑	76T Tim Lollar	.15	.05
❑	77T Fred Lynn	.40	.15
❑	78T Billy Martin MG	.75	.30
❑	79T Ron Mathis	.15	.05
❑	80T Len Matuszek	.15	.05
❑	81T Gene Mauch MG	.15	.05
❑	82T Oddibe McDowell	.50	.20
❑	83T Roger McDowell XRC	.50	.20
❑	84T John McNamara MG	.15	.05
❑	85T Donnie Moore	.15	.05
❑	86T Gene Nelson	.15	.05
❑	87T Steve Nicosia	.15	.05
❑	88T Al Oliver	.40	.15
❑	89T Joe Orsulak XRC	.50	.20
❑	90T Rob Picciolo	.15	.05
❑	91T Chris Pittaro	.15	.05
❑	92T Jim Presley	.50	.20
❑	93T Rick Reuschel	.40	.15
❑	94T Bert Roberge	.15	.05
❑	95T Bob Rodgers MG	.15	.05
❑	96T Jerry Royster	.15	.05
❑	97T Dave Rozema	.15	.05
❑	98T Dave Rucker	.15	.05
❑	99T Vern Ruhle	.15	.05
❑	100T Paul Runge XRC	.25	.08
❑	101T Mark Salas	.15	.05
❑	102T Luis Salazar	.15	.05
❑	103T Joe Sambito	.15	.05
❑	104T Rick Schu	.15	.05
❑	105T Donnie Scott	.15	.05
❑	106T Larry Sheets XRC	.25	.08
❑	107T Don Slaught	.15	.05
❑	108T Roy Smalley	.15	.05
❑	109T Lonnie Smith	.15	.05
❑	110T Nate Snell UER (Headings on back for a batter)	.15	.05
❑	111T Chris Speier	.15	.05
❑	112T Mike Stenhouse	.15	.05
❑	113T Tim Stoddard	.15	.05
❑	114T Jim Sundberg	.40	.15
❑	115T Bruce Sutter	.40	.15
❑	116T Don Sutton	.40	.15
❑	117T Kent Tekulve	.15	.05
❑	118T Tom Tellmann	.15	.05
❑	119T Walt Terrell	.15	.05
❑	120T Mickey Tettleton XRC	.50	.20
❑	121T Derrel Thomas	.15	.05
❑	122T Rich Thompson	.15	.05
❑	123T Alex Trevino	.15	.05
❑	124T John Tudor	.40	.15
❑	125T Jose Uribe	.15	.05
❑	126T Bobby Valentine MG	.40	.15
❑	127T Dave Von Ohlen	.15	.05
❑	128T U.L. Washington	.15	.05
❑	129T Earl Weaver MG	.40	.15
❑	130T Eddie Whitson	.15	.05
❑	131T Herm Winningham	.15	.05
❑	132T Checklist 1-132	.15	.05

1986 Topps

❑	COMPLETE SET (792)	25.00	10.00
❑	COMP.X-MAS.SET (792)	150.00	75.00
❑	1 Pete Rose	2.00	.75
❑	2 Rose Special: '63-'66	.25	.08
❑	3 Rose Special: '67-'70	.25	.08
❑	4 Rose Special: '71-'74	.25	.08
❑	5 Rose Special: '75-'78	.25	.08
❑	6 Rose Special: '79-'82	.25	.08
❑	7 Rose Special: '83-'85	.25	.08
❑	8 Dwayne Murphy	.10	.02
❑	9 Roy Smith	.10	.02
❑	10 Tony Gwynn	.60	.25
❑	11 Bob Ojeda	.10	.02
❑	12 Jose Uribe	.10	.02
❑	13 Bob Kearney	.10	.02
❑	14 Julio Cruz	.10	.02
❑	15 Eddie Whitson	.10	.02
❑	16 Rick Schu	.10	.02
❑	17 Mike Stenhouse	.10	.02
❑	18 Brent Gaff	.10	.02
❑	19 Rich Hebner	.10	.02
❑	20 Lou Whitaker	.15	.05
❑	21 George Bamberger MG	.10	.02
❑	22 Duane Walker	.10	.02
❑	23 Manuel Lee RC*	.10	.02
❑	24 Len Barker	.10	.02
❑	25 Willie Wilson	.15	.05
❑	26 Frank DiPino	.10	.02
❑	27 Ray Knight	.15	.05
❑	28 Eric Davis	.40	.15
❑	29 Tony Phillips	.10	.02
❑	30 Eddie Murray	.40	.15
❑	31 Jamie Easterly	.10	.02
❑	32 Steve Yeager	.15	.05
❑	33 Jeff Lahti	.10	.02
❑	34 Ken Phelps	.10	.02
❑	35 Jeff Reardon	.15	.05
❑	36 Tigers Leaders Lance Parrish	.15	.05
❑	37 Mark Thurmond	.10	.02
❑	38 Glenn Hoffman	.10	.02
❑	39 Dave Rucker	.10	.02
❑	40 Ken Griffey	.15	.05
❑	41 Brad Wellman	.10	.02
❑	42 Geoff Zahn	.10	.02
❑	43 Dave Engle	.10	.02
❑	44 Lance McCullers	.10	.02
❑	45 Damaso Garcia	.10	.02
❑	46 Billy Hatcher	.10	.02
❑	47 Juan Berenguer	.10	.02
❑	48 Bill Almon	.10	.02
❑	49 Rick Manning	.10	.02
❑	50 Dan Quisenberry	.10	.02
❑	51 Bobby Wine MG ERR (Checklist back) (Number of ca	.10	.02
❑	52 Chris Welsh	.10	.02
❑	53 Len Dykstra RC	.75	.30
❑	54 John Franco	.15	.05
❑	55 Fred Lynn	.15	.05
❑	56 Tom Niedenfuer	.10	.02
❑	57 Bill Doran (See also 51)	.10	.02
❑	58 Bill Krueger	.10	.02
❑	59 Andre Thornton	.10	.02
❑	60 Dwight Evans	.25	.08
❑	61 Karl Best	.10	.02
❑	62 Bob Boone	.15	.05
❑	63 Ron Roenicke	.10	.02
❑	64 Floyd Bannister	.10	.02
❑	65 Dan Driessen	.10	.02
❑	66 Cardinals Leaders Bob Forsch	.10	.02
❑	67 Carmelo Martinez	.10	.02
❑	68 Ed Lynch	.10	.02
❑	69 Luis Aguayo	.10	.02
❑	70 Dave Winfield	.15	.05
❑	71 Ken Schrom	.10	.02
❑	72 Shawon Dunston	.15	.05
❑	73 Randy O'Neal	.10	.02
❑	74 Rance Mulliniks	.10	.02
❑	75 Jose DeLeon	.10	.02
❑	76 Dion James	.10	.02
❑	77 Charlie Leibrandt	.10	.02
❑	78 Bruce Benedict	.10	.02
❑	79 Dave Schmidt	.10	.02
❑	80 Darryl Strawberry	.25	.08
❑	81 Gene Mauch MG	.10	.02
❑	82 Tippy Martinez	.10	.02
❑	83 Phil Garner	.15	.05
❑	84 Curt Young	.10	.02
❑	85 Tony Perez w/E.Davis	.15	.05
❑	86 Tom Waddell	.10	.02
❑	87 Candy Maldonado	.10	.02
❑	88 Tom Nieto	.10	.02
❑	89 Randy St.Claire	.10	.02
❑	90 Garry Templeton	.15	.05
❑	91 Steve Crawford	.10	.02
❑	92 Al Cowens	.10	.02
❑	93 Scot Thompson	.10	.02
❑	94 Rich Bordi	.10	.02
❑	95 Ozzie Virgil	.10	.02
❑	96 Blue Jays Leaders Jim Clancy	.10	.02
❑	97 Gary Gaetti	.15	.05
❑	98 Dick Ruthven	.10	.02
❑	99 Buddy Biancalana	.10	.02
❑	100 Nolan Ryan	2.00	.75
❑	101 Dave Bergman	.10	.02
❑	102 Joe Orsulak RC*	.25	.08
❑	103 Luis Salazar	.10	.02
❑	104 Sid Fernandez	.10	.02
❑	105 Gary Ward	.10	.02
❑	106 Ray Burris	.10	.02
❑	107 Rafael Ramirez	.10	.02
❑	108 Ted Power	.10	.02
❑	109 Len Matuszek	.10	.02
❑	110 Scott McGregor	.10	.02
❑	111 Roger Craig MG	.15	.05
❑	112 Bill Campbell	.10	.02
❑	113 U.L. Washington	.10	.02
❑	114 Mike C. Brown	.10	.02
❑	115 Jay Howell	.10	.02
❑	116 Brook Jacoby	.10	.02
❑	117 Bruce Kison	.10	.02
❑	118 Jerry Royster	.10	.02
❑	119 Barry Bonnell	.10	.02
❑	120 Steve Carlton	.15	.05
❑	121 Nelson Simmons	.10	.02
❑	122 Pete Filson	.10	.02
❑	123 Greg Walker	.10	.02
❑	124 Luis Sanchez	.10	.02
❑	125 Dave Lopes	.15	.05
❑	126 Mets Leaders Mookie Wilson	.10	.02
❑	127 Jack Howell	.10	.02
❑	128 John Wathan	.10	.02
❑	129 Jeff Dedmon	.10	.02
❑	130 Alan Trammell	.15	.05
❑	131 Checklist: 1-132	.15	.05
❑	132 Razor Shines	.10	.02
❑	133 Andy McGaffigan	.10	.02
❑	134 Carney Lansford	.15	.05
❑	135 Joe Niekro	.10	.02
❑	136 Mike Hargrove	.10	.02
❑	137 Charlie Moore	.10	.02
❑	138 Mark Davis	.10	.02

❑ 139 Daryl Boston .10 .02
❑ 140 John Candelaria .10 .02
❑ 141 Chuck Cottier MG
See also 171 .10 .02
❑ 142 Bob Jones .10 .02
❑ 143 Dave Van Gorder .10 .02
❑ 144 Doug Sisk .10 .02
❑ 145 Pedro Guerrero .15 .05
❑ 146 Jack Perconte .10 .02
❑ 147 Larry Sheets .10 .02
❑ 148 Mike Heath .10 .02
❑ 149 Brett Butler .15 .05
❑ 150 Joaquin Andujar .15 .05
❑ 151 Dave Stapleton .10 .02
❑ 152 Mike Morgan .10 .02
❑ 153 Ricky Adams .10 .02
❑ 154 Bert Roberge .10 .02
❑ 155 Bob Grich .15 .05
❑ 156 White Sox Leaders
Richard Dotson .10 .02
❑ 157 Ron Hassey .10 .02
❑ 158 Derrel Thomas .10 .02
❑ 159 Orel Hershiser UER .40 .15
❑ 160 Chet Lemon .15 .05
❑ 161 Lee Tunnell .10 .02
❑ 162 Greg Gagne .10 .02
❑ 163 Pete Ladd .10 .02
❑ 164 Steve Balboni .10 .02
❑ 165 Mike Davis .10 .02
❑ 166 Dickie Thon .10 .02
❑ 167 Zane Smith .10 .02
❑ 168 Jeff Burroughs .10 .02
❑ 169 George Wright .10 .02
❑ 170 Gary Carter .15 .05
❑ 171 Bob Rodgers MG ERR
(Checklist back)
(Number of c .10 .02
❑ 172 Jerry Reed .10 .02
❑ 173 Wayne Gross .10 .02
❑ 174 Brian Snyder .10 .02
❑ 175 Steve Sax .10 .02
❑ 176 Jay Tibbs .10 .02
❑ 177 Joel Youngblood .10 .02
❑ 178 Ivan DeJesus .10 .02
❑ 179 Stu Cliburn .10 .02
❑ 180 Don Mattingly 1.25 .50
❑ 181 Al Nipper .10 .02
❑ 182 Bobby Brown .10 .02
❑ 183 Larry Andersen .10 .02
❑ 184 Tim Laudner .10 .02
❑ 185 Rollie Fingers .15 .05
❑ 186 Astros Leaders
Jose Cruz .10 .02
❑ 187 Scott Fletcher .10 .02
❑ 188 Bob Dernier .10 .02
❑ 189 Mike Mason .10 .02
❑ 190 George Hendrick .15 .05
❑ 191 Wally Backman .10 .02
❑ 192 Milt Wilcox .10 .02
❑ 193 Daryl Sconiers .10 .02
❑ 194 Craig McMurtry .10 .02
❑ 195 Dave Concepcion .15 .05
❑ 196 Doyle Alexander .10 .02
❑ 197 Enos Cabell .10 .02
❑ 198 Ken Dixon .10 .02
❑ 199 Dick Howser MG .10 .02
❑ 200 Mike Schmidt 1.00 .40
❑ 201 Vince Coleman RB
Most stolen bases,
season, rook .15 .05
❑ 202 Dwight Gooden RB .25 .08
❑ 203 Keith Hernandez RB .10 .02
❑ 204 Phil Niekro RB
Oldest shutout pitcher .15 .05
❑ 205 Tony Perez RB
Oldest grand slammer .15 .05
❑ 206 Pete Rose RB .40 .15
❑ 207 Fernando Valenzuela RB
Most cons. innings,
start .10 .02
❑ 208 Ramon Romero .10 .02
❑ 209 Randy Ready .10 .02
❑ 210 Calvin Schiraldi .10 .02
❑ 211 Ed Wojna .10 .02
❑ 212 Chris Speier .10 .02
❑ 213 Bob Shirley .10 .02

❑ 214 Randy Bush .10 .02
❑ 215 Frank White .15 .05
❑ 216 A's Leaders
Dwayne Murphy .10 .02
❑ 217 Bill Scherrer .10 .02
❑ 218 Randy Hunt .10 .02
❑ 219 Dennis Lamp .10 .02
❑ 220 Bob Horner .15 .05
❑ 221 Dave Henderson .10 .02
❑ 222 Craig Gerber .10 .02
❑ 223 Atlee Hammaker .10 .02
❑ 224 Cesar Cedeno .15 .05
❑ 225 Ron Darling .15 .05
❑ 226 Lee Lacy .10 .02
❑ 227 Al Jones .10 .02
❑ 228 Tom Lawless .10 .02
❑ 229 Bill Gullickson .10 .02
❑ 230 Terry Kennedy .10 .02
❑ 231 Jim Frey MG .10 .02
❑ 232 Rick Rhoden .10 .02
❑ 233 Steve Lyons .10 .02
❑ 234 Doug Corbett .10 .02
❑ 235 Butch Wynegar .10 .02
❑ 236 Frank Eufemia .10 .02
❑ 237 Ted Simmons .15 .05
❑ 238 Larry Parrish .10 .02
❑ 239 Joel Skinner .10 .02
❑ 240 Tommy John .15 .05
❑ 241 Tony Fernandez .10 .02
❑ 242 Rich Thompson .10 .02
❑ 243 Johnny Grubb .10 .02
❑ 244 Craig Lefferts .10 .02
❑ 245 Jim Sundberg .15 .05
❑ 246 Steve Carlton TL .10 .02
❑ 247 Terry Harper .10 .02
❑ 248 Spike Owen .10 .02
❑ 249 Rob Deer .10 .02
❑ 250 Dwight Gooden .40 .15
❑ 251 Rich Dauer .10 .02
❑ 252 Bobby Castillo .10 .02
❑ 253 Dann Bilardello .10 .02
❑ 254 Ozzie Guillen RC 1.50 .60
❑ 255 Tony Armas .15 .05
❑ 256 Kurt Kepshire .10 .02
❑ 257 Doug DeCinces .10 .02
❑ 258 Tim Burke .10 .02
❑ 259 Dan Pasqua .10 .02
❑ 260 Tony Pena .10 .02
❑ 261 Bobby Valentine MG .15 .05
❑ 262 Mario Ramirez .10 .02
❑ 263 Checklist: 133-264 .15 .05
❑ 264 Darren Daulton RC .50 .20
❑ 265 Ron Davis .10 .02
❑ 266 Keith Moreland .10 .02
❑ 267 Paul Molitor .15 .05
❑ 268 Mike Scott .15 .05
❑ 269 Dane Iorg .10 .02
❑ 270 Jack Morris .15 .05
❑ 271 Dave Collins .10 .02
❑ 272 Tim Tolman .10 .02
❑ 273 Jerry Willard .10 .02
❑ 274 Ron Gardenhire .10 .02
❑ 275 Charlie Hough .15 .05
❑ 276 Yankees Leaders
Willie Randolph .15 .05
❑ 277 Jaime Cocanower .10 .02
❑ 278 Sixto Lezcano .10 .02
❑ 279 Al Pardo .10 .02
❑ 280 Tim Raines .15 .05
❑ 281 Steve Mura .10 .02
❑ 282 Jerry Mumphrey .10 .02
❑ 283 Mike Fischlin .10 .02
❑ 284 Brian Dayett .10 .02
❑ 285 Buddy Bell .15 .05
❑ 286 Luis DeLeon .10 .02
❑ 287 John Christensen .10 .02
❑ 288 Don Aase .10 .02
❑ 289 Johnnie LeMaster .10 .02
❑ 290 Carlton Fisk .25 .08
❑ 291 Tom Lasorda MG .25 .08
❑ 292 Chuck Porter .10 .02
❑ 293 Chris Chambliss .15 .05
❑ 294 Danny Cox .10 .02
❑ 295 Kirk Gibson .15 .05
❑ 296 Geno Petralli .10 .02
❑ 297 Tim Lollar .10 .02

❑ 298 Craig Reynolds .10 .02
❑ 299 Bryn Smith .10 .02
❑ 300 George Brett 1.00 .40
❑ 301 Dennis Rasmussen .10 .02
❑ 302 Greg Gross .10 .02
❑ 303 Curt Wardle .10 .02
❑ 304 Mike Gallego RC .10 .02
❑ 305 Phil Bradley .10 .02
❑ 306 Padres Leaders
Terry Kennedy .10 .02
❑ 307 Dave Sax .10 .02
❑ 308 Ray Fontenot .10 .02
❑ 309 John Shelby .10 .02
❑ 310 Greg Minton .10 .02
❑ 311 Dick Schofield .10 .02
❑ 312 Tom Filer .10 .02
❑ 313 Joe DeSa .10 .02
❑ 314 Frank Pastore .10 .02
❑ 315 Mookie Wilson .15 .05
❑ 316 Sammy Khalifa .10 .02
❑ 317 Ed Romero .10 .02
❑ 318 Terry Whitfield .10 .02
❑ 319 Rick Camp .10 .02
❑ 320 Jim Rice .15 .05
❑ 321 Earl Weaver MG .15 .05
❑ 322 Bob Forsch .10 .02
❑ 323 Jerry Davis .10 .02
❑ 324 Dan Schatzeder .10 .02
❑ 325 Juan Beniquez .10 .02
❑ 326 Kent Tekulve .10 .02
❑ 327 Mike Pagliarulo .10 .02
❑ 328 Pete O'Brien .10 .02
❑ 329 Kirby Puckett 1.00 .40
❑ 330 Rick Sutcliffe .15 .05
❑ 331 Alan Ashby .10 .02
❑ 332 Darryl Motley .10 .02
❑ 333 Tom Henke .15 .05
❑ 334 Ken Oberkfell .10 .02
❑ 335 Don Sutton .15 .05
❑ 336 Indians Leaders
Andre Thornton .15 .05
❑ 337 Darnell Coles .10 .02
❑ 338 Jorge Bell .15 .05
❑ 339 Bruce Berenyi .10 .02
❑ 340 Cal Ripken 1.50 .60
❑ 341 Frank Williams .10 .02
❑ 342 Gary Redus .10 .02
❑ 343 Carlos Diaz .10 .02
❑ 344 Jim Wohlford .10 .02
❑ 345 Donnie Moore .10 .02
❑ 346 Bryan Little .10 .02
❑ 347 Teddy Higuera RC* .25 .08
❑ 348 Cliff Johnson .10 .02
❑ 349 Mark Clear .10 .02
❑ 350 Jack Clark .15 .05
❑ 351 Chuck Tanner MG .10 .02
❑ 352 Harry Spilman .10 .02
❑ 353 Keith Atherton .10 .02
❑ 354 Tony Bernazard .10 .02
❑ 355 Lee Smith .15 .05
❑ 356 Mickey Hatcher .10 .02
❑ 357 Ed VandeBerg .10 .02
❑ 358 Rick Dempsey .10 .02
❑ 359 Mike LaCoss .10 .02
❑ 360 Lloyd Moseby .10 .02
❑ 361 Shane Rawley .10 .02
❑ 362 Tom Paciorek .10 .02
❑ 363 Terry Forster .15 .05
❑ 364 Reid Nichols .10 .02
❑ 365 Mike Flanagan .10 .02
❑ 366 Reds Leaders
Dave Concepcion .15 .05
❑ 367 Aurelio Lopez .10 .02
❑ 368 Greg Brock .10 .02
❑ 369 Al Holland .10 .02
❑ 370 Vince Coleman RC .50 .20
❑ 371 Bill Stein .10 .02
❑ 372 Ben Oglivie .15 .05
❑ 373 Urbano Lugo .10 .02
❑ 374 Terry Francona .15 .05
❑ 375 Rich Gedman .10 .02
❑ 376 Bill Dawley .10 .02
❑ 377 Joe Carter .15 .05
❑ 378 Bruce Bochte .10 .02
❑ 379 Bobby Meacham .10 .02
❑ 380 LaMarr Hoyt .10 .02

❑ 381 Ray Miller MG .10 .02
❑ 382 Ivan Calderon RC* .25 .08
❑ 383 Chris Brown RC .10 .02
❑ 384 Steve Trout .10 .02
❑ 385 Cecil Cooper .15 .05
❑ 386 Cecil Fielder RC 1.00 .40
❑ 387 Steve Kemp .10 .02
❑ 388 Dickie Noles .10 .02
❑ 389 Glenn Davis .10 .02
❑ 390 Tom Seaver .25 .08
❑ 391 Julio Franco .15 .05
❑ 392 John Russell .10 .02
❑ 393 Chris Pittaro .10 .02
❑ 394 Checklist: 265-396 .15 .05
❑ 395 Scott Garrelts .10 .02
❑ 396 Red Sox Leaders
Dwight Evans .25 .08
❑ 397 Steve Buechele RC .25 .08
❑ 398 Earnie Riles .10 .02
❑ 399 Bill Swift .10 .02
❑ 400 Rod Carew .25 .08
❑ 401 Fernando Valenzuela
TBC '81 .10 .02
❑ 402 Tom Seaver TBC .15 .05
❑ 403 Willie Mays TBC .40 .15
❑ 404 Frank Robinson TBC .15 .05
❑ 405 Roger Maris TBC .40 .15
❑ 406 Scott Sanderson .10 .02
❑ 407 Sal Butera .10 .02
❑ 408 Dave Smith .10 .02
❑ 409 Paul Runge RC .10 .02
❑ 410 Dave Kingman .15 .05
❑ 411 Sparky Anderson MG .15 .05
❑ 412 Jim Clancy .10 .02
❑ 413 Tim Flannery .10 .02
❑ 414 Tom Gorman .10 .02
❑ 415 Hal McRae .15 .05
❑ 416 Dennis Martinez .15 .05
❑ 417 R.J. Reynolds .10 .02
❑ 418 Alan Knicely .10 .02
❑ 419 Frank Wills .10 .02
❑ 420 Von Hayes .10 .02
❑ 421 David Palmer .10 .02
❑ 422 Mike Jorgensen .10 .02
❑ 423 Dan Spillner .10 .02
❑ 424 Rick Miller .10 .02
❑ 425 Larry McWilliams .10 .02
❑ 426 Brewers Leaders
Charlie Moore .10 .02
❑ 427 Joe Cowley .10 .02
❑ 428 Max Venable .10 .02
❑ 429 Greg Booker .10 .02
❑ 430 Kent Hrbek .15 .05
❑ 431 George Frazier .10 .02
❑ 432 Mark Bailey .10 .02
❑ 433 Chris Codiroli .10 .02
❑ 434 Curt Wilkerson .10 .02
❑ 435 Bill Caudill .10 .02
❑ 436 Doug Flynn .10 .02
❑ 437 Rick Mahler .10 .02
❑ 438 Clint Hurdle .10 .02
❑ 439 Rick Honeycutt .10 .02
❑ 440 Alvin Davis .10 .02
❑ 441 Whitey Herzog MG .25 .08
❑ 442 Ron Robinson .10 .02
❑ 443 Bill Buckner .15 .05
❑ 444 Alex Trevino .10 .02
❑ 445 Bert Blyleven .15 .05
❑ 446 Lenn Sakata .10 .02
❑ 447 Jerry Don Gleaton .10 .02
❑ 448 Herm Winningham .10 .02
❑ 449 Rod Scurry .10 .02
❑ 450 Graig Nettles .15 .05
❑ 451 Mark Brown .10 .02
❑ 452 Bob Clark .10 .02
❑ 453 Steve Jeltz .10 .02
❑ 454 Burt Hooton .10 .02
❑ 455 Willie Randolph .15 .05
❑ 456 Braves Leaders
Dale Murphy .25 .08
❑ 457 Mickey Tettleton RC .25 .08
❑ 458 Kevin Bass .10 .02
❑ 459 Luis Leal .10 .02
❑ 460 Leon Durham .10 .02
❑ 461 Walt Terrell .10 .02
❑ 462 Domingo Ramos .10 .02
❑ 463 Jim Gott .10 .02
❑ 464 Ruppert Jones .10 .02
❑ 465 Jesse Orosco .10 .02
❑ 466 Tom Foley .10 .02
❑ 467 Bob James .10 .02
❑ 468 Mike Scioscia .15 .05
❑ 469 Storm Davis .10 .02
❑ 470 Bill Madlock .15 .05
❑ 471 Bobby Cox MG .15 .05
❑ 472 Joe Hesketh .10 .02
❑ 473 Mark Brouhard .10 .02
❑ 474 John Tudor .15 .05
❑ 475 Juan Samuel .10 .02
❑ 476 Ron Mathis .10 .02
❑ 477 Mike Easler .10 .02
❑ 478 Andy Hawkins .10 .02
❑ 479 Bob Melvin .10 .02
❑ 480 Oddibe McDowell .10 .02
❑ 481 Scott Bradley .10 .02
❑ 482 Rick Lysander .10 .02
❑ 483 George Vukovich .10 .02
❑ 484 Donnie Hill .10 .02
❑ 485 Gary Matthews .15 .05
❑ 486 Angels Leaders
Bobby Grich .10 .02
❑ 487 Bret Saberhagen .15 .05
❑ 488 Lou Thornton .10 .02
❑ 489 Jim Winn .10 .02
❑ 490 Jeff Leonard .10 .02
❑ 491 Pascual Perez .10 .02
❑ 492 Kelvin Chapman .10 .02
❑ 493 Gene Nelson .10 .02
❑ 494 Gary Roenicke .10 .02
❑ 495 Mark Langston .15 .05
❑ 496 Jay Johnstone .10 .02
❑ 497 John Stuper .10 .02
❑ 498 Tito Landrum .10 .02
❑ 499 Bob L. Gibson .10 .02
❑ 500 Rickey Henderson .40 .15
❑ 501 Dave Johnson MG .10 .02
❑ 502 Glen Cook .10 .02
❑ 503 Mike Fitzgerald .10 .02
❑ 504 Denny Walling .10 .02
❑ 505 Jerry Koosman .15 .05
❑ 506 Bill Russell .15 .05
❑ 507 Steve Ontiveros RC .10 .02
❑ 508 Alan Wiggins .10 .02
❑ 509 Ernie Camacho .10 .02
❑ 510 Wade Boggs .25 .08
❑ 511 Ed Nunez .10 .02
❑ 512 Thad Bosley .10 .02
❑ 513 Ron Washington .10 .02
❑ 514 Mike Jones .10 .02
❑ 515 Darrell Evans .15 .05
❑ 516 Giants Leaders
Greg Minton .10 .02
❑ 517 Milt Thompson RC .25 .08
❑ 518 Buck Martinez .10 .02
❑ 519 Danny Darwin .10 .02
❑ 520 Keith Hernandez .15 .05
❑ 521 Nate Snell .10 .02
❑ 522 Bob Bailor .10 .02
❑ 523 Joe Price .10 .02
❑ 524 Darrell Miller .10 .02
❑ 525 Marvell Wynne .10 .02
❑ 526 Charlie Lea .10 .02
❑ 527 Checklist: 397-528 .15 .05
❑ 528 Terry Pendleton .15 .05
❑ 529 Marc Sullivan .10 .02
❑ 530 Rich Gossage .15 .05
❑ 531 Tony LaRussa MG .15 .05
❑ 532 Don Carman .10 .02
❑ 533 Billy Sample .10 .02
❑ 534 Jeff Calhoun .10 .02
❑ 535 Toby Harrah .15 .05
❑ 536 Jose Rijo .15 .05
❑ 537 Mark Salas .10 .02
❑ 538 Dennis Eckersley .25 .08
❑ 539 Glenn Hubbard .10 .02
❑ 540 Dan Petry .10 .02
❑ 541 Jorge Orta .10 .02
❑ 542 Don Schulze .10 .02
❑ 543 Jerry Narron .10 .02
❑ 544 Eddie Milner .10 .02
❑ 545 Jimmy Key .15 .05
❑ 546 Mariners Leaders
Dave Henderson .10 .02
❑ 547 Roger McDowell RC* .25 .08
❑ 548 Mike Young .10 .02
❑ 549 Bob Welch .15 .05
❑ 550 Tom Herr .10 .02
❑ 551 Dave LaPoint .10 .02
❑ 552 Marc Hill .10 .02
❑ 553 Jim Morrison .10 .02
❑ 554 Paul Householder .10 .02
❑ 555 Hubie Brooks .10 .02
❑ 556 John Denny .10 .02
❑ 557 Gerald Perry .10 .02
❑ 558 Tim Stoddard .10 .02
❑ 559 Tommy Dunbar .10 .02
❑ 560 Dave Righetti .15 .05
❑ 561 Bob Lillis MG .10 .02
❑ 562 Joe Beckwith .10 .02
❑ 563 Alejandro Sanchez .10 .02
❑ 564 Warren Brusstar .10 .02
❑ 565 Tom Brunansky .10 .02
❑ 566 Alfredo Griffin .10 .02
❑ 567 Jeff Barkley .10 .02
❑ 568 Donnie Scott .10 .02
❑ 569 Jim Acker .10 .02
❑ 570 Rusty Staub .15 .05
❑ 571 Mike Jeffcoat .10 .02
❑ 572 Paul Zuvella .10 .02
❑ 573 Tom Hume .10 .02
❑ 574 Ron Kittle .10 .02
❑ 575 Mike Boddicker .10 .02
❑ 576 Andre Dawson TL .10 .02
❑ 577 Jerry Reuss .10 .02
❑ 578 Lee Mazzilli .15 .05
❑ 579 Jim Slaton .10 .02
❑ 580 Willie McGee .15 .05
❑ 581 Bruce Hurst .10 .02
❑ 582 Jim Gantner .10 .02
❑ 583 Al Bumbry .10 .02
❑ 584 Brian Fisher RC .10 .02
❑ 585 Garry Maddox .10 .02
❑ 586 Greg Harris .10 .02
❑ 587 Rafael Santana .10 .02
❑ 588 Steve Lake .10 .02
❑ 589 Sid Bream .10 .02
❑ 590 Bob Knepper .10 .02
❑ 591 Jackie Moore MG .10 .02
❑ 592 Frank Tanana .15 .05
❑ 593 Jesse Barfield .15 .05
❑ 594 Chris Bando .10 .02
❑ 595 Dave Parker .15 .05
❑ 596 Onix Concepcion .10 .02
❑ 597 Sammy Stewart .10 .02
❑ 598 Jim Presley .10 .02
❑ 599 Rick Aguilera RC .25 .08
❑ 600 Dale Murphy .25 .08
❑ 601 Gary Lucas .10 .02
❑ 602 Mariano Duncan RC .25 .08
❑ 603 Bill Laskey .10 .02
❑ 604 Gary Pettis .10 .02
❑ 605 Dennis Boyd .10 .02
❑ 606 Royals Leaders
Hal McRae .15 .05
❑ 607 Ken Dayley .10 .02
❑ 608 Bruce Bochy .10 .02
❑ 609 Barbaro Garbey .10 .02
❑ 610 Ron Guidry .15 .05
❑ 611 Gary Woods .10 .02
❑ 612 Richard Dotson .10 .02
❑ 613 Roy Smalley .10 .02
❑ 614 Rick Waits .10 .02
❑ 615 Johnny Ray .10 .02
❑ 616 Glenn Brummer .10 .02
❑ 617 Lonnie Smith .10 .02
❑ 618 Jim Pankovits .10 .02
❑ 619 Danny Heep .10 .02
❑ 620 Bruce Sutter .15 .05
❑ 621 John Felske MG .10 .02
❑ 622 Gary Lavelle .10 .02
❑ 623 Floyd Rayford .10 .02
❑ 624 Steve McCatty .10 .02
❑ 625 Bob Brenly .10 .02
❑ 626 Roy Thomas .10 .02
❑ 627 Ron Oester .10 .02
❑ 628 Kirk McCaskill RC .25 .08
❑ 629 Mitch Webster .10 .02
❑ 630 Fernando Valenzuela .15 .05

❑ 631 Steve Braun	.10	.02
❑ 632 Dave Von Ohlen	.10	.02
❑ 633 Jackie Gutierrez	.10	.02
❑ 634 Roy Lee Jackson	.10	.02
❑ 635 Jason Thompson	.10	.02
❑ 636 Lee Smith TL	.10	.02
❑ 637 Rudy Law	.10	.02
❑ 638 John Butcher	.10	.02
❑ 639 Bo Diaz	.10	.02
❑ 640 Jose Cruz	.15	.05
❑ 641 Wayne Tolleson	.10	.02
❑ 642 Ray Searage	.10	.02
❑ 643 Tom Brookens	.10	.02
❑ 644 Mark Gubicza	.10	.02
❑ 645 Dusty Baker	.15	.05
❑ 646 Mike Moore	.10	.02
❑ 647 Mel Hall	.10	.02
❑ 648 Steve Bedrosian	.10	.02
❑ 649 Ronn Reynolds	.10	.02
❑ 650 Dave Stieb	.15	.05
❑ 651 Billy Martin MG/TC	.25	.08
❑ 652 Tom Browning	.10	.02
❑ 653 Jim Dwyer	.10	.02
❑ 654 Ken Howell	.10	.02
❑ 655 Manny Trillo	.10	.02
❑ 656 Brian Harper	.10	.02
❑ 657 Juan Agosto	.10	.02
❑ 658 Rob Wilfong	.10	.02
❑ 659 Checklist: 529-660	.15	.05
❑ 660 Steve Garvey	.15	.05
❑ 661 Roger Clemens	4.00	1.50
❑ 662 Bill Schroeder	.10	.02
❑ 663 Neil Allen	.10	.02
❑ 664 Tim Corcoran	.10	.02
❑ 665 Alejandro Pena	.10	.02
❑ 666 Rangers Leaders		
Charlie Hough	.15	.05
❑ 667 Tim Teufel	.10	.02
❑ 668 Cecilio Guante	.10	.02
❑ 669 Ron Cey	.15	.05
❑ 670 Willie Hernandez	.10	.02
❑ 671 Lynn Jones	.10	.02
❑ 672 Rob Picciolo	.10	.02
❑ 673 Ernie Whitt	.10	.02
❑ 674 Pat Tabler	.10	.02
❑ 675 Claudell Washington	.10	.02
❑ 676 Matt Young	.10	.02
❑ 677 Nick Esasky	.10	.02
❑ 678 Dan Gladden	.10	.02
❑ 679 Britt Burns	.10	.02
❑ 680 George Foster	.15	.05
❑ 681 Dick Williams MG	.10	.02
❑ 682 Junior Ortiz	.10	.02
❑ 683 Andy Van Slyke	.25	.08
❑ 684 Bob McClure	.10	.02
❑ 685 Tim Wallach	.10	.02
❑ 686 Jeff Stone	.10	.02
❑ 687 Mike Trujillo	.10	.02
❑ 688 Larry Herndon	.10	.02
❑ 689 Dave Stewart	.15	.05
❑ 690 Ryne Sandberg	.75	.30
❑ 691 Mike Madden	.10	.02
❑ 692 Dale Berra	.10	.02
❑ 693 Tom Tellmann	.10	.02
❑ 694 Garth Iorg	.10	.02
❑ 695 Mike Smithson	.10	.02
❑ 696 Dodgers Leaders		
Bill Russell	.15	.05
❑ 697 Bud Black	.10	.02
❑ 698 Brad Komminsk	.10	.02
❑ 699 Pat Corrales MG	.10	.02
❑ 700 Reggie Jackson	.25	.08
❑ 701 Keith Hernandez AS	.10	.02
❑ 702 Tom Herr AS	.10	.02
❑ 703 Tim Wallach AS	.10	.02
❑ 704 Ozzie Smith AS	.40	.15
❑ 705 Dale Murphy AS	.15	.05
❑ 706 Pedro Guerrero AS	.10	.02
❑ 707 Willie McGee AS	.10	.02
❑ 708 Gary Carter AS	.10	.02
❑ 709 Dwight Gooden AS	.25	.08
❑ 710 John Tudor AS	.10	.02
❑ 711 Jeff Reardon AS	.10	.02
❑ 712 Don Mattingly AS	.60	.25
❑ 713 Damaso Garcia AS	.10	.02
❑ 714 George Brett AS	.40	.15
❑ 715 Cal Ripken AS	.40	.15
❑ 716 Rickey Henderson AS	.25	.08
❑ 717 Dave Winfield AS	.10	.02
❑ 718 George Bell AS	.10	.02
❑ 719 Carlton Fisk AS	.15	.05
❑ 720 Bret Saberhagen AS	.10	.02
❑ 721 Ron Guidry AS	.10	.02
❑ 722 Dan Quisenberry AS	.10	.02
❑ 723 Marty Bystrom	.10	.02
❑ 724 Tim Hulett	.10	.02
❑ 725 Mario Soto	.15	.05
❑ 726 Orioles Leaders		
Rick Dempsey	.15	.05
❑ 727 David Green	.10	.02
❑ 728 Mike Marshall	.10	.02
❑ 729 Jim Beattie	.10	.02
❑ 730 Ozzie Smith	.60	.25
❑ 731 Don Robinson	.10	.02
❑ 732 Floyd Youmans	.10	.02
❑ 733 Ron Romanick	.10	.02
❑ 734 Marty Barrett	.10	.02
❑ 735 Dave Dravecky	.10	.02
❑ 736 Glenn Wilson	.10	.02
❑ 737 Pete Vuckovich	.10	.02
❑ 738 Andre Robertson	.10	.02
❑ 739 Dave Rozema	.10	.02
❑ 740 Lance Parrish	.15	.05
❑ 741 Pete Rose MG/TC	.40	.15
❑ 742 Frank Viola	.15	.05
❑ 743 Pat Sheridan	.10	.02
❑ 744 Lary Sorensen	.10	.02
❑ 745 Willie Upshaw	.10	.02
❑ 746 Denny Gonzalez	.10	.02
❑ 747 Rick Cerone	.10	.02
❑ 748 Steve Henderson	.10	.02
❑ 749 Ed Jurak	.10	.02
❑ 750 Gorman Thomas	.15	.05
❑ 751 Howard Johnson	.15	.05
❑ 752 Mike Krukow	.10	.02
❑ 753 Dan Ford	.10	.02
❑ 754 Pat Clements	.10	.02
❑ 755 Harold Baines	.15	.05
❑ 756 Pirates Leaders		
Rick Rhoden	.10	.02
❑ 757 Darrell Porter	.10	.02
❑ 758 Dave Anderson	.10	.02
❑ 759 Moose Haas	.10	.02
❑ 760 Andre Dawson	.15	.05
❑ 761 Don Slaught	.10	.02
❑ 762 Eric Show	.10	.02
❑ 763 Terry Puhl	.10	.02
❑ 764 Kevin Gross	.10	.02
❑ 765 Don Baylor	.15	.05
❑ 766 Rick Langford	.10	.02
❑ 767 Jody Davis	.10	.02
❑ 768 Vern Ruhle	.10	.02
❑ 769 Harold Reynolds RC	.75	.30
❑ 770 Vida Blue	.15	.05
❑ 771 John McNamara MG	.10	.02
❑ 772 Brian Downing	.15	.05
❑ 773 Greg Pryor	.10	.02
❑ 774 Terry Leach	.10	.02
❑ 775 Al Oliver	.15	.05
❑ 776 Gene Garber	.10	.02
❑ 777 Wayne Krenchicki	.10	.02
❑ 778 Jerry Hairston	.10	.02
❑ 779 Rick Reuschel	.15	.05
❑ 780 Robin Yount	.60	.25
❑ 781 Joe Nolan	.10	.02
❑ 782 Ken Landreaux	.10	.02
❑ 783 Ricky Horton	.10	.02
❑ 784 Alan Bannister	.10	.02
❑ 785 Bob Stanley	.10	.02
❑ 786 Twins Leaders		
Mickey Hatcher	.10	.02
❑ 787 Vance Law	.10	.02
❑ 788 Marty Castillo	.10	.02
❑ 789 Kurt Bevacqua	.10	.02
❑ 790 Phil Niekro	.15	.05
❑ 791 Checklist: 661-792	.15	.05
❑ 792 Charles Hudson	.10	.02

1986 Topps Traded

❑ COMP.FACT.SET (132)	40.00	15.00
❑ 1T Andy Allanson XRC	.10	.02
❑ 2T Neil Allen	.10	.02
❑ 3T Joaquin Andujar	.15	.05
❑ 4T Paul Assenmacher	.40	.15
❑ 5T Scott Bailes	.10	.02
❑ 6T Don Baylor	.15	.05
❑ 7T Steve Bedrosian	.10	.02
❑ 8T Juan Beniquez	.10	.02
❑ 9T Juan Berenguer	.10	.02
❑ 10T Mike Bielecki	.10	.02
❑ 11T Barry Bonds XRC	20.00	8.00
❑ 12T Bobby Bonilla XRC	.75	.30
❑ 13T Juan Bonilla	.10	.02
❑ 14T Rich Bordi	.10	.02
❑ 15T Steve Boros MG	.10	.02
❑ 16T Rick Burleson	.10	.02
❑ 17T Bill Campbell	.10	.02
❑ 18T Tom Candiotti	.10	.02
❑ 19T John Cangelosi	.10	.02
❑ 20T Jose Canseco XRC	4.00	1.50
❑ 21T Carmen Castillo	.10	.02
❑ 22T Rick Cerone	.10	.02
❑ 23T John Cerutti	.10	.02
❑ 24T Will Clark XRC	1.50	.60
❑ 25T Mark Clear	.10	.02
❑ 26T Darnell Coles	.10	.02
❑ 27T Dave Collins	.10	.02
❑ 28T Tim Conroy	.10	.02
❑ 29T Joe Cowley	.10	.02
❑ 30T Joel Davis	.10	.02
❑ 31T Rob Deer	.10	.02
❑ 32T John Denny	.10	.02
❑ 33T Mike Easler	.10	.02
❑ 34T Mark Eichhorn	.10	.02
❑ 35T Steve Farr	.10	.02
❑ 36T Scott Fletcher	.10	.02
❑ 37T Terry Forster	.15	.05
❑ 38T Terry Francona	.15	.05
❑ 39T Jim Fregosi MG	.10	.02
❑ 40T Andres Galarraga XRC	1.00	.40
❑ 41T Ken Griffey	.15	.05
❑ 42T Bill Gullickson	.10	.02
❑ 43T Jose Guzman XRC	.10	.02
❑ 44T Moose Haas	.10	.02
❑ 45T Billy Hatcher	.10	.02
❑ 46T Mike Heath	.10	.02
❑ 47T Tom Hume	.10	.02
❑ 48T Pete Incaviglia XRC	.40	.15
❑ 49T Dane Iorg	.10	.02
❑ 50T Bo Jackson XRC	5.00	2.00
❑ 51T Wally Joyner XRC	.75	.30
❑ 52T Charlie Kerfeld	.10	.02
❑ 53T Eric King	.10	.02
❑ 54T Bob Kipper	.10	.02
❑ 55T Wayne Krenchicki	.10	.02
❑ 56T John Kruk XRC	1.00	.40
❑ 57T Mike LaCoss	.10	.02
❑ 58T Pete Ladd	.10	.02
❑ 59T Mike Laga	.10	.02
❑ 60T Hal Lanier MG	.10	.02
❑ 61T Dave LaPoint	.10	.02
❑ 62T Rudy Law	.10	.02
❑ 63T Rick Leach	.10	.02
❑ 64T Tim Leary	.10	.02
❑ 65T Dennis Leonard	.10	.02
❑ 66T Jim Leyland MG XRC	.50	.20
❑ 67T Steve Lyons	.10	.02
❑ 68T Mickey Mahler	.10	.02
❑ 69T Candy Maldonado	.10	.02
❑ 70T Roger Mason XRC	.10	.02

❑ 71T Bob McClure .10 .02
❑ 72T Andy McGaffigan .10 .02
❑ 73T Gene Michael MG .10 .02
❑ 74T Kevin Mitchell XRC .75 .30
❑ 75T Omar Moreno .10 .02
❑ 76T Jerry Mumphrey .10 .02
❑ 77T Phil Niekro .15 .05
❑ 78T Randy Niemann .10 .02
❑ 79T Juan Nieves .10 .02
❑ 80T Otis Nixon XRC .75 .30
❑ 81T Bob Ojeda .10 .02
❑ 82T Jose Oquendo .10 .02
❑ 83T Tom Paciorek .10 .02
❑ 84T David Palmer .10 .02
❑ 85T Frank Pastore .10 .02
❑ 86T Lou Piniella MG .15 .05
❑ 87T Dan Plesac .40 .15
❑ 88T Darrell Porter .10 .02
❑ 89T Rey Quinones .10 .02
❑ 90T Gary Redus .10 .02
❑ 91T Bip Roberts XRC .40 .15
❑ 92T Billy Joe Robidoux XRC .10 .02
❑ 93T Jeff D. Robinson .10 .02
❑ 94T Gary Roenicke .10 .02
❑ 95T Ed Romero .10 .02
❑ 96T Angel Salazar .10 .02
❑ 97T Joe Sambito .10 .02
❑ 98T Billy Sample .10 .02
❑ 99T Dave Schmidt .10 .02
❑ 100T Ken Schrom .10 .02
❑ 101T Tom Seaver .25 .08
❑ 102T Ted Simmons .15 .05
❑ 103T Sammy Stewart .10 .02
❑ 104T Kurt Stillwell .10 .02
❑ 105T Franklin Stubbs .10 .02
❑ 106T Dale Sveum .10 .02
❑ 107T Chuck Tanner MG .10 .02
❑ 108T Danny Tartabull .15 .05
❑ 109T Tim Teufel .10 .02
❑ 110T Bob Tewksbury XRC .40 .15
❑ 111T Andres Thomas .10 .02
❑ 112T Milt Thompson .40 .15
❑ 113T Robby Thompson XRC .40 .15
❑ 114T Jay Tibbs .10 .02
❑ 115T Wayne Tolleson .10 .02
❑ 116T Alex Trevino .10 .02
❑ 117T Manny Trillo .10 .02
❑ 118T Ed VandeBerg .10 .02
❑ 119T Ozzie Virgil .10 .02
❑ 120T Bob Walk .10 .02
❑ 121T Gene Walter .10 .02
❑ 122T Claudell Washington .10 .02
❑ 123T Bill Wegman XRC .10 .02
❑ 124T Dick Williams MG .10 .02
❑ 125T Mitch Williams XRC .40 .15
❑ 126T Bobby Witt XRC .40 .15
❑ 127T Todd Worrell XRC .40 .15
❑ 128T George Wright .10 .02
❑ 129T Ricky Wright .10 .02
❑ 130T Steve Yeager .15 .05
❑ 131T Paul Zuvella .10 .02
❑ 132T Checklist 1T-132T .10 .02

1987 Topps

❑ COMPLETE SET (792) 25.00 10.00
❑ COMP.FACT SET (792) 40.00 15.00
❑ COMP.HOBBY SET (792) 40.00 15.00
❑ COMP.X-MAS.SET (792) 40.00 15.00

❑ 1 Roger Clemens RB 1.00 .40
❑ 2 Jim Deshaies RB Most cons. K's, start of game .05 .01
❑ 3 Dwight Evans RB Earliest home run, season .15 .05
❑ 4 Davey Lopes RB Most steals, season, 40-year-old .05 .01
❑ 5 Dave Righetti RB Most saves, season .05 .01
❑ 6 Ruben Sierra RB .25 .08
❑ 7 Todd Worrell RB Most saves, season, rookie .05 .01
❑ 8 Terry Pendleton .10 .02
❑ 9 Jay Tibbs .05 .01
❑ 10 Cecil Cooper .10 .02
❑ 11 Indians Team (Mound conference) .05 .01
❑ 12 Jeff Sellers .05 .01
❑ 13 Nick Esasky .05 .01
❑ 14 Dave Stewart .10 .02
❑ 15 Claudell Washington .05 .01
❑ 16 Pat Clements .05 .01
❑ 17 Pete O'Brien .05 .01
❑ 18 Dick Howser MG .05 .01
❑ 19 Matt Young .05 .01
❑ 20 Gary Carter .10 .02
❑ 21 Mark Davis .05 .01
❑ 22 Doug DeCinces .05 .01
❑ 23 Lee Smith .10 .02
❑ 24 Tony Walker .05 .01
❑ 25 Bert Blyleven .10 .02
❑ 26 Greg Brock .05 .01
❑ 27 Joe Cowley .05 .01
❑ 28 Rick Dempsey .05 .01
❑ 29 Jimmy Key .10 .02
❑ 30 Tim Raines .10 .02
❑ 31 Braves Team (Glenn Hubbard and Rafael Ramirez) .05 .01
❑ 32 Tim Leary .05 .01
❑ 33 Andy Van Slyke .15 .05
❑ 34 Jose Rijo .10 .02
❑ 35 Sid Bream .05 .01
❑ 36 Eric King .05 .01
❑ 37 Marvell Wynne .05 .01
❑ 38 Dennis Leonard .05 .01
❑ 39 Marty Barrett .05 .01
❑ 40 Dave Righetti .10 .02
❑ 41 Bo Diaz .05 .01
❑ 42 Gary Redus .05 .01
❑ 43 Gene Michael MG .05 .01
❑ 44 Greg Harris .05 .01
❑ 45 Jim Presley .05 .01
❑ 46 Dan Gladden .05 .01
❑ 47 Dennis Powell .05 .01
❑ 48 Wally Backman .05 .01
❑ 49 Terry Harper .05 .01
❑ 50 Dave Smith .05 .01
❑ 51 Mel Hall .05 .01
❑ 52 Keith Atherton .05 .01
❑ 53 Ruppert Jones .05 .01
❑ 54 Bill Dawley .05 .01
❑ 55 Tim Wallach .05 .01
❑ 56 Brewers Team (Mound conference) .10 .02
❑ 57 Scott Nielsen .05 .01
❑ 58 Thad Bosley .05 .01
❑ 59 Ken Dayley .05 .01
❑ 60 Tony Pena .05 .01
❑ 61 Bobby Thigpen RC .25 .08
❑ 62 Bobby Meacham .05 .01
❑ 63 Fred Toliver .05 .01
❑ 64 Harry Spilman .05 .01
❑ 65 Tom Browning .05 .01
❑ 66 Marc Sullivan .05 .01
❑ 67 Bill Swift .05 .01
❑ 68 Tony LaRussa MG .10 .02
❑ 69 Lonnie Smith .05 .01
❑ 70 Charlie Hough .10 .02
❑ 71 Mike Aldrete .05 .01
❑ 72 Walt Terrell .05 .01
❑ 73 Dave Anderson .05 .01

❑ 74 Dan Pasqua .05 .01
❑ 75 Ron Darling .10 .02
❑ 76 Rafael Ramirez .05 .01
❑ 77 Bryan Oelkers .05 .01
❑ 78 Tom Foley .05 .01
❑ 79 Juan Nieves .05 .01
❑ 80 Wally Joyner RC .40 .15
❑ 81 Padres Team (Andy Hawkins and Terry Kennedy) .05 .01
❑ 82 Rob Murphy .05 .01
❑ 83 Mike Davis .05 .01
❑ 84 Steve Lake .05 .01
❑ 85 Kevin Bass .05 .01
❑ 86 Nate Snell .05 .01
❑ 87 Mark Salas .05 .01
❑ 88 Ed Wojna .05 .01
❑ 89 Ozzie Guillen .15 .05
❑ 90 Dave Stieb .10 .02
❑ 91 Harold Reynolds .10 .02
❑ 92A Urbano Lugo ERR (no trademark) .15 .05
❑ 92B Urbano Lugo COR .05 .01
❑ 93 Jim Leyland MG/TC RC * .25 .08
❑ 94 Calvin Schiraldi .05 .01
❑ 95 Oddibe McDowell .05 .01
❑ 96 Frank Williams .05 .01
❑ 97 Glenn Wilson .05 .01
❑ 98 Bill Scherrer .05 .01
❑ 99 Darryl Motley (Now with Braves on card front) .05 .01
❑ 100 Steve Garvey .10 .02
❑ 101 Carl Willis RC .10 .02
❑ 102 Paul Zuvella .05 .01
❑ 103 Rick Aguilera .05 .01
❑ 104 Billy Sample .05 .01
❑ 105 Floyd Youmans .05 .01
❑ 106 Blue Jays Team (George Bell and Jesse Barfield) .05 .01
❑ 107 John Butcher .05 .01
❑ 108 Jim Gantner UER (Brewers logo reversed) .05 .01
❑ 109 R.J. Reynolds .05 .01
❑ 110 John Tudor .10 .02
❑ 111 Alfredo Griffin .05 .01
❑ 112 Alan Ashby .05 .01
❑ 113 Neil Allen .05 .01
❑ 114 Billy Beane .10 .02
❑ 115 Donnie Moore .05 .01
❑ 116 Bill Russell .10 .02
❑ 117 Jim Beattie .05 .01
❑ 118 Bobby Valentine MG .10 .02
❑ 119 Ron Robinson .05 .01
❑ 120 Eddie Murray .25 .08
❑ 121 Kevin Romine .05 .01
❑ 122 Jim Clancy .05 .01
❑ 123 John Kruk RC .50 .20
❑ 124 Ray Fontenot .05 .01
❑ 125 Bob Brenly .05 .01
❑ 126 Mike Loynd RC .10 .02
❑ 127 Vance Law .05 .01
❑ 128 Checklist 1-132 .05 .01
❑ 129 Rick Cerone .05 .01
❑ 130 Dwight Gooden .15 .05
❑ 131 Pirates Team (Sid Bream and Tony Pena) .05 .01
❑ 132 Paul Assenmacher .25 .08
❑ 133 Jose Oquendo .05 .01
❑ 134 Rich Yett .05 .01
❑ 135 Mike Easler .05 .01
❑ 136 Ron Romanick .05 .01
❑ 137 Jerry Willard .05 .01
❑ 138 Roy Lee Jackson .05 .01
❑ 139 Devon White RC .40 .15
❑ 140 Bret Saberhagen .10 .02
❑ 141 Herm Winningham .05 .01
❑ 142 Rick Sutcliffe .10 .02
❑ 143 Steve Boros MG .05 .01
❑ 144 Mike Scioscia .10 .02
❑ 145 Charlie Kerfeld .05 .01
❑ 146 Tracy Jones .05 .01
❑ 147 Randy Niemann .05 .01

No.	Card	Price	Price
❑ 148	Dave Collins	.05	.01
❑ 149	Ray Searage	.05	.01
❑ 150	Wade Boggs	.15	.05
❑ 151	Mike LaCoss	.05	.01
❑ 152	Toby Harrah	.10	.02
❑ 153	Duane Ward RC *	.25	.08
❑ 154	Tom O'Malley	.05	.01
❑ 155	Eddie Whitson	.05	.01
❑ 156	Mariners Team (Mound conference)	.05	.01
❑ 157	Danny Darwin	.05	.01
❑ 158	Tim Teufel	.05	.01
❑ 159	Ed Olwine	.05	.01
❑ 160	Julio Franco	.10	.02
❑ 161	Steve Ontiveros	.05	.01
❑ 162	Mike LaValliere RC *	.25	.08
❑ 163	Kevin Gross	.05	.01
❑ 164	Sammy Khalifa	.05	.01
❑ 165	Jeff Reardon	.10	.02
❑ 166	Bob Boone	.10	.02
❑ 167	Jim Deshaies RC *	.10	.02
❑ 168	Lou Piniella MG	.10	.02
❑ 169	Ron Washington	.05	.01
❑ 170	Bo Jackson RC	3.00	1.25
❑ 171	Chuck Cary	.05	.01
❑ 172	Ron Oester	.05	.01
❑ 173	Alex Trevino	.05	.01
❑ 174	Henry Cotto	.05	.01
❑ 175	Bob Stanley	.05	.01
❑ 176	Steve Buechele	.05	.01
❑ 177	Keith Moreland	.05	.01
❑ 178	Cecil Fielder	.10	.02
❑ 179	Bill Wegman	.05	.01
❑ 180	Chris Brown	.05	.01
❑ 181	Cardinals Team (Mound conference)	.05	.01
❑ 182	Lee Lacy	.05	.01
❑ 183	Andy Hawkins	.05	.01
❑ 184	Bobby Bonilla RC	.40	.15
❑ 185	Roger McDowell	.05	.01
❑ 186	Bruce Benedict	.05	.01
❑ 187	Mark Huismann	.05	.01
❑ 188	Tony Phillips	.05	.01
❑ 189	Joe Hesketh	.05	.01
❑ 190	Jim Sundberg	.10	.02
❑ 191	Charles Hudson	.05	.01
❑ 192	Cory Snyder	.05	.01
❑ 193	Roger Craig MG	.10	.02
❑ 194	Kirk McCaskill	.05	.01
❑ 195	Mike Pagliarulo	.05	.01
❑ 196	Randy O'Neal UER (Wrong ML career W-L totals)	.05	.01
❑ 197	Mark Bailey	.05	.01
❑ 198	Lee Mazzilli	.10	.02
❑ 199	Mariano Duncan	.05	.01
❑ 200	Pete Rose	.60	.25
❑ 201	John Cangelosi	.05	.01
❑ 202	Ricky Wright	.05	.01
❑ 203	Mike Kingery RC	.10	.02
❑ 204	Sammy Stewart	.05	.01
❑ 205	Graig Nettles	.10	.02
❑ 206	Twins Team (Frank Viola and Tim Laudner)	.05	.01
❑ 207	George Frazier	.05	.01
❑ 208	John Shelby	.05	.01
❑ 209	Rick Schu	.05	.01
❑ 210	Lloyd Moseby	.05	.01
❑ 211	John Morris	.05	.01
❑ 212	Mike Fitzgerald	.05	.01
❑ 213	Randy Myers RC	.40	.15
❑ 214	Omar Moreno	.05	.01
❑ 215	Mark Langston	.05	.01
❑ 216	B.J. Surhoff RC	.40	.15
❑ 217	Chris Codiroli	.05	.01
❑ 218	Sparky Anderson MG	.10	.02
❑ 219	Cecilio Guante	.05	.01
❑ 220	Joe Carter	.10	.02
❑ 221	Vern Ruhle	.05	.01
❑ 222	Denny Walling	.05	.01
❑ 223	Charlie Leibrandt	.05	.01
❑ 224	Wayne Tolleson	.05	.01
❑ 225	Mike Smithson	.05	.01
❑ 226	Max Venable	.05	.01
❑ 227	Jamie Moyer RC	.50	.20
❑ 228	Curt Wilkerson	.05	.01
❑ 229	Mike Birkbeck	.10	.02
❑ 230	Don Baylor	.10	.02
❑ 231	Giants Team (Bob Brenly and Jim Gott)	.05	.01
❑ 232	Reggie Williams	.05	.01
❑ 233	Russ Morman	.05	.01
❑ 234	Pat Sheridan	.05	.01
❑ 235	Alvin Davis	.05	.01
❑ 236	Tommy John	.10	.02
❑ 237	Jim Morrison	.05	.01
❑ 238	Bill Krueger	.05	.01
❑ 239	Juan Espino	.05	.01
❑ 240	Steve Balboni	.05	.01
❑ 241	Danny Heep	.05	.01
❑ 242	Rick Mahler	.05	.01
❑ 243	Whitey Herzog MG	.10	.02
❑ 244	Dickie Noles	.05	.01
❑ 245	Willie Upshaw	.05	.01
❑ 246	Jim Dwyer	.05	.01
❑ 247	Jeff Reed	.05	.01
❑ 248	Gene Walter	.05	.01
❑ 249	Jim Pankovits	.05	.01
❑ 250	Teddy Higuera	.05	.01
❑ 251	Rob Wilfong	.05	.01
❑ 252	Dennis Martinez	.10	.02
❑ 253	Eddie Milner	.05	.01
❑ 254	Bob Tewksbury RC *	.25	.08
❑ 255	Juan Samuel	.05	.01
❑ 256	Royals TL/George Brett	.15	.05
❑ 257	Bob Forsch	.05	.01
❑ 258	Steve Yeager	.10	.02
❑ 259	Mike Greenwell RC	.25	.08
❑ 260	Vida Blue	.10	.02
❑ 261	Ruben Sierra RC	.50	.20
❑ 262	Jim Winn	.05	.01
❑ 263	Stan Javier	.05	.01
❑ 264	Checklist 133-264	.05	.01
❑ 265	Darrell Evans	.10	.02
❑ 266	Jeff Hamilton	.05	.01
❑ 267	Howard Johnson	.10	.02
❑ 268	Pat Corrales MG	.05	.01
❑ 269	Cliff Speck	.05	.01
❑ 270	Jody Davis	.05	.01
❑ 271	Mike G. Brown	.05	.01
❑ 272	Andres Galarraga	.10	.02
❑ 273	Gene Nelson	.05	.01
❑ 274	Jeff Hearron UER (Duplicate 1986 stat line on ba	.05	.01
❑ 275	LaMarr Hoyt	.05	.01
❑ 276	Jackie Gutierrez	.05	.01
❑ 277	Juan Agosto	.05	.01
❑ 278	Gary Pettis	.05	.01
❑ 279	Dan Plesac	.05	.01
❑ 280	Jeff Leonard	.05	.01
❑ 281	Reds TL/Rose	.25	.08
❑ 282	Jeff Calhoun	.05	.01
❑ 283	Doug Drabek RC	.40	.15
❑ 284	John Moses	.05	.01
❑ 285	Dennis Boyd	.05	.01
❑ 286	Mike Woodard	.05	.01
❑ 287	Dave Von Ohlen	.05	.01
❑ 288	Tito Landrum	.05	.01
❑ 289	Bob Kipper	.05	.01
❑ 290	Leon Durham	.05	.01
❑ 291	Mitch Williams RC *	.25	.08
❑ 292	Franklin Stubbs	.05	.01
❑ 293	Bob Rodgers MG (Checklist back, inconsistent des	.05	.01
❑ 294	Steve Jeltz	.05	.01
❑ 295	Len Dykstra	.10	.02
❑ 296	Andres Thomas	.05	.01
❑ 297	Don Schulze	.05	.01
❑ 298	Larry Herndon	.05	.01
❑ 299	Joel Davis	.05	.01
❑ 300	Reggie Jackson	.15	.05
❑ 301	Luis Aquino UER (No trademark never corrected)	.05	.01
❑ 302	Bill Schroeder	.05	.01
❑ 303	Juan Berenguer	.05	.01
❑ 304	Phil Garner	.10	.02
❑ 305	John Franco	.10	.02
❑ 306	Red Sox TL/Seaver	.10	.02
❑ 307	Lee Guetterman	.05	.01
❑ 308	Don Slaught	.05	.01
❑ 309	Mike Young	.05	.01
❑ 310	Frank Viola	.10	.02
❑ 311	Rickey Henderson TBC	.15	.05
❑ 312	Reggie Jackson TBC	.10	.02
❑ 313	Roberto Clemente TBC	.25	.08
❑ 314	Carl Yastrzemski TBC	.25	.08
❑ 315	Maury Wills TBC '62	.10	.02
❑ 316	Brian Fisher	.05	.01
❑ 317	Clint Hurdle	.05	.01
❑ 318	Jim Fregosi MG	.05	.01
❑ 319	Greg Swindell RC	.25	.08
❑ 320	Barry Bonds RC	10.00	4.00
❑ 321	Mike Laga	.05	.01
❑ 322	Chris Bando	.05	.01
❑ 323	Al Newman RC	.05	.01
❑ 324	David Palmer	.05	.01
❑ 325	Garry Templeton	.10	.02
❑ 326	Mark Gubicza	.05	.01
❑ 327	Dale Sveum	.05	.01
❑ 328	Bob Welch	.10	.02
❑ 329	Ron Roenicke	.05	.01
❑ 330	Mike Scott	.10	.02
❑ 331	Mets TL/Carter/Straw	.10	.02
❑ 332	Joe Price	.05	.01
❑ 333	Ken Phelps	.05	.01
❑ 334	Ed Correa	.05	.01
❑ 335	Candy Maldonado	.05	.01
❑ 336	Allan Anderson RC	.05	.01
❑ 337	Darrell Miller	.05	.01
❑ 338	Tim Conroy	.05	.01
❑ 339	Donnie Hill	.05	.01
❑ 340	Roger Clemens	1.50	.60
❑ 341	Mike C. Brown	.05	.01
❑ 342	Bob James	.05	.01
❑ 343	Hal Lanier MG	.05	.01
❑ 344A	Joe Niekro (Copyright inside righthand border)	.05	.01
❑ 344B	Joe Niekro (Copyright outside righthand border)	.05	.01
❑ 345	Andre Dawson	.10	.02
❑ 346	Shawon Dunston	.05	.01
❑ 347	Mickey Brantley	.05	.01
❑ 348	Carmelo Martinez	.05	.01
❑ 349	Storm Davis	.05	.01
❑ 350	Keith Hernandez	.10	.02
❑ 351	Gene Garber	.05	.01
❑ 352	Mike Felder	.05	.01
❑ 353	Ernie Camacho	.05	.01
❑ 354	Jamie Quirk	.05	.01
❑ 355	Don Carman	.05	.01
❑ 356	White Sox Team (Mound conference)	.05	.01
❑ 357	Steve Fireovid	.05	.01
❑ 358	Sal Butera	.05	.01
❑ 359	Doug Corbett	.05	.01
❑ 360	Pedro Guerrero	.10	.02
❑ 361	Mark Thurmond	.05	.01
❑ 362	Luis Quinones	.05	.01
❑ 363	Jose Guzman	.05	.01
❑ 364	Randy Bush	.05	.01
❑ 365	Rick Rhoden	.05	.01
❑ 366	Mark McGwire	4.00	1.50
❑ 367	Jeff Lahti	.05	.01
❑ 368	John McNamara MG	.05	.01
❑ 369	Brian Dayett	.05	.01
❑ 370	Fred Lynn	.10	.02
❑ 371	Mark Eichhorn	.05	.01
❑ 372	Jerry Mumphrey	.05	.01
❑ 373	Jeff Dedmon	.05	.01
❑ 374	Glenn Hoffman	.05	.01
❑ 375	Ron Guidry	.10	.02
❑ 376	Scott Bradley	.05	.01
❑ 377	John Henry Johnson	.05	.01
❑ 378	Rafael Santana	.05	.01
❑ 379	John Russell	.05	.01
❑ 380	Rich Gossage	.10	.02
❑ 381	Expos Team (Mound conference)	.05	.01
❑ 382	Rudy Law	.05	.01
❑ 383	Ron Davis	.05	.01
❑ 384	Johnny Grubb	.05	.01

❑ 385 Orel Hershiser .15 .05
❑ 386 Dickie Thon .05 .01
❑ 387 T.R. Bryden .05 .01
❑ 388 Geno Petralli .05 .01
❑ 389 Jeff D. Robinson .05 .01
❑ 390 Gary Matthews .10 .02
❑ 391 Jay Howell .05 .01
❑ 392 Checklist 265-396 .05 .01
❑ 393 Pete Rose MG/TC .15 .05
❑ 394 Mike Bielecki .05 .01
❑ 395 Damaso Garcia .05 .01
❑ 396 Tim Lollar .05 .01
❑ 397 Greg Walker .05 .01
❑ 398 Brad Havens .05 .01
❑ 399 Curt Ford .05 .01
❑ 400 George Brett .60 .25
❑ 401 Billy Joe Robidoux .05 .01
❑ 402 Mike Trujillo .05 .01
❑ 403 Jerry Royster .05 .01
❑ 404 Doug Sisk .05 .01
❑ 405 Brook Jacoby .05 .01
❑ 406 Yankees TL/Hend/Matt .50 .20
❑ 407 Jim Acker .05 .01
❑ 408 John Mizerock .05 .01
❑ 409 Milt Thompson .05 .01
❑ 410 Fernando Valenzuela .10 .02
❑ 411 Darnell Coles .05 .01
❑ 412 Eric Davis .15 .05
❑ 413 Moose Haas .05 .01
❑ 414 Joe Orsulak .05 .01
❑ 415 Bobby Witt RC .25 .08
❑ 416 Tom Nieto .05 .01
❑ 417 Pat Perry .05 .01
❑ 418 Dick Williams MG .05 .01
❑ 419 Mark Portugal RC * .25 .08
❑ 420 Will Clark RC 1.00 .40
❑ 421 Jose DeLeon .05 .01
❑ 422 Jack Howell .05 .01
❑ 423 Jaime Cocanower .05 .01
❑ 424 Chris Speier .05 .01
❑ 425 Tom Seaver .15 .05
❑ 426 Floyd Rayford .05 .01
❑ 427 Edwin Nunez .05 .01
❑ 428 Bruce Bochy .05 .01
❑ 429 Tim Pyznarski .05 .01
❑ 430 Mike Schmidt .50 .20
❑ 431 Dodgers Team
(Mound conference) .05 .01
❑ 432 Jim Slaton .05 .01
❑ 433 Ed Hearn RC .05 .01
❑ 434 Mike Fischlin .05 .01
❑ 435 Bruce Sutter .10 .02
❑ 436 Andy Allanson RC .05 .01
❑ 437 Ted Power .05 .01
❑ 438 Kelly Downs RC .10 .02
❑ 439 Karl Best .05 .01
❑ 440 Willie McGee .10 .02
❑ 441 Dave Leiper .05 .01
❑ 442 Mitch Webster .05 .01
❑ 443 John Felske MG .05 .01
❑ 444 Jeff Russell .05 .01
❑ 445 Dave Lopes .10 .02
❑ 446 Chuck Finley RC .40 .15
❑ 447 Bill Almon .05 .01
❑ 448 Chris Bosio RC .25 .08
❑ 449 Pat Dodson .10 .02
❑ 450 Kirby Puckett .50 .20
❑ 451 Joe Sambito .05 .01
❑ 452 Dave Henderson .05 .01
❑ 453 Scott Terry RC .10 .02
❑ 454 Luis Salazar .05 .01
❑ 455 Mike Boddicker .05 .01
❑ 456 A's Team
(Mound conference) .05 .01
❑ 457 Len Matuszek .05 .01
❑ 458 Kelly Gruber .05 .01
❑ 459 Dennis Eckersley .15 .05
❑ 460 Darryl Strawberry .10 .02
❑ 461 Craig McMurtry .05 .01
❑ 462 Scott Fletcher .05 .01
❑ 463 Tom Candiotti .05 .01
❑ 464 Butch Wynegar .05 .01
❑ 465 Todd Worrell .05 .01
❑ 466 Kal Daniels .05 .01
❑ 467 Randy St.Claire .05 .01
❑ 468 George Bamberger MG .05 .01
❑ 469 Mike Diaz .05 .01
❑ 470 Dave Dravecky .05 .01
❑ 471 Ronn Reynolds .05 .01
❑ 472 Bill Doran .05 .01
❑ 473 Steve Farr .05 .01
❑ 474 Jerry Narron .05 .01
❑ 475 Scott Garrelts .05 .01
❑ 476 Danny Tartabull .05 .01
❑ 477 Ken Howell .05 .01
❑ 478 Tim Laudner .05 .01
❑ 479 Bob Sebra .05 .01
❑ 480 Jim Rice .10 .02
❑ 481 Phillies Team
(Glenn Wilson,
Juan Samuel, and
V .05 .01
❑ 482 Daryl Boston .05 .01
❑ 483 Dwight Lowry .05 .01
❑ 484 Jim Traber .05 .01
❑ 485 Tony Fernandez .05 .01
❑ 486 Otis Nixon .05 .01
❑ 487 Dave Gumpert .05 .01
❑ 488 Ray Knight .10 .02
❑ 489 Bill Gullickson .05 .01
❑ 490 Dale Murphy .15 .05
❑ 491 Ron Karkovice RC .25 .08
❑ 492 Mike Heath .05 .01
❑ 493 Tom Lasorda MG .15 .05
❑ 494 Barry Jones .05 .01
❑ 495 Gorman Thomas .10 .02
❑ 496 Bruce Bochte .05 .01
❑ 497 Dale Mohorcic .05 .01
❑ 498 Bob Kearney .05 .01
❑ 499 Bruce Ruffin RC .10 .02
❑ 500 Don Mattingly .60 .25
❑ 501 Craig Lefferts .05 .01
❑ 502 Dick Schofield .05 .01
❑ 503 Larry Andersen .05 .01
❑ 504 Mickey Hatcher .05 .01
❑ 505 Bryn Smith .05 .01
❑ 506 Orioles Team
(Mound conference) .05 .01
❑ 507 Dave L. Stapleton .05 .01
❑ 508 Scott Bankhead .05 .01
❑ 509 Enos Cabell .05 .01
❑ 510 Tom Henke .05 .01
❑ 511 Steve Lyons .05 .01
❑ 512 Dave Magadan RC .25 .08
❑ 513 Carmen Castillo .05 .01
❑ 514 Orlando Mercado .05 .01
❑ 515 Willie Hernandez .05 .01
❑ 516 Ted Simmons .10 .02
❑ 517 Mario Soto .10 .02
❑ 518 Gene Mauch MG .05 .01
❑ 519 Curt Young .05 .01
❑ 520 Jack Clark .10 .02
❑ 521 Rick Reuschel .10 .02
❑ 522 Checklist 397-528 .05 .01
❑ 523 Earnie Riles .05 .01
❑ 524 Bob Shirley .05 .01
❑ 525 Phil Bradley .05 .01
❑ 526 Roger Mason .05 .01
❑ 527 Jim Wohlford .05 .01
❑ 528 Ken Dixon .05 .01
❑ 529 Alvaro Espinoza RC .10 .02
❑ 530 Tony Gwynn .30 .10
❑ 531 Astros TL/Y.Berra .10 .02
❑ 532 Jeff Stone .05 .01
❑ 533 Angel Salazar .05 .01
❑ 534 Scott Sanderson .05 .01
❑ 535 Tony Armas .10 .02
❑ 536 Terry Mulholland RC .25 .08
❑ 537 Rance Mulliniks .05 .01
❑ 538 Tom Niedenfuer .05 .01
❑ 539 Reid Nichols .05 .01
❑ 540 Terry Kennedy .05 .01
❑ 541 Rafael Belliard RC .25 .08
❑ 542 Ricky Horton .05 .01
❑ 543 Dave Johnson MG .05 .01
❑ 544 Zane Smith .05 .01
❑ 545 Buddy Bell .10 .02
❑ 546 Mike Morgan .05 .01
❑ 547 Rob Deer .05 .01
❑ 548 Bill Mooneyham .05 .01
❑ 549 Bob Melvin .05 .01
❑ 550 Pete Incaviglia RC * .25 .08
❑ 551 Frank Wills .05 .01
❑ 552 Larry Sheets .05 .01
❑ 553 Mike Maddux .05 .01
❑ 554 Buddy Biancalana .05 .01
❑ 555 Dennis Rasmussen .05 .01
❑ 556 Angels Team
(Rene Lachemann CO,
Mike Witt, and .05 .01
❑ 557 John Cerutti .05 .01
❑ 558 Greg Gagne .05 .01
❑ 559 Lance McCullers .05 .01
❑ 560 Glenn Davis .05 .01
❑ 561 Rey Quinones .05 .01
❑ 562 Bryan Clutterbuck .05 .01
❑ 563 John Stefero .05 .01
❑ 564 Larry McWilliams .05 .01
❑ 565 Dusty Baker .10 .02
❑ 566 Tim Hulett .05 .01
❑ 567 Greg Mathews .05 .01
❑ 568 Earl Weaver MG .10 .02
❑ 569 Wade Rowdon .05 .01
❑ 570 Sid Fernandez .05 .01
❑ 571 Ozzie Virgil .05 .01
❑ 572 Pete Ladd .05 .01
❑ 573 Hal McRae .10 .02
❑ 574 Manny Lee .05 .01
❑ 575 Pat Tabler .05 .01
❑ 576 Frank Pastore .05 .01
❑ 577 Dann Bilardello .05 .01
❑ 578 Billy Hatcher .05 .01
❑ 579 Rick Burleson .05 .01
❑ 580 Mike Krukow .05 .01
❑ 581 Cubs Team
(Ron Cey and
Steve Trout) .05 .01
❑ 582 Bruce Berenyi .05 .01
❑ 583 Junior Ortiz .05 .01
❑ 584 Ron Kittle .05 .01
❑ 585 Scott Bailes .05 .01
❑ 586 Ben Oglivie .10 .02
❑ 587 Eric Plunk .05 .01
❑ 588 Wallace Johnson .05 .01
❑ 589 Steve Crawford .05 .01
❑ 590 Vince Coleman .05 .01
❑ 591 Spike Owen .05 .01
❑ 592 Chris Welsh .05 .01
❑ 593 Chuck Tanner MG .05 .01
❑ 594 Rick Anderson .05 .01
❑ 595 Keith Hernandez AS .05 .01
❑ 596 Steve Sax AS .05 .01
❑ 597 Mike Schmidt AS .25 .08
❑ 598 Ozzie Smith AS .25 .08
❑ 599 Tony Gwynn AS .15 .05
❑ 600 Dave Parker AS .05 .01
❑ 601 Darryl Strawberry AS .05 .01
❑ 602 Gary Carter AS .05 .01
❑ 603A Dwight Gooden AS NoTM .10 .02
❑ 603B Dwight Gooden AS TM .10 .02
❑ 604 Fernando Valenzuela AS .05 .01
❑ 605 Todd Worrell AS .05 .01
❑ 606 Don Mattingly AS .30 .10
❑ 606A Don Mattingly AS NoTM 1.00 .40
❑ 607 Tony Bernazard AS .05 .01
❑ 608 Wade Boggs AS .10 .02
❑ 609 Cal Ripken AS .25 .08
❑ 610 Jim Rice AS .05 .01
❑ 611 Kirby Puckett AS .25 .08
❑ 612 George Bell AS .05 .01
❑ 613 Lance Parrish AS UER
(Pitcher heading
on back) .05 .01
❑ 614 Roger Clemens AS 1.00 .40
❑ 615 Teddy Higuera AS .05 .01
❑ 616 Dave Righetti AS .05 .01
❑ 617 Al Nipper .05 .01
❑ 618 Tom Kelly MG .05 .01
❑ 619 Jerry Reed .05 .01
❑ 620 Jose Canseco 1.00 .40
❑ 621 Danny Cox .05 .01
❑ 622 Glenn Braggs RC .10 .02
❑ 623 Kurt Stillwell .05 .01
❑ 624 Tim Burke .05 .01
❑ 625 Mookie Wilson .10 .02
❑ 626 Joel Skinner .05 .01
❑ 627 Ken Oberkfell .05 .01
❑ 628 Bob Walk .05 .01

❑ 629 Larry Parrish .05 .01
❑ 630 John Candelaria .05 .01
❑ 631 Tigers Team
(Mound conference) .05 .01
❑ 632 Rob Woodward .05 .01
❑ 633 Jose Uribe .05 .01
❑ 634 Rafael Palmeiro RC 1.50 .60
❑ 635 Ken Schrom .05 .01
❑ 636 Darren Daulton .10 .02
❑ 637 Bip Roberts RC .25 .08
❑ 638 Rich Bordi .05 .01
❑ 639 Gerald Perry .05 .01
❑ 640 Mark Clear .05 .01
❑ 641 Domingo Ramos .05 .01
❑ 642 Al Pulido .05 .01
❑ 643 Ron Shepherd .05 .01
❑ 644 John Denny .05 .01
❑ 645 Dwight Evans .15 .05
❑ 646 Mike Mason .05 .01
❑ 647 Tom Lawless .05 .01
❑ 648 Barry Larkin RC 1.00 .40
❑ 649 Mickey Tettleton .05 .01
❑ 650 Hubie Brooks .05 .01
❑ 651 Benny Distefano .05 .01
❑ 652 Terry Forster .10 .02
❑ 653 Kevin Mitchell RC * .40 .15
❑ 654 Checklist 529-660 .10 .02
❑ 655 Jesse Barfield .10 .02
❑ 656 Rangers Team
(Bobby Valentine MG
and Ricky Wrigh .05 .01
❑ 657 Tom Waddell .05 .01
❑ 658 Robby Thompson RC * .25 .08
❑ 659 Aurelio Lopez .05 .01
❑ 660 Bob Horner .10 .02
❑ 661 Lou Whitaker .10 .02
❑ 662 Frank DiPino .05 .01
❑ 663 Cliff Johnson .05 .01
❑ 664 Mike Marshall .05 .01
❑ 665 Rod Scurry .05 .01
❑ 666 Von Hayes .05 .01
❑ 667 Ron Hassey .05 .01
❑ 668 Juan Bonilla .05 .01
❑ 669 Bud Black .05 .01
❑ 670 Jose Cruz .10 .02
❑ 671A Ray Soff ERR
(No D* before
copyright line) .05 .01
❑ 671B Ray Soff COR
(D* before
copyright line) .05 .01
❑ 672 Chili Davis .10 .02
❑ 673 Don Sutton .10 .02
❑ 674 Bill Campbell .05 .01
❑ 675 Ed Romero .05 .01
❑ 676 Charlie Moore .05 .01
❑ 677 Bob Grich .10 .02
❑ 678 Carney Lansford .10 .02
❑ 679 Kent Hrbek .10 .02
❑ 680 Ryne Sandberg .40 .15
❑ 681 George Bell .10 .02
❑ 682 Jerry Reuss .05 .01
❑ 683 Gary Roenicke .05 .01
❑ 684 Kent Tekulve .05 .01
❑ 685 Jerry Hairston .05 .01
❑ 686 Doyle Alexander .05 .01
❑ 687 Alan Trammell .10 .02
❑ 688 Juan Beniquez .05 .01
❑ 689 Darrell Porter .05 .01
❑ 690 Dane Iorg .05 .01
❑ 691 Dave Parker .10 .02
❑ 692 Frank White .10 .02
❑ 693 Terry Puhl .05 .01
❑ 694 Phil Niekro .10 .02
❑ 695 Chico Walker .05 .01
❑ 696 Gary Lucas .05 .01
❑ 697 Ed Lynch .05 .01
❑ 698 Ernie Whitt .05 .01
❑ 699 Ken Landreaux .05 .01
❑ 700 Dave Bergman .05 .01
❑ 701 Willie Randolph .10 .02
❑ 702 Greg Gross .05 .01
❑ 703 Dave Schmidt .05 .01
❑ 704 Jesse Orosco .05 .01
❑ 705 Bruce Hurst .05 .01
❑ 706 Rick Manning .05 .01
❑ 707 Bob McClure .05 .01
❑ 708 Scott McGregor .05 .01
❑ 709 Dave Kingman .10 .02
❑ 710 Gary Gaetti .10 .02
❑ 711 Ken Griffey .10 .02
❑ 712 Don Robinson .05 .01
❑ 713 Tom Brookens .05 .01
❑ 714 Dan Quisenberry .05 .01
❑ 715 Bob Dernier .05 .01
❑ 716 Rick Leach .05 .01
❑ 717 Ed VandeBerg .05 .01
❑ 718 Steve Carlton .10 .02
❑ 719 Tom Hume .05 .01
❑ 720 Richard Dotson .05 .01
❑ 721 Tom Herr .05 .01
❑ 722 Bob Knepper .05 .01
❑ 723 Brett Butler .10 .02
❑ 724 Greg Minton .05 .01
❑ 725 George Hendrick .10 .02
❑ 726 Frank Tanana .10 .02
❑ 727 Mike Moore .05 .01
❑ 728 Tippy Martinez .05 .01
❑ 729 Tom Paciorek .05 .01
❑ 730 Eric Show .05 .01
❑ 731 Dave Concepcion .10 .02
❑ 732 Manny Trillo .05 .01
❑ 733 Bill Caudill .05 .01
❑ 734 Bill Madlock .10 .02
❑ 735 Rickey Henderson .25 .08
❑ 736 Steve Bedrosian .05 .01
❑ 737 Floyd Bannister .05 .01
❑ 738 Jorge Orta .05 .01
❑ 739 Chet Lemon .10 .02
❑ 740 Rich Gedman .05 .01
❑ 741 Paul Molitor .10 .02
❑ 742 Andy McGaffigan .05 .01
❑ 743 Dwayne Murphy .05 .01
❑ 744 Roy Smalley .05 .01
❑ 745 Glenn Hubbard .05 .01
❑ 746 Bob Ojeda .05 .01
❑ 747 Johnny Ray .05 .01
❑ 748 Mike Flanagan .05 .01
❑ 749 Ozzie Smith .40 .15
❑ 750 Steve Trout .05 .01
❑ 751 Garth Iorg .05 .01
❑ 752 Dan Petry .05 .01
❑ 753 Rick Honeycutt .05 .01
❑ 754 Dave LaPoint .05 .01
❑ 755 Luis Aguayo .05 .01
❑ 756 Carlton Fisk .15 .05
❑ 757 Nolan Ryan 1.00 .40
❑ 758 Tony Bernazard .05 .01
❑ 759 Joel Youngblood .05 .01
❑ 760 Mike Witt .05 .01
❑ 761 Greg Pryor .05 .01
❑ 762 Gary Ward .05 .01
❑ 763 Tim Flannery .05 .01
❑ 764 Bill Buckner .10 .02
❑ 765 Kirk Gibson .10 .02
❑ 766 Don Aase .05 .01
❑ 767 Ron Cey .10 .02
❑ 768 Dennis Lamp .05 .01
❑ 769 Steve Sax .05 .01
❑ 770 Dave Winfield .10 .02
❑ 771 Shane Rawley .05 .01
❑ 772 Harold Baines .10 .02
❑ 773 Robin Yount .40 .15
❑ 774 Wayne Krenchicki .05 .01
❑ 775 Joaquin Andujar .10 .02
❑ 776 Tom Brunansky .05 .01
❑ 777 Chris Chambliss .10 .02
❑ 778 Jack Morris .10 .02
❑ 779 Craig Reynolds .05 .01
❑ 780 Andre Thornton .05 .01
❑ 781 Atlee Hammaker .05 .01
❑ 782 Brian Downing .10 .02
❑ 783 Willie Wilson .10 .02
❑ 784 Cal Ripken .75 .30
❑ 785 Terry Francona .10 .02
❑ 786 Jimy Williams MG .05 .01
❑ 787 Alejandro Pena .05 .01
❑ 788 Tim Stoddard .05 .01
❑ 789 Dan Schatzeder .05 .01
❑ 790 Julio Cruz .05 .01
❑ 791 Lance Parrish UER
(No trademark,
never corrected .10 .02
❑ 792 Checklist 661-792 .05 .01

1987 Topps Traded

❑ COMP.FACT.SET (132) 8.00 3.00
❑ 1T Bill Almon .05 .01
❑ 2T Scott Bankhead .05 .01
❑ 3T Eric Bell .10 .02
❑ 4T Juan Beniquez .05 .01
❑ 5T Juan Berenguer .05 .01
❑ 6T Greg Booker .05 .01
❑ 7T Thad Bosley .05 .01
❑ 8T Larry Bowa MG .10 .02
❑ 9T Greg Brock .05 .01
❑ 10T Bob Brower .05 .01
❑ 11T Jerry Browne .10 .02
❑ 12T Ralph Bryant .05 .01
❑ 13T DeWayne Buice .05 .01
❑ 14T Ellis Burks XRC .50 .20
❑ 15T Ivan Calderon .05 .01
❑ 16T Jeff Calhoun .05 .01
❑ 17T Casey Candaele .05 .01
❑ 18T John Cangelosi .05 .01
❑ 19T Steve Carlton .10 .02
❑ 20T Juan Castillo .10 .02
❑ 21T Rick Cerone .05 .01
❑ 22T Ron Cey .10 .02
❑ 23T John Christensen .05 .01
❑ 24T David Cone XRC .75 .30
❑ 25T Chuck Crim .05 .01
❑ 26T Storm Davis .05 .01
❑ 27T Andre Dawson .10 .02
❑ 28T Rick Dempsey .05 .01
❑ 29T Doug Drabek .50 .20
❑ 30T Mike Dunne .05 .01
❑ 31T Dennis Eckersley .15 .05
❑ 32T Lee Elia MG .05 .01
❑ 33T Brian Fisher .05 .01
❑ 34T Terry Francona .10 .02
❑ 35T Willie Fraser .10 .02
❑ 36T Billy Gardner MG .05 .01
❑ 37T Ken Gerhart .05 .01
❑ 38T Dan Gladden .05 .01
❑ 39T Jim Gott .05 .01
❑ 40T Cecilio Guante .05 .01
❑ 41T Albert Hall .05 .01
❑ 42T Terry Harper .05 .01
❑ 43T Mickey Hatcher .05 .01
❑ 44T Brad Havens .05 .01
❑ 45T Neal Heaton .05 .01
❑ 46T Mike Henneman XRC .25 .08
❑ 47T Donnie Hill .05 .01
❑ 48T Guy Hoffman .05 .01
❑ 49T Brian Holton .05 .01
❑ 50T Charles Hudson .05 .01
❑ 51T Danny Jackson .05 .01
❑ 52T Reggie Jackson .15 .05
❑ 53T Chris James XRC .10 .02
❑ 54T Dion James .05 .01
❑ 55T Stan Jefferson .05 .01
❑ 56T Joe Johnson .05 .01
❑ 57T Terry Kennedy .05 .01
❑ 58T Mike Kingery .10 .02
❑ 59T Ray Knight .10 .02
❑ 60T Gene Larkin XRC .25 .08
❑ 61T Mike LaValliere .25 .08
❑ 62T Jack Lazorko .05 .01
❑ 63T Terry Leach .05 .01

❑ 64T	Tim Leary	.05	.01
❑ 65T	Jim Lindeman	.10	.02
❑ 66T	Steve Lombardozzi	.05	.01
❑ 67T	Bill Long	.05	.01
❑ 68T	Barry Lyons	.05	.01
❑ 69T	Shane Mack	.05	.01
❑ 70T	Greg Maddux XRC	5.00	2.00
❑ 71T	Bill Madlock	.10	.02
❑ 72T	Joe Magrane XRC	.10	.02
❑ 73T	Dave Martinez XRC	.25	.08
❑ 74T	Fred McGriff	.60	.25
❑ 75T	Mark McLemore	.10	.02
❑ 76T	Kevin McReynolds	.05	.01
❑ 77T	Dave Meads	.05	.01
❑ 78T	Eddie Milner	.05	.01
❑ 79T	Greg Minton	.05	.01
❑ 80T	John Mitchell XRC	.10	.02
❑ 81T	Kevin Mitchell	.15	.05
❑ 82T	Charlie Moore	.05	.01
❑ 83T	Jeff Musselman	.05	.01
❑ 84T	Gene Nelson	.05	.01
❑ 85T	Graig Nettles	.10	.02
❑ 86T	Al Newman	.05	.01
❑ 87T	Reid Nichols	.05	.01
❑ 88T	Tom Niedenfuer	.05	.01
❑ 89T	Joe Niekro	.05	.01
❑ 90T	Tom Nieto	.05	.01
❑ 91T	Matt Nokes XRC	.25	.08
❑ 92T	Dickie Noles	.05	.01
❑ 93T	Pat Pacillo	.05	.01
❑ 94T	Lance Parrish	.10	.02
❑ 95T	Tony Pena	.05	.01
❑ 96T	Luis Polonia XRC	.25	.08
❑ 97T	Randy Ready	.05	.01
❑ 98T	Jeff Reardon	.10	.02
❑ 99T	Gary Redus	.05	.01
❑ 100T	Jeff Reed	.05	.01
❑ 101T	Rick Rhoden	.05	.01
❑ 102T	Cal Ripken Sr. MG	.05	.01
❑ 103T	Wally Ritchie	.05	.01
❑ 104T	Jeff M. Robinson	.05	.01
❑ 105T	Gary Roenicke	.05	.01
❑ 106T	Jerry Royster	.05	.01
❑ 107T	Mark Salas	.05	.01
❑ 108T	Luis Salazar	.05	.01
❑ 109T	Benito Santiago	.10	.02
❑ 110T	Dave Schmidt	.05	.01
❑ 111T	Kevin Seitzer XRC	.25	.08
❑ 112T	John Shelby	.05	.01
❑ 113T	Steve Shields	.05	.01
❑ 114T	John Smiley XRC	.25	.08
❑ 115T	Chris Speier	.05	.01
❑ 116T	Mike Stanley XRC	.25	.08
❑ 117T	Terry Steinbach XRC	.50	.20
❑ 118T	Les Straker	.05	.01
❑ 119T	Jim Sundberg	.10	.02
❑ 120T	Danny Tartabull	.05	.01
❑ 121T	Tom Trebelhorn MG	.05	.01
❑ 122T	Dave Valle XRC	.10	.02
❑ 123T	Ed VandeBerg	.05	.01
❑ 124T	Andy Van Slyke	.15	.05
❑ 125T	Gary Ward	.05	.01
❑ 126T	Alan Wiggins	.05	.01
❑ 127T	Bill Wilkinson	.05	.01
❑ 128T	Frank Williams	.05	.01
❑ 129T	Matt Williams XRC	1.00	.40
❑ 130T	Jim Winn	.05	.01
❑ 131T	Matt Young	.05	.01
❑ 132T	Checklist 1T-132T	.05	.01

1988 Topps

❑	COMPLETE SET (792)	15.00	6.00
❑	COMP.FACT SET (792)	15.00	6.00
❑	COMP.X-MAS.SET (792)	40.00	15.00
❑ 1	Vince Coleman RB 100 Steals for Third Cons. Seas	.05	.01
❑ 2	Don Mattingly RB	.30	.10
❑ 3	Mark McGwire RB	.75	.30
❑ 3A	Mark McGwire ERR RB	.75	.30
❑ 4	Eddie Murray RB	.15	.05
❑ 4A	Eddie Murray ERR RB	.50	.20
❑ 5	Phil Niekro Joe Niekro RB Brothers Win Record	.10	.02
❑ 6	Nolan Ryan RB	.40	.15
❑ 7	Benito Santiago RB	.05	.01
❑ 8	Kevin Elster	.05	.01
❑ 9	Andy Hawkins	.05	.01
❑ 10	Ryne Sandberg	.40	.15
❑ 11	Mike Young	.05	.01
❑ 12	Bill Schroeder	.05	.01
❑ 13	Andres Thomas	.05	.01
❑ 14	Sparky Anderson MG	.10	.02
❑ 15	Chili Davis	.10	.02
❑ 16	Kirk McCaskill	.05	.01
❑ 17	Ron Oester	.05	.01
❑ 18A	Al Leiter ERR RC	.50	.20
❑ 18B	Al Leiter RC	.50	.20
❑ 19	Mark Davidson	.05	.01
❑ 20	Kevin Gross	.05	.01
❑ 21	Wade Boggs Spike Owen TL	.10	.02
❑ 22	Greg Swindell	.05	.01
❑ 23	Ken Landreaux	.05	.01
❑ 24	Jim Deshaies	.05	.01
❑ 25	Andres Galarraga	.10	.02
❑ 26	Mitch Williams	.05	.01
❑ 27	R.J. Reynolds	.05	.01
❑ 28	Jose Nunez	.05	.01
❑ 29	Angel Salazar	.05	.01
❑ 30	Sid Fernandez	.05	.01
❑ 31	Bruce Bochy	.05	.01
❑ 32	Mike Morgan	.05	.01
❑ 33	Rob Deer	.05	.01
❑ 34	Ricky Horton	.05	.01
❑ 35	Harold Baines	.10	.02
❑ 36	Jamie Moyer	.10	.02
❑ 37	Ed Romero	.05	.01
❑ 38	Jeff Calhoun	.05	.01
❑ 39	Gerald Perry	.05	.01
❑ 40	Orel Hershiser	.10	.02
❑ 41	Bob Melvin	.05	.01
❑ 42	Bill Landrum	.05	.01
❑ 43	Dick Schofield	.05	.01
❑ 44	Lou Piniella MG	.10	.02
❑ 45	Kent Hrbek	.10	.02
❑ 46	Darnell Coles	.05	.01
❑ 47	Joaquin Andujar	.10	.02
❑ 48	Alan Ashby	.05	.01
❑ 49	Dave Clark	.05	.01
❑ 50	Hubie Brooks	.05	.01
❑ 51	C.Ripken/E.Murray TL	.40	.15
❑ 52	Don Robinson	.05	.01
❑ 53	Curt Wilkerson	.05	.01
❑ 54	Jim Clancy	.05	.01
❑ 55	Phil Bradley	.05	.01
❑ 56	Ed Hearn	.05	.01
❑ 57	Tim Crews RC	.25	.08
❑ 58	Dave Magadan	.05	.01
❑ 59	Danny Cox	.05	.01
❑ 60	Rickey Henderson	.20	.07
❑ 61	Mark Knudson	.05	.01
❑ 62	Jeff Hamilton	.05	.01
❑ 63	Jimmy Jones	.05	.01
❑ 64	Ken Caminiti RC	2.00	.75
❑ 65	Leon Durham	.05	.01
❑ 66	Shane Rawley	.05	.01
❑ 67	Ken Oberkfell	.05	.01
❑ 68	Dave Dravecky	.05	.01
❑ 69	Mike Hart	.05	.01
❑ 70	Roger Clemens	1.00	.40
❑ 71	Gary Pettis	.05	.01
❑ 72	Dennis Eckersley	.15	.05
❑ 73	Randy Bush	.05	.01
❑ 74	Tom Lasorda MG	.15	.05
❑ 75	Joe Carter	.10	.02
❑ 76	Dennis Martinez	.10	.02
❑ 77	Tom O'Malley	.05	.01
❑ 78	Dan Petry	.05	.01
❑ 79	Ernie Whitt	.05	.01
❑ 80	Mark Langston	.05	.01
❑ 81	Ron Robinson John Franco TL	.05	.01
❑ 82	Darrel Akerfelds	.05	.01
❑ 83	Jose Oquendo	.05	.01
❑ 84	Cecilio Guante	.05	.01
❑ 85	Howard Johnson	.10	.02
❑ 86	Ron Karkovice	.05	.01
❑ 87	Mike Mason	.05	.01
❑ 88	Earnie Riles	.05	.01
❑ 89	Gary Thurman	.05	.01
❑ 90	Dale Murphy	.15	.05
❑ 91	Joey Cora RC	.25	.08
❑ 92	Len Matuszek	.05	.01
❑ 93	Bob Sebra	.05	.01
❑ 94	Chuck Jackson	.05	.01
❑ 95	Lance Parrish	.10	.02
❑ 96	Todd Benzinger RC*	.25	.08
❑ 97	Scott Garrelts	.05	.01
❑ 98	Rene Gonzales RC	.10	.02
❑ 99	Chuck Finley	.10	.02
❑ 100	Jack Clark	.10	.02
❑ 101	Allan Anderson	.05	.01
❑ 102	Barry Larkin	.15	.05
❑ 103	Curt Young	.05	.01
❑ 104	Dick Williams MG	.05	.01
❑ 105	Jesse Orosco	.05	.01
❑ 106	Jim Walewander	.05	.01
❑ 107	Scott Bailes	.05	.01
❑ 108	Steve Lyons	.05	.01
❑ 109	Joel Skinner	.05	.01
❑ 110	Teddy Higuera	.05	.01
❑ 111	Hubie Brooks Vance Law TL	.05	.01
❑ 112	Les Lancaster	.05	.01
❑ 113	Kelly Gruber	.05	.01
❑ 114	Jeff Russell	.05	.01
❑ 115	Johnny Ray	.05	.01
❑ 116	Jerry Don Gleaton	.05	.01
❑ 117	James Steels	.05	.01
❑ 118	Bob Welch	.10	.02
❑ 119	Robbie Wine	.05	.01
❑ 120	Kirby Puckett	.20	.07
❑ 121	Checklist 1-132	.05	.01
❑ 122	Tony Bernazard	.05	.01
❑ 123	Tom Candiotti	.05	.01
❑ 124	Ray Knight	.10	.02
❑ 125	Bruce Hurst	.05	.01
❑ 126	Steve Jeltz	.05	.01
❑ 127	Jim Gott	.05	.01
❑ 128	Johnny Grubb	.05	.01
❑ 129	Greg Minton	.05	.01
❑ 130	Buddy Bell	.10	.02
❑ 131	Don Schulze	.05	.01
❑ 132	Donnie Hill	.05	.01
❑ 133	Greg Mathews	.05	.01
❑ 134	Chuck Tanner MG	.05	.01
❑ 135	Dennis Rasmussen	.05	.01
❑ 136	Brian Dayett	.05	.01
❑ 137	Chris Bosio	.05	.01
❑ 138	Mitch Webster	.05	.01
❑ 139	Jerry Browne	.05	.01
❑ 140	Jesse Barfield	.10	.02
❑ 141	G.Brett/B.Saberhagen TL	.20	.07
❑ 142	Andy Van Slyke	.15	.05
❑ 143	Mickey Tettleton	.05	.01
❑ 144	Don Gordon	.05	.01
❑ 145	Bill Madlock	.10	.02
❑ 146	Donell Nixon	.05	.01
❑ 147	Bill Buckner	.10	.02
❑ 148	Carmelo Martinez	.05	.01
❑ 149	Ken Howell	.05	.01
❑ 150	Eric Davis	.10	.02
❑ 151	Bob Knepper	.05	.01
❑ 152	Jody Reed RC	.25	.08
❑ 153	John Habyan	.05	.01
❑ 154	Jeff Stone	.05	.01
❑ 155	Bruce Sutter	.10	.02
❑ 156	Gary Matthews	.10	.02

Card		
❑ 157 Atlee Hammaker	.05	.01
❑ 158 Tim Hulett	.05	.01
❑ 159 Brad Arnsberg	.05	.01
❑ 160 Willie McGee	.10	.02
❑ 161 Bryn Smith	.05	.01
❑ 162 Mark McLemore	.05	.01
❑ 163 Dale Mohorcic	.05	.01
❑ 164 Dave Johnson MG	.05	.01
❑ 165 Robin Yount	.30	.10
❑ 166 Rick Rodriquez	.05	.01
❑ 167 Rance Mulliniks	.05	.01
❑ 168 Barry Jones	.05	.01
❑ 169 Ross Jones	.05	.01
❑ 170 Rich Gossage	.10	.02
❑ 171 Shawon Dunston Manny Trillo TL	.05	.01
❑ 172 Lloyd McClendon RC	.25	.08
❑ 173 Eric Plunk	.05	.01
❑ 174 Phil Garner	.10	.02
❑ 175 Kevin Bass	.05	.01
❑ 176 Jeff Reed	.05	.01
❑ 177 Frank Tanana	.10	.02
❑ 178 Dwayne Henry	.05	.01
❑ 179 Charlie Puleo	.05	.01
❑ 180 Terry Kennedy	.05	.01
❑ 181 David Cone	.10	.02
❑ 182 Ken Phelps	.05	.01
❑ 183 Tom Lawless	.05	.01
❑ 184 Ivan Calderon	.05	.01
❑ 185 Rick Rhoden	.05	.01
❑ 186 Rafael Palmeiro	.40	.15
❑ 187 Steve Kiefer	.05	.01
❑ 188 John Russell	.05	.01
❑ 189 Wes Gardner	.05	.01
❑ 190 Candy Maldonado	.05	.01
❑ 191 John Cerutti	.05	.01
❑ 192 Devon White	.10	.02
❑ 193 Brian Fisher	.05	.01
❑ 194 Tom Kelly MG	.05	.01
❑ 195 Dan Quisenberry	.05	.01
❑ 196 Dave Engle	.05	.01
❑ 197 Lance McCullers	.05	.01
❑ 198 Franklin Stubbs	.05	.01
❑ 199 Dave Meads	.05	.01
❑ 200 Wade Boggs	.15	.05
❑ 201 Rangers TL Bobby Valentine MG, Pete O'Brien, Pe	.05	.01
❑ 202 Glenn Hoffman	.05	.01
❑ 203 Fred Toliver	.05	.01
❑ 204 Paul O'Neill	.15	.05
❑ 205 Nelson Liriano	.05	.01
❑ 206 Domingo Ramos	.05	.01
❑ 207 John Mitchell RC	.10	.02
❑ 208 Steve Lake	.05	.01
❑ 209 Richard Dotson	.05	.01
❑ 210 Willie Randolph	.10	.02
❑ 211 Frank DiPino	.05	.01
❑ 212 Greg Brock	.05	.01
❑ 213 Albert Hall	.05	.01
❑ 214 Dave Schmidt	.05	.01
❑ 215 Von Hayes	.05	.01
❑ 216 Jerry Reuss	.05	.01
❑ 217 Harry Spilman	.05	.01
❑ 218 Dan Schatzeder	.05	.01
❑ 219 Mike Stanley	.05	.01
❑ 220 Tom Henke	.05	.01
❑ 221 Rafael Belliard	.05	.01
❑ 222 Steve Farr	.05	.01
❑ 223 Stan Jefferson	.05	.01
❑ 224 Tom Trebelhorn MG	.05	.01
❑ 225 Mike Scioscia	.10	.02
❑ 226 Dave Lopes	.10	.02
❑ 227 Ed Correa	.05	.01
❑ 228 Wallace Johnson	.05	.01
❑ 229 Jeff Musselman	.05	.01
❑ 230 Pat Tabler	.05	.01
❑ 231 B.Bonds/B.Bonilla TL	1.00	.40
❑ 232 Bob James	.05	.01
❑ 233 Rafael Santana	.05	.01
❑ 234 Ken Dayley	.05	.01
❑ 235 Gary Ward	.05	.01
❑ 236 Ted Power	.05	.01
❑ 237 Mike Heath	.05	.01
❑ 238 Luis Polonia RC*	.25	.08
❑ 239 Roy Smalley	.05	.01
❑ 240 Lee Smith	.10	.02
❑ 241 Damaso Garcia	.05	.01
❑ 242 Tom Niedenfuer	.05	.01
❑ 243 Mark Ryal	.05	.01
❑ 244 Jeff D. Robinson	.05	.01
❑ 245 Rich Gedman	.05	.01
❑ 246 Mike Campbell	.05	.01
❑ 247 Thad Bosley	.05	.01
❑ 248 Storm Davis	.05	.01
❑ 249 Mike Marshall	.05	.01
❑ 250 Nolan Ryan	1.00	.40
❑ 251 Tom Foley	.05	.01
❑ 252 Bob Brower	.05	.01
❑ 253 Checklist 133-264	.05	.01
❑ 254 Lee Elia MG	.05	.01
❑ 255 Mookie Wilson	.10	.02
❑ 256 Ken Schrom	.05	.01
❑ 257 Jerry Royster	.05	.01
❑ 258 Ed Nunez	.05	.01
❑ 259 Ron Kittle	.05	.01
❑ 260 Vince Coleman	.05	.01
❑ 261 Giants TL (Five players)	.05	.01
❑ 262 Drew Hall	.05	.01
❑ 263 Glenn Braggs	.05	.01
❑ 264 Les Straker	.05	.01
❑ 265 Bo Diaz	.05	.01
❑ 266 Paul Assenmacher	.05	.01
❑ 267 Billy Bean RC	.10	.02
❑ 268 Bruce Ruffin	.05	.01
❑ 269 Ellis Burks RC	.40	.15
❑ 270 Mike Witt	.05	.01
❑ 271 Ken Gerhart	.05	.01
❑ 272 Steve Ontiveros	.05	.01
❑ 273 Garth Iorg	.05	.01
❑ 274 Junior Ortiz	.05	.01
❑ 275 Kevin Seitzer	.05	.01
❑ 276 Luis Salazar	.05	.01
❑ 277 Alejandro Pena	.05	.01
❑ 278 Jose Cruz	.10	.02
❑ 279 Randy St.Claire	.05	.01
❑ 280 Pete Incaviglia	.05	.01
❑ 281 Jerry Hairston	.05	.01
❑ 282 Pat Perry	.05	.01
❑ 283 Phil Lombardi	.05	.01
❑ 284 Larry Bowa MG	.10	.02
❑ 285 Jim Presley	.05	.01
❑ 286 Chuck Crim	.05	.01
❑ 287 Manny Trillo	.05	.01
❑ 288 Pat Pacillo	.05	.01
❑ 289 Dave Bergman	.05	.01
❑ 290 Tony Fernandez	.05	.01
❑ 291 Billy Hatcher Kevin Bass TL	.05	.01
❑ 292 Carney Lansford	.10	.02
❑ 293 Doug Jones RC	.25	.08
❑ 294 Al Pedrique	.05	.01
❑ 295 Bert Blyleven	.10	.02
❑ 296 Floyd Rayford	.05	.01
❑ 297 Zane Smith	.05	.01
❑ 298 Milt Thompson	.05	.01
❑ 299 Steve Crawford	.05	.01
❑ 300 Don Mattingly	.60	.25
❑ 301 Bud Black	.05	.01
❑ 302 Jose Uribe	.05	.01
❑ 303 Eric Show	.05	.01
❑ 304 George Hendrick	.10	.02
❑ 305 Steve Sax	.05	.01
❑ 306 Billy Hatcher	.05	.01
❑ 307 Mike Trujillo	.05	.01
❑ 308 Lee Mazzilli	.10	.02
❑ 309 Bill Long	.05	.01
❑ 310 Tom Herr	.05	.01
❑ 311 Scott Sanderson	.05	.01
❑ 312 Joey Meyer	.05	.01
❑ 313 Bob McClure	.05	.01
❑ 314 Jimy Williams MG	.05	.01
❑ 315 Dave Parker	.10	.02
❑ 316 Jose Rijo	.10	.02
❑ 317 Tom Nieto	.05	.01
❑ 318 Mel Hall	.05	.01
❑ 319 Mike Loynd	.05	.01
❑ 320 Alan Trammell	.10	.02
❑ 321 Harold Baines Carlton Fisk TL	.10	.02
❑ 322 Vicente Palacios	.05	.01
❑ 323 Rick Leach	.05	.01
❑ 324 Danny Jackson	.05	.01
❑ 325 Glenn Hubbard	.05	.01
❑ 326 Al Nipper	.05	.01
❑ 327 Larry Sheets	.05	.01
❑ 328 Greg Cadaret	.05	.01
❑ 329 Chris Speier	.05	.01
❑ 330 Eddie Whitson	.05	.01
❑ 331 Brian Downing	.10	.02
❑ 332 Jerry Reed	.05	.01
❑ 333 Wally Backman	.05	.01
❑ 334 Dave LaPoint	.05	.01
❑ 335 Claudell Washington	.05	.01
❑ 336 Ed Lynch	.05	.01
❑ 337 Jim Gantner	.05	.01
❑ 338 Brian Holton UER (1987 ERA .389, should be 3.89)	.05	.01
❑ 339 Kurt Stillwell	.05	.01
❑ 340 Jack Morris	.10	.02
❑ 341 Carmen Castillo	.05	.01
❑ 342 Larry Andersen	.05	.01
❑ 343 Greg Gagne	.05	.01
❑ 344 Tony LaRussa MG	.10	.02
❑ 345 Scott Fletcher	.05	.01
❑ 346 Vance Law	.05	.01
❑ 347 Joe Johnson	.05	.01
❑ 348 Jim Eisenreich	.05	.01
❑ 349 Bob Walk	.05	.01
❑ 350 Will Clark	.20	.07
❑ 351 Red Schoendienst CO Tony Pena TL	.10	.02
❑ 352 Bill Ripken RC*	.05	.01
❑ 353 Ed Olwine	.05	.01
❑ 354 Marc Sullivan	.05	.01
❑ 355 Roger McDowell	.05	.01
❑ 356 Luis Aguayo	.05	.01
❑ 357 Floyd Bannister	.05	.01
❑ 358 Rey Quinones	.05	.01
❑ 359 Tim Stoddard	.05	.01
❑ 360 Tony Gwynn	.30	.10
❑ 361 Greg Maddux	1.00	.40
❑ 362 Juan Castillo	.05	.01
❑ 363 Willie Fraser	.05	.01
❑ 364 Nick Esasky	.05	.01
❑ 365 Floyd Youmans	.05	.01
❑ 366 Chet Lemon	.10	.02
❑ 367 Tim Leary	.05	.01
❑ 368 Gerald Young	.05	.01
❑ 369 Greg Harris	.05	.01
❑ 370 Jose Canseco	.50	.20
❑ 371 Joe Hesketh	.05	.01
❑ 372 Matt Williams RC	.75	.30
❑ 373 Checklist 265-396	.05	.01
❑ 374 Doc Edwards MG	.05	.01
❑ 375 Tom Brunansky	.05	.01
❑ 376 Bill Wilkinson	.05	.01
❑ 377 Sam Horn RC	.10	.02
❑ 378 Todd Frohwirth	.05	.01
❑ 379 Rafael Ramirez	.05	.01
❑ 380 Joe Magrane RC*	.05	.01
❑ 381 Wally Joyner Jack Howell TL	.10	.02
❑ 382 Keith Miller RC	.25	.08
❑ 383 Eric Bell	.05	.01
❑ 384 Neil Allen	.05	.01
❑ 385 Carlton Fisk	.15	.05
❑ 386 Don Mattingly AS	.30	.10
❑ 387 Willie Randolph AS	.05	.01
❑ 388 Wade Boggs AS	.10	.02
❑ 389 Alan Trammell AS	.05	.01
❑ 390 George Bell AS	.05	.01
❑ 391 Kirby Puckett AS	.15	.05
❑ 392 Dave Winfield AS	.05	.01
❑ 393 Matt Nokes AS	.05	.01
❑ 394 Roger Clemens AS	.50	.20
❑ 395 Jimmy Key AS	.05	.01
❑ 396 Tom Henke AS	.05	.01
❑ 397 Jack Clark AS	.05	.01
❑ 398 Juan Samuel AS	.05	.01
❑ 399 Tim Wallach AS	.05	.01
❑ 400 Ozzie Smith AS	.20	.07
❑ 401 Andre Dawson AS	.05	.01
❑ 402 Tony Gwynn AS	.15	.05
❑ 403 Tim Raines AS	.05	.01

404	Benny Santiago AS	.05	.01
405	Dwight Gooden AS	.05	.01
406	Shane Rawley AS	.05	.01
407	Steve Bedrosian AS	.05	.01
408	Dion James	.05	.01
409	Joel McKeon	.05	.01
410	Tony Pena	.05	.01
411	Wayne Tolleson	.05	.01
412	Randy Myers	.10	.02
413	John Christensen	.05	.01
414	John McNamara MG	.05	.01
415	Don Carman	.05	.01
416	Keith Moreland	.05	.01
417	Mark Ciardi	.05	.01
418	Joel Youngblood	.05	.01
419	Scott McGregor	.05	.01
420	Wally Joyner	.10	.02
421	Ed VandeBerg	.05	.01
422	Dave Concepcion	.10	.02
423	John Smiley RC*	.25	.08
424	Dwayne Murphy	.05	.01
425	Jeff Reardon	.10	.02
426	Randy Ready	.05	.01
427	Paul Kilgus	.05	.01
428	John Shelby	.05	.01
429	A.Trammell/K.Gibson TL	.10	.02
430	Glenn Davis	.05	.01
431	Casey Candaele	.05	.01
432	Mike Moore	.05	.01
433	Bill Pecota RC*	.05	.01
434	Rick Aguilera	.05	.01
435	Mike Pagliarulo	.05	.01
436	Mike Bielecki	.05	.01
437	Fred Manrique	.05	.01
438	Rob Ducey	.05	.01
439	Dave Martinez	.05	.01
440	Steve Bedrosian	.05	.01
441	Rick Manning	.05	.01
442	Tom Bolton	.05	.01
443	Ken Griffey	.10	.02
444	Cal Ripken, Sr. MG (Checklist back) UER (two cop	.05	.01
445	Mike Krukow	.05	.01
446	Doug DeCinces (Now with Cardinals on card front)	.05	.01
447	Jeff Montgomery RC	.25	.08
448	Mike Davis	.05	.01
449	Jeff M. Robinson	.05	.01
450	Barry Bonds	2.00	.75
451	Keith Atherton	.05	.01
452	Willie Wilson	.10	.02
453	Dennis Powell	.05	.01
454	Marvell Wynne	.05	.01
455	Shawn Hillegas	.05	.01
456	Dave Anderson	.05	.01
457	Terry Leach	.05	.01
458	Ron Hassey	.05	.01
459	Dave Winfield Willie Randolph TL	.05	.01
460	Ozzie Smith	.30	.10
461	Danny Darwin	.05	.01
462	Don Slaught	.05	.01
463	Fred McGriff	.20	.07
464	Jay Tibbs	.05	.01
465	Paul Molitor	.10	.02
466	Jerry Mumphrey	.05	.01
467	Don Aase	.05	.01
468	Darren Daulton	.10	.02
469	Jeff Dedmon	.05	.01
470	Dwight Evans	.15	.05
471	Donnie Moore	.05	.01
472	Robby Thompson	.05	.01
473	Joe Niekro	.05	.01
474	Tom Brookens	.05	.01
475	Pete Rose MG/TC	.50	.20
476	Dave Stewart	.10	.02
477	Jamie Quirk	.05	.01
478	Sid Bream	.05	.01
479	Brett Butler	.10	.02
480	Dwight Gooden	.10	.02
481	Mariano Duncan	.05	.01
482	Mark Davis	.05	.01
483	Rod Booker	.05	.01
484	Pat Clements	.05	.01
485	Harold Reynolds	.10	.02
486	Pat Keedy	.05	.01
487	Jim Pankovits	.05	.01
488	Andy McGaffigan	.05	.01
489	Dodgers TL Pedro Guerrero and Fernando Valenzuel	.05	.01
490	Larry Parrish	.05	.01
491	B.J. Surhoff	.10	.02
492	Doyle Alexander	.05	.01
493	Mike Greenwell	.05	.01
494	Wally Ritchie	.05	.01
495	Eddie Murray	.20	.07
496	Guy Hoffman	.05	.01
497	Kevin Mitchell	.10	.02
498	Bob Boone	.10	.02
499	Eric King	.05	.01
500	Andre Dawson	.10	.02
501	Tim Birtsas	.05	.01
502	Dan Gladden	.05	.01
503	Junior Noboa	.05	.01
504	Bob Rodgers MG	.05	.01
505	Willie Upshaw	.05	.01
506	John Cangelosi	.05	.01
507	Mark Gubicza	.05	.01
508	Tim Teufel	.05	.01
509	Bill Dawley	.05	.01
510	Dave Winfield	.10	.02
511	Joel Davis	.05	.01
512	Alex Trevino	.05	.01
513	Tim Flannery	.05	.01
514	Pat Sheridan	.05	.01
515	Juan Nieves	.05	.01
516	Jim Sundberg	.10	.02
517	Ron Robinson	.05	.01
518	Greg Gross	.05	.01
519	Harold Reynolds Phil Bradley TL	.05	.01
520	Dave Smith	.05	.01
521	Jim Dwyer	.05	.01
522	Bob Patterson	.05	.01
523	Gary Roenicke	.05	.01
524	Gary Lucas	.05	.01
525	Marty Barrett	.05	.01
526	Juan Berenguer	.05	.01
527	Steve Henderson	.05	.01
528A	Checklist 397-528 ERR (455 S. Carlton)	.15	.05
528B	Checklist 397-528 COR (455 S. Hillegas)	.10	.02
529	Tim Burke	.05	.01
530	Gary Carter	.10	.02
531	Rich Yett	.05	.01
532	Mike Kingery	.05	.01
533	John Farrell RC	.10	.02
534	John Wathan MG	.05	.01
535	Ron Guidry	.10	.02
536	John Morris	.05	.01
537	Steve Buechele	.05	.01
538	Bill Wegman	.05	.01
539	Mike LaValliere	.05	.01
540	Bret Saberhagen	.10	.02
541	Juan Beniquez	.05	.01
542	Paul Noce	.05	.01
543	Kent Tekulve	.05	.01
544	Jim Traber	.05	.01
545	Don Baylor	.10	.02
546	John Candelaria	.05	.01
547	Felix Fermin	.05	.01
548	Shane Mack	.05	.01
549	Braves TL Albert Hall, Dale Murphy, Ken Griffey	.10	.02
550	Pedro Guerrero	.10	.02
551	Terry Steinbach	.10	.02
552	Mark Thurmond	.05	.01
553	Tracy Jones	.05	.01
554	Mike Smithson	.05	.01
555	Brook Jacoby	.05	.01
556	Stan Clarke	.05	.01
557	Craig Reynolds	.05	.01
558	Bob Ojeda	.05	.01
559	Ken Williams	.05	.01
560	Tim Wallach	.05	.01
561	Rick Cerone	.05	.01
562	Jim Lindeman	.05	.01
563	Jose Guzman	.05	.01
564	Frank Lucchesi MG	.05	.01
565	Lloyd Moseby	.05	.01
566	Charlie O'Brien	.05	.01
567	Mike Diaz	.05	.01
568	Chris Brown	.05	.01
569	Charlie Leibrandt	.05	.01
570	Jeffrey Leonard	.05	.01
571	Mark Williamson	.05	.01
572	Chris James	.05	.01
573	Bob Stanley	.05	.01
574	Graig Nettles	.10	.02
575	Don Sutton	.10	.02
576	Tommy Hinzo	.05	.01
577	Tom Browning	.05	.01
578	Gary Gaetti	.10	.02
579	Gary Carter Kevin McReynolds TL	.05	.01
580	Mark McGwire	1.50	.60
581	Tito Landrum	.05	.01
582	Mike Henneman RC*	.25	.08
583	Dave Valle	.05	.01
584	Steve Trout	.05	.01
585	Ozzie Guillen	.10	.02
586	Bob Forsch	.05	.01
587	Terry Puhl	.05	.01
588	Jeff Parrett	.05	.01
589	Geno Petralli	.05	.01
590	George Bell	.10	.02
591	Doug Drabek	.05	.01
592	Dale Sveum	.05	.01
593	Bob Tewksbury	.05	.01
594	Bobby Valentine MG	.10	.02
595	Frank White	.10	.02
596	John Kruk	.10	.02
597	Gene Garber	.05	.01
598	Lee Lacy	.05	.01
599	Calvin Schiraldi	.05	.01
600	Mike Schmidt	.50	.20
601	Jack Lazorko	.05	.01
602	Mike Aldrete	.05	.01
603	Rob Murphy	.05	.01
604	Chris Bando	.05	.01
605	Kirk Gibson	.20	.07
606	Moose Haas	.05	.01
607	Mickey Hatcher	.05	.01
608	Charlie Kerfeld	.05	.01
609	Gary Gaetti Kent Hrbek TL	.10	.02
610	Keith Hernandez	.10	.02
611	Tommy John	.10	.02
612	Curt Ford	.05	.01
613	Bobby Thigpen	.05	.01
614	Herm Winningham	.05	.01
615	Jody Davis	.05	.01
616	Jay Aldrich	.05	.01
617	Oddibe McDowell	.05	.01
618	Cecil Fielder	.10	.02
619	Mike Dunne (Inconsistent design, black name on f	.05	.01
620	Cory Snyder	.05	.01
621	Gene Nelson	.05	.01
622	Kal Daniels	.05	.01
623	Mike Flanagan	.05	.01
624	Jim Leyland MG	.10	.02
625	Frank Viola	.10	.02
626	Glenn Wilson	.05	.01
627	Joe Boever	.05	.01
628	Dave Henderson	.05	.01
629	Kelly Downs	.05	.01
630	Darrell Evans	.10	.02
631	Jack Howell	.05	.01
632	Steve Shields	.05	.01
633	Barry Lyons	.05	.01
634	Jose DeLeon	.05	.01
635	Terry Pendleton	.10	.02
636	Charles Hudson	.05	.01
637	Jay Bell RC	.40	.15
638	Steve Balboni	.05	.01
639	Glenn Braggs Tony Muser CO TL	.05	.01
640	Garry Templeton (Inconsistent design, green bord	.10	.02

❑ 641 Rick Honeycutt .05 .01
❑ 642 Bob Dernier .05 .01
❑ 643 Rocky Childress .05 .01
❑ 644 Terry McGriff .05 .01
❑ 645 Matt Nokes RC* .25 .08
❑ 646 Checklist 529-660 .05 .01
❑ 647 Pascual Perez .05 .01
❑ 648 Al Newman .05 .01
❑ 649 DeWayne Buice .05 .01
❑ 650 Cal Ripken .75 .30
❑ 651 Mike Jackson RC* .25 .08
❑ 652 Bruce Benedict .05 .01
❑ 653 Jeff Sellers .05 .01
❑ 654 Roger Craig MG .10 .02
❑ 655 Len Dykstra .10 .02
❑ 656 Lee Guetterman .05 .01
❑ 657 Gary Redus .05 .01
❑ 658 Tim Conroy (Inconsistent design, name in white) .05 .01
❑ 659 Bobby Meacham .05 .01
❑ 660 Rick Reuschel .10 .02
❑ 661 Nolan Ryan TBC .50 .20
❑ 662 Jim Rice TBC .05 .01
❑ 663 Ron Blomberg TBC .05 .01
❑ 664 Bob Gibson TBC .25 .08
❑ 665 Stan Musial TBC .20 .07
❑ 666 Mario Soto .10 .02
❑ 667 Luis Quinones .05 .01
❑ 668 Walt Terrell .05 .01
❑ 669 Lance Parrish Mike Ryan CO TL .05 .01
❑ 670 Dan Plesac .05 .01
❑ 671 Tim Laudner .05 .01
❑ 672 John Davis .05 .01
❑ 673 Tony Phillips .05 .01
❑ 674 Mike Fitzgerald .05 .01
❑ 675 Jim Rice .10 .02
❑ 676 Ken Dixon .05 .01
❑ 677 Eddie Milner .05 .01
❑ 678 Jim Acker .05 .01
❑ 679 Darrell Miller .05 .01
❑ 680 Charlie Hough .10 .02
❑ 681 Bobby Bonilla .10 .02
❑ 682 Jimmy Key .10 .02
❑ 683 Julio Franco .10 .02
❑ 684 Hal Lanier MG .05 .01
❑ 685 Ron Darling .10 .02
❑ 686 Terry Francona .10 .02
❑ 687 Mickey Brantley .05 .01
❑ 688 Jim Winn .05 .01
❑ 689 Tom Pagnozzi RC .10 .02
❑ 690 Jay Howell .05 .01
❑ 691 Dan Pasqua .05 .01
❑ 692 Mike Birkbeck .05 .01
❑ 693 Benito Santiago .10 .02
❑ 694 Eric Nolte .05 .01
❑ 695 Shawon Dunston .05 .01
❑ 696 Duane Ward .05 .01
❑ 697 Steve Lombardozzi .05 .01
❑ 698 Brad Havens .05 .01
❑ 699 B.Santiago/T.Gwynn TL .10 .02
❑ 700 George Brett .50 .20
❑ 701 Sammy Stewart .05 .01
❑ 702 Mike Gallego .05 .01
❑ 703 Bob Brenly .05 .01
❑ 704 Dennis Boyd .05 .01
❑ 705 Juan Samuel .05 .01
❑ 706 Rick Mahler .05 .01
❑ 707 Fred Lynn .10 .02
❑ 708 Gus Polidor .05 .01
❑ 709 George Frazier .05 .01
❑ 710 Darryl Strawberry .10 .02
❑ 711 Bill Gullickson .05 .01
❑ 712 John Moses .05 .01
❑ 713 Willie Hernandez .05 .01
❑ 714 Jim Fregosi MG .05 .01
❑ 715 Todd Worrell .05 .01
❑ 716 Lenn Sakata .05 .01
❑ 717 Jay Baller .05 .01
❑ 718 Mike Felder .05 .01
❑ 719 Denny Walling .05 .01
❑ 720 Tim Raines .10 .02
❑ 721 Pete O'Brien .05 .01
❑ 722 Manny Lee .05 .01
❑ 723 Bob Kipper .05 .01
❑ 724 Danny Tartabull .05 .01
❑ 725 Mike Boddicker .05 .01
❑ 726 Alfredo Griffin .05 .01
❑ 727 Greg Booker .05 .01
❑ 728 Andy Allanson .05 .01
❑ 729 G.Bell/F.McGriff TL .10 .02
❑ 730 John Franco .10 .02
❑ 731 Rick Schu .05 .01
❑ 732 David Palmer .05 .01
❑ 733 Spike Owen .05 .01
❑ 734 Craig Lefferts .05 .01
❑ 735 Kevin McReynolds .05 .01
❑ 736 Matt Young .05 .01
❑ 737 Butch Wynegar .05 .01
❑ 738 Scott Bankhead .05 .01
❑ 739 Daryl Boston .05 .01
❑ 740 Rick Sutcliffe .10 .02
❑ 741 Mike Easler .05 .01
❑ 742 Mark Clear .05 .01
❑ 743 Larry Herndon .05 .01
❑ 744 Whitey Herzog MG .10 .02
❑ 745 Bill Doran .05 .01
❑ 746 Gene Larkin RC* .25 .08
❑ 747 Bobby Witt .05 .01
❑ 748 Reid Nichols .05 .01
❑ 749 Mark Eichhorn .05 .01
❑ 750 Bo Jackson .20 .07
❑ 751 Jim Morrison .05 .01
❑ 752 Mark Grant .05 .01
❑ 753 Danny Heep .05 .01
❑ 754 Mike LaCoss .05 .01
❑ 755 Ozzie Virgil .05 .01
❑ 756 Mike Maddux .05 .01
❑ 757 John Marzano .05 .01
❑ 758 Eddie Williams RC .10 .02
❑ 759 M.McGwire/J.Canseco TL 1.00 .40
❑ 760 Mike Scott .10 .02
❑ 761 Tony Armas .10 .02
❑ 762 Scott Bradley .05 .01
❑ 763 Doug Sisk .05 .01
❑ 764 Greg Walker .05 .01
❑ 765 Neal Heaton .05 .01
❑ 766 Henry Cotto .05 .01
❑ 767 Jose Lind RC .25 .08
❑ 768 Dickie Noles (Now with Tigers on card front) .05 .01
❑ 769 Cecil Cooper .10 .02
❑ 770 Lou Whitaker .10 .02
❑ 771 Ruben Sierra .10 .02
❑ 772 Sal Butera .05 .01
❑ 773 Frank Williams .05 .01
❑ 774 Gene Mauch MG .05 .01
❑ 775 Dave Stieb .10 .02
❑ 776 Checklist 661-792 .05 .01
❑ 777 Lonnie Smith .05 .01
❑ 778A Keith Comstock ERR WL 2.00 .75
❑ 778B Keith Comstock COR (Blue "Padres") .05 .01
❑ 779 Tom Glavine RC 2.50 1.00
❑ 780 Fernando Valenzuela .10 .02
❑ 781 Keith Hughes .05 .01
❑ 782 Jeff Ballard .05 .01
❑ 783 Ron Roenicke .05 .01
❑ 784 Joe Sambito .05 .01
❑ 785 Alvin Davis .05 .01
❑ 786 Joe Price (Inconsistent design, orange team name .05 .01
❑ 787 Bill Almon .05 .01
❑ 788 Ray Searage .05 .01
❑ 789 Joe Carter TL .05 .01
❑ 790 Dave Righetti .10 .02
❑ 791 Ted Simmons .10 .02
❑ 792 John Tudor .10 .02

1988 Topps Traded

❑ COMP.FACT.SET (132) 8.00 3.00
❑ 1T Jim Abbott OLY XRC 2.00 .75
❑ 2T Juan Agosto .10 .02
❑ 3T Luis Alicea XRC .50 .20
❑ 4T Roberto Alomar XRC 2.00 .75
❑ 5T Brady Anderson XRC .75 .30
❑ 6T Jack Armstrong XRC .50 .20
❑ 7T Don August .10 .02
❑ 8T Floyd Bannister .10 .02
❑ 9T Bret Barberie OLY XRC .25 .08
❑ 10T Jose Bautista XRC .25 .08
❑ 11T Don Baylor .20 .07
❑ 12T Tim Belcher .10 .02
❑ 13T Buddy Bell .20 .07
❑ 14T Andy Benes OLY XRC .75 .30
❑ 15T Damon Berryhill XRC* .50 .20
❑ 16T Bud Black .10 .02
❑ 17T Pat Borders XRC .50 .20
❑ 18T Phil Bradley .10 .02
❑ 19T Jeff Branson XRC OLY .50 .20
❑ 20T Tom Brunansky .10 .02
❑ 21T Jay Buhner XRC 1.00 .40
❑ 22T Brett Butler .20 .07
❑ 23T Jim Campanis OLY XRC .10 .02
❑ 24T Sil Campusano .10 .02
❑ 25T John Candelaria .10 .02
❑ 26T Jose Cecena .10 .02
❑ 27T Rick Cerone .10 .02
❑ 28T Jack Clark .20 .07
❑ 29T Kevin Coffman .10 .02
❑ 30T Pat Combs OLY XRC .25 .08
❑ 31T Henry Cotto .10 .02
❑ 32T Chili Davis .20 .07
❑ 33T Mike Davis .10 .02
❑ 34T Jose DeLeon .10 .02
❑ 35T Richard Dotson .10 .02
❑ 36T Cecil Espy XRC .10 .02
❑ 37T Tom Filer .10 .02
❑ 38T Mike Fiore OLY .10 .02
❑ 39T Ron Gant XRC .75 .30
❑ 40T Kirk Gibson .50 .20
❑ 41T Rich Gossage .20 .07
❑ 42T Mark Grace XRC 2.00 .75
❑ 43T Alfredo Griffin .10 .02
❑ 44T Ty Griffin OLY .10 .02
❑ 45T Bryan Harvey XRC .50 .20
❑ 46T Ron Hassey .10 .02
❑ 47T Ray Hayward .10 .02
❑ 48T Dave Henderson .10 .02
❑ 49T Tom Herr .10 .02
❑ 50T Bob Horner .20 .07
❑ 51T Ricky Horton .10 .02
❑ 52T Jay Howell .10 .02
❑ 53T Glenn Hubbard .10 .02
❑ 54T Jeff Innis .10 .02
❑ 55T Danny Jackson .10 .02
❑ 56T Darrin Jackson XRC .25 .08
❑ 57T Roberto Kelly XRC .50 .20
❑ 58T Ron Kittle .10 .02
❑ 59T Ray Knight .20 .07
❑ 60T Vance Law .10 .02
❑ 61T Jeffrey Leonard .10 .02
❑ 62T Mike Macfarlane XRC .50 .20
❑ 63T Scotti Madison .10 .02
❑ 64T Kirt Manwaring .10 .02
❑ 65T Mark Marquess OLY CO .10 .02
❑ 66T Tino Martinez OLY XRC 3.00 1.25
❑ 67T Billy Masse OLY XRC .25 .08
❑ 68T Jack McDowell XRC .75 .30
❑ 69T Jack McKeon MG .20 .07
❑ 70T Larry McWilliams .10 .02
❑ 71T Mickey Morandini OLY XRC .50 .20
❑ 72T Keith Moreland .10 .02
❑ 73T Mike Morgan .10 .02
❑ 74T Charles Nagy OLY XRC .50 .20
❑ 75T Al Nipper .10 .02
❑ 76T Russ Nixon MG .10 .02

❑ 77T Jesse Orosco .10 .02
❑ 78T Joe Orsulak .10 .02
❑ 79T Dave Palmer .10 .02
❑ 80T Mark Parent .10 .02
❑ 81T Dave Parker .20 .07
❑ 82T Dan Pasqua .10 .02
❑ 83T Melido Perez XRC .50 .20
❑ 84T Steve Peters .10 .02
❑ 85T Dan Petry .10 .02
❑ 86T Gary Pettis .10 .02
❑ 87T Jeff Pico .10 .02
❑ 88T Jim Poole OLY XRC .25 .08
❑ 89T Ted Power .10 .02
❑ 90T Rafael Ramirez .10 .02
❑ 91T Dennis Rasmussen .10 .02
❑ 92T Jose Rijo .20 .07
❑ 93T Ernie Riles .10 .02
❑ 94T Luis Rivera .10 .02
❑ 95T Doug Robbins OLY XRC .25 .08
❑ 96T Frank Robinson MG .30 .10
❑ 97T Cookie Rojas MG .10 .02
❑ 98T Chris Sabo XRC .75 .30
❑ 99T Mark Salas .10 .02
❑ 100T Luis Salazar .10 .02
❑ 101T Rafael Santana .10 .02
❑ 102T Nelson Santovenia .10 .02
❑ 103T Mackey Sasser XRC .50 .20
❑ 104T Calvin Schiraldi .10 .02
❑ 105T Mike Schooler .10 .02
❑ 106T Scott Servais OLY XRC .50 .20
❑ 107T Dave Silvestri OLY XRC .25 .08
❑ 108T Don Slaught .10 .02
❑ 109T Joe Slusarski OLY XRC .25 .08
❑ 110T Lee Smith .20 .07
❑ 111T Pete Smith XRC .25 .08
❑ 112T Jim Snyder MG .10 .02
❑ 113T Ed Sprague OLY XRC .50 .20
❑ 114T Pete Stanicek .10 .02
❑ 115T Kurt Stillwell .10 .02
❑ 116T Todd Stottlemyre XRC .50 .20
❑ 117T Bill Swift .10 .02
❑ 118T Pat Tabler .10 .02
❑ 119T Scott Terry .10 .02
❑ 120T Mickey Tettleton .10 .02
❑ 121T Dickie Thon .10 .02
❑ 122T Jeff Treadway XRC .50 .20
❑ 123T Willie Upshaw .10 .02
❑ 124T Robin Ventura OLY XRC 1.50 .60
❑ 125T Ron Washington .10 .02
❑ 126T Walt Weiss XRC .75 .30
❑ 127T Bob Welch .20 .07
❑ 128T David Wells XRC 1.50 .60
❑ 129T Glenn Wilson .10 .02
❑ 130T Ted Wood OLY XRC .25 .08
❑ 131T Don Zimmer MG .20 .07
❑ 132T Checklist 1T-132T .10 .02

1989 Topps

❑ COMPLETE SET (792) 20.00 8.00
❑ COMP.FACT SET (792) 25.00 10.00
❑ COMP.X-MAS.SET (792) 25.00 10.00
❑ FS SUBSET VARIATIONS EXIST
❑ FS PHOTOS ARE PLACED HIGHER/LOWER
❑ 1 George Bell RB .05 .01
❑ 2 Wade Boggs RB .10 .02
❑ 3 Gary Carter RB .05 .01
❑ 4 Andre Dawson RB .05 .01
❑ 5 Orel Hershiser RB .05 .01
❑ 6 Doug Jones RB UER .05 .01
❑ 7 Kevin McReynolds RB .05 .01
❑ 8 Dave Eiland .05 .01
❑ 9 Tim Teufel .05 .01
❑ 10 Andre Dawson .10 .02
❑ 11 Bruce Sutter .10 .02
❑ 12 Dale Sveum .05 .01
❑ 13 Doug Sisk .05 .01
❑ 14 Tom Kelly MG .05 .01
❑ 15 Robby Thompson .05 .01
❑ 16 Ron Robinson .05 .01
❑ 17 Brian Downing .10 .02
❑ 18 Rick Rhoden .05 .01
❑ 19 Greg Gagne .05 .01
❑ 20 Steve Bedrosian .05 .01
❑ 21 Greg Walker TL .05 .01
❑ 22 Tim Crews .05 .01
❑ 23 Mike Fitzgerald .05 .01
❑ 24 Larry Andersen .05 .01
❑ 25 Frank White .10 .02
❑ 26 Dale Mohorcic .05 .01
❑ 27A Orestes Destrade RC * .10 .02
❑ 27B Orestes Destrade VAR .10 .02
❑ 28 Mike Moore .05 .01
❑ 29 Kelly Gruber .05 .01
❑ 30 Dwight Gooden .10 .02
❑ 31 Terry Francona .10 .02
❑ 32 Dennis Rasmussen .05 .01
❑ 33 B.J. Surhoff .10 .02
❑ 34 Ken Williams .05 .01
❑ 35 John Tudor UER
(With Red Sox in '84,should be Pir .10 .02
❑ 36 Mitch Webster .05 .01
❑ 37 Bob Stanley .05 .01
❑ 38 Paul Runge .05 .01
❑ 39 Mike Maddux .05 .01
❑ 40 Steve Sax .05 .01
❑ 41 Terry Mulholland .05 .01
❑ 42 Jim Eppard .05 .01
❑ 43 Guillermo Hernandez .05 .01
❑ 44 Jim Snyder MG .05 .01
❑ 45 Kal Daniels .05 .01
❑ 46 Mark Portugal .05 .01
❑ 47 Carney Lansford .10 .02
❑ 48 Tim Burke .05 .01
❑ 49 Craig Biggio RC 3.00 1.25
❑ 50 George Bell .10 .02
❑ 51 Mark McLemore TL .05 .01
❑ 52 Bob Brenly .05 .01
❑ 53 Ruben Sierra .10 .02
❑ 54 Steve Trout .05 .01
❑ 55 Julio Franco .10 .02
❑ 56 Pat Tabler .05 .01
❑ 57 Alejandro Pena .05 .01
❑ 58 Lee Mazzilli .10 .02
❑ 59 Mark Davis .05 .01
❑ 60 Tom Brunansky .05 .01
❑ 61 Neil Allen .05 .01
❑ 62 Alfredo Griffin .05 .01
❑ 63 Mark Clear .05 .01
❑ 64 Alex Trevino .05 .01
❑ 65 Rick Reuschel .10 .02
❑ 66 Manny Trillo .05 .01
❑ 67 Dave Palmer .05 .01
❑ 68 Darrell Miller .05 .01
❑ 69 Jeff Ballard .05 .01
❑ 70 Mark McGwire 1.00 .40
❑ 71 Mike Boddicker .05 .01
❑ 72 John Moses .05 .01
❑ 73 Pascual Perez .05 .01
❑ 74 Nick Leyva MG .05 .01
❑ 75 Tom Henke .05 .01
❑ 76 Terry Blocker .05 .01
❑ 77 Doyle Alexander .05 .01
❑ 78 Jim Sundberg .10 .02
❑ 79 Scott Bankhead .05 .01
❑ 80 Cory Snyder .05 .01
❑ 81 Tim Raines TL .05 .01
❑ 82 Dave Leiper .05 .01
❑ 83 Jeff Blauser .05 .01
❑ 84 Bill Bene FDP .05 .01
❑ 85 Kevin McReynolds .05 .01
❑ 86 Al Nipper .05 .01
❑ 87 Larry Owen .05 .01
❑ 88 Darryl Hamilton RC * .25 .08
❑ 89 Dave LaPoint .05 .01
❑ 90 Vince Coleman UER
(Wrong birth year) .05 .01
❑ 91 Floyd Youmans .05 .01
❑ 92 Jeff Kunkel .05 .01
❑ 93 Ken Howell .05 .01
❑ 94 Chris Speier .05 .01
❑ 95 Gerald Young .05 .01
❑ 96 Rick Cerone .05 .01
❑ 97 Greg Mathews .05 .01
❑ 98 Larry Sheets .05 .01
❑ 99 Sherman Corbett .05 .01
❑ 100 Mike Schmidt .50 .20
❑ 101 Les Straker .05 .01
❑ 102 Mike Gallego .05 .01
❑ 103 Tim Birtsas .05 .01
❑ 104 Dallas Green MG .05 .01
❑ 105 Ron Darling .10 .02
❑ 106 Willie Upshaw .05 .01
❑ 107 Jose DeLeon .05 .01
❑ 108 Fred Manrique .05 .01
❑ 109 Hipolito Pena .05 .01
❑ 110 Paul Molitor .10 .02
❑ 111 Eric Davis TL .05 .01
❑ 112 Jim Presley .05 .01
❑ 113 Lloyd Moseby .05 .01
❑ 114 Bob Kipper .05 .01
❑ 115 Jody Davis .05 .01
❑ 116 Jeff Montgomery .05 .01
❑ 117 Dave Anderson .05 .01
❑ 118 Checklist 1-132 .05 .01
❑ 119 Terry Puhl .05 .01
❑ 120 Frank Viola .10 .02
❑ 121 Garry Templeton .10 .02
❑ 122 Lance Johnson .05 .01
❑ 123 Spike Owen .05 .01
❑ 124 Jim Traber .05 .01
❑ 125 Mike Krukow .05 .01
❑ 126 Sid Bream .05 .01
❑ 127 Walt Terrell .05 .01
❑ 128 Milt Thompson .05 .01
❑ 129 Terry Clark .05 .01
❑ 130 Gerald Perry .05 .01
❑ 131 Dave Otto .05 .01
❑ 132 Curt Ford .05 .01
❑ 133 Bill Long .05 .01
❑ 134 Don Zimmer MG .10 .02
❑ 135 Jose Rijo .10 .02
❑ 136 Joey Meyer .05 .01
❑ 137 Geno Petralli .05 .01
❑ 138 Wallace Johnson .05 .01
❑ 139 Mike Flanagan .05 .01
❑ 140 Shawon Dunston .05 .01
❑ 141 Brook Jacoby TL .05 .01
❑ 142 Mike Diaz .05 .01
❑ 143 Mike Campbell .05 .01
❑ 144 Jay Bell .10 .02
❑ 145 Dave Stewart .10 .02
❑ 146 Gary Pettis .05 .01
❑ 147 DeWayne Buice .05 .01
❑ 148 Bill Pecota .05 .01
❑ 149 Doug Dascenzo .05 .01
❑ 150 Fernando Valenzuela .10 .02
❑ 151 Terry McGriff .05 .01
❑ 152 Mark Thurmond .05 .01
❑ 153 Jim Pankovits .05 .01
❑ 154 Don Carman .05 .01
❑ 155 Marty Barrett .05 .01
❑ 156 Dave Gallagher .05 .01
❑ 157 Tom Glavine .25 .08
❑ 158 Mike Aldrete .05 .01
❑ 159 Pat Clements .05 .01
❑ 160 Jeffrey Leonard .05 .01
❑ 161 Gregg Olson UER RC .25 .08
❑ 162 John Davis .05 .01
❑ 163 Bob Forsch .05 .01
❑ 164 Hal Lanier MG .05 .01
❑ 165 Mike Dunne .05 .01
❑ 166 Doug Jennings .05 .01
❑ 167 Steve Searcy FS .05 .01
❑ 168 Willie Wilson .10 .02
❑ 169 Mike Jackson .05 .01
❑ 170 Tony Fernandez .05 .01
❑ 171 Andres Thomas TL .05 .01
❑ 172 Frank Williams .05 .01
❑ 173 Mel Hall .05 .01
❑ 174 Todd Burns .05 .01
❑ 175 John Shelby .05 .01

❑ 176 Jeff Parrett .05 .01
❑ 177 Monty Fariss FDP .05 .01
❑ 178 Mark Grant .05 .01
❑ 179 Ozzie Virgil .05 .01
❑ 180 Mike Scott .10 .02
❑ 181 Craig Worthington .05 .01
❑ 182 Bob McClure .05 .01
❑ 183 Oddibe McDowell .05 .01
❑ 184 John Costello .05 .01
❑ 185 Claudell Washington .05 .01
❑ 186 Pat Perry .05 .01
❑ 187 Darren Daulton .10 .02
❑ 188 Dennis Lamp .05 .01
❑ 189 Kevin Mitchell .10 .02
❑ 190 Mike Witt .05 .01
❑ 191 Sil Campusano .05 .01
❑ 192 Paul Mirabella .05 .01
❑ 193 Sparky Anderson MG (Team checklist back) UER (55 .10 .02
❑ 194 Greg W.Harris RC .10 .02
❑ 195 Ozzie Guillen .10 .02
❑ 196 Denny Walling .05 .01
❑ 197 Neal Heaton .05 .01
❑ 198 Danny Heep .05 .01
❑ 199 Mike Schooler RC * .10 .02
❑ 200 George Brett .60 .25
❑ 201 Kelly Gruber TL .05 .01
❑ 202 Brad Moore .05 .01
❑ 203 Rob Ducey .05 .01
❑ 204 Brad Havens .05 .01
❑ 205 Dwight Evans .15 .05
❑ 206 Roberto Alomar .25 .08
❑ 207 Terry Leach .05 .01
❑ 208 Tom Pagnozzi .05 .01
❑ 209 Jeff Bittiger .05 .01
❑ 210 Dale Murphy .15 .05
❑ 211 Mike Pagliarulo .05 .01
❑ 212 Scott Sanderson .05 .01
❑ 213 Rene Gonzales .05 .01
❑ 214 Charlie O'Brien .05 .01
❑ 215 Kevin Gross .05 .01
❑ 216 Jack Howell .05 .01
❑ 217 Joe Price .05 .01
❑ 218 Mike LaValliere .05 .01
❑ 219 Jim Clancy .05 .01
❑ 220 Gary Gaetti .10 .02
❑ 221 Cecil Espy .05 .01
❑ 222 Mark Lewis RC .25 .08
❑ 223 Jay Buhner .10 .02
❑ 224 Tony LaRussa MG .10 .02
❑ 225 Ramon Martinez RC .25 .08
❑ 226 Bill Doran .05 .01
❑ 227 John Farrell .05 .01
❑ 228 Nelson Santovenia .05 .01
❑ 229 Jimmy Key .10 .02
❑ 230 Ozzie Smith .40 .15
❑ 231 Padres TL/R.Alomar .25 .08
❑ 232 Ricky Horton .05 .01
❑ 233 Gregg Jefferies .05 .01
❑ 234 Tom Browning .05 .01
❑ 235 John Kruk .10 .02
❑ 236 Charles Hudson .05 .01
❑ 237 Glenn Hubbard .05 .01
❑ 238 Eric King .05 .01
❑ 239 Tim Laudner .05 .01
❑ 240 Greg Maddux .50 .20
❑ 241 Brett Butler .10 .02
❑ 242 Ed VandeBerg .05 .01
❑ 243 Bob Boone .10 .02
❑ 244 Jim Acker .05 .01
❑ 245 Jim Rice .10 .02
❑ 246 Rey Quinones .05 .01
❑ 247 Shawn Hillegas .05 .01
❑ 248 Tony Phillips .05 .01
❑ 249 Tim Leary .05 .01
❑ 250 Cal Ripken .75 .30
❑ 251 John Dopson .05 .01
❑ 252 Billy Hatcher .05 .01
❑ 253 Jose Alvarez RC .10 .02
❑ 254 Tom Lasorda MG .15 .05
❑ 255 Ron Guidry .10 .02
❑ 256 Benny Santiago .10 .02
❑ 257 Rick Aguilera .05 .01
❑ 258 Checklist 133-264 .05 .01
❑ 259 Larry McWilliams .05 .01
❑ 260 Dave Winfield .10 .02
❑ 261 St.Louis Cardinals TL Tom Brunansky (With Luis A .05 .01
❑ 262 Jeff Pico .05 .01
❑ 263 Mike Felder .05 .01
❑ 264 Rob Dibble RC .40 .15
❑ 265 Kent Hrbek .10 .02
❑ 266 Luis Aquino .05 .01
❑ 267 Jeff M. Robinson .05 .01
❑ 268 Keith Miller RC .25 .08
❑ 269 Tom Bolton .05 .01
❑ 270 Wally Joyner .10 .02
❑ 271 Jay Tibbs .05 .01
❑ 272 Ron Hassey .05 .01
❑ 273 Jose Lind .05 .01
❑ 274 Mark Eichhorn .05 .01
❑ 275 Danny Tartabull UER (Born San Juan, PR should be .05 .01
❑ 276 Paul Kilgus .05 .01
❑ 277 Mike Davis .05 .01
❑ 278 Andy McGaffigan .05 .01
❑ 279 Scott Bradley .05 .01
❑ 280 Bob Knepper .05 .01
❑ 281 Gary Redus .05 .01
❑ 282 Cris Carpenter RC * .10 .02
❑ 283 Andy Allanson .05 .01
❑ 284 Jim Leyland MG .10 .02
❑ 285 John Candelaria .05 .01
❑ 286 Darrin Jackson .10 .02
❑ 287 Juan Nieves .05 .01
❑ 288 Pat Sheridan .05 .01
❑ 289 Ernie Whitt .05 .01
❑ 290 John Franco .10 .02
❑ 291 New York Mets TL Darryl Strawberry (With Keith H .05 .01
❑ 292 Jim Corsi .05 .01
❑ 293 Glenn Wilson .05 .01
❑ 294 Juan Berenguer .05 .01
❑ 295 Scott Fletcher .05 .01
❑ 296 Ron Gant .10 .02
❑ 297 Oswald Peraza .05 .01
❑ 298 Chris James .05 .01
❑ 299 Steve Ellsworth .05 .01
❑ 300 Darryl Strawberry .10 .02
❑ 301 Charlie Leibrandt .05 .01
❑ 302 Gary Ward .05 .01
❑ 303 Felix Fermin .05 .01
❑ 304 Joel Youngblood .05 .01
❑ 305 Dave Smith .05 .01
❑ 306 Tracy Woodson .05 .01
❑ 307 Lance McCullers .05 .01
❑ 308 Ron Karkovice .05 .01
❑ 309 Mario Diaz .05 .01
❑ 310 Rafael Palmeiro .25 .08
❑ 311 Chris Bosio .05 .01
❑ 312 Tom Lawless .05 .01
❑ 313 Dennis Martinez .10 .02
❑ 314 Bobby Valentine MG .10 .02
❑ 315 Greg Swindell .05 .01
❑ 316 Walt Weiss .05 .01
❑ 317 Jack Armstrong RC * .25 .08
❑ 318 Gene Larkin .05 .01
❑ 319 Greg Booker .05 .01
❑ 320 Lou Whitaker .10 .02
❑ 321 Jody Reed TL .05 .01
❑ 322 John Smiley .05 .01
❑ 323 Gary Thurman .05 .01
❑ 324 Bob Milacki .05 .01
❑ 325 Jesse Barfield .10 .02
❑ 326 Dennis Boyd .05 .01
❑ 327 Mark Lemke RC .40 .15
❑ 328 Rick Honeycutt .05 .01
❑ 329 Bob Melvin .05 .01
❑ 330 Eric Davis .10 .02
❑ 331 Curt Wilkerson .05 .01
❑ 332 Tony Armas .10 .02
❑ 333 Bob Ojeda .05 .01
❑ 334 Steve Lyons .05 .01
❑ 335 Dave Righetti .10 .02
❑ 336 Steve Balboni .05 .01
❑ 337 Calvin Schiraldi .05 .01
❑ 338 Jim Adduci .05 .01
❑ 339 Scott Bailes .05 .01
❑ 340 Kirk Gibson .10 .02
❑ 341 Jim Deshaies .05 .01
❑ 342 Tom Brookens .05 .01
❑ 343 Gary Sheffield RC 1.50 .60
❑ 344 Tom Trebelhorn MG .05 .01
❑ 345 Charlie Hough .10 .02
❑ 346 Rex Hudler .05 .01
❑ 347 John Cerutti .05 .01
❑ 348 Ed Hearn .05 .01
❑ 349 Ron Jones .10 .02
❑ 350 Andy Van Slyke .15 .05
❑ 351 San Fran. Giants TL Bob Melvin (With Bill Fahey .05 .01
❑ 352 Rick Schu .05 .01
❑ 353 Marvell Wynne .05 .01
❑ 354 Larry Parrish .05 .01
❑ 355 Mark Langston .05 .01
❑ 356 Kevin Elster .05 .01
❑ 357 Jerry Reuss .05 .01
❑ 358 Ricky Jordan RC * .25 .08
❑ 359 Tommy John .10 .02
❑ 360 Ryne Sandberg .40 .15
❑ 361 Kelly Downs .05 .01
❑ 362 Jack Lazorko .05 .01
❑ 363 Rich Yett .05 .01
❑ 364 Rob Deer .05 .01
❑ 365 Mike Henneman .05 .01
❑ 366 Herm Winningham .05 .01
❑ 367 Johnny Paredes .05 .01
❑ 368 Brian Holton .05 .01
❑ 369 Ken Caminiti .15 .05
❑ 370 Dennis Eckersley .15 .05
❑ 371 Manny Lee .05 .01
❑ 372 Craig Lefferts .05 .01
❑ 373 Tracy Jones .05 .01
❑ 374 John Wathan MG .05 .01
❑ 375 Terry Pendleton .10 .02
❑ 376 Steve Lombardozzi .05 .01
❑ 377 Mike Smithson .05 .01
❑ 378 Checklist 265-396 .05 .01
❑ 379 Tim Flannery .05 .01
❑ 380 Rickey Henderson .25 .08
❑ 381 Larry Sheets TL .05 .01
❑ 382 John Smoltz RC 1.50 .60
❑ 383 Howard Johnson .10 .02
❑ 384 Mark Salas .05 .01
❑ 385 Von Hayes .05 .01
❑ 386 Andres Galarraga AS .05 .01
❑ 387 Ryne Sandberg AS .25 .08
❑ 388 Bobby Bonilla AS .05 .01
❑ 389 Ozzie Smith AS .25 .08
❑ 390 Darryl Strawberry AS .05 .01
❑ 391 Andre Dawson AS .05 .01
❑ 392 Andy Van Slyke AS .10 .02
❑ 393 Gary Carter AS .05 .01
❑ 394 Orel Hershiser AS .05 .01
❑ 395 Danny Jackson AS .05 .01
❑ 396 Kirk Gibson AS .10 .02
❑ 397 Don Mattingly AS .30 .10
❑ 398 Julio Franco AS .05 .01
❑ 399 Wade Boggs AS .10 .02
❑ 400 Alan Trammell AS .05 .01
❑ 401 Jose Canseco AS .15 .05
❑ 402 Mike Greenwell AS .05 .01
❑ 403 Kirby Puckett AS .15 .05
❑ 404 Bob Boone AS .05 .01
❑ 405 Roger Clemens AS .50 .20
❑ 406 Frank Viola AS .05 .01
❑ 407 Dave Winfield AS .05 .01
❑ 408 Greg Walker .05 .01
❑ 409 Ken Dayley .05 .01
❑ 410 Jack Clark .10 .02
❑ 411 Mitch Williams .05 .01
❑ 412 Barry Lyons .05 .01
❑ 413 Mike Kingery .05 .01
❑ 414 Jim Fregosi MG .05 .01
❑ 415 Rich Gossage .10 .02
❑ 416 Fred Lynn .10 .02
❑ 417 Mike LaCoss .05 .01
❑ 418 Bob Dernier .05 .01
❑ 419 Tom Filer .05 .01
❑ 420 Joe Carter .10 .02
❑ 421 Kirk McCaskill .05 .01
❑ 422 Bo Diaz .05 .01
❑ 423 Brian Fisher .05 .01

❑ 424 Luis Polonia UER (Wrong birthdate) .05 .01
❑ 425 Jay Howell .05 .01
❑ 426 Dan Gladden .05 .01
❑ 427 Eric Show .05 .01
❑ 428 Craig Reynolds .05 .01
❑ 429 Minnesota Twins TL Greg Gagne (Taking throw at 2 .05 .01
❑ 430 Mark Gubicza .05 .01
❑ 431 Luis Rivera .05 .01
❑ 432 Chad Kreuter RC .25 .08
❑ 433 Albert Hall .05 .01
❑ 434 Ken Patterson .05 .01
❑ 435 Len Dykstra .10 .02
❑ 436 Bobby Meacham .05 .01
❑ 437 Andy Benes RC * .40 .15
❑ 438 Greg Gross .05 .01
❑ 439 Frank DiPino .05 .01
❑ 440 Bobby Bonilla .10 .02
❑ 441 Jerry Reed .05 .01
❑ 442 Jose Oquendo .05 .01
❑ 443 Rod Nichols .05 .01
❑ 444 Moose Stubing MG .05 .01
❑ 445 Matt Nokes .05 .01
❑ 446 Rob Murphy .05 .01
❑ 447 Donell Nixon .05 .01
❑ 448 Eric Plunk .05 .01
❑ 449 Carmelo Martinez .05 .01
❑ 450 Roger Clemens 1.00 .40
❑ 451 Mark Davidson .05 .01
❑ 452 Israel Sanchez .05 .01
❑ 453 Tom Prince .05 .01
❑ 454 Paul Assenmacher .05 .01
❑ 455 Johnny Ray .05 .01
❑ 456 Tim Belcher .05 .01
❑ 457 Mackey Sasser .05 .01
❑ 458 Donn Pall .05 .01
❑ 459 Dave Valle TL .05 .01
❑ 460 Dave Stieb .10 .02
❑ 461 Buddy Bell .10 .02
❑ 462 Jose Guzman .05 .01
❑ 463 Steve Lake .05 .01
❑ 464 Bryn Smith .05 .01
❑ 465 Mark Grace .25 .08
❑ 466 Chuck Crim .05 .01
❑ 467 Jim Walewander .05 .01
❑ 468 Henry Cotto .05 .01
❑ 469 Jose Bautista RC .10 .02
❑ 470 Lance Parrish .10 .02
❑ 471 Steve Curry .05 .01
❑ 472 Brian Harper .05 .01
❑ 473 Don Robinson .05 .01
❑ 474 Bob Rodgers MG .05 .01
❑ 475 Dave Parker .10 .02
❑ 476 Jon Perlman .05 .01
❑ 477 Dick Schofield .05 .01
❑ 478 Doug Drabek .05 .01
❑ 479 Mike Macfarlane RC * .25 .08
❑ 480 Keith Hernandez .10 .02
❑ 481 Chris Brown .05 .01
❑ 482 Steve Peters .05 .01
❑ 483 Mickey Hatcher .05 .01
❑ 484 Steve Shields .05 .01
❑ 485 Hubie Brooks .05 .01
❑ 486 Jack McDowell .10 .02
❑ 487 Scott Lusader .05 .01
❑ 488 Kevin Coffman (%%Now with Cubs~) .05 .01
❑ 489 Phillies TL/M.Schmidt .15 .05
❑ 490 Chris Sabo RC * .40 .15
❑ 491 Mike Birkbeck .05 .01
❑ 492 Alan Ashby .05 .01
❑ 493 Todd Benzinger .05 .01
❑ 494 Shane Rawley .05 .01
❑ 495 Candy Maldonado .05 .01
❑ 496 Dwayne Henry .05 .01
❑ 497 Pete Stanicek .05 .01
❑ 498 Dave Valle .05 .01
❑ 499 Don Heinkel .05 .01
❑ 500 Jose Canseco .25 .08
❑ 501 Vance Law .05 .01
❑ 502 Duane Ward .05 .01
❑ 503 Al Newman .05 .01
❑ 504 Bob Walk .05 .01
❑ 505 Pete Rose MG/TC .50 .20
❑ 506 Kirt Manwaring .05 .01
❑ 507 Steve Farr .05 .01
❑ 508 Wally Backman .05 .01
❑ 509 Bud Black .05 .01
❑ 510 Bob Horner .10 .02
❑ 511 Richard Dotson .05 .01
❑ 512 Donnie Hill .05 .01
❑ 513 Jesse Orosco .05 .01
❑ 514 Chet Lemon .10 .02
❑ 515 Barry Larkin .15 .05
❑ 516 Eddie Whitson .05 .01
❑ 517 Greg Brock .05 .01
❑ 518 Bruce Ruffin .05 .01
❑ 519 Willie Randolph TL .05 .01
❑ 520 Rick Sutcliffe .10 .02
❑ 521 Mickey Tettleton .05 .01
❑ 522 Randy Kramer .05 .01
❑ 523 Andres Thomas .05 .01
❑ 524 Checklist 397-528 .05 .01
❑ 525 Chili Davis .10 .02
❑ 526 Wes Gardner .05 .01
❑ 527 Dave Henderson .05 .01
❑ 528 Luis Medina (Lower left front has white triangle .05 .01
❑ 529 Tom Foley .05 .01
❑ 530 Nolan Ryan 1.00 .40
❑ 531 Dave Hengel .05 .01
❑ 532 Jerry Browne .05 .01
❑ 533 Andy Hawkins .05 .01
❑ 534 Doc Edwards MG .05 .01
❑ 535 Todd Worrell UER (4 wins in '88, should be 5) .05 .01
❑ 536 Joel Skinner .05 .01
❑ 537 Pete Smith .05 .01
❑ 538 Juan Castillo .05 .01
❑ 539 Barry Jones .05 .01
❑ 540 Bo Jackson .25 .08
❑ 541 Cecil Fielder .10 .02
❑ 542 Todd Frohwirth .05 .01
❑ 543 Damon Berryhill .05 .01
❑ 544 Jeff Sellers .05 .01
❑ 545 Mookie Wilson .10 .02
❑ 546 Mark Williamson .05 .01
❑ 547 Mark McLemore .05 .01
❑ 548 Bobby Witt .05 .01
❑ 549 Jamie Moyer TL .05 .01
❑ 550 Orel Hershiser .10 .02
❑ 551 Randy Ready .05 .01
❑ 552 Greg Cadaret .05 .01
❑ 553 Luis Salazar .05 .01
❑ 554 Nick Esasky .05 .01
❑ 555 Bert Blyleven .10 .02
❑ 556 Bruce Fields .05 .01
❑ 557 Keith A. Miller .05 .01
❑ 558 Dan Pasqua .05 .01
❑ 559 Juan Agosto .05 .01
❑ 560 Tim Raines .10 .02
❑ 561 Luis Aguayo .05 .01
❑ 562 Danny Cox .05 .01
❑ 563 Bill Schroeder .05 .01
❑ 564 Russ Nixon MG .05 .01
❑ 565 Jeff Russell .05 .01
❑ 566 Al Pedrique .05 .01
❑ 567 David Wells UER .10 .02
❑ 568 Mickey Brantley .05 .01
❑ 569 German Jimenez .05 .01
❑ 570 Tony Gwynn .30 .10
❑ 571 Billy Ripken .05 .01
❑ 572 Atlee Hammaker .05 .01
❑ 573 Jim Abbott RC 1.00 .40
❑ 574 Dave Clark .05 .01
❑ 575 Juan Samuel .05 .01
❑ 576 Greg Minton .05 .01
❑ 577 Randy Bush .05 .01
❑ 578 John Morris .05 .01
❑ 579 Glenn Davis TL .05 .01
❑ 580 Harold Reynolds .10 .02
❑ 581 Gene Nelson .05 .01
❑ 582 Mike Marshall .05 .01
❑ 583 Paul Gibson .05 .01
❑ 584 Randy Velarde UER (Signed 1935, should be 1985) .05 .01
❑ 585 Harold Baines .10 .02
❑ 586 Joe Boever .05 .01
❑ 587 Mike Stanley .05 .01
❑ 588 Luis Alicea RC * .25 .08
❑ 589 Dave Meads .05 .01
❑ 590 Andres Galarraga .10 .02
❑ 591 Jeff Musselman .05 .01
❑ 592 John Cangelosi .05 .01
❑ 593 Drew Hall .05 .01
❑ 594 Jimy Williams MG .05 .01
❑ 595 Teddy Higuera .05 .01
❑ 596 Kurt Stillwell .05 .01
❑ 597 Terry Taylor RC .10 .02
❑ 598 Ken Gerhart .05 .01
❑ 599 Tom Candiotti .05 .01
❑ 600 Wade Boggs .15 .05
❑ 601 Dave Dravecky .05 .01
❑ 602 Devon White .10 .02
❑ 603 Frank Tanana .10 .02
❑ 604 Paul O'Neill .15 .05
❑ 605A Bob Welch ML Line ERR 10.00 4.00
❑ 605B Bob Welch COR .10 .02
❑ 606 Rick Dempsey .05 .01
❑ 607 Willie Ansley RC .10 .02
❑ 608 Phil Bradley .05 .01
❑ 609 Detroit Tigers TL Frank Tanana (With Alan Tramme .05 .01
❑ 610 Randy Myers .10 .02
❑ 611 Don Slaught .05 .01
❑ 612 Dan Quisenberry .05 .01
❑ 613 Gary Varsho .05 .01
❑ 614 Joe Hesketh .05 .01
❑ 615 Robin Yount .40 .15
❑ 616 Steve Rosenberg .05 .01
❑ 617 Mark Parent .05 .01
❑ 618 Rance Mulliniks .05 .01
❑ 619 Checklist 529-660 .05 .01
❑ 620 Barry Bonds 1.50 .60
❑ 621 Rick Mahler .05 .01
❑ 622 Stan Javier .05 .01
❑ 623 Fred Toliver .05 .01
❑ 624 Jack McKeon MG .10 .02
❑ 625 Eddie Murray .25 .08
❑ 626 Jeff Reed .05 .01
❑ 627 Greg A. Harris .05 .01
❑ 628 Matt Williams .25 .08
❑ 629 Pete O'Brien .05 .01
❑ 630 Mike Greenwell .05 .01
❑ 631 Dave Bergman .05 .01
❑ 632 Bryan Harvey RC * .25 .08
❑ 633 Daryl Boston .05 .01
❑ 634 Marvin Freeman .05 .01
❑ 635 Willie Randolph .10 .02
❑ 636 Bill Wilkinson .05 .01
❑ 637 Carmen Castillo .05 .01
❑ 638 Floyd Bannister .05 .01
❑ 639 Walt Weiss TL .05 .01
❑ 640 Willie McGee .10 .02
❑ 641 Curt Young .05 .01
❑ 642 Angel Salazar .05 .01
❑ 643 Louie Meadows .05 .01
❑ 644 Lloyd McClendon .05 .01
❑ 645 Jack Morris .10 .02
❑ 646 Kevin Bass .05 .01
❑ 647 Randy Johnson RC 2.00 .75
❑ 648 Sandy Alomar Jr. RC .40 .15
❑ 649 Stu Cliburn .05 .01
❑ 650 Kirby Puckett .25 .08
❑ 651 Tom Niedenfuer .05 .01
❑ 652 Rich Gedman .05 .01
❑ 653 Tommy Barrett .05 .01
❑ 654 Whitey Herzog MG .10 .02
❑ 655 Dave Magadan .05 .01
❑ 656 Ivan Calderon .05 .01
❑ 657 Joe Magrane .05 .01
❑ 658 R.J. Reynolds .05 .01
❑ 659 Al Leiter .25 .08
❑ 660 Will Clark .15 .05
❑ 661 Dwight Gooden TBC 84 .05 .01
❑ 662 Lou Brock TBC .10 .02
❑ 663 Hank Aaron TBC .25 .08
❑ 664 Gil Hodges TBC 69 .10 .02
❑ 665A T.Oliva TBC Copyright ERR
❑ 665B Tony Oliva TBC 64 COR (fabricated card) .10 .02

❑ 666 Randy St.Claire .05 .01
❑ 667 Dwayne Murphy .05 .01
❑ 668 Mike Bielecki .05 .01
❑ 669 L.A. Dodgers TL
Orel Hershiser
(Mound conference .10 .02
❑ 670 Kevin Seitzer .05 .01
❑ 671 Jim Gantner .05 .01
❑ 672 Allan Anderson .05 .01
❑ 673 Don Baylor .10 .02
❑ 674 Otis Nixon .05 .01
❑ 675 Bruce Hurst .05 .01
❑ 676 Ernie Riles .05 .01
❑ 677 Dave Schmidt .05 .01
❑ 678 Dion James .05 .01
❑ 679 Willie Fraser .05 .01
❑ 680 Gary Carter .10 .02
❑ 681 Jeff D. Robinson .05 .01
❑ 682 Rick Leach .05 .01
❑ 683 Jose Cecena .05 .01
❑ 684 Dave Johnson MG .05 .01
❑ 685 Jeff Treadway .05 .01
❑ 686 Scott Terry .05 .01
❑ 687 Alvin Davis .05 .01
❑ 688 Zane Smith .05 .01
❑ 689A Stan Jefferson Pink ERR 10.00 4.00
❑ 689B Stan Jefferson
(Violet triangle on
front bottom .05 .01
❑ 690 Doug Jones .05 .01
❑ 691 Roberto Kelly UER .05 .01
❑ 692 Steve Ontiveros .05 .01
❑ 693 Pat Borders RC * .25 .08
❑ 694 Les Lancaster .05 .01
❑ 695 Carlton Fisk .15 .05
❑ 696 Don August .05 .01
❑ 697A Franklin Stubbs White ERR 10.00 4.00
❑ 697B Franklin Stubbs
(Team name on front
in gray) .05 .01
❑ 698 Keith Atherton .05 .01
❑ 699 Pittsburgh Pirates TL
Al Pedrique
(Tony Gwynn sl .05 .01
❑ 700 Don Mattingly .60 .25
❑ 701 Storm Davis .05 .01
❑ 702 Jamie Quirk .05 .01
❑ 703 Scott Garrelts .05 .01
❑ 704 Carlos Quintana RC .10 .02
❑ 705 Terry Kennedy .05 .01
❑ 706 Pete Incaviglia .05 .01
❑ 707 Steve Jeltz .05 .01
❑ 708 Chuck Finley .10 .02
❑ 709 Tom Herr .05 .01
❑ 710 David Cone .10 .02
❑ 711 Candy Sierra .05 .01
❑ 712 Bill Swift .05 .01
❑ 713 Ty Griffin FDP .05 .01
❑ 714 Joe Morgan MG .10 .02
❑ 715 Tony Pena .05 .01
❑ 716 Wayne Tolleson .05 .01
❑ 717 Jamie Moyer .10 .02
❑ 718 Glenn Braggs .05 .01
❑ 719 Danny Darwin .05 .01
❑ 720 Tim Wallach .05 .01
❑ 721 Ron Tingley .05 .01
❑ 722 Todd Stottlemyre .05 .01
❑ 723 Rafael Belliard .05 .01
❑ 724 Jerry Don Gleaton .05 .01
❑ 725 Terry Steinbach .10 .02
❑ 726 Dickie Thon .05 .01
❑ 727 Joe Orsulak .05 .01
❑ 728 Charlie Puleo .05 .01
❑ 729 Texas Rangers TL
Steve Buechele
(Inconsistent de .05 .01
❑ 730 Danny Jackson .05 .01
❑ 731 Mike Young .05 .01
❑ 732 Steve Buechele .05 .01
❑ 733 Randy Bockus .05 .01
❑ 734 Jody Reed .05 .01
❑ 735 Roger McDowell .05 .01
❑ 736 Jeff Hamilton .05 .01
❑ 737 Norm Charlton RC .25 .08
❑ 738 Darnell Coles .05 .01
❑ 739 Brook Jacoby .05 .01
❑ 740 Dan Plesac .05 .01
❑ 741 Ken Phelps .05 .01
❑ 742 Mike Harkey RC .10 .02
❑ 743 Mike Heath .05 .01
❑ 744 Roger Craig MG .10 .02
❑ 745 Fred McGriff .15 .05
❑ 746 German Gonzalez UER
(Wrong birthdate) .05 .01
❑ 747 Wil Tejada .05 .01
❑ 748 Jimmy Jones .05 .01
❑ 749 Rafael Ramirez .05 .01
❑ 750 Bret Saberhagen .10 .02
❑ 751 Ken Oberkfell .05 .01
❑ 752 Jim Gott .05 .01
❑ 753 Jose Uribe .05 .01
❑ 754 Bob Brower .05 .01
❑ 755 Mike Scioscia .10 .02
❑ 756 Scott Medvin .05 .01
❑ 757 Brady Anderson RC .40 .15
❑ 758 Gene Walter .05 .01
❑ 759 Milwaukee Brewers TL
Rob Deer .05 .01
❑ 760 Lee Smith .10 .02
❑ 761 Dante Bichette RC .40 .15
❑ 762 Bobby Thigpen .05 .01
❑ 763 Dave Martinez .05 .01
❑ 764 Robin Ventura RC .75 .30
❑ 765 Glenn Davis .05 .01
❑ 766 Cecilio Guante .05 .01
❑ 767 Mike Capel .05 .01
❑ 768 Bill Wegman .05 .01
❑ 769 Junior Ortiz .05 .01
❑ 770 Alan Trammell .10 .02
❑ 771 Ron Kittle .05 .01
❑ 772 Ron Oester .05 .01
❑ 773 Keith Moreland .05 .01
❑ 774 Frank Robinson MG/TC .15 .05
❑ 775 Jeff Reardon .10 .02
❑ 776 Nelson Liriano .05 .01
❑ 777 Ted Power .05 .01
❑ 778 Bruce Benedict .05 .01
❑ 779 Craig McMurtry .05 .01
❑ 780 Pedro Guerrero .10 .02
❑ 781 Greg Briley .10 .02
❑ 782 Checklist 661-792 .05 .01
❑ 783 Trevor Wilson RC .10 .02
❑ 784 Steve Avery RC .25 .08
❑ 785 Ellis Burks .10 .02
❑ 786 Melido Perez .05 .01
❑ 787 Dave West RC .10 .02
❑ 788 Mike Morgan .05 .01
❑ 789 Royals TL/Bo Jackson .25 .08
❑ 790 Sid Fernandez .05 .01
❑ 791 Jim Lindeman .05 .01
❑ 792 Rafael Santana .05 .01

1989 Topps Traded

❑ COMP.FACT.SET (132) 10.00 4.00
❑ 1T Don Aase .05 .01
❑ 2T Jim Abbott .50 .20
❑ 3T Kent Anderson .05 .01
❑ 4T Keith Atherton .05 .01
❑ 5T Wally Backman .05 .01
❑ 6T Steve Balboni .05 .01
❑ 7T Jesse Barfield .10 .02
❑ 8T Steve Bedrosian .05 .01
❑ 9T Todd Benzinger .05 .01
❑ 10T Geronimo Berroa .05 .01
❑ 11T Bert Blyleven .10 .02
❑ 12T Bob Boone .10 .02
❑ 13T Phil Bradley .05 .01
❑ 14T Jeff Brantley RC .25 .08
❑ 15T Kevin Brown .25 .08
❑ 16T Jerry Browne .05 .01
❑ 17T Chuck Cary .05 .01
❑ 18T Carmen Castillo .05 .01
❑ 19T Jim Clancy .05 .01
❑ 20T Jack Clark .10 .02
❑ 21T Bryan Clutterbuck .05 .01
❑ 22T Jody Davis .05 .01
❑ 23T Mike Devereaux .05 .01
❑ 24T Frank DiPino .05 .01
❑ 25T Benny Distefano .05 .01
❑ 26T John Dopson .05 .01
❑ 27T Len Dykstra .10 .02
❑ 28T Jim Eisenreich .05 .01
❑ 29T Nick Esasky .05 .01
❑ 30T Alvaro Espinoza .05 .01
❑ 31T Darrell Evans UER .10 .02
❑ 32T Junior Felix RC .10 .02
❑ 33T Felix Fermin .05 .01
❑ 34T Julio Franco .10 .02
❑ 35T Terry Francona .10 .02
❑ 36T Cito Gaston MG .05 .01
❑ 37T Bob Geren UER RC .05 .01
❑ 38T Tom Gordon RC .50 .20
❑ 39T Tommy Gregg .05 .01
❑ 40T Ken Griffey Sr. .10 .02
❑ 41T Ken Griffey Jr. RC 6.00 2.50
❑ 42T Kevin Gross .05 .01
❑ 43T Lee Guetterman .05 .01
❑ 44T Mel Hall .05 .01
❑ 45T Erik Hanson RC .25 .08
❑ 46T Gene Harris RC .10 .02
❑ 47T Andy Hawkins .05 .01
❑ 48T Rickey Henderson .25 .08
❑ 49T Tom Herr .05 .01
❑ 50T Ken Hill RC .25 .08
❑ 51T Brian Holman RC .10 .02
❑ 52T Brian Holton .05 .01
❑ 53T Art Howe MG .05 .01
❑ 54T Ken Howell .05 .01
❑ 55T Bruce Hurst .05 .01
❑ 56T Chris James .05 .01
❑ 57T Randy Johnson 1.50 .60
❑ 58T Jimmy Jones .05 .01
❑ 59T Terry Kennedy .05 .01
❑ 60T Paul Kilgus .05 .01
❑ 61T Eric King .05 .01
❑ 62T Ron Kittle .05 .01
❑ 63T John Kruk .10 .02
❑ 64T Randy Kutcher .05 .01
❑ 65T Steve Lake .05 .01
❑ 66T Mark Langston .05 .01
❑ 67T Dave LaPoint .05 .01
❑ 68T Rick Leach .05 .01
❑ 69T Terry Leach .05 .01
❑ 70T Jim Lefebvre MG .05 .01
❑ 71T Al Leiter .25 .08
❑ 72T Jeffrey Leonard .05 .01
❑ 73T Derek Lilliquist RC .10 .02
❑ 74T Rick Mahler .05 .01
❑ 75T Tom McCarthy .05 .01
❑ 76T Lloyd McClendon .05 .01
❑ 77T Lance McCullers .05 .01
❑ 78T Oddibe McDowell .05 .01
❑ 79T Roger McDowell .05 .01
❑ 80T Larry McWilliams .05 .01
❑ 81T Randy Milligan .05 .01
❑ 82T Mike Moore .05 .01
❑ 83T Keith Moreland .05 .01
❑ 84T Mike Morgan .05 .01
❑ 85T Jamie Moyer .10 .02
❑ 86T Rob Murphy .05 .01
❑ 87T Eddie Murray .25 .08
❑ 88T Pete O'Brien .05 .01
❑ 89T Gregg Olson .25 .08
❑ 90T Steve Ontiveros .05 .01
❑ 91T Jesse Orosco .05 .01
❑ 92T Spike Owen .05 .01
❑ 93T Rafael Palmeiro .25 .08
❑ 94T Clay Parker .05 .01
❑ 95T Jeff Parrett .05 .01
❑ 96T Lance Parrish .10 .02

❑ 97T Dennis Powell	.05	.01
❑ 98T Rey Quinones	.05	.01
❑ 99T Doug Rader MG	.05	.01
❑ 100T Willie Randolph	.10	.02
❑ 101T Shane Rawley	.05	.01
❑ 102T Randy Ready	.05	.01
❑ 103T Bip Roberts	.05	.01
❑ 104T Kenny Rogers RC	2.00	.75
❑ 105T Ed Romero	.05	.01
❑ 106T Nolan Ryan	1.50	.60
❑ 107T Luis Salazar	.05	.01
❑ 108T Juan Samuel	.05	.01
❑ 109T Alex Sanchez RC	.05	.01
❑ 110T Deion Sanders RC	1.50	.60
❑ 111T Steve Sax	.05	.01
❑ 112T Rick Schu	.05	.01
❑ 113T Dwight Smith RC	.25	.08
❑ 114T Lonnie Smith	.05	.01
❑ 115T Billy Spiers RC	.25	.08
❑ 116T Kent Tekulve	.05	.01
❑ 117T Walt Terrell	.05	.01
❑ 118T Milt Thompson	.05	.01
❑ 119T Dickie Thon	.05	.01
❑ 120T Jeff Torborg MG	.05	.01
❑ 121T Jeff Treadway	.05	.01
❑ 122T Omar Vizquel RC	1.00	.40
❑ 123T Jerome Walton RC	.25	.08
❑ 124T Gary Ward	.05	.01
❑ 125T Claudell Washington	.05	.01
❑ 126T Curt Wilkerson	.05	.01
❑ 127T Eddie Williams	.05	.01
❑ 128T Frank Williams	.05	.01
❑ 129T Ken Williams	.05	.01
❑ 130T Mitch Williams	.05	.01
❑ 131T Steve Wilson RC	.10	.02
❑ 132T Checklist 1T-132T	.05	.01

1990 Topps

❑ COMPLETE SET (792)	20.00	8.00
❑ COMP.FACT.SET (792)	25.00	10.00
❑ COMP.X-MAS.SET (792)	40.00	15.00
❑ 1 Nolan Ryan	1.00	.40
❑ 2 Nolan Ryan Salute New York Mets	.50	.20
❑ 3 Nolan Ryan Salute California Angels	.50	.20
❑ 4 Nolan Ryan Salute Houston Astros	.50	.20
❑ 5 Nolan Ryan Salute Texas Rangers UER (Says Texas	.50	.20
❑ 6 Vince Coleman RB (50 consecutive stolen bases)	.05	.01
❑ 7 Rickey Henderson RB	.15	.05
❑ 8 Cal Ripken RB	.25	.08
❑ 9 Eric Plunk	.05	.01
❑ 10 Barry Larkin	.15	.05
❑ 11 Paul Gibson	.05	.01
❑ 12 Joe Girardi	.15	.05
❑ 13 Mark Williamson	.05	.01
❑ 14 Mike Fetters RC	.25	.08
❑ 15 Teddy Higuera	.05	.01
❑ 16 Kent Anderson	.05	.01
❑ 17 Kelly Downs	.05	.01
❑ 18 Carlos Quintana	.05	.01
❑ 19 Al Newman	.05	.01
❑ 20 Mark Gubicza	.05	.01
❑ 21 Jeff Torborg MG	.05	.01
❑ 22 Bruce Ruffin	.05	.01
❑ 23 Randy Velarde	.05	.01
❑ 24 Joe Hesketh	.05	.01
❑ 25 Willie Randolph	.10	.02
❑ 26 Don Slaught	.05	.01
❑ 27 Rick Leach	.05	.01
❑ 28 Duane Ward	.05	.01
❑ 29 John Cangelosi	.05	.01
❑ 30 David Cone	.10	.02
❑ 31 Henry Cotto	.05	.01
❑ 32 John Farrell	.05	.01
❑ 33 Greg Walker	.05	.01
❑ 34 Tony Fossas RC	.05	.01
❑ 35 Benito Santiago	.10	.02
❑ 36 John Costello	.05	.01
❑ 37 Domingo Ramos	.05	.01
❑ 38 Wes Gardner	.05	.01
❑ 39 Curt Ford	.05	.01
❑ 40 Jay Howell	.05	.01
❑ 41 Matt Williams	.10	.02
❑ 42 Jeff M. Robinson	.05	.01
❑ 43 Dante Bichette	.10	.02
❑ 44 Roger Salkeld FDP RC	.10	.02
❑ 45 Dave Parker UER	.10	.02
❑ 46 Rob Dibble	.10	.02
❑ 47 Brian Harper	.05	.01
❑ 48 Zane Smith	.05	.01
❑ 49 Tom Lawless	.05	.01
❑ 50 Glenn Davis	.05	.01
❑ 51 Doug Rader MG	.05	.01
❑ 52 Jack Daugherty RC	.05	.01
❑ 53 Mike LaCoss	.05	.01
❑ 54 Joel Skinner	.05	.01
❑ 55 Darrell Evans UER (HR total should be 414, not 4	.10	.02
❑ 56 Franklin Stubbs	.05	.01
❑ 57 Greg Vaughn	.05	.01
❑ 58 Keith Miller	.05	.01
❑ 59 Ted Power	.05	.01
❑ 60 George Brett	.60	.25
❑ 61 Deion Sanders	.25	.08
❑ 62 Ramon Martinez	.05	.01
❑ 63 Mike Pagliarulo	.05	.01
❑ 64 Danny Darwin	.05	.01
❑ 65 Devon White	.10	.02
❑ 66 Greg Litton	.05	.01
❑ 67 Scott Sanderson	.05	.01
❑ 68 Dave Henderson	.05	.01
❑ 69 Todd Frohwirth	.05	.01
❑ 70 Mike Greenwell	.05	.01
❑ 71 Allan Anderson	.05	.01
❑ 72 Jeff Huson RC	.10	.02
❑ 73 Bob Milacki	.05	.01
❑ 74 Jeff Jackson FDP RC	.10	.02
❑ 75 Doug Jones	.05	.01
❑ 76 Dave Valle	.05	.01
❑ 77 Dave Bergman	.05	.01
❑ 78 Mike Flanagan	.05	.01
❑ 79 Ron Kittle	.05	.01
❑ 80 Jeff Russell	.05	.01
❑ 81 Bob Rodgers MG	.05	.01
❑ 82 Scott Terry	.05	.01
❑ 83 Hensley Meulens	.05	.01
❑ 84 Ray Searage	.05	.01
❑ 85 Juan Samuel	.05	.01
❑ 86 Paul Kilgus	.05	.01
❑ 87 Rick Luecken RC	.05	.01
❑ 88 Glenn Braggs	.05	.01
❑ 89 Clint Zavaras RC	.05	.01
❑ 90 Jack Clark	.10	.02
❑ 91 Steve Frey RC	.05	.01
❑ 92 Mike Stanley	.05	.01
❑ 93 Shawn Hillegas	.05	.01
❑ 94 Herm Winningham	.05	.01
❑ 95 Todd Worrell	.05	.01
❑ 96 Jody Reed	.05	.01
❑ 97 Curt Schilling	1.00	.40
❑ 98 Jose Gonzalez	.05	.01
❑ 99 Rich Monteleone	.05	.01
❑ 100 Will Clark	.15	.05
❑ 101 Shane Rawley	.05	.01
❑ 102 Stan Javier	.05	.01
❑ 103 Marvin Freeman	.05	.01
❑ 104 Bob Knepper	.05	.01
❑ 105 Randy Myers	.10	.02
❑ 106 Charlie O'Brien	.05	.01
❑ 107 Fred Lynn	.05	.01
❑ 108 Rod Nichols	.05	.01
❑ 109 Roberto Kelly	.05	.01
❑ 110 Tommy Helms MG	.05	.01
❑ 111 Ed Whited RC	.05	.01
❑ 112 Glenn Wilson	.05	.01
❑ 113 Manny Lee	.05	.01
❑ 114 Mike Bielecki	.05	.01
❑ 115 Tony Pena	.05	.01
❑ 116 Floyd Bannister	.05	.01
❑ 117 Mike Sharperson	.05	.01
❑ 118 Erik Hanson	.05	.01
❑ 119 Billy Hatcher	.05	.01
❑ 120 John Franco	.10	.02
❑ 121 Robin Ventura	.25	.08
❑ 122 Shawn Abner	.05	.01
❑ 123 Rich Gedman	.05	.01
❑ 124 Dave Dravecky	.10	.02
❑ 125 Kent Hrbek	.10	.02
❑ 126 Randy Kramer	.05	.01
❑ 127 Mike Devereaux	.05	.01
❑ 128 Checklist 1	.05	.01
❑ 129 Ron Jones	.05	.01
❑ 130 Bert Blyleven	.10	.02
❑ 131 Matt Nokes	.05	.01
❑ 132 Lance Blankenship	.05	.01
❑ 133 Ricky Horton	.05	.01
❑ 134 Earl Cunningham FDP RC	.10	.02
❑ 135 Dave Magadan	.05	.01
❑ 136 Kevin Brown	.10	.02
❑ 137 Marty Pevey RC	.05	.01
❑ 138 Al Leiter	.25	.08
❑ 139 Greg Brock	.05	.01
❑ 140 Andre Dawson	.10	.02
❑ 141 John Hart MG RC	.05	.01
❑ 142 Jeff Wetherby RC	.05	.01
❑ 143 Rafael Belliard	.05	.01
❑ 144 Bud Black	.05	.01
❑ 145 Terry Steinbach	.05	.01
❑ 146 Rob Richie RC	.05	.01
❑ 147 Chuck Finley	.10	.02
❑ 148 Edgar Martinez	.15	.05
❑ 149 Steve Farr	.05	.01
❑ 150 Kirk Gibson	.10	.02
❑ 151 Rick Mahler	.05	.01
❑ 152 Lonnie Smith	.05	.01
❑ 153 Randy Milligan	.05	.01
❑ 154 Mike Maddux	.05	.01
❑ 155 Ellis Burks	.15	.05
❑ 156 Ken Patterson	.05	.01
❑ 157 Craig Biggio	.25	.08
❑ 158 Craig Lefferts	.05	.01
❑ 159 Mike Felder	.05	.01
❑ 160 Dave Righetti	.05	.01
❑ 161 Harold Reynolds	.10	.02
❑ 162 Todd Zeile	.10	.02
❑ 163 Phil Bradley	.05	.01
❑ 164 Jeff Juden FDP RC	.10	.02
❑ 165 Walt Weiss	.05	.01
❑ 166 Bobby Witt	.05	.01
❑ 167 Kevin Appier	.10	.02
❑ 168 Jose Lind	.05	.01
❑ 169 Richard Dotson	.05	.01
❑ 170 George Bell	.05	.01
❑ 171 Russ Nixon MG	.05	.01
❑ 172 Tom Lampkin	.05	.01
❑ 173 Tim Belcher	.05	.01
❑ 174 Jeff Kunkel	.05	.01
❑ 175 Mike Moore	.05	.01
❑ 176 Luis Quinones	.05	.01
❑ 177 Mike Henneman	.05	.01
❑ 178 Chris James	.05	.01
❑ 179 Brian Holton	.05	.01
❑ 180 Tim Raines	.10	.02
❑ 181 Juan Agosto	.05	.01
❑ 182 Mookie Wilson	.10	.02
❑ 183 Steve Lake	.05	.01
❑ 184 Danny Cox	.05	.01
❑ 185 Ruben Sierra	.10	.02
❑ 186 Dave LaPoint	.05	.01
❑ 187 Rick Wrona	.05	.01
❑ 188 Mike Smithson	.05	.01
❑ 189 Dick Schofield	.05	.01
❑ 190 Rick Reuschel	.05	.01

❑ 191 Pat Borders .05 .01
❑ 192 Don August .05 .01
❑ 193 Andy Benes .10 .02
❑ 194 Glenallen Hill .05 .01
❑ 195 Tim Burke .05 .01
❑ 196 Gerald Young .05 .01
❑ 197 Doug Drabek .05 .01
❑ 198 Mike Marshall .05 .01
❑ 199 Sergio Valdez RC .05 .01
❑ 200 Don Mattingly .60 .25
❑ 201 Cito Gaston MG .05 .01
❑ 202 Mike Macfarlane .05 .01
❑ 203 Mike Roesler RC .05 .01
❑ 204 Bob Dernier .05 .01
❑ 205 Mark Davis .05 .01
❑ 206 Nick Esasky .05 .01
❑ 207 Bob Ojeda .05 .01
❑ 208 Brook Jacoby .05 .01
❑ 209 Greg Mathews .05 .01
❑ 210 Ryne Sandberg .40 .15
❑ 211 John Cerutti .05 .01
❑ 212 Joe Orsulak .05 .01
❑ 213 Scott Bankhead .05 .01
❑ 214 Terry Francona .10 .02
❑ 215 Kirk McCaskill .05 .01
❑ 216 Ricky Jordan .05 .01
❑ 217 Don Robinson .05 .01
❑ 218 Wally Backman .05 .01
❑ 219 Donn Pall .05 .01
❑ 220 Barry Bonds 1.00 .40
❑ 221 Gary Mielke RC .05 .01
❑ 222 Kurt Stillwell UER (Graduate misspelled as gradu .05 .01
❑ 223 Tommy Gregg .05 .01
❑ 224 Delino DeShields RC .25 .08
❑ 225 Jim Deshaies .05 .01
❑ 226 Mickey Hatcher .05 .01
❑ 227 Kevin Tapani RC .25 .08
❑ 228 Dave Martinez .05 .01
❑ 229 David Wells .10 .02
❑ 230 Keith Hernandez .10 .02
❑ 231 Jack McKeon MG .05 .01
❑ 232 Darnell Coles .05 .01
❑ 233 Ken Hill .10 .02
❑ 234 Mariano Duncan .05 .01
❑ 235 Jeff Reardon .10 .02
❑ 236 Hal Morris .05 .01
❑ 237 Kevin Ritz RC .05 .01
❑ 238 Felix Jose .05 .01
❑ 239 Eric Show .05 .01
❑ 240 Mark Grace .15 .05
❑ 241 Mike Krukow .05 .01
❑ 242 Fred Manrique .05 .01
❑ 243 Barry Jones .05 .01
❑ 244 Bill Schroeder .05 .01
❑ 245 Roger Clemens 1.00 .40
❑ 246 Jim Eisenreich .05 .01
❑ 247 Jerry Reed .05 .01
❑ 248 Dave Anderson .05 .01
❑ 249 Mike (Texas) Smith RC .05 .01
❑ 250 Jose Canseco .15 .05
❑ 251 Jeff Blauser .05 .01
❑ 252 Otis Nixon .05 .01
❑ 253 Mark Portugal .05 .01
❑ 254 Francisco Cabrera .05 .01
❑ 255 Bobby Thigpen .05 .01
❑ 256 Marvell Wynne .05 .01
❑ 257 Jose DeLeon .05 .01
❑ 258 Barry Lyons .05 .01
❑ 259 Lance McCullers .05 .01
❑ 260 Eric Davis .10 .02
❑ 261 Whitey Herzog MG .10 .02
❑ 262 Checklist 2 .05 .01
❑ 263 Mel Stottlemyre Jr. .05 .01
❑ 264 Bryan Clutterbuck .05 .01
❑ 265 Pete O'Brien .05 .01
❑ 266 German Gonzalez .05 .01
❑ 267 Mark Davidson .05 .01
❑ 268 Rob Murphy .05 .01
❑ 269 Dickie Thon .05 .01
❑ 270 Dave Stewart .10 .02
❑ 271 Chet Lemon .05 .01
❑ 272 Bryan Harvey .05 .01
❑ 273 Bobby Bonilla .10 .02
❑ 274 Mauro Gozzo RC .05 .01
❑ 275 Mickey Tettleton .05 .01
❑ 276 Gary Thurman .05 .01
❑ 277 Lenny Harris .05 .01
❑ 278 Pascual Perez .05 .01
❑ 279 Steve Buechele .05 .01
❑ 280 Lou Whitaker .10 .02
❑ 281 Kevin Bass .05 .01
❑ 282 Derek Lilliquist .05 .01
❑ 283 Albert Belle .25 .08
❑ 284 Mark Gardner RC .10 .02
❑ 285 Willie McGee .10 .02
❑ 286 Lee Guetterman .05 .01
❑ 287 Vance Law .05 .01
❑ 288 Greg Briley .05 .01
❑ 289 Norm Charlton .05 .01
❑ 290 Robin Yount .40 .15
❑ 291 Dave Johnson MG .10 .02
❑ 292 Jim Gott .05 .01
❑ 293 Mike Gallego .05 .01
❑ 294 Craig McMurtry .05 .01
❑ 295 Fred McGriff .25 .08
❑ 296 Jeff Ballard .05 .01
❑ 297 Tommy Herr .05 .01
❑ 298 Dan Gladden .05 .01
❑ 299 Adam Peterson .05 .01
❑ 300 Bo Jackson .25 .08
❑ 301 Don Aase .05 .01
❑ 302 Marcus Lawton RC .05 .01
❑ 303 Rick Cerone .05 .01
❑ 304 Marty Clary .05 .01
❑ 305 Eddie Murray .25 .08
❑ 306 Tom Niedenfuer .05 .01
❑ 307 Bip Roberts .05 .01
❑ 308 Jose Guzman .05 .01
❑ 309 Eric Yelding RC .05 .01
❑ 310 Steve Bedrosian .05 .01
❑ 311 Dwight Smith .05 .01
❑ 312 Dan Quisenberry .05 .01
❑ 313 Gus Polidor .05 .01
❑ 314 Donald Harris FDP RC .05 .01
❑ 315 Bruce Hurst .05 .01
❑ 316 Carney Lansford .10 .02
❑ 317 Mark Guthrie RC .05 .01
❑ 318 Wallace Johnson .05 .01
❑ 319 Dion James .05 .01
❑ 320 Dave Stieb .10 .02
❑ 321 Joe Morgan MG .05 .01
❑ 322 Junior Ortiz .05 .01
❑ 323 Willie Wilson .05 .01
❑ 324 Pete Harnisch .05 .01
❑ 325 Robby Thompson .05 .01
❑ 326 Tom McCarthy .05 .01
❑ 327 Ken Williams .05 .01
❑ 328 Curt Young .05 .01
❑ 329 Oddibe McDowell .05 .01
❑ 330 Ron Darling .05 .01
❑ 331 Juan Gonzalez RC 1.00 .40
❑ 332 Paul O'Neill .15 .05
❑ 333 Bill Wegman .05 .01
❑ 334 Johnny Ray .05 .01
❑ 335 Andy Hawkins .05 .01
❑ 336 Ken Griffey Jr. .75 .30
❑ 337 Lloyd McClendon .05 .01
❑ 338 Dennis Lamp .05 .01
❑ 339 Dave Clark .05 .01
❑ 340 Fernando Valenzuela .10 .02
❑ 341 Tom Foley .05 .01
❑ 342 Alex Trevino .05 .01
❑ 343 Frank Tanana .05 .01
❑ 344 George Canale RC .05 .01
❑ 345 Harold Baines .10 .02
❑ 346 Jim Presley .05 .01
❑ 347 Junior Felix .05 .01
❑ 348 Gary Wayne .05 .01
❑ 349 Steve Finley .10 .02
❑ 350 Bret Saberhagen .10 .02
❑ 351 Roger Craig MG .05 .01
❑ 352 Bryn Smith .05 .01
❑ 353 Sandy Alomar Jr. (Not listed as Jr. on card fron .10 .02
❑ 354 Stan Belinda RC .10 .02
❑ 355 Marty Barrett .05 .01
❑ 356 Randy Ready .05 .01
❑ 357 Dave West .05 .01
❑ 358 Andres Thomas .05 .01
❑ 359 Jimmy Jones .05 .01
❑ 360 Paul Molitor .10 .02
❑ 361 Randy McCament RC .05 .01
❑ 362 Damon Berryhill .05 .01
❑ 363 Dan Petry .05 .01
❑ 364 Rolando Roomes .05 .01
❑ 365 Ozzie Guillen .10 .02
❑ 366 Mike Heath .05 .01
❑ 367 Mike Morgan .05 .01
❑ 368 Bill Doran .05 .01
❑ 369 Todd Burns .05 .01
❑ 370 Tim Wallach .05 .01
❑ 371 Jimmy Key .10 .02
❑ 372 Terry Kennedy .05 .01
❑ 373 Alvin Davis .05 .01
❑ 374 Steve Cummings RC .05 .01
❑ 375 Dwight Evans .15 .05
❑ 376 Checklist 3 UER (Higuera misalphabet-ized in Br .05 .01
❑ 377 Mickey Weston RC .05 .01
❑ 378 Luis Salazar .05 .01
❑ 379 Steve Rosenberg .05 .01
❑ 380 Dave Winfield .10 .02
❑ 381 Frank Robinson MG .15 .05
❑ 382 Jeff Musselman .05 .01
❑ 383 John Morris .05 .01
❑ 384 Pat Combs .05 .01
❑ 385 Fred McGriff AS .10 .02
❑ 386 Julio Franco AS .05 .01
❑ 387 Wade Boggs AS .10 .02
❑ 388 Cal Ripken AS .40 .15
❑ 389 Robin Yount AS .25 .08
❑ 390 Ruben Sierra AS .05 .01
❑ 391 Kirby Puckett AS .15 .05
❑ 392 Carlton Fisk AS .10 .02
❑ 393 Bret Saberhagen AS .05 .01
❑ 394 Jeff Ballard AS .05 .01
❑ 395 Jeff Russell AS .05 .01
❑ 396 Bart Giamatti MEM .25 .08
❑ 397 Will Clark AS .10 .02
❑ 398 Ryne Sandberg AS .25 .08
❑ 399 Howard Johnson AS .05 .01
❑ 400 Ozzie Smith AS .25 .08
❑ 401 Kevin Mitchell AS .05 .01
❑ 402 Eric Davis AS .05 .01
❑ 403 Tony Gwynn AS .15 .05
❑ 404 Craig Biggio AS .25 .08
❑ 405 Mike Scott AS .05 .01
❑ 406 Joe Magrane AS .05 .01
❑ 407 Mark Davis AS .05 .01
❑ 408 Trevor Wilson .05 .01
❑ 409 Tom Brunansky .05 .01
❑ 410 Joe Boever .05 .01
❑ 411 Ken Phelps .05 .01
❑ 412 Jamie Moyer .10 .02
❑ 413 Brian DuBois RC .05 .01
❑ 414A FrankThomas NNOF ! 700.00 400.00
❑ 414B Frank Thomas RC 2.00 .75
❑ 415 Shawon Dunston .05 .01
❑ 416 Dave Wayne Johnson RC .05 .01
❑ 417 Jim Gantner .05 .01
❑ 418 Tom Browning .05 .01
❑ 419 Beau Allred RC .05 .01
❑ 420 Carlton Fisk .15 .05
❑ 421 Greg Minton .05 .01
❑ 422 Pat Sheridan .05 .01
❑ 423 Fred Toliver .05 .01
❑ 424 Jerry Reuss .05 .01
❑ 425 Bill Landrum .05 .01
❑ 426 Jeff Hamilton UER (Stats say he fanned 197 times .05 .01
❑ 427 Carmen Castillo .05 .01
❑ 428 Steve Davis RC .05 .01
❑ 429 Tom Kelly MG .05 .01
❑ 430 Pete Incaviglia .05 .01
❑ 431 Randy Johnson .50 .20
❑ 432 Damaso Garcia .05 .01
❑ 433 Steve Olin RC .25 .08
❑ 434 Mark Carreon .05 .01
❑ 435 Kevin Seitzer .05 .01
❑ 436 Mel Hall .05 .01
❑ 437 Les Lancaster .05 .01
❑ 438 Greg Myers .05 .01
❑ 439 Jeff Parrett .05 .01

❑ 440 Alan Trammell .10 .02
❑ 441 Bob Kipper .05 .01
❑ 442 Jerry Browne .05 .01
❑ 443 Cris Carpenter .05 .01
❑ 444 Kyle Abbott FDP RC .05 .01
❑ 445 Danny Jackson .05 .01
❑ 446 Dan Pasqua .05 .01
❑ 447 Atlee Hammaker .05 .01
❑ 448 Greg Gagne .05 .01
❑ 449 Dennis Rasmussen .05 .01
❑ 450 Rickey Henderson .25 .08
❑ 451 Mark Lemke .05 .01
❑ 452 Luis DeLosSantos .05 .01
❑ 453 Jody Davis .05 .01
❑ 454 Jeff King .05 .01
❑ 455 Jeffrey Leonard .05 .01
❑ 456 Chris Gwynn .05 .01
❑ 457 Gregg Jefferies .10 .02
❑ 458 Bob McClure .05 .01
❑ 459 Jim Lefebvre MG .05 .01
❑ 460 Mike Scott .05 .01
❑ 461 Carlos Martinez .05 .01
❑ 462 Denny Walling .05 .01
❑ 463 Drew Hall .05 .01
❑ 464 Jerome Walton .05 .01
❑ 465 Kevin Gross .05 .01
❑ 466 Rance Mulliniks .05 .01
❑ 467 Juan Nieves .05 .01
❑ 468 Bill Ripken .05 .01
❑ 469 John Kruk .10 .02
❑ 470 Frank Viola .05 .01
❑ 471 Mike Brumley .05 .01
❑ 472 Jose Uribe .05 .01
❑ 473 Joe Price .05 .01
❑ 474 Rich Thompson .05 .01
❑ 475 Bob Welch .05 .01
❑ 476 Brad Komminsk .05 .01
❑ 477 Willie Fraser .05 .01
❑ 478 Mike LaValliere .05 .01
❑ 479 Frank White .10 .02
❑ 480 Sid Fernandez .05 .01
❑ 481 Garry Templeton .05 .01
❑ 482 Steve Carter .05 .01
❑ 483 Alejandro Pena .05 .01
❑ 484 Mike Fitzgerald .05 .01
❑ 485 John Candelaria .05 .01
❑ 486 Jeff Treadway .05 .01
❑ 487 Steve Searcy .05 .01
❑ 488 Ken Oberkfell .05 .01
❑ 489 Nick Leyva MG .05 .01
❑ 490 Dan Plesac .05 .01
❑ 491 Dave Cochrane RC .05 .01
❑ 492 Ron Oester .05 .01
❑ 493 Jason Grimsley RC .10 .02
❑ 494 Terry Puhl .05 .01
❑ 495 Lee Smith .10 .02
❑ 496 Cecil Espy UER ('88 stats have 3 SB's, should be .05 .01
❑ 497 Dave Schmidt .05 .01
❑ 498 Rick Schu .05 .01
❑ 499 Bill Long .05 .01
❑ 500 Kevin Mitchell .05 .01
❑ 501 Matt Young .05 .01
❑ 502 Mitch Webster .05 .01
❑ 503 Randy St.Claire .05 .01
❑ 504 Tom O'Malley .05 .01
❑ 505 Kelly Gruber .05 .01
❑ 506 Tom Glavine .15 .05
❑ 507 Gary Redus .05 .01
❑ 508 Terry Leach .05 .01
❑ 509 Tom Pagnozzi .05 .01
❑ 510 Dwight Gooden .10 .02
❑ 511 Clay Parker .05 .01
❑ 512 Gary Pettis .05 .01
❑ 513 Mark Eichhorn .05 .01
❑ 514 Andy Allanson .05 .01
❑ 515 Len Dykstra .10 .02
❑ 516 Tim Leary .05 .01
❑ 517 Roberto Alomar .15 .05
❑ 518 Bill Krueger .05 .01
❑ 519 Bucky Dent MG .05 .01
❑ 520 Mitch Williams .05 .01
❑ 521 Craig Worthington .05 .01
❑ 522 Mike Dunne .05 .01
❑ 523 Jay Bell .10 .02
❑ 524 Daryl Boston .05 .01
❑ 525 Wally Joyner .10 .02
❑ 526 Checklist 4 .05 .01
❑ 527 Ron Hassey .05 .01
❑ 528 Kevin Wickander UER (Monthly scoreboard strikeou .05 .01
❑ 529 Greg A. Harris .05 .01
❑ 530 Mark Langston .05 .01
❑ 531 Ken Caminiti .10 .02
❑ 532 Cecilio Guante .05 .01
❑ 533 Tim Jones .05 .01
❑ 534 Louie Meadows .05 .01
❑ 535 John Smoltz .25 .08
❑ 536 Bob Geren .05 .01
❑ 537 Mark Grant .05 .01
❑ 538 Bill Spiers UER (Photo actually George Canale) .05 .01
❑ 539 Neal Heaton .05 .01
❑ 540 Danny Tartabull .05 .01
❑ 541 Pat Perry .05 .01
❑ 542 Darren Daulton .10 .02
❑ 543 Nelson Liriano .05 .01
❑ 544 Dennis Boyd .05 .01
❑ 545 Kevin McReynolds .05 .01
❑ 546 Kevin Hickey .05 .01
❑ 547 Jack Howell .05 .01
❑ 548 Pat Clements .05 .01
❑ 549 Don Zimmer MG .05 .01
❑ 550 Julio Franco .10 .02
❑ 551 Tim Crews .05 .01
❑ 552 Mike (Miss.) Smith RC .05 .01
❑ 553 Scott Scudder UER (Cedar Rap1ds) .05 .01
❑ 554 Jay Buhner .10 .02
❑ 555 Jack Morris .10 .02
❑ 556 Gene Larkin .05 .01
❑ 557 Jeff Innis RC .05 .01
❑ 558 Rafael Ramirez .05 .01
❑ 559 Andy McGaffigan .05 .01
❑ 560 Steve Sax .05 .01
❑ 561 Ken Dayley .05 .01
❑ 562 Chad Kreuter .05 .01
❑ 563 Alex Sanchez .05 .01
❑ 564 Tyler Houston FDP RC .25 .08
❑ 565 Scott Fletcher .05 .01
❑ 566 Mark Knudson .05 .01
❑ 567 Ron Gant .10 .02
❑ 568 John Smiley .05 .01
❑ 569 Ivan Calderon .05 .01
❑ 570 Cal Ripken .75 .30
❑ 571 Brett Butler .10 .02
❑ 572 Greg W. Harris .05 .01
❑ 573 Danny Heep .05 .01
❑ 574 Bill Swift .05 .01
❑ 575 Lance Parrish .05 .01
❑ 576 Mike Dyer RC .05 .01
❑ 577 Charlie Hayes .05 .01
❑ 578 Joe Magrane .05 .01
❑ 579 Art Howe MG .05 .01
❑ 580 Joe Carter .10 .02
❑ 581 Ken Griffey Sr. .10 .02
❑ 582 Rick Honeycutt .05 .01
❑ 583 Bruce Benedict .05 .01
❑ 584 Phil Stephenson .05 .01
❑ 585 Kal Daniels .05 .01
❑ 586 Edwin Nunez .05 .01
❑ 587 Lance Johnson .05 .01
❑ 588 Rick Rhoden .05 .01
❑ 589 Mike Aldrete .05 .01
❑ 590 Ozzie Smith .40 .15
❑ 591 Todd Stottlemyre .10 .02
❑ 592 R.J. Reynolds .05 .01
❑ 593 Scott Bradley .05 .01
❑ 594 Luis Sojo RC .05 .01
❑ 595 Greg Swindell .05 .01
❑ 596 Jose DeJesus .05 .01
❑ 597 Chris Bosio .05 .01
❑ 598 Brady Anderson .10 .02
❑ 599 Frank Williams .05 .01
❑ 600 Darryl Strawberry .10 .02
❑ 601 Luis Rivera .05 .01
❑ 602 Scott Garrelts .05 .01
❑ 603 Tony Armas .05 .01
❑ 604 Ron Robinson .05 .01
❑ 605 Mike Scioscia .05 .01
❑ 606 Storm Davis .05 .01
❑ 607 Steve Jeltz .05 .01
❑ 608 Eric Anthony RC .10 .02
❑ 609 Sparky Anderson MG .10 .02
❑ 610 Pedro Guerrero .05 .01
❑ 611 Walt Terrell .05 .01
❑ 612 Dave Gallagher .05 .01
❑ 613 Jeff Pico .05 .01
❑ 614 Nelson Santovenia .05 .01
❑ 615 Rob Deer .05 .01
❑ 616 Brian Holman .05 .01
❑ 617 Geronimo Berroa .05 .01
❑ 618 Ed Whitson .05 .01
❑ 619 Rob Ducey .05 .01
❑ 620 Tony Castillo .05 .01
❑ 621 Melido Perez .05 .01
❑ 622 Sid Bream .05 .01
❑ 623 Jim Corsi .05 .01
❑ 624 Darrin Jackson .05 .01
❑ 625 Roger McDowell .05 .01
❑ 626 Bob Melvin .05 .01
❑ 627 Jose Rijo .05 .01
❑ 628 Candy Maldonado .05 .01
❑ 629 Eric Hetzel .05 .01
❑ 630 Gary Gaetti .10 .02
❑ 631 John Wetteland .25 .08
❑ 632 Scott Lusader .05 .01
❑ 633 Dennis Cook .05 .01
❑ 634 Luis Polonia .05 .01
❑ 635 Brian Downing .05 .01
❑ 636 Jesse Orosco .05 .01
❑ 637 Craig Reynolds .05 .01
❑ 638 Jeff Montgomery .10 .02
❑ 639 Tony LaRussa MG .10 .02
❑ 640 Rick Sutcliffe .10 .02
❑ 641 Doug Strange RC .05 .01
❑ 642 Jack Armstrong .05 .01
❑ 643 Alfredo Griffin .05 .01
❑ 644 Paul Assenmacher .05 .01
❑ 645 Jose Oquendo .05 .01
❑ 646 Checklist 5 .05 .01
❑ 647 Rex Hudler .05 .01
❑ 648 Jim Clancy .05 .01
❑ 649 Dan Murphy RC .10 .02
❑ 650 Mike Witt .05 .01
❑ 651 Rafael Santana .05 .01
❑ 652 Mike Boddicker .05 .01
❑ 653 John Moses .05 .01
❑ 654 Paul Coleman FDP RC .10 .02
❑ 655 Gregg Olson .10 .02
❑ 656 Mackey Sasser .05 .01
❑ 657 Terry Mulholland .05 .01
❑ 658 Donell Nixon .05 .01
❑ 659 Greg Cadaret .05 .01
❑ 660 Vince Coleman .05 .01
❑ 661 Dick Howser TBC'85 UER (Seaver's 300th on 7/11/8 .05 .01
❑ 662 Mike Schmidt TBC .25 .08
❑ 663 Fred Lynn TBC'75 .05 .01
❑ 664 Johnny Bench TBC .15 .05
❑ 665 Sandy Koufax TBC .50 .20
❑ 666 Brian Fisher .05 .01
❑ 667 Curt Wilkerson .05 .01
❑ 668 Joe Oliver .05 .01
❑ 669 Tom Lasorda MG .25 .08
❑ 670 Dennis Eckersley .10 .02
❑ 671 Bob Boone .10 .02
❑ 672 Roy Smith .05 .01
❑ 673 Joey Meyer .05 .01
❑ 674 Spike Owen .05 .01
❑ 675 Jim Abbott .15 .05
❑ 676 Randy Kutcher .05 .01
❑ 677 Jay Tibbs .05 .01
❑ 678 Kirt Manwaring UER ('88 Phoenix stats repeated) .05 .01
❑ 679 Gary Ward .05 .01
❑ 680 Howard Johnson .05 .01
❑ 681 Mike Schooler .05 .01
❑ 682 Dann Bilardello .05 .01
❑ 683 Kenny Rogers .10 .02
❑ 684 Julio Machado RC .05 .01
❑ 685 Tony Fernandez .05 .01
❑ 686 Carmelo Martinez .05 .01

❑ 687 Tim Birtsas .05 .01
❑ 688 Milt Thompson .05 .01
❑ 689 Rich Yett .05 .01
❑ 690 Mark McGwire .60 .25
❑ 691 Chuck Cary .05 .01
❑ 692 Sammy Sosa RC 2.50 1.00
❑ 693 Calvin Schiraldi .05 .01
❑ 694 Mike Stanton RC .25 .08
❑ 695 Tom Henke .05 .01
❑ 696 B.J. Surhoff .10 .02
❑ 697 Mike Davis .05 .01
❑ 698 Omar Vizquel .25 .08
❑ 699 Jim Leyland MG .05 .01
❑ 700 Kirby Puckett .25 .08
❑ 701 Bernie Williams RC 1.50 .60
❑ 702 Tony Phillips .05 .01
❑ 703 Jeff Brantley .05 .01
❑ 704 Chip Hale RC .05 .01
❑ 705 Claudell Washington .05 .01
❑ 706 Geno Petralli .05 .01
❑ 707 Luis Aquino .05 .01
❑ 708 Larry Sheets .05 .01
❑ 709 Juan Berenguer .05 .01
❑ 710 Von Hayes .05 .01
❑ 711 Rick Aguilera .10 .02
❑ 712 Todd Benzinger .05 .01
❑ 713 Tim Drummond RC .05 .01
❑ 714 Marquis Grissom RC .40 .15
❑ 715 Greg Maddux .40 .15
❑ 716 Steve Balboni .05 .01
❑ 717 Ron Karkovice .05 .01
❑ 718 Gary Sheffield .25 .08
❑ 719 Wally Whitehurst .05 .01
❑ 720 Andres Galarraga .10 .02
❑ 721 Lee Mazzilli .05 .01
❑ 722 Felix Fermin .05 .01
❑ 723 Jeff D. Robinson .05 .01
❑ 724 Juan Bell .05 .01
❑ 725 Terry Pendleton .10 .02
❑ 726 Gene Nelson .05 .01
❑ 727 Pat Tabler .05 .01
❑ 728 Jim Acker .05 .01
❑ 729 Bobby Valentine MG .05 .01
❑ 730 Tony Gwynn .30 .10
❑ 731 Don Carman .05 .01
❑ 732 Ernest Riles .05 .01
❑ 733 John Dopson .05 .01
❑ 734 Kevin Elster .05 .01
❑ 735 Charlie Hough .10 .02
❑ 736 Rick Dempsey .05 .01
❑ 737 Chris Sabo .05 .01
❑ 738 Gene Harris .05 .01
❑ 739 Dale Sveum .05 .01
❑ 740 Jesse Barfield .05 .01
❑ 741 Steve Wilson .05 .01
❑ 742 Ernie Whitt .05 .01
❑ 743 Tom Candiotti .05 .01
❑ 744 Kelly Mann RC .05 .01
❑ 745 Hubie Brooks .05 .01
❑ 746 Dave Smith .05 .01
❑ 747 Randy Bush .05 .01
❑ 748 Doyle Alexander .05 .01
❑ 749 Mark Parent UER
('87 BA .80,
should be .080) .05 .01
❑ 750 Dale Murphy .15 .05
❑ 751 Steve Lyons .05 .01
❑ 752 Tom Gordon .10 .02
❑ 753 Chris Speier .05 .01
❑ 754 Bob Walk .05 .01
❑ 755 Rafael Palmeiro .15 .05
❑ 756 Ken Howell .05 .01
❑ 757 Larry Walker RC 1.00 .40
❑ 758 Mark Thurmond .05 .01
❑ 759 Tom Trebelhorn MG .05 .01
❑ 760 Wade Boggs .15 .05
❑ 761 Mike Jackson .05 .01
❑ 762 Doug Dascenzo .05 .01
❑ 763 Dennis Martinez .10 .02
❑ 764 Tim Teufel .05 .01
❑ 765 Chili Davis .10 .02
❑ 766 Brian Meyer .05 .01
❑ 767 Tracy Jones .05 .01
❑ 768 Chuck Crim .05 .01
❑ 769 Greg Hibbard RC .10 .02
❑ 770 Cory Snyder .05 .01
❑ 771 Pete Smith .05 .01
❑ 772 Jeff Reed .05 .01
❑ 773 Dave Leiper .05 .01
❑ 774 Ben McDonald RC .25 .08
❑ 775 Andy Van Slyke .15 .05
❑ 776 Charlie Leibrandt .05 .01
❑ 777 Tim Laudner .05 .01
❑ 778 Mike Jeffcoat .05 .01
❑ 779 Lloyd Moseby .05 .01
❑ 780 Orel Hershiser .10 .02
❑ 781 Mario Diaz .05 .01
❑ 782 Jose Alvarez .05 .01
❑ 783 Checklist 6 .05 .01
❑ 784 Scott Bailes .05 .01
❑ 785 Jim Rice .10 .02
❑ 786 Eric King .05 .01
❑ 787 Rene Gonzales .05 .01
❑ 788 Frank DiPino .05 .01
❑ 789 John Wathan MG .05 .01
❑ 790 Gary Carter .10 .02
❑ 791 Alvaro Espinoza .05 .01
❑ 792 Gerald Perry .05 .01
❑ XX George Bush PRES

1990 Topps Traded

❑ COMPLETE SET (132) 3.00 1.25
❑ COMP.FACT.SET (132) 3.00 1.25
❑ 1T Darrel Akerfelds .05 .01
❑ 2T Sandy Alomar Jr. .10 .02
❑ 3T Brad Arnsberg .05 .01
❑ 4T Steve Avery .05 .01
❑ 5T Wally Backman .05 .01
❑ 6T Carlos Baerga RC .25 .08
❑ 7T Kevin Bass .05 .01
❑ 8T Willie Blair RC .10 .02
❑ 9T Mike Blowers RC .25 .08
❑ 10T Shawn Boskie RC .10 .02
❑ 11T Daryl Boston .05 .01
❑ 12T Dennis Boyd .05 .01
❑ 13T Glenn Braggs .05 .01
❑ 14T Hubie Brooks .05 .01
❑ 15T Tom Brunansky .05 .01
❑ 16T John Burkett .05 .01
❑ 17T Casey Candaele .05 .01
❑ 18T John Candelaria .05 .01
❑ 19T Gary Carter .10 .02
❑ 20T Joe Carter .10 .02
❑ 21T Rick Cerone .05 .01
❑ 22T Scott Coolbaugh RC .05 .01
❑ 23T Bobby Cox MG .10 .02
❑ 24T Mark Davis .05 .01
❑ 25T Storm Davis .05 .01
❑ 26T Edgar Diaz RC .05 .01
❑ 27T Wayne Edwards RC .05 .01
❑ 28T Mark Eichhorn .05 .01
❑ 29T Scott Erickson RC .25 .08
❑ 30T Nick Esasky .05 .01
❑ 31T Cecil Fielder .10 .02
❑ 32T John Franco .10 .02
❑ 33T Travis Fryman RC .40 .15
❑ 34T Bill Gullickson .05 .01
❑ 35T Darryl Hamilton .05 .01
❑ 36T Mike Harkey .05 .01
❑ 37T Bud Harrelson MG .05 .01
❑ 38T Billy Hatcher .05 .01
❑ 39T Keith Hernandez .10 .02
❑ 40T Joe Hesketh .05 .01
❑ 41T Dave Hollins RC .25 .08
❑ 42T Sam Horn .05 .01
❑ 43T Steve Howard RC .05 .01
❑ 44T Todd Hundley RC .25 .08
❑ 45T Jeff Huson .05 .01
❑ 46T Chris James .05 .01
❑ 47T Stan Javier .05 .01
❑ 48T David Justice RC .50 .20
❑ 49T Jeff Kaiser .05 .01
❑ 50T Dana Kiecker RC .05 .01
❑ 51T Joe Klink RC .05 .01
❑ 52T Brent Knackert RC .10 .02
❑ 53T Brad Komminsk .05 .01
❑ 54T Mark Langston .05 .01
❑ 55T Tim Layana RC .05 .01
❑ 56T Rick Leach .05 .01
❑ 57T Terry Leach .05 .01
❑ 58T Tim Leary .05 .01
❑ 59T Craig Lefferts .05 .01
❑ 60T Charlie Leibrandt .05 .01
❑ 61T Jim Leyritz RC .25 .08
❑ 62T Fred Lynn .05 .01
❑ 63T Kevin Maas RC .25 .08
❑ 64T Shane Mack .05 .01
❑ 65T Candy Maldonado .05 .01
❑ 66T Fred Manrique .05 .01
❑ 67T Mike Marshall .05 .01
❑ 68T Carmelo Martinez .05 .01
❑ 69T John Marzano .05 .01
❑ 70T Ben McDonald .05 .01
❑ 71T Jack McDowell .05 .01
❑ 72T John McNamara MG .05 .01
❑ 73T Orlando Mercado .05 .01
❑ 74T Stump Merrill MG RC .05 .01
❑ 75T Alan Mills RC .10 .02
❑ 76T Hal Morris .05 .01
❑ 77T Lloyd Moseby .05 .01
❑ 78T Randy Myers .10 .02
❑ 79T Tim Naehring RC .10 .02
❑ 80T Junior Noboa .05 .01
❑ 81T Matt Nokes .05 .01
❑ 82T Pete O'Brien .05 .01
❑ 83T John Olerud RC .50 .20
❑ 84T Greg Olson (C) RC .10 .02
❑ 85T Junior Ortiz .05 .01
❑ 86T Dave Parker .10 .02
❑ 87T Rick Parker RC .05 .01
❑ 88T Bob Patterson .05 .01
❑ 89T Alejandro Pena .05 .01
❑ 90T Tony Pena .05 .01
❑ 91T Pascual Perez .05 .01
❑ 92T Gerald Perry .05 .01
❑ 93T Dan Petry .05 .01
❑ 94T Gary Pettis .05 .01
❑ 95T Tony Phillips .05 .01
❑ 96T Lou Piniella MG .10 .02
❑ 97T Luis Polonia .05 .01
❑ 98T Jim Presley .05 .01
❑ 99T Scott Radinsky RC .10 .02
❑ 100T Willie Randolph .10 .02
❑ 101T Jeff Reardon .10 .02
❑ 102T Greg Riddoch MG RC .05 .01
❑ 103T Jeff Robinson .05 .01
❑ 104T Ron Robinson .05 .01
❑ 105T Kevin Romine .05 .01
❑ 106T Scott Ruskin RC .05 .01
❑ 107T John Russell .05 .01
❑ 108T Bill Sampen RC .05 .01
❑ 109T Juan Samuel .05 .01
❑ 110T Scott Sanderson .05 .01
❑ 111T Jack Savage .05 .01
❑ 112T Dave Schmidt .05 .01
❑ 113T Red Schoendienst MG .25 .08
❑ 114T Terry Shumpert RC .05 .01
❑ 115T Matt Sinatro .05 .01
❑ 116T Don Slaught .05 .01
❑ 117T Bryn Smith .05 .01
❑ 118T Lee Smith .10 .02
❑ 119T Paul Sorrento RC .25 .08
❑ 120T Franklin Stubbs UER
('84 says '99 and has
the sa .05 .01
❑ 121T Russ Swan RC .10 .02
❑ 122T Bob Tewksbury .05 .01
❑ 123T Wayne Tolleson .05 .01
❑ 124T John Tudor .05 .01
❑ 125T Randy Veres .05 .01

❑ 126T Hector Villanueva RC .10 .02
❑ 127T Mitch Webster .05 .01
❑ 128T Ernie Whitt .05 .01
❑ 129T Frank Wills .05 .01
❑ 130T Dave Winfield .10 .02
❑ 131T Matt Young .05 .01
❑ 132T Checklist 1T-132T .05 .01

1991 Topps

❑ COMPLETE SET (792) 20.00 8.00
❑ COMP.FACT.SET (792) 25.00 10.00
❑ 1 Nolan Ryan 1.50 .60
❑ 2 George Brett RB .30 .10
❑ 3 Carlton Fisk RB .10 .02
❑ 4 Kevin Maas RB .05 .01
❑ 5 Cal Ripken RB .40 .15
❑ 6 Nolan Ryan RB .50 .20
❑ 7 Ryne Sandberg RB .25 .08
❑ 8 Bobby Thigpen RB .05 .01
❑ 9 Darrin Fletcher .05 .01
❑ 10 Gregg Olson .05 .01
❑ 11 Roberto Kelly .05 .01
❑ 12 Paul Assenmacher .05 .01
❑ 13 Mariano Duncan .05 .01
❑ 14 Dennis Lamp .05 .01
❑ 15 Von Hayes .05 .01
❑ 16 Mike Heath .05 .01
❑ 17 Jeff Brantley .05 .01
❑ 18 Nelson Liriano .05 .01
❑ 19 Jeff D. Robinson .05 .01
❑ 20 Pedro Guerrero .10 .02
❑ 21 Joe Morgan MG .05 .01
❑ 22 Storm Davis .05 .01
❑ 23 Jim Gantner .05 .01
❑ 24 Dave Martinez .05 .01
❑ 25 Tim Belcher .05 .01
❑ 26 Luis Sojo UER
(Born in Barquisimento,
not Carqui .05 .01
❑ 27 Bobby Witt .05 .01
❑ 28 Alvaro Espinoza .05 .01
❑ 29 Bob Walk .05 .01
❑ 30 Gregg Jefferies .05 .01
❑ 31 Colby Ward RC .05 .01
❑ 32 Mike Simms RC .05 .01
❑ 33 Barry Jones .05 .01
❑ 34 Atlee Hammaker .05 .01
❑ 35 Greg Maddux .40 .15
❑ 36 Donnie Hill .05 .01
❑ 37 Tom Bolton .05 .01
❑ 38 Scott Bradley .05 .01
❑ 39 Jim Neidlinger RC .05 .01
❑ 40 Kevin Mitchell .05 .01
❑ 41 Ken Dayley .05 .01
❑ 42 Chris Hoiles .05 .01
❑ 43 Roger McDowell .05 .01
❑ 44 Mike Felder .05 .01
❑ 45 Chris Sabo .05 .01
❑ 46 Tim Drummond .05 .01
❑ 47 Brook Jacoby .05 .01
❑ 48 Dennis Boyd .05 .01
❑ 49A Pat Borders ERR
(40 steals at
Kinston in '86) .25 .08
❑ 49B Pat Borders COR
(0 steals at
Kinston in '86) .05 .01
❑ 50 Bob Welch .05 .01
❑ 51 Art Howe MG .05 .01
❑ 52 Francisco Oliveras .05 .01
❑ 53 Mike Sharperson UER
(Born in 1961, not 1960) .05 .01
❑ 54 Gary Mielke .05 .01
❑ 55 Jeffrey Leonard .05 .01
❑ 56 Jeff Parrett .05 .01
❑ 57 Jack Howell .05 .01
❑ 58 Mel Stottlemyre Jr. .05 .01
❑ 59 Eric Yelding .05 .01
❑ 60 Frank Viola .10 .02
❑ 61 Stan Javier .05 .01
❑ 62 Lee Guetterman .05 .01
❑ 63 Milt Thompson .05 .01
❑ 64 Tom Herr .05 .01
❑ 65 Bruce Hurst .05 .01
❑ 66 Terry Kennedy .05 .01
❑ 67 Rick Honeycutt .05 .01
❑ 68 Gary Sheffield .10 .02
❑ 69 Steve Wilson .05 .01
❑ 70 Ellis Burks .10 .02
❑ 71 Jim Acker .05 .01
❑ 72 Junior Ortiz .05 .01
❑ 73 Craig Worthington .05 .01
❑ 74 Shane Andrews RC .25 .08
❑ 75 Jack Morris .10 .02
❑ 76 Jerry Browne .05 .01
❑ 77 Drew Hall .05 .01
❑ 78 Geno Petralli .05 .01
❑ 79 Frank Thomas .25 .08
❑ 80A Fernando Valenzuela ERR .40 .15
❑ 80B Fernando Valenzuela COR .10 .02
❑ 81 Cito Gaston MG .05 .01
❑ 82 Tom Glavine .15 .05
❑ 83 Daryl Boston .05 .01
❑ 84 Bob McClure .05 .01
❑ 85 Jesse Barfield .05 .01
❑ 86 Les Lancaster .05 .01
❑ 87 Tracy Jones .05 .01
❑ 88 Bob Tewksbury .05 .01
❑ 89 Darren Daulton .10 .02
❑ 90 Danny Tartabull .05 .01
❑ 91 Greg Colbrunn RC .25 .08
❑ 92 Danny Jackson .05 .01
❑ 93 Ivan Calderon .05 .01
❑ 94 John Dopson .05 .01
❑ 95 Paul Molitor .10 .02
❑ 96 Trevor Wilson .05 .01
❑ 97A Brady Anderson ERR .40 .15
❑ 97B Brady Anderson COR .10 .02
❑ 98 Sergio Valdez .05 .01
❑ 99 Chris Gwynn .05 .01
❑ 100 Don Mattingly .60 .25
❑ 100A Don Mattingly ERR 2.00 .75
❑ 101 Rob Ducey .05 .01
❑ 102 Gene Larkin .05 .01
❑ 103 Tim Costo RC .05 .01
❑ 104 Don Robinson .05 .01
❑ 105 Kevin McReynolds .05 .01
❑ 106 Ed Nunez .05 .01
❑ 107 Luis Polonia .05 .01
❑ 108 Matt Young .05 .01
❑ 109 Greg Riddoch MG .05 .01
❑ 110 Tom Henke .05 .01
❑ 111 Andres Thomas .05 .01
❑ 112 Frank DiPino .05 .01
❑ 113 Carl Everett RC .50 .20
❑ 114 Lance Dickson RC .10 .02
❑ 115 Hubie Brooks .05 .01
❑ 116 Mark Davis .05 .01
❑ 117 Dion James .05 .01
❑ 118 Tom Edens RC .05 .01
❑ 119 Carl Nichols .05 .01
❑ 120 Joe Carter .10 .02
❑ 121 Eric King .05 .01
❑ 122 Paul O'Neill .15 .05
❑ 123 Greg A. Harris .05 .01
❑ 124 Randy Bush .05 .01
❑ 125 Steve Bedrosian .05 .01
❑ 126 Bernard Gilkey .05 .01
❑ 127 Joe Price .05 .01
❑ 128 Travis Fryman .10 .02
❑ 129 Mark Eichhorn .05 .01
❑ 130 Ozzie Smith .40 .15
❑ 131A Checklist 1 ERR
727 Phil Bradley .25 .08
❑ 131B Checklist 1 COR
717 Phil Bradley .05 .01
❑ 132 Jamie Quirk .05 .01
❑ 133 Greg Briley .05 .01
❑ 134 Kevin Elster .05 .01
❑ 135 Jerome Walton .05 .01
❑ 136 Dave Schmidt .05 .01
❑ 137 Randy Ready .05 .01
❑ 138 Jamie Moyer .10 .02
❑ 139 Jeff Treadway .05 .01
❑ 140 Fred McGriff .15 .05
❑ 141 Nick Leyva MG .05 .01
❑ 142 Curt Wilkerson .05 .01
❑ 143 John Smiley .05 .01
❑ 144 Dave Henderson .05 .01
❑ 145 Lou Whitaker .10 .02
❑ 146 Dan Plesac .05 .01
❑ 147 Carlos Baerga .05 .01
❑ 148 Rey Palacios .05 .01
❑ 149 Al Osuna UER RC .10 .02
❑ 150 Cal Ripken .75 .30
❑ 151 Tom Browning .05 .01
❑ 152 Mickey Hatcher .05 .01
❑ 153 Bryan Harvey .05 .01
❑ 154 Jay Buhner .10 .02
❑ 155A Dwight Evans ERR .50 .20
❑ 155B Dwight Evans COR .15 .05
❑ 156 Carlos Martinez .05 .01
❑ 157 John Smoltz .15 .05
❑ 158 Jose Uribe .05 .01
❑ 159 Joe Boever .05 .01
❑ 160 Vince Coleman UER
(Wrong birth year,
born 9/22/6 .05 .01
❑ 161 Tim Leary .05 .01
❑ 162 Ozzie Canseco .05 .01
❑ 163 Dave Johnson .05 .01
❑ 164 Edgar Diaz .05 .01
❑ 165 Sandy Alomar Jr. .05 .01
❑ 166 Harold Baines .10 .02
❑ 167A Randy Tomlin ERR .25 .08
❑ 167B Randy Tomlin COR RC .10 .02
❑ 168 John Olerud .10 .02
❑ 169 Luis Aquino .05 .01
❑ 170 Carlton Fisk .15 .05
❑ 171 Tony LaRussa MG .10 .02
❑ 172 Pete Incaviglia .05 .01
❑ 173 Jason Grimsley .05 .01
❑ 174 Ken Caminiti .10 .02
❑ 175 Jack Armstrong .05 .01
❑ 176 John Orton .05 .01
❑ 177 Reggie Harris .05 .01
❑ 178 Dave Valle .05 .01
❑ 179 Pete Harnisch .05 .01
❑ 180 Tony Gwynn .30 .10
❑ 181 Duane Ward .05 .01
❑ 182 Junior Noboa .05 .01
❑ 183 Clay Parker .05 .01
❑ 184 Gary Green .05 .01
❑ 185 Joe Magrane .05 .01
❑ 186 Rod Booker .05 .01
❑ 187 Greg Cadaret .05 .01
❑ 188 Damon Berryhill .05 .01
❑ 189 Daryl Irvine RC .05 .01
❑ 190 Matt Williams .10 .02
❑ 191 Willie Blair .05 .01
❑ 192 Rob Deer .05 .01
❑ 193 Felix Fermin .05 .01
❑ 194 Xavier Hernandez .05 .01
❑ 195 Wally Joyner .10 .02
❑ 196 Jim Vatcher RC .05 .01
❑ 197 Chris Nabholz .05 .01
❑ 198 R.J. Reynolds .05 .01
❑ 199 Mike Hartley .05 .01
❑ 200 Darryl Strawberry .10 .02
❑ 201 Tom Kelly MG .05 .01
❑ 202 Jim Leyritz .05 .01
❑ 203 Gene Harris .05 .01
❑ 204 Herm Winningham .05 .01
❑ 205 Mike Perez RC .10 .02
❑ 206 Carlos Quintana .05 .01
❑ 207 Gary Wayne .05 .01
❑ 208 Willie Wilson .05 .01
❑ 209 Ken Howell .05 .01
❑ 210 Lance Parrish .10 .02
❑ 211 Brian Barnes RC .05 .01

❑ 212 Steve Finley .10 .02
❑ 213 Frank Wills .05 .01
❑ 214 Joe Girardi .05 .01
❑ 215 Dave Smith .05 .01
❑ 216 Greg Gagne .05 .01
❑ 217 Chris Bosio .05 .01
❑ 218 Rick Parker .05 .01
❑ 219 Jack McDowell .05 .01
❑ 220 Tim Wallach .05 .01
❑ 221 Don Slaught .05 .01
❑ 222 Brian McRae RC .25 .08
❑ 223 Allan Anderson .05 .01
❑ 224 Juan Gonzalez .25 .08
❑ 225 Randy Johnson .30 .10
❑ 226 Alfredo Griffin .05 .01
❑ 227 Steve Avery UER .05 .01
❑ 228 Rex Hudler .05 .01
❑ 229 Rance Mulliniks .05 .01
❑ 230 Sid Fernandez .05 .01
❑ 231 Doug Rader MG .05 .01
❑ 232 Jose DeJesus .05 .01
❑ 233 Al Leiter .10 .02
❑ 234 Scott Erickson .05 .01
❑ 235 Dave Parker .10 .02
❑ 236A Frank Tanana ERR (Tied for lead with 269 K's in .25 .08
❑ 236B Frank Tanana COR (Led league with 269 K's in '75 .05 .01
❑ 237 Rick Cerone .05 .01
❑ 238 Mike Dunne .05 .01
❑ 239 Darren Lewis FTC .05 .01
❑ 240 Mike Scott .05 .01
❑ 241 Dave Clark UER (Career totals 19 HR and 5 3B, sh .05 .01
❑ 242 Mike LaCoss .05 .01
❑ 243 Lance Johnson .05 .01
❑ 244 Mike Jeffcoat .05 .01
❑ 245 Kal Daniels .05 .01
❑ 246 Kevin Wickander .05 .01
❑ 247 Jody Reed .05 .01
❑ 248 Tom Gordon .05 .01
❑ 249 Bob Melvin .05 .01
❑ 250 Dennis Eckersley .10 .02
❑ 251 Mark Lemke .05 .01
❑ 252 Mel Rojas .05 .01
❑ 253 Garry Templeton .05 .01
❑ 254 Shawn Boskie .05 .01
❑ 255 Brian Downing .05 .01
❑ 256 Greg Hibbard .05 .01
❑ 257 Tom O'Malley .05 .01
❑ 258 Chris Hammond FTC .05 .01
❑ 259 Hensley Meulens .05 .01
❑ 260 Harold Reynolds .10 .02
❑ 261 Bud Harrelson MG .05 .01
❑ 262 Tim Jones .05 .01
❑ 263 Checklist 2 .05 .01
❑ 264 Dave Hollins .05 .01
❑ 265 Mark Gubicza .05 .01
❑ 266 Carmelo Castillo .05 .01
❑ 267 Mark Knudson .05 .01
❑ 268 Tom Brookens .05 .01
❑ 269 Joe Hesketh .05 .01
❑ 270 Mark McGwire .75 .30
❑ 270A Mark McGwire ERR 2.00 .75
❑ 271 Omar Olivares RC .10 .02
❑ 272 Jeff King .05 .01
❑ 273 Johnny Ray .05 .01
❑ 274 Ken Williams .05 .01
❑ 275 Alan Trammell .10 .02
❑ 276 Bill Swift .05 .01
❑ 277 Scott Coolbaugh .05 .01
❑ 278 Alex Fernandez UER .05 .01
❑ 279A Jose Gonzalez ERR (Photo actually Billy Bean) .25 .08
❑ 279B Jose Gonzalez COR .05 .01
❑ 280 Bret Saberhagen .10 .02
❑ 281 Larry Sheets .05 .01
❑ 282 Don Carman .05 .01
❑ 283 Marquis Grissom .10 .02
❑ 284 Billy Spiers .05 .01
❑ 285 Jim Abbott .15 .05
❑ 286 Ken Oberkfell .05 .01
❑ 287 Mark Grant .05 .01
❑ 288 Derrick May .05 .01
❑ 289 Tim Birtsas .05 .01
❑ 290 Steve Sax .05 .01
❑ 291 John Wathan MG .05 .01
❑ 292 Bud Black .05 .01
❑ 293 Jay Bell .10 .02
❑ 294 Mike Moore .05 .01
❑ 295 Rafael Palmeiro .15 .05
❑ 296 Mark Williamson .05 .01
❑ 297 Manny Lee .05 .01
❑ 298 Omar Vizquel .15 .05
❑ 299 Scott Radinsky .05 .01
❑ 300 Kirby Puckett .25 .08
❑ 301 Steve Farr .05 .01
❑ 302 Tim Teufel .05 .01
❑ 303 Mike Boddicker .05 .01
❑ 304 Kevin Reimer .05 .01
❑ 305 Mike Scioscia .05 .01
❑ 306A Lonnie Smith ERR (136 games in '90) .40 .15
❑ 306B Lonnie Smith COR (135 games in '90) .05 .01
❑ 307 Andy Benes .05 .01
❑ 308 Tom Pagnozzi .05 .01
❑ 309 Norm Charlton .05 .01
❑ 310 Gary Carter .10 .02
❑ 311 Jeff Pico .05 .01
❑ 312 Charlie Hayes .05 .01
❑ 313 Ron Robinson .05 .01
❑ 314 Gary Pettis .05 .01
❑ 315 Roberto Alomar .15 .05
❑ 316 Gene Nelson .05 .01
❑ 317 Mike Fitzgerald .05 .01
❑ 318 Rick Aguilera .10 .02
❑ 319 Jeff McKnight .05 .01
❑ 320 Tony Fernandez .05 .01
❑ 321 Bob Rodgers MG .05 .01
❑ 322 Terry Shumpert .05 .01
❑ 323 Cory Snyder .05 .01
❑ 324A Ron Kittle ERR (Set another standard ...) .40 .15
❑ 324B Ron Kittle COR (Tied another standard ...) .05 .01
❑ 325 Brett Butler .10 .02
❑ 326 Ken Patterson .05 .01
❑ 327 Ron Hassey .05 .01
❑ 328 Walt Terrell .05 .01
❑ 329 David Justice UER .10 .02
❑ 330 Dwight Gooden .10 .02
❑ 331 Eric Anthony .05 .01
❑ 332 Kenny Rogers .10 .02
❑ 333 Chipper Jones RC 4.00 1.50
❑ 334 Todd Benzinger .05 .01
❑ 335 Mitch Williams .05 .01
❑ 336 Matt Nokes .05 .01
❑ 337A Keith Comstock ERR (Cubs logo on front) .25 .08
❑ 337B Keith Comstock COR (Mariners logo on front) .05 .01
❑ 338 Luis Rivera .05 .01
❑ 339 Larry Walker .25 .08
❑ 340 Ramon Martinez .05 .01
❑ 341 John Moses .05 .01
❑ 342 Mickey Morandini .05 .01
❑ 343 Jose Oquendo .05 .01
❑ 344 Jeff Russell .05 .01
❑ 345 Len Dykstra .10 .02
❑ 346 Jesse Orosco .05 .01
❑ 347 Greg Vaughn .05 .01
❑ 348 Todd Stottlemyre .05 .01
❑ 349 Dave Gallagher .05 .01
❑ 350 Glenn Davis .05 .01
❑ 351 Joe Torre MG .10 .02
❑ 352 Frank White .10 .02
❑ 353 Tony Castillo .05 .01
❑ 354 Sid Bream .05 .01
❑ 355 Chili Davis .10 .02
❑ 356 Mike Marshall .05 .01
❑ 357 Jack Savage .05 .01
❑ 358 Mark Parent .05 .01
❑ 359 Chuck Cary .05 .01
❑ 360 Tim Raines .10 .02
❑ 361 Scott Garrelts .05 .01
❑ 362 Hector Villenueva .05 .01
❑ 363 Rick Mahler .05 .01
❑ 364 Dan Pasqua .05 .01
❑ 365 Mike Schooler .05 .01
❑ 366A Checklist 3 ERR 19 Carl Nichols .25 .08
❑ 366B Checklist 3 COR 119 Carl Nichols .05 .01
❑ 367 Dave Walsh RC .05 .01
❑ 368 Felix Jose .05 .01
❑ 369 Steve Searcy .05 .01
❑ 370 Kelly Gruber .05 .01
❑ 371 Jeff Montgomery .05 .01
❑ 372 Spike Owen .05 .01
❑ 373 Darrin Jackson .05 .01
❑ 374 Larry Casian RC .05 .01
❑ 375 Tony Pena .05 .01
❑ 376 Mike Harkey .05 .01
❑ 377 Rene Gonzales .05 .01
❑ 378A Wilson Alvarez ERR .25 .08
❑ 378B Wilson Alvarez FTC COR .05 .01
❑ 379 Randy Velarde .05 .01
❑ 380 Willie McGee .10 .02
❑ 381 Jim Leyland MG .05 .01
❑ 382 Mackey Sasser .05 .01
❑ 383 Pete Smith .05 .01
❑ 384 Gerald Perry .05 .01
❑ 385 Mickey Tettleton .05 .01
❑ 386 Cecil Fielder AS .05 .01
❑ 387 Julio Franco AS .05 .01
❑ 388 Kelly Gruber AS .05 .01
❑ 389 Alan Trammell AS .10 .02
❑ 390 Jose Canseco AS .10 .02
❑ 391 Rickey Henderson AS .15 .05
❑ 392 Ken Griffey Jr. AS .40 .15
❑ 393 Carlton Fisk AS .10 .02
❑ 394 Bob Welch AS .05 .01
❑ 395 Chuck Finley AS .05 .01
❑ 396 Bobby Thigpen AS .05 .01
❑ 397 Eddie Murray AS .15 .05
❑ 398 Ryne Sandberg AS .25 .08
❑ 399 Matt Williams AS .05 .01
❑ 400 Barry Larkin AS .10 .02
❑ 401 Barry Bonds AS .50 .20
❑ 402 Darryl Strawberry AS .05 .01
❑ 403 Bobby Bonilla AS .05 .01
❑ 404 Mike Scioscia AS .05 .01
❑ 405 Doug Drabek AS .05 .01
❑ 406 Frank Viola AS .05 .01
❑ 407 John Franco AS .05 .01
❑ 408 Earnest Riles .05 .01
❑ 409 Mike Stanley .05 .01
❑ 410 Dave Righetti .10 .02
❑ 411 Lance Blankenship .05 .01
❑ 412 Dave Bergman .05 .01
❑ 413 Terry Mulholland .05 .01
❑ 414 Sammy Sosa .25 .08
❑ 415 Rick Sutcliffe .10 .02
❑ 416 Randy Milligan .05 .01
❑ 417 Bill Krueger .05 .01
❑ 418 Nick Esasky .05 .01
❑ 419 Jeff Reed .05 .01
❑ 420 Bobby Thigpen .05 .01
❑ 421 Alex Cole .05 .01
❑ 422 Rick Reuschel .05 .01
❑ 423 Rafael Ramirez UER (Born 1959, not 1958) .05 .01
❑ 424 Calvin Schiraldi .05 .01
❑ 425 Andy Van Slyke .15 .05
❑ 426 Joe Grahe RC .10 .02
❑ 427 Rick Dempsey .05 .01
❑ 428 John Barfield .05 .01
❑ 429 Stump Merrill MG .05 .01
❑ 430 Gary Gaetti .10 .02
❑ 431 Paul Gibson .05 .01
❑ 432 Delino DeShields .10 .02
❑ 433 Pat Tabler .05 .01
❑ 434 Julio Machado .05 .01
❑ 435 Kevin Maas .05 .01
❑ 436 Scott Bankhead .05 .01
❑ 437 Doug Dascenzo .05 .01
❑ 438 Vicente Palacios .05 .01
❑ 439 Dickie Thon .05 .01
❑ 440 George Bell .05 .01
❑ 441 Zane Smith .05 .01
❑ 442 Charlie O'Brien .05 .01

❑ 443 Jeff Innis .05 .01
❑ 444 Glenn Braggs .05 .01
❑ 445 Greg Swindell .05 .01
❑ 446 Craig Grebeck .05 .01
❑ 447 John Burkett .05 .01
❑ 448 Craig Lefferts .05 .01
❑ 449 Juan Berenguer .05 .01
❑ 450 Wade Boggs .15 .05
❑ 451 Neal Heaton .05 .01
❑ 452 Bill Schroeder .05 .01
❑ 453 Lenny Harris .05 .01
❑ 454A Kevin Appier ERR .40 .15
❑ 454B Kevin Appier COR .10 .02
❑ 455 Walt Weiss .05 .01
❑ 456 Charlie Leibrandt .05 .01
❑ 457 Todd Hundley .05 .01
❑ 458 Brian Holman .05 .01
❑ 459 Tom Trebelhorn MG UER
(Pitching and batting
colu .05 .01
❑ 460 Dave Stieb .05 .01
❑ 461 Robin Ventura .10 .02
❑ 462 Steve Frey .05 .01
❑ 463 Dwight Smith .05 .01
❑ 464 Steve Buechele .05 .01
❑ 465 Ken Griffey Sr. .10 .02
❑ 466 Charles Nagy .05 .01
❑ 467 Dennis Cook .05 .01
❑ 468 Tim Hulett .05 .01
❑ 469 Chet Lemon .05 .01
❑ 470 Howard Johnson .05 .01
❑ 471 Mike Lieberthal RC .40 .15
❑ 472 Kirt Manwaring .05 .01
❑ 473 Curt Young .05 .01
❑ 474 Phil Plantier RC .10 .02
❑ 475 Ted Higuera .05 .01
❑ 476 Glenn Wilson .05 .01
❑ 477 Mike Fetters .05 .01
❑ 478 Kurt Stillwell .05 .01
❑ 479 Bob Patterson UER
(Has a decimal point
between 7 .05 .01
❑ 480 Dave Magadan .05 .01
❑ 481 Eddie Whitson .05 .01
❑ 482 Tino Martinez .25 .08
❑ 483 Mike Aldrete .05 .01
❑ 484 Dave LaPoint .05 .01
❑ 485 Terry Pendleton .10 .02
❑ 486 Tommy Greene .05 .01
❑ 487 Rafael Belliard .05 .01
❑ 488 Jeff Manto .05 .01
❑ 489 Bobby Valentine MG .05 .01
❑ 490 Kirk Gibson .10 .02
❑ 491 Kurt Miller RC .05 .01
❑ 492 Ernie Whitt .05 .01
❑ 493 Jose Rijo .05 .01
❑ 494 Chris James .05 .01
❑ 495 Charlie Hough .10 .02
❑ 496 Marty Barrett .05 .01
❑ 497 Ben McDonald .05 .01
❑ 498 Mark Salas .05 .01
❑ 499 Melido Perez .05 .01
❑ 500 Will Clark .15 .05
❑ 501 Mike Bielecki .05 .01
❑ 502 Carney Lansford .10 .02
❑ 503 Roy Smith .05 .01
❑ 504 Julio Valera .05 .01
❑ 505 Chuck Finley .10 .02
❑ 506 Darnell Coles .05 .01
❑ 507 Steve Jeltz .05 .01
❑ 508 Mike York RC .05 .01
❑ 509 Glenallen Hill .05 .01
❑ 510 John Franco .10 .02
❑ 511 Steve Balboni .05 .01
❑ 512 Jose Mesa .05 .01
❑ 513 Jerald Clark .05 .01
❑ 514 Mike Stanton .05 .01
❑ 515 Alvin Davis .05 .01
❑ 516 Karl Rhodes .05 .01
❑ 517 Joe Oliver .05 .01
❑ 518 Cris Carpenter .05 .01
❑ 519 Sparky Anderson MG .10 .02
❑ 520 Mark Grace .15 .05
❑ 521 Joe Orsulak .05 .01
❑ 522 Stan Belinda .05 .01
❑ 523 Rodney McCray RC .05 .01
❑ 524 Darrel Akerfelds .05 .01
❑ 525 Willie Randolph .10 .02
❑ 526A Moises Alou ERR .40 .15
❑ 526B Moises Alou COR .10 .02
❑ 527A Checklist 4 ERR
105 Keith Miller
719 Kevin McRey .25 .08
❑ 527B Checklist 4 COR
105 Kevin McReynolds
719 Keith M .05 .01
❑ 528 Dennis Martinez .10 .02
❑ 529 Marc Newfield RC .10 .02
❑ 530 Roger Clemens .75 .30
❑ 531 Dave Rohde .05 .01
❑ 532 Kirk McCaskill .05 .01
❑ 533 Oddibe McDowell .05 .01
❑ 534 Mike Jackson .05 .01
❑ 535 Ruben Sierra UER .10 .02
❑ 536 Mike Witt .05 .01
❑ 537 Jose Lind .05 .01
❑ 538 Bip Roberts .05 .01
❑ 539 Scott Terry .05 .01
❑ 540 George Brett .60 .25
❑ 541 Domingo Ramos .05 .01
❑ 542 Rob Murphy .05 .01
❑ 543 Junior Felix .05 .01
❑ 544 Alejandro Pena .05 .01
❑ 545 Dale Murphy .15 .05
❑ 546 Jeff Ballard .05 .01
❑ 547 Mike Pagliarulo .05 .01
❑ 548 Jaime Navarro .05 .01
❑ 549 John McNamara MG .05 .01
❑ 550 Eric Davis .10 .02
❑ 551 Bob Kipper .05 .01
❑ 552 Jeff Hamilton .05 .01
❑ 553 Joe Klink .05 .01
❑ 554 Brian Harper .05 .01
❑ 555 Turner Ward RC .10 .02
❑ 556 Gary Ward .05 .01
❑ 557 Wally Whitehurst .05 .01
❑ 558 Otis Nixon .05 .01
❑ 559 Adam Peterson .05 .01
❑ 560 Greg Smith .05 .01
❑ 561 Tim McIntosh .05 .01
❑ 562 Jeff Kunkel .05 .01
❑ 563 Brent Knackert .05 .01
❑ 564 Dante Bichette .10 .02
❑ 565 Craig Biggio .15 .05
❑ 566 Craig Wilson RC .05 .01
❑ 567 Dwayne Henry .05 .01
❑ 568 Ron Karkovice .05 .01
❑ 569 Curt Schilling .25 .08
❑ 570 Barry Bonds 1.00 .40
❑ 571 Pat Combs .05 .01
❑ 572 Dave Anderson .05 .01
❑ 573 Rich Rodriguez UER RC .05 .01
❑ 574 John Marzano .05 .01
❑ 575 Robin Yount .40 .15
❑ 576 Jeff Kaiser .05 .01
❑ 577 Bill Doran .05 .01
❑ 578 Dave West .05 .01
❑ 579 Roger Craig MG .05 .01
❑ 580 Dave Stewart .10 .02
❑ 581 Luis Quinones .05 .01
❑ 582 Marty Clary .05 .01
❑ 583 Tony Phillips .05 .01
❑ 584 Kevin Brown .10 .02
❑ 585 Pete O'Brien .05 .01
❑ 586 Fred Lynn .05 .01
❑ 587 Jose Offerman UER .05 .01
❑ 588 Mark Whiten FTC .05 .01
❑ 589 Scott Ruskin .05 .01
❑ 590 Eddie Murray .25 .08
❑ 591 Ken Hill .05 .01
❑ 592 B.J. Surhoff .10 .02
❑ 593A Mike Walker ERR
('90 Canton-Akron
stat line omit .25 .08
❑ 593B Mike Walker COR .05 .01
❑ 594 Rich Garces RC .10 .02
❑ 595 Bill Landrum .05 .01
❑ 596 Ronnie Walden RC .10 .02
❑ 597 Jerry Don Gleaton .05 .01
❑ 598 Sam Horn .05 .01
❑ 599A Greg Myers ERR
('90 Syracuse
stat line omitted) .25 .08
❑ 599B Greg Myers COR .05 .01
❑ 600 Bo Jackson .25 .08
❑ 601 Bob Ojeda .05 .01
❑ 602 Casey Candaele .05 .01
❑ 603A Wes Chamberlain ERR .40 .15
❑ 603B Wes Chamberlain COR RC .10 .02
❑ 604 Billy Hatcher .05 .01
❑ 605 Jeff Reardon .10 .02
❑ 606 Jim Gott .05 .01
❑ 607 Edgar Martinez .15 .05
❑ 608 Todd Burns .05 .01
❑ 609 Jeff Torborg MG .05 .01
❑ 610 Andres Galarraga .10 .02
❑ 611 Dave Eiland .05 .01
❑ 612 Steve Lyons .05 .01
❑ 613 Eric Show .05 .01
❑ 614 Luis Salazar .05 .01
❑ 615 Bert Blyleven .10 .02
❑ 616 Todd Zeile .05 .01
❑ 617 Bill Wegman .05 .01
❑ 618 Sil Campusano .05 .01
❑ 619 David Wells .10 .02
❑ 620 Ozzie Guillen .10 .02
❑ 621 Ted Power .05 .01
❑ 622 Jack Daugherty .05 .01
❑ 623 Jeff Blauser .05 .01
❑ 624 Tom Candiotti .05 .01
❑ 625 Terry Steinbach .05 .01
❑ 626 Gerald Young .05 .01
❑ 627 Tim Layana .05 .01
❑ 628 Greg Litton .05 .01
❑ 629 Wes Gardner .05 .01
❑ 630 Dave Winfield .10 .02
❑ 631 Mike Morgan .05 .01
❑ 632 Lloyd Moseby .05 .01
❑ 633 Kevin Tapani .05 .01
❑ 634 Henry Cotto .05 .01
❑ 635 Andy Hawkins .05 .01
❑ 636 Geronimo Pena .05 .01
❑ 637 Bruce Ruffin .05 .01
❑ 638 Mike Macfarlane .05 .01
❑ 639 Frank Robinson MG .15 .05
❑ 640 Andre Dawson .10 .02
❑ 641 Mike Henneman .05 .01
❑ 642 Hal Morris .05 .01
❑ 643 Jim Presley .05 .01
❑ 644 Chuck Crim .05 .01
❑ 645 Juan Samuel .05 .01
❑ 646 Andujar Cedeno .05 .01
❑ 647 Mark Portugal .05 .01
❑ 648 Lee Stevens .05 .01
❑ 649 Bill Sampen .05 .01
❑ 650 Jack Clark .10 .02
❑ 651 Alan Mills .05 .01
❑ 652 Kevin Romine .05 .01
❑ 653 Anthony Telford RC .05 .01
❑ 654 Paul Sorrento .05 .01
❑ 655 Erik Hanson .05 .01
❑ 656A Checklist 5 ERR
348 Vicente Palacios
381 Jose Li .25 .08
❑ 656B Checklist 5 ERR
433 Vicente Palacios
(Palacios s .25 .08
❑ 656C Checklist 5 COR
438 Vicente Palacios
537 Jose Li .05 .01
❑ 657 Mike Kingery .05 .01
❑ 658 Scott Aldred .05 .01
❑ 659 Oscar Azocar .05 .01
❑ 660 Lee Smith .10 .02
❑ 661 Steve Lake .05 .01
❑ 662 Ron Dibble .10 .02
❑ 663 Greg Brock .05 .01
❑ 664 John Farrell .05 .01
❑ 665 Mike LaValliere .05 .01
❑ 666 Danny Darwin .05 .01
❑ 667 Kent Anderson .05 .01
❑ 668 Bill Long .05 .01
❑ 669 Lou Piniella MG .10 .02
❑ 670 Rickey Henderson .25 .08
❑ 671 Andy McGaffigan .05 .01
❑ 672 Shane Mack .05 .01
❑ 673 Greg Olson UER
(6 RBI in '88 at Tide-

water and .05 .01
❑ 674A Kevin Gross ERR (89 BB with Phillies in '88 tied .25 .08
❑ 674B Kevin Gross COR (89 BB with Phillies in '88 led .05 .01
❑ 675 Tom Brunansky .05 .01
❑ 676 Scott Chiamparino .05 .01
❑ 677 Billy Ripken .05 .01
❑ 678 Mark Davidson .05 .01
❑ 679 Bill Bathe .05 .01
❑ 680 David Cone .10 .02
❑ 681 Jeff Schaefer .05 .01
❑ 682 Ray Lankford .10 .02
❑ 683 Derek Lilliquist .05 .01
❑ 684 Milt Cuyler .05 .01
❑ 685 Doug Drabek .05 .01
❑ 686 Mike Gallego .05 .01
❑ 687A John Cerutti ERR (4.46 ERA in '90) .25 .08
❑ 687B John Cerutti COR (4.76 ERA in '90) .05 .01
❑ 688 Rosario Rodriguez RC .05 .01
❑ 689 John Kruk .10 .02
❑ 690 Orel Hershiser .10 .02
❑ 691 Mike Blowers .05 .01
❑ 692A Efrain Valdez ERR .25 .08
❑ 692B Efrain Valdez COR RC .05 .01
❑ 693 Francisco Cabrera .05 .01
❑ 694 Randy Veres .05 .01
❑ 695 Kevin Seitzer .05 .01
❑ 696 Steve Olin .05 .01
❑ 697 Shawn Abner .05 .01
❑ 698 Mark Guthrie .05 .01
❑ 699 Jim Lefebvre MG .05 .01
❑ 700 Jose Canseco .15 .05
❑ 701 Pascual Perez .05 .01
❑ 702 Tim Naehring .05 .01
❑ 703 Juan Agosto .05 .01
❑ 704 Devon White .10 .02
❑ 705 Robby Thompson .05 .01
❑ 706A Brad Arnsberg ERR .25 .08
❑ 706B Brad Arnsberg COR .05 .01
❑ 707 Jim Eisenreich .05 .01
❑ 708 John Mitchell .05 .01
❑ 709 Matt Sinatro .05 .01
❑ 710 Kent Hrbek .10 .02
❑ 711 Jose DeLeon .05 .01
❑ 712 Ricky Jordan .05 .01
❑ 713 Scott Scudder .05 .01
❑ 714 Marvell Wynne .05 .01
❑ 715 Tim Burke .05 .01
❑ 716 Bob Geren .05 .01
❑ 717 Phil Bradley .05 .01
❑ 718 Steve Crawford .05 .01
❑ 719 Keith Miller .05 .01
❑ 720 Cecil Fielder .10 .02
❑ 721 Mark Lee RC .05 .01
❑ 722 Wally Backman .05 .01
❑ 723 Candy Maldonado .05 .01
❑ 724 David Segui .05 .01
❑ 725 Ron Gant .10 .02
❑ 726 Phil Stephenson .05 .01
❑ 727 Mookie Wilson .10 .02
❑ 728 Scott Sanderson .05 .01
❑ 729 Don Zimmer MG .10 .02
❑ 730 Barry Larkin .15 .05
❑ 731 Jeff Gray RC .05 .01
❑ 732 Franklin Stubbs .05 .01
❑ 733 Kelly Downs .05 .01
❑ 734 John Russell .05 .01
❑ 735 Ron Darling .05 .01
❑ 736 Dick Schofield .05 .01
❑ 737 Tim Crews .05 .01
❑ 738 Mel Hall .05 .01
❑ 739 Russ Swan .05 .01
❑ 740 Ryne Sandberg .40 .15
❑ 741 Jimmy Key .10 .02
❑ 742 Tommy Gregg .05 .01
❑ 743 Bryn Smith .05 .01
❑ 744 Nelson Santovenia .05 .01
❑ 745 Doug Jones .05 .01
❑ 746 John Shelby .05 .01
❑ 747 Tony Fossas .05 .01
❑ 748 Al Newman .05 .01
❑ 749 Greg W. Harris .05 .01
❑ 750 Bobby Bonilla .10 .02
❑ 751 Wayne Edwards .05 .01
❑ 752 Kevin Bass .05 .01
❑ 753 Paul Marak UER RC .05 .01
❑ 754 Bill Pecota .05 .01
❑ 755 Mark Langston .05 .01
❑ 756 Jeff Huson .05 .01
❑ 757 Mark Gardner .05 .01
❑ 758 Mike Devereaux .05 .01
❑ 759 Bobby Cox MG .05 .01
❑ 760 Benny Santiago .10 .02
❑ 761 Larry Andersen .05 .01
❑ 762 Mitch Webster .05 .01
❑ 763 Dana Kiecker .05 .01
❑ 764 Mark Carreon .05 .01
❑ 765 Shawon Dunston .05 .01
❑ 766 Jeff Robinson .05 .01
❑ 767 Dan Wilson RC .25 .08
❑ 768 Don Pall .05 .01
❑ 769 Tim Sherrill .05 .01
❑ 770 Jay Howell .05 .01
❑ 771 Gary Redus UER (Born in Tanner, should say Athen .05 .01
❑ 772 Kent Mercker (Born in Indianapolis, should say D .05 .01
❑ 773 Tom Foley .05 .01
❑ 774 Dennis Rasmussen .05 .01
❑ 775 Julio Franco .10 .02
❑ 776 Brent Mayne .05 .01
❑ 777 John Candelaria .05 .01
❑ 778 Dan Gladden .05 .01
❑ 779 Carmelo Martinez .05 .01
❑ 780A Randy Myers ERR (15 career losses) .40 .15
❑ 780B Randy Myers COR (19 career losses) .05 .01
❑ 781 Darryl Hamilton .05 .01
❑ 782 Jim Deshaies .05 .01
❑ 783 Joel Skinner .05 .01
❑ 784 Willie Fraser .05 .01
❑ 785 Scott Fletcher .05 .01
❑ 786 Eric Plunk .05 .01
❑ 787 Checklist 6 .05 .01
❑ 788 Bob Milacki .05 .01
❑ 789 Tom Lasorda MG .25 .08
❑ 790 Ken Griffey Jr. .75 .30
❑ 791 Mike Benjamin .05 .01
❑ 792 Mike Greenwell .05 .01

1991 Topps Traded

❑ COMPLETE SET (132) 10.00 4.00
❑ COMP.FACT.SET (132) 10.00 4.00
❑ 1T Juan Agosto .05 .01
❑ 2T Roberto Alomar .15 .05
❑ 3T Wally Backman .05 .01
❑ 4T Jeff Bagwell RC 1.50 .60
❑ 5T Skeeter Barnes .05 .01
❑ 6T Steve Bedrosian .05 .01
❑ 7T Derek Bell .10 .02
❑ 8T George Bell .05 .01
❑ 9T Rafael Belliard .05 .01
❑ 10T Dante Bichette .10 .02
❑ 11T Bud Black .05 .01
❑ 12T Mike Boddicker .05 .01
❑ 13T Sid Bream .05 .01
❑ 14T Hubie Brooks .05 .01
❑ 15T Brett Butler .10 .02
❑ 16T Ivan Calderon .05 .01
❑ 17T John Candelaria .05 .01
❑ 18T Tom Candiotti .05 .01
❑ 19T Gary Carter .10 .02
❑ 20T Joe Carter .10 .02
❑ 21T Rick Cerone .05 .01
❑ 22T Jack Clark .10 .02
❑ 23T Vince Coleman .05 .01
❑ 24T Scott Coolbaugh .05 .01
❑ 25T Danny Cox .05 .01
❑ 26T Danny Darwin .05 .01
❑ 27T Chili Davis .10 .02
❑ 28T Glenn Davis .05 .01
❑ 29T Steve Decker RC .05 .01
❑ 30T Rob Deer .05 .01
❑ 31T Rich DeLucia RC .05 .01
❑ 32T John Dettmer USA RC .25 .08
❑ 33T Brian Downing .05 .01
❑ 34T Darren Dreifort USA RC .25 .08
❑ 35T Kirk Dressendorfer RC .05 .01
❑ 36T Jim Essian MG .05 .01
❑ 37T Dwight Evans .15 .05
❑ 38T Steve Farr .05 .01
❑ 39T Jeff Fassero RC .25 .08
❑ 40T Junior Felix .05 .01
❑ 41T Tony Fernandez .05 .01
❑ 42T Steve Finley .10 .02
❑ 43T Jim Fregosi MG .05 .01
❑ 44T Gary Gaetti .10 .02
❑ 45T Jason Giambi USA RC 5.00 2.00
❑ 46T Kirk Gibson .10 .02
❑ 47T Leo Gomez .05 .01
❑ 48T Luis Gonzalez RC .50 .20
❑ 49T Jeff Granger USA RC .25 .08
❑ 50T Todd Greene USA RC .50 .20
❑ 51T Jeffrey Hammonds USA RC .50 .20
❑ 52T Mike Hargrove MG .05 .01
❑ 53T Pete Harnisch .05 .01
❑ 54T Rick Helling USA RC .50 .20
❑ 55T Glenallen Hill .05 .01
❑ 56T Charlie Hough .10 .02
❑ 57T Pete Incaviglia .05 .01
❑ 58T Bo Jackson .25 .08
❑ 59T Danny Jackson .05 .01
❑ 60T Reggie Jefferson .05 .01
❑ 61T Charles Johnson USA RC .75 .30
❑ 62T Jeff Johnson RC .05 .01
❑ 63T Todd Johnson USA RC .25 .08
❑ 64T Barry Jones .05 .01
❑ 65T Chris Jones RC .10 .02
❑ 66T Scott Kamieniecki RC .10 .02
❑ 67T Pat Kelly RC .10 .02
❑ 68T Darryl Kile .10 .02
❑ 69T Chuck Knoblauch .10 .02
❑ 70T Bill Krueger .05 .01
❑ 71T Scott Leius .05 .01
❑ 72T Donnie Leshnock USA RC .25 .08
❑ 73T Mark Lewis .05 .01
❑ 74T Candy Maldonado .05 .01
❑ 75T Jason McDonald USA RC .25 .08
❑ 76T Willie McGee .10 .02
❑ 77T Fred McGriff .15 .05
❑ 78T Billy McMillon USA RC .25 .08
❑ 79T Hal McRae MG .10 .02
❑ 80T Dan Melendez USA RC .25 .08
❑ 81T Orlando Merced RC .10 .02
❑ 82T Jack Morris .10 .02
❑ 83T Phil Nevin USA RC .75 .30
❑ 84T Otis Nixon .05 .01
❑ 85T Johnny Oates MG .05 .01
❑ 86T Bob Ojeda .05 .01
❑ 87T Mike Pagliarulo .05 .01
❑ 88T Dean Palmer .10 .02
❑ 89T Dave Parker .10 .02
❑ 90T Terry Pendleton .10 .02
❑ 91T Tony Phillips (P) USA RC .25 .08
❑ 92T Doug Piatt RC .05 .01
❑ 93T Ron Polk USA CO .25 .08
❑ 94T Tim Raines .10 .02
❑ 95T Willie Randolph .10 .02
❑ 96T Dave Righetti .10 .02
❑ 97T Ernie Riles .05 .01
❑ 98T Chris Roberts USA RC .25 .08
❑ 99T Jeff D. Robinson .05 .01

100T Jeff M. Robinson .05 .01
101T Ivan Rodriguez RC 3.00 1.25
102T Steve Rodriguez USA RC .25 .08
103T Tom Runnells MG .05 .01
104T Scott Sanderson .05 .01
105T Bob Scanlan RC .05 .01
106T Pete Schourek RC .10 .02
107T Gary Scott RC .05 .01
108T Paul Shuey USA RC .50 .20
109T Doug Simons RC .05 .01
110T Dave Smith .05 .01
111T Cory Snyder .05 .01
112T Luis Sojo .05 .01
113T Kennie Steenstra USA RC .25 .08
114T Darryl Strawberry .10 .02
115T Franklin Stubbs .05 .01
116T Todd Taylor USA RC .25 .08
117T Wade Taylor RC .05 .01
118T Garry Templeton .05 .01
119T Mickey Tettleton .05 .01
120T Tim Teufel .05 .01
121T Mike Timlin RC .25 .08
122T David Tuttle USA RC .25 .08
123T Mo Vaughn .10 .02
124T Jeff Ware USA RC .25 .08
125T Devon White .10 .02
126T Mark Whiten .05 .01
127T Mitch Williams .05 .01
128T Craig Wilson USA RC .25 .08
129T Willie Wilson .05 .01
130T Chris Wimmer USA RC .25 .08
131T Ivan Zweig USA RC .25 .08
132T Checklist 1T-132T .05 .01

1992 Topps

COMPLETE SET (792) 25.00 10.00
COMP.FACT.SET (802) 25.00 10.00
COMP.HOLIDAY SET (811) 40.00 15.00
1 Nolan Ryan 1.00 .40
2 Rickey Henderson RB .15 .05
3 Jeff Reardon RB .05 .01
4 Nolan Ryan RB .50 .20
5 Dave Winfield RB .05 .01
6 Brien Taylor RC .25 .08
7 Jim Olander .05 .01
8 Bryan Hickerson RC .10 .02
9 Jon Farrell RC .10 .02
10 Wade Boggs .15 .05
11 Jack McDowell .05 .01
12 Luis Gonzalez .10 .02
13 Mike Scioscia .05 .01
14 Wes Chamberlain .05 .01
15 Dennis Martinez .10 .02
16 Jeff Montgomery .05 .01
17 Randy Milligan .05 .01
18 Greg Cadaret .05 .01
19 Jamie Quirk .05 .01
20 Bip Roberts .05 .01
21 Buck Rodgers MG .05 .01
22 Bill Wegman .05 .01
23 Chuck Knoblauch .10 .02
24 Randy Myers .05 .01
25 Ron Gant .10 .02
26 Mike Bielecki .05 .01
27 Juan Gonzalez .15 .05
28 Mike Schooler .05 .01
29 Mickey Tettleton .05 .01
30 John Kruk .10 .02
31 Bryn Smith .05 .01
32 Chris Nabholz .05 .01
33 Carlos Baerga .05 .01
34 Jeff Juden .05 .01
35 Dave Righetti .10 .02
36 Scott Ruffcorn RC .10 .02
37 Luis Polonia .05 .01
38 Tom Candiotti .05 .01
39 Greg Olson .05 .01
40 Cal Ripken/Gehrig 2.00 .75
41 Craig Lefferts .05 .01
42 Mike Macfarlane .05 .01
43 Jose Lind .05 .01
44 Rick Aguilera .10 .02
45 Gary Carter .10 .02
46 Steve Farr .05 .01
47 Rex Hudler .05 .01
48 Scott Scudder .05 .01
49 Damon Berryhill .05 .01
50 Ken Griffey Jr. .40 .15
51 Tom Runnells MG .05 .01
52 Juan Bell .05 .01
53 Tommy Gregg .05 .01
54 David Wells .10 .02
55 Rafael Palmeiro .15 .05
56 Charlie O'Brien .05 .01
57 Donn Pall .05 .01
58 Brad Ausmus RC 1.50 .60
59 Mo Vaughn .10 .02
60 Tony Fernandez .05 .01
61 Paul O'Neill .15 .05
62 Gene Nelson .05 .01
63 Randy Ready .05 .01
64 Bob Kipper .05 .01
65 Willie McGee .10 .02
66 Scott Stahoviak RC .10 .02
67 Luis Salazar .05 .01
68 Marvin Freeman .05 .01
69 Kenny Lofton .15 .05
70 Gary Gaetti .10 .02
71 Erik Hanson .05 .01
72 Eddie Zosky .05 .01
73 Brian Barnes .05 .01
74 Scott Leius .05 .01
75 Bret Saberhagen .10 .02
76 Mike Gallego .05 .01
77 Jack Armstrong .05 .01
78 Ivan Rodriguez .25 .08
79 Jesse Orosco .05 .01
80 David Justice .10 .02
81 Ced Landrum .05 .01
82 Doug Simons .05 .01
83 Tommy Greene .05 .01
84 Leo Gomez .05 .01
85 Jose DeLeon .05 .01
86 Steve Finley .10 .02
87 Bob MacDonald .05 .01
88 Darrin Jackson .05 .01
89 Neal Heaton .05 .01
90 Robin Yount .40 .15
91 Jeff Reed .05 .01
92 Lenny Harris .05 .01
93 Reggie Jefferson .05 .01
94 Sammy Sosa .25 .08
95 Scott Bailes .05 .01
96 Tom McKinnon RC .10 .02
97 Luis Rivera .05 .01
98 Mike Harkey .05 .01
99 Jeff Treadway .05 .01
100 Jose Canseco .15 .05
101 Omar Vizquel .15 .05
102 Scott Kamieniecki .05 .01
103 Ricky Jordan .05 .01
104 Jeff Ballard .05 .01
105 Felix Jose .05 .01
106 Mike Boddicker .05 .01
107 Dan Pasqua .05 .01
108 Mike Timlin .05 .01
109 Roger Craig MG .05 .01
110 Ryne Sandberg .40 .15
111 Mark Carreon .05 .01
112 Oscar Azocar .05 .01
113 Mike Greenwell .05 .01
114 Mark Portugal .05 .01
115 Terry Pendleton .10 .02
116 Willie Randolph .10 .02
117 Scott Terry .05 .01
118 Chili Davis .10 .02
119 Mark Gardner .05 .01
120 Alan Trammell .10 .02
121 Derek Bell .10 .02
122 Gary Varsho .05 .01
123 Bob Ojeda .05 .01
124 Shawn Livsey RC .10 .02
125 Chris Hoiles .05 .01
126 Klesko/Jaha/Brogna/Staton .25 .08
127 Carlos Quintana .05 .01
128 Kurt Stillwell .05 .01
129 Melido Perez .05 .01
130 Alvin Davis .05 .01
131 Checklist 1-132 .05 .01
132 Eric Show .05 .01
133 Rance Mulliniks .05 .01
134 Darryl Kile .10 .02
135 Von Hayes .05 .01
136 Bill Doran .05 .01
137 Jeff D. Robinson .05 .01
138 Monty Fariss .05 .01
139 Jeff Innis .05 .01
140 Mark Grace UER .15 .05
141 Jim Leyland MG UER
(No closed parenthesis
after .10 .02
142 Todd Van Poppel .05 .01
143 Paul Gibson .05 .01
144 Bill Swift .05 .01
145 Danny Tartabull .05 .01
146 Al Newman .05 .01
147 Cris Carpenter .05 .01
148 Anthony Young .05 .01
149 Brian Bohanon .05 .01
150 Roger Clemens .50 .20
151 Jeff Hamilton .05 .01
152 Charlie Leibrandt .05 .01
153 Ron Karkovice .05 .01
154 Hensley Meulens .05 .01
155 Scott Bankhead .05 .01
156 Manny Ramirez RC 4.00 1.50
157 Keith Miller .05 .01
158 Todd Frohwirth .05 .01
159 Darrin Fletcher .05 .01
160 Bobby Bonilla .10 .02
161 Casey Candaele .05 .01
162 Paul Faries .05 .01
163 Dana Kiecker .05 .01
164 Shane Mack .05 .01
165 Mark Langston .05 .01
166 Geronimo Pena .05 .01
167 Andy Allanson .05 .01
168 Dwight Smith .05 .01
169 Chuck Crim .05 .01
170 Alex Cole .05 .01
171 Bill Plummer MG .05 .01
172 Juan Berenguer .05 .01
173 Brian Downing .05 .01
174 Steve Frey .05 .01
175 Orel Hershiser .10 .02
176 Ramon Garcia .05 .01
177 Dan Gladden .05 .01
178 Jim Acker .05 .01
179 DeJard/Bern/Moreno/Stank .05 .01
180 Kevin Mitchell .05 .01
181 Hector Villanueva .05 .01
182 Jeff Reardon .10 .02
183 Brent Mayne .05 .01
184 Jimmy Jones .05 .01
185 Benito Santiago .10 .02
186 Cliff Floyd RC .75 .30
187 Ernie Riles .05 .01
188 Jose Guzman .05 .01
189 Junior Felix .05 .01
190 Glenn Davis .05 .01
191 Charlie Hough .10 .02
192 Dave Fleming .05 .01
193 Omar Olivares .05 .01
194 Eric Karros .10 .02
195 David Cone .10 .02
196 Frank Castillo .05 .01
197 Glenn Braggs .05 .01
198 Scott Aldred .05 .01
199 Jeff Blauser .05 .01
200 Len Dykstra .10 .02

❑ 201 Buck Showalter MG RC .25 .08
❑ 202 Rick Honeycutt .05 .01
❑ 203 Greg Myers .05 .01
❑ 204 Trevor Wilson .05 .01
❑ 205 Jay Howell .05 .01
❑ 206 Luis Sojo .05 .01
❑ 207 Jack Clark .10 .02
❑ 208 Julio Machado .05 .01
❑ 209 Lloyd McClendon .05 .01
❑ 210 Ozzie Guillen .10 .02
❑ 211 Jeremy Hernandez RC .10 .02
❑ 212 Randy Velarde .05 .01
❑ 213 Les Lancaster .05 .01
❑ 214 Andy Mota .05 .01
❑ 215 Rich Gossage .10 .02
❑ 216 Brent Gates RC .10 .02
❑ 217 Brian Harper .05 .01
❑ 218 Mike Flanagan .05 .01
❑ 219 Jerry Browne .05 .01
❑ 220 Jose Rijo .05 .01
❑ 221 Skeeter Barnes .05 .01
❑ 222 Jaime Navarro .05 .01
❑ 223 Mel Hall .05 .01
❑ 224 Bret Barberie .05 .01
❑ 225 Roberto Alomar .15 .05
❑ 226 Pete Smith .05 .01
❑ 227 Daryl Boston .05 .01
❑ 228 Eddie Whitson .05 .01
❑ 229 Shawn Boskie .05 .01
❑ 230 Dick Schofield .05 .01
❑ 231 Brian Drahman .05 .01
❑ 232 John Smiley .05 .01
❑ 233 Mitch Webster .05 .01
❑ 234 Terry Steinbach .05 .01
❑ 235 Jack Morris .10 .02
❑ 236 Bill Pecota .05 .01
❑ 237 Jose Hernandez RC .25 .08
❑ 238 Greg Litton .05 .01
❑ 239 Brian Holman .05 .01
❑ 240 Andres Galarraga .10 .02
❑ 241 Gerald Young .05 .01
❑ 242 Mike Mussina .25 .08
❑ 243 Alvaro Espinoza .05 .01
❑ 244 Darren Daulton .10 .02
❑ 245 John Smoltz .15 .05
❑ 246 Jason Pruitt RC .10 .02
❑ 247 Chuck Finley .10 .02
❑ 248 Jim Gantner .05 .01
❑ 249 Tony Fossas .05 .01
❑ 250 Ken Griffey Sr. .10 .02
❑ 251 Kevin Elster .05 .01
❑ 252 Dennis Rasmussen .05 .01
❑ 253 Terry Kennedy .05 .01
❑ 254 Ryan Bowen .05 .01
❑ 255 Robin Ventura .10 .02
❑ 256 Mike Aldrete .05 .01
❑ 257 Jeff Russell .05 .01
❑ 258 Jim Lindeman .05 .01
❑ 259 Ron Darling .05 .01
❑ 260 Devon White .10 .02
❑ 261 Tom Lasorda MG .10 .02
❑ 262 Terry Lee .05 .01
❑ 263 Bob Patterson .05 .01
❑ 264 Checklist 133-264 .05 .01
❑ 265 Teddy Higuera .05 .01
❑ 266 Roberto Kelly .05 .01
❑ 267 Steve Bedrosian .05 .01
❑ 268 Brady Anderson .10 .02
❑ 269 Ruben Amaro .05 .01
❑ 270 Tony Gwynn .30 .10
❑ 271 Tracy Jones .05 .01
❑ 272 Jerry Don Gleaton .05 .01
❑ 273 Craig Grebeck .05 .01
❑ 274 Bob Scanlan .05 .01
❑ 275 Todd Zeile .05 .01
❑ 276 Shawn Green RC 1.00 .40
❑ 277 Scott Chiamparino .05 .01
❑ 278 Darryl Hamilton .05 .01
❑ 279 Jim Clancy .05 .01
❑ 280 Carlos Martinez .05 .01
❑ 281 Kevin Appier .10 .02
❑ 282 John Wehner .05 .01
❑ 283 Reggie Sanders .10 .02
❑ 284 Gene Larkin .05 .01
❑ 285 Bob Welch .05 .01
❑ 286 Gilberto Reyes .05 .01
❑ 287 Pete Schourek .05 .01
❑ 288 Andujar Cedeno .05 .01
❑ 289 Mike Morgan .05 .01
❑ 290 Bo Jackson .25 .08
❑ 291 Phil Garner MG .10 .02
❑ 292 Ray Lankford .10 .02
❑ 293 Mike Henneman .05 .01
❑ 294 Dave Valle .05 .01
❑ 295 Alonzo Powell .05 .01
❑ 296 Tom Brunansky .05 .01
❑ 297 Kevin Brown .10 .02
❑ 298 Kelly Gruber .05 .01
❑ 299 Charles Nagy .05 .01
❑ 300 Don Mattingly .60 .25
❑ 301 Kirk McCaskill .05 .01
❑ 302 Joey Cora .05 .01
❑ 303 Dan Plesac .05 .01
❑ 304 Joe Oliver .05 .01
❑ 305 Tom Glavine .15 .05
❑ 306 Al Shirley RC .10 .02
❑ 307 Bruce Ruffin .05 .01
❑ 308 Craig Shipley .05 .01
❑ 309 Dave Martinez .05 .01
❑ 310 Jose Mesa .05 .01
❑ 311 Henry Cotto .05 .01
❑ 312 Mike LaValliere .05 .01
❑ 313 Kevin Tapani .05 .01
❑ 314 Jeff Huson .05 .01
❑ 315 Juan Samuel .05 .01
❑ 316 Curt Schilling .15 .05
❑ 317 Mike Bordick .05 .01
❑ 318 Steve Howe .05 .01
❑ 319 Tony Phillips .05 .01
❑ 320 George Bell .05 .01
❑ 321 Lou Piniella MG .10 .02
❑ 322 Tim Burke .05 .01
❑ 323 Milt Thompson .05 .01
❑ 324 Danny Darwin .05 .01
❑ 325 Joe Orsulak .05 .01
❑ 326 Eric King .05 .01
❑ 327 Jay Buhner .10 .02
❑ 328 Joel Johnston .05 .01
❑ 329 Franklin Stubbs .05 .01
❑ 330 Will Clark .15 .05
❑ 331 Steve Lake .05 .01
❑ 332 Chris Jones .05 .01
❑ 333 Pat Tabler .05 .01
❑ 334 Kevin Gross .05 .01
❑ 335 Dave Henderson .05 .01
❑ 336 Greg Anthony RC .10 .02
❑ 337 Alejandro Pena .05 .01
❑ 338 Shawn Abner .05 .01
❑ 339 Tom Browning .05 .01
❑ 340 Otis Nixon .05 .01
❑ 341 Bob Geren .05 .01
❑ 342 Tim Spehr .05 .01
❑ 343 John Vander Wal .05 .01
❑ 344 Jack Daugherty .05 .01
❑ 345 Zane Smith .05 .01
❑ 346 Rheal Cormier .05 .01
❑ 347 Kent Hrbek .10 .02
❑ 348 Rick Wilkins .05 .01
❑ 349 Steve Lyons .05 .01
❑ 350 Gregg Olson .05 .01
❑ 351 Greg Riddoch MG .05 .01
❑ 352 Ed Nunez .05 .01
❑ 353 Braulio Castillo .05 .01
❑ 354 Dave Bergman .05 .01
❑ 355 Warren Newson .05 .01
❑ 356 Luis Quinones .05 .01
❑ 357 Mike Witt .05 .01
❑ 358 Ted Wood .05 .01
❑ 359 Mike Moore .05 .01
❑ 360 Lance Parrish .10 .02
❑ 361 Barry Jones .05 .01
❑ 362 Javier Ortiz .05 .01
❑ 363 John Candelaria .05 .01
❑ 364 Glenallen Hill .05 .01
❑ 365 Duane Ward .05 .01
❑ 366 Checklist 265-396 .05 .01
❑ 367 Rafael Belliard .05 .01
❑ 368 Bill Krueger .05 .01
❑ 369 Steve Whitaker RC .10 .02
❑ 370 Shawon Dunston .05 .01
❑ 371 Dante Bichette .10 .02
❑ 372 Kip Gross .05 .01
❑ 373 Don Robinson .05 .01
❑ 374 Bernie Williams .15 .05
❑ 375 Bert Blyleven .10 .02
❑ 376 Chris Donnels .05 .01
❑ 377 Bob Zupcic RC .10 .02
❑ 378 Joel Skinner .05 .01
❑ 379 Steve Chitren .05 .01
❑ 380 Barry Bonds 1.00 .40
❑ 381 Sparky Anderson MG .10 .02
❑ 382 Sid Fernandez .05 .01
❑ 383 Dave Hollins .05 .01
❑ 384 Mark Lee .05 .01
❑ 385 Tim Wallach .05 .01
❑ 386 Will Clark AS .10 .02
❑ 387 Ryne Sandberg AS .25 .08
❑ 388 Howard Johnson AS .05 .01
❑ 389 Barry Larkin AS .10 .02
❑ 390 Barry Bonds AS .50 .20
❑ 391 Ron Gant AS .05 .01
❑ 392 Bobby Bonilla AS .05 .01
❑ 393 Craig Biggio AS .10 .02
❑ 394 Dennis Martinez AS .05 .01
❑ 395 Tom Glavine AS .10 .02
❑ 396 Lee Smith AS .05 .01
❑ 397 Cecil Fielder AS .05 .01
❑ 398 Julio Franco AS .05 .01
❑ 399 Wade Boggs AS .10 .02
❑ 400 Cal Ripken AS .40 .15
❑ 401 Jose Canseco AS .15 .05
❑ 402 Joe Carter AS .05 .01
❑ 403 Ruben Sierra AS .05 .01
❑ 404 Matt Nokes AS .05 .01
❑ 405 Roger Clemens AS .25 .08
❑ 406 Jim Abbott AS .10 .02
❑ 407 Bryan Harvey AS .05 .01
❑ 408 Bob Milacki .05 .01
❑ 409 Geno Petralli .05 .01
❑ 410 Dave Stewart .10 .02
❑ 411 Mike Jackson .05 .01
❑ 412 Luis Aquino .05 .01
❑ 413 Tim Teufel .05 .01
❑ 414 Jeff Ware .05 .01
❑ 415 Jim Deshaies .05 .01
❑ 416 Ellis Burks .10 .02
❑ 417 Allan Anderson .05 .01
❑ 418 Alfredo Griffin .05 .01
❑ 419 Wally Whitehurst .05 .01
❑ 420 Sandy Alomar Jr. .05 .01
❑ 421 Juan Agosto .05 .01
❑ 422 Sam Horn .05 .01
❑ 423 Jeff Fassero .05 .01
❑ 424 Paul McClellan .05 .01
❑ 425 Cecil Fielder .10 .02
❑ 426 Tim Raines .10 .02
❑ 427 Eddie Taubensee RC .25 .08
❑ 428 Dennis Boyd .05 .01
❑ 429 Tony LaRussa MG .10 .02
❑ 430 Steve Sax .05 .01
❑ 431 Tom Gordon .05 .01
❑ 432 Billy Hatcher .05 .01
❑ 433 Cal Eldred .05 .01
❑ 434 Wally Backman .05 .01
❑ 435 Mark Eichhorn .05 .01
❑ 436 Mookie Wilson .10 .02
❑ 437 Scott Servais .05 .01
❑ 438 Mike Maddux .05 .01
❑ 439 Chico Walker .05 .01
❑ 440 Doug Drabek .05 .01
❑ 441 Rob Deer .05 .01
❑ 442 Dave West .05 .01
❑ 443 Spike Owen .05 .01
❑ 444 Tyrone Hill RC .10 .02
❑ 445 Matt Williams .10 .02
❑ 446 Mark Lewis .05 .01
❑ 447 David Segui .05 .01
❑ 448 Tom Pagnozzi .05 .01
❑ 449 Jeff Johnson .05 .01
❑ 450 Mark McGwire .60 .25
❑ 451 Tom Henke .05 .01
❑ 452 Wilson Alvarez .05 .01
❑ 453 Gary Redus .05 .01
❑ 454 Darren Holmes .05 .01
❑ 455 Pete O'Brien .05 .01
❑ 456 Pat Combs .05 .01
❑ 457 Hubie Brooks .05 .01
❑ 458 Frank Tanana .05 .01

❑	459	Tom Kelly MG	.05	.01
❑	460	Andre Dawson	.10	.02
❑	461	Doug Jones	.05	.01
❑	462	Rich Rodriguez	.05	.01
❑	463	Mike Simms	.05	.01
❑	464	Mike Jeffcoat	.05	.01
❑	465	Barry Larkin	.15	.05
❑	466	Stan Belinda	.05	.01
❑	467	Lonnie Smith	.05	.01
❑	468	Greg Harris	.05	.01
❑	469	Jim Eisenreich	.05	.01
❑	470	Pedro Guerrero	.10	.02
❑	471	Jose DeJesus	.05	.01
❑	472	Rich Rowland RC	.10	.02
❑	473	Bolick/Paquette/Red/Russo	.05	.01
❑	474	Mike Rossiter RC	.10	.02
❑	475	Robby Thompson	.05	.01
❑	476	Randy Bush	.05	.01
❑	477	Greg Hibbard	.05	.01
❑	478	Dale Sveum	.05	.01
❑	479	Chito Martinez	.05	.01
❑	480	Scott Sanderson	.05	.01
❑	481	Tino Martinez	.15	.05
❑	482	Jimmy Key	.10	.02
❑	483	Terry Shumpert	.05	.01
❑	484	Mike Hartley	.05	.01
❑	485	Chris Sabo	.05	.01
❑	486	Bob Walk	.05	.01
❑	487	John Cerutti	.05	.01
❑	488	Scott Cooper	.05	.01
❑	489	Bobby Cox MG	.10	.02
❑	490	Julio Franco	.10	.02
❑	491	Jeff Brantley	.05	.01
❑	492	Mike Devereaux	.05	.01
❑	493	Jose Offerman	.05	.01
❑	494	Gary Thurman	.05	.01
❑	495	Carney Lansford	.10	.02
❑	496	Joe Grahe	.05	.01
❑	497	Andy Ashby	.05	.01
❑	498	Gerald Perry	.05	.01
❑	499	Dave Otto	.05	.01
❑	500	Vince Coleman	.05	.01
❑	501	Rob Mallicoat	.05	.01
❑	502	Greg Briley	.05	.01
❑	503	Pascual Perez	.05	.01
❑	504	Aaron Sele RC	.25	.08
❑	505	Bobby Thigpen	.05	.01
❑	506	Todd Benzinger	.05	.01
❑	507	Candy Maldonado	.05	.01
❑	508	Bill Gullickson	.05	.01
❑	509	Doug Dascenzo	.05	.01
❑	510	Frank Viola	.10	.02
❑	511	Kenny Rogers	.10	.02
❑	512	Mike Heath	.05	.01
❑	513	Kevin Bass	.05	.01
❑	514	Kim Batiste	.05	.01
❑	515	Delino DeShields	.05	.01
❑	516	Ed Sprague	.05	.01
❑	517	Jim Gott	.05	.01
❑	518	Jose Melendez	.05	.01
❑	519	Hal McRae MG	.10	.02
❑	520	Jeff Bagwell	.25	.08
❑	521	Joe Hesketh	.05	.01
❑	522	Milt Cuyler	.05	.01
❑	523	Shawn Hillegas	.05	.01
❑	524	Don Slaught	.05	.01
❑	525	Randy Johnson	.25	.08
❑	526	Doug Piatt	.05	.01
❑	527	Checklist 397-528	.05	.01
❑	528	Steve Foster	.05	.01
❑	529	Joe Girardi	.05	.01
❑	530	Jim Abbott	.15	.05
❑	531	Larry Walker	.15	.05
❑	532	Mike Huff	.05	.01
❑	533	Mackey Sasser	.05	.01
❑	534	Benji Gil RC	.25	.08
❑	535	Dave Stieb	.05	.01
❑	536	Willie Wilson	.05	.01
❑	537	Mark Leiter	.05	.01
❑	538	Jose Uribe	.05	.01
❑	539	Thomas Howard	.05	.01
❑	540	Ben McDonald	.05	.01
❑	541	Jose Tolentino	.05	.01
❑	542	Keith Mitchell	.05	.01
❑	543	Jerome Walton	.05	.01
❑	544	Cliff Brantley	.05	.01
❑	545	Andy Van Slyke	.15	.05
❑	546	Paul Sorrento	.05	.01
❑	547	Herm Winningham	.05	.01
❑	548	Mark Guthrie	.05	.01
❑	549	Joe Torre MG	.10	.02
❑	550	Darryl Strawberry	.10	.02
❑	551	Chipper Jones	.25	.08
❑	552	Dave Gallagher	.05	.01
❑	553	Edgar Martinez	.15	.05
❑	554	Donald Harris	.05	.01
❑	555	Frank Thomas	.25	.08
❑	556	Storm Davis	.05	.01
❑	557	Dickie Thon	.05	.01
❑	558	Scott Garrelts	.05	.01
❑	559	Steve Olin	.05	.01
❑	560	Rickey Henderson	.25	.08
❑	561	Jose Vizcaino	.05	.01
❑	562	Wade Taylor	.05	.01
❑	563	Pat Borders	.05	.01
❑	564	Jimmy Gonzalez RC	.10	.02
❑	565	Lee Smith	.10	.02
❑	566	Bill Sampen	.05	.01
❑	567	Dean Palmer	.10	.02
❑	568	Bryan Harvey	.05	.01
❑	569	Tony Pena	.05	.01
❑	570	Lou Whitaker	.10	.02
❑	571	Randy Tomlin	.05	.01
❑	572	Greg Vaughn	.05	.01
❑	573	Kelly Downs	.05	.01
❑	574	Steve Avery UER	.05	.01
❑	575	Kirby Puckett	.25	.08
❑	576	Heathcliff Slocumb	.05	.01
❑	577	Kevin Seitzer	.05	.01
❑	578	Lee Guetterman	.05	.01
❑	579	Johnny Oates MG	.05	.01
❑	580	Greg Maddux	.40	.15
❑	581	Stan Javier	.05	.01
❑	582	Vicente Palacios	.05	.01
❑	583	Mel Rojas	.05	.01
❑	584	Wayne Rosenthal RC	.10	.02
❑	585	Lenny Webster	.05	.01
❑	586	Rod Nichols	.05	.01
❑	587	Mickey Morandini	.05	.01
❑	588	Russ Swan	.05	.01
❑	589	Mariano Duncan	.05	.01
❑	590	Howard Johnson	.05	.01
❑	591	Burnitz/Brum/Coc/Dozier	.10	.02
❑	592	Denny Neagle	.10	.02
❑	593	Steve Decker	.05	.01
❑	594	Brian Barber RC	.10	.02
❑	595	Bruce Hurst	.05	.01
❑	596	Kent Mercker	.05	.01
❑	597	Mike Magnante RC	.10	.02
❑	598	Jody Reed	.05	.01
❑	599	Steve Searcy	.05	.01
❑	600	Paul Molitor	.10	.02
❑	601	Dave Smith	.05	.01
❑	602	Mike Fetters	.05	.01
❑	603	Luis Mercedes	.05	.01
❑	604	Chris Gwynn	.05	.01
❑	605	Scott Erickson	.05	.01
❑	606	Brook Jacoby	.05	.01
❑	607	Todd Stottlemyre	.05	.01
❑	608	Scott Bradley	.05	.01
❑	609	Mike Hargrove MG	.10	.02
❑	610	Eric Davis	.10	.02
❑	611	Brian Hunter	.05	.01
❑	612	Pat Kelly	.05	.01
❑	613	Pedro Munoz	.05	.01
❑	614	Al Osuna	.05	.01
❑	615	Matt Merullo	.05	.01
❑	616	Larry Andersen	.05	.01
❑	617	Junior Ortiz	.05	.01
❑	618	Hern/Hosey/McNeely/Pelt	.05	.01
❑	619	Danny Jackson	.05	.01
❑	620	George Brett	.60	.25
❑	621	Dan Gakeler	.05	.01
❑	622	Steve Buechele	.05	.01
❑	623	Bob Tewksbury	.05	.01
❑	624	Shawn Estes RC	.25	.08
❑	625	Kevin McReynolds	.05	.01
❑	626	Chris Haney	.05	.01
❑	627	Mike Sharperson	.05	.01
❑	628	Mark Williamson	.05	.01
❑	629	Wally Joyner	.10	.02
❑	630	Carlton Fisk	.15	.05
❑	631	Armando Reynoso RC	.25	.08
❑	632	Felix Fermin	.05	.01
❑	633	Mitch Williams	.05	.01
❑	634	Manuel Lee	.05	.01
❑	635	Harold Baines	.10	.02
❑	636	Greg Harris	.05	.01
❑	637	Orlando Merced	.05	.01
❑	638	Chris Bosio	.05	.01
❑	639	Wayne Housie	.05	.01
❑	640	Xavier Hernandez	.05	.01
❑	641	David Howard	.05	.01
❑	642	Tim Crews	.05	.01
❑	643	Rick Cerone	.05	.01
❑	644	Terry Leach	.05	.01
❑	645	Deion Sanders	.15	.05
❑	646	Craig Wilson	.05	.01
❑	647	Marquis Grissom	.10	.02
❑	648	Scott Fletcher	.05	.01
❑	649	Norm Charlton	.05	.01
❑	650	Jesse Barfield	.05	.01
❑	651	Joe Slusarski	.05	.01
❑	652	Bobby Rose	.05	.01
❑	653	Dennis Lamp	.05	.01
❑	654	Allen Watson RC	.10	.02
❑	655	Brett Butler	.10	.02
❑	656	Pem/H.Rod/Tinsley/G.Will	.10	.02
❑	657	Dave Johnson	.05	.01
❑	658	Checklist 529-660	.05	.01
❑	659	Brian McRae	.05	.01
❑	660	Fred McGriff	.15	.05
❑	661	Bill Landrum	.05	.01
❑	662	Juan Guzman	.05	.01
❑	663	Greg Gagne	.05	.01
❑	664	Ken Hill	.05	.01
❑	665	Dave Haas	.05	.01
❑	666	Tom Foley	.05	.01
❑	667	Roberto Hernandez	.05	.01
❑	668	Dwayne Henry	.05	.01
❑	669	Jim Fregosi MG	.05	.01
❑	670	Harold Reynolds	.10	.02
❑	671	Mark Whiten	.05	.01
❑	672	Eric Plunk	.05	.01
❑	673	Todd Hundley	.05	.01
❑	674	Mo Sanford	.05	.01
❑	675	Bobby Witt	.05	.01
❑	676	Mil/Mahomes/Wendell/Salk	.25	.08
❑	677	John Marzano	.05	.01
❑	678	Joe Klink	.05	.01
❑	679	Pete Incaviglia	.05	.01
❑	680	Dale Murphy	.15	.05
❑	681	Rene Gonzales	.05	.01
❑	682	Andy Benes	.05	.01
❑	683	Jim Poole	.05	.01
❑	684	Trever Miller RC	.10	.02
❑	685	Scott Livingstone	.05	.01
❑	686	Rich DeLucia	.05	.01
❑	687	Harvey Pulliam	.05	.01
❑	688	Tim Belcher	.05	.01
❑	689	Mark Lemke	.05	.01
❑	690	John Franco	.10	.02
❑	691	Walt Weiss	.05	.01
❑	692	Scott Ruskin	.05	.01
❑	693	Jeff King	.05	.01
❑	694	Mike Gardiner	.05	.01
❑	695	Gary Sheffield	.10	.02
❑	696	Joe Boever	.05	.01
❑	697	Mike Felder	.05	.01
❑	698	John Habyan	.05	.01
❑	699	Cito Gaston MG	.05	.01
❑	700	Ruben Sierra	.10	.02
❑	701	Scott Radinsky	.05	.01
❑	702	Lee Stevens	.05	.01
❑	703	Mark Wohlers	.05	.01
❑	704	Curt Young	.05	.01
❑	705	Dwight Evans	.15	.05
❑	706	Rob Murphy	.05	.01
❑	707	Gregg Jefferies	.05	.01
❑	708	Tom Bolton	.05	.01
❑	709	Chris James	.05	.01
❑	710	Kevin Maas	.05	.01
❑	711	Ricky Bones	.05	.01
❑	712	Curt Wilkerson	.05	.01
❑	713	Roger McDowell	.05	.01
❑	714	Pokey Reese RC	.25	.08
❑	715	Craig Biggio	.15	.05
❑	716	Kirk Dressendorfer	.05	.01

	Card	Player		
❑	717	Ken Dayley	.05	.01
❑	718	B.J. Surhoff	.10	.02
❑	719	Terry Mulholland	.05	.01
❑	720	Kirk Gibson	.10	.02
❑	721	Mike Pagliarulo	.05	.01
❑	722	Walt Terrell	.05	.01
❑	723	Jose Oquendo	.05	.01
❑	724	Kevin Morton	.05	.01
❑	725	Dwight Gooden	.10	.02
❑	726	Kirt Manwaring	.05	.01
❑	727	Chuck McElroy	.05	.01
❑	728	Dave Burba	.05	.01
❑	729	Art Howe MG	.05	.01
❑	730	Ramon Martinez	.05	.01
❑	731	Donnie Hill	.05	.01
❑	732	Nelson Santovenia	.05	.01
❑	733	Bob Melvin	.05	.01
❑	734	Scott Hatteberg RC	.25	.08
❑	735	Greg Swindell	.05	.01
❑	736	Lance Johnson	.05	.01
❑	737	Kevin Reimer	.05	.01
❑	738	Dennis Eckersley	.10	.02
❑	739	Rob Ducey	.05	.01
❑	740	Ken Caminiti	.10	.02
❑	741	Mark Gubicza	.05	.01
❑	742	Bill Spiers	.05	.01
❑	743	Darren Lewis	.05	.01
❑	744	Chris Hammond	.05	.01
❑	745	Dave Magadan	.05	.01
❑	746	Bernard Gilkey	.05	.01
❑	747	Willie Banks	.05	.01
❑	748	Matt Nokes	.05	.01
❑	749	Jerald Clark	.05	.01
❑	750	Travis Fryman	.10	.02
❑	751	Steve Wilson	.05	.01
❑	752	Billy Ripken	.05	.01
❑	753	Paul Assenmacher	.05	.01
❑	754	Charlie Hayes	.05	.01
❑	755	Alex Fernandez	.05	.01
❑	756	Gary Pettis	.05	.01
❑	757	Rob Dibble	.10	.02
❑	758	Tim Naehring	.05	.01
❑	759	Jeff Torborg MG	.05	.01
❑	760	Ozzie Smith	.40	.15
❑	761	Mike Fitzgerald	.05	.01
❑	762	John Burkett	.05	.01
❑	763	Kyle Abbott	.05	.01
❑	764	Tyler Green RC	.10	.02
❑	765	Pete Harnisch	.05	.01
❑	766	Mark Davis	.05	.01
❑	767	Kal Daniels	.05	.01
❑	768	Jim Thome	.25	.08
❑	769	Jack Howell	.05	.01
❑	770	Sid Bream	.05	.01
❑	771	Arthur Rhodes	.05	.01
❑	772	Garry Templeton UER (Stat heading in for pitchers	.05	.01
❑	773	Hal Morris	.05	.01
❑	774	Bud Black	.05	.01
❑	775	Ivan Calderon	.05	.01
❑	776	Doug Henry RC	.10	.02
❑	777	John Olerud	.10	.02
❑	778	Tim Leary	.05	.01
❑	779	Jay Bell	.10	.02
❑	780	Eddie Murray	.25	.08
❑	781	Paul Abbott	.05	.01
❑	782	Phil Plantier	.05	.01
❑	783	Joe Magrane	.05	.01
❑	784	Ken Patterson	.05	.01
❑	785	Albert Belle	.10	.02
❑	786	Royce Clayton	.05	.01
❑	787	Checklist 661-792	.05	.01
❑	788	Mike Stanton	.05	.01
❑	789	Bobby Valentine MG	.05	.01
❑	790	Joe Carter	.10	.02
❑	791	Danny Cox	.05	.01
❑	792	Dave Winfield	.10	.02

1992 Topps Traded

	Card	Player		
❑		COMP.FACT.SET (132)	50.00	20.00
❑	1T	Willie Adams USA RC	.25	.08
❑	2T	Jeff Alkire USA RC	.25	.08
❑	3T	Felipe Alou MG	.20	.07
❑	4T	Moises Alou	.20	.07
❑	5T	Ruben Amaro	.10	.02
❑	6T	Jack Armstrong	.10	.02
❑	7T	Scott Bankhead	.10	.02
❑	8T	Tim Belcher	.10	.02
❑	9T	George Bell	.10	.02
❑	10T	Freddie Benavides	.10	.02
❑	11T	Todd Benzinger	.10	.02
❑	12T	Joe Boever	.10	.02
❑	13T	Ricky Bones	.10	.02
❑	14T	Bobby Bonilla	.20	.07
❑	15T	Hubie Brooks	.10	.02
❑	16T	Jerry Browne	.10	.02
❑	17T	Jim Bullinger	.10	.02
❑	18T	Dave Burba	.10	.02
❑	19T	Kevin Campbell	.10	.02
❑	20T	Tom Candiotti	.10	.02
❑	21T	Mark Carreon	.10	.02
❑	22T	Gary Carter	.20	.07
❑	23T	Archi Cianfrocco RC	.10	.02
❑	24T	Phil Clark	.10	.02
❑	25T	Chad Curtis RC	.40	.15
❑	26T	Eric Davis	.20	.07
❑	27T	Tim Davis USA RC	.25	.08
❑	28T	Gary DiSarcina	.10	.02
❑	29T	Darren Dreifort USA	.10	.02
❑	30T	Mariano Duncan	.10	.02
❑	31T	Mike Fitzgerald	.10	.02
❑	32T	John Flaherty	.10	.02
❑	33T	Darrin Fletcher	.10	.02
❑	34T	Scott Fletcher	.10	.02
❑	35T	Ron Fraser USA CO RC	.25	.08
❑	36T	Andres Galarraga	.20	.07
❑	37T	Dave Gallagher	.10	.02
❑	38T	Mike Gallego	.10	.02
❑	39T	Nomar Garciaparra USA RC	20.00	8.00
❑	40T	Jason Giambi USA	1.00	.40
❑	41T	Danny Gladden	.10	.02
❑	42T	Rene Gonzales	.10	.02
❑	43T	Jeff Granger USA	.10	.02
❑	44T	Rick Greene USA RC	.25	.08
❑	45T	Jeffrey Hammonds USA	.20	.07
❑	46T	Charlie Hayes	.10	.02
❑	47T	Von Hayes	.10	.02
❑	48T	Rick Helling USA	.10	.02
❑	49T	Butch Henry RC	.10	.02
❑	50T	Carlos Hernandez	.10	.02
❑	51T	Ken Hill	.10	.02
❑	52T	Butch Hobson	.10	.02
❑	53T	Vince Horsman	.10	.02
❑	54T	Pete Incaviglia	.10	.02
❑	55T	Gregg Jefferies	.10	.02
❑	56T	Charles Johnson USA	.20	.07
❑	57T	Doug Jones	.10	.02
❑	58T	Brian Jordan RC	.75	.30
❑	59T	Wally Joyner	.20	.07
❑	60T	Daron Kirkreit USA RC	.25	.08
❑	61T	Bill Krueger	.10	.02
❑	62T	Gene Lamont MG	.10	.02
❑	63T	Jim Lefebvre MG	.10	.02
❑	64T	Danny Leon	.10	.02
❑	65T	Pat Listach RC	.40	.15
❑	66T	Kenny Lofton	.30	.10
❑	67T	Dave Martinez	.10	.02
❑	68T	Derrick May	.10	.02
❑	69T	Kirk McCaskill	.10	.02
❑	70T	Chad McConnell USA RC	.25	.08
❑	71T	Kevin McReynolds	.10	.02
❑	72T	Rusty Meacham	.10	.02
❑	73T	Keith Miller	.10	.02
❑	74T	Kevin Mitchell	.10	.02
❑	75T	Jason Moler USA RC	.25	.08
❑	76T	Mike Morgan	.10	.02
❑	77T	Jack Morris	.20	.07
❑	78T	Calvin Murray USA RC	.75	.30
❑	79T	Eddie Murray	.50	.20
❑	80T	Randy Myers	.10	.02
❑	81T	Denny Neagle	.20	.07
❑	82T	Phil Nevin USA	.20	.07
❑	83T	Dave Nilsson	.10	.02
❑	84T	Junior Ortiz	.10	.02
❑	85T	Donovan Osborne	.10	.02
❑	86T	Bill Pecota	.10	.02
❑	87T	Melido Perez	.10	.02
❑	88T	Mike Perez	.10	.02
❑	89T	Hipolito Pichardo RC	.10	.02
❑	90T	Willie Randolph	.20	.07
❑	91T	Darren Reed	.10	.02
❑	92T	Bip Roberts	.10	.02
❑	93T	Chris Roberts USA	.10	.02
❑	94T	Steve Rodriguez USA	.10	.02
❑	95T	Bruce Ruffin	.10	.02
❑	96T	Scott Ruskin	.10	.02
❑	97T	Bret Saberhagen	.20	.07
❑	98T	Rey Sanchez RC	.40	.15
❑	99T	Steve Sax	.10	.02
❑	100T	Curt Schilling	.30	.10
❑	101T	Dick Schofield	.10	.02
❑	102T	Gary Scott	.10	.02
❑	103T	Kevin Seitzer	.10	.02
❑	104T	Frank Seminara RC	.10	.02
❑	105T	Gary Sheffield	.20	.07
❑	106T	John Smiley	.10	.02
❑	107T	Cory Snyder	.10	.02
❑	108T	Paul Sorrento	.10	.02
❑	109T	Sammy Sosa Cubs	1.50	.60
❑	110T	Matt Stairs RC	.50	.20
❑	111T	Andy Stankiewicz	.10	.02
❑	112T	Kurt Stillwell	.10	.02
❑	113T	Rick Sutcliffe	.20	.07
❑	114T	Bill Swift	.10	.02
❑	115T	Jeff Tackett	.10	.02
❑	116T	Danny Tartabull	.10	.02
❑	117T	Eddie Taubensee	.20	.07
❑	118T	Dickie Thon	.10	.02
❑	119T	Michael Tucker USA RC	.75	.30
❑	120T	Scooter Tucker	.10	.02
❑	121T	Marc Valdes USA RC	.25	.08
❑	122T	Julio Valera	.10	.02
❑	123T	Jason Varitek USA RC	12.00	5.00
❑	124T	Ron Villone USA RC	.25	.08
❑	125T	Frank Viola	.20	.07
❑	126T	B.J.Wallace USA RC	.25	.08
❑	127T	Dan Walters	.10	.02
❑	128T	Craig Wilson USA	.10	.02
❑	129T	Chris Wimmer USA	.10	.02
❑	130T	Dave Winfield	.20	.07
❑	131T	Herm Winningham	.10	.02
❑	132T	Checklist 1T-132T	.10	.02

1993 Topps

	Card	Player		
❑		COMPLETE SET (825)	40.00	15.00
❑		COMP.HOBBY SET (847)	60.00	30.00
❑		COMP.RETAIL SET (838)	50.00	20.00
❑		COMPLETE SERIES 1 (396)	25.00	10.00
❑		COMPLETE SERIES 2 (429)	25.00	10.00
❑	1	Robin Yount	.75	.30
❑	2	Barry Bonds	1.50	.60
❑	3	Ryne Sandberg	.75	.30

❑	4	Roger Clemens	1.00	.40
❑	5	Tony Gwynn	.60	.25
❑	6	Jeff Tackett	.10	.02
❑	7	Pete Incaviglia	.10	.02
❑	8	Mark Wohlers	.10	.02
❑	9	Kent Hrbek	.20	.07
❑	10	Will Clark	.30	.10
❑	11	Eric Karros	.20	.07
❑	12	Lee Smith	.20	.07
❑	13	Esteban Beltre	.10	.02
❑	14	Greg Briley	.10	.02
❑	15	Marquis Grissom	.20	.07
❑	16	Dan Plesac	.10	.02
❑	17	Dave Hollins	.10	.02
❑	18	Terry Steinbach	.10	.02
❑	19	Ed Nunez	.10	.02
❑	20	Tim Salmon	.30	.10
❑	21	Luis Salazar	.10	.02
❑	22	Jim Eisenreich	.10	.02
❑	23	Todd Stottlemyre	.10	.02
❑	24	Tim Naehring	.10	.02
❑	25	John Franco	.20	.07
❑	26	Skeeter Barnes	.10	.02
❑	27	Carlos Garcia	.10	.02
❑	28	Joe Orsulak	.10	.02
❑	29	Dwayne Henry	.10	.02
❑	30	Fred McGriff	.30	.10
❑	31	Derek Lilliquist	.10	.02
❑	32	Don Mattingly	1.25	.50
❑	33	B.J.Wallace	.10	.02
❑	34	Juan Gonzalez	.20	.07
❑	35	John Smoltz	.30	.10
❑	36	Scott Servais	.10	.02
❑	37	Lenny Webster	.10	.02
❑	38	Chris James	.10	.02
❑	39	Roger McDowell	.10	.02
❑	40	Ozzie Smith	.75	.30
❑	41	Alex Fernandez	.10	.02
❑	42	Spike Owen	.10	.02
❑	43	Ruben Amaro	.10	.02
❑	44	Kevin Seitzer	.10	.02
❑	45	Dave Fleming	.10	.02
❑	46	Eric Fox	.10	.02
❑	47	Bob Scanlan	.10	.02
❑	48	Bert Blyleven	.20	.07
❑	49	Brian McRae	.10	.02
❑	50	Roberto Alomar	.30	.10
❑	51	Mo Vaughn	.20	.07
❑	52	Bobby Bonilla	.20	.07
❑	53	Frank Tanana	.10	.02
❑	54	Mike LaValliere	.10	.02
❑	55	Mark McLemore	.10	.02
❑	56	Chad Mottola RC	.10	.02
❑	57	Norm Charlton	.10	.02
❑	58	Jose Melendez	.10	.02
❑	59	Carlos Martinez	.10	.02
❑	60	Roberto Kelly	.10	.02
❑	61	Gene Larkin	.10	.02
❑	62	Rafael Belliard	.10	.02
❑	63	Al Osuna	.10	.02
❑	64	Scott Chiamparino	.10	.02
❑	65	Brett Butler	.20	.07
❑	66	John Burkett	.10	.02
❑	67	Felix Jose	.10	.02
❑	68	Omar Vizquel	.30	.10
❑	69	John Vander Wal	.10	.02
❑	70	Roberto Hernandez	.10	.02
❑	71	Ricky Bones	.10	.02
❑	72	Jeff Grotewold	.10	.02
❑	73	Mike Moore	.10	.02
❑	74	Steve Buechele	.10	.02
❑	75	Juan Guzman	.10	.02
❑	76	Kevin Appier	.20	.07
❑	77	Junior Felix	.10	.02
❑	78	Greg W. Harris	.10	.02
❑	79	Dick Schofield	.10	.02
❑	80	Cecil Fielder	.20	.07
❑	81	Lloyd McClendon	.10	.02
❑	82	David Segui	.10	.02
❑	83	Reggie Sanders	.20	.07
❑	84	Kurt Stillwell	.10	.02
❑	85	Sandy Alomar Jr.	.10	.02
❑	86	John Habyan	.10	.02
❑	87	Kevin Reimer	.10	.02
❑	88	Mike Stanton	.10	.02
❑	89	Eric Anthony	.10	.02
❑	90	Scott Erickson	.10	.02
❑	91	Craig Colbert	.10	.02
❑	92	Tom Pagnozzi	.10	.02
❑	93	Pedro Astacio	.10	.02
❑	94	Lance Johnson	.10	.02
❑	95	Larry Walker	.20	.07
❑	96	Russ Swan	.10	.02
❑	97	Scott Fletcher	.10	.02
❑	98	Derek Jeter RC	12.00	5.00
❑	99	Mike Williams	.10	.02
❑	100	Mark McGwire	1.25	.50
❑	101	Jim Bullinger	.10	.02
❑	102	Brian Hunter	.10	.02
❑	103	Jody Reed	.10	.02
❑	104	Mike Butcher	.10	.02
❑	105	Gregg Jefferies	.10	.02
❑	106	Howard Johnson	.10	.02
❑	107	John Kiely	.10	.02
❑	108	Jose Lind	.10	.02
❑	109	Sam Horn	.10	.02
❑	110	Barry Larkin	.30	.10
❑	111	Bruce Hurst	.10	.02
❑	112	Brian Barnes	.10	.02
❑	113	Thomas Howard	.10	.02
❑	114	Mel Hall	.10	.02
❑	115	Robby Thompson	.10	.02
❑	116	Mark Lemke	.10	.02
❑	117	Eddie Taubensee	.10	.02
❑	118	David Hulse RC	.10	.02
❑	119	Pedro Munoz	.10	.02
❑	120	Ramon Martinez	.10	.02
❑	121	Todd Worrell	.10	.02
❑	122	Joey Cora	.10	.02
❑	123	Moises Alou	.20	.07
❑	124	Franklin Stubbs	.10	.02
❑	125	Pete O'Brien	.10	.02
❑	126	Bob Ayrault	.10	.02
❑	127	Carney Lansford	.20	.07
❑	128	Kal Daniels	.10	.02
❑	129	Joe Grahe	.10	.02
❑	130	Jeff Montgomery	.10	.02
❑	131	Dave Winfield	.20	.07
❑	132	Preston Wilson RC	.75	.30
❑	133	Steve Wilson	.10	.02
❑	134	Lee Guetterman	.10	.02
❑	135	Mickey Tettleton	.10	.02
❑	136	Jeff King	.10	.02
❑	137	Alan Mills	.10	.02
❑	138	Joe Oliver	.10	.02
❑	139	Gary Gaetti	.20	.07
❑	140	Gary Sheffield	.20	.07
❑	141	Dennis Cook	.10	.02
❑	142	Charlie Hayes	.10	.02
❑	143	Jeff Huson	.10	.02
❑	144	Kent Mercker	.10	.02
❑	145	Eric Young	.10	.02
❑	146	Scott Leius	.10	.02
❑	147	Bryan Hickerson	.10	.02
❑	148	Steve Finley	.20	.07
❑	149	Rheal Cormier	.10	.02
❑	150	Frank Thomas	.50	.20
❑	151	Archi Cianfrocco	.10	.02
❑	152	Rich DeLucia	.10	.02
❑	153	Greg Vaughn	.10	.02
❑	154	Wes Chamberlain	.10	.02
❑	155	Dennis Eckersley	.20	.07
❑	156	Sammy Sosa	.50	.20
❑	157	Gary DiSarcina	.10	.02
❑	158	Kevin Koslofski	.10	.02
❑	159	Doug Linton	.10	.02
❑	160	Lou Whitaker	.20	.07
❑	161	Chad McConnell	.10	.02
❑	162	Joe Hesketh	.10	.02
❑	163	Tim Wakefield	.50	.20
❑	164	Leo Gomez	.10	.02
❑	165	Jose Rijo	.10	.02
❑	166	Tim Scott	.10	.02
❑	167	Steve Olin UER	.10	.02
❑	168	Kevin Maas	.10	.02
❑	169	Kenny Rogers	.20	.07
❑	170	David Justice	.20	.07
❑	171	Doug Jones	.10	.02
❑	172	Jeff Reboulet	.10	.02
❑	173	Andres Galarraga	.20	.07
❑	174	Randy Velarde	.10	.02
❑	175	Kirk McCaskill	.10	.02
❑	176	Darren Lewis	.10	.02
❑	177	Lenny Harris	.10	.02
❑	178	Jeff Fassero	.10	.02
❑	179	Ken Griffey Jr.	.75	.30
❑	180	Darren Daulton	.20	.07
❑	181	John Jaha	.10	.02
❑	182	Ron Darling	.10	.02
❑	183	Greg Maddux	.75	.30
❑	184	Damion Easley	.10	.02
❑	185	Jack Morris	.20	.07
❑	186	Mike Magnante	.10	.02
❑	187	John Dopson	.10	.02
❑	188	Sid Fernandez	.10	.02
❑	189	Tony Phillips	.10	.02
❑	190	Doug Drabek	.10	.02
❑	191	Sean Lowe RC	.10	.02
❑	192	Bob Milacki	.10	.02
❑	193	Steve Foster	.10	.02
❑	194	Jerald Clark	.10	.02
❑	195	Pete Harnisch	.10	.02
❑	196	Pat Kelly	.10	.02
❑	197	Jeff Frye	.10	.02
❑	198	Alejandro Pena	.10	.02
❑	199	Junior Ortiz	.10	.02
❑	200	Kirby Puckett	.50	.20
❑	201	Jose Uribe	.10	.02
❑	202	Mike Scioscia	.10	.02
❑	203	Bernard Gilkey	.10	.02
❑	204	Dan Pasqua	.10	.02
❑	205	Gary Carter	.20	.07
❑	206	Henry Cotto	.10	.02
❑	207	Paul Molitor	.20	.07
❑	208	Mike Hartley	.10	.02
❑	209	Jeff Parrett	.10	.02
❑	210	Mark Langston	.10	.02
❑	211	Doug Dascenzo	.10	.02
❑	212	Rick Reed	.10	.02
❑	213	Candy Maldonado	.10	.02
❑	214	Danny Darwin	.10	.02
❑	215	Pat Howell	.10	.02
❑	216	Mark Leiter	.10	.02
❑	217	Kevin Mitchell	.10	.02
❑	218	Ben McDonald	.10	.02
❑	219	Bip Roberts	.10	.02
❑	220	Benny Santiago	.20	.07
❑	221	Carlos Baerga	.10	.02
❑	222	Bernie Williams	.30	.10
❑	223	Roger Pavlik	.10	.02
❑	224	Sid Bream	.10	.02
❑	225	Matt Williams	.20	.07
❑	226	Willie Banks	.10	.02
❑	227	Jeff Bagwell	.30	.10
❑	228	Tom Goodwin	.10	.02
❑	229	Mike Perez	.10	.02
❑	230	Carlton Fisk	.30	.10
❑	231	John Wetteland	.20	.07
❑	232	Tino Martinez	.30	.10
❑	233	Rick Greene	.10	.02
❑	234	Tim McIntosh	.10	.02
❑	235	Mitch Williams	.10	.02
❑	236	Kevin Campbell	.10	.02
❑	237	Jose Vizcaino	.10	.02
❑	238	Chris Donnels	.10	.02
❑	239	Mike Boddicker	.10	.02
❑	240	John Olerud	.20	.07
❑	241	Mike Gardiner	.10	.02
❑	242	Charlie O'Brien	.10	.02
❑	243	Rob Deer	.10	.02
❑	244	Denny Neagle	.20	.07
❑	245	Chris Sabo	.10	.02
❑	246	Gregg Olson	.10	.02
❑	247	Frank Seminara UER	.10	.02
❑	248	Scott Scudder	.10	.02
❑	249	Tim Burke	.10	.02
❑	250	Chuck Knoblauch	.20	.07
❑	251	Mike Bielecki	.10	.02
❑	252	Xavier Hernandez	.10	.02
❑	253	Jose Guzman	.10	.02
❑	254	Cory Snyder	.10	.02
❑	255	Orel Hershiser	.20	.07
❑	256	Wil Cordero	.10	.02
❑	257	Luis Alicea	.10	.02
❑	258	Mike Schooler	.10	.02
❑	259	Craig Grebeck	.10	.02
❑	260	Duane Ward	.10	.02
❑	261	Bill Wegman	.10	.02

❑ 262 Mickey Morandini .10 .02
❑ 263 Vince Horsman .10 .02
❑ 264 Paul Sorrento .10 .02
❑ 265 Andre Dawson .20 .07
❑ 266 Rene Gonzales .10 .02
❑ 267 Keith Miller .10 .02
❑ 268 Derek Bell .10 .02
❑ 269 Todd Steverson RC .10 .02
❑ 270 Frank Viola .20 .07
❑ 271 Wally Whitehurst .10 .02
❑ 272 Kurt Knudsen .10 .02
❑ 273 Dan Walters .10 .02
❑ 274 Rick Sutcliffe .20 .07
❑ 275 Andy Van Slyke .30 .10
❑ 276 Paul O'Neill .30 .10
❑ 277 Mark Whiten .10 .02
❑ 278 Chris Nabholz .10 .02
❑ 279 Todd Burns .10 .02
❑ 280 Tom Glavine .30 .10
❑ 281 Butch Henry .10 .02
❑ 282 Shane Mack .10 .02
❑ 283 Mike Jackson .10 .02
❑ 284 Henry Rodriguez .10 .02
❑ 285 Bob Tewksbury .10 .02
❑ 286 Ron Karkovice .10 .02
❑ 287 Mike Gallego .10 .02
❑ 288 Dave Cochrane .10 .02
❑ 289 Jesse Orosco .10 .02
❑ 290 Dave Stewart .20 .07
❑ 291 Tommy Greene .10 .02
❑ 292 Rey Sanchez .10 .02
❑ 293 Rob Ducey .10 .02
❑ 294 Brent Mayne .10 .02
❑ 295 Dave Stieb .10 .02
❑ 296 Luis Rivera .10 .02
❑ 297 Jeff Innis .10 .02
❑ 298 Scott Livingstone .10 .02
❑ 299 Bob Patterson .10 .02
❑ 300 Cal Ripken 1.50 .60
❑ 301 Cesar Hernandez .10 .02
❑ 302 Randy Myers .10 .02
❑ 303 Brook Jacoby .10 .02
❑ 304 Melido Perez .10 .02
❑ 305 Rafael Palmeiro .30 .10
❑ 306 Damon Berryhill .10 .02
❑ 307 Dan Serafini RC .10 .02
❑ 308 Darryl Kile .20 .07
❑ 309 J.T. Bruett .10 .02
❑ 310 Dave Righetti .20 .07
❑ 311 Jay Howell .10 .02
❑ 312 Geronimo Pena .10 .02
❑ 313 Greg Hibbard .10 .02
❑ 314 Mark Gardner .10 .02
❑ 315 Edgar Martinez .30 .10
❑ 316 Dave Nilsson .10 .02
❑ 317 Kyle Abbott .10 .02
❑ 318 Willie Wilson .10 .02
❑ 319 Paul Assenmacher .10 .02
❑ 320 Tim Fortugno .10 .02
❑ 321 Rusty Meacham .10 .02
❑ 322 Pat Borders .10 .02
❑ 323 Mike Greenwell .10 .02
❑ 324 Willie Randolph .20 .07
❑ 325 Bill Gullickson .10 .02
❑ 326 Gary Varsho .10 .02
❑ 327 Tim Hulett .10 .02
❑ 328 Scott Ruskin .10 .02
❑ 329 Mike Maddux .10 .02
❑ 330 Danny Tartabull .10 .02
❑ 331 Kenny Lofton .20 .07
❑ 332 Geno Petralli .10 .02
❑ 333 Otis Nixon .10 .02
❑ 334 Jason Kendall RC 1.00 .40
❑ 335 Mark Portugal .10 .02
❑ 336 Mike Pagliarulo .10 .02
❑ 337 Kirt Manwaring .10 .02
❑ 338 Bob Ojeda .10 .02
❑ 339 Mark Clark .10 .02
❑ 340 John Kruk .20 .07
❑ 341 Mel Rojas .10 .02
❑ 342 Erik Hanson .10 .02
❑ 343 Doug Henry .10 .02
❑ 344 Jack McDowell .10 .02
❑ 345 Harold Baines .20 .07
❑ 346 Chuck McElroy .10 .02
❑ 347 Luis Sojo .10 .02
❑ 348 Andy Stankiewicz .10 .02
❑ 349 Hipolito Pichardo .10 .02
❑ 350 Joe Carter .20 .07
❑ 351 Ellis Burks .20 .07
❑ 352 Pete Schourek .10 .02
❑ 353 Buddy Groom .10 .02
❑ 354 Jay Bell .20 .07
❑ 355 Brady Anderson .20 .07
❑ 356 Freddie Benavides .10 .02
❑ 357 Phil Stephenson .10 .02
❑ 358 Kevin Wickander .10 .02
❑ 359 Mike Stanley .10 .02
❑ 360 Ivan Rodriguez .30 .10
❑ 361 Scott Bankhead .10 .02
❑ 362 Luis Gonzalez .20 .07
❑ 363 John Smiley .10 .02
❑ 364 Trevor Wilson .10 .02
❑ 365 Tom Candiotti .10 .02
❑ 366 Craig Wilson .10 .02
❑ 367 Steve Sax .10 .02
❑ 368 Delino DeShields .10 .02
❑ 369 Jaime Navarro .10 .02
❑ 370 Dave Valle .10 .02
❑ 371 Mariano Duncan .10 .02
❑ 372 Rod Nichols .10 .02
❑ 373 Mike Morgan .10 .02
❑ 374 Julio Valera .10 .02
❑ 375 Wally Joyner .20 .07
❑ 376 Tom Henke .10 .02
❑ 377 Herm Winningham .10 .02
❑ 378 Orlando Merced .10 .02
❑ 379 Mike Munoz .10 .02
❑ 380 Todd Hundley .10 .02
❑ 381 Mike Flanagan .10 .02
❑ 382 Tim Belcher .10 .02
❑ 383 Jerry Browne .10 .02
❑ 384 Mike Benjamin .10 .02
❑ 385 Jim Leyritz .10 .02
❑ 386 Ray Lankford .20 .07
❑ 387 Devon White .20 .07
❑ 388 Jeremy Hernandez .10 .02
❑ 389 Brian Harper .10 .02
❑ 390 Wade Boggs .30 .10
❑ 391 Derrick May .10 .02
❑ 392 Travis Fryman .20 .07
❑ 393 Ron Gant .20 .07
❑ 394 Checklist 1-132 .10 .02
❑ 395 Checklist 133-264 UER .10 .02
❑ 396 Checklist 265-396 .10 .02
❑ 397 George Brett 1.25 .50
❑ 398 Bobby Witt .10 .02
❑ 399 Daryl Boston .10 .02
❑ 400 Bo Jackson .50 .20
❑ 401 F.McGriff/F.Thomas AS .30 .10
❑ 402 R.Sandberg/C.Baerga AS .50 .20
❑ 403 G.Sheffield/E.Martinez AS .20 .07
❑ 404 B.Larkin/T.Fryman AS .20 .07
❑ 405 K.Griffey Jr./A.Van Slyke AS .50 .20
❑ 406 L.Walker/K.Puckett AS .30 .10
❑ 407 B.Bonds/J.Carter AS .75 .30
❑ 408 D.Daulton/B.Harper AS .20 .07
❑ 409 G.Maddux/R.Clemens AS .50 .20
❑ 410 T.Glavine/D.Fleming AS .20 .07
❑ 411 L.Smith/D.Eckersley AS .20 .07
❑ 412 Jamie McAndrew .10 .02
❑ 413 Pete Smith .10 .02
❑ 414 Juan Guerrero .10 .02
❑ 415 Todd Frohwirth .10 .02
❑ 416 Randy Tomlin .10 .02
❑ 417 B.J. Surhoff .20 .07
❑ 418 Jim Gott .10 .02
❑ 419 Mark Thompson RC .10 .02
❑ 420 Kevin Tapani .10 .02
❑ 421 Curt Schilling .20 .07
❑ 422 J.T.Snow RC .50 .20
❑ 423 Ryan Klesko .20 .07
❑ 424 John Valentin .10 .02
❑ 425 Joe Girardi .10 .02
❑ 426 Nigel Wilson .10 .02
❑ 427 Bob MacDonald .10 .02
❑ 428 Todd Zeile .10 .02
❑ 429 Milt Cuyler .10 .02
❑ 430 Eddie Murray .50 .20
❑ 431 Rich Amaral .10 .02
❑ 432 Pete Young .10 .02
❑ 433 Tom Schmidt RC .10 .02
❑ 434 Jack Armstrong .10 .02
❑ 435 Willie McGee .20 .07
❑ 436 Greg W. Harris .10 .02
❑ 437 Chris Hammond .10 .02
❑ 438 Ritchie Moody RC .10 .02
❑ 439 Bryan Harvey .10 .02
❑ 440 Ruben Sierra .20 .07
❑ 441 Todd Pridy RC .10 .02
❑ 442 Kevin McReynolds .10 .02
❑ 443 Terry Leach .10 .02
❑ 444 David Nied .10 .02
❑ 445 Dale Murphy .30 .10
❑ 446 Luis Mercedes .10 .02
❑ 447 Keith Shepherd RC .10 .02
❑ 448 Ken Caminiti .20 .07
❑ 449 Jim Austin .10 .02
❑ 450 Darryl Strawberry .20 .07
❑ 451 Quinton McCracken RC .25 .08
❑ 452 Bob Wickman .10 .02
❑ 453 Victor Cole .10 .02
❑ 454 John Johnstone RC .10 .02
❑ 455 Chili Davis .20 .07
❑ 456 Scott Taylor .10 .02
❑ 457 Tracy Woodson .10 .02
❑ 458 David Wells .20 .07
❑ 459 Derek Wallace RC .10 .02
❑ 460 Randy Johnson .50 .20
❑ 461 Steve Reed RC .10 .02
❑ 462 Felix Fermin .10 .02
❑ 463 Scott Aldred .10 .02
❑ 464 Greg Colbrunn .10 .02
❑ 465 Tony Fernandez .10 .02
❑ 466 Mike Felder .10 .02
❑ 467 Lee Stevens .10 .02
❑ 468 Matt Whiteside RC .10 .02
❑ 469 Dave Hansen .10 .02
❑ 470 Rob Dibble .20 .07
❑ 471 Dave Gallagher .10 .02
❑ 472 Chris Gwynn .10 .02
❑ 473 Dave Henderson .10 .02
❑ 474 Ozzie Guillen .20 .07
❑ 475 Jeff Reardon .20 .07
❑ 476 Will Scalzitti RC .10 .02
❑ 477 Jimmy Jones .10 .02
❑ 478 Greg Cadaret .10 .02
❑ 479 Todd Pratt RC .10 .02
❑ 480 Pat Listach .10 .02
❑ 481 Ryan Luzinski RC .10 .02
❑ 482 Darren Reed .10 .02
❑ 483 Brian Griffiths RC .10 .02
❑ 484 John Wehner .10 .02
❑ 485 Glenn Davis .10 .02
❑ 486 Eric Wedge RC .10 .02
❑ 487 Jesse Hollins .10 .02
❑ 488 Manuel Lee .10 .02
❑ 489 Scott Fredrickson RC .10 .02
❑ 490 Omar Olivares .10 .02
❑ 491 Shawn Hare .10 .02
❑ 492 Tom Lampkin .10 .02
❑ 493 Jeff Nelson .10 .02
❑ 494 L.Lucca RC/E.Perez .10 .02
❑ 495 Ken Hill .10 .02
❑ 496 Reggie Jefferson .10 .02
❑ 497 Willie Brown RC .10 .02
❑ 498 Bud Black .10 .02
❑ 499 Chuck Crim .10 .02
❑ 500 Jose Canseco .30 .10
❑ 501 Johnny Oates MG
Bobby Cox MG .20 .07
❑ 502 Butch Hobson MG
Jim Lefebvre MG .10 .02
❑ 503 Buck Rodgers MG
Tony Perez MG .20 .07
❑ 504 Gene Lamont MG
Don Baylor MG .20 .07
❑ 505 Mike Hargrove MG
Rene Lachemann MG .20 .07
❑ 506 Sparky Anderson MG
Art Howe MG .20 .07
❑ 507 Hal McRae MG
Tom Lasorda MG .20 .07
❑ 508 Phil Garner MG
Felipe Alou MG .20 .07
❑ 509 Tom Kelly MG
Jeff Torborg MG .10 .02
❑ 510 Buck Showalter MG

	Jim Fregosi MG	.20	.07
❑ 511	Tony LaRussa MG Jim Leyland MG	.20	.07
❑ 512	Lou Piniella MG Joe Torre MG	.20	.07
❑ 513	Kevin Kennedy MG Jim Riggleman MG	.10	.02
❑ 514	Cito Gaston MG Dusty Baker MG	.20	.07
❑ 515	Greg Swindell	.10	.02
❑ 516	Alex Arias	.10	.02
❑ 517	Bill Pecota	.10	.02
❑ 518	Benji Grigsby RC	.10	.02
❑ 519	David Howard	.10	.02
❑ 520	Charlie Hough	.20	.07
❑ 521	Kevin Flora	.10	.02
❑ 522	Shane Reynolds	.10	.02
❑ 523	Doug Bochtler RC	.10	.02
❑ 524	Chris Hoiles	.10	.02
❑ 525	Scott Sanderson	.10	.02
❑ 526	Mike Sharperson	.10	.02
❑ 527	Mike Fetters	.10	.02
❑ 528	Paul Quantrill	.10	.02
❑ 529	Chipper Jones	.50	.20
❑ 530	Sterling Hitchcock RC	.25	.08
❑ 531	Joe Millette	.10	.02
❑ 532	Tom Brunansky	.10	.02
❑ 533	Frank Castillo	.10	.02
❑ 534	Randy Knorr	.10	.02
❑ 535	Jose Oquendo	.10	.02
❑ 536	Dave Haas	.10	.02
❑ 537	Jason Hutchins RC	.10	.02
❑ 538	Jimmy Baron RC	.10	.02
❑ 539	Kerry Woodson	.10	.02
❑ 540	Ivan Calderon	.10	.02
❑ 541	Denis Boucher	.10	.02
❑ 542	Royce Clayton	.10	.02
❑ 543	Reggie Williams	.10	.02
❑ 544	Steve Decker	.10	.02
❑ 545	Dean Palmer	.20	.07
❑ 546	Hal Morris	.10	.02
❑ 547	Ryan Thompson	.10	.02
❑ 548	Lance Blankenship	.10	.02
❑ 549	Hensley Meulens	.10	.02
❑ 550	Scott Radinsky	.10	.02
❑ 551	Eric Young	.10	.02
❑ 552	Jeff Blauser	.10	.02
❑ 553	Andujar Cedeno	.10	.02
❑ 554	Arthur Rhodes	.10	.02
❑ 555	Terry Mulholland	.10	.02
❑ 556	Darryl Hamilton	.10	.02
❑ 557	Pedro Martinez	1.00	.40
❑ 558	Ryan Whitman RC	.10	.02
❑ 559	Jamie Arnold RC	.10	.02
❑ 560	Zane Smith	.10	.02
❑ 561	Matt Nokes	.10	.02
❑ 562	Bob Zupcic	.10	.02
❑ 563	Shawn Boskie	.10	.02
❑ 564	Mike Timlin	.10	.02
❑ 565	Jerald Clark	.10	.02
❑ 566	Rod Brewer	.10	.02
❑ 567	Mark Carreon	.10	.02
❑ 568	Andy Benes	.10	.02
❑ 569	Shawn Barton RC	.10	.02
❑ 570	Tim Wallach	.10	.02
❑ 571	Dave Mlicki	.10	.02
❑ 572	Trevor Hoffman	.50	.20
❑ 573	John Patterson	.10	.02
❑ 574	DeShawn Warren RC	.10	.02
❑ 575	Monty Fariss	.10	.02
❑ 576	Cliff Floyd	.20	.07
❑ 577	Tim Costo	.10	.02
❑ 578	Dave Magadan	.10	.02
❑ 579	Jason Bates RC	.10	.02
❑ 580	Walt Weiss	.10	.02
❑ 581	Chris Haney	.10	.02
❑ 582	Shawn Abner	.10	.02
❑ 583	Marvin Freeman	.10	.02
❑ 584	Casey Candaele	.10	.02
❑ 585	Ricky Jordan	.10	.02
❑ 586	Jeff Tabaka RC	.10	.02
❑ 587	Manny Alexander	.10	.02
❑ 588	Mike Trombley	.10	.02
❑ 589	Carlos Hernandez	.10	.02
❑ 590	Cal Eldred	.10	.02
❑ 591	Alex Cole	.10	.02
❑ 592	Phil Plantier	.10	.02
❑ 593	Brett Merriman RC	.10	.02
❑ 594	Jerry Nielsen	.10	.02
❑ 595	Shawon Dunston	.10	.02
❑ 596	Jimmy Key	.20	.07
❑ 597	Gerald Perry	.10	.02
❑ 598	Rico Brogna	.10	.02
❑ 599	Clemente Nunez	.10	.02
❑ 600	Bret Saberhagen	.20	.07
❑ 601	Craig Shipley	.10	.02
❑ 602	Henry Mercedes	.10	.02
❑ 603	Jim Thome	.30	.10
❑ 604	Rod Beck	.10	.02
❑ 605	Chuck Finley	.20	.07
❑ 606	Jayhawk Owens RC	.10	.02
❑ 607	Dan Smith	.10	.02
❑ 608	Bill Doran	.10	.02
❑ 609	Lance Parrish	.20	.07
❑ 610	Dennis Martinez	.20	.07
❑ 611	Tom Gordon	.10	.02
❑ 612	Byron Mathews RC	.10	.02
❑ 613	Joel Adamson RC	.10	.02
❑ 614	Brian Williams	.10	.02
❑ 615	Steve Avery	.10	.02
❑ 616	Midre Cummings RC	.10	.02
❑ 617	Craig Lefferts	.10	.02
❑ 618	Tony Pena	.10	.02
❑ 619	Billy Spiers	.10	.02
❑ 620	Todd Benzinger	.10	.02
❑ 621	Greg Boyd RC	.10	.02
❑ 622	Ben Rivera	.10	.02
❑ 623	Al Martin	.10	.02
❑ 624	Sam Militello UER	.10	.02
❑ 625	Rick Aguilera	.10	.02
❑ 626	Dan Gladden	.10	.02
❑ 627	Andres Berumen RC	.10	.02
❑ 628	Kelly Gruber	.10	.02
❑ 629	Cris Carpenter	.10	.02
❑ 630	Mark Grace	.30	.10
❑ 631	Jeff Brantley	.10	.02
❑ 632	Chris Widger RC	.25	.08
❑ 633	Three Russians	.10	.02
❑ 634	Mo Sanford	.10	.02
❑ 635	Albert Belle	.20	.07
❑ 636	Tim Teufel	.10	.02
❑ 637	Greg Myers	.10	.02
❑ 638	Brian Bohanon	.10	.02
❑ 639	Mike Bordick	.10	.02
❑ 640	Dwight Gooden	.20	.07
❑ 641	P.Leahy/G.Baugh RC	.10	.02
❑ 642	Milt Hill	.10	.02
❑ 643	Luis Aquino	.10	.02
❑ 644	Dante Bichette	.20	.07
❑ 645	Bobby Thigpen	.10	.02
❑ 646	Rich Scheid RC	.10	.02
❑ 647	Brian Sackinsky RC	.10	.02
❑ 648	Ryan Hawblitzel	.10	.02
❑ 649	Tom Marsh	.10	.02
❑ 650	Terry Pendleton	.20	.07
❑ 651	Rafael Bournigal	.10	.02
❑ 652	Dave West	.10	.02
❑ 653	Steve Hosey	.10	.02
❑ 654	Gerald Williams	.10	.02
❑ 655	Scott Cooper	.10	.02
❑ 656	Gary Scott	.10	.02
❑ 657	Mike Harkey	.10	.02
❑ 658	J.Burnitz/S.Walker RC	.20	.07
❑ 659	Ed Sprague	.10	.02
❑ 660	Alan Trammell	.20	.07
❑ 661	Garvin Alston RC	.10	.02
❑ 662	Donovan Osborne	.10	.02
❑ 663	Jeff Gardner	.10	.02
❑ 664	Calvin Jones	.10	.02
❑ 665	Darrin Fletcher	.10	.02
❑ 666	Glenallen Hill	.10	.02
❑ 667	Jim Rosenbohm RC	.10	.02
❑ 668	Scott Lewis	.10	.02
❑ 669	Kip Yaughn RC	.10	.02
❑ 670	Julio Franco	.20	.07
❑ 671	Dave Martinez	.10	.02
❑ 672	Kevin Bass	.10	.02
❑ 673	Todd Van Poppel	.10	.02
❑ 674	Mark Gubicza	.10	.02
❑ 675	Tim Raines	.20	.07
❑ 676	Rudy Seanez	.10	.02
❑ 677	Charlie Leibrandt	.10	.02
❑ 678	Randy Milligan	.10	.02
❑ 679	Kim Batiste	.10	.02
❑ 680	Craig Biggio	.30	.10
❑ 681	Darren Holmes	.10	.02
❑ 682	John Candelaria	.10	.02
❑ 683	Eddie Christian RC	.10	.02
❑ 684	Pat Mahomes	.10	.02
❑ 685	Bob Walk	.10	.02
❑ 686	Russ Springer	.10	.02
❑ 687	Tony Sheffield RC	.10	.02
❑ 688	Dwight Smith	.10	.02
❑ 689	Eddie Zosky	.10	.02
❑ 690	Bien Figueroa	.10	.02
❑ 691	Jim Tatum RC	.10	.02
❑ 692	Chad Kreuter	.10	.02
❑ 693	Rich Rodriguez	.10	.02
❑ 694	Shane Turner	.10	.02
❑ 695	Kent Bottenfield	.10	.02
❑ 696	Jose Mesa	.10	.02
❑ 697	Darrell Whitmore RC	.10	.02
❑ 698	Ted Wood	.10	.02
❑ 699	Chad Curtis	.10	.02
❑ 700	Nolan Ryan	2.00	.75
❑ 701	M.Piazza/C.Delgado	3.00	1.25
❑ 702	Tim Pugh RC	.10	.02
❑ 703	Jeff Kent	.50	.20
❑ 704	J.Goodrich/D.Figueroa RC	.10	.02
❑ 705	Bob Welch	.10	.02
❑ 706	Sherard Clinkscales RC	.10	.02
❑ 707	Donn Pall	.10	.02
❑ 708	Greg Olson	.10	.02
❑ 709	Jeff Juden	.10	.02
❑ 710	Mike Mussina	.30	.10
❑ 711	Scott Chiamparino	.10	.02
❑ 712	Stan Javier	.10	.02
❑ 713	John Doherty	.10	.02
❑ 714	Kevin Gross	.10	.02
❑ 715	Greg Gagne	.10	.02
❑ 716	Steve Cooke	.10	.02
❑ 717	Steve Farr	.10	.02
❑ 718	Jay Buhner	.20	.07
❑ 719	Butch Henry	.10	.02
❑ 720	David Cone	.20	.07
❑ 721	Rick Wilkins	.10	.02
❑ 722	Chuck Carr	.10	.02
❑ 723	Kenny Felder RC	.10	.02
❑ 724	Guillermo Velasquez	.10	.02
❑ 725	Billy Hatcher	.10	.02
❑ 726	Mike Veneziale RC	.10	.02
❑ 727	Jonathan Hurst	.10	.02
❑ 728	Steve Frey	.10	.02
❑ 729	Mark Leonard	.10	.02
❑ 730	Charles Nagy	.10	.02
❑ 731	Donald Harris	.10	.02
❑ 732	Travis Buckley RC	.10	.02
❑ 733	Tom Browning	.10	.02
❑ 734	Anthony Young	.10	.02
❑ 735	Steve Shifflett	.10	.02
❑ 736	Jeff Russell	.10	.02
❑ 737	Wilson Alvarez	.10	.02
❑ 738	Lance Painter RC	.10	.02
❑ 739	Dave Weathers	.10	.02
❑ 740	Len Dykstra	.20	.07
❑ 741	Mike Devereaux	.10	.02
❑ 742	R.Arocha RC/A.Embree	.25	.08
❑ 743	Dave Landaker RC	.10	.02
❑ 744	Chris George	.10	.02
❑ 745	Eric Davis	.20	.07
❑ 746	Lamar Rogers RC	.10	.02
❑ 747	Carl Willis	.10	.02
❑ 748	Stan Belinda	.10	.02
❑ 749	Scott Kamieniecki	.10	.02
❑ 750	Rickey Henderson	.50	.20
❑ 751	Eric Hillman	.10	.02
❑ 752	Pat Hentgen	.10	.02
❑ 753	Jim Corsi	.10	.02
❑ 754	Brian Jordan	.20	.07
❑ 755	Bill Swift	.10	.02
❑ 756	Mike Henneman	.10	.02
❑ 757	Harold Reynolds	.20	.07
❑ 758	Sean Berry	.10	.02
❑ 759	Charlie Hayes	.10	.02
❑ 760	Luis Polonia	.10	.02
❑ 761	Darrin Jackson	.10	.02
❑ 762	Mark Lewis	.10	.02
❑ 763	Rob Maurer	.10	.02

❑	764 Willie Greene	.10	.02
❑	765 Vince Coleman	.10	.02
❑	766 Todd Revenig	.10	.02
❑	767 Rich Ireland RC	.10	.02
❑	768 Mike Macfarlane	.10	.02
❑	769 Francisco Cabrera	.10	.02
❑	770 Robin Ventura	.20	.07
❑	771 Kevin Ritz	.10	.02
❑	772 Chito Martinez	.10	.02
❑	773 Cliff Brantley	.10	.02
❑	774 Curt Leskanic RC	.25	.08
❑	775 Chris Bosio	.10	.02
❑	776 Jose Offerman	.10	.02
❑	777 Mark Guthrie	.10	.02
❑	778 Don Slaught	.10	.02
❑	779 Rich Monteleone	.10	.02
❑	780 Jim Abbott	.30	.10
❑	781 Jack Clark	.20	.07
❑	782 R.Mendoza/D.Roman RC	.10	.02
❑	783 Heathcliff Slocumb	.10	.02
❑	784 Jeff Branson	.10	.02
❑	785 Kevin Brown	.20	.07
❑	786 K.Ryan/Gandarillas RC	.10	.02
❑	787 Mike Matthews RC	.10	.02
❑	788 Mackey Sasser	.10	.02
❑	789 Jeff Conine UER	.20	.07
❑	790 George Bell	.10	.02
❑	791 Pat Rapp	.10	.02
❑	792 Joe Boever	.10	.02
❑	793 Jim Poole	.10	.02
❑	794 Andy Ashby	.10	.02
❑	795 Deion Sanders	.30	.10
❑	796 Scott Brosius	.20	.07
❑	797 Brad Pennington	.10	.02
❑	798 Greg Blosser	.10	.02
❑	799 Jim Edmonds RC	2.00	.75
❑	800 Shawn Jeter	.10	.02
❑	801 Jesse Levis	.10	.02
❑	802 Phil Clark UER	.10	.02
❑	803 Eddie Pierce RC	.10	.02
❑	804 Jose Valentin RC	.25	.08
❑	805 Terry Jorgensen	.10	.02
❑	806 Mark Hutton	.10	.02
❑	807 Troy Neel	.10	.02
❑	808 Bret Boone	.20	.07
❑	809 Cris Colon	.10	.02
❑	810 Domingo Martinez RC	.10	.02
❑	811 Javier Lopez	.30	.10
❑	812 Matt Walbeck RC	.10	.02
❑	813 Dan Wilson	.20	.07
❑	814 Scooter Tucker	.10	.02
❑	815 Billy Ashley	.10	.02
❑	816 Tim Laker RC	.10	.02
❑	817 Bobby Jones	.20	.07
❑	818 Brad Brink	.10	.02
❑	819 William Pennyfeather	.10	.02
❑	820 Stan Royer	.10	.02
❑	821 Doug Brocail	.10	.02
❑	822 Kevin Rogers	.10	.02
❑	823 Checklist 397-540	.10	.02
❑	824 Checklist 541-691	.10	.02
❑	825 Checklist 692-825	.10	.02

1993 Topps Traded

❑	COMP.FACT.SET (132)	25.00	10.00
❑	1T Barry Bonds	1.50	.60
❑	2T Rich Renteria	.10	.02
❑	3T Aaron Sele	.10	.02
❑	4T Carlton Loewer USA RC	.25	.08
❑	5T Erik Pappas	.10	.02
❑	6T Greg McMichael RC	.25	.08
❑	7T Freddie Benavides	.10	.02
❑	8T Kirk Gibson	.20	.07
❑	9T Tony Fernandez	.10	.02
❑	10T Jay Gainer RC	.25	.08
❑	11T Orestes Destrade	.10	.02
❑	12T A.J. Hinch USA RC	.50	.20
❑	13T Bobby Munoz	.10	.02
❑	14T Tom Henke	.10	.02
❑	15T Rob Butler	.10	.02
❑	16T Gary Wayne	.10	.02
❑	17T David McCarty	.10	.02
❑	18T Walt Weiss	.10	.02
❑	19T Todd Helton USA RC	12.00	5.00
❑	20T Mark Whiten	.10	.02
❑	21T Ricky Gutierrez	.10	.02
❑	22T Dustin Hermanson USA RC	1.00	.40
❑	23T Sherman Obando RC	.25	.08
❑	24T Mike Piazza	3.00	1.25
❑	25T Jeff Russell	.10	.02
❑	26T Jason Bere	.10	.02
❑	27T Jack Voigt RC	.25	.08
❑	28T Chris Bosio	.10	.02
❑	29T Phil Hiatt	.10	.02
❑	30T Matt Beaumont USA RC	.25	.08
❑	31T Andres Galarraga	.20	.07
❑	32T Greg Swindell	.10	.02
❑	33T Vinny Castilla	.50	.20
❑	34T Pat Clougherty RC USA	.25	.08
❑	35T Greg Briley	.10	.02
❑	36T Dallas Green MG Davey Johnson MG	.10	.02
❑	37T Tyler Green	.10	.02
❑	38T Craig Paquette	.10	.02
❑	39T Danny Sheaffer RC	.25	.08
❑	40T Jim Converse RC	.25	.08
❑	41T Terry Harvey USA RC	.25	.08
❑	42T Phil Plantier	.10	.02
❑	43T Doug Saunders RC	.25	.08
❑	44T Benny Santiago	.20	.07
❑	45T Dante Powell USA RC	.25	.08
❑	46T Jeff Parrett	.10	.02
❑	47T Wade Boggs	.30	.10
❑	48T Paul Molitor	.20	.07
❑	49T Turk Wendell	.10	.02
❑	50T David Wells	.20	.07
❑	51T Gary Sheffield	.20	.07
❑	52T Kevin Young	.20	.07
❑	53T Nelson Liriano	.10	.02
❑	54T Greg Maddux	.75	.30
❑	55T Derek Bell	.10	.02
❑	56T Matt Turner RC	.25	.08
❑	57T Charlie Nelson USA RC	.25	.08
❑	58T Mike Hampton	.20	.07
❑	59T Troy O'Leary RC	.50	.20
❑	60T Benji Gil	.10	.02
❑	61T Mitch Lyden RC	.25	.08
❑	62T J.T.Snow	.30	.10
❑	63T Damon Buford	.10	.02
❑	64T Gene Harris	.10	.02
❑	65T Randy Myers	.10	.02
❑	66T Felix Jose	.10	.02
❑	67T Todd Dunn USA RC	.25	.08
❑	68T Jimmy Key	.20	.07
❑	69T Pedro Castellano	.10	.02
❑	70T Mark Merila USA RC	.25	.08
❑	71T Rich Rodriguez	.10	.02
❑	72T Matt Mieske	.10	.02
❑	73T Pete Incaviglia	.10	.02
❑	74T Carl Everett	.20	.07
❑	75T Jim Abbott	.30	.10
❑	76T Luis Aquino	.10	.02
❑	77T Rene Arocha	.20	.07
❑	78T Jon Shave	.10	.02
❑	79T Todd Walker USA RC	1.00	.40
❑	80T Jack Armstrong	.10	.02
❑	81T Jeff Richardson	.10	.02
❑	82T Blas Minor	.10	.02
❑	83T Dave Winfield	.20	.07
❑	84T Paul O'Neill	.30	.10
❑	85T Steve Reich USA RC	.25	.08
❑	86T Chris Hammond	.10	.02
❑	87T Hilly Hathaway RC	.25	.08
❑	88T Fred McGriff	.30	.10
❑	89T Dave Telgheder RC	.25	.08
❑	90T Richie Lewis RC	.25	.08
❑	91T Brent Gates	.10	.02
❑	92T Andre Dawson	.20	.07
❑	93T Andy Barkett USA RC	.25	.08
❑	94T Doug Drabek	.10	.02
❑	95T Joe Klink	.10	.02
❑	96T Willie Blair	.10	.02
❑	97T Danny Graves USA RC	.50	.20
❑	98T Pat Meares RC	.50	.20
❑	99T Mike Lansing RC	.50	.20
❑	100T Marcos Armas RC	.25	.08
❑	101T Darren Grass USA RC	.25	.08
❑	102T Chris Jones	.10	.02
❑	103T Ken Ryan RC	.25	.08
❑	104T Ellis Burks	.20	.07
❑	105T Roberto Kelly	.10	.02
❑	106T Dave Magadan	.10	.02
❑	107T Paul Wilson USA RC	.50	.20
❑	108T Rob Natal	.10	.02
❑	109T Paul Wagner	.10	.02
❑	110T Jeromy Burnitz	.20	.07
❑	111T Monty Fariss	.10	.02
❑	112T Kevin Mitchell	.10	.02
❑	113T Scott Pose RC	.25	.08
❑	114T Dave Stewart	.20	.07
❑	115T Russ Johnson USA RC	.25	.08
❑	116T Armando Reynoso	.10	.02
❑	117T Geronimo Berroa	.10	.02
❑	118T Woody Williams RC	1.00	.40
❑	119T Tim Bogar RC	.25	.08
❑	120T Bob Scafa USA RC	.25	.08
❑	121T Henry Cotto	.10	.02
❑	122T Gregg Jefferies	.10	.02
❑	123T Norm Charlton	.10	.02
❑	124T Bret Wagner USA RC	.25	.08
❑	125T David Cone	.20	.07
❑	126T Daryl Boston	.10	.02
❑	127T Tim Wallach	.10	.02
❑	128T Mike Martin USA RC	.25	.08
❑	129T John Cummings RC	.25	.08
❑	130T Ryan Bowen	.10	.02
❑	131T John Powell USA RC	.25	.08
❑	132T Checklist 1-132	.10	.02

1994 Topps

❑	COMPLETE SET (792)	50.00	20.00
❑	COMP.FACT.SET (808)	80.00	40.00
❑	COMP.BAKER SET (818)	80.00	40.00
❑	COMPLETE SERIES 1 (396)	25.00	10.00
❑	COMPLETE SERIES 2 (396)	25.00	10.00
❑	1 Mike Piazza	1.00	.40
❑	2 Bernie Williams	.30	.10
❑	3 Kevin Rogers	.10	.02
❑	4 Paul Carey	.10	.02
❑	5 Ozzie Guillen	.20	.07
❑	6 Derrick May	.10	.02
❑	7 Jose Mesa	.10	.02
❑	8 Todd Hundley	.10	.02
❑	9 Chris Haney	.10	.02
❑	10 John Olerud	.20	.07
❑	11 Andujar Cedeno	.10	.02
❑	12 John Smiley	.10	.02
❑	13 Phil Plantier	.10	.02
❑	14 Willie Banks	.10	.02
❑	15 Jay Bell	.20	.07
❑	16 Doug Henry	.10	.02
❑	17 Lance Blankenship	.10	.02
❑	18 Greg W. Harris	.10	.02

- ❑ 19 Scott Livingstone .10 .02
- ❑ 20 Bryan Harvey .10 .02
- ❑ 21 Wil Cordero .10 .02
- ❑ 22 Roger Pavlik .10 .02
- ❑ 23 Mark Lemke .10 .02
- ❑ 24 Jeff Nelson .10 .02
- ❑ 25 Todd Zeile .10 .02
- ❑ 26 Billy Hatcher .10 .02
- ❑ 27 Joe Magrane .10 .02
- ❑ 28 Tony Longmire .10 .02
- ❑ 29 Omar Daal .10 .02
- ❑ 30 Kirt Manwaring .10 .02
- ❑ 31 Melido Perez .10 .02
- ❑ 32 Tim Hulett .10 .02
- ❑ 33 Jeff Schwarz .10 .02
- ❑ 34 Nolan Ryan 2.00 .75
- ❑ 35 Jose Guzman .10 .02
- ❑ 36 Felix Fermin .10 .02
- ❑ 37 Jeff Innis .10 .02
- ❑ 38 Brett Mayne .10 .02
- ❑ 39 Huck Flener RC .10 .02
- ❑ 40 Jeff Bagwell .30 .10
- ❑ 41 Kevin Wickander .10 .02
- ❑ 42 Ricky Gutierrez .10 .02
- ❑ 43 Pat Mahomes .10 .02
- ❑ 44 Jeff King .10 .02
- ❑ 45 Cal Eldred .10 .02
- ❑ 46 Craig Paquette .10 .02
- ❑ 47 Richie Lewis .10 .02
- ❑ 48 Tony Phillips .10 .02
- ❑ 49 Armando Reynoso .10 .02
- ❑ 50 Moises Alou .20 .07
- ❑ 51 Manuel Lee .10 .02
- ❑ 52 Otis Nixon .10 .02
- ❑ 53 Billy Ashley .10 .02
- ❑ 54 Mark Whiten .10 .02
- ❑ 55 Jeff Russell .10 .02
- ❑ 56 Chad Curtis .10 .02
- ❑ 57 Kevin Stocker .10 .02
- ❑ 58 Mike Jackson .10 .02
- ❑ 59 Matt Nokes .10 .02
- ❑ 60 Chris Bosio .10 .02
- ❑ 61 Damon Buford .10 .02
- ❑ 62 Tim Belcher .10 .02
- ❑ 63 Glenallen Hill .10 .02
- ❑ 64 Bill Wertz .10 .02
- ❑ 65 Eddie Murray .50 .20
- ❑ 66 Tom Gordon .10 .02
- ❑ 67 Alex Gonzalez .10 .02
- ❑ 68 Eddie Taubensee .10 .02
- ❑ 69 Jacob Brumfield .10 .02
- ❑ 70 Andy Benes .10 .02
- ❑ 71 Rich Becker .10 .02
- ❑ 72 Steve Cooke .10 .02
- ❑ 73 Billy Spiers .10 .02
- ❑ 74 Scott Brosius .20 .07
- ❑ 75 Alan Trammell .20 .07
- ❑ 76 Luis Aquino .10 .02
- ❑ 77 Jerald Clark .10 .02
- ❑ 78 Mel Rojas .10 .02
- ❑ 79 Craig McClure RC .10 .02
- ❑ 80 Jose Canseco .30 .10
- ❑ 81 Greg McMichael .10 .02
- ❑ 82 Brian Turang RC .10 .02
- ❑ 83 Tom Urbani .10 .02
- ❑ 84 Garret Anderson .50 .20
- ❑ 85 Tony Pena .10 .02
- ❑ 86 Ricky Jordan .10 .02
- ❑ 87 Jim Gott .10 .02
- ❑ 88 Pat Kelly .10 .02
- ❑ 89 Bud Black .10 .02
- ❑ 90 Robin Ventura .20 .07
- ❑ 91 Rick Sutcliffe .20 .07
- ❑ 92 Jose Bautista .10 .02
- ❑ 93 Bob Ojeda .10 .02
- ❑ 94 Phil Hiatt .10 .02
- ❑ 95 Tim Pugh .10 .02
- ❑ 96 Randy Knorr .10 .02
- ❑ 97 Todd Jones .10 .02
- ❑ 98 Ryan Thompson .10 .02
- ❑ 99 Tim Mauser .10 .02
- ❑ 100 Kirby Puckett .50 .20
- ❑ 101 Mark Dewey .10 .02
- ❑ 102 B.J. Surhoff .20 .07
- ❑ 103 Sterling Hitchcock .10 .02
- ❑ 104 Alex Arias .10 .02
- ❑ 105 David Wells .20 .07
- ❑ 106 Daryl Boston .10 .02
- ❑ 107 Mike Stanton .10 .02
- ❑ 108 Gary Redus .10 .02
- ❑ 109 Delino DeShields .10 .02
- ❑ 110 Lee Smith .20 .07
- ❑ 111 Greg Litton .10 .02
- ❑ 112 Frankie Rodriguez .10 .02
- ❑ 113 Russ Springer .10 .02
- ❑ 114 Mitch Williams .10 .02
- ❑ 115 Eric Karros .20 .07
- ❑ 116 Jeff Brantley .10 .02
- ❑ 117 Jack Voigt .10 .02
- ❑ 118 Jason Bere .10 .02
- ❑ 119 Kevin Roberson .10 .02
- ❑ 120 Jimmy Key .20 .07
- ❑ 121 Reggie Jefferson .10 .02
- ❑ 122 Jeromy Burnitz .20 .07
- ❑ 123 Billy Brewer .10 .02
- ❑ 124 Willie Canate .10 .02
- ❑ 125 Greg Swindell .10 .02
- ❑ 126 Hal Morris .10 .02
- ❑ 127 Brad Ausmus .30 .10
- ❑ 128 George Tsamis .10 .02
- ❑ 129 Denny Neagle .20 .07
- ❑ 130 Pat Listach .10 .02
- ❑ 131 Steve Karsay .10 .02
- ❑ 132 Bret Barberie .10 .02
- ❑ 133 Mark Leiter .10 .02
- ❑ 134 Greg Colbrunn .10 .02
- ❑ 135 David Nied .10 .02
- ❑ 136 Dean Palmer .20 .07
- ❑ 137 Steve Avery .10 .02
- ❑ 138 Bill Haselman .10 .02
- ❑ 139 Tripp Cromer .10 .02
- ❑ 140 Frank Viola .20 .07
- ❑ 141 Rene Gonzales .10 .02
- ❑ 142 Curt Schilling .20 .07
- ❑ 143 Tim Wallach .10 .02
- ❑ 144 Bobby Munoz .10 .02
- ❑ 145 Brady Anderson .20 .07
- ❑ 146 Rod Beck .10 .02
- ❑ 147 Mike LaValliere .10 .02
- ❑ 148 Greg Hibbard .10 .02
- ❑ 149 Kenny Lofton .20 .07
- ❑ 150 Dwight Gooden .20 .07
- ❑ 151 Greg Gagne .10 .02
- ❑ 152 Ray McDavid .10 .02
- ❑ 153 Chris Donnels .10 .02
- ❑ 154 Dan Wilson .10 .02
- ❑ 155 Todd Stottlemyre .10 .02
- ❑ 156 David McCarty .10 .02
- ❑ 157 Paul Wagner .10 .02
- ❑ 158 Derek Jeter 1.50 .60
- ❑ 159 Mike Fetters .10 .02
- ❑ 160 Scott Lydy .10 .02
- ❑ 161 Darrell Whitmore .10 .02
- ❑ 162 Bob MacDonald .10 .02
- ❑ 163 Vinny Castilla .20 .07
- ❑ 164 Denis Boucher .10 .02
- ❑ 165 Ivan Rodriguez .30 .10
- ❑ 166 Ron Gant .20 .07
- ❑ 167 Tim Davis .10 .02
- ❑ 168 Steve Dixon .10 .02
- ❑ 169 Scott Fletcher .10 .02
- ❑ 170 Terry Mulholland .10 .02
- ❑ 171 Greg Myers .10 .02
- ❑ 172 Brett Butler .20 .07
- ❑ 173 Bob Wickman .10 .02
- ❑ 174 Dave Martinez .10 .02
- ❑ 175 Fernando Valenzuela .20 .07
- ❑ 176 Craig Grebeck .10 .02
- ❑ 177 Shawn Boskie .10 .02
- ❑ 178 Albie Lopez .10 .02
- ❑ 179 Butch Huskey .10 .02
- ❑ 180 George Brett 1.25 .50
- ❑ 181 Juan Guzman .10 .02
- ❑ 182 Eric Anthony .10 .02
- ❑ 183 Rob Dibble .20 .07
- ❑ 184 Craig Shipley .10 .02
- ❑ 185 Kevin Tapani .10 .02
- ❑ 186 Marcus Moore .10 .02
- ❑ 187 Graeme Lloyd .10 .02
- ❑ 188 Mike Bordick .10 .02
- ❑ 189 Chris Hammond .10 .02
- ❑ 190 Cecil Fielder .20 .07
- ❑ 191 Curt Leskanic .10 .02
- ❑ 192 Lou Frazier .10 .02
- ❑ 193 Steve Dreyer RC .10 .02
- ❑ 194 Javier Lopez .20 .07
- ❑ 195 Edgar Martinez .30 .10
- ❑ 196 Allen Watson .10 .02
- ❑ 197 John Flaherty .10 .02
- ❑ 198 Kurt Stillwell .10 .02
- ❑ 199 Danny Jackson .10 .02
- ❑ 200 Cal Ripken 1.50 .60
- ❑ 201 Mike Bell RC .10 .02
- ❑ 202 Alan Benes RC .25 .08
- ❑ 203 Matt Farner RC .10 .02
- ❑ 204 Jeff Granger .10 .02
- ❑ 205 Brooks Kieschnick RC .10 .02
- ❑ 206 Jeremy Lee RC .10 .02
- ❑ 207 Charles Peterson RC .10 .02
- ❑ 208 Andy Rice RC .10 .02
- ❑ 209 Billy Wagner RC 1.50 .60
- ❑ 210 Kelly Wunsch RC .25 .08
- ❑ 211 Tom Candiotti .10 .02
- ❑ 212 Domingo Jean .10 .02
- ❑ 213 John Burkett .10 .02
- ❑ 214 George Bell .10 .02
- ❑ 215 Dan Plesac .10 .02
- ❑ 216 Manny Ramirez .50 .20
- ❑ 217 Mike Maddux .10 .02
- ❑ 218 Kevin McReynolds .10 .02
- ❑ 219 Pat Borders .10 .02
- ❑ 220 Doug Drabek .10 .02
- ❑ 221 Larry Luebbers RC .10 .02
- ❑ 222 Trevor Hoffman .30 .10
- ❑ 223 Pat Meares .10 .02
- ❑ 224 Danny Miceli .10 .02
- ❑ 225 Greg Vaughn .10 .02
- ❑ 226 Scott Hemond .10 .02
- ❑ 227 Pat Rapp .10 .02
- ❑ 228 Kirk Gibson .20 .07
- ❑ 229 Lance Painter .10 .02
- ❑ 230 Larry Walker .20 .07
- ❑ 231 Benji Gil .10 .02
- ❑ 232 Mark Wohlers .10 .02
- ❑ 233 Rich Amaral .10 .02
- ❑ 234 Eric Pappas .10 .02
- ❑ 235 Scott Cooper .10 .02
- ❑ 236 Mike Butcher .10 .02
- ❑ 237 Pride RC/Green/Sweeney RC .50 .20
- ❑ 238 Kim Batiste .10 .02
- ❑ 239 Paul Assenmacher .10 .02
- ❑ 240 Will Clark .30 .10
- ❑ 241 Jose Offerman .10 .02
- ❑ 242 Todd Frohwirth .10 .02
- ❑ 243 Tim Raines .20 .07
- ❑ 244 Rick Wilkins .10 .02
- ❑ 245 Bret Saberhagen .20 .07
- ❑ 246 Thomas Howard .10 .02
- ❑ 247 Stan Belinda .10 .02
- ❑ 248 Rickey Henderson .50 .20
- ❑ 249 Brian Williams .10 .02
- ❑ 250 Barry Larkin .30 .10
- ❑ 251 Jose Valentin .10 .02
- ❑ 252 Lenny Webster .10 .02
- ❑ 253 Blas Minor .10 .02
- ❑ 254 Tim Teufel .10 .02
- ❑ 255 Bobby Witt .10 .02
- ❑ 256 Walt Weiss .10 .02
- ❑ 257 Chad Kreuter .10 .02
- ❑ 258 Roberto Mejia .10 .02
- ❑ 259 Cliff Floyd .20 .07
- ❑ 260 Julio Franco .20 .07
- ❑ 261 Rafael Belliard .10 .02
- ❑ 262 Marc Newfield .10 .02
- ❑ 263 Gerald Perry .10 .02
- ❑ 264 Ken Ryan .10 .02
- ❑ 265 Chili Davis .20 .07
- ❑ 266 Dave West .10 .02
- ❑ 267 Royce Clayton .10 .02
- ❑ 268 Pedro Martinez .50 .20
- ❑ 269 Mark Hutton .10 .02
- ❑ 270 Frank Thomas .50 .20
- ❑ 271 Brad Pennington .10 .02
- ❑ 272 Mike Harkey .10 .02
- ❑ 273 Sandy Alomar Jr. .10 .02
- ❑ 274 Dave Gallagher .10 .02
- ❑ 275 Wally Joyner .20 .07
- ❑ 276 Ricky Trlicek .10 .02

❑ 277 Al Osuna	.10	.02
❑ 278 Pokey Reese	.10	.02
❑ 279 Kevin Higgins	.10	.02
❑ 280 Rick Aguilera	.10	.02
❑ 281 Orlando Merced	.10	.02
❑ 282 Mike Mohler	.10	.02
❑ 283 John Jaha	.10	.02
❑ 284 Robb Nen	.20	.07
❑ 285 Travis Fryman	.20	.07
❑ 286 Mark Thompson	.10	.02
❑ 287 Mike Lansing	.10	.02
❑ 288 Craig Lefferts	.10	.02
❑ 289 Damon Berryhill	.10	.02
❑ 290 Randy Johnson	.50	.20
❑ 291 Jeff Reed	.10	.02
❑ 292 Danny Darwin	.10	.02
❑ 293 J.T.Snow	.20	.07
❑ 294 Tyler Green	.10	.02
❑ 295 Chris Hoiles	.10	.02
❑ 296 Roger McDowell	.10	.02
❑ 297 Spike Owen	.10	.02
❑ 298 Salomon Torres	.10	.02
❑ 299 Wilson Alvarez	.10	.02
❑ 300 Ryne Sandberg	.75	.30
❑ 301 Derek Lilliquist	.10	.02
❑ 302 Howard Johnson	.10	.02
❑ 303 Greg Cadaret	.10	.02
❑ 304 Pat Hentgen	.10	.02
❑ 305 Craig Biggio	.30	.10
❑ 306 Scott Service	.10	.02
❑ 307 Melvin Nieves	.10	.02
❑ 308 Mike Trombley	.10	.02
❑ 309 Carlos Garcia	.10	.02
❑ 310 Robin Yount	.75	.30
❑ 311 Marcos Armas	.10	.02
❑ 312 Rich Rodriguez	.10	.02
❑ 313 Justin Thompson	.10	.02
❑ 314 Danny Sheaffer	.10	.02
❑ 315 Ken Hill	.10	.02
❑ 316 Terrell Wade RC	.10	.02
❑ 317 Cris Carpenter	.10	.02
❑ 318 Jeff Blauser	.10	.02
❑ 319 Ted Power	.10	.02
❑ 320 Ozzie Smith	.75	.30
❑ 321 John Dopson	.10	.02
❑ 322 Chris Turner	.10	.02
❑ 323 Pete Incaviglia	.10	.02
❑ 324 Alan Mills	.10	.02
❑ 325 Jody Reed	.10	.02
❑ 326 Rich Monteleone	.10	.02
❑ 327 Mark Carreon	.10	.02
❑ 328 Donn Pall	.10	.02
❑ 329 Matt Walbeck	.10	.02
❑ 330 Charley Nagy	.10	.02
❑ 331 Jeff McKnight	.10	.02
❑ 332 Jose Lind	.10	.02
❑ 333 Mike Timlin	.10	.02
❑ 334 Doug Jones	.10	.02
❑ 335 Kevin Mitchell	.10	.02
❑ 336 Luis Lopez	.10	.02
❑ 337 Shane Mack	.10	.02
❑ 338 Randy Tomlin	.10	.02
❑ 339 Matt Mieske	.10	.02
❑ 340 Mark McGwire	1.25	.50
❑ 341 Nigel Wilson	.10	.02
❑ 342 Danny Gladden	.10	.02
❑ 343 Mo Sanford	.10	.02
❑ 344 Sean Berry	.10	.02
❑ 345 Kevin Brown	.20	.07
❑ 346 Greg Olson	.10	.02
❑ 347 Dave Magadan	.10	.02
❑ 348 Rene Arocha	.10	.02
❑ 349 Carlos Quintana	.10	.02
❑ 350 Jim Abbott	.30	.10
❑ 351 Gary DiSarcina	.10	.02
❑ 352 Ben Rivera	.10	.02
❑ 353 Carlos Hernandez	.10	.02
❑ 354 Darren Lewis	.10	.02
❑ 355 Harold Reynolds	.20	.07
❑ 356 Scott Ruffcorn	.10	.02
❑ 357 Mark Gubicza	.10	.02
❑ 358 Paul Sorrento	.10	.02
❑ 359 Anthony Young	.10	.02
❑ 360 Mark Grace	.30	.10
❑ 361 Rob Butler	.10	.02
❑ 362 Kevin Bass	.10	.02
❑ 363 Eric Helfand	.10	.02
❑ 364 Derek Bell	.10	.02
❑ 365 Scott Erickson	.10	.02
❑ 366 Al Martin	.10	.02
❑ 367 Ricky Bones	.10	.02
❑ 368 Jeff Branson	.10	.02
❑ 369 J.Giambi/D.Bell RC	.50	.20
❑ 370 Benito Santiago	.20	.07
❑ 371 John Doherty	.10	.02
❑ 372 Joe Girardi	.10	.02
❑ 373 Tim Scott	.10	.02
❑ 374 Marvin Freeman	.10	.02
❑ 375 Deion Sanders	.30	.10
❑ 376 Roger Salkeld	.10	.02
❑ 377 Bernard Gilkey	.10	.02
❑ 378 Tony Fossas	.10	.02
❑ 379 Mark McLemore UER	.10	.02
❑ 380 Darren Daulton	.20	.07
❑ 381 Chuck Finley	.20	.07
❑ 382 Mitch Webster	.10	.02
❑ 383 Gerald Williams	.10	.02
❑ 384 F.Thomas/F.McGriff AS	.30	.10
❑ 385 R.Alomar/R.Thompson AS	.20	.07
❑ 386 W.Boggs/M.Williams AS	.20	.07
❑ 387 C.Ripken/J.Blauser AS	.50	.20
❑ 388 K.Griffey/L.Dykstra AS	.50	.20
❑ 389 J.Gonzalez/D.Justice AS	.20	.07
❑ 390 A.Belle/B.Bonds AS	.75	.30
❑ 391 M.Stanley/M.Piazza AS	.50	.20
❑ 392 J.McDowell/G.Maddux AS	.30	.10
❑ 393 J.Key/T.Glavine AS	.20	.07
❑ 394 J.Montgomery/R.Myers AS	.10	.02
❑ 395 Checklist 1-198	.10	.02
❑ 396 Checklist 199-396	.10	.02
❑ 397 Tim Salmon	.30	.10
❑ 398 Todd Benzinger	.10	.02
❑ 399 Frank Castillo	.10	.02
❑ 400 Ken Griffey Jr.	.75	.30
❑ 401 John Kruk	.20	.07
❑ 402 Dave Telgheder	.10	.02
❑ 403 Gary Gaetti	.20	.07
❑ 404 Jim Edmonds	.50	.20
❑ 405 Don Slaught	.10	.02
❑ 406 Jose Oquendo	.10	.02
❑ 407 Bruce Ruffin	.10	.02
❑ 408 Phil Clark	.10	.02
❑ 409 Joe Klink	.10	.02
❑ 410 Lou Whitaker	.20	.07
❑ 411 Kevin Seitzer	.10	.02
❑ 412 Darrin Fletcher	.10	.02
❑ 413 Kenny Rogers	.20	.07
❑ 414 Bill Pecota	.10	.02
❑ 415 Dave Fleming	.10	.02
❑ 416 Luis Alicea	.10	.02
❑ 417 Paul Quantrill	.10	.02
❑ 418 Damion Easley	.10	.02
❑ 419 Wes Chamberlain	.10	.02
❑ 420 Harold Baines	.20	.07
❑ 421 Scott Radinsky	.10	.02
❑ 422 Rey Sanchez	.10	.02
❑ 423 Junior Ortiz	.10	.02
❑ 424 Jeff Kent	.30	.10
❑ 425 Brian McRae	.10	.02
❑ 426 Ed Sprague	.10	.02
❑ 427 Tom Edens	.10	.02
❑ 428 Willie Greene	.10	.02
❑ 429 Bryan Hickerson	.10	.02
❑ 430 Dave Winfield	.20	.07
❑ 431 Pedro Astacio	.10	.02
❑ 432 Mike Gallego	.10	.02
❑ 433 Dave Burba	.10	.02
❑ 434 Bob Walk	.10	.02
❑ 435 Darryl Hamilton	.10	.02
❑ 436 Vince Horsman	.10	.02
❑ 437 Bob Natal	.10	.02
❑ 438 Mike Henneman	.10	.02
❑ 439 Willie Blair	.10	.02
❑ 440 Dennis Martinez	.20	.07
❑ 441 Dan Peltier	.10	.02
❑ 442 Tony Tarasco	.10	.02
❑ 443 John Cummings	.10	.02
❑ 444 Geronimo Pena	.10	.02
❑ 445 Aaron Sele	.10	.02
❑ 446 Stan Javier	.10	.02
❑ 447 Mike Williams	.10	.02
❑ 448 D.J. Boston RC	.10	.02
❑ 449 Jim Poole	.10	.02
❑ 450 Carlos Baerga	.10	.02
❑ 451 Bob Scanlan	.10	.02
❑ 452 Lance Johnson	.10	.02
❑ 453 Eric Hillman	.10	.02
❑ 454 Keith Miller	.10	.02
❑ 455 Dave Stewart	.20	.07
❑ 456 Pete Harnisch	.10	.02
❑ 457 Roberto Kelly	.10	.02
❑ 458 Tim Worrell	.10	.02
❑ 459 Pedro Munoz	.10	.02
❑ 460 Orel Hershiser	.20	.07
❑ 461 Randy Velarde	.10	.02
❑ 462 Trevor Wilson	.10	.02
❑ 463 Jerry Goff	.10	.02
❑ 464 Bill Wegman	.10	.02
❑ 465 Dennis Eckersley	.20	.07
❑ 466 Jeff Conine	.20	.07
❑ 467 Joe Boever	.10	.02
❑ 468 Dante Bichette	.20	.07
❑ 469 Jeff Shaw	.10	.02
❑ 470 Rafael Palmeiro	.30	.10
❑ 471 Phil Leftwich RC	.10	.02
❑ 472 Jay Buhner	.20	.07
❑ 473 Bob Tewksbury	.10	.02
❑ 474 Tim Naehring	.10	.02
❑ 475 Tom Glavine	.30	.10
❑ 476 Dave Hollins	.10	.02
❑ 477 Arthur Rhodes	.10	.02
❑ 478 Joey Cora	.10	.02
❑ 479 Mike Morgan	.10	.02
❑ 480 Albert Belle	.20	.07
❑ 481 John Franco	.20	.07
❑ 482 Hipolito Pichardo	.10	.02
❑ 483 Duane Ward	.10	.02
❑ 484 Luis Gonzalez	.20	.07
❑ 485 Joe Oliver	.10	.02
❑ 486 Wally Whitehurst	.10	.02
❑ 487 Mike Benjamin	.10	.02
❑ 488 Eric Davis	.20	.07
❑ 489 Scott Kamieniecki	.10	.02
❑ 490 Kent Hrbek	.20	.07
❑ 491 John Hope RC	.10	.02
❑ 492 Jesse Orosco	.10	.02
❑ 493 Troy Neel	.10	.02
❑ 494 Ryan Bowen	.10	.02
❑ 495 Mickey Tettleton	.10	.02
❑ 496 Chris Jones	.10	.02
❑ 497 John Wetteland	.20	.07
❑ 498 David Hulse	.10	.02
❑ 499 Greg Maddux	.75	.30
❑ 500 Bo Jackson	.50	.20
❑ 501 Donovan Osborne	.10	.02
❑ 502 Mike Greenwell	.10	.02
❑ 503 Steve Frey	.10	.02
❑ 504 Jim Eisenreich	.10	.02
❑ 505 Robby Thompson	.10	.02
❑ 506 Leo Gomez	.10	.02
❑ 507 Dave Staton	.10	.02
❑ 508 Wayne Kirby	.10	.02
❑ 509 Tim Bogar	.10	.02
❑ 510 David Cone	.20	.07
❑ 511 Devon White	.20	.07
❑ 512 Xavier Hernandez	.10	.02
❑ 513 Tim Costo	.10	.02
❑ 514 Gene Harris	.10	.02
❑ 515 Jack McDowell	.10	.02
❑ 516 Kevin Gross	.10	.02
❑ 517 Scott Leius	.10	.02
❑ 518 Lloyd McClendon	.10	.02
❑ 519 Alex Diaz RC	.10	.02
❑ 520 Wade Boggs	.30	.10
❑ 521 Bob Welch	.10	.02
❑ 522 Henry Cotto	.10	.02
❑ 523 Mike Moore	.10	.02
❑ 524 Tim Laker	.10	.02
❑ 525 Andres Galarraga	.20	.07
❑ 526 Jamie Moyer	.20	.07
❑ 527 J.Hardtke RC/C.Sexton RC	.10	.02
❑ 528 Sid Bream	.10	.02
❑ 529 Erik Hanson	.10	.02
❑ 530 Ray Lankford	.20	.07
❑ 531 Rob Deer	.10	.02
❑ 532 Rod Correia	.10	.02
❑ 533 Roger Mason	.10	.02
❑ 534 Mike Devereaux	.10	.02

❑ 535 Jeff Montgomery .10 .02
❑ 536 Dwight Smith .10 .02
❑ 537 Jeremy Hernandez .10 .02
❑ 538 Ellis Burks .20 .07
❑ 539 Bobby Jones .10 .02
❑ 540 Paul Molitor .20 .07
❑ 541 Jeff Juden .10 .02
❑ 542 Chris Sabo .10 .02
❑ 543 Larry Casian .10 .02
❑ 544 Jeff Gardner .10 .02
❑ 545 Ramon Martinez .10 .02
❑ 546 Paul O'Neill .30 .10
❑ 547 Steve Hosey .10 .02
❑ 548 Dave Nilsson .10 .02
❑ 549 Ron Darling .10 .02
❑ 550 Matt Williams .20 .07
❑ 551 Jack Armstrong .10 .02
❑ 552 Bill Krueger .10 .02
❑ 553 Freddie Benavides .10 .02
❑ 554 Jeff Fassero .10 .02
❑ 555 Chuck Knoblauch .20 .07
❑ 556 Guillermo Velasquez .10 .02
❑ 557 Joel Johnston .10 .02
❑ 558 Tom Lampkin .10 .02
❑ 559 Todd Van Poppel .10 .02
❑ 560 Gary Sheffield .20 .07
❑ 561 Skeeter Barnes .10 .02
❑ 562 Darren Holmes .10 .02
❑ 563 John Vander Wal .10 .02
❑ 564 Mike Ignasiak .10 .02
❑ 565 Fred McGriff .30 .10
❑ 566 Luis Polonia .10 .02
❑ 567 Mike Perez .10 .02
❑ 568 John Valentin .10 .02
❑ 569 Mike Felder .10 .02
❑ 570 Tommy Greene .10 .02
❑ 571 David Segui .10 .02
❑ 572 Roberto Hernandez .10 .02
❑ 573 Steve Wilson .10 .02
❑ 574 Willie McGee .20 .07
❑ 575 Randy Myers .10 .02
❑ 576 Darrin Jackson .10 .02
❑ 577 Eric Plunk .10 .02
❑ 578 Mike Macfarlane .10 .02
❑ 579 Doug Brocail .10 .02
❑ 580 Steve Finley .20 .07
❑ 581 John Roper .10 .02
❑ 582 Danny Cox .10 .02
❑ 583 Chip Hale .10 .02
❑ 584 Scott Bullett .10 .02
❑ 585 Kevin Reimer .10 .02
❑ 586 Brent Gates .10 .02
❑ 587 Matt Turner .10 .02
❑ 588 Rich Rowland .10 .02
❑ 589 Kent Bottenfield .10 .02
❑ 590 Marquis Grissom .20 .07
❑ 591 Doug Strange .10 .02
❑ 592 Jay Howell .10 .02
❑ 593 Omar Vizquel .30 .10
❑ 594 Rheal Cormier .10 .02
❑ 595 Andre Dawson .20 .07
❑ 596 Hilly Hathaway .10 .02
❑ 597 Todd Pratt .10 .02
❑ 598 Mike Mussina .30 .10
❑ 599 Alex Fernandez .10 .02
❑ 600 Don Mattingly 1.25 .50
❑ 601 Frank Thomas MOG .30 .10
❑ 602 Ryne Sandberg MOG .50 .20
❑ 603 Wade Boggs MOG .20 .07
❑ 604 Cal Ripken MOG .75 .30
❑ 605 Barry Bonds MOG .75 .30
❑ 606 Ken Griffey Jr. MOG .50 .20
❑ 607 Kirby Puckett MOG .30 .10
❑ 608 Darren Daulton MOG .10 .02
❑ 609 Paul Molitor MOG .10 .02
❑ 610 Terry Steinbach .10 .02
❑ 611 Todd Worrell .10 .02
❑ 612 Jim Thome .30 .10
❑ 613 Chuck McElroy .10 .02
❑ 614 John Habyan .10 .02
❑ 615 Sid Fernandez .10 .02
❑ 616 Jermaine Allensworth RC .10 .02
❑ 617 Steve Bedrosian .10 .02
❑ 618 Rob Ducey .10 .02
❑ 619 Tom Browning .10 .02
❑ 620 Tony Gwynn .60 .25
❑ 621 Carl Willis .10 .02
❑ 622 Kevin Young .10 .02
❑ 623 Rafael Novoa .10 .02
❑ 624 Jerry Browne .10 .02
❑ 625 Charlie Hough .20 .07
❑ 626 Chris Gomez .10 .02
❑ 627 Steve Reed .10 .02
❑ 628 Kirk Rueter .10 .02
❑ 629 Matt Whiteside .10 .02
❑ 630 David Justice .20 .07
❑ 631 Brad Holman .10 .02
❑ 632 Brian Jordan .20 .07
❑ 633 Scott Bankhead .10 .02
❑ 634 Torey Lovullo .10 .02
❑ 635 Len Dykstra .20 .07
❑ 636 Ben McDonald .10 .02
❑ 637 Steve Howe .10 .02
❑ 638 Jose Vizcaino .10 .02
❑ 639 Bill Swift .10 .02
❑ 640 Darryl Strawberry .20 .07
❑ 641 Steve Farr .10 .02
❑ 642 Tom Kramer .10 .02
❑ 643 Joe Orsulak .10 .02
❑ 644 Tom Henke .10 .02
❑ 645 Joe Carter .20 .07
❑ 646 Ken Caminiti .20 .07
❑ 647 Reggie Sanders .20 .07
❑ 648 Andy Ashby .10 .02
❑ 649 Derek Parks .10 .02
❑ 650 Andy Van Slyke .30 .10
❑ 651 Juan Bell .10 .02
❑ 652 Roger Smithberg .10 .02
❑ 653 Chuck Carr .10 .02
❑ 654 Bill Gullickson .10 .02
❑ 655 Charlie Hayes .10 .02
❑ 656 Chris Nabholz .10 .02
❑ 657 Karl Rhodes .10 .02
❑ 658 Pete Smith .10 .02
❑ 659 Bret Boone .20 .07
❑ 660 Gregg Jefferies .10 .02
❑ 661 Bob Zupcic .10 .02
❑ 662 Steve Sax .10 .02
❑ 663 Mariano Duncan .10 .02
❑ 664 Jeff Tackett .10 .02
❑ 665 Mark Langston .10 .02
❑ 666 Steve Buechele .10 .02
❑ 667 Candy Maldonado .10 .02
❑ 668 Woody Williams .20 .07
❑ 669 Tim Wakefield .30 .10
❑ 670 Danny Tartabull .10 .02
❑ 671 Charlie O'Brien .10 .02
❑ 672 Felix Jose .10 .02
❑ 673 Bobby Ayala .10 .02
❑ 674 Scott Servais .10 .02
❑ 675 Roberto Alomar .30 .10
❑ 676 Pedro A.Martinez RC .10 .02
❑ 677 Eddie Guardado .20 .07
❑ 678 Mark Lewis .10 .02
❑ 679 Jaime Navarro .10 .02
❑ 680 Ruben Sierra .20 .07
❑ 681 Rick Renteria .10 .02
❑ 682 Storm Davis .10 .02
❑ 683 Cory Snyder .10 .02
❑ 684 Ron Karkovice .10 .02
❑ 685 Juan Gonzalez .20 .07
❑ 686 Carlos Delgado .30 .10
❑ 687 John Smoltz .30 .10
❑ 688 Brian Dorsett .10 .02
❑ 689 Omar Olivares .10 .02
❑ 690 Mo Vaughn .20 .07
❑ 691 Joe Grahe .10 .02
❑ 692 Mickey Morandini .10 .02
❑ 693 Tino Martinez .30 .10
❑ 694 Brian Barnes .10 .02
❑ 695 Mike Stanley .10 .02
❑ 696 Mark Clark .10 .02
❑ 697 Dave Hansen .10 .02
❑ 698 Willie Wilson .10 .02
❑ 699 Pete Schourek .10 .02
❑ 700 Barry Bonds 1.50 .60
❑ 701 Kevin Appier .20 .07
❑ 702 Tony Fernandez .10 .02
❑ 703 Darryl Kile .20 .07
❑ 704 Archi Cianfrocco .10 .02
❑ 705 Jose Rijo .10 .02
❑ 706 Brian Harper .10 .02
❑ 707 Zane Smith .10 .02
❑ 708 Dave Henderson .10 .02
❑ 709 Angel Miranda UER .10 .02
❑ 710 Orestes Destrade .10 .02
❑ 711 Greg Gohr .10 .02
❑ 712 Eric Young .10 .02
❑ 713 Bullinger/Will/Wat/Welch .10 .02
❑ 714 Tim Spehr .10 .02
❑ 715 Hank Aaron 715 HR .50 .20
❑ 716 Nate Minchey .10 .02
❑ 717 Mike Blowers .10 .02
❑ 718 Kent Mercker .10 .02
❑ 719 Tom Pagnozzi .10 .02
❑ 720 Roger Clemens 1.00 .40
❑ 721 Eduardo Perez .10 .02
❑ 722 Milt Thompson .10 .02
❑ 723 Gregg Olson .10 .02
❑ 724 Kirk McCaskill .10 .02
❑ 725 Sammy Sosa .50 .20
❑ 726 Alvaro Espinoza .10 .02
❑ 727 Henry Rodriguez .10 .02
❑ 728 Jim Leyritz .10 .02
❑ 729 Steve Scarsone .10 .02
❑ 730 Bobby Bonilla .20 .07
❑ 731 Chris Gwynn .10 .02
❑ 732 Al Leiter .20 .07
❑ 733 Bip Roberts .10 .02
❑ 734 Mark Portugal .10 .02
❑ 735 Terry Pendleton .20 .07
❑ 736 Dave Valle .10 .02
❑ 737 Paul Kilgus .10 .02
❑ 738 Greg A. Harris .10 .02
❑ 739 Jon Ratliff RC .10 .02
❑ 740 Kirk Presley RC .10 .02
❑ 741 Josue Estrada RC .10 .02
❑ 742 Wayne Gomes RC .10 .02
❑ 743 Pat Watkins RC .10 .02
❑ 744 Jamey Wright RC .25 .08
❑ 745 Jay Powell RC .10 .02
❑ 746 Ryan McGuire RC .10 .02
❑ 747 Marc Barcelo RC .10 .02
❑ 748 Sloan Smith RC .10 .02
❑ 749 John Wasdin RC .10 .02
❑ 750 Marc Valdes .10 .02
❑ 751 Dan Ehler RC .10 .02
❑ 752 Andre King RC .10 .02
❑ 753 Greg Keagle RC .10 .02
❑ 754 Jason Myers RC .10 .02
❑ 755 Dax Winslett RC .10 .02
❑ 756 Casey Whitten RC .10 .02
❑ 757 Tony Fuduric RC .10 .02
❑ 758 Greg Norton RC .25 .08
❑ 759 Jeff D'Amico RC .10 .02
❑ 760 Ryan Hancock RC .10 .02
❑ 761 David Cooper RC .10 .02
❑ 762 Kevin Orie RC .10 .02
❑ 763 J.O'Donoghue/M.Oquist .10 .02
❑ 764 C.Bailey RC/S.Hatteberg .10 .02
❑ 765 M.Holzemer/P.Swingle RC .10 .02
❑ 766 J.Baldwin/R.Bolton .10 .02
❑ 767 J.Tavarez RC/J.DiPoto .25 .08
❑ 768 D.Bautista/S.Bergman .10 .02
❑ 769 B.Hamelin/J.Vitiello .10 .02
❑ 770 M.Kiefer/T.O'Leary .10 .02
❑ 771 D.Hocking/O.Munoz RC .10 .02
❑ 772 Russ Davis/B.Taylor .10 .02
❑ 773 K.Abbott/M.Jimenez .25 .08
❑ 774 K.King RC/Plantenberg RC .10 .02
❑ 775 J.Shave/D.Wilson .10 .02
❑ 776 D.Cedeno/P.Spoljaric .10 .02
❑ 777 C.Jones/R.Klesko .50 .20
❑ 778 S.Trachsel/T.Wendell .10 .02
❑ 779 J.Spradlin RC/J.Ruffin .10 .02
❑ 780 J.Bates/J.Burke .10 .02
❑ 781 C.Everett/D.Weathers .20 .07
❑ 782 J.Mouton/G.Mota .10 .02
❑ 783 R.Mondesi/B.Van Ryn .20 .07
❑ 784 R.White/G.White .20 .07
❑ 785 B.Pulsipher/B.Fordyce .20 .07
❑ 786 K.Foster RC/G.Schall .10 .02
❑ 787 Rich Aude RC/M.Cummings .10 .02
❑ 788 B.Barber/R.Batchelor .10 .02
❑ 789 B.Johnson RC/S.Sanders .10 .02
❑ 790 J.Phillips/R.Faneyte .10 .02
❑ 791 Checklist 3 .10 .02
❑ 792 Checklist 4 .10 .02

1994 Topps Traded

Card		
❑ COMP.FACT.SET (140)	40.00	20.00
❑ 1T Paul Wilson	.10	.02
❑ 2T Bill Taylor RC	1.00	.40
❑ 3T Dan Wilson	.10	.02
❑ 4T Mark Smith	.10	.02
❑ 5T Toby Borland RC	.25	.08
❑ 6T Dave Clark	.10	.02
❑ 7T Dennis Martinez	.20	.07
❑ 8T Dave Gallagher	.10	.02
❑ 9T Josias Manzanillo	.10	.02
❑ 10T Brian Anderson RC	1.00	.40
❑ 11T Damon Berryhill	.10	.02
❑ 12T Alex Cole	.10	.02
❑ 13T Jacob Shumate RC	.25	.08
❑ 14T Oddibe McDowell	.10	.02
❑ 15T Willie Banks	.10	.02
❑ 16T Jerry Browne	.10	.02
❑ 17T Donnie Elliott	.10	.02
❑ 18T Ellis Burks	.20	.07
❑ 19T Chuck McElroy	.10	.02
❑ 20T Luis Polonia	.10	.02
❑ 21T Brian Harper	.10	.02
❑ 22T Mark Portugal	.10	.02
❑ 23T Dave Henderson	.10	.02
❑ 24T Mark Acre RC	.25	.08
❑ 25T Julio Franco	.20	.07
❑ 26T Darren Hall RC	.25	.08
❑ 27T Eric Anthony	.10	.02
❑ 28T Sid Fernandez	.10	.02
❑ 29T Rusty Greer RC	1.50	.60
❑ 30T Riccardo Ingram RC	.25	.08
❑ 31T Gabe White	.10	.02
❑ 32T Tim Belcher	.10	.02
❑ 33T Terrence Long RC	1.00	.40
❑ 34T Mark Dalesandro RC	.25	.08
❑ 35T Mike Kelly	.10	.02
❑ 36T Jack Morris	.20	.07
❑ 37T Jeff Brantley	.10	.02
❑ 38T Larry Barnes RC	.25	.08
❑ 39T Brian R. Hunter	.10	.02
❑ 40T Otis Nixon	.10	.02
❑ 41T Bret Wagner	.10	.02
❑ 42T P.Martinez/D.Deshields TR	.50	.20
❑ 43T Heathcliff Slocumb	.10	.02
❑ 44T Ben Grieve RC	1.00	.40
❑ 45T John Hudek RC	.25	.08
❑ 46T Shawon Dunston	.10	.02
❑ 47T Greg Colbrunn	.10	.02
❑ 48T Joey Hamilton	.10	.02
❑ 49T Marvin Freeman	.10	.02
❑ 50T Terry Mulholland	.10	.02
❑ 51T Keith Mitchell	.10	.02
❑ 52T Dwight Smith	.10	.02
❑ 53T Shawn Boskie	.10	.02
❑ 54T Kevin Witt RC	1.00	.40
❑ 55T Ron Gant	.20	.07
❑ 56T Jason Schmidt RC	10.00	4.00
❑ 57T Jody Reed	.10	.02
❑ 58T Rick Helling	.10	.02
❑ 59T John Powell	.10	.02
❑ 60T Eddie Murray	.50	.20
❑ 61T Joe Hall RC	.25	.08
❑ 62T Jorge Fabregas	.10	.02
❑ 63T Mike Mordecai RC	.25	.08
❑ 64T Ed Vosberg	.10	.02
❑ 65T Rickey Henderson	.50	.20
❑ 66T Tim Grieve RC	.25	.08
❑ 67T Jon Lieber	.20	.07
❑ 68T Chris Howard	.10	.02
❑ 69T Matt Walbeck	.10	.02
❑ 70T Chan Ho Park RC	1.50	.60
❑ 71T Bryan Eversgerd RC	.25	.08
❑ 72T John Dettmer	.10	.02
❑ 73T Erik Hanson	.10	.02
❑ 74T Mike Thurman RC	.25	.08
❑ 75T Bobby Ayala	.10	.02
❑ 76T Rafael Palmeiro	.30	.10
❑ 77T Bret Boone	.20	.07
❑ 78T Paul Shuey	.10	.02
❑ 79T Kevin Foster RC	.25	.08
❑ 80T Dave Magadan	.10	.02
❑ 81T Bip Roberts	.10	.02
❑ 82T Howard Johnson	.10	.02
❑ 83T Xavier Hernandez	.10	.02
❑ 84T Ross Powell RC	.25	.08
❑ 85T Doug Million RC	.25	.08
❑ 86T Geronimo Berroa	.10	.02
❑ 87T Mark Farris RC	.25	.08
❑ 88T Butch Henry	.10	.02
❑ 89T Junior Felix	.10	.02
❑ 90T Bo Jackson	.50	.20
❑ 91T Hector Carrasco	.10	.02
❑ 92T Charlie O'Brien	.10	.02
❑ 93T Omar Vizquel	.30	.10
❑ 94T David Segui	.10	.02
❑ 95T Dustin Hermanson	.10	.02
❑ 96T Gar Finnvold RC	.25	.08
❑ 97T Dave Stevens	.10	.02
❑ 98T Corey Pointer RC	.25	.08
❑ 99T Felix Fermin	.10	.02
❑ 100T Lee Smith	.20	.07
❑ 101T Reid Ryan RC	1.00	.40
❑ 102T Bobby Munoz	.10	.02
❑ 103T D.Sanders/R.Kelly TR	.30	.10
❑ 104T Turner Ward	.10	.02
❑ 105T W.VanLandingham RC	.25	.08
❑ 106T Vince Coleman	.10	.02
❑ 107T Stan Javier	.10	.02
❑ 108T Darrin Jackson	.10	.02
❑ 109T C.J.Nitkowski RC	.25	.08
❑ 110T Anthony Young	.10	.02
❑ 111T Kurt Miller	.10	.02
❑ 112T Paul Konerko RC	15.00	6.00
❑ 113T Walt Weiss	.10	.02
❑ 114T Daryl Boston	.10	.02
❑ 115T Will Clark	.30	.10
❑ 116T Matt Smith RC	.25	.08
❑ 117T Mark Leiter	.10	.02
❑ 118T Gregg Olson	.10	.02
❑ 119T Tony Pena	.10	.02
❑ 120T Jose Vizcaino	.10	.02
❑ 121T Rick White RC	.25	.08
❑ 122T Rich Rowland	.10	.02
❑ 123T Jeff Reboulet	.10	.02
❑ 124T Greg Hibbard	.10	.02
❑ 125T Chris Sabo	.10	.02
❑ 126T Doug Jones	.10	.02
❑ 127T Tony Fernandez	.10	.02
❑ 128T Carlos Reyes RC	.25	.08
❑ 129T Kevin L.Brown RC	1.00	.40
❑ 130T Ryne Sandberg HL	1.25	.50
❑ 131T Ryne Sandberg HL	1.25	.50
❑ 132T Checklist 1-132	.10	.02

1995 Topps

Card		
❑ COMPLETE SET (660)	80.00	50.00
❑ COMP.HOBBY SET (677)	120.00	60.00
❑ COMP.RETAIL SET (677)	120.00	60.00
❑ COMPLETE SERIES 1 (396)	40.00	25.00
❑ COMPLETE SERIES 2 (264)	40.00	25.00
❑ 1 Frank Thomas	.75	.30
❑ 2 Mickey Morandini	.15	.05
❑ 3 Babe Ruth 100th B-Day	2.00	.75
❑ 4 Scott Cooper	.15	.05
❑ 5 David Cone	.30	.10
❑ 6 Jacob Shumate	.15	.05
❑ 7 Trevor Hoffman	.30	.10
❑ 8 Shane Mack	.15	.05
❑ 9 Delino DeShields	.15	.05
❑ 10 Matt Williams	.30	.10
❑ 11 Sammy Sosa	.75	.30
❑ 12 Gary DiSarcina	.15	.05
❑ 13 Kenny Rogers	.30	.10
❑ 14 Jose Vizcaino	.15	.05
❑ 15 Lou Whitaker	.30	.10
❑ 16 Ron Darling	.15	.05
❑ 17 Dave Nilsson	.15	.05
❑ 18 Chris Hammond	.15	.05
❑ 19 Sid Bream	.15	.05
❑ 20 Denny Martinez	.30	.10
❑ 21 Orlando Merced	.15	.05
❑ 22 John Wetteland	.30	.10
❑ 23 Mike Devereaux	.15	.05
❑ 24 Rene Arocha	.15	.05
❑ 25 Jay Buhner	.30	.10
❑ 26 Darren Holmes	.15	.05
❑ 27 Hal Morris	.15	.05
❑ 28 Brian Buchanan RC	.15	.05
❑ 29 Keith Miller	.15	.05
❑ 30 Paul Molitor	.30	.10
❑ 31 Dave West	.15	.05
❑ 32 Tony Tarasco	.15	.05
❑ 33 Scott Sanders	.15	.05
❑ 34 Eddie Zambrano	.15	.05
❑ 35 Ricky Bones	.15	.05
❑ 36 John Valentin	.15	.05
❑ 37 Kevin Tapani	.15	.05
❑ 38 Tim Wallach	.15	.05
❑ 39 Darren Lewis	.15	.05
❑ 40 Travis Fryman	.30	.10
❑ 41 Mark Leiter	.15	.05
❑ 42 Jose Bautista	.15	.05
❑ 43 Pete Smith	.15	.05
❑ 44 Bret Barberie	.15	.05
❑ 45 Dennis Eckersley	.30	.10
❑ 46 Ken Hill	.15	.05
❑ 47 Chad Ogea	.15	.05
❑ 48 Pete Harnisch	.15	.05
❑ 49 James Baldwin	.15	.05
❑ 50 Mike Mussina	.50	.20
❑ 51 Al Martin	.15	.05
❑ 52 Mark Thompson	.15	.05
❑ 53 Matt Smith	.15	.05
❑ 54 Joey Hamilton	.15	.05
❑ 55 Edgar Martinez	.50	.20
❑ 56 John Smiley	.15	.05
❑ 57 Rey Sanchez	.15	.05
❑ 58 Mike Timlin	.15	.05
❑ 59 Ricky Bottalico	.15	.05
❑ 60 Jim Abbott	.50	.20
❑ 61 Mike Kelly	.15	.05
❑ 62 Brian Jordan	.30	.10
❑ 63 Ken Ryan	.15	.05
❑ 64 Matt Mieske	.15	.05
❑ 65 Rick Aguilera	.15	.05
❑ 66 Ismael Valdes	.15	.05
❑ 67 Royce Clayton	.15	.05
❑ 68 Junior Felix	.15	.05
❑ 69 Harold Reynolds	.30	.10
❑ 70 Juan Gonzalez	.30	.10
❑ 71 Kelly Stinnett	.15	.05
❑ 72 Carlos Reyes	.15	.05
❑ 73 Dave Weathers	.15	.05
❑ 74 Mel Rojas	.15	.05
❑ 75 Doug Drabek	.15	.05
❑ 76 Charles Nagy	.15	.05
❑ 77 Tim Raines	.30	.10
❑ 78 Midre Cummings	.15	.05
❑ 79 Ray Brown RC	.15	.05
❑ 80 Rafael Palmeiro	.50	.20
❑ 81 Charlie Hayes	.15	.05

82	Ray Lankford	.30	.10
83	Tim Davis	.15	.05
84	C.J. Nitkowski	.15	.05
85	Andy Ashby	.15	.05
86	Gerald Williams	.15	.05
87	Terry Shumpert	.15	.05
88	Heathcliff Slocumb	.15	.05
89	Domingo Cedeno	.15	.05
90	Mark Grace	.50	.20
91	Brad Woodall RC	.15	.05
92	Gar Finnvold	.15	.05
93	Jaime Navarro	.15	.05
94	Carlos Hernandez	.15	.05
95	Mark Langston	.15	.05
96	Chuck Carr	.15	.05
97	Mike Gardiner	.15	.05
98	Dave McCarty	.15	.05
99	Cris Carpenter	.15	.05
100	Barry Bonds	2.00	.75
101	David Segui	.15	.05
102	Scott Brosius	.30	.10
103	Mariano Duncan	.15	.05
104	Kenny Lofton	.30	.10
105	Ken Caminiti	.30	.10
106	Darrin Jackson	.15	.05
107	Jim Poole	.15	.05
108	Wil Cordero	.15	.05
109	Danny Miceli	.15	.05
110	Walt Weiss	.15	.05
111	Tom Pagnozzi	.15	.05
112	Terrence Long	.15	.05
113	Bret Boone	.30	.10
114	Daryl Boston	.15	.05
115	Wally Joyner	.30	.10
116	Rob Butler	.15	.05
117	Rafael Belliard	.15	.05
118	Luis Lopez	.15	.05
119	Tony Fossas	.15	.05
120	Len Dykstra	.30	.10
121	Mike Morgan	.15	.05
122	Denny Hocking	.15	.05
123	Kevin Gross	.15	.05
124	Todd Benzinger	.15	.05
125	John Doherty	.15	.05
126	Eduardo Perez	.15	.05
127	Dan Smith	.15	.05
128	Joe Orsulak	.15	.05
129	Brent Gates	.15	.05
130	Jeff Conine	.30	.10
131	Doug Henry	.15	.05
132	Paul Sorrento	.15	.05
133	Mike Hampton	.30	.10
134	Tim Spehr	.15	.05
135	Julio Franco	.30	.10
136	Mike Dyer	.15	.05
137	Chris Sabo	.15	.05
138	Rheal Cormier	.15	.05
139	Paul Konerko	1.00	.40
140	Dante Bichette	.30	.10
141	Chuck McElroy	.15	.05
142	Mike Stanley	.15	.05
143	Bob Hamelin	.15	.05
144	Tommy Greene	.15	.05
145	John Smoltz	.50	.20
146	Ed Sprague	.15	.05
147	Ray McDavid	.15	.05
148	Otis Nixon	.15	.05
149	Turk Wendell	.15	.05
150	Chris James	.15	.05
151	Derek Parks	.15	.05
152	Jose Offerman	.15	.05
153	Tony Clark	.15	.05
154	Chad Curtis	.15	.05
155	Mark Portugal	.15	.05
156	Bill Pulsipher	.15	.05
157	Troy Neel	.15	.05
158	Dave Winfield	.30	.10
159	Bill Wegman	.15	.05
160	Benito Santiago	.30	.10
161	Jose Mesa	.15	.05
162	Luis Gonzalez	.30	.10
163	Alex Fernandez	.15	.05
164	Freddie Benavides	.15	.05
165	Ben McDonald	.15	.05
166	Blas Minor	.15	.05
167	Bret Wagner	.15	.05
168	Mac Suzuki	.15	.05
169	Roberto Mejia	.15	.05
170	Wade Boggs	.50	.20
171	Pokey Reese	.15	.05
172	Hipolito Pichardo	.15	.05
173	Kim Batiste	.15	.05
174	Darren Hall	.15	.05
175	Tom Glavine	.50	.20
176	Phil Plantier	.15	.05
177	Chris Howard	.15	.05
178	Karl Rhodes	.15	.05
179	LaTroy Hawkins	.15	.05
180	Raul Mondesi	.30	.10
181	Jeff Reed	.15	.05
182	Milt Cuyler	.15	.05
183	Jim Edmonds	.50	.20
184	Hector Fajardo	.15	.05
185	Jeff Kent	.30	.10
186	Wilson Alvarez	.15	.05
187	Geronimo Berroa	.15	.05
188	Billy Spiers	.15	.05
189	Derek Lilliquist	.15	.05
190	Craig Biggio	.50	.20
191	Roberto Hernandez	.15	.05
192	Bob Natal	.15	.05
193	Bobby Ayala	.15	.05
194	Travis Miller RC	.15	.05
195	Bob Tewksbury	.15	.05
196	Rondell White	.30	.10
197	Steve Cooke	.15	.05
198	Jeff Branson	.15	.05
199	Derek Jeter	2.00	.75
200	Tim Salmon	.50	.20
201	Steve Frey	.15	.05
202	Kent Mercker	.15	.05
203	Randy Johnson	.75	.30
204	Todd Worrell	.15	.05
205	Mo Vaughn	.30	.10
206	Howard Johnson	.15	.05
207	John Wasdin	.15	.05
208	Eddie Williams	.15	.05
209	Tim Belcher	.15	.05
210	Jeff Montgomery	.15	.05
211	Kirt Manwaring	.15	.05
212	Ben Grieve	.15	.05
213	Pat Hentgen	.15	.05
214	Shawon Dunston	.15	.05
215	Mike Greenwell	.15	.05
216	Alex Diaz	.15	.05
217	Pat Mahomes	.15	.05
218	Dave Hansen	.15	.05
219	Kevin Rogers	.15	.05
220	Cecil Fielder	.30	.10
221	Andrew Lorraine	.15	.05
222	Jack Armstrong	.15	.05
223	Todd Hundley	.15	.05
224	Mark Acre	.15	.05
225	Darrell Whitmore	.15	.05
226	Randy Milligan	.15	.05
227	Wayne Kirby	.15	.05
228	Darryl Kile	.30	.10
229	Bob Zupcic	.15	.05
230	Jay Bell	.30	.10
231	Dustin Hermanson	.15	.05
232	Harold Baines	.30	.10
233	Alan Benes	.15	.05
234	Felix Fermin	.15	.05
235	Ellis Burks	.30	.10
236	Jeff Brantley	.15	.05
237	Karim Garcia RC	.15	.05
238	Matt Nokes	.15	.05
239	Ben Rivera	.15	.05
240	Joe Carter	.30	.10
241	Jeff Granger	.15	.05
242	Terry Pendleton	.30	.10
243	Melvin Nieves	.15	.05
244	Frankie Rodriguez	.15	.05
245	Darryl Hamilton	.15	.05
246	Brooks Kieschnick	.15	.05
247	Todd Hollandsworth	.15	.05
248	Joe Rosselli	.15	.05
249	Bill Gullickson	.15	.05
250	Chuck Knoblauch	.30	.10
251	Kurt Miller	.15	.05
252	Bobby Jones	.15	.05
253	Lance Blankenship	.15	.05
254	Matt Whiteside	.15	.05
255	Darrin Fletcher	.15	.05
256	Eric Plunk	.15	.05
257	Shane Reynolds	.15	.05
258	Norberto Martin	.15	.05
259	Mike Thurman	.15	.05
260	Andy Van Slyke	.50	.20
261	Dwight Smith	.15	.05
262	Allen Watson	.15	.05
263	Dan Wilson	.15	.05
264	Brent Mayne	.15	.05
265	Bip Roberts	.15	.05
266	Sterling Hitchcock	.15	.05
267	Alex Gonzalez	.15	.05
268	Greg Harris	.15	.05
269	Ricky Jordan	.15	.05
270	Johnny Ruffin	.15	.05
271	Mike Stanton	.15	.05
272	Rich Rowland	.15	.05
273	Steve Trachsel	.15	.05
274	Pedro Munoz	.15	.05
275	Ramon Martinez	.15	.05
276	Dave Henderson	.15	.05
277	Chris Gomez	.15	.05
278	Joe Grahe	.15	.05
279	Rusty Greer	.30	.10
280	John Franco	.30	.10
281	Mike Bordick	.15	.05
282	Jeff D'Amico	.15	.05
283	Dave Magadan	.15	.05
284	Tony Pena	.15	.05
285	Greg Swindell	.15	.05
286	Doug Million	.15	.05
287	Gabe White	.15	.05
288	Trey Beamon	.15	.05
289	Arthur Rhodes	.15	.05
290	Juan Guzman	.15	.05
291	Jose Oquendo	.15	.05
292	Willie Blair	.15	.05
293	Eddie Taubensee	.15	.05
294	Steve Howe	.15	.05
295	Greg Maddux	1.25	.50
296	Mike Macfarlane	.15	.05
297	Curt Schilling	.30	.10
298	Phil Clark	.15	.05
299	Woody Williams	.15	.05
300	Jose Canseco	.50	.20
301	Aaron Sele	.15	.05
302	Carl Willis	.15	.05
303	Steve Buechele	.15	.05
304	Dave Burba	.15	.05
305	Orel Hershiser	.30	.10
306	Damion Easley	.15	.05
307	Mike Henneman	.15	.05
308	Josias Manzanillo	.15	.05
309	Kevin Seitzer	.15	.05
310	Ruben Sierra	.30	.10
311	Bryan Harvey	.15	.05
312	Jim Thome	.50	.20
313	Ramon Castro RC	.40	.15
314	Lance Johnson	.15	.05
315	Marquis Grissom	.30	.10
316	Eddie Priest RC	.15	.05
317	Paul Wagner	.15	.05
318	Jamie Moyer	.30	.10
319	Todd Zeile	.15	.05
320	Chris Bosio	.15	.05
321	Steve Reed	.15	.05
322	Erik Hanson	.15	.05
323	Luis Polonia	.15	.05
324	Ryan Klesko	.30	.10
325	Kevin Appier	.30	.10
326	Jim Eisenreich	.15	.05
327	Randy Knorr	.15	.05
328	Craig Shipley	.15	.05
329	Tim Naehring	.15	.05
330	Randy Myers	.15	.05
331	Alex Cole	.15	.05
332	Jim Gott	.15	.05
333	Mike Jackson	.15	.05
334	John Flaherty	.15	.05
335	Chili Davis	.30	.10
336	Benji Gil	.15	.05
337	Jason Jacome	.15	.05
338	Stan Javier	.15	.05
339	Mike Fetters	.15	.05

❑ 340 Rich Renteria .15 .05
❑ 341 Kevin Witt .15 .05
❑ 342 Scott Servais .15 .05
❑ 343 Craig Grebeck .15 .05
❑ 344 Kirk Rueter .15 .05
❑ 345 Don Slaught .15 .05
❑ 346 Armando Benitez .15 .05
❑ 347 Ozzie Smith 1.25 .50
❑ 348 Mike Blowers .15 .05
❑ 349 Armando Reynoso .15 .05
❑ 350 Barry Larkin .50 .20
❑ 351 Mike Williams .15 .05
❑ 352 Scott Kamieniecki .15 .05
❑ 353 Gary Gaetti .30 .10
❑ 354 Todd Stottlemyre .15 .05
❑ 355 Fred McGriff .50 .20
❑ 356 Tim Mauser .15 .05
❑ 357 Chris Gwynn .15 .05
❑ 358 Frank Castillo .15 .05
❑ 359 Jeff Reboulet .15 .05
❑ 360 Roger Clemens 1.50 .60
❑ 361 Mark Carreon .15 .05
❑ 362 Chad Kreuter .15 .05
❑ 363 Mark Farris .15 .05
❑ 364 Bob Welch .15 .05
❑ 365 Dean Palmer .30 .10
❑ 366 Jeromy Burnitz .30 .10
❑ 367 B.J. Surhoff .30 .10
❑ 368 Mike Butcher .15 .05
❑ 369 B.Buckles RC/B.Clontz .15 .05
❑ 370 Eddie Murray .75 .30
❑ 371 Orlando Miller .15 .05
❑ 372 Ron Karkovice .15 .05
❑ 373 Richie Lewis .15 .05
❑ 374 Lenny Webster .15 .05
❑ 375 Jeff Tackett .15 .05
❑ 376 Tom Urbani .15 .05
❑ 377 Tino Martinez .50 .20
❑ 378 Mark Dewey .15 .05
❑ 379 Charles O'Brien .15 .05
❑ 380 Terry Mulholland .15 .05
❑ 381 Thomas Howard .15 .05
❑ 382 Chris Haney .15 .05
❑ 383 Billy Hatcher .15 .05
❑ 384 F.Thomas/J.Bagwell AS .50 .20
❑ 385 B.Boone/C.Baerga AS .30 .10
❑ 386 M.Williams/W.Boggs AS .30 .10
❑ 387 C.Ripken/W.Cordero AS .75 .30
❑ 388 K.Griffey Jr./B.Bonds AS 1.00 .40
❑ 389 T.Gwynn/A.Belle AS .30 .10
❑ 390 D.Bichette/K.Puckett AS .50 .20
❑ 391 M.Piazza/M.Stanley AS .75 .30
❑ 392 G.Maddux/D.Cone AS .75 .30
❑ 393 D.Jackson/J.Key AS .15 .05
❑ 394 J.Franco/L.Smith AS .15 .05
❑ 395 Checklist 1-198 .15 .05
❑ 396 Checklist 199-396 .15 .05
❑ 397 Ken Griffey Jr. 1.25 .50
❑ 398 Rick Heiserman RC .15 .05
❑ 399 Don Mattingly 2.00 .75
❑ 400 Henry Rodriguez .15 .05
❑ 401 Lenny Harris .15 .05
❑ 402 Ryan Thompson .15 .05
❑ 403 Darren Oliver .15 .05
❑ 404 Omar Vizquel .50 .20
❑ 405 Jeff Bagwell .50 .20
❑ 406 Doug Webb RC .15 .05
❑ 407 Todd Van Poppel .15 .05
❑ 408 Leo Gomez .15 .05
❑ 409 Mark Whiten .15 .05
❑ 410 Pedro A.Martinez .15 .05
❑ 411 Reggie Sanders .30 .10
❑ 412 Kevin Foster .15 .05
❑ 413 Danny Tartabull .15 .05
❑ 414 Jeff Blauser .15 .05
❑ 415 Mike Magnante .15 .05
❑ 416 Tom Candiotti .15 .05
❑ 417 Rod Beck .15 .05
❑ 418 Jody Reed .15 .05
❑ 419 Vince Coleman .15 .05
❑ 420 Danny Jackson .15 .05
❑ 421 Ryan Nye RC .15 .05
❑ 422 Larry Walker .30 .10
❑ 423 Russ Johnson DP .15 .05
❑ 424 Pat Borders .15 .05
❑ 425 Lee Smith .30 .10
❑ 426 Paul O'Neill .50 .20
❑ 427 Devon White .30 .10
❑ 428 Jim Bullinger .15 .05
❑ 429 Rob Welch RC .15 .05
❑ 430 Steve Avery .15 .05
❑ 431 Tony Gwynn 1.00 .40
❑ 432 Pat Meares .15 .05
❑ 433 Bill Swift .15 .05
❑ 434 David Wells .30 .10
❑ 435 John Briscoe .15 .05
❑ 436 Roger Pavlik .15 .05
❑ 437 Jayson Peterson RC .15 .05
❑ 438 Roberto Alomar .50 .20
❑ 439 Billy Brewer .15 .05
❑ 440 Gary Sheffield .30 .10
❑ 441 Lou Frazier .15 .05
❑ 442 Terry Steinbach .15 .05
❑ 443 Jay Payton RC .75 .30
❑ 444 Jason Bere .15 .05
❑ 445 Denny Neagle .30 .10
❑ 446 Andres Galarraga .30 .10
❑ 447 Hector Carrasco .15 .05
❑ 448 Bill Risley .15 .05
❑ 449 Andy Benes .15 .05
❑ 450 Jim Leyritz .15 .05
❑ 451 Jose Oliva .15 .05
❑ 452 Greg Vaughn .15 .05
❑ 453 Rich Monteleone .15 .05
❑ 454 Tony Eusebio .15 .05
❑ 455 Chuck Finley .30 .10
❑ 456 Kevin Brown .30 .10
❑ 457 Joe Boever .15 .05
❑ 458 Bobby Munoz .15 .05
❑ 459 Bret Saberhagen .30 .10
❑ 460 Kurt Abbott .15 .05
❑ 461 Bobby Witt .15 .05
❑ 462 Cliff Floyd .30 .10
❑ 463 Mark Clark .15 .05
❑ 464 Andujar Cedeno .15 .05
❑ 465 Marvin Freeman .15 .05
❑ 466 Mike Piazza 1.25 .50
❑ 467 Willie Greene .15 .05
❑ 468 Pat Kelly .15 .05
❑ 469 Carlos Delgado .30 .10
❑ 470 Willie Banks .15 .05
❑ 471 Matt Walbeck .15 .05
❑ 472 Mark McGwire 2.00 .75
❑ 473 McKay Christensen RC .15 .05
❑ 474 Alan Trammell .30 .10
❑ 475 Tom Gordon .15 .05
❑ 476 Greg Colbrunn .15 .05
❑ 477 Darren Daulton .30 .10
❑ 478 Albie Lopez .15 .05
❑ 479 Robin Ventura .30 .10
❑ 480 Eddie Perez RC .40 .15
❑ 481 Bryan Eversgerd .15 .05
❑ 482 Dave Fleming .15 .05
❑ 483 Scott Livingstone .15 .05
❑ 484 Pete Schourek .15 .05
❑ 485 Bernie Williams .50 .20
❑ 486 Mark Lemke .15 .05
❑ 487 Eric Karros .30 .10
❑ 488 Scott Ruffcorn .15 .05
❑ 489 Billy Ashley .15 .05
❑ 490 Rico Brogna .15 .05
❑ 491 John Burkett .15 .05
❑ 492 Cade Gaspar RC .15 .05
❑ 493 Jorge Fabregas .15 .05
❑ 494 Greg Gagne .15 .05
❑ 495 Doug Jones .15 .05
❑ 496 Troy O'Leary .15 .05
❑ 497 Pat Rapp .15 .05
❑ 498 Butch Henry .15 .05
❑ 499 John Olerud .30 .10
❑ 500 John Hudek .15 .05
❑ 501 Jeff King .15 .05
❑ 502 Bobby Bonilla .30 .10
❑ 503 Albert Belle .30 .10
❑ 504 Rick Wilkins .15 .05
❑ 505 John Jaha .15 .05
❑ 506 Nigel Wilson .15 .05
❑ 507 Sid Fernandez .15 .05
❑ 508 Deion Sanders .50 .20
❑ 509 Gil Heredia .15 .05
❑ 510 Scott Elarton RC .40 .15
❑ 511 Melido Perez .15 .05
❑ 512 Greg McMichael .15 .05
❑ 513 Rusty Meacham .15 .05
❑ 514 Shawn Green .30 .10
❑ 515 Carlos Garcia .15 .05
❑ 516 Dave Stevens .15 .05
❑ 517 Eric Young .15 .05
❑ 518 Omar Daal .15 .05
❑ 519 Kirk Gibson .30 .10
❑ 520 Spike Owen .15 .05
❑ 521 Jacob Cruz RC .30 .10
❑ 522 Sandy Alomar Jr. .15 .05
❑ 523 Steve Bedrosian .15 .05
❑ 524 Ricky Gutierrez .15 .05
❑ 525 Dave Veres .15 .05
❑ 526 Gregg Jefferies .15 .05
❑ 527 Jose Valentin .15 .05
❑ 528 Robb Nen .30 .10
❑ 529 Jose Rijo .15 .05
❑ 530 Sean Berry .15 .05
❑ 531 Mike Gallego .15 .05
❑ 532 Roberto Kelly .15 .05
❑ 533 Kevin Stocker .15 .05
❑ 534 Kirby Puckett .75 .30
❑ 535 Chipper Jones .75 .30
❑ 536 Russ Davis .15 .05
❑ 537 Jon Lieber .15 .05
❑ 538 Trey Moore RC .15 .05
❑ 539 Joe Girardi .15 .05
❑ 540 Miguel Cairo RC .15 .05
❑ 541 Tony Phillips .15 .05
❑ 542 Brian Anderson .15 .05
❑ 543 Ivan Rodriguez .50 .20
❑ 544 Jeff Cirillo .15 .05
❑ 545 Joey Cora .15 .05
❑ 546 Chris Hoiles .15 .05
❑ 547 Bernard Gilkey .15 .05
❑ 548 Mike Lansing .15 .05
❑ 549 Jimmy Key .30 .10
❑ 550 Mark Wohlers .15 .05
❑ 551 Chris Clemons RC .15 .05
❑ 552 Vinny Castilla .30 .10
❑ 553 Mark Guthrie .15 .05
❑ 554 Mike Lieberthal .30 .10
❑ 555 Tommy Davis RC .15 .05
❑ 556 Robby Thompson .15 .05
❑ 557 Danny Bautista .15 .05
❑ 558 Will Clark .50 .20
❑ 559 Rickey Henderson .75 .30
❑ 560 Todd Jones .15 .05
❑ 561 Jack McDowell .15 .05
❑ 562 Carlos Rodriguez .15 .05
❑ 563 Mark Eichhorn .15 .05
❑ 564 Jeff Nelson .15 .05
❑ 565 Eric Anthony .15 .05
❑ 566 Randy Velarde .15 .05
❑ 567 Javier Lopez .30 .10
❑ 568 Kevin Mitchell .15 .05
❑ 569 Steve Karsay .15 .05
❑ 570 Brian Meadows RC .15 .05
❑ 571 Rey Ordonez RC .75 .30
❑ 572 John Kruk .30 .10
❑ 573 Scott Leius .15 .05
❑ 574 John Patterson .15 .05
❑ 575 Kevin Brown .30 .10
❑ 576 Mike Moore .15 .05
❑ 577 Manny Ramirez .50 .20
❑ 578 Jose Lind .15 .05
❑ 579 Derrick May .15 .05
❑ 580 Cal Eldred .15 .05
❑ 581 A.Boone RC/D.Bell .75 .30
❑ 582 J.T. Snow .30 .10
❑ 583 Luis Sojo .15 .05
❑ 584 Moises Alou .30 .10
❑ 585 Dave Clark .15 .05
❑ 586 Dave Hollins .15 .05
❑ 587 Nomar Garciaparra 2.00 .75
❑ 588 Cal Ripken 2.50 1.00
❑ 589 Pedro Astacio .15 .05
❑ 590 J.R. Phillips .15 .05
❑ 591 Jeff Frye .15 .05
❑ 592 Bo Jackson .75 .30
❑ 593 Steve Ontiveros .15 .05
❑ 594 David Nied .15 .05
❑ 595 Brad Ausmus .30 .10
❑ 596 Carlos Baerga .15 .05
❑ 597 James Mouton .15 .05

Card	Player		
❑ 598	Ozzie Guillen	.30	.10
❑ 599	Johnny Damon	.75	.30
❑ 600	Yorkis Perez	.15	.05
❑ 601	Rich Rodriguez	.15	.05
❑ 602	Mark McLemore	.15	.05
❑ 603	Jeff Fassero	.15	.05
❑ 604	John Roper	.15	.05
❑ 605	Mark Johnson RC	.40	.15
❑ 606	Wes Chamberlain	.15	.05
❑ 607	Felix Jose	.15	.05
❑ 608	Tony Longmire	.15	.05
❑ 609	Duane Ward	.15	.05
❑ 610	Brett Butler	.30	.10
❑ 611	William VanLandingham	.15	.05
❑ 612	Mickey Tettleton	.15	.05
❑ 613	Brady Anderson	.30	.10
❑ 614	Reggie Jefferson	.15	.05
❑ 615	Mike Kingery	.15	.05
❑ 616	Derek Bell	.15	.05
❑ 617	Scott Erickson	.15	.05
❑ 618	Bob Wickman	.15	.05
❑ 619	Phil Leftwich	.15	.05
❑ 620	David Justice	.30	.10
❑ 621	Paul Wilson	.15	.05
❑ 622	Pedro Martinez	.50	.20
❑ 623	Terry Mathews	.15	.05
❑ 624	Brian McRae	.15	.05
❑ 625	Bruce Ruffin	.15	.05
❑ 626	Steve Finley	.30	.10
❑ 627	Ron Gant	.30	.10
❑ 628	Rafael Bournigal	.15	.05
❑ 629	Darryl Strawberry	.30	.10
❑ 630	Luis Alicea	.15	.05
❑ 631	Mark Smith	.15	.05
❑ 632	C.Bailey/S.Hatteberg	.15	.05
❑ 633	Todd Greene	.30	.10
❑ 634	Rod Bolton	.15	.05
❑ 635	Herbert Perry	.15	.05
❑ 636	Sean Bergman	.15	.05
❑ 637	J.Randa/J.Vitiello	.30	.10
❑ 638	Jose Mercedes	.15	.05
❑ 639	Marty Cordova	.15	.05
❑ 640	R.Rivera/A.Pettitte	.30	.10
❑ 641	W.Adams/S.Spiezio	.15	.05
❑ 642	Eddy Diaz RC	.15	.05
❑ 643	Jon Shave	.15	.05
❑ 644	Paul Spoljaric	.15	.05
❑ 645	Damon Hollins	.15	.05
❑ 646	Doug Glanville	.15	.05
❑ 647	Tim Belk	.15	.05
❑ 648	Rod Pedraza	.15	.05
❑ 649	Marc Valdes	.15	.05
❑ 650	Rick Huisman	.15	.05
❑ 651	Ron Coomer RC	.15	.05
❑ 652	Carlos Perez RC	.40	.15
❑ 653	Jason Isringhausen	.30	.10
❑ 654	Kevin Jordan	.15	.05
❑ 655	Esteban Loaiza	.15	.05
❑ 656	John Frascatore	.15	.05
❑ 657	Bryce Florie	.15	.05
❑ 658	Keith Williams	.15	.05
❑ 659	Checklist	.15	.05
❑ 660	Checklist	.15	.05

1995 Topps Traded

Card	Player		
❑	COMPLETE SET (165)	40.00	15.00
❑ 1T	Frank Thomas AB	.60	.25
❑ 2T	Ken Griffey Jr. AB	1.00	.40
❑ 3T	Barry Bonds AB	1.25	.50
❑ 4T	Albert Belle AB	.40	.15
❑ 5T	Cal Ripken AB	1.50	.60
❑ 6T	Mike Piazza AB	1.00	.40
❑ 7T	Tony Gwynn AB	.60	.25
❑ 8T	Jeff Bagwell AB	.40	.15
❑ 9T	Mo Vaughn AB	.20	.07
❑ 10T	Matt Williams AB	.20	.07
❑ 11T	Ray Durham	.40	.15
❑ 12T	J.LeBron RC UER Beltran	6.00	2.50
❑ 13T	Shawn Green	.40	.15
❑ 14T	Kevin Gross	.20	.07
❑ 15T	Jon Nunnally	.20	.07
❑ 16T	Brian Maxcy RC	.25	.08
❑ 17T	Mark Kiefer	.20	.07
❑ 18T	C.Beltran RC UER LeBron	15.00	6.00
❑ 19T	Michael Mimbs RC	.25	.08
❑ 20T	Larry Walker	.40	.15
❑ 21T	Chad Curtis	.20	.07
❑ 22T	Jeff Barry	.20	.07
❑ 23T	Joe Oliver	.20	.07
❑ 24T	Tomas Perez RC	.25	.08
❑ 25T	Michael Barrett RC	1.00	.40
❑ 26T	Brian McRae	.20	.07
❑ 27T	Derek Bell	.20	.07
❑ 28T	Ray Durham	.40	.15
❑ 29T	Todd Williams	.20	.07
❑ 30T	Ryan Jaroncyk RC	.25	.08
❑ 31T	Todd Steverson	.20	.07
❑ 32T	Mike Devereaux	.20	.07
❑ 33T	Rheal Cormier	.20	.07
❑ 34T	Benny Santiago	.40	.15
❑ 35T	Bob Higginson RC	1.00	.40
❑ 36T	Jack McDowell	.20	.07
❑ 37T	Mike MacFarlane	.20	.07
❑ 38T	Tony McKnight RC	.25	.08
❑ 39T	Brian L.Hunter	.20	.07
❑ 40T	Hideo Nomo RC	4.00	1.50
❑ 41T	Brett Butler	.40	.15
❑ 42T	Donovan Osborne	.20	.07
❑ 43T	Scott Karl	.20	.07
❑ 44T	Tony Phillips	.20	.07
❑ 45T	Marty Cordova	.20	.07
❑ 46T	Dave Mlicki	.20	.07
❑ 47T	Bronson Arroyo RC	6.00	2.50
❑ 48T	John Burkett	.20	.07
❑ 49T	J.D.Smart RC	.25	.08
❑ 50T	Mickey Tettleton	.20	.07
❑ 51T	Todd Stottlemyre	.20	.07
❑ 52T	Mike Perez	.20	.07
❑ 53T	Terry Mulholland	.20	.07
❑ 54T	Edgardo Alfonzo	.20	.07
❑ 55T	Zane Smith	.20	.07
❑ 56T	Jacob Brumfield	.20	.07
❑ 57T	Andujar Cedeno	.20	.07
❑ 58T	Jose Parra	.20	.07
❑ 59T	Manny Alexander	.20	.07
❑ 60T	Tony Tarasco	.20	.07
❑ 61T	Orel Hershiser	.40	.15
❑ 62T	Tim Scott	.20	.07
❑ 63T	Felix Rodriguez RC	.25	.08
❑ 64T	Ken Hill	.20	.07
❑ 65T	Marquis Grissom	.40	.15
❑ 66T	Lee Smith	.40	.15
❑ 67T	Jason Bates	.20	.07
❑ 68T	Felipe Lira	.20	.07
❑ 69T	Alex Hernandez RC	.25	.08
❑ 70T	Tony Fernandez	.20	.07
❑ 71T	Scott Radinsky	.20	.07
❑ 72T	Jose Canseco	.60	.25
❑ 73T	Mark Grudzielanek RC	1.00	.40
❑ 74T	Ben Davis RC	.25	.08
❑ 75T	Jim Abbott	.60	.25
❑ 76T	Roger Bailey	.20	.07
❑ 77T	Gregg Jefferies	.20	.07
❑ 78T	Erik Hanson	.20	.07
❑ 79T	Brad Radke RC	1.00	.40
❑ 80T	Jaime Navarro	.20	.07
❑ 81T	John Wetteland	.40	.15
❑ 82T	Chad Fonville RC	.25	.08
❑ 83T	John Mabry	.20	.07
❑ 84T	Glenallen Hill	.20	.07
❑ 85T	Ken Caminiti	.40	.15
❑ 86T	Tom Goodwin	.20	.07
❑ 87T	Darren Bragg	.20	.07
❑ 88T	Robbie Bell RC	.25	.08
❑ 89T	Jeff Russell	.20	.07
❑ 90T	Dave Gallagher	.20	.07
❑ 91T	Steve Finley	.40	.15
❑ 92T	Vaughn Eshelman	.20	.07
❑ 93T	Kevin Jarvis	.20	.07
❑ 94T	Mark Gubicza	.20	.07
❑ 95T	Tim Wakefield	.40	.15
❑ 96T	Bob Tewksbury	.20	.07
❑ 97T	Sid Roberson RC	.25	.08
❑ 98T	Tom Henke	.20	.07
❑ 99T	Michael Tucker	.20	.07
❑ 100T	Jason Bates	.20	.07
❑ 101T	Otis Nixon	.20	.07
❑ 102T	Mark Whiten	.20	.07
❑ 103T	Dilson Torres RC	.25	.08
❑ 104T	Melvin Bunch RC	.25	.08
❑ 105T	Terry Pendleton	.40	.15
❑ 106T	Corey Jenkins RC	.25	.08
❑ 107T	Glenn Dishman RC	.25	.08
❑ 108T	Reggie Taylor RC	.25	.08
❑ 109T	Curtis Goodwin	.20	.07
❑ 110T	David Cone	.40	.15
❑ 111T	Antonio Osuna	.20	.07
❑ 112T	Paul Shuey	.20	.07
❑ 113T	Doug Jones	.20	.07
❑ 114T	Mark McLemore	.20	.07
❑ 115T	Kevin Ritz	.20	.07
❑ 116T	John Kruk	.40	.15
❑ 117T	Trevor Wilson	.20	.07
❑ 118T	Jerald Clark	.20	.07
❑ 119T	Julian Tavarez	.20	.07
❑ 120T	Tim Pugh	.20	.07
❑ 121T	Todd Zeile	.20	.07
❑ 122T	R.Sexson/B.Schneider RC	4.00	1.50
❑ 123T	Bobby Witt	.20	.07
❑ 124T	Hideo Nomo ROY	1.50	.60
❑ 125T	Joey Cora	.20	.07
❑ 126T	Jim Scharrer RC	.25	.08
❑ 127T	Paul Quantrill	.20	.07
❑ 128T	Chipper Jones ROY	.60	.25
❑ 129T	Kenny James RC	.25	.08
❑ 130T	Mariano Rivera	1.25	.50
❑ 131T	Tyler Green	.20	.07
❑ 132T	Brad Clontz	.20	.07
❑ 133T	Jon Nunnally	.20	.07
❑ 134T	Dave Magadan	.20	.07
❑ 135T	Al Leiter	.40	.15
❑ 136T	Bret Barberie	.20	.07
❑ 137T	Bill Swift	.20	.07
❑ 138T	Scott Cooper	.20	.07
❑ 139T	Roberto Kelly	.20	.07
❑ 140T	Charlie Hayes	.20	.07
❑ 141T	Pete Harnisch	.20	.07
❑ 142T	Rich Amaral	.20	.07
❑ 143T	Rudy Seanez	.20	.07
❑ 144T	Pat Listach	.20	.07
❑ 145T	Quilvio Veras	.20	.07
❑ 146T	Jose Olmeda RC	.25	.08
❑ 147T	Roberto Petagine	.20	.07
❑ 148T	Kevin Brown	.40	.15
❑ 149T	Phil Plantier	.20	.07
❑ 150T	Carlos Perez	.40	.15
❑ 151T	Pat Borders	.20	.07
❑ 152T	Tyler Green	.20	.07
❑ 153T	Stan Belinda	.20	.07
❑ 154T	Dave Stewart	.40	.15
❑ 155T	Andre Dawson	.40	.15
❑ 156T	F.Thomas/F.McGriff AS	.60	.25
❑ 157T	C.Baerga/C.Biggio AS	.40	.15
❑ 158T	W.Boggs/M.Williams AS	.40	.15
❑ 159T	C.Ripken/O.Smith AS	1.00	.40
❑ 160T	K.Griffey/T.Gwynn AS	1.00	.40
❑ 161T	A.Belle/B.Bonds AS	1.25	.50
❑ 162T	K.Puckett/L.Dykstra AS	.60	.25
❑ 163T	I.Rodriguez/M.Piazza AS	1.00	.40
❑ 164T	H.Nomo/R.Johnson AS	1.50	.60
❑ 165T	Checklist	.20	.07

1996 Topps

Card	Player		
❑	COMPLETE SET (440)	40.00	15.00
❑	COMP.HOBBY SET (449)	40.00	15.00
❑	COMP.CEREAL SET (444)	50.00	25.00
❑	COMPLETE SERIES 1 (220)	20.00	8.00
❑	COMPLETE SERIES 2 (220)	20.00	8.00
❑	COMMON CARD (1-440)	.20	.07
❑	COMMON RC	.25	.08
❑ 1	Tony Gwynn STP	.30	.10

- ❑ 2 Mike Piazza STP .50 .20
- ❑ 3 Greg Maddux STP .50 .20
- ❑ 4 Jeff Bagwell STP .20 .07
- ❑ 5 Larry Walker STP .20 .07
- ❑ 6 Barry Larkin STP .20 .07
- ❑ 7 Mickey Mantle 4.00 1.50
- ❑ 8 Tom Glavine STP .20 .07
- ❑ 9 Craig Biggio STP .20 .07
- ❑ 10 Barry Bonds STP .75 .30
- ❑ 11 Heathcliff Slocumb STP .20 .07
- ❑ 12 Matt Williams STP .20 .07
- ❑ 13 Todd Helton 1.00 .40
- ❑ 14 Mark Redman .25 .08
- ❑ 15 Michael Barrett .25 .08
- ❑ 16 Ben Davis .25 .08
- ❑ 17 Juan LeBron .25 .08
- ❑ 18 Tony McKnight .25 .08
- ❑ 19 Ryan Jaroncyk .25 .08
- ❑ 20 Corey Jenkins .25 .08
- ❑ 21 Jim Scharrer .25 .08
- ❑ 22 Mark Bellhorn RC 1.00 .40
- ❑ 23 Jarrod Washburn RC .75 .30
- ❑ 24 Geoff Jenkins RC .75 .30
- ❑ 25 Sean Casey RC 4.00 1.50
- ❑ 26 Brett Tomko RC .40 .15
- ❑ 27 Tony Fernandez .20 .07
- ❑ 28 Rich Becker .20 .07
- ❑ 29 Andujar Cedeno .20 .07
- ❑ 30 Paul Molitor .20 .07
- ❑ 31 Brent Gates .20 .07
- ❑ 32 Glenallen Hill .20 .07
- ❑ 33 Mike Macfarlane .20 .07
- ❑ 34 Manny Alexander .20 .07
- ❑ 35 Todd Zeile .20 .07
- ❑ 36 Joe Girardi .20 .07
- ❑ 37 Tony Tarasco .20 .07
- ❑ 38 Tim Belcher .20 .07
- ❑ 39 Tom Goodwin .20 .07
- ❑ 40 Orel Hershiser .20 .07
- ❑ 41 Tripp Cromer .20 .07
- ❑ 42 Sean Bergman .20 .07
- ❑ 43 Troy Percival .20 .07
- ❑ 44 Kevin Stocker .20 .07
- ❑ 45 Albert Belle .20 .07
- ❑ 46 Tony Eusebio .20 .07
- ❑ 47 Sid Roberson .20 .07
- ❑ 48 Todd Hollandsworth .20 .07
- ❑ 49 Mark Wohlers .20 .07
- ❑ 50 Kirby Puckett .50 .20
- ❑ 51 Darren Holmes .20 .07
- ❑ 52 Ron Karkovice .20 .07
- ❑ 53 Al Martin .20 .07
- ❑ 54 Pat Rapp .20 .07
- ❑ 55 Mark Grace .30 .10
- ❑ 56 Greg Gagne .20 .07
- ❑ 57 Stan Javier .20 .07
- ❑ 58 Scott Sanders .20 .07
- ❑ 59 J.T. Snow .20 .07
- ❑ 60 David Justice .20 .07
- ❑ 61 Royce Clayton .20 .07
- ❑ 62 Kevin Foster .20 .07
- ❑ 63 Tim Naehring .20 .07
- ❑ 64 Orlando Miller .20 .07
- ❑ 65 Mike Mussina .30 .10
- ❑ 66 Jim Eisenreich .20 .07
- ❑ 67 Felix Fermin .20 .07
- ❑ 68 Bernie Williams .30 .10
- ❑ 69 Robb Nen .20 .07
- ❑ 70 Ron Gant .20 .07
- ❑ 71 Felipe Lira .20 .07
- ❑ 72 Jacob Brumfield .20 .07
- ❑ 73 John Mabry .20 .07
- ❑ 74 Mark Carreon .20 .07
- ❑ 75 Carlos Baerga .20 .07
- ❑ 76 Jim Dougherty .20 .07
- ❑ 77 Ryan Thompson .20 .07
- ❑ 78 Scott Leius .20 .07
- ❑ 79 Roger Pavlik .20 .07
- ❑ 80 Gary Sheffield .20 .07
- ❑ 81 Julian Tavarez .20 .07
- ❑ 82 Andy Ashby .20 .07
- ❑ 83 Mark Lemke .20 .07
- ❑ 84 Omar Vizquel .30 .10
- ❑ 85 Darren Daulton .20 .07
- ❑ 86 Mike Lansing .20 .07
- ❑ 87 Rusty Greer .20 .07
- ❑ 88 Dave Stevens .20 .07
- ❑ 89 Jose Offerman .20 .07
- ❑ 90 Tom Henke .20 .07
- ❑ 91 Troy O'Leary .20 .07
- ❑ 92 Michael Tucker .20 .07
- ❑ 93 Marvin Freeman .20 .07
- ❑ 94 Alex Diaz .20 .07
- ❑ 95 John Wetteland .20 .07
- ❑ 96 Cal Ripken 2131 2.00 .75
- ❑ 97 Mike Mimbs .20 .07
- ❑ 98 Bobby Higginson .20 .07
- ❑ 99 Edgardo Alfonzo .20 .07
- ❑ 100 Frank Thomas .50 .20
- ❑ 101 Bob Abreu .50 .20
- ❑ 102 B.Givens/T.J.Mathews .25 .08
- ❑ 103 C.Pritchett/T.Hubbard .25 .08
- ❑ 104 E.Owens/B.Huskey .25 .08
- ❑ 105 Doug Drabek .20 .07
- ❑ 106 Tomas Perez .20 .07
- ❑ 107 Mark Leiter .20 .07
- ❑ 108 Joe Oliver .20 .07
- ❑ 109 Tony Castillo .20 .07
- ❑ 110 Checklist (1-110) .20 .07
- ❑ 111 Kevin Seitzer .20 .07
- ❑ 112 Pete Schourek .20 .07
- ❑ 113 Sean Berry .20 .07
- ❑ 114 Todd Stottlemyre .20 .07
- ❑ 115 Joe Carter .20 .07
- ❑ 116 Jeff King .20 .07
- ❑ 117 Dan Wilson .20 .07
- ❑ 118 Kurt Abbott .20 .07
- ❑ 119 Lyle Mouton .20 .07
- ❑ 120 Jose Rijo .20 .07
- ❑ 121 Curtis Goodwin .20 .07
- ❑ 122 Jose Valentin .20 .07
- ❑ 123 Ellis Burks .20 .07
- ❑ 124 David Cone .20 .07
- ❑ 125 Eddie Murray .50 .20
- ❑ 126 Brian Jordan .20 .07
- ❑ 127 Darrin Fletcher .20 .07
- ❑ 128 Curt Schilling .20 .07
- ❑ 129 Ozzie Guillen .20 .07
- ❑ 130 Kenny Rogers .20 .07
- ❑ 131 Tom Pagnozzi .20 .07
- ❑ 132 Garret Anderson .20 .07
- ❑ 133 Bobby Jones .20 .07
- ❑ 134 Chris Gomez .20 .07
- ❑ 135 Mike Stanley .20 .07
- ❑ 136 Hideo Nomo .50 .20
- ❑ 137 Jon Nunnally .20 .07
- ❑ 138 Tim Wakefield .20 .07
- ❑ 139 Steve Finley .20 .07
- ❑ 140 Ivan Rodriguez .30 .10
- ❑ 141 Quilvio Veras .20 .07
- ❑ 142 Mike Fetters .20 .07
- ❑ 143 Mike Greenwell .20 .07
- ❑ 144 Bill Pulsipher .20 .07
- ❑ 145 Mark McGwire 1.25 .50
- ❑ 146 Frank Castillo .20 .07
- ❑ 147 Greg Vaughn .20 .07
- ❑ 148 Pat Hentgen .20 .07
- ❑ 149 Walt Weiss .20 .07
- ❑ 150 Randy Johnson .50 .20
- ❑ 151 David Segui .20 .07
- ❑ 152 Benji Gil .20 .07
- ❑ 153 Tom Candiotti .20 .07
- ❑ 154 Geronimo Berroa .20 .07
- ❑ 155 John Franco .20 .07
- ❑ 156 Jay Bell .20 .07
- ❑ 157 Mark Gubicza .20 .07
- ❑ 158 Hal Morris .20 .07
- ❑ 159 Wilson Alvarez .20 .07
- ❑ 160 Derek Bell .20 .07
- ❑ 161 Ricky Bottalico .20 .07
- ❑ 162 Bret Boone .20 .07
- ❑ 163 Brad Radke .20 .07
- ❑ 164 John Valentin .20 .07
- ❑ 165 Steve Avery .20 .07
- ❑ 166 Mark McLemore .20 .07
- ❑ 167 Danny Jackson .20 .07
- ❑ 168 Tino Martinez .30 .10
- ❑ 169 Shane Reynolds .20 .07
- ❑ 170 Terry Pendleton .20 .07
- ❑ 171 Jim Edmonds .20 .07
- ❑ 172 Esteban Loaiza .20 .07
- ❑ 173 Ray Durham .20 .07
- ❑ 174 Carlos Perez .20 .07
- ❑ 175 Raul Mondesi .20 .07
- ❑ 176 Steve Ontiveros .20 .07
- ❑ 177 Chipper Jones .50 .20
- ❑ 178 Otis Nixon .20 .07
- ❑ 179 John Burkett .20 .07
- ❑ 180 Gregg Jefferies .20 .07
- ❑ 181 Denny Martinez .20 .07
- ❑ 182 Ken Caminiti .20 .07
- ❑ 183 Doug Jones .20 .07
- ❑ 184 Brian McRae .20 .07
- ❑ 185 Don Mattingly 1.25 .50
- ❑ 186 Mel Rojas .20 .07
- ❑ 187 Marty Cordova .20 .07
- ❑ 188 Vinny Castilla .20 .07
- ❑ 189 John Smoltz .30 .10
- ❑ 190 Travis Fryman .20 .07
- ❑ 191 Chris Hoiles .20 .07
- ❑ 192 Chuck Finley .20 .07
- ❑ 193 Ryan Klesko .20 .07
- ❑ 194 Alex Fernandez .20 .07
- ❑ 195 Dante Bichette .20 .07
- ❑ 196 Eric Karros .20 .07
- ❑ 197 Roger Clemens 1.00 .40
- ❑ 198 Randy Myers .20 .07
- ❑ 199 Tony Phillips .20 .07
- ❑ 200 Cal Ripken 1.50 .60
- ❑ 201 Rod Beck .20 .07
- ❑ 202 Chad Curtis .20 .07
- ❑ 203 Jack McDowell .20 .07
- ❑ 204 Gary Gaetti .20 .07
- ❑ 205 Ken Griffey Jr. .75 .30
- ❑ 206 Ramon Martinez .20 .07
- ❑ 207 Jeff Kent .20 .07
- ❑ 208 Brad Ausmus .20 .07
- ❑ 209 Devon White .20 .07
- ❑ 210 Jason Giambi .20 .07
- ❑ 211 Nomar Garciaparra .75 .30
- ❑ 212 Billy Wagner .20 .07
- ❑ 213 Todd Greene .20 .07
- ❑ 214 Paul Wilson .20 .07
- ❑ 215 Johnny Damon .30 .10
- ❑ 216 Alan Benes .20 .07
- ❑ 217 Karim Garcia .20 .07
- ❑ 218 Dustin Hermanson .20 .07
- ❑ 219 Derek Jeter 1.25 .50
- ❑ 220 Checklist (111-220) .20 .07
- ❑ 221 Kirby Puckett STP .30 .10
- ❑ 222 Cal Ripken STP .75 .30
- ❑ 223 Albert Belle STP .20 .07
- ❑ 224 Randy Johnson STP .30 .10
- ❑ 225 Wade Boggs STP .20 .07
- ❑ 226 Carlos Baerga STP .20 .07
- ❑ 227 Ivan Rodriguez STP .20 .07
- ❑ 228 Mike Mussina STP .20 .07
- ❑ 229 Frank Thomas STP .30 .10
- ❑ 230 Ken Griffey Jr. STP .50 .20
- ❑ 231 Jose Mesa STP .20 .07
- ❑ 232 Matt Morris RC 1.50 .60
- ❑ 233 Craig Wilson RC .75 .30
- ❑ 234 Alvie Shepherd .25 .08
- ❑ 235 Randy Winn RC .75 .30
- ❑ 236 David Yocum RC .25 .08
- ❑ 237 Jason Brester RC .25 .08
- ❑ 238 Shane Monahan RC .25 .08
- ❑ 239 Brian McNichol RC .25 .08
- ❑ 240 Reggie Taylor .25 .08
- ❑ 241 Garrett Long .25 .08

❑	242	Jonathan Johnson	.25	.08
❑	243	Jeff Liefer RC	.25	.08
❑	244	Brian Powell	.25	.08
❑	245	Brian Buchanan RC	.25	.08
❑	246	Mike Piazza	.75	.30
❑	247	Edgar Martinez	.30	.10
❑	248	Chuck Knoblauch	.20	.07
❑	249	Andres Galarraga	.20	.07
❑	250	Tony Gwynn	.60	.25
❑	251	Lee Smith	.20	.07
❑	252	Sammy Sosa	.50	.20
❑	253	Jim Thome	.30	.10
❑	254	Frank Rodriguez	.20	.07
❑	255	Charlie Hayes	.20	.07
❑	256	Bernard Gilkey	.20	.07
❑	257	John Smiley	.20	.07
❑	258	Brady Anderson	.20	.07
❑	259	Rico Brogna	.20	.07
❑	260	Kirt Manwaring	.20	.07
❑	261	Len Dykstra	.20	.07
❑	262	Tom Glavine	.30	.10
❑	263	Vince Coleman	.20	.07
❑	264	John Olerud	.20	.07
❑	265	Orlando Merced	.20	.07
❑	266	Kent Mercker	.20	.07
❑	267	Terry Steinbach	.20	.07
❑	268	Brian L. Hunter	.20	.07
❑	269	Jeff Fassero	.20	.07
❑	270	Jay Buhner	.20	.07
❑	271	Jeff Brantley	.20	.07
❑	272	Tim Raines	.20	.07
❑	273	Jimmy Key	.20	.07
❑	274	Mo Vaughn	.20	.07
❑	275	Andre Dawson	.20	.07
❑	276	Jose Mesa	.20	.07
❑	277	Brett Butler	.20	.07
❑	278	Luis Gonzalez	.20	.07
❑	279	Steve Sparks	.20	.07
❑	280	Chili Davis	.20	.07
❑	281	Carl Everett	.20	.07
❑	282	Jeff Cirillo	.20	.07
❑	283	Thomas Howard	.20	.07
❑	284	Paul O'Neill	.30	.10
❑	285	Pat Meares	.20	.07
❑	286	Mickey Tettleton	.20	.07
❑	287	Rey Sanchez	.20	.07
❑	288	Bip Roberts	.20	.07
❑	289	Roberto Alomar	.30	.10
❑	290	Ruben Sierra	.20	.07
❑	291	John Flaherty	.20	.07
❑	292	Bret Saberhagen	.20	.07
❑	293	Barry Larkin	.30	.10
❑	294	Sandy Alomar Jr.	.20	.07
❑	295	Ed Sprague	.20	.07
❑	296	Gary DiSarcina	.20	.07
❑	297	Marquis Grissom	.20	.07
❑	298	John Frascatore	.20	.07
❑	299	Will Clark	.30	.10
❑	300	Barry Bonds	1.50	.60
❑	301	Ozzie Smith	.75	.30
❑	302	Dave Nilsson	.20	.07
❑	303	Pedro Martinez	.30	.10
❑	304	Joey Cora	.20	.07
❑	305	Rick Aguilera	.20	.07
❑	306	Craig Biggio	.30	.10
❑	307	Jose Vizcaino	.20	.07
❑	308	Jeff Montgomery	.20	.07
❑	309	Moises Alou	.20	.07
❑	310	Robin Ventura	.20	.07
❑	311	David Wells	.20	.07
❑	312	Delino DeShields	.20	.07
❑	313	Trevor Hoffman	.20	.07
❑	314	Andy Benes	.20	.07
❑	315	Deion Sanders	.30	.10
❑	316	Jim Bullinger	.20	.07
❑	317	John Jaha	.20	.07
❑	318	Greg Maddux	.75	.30
❑	319	Tim Salmon	.30	.10
❑	320	Ben McDonald	.20	.07
❑	321	Sandy Martinez	.20	.07
❑	322	Dan Miceli	.20	.07
❑	323	Wade Boggs	.30	.10
❑	324	Ismael Valdes	.20	.07
❑	325	Juan Gonzalez	.20	.07
❑	326	Charles Nagy	.20	.07
❑	327	Ray Lankford	.20	.07
❑	328	Mark Portugal	.20	.07
❑	329	Bobby Bonilla	.20	.07
❑	330	Reggie Sanders	.20	.07
❑	331	Jamie Brewington RC	.25	.08
❑	332	Aaron Sele	.20	.07
❑	333	Pete Harnisch	.20	.07
❑	334	Cliff Floyd	.20	.07
❑	335	Cal Eldred	.20	.07
❑	336	Jason Bates	.20	.07
❑	337	Tony Clark	.20	.07
❑	338	Jose Herrera	.20	.07
❑	339	Alex Ochoa	.20	.07
❑	340	Mark Loretta	.20	.07
❑	341	Donne Wall	.20	.07
❑	342	Jason Kendall	.20	.07
❑	343	Shannon Stewart	.20	.07
❑	344	Brooks Kieschnick	.20	.07
❑	345	Chris Snopek	.20	.07
❑	346	Ruben Rivera	.20	.07
❑	347	Jeff Suppan	.20	.07
❑	348	Phil Nevin	.20	.07
❑	349	John Wasdin	.20	.07
❑	350	Jay Payton	.20	.07
❑	351	Tim Crabtree	.20	.07
❑	352	Rick Krivda	.20	.07
❑	353	Bob Wolcott	.20	.07
❑	354	Jimmy Haynes	.20	.07
❑	355	Herb Perry	.20	.07
❑	356	Ryne Sandberg	.75	.30
❑	357	Harold Baines	.20	.07
❑	358	Chad Ogea	.20	.07
❑	359	Lee Tinsley	.20	.07
❑	360	Matt Williams	.20	.07
❑	361	Randy Velarde	.20	.07
❑	362	Jose Canseco	.30	.10
❑	363	Larry Walker	.20	.07
❑	364	Kevin Appier	.20	.07
❑	365	Darryl Hamilton	.20	.07
❑	366	Jose Lima	.20	.07
❑	367	Javy Lopez	.20	.07
❑	368	Dennis Eckersley	.20	.07
❑	369	Jason Isringhausen	.20	.07
❑	370	Mickey Morandini	.20	.07
❑	371	Scott Cooper	.20	.07
❑	372	Jim Abbott	.30	.10
❑	373	Paul Sorrento	.20	.07
❑	374	Chris Hammond	.20	.07
❑	375	Lance Johnson	.20	.07
❑	376	Kevin Brown	.20	.07
❑	377	Luis Alicea	.20	.07
❑	378	Andy Pettitte	.30	.10
❑	379	Dean Palmer	.20	.07
❑	380	Jeff Bagwell	.30	.10
❑	381	Jaime Navarro	.20	.07
❑	382	Rondell White	.20	.07
❑	383	Erik Hanson	.20	.07
❑	384	Pedro Munoz	.20	.07
❑	385	Heathcliff Slocumb	.20	.07
❑	386	Wally Joyner	.20	.07
❑	387	Bob Tewksbury	.20	.07
❑	388	David Bell	.20	.07
❑	389	Fred McGriff	.30	.10
❑	390	Mike Henneman	.20	.07
❑	391	Robby Thompson	.20	.07
❑	392	Norm Charlton	.20	.07
❑	393	Cecil Fielder	.20	.07
❑	394	Benito Santiago	.20	.07
❑	395	Rafael Palmeiro	.30	.10
❑	396	Ricky Bones	.20	.07
❑	397	Rickey Henderson	.50	.20
❑	398	C.J. Nitkowski	.20	.07
❑	399	Shawon Dunston	.20	.07
❑	400	Manny Ramirez	.30	.10
❑	401	Bill Swift	.20	.07
❑	402	Chad Fonville	.20	.07
❑	403	Joey Hamilton	.20	.07
❑	404	Alex Gonzalez	.20	.07
❑	405	Roberto Hernandez	.20	.07
❑	406	Jeff Blauser	.20	.07
❑	407	LaTroy Hawkins	.20	.07
❑	408	Greg Colbrunn	.20	.07
❑	409	Todd Hundley	.20	.07
❑	410	Glenn Dishman	.20	.07
❑	411	Joe Vitiello	.20	.07
❑	412	Todd Worrell	.20	.07
❑	413	Wil Cordero	.20	.07
❑	414	Ken Hill	.20	.07
❑	415	Carlos Garcia	.20	.07
❑	416	Bryan Rekar	.20	.07
❑	417	Shawn Green	.20	.07
❑	418	Tyler Green	.20	.07
❑	419	Mike Blowers	.20	.07
❑	420	Kenny Lofton	.20	.07
❑	421	Denny Neagle	.20	.07
❑	422	Jeff Conine	.20	.07
❑	423	Mark Langston	.20	.07
❑	424	Ron Wright RC/D.Lee	.75	.30
❑	425	D.Ward RC/R.Sexson	1.00	.40
❑	426	Adam Riggs RC	.25	.08
❑	427	N.Perez/E.Wilson	.25	.08
❑	428	Bartolo Colon	.50	.20
❑	429	Marty Janzen RC	.25	.08
❑	430	Rich Hunter RC	.25	.08
❑	431	Dave Coggin RC	.25	.08
❑	432	R.Ibanez RC/P.Konerko	1.50	.60
❑	433	Marc Kroon	.20	.07
❑	434	S.Rolen/S.Spiezio	.50	.20
❑	435	V.Guerrero/A.Jones	2.50	1.00
❑	436	Shane Spencer RC	.40	.15
❑	437	A.French/D.Stovall RC	.25	.08
❑	438	M.Coleman RC/R.Hidalgo	.25	.08
❑	439	Jermaine Dye	.20	.07
❑	440	Checklist	.20	.07
❑	F7	Mickey Mantle Last Day	5.00	2.00
❑	NNO	Mickey Mantle Tribute Card, promotes the Mantle F	3.00	1.25

1997 Topps

❑		COMPLETE SET (495)	80.00	40.00
❑		COMPLETE SERIES 1 (276)	40.00	20.00
❑		COMPLETE SERIES 2 (220)	40.00	20.00
❑	1	Barry Bonds	1.50	.60
❑	2	Tom Pagnozzi	.20	.07
❑	3	Terrell Wade	.20	.07
❑	4	Jose Valentin	.20	.07
❑	5	Mark Clark	.20	.07
❑	6	Brady Anderson	.20	.07
❑	8	Wade Boggs	.30	.10
❑	9	Scott Stahoviak	.20	.07
❑	10	Andres Galarraga	.20	.07
❑	11	Steve Avery	.20	.07
❑	12	Rusty Greer	.20	.07
❑	13	Derek Jeter	1.25	.50
❑	14	Ricky Bottalico	.20	.07
❑	15	Andy Ashby	.20	.07
❑	16	Paul Shuey	.20	.07
❑	17	F.P. Santangelo	.20	.07
❑	18	Royce Clayton	.20	.07
❑	19	Mike Mohler	.20	.07
❑	20	Mike Piazza	.75	.30
❑	21	Jaime Navarro	.20	.07
❑	22	Billy Wagner	.20	.07
❑	23	Mike Timlin	.20	.07
❑	24	Garret Anderson	.20	.07
❑	25	Ben McDonald	.20	.07
❑	26	Mel Rojas	.20	.07
❑	27	John Burkett	.20	.07
❑	28	Jeff King	.20	.07
❑	29	Reggie Jefferson	.20	.07
❑	30	Kevin Appier	.20	.07
❑	31	Felipe Lira	.20	.07
❑	32	Kevin Tapani	.20	.07
❑	33	Mark Portugal	.20	.07

❑ 34 Carlos Garcia	.20	.07
❑ 35 Joey Cora	.20	.07
❑ 36 David Segui	.20	.07
❑ 37 Mark Grace	.30	.10
❑ 38 Erik Hanson	.20	.07
❑ 39 Jeff D'Amico	.20	.07
❑ 40 Jay Buhner	.20	.07
❑ 41 B.J. Surhoff	.20	.07
❑ 42 Jackie Robinson TRIB	.50	.20
❑ 43 Roger Pavlik	.20	.07
❑ 44 Hal Morris	.20	.07
❑ 45 Mariano Duncan	.20	.07
❑ 46 Harold Baines	.20	.07
❑ 47 Jorge Fabregas	.20	.07
❑ 48 Jose Herrera	.20	.07
❑ 49 Jeff Cirillo	.20	.07
❑ 50 Tom Glavine	.30	.10
❑ 51 Pedro Astacio	.20	.07
❑ 52 Mark Gardner	.20	.07
❑ 53 Arthur Rhodes	.20	.07
❑ 54 Troy O'Leary	.20	.07
❑ 55 Bip Roberts	.20	.07
❑ 56 Mike Lieberthal	.20	.07
❑ 57 Shane Andrews	.20	.07
❑ 58 Scott Karl	.20	.07
❑ 59 Gary DiSarcina	.20	.07
❑ 60 Andy Pettitte	.30	.10
❑ 61 Kevin Elster	.20	.07
❑ 61B Mike Fetters UER	.20	.07
❑ 62 Mark McGwire	1.25	.50
❑ 63 Dan Wilson	.20	.07
❑ 64 Mickey Morandini	.20	.07
❑ 65 Chuck Knoblauch	.20	.07
❑ 66 Tim Wakefield	.20	.07
❑ 67 Raul Mondesi	.20	.07
❑ 68 Todd Jones	.20	.07
❑ 69 Albert Belle	.20	.07
❑ 70 Trevor Hoffman	.20	.07
❑ 71 Eric Young	.20	.07
❑ 72 Robert Perez	.20	.07
❑ 73 Butch Huskey	.20	.07
❑ 74 Brian McRae	.20	.07
❑ 75 Jim Edmonds	.20	.07
❑ 76 Mike Henneman	.20	.07
❑ 77 Frank Rodriguez	.20	.07
❑ 78 Danny Tartabull	.20	.07
❑ 79 Robb Nen	.20	.07
❑ 80 Reggie Sanders	.20	.07
❑ 81 Ron Karkovice	.20	.07
❑ 82 Benito Santiago	.20	.07
❑ 83 Mike Lansing	.20	.07
❑ 85 Craig Biggio	.30	.10
❑ 86 Mike Bordick	.20	.07
❑ 87 Ray Lankford	.20	.07
❑ 88 Charles Nagy	.20	.07
❑ 89 Paul Wilson	.20	.07
❑ 90 John Wetteland	.20	.07
❑ 91 Tom Candiotti	.20	.07
❑ 92 Carlos Delgado	.20	.07
❑ 93 Derek Bell	.20	.07
❑ 94 Mark Lemke	.20	.07
❑ 95 Edgar Martinez	.30	.10
❑ 96 Rickey Henderson	.50	.20
❑ 97 Greg Myers	.20	.07
❑ 98 Jim Leyritz	.20	.07
❑ 99 Mark Johnson	.20	.07
❑ 100 Dwight Gooden HL	.20	.07
❑ 101 Al Leiter HL	.20	.07
❑ 102 John Mabry HL	.20	.07
❑ 103 Alex Ochoa HL	.20	.07
❑ 104 Mike Piazza HL	.50	.20
❑ 105 Jim Thome	.30	.10
❑ 106 Ricky Otero	.20	.07
❑ 107 Jamey Wright	.20	.07
❑ 108 Frank Thomas	.50	.20
❑ 109 Jody Reed	.20	.07
❑ 110 Orel Hershiser	.20	.07
❑ 111 Terry Steinbach	.20	.07
❑ 112 Mark Loretta	.20	.07
❑ 113 Turk Wendell	.20	.07
❑ 114 Marvin Benard	.20	.07
❑ 115 Kevin Brown	.20	.07
❑ 116 Robert Person	.20	.07
❑ 117 Joey Hamilton	.20	.07
❑ 118 Francisco Cordova	.20	.07
❑ 119 John Smiley	.20	.07
❑ 120 Travis Fryman	.20	.07
❑ 121 Jimmy Key	.20	.07
❑ 122 Tom Goodwin	.20	.07
❑ 123 Mike Greenwell	.20	.07
❑ 124 Juan Gonzalez	.20	.07
❑ 125 Pete Harnisch	.20	.07
❑ 126 Roger Cedeno	.20	.07
❑ 127 Ron Gant	.20	.07
❑ 128 Mark Langston	.20	.07
❑ 129 Tim Crabtree	.20	.07
❑ 130 Greg Maddux	.75	.30
❑ 131 William VanLandingham	.20	.07
❑ 132 Wally Joyner	.20	.07
❑ 133 Randy Myers	.20	.07
❑ 134 John Valentin	.20	.07
❑ 135 Bret Boone	.20	.07
❑ 136 Bruce Ruffin	.20	.07
❑ 137 Chris Snopek	.20	.07
❑ 138 Paul Molitor	.20	.07
❑ 139 Mark McLemore	.20	.07
❑ 140 Rafael Palmeiro	.30	.10
❑ 141 Herb Perry	.20	.07
❑ 142 Luis Gonzalez	.20	.07
❑ 143 Doug Drabek	.20	.07
❑ 144 Ken Ryan	.20	.07
❑ 145 Todd Hundley	.20	.07
❑ 146 Ellis Burks	.20	.07
❑ 147 Ozzie Guillen	.20	.07
❑ 148 Rich Becker	.20	.07
❑ 149 Sterling Hitchcock	.20	.07
❑ 150 Bernie Williams	.30	.10
❑ 151 Mike Stanley	.20	.07
❑ 152 Roberto Alomar	.30	.10
❑ 153 Jose Mesa	.20	.07
❑ 154 Steve Trachsel	.20	.07
❑ 155 Alex Gonzalez	.20	.07
❑ 156 Troy Percival	.20	.07
❑ 157 John Smoltz	.30	.10
❑ 158 Pedro Martinez	.30	.10
❑ 159 Jeff Conine	.20	.07
❑ 160 Bernard Gilkey	.20	.07
❑ 161 Jim Eisenreich	.20	.07
❑ 162 Mickey Tettleton	.20	.07
❑ 163 Justin Thompson	.20	.07
❑ 164 Jose Offerman	.20	.07
❑ 165 Tony Phillips	.20	.07
❑ 166 Ismael Valdes	.20	.07
❑ 167 Ryne Sandberg	.75	.30
❑ 168 Matt Mieske	.20	.07
❑ 169 Geronimo Berroa	.20	.07
❑ 170 Otis Nixon	.20	.07
❑ 171 John Mabry	.20	.07
❑ 172 Shawon Dunston	.20	.07
❑ 173 Omar Vizquel	.30	.10
❑ 174 Chris Hoiles	.20	.07
❑ 175 Dwight Gooden	.20	.07
❑ 176 Wilson Alvarez	.20	.07
❑ 177 Todd Hollandsworth	.20	.07
❑ 178 Roger Salkeld	.20	.07
❑ 179 Rey Sanchez	.20	.07
❑ 180 Rey Ordonez	.20	.07
❑ 181 Denny Martinez	.20	.07
❑ 182 Ramon Martinez	.20	.07
❑ 183 Dave Nilsson	.20	.07
❑ 184 Marquis Grissom	.20	.07
❑ 185 Randy Velarde	.20	.07
❑ 186 Ron Coomer	.20	.07
❑ 187 Tino Martinez	.30	.10
❑ 188 Jeff Brantley	.20	.07
❑ 189 Steve Finley	.20	.07
❑ 190 Andy Benes	.20	.07
❑ 191 Terry Adams	.20	.07
❑ 192 Mike Blowers	.20	.07
❑ 193 Russ Davis	.20	.07
❑ 194 Darryl Hamilton	.20	.07
❑ 195 Jason Kendall	.20	.07
❑ 196 Johnny Damon	.30	.10
❑ 197 Dave Martinez	.20	.07
❑ 198 Mike Macfarlane	.20	.07
❑ 199 Norm Charlton	.20	.07
❑ 200 Damian Moss	.25	.08
❑ 201 Jenkins/Ibanez/Cameron	.20	.07
❑ 202 Sean Casey	.30	.10
❑ 203 J.Hansen/H.Bush/F.Crespo	.20	.07
❑ 204 K.Orie/G.Alvarez/A.Boone	.20	.07
❑ 205 B.Davis/K.Brown/B.Estalella	.20	.07
❑ 206 Bubba Trammell RC	.40	.15
❑ 207 Jarrod Washburn	.20	.07
❑ 208 Brian Hunter	.20	.07
❑ 209 Jason Giambi	.20	.07
❑ 210 Henry Rodriguez	.20	.07
❑ 211 Edgar Renteria	.20	.07
❑ 212 Edgardo Alfonzo	.20	.07
❑ 213 Fernando Vina	.20	.07
❑ 214 Shawn Green	.20	.07
❑ 215 Ray Durham	.20	.07
❑ 216 Joe Randa	.20	.07
❑ 217 Armando Reynoso	.20	.07
❑ 218 Eric Davis	.20	.07
❑ 219 Bob Tewksbury	.20	.07
❑ 220 Jacob Cruz	.20	.07
❑ 221 Glenallen Hill	.20	.07
❑ 222 Gary Gaetti	.20	.07
❑ 223 Donne Wall	.20	.07
❑ 224 Brad Clontz	.20	.07
❑ 225 Marty Janzen	.20	.07
❑ 226 Todd Worrell	.20	.07
❑ 227 John Franco	.20	.07
❑ 228 David Wells	.20	.07
❑ 229 Gregg Jefferies	.20	.07
❑ 230 Tim Naehring	.20	.07
❑ 231 Thomas Howard	.20	.07
❑ 232 Roberto Hernandez	.20	.07
❑ 233 Kevin Ritz	.20	.07
❑ 234 Julian Tavarez	.20	.07
❑ 235 Ken Hill	.20	.07
❑ 236 Greg Gagne	.20	.07
❑ 237 Bobby Chouinard	.20	.07
❑ 238 Joe Carter	.20	.07
❑ 239 Jermaine Dye	.20	.07
❑ 240 Antonio Osuna	.20	.07
❑ 241 Julio Franco	.20	.07
❑ 242 Mike Grace	.20	.07
❑ 243 Aaron Sele	.20	.07
❑ 244 David Justice	.20	.07
❑ 245 Sandy Alomar Jr.	.20	.07
❑ 246 Jose Canseco	.30	.10
❑ 247 Paul O'Neill	.30	.10
❑ 248 Sean Berry	.20	.07
❑ 249 N.Bierbrodt/K.Sweeney RC	.25	.08
❑ 250 Vladimir Nunez RC	.25	.08
❑ 251 R.Hartman/D.Hayman RC	.25	.08
❑ 252 A.Sanchez/M.Quatraro RC	.40	.15
❑ 253 Ronni Seberino RC	.25	.08
❑ 254 Rex Hudler	.20	.07
❑ 255 Orlando Miller	.20	.07
❑ 256 Mariano Rivera	.50	.20
❑ 257 Brad Radke	.20	.07
❑ 258 Bobby Higginson	.20	.07
❑ 259 Jay Bell	.20	.07
❑ 260 Mark Grudzielanek	.20	.07
❑ 261 Lance Johnson	.20	.07
❑ 262 Ken Caminiti	.20	.07
❑ 263 J.T. Snow	.20	.07
❑ 264 Gary Sheffield	.20	.07
❑ 265 Darrin Fletcher	.20	.07
❑ 266 Eric Owens	.20	.07
❑ 267 Luis Castillo	.20	.07
❑ 268 Scott Rolen	.30	.10
❑ 269 T.Noel/J.Oliver RC	.25	.08
❑ 270 Robert Stratton RC	.40	.15
❑ 271 Gil Meche RC	1.00	.40
❑ 272 E.Milton RC/D.Brown RC	.40	.15
❑ 273 Chris Reitsma RC	.40	.15
❑ 274 J.Marquis/A.J.Zapp RC	.50	.20
❑ 275 Checklist	.20	.07
❑ 276 Checklist	.20	.07
❑ 277 Chipper Jones UER276	.50	.20
❑ 278 Orlando Merced	.20	.07
❑ 279 Ariel Prieto	.20	.07
❑ 280 Al Leiter	.20	.07
❑ 281 Pat Meares	.20	.07
❑ 282 Darryl Strawberry	.20	.07
❑ 283 Jamie Moyer	.20	.07
❑ 284 Scott Servais	.20	.07
❑ 285 Delino DeShields	.20	.07
❑ 286 Danny Graves	.20	.07
❑ 287 Gerald Williams	.20	.07
❑ 288 Todd Greene	.20	.07
❑ 289 Rico Brogna	.20	.07
❑ 290 Derrick Gibson	.20	.07
❑ 291 Joe Girardi	.20	.07

	Card	Player	Mint	NrMt
❑	292	Darren Lewis	.20	.07
❑	293	Nomar Garciaparra	.75	.30
❑	294	Greg Colbrunn	.20	.07
❑	295	Jeff Bagwell	.30	.10
❑	296	Brent Gates	.20	.07
❑	297	Jose Vizcaino	.20	.07
❑	298	Alex Ochoa	.20	.07
❑	299	Sid Fernandez	.20	.07
❑	300	Ken Griffey Jr.	.75	.30
❑	301	Chris Gomez	.20	.07
❑	302	Wendell Magee	.20	.07
❑	303	Darren Oliver	.20	.07
❑	304	Mel Nieves	.20	.07
❑	305	Sammy Sosa	.50	.20
❑	306	George Arias	.20	.07
❑	307	Jack McDowell	.20	.07
❑	308	Stan Javier	.20	.07
❑	309	Kimera Bartee	.20	.07
❑	310	James Baldwin	.20	.07
❑	311	Rocky Coppinger	.20	.07
❑	312	Keith Lockhart	.20	.07
❑	313	C.J. Nitkowski	.20	.07
❑	314	Allen Watson	.20	.07
❑	315	Darryl Kile	.20	.07
❑	316	Amaury Telemaco	.20	.07
❑	317	Jason Isringhausen	.20	.07
❑	318	Manny Ramirez	.30	.10
❑	319	Terry Pendleton	.20	.07
❑	320	Tim Salmon	.30	.10
❑	321	Eric Karros	.20	.07
❑	322	Mark Whiten	.20	.07
❑	323	Rick Krivda	.20	.07
❑	324	Brett Butler	.20	.07
❑	325	Randy Johnson	.50	.20
❑	326	Eddie Taubensee	.20	.07
❑	327	Mark Leiter	.20	.07
❑	328	Kevin Gross	.20	.07
❑	329	Ernie Young	.20	.07
❑	330	Pat Hentgen	.20	.07
❑	331	Rondell White	.20	.07
❑	332	Bobby Witt	.20	.07
❑	333	Eddie Murray	.50	.20
❑	334	Tim Raines	.20	.07
❑	335	Jeff Fassero	.20	.07
❑	336	Chuck Finley	.20	.07
❑	337	Willie Adams	.20	.07
❑	338	Chan Ho Park	.20	.07
❑	339	Jay Powell	.20	.07
❑	340	Ivan Rodriguez	.30	.10
❑	341	Jermaine Allensworth	.20	.07
❑	342	Jay Payton	.20	.07
❑	343	T.J. Mathews	.20	.07
❑	344	Tony Batista	.20	.07
❑	345	Ed Sprague	.20	.07
❑	346	Jeff Kent	.20	.07
❑	347	Scott Erickson	.20	.07
❑	348	Jeff Suppan	.20	.07
❑	349	Pete Schourek	.20	.07
❑	350	Kenny Lofton	.20	.07
❑	351	Alan Benes	.20	.07
❑	352	Fred McGriff	.30	.10
❑	353	Charlie O'Brien	.20	.07
❑	354	Darren Bragg	.20	.07
❑	355	Alex Fernandez	.20	.07
❑	356	Al Martin	.20	.07
❑	357	Bob Wells	.20	.07
❑	358	Chad Mottola	.20	.07
❑	359	Devon White	.20	.07
❑	360	David Cone	.20	.07
❑	361	Bobby Jones	.20	.07
❑	362	Scott Sanders	.20	.07
❑	363	Karim Garcia	.20	.07
❑	364	Kirt Manwaring	.20	.07
❑	365	Chili Davis	.20	.07
❑	366	Mike Hampton	.20	.07
❑	367	Chad Ogea	.20	.07
❑	368	Curt Schilling	.20	.07
❑	369	Phil Nevin	.20	.07
❑	370	Roger Clemens	1.00	.40
❑	371	Willie Greene	.20	.07
❑	372	Kenny Rogers	.20	.07
❑	373	Jose Rijo	.20	.07
❑	374	Bobby Bonilla	.20	.07
❑	375	Mike Mussina	.30	.10
❑	376	Curtis Pride	.20	.07
❑	377	Todd Walker	.20	.07
❑	378	Jason Bere	.20	.07
❑	379	Heathcliff Slocumb	.20	.07
❑	380	Dante Bichette	.20	.07
❑	381	Carlos Baerga	.20	.07
❑	382	Livan Hernandez	.20	.07
❑	383	Jason Schmidt	.20	.07
❑	384	Kevin Stocker	.20	.07
❑	385	Matt Williams	.20	.07
❑	386	Bartolo Colon	.20	.07
❑	387	Will Clark	.30	.10
❑	388	Dennis Eckersley	.20	.07
❑	389	Brooks Kieschnick	.20	.07
❑	390	Ryan Klesko	.20	.07
❑	391	Mark Carreon	.20	.07
❑	392	Tim Worrell	.20	.07
❑	393	Dean Palmer	.20	.07
❑	394	Wil Cordero	.20	.07
❑	395	Javy Lopez	.20	.07
❑	396	Rich Aurilia	.20	.07
❑	397	Greg Vaughn	.20	.07
❑	398	Vinny Castilla	.20	.07
❑	399	Jeff Montgomery	.20	.07
❑	400	Cal Ripken	1.50	.60
❑	401	Walt Weiss	.20	.07
❑	402	Brad Ausmus	.20	.07
❑	403	Ruben Rivera	.20	.07
❑	404	Mark Wohlers	.20	.07
❑	405	Rick Aguilera	.20	.07
❑	406	Tony Clark	.20	.07
❑	407	Lyle Mouton	.20	.07
❑	408	Bill Pulsipher	.20	.07
❑	409	Jose Rosado	.20	.07
❑	410	Tony Gwynn	.60	.25
❑	411	Cecil Fielder	.20	.07
❑	412	John Flaherty	.20	.07
❑	413	Lenny Dykstra	.20	.07
❑	414	Ugueth Urbina	.20	.07
❑	415	Brian Jordan	.20	.07
❑	416	Bob Abreu	.30	.10
❑	417	Craig Paquette	.20	.07
❑	418	Sandy Martinez	.20	.07
❑	419	Jeff Blauser	.20	.07
❑	420	Barry Larkin	.30	.10
❑	421	Kevin Seitzer	.20	.07
❑	422	Tim Belcher	.20	.07
❑	423	Paul Sorrento	.20	.07
❑	424	Cal Eldred	.20	.07
❑	425	Robin Ventura	.20	.07
❑	426	John Olerud	.20	.07
❑	427	Bob Wolcott	.20	.07
❑	428	Matt Lawton	.20	.07
❑	429	Rod Beck	.20	.07
❑	430	Shane Reynolds	.20	.07
❑	431	Mike James	.20	.07
❑	432	Steve Wojciechowski	.20	.07
❑	433	Vladimir Guerrero	.50	.20
❑	434	Dustin Hermanson	.20	.07
❑	435	Marty Cordova	.20	.07
❑	436	Marc Newfield	.20	.07
❑	437	Todd Stottlemyre	.20	.07
❑	438	Jeffrey Hammonds	.20	.07
❑	439	Dave Stevens	.20	.07
❑	440	Hideo Nomo	.50	.20
❑	441	Mark Thompson	.20	.07
❑	442	Mark Lewis	.20	.07
❑	443	Quinton McCracken	.20	.07
❑	444	Cliff Floyd	.20	.07
❑	445	Denny Neagle	.20	.07
❑	446	John Jaha	.20	.07
❑	447	Mike Sweeney	.20	.07
❑	448	John Wasdin	.20	.07
❑	449	Chad Curtis	.20	.07
❑	450	Mo Vaughn	.20	.07
❑	451	Donovan Osborne	.20	.07
❑	452	Ruben Sierra	.20	.07
❑	453	Michael Tucker	.20	.07
❑	454	Kurt Abbott	.20	.07
❑	455	Andruw Jones UER	.30	.10
❑	456	Shannon Stewart	.20	.07
❑	457	Scott Brosius	.20	.07
❑	458	Juan Guzman	.20	.07
❑	459	Ron Villone	.20	.07
❑	460	Moises Alou	.20	.07
❑	461	Larry Walker	.20	.07
❑	462	Eddie Murray SH	.30	.10
❑	463	Paul Molitor SH	.20	.07
❑	464	Hideo Nomo SH	.20	.07
❑	465	Barry Bonds SH	.75	.30
❑	466	Todd Hundley SH	.20	.07
❑	467	Rheal Cormier	.20	.07
❑	468	J.Sandoval/J.Conti RC	.25	.08
❑	469	R.Barajas/J.Rexrode RC	1.50	.60
❑	470	Jared Sandberg RC	.25	.08
❑	471	P.Wilder/C.Gunner RC	.25	.08
❑	472	M.DeCelle/M.McCain RC	.25	.08
❑	473	Todd Zeile	.20	.07
❑	474	Neifi Perez	.20	.07
❑	475	Jeromy Burnitz	.20	.07
❑	476	Trey Beamon	.20	.07
❑	477	J.Patterson/B.Looper RC	.75	.30
❑	478	Jake Westbrook RC	.50	.20
❑	479	E.Chavez/A.Eaton RC	2.00	.75
❑	480	P.Tucci/J.Lawrence RC	.25	.08
❑	481	K.Benson/B.Koch RC	.50	.20
❑	482	J.Nicholson/A.Prater RC	.25	.08
❑	483	M.Kotsay/M.Johnson RC	.75	.30
❑	484	Armando Benitez	.20	.07
❑	485	Mike Matheny	.20	.07
❑	486	Jeff Reed	.20	.07
❑	487	M.Bellhorn/R.Johnson/E.Wilson	.20	.07
❑	488	R.Hidalgo/B.Grieve	.20	.07
❑	489	Konerko/D.Lee/Wright	.30	.10
❑	490	Bill Mueller RC	1.25	.50
❑	491	J.Abbott/S.Monahan/E.Velazquez	.20	.07
❑	492	Jimmy Anderson RC	.25	.08
❑	493	Carl Pavano	.20	.07
❑	494	Nelson Figueroa RC	.25	.08
❑	495	Checklist (277-400)	.20	.07
❑	496	Checklist (401-496)	.20	.07
❑	NNO	Derek Jeter AU	150.00	75.00

1998 Topps

	Card	Player	Mint	NrMt
❑		COMPLETE SET (503)	80.00	40.00
❑		COMP.HOBBY SET (511)	120.00	60.00
❑		COMP.RETAIL SET (511)	120.00	60.00
❑		COMPLETE SERIES 1 (282)	40.00	20.00
❑		COMPLETE SERIES 2 (221)	40.00	20.00
❑	1	Tony Gwynn	.60	.25
❑	2	Larry Walker	.20	.07
❑	3	Billy Wagner	.20	.07
❑	4	Denny Neagle	.20	.07
❑	5	Vladimir Guerrero	.50	.20
❑	6	Kevin Brown	.30	.10
❑	8	Mariano Rivera	.50	.20
❑	9	Tony Clark	.20	.07
❑	10	Deion Sanders	.30	.10
❑	11	Francisco Cordova	.20	.07
❑	12	Matt Williams	.20	.07
❑	13	Carlos Baerga	.20	.07
❑	14	Mo Vaughn	.20	.07
❑	15	Bobby Witt	.20	.07
❑	16	Matt Stairs	.20	.07
❑	17	Chan Ho Park	.20	.07
❑	18	Mike Bordick	.20	.07
❑	19	Michael Tucker	.20	.07
❑	20	Frank Thomas	.50	.20
❑	21	Roberto Clemente	1.00	.40
❑	22	Dmitri Young	.20	.07
❑	23	Steve Trachsel	.20	.07
❑	24	Jeff Kent	.20	.07
❑	25	Scott Rolen	.30	.10
❑	26	John Thomson	.20	.07
❑	27	Joe Vitiello	.20	.07
❑	28	Eddie Guardado	.20	.07

❑ 29 Charlie Hayes .20 .07
❑ 30 Juan Gonzalez .20 .07
❑ 31 Garret Anderson .20 .07
❑ 32 John Jaha .20 .07
❑ 33 Omar Vizquel .30 .10
❑ 34 Brian Hunter .20 .07
❑ 35 Jeff Bagwell .30 .10
❑ 36 Mark Lemke .20 .07
❑ 37 Doug Glanville .20 .07
❑ 38 Dan Wilson .20 .07
❑ 39 Steve Cooke .20 .07
❑ 40 Chili Davis .20 .07
❑ 41 Mike Cameron .20 .07
❑ 42 F.P. Santangelo .20 .07
❑ 43 Brad Ausmus .20 .07
❑ 44 Gary DiSarcina .20 .07
❑ 45 Pat Hentgen .20 .07
❑ 46 Wilton Guerrero .20 .07
❑ 47 Devon White .20 .07
❑ 48 Danny Patterson .20 .07
❑ 49 Pat Meares .20 .07
❑ 50 Rafael Palmeiro .30 .10
❑ 51 Mark Gardner .20 .07
❑ 52 Jeff Blauser .20 .07
❑ 53 Dave Hollins .20 .07
❑ 54 Carlos Garcia .20 .07
❑ 55 Ben McDonald .20 .07
❑ 56 John Mabry .20 .07
❑ 57 Trevor Hoffman .20 .07
❑ 58 Tony Fernandez .20 .07
❑ 59 Rich Loiselle .20 .07
❑ 60 Mark Leiter .20 .07
❑ 61 Pat Kelly .20 .07
❑ 62 John Flaherty .20 .07
❑ 63 Roger Bailey .20 .07
❑ 64 Tom Gordon .20 .07
❑ 65 Ryan Klesko .20 .07
❑ 66 Darryl Hamilton .20 .07
❑ 67 Jim Eisenreich .20 .07
❑ 68 Butch Huskey .20 .07
❑ 69 Mark Grudzielanek .20 .07
❑ 70 Marquis Grissom .20 .07
❑ 71 Mark McLemore .20 .07
❑ 72 Gary Gaetti .20 .07
❑ 73 Greg Gagne .20 .07
❑ 74 Lyle Mouton .20 .07
❑ 75 Jim Edmonds .20 .07
❑ 76 Shawn Green .20 .07
❑ 77 Greg Vaughn .20 .07
❑ 78 Terry Adams .20 .07
❑ 79 Kevin Polcovich .20 .07
❑ 80 Troy O'Leary .20 .07
❑ 81 Jeff Shaw .20 .07
❑ 82 Rich Becker .20 .07
❑ 83 David Wells .20 .07
❑ 84 Steve Karsay .20 .07
❑ 85 Charles Nagy .20 .07
❑ 86 B.J. Surhoff .20 .07
❑ 87 Jamey Wright .20 .07
❑ 88 James Baldwin .20 .07
❑ 89 Edgardo Alfonzo .20 .07
❑ 90 Jay Buhner .20 .07
❑ 91 Brady Anderson .20 .07
❑ 92 Scott Servais .20 .07
❑ 93 Edgar Renteria .20 .07
❑ 94 Mike Lieberthal .20 .07
❑ 95 Rick Aguilera .20 .07
❑ 96 Walt Weiss .20 .07
❑ 97 Deivi Cruz .20 .07
❑ 98 Kurt Abbott .20 .07
❑ 99 Henry Rodriguez .20 .07
❑ 100 Mike Piazza .75 .30
❑ 101 Bill Taylor .20 .07
❑ 102 Todd Zeile .20 .07
❑ 103 Rey Ordonez .20 .07
❑ 104 Willie Greene .20 .07
❑ 105 Tony Womack .20 .07
❑ 106 Mike Sweeney .20 .07
❑ 107 Jeffrey Hammonds .20 .07
❑ 108 Kevin Orie .20 .07
❑ 109 Alex Gonzalez .20 .07
❑ 110 Jose Canseco .30 .10
❑ 111 Paul Sorrento .20 .07
❑ 112 Joey Hamilton .20 .07
❑ 113 Brad Radke .20 .07
❑ 114 Steve Avery .20 .07
❑ 115 Esteban Loaiza .20 .07
❑ 116 Stan Javier .20 .07
❑ 117 Chris Gomez .20 .07
❑ 118 Royce Clayton .20 .07
❑ 119 Orlando Merced .20 .07
❑ 120 Kevin Appier .20 .07
❑ 121 Mel Nieves .20 .07
❑ 122 Joe Girardi .20 .07
❑ 123 Rico Brogna .20 .07
❑ 124 Kent Mercker .20 .07
❑ 125 Manny Ramirez .30 .10
❑ 126 Jeromy Burnitz .20 .07
❑ 127 Kevin Foster .20 .07
❑ 128 Matt Morris .20 .07
❑ 129 Jason Dickson .20 .07
❑ 130 Tom Glavine .30 .10
❑ 131 Wally Joyner .20 .07
❑ 132 Rick Reed .20 .07
❑ 133 Todd Jones .20 .07
❑ 134 Dave Martinez .20 .07
❑ 135 Sandy Alomar Jr. .20 .07
❑ 136 Mike Lansing .20 .07
❑ 137 Sean Berry .20 .07
❑ 138 Doug Jones .20 .07
❑ 139 Todd Stottlemyre .20 .07
❑ 140 Jay Bell .20 .07
❑ 141 Jaime Navarro .20 .07
❑ 142 Chris Hoiles .20 .07
❑ 143 Joey Cora .20 .07
❑ 144 Scott Spiezio .20 .07
❑ 145 Joe Carter .20 .07
❑ 146 Jose Guillen .20 .07
❑ 147 Damion Easley .20 .07
❑ 148 Lee Stevens .20 .07
❑ 149 Alex Fernandez .20 .07
❑ 150 Randy Johnson .50 .20
❑ 151 J.T. Snow .20 .07
❑ 152 Chuck Finley .20 .07
❑ 153 Bernard Gilkey .20 .07
❑ 154 David Segui .20 .07
❑ 155 Dante Bichette .20 .07
❑ 156 Kevin Stocker .20 .07
❑ 157 Carl Everett .20 .07
❑ 158 Jose Valentin .20 .07
❑ 159 Pokey Reese .20 .07
❑ 160 Derek Jeter 1.25 .50
❑ 161 Roger Pavlik .20 .07
❑ 162 Mark Wohlers .20 .07
❑ 163 Ricky Bottalico .20 .07
❑ 164 Ozzie Guillen .20 .07
❑ 165 Mike Mussina .30 .10
❑ 166 Gary Sheffield .20 .07
❑ 167 Hideo Nomo .50 .20
❑ 168 Mark Grace .30 .10
❑ 169 Aaron Sele .20 .07
❑ 170 Darryl Kile .20 .07
❑ 171 Shawn Estes .20 .07
❑ 172 Vinny Castilla .20 .07
❑ 173 Ron Coomer .20 .07
❑ 174 Jose Rosado .20 .07
❑ 175 Kenny Lofton .20 .07
❑ 176 Jason Giambi .20 .07
❑ 177 Hal Morris .20 .07
❑ 178 Darren Bragg .20 .07
❑ 179 Orel Hershiser .20 .07
❑ 180 Ray Lankford .20 .07
❑ 181 Hideki Irabu .20 .07
❑ 182 Kevin Young .20 .07
❑ 183 Javy Lopez .20 .07
❑ 184 Jeff Montgomery .20 .07
❑ 185 Mike Holtz .20 .07
❑ 186 George Williams .20 .07
❑ 187 Cal Eldred .20 .07
❑ 188 Tom Candiotti .20 .07
❑ 189 Glenallen Hill .20 .07
❑ 190 Brian Giles .20 .07
❑ 191 Dave Mlicki .20 .07
❑ 192 Garrett Stephenson .20 .07
❑ 193 Jeff Frye .20 .07
❑ 194 Joe Oliver .20 .07
❑ 195 Bob Hamelin .20 .07
❑ 196 Luis Sojo .20 .07
❑ 197 LaTroy Hawkins .20 .07
❑ 198 Kevin Elster .20 .07
❑ 199 Jeff Reed .20 .07
❑ 200 Dennis Eckersley .20 .07
❑ 201 Bill Mueller .20 .07
❑ 202 Russ Davis .20 .07
❑ 203 Armando Benitez .20 .07
❑ 204 Quilvio Veras .20 .07
❑ 205 Tim Naehring .20 .07
❑ 206 Quinton McCracken .20 .07
❑ 207 Raul Casanova .20 .07
❑ 208 Matt Lawton .20 .07
❑ 209 Luis Alicea .20 .07
❑ 210 Luis Gonzalez .20 .07
❑ 211 Allen Watson .20 .07
❑ 212 Gerald Williams .20 .07
❑ 213 David Bell .20 .07
❑ 214 Todd Hollandsworth .20 .07
❑ 215 Wade Boggs .30 .10
❑ 216 Jose Mesa .20 .07
❑ 217 Jamie Moyer .20 .07
❑ 218 Darren Daulton .20 .07
❑ 219 Mickey Morandini .20 .07
❑ 220 Rusty Greer .20 .07
❑ 221 Jim Bullinger .20 .07
❑ 222 Jose Offerman .20 .07
❑ 223 Matt Karchner .20 .07
❑ 224 Woody Williams .20 .07
❑ 225 Mark Loretta .20 .07
❑ 226 Mike Hampton .20 .07
❑ 227 Willie Adams .20 .07
❑ 228 Scott Hatteberg .20 .07
❑ 229 Rich Amaral .20 .07
❑ 230 Terry Steinbach .20 .07
❑ 231 Glendon Rusch .20 .07
❑ 232 Bret Boone .20 .07
❑ 233 Robert Person .20 .07
❑ 234 Jose Hernandez .20 .07
❑ 235 Doug Drabek .20 .07
❑ 236 Jason McDonald .20 .07
❑ 237 Chris Widger .20 .07
❑ 238 Tom Martin .20 .07
❑ 239 Dave Burba .20 .07
❑ 240 Pete Rose Jr. .20 .07
❑ 241 Bobby Ayala .20 .07
❑ 242 Tim Wakefield .20 .07
❑ 243 Dennis Springer .20 .07
❑ 244 Tim Belcher .20 .07
❑ 245 J.Garland/G.Goetz .30 .10
❑ 246 L.Berkman/G.Davis .30 .10
❑ 247 V.Wells/A.Akin .30 .10
❑ 248 A.Kennedy/J.Romano .20 .07
❑ 249 J.Dellaero/T.Cameron .20 .07
❑ 250 J.Sandberg/A.Sanchez .20 .07
❑ 251 P.Ortega/J.Manias .20 .07
❑ 252 Mike Stoner RC .20 .07
❑ 253 J.Patterson/L.Rodriguez .20 .07
❑ 254 R.Minor RC/A.Beltre .30 .10
❑ 255 B.Grieve/D.Brown .20 .07
❑ 256 Wood/Pavano/Meche .30 .10
❑ 257 D.Ortiz/Sexson/Ward 2.50 1.00
❑ 258 J.Encarn/Winn/Vessel .20 .07
❑ 259 Bens/T.Smith RC/C.Dunc RC .20 .07
❑ 260 Warren Morris RC .20 .07
❑ 261 R.Hernandez/B.Davis/E.Marrero .20 .07
❑ 262 E.Chavez/R.Branyan .30 .10
❑ 263 Ryan Jackson RC .20 .07
❑ 264 B.Fuentes RC/Clement/Halladay .30 .10
❑ 265 Randy Johnson SH .30 .10
❑ 266 Kevin Brown SH .20 .07
❑ 267 R.Rincon/F.Cordova SH .20 .07
❑ 268 Nomar Garciaparra SH .50 .20
❑ 269 Tino Martinez SH .20 .07
❑ 270 Chuck Knoblauch IL .20 .07
❑ 271 Pedro Martinez IL .30 .10
❑ 272 Denny Neagle IL .20 .07
❑ 273 Juan Gonzalez IL .20 .07
❑ 274 Andres Galarraga IL .20 .07
❑ 275 Checklist (1-195) .20 .07
❑ 276 Checklist (196-283/inserts) .20 .07
❑ 277 Moises Alou WS .20 .07
❑ 278 Sandy Alomar Jr. WS .20 .07
❑ 279 Gary Sheffield WS .20 .07
❑ 280 Matt Williams WS .20 .07
❑ 281 Livan Hernandez WS .20 .07
❑ 282 Chad Ogea WS .20 .07
❑ 283 Marlins Champs .20 .07
❑ 284 Tino Martinez .30 .10
❑ 285 Roberto Alomar .30 .10
❑ 286 Jeff King .20 .07

Item	Hi	Lo
❑ 287 Brian Jordan	.20	.07
❑ 288 Darin Erstad	.20	.07
❑ 289 Ken Caminiti	.20	.07
❑ 290 Jim Thome	.30	.10
❑ 291 Paul Molitor	.20	.07
❑ 292 Ivan Rodriguez	.30	.10
❑ 293 Bernie Williams	.30	.10
❑ 294 Todd Hundley	.20	.07
❑ 295 Andres Galarraga	.20	.07
❑ 296 Greg Maddux	.75	.30
❑ 297 Edgar Martinez	.30	.10
❑ 298 Ron Gant	.20	.07
❑ 299 Derek Bell	.20	.07
❑ 300 Roger Clemens	1.00	.40
❑ 301 Rondell White	.20	.07
❑ 302 Barry Larkin	.30	.10
❑ 303 Robin Ventura	.20	.07
❑ 304 Jason Kendall	.20	.07
❑ 305 Chipper Jones	.50	.20
❑ 306 John Franco	.20	.07
❑ 307 Sammy Sosa	.50	.20
❑ 308 Troy Percival	.20	.07
❑ 309 Chuck Knoblauch	.20	.07
❑ 310 Ellis Burks	.20	.07
❑ 311 Al Martin	.20	.07
❑ 312 Tim Salmon	.30	.10
❑ 313 Moises Alou	.20	.07
❑ 314 Lance Johnson	.20	.07
❑ 315 Justin Thompson	.20	.07
❑ 316 Will Clark	.30	.10
❑ 317 Barry Bonds	1.50	.60
❑ 318 Craig Biggio	.30	.10
❑ 319 John Smoltz	.30	.10
❑ 320 Cal Ripken	1.50	.60
❑ 321 Ken Griffey Jr.	.75	.30
❑ 322 Paul O'Neill	.30	.10
❑ 323 Todd Helton	.30	.10
❑ 324 John Olerud	.20	.07
❑ 325 Mark McGwire	1.25	.50
❑ 326 Jose Cruz Jr.	.20	.07
❑ 327 Jeff Cirillo	.20	.07
❑ 328 Dean Palmer	.20	.07
❑ 329 John Wetteland	.20	.07
❑ 330 Steve Finley	.20	.07
❑ 331 Albert Belle	.20	.07
❑ 332 Curt Schilling	.20	.07
❑ 333 Raul Mondesi	.20	.07
❑ 334 Andruw Jones	.30	.10
❑ 335 Nomar Garciaparra	.75	.30
❑ 336 David Justice	.20	.07
❑ 337 Andy Pettitte	.30	.10
❑ 338 Pedro Martinez	.30	.10
❑ 339 Travis Miller	.20	.07
❑ 340 Chris Stynes	.20	.07
❑ 341 Gregg Jefferies	.20	.07
❑ 342 Jeff Fassero	.20	.07
❑ 343 Craig Counsell	.20	.07
❑ 344 Wilson Alvarez	.20	.07
❑ 345 Bip Roberts	.20	.07
❑ 346 Kelvim Escobar	.20	.07
❑ 347 Mark Bellhorn	.20	.07
❑ 348 Cory Lidle RC	1.50	.60
❑ 349 Fred McGriff	.30	.10
❑ 350 Chuck Carr	.20	.07
❑ 351 Bob Abreu	.20	.07
❑ 352 Juan Guzman	.20	.07
❑ 353 Fernando Vina	.20	.07
❑ 354 Andy Benes	.20	.07
❑ 355 Dave Nilsson	.20	.07
❑ 356 Bobby Bonilla	.20	.07
❑ 357 Ismael Valdes	.20	.07
❑ 358 Carlos Perez	.20	.07
❑ 359 Kirk Rueter	.20	.07
❑ 360 Bartolo Colon	.20	.07
❑ 361 Mel Rojas	.20	.07
❑ 362 Johnny Damon	.30	.10
❑ 363 Geronimo Berroa	.20	.07
❑ 364 Reggie Sanders	.20	.07
❑ 365 Jermaine Allensworth	.20	.07
❑ 366 Orlando Cabrera	.20	.07
❑ 367 Jorge Fabregas	.20	.07
❑ 368 Scott Stahoviak	.20	.07
❑ 369 Ken Cloude	.20	.07
❑ 370 Donovan Osborne	.20	.07
❑ 371 Roger Cedeno	.20	.07
❑ 372 Neifi Perez	.20	.07
❑ 373 Chris Holt	.20	.07
❑ 374 Cecil Fielder	.20	.07
❑ 375 Marty Cordova	.20	.07
❑ 376 Tom Goodwin	.20	.07
❑ 377 Jeff Suppan	.20	.07
❑ 378 Jeff Brantley	.20	.07
❑ 379 Mark Langston	.20	.07
❑ 380 Shane Reynolds	.20	.07
❑ 381 Mike Fetters	.20	.07
❑ 382 Todd Greene	.20	.07
❑ 383 Ray Durham	.20	.07
❑ 384 Carlos Delgado	.20	.07
❑ 385 Jeff D'Amico	.20	.07
❑ 386 Brian McRae	.20	.07
❑ 387 Alan Benes	.20	.07
❑ 388 Heathcliff Slocumb	.20	.07
❑ 389 Eric Young	.20	.07
❑ 390 Travis Fryman	.20	.07
❑ 391 David Cone	.20	.07
❑ 392 Otis Nixon	.20	.07
❑ 393 Jeremi Gonzalez	.20	.07
❑ 394 Jeff Juden	.20	.07
❑ 395 Jose Vizcaino	.20	.07
❑ 396 Ugueth Urbina	.20	.07
❑ 397 Ramon Martinez	.20	.07
❑ 398 Robb Nen	.20	.07
❑ 399 Harold Baines	.20	.07
❑ 400 Delino DeShields	.20	.07
❑ 401 John Burkett	.20	.07
❑ 402 Sterling Hitchcock	.20	.07
❑ 403 Mark Clark	.20	.07
❑ 404 Terrell Wade	.20	.07
❑ 405 Scott Brosius	.20	.07
❑ 406 Chad Curtis	.20	.07
❑ 407 Brian Johnson	.20	.07
❑ 408 Roberto Kelly	.20	.07
❑ 409 Dave Dellucci RC	.40	.15
❑ 410 Michael Tucker	.20	.07
❑ 411 Mark Kotsay	.20	.07
❑ 412 Mark Lewis	.20	.07
❑ 413 Ryan McGuire	.20	.07
❑ 414 Shawon Dunston	.20	.07
❑ 415 Brad Rigby	.20	.07
❑ 416 Scott Erickson	.20	.07
❑ 417 Bobby Jones	.20	.07
❑ 418 Darren Oliver	.20	.07
❑ 419 John Smiley	.20	.07
❑ 420 T.J. Mathews	.20	.07
❑ 421 Dustin Hermanson	.20	.07
❑ 422 Mike Timlin	.20	.07
❑ 423 Willie Blair	.20	.07
❑ 424 Manny Alexander	.20	.07
❑ 425 Bob Tewksbury	.20	.07
❑ 426 Pete Schourek	.20	.07
❑ 427 Reggie Jefferson	.20	.07
❑ 428 Ed Sprague	.20	.07
❑ 429 Jeff Conine	.20	.07
❑ 430 Roberto Hernandez	.20	.07
❑ 431 Tom Pagnozzi	.20	.07
❑ 432 Jaret Wright	.20	.07
❑ 433 Livan Hernandez	.20	.07
❑ 434 Andy Ashby	.20	.07
❑ 435 Todd Dunn	.20	.07
❑ 436 Bobby Higginson	.20	.07
❑ 437 Rod Beck	.20	.07
❑ 438 Jim Leyritz	.20	.07
❑ 439 Matt Williams	.20	.07
❑ 440 Brett Tomko	.20	.07
❑ 441 Joe Randa	.20	.07
❑ 442 Chris Carpenter	.20	.07
❑ 443 Dennis Reyes	.20	.07
❑ 444 Al Leiter	.20	.07
❑ 445 Jason Schmidt	.20	.07
❑ 446 Ken Hill	.20	.07
❑ 447 Shannon Stewart	.20	.07
❑ 448 Enrique Wilson	.20	.07
❑ 449 Fernando Tatis	.20	.07
❑ 450 Jimmy Key	.20	.07
❑ 451 Darrin Fletcher	.20	.07
❑ 452 John Valentin	.20	.07
❑ 453 Kevin Tapani	.20	.07
❑ 454 Eric Karros	.20	.07
❑ 455 Jay Bell	.20	.07
❑ 456 Walt Weiss	.20	.07
❑ 457 Devon White	.20	.07
❑ 458 Carl Pavano	.20	.07
❑ 459 Mike Lansing	.20	.07
❑ 460 John Flaherty	.20	.07
❑ 461 Richard Hidalgo	.20	.07
❑ 462 Quinton McCracken	.20	.07
❑ 463 Karim Garcia	.20	.07
❑ 464 Miguel Cairo	.20	.07
❑ 465 Edwin Diaz	.20	.07
❑ 466 Bobby Smith	.20	.07
❑ 467 Yamil Benitez	.20	.07
❑ 468 Rich Butler	.20	.07
❑ 469 Ben Ford RC	.20	.07
❑ 470 Bubba Trammell	.20	.07
❑ 471 Brent Brede	.20	.07
❑ 472 Brooks Kieschnick	.20	.07
❑ 473 Carlos Castillo	.20	.07
❑ 474 Brad Radke SH	.20	.07
❑ 475 Roger Clemens SH	.50	.20
❑ 476 Curt Schilling SH	.20	.07
❑ 477 John Olerud SH	.20	.07
❑ 478 Mark McGwire SH	.60	.25
❑ 479 M.Piazza/K.Griffey Jr. IL	.50	.20
❑ 480 J.Bagwell/F.Thomas IL	.30	.10
❑ 481 C.Jones/N.Garciaparra IL	.30	.10
❑ 482 L.Walker/J.Gonzalez IL	.20	.07
❑ 483 G.Sheffield/T.Martinez IL	.20	.07
❑ 484 D.Gib/M.Colem/Hutchins	.20	.07
❑ 485 B.Rose/Looper/Politte	.20	.07
❑ 486 E.Milton/Marquis/C.Lee	.20	.07
❑ 487 Robert Fick RC	.30	.10
❑ 488 A.Ramirez/A.Gonz/Casey	.30	.10
❑ 489 D.Bridges/T.Drew RC	.20	.07
❑ 490 D.McDonald/N.Ndungidi RC	.20	.07
❑ 491 Ryan Anderson RC	.20	.07
❑ 492 Troy Glaus RC	1.25	.50
❑ 493 J.Werth/D.Reichert RC	.20	.07
❑ 494 Michael Cuddyer RC	.75	.30
❑ 495 Jack Cust RC	.50	.20
❑ 496 Brian Anderson	.20	.07
❑ 497 Tony Saunders	.20	.07
❑ 498 J.Sandoval/V.Nunez	.20	.07
❑ 499 B.Penny/N.Bierbrodt	.30	.10
❑ 500 D.Carr/L.Cruz RC	.20	.07
❑ 501 C.Bowers/M.McCain	.20	.07
❑ 502 Checklist	.20	.07
❑ 503 Checklist	.20	.07
❑ 504 Alex Rodriguez	2.00	.75

1999 Topps

Item	Hi	Lo
❑ COMPLETE SET (462)	80.00	30.00
❑ COMP.HOBBY SET (462)	80.00	40.00
❑ COMP.X-MAS SET (463)	80.00	40.00
❑ COMPLETE SERIES 1 (241)	40.00	15.00
❑ COMPLETE SERIES 2 (221)	40.00	15.00
❑ COMP.MAC HR SET (70)	500.00	250.00
❑ COMP.SOSA HR SET (66)	250.00	100.00
❑ 1 Roger Clemens	1.00	.40
❑ 2 Andres Galarraga	.20	.07
❑ 3 Scott Brosius	.20	.07
❑ 4 John Flaherty	.20	.07
❑ 5 Jim Leyritz	.20	.07
❑ 6 Ray Durham	.20	.07
❑ 8 Jose Vizcaino	.20	.07
❑ 9 Will Clark	.30	.10
❑ 10 David Wells	.20	.07
❑ 11 Jose Guillen	.20	.07
❑ 12 Scott Hatteberg	.20	.07
❑ 13 Edgardo Alfonzo	.20	.07
❑ 14 Mike Bordick	.20	.07

❑ 15 Manny Ramirez .30 .10
❑ 16 Greg Maddux .75 .30
❑ 17 David Segui .20 .07
❑ 18 Darryl Strawberry .20 .07
❑ 19 Brad Radke .20 .07
❑ 20 Kerry Wood .20 .07
❑ 21 Matt Anderson .20 .07
❑ 22 Derrek Lee .30 .10
❑ 23 Mickey Morandini .20 .07
❑ 24 Paul Konerko .20 .07
❑ 25 Travis Lee .20 .07
❑ 26 Ken Hill .20 .07
❑ 27 Kenny Rogers .20 .07
❑ 28 Paul Sorrento .20 .07
❑ 29 Quilvio Veras .20 .07
❑ 30 Todd Walker .20 .07
❑ 31 Ryan Jackson .20 .07
❑ 32 John Olerud .20 .07
❑ 33 Doug Glanville .20 .07
❑ 34 Nolan Ryan 2.00 .75
❑ 35 Ray Lankford .20 .07
❑ 36 Mark Loretta .20 .07
❑ 37 Jason Dickson .20 .07
❑ 38 Sean Bergman .20 .07
❑ 39 Quinton McCracken .20 .07
❑ 40 Bartolo Colon .20 .07
❑ 41 Brady Anderson .20 .07
❑ 42 Chris Stynes .20 .07
❑ 43 Jorge Posada .30 .10
❑ 44 Justin Thompson .20 .07
❑ 45 Johnny Damon .30 .10
❑ 46 Armando Benitez .20 .07
❑ 47 Brant Brown .20 .07
❑ 48 Charlie Hayes .20 .07
❑ 49 Darren Dreifort .20 .07
❑ 50 Juan Gonzalez .20 .07
❑ 51 Chuck Knoblauch .20 .07
❑ 52 Todd Helton .30 .10
❑ 53 Rick Reed .20 .07
❑ 54 Chris Gomez .20 .07
❑ 55 Gary Sheffield .20 .07
❑ 56 Rod Beck .20 .07
❑ 57 Rey Sanchez .20 .07
❑ 58 Garret Anderson .20 .07
❑ 59 Jimmy Haynes .20 .07
❑ 60 Steve Woodard .20 .07
❑ 61 Rondell White .20 .07
❑ 62 Vladimir Guerrero .50 .20
❑ 63 Eric Karros .20 .07
❑ 64 Russ Davis .20 .07
❑ 65 Mo Vaughn .20 .07
❑ 66 Sammy Sosa .50 .20
❑ 67 Troy Percival .20 .07
❑ 68 Kenny Lofton .20 .07
❑ 69 Bill Taylor .20 .07
❑ 70 Mark McGwire 1.25 .50
❑ 71 Roger Cedeno .20 .07
❑ 72 Javy Lopez .20 .07
❑ 73 Damion Easley .20 .07
❑ 74 Andy Pettitte .30 .10
❑ 75 Tony Gwynn .60 .25
❑ 76 Ricardo Rincon .20 .07
❑ 77 F.P. Santangelo .20 .07
❑ 78 Jay Bell .20 .07
❑ 79 Scott Servais .20 .07
❑ 80 Jose Canseco .30 .10
❑ 81 Roberto Hernandez .20 .07
❑ 82 Todd Dunwoody .20 .07
❑ 83 John Wetteland .20 .07
❑ 84 Mike Caruso .20 .07
❑ 85 Derek Jeter 1.25 .50
❑ 86 Aaron Sele .20 .07
❑ 87 Jose Lima .20 .07
❑ 88 Ryan Christenson .20 .07
❑ 89 Jeff Cirillo .20 .07
❑ 90 Jose Hernandez .20 .07
❑ 91 Mark Kotsay .20 .07
❑ 92 Darren Bragg .20 .07
❑ 93 Albert Belle .20 .07
❑ 94 Matt Lawton .20 .07
❑ 95 Pedro Martinez .30 .10
❑ 96 Greg Vaughn .20 .07
❑ 97 Neifi Perez .20 .07
❑ 98 Gerald Williams .20 .07
❑ 99 Derek Bell .20 .07
❑ 100 Ken Griffey Jr. .75 .30
❑ 101 David Cone .20 .07
❑ 102 Brian Johnson .20 .07
❑ 103 Dean Palmer .20 .07
❑ 104 Javier Valentin .20 .07
❑ 105 Trevor Hoffman .20 .07
❑ 106 Butch Huskey .20 .07
❑ 107 Dave Martinez .20 .07
❑ 108 Billy Wagner .20 .07
❑ 109 Shawn Green .20 .07
❑ 110 Ben Grieve .20 .07
❑ 111 Tom Goodwin .20 .07
❑ 112 Jaret Wright .20 .07
❑ 113 Aramis Ramirez .20 .07
❑ 114 Dmitri Young .20 .07
❑ 115 Hideki Irabu .20 .07
❑ 116 Roberto Kelly .20 .07
❑ 117 Jeff Fassero .20 .07
❑ 118 Mark Clark .20 .07
❑ 119 Jason McDonald .20 .07
❑ 120 Matt Williams .20 .07
❑ 121 Dave Burba .20 .07
❑ 122 Bret Saberhagen .20 .07
❑ 123 Deivi Cruz .20 .07
❑ 124 Chad Curtis .20 .07
❑ 125 Scott Rolen .30 .10
❑ 126 Lee Stevens .20 .07
❑ 127 J.T. Snow .20 .07
❑ 128 Rusty Greer .20 .07
❑ 129 Brian Meadows .20 .07
❑ 130 Jim Edmonds .20 .07
❑ 131 Ron Gant .20 .07
❑ 132 A.J. Hinch .20 .07
❑ 133 Shannon Stewart .20 .07
❑ 134 Brad Fullmer .20 .07
❑ 135 Cal Eldred .20 .07
❑ 136 Matt Walbeck .20 .07
❑ 137 Carl Everett .20 .07
❑ 138 Walt Weiss .20 .07
❑ 139 Fred McGriff .30 .10
❑ 140 Darin Erstad .20 .07
❑ 141 Dave Nilsson .20 .07
❑ 142 Eric Young .20 .07
❑ 143 Dan Wilson .20 .07
❑ 144 Jeff Reed .20 .07
❑ 145 Brett Tomko .20 .07
❑ 146 Terry Steinbach .20 .07
❑ 147 Seth Greisinger .20 .07
❑ 148 Pat Meares .20 .07
❑ 149 Livan Hernandez .20 .07
❑ 150 Jeff Bagwell .30 .10
❑ 151 Bob Wickman .20 .07
❑ 152 Omar Vizquel .30 .10
❑ 153 Eric Davis .20 .07
❑ 154 Larry Sutton .20 .07
❑ 155 Magglio Ordonez .20 .07
❑ 156 Eric Milton .20 .07
❑ 157 Darren Lewis .20 .07
❑ 158 Rick Aguilera .20 .07
❑ 159 Mike Lieberthal .20 .07
❑ 160 Robb Nen .20 .07
❑ 161 Brian Giles .20 .07
❑ 162 Jeff Brantley .20 .07
❑ 163 Gary DiSarcina .20 .07
❑ 164 John Valentin .20 .07
❑ 165 David Dellucci .20 .07
❑ 166 Chan Ho Park .20 .07
❑ 167 Masato Yoshii .20 .07
❑ 168 Jason Schmidt .20 .07
❑ 169 LaTroy Hawkins .20 .07
❑ 170 Bret Boone .20 .07
❑ 171 Jerry DiPoto .20 .07
❑ 172 Mariano Rivera .50 .20
❑ 173 Mike Cameron .20 .07
❑ 174 Scott Erickson .20 .07
❑ 175 Charles Johnson .20 .07
❑ 176 Bobby Jones .20 .07
❑ 177 Francisco Cordova .20 .07
❑ 178 Todd Jones .20 .07
❑ 179 Jeff Montgomery .20 .07
❑ 180 Mike Mussina .30 .10
❑ 181 Bob Abreu .20 .07
❑ 182 Ismael Valdes .20 .07
❑ 183 Andy Fox .20 .07
❑ 184 Woody Williams .20 .07
❑ 185 Denny Neagle .20 .07
❑ 186 Jose Valentin .20 .07
❑ 187 Darrin Fletcher .20 .07
❑ 188 Gabe Alvarez .20 .07
❑ 189 Eddie Taubensee .20 .07
❑ 190 Edgar Martinez .30 .10
❑ 191 Jason Kendall .20 .07
❑ 192 Darryl Kile .20 .07
❑ 193 Jeff King .20 .07
❑ 194 Rey Ordonez .20 .07
❑ 195 Andruw Jones .30 .10
❑ 196 Tony Fernandez .20 .07
❑ 197 Jamey Wright .20 .07
❑ 198 B.J. Surhoff .20 .07
❑ 199 Vinny Castilla .20 .07
❑ 200 David Wells HL .20 .07
❑ 201 Mark McGwire HL .60 .25
❑ 202 Sammy Sosa HL .30 .10
❑ 203 Roger Clemens HL .50 .20
❑ 204 Kerry Wood HL .20 .07
❑ 205 L.Berkman/G.Kapler .40 .15
❑ 206 Alex Escobar RC .40 .15
❑ 207 Peter Bergeron RC .25 .08
❑ 208 M.Barrett/B.Davis/R.Fick .25 .08
❑ 209 P.Cline/R.Hernandez/J.Werth .25 .08
❑ 210 R.Anderson/Chen/Enochs .25 .08
❑ 211 B.Penny/Dotel/Lincoln .25 .08
❑ 212 Chuck Abbott RC .25 .08
❑ 213 C.Jones/J.Urban RC .25 .08
❑ 214 T.Torcato/A.McDowell RC .25 .08
❑ 215 J.Tyner/J.McKinley RC .25 .08
❑ 216 M.Burch/S.Etherton RC .25 .08
❑ 217 R.Elder/M.Tucker RC .25 .08
❑ 218 J.M.Gold/R.Mills RC .25 .08
❑ 219 A.Brown/C.Freeman RC .25 .08
❑ 220A Mark McGwire HR 1 40.00 15.00
❑ 220B Mark McGwire HR 2 15.00 6.00
❑ 220C Mark McGwire HR 3 15.00 6.00
❑ 220D Mark McGwire HR 4 15.00 6.00
❑ 220E Mark McGwire HR 5 15.00 6.00
❑ 220F Mark McGwire HR 6 15.00 6.00
❑ 220G Mark McGwire HR 7 15.00 6.00
❑ 220H Mark McGwire HR 8 15.00 6.00
❑ 220I Mark McGwire HR 9 15.00 6.00
❑ 220J Mark McGwire HR 10 15.00 6.00
❑ 220K Mark McGwire HR 11 15.00 6.00
❑ 220L Mark McGwire HR 12 15.00 6.00
❑ 220M Mark McGwire HR 13 15.00 6.00
❑ 220N Mark McGwire HR 14 15.00 6.00
❑ 220O Mark McGwire HR 15 15.00 6.00
❑ 220P Mark McGwire HR 16 15.00 6.00
❑ 220Q Mark McGwire HR 17 15.00 6.00
❑ 220R Mark McGwire HR 18 15.00 6.00
❑ 220S Mark McGwire HR 19 15.00 6.00
❑ 220T Mark McGwire HR 20 15.00 6.00
❑ 220U Mark McGwire HR 21 15.00 6.00
❑ 220V Mark McGwire HR 22 15.00 6.00
❑ 220W Mark McGwire HR 23 15.00 6.00
❑ 220X Mark McGwire HR 24 15.00 6.00
❑ 220Y Mark McGwire HR 25 15.00 6.00
❑ 220Z Mark McGwire HR 26 15.00 6.00
❑ 220AA Mark McGwire HR 27 15.00 6.00
❑ 220AB Mark McGwire HR 28 15.00 6.00
❑ 220AC Mark McGwire HR 29 15.00 6.00
❑ 220AD Mark McGwire HR 30 15.00 6.00
❑ 220AE Mark McGwire HR 31 15.00 6.00
❑ 220AF Mark McGwire HR 32 15.00 6.00
❑ 220AG Mark McGwire HR 33 15.00 6.00
❑ 220AH Mark McGwire HR 34 15.00 6.00
❑ 220AI Mark McGwire HR 35 15.00 6.00
❑ 220AJ Mark McGwire HR 36 15.00 6.00
❑ 220AK Mark McGwire HR 37 15.00 6.00
❑ 220AL Mark McGwire HR 38 15.00 6.00
❑ 220AM Mark McGwire HR 39 15.00 6.00
❑ 220AN Mark McGwire HR 40 15.00 6.00
❑ 220AO Mark McGwire HR 41 15.00 6.00
❑ 220AP Mark McGwire HR 42 15.00 6.00
❑ 220AQ Mark McGwire HR 43 15.00 6.00
❑ 220AR Mark McGwire HR 44 15.00 6.00
❑ 220AS Mark McGwire HR 45 15.00 6.00
❑ 220AT Mark McGwire HR 46 15.00 6.00
❑ 220AU Mark McGwire HR 47 15.00 6.00
❑ 220AV Mark McGwire HR 48 15.00 6.00
❑ 220AW Mark McGwire HR 49 15.00 6.00
❑ 220AX Mark McGwire HR 50 15.00 6.00
❑ 220AY Mark McGwire HR 51 15.00 6.00
❑ 220AZ Mark McGwire HR 52 15.00 6.00
❑ 220BB Mark McGwire HR 53 15.00 6.00

❑ 220CC	Mark McGwire HR 54	15.00	6.00
❑ 220DD	Mark McGwire HR 55	15.00	6.00
❑ 220EE	Mark McGwire HR 56	15.00	6.00
❑ 220FF	Mark McGwire HR 57	15.00	6.00
❑ 220GG	Mark McGwire HR 58	15.00	6.00
❑ 220HH	Mark McGwire HR 59	15.00	6.00
❑ 220II	Mark McGwire HR 60	15.00	6.00
❑ 220JJ	Mark McGwire HR 61	30.00	12.50
❑ 220KK	Mark McGwire HR 62	40.00	15.00
❑ 220LL	Mark McGwire HR 63	15.00	6.00
❑ 220MM	Mark McGwire HR 64	15.00	6.00
❑ 220NN	Mark McGwire HR 65	15.00	6.00
❑ 220OO	Mark McGwire HR 66	15.00	6.00
❑ 220PP	Mark McGwire HR 67	15.00	6.00
❑ 220QQ	Mark McGwire HR 68	15.00	6.00
❑ 220RR	Mark McGwire HR 69	15.00	6.00
❑ 220SS	Mark McGwire HR 70	100.00	50.00
❑ 221	Larry Walker LL	.20	.07
❑ 222	Bernie Williams LL	.20	.07
❑ 223	Mark McGwire LL	.60	.25
❑ 224	Ken Griffey Jr. LL	.50	.20
❑ 225	Sammy Sosa LL	.30	.10
❑ 226	Juan Gonzalez LL	.20	.07
❑ 227	Dante Bichette LL	.20	.07
❑ 228	Alex Rodriguez LL	.50	.20
❑ 229	Sammy Sosa LL	.30	.10
❑ 230	Derek Jeter LL	.60	.25
❑ 231	Greg Maddux LL	.50	.20
❑ 232	Roger Clemens LL	.50	.20
❑ 233	Ricky Ledee WS	.20	.07
❑ 234	Chuck Knoblauch WS	.20	.07
❑ 235	Bernie Williams WS	.20	.07
❑ 236	Tino Martinez WS	.20	.07
❑ 237	Orlando Hernandez WS	.20	.07
❑ 238	Scott Brosius WS	.20	.07
❑ 239	Andy Pettitte WS	.20	.07
❑ 240	Mariano Rivera WS	.30	.10
❑ 241	Checklist 1	.20	.07
❑ 242	Checklist 2	.20	.07
❑ 243	Tom Glavine	.30	.10
❑ 244	Andy Benes	.20	.07
❑ 245	Sandy Alomar Jr.	.20	.07
❑ 246	Wilton Guerrero	.20	.07
❑ 247	Alex Gonzalez	.20	.07
❑ 248	Roberto Alomar	.30	.10
❑ 249	Ruben Rivera	.20	.07
❑ 250	Eric Chavez	.20	.07
❑ 251	Ellis Burks	.20	.07
❑ 252	Richie Sexson	.20	.07
❑ 253	Steve Finley	.20	.07
❑ 254	Dwight Gooden	.20	.07
❑ 255	Dustin Hermanson	.20	.07
❑ 256	Kirk Rueter	.20	.07
❑ 257	Steve Trachsel	.20	.07
❑ 258	Gregg Jefferies	.20	.07
❑ 259	Matt Stairs	.20	.07
❑ 260	Shane Reynolds	.20	.07
❑ 261	Gregg Olson	.20	.07
❑ 262	Kevin Tapani	.20	.07
❑ 263	Matt Morris	.20	.07
❑ 264	Carl Pavano	.20	.07
❑ 265	Nomar Garciaparra	.75	.30
❑ 266	Kevin Young	.20	.07
❑ 267	Rick Helling	.20	.07
❑ 268	Matt Franco	.20	.07
❑ 269	Brian McRae	.20	.07
❑ 270	Cal Ripken	1.50	.60
❑ 271	Jeff Abbott	.20	.07
❑ 272	Tony Batista	.20	.07
❑ 273	Bill Simas	.20	.07
❑ 274	Brian Hunter	.20	.07
❑ 275	John Franco	.20	.07
❑ 276	Devon White	.20	.07
❑ 277	Rickey Henderson	.50	.20
❑ 278	Chuck Finley	.20	.07
❑ 279	Mike Blowers	.20	.07
❑ 280	Mark Grace	.30	.10
❑ 281	Randy Winn	.20	.07
❑ 282	Bobby Bonilla	.20	.07
❑ 283	David Justice	.20	.07
❑ 284	Shane Monahan	.20	.07
❑ 285	Kevin Brown	.30	.10
❑ 286	Todd Zeile	.20	.07
❑ 287	Al Martin	.20	.07
❑ 288	Troy O'Leary	.20	.07
❑ 289	Darryl Hamilton	.20	.07
❑ 290	Tino Martinez	.30	.10
❑ 291	David Ortiz	.50	.20
❑ 292	Tony Clark	.20	.07
❑ 293	Ryan Minor	.20	.07
❑ 294	Mark Leiter	.20	.07
❑ 295	Wally Joyner	.20	.07
❑ 296	Cliff Floyd	.20	.07
❑ 297	Shawn Estes	.20	.07
❑ 298	Pat Hentgen	.20	.07
❑ 299	Scott Elarton	.20	.07
❑ 300	Alex Rodriguez	.75	.30
❑ 301	Ozzie Guillen	.20	.07
❑ 302	Hideo Nomo	.50	.20
❑ 303	Ryan McGuire	.20	.07
❑ 304	Brad Ausmus	.20	.07
❑ 305	Alex Gonzalez	.20	.07
❑ 306	Brian Jordan	.20	.07
❑ 307	John Jaha	.20	.07
❑ 308	Mark Grudzielanek	.20	.07
❑ 309	Juan Guzman	.20	.07
❑ 310	Tony Womack	.20	.07
❑ 311	Dennis Reyes	.20	.07
❑ 312	Marty Cordova	.20	.07
❑ 313	Ramiro Mendoza	.20	.07
❑ 314	Robin Ventura	.20	.07
❑ 315	Rafael Palmeiro	.30	.10
❑ 316	Ramon Martinez	.20	.07
❑ 317	Pedro Astacio	.20	.07
❑ 318	Dave Hollins	.20	.07
❑ 319	Tom Candiotti	.20	.07
❑ 320	Al Leiter	.20	.07
❑ 321	Rico Brogna	.20	.07
❑ 322	Reggie Jefferson	.20	.07
❑ 323	Bernard Gilkey	.20	.07
❑ 324	Jason Giambi	.20	.07
❑ 325	Craig Biggio	.30	.10
❑ 326	Troy Glaus	.30	.10
❑ 327	Delino DeShields	.20	.07
❑ 328	Fernando Vina	.20	.07
❑ 329	John Smoltz	.30	.10
❑ 330	Jeff Kent	.20	.07
❑ 331	Roy Halladay	.20	.07
❑ 332	Andy Ashby	.20	.07
❑ 333	Tim Wakefield	.20	.07
❑ 334	Roger Clemens	1.00	.40
❑ 335	Bernie Williams	.30	.10
❑ 336	Desi Relaford	.20	.07
❑ 337	John Burkett	.20	.07
❑ 338	Mike Hampton	.20	.07
❑ 339	Royce Clayton	.20	.07
❑ 340	Mike Piazza	.75	.30
❑ 341	Jeremi Gonzalez	.20	.07
❑ 342	Mike Lansing	.20	.07
❑ 343	Jamie Moyer	.20	.07
❑ 344	Ron Coomer	.20	.07
❑ 345	Barry Larkin	.30	.10
❑ 346	Fernando Tatis	.20	.07
❑ 347	Chili Davis	.20	.07
❑ 348	Bobby Higginson	.20	.07
❑ 349	Hal Morris	.20	.07
❑ 350	Larry Walker	.20	.07
❑ 351	Carlos Guillen	.20	.07
❑ 352	Miguel Tejada	.20	.07
❑ 353	Travis Fryman	.20	.07
❑ 354	Jarrod Washburn	.20	.07
❑ 355	Chipper Jones	.50	.20
❑ 356	Todd Stottlemyre	.20	.07
❑ 357	Henry Rodriguez	.20	.07
❑ 358	Eli Marrero	.20	.07
❑ 359	Alan Benes	.20	.07
❑ 360	Tim Salmon	.30	.10
❑ 361	Luis Gonzalez	.20	.07
❑ 362	Scott Spiezio	.20	.07
❑ 363	Chris Carpenter	.20	.07
❑ 364	Bobby Howry	.20	.07
❑ 365	Raul Mondesi	.20	.07
❑ 366	Ugueth Urbina	.20	.07
❑ 367	Tom Evans	.20	.07
❑ 368	Kerry Ligtenberg RC	.25	.08
❑ 369	Adrian Beltre	.20	.07
❑ 370	Ryan Klesko	.20	.07
❑ 371	Wilson Alvarez	.20	.07
❑ 372	John Thomson	.20	.07
❑ 373	Tony Saunders	.20	.07
❑ 374	Dave Mlicki	.20	.07
❑ 375	Ken Caminiti	.20	.07
❑ 376	Jay Buhner	.20	.07
❑ 377	Bill Mueller	.20	.07
❑ 378	Jeff Blauser	.20	.07
❑ 379	Edgar Renteria	.20	.07
❑ 380	Jim Thome	.30	.10
❑ 381	Joey Hamilton	.20	.07
❑ 382	Calvin Pickering	.20	.07
❑ 383	Marquis Grissom	.20	.07
❑ 384	Omar Daal	.20	.07
❑ 385	Curt Schilling	.20	.07
❑ 386	Jose Cruz Jr.	.20	.07
❑ 387	Chris Widger	.20	.07
❑ 388	Pete Harnisch	.20	.07
❑ 389	Charles Nagy	.20	.07
❑ 390	Tom Gordon	.20	.07
❑ 391	Bobby Smith	.20	.07
❑ 392	Derrick Gibson	.20	.07
❑ 393	Jeff Conine	.20	.07
❑ 394	Carlos Perez	.20	.07
❑ 395	Barry Bonds	1.50	.60
❑ 396	Mark McLemore	.20	.07
❑ 397	Juan Encarnacion	.20	.07
❑ 398	Wade Boggs	.30	.10
❑ 399	Ivan Rodriguez	.30	.10
❑ 400	Moises Alou	.20	.07
❑ 401	Jeromy Burnitz	.20	.07
❑ 402	Sean Casey	.20	.07
❑ 403	Jose Offerman	.20	.07
❑ 404	Joe Fontenot	.20	.07
❑ 405	Kevin Millwood	.20	.07
❑ 406	Lance Johnson	.20	.07
❑ 407	Richard Hidalgo	.20	.07
❑ 408	Mike Jackson	.20	.07
❑ 409	Brian Anderson	.20	.07
❑ 410	Jeff Shaw	.20	.07
❑ 411	Preston Wilson	.20	.07
❑ 412	Todd Hundley	.20	.07
❑ 413	Jim Parque	.20	.07
❑ 414	Justin Baughman	.20	.07
❑ 415	Dante Bichette	.20	.07
❑ 416	Paul O'Neill	.30	.10
❑ 417	Miguel Cairo	.20	.07
❑ 418	Randy Johnson	.50	.20
❑ 419	Jesus Sanchez	.20	.07
❑ 420	Carlos Delgado	.20	.07
❑ 421	Ricky Ledee	.20	.07
❑ 422	Orlando Hernandez	.20	.07
❑ 423	Frank Thomas	.50	.20
❑ 424	Pokey Reese	.20	.07
❑ 425	C.Lee/M.Lowell	.40	.15
❑ 426	M.Cuddyer/DeRosa/Hairston	.25	.08
❑ 427	M.Anderson/Belliard/Cabrera	.40	.15
❑ 428	M.Bowie/P.Norton RC/Wolf	.25	.08
❑ 429	J.Cressend RC/Rocker	.40	.15
❑ 430	R.Mateo/M.Zywica RC	.25	.08
❑ 431	J.LaRue/LeCroy/Meluskey	.25	.08
❑ 432	Gabe Kapler	.40	.15
❑ 433	A.Kennedy/M.Lopez RC	.25	.08
❑ 434	Jose Fernandez RC/C.Truby	.25	.08
❑ 435	Doug Mientkiewicz RC	.50	.20
❑ 436	R.Brown RC/V.Wells	.25	.08
❑ 437	A.J. Burnett RC	.75	.30
❑ 438	M.Belisle/M.Roney RC	.25	.08
❑ 439	A.Kearns/C.George RC	1.50	.60
❑ 440	N.Cornejo/N.Bump RC	.25	.08
❑ 441	B.Lidge/M.Nannini RC	1.50	.60
❑ 442	M.Holliday/J.Winchester RC	4.00	1.50
❑ 443	A.Everett/C.Ambres RC	.50	.20
❑ 444	P.Burrell/E.Valent RC	1.50	.60
❑ 445	Roger Clemens SK	.50	.20
❑ 446	Kerry Wood SK	.20	.07
❑ 447	Curt Schilling SK	.20	.07
❑ 448	Randy Johnson SK	.30	.10
❑ 449	Pedro Martinez SK	.30	.10
❑ 450	Bagwell/Galar/McGwire AT	.50	.20
❑ 451	Olerud/Thome/Martinez AT	.20	.07
❑ 452	ARod/Nomar/Jeter AT	.60	.25
❑ 453	Castilla/Jones/Rolen AT	.30	.10
❑ 454	Sosa/Griffey/Gonzalez AT	.50	.20
❑ 455	Bonds/Ramirez/Walker AT	.75	.30
❑ 456	Thomas/Salmon/Justice AT	.50	.20
❑ 457	Lee/Helton/Grieve AT	.20	.07
❑ 458	Guerrero/Vaughn/B.Will AT	.20	.07
❑ 459	Piazza/IRod/Kendall AT	.50	.20
❑ 460	Clemens/Wood/Maddux AT	.50	.20
❑ 461A	Sammy Sosa HR 1	15.00	6.00

❑ 461B Sammy Sosa HR 2	6.00	2.50
❑ 461C Sammy Sosa HR 3	6.00	2.50
❑ 461D Sammy Sosa HR 4	6.00	2.50
❑ 461E Sammy Sosa HR 5	6.00	2.50
❑ 461F Sammy Sosa HR 6	6.00	2.50
❑ 461G Sammy Sosa HR 7	6.00	2.50
❑ 461H Sammy Sosa HR 8	6.00	2.50
❑ 461I Sammy Sosa HR 9	6.00	2.50
❑ 461J Sammy Sosa HR 10	6.00	2.50
❑ 461K Sammy Sosa HR 11	6.00	2.50
❑ 461L Sammy Sosa HR 12	6.00	2.50
❑ 461M Sammy Sosa HR 13	6.00	2.50
❑ 461N Sammy Sosa HR 14	6.00	2.50
❑ 461O Sammy Sosa HR 15	6.00	2.50
❑ 461P Sammy Sosa HR 16	6.00	2.50
❑ 461Q Sammy Sosa HR 17	6.00	2.50
❑ 461R Sammy Sosa HR 18	6.00	2.50
❑ 461S Sammy Sosa HR 19	6.00	2.50
❑ 461T Sammy Sosa HR 20	6.00	2.50
❑ 461U Sammy Sosa HR 21	6.00	2.50
❑ 461V Sammy Sosa HR 22	6.00	2.50
❑ 461W Sammy Sosa HR 23	6.00	2.50
❑ 461X Sammy Sosa HR 24	6.00	2.50
❑ 461Y Sammy Sosa HR 25	6.00	2.50
❑ 461Z Sammy Sosa HR 26	6.00	2.50
❑ 461AA Sammy Sosa HR 27	6.00	2.50
❑ 461AB Sammy Sosa HR 28	6.00	2.50
❑ 461AC Sammy Sosa HR 29	6.00	2.50
❑ 461AD Sammy Sosa HR 30	6.00	2.50
❑ 461AE Sammy Sosa HR 31	6.00	2.50
❑ 461AF Sammy Sosa HR 32	6.00	2.50
❑ 461AG Sammy Sosa HR 33	6.00	2.50
❑ 461AH Sammy Sosa HR 34	6.00	2.50
❑ 461AI Sammy Sosa HR 35	6.00	2.50
❑ 461AJ Sammy Sosa HR 36	6.00	2.50
❑ 461AK Sammy Sosa HR 37	6.00	2.50
❑ 461AL Sammy Sosa HR 38	6.00	2.50
❑ 461AM Sammy Sosa HR 39	6.00	2.50
❑ 461AN Sammy Sosa HR 40	6.00	2.50
❑ 461AO Sammy Sosa HR 41	6.00	2.50
❑ 461AP Sammy Sosa HR 42	6.00	2.50
❑ 461AR Sammy Sosa HR 43	6.00	2.50
❑ 461AS Sammy Sosa HR 44	6.00	2.50
❑ 461AT Sammy Sosa HR 45	6.00	2.50
❑ 461AU Sammy Sosa HR 46	6.00	2.50
❑ 461AV Sammy Sosa HR 47	6.00	2.50
❑ 461AW Sammy Sosa HR 48	6.00	2.50
❑ 461AX Sammy Sosa HR 49	6.00	2.50
❑ 461AY Sammy Sosa HR 50	6.00	2.50
❑ 461AZ Sammy Sosa HR 51	6.00	2.50
❑ 461BB Sammy Sosa HR 52	6.00	2.50
❑ 461CC Sammy Sosa HR 53	6.00	2.50
❑ 461DD Sammy Sosa HR 54	6.00	2.50
❑ 461EE Sammy Sosa HR 55	6.00	2.50
❑ 461FF Sammy Sosa HR 56	6.00	2.50
❑ 461GG Sammy Sosa HR 57	6.00	2.50
❑ 461HH Sammy Sosa HR 58	6.00	2.50
❑ 461II Sammy Sosa HR 59	6.00	2.50
❑ 461JJ Sammy Sosa HR 60	6.00	2.50
❑ 461KK Sammy Sosa HR 61	15.00	6.00
❑ 461LL Sammy Sosa HR 62	20.00	8.00
❑ 461MM Sammy Sosa HR 63	8.00	3.00
❑ 461NN Sammy Sosa HR 64	8.00	3.00
❑ 461OO Sammy Sosa HR 65	8.00	3.00
❑ 461PP Sammy Sosa HR 66	25.00	10.00
❑ 462 Checklist	.20	.07
❑ 463 Checklist	.20	.07

1999 Topps Traded

❑ COMP.FACT.SET (122)	40.00	15.00
❑ COMPLETE SET (121)	25.00	10.00
❑ T1 Seth Etherton	.20	.07
❑ T2 Mark Harriger RC	.25	.08
❑ T3 Matt Wise RC	.25	.08
❑ T4 Carlos Eduardo Hernandez RC	.40	.15
❑ T5 Julio Lugo RC	.75	.30
❑ T6 Mike Nannini	.20	.07
❑ T7 Justin Bowles RC	.25	.08
❑ T8 Mark Mulder RC	1.50	.60
❑ T9 Roberto Vaz RC	.25	.08
❑ T10 Felipe Lopez RC	1.50	.60
❑ T11 Matt Belisle	.50	.20
❑ T12 Micah Bowie	.20	.07
❑ T13 Ruben Quevedo RC	.25	.08
❑ T14 Jose Garcia RC	.25	.08
❑ T15 David Kelton RC	.25	.08

❑ T16 Phil Norton	.20	.07
❑ T17 Corey Patterson RC	1.00	.40
❑ T18 Ron Walker RC	.25	.08
❑ T19 Paul Hoover RC	.25	.08
❑ T20 Ryan Rupe RC	.25	.08
❑ T21 J.D. Closser RC	.40	.15
❑ T22 Rob Ryan RC	.25	.08
❑ T23 Steve Colyer RC	.25	.08
❑ T24 Bubba Crosby RC	.60	.25
❑ T25 Luke Prokopec RC	.25	.08
❑ T26 Matt Blank RC	.25	.08
❑ T27 Josh McKinley	.20	.07
❑ T28 Nate Bump	.20	.07
❑ T29 Giuseppe Chiaramonte RC	.25	.08
❑ T30 Arturo McDowell	.20	.07
❑ T31 Tony Torcato	.20	.07
❑ T32 Dave Roberts RC	.60	.25
❑ T33 C.C. Sabathia RC	1.50	.60
❑ T34 Sean Spencer RC	.25	.08
❑ T35 Chip Ambres	.20	.07
❑ T36 A.J. Burnett	1.00	.40
❑ T37 Mo Bruce RC	.25	.08
❑ T38 Jason Tyner	.20	.07
❑ T39 Mamon Tucker	.20	.07
❑ T40 Sean Burroughs RC	.60	.25
❑ T41 Kevin Eberwein RC	.25	.08
❑ T42 Junior Herndon RC	.25	.08
❑ T43 Bryan Wolff RC	.25	.08
❑ T44 Pat Burrell	1.25	.50
❑ T45 Eric Valent	.20	.07
❑ T46 Carlos Pena RC	.50	.20
❑ T47 Mike Zywica	.20	.07
❑ T48 Adam Everett	.30	.10
❑ T49 Juan Pena RC	.40	.15
❑ T50 Adam Dunn RC	4.00	1.50
❑ T51 Austin Kearns	1.25	.50
❑ T52 Jacobo Sequea RC	.25	.08
❑ T53 Choo Freeman	.20	.07
❑ T54 Jeff Winchester	.20	.07
❑ T55 Matt Burch	.20	.07
❑ T56 Chris George	.20	.07
❑ T57 Scott Mullen RC	.25	.08
❑ T58 Kit Pellow	.20	.07
❑ T59 Mark Quinn RC	.25	.08
❑ T60 Nate Cornejo	.25	.08
❑ T61 Ryan Mills	.20	.07
❑ T62 Kevin Beirne RC	.25	.08
❑ T63 Kip Wells RC	.40	.15
❑ T64 Juan Rivera RC	1.00	.40
❑ T65 Alfonso Soriano RC	5.00	2.00
❑ T66 Josh Hamilton RC	5.00	2.00
❑ T67 Josh Girdley RC	.25	.08
❑ T68 Kyle Snyder RC	.25	.08
❑ T69 Mike Paradis RC	.25	.08
❑ T70 Jason Jennings RC	.60	.25
❑ T71 David Walling RC	.25	.08
❑ T72 Omar Ortiz RC	.25	.08
❑ T73 Jay Gehrke RC	.40	.15
❑ T74 Casey Burns RC	.40	.15
❑ T75 Carl Crawford RC	4.00	1.50
❑ T76 Reggie Sanders	.20	.07
❑ T77 Will Clark	.30	.10
❑ T78 David Wells	.20	.07
❑ T79 Paul Konerko	.20	.07
❑ T80 Armando Benitez	.20	.07
❑ T81 Brant Brown	.20	.07
❑ T82 Mo Vaughn	.20	.07
❑ T83 Jose Canseco	.30	.10
❑ T84 Albert Belle	.20	.07
❑ T85 Dean Palmer	.20	.07
❑ T86 Greg Vaughn	.20	.07
❑ T87 Mark Clark	.20	.07
❑ T88 Pat Meares	.20	.07
❑ T89 Eric Davis	.20	.07
❑ T90 Brian Giles	.20	.07
❑ T91 Jeff Brantley	.20	.07
❑ T92 Bret Boone	.20	.07
❑ T93 Ron Gant	.20	.07
❑ T94 Mike Cameron	.20	.07
❑ T95 Charles Johnson	.20	.07
❑ T96 Denny Neagle	.20	.07
❑ T97 Brian Hunter	.20	.07
❑ T98 Jose Hernandez	.20	.07
❑ T99 Rick Aguilera	.20	.07
❑ T100 Tony Batista	.20	.07
❑ T101 Roger Cedeno	.20	.07
❑ T102 Creighton Gubanich RC	.25	.08
❑ T103 Tim Belcher	.20	.07
❑ T104 Bruce Aven	.20	.07
❑ T105 Brian Daubach RC	.40	.15
❑ T106 Ed Sprague	.20	.07
❑ T107 Michael Tucker	.20	.07
❑ T108 Homer Bush	.20	.07
❑ T109 Armando Reynoso	.20	.07
❑ T110 Brook Fordyce	.20	.07
❑ T111 Matt Mantei	.20	.07
❑ T112 Dave Mlicki	.20	.07
❑ T113 Kenny Rogers	.20	.07
❑ T114 Livan Hernandez	.20	.07
❑ T115 Butch Huskey	.20	.07
❑ T116 David Segui	.20	.07
❑ T117 Darryl Hamilton	.20	.07
❑ T118 Terry Mulholland	.20	.07
❑ T119 Randy Velarde	.20	.07
❑ T120 Bill Taylor	.20	.07
❑ T121 Kevin Appier	.20	.07

2000 Topps

❑ COMPLETE SET (478)	50.00	20.00
❑ COMP.HOBBY SET (478)	60.00	30.00
❑ COMPLETE SERIES 1 (239)	25.00	10.00
❑ COMPLETE SERIES 2 (240)	25.00	10.00
❑ MCGWIRE MM SET (5)	12.00	5.00
❑ AARON MM SET (5)	10.00	4.00
❑ RIPKEN MM SET (5)	15.00	6.00
❑ BOGGS MM SET (5)	3.00	1.25
❑ GWYNN MM SET (5)	6.00	2.50
❑ GRIFFEY MM SET (5)	8.00	3.00
❑ BONDS MM SET (5)	12.00	5.00
❑ SOSA MM SET (5)	8.00	3.00
❑ JETER MM SET (5)	12.00	5.00
❑ A.ROD MM SET (5)	8.00	3.00
❑ 1 Mark McGwire	1.25	.50
❑ 2 Tony Gwynn	.60	.25
❑ 3 Wade Boggs	.30	.10
❑ 4 Cal Ripken	1.50	.60
❑ 5 Matt Williams	.20	.07
❑ 6 Jay Buhner	.20	.07
❑ 8 Jeff Conine	.20	.07
❑ 9 Todd Greene	.20	.07
❑ 10 Mike Lieberthal	.20	.07
❑ 11 Steve Avery	.20	.07
❑ 12 Bret Saberhagen	.20	.07
❑ 13 Magglio Ordonez	.20	.07
❑ 14 Brad Radke	.20	.07
❑ 15 Derek Jeter	1.25	.50

❑ 16	Javy Lopez	.20	.07
❑ 17	Russ Davis	.20	.07
❑ 18	Armando Benitez	.20	.07
❑ 19	B.J. Surhoff	.20	.07
❑ 20	Darryl Kile	.20	.07
❑ 21	Mark Lewis	.20	.07
❑ 22	Mike Williams	.20	.07
❑ 23	Mark McLemore	.20	.07
❑ 24	Sterling Hitchcock	.20	.07
❑ 25	Darin Erstad	.20	.07
❑ 26	Ricky Gutierrez	.20	.07
❑ 27	John Jaha	.20	.07
❑ 28	Homer Bush	.20	.07
❑ 29	Darrin Fletcher	.20	.07
❑ 30	Mark Grace	.30	.10
❑ 31	Fred McGriff	.30	.10
❑ 32	Omar Daal	.20	.07
❑ 33	Eric Karros	.20	.07
❑ 34	Orlando Cabrera	.20	.07
❑ 35	J.T. Snow	.20	.07
❑ 36	Luis Castillo	.20	.07
❑ 37	Rey Ordonez	.20	.07
❑ 38	Bob Abreu	.20	.07
❑ 39	Warren Morris	.20	.07
❑ 40	Juan Gonzalez	.20	.07
❑ 41	Mike Lansing	.20	.07
❑ 42	Chili Davis	.20	.07
❑ 43	Dean Palmer	.20	.07
❑ 44	Hank Aaron	.75	.30
❑ 45	Jeff Bagwell	.30	.10
❑ 46	Jose Valentin	.20	.07
❑ 47	Shannon Stewart	.20	.07
❑ 48	Kent Bottenfield	.20	.07
❑ 49	Jeff Shaw	.20	.07
❑ 50	Sammy Sosa	.50	.20
❑ 51	Randy Johnson	.50	.20
❑ 52	Benny Agbayani	.20	.07
❑ 53	Dante Bichette	.20	.07
❑ 54	Pete Harnisch	.20	.07
❑ 55	Frank Thomas	.50	.20
❑ 56	Jorge Posada	.30	.10
❑ 57	Todd Walker	.20	.07
❑ 58	Juan Encarnacion	.20	.07
❑ 59	Mike Sweeney	.20	.07
❑ 60	Pedro Martinez	.30	.10
❑ 61	Lee Stevens	.20	.07
❑ 62	Brian Giles	.20	.07
❑ 63	Chad Ogea	.20	.07
❑ 64	Ivan Rodriguez	.30	.10
❑ 65	Roger Cedeno	.20	.07
❑ 66	David Justice	.20	.07
❑ 67	Steve Trachsel	.20	.07
❑ 68	Eli Marrero	.20	.07
❑ 69	Dave Nilsson	.20	.07
❑ 70	Ken Caminiti	.20	.07
❑ 71	Tim Raines	.20	.07
❑ 72	Brian Jordan	.20	.07
❑ 73	Jeff Blauser	.20	.07
❑ 74	Bernard Gilkey	.20	.07
❑ 75	John Flaherty	.20	.07
❑ 76	Brent Mayne	.20	.07
❑ 77	Jose Vidro	.20	.07
❑ 78	David Bell	.20	.07
❑ 79	Bruce Aven	.20	.07
❑ 80	John Olerud	.20	.07
❑ 81	Pokey Reese	.20	.07
❑ 82	Woody Williams	.20	.07
❑ 83	Ed Sprague	.20	.07
❑ 84	Joe Girardi	.20	.07
❑ 85	Barry Larkin	.30	.10
❑ 86	Mike Caruso	.20	.07
❑ 87	Bobby Higginson	.20	.07
❑ 88	Roberto Kelly	.20	.07
❑ 89	Edgar Martinez	.30	.10
❑ 90	Mark Kotsay	.20	.07
❑ 91	Paul Sorrento	.20	.07
❑ 92	Eric Young	.20	.07
❑ 93	Carlos Delgado	.20	.07
❑ 94	Troy Glaus	.20	.07
❑ 95	Ben Grieve	.20	.07
❑ 96	Jose Lima	.20	.07
❑ 97	Garret Anderson	.20	.07
❑ 98	Luis Gonzalez	.20	.07
❑ 99	Carl Pavano	.20	.07
❑ 100	Alex Rodriguez	.75	.30
❑ 101	Preston Wilson	.20	.07
❑ 102	Ron Gant	.20	.07
❑ 103	Brady Anderson	.20	.07
❑ 104	Rickey Henderson	.50	.20
❑ 105	Gary Sheffield	.20	.07
❑ 106	Mickey Morandini	.20	.07
❑ 107	Jim Edmonds	.20	.07
❑ 108	Kris Benson	.20	.07
❑ 109	Adrian Beltre	.20	.07
❑ 110	Alex Fernandez	.20	.07
❑ 111	Dan Wilson	.20	.07
❑ 112	Mark Clark	.20	.07
❑ 113	Greg Vaughn	.20	.07
❑ 114	Neifi Perez	.20	.07
❑ 115	Paul O'Neill	.30	.10
❑ 116	Jermaine Dye	.20	.07
❑ 117	Todd Jones	.20	.07
❑ 118	Terry Steinbach	.20	.07
❑ 119	Greg Norton	.20	.07
❑ 120	Curt Schilling	.20	.07
❑ 121	Todd Zeile	.20	.07
❑ 122	Edgardo Alfonzo	.20	.07
❑ 123	Ryan McGuire	.20	.07
❑ 124	Rich Aurilia	.20	.07
❑ 125	John Smoltz	.30	.10
❑ 126	Bob Wickman	.20	.07
❑ 127	Richard Hidalgo	.20	.07
❑ 128	Chuck Finley	.20	.07
❑ 129	Billy Wagner	.20	.07
❑ 130	Todd Hundley	.20	.07
❑ 131	Dwight Gooden	.20	.07
❑ 132	Russ Ortiz	.20	.07
❑ 133	Mike Lowell	.20	.07
❑ 134	Reggie Sanders	.20	.07
❑ 135	John Valentin	.20	.07
❑ 136	Brad Ausmus	.20	.07
❑ 137	Chad Kreuter	.20	.07
❑ 138	David Cone	.20	.07
❑ 139	Brook Fordyce	.20	.07
❑ 140	Roberto Alomar	.30	.10
❑ 141	Charles Nagy	.20	.07
❑ 142	Brian Hunter	.20	.07
❑ 143	Mike Mussina	.30	.10
❑ 144	Robin Ventura	.30	.10
❑ 145	Kevin Brown	.30	.10
❑ 146	Pat Hentgen	.20	.07
❑ 147	Ryan Klesko	.20	.07
❑ 148	Derek Bell	.20	.07
❑ 149	Andy Sheets	.20	.07
❑ 150	Larry Walker	.20	.07
❑ 151	Scott Williamson	.20	.07
❑ 152	Jose Offerman	.20	.07
❑ 153	Doug Mientkiewicz	.20	.07
❑ 154	John Snyder RC	.40	.15
❑ 155	Sandy Alomar Jr.	.20	.07
❑ 156	Joe Nathan	.20	.07
❑ 157	Lance Johnson	.20	.07
❑ 158	Odalis Perez	.20	.07
❑ 159	Hideo Nomo	.50	.20
❑ 160	Steve Finley	.20	.07
❑ 161	Dave Martinez	.20	.07
❑ 162	Matt Walbeck	.20	.07
❑ 163	Bill Spiers	.20	.07
❑ 164	Fernando Tatis	.20	.07
❑ 165	Kenny Lofton	.20	.07
❑ 166	Paul Byrd	.20	.07
❑ 167	Aaron Sele	.20	.07
❑ 168	Eddie Taubensee	.20	.07
❑ 169	Reggie Jefferson	.20	.07
❑ 170	Roger Clemens	1.00	.40
❑ 171	Francisco Cordova	.20	.07
❑ 172	Mike Bordick	.20	.07
❑ 173	Wally Joyner	.20	.07
❑ 174	Marvin Benard	.20	.07
❑ 175	Jason Kendall	.20	.07
❑ 176	Mike Stanley	.20	.07
❑ 177	Chad Allen	.20	.07
❑ 178	Carlos Beltran	.20	.07
❑ 179	Deivi Cruz	.20	.07
❑ 180	Chipper Jones	.50	.20
❑ 181	Vladimir Guerrero	.50	.20
❑ 182	Dave Burba	.20	.07
❑ 183	Tom Goodwin	.20	.07
❑ 184	Brian Daubach	.20	.07
❑ 185	Jay Bell	.20	.07
❑ 186	Roy Halladay	.20	.07
❑ 187	Miguel Tejada	.20	.07
❑ 188	Armando Rios	.20	.07
❑ 189	Fernando Vina	.20	.07
❑ 190	Eric Davis	.20	.07
❑ 191	Henry Rodriguez	.20	.07
❑ 192	Joe McEwing	.20	.07
❑ 193	Jeff Kent	.20	.07
❑ 194	Mike Jackson	.20	.07
❑ 195	Mike Morgan	.20	.07
❑ 196	Jeff Montgomery	.20	.07
❑ 197	Jeff Zimmerman	.20	.07
❑ 198	Tony Fernandez	.20	.07
❑ 199	Jason Giambi	.20	.07
❑ 200	Jose Canseco	.30	.10
❑ 201	Alex Gonzalez	.20	.07
❑ 202	J.Cust/Colangelo/D.Brown	.40	.15
❑ 203	A.Soriano/F.Lopez	.50	.20
❑ 204	Durazo/Burrell/Johnson	.40	.15
❑ 205	John Sneed RC/K.Wells	.40	.15
❑ 206	Kalinowski/Tejera/Mears RC	.40	.15
❑ 207	L.Berkman/C.Patterson	.40	.15
❑ 208	K.Pellow/K.Barker/R.Branyan	.40	.15
❑ 209	B.Garbe/L.Bigbie RC	.50	.20
❑ 210	B.Bradley RC/E.Munson	.40	.15
❑ 211	J.Girdley/K.Snyder	.40	.15
❑ 212	Chance Caple RC/J.Jennings	.40	.15
❑ 213	B.Myers/R.Christianson RC	1.00	.40
❑ 214	J.Stumm/R.Purvis RC	.40	.15
❑ 215	D.Walling/M.Paradis	.40	.15
❑ 216	O.Ortiz/J.Gehrke	.40	.15
❑ 217	David Cone HL	.20	.07
❑ 218	Jose Jimenez HL	.20	.07
❑ 219	Chris Singleton HL	.20	.07
❑ 220	Fernando Tatis HL	.20	.07
❑ 221	Todd Helton HL	.20	.07
❑ 222	Kevin Millwood DIV	.20	.07
❑ 223	Todd Pratt DIV	.20	.07
❑ 224	Orlando Hernandez DIV	.20	.07
❑ 225	Pedro Martinez DIV	.30	.10
❑ 226	Tom Glavine LCS	.20	.07
❑ 227	Bernie Williams LCS	.20	.07
❑ 228	Mariano Rivera WS	.30	.10
❑ 229	Tony Gwynn 20CB	.60	.25
❑ 230	Wade Boggs 20CB	.30	.10
❑ 231	Lance Johnson CB	.20	.07
❑ 232	Mark McGwire 20CB	1.25	.50
❑ 233	Rickey Henderson 20CB	.50	.20
❑ 234	Rickey Henderson 20CB	.50	.20
❑ 235	Roger Clemens 20CB	1.00	.40
❑ 236A	M.McGwire MM 1st HR	2.00	.75
❑ 236B	M.McGwire MM 1987 ROY	2.00	.75
❑ 236C	M.McGwire MM 62nd HR	2.00	.75
❑ 236D	M.McGwire MM 70th HR	2.00	.75
❑ 236E	M.McGwire MM 500th HR	2.00	.75
❑ 237A	H.Aaron MM 1st Career HR	2.00	.75
❑ 237B	H.Aaron MM 1957 MVP	2.00	.75
❑ 237C	H.Aaron MM 3000th Hit	2.00	.75
❑ 237D	H.Aaron MM 715th HR	2.00	.75
❑ 237E	H.Aaron MM 755th HR	2.00	.75
❑ 238A	C.Ripken MM 1982 ROY	4.00	1.50
❑ 238B	C.Ripken MM 1991 MVP	4.00	1.50
❑ 238C	C.Ripken MM 2131 Game	4.00	1.50
❑ 238D	C.Ripken MM Streak Ends	4.00	1.50
❑ 238E	C.Ripken MM 400th HR	4.00	1.50
❑ 239A	W.Boggs MM 1983 Batting	.75	.30
❑ 239B	W.Boggs MM 1988 Batting	.75	.30
❑ 239C	W.Boggs MM 2000th Hit	.75	.30
❑ 239D	W.Boggs MM 1996 Champs	.75	.30
❑ 239E	W.Boggs MM 3000th Hit	.75	.30
❑ 240A	T.Gwynn MM 1984 Batting	1.50	.60
❑ 240B	T.Gwynn MM 1984 NLCS	1.50	.60
❑ 240C	T.Gwynn MM 1995 Batting	1.50	.60
❑ 240D	T.Gwynn MM 1998 NLCS	1.50	.60
❑ 240E	T.Gwynn MM 3000th Hit	1.50	.60
❑ 241	Tom Glavine	.30	.10
❑ 242	David Wells	.20	.07
❑ 243	Kevin Appier	.20	.07
❑ 244	Troy Percival	.20	.07
❑ 245	Ray Lankford	.20	.07
❑ 246	Marquis Grissom	.20	.07
❑ 247	Randy Winn	.20	.07
❑ 248	Miguel Batista	.20	.07
❑ 249	Darren Dreifort	.20	.07
❑ 250	Barry Bonds	1.50	.60
❑ 251	Harold Baines	.20	.07
❑ 252	Cliff Floyd	.20	.07
❑ 253	Freddy Garcia	.20	.07

❑	254	Kenny Rogers	.20	.07
❑	255	Ben Davis	.20	.07
❑	256	Charles Johnson	.20	.07
❑	257	Bubba Trammell	.20	.07
❑	258	Desi Relaford	.20	.07
❑	259	Al Martin	.20	.07
❑	260	Andy Pettitte	.30	.10
❑	261	Carlos Lee	.20	.07
❑	262	Matt Lawton	.20	.07
❑	263	Andy Fox	.20	.07
❑	264	Chan Ho Park	.20	.07
❑	265	Billy Koch	.20	.07
❑	266	Dave Roberts	.20	.07
❑	267	Carl Everett	.20	.07
❑	268	Orel Hershiser	.20	.07
❑	269	Trot Nixon	.20	.07
❑	270	Rusty Greer	.20	.07
❑	271	Will Clark	.30	.10
❑	272	Quilvio Veras	.20	.07
❑	273	Rico Brogna	.20	.07
❑	274	Devon White	.20	.07
❑	275	Tim Hudson	.20	.07
❑	276	Mike Hampton	.20	.07
❑	277	Miguel Cairo	.20	.07
❑	278	Darren Oliver	.20	.07
❑	279	Jeff Cirillo	.20	.07
❑	280	Al Leiter	.20	.07
❑	281	Shane Andrews	.20	.07
❑	282	Carlos Febles	.20	.07
❑	283	Pedro Astacio	.20	.07
❑	284	Juan Guzman	.20	.07
❑	285	Orlando Hernandez	.20	.07
❑	286	Paul Konerko	.20	.07
❑	287	Tony Clark	.20	.07
❑	288	Aaron Boone	.20	.07
❑	289	Ismael Valdes	.20	.07
❑	290	Moises Alou	.20	.07
❑	291	Kevin Tapani	.20	.07
❑	292	John Franco	.20	.07
❑	293	Todd Zeile	.20	.07
❑	294	Jason Schmidt	.20	.07
❑	295	Johnny Damon	.30	.10
❑	296	Scott Brosius	.20	.07
❑	297	Travis Fryman	.20	.07
❑	298	Jose Vizcaino	.20	.07
❑	299	Eric Chavez	.20	.07
❑	300	Mike Piazza	.75	.30
❑	301	Matt Clement	.20	.07
❑	302	Cristian Guzman	.20	.07
❑	303	C.J. Nitkowski	.20	.07
❑	304	Michael Tucker	.20	.07
❑	305	Brett Tomko	.20	.07
❑	306	Mike Lansing	.20	.07
❑	307	Eric Owens	.20	.07
❑	308	Livan Hernandez	.20	.07
❑	309	Rondell White	.20	.07
❑	310	Todd Stottlemyre	.20	.07
❑	311	Chris Carpenter	.20	.07
❑	312	Ken Hill	.20	.07
❑	313	Mark Loretta	.20	.07
❑	314	John Rocker	.20	.07
❑	315	Richie Sexson	.20	.07
❑	316	Ruben Mateo	.20	.07
❑	317	Joe Randa	.20	.07
❑	318	Mike Sirotka	.20	.07
❑	319	Jose Rosado	.20	.07
❑	320	Matt Mantei	.20	.07
❑	321	Kevin Millwood	.20	.07
❑	322	Gary Disarcina	.20	.07
❑	323	Dustin Hermanson	.20	.07
❑	324	Mike Stanton	.20	.07
❑	325	Kirk Rueter	.20	.07
❑	326	Damian Miller RC	.40	.15
❑	327	Doug Glanville	.20	.07
❑	328	Scott Rolen	.30	.10
❑	329	Ray Durham	.20	.07
❑	330	Butch Huskey	.20	.07
❑	331	Mariano Rivera	.50	.20
❑	332	Darren Lewis	.20	.07
❑	333	Mike Timlin	.20	.07
❑	334	Mark Grudzielanek	.20	.07
❑	335	Mike Cameron	.20	.07
❑	336	Kelvim Escobar	.20	.07
❑	337	Bret Boone	.20	.07
❑	338	Mo Vaughn	.20	.07
❑	339	Craig Biggio	.30	.10
❑	340	Michael Barrett	.20	.07
❑	341	Marlon Anderson	.20	.07
❑	342	Bobby Jones	.20	.07
❑	343	John Halama	.20	.07
❑	344	Todd Ritchie	.20	.07
❑	345	Chuck Knoblauch	.20	.07
❑	346	Rick Reed	.20	.07
❑	347	Kelly Stinnett	.20	.07
❑	348	Tim Salmon	.30	.10
❑	349	A.J. Hinch	.20	.07
❑	350	Jose Cruz Jr.	.20	.07
❑	351	Roberto Hernandez	.20	.07
❑	352	Edgar Renteria	.20	.07
❑	353	Jose Hernandez	.20	.07
❑	354	Brad Fullmer	.20	.07
❑	355	Trevor Hoffman	.20	.07
❑	356	Troy O'Leary	.20	.07
❑	357	Justin Thompson	.20	.07
❑	358	Kevin Young	.20	.07
❑	359	Hideki Irabu	.20	.07
❑	360	Jim Thome	.30	.10
❑	361	Steve Karsay	.20	.07
❑	362	Octavio Dotel	.20	.07
❑	363	Omar Vizquel	.30	.10
❑	364	Raul Mondesi	.20	.07
❑	365	Shane Reynolds	.20	.07
❑	366	Bartolo Colon	.20	.07
❑	367	Chris Widger	.20	.07
❑	368	Gabe Kapler	.20	.07
❑	369	Bill Simas	.20	.07
❑	370	Tino Martinez	.30	.10
❑	371	John Thomson	.20	.07
❑	372	Delino Deshields	.20	.07
❑	373	Carlos Perez	.20	.07
❑	374	Eddie Perez	.20	.07
❑	375	Jeromy Burnitz	.20	.07
❑	376	Jimmy Haynes	.20	.07
❑	377	Travis Lee	.20	.07
❑	378	Darryl Hamilton	.20	.07
❑	379	Jamie Moyer	.20	.07
❑	380	Alex Gonzalez	.20	.07
❑	381	John Wetteland	.20	.07
❑	382	Vinny Castilla	.20	.07
❑	383	Jeff Suppan	.20	.07
❑	384	Jim Leyritz	.20	.07
❑	385	Robb Nen	.20	.07
❑	386	Wilson Alvarez	.20	.07
❑	387	Andres Galarraga	.20	.07
❑	388	Mike Remlinger	.20	.07
❑	389	Geoff Jenkins	.20	.07
❑	390	Matt Stairs	.20	.07
❑	391	Bill Mueller	.20	.07
❑	392	Mike Lowell	.20	.07
❑	393	Andy Ashby	.20	.07
❑	394	Ruben Rivera	.20	.07
❑	395	Todd Helton	.30	.10
❑	396	Bernie Williams	.30	.10
❑	397	Royce Clayton	.20	.07
❑	398	Manny Ramirez	.30	.10
❑	399	Kerry Wood	.20	.07
❑	400	Ken Griffey Jr.	.75	.30
❑	401	Enrique Wilson	.20	.07
❑	402	Joey Hamilton	.20	.07
❑	403	Shawn Estes	.20	.07
❑	404	Ugueth Urbina	.20	.07
❑	405	Albert Belle	.20	.07
❑	406	Rick Helling	.20	.07
❑	407	Steve Parris	.20	.07
❑	408	Eric Milton	.20	.07
❑	409	Dave Mlicki	.20	.07
❑	410	Shawn Green	.20	.07
❑	411	Jaret Wright	.20	.07
❑	412	Tony Womack	.20	.07
❑	413	Vernon Wells	.20	.07
❑	414	Ron Belliard	.20	.07
❑	415	Ellis Burks	.20	.07
❑	416	Scott Erickson	.20	.07
❑	417	Rafael Palmeiro	.30	.10
❑	418	Damion Easley	.20	.07
❑	419	Jamey Wright	.20	.07
❑	420	Corey Koskie	.20	.07
❑	421	Bobby Howry	.20	.07
❑	422	Ricky Ledee	.20	.07
❑	423	Dmitri Young	.20	.07
❑	424	Sidney Ponson	.20	.07
❑	425	Greg Maddux	.75	.30
❑	426	Jose Guillen	.20	.07
❑	427	Jon Lieber	.20	.07
❑	428	Andy Benes	.20	.07
❑	429	Randy Velarde	.20	.07
❑	430	Sean Casey	.20	.07
❑	431	Torii Hunter	.20	.07
❑	432	Ryan Rupe	.20	.07
❑	433	David Segui	.20	.07
❑	434	Todd Pratt	.20	.07
❑	435	Nomar Garciaparra	.75	.30
❑	436	Denny Neagle	.20	.07
❑	437	Ron Coomer	.20	.07
❑	438	Chris Singleton	.20	.07
❑	439	Tony Batista	.20	.07
❑	440	Andruw Jones	.30	.10
❑	441	Burroughs/Piatt/Huff	.20	.07
❑	442	Rafael Furcal	.40	.15
❑	443	M.Lamb RC/J.Crede	1.00	.40
❑	444	Julio Zuleta RC	.40	.15
❑	445	Garry Maddox Jr. RC	.40	.15
❑	446	Riley/Sabathia/Mulder	.40	.15
❑	447	Scott Downs RC	.40	.15
❑	448	D.Mirabelli/B.Petrick/J.Werth	.40	.15
❑	449	C.Myers RC/J.Hamilton	.50	.20
❑	450	B.Christensen/R.Stahl RC	.40	.15
❑	451	B.Zito/B.Sheets RC	2.50	1.00
❑	452	K.Ainsworth/Howington RC	.40	.15
❑	453	R.Asadoorian/V.Faison RC	.40	.15
❑	454	K.Reed/J.Heaverlo RC	.40	.15
❑	455	M.MacDougal/B.Baker RC	.40	.15
❑	456	Mark McGwire SH	.60	.25
❑	457	Cal Ripken SH	.75	.30
❑	458	Wade Boggs SH	.20	.07
❑	459	Tony Gwynn SH	.30	.10
❑	460	Jesse Orosco SH	.20	.07
❑	461	L.Walker/N.Garciaparra LL	.30	.10
❑	462	K.Griffey Jr./M.McGwire LL	.50	.20
❑	463	M.Ramirez/M.McGwire LL	.50	.20
❑	464	P.Martinez/R.Johnson LL	.30	.10
❑	465	P.Martinez/R.Johnson LL	.30	.10
❑	466	D.Jeter/L.Gonzalez LL	.50	.20
❑	467	L.Walker/M.Ramirez LL	.30	.10
❑	468	Tony Gwynn 20CB	.60	.25
❑	469	Mark McGwire 20CB	1.25	.50
❑	470	Frank Thomas 20CB	.30	.10
❑	471	Harold Baines 20CB	.20	.07
❑	472	Roger Clemens 20CB	1.00	.40
❑	473	John Franco 20CB	.20	.07
❑	474	John Franco 20CB	.20	.07
❑	475A	K.Griffey Jr. MM 350th HR	2.00	.75
❑	475B	K.Griffey Jr. MM 1997 MVP	2.00	.75
❑	475C	K.Griffey Jr. MM HR Dad	2.00	.75
❑	475D	K.Griffey Jr. MM 1992 AS MVP	2.00	.75
❑	475E	K.Griffey Jr. MM 50 HR 1997	2.00	.75
❑	476A	B.Bonds MM 400HR/400SB	3.00	1.25
❑	476B	B.Bonds MM 40HR/40SB	3.00	1.25
❑	476C	B.Bonds MM 1993 MVP	3.00	1.25
❑	476D	B.Bonds MM 1990 MVP	3.00	1.25
❑	476E	B.Bonds MM 1992 MVP	3.00	1.25
❑	477A	S.Sosa MM 20 HR June	2.00	.75
❑	477B	S.Sosa MM 66 HR 1998	2.00	.75
❑	477C	S.Sosa MM 60 HR 1999	2.00	.75
❑	477D	S.Sosa MM 1998 MVP	2.00	.75
❑	477E	S.Sosa MM HR's 61/62	2.00	.75
❑	478A	D.Jeter MM 1996 ROY	3.00	1.25
❑	478B	D.Jeter MM Wins 1999 WS	3.00	1.25
❑	478C	D.Jeter MM Wins 1998 WS	3.00	1.25
❑	478D	D.Jeter MM Wins 1996 WS	3.00	1.25
❑	478E	D.Jeter MM 17 GM Hit Streak	3.00	1.25
❑	479A	A.Rodriguez MM 40HR/40SB	2.00	.75
❑	479B	A.Rodriguez MM 100th HR	2.00	.75
❑	479C	A.Rodriguez MM 1996 POY	2.00	.75
❑	479D	A.Rodriguez MM Wins 1 Million	2.00	.75
❑	479E	A.Rodriguez MM 1996 Batting Leader	2.00	.75
❑	NNO	M.McGwire 85 Reprint	5.00	2.00

2000 Topps Traded

❑		COMP.FACT.SET (136)	40.00	25.00
❑		COMPLETE SET (135)	30.00	15.00
❑		FACT.SET PRICE IS FOR SEALED SETS		
❑	T1	Mike MacDougal	.30	.10
❑	T2	Andy Tracy RC	.30	.10
❑	T3	Brandon Phillips RC	1.00	.40
❑	T4	Brandon Inge RC	2.00	.75
❑	T5	Robbie Morrison RC	.30	.10

❑ T6 Josh Pressley RC .30 .10
❑ T7 Todd Moser RC .30 .10
❑ T8 Rob Purvis .30 .10
❑ T9 Chance Caple .20 .07
❑ T10 Ben Sheets 1.00 .40
❑ T11 Russ Jacobson RC .30 .10
❑ T12 Brian Cole RC .30 .10
❑ T13 Brad Baker .20 .07
❑ T14 Alex Cintron RC .30 .10
❑ T15 Lyle Overbay RC .75 .30
❑ T16 Mike Edwards RC .30 .10
❑ T17 Sean McGowan RC .30 .10
❑ T18 Jose Molina .20 .07
❑ T19 Marcos Castillo RC .30 .10
❑ T20 Josue Espada RC .30 .10
❑ T21 Alex Gordon RC .30 .10
❑ T22 Rob Pugmire RC .30 .10
❑ T23 Jason Stumm .20 .07
❑ T24 Ty Howington .20 .07
❑ T25 Brett Myers .60 .25
❑ T26 Maicer Izturis RC .30 .10
❑ T27 John McDonald .20 .07
❑ T28 Wilfredo Rodriguez RC .30 .10
❑ T29 Carlos Zambrano RC 4.00 1.50
❑ T30 Alejandro Diaz RC .30 .10
❑ T31 Geraldo Guzman RC .30 .10
❑ T32 J.R. House RC .30 .10
❑ T33 Elvin Nina RC .30 .10
❑ T34 Juan Pierre RC .60 .25
❑ T35 Ben Johnson RC 1.25 .50
❑ T36 Jeff Bailey RC .30 .10
❑ T37 Miguel Olivo RC .50 .20
❑ T38 Francisco Rodriguez RC 1.50 .60
❑ T39 Tony Pena Jr. RC .30 .10
❑ T40 Miguel Cabrera RC 15.00 6.00
❑ T41 Asdrubal Oropeza RC .30 .10
❑ T42 Junior Zamora RC .30 .10
❑ T43 Jovanny Cedeno RC .30 .10
❑ T44 John Sneed .30 .10
❑ T45 Josh Kalinowski .30 .10
❑ T46 Mike Young RC 4.00 1.50
❑ T47 Rico Washington RC .30 .10
❑ T48 Chad Durbin RC .30 .10
❑ T49 Junior Brignac RC .30 .10
❑ T50 Carlos Hernandez RC .30 .10
❑ T51 Cesar Izturis RC .50 .20
❑ T52 Oscar Salazar RC .30 .10
❑ T53 Pat Strange RC .30 .10
❑ T54 Rick Asadoorian .30 .10
❑ T55 Keith Reed .20 .07
❑ T56 Leo Estrella RC .30 .10
❑ T57 Wascar Serrano RC .30 .10
❑ T58 Richard Gomez RC .30 .10
❑ T59 Ramon Santiago RC .30 .10
❑ T60 Jovanny Sosa RC .30 .10
❑ T61 Aaron Rowand RC 1.25 .50
❑ T62 Junior Guerrero RC .30 .10
❑ T63 Luis Terrero RC .30 .10
❑ T64 Brian Sanches RC .30 .10
❑ T65 Scott Sobkowiak RC .30 .10
❑ T66 Gary Majewski RC .30 .10
❑ T67 Barry Zito 1.25 .50
❑ T68 Ryan Christianson .20 .07
❑ T69 Cristian Guerrero RC .30 .10
❑ T70 Tomas De La Rosa RC .30 .10
❑ T71 Andrew Beinbrink RC .30 .10
❑ T72 Ryan Knox RC .30 .10
❑ T73 Alex Graman RC .30 .10
❑ T74 Juan Guzman RC .30 .10
❑ T75 Ruben Salazar RC .30 .10
❑ T76 Luis Matos RC .30 .10
❑ T77 Tony Mota RC .30 .10
❑ T78 Doug Davis .30 .10
❑ T79 Ben Christensen .20 .07
❑ T80 Mike Lamb .50 .20
❑ T81 Adrian Gonzalez RC 2.50 1.00
❑ T82 Mike Stodolka RC .30 .10
❑ T83 Adam Johnson RC .30 .10
❑ T84 Matt Wheatland RC .30 .10
❑ T85 Corey Smith RC .30 .10
❑ T86 Rocco Baldelli RC 1.25 .50
❑ T87 Keith Bucktrot RC .30 .10
❑ T88 Adam Wainwright RC 1.00 .40
❑ T89 Scott Thorman RC .75 .30
❑ T90 Tripper Johnson RC .30 .10
❑ T91 Jim Edmonds Cards .30 .10
❑ T92 Masato Yoshii .20 .07
❑ T93 Adam Kennedy .20 .07
❑ T94 Darryl Kile .30 .10
❑ T95 Mark McLemore .20 .07
❑ T96 Ricky Gutierrez .20 .07
❑ T97 Juan Gonzalez .30 .10
❑ T98 Melvin Mora .30 .10
❑ T99 Dante Bichette .30 .10
❑ T100 Lee Stevens .20 .07
❑ T101 Roger Cedeno .20 .07
❑ T102 John Olerud .30 .10
❑ T103 Eric Young .20 .07
❑ T104 Mickey Morandini .20 .07
❑ T105 Travis Lee .20 .07
❑ T106 Greg Vaughn .20 .07
❑ T107 Todd Zeile .30 .10
❑ T108 Chuck Finley .30 .10
❑ T109 Ismael Valdes .20 .07
❑ T110 Reggie Sanders .30 .10
❑ T111 Pat Hentgen .20 .07
❑ T112 Ryan Klesko .30 .10
❑ T113 Derek Bell .20 .07
❑ T114 Hideo Nomo .75 .30
❑ T115 Aaron Sele .20 .07
❑ T116 Fernando Vina .20 .07
❑ T117 Wally Joyner .30 .10
❑ T118 Brian Hunter .20 .07
❑ T119 Joe Girardi .20 .07
❑ T120 Omar Daal .20 .07
❑ T121 Brook Fordyce .20 .07
❑ T122 Jose Valentin .20 .07
❑ T123 Curt Schilling .30 .10
❑ T124 B.J. Surhoff .30 .10
❑ T125 Henry Rodriguez .20 .07
❑ T126 Mike Bordick .20 .07
❑ T127 David Justice .30 .10
❑ T128 Charles Johnson .30 .10
❑ T129 Will Clark .50 .20
❑ T130 Dwight Gooden .30 .10
❑ T131 David Segui .20 .07
❑ T132 Denny Neagle .30 .10
❑ T133 Jose Canseco .50 .20
❑ T134 Bruce Chen .20 .07
❑ T135 Jason Bere .20 .07

2001 Topps

❑ COMPLETE SET (790) 80.00 40.00
❑ COMP.FACT.BLUE SET (795) 120.0060.00
❑ COMPLETE SERIES 1 (405) 40.00 20.00
❑ COMPLETE SERIES 2 (385) 40.00 20.00
❑ COMMON CARD (1-6/8-791) .20 .07
❑ COMMON (352-376/727-751) .25 .08
❑ 1 Cal Ripken 1.50 .60
❑ 2 Chipper Jones .50 .20
❑ 3 Roger Cedeno .20 .07
❑ 4 Garret Anderson .20 .07
❑ 5 Robin Ventura .20 .07
❑ 6 Daryle Ward .20 .07
❑ 7 Does Not Exist
❑ 8 Craig Paquette .20 .07
❑ 9 Phil Nevin .20 .07
❑ 10 Jermaine Dye .20 .07
❑ 11 Chris Singleton .20 .07
❑ 12 Mike Stanton .20 .07
❑ 13 Brian Hunter .20 .07
❑ 14 Mike Redmond .20 .07
❑ 15 Jim Thome .30 .10
❑ 16 Brian Jordan .20 .07
❑ 17 Joe Girardi .20 .07
❑ 18 Steve Woodard .20 .07
❑ 19 Dustin Hermanson .20 .07
❑ 20 Shawn Green .20 .07
❑ 21 Todd Stottlemyre .20 .07
❑ 22 Dan Wilson .20 .07
❑ 23 Todd Pratt .20 .07
❑ 24 Derek Lowe .20 .07
❑ 25 Juan Gonzalez .20 .07
❑ 26 Clay Bellinger .20 .07
❑ 27 Jeff Fassero .20 .07
❑ 28 Pat Meares .20 .07
❑ 29 Eddie Taubensee .20 .07
❑ 30 Paul O'Neill .30 .10
❑ 31 Jeffrey Hammonds .20 .07
❑ 32 Pokey Reese .20 .07
❑ 33 Mike Mussina .30 .10
❑ 34 Rico Brogna .20 .07
❑ 35 Jay Buhner .20 .07
❑ 36 Steve Cox .20 .07
❑ 37 Quilvio Veras .20 .07
❑ 38 Marquis Grissom .20 .07
❑ 39 Shigetoshi Hasegawa .20 .07
❑ 40 Shane Reynolds .20 .07
❑ 41 Adam Piatt .20 .07
❑ 42 Luis Polonia .20 .07
❑ 43 Brook Fordyce .20 .07
❑ 44 Preston Wilson .20 .07
❑ 45 Ellis Burks .20 .07
❑ 46 Armando Rios .20 .07
❑ 47 Chuck Finley .20 .07
❑ 48 Dan Plesac .20 .07
❑ 49 Shannon Stewart .20 .07
❑ 50 Mark McGwire 1.25 .50
❑ 51 Mark Loretta .20 .07
❑ 52 Gerald Williams .20 .07
❑ 53 Eric Young .20 .07
❑ 54 Peter Bergeron .20 .07
❑ 55 Dave Hansen .20 .07
❑ 56 Arthur Rhodes .20 .07
❑ 57 Bobby Jones .20 .07
❑ 58 Matt Clement .20 .07
❑ 59 Mike Benjamin .20 .07
❑ 60 Pedro Martinez .30 .10
❑ 61 Jose Canseco .30 .10
❑ 62 Matt Anderson .20 .07
❑ 63 Torii Hunter .20 .07
❑ 64 Carlos Lee .20 .07
❑ 65 David Cone .20 .07
❑ 66 Rey Sanchez .20 .07
❑ 67 Eric Chavez .20 .07
❑ 68 Rick Helling .20 .07
❑ 69 Manny Alexander .20 .07
❑ 70 John Franco .20 .07
❑ 71 Mike Bordick .20 .07
❑ 72 Andres Galarraga .20 .07
❑ 73 Jose Cruz Jr. .20 .07
❑ 74 Mike Matheny .20 .07
❑ 75 Randy Johnson .50 .20
❑ 76 Richie Sexson .20 .07
❑ 77 Vladimir Nunez .20 .07
❑ 78 Harold Baines .20 .07
❑ 79 Aaron Boone .20 .07
❑ 80 Darin Erstad .20 .07
❑ 81 Alex Gonzalez .20 .07
❑ 82 Gil Heredia .20 .07
❑ 83 Shane Andrews .20 .07
❑ 84 Todd Hundley .20 .07

❑ 85 Bill Mueller .20 .07
❑ 86 Mark McLemore .20 .07
❑ 87 Scott Spiezio .20 .07
❑ 88 Kevin McGlinchy .20 .07
❑ 89 Bubba Trammell .20 .07
❑ 90 Manny Ramirez .30 .10
❑ 91 Mike Lamb .20 .07
❑ 92 Scott Karl .20 .07
❑ 93 Brian Buchanan .20 .07
❑ 94 Chris Turner .20 .07
❑ 95 Mike Sweeney .20 .07
❑ 96 John Wetteland .20 .07
❑ 97 Rob Bell .20 .07
❑ 98 Pat Rapp .20 .07
❑ 99 John Burkett .20 .07
❑ 100 Derek Jeter 1.25 .50
❑ 101 J.D. Drew .20 .07
❑ 102 Jose Offerman .20 .07
❑ 103 Rick Reed .20 .07
❑ 104 Will Clark .30 .10
❑ 105 Rickey Henderson .50 .20
❑ 106 Dave Berg .20 .07
❑ 107 Kirk Rueter .20 .07
❑ 108 Lee Stevens .20 .07
❑ 109 Jay Bell .20 .07
❑ 110 Fred McGriff .30 .10
❑ 111 Julio Zuleta .20 .07
❑ 112 Brian Anderson .20 .07
❑ 113 Orlando Cabrera .20 .07
❑ 114 Alex Fernandez .20 .07
❑ 115 Derek Bell .20 .07
❑ 116 Eric Owens .20 .07
❑ 117 Brian Bohanon .20 .07
❑ 118 Dennys Reyes .20 .07
❑ 119 Mike Stanley .20 .07
❑ 120 Jorge Posada .30 .10
❑ 121 Rich Becker .20 .07
❑ 122 Paul Konerko .20 .07
❑ 123 Mike Remlinger .20 .07
❑ 124 Travis Lee .20 .07
❑ 125 Ken Caminiti .20 .07
❑ 126 Kevin Barker .20 .07
❑ 127 Paul Quantrill .20 .07
❑ 128 Ozzie Guillen .20 .07
❑ 129 Kevin Tapani .20 .07
❑ 130 Mark Johnson .20 .07
❑ 131 Randy Wolf .20 .07
❑ 132 Michael Tucker .20 .07
❑ 133 Darren Lewis .20 .07
❑ 134 Joe Randa .20 .07
❑ 135 Jeff Cirillo .20 .07
❑ 136 David Ortiz .50 .20
❑ 137 Herb Perry .20 .07
❑ 138 Jeff Nelson .20 .07
❑ 139 Chris Stynes .20 .07
❑ 140 Johnny Damon .30 .10
❑ 141 Jeff Reboulet .20 .07
❑ 142 Jason Schmidt .20 .07
❑ 143 Charles Johnson .20 .07
❑ 144 Pat Burrell .20 .07
❑ 145 Gary Sheffield .20 .07
❑ 146 Tom Glavine .30 .10
❑ 147 Jason Isringhausen .20 .07
❑ 148 Chris Carpenter .20 .07
❑ 149 Jeff Suppan .20 .07
❑ 150 Ivan Rodriguez .30 .10
❑ 151 Luis Sojo .20 .07
❑ 152 Ron Villone .20 .07
❑ 153 Mike Sirotka .20 .07
❑ 154 Chuck Knoblauch .20 .07
❑ 155 Jason Kendall .20 .07
❑ 156 Dennis Cook .20 .07
❑ 157 Bobby Estalella .20 .07
❑ 158 Jose Guillen .20 .07
❑ 159 Thomas Howard .20 .07
❑ 160 Carlos Delgado .20 .07
❑ 161 Benji Gil .20 .07
❑ 162 Tim Bogar .20 .07
❑ 163 Kevin Elster .20 .07
❑ 164 Einar Diaz .20 .07
❑ 165 Andy Benes .20 .07
❑ 166 Adrian Beltre .20 .07
❑ 167 David Bell .20 .07
❑ 168 Turk Wendell .20 .07
❑ 169 Pete Harnisch .20 .07
❑ 170 Roger Clemens 1.00 .40
❑ 171 Scott Williamson .20 .07
❑ 172 Kevin Jordan .20 .07
❑ 173 Brad Penny .20 .07
❑ 174 John Flaherty .20 .07
❑ 175 Troy Glaus .20 .07
❑ 176 Kevin Appier .20 .07
❑ 177 Walt Weiss .20 .07
❑ 178 Tyler Houston .20 .07
❑ 179 Michael Barrett .20 .07
❑ 180 Mike Hampton .20 .07
❑ 181 Francisco Cordova .20 .07
❑ 182 Mike Jackson .20 .07
❑ 183 David Segui .20 .07
❑ 184 Carlos Febles .20 .07
❑ 185 Roy Halladay .20 .07
❑ 186 Seth Etherton .20 .07
❑ 187 Charlie Hayes .20 .07
❑ 188 Fernando Tatis .20 .07
❑ 189 Steve Trachsel .20 .07
❑ 190 Livan Hernandez .20 .07
❑ 191 Joe Oliver .20 .07
❑ 192 Stan Javier .20 .07
❑ 193 B.J. Surhoff .20 .07
❑ 194 Rob Ducey .20 .07
❑ 195 Barry Larkin .30 .10
❑ 196 Danny Patterson .20 .07
❑ 197 Bobby Howry .20 .07
❑ 198 Dmitri Young .20 .07
❑ 199 Brian Hunter .20 .07
❑ 200 Alex Rodriguez .75 .30
❑ 201 Hideo Nomo .50 .20
❑ 202 Luis Alicea .20 .07
❑ 203 Warren Morris .20 .07
❑ 204 Antonio Alfonseca .20 .07
❑ 205 Edgardo Alfonzo .20 .07
❑ 206 Mark Grudzielanek .20 .07
❑ 207 Fernando Vina .20 .07
❑ 208 Willie Greene .20 .07
❑ 209 Homer Bush .20 .07
❑ 210 Jason Giambi .20 .07
❑ 211 Mike Morgan .20 .07
❑ 212 Steve Karsay .20 .07
❑ 213 Matt Lawton .20 .07
❑ 214 Wendell Magee Jr. .20 .07
❑ 215 Rusty Greer .20 .07
❑ 216 Keith Lockhart .20 .07
❑ 217 Billy Koch .20 .07
❑ 218 Todd Hollandsworth .20 .07
❑ 219 Raul Ibanez .20 .07
❑ 220 Tony Gwynn .60 .25
❑ 221 Carl Everett .20 .07
❑ 222 Hector Carrasco .20 .07
❑ 223 Jose Valentin .20 .07
❑ 224 Deivi Cruz .20 .07
❑ 225 Bret Boone .20 .07
❑ 226 Kurt Abbott .20 .07
❑ 227 Melvin Mora .20 .07
❑ 228 Danny Graves .20 .07
❑ 229 Jose Jimenez .20 .07
❑ 230 James Baldwin .20 .07
❑ 231 C.J. Nitkowski .20 .07
❑ 232 Jeff Zimmerman .20 .07
❑ 233 Mike Lowell .20 .07
❑ 234 Hideki Irabu .20 .07
❑ 235 Greg Vaughn .20 .07
❑ 236 Omar Daal .20 .07
❑ 237 Darren Dreifort .20 .07
❑ 238 Gil Meche .20 .07
❑ 239 Damian Jackson .20 .07
❑ 240 Frank Thomas .50 .20
❑ 241 Travis Miller .20 .07
❑ 242 Jeff Frye .20 .07
❑ 243 Dave Magadan .20 .07
❑ 244 Luis Castillo .20 .07
❑ 245 Bartolo Colon .20 .07
❑ 246 Steve Kline .20 .07
❑ 247 Shawon Dunston .20 .07
❑ 248 Rick Aguilera .20 .07
❑ 249 Omar Olivares .20 .07
❑ 250 Craig Biggio .30 .10
❑ 251 Scott Schoeneweis .20 .07
❑ 252 Dave Veres .20 .07
❑ 253 Ramon Martinez .20 .07
❑ 254 Jose Vidro .20 .07
❑ 255 Todd Helton .30 .10
❑ 256 Greg Norton .20 .07
❑ 257 Jacque Jones .20 .07
❑ 258 Jason Grimsley .20 .07
❑ 259 Dan Reichert .20 .07
❑ 260 Robb Nen .20 .07
❑ 261 Mark Clark .20 .07
❑ 262 Scott Hatteberg .20 .07
❑ 263 Doug Brocail .20 .07
❑ 264 Mark Johnson .20 .07
❑ 265 Eric Davis .20 .07
❑ 266 Terry Shumpert .20 .07
❑ 267 Kevin Millar .20 .07
❑ 268 Ismael Valdes .20 .07
❑ 269 Richard Hidalgo .20 .07
❑ 270 Randy Velarde .20 .07
❑ 271 Bengie Molina .20 .07
❑ 272 Tony Womack .20 .07
❑ 273 Enrique Wilson .20 .07
❑ 274 Jeff Brantley .20 .07
❑ 275 Rick Ankiel .20 .07
❑ 276 Terry Mulholland .20 .07
❑ 277 Ron Belliard .20 .07
❑ 278 Terrence Long .20 .07
❑ 279 Alberto Castillo .20 .07
❑ 280 Royce Clayton .20 .07
❑ 281 Joe McEwing .20 .07
❑ 282 Jason McDonald .20 .07
❑ 283 Ricky Bottalico .20 .07
❑ 284 Keith Foulke .20 .07
❑ 285 Brad Radke .20 .07
❑ 286 Gabe Kapler .20 .07
❑ 287 Pedro Astacio .20 .07
❑ 288 Armando Reynoso .20 .07
❑ 289 Darryl Kile .20 .07
❑ 290 Reggie Sanders .20 .07
❑ 291 Esteban Yan .20 .07
❑ 292 Joe Nathan .20 .07
❑ 293 Jay Payton .20 .07
❑ 294 Francisco Cordero .20 .07
❑ 295 Gregg Jefferies .20 .07
❑ 296 LaTroy Hawkins .20 .07
❑ 297 Jeff Tam RC .40 .15
❑ 298 Jacob Cruz .20 .07
❑ 299 Chris Holt .20 .07
❑ 300 Vladimir Guerrero .50 .20
❑ 301 Marvin Benard .20 .07
❑ 302 Alex Ramirez .20 .07
❑ 303 Mike Williams .20 .07
❑ 304 Sean Bergman .20 .07
❑ 305 Juan Encarnacion .20 .07
❑ 306 Russ Davis .20 .07
❑ 307 Hanley Frias .20 .07
❑ 308 Ramon Hernandez .20 .07
❑ 309 Matt Walbeck .20 .07
❑ 310 Bill Spiers .20 .07
❑ 311 Bob Wickman .20 .07
❑ 312 Sandy Alomar Jr. .20 .07
❑ 313 Eddie Guardado .20 .07
❑ 314 Shane Halter .20 .07
❑ 315 Geoff Jenkins .20 .07
❑ 316 Brian Meadows .20 .07
❑ 317 Damian Miller .20 .07
❑ 318 Darrin Fletcher .20 .07
❑ 319 Rafael Furcal .20 .07
❑ 320 Mark Grace .30 .10
❑ 321 Mark Mulder .20 .07
❑ 322 Joe Torre MG .30 .10
❑ 323 Bobby Cox MG .20 .07
❑ 324 Mike Scioscia MG .20 .07
❑ 325 Mike Hargrove MG .20 .07
❑ 326 Jimy Williams MG .20 .07
❑ 327 Jerry Manuel MG .20 .07
❑ 328 Buck Showalter MG .20 .07
❑ 329 Charlie Manuel MG .20 .07
❑ 330 Don Baylor MG .20 .07
❑ 331 Phil Garner MG .20 .07
❑ 332 Jack McKeon MG .20 .07
❑ 333 Tony Muser MG .20 .07
❑ 334 Buddy Bell MG .20 .07
❑ 335 Tom Kelly MG .20 .07
❑ 336 John Boles MG .20 .07
❑ 337 Art Howe MG .20 .07
❑ 338 Larry Dierker MG .20 .07
❑ 339 Lou Piniella MG .20 .07
❑ 340 Davey Johnson MG .20 .07
❑ 341 Larry Rothschild MG .20 .07
❑ 342 Davey Lopes MG .20 .07

❑ 343 Johnny Oates MG .20 .07
❑ 344 Felipe Alou MG .20 .07
❑ 345 Jim Fregosi MG .20 .07
❑ 346 Bobby Valentine MG .20 .07
❑ 347 Terry Francona MG .20 .07
❑ 348 Gene Lamont MG .20 .07
❑ 349 Tony LaRussa MG .20 .07
❑ 350 Bruce Bochy MG .20 .07
❑ 351 Dusty Baker MG .20 .07
❑ 352 A.Gonzalez/A.Johnson .25 .08
❑ 353 M.Wheatland/B.Digby .25 .08
❑ 354 T.Johnson/S.Thorman .25 .08
❑ 355 P.Dumatrait/A.Wainwright .25 .08
❑ 356 David Parrish RC .25 .08
❑ 357 M.Folsom RC/R.Baldelli .40 .15
❑ 358 Dominic Rich RC .25 .08
❑ 359 M.Stodolka/S.Burnett .25 .08
❑ 360 D.Thompson/C.Smith .25 .08
❑ 361 D.Borrell RC/J.Bourgeois RC .25 .08
❑ 362 Chen/Patterson/Hamilton .25 .08
❑ 363 B.Zito/C.Sabathia .50 .20
❑ 364 Ben Sheets .50 .20
❑ 365 Howington/Kalinowski/Girdley .25 .08
❑ 366 Hee Seop Choi RC .50 .20
❑ 367 Bradley/Ainsworth/Tsao .40 .15
❑ 368 Glendenning/Kelly/Silvestre .25 .08
❑ 369 J.R. House .25 .08
❑ 370 Rafael Soriano RC .40 .15
❑ 371 T.Hafner RC/B.Jacobsen 4.00 1.50
❑ 372 Conti/Wakeland/Cole .25 .08
❑ 373 Seabol/Huff/Crede .75 .30
❑ 374 Everett/Ortiz/Ginter .25 .08
❑ 375 Hernandez/Guzman/Eaton .25 .08
❑ 376 Kielty/Bradley/J.Rivera .40 .15
❑ 377 Mark McGwire GM .60 .25
❑ 378 Don Larsen GM .20 .07
❑ 379 Bobby Thomson GM .20 .07
❑ 380 Bill Mazeroski GM .20 .07
❑ 381 Reggie Jackson GM .30 .10
❑ 382 Kirk Gibson GM .20 .07
❑ 383 Roger Maris GM .30 .10
❑ 384 Cal Ripken GM .75 .30
❑ 385 Hank Aaron GM .50 .20
❑ 386 Joe Carter GM .20 .07
❑ 387 Cal Ripken SH 1.50 .60
❑ 388 Randy Johnson SH .30 .10
❑ 389 Ken Griffey Jr. SH .75 .30
❑ 390 Troy Glaus SH .20 .07
❑ 391 Kazuhiro Sasaki SH .20 .07
❑ 392 S.Sosa/T.Glaus LL .30 .10
❑ 393 T.Helton/E.Martinez LL .20 .07
❑ 394 T.Helton/N.Garciaparra LL .50 .20
❑ 395 B.Bonds/J.Giambi LL .75 .30
❑ 396 T.Helton/M.Ramirez LL .20 .07
❑ 397 T.Helton/D.Erstad LL .20 .07
❑ 398 K.Brown/P.Martinez LL .30 .10
❑ 399 R.Johnson/P.Martinez LL .30 .10
❑ 400 Will Clark HL .30 .10
❑ 401 New York Mets HL .50 .20
❑ 402 New York Yankees HL .75 .30
❑ 403 Seattle Mariners HL .20 .07
❑ 404 Mike Hampton HL .20 .07
❑ 405 New York Yankees HL 1.00 .40
❑ 406 New York Yankees Champs 2.00 .75
❑ 407 Jeff Bagwell .30 .10
❑ 408 Brant Brown .20 .07
❑ 409 Brad Fullmer .20 .07
❑ 410 Dean Palmer .20 .07
❑ 411 Greg Zaun .20 .07
❑ 412 Jose Vizcaino .20 .07
❑ 413 Jeff Abbott .20 .07
❑ 414 Travis Fryman .20 .07
❑ 415 Mike Cameron .20 .07
❑ 416 Matt Mantei .20 .07
❑ 417 Alan Benes .20 .07
❑ 418 Mickey Morandini .20 .07
❑ 419 Troy Percival .20 .07
❑ 420 Eddie Perez .20 .07
❑ 421 Vernon Wells .20 .07
❑ 422 Ricky Gutierrez .20 .07
❑ 423 Carlos Hernandez .20 .07
❑ 424 Chan Ho Park .20 .07
❑ 425 Armando Benitez .20 .07
❑ 426 Sidney Ponson .20 .07
❑ 427 Adrian Brown .20 .07
❑ 428 Ruben Mateo .20 .07
❑ 429 Alex Ochoa .20 .07
❑ 430 Jose Rosado .20 .07
❑ 431 Masato Yoshii .20 .07
❑ 432 Corey Koskie .20 .07
❑ 433 Andy Pettitte .30 .10
❑ 434 Brian Daubach .20 .07
❑ 435 Sterling Hitchcock .20 .07
❑ 436 Timo Perez .20 .07
❑ 437 Shawn Estes .20 .07
❑ 438 Tony Armas Jr. .20 .07
❑ 439 Danny Bautista .20 .07
❑ 440 Randy Winn .20 .07
❑ 441 Wilson Alvarez .20 .07
❑ 442 Rondell White .20 .07
❑ 443 Jeromy Burnitz .20 .07
❑ 444 Kelvim Escobar .20 .07
❑ 445 Paul Bako .20 .07
❑ 446 Javier Vazquez .20 .07
❑ 447 Eric Gagne .20 .07
❑ 448 Kenny Lofton .20 .07
❑ 449 Mark Kotsay .20 .07
❑ 450 Jamie Moyer .20 .07
❑ 451 Delino DeShields .20 .07
❑ 452 Rey Ordonez .20 .07
❑ 453 Russ Ortiz .20 .07
❑ 454 Dave Burba .20 .07
❑ 455 Eric Karros .20 .07
❑ 456 Felix Martinez .20 .07
❑ 457 Tony Batista .20 .07
❑ 458 Bobby Higginson .20 .07
❑ 459 Jeff D'Amico .20 .07
❑ 460 Shane Spencer .20 .07
❑ 461 Brent Mayne .20 .07
❑ 462 Glendon Rusch .20 .07
❑ 463 Chris Gomez .20 .07
❑ 464 Jeff Shaw .20 .07
❑ 465 Damon Buford .20 .07
❑ 466 Mike DiFelice .20 .07
❑ 467 Jimmy Haynes .20 .07
❑ 468 Billy Wagner .20 .07
❑ 469 A.J. Hinch .20 .07
❑ 470 Gary DiSarcina .20 .07
❑ 471 Tom Lampkin .20 .07
❑ 472 Adam Eaton .20 .07
❑ 473 Brian Giles .20 .07
❑ 474 John Thomson .20 .07
❑ 475 Cal Eldred .20 .07
❑ 476 Ramiro Mendoza .20 .07
❑ 477 Scott Sullivan .20 .07
❑ 478 Scott Rolen .30 .10
❑ 479 Todd Ritchie .20 .07
❑ 480 Pablo Ozuna .20 .07
❑ 481 Carl Pavano .20 .07
❑ 482 Matt Morris .20 .07
❑ 483 Matt Stairs .20 .07
❑ 484 Tim Belcher .20 .07
❑ 485 Lance Berkman .20 .07
❑ 486 Brian Meadows .20 .07
❑ 487 Bob Abreu .20 .07
❑ 488 John VanderWal .20 .07
❑ 489 Donnie Sadler .20 .07
❑ 490 Damion Easley .20 .07
❑ 491 David Justice .20 .07
❑ 492 Ray Durham .20 .07
❑ 493 Todd Zeile .20 .07
❑ 494 Desi Relaford .20 .07
❑ 495 Cliff Floyd .20 .07
❑ 496 Scott Downs .20 .07
❑ 497 Barry Bonds 1.25 .50
❑ 498 Jeff D'Amico .20 .07
❑ 499 Octavio Dotel .20 .07
❑ 500 Kent Mercker .20 .07
❑ 501 Craig Grebeck .20 .07
❑ 502 Roberto Hernandez .20 .07
❑ 503 Matt Williams .20 .07
❑ 504 Bruce Aven .20 .07
❑ 505 Brett Tomko .20 .07
❑ 506 Kris Benson .20 .07
❑ 507 Neifi Perez .20 .07
❑ 508 Alfonso Soriano .30 .10
❑ 509 Keith Osik .20 .07
❑ 510 Matt Franco .20 .07
❑ 511 Steve Finley .20 .07
❑ 512 Olmedo Saenz .20 .07
❑ 513 Esteban Loaiza .20 .07
❑ 514 Adam Kennedy .20 .07
❑ 515 Scott Elarton .20 .07
❑ 516 Moises Alou .20 .07
❑ 517 Bryan Rekar .20 .07
❑ 518 Darryl Hamilton .20 .07
❑ 519 Osvaldo Fernandez .20 .07
❑ 520 Kip Wells .20 .07
❑ 521 Bernie Williams .30 .10
❑ 522 Mike Darr .20 .07
❑ 523 Marlon Anderson .20 .07
❑ 524 Derrek Lee .30 .10
❑ 525 Ugueth Urbina .20 .07
❑ 526 Vinny Castilla .20 .07
❑ 527 David Wells .20 .07
❑ 528 Jason Marquis .20 .07
❑ 529 Orlando Palmeiro .20 .07
❑ 530 Carlos Perez .20 .07
❑ 531 J.T. Snow .20 .07
❑ 532 Al Leiter .20 .07
❑ 533 Jimmy Anderson .20 .07
❑ 534 Brett Laxton .20 .07
❑ 535 Butch Huskey .20 .07
❑ 536 Orlando Hernandez .20 .07
❑ 537 Magglio Ordonez .20 .07
❑ 538 Willie Blair .20 .07
❑ 539 Kevin Sefcik .20 .07
❑ 540 Chad Curtis .20 .07
❑ 541 John Halama .20 .07
❑ 542 Andy Fox .20 .07
❑ 543 Juan Guzman .20 .07
❑ 544 Frank Menechino RC .20 .07
❑ 545 Raul Mondesi .20 .07
❑ 546 Tim Salmon .30 .10
❑ 547 Ryan Rupe .20 .07
❑ 548 Jeff Reed .20 .07
❑ 549 Mike Mordecai .20 .07
❑ 550 Jeff Kent .20 .07
❑ 551 Wiki Gonzalez .20 .07
❑ 552 Kenny Rogers .20 .07
❑ 553 Kevin Young .20 .07
❑ 554 Brian Johnson .20 .07
❑ 555 Tom Goodwin .20 .07
❑ 556 Tony Clark .20 .07
❑ 557 Mac Suzuki .20 .07
❑ 558 Brian Moehler .20 .07
❑ 559 Jim Parque .20 .07
❑ 560 Mariano Rivera .50 .20
❑ 561 Trot Nixon .20 .07
❑ 562 Mike Mussina .30 .10
❑ 563 Nelson Figueroa .20 .07
❑ 564 Alex Gonzalez .20 .07
❑ 565 Benny Agbayani .20 .07
❑ 566 Ed Sprague .20 .07
❑ 567 Scott Erickson .20 .07
❑ 568 Abraham Nunez .20 .07
❑ 569 Jerry DiPoto .20 .07
❑ 570 Sean Casey .20 .07
❑ 571 Wilton Veras .20 .07
❑ 572 Joe Mays .20 .07
❑ 573 Bill Simas .20 .07
❑ 574 Doug Glanville .20 .07
❑ 575 Scott Sauerbeck .20 .07
❑ 576 Ben Davis .20 .07
❑ 577 Jesus Sanchez .20 .07
❑ 578 Ricardo Rincon .20 .07
❑ 579 John Olerud .20 .07
❑ 580 Curt Schilling .20 .07
❑ 581 Alex Cora .20 .07
❑ 582 Pat Hentgen .20 .07
❑ 583 Javy Lopez .20 .07
❑ 584 Ben Grieve .20 .07
❑ 585 Frank Castillo .20 .07
❑ 586 Kevin Stocker .20 .07
❑ 587 Mark Sweeney .20 .07
❑ 588 Ray Lankford .20 .07
❑ 589 Turner Ward .20 .07
❑ 590 Felipe Crespo .20 .07
❑ 591 Omar Vizquel .30 .10
❑ 592 Mike Lieberthal .20 .07
❑ 593 Ken Griffey Jr. .75 .30
❑ 594 Troy O'Leary .20 .07
❑ 595 Dave Mlicki .20 .07
❑ 596 Manny Ramirez Sox .30 .10
❑ 597 Mike Lansing .20 .07
❑ 598 Rich Aurilia .20 .07
❑ 599 Russell Branyan .20 .07
❑ 600 Russ Johnson .20 .07

- ❑ 601 Greg Colbrunn .20 .07
- ❑ 602 Andruw Jones .30 .10
- ❑ 603 Henry Blanco .20 .07
- ❑ 604 Jarrod Washburn .20 .07
- ❑ 605 Tony Eusebio .20 .07
- ❑ 606 Aaron Sele .20 .07
- ❑ 607 Charles Nagy .20 .07
- ❑ 608 Ryan Klesko .20 .07
- ❑ 609 Dante Bichette .20 .07
- ❑ 610 Bill Haselman .20 .07
- ❑ 611 Jerry Spradlin .20 .07
- ❑ 612 Alex Rodriguez Rangers .75 .30
- ❑ 613 Jose Silva .20 .07
- ❑ 614 Darren Oliver .20 .07
- ❑ 615 Pat Mahomes .20 .07
- ❑ 616 Roberto Alomar .30 .10
- ❑ 617 Edgar Renteria .20 .07
- ❑ 618 Jon Lieber .20 .07
- ❑ 619 John Rocker .20 .07
- ❑ 620 Miguel Tejada .20 .07
- ❑ 621 Mo Vaughn .20 .07
- ❑ 622 Jose Lima .20 .07
- ❑ 623 Kerry Wood .20 .07
- ❑ 624 Mike Timlin .20 .07
- ❑ 625 Wil Cordero .20 .07
- ❑ 626 Albert Belle .20 .07
- ❑ 627 Bobby Jones .20 .07
- ❑ 628 Doug Mirabelli .20 .07
- ❑ 629 Jason Tyner .20 .07
- ❑ 630 Andy Ashby .20 .07
- ❑ 631 Jose Hernandez .20 .07
- ❑ 632 Devon White .20 .07
- ❑ 633 Ruben Rivera .20 .07
- ❑ 634 Steve Parris .20 .07
- ❑ 635 David McCarty .20 .07
- ❑ 636 Jose Canseco .30 .10
- ❑ 637 Todd Walker .20 .07
- ❑ 638 Stan Spencer .20 .07
- ❑ 639 Wayne Gomes .20 .07
- ❑ 640 Freddy Garcia .20 .07
- ❑ 641 Jeremy Giambi .20 .07
- ❑ 642 Luis Lopez .20 .07
- ❑ 643 John Smoltz .30 .10
- ❑ 644 Kelly Stinnett .20 .07
- ❑ 645 Kevin Brown .20 .07
- ❑ 646 Wilton Guerrero .20 .07
- ❑ 647 Al Martin .20 .07
- ❑ 648 Woody Williams .20 .07
- ❑ 649 Brian Rose .20 .07
- ❑ 650 Rafael Palmeiro .30 .10
- ❑ 651 Pete Schourek .20 .07
- ❑ 652 Kevin Jarvis .20 .07
- ❑ 653 Mark Redman .20 .07
- ❑ 654 Ricky Ledee .20 .07
- ❑ 655 Larry Walker .20 .07
- ❑ 656 Paul Byrd .20 .07
- ❑ 657 Jason Bere .20 .07
- ❑ 658 Rick White .20 .07
- ❑ 659 Calvin Murray .20 .07
- ❑ 660 Greg Maddux .75 .30
- ❑ 661 Ron Gant .20 .07
- ❑ 662 Eli Marrero .20 .07
- ❑ 663 Graeme Lloyd .20 .07
- ❑ 664 Trevor Hoffman .20 .07
- ❑ 665 Nomar Garciaparra .75 .30
- ❑ 666 Glenallen Hill .20 .07
- ❑ 667 Matt LeCroy .20 .07
- ❑ 668 Justin Thompson .20 .07
- ❑ 669 Brady Anderson .20 .07
- ❑ 670 Miguel Batista .20 .07
- ❑ 671 Erubiel Durazo .20 .07
- ❑ 672 Kevin Millwood .20 .07
- ❑ 673 Mitch Meluskey .20 .07
- ❑ 674 Luis Gonzalez .20 .07
- ❑ 675 Edgar Martinez .30 .10
- ❑ 676 Robert Person .20 .07
- ❑ 677 Benito Santiago .20 .07
- ❑ 678 Todd Jones .20 .07
- ❑ 679 Tino Martinez .30 .10
- ❑ 680 Carlos Beltran .20 .07
- ❑ 681 Gabe White .20 .07
- ❑ 682 Bret Saberhagen .20 .07
- ❑ 683 Jeff Conine .20 .07
- ❑ 684 Jaret Wright .20 .07
- ❑ 685 Bernard Gilkey .20 .07
- ❑ 686 Garrett Stephenson .20 .07
- ❑ 687 Jamey Wright .20 .07
- ❑ 688 Sammy Sosa .50 .20
- ❑ 689 John Jaha .20 .07
- ❑ 690 Ramon Martinez .20 .07
- ❑ 691 Robert Fick .20 .07
- ❑ 692 Eric Milton .20 .07
- ❑ 693 Denny Neagle .20 .07
- ❑ 694 Ron Coomer .20 .07
- ❑ 695 John Valentin .20 .07
- ❑ 696 Placido Polanco .20 .07
- ❑ 697 Tim Hudson .20 .07
- ❑ 698 Marty Cordova .20 .07
- ❑ 699 Chad Kreuter .20 .07
- ❑ 700 Frank Catalanotto .20 .07
- ❑ 701 Tim Wakefield .20 .07
- ❑ 702 Jim Edmonds .20 .07
- ❑ 703 Michael Tucker .20 .07
- ❑ 704 Cristian Guzman .20 .07
- ❑ 705 Joey Hamilton .20 .07
- ❑ 706 Mike Piazza .75 .30
- ❑ 707 Dave Martinez .20 .07
- ❑ 708 Mike Hampton .20 .07
- ❑ 709 Bobby Bonilla .20 .07
- ❑ 710 Juan Pierre .20 .07
- ❑ 711 John Parrish .20 .07
- ❑ 712 Kory DeHaan .20 .07
- ❑ 713 Brian Tollberg .20 .07
- ❑ 714 Chris Truby .20 .07
- ❑ 715 Emil Brown .20 .07
- ❑ 716 Ryan Dempster .20 .07
- ❑ 717 Rich Garces .20 .07
- ❑ 718 Mike Myers .20 .07
- ❑ 719 Luis Ordaz .20 .07
- ❑ 720 Kazuhiro Sasaki .20 .07
- ❑ 721 Mark Quinn .20 .07
- ❑ 722 Ramon Ortiz .20 .07
- ❑ 723 Kerry Ligtenberg .20 .07
- ❑ 724 Rolando Arrojo .20 .07
- ❑ 725 Tsuyoshi Shinjo RC .50 .20
- ❑ 726 Ichiro Suzuki RC 12.00 5.00
- ❑ 727 Oswalt/Strange/Rauch .75 .30
- ❑ 728 Jake Peavy RC 3.00 1.25
- ❑ 729 S.Smyth RC/Bynum/Haynes .25 .08
- ❑ 730 Cuddyer/Lawrence/Freeman .25 .08
- ❑ 731 C.Pena/Barnes/Wise .25 .08
- ❑ 732 Dawkins/Almonte/Lopez .25 .08
- ❑ 733 Escobar/Valent/Wilkerson .25 .08
- ❑ 734 Hall/Barajas/Goldbach .25 .08
- ❑ 735 Romano/Giles/Ozuna .40 .15
- ❑ 736 D.Brown/Cust/V.Wells .25 .08
- ❑ 737 L.Montanez RC/D.Espinosa .25 .08
- ❑ 738 J.Wayne RC/A.Pluta RC .25 .08
- ❑ 739 J.Axelson RC/C.Cali RC .25 .08
- ❑ 740 S.Boyd RC/C.Morris RC .25 .08
- ❑ 741 T.Arko RC/D.Moylan RC .25 .08
- ❑ 742 L.Cotto RC/L.Escobar .25 .08
- ❑ 743 B.Mims RC/B.Williams RC .25 .08
- ❑ 744 C.Russ RC/B.Edwards .25 .08
- ❑ 745 J.Torres/B.Diggins .25 .08
- ❑ 746 Edwin Encarnacion RC 3.00 1.25
- ❑ 747 B.Bass RC/O.Ayala RC .25 .08
- ❑ 748 M.Matthews RC/J.Kaanoi .25 .08
- ❑ 749 S.McFarland RC/A.Sterrett RC .25 .08
- ❑ 750 D.Krynzel/G.Sizemore 1.50 .60
- ❑ 751 K.Bucktrot/D.Sardinha .25 .08
- ❑ 752 Anaheim Angels TC .20 .07
- ❑ 753 Arizona Diamondbacks TC .20 .07
- ❑ 754 Atlanta Braves TC .20 .07
- ❑ 755 Baltimore Orioles TC .20 .07
- ❑ 756 Boston Red Sox TC .20 .07
- ❑ 757 Chicago Cubs TC .20 .07
- ❑ 758 Chicago White Sox TC .20 .07
- ❑ 759 Cincinnati Reds TC .20 .07
- ❑ 760 Cleveland Indians TC .20 .07
- ❑ 761 Colorado Rockies TC .20 .07
- ❑ 762 Detroit Tigers TC .20 .07
- ❑ 763 Florida Marlins TC .20 .07
- ❑ 764 Houston Astros TC .20 .07
- ❑ 765 Kansas City Royals TC .20 .07
- ❑ 766 Los Angeles Dodgers TC .20 .07
- ❑ 767 Milwaukee Brewers TC .20 .07
- ❑ 768 Minnesota Twins TC .20 .07
- ❑ 769 Montreal Expos TC .20 .07
- ❑ 770 New York Mets TC .20 .07
- ❑ 771 New York Yankees TC 1.00 .40
- ❑ 772 Oakland Athletics TC .20 .07
- ❑ 773 Philadelphia Phillies TC .20 .07
- ❑ 774 Pittsburgh Pirates TC .20 .07
- ❑ 775 San Diego Padres TC .20 .07
- ❑ 776 San Francisco Giants TC .20 .07
- ❑ 777 Seattle Mariners TC .20 .07
- ❑ 778 St. Louis Cardinals TC .20 .07
- ❑ 779 Tampa Bay Devil Rays TC .20 .07
- ❑ 780 Texas Rangers TC .20 .07
- ❑ 781 Toronto Blue Jays TC .20 .07
- ❑ 782 Bucky Dent GM .20 .07
- ❑ 783 Jackie Robinson GM .50 .20
- ❑ 784 Roberto Clemente GM .60 .25
- ❑ 785 Nolan Ryan GM .75 .30
- ❑ 786 Kerry Wood GM .20 .07
- ❑ 787 Rickey Henderson GM .20 .07
- ❑ 788 Lou Brock GM .30 .10
- ❑ 789 David Wells GM .20 .07
- ❑ 790 Andruw Jones GM .20 .07
- ❑ 791 Carlton Fisk GM .20 .07
- ❑ TK B.Jackson/D.Sanders Bat 120.00 60.00
- ❑ NNO B.Thomson/R.Branca AU 60.00 30.00

2001 Topps Traded

- ❑ COMPLETE SET (265) 175.00 100.00
- ❑ COMMON CARD (1-99/145-265) .40 .15
- ❑ COMMON REPRINT (100-144) 1.00 .40
- ❑ T1 Sandy Alomar Jr. .40 .15
- ❑ T2 Kevin Appier .50 .20
- ❑ T3 Brad Ausmus .50 .20
- ❑ T4 Derek Bell .40 .15
- ❑ T5 Bret Boone .50 .20
- ❑ T6 Rico Brogna .40 .15
- ❑ T7 Ellis Burks .50 .20
- ❑ T8 Ken Caminiti .50 .20
- ❑ T9 Roger Cedeno .40 .15
- ❑ T10 Royce Clayton .40 .15
- ❑ T11 Enrique Wilson .40 .15
- ❑ T12 Rheal Cormier .40 .15
- ❑ T13 Eric Davis .50 .20
- ❑ T14 Shawon Dunston .40 .15
- ❑ T15 Andres Galarraga .50 .20
- ❑ T16 Tom Gordon .40 .15
- ❑ T17 Mark Grace .75 .30
- ❑ T18 Jeffrey Hammonds .40 .15
- ❑ T19 Dustin Hermanson .40 .15
- ❑ T20 Quinton McCracken .40 .15
- ❑ T21 Todd Hundley .40 .15
- ❑ T22 Charles Johnson .50 .20
- ❑ T23 Marquis Grissom .50 .20
- ❑ T24 Jose Mesa .40 .15
- ❑ T25 Brian Boehringer .40 .15
- ❑ T26 John Rocker .50 .20
- ❑ T27 Jeff Frye .40 .15
- ❑ T28 Reggie Sanders .50 .20
- ❑ T29 David Segui .40 .15
- ❑ T30 Mike Sirotka .40 .15
- ❑ T31 Fernando Tatis .40 .15
- ❑ T32 Steve Trachsel .40 .15
- ❑ T33 Ismael Valdes .40 .15
- ❑ T34 Randy Velarde .40 .15
- ❑ T35 Ryan Kohlmeier .40 .15
- ❑ T36 Mike Bordick .50 .20
- ❑ T37 Kent Bottenfield .40 .15
- ❑ T38 Pat Rapp .40 .15
- ❑ T39 Jeff Nelson .40 .15
- ❑ T40 Ricky Bottalico .40 .15
- ❑ T41 Luke Prokopec .40 .15
- ❑ T42 Hideo Nomo 1.25 .50

❑ T43 Bill Mueller .50 .20
❑ T44 Roberto Kelly .40 .15
❑ T45 Chris Holt .40 .15
❑ T46 Mike Jackson .40 .15
❑ T47 Devon White .50 .20
❑ T48 Gerald Williams .40 .15
❑ T49 Eddie Taubensee .40 .15
❑ T50 Brian Hunter .40 .15
❑ T51 Nelson Cruz .40 .15
❑ T52 Jeff Fassero .40 .15
❑ T53 Bubba Trammell .40 .15
❑ T54 Bo Porter .40 .15
❑ T55 Greg Norton .40 .15
❑ T56 Benito Santiago .50 .20
❑ T57 Ruben Rivera .40 .15
❑ T58 Dee Brown .40 .15
❑ T59 Jose Canseco .75 .30
❑ T60 Chris Michalak .40 .15
❑ T61 Tim Worrell .40 .15
❑ T62 Matt Clement .50 .20
❑ T63 Bill Pulsipher .40 .15
❑ T64 Troy Brohawn RC .40 .15
❑ T65 Mark Kotsay .50 .20
❑ T66 Jimmy Rollins .50 .20
❑ T67 Shea Hillenbrand .50 .20
❑ T68 Ted Lilly .40 .15
❑ T69 Jermaine Dye .50 .20
❑ T70 Jerry Hairston Jr. .40 .15
❑ T71 John Mabry .40 .15
❑ T72 Kurt Abbott .40 .15
❑ T73 Eric Owens .40 .15
❑ T74 Jeff Brantley .40 .15
❑ T75 Roy Oswalt 1.25 .50
❑ T76 Doug Mientkiewicz .50 .20
❑ T77 Rickey Henderson 1.25 .50
❑ T78 Jason Grimsley .40 .15
❑ T79 Christian Parker RC .40 .15
❑ T80 Donne Wall .40 .15
❑ T81 Alex Arias .40 .15
❑ T82 Willis Roberts .40 .15
❑ T83 Ryan Minor .40 .15
❑ T84 Jason LaRue .40 .15
❑ T85 Ruben Sierra .50 .20
❑ T86 Johnny Damon .75 .30
❑ T87 Juan Gonzalez .50 .20
❑ T88 C.C. Sabathia .50 .20
❑ T89 Tony Batista .40 .15
❑ T90 Jay Witasick .40 .15
❑ T91 Brent Abernathy .40 .15
❑ T92 Paul LoDuca .50 .20
❑ T93 Wes Helms .40 .15
❑ T94 Mark Wohlers .40 .15
❑ T95 Rob Bell .40 .15
❑ T96 Tim Redding .40 .15
❑ T97 Bud Smith RC .40 .15
❑ T98 Adam Dunn .75 .30
❑ T99 I.Suzuki/A.Pujols ROY 15.00 6.00
❑ T100 Carlton Fisk 81 1.25 .50
❑ T101 Tim Raines 81 1.00 .40
❑ T102 Juan Marichal 74 1.00 .40
❑ T103 Dave Winfield 81 1.00 .40
❑ T104 Reggie Jackson 82 1.25 .50
❑ T105 Cal Ripken 82 6.00 2.50
❑ T106 Ozzie Smith 82 3.00 1.25
❑ T107 Tom Seaver 83 1.25 .50
❑ T108 Lou Piniella 74 1.00 .40
❑ T109 Dwight Gooden 84 1.00 .40
❑ T110 Bret Saberhagen 84 1.00 .40
❑ T111 Gary Carter 85 1.00 .40
❑ T112 Jack Clark 85 1.00 .40
❑ T113 Rickey Henderson 85 2.00 .75
❑ T114 Barry Bonds 86 5.00 2.00
❑ T115 Bobby Bonilla 86 1.00 .40
❑ T116 Jose Canseco 86 1.25 .50
❑ T117 Will Clark 86 1.25 .50
❑ T118 Andres Galarraga 86 1.00 .40
❑ T119 Bo Jackson 86 2.00 .75
❑ T120 Wally Joyner 86 1.00 .40
❑ T121 Ellis Burks 87 1.00 .40
❑ T122 David Cone 87 1.00 .40
❑ T123 Greg Maddux 87 3.00 1.25
❑ T124 Willie Randolph 76 1.00 .40
❑ T125 Dennis Eckersley 87 1.00 .40
❑ T126 Matt Williams 87 1.00 .40
❑ T127 Joe Morgan 81 1.00 .40
❑ T128 Fred McGriff 87 1.25 .50
❑ T129 Roberto Alomar 88 1.25 .50
❑ T130 Lee Smith 88 1.00 .40
❑ T131 David Wells 88 1.00 .40
❑ T132 Ken Griffey Jr. 89 3.00 1.25
❑ T133 Deion Sanders 89 1.25 .50
❑ T134 Nolan Ryan 89 4.00 1.50
❑ T135 David Justice 90 1.00 .40
❑ T136 Joe Carter 91 1.00 .40
❑ T137 Jack Morris 92 1.00 .40
❑ T138 Mike Piazza 93 3.00 1.25
❑ T139 Barry Bonds 93 5.00 2.00
❑ T140 Terrence Long 94 1.00 .40
❑ T141 Ben Grieve 94 1.00 .40
❑ T142 Richie Sexson 95 1.00 .40
❑ T143 Sean Burroughs 99 1.00 .40
❑ T144 Alfonso Soriano 99 1.25 .50
❑ T145 Bob Boone MG .50 .20
❑ T146 Larry Bowa MG .50 .20
❑ T147 Bob Brenly MG .40 .15
❑ T148 Buck Martinez MG .40 .15
❑ T149 Lloyd McClendon MG .40 .15
❑ T150 Jim Tracy MG .40 .15
❑ T151 Jared Abruzzo RC .40 .15
❑ T152 Kurt Ainsworth .40 .15
❑ T153 Willie Bloomquist .50 .20
❑ T154 Ben Broussard .40 .15
❑ T155 Bobby Bradley .40 .15
❑ T156 Mike Bynum .40 .15
❑ T157 A.J. Hinch .40 .15
❑ T158 Ryan Christianson .40 .15
❑ T159 Carlos Silva .40 .15
❑ T160 Joe Crede 1.25 .50
❑ T161 Jack Cust .40 .15
❑ T162 Ben Diggins .40 .15
❑ T163 Phil Dumatrait .40 .15
❑ T164 Alex Escobar .40 .15
❑ T165 Miguel Olivo .40 .15
❑ T166 Chris George .40 .15
❑ T167 Marcus Giles .50 .20
❑ T168 Keith Ginter .40 .15
❑ T169 Josh Girdley .40 .15
❑ T170 Tony Alvarez .40 .15
❑ T171 Scott Seabol .40 .15
❑ T172 Josh Hamilton .40 .15
❑ T173 Jason Hart .40 .15
❑ T174 Israel Alcantara .40 .15
❑ T175 Jake Peavy 2.00 .75
❑ T176 Stubby Clapp RC .40 .15
❑ T177 D'Angelo Jimenez .40 .15
❑ T178 Nick Johnson .50 .20
❑ T179 Ben Johnson .50 .20
❑ T180 Larry Bigbie .40 .15
❑ T181 Allen Levrault .40 .15
❑ T182 Felipe Lopez .50 .20
❑ T183 Sean Burnett .40 .15
❑ T184 Nick Neugebauer .40 .15
❑ T185 Austin Kearns .50 .20
❑ T186 Corey Patterson .40 .15
❑ T187 Carlos Pena .40 .15
❑ T188 Ricardo Rodriguez RC .40 .15
❑ T189 Juan Rivera .40 .15
❑ T190 Grant Roberts .40 .15
❑ T191 Adam Pettyjohn RC .40 .15
❑ T192 Jared Sandberg .40 .15
❑ T193 Xavier Nady .40 .15
❑ T194 Dane Sardinha .40 .15
❑ T195 Shawn Sonnier .40 .15
❑ T196 Rafael Soriano .40 .15
❑ T197 Brian Specht RC .40 .15
❑ T198 Aaron Myette .40 .15
❑ T199 Juan Uribe RC .50 .20
❑ T200 Jayson Werth .40 .15
❑ T201 Brad Wilkerson .40 .15
❑ T202 Horacio Estrada .40 .15
❑ T203 Joel Pineiro .50 .20
❑ T204 Matt LeCroy .40 .15
❑ T205 Michael Coleman .40 .15
❑ T206 Ben Sheets .75 .30
❑ T207 Eric Byrnes .40 .15
❑ T208 Sean Burroughs .40 .15
❑ T209 Ken Harvey .40 .15
❑ T210 Travis Hafner 4.00 1.50
❑ T211 Erick Almonte .40 .15
❑ T212 Jason Belcher RC .40 .15
❑ T213 Wilson Betemit RC 1.50 .60
❑ T214 Hank Blalock RC 2.50 1.00
❑ T215 Danny Borrell .40 .15
❑ T216 John Buck RC .50 .20
❑ T217 Freddie Bynum RC .40 .15
❑ T218 Noel Devarez RC .40 .15
❑ T219 Juan Diaz RC .40 .15
❑ T220 Felix Diaz RC .40 .15
❑ T221 Josh Fogg RC .40 .15
❑ T222 Matt Ford RC .40 .15
❑ T223 Scott Heard .40 .15
❑ T224 Ben Hendrickson RC .40 .15
❑ T225 Cody Ross RC .40 .15
❑ T226 Adrian Hernandez RC .40 .15
❑ T227 Alfredo Amezaga RC .40 .15
❑ T228 Bob Keppel RC .40 .15
❑ T229 Ryan Madson RC .75 .30
❑ T230 Octavio Martinez RC .40 .15
❑ T231 Hee Seop Choi .50 .20
❑ T232 Thomas Mitchell .40 .15
❑ T233 Luis Montanez .40 .15
❑ T234 Andy Morales RC .40 .15
❑ T235 Justin Morneau RC 8.00 3.00
❑ T236 Toe Nash RC .40 .15
❑ T237 Valentino Pascucci RC .40 .15
❑ T238 Roy Smith RC .40 .15
❑ T239 Antonio Perez RC .50 .20
❑ T240 Chad Petty RC .40 .15
❑ T241 Steve Smyth .40 .15
❑ T242 Jose Reyes RC 25.00 10.00
❑ T243 Eric Reynolds RC .40 .15
❑ T244 Dominic Rich .40 .15
❑ T245 Jason Richardson RC .40 .15
❑ T246 Ed Rogers RC .40 .15
❑ T247 Albert Pujols RC 50.00 20.00
❑ T248 Esix Snead RC .40 .15
❑ T249 Luis Torres RC .40 .15
❑ T250 Matt White RC .40 .15
❑ T251 Blake Williams .40 .15
❑ T252 Chris Russ .40 .15
❑ T253 Joe Kennedy RC .50 .20
❑ T254 Jeff Randazzo RC .40 .15
❑ T255 Beau Hale RC .40 .15
❑ T256 Brad Hennessey RC 1.25 .50
❑ T257 Jake Gautreau RC .40 .15
❑ T258 Jeff Mathis RC .50 .20
❑ T259 Aaron Heilman RC .50 .20
❑ T260 Bronson Sardinha RC .40 .15
❑ T261 Irvin Guzman RC 4.00 1.50
❑ T262 Gabe Gross RC .50 .20
❑ T263 J.D. Martin RC .40 .15
❑ T264 Chris Smith RC .40 .15
❑ T265 Kenny Baugh RC .40 .15

2002 Topps

❑ COMPLETE SET (718) 80.00 30.00
❑ COMP.FACT.BROWN SET (723) 80.00 40.00
❑ COMP.FACT.GREEN SET (723) 80.0040.00
❑ COMPLETE SERIES 1 (364) 40.00 15.00
❑ COMPLETE SERIES 2 (354) 40.00 15.00
❑ COMMON CARD (1-6/8-719) .20 .07
❑ COMMON (307-331/671-695) .50 .20
❑ COMMON CARD (332-364) .50 .20
❑ 1 Pedro Martinez .30 .10
❑ 2 Mike Stanton .20 .07
❑ 3 Brad Penny .20 .07
❑ 4 Mike Matheny .20 .07
❑ 5 Johnny Damon .30 .10
❑ 6 Bret Boone .20 .07
❑ 7 Does Not Exist

❑ 8	Chris Truby	.20	.07
❑ 9	B.J. Surhoff	.20	.07
❑ 10	Mike Hampton	.20	.07
❑ 11	Juan Pierre	.20	.07
❑ 12	Mark Buehrle	.20	.07
❑ 13	Bob Abreu	.20	.07
❑ 14	David Cone	.20	.07
❑ 15	Aaron Sele	.20	.07
❑ 16	Fernando Tatis	.20	.07
❑ 17	Bobby Jones	.20	.07
❑ 18	Rick Helling	.20	.07
❑ 19	Dmitri Young	.20	.07
❑ 20	Mike Mussina	.30	.10
❑ 21	Mike Sweeney	.20	.07
❑ 22	Cristian Guzman	.20	.07
❑ 23	Ryan Kohlmeier	.20	.07
❑ 24	Adam Kennedy	.20	.07
❑ 25	Larry Walker	.20	.07
❑ 26	Eric Davis	.20	.07
❑ 27	Jason Tyner	.20	.07
❑ 28	Eric Young	.20	.07
❑ 29	Jason Marquis	.20	.07
❑ 30	Luis Gonzalez	.20	.07
❑ 31	Kevin Tapani	.20	.07
❑ 32	Orlando Cabrera	.20	.07
❑ 33	Marty Cordova	.20	.07
❑ 34	Brad Ausmus	.20	.07
❑ 35	Livan Hernandez	.20	.07
❑ 36	Alex Gonzalez	.20	.07
❑ 37	Edgar Renteria	.20	.07
❑ 38	Bengie Molina	.20	.07
❑ 39	Frank Menechino	.20	.07
❑ 40	Rafael Palmeiro	.30	.10
❑ 41	Brad Fullmer	.20	.07
❑ 42	Julio Zuleta	.20	.07
❑ 43	Darren Dreifort	.20	.07
❑ 44	Trot Nixon	.20	.07
❑ 45	Trevor Hoffman	.20	.07
❑ 46	Vladimir Nunez	.20	.07
❑ 47	Mark Kotsay	.20	.07
❑ 48	Kenny Rogers	.20	.07
❑ 49	Ben Petrick	.20	.07
❑ 50	Jeff Bagwell	.30	.10
❑ 51	Juan Encarnacion	.20	.07
❑ 52	Ramiro Mendoza	.20	.07
❑ 53	Brian Meadows	.20	.07
❑ 54	Chad Curtis	.20	.07
❑ 55	Aramis Ramirez	.20	.07
❑ 56	Mark McLemore	.20	.07
❑ 57	Dante Bichette	.20	.07
❑ 58	Scott Schoeneweis	.20	.07
❑ 59	Jose Cruz Jr.	.20	.07
❑ 60	Roger Clemens	1.00	.40
❑ 61	Jose Guillen	.20	.07
❑ 62	Darren Oliver	.20	.07
❑ 63	Chris Reitsma	.20	.07
❑ 64	Jeff Abbott	.20	.07
❑ 65	Robin Ventura	.20	.07
❑ 66	Denny Neagle	.20	.07
❑ 67	Al Martin	.20	.07
❑ 68	Benito Santiago	.20	.07
❑ 69	Roy Oswalt	.20	.07
❑ 70	Juan Gonzalez	.20	.07
❑ 71	Garret Anderson	.20	.07
❑ 72	Bobby Bonilla	.20	.07
❑ 73	Danny Bautista	.20	.07
❑ 74	J.T. Snow	.20	.07
❑ 75	Derek Jeter	1.25	.50
❑ 76	John Olerud	.20	.07
❑ 77	Kevin Appier	.20	.07
❑ 78	Phil Nevin	.20	.07
❑ 79	Sean Casey	.20	.07
❑ 80	Troy Glaus	.20	.07
❑ 81	Joe Randa	.20	.07
❑ 82	Jose Valentin	.20	.07
❑ 83	Ricky Bottalico	.20	.07
❑ 84	Todd Zeile	.20	.07
❑ 85	Barry Larkin	.30	.10
❑ 86	Bob Wickman	.20	.07
❑ 87	Jeff Shaw	.20	.07
❑ 88	Greg Vaughn	.20	.07
❑ 89	Fernando Vina	.20	.07
❑ 90	Mark Mulder	.20	.07
❑ 91	Paul Bako	.20	.07
❑ 92	Aaron Boone	.20	.07
❑ 93	Esteban Loaiza	.20	.07
❑ 94	Richie Sexson	.20	.07
❑ 95	Alfonso Soriano	.20	.07
❑ 96	Tony Womack	.20	.07
❑ 97	Paul Shuey	.20	.07
❑ 98	Melvin Mora	.20	.07
❑ 99	Tony Gwynn	.60	.25
❑ 100	Vladimir Guerrero	.50	.20
❑ 101	Keith Osik	.20	.07
❑ 102	Bud Smith	.20	.07
❑ 103	Scott Williamson	.20	.07
❑ 104	Daryle Ward	.20	.07
❑ 105	Doug Mientkiewicz	.20	.07
❑ 106	Stan Javier	.20	.07
❑ 107	Russ Ortiz	.20	.07
❑ 108	Wade Miller	.20	.07
❑ 109	Luke Prokopec	.20	.07
❑ 110	Andruw Jones	.30	.10
❑ 111	Ron Coomer	.20	.07
❑ 112	Dan Wilson	.20	.07
❑ 113	Luis Castillo	.20	.07
❑ 114	Derek Bell	.20	.07
❑ 115	Gary Sheffield	.20	.07
❑ 116	Ruben Rivera	.20	.07
❑ 117	Paul O'Neill	.30	.10
❑ 118	Craig Paquette	.20	.07
❑ 119	Kelvin Escobar	.20	.07
❑ 120	Brad Radke	.20	.07
❑ 121	Jorge Fabregas	.20	.07
❑ 122	Randy Winn	.20	.07
❑ 123	Tom Goodwin	.20	.07
❑ 124	Jaret Wright	.20	.07
❑ 125	Manny Ramirez	.30	.10
❑ 126	Al Leiter	.20	.07
❑ 127	Ben Davis	.20	.07
❑ 128	Frank Catalanotto	.20	.07
❑ 129	Jose Cabrera	.20	.07
❑ 130	Magglio Ordonez	.20	.07
❑ 131	Jose Macias	.20	.07
❑ 132	Ted Lilly	.20	.07
❑ 133	Chris Holt	.20	.07
❑ 134	Eric Milton	.20	.07
❑ 135	Shannon Stewart	.20	.07
❑ 136	Omar Olivares	.20	.07
❑ 137	David Segui	.20	.07
❑ 138	Jeff Nelson	.20	.07
❑ 139	Matt Williams	.20	.07
❑ 140	Ellis Burks	.20	.07
❑ 141	Jason Bere	.20	.07
❑ 142	Jimmy Haynes	.20	.07
❑ 143	Ramon Hernandez	.20	.07
❑ 144	Craig Counsell	.20	.07
❑ 145	John Smoltz	.30	.10
❑ 146	Homer Bush	.20	.07
❑ 147	Quilvio Veras	.20	.07
❑ 148	Esteban Yan	.20	.07
❑ 149	Ramon Ortiz	.20	.07
❑ 150	Carlos Delgado	.20	.07
❑ 151	Lee Stevens	.20	.07
❑ 152	Wil Cordero	.20	.07
❑ 153	Mike Bordick	.20	.07
❑ 154	John Flaherty	.20	.07
❑ 155	Omar Daal	.20	.07
❑ 156	Todd Ritchie	.20	.07
❑ 157	Carl Everett	.20	.07
❑ 158	Scott Sullivan	.20	.07
❑ 159	Deivi Cruz	.20	.07
❑ 160	Albert Pujols	1.00	.40
❑ 160A	Albert Pujols COR		
❑ 161	Royce Clayton	.20	.07
❑ 162	Jeff Suppan	.20	.07
❑ 163	C.C. Sabathia	.20	.07
❑ 164	Jimmy Rollins	.20	.07
❑ 165	Rickey Henderson	.50	.20
❑ 166	Rey Ordonez	.20	.07
❑ 167	Shawn Estes	.20	.07
❑ 168	Reggie Sanders	.20	.07
❑ 169	Jon Lieber	.20	.07
❑ 170	Armando Benitez	.20	.07
❑ 171	Mike Remlinger	.20	.07
❑ 172	Billy Wagner	.20	.07
❑ 173	Troy Percival	.20	.07
❑ 174	Devon White	.20	.07
❑ 175	Ivan Rodriguez	.30	.10
❑ 176	Dustin Hermanson	.20	.07
❑ 177	Brian Anderson	.20	.07
❑ 178	Graeme Lloyd	.20	.07
❑ 179	Russell Branyan	.20	.07
❑ 180	Bobby Higginson	.20	.07
❑ 181	Alex Gonzalez	.20	.07
❑ 182	John Franco	.20	.07
❑ 183	Sidney Ponson	.20	.07
❑ 184	Jose Mesa	.20	.07
❑ 185	Todd Hollandsworth	.20	.07
❑ 186	Kevin Young	.20	.07
❑ 187	Tim Wakefield	.20	.07
❑ 188	Craig Biggio	.30	.10
❑ 189	Jason Isringhausen	.20	.07
❑ 190	Mark Quinn	.20	.07
❑ 191	Glendon Rusch	.20	.07
❑ 192	Damian Miller	.20	.07
❑ 193	Sandy Alomar Jr.	.20	.07
❑ 194	Scott Brosius	.20	.07
❑ 195	Dave Martinez	.20	.07
❑ 196	Danny Graves	.20	.07
❑ 197	Shea Hillenbrand	.20	.07
❑ 198	Jimmy Anderson	.20	.07
❑ 199	Travis Lee	.20	.07
❑ 200	Randy Johnson	.50	.20
❑ 201	Carlos Beltran	.20	.07
❑ 202	Jerry Hairston	.20	.07
❑ 203	Jesus Sanchez	.20	.07
❑ 204	Eddie Taubensee	.20	.07
❑ 205	David Wells	.20	.07
❑ 206	Russ Davis	.20	.07
❑ 207	Michael Barrett	.20	.07
❑ 208	Marquis Grissom	.20	.07
❑ 209	Byung-Hyun Kim	.20	.07
❑ 210	Hideo Nomo	.50	.20
❑ 211	Ryan Rupe	.20	.07
❑ 212	Ricky Gutierrez	.20	.07
❑ 213	Darryl Kile	.20	.07
❑ 214	Rico Brogna	.20	.07
❑ 215	Terrence Long	.20	.07
❑ 216	Mike Jackson	.20	.07
❑ 217	Jamey Wright	.20	.07
❑ 218	Adrian Beltre	.20	.07
❑ 219	Benny Agbayani	.20	.07
❑ 220	Chuck Knoblauch	.20	.07
❑ 221	Randy Wolf	.20	.07
❑ 222	Andy Ashby	.20	.07
❑ 223	Corey Koskie	.20	.07
❑ 224	Roger Cedeno	.20	.07
❑ 225	Ichiro Suzuki	1.00	.40
❑ 226	Keith Foulke	.20	.07
❑ 227	Ryan Minor	.20	.07
❑ 228	Shawon Dunston	.20	.07
❑ 229	Alex Cora	.20	.07
❑ 230	Jeromy Burnitz	.20	.07
❑ 231	Mark Grace	.30	.10
❑ 232	Aubrey Huff	.20	.07
❑ 233	Jeffrey Hammonds	.20	.07
❑ 234	Olmedo Saenz	.20	.07
❑ 235	Brian Jordan	.20	.07
❑ 236	Jeremy Giambi	.20	.07
❑ 237	Joe Girardi	.20	.07
❑ 238	Eric Gagne	.20	.07
❑ 239	Masato Yoshii	.20	.07
❑ 240	Greg Maddux	.75	.30
❑ 241	Bryan Rekar	.20	.07
❑ 242	Ray Durham	.20	.07
❑ 243	Torii Hunter	.20	.07
❑ 244	Derrek Lee	.30	.10
❑ 245	Jim Edmonds	.20	.07
❑ 246	Einar Diaz	.20	.07
❑ 247	Brian Bohanon	.20	.07
❑ 248	Ron Belliard	.20	.07
❑ 249	Mike Lowell	.20	.07
❑ 250	Sammy Sosa	.50	.20
❑ 251	Richard Hidalgo	.20	.07
❑ 252	Bartolo Colon	.20	.07
❑ 253	Jorge Posada	.30	.10
❑ 254	LaTroy Hawkins	.20	.07
❑ 255	Paul LoDuca	.20	.07
❑ 256	Carlos Febles	.20	.07
❑ 257	Nelson Cruz	.20	.07
❑ 258	Edgardo Alfonzo	.20	.07
❑ 259	Joey Hamilton	.20	.07
❑ 260	Cliff Floyd	.20	.07
❑ 261	Wes Helms	.20	.07
❑ 262	Jay Bell	.20	.07
❑ 263	Mike Cameron	.20	.07
❑ 264	Paul Konerko	.20	.07

	No.	Card		
❑	265	Jeff Kent	.20	.07
❑	266	Robert Fick	.20	.07
❑	267	Allen Levrault	.20	.07
❑	268	Placido Polanco	.20	.07
❑	269	Marlon Anderson	.20	.07
❑	270	Mariano Rivera	.50	.20
❑	271	Chan Ho Park	.20	.07
❑	272	Jose Vizcaino	.20	.07
❑	273	Jeff D'Amico	.20	.07
❑	274	Mark Gardner	.20	.07
❑	275	Travis Fryman	.20	.07
❑	276	Darren Lewis	.20	.07
❑	277	Bruce Bochy MG	.20	.07
❑	278	Jerry Manuel MG	.20	.07
❑	279	Bob Brenly MG	.20	.07
❑	280	Don Baylor MG	.20	.07
❑	281	Davey Lopes MG	.20	.07
❑	282	Jerry Narron MG	.20	.07
❑	283	Tony Muser MG	.20	.07
❑	284	Hal McRae MG	.20	.07
❑	285	Bobby Cox MG	.20	.07
❑	286	Larry Dierker MG	.20	.07
❑	287	Phil Garner MG	.20	.07
❑	288	Joe Kerrigan MG	.20	.07
❑	289	Bobby Valentine MG	.20	.07
❑	290	Dusty Baker MG	.20	.07
❑	291	Lloyd McClendon MG	.20	.07
❑	292	Mike Scioscia MG	.20	.07
❑	293	Buck Martinez MG	.20	.07
❑	294	Larry Bowa MG	.20	.07
❑	295	Tony LaRussa MG	.20	.07
❑	296	Jeff Torborg MG	.20	.07
❑	297	Tom Kelly MG	.20	.07
❑	298	Mike Hargrove MG	.20	.07
❑	299	Art Howe MG	.20	.07
❑	300	Lou Piniella MG	.20	.07
❑	301	Charlie Manuel MG	.20	.07
❑	302	Buddy Bell MG	.20	.07
❑	303	Tony Perez MG	.20	.07
❑	304	Bob Boone MG	.20	.07
❑	305	Joe Torre MG	.30	.10
❑	306	Jim Tracy MG	.20	.07
❑	307	Jason Lane PROS	.50	.20
❑	308	Chris George PROS	.50	.20
❑	309	Hank Blalock PROS	1.00	.40
❑	310	Joe Borchard PROS	.50	.20
❑	311	Marlon Byrd PROS	.50	.20
❑	312	Raymond Cabrera PROS RC	.50	.20
❑	313	Freddy Sanchez PROS RC	2.00	.75
❑	314	Scott Wiggins PROS RC	.50	.20
❑	315	Jason Maule PROS RC	.50	.20
❑	316	Dionys Cesar PROS RC	.50	.20
❑	317	Boof Bonser PROS	.50	.20
❑	318	Juan Tolentino PROS RC	.50	.20
❑	319	Earl Snyder PROS RC	.50	.20
❑	320	Travis Wade PROS RC	.50	.20
❑	321	Napoleon Calzado PROS RC	.50	.20
❑	322	Eric Glaser PROS RC	.50	.20
❑	323	Craig Kuzmic PROS RC	.50	.20
❑	324	Nic Jackson PROS RC	.50	.20
❑	325	Mike Rivera PROS	.50	.20
❑	326	Jason Bay PROS RC	3.00	1.25
❑	327	Chris Smith DP	.50	.20
❑	328	Jake Gautreau DP	.50	.20
❑	329	Gabe Gross DP	.50	.20
❑	330	Kenny Baugh DP	.50	.20
❑	331	J.D. Martin DP	.50	.20
❑	332	Barry Bonds HL	1.25	.50
❑	333	Rickey Henderson HL	.50	.20
❑	334	Bud Smith HL	.50	.20
❑	335	Rickey Henderson HL	.50	.20
❑	336	Barry Bonds HL	1.25	.50
❑	337	Ichiro/Giambi/Alomar LL	.50	.20
❑	338	A.Rod/Ichiro/Boone LL	.50	.20
❑	339	A.Rod/Thome/Palmeiro LL	.50	.20
❑	340	Boone/J.Gonz/A.Rod LL	.50	.20
❑	341	Garcia/Mussina/Mays LL	.50	.20
❑	342	Nomo/Mussina/Clemens LL	.50	.20
❑	343	Walker/Helton/Alou/Berk LL	.50	.20
❑	344	Sosa/Helton/Bonds LL	.75	.30
❑	345	Bonds/Sosa/L.Gonz LL	.75	.30
❑	346	Sosa/Helton/L.Gonz LL	.50	.20
❑	347	R.John/Schilling/Burkett LL	.50	.20
❑	348	R.John/Schilling/Park LL	.50	.20
❑	349	Seattle Mariners PB	.50	.20
❑	350	Oakland Athletics PB	.50	.20
❑	351	New York Yankees PB	.50	.20
❑	352	Cleveland Indians PB	.50	.20
❑	353	Arizona Diamondbacks PB	.50	.20
❑	354	Atlanta Braves PB	.50	.20
❑	355	St. Louis Cardinals PB	.50	.20
❑	356	Houston Astros PB	.50	.20
❑	357	Diamondbacks-Astros UWS	.50	.20
❑	358	Mike Piazza UWS	.50	.20
❑	359	Braves-Phillies UWS	.50	.20
❑	360	Curt Schilling UWS	.50	.20
❑	361	R.Clemens/L.Mazzilli UWS	.50	.20
❑	362	Sammy Sosa UWS	.30	.10
❑	363	Lampkin/Ichiro/Boone UWS	.50	.20
❑	364	B.Bonds/J.Bagwell UWS	.75	.30
❑	365	Barry Bonds HR 1	15.00	6.00
❑	365	Barry Bonds HR 2	10.00	4.00
❑	365	Barry Bonds HR 3	10.00	4.00
❑	365	Barry Bonds HR 4	10.00	4.00
❑	365	Barry Bonds HR 5	10.00	4.00
❑	365	Barry Bonds HR 6	10.00	4.00
❑	365	Barry Bonds HR 7	10.00	4.00
❑	365	Barry Bonds HR 8	10.00	4.00
❑	365	Barry Bonds HR 9	10.00	4.00
❑	365	Barry Bonds HR 10	10.00	4.00
❑	365	Barry Bonds HR 11	10.00	4.00
❑	365	Barry Bonds HR 12	10.00	4.00
❑	365	Barry Bonds HR 13	10.00	4.00
❑	365	Barry Bonds HR 14	10.00	4.00
❑	365	Barry Bonds HR 15	10.00	4.00
❑	365	Barry Bonds HR 16	10.00	4.00
❑	365	Barry Bonds HR 17	10.00	4.00
❑	365	Barry Bonds HR 18	10.00	4.00
❑	365	Barry Bonds HR 19	10.00	4.00
❑	365	Barry Bonds HR 20	10.00	4.00
❑	365	Barry Bonds HR 21	10.00	4.00
❑	365	Barry Bonds HR 22	10.00	4.00
❑	365	Barry Bonds HR 23	10.00	4.00
❑	365	Barry Bonds HR 24	10.00	4.00
❑	365	Barry Bonds HR 25	10.00	4.00
❑	365	Barry Bonds HR 26	10.00	4.00
❑	365	Barry Bonds HR 27	10.00	4.00
❑	365	Barry Bonds HR 28	10.00	4.00
❑	365	Barry Bonds HR 29	10.00	4.00
❑	365	Barry Bonds HR 30	10.00	4.00
❑	365	Barry Bonds HR 31	10.00	4.00
❑	365	Barry Bonds HR 32	10.00	4.00
❑	365	Barry Bonds HR 33	10.00	4.00
❑	365	Barry Bonds HR 34	10.00	4.00
❑	365	Barry Bonds HR 35	10.00	4.00
❑	365	Barry Bonds HR 36	10.00	4.00
❑	365	Barry Bonds HR 37	10.00	4.00
❑	365	Barry Bonds HR 38	10.00	4.00
❑	365	Barry Bonds HR 39	10.00	4.00
❑	365	Barry Bonds HR 40	10.00	4.00
❑	365	Barry Bonds HR 41	10.00	4.00
❑	365	Barry Bonds HR 42	10.00	4.00
❑	365	Barry Bonds HR 43	10.00	4.00
❑	365	Barry Bonds HR 44	10.00	4.00
❑	365	Barry Bonds HR 45	10.00	4.00
❑	365	Barry Bonds HR 46	10.00	4.00
❑	365	Barry Bonds HR 47	10.00	4.00
❑	365	Barry Bonds HR 48	10.00	4.00
❑	365	Barry Bonds HR 49	10.00	4.00
❑	365	Barry Bonds HR 50	10.00	4.00
❑	365	Barry Bonds HR 51	10.00	4.00
❑	365	Barry Bonds HR 52	10.00	4.00
❑	365	Barry Bonds HR 53	10.00	4.00
❑	365	Barry Bonds HR 54	10.00	4.00
❑	365	Barry Bonds HR 55	10.00	4.00
❑	365	Barry Bonds HR 56	10.00	4.00
❑	365	Barry Bonds HR 57	10.00	4.00
❑	365	Barry Bonds HR 58	10.00	4.00
❑	365	Barry Bonds HR 59	10.00	4.00
❑	365	Barry Bonds HR 60	10.00	4.00
❑	365	Barry Bonds HR 61	15.00	6.00
❑	365	Barry Bonds HR 62	10.00	4.00
❑	365	Barry Bonds HR 63	10.00	4.00
❑	365	Barry Bonds HR 64	10.00	4.00
❑	365	Barry Bonds HR 65	10.00	4.00
❑	365	Barry Bonds HR 66	10.00	4.00
❑	365	Barry Bonds HR 67	10.00	4.00
❑	365	Barry Bonds HR 68	10.00	4.00
❑	365	Barry Bonds HR 69	10.00	4.00
❑	365	Barry Bonds HR 70	15.00	6.00
❑	365	Barry Bonds HR 71	10.00	4.00
❑	365	Barry Bonds HR 72	10.00	4.00
❑	365	Barry Bonds HR 73	50.00	20.00
❑	366	Pat Meares	.20	.07
❑	367	Mike Lieberthal	.20	.07
❑	368	Larry Bigbie	.20	.07
❑	369	Ron Gant	.20	.07
❑	370	Moises Alou	.20	.07
❑	371	Chad Kreuter	.20	.07
❑	372	Willis Roberts	.20	.07
❑	373	Toby Hall	.20	.07
❑	374	Miguel Batista	.20	.07
❑	375	John Burkett	.20	.07
❑	376	Cory Lidle	.20	.07
❑	377	Nick Neugebauer	.20	.07
❑	378	Jay Payton	.20	.07
❑	379	Steve Karsay	.20	.07
❑	380	Eric Chavez	.20	.07
❑	381	Kelly Stinnett	.20	.07
❑	382	Jarrod Washburn	.20	.07
❑	383	Rick White	.20	.07
❑	384	Jeff Conine	.20	.07
❑	385	Fred McGriff	.30	.10
❑	386	Marvin Benard	.20	.07
❑	387	Joe Crede	.20	.07
❑	388	Dennis Cook	.20	.07
❑	389	Rick Reed	.20	.07
❑	390	Tom Glavine	.30	.10
❑	391	Rondell White	.20	.07
❑	392	Matt Morris	.20	.07
❑	393	Pat Rapp	.20	.07
❑	394	Robert Person	.20	.07
❑	395	Omar Vizquel	.30	.10
❑	396	Jeff Cirillo	.20	.07
❑	397	Dave Mlicki	.20	.07
❑	398	Jose Ortiz	.20	.07
❑	399	Ryan Dempster	.20	.07
❑	400	Curt Schilling	.20	.07
❑	401	Peter Bergeron	.20	.07
❑	402	Kyle Lohse	.20	.07
❑	403	Craig Wilson	.20	.07
❑	404	David Justice	.20	.07
❑	405	Darin Erstad	.20	.07
❑	406	Jose Mercedes	.20	.07
❑	407	Carl Pavano	.20	.07
❑	408	Albie Lopez	.20	.07
❑	409	Alex Ochoa	.20	.07
❑	410	Chipper Jones	.50	.20
❑	411	Tyler Houston	.20	.07
❑	412	Dean Palmer	.20	.07
❑	413	Damian Jackson	.20	.07
❑	414	Josh Towers	.20	.07
❑	415	Rafael Furcal	.20	.07
❑	416	Mike Morgan	.20	.07
❑	417	Herb Perry	.20	.07
❑	418	Mike Sirotka	.20	.07
❑	419	Mark Wohlers	.20	.07
❑	420	Nomar Garciaparra	.75	.30
❑	421	Felipe Lopez	.20	.07
❑	422	Joe McEwing	.20	.07
❑	423	Jacque Jones	.20	.07
❑	424	Julio Franco	.20	.07
❑	425	Frank Thomas	.50	.20
❑	426	So Taguchi RC	.75	.30
❑	427	Kazuhisa Ishii RC	.50	.20
❑	428	D'Angelo Jimenez	.20	.07
❑	429	Chris Stynes	.20	.07
❑	430	Kerry Wood	.20	.07
❑	431	Chris Singleton	.20	.07
❑	432	Erubiel Durazo	.20	.07
❑	433	Matt Lawton	.20	.07
❑	434	Bill Mueller	.20	.07
❑	435	Jose Canseco	.30	.10
❑	436	Ben Grieve	.20	.07
❑	437	Terry Mulholland	.20	.07
❑	438	David Bell	.20	.07
❑	439	A.J. Pierzynski	.20	.07
❑	440	Adam Dunn	.20	.07
❑	441	Jon Garland	.20	.07
❑	442	Jeff Fassero	.20	.07
❑	443	Julio Lugo	.20	.07
❑	444	Carlos Guillen	.20	.07
❑	445	Orlando Hernandez	.20	.07
❑	446	M.Loretta UER Leskanic	.20	.07
❑	447	Scott Spiezio	.20	.07
❑	448	Kevin Millwood	.20	.07
❑	449	Jamie Moyer	.20	.07
❑	450	Todd Helton	.30	.10

❑ 451 Todd Walker .20 .07
❑ 452 Jose Lima .20 .07
❑ 453 Brook Fordyce .20 .07
❑ 454 Aaron Rowand .20 .07
❑ 455 Barry Zito .20 .07
❑ 456 Eric Owens .20 .07
❑ 457 Charles Nagy .20 .07
❑ 458 Raul Ibanez .20 .07
❑ 459 Joe Mays .20 .07
❑ 460 Jim Thome .30 .10
❑ 461 Adam Eaton .20 .07
❑ 462 Felix Martinez .20 .07
❑ 463 Vernon Wells .20 .07
❑ 464 Donnie Sadler .20 .07
❑ 465 Tony Clark .20 .07
❑ 466 Jose Hernandez .20 .07
❑ 467 Ramon Martinez .20 .07
❑ 468 Rusty Greer .20 .07
❑ 469 Rod Barajas .20 .07
❑ 470 Lance Berkman .20 .07
❑ 471 Brady Anderson .20 .07
❑ 472 Pedro Astacio .20 .07
❑ 473 Shane Halter .20 .07
❑ 474 Bret Prinz .20 .07
❑ 475 Edgar Martinez .30 .10
❑ 476 Steve Trachsel .20 .07
❑ 477 Gary Matthews Jr. .20 .07
❑ 478 Ismael Valdes .20 .07
❑ 479 Juan Uribe .20 .07
❑ 480 Shawn Green .20 .07
❑ 481 Kirk Rueter .20 .07
❑ 482 Damion Easley .20 .07
❑ 483 Chris Carpenter .20 .07
❑ 484 Kris Benson .20 .07
❑ 485 Antonio Alfonseca .20 .07
❑ 486 Kyle Farnsworth .20 .07
❑ 487 Brandon Lyon .20 .07
❑ 488 Hideki Irabu .20 .07
❑ 489 David Ortiz .50 .20
❑ 490 Mike Piazza .75 .30
❑ 491 Derek Lowe .20 .07
❑ 492 Chris Gomez .20 .07
❑ 493 Mark Johnson .20 .07
❑ 494 John Rocker .20 .07
❑ 495 Eric Karros .20 .07
❑ 496 Bill Haselman .20 .07
❑ 497 Dave Veres .20 .07
❑ 498 Pete Harnisch .20 .07
❑ 499 Tomokazu Ohka .20 .07
❑ 500 Barry Bonds 1.25 .50
❑ 501 David Dellucci .20 .07
❑ 502 Wendell Magee .20 .07
❑ 503 Tom Gordon .20 .07
❑ 504 Javier Vazquez .20 .07
❑ 505 Ben Sheets .20 .07
❑ 506 Wilton Guerrero .20 .07
❑ 507 John Halama .20 .07
❑ 508 Mark Redman .20 .07
❑ 509 Jack Wilson .20 .07
❑ 510 Bernie Williams .30 .10
❑ 511 Miguel Cairo .20 .07
❑ 512 Denny Hocking .20 .07
❑ 513 Tony Batista .20 .07
❑ 514 Mark Grudzielanek .20 .07
❑ 515 Jose Vidro .20 .07
❑ 516 Sterling Hitchcock .20 .07
❑ 517 Billy Koch .20 .07
❑ 518 Matt Clement .20 .07
❑ 519 Bruce Chen .20 .07
❑ 520 Roberto Alomar .30 .10
❑ 521 Orlando Palmeiro .20 .07
❑ 522 Steve Finley .20 .07
❑ 523 Danny Patterson .20 .07
❑ 524 Terry Adams .20 .07
❑ 525 Tino Martinez .30 .10
❑ 526 Tony Armas Jr. .20 .07
❑ 527 Geoff Jenkins .20 .07
❑ 528 Kerry Robinson .20 .07
❑ 529 Corey Patterson .20 .07
❑ 530 Brian Giles .20 .07
❑ 531 Jose Jimenez .20 .07
❑ 532 Joe Kennedy .20 .07
❑ 533 Armando Rios .20 .07
❑ 534 Osvaldo Fernandez .20 .07
❑ 535 Ruben Sierra .20 .07
❑ 536 Octavio Dotel .20 .07
❑ 537 Luis Sojo .20 .07
❑ 538 Brent Butler .20 .07
❑ 539 Pablo Ozuna .20 .07
❑ 540 Freddy Garcia .20 .07
❑ 541 Chad Durbin .20 .07
❑ 542 Orlando Merced .20 .07
❑ 543 Michael Tucker .20 .07
❑ 544 Roberto Hernandez .20 .07
❑ 545 Pat Burrell .20 .07
❑ 546 A.J. Burnett .20 .07
❑ 547 Bubba Trammell .20 .07
❑ 548 Scott Elarton .20 .07
❑ 549 Mike Darr .20 .07
❑ 550 Ken Griffey Jr. .75 .30
❑ 551 Ugueth Urbina .20 .07
❑ 552 Todd Jones .20 .07
❑ 553 Delino Deshields .20 .07
❑ 554 Adam Piatt .20 .07
❑ 555 Jason Kendall .20 .07
❑ 556 Hector Ortiz .20 .07
❑ 557 Turk Wendell .20 .07
❑ 558 Rob Bell .20 .07
❑ 559 Sun Woo Kim .20 .07
❑ 560 Raul Mondesi .20 .07
❑ 561 Brent Abernathy .20 .07
❑ 562 Seth Etherton .20 .07
❑ 563 Shawn Wooten .20 .07
❑ 564 Jay Buhner .20 .07
❑ 565 Andres Galarraga .20 .07
❑ 566 Shane Reynolds .20 .07
❑ 567 Rod Beck .20 .07
❑ 568 Dee Brown .20 .07
❑ 569 Pedro Feliz .20 .07
❑ 570 Ryan Klesko .20 .07
❑ 571 John Vander Wal .20 .07
❑ 572 Nick Bierbrodt .20 .07
❑ 573 Joe Nathan .20 .07
❑ 574 James Baldwin .20 .07
❑ 575 J.D. Drew .20 .07
❑ 576 Greg Colbrunn .20 .07
❑ 577 Doug Glanville .20 .07
❑ 578 Brandon Duckworth .20 .07
❑ 579 Shawn Chacon .20 .07
❑ 580 Rich Aurilia .20 .07
❑ 581 Chuck Finley .20 .07
❑ 582 Abraham Nunez .20 .07
❑ 583 Kenny Lofton .20 .07
❑ 584 Brian Daubach .20 .07
❑ 585 Miguel Tejada .20 .07
❑ 586 Nate Cornejo .20 .07
❑ 587 Kazuhiro Sasaki .20 .07
❑ 588 Chris Richard .20 .07
❑ 589 Armando Reynoso .20 .07
❑ 590 Tim Hudson .20 .07
❑ 591 Neifi Perez .20 .07
❑ 592 Steve Cox .20 .07
❑ 593 Henry Blanco .20 .07
❑ 594 Ricky Ledee .20 .07
❑ 595 Tim Salmon .30 .10
❑ 596 Luis Rivas .20 .07
❑ 597 Jeff Zimmerman .20 .07
❑ 598 Matt Stairs .20 .07
❑ 599 Preston Wilson .20 .07
❑ 600 Mark McGwire 1.25 .50
❑ 601 Timo Perez .20 .07
❑ 602 Matt Anderson .20 .07
❑ 603 Todd Hundley .20 .07
❑ 604 Rick Ankiel .20 .07
❑ 605 Tsuyoshi Shinjo .20 .07
❑ 606 Woody Williams .20 .07
❑ 607 Jason LaRue .20 .07
❑ 608 Carlos Lee .20 .07
❑ 609 Russ Johnson .20 .07
❑ 610 Scott Rolen .30 .10
❑ 611 Brent Mayne .20 .07
❑ 612 Darrin Fletcher .20 .07
❑ 613 Ray Lankford .20 .07
❑ 614 Troy O'Leary .20 .07
❑ 615 Javier Lopez .20 .07
❑ 616 Randy Velarde .20 .07
❑ 617 Vinny Castilla .20 .07
❑ 618 Milton Bradley .20 .07
❑ 619 Ruben Mateo .20 .07
❑ 620 Jason Giambi Yankees .20 .07
❑ 621 Andy Benes .20 .07
❑ 622 Joe Mauer RC 10.00 4.00
❑ 623 Andy Pettitte .30 .10
❑ 624 Jose Offerman .20 .07
❑ 625 Mo Vaughn .20 .07
❑ 626 Steve Sparks .20 .07
❑ 627 Mike Matthews .20 .07
❑ 628 Robb Nen .20 .07
❑ 629 Kip Wells .20 .07
❑ 630 Kevin Brown .20 .07
❑ 631 Arthur Rhodes .20 .07
❑ 632 Gabe Kapler .20 .07
❑ 633 Jermaine Dye .20 .07
❑ 634 Josh Beckett .20 .07
❑ 635 Pokey Reese .20 .07
❑ 636 Benji Gil .20 .07
❑ 637 Marcus Giles .20 .07
❑ 638 Julian Tavarez .20 .07
❑ 639 Jason Schmidt .20 .07
❑ 640 Alex Rodriguez .75 .30
❑ 641 Anaheim Angels TC .20 .07
❑ 642 Arizona Diamondbacks TC .30 .10
❑ 643 Atlanta Braves TC .20 .07
❑ 644 Baltimore Orioles TC .20 .07
❑ 645 Boston Red Sox TC .20 .07
❑ 646 Chicago Cubs TC .20 .07
❑ 647 Chicago White Sox TC .20 .07
❑ 648 Cincinnati Reds TC .20 .07
❑ 649 Cleveland Indians TC .20 .07
❑ 650 Colorado Rockies TC .20 .07
❑ 651 Detroit Tigers TC .20 .07
❑ 652 Florida Marlins TC .20 .07
❑ 653 Houston Astros TC .20 .07
❑ 654 Kansas City Royals TC .20 .07
❑ 655 Los Angeles Dodgers TC .20 .07
❑ 656 Milwaukee Brewers TC .20 .07
❑ 657 Minnesota Twins TC .20 .07
❑ 658 Montreal Expos TC .20 .07
❑ 659 New York Mets TC .20 .07
❑ 660 New York Yankees TC .50 .20
❑ 661 Oakland Athletics TC .20 .07
❑ 662 Philadelphia Phillies TC .20 .07
❑ 663 Pittsburgh Pirates TC .20 .07
❑ 664 San Diego Padres TC .20 .07
❑ 665 San Francisco Giants TC .20 .07
❑ 666 Seattle Mariners TC .30 .10
❑ 667 St. Louis Cardinals TC .20 .07
❑ 668 Tampa Bay Devil Rays TC .20 .07
❑ 669 Texas Rangers TC .20 .07
❑ 670 Toronto Blue Jays TC .20 .07
❑ 671 Juan Cruz PROS .50 .20
❑ 672 Kevin Cash PROS RC .50 .20
❑ 673 Jimmy Gobble PROS RC .50 .20
❑ 674 Mike Hill PROS RC .50 .20
❑ 675 Taylor Buchholz PROS RC .50 .20
❑ 676 Bill Hall PROS .50 .20
❑ 677 Brett Roneberg PROS RC .50 .20
❑ 678 Royce Huffman PROS RC .50 .20
❑ 679 Chris Tritle PROS RC .50 .20
❑ 680 Nate Espy PROS RC .50 .20
❑ 681 Nick Alvarez PROS RC .50 .20
❑ 682 Jason Botts PROS RC .50 .20
❑ 683 Ryan Gripp PROS RC .50 .20
❑ 684 Dan Phillips PROS RC .50 .20
❑ 685 Pablo Arias PROS RC .50 .20
❑ 686 John Rodriguez PROS RC .50 .20
❑ 687 Rich Harden PROS RC 3.00 1.25
❑ 688 Neal Frendling PROS RC .50 .20
❑ 689 Rich Thompson PROS RC .50 .20
❑ 690 Greg Montalbano PROS RC .50 .20
❑ 691 Len Dinardo DP RC .50 .20
❑ 692 Ryan Raburn DP RC .50 .20
❑ 693 Josh Barfield DP RC 2.50 1.00
❑ 694 David Bacani DP RC .50 .20
❑ 695 Dan Johnson DP RC 1.00 .40
❑ 696 Mike Mussina GG .20 .07
❑ 697 Ivan Rodriguez GG .30 .10
❑ 698 Doug Mientkiewicz GG .20 .07
❑ 699 Roberto Alomar GG .20 .07
❑ 700 Eric Chavez GG .20 .07
❑ 701 Omar Vizquel GG .20 .07
❑ 702 Mike Cameron GG .20 .07
❑ 703 Torii Hunter GG .20 .07
❑ 704 Ichiro Suzuki GG .50 .20
❑ 705 Greg Maddux GG .50 .20
❑ 706 Brad Ausmus GG .20 .07
❑ 707 Todd Helton GG .20 .07
❑ 708 Fernando Vina GG .20 .07

❑ 709 Scott Rolen GG	.20	.07
❑ 710 Orlando Cabrera GG	.20	.07
❑ 711 Andruw Jones GG	.20	.07
❑ 712 Jim Edmonds GG	.20	.07
❑ 713 Larry Walker GG	.20	.07
❑ 714 Roger Clemens CY	.50	.20
❑ 715 Randy Johnson CY	.30	.10
❑ 716 Ichiro Suzuki MVP	.50	.20
❑ 717 Barry Bonds MVP	.75	.30
❑ 718 Ichiro Suzuki ROY	.50	.20
❑ 719 Albert Pujols ROY	.50	.20

2002 Topps Traded

❑ COMPLETE SET (275)	200.00	100.00
❑ COMMON CARD (T1-T110)	2.00	.75
❑ COMMON CARD (T111-T275)	.40	.15
❑ T1 Jeff Weaver	2.00	.75
❑ T2 Jay Powell	2.00	.75
❑ T3 Alex Gonzalez	2.00	.75
❑ T4 Jason Isringhausen	2.00	.75
❑ T5 Tyler Houston	2.00	.75
❑ T6 Ben Broussard	2.00	.75
❑ T7 Chuck Knoblauch	2.00	.75
❑ T8 Brian L. Hunter	2.00	.75
❑ T9 Dustan Mohr	2.00	.75
❑ T10 Eric Hinske	2.00	.75
❑ T11 Roger Cedeno	2.00	.75
❑ T12 Eddie Perez	2.00	.75
❑ T13 Jeromy Burnitz	2.00	.75
❑ T14 Bartolo Colon	2.00	.75
❑ T15 Rick Helling	2.00	.75
❑ T16 Dan Plesac	2.00	.75
❑ T17 Scott Strickland	2.00	.75
❑ T18 Antonio Alfonseca	2.00	.75
❑ T19 Ricky Gutierrez	2.00	.75
❑ T20 John Valentin	2.00	.75
❑ T21 Raul Mondesi	2.00	.75
❑ T22 Ben Davis	2.00	.75
❑ T23 Nelson Figueroa	2.00	.75
❑ T24 Earl Snyder	2.00	.75
❑ T25 Robin Ventura	2.00	.75
❑ T26 Jimmy Haynes	2.00	.75
❑ T27 Kenny Kelly	2.00	.75
❑ T28 Morgan Ensberg	1.00	.40
❑ T29 Reggie Sanders	2.00	.75
❑ T30 Shigetoshi Hasegawa	2.00	.75
❑ T31 Mike Timlin	2.00	.75
❑ T32 Russell Branyan	2.00	.75
❑ T33 Alan Embree	2.00	.75
❑ T34 D'Angelo Jimenez	2.00	.75
❑ T35 Kent Mercker	2.00	.75
❑ T36 Jesse Orosco	2.00	.75
❑ T37 Gregg Zaun	2.00	.75
❑ T38 Reggie Taylor	2.00	.75
❑ T39 Andres Galarraga	2.00	.75
❑ T40 Chris Truby	2.00	.75
❑ T41 Bruce Chen	2.00	.75
❑ T42 Darren Lewis	2.00	.75
❑ T43 Ryan Kohlmeier	2.00	.75
❑ T44 John McDonald	2.00	.75
❑ T45 Omar Daal	2.00	.75
❑ T46 Matt Clement	2.00	.75
❑ T47 Glendon Rusch	2.00	.75
❑ T48 Chan Ho Park	2.00	.75
❑ T49 Benny Agbayani	2.00	.75
❑ T50 Juan Gonzalez	2.00	.75
❑ T51 Carlos Baerga	2.00	.75
❑ T52 Tim Raines	2.00	.75
❑ T53 Kevin Appier	2.00	.75
❑ T54 Marty Cordova	2.00	.75
❑ T55 Jeff D'Amico	2.00	.75
❑ T56 Dmitri Young	2.00	.75
❑ T57 Roosevelt Brown	2.00	.75
❑ T58 Dustin Hermanson	2.00	.75
❑ T59 Jose Rijo	2.00	.75
❑ T60 Todd Ritchie	2.00	.75
❑ T61 Lee Stevens	2.00	.75
❑ T62 Placido Polanco	2.00	.75
❑ T63 Eric Young	2.00	.75
❑ T64 Chuck Finley	2.00	.75
❑ T65 Dicky Gonzalez	2.00	.75
❑ T66 Jose Macias	2.00	.75
❑ T67 Gabe Kapler	2.00	.75
❑ T68 Sandy Alomar Jr.	2.00	.75
❑ T69 Henry Blanco	2.00	.75
❑ T70 Julian Tavarez	2.00	.75
❑ T71 Paul Bako	2.00	.75
❑ T72 Scott Rolen	3.00	1.25
❑ T73 Brian Jordan	2.00	.75
❑ T74 Rickey Henderson	4.00	1.50
❑ T75 Kevin Mench	2.00	.75
❑ T76 Hideo Nomo	4.00	1.50
❑ T77 Jeremy Giambi	2.00	.75
❑ T78 Brad Fullmer	2.00	.75
❑ T79 Carl Everett	2.00	.75
❑ T80 David Wells	2.00	.75
❑ T81 Aaron Sele	2.00	.75
❑ T82 Todd Hollandsworth	2.00	.75
❑ T83 Vicente Padilla	2.00	.75
❑ T84 Kenny Lofton	2.00	.75
❑ T85 Corky Miller	2.00	.75
❑ T86 Josh Fogg	2.00	.75
❑ T87 Cliff Floyd	2.00	.75
❑ T88 Craig Paquette	2.00	.75
❑ T89 Jay Payton	2.00	.75
❑ T90 Carlos Pena	2.00	.75
❑ T91 Juan Encarnacion	2.00	.75
❑ T92 Rey Sanchez	2.00	.75
❑ T93 Ryan Dempster	2.00	.75
❑ T94 Mario Encarnacion	2.00	.75
❑ T95 Jorge Julio	2.00	.75
❑ T96 John Mabry	2.00	.75
❑ T97 Todd Zeile	2.00	.75
❑ T98 Johnny Damon Sox	3.00	1.25
❑ T99 Deivi Cruz	2.00	.75
❑ T100 Gary Sheffield	2.00	.75
❑ T101 Ted Lilly	2.00	.75
❑ T102 Todd Van Poppel	2.00	.75
❑ T103 Shawn Estes	2.00	.75
❑ T104 Cesar Izturis	2.00	.75
❑ T105 Ron Coomer	2.00	.75
❑ T106 Grady Little MG RC	2.00	.75
❑ T107 Jimy Williams MG	2.00	.75
❑ T108 Tony Pena MG	2.00	.75
❑ T109 Frank Robinson MG	3.00	1.25
❑ T110 Ron Gardenhire MG	2.00	.75
❑ T111 Dennis Tankersley	.40	.15
❑ T112 Alejandro Cadena RC	.40	.15
❑ T113 Justin Reid RC	.40	.15
❑ T114 Nate Field RC	.40	.15
❑ T115 Rene Reyes RC	.40	.15
❑ T116 Nelson Castro RC	.40	.15
❑ T117 Miguel Olivo	.40	.15
❑ T118 David Espinosa	.40	.15
❑ T119 Chris Bootcheck RC	.40	.15
❑ T120 Rob Henkel RC	.40	.15
❑ T121 Steve Bechler RC	.40	.15
❑ T122 Mark Outlaw RC	.40	.15
❑ T123 Henry Pichardo RC	.40	.15
❑ T124 Michael Floyd RC	.40	.15
❑ T125 Richard Lane RC	.40	.15
❑ T126 Pete Zamora RC	.40	.15
❑ T127 Javier Colina	.40	.15
❑ T128 Greg Sain RC	.40	.15
❑ T129 Ronnie Merrill	.40	.15
❑ T130 Gavin Floyd RC	1.00	.40
❑ T131 Josh Bonifay RC	.40	.15
❑ T132 Tommy Marx RC	.40	.15
❑ T133 Gary Cates Jr. RC	.40	.15
❑ T134 Neal Cotts RC	1.00	.40
❑ T135 Angel Berroa	.40	.15
❑ T136 Elio Serrano RC	.40	.15
❑ T137 J.J. Putz RC	.50	.20
❑ T138 Ruben Gotay RC	.50	.20
❑ T139 Eddie Rogers	.40	.15
❑ T140 Wily Mo Pena	.40	.15
❑ T141 Tyler Yates RC	.40	.15
❑ T142 Colin Young RC	.40	.15
❑ T143 Chance Caple	.40	.15
❑ T144 Ben Howard RC	.40	.15
❑ T145 Ryan Bukvich RC	.40	.15
❑ T146 Cliff Bartosh RC	.40	.15
❑ T147 Brandon Claussen	.40	.15
❑ T148 Cristian Guerrero	.40	.15
❑ T149 Derrick Lewis	.40	.15
❑ T150 Eric Miller RC	.40	.15
❑ T151 Justin Huber RC	.75	.30
❑ T152 Adrian Gonzalez	.40	.15
❑ T153 Brian West RC	.40	.15
❑ T154 Chris Baker RC	.40	.15
❑ T155 Drew Henson	.40	.15
❑ T156 Scott Hairston RC	.50	.20
❑ T157 Jason Simontacchi RC	.40	.15
❑ T158 Jason Arnold RC	.40	.15
❑ T159 Brandon Phillips	.40	.15
❑ T160 Adam Roller RC	.40	.15
❑ T161 Scotty Layfield RC	.40	.15
❑ T162 Freddie Money RC	.40	.15
❑ T163 Noochie Varner RC	.40	.15
❑ T164 Terrance Hill RC	.40	.15
❑ T165 Jeremy Hill RC	.40	.15
❑ T166 Carlos Cabrera RC	.40	.15
❑ T167 Jose Morban RC	.40	.15
❑ T168 Kevin Frederick RC	.40	.15
❑ T169 Mark Teixeira	1.50	.60
❑ T170 Brian Rogers	.40	.15
❑ T171 Anastacio Martinez RC	.40	.15
❑ T172 Bobby Jenks RC	1.50	.60
❑ T173 David Gil RC	.40	.15
❑ T174 Andres Torres	.40	.15
❑ T175 James Barrett RC	.40	.15
❑ T176 Jimmy Journell	.40	.15
❑ T177 Brett Kay RC	.40	.15
❑ T178 Jason Young RC	.40	.15
❑ T179 Mark Hamilton RC	.40	.15
❑ T180 Jose Bautista RC	1.00	.40
❑ T181 Blake McGinley RC	.40	.15
❑ T182 Ryan Mottl RC	.40	.15
❑ T183 Jeff Austin RC	.40	.15
❑ T184 Xavier Nady	.40	.15
❑ T185 Kyle Kane RC	.40	.15
❑ T186 Travis Foley RC	.40	.15
❑ T187 Nathan Kaup RC	.40	.15
❑ T188 Eric Cyr	.40	.15
❑ T189 Josh Cisneros RC	.40	.15
❑ T190 Brad Nelson RC	.40	.15
❑ T191 Clint Weibl RC	.40	.15
❑ T192 Ron Calloway RC	.40	.15
❑ T193 Jung Bong	.40	.15
❑ T194 Rolando Viera RC	.40	.15
❑ T195 Jason Bulger RC	.40	.15
❑ T196 Chone Figgins RC	1.50	.60
❑ T197 Jimmy Alvarez RC	.40	.15
❑ T198 Joel Crump RC	.40	.15
❑ T199 Ryan Doumit RC	.60	.25
❑ T200 Demetrius Heath RC	.40	.15
❑ T201 John Ennis RC	.40	.15
❑ T202 Doug Sessions RC	.40	.15
❑ T203 Clinton Hosford RC	.40	.15
❑ T204 Chris Narveson RC	.40	.15
❑ T205 Ross Peeples RC	.40	.15
❑ T206 Alex Requena RC	.40	.15
❑ T207 Matt Erickson RC	.40	.15
❑ T208 Brian Forystek RC	.40	.15
❑ T209 Dewon Brazelton	.40	.15
❑ T210 Nathan Haynes	.40	.15
❑ T211 Jack Cust	.40	.15
❑ T212 Jesse Foppert RC	.50	.20
❑ T213 Jesus Cota RC	.40	.15
❑ T214 Juan M. Gonzalez RC	.40	.15
❑ T215 Tim Kalita RC	.40	.15
❑ T216 Manny Delcarmen RC	.50	.20
❑ T217 Jim Kavourias RC	.40	.15
❑ T218 C.J. Wilson RC	.40	.15
❑ T219 Edwin Yan RC	.40	.15
❑ T220 Andy Van Hekken	.40	.15
❑ T221 Michael Cuddyer	.40	.15
❑ T222 Jeff Verplancke RC	.40	.15
❑ T223 Mike Wilson RC	.40	.15
❑ T224 Corwin Malone RC	.40	.15

❑ T225 Chris Snelling RC	.60	.25
❑ T226 Joe Rogers RC	.40	.15
❑ T227 Jason Bay	4.00	1.50
❑ T228 Ezequiel Astacio RC	.40	.15
❑ T229 Joey Hammond RC	.40	.15
❑ T230 Chris Duffy RC	.50	.20
❑ T231 Mark Prior	1.50	.60
❑ T232 Hansel Izquierdo RC	.40	.15
❑ T233 Franklyn German RC	.40	.15
❑ T234 Alexis Gomez	.40	.15
❑ T235 Jorge Padilla RC	.40	.15
❑ T236 Ryan Snare RC	.40	.15
❑ T237 Deivis Santos	.40	.15
❑ T238 Taggert Bozied RC	.50	.20
❑ T239 Mike Peeples RC	.40	.15
❑ T240 Ronald Acuna RC	.40	.15
❑ T241 Koyie Hill	.40	.15
❑ T242 Garrett Guzman RC	.40	.15
❑ T243 Ryan Church RC	1.00	.40
❑ T244 Tony Fontana RC	.40	.15
❑ T245 Keto Anderson RC	.40	.15
❑ T246 Brad Bouras RC	.40	.15
❑ T247 Jason Dubois RC	.50	.20
❑ T248 Angel Guzman RC	.75	.30
❑ T249 Joel Hanrahan RC	.40	.15
❑ T250 Joe Jiannetti RC	.40	.15
❑ T251 Sean Pierce RC	.40	.15
❑ T252 Jake Mauer RC	.40	.15
❑ T253 Marshall McDougall RC	.40	.15
❑ T254 Edwin Almonte RC	.40	.15
❑ T255 Shawn Riggans RC	.40	.15
❑ T256 Steven Shell RC	.40	.15
❑ T257 Kevin Hooper RC	.40	.15
❑ T258 Michael Frick RC	.40	.15
❑ T259 Travis Chapman RC	.40	.15
❑ T260 Tim Hummel RC	.40	.15
❑ T261 Adam Morrissey RC	.40	.15
❑ T262 Dontrelle Willis RC	5.00	2.00
❑ T263 Justin Sherrod RC	.40	.15
❑ T264 Gerald Smiley RC	.40	.15
❑ T265 Tony Miller RC	.40	.15
❑ T266 Nolan Ryan WW	2.50	1.00
❑ T267 Reggie Jackson WW	.60	.25
❑ T268 Steve Garvey WW	.40	.15
❑ T269 Wade Boggs WW	.60	.25
❑ T270 Sammy Sosa WW	1.00	.40
❑ T271 Curt Schilling WW	.40	.15
❑ T272 Mark Grace WW	.60	.25
❑ T273 Jason Giambi WW	.40	.15
❑ T274 Ken Griffey Jr. WW	1.50	.60
❑ T275 Roberto Alomar WW	.60	.25

2003 Topps

❑ COMPLETE SET (720)	80.00	40.00
❑ COMPLETE SERIES 1 (366)	40.00	20.00
❑ COMPLETE SERIES 2 (354)	40.00	20.00
❑ COMMON CARD (1-6/8-721)	.20	.07
❑ COMMON (292-331/660-684)	.50	.20
❑ 1 Alex Rodriguez	.75	.30
❑ 2 Dan Wilson	.20	.07
❑ 3 Jimmy Rollins	.20	.07
❑ 4 Jermaine Dye	.20	.07
❑ 5 Steve Karsay	.20	.07
❑ 6 Timo Perez	.20	.07
❑ 8 Jose Vidro	.20	.07
❑ 9 Eddie Guardado	.20	.07
❑ 10 Mark Prior	.30	.10
❑ 11 Curt Schilling	.20	.07
❑ 12 Dennis Cook	.20	.07
❑ 13 Andruw Jones	.30	.10
❑ 14 David Segui	.20	.07
❑ 15 Trot Nixon	.20	.07
❑ 16 Kerry Wood	.20	.07
❑ 17 Magglio Ordonez	.20	.07
❑ 18 Jason LaRue	.20	.07
❑ 19 Danys Baez	.20	.07
❑ 20 Todd Helton	.30	.10
❑ 21 Denny Neagle	.20	.07
❑ 22 Dave Mlicki	.20	.07
❑ 23 Roberto Hernandez	.20	.07
❑ 24 Odalis Perez	.20	.07
❑ 25 Nick Neugebauer	.20	.07
❑ 26 David Ortiz	.50	.20
❑ 27 Andres Galarraga	.20	.07
❑ 28 Edgardo Alfonzo	.20	.07
❑ 29 Chad Bradford	.20	.07
❑ 30 Jason Giambi	.20	.07
❑ 31 Brian Giles	.20	.07
❑ 32 Deivi Cruz	.20	.07
❑ 33 Robb Nen	.20	.07
❑ 34 Jeff Nelson	.20	.07
❑ 35 Edgar Renteria	.20	.07
❑ 36 Aubrey Huff	.20	.07
❑ 37 Brandon Duckworth	.20	.07
❑ 38 Juan Gonzalez	.20	.07
❑ 39 Sidney Ponson	.20	.07
❑ 40 Eric Hinske	.20	.07
❑ 41 Kevin Appier	.20	.07
❑ 42 Danny Bautista	.20	.07
❑ 43 Javier Lopez	.20	.07
❑ 44 Jeff Conine	.20	.07
❑ 45 Carlos Baerga	.20	.07
❑ 46 Ugueth Urbina	.20	.07
❑ 47 Mark Buehrle	.20	.07
❑ 48 Aaron Boone	.20	.07
❑ 49 Jason Simontacchi	.20	.07
❑ 50 Sammy Sosa	.50	.20
❑ 51 Jose Jimenez	.20	.07
❑ 52 Bobby Higginson	.20	.07
❑ 53 Luis Castillo	.20	.07
❑ 54 Orlando Merced	.20	.07
❑ 55 Brian Jordan	.20	.07
❑ 56 Eric Young	.20	.07
❑ 57 Bobby Kielty	.20	.07
❑ 58 Luis Rivas	.20	.07
❑ 59 Brad Wilkerson	.20	.07
❑ 60 Roberto Alomar	.30	.10
❑ 61 Roger Clemens	1.00	.40
❑ 62 Scott Hatteberg	.20	.07
❑ 63 Andy Ashby	.20	.07
❑ 64 Mike Williams	.20	.07
❑ 65 Ron Gant	.20	.07
❑ 66 Benito Santiago	.20	.07
❑ 67 Bret Boone	.20	.07
❑ 68 Matt Morris	.20	.07
❑ 69 Troy Glaus	.20	.07
❑ 70 Austin Kearns	.20	.07
❑ 71 Jim Thome	.30	.10
❑ 72 Rickey Henderson	.50	.20
❑ 73 Luis Gonzalez	.20	.07
❑ 74 Brad Fullmer	.20	.07
❑ 75 Herbert Perry	.20	.07
❑ 76 Randy Wolf	.20	.07
❑ 77 Miguel Tejada	.20	.07
❑ 78 Jimmy Anderson	.20	.07
❑ 79 Ramon Martinez	.20	.07
❑ 80 Ivan Rodriguez	.30	.10
❑ 81 John Flaherty	.20	.07
❑ 82 Shannon Stewart	.20	.07
❑ 83 Orlando Palmeiro	.20	.07
❑ 84 Rafael Furcal	.20	.07
❑ 85 Kenny Rogers	.20	.07
❑ 86 Terry Adams	.20	.07
❑ 87 Mo Vaughn	.20	.07
❑ 88 Jose Cruz Jr.	.20	.07
❑ 89 Mike Matheny	.20	.07
❑ 90 Alfonso Soriano	.20	.07
❑ 91 Orlando Cabrera	.20	.07
❑ 92 Jeffrey Hammonds	.20	.07
❑ 93 Hideo Nomo	.50	.20
❑ 94 Carlos Febles	.20	.07
❑ 95 Billy Wagner	.20	.07
❑ 96 Alex Gonzalez	.20	.07
❑ 97 Todd Zeile	.20	.07
❑ 98 Omar Vizquel	.30	.10
❑ 99 Jose Rijo	.20	.07
❑ 100 Ichiro Suzuki	1.00	.40
❑ 101 Steve Cox	.20	.07
❑ 102 Hideki Irabu	.20	.07
❑ 103 Roy Halladay	.20	.07
❑ 104 David Eckstein	.20	.07
❑ 105 Greg Maddux	.75	.30
❑ 106 Jay Gibbons	.20	.07
❑ 107 Travis Driskill	.20	.07
❑ 108 Fred McGriff	.30	.10
❑ 109 Frank Thomas	.50	.20
❑ 110 Shawn Green	.20	.07
❑ 111 Ruben Quevedo	.20	.07
❑ 112 Jacque Jones	.20	.07
❑ 113 Tomo Ohka	.20	.07
❑ 114 Joe McEwing	.20	.07
❑ 115 Ramiro Mendoza	.20	.07
❑ 116 Mark Mulder	.20	.07
❑ 117 Mike Lieberthal	.20	.07
❑ 118 Jack Wilson	.20	.07
❑ 119 Randall Simon	.20	.07
❑ 120 Bernie Williams	.30	.10
❑ 121 Marvin Benard	.20	.07
❑ 122 Jamie Moyer	.20	.07
❑ 123 Andy Benes	.20	.07
❑ 124 Tino Martinez	.30	.10
❑ 125 Esteban Yan	.20	.07
❑ 126 Juan Uribe	.20	.07
❑ 127 Jason Isringhausen	.20	.07
❑ 128 Chris Carpenter	.20	.07
❑ 129 Mike Cameron	.20	.07
❑ 130 Gary Sheffield	.20	.07
❑ 131 Geronimo Gil	.20	.07
❑ 132 Brian Daubach	.20	.07
❑ 133 Corey Patterson	.20	.07
❑ 134 Aaron Rowand	.20	.07
❑ 135 Chris Reitsma	.20	.07
❑ 136 Bob Wickman	.20	.07
❑ 137 Cesar Izturis	.20	.07
❑ 138 Jason Jennings	.20	.07
❑ 139 Brandon Inge	.20	.07
❑ 140 Larry Walker	.20	.07
❑ 141 Ramon Santiago	.20	.07
❑ 142 Vladimir Nunez	.20	.07
❑ 143 Jose Vizcaino	.20	.07
❑ 144 Mark Quinn	.20	.07
❑ 145 Michael Tucker	.20	.07
❑ 146 Darren Dreifort	.20	.07
❑ 147 Ben Sheets	.20	.07
❑ 148 Corey Koskie	.20	.07
❑ 149 Tony Armas Jr.	.20	.07
❑ 150 Kazuhisa Ishii	.20	.07
❑ 151 Al Leiter	.20	.07
❑ 152 Steve Trachsel	.20	.07
❑ 153 Mike Stanton	.20	.07
❑ 154 David Justice	.20	.07
❑ 155 Marlon Anderson	.20	.07
❑ 156 Jason Kendall	.20	.07
❑ 157 Brian Lawrence	.20	.07
❑ 158 J.T. Snow	.20	.07
❑ 159 Edgar Martinez	.30	.10
❑ 160 Pat Burrell	.20	.07
❑ 161 Kerry Robinson	.20	.07
❑ 162 Greg Vaughn	.20	.07
❑ 163 Carl Everett	.20	.07
❑ 164 Vernon Wells	.20	.07
❑ 165 Jose Mesa	.20	.07
❑ 166 Troy Percival	.20	.07
❑ 167 Erubiel Durazo	.20	.07
❑ 168 Jason Marquis	.20	.07
❑ 169 Jerry Hairston Jr.	.20	.07
❑ 170 Vladimir Guerrero	.50	.20
❑ 171 Byung-Hyun Kim	.20	.07
❑ 172 Marcus Giles	.20	.07
❑ 173 Johnny Damon	.30	.10
❑ 174 Jon Lieber	.20	.07
❑ 175 Terrence Long	.20	.07
❑ 176 Sean Casey	.20	.07
❑ 177 Adam Dunn	.20	.07
❑ 178 Juan Pierre	.20	.07
❑ 179 Wendell Magee	.20	.07
❑ 180 Barry Zito	.20	.07
❑ 181 Aramis Ramirez	.20	.07
❑ 182 Pokey Reese	.20	.07
❑ 183 Jeff Kent	.20	.07

❏ 184	Russ Ortiz	.20	.07
❏ 185	Ruben Sierra	.20	.07
❏ 186	Brent Abernathy	.20	.07
❏ 187	Ismael Valdes	.20	.07
❏ 188	Tom Wilson	.20	.07
❏ 189	Craig Counsell	.20	.07
❏ 190	Mike Mussina	.30	.10
❏ 191	Ramon Hernandez	.20	.07
❏ 192	Adam Kennedy	.20	.07
❏ 193	Tony Womack	.20	.07
❏ 194	Wes Helms	.20	.07
❏ 195	Tony Batista	.20	.07
❏ 196	Rolando Arrojo	.20	.07
❏ 197	Kyle Farnsworth	.20	.07
❏ 198	Gary Bennett	.20	.07
❏ 199	Scott Sullivan	.20	.07
❏ 200	Albert Pujols	1.00	.40
❏ 201	Kirk Rueter	.20	.07
❏ 202	Phil Nevin	.20	.07
❏ 203	Kip Wells	.20	.07
❏ 204	Ron Coomer	.20	.07
❏ 205	Jeromy Burnitz	.20	.07
❏ 206	Kyle Lohse	.20	.07
❏ 207	Mike DeJean	.20	.07
❏ 208	Paul Lo Duca	.20	.07
❏ 209	Carlos Beltran	.20	.07
❏ 210	Roy Oswalt	.20	.07
❏ 211	Mike Lowell	.20	.07
❏ 212	Robert Fick	.20	.07
❏ 213	Todd Jones	.20	.07
❏ 214	C.C. Sabathia	.20	.07
❏ 215	Danny Graves	.20	.07
❏ 216	Todd Hundley	.20	.07
❏ 217	Tim Wakefield	.20	.07
❏ 218	Derek Lowe	.20	.07
❏ 219	Kevin Millwood	.20	.07
❏ 220	Jorge Posada	.30	.10
❏ 221	Bobby J. Jones	.20	.07
❏ 222	Carlos Guillen	.20	.07
❏ 223	Fernando Vina	.20	.07
❏ 224	Ryan Rupe	.20	.07
❏ 225	Kelvim Escobar	.20	.07
❏ 226	Ramon Ortiz	.20	.07
❏ 227	Junior Spivey	.20	.07
❏ 228	Juan Cruz	.20	.07
❏ 229	Melvin Mora	.20	.07
❏ 230	Lance Berkman	.20	.07
❏ 231	Brent Butler	.20	.07
❏ 232	Shane Halter	.20	.07
❏ 233	Derrek Lee	.30	.10
❏ 234	Matt Lawton	.20	.07
❏ 235	Chuck Knoblauch	.20	.07
❏ 236	Eric Gagne	.20	.07
❏ 237	Alex Sanchez	.20	.07
❏ 238	Denny Hocking	.20	.07
❏ 239	Eric Milton	.20	.07
❏ 240	Rey Ordonez	.20	.07
❏ 241	Orlando Hernandez	.20	.07
❏ 242	Robert Person	.20	.07
❏ 243	Sean Burroughs	.20	.07
❏ 244	Jeff Cirillo	.20	.07
❏ 245	Mike Lamb	.20	.07
❏ 246	Jose Valentin	.20	.07
❏ 247	Ellis Burks	.20	.07
❏ 248	Shawn Chacon	.20	.07
❏ 249	Josh Beckett	.20	.07
❏ 250	Nomar Garciaparra	.75	.30
❏ 251	Craig Biggio	.30	.10
❏ 252	Joe Randa	.20	.07
❏ 253	Mark Grudzielanek	.20	.07
❏ 254	Glendon Rusch	.20	.07
❏ 255	Michael Barrett	.20	.07
❏ 256	Omar Daal	.20	.07
❏ 257	Elmer Dessens	.20	.07
❏ 258	Wade Miller	.20	.07
❏ 259	Adrian Beltre	.20	.07
❏ 260	Vicente Padilla	.20	.07
❏ 261	Kazuhiro Sasaki	.20	.07
❏ 262	Mike Scioscia MG	.20	.07
❏ 263	Bobby Cox MG	.20	.07
❏ 264	Mike Hargrove MG	.20	.07
❏ 265	Grady Little MG RC	.20	.07
❏ 266	Alex Gonzalez	.20	.07
❏ 267	Jerry Manuel MG	.20	.07
❏ 268	Bob Boone MG	.20	.07
❏ 269	Joel Skinner MG	.20	.07
❏ 270	Clint Hurdle MG	.20	.07
❏ 271	Miguel Batista	.20	.07
❏ 272	Bob Brenly MG	.20	.07
❏ 273	Jeff Torborg MG	.20	.07
❏ 274	Jimy Williams MG	.20	.07
❏ 275	Tony Pena MG	.20	.07
❏ 276	Jim Tracy MG	.20	.07
❏ 277	Jerry Royster MG	.20	.07
❏ 278	Ron Gardenhire MG	.20	.07
❏ 279	Frank Robinson MG	.30	.10
❏ 280	John Halama	.20	.07
❏ 281	Joe Torre MG	.30	.10
❏ 282	Art Howe MG	.20	.07
❏ 283	Larry Bowa MG	.20	.07
❏ 284	Lloyd McClendon MG	.20	.07
❏ 285	Bruce Bochy MG	.20	.07
❏ 286	Dusty Baker MG	.20	.07
❏ 287	Lou Piniella MG	.20	.07
❏ 288	Tony LaRussa MG	.20	.07
❏ 289	Todd Walker	.20	.07
❏ 290	Jerry Narron MG	.20	.07
❏ 291	Carlos Tosca MG	.20	.07
❏ 292	Chris Duncan FY RC	5.00	2.00
❏ 293	Franklin Gutierrez FY RC	1.00	.40
❏ 294	Adam LaRoche FY	.50	.20
❏ 295	Manuel Ramirez FY RC	.50	.20
❏ 296	Il Kim FY RC	.50	.20
❏ 297	Wayne Lydon FY RC	.50	.20
❏ 298	Daryl Clark FY RC	.50	.20
❏ 299	Sean Pierce FY	.50	.20
❏ 300	Andy Marte FY RC	3.00	1.25
❏ 301	Matthew Peterson FY RC	.50	.20
❏ 302	Gonzalo Lopez FY RC	.50	.20
❏ 303	Bernie Castro FY RC	.50	.20
❏ 304	Cliff Lee FY	.50	.20
❏ 305	Jason Perry FY RC	.50	.20
❏ 306	Jaime Bubela FY RC	.50	.20
❏ 307	Alexis Rios FY	1.00	.40
❏ 308	Brendan Harris FY RC	.50	.20
❏ 309	Ramon Nivar-Martinez FY RC	.50	.20
❏ 310	Terry Tiffee FY RC	.50	.20
❏ 311	Kevin Youkilis FY RC	2.00	.75
❏ 312	Ruddy Lugo FY RC	.50	.20
❏ 313	C.J. Wilson FY	.50	.20
❏ 314	Mike McNutt FY RC	.50	.20
❏ 315	Jeff Clark FY RC	.50	.20
❏ 316	Mark Malaska FY RC	.50	.20
❏ 317	Doug Waechter FY RC	.50	.20
❏ 318	Derell McCall FY RC	.50	.20
❏ 319	Scott Tyler FY RC	.50	.20
❏ 320	Craig Brazell FY RC	.50	.20
❏ 321	Walter Young FY	.50	.20
❏ 322	M.Byrd/J.Padilla FS	.50	.20
❏ 323	C.Snelling/S.Choo FS	.50	.20
❏ 324	H.Blalock/M.Teixeira FS	.50	.20
❏ 325	J.Hamilton/C.Crawford FS	.50	.20
❏ 326	O.Hudson/J.Phelps FS	.50	.20
❏ 327	J.Cust/R.Reyes FS	.50	.20
❏ 328	A.Berroa/A.Gomez FS	.50	.20
❏ 329	M.Cuddyer/M.Restovich FS	.50	.20
❏ 330	J.Rivera/M.Thames FS	.50	.20
❏ 331	B.Puffer/J.Bong FS	.50	.20
❏ 332	Mike Cameron SH	.20	.07
❏ 333	Shawn Green SH	.20	.07
❏ 334	Oakland A's SH	.20	.07
❏ 335	Jason Giambi SH	.20	.07
❏ 336	Derek Lowe SH	.20	.07
❏ 337	AL Batting Average LL	.30	.10
❏ 338	AL Runs Scored LL	.20	.07
❏ 339	AL Home Runs LL	.30	.10
❏ 340	AL RBI's LL	.50	.20
❏ 341	AL ERA LL	.20	.07
❏ 342	AL Strikeouts LL	.30	.10
❏ 343	NL Batting Average LL	.50	.20
❏ 344	NL Runs Scored LL	.50	.20
❏ 345	NL Home Runs LL	.50	.20
❏ 346	NL RBI's LL	.20	.07
❏ 347	NL ERA LL	.30	.10
❏ 348	NL Strikeouts LL	.30	.10
❏ 349	AL Division Angels	.20	.07
❏ 350	AL/NL Division Twins/Cards	.30	.10
❏ 351	AL/NL Division Angels/Giants	.30	.10
❏ 352	NL Division Cardinals	.30	.10
❏ 353	Adam Kennedy ALCS	.20	.07
❏ 354	J.T. Snow WS	.30	.10
❏ 355	David Bell NLCS	.30	.10
❏ 356	Jason Giambi AS	.20	.07
❏ 357	Alfonso Soriano AS	.20	.07
❏ 358	Alex Rodriguez AS	.50	.20
❏ 359	Eric Chavez AS	.20	.07
❏ 360	Torii Hunter AS	.20	.07
❏ 361	Bernie Williams AS	.20	.07
❏ 362	Garret Anderson AS	.20	.07
❏ 363	Jorge Posada AS	.20	.07
❏ 364	Derek Lowe AS	.20	.07
❏ 365	Barry Zito AS	.20	.07
❏ 366	Manny Ramirez AS	.30	.10
❏ 367	Mike Scioscia AS	.20	.07
❏ 368	Francisco Rodriguez	.20	.07
❏ 369	Chris Hammond	.20	.07
❏ 370	Chipper Jones	.50	.20
❏ 371	Chris Singleton	.20	.07
❏ 372	Cliff Floyd	.20	.07
❏ 373	Bobby Hill	.20	.07
❏ 374	Antonio Osuna	.20	.07
❏ 375	Barry Larkin	.30	.10
❏ 376	Charles Nagy	.20	.07
❏ 377	Denny Stark	.20	.07
❏ 378	Dean Palmer	.20	.07
❏ 379	Eric Owens	.20	.07
❏ 380	Randy Johnson	.50	.20
❏ 381	Jeff Suppan	.20	.07
❏ 382	Eric Karros	.20	.07
❏ 383	Luis Vizcaino	.20	.07
❏ 384	Johan Santana	.75	.30
❏ 385	Javier Vazquez	.20	.07
❏ 386	John Thomson	.20	.07
❏ 387	Nick Johnson	.20	.07
❏ 388	Mark Ellis	.20	.07
❏ 389	Doug Glanville	.20	.07
❏ 390	Ken Griffey Jr.	.75	.30
❏ 391	Bubba Trammell	.20	.07
❏ 392	Livan Hernandez	.20	.07
❏ 393	Desi Relaford	.20	.07
❏ 394	Eli Marrero	.20	.07
❏ 395	Jared Sandberg	.20	.07
❏ 396	Barry Bonds	1.25	.50
❏ 397	Esteban Loaiza	.20	.07
❏ 398	Aaron Sele	.20	.07
❏ 399	Geoff Blum	.20	.07
❏ 400	Derek Jeter	1.25	.50
❏ 401	Eric Byrnes	.20	.07
❏ 402	Mike Timlin	.20	.07
❏ 403	Mark Kotsay	.20	.07
❏ 404	Rich Aurilia	.20	.07
❏ 405	Joel Pineiro	.20	.07
❏ 406	Chuck Finley	.20	.07
❏ 407	Bengie Molina	.20	.07
❏ 408	Steve Finley	.20	.07
❏ 409	Julio Franco	.20	.07
❏ 410	Marty Cordova	.20	.07
❏ 411	Shea Hillenbrand	.20	.07
❏ 412	Mark Bellhorn	.20	.07
❏ 413	Jon Garland	.20	.07
❏ 414	Reggie Taylor	.20	.07
❏ 415	Milton Bradley	.20	.07
❏ 416	Carlos Pena	.20	.07
❏ 417	Andy Fox	.20	.07
❏ 418	Brad Ausmus	.20	.07
❏ 419	Brent Mayne	.20	.07
❏ 420	Paul Quantrill	.20	.07
❏ 421	Carlos Delgado	.20	.07
❏ 422	Kevin Mench	.20	.07
❏ 423	Joe Kennedy	.20	.07
❏ 424	Mike Crudale	.20	.07
❏ 425	Mark McLemore	.20	.07
❏ 426	Bill Mueller	.20	.07
❏ 427	Rob Mackowiak	.20	.07
❏ 428	Ricky Ledee	.20	.07
❏ 429	Ted Lilly	.20	.07
❏ 430	Sterling Hitchcock	.20	.07
❏ 431	Scott Strickland	.20	.07
❏ 432	Damion Easley	.20	.07
❏ 433	Torii Hunter	.20	.07
❏ 434	Brad Radke	.20	.07
❏ 435	Geoff Jenkins	.20	.07
❏ 436	Paul Byrd	.20	.07
❏ 437	Morgan Ensberg	.20	.07
❏ 438	Mike Maroth	.20	.07
❏ 439	Mike Hampton	.20	.07
❏ 440	Adam Hyzdu	.20	.07
❏ 441	Vance Wilson	.20	.07

❑	442	Todd Ritchie	.20	.07
❑	443	Tom Gordon	.20	.07
❑	444	John Burkett	.20	.07
❑	445	Rodrigo Lopez	.20	.07
❑	446	Tim Spooneybarger	.20	.07
❑	447	Quinton Mccracken	.20	.07
❑	448	Tim Salmon	.30	.10
❑	449	Jarrod Washburn	.20	.07
❑	450	Pedro Martinez	.30	.10
❑	451	Dustan Mohr	.20	.07
❑	452	Julio Lugo	.20	.07
❑	453	Scott Stewart	.20	.07
❑	454	Armando Benitez	.20	.07
❑	455	Raul Mondesi	.20	.07
❑	456	Robin Ventura	.20	.07
❑	457	Bobby Abreu	.20	.07
❑	458	Josh Fogg	.20	.07
❑	459	Ryan Klesko	.20	.07
❑	460	Tsuyoshi Shinjo	.20	.07
❑	461	Jim Edmonds	.20	.07
❑	462	Cliff Politte	.20	.07
❑	463	Chan Ho Park	.20	.07
❑	464	John Mabry	.20	.07
❑	465	Woody Williams	.20	.07
❑	466	Jason Michaels	.20	.07
❑	467	Scott Schoeneweis	.20	.07
❑	468	Brian Anderson	.20	.07
❑	469	Brett Tomko	.20	.07
❑	470	Scott Erickson	.20	.07
❑	471	Kevin Millar Sox	.20	.07
❑	472	Danny Wright	.20	.07
❑	473	Jason Schmidt	.20	.07
❑	474	Scott Williamson	.20	.07
❑	475	Einar Diaz	.20	.07
❑	476	Jay Payton	.20	.07
❑	477	Juan Acevedo	.20	.07
❑	478	Ben Grieve	.20	.07
❑	479	Raul Ibanez	.20	.07
❑	480	Richie Sexson	.20	.07
❑	481	Rick Reed	.20	.07
❑	482	Pedro Astacio	.20	.07
❑	483	Adam Piatt	.20	.07
❑	484	Bud Smith	.20	.07
❑	485	Tomas Perez	.20	.07
❑	486	Adam Eaton	.20	.07
❑	487	Rafael Palmeiro	.30	.10
❑	488	Jason Tyner	.20	.07
❑	489	Scott Rolen	.30	.10
❑	490	Randy Winn	.20	.07
❑	491	Ryan Jensen	.20	.07
❑	492	Trevor Hoffman	.20	.07
❑	493	Craig Wilson	.20	.07
❑	494	Jeremy Giambi	.20	.07
❑	495	Daryle Ward	.20	.07
❑	496	Shane Spencer	.20	.07
❑	497	Andy Pettitte	.30	.10
❑	498	John Franco	.20	.07
❑	499	Felipe Lopez	.20	.07
❑	500	Mike Piazza	.75	.30
❑	501	Cristian Guzman	.20	.07
❑	502	Jose Hernandez	.20	.07
❑	503	Octavio Dotel	.20	.07
❑	504	Brad Penny	.20	.07
❑	505	Dave Veres	.20	.07
❑	506	Ryan Dempster	.20	.07
❑	507	Joe Crede	.20	.07
❑	508	Chad Hermansen	.20	.07
❑	509	Gary Matthews Jr.	.20	.07
❑	510	Matt Franco	.20	.07
❑	511	Ben Weber	.20	.07
❑	512	Dave Berg	.20	.07
❑	513	Michael Young	.30	.10
❑	514	Frank Catalanotto	.20	.07
❑	515	Darin Erstad	.20	.07
❑	516	Matt Williams	.20	.07
❑	517	B.J. Surhoff	.20	.07
❑	518	Kerry Ligtenberg	.20	.07
❑	519	Mike Bordick	.20	.07
❑	520	Arthur Rhodes	.20	.07
❑	521	Joe Girardi	.20	.07
❑	522	D'Angelo Jimenez	.20	.07
❑	523	Paul Konerko	.20	.07
❑	524	Jose Macias	.20	.07
❑	525	Joe Mays	.20	.07
❑	526	Marquis Grissom	.20	.07
❑	527	Neifi Perez	.20	.07
❑	528	Preston Wilson	.20	.07
❑	529	Jeff Weaver	.20	.07
❑	530	Eric Chavez	.20	.07
❑	531	Placido Polanco	.20	.07
❑	532	Matt Mantei	.20	.07
❑	533	James Baldwin	.20	.07
❑	534	Toby Hall	.20	.07
❑	535	Brendan Donnelly	.20	.07
❑	536	Benji Gil	.20	.07
❑	537	Damian Moss	.20	.07
❑	538	Jorge Julio	.20	.07
❑	539	Matt Clement	.20	.07
❑	540	Brian Moehler	.20	.07
❑	541	Lee Stevens	.20	.07
❑	542	Jimmy Haynes	.20	.07
❑	543	Terry Mulholland	.20	.07
❑	544	Dave Roberts	.20	.07
❑	545	J.C. Romero	.20	.07
❑	546	Bartolo Colon	.20	.07
❑	547	Roger Cedeno	.20	.07
❑	548	Mariano Rivera	.50	.20
❑	549	Billy Koch	.20	.07
❑	550	Manny Ramirez	.30	.10
❑	551	Travis Lee	.20	.07
❑	552	Oliver Perez	.20	.07
❑	553	Tim Worrell	.20	.07
❑	554	Rafael Soriano	.20	.07
❑	555	Damian Miller	.20	.07
❑	556	John Smoltz	.30	.10
❑	557	Willis Roberts	.20	.07
❑	558	Tim Hudson	.20	.07
❑	559	Moises Alou	.20	.07
❑	560	Gary Glover	.20	.07
❑	561	Corky Miller	.20	.07
❑	562	Ben Broussard	.20	.07
❑	563	Gabe Kapler	.20	.07
❑	564	Chris Woodward	.20	.07
❑	565	Paul Wilson	.20	.07
❑	566	Todd Hollandsworth	.20	.07
❑	567	So Taguchi	.20	.07
❑	568	John Olerud	.20	.07
❑	569	Reggie Sanders	.20	.07
❑	570	Jake Peavy	.20	.07
❑	571	Kris Benson	.20	.07
❑	572	Todd Pratt	.20	.07
❑	573	Ray Durham	.20	.07
❑	574	Boomer Wells	.20	.07
❑	575	Chris Widger	.20	.07
❑	576	Shawn Wooten	.20	.07
❑	577	Tom Glavine	.30	.10
❑	578	Antonio Alfonseca	.20	.07
❑	579	Keith Foulke	.20	.07
❑	580	Shawn Estes	.20	.07
❑	581	Mark Grace	.30	.10
❑	582	Dmitri Young	.20	.07
❑	583	A.J. Burnett	.20	.07
❑	584	Richard Hidalgo	.20	.07
❑	585	Mike Sweeney	.20	.07
❑	586	Alex Cora	.20	.07
❑	587	Matt Stairs	.20	.07
❑	588	Doug Mientkiewicz	.20	.07
❑	589	Fernando Tatis	.20	.07
❑	590	David Weathers	.20	.07
❑	591	Cory Lidle	.20	.07
❑	592	Dan Plesac	.20	.07
❑	593	Jeff Bagwell	.30	.10
❑	594	Steve Sparks	.20	.07
❑	595	Sandy Alomar Jr.	.20	.07
❑	596	John Lackey	.20	.07
❑	597	Rick Helling	.20	.07
❑	598	Mark DeRosa	.20	.07
❑	599	Carlos Lee	.20	.07
❑	600	Garret Anderson	.20	.07
❑	601	Vinny Castilla	.20	.07
❑	602	Ryan Drese	.20	.07
❑	603	LaTroy Hawkins	.20	.07
❑	604	David Bell	.20	.07
❑	605	Freddy Garcia	.20	.07
❑	606	Miguel Cairo	.20	.07
❑	607	Scott Spiezio	.20	.07
❑	608	Mike Remlinger	.20	.07
❑	609	Tony Graffanino	.20	.07
❑	610	Russell Branyan	.20	.07
❑	611	Chris Magruder	.20	.07
❑	612	Jose Contreras RC	1.00	.40
❑	613	Carl Pavano	.20	.07
❑	614	Kevin Brown	.20	.07
❑	615	Tyler Houston	.20	.07
❑	616	A.J. Pierzynski	.20	.07
❑	617	Tony Fiore	.20	.07
❑	618	Peter Bergeron	.20	.07
❑	619	Rondell White	.20	.07
❑	620	Brett Myers	.20	.07
❑	621	Kevin Young	.20	.07
❑	622	Kenny Lofton	.20	.07
❑	623	Ben Davis	.20	.07
❑	624	J.D. Drew	.20	.07
❑	625	Chris Gomez	.20	.07
❑	626	Karim Garcia	.20	.07
❑	627	Ricky Gutierrez	.20	.07
❑	628	Mark Redman	.20	.07
❑	629	Juan Encarnacion	.20	.07
❑	630	Anaheim Angels TC	.30	.10
❑	631	Arizona Diamondbacks TC	.20	.07
❑	632	Atlanta Braves TC	.20	.07
❑	633	Baltimore Orioles TC	.20	.07
❑	634	Boston Red Sox TC	.20	.07
❑	635	Chicago Cubs TC	.20	.07
❑	636	Chicago White Sox TC	.20	.07
❑	637	Cincinnati Reds TC	.20	.07
❑	638	Cleveland Indians TC	.20	.07
❑	639	Colorado Rockies TC	.20	.07
❑	640	Detroit Tigers TC	.20	.07
❑	641	Florida Marlins TC	.20	.07
❑	642	Houston Astros TC	.20	.07
❑	643	Kansas City Royals TC	.20	.07
❑	644	Los Angeles Dodgers TC	.20	.07
❑	645	Milwaukee Brewers TC	.20	.07
❑	646	Minnesota Twins TC	.20	.07
❑	647	Montreal Expos TC	.20	.07
❑	648	New York Mets TC	.20	.07
❑	649	New York Yankees TC	.30	.10
❑	650	Oakland Athletics TC	.20	.07
❑	651	Philadelphia Phillies TC	.20	.07
❑	652	Pittsburgh Pirates TC	.20	.07
❑	653	San Diego Padres TC	.20	.07
❑	654	San Francisco Giants TC	.20	.07
❑	655	Seattle Mariners TC	.20	.07
❑	656	St. Louis Cardinals TC	.20	.07
❑	657	Tampa Bay Devil Rays TC	.20	.07
❑	658	Texas Rangers TC	.20	.07
❑	659	Toronto Blue Jays TC	.20	.07
❑	660	Bryan Bullington DP RC	.50	.20
❑	661	Jeremy Guthrie DP	.50	.20
❑	662	Joey Gomes DP RC	.50	.20
❑	663	Evel Bastida-Martinez DP RC	.50	.20
❑	664	Brian Wright DP RC	.50	.20
❑	665	B.J. Upton DP	.75	.30
❑	666	Jeff Francis DP	.50	.20
❑	667	Drew Meyer DP	.50	.20
❑	668	Jeremy Hermida DP	.75	.30
❑	669	Khalil Greene DP	.75	.30
❑	670	Darrell Rasner DP RC	.50	.20
❑	671	Cole Hamels DP	2.00	.75
❑	672	James Loney DP	.60	.25
❑	673	Sergio Santos DP	.50	.20
❑	674	Jason Pridie DP	.50	.20
❑	675	B.Phillips/V.Martinez	.50	.20
❑	676	H.Choi/N.Jackson	.50	.20
❑	677	D.Willis/J.Stokes	.75	.30
❑	678	C.Tracy/L.Overbay	.50	.20
❑	679	J.Borchard/C.Malone	.50	.20
❑	680	J.Mauer/J.Morneau	.75	.30
❑	681	D.Henson/B.Claussen	.50	.20
❑	682	C.Utley/G.Floyd	.75	.30
❑	683	T.Bozied/X.Nady	.50	.20
❑	684	A.Heilman/J.Reyes	.50	.20
❑	685	Kenny Rogers AW	.20	.07
❑	686	Bengie Molina AW	.20	.07
❑	687	John Olerud AW	.20	.07
❑	688	Bret Boone AW	.20	.07
❑	689	Eric Chavez AW	.20	.07
❑	690	Alex Rodriguez AW	.50	.20
❑	691	Darin Erstad AW	.20	.07
❑	692	Ichiro Suzuki AW	.50	.20
❑	693	Torii Hunter AW	.20	.07
❑	694	Greg Maddux AW	.50	.20
❑	695	Brad Ausmus AW	.20	.07
❑	696	Todd Helton AW	.20	.07
❑	697	Fernando Vina AW	.20	.07
❑	698	Scott Rolen AW	.20	.07
❑	699	Edgar Renteria AW	.20	.07

❑ 700 Andruw Jones AW .20 .07
❑ 701 Larry Walker AW .20 .07
❑ 702 Jim Edmonds AW .20 .07
❑ 703 Barry Zito AW .20 .07
❑ 704 Randy Johnson AW .30 .10
❑ 705 Miguel Tejada AW .20 .07
❑ 706 Barry Bonds AW .75 .30
❑ 707 Eric Hinske AW .20 .07
❑ 708 Jason Jennings AW .20 .07
❑ 709 Todd Helton AS .20 .07
❑ 710 Jeff Kent AS .20 .07
❑ 711 Edgar Renteria AS .20 .07
❑ 712 Scott Rolen AS .20 .07
❑ 713 Barry Bonds AS .75 .30
❑ 714 Sammy Sosa AS .30 .10
❑ 715 Vladimir Guerrero AS .30 .10
❑ 716 Mike Piazza AS .50 .20
❑ 717 Curt Schilling AS .20 .07
❑ 718 Randy Johnson AS .30 .10
❑ 719 Bobby Cox AS .20 .07
❑ 720 Anaheim Angels WS .30 .10
❑ 721 Anaheim Angels WS .50 .20

2003 Topps Traded

❑ COMPLETE SET (275) 50.00 20.00
❑ COMMON CARD (T1-T120) .20 .07
❑ COMMON CARD (121-165) .40 .15
❑ T1 Juan Pierre .20 .07
❑ T2 Mark Grudzielanek .20 .07
❑ T3 Tanyon Sturtze .20 .07
❑ T4 Greg Vaughn .20 .07
❑ T5 Greg Myers .20 .07
❑ T6 Randall Simon .20 .07
❑ T7 Todd Hundley .20 .07
❑ T8 Marlon Anderson .20 .07
❑ T9 Jeff Reboulet .20 .07
❑ T10 Alex Sanchez .20 .07
❑ T11 Mike Rivera .20 .07
❑ T12 Todd Walker .20 .07
❑ T13 Ray King .20 .07
❑ T14 Shawn Estes .20 .07
❑ T15 Gary Matthews Jr. .20 .07
❑ T16 Jaret Wright .20 .07
❑ T17 Edgardo Alfonzo .20 .07
❑ T18 Omar Daal .20 .07
❑ T19 Ryan Rupe .20 .07
❑ T20 Tony Clark .20 .07
❑ T21 Jeff Suppan .20 .07
❑ T22 Mike Stanton .20 .07
❑ T23 Ramon Martinez .20 .07
❑ T24 Armando Rios .20 .07
❑ T25 Johnny Estrada .20 .07
❑ T26 Joe Girardi .20 .07
❑ T27 Ivan Rodriguez .30 .10
❑ T28 Robert Fick .20 .07
❑ T29 Rick White .20 .07
❑ T30 Robert Person .20 .07
❑ T31 Alan Benes .20 .07
❑ T32 Chris Carpenter .20 .07
❑ T33 Chris Widger .20 .07
❑ T34 Travis Hafner .20 .07
❑ T35 Mike Venafro .20 .07
❑ T36 Jon Lieber .20 .07
❑ T37 Orlando Hernandez .20 .07
❑ T38 Aaron Myette .20 .07
❑ T39 Paul Bako .20 .07
❑ T40 Erubiel Durazo .20 .07
❑ T41 Mark Guthrie .20 .07
❑ T42 Steve Avery .20 .07
❑ T43 Damian Jackson .20 .07
❑ T44 Rey Ordonez .20 .07
❑ T45 John Flaherty .20 .07
❑ T46 Byung-Hyun Kim .20 .07
❑ T47 Tom Goodwin .20 .07
❑ T48 Elmer Dessens .20 .07
❑ T49 Al Martin .20 .07
❑ T50 Gene Kingsale .20 .07
❑ T51 Lenny Harris .20 .07
❑ T52 David Ortiz Sox .50 .20
❑ T53 Jose Lima .20 .07
❑ T54 Mike Difelice .20 .07
❑ T55 Jose Hernandez .20 .07
❑ T56 Todd Zeile .20 .07
❑ T57 Roberto Hernandez .20 .07
❑ T58 Albie Lopez .20 .07
❑ T59 Roberto Alomar .30 .10
❑ T60 Russ Ortiz .20 .07
❑ T61 Brian Daubach .20 .07
❑ T62 Carl Everett .20 .07
❑ T63 Jeromy Burnitz .20 .07
❑ T64 Mark Bellhorn .20 .07
❑ T65 Ruben Sierra .20 .07
❑ T66 Mike Fetters .20 .07
❑ T67 Armando Benitez .20 .07
❑ T68 Deivi Cruz .20 .07
❑ T69 Jose Cruz Jr. .20 .07
❑ T70 Jeremy Fikac .20 .07
❑ T71 Jeff Kent .20 .07
❑ T72 Andres Galarraga .20 .07
❑ T73 Rickey Henderson .50 .20
❑ T74 Royce Clayton .20 .07
❑ T75 Troy O'Leary .20 .07
❑ T76 Ron Coomer .20 .07
❑ T77 Greg Colbrunn .20 .07
❑ T78 Wes Helms .20 .07
❑ T79 Kevin Millwood .20 .07
❑ T80 Damion Easley .20 .07
❑ T81 Bobby Kielty .20 .07
❑ T82 Keith Osik .20 .07
❑ T83 Ramiro Mendoza .20 .07
❑ T84 Shea Hillenbrand .20 .07
❑ T85 Shannon Stewart .20 .07
❑ T86 Eddie Perez .20 .07
❑ T87 Ugueth Urbina .20 .07
❑ T88 Orlando Palmeiro .20 .07
❑ T89 Graeme Lloyd .20 .07
❑ T90 John Vander Wal .20 .07
❑ T91 Gary Bennett .20 .07
❑ T92 Shane Reynolds .20 .07
❑ T93 Steve Parris .20 .07
❑ T94 Julio Lugo .20 .07
❑ T95 John Halama .20 .07
❑ T96 Carlos Baerga .20 .07
❑ T97 Jim Parque .20 .07
❑ T98 Mike Williams .20 .07
❑ T99 Fred McGriff .30 .10
❑ T100 Kenny Rogers .20 .07
❑ T101 Matt Herges .20 .07
❑ T102 Jay Bell .20 .07
❑ T103 Esteban Yan .20 .07
❑ T104 Eric Owens .20 .07
❑ T105 Aaron Fultz .20 .07
❑ T106 Rey Sanchez .20 .07
❑ T107 Jim Thome .30 .10
❑ T108 Aaron Boone .20 .07
❑ T109 Raul Mondesi .20 .07
❑ T110 Kenny Lofton .20 .07
❑ T111 Jose Guillen .20 .07
❑ T112 Aramis Ramirez .20 .07
❑ T113 Sidney Ponson .20 .07
❑ T114 Scott Williamson .20 .07
❑ T115 Robin Ventura .20 .07
❑ T116 Dusty Baker MG .20 .07
❑ T117 Felipe Alou MG .20 .07
❑ T118 Buck Showalter MG .20 .07
❑ T119 Jack McKeon MG .20 .07
❑ T120 Art Howe MG .20 .07
❑ T121 Bobby Crosby PROS .40 .15
❑ T122 Adrian Gonzalez PROS .40 .15
❑ T123 Kevin Cash PROS .40 .15
❑ T124 Shin-Soo Choo PROS .40 .15
❑ T125 Chin-Feng Chen PROS 1.00 .40
❑ T126 Miguel Cabrera PROS 1.00 .40
❑ T127 Jason Young PROS .40 .15
❑ T128 Alex Herrera PROS .40 .15
❑ T129 Jason Dubois PROS .40 .15
❑ T130 Jeff Mathis PROS .40 .15
❑ T131 Casey Kotchman PROS .40 .15
❑ T132 Ed Rogers PROS .40 .15
❑ T133 Wilson Betemit PROS .40 .15
❑ T134 Jim Kavourias PROS .40 .15
❑ T135 Taylor Buchholz PROS .40 .15
❑ T136 Adam LaRoche PROS .40 .15
❑ T137 Dallas McPherson PROS .40 .15
❑ T138 Jesus Cota PROS .40 .15
❑ T139 Clint Nageotte PROS .40 .15
❑ T140 Boof Bonser PROS .40 .15
❑ T141 Walter Young PROS .40 .15
❑ T142 Joe Crede PROS .40 .15
❑ T143 Denny Bautista PROS .40 .15
❑ T144 Victor Diaz PROS .40 .15
❑ T145 Chris Narveson PROS .40 .15
❑ T146 Gabe Gross PROS .40 .15
❑ T147 Jimmy Journell PROS .40 .15
❑ T148 Rafael Soriano PROS .40 .15
❑ T149 Jerome Williams PROS .40 .15
❑ T150 Aaron Cook PROS .40 .15
❑ T151 Anastacio Martinez PROS .40 .15
❑ T152 Scott Hairston PROS .40 .15
❑ T153 John Buck PROS .40 .15
❑ T154 Ryan Ludwick PROS .40 .15
❑ T155 Chris Bootcheck PROS .40 .15
❑ T156 John Rheinecker PROS .40 .15
❑ T157 Jason Lane PROS .40 .15
❑ T159 Adam Wainwright PROS .40 .15
❑ T160 Jason Arnold PROS .40 .15
❑ T161 Jonny Gomes PROS .60 .25
❑ T162 James Loney PROS .50 .20
❑ T163 Mike Fontenot PROS .40 .15
❑ T164 Khalil Greene PROS 1.00 .40
❑ T165 Sean Burnett PROS .40 .15
❑ T166 David Martinez FY RC .40 .15
❑ T167 Felix Pie FY RC 4.00 1.50
❑ T168 Joe Valentine FY RC .40 .15
❑ T169 Brandon Webb FY RC 2.50 1.00
❑ T170 Matt Diaz FY RC .75 .30
❑ T171 Lew Ford FY RC .50 .20
❑ T172 Jeremy Griffiths FY RC .40 .15
❑ T173 Matt Hensley FY RC .40 .15
❑ T174 Charlie Manning FY RC .40 .15
❑ T175 Elizardo Ramirez FY RC .50 .20
❑ T176 Greg Aquino FY RC .40 .15
❑ T177 Felix Sanchez FY RC .40 .15
❑ T178 Kelly Shoppach FY RC .75 .30
❑ T179 Bubba Nelson FY RC .50 .20
❑ T180 Mike Oâ ™Keefe FY RC .40 .15
❑ T181 Hanley Ramirez FY RC 5.00 2.00
❑ T182 Todd Wellemeyer FY RC .40 .15
❑ T183 Dustin Moseley FY RC .40 .15
❑ T184 Eric Crozier FY RC .50 .20
❑ T185 Ryan Shealy FY RC 2.50 1.00
❑ T186 Jeremy Bonderman FY RC 3.00 1.25
❑ T187 T.Story-Harden FY RC .40 .15
❑ T188 Dusty Brown FY RC .40 .15
❑ T189 Rob Hammock FY RC .40 .15
❑ T190 Jorge Piedra FY RC .50 .20
❑ T191 Chris De La Cruz FY RC .40 .15
❑ T192 Eli Whiteside FY RC .40 .15
❑ T193 Jason Kubel FY RC 1.00 .40
❑ T194 Jon Schuerholz FY RC .40 .15
❑ T195 Stephen Randolph FY RC .40 .15
❑ T196 Andy Sisco FY RC .40 .15
❑ T197 Sean Smith FY RC .50 .20
❑ T198 Jon-Mark Sprowl FY RC .40 .15
❑ T199 Matt Kata FY RC .40 .15
❑ T200 Robinson Cano FY RC 8.00 3.00
❑ T201 Nook Logan FY RC .50 .20
❑ T202 Ben Francisco FY RC .40 .15
❑ T203 Arnie Munoz FY RC .40 .15
❑ T204 Ozzie Chavez FY RC .40 .15
❑ T205 Eric Riggs FY RC .50 .20
❑ T206 Beau Kemp FY RC .40 .15
❑ T207 Travis Wong FY RC .50 .20
❑ T208 Dustin Yount FY RC .50 .20
❑ T209 Brian McCann FY RC 6.00 2.50
❑ T210 Wilton Reynolds FY RC .50 .20
❑ T211 Matt Bruback FY RC .40 .15
❑ T212 Andrew Brown FY RC .50 .20
❑ T213 Edgar Gonzalez FY RC .40 .15
❑ T214 Eider Torres FY RC .40 .15

❑ T215 Aquilino Lopez FY RC .40 .15
❑ T216 Bobby Basham FY RC .40 .15
❑ T217 Tim Olson FY RC .40 .15
❑ T218 Nathan Panther FY RC .40 .15
❑ T219 Bryan Grace FY RC .40 .15
❑ T220 Dusty Gomon FY RC .50 .20
❑ T221 Wil Ledezma FY RC .40 .15
❑ T222 Josh Willingham FY RC 1.00 .40
❑ T223 David Cash FY RC .40 .15
❑ T224 Oscar Villarreal FY RC .40 .15
❑ T225 Jeff Duncan FY RC .40 .15
❑ T226 Kade Johnson FY RC .40 .15
❑ T227 Luke Steidlmayer FY RC .40 .15
❑ T228 Brandon Watson FY RC .40 .15
❑ T229 Jose Morales FY RC .40 .15
❑ T230 Mike Gallo FY RC .40 .15
❑ T231 Tyler Adamczyk FY RC .40 .15
❑ T232 Adam Stern FY RC .40 .15
❑ T233 Brennan King FY RC .40 .15
❑ T234 Dan Haren FY RC .75 .30
❑ T235 Michel Hernandez FY RC .40 .15
❑ T236 Ben Fritz FY RC .40 .15
❑ T237 Clay Hensley FY RC .40 .15
❑ T238 Tyler Johnson FY RC .40 .15
❑ T239 Pete LaForest FY RC .40 .15
❑ T240 Tyler Martin FY RC .40 .15
❑ T241 J.D. Durbin FY RC .40 .15
❑ T242 Shane Victorino FY RC .75 .30
❑ T243 Rajai Davis FY RC .40 .15
❑ T244 Ismael Castro FY RC .40 .15
❑ T245 Chien-Ming Wang FY RC 6.00 2.50
❑ T246 Travis Ishikawa FY RC .75 .30
❑ T247 Corey Shafer FY RC .40 .15
❑ T248 Gary Schneidmiller FY RC .40 .15
❑ T249 Dave Pember FY RC .40 .15
❑ T250 Keith Stamler FY RC .40 .15
❑ T251 Tyson Graham FY RC .40 .15
❑ T252 Ryan Cameron FY RC .40 .15
❑ T253 Eric Eckenstahler FY .40 .15
❑ T254 Matthew Peterson FY RC .40 .15
❑ T255 Dustin McGowan FY RC .50 .20
❑ T256 Prentice Redman FY RC .40 .15
❑ T257 Haj Turay FY RC .40 .15
❑ T258 Carlos Guzman FY RC .50 .20
❑ T259 Matt DeMarco FY RC .40 .15
❑ T260 Derek Michaelis FY RC .40 .15
❑ T261 Brian Burgamy FY RC .40 .15
❑ T262 Jay Sitzman FY RC .40 .15
❑ T263 Chris Fallon FY RC .40 .15
❑ T264 Mike Adams FY RC .40 .15
❑ T265 Clint Barmes FY RC 1.00 .40
❑ T266 Eric Reed FY RC .40 .15
❑ T267 Willie Eyre FY RC .40 .15
❑ T268 Carlos Duran FY RC .40 .15
❑ T269 Nick Trzesniak FY RC .40 .15
❑ T270 Ferdin Tejeda FY RC .40 .15
❑ T271 Michael Garciaparra FY RC .40 .15
❑ T272 Michael Hinckley FY RC .50 .20
❑ T273 Branden Florence FY RC .40 .15
❑ T274 Trent Oeltjen FY RC .50 .20
❑ T275 Mike Neu FY RC .40 .15

2004 Topps

❑ COMP.HOBBY SET (737) 80.00 40.00
❑ COMP.HOLIDAY SET (742) 80.00 40.00
❑ COMP.RETAIL SET (737) 80.00 40.00
❑ COMP.ASTROS SET (737) 80.00 40.00
❑ COMP.CUBS SET (737) 80.00 40.00
❑ COMP.RED SOX SET (737) 80.00 40.00
❑ COMP.YANKEES SET (737) 80.00 40.00
❑ COMPLETE SET (732) 80.00 30.00
❑ COMPLETE SERIES 1 (366) 40.00 15.00
❑ COMPLETE SERIES 2 (366) 40.00 15.00
❑ COMMON CARD (1-6/8-732) .20 .07
❑ COMMON (297-326/668-687) .50 .20
❑ COMMON (327-331/688-692) .50 .20
❑ 1 Jim Thome .30 .10
❑ 2 Reggie Sanders .20 .07
❑ 3 Mark Kotsay .20 .07
❑ 4 Edgardo Alfonzo .20 .07
❑ 5 Ben Davis .20 .07
❑ 6 Mike Matheny .20 .07
❑ 8 Marlon Anderson .20 .07
❑ 9 Chan Ho Park .20 .07
❑ 10 Ichiro Suzuki 1.00 .40
❑ 11 Kevin Millwood .20 .07
❑ 12 Bengie Molina .20 .07
❑ 13 Tom Glavine .30 .10
❑ 14 Junior Spivey .20 .07
❑ 15 Marcus Giles .20 .07
❑ 16 David Segui .20 .07
❑ 17 Kevin Millar .20 .07
❑ 18 Corey Patterson .20 .07
❑ 19 Aaron Rowand .20 .07
❑ 20 Derek Jeter 1.00 .40
❑ 21 Jason LaRue .20 .07
❑ 22 Chris Hammond .20 .07
❑ 23 Jay Payton .20 .07
❑ 24 Bobby Higginson .20 .07
❑ 25 Lance Berkman .20 .07
❑ 26 Juan Pierre .20 .07
❑ 27 Brent Mayne .20 .07
❑ 28 Fred McGriff .30 .10
❑ 29 Richie Sexson .20 .07
❑ 30 Tim Hudson .20 .07
❑ 31 Mike Piazza .75 .30
❑ 32 Brad Radke .20 .07
❑ 33 Jeff Weaver .20 .07
❑ 34 Ramon Hernandez .20 .07
❑ 35 David Bell .20 .07
❑ 36 Craig Wilson .20 .07
❑ 37 Jake Peavy .20 .07
❑ 38 Tim Worrell .20 .07
❑ 39 Gil Meche .20 .07
❑ 40 Albert Pujols 1.00 .40
❑ 41 Michael Young .20 .07
❑ 42 Josh Phelps .20 .07
❑ 43 Brendan Donnelly .20 .07
❑ 44 Steve Finley .20 .07
❑ 45 John Smoltz .30 .10
❑ 46 Jay Gibbons .20 .07
❑ 47 Trot Nixon .20 .07
❑ 48 Carl Pavano .20 .07
❑ 49 Frank Thomas .50 .20
❑ 50 Mark Prior .30 .10
❑ 51 Danny Graves .20 .07
❑ 52 Milton Bradley UER .20 .07
❑ 53 Jose Jimenez .20 .07
❑ 54 Shane Halter .20 .07
❑ 55 Mike Lowell .20 .07
❑ 56 Geoff Blum .20 .07
❑ 57 Michael Tucker UER .20 .07
❑ 58 Paul Lo Duca .20 .07
❑ 59 Vicente Padilla .20 .07
❑ 60 Jacque Jones .20 .07
❑ 61 Fernando Tatis .20 .07
❑ 62 Ty Wigginton .20 .07
❑ 63 Pedro Astacio .20 .07
❑ 64 Andy Pettitte .30 .10
❑ 65 Terrence Long .20 .07
❑ 66 Cliff Floyd .20 .07
❑ 67 Mariano Rivera .50 .20
❑ 68 Carlos Silva .20 .07
❑ 69 Marlon Byrd .20 .07
❑ 70 Mark Mulder .20 .07
❑ 71 Kerry Ligtenberg .20 .07
❑ 72 Carlos Guillen .20 .07
❑ 73 Fernando Vina .20 .07
❑ 74 Lance Carter .20 .07
❑ 75 Hank Blalock .20 .07
❑ 76 Jimmy Rollins .20 .07
❑ 77 Francisco Rodriguez .20 .07
❑ 78 Javy Lopez .20 .07
❑ 79 Jerry Hairston Jr. .20 .07
❑ 80 Andruw Jones .30 .10
❑ 81 Rodrigo Lopez .20 .07
❑ 82 Johnny Damon .30 .10
❑ 83 Hee Seop Choi .20 .07
❑ 84 Miguel Olivo .20 .07
❑ 85 Jon Garland .20 .07
❑ 86 Matt Lawton .20 .07
❑ 87 Juan Uribe .20 .07
❑ 88 Steve Sparks .20 .07
❑ 89 Tim Spooneybarger .20 .07
❑ 90 Jose Vidro .20 .07
❑ 91 Luis Rivas .20 .07
❑ 92 Hideo Nomo .50 .20
❑ 93 Javier Vazquez .20 .07
❑ 94 Al Leiter .20 .07
❑ 95 Darren Dreifort .20 .07
❑ 96 Alex Cintron .20 .07
❑ 97 Zach Day .20 .07
❑ 98 Jorge Posada .30 .10
❑ 99 John Halama .20 .07
❑ 100 Alex Rodriguez .75 .30
❑ 101 Orlando Palmeiro .20 .07
❑ 102 Dave Berg .20 .07
❑ 103 Brad Fullmer .20 .07
❑ 104 Mike Hampton .20 .07
❑ 105 Willis Roberts .20 .07
❑ 106 Ramiro Mendoza .20 .07
❑ 107 Juan Cruz .20 .07
❑ 108 Esteban Loaiza .20 .07
❑ 109 Russell Branyan .20 .07
❑ 110 Todd Helton .30 .10
❑ 111 Braden Looper .20 .07
❑ 112 Octavio Dotel .20 .07
❑ 113 Mike MacDougal .20 .07
❑ 114 Cesar Izturis .20 .07
❑ 115 Johan Santana .50 .20
❑ 116 Jose Contreras .20 .07
❑ 117 Placido Polanco .20 .07
❑ 118 Jason Phillips .20 .07
❑ 119 Adam Eaton .20 .07
❑ 120 Vernon Wells .20 .07
❑ 121 Ben Grieve .20 .07
❑ 122 Randy Winn .20 .07
❑ 123 Ismael Valdes .20 .07
❑ 124 Eric Owens .20 .07
❑ 125 Curt Schilling .20 .07
❑ 126 Russ Ortiz .20 .07
❑ 127 Mark Buehrle .20 .07
❑ 128 Danys Baez .20 .07
❑ 129 Dmitri Young .20 .07
❑ 130 Kazuhisa Ishii .20 .07
❑ 131 A.J. Pierzynski .20 .07
❑ 132 Michael Barrett .20 .07
❑ 133 Joe McEwing .20 .07
❑ 134 Alex Cora .20 .07
❑ 135 Tom Wilson .20 .07
❑ 136 Carlos Zambrano .20 .07
❑ 137 Brett Tomko .20 .07
❑ 138 Shigetoshi Hasegawa .20 .07
❑ 139 Jarrod Washburn .20 .07
❑ 140 Greg Maddux .75 .30
❑ 141 Craig Counsell .20 .07
❑ 142 Reggie Taylor .20 .07
❑ 143 Omar Vizquel .30 .10
❑ 144 Alex Gonzalez .20 .07
❑ 145 Billy Wagner .20 .07
❑ 146 Brian Jordan .20 .07
❑ 147 Wes Helms .20 .07
❑ 148 Kyle Lohse .20 .07
❑ 149 Timo Perez .20 .07
❑ 150 Jason Giambi .20 .07
❑ 151 Erubiel Durazo .20 .07
❑ 152 Mike Lieberthal .20 .07
❑ 153 Jason Kendall .20 .07
❑ 154 Xavier Nady .20 .07
❑ 155 Kirk Rueter .20 .07
❑ 156 Mike Cameron .20 .07
❑ 157 Miguel Cairo .20 .07
❑ 158 Woody Williams .20 .07
❑ 159 Toby Hall .20 .07
❑ 160 Bernie Williams .30 .10
❑ 161 Darin Erstad .20 .07
❑ 162 Matt Mantei .20 .07
❑ 163 Geronimo Gil .20 .07
❑ 164 Bill Mueller .20 .07
❑ 165 Damian Miller .20 .07

❑ 166 Tony Graffanino .20 .07
❑ 167 Sean Casey .20 .07
❑ 168 Brandon Phillips .20 .07
❑ 169 Mike Remlinger .20 .07
❑ 170 Adam Dunn .20 .07
❑ 171 Carlos Lee .20 .07
❑ 172 Juan Encarnacion .20 .07
❑ 173 Angel Berroa .20 .07
❑ 174 Desi Relaford .20 .07
❑ 175 Paul Quantrill .20 .07
❑ 176 Ben Sheets .20 .07
❑ 177 Eddie Guardado .20 .07
❑ 178 Rocky Biddle .20 .07
❑ 179 Mike Stanton .20 .07
❑ 180 Eric Chavez .20 .07
❑ 181 Jason Michaels .20 .07
❑ 182 Terry Adams .20 .07
❑ 183 Kip Wells .20 .07
❑ 184 Brian Lawrence .20 .07
❑ 185 Bret Boone .20 .07
❑ 186 Tino Martinez .30 .10
❑ 187 Aubrey Huff .20 .07
❑ 188 Kevin Mench .20 .07
❑ 189 Tim Salmon .30 .10
❑ 190 Carlos Delgado .20 .07
❑ 191 John Lackey .20 .07
❑ 192 Oscar Villarreal .20 .07
❑ 193 Luis Matos .20 .07
❑ 194 Derek Lowe .20 .07
❑ 195 Mark Grudzielanek .20 .07
❑ 196 Tom Gordon .20 .07
❑ 197 Matt Clement .20 .07
❑ 198 Byung-Hyun Kim .20 .07
❑ 199 Brandon Inge .20 .07
❑ 200 Nomar Garciaparra .75 .30
❑ 201 Antonio Osuna .20 .07
❑ 202 Jose Mesa .20 .07
❑ 203 Bo Hart .20 .07
❑ 204 Jack Wilson .20 .07
❑ 205 Ray Durham .20 .07
❑ 206 Freddy Garcia .20 .07
❑ 207 J.D. Drew .20 .07
❑ 208 Einar Diaz .20 .07
❑ 209 Roy Halladay .20 .07
❑ 210 David Eckstein UER .20 .07
❑ 211 Jason Marquis .20 .07
❑ 212 Jorge Julio .20 .07
❑ 213 Tim Wakefield .20 .07
❑ 214 Moises Alou .20 .07
❑ 215 Bartolo Colon .20 .07
❑ 216 Jimmy Haynes .20 .07
❑ 217 Preston Wilson .20 .07
❑ 218 Luis Castillo .20 .07
❑ 219 Richard Hidalgo .20 .07
❑ 220 Manny Ramirez .30 .10
❑ 221 Mike Mussina .30 .10
❑ 222 Randy Wolf .20 .07
❑ 223 Kris Benson .20 .07
❑ 224 Ryan Klesko .20 .07
❑ 225 Rich Aurilia .20 .07
❑ 226 Kelvim Escobar .20 .07
❑ 227 Francisco Cordero .20 .07
❑ 228 Kazuhiro Sasaki .20 .07
❑ 229 Danny Bautista .20 .07
❑ 230 Rafael Furcal .20 .07
❑ 231 Travis Driskill .20 .07
❑ 232 Kyle Farnsworth .20 .07
❑ 233 Jose Valentin .20 .07
❑ 234 Felipe Lopez .20 .07
❑ 235 C.C. Sabathia .20 .07
❑ 236 Brad Penny .20 .07
❑ 237 Brad Ausmus .20 .07
❑ 238 Raul Ibanez .20 .07
❑ 239 Adrian Beltre .20 .07
❑ 240 Rocco Baldelli .20 .07
❑ 241 Orlando Hudson .20 .07
❑ 242 Dave Roberts .20 .07
❑ 243 Doug Mientkiewicz .20 .07
❑ 244 Brad Wilkerson .20 .07
❑ 245 Scott Strickland .20 .07
❑ 246 Ryan Franklin .20 .07
❑ 247 Chad Bradford .20 .07
❑ 248 Gary Bennett .20 .07
❑ 249 Jose Cruz Jr. .20 .07
❑ 250 Jeff Kent .20 .07
❑ 251 Josh Beckett .20 .07
❑ 252 Ramon Ortiz .20 .07
❑ 253 Miguel Batista .20 .07
❑ 254 Jung Bong .20 .07
❑ 255 Deivi Cruz .20 .07
❑ 256 Alex Gonzalez .20 .07
❑ 257 Shawn Chacon .20 .07
❑ 258 Runelvys Hernandez .20 .07
❑ 259 Joe Mays .20 .07
❑ 260 Eric Gagne .20 .07
❑ 261 Dustan Mohr .20 .07
❑ 262 Tomokazu Ohka .20 .07
❑ 263 Eric Byrnes .20 .07
❑ 264 Frank Catalanotto .20 .07
❑ 265 Cristian Guzman .20 .07
❑ 266 Orlando Cabrera .20 .07
❑ 267A Juan Castro .20 .07
❑ 267B Mike Scioscia MG UER 274 .20 .07
❑ 268 Bob Brenly MG .20 .07
❑ 269 Bobby Cox MG .20 .07
❑ 270 Mike Hargrove MG .20 .07
❑ 271 Grady Little MG .20 .07
❑ 272 Dusty Baker MG .20 .07
❑ 273 Jerry Manuel MG .20 .07
❑ 275 Eric Wedge MG .20 .07
❑ 276 Clint Hurdle MG .20 .07
❑ 277 Alan Trammell MG .20 .07
❑ 278 Jack McKeon MG .20 .07
❑ 279 Jimy Williams MG .20 .07
❑ 280 Tony Pena MG .20 .07
❑ 281 Jim Tracy MG .20 .07
❑ 282 Ned Yost MG .20 .07
❑ 283 Ron Gardenhire MG .20 .07
❑ 284 Frank Robinson MG .20 .07
❑ 285 Art Howe MG .20 .07
❑ 286 Joe Torre MG .30 .10
❑ 287 Ken Macha MG .20 .07
❑ 288 Larry Bowa MG .20 .07
❑ 289 Lloyd McClendon MG .20 .07
❑ 290 Bruce Bochy MG .20 .07
❑ 291 Felipe Alou MG .20 .07
❑ 292 Bob Melvin MG .20 .07
❑ 293 Tony LaRussa MG .20 .07
❑ 294 Lou Piniella MG .20 .07
❑ 295 Buck Showalter MG .20 .07
❑ 296 Carlos Tosca MG .20 .07
❑ 297 Anthony Acevedo FY RC .50 .20
❑ 298 Anthony Lerew FY RC .75 .30
❑ 299 Blake Hawksworth FY RC .50 .20
❑ 300 Brayan Pena FY RC .50 .20
❑ 301 Casey Myers FY RC .50 .20
❑ 302 Craig Ansman FY RC .50 .20
❑ 303 David Murphy FY RC .75 .30
❑ 304 Dave Crouthers FY RC .50 .20
❑ 305 Dioner Navarro FY RC .75 .30
❑ 306 Donald Levinski FY RC .50 .20
❑ 307 Jesse Roman FY RC .50 .20
❑ 308 Sung Jung FY RC .50 .20
❑ 309 Jon Knott FY RC .50 .20
❑ 310 Josh Labandeira FY RC .50 .20
❑ 311 Kenny Perez FY RC .50 .20
❑ 312 Khalid Ballouli FY RC .50 .20
❑ 313 Kyle Davies FY RC 2.50 1.00
❑ 314 Marcus McBeth FY RC .50 .20
❑ 315 Matt Creighton FY RC .50 .20
❑ 316 Chris O'Riordan FY RC .50 .20
❑ 317 Mike Gosling FY RC .50 .20
❑ 318 Nic Ungs FY RC .50 .20
❑ 319 Omar Falcon FY RC .50 .20
❑ 320 Rodney Choy Foo FY RC .50 .20
❑ 321 Tim Frend FY RC .50 .20
❑ 322 Todd Self FY RC .50 .20
❑ 323 Tydus Meadows FY RC .50 .20
❑ 324 Yadier Molina FY RC 2.00 .75
❑ 325 Zach Duke FY RC 2.00 .75
❑ 326 Zach Miner FY RC 1.25 .50
❑ 327 B.Castro/K.Greene FS .50 .20
❑ 328 R.Madson/E.Ramirez FS .50 .20
❑ 329 R.Harden/B.Crosby FS .50 .20
❑ 330 Z.Greinke/J.Gobble FS .50 .20
❑ 331 B.Jenks/C.Kotchman FS .50 .20
❑ 332 Sammy Sosa HL .30 .10
❑ 333 Kevin Millwood HL .20 .07
❑ 334 Rafael Palmeiro HL .20 .07
❑ 335 Roger Clemens HL .50 .20
❑ 336 Eric Gagne HL .20 .07
❑ 337 Mueller/Manny/Jeter LL .30 .10
❑ 338 V.Wells/Ichiro/M.Young LL .50 .20
❑ 339 A-Rod/Thomas/Delgado LL .50 .20
❑ 340 Delgado/A-Rod/Boone LL .50 .20
❑ 341 Pedro/Hudson/Loaiza LL .30 .10
❑ 342 Loaiza/Pedro/Halladay LL .30 .10
❑ 343 Pujols/Helton/Renteria LL .50 .20
❑ 344 Pujols/Helton/Pierre LL .50 .20
❑ 345 Thome/Sexson/J.Lopez LL .20 .07
❑ 346 P.Wilson/Sheff/Thome LL .20 .07
❑ 347 Schmidt/K.Brown/Prior LL .30 .10
❑ 348 Wood/Prior/Vazquez LL .30 .10
❑ 349 R.Clemens/D.Wells ALDS .50 .20
❑ 350 K.Wood/M.Prior NLDS .30 .10
❑ 351 Beckett/Cabrera/I.Rod NLCS .50 .20
❑ 352 Giambi/Rivera/Boone ALCS .50 .20
❑ 353 D.Lowe/I.Rod AL/NLDS .50 .20
❑ 354 Pedro/Posa/Clemens ALCS .50 .20
❑ 355 Juan Pierre WS .20 .07
❑ 356 Carlos Delgado AS .20 .07
❑ 357 Bret Boone AS .20 .07
❑ 358 Alex Rodriguez AS .50 .20
❑ 359 Bill Mueller AS .20 .07
❑ 360 Vernon Wells AS .20 .07
❑ 361 Garret Anderson AS .20 .07
❑ 362 Maggio Ordonez AS .20 .07
❑ 363 Jorge Posada AS .20 .07
❑ 364 Roy Halladay AS .20 .07
❑ 365 Andy Pettitte AS .20 .07
❑ 366 Frank Thomas AS .30 .10
❑ 367 Jody Gerut AS .20 .07
❑ 368 Sammy Sosa .50 .20
❑ 369 Joe Crede .20 .07
❑ 370 Gary Sheffield .20 .07
❑ 371 Coco Crisp .20 .07
❑ 372 Torii Hunter .20 .07
❑ 373 Derrek Lee .30 .10
❑ 374 Adam Everett .20 .07
❑ 375 Miguel Tejada .20 .07
❑ 376 Jeremy Affeldt .20 .07
❑ 377 Robin Ventura .20 .07
❑ 378 Scott Podsednik .20 .07
❑ 379 Matthew LeCroy .20 .07
❑ 380 Vladimir Guerrero .50 .20
❑ 381 Tike Redman .20 .07
❑ 382 Jeff Nelson .20 .07
❑ 383 Cliff Lee .20 .07
❑ 384 Bobby Abreu .20 .07
❑ 385 Josh Fogg .20 .07
❑ 386 Trevor Hoffman .20 .07
❑ 387 Jesse Foppert .20 .07
❑ 388 Edgar Martinez .30 .10
❑ 389 Edgar Renteria .20 .07
❑ 390 Chipper Jones .50 .20
❑ 391 Eric Munson .20 .07
❑ 392 Dewon Brazelton .20 .07
❑ 393 John Thomson .20 .07
❑ 394 Chris Woodward .20 .07
❑ 395 Adam LaRoche .20 .07
❑ 396 Elmer Dessens .20 .07
❑ 397 Johnny Estrada .20 .07
❑ 398 Damian Moss .20 .07
❑ 399 Gabe Kapler .20 .07
❑ 400 Dontrelle Willis .30 .10
❑ 401 Troy Glaus .20 .07
❑ 402 Raul Mondesi .20 .07
❑ 403 Shane Reynolds .20 .07
❑ 404 Kurt Ainsworth .20 .07
❑ 405 Pedro Martinez .30 .10
❑ 406 Eric Karros .20 .07
❑ 407 Billy Koch .20 .07
❑ 408 Scott Schoeneweis .20 .07
❑ 409 Paul Wilson .20 .07
❑ 410 Mike Sweeney .20 .07
❑ 411 Jason Bay .20 .07
❑ 412 Mark Redman .20 .07
❑ 413 Jason Jennings .20 .07
❑ 414 Rondell White .20 .07
❑ 415 Todd Hundley .20 .07
❑ 416 Shannon Stewart .20 .07
❑ 417 Jae Weong Seo .20 .07
❑ 418 Livan Hernandez .20 .07
❑ 419 Mark Ellis .20 .07
❑ 420 Pat Burrell .20 .07
❑ 421 Mark Loretta .20 .07
❑ 422 Robb Nen .20 .07
❑ 423 Joel Pineiro .20 .07

No.	Card		
424	Jason Simontacchi	.20	.07
425	Sterling Hitchcock	.20	.07
426	Rey Ordonez	.20	.07
427	Greg Myers	.20	.07
428	Shane Spencer	.20	.07
429	Carlos Baerga	.20	.07
430	Garret Anderson	.20	.07
431	Horacio Ramirez	.20	.07
432	Brian Roberts	.20	.07
433	Damian Jackson	.20	.07
434	Doug Glanville	.20	.07
435	Brian Daubach	.20	.07
436	Alex Escobar	.20	.07
437	Alex Sanchez	.20	.07
438	Jeff Bagwell	.30	.10
439	Darrell May	.20	.07
440	Shawn Green	.20	.07
441	Geoff Jenkins	.20	.07
442	Endy Chavez	.20	.07
443	Nick Johnson	.20	.07
444	Jose Guillen	.20	.07
445	Tomas Perez	.20	.07
446	Phil Nevin	.20	.07
447	Jason Schmidt	.20	.07
448	Julio Mateo	.20	.07
449	So Taguchi	.20	.07
450	Randy Johnson	.50	.20
451	Paul Byrd	.20	.07
452	Chone Figgins	.20	.07
453	Larry Bigbie	.20	.07
454	Scott Williamson	.20	.07
455	Ramon Martinez	.20	.07
456	Roberto Alomar	.30	.10
457	Ryan Dempster	.20	.07
458	Ryan Ludwick	.20	.07
459	Ramon Santiago	.20	.07
460	Jeff Conine	.20	.07
461	Brad Lidge	.20	.07
462	Ken Harvey	.20	.07
463	Guillermo Mota	.20	.07
464	Rick Reed	.20	.07
465	Joey Eischen	.20	.07
466	Wade Miller	.20	.07
467	Steve Karsay	.20	.07
468	Chase Utley	.30	.10
469	Matt Stairs	.20	.07
470	Yorvit Torrealba	.20	.07
471	Joe Kennedy	.20	.07
472	Reed Johnson	.20	.07
473	Victor Zambrano	.20	.07
474	Jeff Davanon	.20	.07
475	Luis Gonzalez	.20	.07
476	Eli Marrero	.20	.07
477	Ray King	.20	.07
478	Jack Cust	.20	.07
479	Omar Daal	.20	.07
480	Todd Walker	.20	.07
481	Shawn Estes	.20	.07
482	Chris Reitsma	.20	.07
483	Jake Westbrook	.20	.07
484	Jeremy Bonderman	.20	.70
485	A.J. Burnett	.20	.07
486	Roy Oswalt	.20	.07
487	Kevin Brown	.20	.07
488	Eric Milton	.20	.07
489	Claudio Vargas	.20	.07
490	Roger Cedeno	.20	.07
491	David Wells	.20	.07
492	Scott Hatteberg	.20	.07
493	Ricky Ledee	.20	.07
494	Eric Young	.20	.07
495	Armando Benitez	.20	.07
496	Dan Haren	.20	.07
497	Carl Crawford	.20	.07
498	Laynce Nix	.20	.07
499	Eric Hinske	.20	.07
500	Ivan Rodriguez	.30	.10
501	Scot Shields	.20	.07
502	Brandon Webb	.20	.07
503	Mark DeRosa	.20	.07
504	Jhonny Peralta	.20	.07
505	Adam Kennedy	.20	.07
506	Tony Batista	.20	.07
507	Jeff Suppan	.20	.07
508	Kenny Lofton	.20	.07
509	Scott Sullivan	.20	.07
510	Ken Griffey Jr.	.75	.30
511	Billy Traber	.20	.07
512	Larry Walker	.20	.07
513	Mike Maroth	.20	.07
514	Todd Hollandsworth	.20	.07
515	Kirk Saarloos	.20	.07
516	Carlos Beltran	.20	.07
517	Juan Rivera	.20	.07
518	Roger Clemens	1.00	.40
519	Karim Garcia	.20	.07
520	Jose Reyes	.20	.07
521	Brandon Duckworth	.20	.07
522	Brian Giles	.20	.07
523	J.T. Snow	.20	.07
524	Jamie Moyer	.20	.07
525	Jason Isringhausen	.20	.07
526	Julio Lugo	.20	.07
527	Mark Teixeira	.30	.10
528	Cory Lidle	.20	.07
529	Lyle Overbay	.20	.07
530	Troy Percival	.20	.07
531	Robby Hammock	.20	.07
532	Robert Fick	.20	.07
533	Jason Johnson	.20	.07
534	Brandon Lyon	.20	.07
535	Antonio Alfonseca	.20	.07
536	Tom Goodwin	.20	.07
537	Paul Konerko	.20	.07
538	D'Angelo Jimenez	.20	.07
539	Ben Broussard	.20	.07
540	Magglio Ordonez	.20	.07
541	Ellis Burks	.20	.07
542	Carlos Pena	.20	.07
543	Chad Fox	.20	.07
544	Jeriome Robertson	.20	.07
545	Travis Hafner	.20	.07
546	Joe Randa	.20	.07
547	Wil Cordero	.20	.07
548	Brady Clark	.20	.07
549	Ruben Sierra	.20	.07
550	Barry Zito	.20	.07
551	Brett Myers	.20	.07
552	Oliver Perez	.20	.07
553	Trey Hodges	.20	.07
554	Benito Santiago	.20	.07
555	David Ross	.20	.07
556	Ramon Vazquez	.20	.07
557	Joe Nathan	.20	.07
558	Dan Wilson	.20	.07
559	Joe Mauer	.50	.20
560	Jim Edmonds	.20	.07
561	Shawn Wooten	.20	.07
562	Matt Kata	.20	.07
563	Vinny Castilla	.20	.07
564	Marty Cordova	.20	.07
565	Aramis Ramirez	.20	.07
566	Carl Everett	.20	.07
567	Ryan Freel	.20	.07
568	Jason Davis	.20	.07
569	Mark Bellhorn Sox	.20	.07
570	Craig Monroe	.20	.07
571	Roberto Hernandez	.20	.07
572	Tim Redding	.20	.07
573	Kevin Appier	.20	.07
574	Jeromy Burnitz	.20	.07
575	Miguel Cabrera	.30	.10
576	Ramon Nivar	.20	.07
577	Casey Blake	.20	.07
578	Aaron Boone	.20	.07
579	Jermaine Dye	.20	.07
580	Jerome Williams	.20	.07
581	John Olerud	.20	.07
582	Scott Rolen	.30	.10
583	Bobby Kielty	.20	.07
584	Travis Lee	.20	.07
585	Jeff Cirillo	.20	.07
586	Scott Spiezio	.20	.07
587	Stephen Randolph	.20	.07
588	Melvin Mora	.20	.07
589	Mike Timlin	.20	.07
590	Kerry Wood	.20	.07
591	Tony Womack	.20	.07
592	Jody Gerut	.20	.07
593	Franklyn German	.20	.07
594	Morgan Ensberg	.20	.07
595	Odalis Perez	.20	.07
596	Michael Cuddyer	.20	.07
597	Jon Lieber	.20	.07
598	Mike Williams	.20	.07
599	Jose Hernandez	.20	.07
600	Alfonso Soriano	.20	.07
601	Marquis Grissom	.20	.07
602	Matt Morris	.20	.07
603	Damian Rolls	.20	.07
604	Juan Gonzalez	.20	.07
605	Aquilino Lopez	.20	.07
606	Jose Valverde	.20	.07
607	Kenny Rogers	.20	.07
608	Joe Borowski	.20	.07
609	Josh Bard	.20	.07
610	Austin Kearns	.20	.07
611	Chin-Hui Tsao	.20	.07
612	Wil Ledezma	.20	.07
613	Aaron Guiel	.20	.07
614	LaTroy Hawkins	.20	.07
615	Tony Armas Jr.	.20	.07
616	Steve Trachsel	.20	.07
617	Ted Lilly	.20	.07
618	Todd Pratt	.20	.07
619	Sean Burroughs	.20	.07
620	Rafael Palmeiro	.30	.10
621	Jeremi Gonzalez	.20	.07
622	Quinton McCracken	.20	.07
623	David Ortiz	.50	.20
624	Randall Simon	.20	.07
625	Wily Mo Pena	.20	.07
626	Nate Cornejo	.20	.07
627	Brian Anderson	.20	.07
628	Corey Koskie	.20	.07
629	Keith Foulke Sox	.20	.07
630	Rheal Cormier	.20	.07
631	Sidney Ponson	.20	.07
632	Gary Matthews Jr.	.20	.07
633	Herbert Perry	.20	.07
634	Shea Hillenbrand	.20	.07
635	Craig Biggio	.30	.10
636	Barry Larkin	.30	.10
637	Arthur Rhodes	.20	.07
638	Anaheim Angels TC	.20	.07
639	Arizona Diamondbacks TC	.20	.07
640	Atlanta Braves TC	.20	.07
641	Baltimore Orioles TC	.20	.07
642	Boston Red Sox TC	.30	.10
643	Chicago Cubs TC	.20	.07
644	Chicago White Sox TC	.20	.07
645	Cincinnati Reds TC	.20	.07
646	Cleveland Indians TC	.20	.07
647	Colorado Rockies TC	.20	.07
648	Detroit Tigers TC	.20	.07
649	Florida Marlins TC	.20	.07
650	Houston Astros TC	.20	.07
651	Kansas City Royals TC	.20	.07
652	Los Angeles Dodgers TC	.20	.07
653	Milwaukee Brewers TC	.20	.07
654	Minnesota Twins TC	.20	.07
655	Montreal Expos TC	.20	.07
656	New York Mets TC	.20	.07
657	New York Yankees TC	.50	.20
658	Oakland Athletics TC	.20	.07
659	Philadelphia Phillies TC	.20	.07
660	Pittsburgh Pirates TC	.20	.07
661	San Diego Padres TC	.20	.07
662	San Francisco Giants TC	.20	.07
663	Seattle Mariners TC	.20	.07
664	St. Louis Cardinals TC	.20	.07
665	Tampa Bay Devil Rays TC	.20	.07
666	Texas Rangers TC	.20	.07
667	Toronto Blue Jays TC	.20	.07
668	Kyle Sleeth DP RC	.50	.20
669	Bradley Sullivan DP RC	.50	.20
670	Carlos Quentin DP RC	2.50	1.00
671	Conor Jackson DP RC	3.00	1.25
672	Jeffrey Allison DP RC	.50	.20
673	Matthew Moses DP RC	1.00	.40
674	Tim Stauffer DP RC	.75	.30
675	Estee Harris DP RC	.50	.20
676	David Aardsma DP RC	.50	.20
677	Omar Quintanilla DP RC	.50	.20
678	Aaron Hill DP	.50	.20
679	Tony Richie DP RC	.50	.20
680	Lastings Milledge DP RC	4.00	1.50
681	Brad Snyder DP RC	1.00	.40

❑ 682 Jason Hirsh DP RC 1.50 .60
❑ 683 Logan Kensing DP RC .50 .20
❑ 684 Chris Lubanski DP .50 .20
❑ 685 Ryan Harvey DP .50 .20
❑ 686 Ryan Wagner DP .50 .20
❑ 687 Rickie Weeks DP .50 .20
❑ 688 G.Sizemore/J.Guthrie .50 .20
❑ 689 E.Jackson/G.Miller .50 .20
❑ 690 J.Reed/N.Cotts .50 .20
❑ 691 A.Loewen/N.Markakis .50 .20
❑ 692 B.Upton/D.Young .50 .20
❑ 693 A.Rodriguez/D.Jeter 1.50 .60
❑ 694 I.Suzuki/A.Pujols 1.00 .40
❑ 695 J.Thome/M.Schmidt 1.00 .40
❑ 696 Mike Mussina GG .20 .07
❑ 697 Bengie Molina GG .20 .07
❑ 698 John Olerud GG .20 .07
❑ 699 Bret Boone GG .20 .07
❑ 700 Eric Chavez GG .20 .07
❑ 701 Alex Rodriguez GG .50 .20
❑ 702 Mike Cameron GG .20 .07
❑ 703 Ichiro Suzuki GG .50 .20
❑ 704 Torii Hunter GG .20 .07
❑ 705 Mike Hampton GG .20 .07
❑ 706 Mike Matheny GG .20 .07
❑ 707 Derrek Lee GG .20 .07
❑ 708 Luis Castillo GG .20 .07
❑ 709 Scott Rolen GG .20 .07
❑ 710 Edgar Renteria GG .20 .07
❑ 711 Andruw Jones GG .20 .07
❑ 712 Jose Cruz Jr. GG .20 .07
❑ 713 Jim Edmonds GG .20 .07
❑ 714 Roy Halladay CY .20 .07
❑ 715 Eric Gagne CY .20 .07
❑ 716 Alex Rodriguez MVP .50 .20
❑ 717 Angel Berroa ROY .20 .07
❑ 718 Dontrelle Willis ROY .20 .07
❑ 719 Todd Helton AS .20 .07
❑ 720 Marcus Giles AS .20 .07
❑ 721 Edgar Renteria AS .20 .07
❑ 722 Scott Rolen AS .20 .07
❑ 723 Albert Pujols AS .50 .20
❑ 724 Gary Sheffield AS .20 .07
❑ 725 Javy Lopez AS .20 .07
❑ 726 Eric Gagne AS .20 .07
❑ 727 Randy Wolf AS .20 .07
❑ 728 Bobby Cox AS .20 .07
❑ 729 Scott Podsednik AS .20 .07
❑ 730 Alex Gonzalez WS .30 .10
❑ 731 Brad Penny WS .30 .10
❑ 732 Beckett/I.Rod/A.Gonz WS .30 .10
❑ 733 Josh Beckett WS MVP .30 .10

2004 Topps Traded

❑ COMPLETE SET (220) 50.00 20.00
❑ COMMON CARD (1-70) .20 .07
❑ COMMON CARD (71-90) .50 .20
❑ COMMON CARD (91-110) .40 .15
❑ COMMON CARD (111-220) .40 .15
❑ BONDS AVAIL VIA HTA SHOP EXCHANGE
❑ PLATE ODDS 1:1151 H, 1:1173 R, 1:327 HTA
❑ PLATE PRINT RUN 1 SET PER COLOR
❑ BLACK-CYAN-MAGENTA-YELLOW ISSUED
❑ NO PLATE PRICING DUE TO SCARCITY
❑ T1 Pokey Reese .20 .07
❑ T2 Tony Womack .20 .07
❑ T3 Richard Hidalgo .20 .07
❑ T4 Juan Uribe .20 .07
❑ T5 J.D. Drew .20 .07
❑ T6 Alex Gonzalez .20 .07
❑ T7 Carlos Guillen .20 .07
❑ T8 Doug Mientkiewicz .20 .07
❑ T9 Fernando Vina .20 .07
❑ T10 Milton Bradley .20 .07
❑ T11 Kelvim Escobar .20 .07
❑ T12 Ben Grieve .20 .07
❑ T13 Brian Jordan .20 .07
❑ T14 A.J. Pierzynski .20 .07
❑ T15 Billy Wagner .20 .07
❑ T16 Terrence Long .20 .07
❑ T17 Carlos Beltran .20 .07
❑ T18 Carl Everett .20 .07
❑ T19 Reggie Sanders .20 .07
❑ T20 Javy Lopez .20 .07
❑ T21 Jay Payton .20 .07
❑ T22 Octavio Dotel .20 .07
❑ T23 Eddie Guardado .20 .07
❑ T24 Andy Pettitte .30 .10
❑ T25 Richie Sexson .20 .07
❑ T26 Ronnie Belliard .20 .07
❑ T27 Michael Tucker .20 .07
❑ T28 Brad Fullmer .20 .07
❑ T29 Freddy Garcia .20 .07
❑ T30 Bartolo Colon .20 .07
❑ T31 Larry Walker Cards .30 .10
❑ T32 Mark Kotsay .20 .07
❑ T33 Jason Marquis .20 .07
❑ T34 Dustan Mohr .20 .07
❑ T35 Javier Vazquez .20 .07
❑ T36 Nomar Garciaparra .75 .30
❑ T37 Tino Martinez .30 .10
❑ T38 Hee Seop Choi .20 .07
❑ T39 Damian Miller .20 .07
❑ T40 Jose Lima .20 .07
❑ T41 Ty Wigginton .20 .07
❑ T42 Raul Ibanez .20 .07
❑ T43 Danys Baez .20 .07
❑ T44 Tony Clark .20 .07
❑ T45 Greg Maddux .75 .30
❑ T46 Victor Zambrano .20 .07
❑ T47 Orlando Cabrera Sox .20 .07
❑ T48 Jose Cruz Jr. .20 .07
❑ T49 Kris Benson .20 .07
❑ T50 Alex Rodriguez 1.00 .40
❑ T51 Steve Finley .20 .07
❑ T52 Ramon Hernandez .20 .07
❑ T53 Esteban Loaiza .20 .07
❑ T54 Ugueth Urbina .20 .07
❑ T55 Jeff Weaver .20 .07
❑ T56 Flash Gordon .20 .07
❑ T57 Jose Contreras .20 .07
❑ T58 Paul Lo Duca .20 .07
❑ T59 Junior Spivey .20 .07
❑ T60 Curt Schilling .30 .10
❑ T61 Brad Penny .20 .07
❑ T62 Braden Looper .20 .07
❑ T63 Miguel Cairo .20 .07
❑ T64 Juan Encarnacion .20 .07
❑ T65 Miguel Batista .20 .07
❑ T66 Terry Francona MG .20 .07
❑ T67 Lee Mazzilli MG .20 .07
❑ T68 Al Pedrique MG .20 .07
❑ T69 Ozzie Guillen MG .50 .20
❑ T70 Phil Garner MG .20 .07
❑ T71 Matt Bush DP RC 1.50 .60
❑ T72 Homer Bailey DP RC 3.00 1.25
❑ T73 Greg Golson DP RC 1.50 .60
❑ T74 Kyle Waldrop DP RC 1.25 .50
❑ T75 Richie Robnett DP RC 1.25 .50
❑ T76 Jay Rainville DP RC 1.50 .60
❑ T77 Bill Bray DP RC .50 .20
❑ T78 Philip Hughes DP RC 8.00 3.00
❑ T79 Scott Elbert DP RC 1.25 .50
❑ T80 Josh Fields DP RC 2.00 .75
❑ T81 Justin Orenduff DP RC .75 .30
❑ T82 Dan Putnam DP RC .75 .30
❑ T83 Chris Nelson DP RC 2.00 .75
❑ T84 Blake DeWitt DP RC 2.00 .75
❑ T85 J.P. Howell DP RC 1.25 .50
❑ T86 Huston Street DP RC 2.00 .75
❑ T87 Kurt Suzuki DP RC 1.25 .50
❑ T88 Erick San Pedro DP RC .50 .20
❑ T89 Matt Tuiasosopo DP RC 2.00 .75
❑ T90 Matt Macri DP RC 1.00 .40
❑ T91 Chad Tracy PROS .40 .15
❑ T92 Scott Hairston PROS .40 .15
❑ T93 Jonny Gomes PROS .40 .15
❑ T94 Chin-Feng Chen PROS .40 .15
❑ T95 Chien-Ming Wang PROS .75 .30
❑ T96 Dustin McGowan PROS .40 .15
❑ T97 Chris Burke PROS .40 .15
❑ T98 Denny Bautista PROS .40 .15
❑ T99 Preston Larrison PROS .40 .15
❑ T100 Kevin Youkilis PROS .40 .15
❑ T101 John Maine PROS .40 .15
❑ T102 Guillermo Quiroz PROS .40 .15
❑ T103 Dave Krynzel PROS .40 .15
❑ T104 David Kelton PROS .40 .15
❑ T105 Edwin Encarnacion PROS .40 .15
❑ T106 Chad Gaudin PROS .40 .15
❑ T107 Sergio Mitre PROS .40 .15
❑ T108 Laynce Nix PROS .40 .15
❑ T109 David Parrish PROS .40 .15
❑ T110 Brandon Claussen PROS .40 .15
❑ T111 Frank Francisco FY RC .40 .15
❑ T112 Brian Dallimore FY RC .40 .15
❑ T113 Jim Crowell FY RC .50 .20
❑ T114 Andres Blanco FY RC .40 .15
❑ T115 Eduardo Villacis FY RC .40 .15
❑ T116 Kazuhito Tadano FY RC .50 .20
❑ T117 Aarom Baldiris FY RC .50 .20
❑ T118 Justin Germano FY RC .40 .15
❑ T119 Joey Gathright FY RC 1.25 .50
❑ T120 Franklyn Gracesqui FY RC .40 .15
❑ T121 Chin-Lung Hu FY RC 1.25 .50
❑ T122 Scott Olsen FY RC 1.50 .60
❑ T123 Tyler Davidson FY RC .50 .20
❑ T124 Fausto Carmona FY RC 1.50 .60
❑ T125 Tim Hutting FY RC .40 .15
❑ T126 Ryan Meaux FY RC .40 .15
❑ T127 Jon Connolly FY RC 1.00 .40
❑ T128 Hector Made FY RC .75 .30
❑ T129 Jamie Brown FY RC .40 .15
❑ T130 Paul McAnulty FY RC .75 .30
❑ T131 Chris Saenz FY RC .40 .15
❑ T132 Marland Williams FY RC .50 .20
❑ T133 Mike Huggins FY RC .40 .15
❑ T134 Jesse Crain FY RC .75 .30
❑ T135 Chad Bentz FY RC .40 .15
❑ T136 Kazuo Matsui FY RC .75 .30
❑ T137 Paul Maholm FY RC 1.25 .50
❑ T138 Brock Jacobsen FY RC .40 .15
❑ T139 Casey Daigle FY RC .40 .15
❑ T140 Nyjer Morgan FY RC .40 .15
❑ T141 Tom Mastny FY RC .40 .15
❑ T142 Kody Kirkland FY RC .50 .20
❑ T143 Jose Capellan FY RC .50 .20
❑ T144 Felix Hernandez FY RC 8.00 3.00
❑ T145 Shawn Hill FY RC .40 .15
❑ T146 Danny Gonzalez FY RC .40 .15
❑ T147 Scott Dohmann FY RC .40 .15
❑ T148 Tommy Murphy FY RC .40 .15
❑ T149 Akinori Otsuka FY RC .40 .15
❑ T150 Miguel Perez FY RC .40 .15
❑ T151 Mike Rouse FY RC .40 .15
❑ T152 Ramon Ramirez FY RC .40 .15
❑ T153 Luke Hughes FY RC .40 .15
❑ T154 Howie Kendrick FY RC 10.00 4.00
❑ T155 Ryan Budde FY RC .40 .15
❑ T156 Charlie Zink FY RC .40 .15
❑ T157 Warner Madrigal FY RC .75 .30
❑ T158 Jason Szuminski FY RC .40 .15
❑ T159 Chad Chop FY RC .40 .15
❑ T160 Shingo Takatsu FY RC .75 .30
❑ T161 Matt Lemanczyk FY RC .40 .15
❑ T162 Wardell Starling FY RC .40 .15
❑ T163 Nick Gorneault FY RC .50 .20
❑ T164 Scott Proctor FY RC .50 .20
❑ T165 Brooks Conrad FY RC .50 .20
❑ T166 Hector Gimenez FY RC .40 .15
❑ T167 Kevin Howard FY RC .50 .20
❑ T168 Vince Perkins FY RC .50 .20
❑ T169 Brock Peterson FY RC .40 .15
❑ T170 Chris Shelton FY RC 1.25 .50
❑ T171 Erick Aybar FY RC .75 .30
❑ T172 Paul Bacot FY RC .50 .20
❑ T173 Matt Capps FY RC .40 .15
❑ T174 Kory Casto FY RC .50 .20
❑ T175 Juan Cedeno FY RC .40 .15
❑ T176 Vito Chiaravalloti FY RC .40 .15
❑ T177 Alec Zumwalt FY RC .40 .15

Card	Player	Price 1	Price 2
T178	J.J. Furmaniak FY RC	.75	.30
T179	Lee Gwaltney FY RC	.40	.15
T180	Donald Kelly FY RC	.40	.15
T181	Benji DeQuin FY RC	.40	.15
T182	Brant Colamarino FY RC	.75	.30
T183	Juan Gutierrez FY RC	.40	.15
T184	Carl Loadenthal FY RC	.50	.20
T185	Ricky Nolasco FY RC	1.50	.60
T186	Jeff Salazar FY RC	1.00	.40
T187	Rob Tejeda FY RC	.75	.30
T188	Alex Romero FY RC	.40	.15
T189	Yoann Torrealba FY RC	.40	.15
T190	Carlos Sosa FY RC	.40	.15
T191	Tim Bittner FY RC	.40	.15
T192	Chris Aguila FY RC	.40	.15
T193	Jason Frasor FY RC	.40	.15
T194	Reid Gorecki FY RC	.40	.15
T195	Dustin Nippert FY RC	.50	.20
T196	Javier Guzman FY RC	.50	.20
T197	Harvey Garcia FY RC	.40	.15
T198	Ivan Ochoa FY RC	.40	.15
T199	David Wallace FY RC	.50	.20
T200	Joel Zumaya FY RC	4.00	1.50
T201	Casey Kopitzke FY RC	.40	.15
T202	Lincoln Holdzkom FY RC	.40	.15
T203	Chad Santos FY RC	.40	.15
T204	Brian Pilkington FY RC	.40	.15
T205	Terry Jones FY RC	.50	.20
T206	Jerome Gamble FY RC	.40	.15
T207	Brad Eldred FY RC	.50	.20
T208	David Pauley FY RC	1.50	.60
T209	Kevin Davidson FY RC	.40	.15
T210	Damaso Espino FY RC	.40	.15
T211	Tom Farmer FY RC	.40	.15
T212	Michael Mooney FY RC	.40	.15
T213	James Tomlin FY RC	.40	.15
T214	Greg Thissen FY RC	.40	.15
T215	Calvin Hayes FY RC	.50	.20
T216	Fernando Cortez FY RC	.40	.15
T217	Sergio Silva FY RC	.40	.15
T218	Jon de Vries FY RC	.40	.15
T219	Don Sutton FY RC	1.00	.40
T220	Leo Nunez FY RC	.40	.15
T221	Barry Bonds HTA EXCH	8.00	3.00

2005 Topps

Item	Price 1	Price 2
COMP.HOBBY SET (737)	80.00	40.00
COMP.HOLIDAY SET (742)	80.00	40.00
COMP.CUBS SET (737)	80.00	40.00
COMP.GIANTS SET (737)	80.00	40.00
COMP.NATIONALS SET (737)	80.00	40.00
COMP.RED SOX SET (737)	80.00	40.00
COMP.TIGERS SET (737)	80.00	40.00
COMP.YANKEES SET (737)	80.00	40.00
COMPLETE SET (732)	80.00	40.00
COMPLETE SERIES 1 (366)	40.00	20.00
COMPLETE SERIES 2 (366)	40.00	20.00
COMMON CARD (1-6/8-734)	.20	.07
COMMON (297-326/668-687)	.50	.20
COMMON (327-331/688-692)	.50	.20
COM (349-355/368/731-734)	1.00	.40
CARD NUMBER 7 DOES NOT EXIST		
OVERALL PLATE SER.1 ODDS 1:154 HTA		
OVERALL PLATE SER.2 ODDS 1:112 HTA		
PLATE PRINT RUN 1 SET PER COLOR		
BLACK-CYAN-MAGENTA-YELLOW ISSUED		
NO PLATE PRICING DUE TO SCARCITY		

Card	Player	Price 1	Price 2
1	Alex Rodriguez	1.00	.40
2	Placido Polanco	.20	.07
3	Torii Hunter	.20	.07
4	Lyle Overbay	.20	.07
5	Johnny Damon	.30	.10
6	Johnny Estrada	.20	.07
8	Francisco Rodriguez	.20	.07
9	Jason LaRue	.20	.07
10	Sammy Sosa	.50	.20
11	Randy Wolf	.20	.07
12	Jason Bay	.20	.07
13	Tom Glavine	.30	.10
14	Michael Tucker	.20	.07
15	Brian Giles	.20	.07
16	Dan Wilson	.20	.07
17	Jim Edmonds	.20	.07
18	Danys Baez	.20	.07
19	Roy Halladay	.20	.07
20	Hank Blalock	.20	.07
21	Darin Erstad	.20	.07
22	Robby Hammock	.20	.07
23	Mike Hampton	.20	.07
24	Mark Bellhorn	.20	.07
25	Jim Thome	.30	.10
26	Scott Schoeneweis	.20	.07
27	Jody Gerut	.20	.07
28	Vinny Castilla	.20	.07
29	Luis Castillo	.20	.07
30	Ivan Rodriguez	.30	.10
31	Craig Biggio	.30	.10
32	Joe Randa	.20	.07
33	Adrian Beltre	.20	.07
34	Scott Podsednik	.20	.07
35	Cliff Floyd	.20	.07
36	Livan Hernandez	.20	.07
37	Eric Byrnes	.20	.07
38	Gabe Kapler	.20	.07
39	Jack Wilson	.20	.07
40	Gary Sheffield	.20	.07
41	Chan Ho Park	.20	.07
42	Carl Crawford	.20	.07
43	Miguel Batista	.20	.07
44	David Bell	.20	.07
45	Jeff DaVanon	.20	.07
46	Brandon Webb	.20	.07
47	Bronson Arroyo	.20	.07
48	Melvin Mora	.20	.07
49	David Ortiz	.50	.20
50	Andruw Jones	.30	.10
51	Chone Figgins	.20	.07
52	Danny Graves	.20	.07
53	Preston Wilson	.20	.07
54	Jeremy Bonderman	.20	.07
55	Chad Fox	.20	.07
56	Dan Miceli	.20	.07
57	Jimmy Gobble	.20	.07
58	Darren Dreifort	.20	.07
59	Matt LeCroy	.20	.07
60	Jose Vidro	.20	.07
61	Al Leiter	.20	.07
62	Javier Vazquez	.20	.07
63	Erubiel Durazo	.20	.07
64	Doug Glanville	.20	.07
65	Scot Shields	.20	.07
66	Edgardo Alfonzo	.20	.07
67	Ryan Franklin	.20	.07
68	Francisco Cordero	.20	.07
69	Brett Myers	.20	.07
70	Curt Schilling	.30	.10
71	Matt Kata	.20	.07
72	Mark DeRosa	.20	.07
73	Rodrigo Lopez	.20	.07
74	Tim Wakefield	.30	.10
75	Frank Thomas	.50	.20
76	Jimmy Rollins	.20	.07
77	Barry Zito	.20	.07
78	Hideo Nomo	.50	.20
79	Brad Wilkerson	.20	.07
80	Adam Dunn	.20	.07
81	Billy Traber	.20	.07
82	Fernando Vina	.20	.07
83	Nate Robertson	.20	.07
84	Brad Ausmus	.20	.07
85	Mike Sweeney	.20	.07
86	Kip Wells	.20	.07
87	Chris Reitsma	.20	.07
88	Zach Day	.20	.07
89	Tony Clark	.20	.07
90	Bret Boone	.20	.07
91	Mark Loretta	.20	.07
92	Jerome Williams	.20	.07
93	Randy Winn	.20	.07
94	Marlon Anderson	.20	.07
95	Aubrey Huff	.20	.07
96	Kevin Mench	.20	.07
97	Frank Catalanotto	.20	.07
98	Flash Gordon	.20	.07
99	Scott Hatteberg	.20	.07
100	Albert Pujols	1.00	.40
101	Jose/Bengie Molina	.50	.20
102	Oscar Villarreal	.20	.07
103	Jay Gibbons	.20	.07
104	Byung-Hyun Kim	.20	.07
105	Joe Borowski	.20	.07
106	Mark Grudzielanek	.20	.07
107	Mark Buehrle	.20	.07
108	Paul Wilson	.20	.07
109	Ronnie Belliard	.20	.07
110	Reggie Sanders	.20	.07
111	Tim Redding	.20	.07
112	Brian Lawrence	.20	.07
113	Darrell May	.20	.07
114	Jose Hernandez	.20	.07
115	Ben Sheets	.20	.07
116	Johan Santana	.50	.20
117	Billy Wagner	.20	.07
118	Mariano Rivera	.50	.20
119	Steve Trachsel	.20	.07
120	Akinori Otsuka	.20	.07
121	Bobby Kielty	.20	.07
122	Orlando Hernandez	.20	.07
123	Raul Ibanez	.20	.07
124	Mike Matheny	.20	.07
125	Vernon Wells	.20	.07
126	Jason Isringhausen	.20	.07
127	Jose Guillen	.20	.07
128	Danny Bautista	.20	.07
129	Marcus Giles	.20	.07
130	Javy Lopez	.20	.07
131	Kevin Millar	.20	.07
132	Kyle Farnsworth	.20	.07
133	Carl Pavano	.20	.07
134	D'Angelo Jimenez	.20	.07
135	Casey Blake	.20	.07
136	Matt Holliday	.25	.08
137	Bobby Higginson	.20	.07
138	Nate Field	.20	.07
139	Alex Gonzalez	.20	.07
140	Jeff Kent	.20	.07
141	Aaron Guiel	.20	.07
142	Shawn Green	.20	.07
143	Bill Hall	.20	.07
144	Shannon Stewart	.20	.07
145	Juan Rivera	.20	.07
146	Coco Crisp	.20	.07
147	Mike Mussina	.30	.10
148	Eric Chavez	.20	.07
149	Jon Lieber	.20	.07
150	Vladimir Guerrero	.50	.20
151	Alex Cintron	.20	.07
152	Horacio Ramirez	.20	.07
153	Sidney Ponson	.20	.07
154	Trot Nixon	.30	.10
155	Greg Maddux	.75	.30
156	Edgar Renteria	.20	.07
157	Ryan Freel	.20	.07
158	Matt Lawton	.20	.07
159	Shawn Chacon	.20	.07
160	Josh Beckett	.20	.07
161	Ken Harvey	.20	.07
162	Juan Cruz	.20	.07
163	Juan Encarnacion	.20	.07
164	Wes Helms	.20	.07
165	Brad Radke	.20	.07
166	Claudio Vargas	.20	.07
167	Mike Cameron	.20	.07
168	Billy Koch	.20	.07
169	Bobby Crosby	.20	.07
170	Mike Lieberthal	.20	.07
171	Rob Mackowiak	.20	.07
172	Sean Burroughs	.20	.07
173	J.T. Snow Jr.	.20	.07
174	Paul Konerko	.20	.07
175	Luis Gonzalez	.20	.07

❑ 176 John Lackey .20 .07
❑ 177 Antonio Alfonseca .20 .07
❑ 178 Brian Roberts .20 .07
❑ 179 Bill Mueller .20 .07
❑ 180 Carlos Lee .20 .07
❑ 181 Corey Patterson .20 .07
❑ 182 Sean Casey .20 .07
❑ 183 Cliff Lee .20 .07
❑ 184 Jason Jennings .20 .07
❑ 185 Dmitri Young .20 .07
❑ 186 Juan Uribe .20 .07
❑ 187 Andy Pettitte .30 .10
❑ 188 Juan Gonzalez .20 .07
❑ 189 Pokey Reese .20 .07
❑ 190 Jason Phillips .20 .07
❑ 191 Rocky Biddle .20 .07
❑ 192 Lew Ford .20 .07
❑ 193 Mark Mulder .20 .07
❑ 194 Bobby Abreu .20 .07
❑ 195 Jason Kendall .20 .07
❑ 196 Terrence Long .20 .07
❑ 197 A.J. Pierzynski .20 .07
❑ 198 Eddie Guardado .20 .07
❑ 199 So Taguchi .20 .07
❑ 200 Jason Giambi .20 .07
❑ 201 Tony Batista .20 .07
❑ 202 Kyle Lohse .20 .07
❑ 203 Trevor Hoffman .20 .07
❑ 204 Tike Redman .20 .07
❑ 205 Matt Herges .20 .07
❑ 206 Gil Meche .20 .07
❑ 207 Chris Carpenter .20 .07
❑ 208 Ben Broussard .20 .07
❑ 209 Eric Young .20 .07
❑ 210 Doug Waechter .20 .07
❑ 211 Jarrod Washburn .20 .07
❑ 212 Chad Tracy .20 .07
❑ 213 John Smoltz .30 .10
❑ 214 Jorge Julio .20 .07
❑ 215 Todd Walker .20 .07
❑ 216 Shingo Takatsu .20 .07
❑ 217 Jose Acevedo .20 .07
❑ 218 David Riske .20 .07
❑ 219 Shawn Estes .20 .07
❑ 220 Lance Berkman .20 .07
❑ 221 Carlos Guillen .20 .07
❑ 222 Jeremy Affeldt .20 .07
❑ 223 Cesar Izturis .20 .07
❑ 224 Scott Sullivan .20 .07
❑ 225 Kazuo Matsui .20 .07
❑ 226 Josh Fogg .20 .07
❑ 227 Jason Schmidt .20 .07
❑ 228 Jason Marquis .20 .07
❑ 229 Scott Spiezio .20 .07
❑ 230 Miguel Tejada .20 .07
❑ 231 Bartolo Colon .20 .07
❑ 232 Jose Valverde .20 .07
❑ 233 Derrek Lee .30 .10
❑ 234 Scott Williamson .20 .07
❑ 235 Joe Crede .20 .07
❑ 236 John Thomson .20 .07
❑ 237 Mike MacDougal .20 .07
❑ 238 Eric Gagne .20 .07
❑ 239 Alex Sanchez .20 .07
❑ 240 Miguel Cabrera .30 .10
❑ 241 Luis Rivas .20 .07
❑ 242 Adam Everett .20 .07
❑ 243 Jason Johnson .20 .07
❑ 244 Travis Hafner .20 .07
❑ 245 Jose Valentin .20 .07
❑ 246 Stephen Randolph .20 .07
❑ 247 Rafael Furcal .20 .07
❑ 248 Adam Kennedy .20 .07
❑ 249 Luis Matos .20 .07
❑ 250 Mark Prior .30 .10
❑ 251 Angel Berroa .20 .07
❑ 252 Phil Nevin .20 .07
❑ 253 Oliver Perez .20 .07
❑ 254 Orlando Hudson .20 .07
❑ 255 Braden Looper .20 .07
❑ 256 Khalil Greene .30 .10
❑ 257 Tim Worrell .20 .07
❑ 258 Carlos Zambrano .20 .07
❑ 259 Odalis Perez .20 .07
❑ 260 Gerald Laird .20 .07
❑ 261 Jose Cruz Jr. .20 .07
❑ 262 Michael Barrett .20 .07
❑ 263 Michael Young UER .20 .07
❑ 264 Toby Hall .20 .07
❑ 265 Woody Williams .20 .07
❑ 266 Rich Harden .20 .07
❑ 267 Mike Scioscia MG .20 .07
❑ 268 Al Pedrique MG .20 .07
❑ 269 Bobby Cox MG .20 .07
❑ 270 Lee Mazzilli MG .20 .07
❑ 271 Terry Francona MG .30 .10
❑ 272 Dusty Baker MG .20 .07
❑ 273 Ozzie Guillen MG .50 .20
❑ 274 Dave Miley MG .20 .07
❑ 275 Eric Wedge MG .20 .07
❑ 276 Clint Hurdle MG .20 .07
❑ 277 Alan Trammell MG .20 .07
❑ 278 Jack McKeon MG .20 .07
❑ 279 Phil Garner MG .20 .07
❑ 280 Tony Pena MG .20 .07
❑ 281 Jim Tracy MG .20 .07
❑ 282 Ned Yost MG .20 .07
❑ 283 Ron Gardenhire MG .20 .07
❑ 284 Frank Robinson MG .20 .07
❑ 285 Art Howe MG .20 .07
❑ 286 Joe Torre MG .30 .10
❑ 287 Ken Macha MG .20 .07
❑ 288 Larry Bowa MG .20 .07
❑ 289 Lloyd McClendon MG .20 .07
❑ 290 Bruce Bochy MG .20 .07
❑ 291 Felipe Alou MG .20 .07
❑ 292 Bob Melvin MG .20 .07
❑ 293 Tony LaRussa MG .20 .07
❑ 294 Lou Piniella MG .20 .07
❑ 295 Buck Showalter MG .20 .07
❑ 296 John Gibbons MG .20 .07
❑ 297 Steve Doetsch FY RC .75 .30
❑ 298 Melky Cabrera FY RC 2.00 .75
❑ 299 Luis Ramirez FY RC .50 .20
❑ 300 Chris Seddon FY RC .50 .20
❑ 301 Nate Schierholtz FY .75 .30
❑ 302 Ian Kinsler FY RC 2.50 1.00
❑ 303 Brandon Moss FY RC 1.50 .60
❑ 304 Chadd Blasko FY RC .75 .30
❑ 305 Jeremy West FY RC .75 .30
❑ 306 Sean Marshall FY RC 1.50 .60
❑ 307 Matt DeSalvo FY RC .75 .30
❑ 308 Ryan Sweeney FY RC 1.00 .40
❑ 309 Matthew Lindstrom FY RC .50 .20
❑ 310 Ryan Goleski FY RC .75 .30
❑ 311 Brett Harper FY RC .75 .30
❑ 312 Chris Roberson FY RC .50 .20
❑ 313 Andre Ethier FY RC 5.00 2.00
❑ 314 Chris Denorfia FY RC 1.00 .40
❑ 315 Ian Bladergroen FY RC .75 .30
❑ 316 Darren Fenster FY RC .50 .20
❑ 317 Kevin West FY RC .50 .20
❑ 318 Chaz Lytle FY RC .75 .30
❑ 319 James Jurries FY RC .75 .30
❑ 320 Matt Rogelstad FY RC .50 .20
❑ 321 Wade Robinson FY RC .50 .20
❑ 322 Jake Dittler FY .50 .20
❑ 323 Brian Stavisky FY RC .50 .20
❑ 324 Kole Strayhorn FY RC .50 .20
❑ 325 Jose Vaquedano FY RC .50 .20
❑ 326 Elvys Quezada FY RC .50 .20
❑ 327 J.Maine/V.Majewski FS .50 .20
❑ 328 R.Weeks/J.Hardy FS .50 .20
❑ 329 G.Gross/G.Quiroz FS .50 .20
❑ 330 D.Wright/C.Brazell FS 3.00 1.25
❑ 331 D.McPherson/J.Mathis FS .50 .20
❑ 332 Randy Johnson SH .30 .10
❑ 333 Randy Johnson SH .30 .10
❑ 334 Ichiro Suzuki SH .50 .20
❑ 335 Ken Griffey Jr. SH .50 .20
❑ 336 Greg Maddux SH .50 .20
❑ 337 Ichiro/Mora/Guerrero LL .50 .20
❑ 338 Ichiro/Young/Guerrero LL .50 .20
❑ 339 Manny/Konerko/Ortiz LL .30 .10
❑ 340 Tejada/Ortiz/Manny LL .30 .10
❑ 341 Johan/Schill/West LL .30 .10
❑ 342 Johan/Pedro/Schill LL .30 .10
❑ 343 Helton/Loretta/Beltre LL .20 .07
❑ 344 Pierre/Loretta/Wilson LL .20 .07
❑ 345 Beltre/Dunn/Pujols LL .50 .20
❑ 346 Castilla/Rolen/Pujols LL .50 .20
❑ 347 Peavy/Johnson/Sheets LL .30 .10
❑ 348 Johnson/Sheets/Schmidt LL .30 .10
❑ 349 A.Rodriguez/R.Sierra ALDS 1.00 .40
❑ 350 L.Walker/A.Pujols NLDS 1.00 .40
❑ 351 C.Schilling/D.Ortiz ALDS 1.00 .40
❑ 352 Curt Schilling WS2 1.00 .40
❑ 353 Sox Celeb/Ortiz-Schil ALCS 1.00 .40
❑ 354 Cards Celeb/Puj-Edm NLCS 1.00 .40
❑ 355 Mark Bellhorn WS1 1.00 .40
❑ 356 Paul Konerko AS .20 .07
❑ 357 Alfonso Soriano AS .20 .07
❑ 358 Miguel Tejada AS .20 .07
❑ 359 Melvin Mora AS .20 .07
❑ 360 Vladimir Guerrero AS .30 .10
❑ 361 Ichiro Suzuki AS .50 .20
❑ 362 Manny Ramirez AS .30 .10
❑ 363 Ivan Rodriguez AS .20 .07
❑ 364 Johan Santana AS .30 .10
❑ 365 Paul Konerko AS .20 .07
❑ 366 David Ortiz AS .30 .10
❑ 367 Bobby Crosby AS .20 .07
❑ 368 Sox Celeb/Ram-Lowe WS4 1.50 .60
❑ 369 Garret Anderson .20 .07
❑ 370 Randy Johnson .50 .20
❑ 371 Charles Thomas .20 .07
❑ 372 Rafael Palmeiro .30 .10
❑ 373 Kevin Youkilis .20 .07
❑ 374 Freddy Garcia .20 .07
❑ 375 Magglio Ordonez .20 .07
❑ 376 Aaron Harang .20 .07
❑ 377 Grady Sizemore .30 .10
❑ 378 Chin-Hui Tsao .20 .07
❑ 379 Eric Munson .20 .07
❑ 380 Juan Pierre .20 .07
❑ 381 Brad Lidge .20 .07
❑ 382 Brian Anderson .20 .07
❑ 383 Alex Cora .20 .07
❑ 384 Brady Clark .20 .07
❑ 385 Todd Helton .30 .10
❑ 386 Chad Cordero .20 .07
❑ 387 Kris Benson .20 .07
❑ 388 Brad Halsey .20 .07
❑ 389 Jermaine Dye .20 .07
❑ 390 Manny Ramirez .30 .10
❑ 391 Daryle Ward .20 .07
❑ 392 Adam Eaton .20 .07
❑ 393 Brett Tomko .20 .07
❑ 394 Bucky Jacobsen .20 .07
❑ 395 Dontrelle Willis .20 .07
❑ 396 B.J. Upton .20 .07
❑ 397 Rocco Baldelli .20 .07
❑ 398 Ted Lilly .20 .07
❑ 399 Ryan Drese .20 .07
❑ 400 Ichiro Suzuki 1.00 .40
❑ 401 Brendan Donnelly .20 .07
❑ 402 Brandon Lyon .20 .07
❑ 403 Nick Green .20 .07
❑ 404 Jerry Hairston Jr. .20 .07
❑ 405 Mike Lowell .20 .07
❑ 406 Kerry Wood .20 .07
❑ 407 Carl Everett .20 .07
❑ 408 Hideki Matsui .75 .30
❑ 409 Omar Vizquel .30 .10
❑ 410 Joe Kennedy .20 .07
❑ 411 Carlos Pena .20 .07
❑ 412 Armando Benitez .20 .07
❑ 413 Carlos Beltran .20 .07
❑ 414 Kevin Appier .20 .07
❑ 415 Jeff Weaver .20 .07
❑ 416 Chad Moeller .20 .07
❑ 417 Joe Mays .20 .07
❑ 418 Terrmel Sledge .20 .07
❑ 419 Richard Hidalgo .20 .07
❑ 420 Kenny Lofton .20 .07
❑ 421 Justin Duchscherer .20 .07
❑ 422 Eric Milton .20 .07
❑ 423 Jose Mesa .20 .07
❑ 424 Ramon Hernandez .20 .07
❑ 425 Jose Reyes .20 .07
❑ 426 Joel Pineiro .20 .07
❑ 427 Matt Morris .20 .07
❑ 428 John Halama .20 .07
❑ 429 Gary Matthews Jr. .20 .07
❑ 430 Ryan Madson .20 .07
❑ 431 Mark Kotsay .20 .07
❑ 432 Carlos Delgado .20 .07
❑ 433 Casey Kotchman .20 .07

❑	434	Greg Aquino	.20	.07
❑	435	Eli Marrero	.20	.07
❑	436	David Newhan	.20	.07
❑	437	Mike Timlin	.20	.07
❑	438	LaTroy Hawkins	.20	.07
❑	439	Jose Contreras	.20	.07
❑	440	Ken Griffey Jr.	.75	.30
❑	441	C.C. Sabathia	.20	.07
❑	442	Brandon Inge	.20	.07
❑	443	Pete Munro	.20	.07
❑	444	John Buck	.20	.07
❑	445	Hee Seop Choi	.20	.07
❑	446	Chris Capuano	.20	.07
❑	447	Jesse Crain	.20	.07
❑	448	Geoff Jenkins	.20	.07
❑	449	Brian Schneider	.20	.07
❑	450	Mike Piazza	.50	.20
❑	451	Jorge Posada	.30	.10
❑	452	Nick Swisher	.20	.07
❑	453	Kevin Millwood	.20	.07
❑	454	Mike Gonzalez	.20	.07
❑	455	Jake Peavy	.20	.07
❑	456	Dustin Hermanson	.20	.07
❑	457	Jeremy Reed	.20	.07
❑	458	Julian Tavarez	.20	.07
❑	459	Geoff Blum	.20	.07
❑	460	Alfonso Soriano	.20	.07
❑	461	Alexis Rios	.20	.07
❑	462	David Eckstein	.20	.07
❑	463	Shea Hillenbrand	.20	.07
❑	464	Russ Ortiz	.20	.07
❑	465	Kurt Ainsworth	.20	.07
❑	466	Orlando Cabrera	.20	.07
❑	467	Carlos Silva	.20	.07
❑	468	Ross Gload	.20	.07
❑	469	Josh Phelps	.20	.07
❑	470	Marquis Grissom	.20	.07
❑	471	Mike Maroth	.20	.07
❑	472	Guillermo Mota	.20	.07
❑	473	Chris Burke	.20	.07
❑	474	David DeJesus	.20	.07
❑	475	Jose Lima	.20	.07
❑	476	Cristian Guzman	.20	.07
❑	477	Nick Johnson	.20	.07
❑	478	Victor Zambrano	.20	.07
❑	479	Rod Barajas	.20	.07
❑	480	Damian Miller	.20	.07
❑	481	Chase Utley	.30	.10
❑	482	Todd Pratt	.20	.07
❑	483	Sean Burnett	.20	.07
❑	484	Boomer Wells	.20	.07
❑	485	Dustan Mohr	.20	.07
❑	486	Bobby Madritsch	.20	.07
❑	487	Ray King	.20	.07
❑	488	Reed Johnson	.20	.07
❑	489	R.A. Dickey	.20	.07
❑	490	Scott Kazmir	.20	.07
❑	491	Tony Womack	.20	.07
❑	492	Tomas Perez	.20	.07
❑	493	Esteban Loaiza	.20	.07
❑	494	Tomo Ohka	.20	.07
❑	495	Mike Lamb	.20	.07
❑	496	Ramon Ortiz	.20	.07
❑	497	Richie Sexson	.20	.07
❑	498	J.D. Drew	.20	.07
❑	499	David Segui	.20	.07
❑	500	Barry Bonds	2.00	.75
❑	501	Aramis Ramirez	.20	.07
❑	502	Wily Mo Pena	.20	.07
❑	503	Jeromy Burnitz	.20	.07
❑	504	Craig Monroe	.20	.07
❑	505	Nomar Garciaparra	.50	.20
❑	506	Brandon Backe	.20	.07
❑	507	Marcus Thames	.20	.07
❑	508	Derek Lowe	.20	.07
❑	509	Doug Davis	.20	.07
❑	510	Joe Mauer	.50	.20
❑	511	Endy Chavez	.20	.07
❑	512	Bernie Williams	.30	.10
❑	513	Mark Redman	.20	.07
❑	514	Jason Michaels	.20	.07
❑	515	Craig Wilson	.20	.07
❑	516	Ryan Klesko	.20	.07
❑	517	Ray Durham	.20	.07
❑	518	Jose Lopez	.20	.07
❑	519	Jeff Suppan	.20	.07
❑	520	Julio Lugo	.20	.07
❑	521	Mike Wood	.20	.07
❑	522	David Bush	.20	.07
❑	523	Juan Rincon	.20	.07
❑	524	Paul Quantrill	.20	.07
❑	525	Marlon Byrd	.20	.07
❑	526	Roy Oswalt	.20	.07
❑	527	Rondell White	.20	.07
❑	528	Troy Glaus	.20	.07
❑	529	Scott Hairston	.20	.07
❑	530	Chipper Jones	.50	.20
❑	531	Daniel Cabrera	.20	.07
❑	532	Doug Mientkiewicz	.20	.07
❑	533	Glendon Rusch	.20	.07
❑	534	Jon Garland	.20	.07
❑	535	Austin Kearns	.20	.07
❑	536	Jake Westbrook	.20	.07
❑	537	Aaron Miles	.20	.07
❑	538	Omar Infante	.20	.07
❑	539	Paul Lo Duca	.20	.07
❑	540	Morgan Ensberg	.20	.07
❑	541	Tony Graffanino	.20	.07
❑	542	Milton Bradley	.20	.07
❑	543	Keith Ginter	.20	.07
❑	544	Justin Morneau	.20	.07
❑	545	Tony Armas Jr.	.20	.07
❑	546	Mike Stanton	.20	.07
❑	547	Kevin Brown	.20	.07
❑	548	Marco Scutaro	.20	.07
❑	549	Tim Hudson	.20	.07
❑	550	Pat Burrell	.20	.07
❑	551	Ty Wigginton	.20	.07
❑	552	Jeff Cirillo	.20	.07
❑	553	Jim Brower	.20	.07
❑	554	Jamie Moyer	.20	.07
❑	555	Larry Walker	.30	.10
❑	556	Dewon Brazelton	.20	.07
❑	557	Brian Jordan	.20	.07
❑	558	Josh Towers	.20	.07
❑	559	Shigetoshi Hasegawa	.20	.07
❑	560	Octavio Dotel	.20	.07
❑	561	Travis Lee	.20	.07
❑	562	Michael Cuddyer	.20	.07
❑	563	Junior Spivey	.20	.07
❑	564	Zack Greinke	.20	.07
❑	565	Roger Clemens	.75	.30
❑	566	Chris Shelton	.30	.10
❑	567	Ugueth Urbina	.20	.07
❑	568	Rafael Betancourt	.20	.07
❑	569	Willie Harris	.20	.07
❑	570	Todd Hollandsworth	.20	.07
❑	571	Keith Foulke	.20	.07
❑	572	Larry Bigbie	.20	.07
❑	573	Paul Byrd	.20	.07
❑	574	Troy Percival	.20	.07
❑	575	Pedro Martinez	.30	.10
❑	576	Matt Clement	.20	.07
❑	577	Ryan Wagner	.20	.07
❑	578	Jeff Francis	.20	.07
❑	579	Jeff Conine	.20	.07
❑	580	Wade Miller	.20	.07
❑	581	Matt Stairs	.20	.07
❑	582	Gavin Floyd	.20	.07
❑	583	Kazuhisa Ishii	.20	.07
❑	584	Victor Santos	.20	.07
❑	585	Jacque Jones	.20	.07
❑	586	Sunny Kim	.20	.07
❑	587	Dan Kolb	.20	.07
❑	588	Cory Lidle	.20	.07
❑	589	Jose Castillo	.20	.07
❑	590	Alex Gonzalez	.20	.07
❑	591	Kirk Rueter	.20	.07
❑	592	Jolbert Cabrera	.20	.07
❑	593	Erik Bedard	.20	.07
❑	594	Ben Grieve	.20	.07
❑	595	Ricky Ledee	.20	.07
❑	596	Mark Hendrickson	.20	.07
❑	597	Laynce Nix	.20	.07
❑	598	Jason Frasor	.20	.07
❑	599	Kevin Gregg	.20	.07
❑	600	Derek Jeter	1.00	.40
❑	601	Luis Terrero	.20	.07
❑	602	Jaret Wright	.20	.07
❑	603	Edwin Jackson	.20	.07
❑	604	Dave Roberts	.20	.07
❑	605	Moises Alou	.20	.07
❑	606	Aaron Rowand	.20	.07
❑	607	Kazuhito Tadano	.20	.07
❑	608	Luis A. Gonzalez	.20	.07
❑	609	A.J. Burnett	.20	.07
❑	610	Jeff Bagwell	.30	.10
❑	611	Brad Penny	.20	.07
❑	612	Craig Counsell	.20	.07
❑	613	Corey Koskie	.20	.07
❑	614	Mark Ellis	.20	.07
❑	615	Felix Rodriguez	.20	.07
❑	616	Jay Payton	.20	.07
❑	617	Hector Luna	.20	.07
❑	618	Miguel Olivo	.20	.07
❑	619	Rob Bell	.20	.07
❑	620	Scott Rolen	.30	.10
❑	621	Ricardo Rodriguez	.20	.07
❑	622	Eric Hinske	.20	.07
❑	623	Tim Salmon	.30	.10
❑	624	Adam LaRoche	.20	.07
❑	625	B.J. Ryan	.20	.07
❑	626	Roberto Alomar	.30	.10
❑	627	Steve Finley	.20	.07
❑	628	Joe Nathan	.20	.07
❑	629	Scott Linebrink	.20	.07
❑	630	Vicente Padilla	.20	.07
❑	631	Raul Mondesi	.20	.07
❑	632	Yadier Molina	.20	.07
❑	633	Tino Martinez	.30	.10
❑	634	Mark Teixeira	.30	.10
❑	635	Kelvim Escobar	.20	.07
❑	636	Pedro Feliz	.20	.07
❑	637	Rich Aurilia	.20	.07
❑	638	Los Angeles Angels TC	.20	.07
❑	639	Arizona Diamondbacks TC	.20	.07
❑	640	Atlanta Braves TC	.30	.10
❑	641	Baltimore Orioles TC	.20	.07
❑	642	Boston Red Sox TC	.50	.20
❑	643	Chicago Cubs TC	.30	.10
❑	644	Chicago White Sox TC	.20	.07
❑	645	Cincinnati Reds TC	.20	.07
❑	646	Cleveland Indians TC	.20	.07
❑	647	Colorado Rockies TC	.20	.07
❑	648	Detroit Tigers TC	.20	.07
❑	649	Florida Marlins TC	.20	.07
❑	650	Houston Astros TC	.20	.07
❑	651	Kansas City Royals TC	.20	.07
❑	652	Los Angeles Dodgers TC	.20	.07
❑	653	Milwaukee Brewers TC	.20	.07
❑	654	Minnesota Twins TC	.20	.07
❑	655	Montreal Expos TC	.20	.07
❑	656	New York Mets TC	.20	.07
❑	657	New York Yankees TC	.50	.20
❑	658	Oakland Athletics TC	.20	.07
❑	659	Philadelphia Phillies TC	.20	.07
❑	660	Pittsburgh Pirates TC	.20	.07
❑	661	San Diego Padres TC	.20	.07
❑	662	San Francisco Giants TC	.20	.07
❑	663	Seattle Mariners TC	.20	.07
❑	664	St. Louis Cardinals TC	.30	.10
❑	665	Tampa Bay Devil Rays TC	.20	.07
❑	666	Texas Rangers TC	.20	.07
❑	667	Toronto Blue Jays TC	.20	.07
❑	668	Billy Butler FY RC	4.00	1.50
❑	669	Wes Swackhamer FY RC	.50	.20
❑	670	Matt Campbell FY RC	.50	.20
❑	671	Ryan Webb FY	.50	.20
❑	672	Glen Perkins FY RC	.75	.30
❑	673	Michael Rogers FY RC	.50	.20
❑	674	Kevin Melillo FY RC	.75	.30
❑	675	Erik Cordier FY RC	.50	.20
❑	676	Landon Powell FY RC	.75	.30
❑	677	Justin Verlander FY RC	4.00	1.50
❑	678	Eric Nielsen FY RC	.50	.20
❑	679	Alexander Smit FY RC	.50	.20
❑	680	Ryan Garko FY RC	1.50	.60
❑	681	Bobby Livingston FY RC	.50	.20
❑	682	Jeff Niemann FY RC	.75	.30
❑	683	Wladimir Balentien FY RC	.75	.30
❑	684	Chip Cannon FY RC	.75	.30
❑	685	Yorman Bazardo FY RC	.50	.20
❑	686	Mike Bourn FY RC	.75	.30
❑	687	Andy LaRoche FY RC	3.00	1.25
❑	688	F.Hernandez/J.Leone	.50	.20
❑	689	R.Howard/C.Hamels	5.00	2.00
❑	690	M.Cain/M.Valdez	1.00	.40
❑	691	A.Marte/J.Francoeur	2.00	.75

	Card		
❑	692 C.Billingsley/J.Guzman	.50	.20
❑	693 J.Hairston Jr./S.Hairston	.20	.07
❑	694 M.Tejada/L.Berkman	.30	.10
❑	695 Kenny Rogers GG	.20	.07
❑	696 Ivan Rodriguez GG	.20	.07
❑	697 Darin Erstad GG	.20	.07
❑	698 Bret Boone GG	.20	.07
❑	699 Eric Chavez GG	.20	.07
❑	700 Derek Jeter GG	.50	.20
❑	701 Vernon Wells GG	.20	.07
❑	702 Ichiro Suzuki GG	.50	.20
❑	703 Torii Hunter GG	.20	.07
❑	704 Greg Maddux GG	.50	.20
❑	705 Mike Matheny GG	.20	.07
❑	706 Todd Helton GG	.20	.07
❑	707 Luis Castillo GG	.20	.07
❑	708 Scott Rolen GG	.20	.07
❑	709 Cesar Izturis GG	.20	.07
❑	710 Jim Edmonds GG	.20	.07
❑	711 Andruw Jones GG	.20	.07
❑	712 Steve Finley GG	.20	.07
❑	713 Johan Santana CY	.30	.10
❑	714 Roger Clemens CY	.50	.20
❑	715 Vladimir Guerrero MVP	.30	.10
❑	716 Barry Bonds MVP	1.00	.40
❑	717 Bobby Crosby ROY	.20	.07
❑	718 Jason Bay ROY	.20	.07
❑	719 Albert Pujols AS	.50	.20
❑	720 Mark Loretta AS	.20	.07
❑	721 Edgar Renteria AS	.20	.07
❑	722 Scott Rolen AS	.20	.07
❑	723 J.D. Drew AS	.20	.07
❑	724 Jim Edmonds AS	.20	.07
❑	725 Johnny Estrada AS	.20	.07
❑	726 Jason Schmidt AS	.20	.07
❑	727 Chris Carpenter AS	.20	.07
❑	728 Eric Gagne AS	.20	.07
❑	729 Jason Bay AS	.20	.07
❑	730 Bobby Cox MG AS	.20	.07
❑	731 D.Ortiz/M.Bellhorn WS1	1.00	.40
❑	732 Curt Schilling WS2	1.00	.40
❑	733 M.Ramirez/P.Martinez WS3	1.00	.40
❑	734 Sox Win Damon/Lowe WS4	1.50	.60

2005 Topps Update

	Card		
❑	COMPLETE SET (330)	40.00	15.00
❑	COMP.FACT.SET (330)	40.00	25.00
❑	COMMON CARD (1-330)	.20	.07
❑	COM (90-110/203-220)	.50	.20
❑	COMMON (116-134)	.50	.20
❑	COM (14/66/221-310)	.50	.20
❑	COMMON (311-330)	.50	.20
❑	PLATE ODDS 1:2009 H, 1:582 HTA, 1:2009 R		
❑	PLATE PRINT RUN 1 SET PER COLOR		
❑	BLACK-CYAN-MAGENTA-YELLOW ISSUED		
❑	NO PLATE PRICING DUE TO SCARCITY		
❑	1 Sammy Sosa	.50	.20
❑	2 Jeff Francoeur	1.50	.60
❑	3 Tony Clark	.20	.07
❑	4 Michael Tucker	.20	.07
❑	5 Mike Matheny	.20	.07
❑	6 Eric Young	.20	.07
❑	7 Jose Valentin	.20	.07
❑	8 Matt Lawton	.20	.07
❑	9 Juan Rivera	.20	.07
❑	10 Shawn Green	.20	.07
❑	11 Aaron Boone	.20	.07
❑	12 Woody Williams	.20	.07
❑	13 Brad Wilkerson	.20	.07
❑	14 Anthony Reyes RC	1.00	.40
❑	15 Russ Adams	.20	.07
❑	16 Gustavo Chacin	.20	.07
❑	17 Michael Restovich	.20	.07
❑	18 Humberto Quintero	.20	.07
❑	19 Matt Ginter	.20	.07
❑	20 Scott Podsednik	.20	.07
❑	21 Byung-Hyun Kim	.20	.07
❑	22 Orlando Hernandez	.20	.07
❑	23 Mark Grudzielanek	.20	.07
❑	24 Jody Gerut	.20	.07
❑	25 Adrian Beltre	.20	.07
❑	26 Scott Schoeneweis	.20	.07
❑	27 Marlon Anderson	.20	.07
❑	28 Jason Vargas	.20	.07
❑	29 Claudio Vargas	.20	.07
❑	30 Jason Kendall	.20	.07
❑	31 Aaron Small	.20	.07
❑	32 Juan Cruz	.20	.07
❑	33 Placido Polanco	.20	.07
❑	34 Jorge Sosa	.20	.07
❑	35 John Olerud	.20	.07
❑	36 Ryan Langerhans	.20	.07
❑	37 Randy Winn	.20	.07
❑	38 Zach Duke	.30	.10
❑	39 Garrett Atkins	.20	.07
❑	40 Al Leiter	.20	.07
❑	41 Shawn Chacon	.20	.07
❑	42 Mark DeRosa	.20	.07
❑	43 Miguel Ojeda	.20	.07
❑	44 A.J. Pierzynski	.20	.07
❑	45 Carlos Lee	.20	.07
❑	46 LaTroy Hawkins	.20	.07
❑	47 Nick Green	.20	.07
❑	48 Shawn Estes	.20	.07
❑	49 Eli Marrero	.20	.07
❑	50 Jeff Kent	.20	.07
❑	51 Joe Randa	.20	.07
❑	52 Jose Hernandez	.20	.07
❑	53 Joe Blanton	.20	.07
❑	54 Huston Street	.30	.10
❑	55 Marlon Byrd	.20	.07
❑	56 Alex Sanchez	.20	.07
❑	57 Livan Hernandez	.20	.07
❑	58 Chris Young	.20	.07
❑	59 Brad Eldred	.20	.07
❑	60 Terrence Long	.20	.07
❑	61 Phil Nevin	.20	.07
❑	62 Kyle Farnsworth	.20	.07
❑	63 Jon Lieber	.20	.07
❑	64 Antonio Alfonseca	.20	.07
❑	65 Tony Graffanino	.20	.07
❑	66 Tadahito Iguchi RC	1.50	.60
❑	67 Brad Thompson	.20	.07
❑	68 Jose Vidro	.20	.07
❑	69 Jason Phillips	.20	.07
❑	70 Carl Pavano	.20	.07
❑	71 Pokey Reese	.20	.07
❑	72 Jerome Williams	.20	.07
❑	73 Kazuhisa Ishii	.20	.07
❑	74 Zach Day	.20	.07
❑	75 Edgar Renteria	.20	.07
❑	76 Mike Myers	.20	.07
❑	77 Jeff Cirillo	.20	.07
❑	78 Endy Chavez	.20	.07
❑	79 Jose Guillen	.20	.07
❑	80 Ugueth Urbina	.20	.07
❑	81 Vinny Castilla	.20	.07
❑	82 Javier Vazquez	.20	.07
❑	83 Willy Taveras	.20	.07
❑	84 Mark Mulder	.20	.07
❑	85 Mike Hargrove MG	.20	.07
❑	86 Buddy Bell MG	.20	.07
❑	87 Charlie Manuel MG	.20	.07
❑	88 Willie Randolph MG	.20	.07
❑	89 Bob Melvin MG	.20	.07
❑	90 Chris Lambert PROS	.50	.20
❑	91 Homer Bailey PROS	.50	.20
❑	92 Ervin Santana PROS	.50	.20
❑	93 Bill Bray PROS	.50	.20
❑	94 Thomas Diamond PROS	.50	.20
❑	95 Trevor Plouffe PROS	.50	.20
❑	96 James Houser PROS	.50	.20
❑	97 Jake Stevens PROS	.50	.20
❑	98 Anthony Whittington PROS	.50	.20
❑	99 Philip Hughes PROS	.50	.20
❑	100 Greg Golson PROS	.50	.20
❑	101 Paul Maholm PROS	.50	.20
❑	102 Carlos Quentin PROS	.50	.20
❑	103 Dan Johnson PROS	.50	.20
❑	104 Mark Rogers PROS	.50	.20
❑	105 Neil Walker PROS	.50	.20
❑	106 Omar Quintanilla PROS	.50	.20
❑	107 Blake DeWitt PROS	.50	.20
❑	108 Taylor Tankersley PROS	.50	.20
❑	109 David Murphy PROS	.50	.20
❑	110 Felix Hernandez PROS	1.00	.40
❑	111 Craig Biggio HL	.20	.07
❑	112 Greg Maddux HL	.50	.20
❑	113 Bobby Abreu HL	.20	.07
❑	114 Alex Rodriguez HL	.50	.20
❑	115 Trevor Hoffman HL	.20	.07
❑	116 A.Pierzynski/T.Iguchi ALDS	.50	.20
❑	117 Reggie Sanders NLDS	.50	.20
❑	118 B.Molina/E.Santana ALDS	.50	.20
❑	119 Burke/Berkman/LaR NLDS	.50	.20
❑	120 Garret Anderson ALCS	.50	.20
❑	121 A.J. Pierzynski ALCS	.50	.20
❑	122 Paul Konerko ALCS	.50	.20
❑	123 Joe Crede ALCS	.50	.20
❑	124 M.Buehrle/J.Garland ALCS	.50	.20
❑	125 F.Garcia/J.Contreras ALCS	.50	.20
❑	126 Reggie Sanders NLCS	.50	.20
❑	127 Roy Oswalt NLCS	.50	.20
❑	128 Roger Clemens NLCS	1.00	.40
❑	129 Albert Pujols NLCS	1.00	.40
❑	130 Roy Oswalt NLCS	.50	.20
❑	131 J.Crede/B.Jenks WS	.75	.30
❑	132 P.Konerko/S.Podsed WS	.75	.30
❑	133 Geoff Blum WS	.50	.20
❑	134 White Sox Sweep WS	1.00	.40
❑	135 ARod/Ortiz/Manny AL HR	.50	.20
❑	136 Young/ARod/Vlad AL BA	.30	.10
❑	137 Ortiz/Teix/Manny AL RBI	.30	.10
❑	138 Colon/Garland/Lee AL W	.20	.07
❑	139 Mill/Johan/Buehrle AL ERA	.30	.10
❑	140 Johan/Randy/Lackey AL K	.30	.10
❑	141 Andruw/Lee/Pujols NL HR	.50	.20
❑	142 Lee/Pujols/Cabrera NL BA	.50	.20
❑	143 Andruw/Pujols/Burr NL RBI	.50	.20
❑	144 Willis/Carp/Oswalt NL W	.20	.07
❑	145 Roger/Andy/Willis NL ERA	.50	.20
❑	146 Peavy/Carp/Pedro NL K	.20	.07
❑	147 Mark Teixeira AS	.20	.07
❑	148 Brian Roberts AS	.20	.07
❑	149 Michael Young AS	.20	.07
❑	150 Alex Rodriguez AS	.50	.20
❑	151 Johnny Damon AS	.20	.07
❑	152 Vladimir Guerrero AS	.30	.10
❑	153 Manny Ramirez AS	.20	.07
❑	154 David Ortiz AS	.30	.10
❑	155 Mariano Rivera AS	.30	.10
❑	156 Joe Nathan AS	.20	.07
❑	157 Albert Pujols AS	.50	.20
❑	158 Jeff Kent AS	.20	.07
❑	159 Felipe Lopez AS	.20	.07
❑	160 Morgan Ensberg AS	.20	.07
❑	161 Miguel Cabrera AS	.20	.07
❑	162 Ken Griffey Jr. AS	.50	.20
❑	163 Andruw Jones AS	.20	.07
❑	164 Paul Lo Duca AS	.20	.07
❑	165 Chad Cordero AS	.20	.07
❑	166 Ken Griffey Jr. Comeback	.50	.20
❑	167 Jason Giambi Comeback	.20	.07
❑	168 Willy Taveras ROY	.20	.07
❑	169 Huston Street ROY	.20	.07
❑	170 Chris Carpenter AS	.20	.07
❑	171 Bartolo Colon AS	.20	.07
❑	172 Bobby Cox AS MG	.20	.07
❑	173 Ozzie Guillen AS MG	.50	.20
❑	174 Andruw Jones POY	.20	.07
❑	175 Johnny Damon AS	.20	.07
❑	176 Alex Rodriguez AS	.50	.20
❑	177 David Ortiz AS	.30	.10
❑	178 Manny Ramirez AS	.20	.07
❑	179 Miguel Tejada AS	.20	.07
❑	180 Vladimir Guerrero AS	.30	.10
❑	181 Mark Teixeira AS	.20	.07
❑	182 Ivan Rodriguez AS	.20	.07
❑	183 Brian Roberts AS	.20	.07
❑	184 Mark Buehrle AS	.20	.07

❑ 185 Bobby Abreu AS .20 .07
❑ 186 Carlos Beltran AS .20 .07
❑ 187 Albert Pujols AS .50 .20
❑ 188 Derrek Lee AS .20 .07
❑ 189 Jim Edmonds AS .20 .07
❑ 190 Aramis Ramirez AS .20 .07
❑ 191 Mike Piazza AS .30 .10
❑ 192 Jeff Kent AS .20 .07
❑ 193 David Eckstein AS .20 .07
❑ 194 Chris Carpenter AS .20 .07
❑ 195 Bobby Abreu HR .20 .07
❑ 196 Ivan Rodriguez HR .20 .07
❑ 197 Carlos Lee HR .20 .07
❑ 198 David Ortiz HR .30 .10
❑ 199 Hee-Seop Choi HR .20 .07
❑ 200 Andruw Jones HR .20 .07
❑ 201 Mark Teixeira HR .20 .07
❑ 202 Jason Bay HR .20 .07
❑ 203 Hanley Ramirez FUT .50 .20
❑ 204 Shin-Soo Choo FUT .50 .20
❑ 205 Justin Huber FUT .50 .20
❑ 206 Nelson Cruz FUT RC 1.25 .50
❑ 207 Edwin Encarnacion FUT .50 .20
❑ 208 Miguel Montero FUT RC 1.25 .50
❑ 209 William Bergolla FUT .50 .20
❑ 210 Luis Montanez FUT .50 .20
❑ 211 Francisco Liriano FUT 1.50 .60
❑ 212 Kevin Thompson FUT .50 .20
❑ 213 B.J. Upton FUT .50 .20
❑ 214 Conor Jackson FUT .50 .20
❑ 215 Delmon Young FUT .50 .20
❑ 216 Andy LaRoche FUT 1.00 .40
❑ 217 Ryan Garko FUT 1.25 .50
❑ 218 Josh Barfield FUT .50 .20
❑ 219 Chris B.Young FUT .50 .20
❑ 220 Justin Verlander FUT 1.50 .60
❑ 221 Drew Anderson FY RC .50 .20
❑ 222 Luis Hernandez FY RC .50 .20
❑ 223 Jim Burt FY RC .50 .20
❑ 224 Mike Morse FY RC .50 .20
❑ 225 Elliot Johnson FY RC .50 .20
❑ 226 C.J. Smith FY RC .50 .20
❑ 227 Casey McGehee FY RC .50 .20
❑ 228 Brian Miller FY RC .50 .20
❑ 229 Chris Vines FY RC .50 .20
❑ 230 D.J. Houlton FY RC .50 .20
❑ 231 Chuck Tiffany FY RC 1.00 .40
❑ 232 Humberto Sanchez FY RC 2.00 .75
❑ 233 Baltazar Lopez FY RC .50 .20
❑ 234 Russ Martin FY RC 2.50 1.00
❑ 235 Dana Eveland FY RC .50 .20
❑ 236 Johan Silva FY RC .50 .20
❑ 237 Adam Harben FY RC .75 .30
❑ 238 Brian Bannister FY RC 1.00 .40
❑ 239 Adam Boeve FY RC .50 .20
❑ 240 Thomas Oldham FY RC .50 .20
❑ 241 Cody Haerther FY RC .50 .20
❑ 242 Dan Santin FY RC .50 .20
❑ 243 Daniel Haigwood FY RC .75 .30
❑ 244 Craig Tatum FY RC .50 .20
❑ 245 Martin Prado FY RC .50 .20
❑ 246 Errol Simonitsch FY RC .75 .30
❑ 247 Lorenzo Scott FY RC .50 .20
❑ 248 Hayden Penn FY RC .75 .30
❑ 249 Heath Totten FY RC .50 .20
❑ 250 Nick Masset FY RC .50 .20
❑ 251 Pedro Lopez FY RC .50 .20
❑ 252 Ben Harrison FY .50 .20
❑ 253 Mike Spidale FY RC .50 .20
❑ 254 Jeremy Harts FY RC .50 .20
❑ 255 Danny Zell FY RC .50 .20
❑ 256 Kevin Collins FY RC .50 .20
❑ 257 Tony Arnerich FY RC .50 .20
❑ 258 Matt Albers FY RC 1.25 .50
❑ 259 Ricky Barrett FY RC .50 .20
❑ 260 Hernan Iribarren FY RC .75 .30
❑ 261 Sean Tracey FY RC .50 .20
❑ 262 Jerry Owens FY RC .75 .30
❑ 263 Steve Nelson FY RC .50 .20
❑ 264 Brandon McCarthy FY RC 1.00 .40
❑ 265 David Shepard FY RC .50 .20
❑ 266 Steven Bondurant FY RC .50 .20
❑ 267 Billy Sadler FY RC .50 .20
❑ 268 Ryan Feierabend FY RC .50 .20
❑ 269 Stuart Pomeranz FY RC .50 .20
❑ 270 Shaun Marcum FY .50 .20
❑ 271 Erik Schindewolf FY RC .50 .20
❑ 272 Stefan Bailie FY RC .50 .20
❑ 273 Mike Esposito FY RC .50 .20
❑ 274 Buck Coats FY RC .50 .20
❑ 275 Andy Sides FY RC .50 .20
❑ 276 Micah Schnurstein FY RC .50 .20
❑ 277 Jesse Gutierrez FY RC .50 .20
❑ 278 Jake Postlewait FY RC .50 .20
❑ 279 Willy Mota FY RC .50 .20
❑ 280 Ryan Speier FY RC .50 .20
❑ 281 Frank Mata FY RC .50 .20
❑ 282 Jair Jurrjens FY RC 1.50 .60
❑ 283 Nick Touchstone FY RC .50 .20
❑ 284 Matthew Kemp FY RC 3.00 1.25
❑ 285 Vinny Rottino FY RC .50 .20
❑ 286 J.B. Thurmond FY RC .50 .20
❑ 287 Kelvin Pichardo FY RC .50 .20
❑ 288 Scott Mitchinson FY RC .50 .20
❑ 289 Darwinson Salazar FY RC .50 .20
❑ 290 George Kottaras FY RC .75 .30
❑ 291 Kenny Durost FY RC .50 .20
❑ 292 Jonathan Sanchez FY RC 1.25 .50
❑ 293 Brandon Moorhead FY RC .50 .20
❑ 294 Kennard Bibbs FY RC .50 .20
❑ 295 David Gassner FY RC .50 .20
❑ 296 Micah Furtado FY RC .50 .20
❑ 297 Ismael Ramirez FY RC .50 .20
❑ 298 Carlos Gonzalez FY RC 2.00 .75
❑ 299 Brandon Sing FY RC .75 .30
❑ 300 Jason Motte FY RC .50 .20
❑ 301 Chuck James FY RC 1.25 .50
❑ 302 Andy Santana FY RC .50 .20
❑ 303 Manny Parra FY RC .50 .20
❑ 304 Chris B.Young FY RC 1.25 .50
❑ 305 Juan Senreiso FY RC .50 .20
❑ 306 Franklin Morales FY RC .75 .30
❑ 307 Jared Gothreaux FY RC .50 .20
❑ 308 Jayce Tingler FY RC .50 .20
❑ 309 Matt Brown FY RC .50 .20
❑ 310 Frank Diaz FY RC .50 .20
❑ 311 Stephen Drew DP RC 4.00 1.50
❑ 312 Jered Weaver DP RC 4.00 1.50
❑ 313 Ryan Braun DP RC 10.00 4.00
❑ 314 John Mayberry Jr. DP RC 1.00 .40
❑ 315 Aaron Thompson DP RC .75 .30
❑ 316 Cesar Carrillo DP RC 1.00 .40
❑ 317 Jacoby Ellsbury DP RC 12.00 5.00
❑ 318 Matt Garza DP RC 2.00 .75
❑ 319 Cliff Pennington DP RC .75 .30
❑ 320 Colby Rasmus DP RC 2.00 .75
❑ 321 Chris Volstad DP RC 1.00 .40
❑ 322 Ricky Romero DP RC .75 .30
❑ 323 Ryan Zimmerman DP RC 5.00 2.00
❑ 324 C.J. Henry DP RC 1.50 .60
❑ 325 Jay Bruce DP RC 3.00 1.25
❑ 326 Beau Jones DP RC 1.00 .40
❑ 327 Mark McCormick DP RC .75 .30
❑ 328 Eli Iorg DP RC .75 .30
❑ 329 Andrew McCutchen DP RC 2.00 .75
❑ 330 Mike Costanzo DP RC 1.25 .50

2006 Topps

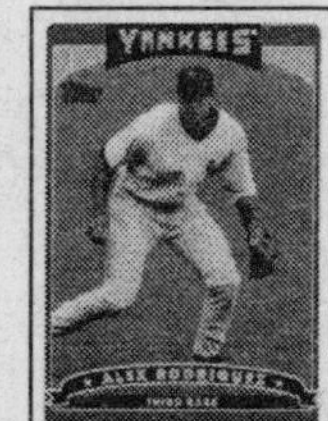

❑ COMP.HOBBY SET (664) 80.00 50.00
❑ COMP.HOLIDAY SET (659) 80.00 50.00
❑ COMP.CARDINALS SET (664) 80.00 50.00
❑ COMP.CUBS SET (664) 80.00 50.00
❑ COMP.PIRATES SET (664) 80.00 50.00
❑ COMP.RED SOX SET (664) 80.00 50.00
❑ COMP.YANKEES SET (664) 80.00 50.00
❑ COMPLETE SET (659) 80.00 30.00
❑ COMPLETE SERIES 1 (329) 40.00 15.00
❑ COMPLETE SERIES 2 (330) 40.00 15.00
❑ COMMON CARD (1-660) .20 .07
❑ COMP.SER.1 SET EXCLUDES CARD 297
❑ CARD 297 NOT INTENDED FOR RELEASE
❑ CARDS 287b AND 312b ISSUED IN FACT.SET
❑ 2 TICKETS EXCH.CARD RANDOM IN PACKS
❑ OVERALL PLATE SER.1 ODDS 1:246 HTA
❑ OVERALL PLATE SER.2 ODDS 1:193 HTA
❑ PLATE PRINT RUN 1 SET PER COLOR
❑ BLACK-CYAN-MAGENTA-YELLOW ISSUED
❑ NO PLATE PRICING DUE TO SCARCITY
❑ 1 Alex Rodriguez .75 .30
❑ 2 Jose Valentin .20 .07
❑ 3 Garrett Atkins .20 .07
❑ 4 Scott Hatteberg .20 .07
❑ 5 Carl Crawford .20 .07
❑ 6 Armando Benitez .20 .07
❑ 7 Mickey Mantle 8.00 3.00
❑ 8 Mike Morse .20 .07
❑ 9 Damian Miller .20 .07
❑ 10 Clint Barmes .20 .07
❑ 11 Michael Barrett .20 .07
❑ 12 Coco Crisp .20 .07
❑ 13 Tadahito Iguchi .20 .07
❑ 14 Chris Snyder .20 .07
❑ 15 Brian Roberts .20 .07
❑ 16 David Wright .75 .30
❑ 17 Victor Santos .20 .07
❑ 18 Trevor Hoffman .20 .07
❑ 19 Jeremy Reed .20 .07
❑ 20 Bobby Abreu .20 .07
❑ 21 Lance Berkman .20 .07
❑ 22 Zach Day .20 .07
❑ 23 Jonny Gomes .20 .07
❑ 24 Jason Marquis .20 .07
❑ 25 Chipper Jones .50 .20
❑ 26 Scott Hairston .20 .07
❑ 27 Ryan Dempster .20 .07
❑ 28 Brandon Inge .20 .07
❑ 29 Aaron Harang .20 .07
❑ 30 Jon Garland .20 .07
❑ 31 Pokey Reese .20 .07
❑ 32 Mike MacDougal .20 .07
❑ 33 Mike Lieberthal .20 .07
❑ 34 Cesar Izturis .20 .07
❑ 35 Brad Wilkerson .20 .07
❑ 36 Jeff Suppan .20 .07
❑ 37 Adam Everett .20 .07
❑ 38 Bengie Molina .20 .07
❑ 39 Rickie Weeks .20 .07
❑ 40 Jorge Posada .30 .10
❑ 41 Rheal Cormier .20 .07
❑ 42 Reed Johnson .20 .07
❑ 43 Laynce Nix .20 .07
❑ 44 Carl Everett .20 .07
❑ 45 Greg Maddux .75 .30
❑ 46 Jeff Francis .20 .07
❑ 47 Felipe Lopez .20 .07
❑ 48 Dan Johnson .20 .07
❑ 49 Humberto Cota .20 .07
❑ 50 Manny Ramirez .30 .10
❑ 51 Juan Uribe .20 .07
❑ 52 Jaret Wright .20 .07
❑ 53 Tomo Ohka .20 .07
❑ 54 Mike Matheny .20 .07
❑ 55 Joe Mauer .50 .20
❑ 56 Jarrod Washburn .20 .07
❑ 57 Randy Winn .20 .07
❑ 58 Pedro Feliz .20 .07
❑ 59 Kenny Rogers .20 .07
❑ 60 Rocco Baldelli .20 .07
❑ 61 Eric Hinske .20 .07
❑ 62 Damaso Marte .20 .07
❑ 63 Desi Relaford .20 .07
❑ 64 Juan Encarnacion .20 .07
❑ 65 Nomar Garciaparra .50 .20
❑ 66 Shawn Estes .20 .07
❑ 67 Brian Jordan .20 .07
❑ 68 Steve Kline .20 .07
❑ 69 Braden Looper .20 .07
❑ 70 Carlos Lee .20 .07
❑ 71 Tom Glavine .30 .10
❑ 72 Craig Biggio .30 .10

No.	Card		
❑ 73	Steve Finley	.20	.07
❑ 74	David Newhan	.20	.07
❑ 75	Eric Gagne	.20	.07
❑ 76	Tony Graffanino	.20	.07
❑ 77	Dallas McPherson	.20	.07
❑ 78	Nick Punto	.20	.07
❑ 79	Mark Kotsay	.20	.07
❑ 80	Kerry Wood	.20	.07
❑ 81	Kyle Farnsworth	.20	.07
❑ 82	Huston Street	.20	.07
❑ 83	Endy Chavez	.20	.07
❑ 84	So Taguchi	.20	.07
❑ 85	Hank Blalock	.20	.07
❑ 86	Brad Radke	.20	.07
❑ 87	Chien-Ming Wang	.75	.30
❑ 88	B.J. Surhoff	.20	.07
❑ 89	Glendon Rusch	.20	.07
❑ 90	Mark Buehrle	.20	.07
❑ 91	Rafael Betancourt	.20	.07
❑ 92	Lance Cormier	.20	.07
❑ 93	Alex Gonzalez	.20	.07
❑ 94	Matt Stairs	.20	.07
❑ 95	Andy Pettitte	.30	.10
❑ 96	Jesse Crain	.20	.07
❑ 97	Kenny Lofton	.20	.07
❑ 98	Geoff Blum	.20	.07
❑ 99	Mark Redman	.20	.07
❑ 100	Barry Bonds	1.00	.40
❑ 101	Chad Orvella	.20	.07
❑ 102	Xavier Nady	.20	.07
❑ 103	Junior Spivey	.20	.07
❑ 104	Bernie Williams	.30	.10
❑ 105	Victor Martinez	.20	.07
❑ 106	Nook Logan	.20	.07
❑ 107	Mark Teahen	.20	.07
❑ 108	Mike Lamb	.20	.07
❑ 109	Jayson Werth	.20	.07
❑ 110	Mariano Rivera	.50	.20
❑ 111	Erubiel Durazo	.20	.07
❑ 112	Ryan Vogelsong	.20	.07
❑ 113	Bobby Madritsch	.20	.07
❑ 114	Travis Lee	.20	.07
❑ 115	Adam Dunn	.20	.07
❑ 116	David Riske	.20	.07
❑ 117	Troy Percival	.20	.07
❑ 118	Chad Tracy	.20	.07
❑ 119	Andy Marte	.20	.07
❑ 120	Edgar Renteria	.20	.07
❑ 121	Jason Giambi	.20	.07
❑ 122	Justin Morneau	.20	.07
❑ 123	J.T. Snow	.20	.07
❑ 124	Danys Baez	.20	.07
❑ 125	Carlos Delgado	.20	.07
❑ 126	John Buck	.20	.07
❑ 127	Shannon Stewart	.20	.07
❑ 128	Mike Cameron	.20	.07
❑ 129	Joe McEwing	.20	.07
❑ 130	Richie Sexson	.20	.07
❑ 131	Rod Barajas	.20	.07
❑ 132	Russ Adams	.20	.07
❑ 133	J.D. Closser	.20	.07
❑ 134	Ramon Ortiz	.20	.07
❑ 135	Josh Beckett	.20	.07
❑ 136	Ryan Freel	.20	.07
❑ 137	Victor Zambrano	.20	.07
❑ 138	Ronnie Belliard	.20	.07
❑ 139	Jason Michaels	.20	.07
❑ 140	Brian Giles	.20	.07
❑ 141	Randy Wolf	.20	.07
❑ 142	Robinson Cano	.30	.10
❑ 143	Joe Blanton	.20	.07
❑ 144	Esteban Loaiza	.20	.07
❑ 145	Troy Glaus	.20	.07
❑ 146	Matt Clement	.20	.07
❑ 147	Geoff Jenkins	.20	.07
❑ 148	John Thomson	.20	.07
❑ 149	A.J. Pierzynski	.20	.07
❑ 150	Pedro Martinez	.30	.10
❑ 151	Roger Clemens	1.00	.40
❑ 152	Jack Wilson	.20	.07
❑ 153	Ray King	.20	.07
❑ 154	Ryan Church	.20	.07
❑ 155	Paul Lo Duca	.20	.07
❑ 156	Dan Wheeler	.20	.07
❑ 157	Carlos Zambrano	.20	.07
❑ 158	Mike Timlin	.20	.07
❑ 159	Brandon Claussen	.20	.07
❑ 160	Travis Hafner	.20	.07
❑ 161	Chris Shelton	.20	.07
❑ 162	Rafael Furcal	.20	.07
❑ 163	Tom Gordon	.20	.07
❑ 164	Noah Lowry	.20	.07
❑ 165	Larry Walker	.30	.10
❑ 166	Dave Roberts	.20	.07
❑ 167	Scott Schoeneweis	.20	.07
❑ 168	Julian Tavarez	.20	.07
❑ 169	Jhonny Peralta	.20	.07
❑ 170	Vernon Wells	.20	.07
❑ 171	Jorge Cantu	.20	.07
❑ 172	Todd Greene	.20	.07
❑ 173	Willy Taveras	.20	.07
❑ 174	Corey Patterson	.20	.07
❑ 175	Ivan Rodriguez	.30	.10
❑ 176	Bobby Kielty	.20	.07
❑ 177	Jose Reyes	.20	.07
❑ 178	Barry Zito	.20	.07
❑ 179	Deivi Cruz	.20	.07
❑ 180	Mark Teixeira	.30	.10
❑ 181	Chone Figgins	.20	.07
❑ 182	Aaron Rowand	.20	.07
❑ 183	Tim Wakefield	.20	.07
❑ 184	Mike Maroth	.20	.07
❑ 185	Johnny Damon	.30	.10
❑ 186	Vicente Padilla	.20	.07
❑ 187	Ryan Klesko	.20	.07
❑ 188	Gary Matthews	.20	.07
❑ 189	Jose Mesa	.20	.07
❑ 190	Nick Johnson	.20	.07
❑ 191	Freddy Garcia	.20	.07
❑ 192	Larry Bigbie	.20	.07
❑ 193	Chris Ray	.20	.07
❑ 194	Torii Hunter	.20	.07
❑ 195	Mike Sweeney	.20	.07
❑ 196	Brad Penny	.20	.07
❑ 197	Jason Frasor	.20	.07
❑ 198	Kevin Mench	.20	.07
❑ 199	Adam Kennedy	.20	.07
❑ 200	Albert Pujols	1.00	.40
❑ 201	Jody Gerut	.20	.07
❑ 202	Luis Gonzalez	.20	.07
❑ 203	Zack Greinke	.20	.07
❑ 204	Miguel Cairo	.20	.07
❑ 205	Jimmy Rollins	.20	.07
❑ 206	Edgardo Alfonzo	.20	.07
❑ 207	Billy Wagner	.20	.07
❑ 208	B.J. Ryan	.20	.07
❑ 209	Orlando Hudson	.20	.07
❑ 210	Preston Wilson	.20	.07
❑ 211	Melvin Mora	.20	.07
❑ 212	Bill Mueller	.20	.07
❑ 213	Javy Lopez	.20	.07
❑ 214	Wilson Betemit	.20	.07
❑ 215	Garret Anderson	.20	.07
❑ 216	Russell Branyan	.20	.07
❑ 217	Jeff Weaver	.20	.07
❑ 218	Doug Mientkiewicz	.20	.07
❑ 219	Mark Ellis	.20	.07
❑ 220	Jason Bay	.20	.07
❑ 221	Adam LaRoche	.20	.07
❑ 222	C.C. Sabathia	.20	.07
❑ 223	Humberto Quintero	.20	.07
❑ 224	Bartolo Colon	.20	.07
❑ 225	Ichiro Suzuki	.75	.30
❑ 226	Brett Tomko	.20	.07
❑ 227	Corey Koskie	.20	.07
❑ 228	David Eckstein	.20	.07
❑ 229	Cristian Guzman	.20	.07
❑ 230	Jeff Kent	.20	.07
❑ 231	Chris Capuano	.20	.07
❑ 232	Rodrigo Lopez	.20	.07
❑ 233	Jason Phillips	.20	.07
❑ 234	Luis Rivas	.20	.07
❑ 235	Cliff Floyd	.20	.07
❑ 236	Gil Meche	.20	.07
❑ 237	Adam Eaton	.20	.07
❑ 238	Matt Morris	.20	.07
❑ 239	Kyle Davies	.20	.07
❑ 240	David Wells	.20	.07
❑ 241	John Smoltz	.30	.10
❑ 242	Felix Hernandez	.50	.20
❑ 243	Kenny Rogers GG	.20	.07
❑ 244	Mark Teixeira GG	.20	.07
❑ 245	Orlando Hudson GG	.20	.07
❑ 246	Derek Jeter GG	.50	.20
❑ 247	Eric Chavez GG	.20	.07
❑ 248	Torii Hunter GG	.20	.07
❑ 249	Vernon Wells GG	.20	.07
❑ 250	Ichiro Suzuki GG	.50	.20
❑ 251	Greg Maddux GG	.50	.20
❑ 252	Mike Matheny GG	.20	.07
❑ 253	Derrek Lee GG	.20	.07
❑ 254	Luis Castillo GG	.20	.07
❑ 255	Omar Vizquel GG	.20	.07
❑ 256	Mike Lowell GG	.20	.07
❑ 257	Andruw Jones GG	.20	.07
❑ 258	Jim Edmonds GG	.20	.07
❑ 259	Bobby Abreu GG	.20	.07
❑ 260	Bartolo Colon CY	.20	.07
❑ 261	Chris Carpenter CY	.20	.07
❑ 262	Alex Rodriguez MVP	.50	.20
❑ 263	Albert Pujols MVP	.50	.20
❑ 264	Huston Street ROY	.20	.07
❑ 265	Ryan Howard ROY	.40	.15
❑ 266	Bob Melvin MG	.20	.07
❑ 267	Bobby Cox MG	.20	.07
❑ 268	Baltimore Orioles TC	.20	.07
❑ 269	Boston Red Sox TC	.50	.20
❑ 270	Chicago White Sox TC	.50	.20
❑ 271	Dusty Baker MG	.20	.07
❑ 272	Jerry Narron MG	.20	.07
❑ 273	Cleveland Indians TC	.20	.07
❑ 274	Clint Hurdle MG	.20	.07
❑ 275	Detroit Tigers TC	.20	.07
❑ 276	Jack McKeon MG	.20	.07
❑ 277	Phil Garner MG	.20	.07
❑ 278	Kansas City Royals TC	.20	.07
❑ 279	Jim Tracy MG	.20	.07
❑ 280	Los Angeles Angels TC	.20	.07
❑ 281	Milwaukee Brewers TC	.20	.07
❑ 282	Minnesota Twins TC	.20	.07
❑ 283	Willie Randolph MG	.20	.07
❑ 284	New York Yankees TC	.50	.20
❑ 285	Oakland Athletics TC	.20	.07
❑ 286	Charlie Manuel MG	.20	.07
❑ 287a	Pete Mackanin MG ERR	.20	.07
❑ 287b	Pete Mackanin MG COR	.20	.07
❑ 288	Bruce Bochy MG	.20	.07
❑ 289	Felipe Alou MG	.20	.07
❑ 290	Seattle Mariners TC	.20	.07
❑ 291	Tony LaRussa MG	.20	.07
❑ 292	Tampa Bay Devil Rays TC	.20	.07
❑ 293	Texas Rangers TC	.20	.07
❑ 294	Toronto Blue Jays TC	.20	.07
❑ 295	Frank Robinson MG	.30	.10
❑ 296	Anderson Hernandez (RC)	.50	.20
❑ 297A	Alex Gordon (RC) Full	1000.00	700.00
❑ 297B	Alex Gordon Cut Out	120.00	60.00
❑ 297C	Alex Gordon Blank Gold	150.00	75.00
❑ 297D	Alex Gordon Blank Silver		
❑ 298	Jason Botts (RC)	.50	.20
❑ 299	Jeff Mathis (RC)	.50	.20
❑ 300	Ryan Garko (RC)	.50	.20
❑ 301	Charlton Jimerson (RC)	.50	.20
❑ 302	Chris Denorfia (RC)	.50	.20
❑ 303	Anthony Reyes (RC)	.50	.20
❑ 304	Bryan Bullington (RC)	.50	.20
❑ 305	Chuck James (RC)	.50	.20
❑ 306	Danny Sandoval RC	.50	.20
❑ 307	Walter Young (RC)	.50	.20
❑ 308	Fausto Carmona (RC)	.50	.20
❑ 309	Francisco Liriano (RC)	2.00	.75
❑ 310	Hong-Chih Kuo (RC)	1.00	.40
❑ 311	Joe Saunders (RC)	.50	.20
❑ 312a	John Koronka Cubs (RC)	.50	.20
❑ 312b	John Koronka Rangers (RC)	.50	.20
❑ 313	Robert Andino RC	.50	.20
❑ 314	Shaun Marcum (RC)	.50	.20
❑ 315	Tom Gorzelanny (RC)	.50	.20
❑ 316	Craig Breslow RC	.50	.20
❑ 317	Chris DeMaria RC	.50	.20
❑ 318	Brayan Pena (RC)	.50	.20
❑ 319	Rich Hill (RC)	.50	.20
❑ 320	Rick Short (RC)	.50	.20
❑ 321	C.J. Wilson (RC)	.50	.20
❑ 322	Marshall McDougall (RC)	.50	.20
❑ 323	Darrell Rasner (RC)	.50	.20
❑ 324	Brandon Watson (RC)	.50	.20
❑ 325	Paul McAnulty (RC)	.50	.20

❑	326	D.Jeter/A.Rodriguez TS	1.00	.40
❑	327	M.Tejada/M.Mora TS	.20	.07
❑	328	M.Giles/C.Jones TS	.30	.10
❑	329	M.Ramirez/D.Ortiz TS	.50	.20
❑	330	M.Barrett/G.Maddux TS	.50	.20
❑	331	Matt Holliday	.25	.08
❑	332	Orlando Cabrera	.20	.07
❑	333	Ryan Langerhans	.20	.07
❑	334	Lew Ford	.20	.07
❑	335	Mark Prior	.30	.10
❑	336	Ted Lilly	.20	.07
❑	337	Michael Young	.20	.07
❑	338	Livan Hernandez	.20	.07
❑	339	Yadier Molina	.20	.07
❑	340	Eric Chavez	.20	.07
❑	341	Miguel Batista	.20	.07
❑	342	Bruce Chen	.20	.07
❑	343	Sean Casey	.20	.07
❑	344	Doug Davis	.20	.07
❑	345	Andruw Jones	.30	.10
❑	346	Hideki Matsui	.50	.20
❑	347	Joe Randa	.20	.07
❑	348	Reggie Sanders	.20	.07
❑	349	Jason Jennings	.20	.07
❑	350	Joe Nathan	.20	.07
❑	351	Jose Lopez	.20	.07
❑	352	John Lackey	.20	.07
❑	353	Claudio Vargas	.20	.07
❑	354	Grady Sizemore	.30	.10
❑	355	Jon Papelbon (RC)	2.00	.75
❑	356	Luis Matos	.20	.07
❑	357	Orlando Hernandez	.20	.07
❑	358	Jamie Moyer	.20	.07
❑	359	Chase Utley	.50	.20
❑	360	Moises Alou	.20	.07
❑	361	Chad Cordero	.20	.07
❑	362	Brian McCann	.20	.07
❑	363	Jermaine Dye	.20	.07
❑	364	Ryan Madson	.20	.07
❑	365	Aramis Ramirez	.20	.07
❑	366	Matt Treanor	.20	.07
❑	367	Ray Durham	.20	.07
❑	368	Khalil Greene	.30	.10
❑	369	Mike Hampton	.20	.07
❑	370	Mike Mussina	.30	.10
❑	371	Brad Hawpe	.20	.07
❑	372	Marlon Byrd	.20	.07
❑	373	Woody Williams	.20	.07
❑	374	Victor Diaz	.20	.07
❑	375	Brady Clark	.20	.07
❑	376	Luis Gonzalez	.20	.07
❑	377	Raul Ibanez	.20	.07
❑	378	Tony Clark	.20	.07
❑	379	Shawn Chacon	.20	.07
❑	380	Marcus Giles	.20	.07
❑	381	Odalis Perez	.20	.07
❑	382	Steve Trachsel	.20	.07
❑	383	Russ Ortiz	.20	.07
❑	384	Toby Hall	.20	.07
❑	385	Bill Hall	.20	.07
❑	386	Luke Hudson	.20	.07
❑	387	Ken Griffey Jr.	.75	.30
❑	388	Tim Hudson	.20	.07
❑	389	Brian Moehler	.20	.07
❑	390	Jake Peavy	.20	.07
❑	391	Casey Blake	.20	.07
❑	392	Sidney Ponson	.20	.07
❑	393	Brian Schneider	.20	.07
❑	394	J.J. Hardy	.20	.07
❑	395	Austin Kearns	.20	.07
❑	396	Pat Burrell	.20	.07
❑	397	Jason Vargas	.20	.07
❑	398	Ryan Howard	.75	.30
❑	399	Joe Crede	.20	.07
❑	400	Vladimir Guerrero	.50	.20
❑	401	Roy Halladay	.20	.07
❑	402	David Dellucci	.20	.07
❑	403	Brandon Webb	.20	.07
❑	404	Marlon Anderson	.20	.07
❑	405	Miguel Tejada	.20	.07
❑	406	Ryan Doumit	.20	.07
❑	407	Kevin Youkilis	.20	.07
❑	408	Jon Lieber	.20	.07
❑	409	Edwin Encarnacion	.20	.07
❑	410	Miguel Cabrera	.30	.10
❑	411	A.J. Burnett	.20	.07
❑	412	David Bell	.20	.07
❑	413	Gregg Zaun	.20	.07
❑	414	Lance Niekro	.20	.07
❑	415	Shawn Green	.20	.07
❑	416	Roberto Hernandez	.20	.07
❑	417	Jay Gibbons	.20	.07
❑	418	Johnny Estrada	.20	.07
❑	419	Omar Vizquel	.30	.10
❑	420	Gary Sheffield	.20	.07
❑	421	Brad Halsey	.20	.07
❑	422	Aaron Cook	.20	.07
❑	423	David Ortiz	.50	.20
❑	424	Tony Womack	.20	.07
❑	425	Joe Kennedy	.20	.07
❑	426	Dustin McGowan	.20	.07
❑	427	Carl Pavano	.20	.07
❑	428	Nick Green	.20	.07
❑	429	Francisco Cordero	.20	.07
❑	430	Octavio Dotel	.20	.07
❑	431	Julio Franco	.20	.07
❑	432	Brett Myers	.20	.07
❑	433	Casey Kotchman	.20	.07
❑	434	Frank Catalanotto	.20	.07
❑	435	Paul Konerko	.20	.07
❑	436	Keith Foulke	.20	.07
❑	437	Juan Rivera	.20	.07
❑	438	Todd Pratt	.20	.07
❑	439	Ben Broussard	.20	.07
❑	440	Scott Kazmir	.30	.10
❑	441	Rich Aurilia	.20	.07
❑	442	Craig Monroe	.20	.07
❑	443	Danny Kolb	.20	.07
❑	444	Curtis Granderson	.20	.07
❑	445	Jeff Francoeur	.50	.20
❑	446	Dustin Hermanson	.20	.07
❑	447	Jacque Jones	.20	.07
❑	448	Bobby Crosby	.20	.07
❑	449	Jason LaRue	.20	.07
❑	450	Derrek Lee	.20	.07
❑	451	Curt Schilling	.30	.10
❑	452	Jake Westbrook	.20	.07
❑	453	Daniel Cabrera	.20	.07
❑	454	Bobby Jenks	.20	.07
❑	455	Dontrelle Willis	.20	.07
❑	456	Brad Lidge	.20	.07
❑	457	Shea Hillenbrand	.20	.07
❑	458	Luis Castillo	.20	.07
❑	459	Mark Hendrickson	.20	.07
❑	460	Randy Johnson	.50	.20
❑	461	Placido Polanco	.20	.07
❑	462	Aaron Boone	.20	.07
❑	463	Todd Walker	.20	.07
❑	464	Nick Swisher	.20	.07
❑	465	Joel Pineiro	.20	.07
❑	466	Jay Payton	.20	.07
❑	467	Cliff Lee	.20	.07
❑	468	Johan Santana	.30	.10
❑	469	Josh Willingham	.20	.07
❑	470	Jeremy Bonderman	.20	.07
❑	471	Runelvys Hernandez	.20	.07
❑	472	Duaner Sanchez	.20	.07
❑	473	Jason Lane	.20	.07
❑	474	Trot Nixon	.20	.07
❑	475	Ramon Hernandez	.20	.07
❑	476	Mike Lowell	.20	.07
❑	477	Chan Ho Park	.20	.07
❑	478	Doug Waechter	.20	.07
❑	479	Carlos Silva	.20	.07
❑	480	Jose Contreras	.20	.07
❑	481	Vinny Castilla	.20	.07
❑	482	Chris Reitsma	.20	.07
❑	483	Jose Guillen	.20	.07
❑	484	Aaron Hill	.20	.07
❑	485	Kevin Millwood	.20	.07
❑	486	Wily Mo Pena	.20	.07
❑	487	Rich Harden	.20	.07
❑	488	Chris Carpenter	.20	.07
❑	489	Jason Bartlett	.20	.07
❑	490	Magglio Ordonez	.20	.07
❑	491	John Rodriguez	.20	.07
❑	492	Bob Wickman	.20	.07
❑	493	Eddie Guardado	.20	.07
❑	494	Kip Wells	.20	.07
❑	495	Adrian Beltre	.20	.07
❑	496	Jose Capellan (RC)	.50	.20
❑	497	Scott Podsednik	.20	.07
❑	498	Brad Thompson	.20	.07
❑	499	Aaron Heilman	.20	.07
❑	500	Derek Jeter	1.25	.50
❑	501	Emil Brown	.20	.07
❑	502	Morgan Ensberg	.20	.07
❑	503	Nate Bump	.20	.07
❑	504	Phil Nevin	.20	.07
❑	505	Jason Schmidt	.20	.07
❑	506	Michael Cuddyer	.20	.07
❑	507	John Patterson	.20	.07
❑	508	Danny Haren	.20	.07
❑	509	Freddy Sanchez	.20	.07
❑	510	J.D. Drew	.20	.07
❑	511	Dmitri Young	.20	.07
❑	512	Eric Milton	.20	.07
❑	513	Ervin Santana	.20	.07
❑	514	Mark Loretta	.20	.07
❑	515	Mark Grudzielanek	.20	.07
❑	516	Derrick Turnbow	.20	.07
❑	517	Denny Bautista	.20	.07
❑	518	Lyle Overbay	.20	.07
❑	519	Julio Lugo	.20	.07
❑	520	Carlos Beltran	.20	.07
❑	521	Jose Cruz Jr.	.20	.07
❑	522	Jason Isringhausen	.20	.07
❑	523	Bronson Arroyo	.20	.07
❑	524	Ben Sheets	.20	.07
❑	525	Zach Duke	.20	.07
❑	526	Ryan Wagner	.20	.07
❑	527	Jose Vidro	.20	.07
❑	528	Doug Mirabelli	.20	.07
❑	529	Kris Benson	.20	.07
❑	530	Carlos Guillen	.20	.07
❑	531	Juan Pierre	.20	.07
❑	532	Scot Shields	.20	.07
❑	533	Scott Hatteberg	.20	.07
❑	534	Tim Stauffer	.20	.07
❑	535	Jim Edmonds	.30	.10
❑	536	Scot Eyre	.20	.07
❑	537	Ben Johnson	.20	.07
❑	538	Mark Mulder	.20	.07
❑	539	Juan Rincon	.20	.07
❑	540	Gustavo Chacin	.20	.07
❑	541	Oliver Perez	.20	.07
❑	542	Chris Young	.20	.07
❑	543	Edinson Volquez	.20	.07
❑	544	Mark Bellhorn	.20	.07
❑	545	Kelvim Escobar	.20	.07
❑	546	Andy Sisco	.20	.07
❑	547	Derek Lowe	.20	.07
❑	548	Sean Burroughs	.20	.07
❑	549	Erik Bedard	.20	.07
❑	550	Alfonso Soriano	.20	.07
❑	551	Matt Murton	.20	.07
❑	552	Eric Byrnes	.20	.07
❑	553	Chris Duffy	.20	.07
❑	554	Kazuo Matsui	.20	.07
❑	555	Scott Rolen	.30	.10
❑	556	Rob Mackowiak	.20	.07
❑	557	Chris Burke	.20	.07
❑	558	Jeromy Burnitz	.20	.07
❑	559	Jerry Hairston Jr.	.20	.07
❑	560	Jim Thome	.30	.10
❑	561	Miguel Olivo	.20	.07
❑	562	Jose Castillo	.20	.07
❑	563	Brad Ausmus	.20	.07
❑	564	Yorvit Torrealba	.20	.07
❑	565	David DeJesus	.20	.07
❑	566	Paul Byrd	.20	.07
❑	567	Brandon Backe	.20	.07
❑	568	Aubrey Huff	.20	.07
❑	569	Mike Jacobs	.20	.07
❑	570	Todd Helton	.30	.10
❑	571	Angel Berroa	.20	.07
❑	572	Todd Jones	.20	.07
❑	573	Jeff Bagwell	.30	.10
❑	574	Darin Erstad	.20	.07
❑	575	Roy Oswalt	.20	.07
❑	576	Rondell White	.20	.07
❑	577	Alex Rios	.20	.07
❑	578	Wes Helms	.20	.07
❑	579	Javier Vazquez	.20	.07
❑	580	Frank Thomas	.50	.20
❑	581	Brian Fuentes	.20	.07
❑	582	Francisco Rodriguez	.20	.07
❑	583	Craig Counsell	.20	.07

❑ 584 Jorge Sosa .20 .07
❑ 585 Mike Piazza .50 .20
❑ 586 Mike Scioscia MG .20 .07
❑ 587 Joe Torre MG .30 .10
❑ 588 Ken Macha MG .20 .07
❑ 589 John Gibbons MG .20 .07
❑ 590 Joe Maddon MG .20 .07
❑ 591 Eric Wedge MG .20 .07
❑ 592 Mike Hargrove MG .20 .07
❑ 593 Sam Perlozzo MG .20 .07
❑ 594 Buck Showalter MG .20 .07
❑ 595 Terry Francona MG .20 .07
❑ 596 Buddy Bell MG .20 .07
❑ 597 Jim Leyland MG .20 .07
❑ 598 Ron Gardenhire MG .20 .07
❑ 599 Ozzie Guillen MG .20 .07
❑ 600 Ned Yost MG .20 .07
❑ 601 Atlanta Braves TC .30 .10
❑ 602 Philadelphia Phillies TC .20 .07
❑ 603 New York Mets TC .20 .07
❑ 604 Washington Nationals TC .20 .07
❑ 605 Florida Marlins TC .20 .07
❑ 606 Houston Astros TC .20 .07
❑ 607 Chicago Cubs TC .30 .10
❑ 608 St. Louis Cardinals TC .30 .10
❑ 609 Pittsburgh Pirates TC .20 .07
❑ 610 Cincinnati Reds TC .20 .07
❑ 611 Colorado Rockies TC .20 .07
❑ 612 Los Angeles Dodgers TC .20 .07
❑ 613 San Francisco Giants TC .20 .07
❑ 614 San Diego Padres TC .20 .07
❑ 615 Arizona Diamondbacks TC .20 .07
❑ 616 Kenji Johjima RC 2.00 .75
❑ 617 Ryan Zimmerman (RC) 2.50 1.00
❑ 618 Craig Hansen RC 1.50 .60
❑ 619 Joey Devine RC .50 .20
❑ 620 Hanley Ramirez (RC) .60 .25
❑ 621 Scott Olsen (RC) .50 .20
❑ 622 Jason Bergmann RC .50 .20
❑ 623 Geovany Soto (RC) .50 .20
❑ 624 J.J. Furmaniak (RC) .50 .20
❑ 625 Jeremy Accardo RC .50 .20
❑ 626 Mark Woodyard (RC) .50 .20
❑ 627 Matt Capps (RC) .50 .20
❑ 628 Tim Corcoran RC .50 .20
❑ 629 Ryan Jorgensen RC .50 .20
❑ 630 Ronny Paulino (RC) .50 .20
❑ 631 Dan Uggla (RC) 1.00 .40
❑ 632 Ian Kinsler (RC) .60 .25
❑ 633 Josh Barfield (RC) .50 .20
❑ 634 Reggie Abercrombie (RC) .50 .20
❑ 635 Joel Zumaya (RC) 1.25 .50
❑ 636 Matt Cain (RC) .75 .30
❑ 637 Conor Jackson (RC) .75 .30
❑ 638 Brian Anderson (RC) .50 .20
❑ 639 Prince Fielder (RC) 1.50 .60
❑ 640 Jeremy Hermida (RC) .75 .30
❑ 641 Justin Verlander (RC) 1.50 .60
❑ 642 Brian Bannister (RC) .50 .20
❑ 643 Willie Eyre (RC) .50 .20
❑ 644 Ricky Nolasco (RC) .50 .20
❑ 645 Paul Maholm (RC) .50 .20
❑ 646 J.Damon/J.Giambi .30 .10
❑ 647 R.White/L.Ford .20 .07
❑ 648 O.Hernandez/O.Hudson .20 .07
❑ 649 A.Dunn/K.Griffey Jr. .75 .30
❑ 650 P.Burrell/M.Lieberthal .20 .07
❑ 651 J.Reyes/K.Matsui .20 .07
❑ 652 H.Blalock/M.Young .20 .07
❑ 653 P.Fielder/R.Weeks .75 .30
❑ 654 T.Lee/R.Baldelli .20 .07
❑ 655 D.Lee/A.Ramirez .20 .07
❑ 656 G.Sizemore/A.Boone .30 .10
❑ 657 Gonzalez/Green/Hill .20 .07
❑ 658 I.Rodriguez/C.Guillen .30 .10
❑ 659 A.Rodriguez/G.Sheffield .75 .30
❑ 660 E.Santana/F.Rodriguez .20 .07
❑ RC1 Alay Soler 60.00 30.00
❑ NNO 2 Tickets EXCH 20.00 8.00

2006 Topps Update

❑ COMPLETE SET (330) 50.00 20.00
❑ COMMON CARD (1-132) .20 .07
❑ SEMISTARS 1-132 .30 .12
❑ UNLISTED STARS 1-132 .50 .20
❑ COMMON ROOKIE (133-170) .50 .20

❑ RC SEMIS 133-170 .75 .30
❑ RC UNLISTED 133-170 1.25 .50
❑ COMMON CARD (171-330) .30 .12
❑ SEMISTARS 171-330 .50 .20
❑ UNLISTED STARS 171-330 .75 .30
❑ 1-330 PLATE ODDS 1:85 HTA
❑ PLATE PRINT RUN 1 SET PER COLOR
❑ BLACK-CYAN-MAGENTA-YELLOW ISSUED
❑ NO PLATE PRICING DUE TO SCARCITY
❑ 1 Austin Kearns .20 .07
❑ 2 Adam Eaton .20 .07
❑ 3 Juan Encarnacion .20 .07
❑ 4 Jarrod Washburn .20 .07
❑ 5 Alex Gonzalez .20 .07
❑ 6 Toby Hall .20 .07
❑ 7 Preston Wilson .20 .07
❑ 8 Ramon Ortiz .20 .07
❑ 9 Jason Michaels .20 .07
❑ 10 Jeff Weaver .20 .07
❑ 11 Russell Branyan .20 .07
❑ 12 Brett Tomko .20 .07
❑ 13 Doug Mientkiewicz .20 .07
❑ 14 David Wells .20 .07
❑ 15 Corey Koskie .20 .07
❑ 16 Russ Ortiz .20 .07
❑ 17 Carlos Pena .20 .07
❑ 18 Mark Hendrickson .20 .07
❑ 19 Julian Tavarez .20 .07
❑ 20 Jeff Conine .20 .07
❑ 21 Dioner Navarro .20 .07
❑ 22 Bob Wickman .20 .07
❑ 23 Felipe Lopez .20 .07
❑ 24 Eddie Guardado .20 .07
❑ 25 David Dellucci .20 .07
❑ 26 Ryan Wagner .20 .07
❑ 27 Nick Green .20 .07
❑ 28 Gary Majewski .20 .07
❑ 29 Shea Hillenbrand .20 .07
❑ 30 Jae Seo .20 .07
❑ 31 Royce Clayton .20 .07
❑ 32 Dave Riske .20 .07
❑ 33 Joey Gathright .20 .07
❑ 34 Robinson Tejada .20 .07
❑ 35 Edwin Jackson .20 .07
❑ 36 Aubrey Huff .20 .07
❑ 37 Akinori Otsuka .20 .07
❑ 38 Juan Castro .20 .07
❑ 39 Zach Day .20 .07
❑ 40 Jeremy Accardo .20 .07
❑ 41 Shawn Green .20 .07
❑ 42 Kazuo Matsui .20 .07
❑ 43 J.J. Putz .20 .07
❑ 44 David Ross .20 .07
❑ 45 Scott Williamson .20 .07
❑ 46 Joe Borchard .20 .07
❑ 47 Elmer Dessens .20 .07
❑ 48 Odalis Perez .20 .07
❑ 49 Kelly Shoppach .20 .07
❑ 50 Brandon Phillips .20 .07
❑ 51 Guillermo Mota .20 .07
❑ 52 Alex Cintron .20 .07
❑ 53 Denny Bautista .20 .07
❑ 54 Josh Bard .20 .07
❑ 55 Julio Lugo .20 .07
❑ 56 Doug Mirabelli .20 .07
❑ 57 Kip Wells .20 .07
❑ 58 Adrian Gonzalez .20 .07
❑ 59 Shawn Chacon .20 .07
❑ 60 Marcus Thames .20 .07
❑ 61 Craig Wilson .20 .07
❑ 62 Cory Sullivan .20 .07
❑ 63 Ben Broussard .20 .07
❑ 64 Todd Walker .20 .07
❑ 65 Greg Maddux .75 .30
❑ 66 Xavier Nady .20 .07
❑ 67 Oliver Perez .20 .07
❑ 68 Sean Casey .20 .07
❑ 69 Kyle Lohse .20 .07
❑ 70 Carlos Lee .20 .07
❑ 71 Rheal Cormier .20 .07
❑ 72 Ronnie Belliard .20 .07
❑ 73 Cory Lidle 4.00 1.50
❑ 74 David Bell .20 .07
❑ 75 Wilson Betemit .20 .07
❑ 76 Danys Baez .20 .07
❑ 77 Mike Stanton .20 .07
❑ 78 Kevin Mench .20 .07
❑ 79 Sandy Alomar Jr. .20 .07
❑ 80 Cesar Izturis .20 .07
❑ 81 Jeremy Affeldt .20 .07
❑ 82 Matt Stairs .20 .07
❑ 83 Hector Luna .20 .07
❑ 84 Tony Graffanino .20 .07
❑ 85 J.P Howell .20 .07
❑ 86 Bengie Molina .20 .07
❑ 87 Maicer Izturis .20 .07
❑ 88 Marco Scutaro .20 .07
❑ 89 Daryle Ward .20 .07
❑ 90 Sal Fasano .20 .07
❑ 91 Oscar Villarreal .20 .07
❑ 92 Gabe Gross .20 .07
❑ 93 Phil Nevin .20 .07
❑ 94 Damon Hollins .20 .07
❑ 95 Juan Cruz .20 .07
❑ 96 Marlon Anderson .20 .07
❑ 97 Jason Davis .20 .07
❑ 98 Ryan Shealy .20 .07
❑ 99 Francisco Cordero .20 .07
❑ 100 Bobby Abreu .20 .07
❑ 101 Roberto Hernandez .20 .07
❑ 102 Gary Bennett .20 .07
❑ 103 Aaron Sele .20 .07
❑ 104 Nook Logan .20 .07
❑ 105 Alfredo Amezaga .20 .07
❑ 106 Chris Woodward .20 .07
❑ 107 Kevin Jarvis .20 .07
❑ 108 B.J. Upton .20 .07
❑ 109 Alan Embree .20 .07
❑ 110 Milton Bradley .20 .07
❑ 111 Pete Orr .20 .07
❑ 112 Jeff Cirillo .20 .07
❑ 113 Corey Patterson .20 .07
❑ 114 Josh Paul .20 .07
❑ 115 Fernando Rodney .20 .07
❑ 116 Jerry Hairston Jr. .20 .07
❑ 117 Scott Proctor .20 .07
❑ 118 Ambiorix Burgos .20 .07
❑ 119 Jose Bautista .20 .07
❑ 120 Livan Hernandez .20 .07
❑ 121 John Mcdonald .20 .07
❑ 122 Ronny Cedeno .20 .07
❑ 123 Nate Robertson .20 .07
❑ 124 Jamey Carroll .20 .07
❑ 125 Alex Escobar .20 .07
❑ 126 Endy Chavez .20 .07
❑ 127 Jorge Julio .20 .07
❑ 128 Kenny Lofton .20 .07
❑ 129 Matt Diaz .20 .07
❑ 130 Dave Bush .20 .07
❑ 131 Jose Molina .20 .07
❑ 132 Mike MacDougal .20 .07
❑ 133 Ben Zobrist (RC) .75 .30
❑ 134 Shane Komine RC .75 .30
❑ 135 Casey Janssen RC .75 .30
❑ 136 Kevin Frandsen (RC) .75 .30
❑ 137 John Rheinecker (RC) .50 .20
❑ 138 Matt Kemp (RC) .75 .30
❑ 139 Scott Mathieson (RC) .50 .20
❑ 140 Jered Weaver (RC) 2.50 1.00
❑ 141 Joel Guzman (RC) .50 .20
❑ 142 Anibal Sanchez (RC) .75 .30
❑ 143 Melky Cabrera (RC) .75 .30
❑ 144 Howie Kendrick (RC) 2.50 1.00
❑ 145 Cole Hamels (RC) 1.25 .50

❑ 146 Willy Aybar (RC) .50 .20
❑ 147 Jamie Shields RC .50 .20
❑ 148 Kevin Thompson (RC) .50 .20
❑ 149 Jon Lester RC 1.50 .60
❑ 150 Stephen Drew (RC) 1.25 .50
❑ 151 Andre Ethier (RC) 1.25 .50
❑ 152 Jordan Tata RC .50 .20
❑ 153 Mike Napoli RC 1.25 .50
❑ 154 Kason Gabbard (RC) .50 .20
❑ 155 Lastings Milledge (RC) .75 .30
❑ 156 Erick Aybar (RC) .50 .20
❑ 157 Fausto Carmona (RC) .50 .20
❑ 158 Russ Martin (RC) .75 .30
❑ 159 David Pauley (RC) .50 .20
❑ 160 Andy Marte (RC) .50 .20
❑ 161 Carlos Quentin (RC) .75 .30
❑ 162 Franklin Gutierrez (RC) .50 .20
❑ 163 Taylor Buchholz (RC) .75 .30
❑ 164 Josh Johnson (RC) .75 .30
❑ 165 Chad Billingsley (RC) .75 .30
❑ 166 Kendry Morales (RC) 1.25 .50
❑ 167 Adam Loewen (RC) .75 .30
❑ 168 Yusmeiro Petit (RC) .50 .20
❑ 169 Matt Albers (RC) .50 .20
❑ 170 John Maine (RC) .75 .30
❑ 171 Alex Rodriguez SH 1.25 .50
❑ 172 Mike Piazza SH .75 .30
❑ 173 Cory Sullivan SH .30 .12
❑ 174 Anibal Sanchez SH .30 .12
❑ 175 Trevor Hoffman SH .30 .12
❑ 176 Barry Bonds SH 1.50 .60
❑ 177 Derek Jeter SH 2.00 .75
❑ 178 Jose Reyes SH .75 .30
❑ 179 Manny Ramirez SH .50 .20
❑ 180 Vladimir Guerrero SH .75 .30
❑ 181 Mariano Rivera SH .75 .30
❑ 182 Mark Kotsay PH .30 .12
❑ 183 Derek Jeter PH 2.00 .75
❑ 184 Carlos Delgado PH .30 .12
❑ 185 Frank Thomas PH .75 .30
❑ 186 Albert Pujols PH 1.50 .60
❑ 187 Magglio Ordonez PH .30 .12
❑ 188 Carlos Delgado PH .30 .12
❑ 189 Kenny Rogers PH .30 .12
❑ 190 Tom Glavine PH .50 .20
❑ 191 P.Polanco/J.Suppan PH .30 .12
❑ 192 Jose Reyes PH .75 .30
❑ 193 E.Chavez/Y.Molina PH .30 .12
❑ 194 Craig Monroe PH .30 .12
❑ 195 J.Verlander/J.Zumaya PH 1.25 .50
❑ 196 P.LoDuca/C.Beltran PH .30 .12
❑ 197 A.Pujols/J.Edmonds/S.Rolen PH 1.50 .60
❑ 198 Anthony Reyes PH .30 .12
❑ 199 Chris Carpenter PH .30 .12
❑ 200 David Eckstein PH .30 .12
❑ 201 Jered Weaver PH 1.50 .60
❑ 202 D.Ortiz/J.Dye/T.Hafner LL .75 .30
❑ 203 J.Mauer/D.Jeter/R.Cano LL 2.00 .75
❑ 204 D.Ortiz/J.Morneau/R.Ibanez LL .75 .30
❑ 205 Crawford/Figgins/Ichiro LL 1.25 .50
❑ 206 J.Santana/C.Wang/J.Garland LL 1.25 .50
❑ 207 J.Santana/R.Halladay/C.Sabathia LL .50 .20
❑ 208 J.Santana/J.Bonderman
J.Lackey LL .50 .20
❑ 209 F.Rodriguez/B.Jenks/B.Ryan LL .30 .12
❑ 210 R.Howard/A.Pujols/A.Soriano LL 1.50 .60
❑ 211 Sanch./Cabrera/Pujols LL 1.50 .60
❑ 212 Howard/Pujols/Berk.LL 1.50 .60
❑ 213 J.Reyes/J.Pierre/H.Ramirez LL .75 .30
❑ 214 D.Lowe/B.Webb/C.Zambrano LL .30 .12
❑ 215 R.Oswalt/C.Carpenter/B.Webb LL .30 .12
❑ 216 A.Harang/J.Peavy/J.Smoltz LL .50 .20
❑ 217 T.Hoffman/B.Wagner/J.Borowski LL .30 .12
❑ 218 Ichiro Suzuki AS 1.25 .50
❑ 219 Derek Jeter AS 2.00 .75
❑ 220 Alex Rodriguez AS 1.25 .50
❑ 221 David Ortiz AS .75 .30
❑ 222 Vladimir Guerrero AS .75 .30
❑ 223 Ivan Rodriguez AS .50 .20
❑ 224 Vernon Wells AS .30 .12
❑ 225 Mark Loretta AS .30 .12
❑ 226 Kenny Rogers AS .30 .12
❑ 227 Alfonso Soriano AS .30 .12
❑ 228 Carlos Beltran AS .30 .12
❑ 229 Albert Pujols AS 1.50 .60
❑ 230 Jason Bay AS .30 .12
❑ 231 Edgar Renteria AS .30 .12
❑ 232 David Wright AS 1.25 .50
❑ 233 Chase Utley AS .75 .30
❑ 234 Paul LoDuca AS .30 .12
❑ 235 Brad Penny AS .30 .12
❑ 236 Derrick Turnbow AS .30 .12
❑ 237 Mark Redman AS .30 .12
❑ 238 Francisco Liriano AS .75 .30
❑ 239 A.J. Pierzynski AS .30 .12
❑ 240 Grady Sizemore AS .50 .20
❑ 241 Jose Contreras AS .30 .12
❑ 242 Jermaine Dye AS .30 .12
❑ 243 Jason Schmidt AS .30 .12
❑ 244 Nomar Garciaparra AS .75 .30
❑ 245 Scott Kazmir AS .50 .20
❑ 246 Johan Santana AS .50 .20
❑ 247 Chris Capuano AS .30 .12
❑ 248 Magglio Ordonez AS .30 .12
❑ 249 Gary Matthews Jr. AS .30 .12
❑ 250 Carlos Lee AS .30 .12
❑ 251 David Eckstein AS .30 .12
❑ 252 Michael Young AS .30 .12
❑ 253 Matt Holliday AS .75 .30
❑ 254 Lance Berkman AS .30 .12
❑ 255 Scott Rolen AS .50 .20
❑ 256 Bronson Arroyo AS .30 .12
❑ 257 Barry Zito AS .30 .12
❑ 258 Brian McCann AS .30 .12
❑ 259 Jose Lopez AS .30 .12
❑ 260 Chris Carpenter AS .30 .12
❑ 261 Roy Halladay AS .30 .12
❑ 262 Jim Thome AS .50 .20
❑ 263 Dan Uggla AS .75 .30
❑ 264 Mariano Rivera AS .75 .30
❑ 265 Roy Oswalt AS .30 .12
❑ 266 Tom Gordon AS .30 .12
❑ 267 Troy Glaus AS .30 .12
❑ 268 Bobby Jenks AS .30 .12
❑ 269 Freddy Sanchez AS .30 .12
❑ 270 Paul Konerko AS .30 .12
❑ 271 Joe Mauer AS .50 .20
❑ 272 B.J. Ryan AS .30 .12
❑ 273 Ryan Howard AS 1.25 .50
❑ 274 Brian Fuentes AS .30 .12
❑ 275 Miguel Cabrera AS .50 .20
❑ 276 Brandon Webb AS .30 .12
❑ 277 Mark Buehrle AS .30 .12
❑ 278 Trevor Hoffman AS .30 .12
❑ 279 Jonathan Papelbon AS 1.50 .60
❑ 280 Andruw Jones AS .50 .20
❑ 281 Miguel Tejada AS .30 .12
❑ 282 Carlos Zambrano AS .30 .12
❑ 283 Ryan Howard HRD 1.25 .50
❑ 284 David Wright HRD 1.25 .50
❑ 285 Miguel Cabrera HRD .50 .20
❑ 286 David Ortiz HRD .75 .30
❑ 287 Jermaine Dye HRD .30 .12
❑ 288 Miguel Tejada HRD .30 .12
❑ 289 Lance Berkman HRD .30 .12
❑ 290 Troy Glaus HRD .30 .12
❑ 291 D.Wright/T.Glavine TL 1.25 .50
❑ 292 R.Howard/T.Gordon TL 1.25 .50
❑ 293 M.Cabrera/D.Willis TL .50 .20
❑ 294 A.Jones/J.Smoltz TL .50 .20
❑ 295 A.Soriano/A.Soriano TL .30 .12
❑ 296 A.Pujols/C.Carpenter TL 1.50 .60
❑ 297 A.Dunn/B.Arroyo TL .30 .12
❑ 298 L.Berkman/R.Oswalt TL .30 .12
❑ 299 C.Capuano/P.Fielder TL 1.25 .50
❑ 300 F.Sanchez/J.Bay TL .30 .12
❑ 301 C.Zambrano/J.Pierre TL .30 .12
❑ 302 A.Gonzalez/T.Hoffman TL .30 .12
❑ 303 D.Lowe/R.Furcal TL .30 .12
❑ 304 O.Vizquel/J.Schmidt TL .50 .20
❑ 305 B.Webb/C.Tracy TL .30 .12
❑ 306 M.Holliday/G.Atkins TL .75 .30
❑ 307 A.Rodriguez/C.Wang TL 1.25 .50
❑ 308 C.Schilling/D.Ortiz TL .75 .30
❑ 309 R.Halladay/V.Wells TL .30 .12
❑ 310 M.Tejada/E.Bedard TL .30 .12
❑ 311 C.Crawford/S.Kazmir TL .50 .20
❑ 312 J.Bonderman/M.Ordonez TL .30 .12
❑ 313 J.Morneau/J.Santana TL .50 .20
❑ 314 J.Garland/J.Dye TL .30 .12
❑ 315 T.Hafner/C.Sabathia TL .30 .12
❑ 316 E.Brown/M.Grudzielanek TL .30 .12
❑ 317 F.Thomas/B.Zito TL .75 .30
❑ 318 J.Weaver/V.Guerrero TL 1.50 .60
❑ 319 M.Young/G.Matthews TL .30 .12
❑ 320 I.Suzuki/J.Putz TL 1.25 .50
❑ 321 D.Jeter/R.Cano CD 2.00 .75
❑ 322 C.Carpenter/M.Mulder CD .30 .12
❑ 323 J.Schmidt/T.Hoffman CD .30 .12
❑ 324 D.Wright/P.LoDuca CD 1.25 .50
❑ 325 L.Berkman/R.Oswalt CD .30 .12
❑ 326 D.Jeter/J.Reyes CD .75 .30
❑ 327 C.Floyd/D.Wright CD 1.25 .50
❑ 328 F.Liriano/J.Santana CD .75 .30
❑ 329 J.Drew/S.Drew CD .75 .30
❑ 330 J.Weaver/J.Weaver CD 1.50 .60

2007 Topps

❑ COMP.HOBBY SET (661) 80.00 40.00
❑ COMP.CARDINALS SET (661) 80.00 40.00
❑ COMP.CUBS SET (661) 80.00 40.00
❑ COMP.DODGERS SET (661) 80.00 40.00
❑ COMP.RED SOX SET (661) 80.00 40.00
❑ COMP.YANKEES SET (661) 80.00 40.00
❑ COMP.SET w/o VAR. (661) 100.00 50.00
❑ COMPLETE SERIES 1 (330) 40.00 15.00
❑ COMP.SERIES 1 w/o #40 (329) 25.00 10.00
❑ COMPLETE SERIES 2 (331) 50.00 25.00
❑ COMMON CARD (1-330) .20 .07
❑ COMMON RC .50 .20
❑ SER.1 VAR. ODDS 1:3700 WAL-MART
❑ SER.2 VAR.ODDS 1:30 HOBBY
❑ NO SER.1 VAR.PRICING DUE TO SCARTIY
❑ OVERALL PLATE SER.1 ODDS 1:98 HTA
❑ OVERALL PLATE SER.2 ODDS 1:139 HTA
❑ PLATE PRINT RUN 1 SET PER COLOR
❑ BLACK-CYAN-MAGENTA-YELLOW ISSUED
❑ NO PLATE PRICING DUE TO SCARCITY
❑ 1 John Lackey .20 .07
❑ 2 Nick Swisher .20 .07
❑ 3 Brad Lidge .20 .07
❑ 4 Bengie Molina .20 .07
❑ 5 Bobby Abreu .20 .07
❑ 6 Edgar Renteria .20 .07
❑ 7 Mickey Mantle 4.00 1.50
❑ 8 Preston Wilson .20 .07
❑ 9 Ryan Dempster .20 .07
❑ 10 C.C. Sabathia .20 .07
❑ 11 Julio Lugo .20 .07
❑ 12 J.D. Drew .20 .07
❑ 13 Miguel Batista .20 .07
❑ 14 Eliezer Alfonzo .20 .07
❑ 15a Andrew Miller RC 3.00 1.25
❑ 15b A.Miller Posed RC 3.00 1.25
❑ 16 Jason Varitek .50 .20
❑ 17 Saul Rivera .20 .07
❑ 18 Orlando Hernandez .20 .07
❑ 19 Alfredo Amezaga .20 .07
❑ 20a D.Young Face Right (RC) 1.25 .50
❑ 20b D.Young Face Left (RC) 1.25 .50
❑ 21 Chris Britton .20 .07
❑ 22 Corey Patterson .20 .07
❑ 23 Josh Bard .20 .07
❑ 24 Tom Gordon .20 .07
❑ 25 Gary Matthews .20 .07
❑ 26 Jason Jennings .20 .07
❑ 27 Joey Gathright .20 .07
❑ 28 Brandon Inge .20 .07
❑ 29 Pat Neshek .75 .30
❑ 30 Bronson Arroyo .20 .07

❑ 31 Jay Payton	.20	.07
❑ 32 Andy Pettitte	.30	.12
❑ 33 Ervin Santana	.20	.07
❑ 34 Paul Konerko	.20	.07
❑ 35 Joel Zumaya	.30	.12
❑ 36 Gregg Zaun	.20	.07
❑ 37 Tony Gwynn Jr.	.20	.07
❑ 38 Adam LaRoche	.20	.07
❑ 39 Jim Edmonds	.30	.12
❑ 40 D.Jeter w Mantle/Bush	15.00	6.00
❑ 41 Rich Hill	.20	.07
❑ 42 Livan Hernandez	.20	.07
❑ 43 Aubrey Huff	.20	.07
❑ 44 Todd Greene	.20	.07
❑ 45 Andre Ethier	.30	.12
❑ 46 Jeremy Sowers	.20	.07
❑ 47 Ben Broussard	.20	.07
❑ 48 Darren Oliver	.20	.07
❑ 49 Nook Logan	.20	.07
❑ 50 Miguel Cabrera	.30	.12
❑ 51 Carlos Lee	.20	.07
❑ 52 Jose Castillo	.20	.07
❑ 53 Mike Piazza	.50	.20
❑ 54 Daniel Cabrera	.20	.07
❑ 55 Cole Hamels	.30	.12
❑ 56 Mark Loretta	.20	.07
❑ 57 Brian Fuentes	.20	.07
❑ 58 Todd Coffey	.20	.07
❑ 59 Brent Clevlen	.20	.07
❑ 60 John Smoltz	.30	.12
❑ 61 Jason Grilli	.20	.07
❑ 62 Dan Wheeler	.20	.07
❑ 63 Scott Proctor	.20	.07
❑ 64 Bobby Kielty	.20	.07
❑ 65 Dan Uggla	.30	.12
❑ 66 Lyle Overbay	.20	.07
❑ 67 Geoff Jenkins	.20	.07
❑ 68 Michael Barrett	.20	.07
❑ 69 Casey Fossum	.20	.07
❑ 70 Ivan Rodriguez	.30	.12
❑ 71 Jose Lopez	.20	.07
❑ 72 Jake Westbrook	.20	.07
❑ 73 Moises Alou	.20	.07
❑ 74 Jose Valverde	.20	.07
❑ 75 Jered Weaver	.30	.12
❑ 76 Lastings Milledge	.30	.12
❑ 77 Austin Kearns	.20	.07
❑ 78 Adam Loewen	.20	.07
❑ 79 Josh Barfield	.20	.07
❑ 80 Johan Santana	.30	.12
❑ 81 Ian Kinsler	.20	.07
❑ 82 Ian Snell	.20	.07
❑ 83 Mike Lowell	.20	.07
❑ 84 Elizardo Ramirez	.20	.07
❑ 85 Scott Rolen	.30	.12
❑ 86 Shannon Stewart	.20	.07
❑ 87 Alexis Gomez	.20	.07
❑ 88 Jimmy Gobble	.20	.07
❑ 89 Jamey Carroll	.20	.07
❑ 90 Chipper Jones	.50	.20
❑ 91 Carlos Silva	.20	.07
❑ 92 Joe Crede	.20	.07
❑ 93 Mike Napoli	.20	.07
❑ 94 Willy Taveras	.20	.07
❑ 95 Rafael Furcal	.20	.07
❑ 96 Phil Nevin	.20	.07
❑ 97 Dave Bush	.20	.07
❑ 98 Marcus Giles	.20	.07
❑ 99 Joe Blanton	.20	.07
❑ 100 Dontrelle Willis	.20	.07
❑ 101 Scott Kazmir	.30	.12
❑ 102 Jeff Kent	.20	.07
❑ 103 Pedro Feliz	.20	.07
❑ 104 Johnny Estrada	.20	.07
❑ 105 Travis Hafner	.20	.07
❑ 106 Ryan Garko	.20	.07
❑ 107 Rafael Soriano	.20	.07
❑ 108 Wes Helms	.20	.07
❑ 109 Billy Wagner	.20	.07
❑ 110 Aaron Rowand	.20	.07
❑ 111 Felipe Lopez	.20	.07
❑ 112 Jeff Conine	.20	.07
❑ 113 Nick Markakis	.30	.12
❑ 114 John Koronka	.20	.07
❑ 115 B.J. Ryan	.20	.07
❑ 116 Tim Wakefield	.20	.07
❑ 117 David Ross	.20	.07
❑ 118 Emil Brown	.20	.07
❑ 119 Michael Cuddyer	.20	.07
❑ 120 Jason Giambi	.20	.07
❑ 121 Alex Cintron	.20	.07
❑ 122 Luke Scott	.20	.07
❑ 123 Chone Figgins	.20	.07
❑ 124 Huston Street	.20	.07
❑ 125 Carlos Delgado	.20	.07
❑ 126 Daryle Ward	.20	.07
❑ 127 Chris Duncan	.20	.07
❑ 128 Damian Miller	.20	.07
❑ 129 Aramis Ramirez	.20	.07
❑ 130 Albert Pujols	1.00	.40
❑ 131 Chris Snyder	.20	.07
❑ 132 Ray Durham	.20	.07
❑ 133 Gary Sheffield	.20	.07
❑ 134 Mike Jacobs	.20	.07
❑ 135a Troy Tulowitzki (RC)	1.25	.50
❑ 135b T.Tulowitzki Throw (RC)	1.25	.50
❑ 136 Jon Rauch	.20	.07
❑ 137 Jay Gibbons	.20	.07
❑ 138 Adrian Gonzalez	.20	.07
❑ 139 Prince Fielder	.50	.20
❑ 140 Freddy Sanchez	.20	.07
❑ 141 Rich Aurilia	.20	.07
❑ 142 Trot Nixon	.20	.07
❑ 143 Vicente Padilla	.20	.07
❑ 144 Jack Wilson	.20	.07
❑ 145 Jake Peavy	.20	.07
❑ 146 Luke Hudson	.20	.07
❑ 147 Javier Vazquez	.20	.07
❑ 148 Scott Podsednik	.20	.07
❑ 149 M.Ordonez/I.Rodriguez CC	.30	.12
❑ 150 Todd Helton	.30	.12
❑ 151 Kendry Morales	.30	.12
❑ 152 Adam Everett	.20	.07
❑ 153 Bob Wickman	.20	.07
❑ 154 Bill Hall	.20	.07
❑ 155 Jeremy Bonderman	.20	.07
❑ 156 Ryan Theriot	.20	.07
❑ 157 Rocco Baldelli	.20	.07
❑ 158 Noah Lowry	.20	.07
❑ 159 Jason Michaels	.20	.07
❑ 160 Justin Verlander	.50	.20
❑ 161 Eduardo Perez	.20	.07
❑ 162 Chris Ray	.20	.07
❑ 163 Dave Roberts	.20	.07
❑ 164 Zach Duke	.20	.07
❑ 165 Mark Buehrle	.20	.07
❑ 166 Hank Blalock	.20	.07
❑ 167 Royce Clayton	.20	.07
❑ 168 Mark Teahen	.20	.07
❑ 169 Todd Jones	.20	.07
❑ 170 Chien-Ming Wang	.75	.30
❑ 171 Nick Punto	.20	.07
❑ 172 Morgan Ensberg	.20	.07
❑ 173 Rob Mackowiak	.20	.07
❑ 174 Frank Catalanotto	.20	.07
❑ 175 Matt Murton	.20	.07
❑ 176 A.Soriano/C.Beltran CC	.20	.07
❑ 177 Francisco Cordero	.20	.07
❑ 178 Jason Marquis	.20	.07
❑ 179 Joe Nathan	.20	.07
❑ 180 Roy Halladay	.20	.07
❑ 181 Melvin Mora	.20	.07
❑ 182 Ramon Ortiz	.20	.07
❑ 183 Jose Valentin	.20	.07
❑ 184 Gil Meche	.20	.07
❑ 185 B.J. Upton	.20	.07
❑ 186 Grady Sizemore	.30	.12
❑ 187 Matt Cain	.30	.12
❑ 188 Eric Byrnes	.20	.07
❑ 189 Carl Crawford	.20	.07
❑ 190 J.J. Putz	.20	.07
❑ 191 Cla Meredith	.20	.07
❑ 192 Matt Capps	.20	.07
❑ 193 Rod Barajas	.20	.07
❑ 194 Edwin Encarnacion	.20	.07
❑ 195 James Loney	.30	.12
❑ 196 Johnny Damon	.30	.12
❑ 197 Freddy Garcia	.20	.07
❑ 198 Mike Redmond	.20	.07
❑ 199 Ryan Shealy	.20	.07
❑ 200 Carlos Beltran	.20	.07
❑ 201 Chuck James	.20	.07
❑ 202 Mark Ellis	.20	.07
❑ 203 Brad Ausmus	.20	.07
❑ 204 Juan Rivera	.20	.07
❑ 205 Cory Sullivan	.20	.07
❑ 206 Ben Sheets	.20	.07
❑ 207 Mark Mulder	.20	.07
❑ 208 Carlos Quentin	.20	.07
❑ 209 Jonathan Broxton	.20	.07
❑ 210 Kazuo Matsui	.20	.07
❑ 211 Armando Benitez	.20	.07
❑ 212 Richie Sexson	.20	.07
❑ 213 Josh Johnson	.20	.07
❑ 214 Brian Schneider	.20	.07
❑ 215 Craig Monroe	.20	.07
❑ 216 Chris Duffy	.20	.07
❑ 217 Chris Coste	.20	.07
❑ 218 Clay Hensley	.20	.07
❑ 219 Chris Gomez	.20	.07
❑ 220 Hideki Matsui	.50	.20
❑ 221 Robinson Tejeda	.20	.07
❑ 222 Scott Hatteberg	.20	.07
❑ 223 Jeff Francis	.20	.07
❑ 224 Matt Thornton	.20	.07
❑ 225 Robinson Cano	.30	.12
❑ 226 Chicago White Sox	.20	.07
❑ 227 Oakland Athletics	.20	.07
❑ 228 St. Louis Cardinals	.20	.07
❑ 229 New York Mets	.20	.07
❑ 230 Barry Zito	.20	.07
❑ 231 Baltimore Orioles	.20	.07
❑ 232 Seattle Mariners	.20	.07
❑ 233 Houston Astros	.20	.07
❑ 234 Pittsburgh Pirates	.20	.07
❑ 235 Reed Johnson	.20	.07
❑ 236 Boston Red Sox	.75	.30
❑ 237 Cincinnati Reds	.20	.07
❑ 238 Philadelphia Phillies	.20	.07
❑ 239 New York Yankees	.50	.20
❑ 240 Chris Carpenter	.20	.07
❑ 241 Atlanta Braves	.30	.12
❑ 242 San Francisco Giants	.20	.07
❑ 243 Joe Torre MG	.30	.12
❑ 244 Tampa Bay Devil Rays	.20	.07
❑ 245 Chad Tracy	.20	.07
❑ 246 Clint Hurdle MG	.20	.07
❑ 247 Mike Scioscia MG	.20	.07
❑ 248 Ron Gardenhire MG	.20	.07
❑ 249 Tony LaRussa MG	.20	.07
❑ 250 Anibal Sanchez	.20	.07
❑ 251 Charlie Manuel MG	.20	.07
❑ 252 John Gibbons MG	.20	.07
❑ 253 Jim Tracy MG	.20	.07
❑ 254 Jerry Narron MG	.20	.07
❑ 255 Brad Penny	.20	.07
❑ 256 Bobby Cox MG	.20	.07
❑ 257 Bob Melvin MG	.20	.07
❑ 258 Mike Hargrove MG	.20	.07
❑ 259 Phil Garner MG	.20	.07
❑ 260 David Wright	.75	.30
❑ 261 Vinny Rottino (RC)	.50	.20
❑ 262 Ryan Braun RC	.50	.20
❑ 263 Kevin Kouzmanoff (RC)	.50	.20
❑ 264 David Murphy (RC)	.50	.20
❑ 265 Jimmy Rollins	.20	.07
❑ 266 Joe Maddon MG	.20	.07
❑ 267 Grady Little MG	.20	.07
❑ 268 Ryan Sweeney (RC)	.50	.20
❑ 269 Fred Lewis (RC)	.50	.20
❑ 270 Alfonso Soriano	.20	.07
❑ 271a Delwyn Young (RC)	.50	.20
❑ 271b D.Young Swing (RC)	.50	.20
❑ 272 Jeff Salazar (RC)	.50	.20
❑ 273 Miguel Montero (RC)	.50	.20
❑ 274 Shawn Riggans (RC)	.50	.20
❑ 275 Greg Maddux	.75	.30
❑ 276 Brian Stokes (RC)	.50	.20
❑ 277 Philip Humber (RC)	.50	.20
❑ 278 Scott Moore (RC)	.50	.20
❑ 279 Adam Lind (RC)	.50	.20
❑ 280 Curt Schilling	.30	.12
❑ 281 Chris Narveson (RC)	.50	.20
❑ 282 Oswaldo Navarro RC	.50	.20
❑ 283 Drew Anderson RC	.50	.20
❑ 284 Jerry Owens (RC)	.50	.20
❑ 285 Stephen Drew	.30	.12
❑ 286 Joaquin Arias (RC)	.50	.20

❑ 287 Jose Garcia RC .50 .20
❑ 288 Shane Youman RC .50 .20
❑ 289 Brian Burres (RC) .50 .20
❑ 290 Matt Holliday .50 .20
❑ 291 Ryan Feierabend (RC) .50 .20
❑ 292a Josh Fields (RC) .50 .20
❑ 292b J.Fields Running (RC) .50 .20
❑ 293 Glen Perkins (RC) .50 .20
❑ 294 Mike Rabelo RC .50 .20
❑ 295 Jorge Posada .30 .12
❑ 296 Ubaldo Jimenez (RC) .50 .20
❑ 297 Brad Ausmus GG .20 .07
❑ 298 Eric Chavez GG .20 .07
❑ 299 Orlando Hudson GG .20 .07
❑ 300 Vladimir Guerrero .50 .20
❑ 301 Derek Jeter GG 1.25 .50
❑ 302 Scott Rolen GG .30 .12
❑ 303 Mark Grudzielanek GG .20 .07
❑ 304 Kenny Rogers GG .20 .07
❑ 305 Frank Thomas .50 .20
❑ 306 Mike Cameron GG .20 .07
❑ 307 Torii Hunter GG .20 .07
❑ 308 Albert Pujols GG 1.00 .40
❑ 309 Mark Teixeira GG .30 .12
❑ 310 Jonathan Papelbon .50 .20
❑ 311 Greg Maddux GG .75 .30
❑ 312 Carlos Beltran GG .20 .07
❑ 313 Ichiro Suzuki GG .75 .30
❑ 314 Andruw Jones GG .30 .12
❑ 315 Manny Ramirez .30 .12
❑ 316 Vernon Wells GG .20 .07
❑ 317 Omar Vizquel GG .30 .12
❑ 318 Ivan Rodriguez GG .30 .12
❑ 319 Brandon Webb CY .20 .07
❑ 320 Magglio Ordonez .20 .07
❑ 321 Johan Santana CY .30 .12
❑ 322 Ryan Howard MVP .75 .30
❑ 323 Justin Morneau MVP .20 .07
❑ 324 Hanley Ramirez ROY .30 .12
❑ 325 Joe Mauer .30 .12
❑ 326 Justin Verlander ROY .50 .20
❑ 327 B.Abreu/D.Jeter CC 1.25 .50
❑ 328 C.Delgado/D.Wright CC .75 .30
❑ 329 Y.Molina/A.Pujols CC 1.00 .40
❑ 330 Ryan Howard .75 .30
❑ 331 Kelly Johnson .20 .07
❑ 332 Chris Young .20 .07
❑ 333 Mark Kotsay .20 .07
❑ 334 A.J. Burnett .20 .07
❑ 335 Brian McCann .20 .07
❑ 336 Woody Williams .20 .07
❑ 337 Jason Isringhausen .20 .07
❑ 338 Juan Pierre .20 .07
❑ 339 Jonny Gomes .20 .07
❑ 340 Roger Clemens 1.00 .40
❑ 341 Akinori Iwamura RC 1.25 .50
❑ 342 Bengie Molina .20 .07
❑ 343 Shin-Soo Choo .30 .12
❑ 344 Kenji Johjima .50 .20
❑ 345 Joe Borowski .20 .07
❑ 346 Shawn Green .20 .07
❑ 347 Chicago Cubs .30 .12
❑ 348 Rodrigo Lopez .20 .07
❑ 349 Brian Giles .20 .07
❑ 350 Chase Utley .50 .20
❑ 351 Mark DeRosa .20 .07
❑ 352 Carl Pavano .20 .07
❑ 353 Kyle Lohse .20 .07
❑ 354 Chris Iannetta .20 .07
❑ 355 Oliver Perez .20 .07
❑ 356 Curtis Granderson .20 .07
❑ 357 Sean Casey .20 .07
❑ 358 Jason Tyner .20 .07
❑ 359 Jon Garland .20 .07
❑ 360 David Ortiz .50 .20
❑ 361 Adam Kennedy .20 .07
❑ 362 Chris Burke .20 .07
❑ 363 Bobby Crosby .20 .07
❑ 364 Conor Jackson .20 .07
❑ 365 Tim Hudson .20 .07
❑ 366 Rickie Weeks .20 .07
❑ 367 Cristian Guzman .20 .07
❑ 368 Mark Prior .30 .12
❑ 369 Ben Zobrist .20 .07
❑ 370 Troy Glaus .20 .07
❑ 371 Kenny Lofton .20 .07
❑ 372 Shane Victorino .20 .07
❑ 373 Cliff Lee .20 .07
❑ 374 Adrian Beltre .20 .07
❑ 375 Miguel Olivo .20 .07
❑ 376 Endy Chavez .20 .07
❑ 377 Zack Segovia (RC) .50 .20
❑ 378 Ramon Hernandez .20 .07
❑ 379 Chris Young .20 .07
❑ 380 Jason Schmidt .20 .07
❑ 381 Ronny Paulino .20 .07
❑ 382 Kevin Millwood .20 .07
❑ 383 Jon Lester .30 .12
❑ 384 Alex Gonzalez .20 .07
❑ 385 Brad Hawpe .20 .07
❑ 386 Placido Polanco .20 .07
❑ 387 Nate Robertson .20 .07
❑ 388 Torii Hunter .20 .07
❑ 389 Gavin Floyd .20 .07
❑ 390 Roy Oswalt .20 .07
❑ 391 Kelvim Escobar .20 .07
❑ 392 Craig Wilson .20 .07
❑ 393 Milton Bradley .20 .07
❑ 394 Aaron Hill .20 .07
❑ 395 Matt Diaz .20 .07
❑ 396 Chris Capuano .20 .07
❑ 397 Juan Encarnacion .20 .07
❑ 398 Jacque Jones .20 .07
❑ 399 James Shields .20 .07
❑ 400 Ichiro Suzuki .75 .30
❑ 401 Matt Kemp .20 .07
❑ 402 Matt Morris .20 .07
❑ 403 Casey Blake .20 .07
❑ 404 Corey Hart .20 .07
❑ 405 Josh Willingham .20 .07
❑ 406 Ryan Madson .20 .07
❑ 407 Nick Johnson .20 .07
❑ 408 Kevin Millar .20 .07
❑ 409 Khalil Greene .30 .12
❑ 410 Tom Glavine .30 .12
❑ 411a Jason Bay .20 .07
❑ 411b Jason Bay No Sig 5.00 2.00
❑ 412 Gerald Laird .20 .07
❑ 413 Coco Crisp .20 .07
❑ 414 Brandon Phillips .20 .07
❑ 415 Aaron Cook .20 .07
❑ 416 Mark Redman .20 .07
❑ 417 Mike Maroth .20 .07
❑ 418 Boof Bonser .20 .07
❑ 419 Jorge Cantu .20 .07
❑ 420 Jeff Weaver .20 .07
❑ 421 Melky Cabrera .20 .07
❑ 422 Francisco Rodriguez .20 .07
❑ 423 Mike Lamb .20 .07
❑ 424 Dan Haren .20 .07
❑ 425 Tomo Ohka .20 .07
❑ 426 Jeff Francoeur .50 .20
❑ 427 Randy Wolf .20 .07
❑ 428 So Taguchi .20 .07
❑ 429 Carlos Zambrano .20 .07
❑ 430 Justin Morneau .20 .07
❑ 431 Luis Gonzalez .20 .07
❑ 432 Takashi Saito .20 .07
❑ 433 Brandon Morrow RC .75 .30
❑ 434 Victor Martinez .20 .07
❑ 435 Felix Hernandez .30 .12
❑ 436 Ricky Nolasco .20 .07
❑ 437 Paul LoDuca .20 .07
❑ 437b Paul LoDuca No Sig 5.00 2.00
❑ 438 Chad Cordero .20 .07
❑ 439 Miguel Tejada .20 .07
❑ 440 Mark Teixeira .30 .12
❑ 441 Pat Burrell .20 .07
❑ 442 Paul Maholm .20 .07
❑ 443 Mike Cameron .20 .07
❑ 444 Josh Beckett .30 .12
❑ 445 Pablo Ozuna .20 .07
❑ 446 Jaret Wright .20 .07
❑ 447 Angel Berroa .20 .07
❑ 448 Fernando Rodney .20 .07
❑ 449 Francisco Liriano .50 .20
❑ 450 Ken Griffey Jr. .75 .30
❑ 451 Bobby Jenks .20 .07
❑ 452 Mike Mussina .30 .12
❑ 453 Howie Kendrick .20 .07
❑ 454 Milwaukee Brewers .20 .07
❑ 455 Dan Johnson .20 .07
❑ 456 Ted Lilly .20 .07
❑ 457 Mike Hampton .20 .07
❑ 458 J.J. Hardy .20 .07
❑ 459 Jeff Suppan .20 .07
❑ 460 Jose Reyes .20 .07
❑ 461 Jae Seo .20 .07
❑ 462 Edgar Gonzalez .20 .07
❑ 463 Russell Martin .20 .07
❑ 464 Omar Vizquel .30 .12
❑ 465 Jhonny Peralta .20 .07
❑ 466 Raul Ibanez .20 .07
❑ 467 Hanley Ramirez .30 .12
❑ 468 Kerry Wood .20 .07
❑ 469 Ryan Church .20 .07
❑ 470 Gary Sheffield .20 .07
❑ 471 David Wells .20 .07
❑ 472 David Dellucci .20 .07
❑ 473 Xavier Nady .20 .07
❑ 474 Michael Young .20 .07
❑ 475 Kevin Youkilis .20 .07
❑ 476 Aaron Harang .20 .07
❑ 477 Brian Lawrence .20 .07
❑ 478 Octavio Dotel .20 .07
❑ 479 Chris Shelton .20 .07
❑ 480 Matt Garza .20 .07
❑ 481a Jim Thome .30 .12
❑ 481b Jim Thome No Sig 5.00 2.00
❑ 482 Jose Contreras .20 .07
❑ 483 Kris Benson .20 .07
❑ 484 John Maine .20 .07
❑ 485 Tadahito Iguchi .20 .07
❑ 486 Wandy Rodriguez .20 .07
❑ 487 Eric Chavez .20 .07
❑ 488 Vernon Wells .20 .07
❑ 489 Doug Davis .20 .07
❑ 490 Andruw Jones .30 .12
❑ 491 David Eckstein .20 .07
❑ 492 Michael Barrett .20 .07
❑ 493 Greg Norton .20 .07
❑ 494 Orlando Hudson .20 .07
❑ 495 Wilson Betemit .20 .07
❑ 496 Ryan Klesko .20 .07
❑ 497 Fausto Carmona .20 .07
❑ 498 Jarrod Washburn .20 .07
❑ 499 Aaron Boone .20 .07
❑ 500 Pedro Martinez .30 .12
❑ 501 Mike O'Connor .20 .07
❑ 502 Brian Roberts .20 .07
❑ 503 Jeff Cirillo .20 .07
❑ 504 Brett Myers .20 .07
❑ 505 Jose Bautista .20 .07
❑ 506 Akinori Otsuka .20 .07
❑ 507 Shea Hillenbrand .20 .07
❑ 508 Ryan Langerhans .20 .07
❑ 509 Josh Fogg .20 .07
❑ 510 Alex Rodriguez .75 .30
❑ 511 Kenny Rogers .20 .07
❑ 512 Jason Kubel .20 .07
❑ 513 Jermaine Dye .20 .07
❑ 514 Mark Grudzielanek .20 .07
❑ 515 Josh Phelps .20 .07
❑ 516 Bartolo Colon .20 .07
❑ 517 Craig Biggio .30 .12
❑ 518 Esteban Loaiza .20 .07
❑ 519 Alex Rios .20 .07
❑ 520 Adam Dunn .20 .07
❑ 521 Derrick Turnbow .20 .07
❑ 522 Anthony Reyes .20 .07
❑ 523 Derrek Lee .20 .07
❑ 524 Ty Wigginton .20 .07
❑ 525 Jeremy Hermida .20 .07
❑ 526 Derek Lowe .20 .07
❑ 527 Randy Winn .20 .07
❑ 528 Paul Byrd .20 .07
❑ 529 Chris Snelling .20 .07
❑ 530 Brandon Webb .20 .07
❑ 531 Julio Franco .20 .07
❑ 532 Jose Vidro .20 .07
❑ 533 Erik Bedard .20 .07
❑ 534 Termel Sledge .20 .07
❑ 535 Jon Lieber .20 .07
❑ 536 Tom Gorzelanny .20 .07
❑ 537 Kip Wells .20 .07
❑ 538 Wily Mo Pena .20 .07
❑ 539 Eric Milton .20 .07
❑ 540 Chad Billingsley .20 .07

❑ 541 David DeJesus .20 .07
❑ 542 Omar Infante .20 .07
❑ 543 Rondell White .20 .07
❑ 544 Juan Uribe .20 .07
❑ 545 Miguel Cairo .20 .07
❑ 546 Orlando Cabrera .20 .07
❑ 547 Byung-Hyun Kim .20 .07
❑ 548 Jason Kendall .20 .07
❑ 549 Horacio Ramirez .20 .07
❑ 550 Trevor Hoffman .20 .07
❑ 551 Ronnie Belliard .20 .07
❑ 552 Chris Woodward .20 .07
❑ 553 Ramon Martinez .20 .07
❑ 554 Elizardo Ramirez .20 .07
❑ 555 Andy Marte .20 .07
❑ 556 John Patterson .20 .07
❑ 557 Scott Olsen .20 .07
❑ 558 Steve Trachsel .20 .07
❑ 559 Doug Mientkiewicz .20 .07
❑ 560 Randy Johnson .50 .20
❑ 561 Chan Ho Park .20 .07
❑ 562 Jamie Moyer .20 .07
❑ 563 Mike Gonzalez .20 .07
❑ 564 Nelson Cruz .20 .07
❑ 565 Alex Cora .20 .07
❑ 566 Ryan Freel .20 .07
❑ 567 Chris Stewart RC .50 .20
❑ 568 Carlos Guillen .20 .07
❑ 569 Jason Bartlett .20 .07
❑ 570 Mariano Rivera .50 .20
❑ 571 Norris Hopper .20 .07
❑ 572 Alex Escobar .20 .07
❑ 573 Gustavo Chacin .20 .07
❑ 574 Brandon McCarthy .20 .07
❑ 575 Seth McClung .20 .07
❑ 576 Yuniesky Betancourt .20 .07
❑ 577 Jason LaRue .20 .07
❑ 578 Dustin Pedroia .20 .07
❑ 579 Taylor Tankersley .20 .07
❑ 580 Garret Anderson .20 .07
❑ 581 Mike Sweeney .20 .07
❑ 582 Scott Thorman .20 .07
❑ 583 Joe Inglett .20 .07
❑ 584 Clint Barmes .20 .07
❑ 585 Willie Bloomquist .20 .07
❑ 586 Willy Aybar .20 .07
❑ 587 Brian Bannister .20 .07
❑ 588 Jose Guillen .20 .07
❑ 589 Brad Wilkerson .20 .07
❑ 590 Lance Berkman .20 .07
❑ 591 Toronto Blue Jays .20 .07
❑ 592 Florida Marlins .20 .07
❑ 593 Washington Nationals .20 .07
❑ 594 Los Angeles Angels .20 .07
❑ 595 Cleveland Indians .20 .07
❑ 596 Texas Rangers .20 .07
❑ 597 Detroit Tigers .20 .07
❑ 598 Arizona Diamondbacks .20 .07
❑ 599 Kansas City Royals .20 .07
❑ 600 Ryan Zimmerman .50 .20
❑ 601 Colorado Rockies .20 .07
❑ 602 Minnesota Twins .20 .07
❑ 603 Los Angeles Dodgers .20 .07
❑ 604 San Diego Padres .20 .07
❑ 605 Bruce Bochy MG .20 .07
❑ 606 Ron Washington MG .20 .07
❑ 607 Manny Acta MG .20 .07
❑ 608 Sam Perlozzo MG .20 .07
❑ 609 Terry Francona MG .20 .07
❑ 610 Jim Leyland MG .20 .07
❑ 611 Eric Wedge MG .20 .07
❑ 612 Ozzie Guillen MG .20 .07
❑ 613 Buddy Bell MG .20 .07
❑ 614 Bob Geren MG .20 .07
❑ 615 Lou Piniella MG .20 .07
❑ 616 Fredi Gonzalez MG .20 .07
❑ 617 Ned Yost MG .20 .07
❑ 618 Willie Randolph MG .20 .07
❑ 619 Bud Black MG .20 .07
❑ 620 Garrett Atkins .20 .07
❑ 621 Alexi Casilla RC .75 .30
❑ 622 Matt Chico (RC) .50 .20
❑ 623 Alejandro De Aza RC .50 .20
❑ 624 Jeremy Brown .20 .07
❑ 625 Josh Hamilton (RC) 1.25 .50
❑ 626 Doug Slaten RC .50 .20
❑ 627 Andy Cannizaro RC .50 .20
❑ 628 Juan Salas (RC) .50 .20
❑ 629 Levale Speigner RC .50 .20
❑ 630a D.Matsuzaka English RC 8.00 3.00
❑ 630b D.Matsuzaka Japanese 12.00 5.00
❑ 630c Daisuke Matsuzaka No Sig 12.00 5.00
❑ 631 Elijah Dukes RC .75 .30
❑ 632 Kevin Cameron RC .50 .20
❑ 633 Juan Perez RC .50 .20
❑ 634a Alex Gordon RC 3.00 1.25
❑ 634b A.Gordon No Sig 8.00 3.00
❑ 635 Juan Lara RC .50 .20
❑ 636 Mike Rabelo RC .50 .20
❑ 637 Justin Hampson (RC) .50 .20
❑ 638 Cesar Jimenez RC .50 .20
❑ 639 Joe Smith RC .50 .20
❑ 640 Kei Igawa RC 1.25 .50
❑ 641 Hideki Okajima RC 2.50 1.00
❑ 642 Sean Henn (RC) .50 .20
❑ 643 Jay Marshall RC .50 .20
❑ 644 Jared Burton RC .50 .20
❑ 645 Angel Sanchez RC .50 .20
❑ 646 Devern Hansack RC .50 .20
❑ 647 Juan Morillo (RC) .50 .20
❑ 648 Hector Gimenez (RC) .50 .20
❑ 649 Brian Barden RC .50 .20
❑ 650 A.Rodriguez/J.Giambi CC .75 .30
❑ 651 J.Michaels/T.Hafner CC .20 .07
❑ 652 J.Johnson/M.Olivo CC .20 .07
❑ 653 S.Casey/P.Polanco CC .20 .07
❑ 654 I.Rodriguez/F.Rodney CC .30 .12
❑ 655 D.Uggla/H.Ramirez CC .30 .12
❑ 656 C.Beltran/J.Reyes CC .20 .07
❑ 657 A.Rodriguez/D.Jeter CC 1.25 .50
❑ 658 A.Rowand/J.Rollins CC .20 .07
❑ 659 A.Berroa/A.Blanco CC .20 .07
❑ 660a Yadier Molina .20 .07
❑ 660b Yadier Molina No Sig 5.00 2.00
❑ 661 Barry Bonds 10.00 4.00

2007 Topps Update

❑ COMP.SET w/o SPs (330) 60.00 30.00
❑ COMMON CARD (1-330) .30 .12
❑ COMMON ROOKIE (1-330) .50 .20
❑ 1-330 PLATE ODDS 1:54 HTA
❑ PLATE PRINT RUN 1 SET PER COLOR
❑ BLACK-CYAN-MAGENTA-YELLOW ISSUED
❑ NO PLATE PRICING DUE TO SCARCITY
❑ 1 Tony Armas Jr. .30 .12
❑ 2 Shannon Stewart .30 .12
❑ 3 Jason Marquis .30 .12
❑ 4 Josh Wilson .30 .12
❑ 5 Steve Trachsel .30 .12
❑ 6 J.D. Drew .30 .12
❑ 7 Ronnie Belliard .30 .12
❑ 8 Trot Nixon .30 .12
❑ 9 Adam LaRoche .30 .12
❑ 10 Mark Loretta .30 .12
❑ 11 Matt Morris .30 .12
❑ 12 Marlon Anderson .30 .12
❑ 13 Jorge Julio .30 .12
❑ 14 Brady Clark .30 .12
❑ 15 David Wells .30 .12
❑ 16 Francisco Rosario .30 .12
❑ 17 Jason Ellison .30 .12
❑ 18 Adam Jones .30 .12
❑ 19 Russell Branyan .30 .12
❑ 20 Rob Bowen .30 .12
❑ 21 J.D. Durbin .30 .12
❑ 22 Jeff Salazar .30 .12
❑ 23 Tadahito Iguchi .30 .12
❑ 24 Brad Hennessey .30 .12
❑ 25 Mark Hendrickson .30 .12
❑ 26 Kameron Loe .30 .12
❑ 27 Yusmeiro Petit .30 .12
❑ 28 Olmedo Saenz .30 .12
❑ 29 Carlos Silva .30 .12
❑ 30 Kevin Frandsen .30 .12
❑ 31 Tony Pena .30 .12
❑ 32 Russ Ortiz .30 .12
❑ 33 Hong-Chih Kuo .30 .12
❑ 34 Paul McAnulty .30 .12
❑ 35 Hiram Bocachica .30 .12
❑ 36 Justin Germano .30 .12
❑ 37 Jason Simontacchi .30 .12
❑ 38 Jose Cruz .30 .12
❑ 39 Wilfredo Ledezma .30 .12
❑ 40 Chris Denorfia .30 .12
❑ 41 Ryan Langerhans .30 .12
❑ 42 Chris Snelling .30 .12
❑ 43 Ubaldo Jimenez .30 .12
❑ 44 Scott Spiezio .30 .12
❑ 45 Byung-Hyun Kim .30 .12
❑ 46 Brandon Lyon .30 .12
❑ 47 Scott Hairston .30 .12
❑ 48 Chad Durbin .30 .12
❑ 49 Sammy Sosa .75 .30
❑ 50 Jason Smith .30 .12
❑ 51 Zack Greinke .30 .12
❑ 52 Armando Benitez .30 .12
❑ 53 Randy Messenger .30 .12
❑ 54 Mark Teixeira .50 .20
❑ 55 Mike Maroth .30 .12
❑ 56 Jamie Burke .30 .12
❑ 57 Carlos Marmol .30 .12
❑ 58 David Weathers .30 .12
❑ 59 Ryan Doumit .30 .12
❑ 60 Michael Barrett .30 .12
❑ 61 Shawn Chacon .30 .12
❑ 62 Mike Fontenot .30 .12
❑ 63 Cesar Izturis .30 .12
❑ 64 Cliff Floyd .30 .12
❑ 65 Angel Pagan .30 .12
❑ 66 Aaron Miles .30 .12
❑ 67 Tony Graffanino .30 .12
❑ 68 Kevin Mench .30 .12
❑ 69 Claudio Vargas .30 .12
❑ 70 Jose Capellan .30 .12
❑ 71 A.J. Pierzynski .30 .12
❑ 72 Darin Erstad .30 .12
❑ 73 Boone Logan .30 .12
❑ 74 Luis Castillo .30 .12
❑ 75 Marcus Thames .30 .12
❑ 76 Neifi Perez .30 .12
❑ 77 Esteban German .30 .12
❑ 78 Tony Pena .30 .12
❑ 79 Adam Wainwright .30 .12
❑ 80 Reggie Sanders .30 .12
❑ 81 Kelly Shoppach .30 .12
❑ 82 Rafael Betancourt .30 .12
❑ 83 Tom Mastny .30 .12
❑ 84 Kyle Farnsworth .30 .12
❑ 85 Rick Ankiel .50 .20
❑ 86 Kevin Thompson .30 .12
❑ 87 Jeff Karstens .30 .12
❑ 88 Eric Hinske .30 .12
❑ 89 Doug Mirabelli .30 .12
❑ 90 Julian Tavarez .30 .12
❑ 91 Carlos Pena .30 .12
❑ 92 Brendan Harris .30 .12
❑ 93 Chris Sampson .30 .12
❑ 94 Al Reyes .30 .12
❑ 95 Dmitri Young .30 .12
❑ 96 Jason Bergmann .30 .12
❑ 97 Shawn Hill .30 .12
❑ 98 Greg Dobbs .30 .12
❑ 99 Carlos Ruiz .30 .12
❑ 100a Abraham Nunez .30 .12
❑ 100b Jacoby Ellsbury (RC) 200.00 100.00
❑ 101 Jayson Werth .30 .12
❑ 102 Adam Eaton .30 .12
❑ 103 Antonio Alfonseca .30 .12
❑ 104 Jorge Sosa .30 .12
❑ 105 Ramon Castro .30 .12

❑ 106 Ruben Gotay .30 .12
❑ 107 Damion Easley .30 .12
❑ 108 David Newhan .30 .12
❑ 109 Jason Wood .30 .12
❑ 110 Reggie Abercrombie .30 .12
❑ 111 Kevin Gregg .30 .12
❑ 112 Henry Owens .30 .12
❑ 113 Willie Harris .30 .12
❑ 114 Pete Orr .30 .12
❑ 115 Casey Janssen .30 .12
❑ 116 Jason Frasor .30 .12
❑ 117 Jeremy Accardo .30 .12
❑ 118 John McDonald .30 .12
❑ 119 Matt Stairs .30 .12
❑ 120 Jason Phillips .30 .12
❑ 121 Justin Duchscherer .30 .12
❑ 122 Rich Harden .30 .12
❑ 123 Jack Cust .30 .12
❑ 124 Lenny DiNardo .30 .12
❑ 125 Joe Kennedy .30 .12
❑ 126 Chad Gaudin .30 .12
❑ 127 Marco Scutaro .30 .12
❑ 128 Brad Thompson .30 .12
❑ 129 Dustin Moseley .30 .12
❑ 130 Eric Gagne .30 .12
❑ 131 Marlon Byrd .30 .12
❑ 132 Scot Shields .30 .12
❑ 133 Victor Diaz .30 .12
❑ 134 Reggie Willits .30 .12
❑ 135 Jose Molina .30 .12
❑ 136 Ramon Vazquez .30 .12
❑ 137 Erick Aybar .30 .12
❑ 138 Sean Marshall .30 .12
❑ 139 Casey Kotchman .30 .12
❑ 140 Ryan Spilborghs .30 .12
❑ 141 Cameron Maybin RC 2.50 1.00
❑ 142 Jeremy Guthrie .30 .12
❑ 143 Jeff Baker .30 .12
❑ 144 Edwin Jackson .30 .12
❑ 145 Macay McBride .30 .12
❑ 146 Freddie Bynum .30 .12
❑ 147 Eric Patterson .30 .12
❑ 148 Dustin McGowan .30 .12
❑ 149 Homer Bailey (RC) .75 .30
❑ 150 Ryan Braun (RC) 3.00 1.25
❑ 151 Tony Abreu RC 1.50 .60
❑ 152 Tyler Clippard (RC) .75 .30
❑ 153 Mark Reynolds RC 1.25 .50
❑ 154 Jesse Litsch RC .75 .30
❑ 155 Carlos Gomez RC .75 .30
❑ 156 Matt DeSalvo (RC) .50 .20
❑ 157 Andy LaRoche (RC) .50 .20
❑ 158 Tim Lincecum RC 5.00 2.00
❑ 159 Jarrod Saltalamacchia (RC) .75 .30
❑ 160 Hunter Pence (RC) 3.00 1.25
❑ 161 Brandon Wood (RC) .50 .20
❑ 162 Phil Hughes (RC) 2.50 1.00
❑ 163 Rocky Cherry RC 1.25 .50
❑ 164 Chase Wright RC 1.25 .50
❑ 165 Dallas Braden RC .75 .30
❑ 166 Felix Pie (RC) .50 .20
❑ 167 Zach McClellan RC .50 .20
❑ 168 Rick Vanden Hurk RC .75 .30
❑ 169 Micah Owings (RC) .50 .20
❑ 170 Jon Coutlangus (RC) .50 .20
❑ 171 Andy Sonnanstine RC .50 .20
❑ 172 Yunel Escobar (RC) .50 .20
❑ 173 Kevin Slowey (RC) 1.25 .50
❑ 174 Curtis Thigpen (RC) .50 .20
❑ 175 Masumi Kuwata RC 4.00 1.50
❑ 176 Kurt Suzuki (RC) .50 .20
❑ 177 Travis Buck (RC) .50 .20
❑ 178 Matt Lindstrom (RC) .50 .20
❑ 179 Jesus Flores RC .50 .20
❑ 180 Joakim Soria RC .50 .20
❑ 181 Nathan Haynes (RC) .50 .20
❑ 182 Matthew Brown RC .75 .30
❑ 183 Travis Metcalf RC .75 .30
❑ 184 Yovani Gallardo (RC) 1.50 .60
❑ 185 Nate Schierholtz (RC) .50 .20
❑ 186 Kyle Kendrick RC 1.25 .50
❑ 187 Kevin Melillo (RC) .50 .20
❑ 188 Ryan Rowland-Smith .30 .12
❑ 189 Lee Gronkiewicz RC .50 .20
❑ 190 Eulogio De La Cruz (RC) .50 .20
❑ 191 Brett Carroll RC .50 .20
❑ 192 Terry Evans RC .50 .20
❑ 193 Chase Headley (RC) .50 .20
❑ 194 Guillermo Rodriguez RC .50 .20
❑ 195 Marcus McBeth (RC) .50 .20
❑ 196 Brian Wolfe (RC) .50 .20
❑ 197 Troy Cate RC .50 .20
❑ 198 Mike Zagurski RC .50 .20
❑ 199 Yoel Hernandez .30 .12
❑ 200 Brad Salmon RC .50 .20
❑ 201 Alberto Arias RC .50 .20
❑ 202 Danny Putnam (RC) .50 .20
❑ 203 Jamie Vermilyea RC .50 .20
❑ 204 Kyle Lohse .30 .12
❑ 205 Sammy Sosa .75 .30
❑ 206 Tom Glavine .50 .20
❑ 207 Prince Fielder .75 .30
❑ 208 Mark Buehrle .30 .12
❑ 209 Troy Tulowitzki .75 .30
❑ 210 Daisuke Matsuzaka RC 5.00 2.00
❑ 211 Randy Johnson .75 .30
❑ 212 Justin Verlander .75 .30
❑ 213 Trevor Hoffman .30 .12
❑ 214 Alex Rodriguez 1.25 .50
❑ 215 Ivan Rodriguez .50 .20
❑ 216 David Ortiz .75 .30
❑ 217 Placido Polanco .30 .12
❑ 218 Derek Jeter 2.00 .75
❑ 219 Alex Rodriguez 1.25 .50
❑ 220 Vladimir Guerrero .75 .30
❑ 221 Magglio Ordonez .30 .12
❑ 222 Ichiro Suzuki 1.25 .50
❑ 223 Russell Martin .30 .12
❑ 224 Prince Fielder .75 .30
❑ 225 Chase Utley .75 .30
❑ 226 Jose Reyes .75 .30
❑ 227 David Wright 1.25 .50
❑ 228 Carlos Beltran .30 .12
❑ 229 Barry Bonds 1.50 .60
❑ 230 Ken Griffey Jr. 1.25 .50
❑ 231 Torii Hunter .30 .12
❑ 232 Jonathan Papelbon .75 .30
❑ 233 J.J. Putz .30 .12
❑ 234 Francisco Rodriguez .30 .12
❑ 235 C.C. Sabathia .30 .12
❑ 236 Johan Santana .50 .20
❑ 237 Justin Verlander .75 .30
❑ 238 Francisco Cordero .30 .12
❑ 239 Mike Lowell .30 .12
❑ 240 Cole Hamels .50 .20
❑ 241 Trevor Hoffman .30 .12
❑ 242 Manny Ramirez .50 .20
❑ 243 Jake Peavy .30 .12
❑ 244 Brad Penny .30 .12
❑ 245 Takashi Saito .30 .12
❑ 246 Ben Sheets .30 .12
❑ 247 Hideki Okajima 1.50 .60
❑ 248 Roy Oswalt .30 .12
❑ 249 Billy Wagner .30 .12
❑ 250 Carl Crawford .30 .12
❑ 251 Chris Young .30 .12
❑ 252 Brian McCann .30 .12
❑ 253 Derrek Lee .30 .12
❑ 254 Albert Pujols 1.50 .60
❑ 255 Dmitri Young .30 .12
❑ 256 Orlando Hudson .30 .12
❑ 257 J.J. Hardy .30 .12
❑ 258 Miguel Cabrera .50 .20
❑ 259 Freddy Sanchez .30 .12
❑ 260 Matt Holliday .75 .30
❑ 261 Carlos Lee .30 .12
❑ 262 Aaron Rowand .30 .12
❑ 263 Alfonso Soriano .30 .12
❑ 264 Victor Martinez .30 .12
❑ 265 Jorge Posada .50 .20
❑ 266 Justin Morneau .30 .12
❑ 267 Brian Roberts .30 .12
❑ 268 Carlos Guillen .30 .12
❑ 269 Grady Sizemore .50 .20
❑ 270 Josh Beckett .50 .20
❑ 271 Dan Haren .30 .12
❑ 272 Bobby Jenks .30 .12
❑ 273 John Lackey .30 .12
❑ 274 Gil Meche .30 .12
❑ 275 M.Fontenot/K.Greene .30 .12
❑ 276 A.Rodriguez/R.Martin 1.25 .50
❑ 277 T.Tulowitzki/J.Reyes .75 .30
❑ 278 Posada/Jeter/ARod 2.00 .75
❑ 279 C.Utley/Ichiro 1.25 .50
❑ 280 C.Crawford/C.Guillen .30 .12
❑ 281 C.Hamels/R.Martin .50 .20
❑ 282 J.Papelbon/J.Posada .75 .30
❑ 283 C.Crawford/V.Martinez .30 .12
❑ 284 A.Soriano/J.Hardy .30 .12
❑ 285 Justin Morneau .30 .12
❑ 286 Prince Fielder .75 .30
❑ 287 Alex Rios .30 .12
❑ 288 Vladimir Guerrero .75 .30
❑ 289 Albert Pujols 1.50 .60
❑ 290 Ryan Howard 1.25 .50
❑ 291 Magglio Ordonez .30 .12
❑ 292 Matt Holliday .75 .30
❑ 293 Wilson Betemit .30 .12
❑ 294 Todd Wellemeyer .30 .12
❑ 295 Scott Baker .30 .12
❑ 296 Edgar Gonzalez .30 .12
❑ 297 J.P. Howell .30 .12
❑ 298 Shaun Marcum .30 .12
❑ 299 Edinson Volquez .30 .12
❑ 300 Kason Gabbard .30 .12
❑ 301 Bob Howry .30 .12
❑ 302 J.A. Happ .30 .12
❑ 303 Scott Feldman .30 .12
❑ 304 D'Angelo Jimenez .30 .12
❑ 305 Orlando Palmeiro .30 .12
❑ 306 Paul Bako .30 .12
❑ 307 Kyle Davies .30 .12
❑ 308 Gabe Gross .30 .12
❑ 309 John Wasdin .30 .12
❑ 310 Jon Knott .30 .12
❑ 311 Josh Phelps .30 .12
❑ 312a J.Chamberlain RC 10.00 4.00
❑ 312b J.Chamberlain Rev.Neg 300.00200.00
❑ 312c J.Chamberlain Hou UER
❑ 313 Octavio Dotel .30 .12
❑ 314 Craig Monroe .30 .12
❑ 315 Edward Mujica .30 .12
❑ 316 Brandon Watson .30 .12
❑ 317 Chris Schroder .30 .12
❑ 318 Scott Proctor .30 .12
❑ 319 Ty Wigginton .30 .12
❑ 320 Troy Percival .30 .12
❑ 321 Scott Linebrink .30 .12
❑ 322 David Murphy .30 .12
❑ 323 Jorge Cantu .30 .12
❑ 324 Dan Wheeler .30 .12
❑ 325 Jason Kendall .30 .12
❑ 326 Milton Bradley .30 .12
❑ 327 Justin Upton RC 4.00 1.50
❑ 328 Kenny Lofton .30 .12
❑ 329 Roger Clemens 1.50 .60
❑ 330 Brian Burres .30 .12
❑ SQ1 Poley Walnuts 50.00 20.00

2003 Topps 205

❑ COMPLETE SERIES 1 (165) 40.00 15.00
❑ COMPLETE SERIES 2 (175) 125.00 75.00
❑ COMP.SERIES 2 w/o SP's (155) 40.0015.00
❑ COM (1-130/161-169/193-315) .50 .20
❑ COMMON (131-145/170-192) .50 .20
❑ COMMON CARD (146-160) 1.00 .40
❑ COMMON SP 2.50 1.00
❑ SERIES 2 SP STATED ODDS 1:5
❑ 1A Barry Bonds w/Cap 3.00 1.25
❑ 1B Barry Bonds w/Helmet 3.00 1.25

	No.	Player	Price	Price
❑	2	Bret Boone	.50	.20
❑	3A	Albert Pujols Clear Logo	2.50	1.00
❑	3B	Albert Pujols White Logo	2.50	1.00
❑	4	Carl Crawford	.50	.20
❑	5	Bartolo Colon	.50	.20
❑	6	Cliff Floyd	.50	.20
❑	7	John Olerud	.50	.20
❑	8A	Jason Giambi Full Jkt	.50	.20
❑	8B	Jason Giambi Partial Jkt	.50	.20
❑	9	Edgardo Alfonzo	.50	.20
❑	10	Ivan Rodriguez	.75	.30
❑	11	Jim Edmonds	.50	.20
❑	12A	Mike Piazza Orange	2.00	.75
❑	12B	Mike Piazza Yellow	2.00	.75
❑	13	Greg Maddux	2.00	.75
❑	14	Jose Vidro	.50	.20
❑	15A	Vlad Guerrero Clear Logo	1.25	.50
❑	15B	Vlad Guerrero White Logo	1.25	.50
❑	16	Bernie Williams	.75	.30
❑	17	Roger Clemens	2.50	1.00
❑	18A	Miguel Tejada Blue	.50	.20
❑	18B	Miguel Tejada Green	.50	.20
❑	19	Carlos Delgado	.50	.20
❑	20A	Alfonso Soriano w/Bat	.50	.20
❑	20B	Alfonso Soriano Sunglasses	.50	.20
❑	21	Bobby Cox MG	.50	.20
❑	22	Mike Scioscia	.50	.20
❑	23	John Smoltz	.75	.30
❑	24	Luis Gonzalez	.50	.20
❑	25	Shawn Green	.50	.20
❑	26	Raul Ibanez	.50	.20
❑	27	Andruw Jones	.75	.30
❑	28	Josh Beckett	.50	.20
❑	29	Derek Lowe	.50	.20
❑	30	Todd Helton	.75	.30
❑	31	Barry Larkin	.75	.30
❑	32	Jason Jennings	.50	.20
❑	33	Darin Erstad	.50	.20
❑	34	Magglio Ordonez	.50	.20
❑	35	Mike Sweeney	.50	.20
❑	36	Kazuhisa Ishii	.50	.20
❑	37	Ron Gardenhire MG	.50	.20
❑	38	Tim Hudson	.50	.20
❑	39	Tim Salmon	.75	.30
❑	40A	Pat Burrell Black Bat	.50	.20
❑	40B	Pat Burrell Brown Bat	.50	.20
❑	41	Manny Ramirez	.75	.30
❑	42	Nick Johnson	.50	.20
❑	43	Tom Glavine	.75	.30
❑	44	Mark Mulder	.50	.20
❑	45	Brian Jordan	.50	.20
❑	46	Rafael Palmeiro	.75	.30
❑	47	Vernon Wells	.50	.20
❑	48	Bob Brenly MG	.50	.20
❑	49	C.C. Sabathia	.50	.20
❑	50A	Alex Rodriguez Look Ahead	2.00	.75
❑	50B	Alex Rodriguez Look Away	2.00	.75
❑	51A	Sammy Sosa Head Duck	1.25	.50
❑	51B	Sammy Sosa Head Left	1.25	.50
❑	52	Paul Konerko	.50	.20
❑	53	Craig Biggio	.75	.30
❑	54	Moises Alou	.50	.20
❑	55	Johnny Damon	.75	.30
❑	56	Torii Hunter	.50	.20
❑	57	Omar Vizquel	.75	.30
❑	58	Orlando Hernandez	.50	.20
❑	59	Barry Zito	.50	.20
❑	60	Lance Berkman	.50	.20
❑	61	Carlos Beltran	.50	.20
❑	62	Edgar Renteria	.50	.20
❑	63	Ben Sheets	.50	.20
❑	64	Doug Mientkiewicz	.50	.20
❑	65	Troy Glaus	.50	.20
❑	66	Preston Wilson	.50	.20
❑	67	Kerry Wood	.50	.20
❑	68	Frank Thomas	1.25	.50
❑	69	Jimmy Rollins	.50	.20
❑	70	Brian Giles	.50	.20
❑	71	Bobby Higginson	.50	.20
❑	72	Larry Walker	.50	.20
❑	73	Randy Johnson	1.25	.50
❑	74	Tony LaRussa MG	.50	.20
❑	75A	Derek Jeter w/Gold Trim	3.00	1.25
❑	75B	Derek Jeter w/o Gold Trim	3.00	1.25
❑	76	Bobby Abreu	.50	.20
❑	77A	Adam Dunn Closed Mouth	.50	.20
❑	77B	Adam Dunn Open Mouth	.50	.20
❑	78	Ryan Klesko	.50	.20
❑	79	Francisco Rodriguez	.50	.20
❑	80	Scott Rolen	.75	.30
❑	81	Roberto Alomar	.75	.30
❑	82	Joe Torre MG	.75	.30
❑	83	Jim Thome	.75	.30
❑	84	Kevin Millwood	.50	.20
❑	85	J.T. Snow	.50	.20
❑	86	Trevor Hoffman	.50	.20
❑	87	Jay Gibbons	.50	.20
❑	88A	Mark Prior New Logo	.75	.30
❑	88B	Mark Prior Old Logo	.75	.30
❑	89	Rich Aurilia	.50	.20
❑	90	Chipper Jones	1.25	.50
❑	91	Richie Sexson	.50	.20
❑	92	Gary Sheffield	.50	.20
❑	93	Pedro Martinez	.75	.30
❑	94	Rodrigo Lopez	.50	.20
❑	95	Al Leiter	.50	.20
❑	96	Jorge Posada	.75	.30
❑	97	Luis Castillo	.50	.20
❑	98	Aubrey Huff	.50	.20
❑	99	A.J. Pierzynski	.50	.20
❑	100A	Ichiro Suzuki Look Ahead	2.50	1.00
❑	100B	Ichiro Suzuki Look Right	2.50	1.00
❑	101	Eric Chavez	.50	.20
❑	102	Brett Myers	.50	.20
❑	103	Jason Kendall	.50	.20
❑	104	Jeff Kent	.50	.20
❑	105	Eric Hinske	.50	.20
❑	106	Jacque Jones	.50	.20
❑	107	Phil Nevin	.50	.20
❑	108	Roy Oswalt	.50	.20
❑	109	Curt Schilling	.50	.20
❑	110A	N.Garciaparra w/Gold Trim	2.00	.75
❑	110B	N.Garciaparra w/o Gold Trim	2.00	.75
❑	111	Garret Anderson	.50	.20
❑	112	Eric Gagne	.50	.20
❑	113	Javier Vazquez	.50	.20
❑	114	Jeff Bagwell	.75	.30
❑	115	Mike Lowell	.50	.20
❑	116	Carlos Pena	.50	.20
❑	117	Ken Griffey Jr.	2.00	.75
❑	118	Tony Batista	.50	.20
❑	119	Edgar Martinez	.75	.30
❑	120	Austin Kearns	.50	.20
❑	121	Jason Stokes PROS	.50	.20
❑	122	Jose Reyes PROS	.50	.20
❑	123	Rocco Baldelli PROS	.50	.20
❑	124	Joe Borchard PROS	.50	.20
❑	125	Joe Mauer PROS	1.25	.50
❑	126	Gavin Floyd PROS	.50	.20
❑	127	Mark Teixeira PROS	.75	.30
❑	128	Jeremy Guthrie PROS	.50	.20
❑	129	B.J. Upton PROS	1.25	.50
❑	130	Khalil Greene PROS	1.25	.50
❑	131	Hanley Ramirez FY RC	5.00	2.00
❑	132	Andy Marte FY RC	4.00	1.50
❑	133	J.D. Durbin FY RC	.50	.20
❑	134	Jason Kubel FY RC	1.25	.50
❑	135	Craig Brazell FY RC	.50	.20
❑	136	Bryan Bullington FY RC	.50	.20
❑	137	Jose Contreras FY RC	1.00	.40
❑	138	Brian Burgamy FY RC	.50	.20
❑	139	Evel Bastida-Martinez FY RC	.50	.20
❑	140	Joey Gomes FY RC	.50	.20
❑	141	Ismael Castro FY RC	.60	.25
❑	142	Travis Wong FY RC	.60	.25
❑	143	Michael Garciaparra FY RC	.50	.20
❑	144	Arnaldo Munoz FY RC	.50	.20
❑	145	Louis Sockalexis FY XRC	.50	.20
❑	146	Richard Hoblitzell REP	1.00	.40
❑	147	George Graham REP	1.00	.40
❑	148	Hal Chase REP	1.00	.40
❑	149	John McGraw REP	1.50	.60
❑	150	Bobby Wallace REP	1.00	.40
❑	151	David Shean REP	1.00	.40
❑	152	Richard Hoblitzell REP SP	2.50	1.00
❑	153	Hal Chase REP	1.00	.40
❑	154	Hooks Wiltse REP	1.00	.40
❑	155	George Brett RET	3.00	1.25
❑	156	Willie Mays RET	3.00	1.25
❑	157	Honus Wagner RET SP	10.00	4.00
❑	158	Nolan Ryan RET	4.00	1.50
❑	159	Reggie Jackson RET	1.50	.60
❑	160	Mike Schmidt RET	3.00	1.25
❑	161	Josh Barfield PROS	.50	.20
❑	162	Grady Sizemore PROS	1.25	.50
❑	163	Justin Morneau PROS	.50	.20
❑	164	Laynce Nix PROS	.50	.20
❑	165	Zack Greinke PROS	.50	.20
❑	166	Victor Martinez PROS	.75	.30
❑	167	Jeff Mathis PROS	.50	.20
❑	168	Casey Kotchman PROS	.50	.20
❑	169	Gabe Gross PROS	.50	.20
❑	170	Edwin Jackson FY RC	.60	.25
❑	171	Delmon Young FY SP RC	10.00	4.00
❑	172	Eric Duncan FY SP RC	6.00	2.50
❑	173	Brian Snyder FY SP RC	5.00	2.00
❑	174	Chris Lubanski FY SP RC	5.00	2.00
❑	175	Ryan Harvey FY SP RC	6.00	2.50
❑	176	Nick Markakis FY SP RC	8.00	3.00
❑	177	Chad Billingsley FY SP RC	8.00	3.00
❑	178	Elizardo Ramirez FY RC	.60	.25
❑	179	Ben Francisco FY RC	.50	.20
❑	180	Franklin Gutierrez FY SP RC	5.00	2.00
❑	181	Aaron Hill FY SP RC	5.00	2.00
❑	182	Kevin Correia FY RC	.50	.20
❑	183	Kelly Shoppach FY RC	1.00	.40
❑	184	Felix Pie FY SP RC	8.00	3.00
❑	185	Adam Loewen FY SP RC	5.00	2.00
❑	186	Danny Garcia FY RC	.50	.20
❑	187	Rickie Weeks FY SP RC	8.00	3.00
❑	188	Robby Hammock FY SP RC	4.00	1.50
❑	189	Ryan Wagner FY SP RC	4.00	1.50
❑	190	Matt Kata FY SP RC	4.00	1.50
❑	191	Bo Hart FY SP RC	4.00	1.50
❑	192	Brandon Webb FY SP RC	6.00	2.50
❑	193	Bengie Molina	.50	.20
❑	194	Junior Spivey	.50	.20
❑	195	Gary Sheffield	.50	.20
❑	196	Jason Johnson	.50	.20
❑	197	David Ortiz	1.25	.50
❑	198	Roberto Alomar	.75	.30
❑	199	Wily Mo Pena	.50	.20
❑	200	Sammy Sosa	1.25	.50
❑	201	Jay Payton	.50	.20
❑	202	Dmitri Young	.50	.20
❑	203	Derrek Lee	.75	.30
❑	204A	Jeff Bagwell w/Hat	.75	.30
❑	204B	Jeff Bagwell w/o Hat	.75	.30
❑	205	Runelvys Hernandez	.50	.20
❑	206	Kevin Brown	.50	.20
❑	207	Wes Helms	.50	.20
❑	208	Eddie Guardado	.50	.20
❑	209	Orlando Cabrera	.50	.20
❑	210	Alfonso Soriano	.50	.20
❑	211	Ty Wigginton	.50	.20
❑	212A	Rich Harden Look Left	.75	.30
❑	212B	Rich Harden Look Right	.75	.30
❑	213	Mike Lieberthal	.50	.20
❑	214	Brian Giles	.50	.20
❑	215	Jason Schmidt	.50	.20
❑	216	Jamie Moyer	.50	.20
❑	217	Matt Morris	.50	.20
❑	218	Victor Zambrano	.50	.20
❑	219	Roy Halladay	.50	.20
❑	220	Mike Hampton	.50	.20
❑	221	Kevin Millar Sox	.50	.20
❑	222	Hideo Nomo	1.25	.50
❑	223	Milton Bradley	.50	.20
❑	224	Jose Guillen	.50	.20
❑	225	Derek Jeter	3.00	1.25
❑	226	Rondell White	.50	.20
❑	227A	Hank Blalock Blue Jsy	.50	.20
❑	227B	Hank Blalock White Jsy	.50	.20
❑	228	Shigetoshi Hasegawa	.50	.20
❑	229	Mike Mussina	.75	.30
❑	230	Cristian Guzman	.50	.20
❑	231A	Todd Helton Blue	.75	.30
❑	231B	Todd Helton Green	.75	.30
❑	232	Kenny Lofton	.50	.20
❑	233	Carl Everett	.50	.20
❑	234	Shea Hillenbrand	.50	.20
❑	235	Brad Fullmer	.50	.20
❑	236	Bernie Williams	.75	.30
❑	237	Vicente Padilla	.50	.20
❑	238	Tim Worrell	.50	.20
❑	239	Juan Gonzalez	.50	.20
❑	240	Ichiro Suzuki	2.50	1.00
❑	241	Aaron Boone	.50	.20

❑ 242 Shannon Stewart .50 .20
❑ 243A Barry Zito Blue .50 .20
❑ 243B Barry Zito Green .50 .20
❑ 244 Reggie Sanders .50 .20
❑ 245 Scott Podsednik .50 .20
❑ 246 Miguel Cabrera 1.25 .50
❑ 247 Angel Berroa .50 .20
❑ 248 Carlos Zambrano .50 .20
❑ 249 Marlon Byrd .50 .20
❑ 250 Mark Prior .75 .30
❑ 251 Esteban Loaiza .50 .20
❑ 252 David Eckstein .50 .20
❑ 253 Alex Cintron .50 .20
❑ 254 Melvin Mora .50 .20
❑ 255 Russ Ortiz .50 .20
❑ 256 Carlos Lee .50 .20
❑ 257 Tino Martinez .75 .30
❑ 258 Randy Wolf .50 .20
❑ 259 Jason Phillips .50 .20
❑ 260 Vladimir Guerrero 1.25 .50
❑ 261 Brad Wilkerson .50 .20
❑ 262 Ivan Rodriguez .75 .30
❑ 263 Matt Lawton .50 .20
❑ 264 Adam Dunn .50 .20
❑ 265 Joe Borowski .50 .20
❑ 266 Jody Gerut .50 .20
❑ 267 Alex Rodriguez 2.00 .75
❑ 268 Brendan Donnelly .50 .20
❑ 269A Randy Johnson Grey 1.25 .50
❑ 269B Randy Johnson Pink 1.25 .50
❑ 270 Nomar Garciaparra 2.00 .75
❑ 271 Javy Lopez .50 .20
❑ 272 Travis Hafner .50 .20
❑ 273 Juan Pierre .50 .20
❑ 274 Morgan Ensberg .50 .20
❑ 275 Albert Pujols 2.50 1.00
❑ 276 Jason LaRue .50 .20
❑ 277 Paul Lo Duca .50 .20
❑ 278 Andy Pettitte .75 .30
❑ 279 Mike Piazza 2.00 .75
❑ 280A Jim Thome Blue .75 .30
❑ 280B Jim Thome Green .75 .30
❑ 281 Marquis Grissom .50 .20
❑ 282 Woody Williams .50 .20
❑ 283A Curt Schilling Look Ahead .50 .20
❑ 283B Curt Schilling Look Right .50 .20
❑ 284A Chipper Jones Blue 1.25 .50
❑ 284B Chipper Jones Yellow 1.25 .50
❑ 285 Deivi Cruz .50 .20
❑ 286 Johnny Damon .75 .30
❑ 287 Chin-Hui Tsao .50 .20
❑ 288 Alex Gonzalez .50 .20
❑ 289 Billy Wagner .50 .20
❑ 290 Jason Giambi .50 .20
❑ 291 Keith Foulke .50 .20
❑ 292 Jerome Williams .50 .20
❑ 293 Livan Hernandez .50 .20
❑ 294 Aaron Guiel .50 .20
❑ 295 Randall Simon .50 .20
❑ 296 Byung-Hyun Kim .50 .20
❑ 297 Jorge Julio .50 .20
❑ 298 Miguel Batista .50 .20
❑ 299 Rafael Furcal .50 .20
❑ 300A Dontrelle Willis No Smile 1.25 .50
❑ 300B Dontrelle Willis Smile SP 4.00 1.50
❑ 301 Alex Sanchez .50 .20
❑ 302 Shawn Chacon .50 .20
❑ 303 Matt Clement .50 .20
❑ 304 Luis Matos .50 .20
❑ 305 Steve Finley .50 .20
❑ 306 Marcus Giles .50 .20
❑ 307 Boomer Wells .50 .20
❑ 308 Jeromy Burnitz .50 .20
❑ 309 Mike MacDougal .50 .20
❑ 310 Mariano Rivera 1.25 .50
❑ 311 Adrian Beltre .50 .20
❑ 312 Mark Loretta .50 .20
❑ 313 Ugueth Urbina .50 .20
❑ 314 Bill Mueller .50 .20
❑ 315 Johan Santana .75 .30
❑ NNO Vintage Buyback

2002 Topps 206

❑ COMPLETE SET (525) 220.00 110.00
❑ COMPLETE SERIES 1 (180) 60.00 25.00
❑ COMPLETE SERIES 2 (180) 60.00 25.00

❑ COMPLETE SERIES 3 (165) 100.00 50.00
❑ COM(1-140/181-270/308-418) .50 .20
❑ COMMON (141-155/271-285) .50 .20
❑ COMMON RC (308-418) .50 .20
❑ COMMON SP (308-398) 2.00 .75
❑ COMMON FYP SP (419-432) 1.00 .40
❑ COMMON RET SP (433-447) 2.00 .75
❑ 1 Vladimir Guerrero 1.25 .50
❑ 2 Sammy Sosa 1.25 .50
❑ 3 Garret Anderson .50 .20
❑ 4 Rafael Palmeiro .75 .30
❑ 5 Juan Gonzalez .50 .20
❑ 6 John Smoltz .75 .30
❑ 7 Mark Mulder .50 .20
❑ 8 Jon Lieber .50 .20
❑ 9 Greg Maddux 2.00 .75
❑ 10 Moises Alou .50 .20
❑ 11 Joe Randa .50 .20
❑ 12 Bobby Abreu .50 .20
❑ 13 Juan Pierre .50 .20
❑ 14 Kerry Wood .50 .20
❑ 15 Craig Biggio .75 .30
❑ 16 Curt Schilling .50 .20
❑ 17 Brian Jordan .50 .20
❑ 18 Edgardo Alfonzo .50 .20
❑ 19 Darren Dreifort .50 .20
❑ 20 Todd Helton .75 .30
❑ 21 Ramon Ortiz .50 .20
❑ 22 Ichiro Suzuki 2.50 1.00
❑ 23 Jimmy Rollins .50 .20
❑ 24 Darin Erstad .50 .20
❑ 25 Shawn Green .50 .20
❑ 26 Tino Martinez .75 .30
❑ 27 Bret Boone .50 .20
❑ 28 Alfonso Soriano .50 .20
❑ 29 Chan Ho Park .50 .20
❑ 30 Roger Clemens 2.50 1.00
❑ 31 Cliff Floyd .50 .20
❑ 32 Johnny Damon .75 .30
❑ 33 Frank Thomas 1.25 .50
❑ 34 Barry Bonds 3.00 1.25
❑ 35 Luis Gonzalez .50 .20
❑ 36 Carlos Lee .50 .20
❑ 37 Roberto Alomar .75 .30
❑ 38 Carlos Delgado .50 .20
❑ 39 Nomar Garciaparra 2.00 .75
❑ 40 Jason Kendall .50 .20
❑ 41 Scott Rolen .75 .30
❑ 42 Tom Glavine .75 .30
❑ 43 Ryan Klesko .50 .20
❑ 44 Brian Giles .50 .20
❑ 45 Bud Smith .50 .20
❑ 46 Charles Nagy .50 .20
❑ 47 Tony Gwynn 1.50 .60
❑ 48 C.C. Sabathia .50 .20
❑ 49 Frank Catalanotto .50 .20
❑ 50 Jerry Hairston .50 .20
❑ 51 Jeromy Burnitz .50 .20
❑ 52 David Justice .50 .20
❑ 53 Bartolo Colon .50 .20
❑ 54 Andres Galarraga .50 .20
❑ 55 Jeff Weaver .50 .20
❑ 56 Terrence Long .50 .20
❑ 57 Tsuyoshi Shinjo .50 .20
❑ 58 Barry Zito .50 .20
❑ 59 Mariano Rivera 1.25 .50
❑ 60 John Olerud .50 .20
❑ 61 Randy Johnson 1.25 .50
❑ 62 Kenny Lofton .50 .20
❑ 63 Jermaine Dye .50 .20
❑ 64 Troy Glaus .50 .20
❑ 65 Larry Walker .50 .20
❑ 66 Hideo Nomo 1.25 .50
❑ 67 Mike Mussina .75 .30
❑ 68 Paul LoDuca .50 .20
❑ 69 Magglio Ordonez .50 .20
❑ 70 Paul O'Neill .75 .30
❑ 71 Sean Casey .50 .20
❑ 72 Lance Berkman .50 .20
❑ 73 Adam Dunn .50 .20
❑ 74 Aramis Ramirez .50 .20
❑ 75 Rafael Furcal .50 .20
❑ 76 Gary Sheffield .50 .20
❑ 77 Todd Hollandsworth .50 .20
❑ 78 Chipper Jones 1.25 .50
❑ 79 Bernie Williams .75 .30
❑ 80 Richard Hidalgo .50 .20
❑ 81 Eric Chavez .50 .20
❑ 82 Mike Piazza 2.00 .75
❑ 83 J.D. Drew .50 .20
❑ 84 Ken Griffey Jr. 2.00 .75
❑ 85 Joe Kennedy .50 .20
❑ 86 Joel Pineiro .50 .20
❑ 87 Josh Towers .50 .20
❑ 88 Andruw Jones .75 .30
❑ 89 Carlos Beltran .50 .20
❑ 90 Mike Cameron .50 .20
❑ 91 Albert Pujols 2.50 1.00
❑ 92 Alex Rodriguez 2.00 .75
❑ 93 Omar Vizquel .75 .30
❑ 94 Juan Encarnacion .50 .20
❑ 95 Jeff Bagwell .75 .30
❑ 96 Jose Canseco .75 .30
❑ 97 Ben Sheets .50 .20
❑ 98 Mark Grace .75 .30
❑ 99 Mike Sweeney .50 .20
❑ 100 Mark McGwire 3.00 1.25
❑ 101 Ivan Rodriguez .75 .30
❑ 102 Rich Aurilia .50 .20
❑ 103 Cristian Guzman .50 .20
❑ 104 Roy Oswalt .50 .20
❑ 105 Tim Hudson .50 .20
❑ 106 Brent Abernathy .50 .20
❑ 107 Mike Hampton .50 .20
❑ 108 Miguel Tejada .50 .20
❑ 109 Bobby Higginson .50 .20
❑ 110 Edgar Martinez .75 .30
❑ 111 Jorge Posada .75 .30
❑ 112 Jason Giambi Yankees .50 .20
❑ 113 Pedro Astacio .50 .20
❑ 114 Kazuhiro Sasaki .50 .20
❑ 115 Preston Wilson .50 .20
❑ 116 Jason Bere .50 .20
❑ 117 Mark Quinn .50 .20
❑ 118 Pokey Reese .50 .20
❑ 119 Derek Jeter 3.00 1.25
❑ 120 Shannon Stewart .50 .20
❑ 121 Jeff Kent .50 .20
❑ 122 Jeremy Giambi .50 .20
❑ 123 Pat Burrell .50 .20
❑ 124 Jim Edmonds .50 .20
❑ 125 Mark Buehrle .50 .20
❑ 126 Kevin Brown .50 .20
❑ 127 Raul Mondesi .50 .20
❑ 128 Pedro Martinez .75 .30
❑ 129 Jim Thome .75 .30
❑ 130 Russ Ortiz .50 .20
❑ 131 Brandon Duckworth PROS .50 .20
❑ 132 Ryan Jamison PROS .50 .20
❑ 133 Brandon Inge PROS .50 .20
❑ 134 Felipe Lopez PROS .50 .20
❑ 135 Jason Lane PROS .50 .20
❑ 136 Forrest Johnson PROS RC .50 .20
❑ 137 Greg Nash PROS .50 .20
❑ 138 Covelli Crisp PROS 2.00 .75
❑ 139 Nick Neugebauer PROS .50 .20
❑ 140 Dustan Mohr PROS .50 .20
❑ 141 Freddy Sanchez FYP RC 2.00 .75
❑ 142 Justin Backsmeyer FYP RC .50 .20
❑ 143 Jorge Julio FYP .50 .20
❑ 144 Ryan Mottl FYP RC .50 .20
❑ 145 Chris Tritle FYP RC .50 .20
❑ 146 Noochie Varner FYP RC .50 .20
❑ 147 Brian Rogers FYP .50 .20

❑ 148 Michael Hill FYP RC .50 .20
❑ 149 Luis Pineda FYP .50 .20
❑ 150 Rich Thompson FYP RC .50 .20
❑ 151 Bill Hall FYP .50 .20
❑ 152 Juan Dominguez FYP RC .50 .20
❑ 153 Justin Woodrow FYP .50 .20
❑ 154 Nic Jackson FYP RC .50 .20
❑ 155 Laynce Nix FYP RC 1.50 .60
❑ 156 Hank Aaron RET 5.00 2.00
❑ 157 Ernie Banks RET 2.50 1.00
❑ 158 Johnny Bench RET 2.50 1.00
❑ 159 George Brett RET 5.00 2.00
❑ 160 Carlton Fisk RET 1.50 .60
❑ 161 Bob Gibson RET 1.50 .60
❑ 162 Reggie Jackson RET 1.50 .60
❑ 163 Don Mattingly RET 5.00 2.00
❑ 164 Kirby Puckett RET 2.50 1.00
❑ 165 Frank Robinson RET 1.50 .60
❑ 166 Nolan Ryan RET 6.00 2.50
❑ 167 Tom Seaver RET 1.50 .60
❑ 168 Mike Schmidt RET 5.00 2.00
❑ 169 Dave Winfield RET 1.00 .40
❑ 170 Carl Yastrzemski RET 3.00 1.25
❑ 171 Frank Chance REP 1.00 .40
❑ 172 Ty Cobb REP 5.00 2.00
❑ 173 Sam Crawford REP 1.00 .40
❑ 174 Johnny Evers REP 1.00 .40
❑ 175 John McGraw REP 1.50 .60
❑ 176 Eddie Plank REP 2.50 1.00
❑ 177 Tris Speaker REP 2.50 1.00
❑ 178 Joe Tinker REP 1.00 .40
❑ 179 H.Wagner Orange REP 8.00 3.00
❑ 180 Cy Young REP 2.50 1.00
❑ 181 Javier Vazquez .50 .20
❑ 182A Mark Mulder Green Jsy .50 .20
❑ 182B Mark Mulder White Jsy .50 .20
❑ 183A Roger Clemens Blue Jsy 2.50 1.00
❑ 183B Roger Clemens Pinstripes 2.50 1.00
❑ 184 Kazuhisa Ishii RC .75 .30
❑ 185 Roberto Alomar .75 .30
❑ 186 Lance Berkman .50 .20
❑ 187A Adam Dunn Arms Folded .50 .20
❑ 187B Adam Dunn w/Bat .50 .20
❑ 188A Aramis Ramirez w/Bat .50 .20
❑ 188B Aramis Ramirez w/o Bat .50 .20
❑ 189 Chuck Knoblauch .50 .20
❑ 190 Nomar Garciaparra 2.00 .75
❑ 191 Brad Penny .50 .20
❑ 192A Gary Sheffield w/Bat .50 .20
❑ 192B Gary Sheffield w/o Bat .50 .20
❑ 193 Alfonso Soriano .50 .20
❑ 194 Andruw Jones .75 .30
❑ 195A Randy Johnson Black Jsy 1.25 .50
❑ 195B Randy Johnson Purple Jsy 1.25 .50
❑ 196A Corey Patterson Blue Jsy .50 .20
❑ 196B Corey Patterson Pinstripes .50 .20
❑ 197 Milton Bradley .50 .20
❑ 198A J.Damon Blue Jsy/Cap .75 .30
❑ 198B J.Damon Blue Jsy/Hlmt .75 .30
❑ 198C J.Damon White Jsy .75 .30
❑ 199A Paul Lo Duca Blue Jsy .50 .20
❑ 199B Paul Lo Duca White Jsy .50 .20
❑ 200A Albert Pujols Red Jsy 2.50 1.00
❑ 200B Albert Pujols Running 2.50 1.00
❑ 200C Albert Pujols w/Bat 2.50 1.00
❑ 201 Scott Rolen .75 .30
❑ 202A J.D. Drew Running .50 .20
❑ 202B J.D. Drew w/Bat .50 .20
❑ 202C J.D. Drew White Jsy .50 .20
❑ 203 Vladimir Guerrero 1.25 .50
❑ 204A Jason Giambi Blue Jsy .50 .20
❑ 204B Jason Giambi Grey Jsy .50 .20
❑ 204C Jason Giambi Pinstripes .50 .20
❑ 205A Moises Alou Grey Jsy .50 .20
❑ 205B Moises Alou Pinstripes .50 .20
❑ 206A Magglio Ordonez Signing .50 .20
❑ 206B Magglio Ordonez w/Bat .50 .20
❑ 207 Carlos Febles .50 .20
❑ 208 So Taguchi RC .75 .30
❑ 209A Rafael Palmeiro One Hand .75 .30
❑ 209B Rafael Palmeiro Two Hands .75 .30
❑ 210 David Wells .50 .20
❑ 211 Orlando Cabrera .50 .20
❑ 212 Sammy Sosa 1.25 .50
❑ 213 Armando Benitez .50 .20
❑ 214 Wes Helms .50 .20
❑ 215A Mariano Rivera Arms Folded 1.25 .50
❑ 215B Mariano Rivera Holding Ball 1.25 .50
❑ 216 Jimmy Rollins .50 .20
❑ 217 Matt Lawton .50 .20
❑ 218A Shawn Green w/Bat .50 .20
❑ 218B Shawn Green w/o Bat .50 .20
❑ 219A Bernie Williams w/Bat .75 .30
❑ 219B Bernie Williams w/o Bat .75 .30
❑ 220A Bret Boone Blue Jsy .50 .20
❑ 220B Bret Boone White Jsy .50 .20
❑ 221A Alex Rodriguez Blue Jsy 2.00 .75
❑ 221B Alex Rodriguez One Hand 2.00 .75
❑ 221C Alex Rodriguez Two Hands 2.00 .75
❑ 222 Roger Cedeno .50 .20
❑ 223 Marty Cordova .50 .20
❑ 224 Fred McGriff .75 .30
❑ 225A Chipper Jones Batting 1.25 .50
❑ 225B Chipper Jones Running 1.25 .50
❑ 226 Kerry Wood .50 .20
❑ 227A Larry Walker Grey Jsy .50 .20
❑ 227B Larry Walker Purple Jsy .50 .20
❑ 228 Robin Ventura .50 .20
❑ 229 Robert Fick .50 .20
❑ 230A Tino Martinez Black Glove .75 .30
❑ 230B Tino Martinez Throwing .75 .30
❑ 230C Tino Martinez w/Bat .75 .30
❑ 231 Ben Petrick .50 .20
❑ 232 Neifi Perez .50 .20
❑ 233 Pedro Martinez .75 .30
❑ 234A Brian Jordan Grey Jsy .50 .20
❑ 234B Brian Jordan White Jsy .50 .20
❑ 235 Freddy Garcia .50 .20
❑ 236A Derek Jeter Batting 3.00 1.25
❑ 236B Derek Jeter Blue Jsy 3.00 1.25
❑ 236C Derek Jeter Kneeling 3.00 1.25
❑ 237 Ben Grieve .50 .20
❑ 238A Barry Bonds Black Jsy 3.00 1.25
❑ 238B Barry Bonds w/Wrist Band 3.00 1.25
❑ 238C B.Bonds w/o Wrist Band 3.00 1.25
❑ 239 Luis Gonzalez .50 .20
❑ 240 Shane Halter .50 .20
❑ 241A Brian Giles Black Jsy .50 .20
❑ 241B Brian Giles Grey Jsy .50 .20
❑ 242 Bud Smith .50 .20
❑ 243 Richie Sexson .50 .20
❑ 244A Barry Zito Green Jsy .50 .20
❑ 244B Barry Zito White Jsy .50 .20
❑ 245 Eric Milton .50 .20
❑ 246A Ivan Rodriguez Blue Jsy .75 .30
❑ 246B Ivan Rodriguez Grey Jsy .75 .30
❑ 246C Ivan Rodriguez White Jsy .75 .30
❑ 247 Toby Hall .50 .20
❑ 248A Mike Piazza Black Jsy 2.00 .75
❑ 248B Mike Piazza Grey Jsy 2.00 .75
❑ 249 Ruben Sierra .50 .20
❑ 250A Tsuyoshi Shinjo Cap .50 .20
❑ 250B Tsuyoshi Shinjo Helmet .50 .20
❑ 251A Jermaine Dye Green Jsy .50 .20
❑ 251B Jermaine Dye White Jsy .50 .20
❑ 252 Roy Oswalt .50 .20
❑ 253 Todd Helton .75 .30
❑ 254 Adrian Beltre .50 .20
❑ 255 Doug Mientkiewicz .50 .20
❑ 256A Ichiro Suzuki Blue Jsy 2.50 1.00
❑ 256B Ichiro Suzuki w/Bat 2.50 1.00
❑ 256C Ichiro Suzuki White Jsy 2.50 1.00
❑ 257A C.C. Sabathia Blue Jsy .50 .20
❑ 257B C.C. Sabathia White Jsy .50 .20
❑ 258 Paul Konerko .50 .20
❑ 259 Ken Griffey Jr. 2.00 .75
❑ 260A Jeromy Burnitz w/Bat .50 .20
❑ 260B Jeromy Burnitz w/o Bat .50 .20
❑ 261 Hank Blalock PROS .75 .30
❑ 262 Mark Prior PROS .75 .30
❑ 263 Josh Beckett PROS .50 .20
❑ 264 Carlos Pena PROS .50 .20
❑ 265 Sean Burroughs PROS .50 .20
❑ 266 Austin Kearns PROS .50 .20
❑ 267 Chin-Hui Tsao PROS .50 .20
❑ 268 Dewon Brazelton PROS .50 .20
❑ 269 J.D. Martin PROS .50 .20
❑ 270 Marlon Byrd PROS .50 .20
❑ 271 Joe Mauer FYP RC 10.00 4.00
❑ 272 Jason Botts FYP RC .50 .20
❑ 273 Mauricio Lara FYP RC .50 .20
❑ 274 Jonny Gomes FYP RC 2.50 1.00
❑ 275 Gavin Floyd FYP RC 1.00 .40
❑ 276 Alex Requena FYP RC .50 .20
❑ 277 Jimmy Gobble FYP RC .50 .20
❑ 278 Chris Duffy FYP RC .50 .20
❑ 279 Colt Griffin FYP RC .50 .20
❑ 280 Ryan Church FYP RC 1.00 .40
❑ 281 Beltran Perez FYP RC .50 .20
❑ 282 Clint Nageotte FYP RC .75 .30
❑ 283 Justin Schuda FYP RC .50 .20
❑ 284 Scott Hairston FYP RC .75 .30
❑ 285 Mario Ramos FYP RC .50 .20
❑ 286A Tom Seaver White Sox RET 1.50 .60
❑ 286B Tom Seaver Mets RET 1.50 .60
❑ 287A Hank Aaron White Jsy RET 5.00 2.00
❑ 287B Hank Aaron Blue Jsy RET 5.00 2.00
❑ 288 Mike Schmidt RET 5.00 2.00
❑ 289A Robin Yount Blue Jsy RET 2.50 1.00
❑ 289B Robin Yount P'stripes RET 2.50 1.00
❑ 290 Joe Morgan RET 1.00 .40
❑ 291 Frank Robinson RET 1.50 .60
❑ 292A Reggie Jackson A's RET 1.50 .60
❑ 292B Reggie Jackson Yanks RET 1.50 .60
❑ 293A Nolan Ryan Astros RET 6.00 2.50
❑ 293B Nolan Ryan Rangers RET 6.00 2.50
❑ 294 Dave Winfield RET 1.00 .40
❑ 295 Willie Mays RET 5.00 2.00
❑ 296 Brooks Robinson RET 1.50 .60
❑ 297A Mark McGwire A's RET 6.00 2.50
❑ 297B Mark McGwire Cards RET 6.00 2.50
❑ 298 Honus Wagner RET 2.50 1.00
❑ 299A Sherry Magee REP 1.00 .40
❑ 299B Sherry Magie UER REP 1.00 .40
❑ 300 Frank Chance REP 1.00 .40
❑ 301A Joe Doyle NY REP 1.00 .40
❑ 301B Joe Doyle NY Nat'l REP 1.00 .40
❑ 302 John McGraw REP 1.50 .60
❑ 303 Jimmy Collins REP 1.00 .40
❑ 304 Buck Herzog REP 1.00 .40
❑ 305 Sam Crawford REP 1.00 .40
❑ 306 Cy Young REP 2.50 1.00
❑ 307 Honus Wagner Blue REP 8.00 3.00
❑ 308A A.Rodriguez Blue Jsy SP 4.00 1.50
❑ 308B A.Rodriguez White Jsy 2.00 .75
❑ 309 Vernon Wells .50 .20
❑ 310A B.Bonds w/Elbow Pad 3.00 1.25
❑ 310B B.Bonds w/o Elbow Pad SP 6.00 2.50
❑ 311 Vicente Padilla .50 .20
❑ 312A A.Soriano w/Wristband .50 .20
❑ 312B A.Soriano w/o Wristband SP 2.00 .75
❑ 313 Mike Piazza 2.00 .75
❑ 314 Jacque Jones .50 .20
❑ 315 Shawn Green SP 2.00 .75
❑ 316 Paul Byrd .50 .20
❑ 317 Lance Berkman .50 .20
❑ 318 Larry Walker .50 .20
❑ 319 Ken Griffey Jr. SP 4.00 1.50
❑ 320 Shea Hillenbrand .50 .20
❑ 321 Jay Gibbons .50 .20
❑ 322 Andruw Jones .75 .30
❑ 323 Luis Gonzalez SP 2.00 .75
❑ 324 Garret Anderson .50 .20
❑ 325 Roy Halladay .50 .20
❑ 326 Randy Winn .50 .20
❑ 327 Matt Morris .50 .20
❑ 328 Robb Nen .50 .20
❑ 329 Trevor Hoffman .50 .20
❑ 330 Kip Wells .50 .20
❑ 331 Orlando Hernandez .50 .20
❑ 332 Rey Ordonez .50 .20
❑ 333 Torii Hunter .50 .20
❑ 334 Geoff Jenkins .50 .20
❑ 335 Eric Karros .50 .20
❑ 336 Mike Lowell .50 .20
❑ 337 Nick Johnson .50 .20
❑ 338 Randall Simon .50 .20
❑ 339 Ellis Burks .50 .20
❑ 340A Sammy Sosa Blue Jsy SP 2.50 1.00
❑ 340B Sammy Sosa White Jsy 1.25 .50
❑ 341 Pedro Martinez .75 .30
❑ 342 Junior Spivey .50 .20
❑ 343 Vinny Castilla .50 .20
❑ 344 Randy Johnson SP 2.50 1.00
❑ 345 Chipper Jones SP 2.50 1.00
❑ 346 Orlando Hudson .50 .20
❑ 347 Albert Pujols SP 5.00 2.00
❑ 348 Rondell White .50 .20

❑ 349 Vladimir Guerrero 1.25 .50
❑ 350A Mark Prior Red SP 1.50 .60
❑ 350B Mark Prior Yellow .75 3.00
❑ 351 Eric Gagne .50 .20
❑ 352 Todd Zeile .50 .20
❑ 353 Manny Ramirez SP 2.00 .75
❑ 354 Kevin Millwood .50 .20
❑ 355 Troy Percival .50 .20
❑ 356A Jason Giambi Batting SP 2.00 .75
❑ 356B Jason Giambi Throwing .50 .20
❑ 357 Bartolo Colon .50 .20
❑ 358 Jeremy Giambi .50 .20
❑ 359 Jose Cruz Jr. .50 .20
❑ 360A I.Suzuki Blue Jsy SP 5.00 2.00
❑ 360B I.Suzuki White Jsy 2.50 1.00
❑ 361 Eddie Guardado .50 .20
❑ 362 Ivan Rodriguez .75 .30
❑ 363 Carl Crawford .50 .20
❑ 364 Jason Simontacchi RC .50 .20
❑ 365 Kenny Lofton .50 .20
❑ 366 Raul Mondesi .50 .20
❑ 367 A.J. Pierzynski .50 .20
❑ 368 Ugueth Urbina .50 .20
❑ 369 Rodrigo Lopez .50 .20
❑ 370A N.Garciaparra One Bat SP 4.00 1.50
❑ 370B N.Garciaparra Two Bats 2.00 .75
❑ 371 Craig Counsell .50 .20
❑ 372 Barry Larkin .75 .30
❑ 373 Carlos Pena .50 .20
❑ 374 Luis Castillo .50 .20
❑ 375 Raul Ibanez .50 .20
❑ 376 Kazuhisa Ishii SP 2.00 .75
❑ 377 Derek Lowe .50 .20
❑ 378 Curt Schilling .50 .20
❑ 379 Jim Thome Phillies .75 .30
❑ 380A Derek Jeter Blue SP 6.00 2.50
❑ 380B Derek Jeter Seats 3.00 1.25
❑ 381 Pat Burrell .50 .20
❑ 382 Jamie Moyer .50 .20
❑ 383 Eric Hinske .50 .20
❑ 384 Scott Rolen .75 .30
❑ 385 Miguel Tejada SP 2.00 .75
❑ 386 Andy Pettitte .75 .30
❑ 387 Mike Lieberthal .50 .20
❑ 388 Al Leiter .50 .20
❑ 389 Todd Helton SP 2.00 .75
❑ 390A Adam Dunn Bat SP 2.00 .75
❑ 390B Adam Dunn Glove .50 .20
❑ 391 Cliff Floyd .50 .20
❑ 392 Tim Salmon .75 .30
❑ 393 Joe Torre MG .75 .30
❑ 394 Bobby Cox MG .50 .20
❑ 395 Tony LaRussa MG .50 .20
❑ 396 Art Howe MG .50 .20
❑ 397 Bob Brenly MG .50 .20
❑ 398 Ron Gardenhire MG .50 .20
❑ 399 Mike Cuddyer PROS .50 .20
❑ 400 Joe Mauer PROS 10.00 4.00
❑ 401 Mark Teixeira PROS 1.25 .50
❑ 402 Hee Seop Choi PROS .50 .20
❑ 403 Angel Berroa PROS .50 .20
❑ 404 Jesse Foppert PROS RC .75 .30
❑ 405 Bobby Crosby PROS 1.25 .50
❑ 406 Jose Reyes PROS .75 .30
❑ 407 Casey Kotchman PROS RC 1.00 .40
❑ 408 Aaron Heilman PROS .50 .20
❑ 409 Adrian Gonzalez PROS .50 .20
❑ 410 Delwyn Young PROS RC 1.00 .40
❑ 411 Brett Myers PROS .50 .20
❑ 412 Justin Huber PROS RC .75 .30
❑ 413 Drew Henson PROS .50 .20
❑ 414 Taggert Bozied PROS RC .75 .30
❑ 415 Dontrelle Willis PROS RC 5.00 2.00
❑ 416 Rocco Baldelli PROS .50 .20
❑ 417 Jason Stokes PROS RC .50 .20
❑ 418 Brandon Phillips PROS .50 .20
❑ 419 Jake Blalock FYP RC .50 .20
❑ 420 Micah Schilling FYP RC 1.00 .40
❑ 421 Denard Span FYP RC 1.00 .40
❑ 422A J.Loney Red FYP RC 4.00 1.50
❑ 422B J.Loney w/Sky FYP RC 4.00 1.50
❑ 423A W.Bankston Blue FYP RC 2.00 .75
❑ 423B W.Bankston w/Sky FYP RC 2.00 .75
❑ 424 Jeremy Hermida FYP RC 5.00 2.00
❑ 425 Curtis Granderson FYP RC 3.00 1.25
❑ 426A J.Pridie Red FYP RC 1.00 .40
❑ 426B J.Pridie w/Sky FYP RC 1.00 .40
❑ 427 Larry Broadway FYP RC .50 .20
❑ 428A K.Greene Green FYP RC 8.00 3.00
❑ 428B K.Greene Red FYP RC 8.00 3.00
❑ 429 Joey Votto FYP RC 3.00 1.25
❑ 430A B.Upton Grey FYP RC 5.00 2.00
❑ 430B B.Upton w/People FYP RC 5.00 2.00
❑ 431A S.Santos Gold FYP RC 1.00 .40
❑ 431B S.Santos Grey FYP RC 1.00 .40
❑ 432 Brian Dopirak FYP RC 1.00 .40
❑ 433 Ozzie Smith RET SP 4.00 1.50
❑ 434 Wade Boggs RET SP 2.50 1.00
❑ 435 Yogi Berra RET SP 4.00 1.50
❑ 436 Al Kaline RET SP 4.00 1.50
❑ 437 Robin Roberts RET SP 2.00 .75
❑ 438 Roberto Clemente RET SP 8.00 3.00
❑ 439 Gary Carter RET SP 2.00 .75
❑ 440 Fergie Jenkins RET SP 2.00 .75
❑ 441 Orlando Cepeda RET SP 2.00 .75
❑ 442 Rod Carew RET SP 2.50 1.00
❑ 443 Harmon Killebrew RET SP 4.00 1.50
❑ 444 Duke Snider RET SP 2.50 1.00
❑ 445 Stan Musial RET SP 6.00 2.50
❑ 446 Hank Greenberg RET SP 4.00 1.50
❑ 447 Lou Brock RET SP 2.50 1.00
❑ 448 Jim Palmer RET 1.00 .40
❑ 449 John McGraw REP 1.50 .60
❑ 450 Mordecai Brown REP 1.00 .40
❑ 451 Christy Mathewson REP 1.50 .60
❑ 452 Sam Crawford REP 1.00 .40
❑ 453 Bill O'Hara REP 1.00 .40
❑ 454 Joe Tinker REP 1.00 .40
❑ 455 Nap Lajoie REP 1.50 .60
❑ 456 Honus Wagner Red REP 8.00 3.00
❑ NNO Repurchased Tobacco Card

2006 Topps 52

❑ COMP.SET w/o SPs (275) 80.00 40.00
❑ COMMON CARD (1-275) .50 .20
❑ COMMON LOGO VAR. 4.00 1.50
❑ LOGO VAR.STATED ODDS 1:5 H,1:5 R
❑ COMMON SP 6.00 2.50
❑ SP STATED ODDS 1:5 H, 1:5 R
❑ 1 Howie Kendrick (RC) 1.25 .50
❑ 2 Enrique Gonzalez (RC) .50 .20
❑ 3 Chuck James (RC) .75 .30
❑ 4 Chris Britton RC .50 .20
❑ 5 David Pauley (RC) .50 .20
❑ 6 Angel Pagan (RC) .50 .20
❑ 7 Pat Neshek RC 5.00 2.00
❑ 8 Walter Young (RC) .50 .20
❑ 9 Chris Denorfia (RC) .50 .20
❑ 10 Rafael Perez RC .50 .20
❑ 11 Ryan Spilborghs (RC) .75 .30
❑ 12 Jon Huber RC .50 .20
❑ 13 Jordan Tata RC .50 .20
❑ 14 Eric Reed (RC) .50 .20
❑ 15 Norris Hopper RC .50 .20
❑ 16 Scott Olsen (RC) .50 .20
❑ 17 Fernando Nieve (RC) .50 .20
❑ 18 Chris Booker (RC) .50 .20
❑ 19 Chad Billingsley (RC) .75 .30
❑ 20 Carlos Villanueva RC .50 .20
❑ 21 Craig Hansen RC 2.00 .75
❑ 22 Dave Gassner (RC) .50 .20
❑ 23 Mike Pelfrey RC 2.00 .75
❑ 24 Matt Smith RC .75 .30
❑ 25 Chris Roberson (RC) .50 .20
❑ 26 John Van Benschoten (RC) .50 .20
❑ 27 Kevin Frandsen (RC) .50 .20
❑ 28 Les Walrond (RC) .50 .20
❑ 29 James Shields RC .50 .20
❑ 30 Russell Martin (RC) .75 .30
❑ 31 Ben Zobrist (RC) .75 .30
❑ 32 John Rheinecker (RC) .50 .20
❑ 33 Francisco Rosario (RC) .50 .20
❑ 34 Santiago Ramirez (RC) .50 .20
❑ 35 Mike Napoli RC 1.25 .50
❑ 36 Tony Pena Jr. (RC) .50 .20
❑ 37A Jeff Karstens RC 1.25 .50
❑ 37B Jeff Karstens 52 Logo 4.00 1.50
❑ 38 Phil Stockman (RC) .50 .20
❑ 39 Kurt Birkins RC .50 .20
❑ 41 Buck Coats (RC) .50 .20
❑ 42 Jim Johnson RC .50 .20
❑ 43 Angel Guzman (RC) .50 .20
❑ 44 Kelly Shoppach (RC) .50 .20
❑ 45 Josh Wilson (RC) .50 .20
❑ 46 Jack Hannahan RC .50 .20
❑ 47 Ricky Nolasco (RC) .50 .20
❑ 48 T.J. Bohn (RC) .50 .20
❑ 49 Joel Zumaya (RC) 1.25 .50
❑ 50 Phil Barzilla RC .50 .20
❑ 51 Justin Huber (RC) .50 .20
❑ 52A Willy Aybar (RC) .50 .20
❑ 52B Willy Aybar 52 Logo 4.00 1.50
❑ 53 Tony Gwynn Jr. (RC) 1.25 .50
❑ 54 Chris Barnwell RC .50 .20
❑ 55 Henry Owens RC .75 .30
❑ 56 Jeff Bajenaru (RC) .50 .20
❑ 57 Jonah Bayliss RC .50 .20
❑ 58 Josh Sharpless RC .50 .20
❑ 59 Eliezer Alfonzo RC .50 .20
❑ 60 Bobby Livingston (RC) .50 .20
❑ 61 John Gall (RC) .50 .20
❑ 62 Ruddy Lugo (RC) .50 .20
❑ 63 Fabio Castro RC .50 .20
❑ 64 Casey Janssen RC .75 .30
❑ 65 Mike O'Connor RC .50 .20
❑ 66 Kendry Morales (RC) .75 .30
❑ 67 James Hoey RC .50 .20
❑ 68 Dustin Moseley (RC) .50 .20
❑ 69 Peter Moylan RC .50 .20
❑ 70 Manny Delcarmen (RC) .50 .20
❑ 71 Rich Hill (RC) .50 .20
❑ 72 Boone Logan RC .50 .20
❑ 73 Cody Ross (RC) .50 .20
❑ 74 Fausto Carmona (RC) .50 .20
❑ 75 Ramon Ramirez (RC) .50 .20
❑ 76 Zach Miner (RC) .50 .20
❑ 77 Hanley Ramirez (RC) 1.25 .50
❑ 78 Josh Johnson (RC) .75 .30
❑ 79 Taylor Buchholz (RC) .50 .20
❑ 80 Joe Nelson (RC) .50 .20
❑ 81 Hong-Chih Kuo (RC) 1.25 .50
❑ 82 Chris Mabeus (RC) .50 .20
❑ 83 Willie Eyre (RC) .50 .20
❑ 84 John Maine (RC) .75 .30
❑ 85 Yurendell DeCaster (RC) .50 .20
❑ 86 Mike Thompson RC .50 .20
❑ 87 Brian Wilson RC .50 .20
❑ 88A Matt Cain (RC) .75 .30
❑ 88B Matt Cain 52 Logo 5.00 2.00
❑ 89 Sean Green RC .50 .20
❑ 90 Tyler Johnson (RC) .50 .20
❑ 91 Jason Childers RC .50 .20
❑ 92 Wes Littleton (RC) .50 .20
❑ 93 Ty Taubenheim RC .75 .30
❑ 94 Saul Rivera (RC) .50 .20
❑ 95 Reggie Willits RC 2.00 .75
❑ 96 Carlos Quentin (RC) .75 .30
❑ 97 Macay McBride (RC) .50 .20
❑ 98 Brandon Fahey RC .50 .20
❑ 99 Sean Marshall (RC) .50 .20
❑ 100 Sean Tracey (RC) .50 .20
❑ 101 Brian Slocum (RC) .50 .20
❑ 102 Choo Freeman (RC) .50 .20
❑ 103 Brent Clevlen (RC) .75 .30
❑ 104 Josh Willingham (RC) .50 .20
❑ 105 Chris Resop (RC) .50 .20
❑ 106 Chris Sampson RC .50 .20
❑ 107A James Loney (RC) .75 .30
❑ 107B James Loney 52 Logo 5.00 2.00
❑ 108 Matt Kemp (RC) .75 .30

❑	109	Jason Kubel (RC)	.50	.20
❑	110	Brian Bannister (RC)	.50	.20
❑	111	Kevin Thompson (RC)	.50	.20
❑	112	Jeremy Brown (RC)	.50	.20
❑	113	Brian Sanches (RC)	.50	.20
❑	114	Nate McLouth (RC)	.50	.20
❑	115	Ben Johnson (RC)	.50	.20
❑	116	Jonathan Sanchez (RC)	.50	.20
❑	117	Mark Lowe (RC)	.50	.20
❑	118	Skip Schumaker (RC)	.50	.20
❑	119	Jason Hammel (RC)	.50	.20
❑	120	Drew Meyer (RC)	.50	.20
❑	121	Melvin Dorta RC	.50	.20
❑	122	Jeff Mathis (RC)	.50	.20
❑	123	Davis Romero (RC)	.50	.20
❑	124	Joey Devine RC	.50	.20
❑	125	Sendy Rleal RC	.50	.20
❑	126	Freddie Bynum (RC)	.50	.20
❑	127	Brian Anderson (RC)	.50	.20
❑	128	Jeremy Sowers (RC)	.50	.20
❑	129	Ryan Shealy (RC)	.50	.20
❑	130	Reggie Abercrombie (RC)	.50	.20
❑	131	Matt Albers (RC)	.50	.20
❑	132	Lastings Milledge (RC)	.75	.30
❑	133	Robert Andino RC	.50	.20
❑	134	Chris Demaria RC	.50	.20
❑	135	Boof Bonser (RC)	.75	.30
❑	136	Alay Soler RC	.50	.20
❑	137	Wil Nieves (RC)	.50	.20
❑	138	Mike Rouse (RC)	.50	.20
❑	139	Carlos Ruiz (RC)	.50	.20
❑	140	Matt Capps (RC)	.50	.20
❑	141	Travis Ishikawa (RC)	.50	.20
❑	142	Josh Kinney RC	.50	.20
❑	143	Josh Rupe (RC)	.50	.20
❑	144	Shaun Marcum (RC)	.50	.20
❑	145	Jason Bergmann RC	.50	.20
❑	146	Tommy Murphy (RC)	.50	.20
❑	147	Martin Prado (RC)	.50	.20
❑	148	Val Majewski (RC)	.50	.20
❑	149	Ian Kinsler (RC)	.75	.30
❑	150	Joe Winkelsas (RC)	.50	.20
❑	151	Agustin Montero (RC)	.50	.20
❑	152	Joe Inglett RC	.50	.20
❑	153	Manuel Corpas RC	.50	.20
❑	154	Yusmeiro Petit (RC)	.50	.20
❑	155	Mark Woodyard (RC)	.50	.20
❑	156	Jeff Fulchino RC	.50	.20
❑	157	Stephen Andrade (RC)	.50	.20
❑	158	Tim Hamulack (RC)	.50	.20
❑	159	Colter Bean (RC)	.50	.20
❑	160	Anderson Hernandez (RC)	.50	.20
❑	161	Kevin Reese (RC)	.50	.20
❑	162	Jason Windsor (RC)	.50	.20
❑	163A	Paul Maholm (RC)	.50	.20
❑	163B	Paul Maholm 52 Logo	5.00	2.00
❑	164	Jeremy Accardo RC	.50	.20
❑	165	Joel Guzman (RC)	.50	.20
❑	166	Erick Aybar (RC)	.50	.20
❑	167	Scott Thorman (RC)	.50	.20
❑	168	Adam Loewen (RC)	.50	.20
❑	169	Carlos Marmol RC	.50	.20
❑	170	Bill Bray (RC)	.50	.20
❑	171	Edward Mujica RC	.50	.20
❑	172	Jeremy Hermida (RC)	.50	.20
❑	173	Taylor Tankersley (RC)	.50	.20
❑	174	Bobby Keppel (RC)	.50	.20
❑	175	Chris B. Young (RC)	.50	.20
❑	176	Josh Rabe RC	.50	.20
❑	177	T.J. Beam (RC)	.50	.20
❑	178A	Shane Komine RC	.75	.30
❑	178B	Shane Komine 52 Logo	5.00	2.00
❑	179	Scott Mathieson (RC)	.50	.20
❑	180	Josh Barfield (RC)	.50	.20
❑	181	Justin Knoedler (RC)	.50	.20
❑	182	Emiliano Fruto RC	.50	.20
❑	183	Adam Wainwright (RC)	.50	.20
❑	184	Nick Masset (RC)	.50	.20
❑	185	Ryan Roberts RC	.50	.20
❑	186	Brandon Watson (RC)	.50	.20
❑	187	Chris Bootcheck (RC)	.50	.20
❑	188	Dan Ortmeier (RC)	.50	.20
❑	189	Kevin Barry (RC)	.50	.20
❑	190	Cory Morris RC	.50	.20
❑	191	Kason Gabbard (RC)	.50	.20
❑	192	Tom Mastny (RC)	.50	.20
❑	193	David Aardsma (RC)	.50	.20
❑	194	Anthony Reyes (RC)	.75	.30
❑	195	Mike Jacobs (RC)	.50	.20
❑	196	Conor Jackson (RC)	.75	.30
❑	197	Kenji Johjima RC	2.50	1.00
❑	198	Jack Taschner (RC)	.50	.20
❑	199	Renyel Pinto (RC)	.50	.20
❑	200	Chad Santos (RC)	.50	.20
❑	201	Aaron Rakers (RC)	.50	.20
❑	202	Franklin Gutierrez (RC)	.50	.20
❑	203	Chris Coste RC	2.00	.75
❑	204	Chris Iannetta RC	.50	.20
❑	205	Mike Vento (RC)	.50	.20
❑	206	Ryan O'Malley RC	.50	.20
❑	207	Jason Botts (RC)	.50	.20
❑	208	John Hattig (RC)	.50	.20
❑	209	Brandon Harper RC	.50	.20
❑	210	Ryan Theriot RC	5.00	2.00
❑	211	Travis Hughes (RC)	.50	.20
❑	212	Paul Hoover (RC)	.50	.20
❑	213	Brayan Pena (RC)	.50	.20
❑	214	Craig Breslow RC	.50	.20
❑	215	Eude Brito (RC)	.50	.20
❑	216A	Melky Cabrera (RC)	.75	.30
❑	216B	Melky Cabrera 52 Logo	5.00	2.00
❑	217A	Jonathan Broxton (RC)	.50	.20
❑	217B	Jonathan Broxton 52 Logo	4.00	1.50
❑	218	Bryan Corey (RC)	.50	.20
❑	219	Ron Flores RC	.50	.20
❑	220	Andrew Brown (RC)	.50	.20
❑	221	Jaime Bubela (RC)	.50	.20
❑	222	Jason Bulger (RC)	.50	.20
❑	223	Alberto Callaspo (RC)	.50	.20
❑	224	Jose Capellan (RC)	.50	.20
❑	225A	Cole Hamels (RC)	1.25	.50
❑	225B	Cole Hamels 52 Logo	8.00	3.00
❑	226	Bernie Castro (RC)	.50	.20
❑	227	Shin-Soo Choo (RC)	.75	.30
❑	228	Doug Clark (RC)	.50	.20
❑	229	Roy Corcoran RC	.50	.20
❑	230	Tim Corcoran RC	.50	.20
❑	231	Nelson Cruz (RC)	.50	.20
❑	232	Rajai Davis (RC)	.50	.20
❑	233A	Chris Duncan (RC)	.75	.30
❑	233B	Chris Duncan 52 Logo	5.00	2.00
❑	234	Scott Dunn (RC)	.50	.20
❑	235	Mike Esposito (RC)	.50	.20
❑	236	Scott Feldman RC	.50	.20
❑	237	Luis Figueroa RC	.50	.20
❑	238	Bartolome Fortunato (RC)	.50	.20
❑	239	Alejandro Freire RC	.50	.20
❑	240	J.J. Furmaniak (RC)	.50	.20
❑	241	Nick Markakis (RC)	.75	.30
❑	242	Matt Garza (RC)	.50	.20
❑	243	Justin Germano (RC)	.50	.20
❑	244	Alexis Gomez (RC)	.50	.20
❑	245	Tom Gorzelanny (RC)	.50	.20
❑	246	Dan Uggla (RC)	1.25	.50
❑	247	Jeremy Guthrie (RC)	.50	.20
❑	248	Stephen Drew (RC)	1.25	.50
❑	249	Brendan Harris (RC)	.50	.20
❑	250	Jeff Harris RC	.50	.20
❑	251	Corey Hart (RC)	.50	.20
❑	252	Chris Heintz RC	.50	.20
❑	253	Prince Fielder (RC)	2.00	.75
❑	254	Francisco Liriano (RC)	2.50	1.00
❑	255	Jason Hirsh (RC)	.50	.20
❑	256	J.R. House (RC)	.50	.20
❑	257	Zach Jackson (RC)	.50	.20
❑	258	Charlton Jimerson (RC)	.50	.20
❑	259	Greg Jones (RC)	.50	.20
❑	260	Mitch Jones (RC)	.50	.20
❑	261	Ryan Jorgensen RC	.50	.20
❑	262	Logan Kensing (RC)	.50	.20
❑	263	John Koronka (RC)	.50	.20
❑	264	Anthony Lerew (RC)	.50	.20
❑	265	Anibal Sanchez (RC)	.75	.30
❑	266	Juan Mateo RC	.50	.20
❑	267	Paul McAnulty (RC)	.50	.20
❑	268	Dustin McGowan (RC)	.50	.20
❑	269	Marty McLeary (RC)	.50	.20
❑	270	Ryan Zimmerman (RC)	3.00	1.25
❑	271	Dustin Nippert (RC)	.50	.20
❑	272	Eric O'Flaherty RC	.50	.20
❑	273	Ronny Paulino (RC)	.50	.20
❑	274	Tony Pena (RC)	.50	.20
❑	275	Hayden Penn (RC)	.50	.20
❑	276	Miguel Perez SP (RC)	6.00	2.50
❑	277	Paul Phillips SP (RC)	6.00	2.50
❑	278	Omar Quintanilla SP (RC)	6.00	2.50
❑	279	Guillermo Quiroz SP (RC)	6.00	2.50
❑	280	Darrell Rasner SP (RC)	6.00	2.50
❑	281	Kenny Ray SP (RC)	6.00	2.50
❑	282	Royce Ring SP (RC)	6.00	2.50
❑	283	Brian Rogers SP RC	8.00	3.00
❑	284	Ed Rogers SP (RC)	6.00	2.50
❑	285	Danny Sandoval SP RC	6.00	2.50
❑	286	Joe Saunders SP (RC)	6.00	2.50
❑	287	Chris Schroder SP RC	6.00	2.50
❑	288	Mike Smith SP (RC)	8.00	3.00
❑	289	Travis Smith SP (RC)	6.00	2.50
❑	290	Geovany Soto SP (RC)	6.00	2.50
❑	291	Brian Sweeney SP (RC)	6.00	2.50
❑	292	Jon Switzer SP (RC)	6.00	2.50
❑	293	Joe Thurston SP (RC)	6.00	2.50
❑	294	Jermaine Van Buren SP (RC)	6.00	2.50
❑	295	Ryan Garko SP (RC)	6.00	2.50
❑	296	Cla Meredith SP (RC)	8.00	3.00
❑	297	Luke Scott SP (RC)	6.00	2.50
❑	298	Andy Marte SP (RC)	6.00	2.50
❑	299	Jered Weaver SP (RC)	10.00	4.00
❑	300	Freddy Guzman SP (RC)	6.00	2.50
❑	301	Jonathan Papelbon SP (RC)	10.00	4.00
❑	302	John-Ford Griffin SP (RC)	6.00	2.50
❑	303	Jon Lester SP RC	10.00	4.00
❑	304	Shawn Hill SP (RC)	6.00	2.50
❑	305	Brian Myrow SP RC	6.00	2.50
❑	306	Anderson Garcia SP RC	6.00	2.50
❑	307	Andre Ethier SP (RC)	8.00	3.00
❑	308	Ben Hendrickson SP (RC)	6.00	2.50
❑	309	Alejandro Machado SP (RC)	6.00	2.50
❑	310	Justin Verlander SP (RC)	10.00	4.00
❑	311A	Mickey Mantle SP Blue	50.00	20.00
❑	311B	Mickey Mantle Black	10.00	4.00
❑	311C	Mickey Mantle Green	10.00	4.00
❑	311D	Mickey Mantle Orange	10.00	4.00
❑	311E	Mickey Mantle Red	10.00	4.00
❑	311F	Mickey Mantle Yellow	10.00	4.00
❑	312	Steve Stemle SP RC	6.00	2.50

2006 Topps Allen and Ginter

❑	COMPLETE SET (350)	120.00	60.00
❑	COMP.SET w/o SP's (300)	40.00	15.00
❑	COMMON SP	3.00	1.25

❑ SP STATED ODDS 1:2 HOBBY, 1:2 RETAIL
❑ SP CL: 5/15/25/35/45/50-59/65/85/105/115
❑ SP CL: 125/135/145/150-159/165/175/185
❑ SP CL: 205/215/235/245/251/255-256/265
❑ SP CL: 285/295/305/315/325/335/345
❑ FRAMED ORIGINALS ODDS 1:3227 H, 1:3227 R

❑	1	Albert Pujols	1.00	.40
❑	2	Aubrey Huff	.20	.10
❑	3	Mark Teixeira	.30	.15
❑	4	Vernon Wells	.20	.10
❑	5	Ken Griffey Jr. SP	5.00	2.00
❑	6	Nick Swisher	.20	.10
❑	7	Jose Reyes	.50	.20
❑	8	David Wright	.75	.30
❑	9	Vladimir Guerrero	.50	.20
❑	10	Andruw Jones	.30	.15
❑	11	Ramon Hernandez	.20	.10
❑	12	Miguel Tejada	.20	.10
❑	13	Juan Pierre	.20	.10

❑ 14 Jim Thome .30 .15
❑ 15 Austin Kearns SP 3.00 1.25
❑ 16 Jhonny Peralta .20 .10
❑ 17 Clint Barmes .20 .10
❑ 18 Angel Berroa .20 .10
❑ 19 Nomar Garciaparra .50 .20
❑ 20 Joe Nathan .20 .10
❑ 21 Brandon Webb .20 .10
❑ 22 Chad Tracy .20 .10
❑ 23 Derek Jeter 1.25 .50
❑ 24 Conor Jackson (RC) .30 .15
❑ 25 Jason Giambi SP 3.00 1.25
❑ 26 Johnny Estrada .20 .10
❑ 27 Luis Gonzalez .20 .10
❑ 28 Javier Vazquez .20 .10
❑ 29 Orlando Hudson .20 .10
❑ 30 Shawn Green .20 .10
❑ 31 Mark Buehrle .20 .10
❑ 32 Wily Mo Pena .20 .10
❑ 33 C.C. Sabathia .20 .10
❑ 34 Ronnie Belliard .20 .10
❑ 35 Travis Hafner SP 3.00 1.25
❑ 36 Mike Jacobs (RC) .20 .10
❑ 37 Roy Oswalt .20 .10
❑ 38 Zack Greinke .20 .10
❑ 39 J.D. Drew .20 .10
❑ 40 Jeff Kent .20 .10
❑ 41 Ben Sheets .20 .10
❑ 42 Luis Castillo .20 .10
❑ 43 Carlos Delgado .20 .10
❑ 44 Cliff Floyd .20 .10
❑ 45 Danny Haren SP 3.00 1.25
❑ 46 Bobby Abreu .20 .10
❑ 47 Jeromy Burnitz .20 .10
❑ 48 Khalil Greene .30 .15
❑ 49 Moises Alou .20 .10
❑ 50 Alex Rodriguez SP 5.00 2.00
❑ 51 Ervin Santana SP 3.00 1.25
❑ 52 Bartolo Colon SP 3.00 1.25
❑ 53 John Smoltz SP 3.00 1.25
❑ 54 David Ortiz SP 3.00 1.25
❑ 55 Hideki Matsui SP 3.00 1.25
❑ 56 Jermaine Dye SP 3.00 1.25
❑ 57 Victor Martinez SP 3.00 1.25
❑ 58 Willy Taveras SP 3.00 1.25
❑ 59 Brady Clark SP 3.00 1.25
❑ 60 Justin Morneau .20 .10
❑ 61 Xavier Nady .20 .10
❑ 62 Rich Harden .20 .10
❑ 63 Jack Wilson .20 .10
❑ 64 Brian Giles .20 .10
❑ 65 Jon Lieber SP 3.00 1.25
❑ 66 Dan Johnson .20 .10
❑ 67 Billy Wagner .20 .10
❑ 68 Rickie Weeks .20 .10
❑ 69 Chris Ray (RC) .20 .10
❑ 70 Chris Shelton .20 .10
❑ 71 Dmitri Young .20 .10
❑ 72 Ivan Rodriguez .30 .15
❑ 73 Jeremy Bonderman .20 .10
❑ 74 Justin Verlander (RC) .75 .30
❑ 75 Randy Johnson .50 .20
❑ 76 Magglio Ordonez .20 .10
❑ 77 Brandon Inge .20 .10
❑ 78 Placido Polanco .20 .10
❑ 79 Ryan Howard .75 .30
❑ 80 Jason Bay .20 .10
❑ 81 Sean Casey .20 .10
❑ 82 Jeremy Hermida (RC) .20 .07
❑ 83 Mike Cameron .20 .10
❑ 84 Trevor Hoffman .20 .10
❑ 85 Mike Matheny SP 3.00 1.25
❑ 86 Steve Finley .20 .10
❑ 87 Adam Everett .20 .10
❑ 88 Jason Isringhausen .20 .10
❑ 89 Jonny Gomes .20 .10
❑ 90 Barry Zito .20 .10
❑ 91 Bobby Crosby .20 .10
❑ 92 Eric Chavez .20 .10
❑ 93 Frank Thomas .50 .20
❑ 94 Huston Street .20 .10
❑ 95 Jorge Posada .30 .15
❑ 96 Casey Kotchman .20 .10
❑ 97 Darin Erstad .20 .10
❑ 98 Chipper Jones .50 .20
❑ 99 Jeff Francoeur .50 .20
❑ 100 Barry Bonds 1.00 .40
❑ 101 Alfonso Soriano .20 .10
❑ 102 Brandon Claussen .20 .10
❑ 103 Aaron Boone .20 .10
❑ 104 Roger Clemens 1.00 .40
❑ 105 Andy Pettitte SP 3.00 1.25
❑ 106 Nick Johnson .20 .10
❑ 107 Tom Gordon .20 .10
❑ 108 Orlando Hernandez .20 .10
❑ 109 Francisco Rodriguez .20 .10
❑ 110 Orlando Cabrera .20 .10
❑ 111 Edgar Renteria .20 .10
❑ 112 Tim Hudson .20 .10
❑ 113 Coco Crisp .20 .10
❑ 114 Matt Clement .20 .10
❑ 115 Greg Maddux SP 5.00 2.00
❑ 116 Paul Konerko .20 .10
❑ 117 Felipe Lopez .20 .10
❑ 118 Garrett Atkins .20 .10
❑ 119 Akinori Otsuka .20 .10
❑ 120 Craig Biggio .30 .15
❑ 121 Danys Baez .20 .10
❑ 122 Brad Penny .20 .10
❑ 123 Eric Gagne .20 .10
❑ 124 Lew Ford .20 .10
❑ 125 Mariano Rivera SP 3.00 1.25
❑ 126 Carlos Beltran .20 .10
❑ 127 Pedro Martinez .30 .15
❑ 128 Todd Helton .30 .15
❑ 129 Aaron Rowand .20 .10
❑ 130 Mike Lieberthal .20 .10
❑ 131 Oliver Perez .20 .10
❑ 132 Ryan Klesko .20 .10
❑ 133 Randy Winn .20 .10
❑ 134 Yuniesky Betancourt .20 .10
❑ 135 David Eckstein SP 3.00 1.25
❑ 136 Chad Orvella .20 .10
❑ 137 Toby Hall .20 .10
❑ 138 Hank Blalock .20 .10
❑ 139 B.J. Ryan .20 .10
❑ 140 Roy Halladay .20 .10
❑ 141 Livan Hernandez .20 .10
❑ 142 John Patterson .20 .10
❑ 143 Bengie Molina .20 .10
❑ 144 Brad Wilkerson .20 .10
❑ 145 Jorge Cantu SP 3.00 1.25
❑ 146 Mark Mulder .20 .10
❑ 147 Felix Hernandez .30 .15
❑ 148 Paul Lo Duca .20 .10
❑ 149 Prince Fielder (RC) .75 .30
❑ 150 Johnny Damon SP 3.00 1.25
❑ 151 Ryan Langerhans SP 3.00 1.25
❑ 152 Kris Benson SP 3.00 1.25
❑ 153 Curt Schilling SP 3.00 1.25
❑ 154 Manny Ramirez SP 3.00 1.25
❑ 155 Robinson Cano SP 3.00 1.25
❑ 156 Derrek Lee SP 3.00 1.25
❑ 157 A.J. Pierzynski SP 3.00 1.25
❑ 158 Adam Dunn SP 3.00 1.25
❑ 159 Cliff Lee SP 3.00 1.25
❑ 160 Grady Sizemore .30 .15
❑ 161 Jeff Francis .20 .10
❑ 162 Dontrelle Willis .20 .10
❑ 163 Brad Ausmus .20 .10
❑ 164 Preston Wilson .20 .10
❑ 165 Derek Lowe SP 3.00 1.25
❑ 166 Chris Capuano .20 .10
❑ 167 Joe Mauer .30 .15
❑ 168 Torii Hunter .20 .10
❑ 169 Chase Utley .50 .20
❑ 170 Zach Duke .20 .10
❑ 171 Jason Schmidt .20 .10
❑ 172 Adrian Beltre .20 .10
❑ 173 Eddie Guardado .20 .10
❑ 174 Richie Sexson .20 .10
❑ 175 Miguel Cabrera SP 3.00 1.25
❑ 176 Julio Lugo .20 .10
❑ 177 Francisco Cordero .20 .10
❑ 178 Kevin Millwood .20 .10
❑ 179 A.J. Burnett .20 .10
❑ 180 Jose Guillen .20 .10
❑ 181 Larry Bigbie .20 .10
❑ 182 Raul Ibanez .20 .10
❑ 183 Jake Peavy .20 .10
❑ 184 Pat Burrell .20 .10
❑ 185 Tom Glavine SP 3.00 1.25
❑ 186 J.J. Hardy .20 .10
❑ 187 Emil Brown .20 .10
❑ 188 Lance Berkman .20 .10
❑ 189 Marcus Giles .20 .10
❑ 190 Scott Podsednik .20 .10
❑ 191 Chone Figgins .20 .10
❑ 192 Melvin Mora .20 .10
❑ 193 Mark Loretta .20 .10
❑ 194 Carlos Zambrano .20 .10
❑ 195 Chien-Ming Wang .75 .30
❑ 196 Mark Prior .30 .15
❑ 197 Bobby Jenks .20 .10
❑ 198 Brian Fuentes .20 .10
❑ 199 Garret Anderson .30 .10
❑ 200 Ichiro Suzuki .75 .30
❑ 201 Brian Roberts .20 .10
❑ 202 Jason Kendall .20 .10
❑ 203 Milton Bradley .20 .10
❑ 204 Jimmy Rollins .20 .10
❑ 205 Brett Myers SP 3.00 1.25
❑ 206 Joe Randa .20 .10
❑ 207 Mike Piazza .50 .20
❑ 208 Matt Morris .20 .10
❑ 209 Omar Vizquel .30 .15
❑ 210 Jeremy Reed .20 .10
❑ 211 Chris Carpenter .20 .10
❑ 212 Jim Edmonds .30 .15
❑ 213 Scott Kazmir .30 .15
❑ 214 Travis Lee .20 .10
❑ 215 Michael Young SP 3.00 1.25
❑ 216 Rod Barajas .20 .10
❑ 217 Gustavo Chacin .20 .10
❑ 218 Lyle Overbay .20 .10
❑ 219 Troy Glaus .20 .10
❑ 220 Chad Cordero .20 .10
❑ 221 Jose Vidro .20 .10
❑ 222 Scott Rolen .30 .15
❑ 223 Carl Crawford .20 .10
❑ 224 Rocco Baldelli .20 .10
❑ 225 Mike Mussina .30 .15
❑ 226 Kelvim Escobar .20 .10
❑ 227 Corey Patterson .20 .10
❑ 228 Javy Lopez .20 .10
❑ 229 Jonathan Papelbon (RC) 1.00 .40
❑ 230 Aramis Ramirez .20 .10
❑ 231 Tadahito Iguchi .20 .10
❑ 232 Morgan Ensberg .20 .10
❑ 233 Mark Grudzielanek .20 .10
❑ 234 Mike Sweeney .20 .10
❑ 235 Shawn Chacon SP 3.00 1.25
❑ 236 Nick Punto .20 .10
❑ 237 Geoff Jenkins .20 .10
❑ 238 Carlos Lee .20 .10
❑ 239 David DeJesus .20 .10
❑ 240 Brad Lidge .20 .10
❑ 241 Bob Wickman .20 .10
❑ 242 Jon Garland .20 .10
❑ 243 Kerry Wood .20 .10
❑ 244 Bronson Arroyo .20 .10
❑ 245 Matt Holliday SP 4.00 1.50
❑ 246 Josh Beckett .20 .07
❑ 247 Johan Santana .30 .15
❑ 248 Rafael Furcal .20 .10
❑ 249 Shannon Stewart .20 .10
❑ 250 Gary Sheffield .20 .10
❑ 251 Josh Barfield SP (RC) 3.00 1.25
❑ 252 Kenji Johjima RC 1.00 .40
❑ 253 Ian Kinsler (RC) .30 .12
❑ 254 Brian Anderson (RC) .20 .10
❑ 255 Matt Cain SP (RC) 3.00 1.25
❑ 256 Josh Willingham SP (RC) 3.00 1.25
❑ 257 John Koronka (RC) .20 .10
❑ 258 Chris Duffy (RC) .20 .10
❑ 259 Brian McCann (RC) .20 .10
❑ 260 Hanley Ramirez (RC) .50 .20
❑ 261 Hong-Chih Kuo (RC) .50 .20
❑ 262 Francisco Liriano (RC) 1.00 .40
❑ 263 Anderson Hernandez (RC) .20 .10
❑ 264 Ryan Zimmerman (RC) 1.25 .50
❑ 265 Brian Bannister SP (RC) 3.00 1.25
❑ 266 Nolan Ryan 1.25 .50
❑ 267 Frank Robinson .20 .10
❑ 268 Roberto Clemente 1.50 .60
❑ 269 Hank Greenberg .50 .20
❑ 270 Napolean Lajoie .30 .10
❑ 271 Lloyd Waner .30 .10

❑ 272 Paul Waner .30 .10
❑ 273 Frankie Frisch .30 .10
❑ 274 Moose Skowron .20 .10
❑ 275 Mickey Mantle 2.50 1.00
❑ 276 Brooks Robinson .30 .15
❑ 277 Carl Yastrzemski .75 .30
❑ 278 Johnny Pesky .20 .10
❑ 279 Stan Musial .75 .30
❑ 280 Bill Mazeroski .30 .15
❑ 281 Harmon Killebrew .50 .20
❑ 282 Monte Irvin .20 .10
❑ 283 Bob Gibson .30 .15
❑ 284 Ted Williams 1.25 .50
❑ 285 Yogi Berra SP 3.00 1.25
❑ 286 Ernie Banks .50 .20
❑ 287 Bobby Doerr .20 .10
❑ 288 Josh Gibson .50 .20
❑ 289 Bob Feller .20 .10
❑ 290 Cal Ripken 2.00 .75
❑ 291 Bobby Cox MG .20 .10
❑ 292 Terry Francona MG .20 .10
❑ 293 Dusty Baker MG .20 .10
❑ 294 Ozzie Guillen MG .20 .10
❑ 295 Jim Leyland MG SP 3.00 1.25
❑ 296 Willie Randolph MG .20 .10
❑ 297 Joe Torre MG .30 .15
❑ 298 Felipe Alou MG .20 .10
❑ 299 Tony La Russa MG .20 .10
❑ 300 Frank Robinson MG .20 .10
❑ 301 Mike Tyson .75 .30
❑ 302 Duke Paoa Kahanamoku .20 .10
❑ 303 Jennie Finch .75 .30
❑ 304 Brandi Chastain .20 .10
❑ 305 Danica Patrick SP 8.00 3.00
❑ 306 Wendy Guey .20 .10
❑ 307 Hulk Hogan .60 .25
❑ 308 Carl Lewis .30 .10
❑ 309 John Wooden .30 .10
❑ 310 Randy Couture .20 .10
❑ 311 Andy Irons .20 .10
❑ 312 Takeru Kobayashi .60 .25
❑ 313 Leon Spinks .20 .10
❑ 314 Jim Thorpe .30 .10
❑ 315 Jerry Bailey SP 3.00 1.25
❑ 316 Adrian C. Anson REP .30 .15
❑ 317 John M. Ward REP .20 .10
❑ 318 Mike Kelly REP .30 .10
❑ 319 Capt. Jack Glasscock REP .20 .10
❑ 320 Aaron Hill .20 .10
❑ 321 Derrick Turnbow .20 .10
❑ 322 Nick Markakis (RC) .30 .15
❑ 323 Brad Hawpe .20 .10
❑ 324 Kevin Mench .20 .10
❑ 325 John Lackey SP 3.00 1.25
❑ 326 Chester A. Arthur .20 .10
❑ 327 Ulysses S. Grant .20 .10
❑ 328 Abraham Lincoln .30 .10
❑ 329 Grover Cleveland .20 .10
❑ 330 Benjamin Harrison .20 .10
❑ 331 Theodore Roosevelt .30 .10
❑ 332 Rutherford B. Hayes .20 .10
❑ 333 Chancellor Otto Von Bismarck .20 .10
❑ 334 Kaiser Wilhelm II .20 .10
❑ 335 Queen Victoria SP 3.00 1.25
❑ 336 Pope Leo XIII .20 .10
❑ 337 Thomas Edison .20 .10
❑ 338 Orville Wright .20 .10
❑ 339 Wilbur Wright .20 .10
❑ 340 Nathaniel Hawthorne .20 .10
❑ 341 Herman Melville .20 .10
❑ 342 Stonewall Jackson .20 .10
❑ 343 Robert E. Lee .20 .10
❑ 344 Andrew Carnegie .20 .10
❑ 345 John Rockefeller SP 3.00 1.25
❑ 346 Bob Fitzsimmons .20 .10
❑ 347 Billy The Kid .20 .10
❑ 348 Buffalo Bill .20 .10
❑ 349 Jesse James .20 .10
❑ 350 Statue Of Liberty .20 .10
❑ NNO Framed Originals 150.00 75.00

2007 Topps Allen and Ginter

❑ COMPLETE SET (350) 120.00 60.00
❑ COMP.SET w/o SP's (300) 50.00 20.00

❑ COMMON CARD .30 .12
❑ COMMON RC .50 .20
❑ COMMON SP 3.00 1.25
❑ SP STATED ODDS 1:2 HOBBY, 1:2 RETAIL
❑ SP CL: 5/43/48/58/63/107/110/119/130/137
❑ SP CL: 152/159/178/193/194/203/219/222
❑ SP CL: 224/243/263/301/302/303/306/307
❑ SP CL: 308/309/310/316/317/318/319/320
❑ SP CL: 321/322/325/326/327/330/331/334
❑ SP CL: 335/336/339/340/345/348/349/350
❑ FRAMED ORIGINALS ODDS 1:17,072 HOBBY
❑ FRAMED ORIGINALS ODDS 1:34,654 RETAIL
❑ 1 Ryan Howard 1.25 .50
❑ 2 Mike Gonzalez .30 .12
❑ 3 Austin Kearns .30 .12
❑ 4 Josh Hamilton (RC) 1.25 .50
❑ 5 Stephen Drew SP 3.00 1.25
❑ 6 Matt Murton .30 .12
❑ 7 Mickey Mantle 4.00 1.50
❑ 8 Howie Kendrick .30 .12
❑ 9 Alexander Graham Bell .30 .12
❑ 10 Jason Bay .30 .12
❑ 11 Hank Blalock .30 .12
❑ 12 Johan Santana .50 .20
❑ 13 Eleanor Roosevelt .30 .12
❑ 14 Kei Igawa RC 1.25 .50
❑ 15 Jeff Francoeur .75 .30
❑ 16 Carl Crawford .30 .12
❑ 17 Jhonny Peralta .30 .12
❑ 18 Mariano Rivera .75 .30
❑ 19 Mario Andretti .75 .30
❑ 20 Vladimir Guerrero .75 .30
❑ 21 Adam Wainwright .30 .12
❑ 22 Huston Street .30 .12
❑ 23 Cael Sanderson .30 .12
❑ 24 Susan B. Anthony .30 .12
❑ 25 Jay Payton .30 .12
❑ 26 P.T. Barnum .30 .12
❑ 27 Scott Podsednik .30 .12
❑ 28 Willie Randolph .30 .12
❑ 29 Sean Casey .30 .12
❑ 30 Eiffel Tower .30 .12
❑ 31 Kenji Johjima .75 .30
❑ 32 Felix Hernandez .50 .20
❑ 33 Elijah Dukes RC .75 .30
❑ 34 Mark Grudzielanek .30 .12
❑ 35 J.D. Drew .30 .12
❑ 36 Kevin Kouzmanoff .30 .12
❑ 37 Jonathan Papelbon .75 .30
❑ 38 Bobby Crosby .30 .12
❑ 39 Brooklyn Bridge .30 .12
❑ 40 Adam Dunn .30 .12
❑ 41 Lyle Overbay .30 .12
❑ 42 Brian Fuentes .30 .12
❑ 43 Scott Rolen SP 3.00 1.25
❑ 44 Matt Lindstrom (RC) .50 .20
❑ 45 Carlos Zambrano .30 .12
❑ 46 Cole Hamels .50 .20
❑ 47 Matt Kemp .30 .12
❑ 48 Gary Matthews SP 3.00 1.25
❑ 49 J.J. Putz .30 .12
❑ 50 Albert Pujols 1.50 .60
❑ 51 Dan Haren .30 .12
❑ 52 Aaron Harang .30 .12
❑ 53 Ferris Wheel .30 .12
❑ 54 Juan Rivera .30 .12
❑ 55 Ken Griffey Jr. 1.25 .50
❑ 56 Chien-Ming Wang 1.25 .50
❑ 57 Sean Henn (RC) .50 .20
❑ 58 Mike Mussina SP 3.00 1.25
❑ 59 Ian Snell .30 .12
❑ 60 Josh Barfield .30 .12
❑ 61 Justin Morneau .30 .12
❑ 62 Dwight D. Eisenhower .30 .12
❑ 63 Bengie Molina SP 3.00 1.25
❑ 64 Brett Myers .30 .12
❑ 65 Andy Marte .30 .12
❑ 66 Bill Hall .30 .12
❑ 67 Ryan Shealy .30 .12
❑ 68 Joe B. Scott .30 .12
❑ 69 Mike Rabelo RC .50 .20
❑ 70 Jermaine Dye .30 .12
❑ 71 Andre Ethier .50 .20
❑ 72 Bruce Lee 1.25 .50
❑ 73 Nick Punto .30 .12
❑ 74 Ervin Santana .30 .12
❑ 75 Troy Tulowitzki (RC) 1.25 .50
❑ 76 Garret Anderson .30 .12
❑ 77 Ryan Freel .30 .12
❑ 78 Carlos Guillen .30 .12
❑ 79 John Smoltz .50 .20
❑ 80 Chase Utley .75 .30
❑ 81 Mike Sweeney .30 .12
❑ 82 Joe Frazier .75 .30
❑ 83 Brad Lidge .30 .12
❑ 84 Casey Blake .30 .12
❑ 85 Ivan Rodriguez .50 .20
❑ 86 Roy Oswalt .30 .12
❑ 87 Akinori Iwamura RC 1.25 .50
❑ 88 Francisco Rodriguez .30 .12
❑ 89 John Lackey .30 .12
❑ 90 Miguel Cabrera .50 .20
❑ 91 Kevin Mench .30 .12
❑ 92 Victor Martinez .30 .12
❑ 93 Chad Tracy .30 .12
❑ 94 Charlie Manuel .30 .12
❑ 95 Hanley Ramirez .50 .20
❑ 96 Dontrelle Willis .30 .12
❑ 97 Doug Slaten RC .50 .20
❑ 98 Noah Lowry .30 .12
❑ 99 Shawn Green .30 .12
❑ 100 David Ortiz .75 .30
❑ 101 Mark Reynolds RC 1.25 .50
❑ 102 Preston Wilson .30 .12
❑ 103 Mohandas Gandhi .30 .12
❑ 104 Jeff Kent .30 .12
❑ 105 Lance Berkman .30 .12
❑ 106 C.C. Sabathia .30 .12
❑ 107 Jason Varitek SP 3.00 1.25
❑ 108 Mark Twain .30 .12
❑ 109 Melvin Mora .30 .12
❑ 110 Michael Young SP 3.00 1.25
❑ 111 Scott Hatteberg .30 .12
❑ 112 Erik Bedard .30 .12
❑ 113 Sitting Bull .30 .12
❑ 114 Homer Bailey (RC) .75 .30
❑ 115 Mark Teahen .30 .12
❑ 116 Ryan Braun (RC) 2.50 1.00
❑ 117 John Miles .30 .12
❑ 118 Coco Crisp .30 .12
❑ 119 Hunter Pence SP (RC) 5.00 2.00
❑ 120 Delmon Young (RC) .75 .30
❑ 121 Aramis Ramirez .30 .12
❑ 122 Magglio Ordonez .30 .12
❑ 123 Tadahito Iguchi .30 .12
❑ 124 Mark Selby .30 .12
❑ 125 Gil Meche .30 .12
❑ 126 Curt Schilling .50 .20
❑ 127 Brandon Phillips .30 .12
❑ 128 Milton Bradley .30 .12
❑ 129 Craig Monroe .30 .12
❑ 130 Jason Schmidt SP 3.00 1.25
❑ 131 Nick Markakis .50 .20
❑ 132 Paul Konerko .30 .12
❑ 133 Carlos Gomez RC .75 .30
❑ 134 Garrett Atkins .30 .12
❑ 135 Jered Weaver .50 .20
❑ 136 Edgar Renteria .30 .12
❑ 137 Jason Isringhausen SP 3.00 1.25
❑ 138 Ray Durham .30 .12
❑ 139 Bob Baffert .30 .12
❑ 140 Nick Swisher .30 .12
❑ 141 Brian McCann .30 .12
❑ 142 Orlando Hudson .30 .12

❑ 143 Brian Bannister .30 .12
❑ 144 Manny Acta .30 .12
❑ 145 Jose Vidro .30 .12
❑ 146 Carlos Quentin .30 .12
❑ 147 Billy Butler (RC) .75 .30
❑ 148 Kenny Rogers .30 .12
❑ 149 Tom Gordon .30 .12
❑ 150 Derek Jeter 2.00 .75
❑ 151 Bob Wickman .30 .12
❑ 152 Carlos Lee SP 3.00 1.25
❑ 153 Willy Taveras .30 .12
❑ 154 Paul LoDuca .30 .12
❑ 155 Ben Sheets .30 .12
❑ 156 Brian Roberts .30 .12
❑ 157 Freddy Adu .75 .30
❑ 158 Jason Kendall .30 .12
❑ 159 Michael Barrett SP 3.00 1.25
❑ 160 Frank Thomas .75 .30
❑ 161 Manny Ramirez .50 .20
❑ 162 Stanley Glenn .30 .12
❑ 163 Robinson Cano .50 .20
❑ 164 Phil Hughes (RC) 2.50 1.00
❑ 165 Joe Mauer .50 .20
❑ 166 Derrek Lee .30 .12
❑ 167 Jeff Weaver .30 .12
❑ 168 Joe Smith RC .30 .12
❑ 169 Louis Pasteur .30 .12
❑ 170 Gary Sheffield .30 .12
❑ 171 Luis Castillo .30 .12
❑ 172 Joe Torre .50 .20
❑ 173 Andy LaRoche (RC) .50 .20
❑ 174 Jamie Fischer .30 .12
❑ 175 Carlos Beltran .30 .12
❑ 176 Bronson Arroyo .30 .12
❑ 177 Rafael Furcal .30 .12
❑ 178 Juan Pierre SP 3.00 1.25
❑ 179 Matt Cain .50 .20
❑ 180 Alfonso Soriano .30 .12
❑ 181 Joe Borowski .30 .12
❑ 182 Conor Jackson .30 .12
❑ 183 Groundhog Day .30 .12
❑ 184 Pat Burrell .30 .12
❑ 185 Troy Glaus .30 .12
❑ 186 Joel Zumaya .50 .20
❑ 187 Russell Martin .30 .12
❑ 188 Josh Willingham .30 .12
❑ 189 Jarrod Saltalamacchia (RC) .75 .30
❑ 190 Scott Kazmir .50 .20
❑ 191 Jeremy Hermida .30 .12
❑ 192 Tower Bridge .30 .12
❑ 193 Rich Hill SP 3.00 1.25
❑ 194 Francisco Cordero SP 3.00 1.25
❑ 195 Mike Piazza .75 .30
❑ 196 Brad Ausmus .30 .12
❑ 197 Greg Louganis .30 .12
❑ 198 Frank Catalanotto .30 .12
❑ 199 Alejandro De Aza RC .75 .30
❑ 200 David Wright 1.25 .50
❑ 201 Freddy Sanchez .30 .12
❑ 202 Shea Hillenbrand .30 .12
❑ 203 Justin Verlander SP 3.00 1.25
❑ 204 Alex Gordon RC 2.50 1.00
❑ 205 Jimmy Rollins .30 .12
❑ 206 Mike Napoli .30 .12
❑ 207 Chris Burke .30 .12
❑ 208 Chipper Jones .75 .30
❑ 209 Randy Johnson .75 .30
❑ 210 Daisuke Matsuzaka RC 5.00 2.00
❑ 211 Orlando Cabrera .30 .12
❑ 212 B.J. Upton .30 .12
❑ 213 Lou Piniella .30 .12
❑ 214 Mike Cameron .30 .12
❑ 215 Luis Gonzalez .30 .12
❑ 216 Rickie Weeks .30 .12
❑ 217 Hideki Okajima RC 2.50 1.00
❑ 218 Johnny Estrada .30 .12
❑ 219 Dan Uggla SP 3.00 1.25
❑ 220 Ryan Zimmerman .75 .30
❑ 221 Tony Gwynn Jr. .30 .12
❑ 222 Rocco Baldelli SP 3.00 1.25
❑ 223 Xavier Nady .30 .12
❑ 224 Josh Bard SP 3.00 1.25
❑ 225 Raul Ibanez .30 .12
❑ 226 Chris Carpenter .30 .12
❑ 227 Matt DeSalvo (RC) .50 .20
❑ 228 Jack the Ripper .30 .12
❑ 229 Eric Chavez .30 .12
❑ 230 Jose Reyes .75 .30
❑ 231 Glen Perkins (RC) .50 .20
❑ 232 Gregg Zaun .30 .12
❑ 233 Jim Thome .50 .20
❑ 234 Joe Crede .30 .12
❑ 235 Barry Zito .30 .12
❑ 236 Yoel Hernandez RC .50 .20
❑ 237 Kelly Johnson .30 .12
❑ 238 Chris Young .30 .12
❑ 239 Fyodor Dostoevsky .30 .12
❑ 240 Miguel Tejada .30 .12
❑ 241 Doug Mientkiewicz .30 .12
❑ 242 Bobby Jenks .30 .12
❑ 243 Brad Hawpe SP 3.00 1.25
❑ 244 Jay Marshall RC .50 .20
❑ 245 Brad Penny .30 .12
❑ 246 Johnny Damon .50 .20
❑ 247 Dave Roberts .30 .12
❑ 248 Ron Washington .30 .12
❑ 249 Mike Aponte .30 .12
❑ 250 Brandon Webb .30 .12
❑ 251 Andy Pettitte .50 .20
❑ 252 Bud Black .30 .12
❑ 253 Michael Cuddyer .30 .12
❑ 254 Chris Stewart RC .50 .20
❑ 255 Mark Teixeira .50 .20
❑ 256 Hideki Matsui .75 .30
❑ 257 Curtis Granderson .30 .12
❑ 258 A.J. Pierzynski .30 .12
❑ 259 Tony La Russa .30 .12
❑ 260 Andruw Jones .50 .20
❑ 261 Torii Hunter .30 .12
❑ 262 Mark Loretta .30 .12
❑ 263 Jim Edmonds SP 3.00 1.25
❑ 264 Aaron Rowand .30 .12
❑ 265 Roy Halladay .30 .12
❑ 266 Freddy Garcia .30 .12
❑ 267 Reggie Sanders .30 .12
❑ 268 Washington Monument .30 .12
❑ 269 Franklin D. Roosevelt .30 .12
❑ 270 Alex Rodriguez 1.25 .50
❑ 271 Wes Helms .30 .12
❑ 272 Mia Hamm .75 .30
❑ 273 Jorge Posada .50 .20
❑ 274 Tim Lincecum RC 5.00 2.00
❑ 275 Bobby Abreu .30 .12
❑ 276 Zach Duke .30 .12
❑ 277 Carlos Delgado .30 .12
❑ 278 Julio Juarez .30 .12
❑ 279 Brandon Inge .30 .12
❑ 280 Todd Helton .50 .20
❑ 281 Marcus Giles .30 .12
❑ 282 Josh Johnson .30 .12
❑ 283 Chris Capuano .30 .12
❑ 284 B.J. Ryan .30 .12
❑ 285 Nick Johnson .30 .12
❑ 286 Khalil Greene .50 .20
❑ 287 Travis Hafner .30 .12
❑ 288 Ted Lilly .30 .12
❑ 289 Jim Leyland .30 .12
❑ 290 Prince Fielder .75 .30
❑ 291 Trevor Hoffman .30 .12
❑ 292 Brian Giles .30 .12
❑ 293 Omar Vizquel .50 .20
❑ 294 Julio Lugo .30 .12
❑ 295 Jake Peavy .30 .12
❑ 296 Adrian Beltre .30 .12
❑ 297 Josh Beckett .50 .20
❑ 298 Harry S. Truman .30 .12
❑ 299 Mark Buehrle .30 .12
❑ 300 Ichiro Suzuki 1.25 .50
❑ 301 Chris Duncan SP 3.00 1.25
❑ 302 Augie Garrido SP 3.00 1.25
❑ 303 Tyler Clippard SP (RC) 3.00 1.25
❑ 304 Ramon Hernandez .30 .12
❑ 305 Jeremy Bonderman .30 .12
❑ 306 Morgan Ensberg SP 3.00 1.25
❑ 307 J.J. Hardy SP 3.00 1.25
❑ 308 Mark Zupan SP 3.00 1.25
❑ 309 Laila Ali SP 3.00 1.25
❑ 310 Greg Maddux SP 4.00 1.50
❑ 311 David Ross .30 .12
❑ 312 Chris Duffy .30 .12
❑ 313 Moises Alou .30 .12
❑ 314 Yadier Molina .30 .12
❑ 315 Corey Patterson .30 .12
❑ 316 Dan O'Brien SP 3.00 1.25
❑ 317 Michael Bourn SP (RC) 3.00 1.25
❑ 318 Jonny Gomes SP 3.00 1.25
❑ 319 Ken Jennings SP 3.00 1.25
❑ 320 Barry Bonds SP 4.00 1.50
❑ 321 Gary Hall Jr. SP 3.00 1.25
❑ 322 Kerri Walsh SP 3.00 1.25
❑ 323 Craig Biggio .50 .20
❑ 324 Ian Kinsler .30 .12
❑ 325 Grady Sizemore SP 3.00 1.25
❑ 326 Alex Rios SP 3.00 1.25
❑ 327 Ted Toles SP 3.00 1.25
❑ 328 Jason Jennings .30 .12
❑ 329 Vernon Wells .30 .12
❑ 330 Bob Geren SP 3.00 1.25
❑ 331 Dennis Rodman SP 3.00 1.25
❑ 332 Tom Glavine .50 .20
❑ 333 Pedro Martinez .50 .20
❑ 334 Gustavo Molina SP RC 3.00 1.25
❑ 335 Bartolo Colon SP 3.00 1.25
❑ 336 Misty May-Treanor SP 3.00 1.25
❑ 337 Randy Winn .30 .12
❑ 338 Eric Byrnes .30 .12
❑ 339 Jason McElwain SP 3.00 1.25
❑ 340 Placido Polanco SP 3.00 1.25
❑ 341 Adrian Gonzalez .30 .12
❑ 342 Chad Cordero .30 .12
❑ 343 Jeff Francis .30 .12
❑ 344 Lastings Milledge .50 .20
❑ 345 Sammy Sosa SP 3.00 1.25
❑ 346 Jacque Jones .30 .12
❑ 347 Anibal Sanchez .30 .12
❑ 348 Roger Clemens SP 4.00 1.50
❑ 349 Jesse Litsch SP RC 3.00 1.25
❑ 350 Adam LaRoche SP 3.00 1.25
❑ NNO Framed Originals 100.00 50.00

1998 Topps Chrome

❑ COMPLETE SET (503) 150.00 60.00
❑ COMPLETE SERIES 1 (282) 80.00 30.00
❑ COMPLETE SERIES 2 (221) 80.00 30.00
❑ 1 Tony Gwynn 2.50 1.00
❑ 2 Larry Walker .75 .30
❑ 3 Billy Wagner .75 .30
❑ 4 Denny Neagle .75 .30
❑ 5 Vladimir Guerrero 2.00 .75
❑ 6 Kevin Brown 1.25 .50
❑ 8 Mariano Rivera 2.00 .75
❑ 9 Tony Clark .75 .30
❑ 10 Deion Sanders 1.25 .50
❑ 11 Francisco Cordova .75 .30
❑ 12 Matt Williams .75 .30
❑ 13 Carlos Baerga .75 .30
❑ 14 Mo Vaughn .75 .30
❑ 15 Bobby Witt .75 .30
❑ 16 Matt Stairs .75 .30
❑ 17 Chan Ho Park .75 .30
❑ 18 Mike Bordick .75 .30
❑ 19 Michael Tucker .75 .30
❑ 20 Frank Thomas 2.00 .75
❑ 21 Roberto Clemente 5.00 2.00
❑ 22 Dmitri Young .75 .30
❑ 23 Steve Trachsel .75 .30
❑ 24 Jeff Kent .75 .30
❑ 25 Scott Rolen 1.25 .50
❑ 26 John Thomson .75 .30
❑ 27 Joe Vitiello .75 .30

❑ 28	Eddie Guardado	.75	.30
❑ 29	Charlie Hayes	.75	.30
❑ 30	Juan Gonzalez	.75	.30
❑ 31	Garret Anderson	.75	.30
❑ 32	John Jaha	.75	.30
❑ 33	Omar Vizquel	1.25	.50
❑ 34	Brian Hunter	.75	.30
❑ 35	Jeff Bagwell	1.25	.50
❑ 36	Mark Lemke	.75	.30
❑ 37	Doug Glanville	.75	.30
❑ 38	Dan Wilson	.75	.30
❑ 39	Steve Cooke	.75	.30
❑ 40	Chili Davis	.75	.30
❑ 41	Mike Cameron	.75	.30
❑ 42	F.P. Santangelo	.75	.30
❑ 43	Brad Ausmus	.75	.30
❑ 44	Gary DiSarcina	.75	.30
❑ 45	Pat Hentgen	.75	.30
❑ 46	Wilton Guerrero	.75	.30
❑ 47	Devon White	.75	.30
❑ 48	Danny Patterson	.75	.30
❑ 49	Pat Meares	.75	.30
❑ 50	Rafael Palmeiro	1.25	.50
❑ 51	Mark Gardner	.75	.30
❑ 52	Jeff Blauser	.75	.30
❑ 53	Dave Hollins	.75	.30
❑ 54	Carlos Garcia	.75	.30
❑ 55	Ben McDonald	.75	.30
❑ 56	John Mabry	.75	.30
❑ 57	Trevor Hoffman	.75	.30
❑ 58	Tony Fernandez	.75	.30
❑ 59	Rich Loiselle RC	.75	.30
❑ 60	Mark Leiter	.75	.30
❑ 61	Pat Kelly	.75	.30
❑ 62	John Flaherty	.75	.30
❑ 63	Roger Bailey	.75	.30
❑ 64	Tom Gordon	.75	.30
❑ 65	Ryan Klesko	.75	.30
❑ 66	Darryl Hamilton	.75	.30
❑ 67	Jim Eisenreich	.75	.30
❑ 68	Butch Huskey	.75	.30
❑ 69	Mark Grudzielanek	.75	.30
❑ 70	Marquis Grissom	.75	.30
❑ 71	Mark McLemore	.75	.30
❑ 72	Gary Gaetti	.75	.30
❑ 73	Greg Gagne	.75	.30
❑ 74	Lyle Mouton	.75	.30
❑ 75	Jim Edmonds	.75	.30
❑ 76	Shawn Green	.75	.30
❑ 77	Greg Vaughn	.75	.30
❑ 78	Terry Adams	.75	.30
❑ 79	Kevin Polcovich	.75	.30
❑ 80	Troy O'Leary	.75	.30
❑ 81	Jeff Shaw	.75	.30
❑ 82	Rich Becker	.75	.30
❑ 83	David Wells	.75	.30
❑ 84	Steve Karsay	.75	.30
❑ 85	Charles Nagy	.75	.30
❑ 86	B.J. Surhoff	.75	.30
❑ 87	Jamey Wright	.75	.30
❑ 88	James Baldwin	.75	.30
❑ 89	Edgardo Alfonzo	.75	.30
❑ 90	Jay Buhner	.75	.30
❑ 91	Brady Anderson	.75	.30
❑ 92	Scott Servais	.75	.30
❑ 93	Edgar Renteria	.75	.30
❑ 94	Mike Lieberthal	.75	.30
❑ 95	Rick Aguilera	.75	.30
❑ 96	Walt Weiss	.75	.30
❑ 97	Deivi Cruz	.75	.30
❑ 98	Kurt Abbott	.75	.30
❑ 99	Henry Rodriguez	.75	.30
❑ 100	Mike Piazza	3.00	1.25
❑ 101	Billy Taylor	.75	.30
❑ 102	Todd Zeile	.75	.30
❑ 103	Rey Ordonez	.75	.30
❑ 104	Willie Greene	.75	.30
❑ 105	Tony Womack	.75	.30
❑ 106	Mike Sweeney	.75	.30
❑ 107	Jeffrey Hammonds	.75	.30
❑ 108	Kevin Orie	.75	.30
❑ 109	Alex Gonzalez	.75	.30
❑ 110	Jose Canseco	1.25	.50
❑ 111	Paul Sorrento	.75	.30
❑ 112	Joey Hamilton	.75	.30
❑ 113	Brad Radke	.75	.30
❑ 114	Steve Avery	.75	.30
❑ 115	Esteban Loaiza	.75	.30
❑ 116	Stan Javier	.75	.30
❑ 117	Chris Gomez	.75	.30
❑ 118	Royce Clayton	.75	.30
❑ 119	Orlando Merced	.75	.30
❑ 120	Kevin Appier	.75	.30
❑ 121	Mel Nieves	.75	.30
❑ 122	Joe Girardi	.75	.30
❑ 123	Rico Brogna	.75	.30
❑ 124	Kent Mercker	.75	.30
❑ 125	Manny Ramirez	1.25	.50
❑ 126	Jeromy Burnitz	.75	.30
❑ 127	Kevin Foster	.75	.30
❑ 128	Matt Morris	.75	.30
❑ 129	Jason Dickson	.75	.30
❑ 130	Tom Glavine	1.25	.50
❑ 131	Wally Joyner	.75	.30
❑ 132	Rick Reed	.75	.30
❑ 133	Todd Jones	.75	.30
❑ 134	Dave Martinez	.75	.30
❑ 135	Sandy Alomar Jr.	.75	.30
❑ 136	Mike Lansing	.75	.30
❑ 137	Sean Berry	.75	.30
❑ 138	Doug Jones	.75	.30
❑ 139	Todd Stottlemyre	.75	.30
❑ 140	Jay Bell	.75	.30
❑ 141	Jaime Navarro	.75	.30
❑ 142	Chris Hoiles	.75	.30
❑ 143	Joey Cora	.75	.30
❑ 144	Scott Spiezio	.75	.30
❑ 145	Joe Carter	.75	.30
❑ 146	Jose Guillen	.75	.30
❑ 147	Damion Easley	.75	.30
❑ 148	Lee Stevens	.75	.30
❑ 149	Alex Fernandez	.75	.30
❑ 150	Randy Johnson	2.00	.75
❑ 151	J.T. Snow	.75	.30
❑ 152	Chuck Finley	.75	.30
❑ 153	Bernard Gilkey	.75	.30
❑ 154	David Segui	.75	.30
❑ 155	Dante Bichette	.75	.30
❑ 156	Kevin Stocker	.75	.30
❑ 157	Carl Everett	.75	.30
❑ 158	Jose Valentin	.75	.30
❑ 159	Pokey Reese	.75	.30
❑ 160	Derek Jeter	5.00	2.00
❑ 161	Roger Pavlik	.75	.30
❑ 162	Mark Wohlers	.75	.30
❑ 163	Ricky Bottalico	.75	.30
❑ 164	Ozzie Guillen	.75	.30
❑ 165	Mike Mussina	1.25	.50
❑ 166	Gary Sheffield	.75	.30
❑ 167	Hideo Nomo	2.00	.75
❑ 168	Mark Grace	1.25	.50
❑ 169	Aaron Sele	.75	.30
❑ 170	Darryl Kile	.75	.30
❑ 171	Shawn Estes	.75	.30
❑ 172	Vinny Castilla	.75	.30
❑ 173	Ron Coomer	.75	.30
❑ 174	Jose Rosado	.75	.30
❑ 175	Kenny Lofton	.75	.30
❑ 176	Jason Giambi	.75	.30
❑ 177	Hal Morris	.75	.30
❑ 178	Darren Bragg	.75	.30
❑ 179	Orel Hershiser	.75	.30
❑ 180	Ray Lankford	.75	.30
❑ 181	Hideki Irabu	.75	.30
❑ 182	Kevin Young	.75	.30
❑ 183	Javy Lopez	.75	.30
❑ 184	Jeff Montgomery	.75	.30
❑ 185	Mike Holtz	.75	.30
❑ 186	George Williams	.75	.30
❑ 187	Cal Eldred	.75	.30
❑ 188	Tom Candiotti	.75	.30
❑ 189	Glenallen Hill	.75	.30
❑ 190	Brian Giles	.75	.30
❑ 191	Dave Mlicki	.75	.30
❑ 192	Garrett Stephenson	.75	.30
❑ 193	Jeff Frye	.75	.30
❑ 194	Joe Oliver	.75	.30
❑ 195	Bob Hamelin	.75	.30
❑ 196	Luis Sojo	.75	.30
❑ 197	LaTroy Hawkins	.75	.30
❑ 198	Kevin Elster	.75	.30
❑ 199	Jeff Reed	.75	.30
❑ 200	Dennis Eckersley	.75	.30
❑ 201	Bill Mueller	.75	.30
❑ 202	Russ Davis	.75	.30
❑ 203	Armando Benitez	.75	.30
❑ 204	Quilvio Veras	.75	.30
❑ 205	Tim Naehring	.75	.30
❑ 206	Quinton McCracken	.75	.30
❑ 207	Raul Casanova	.75	.30
❑ 208	Matt Lawton	.75	.30
❑ 209	Luis Alicea	.75	.30
❑ 210	Luis Gonzalez	.75	.30
❑ 211	Allen Watson	.75	.30
❑ 212	Gerald Williams	.75	.30
❑ 213	David Bell	.75	.30
❑ 214	Todd Hollandsworth	.75	.30
❑ 215	Wade Boggs	1.25	.50
❑ 216	Jose Mesa	.75	.30
❑ 217	Jamie Moyer	.75	.30
❑ 218	Darren Daulton	.75	.30
❑ 219	Mickey Morandini	.75	.30
❑ 220	Rusty Greer	.75	.30
❑ 221	Jim Bullinger	.75	.30
❑ 222	Jose Offerman	.75	.30
❑ 223	Matt Karchner	.75	.30
❑ 224	Woody Williams	.75	.30
❑ 225	Mark Loretta	.75	.30
❑ 226	Mike Hampton	.75	.30
❑ 227	Willie Adams	.75	.30
❑ 228	Scott Hatteberg	.75	.30
❑ 229	Rich Amaral	.75	.30
❑ 230	Terry Steinbach	.75	.30
❑ 231	Glendon Rusch	.75	.30
❑ 232	Bret Boone	.75	.30
❑ 233	Robert Person	.75	.30
❑ 234	Jose Hernandez	.75	.30
❑ 235	Doug Drabek	.75	.30
❑ 236	Jason McDonald	.75	.30
❑ 237	Chris Widger	.75	.30
❑ 238	Tom Martin	.75	.30
❑ 239	Dave Burba	.75	.30
❑ 240	Pete Rose Jr. RC	.75	.30
❑ 241	Bobby Ayala	.75	.30
❑ 242	Tim Wakefield	.75	.30
❑ 243	Dennis Springer	.75	.30
❑ 244	Tim Belcher	.75	.30
❑ 245	J.Garland/G.Goetz	1.00	.40
❑ 246	L.Berkman/G.Davis	1.00	.40
❑ 247	V.Wells/A.Akin	1.00	.40
❑ 248	A.Kennedy/J.Romano	1.00	.40
❑ 249	J.Dellaero/T.Cameron	1.00	.40
❑ 250	J.Sandberg/A.Sanchez	1.00	.40
❑ 251	P.Ortega/J.Manias	1.00	.40
❑ 252	Mike Stoner RC	1.00	.40
❑ 253	J.Patterson/L.Rodriguez	1.00	.40
❑ 254	R.Minor RC/A.Beltre	1.00	.40
❑ 255	B.Grieve/D.Brown	1.00	.40
❑ 256	Wood/Pavano/Meche	1.00	.40
❑ 257	D.Ortiz/Sexson/Ward	5.00	2.00
❑ 258	J.Encarnacion/Winn/Vess	1.00	.40
❑ 259	Bens/T.Smith RC/C.Dunc RC	1.00	.40
❑ 260	Warren Morris RC	1.00	.40
❑ 261	B.Davis/Marrero/R.Hern.	1.00	.40
❑ 262	E.Chavez/R.Branyan	1.00	.40
❑ 263	Ryan Jackson RC	1.00	.40
❑ 264	B.Fuentes RC/Clement/Halladay	1.00	.40
❑ 265	Randy Johnson SH	1.25	.50
❑ 266	Kevin Brown SH	.75	.30
❑ 267	Ricardo Rincon SH	.75	.30
❑ 268	Nomar Garciaparra SH	2.00	.75
❑ 269	Tino Martinez SH	.75	.30
❑ 270	Chuck Knoblauch IL	.75	.30
❑ 271	Pedro Martinez IL	1.25	.50
❑ 272	Denny Neagle IL	.75	.30
❑ 273	Juan Gonzalez IL	.75	.30
❑ 274	Andres Galarraga IL	.75	.30
❑ 275	Checklist	.75	.30
❑ 276	Checklist	.75	.30
❑ 277	Moises Alou WS	.75	.30
❑ 278	Sandy Alomar Jr. WS	.75	.30
❑ 279	Gary Sheffield WS	.75	.30
❑ 280	Matt Williams WS	.75	.30
❑ 281	Livan Hernandez WS	.75	.30
❑ 282	Chad Ogea WS	.75	.30
❑ 283	Marlins Champs	.75	.30
❑ 284	Tino Martinez	1.25	.50
❑ 285	Roberto Alomar	1.25	.50

❑ 286 Jeff King .75 .30
❑ 287 Brian Jordan .75 .30
❑ 288 Darin Erstad .75 .30
❑ 289 Ken Caminiti .75 .30
❑ 290 Jim Thome 1.25 .50
❑ 291 Paul Molitor .75 .30
❑ 292 Ivan Rodriguez 1.25 .50
❑ 293 Bernie Williams 1.25 .50
❑ 294 Todd Hundley .75 .30
❑ 295 Andres Galarraga .75 .30
❑ 296 Greg Maddux 3.00 1.25
❑ 297 Edgar Martinez 1.25 .50
❑ 298 Ron Gant .75 .30
❑ 299 Derek Bell .75 .30
❑ 300 Roger Clemens 4.00 1.50
❑ 301 Rondell White .75 .30
❑ 302 Barry Larkin 1.25 .50
❑ 303 Robin Ventura .75 .30
❑ 304 Jason Kendall .75 .30
❑ 305 Chipper Jones 2.00 .75
❑ 306 John Franco .75 .30
❑ 307 Sammy Sosa 2.00 .75
❑ 308 Troy Percival .75 .30
❑ 309 Chuck Knoblauch .75 .30
❑ 310 Ellis Burks .75 .30
❑ 311 Al Martin .75 .30
❑ 312 Tim Salmon 1.25 .50
❑ 313 Moises Alou .75 .30
❑ 314 Lance Johnson .75 .30
❑ 315 Justin Thompson .75 .30
❑ 316 Will Clark 1.25 .50
❑ 317 Barry Bonds 5.00 2.00
❑ 318 Craig Biggio 1.25 .50
❑ 319 John Smoltz 1.25 .50
❑ 320 Cal Ripken 6.00 2.50
❑ 321 Ken Griffey Jr. 3.00 1.25
❑ 322 Paul O'Neill 1.25 .50
❑ 323 Todd Helton 1.25 .50
❑ 324 John Olerud .75 .30
❑ 325 Mark McGwire 5.00 2.00
❑ 326 Jose Cruz Jr. .75 .30
❑ 327 Jeff Cirillo .75 .30
❑ 328 Dean Palmer .75 .30
❑ 329 John Wetteland .75 .30
❑ 330 Steve Finley .75 .30
❑ 331 Albert Belle .75 .30
❑ 332 Curt Schilling .75 .30
❑ 333 Raul Mondesi .75 .30
❑ 334 Andruw Jones 1.25 .50
❑ 335 Nomar Garciaparra 3.00 1.25
❑ 336 David Justice .75 .30
❑ 337 Andy Pettitte 1.25 .50
❑ 338 Pedro Martinez 1.25 .50
❑ 339 Travis Miller .75 .30
❑ 340 Chris Stynes .75 .30
❑ 341 Gregg Jefferies .75 .30
❑ 342 Jeff Fassero .75 .30
❑ 343 Craig Counsell .75 .30
❑ 344 Wilson Alvarez .75 .30
❑ 345 Bip Roberts .75 .30
❑ 346 Kelvim Escobar .75 .30
❑ 347 Mark Bellhorn .75 .30
❑ 348 Cory Lidle RC 8.00 3.00
❑ 349 Fred McGriff 1.25 .50
❑ 350 Chuck Carr .75 .30
❑ 351 Bob Abreu .75 .30
❑ 352 Juan Guzman .75 .30
❑ 353 Fernando Vina .75 .30
❑ 354 Andy Benes .75 .30
❑ 355 Dave Nilsson .75 .30
❑ 356 Bobby Bonilla .75 .30
❑ 357 Ismael Valdes .75 .30
❑ 358 Carlos Perez .75 .30
❑ 359 Kirk Rueter .75 .30
❑ 360 Bartolo Colon .75 .30
❑ 361 Mel Rojas .75 .30
❑ 362 Johnny Damon 1.25 .50
❑ 363 Geronimo Berroa .75 .30
❑ 364 Reggie Sanders .75 .30
❑ 365 Jermaine Allensworth .75 .30
❑ 366 Orlando Cabrera .75 .30
❑ 367 Jorge Fabregas .75 .30
❑ 368 Scott Stahoviak .75 .30
❑ 369 Ken Cloude .75 .30
❑ 370 Donovan Osborne .75 .30
❑ 371 Roger Cedeno .75 .30
❑ 372 Neifi Perez .75 .30
❑ 373 Chris Holt .75 .30
❑ 374 Cecil Fielder .75 .30
❑ 375 Marty Cordova .75 .30
❑ 376 Tom Goodwin .75 .30
❑ 377 Jeff Suppan .75 .30
❑ 378 Jeff Brantley .75 .30
❑ 379 Mark Langston .75 .30
❑ 380 Shane Reynolds .75 .30
❑ 381 Mike Fetters .75 .30
❑ 382 Todd Greene .75 .30
❑ 383 Ray Durham .75 .30
❑ 384 Carlos Delgado .75 .30
❑ 385 Jeff D'Amico .75 .30
❑ 386 Brian McRae .75 .30
❑ 387 Alan Benes .75 .30
❑ 388 Heathcliff Slocumb .75 .30
❑ 389 Eric Young .75 .30
❑ 390 Travis Fryman .75 .30
❑ 391 David Cone .75 .30
❑ 392 Otis Nixon .75 .30
❑ 393 Jeremi Gonzalez .75 .30
❑ 394 Jeff Juden .75 .30
❑ 395 Jose Vizcaino .75 .30
❑ 396 Ugueth Urbina .75 .30
❑ 397 Ramon Martinez .75 .30
❑ 398 Robb Nen .75 .30
❑ 399 Harold Baines .75 .30
❑ 400 Delino DeShields .75 .30
❑ 401 John Burkett .75 .30
❑ 402 Sterling Hitchcock .75 .30
❑ 403 Mark Clark .75 .30
❑ 404 Terrell Wade .75 .30
❑ 405 Scott Brosius .75 .30
❑ 406 Chad Curtis .75 .30
❑ 407 Brian Johnson .75 .30
❑ 408 Roberto Kelly .75 .30
❑ 409 Dave Dellucci RC 1.25 .50
❑ 410 Michael Tucker .75 .30
❑ 411 Mark Kotsay .75 .30
❑ 412 Mark Lewis .75 .30
❑ 413 Ryan McGuire .75 .30
❑ 414 Shawon Dunston .75 .30
❑ 415 Brad Rigby .75 .30
❑ 416 Scott Erickson .75 .30
❑ 417 Bobby Jones .75 .30
❑ 418 Darren Oliver .75 .30
❑ 419 John Smiley .75 .30
❑ 420 T.J. Mathews .75 .30
❑ 421 Dustin Hermanson .75 .30
❑ 422 Mike Timlin .75 .30
❑ 423 Willie Blair .75 .30
❑ 424 Manny Alexander .75 .30
❑ 425 Bob Tewksbury .75 .30
❑ 426 Pete Schourek .75 .30
❑ 427 Reggie Jefferson .75 .30
❑ 428 Ed Sprague .75 .30
❑ 429 Jeff Conine .75 .30
❑ 430 Roberto Hernandez .75 .30
❑ 431 Tom Pagnozzi .75 .30
❑ 432 Jaret Wright .75 .30
❑ 433 Livan Hernandez .75 .30
❑ 434 Andy Ashby .75 .30
❑ 435 Todd Dunn .75 .30
❑ 436 Bobby Higginson .75 .30
❑ 437 Rod Beck .75 .30
❑ 438 Jim Leyritz .75 .30
❑ 439 Matt Williams .75 .30
❑ 440 Brett Tomko .75 .30
❑ 441 Joe Randa .75 .30
❑ 442 Chris Carpenter .75 .30
❑ 443 Dennis Reyes .75 .30
❑ 444 Al Leiter .75 .30
❑ 445 Jason Schmidt .75 .30
❑ 446 Ken Hill .75 .30
❑ 447 Shannon Stewart .75 .30
❑ 448 Enrique Wilson .75 .30
❑ 449 Fernando Tatis .75 .30
❑ 450 Jimmy Key .75 .30
❑ 451 Darrin Fletcher .75 .30
❑ 452 John Valentin .75 .30
❑ 453 Kevin Tapani .75 .30
❑ 454 Eric Karros .75 .30
❑ 455 Jay Bell .75 .30
❑ 456 Walt Weiss .75 .30
❑ 457 Devon White .75 .30
❑ 458 Carl Pavano .75 .30
❑ 459 Mike Lansing .75 .30
❑ 460 John Flaherty .75 .30
❑ 461 Richard Hidalgo .75 .30
❑ 462 Quinton McCracken .75 .30
❑ 463 Karim Garcia .75 .30
❑ 464 Miguel Cairo .75 .30
❑ 465 Edwin Diaz .75 .30
❑ 466 Bobby Smith .75 .30
❑ 467 Yamil Benitez .75 .30
❑ 468 Rich Butler RC .75 .30
❑ 469 Ben Ford RC .75 .30
❑ 470 Bubba Trammell .75 .30
❑ 471 Brent Brede .75 .30
❑ 472 Brooks Kieschnick .75 .30
❑ 473 Carlos Castillo .75 .30
❑ 474 Brad Radke SH .75 .30
❑ 475 Roger Clemens SH 2.00 .75
❑ 476 Curt Schilling SH .75 .30
❑ 477 John Olerud SH .75 .30
❑ 478 Mark McGwire SH 2.50 1.00
❑ 479 M.Piazza/K.Griffey Jr. IL 2.00 .75
❑ 480 J.Bagwell/F.Thomas IL 1.25 .50
❑ 481 C.Jones/N.Garciaparra IL 1.25 .50
❑ 482 L.Walker/J.Gonzalez IL .75 .30
❑ 483 G.Sheffield/T.Martinez IL .75 .30
❑ 484 D.Gib/M.Colem/Hutchins 1.00 .40
❑ 485 B.Rose/Looper/Politte 1.00 .40
❑ 486 E.Milton/Marquis/C.Lee 1.00 .40
❑ 487 Rob Fick RC 1.00 .40
❑ 488 A.Ramirez/A.Gonz/Casey 1.00 .40
❑ 489 D.Bridges/T.Drew RC 1.00 .40
❑ 490 D.McDonald/N.Ndungidi RC 1.00 .40
❑ 491 Ryan Anderson RC 1.00 .40
❑ 492 Troy Glaus RC 5.00 2.00
❑ 493 Dan Reichert RC 1.00 .40
❑ 494 Michael Cuddyer RC 2.50 1.00
❑ 495 Jack Cust RC 2.00 .75
❑ 496 Brian Anderson 1.00 .40
❑ 497 Tony Saunders 1.00 .40
❑ 498 J.Sandoval/V.Nunez 1.00 .40
❑ 499 B.Penny/N.Bierbrodt 1.00 .40
❑ 500 D.Carr/L.Cruz RC 1.00 .40
❑ 501 C.Bowers/M.McCain 1.00 .40
❑ 502 Checklist .75 .30
❑ 503 Checklist .75 .30
❑ 504 Alex Rodriguez 4.00 1.50

1999 Topps Chrome

❑ COMPLETE SET (462) 120.00 50.00
❑ COMPLETE SERIES 1 (241) 60.00 25.00
❑ COMPLETE SERIES 2 (221) 60.00 25.00
❑ COMMON CARD (1-6/8-463) .50 .20
❑ COMMON (205-212/425-437) 1.00 .40
❑ 1 Roger Clemens 4.00 1.50
❑ 2 Andres Galarraga .75 .30
❑ 3 Scott Brosius .75 .30
❑ 4 John Flaherty .50 .20
❑ 5 Jim Leyritz .50 .20
❑ 6 Ray Durham .75 .30
❑ 8 Jose Vizcaino .50 .20
❑ 9 Will Clark 1.25 .50
❑ 10 David Wells .75 .30
❑ 11 Jose Guillen .75 .30
❑ 12 Scott Hatteberg .50 .20
❑ 13 Edgardo Alfonzo .50 .20
❑ 14 Mike Bordick .50 .20
❑ 15 Manny Ramirez 1.25 .50

❑ 16 Greg Maddux 3.00 1.25
❑ 17 David Segui .50 .20
❑ 18 Darryl Strawberry .75 .30
❑ 19 Brad Radke .75 .30
❑ 20 Kerry Wood .75 .30
❑ 21 Matt Anderson .50 .20
❑ 22 Derrek Lee 1.25 .50
❑ 23 Mickey Morandini .50 .20
❑ 24 Paul Konerko .75 .30
❑ 25 Travis Lee .50 .20
❑ 26 Ken Hill .50 .20
❑ 27 Kenny Rogers .75 .30
❑ 28 Paul Sorrento .50 .20
❑ 29 Quilvio Veras .50 .20
❑ 30 Todd Walker .50 .20
❑ 31 Ryan Jackson .50 .20
❑ 32 John Olerud .75 .30
❑ 33 Doug Glanville .50 .20
❑ 34 Nolan Ryan 6.00 2.50
❑ 35 Ray Lankford .75 .30
❑ 36 Mark Loretta .50 .20
❑ 37 Jason Dickson .50 .20
❑ 38 Sean Bergman .50 .20
❑ 39 Quinton McCracken .50 .20
❑ 40 Bartolo Colon .75 .30
❑ 41 Brady Anderson .75 .30
❑ 42 Chris Stynes .50 .20
❑ 43 Jorge Posada 1.25 .50
❑ 44 Justin Thompson .50 .20
❑ 45 Johnny Damon 1.25 .50
❑ 46 Armando Benitez .50 .20
❑ 47 Brant Brown .50 .20
❑ 48 Charlie Hayes .50 .20
❑ 49 Darren Dreifort .50 .20
❑ 50 Juan Gonzalez .75 .30
❑ 51 Chuck Knoblauch .75 .30
❑ 52 Todd Helton 1.25 .50
❑ 53 Rick Reed .50 .20
❑ 54 Chris Gomez .50 .20
❑ 55 Gary Sheffield .75 .30
❑ 56 Rod Beck .50 .20
❑ 57 Rey Sanchez .50 .20
❑ 58 Garret Anderson .75 .30
❑ 59 Jimmy Haynes .50 .20
❑ 60 Steve Woodard .50 .20
❑ 61 Rondell White .75 .30
❑ 62 Vladimir Guerrero 2.00 .75
❑ 63 Eric Karros .75 .30
❑ 64 Russ Davis .50 .20
❑ 65 Mo Vaughn .75 .30
❑ 66 Sammy Sosa 2.00 .75
❑ 67 Troy Percival .75 .30
❑ 68 Kenny Lofton .75 .30
❑ 69 Bill Taylor .50 .20
❑ 70 Mark McGwire 5.00 2.00
❑ 71 Roger Cedeno .50 .20
❑ 72 Javy Lopez .75 .30
❑ 73 Damion Easley .50 .20
❑ 74 Andy Pettitte 1.25 .50
❑ 75 Tony Gwynn 2.50 1.00
❑ 76 Ricardo Rincon .50 .20
❑ 77 F.P. Santangelo .50 .20
❑ 78 Jay Bell .75 .30
❑ 79 Scott Servais .50 .20
❑ 80 Jose Canseco 1.25 .50
❑ 81 Roberto Hernandez .50 .20
❑ 82 Todd Dunwoody .50 .20
❑ 83 John Wetteland .75 .30
❑ 84 Mike Caruso .50 .20
❑ 85 Derek Jeter 5.00 2.00
❑ 86 Aaron Sele .50 .20
❑ 87 Jose Lima .50 .20
❑ 88 Ryan Christenson .50 .20
❑ 89 Jeff Cirillo .50 .20
❑ 90 Jose Hernandez .50 .20
❑ 91 Mark Kotsay .75 .30
❑ 92 Darren Bragg .50 .20
❑ 93 Albert Belle .75 .30
❑ 94 Matt Lawton .50 .20
❑ 95 Pedro Martinez 1.25 .50
❑ 96 Greg Vaughn .50 .20
❑ 97 Neifi Perez .50 .20
❑ 98 Gerald Williams .50 .20
❑ 99 Derek Bell .50 .20
❑ 100 Ken Griffey Jr. 3.00 1.25
❑ 101 David Cone .75 .30
❑ 102 Brian Johnson .50 .20
❑ 103 Dean Palmer .75 .30
❑ 104 Javier Valentin .50 .20
❑ 105 Trevor Hoffman .75 .30
❑ 106 Butch Huskey .50 .20
❑ 107 Dave Martinez .50 .20
❑ 108 Billy Wagner .75 .30
❑ 109 Shawn Green .75 .30
❑ 110 Ben Grieve .50 .20
❑ 111 Tom Goodwin .50 .20
❑ 112 Jaret Wright .50 .20
❑ 113 Aramis Ramirez .75 .30
❑ 114 Dmitri Young .75 .30
❑ 115 Hideki Irabu .50 .20
❑ 116 Roberto Kelly .50 .20
❑ 117 Jeff Fassero .50 .20
❑ 118 Mark Clark .50 .20
❑ 119 Jason McDonald .50 .20
❑ 120 Matt Williams .75 .30
❑ 121 Dave Burba .50 .20
❑ 122 Bret Saberhagen .75 .30
❑ 123 Deivi Cruz .50 .20
❑ 124 Chad Curtis .50 .20
❑ 125 Scott Rolen 1.25 .50
❑ 126 Lee Stevens .50 .20
❑ 127 J.T. Snow .75 .30
❑ 128 Rusty Greer .75 .30
❑ 129 Brian Meadows .50 .20
❑ 130 Jim Edmonds .75 .30
❑ 131 Ron Gant .75 .30
❑ 132 A.J. Hinch .50 .20
❑ 133 Shannon Stewart .75 .30
❑ 134 Brad Fullmer .50 .20
❑ 135 Cal Eldred .50 .20
❑ 136 Matt Walbeck .50 .20
❑ 137 Carl Everett .75 .30
❑ 138 Walt Weiss .50 .20
❑ 139 Fred McGriff 1.25 .50
❑ 140 Darin Erstad .75 .30
❑ 141 Dave Nilsson .50 .20
❑ 142 Eric Young .50 .20
❑ 143 Dan Wilson .50 .20
❑ 144 Jeff Reed .50 .20
❑ 145 Brett Tomko .50 .20
❑ 146 Terry Steinbach .50 .20
❑ 147 Seth Greisinger .50 .20
❑ 148 Pat Meares .50 .20
❑ 149 Livan Hernandez .75 .30
❑ 150 Jeff Bagwell 1.25 .50
❑ 151 Bob Wickman .50 .20
❑ 152 Omar Vizquel 1.25 .50
❑ 153 Eric Davis .75 .30
❑ 154 Larry Sutton .50 .20
❑ 155 Magglio Ordonez .75 .30
❑ 156 Eric Milton .50 .20
❑ 157 Darren Lewis .50 .20
❑ 158 Rick Aguilera .50 .20
❑ 159 Mike Lieberthal .75 .30
❑ 160 Robb Nen .75 .30
❑ 161 Brian Giles .75 .30
❑ 162 Jeff Brantley .50 .20
❑ 163 Gary DiSarcina .50 .20
❑ 164 John Valentin .50 .20
❑ 165 Dave Dellucci .50 .20
❑ 166 Chan Ho Park .75 .30
❑ 167 Masato Yoshii .50 .20
❑ 168 Jason Schmidt .75 .30
❑ 169 LaTroy Hawkins .50 .20
❑ 170 Bret Boone .75 .30
❑ 171 Jerry DiPoto .50 .20
❑ 172 Mariano Rivera 2.00 .75
❑ 173 Mike Cameron .50 .20
❑ 174 Scott Erickson .50 .20
❑ 175 Charles Johnson .75 .30
❑ 176 Bobby Jones .50 .20
❑ 177 Francisco Cordova .50 .20
❑ 178 Todd Jones .50 .20
❑ 179 Jeff Montgomery .50 .20
❑ 180 Mike Mussina 1.25 .50
❑ 181 Bob Abreu .75 .30
❑ 182 Ismael Valdes .50 .20
❑ 183 Andy Fox .50 .20
❑ 184 Woody Williams .50 .20
❑ 185 Denny Neagle .50 .20
❑ 186 Jose Valentin .50 .20
❑ 187 Darrin Fletcher .50 .20
❑ 188 Gabe Alvarez .50 .20
❑ 189 Eddie Taubensee .50 .20
❑ 190 Edgar Martinez 1.25 .50
❑ 191 Jason Kendall .75 .30
❑ 192 Darryl Kile .75 .30
❑ 193 Jeff King .50 .20
❑ 194 Rey Ordonez .50 .20
❑ 195 Andruw Jones 1.25 .50
❑ 196 Tony Fernandez .50 .20
❑ 197 Jamey Wright .50 .20
❑ 198 B.J. Surhoff .75 .30
❑ 199 Vinny Castilla .75 .30
❑ 200 David Wells HL .50 .20
❑ 201 Mark McGwire HL 2.50 1.00
❑ 202 Sammy Sosa HL 1.25 .50
❑ 203 Roger Clemens HL 2.00 .75
❑ 204 Kerry Wood HL .50 .20
❑ 205 L.Berkman/G.Kapler 1.00 .40
❑ 206 Alex Escobar RC 1.00 .40
❑ 207 Peter Bergeron RC 1.00 .40
❑ 208 M.Barrett/B.Davis/R.Fick 1.00 .40
❑ 209 J.Werth/Hernandez/Cline 1.00 .40
❑ 210 Ryan Anderson 1.00 .40
❑ 211 B.Penny/Dotel/Lincoln 1.00 .40
❑ 212 Chuck Abbott RC 1.00 .40
❑ 213 C.Jones/J.Urban RC 1.00 .40
❑ 214 T.Torcato/A.McDowell RC 1.00 .40
❑ 215 J.Tyner/J.McKinley RC 1.00 .40
❑ 216 M.Burch/S.Etherton RC 1.00 .40
❑ 217 R.Elder/M.Tucker RC 1.00 .40
❑ 218 J.M.Gold/R.Mills RC 1.00 .40
❑ 219 A.Brown/C.Freeman RC 1.00 .40
❑ 220A Mark McGwire HR 1 50.00 20.00
❑ 220B Mark McGwire HR 2 30.00 12.50
❑ 220C Mark McGwire HR 3 30.00 12.50
❑ 220D Mark McGwire HR 4 30.00 12.50
❑ 220E Mark McGwire HR 5 30.00 12.50
❑ 220F Mark McGwire HR 6 30.00 12.50
❑ 220G Mark McGwire HR 7 30.00 12.50
❑ 220H Mark McGwire HR 8 30.00 12.50
❑ 220I Mark McGwire HR 9 30.00 12.50
❑ 220J Mark McGwire HR 10 30.00 12.50
❑ 220K Mark McGwire HR 11 30.00 12.50
❑ 220L Mark McGwire HR 12 30.00 12.50
❑ 220M Mark McGwire HR 13 30.00 12.50
❑ 220N Mark McGwire HR 14 30.00 12.50
❑ 220O Mark McGwire HR 15 30.00 12.50
❑ 220P Mark McGwire HR 16 30.00 12.50
❑ 220Q Mark McGwire HR 17 30.00 12.50
❑ 220R Mark McGwire HR 18 30.00 12.50
❑ 220S Mark McGwire HR 19 30.00 12.50
❑ 220T Mark McGwire HR 20 30.00 12.50
❑ 220U Mark McGwire HR 21 30.00 12.50
❑ 220V Mark McGwire HR 22 30.00 12.50
❑ 220W Mark McGwire HR 23 30.00 12.50
❑ 220X Mark McGwire HR 24 30.00 12.50
❑ 220Y Mark McGwire HR 25 30.00 12.50
❑ 220Z Mark McGwire HR 26 30.00 12.50
❑ 220AA Mark McGwire HR 27 30.00 12.50
❑ 220AB Mark McGwire HR 28 30.00 12.50
❑ 220AC Mark McGwire HR 29 30.00 12.50
❑ 220AD Mark McGwire HR 30 30.00 12.50
❑ 220AE Mark McGwire HR 31 30.00 12.50
❑ 220AF Mark McGwire HR 32 30.00 12.50
❑ 220AG Mark McGwire HR 33 30.00 12.50
❑ 220AH Mark McGwire HR 34 30.00 12.50
❑ 220AI Mark McGwire HR 35 30.00 12.50
❑ 220AJ Mark McGwire HR 36 30.00 12.50
❑ 220AK Mark McGwire HR 37 30.00 12.50
❑ 220AL Mark McGwire HR 38 30.00 12.50
❑ 220AM Mark McGwire HR 39 30.00 12.50
❑ 220AN Mark McGwire HR 40 30.00 12.50
❑ 220AO Mark McGwire HR 41 30.00 12.50
❑ 220AP Mark McGwire HR 42 30.00 12.50
❑ 220AQ Mark McGwire HR 43 30.00 12.50
❑ 220AR Mark McGwire HR 44 30.00 12.50
❑ 220AS Mark McGwire HR 45 30.00 12.50
❑ 220AT Mark McGwire HR 46 30.00 12.50
❑ 220AU Mark McGwire HR 47 30.00 12.50
❑ 220AV Mark McGwire HR 48 30.00 12.50
❑ 220AW Mark McGwire HR 49 30.00 12.50
❑ 220AX Mark McGwire HR 50 30.00 12.50
❑ 220AY Mark McGwire HR 51 30.00 12.50
❑ 220AZ Mark McGwire HR 52 30.00 12.50
❑ 220BB Mark McGwire HR 53 30.00 12.50
❑ 220CC Mark McGwire HR 54 30.00 12.50

❑ 220DD Mark McGwire HR 55 30.00 12.50
❑ 220EE Mark McGwire HR 56 30.00 12.50
❑ 220FF Mark McGwire HR 57 30.00 12.50
❑ 220GG Mark McGwire HR 58 30.00 12.50
❑ 220HH Mark McGwire HR 59 30.00 12.50
❑ 220II Mark McGwire HR 60 30.00 12.50
❑ 220JJ Mark McGwire HR 61 50.00 20.00
❑ 220KK Mark McGwire HR 62 80.00 40.00
❑ 220LL Mark McGwire HR 63 50.00 20.00
❑ 220MM Mark McGwire HR 64 50.00 20.00
❑ 220NN Mark McGwire HR 65 50.00 20.00
❑ 220OO Mark McGwire HR 66 50.00 20.00
❑ 220PP Mark McGwire HR 67 50.00 20.00
❑ 220QQ Mark McGwire HR 68 50.00 20.00
❑ 220RR Mark McGwire HR 69 50.00 20.00
❑ 220SS Mark McGwire HR 70 120.00 60.00
❑ 221 Larry Walker LL .50 .20
❑ 222 Bernie Williams LL .75 .30
❑ 223 Mark McGwire LL 2.50 1.00
❑ 224 Ken Griffey Jr. LL 2.00 .75
❑ 225 Sammy Sosa LL 1.25 .50
❑ 226 Juan Gonzalez LL .50 .20
❑ 227 Dante Bichette LL .50 .20
❑ 228 Alex Rodriguez LL 2.00 .75
❑ 229 Sammy Sosa LL 1.25 .50
❑ 230 Derek Jeter LL 2.50 1.00
❑ 231 Greg Maddux LL 2.00 .75
❑ 232 Roger Clemens LL 2.00 .75
❑ 233 Ricky Ledee WS .50 .20
❑ 234 Chuck Knoblauch WS .50 .20
❑ 235 Bernie Williams WS .75 .30
❑ 236 Tino Martinez WS .75 .30
❑ 237 Orlando Hernandez WS .75 .30
❑ 238 Scott Brosius WS .50 .20
❑ 239 Andy Pettitte WS .75 .30
❑ 240 Mariano Rivera WS 1.25 .50
❑ 241 Checklist .50 .20
❑ 242 Checklist .50 .20
❑ 243 Tom Glavine 1.25 .50
❑ 244 Andy Benes .50 .20
❑ 245 Sandy Alomar Jr. .50 .20
❑ 246 Wilton Guerrero .50 .20
❑ 247 Alex Gonzalez .50 .20
❑ 248 Roberto Alomar 1.25 .50
❑ 249 Ruben Rivera .50 .20
❑ 250 Eric Chavez .75 .30
❑ 251 Ellis Burks .75 .30
❑ 252 Richie Sexson .75 .30
❑ 253 Steve Finley .75 .30
❑ 254 Dwight Gooden .75 .30
❑ 255 Dustin Hermanson .50 .20
❑ 256 Kirk Rueter .50 .20
❑ 257 Steve Trachsel .50 .20
❑ 258 Gregg Jefferies .50 .20
❑ 259 Matt Stairs .50 .20
❑ 260 Shane Reynolds .50 .20
❑ 261 Gregg Olson .50 .20
❑ 262 Kevin Tapani .50 .20
❑ 263 Matt Morris .75 .30
❑ 264 Carl Pavano .75 .30
❑ 265 Nomar Garciaparra 3.00 1.25
❑ 266 Kevin Young .75 .30
❑ 267 Rick Helling .50 .20
❑ 268 Matt Franco .50 .20
❑ 269 Brian McRae .50 .20
❑ 270 Cal Ripken 6.00 2.50
❑ 271 Jeff Abbott .50 .20
❑ 272 Tony Batista .50 .20
❑ 273 Bill Simas .50 .20
❑ 274 Brian Hunter .50 .20
❑ 275 John Franco .75 .30
❑ 276 Devon White .75 .30
❑ 277 Rickey Henderson 2.00 .75
❑ 278 Chuck Finley .75 .30
❑ 279 Mike Blowers .50 .20
❑ 280 Mark Grace 1.25 .50
❑ 281 Randy Winn .50 .20
❑ 282 Bobby Bonilla .75 .30
❑ 283 David Justice .75 .30
❑ 284 Shane Monahan .50 .20
❑ 285 Kevin Brown 1.25 .50
❑ 286 Todd Zeile .75 .30
❑ 287 Al Martin .50 .20
❑ 288 Troy O'Leary .50 .20
❑ 289 Darryl Hamilton .50 .20
❑ 290 Tino Martinez 1.25 .50
❑ 291 David Ortiz 2.00 .75
❑ 292 Tony Clark .50 .20
❑ 293 Ryan Minor .50 .20
❑ 294 Mark Leiter .50 .20
❑ 295 Wally Joyner .75 .30
❑ 296 Cliff Floyd .75 .30
❑ 297 Shawn Estes .50 .20
❑ 298 Pat Hentgen .50 .20
❑ 299 Scott Elarton .50 .20
❑ 300 Alex Rodriguez 3.00 1.25
❑ 301 Ozzie Guillen .75 .30
❑ 302 Hideo Nomo 2.00 .75
❑ 303 Ryan McGuire .50 .20
❑ 304 Brad Ausmus .75 .30
❑ 305 Alex Gonzalez .50 .20
❑ 306 Brian Jordan .75 .30
❑ 307 John Jaha .50 .20
❑ 308 Mark Grudzielanek .50 .20
❑ 309 Juan Guzman .50 .20
❑ 310 Tony Womack .50 .20
❑ 311 Dennis Reyes .50 .20
❑ 312 Marty Cordova .50 .20
❑ 313 Ramiro Mendoza .50 .20
❑ 314 Robin Ventura .75 .30
❑ 315 Rafael Palmeiro 1.25 .50
❑ 316 Ramon Martinez .50 .20
❑ 317 Pedro Astacio .50 .20
❑ 318 Dave Hollins .50 .20
❑ 319 Tom Candiotti .50 .20
❑ 320 Al Leiter .75 .30
❑ 321 Rico Brogna .50 .20
❑ 322 Reggie Jefferson .50 .20
❑ 323 Bernard Gilkey .50 .20
❑ 324 Jason Giambi .75 .30
❑ 325 Craig Biggio 1.25 .50
❑ 326 Troy Glaus 1.25 .50
❑ 327 Delino DeShields .50 .20
❑ 328 Fernando Vina .50 .20
❑ 329 John Smoltz 1.25 .50
❑ 330 Jeff Kent .75 .30
❑ 331 Roy Halladay .75 .30
❑ 332 Andy Ashby .50 .20
❑ 333 Tim Wakefield .75 .30
❑ 334 Roger Clemens 4.00 1.50
❑ 335 Bernie Williams 1.25 .50
❑ 336 Desi Relaford .50 .20
❑ 337 John Burkett .50 .20
❑ 338 Mike Hampton .75 .30
❑ 339 Royce Clayton .50 .20
❑ 340 Mike Piazza 3.00 1.25
❑ 341 Jeremi Gonzalez .50 .20
❑ 342 Mike Lansing .50 .20
❑ 343 Jamie Moyer .75 .30
❑ 344 Ron Coomer .50 .20
❑ 345 Barry Larkin 1.25 .50
❑ 346 Fernando Tatis .50 .20
❑ 347 Chili Davis .75 .30
❑ 348 Bobby Higginson .75 .30
❑ 349 Hal Morris .50 .20
❑ 350 Larry Walker .75 .30
❑ 351 Carlos Guillen .75 .30
❑ 352 Miguel Tejada .75 .30
❑ 353 Travis Fryman .75 .30
❑ 354 Jarrod Washburn .50 .20
❑ 355 Chipper Jones 2.00 .75
❑ 356 Todd Stottlemyre .50 .20
❑ 357 Henry Rodriguez .50 .20
❑ 358 Eli Marrero .50 .20
❑ 359 Alan Benes .50 .20
❑ 360 Tim Salmon 1.25 .50
❑ 361 Luis Gonzalez .75 .30
❑ 362 Scott Spiezio .50 .20
❑ 363 Chris Carpenter .75 .30
❑ 364 Bobby Howry .50 .20
❑ 365 Raul Mondesi .75 .30
❑ 366 Ugueth Urbina .50 .20
❑ 367 Tom Evans .50 .20
❑ 368 Kerry Ligtenberg RC .75 .30
❑ 369 Adrian Beltre .75 .30
❑ 370 Ryan Klesko .75 .30
❑ 371 Wilson Alvarez .50 .20
❑ 372 John Thomson .50 .20
❑ 373 Tony Saunders .50 .20
❑ 374 Dave Mlicki .50 .20
❑ 375 Ken Caminiti .75 .30
❑ 376 Jay Buhner .75 .30
❑ 377 Bill Mueller .75 .30
❑ 378 Jeff Blauser .50 .20
❑ 379 Edgar Renteria .75 .30
❑ 380 Jim Thome 1.25 .50
❑ 381 Joey Hamilton .50 .20
❑ 382 Calvin Pickering .50 .20
❑ 383 Marquis Grissom .75 .30
❑ 384 Omar Daal .50 .20
❑ 385 Curt Schilling .75 .30
❑ 386 Jose Cruz Jr. .50 .20
❑ 387 Chris Widger .50 .20
❑ 388 Pete Harnisch .50 .20
❑ 389 Charles Nagy .50 .20
❑ 390 Tom Gordon .50 .20
❑ 391 Bobby Smith .50 .20
❑ 392 Derrick Gibson .50 .20
❑ 393 Jeff Conine .75 .30
❑ 394 Carlos Perez .50 .20
❑ 395 Barry Bonds 5.00 2.00
❑ 396 Mark McLemore .50 .20
❑ 397 Juan Encarnacion .50 .20
❑ 398 Wade Boggs 1.25 .50
❑ 399 Ivan Rodriguez 1.25 .50
❑ 400 Moises Alou .75 .30
❑ 401 Jeromy Burnitz .75 .30
❑ 402 Sean Casey .75 .30
❑ 403 Jose Offerman .50 .20
❑ 404 Joe Fontenot .50 .20
❑ 405 Kevin Millwood .75 .30
❑ 406 Lance Johnson .50 .20
❑ 407 Richard Hidalgo .50 .20
❑ 408 Mike Jackson .50 .20
❑ 409 Brian Anderson .50 .20
❑ 410 Jeff Shaw .50 .20
❑ 411 Preston Wilson .75 .30
❑ 412 Todd Hundley .50 .20
❑ 413 Jim Parque .50 .20
❑ 414 Justin Baughman .50 .20
❑ 415 Dante Bichette .75 .30
❑ 416 Paul O'Neill 1.25 .50
❑ 417 Miguel Cairo .50 .20
❑ 418 Randy Johnson 2.00 .75
❑ 419 Jesus Sanchez .50 .20
❑ 420 Carlos Delgado .75 .30
❑ 421 Ricky Ledee .50 .20
❑ 422 Orlando Hernandez .75 .30
❑ 423 Frank Thomas 2.00 .75
❑ 424 Pokey Reese .50 .20
❑ 425 C.Lee/M.Lowell 1.00 .40
❑ 426 M.Cuddyer/DeRosa/Hairston 1.00 .40
❑ 427 M.Anderson/Belliard/Cabrera 1.00 .40
❑ 428 M.Bowie/P.Norton RC/Wolf 1.00 .40
❑ 429 J.Cressend RC/Rocker 1.00 .40
❑ 430 R.Mateo/M.Zywica RC 1.00 .40
❑ 431 J.LaRue/LeCroy/Meluskey 1.00 .40
❑ 432 Gabe Kapler 1.00 .40
❑ 433 A.Kennedy/M.Lopez RC 1.00 .40
❑ 434 Jose Fernandez RC/C.Truby 1.00 .40
❑ 435 Doug Mientkiewicz RC 1.50 .60
❑ 436 R.Brown RC/V.Wells 1.00 .40
❑ 437 A.J. Burnett RC 2.00 .75
❑ 438 M.Belisle/M.Roney RC 1.00 .40
❑ 439 A.Kearns/C.George RC 4.00 1.50
❑ 440 N.Cornejo/N.Bump RC 1.00 .40
❑ 441 B.Lidge/M.Nannini RC 4.00 1.50
❑ 442 M.Holliday/J.Winchester RC 8.00 3.00
❑ 443 A.Everett/C.Ambres RC 1.50 .60
❑ 444 P.Burrell/E.Valent RC 4.00 1.50
❑ 445 Roger Clemens SK 2.00 .75
❑ 446 Kerry Wood SK .50 .20
❑ 447 Curt Schilling SK .50 .20
❑ 448 Randy Johnson SK 1.25 .50
❑ 449 Pedro Martinez SK 1.25 .50
❑ 450 Bagwell/Galar/McGwire AT 2.00 .75
❑ 451 Olerud/Thome/Martinez AT .75 .30
❑ 452 ARod/Nomar/Jeter AT 2.50 1.00
❑ 453 Castilla/Jones/Rolen AT 1.25 .50
❑ 454 Sosa/Griffey/Gonzalez AT 2.00 .75
❑ 455 Bonds/Ramirez/Walker AT 2.50 1.00
❑ 456 Thomas/Salmon/Justice AT 2.00 .75
❑ 457 Lee/Helton/Grieve AT .75 .30
❑ 458 Guerrero/Vaughn/B.Will AT .75 .30
❑ 459 Piazza/IRod/Kendall AT 2.00 .75
❑ 460 Clemens/Wood/Maddux AT 2.00 .75
❑ 461A Sammy Sosa HR 1 20.00 8.00
❑ 461B Sammy Sosa HR 2 12.00 5.00

❑ 461C Sammy Sosa HR 3	12.00	5.00
❑ 461D Sammy Sosa HR 4	12.00	5.00
❑ 461E Sammy Sosa HR 5	12.00	5.00
❑ 461F Sammy Sosa HR 6	12.00	5.00
❑ 461G Sammy Sosa HR 7	12.00	5.00
❑ 461H Sammy Sosa HR 8	12.00	5.00
❑ 461I Sammy Sosa HR 9	12.00	5.00
❑ 461J Sammy Sosa HR 10	12.00	5.00
❑ 461K Sammy Sosa HR 11	12.00	5.00
❑ 461L Sammy Sosa HR 12	12.00	5.00
❑ 461M Sammy Sosa HR 13	12.00	5.00
❑ 461N Sammy Sosa HR 14	12.00	5.00
❑ 461O Sammy Sosa HR 15	12.00	5.00
❑ 461P Sammy Sosa HR 16	12.00	5.00
❑ 461Q Sammy Sosa HR 17	12.00	5.00
❑ 461R Sammy Sosa HR 18	12.00	5.00
❑ 461S Sammy Sosa HR 19	12.00	5.00
❑ 461T Sammy Sosa HR 20	12.00	5.00
❑ 461U Sammy Sosa HR 21	12.00	5.00
❑ 461V Sammy Sosa HR 22	12.00	5.00
❑ 461W Sammy Sosa HR 23	12.00	5.00
❑ 461X Sammy Sosa HR 24	12.00	5.00
❑ 461Y Sammy Sosa HR 25	12.00	5.00
❑ 461Z Sammy Sosa HR 26	12.00	5.00
❑ 461AA Sammy Sosa HR 27	12.00	5.00
❑ 461AB Sammy Sosa HR 28	12.00	5.00
❑ 461AC Sammy Sosa HR 29	12.00	5.00
❑ 461AD Sammy Sosa HR 30	12.00	5.00
❑ 461AE Sammy Sosa HR 31	12.00	5.00
❑ 461AF Sammy Sosa HR 32	12.00	5.00
❑ 461AG Sammy Sosa HR 33	12.00	5.00
❑ 461AH Sammy Sosa HR 34	12.00	5.00
❑ 461AI Sammy Sosa HR 35	12.00	5.00
❑ 461AJ Sammy Sosa HR 36	12.00	5.00
❑ 461AK Sammy Sosa HR 37	12.00	5.00
❑ 461AL Sammy Sosa HR 38	12.00	5.00
❑ 461AM Sammy Sosa HR 39	12.00	5.00
❑ 461AN Sammy Sosa HR 40	12.00	5.00
❑ 461AO Sammy Sosa HR 41	12.00	5.00
❑ 461AP Sammy Sosa HR 42	12.00	5.00
❑ 461AR Sammy Sosa HR 43	12.00	5.00
❑ 461AS Sammy Sosa HR 44	12.00	5.00
❑ 461AT Sammy Sosa HR 45	12.00	5.00
❑ 461AU Sammy Sosa HR 46	12.00	5.00
❑ 461AV Sammy Sosa HR 47	12.00	5.00
❑ 461AW Sammy Sosa HR 48	12.00	5.00
❑ 461AX Sammy Sosa HR 49	12.00	5.00
❑ 461AY Sammy Sosa HR 50	12.00	5.00
❑ 461AZ Sammy Sosa HR 51	12.00	5.00
❑ 461BB Sammy Sosa HR 52	12.00	5.00
❑ 461CC Sammy Sosa HR 53	12.00	5.00
❑ 461DD Sammy Sosa HR 54	12.00	5.00
❑ 461EE Sammy Sosa HR 55	12.00	5.00
❑ 461FF Sammy Sosa HR 56	12.00	5.00
❑ 461GG Sammy Sosa HR 57	12.00	5.00
❑ 461HH Sammy Sosa HR 58	12.00	5.00
❑ 461II Sammy Sosa HR 59	12.00	5.00
❑ 461JJ Sammy Sosa HR 60	12.00	5.00
❑ 461KK Sammy Sosa HR 61	20.00	8.00
❑ 461LL Sammy Sosa HR 62	30.00	12.50
❑ 461MM Sammy Sosa HR 63	20.00	8.00
❑ 461NN Sammy Sosa HR 64	20.00	8.00
❑ 461OO Sammy Sosa HR 65	20.00	8.00
❑ 461PP Sammy Sosa HR 66	60.00	30.00
❑ 462 Checklist	.50	.20
❑ 463 Checklist	.50	.20

1999 Topps Chrome Traded

❑ COMP.FACT SET (121)	80.00	40.00
❑ T1 Seth Etherton	.40	.15
❑ T2 Mark Harriger RC	.50	.20
❑ T3 Matt Wise RC	.50	.20
❑ T4 Carlos Eduardo Hernandez RC	.75	.30
❑ T5 Julio Lugo RC	1.25	.50
❑ T6 Mike Nannini	.40	.15
❑ T7 Justin Bowles RC	.50	.20
❑ T8 Mark Mulder RC	3.00	1.25
❑ T9 Roberto Vaz RC	.50	.20
❑ T10 Felipe Lopez RC	3.00	1.25
❑ T11 Matt Belisle	.40	.15
❑ T12 Micah Bowie	.40	.15
❑ T13 Ruben Quevedo RC	.50	.20
❑ T14 Jose Garcia RC	.50	.20
❑ T15 David Kelton RC	.50	.20

❑ T16 Phil Norton	.40	.15
❑ T17 Corey Patterson RC	2.00	.75
❑ T18 Ron Walker RC	.50	.20
❑ T19 Paul Hoover RC	.50	.20
❑ T20 Ryan Rupe RC	.50	.20
❑ T21 J.D. Closser RC	.75	.30
❑ T22 Rob Ryan RC	.50	.20
❑ T23 Steve Colyer RC	.50	.20
❑ T24 Bubba Crosby RC	1.25	.50
❑ T25 Luke Prokopec RC	.50	.20
❑ T26 Matt Blank RC	.50	.20
❑ T27 Josh McKinley	.40	.15
❑ T28 Nate Bump	.50	.20
❑ T29 Giuseppe Chiaramonte RC	.50	.20
❑ T30 Arturo McDowell	.40	.15
❑ T31 Tony Torcato	.40	.15
❑ T32 Dave Roberts RC	1.25	.50
❑ T33 C.C. Sabathia RC	4.00	1.50
❑ T34 Sean Spencer RC	.50	.20
❑ T35 Chip Ambres	.40	.15
❑ T36 A.J. Burnett	2.00	.75
❑ T37 Mo Bruce RC	.50	.20
❑ T38 Jason Tyner	.40	.15
❑ T39 Mamon Tucker	.40	.15
❑ T40 Sean Burroughs RC	1.25	.50
❑ T41 Kevin Eberwein RC	.50	.20
❑ T42 Junior Herndon RC	.50	.20
❑ T43 Bryan Wolff RC	.50	.20
❑ T44 Pat Burrell	3.00	1.25
❑ T45 Eric Valent	.75	.30
❑ T46 Carlos Pena RC	1.00	.40
❑ T47 Mike Zywica	.40	.15
❑ T48 Adam Everett	1.00	.40
❑ T49 Juan Pena RC	.50	.20
❑ T50 Adam Dunn RC	8.00	3.00
❑ T51 Austin Kearns	3.00	1.25
❑ T52 Jacobo Sequea RC	.50	.20
❑ T53 Choo Freeman	.60	.25
❑ T54 Jeff Winchester	.40	.15
❑ T55 Matt Burch	.50	.20
❑ T56 Chris George	.40	.15
❑ T57 Scott Mullen RC	.50	.20
❑ T58 Kit Pellow	.50	.20
❑ T59 Mark Quinn RC	.50	.20
❑ T60 Nate Cornejo	.50	.20
❑ T61 Ryan Mills	.40	.15
❑ T62 Kevin Beirne RC	.50	.20
❑ T63 Kip Wells RC	.75	.30
❑ T64 Juan Rivera RC	2.00	.75
❑ T65 Alfonso Soriano RC	10.00	4.00
❑ T66 Josh Hamilton RC	12.00	5.00
❑ T67 Josh Girdley RC	.50	.20
❑ T68 Kyle Snyder RC	.50	.20
❑ T69 Mike Paradis RC	.50	.20
❑ T70 Jason Jennings RC	1.25	.50
❑ T71 David Walling RC	.50	.20
❑ T72 Omar Ortiz RC	.50	.20
❑ T73 Jay Gehrke RC	.50	.20
❑ T74 Casey Burns RC	.50	.20
❑ T75 Carl Crawford RC	8.00	3.00
❑ T76 Reggie Sanders	.60	.25
❑ T77 Will Clark	1.00	.40
❑ T78 David Wells	.60	.25
❑ T79 Paul Konerko	.60	.25
❑ T80 Armando Benitez	.40	.15
❑ T81 Brant Brown	.40	.15
❑ T82 Mo Vaughn	.60	.25
❑ T83 Jose Canseco	1.00	.40
❑ T84 Albert Belle	.60	.25
❑ T85 Dean Palmer	.60	.25
❑ T86 Greg Vaughn	.40	.15
❑ T87 Mark Clark	.40	.15
❑ T88 Pat Meares	.40	.15
❑ T89 Eric Davis	.60	.25
❑ T90 Brian Giles	.60	.25
❑ T91 Jeff Brantley	.40	.15
❑ T92 Bret Boone	.60	.25
❑ T93 Ron Gant	.60	.25
❑ T94 Mike Cameron	.40	.15
❑ T95 Charles Johnson	.60	.25
❑ T96 Denny Neagle	.40	.15
❑ T97 Brian Hunter	.40	.15
❑ T98 Jose Hernandez	.40	.15
❑ T99 Rick Aguilera	.40	.15
❑ T100 Tony Batista	.40	.15
❑ T101 Roger Cedeno	.40	.15
❑ T102 Creighton Gubanich RC	.50	.20
❑ T103 Tim Belcher	.40	.15
❑ T104 Bruce Aven	.40	.15
❑ T105 Brian Daubach RC	.75	.30
❑ T106 Ed Sprague	.40	.15
❑ T107 Michael Tucker	.40	.15
❑ T108 Homer Bush	.40	.15
❑ T109 Armando Reynoso	.40	.15
❑ T110 Brook Fordyce	.40	.15
❑ T111 Matt Mantei	.40	.15
❑ T112 Dave Mlicki	.40	.15
❑ T113 Kenny Rogers	.60	.25
❑ T114 Livan Hernandez	.60	.25
❑ T115 Butch Huskey	.40	.15
❑ T116 David Segui	.40	.15
❑ T117 Darryl Hamilton	.40	.15
❑ T118 Terry Mulholland	.40	.15
❑ T119 Randy Velarde	.40	.15
❑ T120 Bill Taylor	.40	.15
❑ T121 Kevin Appier	.60	.25

2000 Topps Chrome

❑ COMPLETE SET (478)	160.00	60.00
❑ COMPLETE SERIES 1 (239)	80.00	30.00
❑ COMPLETE SERIES 2 (240)	80.00	30.00
❑ MCGWIRE MM SET (5)	50.00	20.00
❑ AARON MM SET (5)	40.00	15.00
❑ RIPKEN MM SET (5)	60.00	25.00
❑ BOGGS MM SET (5)	12.00	5.00
❑ GWYNN MM SET (5)	25.00	10.00
❑ GRIFFEY MM SET (5)	30.00	12.50
❑ BONDS MM SET (5)	50.00	20.00
❑ SOSA MM SET (5)	30.00	12.50
❑ JETER MM SET (5)	50.00	20.00
❑ A.ROD MM SET (5)	40.00	15.00
❑ 1 Mark McGwire	5.00	2.00
❑ 2 Tony Gwynn	2.50	1.00
❑ 3 Wade Boggs	1.25	.50
❑ 4 Cal Ripken	6.00	2.50
❑ 5 Matt Williams	.75	.30
❑ 6 Jay Buhner	.75	.30
❑ 7 Does Not Exist		
❑ 8 Jeff Conine	.75	.30
❑ 9 Todd Greene	.75	.30
❑ 10 Mike Lieberthal	.75	.30
❑ 11 Steve Avery	.75	.30
❑ 12 Bret Saberhagen	.75	.30
❑ 13 Magglio Ordonez	.75	.30
❑ 14 Brad Radke	.75	.30
❑ 15 Derek Jeter	5.00	2.00

❑ 16 Javy Lopez .75 .30
❑ 17 Russ Davis .75 .30
❑ 18 Armando Benitez .75 .30
❑ 19 B.J. Surhoff .75 .30
❑ 20 Darryl Kile .75 .30
❑ 21 Mark Lewis .75 .30
❑ 22 Mike Williams .75 .30
❑ 23 Mark McLemore .75 .30
❑ 24 Sterling Hitchcock .75 .30
❑ 25 Darin Erstad .75 .30
❑ 26 Ricky Gutierrez .75 .30
❑ 27 John Jaha .75 .30
❑ 28 Homer Bush .75 .30
❑ 29 Darrin Fletcher .75 .30
❑ 30 Mark Grace 1.25 .50
❑ 31 Fred McGriff 1.25 .50
❑ 32 Omar Daal .75 .30
❑ 33 Eric Karros .75 .30
❑ 34 Orlando Cabrera .75 .30
❑ 35 J.T. Snow .75 .30
❑ 36 Luis Castillo .75 .30
❑ 37 Rey Ordonez .75 .30
❑ 38 Bob Abreu .75 .30
❑ 39 Warren Morris .75 .30
❑ 40 Juan Gonzalez .75 .30
❑ 41 Mike Lansing .75 .30
❑ 42 Chili Davis .75 .30
❑ 43 Dean Palmer .75 .30
❑ 44 Hank Aaron 4.00 1.50
❑ 45 Jeff Bagwell 1.25 .50
❑ 46 Jose Valentin .75 .30
❑ 47 Shannon Stewart .75 .30
❑ 48 Kent Bottenfield .75 .30
❑ 49 Jeff Shaw .75 .30
❑ 50 Sammy Sosa 2.00 .75
❑ 51 Randy Johnson 2.00 .75
❑ 52 Benny Agbayani .75 .30
❑ 53 Dante Bichette .75 .30
❑ 54 Pete Harnisch .75 .30
❑ 55 Frank Thomas 2.00 .75
❑ 56 Jorge Posada 1.25 .50
❑ 57 Todd Walker .75 .30
❑ 58 Juan Encarnacion .75 .30
❑ 59 Mike Sweeney .75 .30
❑ 60 Pedro Martinez 1.25 .50
❑ 61 Lee Stevens .75 .30
❑ 62 Brian Giles .75 .30
❑ 63 Chad Ogea .75 .30
❑ 64 Ivan Rodriguez 1.25 .50
❑ 65 Roger Cedeno .75 .30
❑ 66 David Justice .75 .30
❑ 67 Steve Trachsel .75 .30
❑ 68 Eli Marrero .75 .30
❑ 69 Dave Nilsson .75 .30
❑ 70 Ken Caminiti .75 .30
❑ 71 Tim Raines .75 .30
❑ 72 Brian Jordan .75 .30
❑ 73 Jeff Blauser .75 .30
❑ 74 Bernard Gilkey .75 .30
❑ 75 John Flaherty .75 .30
❑ 76 Brent Mayne .75 .30
❑ 77 Jose Vidro .75 .30
❑ 78 David Bell .75 .30
❑ 79 Bruce Aven .75 .30
❑ 80 John Olerud .75 .30
❑ 81 Pokey Reese .75 .30
❑ 82 Woody Williams .75 .30
❑ 83 Ed Sprague .75 .30
❑ 84 Joe Girardi .75 .30
❑ 85 Barry Larkin 1.25 .50
❑ 86 Mike Caruso .75 .30
❑ 87 Bobby Higginson .75 .30
❑ 88 Roberto Kelly .75 .30
❑ 89 Edgar Martinez 1.25 .50
❑ 90 Mark Kotsay .75 .30
❑ 91 Paul Sorrento .75 .30
❑ 92 Eric Young .75 .30
❑ 93 Carlos Delgado .75 .30
❑ 94 Troy Glaus .75 .30
❑ 95 Ben Grieve .75 .30
❑ 96 Jose Lima .75 .30
❑ 97 Garret Anderson .75 .30
❑ 98 Luis Gonzalez .75 .30
❑ 99 Carl Pavano .75 .30
❑ 100 Alex Rodriguez 3.00 1.25
❑ 101 Preston Wilson .75 .30
❑ 102 Ron Gant .75 .30
❑ 103 Brady Anderson .75 .30
❑ 104 Rickey Henderson 2.00 .75
❑ 105 Gary Sheffield .75 .30
❑ 106 Mickey Morandini .75 .30
❑ 107 Jim Edmonds .75 .30
❑ 108 Kris Benson .75 .30
❑ 109 Adrian Beltre .75 .30
❑ 110 Alex Fernandez .75 .30
❑ 111 Dan Wilson .75 .30
❑ 112 Mark Clark .75 .30
❑ 113 Greg Vaughn .75 .30
❑ 114 Neifi Perez .75 .30
❑ 115 Paul O'Neill 1.25 .50
❑ 116 Jermaine Dye .75 .30
❑ 117 Todd Jones .75 .30
❑ 118 Terry Steinbach .75 .30
❑ 119 Greg Norton .75 .30
❑ 120 Curt Schilling .75 .30
❑ 121 Todd Zeile .75 .30
❑ 122 Edgardo Alfonzo .75 .30
❑ 123 Ryan McGuire .75 .30
❑ 124 Rich Aurilia .75 .30
❑ 125 John Smoltz 1.25 .50
❑ 126 Bob Wickman .75 .30
❑ 127 Richard Hidalgo .75 .30
❑ 128 Chuck Finley .75 .30
❑ 129 Billy Wagner .75 .30
❑ 130 Todd Hundley .75 .30
❑ 131 Dwight Gooden .75 .30
❑ 132 Russ Ortiz .75 .30
❑ 133 Mike Lowell .75 .30
❑ 134 Reggie Sanders .75 .30
❑ 135 John Valentin .75 .30
❑ 136 Brad Ausmus .75 .30
❑ 137 Chad Kreuter .75 .30
❑ 138 David Cone .75 .30
❑ 139 Brook Fordyce .75 .30
❑ 140 Roberto Alomar 1.25 .50
❑ 141 Charles Nagy .75 .30
❑ 142 Brian Hunter .75 .30
❑ 143 Mike Mussina 1.25 .50
❑ 144 Robin Ventura 1.25 .50
❑ 145 Kevin Brown 1.25 .50
❑ 146 Pat Hentgen .75 .30
❑ 147 Ryan Klesko .75 .30
❑ 148 Derek Bell .75 .30
❑ 149 Andy Sheets .75 .30
❑ 150 Larry Walker .75 .30
❑ 151 Scott Williamson .75 .30
❑ 152 Jose Offerman .75 .30
❑ 153 Doug Mientkiewicz .75 .30
❑ 154 John Snyder RC 1.00 .40
❑ 155 Sandy Alomar Jr. .75 .30
❑ 156 Joe Nathan .75 .30
❑ 157 Lance Johnson .75 .30
❑ 158 Odalis Perez .75 .30
❑ 159 Hideo Nomo 2.00 .75
❑ 160 Steve Finley .75 .30
❑ 161 Dave Martinez .75 .30
❑ 162 Matt Walbeck .75 .30
❑ 163 Bill Spiers .75 .30
❑ 164 Fernando Tatis .75 .30
❑ 165 Kenny Lofton .75 .30
❑ 166 Paul Byrd .75 .30
❑ 167 Aaron Sele .75 .30
❑ 168 Eddie Taubensee .75 .30
❑ 169 Reggie Jefferson .75 .30
❑ 170 Roger Clemens 4.00 1.50
❑ 171 Francisco Cordova .75 .30
❑ 172 Mike Bordick .75 .30
❑ 173 Wally Joyner .75 .30
❑ 174 Marvin Benard .75 .30
❑ 175 Jason Kendall .75 .30
❑ 176 Mike Stanley .75 .30
❑ 177 Chad Allen .75 .30
❑ 178 Carlos Beltran .75 .30
❑ 179 Deivi Cruz .75 .30
❑ 180 Chipper Jones 2.00 .75
❑ 181 Vladimir Guerrero 2.00 .75
❑ 182 Dave Burba .75 .30
❑ 183 Tom Goodwin .75 .30
❑ 184 Brian Daubach .75 .30
❑ 185 Jay Bell .75 .30
❑ 186 Roy Halladay .75 .30
❑ 187 Miguel Tejada .75 .30
❑ 188 Armando Rios .75 .30
❑ 189 Fernando Vina .75 .30
❑ 190 Eric Davis .75 .30
❑ 191 Henry Rodriguez .75 .30
❑ 192 Joe McEwing .75 .30
❑ 193 Jeff Kent .75 .30
❑ 194 Mike Jackson .75 .30
❑ 195 Mike Morgan .75 .30
❑ 196 Jeff Montgomery .75 .30
❑ 197 Jeff Zimmerman .75 .30
❑ 198 Tony Fernandez .75 .30
❑ 199 Jason Giambi .75 .30
❑ 200 Jose Canseco 1.25 .50
❑ 201 Alex Gonzalez .75 .30
❑ 202 J.Cust/Colangelo/D.Brown 1.00 .40
❑ 203 A.Soriano/F.Lopez 2.00 .75
❑ 204 Durazo/Burrell/Johnson 1.50 .60
❑ 205 John Sneed RC/K.Wells 1.00 .40
❑ 206 Kalinowski/Tejera/Mears RC 1.00 .40
❑ 207 L.Berkman/C.Patterson 1.50 .60
❑ 208 K.Pellow/K.Barker/R.Branyan 1.00 .40
❑ 209 B.Garbe/L.Bigbie RC 2.50 1.00
❑ 210 B.Bradley RC/E.Munson 1.00 .40
❑ 211 J.Girdley/K.Snyder 1.00 .40
❑ 212 Chance Caple RC/J.Jennings 1.00 .40
❑ 213 B.Myers/R.Christianson RC 4.00 1.50
❑ 214 J.Stumm/R.Purvis RC 1.00 .40
❑ 215 D.Walling/M.Paradis 1.00 .40
❑ 216 O.Ortiz/J.Gehrke 1.00 .40
❑ 217 David Cone HL .75 .30
❑ 218 Jose Jimenez HL .75 .30
❑ 219 Chris Singleton HL .75 .30
❑ 220 Fernando Tatis HL .75 .30
❑ 221 Todd Helton HL .75 .30
❑ 222 Kevin Millwood DIV .75 .30
❑ 223 Todd Pratt DIV .75 .30
❑ 224 Orlando Hernandez DIV .75 .30
❑ 225 Pedro Martinez DIV 1.25 .50
❑ 226 Tom Glavine LCS .75 .30
❑ 227 Bernie Williams LCS .75 .30
❑ 228 Mariano Rivera WS 1.25 .50
❑ 229 Tony Gwynn 20CB 2.50 1.00
❑ 230 Wade Boggs 20CB 1.25 .50
❑ 231 Lance Johnson CB .75 .30
❑ 232 Mark McGwire 20CB 5.00 2.00
❑ 233 Rickey Henderson 20CB 2.00 .75
❑ 234 Rickey Henderson 20CB 2.00 .75
❑ 235 Roger Clemens 20CB 4.00 1.50
❑ 236A M.McGwire MM 1st HR 12.00 5.00
❑ 236B M.McGwire MM 1987 ROY 12.005.00
❑ 236C M.McGwire MM 62nd HR 12.00 5.00
❑ 236D M.McGwire MM 70th HR 12.00 5.00
❑ 236E M.McGwire MM 500th HR 12.00 5.00
❑ 237A H.Aaron MM 1st Career HR 10.004.00
❑ 237B H.Aaron MM 1957 MVP 10.00 4.00
❑ 237C H.Aaron MM 3000th Hit 10.00 4.00
❑ 237D H.Aaron MM 715th HR 10.00 4.00
❑ 237E H.Aaron MM 755th HR 10.00 4.00
❑ 238A C.Ripken MM 1982 ROY 15.00 6.00
❑ 238B C.Ripken MM 1991 MVP 15.00 6.00
❑ 238C C.Ripken MM 2131 Game 15.00 6.00
❑ 238D C.Ripken MM Streak Ends 15.006.00
❑ 238E C.Ripken MM 400th HR 15.00 6.00
❑ 239A W.Boggs MM 1983 Batting 3.00 1.25
❑ 239B W.Boggs MM 1988 Batting 3.00 1.25
❑ 239C W.Boggs MM 2000th Hit 3.00 1.25
❑ 239D W.Boggs MM 1996 Champs 3.001.25
❑ 239E W.Boggs MM 3000th Hit 3.00 1.25
❑ 240A T.Gwynn MM 1984 Batting 6.00 2.50
❑ 240B T.Gwynn MM 1984 NLCS 6.00 2.50
❑ 240C T.Gwynn MM 1995 Batting 6.00 2.50
❑ 240D T.Gwynn MM 1998 NLCS 6.00 2.50
❑ 240E T.Gwynn MM 3000th Hit 6.00 2.50
❑ 241 Tom Glavine 1.25 .50
❑ 242 David Wells .75 .30
❑ 243 Kevin Appier .75 .30
❑ 244 Troy Percival .75 .30
❑ 245 Ray Lankford .75 .30
❑ 246 Marquis Grissom .75 .30
❑ 247 Randy Winn .75 .30
❑ 248 Miguel Batista .75 .30
❑ 249 Darren Dreifort .75 .30
❑ 250 Barry Bonds 4.00 1.50
❑ 251 Harold Baines .75 .30
❑ 252 Cliff Floyd .75 .30
❑ 253 Freddy Garcia .75 .30

- ❑ 254 Kenny Rogers .75 .30
- ❑ 255 Ben Davis .75 .30
- ❑ 256 Charles Johnson .75 .30
- ❑ 257 Bubba Trammell .75 .30
- ❑ 258 Desi Relaford .75 .30
- ❑ 259 Al Martin .75 .30
- ❑ 260 Andy Pettitte 1.25 .50
- ❑ 261 Carlos Lee .75 .30
- ❑ 262 Matt Lawton .75 .30
- ❑ 263 Andy Fox .75 .30
- ❑ 264 Chan Ho Park .75 .30
- ❑ 265 Billy Koch .75 .30
- ❑ 266 Dave Roberts .75 .30
- ❑ 267 Carl Everett .75 .30
- ❑ 268 Orel Hershiser .75 .30
- ❑ 269 Trot Nixon .75 .30
- ❑ 270 Rusty Greer .75 .30
- ❑ 271 Will Clark 1.25 .50
- ❑ 272 Quilvio Veras .75 .30
- ❑ 273 Rico Brogna .75 .30
- ❑ 274 Devon White .75 .30
- ❑ 275 Tim Hudson .75 .30
- ❑ 276 Mike Hampton .75 .30
- ❑ 277 Miguel Cairo .75 .30
- ❑ 278 Darren Oliver .75 .30
- ❑ 279 Jeff Cirillo .75 .30
- ❑ 280 Al Leiter .75 .30
- ❑ 281 Shane Andrews .75 .30
- ❑ 282 Carlos Febles .75 .30
- ❑ 283 Pedro Astacio .75 .30
- ❑ 284 Juan Guzman .75 .30
- ❑ 285 Orlando Hernandez .75 .30
- ❑ 286 Paul Konerko .75 .30
- ❑ 287 Tony Clark .75 .30
- ❑ 288 Aaron Boone .75 .30
- ❑ 289 Ismael Valdes .75 .30
- ❑ 290 Moises Alou .75 .30
- ❑ 291 Kevin Tapani .75 .30
- ❑ 292 John Franco .75 .30
- ❑ 293 Todd Zeile .75 .30
- ❑ 294 Jason Schmidt .75 .30
- ❑ 295 Johnny Damon 1.25 .50
- ❑ 296 Scott Brosius .75 .30
- ❑ 297 Travis Fryman .75 .30
- ❑ 298 Jose Vizcaino .75 .30
- ❑ 299 Eric Chavez .75 .30
- ❑ 300 Mike Piazza 3.00 1.25
- ❑ 301 Matt Clement .75 .30
- ❑ 302 Cristian Guzman .75 .30
- ❑ 303 C.J. Nitkowski .75 .30
- ❑ 304 Michael Tucker .75 .30
- ❑ 305 Brett Tomko .75 .30
- ❑ 306 Mike Lansing .75 .30
- ❑ 307 Eric Owens .75 .30
- ❑ 308 Livan Hernandez .75 .30
- ❑ 309 Rondell White .75 .30
- ❑ 310 Todd Stottlemyre .75 .30
- ❑ 311 Chris Carpenter .75 .30
- ❑ 312 Ken Hill .75 .30
- ❑ 313 Mark Loretta .75 .30
- ❑ 314 John Rocker .75 .30
- ❑ 315 Richie Sexson .75 .30
- ❑ 316 Ruben Mateo .75 .30
- ❑ 317 Joe Randa .75 .30
- ❑ 318 Mike Sirotka .75 .30
- ❑ 319 Jose Rosado .75 .30
- ❑ 320 Matt Mantei .75 .30
- ❑ 321 Kevin Millwood .75 .30
- ❑ 322 Gary Disarcina .75 .30
- ❑ 323 Dustin Hermanson .75 .30
- ❑ 324 Mike Stanton .75 .30
- ❑ 325 Kirk Rueter .75 .30
- ❑ 326 Damian Miller RC 1.50 .60
- ❑ 327 Doug Glanville .75 .30
- ❑ 328 Scott Rolen 1.25 .50
- ❑ 329 Ray Durham .75 .30
- ❑ 330 Butch Huskey .75 .30
- ❑ 331 Mariano Rivera 2.00 .75
- ❑ 332 Darren Lewis .75 .30
- ❑ 333 Mike Timlin .75 .30
- ❑ 334 Mark Grudzielanek .75 .30
- ❑ 335 Mike Cameron .75 .30
- ❑ 336 Kelvim Escobar .75 .30
- ❑ 337 Bret Boone .75 .30
- ❑ 338 Mo Vaughn .75 .30
- ❑ 339 Craig Biggio 1.25 .50
- ❑ 340 Michael Barrett .75 .30
- ❑ 341 Marlon Anderson .75 .30
- ❑ 342 Bobby Jones .75 .30
- ❑ 343 John Halama .75 .30
- ❑ 344 Todd Ritchie .75 .30
- ❑ 345 Chuck Knoblauch .75 .30
- ❑ 346 Rick Reed .75 .30
- ❑ 347 Kelly Stinnett .75 .30
- ❑ 348 Tim Salmon 1.25 .50
- ❑ 349 A.J. Hinch .75 .30
- ❑ 350 Jose Cruz Jr. .75 .30
- ❑ 351 Roberto Hernandez .75 .30
- ❑ 352 Edgar Renteria .75 .30
- ❑ 353 Jose Hernandez .75 .30
- ❑ 354 Brad Fullmer .75 .30
- ❑ 355 Trevor Hoffman .75 .30
- ❑ 356 Troy O'Leary .75 .30
- ❑ 357 Justin Thompson .75 .30
- ❑ 358 Kevin Young .75 .30
- ❑ 359 Hideki Irabu .75 .30
- ❑ 360 Jim Thome 1.25 .50
- ❑ 361 Steve Karsay .75 .30
- ❑ 362 Octavio Dotel .75 .30
- ❑ 363 Omar Vizquel 1.25 .50
- ❑ 364 Raul Mondesi .75 .30
- ❑ 365 Shane Reynolds .75 .30
- ❑ 366 Bartolo Colon .75 .30
- ❑ 367 Chris Widger .75 .30
- ❑ 368 Gabe Kapler .75 .30
- ❑ 369 Bill Simas .75 .30
- ❑ 370 Tino Martinez 1.25 .50
- ❑ 371 John Thomson .75 .30
- ❑ 372 Delino Deshields .75 .30
- ❑ 373 Carlos Perez .75 .30
- ❑ 374 Eddie Perez .75 .30
- ❑ 375 Jeromy Burnitz .75 .30
- ❑ 376 Jimmy Haynes .75 .30
- ❑ 377 Travis Lee .75 .30
- ❑ 378 Darryl Hamilton .75 .30
- ❑ 379 Jamie Moyer .75 .30
- ❑ 380 Alex Gonzalez .75 .30
- ❑ 381 John Wetteland .75 .30
- ❑ 382 Vinny Castilla .75 .30
- ❑ 383 Jeff Suppan .75 .30
- ❑ 384 Jim Leyritz .75 .30
- ❑ 385 Robb Nen .75 .30
- ❑ 386 Wilson Alvarez .75 .30
- ❑ 387 Andres Galarraga .75 .30
- ❑ 388 Mike Remlinger .75 .30
- ❑ 389 Geoff Jenkins .75 .30
- ❑ 390 Matt Stairs .75 .30
- ❑ 391 Bill Mueller .75 .30
- ❑ 392 Mike Lowell .75 .30
- ❑ 393 Andy Ashby .75 .30
- ❑ 394 Ruben Rivera .75 .30
- ❑ 395 Todd Helton 1.25 .50
- ❑ 396 Bernie Williams 1.25 .50
- ❑ 397 Royce Clayton .75 .30
- ❑ 398 Manny Ramirez 1.25 .50
- ❑ 399 Kerry Wood .75 .30
- ❑ 400 Ken Griffey Jr. 3.00 1.25
- ❑ 401 Enrique Wilson .75 .30
- ❑ 402 Joey Hamilton .75 .30
- ❑ 403 Shawn Estes .75 .30
- ❑ 404 Ugueth Urbina .75 .30
- ❑ 405 Albert Belle .75 .30
- ❑ 406 Rick Helling .75 .30
- ❑ 407 Steve Parris .75 .30
- ❑ 408 Eric Milton .75 .30
- ❑ 409 Dave Mlicki .75 .30
- ❑ 410 Shawn Green .75 .30
- ❑ 411 Jaret Wright .75 .30
- ❑ 412 Tony Womack .75 .30
- ❑ 413 Vernon Wells .75 .30
- ❑ 414 Ron Belliard .75 .30
- ❑ 415 Ellis Burks .75 .30
- ❑ 416 Scott Erickson .75 .30
- ❑ 417 Rafael Palmeiro 1.25 .50
- ❑ 418 Damion Easley .75 .30
- ❑ 419 Jamey Wright .75 .30
- ❑ 420 Corey Koskie .75 .30
- ❑ 421 Bobby Howry .75 .30
- ❑ 422 Ricky Ledee .75 .30
- ❑ 423 Dmitri Young .75 .30
- ❑ 424 Sidney Ponson .75 .30
- ❑ 425 Greg Maddux 3.00 1.25
- ❑ 426 Jose Guillen .75 .30
- ❑ 427 Jon Lieber .75 .30
- ❑ 428 Andy Benes .75 .30
- ❑ 429 Randy Velarde .75 .30
- ❑ 430 Sean Casey .75 .30
- ❑ 431 Torii Hunter .75 .30
- ❑ 432 Ryan Rupe .75 .30
- ❑ 433 David Segui .75 .30
- ❑ 434 Todd Pratt .75 .30
- ❑ 435 Nomar Garciaparra 3.00 1.25
- ❑ 436 Denny Neagle .75 .30
- ❑ 437 Ron Coomer .75 .30
- ❑ 438 Chris Singleton .75 .30
- ❑ 439 Tony Batista .75 .30
- ❑ 440 Andruw Jones 1.25 .50
- ❑ 441 Burroughs/Piatt/Huff .75 .30
- ❑ 442 Rafael Furcal 1.50 .60
- ❑ 443 M.Lamb RC/J.Crede 4.00 1.50
- ❑ 444 Julio Zuleta RC 1.00 .40
- ❑ 445 Garry Maddox Jr. RC 1.00 .40
- ❑ 446 Riley/Sabathia/Mulder 1.50 .60
- ❑ 447 Scott Downs RC 1.00 .40
- ❑ 448 D.Mirabelli/B.Petrick/J.Werth 1.00 .40
- ❑ 449 C.Myers RC/J.Hamilton 1.50 .60
- ❑ 450 B.Christensen/R.Stahl RC 1.00 .40
- ❑ 451 B.Zito/B.Sheets RC 10.00 4.00
- ❑ 452 K.Ainsworth/Howington RC 1.00 .40
- ❑ 453 R.Asadoorian/V.Faison RC 1.50 .60
- ❑ 454 K.Reed/J.Heaverlo RC 1.00 .40
- ❑ 455 M.MacDougal/B.Baker RC 1.00 .40
- ❑ 456 Mark McGwire SH 2.50 1.00
- ❑ 457 Cal Ripken SH 3.00 1.25
- ❑ 458 Wade Boggs SH .75 .30
- ❑ 459 Tony Gwynn SH 1.25 .50
- ❑ 460 Jesse Orosco SH .75 .30
- ❑ 461 L.Walker/N.Garciaparra LL 1.25 .50
- ❑ 462 K.Griffey Jr./M.McGwire LL 2.00 .75
- ❑ 463 M.Ramirez/M.McGwire LL 2.00 .75
- ❑ 464 P.Martinez/R.Johnson LL 1.25 .50
- ❑ 465 P.Martinez/R.Johnson LL 1.25 .50
- ❑ 466 D.Jeter/L.Gonzalez LL 2.00 .75
- ❑ 467 L.Walker/M.Ramirez LL 1.25 .50
- ❑ 468 Tony Gwynn 20CB 2.50 1.00
- ❑ 469 Mark McGwire 20CB 5.00 2.00
- ❑ 470 Frank Thomas 20CB 1.25 .50
- ❑ 471 Harold Baines 20CB .75 .30
- ❑ 472 Roger Clemens 20CB 4.00 1.50
- ❑ 473 John Franco 20CB .75 .30
- ❑ 474 John Franco 20CB .75 .30
- ❑ 475A K.Griffey Jr. MM 350th HR 8.00 3.00
- ❑ 475B K.Griffey Jr. MM 1997 MVP 8.00 3.00
- ❑ 475C K.Griffey Jr. MM HR Dad 8.00 3.00
- ❑ 475D K.Griffey Jr. MM 1992 AS MVP 8.00 3.00
- ❑ 475E K.Griffey Jr. MM 50 HR 1997 8.00 3.00
- ❑ 476A B.Bonds MM 400HR/400SB 12.00 5.00
- ❑ 476B B.Bonds MM 40HR/40SB 12.00 5.00
- ❑ 476C B.Bonds MM 1993 MVP 12.00 5.00
- ❑ 476D B.Bonds MM 1990 MVP 12.00 5.00
- ❑ 476E B.Bonds MM 1992 MVP 12.00 5.00
- ❑ 477A S.Sosa MM 20 HR June 8.00 3.00
- ❑ 477B S.Sosa MM 66 HR 1998 8.00 3.00
- ❑ 477C S.Sosa MM 60 HR 1999 8.00 3.00
- ❑ 477D S.Sosa MM 1998 MVP 8.00 3.00
- ❑ 477E S.Sosa MM HR's 61/62 8.00 3.00
- ❑ 478A D.Jeter MM 1996 ROY 12.00 5.00
- ❑ 478B D.Jeter MM Wins 1999 WS 12.00 5.00
- ❑ 478C D.Jeter MM Wins 1998 WS 12.00 5.00
- ❑ 478D D.Jeter MM Wins 1996 WS 12.00 5.00
- ❑ 478E D.Jeter MM 17 GM Hit Streak 12.00 5.00
- ❑ 479A A.Rodriguez MM 40HR/40SB 10.00 4.00
- ❑ 479B A.Rodriguez MM 100th HR 10.00 4.00
- ❑ 479C A.Rodriguez MM 1996 POY 10.00 4.00
- ❑ 479D A.Rodriguez MM Wins 1 Million 10.00 4.00
- ❑ 479E A.Rodriguez MM 1996 Batting Leader 10.00 4.00
- ❑ NNO M.McGwire 85 Reprint 8.00 3.00

2000 Topps Chrome Traded

- ❑ COMP.FACT.SET (135) 80.00 40.00
- ❑ T1 Mike MacDougal .75 .30
- ❑ T2 Andy Tracy RC .50 .20
- ❑ T3 Brandon Phillips RC 2.50 1.00
- ❑ T4 Brandon Inge RC 4.00 1.50
- ❑ T5 Robbie Morrison RC .50 .20

❑ T6 Josh Pressley RC .50 .20
❑ T7 Todd Moser RC .50 .20
❑ T8 Rob Purvis .60 .25
❑ T9 Chance Caple .40 .15
❑ T10 Ben Sheets 2.50 1.00
❑ T11 Russ Jacobson RC .50 .20
❑ T12 Brian Cole RC .50 .20
❑ T13 Brad Baker .40 .15
❑ T14 Alex Cintron RC .75 .30
❑ T15 Lyle Overbay RC 2.00 .75
❑ T16 Mike Edwards RC .50 .20
❑ T17 Sean McGowan RC .50 .20
❑ T18 Jose Molina .40 .15
❑ T19 Marcos Castillo RC .50 .20
❑ T20 Josue Espada RC .50 .20
❑ T21 Alex Gordon RC .50 .20
❑ T22 Rob Pugmire RC .50 .20
❑ T23 Jason Stumm .50 .20
❑ T24 Ty Howington .40 .15
❑ T25 Brett Myers 1.50 .60
❑ T26 Maicer Izturis RC .75 .30
❑ T27 John McDonald .40 .15
❑ T28 Wilfredo Rodriguez RC .50 .20
❑ T29 Carlos Zambrano RC 8.00 3.00
❑ T30 Alejandro Diaz RC .50 .20
❑ T31 Geraldo Guzman RC .50 .20
❑ T32 J.R. House RC .50 .20
❑ T33 Elvin Nina RC .50 .20
❑ T34 Juan Pierre RC 2.00 .75
❑ T35 Ben Johnson RC 3.00 1.25
❑ T36 Jeff Bailey RC .50 .20
❑ T37 Miguel Olivo RC 1.25 .50
❑ T38 Francisco Rodriguez RC 4.00 1.50
❑ T39 Tony Pena Jr. RC .50 .20
❑ T40 Miguel Cabrera RC 50.00 25.00
❑ T41 Asdrubal Oropeza RC .50 .20
❑ T42 Junior Zamora RC .75 .30
❑ T43 Jovanny Cedeno RC .50 .20
❑ T44 John Sneed .60 .25
❑ T45 Josh Kalinowski .60 .25
❑ T46 Mike Young RC 10.00 4.00
❑ T47 Rico Washington RC .50 .20
❑ T48 Chad Durbin RC .50 .20
❑ T49 Junior Brignac RC .50 .20
❑ T50 Carlos Hernandez RC .75 .30
❑ T51 Cesar Izturis RC 1.25 .50
❑ T52 Oscar Salazar RC .50 .20
❑ T53 Pat Strange RC .50 .20
❑ T54 Rick Asadoorian .75 .30
❑ T55 Keith Reed .40 .15
❑ T56 Leo Estrella RC .50 .20
❑ T57 Wascar Serrano RC .50 .20
❑ T58 Richard Gomez RC .50 .20
❑ T59 Ramon Santiago RC .50 .20
❑ T60 Jovanny Sosa RC .50 .20
❑ T61 Aaron Rowand RC 3.00 1.25
❑ T62 Junior Guerrero RC .50 .20
❑ T63 Luis Terrero RC .75 .30
❑ T64 Brian Sanches RC .50 .20
❑ T65 Scott Sobkowiak RC .50 .20
❑ T66 Gary Majewski RC .75 .30
❑ T67 Barry Zito 3.00 1.25
❑ T68 Ryan Christianson .50 .20
❑ T69 Cristian Guerrero RC .50 .20
❑ T70 Tomas De La Rosa RC .50 .20
❑ T71 Andrew Beinbrink RC .50 .20
❑ T72 Ryan Knox RC .50 .20
❑ T73 Alex Graman RC .50 .20
❑ T74 Juan Guzman RC .50 .20
❑ T75 Ruben Salazar RC .50 .20
❑ T76 Luis Matos RC .75 .30
❑ T77 Tony Mota RC .50 .20
❑ T78 Doug Davis .60 .25
❑ T79 Ben Christensen .40 .15
❑ T80 Mike Lamb 1.25 .50
❑ T81 Adrian Gonzalez RC 5.00 2.00
❑ T82 Mike Stodolka RC .50 .20
❑ T83 Adam Johnson RC .50 .20
❑ T84 Matt Wheatland RC .50 .20
❑ T85 Corey Smith RC .50 .20
❑ T86 Rocco Baldelli RC 4.00 1.50
❑ T87 Keith Bucktrot RC .50 .20
❑ T88 Adam Wainwright RC 2.00 .75
❑ T89 Scott Thorman RC 2.00 .75
❑ T90 Tripper Johnson RC .50 .20
❑ T91 Jim Edmonds Cards .60 .25
❑ T92 Masato Yoshii .40 .15
❑ T93 Adam Kennedy .40 .15
❑ T94 Darryl Kile .60 .25
❑ T95 Mark McLemore .40 .15
❑ T96 Ricky Gutierrez .40 .15
❑ T97 Juan Gonzalez .60 .25
❑ T98 Melvin Mora .60 .25
❑ T99 Dante Bichette .60 .25
❑ T100 Lee Stevens .40 .15
❑ T101 Roger Cedeno .40 .15
❑ T102 John Olerud .60 .25
❑ T103 Eric Young .40 .15
❑ T104 Mickey Morandini .40 .15
❑ T105 Travis Lee .40 .15
❑ T106 Greg Vaughn .40 .15
❑ T107 Todd Zeile .60 .25
❑ T108 Chuck Finley .60 .25
❑ T109 Ismael Valdes .40 .15
❑ T110 Reggie Sanders .60 .25
❑ T111 Pat Hentgen .40 .15
❑ T112 Ryan Klesko .60 .25
❑ T113 Derek Bell .40 .15
❑ T114 Hideo Nomo 1.50 .60
❑ T115 Aaron Sele .40 .15
❑ T116 Fernando Vina .40 .15
❑ T117 Wally Joyner .60 .25
❑ T118 Brian Hunter .40 .15
❑ T119 Joe Girardi .40 .15
❑ T120 Omar Daal .40 .15
❑ T121 Brook Fordyce .40 .15
❑ T122 Jose Valentin .40 .15
❑ T123 Curt Schilling .60 .25
❑ T124 B.J. Surhoff .60 .25
❑ T125 Henry Rodriguez .40 .15
❑ T126 Mike Bordick .40 .15
❑ T127 David Justice .60 .25
❑ T128 Charles Johnson .60 .25
❑ T129 Will Clark 1.00 .40
❑ T130 Dwight Gooden .60 .25
❑ T131 David Segui .40 .15
❑ T132 Denny Neagle .60 .25
❑ T133 Jose Canseco 1.00 .40
❑ T134 Bruce Chen .40 .15
❑ T135 Jason Bere .40 .15

2001 Topps Chrome

❑ COMPLETE SET (661) 300.00 150.00
❑ COMPLETE SERIES 1 (331) 150.00 75.00
❑ COMPLETE SERIES 2 (330) 150.00 75.00
❑ 1 Cal Ripken 6.00 2.50
❑ 2 Chipper Jones 2.00 .75
❑ 3 Roger Cedeno .50 .20
❑ 4 Garret Anderson .75 .30
❑ 5 Robin Ventura .75 .30
❑ 6 Daryle Ward .50 .20
❑ 7 Does Not Exist
❑ 8 Phil Nevin .75 .30
❑ 9 Jermaine Dye .75 .30
❑ 10 Chris Singleton .50 .20
❑ 11 Mike Redmond .50 .20
❑ 12 Jim Thome 1.25 .50
❑ 13 Brian Jordan .75 .30
❑ 14 Dustin Hermanson .50 .20
❑ 15 Shawn Green .75 .30
❑ 16 Todd Stottlemyre .50 .20
❑ 17 Dan Wilson .50 .20
❑ 18 Derek Lowe .75 .30
❑ 19 Juan Gonzalez .75 .30
❑ 20 Pat Meares .50 .20
❑ 21 Paul O'Neill 1.25 .50
❑ 22 Jeffrey Hammonds .50 .20
❑ 23 Pokey Reese .50 .20
❑ 24 Mike Mussina 1.25 .50
❑ 25 Rico Brogna .50 .20
❑ 26 Jay Buhner .75 .30
❑ 27 Steve Cox .50 .20
❑ 28 Quilvio Veras .50 .20
❑ 29 Marquis Grissom .75 .30
❑ 30 Shigetoshi Hasegawa .75 .30
❑ 31 Shane Reynolds .50 .20
❑ 32 Adam Piatt .50 .20
❑ 33 Preston Wilson .75 .30
❑ 34 Ellis Burks .75 .30
❑ 35 Armando Rios .50 .20
❑ 36 Chuck Finley .75 .30
❑ 37 Shannon Stewart .75 .30
❑ 38 Mark McGwire 5.00 2.00
❑ 39 Gerald Williams .50 .20
❑ 40 Eric Young .50 .20
❑ 41 Peter Bergeron .50 .20
❑ 42 Arthur Rhodes .50 .20
❑ 43 Bobby Jones .50 .20
❑ 44 Matt Clement .75 .30
❑ 45 Pedro Martinez 1.25 .50
❑ 46 Jose Canseco 1.25 .50
❑ 47 Matt Anderson .50 .20
❑ 48 Torii Hunter .75 .30
❑ 49 Carlos Lee .75 .30
❑ 50 Eric Chavez .75 .30
❑ 51 Rick Helling .50 .20
❑ 52 John Franco .75 .30
❑ 53 Mike Bordick .75 .30
❑ 54 Andres Galarraga .75 .30
❑ 55 Jose Cruz Jr. .50 .20
❑ 56 Mike Matheny .50 .20
❑ 57 Randy Johnson 2.00 .75
❑ 58 Richie Sexson .75 .30
❑ 59 Vladimir Nunez .50 .20
❑ 60 Aaron Boone .75 .30
❑ 61 Darin Erstad .75 .30
❑ 62 Alex Gonzalez .50 .20
❑ 63 Gil Heredia .50 .20
❑ 64 Shane Andrews .50 .20
❑ 65 Todd Hundley .50 .20
❑ 66 Bill Mueller .75 .30
❑ 67 Mark McLemore .50 .20
❑ 68 Scott Spiezio .50 .20
❑ 69 Kevin McGlinchy .50 .20
❑ 70 Manny Ramirez 1.25 .50
❑ 71 Mike Lamb .50 .20
❑ 72 Brian Buchanan .50 .20
❑ 73 Mike Sweeney .75 .30
❑ 74 John Wetteland .75 .30
❑ 75 Rob Bell .50 .20
❑ 76 John Burkett .50 .20
❑ 77 Derek Jeter 5.00 2.00
❑ 78 J.D. Drew .75 .30
❑ 79 Jose Offerman .50 .20
❑ 80 Rick Reed .50 .20
❑ 81 Will Clark 1.25 .50
❑ 82 Rickey Henderson 2.00 .75
❑ 83 Kirk Rueter .50 .20
❑ 84 Lee Stevens .50 .20
❑ 85 Jay Bell .75 .30
❑ 86 Fred McGriff 1.25 .50
❑ 87 Julio Zuleta .50 .20

❑ 88	Brian Anderson	.50	.20
❑ 89	Orlando Cabrera	.75	.30
❑ 90	Alex Fernandez	.50	.20
❑ 91	Derek Bell	.50	.20
❑ 92	Eric Owens	.50	.20
❑ 93	Dennys Reyes	.50	.20
❑ 94	Mike Stanley	.50	.20
❑ 95	Jorge Posada	1.25	.50
❑ 96	Paul Konerko	.75	.30
❑ 97	Mike Remlinger	.50	.20
❑ 98	Travis Lee	.50	.20
❑ 99	Ken Caminiti	.75	.30
❑ 100	Kevin Barker	.50	.20
❑ 101	Ozzie Guillen	.75	.30
❑ 102	Randy Wolf	.50	.20
❑ 103	Michael Tucker	.50	.20
❑ 104	Darren Lewis	.50	.20
❑ 105	Joe Randa	.75	.30
❑ 106	Jeff Cirillo	.50	.20
❑ 107	David Ortiz	2.00	.75
❑ 108	Herb Perry	.50	.20
❑ 109	Jeff Nelson	.50	.20
❑ 110	Chris Stynes	.50	.20
❑ 111	Johnny Damon	1.25	.50
❑ 112	Jason Schmidt	.75	.30
❑ 113	Charles Johnson	.50	.20
❑ 114	Pat Burrell	.75	.30
❑ 115	Gary Sheffield	.75	.30
❑ 116	Tom Glavine	1.25	.50
❑ 117	Jason Isringhausen	.75	.30
❑ 118	Chris Carpenter	.75	.30
❑ 119	Jeff Suppan	.50	.20
❑ 120	Ivan Rodriguez	1.25	.50
❑ 121	Luis Sojo	.50	.20
❑ 122	Ron Villone	.50	.20
❑ 123	Mike Sirotka	.50	.20
❑ 124	Chuck Knoblauch	.75	.30
❑ 125	Jason Kendall	.75	.30
❑ 126	Bobby Estalella	.50	.20
❑ 127	Jose Guillen	.75	.30
❑ 128	Carlos Delgado	.75	.30
❑ 129	Benji Gil	.50	.20
❑ 130	Einar Diaz	.50	.20
❑ 131	Andy Benes	.50	.20
❑ 132	Adrian Beltre	.75	.30
❑ 133	Roger Clemens	4.00	1.50
❑ 134	Scott Williamson	.50	.20
❑ 135	Brad Penny	.50	.20
❑ 136	Troy Glaus	.75	.30
❑ 137	Kevin Appier	.75	.30
❑ 138	Walt Weiss	.50	.20
❑ 139	Michael Barrett	.50	.20
❑ 140	Mike Hampton	.75	.30
❑ 141	Francisco Cordova	.50	.20
❑ 142	David Segui	.50	.20
❑ 143	Carlos Febles	.50	.20
❑ 144	Roy Halladay	.75	.30
❑ 145	Seth Etherton	.50	.20
❑ 146	Fernando Tatis	.50	.20
❑ 147	Livan Hernandez	.75	.30
❑ 148	B.J. Surhoff	.75	.30
❑ 149	Barry Larkin	1.25	.50
❑ 150	Bobby Howry	.50	.20
❑ 151	Dmitri Young	.75	.30
❑ 152	Brian Hunter	.50	.20
❑ 153	Alex Rodriguez	3.00	1.25
❑ 154	Hideo Nomo	2.00	.75
❑ 155	Warren Morris	.50	.20
❑ 156	Antonio Alfonseca	.50	.20
❑ 157	Edgardo Alfonzo	.50	.20
❑ 158	Mark Grudzielanek	.50	.20
❑ 159	Fernando Vina	.50	.20
❑ 160	Homer Bush	.50	.20
❑ 161	Jason Giambi	.75	.30
❑ 162	Steve Karsay	.50	.20
❑ 163	Matt Lawton	.50	.20
❑ 164	Rusty Greer	.75	.30
❑ 165	Billy Koch	.50	.20
❑ 166	Todd Hollandsworth	.50	.20
❑ 167	Raul Ibanez	.50	.20
❑ 168	Tony Gwynn	2.50	1.00
❑ 169	Carl Everett	.75	.30
❑ 170	Hector Carrasco	.50	.20
❑ 171	Jose Valentin	.50	.20
❑ 172	Deivi Cruz	.50	.20
❑ 173	Bret Boone	.75	.30
❑ 174	Melvin Mora	.75	.30
❑ 175	Danny Graves	.50	.20
❑ 176	Jose Jimenez	.50	.20
❑ 177	James Baldwin	.50	.20
❑ 178	C.J. Nitkowski	.50	.20
❑ 179	Jeff Zimmerman	.50	.20
❑ 180	Mike Lowell	.75	.30
❑ 181	Hideki Irabu	.50	.20
❑ 182	Greg Vaughn	.50	.20
❑ 183	Omar Daal	.50	.20
❑ 184	Darren Dreifort	.50	.20
❑ 185	Gil Meche	.50	.20
❑ 186	Damian Jackson	.50	.20
❑ 187	Frank Thomas	2.00	.75
❑ 188	Luis Castillo	.50	.20
❑ 189	Bartolo Colon	.75	.30
❑ 190	Craig Biggio	1.25	.50
❑ 191	Scott Schoeneweis	.50	.20
❑ 192	Dave Veres	.50	.20
❑ 193	Ramon Martinez	.50	.20
❑ 194	Jose Vidro	.50	.20
❑ 195	Todd Helton	1.25	.50
❑ 196	Greg Norton	.50	.20
❑ 197	Jacque Jones	.75	.30
❑ 198	Jason Grimsley	.50	.20
❑ 199	Dan Reichert	.50	.20
❑ 200	Robb Nen	.75	.30
❑ 201	Scott Hatteberg	.50	.20
❑ 202	Terry Shumpert	.50	.20
❑ 203	Kevin Millar	.75	.30
❑ 204	Ismael Valdes	.50	.20
❑ 205	Richard Hidalgo	.50	.20
❑ 206	Randy Velarde	.50	.20
❑ 207	Bengie Molina	.50	.20
❑ 208	Tony Womack	.50	.20
❑ 209	Enrique Wilson	.50	.20
❑ 210	Jeff Brantley	.50	.20
❑ 211	Rick Ankiel	.50	.20
❑ 212	Terry Mulholland	.50	.20
❑ 213	Ron Belliard	.50	.20
❑ 214	Terrence Long	.50	.20
❑ 215	Alberto Castillo	.50	.20
❑ 216	Royce Clayton	.50	.20
❑ 217	Joe McEwing	.50	.20
❑ 218	Jason McDonald	.50	.20
❑ 219	Ricky Bottalico	.50	.20
❑ 220	Keith Foulke	.75	.30
❑ 221	Brad Radke	.75	.30
❑ 222	Gabe Kapler	.75	.30
❑ 223	Pedro Astacio	.50	.20
❑ 224	Armando Reynoso	.50	.20
❑ 225	Darryl Kile	.75	.30
❑ 226	Reggie Sanders	.75	.30
❑ 227	Esteban Yan	.50	.20
❑ 228	Joe Nathan	.75	.30
❑ 229	Jay Payton	.50	.20
❑ 230	Francisco Cordero	.50	.20
❑ 231	Gregg Jefferies	.50	.20
❑ 232	LaTroy Hawkins	.50	.20
❑ 233	Jacob Cruz	.50	.20
❑ 234	Chris Holt	.50	.20
❑ 235	Vladimir Guerrero	2.00	.75
❑ 236	Marvin Benard	.50	.20
❑ 237	Alex Ramirez	.50	.20
❑ 238	Mike Williams	.50	.20
❑ 239	Sean Bergman	.50	.20
❑ 240	Juan Encarnacion	.50	.20
❑ 241	Russ Davis	.50	.20
❑ 242	Ramon Hernandez	.50	.20
❑ 243	Sandy Alomar Jr.	.50	.20
❑ 244	Eddie Guardado	.50	.20
❑ 245	Shane Halter	.50	.20
❑ 246	Geoff Jenkins	.50	.20
❑ 247	Brian Meadows	.50	.20
❑ 248	Damian Miller	.50	.20
❑ 249	Darrin Fletcher	.50	.20
❑ 250	Rafael Furcal	.75	.30
❑ 251	Mark Grace	1.25	.50
❑ 252	Mark Mulder	.75	.30
❑ 253	Joe Torre MG	1.25	.50
❑ 254	Bobby Cox MG	.50	.20
❑ 255	Mike Scioscia MG	.50	.20
❑ 256	Mike Hargrove MG	.50	.20
❑ 257	Jimy Williams MG	.50	.20
❑ 258	Jerry Manuel MG	.50	.20
❑ 259	Charlie Manuel MG	.50	.20
❑ 260	Don Baylor MG	.75	.30
❑ 261	Phil Garner MG	.75	.30
❑ 262	Tony Muser MG	.50	.20
❑ 263	Buddy Bell MG	.75	.30
❑ 264	Tom Kelly MG	.50	.20
❑ 265	John Boles MG	.50	.20
❑ 266	Art Howe MG	.50	.20
❑ 267	Larry Dierker MG	.50	.20
❑ 268	Lou Piniella MG	.75	.30
❑ 269	Larry Rothschild MG	.50	.20
❑ 270	Davey Lopes MG	.75	.30
❑ 271	Johnny Oates MG	.50	.20
❑ 272	Felipe Alou MG	.50	.20
❑ 273	Bobby Valentine MG	.50	.20
❑ 274	Tony LaRussa MG	.50	.20
❑ 275	Bruce Bochy MG	.50	.20
❑ 276	Dusty Baker MG	.75	.30
❑ 277	A.Gonzalez/A.Johnson	1.00	.40
❑ 278	M.Wheatland/B.Digby	1.00	.40
❑ 279	T.Johnson/S.Thorman	1.00	.40
❑ 280	P.Dumatrait/A.Wainwright	1.00	.40
❑ 281	David Parrish RC	1.00	.40
❑ 282	M.Folsom RC/R.Baldelli	1.50	.60
❑ 283	Dominic Rich RC	1.00	.40
❑ 284	M.Stodolka/S.Burnett	1.00	.40
❑ 285	D.Thompson/C.Smith	1.00	.40
❑ 286	D.Borrell RC/J.Bourgeois RC	1.00	.40
❑ 287	Chen/Patterson/Hamilton	1.00	.40
❑ 288	B.Zito/C.Sabathia	2.00	.75
❑ 289	Ben Sheets	2.00	.75
❑ 290	Howington/Kalinowski/Girdley	1.00	.40
❑ 291	Hee Seop Choi RC	2.00	.75
❑ 292	Bradley/Ainsworth/Tsao	1.50	.60
❑ 293	Glendenning/Kelly/Silvestre	1.00	.40
❑ 294	J.R. House	1.00	.40
❑ 295	Rafael Soriano RC	1.50	.60
❑ 296	T.Hafner RC/B.Jacobsen	10.00	4.00
❑ 297	Conti/Wakeland/Cole	1.00	.40
❑ 298	Seabol/Huff/Crede	2.50	1.00
❑ 299	Everett/Ortiz/Ginter	1.00	.40
❑ 300	Hernandez/Guzman/Eaton	1.00	.40
❑ 301	Kielty/Bradley/J.Rivera	1.50	.60
❑ 302	Mark McGwire GM	2.50	1.00
❑ 303	Don Larsen GM	.75	.30
❑ 304	Bobby Thomson GM	.75	.30
❑ 305	Bill Mazeroski GM	.75	.30
❑ 306	Reggie Jackson GM	1.25	.50
❑ 307	Kirk Gibson GM	.75	.30
❑ 308	Roger Maris GM	1.25	.50
❑ 309	Cal Ripken GM	3.00	1.25
❑ 310	Hank Aaron GM	2.00	.75
❑ 311	Joe Carter GM	.75	.30
❑ 312	Cal Ripken SH	3.00	1.25
❑ 313	Randy Johnson SH	1.25	.50
❑ 314	Ken Griffey Jr. SH	2.00	.75
❑ 315	Troy Glaus SH	.75	.30
❑ 316	Kazuhiro Sasaki SH	.75	.30
❑ 317	S.Sosa/T.Glaus LL	1.25	.50
❑ 318	T.Helton/E.Martinez LL	.75	.30
❑ 319	T.Helton/N.Garicaparra LL	2.00	.75
❑ 320	B.Bonds/J.Giambi LL	2.00	.75
❑ 321	T.Helton/M.Ramirez LL	.75	.30
❑ 322	T.Helton/D.Erstad LL	.75	.30
❑ 323	K.Brown/P.Martinez LL	1.25	.50
❑ 324	R.Johnson/P.Martinez LL	1.25	.50
❑ 325	Will Clark HL	1.25	.50
❑ 326	New York Mets HL	2.00	.75
❑ 327	New York Yankees HL	3.00	1.25
❑ 328	Seattle Mariners HL	.75	.30
❑ 329	Mike Hampton HL	.75	.30
❑ 330	New York Yankees HL	4.00	1.50
❑ 331	New York Yankees Champs	8.00	3.00
❑ 332	Jeff Bagwell	1.25	.50
❑ 333	Andy Pettitte	1.25	.50
❑ 334	Tony Armas Jr.	.50	.20
❑ 335	Jeromy Burnitz	.75	.30
❑ 336	Javier Vazquez	.75	.30
❑ 337	Eric Karros	.75	.30
❑ 338	Brian Giles	.75	.30
❑ 339	Scott Rolen	1.25	.50
❑ 340	David Justice	.75	.30
❑ 341	Ray Durham	.75	.30
❑ 342	Todd Zeile	.75	.30
❑ 343	Cliff Floyd	.75	.30
❑ 344	Barry Bonds	5.00	2.00
❑ 345	Matt Williams	.75	.30

	No.	Player		
❑	346	Steve Finley	.75	.30
❑	347	Scott Elarton	.50	.20
❑	348	Bernie Williams	1.25	.50
❑	349	David Wells	.75	.30
❑	350	J.T. Snow	.75	.30
❑	351	Al Leiter	.75	.30
❑	352	Magglio Ordonez	.75	.30
❑	353	Raul Mondesi	.75	.30
❑	354	Tim Salmon	1.25	.50
❑	355	Jeff Kent	.75	.30
❑	356	Mariano Rivera	2.00	.75
❑	357	John Olerud	.75	.30
❑	358	Javy Lopez	.75	.30
❑	359	Ben Grieve	.50	.20
❑	360	Ray Lankford	.75	.30
❑	361	Ken Griffey Jr.	3.00	1.25
❑	362	Rich Aurilia	.50	.20
❑	363	Andruw Jones	1.25	.50
❑	364	Ryan Klesko	.75	.30
❑	365	Roberto Alomar	1.25	.50
❑	366	Miguel Tejada	.75	.30
❑	367	Mo Vaughn	.75	.30
❑	368	Albert Belle	.75	.30
❑	369	Jose Canseco	1.25	.50
❑	370	Kevin Brown	.75	.30
❑	371	Rafael Palmeiro	1.25	.50
❑	372	Mark Redman	.50	.20
❑	373	Larry Walker	.75	.30
❑	374	Greg Maddux	3.00	1.25
❑	375	Nomar Garciaparra	3.00	1.25
❑	376	Kevin Millwood	.75	.30
❑	377	Edgar Martinez	1.25	.50
❑	378	Sammy Sosa	2.00	.75
❑	379	Tim Hudson	.75	.30
❑	380	Jim Edmonds	.75	.30
❑	381	Mike Piazza	3.00	1.25
❑	382	Brant Brown	.50	.20
❑	383	Brad Fullmer	.50	.20
❑	384	Alan Benes	.50	.20
❑	385	Mickey Morandini	.50	.20
❑	386	Troy Percival	.75	.30
❑	387	Eddie Perez	.50	.20
❑	388	Vernon Wells	.75	.30
❑	389	Ricky Gutierrez	.50	.20
❑	390	Rondell White	.75	.30
❑	391	Kelvim Escobar	.50	.20
❑	392	Tony Batista	.50	.20
❑	393	Jimmy Haynes	.50	.20
❑	394	Billy Wagner	.75	.30
❑	395	A.J. Hinch	.50	.20
❑	396	Matt Morris	.75	.30
❑	397	Lance Berkman	.75	.30
❑	398	Jeff D'Amico	.50	.20
❑	399	Octavio Dotel	.50	.20
❑	400	Olmedo Saenz	.50	.20
❑	401	Esteban Loaiza	.50	.20
❑	402	Adam Kennedy	.50	.20
❑	403	Moises Alou	.75	.30
❑	404	Orlando Palmeiro	.50	.20
❑	405	Kevin Young	.50	.20
❑	406	Tom Goodwin	.50	.20
❑	407	Mac Suzuki	.75	.30
❑	408	Pat Hentgen	.50	.20
❑	409	Kevin Stocker	.50	.20
❑	410	Mark Sweeney	.50	.20
❑	411	Tony Eusebio	.50	.20
❑	412	Edgar Renteria	.75	.30
❑	413	John Rocker	.75	.30
❑	414	Jose Lima	.50	.20
❑	415	Kerry Wood	.75	.30
❑	416	Mike Timlin	.50	.20
❑	417	Jose Hernandez	.50	.20
❑	418	Jeremy Giambi	.50	.20
❑	419	Luis Lopez	.50	.20
❑	420	Mitch Meluskey	.50	.20
❑	421	Garrett Stephenson	.50	.20
❑	422	Jamey Wright	.50	.20
❑	423	John Jaha	.50	.20
❑	424	Placido Polanco	.50	.20
❑	425	Marty Cordova	.50	.20
❑	426	Joey Hamilton	.50	.20
❑	427	Travis Fryman	.75	.30
❑	428	Mike Cameron	.50	.20
❑	429	Matt Mantei	.50	.20
❑	430	Chan Ho Park	.75	.30
❑	431	Shawn Estes	.50	.20
❑	432	Danny Bautista	.50	.20
❑	433	Wilson Alvarez	.50	.20
❑	434	Kenny Lofton	.75	.30
❑	435	Russ Ortiz	.50	.20
❑	436	Dave Burba	.50	.20
❑	437	Felix Martinez	.50	.20
❑	438	Jeff Shaw	.50	.20
❑	439	Mike DiFelice	.50	.20
❑	440	Roberto Hernandez	.50	.20
❑	441	Bryan Rekar	.50	.20
❑	442	Ugueth Urbina	.50	.20
❑	443	Vinny Castilla	.75	.30
❑	444	Carlos Perez	.50	.20
❑	445	Juan Guzman	.50	.20
❑	446	Ryan Rupe	.50	.20
❑	447	Mike Mordecai	.50	.20
❑	448	Ricardo Rincon	.50	.20
❑	449	Curt Schilling	.75	.30
❑	450	Alex Cora	.50	.20
❑	451	Turner Ward	.50	.20
❑	452	Omar Vizquel	1.25	.50
❑	453	Russ Branyan	.50	.20
❑	454	Russ Johnson	.50	.20
❑	455	Greg Colbrunn	.50	.20
❑	456	Charles Nagy	.50	.20
❑	457	Wil Cordero	.50	.20
❑	458	Jason Tyner	.50	.20
❑	459	Devon White	.75	.30
❑	460	Kelly Stinnett	.50	.20
❑	461	Wilton Guerrero	.50	.20
❑	462	Jason Bere	.50	.20
❑	463	Calvin Murray	.50	.20
❑	464	Miguel Batista	.50	.20
❑	466	Luis Gonzalez	.75	.30
❑	467	Jaret Wright	.50	.20
❑	468	Chad Kreuter	.50	.20
❑	469	Armando Benitez	.50	.20
❑	470	Erubiel Durazo	.50	.20
❑	470	Sidney Ponson	.50	.20
❑	471	Adrian Brown	.50	.20
❑	472	Sterling Hitchcock	.50	.20
❑	473	Timo Perez	.50	.20
❑	474	Jamie Moyer	.75	.30
❑	475	Delino DeShields	.50	.20
❑	476	Glendon Rusch	.50	.20
❑	477	Chris Gomez	.50	.20
❑	478	Adam Eaton	.50	.20
❑	479	Pablo Ozuna	.50	.20
❑	480	Bob Abreu	.75	.30
❑	481	Kris Benson	.50	.20
❑	482	Keith Osik	.50	.20
❑	483	Darryl Hamilton	.50	.20
❑	484	Marlon Anderson	.50	.20
❑	485	Jimmy Anderson	.50	.20
❑	486	John Halama	.50	.20
❑	487	Nelson Figueroa	.50	.20
❑	488	Alex Gonzalez	.50	.20
❑	489	Benny Agbayani	.50	.20
❑	490	Ed Sprague	.50	.20
❑	491	Scott Erickson	.50	.20
❑	492	Doug Glanville	.50	.20
❑	493	Jesus Sanchez	.50	.20
❑	494	Mike Lieberthal	.75	.30
❑	495	Aaron Sele	.50	.20
❑	496	Pat Mahomes	.50	.20
❑	497	Ruben Rivera	.50	.20
❑	498	Wayne Gomes	.50	.20
❑	499	Freddy Garcia	.75	.30
❑	500	Al Martin	.50	.20
❑	501	Woody Williams	.50	.20
❑	502	Paul Byrd	.50	.20
❑	503	Rick White	.50	.20
❑	504	Trevor Hoffman	.75	.30
❑	505	Brady Anderson	.75	.30
❑	506	Robert Person	.50	.20
❑	507	Jeff Conine	.75	.30
❑	508	Chris Truby	.50	.20
❑	509	Emil Brown	.50	.20
❑	510	Ryan Dempster	.50	.20
❑	511	Ruben Mateo	.50	.20
❑	512	Alex Ochoa	.50	.20
❑	513	Jose Rosado	.50	.20
❑	514	Masato Yoshii	.50	.20
❑	515	Brian Daubach	.50	.20
❑	516	Jeff D'Amico	.50	.20
❑	517	Brent Mayne	.50	.20
❑	518	John Thomson	.50	.20
❑	519	Todd Ritchie	.50	.20
❑	520	John VanderWal	.50	.20
❑	521	Neifi Perez	.50	.20
❑	522	Chad Curtis	.50	.20
❑	523	Kenny Rogers	.75	.30
❑	524	Trot Nixon	.75	.30
❑	525	Sean Casey	.75	.30
❑	526	Wilton Veras	.50	.20
❑	527	Troy O'Leary	.50	.20
❑	528	Dante Bichette	.75	.30
❑	529	Jose Silva	.50	.20
❑	530	Darren Oliver	.50	.20
❑	531	Steve Parris	.50	.20
❑	532	David McCarty	.50	.20
❑	533	Todd Walker	.50	.20
❑	534	Brian Rose	.50	.20
❑	535	Pete Schourek	.50	.20
❑	536	Ricky Ledee	.50	.20
❑	537	Justin Thompson	.50	.20
❑	538	Benito Santiago	.75	.30
❑	539	Carlos Beltran	.75	.30
❑	540	Gabe White	.50	.20
❑	541	Bret Saberhagen	.75	.30
❑	542	Ramon Martinez	.50	.20
❑	543	John Valentin	.50	.20
❑	544	Frank Catalanotto	.50	.20
❑	545	Tim Wakefield	.75	.30
❑	546	Michael Tucker	.50	.20
❑	547	Juan Pierre	.75	.30
❑	548	Rich Garces	.50	.20
❑	549	Luis Ordaz	.50	.20
❑	550	Jerry Spradlin	.50	.20
❑	551	Corey Koskie	.50	.20
❑	552	Cal Eldred	.50	.20
❑	553	Alfonso Soriano	1.25	.50
❑	554	Kip Wells	.50	.20
❑	555	Orlando Hernandez	.75	.30
❑	556	Bill Simas	.50	.20
❑	557	Jim Parque	.50	.20
❑	558	Joe Mays	.50	.20
❑	559	Tim Belcher	.50	.20
❑	560	Shane Spencer	.50	.20
❑	561	Glenallen Hill	.50	.20
❑	562	Matt LeCroy	.50	.20
❑	563	Tino Martinez	1.25	.50
❑	564	Eric Milton	.50	.20
❑	565	Ron Coomer	.50	.20
❑	566	Cristian Guzman	.50	.20
❑	567	Kazuhiro Sasaki	.75	.30
❑	568	Mark Quinn	.50	.20
❑	569	Eric Gagne	.75	.30
❑	570	Kerry Ligtenberg	.50	.20
❑	571	Rolando Arrojo	.50	.20
❑	572	Jon Lieber	.50	.20
❑	573	Jose Vizcaino	.50	.20
❑	574	Jeff Abbott	.50	.20
❑	575	Carlos Hernandez	.50	.20
❑	576	Scott Sullivan	.50	.20
❑	577	Matt Stairs	.50	.20
❑	578	Tom Lampkin	.50	.20
❑	579	Donnie Sadler	.50	.20
❑	580	Desi Relaford	.50	.20
❑	581	Scott Downs	.50	.20
❑	582	Mike Mussina	1.25	.50
❑	583	Ramon Ortiz	.50	.20
❑	584	Mike Myers	.50	.20
❑	585	Frank Castillo	.50	.20
❑	586	Manny Ramirez Sox	1.25	.50
❑	587	Alex Rodriguez	3.00	1.25
❑	588	Andy Ashby	.50	.20
❑	589	Felipe Crespo	.50	.20
❑	590	Bobby Bonilla	.75	.30
❑	591	Denny Neagle	.50	.20
❑	592	Dave Martinez	.50	.20
❑	593	Mike Hampton	.75	.30
❑	594	Gary DiSarcina	.50	.20
❑	595	Tsuyoshi Shinjo RC	2.00	.75
❑	596	Albert Pujols RC	80.00	40.00
❑	597	Oswalt/Strange/Rauch	2.50	1.00
❑	598	Jake Peavy RC	10.00	4.00
❑	599	S.Smyth RC/Bynum/Haynes	1.00	.40
❑	600	Cuddyer/Lawrence/Freeman	1.00	.40
❑	601	C.Pena/Barnes/Wise	1.00	.40
❑	602	E.Almonte RC/F.Lopez	1.00	.40
❑	603	Escobar/Valent/Wilkerson	1.00	.40

❑ 604	Hall/Barajas/Goldbach	1.00	.40
❑ 605	Romano/Giles/Ozuna	1.50	.60
❑ 606	D.Brown/Cust/V.Wells	1.00	.40
❑ 607	L.Montanez RC/D.Espinosa	1.00	.40
❑ 608	J.Wayne RC/A.Pluta RC	1.00	.40
❑ 609	J.Axelson RC/C.Cali RC	1.00	.40
❑ 610	S.Boyd RC/C.Morris RC	1.00	.40
❑ 611	T.Arko RC/D.Moylan RC	1.00	.40
❑ 612	L.Cotto RC/L.Escobar	1.00	.40
❑ 613	B.Mims RC/B.Williams RC	1.00	.40
❑ 614	C.Russ RC/B.Edwards	1.00	.40
❑ 615	J.Torres/B.Diggins	1.00	.40
❑ 616	Edwin Encarnacion RC	10.00	4.00
❑ 617	B.Bass RC/O.Ayala RC	1.00	.40
❑ 618	M.Matthews RC/J.Kanooi	1.00	.40
❑ 619	S.McFarland RC/A.Sterrett RC	1.00	.40
❑ 620	D.Krynzel/G.Sizemore	5.00	2.00
❑ 621	K.Bucktrot/D.Sardinha	1.00	.40
❑ 622	Anaheim Angels TC	.75	.30
❑ 623	Arizona Diamondbacks TC	.75	.30
❑ 624	Atlanta Braves TC	.75	.30
❑ 625	Baltimore Orioles TC	.75	.30
❑ 626	Boston Red Sox TC	.75	.30
❑ 627	Chicago Cubs TC	.75	.30
❑ 628	Chicago White Sox TC	.75	.30
❑ 629	Cincinnati Reds TC	.75	.30
❑ 630	Cleveland Indians TC	.75	.30
❑ 631	Colorado Rockies TC	.75	.30
❑ 632	Detroit Tigers TC	.75	.30
❑ 633	Florida Marlins TC	.75	.30
❑ 634	Houston Astros TC	.75	.30
❑ 635	Kansas City Royals TC	.75	.30
❑ 636	Los Angeles Dodgers TC	.75	.30
❑ 637	Milwaukee Brewers TC	.75	.30
❑ 638	Minnesota Twins TC	.75	.30
❑ 639	Montreal Expos TC	.75	.30
❑ 640	New York Mets TC	.75	.30
❑ 641	New York Yankees TC	4.00	1.50
❑ 642	Oakland Athletics TC	.75	.30
❑ 643	Philadelphia Phillies TC	.75	.30
❑ 644	Pittsburgh Pirates TC	.75	.30
❑ 645	San Diego Padres TC	.75	.30
❑ 646	San Francisco Giants TC	.75	.30
❑ 647	Seattle Mariners TC	.75	.30
❑ 648	St. Louis Cardinals TC	.75	.30
❑ 649	Tampa Bay Devil Rays TC	.75	.30
❑ 650	Texas Rangers TC	.75	.30
❑ 651	Toronto Blue Jays TC	.75	.30
❑ 652	Bucky Dent GM	.50	.20
❑ 653	Jackie Robinson GM	2.00	.75
❑ 654	Roberto Clemente GM	2.50	1.00
❑ 655	Nolan Ryan GM	3.00	1.25
❑ 656	Kerry Wood GM	.75	.30
❑ 657	Rickey Henderson GM	2.00	.75
❑ 658	Lou Brock GM	1.25	.50
❑ 659	David Wells GM	.50	.20
❑ 660	Andruw Jones GM	.75	.30
❑ 661	Carlton Fisk GM	.75	.30

2001 Topps Chrome Traded

❑	COMPLETE SET (266)	150.00	75.00
❑	COMMON CARD (1-99/145-266)	.75	.30
❑	COMMON REPRINT (100-144)	1.25	.50
❑ T1	Sandy Alomar Jr.	.75	.30
❑ T2	Kevin Appier	1.25	.50
❑ T3	Brad Ausmus	1.25	.50
❑ T4	Derek Bell	.75	.30
❑ T5	Bret Boone	1.25	.50
❑ T6	Rico Brogna	.75	.30
❑ T7	Ellis Burks	1.25	.50
❑ T8	Ken Caminiti	1.25	.50
❑ T9	Roger Cedeno	.75	.30
❑ T10	Royce Clayton	.75	.30
❑ T11	Enrique Wilson	.75	.30
❑ T12	Rheal Cormier	.75	.30
❑ T13	Eric Davis	1.25	.50
❑ T14	Shawon Dunston	.75	.30
❑ T15	Andres Galarraga	1.25	.50
❑ T16	Tom Gordon	.75	.30
❑ T17	Mark Grace	2.00	.75
❑ T18	Jeffrey Hammonds	.75	.30
❑ T19	Dustin Hermanson	.75	.30
❑ T20	Quinton McCracken	.75	.30
❑ T21	Todd Hundley	.75	.30
❑ T22	Charles Johnson	1.25	.50
❑ T23	Marquis Grissom	1.25	.50
❑ T24	Jose Mesa	.75	.30
❑ T25	Brian Boehringer	.75	.30
❑ T26	John Rocker	1.25	.50
❑ T27	Jeff Frye	.75	.30
❑ T28	Reggie Sanders	1.25	.50
❑ T29	David Segui	.75	.30
❑ T30	Mike Sirotka	.75	.30
❑ T31	Fernando Tatis	.75	.30
❑ T32	Steve Trachsel	.75	.30
❑ T33	Ismael Valdes	.75	.30
❑ T34	Randy Velarde	.75	.30
❑ T35	Ryan Kohlmeier	.75	.30
❑ T36	Mike Bordick	1.25	.50
❑ T37	Kent Bottenfield	.75	.30
❑ T38	Pat Rapp	.75	.30
❑ T39	Jeff Nelson	.75	.30
❑ T40	Ricky Bottalico	.75	.30
❑ T41	Luke Prokopec	.75	.30
❑ T42	Hideo Nomo	3.00	1.25
❑ T43	Bill Mueller	1.25	.50
❑ T44	Roberto Kelly	.75	.30
❑ T45	Chris Holt	.75	.30
❑ T46	Mike Jackson	.75	.30
❑ T47	Devon White	1.25	.50
❑ T48	Gerald Williams	.75	.30
❑ T49	Eddie Taubensee	.75	.30
❑ T50	Brian Hunter	.75	.30
❑ T51	Nelson Cruz	.75	.30
❑ T52	Jeff Fassero	.75	.30
❑ T53	Bubba Trammell	.75	.30
❑ T54	Bo Porter	.75	.30
❑ T55	Greg Norton	.75	.30
❑ T56	Benito Santiago	1.25	.50
❑ T57	Ruben Rivera	.75	.30
❑ T58	Dee Brown	.75	.30
❑ T59	Jose Canseco	2.00	.75
❑ T60	Chris Michalak	.75	.30
❑ T61	Tim Worrell	.75	.30
❑ T62	Matt Clement	1.25	.50
❑ T63	Bill Pulsipher	.75	.30
❑ T64	Troy Brohawn RC	1.00	.40
❑ T65	Mark Kotsay	1.25	.50
❑ T66	Jimmy Rollins	1.25	.50
❑ T67	Shea Hillenbrand	1.25	.50
❑ T68	Ted Lilly	.75	.30
❑ T69	Jermaine Dye	1.25	.50
❑ T70	Jerry Hairston Jr.	.75	.30
❑ T71	John Mabry	.75	.30
❑ T72	Kurt Abbott	.75	.30
❑ T73	Eric Owens	.75	.30
❑ T74	Jeff Brantley	.75	.30
❑ T75	Roy Oswalt	3.00	1.25
❑ T76	Doug Mientkiewicz	1.25	.50
❑ T77	Rickey Henderson	3.00	1.25
❑ T78	Jason Grimsley	.75	.30
❑ T79	Christian Parker RC	1.00	.40
❑ T80	Donne Wall	.75	.30
❑ T81	Alex Arias	.75	.30
❑ T82	Willis Roberts	.75	.30
❑ T83	Ryan Minor	.75	.30
❑ T84	Jason LaRue	.75	.30
❑ T85	Ruben Sierra	1.25	.50
❑ T86	Johnny Damon	2.00	.75
❑ T87	Juan Gonzalez	1.25	.50
❑ T88	C.C. Sabathia	1.25	.50
❑ T89	Tony Batista	.75	.30
❑ T90	Jay Witasick	.75	.30
❑ T91	Brent Abernathy	.75	.30
❑ T92	Paul LoDuca	1.25	.50
❑ T93	Wes Helms	.75	.30
❑ T94	Mark Wohlers	.75	.30
❑ T95	Rob Bell	.75	.30
❑ T96	Tim Redding	.75	.30
❑ T97	Bud Smith RC	1.00	.40
❑ T98	Adam Dunn	2.00	.75
❑ T99	I.Suzuki/A.Pujols ROY	25.00	10.00
❑ T100	Carlton Fisk 81	2.00	.75
❑ T101	Tim Raines 81	1.25	.50
❑ T102	Juan Marichal 74	1.25	.50
❑ T103	Dave Winfield 81	1.25	.50
❑ T104	Reggie Jackson 82	2.00	.75
❑ T105	Cal Ripken 82	10.00	4.00
❑ T106	Ozzie Smith 82	5.00	2.00
❑ T107	Tom Seaver 83	2.00	.75
❑ T108	Lou Piniella 74	1.25	.50
❑ T109	Dwight Gooden 84	1.25	.50
❑ T110	Bret Saberhagen 84	1.25	.50
❑ T111	Gary Carter 85	1.25	.50
❑ T112	Jack Clark 85	1.25	.50
❑ T113	Rickey Henderson 85	3.00	1.25
❑ T114	Barry Bonds 86	8.00	3.00
❑ T115	Bobby Bonilla 86	1.25	.50
❑ T116	Jose Canseco 86	2.00	.75
❑ T117	Will Clark 86	2.00	.75
❑ T118	Andres Galarraga 86	1.25	.50
❑ T119	Bo Jackson 86	3.00	1.25
❑ T120	Wally Joyner 86	1.25	.50
❑ T121	Ellis Burks 87	1.25	.50
❑ T122	David Cone 87	1.25	.50
❑ T123	Greg Maddux 87	5.00	2.00
❑ T124	Willie Randolph 76	1.25	.50
❑ T125	Dennis Eckersley 87	1.25	.50
❑ T126	Matt Williams 87	1.25	.50
❑ T127	Joe Morgan 81	1.25	.50
❑ T128	Fred McGriff 87	2.00	.75
❑ T129	Roberto Alomar 88	2.00	.75
❑ T130	Lee Smith 88	1.25	.50
❑ T131	David Wells 88	1.25	.50
❑ T132	Ken Griffey Jr. 89	5.00	2.00
❑ T133	Deion Sanders 89	2.00	.75
❑ T134	Nolan Ryan 89	8.00	3.00
❑ T135	David Justice 90	1.25	.50
❑ T136	Joe Carter 91	1.25	.50
❑ T137	Jack Morris 92	1.25	.50
❑ T138	Mike Piazza 93	5.00	2.00
❑ T139	Barry Bonds 93	8.00	3.00
❑ T140	Terrence Long 94	1.25	.50
❑ T141	Ben Grieve 94	1.25	.50
❑ T142	Richie Sexson 95	1.25	.50
❑ T143	Sean Burroughs 99	1.25	.50
❑ T144	Alfonso Soriano 99	2.00	.75
❑ T145	Bob Boone MG	1.25	.50
❑ T146	Larry Bowa MG	1.25	.50
❑ T147	Bob Brenly MG	.75	.30
❑ T148	Buck Martinez MG	.75	.30
❑ T149	Lloyd McClendon MG	.75	.30
❑ T150	Jim Tracy MG	.75	.30
❑ T151	Jared Abruzzo RC	1.00	.40
❑ T152	Kurt Ainsworth	.75	.30
❑ T153	Willie Bloomquist	1.25	.50
❑ T154	Ben Broussard	.75	.30
❑ T155	Bobby Bradley	.75	.30
❑ T156	Mike Bynum	.75	.30
❑ T157	A.J. Hinch	.75	.30
❑ T158	Ryan Christianson	.75	.30
❑ T159	Carlos Silva	.75	.30
❑ T160	Joe Crede	3.00	1.25
❑ T161	Jack Cust	.75	.30
❑ T162	Ben Diggins	.75	.30
❑ T163	Phil Dumatrait	.75	.30
❑ T164	Alex Escobar	.75	.30
❑ T165	Miguel Olivo	.75	.30
❑ T166	Chris George	.75	.30
❑ T167	Marcus Giles	1.25	.50
❑ T168	Keith Ginter	.75	.30
❑ T169	Josh Girdley	.75	.30
❑ T170	Tony Alvarez	.75	.30
❑ T171	Scott Seabol	.75	.30
❑ T172	Josh Hamilton	.75	.30
❑ T173	Jason Hart	.75	.30
❑ T174	Israel Alcantara	.75	.30
❑ T175	Jake Peavy	5.00	2.00
❑ T176	Stubby Clapp RC	1.00	.40

❑ T177	D'Angelo Jimenez	.75	.30
❑ T178	Nick Johnson	1.25	.50
❑ T179	Ben Johnson	1.25	.50
❑ T180	Larry Bigbie	.75	.30
❑ T181	Allen Levrault	.75	.30
❑ T182	Felipe Lopez	1.25	.50
❑ T183	Sean Burnett	.75	.30
❑ T184	Nick Neugebauer	.75	.30
❑ T185	Austin Kearns	1.25	.50
❑ T186	Corey Patterson	.75	.30
❑ T187	Carlos Pena	.75	.30
❑ T188	Ricardo Rodriguez RC	1.00	.40
❑ T189	Juan Rivera	.75	.30
❑ T190	Grant Roberts	.75	.30
❑ T191	Adam Pettyjohn RC	1.00	.40
❑ T192	Jared Sandberg	.75	.30
❑ T193	Xavier Nady	.75	.30
❑ T194	Dane Sardinha	.75	.30
❑ T195	Shawn Sonnier	.75	.30
❑ T196	Rafael Soriano	1.00	.40
❑ T197	Brian Specht RC	1.00	.40
❑ T198	Aaron Myette	.75	.30
❑ T199	Juan Uribe RC	1.25	.50
❑ T200	Jayson Werth	.75	.30
❑ T201	Brad Wilkerson	.75	.30
❑ T202	Horacio Estrada	.75	.30
❑ T203	Joel Pineiro	1.25	.50
❑ T204	Matt LeCroy	.75	.30
❑ T205	Michael Coleman	.75	.30
❑ T206	Ben Sheets	2.00	.75
❑ T207	Eric Byrnes	.75	.30
❑ T208	Sean Burroughs	.75	.30
❑ T209	Ken Harvey	.75	.30
❑ T210	Travis Hafner	8.00	3.00
❑ T211	Erick Almonte	1.00	.40
❑ T212	Jason Belcher RC	1.00	.40
❑ T213	Wilson Betemit RC	4.00	1.50
❑ T214	Hank Blalock RC	6.00	2.50
❑ T215	Danny Borrell	1.00	.40
❑ T216	John Buck RC	1.25	.50
❑ T217	Freddie Bynum RC	1.00	.40
❑ T218	Noel Devarez RC	1.00	.40
❑ T219	Juan Diaz RC	1.00	.40
❑ T220	Felix Diaz RC	1.00	.40
❑ T221	Josh Fogg RC	1.00	.40
❑ T222	Matt Ford RC	1.00	.40
❑ T223	Scott Heard	.75	.30
❑ T224	Ben Hendrickson RC	1.00	.40
❑ T225	Cody Ross RC	1.00	.40
❑ T226	Adrian Hernandez RC	1.00	.40
❑ T227	Alfredo Amezaga RC	1.00	.40
❑ T228	Bob Keppel RC	1.00	.40
❑ T229	Ryan Madson RC	2.00	.75
❑ T230	Octavio Martinez RC	1.00	.40
❑ T231	Hee Seop Choi	1.25	.50
❑ T232	Thomas Mitchell	.75	.30
❑ T233	Luis Montanez	1.00	.40
❑ T234	Andy Morales RC	1.00	.40
❑ T235	Justin Morneau RC	12.00	5.00
❑ T236	Toe Nash RC	1.00	.40
❑ T237	Valentino Pascucci RC	1.00	.40
❑ T238	Roy Smith RC	1.00	.40
❑ T239	Antonio Perez RC	1.25	.50
❑ T240	Chad Petty RC	1.00	.40
❑ T241	Steve Smyth	1.00	.40
❑ T242	Jose Reyes RC	30.00	12.50
❑ T243	Eric Reynolds RC	1.00	.40
❑ T244	Dominic Rich	1.00	.40
❑ T245	Jason Richardson RC	1.00	.40
❑ T246	Ed Rogers RC	1.00	.40
❑ T247	Albert Pujols	80.00	40.00
❑ T248	Esix Snead RC	1.00	.40
❑ T249	Luis Torres RC	1.00	.40
❑ T250	Matt White RC	1.00	.40
❑ T251	Blake Williams	1.00	.40
❑ T252	Chris Russ	1.00	.40
❑ T253	Joe Kennedy RC	1.25	.50
❑ T254	Jeff Randazzo RC	1.00	.40
❑ T255	Beau Hale RC	1.00	.40
❑ T256	Brad Hennessey RC	2.00	.75
❑ T257	Jake Gautreau RC	1.00	.40
❑ T258	Jeff Mathis RC	1.25	.50
❑ T259	Aaron Heilman RC	1.25	.50
❑ T260	Bronson Sardinha RC	1.00	.40
❑ T261	Irvin Guzman RC	8.00	3.00
❑ T262	Gabe Gross RC	1.25	.50
❑ T263	J.D. Martin RC	1.00	.40
❑ T264	Chris Smith RC	1.00	.40
❑ T265	Kenny Baugh RC	1.00	.40
❑ T266	Ichiro Suzuki RC	25.00	10.00

2002 Topps Chrome

❑	COMPLETE SET (660)	250.00	100.00
❑	COMPLETE SERIES 1 (330)	125.00	50.00
❑	COMPLETE SERIES 2 (330)	125.00	50.00
❑	COMMON (1-331/366-695)	.50	.20
❑	COMMON (307-326/671-690)	1.50	.60
❑	COMMON (327-331/691-695)	1.50	.60
❑ 1	Pedro Martinez	1.50	.60
❑ 2	Mike Stanton	.50	.20
❑ 3	Brad Penny	.50	.20
❑ 4	Mike Matheny	.50	.20
❑ 5	Johnny Damon	1.50	.60
❑ 6	Bret Boone	1.00	.40
❑ 7	Does Not Exist		
❑ 8	Chris Truby	.50	.20
❑ 9	B.J. Surhoff	1.00	.40
❑ 10	Mike Hampton	1.00	.40
❑ 11	Juan Pierre	1.00	.40
❑ 12	Mark Buehrle	1.00	.40
❑ 13	Bob Abreu	1.00	.40
❑ 14	David Cone	1.00	.40
❑ 15	Aaron Sele	.50	.20
❑ 16	Fernando Tatis	.50	.20
❑ 17	Bobby Jones	.50	.20
❑ 18	Rick Helling	.50	.20
❑ 19	Dmitri Young	1.00	.40
❑ 20	Mike Mussina	1.50	.60
❑ 21	Mike Sweeney	1.00	.40
❑ 22	Cristian Guzman	.50	.20
❑ 23	Ryan Kohlmeier	.50	.20
❑ 24	Adam Kennedy	.50	.20
❑ 25	Larry Walker	1.00	.40
❑ 26	Eric Davis	1.00	.40
❑ 27	Jason Tyner	.50	.20
❑ 28	Eric Young	.50	.20
❑ 29	Jason Marquis	.50	.20
❑ 30	Luis Gonzalez	1.00	.40
❑ 31	Kevin Tapani	.50	.20
❑ 32	Orlando Cabrera	1.00	.40
❑ 33	Marty Cordova	.50	.20
❑ 34	Brad Ausmus	1.00	.40
❑ 35	Livan Hernandez	1.00	.40
❑ 36	Alex Gonzalez	.50	.20
❑ 37	Edgar Renteria	1.00	.40
❑ 38	Bengie Molina	.50	.20
❑ 39	Frank Menechino	.50	.20
❑ 40	Rafael Palmeiro	1.50	.60
❑ 41	Brad Fullmer	.50	.20
❑ 42	Julio Zuleta	.50	.20
❑ 43	Darren Dreifort	.50	.20
❑ 44	Trot Nixon	1.00	.40
❑ 45	Trevor Hoffman	1.00	.40
❑ 46	Vladimir Nunez	.50	.20
❑ 47	Mark Kotsay	1.00	.40
❑ 48	Kenny Rogers	1.00	.40
❑ 49	Ben Petrick	.50	.20
❑ 50	Jeff Bagwell	1.50	.60
❑ 51	Juan Encarnacion	.50	.20
❑ 52	Ramiro Mendoza	.50	.20
❑ 53	Brian Meadows	.50	.20
❑ 54	Chad Curtis	.50	.20
❑ 55	Aramis Ramirez	1.00	.40
❑ 56	Mark McLemore	.50	.20
❑ 57	Dante Bichette	1.00	.40
❑ 58	Scott Schoeneweis	.50	.20
❑ 59	Jose Cruz Jr.	.50	.20
❑ 60	Roger Clemens	5.00	2.00
❑ 61	Jose Guillen	1.00	.40
❑ 62	Darren Oliver	.50	.20
❑ 63	Chris Reitsma	.50	.20
❑ 64	Jeff Abbott	.50	.20
❑ 65	Robin Ventura	1.00	.40
❑ 66	Denny Neagle	.50	.20
❑ 67	Al Martin	.50	.20
❑ 68	Benito Santiago	1.00	.40
❑ 69	Roy Oswalt	1.00	.40
❑ 70	Juan Gonzalez	1.00	.40
❑ 71	Garret Anderson	1.00	.40
❑ 72	Bobby Bonilla	1.00	.40
❑ 73	Danny Bautista	.50	.20
❑ 74	J.T. Snow	1.00	.40
❑ 75	Derek Jeter	6.00	2.50
❑ 76	John Olerud	1.00	.40
❑ 77	Kevin Appier	1.00	.40
❑ 78	Phil Nevin	1.00	.40
❑ 79	Sean Casey	1.00	.40
❑ 80	Troy Glaus	1.00	.40
❑ 81	Joe Randa	1.00	.40
❑ 82	Jose Valentin	.50	.20
❑ 83	Ricky Bottalico	.50	.20
❑ 84	Todd Zeile	1.00	.40
❑ 85	Barry Larkin	1.50	.60
❑ 86	Bob Wickman	.50	.20
❑ 87	Jeff Shaw	.50	.20
❑ 88	Greg Vaughn	.50	.20
❑ 89	Fernando Vina	.50	.20
❑ 90	Mark Mulder	1.00	.40
❑ 91	Paul Bako	.50	.20
❑ 92	Aaron Boone	1.00	.40
❑ 93	Esteban Loaiza	.50	.20
❑ 94	Richie Sexson	1.00	.40
❑ 95	Alfonso Soriano	1.00	.40
❑ 96	Tony Womack	.50	.20
❑ 97	Paul Shuey	.50	.20
❑ 98	Melvin Mora	1.00	.40
❑ 99	Tony Gwynn	3.00	1.25
❑ 100	Vladimir Guerrero	2.50	1.00
❑ 101	Keith Osik	.50	.20
❑ 102	Bud Smith	.50	.20
❑ 103	Scott Williamson	.50	.20
❑ 104	Daryle Ward	.50	.20
❑ 105	Doug Mientkiewicz	1.00	.40
❑ 106	Stan Javier	.50	.20
❑ 107	Russ Ortiz	.50	.20
❑ 108	Wade Miller	.50	.20
❑ 109	Luke Prokopec	.50	.20
❑ 110	Andruw Jones	1.50	.60
❑ 111	Ron Coomer	.50	.20
❑ 112	Dan Wilson	.50	.20
❑ 113	Luis Castillo	.50	.20
❑ 114	Derek Bell	.50	.20
❑ 115	Gary Sheffield	1.00	.40
❑ 116	Ruben Rivera	.50	.20
❑ 117	Paul O'Neill	1.50	.60
❑ 118	Craig Paquette	.50	.20
❑ 119	Kelvim Escobar	.50	.20
❑ 120	Brad Radke	1.00	.40
❑ 121	Jorge Fabregas	.50	.20
❑ 122	Randy Winn	.50	.20
❑ 123	Tom Goodwin	.50	.20
❑ 124	Jaret Wright	.50	.20
❑ 125	Barry Bonds HR 73	40.00	15.00
❑ 126	Al Leiter	.50	.20
❑ 127	Ben Davis	.50	.20
❑ 128	Frank Catalanotto	.50	.20
❑ 129	Jose Cabrera	.50	.20
❑ 130	Magglio Ordonez	1.00	.40
❑ 131	Jose Macias	.50	.20
❑ 132	Ted Lilly	.50	.20
❑ 133	Chris Holt	.50	.20
❑ 134	Eric Milton	.50	.20
❑ 135	Shannon Stewart	1.00	.40
❑ 136	Omar Olivares	.50	.20
❑ 137	David Segui	.50	.20
❑ 138	Jeff Nelson	.50	.20
❑ 139	Matt Williams	1.00	.40
❑ 140	Ellis Burks	1.00	.40
❑ 141	Jason Bere	.50	.20
❑ 142	Jimmy Haynes	.50	.20

❑ 143 Ramon Hernandez .50 .20
❑ 144 Craig Counsell .50 .20
❑ 145 John Smoltz 1.50 .60
❑ 146 Homer Bush .50 .20
❑ 147 Quilvio Veras .50 .20
❑ 148 Esteban Yan .50 .20
❑ 149 Ramon Ortiz .50 .20
❑ 150 Carlos Delgado 1.00 .40
❑ 151 Lee Stevens .50 .20
❑ 152 Wil Cordero .50 .20
❑ 153 Mike Bordick 1.00 .40
❑ 154 John Flaherty .50 .20
❑ 155 Omar Daal .50 .20
❑ 156 Todd Ritchie .50 .20
❑ 157 Carl Everett 1.00 .40
❑ 158 Scott Sullivan .50 .20
❑ 159 Deivi Cruz .50 .20
❑ 160 Albert Pujols 5.00 2.00
❑ 161 Royce Clayton .50 .20
❑ 162 Jeff Suppan .50 .20
❑ 163 C.C. Sabathia 1.00 .40
❑ 164 Jimmy Rollins 1.00 .40
❑ 165 Rickey Henderson 2.50 1.00
❑ 166 Rey Ordonez .50 .20
❑ 167 Shawn Estes .50 .20
❑ 168 Reggie Sanders 1.00 .40
❑ 169 Jon Lieber .50 .20
❑ 170 Armando Benitez .50 .20
❑ 171 Mike Remlinger .50 .20
❑ 172 Billy Wagner 1.00 .40
❑ 173 Troy Percival 1.00 .40
❑ 174 Devon White 1.00 .40
❑ 175 Ivan Rodriguez 1.50 .60
❑ 176 Dustin Hermanson .50 .20
❑ 177 Brian Anderson .50 .20
❑ 178 Graeme Lloyd .50 .20
❑ 179 Russell Branyan .50 .20
❑ 180 Bobby Higginson 1.00 .40
❑ 181 Alex Gonzalez .50 .20
❑ 182 John Franco 1.00 .40
❑ 183 Sidney Ponson .50 .20
❑ 184 Jose Mesa .50 .20
❑ 185 Todd Hollandsworth .50 .20
❑ 186 Kevin Young .50 .20
❑ 187 Tim Wakefield 1.00 .40
❑ 188 Craig Biggio 1.50 .60
❑ 189 Jason Isringhausen 1.00 .40
❑ 190 Mark Quinn .50 .20
❑ 191 Glendon Rusch .50 .20
❑ 192 Damian Miller .50 .20
❑ 193 Sandy Alomar Jr. .50 .20
❑ 194 Scott Brosius 1.00 .40
❑ 195 Dave Martinez .50 .20
❑ 196 Danny Graves .50 .20
❑ 197 Shea Hillenbrand 1.00 .40
❑ 198 Jimmy Anderson .50 .20
❑ 199 Travis Lee .50 .20
❑ 200 Randy Johnson 2.50 1.00
❑ 201 Carlos Beltran 1.00 .40
❑ 202 Jerry Hairston .50 .20
❑ 203 Jesus Sanchez .50 .20
❑ 204 Eddie Taubensee .50 .20
❑ 205 David Wells 1.00 .40
❑ 206 Russ Davis .50 .20
❑ 207 Michael Barrett .50 .20
❑ 208 Marquis Grissom 1.00 .40
❑ 209 Byung-Hyun Kim 1.00 .40
❑ 210 Hideo Nomo 2.50 1.00
❑ 211 Ryan Rupe .50 .20
❑ 212 Ricky Gutierrez .50 .20
❑ 213 Darryl Kile 1.00 .40
❑ 214 Rico Brogna .50 .20
❑ 215 Terrence Long .50 .20
❑ 216 Mike Jackson .50 .20
❑ 217 Jamey Wright .50 .20
❑ 218 Adrian Beltre 1.00 .40
❑ 219 Benny Agbayani .50 .20
❑ 220 Chuck Knoblauch 1.00 .40
❑ 221 Randy Wolf .50 .20
❑ 222 Andy Ashby .50 .20
❑ 223 Corey Koskie .50 .20
❑ 224 Roger Cedeno .50 .20
❑ 225 Ichiro Suzuki 5.00 2.00
❑ 226 Keith Foulke 1.00 .40
❑ 227 Ryan Minor .50 .20
❑ 228 Shawon Dunston .50 .20
❑ 229 Alex Cora .50 .20
❑ 230 Jeromy Burnitz 1.00 .40
❑ 231 Mark Grace 1.50 .60
❑ 232 Aubrey Huff 1.00 .40
❑ 233 Jeffrey Hammonds .50 .20
❑ 234 Olmedo Saenz .50 .20
❑ 235 Brian Jordan 1.00 .40
❑ 236 Jeremy Giambi .50 .20
❑ 237 Joe Girardi .50 .20
❑ 238 Eric Gagne 1.00 .40
❑ 239 Masato Yoshii .50 .20
❑ 240 Greg Maddux 4.00 1.50
❑ 241 Bryan Rekar .50 .20
❑ 242 Ray Durham 1.00 .40
❑ 243 Torii Hunter 1.00 .40
❑ 244 Derrek Lee 1.50 .60
❑ 245 Jim Edmonds 1.00 .40
❑ 246 Einar Diaz .50 .20
❑ 247 Brian Bohanon .50 .20
❑ 248 Ron Belliard .50 .20
❑ 249 Mike Lowell 1.00 .40
❑ 250 Sammy Sosa 2.50 1.00
❑ 251 Richard Hidalgo .50 .20
❑ 252 Bartolo Colon 1.00 .40
❑ 253 Jorge Posada 1.50 .60
❑ 254 Latroy Hawkins .50 .20
❑ 255 Paul LoDuca 1.00 .40
❑ 256 Carlos Febles .50 .20
❑ 257 Nelson Cruz .50 .20
❑ 258 Edgardo Alfonzo .50 .20
❑ 259 Joey Hamilton .50 .20
❑ 260 Cliff Floyd 1.00 .40
❑ 261 Wes Helms .50 .20
❑ 262 Jay Bell 1.00 .40
❑ 263 Mike Cameron .50 .20
❑ 264 Paul Konerko 1.00 .40
❑ 265 Jeff Kent 1.00 .40
❑ 266 Robert Fick .50 .20
❑ 267 Allen Levrault .50 .20
❑ 268 Placido Polanco .50 .20
❑ 269 Marlon Anderson .50 .20
❑ 270 Mariano Rivera 2.50 1.00
❑ 271 Chan Ho Park 1.00 .40
❑ 272 Jose Vizcaino .50 .20
❑ 273 Jeff D'Amico .50 .20
❑ 274 Mark Gardner .50 .20
❑ 275 Travis Fryman 1.00 .40
❑ 276 Darren Lewis .50 .20
❑ 277 Bruce Bochy MG .50 .20
❑ 278 Jerry Manuel MG .50 .20
❑ 279 Bob Brenly MG .50 .20
❑ 280 Don Baylor MG 1.00 .40
❑ 281 Davey Lopes MG 1.00 .40
❑ 282 Jerry Narron MG .50 .20
❑ 283 Tony Muser MG .50 .20
❑ 284 Hal McRae MG 1.00 .40
❑ 285 Bobby Cox MG .50 .20
❑ 286 Larry Dierker MG .50 .20
❑ 287 Phil Garner MG 1.00 .40
❑ 288 Joe Kerrigan MG .50 .20
❑ 289 Bobby Valentine MG .50 .20
❑ 290 Dusty Baker MG 1.00 .40
❑ 291 Lloyd McClendon MG .50 .20
❑ 292 Mike Scioscia MG .50 .20
❑ 293 Buck Martinez MG .50 .20
❑ 294 Larry Bowa MG 1.00 .40
❑ 295 Tony LaRussa MG 1.00 .40
❑ 296 Jeff Torborg MG .50 .20
❑ 297 Tom Kelly MG .50 .20
❑ 298 Mike Hargrove MG .50 .20
❑ 299 Art Howe MG .50 .20
❑ 300 Lou Piniella MG 1.00 .40
❑ 301 Charlie Manuel MG .50 .20
❑ 302 Buddy Bell MG 1.00 .40
❑ 303 Tony Perez MG 1.00 .40
❑ 304 Bob Boone MG 1.00 .40
❑ 305 Joe Torre MG 1.50 .60
❑ 306 Jim Tracy MG .50 .20
❑ 307 Jason Lane PROS 1.50 .60
❑ 308 Chris George PROS 1.50 .60
❑ 309 Hank Blalock PROS 2.50 1.00
❑ 310 Joe Borchard PROS 1.50 .60
❑ 311 Marlon Byrd PROS 1.50 .60
❑ 312 Raymond Cabrera PROS RC 1.50 .60
❑ 313 Freddy Sanchez PROS RC 6.00 2.50
❑ 314 Scott Wiggins PROS RC 1.50 .60
❑ 315 Jason Maule PROS RC 1.50 .60
❑ 316 Dionys Cesar PROS RC 1.50 .60
❑ 317 Boof Bonser PROS 1.50 .60
❑ 318 Juan Tolentino PROS RC 1.50 .60
❑ 319 Earl Snyder PROS RC 1.50 .60
❑ 320 Travis Wade PROS RC 1.50 .60
❑ 321 Napolean Calzado PROS RC 1.50 .60
❑ 322 Eric Glaser PROS RC 1.50 .60
❑ 323 Craig Kuzmic PROS RC 1.50 .60
❑ 324 Nic Jackson PROS RC 1.50 .60
❑ 325 Mike Rivera PROS 1.50 .60
❑ 326 Jason Bay PROS RC 8.00 3.00
❑ 327 Chris Smith DP 1.50 .60
❑ 328 Jake Gautreau DP 1.50 .60
❑ 329 Gabe Gross DP 1.50 .60
❑ 330 Kenny Baugh DP 1.50 .60
❑ 331 J.D. Martin DP 1.50 .60
❑ 366 Pat Meares .50 .20
❑ 367 Mike Lieberthal 1.00 .40
❑ 368 Larry Bigbie .50 .20
❑ 369 Ron Gant 1.00 .40
❑ 370 Moises Alou 1.00 .40
❑ 371 Chad Kreuter .50 .20
❑ 372 Willis Roberts .50 .20
❑ 373 Toby Hall .50 .20
❑ 374 Miguel Batista .50 .20
❑ 375 John Burkett .50 .20
❑ 376 Cory Lidle .50 .20
❑ 377 Nick Neugebauer .50 .20
❑ 378 Jay Payton .50 .20
❑ 379 Steve Karsay .50 .20
❑ 380 Eric Chavez 1.00 .40
❑ 381 Kelly Stinnett .50 .20
❑ 382 Jarrod Washburn .50 .20
❑ 383 Rick White .50 .20
❑ 384 Jeff Conine 1.00 .40
❑ 385 Fred McGriff 1.50 .60
❑ 386 Marvin Benard .50 .20
❑ 387 Joe Crede 1.00 .40
❑ 388 Dennis Cook .50 .20
❑ 389 Rick Reed .50 .20
❑ 390 Tom Glavine 1.50 .60
❑ 391 Rondell White 1.00 .40
❑ 392 Matt Morris 1.00 .40
❑ 393 Pat Rapp .50 .20
❑ 394 Robert Person .50 .20
❑ 395 Omar Vizquel 1.50 .60
❑ 396 Jeff Cirillo .50 .20
❑ 397 Dave Mlicki .50 .20
❑ 398 Jose Ortiz .50 .20
❑ 399 Ryan Dempster .50 .20
❑ 400 Curt Schilling 1.00 .40
❑ 401 Peter Bergeron .50 .20
❑ 402 Kyle Lohse .50 .20
❑ 403 Craig Wilson .50 .20
❑ 404 David Justice 1.00 .40
❑ 405 Darin Erstad 1.00 .40
❑ 406 Jose Mercedes .50 .20
❑ 407 Carl Pavano 1.00 .40
❑ 408 Albie Lopez .50 .20
❑ 409 Alex Ochoa .50 .20
❑ 410 Chipper Jones 2.50 1.00
❑ 411 Tyler Houston .50 .20
❑ 412 Dean Palmer 1.00 .40
❑ 413 Damian Jackson .50 .20
❑ 414 Josh Towers .50 .20
❑ 415 Rafael Furcal 1.00 .40
❑ 416 Mike Morgan .50 .20
❑ 417 Herb Perry .50 .20
❑ 418 Mike Sirotka .50 .20
❑ 419 Mark Wohlers .50 .20
❑ 420 Nomar Garciaparra 4.00 1.50
❑ 421 Felipe Lopez .50 .20
❑ 422 Joe McEwing .50 .20
❑ 423 Jacque Jones 1.00 .40
❑ 424 Julio Franco 1.00 .40
❑ 425 Frank Thomas 2.50 1.00
❑ 426 So Taguchi RC 2.50 1.00
❑ 427 Kazuhisa Ishii RC 2.50 1.00
❑ 428 D'Angelo Jimenez .50 .20
❑ 429 Chris Stynes .50 .20
❑ 430 Kerry Wood 1.00 .40
❑ 431 Chris Singleton .50 .20
❑ 432 Erubiel Durazo .50 .20
❑ 433 Matt Lawton .50 .20
❑ 434 Bill Mueller 1.00 .40

❑ 435 Jose Canseco 1.50 .60
❑ 436 Ben Grieve .50 .20
❑ 437 Terry Mulholland .50 .20
❑ 438 David Bell .50 .20
❑ 439 A.J. Pierzynski 1.00 .40
❑ 440 Adam Dunn 1.00 .40
❑ 441 Jon Garland 1.00 .40
❑ 442 Jeff Fassero .50 .20
❑ 443 Julio Lugo .50 .20
❑ 444 Carlos Guillen 1.00 .40
❑ 445 Orlando Hernandez 1.00 .40
❑ 446 Mark Loretta .50 .20
❑ 447 Scott Spiezio .50 .20
❑ 448 Kevin Millwood 1.00 .40
❑ 449 Jamie Moyer 1.00 .40
❑ 450 Todd Helton 1.50 .60
❑ 451 Todd Walker .50 .20
❑ 452 Jose Lima .50 .20
❑ 453 Brook Fordyce .50 .20
❑ 454 Aaron Rowand 1.00 .40
❑ 455 Barry Zito 1.00 .40
❑ 456 Eric Owens .50 .20
❑ 457 Charles Nagy .50 .20
❑ 458 Raul Ibanez .50 .20
❑ 459 Joe Mays .50 .20
❑ 460 Jim Thome 1.50 .60
❑ 461 Adam Eaton .50 .20
❑ 462 Felix Martinez .50 .20
❑ 463 Vernon Wells 1.00 .40
❑ 464 Donnie Sadler .50 .20
❑ 465 Tony Clark .50 .20
❑ 466 Jose Hernandez .50 .20
❑ 467 Ramon Martinez .50 .20
❑ 468 Rusty Greer 1.00 .40
❑ 469 Rod Barajas .50 .20
❑ 470 Lance Berkman 1.00 .40
❑ 471 Brady Anderson 1.00 .40
❑ 472 Pedro Astacio .50 .20
❑ 473 Shane Halter .50 .20
❑ 474 Bret Prinz .50 .20
❑ 475 Edgar Martinez 1.50 .60
❑ 476 Steve Trachsel .50 .20
❑ 477 Gary Matthews Jr. .50 .20
❑ 478 Ismael Valdes .50 .20
❑ 479 Juan Uribe .50 .20
❑ 480 Shawn Green 1.00 .40
❑ 481 Kirk Rueter .50 .20
❑ 482 Damion Easley .50 .20
❑ 483 Chris Carpenter 1.00 .40
❑ 484 Kris Benson .50 .20
❑ 485 Antonio Alfonseca .50 .20
❑ 486 Kyle Farnsworth .50 .20
❑ 487 Brandon Lyon .50 .20
❑ 488 Hideki Irabu .50 .20
❑ 489 David Ortiz 2.50 1.00
❑ 490 Mike Piazza 4.00 1.50
❑ 491 Derek Lowe 1.00 .40
❑ 492 Chris Gomez .50 .20
❑ 493 Mark Johnson .50 .20
❑ 494 John Rocker 1.00 .40
❑ 495 Eric Karros 1.00 .40
❑ 496 Bill Haselman .50 .20
❑ 497 Dave Veres .50 .20
❑ 498 Pete Harnisch .50 .20
❑ 499 Tomokazu Ohka .50 .20
❑ 500 Barry Bonds 6.00 2.50
❑ 501 David Dellucci .50 .20
❑ 502 Wendell Magee .50 .20
❑ 503 Tom Gordon .50 .20
❑ 504 Javier Vazquez 1.00 .40
❑ 505 Ben Sheets 1.00 .40
❑ 506 Wilton Guerrero .50 .20
❑ 507 John Halama .50 .20
❑ 508 Mark Redman .50 .20
❑ 509 Jack Wilson .50 .20
❑ 510 Bernie Williams 1.50 .60
❑ 511 Miguel Cairo .50 .20
❑ 512 Denny Hocking .50 .20
❑ 513 Tony Batista .50 .20
❑ 514 Mark Grudzielanek .50 .20
❑ 515 Jose Vidro .50 .20
❑ 516 Sterling Hitchcock .50 .20
❑ 517 Billy Koch .50 .20
❑ 518 Matt Clement 1.00 .40
❑ 519 Bruce Chen .50 .20
❑ 520 Roberto Alomar 1.50 .60
❑ 521 Orlando Palmeiro .50 .20
❑ 522 Steve Finley 1.00 .40
❑ 523 Danny Patterson .50 .20
❑ 524 Terry Adams .50 .20
❑ 525 Tino Martinez 1.50 .60
❑ 526 Tony Armas Jr. .50 .20
❑ 527 Geoff Jenkins .50 .20
❑ 528 Kerry Robinson .50 .20
❑ 529 Corey Patterson .50 .20
❑ 530 Brian Giles 1.00 .40
❑ 531 Jose Jimenez .50 .20
❑ 532 Joe Kennedy .50 .20
❑ 533 Armando Rios .50 .20
❑ 534 Osvaldo Fernandez .50 .20
❑ 535 Ruben Sierra 1.00 .40
❑ 536 Octavio Dotel .50 .20
❑ 537 Luis Sojo .50 .20
❑ 538 Brent Butler .50 .20
❑ 539 Pablo Ozuna .50 .20
❑ 540 Freddy Garcia 1.00 .40
❑ 541 Chad Durbin .50 .20
❑ 542 Orlando Merced .50 .20
❑ 543 Michael Tucker .50 .20
❑ 544 Roberto Hernandez .50 .20
❑ 545 Pat Burrell 1.00 .40
❑ 546 A.J. Burnett 1.00 .40
❑ 547 Bubba Trammell .50 .20
❑ 548 Scott Elarton .50 .20
❑ 549 Mike Darr .50 .20
❑ 550 Ken Griffey Jr. 4.00 1.50
❑ 551 Ugueth Urbina .50 .20
❑ 552 Todd Jones .50 .20
❑ 553 Delino Deshields .50 .20
❑ 554 Adam Piatt .50 .20
❑ 555 Jason Kendall 1.00 .40
❑ 556 Hector Ortiz .50 .20
❑ 557 Turk Wendell .50 .20
❑ 558 Rob Bell .50 .20
❑ 559 Sun Woo Kim .50 .20
❑ 560 Raul Mondesi 1.00 .40
❑ 561 Brent Abernathy .50 .20
❑ 562 Seth Etherton .50 .20
❑ 563 Shawn Wooten .50 .20
❑ 564 Jay Buhner 1.00 .40
❑ 565 Andres Galarraga 1.00 .40
❑ 566 Shane Reynolds .50 .20
❑ 567 Rod Beck .50 .20
❑ 568 Dee Brown .50 .20
❑ 569 Pedro Feliz .50 .20
❑ 570 Ryan Klesko 1.00 .40
❑ 571 John Vander Wal .50 .20
❑ 572 Nick Bierbrodt .50 .20
❑ 573 Joe Nathan 1.00 .40
❑ 574 James Baldwin .50 .20
❑ 575 J.D. Drew 1.00 .40
❑ 576 Greg Colbrunn .50 .20
❑ 577 Doug Glanville .50 .20
❑ 578 Brandon Duckworth .50 .20
❑ 579 Shawn Chacon .50 .20
❑ 580 Rich Aurilia .50 .20
❑ 581 Chuck Finley 1.00 .40
❑ 582 Abraham Nunez .50 .20
❑ 583 Kenny Lofton 1.00 .40
❑ 584 Brian Daubach .50 .20
❑ 585 Miguel Tejada 1.00 .40
❑ 586 Nate Cornejo .50 .20
❑ 587 Kazuhiro Sasaki 1.00 .40
❑ 588 Chris Richard .50 .20
❑ 589 Armando Reynoso .50 .20
❑ 590 Tim Hudson 1.00 .40
❑ 591 Neifi Perez .50 .20
❑ 592 Steve Cox .50 .20
❑ 593 Henry Blanco .50 .20
❑ 594 Ricky Ledee .50 .20
❑ 595 Tim Salmon 1.50 .60
❑ 596 Luis Rivas .50 .20
❑ 597 Jeff Zimmerman .50 .20
❑ 598 Matt Stairs .50 .20
❑ 599 Preston Wilson 1.00 .40
❑ 600 Mark McGwire 6.00 2.50
❑ 601 Timo Perez .50 .20
❑ 602 Matt Anderson .50 .20
❑ 603 Todd Hundley .50 .20
❑ 604 Rick Ankiel .50 .20
❑ 605 Tsuyoshi Shinjo 1.00 .40
❑ 606 Woody Williams .50 .20
❑ 607 Jason LaRue .50 .20
❑ 608 Carlos Lee 1.00 .40
❑ 609 Russ Johnson .50 .20
❑ 610 Scott Rolen 1.50 .60
❑ 611 Brent Mayne .50 .20
❑ 612 Darrin Fletcher .50 .20
❑ 613 Ray Lankford 1.00 .40
❑ 614 Troy O'Leary .50 .20
❑ 615 Javier Lopez 1.00 .40
❑ 616 Randy Velarde .50 .20
❑ 617 Vinny Castilla 1.00 .40
❑ 618 Milton Bradley 1.00 .40
❑ 619 Ruben Mateo .50 .20
❑ 620 Jason Giambi Yankees 1.00 .40
❑ 621 Andy Benes .50 .20
❑ 622 Joe Mauer RC 15.00 6.00
❑ 623 Andy Pettitte 1.50 .60
❑ 624 Jose Offerman .50 .20
❑ 625 Mo Vaughn 1.00 .40
❑ 626 Steve Sparks .50 .20
❑ 627 Mike Matthews .50 .20
❑ 628 Robb Nen 1.00 .40
❑ 629 Kip Wells .50 .20
❑ 630 Kevin Brown 1.00 .40
❑ 631 Arthur Rhodes .50 .20
❑ 632 Gabe Kapler 1.00 .40
❑ 633 Jermaine Dye 1.00 .40
❑ 634 Josh Beckett 1.00 .40
❑ 635 Pokey Reese .50 .20
❑ 636 Benji Gil .50 .20
❑ 637 Marcus Giles 1.00 .40
❑ 638 Julian Tavarez .50 .20
❑ 639 Jason Schmidt 1.00 .40
❑ 640 Alex Rodriguez 4.00 1.50
❑ 641 Anaheim Angels TC 1.00 .40
❑ 642 Arizona Diamondbacks TC 1.50 .60
❑ 643 Atlanta Braves TC 1.00 .40
❑ 644 Baltimore Orioles TC 1.00 .40
❑ 645 Boston Red Sox TC 1.00 .40
❑ 646 Chicago Cubs TC 1.00 .40
❑ 647 Chicago White Sox TC 1.00 .40
❑ 648 Cincinnati Reds TC 1.00 .40
❑ 649 Cleveland Indians TC 1.00 .40
❑ 650 Colorado Rockies TC 1.00 .40
❑ 651 Detroit Tigers TC 1.00 .40
❑ 652 Florida Marlins TC 1.00 .40
❑ 653 Houston Astros TC 1.00 .40
❑ 654 Kansas City Royals TC 1.00 .40
❑ 655 Los Angeles Dodgers TC 1.00 .40
❑ 656 Milwaukee Brewers TC 1.00 .40
❑ 657 Minnesota Twins TC 1.00 .40
❑ 658 Montreal Expos TC 1.00 .40
❑ 659 New York Mets TC 1.00 .40
❑ 660 New York Yankees TC 2.50 1.00
❑ 661 Oakland Athletics TC 1.00 .40
❑ 662 Philadelphia Phillies TC 1.00 .40
❑ 663 Pittsburgh Pirates TC 1.00 .40
❑ 664 San Diego Padres TC 1.00 .40
❑ 665 San Francisco Giants TC 1.00 .40
❑ 666 Seattle Mariners TC 1.50 .60
❑ 667 St. Louis Cardinals TC 1.00 .40
❑ 668 Tampa Bay Devil Rays TC 1.00 .40
❑ 669 Texas Rangers TC 1.00 .40
❑ 670 Toronto Blue Jays TC 1.00 .40
❑ 671 Juan Cruz PROS 1.50 .60
❑ 672 Kevin Cash PROS RC 1.50 .60
❑ 673 Jimmy Gobble PROS RC 1.50 .60
❑ 674 Mike Hill PROS RC 1.50 .60
❑ 675 Taylor Buchholz PROS RC 1.50 .60
❑ 676 Bill Hall PROS 1.50 .60
❑ 677 Brett Roneberg PROS RC 1.50 .60
❑ 678 Royce Huffman PROS RC 1.50 .60
❑ 679 Chris Tritle PROS RC 1.50 .60
❑ 680 Nate Espy PROS 1.50 .60
❑ 681 Nick Alvarez PROS RC 1.50 .60
❑ 682 Jason Botts PROS RC 1.50 .60
❑ 683 Ryan Gripp PROS RC 1.50 .60
❑ 684 Dan Phillips PROS RC 1.50 .60
❑ 685 Pablo Arias PROS RC 1.50 .60
❑ 686 John Rodriguez PROS RC 2.50 1.00
❑ 687 Rich Harden PROS RC 8.00 3.00
❑ 688 Neal Frendling PROS RC 1.50 .60
❑ 689 Rich Thompson PROS RC 1.50 .60
❑ 690 Greg Montalbano PROS RC 1.50 .60
❑ 691 Len Dinardo DP RC 1.50 .60
❑ 692 Ryan Raburn DP RC 1.50 .60

❑ 693 Josh Barfield DP RC	5.00	2.00
❑ 694 David Bacani DP RC	1.50	.60
❑ 695 Dan Johnson DP RC	2.50	1.00

2002 Topps Chrome Traded

❑ COMPLETE SET (275)	120.00	60.00
❑ T1 Jeff Weaver	.50	.20
❑ T2 Jay Powell	.50	.20
❑ T3 Alex Gonzalez	.50	.20
❑ T4 Jason Isringhausen	.75	.30
❑ T5 Tyler Houston	.50	.20
❑ T6 Ben Broussard	.50	.20
❑ T7 Chuck Knoblauch	.75	.30
❑ T8 Brian L. Hunter	.50	.20
❑ T9 Dustan Mohr	.50	.20
❑ T10 Eric Hinske	.50	.20
❑ T11 Roger Cedeno	.50	.20
❑ T12 Eddie Perez	.50	.20
❑ T13 Jeromy Burnitz	.75	.30
❑ T14 Bartolo Colon	.75	.30
❑ T15 Rick Helling	.50	.20
❑ T16 Dan Plesac	.50	.20
❑ T17 Scott Strickland	.50	.20
❑ T18 Antonio Alfonseca	.50	.20
❑ T19 Ricky Gutierrez	.50	.20
❑ T20 John Valentin	.50	.20
❑ T21 Raul Mondesi	.75	.30
❑ T22 Ben Davis	.50	.20
❑ T23 Nelson Figueroa	.50	.20
❑ T24 Earl Snyder	.50	.20
❑ T25 Robin Ventura	.75	.30
❑ T26 Jimmy Haynes	.50	.20
❑ T27 Kenny Kelly	.50	.20
❑ T28 Morgan Ensberg	.75	.30
❑ T29 Reggie Sanders	.75	.30
❑ T30 Shigetoshi Hasegawa	.75	.30
❑ T31 Mike Timlin	.50	.20
❑ T32 Russell Branyan	.50	.20
❑ T33 Alan Embree	.50	.20
❑ T34 D'Angelo Jimenez	.50	.20
❑ T35 Kent Mercker	.50	.20
❑ T36 Jesse Orosco	.50	.20
❑ T37 Gregg Zaun	.50	.20
❑ T38 Reggie Taylor	.50	.20
❑ T39 Andres Galarraga	.75	.30
❑ T40 Chris Truby	.50	.20
❑ T41 Bruce Chen	.50	.20
❑ T42 Darren Lewis	.50	.20
❑ T43 Ryan Kohlmeier	.50	.20
❑ T44 John McDonald	.50	.20
❑ T45 Omar Daal	.50	.20
❑ T46 Matt Clement	.75	.30
❑ T47 Glendon Rusch	.50	.20
❑ T48 Chan Ho Park	.75	.30
❑ T49 Benny Agbayani	.50	.20
❑ T50 Juan Gonzalez	.75	.30
❑ T51 Carlos Baerga	.50	.20
❑ T52 Tim Raines	.75	.30
❑ T53 Kevin Appier	.75	.30
❑ T54 Marty Cordova	.50	.20
❑ T55 Jeff D'Amico	.50	.20
❑ T56 Dmitri Young	.75	.30
❑ T57 Roosevelt Brown	.50	.20
❑ T58 Dustin Hermanson	.50	.20
❑ T59 Jose Rijo	.50	.20
❑ T60 Todd Ritchie	.50	.20
❑ T61 Lee Stevens	.50	.20
❑ T62 Placido Polanco	.50	.20
❑ T63 Eric Young	.50	.20
❑ T64 Chuck Finley	.75	.30
❑ T65 Dicky Gonzalez	.50	.20
❑ T66 Jose Macias	.50	.20
❑ T67 Gabe Kapler	.75	.30
❑ T68 Sandy Alomar Jr.	.50	.20
❑ T69 Henry Blanco	.50	.20
❑ T70 Julian Tavarez	.50	.20
❑ T71 Paul Bako	.50	.20
❑ T72 Scott Rolen	1.25	.50
❑ T73 Brian Jordan	.75	.30
❑ T74 Rickey Henderson	2.00	.75
❑ T75 Kevin Mench	.50	.20
❑ T76 Hideo Nomo	2.00	.75
❑ T77 Jeremy Giambi	.50	.20
❑ T78 Brad Fullmer	.50	.20
❑ T79 Carl Everett	.75	.30
❑ T80 David Wells	.75	.30
❑ T81 Aaron Sele	.50	.20
❑ T82 Todd Hollandsworth	.50	.20
❑ T83 Vicente Padilla	.50	.20
❑ T84 Kenny Lofton	.75	.30
❑ T85 Corky Miller	.50	.20
❑ T86 Josh Fogg	.50	.20
❑ T87 Cliff Floyd	.75	.30
❑ T88 Craig Paquette	.50	.20
❑ T89 Jay Payton	.50	.20
❑ T90 Carlos Pena	.50	.20
❑ T91 Juan Encarnacion	.50	.20
❑ T92 Rey Sanchez	.50	.20
❑ T93 Ryan Dempster	.50	.20
❑ T94 Mario Encarnacion	.50	.20
❑ T95 Jorge Julio	.50	.20
❑ T96 John Mabry	.50	.20
❑ T97 Todd Zeile	.75	.30
❑ T98 Johnny Damon	1.25	.50
❑ T99 Deivi Cruz	.50	.20
❑ T100 Gary Sheffield	.75	.30
❑ T101 Ted Lilly	.50	.20
❑ T102 Todd Van Poppel	.50	.20
❑ T103 Shawn Estes	.50	.20
❑ T104 Cesar Izturis	.50	.20
❑ T105 Ron Coomer	.50	.20
❑ T106 Grady Little MG RC	.50	.20
❑ T107 Jimy Williams MGR	.50	.20
❑ T108 Tony Pena MGR	.50	.20
❑ T109 Frank Robinson MGR	1.25	.50
❑ T110 Ron Gardenhire MGR	.50	.20
❑ T111 Dennis Tankersley	.50	.20
❑ T112 Alejandro Cadena RC	1.00	.40
❑ T113 Justin Reid RC	1.00	.40
❑ T114 Nate Field RC	1.00	.40
❑ T115 Rene Reyes RC	1.00	.40
❑ T116 Nelson Castro RC	1.00	.40
❑ T117 Miguel Olivo	.50	.20
❑ T118 David Espinosa	.50	.20
❑ T119 Chris Bootcheck RC	1.00	.40
❑ T120 Rob Henkel RC	1.00	.40
❑ T121 Steve Bechler RC	1.00	.40
❑ T122 Mark Outlaw RC	1.00	.40
❑ T123 Henry Pichardo RC	1.00	.40
❑ T124 Michael Floyd RC	1.00	.40
❑ T125 Richard Lane RC	1.00	.40
❑ T126 Pete Zamora RC	1.00	.40
❑ T127 Javier Colina	.50	.20
❑ T128 Greg Sain RC	1.00	.40
❑ T129 Ronnie Merrill	.50	.20
❑ T130 Gavin Floyd RC	2.50	1.00
❑ T131 Josh Bonifay RC	1.00	.40
❑ T132 Tommy Marx RC	1.00	.40
❑ T133 Gary Cates Jr. RC	1.00	.40
❑ T134 Neal Cotts RC	2.50	1.00
❑ T135 Angel Berroa	.50	.20
❑ T136 Elio Serrano RC	1.00	.40
❑ T137 J.J. Putz RC	1.25	.50
❑ T138 Ruben Gotay RC	1.25	.50
❑ T139 Eddie Rogers	.50	.20
❑ T140 Wily Mo Pena	.75	.30
❑ T141 Tyler Yates RC	1.00	.40
❑ T142 Colin Young RC	.75	.30
❑ T143 Chance Caple	.50	.20
❑ T144 Ben Howard RC	1.00	.40
❑ T145 Ryan Bukvich RC	1.00	.40
❑ T146 Cliff Bartosh RC	1.00	.40
❑ T147 Brandon Claussen	.50	.20
❑ T148 Cristian Guerrero	.50	.20
❑ T149 Derrick Lewis	.50	.20
❑ T150 Eric Miller RC	1.00	.40
❑ T151 Justin Huber RC	2.00	.75
❑ T152 Adrian Gonzalez	.50	.20
❑ T153 Brian West RC	1.00	.40
❑ T154 Chris Baker RC	1.00	.40
❑ T155 Drew Henson	.50	.20
❑ T156 Scott Hairston RC	1.25	.50
❑ T157 Jason Simontacchi RC	1.00	.40
❑ T158 Jason Arnold RC	1.00	.40
❑ T159 Brandon Phillips	.50	.20
❑ T160 Adam Roller RC	1.00	.40
❑ T161 Scotty Layfield RC	1.00	.40
❑ T162 Freddie Money RC	1.00	.40
❑ T163 Noochie Varner RC	1.00	.40
❑ T164 Terrance Hill RC	1.00	.40
❑ T165 Jeremy Hill RC	1.00	.40
❑ T166 Carlos Cabrera RC	1.00	.40
❑ T167 Jose Morban RC	1.00	.40
❑ T168 Kevin Frederick RC	1.00	.40
❑ T169 Mark Teixeira	4.00	1.50
❑ T170 Brian Rogers	.50	.20
❑ T171 Anastacio Martinez RC	1.00	.40
❑ T172 Bobby Jenks RC	4.00	1.50
❑ T173 David Gil RC	1.00	.40
❑ T174 Andres Torres	.50	.20
❑ T175 James Barrett RC	1.00	.40
❑ T176 Jimmy Journell	.50	.20
❑ T177 Brett Kay RC	1.00	.40
❑ T178 Jason Young RC	1.00	.40
❑ T179 Mark Hamilton RC	1.00	.40
❑ T180 Jose Bautista RC	2.50	1.00
❑ T181 Blake McGinley RC	1.00	.40
❑ T182 Ryan Mottl RC	1.00	.40
❑ T183 Jeff Austin RC	1.00	.40
❑ T184 Xavier Nady	.50	.20
❑ T185 Kyle Kane RC	1.00	.40
❑ T186 Travis Foley RC	1.00	.40
❑ T187 Nathan Kaup RC	1.00	.40
❑ T188 Eric Cyr	.50	.20
❑ T189 Josh Cisneros RC	1.00	.40
❑ T190 Brad Nelson RC	1.00	.40
❑ T191 Clint Weibl RC	1.00	.40
❑ T192 Ron Calloway RC	1.00	.40
❑ T193 Jung Bong	.50	.20
❑ T194 Rolando Viera RC	1.00	.40
❑ T195 Jason Bulger RC	1.00	.40
❑ T196 Chone Figgins RC	4.00	1.50
❑ T197 Jimmy Alvarez RC	1.00	.40
❑ T198 Joel Crump RC	1.00	.40
❑ T199 Ryan Doumit RC	1.50	.60
❑ T200 Demetrius Heath RC	1.00	.40
❑ T201 John Ennis RC	1.00	.40
❑ T202 Doug Sessions RC	1.00	.40
❑ T203 Clinton Hosford RC	1.00	.40
❑ T204 Chris Narveson RC	1.00	.40
❑ T205 Ross Peeples RC	1.00	.40
❑ T206 Alex Requena RC	1.00	.40
❑ T207 Matt Erickson RC	1.00	.40
❑ T208 Brian Forystek RC	1.00	.40
❑ T209 Dewon Brazelton	.50	.20
❑ T210 Nathan Haynes	.50	.20
❑ T211 Jack Cust	.50	.20
❑ T212 Jesse Foppert RC	1.25	.50
❑ T213 Jesus Cota RC	1.00	.40
❑ T214 Juan M. Gonzalez RC	1.00	.40
❑ T215 Tim Kalita RC	1.00	.40
❑ T216 Manny Delcarmen RC	1.25	.50
❑ T217 Jim Kavourias RC	1.00	.40
❑ T218 C.J. Wilson RC	1.00	.40
❑ T219 Edwin Yan RC	1.00	.40
❑ T220 Andy Van Hekken	.50	.20
❑ T221 Michael Cuddyer	.50	.20
❑ T222 Jeff Verplancke RC	1.00	.40
❑ T223 Mike Wilson RC	1.00	.40
❑ T224 Corwin Malone RC	1.00	.40
❑ T225 Chris Snelling RC	1.50	.60
❑ T226 Joe Rogers RC	1.00	.40
❑ T227 Jason Bay	8.00	3.00
❑ T228 Ezequiel Astacio RC	1.00	.40
❑ T229 Joey Hammond RC	1.00	.40
❑ T230 Chris Duffy RC	1.00	.40
❑ T231 Mark Prior	1.25	.50
❑ T232 Hansel Izquierdo RC	1.00	.40
❑ T233 Franklyn German RC	1.00	.40

❑ T234 Alexis Gomez	.50	.20
❑ T235 Jorge Padilla RC	1.00	.40
❑ T236 Ryan Snare RC	1.00	.40
❑ T237 Deivis Santos	.50	.20
❑ T238 Taggert Bozied RC	1.25	.50
❑ T239 Mike Peeples RC	1.00	.40
❑ T240 Ronald Acuna RC	1.00	.40
❑ T241 Koyie Hill	.50	.20
❑ T242 Garrett Guzman RC	1.00	.40
❑ T243 Ryan Church RC	2.50	1.00
❑ T244 Tony Fontana RC	1.00	.40
❑ T245 Keto Anderson RC	1.00	.40
❑ T246 Brad Bouras RC	1.00	.40
❑ T247 Jason Dubois RC	1.25	.50
❑ T248 Angel Guzman RC	2.00	.75
❑ T249 Joel Hanrahan RC	1.00	.40
❑ T250 Joe Jiannetti RC	1.00	.40
❑ T251 Sean Pierce RC	1.00	.40
❑ T252 Jake Mauer RC	1.00	.40
❑ T253 Marshall McDougall RC	1.00	.40
❑ T254 Edwin Almonte RC	1.00	.40
❑ T255 Shawn Riggans RC	1.00	.40
❑ T256 Steven Shell RC	1.00	.40
❑ T257 Kevin Hooper RC	1.00	.40
❑ T258 Michael Frick RC	1.00	.40
❑ T259 Travis Chapman RC	1.00	.40
❑ T260 Tim Hummel RC	1.00	.40
❑ T261 Adam Morrissey RC	1.00	.40
❑ T262 Dontrelle Willis RC	10.00	4.00
❑ T263 Justin Sherrod RC	1.00	.40
❑ T264 Gerald Smiley RC	1.00	.40
❑ T265 Tony Miller RC	1.00	.40
❑ T266 Nolan Ryan WW	5.00	2.00
❑ T267 Reggie Jackson WW	1.25	.50
❑ T268 Steve Garvey WW	.75	.30
❑ T269 Wade Boggs WW	1.25	.50
❑ T270 Sammy Sosa WW	2.00	.75
❑ T271 Curt Schilling WW	.75	.30
❑ T272 Mark Grace WW	1.25	.50
❑ T273 Jason Giambi WW	.50	.20
❑ T274 Ken Griffey Jr. WW	3.00	1.25
❑ T275 Roberto Alomar WW	1.25	.50

2003 Topps Chrome

❑ COMPLETE SET (440)	200.00	80.00
❑ COMPLETE SERIES 1 (220)	100.00	40.00
❑ COMPLETE SERIES 2 (220)	100.00	40.00
❑ COMMON (1-200/221-420)	1.00	.40
❑ COMMON (201-220/421-440)	1.50	.60
❑ 1 Alex Rodriguez	4.00	1.50
❑ 2 Eddie Guardado	1.00	.40
❑ 3 Curt Schilling	1.00	.40
❑ 4 Andruw Jones	1.50	.60
❑ 5 Magglio Ordonez	1.00	.40
❑ 6 Todd Helton	1.50	.60
❑ 7 Odalis Perez	1.00	.40
❑ 8 Edgardo Alfonzo	1.00	.40
❑ 9 Eric Hinske	1.00	.40
❑ 10 Danny Bautista	1.00	.40
❑ 11 Sammy Sosa	2.50	1.00
❑ 12 Roberto Alomar	1.50	.60
❑ 13 Roger Clemens	5.00	2.00
❑ 14 Austin Kearns	1.00	.40
❑ 15 Luis Gonzalez	1.00	.40
❑ 16 Mo Vaughn	1.00	.40
❑ 17 Alfonso Soriano	1.00	.40
❑ 18 Orlando Cabrera	1.00	.40
❑ 19 Hideo Nomo	2.50	1.00
❑ 20 Omar Vizquel	1.50	.60
❑ 21 Greg Maddux	4.00	1.50
❑ 22 Fred McGriff	1.50	.60
❑ 23 Frank Thomas	2.50	1.00
❑ 24 Shawn Green	1.00	.40
❑ 25 Jacque Jones	1.00	.40
❑ 26 Bernie Williams	1.50	.60
❑ 27 Corey Patterson	1.00	.40
❑ 28 Cesar Izturis	1.00	.40
❑ 29 Larry Walker	1.00	.40
❑ 30 Darren Dreifort	1.00	.40
❑ 31 Al Leiter	1.00	.40
❑ 32 Jason Marquis	1.00	.40
❑ 33 Sean Casey	1.00	.40
❑ 34 Craig Counsell	1.00	.40
❑ 35 Albert Pujols	5.00	2.00
❑ 36 Kyle Lohse	1.00	.40
❑ 37 Paul Lo Duca	1.00	.40
❑ 38 Roy Oswalt	1.00	.40
❑ 39 Danny Graves	1.00	.40
❑ 40 Kevin Millwood	1.00	.40
❑ 41 Lance Berkman	1.00	.40
❑ 42 Denny Hocking	1.00	.40
❑ 43 Jose Valentin	1.00	.40
❑ 44 Josh Beckett	1.00	.40
❑ 45 Nomar Garciaparra	4.00	1.50
❑ 46 Craig Biggio	1.50	.60
❑ 47 Omar Daal	1.00	.40
❑ 48 Jimmy Rollins	1.00	.40
❑ 49 Jermaine Dye	1.00	.40
❑ 50 Edgar Renteria	1.00	.40
❑ 51 Brandon Duckworth	1.00	.40
❑ 52 Luis Castillo	1.00	.40
❑ 53 Andy Ashby	1.00	.40
❑ 54 Mike Williams	1.00	.40
❑ 55 Benito Santiago	1.00	.40
❑ 56 Bret Boone	1.00	.40
❑ 57 Randy Wolf	1.00	.40
❑ 58 Ivan Rodriguez	1.50	.60
❑ 59 Shannon Stewart	1.00	.40
❑ 60 Jose Cruz Jr.	1.00	.40
❑ 61 Billy Wagner	1.00	.40
❑ 62 Alex Gonzalez	1.00	.40
❑ 63 Ichiro Suzuki	5.00	2.00
❑ 64 Joe McEwing	1.00	.40
❑ 65 Mark Mulder	1.00	.40
❑ 66 Mike Cameron	1.00	.40
❑ 67 Corey Koskie	1.00	.40
❑ 68 Marlon Anderson	1.00	.40
❑ 69 Jason Kendall	1.00	.40
❑ 70 J.T. Snow	1.00	.40
❑ 71 Edgar Martinez	1.50	.60
❑ 72 Vernon Wells	1.00	.40
❑ 73 Vladimir Guerrero	2.50	1.00
❑ 74 Adam Dunn	1.00	.40
❑ 75 Barry Zito	1.00	.40
❑ 76 Jeff Kent	1.00	.40
❑ 77 Russ Ortiz	1.00	.40
❑ 78 Phil Nevin	1.00	.40
❑ 79 Carlos Beltran	1.00	.40
❑ 80 Mike Lowell	1.00	.40
❑ 81 Bob Wickman	1.00	.40
❑ 82 Junior Spivey	1.00	.40
❑ 83 Melvin Mora	1.00	.40
❑ 84 Derrek Lee	1.50	.60
❑ 85 Chuck Knoblauch	1.00	.40
❑ 86 Eric Gagne	1.00	.40
❑ 87 Orlando Hernandez	1.00	.40
❑ 88 Robert Person	1.00	.40
❑ 89 Elmer Dessens	1.00	.40
❑ 90 Wade Miller	1.00	.40
❑ 91 Adrian Beltre	1.00	.40
❑ 92 Kazuhiro Sasaki	1.00	.40
❑ 93 Timo Perez	1.00	.40
❑ 94 Jose Vidro	1.00	.40
❑ 95 Geronimo Gil	1.00	.40
❑ 96 Trot Nixon	1.00	.40
❑ 97 Denny Neagle	1.00	.40
❑ 98 Roberto Hernandez	1.00	.40
❑ 99 David Ortiz	2.50	1.00
❑ 100 Robb Nen	1.00	.40
❑ 101 Sidney Ponson	1.00	.40
❑ 102 Kevin Appier	1.00	.40
❑ 103 Javier Lopez	1.00	.40
❑ 104 Jeff Conine	1.00	.40
❑ 105 Mark Buehrle	1.00	.40
❑ 106 Jason Simontacchi	1.00	.40
❑ 107 Jose Jimenez	1.00	.40
❑ 108 Brian Jordan	1.00	.40
❑ 109 Brad Wilkerson	1.00	.40
❑ 110 Scott Hatteberg	1.00	.40
❑ 111 Matt Morris	1.00	.40
❑ 112 Miguel Tejada	1.00	.40
❑ 113 Rafael Furcal	1.00	.40
❑ 114 Steve Cox	1.00	.40
❑ 115 Roy Halladay	1.00	.40
❑ 116 David Eckstein	1.00	.40
❑ 117 Tomo Ohka	1.00	.40
❑ 118 Jack Wilson	1.00	.40
❑ 119 Randall Simon	1.00	.40
❑ 120 Jamie Moyer	1.00	.40
❑ 121 Andy Benes	1.00	.40
❑ 122 Tino Martinez	1.50	.60
❑ 123 Esteban Yan	1.00	.40
❑ 124 Jason Isringhausen	1.00	.40
❑ 125 Chris Carpenter	1.00	.40
❑ 126 Aaron Rowand	1.00	.40
❑ 127 Brandon Inge	1.00	.40
❑ 128 Jose Vizcaino	1.00	.40
❑ 129 Jose Mesa	1.00	.40
❑ 130 Troy Percival	1.00	.40
❑ 131 Jon Lieber	1.00	.40
❑ 132 Brian Giles	1.00	.40
❑ 133 Aaron Boone	1.00	.40
❑ 134 Bobby Higginson	1.00	.40
❑ 135 Luis Rivas	1.00	.40
❑ 136 Troy Glaus	1.00	.40
❑ 137 Jim Thome	1.50	.60
❑ 138 Ramon Martinez	1.00	.40
❑ 139 Jay Gibbons	1.00	.40
❑ 140 Mike Lieberthal	1.00	.40
❑ 141 Juan Uribe	1.00	.40
❑ 142 Gary Sheffield	1.00	.40
❑ 143 Ramon Santiago	1.00	.40
❑ 144 Ben Sheets	1.00	.40
❑ 145 Tony Armas Jr.	1.00	.40
❑ 146 Kazuhisa Ishii	1.00	.40
❑ 147 Erubiel Durazo	1.00	.40
❑ 148 Jerry Hairston Jr.	1.00	.40
❑ 149 Byung-Hyun Kim	1.00	.40
❑ 150 Marcus Giles	1.00	.40
❑ 151 Johnny Damon	1.50	.60
❑ 152 Terrence Long	1.00	.40
❑ 153 Juan Pierre	1.00	.40
❑ 154 Aramis Ramirez	1.00	.40
❑ 155 Brent Abernathy	1.00	.40
❑ 156 Ismael Valdes	1.00	.40
❑ 157 Mike Mussina	1.50	.60
❑ 158 Ramon Hernandez	1.00	.40
❑ 159 Adam Kennedy	1.00	.40
❑ 160 Tony Womack	1.00	.40
❑ 161 Tony Batista	1.00	.40
❑ 162 Kip Wells	1.00	.40
❑ 163 Jeromy Burnitz	1.00	.40
❑ 164 Todd Hundley	1.00	.40
❑ 165 Tim Wakefield	1.00	.40
❑ 166 Derek Lowe	1.00	.40
❑ 167 Jorge Posada	1.50	.60
❑ 168 Ramon Ortiz	1.00	.40
❑ 169 Brent Butler	1.00	.40
❑ 170 Shane Halter	1.00	.40
❑ 171 Matt Lawton	1.00	.40
❑ 172 Alex Sanchez	1.00	.40
❑ 173 Eric Milton	1.00	.40
❑ 174 Vicente Padilla	1.00	.40
❑ 175 Steve Karsay	1.00	.40
❑ 176 Mark Prior	1.50	.60
❑ 177 Kerry Wood	1.00	.40
❑ 178 Jason LaRue	1.00	.40
❑ 179 Danys Baez	1.00	.40
❑ 180 Nick Neugebauer	1.00	.40
❑ 181 Andres Galarraga	1.00	.40
❑ 182 Jason Giambi	1.00	.40
❑ 183 Aubrey Huff	1.00	.40
❑ 184 Juan Gonzalez	1.00	.40
❑ 185 Ugueth Urbina	1.00	.40
❑ 186 Rickey Henderson	2.50	1.00
❑ 187 Brad Fullmer	1.00	.40
❑ 188 Todd Zeile	1.00	.40
❑ 189 Jason Jennings	1.00	.40
❑ 190 Vladimir Nunez	1.00	.40
❑ 191 David Justice	1.00	.40

❑ 192	Brian Lawrence	1.00	.40
❑ 193	Pat Burrell	1.00	.40
❑ 194	Pokey Reese	1.00	.40
❑ 195	Robert Fick	1.00	.40
❑ 196	C.C. Sabathia	1.00	.40
❑ 197	Fernando Vina	1.00	.40
❑ 198	Sean Burroughs	1.00	.40
❑ 199	Ellis Burks	1.00	.40
❑ 200	Joe Randa	1.00	.40
❑ 201	Chris Duncan FY RC	6.00	2.50
❑ 202	Franklin Gutierrez FY RC	3.00	1.25
❑ 203	Adam LaRoche FY	1.50	.60
❑ 204	Manuel Ramirez FY RC	2.50	1.00
❑ 205	Il Kim FY RC	1.50	.60
❑ 206	Daryl Clark FY RC	1.50	.60
❑ 207	Sean Pierce FY	1.50	.60
❑ 208	Andy Marte FY RC	8.00	3.00
❑ 209	Bernie Castro FY RC	1.50	.60
❑ 210	Jason Perry FY RC	2.50	1.00
❑ 211	Jaime Bubela FY RC	1.50	.60
❑ 212	Alexis Rios FY	2.50	1.00
❑ 213	Brendan Harris FY RC	2.50	1.00
❑ 214	Ramon Nivar-Martinez FY RC	1.50	.60
❑ 215	Terry Tiffee FY RC	1.50	.60
❑ 216	Kevin Youkilis FY RC	4.00	1.50
❑ 217	Derell McCall FY RC	1.50	.60
❑ 218	Scott Tyler FY RC	2.50	1.00
❑ 219	Craig Brazell FY RC	1.50	.60
❑ 220	Walter Young FY	1.50	.60
❑ 221	Francisco Rodriguez	1.00	.40
❑ 222	Chipper Jones	2.50	1.00
❑ 223	Chris Singleton	1.00	.40
❑ 224	Cliff Floyd	1.00	.40
❑ 225	Bobby Hill	1.00	.40
❑ 226	Antonio Osuna	1.00	.40
❑ 227	Barry Larkin	1.50	.60
❑ 228	Dean Palmer	1.00	.40
❑ 229	Eric Owens	1.00	.40
❑ 230	Randy Johnson	2.50	1.00
❑ 231	Jeff Suppan	1.00	.40
❑ 232	Eric Karros	1.00	.40
❑ 233	Johan Santana	1.50	.60
❑ 234	Javier Vazquez	1.00	.40
❑ 235	John Thomson	1.00	.40
❑ 236	Nick Johnson	1.00	.40
❑ 237	Mark Ellis	1.00	.40
❑ 238	Doug Glanville	1.00	.40
❑ 239	Ken Griffey Jr.	4.00	1.50
❑ 240	Bubba Trammell	1.00	.40
❑ 241	Livan Hernandez	1.00	.40
❑ 242	Desi Relaford	1.00	.40
❑ 243	Eli Marrero	1.00	.40
❑ 244	Jared Sandberg	1.00	.40
❑ 245	Barry Bonds	6.00	2.50
❑ 246	Aaron Sele	1.00	.40
❑ 247	Derek Jeter	6.00	2.50
❑ 248	Eric Byrnes	1.00	.40
❑ 249	Rich Aurilia	1.00	.40
❑ 250	Joel Pineiro	1.00	.40
❑ 251	Chuck Finley	1.00	.40
❑ 252	Bengie Molina	1.00	.40
❑ 253	Steve Finley	1.00	.40
❑ 254	Marty Cordova	1.00	.40
❑ 255	Shea Hillenbrand	1.00	.40
❑ 256	Milton Bradley	1.00	.40
❑ 257	Carlos Pena	1.00	.40
❑ 258	Brad Ausmus	1.00	.40
❑ 259	Carlos Delgado	1.00	.40
❑ 260	Kevin Mench	1.00	.40
❑ 261	Joe Kennedy	1.00	.40
❑ 262	Mark McLemore	1.00	.40
❑ 263	Bill Mueller	1.00	.40
❑ 264	Ricky Ledee	1.00	.40
❑ 265	Ted Lilly	1.00	.40
❑ 266	Sterling Hitchcock	1.00	.40
❑ 267	Scott Strickland	1.00	.40
❑ 268	Damion Easley	1.00	.40
❑ 269	Torii Hunter	1.00	.40
❑ 270	Brad Radke	1.00	.40
❑ 271	Geoff Jenkins	1.00	.40
❑ 272	Paul Byrd	1.00	.40
❑ 273	Morgan Ensberg	1.00	.40
❑ 274	Mike Maroth	1.00	.40
❑ 275	Mike Hampton	1.00	.40
❑ 276	Flash Gordon	1.00	.40
❑ 277	John Burkett	1.00	.40
❑ 278	Rodrigo Lopez	1.00	.40
❑ 279	Tim Spooneybarger	1.00	.40
❑ 280	Quinton McCracken	1.00	.40
❑ 281	Tim Salmon	1.50	.60
❑ 282	Jarrod Washburn	1.00	.40
❑ 283	Pedro Martinez	1.50	.60
❑ 284	Julio Lugo	1.00	.40
❑ 285	Armando Benitez	1.00	.40
❑ 286	Raul Mondesi	1.00	.40
❑ 287	Robin Ventura	1.00	.40
❑ 288	Bobby Abreu	1.00	.40
❑ 289	Josh Fogg	1.00	.40
❑ 290	Ryan Klesko	1.00	.40
❑ 291	Tsuyoshi Shinjo	1.00	.40
❑ 292	Jim Edmonds	1.00	.40
❑ 293	Chan Ho Park	1.00	.40
❑ 294	John Mabry	1.00	.40
❑ 295	Woody Williams	1.00	.40
❑ 296	Scott Schoeneweis	1.00	.40
❑ 297	Brian Anderson	1.00	.40
❑ 298	Brett Tomko	1.00	.40
❑ 299	Scott Erickson	1.00	.40
❑ 300	Kevin Millar Sox	1.00	.40
❑ 301	Danny Wright	1.00	.40
❑ 302	Jason Schmidt	1.00	.40
❑ 303	Scott Williamson	1.00	.40
❑ 304	Einar Diaz	1.00	.40
❑ 305	Jay Payton	1.00	.40
❑ 306	Juan Acevedo	1.00	.40
❑ 307	Ben Grieve	1.00	.40
❑ 308	Raul Ibanez	1.00	.40
❑ 309	Richie Sexson	1.00	.40
❑ 310	Rick Reed	1.00	.40
❑ 311	Pedro Astacio	1.00	.40
❑ 312	Bud Smith	1.00	.40
❑ 313	Tomas Perez	1.00	.40
❑ 314	Rafael Palmeiro	1.50	.60
❑ 315	Jason Tyner	1.00	.40
❑ 316	Scott Rolen	1.50	.60
❑ 317	Randy Winn	1.00	.40
❑ 318	Ryan Jensen	1.00	.40
❑ 319	Trevor Hoffman	1.00	.40
❑ 320	Craig Wilson	1.00	.40
❑ 321	Jeremy Giambi	1.00	.40
❑ 322	Andy Pettitte	1.50	.60
❑ 323	John Franco	1.00	.40
❑ 324	Felipe Lopez	1.00	.40
❑ 325	Mike Piazza	4.00	1.50
❑ 326	Cristian Guzman	1.00	.40
❑ 327	Jose Hernandez	1.00	.40
❑ 328	Octavio Dotel	1.00	.40
❑ 329	Brad Penny	1.00	.40
❑ 330	Dave Veres	1.00	.40
❑ 331	Ryan Dempster	1.00	.40
❑ 332	Joe Crede	1.00	.40
❑ 333	Chad Hermansen	1.00	.40
❑ 334	Gary Matthews Jr.	1.00	.40
❑ 335	Frank Catalanotto	1.00	.40
❑ 336	Darin Erstad	1.00	.40
❑ 337	Matt Williams	1.00	.40
❑ 338	B.J. Surhoff	1.00	.40
❑ 339	Kerry Ligtenberg	1.00	.40
❑ 340	Mike Bordick	1.00	.40
❑ 341	Joe Girardi	1.00	.40
❑ 342	D'Angelo Jimenez	1.00	.40
❑ 343	Paul Konerko	1.00	.40
❑ 344	Joe Mays	1.00	.40
❑ 345	Marquis Grissom	1.00	.40
❑ 346	Neifi Perez	1.00	.40
❑ 347	Preston Wilson	1.00	.40
❑ 348	Jeff Weaver	1.00	.40
❑ 349	Eric Chavez	1.00	.40
❑ 350	Placido Polanco	1.00	.40
❑ 351	Matt Mantei	1.00	.40
❑ 352	James Baldwin	1.00	.40
❑ 353	Toby Hall	1.00	.40
❑ 354	Benji Gil	1.00	.40
❑ 355	Damian Moss	1.00	.40
❑ 356	Jorge Julio	1.00	.40
❑ 357	Matt Clement	1.00	.40
❑ 358	Lee Stevens	1.00	.40
❑ 359	Dave Roberts	1.00	.40
❑ 360	J.C. Romero	1.00	.40
❑ 361	Bartolo Colon	1.00	.40
❑ 362	Roger Cedeno	1.00	.40
❑ 363	Mariano Rivera	2.50	1.00
❑ 364	Billy Koch	1.00	.40
❑ 365	Manny Ramirez	1.50	.60
❑ 366	Travis Lee	1.00	.40
❑ 367	Oliver Perez	1.00	.40
❑ 368	Tim Worrell	1.00	.40
❑ 369	Damian Miller	1.00	.40
❑ 370	John Smoltz	1.50	.60
❑ 371	Willis Roberts	1.00	.40
❑ 372	Tim Hudson	1.00	.40
❑ 373	Moises Alou	1.00	.40
❑ 374	Corky Miller	1.00	.40
❑ 375	Ben Broussard	1.00	.40
❑ 376	Gabe Kapler	1.00	.40
❑ 377	Chris Woodward	1.00	.40
❑ 378	Todd Hollandsworth	1.00	.40
❑ 379	So Taguchi	1.00	.40
❑ 380	John Olerud	1.00	.40
❑ 381	Reggie Sanders	1.00	.40
❑ 382	Jake Peavy	1.00	.40
❑ 383	Kris Benson	1.00	.40
❑ 384	Ray Durham	1.00	.40
❑ 385	Boomer Wells	1.00	.40
❑ 386	Tom Glavine	1.50	.60
❑ 387	Antonio Alfonseca	1.00	.40
❑ 388	Keith Foulke	1.00	.40
❑ 389	Shawn Estes	1.00	.40
❑ 390	Mark Grace	1.50	.60
❑ 391	Dmitri Young	1.00	.40
❑ 392	A.J. Burnett	1.00	.40
❑ 393	Richard Hidalgo	1.00	.40
❑ 394	Mike Sweeney	1.00	.40
❑ 395	Doug Mientkiewicz	1.00	.40
❑ 396	Cory Lidle	1.00	.40
❑ 397	Jeff Bagwell	1.50	.60
❑ 398	Steve Sparks	1.00	.40
❑ 399	Sandy Alomar Jr.	1.00	.40
❑ 400	John Lackey	1.00	.40
❑ 401	Rick Helling	1.00	.40
❑ 402	Carlos Lee	1.00	.40
❑ 403	Garret Anderson	1.00	.40
❑ 404	Vinny Castilla	1.00	.40
❑ 405	David Bell	1.00	.40
❑ 406	Freddy Garcia	1.00	.40
❑ 407	Scott Spiezio	1.00	.40
❑ 408	Russell Branyan	1.00	.40
❑ 409	Jose Contreras RC	3.00	1.25
❑ 410	Kevin Brown	1.00	.40
❑ 411	Tyler Houston	1.00	.40
❑ 412	A.J. Pierzynski	1.00	.40
❑ 413	Peter Bergeron	1.00	.40
❑ 414	Brett Myers	1.00	.40
❑ 415	Kenny Lofton	1.00	.40
❑ 416	Ben Davis	1.00	.40
❑ 417	J.D. Drew	1.00	.40
❑ 418	Ricky Gutierrez	1.00	.40
❑ 419	Mark Redman	1.00	.40
❑ 420	Juan Encarnacion	1.00	.40
❑ 421	Bryan Bullington DP RC	1.50	.60
❑ 422	Jeremy Guthrie DP	1.50	.60
❑ 423	Joey Gomes DP RC	1.50	.60
❑ 424	Evel Bastida-Martinez DP RC	1.50	.60
❑ 425	Brian Wright DP RC	1.50	.60
❑ 426	B.J. Upton DP	2.50	1.00
❑ 427	Jeff Francis DP	1.50	.60
❑ 428	Jeremy Hermida DP	2.50	1.00
❑ 429	Khalil Greene DP	2.50	1.00
❑ 430	Darrell Rasner DP RC	1.50	.60
❑ 431	B.Phillips/V.Martinez	2.50	1.00
❑ 432	H.Choi/N.Jackson	1.50	.60
❑ 433	D.Willis/J.Stokes	2.50	1.00
❑ 434	C.Tracy/L.Overbay	1.50	.60
❑ 435	J.Borchard/C.Malone	1.50	.60
❑ 436	J.Mauer/J.Morneau	2.50	1.00
❑ 437	D.Henson/B.Claussen	1.50	.60
❑ 438	C.Utley/G.Floyd	2.50	1.00
❑ 439	T.Bozied/X.Nady	1.50	.60
❑ 440	A.Heilman/J.Reyes	1.50	.60

2003 Topps Chrome Traded

❑ COMPLETE SET (275)	120.00	60.00
❑ COMMON CARD (T1-T120)	.75	.30
❑ COMMON CARD (121-165)	1.00	.40
❑ COMMON CARD (166-275)	1.00	.40

❑ 2 PER 2003 TOPPS TRADED HOBBY PACK

❑ 2 PER 2003 TOPPS TRADED HTA PACK
❑ 2 PER 2003 TOPPS TRADED RETAIL PACK
❑ T1 Juan Pierre .75 .30
❑ T2 Mark Grudzielanek .75 .30
❑ T3 Tanyon Sturtze .75 .30
❑ T4 Greg Vaughn .75 .30
❑ T5 Greg Myers .75 .30
❑ T6 Randall Simon .75 .30
❑ T7 Todd Hundley .75 .30
❑ T8 Marlon Anderson .75 .30
❑ T9 Jeff Reboulet .75 .30
❑ T10 Alex Sanchez .75 .30
❑ T11 Mike Rivera .75 .30
❑ T12 Todd Walker .75 .30
❑ T13 Ray King .75 .30
❑ T14 Shawn Estes .75 .30
❑ T15 Gary Matthews Jr. .75 .30
❑ T16 Jaret Wright .75 .30
❑ T17 Edgardo Alfonzo .75 .30
❑ T18 Omar Daal .75 .30
❑ T19 Ryan Rupe .75 .30
❑ T20 Tony Clark .75 .30
❑ T21 Jeff Suppan .75 .30
❑ T22 Mike Stanton .75 .30
❑ T23 Ramon Martinez .75 .30
❑ T24 Armando Rios .75 .30
❑ T25 Johnny Estrada .75 .30
❑ T26 Joe Girardi .75 .30
❑ T27 Ivan Rodriguez 1.25 .50
❑ T28 Robert Fick .75 .30
❑ T29 Rick White .75 .30
❑ T30 Robert Person .75 .30
❑ T31 Alan Benes .75 .30
❑ T32 Chris Carpenter .75 .30
❑ T33 Chris Widger .75 .30
❑ T34 Travis Hafner .75 .30
❑ T35 Mike Venafro .75 .30
❑ T36 Jon Lieber .75 .30
❑ T37 Orlando Hernandez .75 .30
❑ T38 Aaron Myette .75 .30
❑ T39 Paul Bako .75 .30
❑ T40 Erubiel Durazo .75 .30
❑ T41 Mark Guthrie .75 .30
❑ T42 Steve Avery .75 .30
❑ T43 Damian Jackson .75 .30
❑ T44 Rey Ordonez .75 .30
❑ T45 John Flaherty .75 .30
❑ T46 Byung-Hyun Kim .75 .30
❑ T47 Tom Goodwin .75 .30
❑ T48 Elmer Dessens .75 .30
❑ T49 Al Martin .75 .30
❑ T50 Gene Kingsale .75 .30
❑ T51 Lenny Harris .75 .30
❑ T52 David Ortiz Sox 2.00 .75
❑ T53 Jose Lima .75 .30
❑ T54 Mike Difelice .75 .30
❑ T55 Jose Hernandez .75 .30
❑ T56 Todd Zeile .75 .30
❑ T57 Roberto Hernandez .75 .30
❑ T58 Albie Lopez .75 .30
❑ T59 Roberto Alomar 1.25 .50
❑ T60 Russ Ortiz .75 .30
❑ T61 Brian Daubach .75 .30
❑ T62 Carl Everett .75 .30
❑ T63 Jeromy Burnitz .75 .30
❑ T64 Mark Bellhorn .75 .30
❑ T65 Ruben Sierra .75 .30
❑ T66 Mike Fetters .75 .30
❑ T67 Armando Benitez .75 .30
❑ T68 Deivi Cruz .75 .30
❑ T69 Jose Cruz Jr. .75 .30
❑ T70 Jeremy Fikac .75 .30
❑ T71 Jeff Kent .75 .30
❑ T72 Andres Galarraga .75 .30
❑ T73 Rickey Henderson 2.00 .75
❑ T74 Royce Clayton .75 .30
❑ T75 Troy O'Leary .75 .30
❑ T76 Ron Coomer .75 .30
❑ T77 Greg Colbrunn .75 .30
❑ T78 Wes Helms .75 .30
❑ T79 Kevin Millwood .75 .30
❑ T80 Damion Easley .75 .30
❑ T81 Bobby Kielty .75 .30
❑ T82 Keith Osik .75 .30
❑ T83 Ramiro Mendoza .75 .30
❑ T84 Shea Hillenbrand .75 .30
❑ T85 Shannon Stewart .75 .30
❑ T86 Eddie Perez .75 .30
❑ T87 Ugueth Urbina .75 .30
❑ T88 Orlando Palmeiro .75 .30
❑ T89 Graeme Lloyd .75 .30
❑ T90 John Vander Wal .75 .30
❑ T91 Gary Bennett .75 .30
❑ T92 Shane Reynolds .75 .30
❑ T93 Steve Parris .75 .30
❑ T94 Julio Lugo .75 .30
❑ T95 John Halama .75 .30
❑ T96 Carlos Baerga .75 .30
❑ T97 Jim Parque .75 .30
❑ T98 Mike Williams .75 .30
❑ T99 Fred McGriff 1.25 .50
❑ T100 Kenny Rogers .75 .30
❑ T101 Matt Herges .75 .30
❑ T102 Jay Bell .75 .30
❑ T103 Esteban Yan .75 .30
❑ T104 Eric Owens .75 .30
❑ T105 Aaron Fultz .75 .30
❑ T106 Rey Sanchez .75 .30
❑ T107 Jim Thome 1.25 .50
❑ T108 Aaron Boone .75 .30
❑ T109 Raul Mondesi .75 .30
❑ T110 Kenny Lofton .75 .30
❑ T111 Jose Guillen .75 .30
❑ T112 Aramis Ramirez .75 .30
❑ T113 Sidney Ponson .75 .30
❑ T114 Scott Williamson .75 .30
❑ T115 Robin Ventura .75 .30
❑ T116 Dusty Baker MG .75 .30
❑ T117 Felipe Alou MG .75 .30
❑ T118 Buck Showalter MG .75 .30
❑ T119 Jack McKeon MG .75 .30
❑ T120 Art Howe MG .75 .30
❑ T121 Bobby Crosby PROS 1.00 .40
❑ T122 Adrian Gonzalez PROS 1.00 .40
❑ T123 Kevin Cash PROS 1.00 .40
❑ T124 Shin-Soo Choo PROS 1.00 .40
❑ T125 Chin-Feng Chen PROS 2.50 1.00
❑ T126 Miguel Cabrera PROS 2.50 1.00
❑ T127 Jason Young PROS 1.00 .40
❑ T128 Alex Herrera PROS 1.00 .40
❑ T129 Jason Dubois PROS 1.00 .40
❑ T130 Jeff Mathis PROS 1.00 .40
❑ T131 Casey Kotchman PROS 1.00 .40
❑ T132 Ed Rogers PROS 1.00 .40
❑ T133 Wilson Betemit PROS 1.00 .40
❑ T134 Jim Kavourias PROS 1.00 .40
❑ T135 Taylor Buchholz PROS 1.00 .40
❑ T136 Adam LaRoche PROS 1.00 .40
❑ T137 Dallas McPherson PROS 1.00 .40
❑ T138 Jesus Cota PROS 1.00 .40
❑ T139 Clint Nageotte PROS 1.00 .40
❑ T140 Boof Bonser PROS 1.00 .40
❑ T141 Walter Young PROS 1.00 .40
❑ T142 Joe Crede PROS 1.00 .40
❑ T143 Denny Bautista PROS 1.00 .40
❑ T144 Victor Diaz PROS 1.00 .40
❑ T145 Chris Narveson PROS 1.00 .40
❑ T146 Gabe Gross PROS 1.00 .40
❑ T147 Jimmy Journell PROS 1.00 .40
❑ T148 Rafael Soriano PROS 1.00 .40
❑ T149 Jerome Williams PROS 1.00 .40
❑ T150 Aaron Cook PROS 1.00 .40
❑ T151 Anastacio Martinez PROS 1.00 .40
❑ T152 Scott Hairston PROS 1.00 .40
❑ T153 John Buck PROS 1.00 .40
❑ T154 Ryan Ludwick PROS 1.00 .40
❑ T155 Chris Bootcheck PROS 1.00 .40
❑ T156 John Rheinecker PROS 1.00 .40
❑ T157 Jason Lane PROS 1.00 .40
❑ T159 Adam Wainwright PROS 1.00 .40
❑ T160 Jason Arnold PROS 1.00 .40
❑ T161 Jonny Gomes PROS 1.50 .60
❑ T162 James Loney PROS 1.25 .50
❑ T163 Mike Fontenot PROS 1.00 .40
❑ T164 Khalil Greene PROS 2.50 1.00
❑ T165 Sean Burnett PROS 1.00 .40
❑ T166 David Martinez FY RC 1.00 .40
❑ T167 Felix Pie FY RC 10.00 4.00
❑ T168 Joe Valentine FY RC 1.00 .40
❑ T169 Brandon Webb FY RC 6.00 2.50
❑ T170 Matt Diaz FY RC 1.50 .60
❑ T171 Lew Ford FY RC 1.25 .50
❑ T172 Jeremy Griffiths FY RC 1.00 .40
❑ T173 Matt Hensley FY RC 1.00 .40
❑ T174 Charlie Manning FY RC 1.00 .40
❑ T175 Elizardo Ramirez FY RC 1.25 .50
❑ T176 Greg Aquino FY RC 1.00 .40
❑ T177 Felix Sanchez FY RC 1.00 .40
❑ T178 Kelly Shoppach FY RC 2.00 .75
❑ T179 Bubba Nelson FY RC 1.25 .50
❑ T180 Mike Oâ ™Keefe FY RC 1.00 .40
❑ T181 Hanley Ramirez FY RC 10.00 4.00
❑ T182 Todd Wellemeyer FY RC 1.00 .40
❑ T183 Dustin Moseley FY RC 1.00 .40
❑ T184 Eric Crozier FY RC 1.25 .50
❑ T185 Ryan Shealy FY RC 5.00 2.00
❑ T186 Jeremy Bonderman FY RC 8.00 3.00
❑ T187 T.Story-Harden FY RC 1.00 .40
❑ T188 Dusty Brown FY RC 1.00 .40
❑ T189 Rob Hammock FY RC 1.00 .40
❑ T190 Jorge Piedra FY RC 1.25 .50
❑ T191 Chris De La Cruz FY RC 1.00 .40
❑ T192 Eli Whiteside FY RC 1.00 .40
❑ T193 Jason Kubel FY RC 3.00 1.25
❑ T194 Jon Schuerholz FY RC 1.00 .40
❑ T195 Stephen Randolph FY RC 1.00 .40
❑ T196 Andy Sisco FY RC 1.00 .40
❑ T197 Sean Smith FY RC 1.25 .50
❑ T198 Jon-Mark Sprowl FY RC 1.00 .40
❑ T199 Matt Kata FY RC 1.00 .40
❑ T200 Robinson Cano FY RC 15.00 6.00
❑ T201 Nook Logan FY RC 1.25 .50
❑ T202 Ben Francisco FY RC 1.00 .40
❑ T203 Arnie Munoz FY RC 1.00 .40
❑ T204 Ozzie Chavez FY RC 1.00 .40
❑ T205 Eric Riggs FY RC 1.25 .50
❑ T206 Beau Kemp FY RC 1.00 .40
❑ T207 Travis Wong FY RC 1.25 .50
❑ T208 Dustin Yount FY RC 1.25 .50
❑ T209 Brian McCann FY RC 15.00 6.00
❑ T210 Wilton Reynolds FY RC 1.25 .50
❑ T211 Matt Bruback FY RC 1.00 .40
❑ T212 Andrew Brown FY RC 1.25 .50
❑ T213 Edgar Gonzalez FY RC 1.00 .40
❑ T214 Eider Torres FY RC 1.00 .40
❑ T215 Aquilino Lopez FY RC 1.00 .40
❑ T216 Bobby Basham FY RC 1.00 .40
❑ T217 Tim Olson FY RC 1.00 .40
❑ T218 Nathan Panther FY RC 1.00 .40
❑ T219 Bryan Grace FY RC 1.00 .40
❑ T220 Dusty Gomon FY RC 1.25 .50
❑ T221 Wil Ledezma FY RC 1.00 .40
❑ T222 Josh Willingham FY RC 2.50 1.00
❑ T223 David Cash FY RC 1.00 .40
❑ T224 Oscar Villarreal FY RC 1.00 .40
❑ T225 Jeff Duncan FY RC 1.00 .40
❑ T226 Kade Johnson FY RC 1.00 .40
❑ T227 Luke Steidlmayer FY RC 1.00 .40
❑ T228 Brandon Watson FY RC 1.00 .40
❑ T229 Jose Morales FY RC 1.00 .40
❑ T230 Mike Gallo FY RC 1.00 .40
❑ T231 Tyler Adamczyk FY RC 1.00 .40
❑ T232 Adam Stern FY RC 1.00 .40
❑ T233 Brennan King FY RC 1.00 .40
❑ T234 Dan Haren FY RC 2.00 .75
❑ T235 Michel Hernandez FY RC 1.00 .40
❑ T236 Ben Fritz FY RC 1.00 .40
❑ T237 Clay Hensley FY RC 1.00 .40
❑ T238 Tyler Johnson FY RC 1.00 .40
❑ T239 Pete LaForest FY RC 1.00 .40

Card	Player		
❑ T240	Tyler Martin FY RC	1.00	.40
❑ T241	J.D. Durbin FY RC	1.00	.40
❑ T242	Shane Victorino FY RC	1.50	.60
❑ T243	Rajai Davis FY RC	1.00	.40
❑ T244	Ismael Castro FY RC	1.00	.40
❑ T245	Chien-Ming Wang FY RC	10.00	4.00
❑ T246	Travis Ishikawa FY RC	2.00	.75
❑ T247	Corey Shafer FY RC	1.00	.40
❑ T248	Gary Schneidmiller FY RC	1.00	.40
❑ T249	Dave Pember FY RC	1.00	.40
❑ T250	Keith Stamler FY RC	1.00	.40
❑ T251	Tyson Graham FY RC	1.00	.40
❑ T252	Ryan Cameron FY RC	1.00	.40
❑ T253	Eric Eckenstahler FY	1.00	.40
❑ T254	Matthew Peterson FY RC	1.00	.40
❑ T255	Dustin McGowan FY RC	1.25	.50
❑ T256	Prentice Redman FY RC	1.00	.40
❑ T257	Haj Turay FY RC	1.00	.40
❑ T258	Carlos Guzman FY RC	1.25	.50
❑ T259	Matt DeMarco FY RC	1.00	.40
❑ T260	Derek Michaelis FY RC	1.00	.40
❑ T261	Brian Burgamy FY RC	1.00	.40
❑ T262	Jay Sitzman FY RC	1.00	.40
❑ T263	Chris Fallon FY RC	1.00	.40
❑ T264	Mike Adams FY RC	1.00	.40
❑ T265	Clint Barmes FY RC	2.50	1.00
❑ T266	Eric Reed FY RC	1.00	.40
❑ T267	Willie Eyre FY RC	1.00	.40
❑ T268	Carlos Duran FY RC	1.00	.40
❑ T269	Nick Trzesniak FY RC	1.00	.40
❑ T270	Ferdin Tejeda FY RC	1.00	.40
❑ T271	Michael Garciaparra FY RC	1.00	.40
❑ T272	Michael Hinckley FY RC	1.25	.50
❑ T273	Branden Florence FY RC	1.00	.40
❑ T274	Trent Oeltjen FY RC	1.25	.50
❑ T275	Mike Neu FY RC	1.00	.40

2004 Topps Chrome

Card	Player		
❑	COMP.SERIES 1 w/o SP's (220)	80.00	40.00
❑	COMP.SERIES 2 w/o SP's (220)	80.00	40.00
❑	COMMON (1-210/257-466)	1.00	.40
❑	COMMON (211-220/247-256)	2.00	.75
❑	COMMON AU (221-246)	10.00	4.00
❑ 1	Jim Thome	1.50	.60
❑ 2	Reggie Sanders	1.00	.40
❑ 3	Mark Kotsay	1.00	.40
❑ 4	Edgardo Alfonzo	1.00	.40
❑ 5	Tim Wakefield	1.00	.40
❑ 6	Moises Alou	1.00	.40
❑ 7	Jorge Julio	1.00	.40
❑ 8	Bartolo Colon	1.00	.40
❑ 9	Chan Ho Park	1.00	.40
❑ 10	Ichiro Suzuki	5.00	2.00
❑ 11	Kevin Millwood	1.00	.40
❑ 12	Preston Wilson	1.00	.40
❑ 13	Tom Glavine	1.50	.60
❑ 14	Junior Spivey	1.00	.40
❑ 15	Marcus Giles	1.00	.40
❑ 16	David Segui	1.00	.40
❑ 17	Kevin Millar	1.00	.40
❑ 18	Corey Patterson	1.00	.40
❑ 19	Aaron Rowand	1.00	.40
❑ 20	Derek Jeter	5.00	2.00
❑ 21	Luis Castillo	1.00	.40
❑ 22	Manny Ramirez	1.50	.60
❑ 23	Jay Payton	1.00	.40
❑ 24	Bobby Higginson	1.00	.40
❑ 25	Lance Berkman	1.00	.40
❑ 26	Juan Pierre	1.00	.40
❑ 27	Mike Mussina	1.50	.60
❑ 28	Fred McGriff	1.50	.60
❑ 29	Richie Sexson	1.00	.40
❑ 30	Tim Hudson	1.00	.40
❑ 31	Mike Piazza	4.00	1.50
❑ 32	Brad Radke	1.00	.40
❑ 33	Jeff Weaver	1.00	.40
❑ 34	Ramon Hernandez	1.00	.40
❑ 35	David Bell	1.00	.40
❑ 36	Randy Wolf	1.00	.40
❑ 37	Jake Peavy	1.00	.40
❑ 38	Tim Worrell	1.00	.40
❑ 39	Gil Meche	1.00	.40
❑ 40	Albert Pujols	5.00	2.00
❑ 41	Michael Young	1.00	.40
❑ 42	Josh Phelps	1.00	.40
❑ 43	Brendan Donnelly	1.00	.40
❑ 44	Steve Finley	1.00	.40
❑ 45	John Smoltz	1.50	.60
❑ 46	Jay Gibbons	1.00	.40
❑ 47	Trot Nixon	1.00	.40
❑ 48	Carl Pavano	1.00	.40
❑ 49	Frank Thomas	2.50	1.00
❑ 50	Mark Prior	1.50	.60
❑ 51	Danny Graves	1.00	.40
❑ 52	Milton Bradley	1.00	.40
❑ 53	Kris Benson	1.00	.40
❑ 54	Ryan Klesko	1.00	.40
❑ 55	Mike Lowell	1.00	.40
❑ 56	Geoff Blum	1.00	.40
❑ 57	Michael Tucker	1.00	.40
❑ 58	Paul Lo Duca	1.00	.40
❑ 59	Vicente Padilla	1.00	.40
❑ 60	Jacque Jones	1.00	.40
❑ 61	Fernando Tatis	1.00	.40
❑ 62	Ty Wigginton	1.00	.40
❑ 63	Rich Aurilia	1.00	.40
❑ 64	Andy Pettitte	1.50	.60
❑ 65	Terrence Long	1.00	.40
❑ 66	Cliff Floyd	1.00	.40
❑ 67	Mariano Rivera	2.50	1.00
❑ 68	Kelvim Escobar	1.00	.40
❑ 69	Marlon Byrd	1.00	.40
❑ 70	Mark Mulder	1.00	.40
❑ 71	Francisco Cordero	1.00	.40
❑ 72	Carlos Guillen	1.00	.40
❑ 73	Fernando Vina	1.00	.40
❑ 74	Lance Carter	1.00	.40
❑ 75	Hank Blalock	1.00	.40
❑ 76	Jimmy Rollins	1.00	.40
❑ 77	Francisco Rodriguez	1.00	.40
❑ 78	Javy Lopez	1.00	.40
❑ 79	Jerry Hairston Jr.	1.00	.40
❑ 80	Andruw Jones	1.50	.60
❑ 81	Rodrigo Lopez	1.00	.40
❑ 82	Johnny Damon	1.50	.60
❑ 83	Hee Seop Choi	1.00	.40
❑ 84	Kazuhiro Sasaki	1.00	.40
❑ 85	Danny Bautista	1.00	.40
❑ 86	Matt Lawton	1.00	.40
❑ 87	Juan Uribe	1.00	.40
❑ 88	Rafael Furcal	1.00	.40
❑ 89	Kyle Farnsworth	1.00	.40
❑ 90	Jose Vidro	1.00	.40
❑ 91	Luis Rivas	1.00	.40
❑ 92	Hideo Nomo	2.50	1.00
❑ 93	Javier Vazquez	1.00	.40
❑ 94	Al Leiter	1.00	.40
❑ 95	Jose Valentin	1.00	.40
❑ 96	Alex Cintron	1.00	.40
❑ 97	Zach Day	1.00	.40
❑ 98	Jorge Posada	1.50	.60
❑ 99	C.C. Sabathia	1.00	.40
❑ 100	Alex Rodriguez	4.00	1.50
❑ 101	Brad Penny	1.00	.40
❑ 102	Brad Ausmus	1.00	.40
❑ 103	Raul Ibanez	1.00	.40
❑ 104	Mike Hampton	1.00	.40
❑ 105	Adrian Beltre	1.00	.40
❑ 106	Ramiro Mendoza	1.00	.40
❑ 107	Rocco Baldelli	1.00	.40
❑ 108	Esteban Loaiza	1.00	.40
❑ 109	Russell Branyan	1.00	.40
❑ 110	Todd Helton	1.50	.60
❑ 111	Braden Looper	1.00	.40
❑ 112	Octavio Dotel	1.00	.40
❑ 113	Mike MacDougal	1.00	.40
❑ 114	Cesar Izturis	1.00	.40
❑ 115	Johan Santana	2.50	1.00
❑ 116	Jose Contreras	1.00	.40
❑ 117	Placido Polanco	1.00	.40
❑ 118	Jason Phillips	1.00	.40
❑ 119	Orlando Hudson	1.00	.40
❑ 120	Vernon Wells	1.00	.40
❑ 121	Ben Grieve	1.00	.40
❑ 122	Dave Roberts	1.00	.40
❑ 123	Ismael Valdes	1.00	.40
❑ 124	Eric Owens	1.00	.40
❑ 125	Curt Schilling	1.00	.40
❑ 126	Russ Ortiz	1.00	.40
❑ 127	Mark Buehrle	1.00	.40
❑ 128	Doug Mientkiewicz	1.00	.40
❑ 129	Dmitri Young	1.00	.40
❑ 130	Kazuhisa Ishii	1.00	.40
❑ 131	A.J. Pierzynski	1.00	.40
❑ 132	Brad Wilkerson	1.00	.40
❑ 133	Joe McEwing	1.00	.40
❑ 134	Alex Cora	1.00	.40
❑ 135	Jose Cruz Jr.	1.00	.40
❑ 136	Carlos Zambrano	1.00	.40
❑ 137	Jeff Kent	1.00	.40
❑ 138	Shigetoshi Hasegawa	1.00	.40
❑ 139	Jarrod Washburn	1.00	.40
❑ 140	Greg Maddux	4.00	1.50
❑ 141	Josh Beckett	1.00	.40
❑ 142	Miguel Batista	1.00	.40
❑ 143	Omar Vizquel	1.50	.60
❑ 144	Alex Gonzalez	1.00	.40
❑ 145	Billy Wagner	1.00	.40
❑ 146	Brian Jordan	1.00	.40
❑ 147	Wes Helms	1.00	.40
❑ 148	Deivi Cruz	1.00	.40
❑ 149	Alex Gonzalez	1.00	.40
❑ 150	Jason Giambi	1.00	.40
❑ 151	Erubiel Durazo	1.00	.40
❑ 152	Mike Lieberthal	1.00	.40
❑ 153	Jason Kendall	1.00	.40
❑ 154	Xavier Nady	1.00	.40
❑ 155	Kirk Rueter	1.00	.40
❑ 156	Mike Cameron	1.00	.40
❑ 157	Miguel Cairo	1.00	.40
❑ 158	Woody Williams	1.00	.40
❑ 159	Toby Hall	1.00	.40
❑ 160	Bernie Williams	1.50	.60
❑ 161	Darin Erstad	1.00	.40
❑ 162	Matt Mantei	1.00	.40
❑ 163	Shawn Chacon	1.00	.40
❑ 164	Bill Mueller	1.00	.40
❑ 165	Damian Miller	1.00	.40
❑ 166	Tony Graffanino	1.00	.40
❑ 167	Sean Casey	1.00	.40
❑ 168	Brandon Phillips	1.00	.40
❑ 169	Runelvys Hernandez	1.00	.40
❑ 170	Adam Dunn	1.00	.40
❑ 171	Carlos Lee	1.00	.40
❑ 172	Juan Encarnacion	1.00	.40
❑ 173	Angel Berroa	1.00	.40
❑ 174	Desi Relaford	1.00	.40
❑ 175	Joe Mays	1.00	.40
❑ 176	Ben Sheets	1.00	.40
❑ 177	Eddie Guardado	1.00	.40
❑ 178	Rocky Biddle	1.00	.40
❑ 179	Eric Gagne	1.00	.40
❑ 180	Eric Chavez	1.00	.40
❑ 181	Jason Michaels	1.00	.40
❑ 182	Dustan Mohr	1.00	.40
❑ 183	Kip Wells	1.00	.40
❑ 184	Brian Lawrence	1.00	.40
❑ 185	Bret Boone	1.00	.40
❑ 186	Tino Martinez	1.50	.60
❑ 187	Aubrey Huff	1.00	.40
❑ 188	Kevin Mench	1.00	.40
❑ 189	Tim Salmon	1.50	.60
❑ 190	Carlos Delgado	1.00	.40
❑ 191	John Lackey	1.00	.40
❑ 192	Eric Byrnes	1.00	.40
❑ 193	Luis Matos	1.00	.40
❑ 194	Derek Lowe	1.00	.40
❑ 195	Mark Grudzielanek	1.00	.40
❑ 196	Tom Gordon	1.00	.40
❑ 197	Matt Clement	1.00	.40

198	Byung-Hyun Kim	1.00	.40
199	Brandon Inge	1.00	.40
200	Nomar Garciaparra	4.00	1.50
201	Frank Catalanotto	1.00	.40
202	Cristian Guzman	1.00	.40
203	Bo Hart	1.00	.40
204	Jack Wilson	1.00	.40
205	Ray Durham	1.00	.40
206	Freddy Garcia	1.00	.40
207	J.D. Drew	1.00	.40
208	Orlando Cabrera	1.00	.40
209	Roy Halladay	1.00	.40
210	David Eckstein	1.00	.40
211	Omar Falcon FY RC	2.00	.75
212	Todd Self FY RC	3.00	1.25
213	David Murphy FY RC	3.00	1.25
214	Dioner Navarro FY RC	3.00	1.25
215	Marcus McBeth FY RC	2.00	.75
216	Chris O'Riordan FY RC	2.00	.75
217	Rodney Choy Foo FY RC	2.00	.75
218	Tim Frend FY RC	2.00	.75
219	Yadier Molina FY RC	6.00	2.50
220	Zach Duke FY RC	5.00	2.00
221	Anthony Lerew FY AU RC	15.00	6.00
222	B.Hawksworth FY AU RC	15.00	6.00
223	Brayan Pena FY AU RC	10.00	4.00
224	Craig Ansman FY AU RC	10.00	4.00
225	Jon Knott FY AU RC	10.00	4.00
226	Josh Labandeira FY AU RC	10.00	4.00
227	Khalid Ballouli FY AU RC	10.00	4.00
228	Kyle Davies FY AU RC	25.00	10.00
229	Matt Creighton FY AU RC	10.00	4.00
230	Mike Gosling FY AU RC	10.00	4.00
231	Nic Ungs FY AU RC	10.00	4.00
232	Zach Miner FY AU RC	25.00	10.00
233	Donald Levinski FY AU RC	10.00	4.00
234A	Bradley Sullivan FY AU RC	15.00	6.00
234B	B.Sullivan FY AU ERR 345	25.00	10.00
235	Carlos Quentin FY AU RC	40.00	20.00
236	Conor Jackson FY AU RC	50.00	30.00
237	Estee Harris FY AU RC	15.00	6.00
238	Jeffrey Allison FY AU RC	10.00	4.00
239	Kyle Sleeth FY AU RC	15.00	6.00
240	Matthew Moses FY AU RC	15.00	6.00
241	Tim Stauffer FY AU RC	10.00	4.00
242	Brad Snyder FY AU RC	12.00	5.00
243	Jason Hirsh FY AU RC	25.00	10.00
244	L.Milledge FY AU RC	50.00	20.00
245	Logan Kensing FY AU RC	10.00	4.00
246	Kory Casto FY AU RC	15.00	6.00
247	David Aardsma FY RC	3.00	1.25
248	Omar Quintanilla FY RC	3.00	1.25
249	Ervin Santana FY RC	5.00	2.00
250	Merkin Valdez FY RC	2.00	.75
251	Vito Chiaravalloti FY RC	2.00	.75
252	Travis Blackley FY RC	2.00	.75
253	Chris Shelton FY RC	3.00	1.25
254	Rudy Guillen FY RC	3.00	1.25
255	Bobby Brownlie FY RC	2.50	1.00
256	Paul Maholm FY RC	4.00	1.50
257	Roger Clemens	5.00	2.00
258	Laynce Nix	1.00	.40
259	Eric Hinske	1.00	.40
260	Ivan Rodriguez	1.50	.60
261	Brandon Webb	1.00	.40
262	Jhonny Peralta	1.00	.40
263	Adam Kennedy	1.00	.40
264	Tony Batista	1.00	.40
265	Jeff Suppan	1.00	.40
266	Kenny Lofton	1.00	.40
267	Scott Sullivan	1.00	.40
268	Ken Griffey Jr.	4.00	1.50
269	Juan Rivera	1.00	.40
270	Larry Walker	1.00	.40
271	Todd Hollandsworth	1.00	.40
272	Carlos Beltran	1.00	.40
273	Carl Crawford	1.00	.40
274	Karim Garcia	1.00	.40
275	Jose Reyes	1.00	.40
276	Brandon Duckworth	1.00	.40
277	Brian Giles	1.00	.40
278	J.T. Snow	1.00	.40
279	Jamie Moyer	1.00	.40
280	Julio Lugo	1.00	.40
281	Mark Teixeira	1.50	.60
282	Cory Lidle	1.00	.40
283	Lyle Overbay	1.00	.40
284	Troy Percival	1.00	.40
285	Robby Hammock	1.00	.40
286	Jason Johnson	1.00	.40
287	Damian Rolls	1.00	.40
288	Antonio Alfonseca	1.00	.40
289	Tom Goodwin	1.00	.40
290	Paul Konerko	1.00	.40
291	D'Angelo Jimenez	1.00	.40
292	Ben Broussard	1.00	.40
293	Magglio Ordonez	1.00	.40
294	Carlos Pena	1.00	.40
295	Chad Fox	1.00	.40
296	Jeriome Robertson	1.00	.40
297	Travis Hafner	1.00	.40
298	Joe Randa	1.00	.40
299	Brady Clark	1.00	.40
300	Barry Zito	1.00	.40
301	Ruben Sierra	1.00	.40
302	Brett Myers	1.00	.40
303	Oliver Perez	1.00	.40
304	Benito Santiago	1.00	.40
305	David Ross	1.00	.40
306	Joe Nathan	1.00	.40
307	Jim Edmonds	1.00	.40
308	Matt Kata	1.00	.40
309	Vinny Castilla	1.00	.40
310	Marty Cordova	1.00	.40
311	Aramis Ramirez	1.00	.40
312	Carl Everett	1.00	.40
313	Ryan Freel	1.00	.40
314	Mark Bellhorn Sox	1.00	.40
315	Joe Mauer	2.50	1.00
316	Tim Redding	1.00	.40
317	Jeromy Burnitz	1.00	.40
318	Miguel Cabrera	1.50	.60
319	Ramon Nivar	1.00	.40
320	Casey Blake	1.00	.40
321	Adam LaRoche	1.00	.40
322	Jermaine Dye	1.00	.40
323	Jerome Williams	1.00	.40
324	John Olerud	1.00	.40
325	Scott Rolen	1.50	.60
326	Bobby Kielty	1.00	.40
327	Travis Lee	1.00	.40
328	Jeff Cirillo	1.00	.40
329	Scott Spiezio	1.00	.40
330	Melvin Mora	1.00	.40
331	Mike Timlin	1.00	.40
332	Kerry Wood	1.00	.40
333	Tony Womack	1.00	.40
334	Jody Gerut	1.00	.40
335	Morgan Ensberg	1.00	.40
336	Odalis Perez	1.00	.40
337	Michael Cuddyer	1.00	.40
338	Jose Hernandez	1.00	.40
339	LaTroy Hawkins	1.00	.40
340	Marquis Grissom	1.00	.40
341	Matt Morris	1.00	.40
342	Juan Gonzalez	1.00	.40
343	Jose Valverde	1.00	.40
344	Joe Borowski	1.00	.40
345	Josh Bard	1.00	.40
346	Austin Kearns	1.00	.40
347	Chin-Hui Tsao	1.00	.40
348	Wil Ledezma	1.00	.40
349	Aaron Guiel	1.00	.40
350	Alfonso Soriano	1.00	.40
351	Ted Lilly	1.00	.40
352	Sean Burroughs	1.00	.40
353	Rafael Palmeiro	1.50	.60
354	Quinton McCracken	1.00	.40
355	David Ortiz	2.50	1.00
356	Randall Simon	1.00	.40
357	Wily Mo Pena	1.00	.40
358	Brian Anderson	1.00	.40
359	Corey Koskie	1.00	.40
360	Keith Foulke Sox	1.00	.40
361	Sidney Ponson	1.00	.40
362	Gary Matthews Jr.	1.00	.40
363	Herbert Perry	1.00	.40
364	Shea Hillenbrand	1.00	.40
365	Craig Biggio	1.50	.60
366	Barry Larkin	1.50	.60
367	Arthur Rhodes	1.00	.40
368	Sammy Sosa	2.50	1.00
369	Joe Crede	1.00	.40
370	Gary Sheffield	1.00	.40
371	Coco Crisp	1.00	.40
372	Torii Hunter	1.00	.40
373	Derrek Lee	1.50	.60
374	Adam Everett	1.00	.40
375	Miguel Tejada	1.00	.40
376	Jeremy Affeldt	1.00	.40
377	Robin Ventura	1.00	.40
378	Scott Podsednik	1.00	.40
379	Matthew LeCroy	1.00	.40
380	Vladimir Guerrero	2.50	1.00
381	Steve Karsay	1.00	.40
382	Jeff Nelson	1.00	.40
383	Chase Utley	1.50	.60
384	Bobby Abreu	1.00	.40
385	Josh Fogg	1.00	.40
386	Trevor Hoffman	1.00	.40
387	Matt Stairs	1.00	.40
388	Edgar Martinez	1.50	.60
389	Edgar Renteria	1.00	.40
390	Chipper Jones	2.50	1.00
391	Eric Munson	1.00	.40
392	Dewon Brazelton	1.00	.40
393	John Thomson	1.00	.40
394	Chris Woodward	1.00	.40
395	Joe Kennedy	1.00	.40
396	Reed Johnson	1.00	.40
397	Johnny Estrada	1.00	.40
398	Damian Moss	1.00	.40
399	Victor Zambrano	1.00	.40
400	Dontrelle Willis	1.50	.60
401	Troy Glaus	1.00	.40
402	Raul Mondesi	1.00	.40
403	Jeff Davanon	1.00	.40
404	Kurt Ainsworth	1.00	.40
405	Pedro Martinez	1.50	.60
406	Eric Karros	1.00	.40
407	Billy Koch	1.00	.40
408	Luis Gonzalez	1.00	.40
409	Jack Cust	1.00	.40
410	Mike Sweeney	1.00	.40
411	Jason Bay	1.00	.40
412	Mark Redman	1.00	.40
413	Jason Jennings	1.00	.40
414	Rondell White	1.00	.40
415	Todd Hundley	1.00	.40
416	Shannon Stewart	1.00	.40
417	Jae Weong Seo	1.00	.40
418	Livan Hernandez	1.00	.40
419	Mark Ellis	1.00	.40
420	Pat Burrell	1.00	.40
421	Mark Loretta	1.00	.40
422	Robb Nen	1.00	.40
423	Joel Pineiro	1.00	.40
424	Todd Walker	1.00	.40
425	Jeremy Bonderman	1.00	.40
426	A.J. Burnett	1.00	.40
427	Greg Myers	1.00	.40
428	Roy Oswalt	1.00	.40
429	Carlos Baerga	1.00	.40
430	Garret Anderson	1.00	.40
431	Horacio Ramirez	1.00	.40
432	Brian Roberts	1.00	.40
433	Kevin Brown	1.00	.40
434	Eric Milton	1.00	.40
435	Ramon Vazquez	1.00	.40
436	Alex Escobar	1.00	.40
437	Alex Sanchez	1.00	.40
438	Jeff Bagwell	1.50	.60
439	Claudio Vargas	1.00	.40
440	Shawn Green	1.00	.40
441	Geoff Jenkins	1.00	.40
442	David Wells	1.00	.40
443	Nick Johnson	1.00	.40
444	Jose Guillen	1.00	.40
445	Scott Hatteberg	1.00	.40
446	Phil Nevin	1.00	.40
447	Jason Schmidt	1.00	.40
448	Ricky Ledee	1.00	.40
449	So Taguchi	1.00	.40
450	Randy Johnson	2.50	1.00
451	Eric Young	1.00	.40
452	Chone Figgins	1.00	.40
453	Larry Bigbie	1.00	.40
454	Scott Williamson	1.00	.40

❑	455 Ramon Martinez	1.00	.40
❑	456 Roberto Alomar	1.50	.60
❑	457 Ryan Dempster	1.00	.40
❑	458 Ryan Ludwick	1.00	.40
❑	459 Ramon Santiago	1.00	.40
❑	460 Jeff Conine	1.00	.40
❑	461 Brad Lidge	1.00	.40
❑	462 Ken Harvey	1.00	.40
❑	463 Guillermo Mota	1.00	.40
❑	464 Rick Reed	1.00	.40
❑	465 Armando Benitez	1.00	.40
❑	466 Wade Miller	1.00	.40

2004 Topps Chrome Traded

❑	COMPLETE SET (220)	120.00	60.00
❑	COMMON CARD (1-70)	.75	.30
❑	COMMON CARD (71-90)	1.00	.40
❑	COMMON CARD (91-110)	1.00	.40
❑	COMMON CARD (111-220)	1.00	.40
❑	2 PER 2004 TOPPS TRADED HOBBY PACK		
❑	2 PER 2004 TOPPS TRADED HTA PACK		
❑	2 PER 2004 TOPPS TRADED RETAIL PACK		
❑	PLATE ODDS 1:1151 H, 1:1173 R, 1:327 HTA		
❑	PLATE PRINT RUN 1 SET PER COLOR		
❑	BLACK-CYAN-MAGENTA-YELLOW ISSUED		
❑	NO PLATE PRICING DUE TO SCARCITY		
❑	T1 Pokey Reese	.75	.30
❑	T2 Tony Womack	.75	.30
❑	T3 Richard Hidalgo	.75	.30
❑	T4 Juan Uribe	.75	.30
❑	T5 J.D. Drew	.75	.30
❑	T6 Alex Gonzalez	.75	.30
❑	T7 Carlos Guillen	.75	.30
❑	T8 Doug Mientkiewicz	.75	.30
❑	T9 Fernando Vina	.75	.30
❑	T10 Milton Bradley	.75	.30
❑	T11 Kelvim Escobar	.75	.30
❑	T12 Ben Grieve	.75	.30
❑	T13 Brian Jordan	.75	.30
❑	T14 A.J. Pierzynski	.75	.30
❑	T15 Billy Wagner	.75	.30
❑	T16 Terrence Long	.75	.30
❑	T17 Carlos Beltran	.75	.30
❑	T18 Carl Everett	.75	.30
❑	T19 Reggie Sanders	.75	.30
❑	T20 Javy Lopez	.75	.30
❑	T21 Jay Payton	.75	.30
❑	T22 Octavio Dotel	.75	.30
❑	T23 Eddie Guardado	.75	.30
❑	T24 Andy Pettitte	1.25	.50
❑	T25 Richie Sexson	.75	.30
❑	T26 Ronnie Belliard	.75	.30
❑	T27 Michael Tucker	.75	.30
❑	T28 Brad Fullmer	.75	.30
❑	T29 Freddy Garcia	.75	.30
❑	T30 Bartolo Colon	.75	.30
❑	T31 Larry Walker Cards	1.25	.50
❑	T32 Mark Kotsay	.75	.30
❑	T33 Jason Marquis	.75	.30
❑	T34 Dustan Mohr	.75	.30
❑	T35 Javier Vazquez	.75	.30
❑	T36 Nomar Garciaparra	3.00	1.25
❑	T37 Tino Martinez	1.25	.50
❑	T38 Hee Seop Choi	.75	.30
❑	T39 Damian Miller	.75	.30
❑	T40 Jose Lima	.75	.30
❑	T41 Ty Wigginton	.75	.30
❑	T42 Raul Ibanez	.75	.30
❑	T43 Danys Baez	.75	.30
❑	T44 Tony Clark	.75	.30
❑	T45 Greg Maddux	3.00	1.25
❑	T46 Victor Zambrano	.75	.30
❑	T47 Orlando Cabrera Sox	.75	.30
❑	T48 Jose Cruz Jr.	.75	.30
❑	T49 Kris Benson	.75	.30
❑	T50 Alex Rodriguez	4.00	1.50
❑	T51 Steve Finley	.75	.30
❑	T52 Ramon Hernandez	.75	.30
❑	T53 Esteban Loaiza	.75	.30
❑	T54 Ugueth Urbina	.75	.30
❑	T55 Jeff Weaver	.75	.30
❑	T56 Flash Gordon	.75	.30
❑	T57 Jose Contreras	.75	.30
❑	T58 Paul Lo Duca	.75	.30
❑	T59 Junior Spivey	.75	.30
❑	T60 Curt Schilling	1.25	.50
❑	T61 Brad Penny	.75	.30
❑	T62 Braden Looper	.75	.30
❑	T63 Miguel Cairo	.75	.30
❑	T64 Juan Encarnacion	.75	.30
❑	T65 Miguel Batista	.75	.30
❑	T66 Terry Francona MG	.75	.30
❑	T67 Lee Mazzilli MG	.75	.30
❑	T68 Al Pedrique MG	.75	.30
❑	T69 Ozzie Guillen MG	2.00	.75
❑	T70 Phil Garner MG	.75	.30
❑	T71 Matt Bush DP RC	4.00	1.50
❑	T72 Homer Bailey DP RC	6.00	2.50
❑	T73 Greg Golson DP RC	3.00	1.25
❑	T74 Kyle Waldrop DP RC	2.50	1.00
❑	T75 Richie Robnett DP RC	3.00	1.25
❑	T76 Jay Rainville DP RC	4.00	1.50
❑	T77 Bill Bray DP RC	1.00	.40
❑	T78 Philip Hughes DP RC	15.00	6.00
❑	T79 Scott Elbert DP RC	2.50	1.00
❑	T80 Josh Fields DP RC	5.00	2.00
❑	T81 Justin Orenduff DP RC	2.00	.75
❑	T82 Dan Putnam DP RC	2.00	.75
❑	T83 Chris Nelson DP RC	5.00	2.00
❑	T84 Blake DeWitt DP RC	4.00	1.50
❑	T85 J.P. Howell DP RC	2.50	1.00
❑	T86 Huston Street DP RC	6.00	2.50
❑	T87 Kurt Suzuki DP RC	3.00	1.25
❑	T88 Erick San Pedro DP RC	1.00	.40
❑	T89 Matt Tuiasosopo DP RC	5.00	2.00
❑	T90 Matt Macri DP RC	2.50	1.00
❑	T91 Chad Tracy PROS	1.00	.40
❑	T92 Scott Hairston PROS	1.00	.40
❑	T93 Jonny Gomes PROS	1.00	.40
❑	T94 Chin-Feng Chen PROS	1.00	.40
❑	T95 Chien-Ming Wang PROS	3.00	1.25
❑	T96 Dustin McGowan PROS	1.00	.40
❑	T97 Chris Burke PROS	1.00	.40
❑	T98 Denny Bautista PROS	1.00	.40
❑	T99 Preston Larrison PROS	1.00	.40
❑	T100 Kevin Youkilis PROS	1.00	.40
❑	T101 John Maine PROS	1.00	.40
❑	T102 Guillermo Quiroz PROS	1.00	.40
❑	T103 Dave Krynzel PROS	1.00	.40
❑	T104 David Kelton PROS	1.00	.40
❑	T105 Edwin Encarnacion PROS	1.00	.40
❑	T106 Chad Gaudin PROS	1.00	.40
❑	T107 Sergio Mitre PROS	1.00	.40
❑	T108 Laynce Nix PROS	1.00	.40
❑	T109 David Parrish PROS	1.00	.40
❑	T110 Brandon Claussen PROS	1.00	.40
❑	T111 Frank Francisco FY RC	1.00	.40
❑	T112 Brian Dallimore FY RC	1.00	.40
❑	T113 Jim Crowell FY RC	1.25	.50
❑	T114 Andres Blanco FY RC	1.00	.40
❑	T115 Eduardo Villacis FY RC	1.00	.40
❑	T116 Kazuhito Tadano FY RC	1.25	.50
❑	T117 Aarom Baldiris FY RC	1.25	.50
❑	T118 Justin Germano FY RC	1.00	.40
❑	T119 Joey Gathright FY RC	3.00	1.25
❑	T120 Franklyn Gracesqui FY RC	1.00	.40
❑	T121 Chin-Lung Hu FY RC	3.00	1.25
❑	T122 Scott Olsen FY RC	4.00	1.50
❑	T123 Tyler Davidson FY RC	1.25	.50
❑	T124 Fausto Carmona FY RC	5.00	2.00
❑	T125 Tim Hutting FY RC	1.00	.40
❑	T126 Ryan Meaux FY RC	1.00	.40
❑	T127 Jon Connolly FY RC	2.50	1.00
❑	T128 Hector Made FY RC	2.00	.75
❑	T129 Jamie Brown FY RC	1.00	.40
❑	T130 Paul McAnulty FY RC	2.00	.75
❑	T131 Chris Saenz FY RC	1.00	.40
❑	T132 Marland Williams FY RC	1.25	.50
❑	T133 Mike Huggins FY RC	1.00	.40
❑	T134 Jesse Crain FY RC	2.00	.75
❑	T135 Chad Bentz FY RC	1.00	.40
❑	T136 Kazuo Matsui FY RC	2.00	.75
❑	T137 Paul Maholm FY	2.50	1.00
❑	T138 Brock Jacobsen FY RC	1.00	.40
❑	T139 Casey Daigle FY RC	1.00	.40
❑	T140 Nyjer Morgan FY RC	1.00	.40
❑	T141 Tom Mastny FY RC	1.00	.40
❑	T142 Kody Kirkland FY RC	1.25	.50
❑	T143 Jose Capellan FY RC	1.25	.50
❑	T144 Felix Hernandez FY RC	25.00	10.00
❑	T145 Shawn Hill FY RC	1.00	.40
❑	T146 Danny Gonzalez FY RC	1.00	.40
❑	T147 Scott Dohmann FY RC	1.00	.40
❑	T148 Tommy Murphy FY RC	1.00	.40
❑	T149 Akinori Otsuka FY RC	1.00	.40
❑	T150 Miguel Perez FY RC	1.00	.40
❑	T151 Mike Rouse FY RC	1.00	.40
❑	T152 Ramon Ramirez FY RC	1.00	.40
❑	T153 Luke Hughes FY RC	1.00	.40
❑	T154 Howie Kendrick FY RC	30.00	20.00
❑	T155 Ryan Budde FY RC	1.00	.40
❑	T156 Charlie Zink FY RC	1.00	.40
❑	T157 Warner Madrigal FY RC	2.00	.75
❑	T158 Jason Szuminski FY RC	1.00	.40
❑	T159 Chad Chop FY RC	1.00	.40
❑	T160 Shingo Takatsu FY RC	2.00	.75
❑	T161 Matt Lemanczyk FY RC	1.00	.40
❑	T162 Wardell Starling FY RC	1.00	.40
❑	T163 Nick Gorneault FY RC	1.25	.50
❑	T164 Scott Proctor FY RC	1.25	.50
❑	T165 Brooks Conrad FY RC	1.25	.50
❑	T166 Hector Gimenez FY RC	1.00	.40
❑	T167 Kevin Howard FY RC	1.25	.50
❑	T168 Vince Perkins FY RC	1.25	.50
❑	T169 Brock Peterson FY RC	1.00	.40
❑	T170 Chris Shelton FY	2.00	.75
❑	T171 Erick Aybar FY RC	2.00	.75
❑	T172 Paul Bacot FY RC	1.25	.50
❑	T173 Matt Capps FY RC	1.00	.40
❑	T174 Kory Casto FY	1.25	.50
❑	T175 Juan Cedeno FY RC	1.00	.40
❑	T176 Vito Chiaravalloti FY	1.00	.40
❑	T177 Alec Zumwalt FY RC	1.00	.40
❑	T178 J.J. Furmaniak FY RC	2.00	.75
❑	T179 Lee Gwaltney FY RC	1.00	.40
❑	T180 Donald Kelly FY RC	1.00	.40
❑	T181 Benji DeQuin FY RC	1.00	.40
❑	T182 Brant Colamarino FY RC	2.00	.75
❑	T183 Juan Gutierrez FY RC	1.00	.40
❑	T184 Carl Loadenthal FY RC	1.25	.50
❑	T185 Ricky Nolasco FY RC	3.00	1.25
❑	T186 Jeff Salazar FY RC	2.50	1.00
❑	T187 Rob Tejeda FY RC	2.00	.75
❑	T188 Alex Romero FY RC	1.00	.40
❑	T189 Yoann Torrealba FY RC	1.00	.40
❑	T190 Carlos Sosa FY RC	1.00	.40
❑	T191 Tim Bittner FY RC	1.00	.40
❑	T192 Chris Aguila FY RC	1.00	.40
❑	T193 Jason Frasor FY RC	1.00	.40
❑	T194 Reid Gorecki FY RC	1.00	.40
❑	T195 Dustin Nippert FY RC	1.25	.50
❑	T196 Javier Guzman FY RC	1.25	.50
❑	T197 Harvey Garcia FY RC	1.00	.40
❑	T198 Ivan Ochoa FY RC	1.00	.40
❑	T199 David Wallace FY RC	1.25	.50
❑	T200 Joel Zumaya FY RC	8.00	3.00
❑	T201 Casey Kopitzke FY RC	1.00	.40
❑	T202 Lincoln Holdzkom FY RC	1.00	.40
❑	T203 Chad Santos FY RC	1.00	.40
❑	T204 Brian Pilkington FY RC	1.00	.40
❑	T205 Terry Jones FY RC	1.25	.50
❑	T206 Jerome Gamble FY RC	1.00	.40
❑	T207 Brad Eldred FY RC	1.25	.50
❑	T208 David Pauley FY RC	3.00	1.25
❑	T209 Kevin Davidson FY RC	1.00	.40
❑	T210 Damaso Espino FY RC	1.00	.40
❑	T211 Tom Farmer FY RC	1.00	.40
❑	T212 Michael Mooney FY RC	1.00	.40
❑	T213 James Tomlin FY RC	1.00	.40

❑ T214	Greg Thissen FY RC	1.00	.40
❑ T215	Calvin Hayes FY RC	1.25	.50
❑ T216	Fernando Cortez FY RC	1.00	.40
❑ T217	Sergio Silva FY RC	1.00	.40
❑ T218	Jon de Vries FY RC	1.00	.40
❑ T219	Don Sutton FY RC	2.50	1.00
❑ T220	Leo Nunez FY RC	1.00	.40

2005 Topps Chrome

❑ COMP.SET w/o AU'S (440) 160.00 80.00
❑ COMP.SERIES 1 w/o AU's (220) 80.00 40.00
❑ COMP.SERIES 2 w/o AU's (220) 80.00 40.00
❑ COMMON (1-210/253-467) 1.00 .40
❑ COMMON (211-220/468-472) 2.00 .75
❑ 221-252 PRINT RUN PROVIDED BY TOPPS
❑ EXCHANGE DEADLINE 05/31/07
❑ 1-234 PLATE ODDS 1:310 SER.1 HOBBY
❑ 235-252 PLATE ODDS 1:350 SER.2 MINI BOX
❑ 253-472 PLATE ODDS 1:29 SER.2 MINI BOX
❑ PLATE PRINT RUN 1 SET PER COLOR
❑ BLACK-CYAN-MAGENTA-YELLOW ISSUED
❑ NO PLATE PRICING DUE TO SCARCITY

❑ 1	Alex Rodriguez	4.00	1.50
❑ 2	Placido Polanco	1.00	.40
❑ 3	Torii Hunter	1.00	.40
❑ 4	Lyle Overbay	1.00	.40
❑ 5	Johnny Damon	1.50	.60
❑ 6	Johnny Estrada	1.00	.40
❑ 7	Rich Harden	1.00	.40
❑ 8	Francisco Rodriguez	1.00	.40
❑ 9	Jarrod Washburn	1.00	.40
❑ 10	Sammy Sosa	2.50	1.00
❑ 11	Randy Wolf	1.00	.40
❑ 12	Jason Bay	1.00	.40
❑ 13	Tom Glavine	1.50	.60
❑ 14	Michael Tucker	1.00	.40
❑ 15	Brian Giles	1.00	.40
❑ 16	Chad Tracy	1.00	.40
❑ 17	Jim Edmonds	1.00	.40
❑ 18	John Smoltz	1.50	.60
❑ 19	Roy Halladay	1.00	.40
❑ 20	Hank Blalock	1.00	.40
❑ 21	Darin Erstad	1.00	.40
❑ 22	Todd Walker	1.00	.40
❑ 23	Mike Hampton	1.00	.40
❑ 24	Mark Bellhorn	1.00	.40
❑ 25	Jim Thome	1.50	.60
❑ 26	Shingo Takatsu	1.00	.40
❑ 27	Jody Gerut	1.00	.40
❑ 28	Vinny Castilla	1.00	.40
❑ 29	Luis Castillo	1.00	.40
❑ 30	Ivan Rodriguez	1.50	.60
❑ 31	Craig Biggio	1.50	.60
❑ 32	Joe Randa	1.00	.40
❑ 33	Adrian Beltre	1.00	.40
❑ 34	Scott Podsednik	1.00	.40
❑ 35	Cliff Floyd	1.00	.40
❑ 36	Livan Hernandez	1.00	.40
❑ 37	Eric Byrnes	1.00	.40
❑ 38	Jose Acevedo	1.00	.40
❑ 39	Jack Wilson	1.00	.40
❑ 40	Gary Sheffield	1.00	.40
❑ 41	Chan Ho Park	1.00	.40
❑ 42	Carl Crawford	1.00	.40
❑ 43	Shawn Estes	1.00	.40
❑ 44	David Bell	1.00	.40
❑ 45	Jeff DaVanon	1.00	.40
❑ 46	Brandon Webb	1.00	.40
❑ 47	Lance Berkman	1.00	.40
❑ 48	Melvin Mora	1.00	.40
❑ 49	David Ortiz	2.50	1.00
❑ 50	Andruw Jones	1.50	.60
❑ 51	Chone Figgins	1.00	.40
❑ 52	Danny Graves	1.00	.40
❑ 53	Preston Wilson	1.00	.40
❑ 54	Jeremy Bonderman	1.00	.40
❑ 55	Carlos Guillen	1.00	.40
❑ 56	Cesar Izturis	1.00	.40
❑ 57	Kazuo Matsui	1.00	.40
❑ 58	Jason Schmidt	1.00	.40
❑ 59	Jason Marquis	1.00	.40
❑ 60	Jose Vidro	1.00	.40
❑ 61	Al Leiter	1.00	.40
❑ 62	Javier Vazquez	1.00	.40
❑ 63	Erubiel Durazo	1.00	.40
❑ 64	Scott Spiezio	1.00	.40
❑ 65	Scot Shields	1.00	.40
❑ 66	Edgardo Alfonzo	1.00	.40
❑ 67	Miguel Tejada	1.00	.40
❑ 68	Francisco Cordero	1.00	.40
❑ 69	Brett Myers	1.00	.40
❑ 70	Curt Schilling	1.50	.60
❑ 71	Matt Kata	1.00	.40
❑ 72	Bartolo Colon	1.00	.40
❑ 73	Rodrigo Lopez	1.00	.40
❑ 74	Tim Wakefield	1.00	.40
❑ 75	Frank Thomas	2.50	1.00
❑ 76	Jimmy Rollins	1.00	.40
❑ 77	Barry Zito	1.00	.40
❑ 78	Hideo Nomo	2.50	1.00
❑ 79	Brad Wilkerson	1.00	.40
❑ 80	Adam Dunn	1.00	.40
❑ 81	Derrek Lee	1.50	.60
❑ 82	Joe Crede	1.00	.40
❑ 83	Nate Robertson	1.00	.40
❑ 84	John Thomson	1.00	.40
❑ 85	Mike Sweeney	1.00	.40
❑ 86	Kip Wells	1.00	.40
❑ 87	Eric Gagne	1.00	.40
❑ 88	Zach Day	1.00	.40
❑ 89	Alex Sanchez	1.00	.40
❑ 90	Bret Boone	1.00	.40
❑ 91	Mark Loretta	1.00	.40
❑ 92	Miguel Cabrera	1.50	.60
❑ 93	Randy Winn	1.00	.40
❑ 94	Adam Everett	1.00	.40
❑ 95	Aubrey Huff	1.00	.40
❑ 96	Kevin Mench	1.00	.40
❑ 97	Frank Catalanotto	1.00	.40
❑ 98	Flash Gordon	1.00	.40
❑ 99	Scott Hatteberg	1.00	.40
❑ 100	Albert Pujols	5.00	2.00
❑ 101	J.Molina/B.Molina	1.00	.40
❑ 102	Jason Johnson	1.00	.40
❑ 103	Jay Gibbons	1.00	.40
❑ 104	Byung-Hyun Kim	1.00	.40
❑ 105	Joe Borowski	1.00	.40
❑ 106	Mark Grudzielanek	1.00	.40
❑ 107	Mark Buehrle	1.00	.40
❑ 108	Paul Wilson	1.00	.40
❑ 109	Ronnie Belliard	1.00	.40
❑ 110	Reggie Sanders	1.00	.40
❑ 111	Tim Redding	1.00	.40
❑ 112	Brian Lawrence	1.00	.40
❑ 113	Travis Hafner	1.00	.40
❑ 114	Jose Hernandez	1.00	.40
❑ 115	Ben Sheets	1.00	.40
❑ 116	Johan Santana	2.50	1.00
❑ 117	Billy Wagner	1.00	.40
❑ 118	Mariano Rivera	2.50	1.00
❑ 119	Steve Trachsel	1.00	.40
❑ 120	Akinori Otsuka	1.00	.40
❑ 121	Jose Valentin	1.00	.40
❑ 122	Orlando Hernandez	1.00	.40
❑ 123	Raul Ibanez	1.00	.40
❑ 124	Mike Matheny	1.00	.40
❑ 125	Vernon Wells	1.00	.40
❑ 126	Jason Isringhausen	1.00	.40
❑ 127	Jose Guillen	1.00	.40
❑ 128	Danny Bautista	1.00	.40
❑ 129	Marcus Giles	1.00	.40
❑ 130	Javy Lopez	1.00	.40
❑ 131	Kevin Millar	1.00	.40
❑ 132	Kyle Farnsworth	1.00	.40
❑ 133	Carl Pavano	1.00	.40
❑ 134	Rafael Furcal	1.00	.40
❑ 135	Casey Blake	1.00	.40
❑ 136	Matt Holliday	1.25	.50
❑ 137	Bobby Higginson	1.00	.40
❑ 138	Adam Kennedy	1.00	.40
❑ 139	Alex Gonzalez	1.00	.40
❑ 140	Jeff Kent	1.00	.40
❑ 141	Aaron Guiel	1.00	.40
❑ 142	Shawn Green	1.00	.40
❑ 143	Bill Hall	1.00	.40
❑ 144	Shannon Stewart	1.00	.40
❑ 145	Juan Rivera	1.00	.40
❑ 146	Coco Crisp	1.00	.40
❑ 147	Mike Mussina	1.50	.60
❑ 148	Eric Chavez	1.00	.40
❑ 149	Jon Lieber	1.00	.40
❑ 150	Vladimir Guerrero	2.50	1.00
❑ 151	Alex Cintron	1.00	.40
❑ 152	Luis Matos	1.00	.40
❑ 153	Sidney Ponson	1.00	.40
❑ 154	Trot Nixon	1.00	.40
❑ 155	Greg Maddux	4.00	1.50
❑ 156	Edgar Renteria	1.00	.40
❑ 157	Ryan Freel	1.00	.40
❑ 158	Matt Lawton	1.00	.40
❑ 159	Mark Prior	1.50	.60
❑ 160	Josh Beckett	1.00	.40
❑ 161	Ken Harvey	1.00	.40
❑ 162	Angel Berroa	1.00	.40
❑ 163	Juan Encarnacion	1.00	.40
❑ 164	Wes Helms	1.00	.40
❑ 165	Brad Radke	1.00	.40
❑ 166	Phil Nevin	1.00	.40
❑ 167	Mike Cameron	1.00	.40
❑ 168	Billy Koch	1.00	.40
❑ 169	Bobby Crosby	1.00	.40
❑ 170	Mike Lieberthal	1.00	.40
❑ 171	Rob Mackowiak	1.00	.40
❑ 172	Sean Burroughs	1.00	.40
❑ 173	J.T. Snow	1.00	.40
❑ 174	Paul Konerko	1.00	.40
❑ 175	Luis Gonzalez	1.00	.40
❑ 176	John Lackey	1.00	.40
❑ 177	Oliver Perez	1.00	.40
❑ 178	Brian Roberts	1.00	.40
❑ 179	Bill Mueller	1.00	.40
❑ 180	Carlos Lee	1.00	.40
❑ 181	Corey Patterson	1.00	.40
❑ 182	Sean Casey	1.00	.40
❑ 183	Cliff Lee	1.00	.40
❑ 184	Jason Jennings	1.00	.40
❑ 185	Dmitri Young	1.00	.40
❑ 186	Juan Uribe	1.00	.40
❑ 187	Andy Pettitte	1.50	.60
❑ 188	Juan Gonzalez	1.00	.40
❑ 189	Orlando Hudson	1.00	.40
❑ 190	Jason Phillips	1.00	.40
❑ 191	Braden Looper	1.00	.40
❑ 192	Lew Ford	1.00	.40
❑ 193	Mark Mulder	1.00	.40
❑ 194	Bobby Abreu	1.00	.40
❑ 195	Jason Kendall	1.00	.40
❑ 196	Khalil Greene	1.50	.60
❑ 197	A.J. Pierzynski	1.00	.40
❑ 198	Tim Worrell	1.00	.40
❑ 199	So Taguchi	1.00	.40
❑ 200	Jason Giambi	1.00	.40
❑ 201	Tony Batista	1.00	.40
❑ 202	Carlos Zambrano	1.00	.40
❑ 203	Trevor Hoffman	1.00	.40
❑ 204	Odalis Perez	1.00	.40
❑ 205	Jose Cruz Jr.	1.00	.40
❑ 206	Michael Barrett	1.00	.40
❑ 207	Chris Carpenter	1.00	.40
❑ 208	Michael Young UER	1.00	.40
❑ 209	Toby Hall	1.00	.40
❑ 210	Woody Williams	1.00	.40
❑ 211	Chris Denorfia FY RC	3.00	1.25
❑ 212	Darren Fenster FY RC	2.00	.75
❑ 213	Elvys Quezada FY RC	2.00	.75
❑ 214	Ian Kinsler FY RC	8.00	3.00
❑ 215	Matthew Lindstrom FY RC	2.00	.75
❑ 216	Ryan Goleski FY RC	3.00	1.25
❑ 217	Ryan Sweeney FY RC	4.00	1.50
❑ 218	Sean Marshall FY RC	5.00	2.00

No.	Player		
❑ 219	Steve Doetsch FY RC	3.00	1.25
❑ 220	Wade Robinson FY RC	2.00	.75
❑ 221	Andre Ethier FY AU RC	60.00	40.00
❑ 222	Brandon Moss FY AU RC	20.00	8.00
❑ 223	Chadd Blasko FY AU RC	15.00	6.00
❑ 224	Chris Roberson FY AU RC	10.00	4.00
❑ 225	Chris Seddon FY AU RC	10.00	4.00
❑ 226	Ian Bladergroen FY AU RC	15.00	6.00
❑ 227	Jake Dittler FY AU	10.00	4.00
❑ 228	Jose Vaquedano FY AU RC	10.00	4.00
❑ 229	Jeremy West FY AU RC	15.00	6.00
❑ 230	Kole Strayhorn FY AU RC	10.00	4.00
❑ 231	Kevin West FY AU RC	10.00	4.00
❑ 232	Luis Ramirez FY AU RC	10.00	4.00
❑ 233	Melky Cabrera FY AU RC	40.00	20.00
❑ 234	Nate Schierholtz FY AU	10.00	4.00
❑ 235	Billy Butler FY AU RC	50.00	20.00
❑ 236	B.Szymanski FY AU EXCH	10.00	4.00
❑ 237	Chad Orvella FY AU RC	10.00	4.00
❑ 238	Chip Cannon FY AU RC	20.00	8.00
❑ 239	Eric Nielsen FY AU RC	10.00	4.00
❑ 240	Erik Cordier FY AU RC	10.00	4.00
❑ 241	Glen Perkins FY AU RC	20.00	8.00
❑ 242	Justin Verlander FY AU RC	50.00	30.00
❑ 243	Kevin Melillo FY AU RC	15.00	6.00
❑ 244	Landon Powell FY AU RC	15.00	6.00
❑ 245	Matt Campbell FY AU RC	10.00	4.00
❑ 246	Michael Rogers FY AU RC	10.00	4.00
❑ 247	Nate McLouth FY AU RC	15.00	6.00
❑ 248	Scott Mathieson FY AU RC	10.00	4.00
❑ 249	Shane Costa FY AU RC	10.00	4.00
❑ 250	Tony Giarratano FY AU RC	10.00	4.00
❑ 251	Tyler Pelland FY AU RC	15.00	6.00
❑ 252	Wes Swackhamer FY AU RC	10.00	4.00
❑ 253	Garret Anderson	1.00	.40
❑ 254	Randy Johnson	2.50	1.00
❑ 255	Charles Thomas	1.00	.40
❑ 256	Rafael Palmeiro	1.50	.60
❑ 257	Kevin Youkilis	1.00	.40
❑ 258	Freddy Garcia	1.00	.40
❑ 259	Magglio Ordonez	1.00	.40
❑ 260	Aaron Harang	1.00	.40
❑ 261	Grady Sizemore	1.50	.60
❑ 262	Chin-hui Tsao	1.00	.40
❑ 263	Eric Munson	1.00	.40
❑ 264	Juan Pierre	1.00	.40
❑ 265	Brad Lidge	1.00	.40
❑ 266	Brian Anderson	1.00	.40
❑ 267	Todd Helton	1.50	.60
❑ 268	Chad Cordero	1.00	.40
❑ 269	Kris Benson	1.00	.40
❑ 270	Brad Halsey	1.00	.40
❑ 271	Jermaine Dye	1.00	.40
❑ 272	Manny Ramirez	1.50	.60
❑ 273	Adam Eaton	1.00	.40
❑ 274	Brett Tomko	1.00	.40
❑ 275	Bucky Jacobsen	1.00	.40
❑ 276	Dontrelle Willis	1.00	.40
❑ 277	B.J. Upton	1.00	.40
❑ 278	Rocco Baldelli	1.00	.40
❑ 279	Ryan Drese	1.00	.40
❑ 280	Ichiro Suzuki	5.00	2.00
❑ 281	Brandon Lyon	1.00	.40
❑ 282	Nick Green	1.00	.40
❑ 283	Jerry Hairston Jr.	1.00	.40
❑ 284	Mike Lowell	1.00	.40
❑ 285	Kerry Wood	1.00	.40
❑ 286	Omar Vizquel	1.50	.60
❑ 287	Carlos Beltran	1.00	.40
❑ 288	Carlos Pena	1.00	.40
❑ 289	Jeff Weaver	1.00	.40
❑ 290	Chad Moeller	1.00	.40
❑ 291	Joe Mays	1.00	.40
❑ 292	Termmel Sledge	1.00	.40
❑ 293	Richard Hidalgo	1.00	.40
❑ 294	Justin Duchscherer	1.00	.40
❑ 295	Eric Milton	1.00	.40
❑ 296	Ramon Hernandez	1.00	.40
❑ 297	Jose Reyes	1.00	.40
❑ 298	Joel Pineiro	1.00	.40
❑ 299	Matt Morris	1.00	.40
❑ 300	John Halama	1.00	.40
❑ 301	Gary Matthews Jr.	1.00	.40
❑ 302	Ryan Madson	1.00	.40
❑ 303	Mark Kotsay	1.00	.40
❑ 304	Carlos Delgado	1.00	.40
❑ 305	Casey Kotchman	1.00	.40
❑ 306	Greg Aquino	1.00	.40
❑ 307	LaTroy Hawkins	1.00	.40
❑ 308	Jose Contreras	1.00	.40
❑ 309	Ken Griffey Jr.	4.00	1.50
❑ 310	C.C. Sabathia	1.00	.40
❑ 311	Brandon Inge	1.00	.40
❑ 312	John Buck	1.00	.40
❑ 313	Hee Seop Choi	1.00	.40
❑ 314	Chris Capuano	1.00	.40
❑ 315	Jesse Crain	1.00	.40
❑ 316	Geoff Jenkins	1.00	.40
❑ 317	Mike Piazza	2.50	1.00
❑ 318	Jorge Posada	1.50	.60
❑ 319	Nick Swisher	1.00	.40
❑ 320	Kevin Millwood	1.00	.40
❑ 321	Mike Gonzalez	1.00	.40
❑ 322	Jake Peavy	1.00	.40
❑ 323	Dustin Hermanson	1.00	.40
❑ 324	Jeremy Reed	1.00	.40
❑ 325	Alfonso Soriano	1.00	.40
❑ 326	Alexis Rios	1.00	.40
❑ 327	David Eckstein	1.00	.40
❑ 328	Shea Hillenbrand	1.00	.40
❑ 329	Russ Ortiz	1.00	.40
❑ 330	Kurt Ainsworth	1.00	.40
❑ 331	Orlando Cabrera	1.00	.40
❑ 332	Carlos Silva	1.00	.40
❑ 333	Ross Gload	1.00	.40
❑ 334	Josh Phelps	1.00	.40
❑ 335	Mike Maroth	1.00	.40
❑ 336	Guillermo Mota	1.00	.40
❑ 337	Chris Burke	1.00	.40
❑ 338	David DeJesus	1.00	.40
❑ 339	Jose Lima	1.00	.40
❑ 340	Cristian Guzman	1.00	.40
❑ 341	Nick Johnson	1.00	.40
❑ 342	Victor Zambrano	1.00	.40
❑ 343	Rod Barajas	1.00	.40
❑ 344	Damian Miller	1.00	.40
❑ 345	Chase Utley	1.50	.60
❑ 346	Sean Burnett	1.00	.40
❑ 347	David Wells	1.00	.40
❑ 348	Dustan Mohr	1.00	.40
❑ 349	Bobby Madritsch	1.00	.40
❑ 350	Reed Johnson	1.00	.40
❑ 351	R.A. Dickey	1.00	.40
❑ 352	Scott Kazmir	1.00	.40
❑ 353	Tony Womack	1.00	.40
❑ 354	Tomas Perez	1.00	.40
❑ 355	Esteban Loaiza	1.00	.40
❑ 356	Tomokazu Ohka	1.00	.40
❑ 357	Ramon Ortiz	1.00	.40
❑ 358	Richie Sexson	1.00	.40
❑ 359	J.D. Drew	1.00	.40
❑ 360	Barry Bonds	6.00	2.50
❑ 361	Aramis Ramirez	1.00	.40
❑ 362	Wily Mo Pena	1.00	.40
❑ 363	Jeromy Burnitz	1.00	.40
❑ 364	Nomar Garciaparra	2.50	1.00
❑ 365	Brandon Backe	1.00	.40
❑ 366	Derek Lowe	1.00	.40
❑ 367	Doug Davis	1.00	.40
❑ 368	Joe Mauer	2.50	1.00
❑ 369	Endy Chavez	1.00	.40
❑ 370	Bernie Williams	1.50	.60
❑ 371	Jason Michaels	1.00	.40
❑ 372	Craig Wilson	1.00	.40
❑ 373	Ryan Klesko	1.00	.40
❑ 374	Ray Durham	1.00	.40
❑ 375	Jose Lopez	1.00	.40
❑ 376	Jeff Suppan	1.00	.40
❑ 377	David Bush	1.00	.40
❑ 378	Marlon Byrd	1.00	.40
❑ 379	Roy Oswalt	1.00	.40
❑ 380	Rondell White	1.00	.40
❑ 381	Troy Glaus	1.00	.40
❑ 382	Scott Hairston	1.00	.40
❑ 383	Chipper Jones	2.50	1.00
❑ 384	Daniel Cabrera	1.00	.40
❑ 385	Jon Garland	1.00	.40
❑ 386	Austin Kearns	1.00	.40
❑ 387	Jake Westbrook	1.00	.40
❑ 388	Aaron Miles	1.00	.40
❑ 389	Omar Infante	1.00	.40
❑ 390	Paul Lo Duca	1.00	.40
❑ 391	Morgan Ensberg	1.00	.40
❑ 392	Tony Graffanino	1.00	.40
❑ 393	Milton Bradley	1.00	.40
❑ 394	Keith Ginter	1.00	.40
❑ 395	Justin Morneau	1.00	.40
❑ 396	Tony Armas Jr.	1.00	.40
❑ 397	Kevin Brown	1.00	.40
❑ 398	Marco Scutaro	1.00	.40
❑ 399	Tim Hudson	1.00	.40
❑ 400	Pat Burrell	1.00	.40
❑ 401	Jeff Cirillo	1.00	.40
❑ 402	Larry Walker	1.50	.60
❑ 403	Dewon Brazelton	1.00	.40
❑ 404	Shigetoshi Hasegawa	1.00	.40
❑ 405	Octavio Dotel	1.00	.40
❑ 406	Michael Cuddyer	1.00	.40
❑ 407	Junior Spivey	1.00	.40
❑ 408	Zack Greinke	1.00	.40
❑ 409	Roger Clemens	4.00	1.50
❑ 410	Chris Shelton	1.50	.60
❑ 411	Ugueth Urbina	1.00	.40
❑ 412	Rafael Betancourt	1.00	.40
❑ 413	Willie Harris	1.00	.40
❑ 414	Keith Foulke	1.00	.40
❑ 415	Larry Bigbie	1.00	.40
❑ 416	Paul Byrd	1.00	.40
❑ 417	Troy Percival	1.00	.40
❑ 418	Pedro Martinez	1.50	.60
❑ 419	Matt Clement	1.00	.40
❑ 420	Ryan Wagner	1.00	.40
❑ 421	Jeff Francis	1.00	.40
❑ 422	Jeff Conine	1.00	.40
❑ 423	Wade Miller	1.00	.40
❑ 424	Gavin Floyd	1.00	.40
❑ 425	Kazuhisa Ishii	1.00	.40
❑ 426	Victor Santos	1.00	.40
❑ 427	Jacque Jones	1.00	.40
❑ 428	Hideki Matsui	4.00	1.50
❑ 429	Cory Lidle	1.00	.40
❑ 430	Jose Castillo	1.00	.40
❑ 431	Alex Gonzalez	1.00	.40
❑ 432	Kirk Rueter	1.00	.40
❑ 433	Jolbert Cabrera	1.00	.40
❑ 434	Erik Bedard	1.00	.40
❑ 435	Ricky Ledee	1.00	.40
❑ 436	Mark Hendrickson	1.00	.40
❑ 437	Laynce Nix	1.00	.40
❑ 438	Jason Frasor	1.00	.40
❑ 439	Kevin Gregg	1.00	.40
❑ 440	Derek Jeter	5.00	2.00
❑ 441	Jaret Wright	1.00	.40
❑ 442	Edwin Jackson	1.00	.40
❑ 443	Moises Alou	1.00	.40
❑ 444	Aaron Rowand	1.00	.40
❑ 445	Kazuhito Tadano	1.00	.40
❑ 446	Luis Gonzalez	1.00	.40
❑ 447	A.J. Burnett	1.00	.40
❑ 448	Jeff Bagwell	1.50	.60
❑ 449	Brad Penny	1.00	.40
❑ 450	Corey Koskie	1.00	.40
❑ 451	Mark Ellis	1.00	.40
❑ 452	Hector Luna	1.00	.40
❑ 453	Miguel Olivo	1.00	.40
❑ 454	Scott Rolen	1.50	.60
❑ 455	Ricardo Rodriguez	1.00	.40
❑ 456	Eric Hinske	1.00	.40
❑ 457	Tim Salmon	1.50	.60
❑ 458	Adam LaRoche	1.00	.40
❑ 459	B.J. Ryan	1.00	.40
❑ 460	Steve Finley	1.00	.40
❑ 461	Joe Nathan	1.00	.40
❑ 462	Vicente Padilla	1.00	.40
❑ 463	Yadier Molina	1.00	.40
❑ 464	Tino Martinez	1.50	.60
❑ 465	Mark Teixeira	1.50	.60
❑ 466	Kelvim Escobar	1.00	.40
❑ 467	Pedro Feliz	1.00	.40
❑ 468	Ryan Garko FY RC	5.00	2.00
❑ 469	Bobby Livingston FY RC	2.00	.75
❑ 470	Yorman Bazardo FY RC	2.00	.75
❑ 471	Mike Bourn FY RC	3.00	1.25
❑ 472	Andy LaRoche FY RC	8.00	3.00

2005 Topps Chrome Update

❑ COMPLETE SET (237) 300.00 200.00
❑ COMP.SET w/o SP's (220) 80.00 40.00
❑ COM (1-85/216-220) .75 .30
❑ COMMON (86-105) .75 .30
❑ COM (14/65/106-215) 1.00 .40
❑ 221-237 GROUP A ODDS 1:25 H, 1:49 R
❑ 221-237 GROUP B ODDS 1:29 H, 1:57 R
❑ 1-220 PLATE ODDS 1:347 H
❑ 221-237 PLATE AU ODDS 1:4857 H
❑ PLATE PRINT RUN 1 SET PER COLOR
❑ BLACK-CYAN-MAGENTA-YELLOW ISSUED
❑ NO PLATE PRICING DUE TO SCARCITY
❑ 1 Sammy Sosa 2.00 .75
❑ 2 Jeff Francoeur 2.50 1.00
❑ 3 Tony Clark .75 .30
❑ 4 Michael Tucker .75 .30
❑ 5 Mike Matheny .75 .30
❑ 6 Eric Young .75 .30
❑ 7 Jose Valentin .75 .30
❑ 8 Matt Lawton .75 .30
❑ 9 Juan Rivera .75 .30
❑ 10 Shawn Green .75 .30
❑ 11 Aaron Boone .75 .30
❑ 12 Woody Williams .75 .30
❑ 13 Brad Wilkerson .75 .30
❑ 14 Anthony Reyes RC 5.00 2.00
❑ 15 Gustavo Chacin .75 .30
❑ 16 Michael Restovich .75 .30
❑ 17 Humberto Quintero .75 .30
❑ 18 Matt Ginter .75 .30
❑ 19 Scott Podsednik .75 .30
❑ 20 Byung-Hyun Kim .75 .30
❑ 21 Orlando Hernandez .75 .30
❑ 22 Mark Grudzielanek .75 .30
❑ 23 Jody Gerut .75 .30
❑ 24 Adrian Beltre .75 .30
❑ 25 Scott Schoeneweis .75 .30
❑ 26 Marlon Anderson .75 .30
❑ 27 Jason Vargas .75 .30
❑ 28 Claudio Vargas .75 .30
❑ 29 Jason Kendall .75 .30
❑ 30 Aaron Small .75 .30
❑ 31 Juan Cruz .75 .30
❑ 32 Placido Polanco .75 .30
❑ 33 Jorge Sosa .75 .30
❑ 34 John Olerud .75 .30
❑ 35 Ryan Langerhans .75 .30
❑ 36 Randy Winn .75 .30
❑ 37 Zach Duke 2.00 .75
❑ 38 Garrett Atkins .75 .30
❑ 39 Al Leiter .75 .30
❑ 40 Shawn Chacon .75 .30
❑ 41 Mark DeRosa .75 .30
❑ 42 Miguel Ojeda .75 .30
❑ 43 A.J. Pierzynski .75 .30
❑ 44 Carlos Lee .75 .30
❑ 45 LaTroy Hawkins .75 .30
❑ 46 Nick Green .75 .30
❑ 47 Shawn Estes .75 .30
❑ 48 Eli Marrero .75 .30
❑ 49 Jeff Kent .75 .30
❑ 50 Joe Randa .75 .30
❑ 51 Jose Hernandez .75 .30
❑ 52 Joe Blanton .75 .30
❑ 53 Huston Street 2.00 .75
❑ 54 Marlon Byrd .75 .30
❑ 55 Alex Sanchez .75 .30
❑ 56 Livan Hernandez .75 .30
❑ 57 Chris Young .75 .30
❑ 58 Brad Eldred .75 .30
❑ 59 Terrence Long .75 .30
❑ 60 Phil Nevin .75 .30
❑ 61 Kyle Farnsworth .75 .30
❑ 62 Jon Lieber .75 .30
❑ 63 Antonio Alfonseca .75 .30
❑ 64 Tony Graffanino .75 .30
❑ 65 Tadahito Iguchi RC 3.00 1.25
❑ 66 Brad Thompson .75 .30
❑ 67 Jose Vidro .75 .30
❑ 68 Jason Phillips .75 .30
❑ 69 Carl Pavano .75 .30
❑ 70 Pokey Reese .75 .30
❑ 71 Jerome Williams .75 .30
❑ 72 Kazuhisa Ishii .75 .30
❑ 73 Felix Hernandez 3.00 1.25
❑ 74 Edgar Renteria .75 .30
❑ 75 Mike Myers .75 .30
❑ 76 Jeff Cirillo .75 .30
❑ 77 Endy Chavez .75 .30
❑ 78 Jose Guillen .75 .30
❑ 79 Ugueth Urbina .75 .30
❑ 80 Zach Day .75 .30
❑ 81 Javier Vazquez .75 .30
❑ 82 Willy Taveras .75 .30
❑ 83 Mark Mulder .75 .30
❑ 84 Vinny Castilla .75 .30
❑ 85 Russ Adams .75 .30
❑ 86 Homer Bailey PROS .75 .30
❑ 87 Ervin Santana PROS .75 .30
❑ 88 Bill Bray PROS .75 .30
❑ 89 Thomas Diamond PROS .75 .30
❑ 90 Trevor Plouffe PROS .75 .30
❑ 91 James Houser PROS .75 .30
❑ 92 Jake Stevens PROS .75 .30
❑ 93 Anthony Whittington PROS .75 .30
❑ 94 Philip Hughes PROS .75 .30
❑ 95 Greg Golson PROS .75 .30
❑ 96 Paul Maholm PROS .75 .30
❑ 97 Carlos Quentin PROS .75 .30
❑ 98 Dan Johnson PROS .75 .30
❑ 99 Mark Rogers PROS .75 .30
❑ 100 Neil Walker PROS .75 .30
❑ 101 Omar Quintanilla PROS .75 .30
❑ 102 Blake DeWitt PROS .75 .30
❑ 103 Taylor Tankersley PROS .75 .30
❑ 104 David Murphy PROS .75 .30
❑ 105 Chris Lambert PROS .75 .30
❑ 106 Drew Anderson FY RC 1.00 .40
❑ 107 Luis Hernandez FY RC 1.00 .40
❑ 108 Jim Burt FY RC 1.00 .40
❑ 109 Mike Morse FY RC 2.00 .75
❑ 110 Elliot Johnson FY RC 1.00 .40
❑ 111 C.J. Smith FY RC 1.00 .40
❑ 112 Casey McGehee FY RC 1.00 .40
❑ 113 Brian Miller FY RC 1.00 .40
❑ 114 Chris Vines FY RC 1.00 .40
❑ 115 D.J. Houlton FY RC 1.00 .40
❑ 116 Chuck Tiffany FY RC 3.00 1.25
❑ 117 Humberto Sanchez FY RC 4.00 1.50
❑ 118 Baltazar Lopez FY RC 1.00 .40
❑ 119 Russ Martin FY RC 3.00 1.25
❑ 120 Dana Eveland FY RC 1.00 .40
❑ 121 Johan Silva FY RC 1.00 .40
❑ 122 Adam Harben FY RC 1.25 .50
❑ 123 Brian Bannister FY RC 2.50 1.00
❑ 124 Adam Boeve FY RC 1.00 .40
❑ 125 Thomas Oldham FY RC 1.00 .40
❑ 126 Cody Haerther FY RC 1.00 .40
❑ 127 Dan Santin FY RC 1.00 .40
❑ 128 Daniel Haigwood FY RC 2.00 .75
❑ 129 Craig Tatum FY RC 1.00 .40
❑ 130 Martin Prado FY RC 1.00 .40
❑ 131 Errol Simonitsch FY RC 1.25 .50
❑ 132 Lorenzo Scott FY RC 1.00 .40
❑ 133 Hayden Penn FY RC 2.00 .75
❑ 134 Heath Totten FY RC 1.00 .40
❑ 135 Nick Masset FY RC 1.00 .40
❑ 136 Pedro Lopez FY RC 1.00 .40
❑ 137 Ben Harrison FY 1.00 .40
❑ 138 Mike Spidale FY RC 1.00 .40
❑ 139 Jeremy Harts FY RC 1.00 .40
❑ 140 Danny Zell FY RC 1.00 .40
❑ 141 Kevin Collins FY RC 1.00 .40
❑ 142 Tony Americh FY RC 1.00 .40
❑ 143 Matt Albers FY RC 2.50 1.00
❑ 144 Ricky Barrett FY RC 1.00 .40
❑ 145 Hernan Iribarren FY RC 1.25 .50
❑ 146 Sean Tracey FY RC 1.00 .40
❑ 147 Jerry Owens FY RC 1.25 .50
❑ 148 Steve Nelson FY RC 1.00 .40
❑ 149 Brandon McCarthy FY RC 2.50 1.00
❑ 150 David Shepard FY RC 1.00 .40
❑ 151 Steven Bondurant FY RC 1.00 .40
❑ 152 Billy Sadler FY RC 1.00 .40
❑ 153 Ryan Feierabend FY RC 1.00 .40
❑ 154 Stuart Pomeranz FY RC 1.00 .40
❑ 155 Shaun Marcum FY 1.00 .40
❑ 156 Erik Schindewolf FY RC 1.00 .40
❑ 157 Stefan Bailie FY RC 1.00 .40
❑ 158 Mike Esposito FY RC 1.00 .40
❑ 159 Buck Coats FY RC 1.00 .40
❑ 160 Andy Sides FY RC 1.00 .40
❑ 161 Micah Schnurstein FY RC 1.00 .40
❑ 162 Jesse Gutierrez FY RC 1.00 .40
❑ 163 Jake Postlewait FY RC 1.00 .40
❑ 164 Willy Mota FY RC 1.00 .40
❑ 165 Ryan Speier FY RC 1.00 .40
❑ 166 Frank Mata FY RC 1.00 .40
❑ 167 Jair Jurrjens FY RC 2.50 1.00
❑ 168 Nick Touchstone FY RC 1.00 .40
❑ 169 Matthew Kemp FY RC 8.00 3.00
❑ 170 Vinny Rottino FY RC 1.00 .40
❑ 171 J.B. Thurmond FY RC 1.00 .40
❑ 172 Kelvin Pichardo FY RC 1.00 .40
❑ 173 Scott Mitchinson FY RC 1.00 .40
❑ 174 Darwinson Salazar FY RC 1.00 .40
❑ 175 George Kottaras FY RC 2.00 .75
❑ 176 Kenny Durost FY RC 1.00 .40
❑ 177 Jonathan Sanchez FY RC 3.00 1.25
❑ 178 Brandon Moorhead FY RC 1.00 .40
❑ 179 Kennard Bibbs FY RC 1.00 .40
❑ 180 David Gassner FY RC 1.00 .40
❑ 181 Micah Furtado FY RC 1.00 .40
❑ 182 Ismael Ramirez FY RC 1.00 .40
❑ 183 Carlos Gonzalez FY RC 6.00 2.50
❑ 184 Brandon Sing FY RC 1.25 .50
❑ 185 Jason Motte FY RC 1.00 .40
❑ 186 Chuck James FY RC 5.00 2.00
❑ 187 Andy Santana FY RC 1.00 .40
❑ 188 Manny Parra FY RC 1.25 .50
❑ 189 Chris B.Young FY RC 4.00 1.50
❑ 190 Juan Senreiso FY RC 1.00 .40
❑ 191 Franklin Morales FY RC 2.00 .75
❑ 192 Jared Gothreaux FY RC 1.00 .40
❑ 193 Jayce Tingler FY RC 1.00 .40
❑ 194 Matt Brown FY RC 1.00 .40
❑ 195 Frank Diaz FY RC 1.00 .40
❑ 196 Stephen Drew FY RC 10.00 4.00
❑ 197 Jered Weaver FY RC 10.00 4.00
❑ 198 Ryan Braun FY RC 20.00 8.00
❑ 199 John Mayberry Jr. FY RC 2.50 1.00
❑ 200 Aaron Thompson FY RC 2.00 .75
❑ 201 Ben Copeland FY RC 4.00 1.50
❑ 202 Jacoby Ellsbury FY RC 15.00 6.00
❑ 203 Garrett Olson FY RC 2.00 .75
❑ 204 Cliff Pennington FY RC 2.00 .75
❑ 205 Colby Rasmus FY RC 8.00 3.00
❑ 206 Chris Volstad FY RC 2.50 1.00
❑ 207 Ricky Romero FY RC 2.00 .75
❑ 208 Ryan Zimmerman FY RC 15.00 6.00
❑ 209 C.J. Henry FY RC 4.00 1.50
❑ 210 Nelson Cruz FY RC 3.00 1.25
❑ 211 Josh Wall FY RC 1.25 .50
❑ 212 Nick Webber FY RC 1.00 .40
❑ 213 Paul Kelly FY RC 1.25 .50
❑ 214 Kyle Winters FY RC 1.25 .50
❑ 215 Mitch Boggs FY RC 1.00 .40
❑ 216 Craig Biggio HL .75 .30
❑ 217 Greg Maddux HL 2.00 .75
❑ 218 Bobby Abreu HL .75 .30
❑ 219 Alex Rodriguez HL 2.00 .75
❑ 220 Trevor Hoffman HL .75 .30
❑ 221 Trevor Bell FY AU A RC 15.00 6.00
❑ 222 Jay Bruce FY AU A RC 100.00 50.00
❑ 223 Travis Buck FY AU B RC 15.00 6.00
❑ 224 Cesar Carrillo FY AU B RC 15.00 6.00
❑ 225 Mike Costanzo FY AU A RC 20.00 8.00

	No.	Card		
❑	226	Brent Cox FY AU A RC	10.00	4.00
❑	227	Matt Garza FY AU A RC	40.00	15.00
❑	228	Josh Geer FY AU A RC	10.00	4.00
❑	229	Tyler Greene FY AU A RC	15.00	6.00
❑	230	Eli Iorg FY AU A RC	10.00	4.00
❑	231	Craig Italiano FY AU B RC	10.00	4.00
❑	232	Beau Jones FY AU A RC	15.00	6.00
❑	233	M.McCormick FY AU B RC	10.00	4.00
❑	234	A.McCutchen FY AU B RC	40.00	20.00
❑	235	Micah Owings FY AU B RC	20.00	8.00
❑	236	Cesar Ramos FY AU B RC	10.00	4.00
❑	237	Chaz Roe FY AU A RC	10.00	4.00

2006 Topps Chrome

- ❑ COMP.SET w/o AU's (330) 80.00 40.00
- ❑ COMMON CARD (1-252) .60 .25
- ❑ COMMON CARD (253-275) .40 .15
- ❑ COMMON ROOKIE (276-330) 1.00 .40
- ❑ COMMON AUTO (285b/331-354) 10.00 4.00
- ❑ AU 331-354 ODDS 1:15 HOBBY
- ❑ JOHJIMA AU ODDS 1:1650 HOBBY
- ❑ 1-330 PLATES 1:25 HOBBY BOX LDR
- ❑ 331-354 AU PLATES 1:324 HOBBY BOX LDR
- ❑ PLATE PRINT RUN 1 SET PER COLOR
- ❑ BLACK-CYAN-MAGENTA-YELLOW ISSUED
- ❑ NO PLATE PRICING DUE TO SCARCITY

	No.	Card		
❑	1	Alex Rodriguez	2.50	1.00
❑	2	Garrett Atkins	.60	.25
❑	3	Carl Crawford	.60	.25
❑	4	Clint Barmes	.60	.25
❑	5	Tadahito Iguchi	.60	.25
❑	6	Brian Roberts	.60	.25
❑	7	Mickey Mantle	8.00	3.00
❑	8	David Wright	2.50	1.00
❑	9	Jeremy Reed	.60	.25
❑	10	Bobby Abreu	.60	.25
❑	11	Lance Berkman	.60	.25
❑	12	Jonny Gomes	.60	.25
❑	13	Jason Marquis	.60	.25
❑	14	Chipper Jones	1.50	.60
❑	15	Jon Garland	.60	.25
❑	16	Brad Wilkerson	.60	.25
❑	17	Rickie Weeks	.60	.25
❑	18	Jorge Posada	1.00	.40
❑	19	Greg Maddux	2.50	1.00
❑	20	Jeff Francis	.60	.25
❑	21	Felipe Lopez	.60	.25
❑	22	Dan Johnson	.60	.25
❑	23	Manny Ramirez	1.00	.40
❑	24	Joe Mauer	1.00	.40
❑	25	Randy Winn	.60	.25
❑	26	Pedro Feliz	.60	.25
❑	27	Kenny Rogers	.60	.25
❑	28	Rocco Baldelli	.60	.25
❑	29	Nomar Garciaparra	1.50	.60
❑	30	Carlos Lee	.60	.25
❑	31	Tom Glavine	1.00	.40
❑	32	Craig Biggio	1.00	.40
❑	33	Steve Finley	.60	.25
❑	34	Eric Gagne	.60	.25
❑	35	Dallas McPherson	.60	.25
❑	36	Mark Kotsay	.60	.25
❑	37	Kerry Wood	.60	.25
❑	38	Huston Street	.60	.25
❑	39	Hank Blalock	.60	.25
❑	40	Brad Radke	.60	.25
❑	41	Chien-Ming Wang	2.50	1.00
❑	42	Mark Buehrle	.60	.25
❑	43	Andy Pettitte	1.00	.40
❑	44	Bernie Williams	1.00	.40
❑	45	Victor Martinez	.60	.25
❑	46	Darin Erstad	.60	.25
❑	47	Gustavo Chacin	.60	.25
❑	48	Carlos Guillen	.60	.25
❑	49	Lyle Overbay	.60	.25
❑	50	Barry Bonds	3.00	1.25
❑	51	Nook Logan	.60	.25
❑	52	Mark Teahen	.60	.25
❑	53	Mike Lamb	.60	.25
❑	54	Jayson Werth	.60	.25
❑	55	Mariano Rivera	1.50	.60
❑	56	Julio Lugo	.60	.25
❑	57	Adam Dunn	.60	.25
❑	58	Troy Percival	.60	.25
❑	59	Chad Tracy	.60	.25
❑	60	Edgar Renteria	.60	.25
❑	61	Jason Giambi	.60	.25
❑	62	Justin Morneau	.60	.25
❑	63	Carlos Delgado	.60	.25
❑	64	John Buck	.60	.25
❑	65	Shannon Stewart	.60	.25
❑	66	Mike Cameron	.60	.25
❑	67	Richie Sexson	.60	.25
❑	68	Russ Adams	.60	.25
❑	69	Josh Beckett	.60	.25
❑	70	Ryan Freel	.60	.25
❑	71	Victor Zambrano	.60	.25
❑	72	Ronnie Belliard	.60	.25
❑	73	Brian Giles	.60	.25
❑	74	Randy Wolf	.60	.25
❑	75	Robinson Cano	1.00	.40
❑	76	Joe Blanton	.60	.25
❑	77	Esteban Loaiza	.60	.25
❑	78	Troy Glaus	.60	.25
❑	79	Matt Clement	.60	.25
❑	80	Geoff Jenkins	.60	.25
❑	81	Roy Oswalt	.60	.25
❑	82	A.J. Pierzynski	.60	.25
❑	83	Pedro Martinez	1.00	.40
❑	84	Roger Clemens	3.00	1.25
❑	85	Jack Wilson	.60	.25
❑	86	Mike Piazza	1.50	.60
❑	87	Paul Lo Duca	.60	.25
❑	88	Jeff Bagwell	1.00	.40
❑	89	Carlos Zambrano	.60	.25
❑	90	Brandon Claussen	.60	.25
❑	91	Travis Hafner	.60	.25
❑	92	Chris Shelton	.60	.25
❑	93	Rafael Furcal	.60	.25
❑	94	Frank Thomas	1.50	.60
❑	95	Noah Lowry	.60	.25
❑	96	Jhonny Peralta	.60	.25
❑	97	Vernon Wells	.60	.25
❑	98	Jorge Cantu	.60	.25
❑	99	Willy Taveras	.60	.25
❑	100	Ivan Rodriguez	1.00	.40
❑	101	Jose Reyes	1.50	.60
❑	102	Barry Zito	.60	.25
❑	103	Mark Teixeira	1.00	.40
❑	104	Chone Figgins	.60	.25
❑	105	Todd Helton	1.00	.40
❑	106	Tim Wakefield	.60	.25
❑	107	Mike Maroth	.60	.25
❑	108	Johnny Damon	1.00	.40
❑	109	David DeJesus	.60	.25
❑	110	Ryan Klesko	.60	.25
❑	111	Nick Johnson	.60	.25
❑	112	Freddy Garcia	.60	.25
❑	113	Torii Hunter	.60	.25
❑	114	Mike Sweeney	.60	.25
❑	115	Scott Rolen	1.00	.40
❑	116	Jim Thome	1.00	.40
❑	117	Adam Kennedy	.60	.25
❑	118	Albert Pujols	3.00	1.25
❑	119	Kazuo Matsui	.60	.25
❑	120	Zack Greinke	.60	.25
❑	121	Jimmy Rollins	.60	.25
❑	122	Edgardo Alfonzo	.60	.25
❑	123	Billy Wagner	.60	.25
❑	124	B.J. Ryan	.60	.25
❑	125	Orlando Hudson	.60	.25
❑	126	Preston Wilson	.60	.25
❑	127	Melvin Mora	.60	.25
❑	128	Alfonso Soriano	.60	.25
❑	129	Javy Lopez	.60	.25
❑	130	Wilson Betemit	.60	.25
❑	131	Garret Anderson	.60	.25
❑	132	Jason Bay	.60	.25
❑	133	Adam LaRoche	.60	.25
❑	134	C.C. Sabathia	.60	.25
❑	135	Bartolo Colon	.60	.25
❑	136	Ichiro Suzuki	2.50	1.00
❑	137	Jim Edmonds	1.00	.40
❑	138	David Eckstein	.60	.25
❑	139	Cristian Guzman	.60	.25
❑	140	Jeff Kent	.60	.25
❑	141	Chris Capuano	.60	.25
❑	142	Cliff Floyd	.60	.25
❑	143	Zach Duke	.60	.25
❑	144	Matt Morris	.60	.25
❑	145	Jose Vidro	.60	.25
❑	146	David Wells	.60	.25
❑	147	John Smoltz	1.00	.40
❑	148	Felix Hernandez	1.50	.60
❑	149	Orlando Cabrera	.60	.25
❑	150	Mark Prior	1.00	.40
❑	151	Ted Lilly	.60	.25
❑	152	Michael Young	.60	.25
❑	153	Livan Hernandez	.60	.25
❑	154	Yadier Molina	.60	.25
❑	155	Eric Chavez	.60	.25
❑	156	Miguel Batista	.60	.25
❑	157	Ben Sheets	.60	.25
❑	158	Oliver Perez	.60	.25
❑	159	Doug Davis	.60	.25
❑	160	Andruw Jones	1.00	.40
❑	161	Hideki Matsui	1.50	.60
❑	162	Reggie Sanders	.60	.25
❑	163	Joe Nathan	.60	.25
❑	164	John Lackey	.60	.25
❑	165	Matt Murton	.60	.25
❑	166	Grady Sizemore	1.00	.40
❑	167	Brad Thompson	.60	.25
❑	168	Kevin Millwood	.60	.25
❑	169	Orlando Hernandez	.60	.25
❑	170	Mark Mulder	.60	.25
❑	171	Chase Utley	1.50	.60
❑	172	Moises Alou	.60	.25
❑	173	Wily Mo Pena	.60	.25
❑	174	Brian McCann	.60	.25
❑	175	Jermaine Dye	.60	.25
❑	176	Ryan Madson	.60	.25
❑	177	Aramis Ramirez	.60	.25
❑	178	Khalil Greene	1.00	.40
❑	179	Mike Hampton	.60	.25
❑	180	Mike Mussina	1.00	.40
❑	181	Rich Harden	.60	.25
❑	182	Woody Williams	.60	.25
❑	183	Chris Carpenter	.60	.25
❑	184	Brady Clark	.60	.25
❑	185	Luis Gonzalez	.60	.25
❑	186	Raul Ibanez	.60	.25
❑	187	Magglio Ordonez	.60	.25
❑	188	Adrian Beltre	.60	.25
❑	189	Marcus Giles	.60	.25
❑	190	Odalis Perez	.60	.25
❑	191	Derek Jeter	4.00	1.50
❑	192	Jason Schmidt	.60	.25
❑	193	Toby Hall	.60	.25
❑	194	Danny Haren	.60	.25
❑	195	Tim Hudson	.60	.25
❑	196	Jake Peavy	.60	.25
❑	197	Casey Blake	.60	.25
❑	198	J.D. Drew	.60	.25
❑	199	Ervin Santana	.60	.25
❑	200	J.J. Hardy	.60	.25
❑	201	Austin Kearns	.60	.25
❑	202	Pat Burrell	.60	.25
❑	203	Jason Vargas	.60	.25
❑	204	Ryan Howard	2.50	1.00
❑	205	Joe Crede	.60	.25
❑	206	Vladimir Guerrero	1.50	.60
❑	207	Roy Halladay	.60	.25
❑	208	David Dellucci	.60	.25
❑	209	Brandon Webb	.60	.25
❑	210	Ryan Church	.60	.25
❑	211	Miguel Tejada	.60	.25
❑	212	Mark Loretta	.60	.25
❑	213	Kevin Youkilis	.60	.25
❑	214	Jon Lieber	.60	.25

❑ 215	Miguel Cabrera	1.00	.40
❑ 216	A.J. Burnett	.60	.25
❑ 217	David Bell	.60	.25
❑ 218	Eric Byrnes	.60	.25
❑ 219	Lance Niekro	.60	.25
❑ 220	Shawn Green	.60	.25
❑ 221	Ken Griffey Jr.	2.50	1.00
❑ 222	Johnny Estrada	.60	.25
❑ 223	Omar Vizquel	1.00	.40
❑ 224	Gary Sheffield	.60	.25
❑ 225	Brad Halsey	.60	.25
❑ 226	Aaron Cook	.60	.25
❑ 227	David Ortiz	1.50	.60
❑ 228	Scott Kazmir	1.00	.40
❑ 229	Dustin McGowan	.60	.25
❑ 230	Gregg Zaun	.60	.25
❑ 231	Carlos Beltran	.60	.25
❑ 232	Bob Wickman	.60	.25
❑ 233	Brett Myers	.60	.25
❑ 234	Casey Kotchman	.60	.25
❑ 235	Jeff Francoeur	1.50	.60
❑ 236	Paul Konerko	.60	.25
❑ 237	Juan Rivera	.60	.25
❑ 238	Bobby Crosby	.60	.25
❑ 239	Derrek Lee	.60	.25
❑ 240	Curt Schilling	1.00	.40
❑ 241	Jake Westbrook	.60	.25
❑ 242	Dontrelle Willis	.60	.25
❑ 243	Brad Lidge	.60	.25
❑ 244	Randy Johnson	1.50	.60
❑ 245	Nick Swisher	.60	.25
❑ 246	Johan Santana	1.00	.40
❑ 247	Jeremy Bonderman	.60	.25
❑ 248	Ramon Hernandez	.60	.25
❑ 249	Mike Lowell	.60	.25
❑ 250	Javier Vazquez	.60	.25
❑ 251	Jose Contreras	.60	.25
❑ 252	Aubrey Huff	.60	.25
❑ 253	Kenny Rogers AW	.40	.15
❑ 254	Mark Teixeira AW	.60	.25
❑ 255	Orlando Hudson AW	.40	.15
❑ 256	Derek Jeter AW	2.50	1.00
❑ 257	Eric Chavez AW	.40	.15
❑ 258	Torii Hunter AW	.40	.15
❑ 259	Vernon Wells AW	.40	.15
❑ 260	Ichiro Suzuki AW	1.50	.60
❑ 261	Greg Maddux AW	1.50	.60
❑ 262	Mike Matheny AW	.40	.15
❑ 263	Derrek Lee AW	.40	.15
❑ 264	Luis Castillo AW	.40	.15
❑ 265	Omar Vizquel AW	.60	.25
❑ 266	Mike Lowell AW	.40	.15
❑ 267	Andruw Jones AW	.60	.25
❑ 268	Jim Edmonds AW	.60	.25
❑ 269	Bobby Abreu AW	.40	.15
❑ 270	Bartolo Colon AW	.40	.15
❑ 271	Chris Carpenter AW	.40	.15
❑ 272	Alex Rodriguez AW	1.50	.60
❑ 273	Albert Pujols AW	2.00	.75
❑ 274	Huston Street AW	.40	.15
❑ 275	Ryan Howard AW	1.50	.60
❑ 276	Chris Denorfia (RC)	1.00	.40
❑ 277	John Van Benschoten (RC)	1.00	.40
❑ 278	Russ Martin (RC)	1.50	.60
❑ 279	Fausto Carmona (RC)	1.00	.40
❑ 280	Freddie Bynum (RC)	1.00	.40
❑ 281	Kelly Shoppach (RC)	1.00	.40
❑ 282	Chris Demaria RC	1.00	.40
❑ 283	Jordan Tata RC	1.00	.40
❑ 284	Ryan Zimmerman (RC)	6.00	2.50
❑ 285a	Kenji Johjima RC	5.00	2.00
❑ 285b	Kenji Johjima AU	100.00	50.00
❑ 286	Ruddy Lugo (RC)	1.00	.40
❑ 287	Tommy Murphy (RC)	1.00	.40
❑ 288	Bobby Livingston (RC)	1.00	.40
❑ 289	Anderson Hernandez (RC)	1.00	.40
❑ 290	Brian Slocum (RC)	1.00	.40
❑ 291	Sendy Rleal RC	1.00	.40
❑ 292	Ryan Spilborghs (RC)	1.50	.60
❑ 293	Brandon Fahey RC	1.00	.40
❑ 294	Jason Kubel (RC)	1.00	.40
❑ 295	James Loney (RC)	1.50	.60
❑ 296	Jeremy Accardo RC	1.00	.40
❑ 297	Fabio Castro RC	1.00	.40
❑ 298	Matt Capps (RC)	1.00	.40
❑ 299	Casey Janssen RC	1.00	.40
❑ 300	Martin Prado (RC)	1.00	.40
❑ 301	Ronny Paulino (RC)	1.00	.40
❑ 302	Josh Barfield (RC)	1.00	.40
❑ 303	Joel Zumaya (RC)	2.50	1.00
❑ 304	Matt Cain (RC)	1.50	.60
❑ 305	Conor Jackson (RC)	1.50	.60
❑ 306	Brian Anderson (RC)	1.00	.40
❑ 307	Prince Fielder (RC)	4.00	1.50
❑ 308	Jeremy Hermida (RC)	1.00	.40
❑ 309	Justin Verlander (RC)	4.00	1.50
❑ 310	Brian Bannister (RC)	1.00	.40
❑ 311	Josh Willingham (RC)	1.00	.40
❑ 312	John Rheinecker (RC)	1.00	.40
❑ 313	Nick Markakis (RC)	1.50	.60
❑ 314	Jonathan Papelbon (RC)	5.00	2.00
❑ 315	Mike Jacobs (RC)	1.00	.40
❑ 316	Jose Capellan (RC)	1.00	.40
❑ 317	Mike Napoli RC	2.50	1.00
❑ 318	Ricky Nolasco (RC)	1.00	.40
❑ 319	Ben Johnson (RC)	1.00	.40
❑ 320	Paul Maholm (RC)	1.00	.40
❑ 321	Drew Meyer (RC)	1.00	.40
❑ 322	Jeff Mathis (RC)	1.00	.40
❑ 323	Fernando Nieve (RC)	1.00	.40
❑ 324	John Koronka (RC)	1.00	.40
❑ 325	Wil Nieves (RC)	1.00	.40
❑ 326	Nate McLouth (RC)	1.00	.40
❑ 327	Howie Kendrick (RC)	5.00	2.00
❑ 328	Sean Marshall (RC)	1.00	.40
❑ 329	Brandon Watson (RC)	1.00	.40
❑ 330	Skip Schumaker (RC)	1.00	.40
❑ 331	Ryan Garko AU (RC)	10.00	4.00
❑ 332	Jason Bergmann AU RC	10.00	4.00
❑ 333	Chuck James AU (RC)	15.00	6.00
❑ 334	Adam Wainwright AU (RC)	10.00	4.00
❑ 335	Dan Ortmeier AU (RC)	10.00	4.00
❑ 336	Francisco Liriano AU (RC)	30.00	12.50
❑ 337	Craig Breslow AU RC	10.00	4.00
❑ 338	Darrell Rasner AU (RC)	10.00	4.00
❑ 339	Jason Botts AU (RC)	10.00	4.00
❑ 340	Ian Kinsler AU (RC)	20.00	8.00
❑ 341	Joey Devine AU RC	10.00	4.00
❑ 342	Miguel Perez AU (RC)	10.00	4.00
❑ 343	Scott Olsen AU (RC)	15.00	6.00
❑ 344	Tyler Johnson AU (RC)	10.00	4.00
❑ 345	Anthony Lerew AU (RC)	10.00	4.00
❑ 346	Nelson Cruz AU (RC)	10.00	4.00
❑ 347	Willie Eyre AU (RC)	10.00	4.00
❑ 348	Josh Johnson AU (RC)	20.00	8.00
❑ 349	Shaun Marcum AU (RC)	10.00	4.00
❑ 350	Dustin Nippert AU (RC)	10.00	4.00
❑ 351	Josh Wilson AU (RC)	10.00	4.00
❑ 352	Hanley Ramirez AU (RC)	25.00	10.00
❑ 353	Reggie Abercrombie AU (RC)	10.00	4.00
❑ 354	Dan Uggla AU (RC)	30.00	12.50

2007 Topps Chrome

❑	COMP.SET w/o AU's (330)	80.00	40.00
❑	COMMON CARD	.50	.20
❑	COMMON ROOKIE	1.00	.40
❑	VARIATION ODDS 1:82 HOBBY		
❑	COMMON AUTO	8.00	3.00
❑	AUTO ODDS 1:16 HOBBY, 1:122 RETAIL		
❑	PRINT.PLATE ODDS 1:36 HOBBY BOX LDR		
❑	VAR.PLATES 1:1943 HOBBY BOX LDR		
❑	AU PLATES 1:343 HOBBY BOX LDR		
❑	PLATE PRINT RUN 1 SET PER COLOR		
❑	BLACK-CYAN-MAGENTA-YELLOW ISSUED		
❑	NO PLATE PRICING DUE TO SCARCITY		
❑	EXCHANGE DEADLINE 07/31/09		
❑ 1	Nick Swisher	.50	.20
❑ 2	Bobby Abreu	.50	.20
❑ 3	Edgar Renteria	.50	.20
❑ 4	Mickey Mantle	4.00	1.50
❑ 5	Preston Wilson	.50	.20
❑ 6	C.C. Sabathia	.50	.20
❑ 7	Julio Lugo	.50	.20
❑ 8	J.D. Drew	.50	.20
❑ 9	Jason Varitek	1.25	.50
❑ 10	Orlando Hernandez	.50	.20
❑ 11	Corey Patterson	.50	.20
❑ 12	Josh Bard	.50	.20
❑ 13	Gary Matthews	.50	.20
❑ 14	Jason Jennings	.50	.20
❑ 15	Bronson Arroyo	.50	.20
❑ 16	Andy Pettitte	.75	.30
❑ 17	Ervin Santana	.50	.20
❑ 18	Paul Konerko	.50	.20
❑ 19	Adam LaRoche	.50	.20
❑ 20	Jim Edmonds	.75	.30
❑ 21	Derek Jeter	3.00	1.25
❑ 22	Aubrey Huff	.50	.20
❑ 23	Andre Ethier	.75	.30
❑ 24	Jeremy Sowers	.50	.20
❑ 25	Miguel Cabrera	.75	.30
❑ 26	Carlos Lee	.50	.20
❑ 27	Mike Piazza	1.25	.50
❑ 28	Cole Hamels	.75	.30
❑ 29	Mark Loretta	.50	.20
❑ 30	John Smoltz	.75	.30
❑ 31	Dan Uggla	.75	.30
❑ 32	Lyle Overbay	.50	.20
❑ 33	Michael Barrett	.50	.20
❑ 34	Ivan Rodriguez	.75	.30
❑ 35	Jake Westbrook	.50	.20
❑ 36	Moises Alou	.50	.20
❑ 37	Jered Weaver	.75	.30
❑ 38	Lastings Milledge	.75	.30
❑ 39	Austin Kearns	.50	.20
❑ 40	Adam Loewen	.50	.20
❑ 41	Josh Barfield	.50	.20
❑ 42	Johan Santana	.75	.30
❑ 43	Ian Kinsler	.50	.20
❑ 44	Mike Lowell	.50	.20
❑ 45	Scott Rolen	.75	.30
❑ 46	Chipper Jones	1.25	.50
❑ 47	Joe Crede	.50	.20
❑ 48	Rafael Furcal	.50	.20
❑ 49	Dave Bush	.50	.20
❑ 50	Marcus Giles	.50	.20
❑ 51	Joe Blanton	.50	.20
❑ 52	Dontrelle Willis	.50	.20
❑ 53	Scott Kazmir	.75	.30
❑ 54	Jeff Kent	.50	.20
❑ 55	Travis Hafner	.50	.20
❑ 56	Ryan Garko	.50	.20
❑ 57	Nick Markakis	.75	.30
❑ 58	Michael Cuddyer	.50	.20
❑ 59	Jason Giambi	.50	.20
❑ 60	Chone Figgins	.50	.20
❑ 61	Carlos Delgado	.50	.20
❑ 62	Aramis Ramirez	.50	.20
❑ 63	Albert Pujols	2.50	1.00
❑ 64	Gary Sheffield	.50	.20
❑ 65	Adrian Gonzalez	.50	.20
❑ 66	Prince Fielder	1.25	.50
❑ 67	Freddy Sanchez	.50	.20
❑ 68	Jack Wilson	.50	.20
❑ 69	Jake Peavy	.50	.20
❑ 70	Javier Vazquez	.50	.20
❑ 71	Todd Helton	.75	.30
❑ 72	Bill Hall	.50	.20
❑ 73	Jeremy Bonderman	.50	.20
❑ 74	Rocco Baldelli	.50	.20
❑ 75	Noah Lowry	.50	.20
❑ 76	Justin Verlander	1.25	.50
❑ 77	Mark Buehrle	.50	.20
❑ 78	Hank Blalock	.50	.20
❑ 79	Mark Teahen	.50	.20
❑ 80	Chien-Ming Wang	2.00	.75
❑ 81	Roy Halladay	.50	.20
❑ 82	Melvin Mora	.50	.20
❑ 83	Grady Sizemore	.75	.30
❑ 84	Matt Cain	.75	.30

85	Carl Crawford	.50	.20
86	Johnny Damon	.75	.30
87	Freddy Garcia	.50	.20
88	Ryan Shealy	.50	.20
89	Carlos Beltran	.50	.20
90	Chuck James	.50	.20
91	Ben Sheets	.50	.20
92	Mark Mulder	.50	.20
93	Carlos Quentin	.50	.20
94	Richie Sexson	.50	.20
95	Brian Schneider	.50	.20
96a	Hideki Matsui	1.25	.50
96b	H.Matsui Japanese	5.00	2.00
97	Robinson Tejeda	.50	.20
98	Scott Hatteberg	.50	.20
99	Jeff Francis	.50	.20
100	Robinson Cano	.75	.30
101	Barry Zito	.50	.20
102	Reed Johnson	.50	.20
103	Chris Carpenter	.50	.20
104	Chad Tracy	.50	.20
105	Anibal Sanchez	.50	.20
106	Brad Penny	.50	.20
107	David Wright	2.00	.75
108	Jimmy Rollins	.50	.20
109	Alfonso Soriano	.50	.20
110	Greg Maddux	2.00	.75
111	Curt Schilling	.75	.30
112	Stephen Drew	.75	.30
113	Matt Holliday	1.25	.50
114	Jorge Posada	.75	.30
115	Vladimir Guerrero	1.25	.50
116	Frank Thomas	1.25	.50
117	Jonathan Papelbon	1.25	.50
118	Manny Ramirez	.75	.30
119	Magglio Ordonez	.50	.20
120	Joe Mauer	.75	.30
121	Ryan Howard	2.00	.75
122	Chris Young	.50	.20
123	A.J. Burnett	.50	.20
124	Brian McCann	.50	.20
125	Juan Pierre	.50	.20
126	Jonny Gomes	.50	.20
127	Roger Clemens	2.50	1.00
128	Chad Billingsley	.50	.20
129a	Kenji Johjima	1.25	.50
129b	Kenji Johjima Japanese	5.00	2.00
130	Brian Giles	.50	.20
131	Chase Utley	1.25	.50
132	Carl Pavano	.50	.20
133	Curtis Granderson	.50	.20
134	Sean Casey	.50	.20
135	Jon Garland	.50	.20
136	David Ortiz	1.25	.50
137	Bobby Crosby	.50	.20
138	Conor Jackson	.50	.20
139	Tim Hudson	.50	.20
140	Rickie Weeks	.50	.20
141	Mark Prior	.75	.30
142	Ben Zobrist	.50	.20
143	Troy Glaus	.50	.20
144	Cliff Lee	.50	.20
145	Adrian Beltre	.50	.20
146	Endy Chavez	.50	.20
147	Ramon Hernandez	.50	.20
148	Chris Young	.50	.20
149	Jason Schmidt	.50	.20
150	Kevin Millwood	.50	.20
151	Placido Polanco	.50	.20
152	Torii Hunter	.50	.20
153	Roy Oswalt	.50	.20
154	Kelvim Escobar	.50	.20
155	Milton Bradley	.50	.20
156	Chris Capuano	.50	.20
157	Juan Encarnacion	.50	.20
158a	Ichiro Suzuki	2.00	.75
158b	Ichiro Suzuki Japanese	8.00	3.00
159	Matt Kemp	.50	.20
160	Matt Morris	.50	.20
161	Casey Blake	.50	.20
162	Josh Willingham	.50	.20
163	Nick Johnson	.50	.20
164	Khalil Greene	.75	.30
165	Tom Glavine	.75	.30
166	Jason Bay	.50	.20
167	Brandon Phillips	.50	.20
168	Jorge Cantu	.50	.20
169	Jeff Weaver	.50	.20
170	Melky Cabrera	.50	.20
171	Dan Haren	.50	.20
172	Jeff Francoeur	1.25	.50
173	Randy Wolf	.50	.20
174	Carlos Zambrano	.50	.20
175	Justin Morneau	.50	.20
176	Takashi Saito	.50	.20
177	Victor Martinez	.50	.20
178	Felix Hernandez	.75	.30
179	Paul LoDuca	.50	.20
180	Miguel Tejada	.50	.20
181	Mark Teixeira	.75	.30
182	Pat Burrell	.50	.20
183	Mike Cameron	.50	.20
184	Josh Beckett	.75	.30
185	Francisco Liriano	1.25	.50
186	Ken Griffey Jr.	2.00	.75
187	Mike Mussina	.75	.30
188	Howie Kendrick	.50	.20
189	Ted Lilly	.50	.20
190	Mike Hampton	.50	.20
191	Jeff Suppan	.50	.20
192	Jose Reyes	1.25	.50
193	Russell Martin	.50	.20
194	Jhonny Peralta	.50	.20
195	Raul Ibanez	.50	.20
196	Hanley Ramirez	.75	.30
197	Kerry Wood	.50	.20
198	Gary Sheffield	.50	.20
199	David Dellucci	.50	.20
200	Xavier Nady	.50	.20
201	Michael Young	.50	.20
202	Kevin Youkilis	.50	.20
203	Aaron Harang	.50	.20
204	Matt Garza	.50	.20
205	Jim Thome	.75	.30
206	Jose Contreras	.50	.20
207	Tadahito Iguchi	.50	.20
208	Eric Chavez	.50	.20
209	Vernon Wells	.50	.20
210	Doug Davis	.50	.20
211	Andruw Jones	.75	.30
212	David Eckstein	.50	.20
213	J.J. Hardy	.50	.20
214	Orlando Hudson	.50	.20
215	Pedro Martinez	.75	.30
216	Brian Roberts	.50	.20
217	Brett Myers	.50	.20
218	Alex Rodriguez	2.00	.75
219	Kenny Rogers	.50	.20
220	Jason Kubel	.50	.20
221	Jermaine Dye	.50	.20
222	Bartolo Colon	.50	.20
223	Craig Biggio	.75	.30
224	Alex Rios	.50	.20
225	Adam Dunn	.50	.20
226	Anthony Reyes	.50	.20
227	Derrek Lee	.50	.20
228	Jeremy Hermida	.50	.20
229	Derek Lowe	.50	.20
230	Randy Winn	.50	.20
231	Brandon Webb	.50	.20
232	Jose Vidro	.50	.20
233	Erik Bedard	.50	.20
234	Jon Lieber	.50	.20
235	Wily Mo Pena	.50	.20
236	Kelly Johnson	.50	.20
237	David DeJesus	.50	.20
238	Andy Marte	.50	.20
239	Scott Olsen	.50	.20
240	Randy Johnson	1.25	.50
241	Nelson Cruz	.50	.20
242	Carlos Guillen	.50	.20
243	Brandon McCarthy	.50	.20
244	Garret Anderson	.50	.20
245	Mike Sweeney	.50	.20
246	Brian Bannister	.50	.20
247	Jose Guillen	.50	.20
248	Brad Wilkerson	.50	.20
249	Lance Berkman	.50	.20
250	Ryan Zimmerman	1.25	.50
251	Garrett Atkins	.50	.20
252	Johan Santana	.75	.30
253	Brandon Webb	.50	.20
254	Justin Verlander	1.25	.50
255	Hanley Ramirez	.75	.30
256	Justin Morneau	.50	.20
257	Ryan Howard	2.00	.75
258	Eric Chavez	.50	.20
259	Scott Rolen	.75	.30
260	Derek Jeter	3.00	1.25
261	Omar Vizquel	.75	.30
262	Mark Grudzielanek	.50	.20
263	Orlando Hudson	.50	.20
264	Mark Teixeira	.75	.30
265	Albert Pujols	2.50	1.00
266	Ivan Rodriguez	.75	.30
267	Brad Ausmus	.50	.20
268	Torii Hunter	.50	.20
269	Mike Cameron	.50	.20
270	Ichiro Suzuki	2.00	.75
271	Carlos Beltran	.50	.20
272	Vernon Wells	.50	.20
273	Andruw Jones	.75	.30
274	Kenny Rogers	.50	.20
275	Greg Maddux	2.00	.75
276	Danny Putnam (RC)	1.00	.40
277	Chase Wright RC	2.50	1.00
278	Zach McClellan RC	1.00	.40
279	Jamie Vermilyea RC	1.00	.40
280	Felix Pie (RC)	1.00	.40
281	Phil Hughes (RC)	5.00	2.00
282	Jon Knott (RC)	1.00	.40
283	Micah Owings (RC)	1.00	.40
284	Devern Hansack RC	1.00	.40
285	Andy Cannizaro RC	1.00	.40
286	Lee Gardner (RC)	1.00	.40
287	Josh Hamilton (RC)	2.50	1.00
288	Angel Sanchez AU RC	8.00	3.00
289	J.D. Durbin (RC)	1.00	.40
290	Jaime Burke (RC)	1.00	.40
291	Joe Bisenius RC	1.00	.40
292	Rick Vanden Hurk RC	1.50	.60
293	Brian Barden RC	1.00	.40
294	Levale Speigner RC	1.00	.40
295	Kevin Cameron RC	1.00	.40
296	Don Kelly (RC)	1.00	.40
297a	Hideki Okajima RC	5.00	2.00
297b	Hideki Okajima Japanese	8.00	3.00
298	Andrew Miller RC	6.00	2.50
299	Delmon Young (RC)	2.50	1.00
300	Vinny Rottino (RC)	1.00	.40
301	Philip Humber (RC)	1.00	.40
302	Drew Anderson RC	1.00	.40
303	Jerry Owens (RC)	1.00	.40
304	Jose Garcia RC	1.00	.40
305	Shane Youman RC	1.00	.40
306	Ryan Feierabend (RC)	1.00	.40
307	Mike Rabelo RC	1.00	.40
308	Josh Fields (RC)	1.00	.40
309	Jon Coutlangus (RC)	1.00	.40
310	Travis Buck (RC)	1.00	.40
311	Doug Slaten RC	1.00	.40
312	Ryan Z. Braun RC	1.00	.40
313	Juan Salas (RC)	1.00	.40
314	Matt Lindstrom (RC)	1.00	.40
315	Cesar Jimenez RC	1.00	.40
316	Jay Marshall RC	1.00	.40
317	Jared Burton RC	1.00	.40
318	Juan Perez RC	1.00	.40
319	Elijah Dukes RC	1.50	.60
320	Juan Lara RC	1.00	.40
321	Justin Hampson (RC)	1.00	.40
322a	Kei Igawa RC	2.50	1.00
322b	Kei Igawa Japanese	5.00	2.00
323	Zack Segovia (RC)	1.00	.40
324	Alejandro De Aza RC	1.50	.60
325	Brandon Morrow RC	1.50	.60
326	Gustavo Molina RC	1.00	.40
327	Joe Smith RC	1.00	.40
328	Jesus Flores RC	1.00	.40
329	Jeff Baker (RC)	1.00	.40
330a	Daisuke Matsuzaka RC	10.00	4.00
330b	Daisuke Matsuzaka Japanese	20.00	8.00
331	Troy Tulowitzki AU (RC)	30.00	12.50
332	John Danks AU RC	8.00	3.00
333	Kevin Kouzmanoff AU (RC)	8.00	3.00
334	David Murphy AU (RC)	8.00	3.00
335	Ryan Sweeney AU (RC)	8.00	3.00
336	Fred Lewis AU (RC)	10.00	4.00

❑ 337 Delwyn Young AU (RC) 8.00 3.00
❑ 338 Matt Chico AU (RC) 8.00 3.00
❑ 339 Miguel Montero AU (RC) 8.00 3.00
❑ 340 Shawn Riggans AU (RC) 8.00 3.00
❑ 341 Brian Stokes AU (RC) 8.00 3.00
❑ 342 Scott Moore AU (RC) 8.00 3.00
❑ 343 Adam Lind AU (RC) 8.00 3.00
❑ 344 Chris Narveson AU (RC) 8.00 3.00
❑ 345 Alex Gordon AU RC 40.00 15.00
❑ 346 Joaquin Arias AU (RC) 8.00 3.00
❑ 347 Brian Burres AU (RC) 8.00 3.00
❑ 348 Glen Perkins AU (RC) 8.00 3.00
❑ 349 Ubaldo Jimenez AU (RC) 25.00 10.00
❑ 350 Chris Stewart AU RC 8.00 3.00
❑ 351 Beltran Perez AU (RC) 8.00 3.00
❑ 352 Dennis Sarfate AU (RC) 8.00 3.00
❑ 353 Carlos Maldonado AU (RC) 8.00 3.00
❑ 354 Mitch Maier AU RC 8.00 3.00
❑ 355 Kory Casto AU (RC) 8.00 3.00
❑ 356 Juan Morillo AU (RC) 8.00 3.00
❑ 357 Hector Gimenez AU (RC) 8.00 3.00
❑ 358 Alexi Casilla AU RC 10.00 4.00
❑ 359 Michael Bourn AU (RC) 10.00 4.00
❑ 360 Sean Henn AU (RC) 8.00 3.00
❑ 361 Tim Gradoville AU RC 8.00 3.00
❑ 362 A.Iwamura AU RC EXCH 20.00 8.00
❑ 363 Oswaldo Navarro AU RC 8.00 3.00

2006 Topps Co-Signers

❑ COMP.SET w/o AU's (100) 40.00 15.00
❑ COMMON CARD (1-100) .75 .30
❑ 101-120 GROUP A ODDS 1:2025
❑ 101-120 GROUP B ODDS 1:1625
❑ 101-120 GROUP C ODDS 1:920
❑ 101-120 GROUP D ODDS 1:81
❑ 101-120 GROUP E ODDS 1:270
❑ 101-120 GROUP F ODDS 1:68
❑ 101-120 GROUP G ODDS 1:12
❑ 101-120 GROUP A PRINT RUN 200 CARDS
❑ 101-120 GROUP B PRINT RUN 250 CARDS
❑ 101-120 GROUP C PRINT RUN 440 CARDS
❑ A-C CARDS ARE NOT SERIAL NUMBERED
❑ A-C PRINT RUNS PROVIDED BY TOPPS
❑ 1 Albert Pujols 4.00 1.50
❑ 2 Roger Clemens 4.00 1.50
❑ 3 Paul Konerko .75 .30
❑ 4 Jeff Francouer 2.00 .75
❑ 5 Miguel Tejada .75 .30
❑ 6 Curt Schilling 1.25 .50
❑ 7 Mickey Mantle 5.00 2.00
❑ 8 Miguel Cabrera 1.25 .50
❑ 9 Derrek Lee .75 .30
❑ 10 Jeff Kent .75 .30
❑ 11 Gary Sheffield .75 .30
❑ 12 Rich Harden .75 .30
❑ 13 Scott Rolen 1.25 .50
❑ 14 David Wright 3.00 1.25
❑ 15 Troy Glaus .75 .30
❑ 16 Torii Hunter .75 .30
❑ 17 Nolan Ryan 5.00 2.00
❑ 18 Alfonso Soriano .75 .30
❑ 19 Hank Blalock .75 .30
❑ 20 Chase Utley 2.00 .75
❑ 21 Ryan Howard 3.00 1.25
❑ 22 Robinson Cano 1.25 .50
❑ 23 Derek Jeter 5.00 2.00
❑ 24 Huston Street .75 .30
❑ 25 Jason Giambi .75 .30
❑ 26 Rafael Furcal .75 .30
❑ 27 Rickie Weeks .75 .30
❑ 28 Ivan Rodriguez 1.25 .50
❑ 29 Travis Hafner .75 .30
❑ 30 Greg Maddux 3.00 1.25
❑ 31 Andruw Jones 1.25 .50
❑ 32 Andy Pettitte 1.25 .50
❑ 33 Scott Podsednik .75 .30
❑ 34 Francisco Rodriguez .75 .30
❑ 35 Josh Beckett .75 .30
❑ 36 Lance Berkman .75 .30
❑ 37 Roy Oswalt .75 .30
❑ 38 Pedro Martinez 1.25 .50
❑ 39 Jimmy Rollins .75 .30
❑ 40 Johan Santana 1.25 .50
❑ 41 Randy Johnson 2.00 .75
❑ 42 Mariano Rivera 2.00 .75
❑ 43 Nick Johnson .75 .30
❑ 44 Josh Gibson 2.00 .75
❑ 45 Shawn Green .75 .30
❑ 46 Adrian Beltre .75 .30
❑ 47 Johnny Damon 1.25 .50
❑ 48 Joe Mauer 1.25 .50
❑ 49 Todd Helton 1.25 .50
❑ 50 Alex Rodriguez 3.00 1.25
❑ 51 Jake Peavy .75 .30
❑ 52 David Ortiz 2.00 .75
❑ 53 Mark Buehrle .75 .30
❑ 54 Eric Gagne .75 .30
❑ 55 Hideki Matsui 3.00 1.25
❑ 56 Bobby Abreu .75 .30
❑ 57 Victor Martinez .75 .30
❑ 58 Brian Roberts .75 .30
❑ 59 Chipper Jones 2.00 .75
❑ 60 Carlos Beltran .75 .30
❑ 61 Tim Hudson .75 .30
❑ 62 Carlos Lee .75 .30
❑ 63 Barry Zito .75 .30
❑ 64 Moises Alou .75 .30
❑ 65 Mark Teixeira 1.25 .50
❑ 66 Lyle Overbay .75 .30
❑ 67 Kerry Wood .75 .30
❑ 68 B.J. Ryan .75 .30
❑ 69 Jim Edmonds 1.25 .50
❑ 70 Carlos Delgado .75 .30
❑ 71 Magglio Ordonez .75 .30
❑ 72 Juan Pierre .75 .30
❑ 73 Manny Ramirez 1.25 .50
❑ 74 Dontrelle Willis .75 .30
❑ 75 Ichiro Suzuki 3.00 1.25
❑ 76 Nomar Garciaparra 2.00 .75
❑ 77 Zach Duke .75 .30
❑ 78 Chris Carpenter .75 .30
❑ 79 A.J. Burnett .75 .30
❑ 80 Scott Kazmir 1.25 .50
❑ 81 Carl Crawford .75 .30
❑ 82 Mark Prior 1.25 .50
❑ 83 Adam Dunn .75 .30
❑ 84 Justin Morneau .75 .30
❑ 85 Morgan Ensberg .75 .30
❑ 86 Pat Burrell .75 .30
❑ 87 Paul Lo Duca .75 .30
❑ 88 Jason Bay .75 .30
❑ 89 Aubrey Huff .75 .30
❑ 90 Kevin Millwood .75 .30
❑ 91 Vernon Wells .75 .30
❑ 92 Javy Lopez .75 .30
❑ 93 Michael Young .75 .30
❑ 94 Felix Hernandez 1.25 .50
❑ 95 Ken Griffey Jr. 3.00 1.25
❑ 96 Bartolo Colon .75 .30
❑ 97 Billy Wagner .75 .30
❑ 98 Vladimir Guerrero 2.00 .75
❑ 99 Jose Reyes 2.00 .75
❑ 100 Barry Bonds 5.00 2.00
❑ 101 Anthony LeRew AU G (RC) 10.00 4.00
❑ 102 R.Zimm AU C/440 (RC) * 50.00 20.00
❑ 103 C.Hansen AU B/250 RC * 50.00 20.00
❑ 104 F.Liriano AU G (RC) 40.00 15.00
❑ 105 Jason Botts AU G (RC) 10.00 4.00
❑ 106 Josh Johnson AU G (RC) 15.00 6.00
❑ 107 Hanley Ramirez AU G (RC) 20.00 8.00
❑ 108 A.Wainwright AU G (RC) 15.00 6.00
❑ 109 K.Johjima AU A/200 RC * 100.00 50.00
❑ 110 Dan Ortmeier AU G (RC) 10.00 4.00
❑ 111 Darrell Rasner AU G (RC) 10.00 4.00
❑ 112 Chuck James AU F (RC) 15.00 6.00
❑ 113 Nelson Cruz AU F (RC) 10.00 4.00
❑ 114 Hong-Chih Kuo AU E (RC) 40.00 15.00
❑ 115 Ryan Garko AU G (RC) 10.00 4.00
❑ 116 R.Abercrombie AU D (RC) 10.00 4.00
❑ 117 Ian Kinsler AU D (RC) 20.00 8.00
❑ 118 Joel Zumaya AU D (RC) 25.00 10.00
❑ 119 Willie Eyre AU D (RC) 10.00 4.00
❑ 120 Dan Uggla AU D (RC) 30.00 12.50

2007 Topps Co-Signers

❑ COMP.SET w/o AU's (100) 30.00 12.50
❑ COMMON CARD (1-92) .60 .25
❑ SEMISTARS 1.00 .40
❑ UNLISTED STARS 1.50 .60
❑ COMMON ROOKIE (93-100) 1.50 .60
❑ ROOKIE SEMIS 2.50 1.00
❑ ROOKIE UNLISTED 4.00 1.50
❑ COMMON ROOKIE AU (96-121) 8.00 3.00
❑ ROOKIE AUTO ODDS 1:28
❑ ROOKIE AUTO VARIATION ODDS 1:198
❑ PRINTING PLATE ODDS 1:705
❑ PRINTING PLATE AUTO ODDS 1:21,168
❑ PLATE PRINT RUN 1 SET PER COLOR
❑ BLACK-CYAN-MAGENTA-SPOT-YELLOW ISSUED
❑ NO PLATE PRICING DUE TO SCARCITY
❑ 1 Ryan Howard 2.50 1.00
❑ 2 Jered Weaver 1.00 .40
❑ 3 Brian McCann .60 .25
❑ 4 Garrett Atkins .60 .25
❑ 5 Travis Hafner .60 .25
❑ 6 Jason Schmidt .60 .25
❑ 7 Curtis Granderson .60 .25
❑ 8 Ben Sheets .60 .25
❑ 9 Chien-Ming Wang 2.50 1.00
❑ 10 Francisco Liriano 1.50 .60
❑ 11 Freddy Sanchez .60 .25
❑ 12 Roy Oswalt .60 .25
❑ 13 Jim Edmonds 1.00 .40
❑ 14 Matt Cain 1.00 .40
❑ 15 Jake Peavy .60 .25
❑ 16 Ryan Zimmerman 1.50 .60
❑ 17 Troy Glaus .60 .25
❑ 18 Kenji Johjima 1.50 .60
❑ 19 Curt Schilling 1.00 .40
❑ 20 Alfonso Soriano .60 .25
❑ 21 Adam Dunn .60 .25
❑ 22 Hanley Ramirez 1.00 .40
❑ 23 Mark Teahen .60 .25
❑ 24 Todd Helton 1.00 .40
❑ 25 Alex Rodriguez 2.50 1.00
❑ 26 Mike Mussina 1.00 .40
❑ 27 Jason Bay .60 .25
❑ 28 Carl Crawford .60 .25
❑ 29 Vernon Wells .60 .25
❑ 30 Rich Harden .60 .25
❑ 31 Justin Morneau .60 .25
❑ 32 Andre Ethier 1.00 .40
❑ 33 Ramon Hernandez .60 .25
❑ 34 Erik Bedard .60 .25
❑ 35 Vladimir Guerrero 1.50 .60
❑ 36 Stephen Drew 1.00 .40
❑ 37 Felix Hernandez 1.00 .40
❑ 38 C.C. Sabathia .60 .25
❑ 39 Adrian Gonzalez .60 .25
❑ 40 Prince Fielder 1.50 .60
❑ 41 Carlos Delgado .60 .25
❑ 42 Jimmy Rollins .60 .25

❑ 43 Raul Ibanez	.60	.25
❑ 44 Jorge Cantu	.60	.25
❑ 45 Michael Young	.60	.25
❑ 46 Austin Kearns	.60	.25
❑ 47 Ivan Rodriguez	1.00	.40
❑ 48 Mark Teixeira	.60	.25
❑ 49 David Ortiz	1.50	.60
❑ 50 David Wright	2.50	1.00
❑ 51 Justin Verlander	1.50	.60
❑ 52 Nick Markakis	1.00	.40
❑ 53 Miguel Cabrera	1.00	.40
❑ 54 Lance Berkman	.60	.25
❑ 55 Robinson Cano	1.00	.40
❑ 56 Jon Lieber	.60	.25
❑ 57 Andruw Jones	1.00	.40
❑ 58 Dan Haren	.60	.25
❑ 59 Grady Sizemore	1.00	.40
❑ 60 Gary Sheffield	.60	.25
❑ 61 Paul Lo Duca	.60	.25
❑ 62 Cole Hamels	1.00	.40
❑ 63 Richie Sexson	.60	.25
❑ 64 David Eckstein	.60	.25
❑ 65 Carlos Zambrano	.60	.25
❑ 66 Scott Kazmir	1.00	.40
❑ 67 Anthony Reyes	.60	.25
❑ 68 Mark Kotsay	.60	.25
❑ 69 Miguel Tejada	.60	.25
❑ 70 Pedro Martinez	1.00	.40
❑ 71 Jack Wilson	.60	.25
❑ 72 Joe Mauer	1.00	.40
❑ 73 Brian Giles	.60	.25
❑ 74 Jonathan Papelbon	1.50	.60
❑ 75 Albert Pujols	3.00	1.25
❑ 76 Nick Swisher	.60	.25
❑ 77 Bill Hall	.60	.25
❑ 78 Jose Contreras	.60	.25
❑ 79 David DeJesus	.60	.25
❑ 80 Bobby Abreu	.60	.25
❑ 81 John Smoltz	1.00	.40
❑ 82 Chipper Jones	1.50	.60
❑ 83 Mark Buehrle	.60	.25
❑ 84 Josh Barfield	.60	.25
❑ 85 Derrek Lee	.60	.25
❑ 86 Jim Thome	1.00	.40
❑ 87 Kenny Rogers	.60	.25
❑ 88 Jeremy Sowers	.60	.25
❑ 89 Brandon Webb	.60	.25
❑ 90 Roy Halladay	.60	.25
❑ 91 Tadahito Iguchi	.60	.25
❑ 92 Jeff Kent	.60	.25
❑ 93 Johnny Damon	1.00	.40
❑ 94 Daisuke Matsuzaka RC	8.00	3.00
❑ 95 Kei Igawa RC	2.50	1.00
❑ 96a Delmon Young (RC)	2.00	.75
❑ 96b Delmon Young AU	20.00	8.00
❑ 97a Jeff Baker (RC)	1.50	.60
❑ 97b Jeff Baker AU	8.00	3.00
❑ 98a Michael Bourn (RC)	1.50	.60
❑ 98b Michael Bourn AU	10.00	4.00
❑ 99a Ubaldo Jimenez (RC)	1.50	.60
❑ 99b Ubaldo Jimenez AU	15.00	6.00
❑ 100a Andrew Miller RC	4.00	1.50
❑ 100b Andrew Miller AU	40.00	15.00
❑ 101 Angel Sanchez AU RC	8.00	3.00
❑ 102 Troy Tulowitzki AU (RC)	30.00	12.50
❑ 103 Joaquin Arias AU (RC)	8.00	3.00
❑ 104 Beltran Perez AU (RC)	8.00	3.00
❑ 105 Josh Fields AU (RC)	10.00	4.00
❑ 106 Hector Gimenez AU (RC)	8.00	3.00
❑ 107 Kevin Kouzmanoff AU (RC)	10.00	4.00
❑ 108 Miguel Montero AU (RC)	8.00	3.00
❑ 109 Philip Humber AU (RC)	10.00	4.00
❑ 110 Jerry Owens AU (RC)	8.00	3.00
❑ 111 Shawn Riggans AU (RC)	8.00	3.00
❑ 112 Brian Stokes AU (RC)	8.00	3.00
❑ 113 Scott Moore AU (RC)	8.00	3.00
❑ 114 David Murphy AU (RC)	8.00	3.00
❑ 115 Mitch Maier AU RC	8.00	3.00
❑ 116 Adam Lind AU (RC)	10.00	4.00
❑ 117 Glen Perkins AU (RC)	10.00	4.00
❑ 118 Dennis Sarfate AU (RC)	8.00	3.00
❑ 119 Elijah Dukes AU RC	15.00	6.00
❑ 120 Josh Hamilton AU (RC)	15.00	6.00
❑ 121 Alex Gordon AU RC	40.00	15.00
❑ 122 Barry Bonds	8.00	3.00

2001 Topps Heritage

❑ COMP.MASTER SET (487)	500.00	350.00
❑ COMPLETE SET (407)	400.00	250.00
❑ COMP.BASIC SET (230)	80.00	40.00
❑ COMMON CARD (81-310)	.50	.20
❑ COMMON CARD (1-80)	2.50	1.00
❑ COMMON CARD (311-407)	5.00	2.00
❑ 1 Kris Benson	2.50	1.00
❑ 1 Kris Benson Black	2.50	1.00
❑ 2 Brian Jordan	2.50	1.00
❑ 2 Brian Jordan Black	2.50	1.00
❑ 3 Fernando Vina	2.50	1.00
❑ 3 Fernando Vina Black	2.50	1.00
❑ 4 Mike Sweeney	2.50	1.00
❑ 4 Mike Sweeney Black	2.50	1.00
❑ 5 Rafael Palmeiro	2.50	1.00
❑ 5 Rafael Palmeiro Black	2.50	1.00
❑ 6 Paul O'Neill	2.50	1.00
❑ 6 Paul O'Neill Black	2.50	1.00
❑ 7 Todd Helton	2.50	1.00
❑ 7 Todd Helton Black	2.50	1.00
❑ 8 Ramiro Mendoza	2.50	1.00
❑ 8 Ramiro Mendoza Black	2.50	1.00
❑ 9 Kevin Millwood	2.50	1.00
❑ 9 Kevin Millwood Black	2.50	1.00
❑ 10 Chuck Knoblauch	2.50	1.00
❑ 10 Chuck Knoblauch Black	2.50	1.00
❑ 11 Derek Jeter	10.00	4.00
❑ 11 Derek Jeter Black	10.00	4.00
❑ 12 Alex Rodriguez Rangers	6.00	2.50
❑ 12 A.Rod Black Rangers	6.00	2.50
❑ 13 Geoff Jenkins	2.50	1.00
❑ 13 Geoff Jenkins Black	2.50	1.00
❑ 14 David Justice	2.50	1.00
❑ 14 David Justice Black	2.50	1.00
❑ 15 David Cone	2.50	1.00
❑ 15 David Cone Black	2.50	1.00
❑ 16 Andres Galarraga	2.50	1.00
❑ 16 Andres Galarraga Black	2.50	1.00
❑ 17 Garret Anderson	2.50	1.00
❑ 17 Garret Anderson Black	2.50	1.00
❑ 18 Roger Cedeno	2.50	1.00
❑ 18 Roger Cedeno Black	2.50	1.00
❑ 19 Randy Velarde	2.50	1.00
❑ 19 Randy Velarde Black	2.50	1.00
❑ 20 Carlos Delgado	2.50	1.00
❑ 20 Carlos Delgado Black	2.50	1.00
❑ 21 Quilvio Veras	2.50	1.00
❑ 21 Quilvio Veras Black	2.50	1.00
❑ 22 Jose Vidro	2.50	1.00
❑ 22 Jose Vidro Black	2.50	1.00
❑ 23 Corey Patterson	2.50	1.00
❑ 23 Corey Patterson Black	2.50	1.00
❑ 24 Jorge Posada	2.50	1.00
❑ 24 Jorge Posada Black	2.50	1.00
❑ 25 Eddie Perez	2.50	1.00
❑ 25 Eddie Perez Black	2.50	1.00
❑ 26 Jack Cust	2.50	1.00
❑ 26 Jack Cust Black	2.50	1.00
❑ 27 Sean Burroughs	2.50	1.00
❑ 27 Sean Burroughs Black	2.50	1.00
❑ 28 Randy Wolf	2.50	1.00
❑ 28 Randy Wolf Black	2.50	1.00
❑ 29 Mike Lamb	2.50	1.00
❑ 29 Mike Lamb Black	2.50	1.00
❑ 30 Rafael Furcal	2.50	1.00
❑ 30 Rafael Furcal Black	2.50	1.00
❑ 31 Barry Bonds	10.00	4.00
❑ 31 Barry Bonds Black	10.00	4.00
❑ 32 Tim Hudson	2.50	1.00
❑ 32 Tim Hudson Black	2.50	1.00
❑ 33 Tom Glavine	2.50	1.00
❑ 33 Tom Glavine Black	2.50	1.00
❑ 34 Javy Lopez	2.50	1.00
❑ 34 Javy Lopez Black	2.50	1.00
❑ 35 Aubrey Huff	2.50	1.00
❑ 35 Aubrey Huff Black	2.50	1.00
❑ 36 Wally Joyner	2.50	1.00
❑ 36 Wally Joyner Black	2.50	1.00
❑ 37 Magglio Ordonez	2.50	1.00
❑ 37 Magglio Ordonez Black	2.50	1.00
❑ 38 Matt Lawton	2.50	1.00
❑ 38 Matt Lawton Black	2.50	1.00
❑ 39 Mariano Rivera	4.00	1.50
❑ 39 Mariano Rivera Black	4.00	1.50
❑ 40 Andy Ashby	2.50	1.00
❑ 40 Andy Ashby Black	2.50	1.00
❑ 41 Mark Buehrle	2.50	1.00
❑ 41 Mark Buehrle Black	2.50	1.00
❑ 42 Esteban Loaiza	2.50	1.00
❑ 42 Esteban Loaiza Black	2.50	1.00
❑ 43 Mark Redman	2.50	1.00
❑ 43 Mark Redman Black	2.50	1.00
❑ 44 Mark Quinn	2.50	1.00
❑ 44 Mark Quinn Black	2.50	1.00
❑ 45 Tino Martinez	2.50	1.00
❑ 45 Tino Martinez Black	2.50	1.00
❑ 46 Joe Mays	2.50	1.00
❑ 46 Joe Mays Black	2.50	1.00
❑ 47 Walt Weiss	2.50	1.00
❑ 47 Walt Weiss Black	2.50	1.00
❑ 48 Roger Clemens	8.00	3.00
❑ 48 Roger Clemens Black	8.00	3.00
❑ 49 Greg Maddux	6.00	2.50
❑ 49 Greg Maddux Black	6.00	2.50
❑ 50 Richard Hidalgo	2.50	1.00
❑ 50 Richard Hidalgo Black	2.50	1.00
❑ 51 Orlando Hernandez	2.50	1.00
❑ 51 Orlando Hernandez Black	2.50	1.00
❑ 52 Chipper Jones	4.00	1.50
❑ 52 Chipper Jones Black	4.00	1.50
❑ 53 Ben Grieve	2.50	1.00
❑ 53 Ben Grieve Black	2.50	1.00
❑ 54 Jimmy Haynes	2.50	1.00
❑ 54 Jimmy Haynes Black	2.50	1.00
❑ 55 Ken Caminiti	2.50	1.00
❑ 55 Ken Caminiti Black	2.50	1.00
❑ 56 Tim Salmon	2.50	1.00
❑ 56 Tim Salmon Black	2.50	1.00
❑ 57 Andy Pettitte	2.50	1.00
❑ 57 Andy Pettitte Black	2.50	1.00
❑ 58 Darin Erstad	2.50	1.00
❑ 58 Darin Erstad Black	2.50	1.00
❑ 59 Marquis Grissom	2.50	1.00
❑ 59 Marquis Grissom Black	2.50	1.00
❑ 60 Raul Mondesi	2.50	1.00
❑ 60 Raul Mondesi Black	2.50	1.00
❑ 61 Bengie Molina	2.50	1.00
❑ 61 Bengie Molina Black	2.50	1.00
❑ 62 Miguel Tejada	2.50	1.00
❑ 62 Miguel Tejada Black	2.50	1.00
❑ 63 Jose Cruz Jr.	2.50	1.00
❑ 63 Jose Cruz Jr. Black	2.50	1.00
❑ 64 Billy Koch	2.50	1.00
❑ 64 Billy Koch Black	2.50	1.00
❑ 65 Troy Glaus	2.50	1.00
❑ 65 Troy Glaus Black	2.50	1.00
❑ 66 Cliff Floyd	2.50	1.00
❑ 66 Cliff Floyd Black	2.50	1.00
❑ 67 Tony Batista	2.50	1.00
❑ 67 Tony Batista Black	2.50	1.00
❑ 68 Jeff Bagwell	2.50	1.00
❑ 68 Jeff Bagwell Black	2.50	1.00
❑ 69 Billy Wagner	2.50	1.00
❑ 69 Billy Wagner Black	2.50	1.00
❑ 70 Eric Chavez	2.50	1.00
❑ 70 Eric Chavez Black	2.50	1.00
❑ 71 Troy Percival	2.50	1.00
❑ 71 Troy Percival Black	2.50	1.00
❑ 72 Andruw Jones	2.50	1.00
❑ 72 Andruw Jones Black	2.50	1.00
❑ 73 Shane Reynolds	2.50	1.00
❑ 73 Shane Reynolds Black	2.50	1.00

Card		
❑ 74 Barry Zito	2.50	1.00
❑ 74 Barry Zito Black	2.50	1.00
❑ 75 Roy Halladay	2.50	1.00
❑ 75 Roy Halladay Black	2.50	1.00
❑ 76 David Wells	2.50	1.00
❑ 76 David Wells Black	2.50	1.00
❑ 77 Jason Giambi	2.50	1.00
❑ 77 Jason Giambi Black	2.50	1.00
❑ 78 Scott Elarton	2.50	1.00
❑ 78 Scott Elarton Black	2.50	1.00
❑ 79 Moises Alou	2.50	1.00
❑ 79 Moises Alou Black	2.50	1.00
❑ 80 Adam Piatt	2.50	1.00
❑ 80 Adam Piatt Black	2.50	1.00
❑ 81 Wilton Veras	.50	.20
❑ 82 Darryl Kile	.60	.25
❑ 83 Johnny Damon	1.00	.40
❑ 84 Tony Armas Jr.	.50	.20
❑ 85 Ellis Burks	.60	.25
❑ 86 Jamey Wright	.50	.20
❑ 87 Jose Vizcaino	.50	.20
❑ 88 Bartolo Colon	.60	.25
❑ 89 Carmen Cali RC	.50	.20
❑ 90 Kevin Brown	.60	.25
❑ 91 Josh Hamilton	.50	.20
❑ 92 Jay Buhner	.60	.25
❑ 93 Scott Pratt RC	.60	.25
❑ 94 Alex Cora	.50	.20
❑ 95 Luis Montanez RC	.60	.25
❑ 96 Dmitri Young	.60	.25
❑ 97 J.T. Snow	.60	.25
❑ 98 Damion Easley	.50	.20
❑ 99 Greg Norton	.50	.20
❑ 100 Matt Wheatland	.50	.20
❑ 101 Chin-Feng Chen	.60	.25
❑ 102 Tony Womack	.50	.20
❑ 103 Adam Kennedy Black	.50	.20
❑ 104 J.D. Drew	.60	.25
❑ 105 Carlos Febles	.50	.20
❑ 106 Jim Thome	1.00	.40
❑ 107 Danny Graves	.50	.20
❑ 108 Dave Mlicki	.50	.20
❑ 109 Ron Coomer	.50	.20
❑ 110 James Baldwin	.50	.20
❑ 111 Shaun Boyd RC	.50	.20
❑ 112 Brian Bohanon	.50	.20
❑ 113 Jacque Jones	.60	.25
❑ 114 Alfonso Soriano	1.00	.40
❑ 115 Tony Clark	.50	.20
❑ 116 Terrence Long	.50	.20
❑ 117 Todd Hundley	.50	.20
❑ 118 Kazuhiro Sasaki	.60	.25
❑ 119 Brian Sellier RC	.50	.20
❑ 120 John Olerud	.60	.25
❑ 121 Javier Vazquez	.60	.25
❑ 122 Sean Burnett	.50	.20
❑ 123 Matt LeCroy	.50	.20
❑ 124 Erubiel Durazo	.50	.20
❑ 125 Juan Encarnacion	.50	.20
❑ 126 Pablo Ozuna	.50	.20
❑ 127 Russ Ortiz	.50	.20
❑ 128 David Segui	.50	.20
❑ 129 Mark McGwire	4.00	1.50
❑ 130 Mark Grace	1.00	.40
❑ 131 Fred McGriff	1.00	.40
❑ 132 Carl Pavano	.60	.25
❑ 133 Derek Thompson	.50	.20
❑ 134 Shawn Green	.60	.25
❑ 135 B.J. Surhoff	.60	.25
❑ 136 Michael Tucker	.50	.20
❑ 137 Jason Isringhausen	.60	.25
❑ 138 Eric Milton	.50	.20
❑ 139 Mike Stodolka	.50	.20
❑ 140 Milton Bradley	.60	.25
❑ 141 Curt Schilling	.60	.25
❑ 142 Sandy Alomar Jr.	.50	.20
❑ 143 Brent Mayne	.50	.20
❑ 144 Todd Jones	.50	.20
❑ 145 Charles Johnson	.60	.25
❑ 146 Dean Palmer	.60	.25
❑ 147 Masato Yoshii	.50	.20
❑ 148 Edgar Renteria	.60	.25
❑ 149 Joe Randa	.60	.25
❑ 150 Adam Johnson	.50	.20
❑ 151 Greg Vaughn	.50	.20
❑ 152 Adrian Beltre	.60	.25
❑ 153 Glenallen Hill	.50	.20
❑ 154 David Parrish RC	.50	.20
❑ 155 Neifi Perez	.50	.20
❑ 156 Pete Harnisch	.50	.20
❑ 157 Paul Konerko	.60	.25
❑ 158 Dennys Reyes	.50	.20
❑ 159 Jose Lima Black	.50	.20
❑ 160 Eddie Taubensee	.50	.20
❑ 161 Miguel Cairo	.50	.20
❑ 162 Jeff Kent	.60	.25
❑ 163 Dustin Hermanson	.50	.20
❑ 164 Alex Gonzalez	.50	.20
❑ 165 Hideo Nomo	1.50	.60
❑ 166 Sammy Sosa	1.50	.60
❑ 167 C.J. Nitkowski	.50	.20
❑ 168 Cal Eldred	.50	.20
❑ 169 Jeff Abbott	.50	.20
❑ 170 Jim Edmonds	.60	.25
❑ 171 Mark Mulder Black	.60	.25
❑ 172 Dominic Rich RC	.50	.20
❑ 173 Ray Lankford	.60	.25
❑ 174 Danny Borrell RC	.50	.20
❑ 175 Rick Aguilera	.50	.20
❑ 176 Shannon Stewart Black	.60	.25
❑ 177 Steve Finley	.60	.25
❑ 178 Jim Parque	.50	.20
❑ 179 Kevin Appier Black	.60	.25
❑ 180 Adrian Gonzalez	.50	.20
❑ 181 Tom Goodwin	.50	.20
❑ 182 Kevin Tapani	.50	.20
❑ 183 Fernando Tatis	.50	.20
❑ 184 Mark Grudzielanek	.50	.20
❑ 185 Ryan Anderson	.50	.20
❑ 186 Jeffrey Hammonds	.50	.20
❑ 187 Corey Koskie	.50	.20
❑ 188 Brad Fullmer Black	.50	.20
❑ 189 Rey Sanchez	.50	.20
❑ 190 Michael Barrett	.50	.20
❑ 191 Rickey Henderson	1.50	.60
❑ 192 Jermaine Dye	.60	.25
❑ 193 Scott Brosius	.60	.25
❑ 194 Matt Anderson	.50	.20
❑ 195 Brian Buchanan	.50	.20
❑ 196 Derrek Lee	1.00	.40
❑ 197 Larry Walker	.60	.25
❑ 198 Dan Moylan RC	.50	.20
❑ 199 Vinny Castilla	.60	.25
❑ 200 Ken Griffey Jr.	2.50	1.00
❑ 201 Matt Stairs Black	.50	.20
❑ 202 Ty Howington	.50	.20
❑ 203 Andy Benes	.50	.20
❑ 204 Luis Gonzalez	.60	.25
❑ 205 Brian Moehler	.50	.20
❑ 206 Harold Baines	.60	.25
❑ 207 Pedro Astacio	.50	.20
❑ 208 Cristian Guzman	.50	.20
❑ 209 Kip Wells	.50	.20
❑ 210 Frank Thomas	1.50	.60
❑ 211 Jose Rosado	.50	.20
❑ 212 Vernon Wells Black	.60	.25
❑ 213 Bobby Higginson	.60	.25
❑ 214 Juan Gonzalez	.60	.25
❑ 215 Omar Vizquel	1.00	.40
❑ 216 Bernie Williams	1.00	.40
❑ 217 Aaron Sele	.50	.20
❑ 218 Shawn Estes	.50	.20
❑ 219 Roberto Alomar	1.00	.40
❑ 220 Rick Ankiel	.50	.20
❑ 221 Josh Kalinowski	.50	.20
❑ 222 David Bell	.50	.20
❑ 223 Keith Foulke	.60	.25
❑ 224 Craig Biggio Black	1.00	.40
❑ 225 Josh Axelson RC	.50	.20
❑ 226 Scott Williamson	.50	.20
❑ 227 Ron Belliard	.50	.20
❑ 228 Chris Singleton	.50	.20
❑ 229 Alex Serrano RC	.50	.20
❑ 230 Deivi Cruz	.50	.20
❑ 231 Eric Munson	.50	.20
❑ 232 Luis Castillo	.50	.20
❑ 233 Edgar Martinez	1.00	.40
❑ 234 Jeff Shaw	.50	.20
❑ 235 Jeromy Burnitz	.60	.25
❑ 236 Richie Sexson	.60	.25
❑ 237 Will Clark	1.00	.40
❑ 238 Ron Villone	.50	.20
❑ 239 Kerry Wood	.60	.25
❑ 240 Rich Aurilia	.50	.20
❑ 241 Mo Vaughn Black	.60	.25
❑ 242 Travis Fryman	.60	.25
❑ 243 Manny Ramirez Sox	1.00	.40
❑ 244 Chris Stynes	.50	.20
❑ 245 Ray Durham	.60	.25
❑ 246 Juan Uribe RC	1.00	.40
❑ 247 Juan Guzman	.50	.20
❑ 248 Lee Stevens	.50	.20
❑ 249 Devon White	.60	.25
❑ 250 Kyle Lohse RC	1.00	.40
❑ 251 Bryan Wolff	.50	.20
❑ 252 Matt Galante RC	.60	.25
❑ 253 Eric Young	.50	.20
❑ 254 Freddy Garcia	.60	.25
❑ 255 Jay Bell	.60	.25
❑ 256 Steve Cox	.50	.20
❑ 257 Torii Hunter	.60	.25
❑ 258 Jose Canseco	1.00	.40
❑ 259 Brad Ausmus	.60	.25
❑ 260 Jeff Cirillo	.50	.20
❑ 261 Brad Penny	.50	.20
❑ 262 Antonio Alfonseca	.50	.20
❑ 263 Russ Branyan	.50	.20
❑ 264 Chris Morris RC	.50	.20
❑ 265 John Lackey	.50	.20
❑ 266 Justin Wayne RC	.60	.25
❑ 267 Brad Radke	.60	.25
❑ 268 Todd Stottlemyre	.50	.20
❑ 269 Mark Loretta	.50	.20
❑ 270 Matt Williams	.60	.25
❑ 271 Kenny Lofton	.60	.25
❑ 272 Jeff D'Amico	.50	.20
❑ 273 Jamie Moyer	.60	.25
❑ 274 Darren Dreifort	.50	.20
❑ 275 Denny Neagle	.50	.20
❑ 276 Orlando Cabrera	.60	.25
❑ 277 Chuck Finley	.60	.25
❑ 278 Miguel Batista	.60	.25
❑ 279 Carlos Beltran	.60	.25
❑ 280 Eric Karros	.60	.25
❑ 281 Mark Kotsay	.60	.25
❑ 282 Ryan Dempster	.50	.20
❑ 283 Barry Larkin	1.00	.40
❑ 284 Jeff Suppan	.50	.20
❑ 285 Gary Sheffield	.60	.25
❑ 286 Jose Valentin	.50	.20
❑ 287 Robb Nen	.60	.25
❑ 288 Chan Ho Park	.60	.25
❑ 289 John Halama	.50	.20
❑ 290 Steve Smyth RC	.60	.25
❑ 291 Gerald Williams	.50	.20
❑ 292 Preston Wilson	.60	.25
❑ 293 Victor Hall RC	.60	.25
❑ 294 Ben Sheets	1.00	.40
❑ 295 Eric Davis	.60	.25
❑ 296 Kirk Rueter	.50	.20
❑ 297 Chad Petty RC	.50	.20
❑ 298 Kevin Millar	.60	.25
❑ 299 Marvin Benard	.50	.20
❑ 300 Vladimir Guerrero	1.50	.60
❑ 301 Livan Hernandez	.60	.25
❑ 302 Travis Baptist RC	.50	.20
❑ 303 Bill Mueller	.60	.25
❑ 304 Mike Cameron	.50	.20
❑ 305 Randy Johnson	1.50	.60
❑ 306 Alan Mahaffey RC	.50	.20
❑ 307 Timo Perez UER	.50	.20
❑ 308 Pokey Reese	.50	.20
❑ 309 Ryan Rupe	.50	.20
❑ 310 Carlos Lee	.60	.25
❑ 311 Doug Glanville SP	5.00	2.00
❑ 312 Jay Payton SP	5.00	2.00
❑ 313 Troy O'Leary SP	5.00	2.00
❑ 314 Francisco Cordero SP	5.00	2.00
❑ 315 Rusty Greer SP	5.00	2.00
❑ 316 Cal Ripken SP	25.00	10.00
❑ 317 Ricky Ledee SP	5.00	2.00
❑ 318 Brian Daubach SP	5.00	2.00
❑ 319 Robin Ventura SP	5.00	2.00
❑ 320 Todd Zeile SP	5.00	2.00
❑ 321 Francisco Cordova SP	5.00	2.00
❑ 322 Henry Rodriguez SP	5.00	2.00
❑ 323 Pat Meares SP	5.00	2.00
❑ 324 Glendon Rusch SP	5.00	2.00

Card		
❑ 325 Keith Osik SP	5.00	2.00
❑ 326 Robert Keppel SP RC	5.00	2.00
❑ 327 Bobby Jones SP	5.00	2.00
❑ 328 Alex Ramirez SP	5.00	2.00
❑ 329 Robert Person SP	5.00	2.00
❑ 330 Ruben Mateo SP	5.00	2.00
❑ 331 Rob Bell SP	5.00	2.00
❑ 332 Carl Everett SP	5.00	2.00
❑ 333 Jason Schmidt SP	5.00	2.00
❑ 334 Scott Rolen SP	8.00	3.00
❑ 335 Jimmy Anderson SP	5.00	2.00
❑ 336 Bret Boone SP	5.00	2.00
❑ 337 Delino DeShields SP	5.00	2.00
❑ 338 Trevor Hoffman SP	5.00	2.00
❑ 339 Bob Abreu SP	5.00	2.00
❑ 340 Mike Williams SP	5.00	2.00
❑ 341 Mike Hampton SP	5.00	2.00
❑ 342 John Wetteland SP	5.00	2.00
❑ 343 Scott Erickson SP	5.00	2.00
❑ 344 Enrique Wilson SP	5.00	2.00
❑ 345 Tim Wakefield SP	5.00	2.00
❑ 346 Mike Lowell SP	5.00	2.00
❑ 347 Todd Pratt SP	5.00	2.00
❑ 348 Brook Fordyce SP	5.00	2.00
❑ 349 Benny Agbayani SP	5.00	2.00
❑ 350 Gabe Kapler SP	5.00	2.00
❑ 351 Sean Casey SP	5.00	2.00
❑ 352 Darren Oliver SP	5.00	2.00
❑ 353 Todd Ritchie SP	5.00	2.00
❑ 354 Kenny Rogers SP	5.00	2.00
❑ 355 Jason Kendall SP	5.00	2.00
❑ 356 John Vander Wal SP	5.00	2.00
❑ 357 Ramon Martinez SP	5.00	2.00
❑ 358 Edgardo Alfonzo SP	5.00	2.00
❑ 359 Phil Nevin SP	5.00	2.00
❑ 360 Albert Belle SP	5.00	2.00
❑ 361 Ruben Rivera SP	5.00	2.00
❑ 362 Pedro Martinez SP	8.00	3.00
❑ 363 Derek Lowe SP	5.00	2.00
❑ 364 Pat Burrell SP	5.00	2.00
❑ 365 Mike Mussina SP	8.00	3.00
❑ 366 Brady Anderson SP	5.00	2.00
❑ 367 Darren Lewis SP	5.00	2.00
❑ 368 Sidney Ponson SP	5.00	2.00
❑ 369 Adam Eaton SP	5.00	2.00
❑ 370 Eric Owens SP	5.00	2.00
❑ 371 Aaron Boone SP	5.00	2.00
❑ 372 Matt Clement SP	5.00	2.00
❑ 373 Derek Bell SP	5.00	2.00
❑ 374 Trot Nixon SP	5.00	2.00
❑ 375 Travis Lee SP	5.00	2.00
❑ 376 Mike Benjamin SP	5.00	2.00
❑ 377 Jeff Zimmerman SP	5.00	2.00
❑ 378 Mike Lieberthal SP	5.00	2.00
❑ 379 Rick Reed SP	5.00	2.00
❑ 380 Nomar Garciaparra SP	12.00	5.00
❑ 381 Omar Daal SP	5.00	2.00
❑ 382 Ryan Klesko SP	5.00	2.00
❑ 383 Rey Ordonez SP	5.00	2.00
❑ 384 Kevin Young SP	5.00	2.00
❑ 385 Rick Helling SP	5.00	2.00
❑ 386 Brian Giles SP	5.00	2.00
❑ 387 Tony Gwynn SP	10.00	4.00
❑ 388 Ed Sprague SP	5.00	2.00
❑ 389 J.R. House SP	5.00	2.00
❑ 390 Scott Hatteberg SP	5.00	2.00
❑ 391 John Valentin SP	5.00	2.00
❑ 392 Melvin Mora SP	5.00	2.00
❑ 393 Royce Clayton SP	5.00	2.00
❑ 394 Jeff Fassero SP	5.00	2.00
❑ 395 Manny Alexander SP	5.00	2.00
❑ 396 John Franco SP	5.00	2.00
❑ 397 Luis Alicea SP	5.00	2.00
❑ 398 Ivan Rodriguez SP	8.00	3.00
❑ 399 Kevin Jordan SP	5.00	2.00
❑ 400 Jose Offerman SP	5.00	2.00
❑ 401 Jeff Conine SP	5.00	2.00
❑ 402 Seth Etherton SP	5.00	2.00
❑ 403 Mike Bordick SP	5.00	2.00
❑ 404 Al Leiter SP	5.00	2.00
❑ 405 Mike Piazza SP	12.00	5.00
❑ 406 Armando Benitez SP	5.00	2.00
❑ 407 Warren Morris SP	5.00	2.00
❑ NNO 1952 Card Redemption EXCH		
❑ NNO Replica Hat-Jsy EXCH		

2002 Topps Heritage

Card		
❑ COMPLETE SET (440)	400.00	200.00
❑ COMP.SET w/o SP's (350)	80.00	40.00
❑ COMMON CARD (1-363)	.50	.20
❑ COMMON SP (364-446)	5.00	2.00
❑ 1 Ichiro Suzuki SP	15.00	6.00
❑ 2 Darin Erstad	.60	.25
❑ 3 Rod Beck	.60	.25
❑ 4 Doug Mientkiewicz	.60	.25
❑ 5 Mike Sweeney	.60	.25
❑ 6 Roger Clemens	3.00	1.25
❑ 7 Jason Tyner	.50	.20
❑ 8 Alex Gonzalez	.50	.20
❑ 9 Eric Young	.50	.20
❑ 10 Randy Johnson	1.50	.60
❑ 10N Randy Johnson Night SP	8.00	3.00
❑ 11 Aaron Sele	.50	.20
❑ 12 Tony Clark	.50	.20
❑ 13 C.C. Sabathia	.60	.25
❑ 14 Melvin Mora	.60	.25
❑ 15 Tim Hudson	.60	.25
❑ 16 Ben Petrick	.50	.20
❑ 17 Tom Glavine	1.00	.40
❑ 18 Jason Lane	.60	.25
❑ 19 Larry Walker	.60	.25
❑ 20 Mark Mulder	.60	.25
❑ 21 Steve Finley	.60	.25
❑ 22 Bengie Molina	.50	.20
❑ 23 Rob Bell	.50	.20
❑ 24 Nathan Haynes	.50	.20
❑ 25 Rafael Furcal	.60	.25
❑ 25N Rafael Furcal Night SP	5.00	2.00
❑ 26 Mike Mussina	1.00	.40
❑ 27 Paul LoDuca	.60	.25
❑ 28 Torii Hunter	.60	.25
❑ 29 Carlos Lee	.60	.25
❑ 30 Jimmy Rollins	.60	.25
❑ 31 Arthur Rhodes	.50	.20
❑ 32 Ivan Rodriguez	1.00	.40
❑ 33 Wes Helms	.50	.20
❑ 34 Cliff Floyd	.60	.25
❑ 35 Julian Tavarez	.50	.20
❑ 36 Mark McGwire	4.00	1.50
❑ 37 Chipper Jones SP	8.00	3.00
❑ 38 Denny Neagle	.50	.20
❑ 39 Odalis Perez	.50	.20
❑ 40 Antonio Alfonseca	.50	.20
❑ 41 Edgar Renteria	.60	.25
❑ 42 Troy Glaus	.60	.25
❑ 43 Scott Brosius	.60	.25
❑ 44 Abraham Nunez	.50	.20
❑ 45 Jamey Wright	.50	.20
❑ 46 Bobby Bonilla	.60	.25
❑ 47 Ismael Valdes	.50	.20
❑ 48 Chris Reitsma	.50	.20
❑ 49 Neifi Perez	.50	.20
❑ 50 Juan Cruz	.50	.20
❑ 51 Kevin Brown	.60	.25
❑ 52 Ben Grieve	.50	.20
❑ 53 Alex Rodriguez SP	12.00	5.00
❑ 54 Charles Nagy	.50	.20
❑ 55 Reggie Sanders	.60	.25
❑ 56 Nelson Figueroa	.50	.20
❑ 57 Felipe Lopez	.50	.20
❑ 58 Bill Ortega	.50	.20
❑ 59 Jeffrey Hammonds	.60	.25
❑ 60 Johnny Estrada	.50	.20
❑ 61 Bob Wickman	.50	.20
❑ 62 Doug Glanville	.50	.20
❑ 63 Jeff Cirillo	.50	.20
❑ 63N Jeff Cirillo Night SP	5.00	2.00
❑ 64 Corey Patterson	.50	.20
❑ 65 Aaron Myette	.50	.20
❑ 66 Magglio Ordonez	.60	.25
❑ 67 Ellis Burks	.60	.25
❑ 68 Miguel Tejada	.60	.25
❑ 69 John Olerud	.60	.25
❑ 69N John Olerud Night SP	5.00	2.00
❑ 70 Greg Vaughn	.50	.20
❑ 71 Andy Pettitte	1.00	.40
❑ 72 Mike Matheny	.50	.20
❑ 73 Brandon Duckworth	.50	.20
❑ 74 Scott Schoeneweis	.50	.20
❑ 75 Mike Lowell	.60	.25
❑ 76 Einar Diaz	.50	.20
❑ 77 Tino Martinez	1.00	.40
❑ 78 Matt Williams	.60	.25
❑ 79 Jason Young RC	1.00	.40
❑ 80 Nate Cornejo	.50	.20
❑ 81 Andres Galarraga	.60	.25
❑ 82 Bernie Williams SP	8.00	3.00
❑ 83 Ryan Klesko	.60	.25
❑ 84 Dan Wilson	.50	.20
❑ 85 Henry Pichardo RC	1.00	.40
❑ 86 Ray Durham	.60	.25
❑ 87 Omar Daal	.50	.20
❑ 88 Derrek Lee	1.00	.40
❑ 89 Al Leiter	.60	.25
❑ 90 Darrin Fletcher	.50	.20
❑ 91 Josh Beckett	.60	.25
❑ 92 Johnny Damon	1.00	.40
❑ 92N Johnny Damon Night SP	8.00	3.00
❑ 93 Abraham Nunez	.50	.20
❑ 94 Ricky Ledee	.50	.20
❑ 95 Richie Sexson	.60	.25
❑ 96 Adam Kennedy	.50	.20
❑ 97 Raul Mondesi	.60	.25
❑ 98 John Burkett	.60	.25
❑ 99 Ben Sheets	.60	.25
❑ 99N Ben Sheets Night SP	5.00	2.00
❑ 100 Preston Wilson	.60	.25
❑ 100N Preston Wilson Night SP	5.00	2.00
❑ 101 Boof Bonser	.50	.20
❑ 102 Shigetoshi Hasegawa	.60	.25
❑ 103 Carlos Febles	.50	.20
❑ 104 Jorge Posada SP	8.00	3.00
❑ 105 Michael Tucker	.50	.20
❑ 106 Roberto Hernandez	.60	.25
❑ 107 John Rodriguez RC	1.00	.40
❑ 108 Danny Graves	.50	.20
❑ 109 Rich Aurilia	.50	.20
❑ 110 Jon Lieber	.50	.20
❑ 111 Tim Hummel RC	1.00	.40
❑ 112 J.T. Snow	.60	.25
❑ 113 Kris Benson	.50	.20
❑ 114 Derek Jeter	4.00	1.50
❑ 115 John Franco	.60	.25
❑ 116 Matt Stairs	.50	.20
❑ 117 Ben Davis	.50	.20
❑ 118 Darryl Kile	.60	.25
❑ 119 Mike Peeples RC	1.00	.40
❑ 120 Kevin Tapani	.50	.20
❑ 121 Armando Benitez	.50	.20
❑ 122 Damian Miller	.50	.20
❑ 123 Jose Jimenez	.50	.20
❑ 124 Pedro Astacio	.50	.20
❑ 125 Marlyn Tisdale RC	1.00	.40
❑ 126 Deivi Cruz	.50	.20
❑ 127 Paul O'Neill	1.00	.40
❑ 128 Jermaine Dye	.60	.25
❑ 129 Marcus Giles	.60	.25
❑ 130 Mark Loretta	.50	.20
❑ 131 Garret Anderson	.60	.25
❑ 132 Todd Ritchie	.50	.20
❑ 133 Joe Crede	.60	.25
❑ 134 Kevin Millwood	.60	.25
❑ 135 Shane Reynolds	.50	.20
❑ 136 Mark Grace	1.00	.40
❑ 137 Shannon Stewart	.60	.25
❑ 138 Nick Neugebauer	.50	.20
❑ 139 Nic Jackson RC	1.00	.40
❑ 140 Robb Nen UER	.60	.25
❑ 141 Dmitri Young	.60	.25

No.	Card		
142	Kevin Appier	.60	.25
143	Jack Cust	.50	.20
144	Andres Torres	.50	.20
145	Frank Thomas	1.50	.60
146	Jason Kendall	.60	.25
147	Greg Maddux	2.50	1.00
148	David Justice	.60	.25
149	Hideo Nomo	1.50	.60
150	Bret Boone	.60	.25
151	Wade Miller	.50	.20
152	Jeff Kent	.60	.25
153	Scott Williamson	.50	.20
154	Julio Lugo	.50	.20
155	Bobby Higginson	.60	.25
156	Geoff Jenkins	.50	.20
157	Darren Dreifort	.50	.20
158	Freddy Sanchez RC	3.00	1.25
159	Bud Smith	.50	.20
160	Phil Nevin	.60	.25
161	Cesar Izturis	.50	.20
162	Sean Casey	.60	.25
163	Jose Ortiz	.50	.20
164	Brent Abernathy	.50	.20
165	Kevin Young	.50	.20
166	Daryle Ward	.50	.20
167	Trevor Hoffman	.60	.25
168	Rondell White	.60	.25
169	Kip Wells	.50	.20
170	John Vander Wal	.50	.20
171	Jose Lima	.50	.20
172	Wilton Guerrero	.50	.20
173	Aaron Dean RC	1.00	.40
174	Rick Helling	.50	.20
175	Juan Pierre	.60	.25
176	Jay Bell	.60	.25
177	Craig House	.50	.20
178	David Bell	.50	.20
179	Pat Burrell	.60	.25
180	Eric Gagne	.60	.25
181	Adam Pettyjohn	.50	.20
182	Ugueth Urbina	.50	.20
183	Peter Bergeron	.50	.20
184	Adrian Gonzalez	.50	.20
184N	Adrian Gonzalez Night SP	5.00	2.00
185	Damion Easley	.50	.20
186	Gookie Dawkins	.50	.20
187	Matt Lawton	.50	.20
188	Frank Catalanotto	.50	.20
189	David Wells	.60	.25
190	Roger Cedeno	.50	.20
191	Brian Giles	.60	.25
192	Julio Zuleta	.50	.20
193	Timo Perez	.50	.20
194	Billy Wagner	.60	.25
195	Craig Counsell	.50	.20
196	Bart Miadich	.50	.20
197	Gary Sheffield	.60	.25
198	Richard Hidalgo	.50	.20
199	Juan Uribe	.50	.20
200	Curt Schilling	.60	.25
201	Javy Lopez	.60	.25
202	Jimmy Haynes	.50	.20
203	Jim Edmonds	.60	.25
204	Pokey Reese	.50	.20
204N	Pokey Reese Night SP	5.00	2.00
205	Matt Clement	.60	.25
206	Dean Palmer	.60	.25
207	Nick Johnson	.60	.25
208	Nate Espy RC	1.00	.40
209	Pedro Feliz	.50	.20
210	Aaron Rowand	.60	.25
211	Masato Yoshii	.50	.20
212	Jose Cruz Jr.	.50	.20
213	Paul Byrd	.50	.20
214	Mark Phillips RC	1.00	.40
215	Benny Agbayani	.50	.20
216	Frank Menechino	.50	.20
217	John Flaherty	.50	.20
218	Brian Boehringer	.50	.20
219	Todd Hollandsworth	.50	.20
220	Sammy Sosa SP	8.00	3.00
221	Steve Sparks	.50	.20
222	Homer Bush	.50	.20
223	Mike Hampton	.60	.25
224	Bobby Abreu	.60	.25
225	Barry Larkin	1.00	.40
226	Ryan Rupe	.50	.20
227	Bubba Trammell	.50	.20
228	Todd Zeile	.60	.25
229	Jeff Shaw	.50	.20
230	Alex Ochoa	.50	.20
231	Orlando Cabrera	.60	.25
232	Jeremy Giambi	.50	.20
233	Tomo Ohka	.50	.20
234	Luis Castillo	.50	.20
235	Chris Holt	.50	.20
236	Shawn Green	.60	.25
237	Sidney Ponson	.50	.20
238	Lee Stevens	.50	.20
239	Hank Blalock	1.00	.40
240	Randy Winn	.50	.20
241	Pedro Martinez	1.00	.40
242	Vinny Castilla	.60	.25
243	Steve Karsay	.50	.20
244	Barry Bonds SP	20.00	8.00
245	Jason Bere	.50	.20
246	Scott Rolen	1.00	.40
246N	Scott Rolen Night SP	8.00	3.00
247	Ryan Kohlmeier	.50	.20
248	Kerry Wood	.60	.25
249	Aramis Ramirez	.60	.25
250	Lance Berkman	.60	.25
251	Omar Vizquel	1.00	.40
252	Juan Encarnacion	.50	.20
253	Does Not Exist		
254	David Segui	.50	.20
255	Brian Anderson	.50	.20
256	Jay Payton	.50	.20
257	Mark Grudzielanek	.50	.20
258	Jimmy Anderson	.50	.20
259	Eric Valent	.50	.20
260	Chad Durbin	.50	.20
261	Does Not Exist		
262	Alex Gonzalez	.50	.20
263	Scott Dunn	.50	.20
264	Scott Elarton	.50	.20
265	Tom Gordon	.50	.20
266	Moises Alou	.60	.25
267	Does Not Exist		
268	Does Not Exist		
269	Mark Buehrle	.60	.25
270	Jerry Hairston	.50	.20
271	Does Not Exist		
272	Luke Prokopec	.50	.20
273	Graeme Lloyd	.50	.20
274	Bret Prinz	.50	.20
275	Does Not Exist		
276	Chris Carpenter	.60	.25
277	Ryan Minor	.50	.20
278	Jeff D'Amico	.50	.20
279	Raul Ibanez	.50	.20
280	Joe Mays	.50	.20
281	Livan Hernandez	.60	.25
282	Robin Ventura	.60	.25
283	Gabe Kapler	.60	.25
284	Tony Batista	.50	.20
285	Ramon Hernandez	.50	.20
286	Craig Paquette	.50	.20
287	Mark Kotsay	.60	.25
288	Mike Lieberthal	.60	.25
289	Joe Borchard	.50	.20
290	Cristian Guzman	.50	.20
291	Craig Biggio	1.00	.40
292	Joaquin Benoit	.50	.20
293	Ken Caminiti	.60	.25
294	Sean Burroughs	.50	.20
295	Eric Karros	.60	.25
296	Eric Chavez	.60	.25
297	LaTroy Hawkins	.50	.20
298	Alfonso Soriano	.60	.25
299	John Smoltz	1.00	.40
300	Adam Dunn	.60	.25
301	Ryan Dempster	.50	.20
302	Travis Hafner	.60	.25
303	Russell Branyan	.50	.20
304	Dustin Hermanson	.50	.20
305	Jim Thome	1.00	.40
306	Carlos Beltran	.60	.25
307	Jason Botts RC	.60	.25
308	David Cone	.60	.25
309	Ivanon Coffie	.50	.20
310	Brian Jordan	.60	.25
311	Todd Walker	.50	.20
312	Jeromy Burnitz	.60	.25
313	Tony Armas Jr.	.50	.20
314	Jeff Conine	.60	.25
315	Todd Jones	.50	.20
316	Roy Oswalt	.60	.25
317	Aubrey Huff	.60	.25
318	Josh Fogg	.50	.20
319	Jose Vidro	.50	.20
320	Jace Brewer	.50	.20
321	Mike Redmond	.50	.20
322	Noochie Varner RC	1.00	.40
323	Russ Ortiz	.50	.20
324	Edgardo Alfonzo	.50	.20
325	Ruben Sierra	.60	.25
326	Calvin Murray	.50	.20
327	Marlon Anderson	.50	.20
328	Albie Lopez	.50	.20
329	Chris Gomez	.50	.20
330	Fernando Tatis	.50	.20
331	Stubby Clapp	.50	.20
332	Rickey Henderson	1.50	.60
333	Brad Radke	.60	.25
334	Brent Mayne	.50	.20
335	Cory Lidle	.50	.20
336	Edgar Martinez	1.00	.40
337	Aaron Boone	.60	.25
338	Jay Witasick	.50	.20
339	Benito Santiago	.60	.25
340	Jose Mercedes	.50	.20
341	Fernando Vina	.50	.20
342	A.J. Pierzynski	.60	.25
343	Jeff Bagwell	1.00	.40
344	Brian Bohanon	.50	.20
345	Adrian Beltre	.60	.25
346	Troy Percival	.60	.25
347	Napoleon Calzado RC	1.00	.40
348	Ruben Rivera	.50	.20
349	Rafael Soriano	.50	.20
350	Damian Jackson	.50	.20
351	Joe Randa	.60	.25
352	Chan Ho Park	.60	.25
353	Dante Bichette	.60	.25
354	Bartolo Colon	.60	.25
355	Jason Bay RC	5.00	2.00
356	Shea Hillenbrand	.60	.25
357	Matt Morris	.60	.25
358	Brad Penny	.50	.20
359	Mark Quinn	.50	.20
360	Marquis Grissom	.60	.25
361	Henry Blanco	.50	.20
362	Billy Koch	.50	.20
363	Mike Cameron	.50	.20
364	Albert Pujols SP	15.00	6.00
365	Paul Konerko SP	5.00	2.00
366	Eric Milton SP	5.00	2.00
367	Nick Bierbrodt SP	5.00	2.00
368	Rafael Palmeiro SP	8.00	3.00
369	Jorge Padilla SP RC	5.00	2.00
370	Jason Giambi Yankees SP	5.00	2.00
371	Mike Piazza SP	12.00	5.00
372	Alex Cora SP	5.00	2.00
373	Todd Helton SP	8.00	3.00
374	Juan Gonzalez SP	5.00	2.00
375	Mariano Rivera SP	8.00	3.00
376	Jason LaRue SP	5.00	2.00
377	Tony Gwynn SP	10.00	4.00
378	Wilson Betemit SP	5.00	2.00
379	J.J. Trujillo SP RC	5.00	2.00
380	Brad Ausmus SP	5.00	2.00
381	Chris George SP	5.00	2.00
382	Jose Canseco SP	8.00	3.00
383	Ramon Ortiz SP	5.00	2.00
384	John Rocker SP	5.00	2.00
385	Rey Ordonez SP	5.00	2.00
386	Ken Griffey Jr. SP	12.00	5.00
387	Juan Pena SP	5.00	2.00
388	Michael Barrett SP	5.00	2.00
389	J.D. Drew SP	5.00	2.00
390	Corey Koskie SP	5.00	2.00
391	Vernon Wells SP	5.00	2.00
392	Juan Tolentino SP RC	5.00	2.00
393	Luis Gonzalez SP	5.00	2.00
394	Terrence Long SP	5.00	2.00
395	Travis Lee SP	5.00	2.00
396	Earl Snyder SP RC	5.00	2.00

❑ 397 Nomar Garciaparra SP	12.00	5.00
❑ 398 Jason Schmidt SP	5.00	2.00
❑ 399 David Espinosa SP	5.00	2.00
❑ 400 Steve Green SP	5.00	2.00
❑ 401 Jack Wilson SP	5.00	2.00
❑ 402 Chris Tritle SP RC	5.00	2.00
❑ 403 Angel Berroa SP	5.00	2.00
❑ 404 Josh Towers SP	5.00	2.00
❑ 405 Andruw Jones SP	8.00	3.00
❑ 406 Brent Butler SP	5.00	2.00
❑ 407 Craig Kuzmic SP	5.00	2.00
❑ 408 Derek Bell SP	5.00	2.00
❑ 409 Eric Glaser SP RC	5.00	2.00
❑ 410 Joel Pineiro SP	5.00	2.00
❑ 411 Alexis Gomez SP	5.00	2.00
❑ 412 Mike Rivera SP	5.00	2.00
❑ 413 Shawn Estes SP	5.00	2.00
❑ 414 Milton Bradley SP	5.00	2.00
❑ 415 Carl Everett SP	5.00	2.00
❑ 416 Kazuhiro Sasaki SP	5.00	2.00
❑ 417 Tony Fontana SP RC	5.00	2.00
❑ 418 Josh Pearce SP	5.00	2.00
❑ 419 Gary Matthews Jr. SP	5.00	2.00
❑ 420 Raymond Cabrera SP RC	5.00	2.00
❑ 421 Joe Kennedy SP	5.00	2.00
❑ 422 Jason Maule SP RC	5.00	2.00
❑ 423 Casey Fossum SP	5.00	2.00
❑ 424 Christian Parker SP	5.00	2.00
❑ 425 Laynce Nix SP RC	10.00	4.00
❑ 426 Byung-Hyun Kim SP	5.00	2.00
❑ 427 Freddy Garcia SP	5.00	2.00
❑ 428 Herbert Perry SP	5.00	2.00
❑ 429 Jason Marquis SP	5.00	2.00
❑ 430 Sandy Alomar Jr. SP	5.00	2.00
❑ 431 Roberto Alomar SP	8.00	3.00
❑ 432 Tsuyoshi Shinjo SP	5.00	2.00
❑ 433 Tim Wakefield SP	5.00	2.00
❑ 434 Robert Fick SP	5.00	2.00
❑ 435 Vladimir Guerrero SP	8.00	3.00
❑ 436 Jose Mesa SP	5.00	2.00
❑ 437 Scott Spiezio SP	5.00	2.00
❑ 438 Jose Hernandez SP	5.00	2.00
❑ 439 Jose Acevedo SP	5.00	2.00
❑ 440 Brian West SP RC	5.00	2.00
❑ 441 Barry Zito SP	5.00	2.00
❑ 442 Luis Maza SP	5.00	2.00
❑ 443 Marlon Byrd SP	5.00	2.00
❑ 444 A.J. Burnett SP	5.00	2.00
❑ 445 Dee Brown SP	5.00	2.00
❑ 446 Carlos Delgado SP	5.00	2.00
❑ NNO 1953 Repurchased EXCH.		

2003 Topps Heritage

❑ COMPLETE SET (450)	300.00	175.00
❑ COMP.SET w/o SP's (350)	80.00	40.00
❑ COMMON CARD	.50	.20
❑ COMMON RC	1.00	.40
❑ COMMON SP	5.00	2.00
❑ COMMON SP RC	5.00	2.00
❑ 1A Alex Rodriguez Red	2.50	1.00
❑ 1B Alex Rodriguez Black SP	12.00	5.00
❑ 2 Jose Cruz Jr.	.50	.20
❑ 3 Ichiro Suzuki SP	15.00	6.00
❑ 4 Rich Aurilia	.50	.20
❑ 5 Trevor Hoffman	.60	.25
❑ 6A Brian Giles New Logo	.60	.25
❑ 6B Brian Giles Old Logo SP	5.00	2.00
❑ 7A Albert Pujols Orange	3.00	1.25
❑ 7B Albert Pujols Black SP	15.00	6.00
❑ 8 Vicente Padilla	.50	.20
❑ 9 Bobby Crosby	.60	.25
❑ 10A Derek Jeter New Logo	4.00	1.50
❑ 10B Derek Jeter Old Logo SP	15.00	6.00
❑ 11A Pat Burrell New Logo	.60	.25
❑ 11B Pat Burrell Old Logo SP	5.00	2.00
❑ 12 Armando Benitez	.50	.20
❑ 13 Javier Vazquez	.60	.25
❑ 14 Justin Morneau	.60	.25
❑ 15 Doug Mientkiewicz	.60	.25
❑ 16 Kevin Brown	.60	.25
❑ 17 Alexis Gomez	.50	.20
❑ 18A Lance Berkman Blue	.60	.25
❑ 18B Lance Berkman Black SP	5.00	2.00
❑ 19 Adrian Gonzalez	.50	.20
❑ 20A Todd Helton Green	1.00	.40
❑ 20B Todd Helton Black SP	8.00	3.00
❑ 21 Carlos Pena	.50	.20
❑ 22 Matt Lawton	.50	.20
❑ 23 Elmer Dessens	.50	.20
❑ 24 Hee Seop Choi	.50	.20
❑ 25 Chris Duncan SP RC	12.00	5.00
❑ 26 Ugueth Urbina	.50	.20
❑ 27A Rodrigo Lopez New Logo	.50	.20
❑ 27B Rodrigo Lopez Old Logo SP	5.00	2.00
❑ 28 Damian Moss	.50	.20
❑ 29 Steve Finley	.60	.25
❑ 30A Sammy Sosa New Logo	1.50	.60
❑ 30B Sammy Sosa Old Logo SP	8.00	3.00
❑ 31 Kevin Cash	.50	.20
❑ 32 Kenny Rogers	.60	.25
❑ 33 Ben Grieve	.50	.20
❑ 34 Jason Simontacchi	.50	.20
❑ 35 Shin-Soo Choo	.50	.20
❑ 36 Freddy Garcia	.60	.25
❑ 37 Jesse Foppert	.50	.20
❑ 38 Tony LaRussa MG	.60	.25
❑ 39 Mark Kotsay	.60	.25
❑ 40 Barry Zito	.60	.25
❑ 41 Josh Fogg	.50	.20
❑ 42 Marlon Byrd	.50	.20
❑ 43 Marcus Thames	.50	.20
❑ 44 Al Leiter	.60	.25
❑ 45 Michael Barrett	.50	.20
❑ 46 Jake Peavy	.60	.25
❑ 47 Dustan Mohr	.50	.20
❑ 48 Alex Sanchez	.50	.20
❑ 49 Chin-Feng Chen	.60	.25
❑ 50A Kazuhisa Ishii Blue	.60	.25
❑ 50B Kazuhisa Ishii Black SP	5.00	2.00
❑ 51 Carlos Beltran	.60	.25
❑ 52 Franklin Gutierrez RC	1.00	.40
❑ 53 Miguel Cabrera	1.50	.60
❑ 54 Roger Clemens	3.00	1.25
❑ 55 Juan Cruz	.50	.20
❑ 56 Jason Young	.50	.20
❑ 57 Alex Herrera	.50	.20
❑ 58 Aaron Boone	.60	.25
❑ 59 Mark Buehrle	.60	.25
❑ 60 Larry Walker	.60	.25
❑ 61 Morgan Ensberg	.60	.25
❑ 62 Barry Larkin	1.00	.40
❑ 63 Joe Borchard	.50	.20
❑ 64 Jason Dubois	.50	.20
❑ 65 Shea Hillenbrand	.60	.25
❑ 66 Jay Gibbons	.50	.20
❑ 67 Vinny Castilla	.60	.25
❑ 68 Jeff Mathis	.50	.20
❑ 69 Curt Schilling	.60	.25
❑ 70 Garret Anderson	.60	.25
❑ 71 Josh Phelps	.50	.20
❑ 72 Chan Ho Park	.60	.25
❑ 73 Edgar Renteria	.60	.25
❑ 74 Kazuhiro Sasaki	.60	.25
❑ 75 Lloyd McClendon MG	.50	.20
❑ 76 Jon Lieber	.50	.20
❑ 77 Rolando Viera	.50	.20
❑ 78 Jeff Conine	.60	.25
❑ 79 Kevin Millwood	.60	.25
❑ 80A Randy Johnson Green	1.50	.60
❑ 80B Randy Johnson Black SP	12.00	5.00
❑ 81 Troy Percival	.60	.25
❑ 82 Cliff Floyd	.60	.25
❑ 83 Tony Graffanino	.50	.20
❑ 84 Austin Kearns	.50	.20
❑ 85 Manuel Ramirez SP RC	8.00	3.00
❑ 86 Jim Tracy MG	.50	.20
❑ 87 Rondell White	.60	.25
❑ 88 Trot Nixon	.60	.25
❑ 89 Carlos Lee	.60	.25
❑ 90 Mike Lowell	.60	.25
❑ 91 Raul Ibanez	.50	.20
❑ 92 Ricardo Rodriguez	.50	.20
❑ 93 Ben Sheets	.60	.25
❑ 94 Jason Perry SP RC	8.00	3.00
❑ 95 Mark Teixeira	1.00	.40
❑ 96 Brad Fullmer	.50	.20
❑ 97 Casey Kotchman	.60	.25
❑ 98 Craig Counsell	.50	.20
❑ 99 Jason Marquis	.50	.20
❑ 100A N.Garciaparra New Logo	2.50	1.00
❑ 100B N.Garciaparra Old Logo SP	12.00	5.00
❑ 101 Ed Rogers	.50	.20
❑ 102 Wilson Betemit	.50	.20
❑ 103 Wayne Lydon RC	1.00	.40
❑ 104 Jack Cust	.50	.20
❑ 105 Derrek Lee	1.00	.40
❑ 106 Jim Kavourias	.50	.20
❑ 107 Joe Randa	.60	.25
❑ 108 Taylor Buchholz	.50	.20
❑ 109 Gabe Kapler	.60	.25
❑ 110 Preston Wilson	.60	.25
❑ 111 Craig Biggio	1.00	.40
❑ 112 Paul Lo Duca	.60	.25
❑ 113 Eddie Guardado	.50	.20
❑ 114 Andres Galarraga	1.00	.40
❑ 115 Edgardo Alfonzo	.50	.20
❑ 116 Robin Ventura	.60	.25
❑ 117 Jeremy Giambi	.50	.20
❑ 118 Ray Durham	.60	.25
❑ 119 Mariano Rivera	1.50	.60
❑ 120 Jimmy Rollins	.60	.25
❑ 121 Dennis Tankersley	.50	.20
❑ 122 Jason Schmidt	.60	.25
❑ 123 Bret Boone	.60	.25
❑ 124 Josh Hamilton	.50	.20
❑ 125 Scott Rolen	1.00	.40
❑ 126 Steve Cox	.50	.20
❑ 127 Larry Bowa MG	.60	.25
❑ 128 Adam LaRoche SP	5.00	2.00
❑ 129 Ryan Klesko	.60	.25
❑ 130 Tim Hudson	.60	.25
❑ 131 Brandon Claussen	.50	.20
❑ 132 Craig Brazell SP RC	5.00	2.00
❑ 133 Grady Little MG	.50	.20
❑ 134 Jarrod Washburn	.50	.20
❑ 135 Lyle Overbay	.50	.20
❑ 136 John Burkett	.50	.20
❑ 137 Daryl Clark RC	1.00	.40
❑ 138 Kirk Rueter	.50	.20
❑ 139A Mauer Brothers Green	1.50	.60
❑ 139B Mauer Brothers Black SP	10.00	4.00
❑ 140 Troy Glaus	.60	.25
❑ 141 Trey Hodges SP	5.00	2.00
❑ 142 Dallas McPherson	.60	.25
❑ 143 Art Howe MG	.50	.20
❑ 144 Jesus Cota	.50	.20
❑ 145 J.R. House	.50	.20
❑ 146 Reggie Sanders	.60	.25
❑ 147 Clint Nageotte	.50	.20
❑ 148 Jim Edmonds	.60	.25
❑ 149 Carl Crawford	.60	.25
❑ 150A Mike Piazza Blue	2.50	1.00
❑ 150B Mike Piazza Black SP	12.00	5.00
❑ 151 Seung Song	.50	.20
❑ 152 Roberto Hernandez	.60	.25
❑ 153 Marquis Grissom	.60	.25
❑ 154 Billy Wagner	.60	.25
❑ 155 Josh Beckett	.60	.25
❑ 156A Randall Simon New Logo	.50	.20
❑ 156B Randall Simon Old Logo SP	5.00	2.00
❑ 157 Ben Broussard	.50	.20
❑ 158 Russell Branyan	.50	.20
❑ 159 Frank Thomas	1.50	.60
❑ 160 Alex Escobar	.50	.20
❑ 161 Mark Bellhorn	.60	.25
❑ 162 Melvin Mora	.60	.25
❑ 163 Andruw Jones	1.00	.40
❑ 164 Danny Bautista	.50	.20
❑ 165 Ramon Ortiz	.50	.20
❑ 166 Wily Mo Pena	.60	.25

❑ 167	Jose Jimenez	.50	.20
❑ 168	Mark Redman	.50	.20
❑ 169	Angel Berroa	.50	.20
❑ 170	Andy Marte SP RC	12.00	5.00
❑ 171	Juan Gonzalez	.60	.25
❑ 172	Fernando Vina	.50	.20
❑ 173	Joel Pineiro	.50	.20
❑ 174	Boof Bonser	.50	.20
❑ 175	Bernie Castro SP RC	5.00	2.00
❑ 176	Bobby Cox MG	.50	.20
❑ 177	Jeff Kent	.60	.25
❑ 178	Oliver Perez	.60	.25
❑ 179	Chase Utley	1.50	.60
❑ 180	Mark Mulder	.60	.25
❑ 181	Bobby Abreu	.60	.25
❑ 182	Ramiro Mendoza	.50	.20
❑ 183	Aaron Heilman	.50	.20
❑ 184	A.J. Pierzynski	.60	.25
❑ 185	Eric Gagne	.60	.25
❑ 186	Kirk Saarloos	.50	.20
❑ 187	Ron Gardenhire MG	.50	.20
❑ 188	Dmitri Young	.60	.25
❑ 189	Todd Zeile	.60	.25
❑ 190A	Jim Thome New Logo	1.00	.40
❑ 190B	Jim Thome Old Logo SP	8.00	3.00
❑ 191	Cliff Lee	.50	.20
❑ 192	Matt Morris	.60	.25
❑ 193	Robert Fick	.50	.20
❑ 194	C.C. Sabathia	.60	.25
❑ 195	Alexis Rios	.60	.25
❑ 196	D'Angelo Jimenez	.50	.20
❑ 197	Edgar Martinez	1.00	.40
❑ 198	Robb Nen	.60	.25
❑ 199	Taggert Bozied	.50	.20
❑ 200	Vladimir Guerrero SP	8.00	3.00
❑ 201	Walter Young SP	5.00	2.00
❑ 202	Brendan Harris RC	1.00	.40
❑ 203	Mike Hargrove MG	.50	.20
❑ 204	Vernon Wells	.60	.25
❑ 205	Hank Blalock	.60	.25
❑ 206	Mike Cameron	.50	.20
❑ 207	Tony Batista	.50	.20
❑ 208	Matt Williams	.60	.25
❑ 209	Tony Womack	.50	.20
❑ 210	Ramon Nivar-Martinez RC	1.00	.40
❑ 211	Aaron Sele	.50	.20
❑ 212	Mark Grace	1.00	.40
❑ 213	Joe Crede	.60	.25
❑ 214	Ryan Dempster	.50	.20
❑ 215	Omar Vizquel	1.00	.40
❑ 216	Juan Pierre	.60	.25
❑ 217	Denny Bautista	.50	.20
❑ 218	Chuck Knoblauch	.60	.25
❑ 219	Eric Karros	.60	.25
❑ 220	Victor Diaz	.60	.25
❑ 221	Jacque Jones	.60	.25
❑ 222	Jose Vidro	.50	.20
❑ 223	Joe McEwing	.50	.20
❑ 224	Nick Johnson	.60	.25
❑ 225	Eric Chavez	.60	.25
❑ 226	Jose Mesa	.50	.20
❑ 227	Aramis Ramirez	.60	.25
❑ 228	John Lackey	.50	.20
❑ 229	David Bell	.50	.20
❑ 230	John Olerud	.60	.25
❑ 231	Tino Martinez	1.00	.40
❑ 232	Randy Winn	.50	.20
❑ 233	Todd Hollandsworth	.50	.20
❑ 234	Ruddy Lugo RC	1.00	.40
❑ 235	Carlos Delgado	.60	.25
❑ 236	Chris Narveson	.50	.20
❑ 237	Tim Salmon	1.00	.40
❑ 238	Orlando Palmeiro	.50	.20
❑ 239	Jeff Clark SP RC	5.00	2.00
❑ 240	Byung-Hyun Kim	.60	.25
❑ 241	Mike Remlinger	.50	.20
❑ 242	Johnny Damon	1.00	.40
❑ 243	Corey Patterson	.50	.20
❑ 244	Paul Konerko	.60	.25
❑ 245	Danny Graves	.50	.20
❑ 246	Ellis Burks	.60	.25
❑ 247	Gavin Floyd	.50	.20
❑ 248	Jaime Bubela RC	1.00	.40
❑ 249	Sean Burroughs	.50	.20
❑ 250	Alex Rodriguez SP	12.00	5.00
❑ 251	Gabe Gross	.50	.20
❑ 252	Rafael Palmeiro	1.00	.40
❑ 253	Dewon Brazelton	.50	.20
❑ 254	Jimmy Journell	.50	.20
❑ 255	Rafael Soriano	.50	.20
❑ 256	Jerome Williams	.50	.20
❑ 257	Xavier Nady	.50	.20
❑ 258	Mike Williams	.50	.20
❑ 259	Randy Wolf	.50	.20
❑ 260A	Miguel Tejada Orange	.60	.25
❑ 260B	Miguel Tejada Black SP	5.00	2.00
❑ 261	Juan Rivera	.50	.20
❑ 262	Rey Ordonez	.50	.20
❑ 263	Bartolo Colon	.60	.25
❑ 264	Eric Milton	.50	.20
❑ 265	Jeffrey Hammonds	.50	.20
❑ 266	Odalis Perez	.50	.20
❑ 267	Mike Sweeney	.60	.25
❑ 268	Richard Hidalgo	.50	.20
❑ 269	Alex Gonzalez	.50	.20
❑ 270	Aaron Cook	.50	.20
❑ 271	Earl Snyder	.50	.20
❑ 272	Todd Walker	.50	.20
❑ 273	Aaron Rowand	.60	.25
❑ 274	Matt Clement	.60	.25
❑ 275	Anastacio Martinez	.50	.20
❑ 276	Mike Bordick	.60	.25
❑ 277	John Smoltz	1.00	.40
❑ 278	Scott Hairston	.50	.20
❑ 279	David Eckstein	.60	.25
❑ 280	Shannon Stewart	.60	.25
❑ 281	Carl Everett	.60	.25
❑ 282	Aubrey Huff	.60	.25
❑ 283	Mike Mussina	1.00	.40
❑ 284	Ruben Sierra	.60	.25
❑ 285	Russ Ortiz	.50	.20
❑ 286	Brian Lawrence	.50	.20
❑ 287	Kip Wells	.50	.20
❑ 288	Placido Polanco	.50	.20
❑ 289	Ted Lilly	.50	.20
❑ 290	Andy Pettitte	1.00	.40
❑ 291	John Buck	.50	.20
❑ 292	Orlando Cabrera	.60	.25
❑ 293	Cristian Guzman	.50	.20
❑ 294	Ruben Quevedo	.50	.20
❑ 295	Cesar Izturis	.50	.20
❑ 296	Ryan Ludwick	.50	.20
❑ 297	Roy Oswalt	.60	.25
❑ 298	Jason Stokes	.50	.20
❑ 299	Mike Hampton	.60	.25
❑ 300	Pedro Martinez	1.00	.40
❑ 301	Nic Jackson	.50	.20
❑ 302A	Magglio Ordonez New Logo	.60	.25
❑ 302B	Magglio Ordonez Old Logo SP	5.00	2.00
❑ 303	Manny Ramirez	1.00	.40
❑ 304	Jorge Julio	.50	.20
❑ 305	Javy Lopez	.60	.25
❑ 306	Roy Halladay	.60	.25
❑ 307	Kevin Mench	.50	.20
❑ 308	Jason Isringhausen	.60	.25
❑ 309	Carlos Guillen	.60	.25
❑ 310	Tsuyoshi Shinjo	.60	.25
❑ 311	Phil Nevin	.60	.25
❑ 312	Pokey Reese	.50	.20
❑ 313	Jorge Padilla	.50	.20
❑ 314	Jermaine Dye	.60	.25
❑ 315	David Wells	.60	.25
❑ 316	Mo Vaughn	.60	.25
❑ 317	Bernie Williams	1.00	.40
❑ 318	Michael Restovich	.50	.20
❑ 319	Jose Hernandez	.50	.20
❑ 320	Richie Sexson	.60	.25
❑ 321	Daryle Ward	.50	.20
❑ 322	Luis Castillo	.50	.20
❑ 323	Rene Reyes	.50	.20
❑ 324	Victor Martinez	1.00	.40
❑ 325A	Adam Dunn New Logo	.60	.25
❑ 325B	Adam Dunn Old Logo SP	5.00	2.00
❑ 326	Corwin Malone	.50	.20
❑ 327	Kerry Wood	.60	.25
❑ 328	Rickey Henderson	1.50	.60
❑ 329	Marty Cordova	.50	.20
❑ 330	Greg Maddux	2.50	1.00
❑ 331	Miguel Batista	.50	.20
❑ 332	Chris Bootcheck	.50	.20
❑ 333	Carlos Baerga	.50	.20
❑ 334	Antonio Alfonseca	.50	.20
❑ 335	Shane Halter	.50	.20
❑ 336	Juan Encarnacion	.50	.20
❑ 337	Tom Gordon	.50	.20
❑ 338	Hideo Nomo	1.50	.60
❑ 339	Torii Hunter	.60	.25
❑ 340A	Alfonso Soriano Yellow	.60	.25
❑ 340B	Alfonso Soriano Black SP	5.00	2.00
❑ 341	Roberto Alomar	1.00	.40
❑ 342	David Justice	.60	.25
❑ 343	Mike Lieberthal	.60	.25
❑ 344	Jeff Weaver	.50	.20
❑ 345	Timo Perez	.50	.20
❑ 346	Travis Lee	.50	.20
❑ 347	Sean Casey	.60	.25
❑ 348	Willie Harris	.50	.20
❑ 349	Derek Lowe	.60	.25
❑ 350	Tom Glavine	1.00	.40
❑ 351	Eric Hinske	.50	.20
❑ 352	Rocco Baldelli	.60	.25
❑ 353	J.D. Drew	.60	.25
❑ 354	Jamie Moyer	.60	.25
❑ 355	Todd Linden	.50	.20
❑ 356	Benito Santiago	.60	.25
❑ 357	Brad Baker	.50	.20
❑ 358	Alex Gonzalez	.50	.20
❑ 359	Brandon Duckworth	.50	.20
❑ 360	John Rheinecker	.50	.20
❑ 361	Orlando Hernandez	.60	.25
❑ 362	Pedro Astacio	.50	.20
❑ 363	Brad Wilkerson	.50	.20
❑ 364	David Ortiz SP	8.00	3.00
❑ 365	Geoff Jenkins SP	5.00	2.00
❑ 366	Brian Jordan SP	5.00	2.00
❑ 367	Paul Byrd SP	5.00	2.00
❑ 368	Jason Lane SP	5.00	2.00
❑ 369	Jeff Bagwell SP	8.00	3.00
❑ 370	Bobby Higginson SP	5.00	2.00
❑ 371	Juan Uribe SP	5.00	2.00
❑ 372	Lee Stevens SP	5.00	2.00
❑ 373	Jimmy Haynes SP	5.00	2.00
❑ 374	Jose Valentin SP	5.00	2.00
❑ 375	Ken Griffey Jr. SP	12.00	5.00
❑ 376	Barry Bonds SP	20.00	8.00
❑ 377	Gary Matthews Jr. SP	5.00	2.00
❑ 378	Gary Sheffield SP	5.00	2.00
❑ 379	Rick Helling SP	5.00	2.00
❑ 380	Junior Spivey SP	5.00	2.00
❑ 381	Francisco Rodriguez SP	5.00	2.00
❑ 382	Chipper Jones SP	8.00	3.00
❑ 383	Orlando Hudson SP	5.00	2.00
❑ 384	Ivan Rodriguez SP	8.00	3.00
❑ 385	Chris Snelling SP	5.00	2.00
❑ 386	Kenny Lofton SP	5.00	2.00
❑ 387	Eric Cyr SP	5.00	2.00
❑ 388	Jason Kendall SP	5.00	2.00
❑ 389	Marlon Anderson SP	5.00	2.00
❑ 390	Billy Koch SP	5.00	2.00
❑ 392	Jose Reyes SP	5.00	2.00
❑ 393	Fernando Tatis SP	5.00	2.00
❑ 394	Michael Cuddyer SP	5.00	2.00
❑ 395	Mark Prior SP	8.00	3.00
❑ 396	Dontrelle Willis SP	8.00	3.00
❑ 397	Jay Payton SP	5.00	2.00
❑ 398	Brandon Phillips SP	5.00	2.00
❑ 399	Dustin Moseley SP RC	5.00	2.00
❑ 400	Jason Giambi SP	5.00	2.00
❑ 401	John Mabry SP	5.00	2.00
❑ 402	Ron Gant SP	5.00	2.00
❑ 403	J.T. Snow SP	5.00	2.00
❑ 404	Jeff Cirillo SP	5.00	2.00
❑ 405	Darin Erstad SP	5.00	2.00
❑ 406	Luis Gonzalez SP	5.00	2.00
❑ 407	Marcus Giles SP	5.00	2.00
❑ 408	Brian Daubach SP	5.00	2.00
❑ 409	Moises Alou SP	5.00	2.00
❑ 410	Raul Mondesi SP	5.00	2.00
❑ 411	Adrian Beltre SP	5.00	2.00
❑ 412	A.J. Burnett SP	5.00	2.00
❑ 413	Jason Jennings SP	5.00	2.00
❑ 414	Edwin Almonte SP	5.00	2.00
❑ 415	Fred McGriff SP	8.00	3.00
❑ 416	Tim Raines Jr. SP	5.00	2.00
❑ 417	Rafael Furcal SP	5.00	2.00
❑ 418	Erubiel Durazo SP	5.00	2.00
❑ 419	Drew Henson SP	5.00	2.00
❑ 420	Kevin Appier SP	5.00	2.00

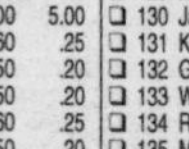

❑ 421 Chad Tracy SP 5.00 2.00
❑ 422 Adam Wainwright SP 5.00 2.00
❑ 423 Choo Freeman SP 5.00 2.00
❑ 424 Sandy Alomar Jr. SP 5.00 2.00
❑ 425 Corey Koskie SP 5.00 2.00
❑ 426 Jeromy Burnitz SP 5.00 2.00
❑ 427 Jorge Posada SP 8.00 3.00
❑ 428 Jason Arnold SP 5.00 2.00
❑ 429 Brett Myers SP 5.00 2.00
❑ 430 Shawn Green SP 5.00 2.00

2004 Topps Heritage

❑ COMPLETE SET (495) 350.00 200.00
❑ COMP.SET w/o SP's (385) 60.00 30.00
❑ 1A Jim Thome Fielding 1.00 .40
❑ 1B Jim Thome Hitting SP 8.00 3.00
❑ 2 Nomar Garciaparra SP 10.00 4.00
❑ 3 Aramis Ramirez .60 .25
❑ 4 Rafael Palmeiro SP 8.00 3.00
❑ 5 Danny Graves .50 .20
❑ 6 Casey Blake .50 .20
❑ 7 Juan Uribe .50 .20
❑ 8A Dmitri Young New Logo .60 .25
❑ 8B Dmitri Young Old Logo SP 5.00 2.00
❑ 9 Billy Wagner .60 .25
❑ 10A Jason Giambi Swinging .60 .25
❑ 10B Jason Giambi Btg Stance SP 5.00 2.00
❑ 11 Carlos Beltran .60 .25
❑ 12 Chad Hermansen .50 .20
❑ 13 B.J. Upton 1.00 .40
❑ 14 Dustan Mohr .50 .20
❑ 15 Endy Chavez .50 .20
❑ 16 Cliff Floyd .60 .25
❑ 17 Bernie Williams 1.00 .40
❑ 18 Eric Chavez .60 .25
❑ 19 Chase Utley 1.00 .40
❑ 20 Randy Johnson 1.50 .60
❑ 21 Vernon Wells .60 .25
❑ 22 Juan Gonzalez .60 .25
❑ 23 Joe Kennedy .50 .20
❑ 24 Bengie Molina .50 .20
❑ 25 Carlos Lee .60 .25
❑ 26 Horacio Ramirez .50 .20
❑ 27 Anthony Acevedo RC .75 .30
❑ 28 Sammy Sosa SP 8.00 3.00
❑ 29 Jon Garland .60 .25
❑ 30A Adam Dunn Fielding .60 .25
❑ 30B Adam Dunn Hitting SP 5.00 2.00
❑ 31 Aaron Rowand .60 .25
❑ 32 Jody Gerut .50 .20
❑ 33 Chin-Hui Tsao .60 .25
❑ 34 Alex Sanchez .50 .20
❑ 35 A.J. Burnett .60 .25
❑ 36 Brad Ausmus .60 .25
❑ 37 Blake Hawksworth RC 1.00 .40
❑ 38 Francisco Rodriguez .60 .25
❑ 39 Alex Cintron .50 .20
❑ 40A Chipper Jones Pointing 1.50 .60
❑ 40B Chipper Jones Fielding SP 8.00 3.00
❑ 41 Deivi Cruz .50 .20
❑ 42 Bill Mueller .60 .25
❑ 43 Joe Borowski .50 .20
❑ 44 Jimmy Haynes .50 .20
❑ 45 Mark Loretta .50 .20
❑ 46 Jerome Williams .50 .20
❑ 47 Gary Sheffield Yanks SP 8.00 3.00
❑ 48 Richard Hidalgo .50 .20
❑ 49A Jason Kendall New Logo .60 .25
❑ 49B Jason Kendall Old Logo SP 5.00 2.00
❑ 50 Ichiro Suzuki SP 12.00 5.00
❑ 51 Jim Edmonds .60 .25
❑ 52 Frank Catalanotto .50 .20
❑ 53 Jose Contreras .50 .20
❑ 54 Mo Vaughn .60 .25
❑ 55 Brendan Donnelly .50 .20
❑ 56 Luis Gonzalez .60 .25
❑ 57 Robert Fick .50 .20
❑ 58 Laynce Nix .50 .20
❑ 59 Johnny Damon 1.00 .40
❑ 60A Magglio Ordonez Running .60 .25
❑ 60B Magglio Ordonez Hitting SP 5.00 2.00
❑ 61 Matt Clement .60 .25
❑ 62 Ryan Ludwick .50 .20
❑ 63 Luis Castillo .50 .20
❑ 64 Dave Crouthers RC .75 .30
❑ 65 Dave Berg .50 .20
❑ 66 Kyle Davies RC 4.00 1.50
❑ 67 Tim Salmon 1.00 .40
❑ 68 Marcus Giles .60 .25
❑ 69 Marty Cordova .50 .20
❑ 70A Todd Helton White Jsy 1.00 .40
❑ 70B Todd Helton Purple Jsy SP 8.00 3.00
❑ 71 Jeff Kent .60 .25
❑ 72 Michael Tucker .50 .20
❑ 73 Cesar Izturis .50 .20
❑ 74 Paul Quantrill .50 .20
❑ 75 Conor Jackson RC 3.00 1.25
❑ 76 Placido Polanco .50 .20
❑ 77 Adam Eaton .50 .20
❑ 78 Ramon Hernandez .60 .25
❑ 79 Edgardo Alfonzo .50 .20
❑ 80 Dioner Navarro RC 1.00 .40
❑ 81 Woody Williams .50 .20
❑ 82 Rey Ordonez .50 .20
❑ 83 Randy Winn .50 .20
❑ 84 Casey Myers RC .75 .30
❑ 85A R.Choy Foo New Logo RC .75 .30
❑ 85B R.Choy Foo Old Logo SP 5.00 2.00
❑ 86 Ray Durham .60 .25
❑ 87 Sean Burroughs .50 .20
❑ 88 Tim Frend RC .75 .30
❑ 89 Shigetoshi Hasegawa .60 .25
❑ 90 Jeffrey Allison RC .75 .30
❑ 91 Orlando Hudson .50 .20
❑ 92 Matt Creighton SP RC 5.00 2.00
❑ 93 Tim Worrell .50 .20
❑ 94 Kris Benson .50 .20
❑ 95 Mike Lieberthal .60 .25
❑ 96 David Wells .60 .25
❑ 97 Jason Phillips .50 .20
❑ 98 Bobby Cox MGR .50 .20
❑ 99 Johan Santana 1.50 .60
❑ 100A Alex Rodriguez Hitting 2.50 1.00
❑ 100B Alex Rodriguez Throwing SP 10.00 4.00
❑ 101 John Vander Wal .50 .20
❑ 102 Orlando Cabrera .60 .25
❑ 103 Hideo Nomo 1.50 .60
❑ 104 Todd Walker .50 .20
❑ 105 Jason Johnson .50 .20
❑ 106 Matt Mantei .50 .20
❑ 107 Jarrod Washburn .50 .20
❑ 108 Preston Wilson .60 .25
❑ 109 Carl Pavano .60 .25
❑ 110 Geoff Blum .50 .20
❑ 111 Eric Gagne .60 .25
❑ 112 Geoff Jenkins .50 .20
❑ 113 Joe Torre MG 1.00 .40
❑ 114 Jon Knott RC .75 .30
❑ 115 Hank Blalock .60 .25
❑ 116 John Olerud .60 .25
❑ 117A Pat Burrell New Logo .60 .25
❑ 117B Pat Burrell Old Logo SP 5.00 2.00
❑ 118 Aaron Boone .60 .25
❑ 119 Zach Day .50 .20
❑ 120A Frank Thomas New Logo 1.50 .60
❑ 120B Frank Thomas Old Logo SP 8.00 3.00
❑ 121 Kyle Farnsworth .50 .20
❑ 122 Derek Lowe .60 .25
❑ 123 Zach Miner SP RC 8.00 3.00
❑ 124 Matthew Moses SP RC 8.00 3.00
❑ 125 Jesse Roman RC .75 .30
❑ 126 Josh Phelps .50 .20
❑ 127 Nic Ungs RC .75 .30
❑ 128 Dan Haren .50 .20
❑ 129 Kirk Rueter .50 .20
❑ 130 Jack McKeon MGR .60 .25
❑ 131 Keith Foulke .60 .25
❑ 132 Garrett Stephenson .50 .20
❑ 133 Wes Helms .50 .20
❑ 134 Raul Ibanez .50 .20
❑ 135 Morgan Ensberg .60 .25
❑ 136 Jay Payton .60 .25
❑ 137 Billy Koch .50 .20
❑ 138 Mark Grudzielanek .50 .20
❑ 139 Rodrigo Lopez .50 .20
❑ 140 Corey Patterson .50 .20
❑ 141 Troy Percival .60 .25
❑ 142 Shea Hillenbrand .60 .25
❑ 143 Brad Fullmer .60 .25
❑ 144 Ricky Nolasco RC 1.50 .60
❑ 145 Mark Teixeira 1.00 .40
❑ 146 Tydus Meadows RC .75 .30
❑ 147 Toby Hall .50 .20
❑ 148 Orlando Palmeiro .50 .20
❑ 149 Khalid Ballouli RC .75 .30
❑ 150 Grady Little MGR .50 .20
❑ 151 David Eckstein .60 .25
❑ 152 Kenny Perez RC .75 .30
❑ 153 Ben Grieve .50 .20
❑ 154 Ismael Valdes .50 .20
❑ 155 Bret Boone .60 .25
❑ 156 Jesse Foppert .50 .20
❑ 157 Vicente Padilla .50 .20
❑ 158 Bobby Abreu .60 .25
❑ 159 Scott Hatteberg .50 .20
❑ 160 Carlos Quentin RC 2.50 1.00
❑ 161 Anthony Lerew RC 1.00 .40
❑ 162 Lance Carter .50 .20
❑ 163 Robb Nen .60 .25
❑ 164 Zach Duke SP RC 10.00 4.00
❑ 165 Xavier Nady .50 .20
❑ 166 Kip Wells .50 .20
❑ 167 Kevin Millwood .60 .25
❑ 168 Jon Lieber .50 .20
❑ 169 Jose Reyes .60 .25
❑ 170 Eric Byrnes .50 .20
❑ 171 Paul Konerko .60 .25
❑ 172 Chris Lubanski .60 .25
❑ 173 Jae Weong Seo .50 .20
❑ 174 Corey Koskie .50 .20
❑ 175 Tim Stauffer RC 1.00 4.00
❑ 176 John Lackey .50 .20
❑ 177 Danny Bautista .50 .20
❑ 178 Shane Reynolds .50 .20
❑ 179 Jorge Julio .50 .20
❑ 180A Manny Ramirez New Logo 1.00 .40
❑ 180B Manny Ramirez Old Logo SP 8.00 3.00
❑ 181 Alex Gonzalez .50 .20
❑ 182A Moises Alou New Logo .60 .25
❑ 182B Moises Alou Old Logo SP 5.00 2.00
❑ 183 Mark Buehrle .60 .25
❑ 184 Carlos Guillen .60 .25
❑ 185 Nate Cornejo .50 .20
❑ 186 Billy Traber .50 .20
❑ 187 Jason Jennings .50 .20
❑ 188 Eric Munson .50 .20
❑ 189 Braden Looper .50 .20
❑ 190 Juan Encarnacion .50 .20
❑ 191 Dusty Baker MGR .60 .25
❑ 192 Travis Lee .50 .20
❑ 193 Miguel Cairo .50 .20
❑ 194 Rich Aurilia SP 5.00 2.00
❑ 195 Tom Gordon .50 .20
❑ 196 Freddy Garcia .60 .25
❑ 197 Brian Lawrence .50 .20
❑ 198 Jorge Posada SP 8.00 3.00
❑ 199 Javier Vazquez .60 .25
❑ 200A Albert Pujols New Logo 3.00 1.25
❑ 200B Albert Pujols Old Logo SP 12.00 5.00
❑ 201 Victor Zambrano .50 .20
❑ 202 Eli Marrero .50 .20
❑ 203 Joel Pineiro .50 .20
❑ 204 Rondell White .60 .25
❑ 205 Craig Ansman RC .75 .30
❑ 206 Michael Young .60 .25
❑ 207 Carlos Baerga .50 .20
❑ 208 Andruw Jones 1.00 .40
❑ 209 Jerry Hairston Jr. .50 .20
❑ 210 Shawn Green SP 5.00 2.00
❑ 211 Ron Gardenhire MGR .50 .20

❑ 212 Darin Erstad .60 .25
❑ 213A Brandon Webb Glove Chest .50 .20
❑ 213B Brandon Webb Glove Out SP 5.00 2.00
❑ 214 Greg Maddux 2.50 1.00
❑ 215 Reed Johnson .50 .20
❑ 216 John Thomson .50 .20
❑ 217 Tino Martinez 1.00 .40
❑ 218 Mike Cameron .50 .20
❑ 219 Edgar Martinez 1.00 .40
❑ 220 Eric Young .50 .20
❑ 221 Reggie Sanders .60 .25
❑ 222 Randy Wolf .50 .20
❑ 223 Erubiel Durazo .50 .20
❑ 224 Mike Mussina 1.00 .40
❑ 225 Tom Glavine 1.00 .40
❑ 226 Troy Glaus .60 .25
❑ 227 Oscar Villarreal .50 .20
❑ 228 David Segui .50 .20
❑ 229 Jeff Suppan .50 .20
❑ 230 Kenny Lofton .60 .25
❑ 231 Esteban Loaiza .50 .20
❑ 232 Felipe Lopez .50 .20
❑ 233 Matt Lawton .50 .20
❑ 234 Mark Bellhorn .60 .25
❑ 235 Wil Ledezma .50 .20
❑ 236 Todd Hollandsworth .50 .20
❑ 237 Octavio Dotel .50 .20
❑ 238 Darren Dreifort .50 .20
❑ 239 Paul Lo Duca .60 .25
❑ 240 Richie Sexson .60 .25
❑ 241 Doug Mientkiewicz .60 .25
❑ 242 Luis Rivas .50 .20
❑ 243 Claudio Vargas .50 .20
❑ 244 Mark Ellis .50 .20
❑ 245 Brett Myers .60 .25
❑ 246 Jake Peavy .60 .25
❑ 247 Marquis Grissom .60 .25
❑ 248 Armando Benitez .50 .20
❑ 249 Ryan Franklin .50 .20
❑ 250A Alfonso Soriano Throwing .60 .25
❑ 250B Alfonso Soriano Fielding SP 5.00 2.00
❑ 251 Tim Hudson .60 .25
❑ 252 Shannon Stewart .60 .25
❑ 253 A.J. Pierzynski .60 .25
❑ 254 Runelvys Hernandez .50 .20
❑ 255 Roy Oswalt .60 .25
❑ 256 Shawn Chacon .50 .20
❑ 257 Tony Graffanino .50 .20
❑ 258 Tim Wakefield .60 .25
❑ 259 Damian Miller .50 .20
❑ 260 Joe Crede .60 .25
❑ 261 Jason LaRue .50 .20
❑ 262 Jose Jimenez .50 .20
❑ 263 Juan Pierre .60 .25
❑ 264 Wade Miller .50 .20
❑ 265 Odalis Perez .50 .20
❑ 266 Eddie Guardado .50 .20
❑ 267 Rocky Biddle .50 .20
❑ 268 Jeff Nelson .50 .20
❑ 269 Terrence Long .50 .20
❑ 270 Ramon Ortiz .50 .20
❑ 271 Raul Mondesi .60 .25
❑ 272 Ugueth Urbina .50 .20
❑ 273 Jeromy Burnitz .60 .25
❑ 274 Brad Radke .60 .25
❑ 275 Jose Vidro .50 .20
❑ 276 Bobby Jenks .60 .25
❑ 277 Ty Wigginton .50 .20
❑ 278 Jose Guillen .60 .25
❑ 279 Delmon Young 1.00 .40
❑ 280 Brian Giles .60 .25
❑ 281 Jason Schmidt .60 .25
❑ 282 Nick Markakis .60 .25
❑ 283 Felipe Alou MGR .60 .25
❑ 284 Carl Crawford .60 .25
❑ 285 Neifi Perez .50 .20
❑ 286 Miguel Tejada .60 .25
❑ 287 Victor Martinez .60 .25
❑ 288 Adam Kennedy .50 .20
❑ 289 Kerry Ligtenberg .50 .20
❑ 290 Scott Williamson .50 .20
❑ 291 Tony Womack .50 .20
❑ 292 Travis Hafner .60 .25
❑ 293 Bobby Crosby .60 .25
❑ 294 Chad Billingsley .60 .25
❑ 295 Russ Ortiz .50 .20
❑ 296 John Burkett .50 .20
❑ 297 Carlos Zambrano .60 .25
❑ 298 Randall Simon .50 .20
❑ 299 Juan Castro .50 .20
❑ 300 Mike Lowell .60 .25
❑ 301 Fred McGriff 1.00 .40
❑ 302 Glendon Rusch .50 .20
❑ 303 Sung Jung RC .75 .30
❑ 304 Rocco Baldelli .60 .25
❑ 305 Fernando Vina .50 .20
❑ 306 Gil Meche .50 .20
❑ 307 Jose Cruz Jr. .50 .20
❑ 308 Bernie Castro .50 .20
❑ 309 Scott Spiezio .50 .20
❑ 310 Paul Byrd .50 .20
❑ 311A Jay Gibbons New Logo .50 .20
❑ 311B Jay Gibbons Old Logo SP 5.00 2.00
❑ 312 Trot Nixon .60 .25
❑ 313 Chris O'Riordan RC .75 .30
❑ 314 Julio Lugo .50 .20
❑ 315 Ben Davis .50 .20
❑ 316 Mike Williams .50 .20
❑ 317 Trevor Hoffman .60 .25
❑ 318 Andy Pettitte 1.00 .40
❑ 319 Orlando Hernandez .60 .25
❑ 320 Juan Rivera .50 .20
❑ 321 Elizardo Ramirez .50 .20
❑ 322 Junior Spivey .50 .20
❑ 323 Tony Batista .50 .20
❑ 324 Mike Remlinger .50 .20
❑ 325 Alex Gonzalez .50 .20
❑ 326 Aaron Hill .50 .20
❑ 327 Steve Finley .60 .25
❑ 328 Vinny Castilla .60 .25
❑ 329 Eric Duncan .60 .25
❑ 330 Mike Gosling RC .75 .30
❑ 331 Eric Hinske .50 .20
❑ 332 Scott Rolen 1.00 .40
❑ 333 Benito Santiago .60 .25
❑ 334 Jimmy Gobble .50 .20
❑ 335 Bobby Higginson .60 .25
❑ 336 Kelvim Escobar .50 .20
❑ 337 Mike DeJean .50 .20
❑ 338 Sidney Ponson .50 .20
❑ 339 Todd Self RC 1.00 .40
❑ 340 Jeff Cirillo .50 .20
❑ 341 Jimmy Rollins .60 .25
❑ 342A Barry Zito White Jsy .60 .25
❑ 342B Barry Zito Green Jsy SP 5.00 2.00
❑ 343 Felix Pie 1.00 .40
❑ 344 Matt Morris .60 .25
❑ 345 Kazuhiro Sasaki .60 .25
❑ 346 Jack Wilson .50 .20
❑ 347 Nick Johnson .60 .25
❑ 348 Wil Cordero .50 .20
❑ 349 Ryan Madson .50 .20
❑ 350 Torii Hunter .60 .25
❑ 351 Andy Ashby .50 .20
❑ 352 Aubrey Huff .60 .25
❑ 353 Brad Lidge .60 .25
❑ 354 Derrek Lee 1.00 .40
❑ 355 Yadier Molina RC 2.50 1.00
❑ 356 Paul Wilson .50 .20
❑ 357 Omar Vizquel 1.00 .40
❑ 358 Rene Reyes .50 .20
❑ 359 Marlon Anderson .50 .20
❑ 360 Bobby Kielty .50 .20
❑ 361A Ryan Wagner New Logo .50 .20
❑ 361B Ryan Wagner Old Logo SP 5.00 2.00
❑ 362 Justin Morneau .60 .25
❑ 363 Shane Spencer .50 .20
❑ 364 David Bell .50 .20
❑ 365 Matt Stairs .50 .20
❑ 366 Joe Borchard .50 .20
❑ 367 Mark Redman .50 .20
❑ 368 Dave Roberts .50 .20
❑ 369 Desi Relaford .50 .20
❑ 370 Rich Harden .60 .25
❑ 371 Fernando Tatis .50 .20
❑ 372 Eric Karros .60 .25
❑ 373 Eric Milton .50 .20
❑ 374 Mike Sweeney .60 .25
❑ 375 Brian Daubach .50 .20
❑ 376 Brian Snyder .50 .20
❑ 377 Chris Reitsma .50 .20
❑ 378 Kyle Lohse .50 .20
❑ 379 Livan Hernandez .60 .25
❑ 380 Robin Ventura .60 .25
❑ 381 Jacque Jones .60 .25
❑ 382 Danny Kolb .50 .20
❑ 383 Casey Kotchman .60 .25
❑ 384 Cristian Guzman .50 .20
❑ 385 Josh Beckett .60 .25
❑ 386 Khalil Greene 1.00 .40
❑ 387 Greg Myers .50 .20
❑ 388 Francisco Cordero .50 .20
❑ 389 Donald Levinski RC .75 .30
❑ 390 Roy Halladay .60 .25
❑ 391 J.D. Drew .60 .25
❑ 392 Jamie Moyer .60 .25
❑ 393 Ken Macha MGR .50 .20
❑ 394 Jeff Davanon .50 .20
❑ 395 Matt Kata .50 .20
❑ 396 Jack Cust .50 .20
❑ 397 Mike Timlin .50 .20
❑ 398 Zack Greinke SP 5.00 2.00
❑ 399 Byung-Hyun Kim SP 5.00 2.00
❑ 400 Kazuhisa Ishii SP 5.00 2.00
❑ 401 Brayan Pena SP RC 5.00 2.00
❑ 402 Garret Anderson SP 5.00 2.00
❑ 403 Kyle Sleeth SP RC 8.00 3.00
❑ 404 Javy Lopez SP 5.00 2.00
❑ 405 Damian Moss SP 5.00 2.00
❑ 406 David Ortiz SP 8.00 3.00
❑ 407 Pedro Martinez SP 8.00 3.00
❑ 408 Hee Seop Choi SP 5.00 2.00
❑ 409 Carl Everett SP 5.00 2.00
❑ 410 Dontrelle Willis SP 8.00 3.00
❑ 411 Ryan Harvey SP 5.00 2.00
❑ 412 Russell Branyan SP 5.00 2.00
❑ 413 Milton Bradley SP 5.00 2.00
❑ 414 Marcus McBeth SP RC 5.00 2.00
❑ 415 Carlos Pena SP 5.00 2.00
❑ 416 Ivan Rodriguez SP 8.00 3.00
❑ 417 Craig Biggio SP 8.00 3.00
❑ 418 Angel Berroa SP 5.00 2.00
❑ 419 Brian Jordan SP 5.00 2.00
❑ 420 Scott Podsednik SP 5.00 2.00
❑ 421 Omar Falcon SP RC 5.00 2.00
❑ 422 Joe Mays SP 5.00 2.00
❑ 423 Brad Wilkerson SP 5.00 2.00
❑ 424 Al Leiter SP 5.00 2.00
❑ 425 Derek Jeter SP 12.00 5.00
❑ 426 Mark Mulder SP 5.00 2.00
❑ 427 Marlon Byrd SP 5.00 2.00
❑ 428 David Murphy SP RC 8.00 3.00
❑ 429 Phil Nevin SP 5.00 2.00
❑ 430 J.T. Snow SP 5.00 2.00
❑ 431 Brad Sullivan SP RC 8.00 3.00
❑ 432 Bo Hart SP 5.00 2.00
❑ 433 Josh Labandeira SP RC 5.00 2.00
❑ 434 Chan Ho Park SP 5.00 2.00
❑ 435 Carlos Delgado SP 5.00 2.00
❑ 436 Curt Schilling Sox SP 8.00 3.00
❑ 437 John Smoltz SP 8.00 3.00
❑ 438 Luis Matos SP 5.00 2.00
❑ 439 Mark Prior SP 8.00 3.00
❑ 440 Roberto Alomar SP 8.00 3.00
❑ 441 Coco Crisp SP 5.00 2.00
❑ 442 Austin Kearns SP 5.00 2.00
❑ 443 Larry Walker SP 5.00 2.00
❑ 444 Neal Cotts SP 5.00 2.00
❑ 445 Jeff Bagwell SP 8.00 3.00
❑ 446 Adrian Beltre SP 5.00 2.00
❑ 447 Grady Sizemore SP 8.00 3.00
❑ 448 Keith Ginter SP 5.00 2.00
❑ 449 Vladimir Guerrero SP 8.00 3.00
❑ 450 Lyle Overbay SP 5.00 2.00
❑ 451 Rafael Furcal SP 5.00 2.00
❑ 452 Melvin Mora SP 5.00 2.00
❑ 453 Kerry Wood SP 5.00 2.00
❑ 454 Jose Valentin SP 5.00 2.00
❑ 455 Ken Griffey Jr. SP 10.00 4.00
❑ 456 Brandon Phillips SP 5.00 2.00
❑ 457 Miguel Cabrera SP 8.00 3.00
❑ 458 Edwin Jackson SP 5.00 2.00
❑ 459 Eric Owens SP 5.00 2.00
❑ 460 Miguel Batista SP 5.00 2.00
❑ 461 Mike Hampton SP 5.00 2.00
❑ 462 Kevin Millar SP 5.00 2.00
❑ 463 Bartolo Colon SP 5.00 2.00
❑ 464 Sean Casey SP 5.00 2.00

Card		
❑ 465 C.C. Sabathia SP	5.00	2.00
❑ 466 Rickie Weeks SP	5.00	2.00
❑ 467 Brad Penny SP	5.00	2.00
❑ 468 Mike MacDougal SP	5.00	2.00
❑ 469 Kevin Brown SP	5.00	2.00
❑ 470 Lance Berkman SP	5.00	2.00
❑ 471 Ben Sheets SP	5.00	2.00
❑ 472 Mariano Rivera SP	8.00	3.00
❑ 473 Mike Piazza SP	10.00	4.00
❑ 474 Ryan Klesko SP	5.00	2.00
❑ 475 Edgar Renteria SP	5.00	2.00

2005 Topps Heritage

Card		
❑ COMPLETE SET (495)	400.00	250.00
❑ COMP.SET w/o SP's (385)	60.00	30.00
❑ COMMON CARD	.50	.20
❑ COMMON RC	.50	.20
❑ COMMON TEAM CARD	.50	.20
❑ COMMON SP	8.00	3.00
❑ COMMON SP RC	8.00	3.00
❑ SP STATED ODDS 1:2 HOBBY/RETAIL		
❑ BASIC SP: 5/20/30/31/33/79/101/110/130		
❑ BASIC SP: 135/260/292/398-475		
❑ VARIATION SP: 3/6/7/31/50/69/78/82/118		
❑ VARIATION SP: 125/135/155/261/273/286		
❑ VARIATION SP: 296/300/312/353/389		
❑ SEE BECKETT.COM FOR VAR.DESCRIPTIONS		
❑ 1 Will Harridge	.50	.20
❑ 2 Warren Giles	.50	.20
❑ 3A Alfonso Soriano Fldg	.50	.20
❑ 3B Alfonso Soriano Running SP	8.00	3.00
❑ 4 Mark Mulder	.50	.20
❑ 5 Todd Helton SP	8.00	3.00
❑ 6A Jason Bay Black Cap	.50	.20
❑ 6B Jason Bay Yellow Cap SP	8.00	3.00
❑ 7A Ichiro Suzuki Running	1.50	.60
❑ 7B Ichiro Suzuki Crouch SP	10.00	4.00
❑ 8 Jim Tracy MG	.50	.20
❑ 9 Gavin Floyd	.50	.20
❑ 10 John Smoltz	.75	.30
❑ 11 Chicago Cubs TC	.75	.30
❑ 12 Darin Erstad	.50	.20
❑ 13 Chad Tracy	.50	.20
❑ 14 Charles Thomas	.50	.20
❑ 15 Miguel Tejada	.50	.20
❑ 16 Andre Ethier RC	5.00	2.00
❑ 17 Jeff Francis	.50	.20
❑ 18 Derrek Lee	.75	.30
❑ 19 Juan Uribe	.50	.20
❑ 20 Jim Edmonds SP	8.00	3.00
❑ 21 Kenny Lofton	.50	.20
❑ 22 Brad Ausmus	.50	.20
❑ 23 Jon Garland	.50	.20
❑ 24 Edwin Jackson	.50	.20
❑ 25 Joe Mauer	1.00	.40
❑ 26 Wes Helms	.50	.20
❑ 27 Brian Schneider	.50	.20
❑ 28 Kazuo Matsui	.50	.20
❑ 29 Flash Gordon	.50	.20
❑ 30 Hideo Nomo SP	8.00	3.00
❑ 31A Albert Pujols Red Hat SP	12.00	5.00
❑ 31B Albert Pujols Blue Hat SP	12.00	5.00
❑ 32 Carl Crawford	.50	.20
❑ 33 Vladimir Guerrero SP	8.00	3.00
❑ 34 Nick Green	.50	.20
❑ 35 Jay Gibbons	.50	.20
❑ 36 Kevin Youkilis	.50	.20
❑ 37 Billy Wagner	.50	.20
❑ 38 Terrence Long	.50	.20
❑ 39 Kevin Mench	.50	.20
❑ 40 Garret Anderson	.50	.20
❑ 41 Reed Johnson	.50	.20
❑ 42 Reggie Sanders	.50	.20
❑ 43 Kirk Rueter	.50	.20
❑ 44 Jay Payton	.50	.20
❑ 45 Tike Redman	.50	.20
❑ 46 Mike Lieberthal	.50	.20
❑ 47 Damian Miller	.50	.20
❑ 48 Zach Day	.50	.20
❑ 49 Juan Rincon	.50	.20
❑ 50A Jim Thome At Bat	.75	.30
❑ 50B Jim Thome Fldg SP	8.00	3.00
❑ 51 Jose Guillen	.50	.20
❑ 52 Richie Sexson	.50	.20
❑ 53 Juan Cruz	.50	.20
❑ 54 Byung-Hyun Kim	.50	.20
❑ 55 Carlos Zambrano	.50	.20
❑ 56 Carlos Lee	.50	.20
❑ 57 Adam Dunn	.50	.20
❑ 58 David Riske	.50	.20
❑ 59 Carlos Guillen	.50	.20
❑ 60 Larry Bowa MG	.50	.20
❑ 61 Barry Bonds	8.00	3.00
❑ 62 Chris Woodward	.50	.20
❑ 63 Matt DeSalvo RC	.75	.30
❑ 64 Brian Stavisky RC	.50	.20
❑ 65 Scot Shields	.50	.20
❑ 66 J.D. Drew	.50	.20
❑ 67 Erik Bedard	.50	.20
❑ 68 Scott Williamson	.50	.20
❑ 69A M.Prior New C on Cap	.75	.30
❑ 69B M.Prior Old C on Cap SP	8.00	3.00
❑ 70 Ken Griffey Jr.	1.50	.60
❑ 71 Kazuhito Tadano	.50	.20
❑ 72 Philadelphia Phillies TC	.50	.20
❑ 73 Jeremy Reed	.50	.20
❑ 74 Ricardo Rodriguez	.50	.20
❑ 75 Carlos Delgado	.50	.20
❑ 76 Eric Milton	.50	.20
❑ 77 Miguel Olivo	.50	.20
❑ 78A E.Alfonzo No Socks	.50	.20
❑ 78B E.Alfonzo Black Socks SP	8.00	3.00
❑ 79 Kazuhisa Ishii SP	8.00	3.00
❑ 80 Jason Giambi	.50	.20
❑ 81 Cliff Floyd	.50	.20
❑ 82A Torii Hunter Twins Cap	.50	.20
❑ 82B Torii Hunter Wash Cap SP	8.00	3.00
❑ 83 Odalis Perez	.50	.20
❑ 84 Scott Podsednik	.50	.20
❑ 85 Cleveland Indians TC	.50	.20
❑ 86 Jeff Suppan	.50	.20
❑ 87 Ray Durham	.50	.20
❑ 88 Tyler Clippard RC	20.00	8.00
❑ 89 Ryan Howard	2.50	1.00
❑ 90 Cincinnati Reds TC	.50	.20
❑ 91 Bengie Molina	.50	.20
❑ 92 Danny Bautista	.50	.20
❑ 93 Eli Marrero	.50	.20
❑ 94 Larry Bigbie	.50	.20
❑ 95 Atlanta Braves TC	.50	.20
❑ 96 Merkin Valdez	.50	.20
❑ 97 Rocco Baldelli	.50	.20
❑ 98 Woody Williams	.50	.20
❑ 99 Jason Frasor	.50	.20
❑ 100 Baltimore Orioles TC	.50	.20
❑ 101 Ivan Rodriguez SP	8.00	3.00
❑ 102 Joe Kennedy	.50	.20
❑ 103 Mike Lowell	.50	.20
❑ 104 Armando Benitez	.50	.20
❑ 105 Craig Biggio	.75	.30
❑ 106 David DeJesus	.50	.20
❑ 107 Adrian Beltre	.50	.20
❑ 108 Phil Nevin	.50	.20
❑ 109 Cristian Guzman	.50	.20
❑ 110 Jorge Posada SP	8.00	3.00
❑ 111 Boston Red Sox TC	1.00	.40
❑ 112 Jeff Mathis	.50	.20
❑ 113 Bartolo Colon	.50	.20
❑ 114 Alex Cintron	.50	.20
❑ 115 Russ Ortiz	.50	.20
❑ 116 Doug Mientkiewicz	.50	.20
❑ 117 Placido Polanco	.50	.20
❑ 118A M.Ordonez Black Uni	.50	.20
❑ 118B M.Ordonez White Uni SP	8.00	3.00
❑ 119 Chris Seddon RC	.50	.20
❑ 120 Bobby Abreu	.50	.20
❑ 121 Pittsburgh Pirates TC	.50	.20
❑ 122 Dallas McPherson	.50	.20
❑ 123 Rodrigo Lopez	.50	.20
❑ 124 Mark Bellhorn	.50	.20
❑ 125A N.Garciaparra Red Cap	1.00	.40
❑ 125B N.Garciaparra Blue Cap SP	8.00	3.00
❑ 126 Sean Casey	.50	.20
❑ 127 Ronnie Belliard	.50	.20
❑ 128 Tom Goodwin	.50	.20
❑ 129 Preston Wilson	.50	.20
❑ 130 Andruw Jones SP	8.00	3.00
❑ 131 Roberto Alomar	.75	.30
❑ 132 John Buck	.50	.20
❑ 133 Jason LaRue	.50	.20
❑ 134 St. Louis Cardinals TC	.75	.30
❑ 135A Alex Rodriguez Fldg SP	10.00	4.00
❑ 135B Alex Rodriguez At Bat SP	10.00	4.00
❑ 136 Nate Robertson	.50	.20
❑ 137 Juan Pierre	.50	.20
❑ 138 Morgan Ensberg	.50	.20
❑ 139 Vinny Castilla	.50	.20
❑ 140 Jake Dittler	.50	.20
❑ 141 Chan Ho Park	.50	.20
❑ 142 Felix Hernandez	3.00	1.25
❑ 143 Jason Isringhausen	.50	.20
❑ 144 Dustan Mohr	.50	.20
❑ 145 Khalil Greene	.75	.30
❑ 146 Minnesota Twins TC	.50	.20
❑ 147 Vicente Padilla	.50	.20
❑ 148 Oliver Perez	.50	.20
❑ 149 Brian Giles	.50	.20
❑ 150 Shawn Green	.50	.20
❑ 151 Matt Lawton	.50	.20
❑ 152 Casey Blake	.50	.20
❑ 153 Frank Thomas	1.00	.40
❑ 154 Orlando Hernandez	.50	.20
❑ 155A Eric Chavez Green Cap	.50	.20
❑ 155B Eric Chavez Blue Cap SP	8.00	3.00
❑ 156 Chase Utley	.75	.30
❑ 157 John Olerud	.50	.20
❑ 158 Adam Eaton	.50	.20
❑ 159 Josh Fogg	.50	.20
❑ 160 Michael Tucker	.50	.20
❑ 161 Kevin Brown	.50	.20
❑ 162 Bobby Crosby	.50	.20
❑ 163 Jason Schmidt	.50	.20
❑ 164 Shannon Stewart	.50	.20
❑ 165 Tony Womack	.50	.20
❑ 166 Los Angeles Dodgers TC	.75	.30
❑ 167 Franklin Gutierrez	.50	.20
❑ 168 Ted Lilly	.50	.20
❑ 169 Mark Teixeira	.75	.30
❑ 170 Matt Morris	.50	.20
❑ 171 Bucky Jacobsen	.50	.20
❑ 172 Steve Doetsch RC	.75	.30
❑ 173 Jeff Weaver	.50	.20
❑ 174 Tony Graffanino	.50	.20
❑ 175 Jeff Bagwell	.75	.30
❑ 176 Carl Pavano	.50	.20
❑ 177 Junior Spivey	.50	.20
❑ 178 Carlos Silva	.50	.20
❑ 179 Tim Redding	.50	.20
❑ 180 Brett Myers	.50	.20
❑ 181 Mike Mussina	.75	.30
❑ 182 Richard Hidalgo	.50	.20
❑ 183 Nick Johnson	.50	.20
❑ 184 Lew Ford	.50	.20
❑ 185 Barry Zito	.50	.20
❑ 186 Jimmy Rollins	.50	.20
❑ 187 Jack Wilson	.50	.20
❑ 188 Chicago White Sox TC	.50	.20
❑ 189 Guillermo Quiroz	.50	.20
❑ 190 Mark Hendrickson	.50	.20
❑ 191 Jeremy Bonderman	.50	.20
❑ 192 Jason Jennings	.50	.20
❑ 193 Paul Lo Duca	.50	.20
❑ 194 A.J. Burnett	.50	.20
❑ 195 Ken Harvey	.50	.20
❑ 196 Geoff Jenkins	.50	.20
❑ 197 Joe Mays	.50	.20
❑ 198 Jose Vidro	.50	.20
❑ 199 David Wright	2.00	.75
❑ 200 Randy Johnson	1.00	.40
❑ 201 Jeff DaVanon	.50	.20

❑ 202 Paul Byrd .50 .20
❑ 203 David Ortiz 1.00 .40
❑ 204 Kyle Farnsworth .50 .20
❑ 205 Keith Foulke .50 .20
❑ 206 Joe Crede .50 .20
❑ 207 Austin Kearns .50 .20
❑ 208 Jody Gerut .50 .20
❑ 209 Shawn Chacon .50 .20
❑ 210 Carlos Pena .50 .20
❑ 211 Luis Castillo .50 .20
❑ 212 Chris Denorfia RC 1.00 .40
❑ 213 Detroit Tigers TC .50 .20
❑ 214 Aubrey Huff .50 .20
❑ 215 Brad Fullmer .50 .20
❑ 216 Frank Catalanotto .50 .20
❑ 217 Raul Ibanez .50 .20
❑ 218 Ryan Klesko .50 .20
❑ 219 Octavio Dotel .50 .20
❑ 220 Rob Mackowiak .50 .20
❑ 221 Scott Hatteberg .50 .20
❑ 222 Pat Burrell .50 .20
❑ 223 Bernie Williams .75 .30
❑ 224 Kris Benson .50 .20
❑ 225 Eric Gagne .50 .20
❑ 226 San Francisco Giants TC .75 .30
❑ 227 Roy Oswalt .50 .20
❑ 228 Josh Beckett .50 .20
❑ 229 Lee Mazzilli MG .50 .20
❑ 230 Rickie Weeks .50 .20
❑ 231 Troy Glaus .50 .20
❑ 232 Chone Figgins .50 .20
❑ 233 John Thomson .50 .20
❑ 234 Trot Nixon .50 .20
❑ 235 Brad Penny .50 .20
❑ 236 Oakland A's TC .50 .20
❑ 237 Miguel Batista .50 .20
❑ 238 Ryan Drese .50 .20
❑ 239 Aaron Miles .50 .20
❑ 240 Randy Wolf .50 .20
❑ 241 Brian Lawrence .50 .20
❑ 242 A.J. Pierzynski .50 .20
❑ 243 Jamie Moyer .50 .20
❑ 244 Chris Carpenter .50 .20
❑ 245 So Taguchi .50 .20
❑ 246 Rob Bell .50 .20
❑ 247 Francisco Cordero .50 .20
❑ 248 Tom Glavine .75 .30
❑ 249 Jermaine Dye .50 .20
❑ 250 Cliff Lee .50 .20
❑ 251 New York Yankees TC 1.00 .40
❑ 252 Vernon Wells .50 .20
❑ 253 R.A. Dickey .50 .20
❑ 254 Larry Walker .75 .30
❑ 255 Randy Winn .50 .20
❑ 256 Pedro Feliz .50 .20
❑ 257 Mark Loretta .50 .20
❑ 258 Tim Worrell .50 .20
❑ 259 Kip Wells .50 .20
❑ 260 Cesar Izturis SP 8.00 3.00
❑ 261A Carlos Beltran Fldg .50 .20
❑ 261B Carlos Beltran At Bat SP 8.00 3.00
❑ 262 Juan Encarnacion .50 .20
❑ 263 Luis A. Gonzalez .50 .20
❑ 264 Grady Sizemore .75 .30
❑ 265 Paul Wilson .50 .20
❑ 266 Mark Buehrle .50 .20
❑ 267 Todd Hollandsworth .50 .20
❑ 268 Orlando Cabrera .50 .20
❑ 269 Sidney Ponson .50 .20
❑ 270 Mike Hampton .50 .20
❑ 271 Luis Gonzalez .50 .20
❑ 272 Brendan Donnelly .50 .20
❑ 273A Chipper Jones Slide 1.00 .40
❑ 273B Chipper Jones Fldg SP 8.00 3.00
❑ 274 Brandon Webb .50 .20
❑ 275 Marty Cordova .50 .20
❑ 276 Greg Maddux 1.50 .60
❑ 277 Jose Contreras .50 .20
❑ 278 Aaron Harang .50 .20
❑ 279 Coco Crisp .50 .20
❑ 280 Bobby Higginson .50 .20
❑ 281 Guillermo Mota .50 .20
❑ 282 Andy Pettitte .75 .30
❑ 283 Jeremy West RC .75 .30
❑ 284 Craig Brazell .50 .20
❑ 285 Eric Hinske .50 .20
❑ 286A Hank Blalock Hitting .50 .20
❑ 286B Hank Blalock Fldg SP 8.00 3.00
❑ 287 B.J. Upton .75 .30
❑ 288 Jason Marquis .50 .20
❑ 289 Matt Herges .50 .20
❑ 290 Ramon Hernandez .50 .20
❑ 291 Marlon Byrd .50 .20
❑ 292 Ryan Sweeney SP RC 8.00 3.00
❑ 293 Esteban Loaiza .50 .20
❑ 294 Al Leiter .50 .20
❑ 295 Alex Gonzalez .50 .20
❑ 296A J.Santana Twins Cap 1.00 .40
❑ 296B J.Santana Wash Cap SP 8.00 3.00
❑ 297 Milton Bradley .50 .20
❑ 298 Mike Sweeney .50 .20
❑ 299 Wade Miller .50 .20
❑ 300A Sammy Sosa Hitting 1.00 .40
❑ 300B Sammy Sosa Standing SP 8.00 3.00
❑ 301 Wily Mo Pena .50 .20
❑ 302 Tim Wakefield .50 .20
❑ 303 Rafael Palmeiro .75 .30
❑ 304 Rafael Furcal .50 .20
❑ 305 David Eckstein .50 .20
❑ 306 David Segui .50 .20
❑ 307 Kevin Millar .50 .20
❑ 308 Matt Clement .50 .20
❑ 309 Wade Robinson RC .50 .20
❑ 310 Brad Radke .50 .20
❑ 311 Steve Finley .50 .20
❑ 312A Lance Berkman Hitting .50 .20
❑ 312B Lance Berkman Fldg SP 8.00 3.00
❑ 313 Joe Randa .50 .20
❑ 314 Miguel Cabrera .75 .30
❑ 315 Billy Koch .50 .20
❑ 316 Alex Sanchez .50 .20
❑ 317 Chin-Hui Tsao .50 .20
❑ 318 Omar Vizquel .75 .30
❑ 319 Ryan Freel .50 .20
❑ 320 LaTroy Hawkins .50 .20
❑ 321 Aaron Rowand .50 .20
❑ 322 Paul Konerko .50 .20
❑ 323 Joe Borowski .50 .20
❑ 324 Jarrod Washburn .50 .20
❑ 325 Jaret Wright .50 .20
❑ 326 Johnny Damon .75 .30
❑ 327 Corey Patterson .50 .20
❑ 328 Travis Hafner .50 .20
❑ 329 Shingo Takatsu .50 .20
❑ 330 Dmitri Young .50 .20
❑ 331 Matt Holliday .60 .25
❑ 332 Jeff Kent .50 .20
❑ 333 Desi Relaford .50 .20
❑ 334 Jose Hernandez .50 .20
❑ 335 Lyle Overbay .50 .20
❑ 336 Jacque Jones .50 .20
❑ 337 Termel Sledge .50 .20
❑ 338 Victor Zambrano .50 .20
❑ 339 Gary Sheffield .50 .20
❑ 340 Brad Wilkerson .50 .20
❑ 341 Ian Kinsler RC 3.00 1.25
❑ 342 Jesse Crain .50 .20
❑ 343 Orlando Hudson .50 .20
❑ 344 Laynce Nix .50 .20
❑ 345 Jose Cruz Jr. .50 .20
❑ 346 Edgar Renteria .50 .20
❑ 347 Eddie Guardado .50 .20
❑ 348 Jerome Williams .50 .20
❑ 349 Trevor Hoffman .50 .20
❑ 350 Mike Piazza 1.00 .40
❑ 351 Jason Kendall .50 .20
❑ 352 Kevin Millwood .50 .20
❑ 353A Tim Hudson Atl Cap .50 .20
❑ 353B Tim Hudson Milw Cap SP 8.00 3.00
❑ 354 Paul Quantrill .50 .20
❑ 355 Jon Lieber .50 .20
❑ 356 Braden Looper .50 .20
❑ 357 Chad Cordero .50 .20
❑ 358 Joe Nathan .50 .20
❑ 359 Doug Davis .50 .20
❑ 360 Ian Bladergroen RC .75 .30
❑ 361 Val Majewski .50 .20
❑ 362 Francisco Rodriguez .50 .20
❑ 363 Kelvim Escobar .50 .20
❑ 364 Marcus Giles .50 .20
❑ 365 Darren Fenster RC .50 .20
❑ 366 David Bell .50 .20
❑ 367 Shea Hillenbrand .50 .20
❑ 368 Manny Ramirez .75 .30
❑ 369 Ben Broussard .50 .20
❑ 370 Luis Ramirez RC .50 .20
❑ 371 Dustin Hermanson .50 .20
❑ 372 Akinori Otsuka .50 .20
❑ 373 Chadd Blasko RC .75 .30
❑ 374 Delmon Young .75 .30
❑ 375 Michael Young .50 .20
❑ 376 Bret Boone .50 .20
❑ 377 Jake Peavy .50 .20
❑ 378 Matthew Lindstrom RC .50 .20
❑ 379 Sean Burroughs .50 .20
❑ 380 Rich Harden .50 .20
❑ 381 Chris Roberson RC .50 .20
❑ 382 John Lackey .50 .20
❑ 383 Johnny Estrada .50 .20
❑ 384 Matt Rogelstad RC .50 .20
❑ 385 Toby Hall .50 .20
❑ 386 Adam LaRoche .50 .20
❑ 387 Bill Hall .50 .20
❑ 388 Tim Salmon .50 .20
❑ 389A Curt Schilling Throw .75 .30
❑ 389B Curt Schilling Glove Up SP 8.00 3.00
❑ 390 Michael Barrett .50 .20
❑ 391 Jose Acevedo .50 .20
❑ 392 Nate Schierholtz .75 .30
❑ 393 J.T. Snow Jr. .50 .20
❑ 394 Mark Redman .50 .20
❑ 395 Ryan Madson .50 .20
❑ 396 Kevin West RC .50 .20
❑ 397 Ramon Ortiz .50 .20
❑ 398 Derek Lowe SP 8.00 3.00
❑ 399 Kerry Wood SP 8.00 3.00
❑ 400 Derek Jeter SP 12.00 5.00
❑ 401 Livan Hernandez SP 8.00 3.00
❑ 402 Casey Kotchman SP 8.00 3.00
❑ 403 Chaz Lytle SP RC 8.00 3.00
❑ 404 Alexis Rios SP 8.00 3.00
❑ 405 Scott Spiezio SP 8.00 3.00
❑ 406 Craig Wilson SP 8.00 3.00
❑ 407 Felix Rodriguez SP 8.00 3.00
❑ 408 D'Angelo Jimenez SP 8.00 3.00
❑ 409 Rondell White SP 8.00 3.00
❑ 410 Shawn Estes SP 8.00 3.00
❑ 411 Troy Percival SP 8.00 3.00
❑ 412 Melvin Mora SP 8.00 3.00
❑ 413 Aramis Ramirez SP 8.00 3.00
❑ 414 Carl Everett SP 8.00 3.00
❑ 415 Elvys Quezada SP RC 8.00 3.00
❑ 416 Ben Sheets SP 8.00 3.00
❑ 417 Matt Stairs SP 8.00 3.00
❑ 418 Adam Everett SP 8.00 3.00
❑ 419 Jason Johnson SP 8.00 3.00
❑ 420 Billy Butler SP RC 10.00 4.00
❑ 421 Justin Morneau SP 8.00 3.00
❑ 422 Jose Reyes SP 8.00 3.00
❑ 423 Mariano Rivera SP 8.00 3.00
❑ 424 Jose Vaquedano SP RC 8.00 3.00
❑ 425 Gabe Gross SP 8.00 3.00
❑ 426 Scott Rolen SP 8.00 3.00
❑ 427 Ty Wigginton SP 8.00 3.00
❑ 428 James Jurries SP RC 8.00 3.00
❑ 429 Pedro Martinez SP 8.00 3.00
❑ 430 Mark Grudzielanek SP 8.00 3.00
❑ 431 Josh Phelps SP 8.00 3.00
❑ 432 Ryan Goleski SP RC 8.00 3.00
❑ 433 Mike Matheny SP 8.00 3.00
❑ 434 Bobby Kielty SP 8.00 3.00
❑ 435 Tony Batista SP 8.00 3.00
❑ 436 Corey Koskie SP 8.00 3.00
❑ 437 Brad Lidge SP 8.00 3.00
❑ 438 Dontrelle Willis SP 8.00 3.00
❑ 439 Angel Berroa SP 8.00 3.00
❑ 440 Jason Kubel SP 8.00 3.00
❑ 441 Roy Halladay SP 8.00 3.00
❑ 442 Brian Roberts SP 8.00 3.00
❑ 443 Bill Mueller SP 8.00 3.00
❑ 444 Adam Kennedy SP 8.00 3.00
❑ 445 Brandon Moss SP RC 8.00 3.00
❑ 446 Sean Burnett SP 8.00 3.00
❑ 447 Eric Byrnes SP 8.00 3.00
❑ 448 Matt Campbell SP RC 8.00 3.00
❑ 449 Ryan Webb SP 8.00 3.00
❑ 450 Jose Valentin SP 8.00 3.00
❑ 451 Jake Westbrook SP 8.00 3.00

	Card	Player		
❑	452	Glen Perkins SP RC	8.00	3.00
❑	453	Alex Gonzalez SP	8.00	3.00
❑	454	Jeromy Burnitz SP	8.00	3.00
❑	455	Zack Greinke SP	8.00	3.00
❑	456	Sean Marshall SP RC	6.00	2.50
❑	457	Erubiel Durazo SP	8.00	3.00
❑	458	Michael Cuddyer SP	8.00	3.00
❑	459	Hee Seop Choi SP	8.00	3.00
❑	460	Melky Cabrera SP RC	10.00	4.00
❑	461	Jerry Hairston Jr. SP	8.00	3.00
❑	462	Moises Alou SP	8.00	3.00
❑	463	Michael Rogers SP RC	8.00	3.00
❑	464	Javy Lopez SP	8.00	3.00
❑	465	Freddy Garcia SP	8.00	3.00
❑	466	Brett Harper SP RC	8.00	3.00
❑	467	Juan Gonzalez SP	8.00	3.00
❑	468	Kevin Melillo SP RC	8.00	3.00
❑	469	Todd Walker SP	8.00	3.00
❑	470	C.C. Sabathia SP	8.00	3.00
❑	471	Kole Strayhorn SP RC	8.00	3.00
❑	472	Mark Kotsay SP	8.00	3.00
❑	473	Javier Vazquez SP	8.00	3.00
❑	474	Mike Cameron SP	8.00	3.00
❑	475	Wes Swackhamer SP RC	8.00	3.00

2006 Topps Heritage

❑ COMPLETE SET (494) 400.00 250.00
❑ COMP.SET w/o SP's (384) 60.00 30.00
❑ COMMON CARD .50 .20
❑ COMMON RC .50 .20
❑ COMMON TEAM CARD .50 .20
❑ COMMON SP 8.00 3.00
❑ SP STATED ODDS 1:2 HOBBY/RETAIL
❑ SP CL: 1/2/10/18/20B/23B/25/35/55
❑ SP CL: 70/76/80B/91/95A/95B/99/106
❑ SP CL: 123/127/165B/200B/212B/265-269
❑ SP CL: 271-274/276-316/318-323/325A
❑ SP CL: 325B/326-328/330-349/350A/350B
❑ SP CL: 351-352/400/407/475B
❑ VARIATION CL: 20/23/80/95/165/200
❑ VARIATION CL: 212/325/350/475
❑ TWO VERSIONS OF EACH VARIATION EXIST
❑ SEE BECKETT.COM FOR VAR.DESCRIPTIONS
❑ CARD 255 NOT INTENDED FOR RELEASE
❑ COMP.SET EXCLUDES CARD 255 CUT OUT

	Card	Player		
❑	1	David Ortiz SP	8.00	3.00
❑	2	Mike Piazza SP	10.00	4.00
❑	3	Daryle Ward	.50	.20
❑	4	Rafael Furcal	.50	.20
❑	5	Derek Lowe	.50	.20
❑	6	Eric Chavez	.50	.20
❑	7	Juan Uribe	.50	.20
❑	8	C.C. Sabathia	.50	.20
❑	9	Sean Casey	.50	.20
❑	10	Barry Bonds SP	12.00	5.00
❑	11	Gary Sheffield	.50	.20
❑	12	Ted Lilly	.50	.20
❑	13	Lew Ford	.50	.20
❑	14	Tom Gordon	.50	.20
❑	15	Curt Schilling	1.00	.40
❑	16	Jason Kendall	.50	.20
❑	17	Frank Catalanotto	.50	.20
❑	18	Pedro Martinez SP	8.00	3.00
❑	19	David Dellucci	.50	.20
❑	20A	A.Jones w/o Seats	1.00	.40
❑	20B	A.Jones w/Seats SP	8.00	3.00
❑	21	Brad Halsey	.50	.20
❑	22	Vernon Wells	.50	.20
❑	23A	D.Jeter Yellow/White Ltr	4.00	1.50
❑	23B	D.Jeter Blue Ltr SP	12.00	5.00
❑	24	Todd Helton	1.00	.40
❑	25	Randy Johnson SP	10.00	4.00
❑	26	Jay Gibbons	.50	.20
❑	27	Joe Mays	.50	.20
❑	28	Paul Konerko	.50	.20
❑	29	Lyle Overbay	.50	.20
❑	30	Jorge Posada	1.00	.40
❑	31	Brandon Webb	.50	.20
❑	32	Marcus Giles	.50	.20
❑	33	J.T. Snow	.50	.20
❑	34	Todd Walker	.50	.20
❑	35	Wily Mo Pena SP	8.00	3.00
❑	36	Carlos Delgado	.50	.20
❑	37	David Wright	1.50	.60
❑	38	Shea Hillenbrand	.50	.20
❑	39	Daniel Cabrera	.50	.20
❑	40	Trevor Hoffman	.50	.20
❑	41	Matt Morris	.50	.20
❑	42	Mariano Rivera	1.50	.60
❑	43	Jeff Bagwell	1.00	.40
❑	44	J.D. Drew	.50	.20
❑	45	Carl Pavano	.50	.20
❑	46	Placido Polanco	.50	.20
❑	47	Adrian Beltre	.50	.20
❑	48	J.D. Closser	.50	.20
❑	49	Paul Lo Duca	.50	.20
❑	50	Scott Rolen	.50	.20
❑	51	Bernie Williams	1.00	.40
❑	52	Jose Guillen	.50	.20
❑	53	Aubrey Huff	.50	.20
❑	54	Greg Maddux	2.50	1.00
❑	55	Derrek Lee SP	8.00	3.00
❑	56	Hideki Matsui	1.50	.60
❑	57	Jose Bautista	.50	.20
❑	58	Kyle Farnsworth	.50	.20
❑	59	Nate Robertson	.50	.20
❑	60	Sammy Sosa	1.50	.60
❑	61	Javier Vazquez	.50	.20
❑	62	Jeff Mathis	.50	.20
❑	63	Mark Buehrle	.50	.20
❑	64	Orlando Hernandez	.50	.20
❑	65	Brandon Claussen	.50	.20
❑	66	Miguel Batista	.50	.20
❑	67	Eddie Guardado	.50	.20
❑	68	Alex Gonzalez	.50	.20
❑	69	Kris Benson	.50	.20
❑	70	Bobby Abreu SP	8.00	3.00
❑	71	Vinny Castilla	.50	.20
❑	72	Ben Broussard	.50	.20
❑	73	Travis Hafner	.50	.20
❑	74	Dmitri Young	.50	.20
❑	75	Alex S. Gonzalez	.50	.20
❑	76	Jason Bay SP	8.00	3.00
❑	77	Charlton Jimerson	.50	.20
❑	78	Ryan Garko	.50	.20
❑	79	Lance Berkman	.50	.20
❑	80A	T.Hudson Red/Blue Ltr	.50	.20
❑	80B	T.Hudson Blue Ltr SP	8.00	3.00
❑	81	Guillermo Mota	.50	.20
❑	82	Chris B. Young	.50	.20
❑	83	Brad Lidge	.50	.20
❑	84	A.J. Pierzynski	.50	.20
❑	85	Maicer Izturis	.50	.20
❑	86	Vladimir Guerrero	1.50	.60
❑	87	J.J. Hardy	.50	.20
❑	88	Cesar Izturis	.50	.20
❑	89	Mark Ellis	.50	.20
❑	90	Chipper Jones	1.50	.60
❑	91	Chris Snelling SP	8.00	3.00
❑	92	Jose Reyes	.50	.20
❑	93	Mike Lieberthal	.50	.20
❑	94	Octavio Dotel	.50	.20
❑	95A	A.Rodriguez Fielding SP	10.00	4.00
❑	95B	A.Rodriguez w/Bat SP	10.00	4.00
❑	96	Brett Myers	.50	.20
❑	97	New York Yankees TC	1.00	.40
❑	98	Ryan Klesko	.50	.20
❑	99	Brian Jordan SP	8.00	3.00
❑	100	W.Harridge/W.Giles	.50	.20
❑	101	Adam Eaton	.50	.20
❑	102	Aaron Boone	.50	.20
❑	103	Alex Rios	.50	.20
❑	104	Andy Pettitte	1.00	.40
❑	105	Barry Zito	.50	.20
❑	106	Bengie Molina SP	8.00	3.00
❑	107	Austin Kearns	.50	.20
❑	108	Adam Everett	.50	.20
❑	109	A.J. Burnett	.50	.20
❑	110	Mark Prior	1.00	.40
❑	111	Russ Ortiz	.50	.20
❑	112	Adam Dunn	.50	.20
❑	113	Byung-Hyun Kim	.50	.20
❑	114	Atlanta Braves TC	.50	.20
❑	115	Carlos Silva	.50	.20
❑	116	Chad Cordero	.50	.20
❑	117	Chone Figgins	.50	.20
❑	118	Chris Reitsma	.50	.20
❑	119	Coco Crisp	.50	.20
❑	120	David DeJesus	.50	.20
❑	121	Chris Snyder	.50	.20
❑	122	Brad Eldred	.50	.20
❑	123	Humberto Cota SP	8.00	3.00
❑	124	Erubiel Durazo	.50	.20
❑	125	Josh Beckett	.50	.20
❑	126	Kenny Lofton	.50	.20
❑	127	Joe Nathan SP	8.00	3.00
❑	128	Bryan Bullington	.50	.20
❑	129	Jim Thome	1.00	.40
❑	130	Shawn Green	.50	.20
❑	131	LaTroy Hawkins	.50	.20
❑	132	Mark Kotsay	.50	.20
❑	133	Matt Lawton	.50	.20
❑	134	Luis Castillo	.50	.20
❑	135	Michael Barrett	.50	.20
❑	136	Preston Wilson	.50	.20
❑	137	Orlando Cabrera	.50	.20
❑	138	Chuck James	.50	.20
❑	139	Raul Ibanez	.50	.20
❑	140	Frank Thomas	1.50	.60
❑	141	Orlando Hudson	.50	.20
❑	142	Scott Kazmir	.50	.20
❑	143	Steve Finley	.50	.20
❑	144	Danny Sandoval RC	.50	.20
❑	145	Javy Lopez	.50	.20
❑	146	Tony Giarratano	.50	.20
❑	147	Terrence Long	.50	.20
❑	148	Victor Martinez	.50	.20
❑	149	Toby Hall	.50	.20
❑	150	Fausto Carmona	.50	.20
❑	151	Tim Wakefield	.50	.20
❑	152	Troy Percival	.50	.20
❑	153	Chris Denorfia	.50	.20
❑	154	Junior Spivey	.50	.20
❑	155	Desi Relaford	.50	.20
❑	156	Francisco Liriano	3.00	1.25
❑	157	Corey Koskie	.50	.20
❑	158	Chris Carpenter	.50	.20
❑	159	Robert Andino RC	.50	.20
❑	160	Cliff Floyd	.50	.20
❑	161	Pittsburgh Pirates TC	.50	.20
❑	162	Anderson Hernandez	.50	.20
❑	163	Mike Maroth	.50	.20
❑	164	Aaron Rowand	.50	.20
❑	165A	A.Pujols Grey Shirt	3.00	1.25
❑	165B	A.Pujols Red Shirt SP	12.00	5.00
❑	166	David Bell	.50	.20
❑	167	Angel Berroa	.50	.20
❑	168	B.J. Ryan	.50	.20
❑	169	Bartolo Colon	.50	.20
❑	170	Hong-Chih Kuo	1.50	.60
❑	171	Cincinnati Reds TC	.50	.20
❑	172	Bill Mueller	.50	.20
❑	173	John Koronka	.50	.20
❑	174	Billy Wagner	.50	.20
❑	175	Zack Greinke	.50	.20
❑	176	Rick Short	.50	.20
❑	177	Yadier Molina	.50	.20
❑	178	Willy Taveras	.50	.20
❑	179	Wes Helms	.50	.20
❑	180	Wade Miller	.50	.20
❑	181	Luis Gonzalez	.50	.20
❑	182	Victor Zambrano	.50	.20
❑	183	Chicago Cubs TC	.50	.20
❑	184	Victor Santos	.50	.20
❑	185	Tyler Walker	.50	.20
❑	186	Bobby Crosby	.50	.20
❑	187	Trot Nixon	.50	.20
❑	188	Nick Johnson	.50	.20
❑	189	Nick Swisher	.50	.20
❑	190	Brian Roberts	.50	.20

❑ 191 Nomar Garciaparra 1.50 .60
❑ 192 Oliver Perez .50 .20
❑ 193 Ramon Hernandez .50 .20
❑ 194 Randy Winn .50 .20
❑ 195 Ryan Church .50 .20
❑ 196 Ryan Wagner .50 .20
❑ 197 Todd Hollandsworth .50 .20
❑ 198 Detroit Tigers TC .50 .20
❑ 199 Tino Martinez 1.00 .40
❑ 200A R.Clemens On Mound 3.00 1.25
❑ 200B R.Clemens Red Shirt SP 10.00 4.00
❑ 201 Shawn Estes .50 .20
❑ 202 Justin Morneau .50 .20
❑ 203 Jeff Francis .50 .20
❑ 204 Oakland Athletics TC .50 .20
❑ 205 Jeff Francoeur 1.50 .60
❑ 206 C.J. Wilson .50 .20
❑ 207 Francisco Rodriguez .50 .20
❑ 208 Edgardo Alfonzo .50 .20
❑ 209 David Eckstein .50 .20
❑ 210 Cory Lidle .50 .20
❑ 211 Chase Utley 1.00 .40
❑ 212A R.Baldelli Yellow/White Ltr .50 .20
❑ 212B R.Baldelli Blue Ltr SP 8.00 3.00
❑ 213 So Taguchi .50 .20
❑ 214 Philadelphia Phillies TC .50 .20
❑ 215 Brad Hawpe .50 .20
❑ 216 Walter Young .50 .20
❑ 217 Tom Gorzelanny .50 .20
❑ 218 Shaun Marcum .50 .20
❑ 219 Ryan Howard 2.50 1.00
❑ 220 Damian Jackson .50 .20
❑ 221 Craig Counsell .50 .20
❑ 222 Damian Miller .50 .20
❑ 223 Derrick Turnbow .50 .20
❑ 224 Hank Blalock .50 .20
❑ 225 Brayan Pena .50 .20
❑ 226 Grady Sizemore 1.00 .40
❑ 227 Ivan Rodriguez 1.00 .40
❑ 228 Jason Isringhausen .50 .20
❑ 229 Brian Fuentes .50 .20
❑ 230 Jason Phillips .50 .20
❑ 231 Jason Schmidt .50 .20
❑ 232 Javier Valentin .50 .20
❑ 233 Jeff Kent .50 .20
❑ 234 John Buck .50 .20
❑ 235 Mike Matheny .50 .20
❑ 236 Jorge Cantu .50 .20
❑ 237 Jose Castillo .50 .20
❑ 238 Kenny Rogers .50 .20
❑ 239 Kerry Wood .50 .20
❑ 240 Kevin Mench .50 .20
❑ 241 Tim Stauffer .50 .20
❑ 242 Eric Milton .50 .20
❑ 243 St. Louis Cardinals TC .50 .20
❑ 244 Shawn Chacon .50 .20
❑ 245 Mike Jacobs .50 .20
❑ 246 Ryan Dempster .50 .20
❑ 247 Todd Jones .50 .20
❑ 248 Tom Glavine 1.00 .40
❑ 249 Tony Graffanino .50 .20
❑ 250 Ichiro Suzuki 2.50 1.00
❑ 251 Baltimore Orioles TC .50 .20
❑ 252 Brad Radke .50 .20
❑ 253 Brad Wilkerson .50 .20
❑ 254 Carlos Lee .50 .20
❑ 255 Alex Gordon Cut Out 300.00 200.00
❑ 256 Gustavo Chacin .50 .20
❑ 257 Jermaine Dye .50 .20
❑ 258 Jose Mesa .50 .20
❑ 259 Julio Lugo .50 .20
❑ 260 Mark Redman .50 .20
❑ 261 Brandon Watson .50 .20
❑ 262 Pedro Feliz .50 .20
❑ 263 Esteban Loaiza .50 .20
❑ 264 Anthony Reyes 1.00 .40
❑ 265 Jose Contreras SP 8.00 3.00
❑ 266 Tadahito Iguchi SP 8.00 3.00
❑ 267 Mark Loretta SP 8.00 3.00
❑ 268 Ray Durham SP 8.00 3.00
❑ 269 Neifi Perez SP 8.00 3.00
❑ 270 Washington Nationals TC .50 .20
❑ 271 Troy Glaus SP 8.00 3.00
❑ 272 Matt Holliday SP 10.00 4.00
❑ 273 Kevin Millwood SP 8.00 3.00
❑ 274 Jon Lieber SP 8.00 3.00
❑ 275 Cleveland Indians TC .50 .20
❑ 276 Jeremy Reed SP 8.00 3.00
❑ 277 Garrett Atkins SP 8.00 3.00
❑ 278 Geoff Jenkins SP 8.00 3.00
❑ 279 Joey Gathright SP 8.00 3.00
❑ 280 Ben Sheets SP 8.00 3.00
❑ 281 Melvin Mora SP 8.00 3.00
❑ 282 Jonathan Papelbon SP 10.00 4.00
❑ 283 John Smoltz SP 8.00 3.00
❑ 284 Jake Peavy SP 8.00 3.00
❑ 285 Felix Hernandez SP 8.00 3.00
❑ 286 Alfonso Soriano SP 8.00 3.00
❑ 287 Bronson Arroyo SP 8.00 3.00
❑ 288 Adam LaRoche SP 8.00 3.00
❑ 289 Aramis Ramirez SP 8.00 3.00
❑ 290 Brad Hennessey SP 8.00 3.00
❑ 291 Conor Jackson SP 8.00 3.00
❑ 292 Rod Barajas SP 8.00 3.00
❑ 293 Chris R. Young SP 8.00 3.00
❑ 294 Jeremy Bonderman SP 8.00 3.00
❑ 295 Jack Wilson SP 8.00 3.00
❑ 296 Jay Payton SP 8.00 3.00
❑ 297 Danys Baez SP 8.00 3.00
❑ 298 Jose Lima SP 8.00 3.00
❑ 299 Luis A. Gonzalez SP 8.00 3.00
❑ 300 Mike Sweeney SP 8.00 3.00
❑ 301 Nelson Cruz SP 8.00 3.00
❑ 302 Eric Gagne SP 8.00 3.00
❑ 303 Juan Castro SP 8.00 3.00
❑ 304 Joe Mauer SP 8.00 3.00
❑ 305 Richie Sexson SP 8.00 3.00
❑ 306 Roy Oswalt SP 8.00 3.00
❑ 307 Rickie Weeks SP 8.00 3.00
❑ 308 Pat Borders SP 8.00 3.00
❑ 309 Mike Morse SP 8.00 3.00
❑ 310 Matt Stairs SP 8.00 3.00
❑ 311 Chad Tracy SP 8.00 3.00
❑ 312 Matt Cain SP 8.00 3.00
❑ 313 Mark Mulder SP 8.00 3.00
❑ 314 Mark Grudzielanek SP 8.00 3.00
❑ 315 Johnny Damon Yanks SP 10.00 4.00
❑ 316 Casey Kotchman SP 8.00 3.00
❑ 317 San Francisco Giants TC .50 .20
❑ 318 Chris Burke SP 8.00 3.00
❑ 319 Carl Crawford SP 8.00 3.00
❑ 320 Edgar Renteria SP 8.00 3.00
❑ 321 Chan Ho Park SP 8.00 3.00
❑ 322 Boston Red Sox TC SP 8.00 3.00
❑ 323 Robinson Cano SP 8.00 3.00
❑ 324 Los Angeles Dodgers TC .50 .20
❑ 325A M.Tejada w/Bat SP 8.00 3.00
❑ 325B M.Tejada Hand Up SP 8.00 3.00
❑ 326 Jimmy Rollins SP 8.00 3.00
❑ 327 Juan Pierre SP 8.00 3.00
❑ 328 Dan Johnson SP 8.00 3.00
❑ 329 Chicago White Sox TC 1.00 .40
❑ 330 Pat Burrell SP 8.00 3.00
❑ 331 Ramon Ortiz SP 8.00 3.00
❑ 332 Rondell White SP 8.00 3.00
❑ 333 David Wells SP 8.00 3.00
❑ 334 Michael Young SP 8.00 3.00
❑ 335 Mike Mussina SP 8.00 3.00
❑ 336 Moises Alou SP 8.00 3.00
❑ 337 Scott Podsednik SP 8.00 3.00
❑ 338 Rich Harden SP 8.00 3.00
❑ 339 Mark Teahen SP 8.00 3.00
❑ 340 Jacque Jones SP 8.00 3.00
❑ 341 Jason Giambi SP 8.00 3.00
❑ 342 Bill Hall SP 8.00 3.00
❑ 343 Jon Garland SP 8.00 3.00
❑ 344 Dontrelle Willis SP 8.00 3.00
❑ 345 Danny Haren SP 8.00 3.00
❑ 346 Brian Giles SP 8.00 3.00
❑ 347 Brad Penny SP 8.00 3.00
❑ 348 Brandon McCarthy SP 8.00 3.00
❑ 349 Chien-Ming Wang SP 10.00 4.00
❑ 350A T.Hunter Red/Blue Ltr SP 8.00 3.00
❑ 350B T.Hunter Blue Ltr SP 8.00 3.00
❑ 351 Yhency Brazoban SP 8.00 3.00
❑ 352 Rodrigo Lopez SP 8.00 3.00
❑ 353 Paul McAnulty .50 .20
❑ 354 Francisco Cordero .50 .20
❑ 355 Brandon Inge .50 .20
❑ 356 Jason Lane .50 .20
❑ 357 Brian Schneider .50 .20
❑ 358 Dustin Hermanson .50 .20
❑ 359 Eric Hinske .50 .20
❑ 360 Jarrod Washburn .50 .20
❑ 361 Jayson Werth .50 .20
❑ 362 Craig Breslow RC .50 .20
❑ 363 Jeff Weaver .50 .20
❑ 364 Jeromy Burnitz .50 .20
❑ 365 Jhonny Peralta .50 .20
❑ 366 Joe Crede .50 .20
❑ 367 Johan Santana 1.50 .60
❑ 368 Jose Valentin .50 .20
❑ 369 Keith Foulke .50 .20
❑ 370 Larry Bigbie .50 .20
❑ 371 Manny Ramirez 1.00 .40
❑ 372 Jim Edmonds .50 .20
❑ 373 Horacio Ramirez .50 .20
❑ 374 Garret Anderson .50 .20
❑ 375 Felipe Lopez .50 .20
❑ 376 Eric Byrnes .50 .20
❑ 377 Darin Erstad .50 .20
❑ 378 Carlos Zambrano .50 .20
❑ 379 Craig Biggio 1.00 .40
❑ 380 Darrell Rasner .50 .20
❑ 381 Dave Roberts .50 .20
❑ 382 Hanley Ramirez .50 .20
❑ 383 Geoff Blum .50 .20
❑ 384 Joel Pineiro .50 .20
❑ 385 Kip Wells .50 .20
❑ 386 Kelvim Escobar .50 .20
❑ 387 John Patterson .50 .20
❑ 388 Jody Gerut .50 .20
❑ 389 Marshall McDougall .50 .20
❑ 390 Mike MacDougal .50 .20
❑ 391 Orlando Palmeiro .50 .20
❑ 392 Rich Aurilia .50 .20
❑ 393 Ronnie Belliard .50 .20
❑ 394 Rich Hill .50 .20
❑ 395 Scott Hatteberg .50 .20
❑ 396 Ryan Langerhans .50 .20
❑ 397 Richard Hidalgo .50 .20
❑ 398 Omar Vizquel 1.00 .40
❑ 399 Mike Lowell .50 .20
❑ 400 Astros Aces SP 8.00 3.00
❑ 401 Mike Cameron .50 .20
❑ 402 Matt Clement .50 .20
❑ 403 Miguel Cabrera 1.00 .40
❑ 404 Milton Bradley .50 .20
❑ 405 Laynce Nix .50 .20
❑ 406 Rob Mackowiak .50 .20
❑ 407 White Sox Power Hitters SP 8.00 3.00
❑ 408 Mark Teixeira 1.00 .40
❑ 409 Brady Clark .50 .20
❑ 410 Johnny Estrada .50 .20
❑ 411 Juan Encarnacion .50 .20
❑ 412 Morgan Ensberg .50 .20
❑ 413 Nook Logan .50 .20
❑ 414 Phil Nevin .50 .20
❑ 415 Reggie Sanders .50 .20
❑ 416 Roy Halladay .50 .20
❑ 417 Livan Hernandez .50 .20
❑ 418 Jose Vidro .50 .20
❑ 419 Shannon Stewart .50 .20
❑ 420 Brian Bruney .50 .20
❑ 421 Royce Clayton .50 .20
❑ 422 Chris Demaria RC .50 .20
❑ 423 Eduardo Perez .50 .20
❑ 424 Jeff Suppan .50 .20
❑ 425 Jaret Wright .50 .20
❑ 426 Joe Randa .50 .20
❑ 427 Bobby Kielty .50 .20
❑ 428 Jason Ellison .50 .20
❑ 429 Gregg Zaun .50 .20
❑ 430 Runelvys Hernandez .50 .20
❑ 431 Joe McEwing .50 .20
❑ 432 Jason LaRue .50 .20
❑ 433 Aaron Miles .50 .20
❑ 434 Adam Kennedy .50 .20
❑ 435 Ambiorix Burgos .50 .20
❑ 436 Armando Benitez .50 .20
❑ 437 Brad Ausmus .50 .20
❑ 438 Brandon Backe .50 .20
❑ 439 Brian James Anderson .50 .20
❑ 440 Bruce Chen .50 .20
❑ 441 Carlos Guillen .50 .20
❑ 442 Casey Blake .50 .20
❑ 443 Chris Capuano .50 .20
❑ 444 Chris Duffy .50 .20

❑ 445 Chris Ray .50 .20
❑ 446 Clint Barmes .50 .20
❑ 447 Andrew Sisco .50 .20
❑ 448 Dallas McPherson .50 .20
❑ 449 Tanyon Sturtze .50 .20
❑ 450 Carlos Beltran .50 .20
❑ 451 Jason Vargas .50 .20
❑ 452 Ervin Santana .50 .20
❑ 453 Jason Marquis .50 .20
❑ 454 Juan Rivera .50 .20
❑ 455 Jake Westbrook .50 .20
❑ 456 Jason Johnson .50 .20
❑ 457 Joe Blanton .50 .20
❑ 458 Kevin Millar .50 .20
❑ 459 John Thomson .50 .20
❑ 460 J.P. Howell .50 .20
❑ 461 Justin Verlander 2.50 1.00
❑ 462 Kelly Johnson .50 .20
❑ 463 Kyle Davies .50 .20
❑ 464 Lance Niekro .50 .20
❑ 465 Magglio Ordonez .50 .20
❑ 466 Melky Cabrera .50 .20
❑ 467 Nick Punto .50 .20
❑ 468 Paul Byrd .50 .20
❑ 469 Randy Wolf .50 .20
❑ 470 Ruben Gotay .50 .20
❑ 471 Ryan Madson .50 .20
❑ 472 Victor Diaz .50 .20
❑ 473 Xavier Nady .50 .20
❑ 474 Zach Duke .50 .20
❑ 475A H.Street Yellow/White Ltr .50 .20
❑ 475B H.Street Blue Ltr SP 8.00 3.00
❑ 476 Brad Thompson .50 .20
❑ 477 Jonny Gomes .50 .20
❑ 478 B.J. Upton .50 .20
❑ 479 Jamey Carroll .50 .20
❑ 480 Mike Hampton .50 .20
❑ 481 Tony Clark .50 .20
❑ 482 Antonio Alfonseca .50 .20
❑ 483 Justin Duchscherer .50 .20
❑ 484 Mike Timlin .50 .20
❑ 485 Joe Saunders .50 .20

2007 Topps Heritage

❑ COMPLETE SET (527) 400.00 250.00
❑ COMP.SET w/o SP's (384) 60.00 30.00
❑ COMMON CARD .50 .20
❑ COMMON RC .50 .20
❑ COMMON TEAM CARD .50 .20
❑ COMMON SP 6.00 2.50
❑ SP STATED ODDS 1:2 HOBBY/RETAIL
❑ SEE BECKETT.COM FOR SP CHECKLIST
❑ COMMON YELLOW 5.00 2.00
❑ YELLOW STATED ODDS 1:6 HOBBY/RETAIL
❑ SEE BECKETT.COM FOR YELLOW CL
❑ CARD 145 DOES NOT EXIST
❑ 1 David Ortiz 1.25 .50
❑ 2a Roger Clemens 2.50 1.00
❑ 2b Roger Clemens YT 8.00 3.00
❑ 3 David Wells .50 .20
❑ 4 Ronny Paulino SP 6.00 2.50
❑ 5 Derek Jeter SP 15.00 6.00
❑ 6 Felix Hernandez .75 .30
❑ 7 Todd Helton .75 .30
❑ 8a David Eckstein .50 .20
❑ 8b David Eckstein YN 5.00 2.00
❑ 9 Craig Wilson .50 .20
❑ 10 John Smoltz .75 .30
❑ 11a Rob Mackowiak .50 .20
❑ 11b Rob Mackowiak YT 5.00 2.00
❑ 12 Scott Hatteberg .50 .20
❑ 13a Wilfredo Ledezma SP 6.00 2.50
❑ 13b Wilfredo Ledezma YT 5.00 2.00
❑ 14 Bobby Abreu SP 6.00 2.50
❑ 15 Mike Stanton .50 .20
❑ 16 Wilson Betemit .50 .20
❑ 17 Darren Oliver .50 .20
❑ 18 Josh Beckett .75 .30
❑ 19 San Francisco Giants TC .50 .20
❑ 20a Robinson Cano .75 .30
❑ 20b Robinson Cano YT 6.00 2.50
❑ 21 Matt Cain .75 .30
❑ 22 Jason Kendall SP 6.00 2.50
❑ 23a Mark Kotsay SP 6.00 2.50
❑ 23b Mark Kotsay YN 5.00 2.00
❑ 24a Yadier Molina .50 .20
❑ 24b Yadier Molina YN 5.00 2.00
❑ 25 Brad Penny .50 .20
❑ 26 Adrian Gonzalez .50 .20
❑ 27 Danny Haren .50 .20
❑ 28 Brian Giles .50 .20
❑ 29 Jose Lopez .50 .20
❑ 30a Ichiro Suzuki 2.00 .75
❑ 30b Ichiro Suzuki YN 8.00 3.00
❑ 31 Beltran Perez SP (RC) 6.00 2.50
❑ 32 Brad Hawpe SP 6.00 2.50
❑ 33a Jim Thome .75 .30
❑ 33b Jim Thome YT 6.00 2.50
❑ 34 Mark DeRosa .50 .20
❑ 35a Woody Williams .50 .20
❑ 35b Woody Williams YT 5.00 2.00
❑ 36 Luis Gonzalez .50 .20
❑ 37 Billy Sadler (RC) .50 .20
❑ 38 Dave Roberts .50 .20
❑ 39 Mitch Maier RC .50 .20
❑ 40 Francisco Cordero SP 6.00 2.50
❑ 41 Anthony Reyes SP 6.00 2.50
❑ 42 Russell Martin .50 .20
❑ 43 Scott Proctor .50 .20
❑ 44 Washington Nationals TC .50 .20
❑ 45 Shane Victorino .50 .20
❑ 46a Joel Zumaya .75 .30
❑ 46b Joel Zumaya YN 6.00 2.50
❑ 47 Delmon Young (RC) 1.25 .50
❑ 48 Alex Rios .50 .20
❑ 49 Willy Taveras SP 6.00 2.50
❑ 50a Mark Buehrle SP 6.00 2.50
❑ 50b Mark Buehrle YT 5.00 2.00
❑ 51 Livan Hernandez .50 .20
❑ 52a Jason Bay .50 .20
❑ 52b Jason Bay YT 5.00 2.00
❑ 53a Jose Valentin .50 .20
❑ 53b Jose Valentin YN 5.00 2.00
❑ 54 Kevin Reese .50 .20
❑ 55 Felipe Lopez .50 .20
❑ 56 Ryan Sweeney (RC) .50 .20
❑ 57a Kelvim Escobar .50 .20
❑ 57b Kelvim Escobar YN 5.00 2.00
❑ 58a N.Swisher Sm.Print SP 6.00 2.50
❑ 58b N.Swisher Lg.Print YT 5.00 2.00
❑ 59 Kevin Millwood SP 6.00 2.50
❑ 60a Preston Wilson .50 .20
❑ 60b Preston Wilson YN 5.00 2.00
❑ 61a Mariano Rivera 1.25 .50
❑ 61b Mariano Rivera YN 6.00 2.50
❑ 62 Josh Barfield .50 .20
❑ 63 Ryan Freel .50 .20
❑ 64 Tim Hudson .50 .20
❑ 65a Chris Narveson (RC) .50 .20
❑ 65b Chris Narveson YN (RC) 5.00 2.00
❑ 66 Matt Murton .50 .20
❑ 67 Melvin Mora SP 6.00 2.50
❑ 68 Jason Jennings SP 6.00 2.50
❑ 69 Emil Brown .50 .20
❑ 70a Magglio Ordonez .50 .20
❑ 70b Magglio Ordonez YN 5.00 2.00
❑ 71 Los Angeles Dodgers TC .50 .20
❑ 72 Ross Gload .50 .20
❑ 73 David Ross .50 .20
❑ 74 Juan Uribe .50 .20
❑ 75 Scott Podsednik .50 .20
❑ 76a Cole Hamels SP 8.00 3.00
❑ 76b Cole Hamels YT 6.00 2.50
❑ 77a Rafael Furcal SP 6.00 2.50
❑ 77b Rafael Furcal YT 5.00 2.00
❑ 78a Ryan Theriot .50 .20
❑ 78b Ryan Theriot YN 5.00 2.00
❑ 79a Corey Patterson .50 .20
❑ 79b Corey Patterson YT 5.00 2.00
❑ 80 Jered Weaver .75 .30
❑ 81a Stephen Drew .75 .30
❑ 81b Stephen Drew YT 6.00 2.50
❑ 82 Adam Kennedy .50 .20
❑ 83 Tony Gwynn Jr. .50 .20
❑ 84 Kazuo Matsui .50 .20
❑ 85a Omar Vizquel SP 8.00 3.00
❑ 85b Omar Vizquel YT 6.00 2.50
❑ 86 Fred Lewis SP (RC) 6.00 2.50
❑ 87a Shawn Chacon .50 .20
❑ 87b Shawn Chacon YN 5.00 2.00
❑ 88 Frank Catalanotto .50 .20
❑ 89 Orlando Hudson .50 .20
❑ 90 Pat Burrell .50 .20
❑ 91 David DeJesus .50 .20
❑ 92a David Wright 2.00 .75
❑ 92b David Wright YN 8.00 3.00
❑ 93 Conor Jackson .50 .20
❑ 94 Xavier Nady SP 6.00 2.50
❑ 95 Bill Hall SP 6.00 2.50
❑ 96 Kip Wells .50 .20
❑ 97a Jeff Suppan .50 .20
❑ 97b Jeff Suppan YN 5.00 2.00
❑ 98a Ryan Zimmerman 1.25 .50
❑ 98b Ryan Zimmerman YN 6.00 2.50
❑ 99 Wes Helms .50 .20
❑ 100a Jose Contreras .50 .20
❑ 100b Jose Contreras YT 5.00 2.00
❑ 101a Miguel Cairo .50 .20
❑ 101b Miguel Cairo YN 5.00 2.00
❑ 102 Brian Roberts .50 .20
❑ 103 Carl Crawford SP 6.00 2.50
❑ 104 Mike Lamb SP 6.00 2.50
❑ 105 Mark Ellis .50 .20
❑ 106 Scott Rolen .75 .30
❑ 107 Garrett Atkins .50 .20
❑ 108a Hanley Ramirez .75 .30
❑ 108b Hanley Ramirez YT 6.00 2.50
❑ 109 Trot Nixon .50 .20
❑ 110 Edgar Renteria .50 .20
❑ 111 Jeff Francis .50 .20
❑ 112 Marcus Thames SP 6.00 2.50
❑ 113 Brian Burres SP (RC) 6.00 2.50
❑ 114 Brian Schneider .50 .20
❑ 115 Jeremy Bonderman .50 .20
❑ 116 Ryan Madson .50 .20
❑ 117 Gerald Laird .50 .20
❑ 118 Roy Halladay .50 .20
❑ 119 Victor Martinez .50 .20
❑ 120 Greg Maddux 2.00 .75
❑ 121 Jay Payton SP 6.00 2.50
❑ 122 Jacque Jones SP 6.00 2.50
❑ 123 Juan Lara RC .50 .20
❑ 124 Derrick Turnbow .50 .20
❑ 125 Adam Everett .50 .20
❑ 126 Michael Cuddyer .50 .20
❑ 127 Gil Meche .50 .20
❑ 128 Willy Aybar .50 .20
❑ 129 Jerry Owens (RC) .50 .20
❑ 130 Manny Ramirez SP 8.00 3.00
❑ 131 Howie Kendrick SP 6.00 2.50
❑ 132 Byung-Hyun Kim .50 .20
❑ 133 Kevin Kouzmanoff (RC) .50 .20
❑ 134 Philadelphia Phillies TC .50 .20
❑ 135 Joe Blanton .50 .20
❑ 136 Ray Durham .50 .20
❑ 137 Luke Hudson .50 .20
❑ 138 Eric Byrnes .50 .20
❑ 139 Ryan Braun SP RC 6.00 2.50
❑ 140 Johnny Damon SP 8.00 3.00
❑ 141 Ambiorix Burgos .50 .20
❑ 142 Hideki Matsui 1.25 .50
❑ 143 Josh Johnson .50 .20
❑ 144 Miguel Cabrera .75 .30
❑ 146 Delwyn Young (RC) .50 .20
❑ 147 Chuck James .50 .20
❑ 148 Morgan Ensberg .50 .20
❑ 149 Jose Vidro SP 6.00 2.50
❑ 150 Alex Rodriguez SP 12.00 5.00
❑ 151 Carlos Maldonado (RC) .50 .20
❑ 152 Jason Schmidt .50 .20

	No.	Card		
❑	153	Alex Escobar	.50	.20
❑	154	Chris Gomez	.50	.20
❑	155	Endy Chavez	.50	.20
❑	156	Kris Benson	.50	.20
❑	157	Bronson Arroyo	.50	.20
❑	158	Cleveland Indians TC SP	6.00	2.50
❑	159	Chris Ray SP	6.00	2.50
❑	160	Richie Sexson	.50	.20
❑	161	Huston Street	.50	.20
❑	162	Kevin Youkilis	.50	.20
❑	163	Armando Benitez	.50	.20
❑	164	Vinny Rottino (RC)	.50	.20
❑	165	Garret Anderson	.50	.20
❑	166	Todd Greene	.50	.20
❑	167	Brian Stokes SP (RC)	6.00	2.50
❑	168	Albert Pujols SP	15.00	6.00
❑	169	Todd Coffey	.50	.20
❑	170	Jason Michaels	.50	.20
❑	171	David Dellucci	.50	.20
❑	172	Eric Milton	.50	.20
❑	173	Austin Kearns	.50	.20
❑	174	Oakland Athletics TC	.50	.20
❑	175	Andy Cannizaro RC	.50	.20
❑	176	David Weathers SP	6.00	2.50
❑	177	Jermaine Dye SP	6.00	2.50
❑	178	Wily Mo Pena	.50	.20
❑	179	Chris Burke	.50	.20
❑	180	Jeff Weaver	.50	.20
❑	181	Edwin Encarnacion	.50	.20
❑	182	Jeremy Hermida	.50	.20
❑	183	Tim Wakefield	.50	.20
❑	184	Rich Hill	.50	.20
❑	185	Aaron Hill SP	6.00	2.50
❑	186	Scot Shields SP	6.00	2.50
❑	187	Randy Johnson	1.25	.50
❑	188	Dan Johnson	.50	.20
❑	189	Sean Marshall	.50	.20
❑	190	Marcus Giles	.50	.20
❑	191	Jonathan Broxton	.50	.20
❑	192	Mike Piazza	1.25	.50
❑	193	Carlos Quentin	.50	.20
❑	194	Derek Lowe SP	6.00	2.50
❑	195	Russell Branyan SP	6.00	2.50
❑	196	Jason Marquis	.50	.20
❑	197	Khalil Greene	.75	.30
❑	198	Ryan Dempster	.50	.20
❑	199	Ronnie Belliard	.50	.20
❑	200	Josh Fogg	.50	.20
❑	201	Carlos Lee	.50	.20
❑	202	Chris Denorfia	.50	.20
❑	203	Kendry Morales SP	8.00	3.00
❑	204	Rafael Soriano SP	6.00	2.50
❑	205	Brandon Phillips	.50	.20
❑	206	Andrew Miller RC	3.00	1.25
❑	207	John Koronka	.50	.20
❑	208	Luis Castillo	.50	.20
❑	209	Angel Guzman	.50	.20
❑	210	Jim Edmonds	.75	.30
❑	211	Patrick Misch (RC)	.50	.20
❑	212	Ty Wigginton SP	6.00	2.50
❑	213	Brandon Inge SP	6.00	2.50
❑	214	Royce Clayton	.50	.20
❑	215	Ben Broussard	.50	.20
❑	216	St. Louis Cardinals TC	.50	.20
❑	217	Mark Mulder	.50	.20
❑	218	Kenji Johjima	1.25	.50
❑	219	Joe Crede	.50	.20
❑	220	Shea Hillenbrand	.50	.20
❑	221	Josh Fields SP (RC)	6.00	2.50
❑	222	Pat Neshek SP	8.00	3.00
❑	223	Reed Johnson	.50	.20
❑	224	Mike Mussina	.75	.30
❑	225	Randy Winn	.50	.20
❑	226	Brian Rogers	.50	.20
❑	227	Juan Rivera	.50	.20
❑	228	Shawn Green	.50	.20
❑	229	Mike Napoli	.50	.20
❑	230	Chase Utley SP	8.00	3.00
❑	231	John Nelson SP (RC)	6.00	2.50
❑	232	Casey Blake	.50	.20
❑	233	Lyle Overbay	.50	.20
❑	234	Adam LaRoche	.50	.20
❑	235	Julio Lugo	.50	.20
❑	236	Johnny Estrada	.50	.20
❑	237	James Shields	.50	.20
❑	238	Jose Castillo	.50	.20
❑	239	Doug Davis SP	6.00	2.50
❑	240	Jason Giambi SP	6.00	2.50
❑	241	Mike Gonzalez	.50	.20
❑	242	Scott Downs	.50	.20
❑	243	Joe Inglett	.50	.20
❑	244	Matt Kemp	.50	.20
❑	245	Ted Lilly	.50	.20
❑	246	New York Yankees TC	1.25	.50
❑	247	Jamey Carroll	.50	.20
❑	248	Adam Wainwright SP	6.00	2.50
❑	249	Matt Thornton SP	6.00	2.50
❑	250	Alfonso Soriano	.50	.20
❑	251	Tom Gordon	.50	.20
❑	252	Dennis Sarfate (RC)	.50	.20
❑	253	Zach Duke	.50	.20
❑	254	Hank Blalock	.50	.20
❑	255	Johan Santana	.75	.30
❑	256	Chicago White Sox TC	.50	.20
❑	257	Aaron Cook SP	6.00	2.50
❑	258	Cliff Lee SP	6.00	2.50
❑	259	Miguel Tejada	.50	.20
❑	260	Mike Lowell	.50	.20
❑	261	Ian Snell	.50	.20
❑	262	Jason Tyner	.50	.20
❑	263	Troy Tulowitzki (RC)	1.25	.50
❑	264	Ervin Santana	.50	.20
❑	265	Jon Lester	.75	.30
❑	266	Andy Pettitte SP	8.00	3.00
❑	267	A.J. Pierzynski SP	6.00	2.50
❑	268	Rich Aurilia	.50	.20
❑	269	Phil Nevin	.50	.20
❑	270	Tom Glavine	.75	.30
❑	271	Chris Coste	.50	.20
❑	272	Moises Alou	.50	.20
❑	273	J.D. Drew	.50	.20
❑	274	Abraham Nunez	.50	.20
❑	275	Jorge Posada SP	8.00	3.00
❑	276	Jeff Conine SP	6.00	2.50
❑	277	Chad Cordero	.50	.20
❑	278	Nick Johnson	.50	.20
❑	279	Kevin Millar	.50	.20
❑	280	Mark Grudzielanek	.50	.20
❑	281	Chris Stewart RC	.50	.20
❑	282	Nate Robertson	.50	.20
❑	283	Drew Anderson RC	.50	.20
❑	284	Doug Mientkiewicz SP	6.00	2.50
❑	285	Ken Griffey Jr. SP	10.00	4.00
❑	286	Cory Sullivan	.50	.20
❑	287	Chris Carpenter	.50	.20
❑	288	Gary Matthews	.50	.20
❑	289	J.Verlander/Jef.Weaver	1.25	.50
❑	290	Vicente Padilla	.50	.20
❑	291	Chris Roberson	.50	.20
❑	292	Chris R. Young	.50	.20
❑	293	Ryan Garko SP	6.00	2.50
❑	294	Miguel Batista SP	6.00	2.50
❑	295	B.J. Upton	.50	.20
❑	296	Justin Verlander	1.25	.50
❑	297	Ben Zobrist	.50	.20
❑	298	Ben Sheets	.50	.20
❑	299	Eric Chavez	.50	.20
❑	300	Scott Schoeneweis	.50	.20
❑	301	Placido Polanco	.50	.20
❑	302	Angel Sanchez SP RC	6.00	2.50
❑	303	Freddy Sanchez SP	6.00	2.50
❑	304	M.Ordonez/C.Monroe	.50	.20
❑	305	A.J. Burnett	.50	.20
❑	306	Juan Perez RC	.50	.20
❑	307	Chris Britton	.50	.20
❑	308	Jon Garland	.50	.20
❑	309	Pedro Feliz	.50	.20
❑	310	Ryan Howard	2.00	.75
❑	311	Aaron Harang SP	6.00	2.50
❑	312	Boston Red Sox TC SP	8.00	3.00
❑	313	Chad Billingsley	.50	.20
❑	314	C.Jones/B.Cox MG	1.25	.50
❑	315	Bengie Molina	.50	.20
❑	316	Juan Pierre	.50	.20
❑	317	Luke Scott	.50	.20
❑	318	Javier Valentin	.50	.20
❑	319	Mark Loretta	.50	.20
❑	320	Kenny Lofton SP	6.00	2.50
❑	321	V.Guerrero/I.Rodriguez SP	8.00	3.00
❑	322	Josh Willingham	.50	.20
❑	323	Lance Berkman	.50	.20
❑	324	Anibal Sanchez	.50	.20
❑	325	Maicer Izturis	.50	.20
❑	326	Brett Myers	.50	.20
❑	327	Chicago Cubs TC	.75	.30
❑	328	Francisco Liriano	2.50	1.00
❑	329	Craig Monroe SP	6.00	2.50
❑	330	Paul LoDuca SP	6.00	2.50
❑	331	Steve Trachsel	.50	.20
❑	332	Bernie Williams	.75	.30
❑	333	Carlos Guillen	.50	.20
❑	334	C.Wang/M.Mussina	2.00	.75
❑	335	Dave Bush	.50	.20
❑	336	Carlos Beltran	.50	.20
❑	337	Jason Isringhausen	.50	.20
❑	338	Todd Walker SP	6.00	2.50
❑	339	Jarrod Washburn SP	6.00	2.50
❑	340	Brandon Webb	.50	.20
❑	341	Pittsburgh Pirates TC	.50	.20
❑	342	Daryle Ward	.50	.20
❑	343	Chad Santos	.50	.20
❑	344	Brad Lidge	.50	.20
❑	345	Brad Ausmus	.50	.20
❑	346	Carlos Delgado	.50	.20
❑	347	Boone Logan SP	6.00	2.50
❑	348	Jimmy Rollins SP	6.00	2.50
❑	349	Orlando Hernandez	.50	.20
❑	350	Gary Sheffield	.50	.20
❑	351	Pujols/Duncan/Edmonds/Molina	2.50	1.00
❑	352	Jake Peavy	.50	.20
❑	353	Jason Varitek	1.25	.50
❑	354	Freddy Garcia	.50	.20
❑	355	Matt Diaz	.50	.20
❑	356	Bernie Castro SP	6.00	2.50
❑	357	Eric Stults SP RC	6.00	2.50
❑	358	John Lackey	.50	.20
❑	359	Bobby Jenks	.50	.20
❑	360	Mark Teixeira	.75	.30
❑	361	Jonathan Papelbon	1.25	.50
❑	362	Paul Konerko	.50	.20
❑	363	Erik Bedard	.50	.20
❑	364	Eliezer Alfonzo	.50	.20
❑	365	Fernando Rodney SP	6.00	2.50
❑	366	Chris Duncan SP	6.00	2.50
❑	367	Jose Diaz (RC)	.50	.20
❑	368	Travis Hafner	.50	.20
❑	369	Matt Capps	.50	.20
❑	370	Ivan Rodriguez	.75	.30
❑	371	David Murphy (RC)	.50	.20
❑	372	Carlos Zambrano	.50	.20
❑	373	Chris Iannetta	.50	.20
❑	374	Jose Mesa SP	6.00	2.50
❑	375	Michael Young SP	6.00	2.50
❑	376	Bill Bray	.50	.20
❑	377	Atlanta Braves TC	.75	.30
❑	378	Jeff Cirillo	.50	.20
❑	379	Barry Zito	.50	.20
❑	380	Clay Hensley	.50	.20
❑	381	J.J. Putz	.50	.20
❑	382	C.C. Sabathia	.50	.20
❑	383	Eduardo Perez SP	6.00	2.50
❑	384	Scott Moore SP (RC)	6.00	2.50
❑	385	Scott Olsen	.50	.20
❑	386	R.Howard/C.Utley	2.00	.75
❑	387	Aaron Rowand	.50	.20
❑	388	Mike Rouse	.50	.20
❑	389	Alexis Gomez	.50	.20
❑	390	Brian McCann	.50	.20
❑	391	Ryan Shealy	.50	.20
❑	392	Shane Youman SP RC	6.00	2.50
❑	393	Melky Cabrera SP	6.00	2.50
❑	394	Jeremy Sowers	.50	.20
❑	395	Casey Janssen	.50	.20
❑	396	Travis Chick (RC)	.50	.20
❑	397	Detroit Tigers TC	.50	.20
❑	398	Reggie Abercrombie	.50	.20
❑	399	Ricky Nolasco	.50	.20
❑	400	Tadahito Iguchi	.50	.20
❑	401	Jose Reyes SP	6.00	2.50
❑	402	Juan Encarnacion SP	6.00	2.50
❑	403	Brandon Harper	.50	.20
❑	404	Torii Hunter	.50	.20
❑	405	Dan Uggla	.75	.30
❑	406	Orlando Cabrera	.50	.20
❑	407	Jose Capellan	.50	.20
❑	408	Baltimore Orioles TC	.50	.20
❑	409	Frank Thomas	1.25	.50
❑	410	Francisco Rodriguez SP	6.00	2.50

❑ 411 Ian Kinsler SP 8.00 3.00
❑ 412 Billy Wagner .50 .20
❑ 413 Andy Marte .50 .20
❑ 414 Mike Jacobs .50 .20
❑ 415 Raul Ibanez .50 .20
❑ 416 Jhonny Peralta .50 .20
❑ 417 Chris B. Young .50 .20
❑ 418 A.Pujols/M.Ordonez 2.50 1.00
❑ 419 Scott Kazmir SP 8.00 3.00
❑ 420 Norris Hopper SP 6.00 2.50
❑ 421 Chris Capuano .50 .20
❑ 422 Troy Glaus .50 .20
❑ 423 Roy Oswalt .50 .20
❑ 424 Grady Sizemore .75 .30
❑ 425 Chone Figgins .50 .20
❑ 426 Chad Tracy .50 .20
❑ 427 Brian Fuentes .50 .20
❑ 428 Cincinnati Reds TC SP 6.00 2.50
❑ 429 Ramon Hernandez SP 6.00 2.50
❑ 430 Mike Cameron .50 .20
❑ 431 Dontrelle Willis .50 .20
❑ 432 Josh Sharpless .50 .20
❑ 433 Adrian Beltre .50 .20
❑ 434 Curtis Granderson .50 .20
❑ 435 B.J. Ryan .50 .20
❑ 436 D.Wright/R.Howard 2.00 .75
❑ 437 Vernon Wells SP 6.00 2.50
❑ 438 Vladimir Guerrero SP 8.00 3.00
❑ 439 Jake Westbrook .50 .20
❑ 440 Chipper Jones 1.25 .50
❑ 441 James Loney .75 .30
❑ 442 Nook Logan .50 .20
❑ 443 Oswaldo Navarro RC .50 .20
❑ 444 Joe Mauer .75 .30
❑ 445 Miguel Montero (RC) .50 .20
❑ 446 Franklin Gutierrez SP 6.00 2.50
❑ 447 Mark Redman SP 6.00 2.50
❑ 448 Mike Rabelo RC .50 .20
❑ 449 Philip Humber (RC) .75 .30
❑ 450 Justin Morneau .50 .20
❑ 451 Hector Gimenez (RC) .50 .20
❑ 452 Matt Holliday 1.25 .50
❑ 453 Akinori Otsuka .50 .20
❑ 454 Prince Fielder 1.25 .50
❑ 455 Chien-Ming Wang SP 10.00 4.00
❑ 456 Shawn Riggans SP 6.00 2.50
❑ 457 John Maine .50 .20
❑ 458 Adam Lind (RC) .50 .20
❑ 459 Ubaldo Jimenez (RC) .50 .20
❑ 460 Jaret Wright .50 .20
❑ 461 Cla Meredith .50 .20
❑ 462 Joaquin Arias (RC) .50 .20
❑ 463 Kenny Rogers .50 .20
❑ 464 Jose Garcia SP RC 6.00 2.50
❑ 465 Pedro Martinez SP 8.00 3.00
❑ 466 Jeff Salazar (RC) .50 .20
❑ 467 Glen Perkins .50 .20
❑ 468 Travis Ishikawa .50 .20
❑ 469 Joe Borowski .50 .20
❑ 470 Jeremy Brown .50 .20
❑ 471 Andre Ethier .75 .30
❑ 472 Taylor Tankersley .50 .20
❑ 473 Lastings Milledge SP 8.00 3.00
❑ 474 Brian Sanches SP 6.00 2.50
❑ 475 O.Guillen AS MG/P.Garner AS MG .50 .20
❑ 476 Albert Pujols AS 2.50 1.00
❑ 477 David Ortiz AS 1.25 .50
❑ 478 Chase Utley AS 1.25 .50
❑ 479 Mark Loretta AS .50 .20
❑ 480 David Wright AS 2.00 .75
❑ 481 Alex Rodriguez AS 2.00 .75
❑ 482 Edgar Renteria AS SP 6.00 2.50
❑ 483 Derek Jeter AS SP 12.00 5.00
❑ 484 Alfonso Soriano AS .50 .20
❑ 485 Vladimir Guerrero AS 1.25 .50
❑ 486 Carlos Beltran AS .50 .20
❑ 487 Vernon Wells AS .50 .20
❑ 488 Jason Bay AS .50 .20
❑ 489 Ichiro Suzuki AS 2.00 .75
❑ 490 Paul LoDuca AS .50 .20
❑ 491 Ivan Rodriguez AS SP 8.00 3.00
❑ 492 Brad Penny AS SP 6.00 2.50
❑ 493 Roy Halladay AS .50 .20
❑ 494 Brian Fuentes AS .50 .20
❑ 495 Kenny Rogers AS .50 .20

2007 Topps Moments and Milestones

❑ COMMON p/r 11250-54600 .75 .30
❑ COMMON p/r 1650-10350 1.00 .40
❑ COMMON p/r 900-1500 8.00 3.00
❑ COMMON p/r 300-450 10.00 4.00
❑ COMMON ROOKIE 10.00 4.00
❑ STATED PRINT RUN 150 SER. #'d SETS
❑ (# OF VARIATONS/TOTAL PRINT RUN)
❑ PRICING BASED ON TOTAL PRINT RUN
❑ OVERALL PLATE ODDS 1:473 HOBBY
❑ PLATE PRINT RUN 1 SET PER COLOR
❑ BLACK-CYAN-MAGENTA-YELLOW ISSUED
❑ NO PLATE PRICING DUE TO SCARCITY
❑ 1 A.Pujols (37/5550) 2.50 1.00
❑ 2 A.Pujols (130/19500) 2.00 .75
❑ 3 A.Pujols (194/29100) 2.00 .75
❑ 4 A.Pujols (112/16800) 2.00 .75
❑ 5 A.Pujols (47/7050) 2.50 1.00
❑ 6 I.Suzuki (242/36300) 1.50 .60
❑ 7 I.Suzuki (34/5100) 2.00 .75
❑ 8 I.Suzuki (8/1200) 10.00 4.00
❑ 9 I.Suzuki (56/8400) 2.00 .75
❑ 10 I.Suzuki (69/10350) 2.00 .75
❑ 11 I.Suzuki (8/1200) 10.00 4.00
❑ 12 G.Maddux (20/3000) 2.00 .75
❑ 13 G.Maddux (199/29850) 1.50 .60
❑ 14 G.Maddux (20/3000) 2.00 .75
❑ 15 G.Maddux (197/29550) 1.50 .60
❑ 16 R.Clemens (24/3600) 2.50 1.00
❑ 17 R.Clemens (10/1500) 12.00 5.00
❑ 18 R.Clemens (238/35700) 2.00 .75
❑ 19 R.Clemens (20/3000) 2.50 1.00
❑ 20 R.Clemens (256/38400) 2.00 .75
❑ 21 C.Jones (45/6750) 1.50 .60
❑ 22 C.Jones (110/16500) 1.25 .50
❑ 23 C.Jones (181/27150) 1.25 .50
❑ 24 C.Jones (116/17400) 1.25 .50
❑ 25 C.Jones (41/6150) 1.50 .60
❑ 26 C.Jones (25/3750) 1.50 .60
❑ 27 A.Rodriguez (47/7050) 2.00 .75
❑ 28 A.Rodriguez (118/17700) 1.50 .60
❑ 29 A.Rodriguez (181/27150) 1.50 .60
❑ 30 A.Rodriguez (124/18600) 1.50 .60
❑ 31 A.Rodriguez (30/4500) 2.00 .75
❑ 32 A.Rodriguez (17/2550) 2.00 .75
❑ 33 A.Rodriguez (48/7200) 2.00 .75
❑ 34 A.Rodriguez (130/19500) 1.50 .60
❑ 35 A.Rodriguez (194/29100) 1.50 .60
❑ 36 A.Rodriguez (124/18600) 1.50 .60
❑ 37 A.Rodriguez (29/4350) 2.00 .75
❑ 38 A.Rodriguez (21/3150) 2.00 .75
❑ 39 V.Guerrero (39/5850) 1.50 .60
❑ 40 V.Guerrero (126/18900) 1.25 .50
❑ 41 V.Guerrero (206/30900) 1.25 .50
❑ 42 V.Guerrero (124/18600) 1.25 .50
❑ 43 V.Guerrero (39/5850) 1.50 .60
❑ 44 V.Guerrero (13/1950) 1.50 .60
❑ 45 K.Griffey Jr. (56/8400) 2.00 .75
❑ 46 K.Griffey Jr. (147/22050) 1.50 .60
❑ 47 K.Griffey Jr. (185/27750) 1.50 .60
❑ 48 Barry Zito (23/3450) 1.00 .40
❑ 49 Barry Zito (182/27300) .75 .30
❑ 50 R.Johnson (18/2700) 1.50 .60
❑ 51 R.Johnson (294/44100) 1.25 .50
❑ 52 R.Johnson (6/900) 8.00 3.00
❑ 53 R,Johnson (3/450) 60.00 30.00
❑ 54 R.Johnson (17/2550) 1.50 .60
❑ 55 R.Johnson (364/54600) 1.25 .50
❑ 56 R.Johnson (12/1800) 1.50 .60
❑ 57 R.Johnson (2/300) 60.00 30.00
❑ 58 P.Fielder (35/5250) 1.50 .60
❑ 59 P.Fielder (81/12150) 1.25 .50
❑ 60 Dan Uggla (26/3900) 1.50 .60
❑ 61 Dan Uggla (27/4050) 1.50 .60
❑ 62 Dan Uggla (172/25800) 1.25 .50
❑ 63 J.Verlander (17/2550) 1.50 .60
❑ 64 J.Verlander (124/18600) 1.25 .50
❑ 65 F.Liriano (12/1800) 1.50 .60
❑ 66 F.Liriano (144/21600) 1.25 .50
❑ 67 R.Zimmerman (176/26400) 1.25 .50
❑ 68 R.Zimmerman (110/16500) 1.25 .50
❑ 69 R.Zimmerman (84/12600) 1.25 .50
❑ 70 Hanley Ramirez (51/7650) 1.50 .60
❑ 71 Hanley Ramirez (119/17850) 1.25 .50
❑ 72 Hanley Ramirez (185/27750) 1.25 .50
❑ 73 Russ Martin (65/9750) 1.00 .40
❑ 74 Russ Martin (26/3900) 1.00 .40
❑ 75 M.Mantle (173/25950) 5.00 2.00
❑ 76 M.Mantle (121/18150) 5.00 2.00
❑ 77 M.Mantle (146/21900) 5.00 2.00
❑ 78 M.Mantle (94/14100) 5.00 2.00
❑ 79 M.Piazza (35/5250) 1.50 .60
❑ 80 M.Piazza (112/16800) 1.25 .50
❑ 81 D.Jeter (10/1500) 15.00 6.00
❑ 82 D.Jeter (78/11700) 2.50 1.00
❑ 83 D.Jeter (183/27450) 2.50 1.00
❑ 84 Dontrelle Willis (14/2100) 1.00 .40
❑ 85 Dontrelle Willis (142/21300) .75 .30
❑ 86 Dontrelle Willis (2/300) 60.00 30.00
❑ 87 Bobby Crosby (22/3300) 1.00 .40
❑ 88 Bobby Crosby (64/9600) 1.00 .40
❑ 89 R.Howard (22/3300) 2.00 .75
❑ 90 R.Howard (63/9450) 2.00 .75
❑ 91 Curt Schilling (21/3150) 1.50 .60
❑ 92 Curt Schilling (203/30450) 1.25 .50
❑ 93 Andruw Jones (52/7800) 1.50 .60
❑ 94 Andruw Jones (128/19200) 1.25 .50
❑ 95 Andruw Jones (11/1650) 1.50 .60
❑ 96 H.Matsui (23/3450) 1.50 .60
❑ 97 H.Matsui (116/17400) 1.25 .50
❑ 98 H.Matsui (192/28800) 1.25 .50
❑ 99 D.Wright (27/4050) 2.00 .75
❑ 100 D.Wright (102/15300) 1.50 .60
❑ 101 D.Wright (42/6300) 2.00 .75
❑ 102 D.Wright (17/2550) 2.00 .75
❑ 103 D.Ortiz (75/11250) 1.25 .50
❑ 104 D.Ortiz (47/7050) 1.50 .60
❑ 105 D.Ortiz (11/1650) 1.50 .60
❑ 106 F.Thomas (38/5700) 1.50 .60
❑ 107 F.Thomas (101/15150) 1.25 .50
❑ 108 Craig Biggio (40/6000) 1.50 .60
❑ 109 Miguel Cabrera (33/4950) 1.50 .60
❑ 110 Miguel Cabrera (116/17400) 1.25 .50
❑ 111 Vernon Wells (12/1800) 1.00 .40
❑ 112 Michael Young (24/3600) 1.00 .40
❑ 113 Michael Young (40/6000) 1.00 .40
❑ 114 Joe Mauer (144/21600) 1.25 .50
❑ 115 Gary Sheffield (34/5100) 1.00 .40
❑ 116 Jim Edmonds (42/6300) 1.50 .60
❑ 117 Jorge Posada (19/2850) 1.50 .60
❑ 118 Jorge Posada (23/3450) 1.50 .60
❑ 119 Pat Burrell (32/4800) 1.00 .40
❑ 120 Adam Dunn (40/6000) 1.00 .40
❑ 121 Johnny Damon (35/5250) 1.50 .60
❑ 122 Scott Rolen (34/5100) 1.50 .60
❑ 123 Paul Konerko (6/900) 8.00 3.00
❑ 124 Roy Halladay (22/3300) 1.00 .40
❑ 125 Grady Sizemore (22/3300) 1.50 .60
❑ 126 Grady Sizemore (37/5550) 1.50 .60
❑ 127 John Smoltz (24/3600) 1.50 .60
❑ 128 Jeff Kent (29/4350) 1.00 .40
❑ 129 Billy Wagner (38/5700) 1.00 .40
❑ 130 Mark Prior (18/2700) 1.50 .60
❑ 131 Eric Chavez (32/4800) 1.00 .40
❑ 132 Jimmy Rollins (41/6150) 1.00 .40
❑ 133 Manny Ramirez (7/1050) 8.00 3.00
❑ 134 Manny Ramirez (45/6750) 1.50 .60
❑ 135 Manny Ramirez (144/21600) 1.25 .50
❑ 136 Derrek Lee (46/6900) 1.00 .40
❑ 137 Derrek Lee (107/16050) .75 .30
❑ 138 Tom Glavine (14/2100) 1.50 .60
❑ 139 Tom Glavine (20/3000) 1.50 .60

	#	Card		
❑	140	Jose Reyes (17/2550)	1.00	.40
❑	141	Pedro Martinez (15/2250)	1.50	.60
❑	142	Pedro Martinez (208/31200)	1.25	.50
❑	143	Mark Teixeira (43/6450)	1.50	.60
❑	144	Jake Peavy (13/1950)	1.00	.40
❑	145	Carlos Lee (32/4800)	1.00	.40
❑	146	Josh Beckett (16/2400)	1.50	.60
❑	147	Johan Santana (20/3000)	1.50	.60
❑	148	Todd Helton (33/4950)	1.50	.60
❑	149	M.Rivera (43/6450)	1.50	.60
❑	150	Travis Hafner (33/4950)	1.00	.40
❑	151	Jason Bay (24/3600)	1.00	.40
❑	152	Bobby Abreu (30/4500)	1.00	.40
❑	153	Mike Mussina (13/1950)	1.50	.60
❑	154	Miguel Tejada (34/5100)	1.00	.40
❑	155	Miguel Tejada (150/22500)	.75	.30
❑	156	Robinson Cano (14/2100)	1.50	.60
❑	157	Robinson Cano (34/5100)	1.50	.60
❑	158	R.Zimmerman (23/3450)	1.50	.60
❑	159	Carlos Beltran (16/2400)	1.00	.40
❑	160	Carlos Beltran (17/2550)	1.00	.40
❑	161	R.Clemens (18/2700)	2.50	1.00
❑	162	R.Clemens (218/32700)	2.00	.75
❑	163	M.Mantle (52/7800)	6.00	2.50
❑	164	M.Mantle (130/19500)	5.00	2.00
❑	165	M.Mantle (188/28200)	5.00	2.00
❑	166	M.Mantle (132/19800)	5.00	2.00
❑	167	M.Mantle (42/6300)	6.00	2.50
❑	168	M.Mantle (97/14550)	5.00	2.00
❑	169	M.Mantle (127/19050)	5.00	2.00
❑	170	Daisuke Matsuzaka RC	120.00	60.00
❑	171	Daisuke Matsuzaka RC	120.00	60.00
❑	172	Daisuke Matsuzaka RC	120.00	60.00
❑	173	Delmon Young (RC)	12.00	5.00
❑	174	Delmon Young (RC)	12.00	5.00
❑	175	Delmon Young (RC)	12.00	5.00
❑	176	Andrew Miller RC	25.00	10.00
❑	177	Andrew Miller RC	25.00	10.00
❑	178	Andrew Miller RC	25.00	10.00
❑	179	Troy Tulowitzki (RC)	12.00	5.00
❑	180	Troy Tulowitzki (RC)	12.00	5.00
❑	181	Troy Tulowitzki (RC)	12.00	5.00
❑	182	Josh Fields (RC)	10.00	4.00
❑	183	Josh Fields (RC)	10.00	4.00
❑	184	Josh Fields (RC)	10.00	4.00
❑	185	Jeff Baker (RC)	10.00	4.00
❑	186	Jeff Baker (RC)	10.00	4.00
❑	187	Jeff Baker (RC)	10.00	4.00
❑	188	Philip Humber (RC)	10.00	4.00
❑	189	Philip Humber (RC)	10.00	4.00
❑	190	Philip Humber (RC)	10.00	4.00
❑	191	Kevin Kouzmanoff (RC)	10.00	4.00
❑	192	Kevin Kouzmanoff (RC)	10.00	4.00
❑	193	Kevin Kouzmanoff (RC)	10.00	4.00

2005 Topps Opening Day

	#	Card		
❑		COMPLETE SET (165)	40.00	15.00
❑		COMMON CARD (1-165)	.40	.15
❑		ISSUED IN OPENING DAY PACKS		
❑	1	Alex Rodriguez	1.50	.60
❑	2	Placido Polanco	.40	.15
❑	3	Torii Hunter	.40	.15
❑	4	Lyle Overbay	.40	.15
❑	5	Johnny Damon	.60	.25
❑	6	Mike Cameron	.40	.15
❑	7	Ichiro Suzuki	2.00	.75
❑	8	Francisco Rodriguez	.40	.15
❑	9	Bobby Crosby	.40	.15
❑	10	Sammy Sosa	1.00	.40
❑	11	Randy Wolf	.40	.15
❑	12	Jason Bay	.40	.15
❑	13	Mike Lieberthal	.40	.15
❑	14	Paul Konerko	.40	.15
❑	15	Brian Giles	.40	.15
❑	16	Luis Gonzalez	.40	.15
❑	17	Jim Edmonds	.40	.15
❑	18	Carlos Lee	.40	.15
❑	19	Corey Patterson	.40	.15
❑	20	Hank Blalock	.40	.15
❑	21	Sean Casey	.40	.15
❑	22	Dmitri Young	.40	.15
❑	23	Mark Mulder	.40	.15
❑	24	Bobby Abreu	.40	.15
❑	25	Jim Thome	.60	.25
❑	26	Jason Kendall	.40	.15
❑	27	Jason Giambi	.40	.15
❑	28	Vinny Castilla	.40	.15
❑	29	Tony Batista	.40	.15
❑	30	Ivan Rodriguez	.60	.25
❑	31	Craig Biggio	.60	.25
❑	32	Chris Carpenter	.40	.15
❑	33	Adrian Beltre	.40	.15
❑	34	Scott Podsednik	.40	.15
❑	35	Cliff Floyd	.40	.15
❑	36	Chad Tracy	.40	.15
❑	37	John Smoltz	.60	.25
❑	38	Shingo Takatsu	.40	.15
❑	39	Jack Wilson	.40	.15
❑	40	Gary Sheffield	.40	.15
❑	41	Lance Berkman	.40	.15
❑	42	Carl Crawford	.40	.15
❑	43	Carlos Guillen	.40	.15
❑	44	David Bell	.40	.15
❑	45	Kazuo Matsui	.40	.15
❑	46	Jason Schmidt	.40	.15
❑	47	Jason Marquis	.40	.15
❑	48	Melvin Mora	.40	.15
❑	49	David Ortiz	1.00	.40
❑	50	Andruw Jones	.60	.25
❑	51	Miguel Tejada	.40	.15
❑	52	Bartolo Colon	.40	.15
❑	53	Derrek Lee	.60	.25
❑	54	Eric Gagne	.40	.15
❑	55	Miguel Cabrera	.60	.25
❑	56	Travis Hafner	.40	.15
❑	57	Jose Valentin	.40	.15
❑	58	Mark Prior	.60	.25
❑	59	Phil Nevin	.40	.15
❑	60	Jose Vidro	.40	.15
❑	61	Khalil Greene	.60	.25
❑	62	Carlos Zambrano	.40	.15
❑	63	Erubiel Durazo	.40	.15
❑	64	Michael Young UER	.40	.15
❑	65	Woody Williams	.40	.15
❑	66	Edgardo Alfonzo	.40	.15
❑	67	Troy Glaus	.40	.15
❑	68	Garret Anderson	.40	.15
❑	69	Richie Sexson	.40	.15
❑	70	Curt Schilling	.60	.25
❑	71	Randy Johnson	1.00	.40
❑	72	Chipper Jones	1.00	.40
❑	73	J.D. Drew	.40	.15
❑	74	Russ Ortiz	.40	.15
❑	75	Frank Thomas	1.00	.40
❑	76	Jimmy Rollins	.40	.15
❑	77	Barry Zito	.40	.15
❑	78	Rafael Palmeiro	.60	.25
❑	79	Brad Wilkerson	.40	.15
❑	80	Adam Dunn	.40	.15
❑	81	Doug Mientkiewicz	.40	.15
❑	82	Manny Ramirez	.60	.25
❑	83	Pedro Martinez	.60	.25
❑	84	Moises Alou	.40	.15
❑	85	Mike Sweeney	.40	.15
❑	86	Boston Red Sox WC	1.00	.40
❑	87	Matt Clement	.40	.15
❑	88	Nomar Garciaparra	1.00	.40
❑	89	Magglio Ordonez	.40	.15
❑	90	Bret Boone	.40	.15
❑	91	Mark Loretta	.40	.15
❑	92	Jose Contreras	.40	.15
❑	93	Randy Winn	.40	.15
❑	94	Austin Kearns	.40	.15
❑	95	Ken Griffey Jr.	1.50	.60
❑	96	Jake Westbrook	.40	.15
❑	97	Kazuhito Tadano	.40	.15
❑	98	C.C. Sabathia	.40	.15
❑	99	Todd Helton	.60	.25
❑	100	Albert Pujols	2.00	.75
❑	101	Jose Molina Bengie Molina	.40	.15
❑	102	Aaron Miles	.40	.15
❑	103	Mike Lowell	.40	.15
❑	104	Paul Lo Duca	.40	.15
❑	105	Juan Pierre	.40	.15
❑	106	Dontrelle Willis	.40	.15
❑	107	Jeff Bagwell	.60	.25
❑	108	Carlos Beltran	.40	.15
❑	109	Ronnie Belliard	.40	.15
❑	110	Roy Oswalt	.40	.15
❑	111	Zack Greinke	.40	.15
❑	112	Steve Finley	.40	.15
❑	113	Kazuhisa Ishii	.40	.15
❑	114	Justin Morneau	.40	.15
❑	115	Ben Sheets	.40	.15
❑	116	Johan Santana	1.00	.40
❑	117	Billy Wagner	.40	.15
❑	118	Mariano Rivera	1.00	.40
❑	119	Corey Koskie	.40	.15
❑	120	Akinori Otsuka	.40	.15
❑	121	Joe Mauer	1.00	.40
❑	122	Jacque Jones	.40	.15
❑	123	Joe Nathan	.40	.15
❑	124	Nick Johnson	.40	.15
❑	125	Vernon Wells	.40	.15
❑	126	Mike Piazza	1.00	.40
❑	127	Jose Guillen	.40	.15
❑	128	Jose Reyes	.40	.15
❑	129	Marcus Giles	.40	.15
❑	130	Javy Lopez	.40	.15
❑	131	Kevin Millar	.40	.15
❑	132	Jorge Posada	.60	.25
❑	133	Carl Pavano	.40	.15
❑	134	Bernie Williams	.60	.25
❑	135	Kerry Wood	.40	.15
❑	136	Matt Holliday	.50	.20
❑	137	Kevin Brown	.40	.15
❑	138	Derek Jeter	2.00	.75
❑	139	Barry Bonds	2.50	1.00
❑	140	Jeff Kent	.40	.15
❑	141	Mark Kotsay	.40	.15
❑	142	Shawn Green	.40	.15
❑	143	Tim Hudson	.40	.15
❑	144	Shannon Stewart	.40	.15
❑	145	Pat Burrell	.40	.15
❑	146	Gavin Floyd	.40	.15
❑	147	Mike Mussina	.60	.25
❑	148	Eric Chavez	.40	.15
❑	149	Jon Lieber	.40	.15
❑	150	Vladimir Guerrero	1.00	.40
❑	151	Vicente Padilla	.40	.15
❑	152	Ryan Klesko	.40	.15
❑	153	Jake Peavy	.40	.15
❑	154	Scott Rolen	.60	.25
❑	155	Greg Maddux	1.50	.60
❑	156	Edgar Renteria	.40	.15
❑	157	Larry Walker	.60	.25
❑	158	Scott Kazmir	.40	.15
❑	159	B.J. Upton	.60	.25
❑	160	Mark Teixeira	.60	.25
❑	161	Ken Harvey	.40	.15
❑	162	Alfonso Soriano	.40	.15
❑	163	Carlos Delgado	.40	.15
❑	164	Alexis Rios	.40	.15
❑	165	Checklist	.40	.15

2006 Topps Opening Day

- ❑ COMPLETE SET (165) 40.00 15.00
- ❑ COMMON CARD (1-165) .40 .15
- ❑ OVERALL PLATE SER.1 ODDS 1:246 HTA
- ❑ PLATE PRINT RUN 1 SET PER COLOR
- ❑ BLACK-CYAN-MAGENTA-YELLOW ISSUED
- ❑ NO PLATE PRICING DUE TO SCARCITY
- ❑ 1 Alex Rodriguez 1.50 .60
- ❑ 2 Jhonny Peralta .50 .20
- ❑ 3 Garrett Atkins .40 .15
- ❑ 4 Vernon Wells .40 .15
- ❑ 5 Carl Crawford .40 .15
- ❑ 6 Josh Beckett .40 .15
- ❑ 7 Mickey Mantle 8.00 3.00
- ❑ 8 Willy Taveras .40 .15
- ❑ 9 Ivan Rodriguez .60 .25
- ❑ 10 Clint Barmes .40 .15
- ❑ 11 Jose Reyes 1.00 .40
- ❑ 12 Travis Hafner .40 .15
- ❑ 13 Tadahito Iguchi .40 .15
- ❑ 14 Barry Zito .40 .15
- ❑ 15 Brian Roberts .40 .15
- ❑ 16 David Wright 1.50 .60
- ❑ 17 Mark Teixeira .60 .25
- ❑ 18 Roy Halladay .40 .15
- ❑ 19 Scott Rolen .60 .25
- ❑ 20 Bobby Abreu .40 .15
- ❑ 21 Lance Berkman .40 .15
- ❑ 22 Moises Alou .40 .15
- ❑ 23 Chone Figgins .40 .15
- ❑ 24 Aaron Rowand .40 .15
- ❑ 25 Chipper Jones 1.00 .40
- ❑ 26 Johnny Damon .60 .25
- ❑ 27 Matt Clement .40 .15
- ❑ 28 Nick Johnson .40 .15
- ❑ 29 Freddy Garcia .40 .15
- ❑ 30 Jon Garland .40 .15
- ❑ 31 Torii Hunter .40 .15
- ❑ 32 Mike Sweeney .40 .15
- ❑ 33 Mike Lieberthal .40 .15
- ❑ 34 Rafael Furcal .40 .15
- ❑ 35 Brad Wilkerson .40 .15
- ❑ 36 Brad Penny .40 .15
- ❑ 37 Jorge Cantu .40 .15
- ❑ 38 Paul Konerko .40 .15
- ❑ 39 Rickie Weeks .40 .15
- ❑ 40 Jorge Posada .60 .25
- ❑ 41 Albert Pujols 2.00 .75
- ❑ 42 Zack Greinke .40 .15
- ❑ 43 Jimmy Rollins .40 .15
- ❑ 44 Mark Prior .60 .25
- ❑ 45 Greg Maddux 1.50 .60
- ❑ 46 Jeff Francis .40 .15
- ❑ 47 Felipe Lopez .40 .15
- ❑ 48 Dan Johnson .40 .15
- ❑ 49 B.J. Ryan .40 .15
- ❑ 50 Manny Ramirez .60 .25
- ❑ 51 Melvin Mora .40 .15
- ❑ 52 Javy Lopez .40 .15
- ❑ 53 Garret Anderson .40 .15
- ❑ 54 Jason Bay .40 .15
- ❑ 55 Joe Mauer .60 .25
- ❑ 56 C.C. Sabathia .40 .15
- ❑ 57 Bartolo Colon .40 .15
- ❑ 58 Ichiro Suzuki 1.50 .60
- ❑ 59 Andruw Jones .60 .25
- ❑ 60 Rocco Baldelli .40 .15
- ❑ 61 Jeff Kent .40 .15
- ❑ 62 Cliff Floyd .40 .15
- ❑ 63 John Smoltz .60 .25
- ❑ 64 Shawn Green .40 .15
- ❑ 65 Nomar Garciaparra 1.00 .40
- ❑ 66 Miguel Cabrera .60 .25
- ❑ 67 Vladimir Guerrero 1.00 .40
- ❑ 68 Gary Sheffield .40 .15
- ❑ 69 Jake Peavy .40 .15
- ❑ 70 Carlos Lee .40 .15
- ❑ 71 Tom Glavine .60 .25
- ❑ 72 Craig Biggio .60 .25
- ❑ 73 Steve Finley .40 .15
- ❑ 74 Adrian Beltre .40 .15
- ❑ 75 Eric Gagne .40 .15
- ❑ 76 Aubrey Huff .40 .15
- ❑ 77 Livan Hernandez .40 .15
- ❑ 78 Scott Podsednik .40 .15
- ❑ 79 Todd Helton .60 .25
- ❑ 80 Kerry Wood .40 .15
- ❑ 81 Randy Johnson 1.00 .40
- ❑ 82 Huston Street .40 .15
- ❑ 83 Pedro Martinez .60 .25
- ❑ 84 Roger Clemens 2.00 .75
- ❑ 85 Hank Blalock .40 .15
- ❑ 86 Carlos Beltran .40 .15
- ❑ 87 Chien-Ming Wang 1.50 .60
- ❑ 88 Rich Harden .40 .15
- ❑ 89 Mike Mussina .60 .25
- ❑ 90 Mark Buehrle .40 .15
- ❑ 91 Michael Young .40 .15
- ❑ 92 Mark Mulder .40 .15
- ❑ 93 Khalil Greene .60 .25
- ❑ 94 Johan Santana .60 .25
- ❑ 95 Andy Pettitte .60 .25
- ❑ 96 Derek Jeter 2.50 1.00
- ❑ 97 Jack Wilson .40 .15
- ❑ 98 Ben Sheets .40 .15
- ❑ 99 Miguel Tejada .40 .15
- ❑ 100 Barry Bonds 2.50 1.00
- ❑ 101 Dontrelle Willis .40 .15
- ❑ 102 Curt Schilling .60 .25
- ❑ 103 Jose Contreras .40 .15
- ❑ 104 Jeremy Bonderman .40 .15
- ❑ 105 David Ortiz 1.00 .40
- ❑ 106 Lyle Overbay .40 .15
- ❑ 107 Robinson Cano .60 .25
- ❑ 108 Tim Hudson .40 .15
- ❑ 109 Paul Lo Duca .40 .15
- ❑ 110 Mariano Rivera .60 .25
- ❑ 111 Derrek Lee .40 .15
- ❑ 112 Morgan Ensberg .40 .15
- ❑ 113 Wily Mo Pena .40 .15
- ❑ 114 Roy Oswalt .40 .15
- ❑ 115 Adam Dunn .40 .15
- ❑ 116 Hideki Matsui 1.50 .60
- ❑ 117 Pat Burrell .40 .15
- ❑ 118 Jason Schmidt .40 .15
- ❑ 119 Alfonso Soriano .40 .15
- ❑ 120 Aramis Ramirez .40 .15
- ❑ 121 Jason Giambi .40 .15
- ❑ 122 Orlando Hernandez .40 .15
- ❑ 123 Magglio Ordonez .40 .15
- ❑ 124 Troy Glaus .40 .15
- ❑ 125 Carlos Delgado .40 .15
- ❑ 126 Kevin Millwood .40 .15
- ❑ 127 Shannon Stewart .40 .15
- ❑ 128 Luis Castillo .40 .15
- ❑ 129 Jim Edmonds .60 .25
- ❑ 130 Richie Sexson .40 .15
- ❑ 131 Dmitri Young .40 .15
- ❑ 132 Russ Adams .40 .15
- ❑ 133 Nick Swisher .40 .15
- ❑ 134 Jermaine Dye .40 .15
- ❑ 135 Anderson Hernandez (RC) .40 .15
- ❑ 136 Justin Huber (RC) .40 .15
- ❑ 137 Jason Botts (RC) .40 .15
- ❑ 138 Jeff Mathis (RC) .40 .15
- ❑ 139 Ryan Garko (RC) .40 .15
- ❑ 140 Charlton Jimerson (RC) .40 .15
- ❑ 141 Chris Denorfia (RC) .40 .15
- ❑ 142 Anthony Reyes (RC) .40 .15
- ❑ 143 Bryan Bullington (RC) .40 .15
- ❑ 144 Chuck James (RC) .60 .25
- ❑ 145 Danny Sandoval RC .40 .15
- ❑ 146 Walter Young (RC) .40 .15
- ❑ 147 Fausto Carmona (RC) .40 .15
- ❑ 148 Francisco Liriano (RC) 2.00 .75
- ❑ 149 Hong-Chih Kuo (RC) 1.00 .40
- ❑ 150 Joe Saunders (RC) .40 .15
- ❑ 151 John Koronka (RC) .40 .15
- ❑ 152 Robert Andino RC .40 .15
- ❑ 153 Shaun Marcum (RC) .40 .15
- ❑ 154 Tom Gorzelanny (RC) .40 .15
- ❑ 155 Craig Breslow RC .40 .15
- ❑ 156 Chris Demaria RC .40 .15
- ❑ 157 Brayan Pena (RC) .40 .15
- ❑ 158 Rich Hill (RC) .40 .15
- ❑ 159 Rick Short (RC) .40 .15
- ❑ 160 Darrell Rasner (RC) .40 .15
- ❑ 161 C.J. Wilson (RC) .40 .15
- ❑ 162 Brandon Watson (RC) .40 .15
- ❑ 163 Paul McAnulty (RC) .40 .15
- ❑ 164 Marshall McDougall (RC) .40 .15
- ❑ 165 Checklist .40 .15

2007 Topps Opening Day

- ❑ COMPLETE SET (220) 50.00 20.00
- ❑ COMMON CARD (1-220) .40 .15
- ❑ COMMON RC .50 .20
- ❑ 1 Bobby Abreu .40 .15
- ❑ 2 Mike Piazza 1.00 .40
- ❑ 3 Jake Westbrook .40 .15
- ❑ 4 Zach Duke .40 .15
- ❑ 5 David Wright 1.50 .60
- ❑ 6 Adrian Gonzalez .40 .15
- ❑ 7 Mickey Mantle 5.00 2.00
- ❑ 8 Bill Hall .40 .15
- ❑ 9 Robinson Cano .60 .25
- ❑ 10 Dontrelle Willis .40 .15
- ❑ 11 J.D. Drew .40 .15
- ❑ 12 Paul Konerko .40 .15
- ❑ 13 Austin Kearns .40 .15
- ❑ 14 Mike Lowell .40 .15
- ❑ 15 Magglio Ordonez .40 .15
- ❑ 16 Rafael Furcal .40 .15
- ❑ 17 Matt Cain .60 .25
- ❑ 18 Craig Monroe .40 .15
- ❑ 19 Matt Holliday .50 .20
- ❑ 20 Edgar Renteria .40 .15
- ❑ 21 Mark Buehrle .40 .15
- ❑ 22 Carlos Quentin .40 .15
- ❑ 23 C.C. Sabathia .40 .15
- ❑ 24 Nick Markakis .60 .25
- ❑ 25 Chipper Jones 1.00 .40
- ❑ 26 Jason Giambi .40 .15
- ❑ 27 Barry Zito .40 .15
- ❑ 28 Jake Peavy .40 .15
- ❑ 29 Hank Blalock .40 .15
- ❑ 30 Johnny Damon .60 .25
- ❑ 31 Chad Tracy .40 .15
- ❑ 32 Nick Swisher .40 .15
- ❑ 33 Willy Taveras .40 .15
- ❑ 34 Chuck James .40 .15
- ❑ 35 Carlos Delgado .40 .15
- ❑ 36 Livan Hernandez .40 .15
- ❑ 37 Freddy Garcia .40 .15
- ❑ 38 Bronson Arroyo .40 .15
- ❑ 39 Jack Wilson .40 .15
- ❑ 40 Dan Uggla .60 .25
- ❑ 41 Chris Carpenter .40 .15
- ❑ 42 Jorge Posada .60 .25
- ❑ 43 Joe Mauer .60 .25
- ❑ 44 Corey Patterson .40 .15

❑ 45 Chien-Ming Wang 1.50 .60
❑ 46 Derek Jeter 15.00 6.00
❑ 47 Carlos Beltran .40 .15
❑ 48 Jim Edmonds .60 .25
❑ 49 Jeremy Sowers .40 .15
❑ 50 Randy Johnson 1.00 .40
❑ 51 Jered Weaver .60 .25
❑ 52 Josh Barfield .40 .15
❑ 53 Scott Rolen .60 .25
❑ 54 Ryan Shealy .40 .15
❑ 55 Freddy Sanchez .40 .15
❑ 56 Javier Vazquez .40 .15
❑ 57 Jeremy Bonderman .40 .15
❑ 58 Miguel Cabrera .60 .25
❑ 59 Kazuo Matsui .40 .15
❑ 60 Curt Schilling .60 .25
❑ 61 Alfonso Soriano .40 .15
❑ 62 Orlando Hernandez .40 .15
❑ 63 Joe Blanton .40 .15
❑ 64 Aramis Ramirez .40 .15
❑ 65 Ben Sheets .40 .15
❑ 66 Jimmy Rollins .40 .15
❑ 67 Mark Loretta .40 .15
❑ 68 Cole Hamels .60 .25
❑ 69 Albert Pujols 2.00 .75
❑ 70 Moises Alou .40 .15
❑ 71 Mark Teahen .40 .15
❑ 72 Roy Halladay .40 .15
❑ 73 Cory Sullivan .40 .15
❑ 74 Frank Thomas 1.00 .40
❑ 75 Ryan Howard 1.50 .60
❑ 76 Rocco Baldelli .40 .15
❑ 77 Manny Ramirez .60 .25
❑ 78 Ray Durham .40 .15
❑ 79 Gary Sheffield .40 .15
❑ 80 Jay Gibbons .40 .15
❑ 81 Todd Helton .60 .25
❑ 82 Gary Matthews .40 .15
❑ 83 Brandon Inge .40 .15
❑ 84 Jonathan Papelbon 1.00 .40
❑ 85 John Smoltz .60 .25
❑ 86 Chone Figgins .40 .15
❑ 87 Hideki Matsui 1.00 .40
❑ 88 Carlos Lee .40 .15
❑ 89 Jose Reyes .40 .15
❑ 90 Lyle Overbay .40 .15
❑ 91 Johan Santana .60 .25
❑ 92 Ian Kinsler .40 .15
❑ 93 Scott Kazmir .60 .25
❑ 94 Hanley Ramirez .60 .25
❑ 95 Greg Maddux 1.50 .60
❑ 96 Johnny Estrada .40 .15
❑ 97 B.J. Upton .40 .15
❑ 98 Francisco Liriano 1.00 .40
❑ 99 Chase Utley 1.00 .40
❑ 100 Preston Wilson .40 .15
❑ 101 Marcus Giles .40 .15
❑ 102 Jeff Kent .40 .15
❑ 103 Grady Sizemore .60 .25
❑ 104 Ken Griffey 1.50 .60
❑ 105 Garret Anderson .40 .15
❑ 106 Brian McCann .40 .15
❑ 107 Jon Garland .40 .15
❑ 108 Troy Glaus .40 .15
❑ 109 Brandon Webb .40 .15
❑ 110 Jason Schmidt .40 .15
❑ 111 Ramon Hernandez .40 .15
❑ 112 Justin Morneau .40 .15
❑ 113 Mike Cameron .40 .15
❑ 114 Andruw Jones .60 .25
❑ 115 Russell Martin .40 .15
❑ 116 Vernon Wells .40 .15
❑ 117 Orlando Hudson .40 .15
❑ 118 Derek Lowe .40 .15
❑ 119 Alex Rodriguez 1.50 .60
❑ 120 Chad Billingsley .40 .15
❑ 121 Kenji Johjima 1.00 .40
❑ 122 Nick Johnson .40 .15
❑ 123 Dan Haren .40 .15
❑ 124 Mark Teixeira .60 .25
❑ 125 Jeff Francoeur 1.00 .40
❑ 126 Ted Lilly .40 .15
❑ 127 Jhonny Peralta .40 .15
❑ 128 Aaron Harang .40 .15
❑ 129 Ryan Zimmerman 1.00 .40
❑ 130 Jermaine Dye .40 .15
❑ 131 Orlando Cabrera .40 .15
❑ 132 Juan Pierre .40 .15
❑ 133 Brian Giles .40 .15
❑ 134 Jason Bay .40 .15
❑ 135 David Ortiz 1.00 .40
❑ 136 Chris Capuano .40 .15
❑ 137 Carlos Zambrano .40 .15
❑ 138 Luis Gonzalez .40 .15
❑ 139 Jeff Weaver .40 .15
❑ 140 Lance Berkman .40 .15
❑ 141 Raul Ibanez .40 .15
❑ 142 Jim Thome .60 .25
❑ 143 Jose Contreras .40 .15
❑ 144 David Eckstein .40 .15
❑ 145 Adam Dunn .40 .15
❑ 146 Alex Rios .40 .15
❑ 147 Garrett Atkins .40 .15
❑ 148 A.J. Burnett .40 .15
❑ 149 Jeremy Hermida .40 .15
❑ 150 Conor Jackson .40 .15
❑ 151 Adrian Beltre .40 .15
❑ 152 Torii Hunter .40 .15
❑ 153 Andrew Miller RC 4.00 1.50
❑ 154 Ichiro Suzuki 1.50 .60
❑ 155 Mark Redman .40 .15
❑ 156 Paul LoDuca .40 .15
❑ 157 Xavier Nady .40 .15
❑ 158 Stephen Drew .60 .25
❑ 159 Eric Chavez .40 .15
❑ 160 Pedro Martinez .60 .25
❑ 161 Derrek Lee .40 .15
❑ 162 David DeJesus .40 .15
❑ 163 Troy Tulowitzki (RC) 1.25 .50
❑ 164 Vinny Rottino (RC) .50 .20
❑ 165 Philip Humber (RC) .75 .30
❑ 166 Jerry Owens (RC) .50 .20
❑ 167 Ubaldo Jimenez (RC) .50 .20
❑ 168 Michael Young .40 .15
❑ 169 Ryan Braun RC .50 .20
❑ 170 Kevin Kouzmanoff (RC) .50 .20
❑ 171 Oswaldo Navarro RC .50 .20
❑ 172 Miguel Montero (RC) .50 .20
❑ 173 Roy Oswalt .40 .15
❑ 174 Shane Youman RC .50 .20
❑ 175 Josh Fields (RC) .50 .20
❑ 176 Adam Lind (RC) .50 .20
❑ 177 Miguel Tejada .40 .15
❑ 178 Delwyn Young (RC) .50 .20
❑ 179 Scott Moore (RC) .50 .20
❑ 180 Fred Lewis (RC) .50 .20
❑ 181 Glen Perkins (RC) .50 .20
❑ 182 Vladimir Guerrero 1.00 .40
❑ 183 Drew Anderson RC .50 .20
❑ 184 Jeff Salazar (RC) .50 .20
❑ 185 Tom Gordon .40 .15
❑ 186 The Bird .40 .15
❑ 187 Justin Verlander 1.00 .40
❑ 188 Delmon Young (RC) 1.25 .50
❑ 189 Homer .40 .15
❑ 190 Wally the Green Monster .40 .15
❑ 191 Southpaw .40 .15
❑ 192 Dinger .40 .15
❑ 193 Carl Crawford .40 .15
❑ 194 Slider .40 .15
❑ 195 Gapper .40 .15
❑ 196 Paws .40 .15
❑ 197 Billy the Marlin .40 .15
❑ 198 Ivan Rodriguez .60 .25
❑ 199 Slugger .40 .15
❑ 200 Junction Jack .40 .15
❑ 201 Bernie Brewer .40 .15
❑ 202 Travis Hafner .40 .15
❑ 203 Stomper .40 .15
❑ 204 Mr. Met .40 .15
❑ 205 The Moose .40 .15
❑ 206 Phillie Phanatic .40 .15
❑ 207 Prince Fielder 1.00 .40
❑ 208 Julio Lugo .40 .15
❑ 209 Pirate Parrot .40 .15
❑ 210 Joel Zumaya .60 .25
❑ 211 Swinging Friar .40 .15
❑ 212 Jay Payton .40 .15
❑ 213 Lou Seal .40 .15
❑ 214 Fredbird .40 .15
❑ 215 Screech .40 .15
❑ 216 TC Bear .40 .15
❑ 217 Andre Ethier .60 .25
❑ 218 Ervin Santana .40 .15
❑ 219 Melvin Mora .40 .15
❑ 220 Checklist .40 .15

2005 Topps Rookie Cup

❑ COMP.SET w/o AU's (150) 40.00 20.00
❑ COMMON CARD (1-150) .50 .20
❑ AU 151-160 ODDS 1:62 H, 1:155 R
❑ 1-150 OVERALL PLATE ODDS 1:251 H
❑ 151-160 OVERALL AU PLATE ODDS 1:3752 H
❑ BLACK-CYAN-MAGENTA-YELLOW ISSUED
❑ NO PLATE PRICING DUE TO SCARCITY
❑ 1 Pat Corrales .50 .20
❑ 2 Ron Santo 1.50 .60
❑ 3 Joe Torre 1.50 .60
❑ 4 Boog Powell 1.00 .40
❑ 5 Tom Tresh 1.00 .40
❑ 6 Jonny Gomes 1.00 .40
❑ 7 Rico Carty .50 .20
❑ 8 Bert Campaneris 1.00 .40
❑ 9 Tony Oliva 1.00 .40
❑ 10 Ron Swoboda 1.00 .40
❑ 11 Tony Perez 1.00 .40
❑ 12 Joe Morgan 1.00 .40
❑ 13 Davey Johnson .50 .20
❑ 14 Cleon Jones .50 .20
❑ 15 Tom Seaver 1.50 .60
❑ 16 Rod Carew 1.50 .60
❑ 17 Rick Monday 1.00 .40
❑ 18 Johnny Bench 2.50 1.00
❑ 19 Bobby Cox 1.00 .40
❑ 20 Jerry Koosman 1.00 .40
❑ 21 Al Oliver 1.00 .40
❑ 22 Lou Piniella 1.00 .40
❑ 23 Larry Bowa 1.00 .40
❑ 24 Chris Chambliss 1.00 .40
❑ 25 Bill Buckner 1.00 .40
❑ 26 Don Baylor 1.00 .40
❑ 27 Buddy Bell 1.00 .40
❑ 28 Carlton Fisk 1.50 .60
❑ 29 Gary Matthews 1.00 .40
❑ 30 Dave Lopes 1.00 .40
❑ 31 Bob Boone 1.00 .40
❑ 32 Bill Madlock 1.00 .40
❑ 33 Claudell Washington .50 .20
❑ 34 Jim Rice 1.00 .40
❑ 35 Gary Carter 1.00 .40
❑ 36 Willie Randolph 1.00 .40
❑ 37 Chet Lemon .50 .20
❑ 38 Andre Dawson 1.00 .40
❑ 39 Eddie Murray 2.50 1.00
❑ 40 Paul Molitor 1.00 .40
❑ 41 Ozzie Smith 4.00 1.50
❑ 42 Jeffrey Leonard .50 .20
❑ 43 Lonnie Smith .50 .20
❑ 44 Mookie Wilson 1.00 .40
❑ 45 Tim Wallach .50 .20
❑ 46 Tim Raines 1.00 .40
❑ 47 Fernando Valenzuela 1.00 .40
❑ 48 Cal Ripken 8.00 3.00
❑ 49 Ryne Sandberg 5.00 2.00
❑ 50 Willie McGee 1.00 .40
❑ 51 Darryl Strawberry 1.00 .40
❑ 52 Julio Franco 1.00 .40
❑ 53 Brook Jacoby .50 .20
❑ 54 Dwight Gooden 1.00 .40
❑ 55 Roger McDowell .50 .20

❑ 56 Ozzie Guillen 1.00 .40
❑ 57 Vince Coleman .50 .20
❑ 58 Pete Incaviglia .50 .20
❑ 59 Wally Joyner 1.00 .40
❑ 60 Jose Canseco 2.50 1.00
❑ 61 Cory Snyder .50 .20
❑ 62 Devon White .50 .20
❑ 63 Walt Weiss .50 .20
❑ 64 Mark Grace 1.50 .60
❑ 65 Ron Gant 1.00 .40
❑ 66 Chris Sabo 1.00 .40
❑ 67 Jay Buhner 1.00 .40
❑ 68 Gary Sheffield 1.50 .60
❑ 69 Gregg Jefferies .50 .20
❑ 70 Ken Griffey Jr. 4.00 1.50
❑ 71 Tom Gordon .50 .20
❑ 72 Jim Abbott 1.00 .40
❑ 73 Dave Justice 1.50 .60
❑ 74 Larry Walker 1.00 .40
❑ 75 Sandy Alomar Jr. .50 .20
❑ 76 Chuck Knoblauch 1.00 .40
❑ 77 Jeff Bagwell 1.50 .60
❑ 78 Luis Gonzalez 1.00 .40
❑ 79 Ivan Rodriguez 1.50 .60
❑ 80 Eric Karros 1.00 .40
❑ 81 Jeff Kent 1.00 .40
❑ 82 Kenny Lofton 1.00 .40
❑ 83 Moises Alou 1.00 .40
❑ 84 Reggie Sanders 1.00 .40
❑ 85 Jeff Conine 1.00 .40
❑ 86 J.T. Snow 1.00 .40
❑ 87 Tim Salmon 1.00 .40
❑ 88 Mike Piazza 2.50 1.00
❑ 89 Manny Ramirez 1.50 .60
❑ 90 Ryan Klesko 1.00 .40
❑ 91 Javy Lopez 1.00 .40
❑ 92 Chipper Jones 2.50 1.00
❑ 93 Ray Durham 1.00 .40
❑ 94 Garret Anderson 1.00 .40
❑ 95 Shawn Green 1.00 .40
❑ 96 Hideo Nomo 2.50 1.00
❑ 97 Jermaine Dye 1.00 .40
❑ 98 Tony Clark .50 .20
❑ 99 Joe Randa 1.00 .40
❑ 100 Derek Jeter 5.00 2.00
❑ 101 Jason Kendall 1.00 .40
❑ 102 Billy Wagner 1.00 .40
❑ 103 Andruw Jones 1.50 .60
❑ 104 Dmitri Young 1.00 .40
❑ 105 Scott Rolen 1.50 .60
❑ 106 Nomar Garciaparra 2.50 1.00
❑ 107 Jose Cruz Jr. .50 .20
❑ 108 Scott Hatteberg .50 .20
❑ 109 Mark Kotsay 1.00 .40
❑ 110 Todd Helton 1.50 .60
❑ 111 Miguel Cairo .50 .20
❑ 112 Maggio Ordonez 1.00 .40
❑ 113 Kerry Wood 1.00 .40
❑ 114 Preston Wilson 1.00 .40
❑ 115 Alex Gonzalez .50 .20
❑ 116 Carlos Beltran 1.00 .40
❑ 117 Rafael Furcal 1.00 .40
❑ 118 Pat Burrell 1.00 .40
❑ 119 Adam Kennedy .50 .20
❑ 120 Terrence Long .50 .20
❑ 121 Jay Payton .50 .20
❑ 122 Bengie Molina .50 .20
❑ 123 Albert Pujols 5.00 2.00
❑ 124 Craig Wilson .50 .20
❑ 125 Alfonso Soriano 1.00 .40
❑ 126 Jimmy Rollins 1.00 .40
❑ 127 Adam Dunn 1.00 .40
❑ 128 Ichiro Suzuki 4.00 1.50
❑ 129 Roy Oswalt 1.00 .40
❑ 130 C.C. Sabathia 1.00 .40
❑ 131 Brad Wilkerson .50 .20
❑ 132 Nick Johnson 1.00 .40
❑ 133 Eric Hinske .50 .20
❑ 134 Austin Kearns 1.00 .40
❑ 135 Dontrelle Willis 1.00 .40
❑ 136 Mark Teixeira 1.50 .60
❑ 137 Rocco Baldelli 1.00 .40
❑ 138 Scott Podsednik 1.00 .40
❑ 139 Brandon Webb .50 .20
❑ 140 Jason Bay 1.00 .40
❑ 141 Adam LaRoche .50 .20
❑ 142 Khalil Greene 1.50 .60
❑ 143 Joe Mauer 2.50 1.00
❑ 144 Matt Holliday .60 .25
❑ 145 Chad Tracy .50 .20
❑ 146 Garrett Atkins .50 .20
❑ 147 Tadahito Iguchi RC 3.00 1.25
❑ 148 Russ Adams .50 .20
❑ 149 Huston Street 1.50 .60
❑ 150 Dan Johnson 1.00 .40
❑ 151 J. Brent Cox AU RC 15.00 6.00
❑ 152 John Drennen AU RC 25.00 10.00
❑ 153 Ryan Tucker AU RC 15.00 6.00
❑ 154 Yunel Escobar AU RC 20.00 8.00
❑ 155 Jacob Marceaux AU RC 10.00 4.00
❑ 156 Mark Pawelek AU RC 30.00 12.50
❑ 157 Brandon Snyder AU RC 25.00 10.00
❑ 158 Wade Townsend AU RC 15.00 6.00
❑ 159 Troy Tulowitzki AU RC 100.00 50.00
❑ 160 Kevin Whelan AU RC 15.00 6.00

2006 Topps Sterling

❑ B.BONDS (1-19) 12.00 5.00
❑ B.BONDS ODDS 1:10
❑ M.MANTLE (20-39) 15.00 6.00
❑ M.MANTLE ODDS 1:10
❑ J.GIBSON (40-43) 30.00 12.50
❑ J.GIBSON ODDS 1:191
❑ R.HENDERSON (44-53) 10.00 4.00
❑ R.HENDERSON ODDS 1:22
❑ T.WILLIAMS (54-62) 12.00 5.00
❑ T.WILLIAMS ODDS 1:27
❑ R.CLEMENTE (63-67) 25.00 10.00
❑ R.CLEMENTE ODDS 1:40
❑ N.RYAN (68-77) 20.00 8.00
❑ N.RYAN ODDS 1:20
❑ C.RIPKEN (78-96) 20.00 8.00
❑ C.RIPKEN ODDS 1:10
❑ S.MUSIAL (97-101) 10.00 4.00
❑ S.MUSIAL ODDS 1:40
❑ R.JACKSON (102-106) 10.00 4.00
❑ R.JACKSON ODDS 1:40
❑ J.BENCH (107-111) 10.00 4.00
❑ J.BENCH ODDS 1:43
❑ G.BRETT (112-121) 10.00 4.00
❑ G.BRETT ODDS 1:20
❑ D.MATTINGLY (122-131) 12.00 5.00
❑ D.MATTINGLY ODDS 1:20
❑ R.MARIS (132-136) 12.00 5.00
❑ R.MARIS ODDS 1:40
❑ R.CAREW (137-146) 10.00 4.00
❑ R.CAREW ODDS 1:20
❑ Y.BERRA (147-151) 10.00 4.00
❑ Y.BERRA ODDS 1:40
❑ M.SCHMIDT (152-156) 10.00 4.00
❑ M.SCHMIDT ODDS 1:40
❑ C.YASTRZEMSKI (157-175) 10.00 4.00
❑ C.YASTRZEMSKI ODDS 1:10
❑ T.GWYNN (176-185) 10.00 4.00
❑ T.GWYNN ODDS 1:20
❑ R.SANDBERG (186-190) 10.00 4.00
❑ R.SANDBERG ODDS 1:40
❑ O.SMITH (191-200) 10.00 4.00
❑ O.SMITH ODDS 1:20
❑ STATED PRINT RUN 250 SER.#'d SETS

2002 Topps Total

❑ COMPLETE SET (990) 150.00 75.00
❑ 1 Joe Mauer RC 10.00 4.00
❑ 2 Derek Jeter 2.00 .75
❑ 3 Shawn Green .30 .10
❑ 4 Vladimir Guerrero .75 .30
❑ 5 Mike Piazza 1.25 .50
❑ 6 Brandon Duckworth .20 .07
❑ 7 Aramis Ramirez .30 .10
❑ 8 Josh Barfield RC 2.50 1.00
❑ 9 Troy Glaus .30 .10
❑ 10 Sammy Sosa .75 .30
❑ 11 Rod Barajas .20 .07
❑ 12 Tsuyoshi Shinjo .30 .10
❑ 13 Larry Bigbie .20 .07
❑ 14 Tino Martinez .50 .20
❑ 15 Craig Biggio .50 .20
❑ 16 Anastacio Martinez RC .40 .15
❑ 17 John McDonald .20 .07
❑ 18 Kyle Kane RC .25 .08
❑ 19 Aubrey Huff .30 .10
❑ 20 Juan Cruz .20 .07
❑ 21 Doug Creek .20 .07
❑ 22 Luther Hackman .20 .07
❑ 23 Rafael Furcal .30 .10
❑ 24 Andres Torres .20 .07
❑ 25 Jason Giambi .30 .10
❑ 26 Jose Paniagua .20 .07
❑ 27 Jose Offerman .20 .07
❑ 28 Alex Arias .20 .07
❑ 29 J.M. Gold .20 .07
❑ 30 Jeff Bagwell .50 .20
❑ 31 Brent Cookson .20 .07
❑ 32 Kelly Wunsch .20 .07
❑ 33 Larry Walker .30 .10
❑ 34 Luis Gonzalez .30 .10
❑ 35 John Franco .30 .10
❑ 36 Roy Oswalt .30 .10
❑ 37 Tom Glavine .50 .20
❑ 38 C.C. Sabathia .30 .10
❑ 39 Jay Gibbons .20 .07
❑ 40 Wilson Betemit .20 .07
❑ 41 Tony Armas Jr. .20 .07
❑ 42 Mo Vaughn .30 .10
❑ 43 Gerard Oakes RC .40 .15
❑ 44 Dmitri Young .30 .10
❑ 45 Tim Salmon .50 .20
❑ 46 Barry Zito .30 .10
❑ 47 Adrian Gonzalez .20 .07
❑ 48 Joe Davenport .20 .07
❑ 49 Adrian Hernandez .20 .07
❑ 50 Randy Johnson .75 .30
❑ 52 Adam Pettyjohn .20 .07
❑ 53 Alex Escobar .20 .07
❑ 54 Stevenson Agosto RC .25 .08
❑ 55 Omar Daal .20 .07
❑ 56 Mike Buddie .20 .07
❑ 57 Dave Williams .20 .07
❑ 58 Marquis Grissom .30 .10
❑ 59 Pat Burrell .30 .10
❑ 60 Mark Prior .50 .20
❑ 61 Mike Bynum .20 .07
❑ 62 Mike Hill RC .40 .15
❑ 63 Brandon Backe RC .50 .20
❑ 64 Dan Wilson .20 .07
❑ 65 Nick Johnson .30 .10
❑ 66 Jason Grimsley .20 .07

❑ 67 Russ Johnson .20 .07
❑ 68 Todd Walker .20 .07
❑ 69 Kyle Farnsworth .20 .07
❑ 70 Ben Broussard .20 .07
❑ 71 Garrett Guzman RC .40 .15
❑ 72 Terry Mulholland .20 .07
❑ 73 Tyler Houston .20 .07
❑ 74 Jace Brewer .20 .07
❑ 75 Chris Baker RC .40 .15
❑ 76 Frank Catalanotto .20 .07
❑ 77 Mike Redmond .20 .07
❑ 78 Matt Wise .20 .07
❑ 79 Fernando Vina .20 .07
❑ 80 Kevin Brown .30 .10
❑ 81 Grant Balfour .20 .07
❑ 82 Clint Nageotte RC .50 .20
❑ 83 Jeff Tam .20 .07
❑ 84 Steve Trachsel .20 .07
❑ 85 Tomo Ohka .20 .07
❑ 86 Keith McDonald .20 .07
❑ 87 Jose Ortiz .20 .07
❑ 88 Rusty Greer .30 .10
❑ 89 Jeff Suppan .20 .07
❑ 90 Moises Alou .30 .10
❑ 91 Juan Encarnacion .20 .07
❑ 92 Tyler Yates RC .40 .15
❑ 93 Scott Strickland .20 .07
❑ 94 Brent Butler .20 .07
❑ 95 Jon Rauch .20 .07
❑ 96 Brian Mallette RC .25 .08
❑ 97 Joe Randa .30 .10
❑ 98 Cesar Crespo .20 .07
❑ 99 Felix Rodriguez .20 .07
❑ 100 Chipper Jones .75 .30
❑ 101 Victor Martinez .75 .30
❑ 102 Danny Graves .20 .07
❑ 103 Brandon Berger .20 .07
❑ 104 Carlos Garcia .20 .07
❑ 105 Alfonso Soriano .30 .10
❑ 106 Allan Simpson RC .25 .08
❑ 107 Brad Thomas .20 .07
❑ 108 Devon White .30 .10
❑ 109 Scott Chiasson .20 .07
❑ 110 Cliff Floyd .30 .10
❑ 111 Scott Williamson .20 .07
❑ 112 Julio Zuleta .20 .07
❑ 113 Terry Adams .20 .07
❑ 114 Zach Day .20 .07
❑ 115 Ben Grieve .20 .07
❑ 116 Mark Ellis .20 .07
❑ 117 Bobby Jenks RC 1.50 .60
❑ 118 LaTroy Hawkins .20 .07
❑ 119 Tim Raines Jr. .20 .07
❑ 120 Juan Uribe .20 .07
❑ 121 Bob Scanlan .20 .07
❑ 122 Brad Nelson RC .40 .15
❑ 123 Adam Johnson .20 .07
❑ 124 Raul Casanova .20 .07
❑ 125 Jeff D'Amico .20 .07
❑ 126 Aaron Cook RC .40 .15
❑ 127 Alan Benes .20 .07
❑ 128 Mark Little .20 .07
❑ 129 Randy Wolf .20 .07
❑ 130 Phil Nevin .30 .10
❑ 131 Guillermo Mota .20 .07
❑ 132 Nick Neugebauer .20 .07
❑ 133 Pedro Borbon Jr. .20 .07
❑ 134 Doug Mientkiewicz .30 .10
❑ 135 Edgardo Alfonzo .20 .07
❑ 136 Dustan Mohr .20 .07
❑ 137 Dan Reichert .20 .07
❑ 138 Dewon Brazelton .20 .07
❑ 139 Orlando Cabrera .30 .10
❑ 140 Todd Hollandsworth .20 .07
❑ 141 Darren Dreifort .20 .07
❑ 142 Jose Valentin .20 .07
❑ 143 Josh Kalinowski .20 .07
❑ 144 Randy Keisler .20 .07
❑ 145 Bret Boone .30 .10
❑ 146 Roosevelt Brown .20 .07
❑ 147 Brent Abernathy .20 .07
❑ 148 Jorge Julio .20 .07
❑ 149 Alex Gonzalez .20 .07
❑ 150 Juan Pierre .30 .10
❑ 151 Roger Cedeno .20 .07
❑ 152 Javier Vazquez .30 .10
❑ 153 Armando Benitez .20 .07
❑ 154 Dave Burba .20 .07
❑ 155 Brad Penny .20 .07
❑ 156 Ryan Jensen .20 .07
❑ 157 Jeromy Burnitz .30 .10
❑ 158 Matt Childers RC .40 .15
❑ 159 Wilmy Caceres .20 .07
❑ 160 Roger Clemens 1.50 .60
❑ 161 Jamie Cerda RC .40 .15
❑ 162 Jason Christiansen .20 .07
❑ 163 Pokey Reese .20 .07
❑ 164 Ivanon Coffie .20 .07
❑ 165 Joaquin Benoit .20 .07
❑ 166 Mike Matheny .20 .07
❑ 167 Eric Cammack .20 .07
❑ 168 Alex Graman .20 .07
❑ 169 Brook Fordyce .20 .07
❑ 170 Mike Lieberthal .30 .10
❑ 171 Giovanni Carrara .20 .07
❑ 172 Antonio Perez .20 .07
❑ 173 Fernando Tatis .20 .07
❑ 174 Jason Bay RC 5.00 2.00
❑ 175 Jason Botts RC .50 .20
❑ 176 Danys Baez .20 .07
❑ 177 Shea Hillenbrand .30 .10
❑ 178 Jack Cust .20 .07
❑ 179 Clay Bellinger .20 .07
❑ 180 Roberto Alomar .50 .20
❑ 181 Graeme Lloyd .20 .07
❑ 182 Clint Weibl RC .25 .08
❑ 183 Royce Clayton .20 .07
❑ 184 Ben Davis .20 .07
❑ 185 Brian Adams RC .25 .08
❑ 186 Jack Wilson .20 .07
❑ 187 David Coggin .20 .07
❑ 188 Derrick Turnbow .20 .07
❑ 189 Vladimir Nunez .20 .07
❑ 190 Mariano Rivera .75 .30
❑ 191 Wilson Guzman .20 .07
❑ 192 Michael Barrett .20 .07
❑ 193 Corey Patterson .20 .07
❑ 194 Luis Sojo .20 .07
❑ 195 Scott Elarton .20 .07
❑ 196 Charles Thomas RC .40 .15
❑ 197 Ricky Bottalico .20 .07
❑ 198 Wilfredo Rodriguez .20 .07
❑ 199 Ricardo Rincon .20 .07
❑ 200 John Smoltz .50 .20
❑ 201 Travis Miller .20 .07
❑ 202 Ben Weber .20 .07
❑ 203 T.J. Tucker .20 .07
❑ 204 Terry Shumpert .20 .07
❑ 205 Bernie Williams .50 .20
❑ 206 Russ Ortiz .20 .07
❑ 207 Nate Rolison .20 .07
❑ 208 Jose Cruz Jr. .20 .07
❑ 209 Bill Ortega .20 .07
❑ 210 Carl Everett .30 .10
❑ 211 Luis Lopez .20 .07
❑ 212 Brian Wolfe RC .40 .15
❑ 213 Doug Davis .20 .07
❑ 214 Troy Mattes .20 .07
❑ 215 Al Leiter .30 .10
❑ 216 Joe Mays .20 .07
❑ 217 Bobby Smith .20 .07
❑ 218 J.J. Trujillo RC .40 .15
❑ 219 Hideo Nomo .75 .30
❑ 220 Jimmy Rollins .30 .10
❑ 221 Bobby Seay .20 .07
❑ 222 Mike Thurman .20 .07
❑ 223 Bartolo Colon .30 .10
❑ 224 Jesus Sanchez .20 .07
❑ 225 Ray Durham .30 .10
❑ 226 Juan Diaz .20 .07
❑ 227 Lee Stevens .20 .07
❑ 228 Ben Howard RC .40 .15
❑ 229 James Mouton .20 .07
❑ 230 Paul Quantrill .20 .07
❑ 231 Randy Knorr .20 .07
❑ 232 Abraham Nunez .20 .07
❑ 233 Mike Fetters .20 .07
❑ 234 Mario Encarnacion .20 .07
❑ 235 Jeremy Fikac .20 .07
❑ 236 Travis Lee .20 .07
❑ 237 Bob File .20 .07
❑ 238 Pete Harnisch .20 .07
❑ 239 Randy Galvez RC .40 .15
❑ 240 Geoff Goetz .20 .07
❑ 241 Gary Glover .20 .07
❑ 242 Troy Percival .30 .10
❑ 243 Len Dinardo RC .40 .15
❑ 244 Jonny Gomes RC 2.50 1.00
❑ 245 Jesus Medrano RC .40 .15
❑ 246 Rey Ordonez .20 .07
❑ 247 Juan Gonzalez .30 .10
❑ 248 Jose Guillen .30 .10
❑ 249 Franklyn German RC .40 .15
❑ 250 Mike Mussina .50 .20
❑ 251 Ugueth Urbina .20 .07
❑ 252 Melvin Mora .30 .10
❑ 253 Gerald Williams .20 .07
❑ 254 Jared Sandberg .20 .07
❑ 255 Darrin Fletcher .20 .07
❑ 256 A.J. Pierzynski .30 .10
❑ 257 Lenny Harris .20 .07
❑ 258 Blaine Neal .20 .07
❑ 259 Denny Neagle .20 .07
❑ 260 Jason Hart .20 .07
❑ 261 Henry Mateo .20 .07
❑ 262 Rheal Cormier .20 .07
❑ 263 Luis Terrero .20 .07
❑ 264 Shigetoshi Hasegawa .30 .10
❑ 265 Bill Haselman .20 .07
❑ 266 Scott Hatteberg .20 .07
❑ 267 Adam Hyzdu .20 .07
❑ 268 Mike Williams .20 .07
❑ 269 Marlon Anderson .20 .07
❑ 270 Bruce Chen .20 .07
❑ 271 Eli Marrero .20 .07
❑ 272 Jimmy Haynes .20 .07
❑ 273 Bronson Arroyo .30 .10
❑ 274 Kevin Jordan .20 .07
❑ 275 Rick Helling .20 .07
❑ 276 Mark Loretta .20 .07
❑ 277 Dustin Hermanson .20 .07
❑ 278 Pablo Ozuna .20 .07
❑ 279 Keto Anderson RC .40 .15
❑ 280 Jermaine Dye .30 .10
❑ 281 Will Smith .20 .07
❑ 282 Brian Daubach .20 .07
❑ 283 Eric Hinske .20 .07
❑ 284 Joe Jiannetti RC .40 .15
❑ 285 Chan Ho Park .30 .10
❑ 286 Curtis Legendre RC .40 .15
❑ 287 Jeff Reboulet .20 .07
❑ 288 Scott Rolen .50 .20
❑ 289 Chris Richard .20 .07
❑ 290 Eric Chavez .30 .10
❑ 291 Scot Shields .20 .07
❑ 292 Donnie Sadler .20 .07
❑ 293 Dave Veres .20 .07
❑ 294 Craig Counsell .20 .07
❑ 295 Armando Reynoso .20 .07
❑ 296 Kyle Lohse .20 .07
❑ 297 Arthur Rhodes .20 .07
❑ 298 Sidney Ponson .20 .07
❑ 299 Trevor Hoffman .30 .10
❑ 300 Kerry Wood .30 .10
❑ 301 Danny Bautista .20 .07
❑ 302 Scott Sauerbeck .20 .07
❑ 303 Johnny Estrada .20 .07
❑ 304 Mike Timlin .20 .07
❑ 305 Orlando Hernandez .30 .10
❑ 306 Tony Clark .20 .07
❑ 307 Tomas Perez .20 .07
❑ 308 Marcus Giles .30 .10
❑ 309 Mike Bordick .30 .10
❑ 310 Jorge Posada .50 .20
❑ 311 Jason Conti .20 .07
❑ 312 Kevin Millar .30 .10
❑ 313 Paul Shuey .20 .07
❑ 314 Jake Mauer RC .40 .15
❑ 315 Luke Hudson .20 .07
❑ 316 Angel Berroa .20 .07
❑ 317 Fred Bastardo RC .40 .15
❑ 318 Shawn Estes .20 .07
❑ 319 Andy Ashby .20 .07
❑ 320 Ryan Klesko .30 .10
❑ 321 Kevin Appier .30 .10
❑ 322 Juan Pena .20 .07
❑ 323 Alex Herrera .20 .07
❑ 324 Robb Nen .30 .10

❑	325	Orlando Hudson	.20	.07
❑	326	Lyle Overbay	.20	.07
❑	327	Ben Sheets	.30	.10
❑	328	Mike DiFelice	.20	.07
❑	329	Pablo Arias RC	.40	.15
❑	330	Mike Sweeney	.30	.10
❑	331	Rick Ankiel	.20	.07
❑	332	Tomas De La Rosa	.20	.07
❑	333	Kazuhisa Ishii RC	.50	.20
❑	334	Jose Reyes	.50	.20
❑	335	Jeremy Giambi	.20	.07
❑	336	Jose Mesa	.20	.07
❑	337	Ralph Roberts RC	.40	.15
❑	338	Jose Nunez	.20	.07
❑	339	Curt Schilling	.30	.10
❑	340	Sean Casey	.30	.10
❑	341	Bob Wells	.20	.07
❑	342	Carlos Beltran	.30	.10
❑	343	Alexis Gomez	.20	.07
❑	344	Brandon Claussen	.20	.07
❑	345	Buddy Groom	.20	.07
❑	346	Mark Phillips RC	.40	.15
❑	347	Francisco Cordova	.20	.07
❑	348	Joe Oliver	.20	.07
❑	349	Danny Patterson	.20	.07
❑	350	Joel Pineiro	.20	.07
❑	351	J.R. House	.20	.07
❑	352	Benny Agbayani	.20	.07
❑	353	Jose Vidro	.20	.07
❑	354	Reed Johnson RC	1.00	.40
❑	355	Mike Lowell	.30	.10
❑	356	Scott Schoeneweis	.20	.07
❑	357	Brian Jordan	.30	.10
❑	358	Steve Finley	.30	.10
❑	359	Randy Choate	.20	.07
❑	360	Jose Lima	.20	.07
❑	361	Miguel Olivo	.20	.07
❑	362	Kenny Rogers	.30	.10
❑	363	David Justice	.30	.10
❑	364	Brandon Knight	.20	.07
❑	365	Joe Kennedy	.20	.07
❑	366	Eric Valent	.20	.07
❑	367	Nelson Cruz	.20	.07
❑	368	Brian Giles	.30	.10
❑	369	Charles Gipson RC	.25	.08
❑	370	Juan Pena	.20	.07
❑	371	Mark Redman	.20	.07
❑	372	Billy Koch	.20	.07
❑	373	Ted Lilly	.20	.07
❑	374	Craig Paquette	.20	.07
❑	375	Kevin Jarvis	.20	.07
❑	376	Scott Erickson	.20	.07
❑	377	Josh Paul	.20	.07
❑	378	Darwin Cubillan	.20	.07
❑	379	Nelson Figueroa	.20	.07
❑	380	Darin Erstad	.30	.10
❑	381	Jeremy Hill RC	.40	.15
❑	382	Elvin Nina	.20	.07
❑	383	David Wells	.30	.10
❑	384	Jay Caligiuri RC	.40	.15
❑	385	Freddy Garcia	.30	.10
❑	386	Damian Miller	.20	.07
❑	387	Bobby Higginson	.30	.10
❑	388	Alejandro Giron RC	.40	.15
❑	389	Ivan Rodriguez	.50	.20
❑	390	Ed Rogers	.20	.07
❑	391	Andy Benes	.20	.07
❑	392	Matt Blank	.20	.07
❑	393	Ryan Vogelsong	.20	.07
❑	394	Kelly Ramos RC	.25	.08
❑	395	Eric Karros	.30	.10
❑	396	Bobby J. Jones	.20	.07
❑	397	Omar Vizquel	.50	.20
❑	398	Matt Perisho	.20	.07
❑	399	Delino DeShields	.20	.07
❑	400	Carlos Hernandez	.20	.07
❑	401	Derrek Lee	.50	.20
❑	402	Kirk Rueter	.20	.07
❑	403	David Wright RC	30.00	12.50
❑	404	Paul LoDuca	.30	.10
❑	405	Brian Schneider	.20	.07
❑	406	Milton Bradley	.30	.10
❑	407	Daryle Ward	.20	.07
❑	408	Cody Ransom	.20	.07
❑	409	Fernando Rodney	.20	.07
❑	410	John Suomi RC	.40	.15
❑	411	Joe Girardi	.20	.07
❑	412	Demetrius Heath RC	.40	.15
❑	413	John Foster RC	.40	.15
❑	414	Doug Glanville	.20	.07
❑	415	Ryan Kohlmeier	.20	.07
❑	416	Mike Matthews	.20	.07
❑	417	Craig Wilson	.20	.07
❑	418	Jay Witasick	.20	.07
❑	419	Jay Payton	.20	.07
❑	420	Andruw Jones	.50	.20
❑	421	Benji Gil	.20	.07
❑	422	Jeff Liefer	.20	.07
❑	423	Kevin Young	.20	.07
❑	424	Richie Sexson	.30	.10
❑	425	Cory Lidle	.20	.07
❑	426	Shane Halter	.20	.07
❑	427	Jesse Foppert RC	.50	.20
❑	428	Jose Molina	.20	.07
❑	429	Nick Alvarez RC	.40	.15
❑	430	Brian L. Hunter	.20	.07
❑	431	Cliff Bartosh RC	.40	.15
❑	432	Junior Spivey	.20	.07
❑	433	Eric Good RC	.40	.15
❑	434	Chin-Feng Chen	.30	.10
❑	435	T.J. Mathews	.20	.07
❑	436	Rich Rodriguez	.20	.07
❑	437	Bobby Abreu	.30	.10
❑	438	Joe McEwing	.20	.07
❑	439	Michael Tucker	.20	.07
❑	440	Preston Wilson	.30	.10
❑	441	Mike MacDougal	.20	.07
❑	442	Shannon Stewart	.30	.10
❑	443	Bob Howry	.20	.07
❑	444	Mike Benjamin	.20	.07
❑	445	Erik Hiljus	.20	.07
❑	446	Ryan Gripp RC	.40	.15
❑	447	Jose Vizcaino	.20	.07
❑	448	Shawn Wooten	.20	.07
❑	449	Steve Kent RC	.40	.15
❑	450	Ramiro Mendoza	.20	.07
❑	451	Jake Westbrook	.20	.07
❑	452	Joe Lawrence	.20	.07
❑	453	Jae Seo	.20	.07
❑	454	Ryan Fry RC	.40	.15
❑	455	Darren Lewis	.20	.07
❑	456	Brad Wilkerson	.20	.07
❑	457	Gustavo Chacin RC	1.00	.40
❑	458	Adrian Brown	.20	.07
❑	459	Mike Cameron	.20	.07
❑	460	Bud Smith	.20	.07
❑	461	Derrick Lewis	.20	.07
❑	462	Derek Lowe	.30	.10
❑	463	Matt Williams	.30	.10
❑	464	Jason Jennings	.20	.07
❑	465	Albie Lopez	.20	.07
❑	466	Felipe Lopez	.20	.07
❑	467	Luke Allen	.20	.07
❑	468	Brian Anderson	.20	.07
❑	469	Matt Riley	.20	.07
❑	470	Ryan Dempster	.20	.07
❑	471	Matt Ginter	.20	.07
❑	472	David Ortiz	.75	.30
❑	473	Cole Barthel RC	.25	.08
❑	474	Damian Jackson	.20	.07
❑	475	Andy Van Hekken	.20	.07
❑	476	Doug Brocail	.20	.07
❑	477	Denny Hocking	.20	.07
❑	478	Sean Douglass	.20	.07
❑	479	Eric Owens	.20	.07
❑	480	Ryan Ludwick	.20	.07
❑	481	Todd Pratt	.20	.07
❑	482	Aaron Sele	.20	.07
❑	483	Edgar Renteria	.30	.10
❑	484	Raymond Cabrera RC	.40	.15
❑	485	Brandon Lyon	.20	.07
❑	486	Chase Utley	2.50	1.00
❑	487	Robert Fick	.20	.07
❑	488	Wilfredo Cordero	.20	.07
❑	489	Octavio Dotel	.20	.07
❑	490	Paul Abbott	.20	.07
❑	491	Jason Kendall	.30	.10
❑	492	Jarrod Washburn	.20	.07
❑	493	Dane Sardinha	.20	.07
❑	494	Jung Bong	.20	.07
❑	495	J.D. Drew	.30	.10
❑	496	Jason Schmidt	.30	.10
❑	497	Mike Magnante	.20	.07
❑	498	Jorge Padilla RC	.40	.15
❑	499	Eric Gagne	.30	.10
❑	500	Todd Helton	.50	.20
❑	501	Jeff Weaver	.20	.07
❑	502	Alex Sanchez	.20	.07
❑	503	Ken Griffey Jr.	1.25	.50
❑	504	Abraham Nunez	.20	.07
❑	505	Reggie Sanders	.30	.10
❑	506	Casey Kotchman RC	1.00	.40
❑	507	Jim Mann	.20	.07
❑	508	Matt LeCroy	.20	.07
❑	509	Frank Castillo	.20	.07
❑	510	Geoff Jenkins	.20	.07
❑	511	Jayson Durocher RC	.25	.08
❑	512	Ellis Burks	.30	.10
❑	513	Aaron Fultz	.20	.07
❑	514	Hiram Bocachica	.20	.07
❑	515	Nate Espy RC	.40	.15
❑	516	Placido Polanco	.20	.07
❑	517	Kerry Ligtenberg	.20	.07
❑	518	Doug Nickle	.20	.07
❑	519	Ramon Ortiz	.20	.07
❑	520	Greg Swindell	.20	.07
❑	521	J.J. Davis	.20	.07
❑	522	Sandy Alomar Jr.	.20	.07
❑	523	Chris Carpenter	.30	.10
❑	524	Vance Wilson	.20	.07
❑	525	Nomar Garciaparra	1.25	.50
❑	526	Jim Mecir	.20	.07
❑	527	Taylor Buchholz RC	.50	.20
❑	528	Brent Mayne	.20	.07
❑	529	John Rodriguez RC	.50	.20
❑	530	David Segui	.20	.07
❑	531	Nate Cornejo	.20	.07
❑	532	Gil Heredia	.20	.07
❑	533	Esteban Loaiza	.20	.07
❑	534	Pat Mahomes	.20	.07
❑	535	Matt Morris	.30	.10
❑	536	Todd Stottlemyre	.20	.07
❑	537	Brian Lesher	.20	.07
❑	538	Arturo McDowell	.20	.07
❑	539	Felix Diaz	.20	.07
❑	540	Mark Mulder	.30	.10
❑	541	Kevin Frederick RC	.40	.15
❑	542	Andy Fox	.20	.07
❑	543	Dionys Cesar RC	.25	.08
❑	544	Justin Miller	.20	.07
❑	545	Keith Osik	.20	.07
❑	546	Shane Reynolds	.20	.07
❑	547	Mike Myers	.20	.07
❑	548	Raul Chavez RC	.25	.08
❑	549	Joe Nathan	.30	.10
❑	550	Ryan Anderson	.20	.07
❑	551	Jason Marquis	.20	.07
❑	552	Marty Cordova	.20	.07
❑	553	Kevin Tapani	.20	.07
❑	554	Jimmy Anderson	.20	.07
❑	555	Pedro Martinez	.50	.20
❑	556	Rocky Biddle	.20	.07
❑	557	Alex Ochoa	.20	.07
❑	558	D'Angelo Jimenez	.20	.07
❑	559	Wilkin Ruan	.20	.07
❑	560	Terrence Long	.20	.07
❑	561	Mark Lukasiewicz	.20	.07
❑	562	Jose Santiago	.20	.07
❑	563	Brad Fullmer	.20	.07
❑	564	Corky Miller	.20	.07
❑	565	Matt White	.20	.07
❑	566	Mark Grace	.50	.20
❑	567	Raul Ibanez	.20	.07
❑	568	Josh Towers	.20	.07
❑	569	Juan M. Gonzalez RC	.40	.15
❑	570	Brian Buchanan	.20	.07
❑	571	Ken Harvey	.20	.07
❑	572	Jeffrey Hammonds	.20	.07
❑	573	Wade Miller	.20	.07
❑	574	Elpidio Guzman	.20	.07
❑	575	Kevin Olsen	.20	.07
❑	576	Austin Kearns	.20	.07
❑	577	Tim Kalita RC	.40	.15
❑	578	David Dellucci	.20	.07
❑	579	Alex Gonzalez	.20	.07
❑	580	Joe Orloski RC	.40	.15
❑	581	Gary Matthews Jr.	.20	.07
❑	582	Ryan Mills	.20	.07

Card		
❑ 583 Erick Almonte	.20	.07
❑ 584 Jeremy Affeldt	.20	.07
❑ 585 Chris Tritle RC	.25	.08
❑ 586 Michael Cuddyer	.20	.07
❑ 587 Kris Foster	.20	.07
❑ 588 Russell Branyan	.20	.07
❑ 589 Darren Oliver	.20	.07
❑ 590 Freddie Money RC	.40	.15
❑ 591 Carlos Lee	.30	.10
❑ 592 Tim Wakefield	.30	.10
❑ 593 Bubba Trammell	.20	.07
❑ 594 John Koronka RC	1.00	.40
❑ 595 Geoff Blum	.20	.07
❑ 596 Darryl Kile	.30	.10
❑ 597 Neifi Perez	.20	.07
❑ 598 Torii Hunter	.30	.10
❑ 599 Luis Castillo	.20	.07
❑ 600 Mark Buehrle	.30	.10
❑ 601 Jeff Zimmerman	.20	.07
❑ 602 Mike DeJean	.20	.07
❑ 603 Julio Lugo	.20	.07
❑ 604 Chad Hermansen	.20	.07
❑ 605 Keith Foulke	.30	.10
❑ 606 Lance Davis	.20	.07
❑ 607 Jeff Austin RC	.40	.15
❑ 608 Brandon Inge	.20	.07
❑ 609 Orlando Merced	.20	.07
❑ 610 Johnny Damon Sox	.50	.20
❑ 611 Doug Henry	.20	.07
❑ 612 Adam Kennedy	.20	.07
❑ 613 Wiki Gonzalez	.20	.07
❑ 614 Brian West RC	.40	.15
❑ 615 Andy Pettitte	.50	.20
❑ 616 Chone Figgins RC	1.50	.60
❑ 617 Matt Lawton	.20	.07
❑ 618 Paul Rigdon	.20	.07
❑ 619 Keith Lockhart	.20	.07
❑ 620 Tim Redding	.20	.07
❑ 621 John Parrish	.20	.07
❑ 622 Homer Bush	.20	.07
❑ 623 Todd Greene	.20	.07
❑ 624 David Eckstein	.30	.10
❑ 625 Greg Montalbano RC	.40	.15
❑ 626 Joe Beimel	.20	.07
❑ 627 Adrian Beltre	.30	.10
❑ 628 Charles Nagy	.20	.07
❑ 629 Cristian Guzman	.20	.07
❑ 630 Toby Hall	.20	.07
❑ 631 Jose Hernandez	.20	.07
❑ 632 Jose Macias	.30	.10
❑ 633 Jaret Wright	.20	.07
❑ 634 Steve Parris	.20	.07
❑ 635 Gene Kingsale	.20	.07
❑ 636 Tim Worrell	.20	.07
❑ 637 Billy Martin	.20	.07
❑ 638 Jovanny Cedeno	.20	.07
❑ 639 Curtis Leskanic	.20	.07
❑ 640 Tim Hudson	.30	.10
❑ 641 Juan Castro	.20	.07
❑ 642 Rafael Soriano	.20	.07
❑ 643 Juan Rincon	.20	.07
❑ 644 Mark DeRosa	.20	.07
❑ 645 Carlos Pena	.20	.07
❑ 646 Robin Ventura	.30	.10
❑ 647 Odalis Perez	.20	.07
❑ 648 Damion Easley	.20	.07
❑ 649 Benito Santiago	.30	.10
❑ 650 Alex Rodriguez	1.25	.50
❑ 651 Aaron Rowand	.30	.10
❑ 652 Alex Cora	.20	.07
❑ 653 Bobby Kielty	.20	.07
❑ 654 Jose Rodriguez RC	.40	.15
❑ 655 Herbert Perry	.20	.07
❑ 656 Jeff Urban	.20	.07
❑ 657 Paul Bako	.20	.07
❑ 658 Shane Spencer	.20	.07
❑ 659 Pat Hentgen	.20	.07
❑ 660 Jeff Kent	.30	.10
❑ 661 Mark McLemore	.20	.07
❑ 662 Chuck Knoblauch	.30	.10
❑ 663 Blake Stein	.20	.07
❑ 664 Brett Roneberg RC	.40	.15
❑ 665 Josh Phelps	.20	.07
❑ 666 Byung-Hyun Kim	.30	.10
❑ 667 Dave Martinez	.20	.07
❑ 668 Mike Maroth	.20	.07
❑ 669 Shawn Chacon	.20	.07
❑ 670 Billy Wagner	.30	.10
❑ 671 Luis Alicea	.20	.07
❑ 672 Sterling Hitchcock	.20	.07
❑ 673 Adam Piatt	.20	.07
❑ 674 Ryan Franklin	.20	.07
❑ 675 Luke Prokopec	.20	.07
❑ 676 Alfredo Amezaga	.20	.07
❑ 677 Gookie Dawkins	.20	.07
❑ 678 Eric Byrnes	.20	.07
❑ 679 Barry Larkin	.50	.20
❑ 680 Albert Pujols	1.50	.60
❑ 681 Edwards Guzman	.20	.07
❑ 682 Jason Bere	.20	.07
❑ 683 Adam Everett	.20	.07
❑ 684 Greg Colbrunn	.20	.07
❑ 685 Brandon Puffer RC	.40	.15
❑ 686 Mark Kotsay	.30	.10
❑ 687 Willie Bloomquist	.30	.10
❑ 688 Hank Blalock	.50	.20
❑ 689 Travis Hafner	.30	.10
❑ 690 Lance Berkman	.30	.10
❑ 691 Joe Crede	.30	.10
❑ 692 Chuck Finley	.30	.10
❑ 693 John Grabow	.20	.07
❑ 694 Randy Winn	.20	.07
❑ 695 Mike James	.20	.07
❑ 696 Kris Benson	.20	.07
❑ 697 Bret Prinz	.20	.07
❑ 698 Jeff Williams	.20	.07
❑ 699 Eric Munson	.20	.07
❑ 700 Mike Hampton	.30	.10
❑ 701 Ramon E. Martinez	.20	.07
❑ 702 Hansel Izquierdo RC	.40	.15
❑ 703 Nathan Haynes	.20	.07
❑ 704 Eddie Taubensee	.20	.07
❑ 705 Esteban German	.20	.07
❑ 706 Ross Gload	.20	.07
❑ 707 Matt Merricks RC	.40	.15
❑ 708 Chris Piersoll RC	.25	.08
❑ 709 Seth Greisinger	.20	.07
❑ 710 Ichiro Suzuki	1.50	.60
❑ 711 Cesar Izturis	.20	.07
❑ 712 Brad Cresse	.20	.07
❑ 713 Carl Pavano	.30	.10
❑ 714 Steve Sparks	.20	.07
❑ 715 Dennis Tankersley	.20	.07
❑ 716 Kelvim Escobar	.20	.07
❑ 717 Jason LaRue	.20	.07
❑ 718 Corey Koskie	.20	.07
❑ 719 Vinny Castilla	.30	.10
❑ 720 Tim Drew	.20	.07
❑ 721 Chin-Hui Tsao	.30	.10
❑ 722 Paul Byrd	.20	.07
❑ 723 Alex Cintron	.20	.07
❑ 724 Orlando Palmeiro	.20	.07
❑ 725 Ramon Hernandez	.20	.07
❑ 726 Mark Johnson	.20	.07
❑ 727 B.J. Ryan	.20	.07
❑ 728 Wendell Magee	.20	.07
❑ 729 Michael Coleman	.20	.07
❑ 730 Mario Ramos RC	.40	.15
❑ 731 Mike Stanton	.20	.07
❑ 732 Dee Brown	.20	.07
❑ 733 Brad Ausmus	.30	.10
❑ 734 Napoleon Calzado RC	.40	.15
❑ 735 Woody Williams	.20	.07
❑ 736 Paxton Crawford	.20	.07
❑ 737 Jason Karnuth	.20	.07
❑ 738 Michael Restovich	.20	.07
❑ 739 Ramon Castro	.20	.07
❑ 740 Magglio Ordonez	.30	.10
❑ 741 Tom Gordon	.20	.07
❑ 742 Mark Grudzielanek	.20	.07
❑ 743 Jaime Moyer	.30	.10
❑ 744 Marlyn Tisdale RC	.40	.15
❑ 745 Steve Kline	.20	.07
❑ 746 Adam Eaton	.20	.07
❑ 747 Eric Glaser RC	.40	.15
❑ 748 Sean DePaula	.20	.07
❑ 749 Greg Norton	.20	.07
❑ 750 Steve Reed	.20	.07
❑ 751 Ricardo Aramboles	.20	.07
❑ 752 Matt Mantei	.20	.07
❑ 753 Gene Stechschulte	.20	.07
❑ 754 Chuck McElroy	.20	.07
❑ 755 Barry Bonds	2.00	.75
❑ 756 Matt Anderson	.20	.07
❑ 757 Yorvit Torrealba	.20	.07
❑ 758 Jason Standridge	.20	.07
❑ 759 Desi Relaford	.20	.07
❑ 760 Jolbert Cabrera	.20	.07
❑ 761 Chris George	.20	.07
❑ 762 Erubiel Durazo	.20	.07
❑ 763 Paul Konerko	.30	.10
❑ 764 Tike Redman	.20	.07
❑ 765 Chad Ricketts RC	.25	.08
❑ 766 Roberto Hernandez	.20	.07
❑ 767 Mark Lewis	.20	.07
❑ 768 Livan Hernandez	.30	.10
❑ 769 Carlos Brackley RC	.40	.15
❑ 770 Kazuhiro Sasaki	.30	.10
❑ 771 Bill Hall	.30	.10
❑ 772 Nelson Castro RC	.40	.15
❑ 773 Eric Milton	.20	.07
❑ 774 Tom Davey	.20	.07
❑ 775 Todd Ritchie	.20	.07
❑ 776 Seth Etherton	.20	.07
❑ 777 Chris Singleton	.20	.07
❑ 778 Robert Averette RC	.25	.08
❑ 779 Robert Person	.20	.07
❑ 780 Fred McGriff	.50	.20
❑ 781 Richard Hidalgo	.20	.07
❑ 782 Kris Wilson	.20	.07
❑ 783 John Rocker	.30	.10
❑ 784 Justin Kaye	.20	.07
❑ 785 Glendon Rusch	.20	.07
❑ 786 Greg Vaughn	.20	.07
❑ 787 Mike Lamb	.20	.07
❑ 788 Greg Myers	.20	.07
❑ 789 Nate Field RC	.40	.15
❑ 790 Jim Edmonds	.30	.10
❑ 791 Olmedo Saenz	.20	.07
❑ 792 Jason Johnson	.20	.07
❑ 793 Mike Lincoln	.20	.07
❑ 794 Todd Coffey RC	.40	.15
❑ 795 Jesus Sanchez	.20	.07
❑ 796 Aaron Myette	.20	.07
❑ 797 Tony Womack	.20	.07
❑ 798 Chad Kreuter	.20	.07
❑ 799 Brady Clark	.20	.07
❑ 800 Adam Dunn	.30	.10
❑ 801 Jacque Jones	.30	.10
❑ 802 Kevin Millwood	.30	.10
❑ 803 Mike Rivera	.20	.07
❑ 804 Jim Thome	.50	.20
❑ 805 Jeff Conine	.30	.10
❑ 806 Elmer Dessens	.20	.07
❑ 807 Randy Velarde	.20	.07
❑ 808 Carlos Delgado	.30	.10
❑ 809 Steve Karsay	.20	.07
❑ 810 Casey Fossum	.20	.07
❑ 811 J.C. Romero	.20	.07
❑ 812 Chris Truby	.20	.07
❑ 813 Tony Graffanino	.20	.07
❑ 814 Wascar Serrano	.20	.07
❑ 815 Delvin James	.20	.07
❑ 816 Pedro Feliz	.20	.07
❑ 817 Damian Rolls	.20	.07
❑ 818 Scott Linebrink	.20	.07
❑ 819 Rafael Palmeiro	.50	.20
❑ 820 Javy Lopez	.30	.10
❑ 821 Larry Barnes	.20	.07
❑ 822 Brian Lawrence	.20	.07
❑ 823 Scotty Layfield RC	.40	.15
❑ 824 Jeff Cirillo	.20	.07
❑ 825 Willis Roberts	.20	.07
❑ 826 Rich Harden RC	3.00	1.25
❑ 827 Chris Snelling RC	.60	.25
❑ 828 Gary Sheffield	.30	.10
❑ 829 Jeff Heaverlo	.20	.07
❑ 830 Matt Clement	.30	.10
❑ 831 Rich Garces	.20	.07
❑ 832 Rondell White	.30	.10
❑ 833 Henry Pichardo RC	.40	.15
❑ 834 Aaron Boone	.30	.10
❑ 835 Ruben Sierra	.30	.10
❑ 836 Deivis Santos	.20	.07
❑ 837 Tony Batista	.20	.07
❑ 838 Rob Bell	.20	.07
❑ 839 Frank Thomas	.75	.30
❑ 840 Jose Silva	.20	.07

❑ 841 Dan Johnson RC	1.00	.40
❑ 842 Steve Cox	.20	.07
❑ 843 Jose Acevedo	.20	.07
❑ 844 Jay Bell	.30	.10
❑ 845 Mike Sirotka	.20	.07
❑ 846 Garret Anderson	.30	.10
❑ 847 James Shanks RC	.40	.15
❑ 848 Trot Nixon	.30	.10
❑ 849 Keith Ginter	.20	.07
❑ 850 Tim Spooneybarger	.20	.07
❑ 851 Matt Stairs	.20	.07
❑ 852 Chris Stynes	.20	.07
❑ 853 Marvin Benard	.20	.07
❑ 854 Raul Mondesi	.30	.10
❑ 855 Jeremy Owens	.20	.07
❑ 856 Jon Garland	.30	.10
❑ 857 Mitch Meluskey	.20	.07
❑ 858 Chad Durbin	.20	.07
❑ 859 John Burkett	.20	.07
❑ 860 Jon Switzer RC	.40	.15
❑ 861 Peter Bergeron	.20	.07
❑ 862 Jesus Colome	.20	.07
❑ 863 Todd Hundley	.20	.07
❑ 864 Ben Petrick	.20	.07
❑ 865 So Taguchi RC	.50	.20
❑ 866 Ryan Drese	.20	.07
❑ 867 Mike Trombley	.20	.07
❑ 868 Rick Reed	.20	.07
❑ 869 Mark Teixeira	.75	.30
❑ 870 Corey Thurman RC	.40	.15
❑ 871 Brian Roberts	.30	.10
❑ 872 Mike Timlin	.20	.07
❑ 873 Chris Reitsma	.20	.07
❑ 874 Jeff Fassero	.20	.07
❑ 875 Carlos Valderrama	.20	.07
❑ 876 John Lackey	.20	.07
❑ 877 Travis Fryman	.30	.10
❑ 878 Ismael Valdes	.20	.07
❑ 879 Rick White	.20	.07
❑ 880 Edgar Martinez	.50	.20
❑ 881 Dean Palmer	.30	.10
❑ 882 Matt Allegra RC	.40	.15
❑ 883 Greg Sain RC	.40	.15
❑ 884 Carlos Silva	.20	.07
❑ 885 Jose Valverde RC	.40	.15
❑ 886 Dernell Stenson	.20	.07
❑ 887 Todd Van Poppel	.20	.07
❑ 888 Wes Anderson	.20	.07
❑ 889 Bill Mueller	.30	.10
❑ 890 Morgan Ensberg	.30	.10
❑ 891 Marcus Thames	.20	.07
❑ 892 Adam Walker RC	.40	.15
❑ 893 John Halama	.20	.07
❑ 894 Frank Menechino	.20	.07
❑ 895 Greg Maddux	1.25	.50
❑ 896 Gary Bennett	.20	.07
❑ 897 Mauricio Lara RC	.40	.15
❑ 898 Mike Young	.75	.30
❑ 899 Travis Phelps	.20	.07
❑ 900 Rich Aurilia	.20	.07
❑ 901 Henry Blanco	.20	.07
❑ 902 Carlos Febles	.20	.07
❑ 903 Scott MacRae	.20	.07
❑ 904 Lou Merloni	.20	.07
❑ 905 Dicky Gonzalez	.20	.07
❑ 906 Jeff DaVanon	.20	.07
❑ 907 A.J. Burnett	.30	.10
❑ 908 Einar Diaz	.20	.07
❑ 909 Julio Franco	.30	.10
❑ 910 John Olerud	.30	.10
❑ 911 Mark Hamilton RC	.40	.15
❑ 912 David Riske	.20	.07
❑ 913 Jason Tyner	.20	.07
❑ 914 Britt Reames	.20	.07
❑ 915 Vernon Wells	.30	.10
❑ 916 Eddie Perez	.20	.07
❑ 917 Edwin Almonte RC	.40	.15
❑ 918 Enrique Wilson	.20	.07
❑ 919 Chris Gomez	.20	.07
❑ 920 Jayson Werth	.20	.07
❑ 921 Jeff Nelson	.20	.07
❑ 922 Freddy Sanchez RC	2.00	.75
❑ 923 John Vander Wal	.20	.07
❑ 924 Chad Qualls RC	.50	.20
❑ 925 Gabe White	.20	.07
❑ 926 Chad Harville	.20	.07
❑ 927 Ricky Gutierrez	.20	.07
❑ 928 Carlos Guillen	.30	.10
❑ 929 B.J. Surhoff	.30	.10
❑ 930 Chris Woodward	.20	.07
❑ 931 Ricardo Rodriguez	.20	.07
❑ 932 Jimmy Gobble RC	.40	.15
❑ 933 Jon Lieber	.20	.07
❑ 934 Craig Kuzmic RC	.40	.15
❑ 935 Eric Young	.20	.07
❑ 936 Greg Zaun	.20	.07
❑ 937 Miguel Batista	.20	.07
❑ 938 Danny Wright	.20	.07
❑ 939 Todd Zeile	.30	.10
❑ 940 Chad Zerbe	.20	.07
❑ 941 Jason Young RC	.25	.08
❑ 942 Ronnie Belliard	.20	.07
❑ 943 John Ennis RC	.40	.15
❑ 944 John Flaherty	.20	.07
❑ 945 Jerry Hairston Jr.	.20	.07
❑ 946 Al Levine	.20	.07
❑ 947 Antonio Alfonseca	.20	.07
❑ 948 Brian Moehler	.20	.07
❑ 949 Calvin Murray	.20	.07
❑ 950 Nick Bierbrodt	.20	.07
❑ 951 Sun Woo Kim	.20	.07
❑ 952 Noochie Varner RC	.40	.15
❑ 953 Luis Rivas	.20	.07
❑ 954 Donnie Bridges	.20	.07
❑ 955 Ramon Vazquez	.20	.07
❑ 956 Luis Garcia	.20	.07
❑ 957 Mark Quinn	.20	.07
❑ 958 Armando Rios	.20	.07
❑ 959 Chad Fox	.20	.07
❑ 960 Hee Seop Choi	.20	.07
❑ 961 Turk Wendell	.20	.07
❑ 962 Adam Roller RC	.40	.15
❑ 963 Grant Roberts	.20	.07
❑ 964 Ben Molina	.20	.07
❑ 965 Juan Rivera	.20	.07
❑ 966 Matt Kinney	.20	.07
❑ 967 Rod Beck	.20	.07
❑ 968 Xavier Nady	.20	.07
❑ 969 Masato Yoshii	.20	.07
❑ 970 Miguel Tejada	.30	.10
❑ 971 Danny Kolb	.20	.07
❑ 972 Mike Remlinger	.20	.07
❑ 973 Ray Lankford	.30	.10
❑ 974 Ryan Minor	.20	.07
❑ 975 J.T. Snow	.30	.10
❑ 976 Brad Radke	.30	.10
❑ 977 Jason Lane	.30	.10
❑ 978 Jamey Wright	.20	.07
❑ 979 Tom Goodwin	.20	.07
❑ 980 Erik Bedard	.30	.10
❑ 981 Gabe Kapler	.30	.10
❑ 982 Brian Reith	.20	.07
❑ 983 Nic Jackson RC	.40	.15
❑ 984 Kurt Ainsworth	.20	.07
❑ 985 Jason Isringhausen	.30	.10
❑ 986 Willie Harris	.20	.07
❑ 987 David Cone	.30	.10
❑ 988 Bob Wickman	.20	.07
❑ 989 Wes Helms	.20	.07
❑ 990 Josh Beckett	.30	.10

2003 Topps Total

❑ COMPLETE SET (990)	200.00	100.00
❑ COMMON CARD (1-990)	.20	.07
❑ COMMON RC	.25	.08
❑ 1 Brent Abernathy	.20	.07
❑ 2 Bobby Hill	.20	.07
❑ 3 Victor Martinez	.50	.20
❑ 4 Chip Ambres	.20	.07
❑ 5 Matt Anderson	.20	.07
❑ 6 Ricardo Aramboles	.20	.07
❑ 7 Carlos Pena	.20	.07
❑ 8 Aaron Guiel	.20	.07
❑ 9 Luke Allen	.20	.07
❑ 10 Francisco Rodriguez	.30	.10
❑ 11 Jason Marquis	.20	.07
❑ 12 Edwin Almonte	.20	.07
❑ 13 Grant Balfour	.20	.07
❑ 14 Adam Piatt	.20	.07
❑ 15 Andy Phillips	.20	.07
❑ 16 Adrian Beltre	.30	.10
❑ 17 Brandon Backe	.20	.07
❑ 18 Dave Berg	.20	.07
❑ 19 Brett Myers	.30	.10
❑ 20 Brian Meadows	.20	.07
❑ 21 Chin-Feng Chen	.30	.10
❑ 22 Blake Williams	.20	.07
❑ 23 Josh Bard	.20	.07
❑ 24 Josh Beckett	.30	.10
❑ 25 Tommy Whiteman	.20	.07
❑ 26 Matt Childers	.20	.07
❑ 27 Adam Everett	.20	.07
❑ 28 Mike Bordick	.30	.10
❑ 29 Antonio Alfonseca	.20	.07
❑ 30 Doug Creek	.20	.07
❑ 31 J.D. Drew	.30	.10
❑ 32 Milton Bradley	.30	.10
❑ 33 David Wells	.30	.10
❑ 34 Vance Wilson	.20	.07
❑ 35 Jeff Fassero	.20	.07
❑ 36 Sandy Alomar Jr.	.20	.07
❑ 37 Ryan Vogelsong	.20	.07
❑ 38 Roger Clemens	1.50	.60
❑ 39 Juan Gonzalez	.30	.10
❑ 40 Dustin Hermanson	.20	.07
❑ 41 Andy Ashby	.20	.07
❑ 42 Adam Hyzdu	.20	.07
❑ 43 Ben Broussard	.20	.07
❑ 44 Ryan Klesko	.30	.10
❑ 45 Chris Buglovsky FY RC	.40	.15
❑ 46 Bud Smith	.20	.07
❑ 47 Aaron Boone	.30	.10
❑ 48 Cliff Floyd	.30	.10
❑ 49 Alex Cora	.20	.07
❑ 50 Curt Schilling	.30	.10
❑ 51 Michael Cuddyer	.20	.07
❑ 52 Joe Valentine FY RC	.40	.15
❑ 53 Carlos Guillen	.30	.10
❑ 54 Angel Berroa	.20	.07
❑ 55 Eli Marrero	.20	.07
❑ 56 A.J. Burnett	.30	.10
❑ 57 Oliver Perez	.30	.10
❑ 58 Matt Morris	.30	.10
❑ 59 Valerio De Los Santos	.20	.07
❑ 60 Austin Kearns	.20	.07
❑ 61 Darren Dreifort	.20	.07
❑ 62 Jason Standridge	.20	.07
❑ 63 Carlos Silva	.20	.07
❑ 64 Moises Alou	.30	.10
❑ 65 Jason Anderson	.20	.07
❑ 66 Russell Branyan	.20	.07
❑ 67 B.J. Ryan	.20	.07
❑ 68 Cory Aldridge	.20	.07
❑ 69 Ellis Burks	.30	.10
❑ 70 Troy Glaus	.30	.10
❑ 71 Kelly Wunsch	.20	.07
❑ 72 Brad Wilkerson	.20	.07
❑ 73 Jayson Durocher	.20	.07
❑ 74 Tony Fiore	.20	.07
❑ 75 Brian Giles	.30	.10
❑ 76 Billy Wagner	.30	.10
❑ 77 Neifi Perez	.20	.07
❑ 78 Jose Valverde	.20	.07
❑ 79 Brent Butler	.20	.07
❑ 80 Mario Ramos	.20	.07
❑ 81 Kerry Robinson	.20	.07
❑ 82 Brent Mayne	.20	.07
❑ 83 Sean Casey	.30	.10
❑ 84 Danys Baez	.20	.07
❑ 85 Chase Utley	.75	.30

❑ 86	Jared Sandberg	.20	.07
❑ 87	Terrence Long	.20	.07
❑ 88	Kevin Walker	.20	.07
❑ 89	Royce Clayton	.20	.07
❑ 90	Shea Hillenbrand	.30	.10
❑ 91	Brad Lidge	.30	.10
❑ 92	Shawn Chacon	.20	.07
❑ 93	Kenny Rogers	.30	.10
❑ 94	Chris Snelling	.20	.07
❑ 95	Omar Vizquel	.50	.20
❑ 96	Joe Borchard	.20	.07
❑ 97	Matt Belisle	.20	.07
❑ 98	Steve Smyth	.20	.07
❑ 99	Raul Mondesi	.30	.10
❑ 100	Chipper Jones	.75	.30
❑ 101	Victor Alvarez	.20	.07
❑ 102	J.M. Gold	.20	.07
❑ 103	Willis Roberts	.20	.07
❑ 104	Eddie Guardado	.20	.07
❑ 105	Brad Voyles	.20	.07
❑ 106	Bronson Arroyo	.30	.10
❑ 107	Juan Castro	.20	.07
❑ 108	Dan Plesac	.20	.07
❑ 109	Ramon Castro	.20	.07
❑ 110	Tim Salmon	.50	.20
❑ 111	Gene Kingsale	.20	.07
❑ 112	J.D. Closser	.20	.07
❑ 113	Mark Buehrle	.30	.10
❑ 114	Steve Karsay	.20	.07
❑ 115	Cristian Guerrero	.20	.07
❑ 116	Brad Ausmus	.30	.10
❑ 117	Cristian Guzman	.20	.07
❑ 118	Dan Wilson	.20	.07
❑ 119	Jake Westbrook	.20	.07
❑ 120	Manny Ramirez	.50	.20
❑ 121	Jason Giambi	.30	.10
❑ 122	Bob Wickman	.20	.07
❑ 123	Aaron Cook	.20	.07
❑ 124	Alfredo Amezaga	.20	.07
❑ 125	Corey Thurman	.20	.07
❑ 126	Brandon Puffer	.20	.07
❑ 127	Hee Seop Choi	.20	.07
❑ 128	Javier Vazquez	.30	.10
❑ 129	Carlos Valderrama	.20	.07
❑ 130	Jerome Williams	.20	.07
❑ 131	Wilson Betemit	.20	.07
❑ 132	Luke Prokopec	.20	.07
❑ 133	Esteban Yan	.20	.07
❑ 134	Brandon Berger	.20	.07
❑ 135	Bill Hall	.20	.07
❑ 136	LaTroy Hawkins	.20	.07
❑ 137	Nate Cornejo	.20	.07
❑ 138	Jim Mecir	.20	.07
❑ 139	Joe Crede	.30	.10
❑ 140	Andres Galarraga	.30	.10
❑ 141	Reggie Sanders	.30	.10
❑ 142	Joey Eischen	.20	.07
❑ 143	Mike Timlin	.20	.07
❑ 144	Jose Cruz Jr.	.20	.07
❑ 145	Wes Helms	.20	.07
❑ 146	Brian Roberts	.30	.10
❑ 147	Bret Prinz	.20	.07
❑ 148	Brian Hunter	.20	.07
❑ 149	Chad Hermansen	.20	.07
❑ 150	Andruw Jones	.50	.20
❑ 151	Kurt Ainsworth	.20	.07
❑ 152	Cliff Bartosh	.20	.07
❑ 153	Kyle Lohse	.20	.07
❑ 154	Brian Jordan	.30	.10
❑ 155	Coco Crisp	.50	.20
❑ 156	Tomas Perez	.20	.07
❑ 157	Keith Foulke	.30	.10
❑ 158	Chris Carpenter	.30	.10
❑ 159	Mike Remlinger	.20	.07
❑ 160	Dewon Brazelton	.20	.07
❑ 161	Brook Fordyce	.20	.07
❑ 162	Rusty Greer	.30	.10
❑ 163	Scott Downs	.20	.07
❑ 164	Jason Dubois	.20	.07
❑ 165	David Coggin	.20	.07
❑ 166	Mike DeJean	.20	.07
❑ 167	Carlos Hernandez	.20	.07
❑ 168	Matt Williams	.30	.10
❑ 169	Rheal Cormier	.20	.07
❑ 170	Duaner Sanchez	.20	.07
❑ 171	Craig Counsell	.20	.07
❑ 172	Edgar Martinez	.50	.20
❑ 173	Zack Greinke	.30	.10
❑ 174	Pedro Feliz	.20	.07
❑ 175	Randy Choate	.20	.07
❑ 176	Jon Garland	.30	.10
❑ 177	Keith Ginter	.20	.07
❑ 178	Carlos Febles	.20	.07
❑ 179	Kerry Wood	.30	.10
❑ 180	Jack Cust	.20	.07
❑ 181	Koyie Hill	.20	.07
❑ 182	Ricky Gutierrez	.20	.07
❑ 183	Ben Grieve	.20	.07
❑ 184	Scott Eyre	.20	.07
❑ 185	Jason Isringhausen	.30	.10
❑ 186	Gookie Dawkins	.20	.07
❑ 187	Roberto Alomar	.50	.20
❑ 188	Eric Junge	.20	.07
❑ 189	Carlos Beltran	.30	.10
❑ 190	Denny Hocking	.20	.07
❑ 191	Jason Schmidt	.30	.10
❑ 192	Cory Lidle	.20	.07
❑ 193	Rob Mackowiak	.20	.07
❑ 194	Charlton Jimerson RC	.40	.15
❑ 195	Darin Erstad	.30	.10
❑ 196	Jason Davis	.20	.07
❑ 197	Luis Castillo	.20	.07
❑ 198	Juan Encarnacion	.20	.07
❑ 199	Jeffrey Hammonds	.20	.07
❑ 200	Nomar Garciaparra	1.25	.50
❑ 201	Ryan Christianson	.20	.07
❑ 202	Robert Person	.20	.07
❑ 203	Damian Moss	.20	.07
❑ 204	Chris Richard	.20	.07
❑ 205	Todd Hundley	.20	.07
❑ 206	Paul Bako	.20	.07
❑ 207	Adam Kennedy	.20	.07
❑ 208	Scott Hatteberg	.20	.07
❑ 209	Andy Pratt	.20	.07
❑ 210	Ken Griffey Jr.	1.25	.50
❑ 211	Chris George	.20	.07
❑ 212	Lance Niekro	.20	.07
❑ 213	Greg Colbrunn	.20	.07
❑ 214	Herbert Perry	.20	.07
❑ 215	Cody Ransom	.20	.07
❑ 216	Craig Biggio	.50	.20
❑ 217	Miguel Batista	.20	.07
❑ 218	Alex Escobar	.20	.07
❑ 219	Willie Harris	.20	.07
❑ 220	Scott Strickland	.20	.07
❑ 221	Felix Rodriguez	.20	.07
❑ 222	Torii Hunter	.30	.10
❑ 223	Tyler Houston	.20	.07
❑ 224	Darrell May	.20	.07
❑ 225	Benito Santiago	.30	.10
❑ 226	Ryan Dempster	.20	.07
❑ 227	Andy Fox	.20	.07
❑ 228	Jung Bong	.20	.07
❑ 229	Jose Macias	.20	.07
❑ 230	Shannon Stewart	.30	.10
❑ 231	Buddy Groom	.20	.07
❑ 232	Eric Valent	.20	.07
❑ 233	Scott Schoenweis	.20	.07
❑ 234	Corey Hart	.20	.07
❑ 235	Brett Tomko	.20	.07
❑ 236	Shane Bazzell RC	.40	.15
❑ 237	Tim Hummel	.20	.07
❑ 238	Matt Stairs	.20	.07
❑ 239	Pete Munro	.20	.07
❑ 240	Ismael Valdes	.20	.07
❑ 241	Brian Fuentes	.20	.07
❑ 242	Cesar Izturis	.20	.07
❑ 243	Mark Bellhorn	.30	.10
❑ 244	Geoff Jenkins	.20	.07
❑ 245	Derek Jeter	2.00	.75
❑ 246	Anderson Machado	.20	.07
❑ 247	Dave Roberts	.20	.07
❑ 248	Jaime Cerda	.20	.07
❑ 249	Woody Williams	.20	.07
❑ 250	Vernon Wells	.30	.10
❑ 251	Jon Lieber	.20	.07
❑ 252	Franklyn German	.20	.07
❑ 253	David Segui	.20	.07
❑ 254	Freddy Garcia	.30	.10
❑ 255	James Baldwin	.20	.07
❑ 256	Tony Alvarez	.20	.07
❑ 257	Walter Young	.20	.07
❑ 258	Alex Herrera	.20	.07
❑ 259	Robert Fick	.20	.07
❑ 260	Rob Bell	.20	.07
❑ 261	Ben Petrick	.20	.07
❑ 262	Dee Brown	.20	.07
❑ 263	Mike Bacsik	.20	.07
❑ 264	Corey Patterson	.20	.07
❑ 265	Marvin Benard	.20	.07
❑ 266	Eddie Rogers	.20	.07
❑ 267	Elio Serrano	.20	.07
❑ 268	D'Angelo Jimenez	.20	.07
❑ 269	Adam Johnson	.20	.07
❑ 270	Gregg Zaun	.20	.07
❑ 271	Nick Johnson	.30	.10
❑ 272	Geoff Goetz	.20	.07
❑ 273	Ryan Drese	.20	.07
❑ 274	Eric Dubose	.20	.07
❑ 275	Barry Zito	.30	.10
❑ 276	Mike Crudale	.20	.07
❑ 277	Paul Byrd	.20	.07
❑ 278	Eric Gagne	.30	.10
❑ 279	Aramis Ramirez	.30	.10
❑ 280	Ray Durham	.30	.10
❑ 281	Tony Graffanino	.20	.07
❑ 282	Jeremy Guthrie	.20	.07
❑ 283	Erik Bedard	.20	.07
❑ 284	Vince Faison	.20	.07
❑ 285	Bobby Kielty	.20	.07
❑ 286	Francis Beltran	.20	.07
❑ 287	Alexis Gomez	.20	.07
❑ 288	Vladimir Guerrero	.75	.30
❑ 289	Kevin Appier	.30	.10
❑ 290	Gil Meche	.20	.07
❑ 291	Marquis Grissom	.30	.10
❑ 292	John Burkett	.20	.07
❑ 293	Vinny Castilla	.30	.10
❑ 294	Tyler Walker	.20	.07
❑ 295	Shane Halter	.20	.07
❑ 296	Geronimo Gil	.20	.07
❑ 297	Eric Hinske	.20	.07
❑ 298	Adam Dunn	.30	.10
❑ 299	Mike Kinkade	.20	.07
❑ 300	Mark Prior	.50	.20
❑ 301	Corey Koskie	.20	.07
❑ 302	David Dellucci	.20	.07
❑ 303	Todd Helton	.50	.20
❑ 304	Greg Miller	.20	.07
❑ 305	Delvin James	.20	.07
❑ 306	Humberto Cota	.20	.07
❑ 307	Aaron Harang	.20	.07
❑ 308	Jeremy Hill	.20	.07
❑ 309	Billy Koch	.20	.07
❑ 310	Brandon Claussen	.20	.07
❑ 311	Matt Ginter	.20	.07
❑ 312	Jason Lane	.20	.07
❑ 313	Ben Weber	.20	.07
❑ 314	Alan Benes	.20	.07
❑ 315	Matt Walbeck	.20	.07
❑ 316	Danny Graves	.20	.07
❑ 317	Jason Johnson	.20	.07
❑ 318	Jason Grimsley	.20	.07
❑ 319	Steve Kline	.20	.07
❑ 320	Johnny Damon	.50	.20
❑ 321	Jay Gibbons	.20	.07
❑ 322	J.J. Putz	.20	.07
❑ 323	Stephen Randolph RC	.40	.15
❑ 324	Bobby Higginson	.30	.10
❑ 325	Kazuhisa Ishii	.30	.10
❑ 326	Carlos Lee	.30	.10
❑ 327	J.R. House	.20	.07
❑ 328	Mark Loretta	.20	.07
❑ 329	Mike Matheny	.20	.07
❑ 330	Ben Diggins	.20	.07
❑ 331	Seth Etherton	.20	.07
❑ 332	Eli Whiteside FY RC	.40	.15
❑ 333	Juan Rivera	.20	.07
❑ 334	Jeff Conine	.30	.10
❑ 335	John McDonald	.20	.07
❑ 336	Erik Hiljus	.20	.07
❑ 337	David Eckstein	.30	.10
❑ 338	Jeff Bagwell	.50	.20
❑ 339	Matt Holliday	.25	.08
❑ 340	Jeff Liefer	.20	.07
❑ 341	Greg Myers	.20	.07
❑ 342	Scott Sauerbeck	.20	.07
❑ 343	Omar Infante	.20	.07

- ❑ 344 Ryan Langerhans .30 .10
- ❑ 345 Abraham Nunez .20 .07
- ❑ 346 Mike MacDougal .20 .07
- ❑ 347 Travis Phelps .20 .07
- ❑ 348 Terry Shumpert .20 .07
- ❑ 349 Alex Rodriguez 1.25 .50
- ❑ 350 Bobby Seay .20 .07
- ❑ 351 Ichiro Suzuki 1.50 .60
- ❑ 352 Brandon Inge .20 .07
- ❑ 353 Jack Wilson .20 .07
- ❑ 354 John Ennis .20 .07
- ❑ 355 Jamal Strong .20 .07
- ❑ 356 Jason Jennings .20 .07
- ❑ 357 Jeff Kent .30 .10
- ❑ 358 Scott Chiasson .20 .07
- ❑ 359 Jeremy Griffiths RC .40 .15
- ❑ 360 Paul Konerko .30 .10
- ❑ 361 Jeff Austin .20 .07
- ❑ 362 Todd Van Poppel .20 .07
- ❑ 363 Sun Woo Kim .20 .07
- ❑ 364 Jerry Hairston Jr.. .20 .07
- ❑ 365 Tony Torcato .20 .07
- ❑ 366 Arthur Rhodes .20 .07
- ❑ 367 Jose Jimenez .20 .07
- ❑ 368 Matt LeCroy .20 .07
- ❑ 369 Curtis Leskanic .20 .07
- ❑ 370 Ramon Vazquez .20 .07
- ❑ 371 Joe Randa .30 .10
- ❑ 372 John Franco .30 .10
- ❑ 373 Bobby Estalella .20 .07
- ❑ 374 Craig Wilson .20 .07
- ❑ 375 Michael Young .50 .20
- ❑ 376 Mark Ellis .20 .07
- ❑ 377 Joe Mauer .75 .30
- ❑ 378 Checklist 1 .20 .07
- ❑ 379 Jason Kendall .30 .10
- ❑ 380 Checklist 2 .20 .07
- ❑ 381 Alex Gonzalez .20 .07
- ❑ 382 Tom Gordon .20 .07
- ❑ 383 John Buck .20 .07
- ❑ 384 Shigetoshi Hasegawa .30 .10
- ❑ 385 Scott Stewart .20 .07
- ❑ 386 Luke Hudson .20 .07
- ❑ 387 Todd Jones .20 .07
- ❑ 388 Fred McGriff .50 .20
- ❑ 389 Mike Sweeney .30 .10
- ❑ 390 Marlon Anderson .20 .07
- ❑ 391 Terry Adams .20 .07
- ❑ 392 Mark DeRosa .20 .07
- ❑ 393 Doug Mientkiewicz .30 .10
- ❑ 394 Miguel Cairo .20 .07
- ❑ 395 Jamie Moyer .30 .10
- ❑ 396 Jose Leon .20 .07
- ❑ 397 Matt Clement .30 .10
- ❑ 398 Bengie Molina .20 .07
- ❑ 399 Marcus Thames .20 .07
- ❑ 400 Nick Bierbrodt .20 .07
- ❑ 401 Tim Kalita .20 .07
- ❑ 402 Corwin Malone .20 .07
- ❑ 403 Jesse Orosco .20 .07
- ❑ 404 Brandon Phillips .20 .07
- ❑ 405 Eric Cyr .20 .07
- ❑ 406 Jason Michaels .20 .07
- ❑ 407 Julio Lugo .20 .07
- ❑ 408 Gabe Kapler .30 .10
- ❑ 409 Mark Mulder .30 .10
- ❑ 410 Adam Eaton .20 .07
- ❑ 411 Ken Harvey .20 .07
- ❑ 412 Jolbert Cabrera .20 .07
- ❑ 413 Eric Milton .20 .07
- ❑ 414 Josh Hall RC .40 .15
- ❑ 415 Bob File .20 .07
- ❑ 416 Brett Evert .20 .07
- ❑ 417 Ron Chiavacci .20 .07
- ❑ 418 Jorge De La Rosa .20 .07
- ❑ 419 Quinton McCracken .20 .07
- ❑ 420 Luther Hackman .20 .07
- ❑ 421 Gary Knotts .20 .07
- ❑ 422 Kevin Brown .30 .10
- ❑ 423 Jeff Cirillo .20 .07
- ❑ 424 Damaso Marte .20 .07
- ❑ 425 Chan Ho Park .30 .10
- ❑ 426 Nathan Haynes .20 .07
- ❑ 427 Matt Lawton .20 .07
- ❑ 428 Mike Stanton .20 .07
- ❑ 429 Bernie Williams .50 .20
- ❑ 430 Kevin Jarvis .20 .07
- ❑ 431 Joe McEwing .20 .07
- ❑ 432 Mark Kotsay .30 .10
- ❑ 433 Juan Cruz .20 .07
- ❑ 434 Russ Ortiz .20 .07
- ❑ 435 Jeff Nelson .20 .07
- ❑ 436 Alan Embree .20 .07
- ❑ 437 Miguel Tejada .30 .10
- ❑ 438 Kirk Saarloos .20 .07
- ❑ 439 Cliff Lee .20 .07
- ❑ 440 Ryan Ludwick .20 .07
- ❑ 441 Derrek Lee .50 .20
- ❑ 442 Bobby Abreu .30 .10
- ❑ 443 Dustan Mohr .20 .07
- ❑ 444 Nook Logan RC .50 .20
- ❑ 445 Seth McClung .20 .07
- ❑ 446 Miguel Olivo .20 .07
- ❑ 447 Henry Blanco .20 .07
- ❑ 448 Seung Song .20 .07
- ❑ 449 Kris Wilson .20 .07
- ❑ 450 Xavier Nady .20 .07
- ❑ 451 Corky Miller .20 .07
- ❑ 452 Jim Thome .50 .20
- ❑ 453 George Lombard .20 .07
- ❑ 454 Rey Ordonez .20 .07
- ❑ 455 Deivis Santos .20 .07
- ❑ 456 Mike Myers .20 .07
- ❑ 457 Edgar Renteria .30 .10
- ❑ 458 Braden Looper .20 .07
- ❑ 459 Guillermo Mota .20 .07
- ❑ 460 Scott Rolen .50 .20
- ❑ 461 Lance Berkman .30 .10
- ❑ 462 Jeff Heaverlo .20 .07
- ❑ 463 Ramon Hernandez .20 .07
- ❑ 464 Jason Simontacchi .20 .07
- ❑ 465 So Taguchi .30 .10
- ❑ 466 Dave Veres .20 .07
- ❑ 467 Shane Loux .20 .07
- ❑ 468 Rodrigo Lopez .20 .07
- ❑ 469 Bubba Trammell .20 .07
- ❑ 470 Scott Sullivan .20 .07
- ❑ 471 Mike Mussina .50 .20
- ❑ 472 Ramon Ortiz .20 .07
- ❑ 473 Lyle Overbay .20 .07
- ❑ 474 Mike Lowell .30 .10
- ❑ 475 Al Martin .20 .07
- ❑ 476 Larry Bigbie .20 .07
- ❑ 477 Rey Sanchez .20 .07
- ❑ 478 Magglio Ordonez .30 .10
- ❑ 479 Rondell White .30 .10
- ❑ 480 Jay Witasick .20 .07
- ❑ 481 Jimmy Rollins .30 .10
- ❑ 482 Mike Maroth .20 .07
- ❑ 483 Alejandro Machado .20 .07
- ❑ 484 Nick Neugebauer .20 .07
- ❑ 485 Victor Zambrano .20 .07
- ❑ 486 Travis Lee .20 .07
- ❑ 487 Bobby Bradley .20 .07
- ❑ 488 Marcus Giles .30 .10
- ❑ 489 Steve Trachsel .20 .07
- ❑ 490 Derek Lowe .30 .10
- ❑ 491 Hideo Nomo .75 .30
- ❑ 492 Brad Hawpe .30 .10
- ❑ 493 Jesus Medrano .20 .07
- ❑ 494 Rick Ankiel .20 .07
- ❑ 495 Pasqual Coco .20 .07
- ❑ 496 Michael Barrett .20 .07
- ❑ 497 Joe Beimel .20 .07
- ❑ 498 Marty Cordova .20 .07
- ❑ 499 Aaron Sele .20 .07
- ❑ 500 Sammy Sosa .75 .30
- ❑ 501 Ivan Rodriguez .50 .20
- ❑ 502 Keith Osik .20 .07
- ❑ 503 Hank Blalock .30 .10
- ❑ 504 Hiram Bocachica .20 .07
- ❑ 505 Junior Spivey .20 .07
- ❑ 506 Edgardo Alfonzo .20 .07
- ❑ 507 Alex Graman .20 .07
- ❑ 508 J.J. Davis .20 .07
- ❑ 509 Roger Cedeno .20 .07
- ❑ 510 Joe Roa .20 .07
- ❑ 511 Wily Mo Pena .30 .10
- ❑ 512 Eric Munson .20 .07
- ❑ 513 Arnie Munoz RC .40 .15
- ❑ 514 Albie Lopez .20 .07
- ❑ 515 Andy Pettitte .50 .20
- ❑ 516 Jim Edmonds .30 .10
- ❑ 517 Jeff Davanon .20 .07
- ❑ 518 Aaron Myette .20 .07
- ❑ 519 C.C. Sabathia .30 .10
- ❑ 520 Gerardo Garcia .20 .07
- ❑ 521 Brian Schneider .20 .07
- ❑ 522 Wes Obermueller .20 .07
- ❑ 523 John Mabry .20 .07
- ❑ 524 Casey Fossum .20 .07
- ❑ 525 Toby Hall .20 .07
- ❑ 526 Denny Neagle .20 .07
- ❑ 527 Willie Bloomquist .30 .10
- ❑ 528 A.J. Pierzynski .30 .10
- ❑ 529 Bartolo Colon .30 .10
- ❑ 530 Chad Harville .20 .07
- ❑ 531 Blaine Neal .20 .07
- ❑ 532 Luis Terrero .20 .07
- ❑ 533 Reggie Taylor .20 .07
- ❑ 534 Melvin Mora .30 .10
- ❑ 535 Tino Martinez .50 .20
- ❑ 536 Peter Bergeron .20 .07
- ❑ 537 Jorge Padilla .20 .07
- ❑ 538 Oscar Villarreal RC .40 .15
- ❑ 539 David Weathers .20 .07
- ❑ 540 Mike Lamb .20 .07
- ❑ 541 Greg Norton .20 .07
- ❑ 542 Michael Tucker .20 .07
- ❑ 543 Ben Kozlowski .20 .07
- ❑ 544 Alex Sanchez .20 .07
- ❑ 545 Trey Lunsford .20 .07
- ❑ 546 Abraham Nunez .20 .07
- ❑ 547 Mike Lincoln .20 .07
- ❑ 548 Orlando Hernandez .30 .10
- ❑ 549 Kevin Mench .20 .07
- ❑ 550 Garret Anderson .30 .10
- ❑ 551 Kyle Farnsworth .20 .07
- ❑ 552 Kevin Olsen .20 .07
- ❑ 553 Joel Pineiro .20 .07
- ❑ 554 Jorge Julio .20 .07
- ❑ 555 Jose Mesa .20 .07
- ❑ 556 Jorge Posada .50 .20
- ❑ 557 Jose Ortiz .20 .07
- ❑ 558 Mike Tonis .20 .07
- ❑ 559 Gabe White .20 .07
- ❑ 560 Rafael Furcal .30 .10
- ❑ 561 Matt Franco .20 .07
- ❑ 562 Trey Hodges .20 .07
- ❑ 563 Esteban German .20 .07
- ❑ 564 Josh Fogg .20 .07
- ❑ 565 Fernando Tatis .20 .07
- ❑ 566 Alex Cintron .20 .07
- ❑ 567 Grant Roberts .20 .07
- ❑ 568 Gene Stechschulte .20 .07
- ❑ 569 Rafael Palmeiro .50 .20
- ❑ 570 Mike Hampton .30 .10
- ❑ 571 Ben Davis .20 .07
- ❑ 572 Dean Palmer .30 .10
- ❑ 573 Jerrod Riggan .20 .07
- ❑ 574 Nate Frese .20 .07
- ❑ 575 Josh Phelps .20 .07
- ❑ 576 Freddie Bynum .20 .07
- ❑ 577 Morgan Ensberg .30 .10
- ❑ 578 Juan Rincon .20 .07
- ❑ 579 Kazuhiro Sasaki .30 .10
- ❑ 580 Yorvit Torrealba .20 .07
- ❑ 581 Tim Wakefield .30 .10
- ❑ 582 Sterling Hitchcock .20 .07
- ❑ 583 Craig Paquette .20 .07
- ❑ 584 Kevin Millwood .30 .10
- ❑ 585 Damian Rolls .20 .07
- ❑ 586 Brad Baisley .20 .07
- ❑ 587 Kyle Snyder .20 .07
- ❑ 588 Paul Quantrill .20 .07
- ❑ 589 Trot Nixon .30 .10
- ❑ 590 J.T. Snow .30 .10
- ❑ 591 Kevin Young .20 .07
- ❑ 592 Tomo Ohka .20 .07
- ❑ 593 Brian Boehringer .20 .07
- ❑ 594 Danny Patterson .20 .07
- ❑ 595 Jeff Tam .20 .07
- ❑ 596 Anastacio Martinez .20 .07
- ❑ 597 Rod Barajas .20 .07
- ❑ 598 Octavio Dotel .20 .07
- ❑ 599 Jason Tyner .20 .07
- ❑ 600 Gary Sheffield .30 .10
- ❑ 601 Ruben Quevedo .20 .07

❑	602	Jay Payton	.20	.07
❑	603	Mo Vaughn	.30	.10
❑	604	Pat Burrell	.30	.10
❑	605	Fernando Vina	.20	.07
❑	606	Wes Anderson	.20	.07
❑	607	Alex Gonzalez	.20	.07
❑	608	Ted Lilly	.20	.07
❑	609	Nick Punto	.20	.07
❑	610	Ryan Madson	.20	.07
❑	611	Odalis Perez	.20	.07
❑	612	Chris Woodward	.20	.07
❑	613	John Olerud	.30	.10
❑	614	Brad Cresse	.20	.07
❑	615	Chad Zerbe	.20	.07
❑	616	Brad Penny	.20	.07
❑	617	Barry Larkin	.50	.20
❑	618	Brandon Duckworth	.20	.07
❑	619	Brad Radke	.30	.10
❑	620	Troy Brohawn	.20	.07
❑	621	Juan Pierre	.30	.10
❑	622	Rick Reed	.20	.07
❑	623	Omar Daal	.20	.07
❑	624	Jose Hernandez	.20	.07
❑	625	Greg Maddux	1.25	.50
❑	626	Henry Mateo	.20	.07
❑	627	Kip Wells	.20	.07
❑	628	Kevin Cash	.20	.07
❑	629	Wil Ledezma FY RC	.40	.15
❑	630	Luis Gonzalez	.30	.10
❑	631	Jason Conti	.20	.07
❑	632	Ricardo Rincon	.20	.07
❑	633	Mike Bynum	.20	.07
❑	634	Mike Redmond	.20	.07
❑	635	Chance Caple	.20	.07
❑	636	Chris Widger	.20	.07
❑	637	Michael Restovich	.20	.07
❑	638	Mark Grudzielanek	.20	.07
❑	639	Brandon Larson	.20	.07
❑	640	Rocco Baldelli	.30	.10
❑	641	Javy Lopez	.30	.10
❑	642	Rene Reyes	.20	.07
❑	643	Orlando Merced	.20	.07
❑	644	Jason Phillips	.20	.07
❑	645	Luis Ugueto	.20	.07
❑	646	Ron Calloway	.20	.07
❑	647	Josh Paul	.20	.07
❑	648	Todd Greene	.20	.07
❑	649	Joe Girardi	.20	.07
❑	650	Todd Ritchie	.20	.07
❑	651	Kevin Millar Sox	.30	.10
❑	652	Shawn Wooten	.20	.07
❑	653	David Riske	.20	.07
❑	654	Luis Rivas	.20	.07
❑	655	Roy Halladay	.30	.10
❑	656	Travis Driskill	.20	.07
❑	657	Ricky Ledee	.20	.07
❑	658	Timo Perez	.20	.07
❑	659	Fernando Rodney	.20	.07
❑	660	Trevor Hoffman	.30	.10
❑	661	Pat Hentgen	.30	.10
❑	662	Bret Boone	.30	.10
❑	663	Ryan Jensen	.20	.07
❑	664	Ricardo Rodriguez	.20	.07
❑	665	Jeremy Lambert	.20	.07
❑	666	Troy Percival	.30	.10
❑	667	Jon Rauch	.20	.07
❑	668	Mariano Rivera	.75	.30
❑	669	Jason LaRue	.20	.07
❑	670	J.C. Romero	.20	.07
❑	671	Cody Ross	.20	.07
❑	672	Eric Byrnes	.20	.07
❑	673	Paul Lo Duca	.30	.10
❑	674	Brad Fullmer	.20	.07
❑	675	Cliff Politte	.20	.07
❑	676	Justin Miller	.20	.07
❑	677	Nic Jackson	.20	.07
❑	678	Kris Benson	.20	.07
❑	679	Carl Sadler	.20	.07
❑	680	Joe Nathan	.30	.10
❑	681	Julio Santana	.20	.07
❑	682	Wade Miller	.20	.07
❑	683	Josh Pearce	.20	.07
❑	684	Tony Armas Jr.	.20	.07
❑	685	Al Leiter	.30	.10
❑	686	Raul Ibanez	.20	.07
❑	687	Danny Bautista	.20	.07
❑	688	Travis Hafner	.30	.10
❑	689	Carlos Zambrano	.30	.10
❑	690	Pedro Martinez	.50	.20
❑	691	Ramon Santiago	.20	.07
❑	692	Felipe Lopez	.20	.07
❑	693	David Ross	.20	.07
❑	694	Chone Figgins	.20	.07
❑	695	Antonio Osuna	.20	.07
❑	696	Jay Powell	.20	.07
❑	697	Ryan Church	.30	.10
❑	698	Alexis Rios	.30	.10
❑	699	Tanyon Sturtze	.20	.07
❑	700	Turk Wendell	.20	.07
❑	701	Richard Hidalgo	.20	.07
❑	702	Joe Mays	.20	.07
❑	703	Jorge Sosa	.20	.07
❑	704	Eric Karros	.30	.10
❑	705	Steve Finley	.30	.10
❑	706	Sean Smith FY RC	.50	.20
❑	707	Jeremy Giambi	.20	.07
❑	708	Scott Hodges	.20	.07
❑	709	Vicente Padilla	.20	.07
❑	710	Erubiel Durazo	.20	.07
❑	711	Aaron Rowand	.30	.10
❑	712	Dennis Tankersley	.20	.07
❑	713	Rick Bauer	.20	.07
❑	714	Tim Olson FY RC	.40	.15
❑	715	Jeff Urban	.20	.07
❑	716	Steve Sparks	.20	.07
❑	717	Glendon Rusch	.20	.07
❑	718	Ricky Stone	.20	.07
❑	719	Benji Gil	.20	.07
❑	720	Pete Walker	.20	.07
❑	721	Tim Worrell	.20	.07
❑	722	Michael Tejera	.20	.07
❑	723	David Kelton	.20	.07
❑	724	Britt Reames	.20	.07
❑	725	John Stephens	.20	.07
❑	726	Mark McLemore	.20	.07
❑	727	Jeff Zimmerman	.20	.07
❑	728	Checklist 3	.20	.07
❑	729	Andres Torres	.20	.07
❑	730	Checklist 4	.20	.07
❑	731	Johan Santana	.50	.20
❑	732	Dane Sardinha	.20	.07
❑	733	Rodrigo Rosario	.20	.07
❑	734	Frank Thomas	.75	.30
❑	735	Tom Glavine	.50	.20
❑	736	Doug Mirabelli	.20	.07
❑	737	Juan Uribe	.20	.07
❑	738	Ryan Anderson	.20	.07
❑	739	Sean Burroughs	.20	.07
❑	740	Eric Chavez	.30	.10
❑	741	Enrique Wilson	.20	.07
❑	742	Elmer Dessens	.20	.07
❑	743	Marlon Byrd	.20	.07
❑	744	Brendan Donnelly	.20	.07
❑	745	Gary Bennett	.20	.07
❑	746	Roy Oswalt	.30	.10
❑	747	Andy Van Hekken	.20	.07
❑	748	Jesus Colome	.20	.07
❑	749	Erick Almonte	.20	.07
❑	750	Frank Catalanotto	.20	.07
❑	751	Kenny Lofton	.30	.10
❑	752	Carlos Delgado	.30	.10
❑	753	Ryan Franklin	.20	.07
❑	754	Wilkin Ruan	.20	.07
❑	755	Kelvim Escobar	.20	.07
❑	756	Tim Drew	.20	.07
❑	757	Jarrod Washburn	.20	.07
❑	758	Runelvys Hernandez	.20	.07
❑	759	Cory Vance	.20	.07
❑	760	Doug Glanville	.20	.07
❑	761	Ryan Rupe	.20	.07
❑	762	Jermaine Dye	.30	.10
❑	763	Mike Cameron	.20	.07
❑	764	Scott Erickson	.20	.07
❑	765	Richie Sexson	.30	.10
❑	766	Jose Vidro	.20	.07
❑	767	Brian West	.20	.07
❑	768	Shawn Estes	.20	.07
❑	769	Brian Tallet	.20	.07
❑	770	Larry Walker	.30	.10
❑	771	Josh Hamilton	.20	.07
❑	772	Orlando Hudson	.20	.07
❑	773	Justin Morneau	.30	.10
❑	774	Ryan Bukvich	.20	.07
❑	775	Mike Gonzalez	.20	.07
❑	776	Tsuyoshi Shinjo	.30	.10
❑	777	Matt Mantei	.20	.07
❑	778	Jimmy Journell	.20	.07
❑	779	Brian Lawrence	.20	.07
❑	780	Mike Lieberthal	.30	.10
❑	781	Scott Mullen	.20	.07
❑	782	Zach Day	.20	.07
❑	783	John Thomson	.20	.07
❑	784	Ben Sheets	.30	.10
❑	785	Damon Minor	.20	.07
❑	786	Jose Valentin	.20	.07
❑	787	Armando Benitez	.20	.07
❑	788	Jamie Walker RC	.25	.08
❑	789	Preston Wilson	.30	.10
❑	790	Josh Wilson	.20	.07
❑	791	Phil Nevin	.30	.10
❑	792	Roberto Hernandez	.20	.07
❑	793	Mike Williams	.20	.07
❑	794	Jake Peavy	.30	.10
❑	795	Paul Shuey	.20	.07
❑	796	Chad Bradford	.20	.07
❑	797	Bobby Jenks	.30	.10
❑	798	Sean Douglass	.20	.07
❑	799	Damian Miller	.20	.07
❑	800	Mark Wohlers	.20	.07
❑	801	Ty Wigginton	.20	.07
❑	802	Alfonso Soriano	.30	.10
❑	803	Randy Johnson	.75	.30
❑	804	Placido Polanco	.20	.07
❑	805	Drew Henson	.20	.07
❑	806	Tony Womack	.20	.07
❑	807	Pokey Reese	.20	.07
❑	808	Albert Pujols	1.50	.60
❑	809	Henri Stanley	.20	.07
❑	810	Mike Rivera	.20	.07
❑	811	John Lackey	.20	.07
❑	812	Brian Wright FY RC	.40	.15
❑	813	Eric Good	.20	.07
❑	814	Dernell Stenson	.20	.07
❑	815	Kirk Rueter	.20	.07
❑	816	Todd Zeile	.20	.07
❑	817	Brad Thomas	.20	.07
❑	818	Shawn Sedlacek	.20	.07
❑	819	Garrett Stephenson	.20	.07
❑	820	Mark Teixeira	.50	.20
❑	821	Tim Hudson	.30	.10
❑	822	Mike Koplove	.20	.07
❑	823	Chris Reitsma	.20	.07
❑	824	Rafael Soriano	.20	.07
❑	825	Ugueth Urbina	.20	.07
❑	826	Lance Carter	.20	.07
❑	827	Colin Young	.20	.07
❑	828	Pat Strange	.20	.07
❑	829	Juan Pena	.20	.07
❑	830	Joe Thurston	.20	.07
❑	831	Shawn Green	.30	.10
❑	832	Pedro Astacio	.20	.07
❑	833	Danny Wright	.20	.07
❑	834	Wes O'Brien FY RC	.40	.15
❑	835	Luis Lopez	.20	.07
❑	836	Randall Simon	.20	.07
❑	837	Jaret Wright	.20	.07
❑	838	Jayson Werth	.20	.07
❑	839	Endy Chavez	.20	.07
❑	840	Checklist 5	.20	.07
❑	841	Chad Paronto	.20	.07
❑	842	Randy Winn	.20	.07
❑	843	Sidney Ponson	.20	.07
❑	844	Robin Ventura	.30	.10
❑	845	Rich Aurilia	.20	.07
❑	846	Joaquin Benoit	.20	.07
❑	847	Barry Bonds	2.00	.75
❑	848	Carl Crawford	.30	.10
❑	849	Jeromy Burnitz	.30	.10
❑	850	Orlando Cabrera	.30	.10
❑	851	Luis Vizcaino	.20	.07
❑	852	Randy Wolf	.20	.07
❑	853	Todd Walker	.20	.07
❑	854	Jeremy Affeldt	.20	.07
❑	855	Einar Diaz	.20	.07
❑	856	Carl Everett	.30	.10
❑	857	Wiki Gonzalez	.20	.07
❑	858	Mike Paradis	.20	.07
❑	859	Travis Harper	.20	.07

❑ 860 Mike Piazza 1.25 .50
❑ 861 Will Ohman .20 .07
❑ 862 Eric Young .20 .07
❑ 863 Jason Grabowski .20 .07
❑ 864 Rett Johnson RC .40 .15
❑ 865 Aubrey Huff .30 .10
❑ 866 John Smoltz .50 .20
❑ 867 Mickey Callaway .20 .07
❑ 868 Joe Kennedy .20 .07
❑ 869 Tim Redding .20 .07
❑ 870 Colby Lewis .20 .07
❑ 871 Salomon Torres .20 .07
❑ 872 Marco Scutaro .20 .07
❑ 873 Tony Batista .20 .07
❑ 874 Dmitri Young .30 .10
❑ 875 Scott Williamson .20 .07
❑ 876 Scott Spiezio .20 .07
❑ 877 John Webb .20 .07
❑ 878 Jose Acevedo .20 .07
❑ 879 Kevin Orie .20 .07
❑ 880 Jacque Jones .30 .10
❑ 881 Ben Francisco FY RC .40 .15
❑ 882 Bobby Basham FY RC .40 .15
❑ 883 Corey Shafer FY RC .40 .15
❑ 884 J.D. Durbin FY RC .40 .15
❑ 885 Chien-Ming Wang FY RC 8.00 3.00
❑ 886 Adam Stern FY RC .25 .08
❑ 887 Wayne Lydon FY RC .40 .15
❑ 888 Derell McCall FY RC .40 .15
❑ 889 Jon Nelson FY RC .50 .20
❑ 890 Willie Eyre FY RC .40 .15
❑ 891 Ramon Nivar-Martinez FY RC .40 .15
❑ 892 Adrian Myers FY RC .25 .08
❑ 893 Jamie Athas FY RC .40 .15
❑ 894 Ismael Castro FY RC .50 .20
❑ 895 David Martinez FY RC .40 .15
❑ 896 Terry Tiffee FY RC .40 .15
❑ 897 Nathan Panther FY RC .40 .15
❑ 898 Kyle Roat FY RC .40 .15
❑ 899 Kason Gabbard FY RC .40 .15
❑ 900 Hanley Ramirez FY RC 4.00 1.50
❑ 901 Bryan Grace FY RC .40 .15
❑ 902 B.J. Barns FY RC .40 .15
❑ 903 Greg Bruso FY RC .40 .15
❑ 904 Mike Neu FY RC .40 .15
❑ 905 Dustin Yount FY RC .50 .20
❑ 906 Shane Victorino FY RC .75 .30
❑ 907 Brian Burgamy FY RC .40 .15
❑ 908 Beau Kemp FY RC .40 .15
❑ 909 David Corrente FY RC .40 .15
❑ 910 Dexter Cooper FY RC .40 .15
❑ 911 Chris Colton FY RC .40 .15
❑ 912 David Cash FY RC .40 .15
❑ 913 Bernie Castro FY RC .40 .15
❑ 914 Luis Hodge FY RC .40 .15
❑ 915 Jeff Clark FY RC .40 .15
❑ 916 Jason Kubel FY RC 1.00 .40
❑ 917 T.J. Bohn FY RC .40 .15
❑ 918 Luke Steidlmayer FY RC .40 .15
❑ 919 Matthew Peterson FY RC .40 .15
❑ 920 Darrell Rasner FY RC .40 .15
❑ 921 Scott Tyler FY RC .50 .20
❑ 922 Gary Schneidmiller FY RC .40 .15
❑ 923 Gregor Blanco FY RC .40 .15
❑ 924 Ryan Cameron FY RC .40 .15
❑ 925 Wilfredo Rodriguez FY .20 .07
❑ 926 Rajai Davis FY RC .40 .15
❑ 927 Evel Bastida-Martinez FY RC .40 .15
❑ 928 Chris Duncan FY RC 4.00 1.50
❑ 929 Dave Pember FY RC .40 .15
❑ 930 Branden Florence FY RC .40 .15
❑ 931 Eric Eckenstahler FY .20 .07
❑ 932 Hong-Chih Kuo FY RC 5.00 2.00
❑ 933 Il Kim FY RC .40 .15
❑ 934 Michael Garciaparra FY RC .40 .15
❑ 935 Kip Bouknight FY RC .50 .20
❑ 936 Gary Harris FY RC .40 .15
❑ 937 Derry Hammond FY RC .40 .15
❑ 938 Joey Gomes FY RC .40 .15
❑ 939 Donnie Hood FY RC .50 .20
❑ 940 Clay Hensley FY RC .40 .15
❑ 941 David Pahucki FY RC .40 .15
❑ 942 Wilton Reynolds FY RC .40 .15
❑ 943 Michael Hinckley FY RC .50 .20
❑ 944 Josh Willingham FY RC 1.00 .40
❑ 945 Pete LaForest FY RC .40 .15
❑ 946 Pete Smart FY RC .40 .15
❑ 947 Jay Sitzman FY RC .40 .15
❑ 948 Mark Malaska FY RC .40 .15
❑ 949 Mike Gallo FY RC .40 .15
❑ 950 Matt Diaz FY RC .75 .30
❑ 951 Brennan King FY RC .40 .15
❑ 952 Ryan Howard FY RC 30.00 12.50
❑ 953 Daryl Clark FY RC .40 .15
❑ 954 Dayton Buller FY RC .40 .15
❑ 955 Rylan Reed FY RC .40 .15
❑ 956 Chris Booker FY .20 .07
❑ 957 Brandon Watson FY RC .40 .15
❑ 958 Matt DeMarco FY RC .40 .15
❑ 959 Doug Waechter FY RC .50 .20
❑ 960 Callix Crabbe FY RC .50 .20
❑ 961 Jairo Garcia FY RC .50 .20
❑ 962 Jason Perry FY RC .50 .20
❑ 963 Eric Riggs FY RC .50 .20
❑ 964 Travis Ishikawa FY RC .75 .30
❑ 965 Simon Pond FY RC .40 .15
❑ 966 Manuel Ramirez FY RC .50 .20
❑ 967 Tyler Johnson FY RC .40 .15
❑ 968 Jaime Bubela FY RC .40 .15
❑ 969 Haj Turay FY RC .25 .08
❑ 970 Tyson Graham FY RC .40 .15
❑ 971 David DeJesus FY RC .75 .30
❑ 972 Franklin Gutierrez FY RC 1.00 .40
❑ 973 Craig Brazell FY RC .40 .15
❑ 974 Keith Stamler FY RC .40 .15
❑ 975 Jemel Spearman FY RC .40 .15
❑ 976 Ozzie Chavez FY RC .40 .15
❑ 977 Nick Trzesniak FY RC .40 .15
❑ 978 Bill Simon FY RC .40 .15
❑ 979 Matthew Hagen FY RC .40 .15
❑ 980 Chris Kroski FY RC .40 .15
❑ 981 Prentice Redman FY RC .40 .15
❑ 982 Kevin Randel FY RC .40 .15
❑ 983 Thomari Story-Harden FY RC .40 .15
❑ 984 Brian Shackelford FY RC .40 .15
❑ 985 Mike Adams FY RC .40 .15
❑ 986 Brian McCann FY RC 5.00 2.00
❑ 987 Mike McNutt FY RC .40 .15
❑ 988 Aron Weston FY RC .40 .15
❑ 989 Dustin Moseley FY RC .40 .15
❑ 990 Bryan Bullington FY RC .40 .15

2004 Topps Total

❑ COMPLETE SET (880) 150.00 75.00
❑ OVERALL PRESS PLATES ODDS 1:159
❑ PLATES PRINT RUN 1 #'d SET PER COLOR
❑ PLATES: BLACK, CYAN, MAGENTA, YELLOW
❑ NO PLATES PRICING DUE TO SCARCITY
❑ 1 Kevin Brown .30 .10
❑ 2 Mike Mordecai .30 .10
❑ 3 Seung Song .30 .10
❑ 4 Mike Maroth .30 .10
❑ 5 Mike Lieberthal .30 .10
❑ 6 Billy Koch .30 .10
❑ 7 Mike Stanton .30 .10
❑ 8 Brad Penny .30 .10
❑ 9 Brooks Kieschnick .30 .10
❑ 10 Carlos Delgado .30 .10
❑ 11 Brady Clark .30 .10
❑ 12 Ramon Martinez .30 .10
❑ 13 Dan Wilson .30 .10
❑ 14 Guillermo Mota .30 .10
❑ 15 Trevor Hoffman .30 .10
❑ 16 Tony Batista .30 .10
❑ 17 Rusty Greer .30 .10
❑ 18 David Weathers .30 .10
❑ 19 Horacio Ramirez .30 .10
❑ 20 Aubrey Huff .30 .10
❑ 21 Casey Blake .30 .10
❑ 22 Ryan Bukvich .30 .10
❑ 23 Garrett Atkins .30 .10
❑ 24 Jose Contreras .30 .10
❑ 25 Chipper Jones .75 .30
❑ 26 Neifi Perez .30 .10
❑ 27 Scott Linebrink .30 .10
❑ 28 Matt Kinney .30 .10
❑ 29 Michael Restovich .30 .10
❑ 30 Scott Rolen .50 .20
❑ 31 John Franco .30 .10
❑ 32 Toby Hall .30 .10
❑ 33 Wily Mo Pena .30 .10
❑ 34 Dennis Tankersley .30 .10
❑ 35 Robb Nen .30 .10
❑ 36 Jose Valverde .30 .10
❑ 37 Chin-Feng Chen .30 .10
❑ 38 Gary Knotts .30 .10
❑ 39 Mark Sweeney .30 .10
❑ 40 Bret Boone .30 .10
❑ 41 Josh Phelps .30 .10
❑ 42 Jason LaRue .30 .10
❑ 43 Tim Redding .30 .10
❑ 44 Greg Myers .30 .10
❑ 45 Darin Erstad .30 .10
❑ 46 Kip Wells .30 .10
❑ 47 Matt Ford .30 .10
❑ 48 Jerome Williams .30 .10
❑ 49 Brian Meadows .30 .10
❑ 50 Albert Pujols 1.50 .60
❑ 51 Kirk Saarloos .30 .10
❑ 52 Scott Eyre .30 .10
❑ 53 John Flaherty .30 .10
❑ 54 Rafael Soriano .30 .10
❑ 55 Shea Hillenbrand .30 .10
❑ 56 Kyle Farnsworth .30 .10
❑ 57 Nate Cornejo .30 .10
❑ 58 Julian Tavarez .30 .10
❑ 59 Ryan Vogelsong .30 .10
❑ 60 Ryan Klesko .30 .10
❑ 61 Luke Hudson .30 .10
❑ 62 Justin Morneau .30 .10
❑ 63 Frank Catalanotto .30 .10
❑ 64 Derrick Turnbow .30 .10
❑ 65 Marcus Giles .30 .10
❑ 66 Mark Mulder .30 .10
❑ 67 Matt Anderson .30 .10
❑ 68 Mike Matheny .30 .10
❑ 69 Brian Lawrence .30 .10
❑ 70 Bobby Abreu .30 .10
❑ 71 Damian Moss .30 .10
❑ 72 Richard Hidalgo .30 .10
❑ 73 Mark Kotsay .30 .10
❑ 74 Mike Cameron .30 .10
❑ 75 Troy Glaus .30 .10
❑ 76 Matt Holliday .40 .15
❑ 77 Byung-Hyun Kim .30 .10
❑ 78 Aaron Sele .30 .10
❑ 79 Danny Graves .30 .10
❑ 80 Barry Zito .30 .10
❑ 81 Matt LeCroy .30 .10
❑ 82 Jason Isringhausen .30 .10
❑ 83 Colby Lewis .30 .10
❑ 84 Franklyn German .30 .10
❑ 85 Luis Matos .30 .10
❑ 86 Mike Timlin .30 .10
❑ 87 Miguel Batista .30 .10
❑ 88 John McDonald .30 .10
❑ 89 Joey Eischen .30 .10
❑ 90 Mike Mussina .50 .20
❑ 91 Jack Wilson .30 .10
❑ 92 Aaron Cook .30 .10
❑ 93 John Parrish .30 .10
❑ 94 Jose Valentin .30 .10
❑ 95 Johnny Damon .50 .20
❑ 96 Pat Burrell .30 .10
❑ 97 Brendan Donnelly .30 .10
❑ 98 Lance Carter .30 .10
❑ 99 Omar Daal .30 .10
❑ 100 Ichiro Suzuki 1.50 .60
❑ 101 Robin Ventura .30 .10
❑ 102 Brian Shouse .30 .10

❑	103	Kevin Jarvis	.30	.10
❑	104	Jason Young	.30	.10
❑	105	Moises Alou	.30	.10
❑	106	Wes Obermueller	.30	.10
❑	107	David Segui	.30	.10
❑	108	Mike MacDougal	.30	.10
❑	109	John Buck	.30	.10
❑	110	Gary Sheffield	.30	.10
❑	111	Yorvit Torrealba	.30	.10
❑	112	Matt Kata	.30	.10
❑	113	David Bell	.30	.10
❑	114	Juan Gonzalez	.30	.10
❑	115	Kelvim Escobar	.30	.10
❑	116	Ruben Sierra	.30	.10
❑	117	Todd Wellemeyer	.30	.10
❑	118	Jamie Walker	.30	.10
❑	119	Will Cunnane	.30	.10
❑	120	Cliff Floyd	.30	.10
❑	121	Aramis Ramirez	.30	.10
❑	122	Damaso Marte	.30	.10
❑	123	Juan Castro	.30	.10
❑	124	Chris Woodward	.30	.10
❑	125	Andruw Jones	.50	.20
❑	126	Ben Weber	.30	.10
❑	127	Dee Brown	.30	.10
❑	128	Steve Reed	.30	.10
❑	129	Gabe Kapler	.30	.10
❑	130	Miguel Cabrera	.50	.20
❑	131	Billy McMillon	.30	.10
❑	132	Julio Mateo	.30	.10
❑	133	Preston Wilson	.30	.10
❑	134	Tony Clark	.30	.10
❑	135	Carlos Lee	.30	.10
❑	136	Carlos Baerga	.30	.10
❑	137	Mike Crudale	.30	.10
❑	138	David Ross	.30	.10
❑	139	Josh Fogg	.30	.10
❑	140	Dmitri Young	.30	.10
❑	141	Cliff Lee	.30	.10
❑	142	Mike Lowell	.30	.10
❑	143	Jason Lane	.30	.10
❑	144	Pedro Feliz	.30	.10
❑	145	Ken Griffey Jr.	1.25	.50
❑	146	Dustin Hermanson	.30	.10
❑	147	Scott Hodges	.30	.10
❑	148	Aquilino Lopez	.30	.10
❑	149	Wes Helms	.30	.10
❑	150	Jason Giambi	.30	.10
❑	151	Erasmo Ramirez	.30	.10
❑	152	Sean Burroughs	.30	.10
❑	153	J.T. Snow	.30	.10
❑	154	Eddie Guardado	.30	.10
❑	155	C.C. Sabathia	.30	.10
❑	156	Kyle Lohse	.30	.10
❑	157	Roberto Hernandez	.30	.10
❑	158	Jason Simontacchi	.30	.10
❑	159	Tim Spooneybarger	.30	.10
❑	160	Alfonso Soriano	.30	.10
❑	161	Mike Gonzalez	.30	.10
❑	162	Alex Cora	.30	.10
❑	163	Kevin Gryboski	.30	.10
❑	164	Mike Lincoln	.30	.10
❑	165	Luis Castillo	.30	.10
❑	166	Odalis Perez	.30	.10
❑	167	Alex Sanchez	.30	.10
❑	168	Rob Mackowiak	.30	.10
❑	169	Francisco Rodriguez	.30	.10
❑	170	Roy Oswalt	.30	.10
❑	171	Omar Infante	.30	.10
❑	172	Ryan Jensen	.30	.10
❑	173	Ben Broussard	.30	.10
❑	174	Mark Hendrickson	.30	.10
❑	175	Manny Ramirez	.50	.20
❑	176	Rob Bell	.30	.10
❑	177	Adam Everett	.30	.10
❑	178	Chris George	.30	.10
❑	179	Ronnie Belliard	.30	.10
❑	180	Eric Gagne	.30	.10
❑	181	Scott Schoeneweis	.30	.10
❑	182	Kris Benson	.30	.10
❑	183	Amaury Telemaco	.30	.10
❑	184	John Riedling	.30	.10
❑	185	Juan Pierre	.30	.10
❑	186	Ramon Ortiz	.30	.10
❑	187	Luis Rivas	.30	.10
❑	188	Larry Bigbie	.30	.10
❑	189	Robby Hammock	.30	.10
❑	190	Geoff Jenkins	.30	.10
❑	191	Chad Cordero	.30	.10
❑	192	Mark Ellis	.30	.10
❑	193	Mark Loretta	.30	.10
❑	194	Ryan Drese	.30	.10
❑	195	Lance Berkman	.30	.10
❑	196	Kevin Appier	.30	.10
❑	197	Kiko Calero	.30	.10
❑	198	Mickey Callaway	.30	.10
❑	199	Chase Utley	.50	.20
❑	200	Nomar Garciaparra	1.25	.50
❑	201	Kevin Cash	.30	.10
❑	202	Ramiro Mendoza	.30	.10
❑	203	Shane Reynolds	.30	.10
❑	204	Chris Spurling	.30	.10
❑	205	Aaron Guiel	.30	.10
❑	206	Mark DeRosa	.30	.10
❑	207	Adam Kennedy	.30	.10
❑	208	Andy Pettitte	.50	.20
❑	209	Rafael Palmeiro	.50	.20
❑	210	Luis Gonzalez	.30	.10
❑	211	Ryan Franklin	.30	.10
❑	212	Bob Wickman	.30	.10
❑	213	Ron Calloway	.30	.10
❑	214	Jae Weong Seo	.30	.10
❑	215	Kazuhisa Ishii	.30	.10
❑	216	Sterling Hitchcock	.30	.10
❑	217	Jimmy Gobble	.30	.10
❑	218	Chad Moeller	.30	.10
❑	219	Jake Peavy	.30	.10
❑	220	John Smoltz	.50	.20
❑	221	Donovan Osborne	.30	.10
❑	222	David Wells	.30	.10
❑	223	Brad Lidge	.30	.10
❑	224	Carlos Zambrano	.30	.10
❑	225	Kerry Wood	.30	.10
❑	226	Alex Cintron	.30	.10
❑	227	Javier A. Lopez	.30	.10
❑	228	Jeremy Griffiths	.30	.10
❑	229	Jon Garland	.30	.10
❑	230	Curt Schilling	.50	.20
❑	231	Alex Scott Gonzalez	.30	.10
❑	232	Jay Gibbons	.30	.10
❑	233	Aaron Miles	.30	.10
❑	234	Mike Gallo	.30	.10
❑	235	Johan Santana	.75	.30
❑	236	Jose Guillen	.30	.10
❑	237	Jeff Conine	.30	.10
❑	238	Matt Roney	.30	.10
❑	239	Desi Relaford	.30	.10
❑	240	Frank Thomas	.75	.30
❑	241	Danny Patterson	.30	.10
❑	242	Kevin Mench	.30	.10
❑	243	Mike Redmond	.30	.10
❑	244	Jeff Suppan	.30	.10
❑	245	Carl Everett	.30	.10
❑	246	Jack Cressend	.30	.10
❑	247	Matt Mantei	.30	.10
❑	248	Enrique Wilson	.30	.10
❑	249	Craig Counsell	.30	.10
❑	250	Mark Prior	.50	.20
❑	251	Jared Sandberg	.30	.10
❑	252	Scott Strickland	.30	.10
❑	253	Lew Ford	.30	.10
❑	254	Hee Seop Choi	.30	.10
❑	255	Jason Phillips	.30	.10
❑	256	Jason Jennings	.30	.10
❑	257	Todd Pratt	.30	.10
❑	258	Matt Herges	.30	.10
❑	259	Kerry Ligtenberg	.30	.10
❑	260	Austin Kearns	.30	.10
❑	261	Jay Witasick	.30	.10
❑	262	Tony Armas Jr.	.30	.10
❑	263	Tom Martin	.30	.10
❑	264	Oliver Perez	.30	.10
❑	265	Jorge Posada	.50	.20
❑	266	Jason Boyd	.30	.10
❑	267	Ben Hendrickson	.30	.10
❑	268	Reggie Sanders	.30	.10
❑	269	Julio Lugo	.30	.10
❑	270	Pedro Martinez	.50	.20
❑	271	Kyle Snyder	.30	.10
❑	272	Felipe Lopez	.30	.10
❑	273	Kevin Millar	.30	.10
❑	274	Travis Hafner	.30	.10
❑	275	Magglio Ordonez	.30	.10
❑	276	Marlon Byrd	.30	.10
❑	277	Scott Spiezio	.30	.10
❑	278	Mark Corey	.30	.10
❑	279	Tim Salmon	.50	.20
❑	280	Alex Gonzalez	.30	.10
❑	281	Marquis Grissom	.30	.10
❑	282	Miguel Olivo	.30	.10
❑	283	Orlando Hudson	.30	.10
❑	284	Rondell White	.30	.10
❑	285	Jermaine Dye	.30	.10
❑	286	Paul Shuey	.30	.10
❑	287	Brandon Inge	.30	.10
❑	288	B.J. Surhoff	.30	.10
❑	289	Edgar Gonzalez	.30	.10
❑	290	Angel Berroa	.30	.10
❑	291	Claudio Vargas	.30	.10
❑	292	Cesar Izturis	.30	.10
❑	293	Brandon Phillips	.30	.10
❑	294	Jeff Duncan	.30	.10
❑	295	Randy Wolf	.30	.10
❑	296	Barry Larkin	.50	.20
❑	297	Felix Rodriguez	.30	.10
❑	298	Robb Quinlan	.30	.10
❑	299	Brian Jordan	.30	.10
❑	300	Dontrelle Willis	.50	.20
❑	301	Doug Davis	.30	.10
❑	302	Ricky Stone	.30	.10
❑	303	Travis Harper	.30	.10
❑	304	Jaret Wright	.30	.10
❑	305	Edgardo Alfonzo	.30	.10
❑	306	Quinton McCracken	.30	.10
❑	307	Jason Bay	.30	.10
❑	308	Joe Randa	.30	.10
❑	309	Steve Sparks	.30	.10
❑	310	Roy Halladay	.30	.10
❑	311	Antonio Alfonseca	.30	.10
❑	312	Michael Cuddyer	.30	.10
❑	313	John Patterson	.30	.10
❑	314	Chris Widger	.30	.10
❑	315	Shigetoshi Hasegawa	.30	.10
❑	316	Tim Wakefield	.30	.10
❑	317	Scott Hatteberg	.30	.10
❑	318	Mike Remlinger	.30	.10
❑	319	Jose Vizcaino	.30	.10
❑	320	Rocco Baldelli	.30	.10
❑	321	David Riske	.30	.10
❑	322	Steve Karsay	.30	.10
❑	323	Peter Bergeron	.30	.10
❑	324	Jeff Weaver	.30	.10
❑	325	Larry Walker	.30	.10
❑	326	Jack Cust	.30	.10
❑	327	Bo Hart	.30	.10
❑	328	Rod Beck	.30	.10
❑	329	Jose Acevedo	.30	.10
❑	330	Hank Blalock	.30	.10
❑	331	Tom Gordon	.30	.10
❑	332	Brian Fuentes	.30	.10
❑	333	Tomas Perez	.30	.10
❑	334	Lenny Harris	.30	.10
❑	335	Matt Morris	.30	.10
❑	336	Jeremi Gonzalez	.30	.10
❑	337	David Eckstein	.30	.10
❑	338	Aaron Rowand	.30	.10
❑	339	Rick Bauer	.30	.10
❑	340	Jim Edmonds	.30	.10
❑	341	Joe Borowski	.30	.10
❑	342	Eric DuBose	.30	.10
❑	343	D'Angelo Jimenez	.30	.10
❑	344	Tomo Ohka	.30	.10
❑	345	Victor Zambrano	.30	.10
❑	346	Joe McEwing	.30	.10
❑	347	Jorge Sosa	.30	.10
❑	348	Keith Ginter	.30	.10
❑	349	A.J. Pierzynski	.30	.10
❑	350	Mike Sweeney	.30	.10
❑	351	Shawn Chacon	.30	.10
❑	352	Matt Clement	.30	.10
❑	353	Vance Wilson	.30	.10
❑	354	Benito Santiago	.30	.10
❑	355	Eric Hinske	.30	.10
❑	356	Vladimir Guerrero	.75	.30
❑	357	Kenny Rogers	.30	.10
❑	358	Travis Lee	.30	.10
❑	359	Jay Powell	.30	.10
❑	360	Phil Nevin	.30	.10

❏	361	Willie Harris	.30	.10
❏	362	Ty Wigginton	.30	.10
❏	363	Chad Fox	.30	.10
❏	364	Junior Spivey	.30	.10
❏	365	Brandon Webb	.30	.10
❏	366	Brett Myers	.30	.10
❏	367	Alexis Gomez	.30	.10
❏	368	Dave Roberts	.30	.10
❏	369	LaTroy Hawkins	.30	.10
❏	370	Kevin Millwood	.30	.10
❏	371	Brian Schneider	.30	.10
❏	372	Blaine Neal	.30	.10
❏	373	Jeromy Burnitz	.30	.10
❏	374	Ted Lilly	.30	.10
❏	375	Shawn Green	.30	.10
❏	376	Carlos Pena	.30	.10
❏	377	Gil Meche	.30	.10
❏	378	Jeff Bagwell	.50	.20
❏	379	Alex Escobar	.30	.10
❏	380	Erubiel Durazo	.30	.10
❏	381	Cristian Guzman	.30	.10
❏	382	Rocky Biddle	.30	.10
❏	383	Craig Wilson	.30	.10
❏	384	Rey Sanchez	.30	.10
❏	385	Russ Ortiz	.30	.10
❏	386	Freddy Garcia	.30	.10
❏	387	Luis Vizcaino	.30	.10
❏	388	David Ortiz	.75	.30
❏	389	Jose Molina	.30	.10
❏	390	Edgar Martinez	.50	.20
❏	391	Nate Bump	.30	.10
❏	392	Brent Mayne	.30	.10
❏	393	Ray King	.30	.10
❏	394	Paul Wilson	.30	.10
❏	395	Melvin Mora	.30	.10
❏	396	Morgan Ensberg	.30	.10
❏	397	Ramon Hernandez	.30	.10
❏	398	Juan Rincon	.30	.10
❏	399	Ron Mahay	.30	.10
❏	400	Jeff Kent	.30	.10
❏	401	Cal Eldred	.30	.10
❏	402	Mike Difelice	.30	.10
❏	403	Valerio De Los Santos	.30	.10
❏	404	Steve Finley	.30	.10
❏	405	Trot Nixon	.30	.10
❏	406	Akinori Otsuka RC	.40	.15
❏	407	Ryan Freel	.30	.10
❏	408	Ray Durham	.30	.10
❏	409	Aaron Heilman	.30	.10
❏	410	Edgar Renteria	.30	.10
❏	411	Mike Hampton	.30	.10
❏	412	Kirk Rueter	.30	.10
❏	413	Jim Mecir	.30	.10
❏	414	Brian Roberts	.30	.10
❏	415	Paul Konerko	.30	.10
❏	416	Reed Johnson	.30	.10
❏	417	Roger Clemens	1.50	.60
❏	418	Coco Crisp	.30	.10
❏	419	Carlos Hernandez	.30	.10
❏	420	Scott Podsednik	.30	.10
❏	421	Miguel Cairo	.30	.10
❏	422	Abraham Nunez	.30	.10
❏	423	Endy Chavez	.30	.10
❏	424	Eric Munson	.30	.10
❏	425	Torii Hunter	.30	.10
❏	426	Ben Howard	.30	.10
❏	427	Chris Gomez	.30	.10
❏	428	Francisco Cordero	.30	.10
❏	429	Jeffrey Hammonds	.30	.10
❏	430	Shannon Stewart	.30	.10
❏	431	Einar Diaz	.30	.10
❏	432	Eric Byrnes	.30	.10
❏	433	Marty Cordova	.30	.10
❏	434	Matt Ginter	.30	.10
❏	435	Victor Martinez	.30	.10
❏	436	Geronimo Gil	.30	.10
❏	437	Grant Balfour	.30	.10
❏	438	Ramon Vazquez	.30	.10
❏	439	Jose Cruz Jr.	.30	.10
❏	440	Orlando Cabrera	.30	.10
❏	441	Joe Kennedy	.30	.10
❏	442	Scott Williamson	.30	.10
❏	443	Troy Percival	.30	.10
❏	444	Derrek Lee	.50	.20
❏	445	Runelvys Hernandez	.30	.10
❏	446	Mark Grudzielanek	.30	.10
❏	447	Trey Hodges	.30	.10
❏	448	Jimmy Haynes	.30	.10
❏	449	Eric Milton	.30	.10
❏	450	Todd Helton	.50	.20
❏	451	Greg Zaun	.30	.10
❏	452	Woody Williams	.30	.10
❏	453	Todd Walker	.30	.10
❏	454	Juan Cruz	.30	.10
❏	455	Fernando Vina	.30	.10
❏	456	Omar Vizquel	.50	.20
❏	457	Roberto Alomar	.50	.20
❏	458	Bill Hall	.30	.10
❏	459	Juan Rivera	.30	.10
❏	460	Tom Glavine	.50	.20
❏	461	Ramon Castro	.30	.10
❏	462	Cory Vance	.30	.10
❏	463	Dan Miceli	.30	.10
❏	464	Lyle Overbay	.30	.10
❏	465	Craig Biggio	.50	.20
❏	466	Ricky Ledee	.30	.10
❏	467	Michael Barrett	.30	.10
❏	468	Jason Anderson	.30	.10
❏	469	Matt Stairs	.30	.10
❏	470	Jarrod Washburn	.30	.10
❏	471	Todd Hundley	.30	.10
❏	472	Grant Roberts	.30	.10
❏	473	Randy Winn	.30	.10
❏	474	Pat Hentgen	.30	.10
❏	475	Jose Vidro	.30	.10
❏	476	Tony Torcato	.30	.10
❏	477	Jeremy Affeldt	.30	.10
❏	478	Carlos Guillen	.30	.10
❏	479	Paul Quantrill	.30	.10
❏	480	Rafael Furcal	.30	.10
❏	481	Adam Melhuse	.30	.10
❏	482	Jerry Hairston Jr.	.30	.10
❏	483	Adam Bernero	.30	.10
❏	484	Terrence Long	.30	.10
❏	485	Paul Lo Duca	.30	.10
❏	486	Corey Koskie	.30	.10
❏	487	John Lackey	.30	.10
❏	488	Chad Zerbe	.30	.10
❏	489	Vinny Castilla	.30	.10
❏	490	Corey Patterson	.30	.10
❏	491	John Olerud	.30	.10
❏	492	Josh Bard	.30	.10
❏	493	Darren Dreifort	.30	.10
❏	494	Jason Standridge	.30	.10
❏	495	Ben Sheets	.30	.10
❏	496	Jose Castillo	.30	.10
❏	497	Jay Payton	.30	.10
❏	498	Rob Bowen	.30	.10
❏	499	Bobby Higginson	.30	.10
❏	500	Alex Rodriguez Yanks	1.25	.50
❏	501	Octavio Dotel	.30	.10
❏	502	Rheal Cormier	.30	.10
❏	503	Felix Heredia	.30	.10
❏	504	Dan Wright	.30	.10
❏	505	Michael Young	.30	.10
❏	506	Wilfredo Ledezma	.30	.10
❏	507	Sun Woo Kim	.30	.10
❏	508	Michael Tejera	.30	.10
❏	509	Herbert Perry	.30	.10
❏	510	Esteban Loaiza	.30	.10
❏	511	Alan Embree	.30	.10
❏	512	Ben Davis	.30	.10
❏	513	Greg Colbrunn	.30	.10
❏	514	Josh Hall	.30	.10
❏	515	Raul Ibanez	.30	.10
❏	516	Jason Kershner	.30	.10
❏	517	Corky Miller	.30	.10
❏	518	Jason Marquis	.30	.10
❏	519	Roger Cedeno	.30	.10
❏	520	Adam Dunn	.30	.10
❏	521	Paul Byrd	.30	.10
❏	522	Sandy Alomar Jr.	.30	.10
❏	523	Salomon Torres	.30	.10
❏	524	John Halama	.30	.10
❏	525	Mike Piazza	1.25	.50
❏	526	Buddy Groom	.30	.10
❏	527	Adrian Beltre	.30	.10
❏	528	Chad Harville	.30	.10
❏	529	Javier Vazquez	.30	.10
❏	530	Jody Gerut	.30	.10
❏	531	Elmer Dessens	.30	.10
❏	532	B.J. Ryan	.30	.10
❏	533	Chad Durbin	.30	.10
❏	534	Doug Mirabelli	.30	.10
❏	535	Bernie Williams	.50	.20
❏	536	Jeff DaVanon	.30	.10
❏	537	Dave Berg	.30	.10
❏	538	Geoff Blum	.30	.10
❏	539	John Thomson	.30	.10
❏	540	Jeremy Bonderman	.30	.10
❏	541	Jeff Zimmerman	.30	.10
❏	542	Derek Lowe	.30	.10
❏	543	Scot Shields	.30	.10
❏	544	Michael Tucker	.30	.10
❏	545	Tim Hudson	.30	.10
❏	546	Ryan Ludwick	.30	.10
❏	547	Rick Reed	.30	.10
❏	548	Placido Polanco	.30	.10
❏	549	Tony Graffanino	.30	.10
❏	550	Garret Anderson	.30	.10
❏	551	Timo Perez	.30	.10
❏	552	Jesus Colome	.30	.10
❏	553	R.A. Dickey	.30	.10
❏	554	Tim Worrell	.30	.10
❏	555	Jason Kendall	.30	.10
❏	556	Tom Goodwin	.30	.10
❏	557	Joaquin Benoit	.30	.10
❏	558	Stephen Randolph	.30	.10
❏	559	Miguel Tejada	.30	.10
❏	560	A.J. Burnett	.30	.10
❏	561	Ben Diggins	.30	.10
❏	562	Kent Mercker	.30	.10
❏	563	Zach Day	.30	.10
❏	564	Antonio Perez	.30	.10
❏	565	Jason Schmidt	.30	.10
❏	566	Armando Benitez	.30	.10
❏	567	Denny Neagle	.30	.10
❏	568	Eric Eckenstahler	.30	.10
❏	569	Chan Ho Park	.30	.10
❏	570	Carlos Beltran	.30	.10
❏	571	Brett Tomko	.30	.10
❏	572	Henry Mateo	.30	.10
❏	573	Ken Harvey	.30	.10
❏	574	Matt Lawton	.30	.10
❏	575	Mariano Rivera	.75	.30
❏	576	Darrell May	.30	.10
❏	577	Jamie Moyer	.30	.10
❏	578	Paul Bako	.30	.10
❏	579	Cory Lidle	.30	.10
❏	580	Jacque Jones	.30	.10
❏	581	Jolbert Cabrera	.30	.10
❏	582	Jason Grimsley	.30	.10
❏	583	Danny Kolb	.30	.10
❏	584	Billy Wagner	.30	.10
❏	585	Rich Aurilia	.30	.10
❏	586	Vicente Padilla	.30	.10
❏	587	Oscar Villarreal	.30	.10
❏	588	Rene Reyes	.30	.10
❏	589	Jon Lieber	.30	.10
❏	590	Nick Johnson	.30	.10
❏	591	Bobby Crosby	.30	.10
❏	592	Steve Trachsel	.30	.10
❏	593	Brian Boehringer	.30	.10
❏	594	Juan Uribe	.30	.10
❏	595	Bartolo Colon	.30	.10
❏	596	Bobby Hill	.30	.10
❏	597	Chris Shelton RC	1.00	.40
❏	598	Carl Pavano	.30	.10
❏	599	Kurt Ainsworth	.30	.10
❏	600	Derek Jeter	1.50	.60
❏	601	Doug Mientkiewicz	.30	.10
❏	602	Orlando Palmeiro	.30	.10
❏	603	J.C. Romero	.30	.10
❏	604	Scott Sullivan	.30	.10
❏	605	Brad Radke	.30	.10
❏	606	Fernando Rodney	.30	.10
❏	607	Jim Brower	.30	.10
❏	608	Josh Towers	.30	.10
❏	609	Brad Fullmer	.30	.10
❏	610	Jose Reyes	.30	.10
❏	611	Ryan Wagner	.30	.10
❏	612	Joe Mays	.30	.10
❏	613	Jung Bong	.30	.10
❏	614	Curtis Leskanic	.30	.10
❏	615	Al Leiter	.30	.10
❏	616	Wade Miller	.30	.10
❏	617	Keith Foulke Sox	.30	.10
❏	618	Casey Fossum	.30	.10

❑ 619 Craig Monroe	.30	.10
❑ 620 Hideo Nomo	.75	.30
❑ 621 Bob File	.30	.10
❑ 622 Steve Kline	.30	.10
❑ 623 Bobby Kielty	.30	.10
❑ 624 Dewon Brazelton	.30	.10
❑ 625 Eric Chavez	.30	.10
❑ 626 Chris Carpenter	.30	.10
❑ 627 Alexis Rios	.30	.10
❑ 628 Jason Davis	.30	.10
❑ 629 Jose Jimenez	.30	.10
❑ 630 Vernon Wells	.30	.10
❑ 631 Kenny Lofton	.30	.10
❑ 632 Chad Bradford	.30	.10
❑ 633 Brad Wilkerson	.30	.10
❑ 634 Pokey Reese	.30	.10
❑ 635 Richie Sexson	.30	.10
❑ 636 Chin-Hui Tsao	.30	.10
❑ 637 Eli Marrero	.30	.10
❑ 638 Chris Reitsma	.30	.10
❑ 639 Daryle Ward	.30	.10
❑ 640 Mark Teixeira	.50	.20
❑ 641 Corwin Malone	.30	.10
❑ 642 Adam Eaton	.30	.10
❑ 643 Jimmy Rollins	.30	.10
❑ 644 Brian Anderson	.30	.10
❑ 645 Bill Mueller	.30	.10
❑ 646 Jake Westbrook	.30	.10
❑ 647 Bengie Molina	.30	.10
❑ 648 Jorge Julio	.30	.10
❑ 649 Billy Traber	.30	.10
❑ 650 Randy Johnson	.75	.30
❑ 651 Javy Lopez	.30	.10
❑ 652 Doug Glanville	.30	.10
❑ 653 Jeff Cirillo	.30	.10
❑ 654 Tino Martinez	.50	.20
❑ 655 Mark Buehrle	.30	.10
❑ 656 Jason Michaels	.30	.10
❑ 657 Damian Rolls	.30	.10
❑ 658 Rosman Garcia	.30	.10
❑ 659 Scott Hairston	.30	.10
❑ 660 Carl Crawford	.30	.10
❑ 661 Livan Hernandez	.30	.10
❑ 662 Danny Bautista	.30	.10
❑ 663 Brad Ausmus	.30	.10
❑ 664 Juan Acevedo	.30	.10
❑ 665 Sean Casey	.30	.10
❑ 666 Josh Beckett	.30	.10
❑ 667 Milton Bradley	.30	.10
❑ 668 Braden Looper	.30	.10
❑ 669 Paul Abbott	.30	.10
❑ 670 Joel Pineiro	.30	.10
❑ 671 Luis Terrero	.30	.10
❑ 672 Rodrigo Lopez	.30	.10
❑ 673 Joe Crede	.30	.10
❑ 674 Mike Koplove	.30	.10
❑ 675 Brian Giles	.30	.10
❑ 676 Jeff Nelson	.30	.10
❑ 677 Russell Branyan	.30	.10
❑ 678 Mike DeJean	.30	.10
❑ 679 Brian Daubach	.30	.10
❑ 680 Ellis Burks	.30	.10
❑ 681 Ryan Dempster	.30	.10
❑ 682 Cliff Politte	.30	.10
❑ 683 Brian Reith	.30	.10
❑ 684 Scott Stewart	.30	.10
❑ 685 Allan Simpson	.30	.10
❑ 686 Shawn Estes	.30	.10
❑ 687 Jason Johnson	.30	.10
❑ 688 Wil Cordero	.30	.10
❑ 689 Kelly Stinnett	.30	.10
❑ 690 Jose Lima	.30	.10
❑ 691 Gary Bennett	.30	.10
❑ 692 T.J. Tucker	.30	.10
❑ 693 Shane Spencer	.30	.10
❑ 694 Chris Hammond	.30	.10
❑ 695 Raul Mondesi	.30	.10
❑ 696 Xavier Nady	.30	.10
❑ 697 Cody Ransom	.30	.10
❑ 698 Ron Villone	.30	.10
❑ 699 Brook Fordyce	.30	.10
❑ 700 Sammy Sosa	.75	.30
❑ 701 Terry Adams	.30	.10
❑ 702 Ricardo Rincon	.30	.10
❑ 703 Tike Redman	.30	.10
❑ 704 Chris Stynes	.30	.10
❑ 705 Mark Redman	.30	.10
❑ 706 Juan Encarnacion	.30	.10
❑ 707 Jhonny Peralta	.30	.10
❑ 708 Denny Hocking	.30	.10
❑ 709 Ivan Rodriguez	.50	.20
❑ 710 Jose Hernandez	.30	.10
❑ 711 Brandon Duckworth	.30	.10
❑ 712 Dave Burba	.30	.10
❑ 713 Joe Nathan	.30	.10
❑ 714 Dan Smith	.30	.10
❑ 715 Karim Garcia	.30	.10
❑ 716 Arthur Rhodes	.30	.10
❑ 717 Shawn Wooten	.30	.10
❑ 718 Ramon Santiago	.30	.10
❑ 719 Luis Ugueto	.30	.10
❑ 720 Danys Baez	.30	.10
❑ 721 Alfredo Amezaga PROS	.30	.10
❑ 722 Sidney Ponson	.30	.10
❑ 723 Joe Mauer PROS	.75	.30
❑ 724 Jesse Foppert PROS	.30	.10
❑ 725 Todd Greene	.30	.10
❑ 726 Dan Haren PROS	.30	.10
❑ 727 Brandon Larson PROS	.30	.10
❑ 728 Bobby Jenks PROS	.30	.10
❑ 729 Grady Sizemore PROS	.75	.30
❑ 730 Ben Grieve	.30	.10
❑ 731 Khalil Greene PROS	.50	.20
❑ 732 Chad Gaudin PROS	.30	.10
❑ 733 Johnny Estrada PROS	.30	.10
❑ 734 Joe Valentine PROS	.30	.10
❑ 735 Tim Raines Jr. PROS	.30	.10
❑ 736 Brandon Claussen PROS	.30	.10
❑ 737 Sam Marsonek PROS	.30	.10
❑ 738 Delmon Young PROS	.50	.20
❑ 739 David Dellucci	.30	.10
❑ 740 Sergio Mitre PROS	.30	.10
❑ 741 Nick Neugebauer PROS	.30	.10
❑ 742 Laynce Nix PROS	.30	.10
❑ 743 Joe Thurston PROS	.30	.10
❑ 744 Ryan Langerhans PROS	.30	.10
❑ 745 Pete LaForest PROS	.30	.10
❑ 746 Arnie Munoz PROS	.30	.10
❑ 747 Rickie Weeks PROS	.30	.10
❑ 748 Neal Cotts PROS	.30	.10
❑ 749 Jonny Gomes PROS	.30	.10
❑ 750 Jim Thome	.50	.20
❑ 751 Jon Rauch PROS	.30	.10
❑ 752 Edwin Jackson PROS	.30	.10
❑ 753 Ryan Madson PROS	.30	.10
❑ 754 Andrew Good PROS	.30	.10
❑ 755 Eddie Perez	.30	.10
❑ 756 Joe Borchard PROS	.30	.10
❑ 757 Jeremy Guthrie PROS	.30	.10
❑ 758 Jose Mesa	.30	.10
❑ 759 Doug Waechter PROS	.30	.10
❑ 760 J.D. Drew	.30	.10
❑ 761 Adam LaRoche PROS	.30	.10
❑ 762 Rich Harden PROS	.30	.10
❑ 763 Justin Speier	.30	.10
❑ 764 Todd Zeile	.30	.10
❑ 765 Turk Wendell	.30	.10
❑ 766 Mark Bellhorn Sox	.30	.10
❑ 767 Mike Jackson	.30	.10
❑ 768 Chone Figgins	.30	.10
❑ 769 Mike Neu	.30	.10
❑ 770 Greg Maddux	1.25	.50
❑ 771 Frank Menechino	.30	.10
❑ 772 Alec Zumwalt RC	.30	.10
❑ 773 Eric Young	.30	.10
❑ 774 Dustan Mohr	.30	.10
❑ 775 Shane Halter	.30	.10
❑ 776 Brian Buchanan	.30	.10
❑ 777 So Taguchi	.30	.10
❑ 778 Eric Karros	.30	.10
❑ 779 Ramon Nivar	.30	.10
❑ 780 Marlon Anderson	.30	.10
❑ 781 Brayan Pena FY RC	.40	.15
❑ 782 Chris O'Riordan FY RC	.40	.15
❑ 783 Dioner Navarro FY RC	.75	.30
❑ 784 Alberto Callaspo FY RC	.75	.30
❑ 785 Hector Gimenez FY RC	.30	.10
❑ 786 Yadier Molina FY RC	2.00	.75
❑ 787 Kevin Richardson FY RC	.30	.10
❑ 788 Brian Pilkington FY RC	.30	.10
❑ 789 Adam Greenberg FY RC	.75	.30
❑ 790 Ervin Santana FY RC	2.00	.75
❑ 791 Brant Colamarino FY RC	.75	.30
❑ 792 Ben Himes FY RC	.30	.10
❑ 793 Todd Self FY RC	.50	.20
❑ 794 Brad Vericker FY RC	.40	.15
❑ 795 Donald Kelly FY RC	.40	.15
❑ 796 Brock Jacobsen FY RC	.30	.10
❑ 797 Brock Peterson FY RC	.40	.15
❑ 798 Carlos Sosa FY RC	.40	.15
❑ 799 Chad Chop FY RC	.40	.15
❑ 800 Matt Moses FY RC	1.00	.40
❑ 801 Chris Aguila FY RC	.40	.15
❑ 802 David Murphy FY RC	.75	.30
❑ 803 Don Sutton FY RC	1.00	.40
❑ 804 Jereme Milons FY RC	.50	.20
❑ 805 Jon Coutlangus FY RC	.30	.10
❑ 806 Greg Thissen FY RC	.40	.15
❑ 807 Jose Capellan FY RC	.50	.20
❑ 808 Chad Santos FY RC	.40	.15
❑ 809 Wardell Starling FY RC	.40	.15
❑ 810 Kevin Kouzmanoff FY RC	2.00	.75
❑ 811 Kevin Davidson FY RC	.30	.10
❑ 812 Michael Mooney FY RC	.40	.15
❑ 813 Rodney Choy Foo FY RC	.30	.10
❑ 814 Reid Gorecki FY RC	.40	.15
❑ 815 Rudy Guillen FY RC	.75	.30
❑ 816 Harvey Garcia FY RC	.30	.10
❑ 817 Warner Madrigal FY RC	.75	.30
❑ 818 Kenny Perez FY RC	.40	.15
❑ 819 Joaquin Arias FY RC	.75	.30
❑ 820 Benji DeQuin FY RC	.30	.10
❑ 821 Lastings Milledge FY RC	5.00	2.00
❑ 822 Blake Hawksworth FY RC	.50	.20
❑ 823 Estee Harris FY RC	.50	.20
❑ 824 Bobby Brownlie FY RC	1.00	.40
❑ 825 Wanell Severino FY RC	.30	.10
❑ 826 Bobby Madritsch FY	.30	.10
❑ 827 Travis Hanson FY RC	.50	.20
❑ 828 Brandon Medders FY RC	.40	.15
❑ 829 Kevin Howard FY RC	.50	.20
❑ 830 Brian Steffek FY RC	.30	.10
❑ 831 Terry Jones FY RC	.50	.20
❑ 832 Anthony Acevedo FY RC	.40	.15
❑ 833 Kory Casto FY RC	.50	.20
❑ 834 Brooks Conrad FY RC	.40	.15
❑ 835 Juan Gutierrez FY RC	.40	.15
❑ 836 Charlie Zink FY RC	.30	.10
❑ 837 David Aardsma FY RC	.50	.20
❑ 838 Carl Loadenthal FY RC	.50	.20
❑ 839 Donald Levinski FY RC	.30	.10
❑ 840 Dustin Nippert FY RC	.50	.20
❑ 841 Calvin Hayes FY RC	.50	.20
❑ 842 Felix Hernandez FY RC	8.00	3.00
❑ 843 Tyler Davidson FY RC	.50	.20
❑ 844 George Sherrill FY RC	.40	.15
❑ 845 Craig Ansman FY RC	.40	.15
❑ 846 Jeff Allison FY RC	.40	.15
❑ 847 Tommy Murphy FY RC	.40	.15
❑ 848 Jerome Gamble FY RC	.30	.10
❑ 849 Jesse English FY RC	.40	.15
❑ 850 Alex Romero FY RC	.40	.15
❑ 851 Joel Zumaya FY RC	3.00	1.25
❑ 852 Carlos Quentin FY RC	2.50	1.00
❑ 853 Jose Valdez FY RC	.40	.15
❑ 854 J.J. Furmaniak FY RC	.75	.30
❑ 855 Juan Cedeno FY RC	.40	.15
❑ 856 Kyle Sleeth FY RC	.50	.20
❑ 857 Josh Labandeira FY RC	.40	.15
❑ 858 Lee Gwaltney FY RC	.30	.10
❑ 859 Lincoln Holdzkom FY RC	.40	.15
❑ 860 Ivan Ochoa FY RC	.40	.15
❑ 861 Luke Anderson FY RC	.30	.10
❑ 862 Conor Jackson FY RC	3.00	1.25
❑ 863 Matt Capps FY RC	.40	.15
❑ 864 Merkin Valdez FY RC	.50	.20
❑ 865 Paul Bacot FY RC	.50	.20
❑ 866 Erick Aybar FY RC	1.00	.40
❑ 867 Scott Proctor FY RC	.50	.20
❑ 868 Tim Stauffer FY RC	1.00	.40
❑ 869 Matt Creighton FY RC	.40	.15
❑ 870 Zach Miner FY RC	1.25	.50
❑ 871 Danny Gonzalez FY RC	.30	.10
❑ 872 Tom Farmer FY RC	.40	.15
❑ 873 John Santor FY RC	.30	.10
❑ 874 Logan Kensing FY RC	.40	.15
❑ 875 Vito Chiaravalloti FY RC	.40	.15
❑ 876 Checklist	.30	.10

❑ 877	Checklist	.30	.10
❑ 878	Checklist	.30	.10
❑ 879	Checklist	.30	.10
❑ 880	Checklist	.30	.10

2005 Topps Total

❑	COMPLETE SET (770)	150.00	75.00
❑	COMMON (1-575/666)	.30	.10
❑	COMMON CARD (576-690)	.30	.10
❑	COM (269/588/691-765)	.50	.20
❑	COMMON CL (766-770)	.30	.10
❑	OVERALL PLATE ODDS 1:85 HOBBY		
❑	PLATE PRINT RUN 1 SET PER COLOR		
❑	BLACK-CYAN-MAGENTA-YELLOW ISSUED		
❑	FRONT AND BACK PLATES PRODUCED		
❑	NO PLATE PRICING DUE TO SCARCITY		
❑ 1	Rafael Furcal	.30	.10
❑ 2	Tony Clark	.30	.10
❑ 3	Hideki Matsui	1.25	.50
❑ 4	Zach Day	.30	.10
❑ 5	Garret Anderson	.30	.10
❑ 6	B.J. Surhoff	.30	.10
❑ 7	Trevor Hoffman	.30	.10
❑ 8	Kenny Lofton	.30	.10
❑ 9	Ross Gload	.30	.10
❑ 10	Jorge Cantu	.30	.10
❑ 11	Joel Pineiro	.30	.10
❑ 12	Alex Cintron	.30	.10
❑ 13	Mike Matheny	.30	.10
❑ 14	Rod Barajas	.30	.10
❑ 15	Ray Durham	.30	.10
❑ 16	Danys Baez	.30	.10
❑ 17	Brian Schneider	.30	.10
❑ 18	Tike Redman	.30	.10
❑ 19	Ricardo Rodriguez	.30	.10
❑ 20	Mike Sweeney	.30	.10
❑ 21	Greg Myers	.30	.10
❑ 22	Chone Figgins	.30	.10
❑ 23	Brian Lawrence	.30	.10
❑ 24	Joe Nathan	.30	.10
❑ 25	Placido Polanco	.30	.10
❑ 26	Yadier Molina	.30	.10
❑ 27	Gary Bennett	.30	.10
❑ 28	Yorvit Torrealba	.30	.10
❑ 29	Javier Valentin	.30	.10
❑ 30	Jason Giambi	.30	.10
❑ 31	Brandon Claussen	.30	.10
❑ 32	Miguel Olivo	.30	.10
❑ 33	Josh Bard	.30	.10
❑ 34	Ramon Hernandez	.30	.10
❑ 35	Geoff Jenkins	.30	.10
❑ 36	Bobby Kielty	.30	.10
❑ 37	Luis A. Gonzalez	.30	.10
❑ 38	Benito Santiago	.30	.10
❑ 39	Brandon Inge	.30	.10
❑ 40	Mark Prior	.50	.20
❑ 41	Mike Lieberthal	.30	.10
❑ 42	Toby Hall	.30	.10
❑ 43	Brad Ausmus	.30	.10
❑ 44	Damian Miller	.30	.10
❑ 45	Mark Kotsay	.30	.10
❑ 46	John Buck	.30	.10
❑ 47	Oliver Perez	.30	.10
❑ 48	Matt Morris	.30	.10
❑ 49	Raul Chavez	.30	.10
❑ 50	Randy Johnson	.75	.30
❑ 51	Dave Bush	.30	.10
❑ 52	Jose Macias	.30	.10
❑ 53	Paul Wilson	.30	.10
❑ 54	Wilfredo Ledezma	.30	.10
❑ 55	J.D. Drew	.30	.10
❑ 56	Pedro Martinez	.50	.20
❑ 57	Josh Towers	.30	.10
❑ 58	Jamie Moyer	.30	.10
❑ 59	Scott Elarton	.30	.10
❑ 60	Ken Griffey Jr.	1.25	.50
❑ 61	Steve Trachsel	.30	.10
❑ 62	Bubba Crosby	.30	.10
❑ 63	Michael Barrett	.30	.10
❑ 64	Odalis Perez	.30	.10
❑ 65	B.J. Upton	.30	.10
❑ 66	Eric Bruntlett	.30	.10
❑ 67	Victor Zambrano	.30	.10
❑ 68	Brandon League	.30	.10
❑ 69	Carlos Silva	.30	.10
❑ 70	Lyle Overbay	.30	.10
❑ 71	Runelvys Hernandez	.30	.10
❑ 72	Brad Penny	.30	.10
❑ 73	Ty Wigginton	.30	.10
❑ 74	Orlando Hudson	.30	.10
❑ 75	Roy Oswalt	.30	.10
❑ 76	Jason LaRue	.30	.10
❑ 77	Ismael Valdez	.30	.10
❑ 78	Calvin Pickering	.30	.10
❑ 79	Bill Hall	.30	.10
❑ 80	Carl Crawford	.30	.10
❑ 81	Tomas Perez	.30	.10
❑ 82	Joe Kennedy	.30	.10
❑ 83	Chris Woodward	.30	.10
❑ 84	Jason Lane	.30	.10
❑ 85	Steve Finley	.30	.10
❑ 86	Jeff Francis	.30	.10
❑ 87	Felipe Lopez	.30	.10
❑ 88	Chan Ho Park	.30	.10
❑ 89	Joe Crede	.30	.10
❑ 90	Jose Vidro	.30	.10
❑ 91	Casey Kotchman	.30	.10
❑ 92	Brandon Backe	.30	.10
❑ 93	Mike Hampton	.30	.10
❑ 94	Ryan Dempster	.30	.10
❑ 95	Wily Mo Pena	.30	.10
❑ 96	Matt Holliday	.40	.15
❑ 97	A.J. Pierzynski	.30	.10
❑ 98	Jason Jennings	.30	.10
❑ 99	Eli Marrero	.30	.10
❑ 100	Carlos Beltran	.30	.10
❑ 101	Scott Kazmir	.30	.10
❑ 102	Kenny Rogers	.30	.10
❑ 103	Roy Halladay	.30	.10
❑ 104	Alex Cora	.30	.10
❑ 105	Richie Sexson	.30	.10
❑ 106	Ben Sheets	.30	.10
❑ 107	Bartolo Colon	.30	.10
❑ 108	Eddie Perez	.30	.10
❑ 109	Vicente Padilla	.30	.10
❑ 110	Sammy Sosa	.75	.30
❑ 111	Mark Ellis	.30	.10
❑ 112	Woody Williams	.30	.10
❑ 113	Todd Greene	.30	.10
❑ 114	Nook Logan	.30	.10
❑ 115	Francisco Rodriguez	.30	.10
❑ 116	Miguel Batista	.30	.10
❑ 117	Livan Hernandez	.30	.10
❑ 118	Chris Aguila	.30	.10
❑ 119	Coco Crisp	.30	.10
❑ 120	Jose Reyes	.30	.10
❑ 121	Ricky Ledee	.30	.10
❑ 122	Brad Radke	.30	.10
❑ 123	Carlos Guillen	.30	.10
❑ 124	Paul Bako	.30	.10
❑ 125	Tom Glavine	.50	.20
❑ 126	Chad Moeller	.30	.10
❑ 127	Mark Buehrle	.30	.10
❑ 128	Casey Blake	.30	.10
❑ 129	Juan Rivera	.30	.10
❑ 130	Preston Wilson	.30	.10
❑ 131	Nate Robertson	.30	.10
❑ 132	Julio Franco	.30	.10
❑ 133	Derek Lowe	.30	.10
❑ 134	Rob Bell	.30	.10
❑ 135	Javy Lopez	.30	.10
❑ 136	Javier Vazquez	.30	.10
❑ 137	Desi Relaford	.30	.10
❑ 138	Danny Graves	.30	.10
❑ 139	Josh Fogg	.30	.10
❑ 140	Bobby Crosby	.30	.10
❑ 141	Ramon Castro	.30	.10
❑ 142	Jerry Hairston Jr.	.30	.10
❑ 143	Morgan Ensberg	.30	.10
❑ 144	Brandon Webb	.30	.10
❑ 145	Jack Wilson	.30	.10
❑ 146	Bill Mueller	.30	.10
❑ 147	Troy Glaus	.30	.10
❑ 148	Armando Benitez	.30	.10
❑ 149	Adam LaRoche	.30	.10
❑ 150	Hank Blalock	.30	.10
❑ 151	Ryan Franklin	.30	.10
❑ 152	Kevin Millwood	.30	.10
❑ 153	Jason Marquis	.30	.10
❑ 154	Dewon Brazelton	.30	.10
❑ 155	Al Leiter	.30	.10
❑ 156	Garrett Atkins	.30	.10
❑ 157	Todd Walker	.30	.10
❑ 158	Kris Benson	.30	.10
❑ 159	Eric Milton	.30	.10
❑ 160	Bret Boone	.30	.10
❑ 161	Matt LeCroy	.30	.10
❑ 162	Chris Widger	.30	.10
❑ 163	Ruben Gotay	.30	.10
❑ 164	Craig Monroe	.30	.10
❑ 165	Travis Hafner	.30	.10
❑ 166	Vance Wilson	.30	.10
❑ 167	Jason Grabowski	.30	.10
❑ 168	Tim Salmon	.50	.20
❑ 169	Henry Blanco	.30	.10
❑ 170	Josh Beckett	.30	.10
❑ 171	Jake Westbrook	.30	.10
❑ 172	Paul Lo Duca	.30	.10
❑ 173	Julio Lugo	.30	.10
❑ 174	Juan Cruz	.30	.10
❑ 175	Mark Mulder	.30	.10
❑ 176	Juan Castro	.30	.10
❑ 177	Damion Easley	.30	.10
❑ 178	LaTroy Hawkins	.30	.10
❑ 179	Jon Lieber	.30	.10
❑ 180	Vernon Wells	.30	.10
❑ 181	Jeff DaVanon	.30	.10
❑ 182	Dustan Mohr	.30	.10
❑ 183	Ryan Freel	.30	.10
❑ 184	Doug Davis	.30	.10
❑ 185	Sean Casey	.30	.10
❑ 186	Robb Quinlan	.30	.10
❑ 187	J.D. Closser	.30	.10
❑ 188	Tim Wakefield	.30	.10
❑ 189	Brian Jordan	.30	.10
❑ 190	Adam Dunn	.30	.10
❑ 191	Antonio Perez	.30	.10
❑ 192	Brett Tomko	.30	.10
❑ 193	John Flaherty	.30	.10
❑ 194	Michael Cuddyer	.30	.10
❑ 195	Ronnie Belliard	.30	.10
❑ 196	Tony Womack	.30	.10
❑ 197	Jason Johnson	.30	.10
❑ 198	Victor Santos	.30	.10
❑ 199	Danny Haren	.30	.10
❑ 200	Derek Jeter	1.50	.60
❑ 201	Brian Anderson	.30	.10
❑ 202	Carlos Pena	.30	.10
❑ 203	Jaret Wright	.30	.10
❑ 204	Paul Byrd	.30	.10
❑ 205	Shannon Stewart	.30	.10
❑ 206	Chris Carpenter	.30	.10
❑ 207	Matt Stairs	.30	.10
❑ 208	Brad Hawpe	.30	.10
❑ 209	Bobby Higginson	.30	.10
❑ 210	Torii Hunter	.30	.10
❑ 211	Shawn Green	.30	.10
❑ 212	Todd Hollandsworth	.30	.10
❑ 213	Scott Erickson	.30	.10
❑ 214	C.C. Sabathia	.30	.10
❑ 215	Mike Mussina	.50	.20
❑ 216	Jason Kendall	.30	.10
❑ 217	Todd Pratt	.30	.10
❑ 218	Danny Kolb	.30	.10
❑ 219	Tony Armas	.30	.10
❑ 220	Edgar Renteria	.30	.10
❑ 221	Dave Roberts	.30	.10
❑ 222	Luis Rivas	.30	.10
❑ 223	Adam Everett	.30	.10
❑ 224	Jeff Cirillo	.30	.10

❑ 225 Orlando Hernandez .30 .10
❑ 226 Ken Harvey .30 .10
❑ 227 Corey Patterson .30 .10
❑ 228 Humberto Cota .30 .10
❑ 229 A.J. Burnett .30 .10
❑ 230 Roger Clemens 1.25 .50
❑ 231 Joe Randa .30 .10
❑ 232 David Dellucci .30 .10
❑ 233 Troy Percival .30 .10
❑ 234 Dustin Hermanson .30 .10
❑ 235 Eric Gagne .30 .10
❑ 236 Terry Tiffee .30 .10
❑ 237 Tony Graffanino .30 .10
❑ 238 Jayson Werth .30 .10
❑ 239 Mark Sweeney .30 .10
❑ 240 Chipper Jones .75 .30
❑ 241 Aramis Ramirez .30 .10
❑ 242 Frank Catalanotto .30 .10
❑ 243 Mike Maroth .30 .10
❑ 244 Kelvim Escobar .30 .10
❑ 245 Bobby Abreu .30 .10
❑ 246 Kyle Lohse .30 .10
❑ 247 Jason Isringhausen .30 .10
❑ 248 Jose Lima .30 .10
❑ 249 Adrian Gonzalez .30 .10
❑ 250 Alex Rodriguez 1.25 .50
❑ 251 Ramon Ortiz .30 .10
❑ 252 Frank Menechino .30 .10
❑ 253 Keith Ginter .30 .10
❑ 254 Kip Wells .30 .10
❑ 255 Dmitri Young .30 .10
❑ 256 Craig Biggio .50 .20
❑ 257 Ramon E. Martinez .30 .10
❑ 258 Jason Bartlett .30 .10
❑ 259 Brad Lidge .30 .10
❑ 260 Brian Giles .30 .10
❑ 261 Luis Terrero .30 .10
❑ 262 Miguel Ojeda .30 .10
❑ 263 Rich Harden .30 .10
❑ 264 Jacque Jones .30 .10
❑ 265 Marcus Giles .30 .10
❑ 266 Carlos Zambrano .30 .10
❑ 267 Michael Tucker .30 .10
❑ 268 Wes Obermueller .30 .10
❑ 269 Pete Orr RC .50 .20
❑ 270 Jim Thome .50 .20
❑ 271 Omar Vizquel .50 .20
❑ 272 Jose Valentin .30 .10
❑ 273 Juan Uribe .30 .10
❑ 274 Doug Mirabelli .30 .10
❑ 275 Jeff Kent .30 .10
❑ 276 Brad Wilkerson .30 .10
❑ 277 Chris Burke .30 .10
❑ 278 Endy Chavez .30 .10
❑ 279 Richard Hidalgo .30 .10
❑ 280 John Smoltz .50 .20
❑ 281 Jarrod Washburn .30 .10
❑ 282 Larry Bigbie .30 .10
❑ 283 Edgardo Alfonzo .30 .10
❑ 284 Cliff Lee .30 .10
❑ 285 Carlos Lee .30 .10
❑ 286 Olmedo Saenz .30 .10
❑ 287 Tomo Ohka .30 .10
❑ 288 Ruben Sierra .30 .10
❑ 289 Nick Swisher .30 .10
❑ 290 Frank Thomas .75 .30
❑ 291 Aaron Cook .30 .10
❑ 292 Cody McKay .30 .10
❑ 293 Hee-Seop Choi .30 .10
❑ 294 Carl Pavano .30 .10
❑ 295 Scott Rolen .50 .20
❑ 296 Matt Kata .30 .10
❑ 297 Terrence Long .30 .10
❑ 298 Jimmy Gobble .30 .10
❑ 299 Jason Repko .30 .10
❑ 300 Manny Ramirez .50 .20
❑ 301 Dan Wilson .30 .10
❑ 302 Jhonny Peralta .30 .10
❑ 303 John Mabry .30 .10
❑ 304 Adam Melhuse .30 .10
❑ 305 Kerry Wood .30 .10
❑ 306 Ryan Langerhans .30 .10
❑ 307 Antonio Alfonseca .30 .10
❑ 308 Marco Scutaro .30 .10
❑ 309 Jamey Carroll .30 .10
❑ 310 Lance Berkman .30 .10
❑ 311 Willie Harris .30 .10
❑ 312 Phil Nevin .30 .10
❑ 313 Gregg Zaun .30 .10
❑ 314 Michael Ryan .30 .10
❑ 315 Zack Greinke .30 .10
❑ 316 Ted Lilly .30 .10
❑ 317 David Eckstein .30 .10
❑ 318 Tony Torcato .30 .10
❑ 319 Rob Mackowiak .30 .10
❑ 320 Mark Teixeira .50 .20
❑ 321 Jason Phillips .30 .10
❑ 322 Jeremy Reed .30 .10
❑ 323 Bengie Molina .30 .10
❑ 324 Terrmel Sledge .30 .10
❑ 325 Justin Morneau .30 .10
❑ 326 Sandy Alomar Jr. .30 .10
❑ 327 Jon Garland .30 .10
❑ 328 Jay Payton .30 .10
❑ 329 Tino Martinez .50 .20
❑ 330 Jason Bay .30 .10
❑ 331 Jeff Conine .30 .10
❑ 332 Shawn Chacon .30 .10
❑ 333 Angel Berroa .30 .10
❑ 334 Reggie Sanders .30 .10
❑ 335 Kevin Brown .30 .10
❑ 336 Brady Clark .30 .10
❑ 337 Casey Fossum .30 .10
❑ 338 Raul Ibanez .30 .10
❑ 339 Derrek Lee .50 .20
❑ 340 Victor Martinez .30 .10
❑ 341 Kazuhisa Ishii .30 .10
❑ 342 Royce Clayton .30 .10
❑ 343 Trot Nixon .30 .10
❑ 344 Eric Young .30 .10
❑ 345 Aubrey Huff .30 .10
❑ 346 Brett Myers .30 .10
❑ 347 Joey Gathright .30 .10
❑ 348 Mark Grudzielanek .30 .10
❑ 349 Scott Spiezio .30 .10
❑ 350 Eric Chavez .30 .10
❑ 351 Einar Diaz .30 .10
❑ 352 Dallas McPherson .30 .10
❑ 353 John Thomson .30 .10
❑ 354 Neifi Perez .30 .10
❑ 355 Larry Walker .50 .20
❑ 356 Billy Wagner .30 .10
❑ 357 Mike Cameron .30 .10
❑ 358 Jimmy Rollins .30 .10
❑ 359 Kevin Mench .30 .10
❑ 360 Joe Mauer .75 .30
❑ 361 Jose Molina .30 .10
❑ 362 Joe Borchard .30 .10
❑ 363 Kevin Cash .30 .10
❑ 364 Jay Gibbons .30 .10
❑ 365 Khalil Greene .50 .20
❑ 366 Justin Leone .30 .10
❑ 367 Eddie Guardado .30 .10
❑ 368 Mike Lamb .30 .10
❑ 369 Matt Riley .30 .10
❑ 370 Luis Gonzalez .30 .10
❑ 371 Alfredo Amezaga .30 .10
❑ 372 J.J. Hardy .30 .10
❑ 373 Hector Luna .30 .10
❑ 374 Greg Aquino .30 .10
❑ 375 Jim Edmonds .30 .10
❑ 376 Joe Blanton .30 .10
❑ 377 Russell Branyan .30 .10
❑ 378 J.T. Snow .30 .10
❑ 379 Magglio Ordonez .30 .10
❑ 380 Rafael Palmeiro .50 .20
❑ 381 Andruw Jones .50 .20
❑ 382 David DeJesus .30 .10
❑ 383 Marquis Grissom .30 .10
❑ 384 Bobby Hill .30 .10
❑ 385 Kazuo Matsui .30 .10
❑ 386 Mark Loretta .30 .10
❑ 387 Chris Shelton .40 .15
❑ 388 Johnny Estrada .30 .10
❑ 389 Adam Hyzdu .30 .10
❑ 390 Nomar Garciaparra .75 .30
❑ 391 Mark Teahen .30 .10
❑ 392 Chris Capuano .30 .10
❑ 393 Ben Broussard .30 .10
❑ 394 Daniel Cabrera .30 .10
❑ 395 Jeremy Bonderman .30 .10
❑ 396 Darin Erstad .30 .10
❑ 397 Alex S. Gonzalez .30 .10
❑ 398 Kevin Millar .30 .10
❑ 399 Freddy Garcia .30 .10
❑ 400 Alfonso Soriano .30 .10
❑ 401 Koyie Hill .30 .10
❑ 402 Omar Infante .30 .10
❑ 403 Alex Gonzalez .30 .10
❑ 404 Pat Burrell .30 .10
❑ 405 Wes Helms .30 .10
❑ 406 Junior Spivey .30 .10
❑ 407 Joe Mays .30 .10
❑ 408 Jason Stanford .30 .10
❑ 409 Gil Meche .30 .10
❑ 410 Tim Hudson .30 .10
❑ 411 Chase Utley .50 .20
❑ 412 Matt Clement .30 .10
❑ 413 Nick Green .30 .10
❑ 414 Jose Vizcaino .30 .10
❑ 415 Ryan Klesko .30 .10
❑ 416 Vinny Castilla .30 .10
❑ 417 Brian Roberts .30 .10
❑ 418 Geronimo Gil .30 .10
❑ 419 Gary Matthews .30 .10
❑ 420 Jeff Weaver .30 .10
❑ 421 Jerome Williams .30 .10
❑ 422 Andy Pettitte .50 .20
❑ 423 Randy Wolf .30 .10
❑ 424 D'Angelo Jimenez .30 .10
❑ 425 Moises Alou .30 .10
❑ 426 Eric Byrnes .30 .10
❑ 427 Mark Redman .30 .10
❑ 428 Jermaine Dye .30 .10
❑ 429 Cory Lidle .30 .10
❑ 430 Jason Schmidt .30 .10
❑ 431 Jason W. Smith .30 .10
❑ 432 Jose Castillo .30 .10
❑ 433 Pokey Reese .30 .10
❑ 434 Matt Lawton .30 .10
❑ 435 Jose Guillen .30 .10
❑ 436 Craig Counsell .30 .10
❑ 437 Jose Hernandez .30 .10
❑ 438 Braden Looper .30 .10
❑ 439 Scott Hatteberg .30 .10
❑ 440 Gary Sheffield .30 .10
❑ 441 Gabe Gross .30 .10
❑ 442 Chris Gomez .30 .10
❑ 443 Dontrelle Willis .30 .10
❑ 444 Jamey Wright .30 .10
❑ 445 Rocco Baldelli .30 .10
❑ 446 Bernie Williams .50 .20
❑ 447 Sean Burroughs .30 .10
❑ 448 Willie Bloomquist .30 .10
❑ 449 Luis Castillo .30 .10
❑ 450 Mike Piazza .75 .30
❑ 451 Ryan Drese .30 .10
❑ 452 Pedro Feliz .30 .10
❑ 453 Horacio Ramirez .30 .10
❑ 454 Luis Matos .30 .10
❑ 455 Craig Wilson .30 .10
❑ 456 Russ Ortiz .30 .10
❑ 457 Xavier Nady .30 .10
❑ 458 Hideo Nomo .75 .30
❑ 459 Miguel Cairo .30 .10
❑ 460 Mike Lowell .30 .10
❑ 461 Corky Miller .30 .10
❑ 462 Bobby Madritsch .30 .10
❑ 463 Jose Contreras .30 .10
❑ 464 Johnny Damon .50 .20
❑ 465 Miguel Cabrera .50 .20
❑ 466 Eric Hinske .30 .10
❑ 467 Marlon Byrd .30 .10
❑ 468 Aaron Miles .30 .10
❑ 469 Ramon Vazquez .30 .10
❑ 470 Michael Young .30 .10
❑ 471 Alex Sanchez .30 .10
❑ 472 Shea Hillenbrand .30 .10
❑ 473 Jeff Bagwell .50 .20
❑ 474 Erik Bedard .30 .10
❑ 475 Jake Peavy .30 .10
❑ 476 Jody Gerut .30 .10
❑ 477 Randy Winn .30 .10
❑ 478 Kevin Youkilis .30 .10
❑ 479 Eric Dubose .30 .10
❑ 480 David Wright 1.25 .50
❑ 481 Wilson Valdez .30 .10
❑ 482 Cliff Floyd .30 .10

❑	483	Jose Mesa	.30	.10
❑	484	Doug Mientkiewicz	.30	.10
❑	485	Jorge Posada	.50	.20
❑	486	Sidney Ponson	.30	.10
❑	487	Dave Krynzel	.30	.10
❑	488	Octavio Dotel	.30	.10
❑	489	Matt Treanor	.30	.10
❑	490	Johan Santana	.75	.30
❑	491	John Patterson	.30	.10
❑	492	So Taguchi	.30	.10
❑	493	Carl Everett	.30	.10
❑	494	Jason Dubois	.30	.10
❑	495	Albert Pujols	1.50	.60
❑	496	Kirk Rueter	.30	.10
❑	497	Geoff Blum	.30	.10
❑	498	Juan Encarnacion	.30	.10
❑	499	Mark Hendrickson	.30	.10
❑	500	Barry Bonds	2.00	.75
❑	501	Cesar Izturis	.30	.10
❑	502	David Wells	.30	.10
❑	503	Jorge Julio	.30	.10
❑	504	Cristian Guzman	.30	.10
❑	505	Juan Pierre	.30	.10
❑	506	Adam Eaton	.30	.10
❑	507	Nick Johnson	.30	.10
❑	508	Mike Redmond	.30	.10
❑	509	Daryle Ward	.30	.10
❑	510	Adrian Beltre	.30	.10
❑	511	Laynce Nix	.30	.10
❑	512	Reed Johnson	.30	.10
❑	513	Jeremy Affeldt	.30	.10
❑	514	R.A. Dickey	.30	.10
❑	515	Alex Rios	.30	.10
❑	516	Orlando Palmeiro	.30	.10
❑	517	Mark Bellhorn	.30	.10
❑	518	Adam Kennedy	.30	.10
❑	519	Curtis Granderson	.30	.10
❑	520	Todd Helton	.50	.20
❑	521	Aaron Boone	.30	.10
❑	522	Milton Bradley	.30	.10
❑	523	Timo Perez	.30	.10
❑	524	Jeff Suppan	.30	.10
❑	525	Austin Kearns	.30	.10
❑	526	Charles Thomas	.30	.10
❑	527	Bronson Arroyo	.30	.10
❑	528	Roger Cedeno	.30	.10
❑	529	Russ Adams	.30	.10
❑	530	Barry Zito	.30	.10
❑	531	Bob Wickman	.30	.10
❑	532	Deivi Cruz	.30	.10
❑	533	Mariano Rivera	.75	.30
❑	534	J.J. Davis	.30	.10
❑	535	Greg Maddux	1.25	.50
❑	536	Ryan Vogelsong	.30	.10
❑	537	Josh Phelps	.30	.10
❑	538	Scott Hairston	.30	.10
❑	539	Vladimir Guerrero	.75	.30
❑	540	Ivan Rodriguez	.50	.20
❑	541	David Newhan	.30	.10
❑	542	David Bell	.30	.10
❑	543	Lew Ford	.30	.10
❑	544	Grady Sizemore	.50	.20
❑	545	David Ortiz	.75	.30
❑	546	Jose Cruz Jr.	.30	.10
❑	547	Aaron Rowand	.30	.10
❑	548	Marcus Thames	.30	.10
❑	549	Scott Podsednik	.30	.10
❑	550	Ichiro Suzuki	1.50	.60
❑	551	Eduardo Perez	.30	.10
❑	552	Chris Snyder	.30	.10
❑	553	Corey Koskie	.30	.10
❑	554	Miguel Tejada	.30	.10
❑	555	Orlando Cabrera	.30	.10
❑	556	Rondell White	.30	.10
❑	557	Wade Miller	.30	.10
❑	558	Rodrigo Lopez	.30	.10
❑	559	Chad Tracy	.30	.10
❑	560	Paul Konerko	.30	.10
❑	561	Wil Cordero	.30	.10
❑	562	John McDonald	.30	.10
❑	563	Jason Ellison	.30	.10
❑	564	Jason Michaels	.30	.10
❑	565	Melvin Mora	.30	.10
❑	566	Ryan Church	.30	.10
❑	567	Ryan Ludwick	.30	.10
❑	568	Erubiel Durazo	.30	.10
❑	569	Noah Lowry	.30	.10
❑	570	Curt Schilling	.50	.20
❑	571	Esteban Loaiza	.30	.10
❑	572	Freddy Sanchez	.30	.10
❑	573	Rich Aurilia	.30	.10
❑	574	Travis Lee	.30	.10
❑	575	Nick Punto	.30	.10
❑	576	J.Christiansen/K.Correia	.30	.10
❑	577	B.Baker/T.Redding	.30	.10
❑	578	T.Adams/G.Floyd	.30	.10
❑	579	S.Etherton/D.Meyer	.30	.10
❑	580	J.Lehr/D.Turnbow	.30	.10
❑	581	M.Gosling/B.Halsey	.30	.10
❑	582	J.Mecir/L.Kensing	.30	.10
❑	583	B.Hennessey/J.Fassero	.30	.10
❑	584	J.Adkins/F.Diaz	.30	.10
❑	585	J.Crain/J.Rincon	.30	.10
❑	586	J.Cerda/N.Field	.30	.10
❑	587	B.Fortunato/J.Seo	.30	.10
❑	588	S.Schmoll RC/Y.Brazoban	.50	.20
❑	589	U.Urbina/J.Walker	.30	.10
❑	590	J.De Paula/S.Proctor	.30	.10
❑	591	J.Davis/B.Howry	.30	.10
❑	592	T.Worrell/P.Liriano	.30	.10
❑	593	J.Acevedo/K.Mercker	.30	.10
❑	594	C.Hammond/S.Linebrink	.30	.10
❑	595	F.Nieve/J.Franco	.30	.10
❑	596	R.Flores/M.Lincoln	.30	.10
❑	597	J.Borowski/S.Mitre	.30	.10
❑	598	L.Carter/J.Colome	.30	.10
❑	599	J.Halama/L.DiNardo	.30	.10
❑	600	C.Bradford/K.Calero	.30	.10
❑	601	D.Aardsma/J.Brower	.30	.10
❑	602	G.Geary/R.Madson	.30	.10
❑	603	B.Moehler/N.Bump	.30	.10
❑	604	C.Tsao/R.Speier	.30	.10
❑	605	R.Wagner/A.Harang	.30	.10
❑	606	S.Kline/R.Bauer	.30	.10
❑	607	L.Cormier/R.Choate	.30	.10
❑	608	J.Leicester/T.Wellemeyer	.30	.10
❑	609	V.Chulk/J.Frasor	.30	.10
❑	610	S.Dohmann/B.Fuentes	.30	.10
❑	611	S.Colyer/R.Hernandez	.30	.10
❑	612	I.Snell/S.Torres	.30	.10
❑	613	C.Eldred/A.Wainwright	.30	.10
❑	614	R.Bukvich/D.Brocail	.30	.10
❑	615	J.Putz/A.Sele	.30	.10
❑	616	B.Chen/T.Williams	.30	.10
❑	617	D.Weathers/B.Weber	.30	.10
❑	618	D.Reyes/R.Seanez	.30	.10
❑	619	T.Harikkala/R.Rincon	.30	.10
❑	620	S.Camp/D.Bautista	.30	.10
❑	621	J.Lopez/A.Simpson	.30	.10
❑	622	M.Remlinger/G.Rusch	.30	.10
❑	623	R.Colon/K.Gryboski	.30	.10
❑	624	T.Martin/C.Reitsma	.30	.10
❑	625	C.Qualls/D.Wheeler	.30	.10
❑	626	T.Phelps/M.Wise	.30	.10
❑	627	S.Schoeneweis/J.Speier	.30	.10
❑	628	F.Cordero/F.Francisco	.30	.10
❑	629	R.Soriano/M.Thornton	.30	.10
❑	630	M.Stanton/S.Karsay	.30	.10
❑	631	M.MacDougal/S.Sullivan	.30	.10
❑	632	B.Bruney/O.Villarreal	.30	.10
❑	633	M.Adams/R.Bottalico	.30	.10
❑	634	E.Rodriguez/D.Borkowski	.30	.10
❑	635	R.Betancourt/D.Riske	.30	.10
❑	636	J.De La Rosa/G.Glover	.30	.10
❑	637	M.Perisho/B.Howard	.30	.10
❑	638	J.Bajenaru/L.Vizcaino	.30	.10
❑	639	R.Mahay/E.Ramirez	.30	.10
❑	640	J.Grabow/M.Gonzalez	.30	.10
❑	641	J.Romero/M.Guerrier	.30	.10
❑	642	C.Hernandez/B.Duckworth	.30	.10
❑	643	T.Harper/S.McClung	.30	.10
❑	644	M.Herges/T.Walker	.30	.10
❑	645	K.Wunsch/E.Dessens	.30	.10
❑	646	M.Malaska/M.Myers	.30	.10
❑	647	K.Farnsworth/G.Knotts	.30	.10
❑	648	J.Duchscherer/J.Garcia	.30	.10
❑	649	A.Rakers/S.Reed	.30	.10
❑	650	T.Gordon/P.Quantrill	.30	.10
❑	651	B.Lyon/S.Estes	.30	.10
❑	652	P.Walker/G.Chacin	.30	.10
❑	653	J.Lackey/S.Shields	.30	.10
❑	654	D.Waechter/T.Miller	.30	.10
❑	655	L.Ayala/C.Cordero	.30	.10
❑	656	R.Villone/J.Mateo	.30	.10
❑	657	M.Mantei/B.Neal	.30	.10
❑	658	D.Marte/C.Politte	.30	.10
❑	659	J.Valentine/L.Hudson	.30	.10
❑	660	T.Jones/J.Riedling	.30	.10
❑	661	H.Bell/A.Heilman	.30	.10
❑	662	D.May/A.Otsuka	.30	.10
❑	663	J.Eischen/J.Horgan	.30	.10
❑	664	A.Sisco/M.Wood	.30	.10
❑	665	A.Embree/M.Timlin	.30	.10
❑	666	Keith Foulke	.30	.10
❑	667	R.Cormier/A.Fultz	.30	.10
❑	668	J.Woods/K.Gregg	.30	.10
❑	669	M.Ginter/F.German	.30	.10
❑	670	S.Eyre/M.Valdez	.30	.10
❑	671	B.Meadows/R.White	.30	.10
❑	672	G.Mota/T.Spooneybarger	.30	.10
❑	673	J.Grimsley/B.Ryan	.30	.10
❑	674	N.Cotts/S.Takatsu	.30	.10
❑	675	M.DeJean/F.Heredia	.30	.10
❑	676	M.Belisle/J.Hancock	.30	.10
❑	677	J.Rauch/T.Tucker	.30	.10
❑	678	N.Regilio/B.Shouse	.30	.10
❑	679	J.Tavarez/R.King	.30	.10
❑	680	C.Fox/M.Wuertz	.30	.10
❑	681	J.Sosa/A.Bernero	.30	.10
❑	682	J.Valverde/M.Koplove	.30	.10
❑	683	A.Rhodes/S.Sauerbeck	.30	.10
❑	684	F.Rodriguez/T.Sturtze	.30	.10
❑	685	G.Carrara/D.Sanchez	.30	.10
❑	686	M.Gallo/C.Harville	.30	.10
❑	687	M.Johnston/S.Burnett	.30	.10
❑	688	J.Nelson/S.Hasegawa	.30	.10
❑	689	C.Vargas/A.Osuna	.30	.10
❑	690	B.Donnelly/E.Yan	.30	.10
❑	691	J.Mathis/E.Santana	.50	.20
❑	692	C.Everts/B.Bray	.50	.20
❑	693	J.Kubel/T.Plouffe	.50	.20
❑	694	J.Stevens/A.Marte	.50	.20
❑	695	A.Hill/C.Gaudin	.50	.20
❑	696	C.Quentin/J.Cota	.50	.20
❑	697	T.Diamond/C.Young	.50	.20
❑	698	O.Quintanilla/D.Johnson	.50	.20
❑	699	J.Maine/V.Majewski	.50	.20
❑	700	J.Houser/J.Gomes	.50	.20
❑	701	D.Murphy/H.Ramirez	.50	.20
❑	702	C.Lambert/R.Ankiel	.50	.20
❑	703	F.Pie/A.Guzman	.50	.20
❑	704	F.Lewis/N.Schierholtz	.50	.20
❑	705	A.Munoz/G.Gonzalez	.50	.20
❑	706	F.Hernandez/T.Blackley	1.50	.60
❑	707	R.Olmedo/E.Encarnacion	.50	.20
❑	708	T.Stauffer/J.Germano	.50	.20
❑	709	J.Guthrie/J.Sowers	.50	.20
❑	710	J.Cortes/T.Gorzelanny	.50	.20
❑	711	T.Tankersley/E.Reed	.50	.20
❑	712	N.Walker/P.Maholm	.50	.20
❑	713	W.Taveras/L.Scott RC	1.50	.60
❑	714	R.Howard/G.Golson	2.00	.75
❑	715	B.DeWitt/E.Jackson	.50	.20
❑	716	H.Street/D.Putnam	.50	.20
❑	717	R.Weeks/M.Rogers	.50	.20
❑	718	R.Cano/P.Hughes	.50	.20
❑	719	K.Waldrop/J.Rainville	.50	.20
❑	720	C.Brazell/Y.Petit	.50	.20
❑	721	B.Lopez RC/M.Brown RC	.50	.20
❑	722	D.Thomp RC/E.Chavez RC	.50	.20
❑	723	D.Uggla RC/E.Sch'wolf RC	10.00	4.00
❑	724	I.Ramirez RC/J.Tingler RC	.50	.20
❑	725	T.G'tano RC/E.de la Cruz RC	.50	.20
❑	726	M.Campbell RC/S.Costa RC	.50	.20
❑	727	M.Prado RC/Bi.McCarthy RC	.50	.20
❑	728	I.Kinsler RC/J.Senreiso RC	2.50	1.00
❑	729	L.Ramirez RC/Lo.Scott RC	.50	.20
❑	730	C.Seddon RC/E.Johnson RC	.50	.20
❑	731	C.Tatum RC/J.Moran RC	.50	.20
❑	732	S.Pomeranz RC/J.Motte RC	.50	.20
❑	733	J.Vaquedano RC/S.Bailie RC	.50	.20
❑	734	M.Albers RC/W.Robinson RC	1.25	.50
❑	735	M.DeSalvo RC/Me.Cabr RC	2.00	.75
❑	736	B.Stavisky RC/L.Powell RC	.50	.20
❑	737	S.Mathieson RC/S.Mitch RC	.75	.30
❑	738	S.Marshall RC/B.Bay RC	1.50	.60
❑	739	B.McCarthy RC/P.Lopez RC	1.25	.50
❑	740	A.Smit RC/R.Barrett RC	.50	.20

❑ 741 M.R'stad RC/R.F'bend RC .50 .20
❑ 742 N.McLouth RC/A.Boeve RC .50 .20
❑ 743 K.Melillo RC/M.Rogers RC .75 .30
❑ 744 M.Kemp RC/H.Totten RC 4.00 1.50
❑ 745 J.Miller RC/T.Americh RC .50 .20
❑ 746 T.Pelland RC/J.Gutierrez RC .50 .20
❑ 747 J.West RC/W.Mota RC .50 .20
❑ 748 R.Goleski RC/R.Garko RC 1.50 .60
❑ 749 B.Triplett RC/J.Gothreaux RC .50 .20
❑ 750 K.West RC/G.Perkins RC .75 .30
❑ 751 M.Esposito RC/Z.Parker RC .50 .20
❑ 752 R.Sweeney RC/B.Miller RC 1.00 .40
❑ 753 C.McGehee RC/B.Coats RC .50 .20
❑ 754 M.Bourn RC/K.Pichardo RC .75 .30
❑ 755 M.Morse RC/B.Livingston RC .75 .30
❑ 756 W.Swack RC/B.Ryan RC .50 .20
❑ 757 M.Furtado RC/N.Masset RC .50 .20
❑ 758 P.Ramos RC/G.Kottaras RC .75 .30
❑ 759 E.Quezada RC/T.Beam RC .75 .30
❑ 760 D.Eveland RC/T.Hinton RC .50 .20
❑ 761 J.Jurries RC/C.Vines RC .50 .20
❑ 762 H.Sanch RC/J.Verlander RC 5.00 2.00
❑ 763 P.Humber RC/S.Bowman RC .75 .30
❑ 764 P.Misch RC/J.Thurmond RC .50 .20
❑ 765 C.Colonel RC/N.Wilson RC .50 .20
❑ 766 Checklist 1 .30 .10
❑ 767 Checklist 2 .30 .10
❑ 768 Checklist 3 .30 .10
❑ 769 Checklist 4 .30 .10
❑ 770 Checklist 5 .30 .10

2006 Topps Triple Threads

❑ COMMON CARD (1-100) 4.00 1.50
❑ 1-100 THREE PER PACK
❑ COMMON CARD (101-120) 15.00 6.00
❑ MINOR STARS 101-112 25.00 10.00
❑ SEMISTARS 101-112 40.00 15.00
❑ COMMON CARD (113-120) 15.00 6.00
❑ MINOR STARS 113-120 25.00 10.00
❑ SEMISTARS 113-120 40.00 15.00
❑ 101-120 ODDS 1:7 MINI
❑ 101-120 PRINT RUN 225 SERIAL #'d SETS
❑ OVERALL 1-100 PLATE ODDS 1:80 MINI
❑ PLATE PRINT RUN 1 SET PER COLOR
❑ BLACK-CYAN-MAGENTA-YELLOW ISSUED
❑ NO PLATE PRICING DUE TO SCARCITY
❑ 1 Hideki Matsui 5.00 2.00
❑ 2 Josh Gibson HOF 5.00 2.00
❑ 3 Roger Clemens 8.00 3.00
❑ 4 Paul Konerko 3.00 1.25
❑ 5 Brooks Robinson HOF 4.00 1.50
❑ 6 Stan Musial HOF 5.00 2.00
❑ 7 Dontrelle Willis 3.00 1.25
❑ 8 Yogi Berra HOF 5.00 2.00
❑ 9 John Smoltz 4.00 1.50
❑ 10 Brian Roberts 3.00 1.25
❑ 11 Gary Sheffield 3.00 1.25
❑ 12 Wade Boggs HOF 4.00 1.50
❑ 13 Alex Rodriguez 8.00 3.00
❑ 14 Ernie Banks HOF 5.00 2.00
❑ 15 Ichiro Suzuki 8.00 3.00
❑ 16 Whitey Ford HOF 4.00 1.50
❑ 17 Vladimir Guerrero 5.00 2.00
❑ 18 Tadahito Iguchi 3.00 1.25
❑ 19 Robin Yount HOF 5.00 2.00
❑ 20 Jason Schmidt 3.00 1.25
❑ 21 Roberto Clemente HOF 10.00 4.00
❑ 22 Andruw Jones 4.00 1.50
❑ 23 Don Mattingly HOF 10.00 4.00
❑ 24 Joe Mauer 4.00 1.50
❑ 25 Barry Bonds 12.00 5.00
❑ 26 Johnny Damon 4.00 1.50
❑ 27 Chris Carpenter 3.00 1.25
❑ 28 Garret Anderson 3.00 1.25
❑ 29 Scott Rolen 4.00 1.50
❑ 30 Tim Hudson 3.00 1.25
❑ 31 Dave Winfield HOF 3.00 1.25
❑ 32 Steve Carlton HOF 3.00 1.25
❑ 33 Miguel Tejada 3.00 1.25
❑ 34 Nolan Ryan HOF 10.00 4.00
❑ 35 Mark Buehrle 3.00 1.25
❑ 36 Travis Hafner 3.00 1.25
❑ 37 Rickie Weeks 3.00 1.25
❑ 38 Sammy Sosa 5.00 2.00
❑ 39 Carlos Beltran 3.00 1.25
❑ 40 Todd Helton 4.00 1.50
❑ 41 Tom Seaver HOF 4.00 1.50
❑ 42 Ted Williams HOF 6.00 2.50
❑ 43 Alfonso Soriano 3.00 1.25
❑ 44 Reggie Jackson HOF 4.00 1.50
❑ 45 Pedro Martinez 4.00 1.50
❑ 46 Randy Johnson 5.00 2.00
❑ 47 Ted Williams HOF 6.00 2.50
❑ 48 Torii Hunter 3.00 1.25
❑ 49 Manny Ramirez 4.00 1.50
❑ 50 George Brett HOF 6.00 2.50
❑ 51 Chipper Jones 5.00 2.00
❑ 52 Nomar Garciaparra 4.00 1.50
❑ 53 Richie Sexson 3.00 1.25
❑ 54 David Ortiz 5.00 2.00
❑ 55 Derek Jeter 15.00 6.00
❑ 56 Mickey Mantle HOF 15.00 6.00
❑ 57 Michael Young 3.00 1.25
❑ 58 Aramis Ramirez 3.00 1.25
❑ 59 Bartolo Colon 3.00 1.25
❑ 60 Troy Glaus 3.00 1.25
❑ 61 Carlos Delgado 3.00 1.25
❑ 62 Mike Sweeney 3.00 1.25
❑ 63 Jorge Cantu 3.00 1.25
❑ 64 Mike Mussina 4.00 1.50
❑ 65 Hank Blalock 3.00 1.25
❑ 66 Frank Robinson HOF 3.00 1.25
❑ 67 Carl Yastrzemski HOF 5.00 2.00
❑ 68 Adam Dunn 3.00 1.25
❑ 69 Eric Chavez 3.00 1.25
❑ 70 Curt Schilling 4.00 1.50
❑ 71 Jeff Francoeur 6.00 2.50
❑ 72 C.C. Sabathia 3.00 1.25
❑ 73 Roy Oswalt 3.00 1.25
❑ 74 Carlos Lee 3.00 1.25
❑ 75 Barry Zito 3.00 1.25
❑ 76 Derrek Lee 4.00 1.50
❑ 77 Greg Maddux 6.00 2.50
❑ 78 Ivan Rodriguez 4.00 1.50
❑ 79 Jeff Kent 3.00 1.25
❑ 80 Gary Carter HOF 3.00 1.25
❑ 81 Jose Reyes 3.00 1.25
❑ 82 Johan Santana 4.00 1.50
❑ 83 Magglio Ordonez 3.00 1.25
❑ 84 Mark Prior 4.00 1.50
❑ 85 Johnny Bench HOF 5.00 2.00
❑ 86 Vernon Wells 3.00 1.25
❑ 87 Mark Mulder 3.00 1.25
❑ 88 Cal Ripken 15.00 6.00
❑ 89 Mark Teixeira 4.00 1.50
❑ 90 Miguel Cabrera 4.00 1.50
❑ 91 Duke Snider HOF 4.00 1.50
❑ 92 Jason Giambi 3.00 1.25
❑ 93 Albert Pujols 8.00 3.00
❑ 94 Carl Crawford 3.00 1.25
❑ 95 Jim Edmonds 3.00 1.25
❑ 96 Jose Contreras 3.00 1.25
❑ 97 Victor Martinez 3.00 1.25
❑ 98 Jeremy Bonderman 3.00 1.25
❑ 99 Lance Berkman 3.00 1.25
❑ 100 Rocco Baldelli 3.00 1.25
❑ 101 Zach Duke AU J-J 25.00 10.00
❑ 102 Felix Hernandez AU J-J 40.00 15.00
❑ 103 Dan Johnson AU J-J 15.00 6.00
❑ 104 Brandon McCarthy AU J-J 25.00 10.00
❑ 105 Huston Street AU J-J 25.00 10.00
❑ 106 Robinson Cano AU J-J 50.00 20.00
❑ 107 Jason Bay AU J-J 25.00 10.00
❑ 108 Ryan Howard AU B-B 120.00 60.00
❑ 109 Ervin Santana AU J-J 15.00 6.00
❑ 110 Rich Harden AU J-J 15.00 6.00
❑ 111 Aaron Hill AU J-J 15.00 6.00
❑ 112 David Wright AU J-J 60.00 30.00
❑ 114 Nelson Cruz AU J-J (RC) 15.00 6.00
❑ 115 F.Liriano AU J-J (RC) 100.00 50.00
❑ 116 Hong-Chih Kuo AU J-J (RC) 120.00 60.00
❑ 117 Ryan Garko AU J-J (RC) 25.00 10.00
❑ 118 Craig Hansen AU J-J RC 50.00 20.00
❑ 119 Shin-Soo Choo AU J-J (RC) 15.006.00
❑ 120 Darrell Rasner AU J-J (RC) 15.00 6.00

2007 Topps Triple Threads

❑ COMP.SET w/o AU's (125) 200.00 125.00
❑ COMMON CARD (1-125) 1.00 .40
❑ 1-125 STATED PRINT RUN 1350 SER.#'d SETS
❑ COMMON JSY AU 12.00 5.00
❑ 126-189 JSY AU ODDS 1:9 MINI
❑ 126-189 JSY AU VARIATION ODDS 1:38 MINI
❑ 126-189 JSY AU PRINT RUN 99 SER.#'d SETS
❑ TEAM INITIAL DIECUTS ARE VARIATIONS
❑ OVERALL 1-125 PLATE ODDS 1:113 MINI
❑ PLATE PRINT RUN 1 SET PER COLOR
❑ BLACK-CYAN-MAGENTA-YELLOW ISSUED
❑ NO PLATE PRICING DUE TO SCARCITY
❑ 1 Alex Rodriguez 3.00 1.25
❑ 2 Barry Zito 1.00 .40
❑ 3 Corey Patterson 1.00 .40
❑ 4 Roberto Clemente 6.00 2.50
❑ 5 David Wright 3.00 1.25
❑ 6 Dontrelle Willis 1.00 .40
❑ 7 Mickey Mantle 8.00 3.00
❑ 8 Adam Dunn 1.00 .40
❑ 9 Richie Ashburn 1.50 .60
❑ 10 Ryan Howard 3.00 1.25
❑ 11 Miguel Tejada 1.00 .40
❑ 12 Ernie Banks 2.50 1.00
❑ 13 Ken Griffey Jr. 3.00 1.25
❑ 14 Johnny Bench 2.50 1.00
❑ 15 Ichiro Suzuki 3.00 1.25
❑ 16 Gil Meche 1.00 .40
❑ 17 Kazuo Matsui 1.00 .40
❑ 18 Matt Holliday 1.25 .50
❑ 19 Juan Pierre 1.00 .40
❑ 20 Yogi Berra 2.50 1.00
❑ 21 Bill Hall 1.00 .40
❑ 22 Wade Boggs 1.50 .60
❑ 23 Jason Bay 1.00 .40
❑ 24 Troy Glaus 1.00 .40
❑ 25 Paul Konerko 1.00 .40
❑ 26 Rod Carew 1.50 .60
❑ 27 Jay Gibbons 1.00 .40
❑ 28 Frank Thomas 2.50 1.00
❑ 29 Joe Mauer 1.50 .60
❑ 30 Carlos Beltran 1.00 .40
❑ 31 Frank Robinson 1.00 .40
❑ 32 Bobby Abreu 1.00 .40
❑ 33 Roy Oswalt 1.00 .40
❑ 34 Edgar Renteria 1.00 .40
❑ 35 Magglio Ordonez 1.00 .40
❑ 36 Mike Piazza 2.50 1.00
❑ 37 Trevor Hoffman 1.00 .40
❑ 38 Eddie Mathews 2.50 1.00
❑ 39 Albert Pujols 4.00 1.50
❑ 40 Dennis Eckersley 1.00 .40
❑ 41 Andruw Jones 1.50 .60

❑ 42 Alfonso Soriano	1.00	.40
❑ 43 Bob Feller	1.00	.40
❑ 44 J.D. Drew	1.00	.40
❑ 45 Jason Schmidt	1.00	.40
❑ 46 Vladimir Guerrero	2.50	1.00
❑ 47 Reggie Jackson	1.50	.60
❑ 48 Lance Berkman	1.00	.40
❑ 49 Michael Young	1.00	.40
❑ 50 Carlton Fisk	1.50	.60
❑ 51 Brandon Webb	1.00	.40
❑ 52 Adrian Beltre	1.00	.40
❑ 53 Hideki Matsui	2.50	1.00
❑ 54 Bronson Arroyo	1.00	.40
❑ 55 Tony Gwynn	2.50	1.00
❑ 56 Ray Durham	1.00	.40
❑ 57 Garrett Atkins	1.00	.40
❑ 58 Nolan Ryan	5.00	2.00
❑ 59 Daisuke Matsuzaka RC	15.00	6.00
❑ 60 Todd Helton	1.50	.60
❑ 61 Carl Crawford	1.00	.40
❑ 62 Jake Peavy	1.00	.40
❑ 63 Rafael Furcal	1.00	.40
❑ 64 Joe Morgan	1.00	.40
❑ 65 Greg Maddux	3.00	1.25
❑ 66 Luis Aparicio	1.00	.40
❑ 67 Derrek Lee	1.00	.40
❑ 68 Johnny Damon	1.50	.60
❑ 69 Mike Lowell	1.00	.40
❑ 70 Roger Maris	2.50	1.00
❑ 71 Vernon Wells	1.00	.40
❑ 72 Monte Irvin	1.00	.40
❑ 73 Jermaine Dye	1.00	.40
❑ 74 Miguel Cabrera	1.50	.60
❑ 75 Barry Bonds	4.00	1.50
❑ 76 Stan Musial	3.00	1.25
❑ 77 Derek Lowe	1.00	.40
❑ 78 Don Mattingly	4.00	1.50
❑ 79 Lyle Overbay	1.00	.40
❑ 80 Chien-Ming Wang	3.00	1.25
❑ 81 Carlos Zambrano	1.00	.40
❑ 82 Kei Igawa RC	3.00	1.25
❑ 83 Cole Hamels	1.50	.60
❑ 84 Gary Sheffield	1.00	.40
❑ 85 Nick Johnson	1.00	.40
❑ 86 Brooks Robinson	1.50	.60
❑ 87 Curt Schilling	1.50	.60
❑ 88 Ryne Sandberg	4.00	1.50
❑ 89 Mike Cameron	1.00	.40
❑ 90 Mike Schmidt	3.00	1.25
❑ 91 Chris Carpenter	1.00	.40
❑ 92 Scott Rolen	1.50	.60
❑ 93 Rocco Baldelli	1.00	.40
❑ 94 C.C. Sabathia	1.00	.40
❑ 95 Jeff Francis	1.00	.40
❑ 96 Ozzie Smith	3.00	1.25
❑ 97 Aramis Ramirez	1.00	.40
❑ 98 Aaron Harang	1.00	.40
❑ 99 Duke Snider	1.50	.60
❑ 100 David Ortiz	2.50	1.00
❑ 101 Raul Ibanez	1.00	.40
❑ 102 Bruce Sutter	1.00	.40
❑ 103 Gary Matthews	1.00	.40
❑ 104 Chipper Jones	2.50	1.00
❑ 105 Craig Biggio	1.50	.60
❑ 106 Roy Halladay	1.00	.40
❑ 107 Hoyt Wilhelm	1.00	.40
❑ 108 Manny Ramirez	1.50	.60
❑ 109 Randy Johnson	2.50	1.00
❑ 110 Carl Yastrzemski	3.00	1.25
❑ 111 Mark Teixeira	1.50	.60
❑ 112 Derek Jeter	5.00	2.00
❑ 113 Stephen Drew	1.50	.60
❑ 114 Darryl Strawberry	1.00	.40
❑ 115 Travis Hafner	1.00	.40
❑ 116 Torii Hunter	1.00	.40
❑ 117 Jim Edmonds	1.50	.60
❑ 118 John Smoltz	1.50	.60
❑ 119 Bo Jackson	2.50	1.00
❑ 120 Roger Clemens	4.00	1.50
❑ 121 Pedro Martinez	1.50	.60
❑ 122 Rickey Henderson	2.50	1.00
❑ 123 Ivan Rodriguez	1.50	.60
❑ 124 Robin Yount	2.50	1.00
❑ 125 Johan Santana	1.50	.60
❑ 126a Robinson Cano Jsy AU	40.00	15.00
❑ 126b Robinson Cano Jsy AU	40.00	15.00
❑ 127a Jose Reyes Jsy AU	60.00	30.00
❑ 127b Jose Reyes Jsy AU	60.00	30.00
❑ 128a Justin Morneau Jsy AU	25.00	10.00
❑ 128b Justin Morneau Jsy AU	25.00	10.00
❑ 129a Curtis Granderson Jsy AU	30.00	12.50
❑ 129b Curtis Granderson Jsy AU	30.00	12.50
❑ 130a Justin Verlander Jsy AU	40.00	15.00
❑ 130b Justin Verlander Jsy AU	40.00	15.00
❑ 131 Prince Fielder Jsy AU	60.00	30.00
❑ 132a Ryan Zimmerman Jsy AU	40.00	15.00
❑ 132b Ryan Zimmerman Jsy AU	40.00	15.00
❑ 133 Mike Napoli Jsy AU	12.00	5.00
❑ 134 Melky Cabrera Jsy AU	25.00	10.00
❑ 135 Jonathan Papelbon Jsy AU	40.00	15.00
❑ 136a Nick Markakis Jsy AU	25.00	10.00
❑ 136b Nick Markakis Jsy AU	25.00	10.00
❑ 137 B.J. Upton Jsy AU	20.00	8.00
❑ 138a Joel Zumaya Jsy AU	25.00	10.00
❑ 138b Joel Zumaya Jsy AU	25.00	10.00
❑ 140 Nick Swisher Jsy AU	25.00	10.00
❑ 141 Andre Ethier Jsy AU	20.00	8.00
❑ 142a Jered Weaver Jsy AU	25.00	10.00
❑ 142b Jered Weaver Jsy AU	25.00	10.00
❑ 143 Matt Cain Jsy AU	30.00	12.50
❑ 144 Lastings Milledge Jsy AU	20.00	8.00
❑ 145 Brian McCann Jsy AU	40.00	15.00
❑ 146 Shin-Soo Choo Jsy AU	15.00	6.00
❑ 147a Dan Uggla Jsy AU	25.00	10.00
❑ 147b Dan Uggla Jsy AU	25.00	10.00
❑ 148 Hanley Ramirez Jsy AU	40.00	15.00
❑ 149 Russell Martin Jsy AU	40.00	15.00
❑ 150 Francisco Liriano Jsy AU	25.00	10.00
❑ 151 Anthony Reyes Jsy AU	12.00	5.00
❑ 152 Josh Barfield Jsy AU	15.00	6.00
❑ 153 Anibal Sanchez Jsy AU	12.00	5.00
❑ 154 Jeremy Hermida Jsy AU	15.00	6.00
❑ 155 Kendry Morales Jsy AU	12.00	5.00
❑ 156 Matt Kemp Jsy AU	25.00	10.00
❑ 157 Freddy Sanchez Jsy AU	15.00	6.00
❑ 158 Howie Kendrick Jsy AU	20.00	8.00
❑ 159 Scott Thorman Jsy AU	20.00	8.00
❑ 160 Franklin Gutierrez Bat AU	15.00	6.00
❑ 161 Jason Bartlett Jsy AU	15.00	6.00
❑ 162 Chris Duncan Jsy AU	50.00	20.00
❑ 163 Maicer Izturis Jsy AU	12.00	5.00
❑ 164 Jason Botts Jsy AU	12.00	5.00
❑ 165 Tony Gwynn Jr. Jsy AU	40.00	15.00
❑ 166 Jorge Cantu Jsy AU	12.00	5.00
❑ 167 Adam Jones Jsy AU	40.00	15.00
❑ 168 Edinson Volquez Jsy AU	12.00	5.00
❑ 169 Joey Gathright Jsy AU	12.00	5.00
❑ 170 Carlos Marmol Jsy AU	20.00	8.00
❑ 171 Ben Zobrist Jsy AU	15.00	6.00
❑ 172 Josh Willingham Jsy AU	12.00	5.00
❑ 173 Brad Thompson Jsy AU	25.00	10.00
❑ 174a Chris Ray Jsy AU	15.00	6.00
❑ 174b Ervin Santana Jsy AU	15.00	6.00
❑ 175 Ronny Paulino Jsy AU	12.00	5.00
❑ 176 Tyler Johnson Jsy AU	12.00	5.00
❑ 177 J.J. Hardy Jsy AU	30.00	12.50
❑ 178 Adrian Gonzalez Jsy AU	20.00	8.00
❑ 179 Scott Kazmir Jsy AU	25.00	10.00
❑ 180 Juan Morillo Jsy AU (RC)	12.00	5.00
❑ 181a Shawn Riggans JSY AU (RC)	12.00	5.00
❑ 181b Shawn Riggans JSY AU (RC)	12.00	5.00
❑ 182 Brian Stokes JSY AU (RC)	12.00	5.00
❑ 183 Delmon Young JSY AU (RC)	30.00	12.50
❑ 184a Troy Tulowitzki JSY AU (RC)	60.00	30.00
❑ 184b Troy Tulowitzki JSY AU (RC)	60.00	30.00
❑ 185 Adam Lind JSY AU (RC)	15.00	6.00
❑ 186 David Murphy JSY AU (RC)	15.00	6.00
❑ 187a Philip Humber JSY AU (RC)	15.00	6.00
❑ 187b Philip Humber JSY AU (RC)	15.00	6.00
❑ 188a Andrew Miller JSY AU RC	60.00	30.00
❑ 188b Andrew Miller JSY AU RC	60.00	30.00
❑ 189a Glen Perkins JSY AU (RC)	12.00	5.00
❑ 189b Glen Perkins JSY AU (RC)	12.00	5.00

2005 Topps Turkey Red

❑ COMPLETE SET (330)	300.00	200.00
❑ COMP.SET w/o SP's (275)	50.00	20.00
❑ COMMON CARD (1-270)	.40	.15
❑ COMMON SP (1-270)	8.00	3.00
❑ SP CL: 160A/160B/170/175/181/184/185/193		
❑ COMMON REPRINT	.75	.30
❑ COMMON RC (271-300)	1.00	.40
❑ COMMON RET (301-315)	1.00	.40
❑ VAR CL: 1/5/10/16/75/83/100/102/120/125		
❑ VAR CL: 130/160/225/230/270		
❑ TWO VERSIONS OF EACH VARIATION EXIST		
❑ 1A B.Bonds Grey Uni SP	15.00	6.00
❑ 1B B.Bonds White Uni	2.50	1.00
❑ 2 Michael Young	.40	.15
❑ 3 Jim Edmonds	.40	.15
❑ 4 Cliff Floyd	.40	.15
❑ 5A R.Clemens Blue Sky SP	10.00	4.00
❑ 5B R.Clemens Yellow Sky SP	10.00	4.00
❑ 6 Hal Chase REP	.75	.30
❑ 7 Shannon Stewart	.40	.15
❑ 8 Fred Clarke REP	.75	.30
❑ 9 Travis Hafner	.40	.15
❑ 10A S.Sosa w/Name SP	8.00	3.00
❑ 10B S.Sosa w/o Name SP	8.00	3.00
❑ 11 Jermaine Dye	.40	.15
❑ 12 Lyle Overbay	.40	.15
❑ 13 Oliver Perez	.40	.15
❑ 14 Red Dooin REP	.75	.30
❑ 15 Kid Elberfeld REP	.75	.30
❑ 16A M.Piazza Blue Uni SP	8.00	3.00
❑ 16B M.Piazza Pinstripe	1.00	.40
❑ 17 Bret Boone	.40	.15
❑ 18 Hughie Jennings REP	.75	.30
❑ 19 Jeff Francis	.40	.15
❑ 20 Manny Ramirez SP	8.00	3.00
❑ 21 Russ Ortiz	.40	.15
❑ 22 Carlos Zambrano	.40	.15
❑ 23 Luis Castillo	.40	.15
❑ 24 David DeJesus	.40	.15
❑ 25 Carlos Beltran SP	8.00	3.00
❑ 26 Doug Davis	.40	.15
❑ 27 Bobby Abreu	.40	.15
❑ 28 Rich Harden SP	8.00	3.00
❑ 29 Brian Giles	.40	.15
❑ 30 Richie Sexson SP	8.00	3.00
❑ 31 Nick Johnson	.40	.15
❑ 32 Roy Halladay	.40	.15
❑ 33 Andy Pettitte	.60	.25
❑ 34 Miguel Cabrera	.60	.25
❑ 35 Jeff Kent	.40	.15
❑ 36 Chone Figgins	.40	.15
❑ 37 Carlos Lee	.40	.15
❑ 38 Greg Maddux	1.50	.60
❑ 39 Preston Wilson	.40	.15
❑ 40 Chipper Jones	1.00	.40
❑ 41 Coco Crisp	.40	.15
❑ 42 Adam Dunn	.40	.15
❑ 43 Out At Second M.Tejada CL	.40	.15
❑ 44 Sheffield At Bat CL	.40	.15
❑ 45 Play At the Plate J.Lopez CL	.40	.15
❑ 46 Rolen Diggin' In CL	.40	.15
❑ 47 Helton With the Slap Tag CL	.40	.15
❑ 48 Clemens Bringing Heat CL	1.00	.40
❑ 49 A Close Play J.Rollins CL	.40	.15
❑ 50 Ichiro At Bat CL	1.00	.40
❑ 51 Can of Corn C.Floyd CL	.40	.15
❑ 52 Pulling String J.Santana CL	1.00	.40
❑ 53 Mark Teixeira	.60	.25
❑ 54 Chris Carpenter	.40	.15
❑ 55 Roy Oswalt SP	8.00	3.00
❑ 56 Casey Kotchman	.40	.15
❑ 57 Torii Hunter	.40	.15
❑ 58 Jose Reyes	.40	.15
❑ 59 Wily Mo Pena SP	8.00	3.00

❑	60	Magglio Ordonez SP	8.00	3.00
❑	61	Aaron Miles	.40	.15
❑	62	Dallas McPherson	.40	.15
❑	63	Javy Lopez	.40	.15
❑	64	Luis Gonzalez	.40	.15
❑	65	David Ortiz	1.00	.40
❑	66	Jorge Posada	.60	.25
❑	67	Xavier Nady	.40	.15
❑	68	Larry Walker	.60	.25
❑	69	Mark Loretta	.40	.15
❑	70	Jim Thome SP	8.00	3.00
❑	71	Livan Hernandez	.40	.15
❑	72	Garrett Atkins	.40	.15
❑	73	Milton Bradley	.40	.15
❑	74	B.J. Upton	.40	.15
❑	75A	I.Suzuki w/Name SP	10.00	4.00
❑	75B	I.Suzuki w/o Name SP	10.00	4.00
❑	76	Aramis Ramirez	.40	.15
❑	77	Eric Milton	.40	.15
❑	78	Troy Glaus SP	8.00	3.00
❑	79	David Newhan	.40	.15
❑	80	Delmon Young	.60	.25
❑	81	Justin Morneau	.40	.15
❑	82	Ramon Ortiz	.40	.15
❑	83A	E.Chavez Blue Sky	.40	.15
❑	83B	E.Chavez Purple Sky SP	8.00	3.00
❑	84	Sean Burroughs	.40	.15
❑	85	Scott Rolen SP	8.00	3.00
❑	86	Rocco Baldelli	.40	.15
❑	87	Joe Mauer SP	10.00	4.00
❑	88	Tony Womack	.40	.15
❑	89	Ken Griffey Jr.	1.50	.60
❑	90	Alfonso Soriano SP	8.00	3.00
❑	91	Paul Konerko	.40	.15
❑	92	Guillermo Mota	.40	.15
❑	93	Lance Berkman	.40	.15
❑	94	Mark Buehrle	.40	.15
❑	95	Matt Clement	.40	.15
❑	96	Melvin Mora	.40	.15
❑	97	Khalil Greene	.60	.25
❑	98	David Wright	1.50	.60
❑	99	Jack Wilson	.40	.15
❑	100A	A.Rodriguez w/Bat SP	10.00	4.00
❑	100B	A.Rodriguez w/Glove SP	10.00	4.00
❑	101	Joe Nathan	.40	.15
❑	102A	A.Beltre Grey Uni SP	8.00	3.00
❑	102B	A.Beltre White Uni	.40	.15
❑	103	Mike Sweeney	.40	.15
❑	104	Brad Lidge	.40	.15
❑	105	Shawn Green	.40	.15
❑	106	Miguel Tejada SP	8.00	3.00
❑	107	Derrek Lee	.60	.25
❑	108	Eric Hinske	.40	.15
❑	109	Eric Byrnes	.40	.15
❑	110	Hideki Matsui SP	8.00	3.00
❑	111	Tom Glavine	.60	.25
❑	112	Jimmy Rollins	.40	.15
❑	113	Ryan Drese	.40	.15
❑	114	Josh Beckett	.40	.15
❑	115	Curt Schilling SP	8.00	3.00
❑	116	Jeremy Bonderman	.40	.15
❑	117	Kazuo Matsui	.40	.15
❑	118	Chase Utley	.60	.25
❑	119	Troy Percival	.40	.15
❑	120A	V.Guerrero w/Bat SP	8.00	3.00
❑	120B	V.Guerrero w/Glove SP	8.00	3.00
❑	121	Gary Sheffield	.40	.15
❑	122	Jeromy Burnitz	.40	.15
❑	123	Javier Vazquez	.40	.15
❑	124	Kevin Millar	.40	.15
❑	125A	R.Johnson Blue Sky	1.00	.40
❑	125B	R.Johnson Purple Sky SP	8.00	3.00
❑	126	Pat Burrell	.40	.15
❑	127	Jason Schmidt	.40	.15
❑	128	Jose Vidro	.40	.15
❑	129	Kip Wells	.40	.15
❑	130A	I.Rodriguez w/Cap	.60	.25
❑	130B	I.Rodriguez w/Helmet SP	8.00	3.00
❑	131	C.C. Sabathia	.40	.15
❑	132	Carlos Delgado SP	8.00	3.00
❑	133	Bartolo Colon	.40	.15
❑	134	Andruw Jones	.60	.25
❑	135	Kerry Wood	.40	.15
❑	136	Sidney Ponson	.40	.15
❑	137	Eric Gagne	.40	.15
❑	138	Rickie Weeks	.40	.15
❑	139	Mariano Rivera	1.00	.40
❑	140	Bobby Crosby	.40	.15
❑	141	Jamie Moyer	.40	.15
❑	142	Corey Koskie	.40	.15
❑	143	John Smoltz	.60	.25
❑	144	Frank Thomas	1.00	.40
❑	145	Cristian Guzman	.40	.15
❑	146	Paul Lo Duca	.40	.15
❑	147	Geoff Jenkins	.40	.15
❑	148	Nick Swisher	.40	.15
❑	149	Jason Bay SP	8.00	3.00
❑	150	Albert Pujols SP	15.00	6.00
❑	151	Edwin Jackson	.40	.15
❑	152	Carl Crawford	.40	.15
❑	153	Mark Mulder	.40	.15
❑	154	Rafael Palmeiro	.60	.25
❑	155	Pedro Martinez SP	8.00	3.00
❑	156	Jake Westbrook	.40	.15
❑	157	Sean Casey	.40	.15
❑	158	Aaron Rowand	.40	.15
❑	159	J.D. Drew	.40	.15
❑	160A	J.Sant Glove on Knee SP	8.00	3.00
❑	160B	J.Santana Throwing SP	8.00	3.00
❑	161	Gavin Floyd	.40	.15
❑	162	Vernon Wells	.40	.15
❑	163	Aubrey Huff	.40	.15
❑	164	Jeff Bagwell	.60	.25
❑	165	Boomer Wells	.40	.15
❑	166	Brad Penny	.40	.15
❑	167	Austin Kearns	.40	.15
❑	168	Mike Mussina	.60	.25
❑	169	Randy Wolf	.40	.15
❑	170	Tim Hudson SP	8.00	3.00
❑	171	Casey Blake	.40	.15
❑	172	Edgar Renteria	.40	.15
❑	173	Ben Sheets	.40	.15
❑	174	Kevin Brown	.40	.15
❑	175	Nomar Garciaparra SP	8.00	3.00
❑	176	Armando Benitez	.40	.15
❑	177	Jody Gerut	.40	.15
❑	178	Craig Biggio	.60	.25
❑	179	Omar Vizquel	.60	.25
❑	180	Jake Peavy	.40	.15
❑	181	Gustavo Chacin SP	8.00	3.00
❑	182	Johnny Damon	.60	.25
❑	183	Mike Lieberthal	.40	.15
❑	184	Felix Hernandez SP	15.00	6.00
❑	185	Zach Day SP	8.00	3.00
❑	186	Matt Cain	1.00	.40
❑	187	Erubiel Durazo	.40	.15
❑	188	Zack Greinke	.40	.15
❑	189	Matt Morris	.40	.15
❑	190	Billy Wagner	.40	.15
❑	191	Al Leiter	.40	.15
❑	192	Miguel Olivo	.40	.15
❑	193	Jose Capellan SP	8.00	3.00
❑	194	Adam Eaton	.40	.15
❑	195	Steven White SP RC	8.00	3.00
❑	196	Joe Randa	.40	.15
❑	197	Richard Hidalgo	.40	.15
❑	198	Orlando Cabrera	.40	.15
❑	199	Joel Guzman SP	8.00	3.00
❑	200	Garret Anderson	.40	.15
❑	201	Endy Chavez	.40	.15
❑	202	Andy Marte	.40	.15
❑	203	Jose Guillen	.40	.15
❑	204	Victor Martinez	.40	.15
❑	205	Johnny Estrada	.40	.15
❑	206	Damian Miller	.40	.15
❑	207	Ken Harvey	.40	.15
❑	208	Ronnie Belliard	.40	.15
❑	209	Chan Ho Park	.40	.15
❑	210	Laynce Nix	.40	.15
❑	211	Lew Ford	.40	.15
❑	212	Moises Alou	.40	.15
❑	213	Kris Benson	.40	.15
❑	214	Mike Gonzalez SP	8.00	3.00
❑	215	Chris Burke	.40	.15
❑	216	Juan Pierre	.40	.15
❑	217	Phil Nevin	.40	.15
❑	218	Jerry Hairston Jr.	.40	.15
❑	219	Jeremy Reed	.40	.15
❑	220	Scott Kazmir SP	8.00	3.00
❑	221	Mike Maroth	.40	.15
❑	222	Alex Rios	.40	.15
❑	223	Esteban Loaiza	.40	.15
❑	224	Termel Sledge	.40	.15
❑	225A	M.Prior Blue Sky SP	8.00	3.00
❑	225B	M.Prior Yellow Sky SP	8.00	3.00
❑	226	Hank Blalock	.40	.15
❑	227	Craig Wilson	.40	.15
❑	228	Cesar Izturis	.40	.15
❑	229	Dmitri Young	.40	.15
❑	230A	D.Jeter Blue Sky SP	15.00	6.00
❑	230B	D.Jeter Purple Sky SP	15.00	6.00
❑	231	Mark Kotsay	.40	.15
❑	232	Darin Erstad	.40	.15
❑	233	Brandon Backe SP	8.00	3.00
❑	234	Mike Lowell	.40	.15
❑	235	Scott Podsednik	.40	.15
❑	236	Michael Barrett	.40	.15
❑	237	Chad Tracy	.40	.15
❑	238	David Dellucci	.40	.15
❑	239	Brady Clark	.40	.15
❑	240	Jorge Cantu	.40	.15
❑	241	Wil Ledezma	.40	.15
❑	242	Morgan Ensberg	.40	.15
❑	243	Omar Infante	.40	.15
❑	244	Corey Patterson	.40	.15
❑	245	Matt Holliday	.50	.20
❑	246	Vinny Castilla	.40	.15
❑	247	Jason Bartlett	.40	.15
❑	248	Noah Lowry	.40	.15
❑	249	Huston Street	.60	.25
❑	250	Russell Branyan	.40	.15
❑	251	Juan Uribe	.40	.15
❑	252	Larry Bigbie	.40	.15
❑	253	Grady Sizemore	.60	.25
❑	254	Pedro Feliz	.40	.15
❑	255	Brad Wilkerson	.40	.15
❑	256	Brandon Inge	.40	.15
❑	257	Dewon Brazelton	.40	.15
❑	258	Rodrigo Lopez	.40	.15
❑	259	Jacque Jones	.40	.15
❑	260	Jason Giambi	.40	.15
❑	261	Clint Barmes	.40	.15
❑	262	Willy Taveras	.40	.15
❑	263	Marcus Giles	.40	.15
❑	264	Joe Blanton	.40	.15
❑	265	John Thomson	.40	.15
❑	266	Steve Finley SP	8.00	3.00
❑	267	Kevin Millwood	.40	.15
❑	268	David Eckstein	.40	.15
❑	269	Barry Zito	.40	.15
❑	270A	T.Helton Purple Sky SP	8.00	3.00
❑	270B	T.Helton Yellow Sky SP	8.00	3.00
❑	271	Landon Powell RC	1.00	.40
❑	272	Justin Verlander RC	4.00	1.50
❑	273	Wes Swackhamer RC	1.00	.40
❑	274	Wladimir Balentien RC	1.00	.40
❑	275	Philip Humber RC	1.00	.40
❑	276	Kevin Melillo RC	1.00	.40
❑	277	Billy Butler RC	4.00	1.50
❑	278	Michael Rogers RC	1.00	.40
❑	279	Bobby Livingston RC	1.00	.40
❑	280	Glen Perkins RC	1.00	.40
❑	281	Mike Bourn RC	1.00	.40
❑	282	Tyler Pelland RC	1.00	.40
❑	283	Jeremy West RC	1.00	.40
❑	284	Brandon McCarthy RC	1.50	.60
❑	285	Ian KinslerÂ RC	2.50	1.00
❑	286	Chris Roberson RC	1.00	.40
❑	287	Melky Cabrera RC	2.00	.75
❑	288	Ryan Sweeney RC	1.00	.40
❑	289	Chip Cannon RC	1.25	.50
❑	290	Andy LaRoche RC	4.00	1.50
❑	291	Chuck Tiffany RC	1.25	.50
❑	292	Ian Bladergroen RC	1.00	.40
❑	293	Bear Bay RC	1.00	.40
❑	294	Hernan Iribarren RC	1.25	.50
❑	295	Stuart Pomeranz RC	1.00	.40
❑	296	Luke Scott RC	2.00	.75
❑	297	Chuck James RC	2.00	.75
❑	298	Kennard Bibbs RC	1.00	.40
❑	299	Steven Bondurant RC	1.00	.40
❑	300	Thomas Oldham RC	1.00	.40
❑	301	Nolan Ryan RET	5.00	2.00
❑	302	Reggie Jackson RET	1.25	.50
❑	303	Tom Seaver RET	1.25	.50
❑	304	Al Kaline RET	2.00	.75
❑	305	Cal Ripken RET	6.00	2.50
❑	306	Josh Gibson RET	2.00	.75

❑ 307	Frank Robinson RET	1.00	.40
❑ 308	Duke Snider RET	1.25	.50
❑ 309	Wade Boggs RET	1.25	.50
❑ 310	Tony Gwynn RET	2.50	1.00
❑ 311	Carl Yastrzemski RET	2.00	.75
❑ 312	Ryne Sandberg RET	3.00	1.25
❑ 313	Gary Carter RET	1.00	.40
❑ 314	Brooks Robinson RET	1.25	.50
❑ 315	Ernie Banks RET	2.00	.75

2006 Topps Turkey Red

❑	COMPLETE SET (330)	250.00	150.00
❑	COMP.SET w/o SP's (275)	40.00	15.00
❑	COMMON CARD (316-580)	.40	.15
❑	COMMON SP (316-580)	8.00	3.00
❑	SP STATED ODDS 1:4 HOBBY, 1:4 RETAIL		
❑	SEE BECKETT.COM FOR SP CHECKLIST		
❑	COMMON CL (571-580)	.20	.07
❑	CL SEMIS 571-580	.30	.12
❑	COMMON RET (581-590)	.75	.30
❑	COMMON RC (591-630)	1.00	.40
❑	OVERALL PLATE ODDS 1:477 H		
❑	PLATE PRINT RUN 1 SET PER COLOR		
❑	BLACK-CYAN-MAGENTA-YELLOW ISSUED		
❑	NO PLATE PRICING DUE TO SCARCITY		
❑ 316A	A.Rodriguez Yanks	1.50	.60
❑ 316B	A.Rodriguez Rangers SP	10.00	4.00
❑ 316C	Alex Rodriguez M's SP	10.00	4.00
❑ 317	Jeff Francoeur SP	8.00	3.00
❑ 318	Shawn Green	.40	.15
❑ 319	Daniel Cabrera	.40	.15
❑ 320	Craig Biggio	.60	.25
❑ 321	Jeremy Bonderman	.40	.15
❑ 322	Mark Kotsay	.40	.15
❑ 323	Cliff Floyd	.40	.15
❑ 324	Jimmy Rollins	.40	.15
❑ 325A	M.Ordonez Tigers	.40	.15
❑ 325B	M.Ordonez W.Sox SP	8.00	3.00
❑ 326	C.C. Sabathia	.40	.15
❑ 327	Oliver Perez	.40	.15
❑ 328	Orlando Hudson	.40	.15
❑ 329	Chris Ray	.40	.15
❑ 330	Manny Ramirez	.60	.25
❑ 331	Paul Konerko	.40	.15
❑ 332	Joe Mauer SP	8.00	3.00
❑ 333	Jorge Posada	.60	.25
❑ 334	Mark Ellis	.40	.15
❑ 335	A.J. Burnett	.40	.15
❑ 336	Mike Sweeney	.40	.15
❑ 337	Shannon Stewart	.40	.15
❑ 338	Jake Peavy SP	8.00	3.00
❑ 339A	C.Delgado Mets SP	8.00	3.00
❑ 339B	C.Delgado B.Jays SP	8.00	3.00
❑ 340	Brian Roberts	.40	.15
❑ 341	Dontrelle Willis	.40	.15
❑ 342	Aaron Rowand	.40	.15
❑ 343A	R.Sexson M's	.40	.15
❑ 343B	R.Sexson Brewers SP	8.00	3.00
❑ 344	Chris Carpenter	.40	.15
❑ 345	Carlos Zambrano	.40	.15
❑ 346	Nomar Garciaparra	1.00	.40
❑ 347	Carlos Lee	.40	.15
❑ 348A	P.Wilson Astros	.40	.15
❑ 348B	P.Wilson Marlins SP	8.00	3.00
❑ 349	Mariano Rivera	1.00	.40
❑ 350	Ichiro Suzuki SP	10.00	4.00
❑ 351A	M.Piazza Padres	1.00	.40
❑ 351B	Mike Piazza Mets SP	8.00	3.00
❑ 352	Jason Schmidt	.40	.15
❑ 353	Jeff Weaver	.40	.15
❑ 354	Rocco Baldelli	.40	.15
❑ 355	Adam Dunn	.40	.15
❑ 356	Jeromy Burnitz	.40	.15
❑ 357	Chris Shelton SP	8.00	3.00
❑ 358	Chone Figgins SP	8.00	3.00
❑ 359	Javier Vazquez	.40	.15
❑ 360	Chipper Jones	1.00	.40
❑ 361	Frank Thomas	1.00	.40
❑ 362	Mark Loretta	.40	.15
❑ 363	Hideki Matsui	1.00	.40
❑ 364	J.J. Hardy SP	8.00	3.00
❑ 365	Todd Helton	.60	.25
❑ 366	Reggie Sanders	.40	.15
❑ 367	Jay Gibbons	.40	.15
❑ 368	Johnny Estrada	.40	.15
❑ 369	Grady Sizemore	.60	.25
❑ 370	Jim Thome	.60	.25
❑ 371	Ivan Rodriguez	.60	.25
❑ 372	Jason Bay	.40	.15
❑ 373	Carl Crawford	.40	.15
❑ 374	Adrian Beltre	.40	.15
❑ 375	Derrek Lee SP	8.00	3.00
❑ 376	Miguel Olivo	.40	.15
❑ 377	Roy Oswalt	.40	.15
❑ 378	Coco Crisp	.40	.15
❑ 379	Moises Alou	.40	.15
❑ 380	Kevin Millwood	.40	.15
❑ 381	Mark Grudzielanek	.40	.15
❑ 382	Justin Morneau	.40	.15
❑ 383	Austin Kearns	.40	.15
❑ 384	Brad Penny	.40	.15
❑ 385	Troy Glaus	.40	.15
❑ 386	Cliff Lee	.40	.15
❑ 387	Armando Benitez	.40	.15
❑ 388	Clint Barmes	.40	.15
❑ 389	Orlando Cabrera	.40	.15
❑ 390	Jim Edmonds SP	8.00	3.00
❑ 391	Jermaine Dye	.40	.15
❑ 392	Morgan Ensberg SP	8.00	3.00
❑ 393	Paul LoDuca	.40	.15
❑ 394	Eric Chavez	.40	.15
❑ 395	Greg Maddux SP	10.00	4.00
❑ 396	Jack Wilson	.40	.15
❑ 397	Omar Vizquel	.60	.25
❑ 398	Joe Nathan	.40	.15
❑ 399	Bobby Abreu	.40	.15
❑ 400	Barry Bonds SP	15.00	6.00
❑ 401	Gary Sheffield	.40	.15
❑ 402	John Patterson	.40	.15
❑ 403	J.D. Drew	.40	.15
❑ 404	Bruce Chen	.40	.15
❑ 405	Johnny Damon SP	8.00	3.00
❑ 406	Aubrey Huff	.40	.15
❑ 407	Mark Mulder	.40	.15
❑ 408	Jamie Moyer	.40	.15
❑ 409	Carlos Guillen	.40	.15
❑ 410	Andruw Jones SP	8.00	3.00
❑ 411	Jhonny Peralta SP	8.00	3.00
❑ 412	Doug Davis	.40	.15
❑ 413	Aaron Miles	.40	.15
❑ 414	Jon Lieber	.40	.15
❑ 415	Aaron Hill	.40	.15
❑ 416	Josh Beckett SP	8.00	3.00
❑ 417	Bobby Crosby	.40	.15
❑ 418	Noah Lowry SP	8.00	3.00
❑ 419	Sidney Ponson	.40	.15
❑ 420	Luis Castillo	.40	.15
❑ 421	Brad Wilkerson	.40	.15
❑ 422	Felix Hernandez SP	8.00	3.00
❑ 423	Vinny Castilla	.40	.15
❑ 424	Tom Glavine	.60	.25
❑ 425	Vladimir Guerrero	1.00	.40
❑ 426	Javy Lopez	.40	.15
❑ 427	Ronnie Belliard	.40	.15
❑ 428	Dmitri Young	.40	.15
❑ 429	Johan Santana	.60	.25
❑ 430A	D.Ortiz Red Sox SP	8.00	3.00
❑ 430B	D.Ortiz Twins SP	8.00	3.00
❑ 431	Ben Sheets	.40	.15
❑ 432	Matt Holliday	1.00	.40
❑ 433	Brian McCann	.40	.15
❑ 434	Joe Blanton	.40	.15
❑ 435	Sean Casey	.40	.15
❑ 436	Brad Lidge	.40	.15
❑ 437	Chad Tracy	.40	.15
❑ 438	Brett Myers	.40	.15
❑ 439	Matt Morris	.40	.15
❑ 440	Brian Giles	.40	.15
❑ 441	Zach Duke	.40	.15
❑ 442	Jose Lopez	.40	.15
❑ 443	Kris Benson	.40	.15
❑ 444	Jose Reyes SP	8.00	3.00
❑ 445	Travis Hafner	.40	.15
❑ 446	Orlando Hernandez	.40	.15
❑ 447	Edgar Renteria	.40	.15
❑ 448	Scott Podsednik	.40	.15
❑ 449	Nick Swisher SP	8.00	3.00
❑ 450	Derek Jeter SP	15.00	6.00
❑ 451	Scott Kazmir SP	8.00	3.00
❑ 452	Hank Blalock	.40	.15
❑ 453	Jake Westbrook	.40	.15
❑ 454	Miguel Cabrera	.60	.25
❑ 455A	K.Griffey Jr. Reds	1.50	.60
❑ 455B	K.Griffey Jr. M's SP	10.00	4.00
❑ 456	Rafael Furcal	.40	.15
❑ 457	Lance Berkman	.40	.15
❑ 458	Aramis Ramirez	.40	.15
❑ 459A	X.Nady Mets	.40	.15
❑ 459B	X.Nady Padres SP	8.00	3.00
❑ 460A	R.Johnson Yanks	1.00	.40
❑ 460B	R.Johnson Astros SP	8.00	3.00
❑ 461	Khalil Greene	.60	.25
❑ 462	Bartolo Colon	.40	.15
❑ 463	Mike Lowell	.40	.15
❑ 464	David DeJesus	.40	.15
❑ 465	Ryan Howard SP	10.00	4.00
❑ 466	Tim Salmon SP	8.00	3.00
❑ 467	Mark Buehrle SP	8.00	3.00
❑ 468	Curtis Granderson	.40	.15
❑ 469	Kerry Wood	.40	.15
❑ 470	Miguel Tejada	.40	.15
❑ 471	Geoff Jenkins	.40	.15
❑ 472	Jeremy Reed	.40	.15
❑ 473	David Eckstein	.40	.15
❑ 474	Lyle Overbay	.40	.15
❑ 475	Michael Young	.40	.15
❑ 476A	N.Johnson Nats SP	8.00	3.00
❑ 476B	N.Johnson Yanks SP	8.00	3.00
❑ 477	Carlos Beltran	.40	.15
❑ 478	Huston Street	.40	.15
❑ 479	Brandon Webb	.40	.15
❑ 480	Phil Nevin	.40	.15
❑ 481	Ryan Madson SP	8.00	3.00
❑ 482	Jason Giambi	.40	.15
❑ 483	Angel Berroa	.40	.15
❑ 484	Casey Blake	.40	.15
❑ 485	Pat Burrell	.40	.15
❑ 486	B.J. Ryan	.40	.15
❑ 487	Torii Hunter	.40	.15
❑ 488	Garret Anderson	.40	.15
❑ 489	Chase Utley SP	8.00	3.00
❑ 490	Matt Murton	.40	.15
❑ 491	Rich Harden	.40	.15
❑ 492	Garrett Atkins	.40	.15
❑ 493	Tadahito Iguchi SP	8.00	3.00
❑ 494	Jarrod Washburn	.40	.15
❑ 495	Carl Everett	.40	.15
❑ 496	Kameron Loe	.40	.15
❑ 497	Jorge Cantu SP	8.00	3.00
❑ 498	Chris Young	.40	.15
❑ 499	Marcus Giles	.40	.15
❑ 500	Albert Pujols	2.00	.75
❑ 501A	A.Soriano Nats SP	8.00	3.00
❑ 501B	A.Soriano Yanks SP	8.00	3.00
❑ 502	Randy Winn	.40	.15
❑ 503	Roy Halladay	.40	.15
❑ 504	Victor Martinez	.40	.15
❑ 505	Pedro Martinez	.60	.25
❑ 506	Rickie Weeks	.40	.15
❑ 507	Dan Johnson	.40	.15
❑ 508A	T.Hudson Braves	.40	.15
❑ 508B	T.Hudson A's SP	8.00	3.00
❑ 509	Mark Prior	.60	.25
❑ 510	Melvin Mora	.40	.15
❑ 511	Matt Clement	.40	.15
❑ 512	Brandon Inge	.40	.15
❑ 513	Mike Mussina	.60	.25
❑ 514	Mike Cameron	.40	.15
❑ 515	Barry Zito	.40	.15
❑ 516	Luis Gonzalez	.40	.15

❑ 517 Jose Castillo .40 .15
❑ 518 Andy Pettitte .60 .25
❑ 519 Wily Mo Pena .40 .15
❑ 520 Billy Wagner .40 .15
❑ 521 Ervin Santana SP 8.00 3.00
❑ 522 Juan Pierre .40 .15
❑ 523 Dan Haren .40 .15
❑ 524 Adrian Gonzalez SP 8.00 3.00
❑ 525 Robinson Cano .60 .25
❑ 526 Jeff Kent .40 .15
❑ 527 Cory Sullivan .40 .15
❑ 528 Joe Crede SP 8.00 3.00
❑ 529 John Smoltz .60 .25
❑ 530 David Wright 1.50 .60
❑ 531 Chad Cordero .40 .15
❑ 532 Scott Rolen SP 8.00 3.00
❑ 533 Edwin Jackson .40 .15
❑ 534 Doug Mientkiewicz .40 .15
❑ 535 Mark Teixeira SP 8.00 3.00
❑ 536 Kelvim Escobar .40 .15
❑ 537 Alex Rios .40 .15
❑ 538 Jose Vidro .40 .15
❑ 539 Alex Gonzalez .40 .15
❑ 540 Yadier Molina .40 .15
❑ 541 Ronny Cedeno SP 8.00 3.00
❑ 542 Mark Hendrickson .40 .15
❑ 543 Russ Adams .40 .15
❑ 544 Chris Capuano .40 .15
❑ 545 Raul Ibanez .40 .15
❑ 546 Vicente Padilla .40 .15
❑ 547 Chris Duffy .40 .15
❑ 548 Bengie Molina .40 .15
❑ 549 Chien-Ming Wang 1.50 .60
❑ 550 Curt Schilling .60 .25
❑ 551 Craig Wilson .40 .15
❑ 552 Mike Lieberthal .40 .15
❑ 553 Kazuo Matsui .40 .15
❑ 554 Jeff Francis .40 .15
❑ 555 Brady Clark .40 .15
❑ 556 Willy Taveras .40 .15
❑ 557 Mike Maroth .40 .15
❑ 558 Bernie Williams .60 .25
❑ 559 Edwin Encarnacion .40 .15
❑ 560 Vernon Wells .40 .15
❑ 561A L.Hernandez Nats .40 .15
❑ 561B L.Hernandez Giants SP 8.00 3.00
❑ 562 Kenny Rogers .40 .15
❑ 563 Steve Finley .40 .15
❑ 564 Trot Nixon .40 .15
❑ 565 Jonny Gomes SP 8.00 3.00
❑ 566 Brandon Phillips .40 .15
❑ 567 Shawn Chacon .40 .15
❑ 568 Dave Bush .40 .15
❑ 569 Jose Guillen .40 .15
❑ 570 Gustavo Chacin .40 .15
❑ 571 A.Rod Safe at the Plate CL .75 .30
❑ 572 Pujols At Bat CL 1.00 .40
❑ 573 Bonds On Deck CL 1.00 .40
❑ 574 Breaking Up Two CL .20 .07
❑ 575 Conference On The Mound CL .50 .20
❑ 576 Touch Em All CL .75 .30
❑ 577 Avoiding The Runner CL .20 .07
❑ 578 Bunting The Runner Over CL .20 .07
❑ 579 In The Hole CL .20 .07
❑ 580 Jeter Steals Third CL 1.25 .50
❑ 581 Nolan Ryan RET 5.00 2.00
❑ 582 Cal Ripken RET 8.00 3.00
❑ 583 Carl Yastrzemski RET 3.00 1.25
❑ 584 Duke Snider RET 1.25 .50
❑ 585 Tom Seaver RET 1.25 .50
❑ 586 Mickey Mantle RET 10.00 4.00
❑ 587 Jim Palmer RET .75 .30
❑ 588 Gary Carter RET .75 .30
❑ 589 Stan Musial RET 3.00 1.25
❑ 590 Luis Aparicio RET .75 .30
❑ 591 Prince Fielder (RC) 4.00 1.50
❑ 592 Conor Jackson (RC) 1.50 .60
❑ 593 Jeremy Hermida (RC) 1.00 .40
❑ 594 Jeff Mathis (RC) 1.00 .40
❑ 595 Alay Soler RC 1.00 .40
❑ 596 Ryan Spilborghs (RC) 1.50 .60
❑ 597 Chuck James (RC) 1.50 .60
❑ 598 Josh Barfield (RC) 1.00 .40
❑ 599 Ian Kinsler (RC) 1.50 .60
❑ 600 Val Majewski (RC) 1.00 .40
❑ 601 Brian Slocum (RC) 1.00 .40
❑ 602 Matt Kemp (RC) 1.50 .60
❑ 603 Nate McLouth (RC) 1.00 .40
❑ 604 Sean Marshall (RC) 1.00 .40
❑ 605 Brian Bannister (RC) 1.00 .40
❑ 606 Ryan Zimmerman (RC) 6.00 2.50
❑ 607 Kendry Morales (RC) 2.50 1.00
❑ 608 Jonathan Papelbon (RC) 5.00 2.00
❑ 609 Matt Cain (RC) 1.50 .60
❑ 610 Anderson Hernandez (RC) 1.00 .40
❑ 611 Jose Capellan (RC) 1.00 .40
❑ 612 Lastings Milledge (RC) 1.50 .60
❑ 613 Francisco Liriano (RC) 5.00 2.00
❑ 614 Hanley Ramirez (RC) 2.50 1.00
❑ 615 Brian Anderson (RC) 1.00 .40
❑ 616 Reggie Abercrombie (RC) 1.00 .40
❑ 617 Erick Aybar (RC) 1.00 .40
❑ 618 James Loney (RC) 1.50 .60
❑ 619 Joel Zumaya (RC) 2.50 1.00
❑ 620 Travis Ishikawa (RC) 1.00 .40
❑ 621 Jason Kubel (RC) 1.00 .40
❑ 622 Drew Meyer (RC) 1.00 .40
❑ 623 Kenji Johjima RC 5.00 2.00
❑ 624 Fausto Carmona (RC) 1.00 .40
❑ 625 Nick Markakis (RC) 1.50 .60
❑ 626 John Rheinecker (RC) 1.00 .40
❑ 627 Melky Cabrera (RC) 1.50 .60
❑ 628 Michael Pelfrey RC 4.00 1.50
❑ 629 Dan Uggla (RC) 2.50 1.00
❑ 630 Justin Verlander (RC) 4.00 1.50

2007 Topps Turkey Red

❑ COMPLETE SET (200) 200.00 150.00
❑ COMP.SET w/o SP's (150) 30.00 12.50
❑ COMMON CARD (1-186) .30 .12
❑ COMMON RC (1-186) .40 .15
❑ COMMON SP (1-186) 6.00 2.50
❑ SP ODDS 1:4 HOBBY, 1:4 RETAIL
❑ COMMON AD BACK (1-186) 6.00 2.50
❑ AD BACK ODDS 1:4 HOBBY,1:4 RETAIL
❑ 1 Ryan Howard 1.25 .50
❑ 1b R.Howard Ad Back SP 10.00 4.00
❑ 2 Dontrelle Willis .30 .12
❑ 3 Matt Cain .50 .20
❑ 4 John Maine .30 .12
❑ 5 Cole Hamels .50 .20
❑ 6 Corey Patterson .30 .12
❑ 7 Mickey Mantle SP 25.00 10.00
❑ 8 Servin Up Strikes Johan Santana CL .50 .20
❑ 9 Josh Beckett .30 .12
❑ 10 Jimmy Rollins .30 .12
❑ 11 Kenji Johjima .75 .30
❑ 12 Orlando Hernandez .30 .12
❑ 13 Jorge Posada Play at the Plate CL .50 .20
❑ 14 Ivan Rodriguez .50 .20
❑ 15 Ichiro Suzuki 1.25 .50
❑ 15b I.Suzuki Ad Back SP 10.00 4.00
❑ 16 Double Griffey CL 1.25 .50
❑ 17 Stephen Drew .50 .20
❑ 18 B.J. Upton .30 .12
❑ 19 Mickey Mantle 2.50 1.00
❑ 20 Alex Rodriguez 1.25 .50
❑ 20b A.Rod Ad Back SP 10.00 4.00
❑ 21 Adam Dunn .30 .12
❑ 22 Adam Lind SP (RC) 6.00 2.50
❑ 23 Adrian Gonzalez .30 .12
❑ 24 Akinori Iwamura RC 1.00 .40
❑ 25 Albert Pujols 1.50 .60
❑ 25b A.Pujols Ad Back SP 10.00 4.00
❑ 26 Frank Thomas .75 .30
❑ 27 Roy Halladay .30 .12
❑ 28 Alejandro De Aza RC .60 .25
❑ 29 Alex Gordon RC 2.00 .75
❑ 30 Barry Bonds 1.50 .60
❑ 31 Andrew Miller RC 2.50 1.00
❑ 32 Andruw Jones .50 .20
❑ 33 Kurt Suzuki SP (RC) 6.00 2.50
❑ 34 Mickey Mantle 2.50 1.00
❑ 35 Andy Pettitte .50 .20
❑ 36 Tadahito Iguchi .30 .12
❑ 37 Edgar Renteria .30 .12
❑ 38 Tim Hudson .30 .12
❑ 39 Micah Owings (RC) .40 .15
❑ 40 Chipper Jones .75 .30
❑ 40b C.Jones Ad Back SP 8.00 3.00
❑ 41 Barry Zito .30 .12
❑ 42 Dice-K CL 3.00 1.25
❑ 43 Jarrod Saltalamacchia SP (RC) 6.00 2.50
❑ 44 Bill Hall .30 .12
❑ 45 Billy Butler (RC) .60 .25
❑ 46 Billy Wagner .30 .12
❑ 47 Rich Harden SP 6.00 2.50
❑ 48 Prince Albert CL 1.50 .60
❑ 49 Brandon Inge .30 .12
❑ 50 Jason Giambi .30 .12
❑ 51 Brandon Webb .30 .12
❑ 52 Brandon Wood (RC) .40 .15
❑ 53 Swiping Second Carl Crawford CL .30 .12
❑ 54 Brian Giles .30 .12
❑ 55 Josh Hamilton (RC) 1.00 .40
❑ 56 C.Utley Ad Back SP 8.00 3.00
❑ 57 Miguel Montero (RC) .40 .15
❑ 58 Carl Crawford .30 .12
❑ 59 Carlos Beltran .30 .12
❑ 60 Mariano Rivera .75 .30
❑ 61 Carlos Delgado .30 .12
❑ 62 Carlos Lee SP 6.00 2.50
❑ 63 Carlos Zambrano SP 6.00 2.50
❑ 64 Miguel Tejada .30 .12
❑ 65 Mike Cameron .30 .12
❑ 66 Chase Utley SP 8.00 3.00
❑ 67 Chase Wright RC 1.00 .40
❑ 68 Chien-Ming Wang 1.25 .50
❑ 69 Nick Swisher .30 .12
❑ 70 David Wright 1.25 .50
❑ 71 Mike Piazza SP 8.00 3.00
❑ 72 Chris Carpenter .30 .12
❑ 73 Mark Buehrle SP 6.00 2.50
❑ 74 Torii Hunter SP 6.00 2.50
❑ 75 Tyler Clippard (RC) .60 .25
❑ 76 Nick Markakis .50 .20
❑ 77 Mickey Mantle 2.50 1.00
❑ 78 Curt Schilling .50 .20
❑ 79 Curtis Granderson .30 .12
❑ 80 Craig Biggio .50 .20
❑ 81 Juan Pierre .30 .12
❑ 82 Dallas Braden SP RC 6.00 2.50
❑ 83 Dan Haren SP 6.00 2.50
❑ 84 Dan Uggla .50 .20
❑ 85 Danny Putnam (RC) .40 .15
❑ 86 David DeJesus .30 .12
❑ 87 David Eckstein .30 .12
❑ 88 Tim Lincecum RC 3.00 1.25
❑ 89 Johnny Damon SP 6.00 2.50
❑ 90 Justin Morneau .30 .12
❑ 91 Delmon Young (RC) .60 .25
❑ 92 Homer Bailey (RC) .60 .25
❑ 93 Carlos Gomez RC .60 .25
❑ 94 Josh Fields SP (RC) 6.00 2.50
❑ 95 Derek Jeter 2.00 .75
❑ 95b D.Jeter Ad Back SP 15.00 6.00
❑ 96 Derek Lee .30 .12
❑ 97 Don Kelly (RC) .40 .15
❑ 98 Doug Slaten RC .40 .15
❑ 99 Dustin Moseley .30 .12
❑ 100 Gary Sheffield .30 .12
❑ 101 Orlando Hudson SP 6.00 2.50
❑ 102 Elijah Dukes RC .60 .25
❑ 103 Eric Byrnes SP 6.00 2.50
❑ 104 Eric Chavez .30 .12
❑ 105 Phil Hughes (RC) 2.00 .75
❑ 105b Hughes Ad Back SP (RC) 10.00 4.00
❑ 106 Felix Hernandez SP 6.00 2.50
❑ 106b Felix Hernandez Ad Back SP 6.00 2.50
❑ 107 Mickey Mantle 2.50 1.00

❑ 108 Felix Pie (RC)	.40	.15
❑ 109 Captain Jeter CL	2.00	.75
❑ 110 Daisuke Matsuzaka RC	4.00	1.50
❑ 110b Dice-K Ad Back SP RC	15.00	6.00
❑ 111 Francisco Rodriguez	.30	.12
❑ 112 Ramon Hernandez	.30	.12
❑ 113 Randy Johnson	.75	.30
❑ 114 Gary Matthews	.30	.12
❑ 115 Prince Fielder	.75	.30
❑ 116 Vladdy Yard CL	.75	.30
❑ 117 Mickey Mantle	2.50	1.00
❑ 118 Hideki Matsui	.75	.30
❑ 119 Hideki Okajima RC	2.00	.75
❑ 120 Manny Ramirez	.50	.20
❑ 121 H.Pence SP (RC)	15.00	6.00
❑ 122 Roy Oswalt	.30	.12
❑ 123 Josh Willingham SP	6.00	2.50
❑ 124 Tom Gordon SP	6.00	2.50
❑ 125 Michael Young	.30	.12
❑ 126 J.D. Drew	.30	.12
❑ 127 Ryan Zimmerman	.75	.30
❑ 128 James Shields SP	6.00	2.50
❑ 129 Jack Wilson	.30	.12
❑ 130 David Ortiz	.75	.30
❑ 130b D.Ortiz Ad Back SP	8.00	3.00
❑ 131 Jose Reyes CL	.75	.30
❑ 132 Jamie Vermilyea RC	.40	.15
❑ 133 Jason Bay	.30	.12
❑ 134 Scott Kazmir SP	6.00	2.50
❑ 135 Jason Isringhausen SP	6.00	2.50
❑ 136 Jason Marquis SP	6.00	2.50
❑ 137 Jason Schmidt	.30	.12
❑ 138 Shawn Green	.30	.12
❑ 139 Jeff Francoeur SP	8.00	3.00
❑ 140 Alfonso Soriano	.30	.12
❑ 141 Kevin Kouzmanoff (RC)	.40	.15
❑ 142 Jered Weaver	.50	.20
❑ 143 Todd Helton SP	6.00	2.50
❑ 144 Jermaine Dye	.30	.12
❑ 145 Jim Thome	.50	.20
❑ 146 Tom Glavine SP	6.00	2.50
❑ 147 Joe Mauer	.50	.20
❑ 148 Joe Nathan	.30	.12
❑ 149 Joe Smith RC	.40	.15
❑ 150 Ken Griffey Jr.	1.25	.50
❑ 150b Griffey Ad Back SP	10.00	4.00
❑ 151 Grady Sizemore	.50	.20
❑ 152 Sammy Sosa SP	8.00	3.00
❑ 153 Andy LaRoche (RC)	.40	.15
❑ 154 Travis Buck (RC)	.40	.15
❑ 155 Alex Rios	.30	.12
❑ 156 Travis Hafner	.30	.12
❑ 157 Jake Peavy	.30	.12
❑ 158 Jeff Kent	.30	.12
❑ 159 Johan Santana	.50	.20
❑ 159b Johan Santana Ad Back SP	6.00	2.50
❑ 160 Ivan Rodriguez	.50	.20
❑ 161 Trevor Hoffman	.30	.12
❑ 162 Troy Glaus	.30	.12
❑ 163 Troy Tulowitzki (RC)	1.00	.40
❑ 164 Jorge Posada	.50	.20
❑ 165 Kei Igawa SP RC	8.00	3.00
❑ 166 Jose Reyes	.75	.30
❑ 167 Mickey Mantle	2.50	1.00
❑ 168 Utley Streak CL	.75	.30
❑ 169 Justin Verlander	.75	.30
❑ 170 Hanley Ramirez	.50	.20
❑ 171 Kelly Johnson SP	6.00	2.50
❑ 172 Kelvin Jimenez RC	.40	.15
❑ 173 Roger Clemens	1.50	.60
❑ 174 Khalil Greene SP	6.00	2.50
❑ 175 Lance Berkman	.30	.12
❑ 176 Turning Two Hanley Ramirez CL	.50	.20
❑ 177 Kyle Kendrick RC	1.00	.40
❑ 178 Magglio Ordonez	.30	.12
❑ 179 Marcus Giles SP	6.00	2.50
❑ 180 Miguel Cabrera	.50	.20
❑ 180b Miguel Cabrera Ad Back SP	6.00	2.50
❑ 181 Mark Teahen	.30	.12
❑ 182 Mark Teixeira SP	6.00	2.50
❑ 183 Matt Chico SP (RC)	6.00	2.50
❑ 184 Matt Holliday	.40	.15
❑ 185 Vladimir Guerrero	.75	.30
❑ 185b V. Guerrero Ad Back SP	8.00	3.00
❑ 186 Yovani Gallardo (RC)	1.00	.40

2007 UD Masterpieces

❑ COMPLETE SET (90)	60.00	30.00
❑ COMMON CARD (1-90)	.60	.25
❑ COMMON ROOKIE (1-90)	.60	.25
❑ PRINTING PLATES RANDOMLY INSERTED		
❑ PLATE PRINT RUN 1 SET PER COLOR		
❑ BLACK-CYAN-MAGENTA-YELLOW ISSUED		
❑ NO PLATE PRICING DUE TO SCARCITY		
❑ 1 Babe Ruth	4.00	1.50
❑ 2 Babe Ruth	4.00	1.50
❑ 3 Bobby Thomson	1.00	.40
❑ 4 Bill Mazeroski	1.00	.40
❑ 5 Carlton Fisk	1.00	.40
❑ 6 Kirk Gibson	.60	.25
❑ 7 Don Larsen	.60	.25
❑ 8 Lou Gehrig	3.00	1.25
❑ 9 Roger Maris	1.50	.60
❑ 10 Cal Ripken Jr.	6.00	2.50
❑ 11 Bucky Dent	.60	.25
❑ 12 Ryan Howard	2.50	1.00
❑ 13 Brooks Robinson	1.00	.40
❑ 14 David Ortiz	1.50	.60
❑ 15 Hideki Matsui	1.50	.60
❑ 16 Roger Clemens	3.00	1.25
❑ 17 Sandy Koufax	5.00	2.00
❑ 18 Reggie Jackson	1.00	.40
❑ 19 Ozzie Smith	2.50	1.00
❑ 20 Ty Cobb	2.50	1.00
❑ 21 Walter Johnson	1.50	.60
❑ 22 Babe Ruth	4.00	1.50
❑ 23 Roy Campanella	1.50	.60
❑ 24 Jackie Robinson	1.50	.60
❑ 25 Carl Yastrzemski	2.50	1.00
❑ 26 Sandy Koufax	5.00	2.00
❑ 27 Daisuke Matsuzaka RC	6.00	2.50
❑ 28 Kei Igawa RC	1.50	.60
❑ 29 Ken Griffey Jr.	2.50	1.00
❑ 30 Derek Jeter	4.00	1.50
❑ 31 David Ortiz	1.50	.60
❑ 32 Vladimir Guerrero	1.50	.60
❑ 33 Chase Utley	1.50	.60
❑ 34 Troy Tulowitzki (RC)	1.50	.60
❑ 35 Joe Mauer	1.00	.40
❑ 36 Travis Hafner	.60	.25
❑ 37 Miguel Cabrera	1.00	.40
❑ 38 Albert Pujols	3.00	1.25
❑ 39 Frank Thomas	1.50	.60
❑ 40 Mike Piazza	1.50	.60
❑ 41 Josh Hamilton	1.50	.60
❑ 42 T.Gwynn/C.Ripken Jr.	6.00	2.50
❑ 43 Ichiro Suzuki	2.50	1.00
❑ 44 Hideki Matsui	1.50	.60
❑ 45 Ken Griffey Jr.	2.50	1.00
❑ 46 Michael Jordan	4.00	1.50
❑ 47 John F. Kennedy	2.50	1.00
❑ 48 Randy Johnson	1.50	.60
❑ 49 Albert Pujols	3.00	1.25
❑ 50 Carlos Beltran	.60	.25
❑ 51 Delmon Young (RC)	1.00	.40
❑ 52 Johan Santana	1.00	.40
❑ 53 Cal Ripken Jr.	6.00	2.50
❑ 54 Y.Berra/J.Robinson	1.50	.60
❑ 55 Cal Ripken Jr.	6.00	2.50
❑ 56 Hanley Ramirez	1.00	.40
❑ 57 Victor Martinez	.60	.25
❑ 58 Cole Hamels	1.00	.40
❑ 59 Bobby Doerr	.60	.25
❑ 60 Bruce Sutter	.60	.25
❑ 61 Jason Bay	.60	.25
❑ 62 Luis Aparicio	.60	.25
❑ 63 Stephen Drew	1.00	.40
❑ 64 Jered Weaver	1.00	.40
❑ 65 Alex Gordon RC	3.00	1.25
❑ 66 Howie Kendrick	.60	.25
❑ 67 Ryan Zimmerman	1.50	.60
❑ 68 Akinori Iwamura RC	1.50	.60
❑ 69 Chien-Ming Wang	2.50	1.00
❑ 70 David Wright	2.50	1.00
❑ 71 Ryan Howard	2.50	1.00
❑ 72 Alex Rodriguez	2.50	1.00
❑ 73 Justin Morneau	.60	.25
❑ 74 Andrew Miller RC	4.00	1.50
❑ 75 Richard Nixon	1.50	.60
❑ 76 Bill Clinton	2.50	1.00
❑ 77 Phil Hughes (RC)	3.00	1.25
❑ 78 Tom Glavine	1.00	.40
❑ 79 Chipper Jones	1.50	.60
❑ 80 Craig Biggio	1.00	.40
❑ 81 Chris Chambliss	.60	.25
❑ 82 Tim Lincecum RC	6.00	2.50
❑ 83 Billy Butler (RC)	1.00	.40
❑ 84 Andy LaRoche (RC)	.60	.25
❑ 85 1969 New York Mets	.60	.25
❑ 86 2004 Boston Red Sox	2.50	1.00
❑ 87 Roberto Clemente	5.00	2.00
❑ 88 Chase Utley	1.50	.60
❑ 89 Reggie Jackson	1.00	.40
❑ 90 Curt Schilling	1.00	.40

2001 Ultimate Collection

❑ COMMON CARD (1-90)	4.00	1.50
❑ COMMON CARD (91-100)	10.00	4.00
❑ COMMON CARD (101-110)	10.00	4.00
❑ COMMON CARD (111-120)	15.00	6.00
❑ 1 Troy Glaus	4.00	1.50
❑ 2 Darin Erstad	4.00	1.50
❑ 3 Jason Giambi	4.00	1.50
❑ 4 Barry Zito	4.00	1.50
❑ 5 Tim Hudson	4.00	1.50
❑ 6 Miguel Tejada	4.00	1.50
❑ 7 Carlos Delgado	4.00	1.50
❑ 8 Shannon Stewart	4.00	1.50
❑ 9 Greg Vaughn	4.00	1.50
❑ 10 Toby Hall	4.00	1.50
❑ 11 Roberto Alomar	4.00	1.50
❑ 12 Juan Gonzalez	4.00	1.50
❑ 13 Jim Thome	4.00	1.50
❑ 14 Edgar Martinez	4.00	1.50
❑ 15 Freddy Garcia	4.00	1.50
❑ 16 Bret Boone	4.00	1.50
❑ 17 Kazuhiro Sasaki	4.00	1.50
❑ 18 Cal Ripken	20.00	8.00
❑ 19 Tim Raines Jr.	4.00	1.50
❑ 20 Alex Rodriguez	10.00	4.00
❑ 21 Ivan Rodriguez	4.00	1.50
❑ 22 Rafael Palmeiro	4.00	1.50
❑ 23 Pedro Martinez	4.00	1.50
❑ 24 Nomar Garciaparra	10.00	4.00
❑ 25 Manny Ramirez Sox	4.00	1.50
❑ 26 Hideo Nomo	6.00	2.50
❑ 27 Mike Sweeney	4.00	1.50
❑ 28 Carlos Beltran	4.00	1.50
❑ 29 Tony Clark	4.00	1.50
❑ 30 Dean Palmer	4.00	1.50
❑ 31 Doug Mientkiewicz	4.00	1.50

❑ 32 Cristian Guzman 4.00 1.50
❑ 33 Corey Koskie 4.00 1.50
❑ 34 Frank Thomas 6.00 2.50
❑ 35 Magglio Ordonez 4.00 1.50
❑ 36 Jose Canseco 4.00 1.50
❑ 37 Roger Clemens 12.00 5.00
❑ 38 Derek Jeter 15.00 6.00
❑ 39 Bernie Williams 4.00 1.50
❑ 40 Mike Mussina 4.00 1.50
❑ 41 Tino Martinez 4.00 1.50
❑ 42 Jeff Bagwell 4.00 1.50
❑ 43 Lance Berkman 4.00 1.50
❑ 44 Roy Oswalt 6.00 2.50
❑ 45 Chipper Jones 6.00 2.50
❑ 46 Greg Maddux 10.00 4.00
❑ 47 Andruw Jones 4.00 1.50
❑ 48 Tom Glavine 4.00 1.50
❑ 49 Richie Sexson 4.00 1.50
❑ 50 Jeromy Burnitz 4.00 1.50
❑ 51 Ben Sheets 4.00 1.50
❑ 52 Mark McGwire 15.00 6.00
❑ 53 Matt Morris 4.00 1.50
❑ 54 Jim Edmonds 4.00 1.50
❑ 55 J.D. Drew 4.00 1.50
❑ 56 Sammy Sosa 6.00 2.50
❑ 57 Fred McGriff 4.00 1.50
❑ 58 Kerry Wood 4.00 1.50
❑ 59 Randy Johnson 6.00 2.50
❑ 60 Luis Gonzalez 4.00 1.50
❑ 61 Curt Schilling 4.00 1.50
❑ 62 Shawn Green 4.00 1.50
❑ 63 Kevin Brown 4.00 1.50
❑ 64 Gary Sheffield 4.00 1.50
❑ 65 Vladimir Guerrero 6.00 2.50
❑ 66 Barry Bonds 15.00 6.00
❑ 67 Jeff Kent 4.00 1.50
❑ 68 Rich Aurilia 4.00 1.50
❑ 69 Cliff Floyd 4.00 1.50
❑ 70 Charles Johnson 4.00 1.50
❑ 71 Josh Beckett 4.00 1.50
❑ 72 Mike Piazza 10.00 4.00
❑ 73 Edgardo Alfonzo 4.00 1.50
❑ 74 Robin Ventura 4.00 1.50
❑ 75 Tony Gwynn 8.00 3.00
❑ 76 Ryan Klesko 4.00 1.50
❑ 77 Phil Nevin 4.00 1.50
❑ 78 Scott Rolen 4.00 1.50
❑ 79 Bobby Abreu 4.00 1.50
❑ 80 Jimmy Rollins 4.00 1.50
❑ 81 Brian Giles 4.00 1.50
❑ 82 Jason Kendall 4.00 1.50
❑ 83 Aramis Ramirez 4.00 1.50
❑ 84 Ken Griffey Jr. 10.00 4.00
❑ 85 Adam Dunn 4.00 1.50
❑ 86 Sean Casey 4.00 1.50
❑ 87 Barry Larkin 4.00 1.50
❑ 88 Larry Walker 4.00 1.50
❑ 89 Mike Hampton 4.00 1.50
❑ 90 Todd Helton 4.00 1.50
❑ 91 Ken Harvey T1 10.00 4.00
❑ 92 Bill Ortega T1 RC 10.00 4.00
❑ 93 Juan Diaz T1 RC 10.00 4.00
❑ 94 Greg Miller T1 RC 10.00 4.00
❑ 95 Brandon Berger T1 RC 10.00 4.00
❑ 96 Brandon Lyon T1 RC 10.00 4.00
❑ 97 Jay Gibbons T1 RC 15.00 6.00
❑ 98 Rob Mackowiak T1 RC 15.00 6.00
❑ 99 Erick Almonte T1 RC 10.00 4.00
❑ 100 Jason Middlebrook T1 RC 10.00 4.00
❑ 101 Johnny Estrada T2 RC 15.00 6.00
❑ 102 Juan Uribe T2 RC 15.00 6.00
❑ 103 Travis Hafner T2 RC 30.00 12.50
❑ 104 Morgan Ensberg T2 RC 15.00 6.00
❑ 105 Mike Rivera T2 RC 10.00 4.00
❑ 106 Josh Towers T2 RC 15.00 6.00
❑ 107 Adrian Hernandez T2 RC 10.00 4.00
❑ 108 Rafael Soriano T2 RC 10.00 4.00
❑ 109 Jackson Melian T2 RC 10.00 4.00
❑ 110 Wilkin Ruan T2 RC 10.00 4.00
❑ 111 Albert Pujols T3 RC 700.00 500.00
❑ 112 Tsuyoshi Shinjo T3 RC 25.00 10.00
❑ 113 Brandon Duckworth T3 RC 15.00 6.00
❑ 114 Juan Cruz T3 RC 15.00 6.00
❑ 115 Dewon Brazelton T3 RC 15.00 6.00
❑ 116 Mark Prior T3 AU RC 200.00 125.00
❑ 117 Mark Teixeira T3 AU RC 300.00 200.00
❑ 118 Wilson Betemit T3 RC 25.00 10.00
❑ 119 Bud Smith T3 RC 15.00 6.00
❑ 120 Ichiro Suzuki T3 AU RC 1800.00 1200.00

2002 Ultimate Collection

❑ COMMON CARD (1-60) 4.00 1.50
❑ COMMON CARD (61-110) 10.00 4.00
❑ 61-110 PRINT RUN 550 SERIAL #'d SETS
❑ COMMON CARD (111-113) 15.00 6.00
❑ COMMON CARD (114-120) 15.00 6.00
❑ 1 Troy Glaus 4.00 1.50
❑ 2 Luis Gonzalez 4.00 1.50
❑ 3 Curt Schilling 4.00 1.50
❑ 4 Randy Johnson 6.00 2.50
❑ 5 Andruw Jones 4.00 1.50
❑ 6 Greg Maddux 10.00 4.00
❑ 7 Chipper Jones 6.00 2.50
❑ 8 Gary Sheffield 4.00 1.50
❑ 9 Cal Ripken 20.00 8.00
❑ 10 Manny Ramirez 4.00 1.50
❑ 11 Pedro Martinez 4.00 1.50
❑ 12 Nomar Garciaparra 10.00 4.00
❑ 13 Sammy Sosa 6.00 2.50
❑ 14 Kerry Wood 4.00 1.50
❑ 15 Mark Prior 6.00 2.50
❑ 16 Magglio Ordonez 4.00 1.50
❑ 17 Frank Thomas 6.00 2.50
❑ 18 Adam Dunn 4.00 1.50
❑ 19 Ken Griffey Jr. 10.00 4.00
❑ 20 Jim Thome 4.00 1.50
❑ 21 Larry Walker 4.00 1.50
❑ 22 Todd Helton 4.00 1.50
❑ 23 Nolan Ryan 15.00 6.00
❑ 24 Jeff Bagwell 4.00 1.50
❑ 25 Roy Oswalt 4.00 1.50
❑ 26 Lance Berkman 4.00 1.50
❑ 27 Mike Sweeney 4.00 1.50
❑ 28 Shawn Green 4.00 1.50
❑ 29 Hideo Nomo 6.00 2.50
❑ 30 Torii Hunter 4.00 1.50
❑ 31 Vladimir Guerrero 6.00 2.50
❑ 32 Tom Seaver 4.00 1.50
❑ 33 Mike Piazza 10.00 4.00
❑ 34 Roberto Alomar 4.00 1.50
❑ 35 Derek Jeter 15.00 6.00
❑ 36 Alfonso Soriano 4.00 1.50
❑ 37 Jason Giambi 4.00 1.50
❑ 38 Roger Clemens 12.00 5.00
❑ 39 Mike Mussina 4.00 1.50
❑ 40 Bernie Williams 4.00 1.50
❑ 41 Joe DiMaggio 12.00 5.00
❑ 42 Mickey Mantle 25.00 10.00
❑ 43 Miguel Tejada 4.00 1.50
❑ 44 Eric Chavez 4.00 1.50
❑ 45 Barry Zito 4.00 1.50
❑ 46 Pat Burrell 4.00 1.50
❑ 47 Jason Kendall 4.00 1.50
❑ 48 Brian Giles 4.00 1.50
❑ 49 Barry Bonds 15.00 6.00
❑ 50 Ichiro Suzuki 12.00 5.00
❑ 51 Stan Musial 10.00 4.00
❑ 52 J.D. Drew 4.00 1.50
❑ 53 Scott Rolen 4.00 1.50
❑ 54 Albert Pujols 12.00 5.00
❑ 55 Mark McGwire 15.00 6.00
❑ 56 Alex Rodriguez 10.00 4.00
❑ 57 Ivan Rodriguez 4.00 1.50
❑ 58 Juan Gonzalez 4.00 1.50
❑ 59 Rafael Palmeiro 4.00 1.50
❑ 60 Carlos Delgado 4.00 1.50
❑ 61 Jose Valverde UR RC 10.00 4.00
❑ 62 Doug Devore UR RC 10.00 4.00
❑ 63 John Ennis UR RC 10.00 4.00
❑ 64 Joey Dawley UR RC 10.00 4.00
❑ 65 Trey Hodges UR RC 10.00 4.00
❑ 66 Mike Mahoney UR 10.00 4.00
❑ 67 Aaron Cook UR RC 10.00 4.00
❑ 68 Rene Reyes UR RC 10.00 4.00
❑ 69 Mark Corey UR RC 10.00 4.00
❑ 70 Hansel Izquierdo UR RC 10.00 4.00
❑ 71 Brandon Puffer UR RC 10.00 4.00
❑ 72 Jeriome Robertson UR RC 10.00 4.00
❑ 73 Jose Diaz UR RC 10.00 4.00
❑ 74 David Ross UR RC 10.00 4.00
❑ 75 Jayson Durocher UR RC 10.00 4.00
❑ 76 Eric Good UR RC 10.00 4.00
❑ 77 Satoru Komiyama UR RC 10.00 4.00
❑ 78 Tyler Yates UR RC 10.00 4.00
❑ 79 Eric Junge UR RC 10.00 4.00
❑ 80 Anderson Machado UR RC 10.00 4.00
❑ 81 Adrian Burnside UR RC 10.00 4.00
❑ 82 Ben Howard UR RC 10.00 4.00
❑ 83 Clay Condrey UR RC 10.00 4.00
❑ 84 Nelson Castro UR RC 10.00 4.00
❑ 85 So Taguchi UR RC 15.00 6.00
❑ 86 Mike Crudale UR RC 10.00 4.00
❑ 87 Scotty Layfield UR RC 10.00 4.00
❑ 88 Steve Bechler UR RC 10.00 4.00
❑ 89 Travis Driskill UR RC 10.00 4.00
❑ 90 Howie Clark UR RC 10.00 4.00
❑ 91 Josh Hancock UR RC 12.00 5.00
❑ 92 Jorge De La Rosa UR RC 10.00 4.00
❑ 93 Anastacio Martinez UR RC 10.00 4.00
❑ 94 Brian Tallet UR RC 10.00 4.00
❑ 95 Carl Sadler UR RC 10.00 4.00
❑ 96 Cliff Lee UR RC 15.00 6.00
❑ 97 Josh Bard UR RC 10.00 4.00
❑ 98 Wes Obermueller UR RC 10.00 4.00
❑ 99 Juan Brito UR RC 10.00 4.00
❑ 100 Aaron Guiel UR RC 10.00 4.00
❑ 101 Jeremy Hill UR RC 10.00 4.00
❑ 102 Kevin Frederick UR RC 10.00 4.00
❑ 103 Nate Field UR RC 10.00 4.00
❑ 104 Julio Mateo UR RC 10.00 4.00
❑ 105 Chris Snelling UR RC 12.00 5.00
❑ 106 Felix Escalona UR RC 10.00 4.00
❑ 107 Reynaldo Garcia UR RC 10.00 4.00
❑ 108 Mike Smith UR RC 10.00 4.00
❑ 109 Ken Huckaby UR RC 10.00 4.00
❑ 110 Kevin Cash UR RC 10.00 4.00
❑ 111 Kazuhisa Ishii UR AU RC 40.00 15.00
❑ 112 Freddy Sanchez UR AU RC 40.00 15.00
❑ 113 Jas Simontacchi UR AU RC 15.00 6.00
❑ 114 Jorge Padilla UR AU RC 15.00 6.00
❑ 115 Kirk Saarloos UR AU RC 15.00 6.00
❑ 116 Rodrigo Rosario UR AU RC 15.00 6.00
❑ 117 Oliver Perez UR AU RC 40.00 15.00
❑ 118 Miguel Asencio UR AU RC 15.00 6.00
❑ 119 Franklyn German UR AU RC 15.00 6.00
❑ 120 Jaime Cerda UR AU RC 15.00 6.00
❑ MM M.McGwire Priority EXCH/100

2003 Ultimate Collection

❑ COMMON CARD (1-84) 3.00 1.25
❑ 1-84 STATED ODDS TWO PER PACK
❑ COMMON CARD (85-117) 5.00 2.00

Card		
❑ COMMON CARD (118-140)	5.00	2.00
❑ 118-140 PRINT RUN 399 SERIAL #'d SETS		
❑ COMMON CARD (141-158)	6.00	2.50
❑ COMMON CARD (159-168)	12.00	5.00
❑ 159-168 PRINT RUN 100 SERIAL #'d SETS		
❑ 85-168 STATED ODDS ONE PER PACK		
❑ COMMON CARD (169-174)	15.00	6.00
❑ 169-174 , ULT.SIG.OVERALL ODDS 1:4		
❑ COMMON CARD (175-180)	15.00	6.00
❑ 175-180 , BUYBACK OVERALL ODDS 1:8		
❑ 169-180 PRINT RUN 250 SERIAL #'d SETS		
❑ MATSUI PART LIVE/ PART EXCH		
❑ EXCHANGE DEADLINE 12/17/06		
❑ 1 Ichiro Suzuki	10.00	4.00
❑ 2 Ken Griffey Jr.	8.00	3.00
❑ 3 Sammy Sosa	5.00	2.00
❑ 4 Jason Giambi	3.00	1.25
❑ 5 Mike Piazza	8.00	3.00
❑ 6 Derek Jeter	10.00	4.00
❑ 7 Randy Johnson	5.00	2.00
❑ 8 Barry Bonds	12.00	5.00
❑ 9 Carlos Delgado	3.00	1.25
❑ 10 Mark Prior	5.00	2.00
❑ 11 Vladimir Guerrero	5.00	2.00
❑ 12 Alfonso Soriano	3.00	1.25
❑ 13 Jim Thome	5.00	2.00
❑ 14 Pedro Martinez	5.00	2.00
❑ 15 Nomar Garciaparra	8.00	3.00
❑ 16 Chipper Jones	5.00	2.00
❑ 17 Rocco Baldelli	3.00	1.25
❑ 18 Dontrelle Willis	5.00	2.00
❑ 19 Garret Anderson	3.00	1.25
❑ 20 Jeff Bagwell	5.00	2.00
❑ 21 Jim Edmonds	3.00	1.25
❑ 22 Rickey Henderson	5.00	2.00
❑ 23 Torii Hunter	3.00	1.25
❑ 24 Tom Glavine	5.00	2.00
❑ 25 Hideo Nomo	5.00	2.00
❑ 26 Luis Gonzalez	3.00	1.25
❑ 27 Alex Rodriguez	8.00	3.00
❑ 28 Albert Pujols	10.00	4.00
❑ 29 Manny Ramirez	5.00	2.00
❑ 30 Rafael Palmeiro	5.00	2.00
❑ 31 Bernie Williams	5.00	2.00
❑ 32 Curt Schilling	3.00	1.25
❑ 33 Roger Clemens	10.00	4.00
❑ 34 Andruw Jones	5.00	2.00
❑ 35 J.D. Drew	3.00	1.25
❑ 36 Kerry Wood	3.00	1.25
❑ 37 Scott Rolen	5.00	2.00
❑ 38 Darin Erstad	3.00	1.25
❑ 39 Joe DiMaggio	8.00	3.00
❑ 40 Magglio Ordonez	3.00	1.25
❑ 41 Todd Helton	5.00	2.00
❑ 42 Barry Zito	3.00	1.25
❑ 43 Mickey Mantle	15.00	6.00
❑ 44 Miguel Tejada	3.00	1.25
❑ 45 Troy Glaus	3.00	1.25
❑ 46 Kazuhisa Ishii	3.00	1.25
❑ 47 Adam Dunn	3.00	1.25
❑ 48 Ted Williams	10.00	4.00
❑ 49 Mike Mussina	5.00	2.00
❑ 50 Ivan Rodriguez	5.00	2.00
❑ 51 Jacque Jones	3.00	1.25
❑ 52 Stan Musial	8.00	3.00
❑ 53 Mariano Rivera	5.00	2.00
❑ 54 Larry Walker	3.00	1.25
❑ 55 Aaron Boone	3.00	1.25
❑ 56 Hank Blalock	3.00	1.25
❑ 57 Rich Harden	5.00	2.00
❑ 58 Lance Berkman	3.00	1.25
❑ 59 Eric Chavez	3.00	1.25
❑ 60 Carlos Beltran	3.00	1.25
❑ 61 Roy Oswalt	3.00	1.25
❑ 62 Moises Alou	3.00	1.25
❑ 63 Nolan Ryan	12.00	5.00
❑ 64 Jeff Kent	3.00	1.25
❑ 65 Roberto Alomar	5.00	2.00
❑ 66 Runelvys Hernandez	3.00	1.25
❑ 67 Roy Halladay	3.00	1.25
❑ 68 Tim Hudson	3.00	1.25
❑ 69 Tom Seaver	5.00	2.00
❑ 70 Edgardo Alfonzo	3.00	1.25
❑ 71 Andy Pettitte	5.00	2.00
❑ 72 Preston Wilson	3.00	1.25
❑ 73 Frank Thomas	5.00	2.00
❑ 74 Jerome Williams	3.00	1.25
❑ 75 Shawn Green	3.00	1.25
❑ 76 David Wells	3.00	1.25
❑ 77 John Smoltz	5.00	2.00
❑ 78 Jorge Posada	5.00	2.00
❑ 79 Marlon Byrd	3.00	1.25
❑ 80 Austin Kearns	3.00	1.25
❑ 81 Bret Boone	3.00	1.25
❑ 82 Rafael Furcal	3.00	1.25
❑ 83 Jay Gibbons	3.00	1.25
❑ 84 Shane Reynolds	3.00	1.25
❑ 85 Nate Bland UR T1 RC	5.00	2.00
❑ 86 Willie Eyre UR T1 RC	5.00	2.00
❑ 87 Jeremy Guthrie UR T1	5.00	2.00
❑ 88 Jeremy Wedel UR T1 RC	5.00	2.00
❑ 89 Jhonny Peralta UR T1	8.00	3.00
❑ 90 Luis Ayala UR T1 RC	5.00	2.00
❑ 91 Michael Hessman UR T1 RC	5.00	2.00
❑ 92 Michael Nakamura UR T1 RC	5.00	2.00
❑ 93 Nook Logan UR T1 RC	8.00	3.00
❑ 94 Rett Johnson UR T1 RC	5.00	2.00
❑ 95 Josh Hall UR T1 RC	5.00	2.00
❑ 96 Julio Manon UR T1 RC	5.00	2.00
❑ 97 Heath Bell UR T1 RC	5.00	2.00
❑ 98 Ian Ferguson UR T1 RC	5.00	2.00
❑ 99 Jason Gilfillan UR T1 RC	5.00	2.00
❑ 100 Jason Roach UR T1 RC	5.00	2.00
❑ 101 Jason Shiell UR T1 RC	5.00	2.00
❑ 102 Termel Sledge UR T1 RC	5.00	2.00
❑ 103 Phil Seibel UR T1 RC	5.00	2.00
❑ 104 Jeff Duncan UR T1 RC	5.00	2.00
❑ 105 Mike Neu UR T1 RC	5.00	2.00
❑ 106 Colin Porter UR T1 RC	5.00	2.00
❑ 107 David Matranga UR T1 RC	5.00	2.00
❑ 108 Aaron Looper UR T1 RC	5.00	2.00
❑ 109 Jeremy Bonderman UR T1 RC	15.00	6.00
❑ 110 Miguel Ojeda UR T1 RC	5.00	2.00
❑ 111 Chad Cordero UR T1 RC	10.00	4.00
❑ 112 Shane Bazzell UR T1 RC	5.00	2.00
❑ 113 Tim Olson UR T1 RC	5.00	2.00
❑ 114 Michel Hernandez UR T1 RC	5.00	2.00
❑ 115 Chien-Ming Wang UR T1 RC	50.00	20.00
❑ 116 Josh Stewart UR T1 RC	5.00	2.00
❑ 117 Clint Barmes UR T1 RC	5.00	2.00
❑ 118 Craig Brazell UR T2 RC	5.00	2.00
❑ 119 Josh Willingham UR T2 RC	10.00	4.00
❑ 120 Brent Hoard UR T2 RC	5.00	2.00
❑ 121 Francisco Rosario UR T2 RC	5.00	2.00
❑ 122 Rick Roberts UR T2 RC	5.00	2.00
❑ 123 Geoff Geary UR T2 RC	5.00	2.00
❑ 124 Edgar Gonzalez UR T2 RC	5.00	2.00
❑ 125 Kevin Correia UR T2 RC	5.00	2.00
❑ 126 Ryan Cameron UR T2 RC	5.00	2.00
❑ 127 Beau Kemp UR T2 RC	5.00	2.00
❑ 128 Tommy Phelps UR T2	5.00	2.00
❑ 129 Mark Malaska UR T2 RC	5.00	2.00
❑ 130 Kevin Ohme UR T2 RC	5.00	2.00
❑ 131 Humberto Quintero UR T2 RC	5.00	2.00
❑ 132 Aquilino Lopez UR T2 RC	5.00	2.00
❑ 133 Andrew Brown UR T2 RC	8.00	3.00
❑ 134 Wilfredo Ledezma UR T2 RC	5.00	2.00
❑ 135 Luis De Los Santos UR T2	5.00	2.00
❑ 136 Garrett Atkins UR T2	5.00	2.00
❑ 137 Fernando Cabrera UR T2 RC	5.00	2.00
❑ 138 D.J. Carrasco UR T2 RC	5.00	2.00
❑ 139 Alfredo Gonzalez UR T2 RC	5.00	2.00
❑ 140 Alex Prieto UR T2 RC	5.00	2.00
❑ 141 Matt Kata UR T3 RC	6.00	2.50
❑ 142 Chris Capuano UR T3 RC	15.00	6.00
❑ 143 Bobby Madritsch UR T3 RC	6.00	2.50
❑ 144 Greg Jones UR T3 RC	6.00	2.50
❑ 145 Pete Zoccolillo UR T3 RC	6.00	2.50
❑ 146 Chad Gaudin UR T3 RC	6.00	2.50
❑ 147 Rosman Garcia UR T3 RC	6.00	2.50
❑ 148 Gerald Laird UR T3	6.00	2.50
❑ 149 Danny Garcia UR T3 RC	6.00	2.50
❑ 150 Stephen Randolph UR T3 RC	6.00	2.50
❑ 151 Pete LaForest UR T3 RC	6.00	2.50
❑ 152 Brian Sweeney UR T3 RC	6.00	2.50
❑ 153 Aaron Miles UR T3 RC	10.00	4.00
❑ 154 Jorge DePaula UR T3 UER	6.00	2.50
❑ 155 Graham Koonce UR T3 RC	6.00	2.50
❑ 156 Tom Gregorio UR T3 RC	6.00	2.50
❑ 157 Javier A. Lopez UR T3 RC	6.00	2.50
❑ 158 Oscar Villarreal UR T3 RC	6.00	2.50
❑ 159 Prentice Redman UR T4 RC	12.00	5.00
❑ 160 Francisco Cruceta UR T4 RC	12.00	5.00
❑ 161 Guillermo Quiroz UR T4 RC	12.00	5.00
❑ 162 Jeremy Griffiths UR T4 RC	12.00	5.00
❑ 163 Lew Ford UR T4 RC	20.00	8.00
❑ 164 Rob Hammock UR T4 RC	12.00	5.00
❑ 165 Todd Wellemeyer UR T4 RC	12.00	5.00
❑ 166 Ryan Wagner UR T4 RC	12.00	5.00
❑ 167 Edwin Jackson UR T4 RC	20.00	8.00
❑ 168 Dan Haren UR T4 RC	20.00	8.00
❑ 169 Hideki Matsui AU RC	350.00	250.00
❑ 170 Jose Contreras AU RC	50.00	20.00
❑ 171 Delmon Young AU RC	325.00	225.00
❑ 172 Rickie Weeks AU RC	100.00	50.00
❑ 173 Brandon Webb AU RC	100.00	50.00
❑ 174 Bo Hart AU RC	15.00	6.00
❑ 175 Rocco Baldelli YS AU	25.00	10.00
❑ 176 Jose Reyes YS AU	25.00	10.00
❑ 177 Dontrelle Willis YS AU	50.00	20.00
❑ 178 Bobby Hill YS AU	15.00	6.00
❑ 179 Jae Weong Seo YS AU	25.00	10.00
❑ 180 Jesse Foppert YS AU	15.00	6.00

2004 Ultimate Collection

Card		
❑ COMMON CARD (1-42)	3.00	1.25
❑ COMMON CARD (43-126)	3.00	1.25
❑ 1-126 STATED ODDS TWO PER PACK		
❑ 1-126 PRINT RUN 675 SERIAL #'d CARDS		
❑ COMMON CARD (127-168)	5.00	2.00
❑ 127-209/222 STATED ODDS 3:4 PACKS		
❑ 127-168 PRINT RUN 525 SERIAL #'d SETS		
❑ COMMON CARD (169-194)	6.00	2.50
❑ 169-194 PRINT RUN 299 SERIAL #'d SETS		
❑ COMMON (195-209/222)	8.00	3.00
❑ 195-209/222 PRINT RUN 199 SER.#'d SETS		
❑ 210-221 STATED ODDS 1:10		
❑ 210-221 PRINT RUN 75 SERIAL #'d SETS		
❑ EXCHANGE DEADLINE 12/28/07		
❑ 1 Al Kaline	5.00	2.00
❑ 2 Billy Williams	3.00	1.25
❑ 3 Bob Feller	3.00	1.25
❑ 4 Bob Gibson	5.00	2.00
❑ 5 Bob Lemon	3.00	1.25
❑ 6 Bobby Doerr	3.00	1.25
❑ 7 Brooks Robinson	5.00	2.00
❑ 8 Cal Ripken	15.00	6.00
❑ 9 Catfish Hunter	5.00	2.00
❑ 10 Eddie Mathews	5.00	2.00
❑ 11 Enos Slaughter	3.00	1.25
❑ 12 Ernie Banks	5.00	2.00
❑ 13 Fergie Jenkins	3.00	1.25
❑ 14 Gaylord Perry	3.00	1.25
❑ 15 Harmon Killebrew	5.00	2.00
❑ 16 Jim Bunning	3.00	1.25
❑ 17 Joe DiMaggio	8.00	3.00
❑ 18 Joe Morgan	3.00	1.25
❑ 19 Juan Marichal	3.00	1.25
❑ 20 Lou Brock	5.00	2.00
❑ 21 Luis Aparicio	3.00	1.25
❑ 22 Mickey Mantle	15.00	6.00
❑ 23 Mike Schmidt	10.00	4.00
❑ 24 Monte Irvin	3.00	1.25
❑ 25 Nolan Ryan	12.00	5.00
❑ 26 Pee Wee Reese	5.00	2.00
❑ 27 Phil Niekro	3.00	1.25
❑ 28 Phil Rizzuto	5.00	2.00
❑ 29 Ralph Kiner	5.00	2.00
❑ 30 Richie Ashburn	5.00	2.00
❑ 31 Robin Roberts	3.00	1.25

❑ 32 Robin Yount 5.00 2.00
❑ 33 Rod Carew 5.00 2.00
❑ 34 Rollie Fingers 3.00 1.25
❑ 35 Stan Musial 8.00 3.00
❑ 36 Ted Williams 10.00 4.00
❑ 37 Tom Seaver 5.00 2.00
❑ 38 Warren Spahn 5.00 2.00
❑ 39 Whitey Ford 5.00 2.00
❑ 40 Willie McCovey 5.00 2.00
❑ 41 Willie Stargell 5.00 2.00
❑ 42 Yogi Berra 5.00 2.00
❑ 43 Adrian Beltre 3.00 1.25
❑ 44 Albert Pujols 10.00 4.00
❑ 45 Alex Rodriguez 8.00 3.00
❑ 46 Alfonso Soriano 3.00 1.25
❑ 47 Andruw Jones 5.00 2.00
❑ 48 Andy Pettitte 5.00 2.00
❑ 49 Aubrey Huff 3.00 1.25
❑ 50 Barry Larkin 5.00 2.00
❑ 51 Ben Sheets 3.00 1.25
❑ 52 Bernie Williams 5.00 2.00
❑ 53 Bobby Abreu 3.00 1.25
❑ 54 Brad Penny 3.00 1.25
❑ 55 Bret Boone 3.00 1.25
❑ 56 Brian Giles 3.00 1.25
❑ 57 Carlos Beltran 3.00 1.25
❑ 58 Carlos Delgado 3.00 1.25
❑ 59 Carlos Guillen 3.00 1.25
❑ 60 Carlos Lee 3.00 1.25
❑ 61 Carlos Zambrano 3.00 1.25
❑ 62 Chipper Jones 5.00 2.00
❑ 63 Craig Biggio 5.00 2.00
❑ 64 Craig Wilson 3.00 1.25
❑ 65 Curt Schilling 5.00 2.00
❑ 66 David Ortiz 5.00 2.00
❑ 67 Derek Jeter 10.00 4.00
❑ 68 Eric Chavez 3.00 1.25
❑ 69 Eric Gagne 3.00 1.25
❑ 70 Frank Thomas 5.00 2.00
❑ 71 Garret Anderson 3.00 1.25
❑ 72 Gary Sheffield 3.00 1.25
❑ 73 Greg Maddux 8.00 3.00
❑ 74 Hank Blalock 3.00 1.25
❑ 75 Hideki Matsui 8.00 3.00
❑ 76 Ichiro Suzuki 10.00 4.00
❑ 77 Ivan Rodriguez 5.00 2.00
❑ 78 J.D. Drew 3.00 1.25
❑ 79 Jake Peavy 3.00 1.25
❑ 80 Jason Schmidt 3.00 1.25
❑ 81 Jeff Bagwell 5.00 2.00
❑ 82 Jeff Kent 3.00 1.25
❑ 83 Jim Thome 5.00 2.00
❑ 84 Joe Mauer 5.00 2.00
❑ 85 Johan Santana 5.00 2.00
❑ 86 Jose Reyes 3.00 1.25
❑ 87 Jose Vidro 3.00 1.25
❑ 88 Ken Griffey Jr. 8.00 3.00
❑ 89 Kerry Wood 3.00 1.25
❑ 90 Larry Walker Cards 5.00 2.00
❑ 91 Luis Gonzalez 3.00 1.25
❑ 92 Lyle Overbay 3.00 1.25
❑ 93 Magglio Ordonez 3.00 1.25
❑ 94 Manny Ramirez 5.00 2.00
❑ 95 Mark Mulder 3.00 1.25
❑ 96 Mark Prior 5.00 2.00
❑ 97 Mark Teixeira 5.00 2.00
❑ 98 Melvin Mora 3.00 1.25
❑ 99 Michael Young 3.00 1.25
❑ 100 Miguel Cabrera 5.00 2.00
❑ 101 Miguel Tejada 3.00 1.25
❑ 102 Mike Lowell 3.00 1.25
❑ 103 Mike Piazza 8.00 3.00
❑ 104 Mike Sweeney 3.00 1.25
❑ 105 Nomar Garciaparra 8.00 3.00
❑ 106 Oliver Perez 3.00 1.25
❑ 107 Pedro Martinez 5.00 2.00
❑ 108 Preston Wilson 3.00 1.25
❑ 109 Rafael Palmeiro 5.00 2.00
❑ 110 Randy Johnson 5.00 2.00
❑ 111 Roger Clemens 10.00 4.00
❑ 112 Roy Halladay 3.00 1.25
❑ 113 Roy Oswalt 3.00 1.25
❑ 114 Sammy Sosa 5.00 2.00
❑ 115 Scott Podsednik 3.00 1.25
❑ 116 Scott Rolen 5.00 2.00
❑ 117 Shawn Green 3.00 1.25
❑ 118 Tim Hudson 3.00 1.25
❑ 119 Todd Helton 5.00 2.00
❑ 120 Tom Glavine 5.00 2.00
❑ 121 Torii Hunter 3.00 1.25
❑ 122 Travis Hafner 3.00 1.25
❑ 123 Troy Glaus 3.00 1.25
❑ 124 Vernon Wells 3.00 1.25
❑ 125 Victor Martinez 3.00 1.25
❑ 126 Vladimir Guerrero 5.00 2.00
❑ 127 Aarom Baldiris UR T1 RC 8.00 3.00
❑ 128 Alfredo Simon UR T1 RC 5.00 2.00
❑ 129 Andres Blanco UR T1 RC 5.00 2.00
❑ 130 Jeff Bajenaru UR T1 RC 5.00 2.00
❑ 131 Bart Fortunato UR T1 RC 5.00 2.00
❑ 132 B.Medders UR T1 RC 5.00 2.00
❑ 133 Brian Dallimore UR T1 RC 5.00 2.00
❑ 134 Carlos Hines UR T1 RC 5.00 2.00
❑ 135 Carlos Vasquez UR T1 RC 8.00 3.00
❑ 136 Casey Daigle UR T1 RC 5.00 2.00
❑ 137 Chad Bentz UR T1 RC 5.00 2.00
❑ 138 Chris Aguila UR T1 RC 5.00 2.00
❑ 139 Chris Saenz UR T1 RC 5.00 2.00
❑ 140 Chris Shelton UR T1 RC 12.00 5.00
❑ 141 Colby Miller UR T1 RC 5.00 2.00
❑ 142 Dave Crouthers UR T1 RC 5.00 2.00
❑ 143 David Aardsma UR T1 RC 8.00 3.00
❑ 144 Dennis Sarfate UR T1 RC 5.00 2.00
❑ 145 Donnie Kelly UR T1 RC 5.00 2.00
❑ 146 Eddy Rodriguez UR T1 RC 8.00 3.00
❑ 147 Eduardo Villacis UR T1 RC 5.00 2.00
❑ 148 Edwardo Sierra UR T1 RC 8.00 3.00
❑ 149 Edwin Moreno UR T1 RC 8.00 3.00
❑ 150 Kyle Denney UR T1 RC 5.00 2.00
❑ 151 Evan Rust UR T1 RC 5.00 2.00
❑ 152 Fernando Nieve UR T1 RC 8.00 3.00
❑ 153 Frank Francisco UR T1 RC 5.00 2.00
❑ 154 Frank Gracesqui UR T1 RC 5.00 2.00
❑ 155 Freddy Guzman UR T1 RC 5.00 2.00
❑ 156 Greg Dobbs UR T1 RC 5.00 2.00
❑ 157 Hector Gimenez UR T1 RC 5.00 2.00
❑ 158 Jason Alfaro UR T1 RC 5.00 2.00
❑ 159 Jake Woods UR T1 RC 5.00 2.00
❑ 160 Andy Green UR T1 RC 5.00 2.00
❑ 161 Jason Bartlett UR T1 RC 8.00 3.00
❑ 162 Jason Frasor UR T1 RC 5.00 2.00
❑ 163 Jeff Bennett UR T1 RC 5.00 2.00
❑ 164 Jerome Gamble UR T1 RC 5.00 2.00
❑ 165 Jerry Gil UR T1 RC 5.00 2.00
❑ 166 Joe Hietpas UR T1 RC 5.00 2.00
❑ 167 Jorge Sequea UR T1 RC 5.00 2.00
❑ 168 Jorge Vasquez UR T1 RC 5.00 2.00
❑ 169 Josh Labandeira UR T2 RC 6.00 2.50
❑ 170 Justin Germano UR T2 RC 6.00 2.50
❑ 171 Justin Hampson UR T2 RC 6.00 2.50
❑ 172 Chris Young UR T2 RC 50.00 20.00
❑ 173 Justin Knoedler UR T2 RC 6.00 2.50
❑ 174 Justin Lehr UR T2 RC 6.00 2.50
❑ 175 Justin Leone UR T2 RC 10.00 4.00
❑ 176 Kaz Tadano UR T2 RC 10.00 4.00
❑ 177 Kevin Cave UR T2 RC 6.00 2.50
❑ 178 Linc Holdzkom UR T2 RC 6.00 2.50
❑ 179 Mike Rose UR T2 RC 6.00 2.50
❑ 180 Luis Gonzalez UR T2 RC 6.00 2.50
❑ 181 Mariano Gomez UR T2 RC 6.00 2.50
❑ 182 Rene Rivera UR T2 RC 6.00 2.50
❑ 183 Michael Wuertz UR T2 RC 10.00 4.00
❑ 184 Mike Gosling UR T2 RC 6.00 2.50
❑ 185 Mike Johnston UR T2 RC 6.00 2.50
❑ 186 Mike Rouse UR T2 RC 6.00 2.50
❑ 187 Nick Regilio UR T2 RC 6.00 2.50
❑ 188 Onil Joseph UR T2 RC 6.00 2.50
❑ 189 Orl Rodriguez UR T2 RC 6.00 2.50
❑ 190 Phil Stockman UR T2 RC 6.00 2.50
❑ 191 Renyel Pinto UR T2 RC 10.00 4.00
❑ 192 Roberto Novoa UR T2 RC 10.00 4.00
❑ 193 Roman Colon UR T2 RC 6.00 2.50
❑ 194 Ronald Belisario UR T2 RC 6.00 2.50
❑ 195 Ronny Cedeno UR T3 RC 10.00 4.00
❑ 196 Ryan Meaux UR T3 RC 8.00 3.00
❑ 197 Ryan Wing UR T3 RC 8.00 3.00
❑ 198 Scott Dohmann UR T3 RC 8.00 3.00
❑ 199 Joey Gathright UR T3 RC 12.00 5.00
❑ 200 Shawn Camp UR T3 RC 8.00 3.00
❑ 201 Shawn Hill UR T3 RC 8.00 3.00
❑ 202 Steve Andrade UR T3 RC 8.00 3.00
❑ 203 Tim Bausher UR T3 RC 8.00 3.00
❑ 204 Tim Bittner UR T3 RC 8.00 3.00
❑ 205 Brad Halsey UR T3 RC 12.00 5.00
❑ 206 William Bergolla UR T3 RC 8.00 3.00
❑ 207 Kameron Loe UR T3 RC 20.00 8.00
❑ 208 Jesse Crain UR T3 RC 12.00 5.00
❑ 209 Scott Kazmir UR T3 RC 30.00 12.50
❑ 210 Akinori Otsuka AU RC 50.00 20.00
❑ 211 Chris Oxspring AU RC 25.00 10.00
❑ 212 Ian Snell AU RC 40.00 15.00
❑ 213 John Gall AU RC 40.00 15.00
❑ 214 Jose Capellan AU RC 25.00 10.00
❑ 215 Yadier Molina AU RC 80.00 50.00
❑ 216 Merkin Valdez AU RC 25.00 10.00
❑ 217 R.Ramirez AU RC EXCH 25.00 10.00
❑ 218 Rusty Tucker AU RC 40.00 15.00
❑ 219 Scott Proctor AU RC 40.00 15.00
❑ 220 Sean Henn AU RC 25.00 10.00
❑ 221 Shingo Takatsu AU RC 40.00 15.00
❑ 222 Kazuo Matsui UR T3 RC 10.00 4.00

2005 Ultimate Collection

❑ COMMON CARD (1-100) 3.00 1.25
❑ 1-100 APPX ODDS 3:2 PACKS
❑ 1-100 PRINT RUN 475 SERIAL #'d SETS
❑ COMMON CARD (101-142) 5.00 2.00
❑ 101-142 APPX. ODDS 1:3
❑ 101-142 PRINT RUN 275 SERIAL #'d SETS
❑ COMMON CARD (143-237) 5.00 2.00
❑ COMMON RC (143-237) 5.00 2.00
❑ 143-237 STATED ODDS 3:4 PACKS
❑ 143-237 PRINT RUN 275 SERIAL #'d SETS
❑ 238-242 OVERALL AU ODDS 1:4
❑ 238-242 PRINT RUN 99 SERIAL #'d SETS
❑ 1 A.J. Burnett 3.00 1.25
❑ 2 Adam Dunn 3.00 1.25
❑ 3 Adrian Beltre 3.00 1.25
❑ 4 Albert Pujols 8.00 3.00
❑ 5 Alex Rodriguez 10.00 4.00
❑ 6 Alfonso Soriano 3.00 1.25
❑ 7 Andruw Jones 5.00 2.00
❑ 8 Andy Pettitte 5.00 2.00
❑ 9 Aramis Ramirez 3.00 1.25
❑ 10 Aubrey Huff 3.00 1.25
❑ 11 Ben Sheets 3.00 1.25
❑ 12 Bobby Abreu 3.00 1.25
❑ 13 Bobby Crosby 3.00 1.25
❑ 14 Chris Carpenter 3.00 1.25
❑ 15 Brian Giles 3.00 1.25
❑ 16 Brian Roberts 3.00 1.25
❑ 17 Carl Crawford 3.00 1.25
❑ 18 Carlos Beltran 3.00 1.25
❑ 19 Carlos Delgado 3.00 1.25
❑ 20 Carlos Zambrano 3.00 1.25
❑ 21 Chipper Jones 5.00 2.00
❑ 22 Corey Patterson 3.00 1.25
❑ 23 Craig Biggio 5.00 2.00
❑ 24 Curt Schilling 5.00 2.00
❑ 25 Dallas McPherson 3.00 1.25
❑ 26 David Ortiz 5.00 2.00
❑ 27 David Wright 8.00 3.00
❑ 28 Delmon Young 5.00 2.00
❑ 29 Derek Jeter 10.00 4.00
❑ 30 Derrek Lee 5.00 2.00
❑ 31 Dontrelle Willis 3.00 1.25
❑ 32 Eric Chavez 3.00 1.25
❑ 33 Eric Gagne 3.00 1.25
❑ 34 Francisco Rodriguez 3.00 1.25
❑ 35 Gary Sheffield 3.00 1.25

Card		
❑ 36 Greg Maddux	8.00	3.00
❑ 37 Hank Blalock	3.00	1.25
❑ 38 Hideki Matsui	6.00	2.50
❑ 39 Ichiro Suzuki	10.00	4.00
❑ 40 Ivan Rodriguez	5.00	2.00
❑ 41 J.D. Drew	3.00	1.25
❑ 42 Jake Peavy	3.00	1.25
❑ 43 Jason Bay	3.00	1.25
❑ 44 Jason Schmidt	3.00	1.25
❑ 45 Jeff Bagwell	5.00	2.00
❑ 46 Jeff Kent	3.00	1.25
❑ 47 Jeremy Bonderman	3.00	1.25
❑ 48 Jim Edmonds	3.00	1.25
❑ 49 Jim Thome	5.00	2.00
❑ 50 Joe Mauer	5.00	2.00
❑ 51 Johan Santana	5.00	2.00
❑ 52 John Smoltz	5.00	2.00
❑ 53 Johnny Damon	5.00	2.00
❑ 54 Jose Reyes	3.00	1.25
❑ 55 Jose Vidro	3.00	1.25
❑ 56 Josh Beckett	3.00	1.25
❑ 57 Justin Morneau	3.00	1.25
❑ 58 Ken Griffey Jr.	8.00	3.00
❑ 59 Kerry Wood	3.00	1.25
❑ 60 Khalil Greene	5.00	2.00
❑ 61 Lance Berkman	3.00	1.25
❑ 62 Larry Walker	5.00	2.00
❑ 63 Luis Gonzalez	3.00	1.25
❑ 64 Manny Ramirez	5.00	2.00
❑ 65 Mark Buehrle	3.00	1.25
❑ 66 Mark Mulder	3.00	1.25
❑ 67 Mark Prior	5.00	2.00
❑ 68 Mark Teixeira	5.00	2.00
❑ 69 Michael Young	3.00	1.25
❑ 70 Miguel Cabrera	5.00	2.00
❑ 71 Miguel Tejada	3.00	1.25
❑ 72 Mike Mussina	5.00	2.00
❑ 73 Mike Piazza	5.00	2.00
❑ 74 Moises Alou	3.00	1.25
❑ 75 Nomar Garciaparra	5.00	2.00
❑ 76 Oliver Perez	3.00	1.25
❑ 77 Pat Burrell	3.00	1.25
❑ 78 Paul Konerko	3.00	1.25
❑ 79 Pedro Feliz	3.00	1.25
❑ 80 Pedro Martinez	5.00	2.00
❑ 81 Randy Johnson	5.00	2.00
❑ 82 Richie Sexson	3.00	1.25
❑ 83 Rickie Weeks	3.00	1.25
❑ 84 Roger Clemens	8.00	3.00
❑ 85 Roy Halladay	3.00	1.25
❑ 86 Roy Oswalt	3.00	1.25
❑ 87 Sammy Sosa	5.00	2.00
❑ 88 Scott Kazmir	3.00	1.25
❑ 89 Scott Rolen	5.00	2.00
❑ 90 Shawn Green	3.00	1.25
❑ 91 Tim Hudson	3.00	1.25
❑ 92 Todd Helton	5.00	2.00
❑ 93 Tom Glavine	5.00	2.00
❑ 94 Torii Hunter	3.00	1.25
❑ 95 Travis Hafner	3.00	1.25
❑ 96 Troy Glaus	3.00	1.25
❑ 97 Vernon Wells	3.00	1.25
❑ 98 Victor Martinez	3.00	1.25
❑ 99 Vladimir Guerrero	5.00	2.00
❑ 100 Zack Greinke	3.00	1.25
❑ 101 Al Kaline RET	8.00	3.00
❑ 102 Babe Ruth RET	10.00	4.00
❑ 103 Bo Jackson RET	8.00	3.00
❑ 104 Bob Gibson RET	8.00	3.00
❑ 105 Brooks Robinson RET	8.00	3.00
❑ 106 Cal Ripken RET	20.00	8.00
❑ 107 Carl Yastrzemski RET	8.00	3.00
❑ 108 Carlton Fisk RET	8.00	3.00
❑ 109 Catfish Hunter RET	5.00	2.00
❑ 110 Christy Mathewson RET	8.00	3.00
❑ 111 Cy Young RET	8.00	3.00
❑ 112 Don Mattingly RET	10.00	4.00
❑ 113 Eddie Mathews RET	8.00	3.00
❑ 114 Eddie Murray RET	8.00	3.00
❑ 115 Gary Carter RET	5.00	2.00
❑ 116 Harmon Killebrew RET	8.00	3.00
❑ 117 Jim Palmer RET	5.00	2.00
❑ 118 Jimmie Foxx RET	8.00	3.00
❑ 119 Joe DiMaggio RET	8.00	3.00
❑ 120 Johnny Bench RET	8.00	3.00
❑ 121 Lefty Grove RET	8.00	3.00
❑ 122 Lou Gehrig RET	8.00	3.00
❑ 123 Mel Ott RET	8.00	3.00
❑ 124 Reggie Jackson RET	8.00	3.00
❑ 125 Mike Schmidt RET	10.00	4.00
❑ 126 Nolan Ryan RET	12.00	5.00
❑ 127 Ozzie Smith RET	8.00	3.00
❑ 128 Paul Molitor RET	5.00	2.00
❑ 129 Pee Wee Reese RET	8.00	3.00
❑ 130 Robin Yount RET	8.00	3.00
❑ 131 Ryne Sandberg RET	10.00	4.00
❑ 132 Ted Williams RET	8.00	3.00
❑ 133 Thurman Munson RET	8.00	3.00
❑ 134 Tom Seaver RET	8.00	3.00
❑ 135 Tony Gwynn RET	8.00	3.00
❑ 136 Wade Boggs RET	8.00	3.00
❑ 137 Walter Johnson RET	8.00	3.00
❑ 138 Warren Spahn RET	8.00	3.00
❑ 139 Will Clark RET	8.00	3.00
❑ 140 Willie McCovey RET	8.00	3.00
❑ 141 Willie Stargell RET	8.00	3.00
❑ 142 Yogi Berra RET	8.00	3.00
❑ 143 Ambiorix Burgos UP RC	5.00	2.00
❑ 144 Ambiorix Concepcion UP RC	5.00	2.00
❑ 145 Anibal Sanchez UP RC	15.00	6.00
❑ 146 Bill McCarthy UP RC	5.00	2.00
❑ 147 Brian Burres UP RC	5.00	2.00
❑ 148 Carlos Ruiz UP RC	5.00	2.00
❑ 149 Casey Rogowski UP RC	8.00	3.00
❑ 150 Chris Resop UP RC	5.00	2.00
❑ 151 Chris Roberson UP RC	5.00	2.00
❑ 152 Chris Seddon UP RC	5.00	2.00
❑ 153 Colter Bean UP RC	5.00	2.00
❑ 154 Dae-Sung Koo UP RC	5.00	2.00
❑ 155 Danny Rueckel UP RC	5.00	2.00
❑ 156 Dave Gassner UP RC	5.00	2.00
❑ 157 Ryan Howard UP	15.00	6.00
❑ 158 D.J. Houlton UP RC	5.00	2.00
❑ 159 Derek Wathan UP RC	5.00	2.00
❑ 160 Devon Lowery UP RC	5.00	2.00
❑ 161 Enrique Gonzalez UP RC	5.00	2.00
❑ 162 Erick Threets UP RC	5.00	2.00
❑ 163 Eude Brito UP RC	5.00	2.00
❑ 164 Francisco Butto UP RC	5.00	2.00
❑ 165 Franquelis Osoria UP RC	5.00	2.00
❑ 166 Garrett Jones UP RC	5.00	2.00
❑ 167 Geovany Soto UP RC	10.00	4.00
❑ 168 Ismael Ramirez UP RC	5.00	2.00
❑ 169 Jared Gothreaux UP RC	5.00	2.00
❑ 170 Jason Hammel UP RC	5.00	2.00
❑ 171 Jeff Housman UP RC	5.00	2.00
❑ 172 Jeff Miller UP RC	5.00	2.00
❑ 173 Jeff Francoeur UP	12.00	5.00
❑ 174 John Hattig UP RC	5.00	2.00
❑ 175 Jorge Campillo UP RC	5.00	2.00
❑ 176 Juan Morillo UP RC	5.00	2.00
❑ 177 Justin Wechsler UP RC	5.00	2.00
❑ 178 Keiichi Yabu UP RC	5.00	2.00
❑ 179 Kendry Morales UP RC	15.00	6.00
❑ 180 Luis Hernandez UP RC	5.00	2.00
❑ 181 Luis Mendoza UP RC	5.00	2.00
❑ 182 Luis Pena UP RC	5.00	2.00
❑ 183 Luis O.Rodriguez UP RC	5.00	2.00
❑ 184 Luke Scott UP RC	10.00	4.00
❑ 185 Marcos Carvajal UP RC	5.00	2.00
❑ 186 Mark Woodyard UP RC	5.00	2.00
❑ 187 Matt Smith UP RC	5.00	2.00
❑ 188 Matthew Lindstrom UP RC	5.00	2.00
❑ 189 Miguel Negron UP RC	8.00	3.00
❑ 190 Mike Morse UP RC	5.00	2.00
❑ 191 Nate McLouth UP RC	5.00	2.00
❑ 192 Nick Masset UP RC	5.00	2.00
❑ 193 Paulino Reynoso UP RC	5.00	2.00
❑ 194 Pedro Lopez UP RC	5.00	2.00
❑ 195 Pete Orr UP RC	5.00	2.00
❑ 196 Randy Messenger UP RC	5.00	2.00
❑ 197 Randy Williams UP RC	5.00	2.00
❑ 198 Raul Tablado UP RC	5.00	2.00
❑ 199 Ronny Paulino UP RC	6.00	2.50
❑ 200 Russ Rohlicek UP RC	5.00	2.00
❑ 201 Russell Martin UP RC	12.00	5.00
❑ 202 Scott Baker UP RC	8.00	3.00
❑ 203 Scott Munter UP RC	5.00	2.00
❑ 204 Sean Thompson UP RC	5.00	2.00
❑ 205 Sean Tracey UP RC	5.00	2.00
❑ 206 Steve Schmoll UP RC	5.00	2.00
❑ 207 Tony Pena UP RC	5.00	2.00
❑ 208 Travis Bowyer UP RC	5.00	2.00
❑ 209 Ubaldo Jimenez UP RC	10.00	4.00
❑ 210 Wladimir Balentien UP RC	10.00	4.00
❑ 211 Yorman Bazardo UP RC	5.00	2.00
❑ 212 Yuniesky Betancourt UP RC	10.00	4.00
❑ 213 Adam Shabala UP RC	5.00	2.00
❑ 214 Brandon McCarthy UP RC	10.00	4.00
❑ 215 Chad Orvella UP RC	5.00	2.00
❑ 216 Jermaine Van Buren UP	5.00	2.00
❑ 217 Anthony Reyes UP RC	25.00	10.00
❑ 218 Dana Eveland UP RC	5.00	2.00
❑ 219 Brian Anderson UP RC	8.00	3.00
❑ 220 Hayden Penn UP RC	8.00	3.00
❑ 221 Chris Denorfia UP RC	10.00	4.00
❑ 222 Joel Peralta UP RC	5.00	2.00
❑ 223 Ryan Garko UP RC	10.00	4.00
❑ 224 Felix Hernandez UP	10.00	4.00
❑ 225 Mark McLemore UP RC	5.00	2.00
❑ 226 Melky Cabrera UP RC	15.00	6.00
❑ 227 Nelson Cruz UP RC	10.00	4.00
❑ 228 Norihiro Nakamura UP RC	8.00	3.00
❑ 229 Oscar Robles UP RC	5.00	2.00
❑ 230 Rick Short UP RC	5.00	2.00
❑ 231 Ryan Zimmerman UP RC	30.00	12.50
❑ 232 Ryan Speier UP RC	5.00	2.00
❑ 233 Ryan Spilborghs UP RC	8.00	3.00
❑ 234 Shane Costa UP RC	5.00	2.00
❑ 235 Zach Duke UP	8.00	3.00
❑ 236 Tony Giarratano UP RC	5.00	2.00
❑ 237 Jeff Niemann UP RC	8.00	3.00
❑ 238 Stephen Drew AU RC	200.00	100.00
❑ 239 Justin Verlander AU RC	300.00	200.00
❑ 240 Prince Fielder AU RC	600.00	500.00
❑ 241 Philip Humber AU RC	80.00	40.00
❑ 242 Tadahito Iguchi AU RC	120.00	60.00

2006 Ultimate Collection

Card		
❑ COMMON CARD (1-274)	2.50	1.00
❑ VETERAN PRINT RUN 799 SER.#'d SETS		
❑ COMMON RC (1-274)	2.50	1.00
❑ RC PRINT RUN 799 SERIAL #'d SETS		
❑ COMMON AU RC (101-175)	10.00	4.00
❑ AU RC MINORS	10.00	4.00
❑ OVERALL AU ODDS 1:2		
❑ AU RC PRINT RUNS B/WN 150-180		
❑ EXCHANGE DEADLINE 12/20/09		
❑ PLATE ODDS APPX. 7:10 BONUS PACKS		
❑ PLATE PRINT RUN 1 SET PER COLOR		
❑ BLACK-CYAN-MAGENTA-YELLOW ISSUED		
❑ NO PLATE PRICING DUE TO SCARCITY		
❑ 1 Babe Ruth	10.00	4.00
❑ 2 Chad Tracy	2.50	1.00
❑ 3 Brandon Webb	2.50	1.00
❑ 4 Andruw Jones	4.00	1.50
❑ 5 Chipper Jones	5.00	2.00
❑ 6 John Smoltz	4.00	1.50
❑ 7 Eddie Mathews	5.00	2.00
❑ 8 Miguel Tejada	2.50	1.00
❑ 9 Brian Roberts	2.50	1.00
❑ 10 Mickey Cochrane	2.50	1.00
❑ 11 Curt Schilling	4.00	1.50
❑ 12 David Ortiz	5.00	2.00
❑ 13 Manny Ramirez	4.00	1.50
❑ 14 Johnny Bench	5.00	2.00
❑ 15 Cy Young	5.00	2.00
❑ 16 Greg Maddux	6.00	2.50
❑ 17 Derrek Lee	2.50	1.00
❑ 18 Yogi Berra	5.00	2.00

❑ 19 Walter Johnson 5.00 2.00
❑ 20 Jim Thome 4.00 1.50
❑ 21 Paul Konerko 2.50 1.00
❑ 22 Lou Gehrig 8.00 3.00
❑ 23 Jose Contreras 2.50 1.00
❑ 24 Ken Griffey Jr. 6.00 2.50
❑ 25 Adam Dunn 2.50 1.00
❑ 26 Reggie Jackson 4.00 1.50
❑ 27 Travis Hafner 2.50 1.00
❑ 28 Victor Martinez 2.50 1.00
❑ 29 Grady Sizemore 4.00 1.50
❑ 30 Casey Stengel 2.50 1.00
❑ 31 Todd Helton 4.00 1.50
❑ 32 Nolan Ryan 10.00 4.00
❑ 33 Clint Barmes 2.50 1.00
❑ 34 Ivan Rodriguez 4.00 1.50
❑ 35 Chris Shelton 2.50 1.00
❑ 36 Ty Cobb 8.00 3.00
❑ 37 Miguel Cabrera 4.00 1.50
❑ 38 Dontrelle Willis 2.50 1.00
❑ 39 Lance Berkman 2.50 1.00
❑ 40 Tom Seaver 4.00 1.50
❑ 41 Roy Oswalt 2.50 1.00
❑ 42 Christy Mathewson 5.00 2.00
❑ 43 Luis Aparicio 2.50 1.00
❑ 44 Vladimir Guerrero 5.00 2.00
❑ 45 Bartolo Colon 2.50 1.00
❑ 46 Roy Campanella 5.00 2.00
❑ 47 George Sisler 2.50 1.00
❑ 48 Jeff Kent 2.50 1.00
❑ 49 J.D. Drew 2.50 1.00
❑ 50 Carlos Lee 2.50 1.00
❑ 51 Willie Stargell 4.00 1.50
❑ 52 Rickie Weeks 2.50 1.00
❑ 53 Johan Santana 4.00 1.50
❑ 54 Torii Hunter 2.50 1.00
❑ 55 Joe Mauer 4.00 1.50
❑ 56 Pedro Martinez 4.00 1.50
❑ 57 David Wright 8.00 3.00
❑ 58 Carlos Beltran 2.50 1.00
❑ 59 Jimmie Foxx 5.00 2.00
❑ 60 Jose Reyes 2.50 1.00
❑ 61 Derek Jeter 10.00 4.00
❑ 62 Alex Rodriguez 8.00 3.00
❑ 63 Randy Johnson 5.00 2.00
❑ 64 Hideki Matsui 5.00 2.00
❑ 65 Thurman Munson 5.00 2.00
❑ 66 Rich Harden 2.50 1.00
❑ 67 Eric Chavez 2.50 1.00
❑ 68 Don Drysdale 4.00 1.50
❑ 69 Bobby Crosby 2.50 1.00
❑ 70 Pee Wee Reese 4.00 1.50
❑ 71 Ryan Howard 8.00 3.00
❑ 72 Chase Utley 5.00 2.00
❑ 73 Jackie Robinson 5.00 2.00
❑ 74 Jason Bay 2.50 1.00
❑ 75 Honus Wagner 5.00 2.00
❑ 76 Lefty Grove 2.50 1.00
❑ 77 Jake Peavy 2.50 1.00
❑ 78 Brian Giles 2.50 1.00
❑ 79 Eddie Murray 5.00 2.00
❑ 80 Omar Vizquel 4.00 1.50
❑ 81 Jason Schmidt 2.50 1.00
❑ 82 Ichiro Suzuki 6.00 2.50
❑ 83 Felix Hernandez 4.00 1.50
❑ 84 Kenji Johjima RC 8.00 3.00
❑ 85 Albert Pujols 8.00 3.00
❑ 86 Chris Carpenter 2.50 1.00
❑ 87 Brooks Robinson 4.00 1.50
❑ 88 Dizzy Dean 4.00 1.50
❑ 89 Carl Crawford 2.50 1.00
❑ 90 Rogers Hornsby 4.00 1.50
❑ 91 Scott Kazmir 4.00 1.50
❑ 92 Mark Teixeira 4.00 1.50
❑ 93 Michael Young 2.50 1.00
❑ 94 Johnny Mize 2.50 1.00
❑ 95 Vernon Wells 2.50 1.00
❑ 96 Roy Halladay 2.50 1.00
❑ 97 Mel Ott 2.50 1.00
❑ 98 Alfonso Soriano 2.50 1.00
❑ 99 Joe Morgan 2.50 1.00
❑ 100 Satchel Paige 5.00 2.00
❑ 101 A.Wainwright AU/180 (RC) 25.00 10.00
❑ 102 A.Hernandez AU/180 (RC) 10.00 4.00
❑ 103 A.Ethier AU/180 (RC) 30.00 12.50
❑ 104 B.Johnson AU/180 (RC) 10.00 4.00
❑ 105 B.Bonser AU/180 (RC) 15.00 6.00
❑ 106 B.Logan AU/180 RC 10.00 4.00
❑ 107 B.Anderson AU/180 (RC) 10.00 4.00
❑ 108 B.Bannister AU/180 (RC) 15.00 6.00
❑ 109 C.Demaria AU/180 RC 10.00 4.00
❑ 110 C.Denorfia AU/180 (RC) 10.00 4.00
❑ 111 C.Ross AU/180 (RC) 10.00 4.00
❑ 112 C.Hamels AU/180 (RC) 80.00 40.00
❑ 113 C.Jackson AU/180 (RC) 15.00 6.00
❑ 114 D.Uggla AU/180 (RC) EXCH 25.00 10.00
❑ 115 D.Gassner AU/180 (RC) 10.00 4.00
❑ 116 E.Reed AU/180 (RC) 10.00 4.00
❑ 118 F.Nieve AU/180 (RC) 10.00 4.00
❑ 119 F.Liriano AU/180 (RC) 60.00 30.00
❑ 120 F.Bynum AU/180 (RC) 10.00 4.00
❑ 121 H.Ramirez AU/180 (RC) 25.00 10.00
❑ 122 H.Kuo AU/180 (RC) EXCH 80.00 40.00
❑ 123 I.Kinsler AU/180 (RC) 60.00 30.00
❑ 124 J.Hammel AU/180 (RC) 10.00 4.00
❑ 125 J.Kubel AU/180 (RC) 10.00 4.00
❑ 126 J.Harris AU/180 RC 10.00 4.00
❑ 127 J.Weaver AU/150 (RC) 50.00 20.00
❑ 128 J.Accardo AU/180 (RC) 10.00 4.00
❑ 129 J.Hermida AU/180 (RC) 15.00 6.00
❑ 130 J.Zumaya AU/180 (RC) 40.00 15.00
❑ 131 J.Devine AU/180 RC 10.00 4.00
❑ 132 J.Koronka AU/180 (RC) 10.00 4.00
❑ 133 J.Van Benschoten AU/180 (RC) 10.00 4.00
❑ 134 J.Papelbon AU/180 (RC) 50.00 20.00
❑ 135 J.Capellan AU/180 (RC) 10.00 4.00
❑ 136 J.Johnson AU/180 (RC) 15.00 6.00
❑ 137 J.Rupe AU/180 (RC) 10.00 4.00
❑ 138 J.Willingham AU/180 (RC) 10.00 4.00
❑ 139 J.Wilson AU/180 (RC) 10.00 4.00
❑ 140 J.Verlander AU/180 (RC) 50.00 20.00
❑ 141 K.Shoppach AU/180 (RC) 10.00 4.00
❑ 142 K.Morales AU/180 (RC) 15.00 6.00
❑ 143 M.McBride AU/180 (RC) 10.00 4.00
❑ 144 M.Prado AU/180 (RC) 10.00 4.00
❑ 145 M.Cain AU/180 (RC) 25.00 10.00
❑ 146 M.Jacobs AU/180 (RC) 10.00 4.00
❑ 147 M.Thompson AU/180 RC 10.00 4.00
❑ 148 N.McLouth AU/180 (RC) 10.00 4.00
❑ 149 P.Maholm AU/180 (RC) 10.00 4.00
❑ 150 P.Fielder AU/180 (RC) EXCH 120.00 60.00
❑ 151 R.Abercrombie AU/180 (RC) 10.00 4.00
❑ 152 R.Hill AU/180 (RC) 40.00 15.00
❑ 153 R.Flores AU/180 RC 10.00 4.00
❑ 154 R.Lugo AU/180 (RC) 10.00 4.00
❑ 155 R.Zimmerman AU/180 (RC) 60.00 30.00
❑ 156 S.Marshall AU/180 (RC) 25.00 10.00
❑ 157 T.Saito AU/180 RC 25.00 10.00
❑ 158 T.Buchholz AU/180 (RC) 10.00 4.00
❑ 159 T.Pena Jr. AU/180 (RC) 10.00 4.00
❑ 160 W.Nieves AU/180 (RC) 10.00 4.00
❑ 161 J.Shields AU/180 RC 10.00 4.00
❑ 162 J.Lester AU/180 RC 50.00 20.00
❑ 163 C.Hansen AU/180 RC 40.00 15.00
❑ 164 A.Rakers AU/180 (RC) 10.00 4.00
❑ 165 Y.Petit AU/180 (RC) EXCH 10.00 4.00
❑ 166 B.Livingston AU/180 (RC) 10.00 4.00
❑ 167 B.Harris AU/180 (RC) 10.00 4.00
❑ 169 C.Ruiz AU/180 (RC) 10.00 4.00
❑ 170 C.Britton AU/180 RC 10.00 4.00
❑ 171 H.Kendrick AU/180 (RC) 40.00 15.00
❑ 172 J.Van Buren AU/180 (RC) 10.00 4.00
❑ 173 K.Frandsen AU/180 (RC) 15.00 6.00
❑ 174 M.Capps AU/180 (RC) 10.00 4.00
❑ 175 P.Moylan AU/180 RC 10.00 4.00
❑ 191 Richie Ashburn 4.00 1.50
❑ 192 Lou Brock 4.00 1.50
❑ 193 Lou Boudreau 2.50 1.00
❑ 194 Orlando Cepeda 2.50 1.00
❑ 195 Bobby Doerr 2.50 1.00
❑ 196 Dennis Eckersley 2.50 1.00
❑ 197 Bob Feller 2.50 1.00
❑ 198 Rollie Fingers 2.50 1.00
❑ 199 Carlton Fisk 4.00 1.50
❑ 200 Bob Gibson 4.00 1.50
❑ 201 Catfish Hunter 2.50 1.00
❑ 202 Fergie Jenkins 2.50 1.00
❑ 203 Al Kaline 5.00 2.00
❑ 204 Harmon Killebrew 5.00 2.00
❑ 205 Ralph Kiner 4.00 1.50
❑ 206 Buck Leonard 2.50 1.00
❑ 207 Juan Marichal 2.50 1.00
❑ 208 Bill Mazeroski 4.00 1.50
❑ 209 Willie McCovey 4.00 1.50
❑ 210 Jim Palmer 2.50 1.00
❑ 211 Tony Perez 2.50 1.00
❑ 212 Gaylord Perry 2.50 1.00
❑ 213 Phil Rizzuto 4.00 1.50
❑ 214 Robin Roberts 2.50 1.00
❑ 215 Mike Schmidt 6.00 2.50
❑ 216 Enos Slaughter 2.50 1.00
❑ 217 Ozzie Smith 6.00 2.50
❑ 218 Billy Williams 2.50 1.00
❑ 219 Robin Yount 5.00 2.00
❑ 220 Carlos Quentin (RC) 4.00 1.50
❑ 221 Jeff Francoeur 5.00 2.00
❑ 222 Brian McCann 2.50 1.00
❑ 223 Nick Markakis (RC) 4.00 1.50
❑ 224 Josh Beckett 2.50 1.00
❑ 225 Jason Varitek 5.00 2.00
❑ 226 Mark Prior 4.00 1.50
❑ 227 Aramis Ramirez 2.50 1.00
❑ 228 Jermaine Dye 2.50 1.00
❑ 229 Tadahito Iguchi 2.50 1.00
❑ 230 Bobby Jenks 2.50 1.00
❑ 231 C.C. Sabathia 2.50 1.00
❑ 232 Jeff Francis 2.50 1.00
❑ 233 Matt Holliday 3.00 1.25
❑ 234 Magglio Ordonez 2.50 1.00
❑ 235 Kenny Rogers 2.50 1.00
❑ 236 Roger Clemens 8.00 3.00
❑ 237 Andy Pettitte 2.50 1.00
❑ 238 Craig Biggio 4.00 1.50
❑ 239 Chone Figgins 2.50 1.00
❑ 240 John Lackey 2.50 1.00
❑ 241 Nomar Garciaparra 5.00 2.00
❑ 242 Prince Fielder 6.00 2.50
❑ 243 Ben Sheets 2.50 1.00
❑ 244 Bill Hall 2.50 1.00
❑ 245 Justin Morneau 2.50 1.00
❑ 246 Joe Nathan 2.50 1.00
❑ 247 Carlos Delgado 2.50 1.00
❑ 248 Shawn Green 2.50 1.00
❑ 249 Billy Wagner 2.50 1.00
❑ 250 Jason Giambi 2.50 1.00
❑ 251 Mike Mussina 4.00 1.50
❑ 252 Mariano Rivera 5.00 2.00
❑ 253 Robinson Cano 4.00 1.50
❑ 254 Bobby Abreu 2.50 1.00
❑ 255 Huston Street 2.50 1.00
❑ 256 Frank Thomas 5.00 2.00
❑ 257 Danny Haren 2.50 1.00
❑ 258 Jason Kendall 2.50 1.00
❑ 259 Nick Swisher 2.50 1.00
❑ 260 Pat Burrell 2.50 1.00
❑ 261 Tom Gordon 2.50 1.00
❑ 262 Freddy Sanchez 2.50 1.00
❑ 263 Trevor Hoffman 2.50 1.00
❑ 264 Khalil Greene 4.00 1.50
❑ 265 Adrian Gonzalez 2.50 1.00
❑ 266 Moises Alou 2.50 1.00
❑ 267 Matt Morris 2.50 1.00
❑ 268 Pedro Feliz 2.50 1.00
❑ 269 Richie Sexson 2.50 1.00
❑ 270 Hoyt Wilhelm 2.50 1.00
❑ 271 Adrian Beltre 2.50 1.00
❑ 272 Jim Edmonds 4.00 1.50
❑ 273 Scott Rolen 4.00 1.50
❑ 274 Jason Isringhausen 2.50 1.00
❑ 275 Jorge Cantu 2.50 1.00
❑ 276 Hank Blalock 2.50 1.00
❑ 277 Kevin Millwood 2.50 1.00
❑ 278 Alex Rios 2.50 1.00
❑ 279 Troy Glaus 2.50 1.00
❑ 280 B.J. Ryan 2.50 1.00
❑ 281 Nick Johnson 2.50 1.00
❑ 282 Chad Cordero 2.50 1.00
❑ 283 Austin Kearns 2.50 1.00
❑ 284 Ricky Nolasco (RC) 2.50 1.00
❑ 285 Travis Ishikawa (RC) 2.50 1.00
❑ 286 Lastings Milledge (RC) 4.00 1.50
❑ 287 James Loney (RC) 4.00 1.50
❑ 288 Red Schoendienst 2.50 1.00
❑ 289 Warren Spahn 4.00 1.50
❑ 290 Early Wynn 2.50 1.00

2007 Ultimate Collection

- ❑ COMMON CARD (1-100) 2.00 .75
- ❑ 1-100 PRINT RUN 450 SER.#'d SETS
- ❑ COMMON AU RC (101-141) 10.00 4.00
- ❑ OVERALL AU ODDS ONE PER PACK
- ❑ AU RC PRINT RUNS B/WN 289-299 COPIES PER
- ❑ EXCHANGE DEADLINE 9/24/2009
- ❑ 1 Chipper Jones 5.00 2.00
- ❑ 2 Andruw Jones 3.00 1.25
- ❑ 3 Tim Hudson 2.00 .75
- ❑ 4 Stephen Drew 3.00 1.25
- ❑ 5 Randy Johnson 5.00 2.00
- ❑ 6 Brandon Webb 2.00 .75
- ❑ 7 Alfonso Soriano 2.00 .75
- ❑ 8 Derrek Lee 2.00 .75
- ❑ 9 Aramis Ramirez 2.00 .75
- ❑ 10 Carlos Zambrano 2.00 .75
- ❑ 11 Ken Griffey Jr. 8.00 3.00
- ❑ 12 Adam Dunn 2.00 .75
- ❑ 13 Ryan Freel 2.00 .75
- ❑ 14 Todd Helton 3.00 1.25
- ❑ 15 Garrett Atkins 2.00 .75
- ❑ 16 Matt Holliday 5.00 2.00
- ❑ 17 Hanley Ramirez 3.00 1.25
- ❑ 18 Dontrelle Willis 2.00 .75
- ❑ 19 Miguel Cabrera 3.00 1.25
- ❑ 20 Lance Berkman 2.00 .75
- ❑ 21 Roy Oswalt 2.00 .75
- ❑ 22 Carlos Lee 2.00 .75
- ❑ 23 Nomar Garciaparra 5.00 2.00
- ❑ 24 Jason Schmidt 2.00 .75
- ❑ 25 Juan Pierre 2.00 .75
- ❑ 26 Russell Martin 2.00 .75
- ❑ 27 Rickie Weeks 2.00 .75
- ❑ 28 Prince Fielder 5.00 2.00
- ❑ 29 Ben Sheets 2.00 .75
- ❑ 30 David Wright 8.00 3.00
- ❑ 31 Jose Reyes 5.00 2.00
- ❑ 32 Pedro Martinez 3.00 1.25
- ❑ 33 Carlos Beltran 2.00 .75
- ❑ 34 Brett Myers 2.00 .75
- ❑ 35 Jimmy Rollins 2.00 .75
- ❑ 36 Ryan Howard 8.00 3.00
- ❑ 37 Jason Bay 2.00 .75
- ❑ 38 Freddy Sanchez 2.00 .75
- ❑ 39 Ian Snell 2.00 .75
- ❑ 40 Jake Peavy 2.00 .75
- ❑ 41 Greg Maddux 8.00 3.00
- ❑ 42 Brian Giles 2.00 .75
- ❑ 43 Matt Cain 3.00 1.25
- ❑ 44 Barry Zito 2.00 .75
- ❑ 45 Ray Durham 2.00 .75
- ❑ 46 Albert Pujols 10.00 4.00
- ❑ 47 Chris Carpenter 2.00 .75
- ❑ 48 Chris Duncan 2.00 .75
- ❑ 49 Scott Rolen 3.00 1.25
- ❑ 50 Ryan Zimmerman 5.00 2.00
- ❑ 51 Chad Cordero 2.00 .75
- ❑ 52 Ryan Church 2.00 .75
- ❑ 53 Miguel Tejada 2.00 .75
- ❑ 54 Erik Bedard 2.00 .75
- ❑ 55 Brian Roberts 2.00 .75
- ❑ 56 David Ortiz 5.00 2.00
- ❑ 57 Josh Beckett 3.00 1.25
- ❑ 58 Manny Ramirez 3.00 1.25
- ❑ 59 Daisuke Matsuzaka RC 30.00 12.50
- ❑ 60 Jim Thome 3.00 1.25
- ❑ 61 Paul Konerko 2.00 .75
- ❑ 62 Jermaine Dye 2.00 .75
- ❑ 63 Grady Sizemore 3.00 1.25
- ❑ 64 Victor Martinez 2.00 .75
- ❑ 65 C.C. Sabathia 2.00 .75
- ❑ 66 Ivan Rodriguez 3.00 1.25
- ❑ 67 Justin Verlander 5.00 2.00
- ❑ 68 Gary Sheffield 2.00 .75
- ❑ 69 Jeremy Bonderman 2.00 .75
- ❑ 70 Gil Meche 2.00 .75
- ❑ 71 Mike Sweeney 2.00 .75
- ❑ 72 Mark Teahen 2.00 .75
- ❑ 73 Vladimir Guerrero 5.00 2.00
- ❑ 74 Howie Kendrick 2.00 .75
- ❑ 75 Francisco Rodriguez 2.00 .75
- ❑ 76 Johan Santana 3.00 1.25
- ❑ 77 Justin Morneau 2.00 .75
- ❑ 78 Joe Mauer 3.00 1.25
- ❑ 79 Michael Cuddyer 2.00 .75
- ❑ 80 Alex Rodriguez 8.00 3.00
- ❑ 81 Derek Jeter 12.00 5.00
- ❑ 82 Johnny Damon 3.00 1.25
- ❑ 83 Roger Clemens 10.00 4.00
- ❑ 84 Rich Harden 2.00 .75
- ❑ 85 Mike Piazza 5.00 2.00
- ❑ 86 Huston Street 2.00 .75
- ❑ 87 Ichiro Suzuki 8.00 3.00
- ❑ 88 Felix Hernandez 3.00 1.25
- ❑ 89 Kenji Johjima 5.00 2.00
- ❑ 90 Adrian Beltre 2.00 .75
- ❑ 91 Carl Crawford 2.00 .75
- ❑ 92 Scott Kazmir 3.00 1.25
- ❑ 93 B.J. Upton 2.00 .75
- ❑ 94 Michael Young 2.00 .75
- ❑ 95 Mark Teixeira 3.00 1.25
- ❑ 96 Sammy Sosa 5.00 2.00
- ❑ 97 Hank Blalock 2.00 .75
- ❑ 98 Vernon Wells 2.00 .75
- ❑ 99 Roy Halladay 2.00 .75
- ❑ 100 Frank Thomas 5.00 2.00
- ❑ 101 Adam Lind AU (RC) 10.00 4.00
- ❑ 102 Akinori Iwamura AU RC 30.00 12.50
- ❑ 103 Andrew Miller AU RC 60.00 30.00
- ❑ 104 Michael Bourn AU (RC) 10.00 4.00
- ❑ 105 Kory Casto AU (RC) 10.00 4.00
- ❑ 106 Ryan Braun AU (RC) 100.00 50.00
- ❑ 107 Sean Gallagher AU (RC) 10.00 4.00
- ❑ 108 Billy Butler AU (RC) 40.00 15.00
- ❑ 109 Alexi Casilla AU RC 10.00 4.00
- ❑ 110 Chris Stewart AU RC 10.00 4.00
- ❑ 111 Matt DeSalvo AU (RC) 15.00 6.00
- ❑ 112 Chase Headley AU (RC) 15.00 6.00
- ❑ 113 D.Young AU/292 (RC) 30.00 12.50
- ❑ 114 Homer Bailey AU (RC) 25.00 10.00
- ❑ 115 Kurt Suzuki AU (RC) 15.00 6.00
- ❑ 116 A.Gordon AU/297 RC 60.00 30.00
- ❑ 117 Josh Hamilton AU (RC) 25.00 10.00
- ❑ 118 Fred Lewis AU (RC) 10.00 4.00
- ❑ 119 Glen Perkins AU (RC) 10.00 4.00
- ❑ 120 Hector Gimenez AU (RC) 10.00 4.00
- ❑ 121 Phil Hughes AU (RC) 60.00 30.00
- ❑ 122 Jeff Baker AU (RC) 10.00 4.00
- ❑ 123 Andy LaRoche AU (RC) 10.00 4.00
- ❑ 124 Tim Lincecum AU RC 120.00 60.00
- ❑ 125 Joaquin Arias AU (RC) 10.00 4.00
- ❑ 126 D.Matsuzaka AU EXCH 400.00 250.00
- ❑ 127 Micah Owings AU (RC) 15.00 6.00
- ❑ 128 H.Pence AU/297 (RC) 60.00 30.00
- ❑ 129 Matt Chico AU (RC) 10.00 4.00
- ❑ 130 Kei Igawa AU RC 30.00 12.50
- ❑ 131 Kevin Kouzmanoff AU (RC) 10.00 4.00
- ❑ 132 M.Montero AU/289 (RC) 10.00 4.00
- ❑ 133 Mike Rabelo AU RC 10.00 4.00
- ❑ 134 Felix Pie AU (RC) 10.00 4.00
- ❑ 135 Curtis Thigpen AU (RC) 10.00 4.00
- ❑ 136 Ryan Z. Braun AU RC 15.00 6.00
- ❑ 137 Ryan Sweeney AU (RC) 10.00 4.00
- ❑ 138 Brandon Wood AU (RC) 15.00 6.00
- ❑ 139 Troy Tulowitzki AU (RC) 50.00 20.00
- ❑ 140 Justin Upton AU RC 80.00 40.00
- ❑ 141 J.Chamberlain AU RC EXCH 250.00 200.00

2001 Ultra

- ❑ COMPLETE SET (275) 120.00 60.00
- ❑ COMP.SET w/o SP's (250) 25.00 10.00
- ❑ COMMON CARD (1-250) .30 .10
- ❑ COMMON CARD (251-275) 3.00 1.25
- ❑ COMMON CARD (276-280) 5.00 2.00
- ❑ 1 Pedro Martinez .50 .20
- ❑ 2 Derek Jeter 2.00 .75
- ❑ 3 Cal Ripken 2.50 1.00
- ❑ 4 Alex Rodriguez 1.25 .50
- ❑ 5 Vladimir Guerrero .75 .30
- ❑ 6 Troy Glaus .30 .10
- ❑ 7 Sammy Sosa .75 .30
- ❑ 8 Mike Piazza 1.25 .50
- ❑ 9 Tony Gwynn 1.00 .40
- ❑ 10 Tim Hudson .30 .10
- ❑ 11 John Flaherty .30 .10
- ❑ 12 Jeff Cirillo .30 .10
- ❑ 13 Ellis Burks .30 .10
- ❑ 14 Carlos Lee .30 .10
- ❑ 15 Carlos Beltran .30 .10
- ❑ 16 Ruben Rivera .30 .10
- ❑ 17 Richard Hidalgo .30 .10
- ❑ 18 Omar Vizquel .50 .20
- ❑ 19 Michael Barrett .30 .10
- ❑ 20 Jose Canseco .50 .20
- ❑ 21 Jason Giambi .30 .10
- ❑ 22 Greg Maddux 1.25 .50
- ❑ 23 Charles Johnson .30 .10
- ❑ 24 Sandy Alomar Jr. .30 .10
- ❑ 25 Rick Ankiel .30 .10
- ❑ 26 Richie Sexson .30 .10
- ❑ 27 Matt Williams .30 .10
- ❑ 28 Joe Girardi .30 .10
- ❑ 29 Jason Kendall .30 .10
- ❑ 30 Brad Fullmer .30 .10
- ❑ 31 Alex Gonzalez .30 .10
- ❑ 32 Rick Helling .30 .10
- ❑ 33 Mike Mussina .50 .20
- ❑ 34 Joe Randa .30 .10
- ❑ 35 J.T. Snow .30 .10
- ❑ 36 Edgardo Alfonzo .30 .10
- ❑ 37 Dante Bichette .30 .10
- ❑ 38 Brad Ausmus .30 .10
- ❑ 39 Bobby Abreu .30 .10
- ❑ 40 Warren Morris .30 .10
- ❑ 41 Tony Womack .30 .10
- ❑ 42 Russell Branyan .30 .10
- ❑ 43 Mike Lowell .30 .10
- ❑ 44 Mark Grace .50 .20
- ❑ 45 Jeromy Burnitz .30 .10
- ❑ 46 J.D. Drew .30 .10
- ❑ 47 David Justice .30 .10
- ❑ 48 Alex Gonzalez .30 .10
- ❑ 49 Tino Martinez .50 .20
- ❑ 50 Raul Mondesi .30 .10
- ❑ 51 Rafael Furcal .30 .10
- ❑ 52 Marquis Grissom .30 .10
- ❑ 53 Kevin Young .30 .10
- ❑ 54 Jon Lieber .30 .10
- ❑ 55 Henry Rodriguez .30 .10
- ❑ 56 Dave Burba .30 .10
- ❑ 57 Shannon Stewart .30 .10
- ❑ 58 Preston Wilson .30 .10

❑ 59	Paul O'Neill	.50	.20
❑ 60	Jimmy Haynes	.30	.10
❑ 61	Darryl Kile	.30	.10
❑ 62	Bret Boone	.30	.10
❑ 63	Bartolo Colon	.30	.10
❑ 64	Andres Galarraga	.30	.10
❑ 65	Trot Nixon	.30	.10
❑ 66	Steve Finley	.30	.10
❑ 67	Shawn Green	.30	.10
❑ 68	Robert Person	.30	.10
❑ 69	Kenny Rogers	.30	.10
❑ 70	Bobby Higginson	.30	.10
❑ 71	Barry Larkin	.50	.20
❑ 72	Al Martin	.30	.10
❑ 73	Tom Glavine	.50	.20
❑ 74	Rondell White	.30	.10
❑ 75	Ray Lankford	.30	.10
❑ 76	Moises Alou	.30	.10
❑ 77	Matt Clement	.30	.10
❑ 78	Geoff Jenkins	.30	.10
❑ 79	David Wells	.30	.10
❑ 80	Chuck Finley	.30	.10
❑ 81	Andy Pettitte	.50	.20
❑ 82	Travis Fryman	.30	.10
❑ 83	Ron Coomer	.30	.10
❑ 84	Mark McGwire	2.00	.75
❑ 85	Kerry Wood	.30	.10
❑ 86	Jorge Posada	.50	.20
❑ 87	Jeff Bagwell	.50	.20
❑ 88	Andruw Jones	.50	.20
❑ 89	Ryan Klesko	.30	.10
❑ 90	Mariano Rivera	.75	.30
❑ 91	Lance Berkman	.30	.10
❑ 92	Kenny Lofton	.30	.10
❑ 93	Jacque Jones	.30	.10
❑ 94	Eric Young	.30	.10
❑ 95	Edgar Renteria	.30	.10
❑ 96	Chipper Jones	.75	.30
❑ 97	Todd Helton	.50	.20
❑ 98	Shawn Estes	.30	.10
❑ 99	Mark Mulder	.30	.10
❑ 100	Lee Stevens	.30	.10
❑ 101	Jermaine Dye	.30	.10
❑ 102	Greg Vaughn	.30	.10
❑ 103	Chris Singleton	.30	.10
❑ 104	Brady Anderson	.30	.10
❑ 105	Terrence Long	.30	.10
❑ 106	Quilvio Veras	.30	.10
❑ 107	Magglio Ordonez	.30	.10
❑ 108	Johnny Damon	.50	.20
❑ 109	Jeffrey Hammonds	.30	.10
❑ 110	Fred McGriff	.50	.20
❑ 111	Carl Pavano	.30	.10
❑ 112	Bobby Estalella	.30	.10
❑ 113	Todd Hundley	.30	.10
❑ 114	Scott Rolen	.50	.20
❑ 115	Robin Ventura	.30	.10
❑ 116	Pokey Reese	.30	.10
❑ 117	Luis Gonzalez	.30	.10
❑ 118	Jose Offerman	.30	.10
❑ 119	Edgar Martinez	.50	.20
❑ 120	Dean Palmer	.30	.10
❑ 121	David Segui	.30	.10
❑ 122	Troy O'Leary	.30	.10
❑ 123	Tony Batista	.30	.10
❑ 124	Todd Zeile	.30	.10
❑ 125	Randy Johnson	.75	.30
❑ 126	Luis Castillo	.30	.10
❑ 127	Kris Benson	.30	.10
❑ 128	John Olerud	.30	.10
❑ 129	Eric Karros	.30	.10
❑ 130	Eddie Taubensee	.30	.10
❑ 131	Neifi Perez	.30	.10
❑ 132	Matt Stairs	.30	.10
❑ 133	Luis Alicea	.30	.10
❑ 134	Jeff Kent	.30	.10
❑ 135	Javier Vazquez	.30	.10
❑ 136	Garret Anderson	.30	.10
❑ 137	Frank Thomas	.75	.30
❑ 138	Carlos Febles	.30	.10
❑ 139	Albert Belle	.30	.10
❑ 140	Tony Clark	.30	.10
❑ 141	Pat Burrell	.30	.10
❑ 142	Mike Sweeney	.30	.10
❑ 143	Jay Buhner	.30	.10
❑ 144	Gabe Kapler	.30	.10
❑ 145	Derek Bell	.30	.10
❑ 146	B.J. Surhoff	.30	.10
❑ 147	Adam Kennedy	.30	.10
❑ 148	Aaron Boone	.30	.10
❑ 149	Todd Stottlemyre	.30	.10
❑ 150	Roberto Alomar	.50	.20
❑ 151	Orlando Hernandez	.30	.10
❑ 152	Jason Varitek	.75	.30
❑ 153	Gary Sheffield	.30	.10
❑ 154	Cliff Floyd	.30	.10
❑ 155	Chad Hermansen	.30	.10
❑ 156	Carlos Delgado	.30	.10
❑ 157	Aaron Sele	.30	.10
❑ 158	Sean Casey	.30	.10
❑ 159	Ruben Mateo	.30	.10
❑ 160	Mike Bordick	.30	.10
❑ 161	Mike Cameron	.30	.10
❑ 162	Doug Glanville	.30	.10
❑ 163	Damion Easley	.30	.10
❑ 164	Carl Everett	.30	.10
❑ 165	Bengie Molina	.30	.10
❑ 166	Adrian Beltre	.30	.10
❑ 167	Tom Goodwin	.30	.10
❑ 168	Rickey Henderson	.75	.30
❑ 169	Mo Vaughn	.30	.10
❑ 170	Mike Lieberthal	.30	.10
❑ 171	Ken Griffey Jr.	1.25	.50
❑ 172	Juan Gonzalez	.30	.10
❑ 173	Ivan Rodriguez	.50	.20
❑ 174	Al Leiter	.30	.10
❑ 175	Vinny Castilla	.30	.10
❑ 176	Peter Bergeron	.30	.10
❑ 177	Pedro Astacio	.30	.10
❑ 178	Paul Konerko	.30	.10
❑ 179	Mitch Meluskey	.30	.10
❑ 180	Kevin Millwood	.30	.10
❑ 181	Ben Grieve	.30	.10
❑ 182	Barry Bonds	2.00	.75
❑ 183	Rusty Greer	.30	.10
❑ 184	Miguel Tejada	.30	.10
❑ 185	Mark Quinn	.30	.10
❑ 186	Larry Walker	.30	.10
❑ 187	Jose Valentin	.30	.10
❑ 188	Jose Vidro	.30	.10
❑ 189	Delino DeShields	.30	.10
❑ 190	Darin Erstad	.30	.10
❑ 191	Bill Mueller	.30	.10
❑ 192	Ray Durham	.30	.10
❑ 193	Ken Caminiti	.30	.10
❑ 194	Jim Thome	.50	.20
❑ 195	Javy Lopez	.30	.10
❑ 196	Fernando Vina	.30	.10
❑ 197	Eric Chavez	.30	.10
❑ 198	Eric Owens	.30	.10
❑ 199	Brad Radke	.30	.10
❑ 200	Travis Lee	.30	.10
❑ 201	Tim Salmon	.50	.20
❑ 202	Rafael Palmeiro	.50	.20
❑ 203	Nomar Garciaparra	1.25	.50
❑ 204	Mike Hampton	.30	.10
❑ 205	Kevin Brown	.30	.10
❑ 206	Juan Encarnacion	.30	.10
❑ 207	Danny Graves	.30	.10
❑ 208	Carlos Guillen	.30	.10
❑ 209	Phil Nevin	.30	.10
❑ 210	Matt Lawton	.30	.10
❑ 211	Manny Ramirez	.50	.20
❑ 212	James Baldwin	.30	.10
❑ 213	Fernando Tatis	.30	.10
❑ 214	Craig Biggio	.50	.20
❑ 215	Brian Jordan	.30	.10
❑ 216	Bernie Williams	.50	.20
❑ 217	Ryan Dempster	.30	.10
❑ 218	Roger Clemens	1.50	.60
❑ 219	Jose Cruz Jr.	.30	.10
❑ 220	John Valentin	.30	.10
❑ 221	Dmitri Young	.30	.10
❑ 222	Curt Schilling	.30	.10
❑ 223	Jim Edmonds	.30	.10
❑ 224	Chan Ho Park	.30	.10
❑ 225	Brian Giles	.30	.10
❑ 226	J.Anderson/T.Redman	.30	.10
❑ 227	A.Piatt/J.Ortiz	.30	.10
❑ 228	K.Kelly/A.Huff	.30	.10
❑ 229	R.Choate/C.Dingman	.30	.10
❑ 230	E.Cammack/G.Roberts	.30	.10
❑ 231	Y.Lara/A.Tracy	.30	.10
❑ 232	W.Franklin/S.Linebrink	.30	.10
❑ 233	C.Cairncross/C.Perry	.30	.10
❑ 234	J.Romero/M.LeCroy	.30	.10
❑ 235	G.Guzman/J.Conti	.30	.10
❑ 236	M.Burkhart/P.Crawford	.30	.10
❑ 237	P.Coco/L.Estrella	.30	.10
❑ 238	J.Parrish/F.Lunar	.30	.10
❑ 239	K.McDonald/J.Brunette	.30	.10
❑ 240	C.Casimiro/I.Coffie	.30	.10
❑ 241	D.Garibay/R.Quevedo	.30	.10
❑ 242	S.Lee/T.Ohka	.30	.10
❑ 243	H.Ortiz/J.D'Amico	.30	.10
❑ 244	J.Sparks/T.Harper	.30	.10
❑ 245	J.Boyd/D.Coggin	.30	.10
❑ 246	M.Buehrle/L.Barcelo	.50	.20
❑ 247	A.Melhuse/B.Petrick	.30	.10
❑ 248	K.Davis/P.Rigdon	.30	.10
❑ 249	M.Darr/K.DeHaan	.30	.10
❑ 250	V.Padilla/M.Brownson	3.00	1.25
❑ 251	Barry Zito PROS	5.00	2.00
❑ 252	Tim Drew PROS	3.00	1.25
❑ 253	Luis Matos PROS	3.00	1.25
❑ 254	Alex Cabrera PROS	3.00	1.25
❑ 255	Jon Garland PROS	3.00	1.25
❑ 256	Milton Bradley PROS	3.00	1.25
❑ 257	Juan Pierre PROS	3.00	1.25
❑ 258	Ismael Villegas PROS	3.00	1.25
❑ 259	Eric Munson PROS	3.00	1.25
❑ 260	Tomas De la Rosa PROS	3.00	1.25
❑ 261	Chris Richard PROS	3.00	1.25
❑ 262	Jason Tyner PROS	3.00	1.25
❑ 263	B.J. Waszgis PROS	3.00	1.25
❑ 264	Jason Marquis PROS	3.00	1.25
❑ 265	Dusty Allen PROS	3.00	1.25
❑ 266	Corey Patterson PROS	3.00	1.25
❑ 267	Eric Byrnes PROS	3.00	1.25
❑ 268	Xavier Nady PROS	3.00	1.25
❑ 269	George Lombard PROS	3.00	1.25
❑ 270	Timo Perez PROS	3.00	1.25
❑ 271	Gary Matthews Jr. PROS	3.00	1.25
❑ 272	Chad Durbin PROS	3.00	1.25
❑ 273	Tony Armas Jr. PROS	3.00	1.25
❑ 274	Francisco Cordero PROS	3.00	1.25
❑ 275	Alfonso Soriano PROS	5.00	2.00
❑ 276	J.Spivey RC/J.Uribe RC	8.00	3.00
❑ 277	A.Pujols RC/B.Smith RC	80.00	40.00
❑ 278	I.Suzuki RC/T.Shinjo RC	30.00	12.50
❑ 279	D.Henson RC/J.Melian RC	8.00	3.00
❑ 280	M.White RC/A.Hernandez RC	5.00	2.00

2003 Ultra

❑	COMP.LO SET (250)	100.00	40.00
❑	COMP.LO SET w/o SP's (200)	25.00	10.00
❑	COMMON CARD (201-220)	1.50	.60
❑	COMMON CARD (221-250)	2.00	.75
❑	COMMON CARD (251-265)	3.00	1.25
❑ 1	Barry Bonds	2.00	.75
❑ 2	Derek Jeter	2.00	.75
❑ 3	Ichiro Suzuki	1.50	.60
❑ 4	Mike Lowell	.30	.10
❑ 5	Hideo Nomo	.75	.30
❑ 6	Javier Vazquez	.30	.10
❑ 7	Jeremy Giambi	.30	.10
❑ 8	Jamie Moyer	.30	.10
❑ 9	Rafael Palmeiro	.50	.20
❑ 10	Magglio Ordonez	.30	.10
❑ 11	Trot Nixon	.30	.10

	No.	Player		
☐	12	Luis Castillo	.30	.10
☐	13	Paul Byrd	.30	.10
☐	14	Adam Kennedy	.30	.10
☐	15	Trevor Hoffman	.30	.10
☐	16	Matt Morris	.30	.10
☐	17	Nomar Garciaparra	1.25	.50
☐	18	Matt Lawton	.30	.10
☐	19	Carlos Beltran	.30	.10
☐	20	Jason Giambi	.30	.10
☐	21	Brian Giles	.30	.10
☐	22	Jim Edmonds	.30	.10
☐	23	Garret Anderson	.30	.10
☐	24	Tony Batista	.30	.10
☐	25	Aaron Boone	.30	.10
☐	26	Mike Hampton	.30	.10
☐	27	Billy Wagner	.30	.10
☐	28	Kazuhisa Ishii	.30	.10
☐	29	Al Leiter	.30	.10
☐	30	Pat Burrell	.30	.10
☐	31	Jeff Kent	.30	.10
☐	32	Randy Johnson	.75	.30
☐	33	Ray Durham	.30	.10
☐	34	Josh Beckett	.30	.10
☐	35	Cristian Guzman	.30	.10
☐	36	Roger Clemens	1.50	.60
☐	37	Freddy Garcia	.30	.10
☐	38	Roy Halladay	.30	.10
☐	39	David Eckstein	.30	.10
☐	40	Jerry Hairston	.30	.10
☐	41	Barry Larkin	.50	.20
☐	42	Larry Walker	.30	.10
☐	43	Craig Biggio	.50	.20
☐	44	Edgardo Alfonzo	.30	.10
☐	45	Marlon Byrd	.30	.10
☐	46	J.T. Snow	.30	.10
☐	47	Juan Gonzalez	.30	.10
☐	48	Ramon Ortiz	.30	.10
☐	49	Jay Gibbons	.30	.10
☐	50	Adam Dunn	.30	.10
☐	51	Juan Pierre	.30	.10
☐	52	Jeff Bagwell	.50	.20
☐	53	Kevin Brown	.30	.10
☐	54	Pedro Astacio	.30	.10
☐	55	Mike Lieberthal	.30	.10
☐	56	Johnny Damon	.50	.20
☐	57	Tim Salmon	.50	.20
☐	58	Mike Bordick	.30	.10
☐	59	Ken Griffey Jr.	1.25	.50
☐	60	Jason Jennings	.30	.10
☐	61	Lance Berkman	.30	.10
☐	62	Jeromy Burnitz	.30	.10
☐	63	Jimmy Rollins	.30	.10
☐	64	Tsuyoshi Shinjo	.30	.10
☐	65	Alex Rodriguez	1.25	.50
☐	66	Greg Maddux	1.25	.50
☐	67	Mark Prior	.50	.20
☐	68	Mike Maroth	.30	.10
☐	69	Geoff Jenkins	.30	.10
☐	70	Tony Armas Jr.	.30	.10
☐	71	Jermaine Dye	.30	.10
☐	72	Albert Pujols	1.50	.60
☐	73	Shannon Stewart	.30	.10
☐	74	Troy Glaus	.30	.10
☐	75	Brook Fordyce	.30	.10
☐	76	Juan Encarnacion	.30	.10
☐	77	Todd Hollandsworth	.30	.10
☐	78	Roy Oswalt	.30	.10
☐	79	Paul Lo Duca	.30	.10
☐	80	Mike Piazza	1.25	.50
☐	81	Bobby Abreu	.30	.10
☐	82	Sean Burroughs	.30	.10
☐	83	Randy Winn	.30	.10
☐	84	Curt Schilling	.30	.10
☐	85	Chris Singleton	.30	.10
☐	86	Sean Casey	.30	.10
☐	87	Todd Zeile	.30	.10
☐	88	Richard Hidalgo	.30	.10
☐	89	Roberto Alomar	.50	.20
☐	90	Tim Hudson	.30	.10
☐	91	Ryan Klesko	.30	.10
☐	92	Greg Vaughn	.30	.10
☐	93	Tony Womack	.30	.10
☐	94	Fred McGriff	.50	.20
☐	95	Tom Glavine	.50	.20
☐	96	Todd Walker	.30	.10
☐	97	Travis Fryman	.30	.10
☐	98	Shane Reynolds	.30	.10
☐	99	Shawn Green	.30	.10
☐	100	Mo Vaughn	.30	.10
☐	101	Adam Piatt	.30	.10
☐	102	Deivi Cruz	.30	.10
☐	103	Steve Cox	.30	.10
☐	104	Luis Gonzalez	.30	.10
☐	105	Russell Branyan	.30	.10
☐	106	Daryle Ward	.30	.10
☐	107	Mariano Rivera	.75	.30
☐	108	Phil Nevin	.30	.10
☐	109	Ben Grieve	.30	.10
☐	110	Moises Alou	.30	.10
☐	111	Omar Vizquel	.50	.20
☐	112	Joe Randa	.30	.10
☐	113	Jorge Posada	.50	.20
☐	114	Mark Kotsay	.30	.10
☐	115	Ryan Rupe	.30	.10
☐	116	Javy Lopez	.30	.10
☐	117	Corey Patterson	.30	.10
☐	118	Bobby Higginson	.30	.10
☐	119	Jose Vidro	.30	.10
☐	120	Barry Zito	.30	.10
☐	121	Scott Rolen	.50	.20
☐	122	Gary Sheffield	.30	.10
☐	123	Kerry Wood	.30	.10
☐	124	Brandon Inge	.30	.10
☐	125	Jose Hernandez	.30	.10
☐	126	Michael Barrett	.30	.10
☐	127	Miguel Tejada	.30	.10
☐	128	Edgar Renteria	.30	.10
☐	129	Junior Spivey	.30	.10
☐	130	Jose Valentin	.30	.10
☐	131	Derrek Lee	.50	.20
☐	132	A.J. Pierzynski	.30	.10
☐	133	Mike Mussina	.50	.20
☐	134	Bret Boone	.30	.10
☐	135	Chan Ho Park	.30	.10
☐	136	Steve Finley	.30	.10
☐	137	Mark Buehrle	.30	.10
☐	138	A.J. Burnett	.30	.10
☐	139	Ben Sheets	.30	.10
☐	140	David Ortiz	.75	.30
☐	141	Nick Johnson	.30	.10
☐	142	Randall Simon	.30	.10
☐	143	Carlos Delgado	.30	.10
☐	144	Darin Erstad	.30	.10
☐	145	Shea Hillenbrand	.30	.10
☐	146	Todd Helton	.50	.20
☐	147	Preston Wilson	.30	.10
☐	148	Eric Gagne	.30	.10
☐	149	Vladimir Guerrero	.75	.30
☐	150	Brandon Duckworth	.30	.10
☐	151	Rich Aurilia	.30	.10
☐	152	Ivan Rodriguez	.50	.20
☐	153	Andruw Jones	.50	.20
☐	154	Carlos Lee	.30	.10
☐	155	Robert Fick	.30	.10
☐	156	Jacque Jones	.30	.10
☐	157	Bernie Williams	.50	.20
☐	158	John Olerud	.30	.10
☐	159	Eric Hinske	.30	.10
☐	160	Matt Clement	.30	.10
☐	161	Dmitri Young	.30	.10
☐	162	Torii Hunter	.30	.10
☐	163	Carlos Pena	.30	.10
☐	164	Mike Cameron	.30	.10
☐	165	Raul Mondesi	.30	.10
☐	166	Pedro Martinez	.50	.20
☐	167	Bob Wickman	.30	.10
☐	168	Mike Sweeney	.30	.10
☐	169	David Wells	.30	.10
☐	170	Jason Kendall	.30	.10
☐	171	Tino Martinez	.50	.20
☐	172	Matt Williams	.30	.10
☐	173	Frank Thomas	.75	.30
☐	174	Cliff Floyd	.30	.10
☐	175	Corey Koskie	.30	.10
☐	176	Orlando Hernandez	.30	.10
☐	177	Edgar Martinez	.50	.20
☐	178	Richie Sexson	.30	.10
☐	179	Manny Ramirez	.50	.20
☐	180	Jim Thome	.50	.20
☐	181	Andy Pettitte	.50	.20
☐	182	Aramis Ramirez	.30	.10
☐	183	J.D. Drew	.30	.10
☐	184	Brian Jordan	.30	.10
☐	185	Sammy Sosa	.75	.30
☐	186	Jeff Weaver	.30	.10
☐	187	Jeffrey Hammonds	.30	.10
☐	188	Eric Milton	.30	.10
☐	189	Eric Chavez	.30	.10
☐	190	Kazuhiro Sasaki	.30	.10
☐	191	Jose Cruz Jr.	.30	.10
☐	192	Derek Lowe	.30	.10
☐	193	C.C. Sabathia	.30	.10
☐	194	Adrian Beltre	.30	.10
☐	195	Alfonso Soriano	.30	.10
☐	196	Jack Wilson	.30	.10
☐	197	Fernando Vina	.30	.10
☐	198	Chipper Jones	.75	.30
☐	199	Paul Konerko	.30	.10
☐	200	Rusty Greer	.30	.10
☐	201	Jason Giambi AS	1.50	.60
☐	202	Alfonso Soriano AS	1.50	.60
☐	203	Shea Hillenbrand AS	1.50	.60
☐	204	Alex Rodriguez AS	2.50	1.00
☐	205	Jorge Posada AS	1.50	.60
☐	206	Ichiro Suzuki AS	3.00	1.25
☐	207	Manny Ramirez AS	1.50	.60
☐	208	Torii Hunter AS	1.50	.60
☐	209	Todd Helton AS	1.50	.60
☐	210	Jose Vidro AS	1.50	.60
☐	211	Scott Rolen AS	1.50	.60
☐	212	Jimmy Rollins AS	1.50	.60
☐	213	Mike Piazza AS	2.50	1.00
☐	214	Barry Bonds AS	4.00	1.50
☐	215	Sammy Sosa AS	1.50	.60
☐	216	Vladimir Guerrero AS	1.50	.60
☐	217	Lance Berkman AS	1.50	.60
☐	218	Derek Jeter AS	4.00	1.50
☐	219	Nomar Garciaparra AS	2.50	1.00
☐	220	Luis Gonzalez AS	1.50	.60
☐	221	Kazuhisa Ishii 02R	2.00	.75
☐	222	Satoru Komiyama 02R	2.00	.75
☐	223	So Taguchi 02R	2.00	.75
☐	224	Jorge Padilla 02R	2.00	.75
☐	225	Ben Howard 02R	2.00	.75
☐	226	Jason Simontacchi 02R	2.00	.75
☐	227	Barry Wesson 02R	2.00	.75
☐	228	Howie Clark 02R	2.00	.75
☐	229	Aaron Guiel 02R	2.00	.75
☐	230	Oliver Perez 02R	2.00	.75
☐	231	David Ross 02R	2.00	.75
☐	232	Julius Matos 02R	2.00	.75
☐	233	Chris Snelling 02R	2.00	.75
☐	234	Rodrigo Lopez 02R	2.00	.75
☐	235	Will Nieves 02R	2.00	.75
☐	236	Joe Borchard 02R	2.00	.75
☐	237	Aaron Cook 02R	2.00	.75
☐	238	Anderson Machado 02R	2.00	.75
☐	239	Corey Thurman 02R	2.00	.75
☐	240	Tyler Yates 02R	2.00	.75
☐	241	Coco Crisp 03R	3.00	1.25
☐	242	Andy Van Hekken 03R	2.00	.75
☐	243	Jim Rushford 03R	2.00	.75
☐	244	Jeriome Robertson 03R	2.00	.75
☐	245	Shane Nance 03R	2.00	.75
☐	246	Kevin Cash 03R	2.00	.75
☐	247	Kirk Saarloos 03R	2.00	.75
☐	248	Josh Bard 03R	2.00	.75
☐	249	Dave Pember 03R RC	2.00	.75
☐	250	Freddy Sanchez 03R	2.00	.75
☐	251	Chien-Ming Wang PROS RC	20.00	8.00
☐	252	Rickie Weeks PROS RC	6.00	2.50
☐	253	Brandon Webb PROS RC	8.00	3.00
☐	254	Hideki Matsui PROS RC	10.00	4.00
☐	255	Michael Hessman PROS RC	3.00	1.25
☐	256	Ryan Wagner PROS RC	3.00	1.25
☐	257	Matt Kata PROS RC	3.00	1.25
☐	258	Edwin Jackson PROS RC	4.00	1.50
☐	259	Jose Contreras PROS RC	4.00	1.50
☐	260	Delmon Young PROS RC	10.00	4.00
☐	261	Bo Hart PROS RC	3.00	1.25
☐	262	Jeff Duncan PROS RC	3.00	1.25
☐	263	Robby Hammock PROS RC	3.00	1.25
☐	264	Jeremy Bonderman PROS RC	10.00	4.00
☐	265	Clint Barmes PROS RC	2.50	1.00

2004 Ultra

❑ COMPLETE SERIES 1 (220) 60.00 30.00
❑ COMP.SERIES 1 w/o SP's (200) 25.00 10.00
❑ COMP.SERIES 2 w/o SP's (75) 25.00 10.00
❑ COMP.SERIES 2 w/o L13 (162) 100.00 50.00
❑ COMMON CARD (1-200) .30 .10
❑ COMMON CARD (201-220) 1.25 .50
❑ 201-220 APPROXIMATE ODDS 1:2 HOBBY
❑ 201-220 RANDOM IN RETAIL PACKS
❑ COMMON CARD (296-382) 2.00 .75
❑ 296-382 ODDS TWO PER HOBBY/RETAIL
❑ COMMON CARD (383-395) 12.00 5.00
❑ 383-395 ODDS 1:28 HOBBY, 1:2000 RETAIL
❑ 383-395 PRINT RUN 500 SERIAL #'d SETS

❑ 1	Maggio Ordonez	.30	.10
❑ 2	Bobby Abreu	.30	.10
❑ 3	Eric Munson	.30	.10
❑ 4	Eric Byrnes	.30	.10
❑ 5	Bartolo Colon	.30	.10
❑ 6	Juan Encarnacion	.30	.10
❑ 7	Jody Gerut	.30	.10
❑ 8	Eddie Guardado	.30	.10
❑ 9	Shea Hillenbrand	.30	.10
❑ 10	Andruw Jones	.50	.20
❑ 11	Carlos Lee	.30	.10
❑ 12	Pedro Martinez	.50	.20
❑ 13	Barry Larkin	.50	.20
❑ 14	Angel Berroa	.30	.10
❑ 15	Edgar Martinez	.50	.20
❑ 16	Sidney Ponson	.30	.10
❑ 17	Mariano Rivera	.75	.30
❑ 18	Richie Sexson	.30	.10
❑ 19	Frank Thomas	.75	.30
❑ 20	Jerome Williams	.30	.10
❑ 21	Barry Zito	.30	.10
❑ 22	Roberto Alomar	.50	.20
❑ 23	Rocky Biddle	.30	.10
❑ 24	Orlando Cabrera	.30	.10
❑ 25	Placido Polanco	.30	.10
❑ 26	Morgan Ensberg	.30	.10
❑ 27	Jason Giambi	.30	.10
❑ 28	Jim Thome	.50	.20
❑ 29	Vladimir Guerrero	.75	.30
❑ 30	Tim Hudson	.30	.10
❑ 31	Jacque Jones	.30	.10
❑ 32	Derrek Lee	.50	.20
❑ 33	Rafael Palmeiro	.50	.20
❑ 34	Mike Mussina	.50	.20
❑ 35	Corey Patterson	.30	.10
❑ 36	Mike Cameron	.30	.10
❑ 37	Ivan Rodriguez	.50	.20
❑ 38	Ben Sheets	.30	.10
❑ 39	Woody Williams	.30	.10
❑ 40	Ichiro Suzuki	1.50	.60
❑ 41	Moises Alou	.30	.10
❑ 42	Craig Biggio	.50	.20
❑ 43	Jorge Posada	.50	.20
❑ 44	Craig Monroe	.30	.10
❑ 45	Darin Erstad	.30	.10
❑ 46	Jay Gibbons	.30	.10
❑ 47	Aaron Guiel	.30	.10
❑ 48	Travis Lee	.30	.10
❑ 49	Jorge Julio	.30	.10
❑ 50	Torii Hunter	.30	.10
❑ 51	Luis Matos	.30	.10
❑ 52	Brett Myers	.30	.10
❑ 53	Sean Casey	.30	.10
❑ 54	Mark Prior	.50	.20
❑ 55	Alex Rodriguez	1.25	.50
❑ 56	Gary Sheffield	.30	.10
❑ 57	Jason Varitek	.75	.30
❑ 58	Dontrelle Willis	.50	.20
❑ 59	Garret Anderson	.30	.10
❑ 60	Casey Blake	.30	.10
❑ 61	Jay Payton	.30	.10
❑ 62	Carl Crawford	.30	.10
❑ 63	Carl Everett	.30	.10
❑ 64	Marcus Giles	.30	.10
❑ 65	Jose Guillen	.30	.10
❑ 66	Eric Karros	.30	.10
❑ 67	Mike Lieberthal	.30	.10
❑ 68	Hideki Matsui	1.25	.50
❑ 69	Xavier Nady	.30	.10
❑ 70	Hank Blalock	.30	.10
❑ 71	Albert Pujols	1.50	.60
❑ 72	Jose Cruz Jr.	.30	.10
❑ 73	Randall Simon	.30	.10
❑ 74	Javier Vazquez	.30	.10
❑ 75	Preston Wilson	.30	.10
❑ 76	Danys Baez	.30	.10
❑ 77	Alex Cintron	.30	.10
❑ 78	Jake Peavy	.30	.10
❑ 79	Scott Rolen	.50	.20
❑ 80	Robert Fick	.30	.10
❑ 81	Brian Giles	.30	.10
❑ 82	Roy Halladay	.30	.10
❑ 83	Kazuhisa Ishii	.30	.10
❑ 84	Austin Kearns	.30	.10
❑ 85	Paul Lo Duca	.30	.10
❑ 86	Darrell May	.30	.10
❑ 87	Phil Nevin	.30	.10
❑ 88	Carlos Pena	.30	.10
❑ 89	Manny Ramirez	.50	.20
❑ 90	C.C. Sabathia	.30	.10
❑ 91	John Smoltz	.50	.20
❑ 92	Jose Vidro	.30	.10
❑ 93	Randy Wolf	.30	.10
❑ 94	Jeff Bagwell	.50	.20
❑ 95	Barry Bonds	2.00	.75
❑ 96	Frank Catalanotto	.30	.10
❑ 97	Zach Day	.30	.10
❑ 98	David Ortiz	.75	.30
❑ 99	Troy Glaus	.30	.10
❑ 100	Bo Hart	.30	.10
❑ 101	Geoff Jenkins	.30	.10
❑ 102	Jason Kendall	.30	.10
❑ 103	Esteban Loaiza	.30	.10
❑ 104	Doug Mientkiewicz	.30	.10
❑ 105	Trot Nixon	.30	.10
❑ 106	Troy Percival	.30	.10
❑ 107	Aramis Ramirez	.30	.10
❑ 108	Alex Sanchez	.30	.10
❑ 109	Alfonso Soriano	.30	.10
❑ 110	Omar Vizquel	.50	.20
❑ 111	Kerry Wood	.30	.10
❑ 112	Rocco Baldelli	.30	.10
❑ 113	Bret Boone	.30	.10
❑ 114	Shawn Chacon	.30	.10
❑ 115	Carlos Delgado	.30	.10
❑ 116	Shawn Green	.30	.10
❑ 117	Tim Worrell	.30	.10
❑ 118	Tom Glavine	.50	.20
❑ 119	Shigetoshi Hasegawa	.30	.10
❑ 120	Derek Jeter	1.50	.60
❑ 121	Jeff Kent	.30	.10
❑ 122	Braden Looper	.30	.10
❑ 123	Kevin Millwood	.30	.10
❑ 124	Hideo Nomo	.75	.30
❑ 125	Jason Phillips	.30	.10
❑ 126	Tim Redding	.30	.10
❑ 127	Reggie Sanders	.30	.10
❑ 128	Sammy Sosa	.75	.30
❑ 129	Billy Wagner	.30	.10
❑ 130	Miguel Batista	.30	.10
❑ 131	Milton Bradley	.30	.10
❑ 132	Eric Chavez	.30	.10
❑ 133	J.D. Drew	.30	.10
❑ 134	Keith Foulke	.30	.10
❑ 135	Luis Gonzalez	.30	.10
❑ 136	LaTroy Hawkins	.30	.10
❑ 137	Randy Johnson	.75	.30
❑ 138	Byung-Hyun Kim	.30	.10
❑ 139	Javy Lopez	.30	.10
❑ 140	Melvin Mora	.30	.10
❑ 141	Aubrey Huff	.30	.10
❑ 142	Mike Piazza	1.25	.50
❑ 143	Mark Redman	.30	.10
❑ 144	Kazuhiro Sasaki	.30	.10
❑ 145	Shannon Stewart	.30	.10
❑ 146	Larry Walker	.30	.10
❑ 147	Dmitri Young	.30	.10
❑ 148	Josh Beckett	.30	.10
❑ 149	Jae Weong Seo	.30	.10
❑ 150	Hee Seop Choi	.30	.10
❑ 151	Adam Dunn	.30	.10
❑ 152	Rafael Furcal	.30	.10
❑ 153	Juan Gonzalez	.30	.10
❑ 154	Todd Helton	.50	.20
❑ 155	Carlos Zambrano	.30	.10
❑ 156	Ryan Klesko	.30	.10
❑ 157	Mike Lowell	.30	.10
❑ 158	Jamie Moyer	.30	.10
❑ 159	Russ Ortiz	.30	.10
❑ 160	Juan Pierre	.30	.10
❑ 161	Edgar Renteria	.30	.10
❑ 162	Curt Schilling	.30	.10
❑ 163	Mike Sweeney	.30	.10
❑ 164	Brandon Webb	.30	.10
❑ 165	Michael Young	.30	.10
❑ 166	Carlos Beltran	.30	.10
❑ 167	Sean Burroughs	.30	.10
❑ 168	Luis Castillo	.30	.10
❑ 169	David Eckstein	.30	.10
❑ 170	Eric Gagne	.30	.10
❑ 171	Chipper Jones	.75	.30
❑ 172	Livan Hernandez	.30	.10
❑ 173	Nick Johnson	.30	.10
❑ 174	Corey Koskie	.30	.10
❑ 175	Jason Schmidt	.30	.10
❑ 176	Bill Mueller	.30	.10
❑ 177	Steve Finley	.30	.10
❑ 178	A.J. Pierzynski	.30	.10
❑ 179	Rene Reyes	.30	.10
❑ 180	Jason Johnson	.30	.10
❑ 181	Mark Teixeira	.50	.20
❑ 182	Kip Wells	.30	.10
❑ 183	Mike MacDougal	.30	.10
❑ 184	Lance Berkman	.30	.10
❑ 185	Victor Zambrano	.30	.10
❑ 186	Roger Clemens	1.50	.60
❑ 187	Jim Edmonds	.30	.10
❑ 188	Nomar Garciaparra	1.25	.50
❑ 189	Ken Griffey Jr.	1.25	.50
❑ 190	Richard Hidalgo	.30	.10
❑ 191	Cliff Floyd	.30	.10
❑ 192	Greg Maddux	1.25	.50
❑ 193	Mark Mulder	.30	.10
❑ 194	Roy Oswalt	.30	.10
❑ 195	Marlon Byrd	.30	.10
❑ 196	Jose Reyes	.30	.10
❑ 197	Kevin Brown	.30	.10
❑ 198	Miguel Tejada	.30	.10
❑ 199	Vernon Wells	.30	.10
❑ 200	Joel Pineiro	.30	.10
❑ 201	Rickie Weeks AR	2.00	.75
❑ 202	Chad Gaudin AR	1.25	.50
❑ 203	Ryan Wagner AR	1.25	.50
❑ 204	Chris Bootcheck AR	1.25	.50
❑ 205	Koyie Hill AR	1.25	.50
❑ 206	Jeff Duncan AR	1.25	.50
❑ 207	Rich Harden AR	2.00	.75
❑ 208	Edwin Jackson AR	1.25	.50
❑ 209	Robby Hammock AR	1.25	.50
❑ 210	Khalil Greene AR	3.00	1.25
❑ 211	Chien-Ming Wang AR	5.00	2.00
❑ 212	Prentice Redman AR	1.25	.50
❑ 213	Todd Wellemeyer AR	1.25	.50
❑ 214	Clint Barmes AR	2.00	.75
❑ 215	Matt Kata AR	1.25	.50
❑ 216	Jon Leicester AR	1.25	.50
❑ 217	Jeremy Guthrie AR	1.25	.50
❑ 218	Chin-Hui Tsao AR	2.00	.75
❑ 219	Dan Haren AR	1.25	.50
❑ 220	Delmon Young AR	3.00	1.25
❑ 221	Vladimir Guerrero	1.25	.50
❑ 222	Andy Pettitte	.75	.30
❑ 223	Gary Sheffield	.50	.20
❑ 224	Javier Vazquez	.50	.20
❑ 225	Alex Rodriguez	2.00	.75

❑ 226 Billy Wagner	.50	.20
❑ 227 Miguel Tejada	.50	.20
❑ 228 Greg Maddux	2.00	.75
❑ 229 Ivan Rodriguez	.75	.30
❑ 230 Roger Clemens	2.50	1.00
❑ 231 Alfonso Soriano	.50	.20
❑ 232 Miguel Cabrera	.75	.30
❑ 233 Javy Lopez	.50	.20
❑ 234 David Wells	.50	.20
❑ 235 Eric Milton	.50	.20
❑ 236 Armando Benitez	.50	.20
❑ 237 Mike Cameron	.50	.20
❑ 238 J.D. Drew	.50	.20
❑ 239 Carlos Beltran	.50	.20
❑ 240 Bartolo Colon	.50	.20
❑ 241 Jose Guillen	.50	.20
❑ 242 Kevin Brown	.50	.20
❑ 243 Carlos Guillen	.50	.20
❑ 244 Kenny Lofton	.50	.20
❑ 245 Pokey Reese	.50	.20
❑ 246 Rafael Palmeiro	.75	.30
❑ 247 Nomar Garciaparra	2.00	.75
❑ 248 Hee Seop Choi	.50	.20
❑ 249 Juan Uribe	.50	.20
❑ 250 Nick Johnson	.50	.20
❑ 251 Scott Podsednik	.50	.20
❑ 252 Richie Sexson	.50	.20
❑ 253 Keith Foulke Sox	.50	.20
❑ 254 Jaret Wright	.50	.20
❑ 255 Johnny Estrada	.50	.20
❑ 256 Michael Barrett	.50	.20
❑ 257 Bernie Williams	.75	.30
❑ 258 Octavio Dotel	.50	.20
❑ 259 Jeromy Burnitz	.50	.20
❑ 260 Kevin Youkilis	.50	.20
❑ 261 Derrek Lee	.75	.30
❑ 262 Jack Wilson	.50	.20
❑ 263 Craig Wilson	.50	.20
❑ 264 Richard Hidalgo	.50	.20
❑ 265 Royce Clayton	.50	.20
❑ 266 Curt Schilling	.75	.30
❑ 267 Joe Mauer	.75	.30
❑ 268 Bobby Crosby	.50	.20
❑ 269 Zack Greinke	.50	.20
❑ 270 Victor Martinez	.50	.20
❑ 271 Pedro Feliz	.50	.20
❑ 272 Tony Batista	.50	.20
❑ 273 Casey Kotchman	.50	.20
❑ 274 Freddy Garcia	.50	.20
❑ 275 Adam Everett	.50	.20
❑ 276 Alexis Rios	.50	.20
❑ 277 Lew Ford	.50	.20
❑ 278 Adam LaRoche	.50	.20
❑ 279 Lyle Overbay	.50	.20
❑ 280 Juan Gonzalez	.50	.20
❑ 281 A.J. Pierzynski	.50	.20
❑ 282 Scott Hairston	.50	.20
❑ 283 Danny Bautista	.50	.20
❑ 284 Brad Penny	.50	.20
❑ 285 Paul Konerko	.50	.20
❑ 286 Matt Lawton	.50	.20
❑ 287 Carl Pavano	.50	.20
❑ 288 Pat Burrell	.50	.20
❑ 289 Kenny Rogers	.50	.20
❑ 290 Laynce Nix	.50	.20
❑ 291 Johnny Damon	.75	.30
❑ 292 Paul Wilson	.50	.20
❑ 293 Vinny Castilla	.50	.20
❑ 294 Aaron Miles	.50	.20
❑ 295 Ken Harvey	.50	.20
❑ 296 Onil Joseph RC	2.00	.75
❑ 297 Kazuhito Tadano RC	3.00	1.25
❑ 298 Jeff Bennett RC	2.00	.75
❑ 299 Chad Bentz RC	2.00	.75
❑ 300 Akinori Otsuka RC	2.00	.75
❑ 301 Jon Knott RC	2.00	.75
❑ 302 Ian Snell RC	3.00	1.25
❑ 303 Fernando Nieve RC	3.00	1.25
❑ 304 Mike Rouse RC	2.00	.75
❑ 305 Dennis Sarfate RC	2.00	.75
❑ 306 Josh Labandeira RC	2.00	.75
❑ 307 Chris Oxspring RC	2.00	.75
❑ 308 Alfredo Simon RC	2.00	.75
❑ 309 Rusty Tucker RC	3.00	1.25
❑ 310 Lincoln Holdzkom RC	2.00	.75
❑ 311 Justin Leone RC	3.00	1.25
❑ 312 Jorge Sequea RC	2.00	.75
❑ 313 Brian Dallimore RC	2.00	.75
❑ 314 Tim Bittner RC	2.00	.75
❑ 315 Ronny Cedeno RC	3.00	1.25
❑ 316 Justin Hampson RC	2.00	.75
❑ 317 Ryan Wing RC	2.00	.75
❑ 318 Mariano Gomez RC	2.00	.75
❑ 319 Carlos Vasquez RC	3.00	1.25
❑ 320 Casey Daigle RC	2.00	.75
❑ 321 Renyel Pinto RC	3.00	1.25
❑ 322 Chris Shelton RC	3.00	1.25
❑ 323 Mike Gosling RC	2.00	.75
❑ 324 Aarom Baldiris RC	3.00	1.25
❑ 325 Ramon Ramirez RC	2.00	.75
❑ 326 Roberto Novoa RC	3.00	1.25
❑ 327 Sean Henn RC	2.00	.75
❑ 328 Nick Regilio RC	2.00	.75
❑ 329 Dave Crouthers RC	2.00	.75
❑ 330 Greg Dobbs RC	2.00	.75
❑ 331 Angel Chavez RC	2.00	.75
❑ 332 Luis A. Gonzalez RC	2.00	.75
❑ 333 Justin Knoedler RC	2.00	.75
❑ 334 Jason Frasor RC	2.00	.75
❑ 335 Jerry Gil RC	2.00	.75
❑ 336 Carlos Hines RC	2.00	.75
❑ 337 Ivan Ochoa RC	2.00	.75
❑ 338 Jose Capellan RC	3.00	1.25
❑ 339 Hector Gimenez RC	2.00	.75
❑ 340 Shawn Hill RC	2.00	.75
❑ 341 Freddy Guzman RC	2.00	.75
❑ 342 Scott Proctor RC	3.00	1.25
❑ 343 Frank Francisco RC	2.00	.75
❑ 344 Brandon Medders RC	2.00	.75
❑ 345 Andy Green RC	2.00	.75
❑ 346 Eddy Rodriguez RC	3.00	1.25
❑ 347 Tim Hamulack RC	2.00	.75
❑ 348 Michael Wuertz RC	3.00	1.25
❑ 349 Arnie Munoz	2.00	.75
❑ 350 Enemencio Pacheco RC	2.00	.75
❑ 351 Dusty Bergman RC	2.00	.75
❑ 352 Charles Thomas RC	2.00	.75
❑ 353 William Bergolla RC	2.00	.75
❑ 354 Ramon Castro RC	2.00	.75
❑ 355 Justin Lehr RC	2.00	.75
❑ 356 Lino Urdaneta RC	2.00	.75
❑ 357 Donnie Kelly RC	2.00	.75
❑ 358 Kevin Cave RC	2.00	.75
❑ 359 Franklyn Gracesqui RC	2.00	.75
❑ 360 Chris Aguila RC	2.00	.75
❑ 361 Jorge Vasquez RC	2.00	.75
❑ 362 Andres Blanco RC	2.00	.75
❑ 363 Orlando Rodriguez RC	2.00	.75
❑ 364 Colby Miller RC	2.00	.75
❑ 365 Shawn Camp RC	2.00	.75
❑ 366 Jake Woods RC	2.00	.75
❑ 367 George Sherrill RC	2.00	.75
❑ 368 Justin Huisman RC	2.00	.75
❑ 369 Jimmy Serrano RC	2.00	.75
❑ 370 Mike Johnston RC	2.00	.75
❑ 371 Ryan Meaux RC	2.00	.75
❑ 372 Scott Dohmann RC	2.00	.75
❑ 373 Brad Halsey RC	3.00	1.25
❑ 374 Joey Gathright RC	4.00	1.50
❑ 375 Yadier Molina RC	5.00	2.00
❑ 376 Travis Blackley RC	2.00	.75
❑ 377 Steve Andrade RC	2.00	.75
❑ 378 Phil Stockman RC	2.00	.75
❑ 379 Roman Colon RC	2.00	.75
❑ 380 Jesse Crain RC	3.00	1.25
❑ 381 Edwardo Sierra RC	3.00	1.25
❑ 382 Justin Germano RC	2.00	.75
❑ 383 Kaz Matsui L13 RC	10.00	4.00
❑ 384 Shingo Takatsu L13 RC	10.00	4.00
❑ 385 John Gall L13 RC	12.00	5.00
❑ 386 Chris Saenz L13 RC	12.00	5.00
❑ 387 Merkin Valdez L13 RC	10.00	4.00
❑ 388 Jamie Brown L13 RC	12.00	5.00
❑ 389 Jason Bartlett L13 RC	12.00	5.00
❑ 390 David Aardsma L13 RC	12.00	5.00
❑ 391 Scott Kazmir L13 RC	30.00	12.50
❑ 392 David Wright L13	30.00	12.50
❑ 393 Dioner Navarro L13 RC	10.00	4.00
❑ 394 B.J. Upton L13	12.00	5.00
❑ 395 Gavin Floyd L13	12.00	5.00

2005 Ultra

❑ COMPLETE SET (220)	100.00	40.00
❑ COMP.SET w/o SP's (200)	40.00	15.00
❑ COMMON CARD (1-200)	.30	.10
❑ COMMON CARD (201-220)	2.00	.75
❑ 201-220 ODDS 1:4 HOBBY, 1:5 RETAIL		
❑ 1 Andy Pettitte	.50	.20
❑ 2 Jose Cruz Jr.	.30	.10
❑ 3 Cliff Floyd	.30	.10
❑ 4 Paul Konerko	.30	.10
❑ 5 Joe Mauer	.75	.30
❑ 6 Scott Spiezio	.30	.10
❑ 7 Ben Sheets	.30	.10
❑ 8 Kerry Wood	.30	.10
❑ 9 Carl Pavano	.30	.10
❑ 10 Matt Morris	.30	.10
❑ 11 Kaz Matsui	.30	.10
❑ 12 Ivan Rodriguez	.50	.20
❑ 13 Victor Martinez	.30	.10
❑ 14 Justin Morneau	.30	.10
❑ 15 Adam Everett	.30	.10
❑ 16 Carl Crawford	.30	.10
❑ 17 David Ortiz	.75	.30
❑ 18 Jason Giambi	.30	.10
❑ 19 Derrek Lee	.50	.20
❑ 20 Magglio Ordonez	.30	.10
❑ 21 Bobby Abreu	.30	.10
❑ 22 Milton Bradley	.30	.10
❑ 23 Jeff Bagwell	.50	.20
❑ 24 Jim Edmonds	.30	.10
❑ 25 Garret Anderson	.30	.10
❑ 26 Jacque Jones	.30	.10
❑ 27 Ted Lilly	.30	.10
❑ 28 Greg Maddux	1.25	.50
❑ 29 Jermaine Dye	.30	.10
❑ 30 Bill Mueller	.30	.10
❑ 31 Roy Oswalt	.30	.10
❑ 32 Tony Womack	.30	.10
❑ 33 Andruw Jones	.50	.20
❑ 34 Tom Glavine	.50	.20
❑ 35 Mariano Rivera	.75	.30
❑ 36 Sean Casey	.30	.10
❑ 37 Edgardo Alfonzo	.30	.10
❑ 38 Brad Penny	.30	.10
❑ 39 Johan Santana	.75	.30
❑ 40 Mark Teixeira	.50	.20
❑ 41 Manny Ramirez	.50	.20
❑ 42 Gary Sheffield	.30	.10
❑ 43 Matt Lawton	.30	.10
❑ 44 Troy Percival	.30	.10
❑ 45 Rocco Baldelli	.30	.10
❑ 46 Doug Mientkiewicz	.30	.10
❑ 47 Corey Patterson	.30	.10
❑ 48 Austin Kearns	.30	.10
❑ 49 Edgar Martinez	.50	.20
❑ 50 Brad Radke	.30	.10
❑ 51 Barry Larkin	.50	.20
❑ 52 Chone Figgins	.30	.10
❑ 53 Alexis Rios	.30	.10
❑ 54 Alex Rodriguez	1.25	.50
❑ 55 Vinny Castilla	.30	.10
❑ 56 Javier Vazquez	.30	.10
❑ 57 Javy Lopez	.30	.10
❑ 58 Mike Cameron	.30	.10
❑ 59 Brian Giles	.30	.10
❑ 60 Dontrelle Willis	.30	.10
❑ 61 Rafael Furcal	.30	.10

❑ 62 Trot Nixon .30 .10
❑ 63 Mark Mulder .30 .10
❑ 64 Josh Beckett .30 .10
❑ 65 J.D. Drew .30 .10
❑ 66 Brandon Webb .30 .10
❑ 67 Wade Miller .30 .10
❑ 68 Lyle Overbay .30 .10
❑ 69 Pedro Martinez .50 .20
❑ 70 Rich Harden .30 .10
❑ 71 Al Leiter .30 .10
❑ 72 Adam Eaton .30 .10
❑ 73 Mike Sweeney .30 .10
❑ 74 Steve Finley .30 .10
❑ 75 Kris Benson .30 .10
❑ 76 Jim Thome .50 .20
❑ 77 Juan Pierre .30 .10
❑ 78 Bartolo Colon .30 .10
❑ 79 Carlos Delgado .30 .10
❑ 80 Jack Wilson .30 .10
❑ 81 Ken Harvey .30 .10
❑ 82 Nomar Garciaparra .75 .30
❑ 83 Paul Lo Duca .30 .10
❑ 84 Cesar Izturis .30 .10
❑ 85 Adrian Beltre .30 .10
❑ 86 Brian Roberts .30 .10
❑ 87 David Eckstein .30 .10
❑ 88 Jimmy Rollins .30 .10
❑ 89 Roger Clemens 1.25 .50
❑ 90 Randy Johnson .75 .30
❑ 91 Orlando Hudson .30 .10
❑ 92 Tim Hudson .30 .10
❑ 93 Dmitri Young .30 .10
❑ 94 Chipper Jones .75 .30
❑ 95 John Smoltz .50 .20
❑ 96 Billy Wagner .30 .10
❑ 97 Hideo Nomo .75 .30
❑ 98 Sammy Sosa .75 .30
❑ 99 Darin Erstad .30 .10
❑ 100 Todd Helton .50 .20
❑ 101 Aubrey Huff .30 .10
❑ 102 Alfonso Soriano .30 .10
❑ 103 Jose Vidro .30 .10
❑ 104 Carlos Lee .30 .10
❑ 105 Corey Koskie .30 .10
❑ 106 Bret Boone .30 .10
❑ 107 Torii Hunter .30 .10
❑ 108 Aramis Ramirez .30 .10
❑ 109 Chase Utley .50 .20
❑ 110 Reggie Sanders .30 .10
❑ 111 Livan Hernandez .30 .10
❑ 112 Jeromy Burnitz .30 .10
❑ 113 Carlos Zambrano .30 .10
❑ 114 Hank Blalock .30 .10
❑ 115 Sidney Ponson .30 .10
❑ 116 Zack Greinke .30 .10
❑ 117 Trevor Hoffman .30 .10
❑ 118 Jeff Kent .30 .10
❑ 119 Richie Sexson .30 .10
❑ 120 Melvin Mora .30 .10
❑ 121 Eric Chavez .30 .10
❑ 122 Miguel Cabrera .50 .20
❑ 123 Ryan Freel .30 .10
❑ 124 Russ Ortiz .30 .10
❑ 125 Craig Wilson .30 .10
❑ 126 Craig Biggio .50 .20
❑ 127 Curt Schilling .50 .20
❑ 128 Kaz Ishii .30 .10
❑ 129 Marquis Grissom .30 .10
❑ 130 Bernie Williams .50 .20
❑ 131 Travis Hafner .30 .10
❑ 132 Hee Seop Choi .30 .10
❑ 133 Scott Rolen .50 .20
❑ 134 Tony Batista .30 .10
❑ 135 Frank Thomas .75 .30
❑ 136 Jason Varitek .75 .30
❑ 137 Ichiro Suzuki 1.50 .60
❑ 138 Junior Spivey .30 .10
❑ 139 Adam Dunn .30 .10
❑ 140 Jorge Posada .50 .20
❑ 141 Edgar Renteria .30 .10

❑ 142 Hideki Matsui 1.25 .50
❑ 143 Carlos Guillen .30 .10
❑ 144 Jody Gerut .30 .10
❑ 145 Wily Mo Pena .30 .10
❑ 146 Derek Jeter 1.50 .60
❑ 147 C.C. Sabathia .30 .10
❑ 148 Geoff Jenkins .30 .10
❑ 149 Albert Pujols 1.50 .60
❑ 150 Eric Munson .30 .10
❑ 151 Moises Alou .30 .10
❑ 152 Jerry Hairston .30 .10
❑ 153 Ray Durham .30 .10
❑ 154 Mike Piazza .75 .30
❑ 155 Omar Vizquel .30 .10
❑ 156 A.J. Pierzynski .30 .10
❑ 157 Michael Young .30 .10
❑ 158 Jason Bay .30 .10
❑ 159 Mark Loretta .30 .10
❑ 160 Shawn Green .30 .10
❑ 161 Luis Gonzalez .30 .10
❑ 162 Johnny Damon .50 .20
❑ 163 Eric Milton .30 .10
❑ 164 Mike Lowell .30 .10
❑ 165 Jose Guillen .30 .10
❑ 166 Eric Hinske .30 .10
❑ 167 Jason Kendall .30 .10
❑ 168 Carlos Beltran .30 .10
❑ 169 Johnny Estrada .30 .10
❑ 170 Scott Hatteberg .30 .10
❑ 171 Laynce Nix .30 .10
❑ 172 Eric Gagne .30 .10
❑ 173 Richard Hidalgo .30 .10
❑ 174 Bobby Crosby .30 .10
❑ 175 Woody Williams .30 .10
❑ 176 Justin Leone .30 .10
❑ 177 Orlando Cabrera .30 .10
❑ 178 Mark Prior .50 .20
❑ 179 Jorge Julio .30 .10
❑ 180 Jamie Moyer .30 .10
❑ 181 Jose Reyes .30 .10
❑ 182 Ken Griffey Jr. 1.25 .50
❑ 183 Mike Lieberthal .30 .10
❑ 184 Kenny Rogers .30 .10
❑ 185 Mike Mussina .50 .20
❑ 186 Preston Wilson .30 .10
❑ 187 Khalil Greene .50 .20
❑ 188 Angel Berroa .30 .10
❑ 189 Miguel Tejada .30 .10
❑ 190 Freddy Garcia .30 .10
❑ 191 Pat Burrell .30 .10
❑ 192 Luis Castillo .30 .10
❑ 193 Vladimir Guerrero .75 .30
❑ 194 Roy Halladay .30 .10
❑ 195 Barry Zito .30 .10
❑ 196 Lance Berkman .30 .10
❑ 197 Rafael Palmeiro .50 .20
❑ 198 Nate Robertson .30 .10
❑ 199 Jason Schmidt .30 .10
❑ 200 Scott Podsednik .30 .10
❑ 201 Casey Kotchman AR 3.00 1.25
❑ 202 Scott Kazmir AR 5.00 2.00
❑ 203 Bucky Jacobsen AR 2.00 .75
❑ 204 Jeff Keppinger AR 2.00 .75
❑ 205 Dave Bush AR 2.00 .75
❑ 206 Gavin Floyd AR 2.00 .75
❑ 207 David Wright AR 8.00 3.00
❑ 208 B.J. Upton AR 5.00 2.00
❑ 209 David Aardsma AR 2.00 .75
❑ 210 Jason Bartlett AR 2.00 .75
❑ 211 Dioner Navarro AR 3.00 1.25
❑ 212 Jason Kubel AR 2.00 .75
❑ 213 Ryan Howard AR 8.00 3.00
❑ 214 Charles Thomas AR 2.00 .75
❑ 215 Freddy Guzman AR 2.00 .75
❑ 216 Brad Halsey AR 2.00 .75
❑ 217 Joey Gathright AR 3.00 1.25
❑ 218 Jeff Francis AR 2.00 .75
❑ 219 Terry Tiffee AR 2.00 .75
❑ 220 Nick Swisher AR 5.00 2.00

2006 Ultra

❑ COMP.SET w/o RL13 (200) 40.00 15.00
❑ COMMON CARD (1-180) .40 .15
❑ RL13 201-250 ODDS 1:4 HOBBY, 1:4 RETAIL
❑ 251 PRINT RUN 5000 CARDS
❑ 251 JOHJIMA IS NOT SERIAL NUMBERED
❑ 251 PRINT RUN INFO PROVIDED BY UD
❑ 251 JOHJIMA EXCH. DEADLINE 05/25/08
❑ 1 Vladimir Guerrero 1.00 .40
❑ 2 Bartolo Colon .40 .15
❑ 3 Francisco Rodriguez .40 .15
❑ 4 Darin Erstad .40 .15
❑ 5 Chone Figgins .40 .15
❑ 6 Bengie Molina .40 .15
❑ 7 Roger Clemens 2.00 .75
❑ 8 Lance Berkman .40 .15
❑ 9 Morgan Ensberg .40 .15
❑ 10 Roy Oswalt .40 .15
❑ 11 Andy Pettitte .60 .25
❑ 12 Craig Biggio .60 .25
❑ 13 Eric Chavez .40 .15
❑ 14 Barry Zito .40 .15
❑ 15 Huston Street .40 .15
❑ 16 Bobby Crosby .40 .15
❑ 17 Nick Swisher .40 .15
❑ 18 Rich Harden .40 .15
❑ 19 Vernon Wells .40 .15
❑ 20 Roy Halladay .40 .15
❑ 21 Alex Rios .40 .15
❑ 22 Orlando Hudson .40 .15
❑ 23 Shea Hillenbrand .40 .15
❑ 24 Gustavo Chacin .40 .15
❑ 25 Chipper Jones 1.00 .40
❑ 26 Andruw Jones .60 .25
❑ 27 Jeff Francoeur 1.00 .40
❑ 28 John Smoltz .60 .25
❑ 29 Tim Hudson .40 .15
❑ 30 Marcus Giles .40 .15
❑ 31 Carlos Lee .40 .15
❑ 32 Ben Sheets .40 .15
❑ 33 Rickie Weeks .40 .15
❑ 34 Chris Capuano .40 .15
❑ 35 Geoff Jenkins .40 .15
❑ 36 Brady Clark .40 .15
❑ 37 Albert Pujols 2.00 .75
❑ 38 Jim Edmonds .60 .25
❑ 39 Chris Carpenter .40 .15
❑ 40 Mark Mulder .40 .15
❑ 41 Yadier Molina .40 .15
❑ 42 Scott Rolen .60 .25
❑ 43 Derrek Lee .40 .15
❑ 44 Mark Prior .60 .25
❑ 45 Aramis Ramirez .40 .15
❑ 46 Carlos Zambrano .40 .15
❑ 47 Greg Maddux 1.50 .60
❑ 48 Nomar Garciaparra 1.00 .40
❑ 49 Jonny Gomes .40 .15
❑ 50 Carl Crawford .40 .15
❑ 51 Scott Kazmir .60 .25
❑ 52 Jorge Cantu .40 .15
❑ 53 Julio Lugo .40 .15
❑ 54 Aubrey Huff .40 .15
❑ 55 Luis Gonzalez .40 .15
❑ 56 Brandon Webb .40 .15
❑ 57 Troy Glaus .40 .15
❑ 58 Shawn Green .40 .15
❑ 59 Craig Counsell .40 .15

	Card	Hi	Lo
❑	60 Conor Jackson (RC)	1.50	.60
❑	61 Jeff Kent	.40	.15
❑	62 Eric Gagne	.40	.15
❑	63 J.D. Drew	.40	.15
❑	64 Milton Bradley	.40	.15
❑	65 Jeff Weaver	.40	.15
❑	66 Cesar Izturis	.40	.15
❑	67 Jason Schmidt	.40	.15
❑	68 Moises Alou	.40	.15
❑	69 Pedro Feliz	.40	.15
❑	70 Randy Winn	.40	.15
❑	71 Omar Vizquel	.60	.25
❑	72 Noah Lowry	.40	.15
❑	73 Travis Hafner	.40	.15
❑	74 Victor Martinez	.40	.15
❑	75 C.C. Sabathia	.40	.15
❑	76 Grady Sizemore	.60	.25
❑	77 Coco Crisp	.40	.15
❑	78 Cliff Lee	.40	.15
❑	79 Raul IbaÃ±ez	.40	.15
❑	80 Ichiro Suzuki	1.50	.60
❑	81 Richie Sexson	.40	.15
❑	82 Felix Hernandez	.60	.25
❑	83 Adrian Beltre	.40	.15
❑	84 Jamie Moyer	.40	.15
❑	85 Miguel Cabrera	.60	.25
❑	86 A.J. Burnett	.40	.15
❑	87 Juan Pierre	.40	.15
❑	88 Carlos Delgado	.40	.15
❑	89 Dontrelle Willis	.40	.15
❑	90 Juan Encarnacion	.40	.15
❑	91 Carlos Beltran	.40	.15
❑	92 Jose Reyes	1.00	.40
❑	93 David Wright	1.50	.60
❑	94 Tom Glavine	.60	.25
❑	95 Mike Piazza	1.00	.40
❑	96 Pedro Martinez	.60	.25
❑	97 Ryan Zimmerman (RC)	3.00	1.25
❑	98 Nick Johnson	.40	.15
❑	99 Jose Vidro	.40	.15
❑	100 Jose Guillen	.40	.15
❑	101 Livan Hernandez	.40	.15
❑	102 John Patterson	.40	.15
❑	103 Miguel Tejada	.40	.15
❑	104 Melvin Mora	.40	.15
❑	105 Brian Roberts	.40	.15
❑	106 Erik Bedard	.40	.15
❑	107 Javy Lopez	.40	.15
❑	108 Rodrigo Lopez	.40	.15
❑	109 Jake Peavy	.40	.15
❑	110 Mike Cameron	.40	.15
❑	111 Mark Loretta	.40	.15
❑	112 Brian Giles	.40	.15
❑	113 Trevor Hoffman	.40	.15
❑	114 Ramon Hernandez	.40	.15
❑	115 Bobby Abreu	.40	.15
❑	116 Chase Utley	1.00	.40
❑	117 Pat Burrell	.40	.15
❑	118 Jimmy Rollins	.40	.15
❑	119 Ryan Howard	1.50	.60
❑	120 Billy Wagner	.40	.15
❑	121 Jason Bay	.40	.15
❑	122 Oliver Perez	.40	.15
❑	123 Jack Wilson	.40	.15
❑	124 Zach Duke	.40	.15
❑	125 Rob Mackowiak	.40	.15
❑	126 Freddy Sanchez	.40	.15
❑	127 Mark Teixeira	.60	.25
❑	128 Michael Young	.40	.15
❑	129 Alfonso Soriano	.40	.15
❑	130 Hank Blalock	.40	.15
❑	131 Kenny Rogers	.40	.15
❑	132 Kevin Mench	.40	.15
❑	133 Manny Ramirez	.60	.25
❑	134 Josh Beckett	.40	.15
❑	135 David Ortiz	1.00	.40
❑	136 Johnny Damon	.60	.25
❑	137 Edgar Renteria	.40	.15
❑	138 Curt Schilling	.60	.25
❑	139 Ken Griffey Jr.	1.50	.60
❑	140 Adam Dunn	.40	.15
❑	141 Felipe Lopez	.40	.15
❑	142 Wily Mo Pena	.40	.15
❑	143 Aaron Harang	.40	.15
❑	144 Sean Casey	.40	.15
❑	145 Todd Helton	.60	.25
❑	146 Garrett Atkins	.40	.15
❑	147 Matt Holliday	1.00	.40
❑	148 Jeff Francis	.40	.15
❑	149 Clint Barmes	.40	.15
❑	150 Luis Gonzalez	.40	.15
❑	151 Mike Sweeney	.40	.15
❑	152 Zack Greinke	.40	.15
❑	153 Angel Berroa	.40	.15
❑	154 Emil Brown	.40	.15
❑	155 David DeJesus	.40	.15
❑	156 Ivan Rodriguez	.60	.25
❑	157 Jeremy Bonderman	.40	.15
❑	158 Brandon Inge	.40	.15
❑	159 Craig Monroe	.40	.15
❑	160 Chris Shelton	.40	.15
❑	161 Dmitri Young	.40	.15
❑	162 Johan Santana	.60	.25
❑	163 Joe Mauer	.60	.25
❑	164 Torii Hunter	.40	.15
❑	165 Shannon Stewart	.40	.15
❑	166 Scott Baker	.40	.15
❑	167 Brad Radke	.40	.15
❑	168 Jon Garland	.40	.15
❑	169 Tadahito Iguchi	.40	.15
❑	170 Paul Konerko	.40	.15
❑	171 Scott Podsednik	.40	.15
❑	172 Mark Buehrle	.40	.15
❑	173 Joe Crede	.40	.15
❑	174 Derek Jeter	2.50	1.00
❑	175 Alex Rodriguez	1.50	.60
❑	176 Hideki Matsui	1.50	.60
❑	177 Randy Johnson	1.00	.40
❑	178 Gary Sheffield	.40	.15
❑	179 Mariano Rivera	1.00	.40
❑	180 Jason Giambi	.40	.15
❑	181 Joey Devine RC	1.00	.40
❑	182 Alejandro Freire RC	1.00	.40
❑	183 Craig Hansen RC	2.00	.75
❑	184 Robert Andino RC	1.00	.40
❑	185 Ryan Jorgensen RC	1.00	.40
❑	186 Chris Demaria RC	1.00	.40
❑	187 Jonah Bayliss RC	1.00	.40
❑	188 Ryan Theriot RC	1.00	.40
❑	189 Steve Stemle RC	1.00	.40
❑	190 Brian Myrow RC	1.00	.40
❑	191 Chris Heintz RC	1.00	.40
❑	192 Ron Flores RC	1.00	.40
❑	193 Danny Sandoval RC	1.00	.40
❑	194 Craig Breslow RC	1.00	.40
❑	195 Jeremy Accardo RC	1.00	.40
❑	196 Jeff Harris RC	1.00	.40
❑	197 Tim Corcoran RC	1.00	.40
❑	198 Scott Feldman RC	1.00	.40
❑	199 Robinson Cano	.60	.25
❑	200 Jason Bergmann RC	2.00	.75
❑	201 Ken Griffey Jr. RL13	8.00	3.00
❑	202 Frank Thomas RL13	5.00	2.00
❑	203 Chipper Jones RL13	5.00	2.00
❑	204 Tony Clark RL13	2.00	.75
❑	205 Mike Lieberthal RL13	2.00	.75
❑	206 Manny Ramirez RL13	3.00	1.25
❑	207 Phil Nevin RL13	2.00	.75
❑	208 Derek Jeter RL13	10.00	4.00
❑	209 Preston Wilson RL13	2.00	.75
❑	210 Billy Wagner RL13	2.00	.75
❑	211 Alex Rodriguez RL13	8.00	3.00
❑	212 Trot Nixon RL13	2.00	.75
❑	213 Jaret Wright RL13	2.00	.75
❑	214 Nomar Garciaparra RL13	5.00	2.00
❑	215 Paul Konerko RL13	2.00	.75
❑	216 Paul Wilson RL13	2.00	.75
❑	217 Dustin Hermanson RL13	2.00	.75
❑	218 Todd Walker RL13	2.00	.75
❑	219 Matt Morris RL13	2.00	.75
❑	220 Darin Erstad RL13	2.00	.75
❑	221 Todd Helton RL13	3.00	1.25
❑	222 Geoff Jenkins RL13	2.00	.75
❑	223 Eric Chavez RL13	2.00	.75
❑	224 Kris Benson RL13	2.00	.75
❑	225 Jon Garland RL13	2.00	.75
❑	226 Troy Glaus RL13	2.00	.75
❑	227 Vernon Wells RL13	2.00	.75
❑	228 Michael Cuddyer RL13	2.00	.75
❑	229 Justin Verlander RL13	8.00	3.00
❑	230 Pat Burrell RL13	2.00	.75
❑	231 Mark Mulder RL13	2.00	.75
❑	232 Corey Patterson RL13	2.00	.75
❑	233 J.D. Drew RL13	2.00	.75
❑	234 Austin Kearns RL13	2.00	.75
❑	235 Felipe Lopez RL13	2.00	.75
❑	236 Sean Burroughs RL13	2.00	.75
❑	237 Ben Sheets RL13	2.00	.75
❑	238 Brett Myers RL13	2.00	.75
❑	239 Josh Beckett RL13	2.00	.75
❑	240 Barry Zito RL13	2.00	.75
❑	241 Adrian Gonzalez RL13	2.00	.75
❑	242 Rocco Baldelli RL13	2.00	.75
❑	243 Chris Burke RL13	2.00	.75
❑	244 Joe Mauer RL13	3.00	1.25
❑	245 Mark Prior RL13	3.00	1.25
❑	246 Mark Teixiera RL13	3.00	1.25
❑	247 Khalil Greene RL13	3.00	1.25
❑	248 Zack Greinke RL13	2.00	.75
❑	249 Prince Fielder RL13	8.00	3.00
❑	250 Rickie Weeks RL13	2.00	.75
❑	251 Kenji Johjima	15.00	6.00

2007 Ultra

	Card	Hi	Lo
❑	COMP.SET w/o RC's (200)	50.00	20.00
❑	COMMON CARD	.50	.20
❑	COMMON ROOKIE	2.50	1.00
❑	COMMON L13	2.50	1.00
❑	PRINTING PLATE ODDS 1:1252 HOB/RET		
❑	PLATE PRINT RUN 1 SET PER COLOR		
❑	BLACK-CYAN-MAGENTA-YELLOW ISSUED		
❑	NO PLATE PRICING DUE TO SCARCITY		
❑	1 Brandon Webb	.50	.20
❑	2 Randy Johnson	1.25	.50
❑	3 Conor Jackson	.50	.20
❑	4 Stephen Drew	.75	.30
❑	5 Eric Byrnes	.50	.20
❑	6 Carlos Quentin	.50	.20
❑	7 Andruw Jones	.75	.30
❑	8 Chipper Jones	1.25	.50
❑	9 Jeff Francoeur	1.25	.50
❑	10 Tim Hudson	.50	.20
❑	11 John Smoltz	.75	.30
❑	12 Edgar Renteria	.50	.20
❑	13 Erik Bedard	.50	.20
❑	14 Kris Benson	.50	.20
❑	15 Miguel Tejada	.50	.20
❑	16 Nick Markakis	.75	.30
❑	17 Brian Roberts	.50	.20
❑	18 Melvin Mora	.50	.20
❑	19 Aubrey Huff	.50	.20
❑	20 Curt Schilling	.75	.30
❑	21 Jonathan Papelbon	1.25	.50
❑	22 Josh Beckett	.75	.30
❑	23 Jason Varitek	1.25	.50
❑	24 David Ortiz	1.25	.50
❑	25 Manny Ramirez	.75	.30
❑	26 J.D. Drew	.50	.20
❑	27 Carlos Zambrano	.50	.20
❑	28 Derrek Lee	.50	.20
❑	29 Aramis Ramirez	.50	.20
❑	30 Alfonso Soriano	.50	.20
❑	31 Rich Hill	.50	.20
❑	32 Jacque Jones	.50	.20
❑	33 A.J. Pierzynski	.50	.20
❑	34 Jermaine Dye	.50	.20
❑	35 Paul Konerko	.50	.20
❑	36 Bobby Jenks	.50	.20
❑	37 Jon Garland	.50	.20
❑	38 Mark Buehrle	.50	.20

❑ 39	Tadahito Iguchi	.50	.20
❑ 40	Adam Dunn	.50	.20
❑ 41	Ken Griffey Jr.	2.00	.75
❑ 42	Aaron Harang	.50	.20
❑ 43	Bronson Arroyo	.50	.20
❑ 44	Ryan Freel	.50	.20
❑ 45	Brandon Phillips	.50	.20
❑ 46	Grady Sizemore	.75	.30
❑ 47	Travis Hafner	.50	.20
❑ 48	Victor Martinez	.50	.20
❑ 49	Jhonny Peralta	.50	.20
❑ 50	C.C. Sabathia	.50	.20
❑ 51	Jeremy Sowers	.50	.20
❑ 52	Ryan Garko	.50	.20
❑ 53	Garrett Atkins	.50	.20
❑ 54	Willy Taveras	.50	.20
❑ 55	Todd Helton	.75	.30
❑ 56	Jeff Francis	.50	.20
❑ 57	Brad Hawpe	.50	.20
❑ 58	Matt Holliday	1.25	.50
❑ 59	Justin Verlander	1.25	.50
❑ 60	Jeremy Bonderman	.50	.20
❑ 61	Magglio Ordonez	.50	.20
❑ 62	Ivan Rodriguez	.75	.30
❑ 63	Gary Sheffield	.50	.20
❑ 64	Kenny Rogers	.50	.20
❑ 65	Brandon Inge	.50	.20
❑ 66	Anibal Sanchez	.50	.20
❑ 67	Scott Olsen	.50	.20
❑ 68	Dontrelle Willis	.50	.20
❑ 69	Dan Uggla	.75	.30
❑ 70	Hanley Ramirez	.75	.30
❑ 71	Miguel Cabrera	.75	.30
❑ 72	Jeremy Hermida	.50	.20
❑ 73	Roy Oswalt	.50	.20
❑ 74	Brad Lidge	.50	.20
❑ 75	Lance Berkman	.50	.20
❑ 76	Carlos Lee	.50	.20
❑ 77	Morgan Ensberg	.50	.20
❑ 78	Craig Biggio	.75	.30
❑ 79	Reggie Sanders	.50	.20
❑ 80	Mike Sweeney	.50	.20
❑ 81	Mark Teahen	.50	.20
❑ 82	John Buck	.50	.20
❑ 83	Mark Grudzielanek	.50	.20
❑ 84	Gary Matthews	.50	.20
❑ 85	Vladimir Guerrero	1.25	.50
❑ 86	Garret Anderson	.50	.20
❑ 87	Howie Kendrick	.50	.20
❑ 88	Jered Weaver	.75	.30
❑ 89	Chone Figgins	.50	.20
❑ 90	Bartolo Colon	.50	.20
❑ 91	Francisco Rodriguez	.50	.20
❑ 92	Nomar Garciaparra	1.25	.50
❑ 93	Andre Ethier	.75	.30
❑ 94	Rafael Furcal	.50	.20
❑ 95	Jeff Kent	.50	.20
❑ 96	Derek Lowe	.50	.20
❑ 97	Jason Schmidt	.50	.20
❑ 98	Takashi Saito	.50	.20
❑ 99	Ben Sheets	.50	.20
❑ 100	Prince Fielder	1.25	.50
❑ 101	Bill Hall	.50	.20
❑ 102	Rickie Weeks	.50	.20
❑ 103	Francisco Cordero	.50	.20
❑ 104	J.J. Hardy	.50	.20
❑ 105	Johan Santana	.75	.30
❑ 106	Justin Morneau	.50	.20
❑ 107	Joe Mauer	.75	.30
❑ 108	Joe Nathan	.50	.20
❑ 109	Torii Hunter	.50	.20
❑ 110	Michael Cuddyer	.50	.20
❑ 111	Boof Bonser	.50	.20
❑ 112	Tom Glavine	.75	.30
❑ 113	Pedro Martinez	.75	.30
❑ 114	Billy Wagner	.50	.20
❑ 115	Jose Reyes	1.25	.50
❑ 116	David Wright	2.00	.75
❑ 117	Carlos Delgado	.50	.20
❑ 118	Carlos Beltran	.50	.20
❑ 119	Alex Rodriguez	2.00	.75
❑ 120	Chien-Ming Wang	2.00	.75
❑ 121	Mariano Rivera	1.25	.50
❑ 122	Bobby Abreu	.50	.20
❑ 123	Hideki Matsui	1.25	.50
❑ 124	Johnny Damon	.75	.30

❑ 125	Robinson Cano	.75	.30
❑ 126	Derek Jeter	3.00	1.25
❑ 127	Nick Swisher	.50	.20
❑ 128	Eric Chavez	.50	.20
❑ 129	Jason Kendall	.50	.20
❑ 130	Bobby Crosby	.50	.20
❑ 131	Huston Street	.50	.20
❑ 132	Dan Haren	.50	.20
❑ 133	Rich Harden	.50	.20
❑ 134	Mike Piazza	1.25	.50
❑ 135	Chase Utley	1.25	.50
❑ 136	Jimmy Rollins	.50	.20
❑ 137	Aaron Rowand	.50	.20
❑ 138	Jamie Moyer	.50	.20
❑ 139	Cole Hamels	.75	.30
❑ 140	Pat Burrell	.50	.20
❑ 141	Ryan Howard	2.00	.75
❑ 142	Freddy Sanchez	.50	.20
❑ 143	Zach Duke	.50	.20
❑ 144	Ian Snell	.50	.20
❑ 145	Jack Wilson	.50	.20
❑ 146	Jason Bay	.50	.20
❑ 147	Albert Pujols	2.50	1.00
❑ 148	Scott Rolen	.75	.30
❑ 149	Jim Edmonds	.75	.30
❑ 150	Chris Carpenter	.50	.20
❑ 151	Yadier Molina	.50	.20
❑ 152	Adam Wainwright	.50	.20
❑ 153	David Eckstein	.50	.20
❑ 154	Trevor Hoffman	.50	.20
❑ 155	Brian Giles	.50	.20
❑ 156	Adrian Gonzalez	.50	.20
❑ 157	Jake Peavy	.50	.20
❑ 158	Khalil Greene	.75	.30
❑ 159	Chris Young	.50	.20
❑ 160	Greg Maddux	2.00	.75
❑ 161	Mike Cameron	.50	.20
❑ 162	Matt Cain	.75	.30
❑ 163	Matt Morris	.50	.20
❑ 164	Pedro Feliz	.50	.20
❑ 165	Omar Vizquel	.75	.30
❑ 166	Randy Winn	.50	.20
❑ 167	Barry Zito	.50	.20
❑ 168	Adrian Beltre	.50	.20
❑ 169	Yuniesky Betancourt	.50	.20
❑ 170	Richie Sexson	.50	.20
❑ 171	Raul Ibanez	.50	.20
❑ 172	Kenji Johjima	1.25	.50
❑ 173	Ichiro Suzuki	2.00	.75
❑ 174	Felix Hernandez	.75	.30
❑ 175	Scott Kazmir	.75	.30
❑ 176	Carl Crawford	.50	.20
❑ 177	B.J. Upton	.50	.20
❑ 178	James Shields	.50	.20
❑ 179	Rocco Baldelli	.50	.20
❑ 180	Jorge Cantu	.50	.20
❑ 181	Ty Wigginton	.50	.20
❑ 182	Mark Teixeira	.75	.30
❑ 183	Hank Blalock	.50	.20
❑ 184	Ian Kinsler	.50	.20
❑ 185	Michael Young	.50	.20
❑ 186	Vicente Padilla	.50	.20
❑ 187	Akinori Otsuka	.50	.20
❑ 188	Kenny Lofton	.50	.20
❑ 189	A.J. Burnett	.50	.20
❑ 190	Roy Halladay	.50	.20
❑ 191	B.J. Ryan	.50	.20
❑ 192	Vernon Wells	.50	.20
❑ 193	Alex Rios	.50	.20
❑ 194	Troy Glaus	.50	.20
❑ 195	Frank Thomas	1.25	.50
❑ 196	Ryan Zimmerman	1.25	.50
❑ 197	Michael O'Connor	.50	.20
❑ 198	Chad Cordero	.50	.20
❑ 199	Nick Johnson	.50	.20
❑ 200	Felipe Lopez	.50	.20
❑ 201	Miguel Montero (RC)	2.50	1.00
❑ 202	Doug Slaten RC	2.50	1.00
❑ 203	Joseph Bisenius RC	2.50	1.00
❑ 204	Jared Burton RC	2.50	1.00
❑ 205	Kevin Cameron RC	2.50	1.00
❑ 206	Matt Chico (RC)	2.50	1.00
❑ 207	Chris Stewart RC	2.50	1.00
❑ 208	Joe Smith RC	2.50	1.00
❑ 209	Zack Segovia (RC)	2.50	1.00
❑ 210	John Danks RC	2.50	1.00

❑ 211	Lee Gardner (RC)	2.50	1.00
❑ 212	Jeff Baker (RC)	2.50	1.00
❑ 213	Jamie Burke (RC)	2.50	1.00
❑ 214	Phil Hughes (RC)	12.00	5.00
❑ 215	Mike Rabelo RC	2.50	1.00
❑ 216	Jose Garcia RC	2.50	1.00
❑ 217	Hector Gimenez (RC)	2.50	1.00
❑ 218	Jesus Flores RC	2.50	1.00
❑ 219	Brandon Morrow RC	4.00	1.50
❑ 220	Hideki Okajima RC	12.00	5.00
❑ 221	Jay Marshall RC	2.50	1.00
❑ 222	Matt Lindstrom (RC)	2.50	1.00
❑ 223	Juan Salas (RC)	2.50	1.00
❑ 224	Juan Perez RC	2.50	1.00
❑ 225	Sean Henn (RC)	2.50	1.00
❑ 226	Travis Buck (RC)	2.50	1.00
❑ 227	Gustavo Molina RC	2.50	1.00
❑ 228	Hunter Pence (RC)	12.00	5.00
❑ 229	Michael Bourn (RC)	2.50	1.00
❑ 230	Brian Barden RC	2.50	1.00
❑ 231	Don Kelly (RC)	2.50	1.00
❑ 232	Joakim Soria RC	2.50	1.00
❑ 233	Cesar Jimenez RC	2.50	1.00
❑ 234	Levale Speigner RC	2.50	1.00
❑ 235	Micah Owings (RC)	2.50	1.00
❑ 236	Brian Stokes (RC)	2.50	1.00
❑ 237	Joaquin Arias (RC)	2.50	1.00
❑ 238	Josh Hamilton L13 (RC)	6.00	2.50
❑ 239	Daisuke Matsuzaka L13 RC	15.00	6.00
❑ 240	Alejandro De Aza L13 RC	4.00	1.50
❑ 241	Kory Casto L13 (RC)	2.50	1.00
❑ 242	Troy Tulowitzki L13 (RC)	6.00	2.50
❑ 243	Akinori Iwamura L13 RC	6.00	2.50
❑ 244	Angel Sanchez L13 RC	2.50	1.00
❑ 245	Ryan Braun L13 (RC)	15.00	6.00
❑ 246	Alex Gordon L13 RC	12.00	5.00
❑ 247	Elijah Dukes L13 RC	4.00	1.50
❑ 248	Kei Igawa L13 RC	6.00	2.50
❑ 249	Kevin Kouzmanoff L13 (RC)	2.50	1.00
❑ 250	Delmon Young L13 (RC)	4.00	1.50

1989 Upper Deck

❑	COMPLETE SET (800)	80.00	40.00
❑	COMP.FACT.SET (800)	100.00	50.00
❑	COMP.HI FACT.SET (100)	10.00	4.00
❑ 1	Ken Griffey Jr. RC	40.00	15.00
❑ 2	Luis Medina RC	.25	.08
❑ 3	Tony Chance RC	.25	.08
❑ 4	Dave Otto	.25	.08
❑ 5	Sandy Alomar Jr. RC	1.00	.40
❑ 6	Rolando Roomes RC	.25	.08
❑ 7	Dave West RC	.25	.08
❑ 8	Cris Carpenter RC *	.25	.08
❑ 9	Gregg Jefferies	.25	.08
❑ 10	Doug Dascenzo RC	.25	.08
❑ 11	Ron Jones RC	.25	.08
❑ 12	Luis DeLosSantos RC	.25	.08
❑ 13	Gary Sheffield RC	5.00	2.00
❑ 13A	Gary Sheffield ERR	5.00	2.00
❑ 14	Mike Harkey RC	.25	.08
❑ 15	Lance Blankenship RC	.25	.08
❑ 16	William Brennan RC	.25	.08
❑ 17	John Smoltz RC	5.00	2.00
❑ 18	Ramon Martinez RC	.50	.20
❑ 19	Mark Lemke RC	1.00	.40
❑ 20	Juan Bell RC	.25	.08
❑ 21	Rey Palacios RC	.25	.08
❑ 22	Felix Jose RC	.25	.08

❑ 23 Van Snider RC	.25	.08
❑ 24 Dante Bichette RC	1.00	.40
❑ 25 Randy Johnson RC	8.00	3.00
❑ 26 Carlos Quintana RC	.25	.08
❑ 27 Star Rookie CL	.25	.08
❑ 28 Mike Schooler	.25	.08
❑ 29 Randy St.Claire	.25	.08
❑ 30 Jerald Clark RC	.25	.08
❑ 31 Kevin Gross	.25	.08
❑ 32 Dan Firova	.25	.08
❑ 33 Jeff Calhoun	.25	.08
❑ 34 Tommy Hinzo	.25	.08
❑ 35 Ricky Jordan RC *	.50	.20
❑ 36 Larry Parrish	.25	.08
❑ 37 Bret Saberhagen UER (Hit total 931, should be 10	.40	.15
❑ 38 Mike Smithson	.25	.08
❑ 39 Dave Dravecky	.25	.08
❑ 40 Ed Romero	.25	.08
❑ 41 Jeff Musselman	.25	.08
❑ 42 Ed Hearn	.25	.08
❑ 43 Rance Mulliniks	.25	.08
❑ 44 Jim Eisenreich	.25	.08
❑ 45 Sil Campusano	.25	.08
❑ 46 Mike Krukow	.25	.08
❑ 47 Paul Gibson	.25	.08
❑ 48 Mike LaCoss	.25	.08
❑ 49 Larry Herndon	.25	.08
❑ 50 Scott Garrelts	.25	.08
❑ 51 Dwayne Henry	.25	.08
❑ 52 Jim Acker	.25	.08
❑ 53 Steve Sax	.25	.08
❑ 54 Pete O'Brien	.25	.08
❑ 55 Paul Runge	.25	.08
❑ 56 Rick Rhoden	.25	.08
❑ 57 John Dopson	.25	.08
❑ 58 Casey Candaele UER (No stats for Astros for '88	.25	.08
❑ 59 Dave Righetti	.40	.15
❑ 60 Joe Hesketh	.25	.08
❑ 61 Frank DiPino	.25	.08
❑ 62 Tim Laudner	.25	.08
❑ 63 Jamie Moyer	.40	.15
❑ 64 Fred Toliver	.25	.08
❑ 65 Mitch Webster	.25	.08
❑ 66 John Tudor	.40	.15
❑ 67 John Cangelosi	.25	.08
❑ 68 Mike Devereaux	.25	.08
❑ 69 Brian Fisher	.25	.08
❑ 70 Mike Marshall	.25	.08
❑ 71 Zane Smith	.25	.08
❑ 72A Brian Holton ERR	1.00	.40
❑ 72B Brian Holton COR	.40	.15
❑ 73 Jose Guzman	.25	.08
❑ 74 Rick Mahler	.25	.08
❑ 75 John Shelby	.25	.08
❑ 76 Jim Deshaies	.25	.08
❑ 77 Bobby Meacham	.25	.08
❑ 78 Bryn Smith	.25	.08
❑ 79 Joaquin Andujar	.40	.15
❑ 80 Richard Dotson	.25	.08
❑ 81 Charlie Lea	.25	.08
❑ 82 Calvin Schiraldi	.25	.08
❑ 83 Les Straker	.25	.08
❑ 84 Les Lancaster	.25	.08
❑ 85 Allan Anderson	.25	.08
❑ 86 Junior Ortiz	.25	.08
❑ 87 Jesse Orosco	.25	.08
❑ 88 Felix Fermin	.25	.08
❑ 89 Dave Anderson	.25	.08
❑ 90 Rafael Belliard UER (Born '61, not '51)	.25	.08
❑ 91 Franklin Stubbs	.25	.08
❑ 92 Cecil Espy	.25	.08
❑ 93 Albert Hall	.25	.08
❑ 94 Tim Leary	.25	.08
❑ 95 Mitch Williams	.25	.08
❑ 96 Tracy Jones	.25	.08
❑ 97 Danny Darwin	.25	.08
❑ 98 Gary Ward	.25	.08
❑ 99 Neal Heaton	.25	.08
❑ 100 Jim Pankovits	.25	.08
❑ 101 Bill Doran	.25	.08
❑ 102 Tim Wallach	.25	.08
❑ 103 Joe Magrane	.25	.08
❑ 104 Ozzie Virgil	.25	.08
❑ 105 Alvin Davis	.25	.08
❑ 106 Tom Brookens	.25	.08
❑ 107 Shawon Dunston	.25	.08
❑ 108 Tracy Woodson	.25	.08
❑ 109 Nelson Liriano	.25	.08
❑ 110 Devon White	.40	.15
❑ 111 Steve Balboni	.25	.08
❑ 112 Buddy Bell	.40	.15
❑ 113 German Jimenez	.25	.08
❑ 114 Ken Dayley	.25	.08
❑ 115 Andres Galarraga	.40	.15
❑ 116 Mike Scioscia	.40	.15
❑ 117 Gary Pettis	.25	.08
❑ 118 Ernie Whitt	.25	.08
❑ 119 Bob Boone	.40	.15
❑ 120 Ryne Sandberg	1.50	.60
❑ 121 Bruce Benedict	.25	.08
❑ 122 Hubie Brooks	.25	.08
❑ 123 Mike Moore	.25	.08
❑ 124 Wallace Johnson	.25	.08
❑ 125 Bob Horner	.40	.15
❑ 126 Chili Davis	.40	.15
❑ 127 Manny Trillo	.25	.08
❑ 128 Chet Lemon	.40	.15
❑ 129 John Cerutti	.25	.08
❑ 130 Orel Hershiser	.40	.15
❑ 131 Terry Pendleton	.40	.15
❑ 132 Jeff Blauser	.25	.08
❑ 133 Mike Fitzgerald	.25	.08
❑ 134 Henry Cotto	.25	.08
❑ 135 Gerald Young	.25	.08
❑ 136 Luis Salazar	.25	.08
❑ 137 Alejandro Pena	.25	.08
❑ 138 Jack Howell	.25	.08
❑ 139 Tony Fernandez	.25	.08
❑ 140 Mark Grace	1.00	.40
❑ 141 Ken Caminiti	.60	.25
❑ 142 Mike Jackson	.25	.08
❑ 143 Larry McWilliams	.25	.08
❑ 144 Andres Thomas	.25	.08
❑ 145 Nolan Ryan 3X	4.00	1.50
❑ 146 Mike Davis	.25	.08
❑ 147 DeWayne Buice	.25	.08
❑ 148 Jody Davis	.25	.08
❑ 149 Jesse Barfield	.40	.15
❑ 150 Matt Nokes	.25	.08
❑ 151 Jerry Reuss	.25	.08
❑ 152 Rick Cerone	.25	.08
❑ 153 Storm Davis	.25	.08
❑ 154 Marvell Wynne	.25	.08
❑ 155 Will Clark	.60	.25
❑ 156 Luis Aguayo	.25	.08
❑ 157 Willie Upshaw	.25	.08
❑ 158 Randy Bush	.25	.08
❑ 159 Ron Darling	.40	.15
❑ 160 Kal Daniels	.25	.08
❑ 161 Spike Owen	.25	.08
❑ 162 Luis Polonia	.25	.08
❑ 163 Kevin Mitchell UER	.40	.15
❑ 164 Dave Gallagher	.25	.08
❑ 165 Benito Santiago	.40	.15
❑ 166 Greg Gagne	.25	.08
❑ 167 Ken Phelps	.25	.08
❑ 168 Sid Fernandez	.25	.08
❑ 169 Bo Diaz	.25	.08
❑ 170 Cory Snyder	.25	.08
❑ 171 Eric Show	.25	.08
❑ 172 Robby Thompson	.25	.08
❑ 173 Marty Barrett	.25	.08
❑ 174 Dave Henderson	.25	.08
❑ 175 Ozzie Guillen	.40	.15
❑ 176 Barry Lyons	.25	.08
❑ 177 Kelvin Torve	.25	.08
❑ 178 Don Slaught	.25	.08
❑ 179 Steve Lombardozzi	.25	.08
❑ 180 Chris Sabo RC *	1.00	.40
❑ 181 Jose Uribe	.25	.08
❑ 182 Shane Mack	.25	.08
❑ 183 Ron Karkovice	.25	.08
❑ 184 Todd Benzinger	.25	.08
❑ 185 Dave Stewart	.40	.15
❑ 186 Julio Franco	.40	.15
❑ 187 Ron Robinson	.25	.08
❑ 188 Wally Backman	.25	.08
❑ 189 Randy Velarde	.25	.08
❑ 190 Joe Carter	.40	.15
❑ 191 Bob Welch	.40	.15
❑ 192 Kelly Paris	.25	.08
❑ 193 Chris Brown	.25	.08
❑ 194 Rick Reuschel	.40	.15
❑ 195 Roger Clemens	2.00	.75
❑ 196 Dave Concepcion	.40	.15
❑ 197 Al Newman	.25	.08
❑ 198 Brook Jacoby	.25	.08
❑ 199 Mookie Wilson	.40	.15
❑ 200 Don Mattingly	2.50	1.00
❑ 201 Dick Schofield	.25	.08
❑ 202 Mark Gubicza	.25	.08
❑ 203 Gary Gaetti	.40	.15
❑ 204 Dan Pasqua	.25	.08
❑ 205 Andre Dawson	.40	.15
❑ 206 Chris Speier	.25	.08
❑ 207 Kent Tekulve	.25	.08
❑ 208 Rod Scurry	.25	.08
❑ 209 Scott Bailes	.25	.08
❑ 210 Rickey Henderson	1.00	.40
❑ 211 Harold Baines	.40	.15
❑ 212 Tony Armas	.40	.15
❑ 213 Kent Hrbek	.40	.15
❑ 214 Darrin Jackson	.25	.08
❑ 215 George Brett	2.50	1.00
❑ 216 Rafael Santana	.25	.08
❑ 217 Andy Allanson	.25	.08
❑ 218 Brett Butler	.40	.15
❑ 219 Steve Jeltz	.25	.08
❑ 220 Jay Buhner	.40	.15
❑ 221 Bo Jackson	1.00	.40
❑ 222 Angel Salazar	.25	.08
❑ 223 Kirk McCaskill	.25	.08
❑ 224 Steve Lyons	.25	.08
❑ 225 Bert Blyleven	.40	.15
❑ 226 Scott Bradley	.25	.08
❑ 227 Bob Melvin	.25	.08
❑ 228 Ron Kittle	.25	.08
❑ 229 Phil Bradley	.25	.08
❑ 230 Tommy John	.40	.15
❑ 231 Greg Walker	.25	.08
❑ 232 Juan Berenguer	.25	.08
❑ 233 Pat Tabler	.25	.08
❑ 234 Terry Clark	.25	.08
❑ 235 Rafael Palmeiro	1.00	.40
❑ 236 Paul Zuvella	.25	.08
❑ 237 Willie Randolph	.40	.15
❑ 238 Bruce Fields	.25	.08
❑ 239 Mike Aldrete	.25	.08
❑ 240 Lance Parrish	.40	.15
❑ 241 Greg Maddux	2.50	1.00
❑ 242 John Moses	.25	.08
❑ 243 Melido Perez	.25	.08
❑ 244 Willie Wilson	.40	.15
❑ 245 Mark McLemore	.25	.08
❑ 246 Von Hayes	.25	.08
❑ 247 Matt Williams	1.00	.40
❑ 248 John Candelaria UER (Listed as Yankee for part o	.25	.08
❑ 249 Harold Reynolds	.40	.15
❑ 250 Greg Swindell	.25	.08
❑ 251 Juan Agosto	.25	.08
❑ 252 Mike Felder	.25	.08
❑ 253 Vince Coleman	.25	.08
❑ 254 Larry Sheets	.25	.08
❑ 255 George Bell	.40	.15
❑ 256 Terry Steinbach	.40	.15
❑ 257 Jack Armstrong RC *	.50	.20
❑ 258 Dickie Thon	.25	.08
❑ 259 Ray Knight	.40	.15
❑ 260 Darryl Strawberry	.40	.15
❑ 261 Doug Sisk	.25	.08
❑ 262 Alex Trevino	.25	.08
❑ 263 Jeffrey Leonard	.25	.08
❑ 264 Tom Henke	.25	.08
❑ 265 Ozzie Smith	1.50	.60
❑ 266 Dave Bergman	.25	.08
❑ 267 Tony Phillips	.25	.08
❑ 268 Mark Davis	.25	.08
❑ 269 Kevin Elster	.25	.08
❑ 270 Barry Larkin	.60	.25
❑ 271 Manny Lee	.25	.08
❑ 272 Tom Brunansky	.25	.08

❑ 273 Craig Biggio RC 6.00 2.50
❑ 274 Jim Gantner .25 .08
❑ 275 Eddie Murray 1.00 .40
❑ 276 Jeff Reed .25 .08
❑ 277 Tim Teufel .25 .08
❑ 278 Rick Honeycutt .25 .08
❑ 279 Guillermo Hernandez .25 .08
❑ 280 John Kruk .40 .15
❑ 281 Luis Alicea RC * .50 .20
❑ 282 Jim Clancy .25 .08
❑ 283 Billy Ripken .25 .08
❑ 284 Craig Reynolds .25 .08
❑ 285 Robin Yount 1.50 .60
❑ 286 Jimmy Jones .25 .08
❑ 287 Ron Oester .25 .08
❑ 288 Terry Leach .25 .08
❑ 289 Dennis Eckersley .60 .25
❑ 290 Alan Trammell .40 .15
❑ 291 Jimmy Key .40 .15
❑ 292 Chris Bosio .25 .08
❑ 293 Jose DeLeon .25 .08
❑ 294 Jim Traber .25 .08
❑ 295 Mike Scott .40 .15
❑ 296 Roger McDowell .25 .08
❑ 297 Garry Templeton .40 .15
❑ 298 Doyle Alexander .25 .08
❑ 299 Nick Esasky .25 .08
❑ 300 Mark McGwire 5.00 2.00
❑ 301 Darryl Hamilton RC * .50 .20
❑ 302 Dave Smith .25 .08
❑ 303 Rick Sutcliffe .40 .15
❑ 304 Dave Stapleton .25 .08
❑ 305 Alan Ashby .25 .08
❑ 306 Pedro Guerrero .40 .15
❑ 307 Ron Guidry .40 .15
❑ 308 Steve Farr .25 .08
❑ 309 Curt Ford .25 .08
❑ 310 Claudell Washington .25 .08
❑ 311 Tom Prince .25 .08
❑ 312 Chad Kreuter RC .50 .20
❑ 313 Ken Oberkfell .25 .08
❑ 314 Jerry Browne .25 .08
❑ 315 R.J. Reynolds .25 .08
❑ 316 Scott Bankhead .25 .08
❑ 317 Milt Thompson .25 .08
❑ 318 Mario Diaz .25 .08
❑ 319 Bruce Ruffin .25 .08
❑ 320 Dave Valle .25 .08
❑ 321A Gary Varsho ERR 2.00 .75
❑ 321B Gary Varsho COR
(In road uniform) .25 .08
❑ 322 Paul Mirabella .25 .08
❑ 323 Chuck Jackson .25 .08
❑ 324 Drew Hall .25 .08
❑ 325 Don August .25 .08
❑ 326 Israel Sanchez .25 .08
❑ 327 Denny Walling .25 .08
❑ 328 Joel Skinner .25 .08
❑ 329 Danny Tartabull .25 .08
❑ 330 Tony Pena .25 .08
❑ 331 Jim Sundberg .40 .15
❑ 332 Jeff D. Robinson .25 .08
❑ 333 Oddibe McDowell .25 .08
❑ 334 Jose Lind .25 .08
❑ 335 Paul Kilgus .25 .08
❑ 336 Juan Samuel .25 .08
❑ 337 Mike Campbell .25 .08
❑ 338 Mike Maddux .25 .08
❑ 339 Darnell Coles .25 .08
❑ 340 Bob Dernier .25 .08
❑ 341 Rafael Ramirez .25 .08
❑ 342 Scott Sanderson .25 .08
❑ 343 B.J. Surhoff .40 .15
❑ 344 Billy Hatcher .25 .08
❑ 345 Pat Perry .25 .08
❑ 346 Jack Clark .40 .15
❑ 347 Gary Thurman .25 .08
❑ 348 Tim Jones .25 .08
❑ 349 Dave Winfield .40 .15
❑ 350 Frank White .40 .15
❑ 351 Dave Collins .25 .08
❑ 352 Jack Morris .40 .15
❑ 353 Eric Plunk .25 .08
❑ 354 Leon Durham .25 .08
❑ 355 Ivan DeJesus .25 .08
❑ 356 Brian Holman RC * .25 .08
❑ 357A Dale Murphy RevNeg 30.00 12.50
❑ 357B Dale Murphy COR .60 .25
❑ 358 Mark Portugal .25 .08
❑ 359 Andy McGaffigan .25 .08
❑ 360 Tom Glavine 1.00 .40
❑ 361 Keith Moreland .25 .08
❑ 362 Todd Stottlemyre .25 .08
❑ 363 Dave Leiper .25 .08
❑ 364 Cecil Fielder .40 .15
❑ 365 Carmelo Martinez .25 .08
❑ 366 Dwight Evans .60 .25
❑ 367 Kevin McReynolds .25 .08
❑ 368 Rich Gedman .25 .08
❑ 369 Len Dykstra .40 .15
❑ 370 Jody Reed .25 .08
❑ 371 Jose Canseco 1.00 .40
❑ 372 Rob Murphy .25 .08
❑ 373 Mike Henneman .25 .08
❑ 374 Walt Weiss .25 .08
❑ 375 Rob Dibble RC 1.00 .40
❑ 376 Kirby Puckett 1.00 .40
❑ 377 Dennis Martinez .40 .15
❑ 378 Ron Gant .40 .15
❑ 379 Brian Harper .25 .08
❑ 380 Nelson Santovenia .25 .08
❑ 381 Lloyd Moseby .25 .08
❑ 382 Lance McCullers .25 .08
❑ 383 Dave Stieb .40 .15
❑ 384 Tony Gwynn 1.25 .50
❑ 385 Mike Flanagan .25 .08
❑ 386 Bob Ojeda .25 .08
❑ 387 Bruce Hurst .25 .08
❑ 388 Dave Magadan .25 .08
❑ 389 Wade Boggs .60 .25
❑ 390 Gary Carter .40 .15
❑ 391 Frank Tanana .40 .15
❑ 392 Curt Young .25 .08
❑ 393 Jeff Treadway .25 .08
❑ 394 Darrell Evans .40 .15
❑ 395 Glenn Hubbard .25 .08
❑ 396 Chuck Cary .25 .08
❑ 397 Frank Viola .40 .15
❑ 398 Jeff Parrett .25 .08
❑ 399 Terry Blocker .25 .08
❑ 400 Dan Gladden .25 .08
❑ 401 Louie Meadows .25 .08
❑ 402 Tim Raines .40 .15
❑ 403 Joey Meyer .25 .08
❑ 404 Larry Andersen .25 .08
❑ 405 Rex Hudler .25 .08
❑ 406 Mike Schmidt 2.00 .75
❑ 407 John Franco .40 .15
❑ 408 Brady Anderson RC 1.00 .40
❑ 409 Don Carman .25 .08
❑ 410 Eric Davis .40 .15
❑ 411 Bob Stanley .25 .08
❑ 412 Pete Smith .25 .08
❑ 413 Jim Rice .40 .15
❑ 414 Bruce Sutter .40 .15
❑ 415 Oil Can Boyd .25 .08
❑ 416 Ruben Sierra .40 .15
❑ 417 Mike LaValliere .25 .08
❑ 418 Steve Buechele .25 .08
❑ 419 Gary Redus .25 .08
❑ 420 Scott Fletcher .25 .08
❑ 421 Dale Sveum .25 .08
❑ 422 Bob Knepper .25 .08
❑ 423 Luis Rivera .25 .08
❑ 424 Ted Higuera .25 .08
❑ 425 Kevin Bass .25 .08
❑ 426 Ken Gerhart .25 .08
❑ 427 Shane Rawley .25 .08
❑ 428 Paul O'Neill .60 .25
❑ 429 Joe Orsulak .25 .08
❑ 430 Jackie Gutierrez .25 .08
❑ 431 Gerald Perry .25 .08
❑ 432 Mike Greenwell .25 .08
❑ 433 Jerry Royster .25 .08
❑ 434 Ellis Burks .40 .15
❑ 435 Ed Olwine .25 .08
❑ 436 Dave Rucker .25 .08
❑ 437 Charlie Hough .40 .15
❑ 438 Bob Walk .25 .08
❑ 439 Bob Brower .25 .08
❑ 440 Barry Bonds 5.00 2.00
❑ 441 Tom Foley .25 .08
❑ 442 Rob Deer .25 .08
❑ 443 Glenn Davis .25 .08
❑ 444 Dave Martinez .25 .08
❑ 445 Bill Wegman .25 .08
❑ 446 Lloyd McClendon .25 .08
❑ 447 Dave Schmidt .25 .08
❑ 448 Darren Daulton .40 .15
❑ 449 Frank Williams .25 .08
❑ 450 Don Aase .25 .08
❑ 451 Lou Whitaker .40 .15
❑ 452 Rich Gossage .40 .15
❑ 453 Ed Whitson .25 .08
❑ 454 Jim Walewander .25 .08
❑ 455 Damon Berryhill .25 .08
❑ 456 Tim Burke .25 .08
❑ 457 Barry Jones .25 .08
❑ 458 Joel Youngblood .25 .08
❑ 459 Floyd Youmans .25 .08
❑ 460 Mark Salas .25 .08
❑ 461 Jeff Russell .25 .08
❑ 462 Darrell Miller .25 .08
❑ 463 Jeff Kunkel .25 .08
❑ 464 Sherman Corbett .25 .08
❑ 465 Curtis Wilkerson .25 .08
❑ 466 Bud Black .25 .08
❑ 467 Cal Ripken 3.00 1.25
❑ 468 John Farrell .25 .08
❑ 469 Terry Kennedy .25 .08
❑ 470 Tom Candiotti .25 .08
❑ 471 Roberto Alomar 1.00 .40
❑ 472 Jeff M. Robinson .25 .08
❑ 473 Vance Law .25 .08
❑ 474 Randy Ready UER
(Strikeout total 136,
should be .25 .08
❑ 475 Walt Terrell .25 .08
❑ 476 Kelly Downs .25 .08
❑ 477 Johnny Paredes .25 .08
❑ 478 Shawn Hillegas .25 .08
❑ 479 Bob Brenly .25 .08
❑ 480 Otis Nixon .25 .08
❑ 481 Johnny Ray .25 .08
❑ 482 Geno Petralli .25 .08
❑ 483 Stu Cliburn .25 .08
❑ 484 Pete Incaviglia .25 .08
❑ 485 Brian Downing .40 .15
❑ 486 Jeff Stone .25 .08
❑ 487 Carmen Castillo .25 .08
❑ 488 Tom Niedenfuer .25 .08
❑ 489 Jay Bell .40 .15
❑ 490 Rick Schu .25 .08
❑ 491 Jeff Pico .25 .08
❑ 492 Mark Parent .25 .08
❑ 493 Eric King .25 .08
❑ 494 Al Nipper .25 .08
❑ 495 Andy Hawkins .25 .08
❑ 496 Daryl Boston .25 .08
❑ 497 Ernie Riles .25 .08
❑ 498 Pascual Perez .25 .08
❑ 499 Bill Long UER
(Games started total
70, should be .25 .08
❑ 500 Kirt Manwaring .25 .08
❑ 501 Chuck Crim .25 .08
❑ 502 Candy Maldonado .25 .08
❑ 503 Dennis Lamp .25 .08
❑ 504 Glenn Braggs .25 .08
❑ 505 Joe Price .25 .08
❑ 506 Ken Williams .25 .08
❑ 507 Bill Pecota .25 .08
❑ 508 Rey Quinones .25 .08
❑ 509 Jeff Bittiger .25 .08
❑ 510 Kevin Seitzer .25 .08
❑ 511 Steve Bedrosian .25 .08
❑ 512 Todd Worrell .25 .08
❑ 513 Chris James .25 .08
❑ 514 Jose Oquendo .25 .08
❑ 515 David Palmer .25 .08
❑ 516 John Smiley .25 .08
❑ 517 Dave Clark .25 .08
❑ 518 Mike Dunne .25 .08
❑ 519 Ron Washington .25 .08
❑ 520 Bob Kipper .25 .08
❑ 521 Lee Smith .40 .15
❑ 522 Juan Castillo .25 .08
❑ 523 Don Robinson .25 .08

❑ 524 Kevin Romine	.25	.08
❑ 525 Paul Molitor	.40	.15
❑ 526 Mark Langston	.25	.08
❑ 527 Donnie Hill	.25	.08
❑ 528 Larry Owen	.25	.08
❑ 529 Jerry Reed	.25	.08
❑ 530 Jack McDowell	.40	.15
❑ 531 Greg Mathews	.25	.08
❑ 532 John Russell	.25	.08
❑ 533 Dan Quisenberry	.25	.08
❑ 534 Greg Gross	.25	.08
❑ 535 Danny Cox	.25	.08
❑ 536 Terry Francona	.40	.15
❑ 537 Andy Van Slyke	.60	.25
❑ 538 Mel Hall	.25	.08
❑ 539 Jim Gott	.25	.08
❑ 540 Doug Jones	.25	.08
❑ 541 Craig Lefferts	.25	.08
❑ 542 Mike Boddicker	.25	.08
❑ 543 Greg Brock	.25	.08
❑ 544 Atlee Hammaker	.25	.08
❑ 545 Tom Bolton	.25	.08
❑ 546 Mike Macfarlane RC *	.50	.20
❑ 547 Rich Renteria	.25	.08
❑ 548 John Davis	.25	.08
❑ 549 Floyd Bannister	.25	.08
❑ 550 Mickey Brantley	.25	.08
❑ 551 Duane Ward	.25	.08
❑ 552 Dan Petry	.25	.08
❑ 553 Mickey Tettleton	.25	.08
❑ 554 Rick Leach	.25	.08
❑ 555 Mike Witt	.25	.08
❑ 556 Sid Bream	.25	.08
❑ 557 Bobby Witt	.25	.08
❑ 558 Tommy Herr	.25	.08
❑ 559 Randy Milligan	.25	.08
❑ 560 Jose Cecena	.25	.08
❑ 561 Mackey Sasser	.25	.08
❑ 562 Carney Lansford	.40	.15
❑ 563 Rick Aguilera	.25	.08
❑ 564 Ron Hassey	.25	.08
❑ 565 Dwight Gooden	.40	.15
❑ 566 Paul Assenmacher	.25	.08
❑ 567 Neil Allen	.25	.08
❑ 568 Jim Morrison	.25	.08
❑ 569 Mike Pagliarulo	.25	.08
❑ 570 Ted Simmons	.40	.15
❑ 571 Mark Thurmond	.25	.08
❑ 572 Fred McGriff	.60	.25
❑ 573 Wally Joyner	.40	.15
❑ 574 Jose Bautista RC	.25	.08
❑ 575 Kelly Gruber	.25	.08
❑ 576 Cecilio Guante	.25	.08
❑ 577 Mark Davidson	.25	.08
❑ 578 Bobby Bonilla UER	.40	.15
❑ 579 Mike Stanley	.25	.08
❑ 580 Gene Larkin	.25	.08
❑ 581 Stan Javier	.25	.08
❑ 582 Howard Johnson	.40	.15
❑ 583A Mike Gallego Rev Ng	1.00	.40
❑ 583B Mike Gallego COR	1.00	.40
❑ 584 David Cone	.40	.15
❑ 585 Doug Jennings	.25	.08
❑ 586 Charles Hudson	.25	.08
❑ 587 Dion James	.25	.08
❑ 588 Al Leiter	1.00	.40
❑ 589 Charlie Puleo	.25	.08
❑ 590 Roberto Kelly	.25	.08
❑ 591 Thad Bosley	.25	.08
❑ 592 Pete Stanicek	.25	.08
❑ 593 Pat Borders RC *	.50	.20
❑ 594 Bryan Harvey RC *	.50	.20
❑ 595 Jeff Ballard	.25	.08
❑ 596 Jeff Reardon	.40	.15
❑ 597 Doug Drabek	.25	.08
❑ 598 Edwin Correa	.25	.08
❑ 599 Keith Atherton	.25	.08
❑ 600 Dave LaPoint	.25	.08
❑ 601 Don Baylor	.40	.15
❑ 602 Tom Pagnozzi	.25	.08
❑ 603 Tim Flannery	.25	.08
❑ 604 Gene Walter	.25	.08
❑ 605 Dave Parker	.40	.15
❑ 606 Mike Diaz	.25	.08
❑ 607 Chris Gwynn	.25	.08
❑ 608 Odell Jones	.25	.08
❑ 609 Carlton Fisk	.60	.25
❑ 610 Jay Howell	.25	.08
❑ 611 Tim Crews	.25	.08
❑ 612 Keith Hernandez	.40	.15
❑ 613 Willie Fraser	.25	.08
❑ 614 Jim Eppard	.25	.08
❑ 615 Jeff Hamilton	.25	.08
❑ 616 Kurt Stillwell	.25	.08
❑ 617 Tom Browning	.25	.08
❑ 618 Jeff Montgomery	.25	.08
❑ 619 Jose Rijo	.40	.15
❑ 620 Jamie Quirk	.25	.08
❑ 621 Willie McGee	.40	.15
❑ 622 Mark Grant UER (Glove on wrong hand)	.25	.08
❑ 623 Bill Swift	.25	.08
❑ 624 Orlando Mercado	.25	.08
❑ 625 John Costello	.25	.08
❑ 626 Jose Gonzalez	.25	.08
❑ 627A Bill Schroeder ERR	.60	.25
❑ 627B Bill Schroeder COR	.60	.25
❑ 628A Fred Manrique ERR Guillen	.60	.25
❑ 628B Fred Manrique COR (Swinging bat on back)	.25	.08
❑ 629 Ricky Horton	.25	.08
❑ 630 Dan Plesac	.25	.08
❑ 631 Alfredo Griffin	.25	.08
❑ 632 Chuck Finley	.40	.15
❑ 633 Kirk Gibson	.40	.15
❑ 634 Randy Myers	.40	.15
❑ 635 Greg Minton	.25	.08
❑ 636A Herm Winningham ERR (W1nningham on back)	1.00	.40
❑ 636B Herm Winningham COR	.25	.08
❑ 637 Charlie Leibrandt	.25	.08
❑ 638 Tim Birtsas	.25	.08
❑ 639 Bill Buckner	.40	.15
❑ 640 Danny Jackson	.25	.08
❑ 641 Greg Booker	.25	.08
❑ 642 Jim Presley	.25	.08
❑ 643 Gene Nelson	.25	.08
❑ 644 Rod Booker	.25	.08
❑ 645 Dennis Rasmussen	.25	.08
❑ 646 Juan Nieves	.25	.08
❑ 647 Bobby Thigpen	.25	.08
❑ 648 Tim Belcher	.25	.08
❑ 649 Mike Young	.25	.08
❑ 650 Ivan Calderon	.25	.08
❑ 651 Oswald Peraza	.25	.08
❑ 652A Pat Sheridan ERR NPO	15.00	6.00
❑ 652B Pat Sheridan COR	.25	.08
❑ 653 Mike Morgan	.25	.08
❑ 654 Mike Heath	.25	.08
❑ 655 Jay Tibbs	.25	.08
❑ 656 Fernando Valenzuela	.40	.15
❑ 657 Lee Mazzilli	.40	.15
❑ 658 Frank Viola AL CY	.25	.08
❑ 659A Jose Canseco MVP	.60	.25
❑ 659B Jose Canseco MVP	.60	.25
❑ 660 Walt Weiss AL ROY	.25	.08
❑ 661 Orel Hershiser NL CY	.25	.08
❑ 662 Kirk Gibson NL MVP	.40	.15
❑ 663 Chris Sabo NL ROY	.40	.15
❑ 664 D.Eckersley ALCS MVP	.40	.15
❑ 665 O.Hershiser NLCS MVP	.40	.15
❑ 666 Kirk Gibson WS	1.00	.40
❑ 667 Orel Hershiser WS MVP	.25	.08
❑ 668 Wally Joyner TC California Angels	.25	.08
❑ 669 Nolan Ryan TC	1.25	.50
❑ 670 Jose Canseco TC	.60	.25
❑ 671 Fred McGriff TC	.40	.15
❑ 672 Dale Murphy TC Atlanta Braves	.40	.15
❑ 673 Paul Molitor TC	.25	.08
❑ 674 Ozzie Smith TC	1.00	.40
❑ 675 Ryne Sandberg TC	1.00	.40
❑ 676 Kirk Gibson TC	.40	.15
❑ 677 Andres Galarraga TC	.25	.08
❑ 678 Will Clark TC	.40	.15
❑ 679 Cory Snyder TC Cleveland Indians	.25	.08
❑ 680 Alvin Davis TC Seattle Mariners	.25	.08
❑ 681 Darryl Strawberry TC		
New York Mets	.25	.08
❑ 682 Cal Ripken TC	1.00	.40
❑ 683 Tony Gwynn TC	.60	.25
❑ 684 Mike Schmidt TC	1.00	.40
❑ 685 Andy Van Slyke TC Pittsburgh Pirates UER (96 Jun	.40	.15
❑ 686 Ruben Sierra TC	.25	.08
❑ 687 Wade Boggs TC	.40	.15
❑ 688 Eric Davis TC Cincinnati Reds	.25	.08
❑ 689 George Brett TC	1.00	.40
❑ 690 Alan Trammell TC Detroit Tigers	.25	.08
❑ 691 Frank Viola TC Minnesota Twins	.25	.08
❑ 692 Harold Baines TC Chicago White Sox	.25	.08
❑ 693 Don Mattingly TC	1.00	.40
❑ 694 Checklist 1-100	.25	.08
❑ 695 Checklist 101-200	.25	.08
❑ 696 Checklist 201-300	.25	.08
❑ 697 Checklist 301-400	.25	.08
❑ 698 Checklist UER	.25	.08
❑ 699 Checklist 501-600 UER		
(543 Greg Booker)	.25	.08
❑ 700 Checklist 601-700	.25	.08
❑ 701 Checklist 701-800	.25	.08
❑ 702 Jesse Barfield	.40	.15
❑ 703 Walt Terrell	.25	.08
❑ 704 Dickie Thon	.25	.08
❑ 705 Al Leiter	1.00	.40
❑ 706 Dave LaPoint	.25	.08
❑ 707 Charlie Hayes RC	.50	.20
❑ 708 Andy Hawkins	.25	.08
❑ 709 Mickey Hatcher	.25	.08
❑ 710 Lance McCullers	.25	.08
❑ 711 Ron Kittle	.25	.08
❑ 712 Bert Blyleven	.40	.15
❑ 713 Rick Dempsey	.25	.08
❑ 714 Ken Williams	.25	.08
❑ 715 Steve Rosenberg	.25	.08
❑ 716 Joe Skalski	.25	.08
❑ 717 Spike Owen	.25	.08
❑ 718 Todd Burns	.25	.08
❑ 719 Kevin Gross	.25	.08
❑ 720 Tommy Herr	.25	.08
❑ 721 Rob Ducey	.25	.08
❑ 722 Gary Green	.25	.08
❑ 723 Gregg Olson RC	.50	.20
❑ 724 Greg W.Harris RC	.25	.08
❑ 725 Craig Worthington	.25	.08
❑ 726 Thomas Howard RC	.25	.08
❑ 727 Dale Mohorcic	.25	.08
❑ 728 Rich Yett	.25	.08
❑ 729 Mel Hall	.25	.08
❑ 730 Floyd Youmans	.25	.08
❑ 731 Lonnie Smith	.25	.08
❑ 732 Wally Backman	.25	.08
❑ 733 Trevor Wilson RC	.25	.08
❑ 734 Jose Alvarez RC	.25	.08
❑ 735 Bob Milacki	.25	.08
❑ 736 Tom Gordon RC	1.50	.60
❑ 737 Wally Whitehurst RC	.25	.08
❑ 738 Mike Aldrete	.25	.08
❑ 739 Keith Miller	.25	.08
❑ 740 Randy Milligan	.25	.08
❑ 741 Jeff Parrett	.25	.08
❑ 742 Steve Finley RC	2.00	.75
❑ 743 Junior Felix RC	.25	.08
❑ 744 Pete Harnisch RC	.50	.20
❑ 745 Billy Spiers RC	.50	.20
❑ 746 Hensley Meulens RC	.25	.08
❑ 747 Juan Bell RC	.25	.08
❑ 748 Steve Sax	.25	.08
❑ 749 Phil Bradley	.25	.08
❑ 750 Rey Quinones	.25	.08
❑ 751 Tommy Gregg	.25	.08
❑ 752 Kevin Brown	1.00	.40
❑ 753 Derek Lilliquist RC	.25	.08
❑ 754 Todd Zeile RC	1.00	.40
❑ 755 Jim Abbott RC	2.00	.75
❑ 756 Ozzie Canseco	.25	.08
❑ 757 Nick Esasky	.25	.08
❑ 758 Mike Moore	.25	.08
❑ 759 Rob Murphy	.25	.08

- ❑ 760 Rick Mahler .25 .08
- ❑ 761 Fred Lynn .40 .15
- ❑ 762 Kevin Blankenship .25 .08
- ❑ 763 Eddie Murray 1.00 .40
- ❑ 764 Steve Searcy .25 .08
- ❑ 765 Jerome Walton RC .50 .20
- ❑ 766 Erik Hanson RC .50 .20
- ❑ 767 Bob Boone .40 .15
- ❑ 768 Edgar Martinez 1.00 .40
- ❑ 769 Jose DeJesus .25 .08
- ❑ 770 Greg Briley .25 .08
- ❑ 771 Steve Peters .25 .08
- ❑ 772 Rafael Palmeiro 1.00 .40
- ❑ 773 Jack Clark .40 .15
- ❑ 774 Nolan Ryan w/FB 4.00 1.50
- ❑ 775 Lance Parrish .40 .15
- ❑ 776 Joe Girardi RC 1.00 .40
- ❑ 777 Willie Randolph .40 .15
- ❑ 778 Mitch Williams .25 .08
- ❑ 779 Dennis Cook RC .50 .20
- ❑ 780 Dwight Smith RC .50 .20
- ❑ 781 Lenny Harris RC .50 .20
- ❑ 782 Torey Lovullo RC .25 .08
- ❑ 783 Norm Charlton RC .50 .20
- ❑ 784 Chris Brown .25 .08
- ❑ 785 Todd Benzinger .25 .08
- ❑ 786 Shane Rawley .25 .08
- ❑ 787 Omar Vizquel RC 3.00 1.25
- ❑ 788 LaVel Freeman .25 .08
- ❑ 789 Jeffrey Leonard .25 .08
- ❑ 790 Eddie Williams .25 .08
- ❑ 791 Jamie Moyer .40 .15
- ❑ 792 Bruce Hurst UER (Workd Series) .25 .08
- ❑ 793 Julio Franco .40 .15
- ❑ 794 Claudell Washington .25 .08
- ❑ 795 Jody Davis .25 .08
- ❑ 796 Oddibe McDowell .25 .08
- ❑ 797 Paul Kilgus .25 .08
- ❑ 798 Tracy Jones .25 .08
- ❑ 799 Steve Wilson .25 .08
- ❑ 800 Pete O'Brien .25 .08

1990 Upper Deck

Kevin Maas

- ❑ COMPLETE SET (800) 25.00 10.00
- ❑ COMP.FACT.SET (800) 25.00 10.00
- ❑ COMPLETE LO SET (700) 25.00 15.00
- ❑ COMPLETE HI SET (100) 5.00 2.00
- ❑ COMP.HI FACT.SET (100) 4.00 2.00
- ❑ 1 Star Rookie Checklist .10 .02
- ❑ 2 Randy Nosek RC .10 .02
- ❑ 3 Tom Drees RC .10 .02
- ❑ 4 Curt Young .10 .02
- ❑ 5 Devon White TC .10 .02
- ❑ 6 Luis Salazar .10 .02
- ❑ 7 Von Hayes TC .10 .02
- ❑ 8 Jose Bautista .10 .02
- ❑ 9 Marquis Grissom RC .50 .20
- ❑ 10 Orel Hershiser TC .10 .02
- ❑ 11 Rick Aguilera .20 .07
- ❑ 12 Benito Santiago TC .10 .02
- ❑ 13 Deion Sanders .50 .20
- ❑ 14 Marvell Wynne .10 .02
- ❑ 15 Dave West .10 .02
- ❑ 16 Bobby Bonilla TC .10 .02
- ❑ 17 Sammy Sosa RC 3.00 1.25
- ❑ 18 Steve Sax TC .10 .02
- ❑ 19 Jack Howell .10 .02
- ❑ 20 Mike Schmidt SPEC 1.00 .40
- ❑ 21 Robin Ventura .50 .20
- ❑ 22 Brian Meyer .10 .02
- ❑ 23 Blaine Beatty RC .10 .02
- ❑ 24 Ken Griffey Jr. TC .60 .25
- ❑ 25 Greg Vaughn .10 .02
- ❑ 26 Xavier Hernandez RC .10 .02
- ❑ 27 Jason Grimsley RC .10 .02
- ❑ 28 Eric Anthony RC .10 .02
- ❑ 29 Tim Raines TC UER .10 .02
- ❑ 30 David Wells .20 .07
- ❑ 31 Hal Morris .10 .02
- ❑ 32 Bo Jackson TC .20 .07
- ❑ 33 Kelly Mann RC .10 .02
- ❑ 34 Nolan Ryan SPEC 1.00 .40
- ❑ 35 Scott Service UER (Born Cincinatti on 7/27/67, s .10 .02
- ❑ 36 Mark McGwire TC .75 .30
- ❑ 37 Tino Martinez 1.00 .40
- ❑ 38 Chili Davis .20 .07
- ❑ 39 Scott Sanderson .10 .02
- ❑ 40 Kevin Mitchell TC .10 .02
- ❑ 41 Lou Whitaker TC .10 .02
- ❑ 42 Scott Coolbaugh RC .10 .02
- ❑ 43 Jose Cano RC .10 .02
- ❑ 44 Jose Vizcaino RC .25 .08
- ❑ 45 Bob Hamelin RC .25 .08
- ❑ 46 Jose Offerman RC .25 .08
- ❑ 47 Kevin Blankenship .10 .02
- ❑ 48 Kirby Puckett TC .30 .10
- ❑ 49 Tommy Greene UER RC .10 .02
- ❑ 50 Will Clark SPEC .20 .07
- ❑ 51 Rob Nelson .10 .02
- ❑ 52 Chris Hammond UER RC .10 .02
- ❑ 53 Joe Carter TC .10 .02
- ❑ 54A Ben McDonald ERR 2.00 .75
- ❑ 54B Ben McDonald COR RC .25 .08
- ❑ 55 Andy Benes UER .20 .07
- ❑ 56 John Olerud RC .75 .30
- ❑ 57 Roger Clemens TC .75 .30
- ❑ 58 Tony Armas .10 .02
- ❑ 59 George Canale RC .10 .02
- ❑ 60A Mickey Tettleton TC ERR 2.00 .75
- ❑ 60B Mickey Tettleton TC COR .10 .02
- ❑ 61 Mike Stanton RC .25 .08
- ❑ 62 Dwight Gooden TC .10 .02
- ❑ 63 Kent Mercker RC .25 .08
- ❑ 64 Francisco Cabrera .10 .02
- ❑ 65 Steve Avery .10 .02
- ❑ 66 Jose Canseco .30 .10
- ❑ 67 Matt Merullo .10 .02
- ❑ 68 Vince Coleman TC UER .10 .02
- ❑ 69 Ron Karkovice .10 .02
- ❑ 70 Kevin Maas RC .25 .08
- ❑ 71 Dennis Cook UER (Shown with righty glove on card .10 .02
- ❑ 72 Juan Gonzalez RC 1.50 .60
- ❑ 73 Andre Dawson TC .10 .02
- ❑ 74 Dean Palmer RC .25 .08
- ❑ 75 Bo Jackson SPEC .20 .07
- ❑ 76 Rob Richie RC .10 .02
- ❑ 77 Bobby Rose UER (Pickin, should be pick in) .10 .02
- ❑ 78 Brian DuBois UER RC .10 .02
- ❑ 79 Ozzie Guillen TC .10 .02
- ❑ 80 Gene Nelson .10 .02
- ❑ 81 Bob McClure .10 .02
- ❑ 82 Julio Franco TC .10 .02
- ❑ 83 Greg Minton .10 .02
- ❑ 84 John Smoltz TC UER .30 .10
- ❑ 85 Willie Fraser .10 .02
- ❑ 86 Neal Heaton .10 .02
- ❑ 87 Kevin Tapani RC .25 .08
- ❑ 88 Mike Scott TC .10 .02
- ❑ 89A Jim Gott ERR 2.00 .75
- ❑ 89B Jim Gott COR .10 .02
- ❑ 90 Lance Johnson .10 .02
- ❑ 91 Robin Yount TC UER .50 .20
- ❑ 92 Jeff Parrett .10 .02
- ❑ 93 Julio Machado RC .10 .02
- ❑ 94 Ron Jones .10 .02
- ❑ 95 George Bell TC .10 .02
- ❑ 96 Jerry Reuss .10 .02
- ❑ 97 Brian Fisher .10 .02
- ❑ 98 Kevin Ritz RC .10 .02
- ❑ 99 Barry Larkin TC .20 .07
- ❑ 100 Checklist 1-100 .10 .02
- ❑ 101 Gerald Perry .10 .02
- ❑ 102 Kevin Appier .20 .07
- ❑ 103 Julio Franco .20 .07
- ❑ 104 Craig Biggio .50 .20
- ❑ 105 Bo Jackson UER .50 .20
- ❑ 106 Junior Felix .10 .02
- ❑ 107 Mike Harkey .10 .02
- ❑ 108 Fred McGriff .50 .20
- ❑ 109 Rick Sutcliffe .20 .07
- ❑ 110 Pete O'Brien .10 .02
- ❑ 111 Kelly Gruber .10 .02
- ❑ 112 Dwight Evans .30 .10
- ❑ 113 Pat Borders .10 .02
- ❑ 114 Dwight Gooden .20 .07
- ❑ 115 Kevin Batiste RC .10 .02
- ❑ 116 Eric Davis .20 .07
- ❑ 117 Kevin Mitchell UER (Career HR total 99, should b .10 .02
- ❑ 118 Ron Oester .10 .02
- ❑ 119 Brett Butler .20 .07
- ❑ 120 Danny Jackson .10 .02
- ❑ 121 Tommy Gregg .10 .02
- ❑ 122 Ken Caminiti .20 .07
- ❑ 123 Kevin Brown .20 .07
- ❑ 124 George Brett 1.25 .50
- ❑ 125 Mike Scott .10 .02
- ❑ 126 Cory Snyder .10 .02
- ❑ 127 George Bell .10 .02
- ❑ 128 Mark Grace .30 .10
- ❑ 129 Devon White .20 .07
- ❑ 130 Tony Fernandez .10 .02
- ❑ 131 Don Aase .10 .02
- ❑ 132 Rance Mulliniks .10 .02
- ❑ 133 Marty Barrett .10 .02
- ❑ 134 Nelson Liriano .10 .02
- ❑ 135 Mark Carreon .10 .02
- ❑ 136 Candy Maldonado .10 .02
- ❑ 137 Tim Birtsas .10 .02
- ❑ 138 Tom Brookens .10 .02
- ❑ 139 John Franco .20 .07
- ❑ 140 Mike LaCoss .10 .02
- ❑ 141 Jeff Treadway .10 .02
- ❑ 142 Pat Tabler .10 .02
- ❑ 143 Darrell Evans .20 .07
- ❑ 144 Rafael Ramirez .10 .02
- ❑ 145 Oddibe McDowell UER (Misspelled Odibbe) .10 .02
- ❑ 146 Brian Downing .10 .02
- ❑ 147 Curt Wilkerson .10 .02
- ❑ 148 Ernie Whitt .10 .02
- ❑ 149 Bill Schroeder .10 .02
- ❑ 150 Domingo Ramos UER (Says throws right, but shows .10 .02
- ❑ 151 Rick Honeycutt .10 .02
- ❑ 152 Don Slaught .10 .02
- ❑ 153 Mitch Webster .10 .02
- ❑ 154 Tony Phillips .10 .02
- ❑ 155 Paul Kilgus .10 .02
- ❑ 156 Ken Griffey Jr. 1.50 .60
- ❑ 157 Gary Sheffield .50 .20
- ❑ 158 Wally Backman .10 .02
- ❑ 159 B.J. Surhoff .20 .07
- ❑ 160 Louie Meadows .10 .02
- ❑ 161 Paul O'Neill .30 .10
- ❑ 162 Jeff McKnight RC .10 .02
- ❑ 163 Alvaro Espinoza .10 .02
- ❑ 164 Scott Scudder .10 .02
- ❑ 165 Jeff Reed .10 .02
- ❑ 166 Gregg Jefferies .20 .07
- ❑ 167 Barry Larkin .30 .10
- ❑ 168 Gary Carter .20 .07
- ❑ 169 Robby Thompson .10 .02
- ❑ 170 Rolando Roomes .10 .02
- ❑ 171 Mark McGwire 1.50 .60
- ❑ 172 Steve Sax .10 .02
- ❑ 173 Mark Williamson .10 .02
- ❑ 174 Mitch Williams .10 .02
- ❑ 175 Brian Holton .10 .02
- ❑ 176 Rob Deer .10 .02
- ❑ 177 Tim Raines .20 .07

❑ 178 Mike Felder .10 .02
❑ 179 Harold Reynolds .20 .07
❑ 180 Terry Francona .20 .07
❑ 181 Chris Sabo .10 .02
❑ 182 Darryl Strawberry .20 .07
❑ 183 Willie Randolph .20 .07
❑ 184 Bill Ripken .10 .02
❑ 185 Mackey Sasser .10 .02
❑ 186 Todd Benzinger .10 .02
❑ 187 Kevin Elster UER (16 homers in 1989, should be 1 .10 .02
❑ 188 Jose Uribe .10 .02
❑ 189 Tom Browning .10 .02
❑ 190 Keith Miller .10 .02
❑ 191 Don Mattingly 1.25 .50
❑ 192 Dave Parker .20 .07
❑ 193 Roberto Kelly UER .10 .02
❑ 194 Phil Bradley .10 .02
❑ 195 Ron Hassey .10 .02
❑ 196 Gerald Young .10 .02
❑ 197 Hubie Brooks .10 .02
❑ 198 Bill Doran .10 .02
❑ 199 Al Newman .10 .02
❑ 200 Checklist 101-200 .10 .02
❑ 201 Terry Puhl .10 .02
❑ 202 Frank DiPino .10 .02
❑ 203 Jim Clancy .10 .02
❑ 204 Bob Ojeda .10 .02
❑ 205 Alex Trevino .10 .02
❑ 206 Dave Henderson .10 .02
❑ 207 Henry Cotto .10 .02
❑ 208 Rafael Belliard UER (Born 1961, not 1951) .10 .02
❑ 209 Stan Javier .10 .02
❑ 210 Jerry Reed .10 .02
❑ 211 Doug Dascenzo .10 .02
❑ 212 Andres Thomas .10 .02
❑ 213 Greg Maddux .75 .30
❑ 214 Mike Schooler .10 .02
❑ 215 Lonnie Smith .10 .02
❑ 216 Jose Rijo .10 .02
❑ 217 Greg Gagne .10 .02
❑ 218 Jim Gantner .10 .02
❑ 219 Allan Anderson .10 .02
❑ 220 Rick Mahler .10 .02
❑ 221 Jim Deshaies .10 .02
❑ 222 Keith Hernandez .20 .07
❑ 223 Vince Coleman .10 .02
❑ 224 David Cone .20 .07
❑ 225 Ozzie Smith .75 .30
❑ 226 Matt Nokes .10 .02
❑ 227 Barry Bonds 1.50 .60
❑ 228 Felix Jose .10 .02
❑ 229 Dennis Powell .10 .02
❑ 230 Mike Gallego .10 .02
❑ 231 Shawon Dunston UER ('89 stats are Andre Dawson's .10 .02
❑ 232 Ron Gant .20 .07
❑ 233 Omar Vizquel .50 .20
❑ 234 Derek Lilliquist .10 .02
❑ 235 Erik Hanson .10 .02
❑ 236 Kirby Puckett .50 .20
❑ 237 Bill Spiers .10 .02
❑ 238 Dan Gladden .10 .02
❑ 239 Bryan Clutterbuck .10 .02
❑ 240 John Moses .10 .02
❑ 241 Ron Darling .10 .02
❑ 242 Joe Magrane .10 .02
❑ 243 Dave Magadan .10 .02
❑ 244 Pedro Guerrero UER (Misspelled Guererro) .10 .02
❑ 245 Glenn Davis .10 .02
❑ 246 Terry Steinbach .10 .02
❑ 247 Fred Lynn .10 .02
❑ 248 Gary Redus .10 .02
❑ 249 Ken Williams .10 .02
❑ 250 Sid Bream .10 .02
❑ 251 Bob Welch UER (2587 career strike-outs, should .10 .02
❑ 252 Bill Buckner .10 .02
❑ 253 Carney Lansford .20 .07
❑ 254 Paul Molitor .20 .07
❑ 255 Jose DeJesus .10 .02
❑ 256 Orel Hershiser .20 .07
❑ 257 Tom Brunansky .10 .02
❑ 258 Mike Davis .10 .02
❑ 259 Jeff Ballard .10 .02
❑ 260 Scott Terry .10 .02
❑ 261 Sid Fernandez .10 .02
❑ 262 Mike Marshall .10 .02
❑ 263 Howard Johnson UER (192 SO, should be 592) .10 .02
❑ 264 Kirk Gibson UER .20 .07
❑ 265 Kevin McReynolds .10 .02
❑ 266 Cal Ripken 1.50 .60
❑ 267 Ozzie Guillen UER .20 .07
❑ 268 Jim Traber .10 .02
❑ 269 Bobby Thigpen UER (31 saves in 1989, should be 3 .10 .02
❑ 270 Joe Orsulak .10 .02
❑ 271 Bob Boone .20 .07
❑ 272 Dave Stewart UER .20 .07
❑ 273 Tim Wallach .10 .02
❑ 274 Luis Aquino UER (Says throws lefty, but shows hi .10 .02
❑ 275 Mike Moore .10 .02
❑ 276 Tony Pena .10 .02
❑ 277 Eddie Murray .50 .20
❑ 278 Milt Thompson .10 .02
❑ 279 Alejandro Pena .10 .02
❑ 280 Ken Dayley .10 .02
❑ 281 Carmelo Castillo .10 .02
❑ 282 Tom Henke .10 .02
❑ 283 Mickey Hatcher .10 .02
❑ 284 Roy Smith .10 .02
❑ 285 Manny Lee .10 .02
❑ 286 Dan Pasqua .10 .02
❑ 287 Larry Sheets .10 .02
❑ 288 Garry Templeton .10 .02
❑ 289 Eddie Williams .10 .02
❑ 290 Brady Anderson .20 .07
❑ 291 Spike Owen .10 .02
❑ 292 Storm Davis .10 .02
❑ 293 Chris Bosio .10 .02
❑ 294 Jim Eisenreich .10 .02
❑ 295 Don August .10 .02
❑ 296 Jeff Hamilton .10 .02
❑ 297 Mickey Tettleton .10 .02
❑ 298 Mike Scioscia .10 .02
❑ 299 Kevin Hickey .10 .02
❑ 300 Checklist 201-300 .10 .02
❑ 301 Shawn Abner .10 .02
❑ 302 Kevin Bass .10 .02
❑ 303 Bip Roberts .10 .02
❑ 304 Joe Girardi .30 .10
❑ 305 Danny Darwin .10 .02
❑ 306 Mike Heath .10 .02
❑ 307 Mike Macfarlane .10 .02
❑ 308 Ed Whitson .10 .02
❑ 309 Tracy Jones .10 .02
❑ 310 Scott Fletcher .10 .02
❑ 311 Darnell Coles .10 .02
❑ 312 Mike Brumley .10 .02
❑ 313 Bill Swift .10 .02
❑ 314 Charlie Hough .20 .07
❑ 315 Jim Presley .10 .02
❑ 316 Luis Polonia .10 .02
❑ 317 Mike Morgan .10 .02
❑ 318 Lee Guetterman .10 .02
❑ 319 Jose Oquendo .10 .02
❑ 320 Wayne Tolleson .10 .02
❑ 321 Jody Reed .10 .02
❑ 322 Damon Berryhill .10 .02
❑ 323 Roger Clemens 1.50 .60
❑ 324 Ryne Sandberg .75 .30
❑ 325 Benito Santiago UER .20 .07
❑ 326 Bret Saberhagen UER (1140 hits, should be 1240; .20 .07
❑ 327 Lou Whitaker .20 .07
❑ 328 Dave Gallagher .10 .02
❑ 329 Mike Pagliarulo .10 .02
❑ 330 Doyle Alexander .10 .02
❑ 331 Jeffrey Leonard .10 .02
❑ 332 Torey Lovullo .10 .02
❑ 333 Pete Incaviglia .10 .02
❑ 334 Rickey Henderson .50 .20
❑ 335 Rafael Palmeiro .30 .10
❑ 336 Ken Hill .20 .07
❑ 337 Dave Winfield UER .20 .07
❑ 338 Alfredo Griffin .10 .02
❑ 339 Andy Hawkins .10 .02
❑ 340 Ted Power .10 .02
❑ 341 Steve Wilson .10 .02
❑ 342 Jack Clark UER (916 BB, should be 1006; 1142 SO, .20 .07
❑ 343 Ellis Burks .30 .10
❑ 344 Tony Gwynn .60 .25
❑ 345 Jerome Walton UER (Total At Bats 476, should be .10 .02
❑ 346 Roberto Alomar .30 .10
❑ 347 Carlos Martinez UER (Born 8/11/64, should be 8/1 .10 .02
❑ 348 Chet Lemon .10 .02
❑ 349 Willie Wilson .10 .02
❑ 350 Greg Walker .10 .02
❑ 351 Tom Bolton .10 .02
❑ 352 German Gonzalez .10 .02
❑ 353 Harold Baines .20 .07
❑ 354 Mike Greenwell .10 .02
❑ 355 Ruben Sierra .20 .07
❑ 356 Andres Galarraga .20 .07
❑ 357 Andre Dawson .20 .07
❑ 358 Jeff Brantley .10 .02
❑ 359 Mike Bielecki .10 .02
❑ 360 Ken Oberkfell .10 .02
❑ 361 Kurt Stillwell .10 .02
❑ 362 Brian Holman .10 .02
❑ 363 Kevin Seitzer UER (Career triples total does not .10 .02
❑ 364 Alvin Davis .10 .02
❑ 365 Tom Gordon .20 .07
❑ 366 Bobby Bonilla UER (Two steals in 1987, should be .20 .07
❑ 367 Carlton Fisk .30 .10
❑ 368 Steve Carter UER (Charlotesville) .10 .02
❑ 369 Joel Skinner .10 .02
❑ 370 John Cangelosi .10 .02
❑ 371 Cecil Espy .10 .02
❑ 372 Gary Wayne .10 .02
❑ 373 Jim Rice .20 .07
❑ 374 Mike Dyer RC .10 .02
❑ 375 Joe Carter .20 .07
❑ 376 Dwight Smith .10 .02
❑ 377 John Wetteland .50 .20
❑ 378 Earnie Riles .10 .02
❑ 379 Otis Nixon .10 .02
❑ 380 Vance Law .10 .02
❑ 381 Dave Bergman .10 .02
❑ 382 Frank White .20 .07
❑ 383 Scott Bradley .10 .02
❑ 384 Israel Sanchez UER (Totals don't include '89 s .10 .02
❑ 385 Gary Pettis .10 .02
❑ 386 Donn Pall .10 .02
❑ 387 John Smiley .10 .02
❑ 388 Tom Candiotti .10 .02
❑ 389 Junior Ortiz .10 .02
❑ 390 Steve Lyons .10 .02
❑ 391 Brian Harper .10 .02
❑ 392 Fred Manrique .10 .02
❑ 393 Lee Smith .20 .07
❑ 394 Jeff Kunkel .10 .02
❑ 395 Claudell Washington .10 .02
❑ 396 John Tudor .10 .02
❑ 397 Terry Kennedy UER (Career totals all wrong) .10 .02
❑ 398 Lloyd McClendon .10 .02
❑ 399 Craig Lefferts .10 .02
❑ 400 Checklist 301-400 .10 .02
❑ 401 Keith Moreland .10 .02
❑ 402 Rich Gedman .10 .02
❑ 403 Jeff D. Robinson .10 .02
❑ 404 Randy Ready .10 .02
❑ 405 Rick Cerone .10 .02

❑ 406 Jeff Blauser .10 .02
❑ 407 Larry Andersen .10 .02
❑ 408 Joe Boever .10 .02
❑ 409 Felix Fermin .10 .02
❑ 410 Glenn Wilson .10 .02
❑ 411 Rex Hudler .10 .02
❑ 412 Mark Grant .10 .02
❑ 413 Dennis Martinez .20 .07
❑ 414 Darrin Jackson .10 .02
❑ 415 Mike Aldrete .10 .02
❑ 416 Roger McDowell .10 .02
❑ 417 Jeff Reardon .20 .07
❑ 418 Darren Daulton .20 .07
❑ 419 Tim Laudner .10 .02
❑ 420 Don Carman .10 .02
❑ 421 Lloyd Moseby .10 .02
❑ 422 Doug Drabek .10 .02
❑ 423 Lenny Harris UER
(Walks 2 in '89,
should be 20) .10 .02
❑ 424 Jose Lind .10 .02
❑ 425 Dave Wayne Johnson RC .10 .02
❑ 426 Jerry Browne .10 .02
❑ 427 Eric Yelding RC .10 .02
❑ 428 Brad Komminsk .10 .02
❑ 429 Jody Davis .10 .02
❑ 430 Mariano Duncan .10 .02
❑ 431 Mark Davis .10 .02
❑ 432 Nelson Santovenia .10 .02
❑ 433 Bruce Hurst .10 .02
❑ 434 Jeff Huson RC .10 .02
❑ 435 Chris James .10 .02
❑ 436 Mark Guthrie RC .10 .02
❑ 437 Charlie Hayes .10 .02
❑ 438 Shane Rawley .10 .02
❑ 439 Dickie Thon .10 .02
❑ 440 Juan Berenguer .10 .02
❑ 441 Kevin Romine .10 .02
❑ 442 Bill Landrum .10 .02
❑ 443 Todd Frohwirth .10 .02
❑ 444 Craig Worthington .10 .02
❑ 445 Fernando Valenzuela .20 .07
❑ 446 Albert Belle .50 .20
❑ 447 Ed Whited UER RC .10 .02
❑ 448 Dave Smith .10 .02
❑ 449 Dave Clark .10 .02
❑ 450 Juan Agosto .10 .02
❑ 451 Dave Valle .10 .02
❑ 452 Kent Hrbek .20 .07
❑ 453 Von Hayes .10 .02
❑ 454 Gary Gaetti .20 .07
❑ 455 Greg Briley .10 .02
❑ 456 Glenn Braggs .10 .02
❑ 457 Kirt Manwaring .10 .02
❑ 458 Mel Hall .10 .02
❑ 459 Brook Jacoby .10 .02
❑ 460 Pat Sheridan .10 .02
❑ 461 Rob Murphy .10 .02
❑ 462 Jimmy Key .20 .07
❑ 463 Nick Esasky .10 .02
❑ 464 Rob Ducey .10 .02
❑ 465 Carlos Quintana UER
(Internatinoal) .10 .02
❑ 466 Larry Walker RC 1.50 .60
❑ 467 Todd Worrell .10 .02
❑ 468 Kevin Gross .10 .02
❑ 469 Terry Pendleton .20 .07
❑ 470 Dave Martinez .10 .02
❑ 471 Gene Larkin .10 .02
❑ 472 Len Dykstra UER .20 .07
❑ 473 Barry Lyons .10 .02
❑ 474 Terry Mulholland .10 .02
❑ 475 Chip Hale RC .10 .02
❑ 476 Jesse Barfield .10 .02
❑ 477 Dan Plesac .10 .02
❑ 478A Scott Garrelts ERR 2.00 .75
❑ 478B Scott Garrelts COR .10 .02
❑ 479 Dave Righetti .10 .02
❑ 480 Gus Polidor UER
(Wearing 14 on front,
but 10 on .10 .02
❑ 481 Mookie Wilson .20 .07
❑ 482 Luis Rivera .10 .02
❑ 483 Mike Flanagan .10 .02
❑ 484 Dennis Boyd .10 .02
❑ 485 John Cerutti .10 .02
❑ 486 John Costello .10 .02
❑ 487 Pascual Perez .10 .02
❑ 488 Tommy Herr .10 .02
❑ 489 Tom Foley .10 .02
❑ 490 Curt Ford .10 .02
❑ 491 Steve Lake .10 .02
❑ 492 Tim Teufel .10 .02
❑ 493 Randy Bush .10 .02
❑ 494 Mike Jackson .10 .02
❑ 495 Steve Jeltz .10 .02
❑ 496 Paul Gibson .10 .02
❑ 497 Steve Balboni .10 .02
❑ 498 Bud Black .10 .02
❑ 499 Dale Sveum .10 .02
❑ 500 Checklist 401-500 .10 .02
❑ 501 Tim Jones .10 .02
❑ 502 Mark Portugal .10 .02
❑ 503 Ivan Calderon .10 .02
❑ 504 Rick Rhoden .10 .02
❑ 505 Willie McGee .20 .07
❑ 506 Kirk McCaskill .10 .02
❑ 507 Dave LaPoint .10 .02
❑ 508 Jay Howell .10 .02
❑ 509 Johnny Ray .10 .02
❑ 510 Dave Anderson .10 .02
❑ 511 Chuck Crim .10 .02
❑ 512 Joe Hesketh .10 .02
❑ 513 Dennis Eckersley .20 .07
❑ 514 Greg Brock .10 .02
❑ 515 Tim Burke .10 .02
❑ 516 Frank Tanana .10 .02
❑ 517 Jay Bell .20 .07
❑ 518 Guillermo Hernandez .10 .02
❑ 519 Randy Kramer UER
(Codiroli misspelled
as Codorol .10 .02
❑ 520 Charles Hudson .10 .02
❑ 521 Jim Corsi
(Word %%originally~ is
misspelled on b .10 .02
❑ 522 Steve Rosenberg .10 .02
❑ 523 Cris Carpenter .10 .02
❑ 524 Matt Winters RC .10 .02
❑ 525 Melido Perez .10 .02
❑ 526 Chris Gwynn UER
(Albeguergue) .10 .02
❑ 527 Bert Blyleven UER
(Games career total is
wrong, .20 .07
❑ 528 Chuck Cary .10 .02
❑ 529 Daryl Boston .10 .02
❑ 530 Dale Mohorcic .10 .02
❑ 531 Geronimo Berroa .10 .02
❑ 532 Edgar Martinez .30 .10
❑ 533 Dale Murphy .30 .10
❑ 534 Jay Buhner .20 .07
❑ 535 John Smoltz .50 .20
❑ 536 Andy Van Slyke .30 .10
❑ 537 Mike Henneman .10 .02
❑ 538 Miguel Garcia .10 .02
❑ 539 Frank Williams .10 .02
❑ 540 R.J. Reynolds .10 .02
❑ 541 Shawn Hillegas .10 .02
❑ 542 Walt Weiss .10 .02
❑ 543 Greg Hibbard RC .10 .02
❑ 544 Nolan Ryan 2.00 .75
❑ 545 Todd Zeile .20 .07
❑ 546 Hensley Meulens .10 .02
❑ 547 Tim Belcher .10 .02
❑ 548 Mike Witt .10 .02
❑ 549 Greg Cadaret UER
(Aquiring, should
be Acquiring) .10 .02
❑ 550 Franklin Stubbs .10 .02
❑ 551 Tony Castillo .10 .02
❑ 552 Jeff M. Robinson .10 .02
❑ 553 Steve Olin RC .25 .08
❑ 554 Alan Trammell .20 .07
❑ 555 Wade Boggs 4X .30 .10
❑ 556 Will Clark .30 .10
❑ 557 Jeff King .10 .02
❑ 558 Mike Fitzgerald .10 .02
❑ 559 Ken Howell .10 .02
❑ 560 Bob Kipper .10 .02
❑ 561 Scott Bankhead .10 .02
❑ 562A Jeff Innis ERR 2.00 .75
❑ 562B Jeff Innis COR RC .10 .02
❑ 563 Randy Johnson 1.00 .40
❑ 564 Wally Whitehurst .10 .02
❑ 565 Gene Harris .10 .02
❑ 566 Norm Charlton .10 .02
❑ 567 Robin Yount UER .75 .30
❑ 568 Joe Oliver .10 .02
❑ 569 Mark Parent .10 .02
❑ 570 John Farrell UER
(Loss total added wrong) .10 .02
❑ 571 Tom Glavine .30 .10
❑ 572 Rod Nichols .10 .02
❑ 573 Jack Morris .20 .07
❑ 574 Greg Swindell .10 .02
❑ 575 Steve Searcy .10 .02
❑ 576 Ricky Jordan .10 .02
❑ 577 Matt Williams .20 .07
❑ 578 Mike LaValliere .10 .02
❑ 579 Bryn Smith .10 .02
❑ 580 Bruce Ruffin .10 .02
❑ 581 Randy Myers .20 .07
❑ 582 Rick Wrona .10 .02
❑ 583 Juan Samuel .10 .02
❑ 584 Les Lancaster .10 .02
❑ 585 Jeff Musselman .10 .02
❑ 586 Rob Dibble .20 .07
❑ 587 Eric Show .10 .02
❑ 588 Jesse Orosco .10 .02
❑ 589 Herm Winningham .10 .02
❑ 590 Andy Allanson .10 .02
❑ 591 Dion James .10 .02
❑ 592 Carmelo Martinez .10 .02
❑ 593 Luis Quinones .10 .02
❑ 594 Dennis Rasmussen .10 .02
❑ 595 Rich Yett .10 .02
❑ 596 Bob Walk .10 .02
❑ 597A Andy McGaffigan ERR
(Photo actually
Rich Thompso 2.00 .75
❑ 597B Andy McGaffigan COR .10 .02
❑ 598 Billy Hatcher .10 .02
❑ 599 Bob Knepper .10 .02
❑ 600 Checklist 501-600 UER
(599 Bob Kneppers) .10 .02
❑ 601 Joey Cora .20 .07
❑ 602 Steve Finley .20 .07
❑ 603 Kal Daniels UER
(12 hits in '87, should
be 123; .10 .02
❑ 604 Gregg Olson .20 .07
❑ 605 Dave Stieb .20 .07
❑ 606 Kenny Rogers .20 .07
❑ 607 Zane Smith .10 .02
❑ 608 Bob Geren UER
(Origionally) .10 .02
❑ 609 Chad Kreuter .10 .02
❑ 610 Mike Smithson .10 .02
❑ 611 Jeff Wetherby RC .10 .02
❑ 612 Gary Mielke RC .10 .02
❑ 613 Pete Smith .10 .02
❑ 614 Jack Daugherty RC .10 .02
❑ 615 Lance McCullers .10 .02
❑ 616 Don Robinson .10 .02
❑ 617 Jose Guzman .10 .02
❑ 618 Steve Bedrosian .10 .02
❑ 619 Jamie Moyer .20 .07
❑ 620 Atlee Hammaker .10 .02
❑ 621 Rick Luecken RC .10 .02
❑ 622 Greg W. Harris .10 .02
❑ 623 Pete Harnisch .10 .02
❑ 624 Jerald Clark .10 .02
❑ 625 Jack McDowell .10 .02
❑ 626 Frank Viola .10 .02
❑ 627 Teddy Higuera .10 .02
❑ 628 Marty Pevey RC .10 .02
❑ 629 Bill Wegman .10 .02
❑ 630 Eric Plunk .10 .02
❑ 631 Drew Hall .10 .02
❑ 632 Doug Jones .10 .02
❑ 633 Geno Petralli UER
(Sacremento) .10 .02
❑ 634 Jose Alvarez .10 .02
❑ 635 Bob Milacki .10 .02
❑ 636 Bobby Witt .10 .02
❑ 637 Trevor Wilson .10 .02
❑ 638 Jeff Russell UER

Card		
(Shutout stats wrong)	.10	.02
❑ 639 Mike Krukow	.10	.02
❑ 640 Rick Leach	.10	.02
❑ 641 Dave Schmidt	.10	.02
❑ 642 Terry Leach	.10	.02
❑ 643 Calvin Schiraldi	.10	.02
❑ 644 Bob Melvin	.10	.02
❑ 645 Jim Abbott	.30	.10
❑ 646 Jaime Navarro	.10	.02
❑ 647 Mark Langston UER (Several errors in stats total	.10	.02
❑ 648 Juan Nieves	.10	.02
❑ 649 Damaso Garcia	.10	.02
❑ 650 Charlie O'Brien	.10	.02
❑ 651 Eric King	.10	.02
❑ 652 Mike Boddicker	.10	.02
❑ 653 Duane Ward	.10	.02
❑ 654 Bob Stanley	.10	.02
❑ 655 Sandy Alomar Jr.	.20	.07
❑ 656 Danny Tartabull UER	.10	.02
❑ 657 Randy McCament RC	.10	.02
❑ 658 Charlie Leibrandt	.10	.02
❑ 659 Dan Quisenberry	.10	.02
❑ 660 Paul Assenmacher	.10	.02
❑ 661 Walt Terrell	.10	.02
❑ 662 Tim Leary	.10	.02
❑ 663 Randy Milligan	.10	.02
❑ 664 Bo Diaz	.10	.02
❑ 665 Mark Lemke UER (Richmond misspelled as Richomond	.10	.02
❑ 666 Jose Gonzalez	.10	.02
❑ 667 Chuck Finley UER (Born 11/16/62, should be 11/26	.20	.07
❑ 668 John Kruk	.20	.07
❑ 669 Dick Schofield	.10	.02
❑ 670 Tim Crews	.10	.02
❑ 671 John Dopson	.10	.02
❑ 672 John Orton RC	.10	.02
❑ 673 Eric Hetzel	.10	.02
❑ 674 Lance Parrish	.10	.02
❑ 675 Ramon Martinez	.10	.02
❑ 676 Mark Gubicza	.10	.02
❑ 677 Greg Litton	.10	.02
❑ 678 Greg Mathews	.10	.02
❑ 679 Dave Dravecky	.20	.07
❑ 680 Steve Farr	.10	.02
❑ 681 Mike Devereaux	.10	.02
❑ 682 Ken Griffey Sr.	.20	.07
❑ 683A Jamie Weston ERR	2.00	.75
❑ 683B Mickey Weston COR RC	.10	.02
❑ 684 Jack Armstrong	.10	.02
❑ 685 Steve Buechele	.10	.02
❑ 686 Bryan Harvey	.10	.02
❑ 687 Lance Blankenship	.10	.02
❑ 688 Dante Bichette	.20	.07
❑ 689 Todd Burns	.10	.02
❑ 690 Dan Petry	.10	.02
❑ 691 Kent Anderson	.10	.02
❑ 692 Todd Stottlemyre	.20	.07
❑ 693 Wally Joyner UER (Several stats errors)	.20	.07
❑ 694 Mike Rochford	.10	.02
❑ 695 Floyd Bannister	.10	.02
❑ 696 Rick Reuschel	.10	.02
❑ 697 Jose DeLeon	.10	.02
❑ 698 Jeff Montgomery	.20	.07
❑ 699 Kelly Downs	.10	.02
❑ 700A CL 601-700 ERR	2.00	.75
❑ 700B Checklist 601-700 (683 Mickey Weston)	.10	.02
❑ 701 Jim Gott	.10	.02
❑ 702 L.Walker/Grissom/DeSh	.50	.20
❑ 702A Mike Witt Black	10.00	5.00
❑ 703 Alejandro Pena	.10	.02
❑ 704 Willie Randolph	.20	.07
❑ 705 Tim Leary	.10	.02
❑ 706 Chuck McElroy RC	.10	.02
❑ 707 Gerald Perry	.10	.02
❑ 708 Tom Brunansky	.10	.02
❑ 709 John Franco	.20	.07
❑ 710 Mark Davis	.10	.02
❑ 711 David Justice RC	.75	.30
❑ 712 Storm Davis	.10	.02
❑ 713 Scott Ruskin RC	.10	.02
❑ 714 Glenn Braggs	.10	.02
❑ 715 Kevin Bearse RC	.10	.02
❑ 716 Jose Nunez	.10	.02
❑ 717 Tim Layana RC	.10	.02
❑ 718 Greg Myers	.10	.02
❑ 719 Pete O'Brien	.10	.02
❑ 720 John Candelaria	.10	.02
❑ 721 Craig Grebeck RC	.10	.02
❑ 722 Shawn Boskie RC	.10	.02
❑ 723 Jim Leyritz RC	.25	.08
❑ 724 Bill Sampen RC	.10	.02
❑ 725 Scott Radinsky RC	.10	.02
❑ 726 Todd Hundley RC	.25	.08
❑ 727 Scott Hemond RC	.10	.02
❑ 728 Lenny Webster RC	.10	.02
❑ 729 Jeff Reardon	.20	.07
❑ 730 Mitch Webster	.10	.02
❑ 731 Brian Bohanon RC	.10	.02
❑ 732 Rick Parker RC	.10	.02
❑ 733 Terry Shumpert RC	.10	.02
❑ 734A Nolan Ryan 6th	3.00	1.25
❑ 734B Nolan Ryan 6th/300	1.00	.40
❑ 735 John Burkett	.10	.02
❑ 736 Derrick May RC	.10	.02
❑ 737 Carlos Baerga RC	.25	.08
❑ 738 Greg Smith RC	.10	.02
❑ 739 Scott Sanderson	.10	.02
❑ 740 Joe Kraemer RC	.10	.02
❑ 741 Hector Villanueva RC	.10	.02
❑ 742 Mike Fetters RC	.25	.08
❑ 743 Mark Gardner RC	.10	.02
❑ 744 Matt Nokes	.10	.02
❑ 745 Dave Winfield	.20	.07
❑ 746 Delino DeShields RC	.25	.08
❑ 747 Dann Howitt RC	.10	.02
❑ 748 Tony Pena	.10	.02
❑ 749 Oil Can Boyd	.10	.02
❑ 750 Mike Benjamin RC	.10	.02
❑ 751 Alex Cole RC	.10	.02
❑ 752 Eric Gunderson RC	.10	.02
❑ 753 Howard Farmer RC	.10	.02
❑ 754 Joe Carter	.20	.07
❑ 755 Ray Lankford RC	.50	.20
❑ 756 Sandy Alomar Jr.	.20	.07
❑ 757 Alex Sanchez	.10	.02
❑ 758 Nick Esasky	.10	.02
❑ 759 Stan Belinda RC	.10	.02
❑ 760 Jim Presley	.10	.02
❑ 761 Gary DiSarcina RC	.25	.08
❑ 762 Wayne Edwards RC	.10	.02
❑ 763 Pat Combs	.10	.02
❑ 764 Mickey Pina RC	.10	.02
❑ 765 Wilson Alvarez RC	.25	.08
❑ 766 Dave Parker	.20	.07
❑ 767 Mike Blowers RC	.10	.02
❑ 768 Tony Phillips	.10	.02
❑ 769 Pascual Perez	.10	.02
❑ 770 Gary Pettis	.10	.02
❑ 771 Fred Lynn	.10	.02
❑ 772 Mel Rojas RC	.10	.02
❑ 773 David Segui RC	.50	.20
❑ 774 Gary Carter	.20	.07
❑ 775 Rafael Valdez RC	.10	.02
❑ 776 Glenallen Hill	.10	.02
❑ 777 Keith Hernandez	.20	.07
❑ 778 Billy Hatcher	.10	.02
❑ 779 Marty Clary	.10	.02
❑ 780 Candy Maldonado	.10	.02
❑ 781 Mike Marshall	.10	.02
❑ 782 Billy Joe Robidoux	.10	.02
❑ 783 Mark Langston	.10	.02
❑ 784 Paul Sorrento RC	.25	.08
❑ 785 Dave Hollins RC	.25	.08
❑ 786 Cecil Fielder	.20	.07
❑ 787 Matt Young	.10	.02
❑ 788 Jeff Huson	.10	.02
❑ 789 Lloyd Moseby	.10	.02
❑ 790 Ron Kittle	.10	.02
❑ 791 Hubie Brooks	.10	.02
❑ 792 Craig Lefferts	.10	.02
❑ 793 Kevin Bass	.10	.02
❑ 794 Bryn Smith	.10	.02
❑ 795 Juan Samuel	.10	.02
❑ 796 Sam Horn	.10	.02
❑ 797 Randy Myers	.20	.07
❑ 798 Chris James	.10	.02
❑ 799 Bill Gullickson	.10	.02
❑ 800 Checklist 701-800	.10	.02

1991 Upper Deck

Card		
❑ COMPLETE SET (800)	15.00	6.00
❑ COMP.FACT.SET (800)	20.00	8.00
❑ COMPLETE LO SET (700)	15.00	6.00
❑ COMPLETE HI SET (100)	5.00	2.00
❑ 1 Star Rookie Checklist	.05	.01
❑ 2 Phil Plantier RC	.10	.02
❑ 3 D.J. Dozier	.05	.01
❑ 4 Dave Hansen	.05	.01
❑ 5 Mo Vaughn	.10	.02
❑ 6 Leo Gomez	.05	.01
❑ 7 Scott Aldred	.05	.01
❑ 8 Scott Chiamparino	.05	.01
❑ 9 Lance Dickson RC	.10	.02
❑ 10 Sean Berry RC	.10	.02
❑ 11 Bernie Williams	.25	.08
❑ 12 Brian Barnes UER RC	.10	.02
❑ 13 Narciso Elvira RC	.05	.01
❑ 14 Mike Gardiner RC	.05	.01
❑ 15 Greg Colbrunn RC	.25	.08
❑ 16 Bernard Gilkey	.05	.01
❑ 17 Mark Lewis	.05	.01
❑ 18 Mickey Morandini	.05	.01
❑ 19 Charles Nagy	.05	.01
❑ 20 Geronimo Pena	.05	.01
❑ 21 Henry Rodriguez RC	.25	.08
❑ 22 Scott Cooper FUDC	.05	.01
❑ 23 Andujar Cedeno UER	.05	.01
❑ 24 Eric Karros RC	.75	.30
❑ 25 Steve Decker UER RC	.05	.01
❑ 26 Kevin Belcher RC	.05	.01
❑ 27 Jeff Conine RC	.50	.20
❑ 28 Dave Stewart TC	.05	.01
❑ 29 Carlton Fisk TC	.10	.02
❑ 30 Rafael Palmeiro TC	.10	.02
❑ 31 Chuck Finley TC	.05	.01
❑ 32 Harold Reynolds TC	.05	.01
❑ 33 Bret Saberhagen TC	.05	.01
❑ 34 Gary Gaetti TC	.05	.01
❑ 35 Scott Leius	.05	.01
❑ 36 Neal Heaton	.05	.01
❑ 37 Terry Lee RC	.05	.01
❑ 38 Gary Redus	.05	.01
❑ 39 Barry Jones	.05	.01
❑ 40 Chuck Knoblauch	.10	.02
❑ 41 Larry Andersen	.05	.01
❑ 42 Darryl Hamilton	.05	.01
❑ 43 Mike Greenwell TC	.05	.01
❑ 44 Kelly Gruber TC	.05	.01
❑ 45 Jack Morris TC	.05	.01
❑ 46 Sandy Alomar Jr. TC	.05	.01
❑ 47 Gregg Olson TC	.05	.01
❑ 48 Dave Parker TC	.05	.01
❑ 49 Roberto Kelly TC	.05	.01
❑ 50 Top Prospect Checklist	.05	.01
❑ 51 Kyle Abbott	.05	.01
❑ 52 Jeff Juden	.05	.01
❑ 53 Todd Van Poppel UER RC	.25	.08
❑ 54 Steve Karsay RC	.25	.08
❑ 55 Chipper Jones RC	4.00	1.50
❑ 56 Chris Johnson UER RC	.10	.02
❑ 57 John Ericks	.05	.01
❑ 58 Gary Scott RC	.05	.01
❑ 59 Kiki Jones	.05	.01

Card		
❑ 60 Wil Cordero RC	.10	.02
❑ 61 Royce Clayton	.05	.01
❑ 62 Tim Costo RC	.10	.02
❑ 63 Roger Salkeld FUDC	.05	.01
❑ 64 Brook Fordyce RC	.25	.08
❑ 65 Mike Mussina RC	2.00	.75
❑ 66 Dave Staton RC	.10	.02
❑ 67 Mike Lieberthal RC	.50	.20
❑ 68 Kurt Miller RC	.05	.01
❑ 69 Dan Peltier RC	.10	.02
❑ 70 Greg Blosser FUDC	.05	.01
❑ 71 Reggie Sanders RC	.75	.30
❑ 72 Brent Mayne	.05	.01
❑ 73 Rico Brogna	.05	.01
❑ 74 Willie Banks	.05	.01
❑ 75 Len Brutcher RC	.05	.01
❑ 76 Pat Kelly RC	.10	.02
❑ 77 Chris Sabo TC	.05	.01
❑ 78 Ramon Martinez TC	.05	.01
❑ 79 Matt Williams TC	.05	.01
❑ 80 Roberto Alomar TC	.10	.02
❑ 81 Glenn Davis TC	.05	.01
❑ 82 Ron Gant TC	.05	.01
❑ 83 Cecil Fielder's Feat	.05	.01
❑ 84 Orlando Merced RC	.10	.02
❑ 85 Domingo Ramos	.05	.01
❑ 86 Tom Bolton	.05	.01
❑ 87 Andres Santana	.05	.01
❑ 88 John Dopson	.05	.01
❑ 89 Kenny Williams	.05	.01
❑ 90 Marty Barrett	.05	.01
❑ 91 Tom Pagnozzi	.05	.01
❑ 92 Carmelo Martinez	.05	.01
❑ 93 Bobby Thigpen SAVE	.05	.01
❑ 94 Barry Bonds TC	.50	.20
❑ 95 Gregg Jefferies TC	.05	.01
❑ 96 Tim Wallach TC	.05	.01
❑ 97 Len Dykstra TC	.05	.01
❑ 98 Pedro Guerrero TC	.05	.01
❑ 99 Mark Grace TC	.10	.02
❑ 100 Checklist 1-100	.05	.01
❑ 101 Kevin Elster	.05	.01
❑ 102 Tom Brookens	.05	.01
❑ 103 Mackey Sasser	.05	.01
❑ 104 Felix Fermin	.05	.01
❑ 105 Kevin McReynolds	.05	.01
❑ 106 Dave Stieb	.05	.01
❑ 107 Jeffrey Leonard	.05	.01
❑ 108 Dave Henderson	.05	.01
❑ 109 Sid Bream	.05	.01
❑ 110 Henry Cotto	.05	.01
❑ 111 Shawon Dunston	.05	.01
❑ 112 Mariano Duncan	.05	.01
❑ 113 Joe Girardi	.05	.01
❑ 114 Billy Hatcher	.05	.01
❑ 115 Greg Maddux	.40	.15
❑ 116 Jerry Browne	.05	.01
❑ 117 Juan Samuel	.05	.01
❑ 118 Steve Olin	.05	.01
❑ 119 Alfredo Griffin	.05	.01
❑ 120 Mitch Webster	.05	.01
❑ 121 Joel Skinner	.05	.01
❑ 122 Frank Viola	.10	.02
❑ 123 Cory Snyder	.05	.01
❑ 124 Howard Johnson	.05	.01
❑ 125 Carlos Baerga	.05	.01
❑ 126 Tony Fernandez	.05	.01
❑ 127 Dave Stewart	.10	.02
❑ 128 Jay Buhner	.10	.02
❑ 129 Mike LaValliere	.05	.01
❑ 130 Scott Bradley	.05	.01
❑ 131 Tony Phillips	.05	.01
❑ 132 Ryne Sandberg	.40	.15
❑ 133 Paul O'Neill	.15	.05
❑ 134 Mark Grace	.15	.05
❑ 135 Chris Sabo	.05	.01
❑ 136 Ramon Martinez	.05	.01
❑ 137 Brook Jacoby	.05	.01
❑ 138 Candy Maldonado	.05	.01
❑ 139 Mike Scioscia	.05	.01
❑ 140 Chris James	.05	.01
❑ 141 Craig Worthington	.05	.01
❑ 142 Manny Lee	.05	.01
❑ 143 Tim Raines	.10	.02
❑ 144 Sandy Alomar Jr.	.05	.01
❑ 145 John Olerud	.10	.02
❑ 146 Ozzie Canseco w/Jose	.10	.02
❑ 147 Pat Borders	.05	.01
❑ 148 Harold Reynolds	.10	.02
❑ 149 Tom Henke	.05	.01
❑ 150 R.J. Reynolds	.05	.01
❑ 151 Mike Gallego	.05	.01
❑ 152 Bobby Bonilla	.10	.02
❑ 153 Terry Steinbach	.05	.01
❑ 154 Barry Bonds	1.00	.40
❑ 155 Jose Canseco	.15	.05
❑ 156 Gregg Jefferies	.05	.01
❑ 157 Matt Williams	.10	.02
❑ 158 Craig Biggio	.15	.05
❑ 159 Daryl Boston	.05	.01
❑ 160 Ricky Jordan	.05	.01
❑ 161 Stan Belinda	.05	.01
❑ 162 Ozzie Smith	.40	.15
❑ 163 Tom Brunansky	.05	.01
❑ 164 Todd Zeile	.05	.01
❑ 165 Mike Greenwell	.05	.01
❑ 166 Kal Daniels	.05	.01
❑ 167 Kent Hrbek	.10	.02
❑ 168 Franklin Stubbs	.05	.01
❑ 169 Dick Schofield	.05	.01
❑ 170 Junior Ortiz	.05	.01
❑ 171 Hector Villanueva	.05	.01
❑ 172 Dennis Eckersley	.10	.02
❑ 173 Mitch Williams	.05	.01
❑ 174 Mark McGwire	.75	.30
❑ 175 Fernando Valenzuela 3X	.10	.02
❑ 176 Gary Carter	.10	.02
❑ 177 Dave Magadan	.05	.01
❑ 178 Robby Thompson	.05	.01
❑ 179 Bob Ojeda	.05	.01
❑ 180 Ken Caminiti	.10	.02
❑ 181 Don Slaught	.05	.01
❑ 182 Luis Rivera	.05	.01
❑ 183 Jay Bell	.10	.02
❑ 184 Jody Reed	.05	.01
❑ 185 Wally Backman	.05	.01
❑ 186 Dave Martinez	.05	.01
❑ 187 Luis Polonia	.05	.01
❑ 188 Shane Mack	.05	.01
❑ 189 Spike Owen	.05	.01
❑ 190 Scott Bailes	.05	.01
❑ 191 John Russell	.05	.01
❑ 192 Walt Weiss	.05	.01
❑ 193 Jose Oquendo	.05	.01
❑ 194 Carney Lansford	.10	.02
❑ 195 Jeff Huson	.05	.01
❑ 196 Keith Miller	.05	.01
❑ 197 Eric Yelding	.05	.01
❑ 198 Ron Darling	.05	.01
❑ 199 John Kruk	.10	.02
❑ 200 Checklist 101-200	.05	.01
❑ 201 John Shelby	.05	.01
❑ 202 Bob Geren	.05	.01
❑ 203 Lance McCullers	.05	.01
❑ 204 Alvaro Espinoza	.05	.01
❑ 205 Mark Salas	.05	.01
❑ 206 Mike Pagliarulo	.05	.01
❑ 207 Jose Uribe	.05	.01
❑ 208 Jim Deshaies	.05	.01
❑ 209 Ron Karkovice	.05	.01
❑ 210 Rafael Ramirez	.05	.01
❑ 211 Donnie Hill	.05	.01
❑ 212 Brian Harper	.05	.01
❑ 213 Jack Howell	.05	.01
❑ 214 Wes Gardner	.05	.01
❑ 215 Tim Burke	.05	.01
❑ 216 Doug Jones	.05	.01
❑ 217 Hubie Brooks	.05	.01
❑ 218 Tom Candiotti	.05	.01
❑ 219 Gerald Perry	.05	.01
❑ 220 Jose DeLeon	.05	.01
❑ 221 Wally Whitehurst	.05	.01
❑ 222 Alan Mills	.05	.01
❑ 223 Alan Trammell	.10	.02
❑ 224 Dwight Gooden	.10	.02
❑ 225 Travis Fryman	.10	.02
❑ 226 Joe Carter	.10	.02
❑ 227 Julio Franco	.10	.02
❑ 228 Craig Lefferts	.05	.01
❑ 229 Gary Pettis	.05	.01
❑ 230 Dennis Rasmussen	.05	.01
❑ 231A Brian Downing ERR	.05	.01
❑ 231B Brian Downing COR	.25	.08
❑ 232 Carlos Quintana	.05	.01
❑ 233 Gary Gaetti	.10	.02
❑ 234 Mark Langston	.05	.01
❑ 235 Tim Wallach	.05	.01
❑ 236 Greg Swindell	.05	.01
❑ 237 Eddie Murray	.25	.08
❑ 238 Jeff Manto	.05	.01
❑ 239 Lenny Harris	.05	.01
❑ 240 Jesse Orosco	.05	.01
❑ 241 Scott Lusader	.05	.01
❑ 242 Sid Fernandez	.05	.01
❑ 243 Jim Leyritz	.05	.01
❑ 244 Cecil Fielder	.10	.02
❑ 245 Darryl Strawberry	.10	.02
❑ 246 Frank Thomas	.25	.08
❑ 247 Kevin Mitchell	.05	.01
❑ 248 Lance Johnson	.05	.01
❑ 249 Rick Reuschel	.05	.01
❑ 250 Mark Portugal	.05	.01
❑ 251 Derek Lilliquist	.05	.01
❑ 252 Brian Holman	.05	.01
❑ 253 Rafael Valdez UER	.05	.01
❑ 254 B.J. Surhoff	.10	.02
❑ 255 Tony Gwynn	.30	.10
❑ 256 Andy Van Slyke	.15	.05
❑ 257 Todd Stottlemyre	.05	.01
❑ 258 Jose Lind	.05	.01
❑ 259 Greg Myers	.05	.01
❑ 260 Jeff Ballard	.05	.01
❑ 261 Bobby Thigpen	.05	.01
❑ 262 Jimmy Kremers	.05	.01
❑ 263 Robin Ventura	.10	.02
❑ 264 John Smoltz	.15	.05
❑ 265 Sammy Sosa	.25	.08
❑ 266 Gary Sheffield	.10	.02
❑ 267 Len Dykstra	.10	.02
❑ 268 Bill Spiers	.05	.01
❑ 269 Charlie Hayes	.05	.01
❑ 270 Brett Butler	.10	.02
❑ 271 Bip Roberts	.05	.01
❑ 272 Rob Deer	.05	.01
❑ 273 Fred Lynn	.05	.01
❑ 274 Dave Parker	.10	.02
❑ 275 Andy Benes	.05	.01
❑ 276 Glenallen Hill	.05	.01
❑ 277 Steve Howard	.05	.01
❑ 278 Doug Drabek	.05	.01
❑ 279 Joe Oliver	.05	.01
❑ 280 Todd Benzinger	.05	.01
❑ 281 Eric King	.05	.01
❑ 282 Jim Presley	.05	.01
❑ 283 Ken Patterson	.05	.01
❑ 284 Jack Daugherty	.05	.01
❑ 285 Ivan Calderon	.05	.01
❑ 286 Edgar Diaz	.05	.01
❑ 287 Kevin Bass	.05	.01
❑ 288 Don Carman	.05	.01
❑ 289 Greg Brock	.05	.01
❑ 290 John Franco	.10	.02
❑ 291 Joey Cora	.05	.01
❑ 292 Bill Wegman	.05	.01
❑ 293 Eric Show	.05	.01
❑ 294 Scott Bankhead	.05	.01
❑ 295 Garry Templeton	.05	.01
❑ 296 Mickey Tettleton	.05	.01
❑ 297 Luis Sojo	.05	.01
❑ 298 Jose Rijo	.05	.01
❑ 299 Dave Johnson	.05	.01
❑ 300 Checklist 201-300	.05	.01
❑ 301 Mark Grant	.05	.01
❑ 302 Pete Harnisch	.05	.01
❑ 303 Greg Olson	.05	.01
❑ 304 Anthony Telford RC	.05	.01
❑ 305 Lonnie Smith	.05	.01
❑ 306 Chris Hoiles FUDC	.05	.01
❑ 307 Bryn Smith	.05	.01
❑ 308 Mike Devereaux	.05	.01
❑ 309A Milt Thompson ERR	.25	.08
❑ 309B Milt Thompson COR	.05	.01
❑ 310 Bob Melvin	.05	.01
❑ 311 Luis Salazar	.05	.01
❑ 312 Ed Whitson	.05	.01
❑ 313 Charlie Hough	.10	.02
❑ 314 Dave Clark	.05	.01
❑ 315 Eric Gunderson	.05	.01

❑ 316 Dan Petry .05 .01
❑ 317 Dante Bichette .10 .02
❑ 318 Mike Heath .05 .01
❑ 319 Damon Berryhill .05 .01
❑ 320 Walt Terrell .05 .01
❑ 321 Scott Fletcher .05 .01
❑ 322 Dan Plesac .05 .01
❑ 323 Jack McDowell .05 .01
❑ 324 Paul Molitor .10 .02
❑ 325 Ozzie Guillen .10 .02
❑ 326 Gregg Olson .05 .01
❑ 327 Pedro Guerrero .10 .02
❑ 328 Bob Milacki .05 .01
❑ 329 John Tudor UER .05 .01
❑ 330 Steve Finley UER .10 .02
❑ 331 Jack Clark .10 .02
❑ 332 Jerome Walton .05 .01
❑ 333 Andy Hawkins .05 .01
❑ 334 Derrick May .05 .01
❑ 335 Roberto Alomar .15 .05
❑ 336 Jack Morris .10 .02
❑ 337 Dave Winfield .10 .02
❑ 338 Steve Searcy .05 .01
❑ 339 Chili Davis .10 .02
❑ 340 Larry Sheets .05 .01
❑ 341 Ted Higuera .05 .01
❑ 342 David Segui .05 .01
❑ 343 Greg Cadaret .05 .01
❑ 344 Robin Yount .40 .15
❑ 345 Nolan Ryan 1.00 .40
❑ 346 Ray Lankford .10 .02
❑ 347 Cal Ripken .75 .30
❑ 348 Lee Smith .10 .02
❑ 349 Brady Anderson .10 .02
❑ 350 Frank DiPino .05 .01
❑ 351 Hal Morris .05 .01
❑ 352 Deion Sanders .15 .05
❑ 353 Barry Larkin .15 .05
❑ 354 Don Mattingly .60 .25
❑ 355 Eric Davis .10 .02
❑ 356 Jose Offerman .05 .01
❑ 357 Mel Rojas .05 .01
❑ 358 Rudy Seanez .05 .01
❑ 359 Oil Can Boyd .05 .01
❑ 360 Nelson Liriano .05 .01
❑ 361 Ron Gant .10 .02
❑ 362 Howard Farmer .05 .01
❑ 363 David Justice .10 .02
❑ 364 Delino DeShields .10 .02
❑ 365 Steve Avery .05 .01
❑ 366 David Cone .10 .02
❑ 367 Lou Whitaker .10 .02
❑ 368 Von Hayes .05 .01
❑ 369 Frank Tanana .05 .01
❑ 370 Tim Teufel .05 .01
❑ 371 Randy Myers .05 .01
❑ 372 Roberto Kelly .05 .01
❑ 373 Jack Armstrong .05 .01
❑ 374 Kelly Gruber .05 .01
❑ 375 Kevin Maas .05 .01
❑ 376 Randy Johnson .30 .10
❑ 377 David West .05 .01
❑ 378 Brent Knackert .05 .01
❑ 379 Rick Honeycutt .05 .01
❑ 380 Kevin Gross .05 .01
❑ 381 Tom Foley .05 .01
❑ 382 Jeff Blauser .05 .01
❑ 383 Scott Ruskin .05 .01
❑ 384 Andres Thomas .05 .01
❑ 385 Dennis Martinez .10 .02
❑ 386 Mike Henneman .05 .01
❑ 387 Felix Jose .05 .01
❑ 388 Alejandro Pena .05 .01
❑ 389 Chet Lemon .05 .01
❑ 390 Craig Wilson RC .05 .01
❑ 391 Chuck Crim .05 .01
❑ 392 Mel Hall .05 .01
❑ 393 Mark Knudson .05 .01
❑ 394 Norm Charlton .05 .01
❑ 395 Mike Felder .05 .01
❑ 396 Tim Layana .05 .01
❑ 397 Steve Frey .05 .01
❑ 398 Bill Doran .05 .01
❑ 399 Dion James .05 .01
❑ 400 Checklist 301-400 .05 .01
❑ 401 Ron Hassey .05 .01
❑ 402 Don Robinson .05 .01
❑ 403 Gene Nelson .05 .01
❑ 404 Terry Kennedy .05 .01
❑ 405 Todd Burns .05 .01
❑ 406 Roger McDowell .05 .01
❑ 407 Bob Kipper .05 .01
❑ 408 Darren Daulton .10 .02
❑ 409 Chuck Cary .05 .01
❑ 410 Bruce Ruffin .05 .01
❑ 411 Juan Berenguer .05 .01
❑ 412 Gary Ward .05 .01
❑ 413 Al Newman .05 .01
❑ 414 Danny Jackson .05 .01
❑ 415 Greg Gagne .05 .01
❑ 416 Tom Herr .05 .01
❑ 417 Jeff Parrett .05 .01
❑ 418 Jeff Reardon .10 .02
❑ 419 Mark Lemke .05 .01
❑ 420 Charlie O'Brien .05 .01
❑ 421 Willie Randolph .10 .02
❑ 422 Steve Bedrosian .05 .01
❑ 423 Mike Moore .05 .01
❑ 424 Jeff Brantley .05 .01
❑ 425 Bob Welch .05 .01
❑ 426 Terry Mulholland .05 .01
❑ 427 Willie Blair .05 .01
❑ 428 Darrin Fletcher .05 .01
❑ 429 Mike Witt .05 .01
❑ 430 Joe Boever .05 .01
❑ 431 Tom Gordon .05 .01
❑ 432 Pedro Munoz RC .10 .02
❑ 433 Kevin Seitzer .05 .01
❑ 434 Kevin Tapani .05 .01
❑ 435 Bret Saberhagen .10 .02
❑ 436 Ellis Burks .10 .02
❑ 437 Chuck Finley .10 .02
❑ 438 Mike Boddicker .05 .01
❑ 439 Francisco Cabrera .05 .01
❑ 440 Todd Hundley .05 .01
❑ 441 Kelly Downs .05 .01
❑ 442 Dann Howitt .05 .01
❑ 443 Scott Garrelts .05 .01
❑ 444 Rickey Henderson .25 .08
❑ 445 Will Clark .15 .05
❑ 446 Ben McDonald .05 .01
❑ 447 Dale Murphy .15 .05
❑ 448 Dave Righetti .10 .02
❑ 449 Dickie Thon .05 .01
❑ 450 Ted Power .05 .01
❑ 451 Scott Coolbaugh .05 .01
❑ 452 Dwight Smith .05 .01
❑ 453 Pete Incaviglia .05 .01
❑ 454 Andre Dawson .10 .02
❑ 455 Ruben Sierra .10 .02
❑ 456 Andres Galarraga .10 .02
❑ 457 Alvin Davis .05 .01
❑ 458 Tony Castillo .05 .01
❑ 459 Pete O'Brien .05 .01
❑ 460 Charlie Leibrandt .05 .01
❑ 461 Vince Coleman .05 .01
❑ 462 Steve Sax .05 .01
❑ 463 Omar Olivares RC .10 .02
❑ 464 Oscar Azocar .05 .01
❑ 465 Joe Magrane .05 .01
❑ 466 Karl Rhodes .05 .01
❑ 467 Benito Santiago .10 .02
❑ 468 Joe Klink .05 .01
❑ 469 Sil Campusano .05 .01
❑ 470 Mark Parent .05 .01
❑ 471 Shawn Boskie UER .05 .01
❑ 472 Kevin Brown .10 .02
❑ 473 Rick Sutcliffe .10 .02
❑ 474 Rafael Palmeiro .15 .05
❑ 475 Mike Harkey .05 .01
❑ 476 Jaime Navarro .05 .01
❑ 477 Marquis Grissom .10 .02
❑ 478 Marty Clary .05 .01
❑ 479 Greg Briley .05 .01
❑ 480 Tom Glavine .15 .05
❑ 481 Lee Guetterman .05 .01
❑ 482 Rex Hudler .05 .01
❑ 483 Dave LaPoint .05 .01
❑ 484 Terry Pendleton .10 .02
❑ 485 Jesse Barfield .05 .01
❑ 486 Jose DeJesus .05 .01
❑ 487 Paul Abbott RC .10 .02
❑ 488 Ken Howell .05 .01
❑ 489 Greg W. Harris .05 .01
❑ 490 Roy Smith .05 .01
❑ 491 Paul Assenmacher .05 .01
❑ 492 Geno Petralli .05 .01
❑ 493 Steve Wilson .05 .01
❑ 494 Kevin Reimer .05 .01
❑ 495 Bill Long .05 .01
❑ 496 Mike Jackson .05 .01
❑ 497 Oddibe McDowell .05 .01
❑ 498 Bill Swift .05 .01
❑ 499 Jeff Treadway .05 .01
❑ 500 Checklist 401-500 .05 .01
❑ 501 Gene Larkin .05 .01
❑ 502 Bob Boone .10 .02
❑ 503 Allan Anderson .05 .01
❑ 504 Luis Aquino .05 .01
❑ 505 Mark Guthrie .05 .01
❑ 506 Joe Orsulak .05 .01
❑ 507 Dana Kiecker .05 .01
❑ 508 Dave Gallagher .05 .01
❑ 509 Greg A. Harris .05 .01
❑ 510 Mark Williamson .05 .01
❑ 511 Casey Candaele .05 .01
❑ 512 Mookie Wilson .10 .02
❑ 513 Dave Smith .05 .01
❑ 514 Chuck Carr FUDC .05 .01
❑ 515 Glenn Wilson .05 .01
❑ 516 Mike Fitzgerald .05 .01
❑ 517 Devon White .10 .02
❑ 518 Dave Hollins .05 .01
❑ 519 Mark Eichhorn .05 .01
❑ 520 Otis Nixon .05 .01
❑ 521 Terry Shumpert .05 .01
❑ 522 Scott Erickson .05 .01
❑ 523 Danny Tartabull .05 .01
❑ 524 Orel Hershiser .10 .02
❑ 525 George Brett .60 .25
❑ 526 Greg Vaughn .05 .01
❑ 527 Tim Naehring FUDC .05 .01
❑ 528 Curt Schilling .25 .08
❑ 529 Chris Bosio .05 .01
❑ 530 Sam Horn .05 .01
❑ 531 Mike Scott .05 .01
❑ 532 George Bell .05 .01
❑ 533 Eric Anthony .05 .01
❑ 534 Julio Valera .05 .01
❑ 535 Glenn Davis .05 .01
❑ 536 Larry Walker .25 .08
❑ 537 Pat Combs .05 .01
❑ 538 Chris Nabholz .05 .01
❑ 539 Kirk McCaskill .05 .01
❑ 540 Randy Ready .05 .01
❑ 541 Mark Gubicza .05 .01
❑ 542 Rick Aguilera .10 .02
❑ 543 Brian McRae RC .25 .08
❑ 544 Kirby Puckett .25 .08
❑ 545 Bo Jackson .25 .08
❑ 546 Wade Boggs .15 .05
❑ 547 Tim McIntosh .05 .01
❑ 548 Randy Milligan .05 .01
❑ 549 Dwight Evans .15 .05
❑ 550 Billy Ripken .05 .01
❑ 551 Erik Hanson .05 .01
❑ 552 Lance Parrish .10 .02
❑ 553 Tino Martinez .25 .08
❑ 554 Jim Abbott .15 .05
❑ 555 Ken Griffey Jr. .50 .20
❑ 556 Milt Cuyler .05 .01
❑ 557 Mark Leonard RC .05 .01
❑ 558 Jay Howell .05 .01
❑ 559 Lloyd Moseby .05 .01
❑ 560 Chris Gwynn .05 .01
❑ 561 Mark Whiten FUDC .05 .01
❑ 562 Harold Baines .10 .02
❑ 563 Junior Felix .05 .01
❑ 564 Darren Lewis FUDC .05 .01
❑ 565 Fred McGriff .15 .05
❑ 566 Kevin Appier .10 .02
❑ 567 Luis Gonzalez RC .75 .30
❑ 568 Frank White .10 .02
❑ 569 Juan Agosto .05 .01
❑ 570 Mike Macfarlane .05 .01
❑ 571 Bert Blyleven .10 .02
❑ 572 Ken Griffey Sr./Jr. .25 .08
❑ 573 Lee Stevens .05 .01

❑ 574 Edgar Martinez .15 .05
❑ 575 Wally Joyner .10 .02
❑ 576 Tim Belcher .05 .01
❑ 577 John Burkett .05 .01
❑ 578 Mike Morgan .05 .01
❑ 579 Paul Gibson .05 .01
❑ 580 Jose Vizcaino .05 .01
❑ 581 Duane Ward .05 .01
❑ 582 Scott Sanderson .05 .01
❑ 583 David Wells .10 .02
❑ 584 Willie McGee .10 .02
❑ 585 John Cerutti .05 .01
❑ 586 Danny Darwin .05 .01
❑ 587 Kurt Stillwell .05 .01
❑ 588 Rich Gedman .05 .01
❑ 589 Mark Davis .05 .01
❑ 590 Bill Gullickson .05 .01
❑ 591 Matt Young .05 .01
❑ 592 Bryan Harvey .05 .01
❑ 593 Omar Vizquel .15 .05
❑ 594 Scott Lewis RC .10 .02
❑ 595 Dave Valle .05 .01
❑ 596 Tim Crews .05 .01
❑ 597 Mike Bielecki .05 .01
❑ 598 Mike Sharperson .05 .01
❑ 599 Dave Bergman .05 .01
❑ 600 Checklist 501-600 .05 .01
❑ 601 Steve Lyons .05 .01
❑ 602 Bruce Hurst .05 .01
❑ 603 Donn Pall .05 .01
❑ 604 Jim Vatcher RC .05 .01
❑ 605 Dan Pasqua .05 .01
❑ 606 Kenny Rogers .10 .02
❑ 607 Jeff Schulz RC .05 .01
❑ 608 Brad Arnsberg .05 .01
❑ 609 Willie Wilson .05 .01
❑ 610 Jamie Moyer .10 .02
❑ 611 Ron Oester .05 .01
❑ 612 Dennis Cook .05 .01
❑ 613 Rick Mahler .05 .01
❑ 614 Bill Landrum .05 .01
❑ 615 Scott Scudder .05 .01
❑ 616 Tom Edens RC .05 .01
❑ 617 1917 Revisited .10 .02
❑ 618 Jim Gantner .05 .01
❑ 619 Darrel Akerfelds .05 .01
❑ 620 Ron Robinson .05 .01
❑ 621 Scott Radinsky .05 .01
❑ 622 Pete Smith .05 .01
❑ 623 Melido Perez .05 .01
❑ 624 Jerald Clark .05 .01
❑ 625 Carlos Martinez .05 .01
❑ 626 Wes Chamberlain RC .25 .08
❑ 627 Bobby Witt .05 .01
❑ 628 Ken Dayley .05 .01
❑ 629 John Barfield .05 .01
❑ 630 Bob Tewksbury .05 .01
❑ 631 Glenn Braggs .05 .01
❑ 632 Jim Neidlinger RC .05 .01
❑ 633 Tom Browning .05 .01
❑ 634 Kirk Gibson .10 .02
❑ 635 Rob Dibble .10 .02
❑ 636 R.Henderson/L.Brock .25 .08
❑ 636A R.Henderson/L.Brock .25 .08
❑ 637 Jeff Montgomery .05 .01
❑ 638 Mike Schooler .05 .01
❑ 639 Storm Davis .05 .01
❑ 640 Rich Rodriguez RC .05 .01
❑ 641 Phil Bradley .05 .01
❑ 642 Kent Mercker .05 .01
❑ 643 Carlton Fisk .15 .05
❑ 644 Mike Bell RC .05 .01
❑ 645 Alex Fernandez .05 .01
❑ 646 Juan Gonzalez .25 .08
❑ 647 Ken Hill .05 .01
❑ 648 Jeff Russell .05 .01
❑ 649 Chuck Malone .05 .01
❑ 650 Steve Buechele .05 .01
❑ 651 Mike Benjamin .05 .01
❑ 652 Tony Pena .05 .01
❑ 653 Trevor Wilson .05 .01
❑ 654 Alex Cole .05 .01
❑ 655 Roger Clemens .75 .30
❑ 656 Mark McGwire BASH .40 .15
❑ 657 Joe Grahe RC .10 .02
❑ 658 Jim Eisenreich .05 .01
❑ 659 Dan Gladden .05 .01
❑ 660 Steve Farr .05 .01
❑ 661 Bill Sampen .05 .01
❑ 662 Dave Rohde .05 .01
❑ 663 Mark Gardner .05 .01
❑ 664 Mike Simms RC .05 .01
❑ 665 Moises Alou .10 .02
❑ 666 Mickey Hatcher .05 .01
❑ 667 Jimmy Key .10 .02
❑ 668 John Wetteland .10 .02
❑ 669 John Smiley .05 .01
❑ 670 Jim Acker .05 .01
❑ 671 Pascual Perez .05 .01
❑ 672 Reggie Harris UER .05 .01
❑ 673 Matt Nokes .05 .01
❑ 674 Rafael Novoa RC .05 .01
❑ 675 Hensley Meulens .05 .01
❑ 676 Jeff M. Robinson .05 .01
❑ 677 C.Fisk/R.Ventura .10 .02
❑ 678 Johnny Ray .05 .01
❑ 679 Greg Hibbard .05 .01
❑ 680 Paul Sorrento .05 .01
❑ 681 Mike Marshall .05 .01
❑ 682 Jim Clancy .05 .01
❑ 683 Rob Murphy .05 .01
❑ 684 Dave Schmidt .05 .01
❑ 685 Jeff Gray RC .05 .01
❑ 686 Mike Hartley .05 .01
❑ 687 Jeff King .05 .01
❑ 688 Stan Javier .05 .01
❑ 689 Bob Walk .05 .01
❑ 690 Jim Gott .05 .01
❑ 691 Mike LaCoss .05 .01
❑ 692 John Farrell .05 .01
❑ 693 Tim Leary .05 .01
❑ 694 Mike Walker .05 .01
❑ 695 Eric Plunk .05 .01
❑ 696 Mike Fetters .05 .01
❑ 697 Wayne Edwards .05 .01
❑ 698 Tim Drummond .05 .01
❑ 699 Willie Fraser .05 .01
❑ 700 Checklist 601-700 .05 .01
❑ 701 Mike Heath .05 .01
❑ 702 J.Bagwell/L.Gonz/K.Rhodes 1.00 .40
❑ 703 Jose Mesa .05 .01
❑ 704 Dave Smith .05 .01
❑ 705 Danny Darwin .05 .01
❑ 706 Rafael Belliard .05 .01
❑ 707 Rob Murphy .05 .01
❑ 708 Terry Pendleton .10 .02
❑ 709 Mike Pagliarulo .05 .01
❑ 710 Sid Bream .05 .01
❑ 711 Junior Felix .05 .01
❑ 712 Dante Bichette .10 .02
❑ 713 Kevin Gross .05 .01
❑ 714 Luis Sojo .05 .01
❑ 715 Bob Ojeda .05 .01
❑ 716 Julio Machado .05 .01
❑ 717 Steve Farr .05 .01
❑ 718 Franklin Stubbs .05 .01
❑ 719 Mike Boddicker .05 .01
❑ 720 Willie Randolph .10 .02
❑ 721 Willie McGee .10 .02
❑ 722 Chili Davis .10 .02
❑ 723 Danny Jackson .05 .01
❑ 724 Cory Snyder .05 .01
❑ 725 Dawson/Bell/Sandberg .25 .08
❑ 726 Rob Deer .05 .01
❑ 727 Rich DeLucia RC .05 .01
❑ 728 Mike Perez RC .10 .02
❑ 729 Mickey Tettleton .05 .01
❑ 730 Mike Blowers .05 .01
❑ 731 Gary Gaetti .10 .02
❑ 732 Brett Butler .10 .02
❑ 733 Dave Parker .10 .02
❑ 734 Eddie Zosky .05 .01
❑ 735 Jack Clark .10 .02
❑ 736 Jack Morris .10 .02
❑ 737 Kirk Gibson .10 .02
❑ 738 Steve Bedrosian .05 .01
❑ 739 Candy Maldonado .05 .01
❑ 740 Matt Young .05 .01
❑ 741 Rich Garces RC .10 .02
❑ 742 George Bell .05 .01
❑ 743 Deion Sanders .15 .05
❑ 744 Bo Jackson .25 .08
❑ 745 Luis Mercedes RC .10 .02
❑ 746 Reggie Jefferson .05 .01
❑ 747 Pete Incaviglia .05 .01
❑ 748 Chris Hammond .05 .01
❑ 749 Mike Stanton .05 .01
❑ 750 Scott Sanderson .05 .01
❑ 751 Paul Faries RC .05 .01
❑ 752 Al Osuna RC .05 .01
❑ 753 Steve Chitren RC .05 .01
❑ 754 Tony Fernandez .05 .01
❑ 755 Jeff Bagwell UER RC 1.50 .60
❑ 756 Kirk Dressendorfer RC .10 .02
❑ 757 Glenn Davis .05 .01
❑ 758 Gary Carter .10 .02
❑ 759 Zane Smith .05 .01
❑ 760 Vance Law .05 .01
❑ 761 Denis Boucher RC .10 .02
❑ 762 Turner Ward RC .10 .02
❑ 763 Roberto Alomar .15 .05
❑ 764 Albert Belle .10 .02
❑ 765 Joe Carter .10 .02
❑ 766 Pete Schourek RC .10 .02
❑ 767 Heathcliff Slocumb RC .10 .02
❑ 768 Vince Coleman .05 .01
❑ 769 Mitch Williams .05 .01
❑ 770 Brian Downing .05 .01
❑ 771 Dana Allison RC .05 .01
❑ 772 Pete Harnisch .05 .01
❑ 773 Tim Raines .10 .02
❑ 774 Darryl Kile .10 .02
❑ 775 Fred McGriff .15 .05
❑ 776 Dwight Evans .15 .05
❑ 777 Joe Slusarski RC .05 .01
❑ 778 Dave Righetti .10 .02
❑ 779 Jeff Hamilton .05 .01
❑ 780 Ernest Riles .05 .01
❑ 781 Ken Dayley .05 .01
❑ 782 Eric King .05 .01
❑ 783 Devon White .10 .02
❑ 784 Beau Allred .05 .01
❑ 785 Mike Timlin RC .25 .08
❑ 786 Ivan Calderon .05 .01
❑ 787 Hubie Brooks .05 .01
❑ 788 Juan Agosto .05 .01
❑ 789 Barry Jones .05 .01
❑ 790 Wally Backman .05 .01
❑ 791 Jim Presley .05 .01
❑ 792 Charlie Hough .10 .02
❑ 793 Larry Andersen .05 .01
❑ 794 Steve Finley .10 .02
❑ 795 Shawn Abner .05 .01
❑ 796 Jeff M. Robinson .05 .01
❑ 797 Joe Bitker RC .05 .01
❑ 798 Eric Show .05 .01
❑ 799 Bud Black .05 .01
❑ 800 Checklist 701-800 .05 .01
❑ HH1 Hank Aaron Hologram 1.50 .60
❑ SP1 Michael Jordan 8.00 3.00
❑ SP2 N.Ryan/R.Henderson 2.00 .75

1991 Upper Deck Final Edition

❑ COMP.FACT.SET (100) 8.00 3.00
❑ 1F R.Klesko/R.Sanders CL .25 .08
❑ 2F Pedro Martinez RC 8.00 3.00
❑ 3F Lance Dickson .05 .01
❑ 4F Royce Clayton .05 .01
❑ 5F Scott Bryant .05 .01

Card	Player	Price	Price
❑ 6F	Dan Wilson RC	.25	.08
❑ 7F	Dmitri Young RC	.75	.30
❑ 8F	Ryan Klesko RC	.50	.20
❑ 9F	Tom Goodwin	.05	.01
❑ 10F	Rondell White RC	.50	.20
❑ 11F	Reggie Sanders	.50	.20
❑ 12F	Todd Van Poppel	.05	.01
❑ 13F	Arthur Rhodes RC	.25	.08
❑ 14F	Eddie Zosky	.05	.01
❑ 15F	Gerald Williams RC	.25	.08
❑ 16F	Robert Eenhoorn RC	.10	.02
❑ 17F	Jim Thome RC	4.00	1.50
❑ 18F	Marc Newfield RC	.10	.02
❑ 19F	Kerwin Moore RC	.10	.02
❑ 20F	Jeff McNeely RC	.10	.02
❑ 21F	Frank Rodriguez RC	.10	.02
❑ 22F	Andy Mota RC	.05	.01
❑ 23F	Chris Haney RC	.10	.02
❑ 24F	Kenny Lofton RC	.75	.30
❑ 25F	Dave Nilsson RC	.25	.08
❑ 26F	Derek Bell	.10	.02
❑ 27F	Frank Castillo RC	.25	.08
❑ 28F	Candy Maldonado	.05	.01
❑ 29F	Chuck McElroy	.05	.01
❑ 30F	Chito Martinez RC	.05	.01
❑ 31F	Steve Howe	.05	.01
❑ 32F	Freddie Benavides RC	.05	.01
❑ 33F	Scott Kamieniecki RC	.10	.02
❑ 34F	Denny Neagle RC	.25	.08
❑ 35F	Mike Humphreys RC	.10	.02
❑ 36F	Mike Remlinger	.05	.01
❑ 37F	Scott Coolbaugh	.05	.01
❑ 38F	Darren Lewis	.05	.01
❑ 39F	Thomas Howard	.05	.01
❑ 40F	John Candelaria	.05	.01
❑ 41F	Todd Benzinger	.05	.01
❑ 42F	Wilson Alvarez	.05	.01
❑ 43F	Patrick Lennon RC	.10	.02
❑ 44F	Rusty Meacham RC	.10	.02
❑ 45F	Ryan Bowen RC	.10	.02
❑ 46F	Rick Wilkins RC	.10	.02
❑ 47F	Ed Sprague	.05	.01
❑ 48F	Bob Scanlan RC	.05	.01
❑ 49F	Tom Candiotti	.05	.01
❑ 50F	Dennis Martinez Perfect	.10	.02
❑ 51F	Oil Can Boyd	.05	.01
❑ 52F	Glenallen Hill	.05	.01
❑ 53F	Scott Livingstone RC	.10	.02
❑ 54F	Brian R.Hunter RC	.25	.08
❑ 55F	Ivan Rodriguez RC	2.00	.75
❑ 56F	Keith Mitchell RC	.10	.02
❑ 57F	Roger McDowell	.05	.01
❑ 58F	Otis Nixon	.05	.01
❑ 59F	Juan Bell	.05	.01
❑ 60F	Bill Krueger	.05	.01
❑ 61F	Chris Donnels RC	.05	.01
❑ 62F	Tommy Greene	.05	.01
❑ 63F	Doug Simons RC	.05	.01
❑ 64F	Andy Ashby RC	.25	.08
❑ 65F	Anthony Young RC	.10	.02
❑ 66F	Kevin Morton RC	.05	.01
❑ 67F	Bret Barberie RC	.10	.02
❑ 68F	Scott Servais RC	.25	.08
❑ 69F	Ron Darling	.05	.01
❑ 70F	Tim Burke	.05	.01
❑ 71F	Vicente Palacios	.05	.01
❑ 72F	Gerald Alexander RC	.05	.01
❑ 73F	Reggie Jefferson	.05	.01
❑ 74F	Dean Palmer	.10	.02
❑ 75F	Mark Whiten	.05	.01
❑ 76F	Randy Tomlin RC	.10	.02
❑ 77F	Mark Wohlers RC	.25	.08
❑ 78F	Brook Jacoby	.05	.01
❑ 79F	K.Griffey Jr./R.Sandberg CL	.40	.15
❑ 80F	Jack Morris AS	.05	.01
❑ 81F	Sandy Alomar Jr. AS	.05	.01
❑ 82F	Cecil Fielder AS	.05	.01
❑ 83F	Roberto Alomar AS	.10	.02
❑ 84F	Wade Boggs AS	.10	.02
❑ 85F	Cal Ripken AS	.40	.15
❑ 86F	Rickey Henderson AS	.15	.05
❑ 87F	Ken Griffey Jr. AS	.25	.08
❑ 88F	Dave Henderson AS	.05	.01
❑ 89F	Danny Tartabull AS	.05	.01
❑ 90F	Tom Glavine AS	.10	.02
❑ 91F	Benito Santiago AS	.05	.01
❑ 92F	Will Clark AS	.10	.02
❑ 93F	Ryne Sandberg AS	.25	.08
❑ 94F	Chris Sabo AS	.05	.01
❑ 95F	Ozzie Smith AS	.25	.08
❑ 96F	Ivan Calderon AS	.05	.01
❑ 97F	Tony Gwynn AS	.15	.05
❑ 98F	Andre Dawson AS	.05	.01
❑ 99F	Bobby Bonilla AS	.05	.01
❑ 100F	Checklist 1-100	.05	.01

1992 Upper Deck

Card	Player	Price	Price
❑	COMPLETE SET (800)	25.00	10.00
❑	COMPLETE LO SET (700)	20.00	8.00
❑	COMPLETE HI SET (100)	5.00	2.00
❑ 1	J.Thome/R.Klesko CL	.25	.08
❑ 2	Royce Clayton SR	.05	.01
❑ 3	Brian Jordan RC	.50	.20
❑ 4	Dave Fleming	.05	.01
❑ 5	Jim Thome	.25	.08
❑ 6	Jeff Juden SR	.05	.01
❑ 7	Roberto Hernandez SR	.05	.01
❑ 8	Kyle Abbott SR	.05	.01
❑ 9	Chris George SR	.05	.01
❑ 10	Rob Maurer SR	.05	.01
❑ 11	Donald Harris SR	.05	.01
❑ 12	Ted Wood SR	.05	.01
❑ 13	Patrick Lennon SR	.05	.01
❑ 14	Willie Banks SR	.05	.01
❑ 15	Roger Salkeld SR UER (Bill was his grand-father	.05	.01
❑ 16	Wil Cordero	.05	.01
❑ 17	Arthur Rhodes SR	.05	.01
❑ 18	Pedro Martinez	1.00	.40
❑ 19	Andy Ashby SR	.05	.01
❑ 20	Tom Goodwin SR	.05	.01
❑ 21	Braulio Castillo SR	.05	.01
❑ 22	Todd Van Poppel	.05	.01
❑ 23	Brian Williams RC	.05	.01
❑ 24	Ryan Klesko	.10	.02
❑ 25	Kenny Lofton	.15	.05
❑ 26	Derek Bell	.10	.02
❑ 27	Reggie Sanders	.10	.02
❑ 28	Dave Winfield's 400th	.05	.01
❑ 29	David Justice TC	.05	.01
❑ 30	Rob Dibble TC Cincinnati Reds	.05	.01
❑ 31	Craig Biggio TC	.10	.02
❑ 32	Eddie Murray TC	.15	.05
❑ 33	Fred McGriff TC	.10	.02
❑ 34	Willie McGee TC San Francisco Giants	.05	.01
❑ 35	Shawon Dunston TC Chicago Cubs	.05	.01
❑ 36	Delino DeShields TC	.05	.01
❑ 37	Howard Johnson TC New York Mets	.05	.01
❑ 38	John Kruk TC	.05	.01
❑ 39	Doug Drabek TC Pittsburgh Pirates	.05	.01
❑ 40	Todd Zeile TC	.05	.01
❑ 41	Steve Avery Playoff	.05	.01
❑ 42	Jeremy Hernandez RC	.05	.01
❑ 43	Doug Henry RC	.10	.02
❑ 44	Chris Donnels	.05	.01
❑ 45	Mo Sanford	.05	.01
❑ 46	Scott Kamieniecki	.05	.01
❑ 47	Mark Lemke	.05	.01
❑ 48	Steve Farr	.05	.01
❑ 49	Francisco Oliveras	.05	.01
❑ 50	Ced Landrum	.05	.01
❑ 51	R.White/M.Newfield CL	.10	.02
❑ 52	Eduardo Perez RC	.25	.08
❑ 53	Tom Nevers TP	.05	.01
❑ 54	David Zancanaro TP	.05	.01
❑ 55	Shawn Green RC	1.00	.40
❑ 56	Mark Wohlers TP	.05	.01
❑ 57	Dave Nilsson	.05	.01
❑ 58	Dmitri Young	.10	.02
❑ 59	Ryan Hawblitzel RC	.10	.02
❑ 60	Raul Mondesi	.10	.02
❑ 61	Rondell White	.10	.02
❑ 62	Steve Hosey	.05	.01
❑ 63	Manny Ramirez RC	4.00	1.50
❑ 64	Marc Newfield	.05	.01
❑ 65	Jeromy Burnitz	.10	.02
❑ 66	Mark Smith RC	.10	.02
❑ 67	Joey Hamilton RC	.10	.02
❑ 68	Tyler Green RC	.10	.02
❑ 69	Jon Farrell RC	.10	.02
❑ 70	Kurt Miller TP	.05	.01
❑ 71	Jeff Plympton TP	.05	.01
❑ 72	Dan Wilson TP	.05	.01
❑ 73	Joe Vitiello RC	.10	.02
❑ 74	Rico Brogna TP	.05	.01
❑ 75	David McCarty RC	.25	.08
❑ 76	Bob Wickman	.25	.08
❑ 77	Carlos Rodriguez TP	.05	.01
❑ 78	Jim Abbott Stay In School	.10	.02
❑ 79	P.Martinez/R.Martinez	.25	.08
❑ 80	Kevin Mitchell Keith Mitchell	.05	.01
❑ 81	Sandy/Roberto Alomar	.10	.02
❑ 82	Ripken Brothers	.50	.20
❑ 83	Tony/Chris Gwynn	.15	.05
❑ 84	D.Gooden/G.Sheffield	.10	.02
❑ 85	K.Griffey Jr. w/Family	.25	.08
❑ 86	Jim Abbott TC California Angels	.10	.02
❑ 87	Frank Thomas TC	.15	.05
❑ 88	Danny Tartabull TC Kansas City Royals	.05	.01
❑ 89	Scott Erickson TC Minnesota Twins	.05	.01
❑ 90	Rickey Henderson TC	.15	.05
❑ 91	Edgar Martinez TC	.10	.02
❑ 92	Nolan Ryan TC	.50	.20
❑ 93	Ben McDonald TC Baltimore Orioles	.05	.01
❑ 94	Ellis Burks TC Boston Red Sox	.05	.01
❑ 95	Greg Swindell TC Cleveland Indians	.05	.01
❑ 96	Cecil Fielder TC	.05	.01
❑ 97	Greg Vaughn TC	.05	.01
❑ 98	Kevin Maas TC New York Yankees	.05	.01
❑ 99	Dave Stieb TC Toronto Blue Jays	.05	.01
❑ 100	Checklist 1-100	.05	.01
❑ 101	Joe Oliver	.05	.01
❑ 102	Hector Villanueva	.05	.01
❑ 103	Ed Whitson	.05	.01
❑ 104	Danny Jackson	.05	.01
❑ 105	Chris Hammond	.05	.01
❑ 106	Ricky Jordan	.05	.01
❑ 107	Kevin Bass	.05	.01
❑ 108	Darrin Fletcher	.05	.01
❑ 109	Junior Ortiz	.05	.01
❑ 110	Tom Bolton	.05	.01
❑ 111	Jeff King	.05	.01
❑ 112	Dave Magadan	.05	.01
❑ 113	Mike LaValliere	.05	.01
❑ 114	Hubie Brooks	.05	.01
❑ 115	Jay Bell	.10	.02
❑ 116	David Wells	.10	.02
❑ 117	Jim Leyritz	.05	.01
❑ 118	Manuel Lee	.05	.01
❑ 119	Alvaro Espinoza	.05	.01
❑ 120	B.J. Surhoff	.10	.02
❑ 121	Hal Morris	.05	.01
❑ 122	Shawon Dawson	.05	.01
❑ 123	Chris Sabo	.05	.01

❑ 124 Andre Dawson	.10	.02
❑ 125 Eric Davis	.10	.02
❑ 126 Chili Davis	.10	.02
❑ 127 Dale Murphy	.15	.05
❑ 128 Kirk McCaskill	.05	.01
❑ 129 Terry Mulholland	.05	.01
❑ 130 Rick Aguilera	.10	.02
❑ 131 Vince Coleman	.05	.01
❑ 132 Andy Van Slyke	.15	.05
❑ 133 Gregg Jefferies	.05	.01
❑ 134 Barry Bonds	1.00	.40
❑ 135 Dwight Gooden	.10	.02
❑ 136 Dave Stieb	.05	.01
❑ 137 Albert Belle	.10	.02
❑ 138 Teddy Higuera	.05	.01
❑ 139 Jesse Barfield	.05	.01
❑ 140 Pat Borders	.05	.01
❑ 141 Bip Roberts	.05	.01
❑ 142 Rob Dibble	.10	.02
❑ 143 Mark Grace	.15	.05
❑ 144 Barry Larkin	.15	.05
❑ 145 Ryne Sandberg	.40	.15
❑ 146 Scott Erickson	.05	.01
❑ 147 Luis Polonia	.05	.01
❑ 148 John Burkett	.05	.01
❑ 149 Luis Sojo	.05	.01
❑ 150 Dickie Thon	.05	.01
❑ 151 Walt Weiss	.05	.01
❑ 152 Mike Scioscia	.05	.01
❑ 153 Mark McGwire	.60	.25
❑ 154 Matt Williams	.10	.02
❑ 155 Rickey Henderson	.25	.08
❑ 156 Sandy Alomar Jr.	.05	.01
❑ 157 Brian McRae	.05	.01
❑ 158 Harold Baines	.10	.02
❑ 159 Kevin Appier	.10	.02
❑ 160 Felix Fermin	.05	.01
❑ 161 Leo Gomez	.05	.01
❑ 162 Craig Biggio	.15	.05
❑ 163 Ben McDonald	.05	.01
❑ 164 Randy Johnson	.25	.08
❑ 165 Cal Ripken	.75	.30
❑ 166 Frank Thomas	.25	.08
❑ 167 Delino DeShields	.05	.01
❑ 168 Greg Gagne	.05	.01
❑ 169 Ron Karkovice	.05	.01
❑ 170 Charlie Leibrandt	.05	.01
❑ 171 Dave Righetti	.10	.02
❑ 172 Dave Henderson	.05	.01
❑ 173 Steve Decker	.05	.01
❑ 174 Darryl Strawberry	.10	.02
❑ 175 Will Clark	.15	.05
❑ 176 Ruben Sierra	.10	.02
❑ 177 Ozzie Smith	.40	.15
❑ 178 Charles Nagy	.05	.01
❑ 179 Gary Pettis	.05	.01
❑ 180 Kirk Gibson	.10	.02
❑ 181 Randy Milligan	.05	.01
❑ 182 Dave Valle	.05	.01
❑ 183 Chris Hoiles	.05	.01
❑ 184 Tony Phillips	.05	.01
❑ 185 Brady Anderson	.10	.02
❑ 186 Scott Fletcher	.05	.01
❑ 187 Gene Larkin	.05	.01
❑ 188 Lance Johnson	.05	.01
❑ 189 Greg Olson	.05	.01
❑ 190 Melido Perez	.05	.01
❑ 191 Lenny Harris	.05	.01
❑ 192 Terry Kennedy	.05	.01
❑ 193 Mike Gallego	.05	.01
❑ 194 Willie McGee	.10	.02
❑ 195 Juan Samuel	.05	.01
❑ 196 Jeff Huson	.10	.02
❑ 197 Alex Cole	.05	.01
❑ 198 Ron Robinson	.05	.01
❑ 199 Joel Skinner	.05	.01
❑ 200 Checklist 101-200	.05	.01
❑ 201 Kevin Reimer	.05	.01
❑ 202 Stan Belinda	.05	.01
❑ 203 Pat Tabler	.05	.01
❑ 204 Jose Guzman	.05	.01
❑ 205 Jose Lind	.05	.01
❑ 206 Spike Owen	.05	.01
❑ 207 Joe Orsulak	.05	.01
❑ 208 Charlie Hayes	.05	.01
❑ 209 Mike Devereaux	.05	.01
❑ 210 Mike Fitzgerald	.05	.01
❑ 211 Willie Randolph	.10	.02
❑ 212 Rod Nichols	.05	.01
❑ 213 Mike Boddicker	.05	.01
❑ 214 Bill Spiers	.05	.01
❑ 215 Steve Olin	.05	.01
❑ 216 David Howard	.05	.01
❑ 217 Gary Varsho	.05	.01
❑ 218 Mike Harkey	.05	.01
❑ 219 Luis Aquino	.05	.01
❑ 220 Chuck McElroy	.05	.01
❑ 221 Doug Drabek	.05	.01
❑ 222 Dave Winfield	.10	.02
❑ 223 Rafael Palmeiro	.15	.05
❑ 224 Joe Carter	.10	.02
❑ 225 Bobby Bonilla	.10	.02
❑ 226 Ivan Calderon	.05	.01
❑ 227 Gregg Olson	.05	.01
❑ 228 Tim Wallach	.05	.01
❑ 229 Terry Pendleton	.10	.02
❑ 230 Gilberto Reyes	.05	.01
❑ 231 Carlos Baerga	.05	.01
❑ 232 Greg Vaughn	.05	.01
❑ 233 Bret Saberhagen	.10	.02
❑ 234 Gary Sheffield	.10	.02
❑ 235 Mark Lewis	.05	.01
❑ 236 George Bell	.05	.01
❑ 237 Danny Tartabull	.05	.01
❑ 238 Willie Wilson	.05	.01
❑ 239 Doug Dascenzo	.05	.01
❑ 240 Bill Pecota	.05	.01
❑ 241 Julio Franco	.10	.02
❑ 242 Ed Sprague	.05	.01
❑ 243 Juan Gonzalez	.15	.05
❑ 244 Chuck Finley	.10	.02
❑ 245 Ivan Rodriguez	.25	.08
❑ 246 Len Dykstra	.10	.02
❑ 247 Deion Sanders	.15	.05
❑ 248 Dwight Evans	.15	.05
❑ 249 Larry Walker	.15	.05
❑ 250 Billy Ripken	.05	.01
❑ 251 Mickey Tettleton	.05	.01
❑ 252 Tony Pena	.05	.01
❑ 253 Benito Santiago	.10	.02
❑ 254 Kirby Puckett	.25	.08
❑ 255 Cecil Fielder	.10	.02
❑ 256 Howard Johnson	.05	.01
❑ 257 Andujar Cedeno	.05	.01
❑ 258 Jose Rijo	.05	.01
❑ 259 Al Osuna	.05	.01
❑ 260 Todd Hundley	.05	.01
❑ 261 Orel Hershiser	.10	.02
❑ 262 Ray Lankford	.10	.02
❑ 263 Robin Ventura	.10	.02
❑ 264 Felix Jose	.05	.01
❑ 265 Eddie Murray	.25	.08
❑ 266 Kevin Mitchell	.05	.01
❑ 267 Gary Carter	.10	.02
❑ 268 Mike Benjamin	.05	.01
❑ 269 Dick Schofield	.05	.01
❑ 270 Jose Uribe	.05	.01
❑ 271 Pete Incaviglia	.05	.01
❑ 272 Tony Fernandez	.05	.01
❑ 273 Alan Trammell	.10	.02
❑ 274 Tony Gwynn	.30	.10
❑ 275 Mike Greenwell	.05	.01
❑ 276 Jeff Bagwell	.25	.08
❑ 277 Frank Viola	.10	.02
❑ 278 Randy Myers	.05	.01
❑ 279 Ken Caminiti	.10	.02
❑ 280 Bill Doran	.05	.01
❑ 281 Dan Pasqua	.05	.01
❑ 282 Alfredo Griffin	.05	.01
❑ 283 Jose Oquendo	.05	.01
❑ 284 Kal Daniels	.05	.01
❑ 285 Bobby Thigpen	.05	.01
❑ 286 Robby Thompson	.05	.01
❑ 287 Mark Eichhorn	.05	.01
❑ 288 Mike Felder	.05	.01
❑ 289 Dave Gallagher	.05	.01
❑ 290 Dave Anderson	.05	.01
❑ 291 Mel Hall	.05	.01
❑ 292 Jerald Clark	.05	.01
❑ 293 Al Newman	.05	.01
❑ 294 Rob Deer	.05	.01
❑ 295 Matt Nokes	.05	.01
❑ 296 Jack Armstrong	.05	.01
❑ 297 Jim Deshaies	.05	.01
❑ 298 Jeff Innis	.05	.01
❑ 299 Jeff Reed	.05	.01
❑ 300 Checklist 201-300	.05	.01
❑ 301 Lonnie Smith	.05	.01
❑ 302 Jimmy Key	.10	.02
❑ 303 Junior Felix	.05	.01
❑ 304 Mike Heath	.05	.01
❑ 305 Mark Langston	.05	.01
❑ 306 Greg W. Harris	.05	.01
❑ 307 Brett Butler	.10	.02
❑ 308 Luis Rivera	.05	.01
❑ 309 Bruce Ruffin	.05	.01
❑ 310 Paul Faries	.05	.01
❑ 311 Terry Leach	.05	.01
❑ 312 Scott Brosius RC	.50	.20
❑ 313 Scott Leius	.05	.01
❑ 314 Harold Reynolds	.10	.02
❑ 315 Jack Morris	.10	.02
❑ 316 David Segui	.05	.01
❑ 317 Bill Gullickson	.05	.01
❑ 318 Todd Frohwirth	.05	.01
❑ 319 Mark Leiter	.05	.01
❑ 320 Jeff M. Robinson	.05	.01
❑ 321 Gary Gaetti	.10	.02
❑ 322 John Smoltz	.15	.05
❑ 323 Andy Benes	.05	.01
❑ 324 Kelly Gruber	.05	.01
❑ 325 Jim Abbott	.15	.05
❑ 326 John Kruk	.10	.02
❑ 327 Kevin Seitzer	.05	.01
❑ 328 Darrin Jackson	.05	.01
❑ 329 Kurt Stillwell	.05	.01
❑ 330 Mike Maddux	.05	.01
❑ 331 Dennis Eckersley	.10	.02
❑ 332 Dan Gladden	.05	.01
❑ 333 Jose Canseco	.15	.05
❑ 334 Kent Hrbek	.10	.02
❑ 335 Ken Griffey Sr.	.10	.02
❑ 336 Greg Swindell	.05	.01
❑ 337 Trevor Wilson	.05	.01
❑ 338 Sam Horn	.05	.01
❑ 339 Mike Henneman	.05	.01
❑ 340 Jerry Browne	.05	.01
❑ 341 Glenn Braggs	.05	.01
❑ 342 Tom Glavine	.15	.05
❑ 343 Wally Joyner	.10	.02
❑ 344 Fred McGriff	.15	.05
❑ 345 Ron Gant	.10	.02
❑ 346 Ramon Martinez	.05	.01
❑ 347 Wes Chamberlain	.05	.01
❑ 348 Terry Shumpert	.05	.01
❑ 349 Tim Teufel	.05	.01
❑ 350 Wally Backman	.05	.01
❑ 351 Joe Girardi	.05	.01
❑ 352 Devon White	.10	.02
❑ 353 Greg Maddux	.40	.15
❑ 354 Ryan Bowen	.05	.01
❑ 355 Roberto Alomar	.15	.05
❑ 356 Don Mattingly	.60	.25
❑ 357 Pedro Guerrero	.10	.02
❑ 358 Steve Sax	.05	.01
❑ 359 Joey Cora	.05	.01
❑ 360 Jim Gantner	.05	.01
❑ 361 Brian Barnes	.05	.01
❑ 362 Kevin McReynolds	.05	.01
❑ 363 Bret Barberie	.05	.01
❑ 364 David Cone	.10	.02
❑ 365 Dennis Martinez	.10	.02
❑ 366 Brian Hunter	.05	.01
❑ 367 Edgar Martinez	.15	.05
❑ 368 Steve Finley	.10	.02
❑ 369 Greg Briley	.05	.01
❑ 370 Jeff Blauser	.05	.01
❑ 371 Todd Stottlemyre	.05	.01
❑ 372 Luis Gonzalez	.10	.02
❑ 373 Rick Wilkins	.05	.01
❑ 374 Darryl Kile	.10	.02
❑ 375 John Olerud	.10	.02
❑ 376 Lee Smith	.10	.02
❑ 377 Kevin Maas	.05	.01
❑ 378 Dante Bichette	.10	.02
❑ 379 Tom Pagnozzi	.05	.01
❑ 380 Mike Flanagan	.05	.01
❑ 381 Charlie O'Brien	.05	.01

❑ 382 Dave Martinez .05 .01
❑ 383 Keith Miller .05 .01
❑ 384 Scott Ruskin .05 .01
❑ 385 Kevin Elster .05 .01
❑ 386 Alvin Davis .05 .01
❑ 387 Casey Candaele .05 .01
❑ 388 Pete O'Brien .05 .01
❑ 389 Jeff Treadway .05 .01
❑ 390 Scott Bradley .05 .01
❑ 391 Mookie Wilson .10 .02
❑ 392 Jimmy Jones .05 .01
❑ 393 Candy Maldonado .05 .01
❑ 394 Eric Yelding .05 .01
❑ 395 Tom Henke .05 .01
❑ 396 Franklin Stubbs .05 .01
❑ 397 Milt Thompson .05 .01
❑ 398 Mark Carreon .05 .01
❑ 399 Randy Velarde .05 .01
❑ 400 Checklist 301-400 .05 .01
❑ 401 Omar Vizquel .15 .05
❑ 402 Joe Boever .05 .01
❑ 403 Bill Krueger .05 .01
❑ 404 Jody Reed .05 .01
❑ 405 Mike Schooler .05 .01
❑ 406 Jason Grimsley .05 .01
❑ 407 Greg Myers .05 .01
❑ 408 Randy Ready .05 .01
❑ 409 Mike Timlin .05 .01
❑ 410 Mitch Williams .05 .01
❑ 411 Garry Templeton .05 .01
❑ 412 Greg Cadaret .05 .01
❑ 413 Donnie Hill .05 .01
❑ 414 Wally Whitehurst .05 .01
❑ 415 Scott Sanderson .05 .01
❑ 416 Thomas Howard .05 .01
❑ 417 Neal Heaton .05 .01
❑ 418 Charlie Hough .10 .02
❑ 419 Jack Howell .05 .01
❑ 420 Greg Hibbard .05 .01
❑ 421 Carlos Quintana .05 .01
❑ 422 Kim Batiste .05 .01
❑ 423 Paul Molitor .10 .02
❑ 424 Ken Griffey Jr. .40 .15
❑ 425 Phil Plantier .05 .01
❑ 426 Denny Neagle .10 .02
❑ 427 Von Hayes .05 .01
❑ 428 Shane Mack .05 .01
❑ 429 Darren Daulton .10 .02
❑ 430 Dwayne Henry .05 .01
❑ 431 Lance Parrish .10 .02
❑ 432 Mike Humphreys .05 .01
❑ 433 Tim Burke .05 .01
❑ 434 Bryan Harvey .05 .01
❑ 435 Pat Kelly .05 .01
❑ 436 Ozzie Guillen .10 .02
❑ 437 Bruce Hurst .05 .01
❑ 438 Sammy Sosa .25 .08
❑ 439 Dennis Rasmussen .05 .01
❑ 440 Ken Patterson .05 .01
❑ 441 Jay Buhner .10 .02
❑ 442 Pat Combs .05 .01
❑ 443 Wade Boggs .15 .05
❑ 444 George Brett .60 .25
❑ 445 Mo Vaughn .10 .02
❑ 446 Chuck Knoblauch .10 .02
❑ 447 Tom Candiotti .05 .01
❑ 448 Mark Portugal .05 .01
❑ 449 Mickey Morandini .05 .01
❑ 450 Duane Ward .05 .01
❑ 451 Otis Nixon .05 .01
❑ 452 Bob Welch .05 .01
❑ 453 Rusty Meacham .05 .01
❑ 454 Keith Mitchell .05 .01
❑ 455 Marquis Grissom .10 .02
❑ 456 Robin Yount .40 .15
❑ 457 Harvey Pulliam .05 .01
❑ 458 Jose DeLeon .05 .01
❑ 459 Mark Gubicza .05 .01
❑ 460 Darryl Hamilton .05 .01
❑ 461 Tom Browning .05 .01
❑ 462 Monty Fariss .05 .01
❑ 463 Jerome Walton .05 .01
❑ 464 Paul O'Neill .15 .05
❑ 465 Dean Palmer .10 .02
❑ 466 Travis Fryman .10 .02
❑ 467 John Smiley .05 .01
❑ 468 Lloyd Moseby .05 .01
❑ 469 John Wehner .05 .01
❑ 470 Skeeter Barnes .05 .01
❑ 471 Steve Chitren .05 .01
❑ 472 Kent Mercker .05 .01
❑ 473 Terry Steinbach .05 .01
❑ 474 Andres Galarraga .10 .02
❑ 475 Steve Avery .05 .01
❑ 476 Tom Gordon .05 .01
❑ 477 Cal Eldred .05 .01
❑ 478 Omar Olivares .05 .01
❑ 479 Julio Machado .05 .01
❑ 480 Bob Milacki .05 .01
❑ 481 Les Lancaster .05 .01
❑ 482 John Candelaria .05 .01
❑ 483 Brian Downing .05 .01
❑ 484 Roger McDowell .05 .01
❑ 485 Scott Scudder .05 .01
❑ 486 Zane Smith .05 .01
❑ 487 John Cerutti .05 .01
❑ 488 Steve Buechele .05 .01
❑ 489 Paul Gibson .05 .01
❑ 490 Curtis Wilkerson .05 .01
❑ 491 Marvin Freeman .05 .01
❑ 492 Tom Foley .05 .01
❑ 493 Juan Berenguer .05 .01
❑ 494 Ernest Riles .05 .01
❑ 495 Sid Bream .05 .01
❑ 496 Chuck Crim .05 .01
❑ 497 Mike Macfarlane .05 .01
❑ 498 Dale Sveum .05 .01
❑ 499 Storm Davis .05 .01
❑ 500 Checklist 401-500 .05 .01
❑ 501 Jeff Reardon .10 .02
❑ 502 Shawn Abner .05 .01
❑ 503 Tony Fossas .05 .01
❑ 504 Cory Snyder .05 .01
❑ 505 Matt Young .05 .01
❑ 506 Allan Anderson .05 .01
❑ 507 Mark Lee .05 .01
❑ 508 Gene Nelson .05 .01
❑ 509 Mike Pagliarulo .05 .01
❑ 510 Rafael Belliard .05 .01
❑ 511 Jay Howell .05 .01
❑ 512 Bob Tewksbury .05 .01
❑ 513 Mike Morgan .05 .01
❑ 514 John Franco .10 .02
❑ 515 Kevin Gross .05 .01
❑ 516 Lou Whitaker .10 .02
❑ 517 Orlando Merced .05 .01
❑ 518 Todd Benzinger .05 .01
❑ 519 Gary Redus .05 .01
❑ 520 Walt Terrell .05 .01
❑ 521 Jack Clark .10 .02
❑ 522 Dave Parker .10 .02
❑ 523 Tim Naehring .05 .01
❑ 524 Mark Whiten .05 .01
❑ 525 Ellis Burks .10 .02
❑ 526 Frank Castillo .05 .01
❑ 527 Brian Harper .05 .01
❑ 528 Brook Jacoby .05 .01
❑ 529 Rick Sutcliffe .10 .02
❑ 530 Joe Klink .05 .01
❑ 531 Terry Bross .05 .01
❑ 532 Jose Offerman .05 .01
❑ 533 Todd Zeile .05 .01
❑ 534 Eric Karros .10 .02
❑ 535 Anthony Young .05 .01
❑ 536 Milt Cuyler .05 .01
❑ 537 Randy Tomlin .05 .01
❑ 538 Scott Livingstone .05 .01
❑ 539 Jim Eisenreich .05 .01
❑ 540 Don Slaught .05 .01
❑ 541 Scott Cooper .05 .01
❑ 542 Joe Grahe .05 .01
❑ 543 Tom Brunansky .05 .01
❑ 544 Eddie Zosky .05 .01
❑ 545 Roger Clemens .50 .20
❑ 546 David Justice .10 .02
❑ 547 Dave Stewart .10 .02
❑ 548 David West .05 .01
❑ 549 Dave Smith .05 .01
❑ 550 Dan Plesac .05 .01
❑ 551 Alex Fernandez .05 .01
❑ 552 Bernard Gilkey .05 .01
❑ 553 Jack McDowell .05 .01
❑ 554 Tino Martinez .15 .05
❑ 555 Bo Jackson .25 .08
❑ 556 Bernie Williams .15 .05
❑ 557 Mark Gardner .05 .01
❑ 558 Glenallen Hill .05 .01
❑ 559 Oil Can Boyd .05 .01
❑ 560 Chris James .05 .01
❑ 561 Scott Servais .05 .01
❑ 562 Rey Sanchez RC .25 .08
❑ 563 Paul McClellan .05 .01
❑ 564 Andy Mota .05 .01
❑ 565 Darren Lewis .05 .01
❑ 566 Jose Melendez .05 .01
❑ 567 Tommy Greene .05 .01
❑ 568 Rich Rodriguez .05 .01
❑ 569 Heathcliff Slocumb .05 .01
❑ 570 Joe Hesketh .05 .01
❑ 571 Carlton Fisk .15 .05
❑ 572 Erik Hanson .05 .01
❑ 573 Wilson Alvarez .05 .01
❑ 574 Rheal Cormier .05 .01
❑ 575 Tim Raines .10 .02
❑ 576 Bobby Witt .05 .01
❑ 577 Roberto Kelly .05 .01
❑ 578 Kevin Brown .10 .02
❑ 579 Chris Nabholz .05 .01
❑ 580 Jesse Orosco .05 .01
❑ 581 Jeff Brantley .05 .01
❑ 582 Rafael Ramirez .05 .01
❑ 583 Kelly Downs .05 .01
❑ 584 Mike Simms .05 .01
❑ 585 Mike Remlinger .05 .01
❑ 586 Dave Hollins .05 .01
❑ 587 Larry Andersen .05 .01
❑ 588 Mike Gardiner .05 .01
❑ 589 Craig Lefferts .05 .01
❑ 590 Paul Assenmacher .05 .01
❑ 591 Bryn Smith .05 .01
❑ 592 Donn Pall .05 .01
❑ 593 Mike Jackson .05 .01
❑ 594 Scott Radinsky .05 .01
❑ 595 Brian Holman .05 .01
❑ 596 Geronimo Pena .05 .01
❑ 597 Mike Jeffcoat .05 .01
❑ 598 Carlos Martinez .05 .01
❑ 599 Geno Petralli .05 .01
❑ 600 Checklist 501-600 .05 .01
❑ 601 Jerry Don Gleaton .05 .01
❑ 602 Adam Peterson .05 .01
❑ 603 Craig Grebeck .05 .01
❑ 604 Mark Guthrie .05 .01
❑ 605 Frank Tanana .05 .01
❑ 606 Hensley Meulens .05 .01
❑ 607 Mark Davis .05 .01
❑ 608 Eric Plunk .05 .01
❑ 609 Mark Williamson .05 .01
❑ 610 Lee Guetterman .05 .01
❑ 611 Bobby Rose .05 .01
❑ 612 Bill Wegman .05 .01
❑ 613 Mike Hartley .05 .01
❑ 614 Chris Beasley .05 .01
❑ 615 Chris Bosio .05 .01
❑ 616 Henry Cotto .05 .01
❑ 617 Chico Walker .05 .01
❑ 618 Russ Swan .05 .01
❑ 619 Bob Walk .05 .01
❑ 620 Bill Swift .05 .01
❑ 621 Warren Newson .05 .01
❑ 622 Steve Bedrosian .05 .01
❑ 623 Ricky Bones .05 .01
❑ 624 Kevin Tapani .05 .01
❑ 625 Juan Guzman .05 .01
❑ 626 Jeff Johnson .05 .01
❑ 627 Jeff Montgomery .05 .01
❑ 628 Ken Hill .05 .01
❑ 629 Gary Thurman .05 .01
❑ 630 Steve Howe .05 .01
❑ 631 Jose DeJesus .05 .01
❑ 632 Kirk Dressendorfer .05 .01
❑ 633 Jaime Navarro .05 .01
❑ 634 Lee Stevens .05 .01
❑ 635 Pete Harnisch .05 .01
❑ 636 Bill Landrum .05 .01
❑ 637 Rich DeLucia .05 .01
❑ 638 Luis Salazar .05 .01
❑ 639 Rob Murphy .05 .01

Card		
❑ 640 J.Canseco/R.Henderson CL	.15	.05
❑ 641 Roger Clemens DS	.25	.08
❑ 642 Jim Abbott DS	.10	.02
❑ 643 Travis Fryman DS	.05	.01
❑ 644 Jesse Barfield DS	.05	.01
❑ 645 Cal Ripken DS	.40	.15
❑ 646 Wade Boggs DS	.10	.02
❑ 647 Cecil Fielder DS	.05	.01
❑ 648 Rickey Henderson DS	.15	.05
❑ 649 Jose Canseco DS	.10	.02
❑ 650 Ken Griffey Jr. DS	.25	.08
❑ 651 Kenny Rogers	.10	.02
❑ 652 Luis Mercedes	.05	.01
❑ 653 Mike Stanton	.05	.01
❑ 654 Glenn Davis	.05	.01
❑ 655 Nolan Ryan	1.00	.40
❑ 656 Reggie Jefferson	.05	.01
❑ 657 Javier Ortiz	.05	.01
❑ 658 Greg A. Harris	.05	.01
❑ 659 Mariano Duncan	.05	.01
❑ 660 Jeff Shaw	.05	.01
❑ 661 Mike Moore	.05	.01
❑ 662 Chris Haney	.05	.01
❑ 663 Joe Slusarski	.05	.01
❑ 664 Wayne Housie	.05	.01
❑ 665 Carlos Garcia	.05	.01
❑ 666 Bob Ojeda	.05	.01
❑ 667 Bryan Hickerson RC	.10	.02
❑ 668 Tim Belcher	.05	.01
❑ 669 Ron Darling	.05	.01
❑ 670 Rex Hudler	.05	.01
❑ 671 Sid Fernandez	.05	.01
❑ 672 Chito Martinez	.05	.01
❑ 673 Pete Schourek	.05	.01
❑ 674 Armando Reynoso RC	.25	.08
❑ 675 Mike Mussina	.25	.08
❑ 676 Kevin Morton	.05	.01
❑ 677 Norm Charlton	.05	.01
❑ 678 Danny Darwin	.05	.01
❑ 679 Eric King	.05	.01
❑ 680 Ted Power	.05	.01
❑ 681 Barry Jones	.05	.01
❑ 682 Carney Lansford	.10	.02
❑ 683 Mel Rojas	.05	.01
❑ 684 Rick Honeycutt	.05	.01
❑ 685 Jeff Fassero	.05	.01
❑ 686 Cris Carpenter	.05	.01
❑ 687 Tim Crews	.05	.01
❑ 688 Scott Terry	.05	.01
❑ 689 Chris Gwynn	.05	.01
❑ 690 Gerald Perry	.05	.01
❑ 691 John Barfield	.05	.01
❑ 692 Bob Melvin	.05	.01
❑ 693 Juan Agosto	.05	.01
❑ 694 Alejandro Pena	.05	.01
❑ 695 Jeff Russell	.05	.01
❑ 696 Carmelo Martinez	.05	.01
❑ 697 Bud Black	.05	.01
❑ 698 Dave Otto	.05	.01
❑ 699 Billy Hatcher	.05	.01
❑ 700 Checklist 601-700	.05	.01
❑ 701 Clemente Nunez RC	.05	.01
❑ 702 M.Clark/Osborne/Jordan	.05	.01
❑ 703 Mike Morgan	.05	.01
❑ 704 Keith Miller	.05	.01
❑ 705 Kurt Stillwell	.05	.01
❑ 706 Damon Berryhill	.05	.01
❑ 707 Von Hayes	.05	.01
❑ 708 Rick Sutcliffe	.10	.02
❑ 709 Hubie Brooks	.05	.01
❑ 710 Ryan Turner RC	.10	.02
❑ 711 B.Bonds/A.Van Slyke CL	.50	.20
❑ 712 Jose Rijo DS	.05	.01
❑ 713 Tom Glavine DS	.10	.02
❑ 714 Shawon Dunston DS	.05	.01
❑ 715 Andy Van Slyke DS	.10	.02
❑ 716 Ozzie Smith DS	.25	.08
❑ 717 Tony Gwynn DS	.15	.05
❑ 718 Will Clark DS	.10	.02
❑ 719 Marquis Grissom DS	.05	.01
❑ 720 Howard Johnson DS	.05	.01
❑ 721 Barry Bonds DS	.50	.20
❑ 722 Kirk McCaskill	.05	.01
❑ 723 Sammy Sosa Cubs	.75	.30
❑ 724 George Bell	.05	.01
❑ 725 Gregg Jefferies	.05	.01

Card		
❑ 726 Gary DiSarcina	.05	.01
❑ 727 Mike Bordick	.05	.01
❑ 728 Eddie Murray 400 HR	.15	.05
❑ 729 Rene Gonzales	.05	.01
❑ 730 Mike Bielecki	.05	.01
❑ 731 Calvin Jones	.05	.01
❑ 732 Jack Morris	.10	.02
❑ 733 Frank Viola	.10	.02
❑ 734 Dave Winfield	.10	.02
❑ 735 Kevin Mitchell	.05	.01
❑ 736 Bill Swift	.05	.01
❑ 737 Dan Gladden	.05	.01
❑ 738 Mike Jackson	.05	.01
❑ 739 Mark Carreon	.05	.01
❑ 740 Kirt Manwaring	.05	.01
❑ 741 Randy Myers	.05	.01
❑ 742 Kevin McReynolds	.05	.01
❑ 743 Steve Sax	.05	.01
❑ 744 Wally Joyner	.10	.02
❑ 745 Gary Sheffield	.10	.02
❑ 746 Danny Tartabull	.05	.01
❑ 747 Julio Valera	.05	.01
❑ 748 Denny Neagle	.10	.02
❑ 749 Lance Blankenship	.05	.01
❑ 750 Mike Gallego	.05	.01
❑ 751 Bret Saberhagen	.10	.02
❑ 752 Ruben Amaro	.05	.01
❑ 753 Eddie Murray	.25	.08
❑ 754 Kyle Abbott	.05	.01
❑ 755 Bobby Bonilla	.10	.02
❑ 756 Eric Davis	.10	.02
❑ 757 Eddie Taubensee RC	.25	.08
❑ 758 Andres Galarraga	.10	.02
❑ 759 Pete Incaviglia	.05	.01
❑ 760 Tom Candiotti	.05	.01
❑ 761 Tim Belcher	.05	.01
❑ 762 Ricky Bones	.05	.01
❑ 763 Bip Roberts	.05	.01
❑ 764 Pedro Munoz	.05	.01
❑ 765 Greg Swindell	.05	.01
❑ 766 Kenny Lofton	.15	.05
❑ 767 Gary Carter	.10	.02
❑ 768 Charlie Hayes	.05	.01
❑ 769 Dickie Thon	.05	.01
❑ 770 Donovan Osborne DD CL	.05	.01
❑ 771 Bret Boone	.15	.05
❑ 772 Archi Cianfrocco RC	.10	.02
❑ 773 Mark Clark RC	.10	.02
❑ 774 Chad Curtis RC	.25	.08
❑ 775 Pat Listach RC	.25	.08
❑ 776 Pat Mahomes RC	.25	.08
❑ 777 Donovan Osborne	.05	.01
❑ 778 John Patterson RC	.10	.02
❑ 779 Andy Stankiewicz DD	.05	.01
❑ 780 Turk Wendell RC	.25	.08
❑ 781 Bill Krueger	.05	.01
❑ 782 Rickey Henderson 1000	.15	.05
❑ 783 Kevin Seitzer	.05	.01
❑ 784 Dave Martinez	.05	.01
❑ 785 John Smiley	.05	.01
❑ 786 Matt Stairs RC	.25	.08
❑ 787 Scott Scudder	.05	.01
❑ 788 John Wetteland	.10	.02
❑ 789 Jack Armstrong	.05	.01
❑ 790 Ken Hill	.05	.01
❑ 791 Dick Schofield	.05	.01
❑ 792 Mariano Duncan	.05	.01
❑ 793 Bill Pecota	.05	.01
❑ 794 Mike Kelly RC	.10	.02
❑ 795 Willie Randolph	.10	.02
❑ 796 Butch Henry	.05	.01
❑ 797 Carlos Hernandez	.05	.01
❑ 798 Doug Jones	.05	.01
❑ 799 Melido Perez	.05	.01
❑ 800 Checklist 701-800	.05	.01
❑ HH2 Ted Williams Holo	2.00	.75
❑ SP3 Deion Sanders FB/BB	1.00	.40
❑ SP4 F.Thomas/T.Selleck	1.00	.40

1993 Upper Deck

Card		
❑ COMPLETE SET (840)	40.00	15.00
❑ COMP.FACT.SET (840)	50.00	20.00
❑ COMPLETE SERIES 1 (420)	15.00	6.00
❑ COMPLETE SERIES 2 (420)	25.00	10.00
❑ 1 Tim Salmon CL	.20	.07
❑ 2 Mike Piazza	3.00	1.25
❑ 3 Rene Arocha RC	.50	.20
❑ 4 Willie Greene	.10	.02
❑ 5 Manny Alexander	.10	.02
❑ 6 Dan Wilson	.20	.07
❑ 7 Dan Smith	.10	.02
❑ 8 Kevin Rogers	.10	.02
❑ 9 Nigel Wilson	.10	.02
❑ 10 Joe Vitko	.10	.02
❑ 11 Tim Costo	.10	.02
❑ 12 Alan Embree	.10	.02
❑ 13 Jim Tatum RC	.15	.05
❑ 14 Cris Colon	.10	.02
❑ 15 Steve Hosey	.10	.02
❑ 16 Sterling Hitchcock RC	.50	.20
❑ 17 Dave Mlicki	.10	.02
❑ 18 Jessie Hollins	.10	.02
❑ 19 Bobby Jones	.20	.07
❑ 20 Kurt Miller	.10	.02
❑ 21 Melvin Nieves	.10	.02
❑ 22 Billy Ashley	.10	.02
❑ 23 J.T.Snow RC	.75	.30
❑ 24 Chipper Jones	.50	.20
❑ 25 Tim Salmon	.30	.10
❑ 26 Tim Pugh RC	.15	.05
❑ 27 David Nied	.10	.02
❑ 28 Mike Trombley	.10	.02
❑ 29 Javier Lopez	.30	.10
❑ 30 Jim Abbott CH CL	.20	.07
❑ 31 Jim Abbott CH	.10	.02
❑ 32 Dale Murphy CH	.30	.10
❑ 33 Tony Pena CH	.10	.02
❑ 34 Kirby Puckett CH	.30	.10
❑ 35 Harold Reynolds CH	.10	.02
❑ 36 Cal Ripken CH	.75	.30
❑ 37 Nolan Ryan CH	1.00	.40
❑ 38 Ryne Sandberg CH	.50	.20
❑ 39 Dave Stewart CH	.10	.02
❑ 40 Dave Winfield CH	.10	.02
❑ 41 M.McGwire/J.Carter CL	.50	.20
❑ 42 R.Alomar/J.Carter	.20	.07
❑ 43 Molitor/Listach/Yount	.50	.20
❑ 44 C.Ripken/B.Anderson	.50	.20
❑ 45 Belle/Baerga/Thome/Lofton	.20	.07
❑ 46 C.Fielder/M.Tettleton	.10	.02
❑ 47 R.Kelly/D.Mattingly	.60	.25
❑ 48 R.Clemens/F.Viola	.50	.20
❑ 49 R.Sierra/M.McGwire	.50	.20
❑ 50 K.Puckett/K.Hrbek	.30	.10
❑ 51 F.Thomas/R.Ventura	.30	.10
❑ 52 Cans/IRod/Gonz/Palmeiro	.30	.10
❑ 53 Lethal Lefties Mark Langston Jim Abbott Chuck F	.20	.07
❑ 54 Joyner/Jefferies/Brett	.50	.20
❑ 55 K.Griffey/Buhner/Mitchell	.50	.20
❑ 56 George Brett	1.25	.50
❑ 57 Scott Cooper	.10	.02
❑ 58 Mike Maddux	.10	.02
❑ 59 Rusty Meacham	.10	.02
❑ 60 Wil Cordero	.10	.02
❑ 61 Tim Teufel	.10	.02
❑ 62 Jeff Montgomery	.10	.02
❑ 63 Scott Livingstone	.10	.02
❑ 64 Doug Dascenzo	.10	.02
❑ 65 Bret Boone	.20	.07
❑ 66 Tim Wakefield	.50	.20
❑ 67 Curt Schilling	.20	.07

68	Frank Tanana	.10	.02
69	Len Dykstra	.20	.07
70	Derek Lilliquist	.10	.02
71	Anthony Young	.10	.02
72	Hipolito Pichardo	.10	.02
73	Rod Beck	.10	.02
74	Kent Hrbek	.20	.07
75	Tom Glavine	.30	.10
76	Kevin Brown	.20	.07
77	Chuck Finley	.20	.07
78	Bob Walk	.10	.02
79	Rheal Cormier UER	.10	.02
80	Rick Sutcliffe	.20	.07
81	Harold Baines	.20	.07
82	Lee Smith	.20	.07
83	Geno Petralli	.10	.02
84	Jose Oquendo	.10	.02
85	Mark Gubicza	.10	.02
86	Mickey Tettleton	.10	.02
87	Bobby Witt	.10	.02
88	Mark Lewis	.10	.02
89	Kevin Appier	.20	.07
90	Mike Stanton	.10	.02
91	Rafael Belliard	.10	.02
92	Kenny Rogers	.20	.07
93	Randy Velarde	.10	.02
94	Luis Sojo	.10	.02
95	Mark Leiter	.10	.02
96	Jody Reed	.10	.02
97	Pete Harnisch	.10	.02
98	Tom Candiotti	.10	.02
99	Mark Portugal	.10	.02
100	Dave Valle	.10	.02
101	Shawon Dunston	.10	.02
102	B.J. Surhoff	.20	.07
103	Jay Bell	.20	.07
104	Sid Bream	.10	.02
105	Frank Thomas CL	.30	.10
106	Mike Morgan	.10	.02
107	Bill Doran	.10	.02
108	Lance Blankenship	.10	.02
109	Mark Lemke	.10	.02
110	Brian Harper	.10	.02
111	Brady Anderson	.20	.07
112	Bip Roberts	.10	.02
113	Mitch Williams	.10	.02
114	Craig Biggio	.30	.10
115	Eddie Murray	.50	.20
116	Matt Nokes	.10	.02
117	Lance Parrish	.20	.07
118	Bill Swift	.10	.02
119	Jeff Innis	.10	.02
120	Mike LaValliere	.10	.02
121	Hal Morris	.10	.02
122	Walt Weiss	.10	.02
123	Ivan Rodriguez	.30	.10
124	Andy Van Slyke	.30	.10
125	Roberto Alomar	.30	.10
126	Robby Thompson	.10	.02
127	Sammy Sosa	.50	.20
128	Mark Langston	.10	.02
129	Jerry Browne	.10	.02
130	Chuck McElroy	.10	.02
131	Frank Viola	.20	.07
132	Leo Gomez	.10	.02
133	Ramon Martinez	.10	.02
134	Don Mattingly	1.25	.50
135	Roger Clemens	1.00	.40
136	Rickey Henderson	.50	.20
137	Darren Daulton	.20	.07
138	Ken Hill	.10	.02
139	Ozzie Guillen	.20	.07
140	Jerald Clark	.10	.02
141	Dave Fleming	.10	.02
142	Delino DeShields	.10	.02
143	Matt Williams	.20	.07
144	Larry Walker	.20	.07
145	Ruben Sierra	.20	.07
146	Ozzie Smith	.75	.30
147	Chris Sabo	.10	.02
148	Carlos Hernandez	.10	.02
149	Pat Borders	.10	.02
150	Orlando Merced	.10	.02
151	Royce Clayton	.10	.02
152	Kurt Stillwell	.10	.02
153	Dave Hollins	.10	.02
154	Mike Greenwell	.10	.02
155	Nolan Ryan	2.00	.75
156	Felix Jose	.10	.02
157	Junior Felix	.10	.02
158	Derek Bell	.10	.02
159	Steve Buechele	.10	.02
160	John Burkett	.10	.02
161	Pat Howell	.10	.02
162	Milt Cuyler	.10	.02
163	Terry Pendleton	.20	.07
164	Jack Morris	.20	.07
165	Tony Gwynn	.60	.25
166	Deion Sanders	.30	.10
167	Mike Devereaux	.10	.02
168	Ron Darling	.10	.02
169	Orel Hershiser	.20	.07
170	Mike Jackson	.10	.02
171	Doug Jones	.10	.02
172	Dan Walters	.10	.02
173	Darren Lewis	.10	.02
174	Carlos Baerga	.10	.02
175	Ryne Sandberg	.75	.30
176	Gregg Jefferies	.10	.02
177	John Jaha	.10	.02
178	Luis Polonia	.10	.02
179	Kirt Manwaring	.10	.02
180	Mike Magnante	.10	.02
181	Billy Ripken	.10	.02
182	Mike Moore	.10	.02
183	Eric Anthony	.10	.02
184	Lenny Harris	.10	.02
185	Tony Pena	.10	.02
186	Mike Felder	.10	.02
187	Greg Olson	.10	.02
188	Rene Gonzales	.10	.02
189	Mike Bordick	.10	.02
190	Mel Rojas	.10	.02
191	Todd Frohwirth	.10	.02
192	Darryl Hamilton	.10	.02
193	Mike Fetters	.10	.02
194	Omar Olivares	.10	.02
195	Tony Phillips	.10	.02
196	Paul Sorrento	.10	.02
197	Trevor Wilson	.10	.02
198	Kevin Gross	.10	.02
199	Ron Karkovice	.10	.02
200	Brook Jacoby	.10	.02
201	Mariano Duncan	.10	.02
202	Dennis Cook	.10	.02
203	Daryl Boston	.10	.02
204	Mike Perez	.10	.02
205	Manuel Lee	.10	.02
206	Steve Olin	.10	.02
207	Charlie Hough	.20	.07
208	Scott Scudder	.10	.02
209	Charlie O'Brien	.10	.02
210	Barry Bonds CL	.75	.30
211	Jose Vizcaino	.10	.02
212	Scott Leius	.10	.02
213	Kevin Mitchell	.10	.02
214	Brian Barnes	.10	.02
215	Pat Kelly	.10	.02
216	Chris Hammond	.10	.02
217	Rob Deer	.10	.02
218	Cory Snyder	.10	.02
219	Gary Carter	.20	.07
220	Danny Darwin	.10	.02
221	Tom Gordon	.10	.02
222	Gary Sheffield 2X	.20	.07
223	Joe Carter	.20	.07
224	Jay Buhner	.20	.07
225	Jose Offerman	.10	.02
226	Jose Rijo	.10	.02
227	Mark Whiten	.10	.02
228	Randy Milligan	.10	.02
229	Bud Black	.10	.02
230	Gary DiSarcina	.10	.02
231	Steve Finley	.20	.07
232	Dennis Martinez	.20	.07
233	Mike Mussina	.30	.10
234	Joe Oliver	.10	.02
235	Chad Curtis	.10	.02
236	Shane Mack	.10	.02
237	Jaime Navarro	.10	.02
238	Brian McRae	.10	.02
239	Chili Davis	.20	.07
240	Jeff King	.10	.02
241	Dean Palmer	.20	.07
242	Danny Tartabull	.10	.02
243	Charles Nagy	.10	.02
244	Ray Lankford	.20	.07
245	Barry Larkin	.30	.10
246	Steve Avery	.10	.02
247	John Kruk	.20	.07
248	Derrick May	.10	.02
249	Stan Javier	.10	.02
250	Roger McDowell	.10	.02
251	Dan Gladden	.10	.02
252	Wally Joyner	.20	.07
253	Pat Listach	.10	.02
254	Chuck Knoblauch	.20	.07
255	Sandy Alomar Jr.	.10	.02
256	Jeff Bagwell	.30	.10
257	Andy Stankiewicz	.10	.02
258	Darrin Jackson	.10	.02
259	Brett Butler	.20	.07
260	Joe Orsulak	.10	.02
261	Andy Benes	.10	.02
262	Kenny Lofton	.20	.07
263	Robin Ventura	.20	.07
264	Ron Gant	.20	.07
265	Ellis Burks	.20	.07
266	Juan Guzman	.10	.02
267	Wes Chamberlain	.10	.02
268	John Smiley	.10	.02
269	Franklin Stubbs	.10	.02
270	Tom Browning	.10	.02
271	Dennis Eckersley	.20	.07
272	Carlton Fisk	.30	.10
273	Lou Whitaker	.20	.07
274	Phil Plantier	.10	.02
275	Bobby Bonilla	.20	.07
276	Ben McDonald	.10	.02
277	Bob Zupcic	.10	.02
278	Terry Steinbach	.10	.02
279	Terry Mulholland	.10	.02
280	Lance Johnson	.10	.02
281	Willie McGee	.20	.07
282	Bret Saberhagen	.20	.07
283	Randy Myers	.10	.02
284	Randy Tomlin	.10	.02
285	Mickey Morandini	.10	.02
286	Brian Williams	.10	.02
287	Tino Martinez	.30	.10
288	Jose Melendez	.10	.02
289	Jeff Huson	.10	.02
290	Joe Grahe	.10	.02
291	Mel Hall	.10	.02
292	Otis Nixon	.10	.02
293	Todd Hundley	.10	.02
294	Casey Candaele	.10	.02
295	Kevin Seitzer	.10	.02
296	Eddie Taubensee	.10	.02
297	Moises Alou	.20	.07
298	Scott Radinsky	.10	.02
299	Thomas Howard	.10	.02
300	Kyle Abbott	.10	.02
301	Omar Vizquel	.30	.10
302	Keith Miller	.10	.02
303	Rick Aguilera	.10	.02
304	Bruce Hurst	.10	.02
305	Ken Caminiti	.20	.07
306	Mike Pagliarulo	.10	.02
307	Frank Seminara	.10	.02
308	Andre Dawson	.20	.07
309	Jose Lind	.10	.02
310	Joe Boever	.10	.02
311	Jeff Parrett	.10	.02
312	Alan Mills	.10	.02
313	Kevin Tapani	.10	.02
314	Darryl Kile	.20	.07
315	Checklist 211-315 Will Clark	.20	.07
316	Mike Sharperson	.10	.02
317	John Orton	.10	.02
318	Bob Tewksbury	.10	.02
319	Xavier Hernandez	.10	.02
320	Paul Assenmacher	.10	.02
321	John Franco	.20	.07
322	Mike Timlin	.10	.02
323	Jose Guzman	.10	.02
324	Pedro Martinez	1.00	.40

❑ 325 Bill Spiers .10 .02
❑ 326 Melido Perez .10 .02
❑ 327 Mike Macfarlane .10 .02
❑ 328 Ricky Bones .10 .02
❑ 329 Scott Bankhead .10 .02
❑ 330 Rich Rodriguez .10 .02
❑ 331 Geronimo Pena .10 .02
❑ 332 Bernie Williams .30 .10
❑ 333 Paul Molitor .20 .07
❑ 334 Carlos Garcia .10 .02
❑ 335 David Cone .20 .07
❑ 336 Randy Johnson .50 .20
❑ 337 Pat Mahomes .10 .02
❑ 338 Erik Hanson .10 .02
❑ 339 Duane Ward .10 .02
❑ 340 Al Martin .10 .02
❑ 341 Pedro Munoz .10 .02
❑ 342 Greg Colbrunn .10 .02
❑ 343 Julio Valera .10 .02
❑ 344 John Olerud .20 .07
❑ 345 George Bell .10 .02
❑ 346 Devon White .20 .07
❑ 347 Donovan Osborne .10 .02
❑ 348 Mark Gardner .10 .02
❑ 349 Zane Smith .10 .02
❑ 350 Wilson Alvarez .10 .02
❑ 351 Kevin Koslofski .10 .02
❑ 352 Roberto Hernandez .10 .02
❑ 353 Glenn Davis .10 .02
❑ 354 Reggie Sanders .20 .07
❑ 355 Ken Griffey Jr. .75 .30
❑ 356 Marquis Grissom .20 .07
❑ 357 Jack McDowell .10 .02
❑ 358 Jimmy Key .20 .07
❑ 359 Stan Belinda .10 .02
❑ 360 Gerald Williams .10 .02
❑ 361 Sid Fernandez .10 .02
❑ 362 Alex Fernandez .10 .02
❑ 363 John Smoltz .30 .10
❑ 364 Travis Fryman .20 .07
❑ 365 Jose Canseco .30 .10
❑ 366 David Justice .20 .07
❑ 367 Pedro Astacio .10 .02
❑ 368 Tim Belcher .10 .02
❑ 369 Steve Sax .10 .02
❑ 370 Gary Gaetti .20 .07
❑ 371 Jeff Frye .10 .02
❑ 372 Bob Wickman .10 .02
❑ 373 Ryan Thompson .10 .02
❑ 374 David Hulse RC .15 .05
❑ 375 Cal Eldred .10 .02
❑ 376 Ryan Klesko .20 .07
❑ 377 Damion Easley .10 .02
❑ 378 John Kiely .10 .02
❑ 379 Jim Bullinger .10 .02
❑ 380 Brian Bohanon .10 .02
❑ 381 Rod Brewer .10 .02
❑ 382 Fernando Ramsey RC .15 .05
❑ 383 Sam Militello .10 .02
❑ 384 Arthur Rhodes .10 .02
❑ 385 Eric Karros .20 .07
❑ 386 Rico Brogna .10 .02
❑ 387 John Valentin .10 .02
❑ 388 Kerry Woodson .10 .02
❑ 389 Ben Rivera .10 .02
❑ 390 Matt Whiteside RC .15 .05
❑ 391 Henry Rodriguez .10 .02
❑ 392 John Wetteland .20 .07
❑ 393 Kent Mercker .10 .02
❑ 394 Bernard Gilkey .10 .02
❑ 395 Doug Henry .10 .02
❑ 396 Mo Vaughn .20 .07
❑ 397 Scott Erickson .10 .02
❑ 398 Bill Gullickson .10 .02
❑ 399 Mark Guthrie .10 .02
❑ 400 Dave Martinez .10 .02
❑ 401 Jeff Kent .50 .20
❑ 402 Chris Hoiles .10 .02
❑ 403 Mike Henneman .10 .02
❑ 404 Chris Nabholz .10 .02
❑ 405 Tom Pagnozzi .10 .02
❑ 406 Kelly Gruber .10 .02
❑ 407 Bob Welch .10 .02
❑ 408 Frank Castillo .10 .02
❑ 409 John Dopson .10 .02
❑ 410 Steve Farr .10 .02
❑ 411 Henry Cotto .10 .02
❑ 412 Bob Patterson .10 .02
❑ 413 Todd Stottlemyre .10 .02
❑ 414 Greg A. Harris .10 .02
❑ 415 Denny Neagle .20 .07
❑ 416 Bill Wegman .10 .02
❑ 417 Willie Wilson .10 .02
❑ 418 Terry Leach .10 .02
❑ 419 Willie Randolph .20 .07
❑ 420 Checklist 316-420 McGwire .30 .10
❑ 421 Calvin Murray CL .10 .02
❑ 422 Pete Janicki RC .15 .05
❑ 423 Todd Jones TP .20 .07
❑ 424 Mike Neill .10 .02
❑ 425 Carlos Delgado .50 .20
❑ 426 Jose Oliva .10 .02
❑ 427 Tyrone Hill .10 .02
❑ 428 Dmitri Young .20 .07
❑ 429 Derek Wallace RC .15 .05
❑ 430 Michael Moore RC .15 .05
❑ 431 Cliff Floyd .20 .07
❑ 432 Calvin Murray .10 .02
❑ 433 Manny Ramirez .75 .30
❑ 434 Marc Newfield .10 .02
❑ 435 Charles Johnson .20 .07
❑ 436 Butch Huskey .10 .02
❑ 437 Brad Pennington TP .10 .02
❑ 438 Ray McDavid RC .15 .05
❑ 439 Chad McConnell .10 .02
❑ 440 Midre Cummings RC .15 .05
❑ 441 Benji Gil .10 .02
❑ 442 Frankie Rodriguez .10 .02
❑ 443 Chad Mottola RC .15 .05
❑ 444 John Burke RC .15 .05
❑ 445 Michael Tucker .10 .02
❑ 446 Rick Greene .10 .02
❑ 447 Rich Becker .10 .02
❑ 448 Mike Robertson TP .10 .02
❑ 449 Derek Jeter RC ! 10.00 4.00
❑ 450 I.Rodriguez/D.McCarty CL .30 .10
❑ 451 Jim Abbott IN .20 .07
❑ 452 Jeff Bagwell IN .20 .07
❑ 453 Jason Bere IN .10 .02
❑ 454 Delino DeShields IN .10 .02
❑ 455 Travis Fryman IN .10 .02
❑ 456 Alex Gonzalez IN .10 .02
❑ 457 Phil Hiatt IN .10 .02
❑ 458 Dave Hollins IN .10 .02
❑ 459 Chipper Jones IN .30 .10
❑ 460 David Justice IN .10 .02
❑ 461 Ray Lankford IN .10 .02
❑ 462 David McCarty IN .10 .02
❑ 463 Mike Mussina IN .20 .07
❑ 464 Jose Offerman IN .10 .02
❑ 465 Dean Palmer IN .10 .02
❑ 466 Geronimo Pena IN .10 .02
❑ 467 Eduardo Perez IN .10 .02
❑ 468 Ivan Rodriguez IN .20 .07
❑ 469 Reggie Sanders IN .10 .02
❑ 470 Bernie Williams IN .20 .07
❑ 471 Bonds/Williams/Clark CL .75 .30
❑ 472 Madd/Avery/Smolt/Glav .50 .20
❑ 473 Red October
Jose Rijo
Rob Dibble
Roberto Kelly .20 .07
❑ 474 Sheff/Plant/Gwynn/McGrif .20 .07
❑ 475 Biggio/Drabek/Bagwell .20 .07
❑ 476 Clark/Bonds/Williams .75 .30
❑ 477 Eric Davis
Darryl Strawberry .20 .07
❑ 478 Bich/Nied/Galarraga .20 .07
❑ 479 Maga/Destr/Barbe/Conine .10 .02
❑ 480 Wakefield/Van Slyke/Bell .20 .07
❑ 481 Griss/DeSh/Mart/Walker .30 .10
❑ 482 O.Smith/Redbirds .50 .20
❑ 483 Myers/Sandberg/Grace .50 .20
❑ 484 Big Apple Power Switch .30 .10
❑ 485 Kruk/Holl/Dault/Dyks .10 .02
❑ 486 Barry Bonds AW .75 .30
❑ 487 Dennis Eckersley AW .20 .07
❑ 488 Greg Maddux AW .50 .20
❑ 489 Dennis Eckersley AW .20 .07
❑ 490 Eric Karros AW .10 .02
❑ 491 Pat Listach AW .10 .02
❑ 492 Gary Sheffield AW .10 .02
❑ 493 Mark McGwire AW .60 .25
❑ 494 Gary Sheffield AW .10 .02
❑ 495 Edgar Martinez AW .20 .07
❑ 496 Fred McGriff AW .20 .07
❑ 497 Juan Gonzalez AW .10 .02
❑ 498 Darren Daulton AW .10 .02
❑ 499 Cecil Fielder AW .10 .02
❑ 500 Brent Gates CL .10 .02
❑ 501 Tavo Alvarez .10 .02
❑ 502 Rod Bolton .10 .02
❑ 503 John Cummings RC .15 .05
❑ 504 Brent Gates .10 .02
❑ 505 Tyler Green .10 .02
❑ 506 Jose Martinez RC .15 .05
❑ 507 Troy Percival .30 .10
❑ 508 Kevin Stocker .10 .02
❑ 509 Matt Walbeck RC .15 .05
❑ 510 Rondell White .20 .07
❑ 511 Billy Ripken .10 .02
❑ 512 Mike Moore .10 .02
❑ 513 Jose Lind .10 .02
❑ 514 Chito Martinez .10 .02
❑ 515 Jose Guzman .10 .02
❑ 516 Kim Batiste .10 .02
❑ 517 Jeff Tackett .10 .02
❑ 518 Charlie Hough .20 .07
❑ 519 Marvin Freeman .10 .02
❑ 520 Carlos Martinez .10 .02
❑ 521 Eric Young .10 .02
❑ 522 Pete Incaviglia .10 .02
❑ 523 Scott Fletcher .10 .02
❑ 524 Orestes Destrade .10 .02
❑ 525 Ken Griffey Jr. CL .50 .20
❑ 526 Ellis Burks .20 .07
❑ 527 Juan Samuel .10 .02
❑ 528 Dave Magadan .10 .02
❑ 529 Jeff Parrett .10 .02
❑ 530 Bill Krueger .10 .02
❑ 531 Frank Bolick .10 .02
❑ 532 Alan Trammell .20 .07
❑ 533 Walt Weiss .10 .02
❑ 534 David Cone .20 .07
❑ 535 Greg Maddux .75 .30
❑ 536 Kevin Young .20 .07
❑ 537 Dave Hansen .10 .02
❑ 538 Alex Cole .10 .02
❑ 539 Greg Hibbard .10 .02
❑ 540 Gene Larkin .10 .02
❑ 541 Jeff Reardon .20 .07
❑ 542 Felix Jose .10 .02
❑ 543 Jimmy Key .20 .07
❑ 544 Reggie Jefferson .10 .02
❑ 545 Gregg Jefferies .10 .02
❑ 546 Dave Stewart .20 .07
❑ 547 Tim Wallach .10 .02
❑ 548 Spike Owen .10 .02
❑ 549 Tommy Greene .10 .02
❑ 550 Fernando Valenzuela .20 .07
❑ 551 Rich Amaral .10 .02
❑ 552 Bret Barberie .10 .02
❑ 553 Edgar Martinez .30 .10
❑ 554 Jim Abbott .30 .10
❑ 555 Frank Thomas .50 .20
❑ 556 Wade Boggs .30 .10
❑ 557 Tom Henke .10 .02
❑ 558 Milt Thompson .10 .02
❑ 559 Lloyd McClendon .10 .02
❑ 560 Vinny Castilla .50 .20
❑ 561 Ricky Jordan .10 .02
❑ 562 Andujar Cedeno .10 .02
❑ 563 Greg Vaughn .10 .02
❑ 564 Cecil Fielder .20 .07
❑ 565 Kirby Puckett .50 .20
❑ 566 Mark McGwire 1.25 .50
❑ 567 Barry Bonds 1.50 .60
❑ 568 Jody Reed .10 .02
❑ 569 Todd Zeile .10 .02
❑ 570 Mark Carreon .10 .02
❑ 571 Joe Girardi .10 .02
❑ 572 Luis Gonzalez .20 .07
❑ 573 Mark Grace .30 .10
❑ 574 Rafael Palmeiro .30 .10
❑ 575 Darryl Strawberry .20 .07
❑ 576 Will Clark .30 .10
❑ 577 Fred McGriff .30 .10
❑ 578 Kevin Reimer .10 .02

❑ 579 Dave Righetti .20 .07
❑ 580 Juan Bell .10 .02
❑ 581 Jeff Brantley .10 .02
❑ 582 Brian Hunter .10 .02
❑ 583 Tim Naehring .10 .02
❑ 584 Glenallen Hill .10 .02
❑ 585 Cal Ripken 1.50 .60
❑ 586 Albert Belle .20 .07
❑ 587 Robin Yount .75 .30
❑ 588 Chris Bosio .10 .02
❑ 589 Pete Smith .10 .02
❑ 590 Chuck Carr .10 .02
❑ 591 Jeff Blauser .10 .02
❑ 592 Kevin McReynolds .10 .02
❑ 593 Andres Galarraga .20 .07
❑ 594 Kevin Maas .10 .02
❑ 595 Eric Davis .20 .07
❑ 596 Brian Jordan .20 .07
❑ 597 Tim Raines .20 .07
❑ 598 Rick Wilkins .10 .02
❑ 599 Steve Cooke .10 .02
❑ 600 Mike Gallego .10 .02
❑ 601 Mike Munoz .10 .02
❑ 602 Luis Rivera .10 .02
❑ 603 Junior Ortiz .10 .02
❑ 604 Brent Mayne .10 .02
❑ 605 Luis Alicea .10 .02
❑ 606 Damon Berryhill .10 .02
❑ 607 Dave Henderson .10 .02
❑ 608 Kirk McCaskill .10 .02
❑ 609 Jeff Fassero .10 .02
❑ 610 Mike Harkey .10 .02
❑ 611 Francisco Cabrera .10 .02
❑ 612 Rey Sanchez .10 .02
❑ 613 Scott Servais .10 .02
❑ 614 Darrin Fletcher .10 .02
❑ 615 Felix Fermin .10 .02
❑ 616 Kevin Seitzer .10 .02
❑ 617 Bob Scanlan .10 .02
❑ 618 Billy Hatcher .10 .02
❑ 619 John Vander Wal .10 .02
❑ 620 Joe Hesketh .10 .02
❑ 621 Hector Villanueva .10 .02
❑ 622 Randy Milligan .10 .02
❑ 623 Tony Tarasco RC .15 .05
❑ 624 Russ Swan .10 .02
❑ 625 Willie Wilson .10 .02
❑ 626 Frank Tanana .10 .02
❑ 627 Pete O'Brien .10 .02
❑ 628 Lenny Webster .10 .02
❑ 629 Mark Clark .10 .02
❑ 630 Roger Clemens CL .50 .20
❑ 631 Alex Arias .10 .02
❑ 632 Chris Gwynn .10 .02
❑ 633 Tom Bolton .10 .02
❑ 634 Greg Briley .10 .02
❑ 635 Kent Bottenfield .10 .02
❑ 636 Kelly Downs .10 .02
❑ 637 Manuel Lee .10 .02
❑ 638 Al Leiter .20 .07
❑ 639 Jeff Gardner .10 .02
❑ 640 Mike Gardiner .10 .02
❑ 641 Mark Gardner .10 .02
❑ 642 Jeff Branson .10 .02
❑ 643 Paul Wagner .10 .02
❑ 644 Sean Berry .10 .02
❑ 645 Phil Hiatt .10 .02
❑ 646 Kevin Mitchell .10 .02
❑ 647 Charlie Hayes .10 .02
❑ 648 Jim Deshaies .10 .02
❑ 649 Dan Pasqua .10 .02
❑ 650 Mike Maddux .10 .02
❑ 651 Domingo Martinez RC .15 .05
❑ 652 Greg McMichael RC .15 .05
❑ 653 Eric Wedge RC .50 .20
❑ 654 Mark Whiten .10 .02
❑ 655 Roberto Kelly .10 .02
❑ 656 Julio Franco .20 .07
❑ 657 Gene Harris .10 .02
❑ 658 Pete Schourek .10 .02
❑ 659 Mike Bielecki .10 .02
❑ 660 Ricky Gutierrez .10 .02
❑ 661 Chris Hammond .10 .02
❑ 662 Tim Scott .10 .02
❑ 663 Norm Charlton .10 .02
❑ 664 Doug Drabek .10 .02
❑ 665 Dwight Gooden .20 .07
❑ 666 Jim Gott .10 .02
❑ 667 Randy Myers .10 .02
❑ 668 Darren Holmes .10 .02
❑ 669 Tim Spehr .10 .02
❑ 670 Bruce Ruffin .10 .02
❑ 671 Bobby Thigpen .10 .02
❑ 672 Tony Fernandez .10 .02
❑ 673 Darrin Jackson .10 .02
❑ 674 Gregg Olson .10 .02
❑ 675 Rob Dibble .20 .07
❑ 676 Howard Johnson .10 .02
❑ 677 Mike Lansing RC .50 .20
❑ 678 Charlie Leibrandt .10 .02
❑ 679 Kevin Bass .10 .02
❑ 680 Hubie Brooks .10 .02
❑ 681 Scott Brosius .20 .07
❑ 682 Randy Knorr .10 .02
❑ 683 Dante Bichette .20 .07
❑ 684 Bryan Harvey .10 .02
❑ 685 Greg Gohr .10 .02
❑ 686 Willie Banks .10 .02
❑ 687 Robb Nen .20 .07
❑ 688 Mike Scioscia .10 .02
❑ 689 John Farrell .10 .02
❑ 690 John Candelaria .10 .02
❑ 691 Damon Buford .10 .02
❑ 692 Todd Worrell .10 .02
❑ 693 Pat Hentgen .10 .02
❑ 694 John Smiley .10 .02
❑ 695 Greg Swindell .10 .02
❑ 696 Derek Bell .10 .02
❑ 697 Terry Jorgensen .10 .02
❑ 698 Jimmy Jones .10 .02
❑ 699 David Wells .20 .07
❑ 700 Dave Martinez .10 .02
❑ 701 Steve Bedrosian .10 .02
❑ 702 Jeff Russell .10 .02
❑ 703 Joe Magrane .10 .02
❑ 704 Matt Mieske .10 .02
❑ 705 Paul Molitor .20 .07
❑ 706 Dale Murphy .30 .10
❑ 707 Steve Howe .10 .02
❑ 708 Greg Gagne .10 .02
❑ 709 Dave Eiland .10 .02
❑ 710 David West .10 .02
❑ 711 Luis Aquino .10 .02
❑ 712 Joe Orsulak .10 .02
❑ 713 Eric Plunk .10 .02
❑ 714 Mike Felder .10 .02
❑ 715 Joe Klink .10 .02
❑ 716 Lonnie Smith .10 .02
❑ 717 Monty Fariss .10 .02
❑ 718 Craig Lefferts .10 .02
❑ 719 John Habyan .10 .02
❑ 720 Willie Blair .10 .02
❑ 721 Darnell Coles .10 .02
❑ 722 Mark Williamson .10 .02
❑ 723 Bryn Smith .10 .02
❑ 724 Greg W. Harris .10 .02
❑ 725 Graeme Lloyd RC .50 .20
❑ 726 Cris Carpenter .10 .02
❑ 727 Chico Walker .10 .02
❑ 728 Tracy Woodson .10 .02
❑ 729 Jose Uribe .10 .02
❑ 730 Stan Javier .10 .02
❑ 731 Jay Howell .10 .02
❑ 732 Freddie Benavides .10 .02
❑ 733 Jeff Reboulet .10 .02
❑ 734 Scott Sanderson .10 .02
❑ 735 Ryne Sandberg CL .50 .20
❑ 736 Archi Cianfrocco .10 .02
❑ 737 Daryl Boston .10 .02
❑ 738 Craig Grebeck .10 .02
❑ 739 Doug Dascenzo .10 .02
❑ 740 Gerald Young .10 .02
❑ 741 Candy Maldonado .10 .02
❑ 742 Joey Cora .10 .02
❑ 743 Don Slaught .10 .02
❑ 744 Steve Decker .10 .02
❑ 745 Blas Minor .10 .02
❑ 746 Storm Davis .10 .02
❑ 747 Carlos Quintana .10 .02
❑ 748 Vince Coleman .10 .02
❑ 749 Todd Burns .10 .02
❑ 750 Steve Frey .10 .02
❑ 751 Ivan Calderon .10 .02
❑ 752 Steve Reed RC .15 .05
❑ 753 Danny Jackson .10 .02
❑ 754 Jeff Conine .20 .07
❑ 755 Juan Gonzalez .20 .07
❑ 756 Mike Kelly .10 .02
❑ 757 John Doherty .10 .02
❑ 758 Jack Armstrong .10 .02
❑ 759 John Wehner .10 .02
❑ 760 Scott Bankhead .10 .02
❑ 761 Jim Tatum .10 .02
❑ 762 Scott Pose RC .15 .05
❑ 763 Andy Ashby .10 .02
❑ 764 Ed Sprague .10 .02
❑ 765 Harold Baines .20 .07
❑ 766 Kirk Gibson .20 .07
❑ 767 Troy Neel .10 .02
❑ 768 Dick Schofield .10 .02
❑ 769 Dickie Thon .10 .02
❑ 770 Butch Henry .10 .02
❑ 771 Junior Felix .10 .02
❑ 772 Ken Ryan RC .15 .05
❑ 773 Trevor Hoffman .50 .20
❑ 774 Phil Plantier .10 .02
❑ 775 Bo Jackson .50 .20
❑ 776 Benito Santiago .20 .07
❑ 777 Andre Dawson .20 .07
❑ 778 Bryan Hickerson .10 .02
❑ 779 Dennis Moeller .10 .02
❑ 780 Ryan Bowen .10 .02
❑ 781 Eric Fox .10 .02
❑ 782 Joe Kmak .10 .02
❑ 783 Mike Hampton .20 .07
❑ 784 Darrell Sherman RC .15 .05
❑ 785 J.T.Snow .30 .10
❑ 786 Dave Winfield .20 .07
❑ 787 Jim Austin .10 .02
❑ 788 Craig Shipley .10 .02
❑ 789 Greg Myers .10 .02
❑ 790 Todd Benzinger .10 .02
❑ 791 Cory Snyder .10 .02
❑ 792 David Segui .10 .02
❑ 793 Armando Reynoso .10 .02
❑ 794 Chili Davis .20 .07
❑ 795 Dave Nilsson .10 .02
❑ 796 Paul O'Neill .30 .10
❑ 797 Jerald Clark .10 .02
❑ 798 Jose Mesa .10 .02
❑ 799 Brain Holman .10 .02
❑ 800 Jim Eisenreich .10 .02
❑ 801 Mark McLemore .10 .02
❑ 802 Luis Sojo .10 .02
❑ 803 Harold Reynolds .20 .07
❑ 804 Dan Plesac .10 .02
❑ 805 Dave Stieb .10 .02
❑ 806 Tom Brunansky .10 .02
❑ 807 Kelly Gruber .10 .02
❑ 808 Bob Ojeda .10 .02
❑ 809 Dave Burba .10 .02
❑ 810 Joe Boever .10 .02
❑ 811 Jeremy Hernandez .10 .02
❑ 812 Tim Salmon TC .20 .07
❑ 813 Jeff Bagwell TC .20 .07
❑ 814 Dennis Eckersley TC .20 .07
❑ 815 Roberto Alomar TC .20 .07
❑ 816 Steve Avery TC .10 .02
❑ 817 Pat Listach TC .10 .02
❑ 818 Gregg Jefferies TC .10 .02
❑ 819 Sammy Sosa TC .50 .20
❑ 820 Darryl Strawberry TC .10 .02
❑ 821 Dennis Martinez TC .10 .02
❑ 822 Robby Thompson TC .10 .02
❑ 823 Albert Belle TC .20 .07
❑ 824 Randy Johnson TC .30 .10
❑ 825 Nigel Wilson TC .10 .02
❑ 826 Bobby Bonilla TC .10 .02
❑ 827 Glenn Davis TC .10 .02
❑ 828 Gary Sheffield TC .10 .02
❑ 829 Darren Daulton TC .10 .02
❑ 830 Jay Bell TC .10 .02
❑ 831 Juan Gonzalez TC .10 .02
❑ 832 Andre Dawson TC .10 .02
❑ 833 Hal Morris TC .10 .02
❑ 834 David Nied TC .10 .02
❑ 835 Felix Jose TC .10 .02
❑ 836 Travis Fryman TC .10 .02

❑	Card		
❑	837 Shane Mack TC	.10	.02
❑	838 Robin Ventura TC	.10	.02
❑	839 Danny Tartabull TC	.10	.02
❑	840 Roberto Alomar CL	.20	.07
❑	SP5 G.Brett/R.Yount	1.00	.40
❑	SP6 Nolan Ryan	2.00	.75

1994 Upper Deck

❑	Card		
❑	COMPLETE SET (550)	40.00	15.00
❑	COMPLETE SERIES 1 (280)	25.00	12.50
❑	COMPLETE SERIES 2 (270)	15.00	7.50
❑	1 Brian Anderson RC	.40	.15
❑	2 Shane Andrews	.15	.05
❑	3 James Baldwin	.15	.05
❑	4 Rich Becker	.15	.05
❑	5 Greg Blosser	.15	.05
❑	6 Ricky Bottalico RC	.15	.05
❑	7 Midre Cummings	.15	.05
❑	8 Carlos Delgado	.50	.20
❑	9 Steve Dreyer RC	.15	.05
❑	10 Joey Eischen	.15	.05
❑	11 Carl Everett	.30	.10
❑	12 Cliff Floyd	.30	.10
❑	13 Alex Gonzalez	.15	.05
❑	14 Jeff Granger	.15	.05
❑	15 Shawn Green	.75	.30
❑	16 Brian L.Hunter	.15	.05
❑	17 Butch Huskey	.15	.05
❑	18 Mark Hutton	.15	.05
❑	19 Michael Jordan RC	8.00	3.00
❑	20 Steve Karsay	.15	.05
❑	21 Jeff McNeely	.15	.05
❑	22 Marc Newfield	.15	.05
❑	23 Manny Ramirez	.75	.30
❑	24 Alex Rodriguez RC	25.00	10.00
❑	25 Scott Ruffcorn UER	.15	.05
❑	26 Paul Spoljaric UER	.15	.05
❑	27 Salomon Torres	.15	.05
❑	28 Steve Trachsel	.15	.05
❑	29 Chris Turner	.15	.05
❑	30 Gabe White	.15	.05
❑	31 Randy Johnson FT	.50	.20
❑	32 John Wetteland FT	.15	.05
❑	33 Mike Piazza FT	.75	.30
❑	34 Rafael Palmeiro FT	.30	.10
❑	35 Roberto Alomar FT	.30	.10
❑	36 Matt Williams FT	.15	.05
❑	37 Travis Fryman FT	.15	.05
❑	38 Barry Bonds FT	1.00	.40
❑	39 Marquis Grissom FT	.15	.05
❑	40 Albert Belle FT	.30	.10
❑	41 Steve Avery FUT	.15	.05
❑	42 Jason Bere FUT	.15	.05
❑	43 Alex Fernandez FUT	.15	.05
❑	44 Mike Mussina FUT	.30	.10
❑	45 Aaron Sele FUT	.15	.05
❑	46 Rod Beck FUT	.15	.05
❑	47 Mike Piazza FUT	.75	.30
❑	48 John Olerud FUT	.15	.05
❑	49 Carlos Baerga FUT	.15	.05
❑	50 Gary Sheffield FUT	.15	.05
❑	51 Travis Fryman FUT	.15	.05
❑	52 Juan Gonzalez FUT	.15	.05
❑	53 Ken Griffey Jr. FUT	.75	.30
❑	54 Tim Salmon FUT	.30	.10
❑	55 Frank Thomas FUT	.50	.20
❑	56 Tony Phillips	.15	.05
❑	57 Julio Franco	.30	.10
❑	58 Kevin Mitchell	.15	.05
❑	59 Raul Mondesi	.30	.10
❑	60 Rickey Henderson	.75	.30
❑	61 Jay Buhner	.30	.10
❑	62 Bill Swift	.15	.05
❑	63 Brady Anderson	.30	.10
❑	64 Ryan Klesko	.30	.10
❑	65 Darren Daulton	.30	.10
❑	66 Damion Easley	.15	.05
❑	67 Mark McGwire	2.00	.75
❑	68 John Roper	.15	.05
❑	69 Dave Telgheder	.15	.05
❑	70 David Nied	.15	.05
❑	71 Mo Vaughn	.30	.10
❑	72 Tyler Green	.15	.05
❑	73 Dave Magadan	.15	.05
❑	74 Chili Davis	.30	.10
❑	75 Archi Cianfrocco	.15	.05
❑	76 Joe Girardi	.15	.05
❑	77 Chris Hoiles	.15	.05
❑	78 Ryan Bowen	.15	.05
❑	79 Greg Gagne	.15	.05
❑	80 Aaron Sele	.15	.05
❑	81 Dave Winfield	.30	.10
❑	82 Chad Curtis	.15	.05
❑	83 Andy Van Slyke	.50	.20
❑	84 Kevin Stocker	.15	.05
❑	85 Deion Sanders	.50	.20
❑	86 Bernie Williams	.50	.20
❑	87 John Smoltz	.50	.20
❑	88 Ruben Santana	.15	.05
❑	89 Dave Stewart	.30	.10
❑	90 Don Mattingly	2.00	.75
❑	91 Joe Carter	.30	.10
❑	92 Ryne Sandberg	1.25	.50
❑	93 Chris Gomez	.15	.05
❑	94 Tino Martinez	.50	.20
❑	95 Terry Pendleton	.30	.10
❑	96 Andre Dawson	.30	.10
❑	97 Wil Cordero	.15	.05
❑	98 Kent Hrbek	.30	.10
❑	99 John Olerud	.30	.10
❑	100 Kirt Manwaring	.15	.05
❑	101 Tim Bogar	.15	.05
❑	102 Mike Mussina	.50	.20
❑	103 Nigel Wilson	.15	.05
❑	104 Ricky Gutierrez	.15	.05
❑	105 Roberto Mejia	.15	.05
❑	106 Tom Pagnozzi	.15	.05
❑	107 Mike Macfarlane	.15	.05
❑	108 Jose Bautista	.15	.05
❑	109 Luis Ortiz	.15	.05
❑	110 Brent Gates	.15	.05
❑	111 Tim Salmon	.50	.20
❑	112 Wade Boggs	.50	.20
❑	113 Tripp Cromer	.15	.05
❑	114 Denny Hocking	.15	.05
❑	115 Carlos Baerga	.15	.05
❑	116 J.R. Phillips	.15	.05
❑	117 Bo Jackson	.75	.30
❑	118 Lance Johnson	.15	.05
❑	119 Bobby Jones	.15	.05
❑	120 Bobby Witt	.15	.05
❑	121 Ron Karkovice	.15	.05
❑	122 Jose Vizcaino	.15	.05
❑	123 Danny Darwin	.15	.05
❑	124 Eduardo Perez	.15	.05
❑	125 Brian Looney RC	.15	.05
❑	126 Pat Hentgen	.15	.05
❑	127 Frank Viola	.30	.10
❑	128 Darren Holmes	.15	.05
❑	129 Wally Whitehurst	.15	.05
❑	130 Matt Walbeck	.15	.05
❑	131 Albert Belle	.30	.10
❑	132 Steve Cooke	.15	.05
❑	133 Kevin Appier	.30	.10
❑	134 Joe Oliver	.15	.05
❑	135 Benji Gil	.15	.05
❑	136 Steve Buechele	.15	.05
❑	137 Devon White	.30	.10
❑	138 Sterling Hitchcock UER	.15	.05
❑	139 Phil Leftwich RC	.15	.05
❑	140 Jose Canseco	.50	.20
❑	141 Rick Aguilera	.15	.05
❑	142 Rod Beck	.15	.05
❑	143 Jose Rijo	.15	.05
❑	144 Tom Glavine	.50	.20
❑	145 Phil Plantier	.15	.05
❑	146 Jason Bere	.15	.05
❑	147 Jamie Moyer	.30	.10
❑	148 Wes Chamberlain	.15	.05
❑	149 Glenallen Hill	.15	.05
❑	150 Mark Whiten	.15	.05
❑	151 Bret Barberie	.15	.05
❑	152 Chuck Knoblauch	.30	.10
❑	153 Trevor Hoffman	.50	.20
❑	154 Rick Wilkins	.15	.05
❑	155 Juan Gonzalez	.30	.10
❑	156 Ozzie Guillen	.30	.10
❑	157 Jim Eisenreich	.15	.05
❑	158 Pedro Astacio	.15	.05
❑	159 Joe Magrane	.15	.05
❑	160 Ryan Thompson	.15	.05
❑	161 Jose Lind	.15	.05
❑	162 Jeff Conine	.30	.10
❑	163 Todd Benzinger	.15	.05
❑	164 Roger Salkeld	.15	.05
❑	165 Gary DiSarcina	.15	.05
❑	166 Kevin Gross	.15	.05
❑	167 Charlie Hayes	.15	.05
❑	168 Tim Costo	.15	.05
❑	169 Wally Joyner	.30	.10
❑	170 Johnny Ruffin	.15	.05
❑	171 Kirk Rueter	.15	.05
❑	172 Lenny Dykstra	.30	.10
❑	173 Ken Hill	.15	.05
❑	174 Mike Bordick	.15	.05
❑	175 Billy Hall	.15	.05
❑	176 Rob Butler	.15	.05
❑	177 Jay Bell	.30	.10
❑	178 Jeff Kent	.50	.20
❑	179 David Wells	.30	.10
❑	180 Dean Palmer	.30	.10
❑	181 Mariano Duncan	.15	.05
❑	182 Orlando Merced	.15	.05
❑	183 Brett Butler	.30	.10
❑	184 Milt Thompson	.15	.05
❑	185 Chipper Jones	.75	.30
❑	186 Paul O'Neill	.50	.20
❑	187 Mike Greenwell	.15	.05
❑	188 Harold Baines	.30	.10
❑	189 Todd Stottlemyre	.15	.05
❑	190 Jeromy Burnitz	.30	.10
❑	191 Rene Arocha	.15	.05
❑	192 Jeff Fassero	.15	.05
❑	193 Robby Thompson	.15	.05
❑	194 Greg W. Harris	.15	.05
❑	195 Todd Van Poppel	.15	.05
❑	196 Jose Guzman	.15	.05
❑	197 Shane Mack	.15	.05
❑	198 Carlos Garcia	.15	.05
❑	199 Kevin Roberson	.15	.05
❑	200 David McCarty	.15	.05
❑	201 Alan Trammell	.30	.10
❑	202 Chuck Carr	.15	.05
❑	203 Tommy Greene	.15	.05
❑	204 Wilson Alvarez	.15	.05
❑	205 Dwight Gooden	.30	.10
❑	206 Tony Tarasco	.15	.05
❑	207 Darren Lewis	.15	.05
❑	208 Eric Karros	.30	.10
❑	209 Chris Hammond	.15	.05
❑	210 Jeffrey Hammonds	.15	.05
❑	211 Rich Amaral	.15	.05
❑	212 Danny Tartabull	.15	.05
❑	213 Jeff Russell	.15	.05
❑	214 Dave Staton	.15	.05
❑	215 Kenny Lofton	.30	.10
❑	216 Manuel Lee	.15	.05
❑	217 Brian Koelling	.15	.05
❑	218 Scott Lydy	.15	.05

❑ 219 Tony Gwynn 1.00 .40
❑ 220 Cecil Fielder .30 .10
❑ 221 Royce Clayton .15 .05
❑ 222 Reggie Sanders .30 .10
❑ 223 Brian Jordan .30 .10
❑ 224 Ken Griffey Jr. 1.25 .50
❑ 225 Fred McGriff .50 .20
❑ 226 Felix Jose .15 .05
❑ 227 Brad Pennington .15 .05
❑ 228 Chris Bosio .15 .05
❑ 229 Mike Stanley .15 .05
❑ 230 Willie Greene .15 .05
❑ 231 Alex Fernandez .15 .05
❑ 232 Brad Ausmus .50 .20
❑ 233 Darrell Whitmore .15 .05
❑ 234 Marcus Moore .15 .05
❑ 235 Allen Watson .15 .05
❑ 236 Jose Offerman .15 .05
❑ 237 Rondell White .30 .10
❑ 238 Jeff King .15 .05
❑ 239 Luis Alicea .15 .05
❑ 240 Dan Wilson .15 .05
❑ 241 Ed Sprague .15 .05
❑ 242 Todd Hundley .15 .05
❑ 243 Al Martin .15 .05
❑ 244 Mike Lansing .15 .05
❑ 245 Ivan Rodriguez .50 .20
❑ 246 Dave Fleming .15 .05
❑ 247 John Doherty .15 .05
❑ 248 Mark McLemore .15 .05
❑ 249 Bob Hamelin .15 .05
❑ 250 Curtis Pride RC .40 .15
❑ 251 Zane Smith .15 .05
❑ 252 Eric Young .15 .05
❑ 253 Brian McRae .15 .05
❑ 254 Tim Raines .30 .10
❑ 255 Javier Lopez .30 .10
❑ 256 Melvin Nieves .15 .05
❑ 257 Randy Myers .15 .05
❑ 258 Willie McGee .30 .10
❑ 259 Jimmy Key UER .30 .10
❑ 260 Tom Candiotti .15 .05
❑ 261 Eric Davis .30 .10
❑ 262 Craig Paquette .15 .05
❑ 263 Robin Ventura .30 .10
❑ 264 Pat Kelly .15 .05
❑ 265 Gregg Jefferies .15 .05
❑ 266 Cory Snyder .15 .05
❑ 267 David Justice HFA .15 .05
❑ 268 Sammy Sosa HFA .75 .30
❑ 269 Barry Larkin HFA .30 .10
❑ 270 Andres Galarraga HFA .15 .05
❑ 271 Gary Sheffield HFA .15 .05
❑ 272 Jeff Bagwell HFA .30 .10
❑ 273 Mike Piazza HFA .75 .30
❑ 274 Larry Walker HFA .15 .05
❑ 275 Bobby Bonilla HFA .15 .05
❑ 276 John Kruk HFA .15 .05
❑ 277 Jay Bell HFA .15 .05
❑ 278 Ozzie Smith HFA .75 .30
❑ 279 Tony Gwynn HFA .50 .20
❑ 280 Barry Bonds HFA 1.00 .40
❑ 281 Cal Ripken HFA 1.25 .50
❑ 282 Mo Vaughn HFA .15 .05
❑ 283 Tim Salmon HFA .30 .10
❑ 284 Frank Thomas HFA .50 .20
❑ 285 Albert Belle HFA .30 .10
❑ 286 Cecil Fielder HFA .15 .05
❑ 287 Wally Joyner HFA .15 .05
❑ 288 Greg Vaughn HFA .15 .05
❑ 289 Kirby Puckett HFA .50 .20
❑ 290 Don Mattingly HFA 1.00 .40
❑ 291 Terry Steinbach HFA .15 .05
❑ 292 Ken Griffey Jr. HFA .75 .30
❑ 293 Juan Gonzalez HFA .15 .05
❑ 294 Paul Molitor HFA .15 .05
❑ 295 Tavo Alvarez UDCA .15 .05
❑ 296 Matt Brunson UDCA .15 .05
❑ 297 Shawn Green UDCA .30 .10
❑ 298 Alex Rodriguez UDCA 6.00 2.50
❑ 299 Shannon Stewart UDCA .75 .30
❑ 300 Frank Thomas .75 .30
❑ 301 Mickey Tettleton .15 .05
❑ 302 Pedro Munoz .15 .05
❑ 303 Jose Valentin .15 .05
❑ 304 Orestes Destrade .15 .05
❑ 305 Pat Listach .15 .05
❑ 306 Scott Brosius .30 .10
❑ 307 Kurt Miller .15 .05
❑ 308 Rob Dibble .30 .10
❑ 309 Mike Blowers .15 .05
❑ 310 Jim Abbott .50 .20
❑ 311 Mike Jackson .15 .05
❑ 312 Craig Biggio .50 .20
❑ 313 Kurt Abbott RC .15 .05
❑ 314 Chuck Finley .30 .10
❑ 315 Andres Galarraga .30 .10
❑ 316 Mike Moore .15 .05
❑ 317 Doug Strange .15 .05
❑ 318 Pedro Martinez .75 .30
❑ 319 Kevin McReynolds .15 .05
❑ 320 Greg Maddux 1.25 .50
❑ 321 Mike Henneman .15 .05
❑ 322 Scott Leius .15 .05
❑ 323 John Franco .30 .10
❑ 324 Jeff Blauser .15 .05
❑ 325 Kirby Puckett .75 .30
❑ 326 Darryl Hamilton .15 .05
❑ 327 John Smiley .15 .05
❑ 328 Derrick May .15 .05
❑ 329 Jose Vizcaino .15 .05
❑ 330 Randy Johnson .75 .30
❑ 331 Jack Morris .30 .10
❑ 332 Graeme Lloyd .15 .05
❑ 333 Dave Valle .15 .05
❑ 334 Greg Myers .15 .05
❑ 335 John Wetteland .30 .10
❑ 336 Jim Gott .15 .05
❑ 337 Tim Naehring .15 .05
❑ 338 Mike Kelly .15 .05
❑ 339 Jeff Montgomery .15 .05
❑ 340 Rafael Palmeiro .50 .20
❑ 341 Eddie Murray .75 .30
❑ 342 Xavier Hernandez .15 .05
❑ 343 Bobby Munoz .15 .05
❑ 344 Bobby Bonilla .30 .10
❑ 345 Travis Fryman .30 .10
❑ 346 Steve Finley .30 .10
❑ 347 Chris Sabo .15 .05
❑ 348 Armando Reynoso .15 .05
❑ 349 Ramon Martinez .15 .05
❑ 350 Will Clark .50 .20
❑ 351 Moises Alou .30 .10
❑ 352 Jim Thome .50 .20
❑ 353 Bob Tewksbury .15 .05
❑ 354 Andujar Cedeno .15 .05
❑ 355 Orel Hershiser .30 .10
❑ 356 Mike Devereaux .15 .05
❑ 357 Mike Perez .15 .05
❑ 358 Dennis Martinez .30 .10
❑ 359 Dave Nilsson .15 .05
❑ 360 Ozzie Smith 1.25 .50
❑ 361 Eric Anthony .15 .05
❑ 362 Scott Sanders .15 .05
❑ 363 Paul Sorrento .15 .05
❑ 364 Tim Belcher .15 .05
❑ 365 Dennis Eckersley .30 .10
❑ 366 Mel Rojas .15 .05
❑ 367 Tom Henke .15 .05
❑ 368 Randy Tomlin .15 .05
❑ 369 B.J. Surhoff .30 .10
❑ 370 Larry Walker .30 .10
❑ 371 Joey Cora .15 .05
❑ 372 Mike Harkey .15 .05
❑ 373 John Valentin .15 .05
❑ 374 Doug Jones .15 .05
❑ 375 David Justice .30 .10
❑ 376 Vince Coleman .15 .05
❑ 377 David Hulse .15 .05
❑ 378 Kevin Seitzer .15 .05
❑ 379 Pete Harnisch .15 .05
❑ 380 Ruben Sierra .30 .10
❑ 381 Mark Lewis .15 .05
❑ 382 Bip Roberts .15 .05
❑ 383 Paul Wagner .15 .05
❑ 384 Stan Javier .15 .05
❑ 385 Barry Larkin .50 .20
❑ 386 Mark Portugal .15 .05
❑ 387 Roberto Kelly .15 .05
❑ 388 Andy Benes .15 .05
❑ 389 Felix Fermin .15 .05
❑ 390 Marquis Grissom .30 .10
❑ 391 Troy Neel .15 .05
❑ 392 Chad Kreuter .15 .05
❑ 393 Gregg Olson .15 .05
❑ 394 Charles Nagy .15 .05
❑ 395 Jack McDowell .15 .05
❑ 396 Luis Gonzalez .30 .10
❑ 397 Benito Santiago .30 .10
❑ 398 Chris James .15 .05
❑ 399 Terry Mulholland .15 .05
❑ 400 Barry Bonds 2.00 .75
❑ 401 Joe Grahe .15 .05
❑ 402 Duane Ward .15 .05
❑ 403 John Burkett .15 .05
❑ 404 Scott Servais .15 .05
❑ 405 Bryan Harvey .15 .05
❑ 406 Bernard Gilkey .15 .05
❑ 407 Greg McMichael .15 .05
❑ 408 Tim Wallach .15 .05
❑ 409 Ken Caminiti .30 .10
❑ 410 John Kruk .30 .10
❑ 411 Darrin Jackson .15 .05
❑ 412 Mike Gallego .15 .05
❑ 413 David Cone .30 .10
❑ 414 Lou Whitaker .30 .10
❑ 415 Sandy Alomar Jr. .15 .05
❑ 416 Bill Wegman .15 .05
❑ 417 Pat Borders .15 .05
❑ 418 Roger Pavlik .15 .05
❑ 419 Pete Smith .15 .05
❑ 420 Steve Avery .15 .05
❑ 421 David Segui .15 .05
❑ 422 Rheal Cormier .15 .05
❑ 423 Harold Reynolds .30 .10
❑ 424 Edgar Martinez .50 .20
❑ 425 Cal Ripken 2.50 1.00
❑ 426 Jaime Navarro .15 .05
❑ 427 Sean Berry .15 .05
❑ 428 Bret Saberhagen .30 .10
❑ 429 Bob Welch .15 .05
❑ 430 Juan Guzman .15 .05
❑ 431 Cal Eldred .15 .05
❑ 432 Dave Hollins .15 .05
❑ 433 Sid Fernandez .15 .05
❑ 434 Willie Banks .15 .05
❑ 435 Darryl Kile .30 .10
❑ 436 Henry Rodriguez .15 .05
❑ 437 Tony Fernandez .15 .05
❑ 438 Walt Weiss .15 .05
❑ 439 Kevin Tapani .15 .05
❑ 440 Mark Grace .50 .20
❑ 441 Brian Harper .15 .05
❑ 442 Kent Mercker .15 .05
❑ 443 Anthony Young .15 .05
❑ 444 Todd Zeile .15 .05
❑ 445 Greg Vaughn .15 .05
❑ 446 Ray Lankford .30 .10
❑ 447 Dave Weathers .15 .05
❑ 448 Bret Boone .30 .10
❑ 449 Charlie Hough .30 .10
❑ 450 Roger Clemens 1.50 .60
❑ 451 Mike Morgan .15 .05
❑ 452 Doug Drabek .15 .05
❑ 453 Danny Jackson .15 .05
❑ 454 Dante Bichette .30 .10
❑ 455 Roberto Alomar .50 .20
❑ 456 Ben McDonald .15 .05
❑ 457 Kenny Rogers .30 .10
❑ 458 Bill Gullickson .15 .05
❑ 459 Darrin Fletcher .15 .05
❑ 460 Curt Schilling .30 .10
❑ 461 Billy Hatcher .15 .05
❑ 462 Howard Johnson .15 .05
❑ 463 Mickey Morandini .15 .05
❑ 464 Frank Castillo .15 .05

❑ 465	Delino DeShields	.15	.05
❑ 466	Gary Gaetti	.30	.10
❑ 467	Steve Farr	.15	.05
❑ 468	Roberto Hernandez	.15	.05
❑ 469	Jack Armstrong	.15	.05
❑ 470	Paul Molitor	.30	.10
❑ 471	Melido Perez	.15	.05
❑ 472	Greg Hibbard	.15	.05
❑ 473	Jody Reed	.15	.05
❑ 474	Tom Gordon	.15	.05
❑ 475	Gary Sheffield	.30	.10
❑ 476	John Jaha	.15	.05
❑ 477	Shawon Dunston	.15	.05
❑ 478	Reggie Jefferson	.15	.05
❑ 479	Don Slaught	.15	.05
❑ 480	Jeff Bagwell	.50	.20
❑ 481	Tim Pugh	.15	.05
❑ 482	Kevin Young	.15	.05
❑ 483	Ellis Burks	.30	.10
❑ 484	Greg Swindell	.15	.05
❑ 485	Mark Langston	.15	.05
❑ 486	Omar Vizquel	.50	.20
❑ 487	Kevin Brown	.30	.10
❑ 488	Terry Steinbach	.15	.05
❑ 489	Mark Lemke	.15	.05
❑ 490	Matt Williams	.30	.10
❑ 491	Pete Incaviglia	.15	.05
❑ 492	Karl Rhodes	.15	.05
❑ 493	Shawn Green	.75	.30
❑ 494	Hal Morris	.15	.05
❑ 495	Derek Bell	.15	.05
❑ 496	Luis Polonia	.15	.05
❑ 497	Otis Nixon	.15	.05
❑ 498	Ron Darling	.15	.05
❑ 499	Mitch Williams	.15	.05
❑ 500	Mike Piazza	1.50	.60
❑ 501	Pat Meares	.15	.05
❑ 502	Scott Cooper	.15	.05
❑ 503	Scott Erickson	.15	.05
❑ 504	Jeff Juden	.15	.05
❑ 505	Lee Smith	.30	.10
❑ 506	Bobby Ayala	.15	.05
❑ 507	Dave Henderson	.15	.05
❑ 508	Erik Hanson	.15	.05
❑ 509	Bob Wickman	.15	.05
❑ 510	Sammy Sosa	.75	.30
❑ 511	Hector Carrasco	.15	.05
❑ 512	Tim Davis	.15	.05
❑ 513	Joey Hamilton	.15	.05
❑ 514	Robert Eenhoorn	.15	.05
❑ 515	Jorge Fabregas	.15	.05
❑ 516	Tim Hyers RC	.15	.05
❑ 517	John Hudek RC	.15	.05
❑ 518	James Mouton	.15	.05
❑ 519	Herbert Perry RC	.15	.05
❑ 520	Chan Ho Park RC	.75	.30
❑ 521	W.VanLandingham RC	.15	.05
❑ 522	Paul Shuey DD	.15	.05
❑ 523	Ryan Hancock RC	.15	.05
❑ 524	Billy Wagner RC	2.00	.75
❑ 525	Jason Giambi	.75	.30
❑ 526	Jose Silva RC	.15	.05
❑ 527	Terrell Wade RC	.15	.05
❑ 528	Todd Dunn	.15	.05
❑ 529	Alan Benes RC	.40	.15
❑ 530	Brooks Kieschnick RC	.15	.05
❑ 531	Todd Hollandsworth	.15	.05
❑ 532	Brad Fullmer RC	.40	.15
❑ 533	Steve Soderstrom RC	.15	.05
❑ 534	Daron Kirkreit	.15	.05
❑ 535	Arquimedez Pozo RC	.15	.05
❑ 536	Charles Johnson	.30	.10
❑ 537	Preston Wilson	.30	.10
❑ 538	Alex Ochoa	.15	.05
❑ 539	Derrek Lee RC	4.00	1.50
❑ 540	Wayne Gomes RC	.15	.05
❑ 541	Jermaine Allensworth RC	.15	.05
❑ 542	Mike Bell RC	.15	.05
❑ 543	Trot Nixon RC	2.00	.75
❑ 544	Pokey Reese	.15	.05
❑ 545	Neifi Perez RC	.40	.15
❑ 546	Johnny Damon	.75	.30
❑ 547	Matt Brunson RC	.15	.05
❑ 548	LaTroy Hawkins RC	.40	.15
❑ 549	Eddie Pearson RC	.15	.05
❑ 550	Derek Jeter	2.50	1.00
❑ A298	Alex Rodriguez AU	600.00	300.00
❑ P224	Ken Griffey Jr. Promo	2.00	.75
❑ GM1	Griffey/Mantle AU/1000	1200.00	1000.00
❑ KG1	K.Griffey Jr. AU/1000	300.00	200.00
❑ MM1	M.Mantle AU/1000	750.00	450.00

1995 Upper Deck

❑	COMP.MASTER SET (495)	110.00	55.00
❑	COMPLETE SET (450)	50.00	20.00
❑	COMPLETE SERIES 1 (225)	25.00	10.00
❑	COMPLETE SERIES 2 (225)	25.00	10.00
❑	COMMON CARD (1-450)	.15	.05
❑	COMP.TRADE SET (45)	60.00	30.00
❑	COMMON TRADE (451T-495T)	1.00	.40
❑ 1	Ruben Rivera	.15	.05
❑ 2	Bill Pulsipher	.15	.05
❑ 3	Ben Grieve	.15	.05
❑ 4	Curtis Goodwin	.15	.05
❑ 5	Damon Hollins	.15	.05
❑ 6	Todd Greene	.15	.05
❑ 7	Glenn Williams	.15	.05
❑ 8	Bret Wagner	.15	.05
❑ 9	Karim Garcia RC	.15	.05
❑ 10	Nomar Garciaparra	2.00	.75
❑ 11	Raul Casanova RC	.15	.05
❑ 12	Matt Smith	.15	.05
❑ 13	Paul Wilson	.15	.05
❑ 14	Jason Isringhausen	.30	.10
❑ 15	Reid Ryan	.30	.10
❑ 16	Lee Smith	.30	.10
❑ 17	Chili Davis	.30	.10
❑ 18	Brian Anderson	.15	.05
❑ 19	Gary DiSarcina	.15	.05
❑ 20	Bo Jackson	.75	.30
❑ 21	Chuck Finley	.30	.10
❑ 22	Darryl Kile	.30	.10
❑ 23	Shane Reynolds	.15	.05
❑ 24	Tony Eusebio	.15	.05
❑ 25	Craig Biggio	.50	.20
❑ 26	Doug Drabek	.15	.05
❑ 27	Brian L.Hunter	.15	.05
❑ 28	James Mouton	.15	.05
❑ 29	Geronimo Berroa	.15	.05
❑ 30	Rickey Henderson	.75	.30
❑ 31	Steve Karsay	.15	.05
❑ 32	Steve Ontiveros	.15	.05
❑ 33	Ernie Young	.15	.05
❑ 34	Dennis Eckersley	.30	.10
❑ 35	Mark McGwire	2.00	.75
❑ 36	Dave Stewart	.30	.10
❑ 37	Pat Hentgen	.15	.05
❑ 38	Carlos Delgado	.30	.10
❑ 39	Joe Carter	.30	.10
❑ 40	Roberto Alomar	.50	.20
❑ 41	John Olerud	.30	.10
❑ 42	Devon White	.30	.10
❑ 43	Roberto Kelly	.15	.05
❑ 44	Jeff Blauser	.15	.05
❑ 45	Fred McGriff	.50	.20
❑ 46	Tom Glavine	.50	.20
❑ 47	Mike Kelly	.15	.05
❑ 48	Javier Lopez	.30	.10
❑ 49	Greg Maddux	1.25	.50
❑ 50	Matt Mieske	.15	.05

❑ 51	Troy O'Leary	.15	.05
❑ 52	Jeff Cirillo	.15	.05
❑ 53	Cal Eldred	.15	.05
❑ 54	Pat Listach	.15	.05
❑ 55	Jose Valentin	.15	.05
❑ 56	John Mabry	.15	.05
❑ 57	Bob Tewksbury	.15	.05
❑ 58	Brian Jordan	.30	.10
❑ 59	Gregg Jefferies	.15	.05
❑ 60	Ozzie Smith	1.25	.50
❑ 61	Geronimo Pena	.15	.05
❑ 62	Mark Whiten	.15	.05
❑ 63	Rey Sanchez	.15	.05
❑ 64	Willie Banks	.15	.05
❑ 65	Mark Grace	.50	.20
❑ 66	Randy Myers	.15	.05
❑ 67	Steve Trachsel	.15	.05
❑ 68	Derrick May	.15	.05
❑ 69	Brett Butler	.30	.10
❑ 70	Eric Karros	.30	.10
❑ 71	Tim Wallach	.15	.05
❑ 72	Delino DeShields	.15	.05
❑ 73	Darren Dreifort	.15	.05
❑ 74	Orel Hershiser	.30	.10
❑ 75	Billy Ashley	.15	.05
❑ 76	Sean Berry	.15	.05
❑ 77	Ken Hill	.15	.05
❑ 78	John Wetteland	.30	.10
❑ 79	Moises Alou	.30	.10
❑ 80	Cliff Floyd	.30	.10
❑ 81	Marquis Grissom	.30	.10
❑ 82	Larry Walker	.30	.10
❑ 83	Rondell White	.30	.10
❑ 84	William VanLandingham	.15	.05
❑ 85	Matt Williams	.30	.10
❑ 86	Rod Beck	.15	.05
❑ 87	Darren Lewis	.15	.05
❑ 88	Robby Thompson	.15	.05
❑ 89	Darryl Strawberry	.30	.10
❑ 90	Kenny Lofton	.30	.10
❑ 91	Charles Nagy	.15	.05
❑ 92	Sandy Alomar Jr.	.15	.05
❑ 93	Mark Clark	.15	.05
❑ 94	Dennis Martinez	.30	.10
❑ 95	Dave Winfield	.30	.10
❑ 96	Jim Thome	.50	.20
❑ 97	Manny Ramirez	.50	.20
❑ 98	Goose Gossage	.30	.10
❑ 99	Tino Martinez	.50	.20
❑ 100	Ken Griffey Jr.	1.25	.50
❑ 101	Greg Maddux ANA	.75	.30
❑ 102	Randy Johnson ANA	.50	.20
❑ 103	Barry Bonds ANA	1.00	.40
❑ 104	Juan Gonzalez ANA	.15	.05
❑ 105	Frank Thomas ANA	.50	.20
❑ 106	Matt Williams ANA	.15	.05
❑ 107	Paul Molitor ANA	.15	.05
❑ 108	Fred McGriff ANA	.30	.10
❑ 109	Carlos Baerga ANA	.15	.05
❑ 110	Ken Griffey Jr. ANA	.75	.30
❑ 111	Reggie Jefferson	.15	.05
❑ 112	Randy Johnson	.75	.30
❑ 113	Marc Newfield	.15	.05
❑ 114	Robb Nen	.30	.10
❑ 115	Jeff Conine	.30	.10
❑ 116	Kurt Abbott	.15	.05
❑ 117	Charlie Hough	.30	.10
❑ 118	Dave Weathers	.15	.05
❑ 119	Juan Castillo	.15	.05
❑ 120	Bret Saberhagen	.30	.10
❑ 121	Rico Brogna	.15	.05
❑ 122	John Franco	.30	.10
❑ 123	Todd Hundley	.15	.05
❑ 124	Jason Jacome	.15	.05
❑ 125	Bobby Jones	.15	.05
❑ 126	Bret Barberie	.15	.05
❑ 127	Ben McDonald	.15	.05
❑ 128	Harold Baines	.30	.10
❑ 129	Jeffrey Hammonds	.15	.05
❑ 130	Mike Mussina	.50	.20
❑ 131	Chris Hoiles	.15	.05
❑ 132	Brady Anderson	.30	.10
❑ 133	Eddie Williams	.15	.05
❑ 134	Andy Benes	.15	.05
❑ 135	Tony Gwynn	1.00	.40
❑ 136	Bip Roberts	.15	.05

❑	137	Joey Hamilton	.15	.05
❑	138	Luis Lopez	.15	.05
❑	139	Ray McDavid	.15	.05
❑	140	Lenny Dykstra	.30	.10
❑	141	Mariano Duncan	.15	.05
❑	142	Fernando Valenzuela	.30	.10
❑	143	Bobby Munoz	.15	.05
❑	144	Kevin Stocker	.15	.05
❑	145	John Kruk	.30	.10
❑	146	Jon Lieber	.15	.05
❑	147	Zane Smith	.15	.05
❑	148	Steve Cooke	.15	.05
❑	149	Andy Van Slyke	.50	.20
❑	150	Jay Bell	.30	.10
❑	151	Carlos Garcia	.15	.05
❑	152	John Dettmer	.15	.05
❑	153	Darren Oliver	.15	.05
❑	154	Dean Palmer	.30	.10
❑	155	Otis Nixon	.15	.05
❑	156	Rusty Greer	.30	.10
❑	157	Rick Helling	.15	.05
❑	158	Jose Canseco	.50	.20
❑	159	Roger Clemens	1.50	.60
❑	160	Andre Dawson	.30	.10
❑	161	Mo Vaughn	.30	.10
❑	162	Aaron Sele	.15	.05
❑	163	John Valentin	.15	.05
❑	164	Brian R. Hunter	.15	.05
❑	165	Bret Boone	.30	.10
❑	166	Hector Carrasco	.15	.05
❑	167	Pete Schourek	.15	.05
❑	168	Willie Greene	.15	.05
❑	169	Kevin Mitchell	.15	.05
❑	170	Deion Sanders	.50	.20
❑	171	John Roper	.15	.05
❑	172	Charlie Hayes	.15	.05
❑	173	David Nied	.15	.05
❑	174	Ellis Burks	.30	.10
❑	175	Dante Bichette	.30	.10
❑	176	Marvin Freeman	.15	.05
❑	177	Eric Young	.15	.05
❑	178	David Cone	.30	.10
❑	179	Greg Gagne	.15	.05
❑	180	Bob Hamelin	.15	.05
❑	181	Wally Joyner	.30	.10
❑	182	Jeff Montgomery	.15	.05
❑	183	Jose Lind	.15	.05
❑	184	Chris Gomez	.15	.05
❑	185	Travis Fryman	.30	.10
❑	186	Kirk Gibson	.30	.10
❑	187	Mike Moore	.15	.05
❑	188	Lou Whitaker	.30	.10
❑	189	Sean Bergman	.15	.05
❑	190	Shane Mack	.15	.05
❑	191	Rick Aguilera	.15	.05
❑	192	Denny Hocking	.15	.05
❑	193	Chuck Knoblauch	.30	.10
❑	194	Kevin Tapani	.15	.05
❑	195	Kent Hrbek	.30	.10
❑	196	Ozzie Guillen	.30	.10
❑	197	Wilson Alvarez	.15	.05
❑	198	Tim Raines	.30	.10
❑	199	Scott Ruffcorn	.15	.05
❑	200	Michael Jordan	2.50	1.00
❑	201	Robin Ventura	.30	.10
❑	202	Jason Bere	.15	.05
❑	203	Darrin Jackson	.15	.05
❑	204	Russ Davis	.15	.05
❑	205	Jimmy Key	.30	.10
❑	206	Jack McDowell	.15	.05
❑	207	Jim Abbott	.50	.20
❑	208	Paul O'Neill	.50	.20
❑	209	Bernie Williams	.50	.20
❑	210	Don Mattingly	2.00	.75
❑	211	Orlando Miller	.15	.05
❑	212	Alex Gonzalez	.15	.05
❑	213	Terrell Wade	.15	.05
❑	214	Jose Oliva	.15	.05
❑	215	Alex Rodriguez	2.00	.75
❑	216	Garret Anderson	.30	.10
❑	217	Alan Benes	.15	.05
❑	218	Armando Benitez	.15	.05
❑	219	Dustin Hermanson	.15	.05
❑	220	Charles Johnson	.30	.10
❑	221	Julian Tavarez	.15	.05
❑	222	Jason Giambi	.50	.20
❑	223	LaTroy Hawkins	.15	.05
❑	224	Todd Hollandsworth	.15	.05
❑	225	Derek Jeter	2.00	.75
❑	226	Hideo Nomo RC	2.50	1.00
❑	227	Tony Clark	.15	.05
❑	228	Roger Cedeno	.15	.05
❑	229	Scott Stahoviak	.15	.05
❑	230	Michael Tucker	.15	.05
❑	231	Joe Rosselli	.15	.05
❑	232	Antonio Osuna	.15	.05
❑	233	Bob Higginson RC	.75	.30
❑	234	Mark Grudzielanek RC	.75	.30
❑	235	Ray Durham	.30	.10
❑	236	Frank Rodriguez	.15	.05
❑	237	Quilvio Veras	.15	.05
❑	238	Darren Bragg	.15	.05
❑	239	Ugueth Urbina	.15	.05
❑	240	Jason Bates	.15	.05
❑	241	David Bell	.15	.05
❑	242	Ron Villone	.15	.05
❑	243	Joe Randa	.30	.10
❑	244	Carlos Perez RC	.40	.15
❑	245	Brad Clontz	.15	.05
❑	246	Steve Rodriguez	.15	.05
❑	247	Joe Vitiello	.15	.05
❑	248	Ozzie Timmons	.15	.05
❑	249	Rudy Pemberton	.15	.05
❑	250	Marty Cordova	.15	.05
❑	251	Tony Graffanino	.15	.05
❑	252	Mark Johnson RC	.40	.15
❑	253	Tomas Perez RC	.15	.05
❑	254	Jimmy Hurst	.15	.05
❑	255	Edgardo Alfonzo	.15	.05
❑	256	Jose Malave	.15	.05
❑	257	Brad Radke RC	.75	.30
❑	258	Jon Nunnally	.15	.05
❑	259	Dilson Torres RC	.15	.05
❑	260	Esteban Loaiza	.15	.05
❑	261	Freddy Adrian Garcia RC	.15	.05
❑	262	Don Wengert	.15	.05
❑	263	Robert Person RC	.40	.15
❑	264	Tim Unroe RC	.15	.05
❑	265	Juan Acevedo RC	.15	.05
❑	266	Eduardo Perez	.15	.05
❑	267	Tony Phillips	.15	.05
❑	268	Jim Edmonds	.50	.20
❑	269	Jorge Fabregas	.15	.05
❑	270	Tim Salmon	.50	.20
❑	271	Mark Langston	.15	.05
❑	272	J.T. Snow	.30	.10
❑	273	Phil Plantier	.15	.05
❑	274	Derek Bell	.15	.05
❑	275	Jeff Bagwell	.50	.20
❑	276	Luis Gonzalez	.30	.10
❑	277	John Hudek	.15	.05
❑	278	Todd Stottlemyre	.15	.05
❑	279	Mark Acre	.15	.05
❑	280	Ruben Sierra	.30	.10
❑	281	Mike Bordick	.15	.05
❑	282	Ron Darling	.15	.05
❑	283	Brent Gates	.15	.05
❑	284	Todd Van Poppel	.15	.05
❑	285	Paul Molitor	.30	.10
❑	286	Ed Sprague	.15	.05
❑	287	Juan Guzman	.15	.05
❑	288	David Cone	.30	.10
❑	289	Shawn Green	.30	.10
❑	290	Marquis Grissom	.30	.10
❑	291	Kent Mercker	.15	.05
❑	292	Steve Avery	.15	.05
❑	293	Chipper Jones	.75	.30
❑	294	John Smoltz	.50	.20
❑	295	David Justice	.30	.10
❑	296	Ryan Klesko	.30	.10
❑	297	Joe Oliver	.15	.05
❑	298	Ricky Bones	.15	.05
❑	299	John Jaha	.15	.05
❑	300	Greg Vaughn	.15	.05
❑	301	Dave Nilsson	.15	.05
❑	302	Kevin Seitzer	.15	.05
❑	303	Bernard Gilkey	.15	.05
❑	304	Allen Battle	.15	.05
❑	305	Ray Lankford	.30	.10
❑	306	Tom Pagnozzi	.15	.05
❑	307	Allen Watson	.15	.05
❑	308	Danny Jackson	.15	.05
❑	309	Ken Hill	.15	.05
❑	310	Todd Zeile	.15	.05
❑	311	Kevin Roberson	.15	.05
❑	312	Steve Buechele	.15	.05
❑	313	Rick Wilkins	.15	.05
❑	314	Kevin Foster	.15	.05
❑	315	Sammy Sosa	.75	.30
❑	316	Howard Johnson	.15	.05
❑	317	Greg Hansell	.15	.05
❑	318	Pedro Astacio	.15	.05
❑	319	Rafael Bournigal	.15	.05
❑	320	Mike Piazza	1.25	.50
❑	321	Ramon Martinez	.15	.05
❑	322	Raul Mondesi	.30	.10
❑	323	Ismael Valdes	.15	.05
❑	324	Wil Cordero	.15	.05
❑	325	Tony Tarasco	.15	.05
❑	326	Roberto Kelly	.15	.05
❑	327	Jeff Fassero	.15	.05
❑	328	Mike Lansing	.15	.05
❑	329	Pedro Martinez	.50	.20
❑	330	Kirk Rueter	.15	.05
❑	331	Glenallen Hill	.15	.05
❑	332	Kirt Manwaring	.15	.05
❑	333	Royce Clayton	.15	.05
❑	334	J.R. Phillips	.15	.05
❑	335	Barry Bonds	2.00	.75
❑	336	Mark Portugal	.15	.05
❑	337	Terry Mulholland	.15	.05
❑	338	Omar Vizquel	.50	.20
❑	339	Carlos Baerga	.15	.05
❑	340	Albert Belle	.30	.10
❑	341	Eddie Murray	.75	.30
❑	342	Wayne Kirby	.15	.05
❑	343	Chad Ogea	.15	.05
❑	344	Tim Davis	.15	.05
❑	345	Jay Buhner	.30	.10
❑	346	Bobby Ayala	.15	.05
❑	347	Mike Blowers	.15	.05
❑	348	Dave Fleming	.15	.05
❑	349	Edgar Martinez	.50	.20
❑	350	Andre Dawson	.30	.10
❑	351	Darrell Whitmore	.15	.05
❑	352	Chuck Carr	.15	.05
❑	353	John Burkett	.15	.05
❑	354	Chris Hammond	.15	.05
❑	355	Gary Sheffield	.30	.10
❑	356	Pat Rapp	.15	.05
❑	357	Greg Colbrunn	.15	.05
❑	358	David Segui	.15	.05
❑	359	Jeff Kent	.30	.10
❑	360	Bobby Bonilla	.30	.10
❑	361	Pete Harnisch	.15	.05
❑	362	Ryan Thompson	.15	.05
❑	363	Jose Vizcaino	.15	.05
❑	364	Brett Butler	.30	.10
❑	365	Cal Ripken	2.50	1.00
❑	366	Rafael Palmeiro	.50	.20
❑	367	Leo Gomez	.15	.05
❑	368	Andy Van Slyke	.50	.20
❑	369	Arthur Rhodes	.15	.05
❑	370	Ken Caminiti	.30	.10
❑	371	Steve Finley	.30	.10
❑	372	Melvin Nieves	.15	.05
❑	373	Andujar Cedeno	.15	.05
❑	374	Trevor Hoffman	.30	.10
❑	375	Fernando Valenzuela	.30	.10
❑	376	Ricky Bottalico	.15	.05
❑	377	Dave Hollins	.15	.05
❑	378	Charlie Hayes	.15	.05
❑	379	Tommy Greene	.15	.05
❑	380	Darren Daulton	.30	.10
❑	381	Curt Schilling	.30	.10
❑	382	Midre Cummings	.15	.05
❑	383	Al Martin	.15	.05
❑	384	Jeff King	.15	.05
❑	385	Orlando Merced	.15	.05
❑	386	Denny Neagle	.30	.10
❑	387	Don Slaught	.15	.05
❑	388	Dave Clark	.15	.05
❑	389	Kevin Gross	.15	.05
❑	390	Will Clark	.50	.20
❑	391	Ivan Rodriguez	.50	.20
❑	392	Benji Gil	.15	.05
❑	393	Jeff Frye	.15	.05
❑	394	Kenny Rogers	.30	.10

❑ 395	Juan Gonzalez	.30	.10
❑ 396	Mike Macfarlane	.15	.05
❑ 397	Lee Tinsley	.15	.05
❑ 398	Tim Naehring	.15	.05
❑ 399	Tim Vanegmond	.15	.05
❑ 400	Mike Greenwell	.15	.05
❑ 401	Ken Ryan	.15	.05
❑ 402	John Smiley	.15	.05
❑ 403	Tim Pugh	.15	.05
❑ 404	Reggie Sanders	.30	.10
❑ 405	Barry Larkin	.50	.20
❑ 406	Hal Morris	.15	.05
❑ 407	Jose Rijo	.15	.05
❑ 408	Lance Painter	.15	.05
❑ 409	Joe Girardi	.15	.05
❑ 410	Andres Galarraga	.30	.10
❑ 411	Mike Kingery	.15	.05
❑ 412	Roberto Mejia	.15	.05
❑ 413	Walt Weiss	.15	.05
❑ 414	Bill Swift	.15	.05
❑ 415	Larry Walker	.30	.10
❑ 416	Billy Brewer	.15	.05
❑ 417	Pat Borders	.15	.05
❑ 418	Tom Gordon	.15	.05
❑ 419	Kevin Appier	.30	.10
❑ 420	Gary Gaetti	.30	.10
❑ 421	Greg Gohr	.15	.05
❑ 422	Felipe Lira	.15	.05
❑ 423	John Doherty	.15	.05
❑ 424	Chad Curtis	.15	.05
❑ 425	Cecil Fielder	.30	.10
❑ 426	Alan Trammell	.30	.10
❑ 427	David McCarty	.15	.05
❑ 428	Scott Erickson	.15	.05
❑ 429	Pat Mahomes	.15	.05
❑ 430	Kirby Puckett	.75	.30
❑ 431	Dave Stevens	.15	.05
❑ 432	Pedro Munoz	.15	.05
❑ 433	Chris Sabo	.15	.05
❑ 434	Alex Fernandez	.15	.05
❑ 435	Frank Thomas	.75	.30
❑ 436	Roberto Hernandez	.15	.05
❑ 437	Lance Johnson	.15	.05
❑ 438	Jim Abbott	.50	.20
❑ 439	John Wetteland	.30	.10
❑ 440	Melido Perez	.15	.05
❑ 441	Tony Fernandez	.15	.05
❑ 442	Pat Kelly	.15	.05
❑ 443	Mike Stanley	.15	.05
❑ 444	Danny Tartabull	.15	.05
❑ 445	Wade Boggs	.50	.20
❑ 446	Robin Yount TRIB	1.25	.50
❑ 447	Ryne Sandberg TRIB	1.25	.50
❑ 448	Nolan Ryan TRIB	3.00	1.25
❑ 449	George Brett TRIB	2.00	.75
❑ 450	Mike Schmidt TRIB	1.25	.50
❑ 451	Jim Abbott TRADE	2.00	.75
❑ 452	Danny Tartabull TRADE	1.00	.40
❑ 453	Ariel Prieto TRADE	1.00	.40
❑ 454	Scott Cooper TRADE	1.00	.40
❑ 455	Tom Henke TRADE	1.00	.40
❑ 456	Todd Zeile TRADE	1.00	.40
❑ 457	Brian McRae TRADE	1.00	.40
❑ 458	Luis Gonzalez TRADE	1.50	.60
❑ 459	Jaime Navarro TRADE	1.00	.40
❑ 460	Todd Worrell TRADE	1.00	.40
❑ 461	Roberto Kelly TRADE	1.00	.40
❑ 462	Chad Fonville TRADE	1.00	.40
❑ 463	Shane Andrews TRADE	1.00	.40
❑ 464	David Segui TRADE	1.00	.40
❑ 465	Deion Sanders TRADE	2.00	.75
❑ 466	Orel Hershiser TRADE	1.50	.60
❑ 467	Ken Hill TRADE	1.00	.40
❑ 468	Andy Benes TRADE	1.00	.40
❑ 469	Terry Pendleton TRADE	1.50	.60
❑ 470	Bobby Bonilla TRADE	1.50	.60
❑ 471	Scott Erickson TRADE	1.00	.40
❑ 472	Kevin Brown TRADE	1.50	.60
❑ 473	Glenn Dishman TRADE	1.00	.40
❑ 474	Phil Plantier TRADE	1.00	.40
❑ 475	Gregg Jefferies TRADE	1.00	.40
❑ 476	Tyler Green TRADE	1.00	.40
❑ 477	Heathcliff Slocumb TRADE	1.00	.40
❑ 478	Mark Whiten TRADE	1.00	.40
❑ 479	Mickey Tettleton TRADE	1.00	.40
❑ 480	Tim Wakefield TRADE	1.50	.60
❑ 481	Vaughn Eshelman TRADE	1.00	.40
❑ 482	Rick Aguilera TRADE	1.00	.40
❑ 483	Erik Hanson TRADE	1.00	.40
❑ 484	Willie McGee TRADE	1.50	.60
❑ 485	Troy O'Leary TRADE	1.00	.40
❑ 486	Benito Santiago TRADE	1.50	.60
❑ 487	Darren Lewis TRADE	1.00	.40
❑ 488	Dave Burba TRADE	1.00	.40
❑ 489	Ron Gant TRADE	1.50	.60
❑ 490	Bret Saberhagen TRADE	1.50	.60
❑ 491	Vinny Castilla TRADE	1.50	.60
❑ 492	Frank Rodriguez TRADE	1.00	.40
❑ 493	Andy Pettitte TRADE	2.00	.75
❑ 494	Ruben Sierra TRADE	1.50	.60
❑ 495	David Cone TRADE	1.50	.60
❑ J159	R.Clemens Jumbo AU	100.00	50.00
❑ J215	A.Rodriguez Jumbo AU	120.00	60.00
❑ P100	Ken Griffey Jr. Promo	2.00	.75

1996 Upper Deck

❑	COMPLETE SET (480)	50.00	20.00
❑	COMP.FACT.SET (510)	100.00	50.00
❑	COMPLETE SERIES 1 (240)	25.00	10.00
❑	COMPLETE SERIES 2 (240)	25.00	10.00
❑	COMMON CARD (1-480)	.30	.10
❑	COMP.UPDATE SET (30)	20.00	10.00
❑	COMMON UPDATE (481U-510U)	.50	.20
❑ 1	Cal Ripken 2131	4.00	1.50
❑ 2	Eddie Murray 3000 Hits	.50	.20
❑ 3	Mark Wohlers	.30	.10
❑ 4	David Justice	.30	.10
❑ 5	Chipper Jones	.75	.30
❑ 6	Javier Lopez	.30	.10
❑ 7	Mark Lemke	.30	.10
❑ 8	Marquis Grissom	.30	.10
❑ 9	Tom Glavine	.50	.20
❑ 10	Greg Maddux	1.25	.50
❑ 11	Manny Alexander	.30	.10
❑ 12	Curtis Goodwin	.30	.10
❑ 13	Scott Erickson	.30	.10
❑ 14	Chris Hoiles	.30	.10
❑ 15	Rafael Palmeiro	.50	.20
❑ 16	Rick Krivda	.30	.10
❑ 17	Jeff Manto	.30	.10
❑ 18	Mo Vaughn	.30	.10
❑ 19	Tim Wakefield	.30	.10
❑ 20	Roger Clemens	1.50	.60
❑ 21	Tim Naehring	.30	.10
❑ 22	Troy O'Leary	.30	.10
❑ 23	Mike Greenwell	.30	.10
❑ 24	Stan Belinda	.30	.10
❑ 25	John Valentin	.30	.10
❑ 26	J.T. Snow	.30	.10
❑ 27	Gary DiSarcina	.30	.10
❑ 28	Mark Langston	.30	.10
❑ 29	Brian Anderson	.30	.10
❑ 30	Jim Edmonds	.30	.10
❑ 31	Garret Anderson	.30	.10
❑ 32	Orlando Palmeiro	.30	.10
❑ 33	Brian McRae	.30	.10
❑ 34	Kevin Foster	.30	.10
❑ 35	Sammy Sosa	.75	.30
❑ 36	Todd Zeile	.30	.10
❑ 37	Jim Bullinger	.30	.10
❑ 38	Luis Gonzalez	.30	.10
❑ 39	Lyle Mouton	.30	.10
❑ 40	Ray Durham	.30	.10
❑ 41	Ozzie Guillen	.30	.10
❑ 42	Alex Fernandez	.30	.10
❑ 43	Brian Keyser	.30	.10
❑ 44	Robin Ventura	.30	.10
❑ 45	Reggie Sanders	.30	.10
❑ 46	Pete Schourek	.30	.10
❑ 47	John Smiley	.30	.10
❑ 48	Jeff Brantley	.30	.10
❑ 49	Thomas Howard	.30	.10
❑ 50	Bret Boone	.30	.10
❑ 51	Kevin Jarvis	.30	.10
❑ 52	Jeff Branson	.30	.10
❑ 53	Carlos Baerga	.30	.10
❑ 54	Jim Thome	.50	.20
❑ 55	Manny Ramirez	.50	.20
❑ 56	Omar Vizquel	.50	.20
❑ 57	Jose Mesa	.30	.10
❑ 58	Julian Tavarez UER	.30	.10
❑ 59	Orel Hershiser	.30	.10
❑ 60	Larry Walker	.30	.10
❑ 61	Bret Saberhagen	.30	.10
❑ 62	Vinny Castilla	.30	.10
❑ 63	Eric Young	.30	.10
❑ 64	Bryan Rekar	.30	.10
❑ 65	Andres Galarraga	.30	.10
❑ 66	Steve Reed	.30	.10
❑ 67	Chad Curtis	.30	.10
❑ 68	Bobby Higginson	.30	.10
❑ 69	Phil Nevin	.30	.10
❑ 70	Cecil Fielder	.30	.10
❑ 71	Felipe Lira	.30	.10
❑ 72	Chris Gomez	.30	.10
❑ 73	Charles Johnson	.30	.10
❑ 74	Quilvio Veras	.30	.10
❑ 75	Jeff Conine	.30	.10
❑ 76	John Burkett	.30	.10
❑ 77	Greg Colbrunn	.30	.10
❑ 78	Terry Pendleton	.30	.10
❑ 79	Shane Reynolds	.30	.10
❑ 80	Jeff Bagwell	.50	.20
❑ 81	Orlando Miller	.30	.10
❑ 82	Mike Hampton	.30	.10
❑ 83	James Mouton	.30	.10
❑ 84	Brian L. Hunter	.30	.10
❑ 85	Derek Bell	.30	.10
❑ 86	Kevin Appier	.30	.10
❑ 87	Joe Vitiello	.30	.10
❑ 88	Wally Joyner	.30	.10
❑ 89	Michael Tucker	.30	.10
❑ 90	Johnny Damon	.50	.20
❑ 91	Jon Nunnally	.30	.10
❑ 92	Jason Jacome	.30	.10
❑ 93	Chad Fonville	.30	.10
❑ 94	Chan Ho Park	.30	.10
❑ 95	Hideo Nomo	.75	.30
❑ 96	Ismael Valdes	.30	.10
❑ 97	Greg Gagne	.30	.10
❑ 98	Diamondbacks-Devil Rays	.75	.30
❑ 99	Raul Mondesi	.30	.10
❑ 100	Dave Winfield YH	.30	.10
❑ 101	Dennis Eckersley YH	.30	.10
❑ 102	Andre Dawson YH	.30	.10
❑ 103	Dennis Martinez YH	.30	.10
❑ 104	Lance Parrish YH	.30	.10
❑ 105	Eddie Murray YH	.50	.20
❑ 106	Alan Trammell YH	.30	.10
❑ 107	Lou Whitaker YH	.30	.10
❑ 108	Ozzie Smith YH	.75	.30
❑ 109	Paul Molitor YH	.30	.10
❑ 110	Rickey Henderson YH	.50	.20
❑ 111	Tim Raines YH	.30	.10
❑ 112	Harold Baines YH	.30	.10
❑ 113	Lee Smith YH	.30	.10
❑ 114	Fernando Valenzuela YH	.30	.10
❑ 115	Cal Ripken YH	1.25	.50
❑ 116	Tony Gwynn YH	.50	.20
❑ 117	Wade Boggs	.50	.20
❑ 118	Todd Hollandsworth	.30	.10
❑ 119	Dave Nilsson	.30	.10
❑ 120	Jose Valentin	.30	.10
❑ 121	Steve Sparks	.30	.10
❑ 122	Chuck Carr	.30	.10
❑ 123	John Jaha	.30	.10
❑ 124	Scott Karl	.30	.10
❑ 125	Chuck Knoblauch	.30	.10
❑ 126	Brad Radke	.30	.10
❑ 127	Pat Meares	.30	.10

128	Ron Coomer	.30	.10
129	Pedro Munoz	.30	.10
130	Kirby Puckett	.75	.30
131	David Segui	.30	.10
132	Mark Grudzielanek	.30	.10
133	Mike Lansing	.30	.10
134	Sean Berry	.30	.10
135	Rondell White	.30	.10
136	Pedro Martinez	.50	.20
137	Carl Everett	.30	.10
138	Dave Mlicki	.30	.10
139	Bill Pulsipher	.30	.10
140	Jason Isringhausen	.30	.10
141	Rico Brogna	.30	.10
142	Edgardo Alfonzo	.30	.10
143	Jeff Kent	.30	.10
144	Andy Pettitte	.50	.20
145	Mike Piazza BO	.75	.30
146	Cliff Floyd BO	.30	.10
147	Jason Isringhausen BO	.30	.10
148	Tim Wakefield BO	.30	.10
149	Chipper Jones BO	.50	.20
150	Hideo Nomo BO	.50	.20
151	Mark McGwire BO	1.00	.40
152	Ron Gant BO	.30	.10
153	Gary Gaetti BO	.30	.10
154	Don Mattingly	2.00	.75
155	Paul O'Neill	.50	.20
156	Derek Jeter	2.00	.75
157	Joe Girardi	.30	.10
158	Ruben Sierra	.30	.10
159	Jorge Posada	.50	.20
160	Geronimo Berroa	.30	.10
161	Steve Ontiveros	.30	.10
162	George Williams	.30	.10
163	Doug Johns	.30	.10
164	Ariel Prieto	.30	.10
165	Scott Brosius	.30	.10
166	Mike Bordick	.30	.10
167	Tyler Green	.30	.10
168	Mickey Morandini	.30	.10
169	Darren Daulton	.30	.10
170	Gregg Jefferies	.30	.10
171	Jim Eisenreich	.30	.10
172	Heathcliff Slocumb	.30	.10
173	Kevin Stocker	.30	.10
174	Esteban Loaiza	.30	.10
175	Jeff King	.30	.10
176	Mark Johnson	.30	.10
177	Denny Neagle	.30	.10
178	Orlando Merced	.30	.10
179	Carlos Garcia	.30	.10
180	Brian Jordan	.30	.10
181	Mike Morgan	.30	.10
182	Mark Petkovsek	.30	.10
183	Bernard Gilkey	.30	.10
184	John Mabry	.30	.10
185	Tom Henke	.30	.10
186	Glenn Dishman	.30	.10
187	Andy Ashby	.30	.10
188	Bip Roberts	.30	.10
189	Melvin Nieves	.30	.10
190	Ken Caminiti	.30	.10
191	Brad Ausmus	.30	.10
192	Deion Sanders	.50	.20
193	Jamie Brewington RC	.30	.10
194	Glenallen Hill	.30	.10
195	Barry Bonds	2.00	.75
196	Wm. Van Landingham	.30	.10
197	Mark Carreon	.30	.10
198	Royce Clayton	.30	.10
199	Joey Cora	.30	.10
200	Ken Griffey Jr.	1.25	.50
201	Jay Buhner	.30	.10
202	Alex Rodriguez	1.50	.60
203	Norm Charlton	.30	.10
204	Andy Benes	.30	.10
205	Edgar Martinez	.50	.20
206	Juan Gonzalez	.30	.10
207	Will Clark	.50	.20
208	Kevin Gross	.30	.10
209	Roger Pavlik	.30	.10
210	Ivan Rodriguez	.50	.20
211	Rusty Greer	.30	.10
212	Angel Martinez	.30	.10
213	Tomas Perez	.30	.10
214	Alex Gonzalez	.30	.10
215	Joe Carter	.30	.10
216	Shawn Green	.30	.10
217	Edwin Hurtado	.30	.10
218	E.Martinez/T.Pena CL	.30	.10
219	C.Jones/B.Larkin CL	.50	.20
220	Orel Hershiser CL	.30	.10
221	Mike Devereaux CL	.30	.10
222	Tom Glavine CL	.30	.10
223	Karim Garcia	.30	.10
224	Arquimedez Pozo	.30	.10
225	Billy Wagner	.30	.10
226	John Wasdin	.30	.10
227	Jeff Suppan	.30	.10
228	Steve Gibralter	.30	.10
229	Jimmy Haynes	.30	.10
230	Ruben Rivera	.30	.10
231	Chris Snopek	.30	.10
232	Alex Ochoa	.30	.10
233	Shannon Stewart	.30	.10
234	Quinton McCracken	.30	.10
235	Trey Beamon	.30	.10
236	Billy McMillon	.30	.10
237	Steve Cox	.30	.10
238	George Arias	.30	.10
239	Yamil Benitez	.30	.10
240	Todd Greene	.30	.10
241	Jason Kendall	.30	.10
242	Brooks Kieschnick	.30	.10
243	Osvaldo Fernandez RC	.30	.10
244	Livan Hernandez RC	1.00	.40
245	Rey Ordonez	.30	.10
246	Mike Grace RC	.30	.10
247	Jay Canizaro	.30	.10
248	Bob Wolcott	.30	.10
249	Jermaine Dye	.30	.10
250	Jason Schmidt	.50	.20
251	Mike Sweeney RC	1.00	.40
252	Marcus Jensen	.30	.10
253	Mendy Lopez	.30	.10
254	Wilton Guerrero RC	.30	.10
255	Paul Wilson	.30	.10
256	Edgar Renteria	.30	.10
257	Richard Hidalgo	.30	.10
258	Bob Abreu	.75	.30
259	Robert Smith RC	.30	.10
260	Sal Fasano	.30	.10
261	Enrique Wilson	.30	.10
262	Rich Hunter RC	.30	.10
263	Sergio Nunez	.30	.10
264	Dan Serafini	.30	.10
265	David Doster	.30	.10
266	Ryan McGuire	.30	.10
267	Scott Spiezio	.30	.10
268	Rafael Orellano	.30	.10
269	Steve Avery	.30	.10
270	Fred McGriff	.50	.20
271	John Smoltz	.50	.20
272	Ryan Klesko	.30	.10
273	Jeff Blauser	.30	.10
274	Brad Clontz	.30	.10
275	Roberto Alomar	.50	.20
276	B.J. Surhoff	.30	.10
277	Jeffrey Hammonds	.30	.10
278	Brady Anderson	.30	.10
279	Bobby Bonilla	.30	.10
280	Cal Ripken	2.50	1.00
281	Mike Mussina	.50	.20
282	Wil Cordero	.30	.10
283	Mike Stanley	.30	.10
284	Aaron Sele	.30	.10
285	Jose Canseco	.50	.20
286	Tom Gordon	.30	.10
287	Heathcliff Slocumb	.30	.10
288	Lee Smith	.30	.10
289	Troy Percival	.30	.10
290	Tim Salmon	.50	.20
291	Chuck Finley	.30	.10
292	Jim Abbott	.50	.20
293	Chili Davis	.30	.10
294	Steve Trachsel	.30	.10
295	Mark Grace	.50	.20
296	Rey Sanchez	.30	.10
297	Scott Servais	.30	.10
298	Jaime Navarro	.30	.10
299	Frank Castillo	.30	.10
300	Frank Thomas	.75	.30
301	Jason Bere	.30	.10
302	Danny Tartabull	.30	.10
303	Darren Lewis	.30	.10
304	Roberto Hernandez	.30	.10
305	Tony Phillips	.30	.10
306	Wilson Alvarez	.30	.10
307	Jose Rijo	.30	.10
308	Hal Morris	.30	.10
309	Mark Portugal	.30	.10
310	Barry Larkin	.50	.20
311	Dave Burba	.30	.10
312	Eddie Taubensee	.30	.10
313	Sandy Alomar Jr.	.30	.10
314	Dennis Martinez	.30	.10
315	Albert Belle	.30	.10
316	Eddie Murray	.75	.30
317	Charles Nagy	.30	.10
318	Chad Ogea	.30	.10
319	Kenny Lofton	.30	.10
320	Dante Bichette	.30	.10
321	Armando Reynoso	.30	.10
322	Walt Weiss	.30	.10
323	Ellis Burks	.30	.10
324	Kevin Ritz	.30	.10
325	Bill Swift	.30	.10
326	Jason Bates	.30	.10
327	Tony Clark	.30	.10
328	Travis Fryman	.30	.10
329	Mark Parent	.30	.10
330	Alan Trammell	.30	.10
331	C.J. Nitkowski	.30	.10
332	Jose Lima	.30	.10
333	Phil Plantier	.30	.10
334	Kurt Abbott	.30	.10
335	Andre Dawson	.30	.10
336	Chris Hammond	.30	.10
337	Robb Nen	.30	.10
338	Pat Rapp	.30	.10
339	Al Leiter	.30	.10
340	Gary Sheffield	.30	.10
341	Todd Jones	.30	.10
342	Doug Drabek	.30	.10
343	Greg Swindell	.30	.10
344	Tony Eusebio	.30	.10
345	Craig Biggio	.50	.20
346	Darryl Kile	.30	.10
347	Mike Macfarlane	.30	.10
348	Jeff Montgomery	.30	.10
349	Chris Haney	.30	.10
350	Bip Roberts	.30	.10
351	Tom Goodwin	.30	.10
352	Mark Gubicza	.30	.10
353	Joe Randa	.30	.10
354	Ramon Martinez	.30	.10
355	Eric Karros	.30	.10
356	Delino DeShields	.30	.10
357	Brett Butler	.30	.10
358	Todd Worrell	.30	.10
359	Mike Blowers	.30	.10
360	Mike Piazza	1.25	.50
361	Ben McDonald	.30	.10
362	Ricky Bones	.30	.10
363	Greg Vaughn	.30	.10
364	Matt Mieske	.30	.10
365	Kevin Seitzer	.30	.10
366	Jeff Cirillo	.30	.10
367	LaTroy Hawkins	.30	.10
368	Frank Rodriguez	.30	.10
369	Rick Aguilera	.30	.10
370	Roberto Alomar BG	.30	.10
371	Albert Belle BG	.30	.10
372	Wade Boggs BG	.30	.10
373	Barry Bonds BG	1.00	.40
374	Roger Clemens BG	.75	.30
375	Dennis Eckersley BG	.30	.10
376	Ken Griffey Jr. BG	.75	.30
377	Tony Gwynn BG	.50	.20
378	Rickey Henderson BG	.50	.20
379	Greg Maddux BG	.75	.30
380	Fred McGriff BG	.30	.10
381	Paul Molitor BG	.30	.10
382	Eddie Murray BG	.50	.20
383	Mike Piazza BG	.75	.30
384	Kirby Puckett BG	.50	.20
385	Cal Ripken BG	1.25	.50

386	Ozzie Smith BG	.75	.30
387	Frank Thomas BG	.50	.20
388	Matt Walbeck	.30	.10
389	Dave Stevens	.30	.10
390	Marty Cordova	.30	.10
391	Darrin Fletcher	.30	.10
392	Cliff Floyd	.30	.10
393	Mel Rojas	.30	.10
394	Shane Andrews	.30	.10
395	Moises Alou	.30	.10
396	Carlos Perez	.30	.10
397	Jeff Fassero	.30	.10
398	Bobby Jones	.30	.10
399	Todd Hundley	.30	.10
400	John Franco	.30	.10
401	Jose Vizcaino	.30	.10
402	Bernard Gilkey	.30	.10
403	Pete Harnisch	.30	.10
404	Pat Kelly	.30	.10
405	David Cone	.30	.10
406	Bernie Williams	.50	.20
407	John Wetteland	.30	.10
408	Scott Kamieniecki	.30	.10
409	Tim Raines	.30	.10
410	Wade Boggs	.50	.20
411	Terry Steinbach	.30	.10
412	Jason Giambi	.30	.10
413	Todd Van Poppel	.30	.10
414	Pedro Munoz	.30	.10
415	Eddie Murray SBT	.50	.20
416	Dennis Eckersley SBT	.30	.10
417	Bip Roberts SBT	.30	.10
418	Glenallen Hill SBT	.30	.10
419	John Hudek SBT	.30	.10
420	Derek Bell SBT	.30	.10
421	Larry Walker SBT	.30	.10
422	Greg Maddux SBT	.75	.30
423	Ken Caminiti SBT	.30	.10
424	Brent Gates	.30	.10
425	Mark McGwire	2.00	.75
426	Mark Whiten	.30	.10
427	Sid Fernandez	.30	.10
428	Ricky Bottalico	.30	.10
429	Mike Mimbs	.30	.10
430	Lenny Dykstra	.30	.10
431	Todd Zeile	.30	.10
432	Benito Santiago	.30	.10
433	Danny Miceli	.30	.10
434	Al Martin	.30	.10
435	Jay Bell	.30	.10
436	Charlie Hayes	.30	.10
437	Mike Kingery	.30	.10
438	Paul Wagner	.30	.10
439	Tom Pagnozzi	.30	.10
440	Ozzie Smith	1.25	.50
441	Ray Lankford	.30	.10
442	Dennis Eckersley	.30	.10
443	Ron Gant	.30	.10
444	Alan Benes	.30	.10
445	Rickey Henderson	.75	.30
446	Jody Reed	.30	.10
447	Trevor Hoffman	.30	.10
448	Andujar Cedeno	.30	.10
449	Steve Finley	.30	.10
450	Tony Gwynn	1.00	.40
451	Joey Hamilton	.30	.10
452	Mark Leiter	.30	.10
453	Rod Beck	.30	.10
454	Kirt Manwaring	.30	.10
455	Matt Williams	.30	.10
456	Robby Thompson	.30	.10
457	Shawon Dunston	.30	.10
458	Russ Davis	.30	.10
459	Paul Sorrento	.30	.10
460	Randy Johnson	.75	.30
461	Chris Bosio	.30	.10
462	Luis Sojo	.30	.10
463	Sterling Hitchcock	.30	.10
464	Benji Gil	.30	.10
465	Mickey Tettleton	.30	.10
466	Mark McLemore	.30	.10
467	Darryl Hamilton	.30	.10
468	Ken Hill	.30	.10
469	Dean Palmer	.30	.10
470	Carlos Delgado	.30	.10
471	Ed Sprague	.30	.10
472	Otis Nixon	.30	.10
473	Pat Hentgen	.30	.10
474	Juan Guzman	.30	.10
475	John Olerud	.30	.10
476	Buck Showalter CL	.30	.10
477	Bobby Cox CL	.30	.10
478	Tommy Lasorda CL	.30	.10
479	Buck Showalter CL	.30	.10
480	Sparky Anderson CL	.30	.10
481U	Randy Myers	.50	.20
482U	Kent Mercker	.50	.20
483U	David Wells	.75	.30
484U	Kevin Mitchell	.50	.20
485U	Randy Velarde	.50	.20
486U	Ryne Sandberg	4.00	1.50
487U	Doug Jones	.50	.20
488U	Terry Adams	.50	.20
489U	Kevin Tapani	.50	.20
490U	Harold Baines	.75	.30
491U	Eric Davis	.75	.30
492U	Julio Franco	.75	.30
493U	Jack McDowell	.50	.20
494U	Devon White	.75	.30
495U	Kevin Brown	.75	.30
496U	Rick Wilkins	.50	.20
497U	Sean Berry	.50	.20
498U	Keith Lockhart	.50	.20
499U	Mark Loretta	.50	.20
500U	Paul Molitor	.75	.30
501U	Roberto Kelly	.50	.20
502U	Lance Johnson	.50	.20
503U	Tino Martinez	1.25	.50
504U	Kenny Rogers	.75	.30
505U	Todd Stottlemyre	.50	.20
506U	Gary Gaetti	.75	.30
507U	Royce Clayton	.50	.20
508U	Andy Benes	.50	.20
509U	Wally Joyner	.75	.30
510U	Erik Hanson	.50	.20
P100	Ken Griffey Jr Promo	3.00	1.25

1997 Upper Deck

COMP.MASTER SET (550)	200.00	80.00
COMPLETE SET (490)	100.00	50.00
COMPLETE SERIES 1 (240)	40.00	20.00
COMPLETE SERIES 2 (250)	60.00	30.00
COMP.SER.2 w/o GHL (240)	25.00	10.00
COMMON (1-240/271-520)	.30	.10
COMP.UPDATE SET (30)	80.00	40.00
COMMON UPDATE (241-270)	1.00	.40
1 UPD.SET VIA MAIL PER 10 SER.1 WRAPS		
COMMON GHL (415-424)	1.50	.60
COMP.TRADE SET (30)	20.00	8.00
COMMON TRADE (521-550)	.50	.20

1	Jackie Robinson	.50	.20
2	Jackie Robinson	.50	.20
3	Jackie Robinson	.50	.20
4	Jackie Robinson	.50	.20
5	Jackie Robinson	.50	.20
6	Jackie Robinson	.50	.20
7	Jackie Robinson	.50	.20
8	Jackie Robinson	.50	.20
9	Jackie Robinson	.50	.20
10	Chipper Jones	.75	.30
11	Marquis Grissom	.30	.10
12	Jermaine Dye	.30	.10
13	Mark Lemke	.30	.10
14	Terrell Wade	.30	.10
15	Fred McGriff	.50	.20
16	Tom Glavine	.50	.20
17	Mark Wohlers	.30	.10
18	Randy Myers	.30	.10
19	Roberto Alomar	.50	.20
20	Cal Ripken	2.50	1.00
21	Rafael Palmeiro	.50	.20
22	Mike Mussina	.50	.20
23	Brady Anderson	.30	.10
24	Jose Canseco	.50	.20
25	Mo Vaughn	.30	.10
26	Roger Clemens	1.50	.60
27	Tim Naehring	.30	.10
28	Jeff Suppan	.30	.10
29	Troy Percival	.30	.10
30	Sammy Sosa	.75	.30
31	Amaury Telemaco	.30	.10
32	Rey Sanchez	.30	.10
33	Scott Servais	.30	.10
34	Steve Trachsel	.30	.10
35	Mark Grace	.50	.20
36	Wilson Alvarez	.30	.10
37	Harold Baines	.30	.10
38	Tony Phillips	.30	.10
39	James Baldwin	.30	.10
40	Frank Thomas UER	.75	.30
41	Lyle Mouton	.30	.10
42	Chris Snopek	.30	.10
43	Hal Morris	.30	.10
44	Eric Davis	.30	.10
45	Barry Larkin	.50	.20
46	Reggie Sanders	.30	.10
47	Pete Schourek	.30	.10
48	Lee Smith	.30	.10
49	Charles Nagy	.30	.10
50	Albert Belle	.30	.10
51	Julio Franco	.30	.10
52	Kenny Lofton	.30	.10
53	Orel Hershiser	.30	.10
54	Omar Vizquel	.50	.20
55	Eric Young	.30	.10
56	Curtis Leskanic	.30	.10
57	Quinton McCracken	.30	.10
58	Kevin Ritz	.30	.10
59	Walt Weiss	.30	.10
60	Dante Bichette	.30	.10
61	Mark Lewis	.30	.10
62	Tony Clark	.30	.10
63	Travis Fryman	.30	.10
64	John Smoltz SF	.30	.10
65	Greg Maddux SF	.75	.30
66	Tom Glavine SF	.30	.10
67	Mike Mussina SF	.30	.10
68	Andy Pettitte SF	.30	.10
69	Mariano Rivera SF	.50	.20
70	Hideo Nomo SF	.30	.10
71	Kevin Brown SF	.30	.10
72	Randy Johnson SF	.50	.20
73	Felipe Lira	.30	.10
74	Kimera Bartee	.30	.10
75	Alan Trammell	.30	.10
76	Kevin Brown	.30	.10
77	Edgar Renteria	.30	.10
78	Al Leiter	.30	.10
79	Charles Johnson	.30	.10
80	Andre Dawson	.30	.10
81	Billy Wagner	.30	.10
82	Donne Wall	.30	.10
83	Jeff Bagwell	.50	.20
84	Keith Lockhart	.30	.10
85	Jeff Montgomery	.30	.10
86	Tom Goodwin	.30	.10
87	Tim Belcher	.30	.10
88	Mike Macfarlane	.30	.10
89	Joe Randa	.30	.10
90	Brett Butler	.30	.10
91	Todd Worrell	.30	.10
92	Todd Hollandsworth	.30	.10
93	Ismael Valdes	.30	.10
94	Hideo Nomo	.75	.30
95	Mike Piazza	1.25	.50
96	Jeff Cirillo	.30	.10
97	Ricky Bones	.30	.10
98	Fernando Vina	.30	.10
99	Ben McDonald	.30	.10

❑ 100	John Jaha	.30	.10
❑ 101	Mark Loretta	.30	.10
❑ 102	Paul Molitor	.30	.10
❑ 103	Rick Aguilera	.30	.10
❑ 104	Marty Cordova	.30	.10
❑ 105	Kirby Puckett	.75	.30
❑ 106	Dan Naulty	.30	.10
❑ 107	Frank Rodriguez	.30	.10
❑ 108	Shane Andrews	.30	.10
❑ 109	Henry Rodriguez	.30	.10
❑ 110	Mark Grudzielanek	.30	.10
❑ 111	Pedro Martinez	.50	.20
❑ 112	Ugueth Urbina	.30	.10
❑ 113	David Segui	.30	.10
❑ 114	Rey Ordonez	.30	.10
❑ 115	Bernard Gilkey	.30	.10
❑ 116	Butch Huskey	.30	.10
❑ 117	Paul Wilson	.30	.10
❑ 118	Alex Ochoa	.30	.10
❑ 119	John Franco	.30	.10
❑ 120	Dwight Gooden	.30	.10
❑ 121	Ruben Rivera	.30	.10
❑ 122	Andy Pettitte	.50	.20
❑ 123	Tino Martinez	.50	.20
❑ 124	Bernie Williams	.50	.20
❑ 125	Wade Boggs	.50	.20
❑ 126	Paul O'Neill	.50	.20
❑ 127	Scott Brosius	.30	.10
❑ 128	Ernie Young	.30	.10
❑ 129	Doug Johns	.30	.10
❑ 130	Geronimo Berroa	.30	.10
❑ 131	Jason Giambi	.30	.10
❑ 132	John Wasdin	.30	.10
❑ 133	Jim Eisenreich	.30	.10
❑ 134	Ricky Otero	.30	.10
❑ 135	Ricky Bottalico	.30	.10
❑ 136	Mark Langston DG	.30	.10
❑ 137	Greg Maddux DG	.75	.30
❑ 138	Ivan Rodriguez DG	.30	.10
❑ 139	Charles Johnson DG	.30	.10
❑ 140	J.T. Snow DG	.30	.10
❑ 141	Mark Grace DG	.30	.10
❑ 142	Roberto Alomar DG	.30	.10
❑ 143	Craig Biggio DG	.30	.10
❑ 144	Ken Caminiti DG	.30	.10
❑ 145	Matt Williams DG	.30	.10
❑ 146	Omar Vizquel DG	.30	.10
❑ 147	Cal Ripken DG	1.25	.50
❑ 148	Ozzie Smith DG	.75	.30
❑ 149	Rey Ordonez DG	.30	.10
❑ 150	Ken Griffey Jr. DG	.75	.30
❑ 151	Devon White DG	.30	.10
❑ 152	Barry Bonds DG	1.00	.40
❑ 153	Kenny Lofton DG	.30	.10
❑ 154	Mickey Morandini	.30	.10
❑ 155	Gregg Jefferies	.30	.10
❑ 156	Curt Schilling	.30	.10
❑ 157	Jason Kendall	.30	.10
❑ 158	Francisco Cordova	.30	.10
❑ 159	Dennis Eckersley	.30	.10
❑ 160	Ron Gant	.30	.10
❑ 161	Ozzie Smith	1.25	.50
❑ 162	Brian Jordan	.30	.10
❑ 163	John Mabry	.30	.10
❑ 164	Andy Ashby	.30	.10
❑ 165	Steve Finley	.30	.10
❑ 166	Fernando Valenzuela	.30	.10
❑ 167	Archi Cianfrocco	.30	.10
❑ 168	Wally Joyner	.30	.10
❑ 169	Greg Vaughn	.30	.10
❑ 170	Barry Bonds	2.00	.75
❑ 171	William VanLandingham	.30	.10
❑ 172	Marvin Benard	.30	.10
❑ 173	Rich Aurilia	.30	.10
❑ 174	Jay Canizaro	.30	.10
❑ 175	Ken Griffey Jr.	1.25	.50
❑ 176	Bob Wells	.30	.10
❑ 177	Jay Buhner	.30	.10
❑ 178	Sterling Hitchcock	.30	.10
❑ 179	Edgar Martinez	.50	.20
❑ 180	Rusty Greer	.30	.10
❑ 181	Dave Nilsson GI	.30	.10
❑ 182	Larry Walker GI	.30	.10
❑ 183	Edgar Renteria GI	.30	.10
❑ 184	Rey Ordonez GI	.30	.10
❑ 185	Rafael Palmeiro GI	.30	.10
❑ 186	Osvaldo Fernandez GI	.30	.10
❑ 187	Raul Mondesi GI	.30	.10
❑ 188	Manny Ramirez GI	.30	.10
❑ 189	Sammy Sosa GI	.50	.20
❑ 190	Robert Eenhoorn GI	.30	.10
❑ 191	Devon White GI	.30	.10
❑ 192	Hideo Nomo GI	.30	.10
❑ 193	Mac Suzuki GI	.30	.10
❑ 194	Chan Ho Park GI	.30	.10
❑ 195	Fernando Valenzuela GI	.30	.10
❑ 196	Andruw Jones GI	.30	.10
❑ 197	Vinny Castilla GI	.30	.10
❑ 198	Dennis Martinez GI	.30	.10
❑ 199	Ruben Rivera GI	.30	.10
❑ 200	Juan Gonzalez GI	.30	.10
❑ 201	Roberto Alomar GI	.30	.10
❑ 202	Edgar Martinez GI	.30	.10
❑ 203	Ivan Rodriguez GI	.30	.10
❑ 204	Carlos Delgado GI	.30	.10
❑ 205	Andres Galarraga GI	.30	.10
❑ 206	Ozzie Guillen GI	.30	.10
❑ 207	Midre Cummings GI	.30	.10
❑ 208	Roger Pavlik	.30	.10
❑ 209	Darren Oliver	.30	.10
❑ 210	Dean Palmer	.30	.10
❑ 211	Ivan Rodriguez	.50	.20
❑ 212	Otis Nixon	.30	.10
❑ 213	Pat Hentgen	.30	.10
❑ 214	Ozzie/Dawson/Puckett HL/CL	.50	.20
❑ 215	Bonds/Sheff/Brady HL/CL	1.00	.40
❑ 216	Ken Caminiti SH CL	.30	.10
❑ 217	John Smoltz SH CL	.30	.10
❑ 218	Eric Young SH CL	.30	.10
❑ 219	Juan Gonzalez SH CL	.30	.10
❑ 220	Eddie Murray SH CL	.50	.20
❑ 221	Tommy Lasorda SH CL	.30	.10
❑ 222	Paul Molitor SH CL	.30	.10
❑ 223	Luis Castillo	.30	.10
❑ 224	Justin Thompson	.30	.10
❑ 225	Rocky Coppinger	.30	.10
❑ 226	Jermaine Allensworth	.30	.10
❑ 227	Jeff D'Amico	.30	.10
❑ 228	Jamey Wright	.30	.10
❑ 229	Scott Rolen	.50	.20
❑ 230	Darin Erstad	.30	.10
❑ 231	Marty Janzen	.30	.10
❑ 232	Jacob Cruz	.30	.10
❑ 233	Raul Ibanez	.30	.10
❑ 234	Nomar Garciaparra	1.25	.50
❑ 235	Todd Walker	.30	.10
❑ 236	Brian Giles RC	1.50	.60
❑ 237	Matt Beech	.30	.10
❑ 238	Mike Cameron	.30	.10
❑ 239	Jose Paniagua	.30	.10
❑ 240	Andruw Jones	.50	.20
❑ 241	Brant Brown UPD	1.00	.40
❑ 242	Robin Jennings UPD	1.00	.40
❑ 243	Willie Adams UPD	1.00	.40
❑ 244	Ken Caminiti UPD	1.50	.60
❑ 245	Brian Jordan UPD	1.50	.60
❑ 246	Chipper Jones UPD	4.00	1.50
❑ 247	Juan Gonzalez UPD	1.50	.60
❑ 248	Bernie Williams UPD	2.50	1.00
❑ 249	Roberto Alomar UPD	2.50	1.00
❑ 250	Bernie Williams UPD	2.50	1.00
❑ 251	David Wells UPD	1.50	.60
❑ 252	Cecil Fielder UPD	1.50	.60
❑ 253	Darryl Strawberry UPD	1.50	.60
❑ 254	Andy Pettitte UPD	2.50	1.00
❑ 255	Javier Lopez UPD	1.50	.60
❑ 256	Gary Gaetti UPD	1.50	.60
❑ 257	Ron Gant UPD	1.50	.60
❑ 258	Brian Jordan UPD	1.50	.60
❑ 259	John Smoltz UPD	2.50	1.00
❑ 260	Greg Maddux UPD	8.00	3.00
❑ 261	Tom Glavine UPD	2.50	1.00
❑ 262	Andruw Jones UPD	2.50	1.00
❑ 263	Greg Maddux UPD	8.00	3.00
❑ 264	David Cone UPD	1.50	.60
❑ 265	Jim Leyritz UPD	1.00	.40
❑ 266	Andy Pettitte UPD	2.50	1.00
❑ 267	John Wetteland UPD	1.50	.60
❑ 268	Dario Veras UPD	1.00	.40
❑ 269	Neifi Perez UPD	1.00	.40
❑ 270	Bill Mueller UPD	4.00	1.50
❑ 271	Vladimir Guerrero	.75	.30
❑ 272	Dmitri Young	.30	.10
❑ 273	Nerio Rodriguez RC	.30	.10
❑ 274	Kevin Orie	.30	.10
❑ 275	Felipe Crespo	.30	.10
❑ 276	Danny Graves	.30	.10
❑ 277	Rod Myers	.30	.10
❑ 278	Felix Heredia RC	.30	.10
❑ 279	Ralph Milliard	.30	.10
❑ 280	Greg Norton	.30	.10
❑ 281	Derek Wallace	.30	.10
❑ 282	Trot Nixon	.30	.10
❑ 283	Bobby Chouinard	.30	.10
❑ 284	Jay Witasick	.30	.10
❑ 285	Travis Miller	.30	.10
❑ 286	Brian Bevil	.30	.10
❑ 287	Bobby Estalella	.30	.10
❑ 288	Steve Soderstrom	.30	.10
❑ 289	Mark Langston	.30	.10
❑ 290	Tim Salmon	.50	.20
❑ 291	Jim Edmonds	.30	.10
❑ 292	Garret Anderson	.30	.10
❑ 293	George Arias	.30	.10
❑ 294	Gary DiSarcina	.30	.10
❑ 295	Chuck Finley	.30	.10
❑ 296	Todd Greene	.30	.10
❑ 297	Randy Velarde	.30	.10
❑ 298	David Justice	.30	.10
❑ 299	Ryan Klesko	.30	.10
❑ 300	John Smoltz	.50	.20
❑ 301	Javier Lopez	.30	.10
❑ 302	Greg Maddux	1.25	.50
❑ 303	Denny Neagle	.30	.10
❑ 304	B.J. Surhoff	.30	.10
❑ 305	Chris Hoiles	.30	.10
❑ 306	Eric Davis	.30	.10
❑ 307	Scott Erickson	.30	.10
❑ 308	Mike Bordick	.30	.10
❑ 309	John Valentin	.30	.10
❑ 310	Heathcliff Slocumb	.30	.10
❑ 311	Tom Gordon	.30	.10
❑ 312	Mike Stanley	.30	.10
❑ 313	Reggie Jefferson	.30	.10
❑ 314	Darren Bragg	.30	.10
❑ 315	Troy O'Leary	.30	.10
❑ 316	John Mabry SH CL	.30	.10
❑ 317	Mark Whiten SH CL	.30	.10
❑ 318	Edgar Martinez SH CL	.30	.10
❑ 319	Alex Rodriguez SH CL	.75	.30
❑ 320	Mark McGwire SH CL	1.00	.40
❑ 321	Hideo Nomo SH CL	.30	.10
❑ 322	Todd Hundley SH CL	.30	.10
❑ 323	Barry Bonds SH CL	1.00	.40
❑ 324	Andruw Jones SH CL	.30	.10
❑ 325	Ryne Sandberg	1.25	.50
❑ 326	Brian McRae	.30	.10
❑ 327	Frank Castillo	.30	.10
❑ 328	Shawon Dunston	.30	.10
❑ 329	Ray Durham	.30	.10
❑ 330	Robin Ventura	.30	.10
❑ 331	Ozzie Guillen	.30	.10
❑ 332	Roberto Hernandez	.30	.10
❑ 333	Albert Belle	.30	.10
❑ 334	Dave Martinez	.30	.10
❑ 335	Willie Greene	.30	.10
❑ 336	Jeff Brantley	.30	.10
❑ 337	Kevin Jarvis	.30	.10
❑ 338	John Smiley	.30	.10
❑ 339	Eddie Taubensee	.30	.10
❑ 340	Bret Boone	.30	.10
❑ 341	Kevin Seitzer	.30	.10
❑ 342	Jack McDowell	.30	.10
❑ 343	Sandy Alomar Jr.	.30	.10
❑ 344	Chad Curtis	.30	.10
❑ 345	Manny Ramirez	.50	.20
❑ 346	Chad Ogea	.30	.10
❑ 347	Jim Thome	.50	.20
❑ 348	Mark Thompson	.30	.10
❑ 349	Ellis Burks	.30	.10
❑ 350	Andres Galarraga	.30	.10
❑ 351	Vinny Castilla	.30	.10
❑ 352	Kirt Manwaring	.30	.10
❑ 353	Larry Walker	.30	.10
❑ 354	Omar Olivares	.30	.10
❑ 355	Bobby Higginson	.30	.10
❑ 356	Melvin Nieves	.30	.10
❑ 357	Brian Johnson	.30	.10

❑	358	Devon White	.30	.10
❑	359	Jeff Conine	.30	.10
❑	360	Gary Sheffield	.30	.10
❑	361	Robb Nen	.30	.10
❑	362	Mike Hampton	.30	.10
❑	363	Bob Abreu	.50	.20
❑	364	Luis Gonzalez	.30	.10
❑	365	Derek Bell	.30	.10
❑	366	Sean Berry	.30	.10
❑	367	Craig Biggio	.50	.20
❑	368	Darryl Kile	.30	.10
❑	369	Shane Reynolds	.30	.10
❑	370	Jeff Bagwell CF	.30	.10
❑	371	Ron Gant CF	.30	.10
❑	372	Andy Benes CF	.30	.10
❑	373	Gary Gaetti CF	.30	.10
❑	374	Ramon Martinez CF	.30	.10
❑	375	Raul Mondesi CF	.30	.10
❑	376	Steve Finley CF	.30	.10
❑	377	Ken Caminiti CF	.30	.10
❑	378	Tony Gwynn CF	.50	.20
❑	379	Dario Veras RC	.30	.10
❑	380	Andy Pettitte CF	.30	.10
❑	381	Ruben Rivera CF	.30	.10
❑	382	David Cone CF	.30	.10
❑	383	Roberto Alomar CF	.30	.10
❑	384	Edgar Martinez CF	.30	.10
❑	385	Ken Griffey Jr. CF	.75	.30
❑	386	Mark McGwire CF	1.00	.40
❑	387	Rusty Greer CF	.30	.10
❑	388	Jose Rosado	.30	.10
❑	389	Kevin Appier	.30	.10
❑	390	Johnny Damon	.50	.20
❑	391	Jose Offerman	.30	.10
❑	392	Michael Tucker	.30	.10
❑	393	Craig Paquette	.30	.10
❑	394	Bip Roberts	.30	.10
❑	395	Ramon Martinez	.30	.10
❑	396	Greg Gagne	.30	.10
❑	397	Chan Ho Park	.30	.10
❑	398	Karim Garcia	.30	.10
❑	399	Wilton Guerrero	.30	.10
❑	400	Eric Karros	.30	.10
❑	401	Raul Mondesi	.30	.10
❑	402	Matt Mieske	.30	.10
❑	403	Mike Fetters	.30	.10
❑	404	Dave Nilsson	.30	.10
❑	405	Jose Valentin	.30	.10
❑	406	Scott Karl	.30	.10
❑	407	Marc Newfield	.30	.10
❑	408	Cal Eldred	.30	.10
❑	409	Rich Becker	.30	.10
❑	410	Terry Steinbach	.30	.10
❑	411	Chuck Knoblauch	.30	.10
❑	412	Pat Meares	.30	.10
❑	413	Brad Radke	.30	.10
❑	414	Kirby Puckett UER	.75	.30
❑	415	Andruw Jones GHL SP	1.50	.60
❑	416	Chipper Jones GHL SP	2.50	1.00
❑	417	Mo Vaughn GHL SP	1.50	.60
❑	418	Frank Thomas GHL SP	2.50	1.00
❑	419	Albert Belle GHL SP	1.50	.60
❑	420	Mark McGwire GHL SP	8.00	3.00
❑	421	Derek Jeter GHL SP	8.00	3.00
❑	422	Alex Rodriguez GHL SP	5.00	2.00
❑	423	Juan Gonzalez GHL SP	1.50	.60
❑	424	Ken Griffey Jr. GHL SP	5.00	2.00
❑	425	Rondell White	.30	.10
❑	426	Darrin Fletcher	.30	.10
❑	427	Cliff Floyd	.30	.10
❑	428	Mike Lansing	.30	.10
❑	429	F.P. Santangelo	.30	.10
❑	430	Todd Hundley	.30	.10
❑	431	Mark Clark	.30	.10
❑	432	Pete Harnisch	.30	.10
❑	433	Jason Isringhausen	.30	.10
❑	434	Bobby Jones	.30	.10
❑	435	Lance Johnson	.30	.10
❑	436	Carlos Baerga	.30	.10
❑	437	Mariano Duncan	.30	.10
❑	438	David Cone	.30	.10
❑	439	Mariano Rivera	.75	.30
❑	440	Derek Jeter	2.00	.75
❑	441	Joe Girardi	.30	.10
❑	442	Charlie Hayes	.30	.10
❑	443	Tim Raines	.30	.10
❑	444	Darryl Strawberry	.30	.10
❑	445	Cecil Fielder	.30	.10
❑	446	Ariel Prieto	.30	.10
❑	447	Tony Batista	.30	.10
❑	448	Brent Gates	.30	.10
❑	449	Scott Spiezio	.30	.10
❑	450	Mark McGwire	2.00	.75
❑	451	Don Wengert	.30	.10
❑	452	Mike Lieberthal	.30	.10
❑	453	Lenny Dykstra	.30	.10
❑	454	Rex Hudler	.30	.10
❑	455	Darren Daulton	.30	.10
❑	456	Kevin Stocker	.30	.10
❑	457	Trey Beamon	.30	.10
❑	458	Midre Cummings	.30	.10
❑	459	Mark Johnson	.30	.10
❑	460	Al Martin	.30	.10
❑	461	Kevin Elster	.30	.10
❑	462	Jon Lieber	.30	.10
❑	463	Jason Schmidt	.30	.10
❑	464	Paul Wagner	.30	.10
❑	465	Andy Benes	.30	.10
❑	466	Alan Benes	.30	.10
❑	467	Royce Clayton	.30	.10
❑	468	Gary Gaetti	.30	.10
❑	469	Curt Lyons RC	.30	.10
❑	470	Eugene Kingsale DD	.30	.10
❑	471	Damian Jackson DD	.30	.10
❑	472	Wendell Magee DD	.30	.10
❑	473	Kevin L. Brown DD	.30	.10
❑	474	Raul Casanova DD	.30	.10
❑	475	Ramiro Mendoza RC	.30	.10
❑	476	Todd Dunn DD	.30	.10
❑	477	Chad Mottola DD	.30	.10
❑	478	Andy Larkin DD	.30	.10
❑	479	Jaime Bluma DD	.30	.10
❑	480	Mac Suzuki DD	.30	.10
❑	481	Brian Banks DD	.30	.10
❑	482	Desi Wilson DD	.30	.10
❑	483	Einar Diaz DD	.30	.10
❑	484	Tom Pagnozzi	.30	.10
❑	485	Ray Lankford	.30	.10
❑	486	Todd Stottlemyre	.30	.10
❑	487	Donovan Osborne	.30	.10
❑	488	Trevor Hoffman	.30	.10
❑	489	Chris Gomez	.30	.10
❑	490	Ken Caminiti	.30	.10
❑	491	John Flaherty	.30	.10
❑	492	Tony Gwynn	1.00	.40
❑	493	Joey Hamilton	.30	.10
❑	494	Rickey Henderson	.75	.30
❑	495	Glenallen Hill	.30	.10
❑	496	Rod Beck	.30	.10
❑	497	Osvaldo Fernandez	.30	.10
❑	498	Rick Wilkins	.30	.10
❑	499	Joey Cora	.30	.10
❑	500	Alex Rodriguez	1.25	.50
❑	501	Randy Johnson	.75	.30
❑	502	Paul Sorrento	.30	.10
❑	503	Dan Wilson	.30	.10
❑	504	Jamie Moyer	.30	.10
❑	505	Will Clark	.50	.20
❑	506	Mickey Tettleton	.30	.10
❑	507	John Burkett	.30	.10
❑	508	Ken Hill	.30	.10
❑	509	Mark McLemore	.30	.10
❑	510	Juan Gonzalez	.30	.10
❑	511	Bobby Witt	.30	.10
❑	512	Carlos Delgado	.30	.10
❑	513	Alex Gonzalez	.30	.10
❑	514	Shawn Green	.30	.10
❑	515	Joe Carter	.30	.10
❑	516	Juan Guzman	.30	.10
❑	517	Charlie O'Brien	.30	.10
❑	518	Ed Sprague	.30	.10
❑	519	Mike Timlin	.30	.10
❑	520	Roger Clemens	1.50	.60
❑	521	Eddie Murray TRADE	2.00	.75
❑	522	Jason Dickson TRADE	.50	.20
❑	523	Jim Leyritz TRADE	.50	.20
❑	524	Michael Tucker TRADE	.50	.20
❑	525	Kenny Lofton TRADE	.75	.30
❑	526	Jimmy Key TRADE	.75	.30
❑	527	Mel Rojas TRADE	.50	.20
❑	528	Deion Sanders TRADE	1.25	.50
❑	529	Bartolo Colon TRADE	.75	.30
❑	530	Matt Williams TRADE	.75	.30
❑	531	Marquis Grissom TRADE	.75	.30
❑	532	David Justice TRADE	.75	.30
❑	533	Bubba Trammell TRADE	.75	.30
❑	534	Moises Alou TRADE	.75	.30
❑	535	Bobby Bonilla TRADE	.75	.30
❑	536	Alex Fernandez TRADE	.50	.20
❑	537	Jay Bell TRADE	.75	.30
❑	538	Chili Davis TRADE	.75	.30
❑	539	Jeff King TRADE	.50	.20
❑	540	Todd Zeile TRADE	.50	.20
❑	541	John Olerud TRADE	.75	.30
❑	542	Jose Guillen TRADE	.75	.30
❑	543	Derrek Lee TRADE	1.25	.50
❑	544	Dante Powell TRADE	.50	.20
❑	545	J.T. Snow TRADE	.75	.30
❑	546	Jeff Kent TRADE	.75	.30
❑	547	Jose Cruz Jr. TRADE	.75	.30
❑	548	John Wetteland TRADE	.75	.30
❑	549	Orlando Merced TRADE	.50	.20
❑	550	Hideki Irabu TRADE	.75	.30

1998 Upper Deck

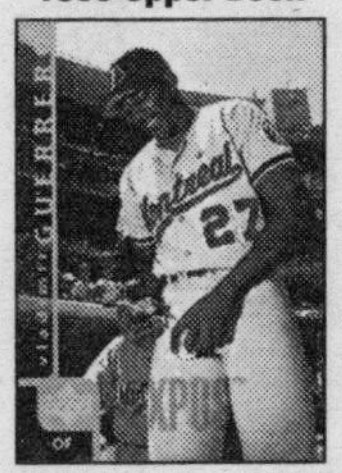

❑	COMPLETE SET (751)	200.00	80.00
❑	COMPLETE SERIES 1 (270)	40.00	15.00
❑	COMPLETE SERIES 2 (270)	40.00	15.00
❑	COMPLETE SERIES 3 (211)	120.00	50.00
❑	COMMON (1-600/631-750)	.30	.10
❑	COMMON EP (601-630)	2.00	.75
❑	EP SER.2 ODDS APPROXIMATELY 1:4		

❑	1	Tino Martinez HIST	.30	.10
❑	2	Jimmy Key HIST	.30	.10
❑	3	Jay Buhner HIST	.30	.10
❑	4	Mark Gardner HIST	.30	.10
❑	5	Greg Maddux HIST	.75	.30
❑	6	Pedro Martinez HIST	.50	.20
❑	7	Hideo Nomo HIST	.50	.20
❑	8	Sammy Sosa HIST	.50	.20
❑	9	Mark McGwire GHL	1.00	.40
❑	10	Ken Griffey Jr. GHL	.75	.30
❑	11	Larry Walker GHL	.30	.10
❑	12	Tino Martinez GHL	.30	.10
❑	13	Mike Piazza GHL	.75	.30
❑	14	Jose Cruz Jr. GHL	.30	.10
❑	15	Tony Gwynn GHL	.50	.20
❑	16	Greg Maddux GHL	.75	.30
❑	17	Roger Clemens GHL	.75	.30
❑	18	Alex Rodriguez GHL	.75	.30
❑	19	Shigetoshi Hasegawa	.30	.10
❑	20	Eddie Murray	.75	.30
❑	21	Jason Dickson	.30	.10
❑	22	Darin Erstad	.30	.10
❑	23	Chuck Finley	.30	.10
❑	24	Dave Hollins	.30	.10
❑	25	Garret Anderson	.30	.10
❑	26	Michael Tucker	.30	.10
❑	27	Kenny Lofton	.30	.10
❑	28	Javier Lopez	.30	.10
❑	29	Fred McGriff	.50	.20
❑	30	Greg Maddux	1.25	.50
❑	31	Jeff Blauser	.30	.10
❑	32	John Smoltz	.50	.20
❑	33	Mark Wohlers	.30	.10
❑	34	Scott Erickson	.30	.10
❑	35	Jimmy Key	.30	.10
❑	36	Harold Baines	.30	.10
❑	37	Randy Myers	.30	.10
❑	38	B.J. Surhoff	.30	.10

❑	39	Eric Davis	.30	.10
❑	40	Rafael Palmeiro	.50	.20
❑	41	Jeffrey Hammonds	.30	.10
❑	42	Mo Vaughn	.30	.10
❑	43	Tom Gordon	.30	.10
❑	44	Tim Naehring	.30	.10
❑	45	Darren Bragg	.30	.10
❑	46	Aaron Sele	.30	.10
❑	47	Troy O'Leary	.30	.10
❑	48	John Valentin	.30	.10
❑	49	Doug Glanville	.30	.10
❑	50	Ryne Sandberg	1.25	.50
❑	51	Steve Trachsel	.30	.10
❑	52	Mark Grace	.50	.20
❑	53	Kevin Foster	.30	.10
❑	54	Kevin Tapani	.30	.10
❑	55	Kevin Orie	.30	.10
❑	56	Lyle Mouton	.30	.10
❑	57	Ray Durham	.30	.10
❑	58	Jaime Navarro	.30	.10
❑	59	Mike Cameron	.30	.10
❑	60	Albert Belle	.30	.10
❑	61	Doug Drabek	.30	.10
❑	62	Chris Snopek	.30	.10
❑	63	Eddie Taubensee	.30	.10
❑	64	Terry Pendleton	.30	.10
❑	65	Barry Larkin	.50	.20
❑	66	Willie Greene	.30	.10
❑	67	Deion Sanders	.50	.20
❑	68	Pokey Reese	.30	.10
❑	69	Jeff Shaw	.30	.10
❑	70	Jim Thome	.50	.20
❑	71	Orel Hershiser	.30	.10
❑	72	Omar Vizquel	.50	.20
❑	73	Brian Giles	.30	.10
❑	74	David Justice	.30	.10
❑	75	Bartolo Colon	.30	.10
❑	76	Sandy Alomar Jr.	.30	.10
❑	77	Neifi Perez	.30	.10
❑	78	Dante Bichette	.30	.10
❑	79	Vinny Castilla	.30	.10
❑	80	Eric Young	.30	.10
❑	81	Quinton McCracken	.30	.10
❑	82	Jamey Wright	.30	.10
❑	83	John Thomson	.30	.10
❑	84	Damion Easley	.30	.10
❑	85	Justin Thompson	.30	.10
❑	86	Willie Blair	.30	.10
❑	87	Raul Casanova	.30	.10
❑	88	Bobby Higginson	.30	.10
❑	89	Bubba Trammell	.30	.10
❑	90	Tony Clark	.30	.10
❑	91	Livan Hernandez	.30	.10
❑	92	Charles Johnson	.30	.10
❑	93	Edgar Renteria	.30	.10
❑	94	Alex Fernandez	.30	.10
❑	95	Gary Sheffield	.30	.10
❑	96	Moises Alou	.30	.10
❑	97	Tony Saunders	.30	.10
❑	98	Robb Nen	.30	.10
❑	99	Darryl Kile	.30	.10
❑	100	Craig Biggio	.50	.20
❑	101	Chris Holt	.30	.10
❑	102	Bob Abreu	.30	.10
❑	103	Luis Gonzalez	.30	.10
❑	104	Billy Wagner	.30	.10
❑	105	Brad Ausmus	.30	.10
❑	106	Chili Davis	.30	.10
❑	107	Tim Belcher	.30	.10
❑	108	Dean Palmer	.30	.10
❑	109	Jeff King	.30	.10
❑	110	Jose Rosado	.30	.10
❑	111	Mike Macfarlane	.30	.10
❑	112	Jay Bell	.30	.10
❑	113	Todd Worrell	.30	.10
❑	114	Chan Ho Park	.30	.10
❑	115	Raul Mondesi	.30	.10
❑	116	Brett Butler	.30	.10
❑	117	Greg Gagne	.30	.10
❑	118	Hideo Nomo	.75	.30
❑	119	Todd Zeile	.30	.10
❑	120	Eric Karros	.30	.10
❑	121	Cal Eldred	.30	.10
❑	122	Jeff D'Amico	.30	.10
❑	123	Antone Williamson	.30	.10
❑	124	Doug Jones	.30	.10
❑	125	Dave Nilsson	.30	.10
❑	126	Gerald Williams	.30	.10
❑	127	Fernando Vina	.30	.10
❑	128	Ron Coomer	.30	.10
❑	129	Matt Lawton	.30	.10
❑	130	Paul Molitor	.30	.10
❑	131	Todd Walker	.30	.10
❑	132	Rick Aguilera	.30	.10
❑	133	Brad Radke	.30	.10
❑	134	Bob Tewksbury	.30	.10
❑	135	Vladimir Guerrero	.75	.30
❑	136	Tony Gwynn DG	.50	.20
❑	137	Roger Clemens DG	.75	.30
❑	138	Dennis Eckersley DG	.30	.10
❑	139	Brady Anderson DG	.30	.10
❑	140	Ken Griffey Jr. DG	.75	.30
❑	141	Derek Jeter DG	1.00	.40
❑	142	Ken Caminiti DG	.30	.10
❑	143	Frank Thomas DG	.50	.20
❑	144	Barry Bonds DG	1.00	.40
❑	145	Cal Ripken DG	1.25	.50
❑	146	Alex Rodriguez DG	.75	.30
❑	147	Greg Maddux DG	.75	.30
❑	148	Kenny Lofton DG	.30	.10
❑	149	Mike Piazza DG	.75	.30
❑	150	Mark McGwire DG	1.00	.40
❑	151	Andruw Jones DG	.30	.10
❑	152	Rusty Greer DG	.30	.10
❑	153	F.P. Santangelo DG	.30	.10
❑	154	Mike Lansing	.30	.10
❑	155	Lee Smith	.30	.10
❑	156	Carlos Perez	.30	.10
❑	157	Pedro Martinez	.50	.20
❑	158	Ryan McGuire	.30	.10
❑	159	F.P. Santangelo	.30	.10
❑	160	Rondell White	.30	.10
❑	161	Takashi Kashiwada RC	.40	.15
❑	162	Butch Huskey	.30	.10
❑	163	Edgardo Alfonzo	.30	.10
❑	164	John Franco	.30	.10
❑	165	Todd Hundley	.30	.10
❑	166	Rey Ordonez	.30	.10
❑	167	Armando Reynoso	.30	.10
❑	168	John Olerud	.30	.10
❑	169	Bernie Williams	.50	.20
❑	170	Andy Pettitte	.50	.20
❑	171	Wade Boggs	.50	.20
❑	172	Paul O'Neill	.50	.20
❑	173	Cecil Fielder	.30	.10
❑	174	Charlie Hayes	.30	.10
❑	175	David Cone	.30	.10
❑	176	Hideki Irabu	.30	.10
❑	177	Mark Bellhorn	.30	.10
❑	178	Steve Karsay	.30	.10
❑	179	Damon Mashore	.30	.10
❑	180	Jason McDonald	.30	.10
❑	181	Scott Spiezio	.30	.10
❑	182	Ariel Prieto	.30	.10
❑	183	Jason Giambi	.30	.10
❑	184	Wendell Magee	.30	.10
❑	185	Rico Brogna	.30	.10
❑	186	Garrett Stephenson	.30	.10
❑	187	Wayne Gomes	.30	.10
❑	188	Ricky Bottalico	.30	.10
❑	189	Mickey Morandini	.30	.10
❑	190	Mike Lieberthal	.30	.10
❑	191	Kevin Polcovich	.30	.10
❑	192	Francisco Cordova	.30	.10
❑	193	Kevin Young	.30	.10
❑	194	Jon Lieber	.30	.10
❑	195	Kevin Elster	.30	.10
❑	196	Tony Womack	.30	.10
❑	197	Lou Collier	.30	.10
❑	198	Mike Difelice RC	.40	.15
❑	199	Gary Gaetti	.30	.10
❑	200	Dennis Eckersley	.30	.10
❑	201	Alan Benes	.30	.10
❑	202	Willie McGee	.30	.10
❑	203	Ron Gant	.30	.10
❑	204	Fernando Valenzuela	.30	.10
❑	205	Mark McGwire	2.00	.75
❑	206	Archi Cianfrocco	.30	.10
❑	207	Andy Ashby	.30	.10
❑	208	Steve Finley	.30	.10
❑	209	Quilvio Veras	.30	.10
❑	210	Ken Caminiti	.30	.10
❑	211	Rickey Henderson	.75	.30
❑	212	Joey Hamilton	.30	.10
❑	213	Derrek Lee	.50	.20
❑	214	Bill Mueller	.30	.10
❑	215	Shawn Estes	.30	.10
❑	216	J.T. Snow	.30	.10
❑	217	Mark Gardner	.30	.10
❑	218	Terry Mulholland	.30	.10
❑	219	Dante Powell	.30	.10
❑	220	Jeff Kent	.30	.10
❑	221	Jamie Moyer	.30	.10
❑	222	Joey Cora	.30	.10
❑	223	Jeff Fassero	.30	.10
❑	224	Dennis Martinez	.30	.10
❑	225	Ken Griffey Jr.	1.25	.50
❑	226	Edgar Martinez	.50	.20
❑	227	Russ Davis	.30	.10
❑	228	Dan Wilson	.30	.10
❑	229	Will Clark	.50	.20
❑	230	Ivan Rodriguez	.50	.20
❑	231	Benji Gil	.30	.10
❑	232	Lee Stevens	.30	.10
❑	233	Mickey Tettleton	.30	.10
❑	234	Julio Santana	.30	.10
❑	235	Rusty Greer	.30	.10
❑	236	Bobby Witt	.30	.10
❑	237	Ed Sprague	.30	.10
❑	238	Pat Hentgen	.30	.10
❑	239	Kelvim Escobar	.30	.10
❑	240	Joe Carter	.30	.10
❑	241	Carlos Delgado	.30	.10
❑	242	Shannon Stewart	.30	.10
❑	243	Benito Santiago	.30	.10
❑	244	Tino Martinez SH	.30	.10
❑	245	Ken Griffey Jr. SH	.75	.30
❑	246	Kevin Brown SH	.30	.10
❑	247	Ryne Sandberg SH	.50	.20
❑	248	Mo Vaughn SH	.30	.10
❑	249	Darryl Hamilton SH	.30	.10
❑	250	Randy Johnson SH	.50	.20
❑	251	Steve Finley SH	.30	.10
❑	252	Bobby Higginson SH	.30	.10
❑	253	Brett Tomko	.30	.10
❑	254	Mark Kotsay	.30	.10
❑	255	Jose Guillen	.30	.10
❑	256	Eli Marrero	.30	.10
❑	257	Dennis Reyes	.30	.10
❑	258	Richie Sexson	.30	.10
❑	259	Pat Cline	.30	.10
❑	260	Todd Helton	.50	.20
❑	261	Juan Melo	.30	.10
❑	262	Matt Morris	.30	.10
❑	263	Jeremi Gonzalez	.30	.10
❑	264	Jeff Abbott	.30	.10
❑	265	Aaron Boone	.30	.10
❑	266	Todd Dunwoody	.30	.10
❑	267	Jaret Wright	.30	.10
❑	268	Derrick Gibson	.30	.10
❑	269	Mario Valdez	.30	.10
❑	270	Fernando Tatis	.30	.10
❑	271	Craig Counsell	.30	.10
❑	272	Brad Rigby	.30	.10
❑	273	Danny Clyburn	.30	.10
❑	274	Brian Rose	.30	.10
❑	275	Miguel Tejada	.75	.30
❑	276	Jason Varitek	.75	.30
❑	277	Dave Dellucci RC	.60	.25
❑	278	Michael Coleman	.30	.10
❑	279	Adam Riggs	.30	.10
❑	280	Ben Grieve	.30	.10
❑	281	Brad Fullmer	.30	.10
❑	282	Ken Cloude	.30	.10
❑	283	Tom Evans	.30	.10
❑	284	Kevin Millwood RC	1.00	.40
❑	285	Paul Konerko	.30	.10
❑	286	Juan Encarnacion	.30	.10
❑	287	Chris Carpenter	.30	.10
❑	288	Tom Fordham	.30	.10
❑	289	Gary DiSarcina	.30	.10
❑	290	Tim Salmon	.50	.20
❑	291	Troy Percival	.30	.10
❑	292	Todd Greene	.30	.10
❑	293	Ken Hill	.30	.10
❑	294	Dennis Springer	.30	.10
❑	295	Jim Edmonds	.30	.10
❑	296	Allen Watson	.30	.10

❑ 297 Brian Anderson .30 .10
❑ 298 Keith Lockhart .30 .10
❑ 299 Tom Glavine .50 .20
❑ 300 Chipper Jones .75 .30
❑ 301 Randall Simon .30 .10
❑ 302 Mark Lemke .30 .10
❑ 303 Ryan Klesko .30 .10
❑ 304 Denny Neagle .30 .10
❑ 305 Andruw Jones .50 .20
❑ 306 Mike Mussina .50 .20
❑ 307 Brady Anderson .30 .10
❑ 308 Chris Hoiles .30 .10
❑ 309 Mike Bordick .30 .10
❑ 310 Cal Ripken 2.50 1.00
❑ 311 Geronimo Berroa .30 .10
❑ 312 Armando Benitez .30 .10
❑ 313 Roberto Alomar .50 .20
❑ 314 Tim Wakefield .30 .10
❑ 315 Reggie Jefferson .30 .10
❑ 316 Jeff Frye .30 .10
❑ 317 Scott Hatteberg .30 .10
❑ 318 Steve Avery .30 .10
❑ 319 Robinson Checo .30 .10
❑ 320 Nomar Garciaparra 1.25 .50
❑ 321 Lance Johnson .30 .10
❑ 322 Tyler Houston .30 .10
❑ 323 Mark Clark .30 .10
❑ 324 Terry Adams .30 .10
❑ 325 Sammy Sosa .75 .30
❑ 326 Scott Servais .30 .10
❑ 327 Manny Alexander .30 .10
❑ 328 Norberto Martin .30 .10
❑ 329 Scott Eyre .30 .10
❑ 330 Frank Thomas .75 .30
❑ 331 Robin Ventura .30 .10
❑ 332 Matt Karchner .30 .10
❑ 333 Keith Foulke .30 .10
❑ 334 James Baldwin .30 .10
❑ 335 Chris Stynes .30 .10
❑ 336 Bret Boone .30 .10
❑ 337 Jon Nunnally .30 .10
❑ 338 Dave Burba .30 .10
❑ 339 Eduardo Perez .30 .10
❑ 340 Reggie Sanders .30 .10
❑ 341 Mike Remlinger .30 .10
❑ 342 Pat Watkins .30 .10
❑ 343 Chad Ogea .30 .10
❑ 344 John Smiley .30 .10
❑ 345 Kenny Lofton .30 .10
❑ 346 Jose Mesa .30 .10
❑ 347 Charles Nagy .30 .10
❑ 348 Enrique Wilson .30 .10
❑ 349 Bruce Aven .30 .10
❑ 350 Manny Ramirez .50 .20
❑ 351 Jerry DiPoto .30 .10
❑ 352 Ellis Burks .30 .10
❑ 353 Kirt Manwaring .30 .10
❑ 354 Vinny Castilla .30 .10
❑ 355 Larry Walker .30 .10
❑ 356 Kevin Ritz .30 .10
❑ 357 Pedro Astacio .30 .10
❑ 358 Scott Sanders .30 .10
❑ 359 Deivi Cruz .30 .10
❑ 360 Brian L. Hunter .30 .10
❑ 361 Pedro Martinez HM .50 .20
❑ 362 Tom Glavine HM .30 .10
❑ 363 Willie McGee HM .30 .10
❑ 364 J.T. Snow HM .30 .10
❑ 365 Rusty Greer HM .30 .10
❑ 366 Mike Grace HM .30 .10
❑ 367 Tony Clark HM .30 .10
❑ 368 Ben Grieve HM .30 .10
❑ 369 Gary Sheffield HM .30 .10
❑ 370 Joe Oliver .30 .10
❑ 371 Todd Jones .30 .10
❑ 372 Frank Catalanotto RC .60 .25
❑ 373 Brian Moehler .30 .10
❑ 374 Cliff Floyd .30 .10
❑ 375 Bobby Bonilla .30 .10
❑ 376 Al Leiter .30 .10
❑ 377 Josh Booty .30 .10
❑ 378 Darren Daulton .30 .10
❑ 379 Jay Powell .30 .10
❑ 380 Felix Heredia .30 .10
❑ 381 Jim Eisenreich .30 .10
❑ 382 Richard Hidalgo .30 .10
❑ 383 Mike Hampton .30 .10
❑ 384 Shane Reynolds .30 .10
❑ 385 Jeff Bagwell .50 .20
❑ 386 Derek Bell .30 .10
❑ 387 Ricky Gutierrez .30 .10
❑ 388 Bill Spiers .30 .10
❑ 389 Jose Offerman .30 .10
❑ 390 Johnny Damon .50 .20
❑ 391 Jermaine Dye .30 .10
❑ 392 Jeff Montgomery .30 .10
❑ 393 Glendon Rusch .30 .10
❑ 394 Mike Sweeney .30 .10
❑ 395 Kevin Appier .30 .10
❑ 396 Joe Vitiello .30 .10
❑ 397 Ramon Martinez .30 .10
❑ 398 Darren Dreifort .30 .10
❑ 399 Wilton Guerrero .30 .10
❑ 400 Mike Piazza 1.25 .50
❑ 401 Eddie Murray .75 .30
❑ 402 Ismael Valdes .30 .10
❑ 403 Todd Hollandsworth .30 .10
❑ 404 Mark Loretta .30 .10
❑ 405 Jeromy Burnitz .30 .10
❑ 406 Jeff Cirillo .30 .10
❑ 407 Scott Karl .30 .10
❑ 408 Mike Matheny .30 .10
❑ 409 Jose Valentin .30 .10
❑ 410 John Jaha .30 .10
❑ 411 Terry Steinbach .30 .10
❑ 412 Torii Hunter .30 .10
❑ 413 Pat Meares .30 .10
❑ 414 Marty Cordova .30 .10
❑ 415 Jaret Wright PH .30 .10
❑ 416 Mike Mussina PH .30 .10
❑ 417 John Smoltz PH .30 .10
❑ 418 Devon White PH .30 .10
❑ 419 Denny Neagle PH .30 .10
❑ 420 Livan Hernandez PH .30 .10
❑ 421 Kevin Brown PH .30 .10
❑ 422 Marquis Grissom PH .30 .10
❑ 423 Mike Mussina PH .30 .10
❑ 424 Eric Davis PH .30 .10
❑ 425 Tony Fernandez PH .30 .10
❑ 426 Moises Alou PH .30 .10
❑ 427 Sandy Alomar Jr. PH .30 .10
❑ 428 Gary Sheffield PH .30 .10
❑ 429 Jaret Wright PH .30 .10
❑ 430 Livan Hernandez PH .30 .10
❑ 431 Chad Ogea PH .30 .10
❑ 432 Edgar Renteria PH .30 .10
❑ 433 LaTroy Hawkins .30 .10
❑ 434 Rich Robertson .30 .10
❑ 435 Chuck Knoblauch .30 .10
❑ 436 Jose Vidro .30 .10
❑ 437 Dustin Hermanson .30 .10
❑ 438 Jim Bullinger .30 .10
❑ 439 Orlando Cabrera .30 .10
❑ 440 Vladimir Guerrero .75 .30
❑ 441 Ugueth Urbina .30 .10
❑ 442 Brian McRae .30 .10
❑ 443 Matt Franco .30 .10
❑ 444 Bobby Jones .30 .10
❑ 445 Bernard Gilkey .30 .10
❑ 446 Dave Mlicki .30 .10
❑ 447 Brian Bohanon .30 .10
❑ 448 Mel Rojas .30 .10
❑ 449 Tim Raines .30 .10
❑ 450 Derek Jeter 2.00 .75
❑ 451 Roger Clemens UE .75 .30
❑ 452 Nomar Garciaparra UE .75 .30
❑ 453 Mike Piazza UE .75 .30
❑ 454 Mark McGwire UE 1.00 .40
❑ 455 Ken Griffey Jr. UE .75 .30
❑ 456 Larry Walker UE .30 .10
❑ 457 Alex Rodriguez UE .75 .30
❑ 458 Tony Gwynn UE .50 .20
❑ 459 Frank Thomas UE .50 .20
❑ 460 Tino Martinez .50 .20
❑ 461 Chad Curtis .30 .10
❑ 462 Ramiro Mendoza .30 .10
❑ 463 Joe Girardi .30 .10
❑ 464 David Wells .30 .10
❑ 465 Mariano Rivera .75 .30
❑ 466 Willie Adams .30 .10
❑ 467 George Williams .30 .10
❑ 468 Dave Telgheder .30 .10
❑ 469 Dave Magadan .30 .10
❑ 470 Matt Stairs .30 .10
❑ 471 Bill Taylor .30 .10
❑ 472 Jimmy Haynes .30 .10
❑ 473 Gregg Jefferies .30 .10
❑ 474 Midre Cummings .30 .10
❑ 475 Curt Schilling .30 .10
❑ 476 Mike Grace .30 .10
❑ 477 Mark Leiter .30 .10
❑ 478 Matt Beech .30 .10
❑ 479 Scott Rolen .50 .20
❑ 480 Jason Kendall .30 .10
❑ 481 Esteban Loaiza .30 .10
❑ 482 Jermaine Allensworth .30 .10
❑ 483 Mark Smith .30 .10
❑ 484 Jason Schmidt .30 .10
❑ 485 Jose Guillen .30 .10
❑ 486 Al Martin .30 .10
❑ 487 Delino DeShields .30 .10
❑ 488 Todd Stottlemyre .30 .10
❑ 489 Brian Jordan .30 .10
❑ 490 Ray Lankford .30 .10
❑ 491 Matt Morris .30 .10
❑ 492 Royce Clayton .30 .10
❑ 493 John Mabry .30 .10
❑ 494 Wally Joyner .30 .10
❑ 495 Trevor Hoffman .30 .10
❑ 496 Chris Gomez .30 .10
❑ 497 Sterling Hitchcock .30 .10
❑ 498 Pete Smith .30 .10
❑ 499 Greg Vaughn .30 .10
❑ 500 Tony Gwynn 1.00 .40
❑ 501 Will Cunnane .30 .10
❑ 502 Darryl Hamilton .30 .10
❑ 503 Brian Johnson .30 .10
❑ 504 Kirk Rueter .30 .10
❑ 505 Barry Bonds 2.00 .75
❑ 506 Osvaldo Fernandez .30 .10
❑ 507 Stan Javier .30 .10
❑ 508 Julian Tavarez .30 .10
❑ 509 Rich Aurilia .30 .10
❑ 510 Alex Rodriguez 1.25 .50
❑ 511 David Segui .30 .10
❑ 512 Rich Amaral .30 .10
❑ 513 Raul Ibanez .30 .10
❑ 514 Jay Buhner .30 .10
❑ 515 Randy Johnson .75 .30
❑ 516 Heathcliff Slocumb .30 .10
❑ 517 Tony Saunders .30 .10
❑ 518 Kevin Elster .30 .10
❑ 519 John Burkett .30 .10
❑ 520 Juan Gonzalez .30 .10
❑ 521 John Wetteland .30 .10
❑ 522 Domingo Cedeno .30 .10
❑ 523 Darren Oliver .30 .10
❑ 524 Roger Pavlik .30 .10
❑ 525 Jose Cruz Jr. .30 .10
❑ 526 Woody Williams .30 .10
❑ 527 Alex Gonzalez .30 .10
❑ 528 Robert Person .30 .10
❑ 529 Juan Guzman .30 .10
❑ 530 Roger Clemens 1.50 .60
❑ 531 Shawn Green .30 .10
❑ 532 F.Cordova/R.Rincon/M.Smith SH .30 .10
❑ 533 Nomar Garciaparra SH .75 .30
❑ 534 Roger Clemens SH .75 .30
❑ 535 Mark McGwire SH 1.00 .40
❑ 536 Larry Walker SH .30 .10
❑ 537 Mike Piazza SH .75 .30
❑ 538 Curt Schilling SH .30 .10
❑ 539 Tony Gwynn SH .50 .20
❑ 540 Ken Griffey Jr. SH .75 .30
❑ 541 Carl Pavano .30 .10
❑ 542 Shane Monahan .30 .10
❑ 543 Gabe Kapler RC .60 .25
❑ 544 Eric Milton .30 .10
❑ 545 Gary Matthews Jr. RC .60 .25
❑ 546 Mike Kinkade RC .30 .10
❑ 547 Ryan Christenson RC .30 .10
❑ 548 Corey Koskie RC .60 .25
❑ 549 Norm Hutchins .30 .10
❑ 550 Russell Branyan .30 .10
❑ 551 Masato Yoshii RC .40 .15
❑ 552 Jesus Sanchez RC .30 .10
❑ 553 Anthony Sanders .30 .10
❑ 554 Edwin Diaz .30 .10

❑ 555 Gabe Alvarez .30 .10
❑ 556 Carlos Lee RC 2.00 .75
❑ 557 Mike Darr .30 .10
❑ 558 Kerry Wood .40 .15
❑ 559 Carlos Guillen .30 .10
❑ 560 Sean Casey .30 .10
❑ 561 Manny Aybar RC .30 .10
❑ 562 Octavio Dotel .30 .10
❑ 563 Jarrod Washburn .30 .10
❑ 564 Mark L. Johnson .30 .10
❑ 565 Ramon Hernandez .30 .10
❑ 566 Rich Butler RC .30 .10
❑ 567 Mike Caruso .30 .10
❑ 568 Cliff Politte .30 .10
❑ 569 Scott Elarton .30 .10
❑ 570 Magglio Ordonez RC 3.00 1.25
❑ 571 Adam Butler RC .30 .10
❑ 572 Marlon Anderson .30 .10
❑ 573 Julio Ramirez RC .30 .10
❑ 574 Darron Ingram RC .30 .10
❑ 575 Bruce Chen .30 .10
❑ 576 Steve Woodard .30 .10
❑ 577 Hiram Bocachica .30 .10
❑ 578 Kevin Witt .30 .10
❑ 579 Javier Vazquez .30 .10
❑ 580 Alex Gonzalez .30 .10
❑ 581 Brian Powell .30 .10
❑ 582 Wes Helms .30 .10
❑ 583 Ron Wright .30 .10
❑ 584 Rafael Medina .30 .10
❑ 585 Daryle Ward .30 .10
❑ 586 Geoff Jenkins .30 .10
❑ 587 Preston Wilson .30 .10
❑ 588 Jim Chamblee RC .30 .10
❑ 589 Mike Lowell RC 1.50 .60
❑ 590 A.J. Hinch .30 .10
❑ 591 Francisco Cordero RC .60 .25
❑ 592 Rolando Arrojo RC .40 .15
❑ 593 Braden Looper .30 .10
❑ 594 Sidney Ponson .30 .10
❑ 595 Matt Clement .30 .10
❑ 596 Carlton Loewer .30 .10
❑ 597 Brian Meadows .30 .10
❑ 598 Danny Klassen .30 .10
❑ 599 Larry Sutton .30 .10
❑ 600 Travis Lee .30 .10
❑ 601 Randy Johnson EP 2.50 1.00
❑ 602 Greg Maddux EP 4.00 1.50
❑ 603 Roger Clemens EP 5.00 2.00
❑ 604 Jaret Wright EP 2.00 .75
❑ 605 Mike Piazza EP 4.00 1.50
❑ 606 Tino Martinez EP 2.00 .75
❑ 607 Frank Thomas EP 2.50 1.00
❑ 608 Mo Vaughn EP 2.00 .75
❑ 609 Todd Helton EP 2.00 .75
❑ 610 Mark McGwire EP 6.00 3.00
❑ 611 Jeff Bagwell EP 2.00 .75
❑ 612 Travis Lee EP 2.00 .75
❑ 613 Scott Rolen EP 2.00 .75
❑ 614 Cal Ripken EP 8.00 3.00
❑ 615 Chipper Jones EP 2.50 1.00
❑ 616 Nomar Garciaparra EP 4.00 1.50
❑ 617 Alex Rodriguez EP 4.00 1.50
❑ 618 Derek Jeter EP 6.00 2.50
❑ 619 Tony Gwynn EP 3.00 1.25
❑ 620 Ken Griffey Jr. EP 4.00 1.50
❑ 621 Kenny Lofton EP 2.00 .75
❑ 622 Juan Gonzalez EP 2.00 .75
❑ 623 Jose Cruz Jr. EP 2.00 .75
❑ 624 Larry Walker EP 2.00 .75
❑ 625 Barry Bonds EP 6.00 2.50
❑ 626 Ben Grieve EP 2.00 .75
❑ 627 Andruw Jones EP 2.00 .75
❑ 628 Vladimir Guerrero EP 2.50 1.00
❑ 629 Paul Konerko EP 2.00 .75
❑ 630 Paul Molitor EP 2.00 .75
❑ 631 Cecil Fielder .30 .10
❑ 632 Jack McDowell .30 .10
❑ 633 Mike James .30 .10
❑ 634 Brian Anderson .30 .10
❑ 635 Jay Bell .30 .10
❑ 636 Devon White .30 .10
❑ 637 Andy Stankiewicz .30 .10
❑ 638 Tony Batista .30 .10
❑ 639 Omar Daal .30 .10
❑ 640 Matt Williams .30 .10
❑ 641 Brent Brede .30 .10
❑ 642 Jorge Fabregas .30 .10
❑ 643 Karim Garcia .30 .10
❑ 644 Felix Rodriguez .30 .10
❑ 645 Andy Benes .30 .10
❑ 646 Willie Blair .30 .10
❑ 647 Jeff Suppan .30 .10
❑ 648 Yamil Benitez .30 .10
❑ 649 Walt Weiss .30 .10
❑ 650 Andres Galarraga .30 .10
❑ 651 Doug Drabek .30 .10
❑ 652 Ozzie Guillen .30 .10
❑ 653 Joe Carter .30 .10
❑ 654 Dennis Eckersley .30 .10
❑ 655 Pedro Martinez .50 .20
❑ 656 Jim Leyritz .30 .10
❑ 657 Henry Rodriguez .30 .10
❑ 658 Rod Beck .30 .10
❑ 659 Mickey Morandini .30 .10
❑ 660 Jeff Blauser .30 .10
❑ 661 Ruben Sierra .30 .10
❑ 662 Mike Sirotka .30 .10
❑ 663 Pete Harnisch .30 .10
❑ 664 Damian Jackson .30 .10
❑ 665 Dmitri Young .30 .10
❑ 666 Steve Cooke .30 .10
❑ 667 Geronimo Berroa .30 .10
❑ 668 Shawon Dunston .30 .10
❑ 669 Mike Jackson .30 .10
❑ 670 Travis Fryman .30 .10
❑ 671 Dwight Gooden .30 .10
❑ 672 Paul Assenmacher .30 .10
❑ 673 Eric Plunk .30 .10
❑ 674 Mike Lansing .30 .10
❑ 675 Darryl Kile .30 .10
❑ 676 Luis Gonzalez .30 .10
❑ 677 Frank Castillo .30 .10
❑ 678 Joe Randa .30 .10
❑ 679 Bip Roberts .30 .10
❑ 680 Derrek Lee .50 .20
❑ 681 M.Piazza Mets SP 3.00 1.25
❑ 681A M.Piazza Marlins SP 3.00 1.25
❑ 682 Sean Berry .30 .10
❑ 683 Ramon Garcia .30 .10
❑ 684 Carl Everett .30 .10
❑ 685 Moises Alou .30 .10
❑ 686 Hal Morris .30 .10
❑ 687 Jeff Conine .30 .10
❑ 688 Gary Sheffield .30 .10
❑ 689 Jose Vizcaino .30 .10
❑ 690 Charles Johnson .30 .10
❑ 691 Bobby Bonilla .30 .10
❑ 692 Marquis Grissom .30 .10
❑ 693 Alex Ochoa .30 .10
❑ 694 Mike Morgan .30 .10
❑ 695 Orlando Merced .30 .10
❑ 696 David Ortiz 1.00 .40
❑ 697 Brent Gates .30 .10
❑ 698 Otis Nixon .30 .10
❑ 699 Trey Moore .30 .10
❑ 700 Derrick May .30 .10
❑ 701 Rich Becker .30 .10
❑ 702 Al Leiter .30 .10
❑ 703 Chili Davis .30 .10
❑ 704 Scott Brosius .30 .10
❑ 705 Chuck Knoblauch .30 .10
❑ 706 Kenny Rogers .30 .10
❑ 707 Mike Blowers .30 .10
❑ 708 Mike Fetters .30 .10
❑ 709 Tom Candiotti .30 .10
❑ 710 Rickey Henderson .75 .30
❑ 711 Bob Abreu .30 .10
❑ 712 Mark Lewis .30 .10
❑ 713 Doug Glanville .30 .10
❑ 714 Desi Relaford .30 .10
❑ 715 Kent Mercker .30 .10
❑ 716 Kevin Brown .50 .20
❑ 717 James Mouton .30 .10
❑ 718 Mark Langston .30 .10
❑ 719 Greg Myers .30 .10
❑ 720 Orel Hershiser .30 .10
❑ 721 Charlie Hayes .30 .10
❑ 722 Robb Nen .30 .10
❑ 723 Glenallen Hill .30 .10
❑ 724 Tony Saunders .30 .10
❑ 725 Wade Boggs .50 .20
❑ 726 Kevin Stocker .30 .10
❑ 727 Wilson Alvarez .30 .10
❑ 728 Albie Lopez .30 .10
❑ 729 Dave Martinez .30 .10
❑ 730 Fred McGriff .50 .20
❑ 731 Quinton McCracken .30 .10
❑ 732 Bryan Rekar .30 .10
❑ 733 Paul Sorrento .30 .10
❑ 734 Roberto Hernandez .30 .10
❑ 735 Bubba Trammell .30 .10
❑ 736 Miguel Cairo .30 .10
❑ 737 John Flaherty .30 .10
❑ 738 Terrell Wade .30 .10
❑ 739 Roberto Kelly .30 .10
❑ 740 Mark McLemore .30 .10
❑ 741 Danny Patterson .30 .10
❑ 742 Aaron Sele .30 .10
❑ 743 Tony Fernandez .30 .10
❑ 744 Randy Myers .30 .10
❑ 745 Jose Canseco .50 .20
❑ 746 Darrin Fletcher .30 .10
❑ 747 Mike Stanley .30 .10
❑ 748 Marquis Grissom SH CL .30 .10
❑ 749 Fred McGriff SH CL .30 .10
❑ 750 Travis Lee SH CL .30 .10

1999 Upper Deck

❑ COMPLETE SET (525) 100.00 50.00
❑ COMPLETE SERIES 1 (255) 60.00 30.00
❑ COMPLETE SERIES 2 (270) 40.00 20.00
❑ COMMON (19-255/293-535) .30 .10
❑ COMMON SER.1 SR (1-18) .50 .20
❑ COMMON SER.2 SR (266-292) .50 .20
❑ 1 Troy Glaus SR 1.00 .40
❑ 2 Adrian Beltre SR .60 .25
❑ 3 Matt Anderson SR .50 .20
❑ 4 Eric Chavez SR .60 .25
❑ 5 Jin Ho Cho SR .50 .20
❑ 6 Robert Smith SR .50 .20
❑ 7 George Lombard SR .50 .20
❑ 8 Mike Kinkade SR .50 .20
❑ 9 Seth Greisinger SR .50 .20
❑ 10 J.D. Drew SR .60 .25
❑ 11 Aramis Ramirez SR .60 .25
❑ 12 Carlos Guillen SR .60 .25
❑ 13 Justin Baughman SR .50 .20
❑ 14 Jim Parque SR .50 .20
❑ 15 Ryan Jackson SR .50 .20
❑ 16 Ramon E.Martinez SR RC .50 .20
❑ 17 Orlando Hernandez SR .60 .25
❑ 18 Jeremy Giambi SR .50 .20
❑ 19 Gary DiSarcina .30 .10
❑ 20 Darin Erstad .30 .10
❑ 21 Troy Glaus .50 .20
❑ 22 Chuck Finley .30 .10
❑ 23 Dave Hollins .30 .10
❑ 24 Troy Percival .30 .10
❑ 25 Tim Salmon .50 .20
❑ 26 Brian Anderson .30 .10
❑ 27 Jay Bell .30 .10
❑ 28 Andy Benes .30 .10
❑ 29 Brent Brede .30 .10
❑ 30 David Dellucci .30 .10
❑ 31 Karim Garcia .30 .10
❑ 32 Travis Lee .30 .10
❑ 33 Andres Galarraga .30 .10
❑ 34 Ryan Klesko .30 .10
❑ 35 Keith Lockhart .30 .10

❑ 36 Kevin Millwood .30 .10
❑ 37 Denny Neagle .30 .10
❑ 38 John Smoltz .50 .20
❑ 39 Michael Tucker .30 .10
❑ 40 Walt Weiss .30 .10
❑ 41 Dennis Martinez .30 .10
❑ 42 Javy Lopez .30 .10
❑ 43 Brady Anderson .30 .10
❑ 44 Harold Baines .30 .10
❑ 45 Mike Bordick .30 .10
❑ 46 Roberto Alomar .50 .20
❑ 47 Scott Erickson .30 .10
❑ 48 Mike Mussina .50 .20
❑ 49 Cal Ripken 2.50 1.00
❑ 50 Darren Bragg .30 .10
❑ 51 Dennis Eckersley .30 .10
❑ 52 Nomar Garciaparra 1.25 .50
❑ 53 Scott Hatteberg .30 .10
❑ 54 Troy O'Leary .30 .10
❑ 55 Bret Saberhagen .30 .10
❑ 56 John Valentin .30 .10
❑ 57 Rod Beck .30 .10
❑ 58 Jeff Blauser .30 .10
❑ 59 Brant Brown .30 .10
❑ 60 Mark Clark .30 .10
❑ 61 Mark Grace .50 .20
❑ 62 Kevin Tapani .30 .10
❑ 63 Henry Rodriguez .30 .10
❑ 64 Mike Cameron .30 .10
❑ 65 Mike Caruso .30 .10
❑ 66 Ray Durham .30 .10
❑ 67 Jaime Navarro .30 .10
❑ 68 Magglio Ordonez .30 .10
❑ 69 Mike Sirotka .30 .10
❑ 70 Sean Casey .30 .10
❑ 71 Barry Larkin .50 .20
❑ 72 Jon Nunnally .30 .10
❑ 73 Paul Konerko .30 .10
❑ 74 Chris Stynes .30 .10
❑ 75 Brett Tomko .30 .10
❑ 76 Dmitri Young .30 .10
❑ 77 Sandy Alomar Jr. .30 .10
❑ 78 Bartolo Colon .30 .10
❑ 79 Travis Fryman .30 .10
❑ 80 Brian Giles .30 .10
❑ 81 David Justice .30 .10
❑ 82 Omar Vizquel .50 .20
❑ 83 Jaret Wright .30 .10
❑ 84 Jim Thome .50 .20
❑ 85 Charles Nagy .30 .10
❑ 86 Pedro Astacio .30 .10
❑ 87 Todd Helton .50 .20
❑ 88 Darryl Kile .30 .10
❑ 89 Mike Lansing .30 .10
❑ 90 Neifi Perez .30 .10
❑ 91 John Thomson .30 .10
❑ 92 Larry Walker .30 .10
❑ 93 Tony Clark .30 .10
❑ 94 Deivi Cruz .30 .10
❑ 95 Damion Easley .30 .10
❑ 96 Brian L.Hunter .30 .10
❑ 97 Todd Jones .30 .10
❑ 98 Brian Moehler .30 .10
❑ 99 Gabe Alvarez .30 .10
❑ 100 Craig Counsell .30 .10
❑ 101 Cliff Floyd .30 .10
❑ 102 Livan Hernandez .30 .10
❑ 103 Andy Larkin .30 .10
❑ 104 Derrek Lee .50 .20
❑ 105 Brian Meadows .30 .10
❑ 106 Moises Alou .30 .10
❑ 107 Sean Berry .30 .10
❑ 108 Craig Biggio .50 .20
❑ 109 Ricky Gutierrez .30 .10
❑ 110 Mike Hampton .30 .10
❑ 111 Jose Lima .30 .10
❑ 112 Billy Wagner .30 .10
❑ 113 Hal Morris .30 .10
❑ 114 Johnny Damon .50 .20
❑ 115 Jeff King .30 .10
❑ 116 Jeff Montgomery .30 .10
❑ 117 Glendon Rusch .30 .10
❑ 118 Larry Sutton .30 .10
❑ 119 Bobby Bonilla .30 .10
❑ 120 Jim Eisenreich .30 .10
❑ 121 Eric Karros .30 .10
❑ 122 Matt Luke .30 .10
❑ 123 Ramon Martinez .30 .10
❑ 124 Gary Sheffield .30 .10
❑ 125 Eric Young .30 .10
❑ 126 Charles Johnson .30 .10
❑ 127 Jeff Cirillo .30 .10
❑ 128 Marquis Grissom .30 .10
❑ 129 Jeromy Burnitz .30 .10
❑ 130 Bob Wickman .30 .10
❑ 131 Scott Karl .30 .10
❑ 132 Mark Loretta .30 .10
❑ 133 Fernando Vina .30 .10
❑ 134 Matt Lawton .30 .10
❑ 135 Pat Meares .30 .10
❑ 136 Eric Milton .30 .10
❑ 137 Paul Molitor .30 .10
❑ 138 David Ortiz .75 .30
❑ 139 Todd Walker .30 .10
❑ 140 Shane Andrews .30 .10
❑ 141 Brad Fullmer .30 .10
❑ 142 Vladimir Guerrero .75 .30
❑ 143 Dustin Hermanson .30 .10
❑ 144 Ryan McGuire .30 .10
❑ 145 Ugueth Urbina .30 .10
❑ 146 John Franco .30 .10
❑ 147 Butch Huskey .30 .10
❑ 148 Bobby Jones .30 .10
❑ 149 John Olerud .30 .10
❑ 150 Rey Ordonez .30 .10
❑ 151 Mike Piazza 1.25 .50
❑ 152 Hideo Nomo .75 .30
❑ 153 Masato Yoshii .30 .10
❑ 154 Derek Jeter 2.00 .75
❑ 155 Chuck Knoblauch .30 .10
❑ 156 Paul O'Neill .50 .20
❑ 157 Andy Pettitte .50 .20
❑ 158 Mariano Rivera .75 .30
❑ 159 Darryl Strawberry .30 .10
❑ 160 David Wells .30 .10
❑ 161 Jorge Posada .50 .20
❑ 162 Ramiro Mendoza .30 .10
❑ 163 Miguel Tejada .30 .10
❑ 164 Ryan Christenson .30 .10
❑ 165 Rickey Henderson .75 .30
❑ 166 A.J. Hinch .30 .10
❑ 167 Ben Grieve .30 .10
❑ 168 Kenny Rogers .30 .10
❑ 169 Matt Stairs .30 .10
❑ 170 Bob Abreu .30 .10
❑ 171 Rico Brogna .30 .10
❑ 172 Doug Glanville .30 .10
❑ 173 Mike Grace .30 .10
❑ 174 Desi Relaford .30 .10
❑ 175 Scott Rolen .50 .20
❑ 176 Jose Guillen .30 .10
❑ 177 Francisco Cordova .30 .10
❑ 178 Al Martin .30 .10
❑ 179 Jason Schmidt .30 .10
❑ 180 Turner Ward .30 .10
❑ 181 Kevin Young .30 .10
❑ 182 Mark McGwire 2.00 .75
❑ 183 Delino DeShields .30 .10
❑ 184 Eli Marrero .30 .10
❑ 185 Tom Lampkin .30 .10
❑ 186 Ray Lankford .30 .10
❑ 187 Willie McGee .30 .10
❑ 188 Matt Morris .30 .10
❑ 189 Andy Ashby .30 .10
❑ 190 Kevin Brown .50 .20
❑ 191 Ken Caminiti .30 .10
❑ 192 Trevor Hoffman .30 .10
❑ 193 Wally Joyner .30 .10
❑ 194 Greg Vaughn .30 .10
❑ 195 Danny Darwin .30 .10
❑ 196 Shawn Estes .30 .10
❑ 197 Orel Hershiser .30 .10
❑ 198 Jeff Kent .30 .10
❑ 199 Bill Mueller .30 .10
❑ 200 Robb Nen .30 .10
❑ 201 J.T. Snow .30 .10
❑ 202 Ken Cloude .30 .10
❑ 203 Russ Davis .30 .10
❑ 204 Jeff Fassero .30 .10
❑ 205 Ken Griffey Jr. 1.25 .50
❑ 206 Shane Monahan .30 .10
❑ 207 David Segui .30 .10
❑ 208 Dan Wilson .30 .10
❑ 209 Wilson Alvarez .30 .10
❑ 210 Wade Boggs .50 .20
❑ 211 Miguel Cairo .30 .10
❑ 212 Bubba Trammell .30 .10
❑ 213 Quinton McCracken .30 .10
❑ 214 Paul Sorrento .30 .10
❑ 215 Kevin Stocker .30 .10
❑ 216 Will Clark .50 .20
❑ 217 Rusty Greer .30 .10
❑ 218 Rick Helling .30 .10
❑ 219 Mark McLemore .30 .10
❑ 220 Ivan Rodriguez .50 .20
❑ 221 John Wetteland .30 .10
❑ 222 Jose Canseco .50 .20
❑ 223 Roger Clemens 1.50 .60
❑ 224 Carlos Delgado .30 .10
❑ 225 Darrin Fletcher .30 .10
❑ 226 Alex Gonzalez .30 .10
❑ 227 Jose Cruz Jr. .30 .10
❑ 228 Shannon Stewart .30 .10
❑ 229 Rolando Arrojo FF .30 .10
❑ 230 Livan Hernandez FF .30 .10
❑ 231 Orlando Hernandez FF .30 .10
❑ 232 Raul Mondesi FF .30 .10
❑ 233 Moises Alou FF .30 .10
❑ 234 Pedro Martinez FF .50 .20
❑ 235 Sammy Sosa FF .50 .20
❑ 236 Vladimir Guerrero FF .75 .30
❑ 237 Bartolo Colon FF .30 .10
❑ 238 Miguel Tejada FF .30 .10
❑ 239 Ismael Valdes FF .30 .10
❑ 240 Mariano Rivera FF .50 .20
❑ 241 Jose Cruz Jr. FF .30 .10
❑ 242 Juan Gonzalez FF .30 .10
❑ 243 Ivan Rodriguez FF .50 .20
❑ 244 Sandy Alomar Jr. FF .30 .10
❑ 245 Roberto Alomar FF .50 .20
❑ 246 Magglio Ordonez FF .30 .10
❑ 247 Kerry Wood SH CL .30 .10
❑ 248 Mark McGwire SH CL 2.00 .75
❑ 249 David Wells SH CL .30 .10
❑ 250 Rolando Arrojo SH CL .30 .10
❑ 251 Ken Griffey Jr. SH CL 1.25 .50
❑ 252 Trevor Hoffman SH CL .30 .10
❑ 253 Travis Lee SH CL .30 .10
❑ 254 Roberto Alomar SH CL .30 .10
❑ 255 Sammy Sosa SH CL .50 .20
❑ 266 Pat Burrell SR RC 3.00 1.25
❑ 267 Shea Hillenbrand SR RC 1.50 .60
❑ 268 Robert Fick SR .50 .20
❑ 269 Roy Halladay SR .60 .25
❑ 270 Ruben Mateo SR .50 .20
❑ 271 Bruce Chen SR .50 .20
❑ 272 Angel Pena SR .50 .20
❑ 273 Michael Barrett SR .50 .20
❑ 274 Kevin Witt SR .50 .20
❑ 275 Damon Minor SR .50 .20
❑ 276 Ryan Minor SR .50 .20
❑ 277 A.J. Pierzynski SR .60 .25
❑ 278 A.J. Burnett SR RC 1.50 .60
❑ 279 Dermal Brown SR .50 .20
❑ 280 Joe Lawrence SR .50 .20
❑ 281 Derrick Gibson SR .50 .20
❑ 282 Carlos Febles SR .50 .20
❑ 283 Chris Haas SR .50 .20
❑ 284 Cesar King SR .50 .20
❑ 285 Calvin Pickering SR .50 .20
❑ 286 Mitch Meluskey SR .50 .20
❑ 287 Carlos Beltran SR 1.00 .40
❑ 288 Ron Belliard SR .50 .20
❑ 289 Jerry Hairston Jr. SR .50 .20
❑ 290 Fernando Seguignol SR .50 .20
❑ 291 Kris Benson SR .50 .20
❑ 292 Chad Hutchinson SR RC .60 .25
❑ 293 Jarrod Washburn .30 .10
❑ 294 Jason Dickson .30 .10
❑ 295 Mo Vaughn .30 .10
❑ 296 Garret Anderson .30 .10
❑ 297 Jim Edmonds .30 .10
❑ 298 Ken Hill .30 .10
❑ 299 Shigetoshi Hasegawa .30 .10
❑ 300 Todd Stottlemyre .30 .10
❑ 301 Randy Johnson .75 .30
❑ 302 Omar Daal .30 .10
❑ 303 Steve Finley .30 .10

❑ 304 Matt Williams .30 .10
❑ 305 Danny Klassen .30 .10
❑ 306 Tony Batista .30 .10
❑ 307 Brian Jordan .30 .10
❑ 308 Greg Maddux 1.25 .50
❑ 309 Chipper Jones .75 .30
❑ 310 Bret Boone .30 .10
❑ 311 Ozzie Guillen .30 .10
❑ 312 John Rocker .30 .10
❑ 313 Tom Glavine .50 .20
❑ 314 Andruw Jones .50 .20
❑ 315 Albert Belle .30 .10
❑ 316 Charles Johnson .30 .10
❑ 317 Will Clark .50 .20
❑ 318 B.J. Surhoff .30 .10
❑ 319 Delino DeShields .30 .10
❑ 320 Heathcliff Slocumb .30 .10
❑ 321 Sidney Ponson .30 .10
❑ 322 Juan Guzman .30 .10
❑ 323 Reggie Jefferson .30 .10
❑ 324 Mark Portugal .30 .10
❑ 325 Tim Wakefield .30 .10
❑ 326 Jason Varitek .75 .30
❑ 327 Jose Offerman .30 .10
❑ 328 Pedro Martinez .50 .20
❑ 329 Trot Nixon .30 .10
❑ 330 Kerry Wood .30 .10
❑ 331 Sammy Sosa .75 .30
❑ 332 Glenallen Hill .30 .10
❑ 333 Gary Gaetti .30 .10
❑ 334 Mickey Morandini .30 .10
❑ 335 Benito Santiago .30 .10
❑ 336 Jeff Blauser .30 .10
❑ 337 Frank Thomas .75 .30
❑ 338 Paul Konerko .30 .10
❑ 339 Jaime Navarro .30 .10
❑ 340 Carlos Lee .30 .10
❑ 341 Brian Simmons .30 .10
❑ 342 Mark Johnson .30 .10
❑ 343 Jeff Abbott .30 .10
❑ 344 Steve Avery .30 .10
❑ 345 Mike Cameron .30 .10
❑ 346 Michael Tucker .30 .10
❑ 347 Greg Vaughn .30 .10
❑ 348 Hal Morris .30 .10
❑ 349 Pete Harnisch .30 .10
❑ 350 Denny Neagle .30 .10
❑ 351 Manny Ramirez .50 .20
❑ 352 Roberto Alomar .50 .20
❑ 353 Dwight Gooden .30 .10
❑ 354 Kenny Lofton .30 .10
❑ 355 Mike Jackson .30 .10
❑ 356 Charles Nagy .30 .10
❑ 357 Enrique Wilson .30 .10
❑ 358 Russ Branyan .30 .10
❑ 359 Richie Sexson .30 .10
❑ 360 Vinny Castilla .30 .10
❑ 361 Dante Bichette .30 .10
❑ 362 Kirt Manwaring .30 .10
❑ 363 Darryl Hamilton .30 .10
❑ 364 Jamey Wright .30 .10
❑ 365 Curtis Leskanic .30 .10
❑ 366 Jeff Reed .30 .10
❑ 367 Bobby Higginson .30 .10
❑ 368 Justin Thompson .30 .10
❑ 369 Brad Ausmus .30 .10
❑ 370 Dean Palmer .30 .10
❑ 371 Gabe Kapler .30 .10
❑ 372 Juan Encarnacion .30 .10
❑ 373 Karim Garcia .30 .10
❑ 374 Alex Gonzalez .30 .10
❑ 375 Braden Looper .30 .10
❑ 376 Preston Wilson .30 .10
❑ 377 Todd Dunwoody .30 .10
❑ 378 Alex Fernandez .30 .10
❑ 379 Mark Kotsay .30 .10
❑ 380 Matt Mantei .30 .10
❑ 381 Ken Caminiti .30 .10
❑ 382 Scott Elarton .30 .10
❑ 383 Jeff Bagwell .50 .20
❑ 384 Derek Bell .30 .10
❑ 385 Ricky Gutierrez .30 .10
❑ 386 Richard Hidalgo .30 .10
❑ 387 Shane Reynolds .30 .10
❑ 388 Carl Everett .30 .10
❑ 389 Scott Service .30 .10
❑ 390 Jeff Suppan .30 .10
❑ 391 Joe Randa .30 .10
❑ 392 Kevin Appier .30 .10
❑ 393 Shane Halter .30 .10
❑ 394 Chad Kreuter .30 .10
❑ 395 Mike Sweeney .30 .10
❑ 396 Kevin Brown .50 .20
❑ 397 Devon White .30 .10
❑ 398 Todd Hollandsworth .30 .10
❑ 399 Todd Hundley .30 .10
❑ 400 Chan Ho Park .30 .10
❑ 401 Mark Grudzielanek .30 .10
❑ 402 Raul Mondesi .30 .10
❑ 403 Ismael Valdes .30 .10
❑ 404 Rafael Roque RC .30 .10
❑ 405 Sean Berry .30 .10
❑ 406 Kevin Barker .30 .10
❑ 407 Dave Nilsson .30 .10
❑ 408 Geoff Jenkins .30 .10
❑ 409 Jim Abbott .50 .20
❑ 410 Bobby Hughes .30 .10
❑ 411 Corey Koskie .30 .10
❑ 412 Rick Aguilera .30 .10
❑ 413 LaTroy Hawkins .30 .10
❑ 414 Ron Coomer .30 .10
❑ 415 Denny Hocking .30 .10
❑ 416 Marty Cordova .30 .10
❑ 417 Terry Steinbach .30 .10
❑ 418 Rondell White .30 .10
❑ 419 Wilton Guerrero .30 .10
❑ 420 Shane Andrews .30 .10
❑ 421 Orlando Cabrera .30 .10
❑ 422 Carl Pavano .30 .10
❑ 423 Javier Vazquez .30 .10
❑ 424 Chris Widger .30 .10
❑ 425 Robin Ventura .30 .10
❑ 426 Rickey Henderson .75 .30
❑ 427 Al Leiter .30 .10
❑ 428 Bobby Jones .30 .10
❑ 429 Brian McRae .30 .10
❑ 430 Roger Cedeno .30 .10
❑ 431 Bobby Bonilla .30 .10
❑ 432 Edgardo Alfonzo .30 .10
❑ 433 Bernie Williams .50 .20
❑ 434 Ricky Ledee .30 .10
❑ 435 Chili Davis .30 .10
❑ 436 Tino Martinez .50 .20
❑ 437 Scott Brosius .30 .10
❑ 438 David Cone .30 .10
❑ 439 Joe Girardi .30 .10
❑ 440 Roger Clemens 1.50 .60
❑ 441 Chad Curtis .30 .10
❑ 442 Hideki Irabu .30 .10
❑ 443 Jason Giambi .30 .10
❑ 444 Scott Spiezio .30 .10
❑ 445 Tony Phillips .30 .10
❑ 446 Ramon Hernandez .30 .10
❑ 447 Mike Macfarlane .30 .10
❑ 448 Tom Candiotti .30 .10
❑ 449 Billy Taylor .30 .10
❑ 450 Bobby Estalella .30 .10
❑ 451 Curt Schilling .30 .10
❑ 452 Carlton Loewer .30 .10
❑ 453 Marlon Anderson .30 .10
❑ 454 Kevin Jordan .30 .10
❑ 455 Ron Gant .30 .10
❑ 456 Chad Ogea .30 .10
❑ 457 Abraham Nunez .30 .10
❑ 458 Jason Kendall .30 .10
❑ 459 Pat Meares .30 .10
❑ 460 Brant Brown .30 .10
❑ 461 Brian Giles .30 .10
❑ 462 Chad Hermansen .30 .10
❑ 463 Freddy Adrian Garcia .30 .10
❑ 464 Edgar Renteria .30 .10
❑ 465 Fernando Tatis .30 .10
❑ 466 Eric Davis .30 .10
❑ 467 Darren Bragg .30 .10
❑ 468 Donovan Osborne .30 .10
❑ 469 Manny Aybar .30 .10
❑ 470 Jose Jimenez .30 .10
❑ 471 Kent Mercker .30 .10
❑ 472 Reggie Sanders .30 .10
❑ 473 Ruben Rivera .30 .10
❑ 474 Tony Gwynn 1.00 .40
❑ 475 Jim Leyritz .30 .10
❑ 476 Chris Gomez .30 .10
❑ 477 Matt Clement .30 .10
❑ 478 Carlos Hernandez .30 .10
❑ 479 Sterling Hitchcock .30 .10
❑ 480 Ellis Burks .30 .10
❑ 481 Barry Bonds 2.00 .75
❑ 482 Marvin Benard .30 .10
❑ 483 Kirk Rueter .30 .10
❑ 484 F.P. Santangelo .30 .10
❑ 485 Stan Javier .30 .10
❑ 486 Jeff Kent .30 .10
❑ 487 Alex Rodriguez 1.25 .50
❑ 488 Tom Lampkin .30 .10
❑ 489 Jose Mesa .30 .10
❑ 490 Jay Buhner .30 .10
❑ 491 Edgar Martinez .50 .20
❑ 492 Butch Huskey .30 .10
❑ 493 John Mabry .30 .10
❑ 494 Jamie Moyer .30 .10
❑ 495 Roberto Hernandez .30 .10
❑ 496 Tony Saunders .30 .10
❑ 497 Fred McGriff .50 .20
❑ 498 Dave Martinez .30 .10
❑ 499 Jose Canseco .50 .20
❑ 500 Rolando Arrojo .30 .10
❑ 501 Esteban Yan .30 .10
❑ 502 Juan Gonzalez .30 .10
❑ 503 Rafael Palmeiro .50 .20
❑ 504 Aaron Sele .30 .10
❑ 505 Royce Clayton .30 .10
❑ 506 Todd Zeile .30 .10
❑ 507 Tom Goodwin .30 .10
❑ 508 Lee Stevens .30 .10
❑ 509 Esteban Loaiza .30 .10
❑ 510 Joey Hamilton .30 .10
❑ 511 Homer Bush .30 .10
❑ 512 Willie Greene .30 .10
❑ 513 Shawn Green .30 .10
❑ 514 David Wells .30 .10
❑ 515 Kelvim Escobar .30 .10
❑ 516 Tony Fernandez .30 .10
❑ 517 Pat Hentgen .30 .10
❑ 518 Mark McGwire AR 1.00 .40
❑ 519 Ken Griffey Jr. AR .75 .30
❑ 520 Sammy Sosa AR .50 .20
❑ 521 Juan Gonzalez AR .30 .10
❑ 522 J.D. Drew AR .30 .10
❑ 523 Chipper Jones AR .50 .20
❑ 524 Alex Rodriguez AR .75 .30
❑ 525 Mike Piazza AR .75 .30
❑ 526 Nomar Garciaparra AR .75 .30
❑ 527 Mark McGwire SH CL 1.00 .40
❑ 528 Sammy Sosa SH CL .50 .20
❑ 529 Scott Brosius SH CL .30 .10
❑ 530 Cal Ripken SH CL 1.25 .50
❑ 531 Barry Bonds SH CL 1.00 .40
❑ 532 Roger Clemens SH CL .75 .30
❑ 533 Ken Griffey Jr. SH CL .75 .30
❑ 534 Alex Rodriguez SH CL .75 .30
❑ 535 Curt Schilling SH CL .30 .10
❑ NNO K.Griffey Jr. '89 AU/100 1250.00 1000.00

2000 Upper Deck

❑ COMPLETE SET (540) 100.00 40.00
❑ COMPLETE SERIES 1 (270) 50.00 20.00
❑ COMPLETE SERIES 2 (270) 50.00 20.00
❑ COMMON CARD (1-540) .30 .10

❑ COMMON SR (1-28/271-297) .50 .20
❑ 1 Rick Ankiel SR .50 .20
❑ 2 Vernon Wells SR .75 .30
❑ 3 Ryan Anderson SR .50 .20
❑ 4 Ed Yarnall SR .50 .20
❑ 5 Brian McNichol SR .50 .20
❑ 6 Ben Petrick SR .50 .20
❑ 7 Kip Wells SR .50 .20
❑ 8 Eric Munson SR .50 .20
❑ 9 Matt Riley SR .50 .20
❑ 10 Peter Bergeron SR .50 .20
❑ 11 Eric Gagne SR 2.00 .75
❑ 12 Ramon Ortiz SR .50 .20
❑ 13 Josh Beckett SR 2.00 .75
❑ 14 Alfonso Soriano SR 2.00 .75
❑ 15 Jorge Toca SR .50 .20
❑ 16 Buddy Carlyle SR .50 .20
❑ 17 Chad Hermansen SR .50 .20
❑ 18 Matt Perisho SR .50 .20
❑ 19 Tomokazu Ohka SR RC .75 .30
❑ 20 Jacque Jones SR .75 .30
❑ 21 Josh Paul SR .50 .20
❑ 22 Dermal Brown SR .50 .20
❑ 23 Adam Kennedy SR .50 .20
❑ 24 Chad Harville SR .50 .20
❑ 25 Calvin Murray SR .50 .20
❑ 26 Chad Meyers SR .50 .20
❑ 27 Brian Cooper SR .50 .20
❑ 28 Troy Glaus .30 .10
❑ 29 Ben Molina .30 .10
❑ 30 Troy Percival .30 .10
❑ 31 Ken Hill .30 .10
❑ 32 Chuck Finley .30 .10
❑ 33 Todd Greene .30 .10
❑ 34 Tim Salmon .50 .20
❑ 35 Gary DiSarcina .30 .10
❑ 36 Luis Gonzalez .30 .10
❑ 37 Tony Womack .30 .10
❑ 38 Omar Daal .30 .10
❑ 39 Randy Johnson .75 .30
❑ 40 Erubiel Durazo .30 .10
❑ 41 Jay Bell .30 .10
❑ 42 Steve Finley .30 .10
❑ 43 Travis Lee .30 .10
❑ 44 Greg Maddux 1.25 .50
❑ 45 Bret Boone .30 .10
❑ 46 Brian Jordan .30 .10
❑ 47 Kevin Millwood .30 .10
❑ 48 Odalis Perez .30 .10
❑ 49 Javy Lopez .30 .10
❑ 50 John Smoltz .50 .20
❑ 51 Bruce Chen .30 .10
❑ 52 Albert Belle .30 .10
❑ 53 Jerry Hairston Jr. .30 .10
❑ 54 Will Clark .50 .20
❑ 55 Sidney Ponson .30 .10
❑ 56 Charles Johnson .30 .10
❑ 57 Cal Ripken 2.50 1.00
❑ 58 Ryan Minor .30 .10
❑ 59 Mike Mussina .50 .20
❑ 60 Tom Gordon .30 .10
❑ 61 Jose Offerman .30 .10
❑ 62 Trot Nixon .30 .10
❑ 63 Pedro Martinez .50 .20
❑ 64 John Valentin .30 .10
❑ 65 Jason Varitek .75 .30
❑ 66 Juan Pena .30 .10
❑ 67 Troy O'Leary .30 .10
❑ 68 Sammy Sosa .75 .30
❑ 69 Henry Rodriguez .30 .10
❑ 70 Kyle Farnsworth .30 .10
❑ 71 Glenallen Hill .30 .10
❑ 72 Lance Johnson .30 .10
❑ 73 Mickey Morandini .30 .10
❑ 74 Jon Lieber .30 .10
❑ 75 Kevin Tapani .30 .10
❑ 76 Carlos Lee .30 .10
❑ 77 Ray Durham .30 .10
❑ 78 Jim Parque .30 .10
❑ 79 Bob Howry .30 .10
❑ 80 Maggio Ordonez .30 .10
❑ 81 Paul Konerko .30 .10
❑ 82 Mike Caruso .30 .10
❑ 83 Chris Singleton .30 .10
❑ 84 Sean Casey .30 .10
❑ 85 Barry Larkin .50 .20
❑ 86 Pokey Reese .30 .10
❑ 87 Eddie Taubensee .30 .10
❑ 88 Scott Williamson .30 .10
❑ 89 Jason LaRue .30 .10
❑ 90 Aaron Boone .30 .10
❑ 91 Jeffrey Hammonds .30 .10
❑ 92 Omar Vizquel .50 .20
❑ 93 Manny Ramirez .50 .20
❑ 94 Kenny Lofton .30 .10
❑ 95 Jaret Wright .30 .10
❑ 96 Einar Diaz .30 .10
❑ 97 Charles Nagy .30 .10
❑ 98 David Justice .30 .10
❑ 99 Richie Sexson .30 .10
❑ 100 Steve Karsay .30 .10
❑ 101 Todd Helton .50 .20
❑ 102 Dante Bichette .30 .10
❑ 103 Larry Walker .30 .10
❑ 104 Pedro Astacio .30 .10
❑ 105 Neifi Perez .30 .10
❑ 106 Brian Bohanon .30 .10
❑ 107 Edgard Clemente .30 .10
❑ 108 Dave Veres .30 .10
❑ 109 Gabe Kapler .30 .10
❑ 110 Juan Encarnacion .30 .10
❑ 111 Jeff Weaver .30 .10
❑ 112 Damion Easley .30 .10
❑ 113 Justin Thompson .30 .10
❑ 114 Brad Ausmus .30 .10
❑ 115 Frank Catalanotto .30 .10
❑ 116 Todd Jones .30 .10
❑ 117 Preston Wilson .30 .10
❑ 118 Cliff Floyd .30 .10
❑ 119 Mike Lowell .30 .10
❑ 120 Antonio Alfonseca .30 .10
❑ 121 Alex Gonzalez .30 .10
❑ 122 Braden Looper .30 .10
❑ 123 Bruce Aven .30 .10
❑ 124 Richard Hidalgo .30 .10
❑ 125 Mitch Meluskey .30 .10
❑ 126 Jeff Bagwell .50 .20
❑ 127 Jose Lima .30 .10
❑ 128 Derek Bell .30 .10
❑ 129 Billy Wagner .30 .10
❑ 130 Shane Reynolds .30 .10
❑ 131 Moises Alou .30 .10
❑ 132 Carlos Beltran .30 .10
❑ 133 Carlos Febles .30 .10
❑ 134 Jermaine Dye .30 .10
❑ 135 Jeremy Giambi .30 .10
❑ 136 Joe Randa .30 .10
❑ 137 Jose Rosado .30 .10
❑ 138 Chad Kreuter .30 .10
❑ 139 Jose Vizcaino .30 .10
❑ 140 Adrian Beltre .30 .10
❑ 141 Kevin Brown .50 .20
❑ 142 Ismael Valdes .30 .10
❑ 143 Angel Pena .30 .10
❑ 144 Chan Ho Park .30 .10
❑ 145 Mark Grudzielanek .30 .10
❑ 146 Jeff Shaw .30 .10
❑ 147 Geoff Jenkins .30 .10
❑ 148 Jeromy Burnitz .30 .10
❑ 149 Hideo Nomo .75 .30
❑ 150 Ron Belliard .30 .10
❑ 151 Sean Berry .30 .10
❑ 152 Mark Loretta .30 .10
❑ 153 Steve Woodard .30 .10
❑ 154 Joe Mays .30 .10
❑ 155 Eric Milton .30 .10
❑ 156 Corey Koskie .30 .10
❑ 157 Ron Coomer .30 .10
❑ 158 Brad Radke .30 .10
❑ 159 Terry Steinbach .30 .10
❑ 160 Cristian Guzman .30 .10
❑ 161 Vladimir Guerrero .75 .30
❑ 162 Wilton Guerrero .30 .10
❑ 163 Michael Barrett .30 .10
❑ 164 Chris Widger .30 .10
❑ 165 Fernando Seguignol .30 .10
❑ 166 Ugueth Urbina .30 .10
❑ 167 Dustin Hermanson .30 .10
❑ 168 Kenny Rogers .30 .10
❑ 169 Edgardo Alfonzo .30 .10
❑ 170 Orel Hershiser .30 .10
❑ 171 Robin Ventura .30 .10
❑ 172 Octavio Dotel .30 .10
❑ 173 Rickey Henderson .75 .30
❑ 174 Roger Cedeno .30 .10
❑ 175 John Olerud .30 .10
❑ 176 Derek Jeter 2.00 .75
❑ 177 Tino Martinez .50 .20
❑ 178 Orlando Hernandez .30 .10
❑ 179 Chuck Knoblauch .30 .10
❑ 180 Bernie Williams .50 .20
❑ 181 Chili Davis .30 .10
❑ 182 David Cone .30 .10
❑ 183 Ricky Ledee .30 .10
❑ 184 Paul O'Neill .50 .20
❑ 185 Jason Giambi .30 .10
❑ 186 Eric Chavez .30 .10
❑ 187 Matt Stairs .30 .10
❑ 188 Miguel Tejada .30 .10
❑ 189 Olmedo Saenz .30 .10
❑ 190 Tim Hudson .30 .10
❑ 191 John Jaha .30 .10
❑ 192 Randy Velarde .30 .10
❑ 193 Rico Brogna .30 .10
❑ 194 Mike Lieberthal .30 .10
❑ 195 Marlon Anderson .30 .10
❑ 196 Bob Abreu .30 .10
❑ 197 Ron Gant .30 .10
❑ 198 Randy Wolf .30 .10
❑ 199 Desi Relaford .30 .10
❑ 200 Doug Glanville .30 .10
❑ 201 Warren Morris .30 .10
❑ 202 Kris Benson .30 .10
❑ 203 Kevin Young .30 .10
❑ 204 Brian Giles .30 .10
❑ 205 Jason Schmidt .30 .10
❑ 206 Ed Sprague .30 .10
❑ 207 Francisco Cordova .30 .10
❑ 208 Mark McGwire 2.00 .75
❑ 209 Jose Jimenez .30 .10
❑ 210 Fernando Tatis .30 .10
❑ 211 Kent Bottenfield .30 .10
❑ 212 Eli Marrero .30 .10
❑ 213 Edgar Renteria .30 .10
❑ 214 Joe McEwing .30 .10
❑ 215 J.D. Drew .30 .10
❑ 216 Tony Gwynn 1.00 .40
❑ 217 Gary Matthews Jr. .30 .10
❑ 218 Eric Owens .30 .10
❑ 219 Damian Jackson .30 .10
❑ 220 Reggie Sanders .30 .10
❑ 221 Trevor Hoffman .30 .10
❑ 222 Ben Davis .30 .10
❑ 223 Shawn Estes .30 .10
❑ 224 F.P. Santangelo .30 .10
❑ 225 Livan Hernandez .30 .10
❑ 226 Ellis Burks .30 .10
❑ 227 J.T. Snow .30 .10
❑ 228 Jeff Kent .30 .10
❑ 229 Robb Nen .30 .10
❑ 230 Marvin Benard .30 .10
❑ 231 Ken Griffey Jr. 1.25 .50
❑ 232 John Halama .30 .10
❑ 233 Gil Meche .30 .10
❑ 234 David Bell .30 .10
❑ 235 Brian Hunter .30 .10
❑ 236 Jay Buhner .30 .10
❑ 237 Edgar Martinez .50 .20
❑ 238 Jose Mesa .30 .10
❑ 239 Wilson Alvarez .30 .10
❑ 240 Wade Boggs .50 .20
❑ 241 Fred McGriff .50 .20
❑ 242 Jose Canseco .50 .20
❑ 243 Kevin Stocker .30 .10
❑ 244 Roberto Hernandez .30 .10
❑ 245 Bubba Trammell .30 .10
❑ 246 John Flaherty .30 .10
❑ 247 Ivan Rodriguez .50 .20
❑ 248 Rusty Greer .30 .10
❑ 249 Rafael Palmeiro .50 .20
❑ 250 Jeff Zimmerman .30 .10
❑ 251 Royce Clayton .30 .10
❑ 252 Todd Zeile .30 .10
❑ 253 John Wetteland .30 .10
❑ 254 Ruben Mateo .30 .10
❑ 255 Kelvim Escobar .30 .10
❑ 256 David Wells .30 .10
❑ 257 Shawn Green .30 .10

❑	258	Homer Bush	.30	.10
❑	259	Shannon Stewart	.30	.10
❑	260	Carlos Delgado	.30	.10
❑	261	Roy Halladay	.30	.10
❑	262	Fernando Tatis SH CL	.30	.10
❑	263	Jose Jimenez SH CL	.30	.10
❑	264	Tony Gwynn SH CL	.50	.20
❑	265	Wade Boggs SH CL	.30	.10
❑	266	Cal Ripken SH CL	1.25	.50
❑	267	David Cone SH CL	.30	.10
❑	268	Mark McGwire SH CL	1.25	.50
❑	269	Pedro Martinez SH CL	.50	.20
❑	270	Nomar Garciaparra SH CL	.75	.30
❑	271	Nick Johnson SR	.75	.30
❑	272	Mark Quinn SR	.50	.20
❑	273	Roosevelt Brown SR	.50	.20
❑	274	Terrence Long SR	.50	.20
❑	275	Jason Marquis SR	.50	.20
❑	276	Kazuhiro Sasaki SR RC	1.25	.50
❑	277	Aaron Myette SR	.50	.20
❑	278	Danys Baez SR RC	.75	.30
❑	279	Travis Dawkins SR	.50	.20
❑	280	Mark Mulder SR	.75	.30
❑	281	Chris Haas SR	.50	.20
❑	282	Milton Bradley SR	.75	.30
❑	283	Brad Penny SR	.50	.20
❑	284	Rafael Furcal SR	.75	.30
❑	285	Luis Matos SR RC	.75	.30
❑	286	Victor Santos SR RC	.75	.30
❑	287	Rico Washington SR RC	.50	.20
❑	288	Rob Bell SR	.50	.20
❑	289	Joe Crede SR	2.50	1.00
❑	290	Pablo Ozuna SR	.50	.20
❑	291	Wascar Serrano SR RC	.50	.20
❑	292	Sang-Hoon Lee SR RC	.50	.20
❑	293	Chris Wakeland SR RC	.50	.20
❑	294	Luis Rivera SR RC	.50	.20
❑	295	Mike Lamb SR RC	1.25	.50
❑	296	Wily Mo Pena SR	.75	.30
❑	297	Mike Meyers SR RC	.75	.30
❑	298	Mo Vaughn	.30	.10
❑	299	Darin Erstad	.30	.10
❑	300	Garret Anderson	.30	.10
❑	301	Tim Belcher	.30	.10
❑	302	Scott Spiezio	.30	.10
❑	303	Kent Bottenfield	.30	.10
❑	304	Orlando Palmeiro	.30	.10
❑	305	Jason Dickson	.30	.10
❑	306	Matt Williams	.30	.10
❑	307	Brian Anderson	.30	.10
❑	308	Hanley Frias	.30	.10
❑	309	Todd Stottlemyre	.30	.10
❑	310	Matt Mantei	.30	.10
❑	311	David Dellucci	.30	.10
❑	312	Armando Reynoso	.30	.10
❑	313	Bernard Gilkey	.30	.10
❑	314	Chipper Jones	.75	.30
❑	315	Tom Glavine	.50	.20
❑	316	Quilvio Veras	.30	.10
❑	317	Andruw Jones	.50	.20
❑	318	Bobby Bonilla	.30	.10
❑	319	Reggie Sanders	.30	.10
❑	320	Andres Galarraga	.30	.10
❑	321	George Lombard	.30	.10
❑	322	John Rocker	.30	.10
❑	323	Wally Joyner	.30	.10
❑	324	B.J. Surhoff	.30	.10
❑	325	Scott Erickson	.30	.10
❑	326	Delino DeShields	.30	.10
❑	327	Jeff Conine	.30	.10
❑	328	Mike Timlin	.30	.10
❑	329	Brady Anderson	.30	.10
❑	330	Mike Bordick	.30	.10
❑	331	Harold Baines	.30	.10
❑	332	Nomar Garciaparra	1.25	.50
❑	333	Bret Saberhagen	.30	.10
❑	334	Ramon Martinez	.30	.10
❑	335	Donnie Sadler	.30	.10
❑	336	Wilton Veras	.30	.10
❑	337	Mike Stanley	.30	.10
❑	338	Brian Rose	.30	.10
❑	339	Carl Everett	.30	.10
❑	340	Tim Wakefield	.30	.10
❑	341	Mark Grace	.50	.20
❑	342	Kerry Wood	.30	.10
❑	343	Eric Young	.30	.10
❑	344	Jose Nieves	.30	.10
❑	345	Ismael Valdes	.30	.10
❑	346	Joe Girardi	.30	.10
❑	347	Damon Buford	.30	.10
❑	348	Ricky Gutierrez	.30	.10
❑	349	Frank Thomas	.75	.30
❑	350	Brian Simmons	.30	.10
❑	351	James Baldwin	.30	.10
❑	352	Brook Fordyce	.30	.10
❑	353	Jose Valentin	.30	.10
❑	354	Mike Sirotka	.30	.10
❑	355	Greg Norton	.30	.10
❑	356	Dante Bichette	.30	.10
❑	357	Deion Sanders	.50	.20
❑	358	Ken Griffey Jr.	1.25	.50
❑	359	Denny Neagle	.30	.10
❑	360	Dmitri Young	.30	.10
❑	361	Pete Harnisch	.30	.10
❑	362	Michael Tucker	.30	.10
❑	363	Roberto Alomar	.50	.20
❑	364	Dave Roberts	.30	.10
❑	365	Jim Thome	.50	.20
❑	366	Bartolo Colon	.30	.10
❑	367	Travis Fryman	.30	.10
❑	368	Chuck Finley	.30	.10
❑	369	Russell Branyan	.30	.10
❑	370	Alex Ramirez	.30	.10
❑	371	Jeff Cirillo	.30	.10
❑	372	Jeffrey Hammonds	.30	.10
❑	373	Scott Karl	.30	.10
❑	374	Brent Mayne	.30	.10
❑	375	Tom Goodwin	.30	.10
❑	376	Jose Jimenez	.30	.10
❑	377	Rolando Arrojo	.30	.10
❑	378	Terry Shumpert	.30	.10
❑	379	Juan Gonzalez	.30	.10
❑	380	Bobby Higginson	.30	.10
❑	381	Tony Clark	.30	.10
❑	382	Dave Mlicki	.30	.10
❑	383	Deivi Cruz	.30	.10
❑	384	Brian Moehler	.30	.10
❑	385	Dean Palmer	.30	.10
❑	386	Luis Castillo	.30	.10
❑	387	Mike Redmond	.30	.10
❑	388	Alex Fernandez	.30	.10
❑	389	Brant Brown	.30	.10
❑	390	Dave Berg	.30	.10
❑	391	A.J. Burnett	.30	.10
❑	392	Mark Kotsay	.30	.10
❑	393	Craig Biggio	.50	.20
❑	394	Daryle Ward	.30	.10
❑	395	Lance Berkman	.30	.10
❑	396	Roger Cedeno	.30	.10
❑	397	Scott Elarton	.30	.10
❑	398	Octavio Dotel	.30	.10
❑	399	Ken Caminiti	.30	.10
❑	400	Johnny Damon	.50	.20
❑	401	Mike Sweeney	.30	.10
❑	402	Jeff Suppan	.30	.10
❑	403	Rey Sanchez	.30	.10
❑	404	Blake Stein	.30	.10
❑	405	Ricky Bottalico	.30	.10
❑	406	Jay Witasick	.30	.10
❑	407	Shawn Green	.30	.10
❑	408	Orel Hershiser	.30	.10
❑	409	Gary Sheffield	.30	.10
❑	410	Todd Hollandsworth	.30	.10
❑	411	Terry Adams	.30	.10
❑	412	Todd Hundley	.30	.10
❑	413	Eric Karros	.30	.10
❑	414	F.P. Santangelo	.30	.10
❑	415	Alex Cora	.30	.10
❑	416	Marquis Grissom	.30	.10
❑	417	Henry Blanco	.30	.10
❑	418	Jose Hernandez	.30	.10
❑	419	Kyle Peterson	.30	.10
❑	420	John Snyder RC	.30	.10
❑	421	Bob Wickman	.30	.10
❑	422	Jamey Wright	.30	.10
❑	423	Chad Allen	.30	.10
❑	424	Todd Walker	.30	.10
❑	425	J.C. Romero RC	.30	.10
❑	426	Butch Huskey	.30	.10
❑	427	Jacque Jones	.30	.10
❑	428	Matt Lawton	.30	.10
❑	429	Rondell White	.30	.10
❑	430	Jose Vidro	.30	.10
❑	431	Hideki Irabu	.30	.10
❑	432	Javier Vazquez	.30	.10
❑	433	Lee Stevens	.30	.10
❑	434	Mike Thurman	.30	.10
❑	435	Geoff Blum	.30	.10
❑	436	Mike Hampton	.30	.10
❑	437	Mike Piazza	1.25	.50
❑	438	Al Leiter	.30	.10
❑	439	Derek Bell	.30	.10
❑	440	Armando Benitez	.30	.10
❑	441	Rey Ordonez	.30	.10
❑	442	Todd Zeile	.30	.10
❑	443	Roger Clemens	1.50	.60
❑	444	Ramiro Mendoza	.30	.10
❑	445	Andy Pettitte	.50	.20
❑	446	Scott Brosius	.30	.10
❑	447	Mariano Rivera	.75	.30
❑	448	Jim Leyritz	.30	.10
❑	449	Jorge Posada	.50	.20
❑	450	Omar Olivares	.30	.10
❑	451	Ben Grieve	.30	.10
❑	452	A.J. Hinch	.30	.10
❑	453	Gil Heredia	.30	.10
❑	454	Kevin Appier	.30	.10
❑	455	Ryan Christenson	.30	.10
❑	456	Ramon Hernandez	.30	.10
❑	457	Scott Rolen	.50	.20
❑	458	Alex Arias	.30	.10
❑	459	Andy Ashby	.30	.10
❑	460	Kevin Jordan UER 474	.30	.10
❑	461	Robert Person	.30	.10
❑	462	Paul Byrd	.30	.10
❑	463	Curt Schilling	.30	.10
❑	464	Mike Jackson	.30	.10
❑	465	Jason Kendall	.30	.10
❑	466	Pat Meares	.30	.10
❑	467	Bruce Aven	.30	.10
❑	468	Todd Ritchie	.30	.10
❑	469	Wil Cordero	.30	.10
❑	470	Aramis Ramirez	.30	.10
❑	471	Andy Benes	.30	.10
❑	472	Ray Lankford	.30	.10
❑	473	Fernando Vina	.30	.10
❑	474	Jim Edmonds	.30	.10
❑	475	Craig Paquette	.30	.10
❑	476	Pat Hentgen	.30	.10
❑	477	Darryl Kile	.30	.10
❑	478	Sterling Hitchcock	.30	.10
❑	479	Ruben Rivera	.30	.10
❑	480	Ryan Klesko	.30	.10
❑	481	Phil Nevin	.30	.10
❑	482	Woody Williams	.30	.10
❑	483	Carlos Hernandez	.30	.10
❑	484	Brian Meadows	.30	.10
❑	485	Bret Boone	.30	.10
❑	486	Barry Bonds	2.00	.75
❑	487	Russ Ortiz	.30	.10
❑	488	Bobby Estalella	.30	.10
❑	489	Rich Aurilia	.30	.10
❑	490	Bill Mueller	.30	.10
❑	491	Joe Nathan	.30	.10
❑	492	Russ Davis	.30	.10
❑	493	John Olerud	.30	.10
❑	494	Alex Rodriguez	1.25	.50
❑	495	Freddy Garcia	.30	.10
❑	496	Carlos Guillen	.30	.10
❑	497	Aaron Sele	.30	.10
❑	498	Brett Tomko	.30	.10
❑	499	Jamie Moyer	.30	.10
❑	500	Mike Cameron	.30	.10
❑	501	Vinny Castilla	.30	.10
❑	502	Gerald Williams	.30	.10
❑	503	Mike DiFelice	.30	.10
❑	504	Ryan Rupe	.30	.10
❑	505	Greg Vaughn	.30	.10
❑	506	Miguel Cairo	.30	.10
❑	507	Juan Guzman	.30	.10
❑	508	Jose Guillen	.30	.10
❑	509	Gabe Kapler	.30	.10
❑	510	Rick Helling	.30	.10
❑	511	David Segui	.30	.10
❑	512	Doug Davis	.30	.10
❑	513	Justin Thompson	.30	.10
❑	514	Chad Curtis	.30	.10
❑	515	Tony Batista	.30	.10

Card		
❑ 516 Billy Koch	.30	.10
❑ 517 Raul Mondesi	.30	.10
❑ 518 Joey Hamilton	.30	.10
❑ 519 Darrin Fletcher	.30	.10
❑ 520 Brad Fullmer	.30	.10
❑ 521 Jose Cruz Jr.	.30	.10
❑ 522 Kevin Witt	.30	.10
❑ 523 Mark McGwire AUT	1.00	.40
❑ 524 Roberto Alomar AUT	.30	.10
❑ 525 Chipper Jones AUT	.50	.20
❑ 526 Derek Jeter AUT	1.00	.40
❑ 527 Ken Griffey Jr. AUT	.75	.30
❑ 528 Sammy Sosa AUT	.50	.20
❑ 529 Manny Ramirez AUT	.50	.20
❑ 530 Ivan Rodriguez AUT	.30	.10
❑ 531 Pedro Martinez AUT	.50	.20
❑ 532 Mariano Rivera CL	.50	.20
❑ 533 Sammy Sosa CL	.50	.20
❑ 534 Cal Ripken CL	1.25	.50
❑ 535 Vladimir Guerrero CL	.50	.20
❑ 536 Tony Gwynn CL	.50	.20
❑ 537 Mark McGwire CL	1.00	.40
❑ 538 Bernie Williams CL	.30	.10
❑ 539 Pedro Martinez CL	.50	.20
❑ 540 Ken Griffey Jr. CL	.75	.30

2001 Upper Deck

Card		
❑ COMPLETE SET (450)	150.00	90.00
❑ COMPLETE SERIES 1 (270)	40.00	20.00
❑ COMPLETE SERIES 2 (180)	100.00	60.00
❑ COMMON (46-270/300-450)	.30	.10
❑ COMMON SR (1-45/271-300)	.50	.20
❑ 1 Jeff DaVanon SR	.50	.20
❑ 2 Aubrey Huff SR	.50	.20
❑ 3 Pasqual Coco SR	.50	.20
❑ 4 Barry Zito SR	.60	.25
❑ 5 Augie Ojeda SR	.50	.20
❑ 6 Chris Richard SR	.50	.20
❑ 7 Josh Phelps SR	.50	.20
❑ 8 Kevin Nicholson SR	.50	.20
❑ 9 Juan Guzman SR	.50	.20
❑ 10 Brandon Kolb SR	.50	.20
❑ 11 Johan Santana SR	5.00	2.00
❑ 12 Josh Kalinowski SR	.50	.20
❑ 13 Tike Redman SR	.50	.20
❑ 14 Ivanon Coffie SR	.50	.20
❑ 15 Chad Durbin SR	.50	.20
❑ 16 Derrick Turnbow SR	.50	.20
❑ 17 Scott Downs SR	.50	.20
❑ 18 Jason Grilli SR	.50	.20
❑ 19 Mark Buehrle SR	.60	.25
❑ 20 Paxton Crawford SR	.50	.20
❑ 21 Bronson Arroyo SR	1.00	.40
❑ 22 Tomas De la Rosa SR	.50	.20
❑ 23 Paul Rigdon SR	.50	.20
❑ 24 Rob Ramsay SR	.50	.20
❑ 25 Damian Rolls SR	.50	.20
❑ 26 Jason Conti SR	.50	.20
❑ 27 John Parrish SR	.50	.20
❑ 28 Geraldo Guzman SR	.50	.20
❑ 29 Tony Mota SR	.50	.20
❑ 30 Luis Rivas SR	.50	.20
❑ 31 Brian Tollberg SR	.50	.20
❑ 32 Adam Bernero SR	.50	.20
❑ 33 Michael Cuddyer SR	.50	.20
❑ 34 Josue Espada SR	.50	.20
❑ 35 Joe Lawrence SR	.50	.20
❑ 36 Chad Moeller SR	.50	.20
❑ 37 Nick Bierbrodt SR	.50	.20
❑ 38 DeWayne Wise SR	.50	.20
❑ 39 Javier Cardona SR	.50	.20
❑ 40 Hiram Bocachica SR	.50	.20
❑ 41 Giuseppe Chiaramonte SR	.50	.20
❑ 42 Alex Cabrera SR	.50	.20
❑ 43 Jimmy Rollins SR	.50	.20
❑ 44 Pat Flury SR RC	.50	.20
❑ 45 Leo Estrella SR	.50	.20
❑ 46 Darin Erstad	.30	.10
❑ 47 Seth Etherton	.30	.10
❑ 48 Troy Glaus	.30	.10
❑ 49 Brian Cooper	.30	.10
❑ 50 Tim Salmon	.50	.20
❑ 51 Adam Kennedy	.30	.10
❑ 52 Bengie Molina	.30	.10
❑ 53 Jason Giambi	.30	.10
❑ 54 Miguel Tejada	.30	.10
❑ 55 Tim Hudson	.30	.10
❑ 56 Eric Chavez	.30	.10
❑ 57 Terrence Long	.30	.10
❑ 58 Jason Isringhausen	.30	.10
❑ 59 Ramon Hernandez	.30	.10
❑ 60 Raul Mondesi	.30	.10
❑ 61 David Wells	.30	.10
❑ 62 Shannon Stewart	.30	.10
❑ 63 Tony Batista	.30	.10
❑ 64 Brad Fullmer	.30	.10
❑ 65 Chris Carpenter	.30	.10
❑ 66 Homer Bush	.30	.10
❑ 67 Gerald Williams	.30	.10
❑ 68 Miguel Cairo	.30	.10
❑ 69 Ryan Rupe	.30	.10
❑ 70 Greg Vaughn	.30	.10
❑ 71 John Flaherty	.30	.10
❑ 72 Dan Wheeler	.30	.10
❑ 73 Fred McGriff	.50	.20
❑ 74 Roberto Alomar	.50	.20
❑ 75 Bartolo Colon	.30	.10
❑ 76 Kenny Lofton	.30	.10
❑ 77 David Segui	.30	.10
❑ 78 Omar Vizquel	.50	.20
❑ 79 Russ Branyan	.30	.10
❑ 80 Chuck Finley	.30	.10
❑ 81 Manny Ramirez UER	.50	.20
❑ 82 Alex Rodriguez	1.25	.50
❑ 83 John Halama	.30	.10
❑ 84 Mike Cameron	.30	.10
❑ 85 David Bell	.30	.10
❑ 86 Jay Buhner	.30	.10
❑ 87 Aaron Sele	.30	.10
❑ 88 Rickey Henderson	.75	.30
❑ 89 Brook Fordyce	.30	.10
❑ 90 Cal Ripken	2.50	1.00
❑ 91 Mike Mussina	.50	.20
❑ 92 Delino DeShields	.30	.10
❑ 93 Melvin Mora	.30	.10
❑ 94 Sidney Ponson	.30	.10
❑ 95 Brady Anderson	.30	.10
❑ 96 Ivan Rodriguez	.50	.20
❑ 97 Ricky Ledee	.30	.10
❑ 98 Rick Helling	.30	.10
❑ 99 Ruben Mateo	.30	.10
❑ 100 Luis Alicea	.30	.10
❑ 101 John Wetteland	.30	.10
❑ 102 Mike Lamb	.30	.10
❑ 103 Carl Everett	.30	.10
❑ 104 Troy O'Leary	.30	.10
❑ 105 Wilton Veras	.30	.10
❑ 106 Pedro Martinez	.50	.20
❑ 107 Rolando Arrojo	.30	.10
❑ 108 Scott Hatteberg	.30	.10
❑ 109 Jason Varitek	.75	.30
❑ 110 Jose Offerman	.30	.10
❑ 111 Carlos Beltran	.30	.10
❑ 112 Johnny Damon	.50	.20
❑ 113 Mark Quinn	.30	.10
❑ 114 Rey Sanchez	.30	.10
❑ 115 Mac Suzuki	.30	.10
❑ 116 Jermaine Dye	.30	.10
❑ 117 Chris Fussell	.30	.10
❑ 118 Jeff Weaver	.30	.10
❑ 119 Dean Palmer	.30	.10
❑ 120 Robert Fick	.30	.10
❑ 121 Brian Moehler	.30	.10
❑ 122 Damion Easley	.30	.10
❑ 123 Juan Encarnacion	.30	.10
❑ 124 Tony Clark	.30	.10
❑ 125 Cristian Guzman	.30	.10
❑ 126 Matt LeCroy	.30	.10
❑ 127 Eric Milton	.30	.10
❑ 128 Jay Canizaro	.30	.10
❑ 129 David Ortiz	.75	.30
❑ 130 Brad Radke	.30	.10
❑ 131 Jacque Jones	.30	.10
❑ 132 Magglio Ordonez	.30	.10
❑ 133 Carlos Lee	.30	.10
❑ 134 Mike Sirotka	.30	.10
❑ 135 Ray Durham	.30	.10
❑ 136 Paul Konerko	.30	.10
❑ 137 Charles Johnson	.30	.10
❑ 138 James Baldwin	.30	.10
❑ 139 Jeff Abbott	.30	.10
❑ 140 Roger Clemens	1.50	.60
❑ 141 Derek Jeter	2.00	.75
❑ 142 David Justice	.30	.10
❑ 143 Ramiro Mendoza	.30	.10
❑ 144 Chuck Knoblauch	.30	.10
❑ 145 Orlando Hernandez	.30	.10
❑ 146 Alfonso Soriano	.50	.20
❑ 147 Jeff Bagwell	.50	.20
❑ 148 Julio Lugo	.30	.10
❑ 149 Mitch Meluskey	.30	.10
❑ 150 Jose Lima	.30	.10
❑ 151 Richard Hidalgo	.30	.10
❑ 152 Moises Alou	.30	.10
❑ 153 Scott Elarton	.30	.10
❑ 154 Andruw Jones	.50	.20
❑ 155 Quilvio Veras	.30	.10
❑ 156 Greg Maddux	1.25	.50
❑ 157 Brian Jordan	.30	.10
❑ 158 Andres Galarraga	.30	.10
❑ 159 Kevin Millwood	.30	.10
❑ 160 Rafael Furcal	.30	.10
❑ 161 Jeromy Burnitz	.30	.10
❑ 162 Jimmy Haynes	.30	.10
❑ 163 Mark Loretta	.30	.10
❑ 164 Ron Belliard	.30	.10
❑ 165 Richie Sexson	.30	.10
❑ 166 Kevin Barker	.30	.10
❑ 167 Jeff D'Amico	.30	.10
❑ 168 Rick Ankiel	.30	.10
❑ 169 Mark McGwire	2.00	.75
❑ 170 J.D. Drew	.30	.10
❑ 171 Eli Marrero	.30	.10
❑ 172 Darryl Kile	.30	.10
❑ 173 Edgar Renteria	.30	.10
❑ 174 Will Clark	.50	.20
❑ 175 Eric Young	.30	.10
❑ 176 Mark Grace	.50	.20
❑ 177 Jon Lieber	.30	.10
❑ 178 Damon Buford	.30	.10
❑ 179 Kerry Wood	.30	.10
❑ 180 Rondell White	.30	.10
❑ 181 Joe Girardi	.30	.10
❑ 182 Curt Schilling	.30	.10
❑ 183 Randy Johnson	.75	.30
❑ 184 Steve Finley	.30	.10
❑ 185 Kelly Stinnett	.30	.10
❑ 186 Jay Bell	.30	.10
❑ 187 Matt Mantei	.30	.10
❑ 188 Luis Gonzalez	.30	.10
❑ 189 Shawn Green	.30	.10
❑ 190 Todd Hundley	.30	.10
❑ 191 Chan Ho Park	.30	.10
❑ 192 Adrian Beltre	.30	.10
❑ 193 Mark Grudzielanek	.30	.10
❑ 194 Gary Sheffield	.30	.10
❑ 195 Tom Goodwin	.30	.10
❑ 196 Lee Stevens	.30	.10
❑ 197 Javier Vazquez	.30	.10
❑ 198 Milton Bradley	.30	.10
❑ 199 Vladimir Guerrero	.75	.30
❑ 200 Carl Pavano	.30	.10
❑ 201 Orlando Cabrera	.30	.10
❑ 202 Tony Armas Jr.	.30	.10
❑ 203 Jeff Kent	.30	.10
❑ 204 Calvin Murray	.30	.10
❑ 205 Ellis Burks	.30	.10
❑ 206 Barry Bonds	2.00	.75
❑ 207 Russ Ortiz	.30	.10
❑ 208 Marvin Benard	.30	.10

❑ 209	Joe Nathan	.30	.10
❑ 210	Preston Wilson	.30	.10
❑ 211	Cliff Floyd	.30	.10
❑ 212	Mike Lowell	.30	.10
❑ 213	Ryan Dempster	.30	.10
❑ 214	Brad Penny	.30	.10
❑ 215	Mike Redmond	.30	.10
❑ 216	Luis Castillo	.30	.10
❑ 217	Derek Bell	.30	.10
❑ 218	Mike Hampton	.30	.10
❑ 219	Todd Zeile	.30	.10
❑ 220	Robin Ventura	.30	.10
❑ 221	Mike Piazza	1.25	.50
❑ 222	Al Leiter	.30	.10
❑ 223	Edgardo Alfonzo	.30	.10
❑ 224	Mike Bordick	.30	.10
❑ 225	Phil Nevin	.30	.10
❑ 226	Ryan Klesko	.30	.10
❑ 227	Adam Eaton	.30	.10
❑ 228	Eric Owens	.30	.10
❑ 229	Tony Gwynn	1.00	.40
❑ 230	Matt Clement	.30	.10
❑ 231	Wiki Gonzalez	.30	.10
❑ 232	Robert Person	.30	.10
❑ 233	Doug Glanville	.30	.10
❑ 234	Scott Rolen	.50	.20
❑ 235	Mike Lieberthal	.30	.10
❑ 236	Randy Wolf	.30	.10
❑ 237	Bob Abreu	.30	.10
❑ 238	Pat Burrell	.30	.10
❑ 239	Bruce Chen	.30	.10
❑ 240	Kevin Young	.30	.10
❑ 241	Todd Ritchie	.30	.10
❑ 242	Adrian Brown	.30	.10
❑ 243	Chad Hermansen	.30	.10
❑ 244	Warren Morris	.30	.10
❑ 245	Kris Benson	.30	.10
❑ 246	Jason Kendall	.30	.10
❑ 247	Pokey Reese	.30	.10
❑ 248	Rob Bell	.30	.10
❑ 249	Ken Griffey Jr.	1.25	.50
❑ 250	Sean Casey	.30	.10
❑ 251	Aaron Boone	.30	.10
❑ 252	Pete Harnisch	.30	.10
❑ 253	Barry Larkin	.50	.20
❑ 254	Dmitri Young	.30	.10
❑ 255	Todd Hollandsworth	.30	.10
❑ 256	Pedro Astacio	.30	.10
❑ 257	Todd Helton	.50	.20
❑ 258	Terry Shumpert	.30	.10
❑ 259	Neifi Perez	.30	.10
❑ 260	Jeffrey Hammonds	.30	.10
❑ 261	Ben Petrick	.30	.10
❑ 262	Mark McGwire SH	1.00	.40
❑ 263	Derek Jeter SH	1.00	.40
❑ 264	Sammy Sosa SH	.50	.20
❑ 265	Cal Ripken SH	1.25	.50
❑ 266	Pedro Martinez SH	.50	.20
❑ 267	Barry Bonds SH	1.00	.40
❑ 268	Fred McGriff SH	.30	.10
❑ 269	Randy Johnson SH	.50	.20
❑ 270	Darin Erstad SH	.30	.10
❑ 271	Ichiro Suzuki SR RC	15.00	6.00
❑ 272	Wilson Betemit SR RC	2.00	.75
❑ 273	Corey Patterson SR	.50	.20
❑ 274	Sean Douglass SR RC	.50	.20
❑ 275	Mike Penney SR RC	.50	.20
❑ 276	Nate Teut SR RC	.50	.20
❑ 277	Ricardo Rodriguez SR RC	.50	.20
❑ 278	Brandon Duckworth SR RC	.50	.20
❑ 279	Rafael Soriano SR RC	.50	.20
❑ 280	Juan Diaz SR RC	.50	.20
❑ 281	Horacio Ramirez SR RC	.60	.25
❑ 282	Tsuyoshi Shinjo SR RC	.60	.25
❑ 283	Keith Ginter SR	.50	.20
❑ 284	Esix Snead SR RC	.50	.20
❑ 285	Erick Almonte SR RC	.50	.20
❑ 286	Travis Hafner SR RC	5.00	2.00
❑ 287	Jason Smith SR RC	.50	.20
❑ 288	Jackson Melian SR RC	.50	.20
❑ 289	Tyler Walker SR RC	.50	.20
❑ 290	Jason Standridge SR	.50	.20
❑ 291	Juan Uribe SR RC	.60	.25
❑ 292	Adrian Hernandez SR RC	.50	.20
❑ 293	Jason Michaels SR RC	.50	.20
❑ 294	Jason Hart SR	.50	.20
❑ 295	Albert Pujols SR RC	60.00	30.00
❑ 296	Morgan Ensberg SR RC	2.00	.75
❑ 297	Brandon Inge SR	.50	.20
❑ 298	Jesus Colome SR	.50	.20
❑ 299	Kyle Kessel SR RC	.50	.20
❑ 300	Timo Perez SR	.50	.20
❑ 301	Mo Vaughn	.30	.10
❑ 302	Ismael Valdes	.30	.10
❑ 303	Glenallen Hill	.30	.10
❑ 304	Garret Anderson	.30	.10
❑ 305	Johnny Damon	.50	.20
❑ 306	Jose Ortiz	.30	.10
❑ 307	Mark Mulder	.30	.10
❑ 308	Adam Piatt	.30	.10
❑ 309	Gil Heredia	.30	.10
❑ 310	Mike Sirotka	.30	.10
❑ 311	Carlos Delgado	.30	.10
❑ 312	Alex Gonzalez	.30	.10
❑ 313	Jose Cruz Jr.	.30	.10
❑ 314	Darrin Fletcher	.30	.10
❑ 315	Ben Grieve	.30	.10
❑ 316	Vinny Castilla	.30	.10
❑ 317	Wilson Alvarez	.30	.10
❑ 318	Brent Abernathy	.30	.10
❑ 319	Ellis Burks	.30	.10
❑ 320	Jim Thome	.50	.20
❑ 321	Juan Gonzalez	.30	.10
❑ 322	Ed Taubensee	.30	.10
❑ 323	Travis Fryman	.30	.10
❑ 324	John Olerud	.30	.10
❑ 325	Edgar Martinez	.50	.20
❑ 326	Freddy Garcia	.30	.10
❑ 327	Bret Boone	.50	.20
❑ 328	Kazuhiro Sasaki	.30	.10
❑ 329	Albert Belle	.30	.10
❑ 330	Mike Bordick	.30	.10
❑ 331	David Segui	.30	.10
❑ 332	Pat Hentgen	.30	.10
❑ 333	Alex Rodriguez	1.25	.50
❑ 334	Andres Galarraga	.30	.10
❑ 335	Gabe Kapler	.30	.10
❑ 336	Ken Caminiti	.30	.10
❑ 337	Rafael Palmeiro	.50	.20
❑ 338	Manny Ramirez Sox	.50	.20
❑ 339	David Cone	.30	.10
❑ 340	Nomar Garciaparra	1.25	.50
❑ 341	Trot Nixon	.30	.10
❑ 342	Derek Lowe	.30	.10
❑ 343	Roberto Hernandez	.30	.10
❑ 344	Mike Sweeney	.30	.10
❑ 345	Carlos Febles	.30	.10
❑ 346	Jeff Suppan	.30	.10
❑ 347	Roger Cedeno	.30	.10
❑ 348	Bobby Higginson	.30	.10
❑ 349	Deivi Cruz	.30	.10
❑ 350	Mitch Meluskey	.30	.10
❑ 351	Matt Lawton	.30	.10
❑ 352	Mark Redman	.30	.10
❑ 353	Jay Canizaro	.30	.10
❑ 354	Corey Koskie	.30	.10
❑ 355	Matt Kinney	.30	.10
❑ 356	Frank Thomas	.75	.30
❑ 357	Sandy Alomar Jr.	.30	.10
❑ 358	David Wells	.30	.10
❑ 359	Jim Parque	.30	.10
❑ 360	Chris Singleton	.30	.10
❑ 361	Tino Martinez	.50	.20
❑ 362	Paul O'Neill	.50	.20
❑ 363	Mike Mussina	.50	.20
❑ 364	Bernie Williams	.50	.20
❑ 365	Andy Pettitte	.50	.20
❑ 366	Mariano Rivera	.75	.30
❑ 367	Brad Ausmus	.30	.10
❑ 368	Craig Biggio	.50	.20
❑ 369	Lance Berkman	.30	.10
❑ 370	Shane Reynolds	.30	.10
❑ 371	Chipper Jones	.75	.30
❑ 372	Tom Glavine	.50	.20
❑ 373	B.J. Surhoff	.30	.10
❑ 374	John Smoltz	.50	.20
❑ 375	Rico Brogna	.30	.10
❑ 376	Geoff Jenkins	.30	.10
❑ 377	Jose Hernandez	.30	.10
❑ 378	Tyler Houston	.30	.10
❑ 379	Henry Blanco	.30	.10
❑ 380	Jeffrey Hammonds	.30	.10
❑ 381	Jim Edmonds	.30	.10
❑ 382	Fernando Vina	.30	.10
❑ 383	Andy Benes	.30	.10
❑ 384	Ray Lankford	.30	.10
❑ 385	Dustin Hermanson	.30	.10
❑ 386	Todd Hundley	.30	.10
❑ 387	Sammy Sosa	.75	.30
❑ 388	Tom Gordon	.30	.10
❑ 389	Bill Mueller	.30	.10
❑ 390	Ron Coomer	.30	.10
❑ 391	Matt Stairs	.30	.10
❑ 392	Mark Grace	.50	.20
❑ 393	Matt Williams	.30	.10
❑ 394	Todd Stottlemyre	.30	.10
❑ 395	Tony Womack	.30	.10
❑ 396	Erubiel Durazo	.30	.10
❑ 397	Reggie Sanders	.30	.10
❑ 398	Andy Ashby	.30	.10
❑ 399	Eric Karros	.30	.10
❑ 400	Kevin Brown	.30	.10
❑ 401	Darren Dreifort	.30	.10
❑ 402	Fernando Tatis	.30	.10
❑ 403	Jose Vidro	.30	.10
❑ 404	Peter Bergeron	.30	.10
❑ 405	Geoff Blum	.30	.10
❑ 406	J.T. Snow	.30	.10
❑ 407	Livan Hernandez	.30	.10
❑ 408	Robb Nen	.30	.10
❑ 409	Bobby Estalella	.30	.10
❑ 410	Rich Aurilia	.30	.10
❑ 411	Eric Davis	.30	.10
❑ 412	Charles Johnson	.30	.10
❑ 413	Alex Gonzalez	.30	.10
❑ 414	A.J. Burnett	.30	.10
❑ 415	Antonio Alfonseca	.30	.10
❑ 416	Derrek Lee	.50	.20
❑ 417	Jay Payton	.30	.10
❑ 418	Kevin Appier	.30	.10
❑ 419	Steve Trachsel	.30	.10
❑ 420	Rey Ordonez	.30	.10
❑ 421	Darryl Hamilton	.30	.10
❑ 422	Ben Davis	.30	.10
❑ 423	Damian Jackson	.30	.10
❑ 424	Mark Kotsay	.30	.10
❑ 425	Trevor Hoffman	.30	.10
❑ 426	Travis Lee	.30	.10
❑ 427	Omar Daal	.30	.10
❑ 428	Paul Byrd	.30	.10
❑ 429	Reggie Taylor	.30	.10
❑ 430	Brian Giles	.30	.10
❑ 431	Derek Bell	.30	.10
❑ 432	Francisco Cordova	.30	.10
❑ 433	Pat Meares	.30	.10
❑ 434	Scott Williamson	.30	.10
❑ 435	Jason LaRue	.30	.10
❑ 436	Michael Tucker	.30	.10
❑ 437	Wilton Guerrero	.30	.10
❑ 438	Mike Hampton	.30	.10
❑ 439	Ron Gant	.30	.10
❑ 440	Jeff Cirillo	.30	.10
❑ 441	Denny Neagle	.30	.10
❑ 442	Larry Walker	.30	.10
❑ 443	Juan Pierre	.30	.10
❑ 444	Todd Walker	.30	.10
❑ 445	Jason Giambi SH CL	.30	.10
❑ 446	Jeff Kent SH CL	.30	.10
❑ 447	Mariano Rivera SH CL	.50	.20
❑ 448	Edgar Martinez SH CL	.30	.10
❑ 449	Troy Glaus SH CL	.30	.10
❑ 450	Alex Rodriguez SH CL	.75	.30

2002 Upper Deck

❑ COMPLETE SET (745)	160.00	85.00
❑ COMPLETE SERIES 1 (500)	110.00	60.00
❑ COMPLETE SERIES 2 (245)	50.00	25.00
❑ COMMON (51-500/546-745)	.30	.10
❑ COMMON SR (1-50/501-545)	1.00	.40
❑ 1 Mark Prior SR	2.00	.75
❑ 2 Mark Teixeira SR	5.00	2.00
❑ 3 Brian Roberts SR	2.00	.75
❑ 4 Jason Romano SR	1.00	.40
❑ 5 Dennis Stark SR	1.00	.40
❑ 6 Oscar Salazar SR	1.00	.40
❑ 7 John Patterson SR	1.00	.40
❑ 8 Shane Loux SR	1.00	.40
❑ 9 Marcus Giles SR	1.00	.40
❑ 10 Juan Cruz SR	1.00	.40
❑ 11 Jorge Julio SR	1.00	.40
❑ 12 Adam Dunn SR	1.00	.40
❑ 13 Delvin James SR	1.00	.40
❑ 14 Jeremy Affeldt SR	1.00	.40
❑ 15 Tim Raines Jr. SR	1.00	.40
❑ 16 Luke Hudson SR	1.00	.40
❑ 17 Todd Sears SR	1.00	.40
❑ 18 George Perez SR	1.00	.40
❑ 19 Wilmy Caceres SR	1.00	.40
❑ 20 Abraham Nunez SR	1.00	.40
❑ 21 Mike Amrhein SR RC	1.00	.40
❑ 22 Carlos Hernandez SR	1.00	.40
❑ 23 Scott Hodges SR	1.00	.40
❑ 24 Brandon Knight SR	1.00	.40
❑ 25 Geoff Goetz SR	1.00	.40
❑ 26 Carlos Garcia SR	1.00	.40
❑ 27 Luis Pineda SR	1.00	.40
❑ 28 Chris Gissell SR	1.00	.40
❑ 29 Jae Weong Seo SR	1.00	.40
❑ 30 Paul Phillips SR	1.00	.40
❑ 31 Cory Aldridge SR	1.00	.40
❑ 32 Aaron Cook SR RC	1.00	.40
❑ 33 Rendy Espina SR RC	1.00	.40
❑ 34 Jason Phillips SR	1.00	.40
❑ 35 Carlos Silva SR	1.00	.40
❑ 36 Ryan Mills SR	1.00	.40
❑ 37 Pedro Santana SR	1.00	.40
❑ 38 John Grabow SR	1.00	.40
❑ 39 Cody Ransom SR	1.00	.40
❑ 40 Orlando Woodards SR	1.00	.40
❑ 41 Bud Smith SR	1.00	.40
❑ 42 Junior Guerrero SR	1.00	.40
❑ 43 David Brous SR	1.00	.40
❑ 44 Steve Green SR	1.00	.40
❑ 45 Brian Rogers SR	1.00	.40
❑ 46 Juan Figueroa SR RC	1.00	.40
❑ 47 Nick Punto SR	1.00	.40
❑ 48 Junior Herndon SR	1.00	.40
❑ 49 Justin Kaye SR	1.00	.40
❑ 50 Jason Karnuth SR	1.00	.40
❑ 51 Troy Glaus	.30	.10
❑ 52 Bengie Molina	.30	.10
❑ 53 Ramon Ortiz	.30	.10
❑ 54 Adam Kennedy	.30	.10
❑ 55 Jarrod Washburn	.30	.10
❑ 56 Troy Percival	.30	.10
❑ 57 David Eckstein	.30	.10
❑ 58 Ben Weber	.30	.10
❑ 59 Larry Barnes	.30	.10
❑ 60 Ismael Valdes	.30	.10
❑ 61 Benji Gil	.30	.10
❑ 62 Scott Schoeneweis	.30	.10
❑ 63 Pat Rapp	.30	.10
❑ 64 Jason Giambi	.30	.10
❑ 65 Mark Mulder	.30	.10
❑ 66 Ron Gant	.30	.10
❑ 67 Johnny Damon	.50	.20
❑ 68 Adam Piatt	.30	.10
❑ 69 Jermaine Dye	.30	.10
❑ 70 Jason Hart	.30	.10
❑ 71 Eric Chavez	.30	.10
❑ 72 Jim Mecir	.30	.10
❑ 73 Barry Zito	.30	.10
❑ 74 Jason Isringhausen	.30	.10
❑ 75 Jeremy Giambi	.30	.10
❑ 76 Olmedo Saenz	.30	.10
❑ 77 Terrence Long	.30	.10
❑ 78 Ramon Hernandez	.30	.10
❑ 79 Chris Carpenter	.30	.10
❑ 80 Raul Mondesi	.30	.10
❑ 81 Carlos Delgado	.30	.10
❑ 82 Billy Koch	.30	.10
❑ 83 Vernon Wells	.30	.10
❑ 84 Darrin Fletcher	.30	.10
❑ 85 Homer Bush	.30	.10
❑ 86 Pasqual Coco	.30	.10
❑ 87 Shannon Stewart	.30	.10
❑ 88 Chris Woodward	.30	.10
❑ 89 Joe Lawrence	.30	.10
❑ 90 Esteban Loaiza	.30	.10
❑ 91 Cesar Izturis	.30	.10
❑ 92 Kelvim Escobar	.30	.10
❑ 93 Greg Vaughn	.30	.10
❑ 94 Brent Abernathy	.30	.10
❑ 95 Tanyon Sturtze	.30	.10
❑ 96 Steve Cox	.30	.10
❑ 97 Aubrey Huff	.30	.10
❑ 98 Jesus Colome	.30	.10
❑ 99 Ben Grieve	.30	.10
❑ 100 Esteban Yan	.30	.10
❑ 101 Joe Kennedy	.30	.10
❑ 102 Felix Martinez	.30	.10
❑ 103 Nick Bierbrodt	.30	.10
❑ 104 Damian Rolls	.30	.10
❑ 105 Russ Johnson	.30	.10
❑ 106 Toby Hall	.30	.10
❑ 107 Roberto Alomar	.50	.20
❑ 108 Bartolo Colon	.30	.10
❑ 109 John Rocker	.30	.10
❑ 110 Juan Gonzalez	.30	.10
❑ 111 Einar Diaz	.30	.10
❑ 112 Chuck Finley	.30	.10
❑ 113 Kenny Lofton	.30	.10
❑ 114 Danys Baez	.30	.10
❑ 115 Travis Fryman	.30	.10
❑ 116 C.C. Sabathia	.30	.10
❑ 117 Paul Shuey	.30	.10
❑ 118 Marty Cordova	.30	.10
❑ 119 Ellis Burks	.30	.10
❑ 120 Bob Wickman	.30	.10
❑ 121 Edgar Martinez	.50	.20
❑ 122 Freddy Garcia	.30	.10
❑ 123 Ichiro Suzuki	1.50	.60
❑ 124 John Olerud	.30	.10
❑ 125 Gil Meche	.30	.10
❑ 126 Dan Wilson	.30	.10
❑ 127 Aaron Sele	.30	.10
❑ 128 Kazuhiro Sasaki	.30	.10
❑ 129 Mark McLemore	.30	.10
❑ 130 Carlos Guillen	.30	.10
❑ 131 Al Martin	.30	.10
❑ 132 David Bell	.30	.10
❑ 133 Jay Buhner	.30	.10
❑ 134 Stan Javier	.30	.10
❑ 135 Tony Batista	.30	.10
❑ 136 Jason Johnson	.30	.10
❑ 137 Brook Fordyce	.30	.10
❑ 138 Mike Kinkade	.30	.10
❑ 139 Willis Roberts	.30	.10
❑ 140 David Segui	.30	.10
❑ 141 Josh Towers	.30	.10
❑ 142 Jeff Conine	.30	.10
❑ 143 Chris Richard	.30	.10
❑ 144 Pat Hentgen	.30	.10
❑ 145 Melvin Mora	.30	.10
❑ 146 Jerry Hairston Jr.	.30	.10
❑ 147 Calvin Maduro	.30	.10
❑ 148 Brady Anderson	.30	.10
❑ 149 Alex Rodriguez	1.25	.50
❑ 150 Kenny Rogers	.30	.10
❑ 151 Chad Curtis	.30	.10
❑ 152 Ricky Ledee	.30	.10
❑ 153 Rafael Palmeiro	.50	.20
❑ 154 Rob Bell	.30	.10
❑ 155 Rick Helling	.30	.10
❑ 156 Doug Davis	.30	.10
❑ 157 Mike Lamb	.30	.10
❑ 158 Gabe Kapler	.30	.10
❑ 159 Jeff Zimmerman	.30	.10
❑ 160 Bill Haselman	.30	.10
❑ 161 Tim Crabtree	.30	.10
❑ 162 Carlos Pena	.30	.10
❑ 163 Nomar Garciaparra	1.25	.50
❑ 164 Shea Hillenbrand	.30	.10
❑ 165 Hideo Nomo	.75	.30
❑ 166 Manny Ramirez	.50	.20
❑ 167 Jose Offerman	.30	.10
❑ 168 Scott Hatteberg	.30	.10
❑ 169 Trot Nixon	.30	.10
❑ 170 Darren Lewis	.30	.10
❑ 171 Derek Lowe	.30	.10
❑ 172 Troy O'Leary	.30	.10
❑ 173 Tim Wakefield	.30	.10
❑ 174 Chris Stynes	.30	.10
❑ 175 John Valentin	.30	.10
❑ 176 David Cone	.30	.10
❑ 177 Neifi Perez	.30	.10
❑ 178 Brent Mayne	.30	.10
❑ 179 Dan Reichert	.30	.10
❑ 180 A.J. Hinch	.30	.10
❑ 181 Chris George	.30	.10
❑ 182 Mike Sweeney	.30	.10
❑ 183 Jeff Suppan	.30	.10
❑ 184 Roberto Hernandez	.30	.10
❑ 185 Joe Randa	.30	.10
❑ 186 Paul Byrd	.30	.10
❑ 187 Luis Ordaz	.30	.10
❑ 188 Kris Wilson	.30	.10
❑ 189 Dee Brown	.30	.10
❑ 190 Tony Clark	.30	.10
❑ 191 Matt Anderson	.30	.10
❑ 192 Robert Fick	.30	.10
❑ 193 Juan Encarnacion	.30	.10
❑ 194 Dean Palmer	.30	.10
❑ 195 Victor Santos	.30	.10
❑ 196 Damion Easley	.30	.10
❑ 197 Jose Lima	.30	.10
❑ 198 Deivi Cruz	.30	.10
❑ 199 Roger Cedeno	.30	.10
❑ 200 Jose Macias	.30	.10
❑ 201 Jeff Weaver	.30	.10
❑ 202 Brandon Inge	.30	.10
❑ 203 Brian Moehler	.30	.10
❑ 204 Brad Radke	.30	.10
❑ 205 Doug Mientkiewicz	.30	.10
❑ 206 Cristian Guzman	.30	.10
❑ 207 Corey Koskie	.30	.10
❑ 208 LaTroy Hawkins	.30	.10
❑ 209 J.C. Romero	.30	.10
❑ 210 Chad Allen	.30	.10
❑ 211 Torii Hunter	.30	.10
❑ 212 Travis Miller	.30	.10
❑ 213 Joe Mays	.30	.10
❑ 214 Todd Jones	.30	.10
❑ 215 David Ortiz	.75	.30
❑ 216 Brian Buchanan	.30	.10
❑ 217 A.J. Pierzynski	.30	.10
❑ 218 Carlos Lee	.30	.10
❑ 219 Gary Glover	.30	.10
❑ 220 Jose Valentin	.30	.10
❑ 221 Aaron Rowand	.30	.10
❑ 222 Sandy Alomar Jr.	.30	.10
❑ 223 Herbert Perry	.30	.10
❑ 224 Jon Garland	.30	.10
❑ 225 Mark Buehrle	.30	.10
❑ 226 Chris Singleton	.30	.10
❑ 227 Kip Wells	.30	.10
❑ 228 Ray Durham	.30	.10
❑ 229 Joe Crede	.30	.10
❑ 230 Keith Foulke	.30	.10
❑ 231 Royce Clayton	.30	.10
❑ 232 Andy Pettitte	.50	.20
❑ 233 Derek Jeter	2.00	.75

❑	234	Jorge Posada	.50	.20
❑	235	Roger Clemens	1.50	.60
❑	236	Paul O'Neill	.50	.20
❑	237	Nick Johnson	.30	.10
❑	238	Gerald Williams	.30	.10
❑	239	Mariano Rivera	.75	.30
❑	240	Alfonso Soriano	.30	.10
❑	241	Ramiro Mendoza	.30	.10
❑	242	Mike Mussina	.50	.20
❑	243	Luis Sojo	.30	.10
❑	244	Scott Brosius	.30	.10
❑	245	David Justice	.30	.10
❑	246	Wade Miller	.30	.10
❑	247	Brad Ausmus	.30	.10
❑	248	Jeff Bagwell	.50	.20
❑	249	Daryle Ward	.30	.10
❑	250	Shane Reynolds	.30	.10
❑	251	Chris Truby	.30	.10
❑	252	Billy Wagner	.30	.10
❑	253	Craig Biggio	.50	.20
❑	254	Moises Alou	.30	.10
❑	255	Vinny Castilla	.30	.10
❑	256	Tim Redding	.30	.10
❑	257	Roy Oswalt	.30	.10
❑	258	Julio Lugo	.30	.10
❑	259	Chipper Jones	.75	.30
❑	260	Greg Maddux	1.25	.50
❑	261	Ken Caminiti	.30	.10
❑	262	Kevin Millwood	.30	.10
❑	263	Keith Lockhart	.30	.10
❑	264	Rey Sanchez	.30	.10
❑	265	Jason Marquis	.30	.10
❑	266	Brian Jordan	.30	.10
❑	267	Steve Karsay	.30	.10
❑	268	Wes Helms	.30	.10
❑	269	B.J. Surhoff	.30	.10
❑	270	Wilson Betemit	.30	.10
❑	271	John Smoltz	.50	.20
❑	272	Rafael Furcal	.30	.10
❑	273	Jeromy Burnitz	.30	.10
❑	274	Jimmy Haynes	.30	.10
❑	275	Mark Loretta	.30	.10
❑	276	Jose Hernandez	.30	.10
❑	277	Paul Rigdon	.30	.10
❑	278	Alex Sanchez	.30	.10
❑	279	Chad Fox	.30	.10
❑	280	Devon White	.30	.10
❑	281	Tyler Houston	.30	.10
❑	282	Ronnie Belliard	.30	.10
❑	283	Luis Lopez	.30	.10
❑	284	Ben Sheets	.30	.10
❑	285	Curtis Leskanic	.30	.10
❑	286	Henry Blanco	.30	.10
❑	287	Mark McGwire	2.00	.75
❑	288	Edgar Renteria	.30	.10
❑	289	Matt Morris	.30	.10
❑	290	Gene Stechschulte	.30	.10
❑	291	Dustin Hermanson	.30	.10
❑	292	Eli Marrero	.30	.10
❑	293	Albert Pujols	1.50	.60
❑	294	Luis Saturria	.30	.10
❑	295	Bobby Bonilla	.30	.10
❑	296	Garrett Stephenson	.30	.10
❑	297	Jim Edmonds	.30	.10
❑	298	Rick Ankiel	.30	.10
❑	299	Placido Polanco	.30	.10
❑	300	Dave Veres	.30	.10
❑	301	Sammy Sosa	.75	.30
❑	302	Eric Young	.30	.10
❑	303	Kerry Wood	.30	.10
❑	304	Jon Lieber	.30	.10
❑	305	Joe Girardi	.30	.10
❑	306	Fred McGriff	.50	.20
❑	307	Jeff Fassero	.30	.10
❑	308	Julio Zuleta	.30	.10
❑	309	Kevin Tapani	.30	.10
❑	310	Rondell White	.30	.10
❑	311	Julian Tavarez	.30	.10
❑	312	Tom Gordon	.30	.10
❑	313	Corey Patterson	.30	.10
❑	314	Bill Mueller	.30	.10
❑	315	Randy Johnson	.75	.30
❑	316	Chad Moeller	.30	.10
❑	317	Tony Womack	.30	.10
❑	318	Erubiel Durazo	.30	.10
❑	319	Luis Gonzalez	.30	.10
❑	320	Brian Anderson	.30	.10
❑	321	Reggie Sanders	.30	.10
❑	322	Greg Colbrunn	.30	.10
❑	323	Robert Ellis	.30	.10
❑	324	Jack Cust	.30	.10
❑	325	Bret Prinz	.30	.10
❑	326	Steve Finley	.30	.10
❑	327	Byung-Hyun Kim	.30	.10
❑	328	Albie Lopez	.30	.10
❑	329	Gary Sheffield	.30	.10
❑	330	Mark Grudzielanek	.30	.10
❑	331	Paul LoDuca	.30	.10
❑	332	Tom Goodwin	.30	.10
❑	333	Andy Ashby	.30	.10
❑	334	Hiram Bocachica	.30	.10
❑	335	Dave Hansen	.30	.10
❑	336	Kevin Brown	.30	.10
❑	337	Marquis Grissom	.30	.10
❑	338	Terry Adams	.30	.10
❑	339	Chan Ho Park	.30	.10
❑	340	Adrian Beltre	.30	.10
❑	341	Luke Prokopec	.30	.10
❑	342	Jeff Shaw	.30	.10
❑	343	Vladimir Guerrero	.75	.30
❑	344	Orlando Cabrera	.30	.10
❑	345	Tony Armas Jr.	.30	.10
❑	346	Michael Barrett	.30	.10
❑	347	Geoff Blum	.30	.10
❑	348	Ryan Minor	.30	.10
❑	349	Peter Bergeron	.30	.10
❑	350	Graeme Lloyd	.30	.10
❑	351	Jose Vidro	.30	.10
❑	352	Javier Vazquez	.30	.10
❑	353	Matt Blank	.30	.10
❑	354	Masato Yoshii	.30	.10
❑	355	Carl Pavano	.30	.10
❑	356	Barry Bonds	2.00	.75
❑	357	Shawon Dunston	.30	.10
❑	358	Livan Hernandez	.30	.10
❑	359	Felix Rodriguez	.30	.10
❑	360	Pedro Feliz	.30	.10
❑	361	Calvin Murray	.30	.10
❑	362	Robb Nen	.30	.10
❑	363	Marvin Benard	.30	.10
❑	364	Russ Ortiz	.30	.10
❑	365	Jason Schmidt	.30	.10
❑	366	Rich Aurilia	.30	.10
❑	367	John Vander Wal	.30	.10
❑	368	Benito Santiago	.30	.10
❑	369	Ryan Dempster	.30	.10
❑	370	Charles Johnson	.30	.10
❑	371	Alex Gonzalez	.30	.10
❑	372	Luis Castillo	.30	.10
❑	373	Mike Lowell	.30	.10
❑	374	Antonio Alfonseca	.30	.10
❑	375	A.J. Burnett	.30	.10
❑	376	Brad Penny	.30	.10
❑	377	Jason Grilli	.30	.10
❑	378	Derrek Lee	.50	.20
❑	379	Matt Clement	.30	.10
❑	380	Eric Owens	.30	.10
❑	381	Vladimir Nunez	.30	.10
❑	382	Cliff Floyd	.30	.10
❑	383	Mike Piazza	1.25	.50
❑	384	Lenny Harris	.30	.10
❑	385	Glendon Rusch	.30	.10
❑	386	Todd Zeile	.30	.10
❑	387	Al Leiter	.30	.10
❑	388	Armando Benitez	.30	.10
❑	389	Alex Escobar	.30	.10
❑	390	Kevin Appier	.30	.10
❑	391	Matt Lawton	.30	.10
❑	392	Bruce Chen	.30	.10
❑	393	John Franco	.30	.10
❑	394	Tsuyoshi Shinjo	.30	.10
❑	395	Rey Ordonez	.30	.10
❑	396	Joe McEwing	.30	.10
❑	397	Ryan Klesko	.30	.10
❑	398	Brian Lawrence	.30	.10
❑	399	Kevin Walker	.30	.10
❑	400	Phil Nevin	.30	.10
❑	401	Bubba Trammell	.30	.10
❑	402	Wiki Gonzalez	.30	.10
❑	403	D'Angelo Jimenez	.30	.10
❑	404	Rickey Henderson	.75	.30
❑	405	Mike Darr	.30	.10
❑	406	Trevor Hoffman	.30	.10
❑	407	Damian Jackson	.30	.10
❑	408	Santiago Perez	.30	.10
❑	409	Cesar Crespo	.30	.10
❑	410	Robert Person	.30	.10
❑	411	Travis Lee	.30	.10
❑	412	Scott Rolen	.50	.20
❑	413	Turk Wendell	.30	.10
❑	414	Randy Wolf	.30	.10
❑	415	Kevin Jordan	.30	.10
❑	416	Jose Mesa	.30	.10
❑	417	Mike Lieberthal	.30	.10
❑	418	Bobby Abreu	.30	.10
❑	419	Tomas Perez	.30	.10
❑	420	Doug Glanville	.30	.10
❑	421	Reggie Taylor	.30	.10
❑	422	Jimmy Rollins	.30	.10
❑	423	Brian Giles	.30	.10
❑	424	Rob Mackowiak	.30	.10
❑	425	Bronson Arroyo	.30	.10
❑	426	Kevin Young	.30	.10
❑	427	Jack Wilson	.30	.10
❑	428	Adrian Brown	.30	.10
❑	429	Chad Hermansen	.30	.10
❑	430	Jimmy Anderson	.30	.10
❑	431	Aramis Ramirez	.30	.10
❑	432	Todd Ritchie	.30	.10
❑	433	Pat Meares	.30	.10
❑	434	Warren Morris	.30	.10
❑	435	Derek Bell	.30	.10
❑	436	Ken Griffey Jr.	1.25	.50
❑	437	Elmer Dessens	.30	.10
❑	438	Ruben Rivera	.30	.10
❑	439	Jason LaRue	.30	.10
❑	440	Sean Casey	.30	.10
❑	441	Pete Harnisch	.30	.10
❑	442	Danny Graves	.30	.10
❑	443	Aaron Boone	.30	.10
❑	444	Dmitri Young	.30	.10
❑	445	Brandon Larson	.30	.10
❑	446	Pokey Reese	.30	.10
❑	447	Todd Walker	.30	.10
❑	448	Juan Castro	.30	.10
❑	449	Todd Helton	.50	.20
❑	450	Ben Petrick	.30	.10
❑	451	Juan Pierre	.30	.10
❑	452	Jeff Cirillo	.30	.10
❑	453	Juan Uribe	.30	.10
❑	454	Brian Bohanon	.30	.10
❑	455	Terry Shumpert	.30	.10
❑	456	Mike Hampton	.30	.10
❑	457	Shawn Chacon	.30	.10
❑	458	Adam Melhuse	.30	.10
❑	459	Greg Norton	.30	.10
❑	460	Gabe White	.30	.10
❑	461	Ichiro Suzuki WS	.75	.30
❑	462	Carlos Delgado WS	.30	.10
❑	463	Manny Ramirez WS	.50	.20
❑	464	Miguel Tejada WS	.30	.10
❑	465	Tsuyoshi Shinjo WS	.30	.10
❑	466	Bernie Williams WS	.30	.10
❑	467	Juan Gonzalez WS	.30	.10
❑	468	Andruw Jones WS	.30	.10
❑	469	Ivan Rodriguez WS	.30	.10
❑	470	Larry Walker WS	.30	.10
❑	471	Hideo Nomo WS	.30	.10
❑	472	Albert Pujols WS	.75	.30
❑	473	Pedro Martinez WS	.50	.20
❑	474	Vladimir Guerrero WS	.50	.20
❑	475	Tony Batista WS	.30	.10
❑	476	Kazuhiro Sasaki WS	.30	.10
❑	477	Richard Hidalgo WS	.30	.10
❑	478	Carlos Lee WS	.30	.10
❑	479	Roberto Alomar WS	.30	.10
❑	480	Rafael Palmeiro WS	.30	.10
❑	481	Ken Griffey Jr. GG	.75	.30
❑	482	Ken Griffey Jr. GG	.75	.30
❑	483	Ken Griffey Jr. GG	.75	.30
❑	484	Ken Griffey Jr. GG	.75	.30
❑	485	Ken Griffey Jr. GG	.75	.30
❑	486	Ken Griffey Jr. GG	.75	.30
❑	487	Ken Griffey Jr. GG	.75	.30
❑	488	Ken Griffey Jr. GG	.75	.30
❑	489	Ken Griffey Jr. GG	.75	.30
❑	490	Ken Griffey Jr. GG	.75	.30
❑	491	Barry Bonds CL	1.00	.40

❑ 492 Hideo Nomo CL .30 .10
❑ 493 Ichiro Suzuki CL .75 .30
❑ 494 Cal Ripken CL 1.25 .50
❑ 495 Tony Gwynn CL .50 .20
❑ 496 Randy Johnson CL .50 .20
❑ 497 A.J. Burnett CL .30 .10
❑ 498 Rickey Henderson CL .50 .20
❑ 499 Albert Pujols CL .75 .30
❑ 500 Luis Gonzalez CL .30 .10
❑ 501 Brandon Puffer SR RC 1.00 .40
❑ 502 Rodrigo Rosario SR RC 1.00 .40
❑ 503 Tom Shearn SR RC 1.00 .40
❑ 504 Reed Johnson SR RC 1.50 .60
❑ 505 Chris Baker SR RC 1.00 .40
❑ 506 John Ennis SR RC 1.00 .40
❑ 507 Luis Martinez SR RC 1.00 .40
❑ 508 So Taguchi SR RC 1.50 .60
❑ 509 Scotty Layfield SR RC 1.00 .40
❑ 510 Francis Beltran SR RC 1.00 .40
❑ 511 Brandon Backe SR RC 1.50 .60
❑ 512 Doug Devore SR RC 1.00 .40
❑ 513 Jeremy Ward SR RC 1.00 .40
❑ 514 Jose Valverde SR RC 1.00 .40
❑ 515 P.J. Bevis SR RC 1.00 .40
❑ 516 Victor Alvarez SR RC 1.00 .40
❑ 517 Kazuhisa Ishii SR RC 1.50 .60
❑ 518 Jorge Nunez SR RC 1.00 .40
❑ 519 Eric Good SR RC 1.00 .40
❑ 520 Ron Calloway SR RC 1.00 .40
❑ 521 Val Pascucci SR 1.00 .40
❑ 522 Nelson Castro SR RC 1.00 .40
❑ 523 Deivis Santos SR 1.00 .40
❑ 524 Luis Ugueto SR RC 1.00 .40
❑ 525 Matt Thornton SR RC 1.00 .40
❑ 526 Hansel Izquierdo SR RC 1.00 .40
❑ 527 Tyler Yates SR RC 1.00 .40
❑ 528 Mark Corey SR RC 1.00 .40
❑ 529 Jaime Cerda SR RC 1.00 .40
❑ 530 Satoru Komiyama SR RC 1.00 .40
❑ 531 Steve Bechler SR RC 1.00 .40
❑ 532 Ben Howard SR RC 1.00 .40
❑ 533 Anderson Machado SR RC 1.00 .40
❑ 534 Jorge Padilla SR RC 1.00 .40
❑ 535 Eric Junge SR RC 1.00 .40
❑ 536 Adrian Burnside SR RC 1.00 .40
❑ 537 Mike Gonzalez SR RC 1.00 .40
❑ 538 Josh Hancock SR RC 1.25 .50
❑ 539 Colin Young SR RC 1.00 .40
❑ 540 Rene Reyes SR RC 1.00 .40
❑ 541 Cam Esslinger SR RC 1.00 .40
❑ 542 Tim Kalita SR RC 1.00 .40
❑ 543 Kevin Frederick SR RC 1.00 .40
❑ 544 Kyle Kane SR RC 1.00 .40
❑ 545 Edwin Almonte SR RC 1.00 .40
❑ 546 Aaron Sele .30 .10
❑ 547 Garret Anderson .30 .10
❑ 548 Darin Erstad .30 .10
❑ 549 Brad Fullmer .30 .10
❑ 550 Kevin Appier .30 .10
❑ 551 Tim Salmon .50 .20
❑ 552 David Justice .30 .10
❑ 553 Billy Koch .30 .10
❑ 554 Scott Hatteberg .30 .10
❑ 555 Tim Hudson .30 .10
❑ 556 Miguel Tejada .30 .10
❑ 557 Carlos Pena .30 .10
❑ 558 Mike Sirotka .30 .10
❑ 559 Jose Cruz Jr. .30 .10
❑ 560 Josh Phelps .30 .10
❑ 561 Brandon Lyon .30 .10
❑ 562 Luke Prokopec .30 .10
❑ 563 Felipe Lopez .30 .10
❑ 564 Jason Standridge .30 .10
❑ 565 Chris Gomez .30 .10
❑ 566 John Flaherty .30 .10
❑ 567 Jason Tyner .30 .10
❑ 568 Bobby Smith .30 .10
❑ 569 Wilson Alvarez .30 .10
❑ 570 Matt Lawton .30 .10
❑ 571 Omar Vizquel .50 .20
❑ 572 Jim Thome .50 .20
❑ 573 Brady Anderson .30 .10
❑ 574 Alex Escobar .30 .10
❑ 575 Russell Branyan .30 .10
❑ 576 Bret Boone .30 .10
❑ 577 Ben Davis .30 .10
❑ 578 Mike Cameron .30 .10
❑ 579 Jamie Moyer .30 .10
❑ 580 Ruben Sierra .30 .10
❑ 581 Jeff Cirillo .30 .10
❑ 582 Marty Cordova .30 .10
❑ 583 Mike Bordick .30 .10
❑ 584 Brian Roberts .30 .10
❑ 585 Luis Matos .30 .10
❑ 586 Geronimo Gil .30 .10
❑ 587 Jay Gibbons .30 .10
❑ 588 Carl Everett .30 .10
❑ 589 Ivan Rodriguez .50 .20
❑ 590 Chan Ho Park .30 .10
❑ 591 Juan Gonzalez .30 .10
❑ 592 Hank Blalock .50 .20
❑ 593 Todd Van Poppel .30 .10
❑ 594 Pedro Martinez .50 .20
❑ 595 Jason Varitek .75 .30
❑ 596 Tony Clark .30 .10
❑ 597 Johnny Damon Sox .50 .20
❑ 598 Dustin Hermanson .30 .10
❑ 599 John Burkett .30 .10
❑ 600 Carlos Beltran .30 .10
❑ 601 Mark Quinn .30 .10
❑ 602 Chuck Knoblauch .30 .10
❑ 603 Michael Tucker .30 .10
❑ 604 Carlos Febles .30 .10
❑ 605 Jose Rosado .30 .10
❑ 606 Dmitri Young .30 .10
❑ 607 Bobby Higginson .30 .10
❑ 608 Craig Paquette .30 .10
❑ 609 Mitch Meluskey .30 .10
❑ 610 Wendell Magee .30 .10
❑ 611 Mike Rivera .30 .10
❑ 612 Jacque Jones .30 .10
❑ 613 Luis Rivas .30 .10
❑ 614 Eric Milton .30 .10
❑ 615 Eddie Guardado .30 .10
❑ 616 Matt LeCroy .30 .10
❑ 617 Mike Jackson .30 .10
❑ 618 Magglio Ordonez .30 .10
❑ 619 Frank Thomas .75 .30
❑ 620 Rocky Biddle .30 .10
❑ 621 Paul Konerko .30 .10
❑ 622 Todd Ritchie .30 .10
❑ 623 Jon Rauch .30 .10
❑ 624 John Vander Wal .30 .10
❑ 625 Rondell White .30 .10
❑ 626 Jason Giambi .30 .10
❑ 627 Robin Ventura .30 .10
❑ 628 David Wells .30 .10
❑ 629 Bernie Williams .50 .20
❑ 630 Lance Berkman .30 .10
❑ 631 Richard Hidalgo .30 .10
❑ 632 Greg Zaun .30 .10
❑ 633 Jose Vizcaino .30 .10
❑ 634 Octavio Dotel .30 .10
❑ 635 Morgan Ensberg .30 .10
❑ 636 Andruw Jones .50 .20
❑ 637 Tom Glavine .50 .20
❑ 638 Gary Sheffield .30 .10
❑ 639 Vinny Castilla .30 .10
❑ 640 Javy Lopez .30 .10
❑ 641 Albie Lopez .30 .10
❑ 642 Geoff Jenkins .30 .10
❑ 643 Jeffrey Hammonds .30 .10
❑ 644 Alex Ochoa .30 .10
❑ 645 Richie Sexson .30 .10
❑ 646 Eric Young .30 .10
❑ 647 Glendon Rusch .30 .10
❑ 648 Tino Martinez .50 .20
❑ 649 Fernando Vina .30 .10
❑ 650 J.D. Drew .30 .10
❑ 651 Woody Williams .30 .10
❑ 652 Darryl Kile .30 .10
❑ 653 Jason Isringhausen .30 .10
❑ 654 Moises Alou .30 .10
❑ 655 Alex Gonzalez .30 .10
❑ 656 Delino DeShields .30 .10
❑ 657 Todd Hundley .30 .10
❑ 658 Chris Stynes .30 .10
❑ 659 Jason Bere .30 .10
❑ 660 Curt Schilling .30 .10
❑ 661 Craig Counsell .30 .10
❑ 662 Mark Grace .50 .20
❑ 663 Matt Williams .30 .10
❑ 664 Jay Bell .30 .10
❑ 665 Rick Helling .30 .10
❑ 666 Shawn Green .30 .10
❑ 667 Eric Karros .30 .10
❑ 668 Hideo Nomo .75 .30
❑ 669 Omar Daal .30 .10
❑ 670 Brian Jordan .30 .10
❑ 671 Cesar Izturis .30 .10
❑ 672 Fernando Tatis .30 .10
❑ 673 Lee Stevens .30 .10
❑ 674 Tomo Ohka .30 .10
❑ 675 Brian Schneider .30 .10
❑ 676 Brad Wilkerson .30 .10
❑ 677 Bruce Chen .30 .10
❑ 678 Tsuyoshi Shinjo .30 .10
❑ 679 Jeff Kent .30 .10
❑ 680 Kirk Rueter .30 .10
❑ 681 J.T. Snow .30 .10
❑ 682 David Bell .30 .10
❑ 683 Reggie Sanders .30 .10
❑ 684 Preston Wilson .30 .10
❑ 685 Vic Darensbourg .30 .10
❑ 686 Josh Beckett .30 .10
❑ 687 Pablo Ozuna .30 .10
❑ 688 Mike Redmond .30 .10
❑ 689 Scott Strickland .30 .10
❑ 690 Mo Vaughn .30 .10
❑ 691 Roberto Alomar .50 .20
❑ 692 Edgardo Alfonzo .30 .10
❑ 693 Shawn Estes .30 .10
❑ 694 Roger Cedeno .30 .10
❑ 695 Jeromy Burnitz .30 .10
❑ 696 Ray Lankford .30 .10
❑ 697 Mark Kotsay .30 .10
❑ 698 Kevin Jarvis .30 .10
❑ 699 Bobby Jones .30 .10
❑ 700 Sean Burroughs .30 .10
❑ 701 Ramon Vazquez .30 .10
❑ 702 Pat Burrell .30 .10
❑ 703 Marlon Byrd .30 .10
❑ 704 Brandon Duckworth .30 .10
❑ 705 Marlon Anderson .30 .10
❑ 706 Vicente Padilla .30 .10
❑ 707 Kip Wells .30 .10
❑ 708 Jason Kendall .30 .10
❑ 709 Pokey Reese .30 .10
❑ 710 Pat Meares .30 .10
❑ 711 Kris Benson .30 .10
❑ 712 Armando Rios .30 .10
❑ 713 Mike Williams .30 .10
❑ 714 Barry Larkin .50 .20
❑ 715 Adam Dunn .30 .10
❑ 716 Juan Encarnacion .30 .10
❑ 717 Scott Williamson .30 .10
❑ 718 Wilton Guerrero .30 .10
❑ 719 Chris Reitsma .30 .10
❑ 720 Larry Walker .30 .10
❑ 721 Denny Neagle .30 .10
❑ 722 Todd Zeile .30 .10
❑ 723 Jose Ortiz .30 .10
❑ 724 Jason Jennings .30 .10
❑ 725 Tony Eusebio .30 .10
❑ 726 Ichiro Suzuki YR .75 .30
❑ 727 Barry Bonds YR 1.00 .40
❑ 728 Randy Johnson YR .50 .20
❑ 729 Albert Pujols YR .75 .30
❑ 730 Roger Clemens YR .75 .30
❑ 731 Sammy Sosa YR .50 .20
❑ 732 Alex Rodriguez YR .75 .30
❑ 733 Chipper Jones YR .50 .20
❑ 734 Rickey Henderson YR .50 .20
❑ 735 Ichiro Suzuki YR .75 .30
❑ 736 Luis Gonzalez SH CL .30 .10
❑ 737 Derek Jeter SH CL 1.00 .40
❑ 738 Ichiro Suzuki SH CL .75 .30
❑ 739 Barry Bonds SH CL 1.00 .40
❑ 740 Curt Schilling SH CL .30 .10
❑ 741 Shawn Green SH CL .30 .10
❑ 742 Jason Giambi SH CL .30 .10
❑ 743 Roberto Alomar SH CL .30 .10
❑ 744 Larry Walker SH CL .30 .10
❑ 745 Mark McGwire SH CL 1.00 .40

2003 Upper Deck

Card		
❑ COMPLETE SERIES 1 (270)	50.00	20.00
❑ COMPLETE SERIES 2 (270)	50.00	20.00
❑ COMP.UPDATE SET (60)	20.00	10.00
❑ COMMON (31-500/531-600)	.30	.10
❑ COMMON (1-30/501-530)	1.00	.40
❑ COMMON RC (541-600)	.50	.20
❑ SR 1-30/501-530 ARE NOT SHORT PRINTS		
❑ CARD 19 DOES NOT EXIST		
❑ SCUTARO/NOMAR ARE BOTH CARD 96		
❑ 541-600 ISSUED IN 04 UD1 HOBBY BOXES		
❑ UPDATE SET EXCH 1:240 '04 UD1 RETAIL		
❑ UPDATE SET EXCH.DEADLINE 11/10/06		
❑ 1 John Lackey SR	1.00	.40
❑ 2 Alex Cintron SR	1.00	.40
❑ 3 Jose Leon SR	1.00	.40
❑ 4 Bobby Hill SR	1.00	.40
❑ 5 Brandon Larson SR	1.00	.40
❑ 6 Raul Gonzalez SR	1.00	.40
❑ 7 Ben Broussard SR	1.00	.40
❑ 8 Earl Snyder SR	1.00	.40
❑ 9 Ramon Santiago SR	1.00	.40
❑ 10 Jason Lane SR	1.00	.40
❑ 11 Keith Ginter SR	1.00	.40
❑ 12 Kirk Saarloos SR	1.00	.40
❑ 13 Juan Brito SR	1.00	.40
❑ 14 Runelvys Hernandez SR	1.00	.40
❑ 15 Shawn Sedlacek SR	1.00	.40
❑ 16 Jayson Durocher SR	1.00	.40
❑ 17 Kevin Frederick SR	1.00	.40
❑ 18 Zach Day SR	1.00	.40
❑ 19 Marcos Scutaro SR	1.00	.40
❑ 20 Marcus Thames SR	1.00	.40
❑ 21 Esteban German SR	1.00	.40
❑ 22 Brett Myers SR	1.00	.40
❑ 23 Oliver Perez SR	1.00	.40
❑ 24 Dennis Tankersley SR	1.00	.40
❑ 25 Julius Matos SR	1.00	.40
❑ 26 Jake Peavy SR	1.00	.40
❑ 27 Eric Cyr SR	1.00	.40
❑ 28 Mike Crudale SR	1.00	.40
❑ 29 Josh Pearce SR	1.00	.40
❑ 30 Carl Crawford SR	1.00	.40
❑ 31 Tim Salmon	.50	.20
❑ 32 Troy Glaus	.30	.10
❑ 33 Adam Kennedy	.30	.10
❑ 34 David Eckstein	.30	.10
❑ 35 Ben Molina	.30	.10
❑ 36 Jarrod Washburn	.30	.10
❑ 37 Ramon Ortiz	.30	.10
❑ 38 Eric Chavez	.30	.10
❑ 39 Miguel Tejada	.30	.10
❑ 40 Adam Piatt	.30	.10
❑ 41 Jermaine Dye	.30	.10
❑ 42 Olmedo Saenz	.30	.10
❑ 43 Tim Hudson	.30	.10
❑ 44 Barry Zito	.30	.10
❑ 45 Billy Koch	.30	.10
❑ 46 Shannon Stewart	.30	.10
❑ 47 Kelvim Escobar	.30	.10
❑ 48 Jose Cruz Jr.	.30	.10
❑ 49 Vernon Wells	.30	.10
❑ 50 Roy Halladay	.30	.10
❑ 51 Esteban Loaiza	.30	.10
❑ 52 Eric Hinske	.30	.10
❑ 53 Steve Cox	.30	.10
❑ 54 Brent Abernathy	.30	.10
❑ 55 Ben Grieve	.30	.10
❑ 56 Aubrey Huff	.30	.10
❑ 57 Jared Sandberg	.30	.10
❑ 58 Paul Wilson	.30	.10
❑ 59 Tanyon Sturtze	.30	.10
❑ 60 Jim Thome	.50	.20
❑ 61 Omar Vizquel	.50	.20
❑ 62 C.C. Sabathia	.30	.10
❑ 63 Chris Magruder	.30	.10
❑ 64 Ricky Gutierrez	.30	.10
❑ 65 Einar Diaz	.30	.10
❑ 66 Danys Baez	.30	.10
❑ 67 Ichiro Suzuki	1.50	.60
❑ 68 Ruben Sierra	.30	.10
❑ 69 Carlos Guillen	.30	.10
❑ 70 Mark McLemore	.30	.10
❑ 71 Dan Wilson	.30	.10
❑ 72 Jamie Moyer	.30	.10
❑ 73 Joel Pineiro	.30	.10
❑ 74 Edgar Martinez	.50	.20
❑ 75 Tony Batista	.30	.10
❑ 76 Jay Gibbons	.30	.10
❑ 77 Chris Singleton	.30	.10
❑ 78 Melvin Mora	.30	.10
❑ 79 Geronimo Gil	.30	.10
❑ 80 Rodrigo Lopez	.30	.10
❑ 81 Jorge Julio	.30	.10
❑ 82 Rafael Palmeiro	.50	.20
❑ 83 Juan Gonzalez	.30	.10
❑ 84 Mike Young	.50	.20
❑ 85 Hideki Irabu	.30	.10
❑ 86 Chan Ho Park	.30	.10
❑ 87 Kevin Mench	.30	.10
❑ 88 Doug Davis	.30	.10
❑ 89 Pedro Martinez	.50	.20
❑ 90 Shea Hillenbrand	.30	.10
❑ 91 Derek Lowe	.30	.10
❑ 92 Jason Varitek	.75	.30
❑ 93 Tony Clark	.30	.10
❑ 94 John Burkett	.30	.10
❑ 95 Frank Castillo	.30	.10
❑ 96 Nomar Garciaparra	1.25	.50
❑ 97 Rickey Henderson	.75	.30
❑ 98 Mike Sweeney	.30	.10
❑ 99 Carlos Febles	.30	.10
❑ 100 Mark Quinn	.30	.10
❑ 101 Raul Ibanez	.30	.10
❑ 102 A.J. Hinch	.30	.10
❑ 103 Paul Byrd	.30	.10
❑ 104 Chuck Knoblauch	.30	.10
❑ 105 Dmitri Young	.30	.10
❑ 106 Randall Simon	.30	.10
❑ 107 Brandon Inge	.30	.10
❑ 108 Damion Easley	.30	.10
❑ 109 Carlos Pena	.30	.10
❑ 110 George Lombard	.30	.10
❑ 111 Juan Acevedo	.30	.10
❑ 112 Torii Hunter	.30	.10
❑ 113 Doug Mientkiewicz	.30	.10
❑ 114 David Ortiz	.50	.20
❑ 115 Eric Milton	.30	.10
❑ 116 Eddie Guardado	.30	.10
❑ 117 Cristian Guzman	.30	.10
❑ 118 Corey Koskie	.30	.10
❑ 119 Magglio Ordonez	.30	.10
❑ 120 Mark Buehrle	.30	.10
❑ 121 Todd Ritchie	.30	.10
❑ 122 Jose Valentin	.30	.10
❑ 123 Paul Konerko	.30	.10
❑ 124 Carlos Lee	.30	.10
❑ 125 Jon Garland	.30	.10
❑ 126 Jason Giambi	.30	.10
❑ 127 Derek Jeter	2.00	.75
❑ 128 Roger Clemens	1.50	.60
❑ 129 Raul Mondesi	.30	.10
❑ 130 Jorge Posada	.50	.20
❑ 131 Rondell White	.30	.10
❑ 132 Robin Ventura	.30	.10
❑ 133 Mike Mussina	.50	.20
❑ 134 Jeff Bagwell	.50	.20
❑ 135 Craig Biggio	.50	.20
❑ 136 Morgan Ensberg	.30	.10
❑ 137 Richard Hidalgo	.30	.10
❑ 138 Brad Ausmus	.30	.10
❑ 139 Roy Oswalt	.30	.10
❑ 140 Carlos Hernandez	.30	.10
❑ 141 Shane Reynolds	.30	.10
❑ 142 Gary Sheffield	.30	.10
❑ 143 Andruw Jones	.50	.20
❑ 144 Tom Glavine	.50	.20
❑ 145 Rafael Furcal	.30	.10
❑ 146 Javy Lopez	.30	.10
❑ 147 Vinny Castilla	.30	.10
❑ 148 Marcus Giles	.30	.10
❑ 149 Kevin Millwood	.30	.10
❑ 150 Jason Marquis	.30	.10
❑ 151 Ruben Quevedo	.30	.10
❑ 152 Ben Sheets	.30	.10
❑ 153 Geoff Jenkins	.30	.10
❑ 154 Jose Hernandez	.30	.10
❑ 155 Glendon Rusch	.30	.10
❑ 156 Jeffrey Hammonds	.30	.10
❑ 157 Alex Sanchez	.30	.10
❑ 158 Jim Edmonds	.30	.10
❑ 159 Tino Martinez	.50	.20
❑ 160 Albert Pujols	1.50	.60
❑ 161 Eli Marrero	.30	.10
❑ 162 Woody Williams	.30	.10
❑ 163 Fernando Vina	.30	.10
❑ 164 Jason Isringhausen	.30	.10
❑ 165 Jason Simontacchi	.30	.10
❑ 166 Kerry Robinson	.30	.10
❑ 167 Sammy Sosa	.75	.30
❑ 168 Juan Cruz	.30	.10
❑ 169 Fred McGriff	.50	.20
❑ 170 Antonio Alfonseca	.30	.10
❑ 171 Jon Lieber	.30	.10
❑ 172 Mark Prior	.50	.20
❑ 173 Moises Alou	.30	.10
❑ 174 Matt Clement	.30	.10
❑ 175 Mark Bellhorn	.30	.10
❑ 176 Randy Johnson	.75	.30
❑ 177 Luis Gonzalez	.30	.10
❑ 178 Tony Womack	.30	.10
❑ 179 Mark Grace	.50	.20
❑ 180 Junior Spivey	.30	.10
❑ 181 Byung Hyun Kim	.30	.10
❑ 182 Danny Bautista	.30	.10
❑ 183 Brian Anderson	.30	.10
❑ 184 Shawn Green	.30	.10
❑ 185 Brian Jordan	.30	.10
❑ 186 Eric Karros	.30	.10
❑ 187 Andy Ashby	.30	.10
❑ 188 Cesar Izturis	.30	.10
❑ 189 Dave Roberts	.30	.10
❑ 190 Eric Gagne	.30	.10
❑ 191 Kazuhisa Ishii	.30	.10
❑ 192 Adrian Beltre	.30	.10
❑ 193 Vladimir Guerrero	.75	.30
❑ 194 Tony Armas Jr.	.30	.10
❑ 195 Bartolo Colon	.30	.10
❑ 196 Troy O'Leary	.30	.10
❑ 197 Tomo Ohka	.30	.10
❑ 198 Brad Wilkerson	.30	.10
❑ 199 Orlando Cabrera	.30	.10
❑ 200 Barry Bonds	2.00	.75
❑ 201 David Bell	.30	.10
❑ 202 Tsuyoshi Shinjo	.30	.10
❑ 203 Benito Santiago	.30	.10
❑ 204 Livan Hernandez	.30	.10
❑ 205 Jason Schmidt	.30	.10
❑ 206 Kirk Rueter	.30	.10
❑ 207 Ramon E. Martinez	.30	.10
❑ 208 Mike Lowell	.30	.10
❑ 209 Luis Castillo	.30	.10
❑ 210 Derrek Lee	.50	.20
❑ 211 Andy Fox	.30	.10
❑ 212 Eric Owens	.30	.10
❑ 213 Charles Johnson	.30	.10
❑ 214 Brad Penny	.30	.10
❑ 215 A.J. Burnett	.30	.10
❑ 216 Edgardo Alfonzo	.30	.10
❑ 217 Roberto Alomar	.50	.20
❑ 218 Rey Ordonez	.30	.10
❑ 219 Al Leiter	.30	.10
❑ 220 Roger Cedeno	.30	.10
❑ 221 Timo Perez	.30	.10
❑ 222 Jeromy Burnitz	.30	.10
❑ 223 Pedro Astacio	.30	.10
❑ 224 Joe McEwing	.30	.10
❑ 225 Ryan Klesko	.30	.10
❑ 226 Ramon Vazquez	.30	.10

❑ 227	Mark Kotsay	.30	.10
❑ 228	Bubba Trammell	.30	.10
❑ 229	Wiki Gonzalez	.30	.10
❑ 230	Trevor Hoffman	.30	.10
❑ 231	Ron Gant	.30	.10
❑ 232	Bob Abreu	.30	.10
❑ 233	Marlon Anderson	.30	.10
❑ 234	Jeremy Giambi	.30	.10
❑ 235	Jimmy Rollins	.30	.10
❑ 236	Mike Lieberthal	.30	.10
❑ 237	Vicente Padilla	.30	.10
❑ 238	Randy Wolf	.30	.10
❑ 239	Pokey Reese	.30	.10
❑ 240	Brian Giles	.30	.10
❑ 241	Jack Wilson	.30	.10
❑ 242	Mike Williams	.30	.10
❑ 243	Kip Wells	.30	.10
❑ 244	Rob Mackowiak	.30	.10
❑ 245	Craig Wilson	.30	.10
❑ 246	Adam Dunn	.30	.10
❑ 247	Sean Casey	.30	.10
❑ 248	Todd Walker	.30	.10
❑ 249	Corky Miller	.30	.10
❑ 250	Ryan Dempster	.30	.10
❑ 251	Reggie Taylor	.30	.10
❑ 252	Aaron Boone	.30	.10
❑ 253	Larry Walker	.30	.10
❑ 254	Jose Ortiz	.30	.10
❑ 255	Todd Zeile	.30	.10
❑ 256	Bobby Estalella	.30	.10
❑ 257	Juan Pierre	.30	.10
❑ 258	Terry Shumpert	.30	.10
❑ 259	Mike Hampton	.30	.10
❑ 260	Denny Stark	.30	.10
❑ 261	Shawn Green SH CL	.30	.10
❑ 262	Derek Lowe SH CL	.30	.10
❑ 263	Barry Bonds SH CL	1.00	.40
❑ 264	Mike Cameron SH CL	.30	.10
❑ 265	Luis Castillo SH CL	.30	.10
❑ 266	Vladimir Guerrero SH CL	.50	.20
❑ 267	Jason Giambi SH CL	.30	.10
❑ 268	Eric Gagne SH CL	.30	.10
❑ 269	Magglio Ordonez SH CL	.30	.10
❑ 270	Jim Thome SH CL	.30	.10
❑ 271	Garret Anderson	.30	.10
❑ 272	Troy Percival	.30	.10
❑ 273	Brad Fullmer	.30	.10
❑ 274	Scott Spiezio	.30	.10
❑ 275	Darin Erstad	.30	.10
❑ 276	Francisco Rodriguez	.30	.10
❑ 277	Kevin Appier	.30	.10
❑ 278	Shawn Wooten	.30	.10
❑ 279	Eric Owens	.30	.10
❑ 280	Scott Hatteberg	.30	.10
❑ 281	Terrence Long	.30	.10
❑ 282	Mark Mulder	.30	.10
❑ 283	Ramon Hernandez	.30	.10
❑ 284	Ted Lilly	.30	.10
❑ 285	Erubiel Durazo	.30	.10
❑ 286	Mark Ellis	.30	.10
❑ 287	Carlos Delgado	.30	.10
❑ 288	Orlando Hudson	.30	.10
❑ 289	Chris Woodward	.30	.10
❑ 290	Mark Hendrickson	.30	.10
❑ 291	Josh Phelps	.30	.10
❑ 292	Ken Huckaby	.30	.10
❑ 293	Justin Miller	.30	.10
❑ 294	Travis Lee	.30	.10
❑ 295	Jorge Sosa	.30	.10
❑ 296	Joe Kennedy	.30	.10
❑ 297	Carl Crawford	.30	.10
❑ 298	Toby Hall	.30	.10
❑ 299	Rey Ordonez	.30	.10
❑ 300	Brandon Phillips	.30	.10
❑ 301	Matt Lawton	.30	.10
❑ 302	Ellis Burks	.30	.10
❑ 303	Bill Selby	.30	.10
❑ 304	Travis Hafner	.30	.10
❑ 305	Milton Bradley	.30	.10
❑ 306	Karim Garcia	.30	.10
❑ 307	Cliff Lee	.30	.10
❑ 308	Jeff Cirillo	.30	.10
❑ 309	John Olerud	.30	.10
❑ 310	Kazuhiro Sasaki	.30	.10
❑ 311	Freddy Garcia	.30	.10
❑ 312	Bret Boone	.30	.10
❑ 313	Mike Cameron	.30	.10
❑ 314	Ben Davis	.30	.10
❑ 315	Randy Winn	.30	.10
❑ 316	Gary Matthews Jr.	.30	.10
❑ 317	Jeff Conine	.30	.10
❑ 318	Sidney Ponson	.30	.10
❑ 319	Jerry Hairston	.30	.10
❑ 320	David Segui	.30	.10
❑ 321	Scott Erickson	.30	.10
❑ 322	Marty Cordova	.30	.10
❑ 323	Hank Blalock	.30	.10
❑ 324	Herbert Perry	.30	.10
❑ 325	Alex Rodriguez	1.25	.50
❑ 326	Carl Everett	.30	.10
❑ 327	Einar Diaz	.30	.10
❑ 328	Ugueth Urbina	.30	.10
❑ 329	Mark Teixeira	.50	.20
❑ 330	Manny Ramirez	.50	.20
❑ 331	Johnny Damon	.50	.20
❑ 332	Trot Nixon	.30	.10
❑ 333	Tim Wakefield	.30	.10
❑ 334	Casey Fossum	.30	.10
❑ 335	Todd Walker	.30	.10
❑ 336	Jeremy Giambi	.30	.10
❑ 337	Bill Mueller	.30	.10
❑ 338	Ramiro Mendoza	.30	.10
❑ 339	Carlos Beltran	.30	.10
❑ 340	Jason Grimsley	.30	.10
❑ 341	Brent Mayne	.30	.10
❑ 342	Angel Berroa	.30	.10
❑ 343	Albie Lopez	.30	.10
❑ 344	Michael Tucker	.30	.10
❑ 345	Bobby Higginson	.30	.10
❑ 346	Shane Halter	.30	.10
❑ 347	Jeremy Bonderman RC	4.00	1.50
❑ 348	Eric Munson	.30	.10
❑ 349	Andy Van Hekken	.30	.10
❑ 350	Matt Anderson	.30	.10
❑ 351	Jacque Jones	.30	.10
❑ 352	A.J. Pierzynski	.30	.10
❑ 353	Joe Mays	.30	.10
❑ 354	Brad Radke	.30	.10
❑ 355	Dustan Mohr	.30	.10
❑ 356	Bobby Kielty	.30	.10
❑ 357	Michael Cuddyer	.30	.10
❑ 358	Luis Rivas	.30	.10
❑ 359	Frank Thomas	.75	.30
❑ 360	Joe Borchard	.30	.10
❑ 361	D'Angelo Jimenez	.30	.10
❑ 362	Bartolo Colon	.30	.10
❑ 363	Joe Crede	.30	.10
❑ 364	Miguel Olivo	.30	.10
❑ 365	Billy Koch	.30	.10
❑ 366	Bernie Williams	.50	.20
❑ 367	Nick Johnson	.30	.10
❑ 368	Andy Pettitte	.50	.20
❑ 369	Mariano Rivera	.75	.30
❑ 370	Alfonso Soriano	.30	.10
❑ 371	David Wells	.30	.10
❑ 372	Drew Henson	.30	.10
❑ 373	Juan Rivera	.30	.10
❑ 374	Steve Karsay	.30	.10
❑ 375	Jeff Kent	.30	.10
❑ 376	Lance Berkman	.30	.10
❑ 377	Octavio Dotel	.30	.10
❑ 378	Julio Lugo	.30	.10
❑ 379	Jason Lane	.30	.10
❑ 380	Wade Miller	.30	.10
❑ 381	Billy Wagner	.30	.10
❑ 382	Brad Ausmus	.30	.10
❑ 383	Mike Hampton	.30	.10
❑ 384	Chipper Jones	.75	.30
❑ 385	John Smoltz	.50	.20
❑ 386	Greg Maddux	1.25	.50
❑ 387	Javy Lopez	.30	.10
❑ 388	Robert Fick	.30	.10
❑ 389	Mark DeRosa	.30	.10
❑ 390	Russ Ortiz	.30	.10
❑ 391	Julio Franco	.30	.10
❑ 392	Richie Sexson	.30	.10
❑ 393	Eric Young	.30	.10
❑ 394	Robert Machado	.30	.10
❑ 395	Mike DeJean	.30	.10
❑ 396	Todd Ritchie	.30	.10
❑ 397	Royce Clayton	.30	.10
❑ 398	Nick Neugebauer	.30	.10
❑ 399	J.D. Drew	.30	.10
❑ 400	Edgar Renteria	.30	.10
❑ 401	Scott Rolen	.50	.20
❑ 402	Matt Morris	.30	.10
❑ 403	Garrett Stephenson	.30	.10
❑ 404	Eduardo Perez	.30	.10
❑ 405	Mike Matheny	.30	.10
❑ 406	Miguel Cairo	.30	.10
❑ 407	Brett Tomko	.30	.10
❑ 408	Bobby Hill	.30	.10
❑ 409	Troy O'Leary	.30	.10
❑ 410	Corey Patterson	.30	.10
❑ 411	Kerry Wood	.30	.10
❑ 412	Eric Karros	.30	.10
❑ 413	Hee Seop Choi	.30	.10
❑ 414	Alex Gonzalez	.30	.10
❑ 415	Matt Clement	.30	.10
❑ 416	Mark Grudzielanek	.30	.10
❑ 417	Curt Schilling	.30	.10
❑ 418	Steve Finley	.30	.10
❑ 419	Craig Counsell	.30	.10
❑ 420	Matt Williams	.30	.10
❑ 421	Quinton McCracken	.30	.10
❑ 422	Chad Moeller	.30	.10
❑ 423	Lyle Overbay	.30	.10
❑ 424	Miguel Batista	.30	.10
❑ 425	Paul Lo Duca	.30	.10
❑ 426	Kevin Brown	.30	.10
❑ 427	Hideo Nomo	.75	.30
❑ 428	Fred McGriff	.50	.20
❑ 429	Joe Thurston	.30	.10
❑ 430	Odalis Perez	.30	.10
❑ 431	Darren Dreifort	.30	.10
❑ 432	Todd Hundley	.30	.10
❑ 433	Dave Roberts	.30	.10
❑ 434	Jose Vidro	.30	.10
❑ 435	Javier Vazquez	.30	.10
❑ 436	Michael Barrett	.30	.10
❑ 437	Fernando Tatis	.30	.10
❑ 438	Peter Bergeron	.30	.10
❑ 439	Endy Chavez	.30	.10
❑ 440	Orlando Hernandez	.30	.10
❑ 441	Marvin Benard	.30	.10
❑ 442	Rich Aurilia	.30	.10
❑ 443	Pedro Feliz	.30	.10
❑ 444	Robb Nen	.30	.10
❑ 445	Ray Durham	.30	.10
❑ 446	Marquis Grissom	.30	.10
❑ 447	Damian Moss	.30	.10
❑ 448	Edgardo Alfonzo	.30	.10
❑ 449	Juan Pierre	.30	.10
❑ 450	Braden Looper	.30	.10
❑ 451	Alex Gonzalez	.30	.10
❑ 452	Justin Wayne	.30	.10
❑ 453	Josh Beckett	.30	.10
❑ 454	Juan Encarnacion	.30	.10
❑ 455	Ivan Rodriguez	.50	.20
❑ 456	Todd Hollandsworth	.30	.10
❑ 457	Cliff Floyd	.30	.10
❑ 458	Rey Sanchez	.30	.10
❑ 459	Mike Piazza	1.25	.50
❑ 460	Mo Vaughn	.30	.10
❑ 461	Armando Benitez	.30	.10
❑ 462	Tsuyoshi Shinjo	.30	.10
❑ 463	Tom Glavine	.50	.20
❑ 464	David Cone	.30	.10
❑ 465	Phil Nevin	.30	.10
❑ 466	Sean Burroughs	.30	.10
❑ 467	Jake Peavy	.30	.10
❑ 468	Brian Lawrence	.30	.10
❑ 469	Mark Loretta	.30	.10
❑ 470	Dennis Tankersley	.30	.10
❑ 471	Jesse Orosco	.30	.10
❑ 472	Jim Thome	.50	.20
❑ 473	Kevin Millwood	.30	.10
❑ 474	David Bell	.30	.10
❑ 475	Pat Burrell	.30	.10
❑ 476	Brandon Duckworth	.30	.10
❑ 477	Jose Mesa	.30	.10
❑ 478	Marlon Byrd	.30	.10
❑ 479	Reggie Sanders	.30	.10
❑ 480	Jason Kendall	.30	.10
❑ 481	Aramis Ramirez	.30	.10
❑ 482	Kris Benson	.30	.10
❑ 483	Matt Stairs	.30	.10
❑ 484	Kevin Young	.30	.10

❑ 485 Kenny Lofton .30 .10
❑ 486 Austin Kearns .30 .10
❑ 487 Barry Larkin .50 .20
❑ 488 Jason LaRue .30 .10
❑ 489 Ken Griffey Jr. 1.25 .50
❑ 490 Danny Graves .30 .10
❑ 491 Russell Branyan .30 .10
❑ 492 Reggie Taylor .30 .10
❑ 493 Jimmy Haynes .30 .10
❑ 494 Charles Johnson .30 .10
❑ 495 Todd Helton .50 .20
❑ 496 Juan Uribe .30 .10
❑ 497 Preston Wilson .30 .10
❑ 498 Chris Stynes .30 .10
❑ 499 Jason Jennings .30 .10
❑ 500 Jay Payton .30 .10
❑ 501 Hideki Matsui SR RC 5.00 2.00
❑ 502 Jose Contreras SR RC 1.50 .60
❑ 503 Brandon Webb SR RC 3.00 1.25
❑ 504 Robby Hammock SR RC 1.00 .40
❑ 505 Matt Kata SR RC 1.00 .40
❑ 506 Tim Olson SR RC 1.00 .40
❑ 507 Michael Hessman SR RC 1.00 .40
❑ 508 Jon Leicester SR RC 1.00 .40
❑ 509 Todd Wellemeyer SR RC 1.00 .40
❑ 510 David Sanders SR RC 1.00 .40
❑ 511 Josh Stewart SR RC 1.00 .40
❑ 512 Luis Ayala SR RC 1.00 .40
❑ 513 Clint Barmes SR RC 1.25 .50
❑ 514 Josh Willingham SR RC 2.00 .75
❑ 515 Alejandro Machado SR RC 1.00 .40
❑ 516 Felix Sanchez SR RC 1.00 .40
❑ 517 Willie Eyre SR RC 1.00 .40
❑ 518 Brent Hoard SR RC 1.00 .40
❑ 519 Lew Ford SR RC 1.50 .60
❑ 520 Terrmel Sledge SR RC 1.00 .40
❑ 521 Jeremy Griffiths SR RC 1.00 .40
❑ 522 Phil Seibel SR RC 1.00 .40
❑ 523 Craig Brazell SR RC 1.00 .40
❑ 524 Prentice Redman SR RC 1.00 .40
❑ 525 Jeff Duncan SR RC 1.00 .40
❑ 526 Shane Bazzell SR RC 1.00 .40
❑ 527 Bernie Castro SR RC 1.00 .40
❑ 528 Rett Johnson SR RC 1.00 .40
❑ 529 Bobby Madritsch SR RC 1.00 .40
❑ 530 Rocco Baldelli SR 1.00 .40
❑ 531 Alex Rodriguez SH CL .75 .30
❑ 532 Eric Chavez SH CL .30 .10
❑ 533 Miguel Tejada SH CL .30 .10
❑ 534 Ichiro Suzuki SH CL .75 .30
❑ 535 Sammy Sosa SH CL .50 .20
❑ 536 Barry Zito SH CL .30 .10
❑ 537 Darin Erstad SH CL .30 .10
❑ 538 Alfonso Soriano SH CL .30 .10
❑ 539 Troy Glaus SH CL .30 .10
❑ 540 Nomar Garciaparra SH CL .75 .30
❑ 541 Bo Hart RC .50 .20
❑ 542 Dan Haren RC .75 .30
❑ 543 Ryan Wagner RC .50 .20
❑ 544 Rich Harden .50 .20
❑ 545 Dontrelle Willis .75 .30
❑ 546 Jerome Williams .30 .10
❑ 547 Bobby Crosby .30 .10
❑ 548 Greg Jones RC .50 .20
❑ 549 Todd Linden .30 .10
❑ 550 Byung-Hyun Kim .30 .10
❑ 551 Rickie Weeks RC 3.00 1.25
❑ 552 Jason Roach RC .50 .20
❑ 553 Oscar Villarreal RC .50 .20
❑ 554 Justin Duchscherer .30 .10
❑ 555 Chris Capuano RC 1.50 .60
❑ 556 Josh Hall RC .50 .20
❑ 557 Luis Matos .30 .10
❑ 558 Miguel Ojeda RC .50 .20
❑ 559 Kevin Ohme RC .50 .20
❑ 560 Julio Manon RC .50 .20
❑ 561 Kevin Correia RC .50 .20
❑ 562 Delmon Young RC 5.00 2.00
❑ 563 Aaron Boone .30 .10
❑ 564 Aaron Looper RC .50 .20
❑ 565 Mike Neu RC .50 .20
❑ 566 Aquilino Lopez RC .50 .20
❑ 567 Jhonny Peralta .75 .30
❑ 568 Duaner Sanchez .30 .10
❑ 569 Stephen Randolph RC .50 .20
❑ 570 Nate Bland RC .50 .20
❑ 571 Chin-Hui Tsao .30 .10
❑ 572 Michel Hernandez RC .50 .20
❑ 573 Rocco Baldelli .30 .10
❑ 574 Robb Quinlan .30 .10
❑ 575 Aaron Heilman .30 .10
❑ 576 Jae Weong Seo .30 .10
❑ 577 Joe Borowski .30 .10
❑ 578 Chris Bootcheck .30 .10
❑ 579 Michael Ryan RC .50 .20
❑ 580 Mark Malaska RC .50 .20
❑ 581 Jose Guillen .30 .10
❑ 582 Josh Towers .30 .10
❑ 583 Tom Gregorio RC .50 .20
❑ 584 Edwin Jackson RC .50 .20
❑ 585 Jason Anderson .30 .10
❑ 586 Jose Reyes .30 .10
❑ 587 Miguel Cabrera .75 .30
❑ 588 Nate Bump .30 .10
❑ 589 Jeromy Burnitz .30 .10
❑ 590 David Ross .30 .10
❑ 591 Chase Utley .75 .30
❑ 592 Brandon Webb 1.50 .60
❑ 593 Masao Kida .30 .10
❑ 594 Jimmy Journell .30 .10
❑ 595 Eric Young .30 .10
❑ 596 Tony Womack .30 .10
❑ 597 Amaury Telemaco .30 .10
❑ 598 Rickey Henderson .75 .30
❑ 599 Esteban Loaiza .30 .10
❑ 600 Sidney Ponson .30 .10
❑ NNO Update Set Exchange Card

2004 Upper Deck

❑ COMPLETE SERIES 1 (270) 50.00 20.00
❑ COMPLETE SERIES 2 (270) 50.00 20.00
❑ COMP.UPDATE SET (50) 15.00 7.50
❑ COMMON (31-480/541-565) .30 .10
❑ COMMON (1-30/481-540) 1.00 .40
❑ COMMON CARD (566-590) .50 .20
❑ 541-590 ONE SET PER '05 UD1 HOBBY BOX
❑ UPDATE SET EXCH 1:480 '05 UD1 RETAIL
❑ UPDATE SET EXCH.DEADLINE TBD
❑ 1 Dontrelle Willis SR 1.50 .60
❑ 2 Edgar Gonzalez SR 1.00 .40
❑ 3 Jose Reyes SR 1.00 .40
❑ 4 Jae Weong Seo SR 1.00 .40
❑ 5 Miguel Cabrera SR 1.50 .60
❑ 6 Jesse Foppert SR 1.00 .40
❑ 7 Mike Neu SR 1.00 .40
❑ 8 Michael Nakamura SR 1.00 .40
❑ 9 Luis Ayala SR 1.00 .40
❑ 10 Jared Sandberg SR 1.00 .40
❑ 11 Jhonny Peralta SR 1.00 .40
❑ 12 Wil Ledezma SR 1.00 .40
❑ 13 Jason Roach SR 1.00 .40
❑ 14 Kirk Saarloos SR 1.00 .40
❑ 15 Cliff Lee SR 1.00 .40
❑ 16 Bobby Hill SR 1.00 .40
❑ 17 Lyle Overbay SR 1.00 .40
❑ 18 Josh Hall SR 1.00 .40
❑ 19 Joe Thurston SR 1.00 .40
❑ 20 Matt Kata SR 1.00 .40
❑ 21 Jeremy Bonderman SR 1.00 .40
❑ 22 Julio Manon SR 1.00 .40
❑ 23 Rodrigo Rosario SR 1.00 .40
❑ 24 Robby Hammock SR 1.00 .40
❑ 25 David Sanders SR 1.00 .40
❑ 26 Miguel Ojeda SR 1.00 .40
❑ 27 Mark Teixeira SR 1.50 .60
❑ 28 Franklyn German SR 1.00 .40
❑ 29 Ken Harvey SR 1.00 .40
❑ 30 Xavier Nady SR 1.00 .40
❑ 31 Tim Salmon .50 .20
❑ 32 Troy Glaus .30 .10
❑ 33 Adam Kennedy .30 .10
❑ 34 David Eckstein .30 .10
❑ 35 Ben Molina .30 .10
❑ 36 Jarrod Washburn .30 .10
❑ 37 Ramon Ortiz .30 .10
❑ 38 Eric Chavez .30 .10
❑ 39 Miguel Tejada .30 .10
❑ 40 Chris Singleton .30 .10
❑ 41 Jermaine Dye .30 .10
❑ 42 John Halama .30 .10
❑ 43 Tim Hudson .30 .10
❑ 44 Barry Zito .30 .10
❑ 45 Ted Lilly .30 .10
❑ 46 Bobby Kielty .30 .10
❑ 47 Kelvim Escobar .30 .10
❑ 48 Josh Phelps .30 .10
❑ 49 Vernon Wells .30 .10
❑ 50 Roy Halladay .30 .10
❑ 51 Orlando Hudson .30 .10
❑ 52 Eric Hinske .30 .10
❑ 53 Brandon Backe .30 .10
❑ 54 Dewon Brazelton .30 .10
❑ 55 Ben Grieve .30 .10
❑ 56 Aubrey Huff .30 .10
❑ 57 Toby Hall .30 .10
❑ 58 Rocco Baldelli .30 .10
❑ 59 Al Martin .30 .10
❑ 60 Brandon Phillips .30 .10
❑ 61 Omar Vizquel .50 .20
❑ 62 C.C. Sabathia .30 .10
❑ 63 Milton Bradley .30 .10
❑ 64 Ricky Gutierrez .30 .10
❑ 65 Matt Lawton .30 .10
❑ 66 Danys Baez .30 .10
❑ 67 Ichiro Suzuki 1.50 .60
❑ 68 Randy Winn .30 .10
❑ 69 Carlos Guillen .30 .10
❑ 70 Mark McLemore .30 .10
❑ 71 Dan Wilson .30 .10
❑ 72 Jamie Moyer .30 .10
❑ 73 Joel Pineiro .30 .10
❑ 74 Edgar Martinez .50 .20
❑ 75 Tony Batista .30 .10
❑ 76 Jay Gibbons .30 .10
❑ 77 Jeff Conine .30 .10
❑ 78 Melvin Mora .30 .10
❑ 79 Geronimo Gil .30 .10
❑ 80 Rodrigo Lopez .30 .10
❑ 81 Jorge Julio .30 .10
❑ 82 Rafael Palmeiro .50 .20
❑ 83 Juan Gonzalez .30 .10
❑ 84 Mike Young .30 .10
❑ 85 Alex Rodriguez 1.25 .50
❑ 86 Einar Diaz .30 .10
❑ 87 Kevin Mench .30 .10
❑ 88 Hank Blalock .30 .10
❑ 89 Pedro Martinez .50 .20
❑ 90 Byung-Hyun Kim .30 .10
❑ 91 Derek Lowe .30 .10
❑ 92 Jason Varitek .75 .30
❑ 93 Manny Ramirez .50 .20
❑ 94 John Burkett .30 .10
❑ 95 Todd Walker .30 .10
❑ 96 Nomar Garciaparra 1.25 .50
❑ 97 Trot Nixon .30 .10
❑ 98 Mike Sweeney .30 .10
❑ 99 Carlos Febles .30 .10
❑ 100 Mike MacDougal .30 .10
❑ 101 Raul Ibanez .30 .10
❑ 102 Jason Grimsley .30 .10
❑ 103 Chris George .30 .10
❑ 104 Brent Mayne .30 .10
❑ 105 Dmitri Young .30 .10
❑ 106 Eric Munson .30 .10
❑ 107 A.J. Hinch .30 .10
❑ 108 Andres Torres .30 .10
❑ 109 Bobby Higginson .30 .10
❑ 110 Shane Halter .30 .10
❑ 111 Matt Walbeck .30 .10
❑ 112 Torii Hunter .30 .10

❑	113	Doug Mientkiewicz	.30	.10
❑	114	Lew Ford	.30	.10
❑	115	Eric Milton	.30	.10
❑	116	Eddie Guardado	.30	.10
❑	117	Cristian Guzman	.30	.10
❑	118	Corey Koskie	.30	.10
❑	119	Magglio Ordonez	.30	.10
❑	120	Mark Buehrle	.30	.10
❑	121	Billy Koch	.30	.10
❑	122	Jose Valentin	.30	.10
❑	123	Paul Konerko	.30	.10
❑	124	Carlos Lee	.30	.10
❑	125	Jon Garland	.30	.10
❑	126	Jason Giambi	.30	.10
❑	127	Derek Jeter	1.50	.60
❑	128	Roger Clemens	1.50	.60
❑	129	Andy Pettitte	.50	.20
❑	130	Jorge Posada	.50	.20
❑	131	David Wells	.30	.10
❑	132	Hideki Matsui	1.25	.50
❑	133	Mike Mussina	.50	.20
❑	134	Jeff Bagwell	.50	.20
❑	135	Craig Biggio	.50	.20
❑	136	Morgan Ensberg	.30	.10
❑	137	Richard Hidalgo	.30	.10
❑	138	Brad Ausmus	.30	.10
❑	139	Roy Oswalt	.30	.10
❑	140	Billy Wagner	.30	.10
❑	141	Octavio Dotel	.30	.10
❑	142	Gary Sheffield	.30	.10
❑	143	Andruw Jones	.50	.20
❑	144	John Smoltz	.50	.20
❑	145	Rafael Furcal	.30	.10
❑	146	Javy Lopez	.30	.10
❑	147	Shane Reynolds	.30	.10
❑	148	Horacio Ramirez	.30	.10
❑	149	Mike Hampton	.30	.10
❑	150	Jung Bong	.30	.10
❑	151	Ruben Quevedo	.30	.10
❑	152	Ben Sheets	.30	.10
❑	153	Geoff Jenkins	.30	.10
❑	154	Royce Clayton	.30	.10
❑	155	Glendon Rusch	.30	.10
❑	156	John Vander Wal	.30	.10
❑	157	Scott Podsednik	.30	.10
❑	158	Jim Edmonds	.30	.10
❑	159	Tino Martinez	.50	.20
❑	160	Albert Pujols	1.50	.60
❑	161	Matt Morris	.30	.10
❑	162	Woody Williams	.30	.10
❑	163	Edgar Renteria	.30	.10
❑	164	Jason Isringhausen	.30	.10
❑	165	Jason Simontacchi	.30	.10
❑	166	Kerry Robinson	.30	.10
❑	167	Sammy Sosa	.75	.30
❑	168	Joe Borowski	.30	.10
❑	169	Tony Womack	.30	.10
❑	170	Antonio Alfonseca	.30	.10
❑	171	Corey Patterson	.30	.10
❑	172	Mark Prior	.50	.20
❑	173	Moises Alou	.30	.10
❑	174	Matt Clement	.30	.10
❑	175	Randall Simon	.30	.10
❑	176	Randy Johnson	.75	.30
❑	177	Luis Gonzalez	.30	.10
❑	178	Craig Counsell	.30	.10
❑	179	Miguel Batista	.30	.10
❑	180	Steve Finley	.30	.10
❑	181	Brandon Webb	.30	.10
❑	182	Danny Bautista	.30	.10
❑	183	Oscar Villarreal	.30	.10
❑	184	Shawn Green	.30	.10
❑	185	Brian Jordan	.30	.10
❑	186	Fred McGriff	.50	.20
❑	187	Andy Ashby	.30	.10
❑	188	Rickey Henderson	.75	.30
❑	189	Dave Roberts	.30	.10
❑	190	Eric Gagne	.30	.10
❑	191	Kazuhisa Ishii	.30	.10
❑	192	Adrian Beltre	.30	.10
❑	193	Vladimir Guerrero	.75	.30
❑	194	Livan Hernandez	.30	.10
❑	195	Ron Calloway	.30	.10
❑	196	Sun Woo Kim	.30	.10
❑	197	Wil Cordero	.30	.10
❑	198	Brad Wilkerson	.30	.10
❑	199	Orlando Cabrera	.30	.10
❑	200	Barry Bonds	2.00	.75
❑	201	Ray Durham	.30	.10
❑	202	Andres Galarraga	.30	.10
❑	203	Benito Santiago	.30	.10
❑	204	Jose Cruz Jr.	.30	.10
❑	205	Jason Schmidt	.30	.10
❑	206	Kirk Rueter	.30	.10
❑	207	Felix Rodriguez	.30	.10
❑	208	Mike Lowell	.30	.10
❑	209	Luis Castillo	.30	.10
❑	210	Derrek Lee	.50	.20
❑	211	Andy Fox	.30	.10
❑	212	Tommy Phelps	.30	.10
❑	213	Todd Hollandsworth	.30	.10
❑	214	Brad Penny	.30	.10
❑	215	Juan Pierre	.30	.10
❑	216	Mike Piazza	1.25	.50
❑	217	Jae Weong Seo	.30	.10
❑	218	Ty Wigginton	.30	.10
❑	219	Al Leiter	.30	.10
❑	220	Roger Cedeno	.30	.10
❑	221	Timo Perez	.30	.10
❑	222	Aaron Heilman	.30	.10
❑	223	Pedro Astacio	.30	.10
❑	224	Joe McEwing	.30	.10
❑	225	Ryan Klesko	.30	.10
❑	226	Brian Giles	.30	.10
❑	227	Mark Kotsay	.30	.10
❑	228	Brian Lawrence	.30	.10
❑	229	Rod Beck	.30	.10
❑	230	Trevor Hoffman	.30	.10
❑	231	Sean Burroughs	.30	.10
❑	232	Bob Abreu	.30	.10
❑	233	Jim Thome	.50	.20
❑	234	David Bell	.30	.10
❑	235	Jimmy Rollins	.30	.10
❑	236	Mike Lieberthal	.30	.10
❑	237	Vicente Padilla	.30	.10
❑	238	Randy Wolf	.30	.10
❑	239	Reggie Sanders	.30	.10
❑	240	Jason Kendall	.30	.10
❑	241	Jack Wilson	.30	.10
❑	242	Jose Hernandez	.30	.10
❑	243	Kip Wells	.30	.10
❑	244	Carlos Rivera	.30	.10
❑	245	Craig Wilson	.30	.10
❑	246	Adam Dunn	.30	.10
❑	247	Sean Casey	.30	.10
❑	248	Danny Graves	.30	.10
❑	249	Ryan Dempster	.30	.10
❑	250	Barry Larkin	.50	.20
❑	251	Reggie Taylor	.30	.10
❑	252	Wily Mo Pena	.30	.10
❑	253	Larry Walker	.30	.10
❑	254	Mark Sweeney	.30	.10
❑	255	Preston Wilson	.30	.10
❑	256	Jason Jennings	.30	.10
❑	257	Charles Johnson	.30	.10
❑	258	Jay Payton	.30	.10
❑	259	Chris Stynes	.30	.10
❑	260	Juan Uribe	.30	.10
❑	261	Hideki Matsui SH CL	.75	.30
❑	262	Barry Bonds SH CL	1.00	.40
❑	263	Dontrelle Willis SH CL	.30	.10
❑	264	Kevin Millwood SH CL	.30	.10
❑	265	Billy Wagner SH CL	.30	.10
❑	266	Rocco Baldelli SH CL	.30	.10
❑	267	Roger Clemens SH CL	.75	.30
❑	268	Rafael Palmeiro SH CL	.30	.10
❑	269	Miguel Cabrera SH CL	.50	.20
❑	270	Jose Contreras SH CL	.30	.10
❑	271	Aaron Sele	.30	.10
❑	272	Bartolo Colon	.30	.10
❑	273	Darin Erstad	.30	.10
❑	274	Francisco Rodriguez	.30	.10
❑	275	Garret Anderson	.30	.10
❑	276	Jose Guillen	.30	.10
❑	277	Troy Percival	.30	.10
❑	278	Alex Cintron	.30	.10
❑	279	Casey Fossum	.30	.10
❑	280	Elmer Dessens	.30	.10
❑	281	Jose Valverde	.30	.10
❑	282	Matt Mantei	.30	.10
❑	283	Richie Sexson	.30	.10
❑	284	Roberto Alomar	.50	.20
❑	285	Shea Hillenbrand	.30	.10
❑	286	Chipper Jones	.75	.30
❑	287	Greg Maddux	1.25	.50
❑	288	J.D. Drew	.30	.10
❑	289	Marcus Giles	.30	.10
❑	290	Mike Hessman	.30	.10
❑	291	John Thomson	.30	.10
❑	292	Russ Ortiz	.30	.10
❑	293	Adam Loewen	.30	.10
❑	294	Jack Cust	.30	.10
❑	295	Jerry Hairston Jr.	.30	.10
❑	296	Kurt Ainsworth	.30	.10
❑	297	Luis Matos	.30	.10
❑	298	Marty Cordova	.30	.10
❑	299	Sidney Ponson	.30	.10
❑	300	Bill Mueller	.30	.10
❑	301	Curt Schilling	.30	.10
❑	302	David Ortiz	.50	.20
❑	303	Johnny Damon	.50	.20
❑	304	Keith Foulke Sox	.30	.10
❑	305	Pokey Reese	.30	.10
❑	306	Scott Williamson	.30	.10
❑	307	Tim Wakefield	.30	.10
❑	308	Alex S. Gonzalez	.30	.10
❑	309	Aramis Ramirez	.30	.10
❑	310	Carlos Zambrano	.30	.10
❑	311	Juan Cruz	.30	.10
❑	312	Kerry Wood	.30	.10
❑	313	Kyle Farnsworth	.30	.10
❑	314	Aaron Rowand	.30	.10
❑	315	Esteban Loaiza	.30	.10
❑	316	Frank Thomas	.75	.30
❑	317	Joe Borchard	.30	.10
❑	318	Joe Crede	.30	.10
❑	319	Miguel Olivo	.30	.10
❑	320	Willie Harris	.30	.10
❑	321	Aaron Harang	.30	.10
❑	322	Austin Kearns	.30	.10
❑	323	Brandon Claussen	.30	.10
❑	324	Brandon Larson	.30	.10
❑	325	Ryan Freel	.30	.10
❑	326	Ken Griffey Jr.	1.25	.50
❑	327	Ryan Wagner	.30	.10
❑	328	Alex Escobar	.30	.10
❑	329	Coco Crisp	.30	.10
❑	330	David Riske	.30	.10
❑	331	Jody Gerut	.30	.10
❑	332	Josh Bard	.30	.10
❑	333	Travis Hafner	.30	.10
❑	334	Chin-Hui Tsao	.30	.10
❑	335	Denny Stark	.30	.10
❑	336	Jeromy Burnitz	.30	.10
❑	337	Shawn Chacon	.30	.10
❑	338	Todd Helton	.50	.20
❑	339	Vinny Castilla	.30	.10
❑	340	Alex Sanchez	.30	.10
❑	341	Carlos Pena	.30	.10
❑	342	Fernando Vina	.30	.10
❑	343	Jason Johnson	.30	.10
❑	344	Matt Anderson	.30	.10
❑	345	Mike Maroth	.30	.10
❑	346	Rondell White	.30	.10
❑	347	A.J. Burnett	.30	.10
❑	348	Alex Gonzalez	.30	.10
❑	349	Armando Benitez	.30	.10
❑	350	Carl Pavano	.30	.10
❑	351	Hee Seop Choi	.30	.10
❑	352	Ivan Rodriguez	.50	.20
❑	353	Josh Beckett	.30	.10
❑	354	Josh Willingham	.30	.10
❑	355	Adam Everett	.30	.10
❑	356	Brandon Duckworth	.30	.10
❑	357	Jason Lane	.30	.10
❑	358	Jeff Kent	.30	.10
❑	359	Jeriome Robertson	.30	.10
❑	360	Lance Berkman	.30	.10
❑	361	Wade Miller	.30	.10
❑	362	Aaron Guiel	.30	.10
❑	363	Angel Berroa	.30	.10
❑	364	Carlos Beltran	.30	.10
❑	365	David DeJesus	.30	.10
❑	366	Desi Relaford	.30	.10
❑	367	Joe Randa	.30	.10
❑	368	Runelvys Hernandez	.30	.10
❑	369	Edwin Jackson	.30	.10
❑	370	Hideo Nomo	.75	.30

❑ 371 Jeff Weaver .30 .10
❑ 372 Juan Encarnacion .30 .10
❑ 373 Odalis Perez .30 .10
❑ 374 Paul Lo Duca .30 .10
❑ 375 Robin Ventura .30 .10
❑ 376 Bill Hall .30 .10
❑ 377 Chad Moeller .30 .10
❑ 378 Chris Capuano .30 .10
❑ 379 Junior Spivey .30 .10
❑ 380 Rickie Weeks .30 .10
❑ 381 Wes Helms .30 .10
❑ 382 Brad Radke .30 .10
❑ 383 Jacque Jones .30 .10
❑ 384 Joe Mays .30 .10
❑ 385 Joe Nathan .30 .10
❑ 386 Johan Santana .75 .30
❑ 387 Nick Punto .30 .10
❑ 388 Shannon Stewart .30 .10
❑ 389 Carl Everett .30 .10
❑ 390 Claudio Vargas .30 .10
❑ 391 Jose Vidro .30 .10
❑ 392 Nick Johnson .30 .10
❑ 393 Rocky Biddle .30 .10
❑ 394 Tony Armas Jr. .30 .10
❑ 395 Braden Looper .30 .10
❑ 396 Cliff Floyd .30 .10
❑ 397 Jason Phillips .30 .10
❑ 398 Mike Cameron .30 .10
❑ 399 Tom Glavine .50 .20
❑ 400 Kenny Lofton .30 .10
❑ 401 Alfonso Soriano .30 .10
❑ 402 Bernie Williams .50 .20
❑ 403 Javier Vazquez .30 .10
❑ 404 Jon Lieber .30 .10
❑ 405 Jose Contreras .30 .10
❑ 406 Kevin Brown .30 .10
❑ 407 Mariano Rivera .75 .30
❑ 408 Arthur Rhodes .30 .10
❑ 409 Eric Byrnes .30 .10
❑ 410 Erubiel Durazo .30 .10
❑ 411 Graham Koonce .30 .10
❑ 412 Marco Scutaro .30 .10
❑ 413 Mark Mulder .30 .10
❑ 414 Mark Redman .30 .10
❑ 415 Rich Harden .30 .10
❑ 416 Brett Myers .30 .10
❑ 417 Chase Utley .50 .20
❑ 418 Kevin Millwood .30 .10
❑ 419 Marlon Byrd .30 .10
❑ 420 Pat Burrell .30 .10
❑ 421 Placido Polanco .30 .10
❑ 422 Tim Worrell .30 .10
❑ 423 Jason Bay .30 .10
❑ 424 Josh Fogg .30 .10
❑ 425 Kris Benson .30 .10
❑ 426 Mike Gonzalez .30 .10
❑ 427 Oliver Perez .30 .10
❑ 428 Tike Redman .30 .10
❑ 429 Adam Eaton .30 .10
❑ 430 Ismael Valdes .30 .10
❑ 431 Jake Peavy .30 .10
❑ 432 Khalil Greene .50 .20
❑ 433 Mark Loretta .30 .10
❑ 434 Phil Nevin .30 .10
❑ 435 Ramon Hernandez .30 .10
❑ 436 A.J. Pierzynski .30 .10
❑ 437 Edgardo Alfonzo .30 .10
❑ 438 J.T. Snow .30 .10
❑ 439 Jerome Williams .30 .10
❑ 440 Marquis Grissom .30 .10
❑ 441 Robb Nen .30 .10
❑ 442 Bret Boone .30 .10
❑ 443 Freddy Garcia .30 .10
❑ 444 Gil Meche .30 .10
❑ 445 John Olerud .30 .10
❑ 446 Rich Aurilia .30 .10
❑ 447 Shigetoshi Hasegawa .30 .10
❑ 448 Bo Hart .30 .10
❑ 449 Danny Haren .30 .10
❑ 450 Jason Marquis .30 .10
❑ 451 Marlon Anderson .30 .10
❑ 452 Scott Rolen .50 .20
❑ 453 So Taguchi .30 .10
❑ 454 Carl Crawford .30 .10
❑ 455 Delmon Young .50 .20
❑ 456 Geoff Blum .30 .10
❑ 457 Jesus Colome .30 .10
❑ 458 Jonny Gomes .30 .10
❑ 459 Lance Carter .30 .10
❑ 460 Robert Fick .30 .10
❑ 461 Chan Ho Park .30 .10
❑ 462 Francisco Cordero .30 .10
❑ 463 Jeff Nelson .30 .10
❑ 464 Jeff Zimmerman .30 .10
❑ 465 Kenny Rogers .30 .10
❑ 466 Aquilino Lopez .30 .10
❑ 467 Carlos Delgado .30 .10
❑ 468 Frank Catalanotto .30 .10
❑ 469 Reed Johnson .30 .10
❑ 470 Pat Hentgen .30 .10
❑ 471 Curt Schilling SH CL .30 .10
❑ 472 Gary Sheffield SH CL .30 .10
❑ 473 Javier Vazquez SH CL .30 .10
❑ 474 Kazuo Matsui SH CL .50 .20
❑ 475 Kevin Brown SH CL .30 .10
❑ 476 Rafael Palmeiro SH CL .30 .10
❑ 477 Richie Sexson SH CL .30 .10
❑ 478 Roger Clemens SH CL .75 .30
❑ 479 Vladimir Guerrero SH CL .50 .20
❑ 480 Alex Rodriguez SH CL .75 .30
❑ 481 Jake Woods SR RC 1.00 .40
❑ 482 Tim Bittner SR RC 1.00 .40
❑ 483 Brandon Medders SR RC 1.00 .40
❑ 484 Casey Daigle SR RC 1.00 .40
❑ 485 Jerry Gil SR RC 1.00 .40
❑ 486 Mike Gosling SR RC 1.00 .40
❑ 487 Jose Capellan SR RC 1.50 .60
❑ 488 Onil Joseph SR RC 1.00 .40
❑ 489 Roman Colon SR RC 1.00 .40
❑ 490 Dave Crouthers SR RC 1.00 .40
❑ 491 Eddy Rodriguez SR RC 1.50 .60
❑ 492 Franklyn Gracesqui SR RC 1.00 .40
❑ 493 Jamie Brown SR RC 1.00 .40
❑ 494 Jerome Gamble SR RC 1.00 .40
❑ 495 Tim Hamulack SR RC 1.00 .40
❑ 496 Carlos Vasquez SR RC 1.50 .60
❑ 497 Renyel Pinto SR RC 1.50 .60
❑ 498 Ronny Cedeno SR RC 2.00 .75
❑ 499 Enemencio Pacheco SR RC 1.00 .40
❑ 500 Ryan Meaux SR RC 1.00 .40
❑ 501 Ryan Wing SR RC 1.00 .40
❑ 502 Shingo Takatsu SR RC 1.50 .60
❑ 503 William Bergolla SR RC 1.00 .40
❑ 504 Ivan Ochoa SR RC 1.00 .40
❑ 505 Mariano Gomez SR RC 1.00 .40
❑ 506 Justin Hampson SR RC 1.00 .40
❑ 507 Justin Huisman SR RC 1.00 .40
❑ 508 Scott Dohmann SR RC 1.00 .40
❑ 509 Donnie Kelly SR RC 1.00 .40
❑ 510 Chris Aguila SR RC 1.00 .40
❑ 511 Lincoln Holdzkom SR RC 1.00 .40
❑ 512 Freddy Guzman SR RC 1.00 .40
❑ 513 Hector Gimenez SR RC 1.00 .40
❑ 514 Jorge Vasquez SR RC 1.00 .40
❑ 515 Jason Frasor SR RC 1.00 .40
❑ 516 Chris Saenz SR RC 1.00 .40
❑ 517 Dennis Sarfate SR RC 1.00 .40
❑ 518 Colby Miller SR RC 1.00 .40
❑ 519 Jason Bartlett SR RC 1.50 .60
❑ 520 Chad Bentz SR RC 1.00 .40
❑ 521 Josh Labandeira SR RC 1.00 .40
❑ 522 Shawn Hill SR RC 1.00 .40
❑ 523 Kazuo Matsui SR RC 1.50 .60
❑ 524 Carlos Hines SR RC 1.00 .40
❑ 525 Mike Vento SR RC 1.50 .60
❑ 526 Scott Proctor SR RC 1.50 .60
❑ 527 Sean Henn SR RC 1.00 .40
❑ 528 David Aardsma SR RC 1.50 .60
❑ 529 Ian Snell SR RC 2.00 .75
❑ 530 Mike Johnston SR RC 1.00 .40
❑ 531 Akinori Otsuka SR RC 1.00 .40
❑ 532 Rusty Tucker SR RC 1.50 .60
❑ 533 Justin Knoedler SR RC 1.00 .40
❑ 534 Merkin Valdez SR RC 1.50 .60
❑ 535 Greg Dobbs SR RC 1.00 .40
❑ 536 Justin Leone SR RC 1.50 .60
❑ 537 Shawn Camp SR RC 1.00 .40
❑ 538 Edwin Moreno SR RC 1.00 .40
❑ 539 Angel Chavez SR RC 1.00 .40
❑ 540 Jesse Harper SR RC 1.00 .40
❑ 541 Alex Rodriguez 1.25 .50
❑ 542 Roger Clemens 1.50 .60
❑ 543 Andy Pettitte .50 .20
❑ 544 Vladimir Guerrero .75 .30
❑ 545 David Wells .30 .10
❑ 546 Derrek Lee .50 .20
❑ 547 Carlos Beltran .30 .10
❑ 548 Orlando Cabrera Sox .30 .10
❑ 549 Paul Lo Duca .30 .10
❑ 550 Dave Roberts .30 .10
❑ 551 Guillermo Mota .30 .10
❑ 552 Steve Finley .30 .10
❑ 553 Juan Encarnacion .30 .10
❑ 554 Larry Walker .30 .10
❑ 555 Ty Wigginton .30 .10
❑ 556 Doug Mientkiewicz .30 .10
❑ 557 Roberto Alomar .50 .20
❑ 558 B.J. Upton .50 .20
❑ 559 Brad Penny .30 .10
❑ 560 Hee Seop Choi .30 .10
❑ 561 David Wright 3.00 1.25
❑ 562 Nomar Garciaparra 1.25 .50
❑ 563 Felix Rodriguez .30 .10
❑ 564 Victor Zambrano .30 .10
❑ 565 Kris Benson .30 .10
❑ 566 Aarom Baldiris SR RC .50 .20
❑ 567 Joey Gathright SR RC 1.00 .40
❑ 568 Charles Thomas SR RC .50 .20
❑ 569 Brian Dallimore SR RC .50 .20
❑ 570 Chris Oxspring SR RC .50 .20
❑ 571 Chris Shelton SR RC 2.00 .75
❑ 572 Dioner Navarro SR RC 1.25 .50
❑ 573 Edwardo Sierra SR RC .50 .20
❑ 574 Fernando Nieve SR RC .75 .30
❑ 575 Frank Francisco SR RC .50 .20
❑ 576 Jeff Bennett SR RC .50 .20
❑ 577 Justin Lehr SR RC .50 .20
❑ 578 John Gall SR RC .50 .20
❑ 579 Jorge Sequea SR RC .50 .20
❑ 580 Justin Germano SR RC .50 .20
❑ 581 Kazuhito Tadano SR RC .50 .20
❑ 582 Kevin Cave SR RC .50 .20
❑ 583 Jesse Crain SR RC .75 .30
❑ 584 Luis A. Gonzalez SR RC .50 .20
❑ 585 Michael Wuertz SR RC .50 .20
❑ 586 Orlando Rodriguez SR RC .50 .20
❑ 587 Phil Stockman SR RC .50 .20
❑ 588 Ramon Ramirez SR RC .50 .20
❑ 589 Roberto Novoa SR RC .50 .20
❑ 590 Scott Kazmir SR RC 4.00 1.50
❑ NNO Update Set Exchange Card

2005 Upper Deck

❑ COMPLETE SERIES 1 (300) 50.00 30.00
❑ COMMON CARD (1-500) .30 .10
❑ COMMON (211-250/426-450) 1.00 .40
❑ OVERALL PLATES SER.1 ODDS 1:1080 H
❑ PLATES PRINT RUN 1 #'d SET PER COLOR
❑ BLACK-CYAN-MAGENTA-YELLOW ISSUED
❑ NO PLATES PRICING DUE TO SCARCITY
❑ 1 Casey Kotchman .30 .10
❑ 2 Chone Figgins .30 .10
❑ 3 David Eckstein .30 .10
❑ 4 Jarrod Washburn .30 .10
❑ 5 Robb Quinlan .30 .10
❑ 6 Troy Glaus .30 .10
❑ 7 Vladimir Guerrero .75 .30
❑ 8 Brandon Webb .30 .10
❑ 9 Danny Bautista .30 .10
❑ 10 Luis Gonzalez .30 .10

❑	11 Matt Kata	.30	.10
❑	12 Randy Johnson	.75	.30
❑	13 Robby Hammock	.30	.10
❑	14 Shea Hillenbrand	.30	.10
❑	15 Adam LaRoche	.30	.10
❑	16 Andruw Jones	.50	.20
❑	17 Horacio Ramirez	.30	.10
❑	18 John Smoltz	.50	.20
❑	19 Johnny Estrada	.30	.10
❑	20 Mike Hampton	.30	.10
❑	21 Rafael Furcal	.30	.10
❑	22 Brian Roberts	.30	.10
❑	23 Javy Lopez	.30	.10
❑	24 Jay Gibbons	.30	.10
❑	25 Jorge Julio	.30	.10
❑	26 Melvin Mora	.30	.10
❑	27 Miguel Tejada	.30	.10
❑	28 Rafael Palmeiro	.50	.20
❑	29 Derek Lowe	.30	.10
❑	30 Jason Varitek	.75	.30
❑	31 Kevin Youkilis	.30	.10
❑	32 Manny Ramirez	.50	.20
❑	33 Curt Schilling	.50	.20
❑	34 Pedro Martinez	.50	.20
❑	35 Trot Nixon	.30	.10
❑	36 Corey Patterson	.30	.10
❑	37 Derrek Lee	.50	.20
❑	38 LaTroy Hawkins	.30	.10
❑	39 Mark Prior	.50	.20
❑	40 Matt Clement	.30	.10
❑	41 Moises Alou	.30	.10
❑	42 Sammy Sosa	.75	.30
❑	43 Aaron Rowand	.30	.10
❑	44 Carlos Lee	.30	.10
❑	45 Jose Valentin	.30	.10
❑	46 Juan Uribe	.30	.10
❑	47 Magglio Ordonez	.30	.10
❑	48 Mark Buehrle	.30	.10
❑	49 Paul Konerko	.30	.10
❑	50 Adam Dunn	.30	.10
❑	51 Barry Larkin	.50	.20
❑	52 D'Angelo Jimenez	.30	.10
❑	53 Danny Graves	.30	.10
❑	54 Paul Wilson	.30	.10
❑	55 Sean Casey	.30	.10
❑	56 Wily Mo Pena	.30	.10
❑	57 Ben Broussard	.30	.10
❑	58 C.C. Sabathia	.30	.10
❑	59 Casey Blake	.30	.10
❑	60 Cliff Lee	.30	.10
❑	61 Matt Lawton	.30	.10
❑	62 Omar Vizquel	.30	.10
❑	63 Victor Martinez	.30	.10
❑	64 Charles Johnson	.30	.10
❑	65 Joe Kennedy	.30	.10
❑	66 Jeromy Burnitz	.30	.10
❑	67 Matt Holliday	.40	.15
❑	68 Preston Wilson	.30	.10
❑	69 Royce Clayton	.30	.10
❑	70 Shawn Estes	.30	.10
❑	71 Bobby Higginson	.30	.10
❑	72 Brandon Inge	.30	.10
❑	73 Carlos Guillen	.30	.10
❑	74 Dmitri Young	.30	.10
❑	75 Eric Munson	.30	.10
❑	76 Jeremy Bonderman	.30	.10
❑	77 Ugueth Urbina	.30	.10
❑	78 Josh Beckett	.30	.10
❑	79 Dontrelle Willis	.30	.10
❑	80 Jeff Conine	.30	.10
❑	81 Juan Pierre	.30	.10
❑	82 Luis Castillo	.30	.10
❑	83 Miguel Cabrera	.50	.20
❑	84 Mike Lowell	.30	.10
❑	85 Andy Pettitte	.50	.20
❑	86 Brad Lidge	.30	.10
❑	87 Carlos Beltran	.30	.10
❑	88 Craig Biggio	.50	.20
❑	89 Jeff Bagwell	.50	.20
❑	90 Roger Clemens	1.25	.50
❑	91 Roy Oswalt	.30	.10
❑	92 Benito Santiago	.30	.10
❑	93 Jeremy Affeldt	.30	.10
❑	94 Juan Gonzalez	.30	.10
❑	95 Ken Harvey	.30	.10
❑	96 Mike MacDougal	.30	.10
❑	97 Mike Sweeney	.30	.10
❑	98 Zack Greinke	.30	.10
❑	99 Adrian Beltre	.30	.10
❑	100 Alex Cora	.30	.10
❑	101 Cesar Izturis	.30	.10
❑	102 Eric Gagne	.30	.10
❑	103 Kazuhisa Ishii	.30	.10
❑	104 Milton Bradley	.30	.10
❑	105 Shawn Green	.30	.10
❑	106 Danny Kolb	.30	.10
❑	107 Ben Sheets	.30	.10
❑	108 Brooks Kieschnick	.30	.10
❑	109 Craig Counsell	.30	.10
❑	110 Geoff Jenkins	.30	.10
❑	111 Lyle Overbay	.30	.10
❑	112 Scott Podsednik	.30	.10
❑	113 Corey Koskie	.30	.10
❑	114 Johan Santana	.75	.30
❑	115 Joe Mauer	.75	.30
❑	116 Justin Morneau	.30	.10
❑	117 Lew Ford	.30	.10
❑	118 Matt LeCroy	.30	.10
❑	119 Torii Hunter	.30	.10
❑	120 Brad Wilkerson	.30	.10
❑	121 Chad Cordero	.30	.10
❑	122 Livan Hernandez	.30	.10
❑	123 Jose Vidro	.30	.10
❑	124 Termel Sledge	.30	.10
❑	125 Tony Batista	.30	.10
❑	126 Zach Day	.30	.10
❑	127 Al Leiter	.30	.10
❑	128 Jae Weong Seo	.30	.10
❑	129 Jose Reyes	.30	.10
❑	130 Kazuo Matsui	.30	.10
❑	131 Mike Piazza	.75	.30
❑	132 Todd Zeile	.30	.10
❑	133 Cliff Floyd	.30	.10
❑	134 Alex Rodriguez	1.25	.50
❑	135 Derek Jeter	1.50	.60
❑	136 Gary Sheffield	.30	.10
❑	137 Hideki Matsui	1.25	.50
❑	138 Jason Giambi	.30	.10
❑	139 Jorge Posada	.50	.20
❑	140 Mike Mussina	.50	.20
❑	141 Barry Zito	.30	.10
❑	142 Bobby Crosby	.30	.10
❑	143 Octavio Dotel	.30	.10
❑	144 Eric Chavez	.30	.10
❑	145 Jermaine Dye	.30	.10
❑	146 Mark Kotsay	.30	.10
❑	147 Tim Hudson	.30	.10
❑	148 Billy Wagner	.30	.10
❑	149 Bobby Abreu	.30	.10
❑	150 David Bell	.30	.10
❑	151 Jim Thome	.50	.20
❑	152 Jimmy Rollins	.30	.10
❑	153 Mike Lieberthal	.30	.10
❑	154 Randy Wolf	.30	.10
❑	155 Craig Wilson	.30	.10
❑	156 Daryle Ward	.30	.10
❑	157 Jack Wilson	.30	.10
❑	158 Jason Kendall	.30	.10
❑	159 Kip Wells	.30	.10
❑	160 Oliver Perez	.30	.10
❑	161 Rob Mackowiak	.30	.10
❑	162 Brian Giles	.30	.10
❑	163 Brian Lawrence	.30	.10
❑	164 David Wells	.30	.10
❑	165 Jay Payton	.30	.10
❑	166 Ryan Klesko	.30	.10
❑	167 Sean Burroughs	.30	.10
❑	168 Trevor Hoffman	.30	.10
❑	169 Brett Tomko	.30	.10
❑	170 J.T. Snow	.30	.10
❑	171 Jason Schmidt	.30	.10
❑	172 Kirk Rueter	.30	.10
❑	173 A.J. Pierzynski	.30	.10
❑	174 Pedro Feliz	.30	.10
❑	175 Ray Durham	.30	.10
❑	176 Eddie Guardado	.30	.10
❑	177 Edgar Martinez	.50	.20
❑	178 Ichiro Suzuki	1.50	.60
❑	179 Jamie Moyer	.30	.10
❑	180 Joel Pineiro	.30	.10
❑	181 Randy Winn	.30	.10
❑	182 Raul Ibanez	.30	.10
❑	183 Albert Pujols	1.50	.60
❑	184 Edgar Renteria	.30	.10
❑	185 Jason Isringhausen	.30	.10
❑	186 Jim Edmonds	.30	.10
❑	187 Matt Morris	.30	.10
❑	188 Reggie Sanders	.30	.10
❑	189 Tony Womack	.30	.10
❑	190 Aubrey Huff	.30	.10
❑	191 Danys Baez	.30	.10
❑	192 Carl Crawford	.30	.10
❑	193 Jose Cruz Jr.	.30	.10
❑	194 Rocco Baldelli	.30	.10
❑	195 Tino Martinez	.50	.20
❑	196 Dewon Brazelton	.30	.10
❑	197 Alfonso Soriano	.30	.10
❑	198 Brad Fullmer	.30	.10
❑	199 Gerald Laird	.30	.10
❑	200 Hank Blalock	.30	.10
❑	201 Laynce Nix	.30	.10
❑	202 Mark Teixeira	.50	.20
❑	203 Michael Young	.30	.10
❑	204 Alexis Rios	.30	.10
❑	205 Eric Hinske	.30	.10
❑	206 Miguel Batista	.30	.10
❑	207 Orlando Hudson	.30	.10
❑	208 Roy Halladay	.30	.10
❑	209 Ted Lilly	.30	.10
❑	210 Vernon Wells	.30	.10
❑	211 Aarom Baldiris SR	1.00	.40
❑	212 B.J. Upton SR	1.00	.40
❑	213 Dallas McPherson SR	1.00	.40
❑	214 Brian Dallimore SR	1.00	.40
❑	215 Chris Oxspring SR	1.00	.40
❑	216 Chris Shelton SR	1.50	.60
❑	217 David Wright SR	2.00	.75
❑	218 Edwardo Sierra SR	1.00	.40
❑	219 Fernando Nieve SR	1.00	.40
❑	220 Frank Francisco SR	1.00	.40
❑	221 Jeff Bennett SR	1.00	.40
❑	222 Justin Lehr SR	1.00	.40
❑	223 John Gall SR	1.00	.40
❑	224 Jorge Sequea SR	1.00	.40
❑	225 Justin Germano SR	1.00	.40
❑	226 Kazuhito Tadano SR	1.00	.40
❑	227 Kevin Cave SR	1.00	.40
❑	228 Joe Blanton SR	1.00	.40
❑	229 Luis A. Gonzalez SR	1.00	.40
❑	230 Michael Wuertz SR	1.00	.40
❑	231 Mike Rouse SR	1.00	.40
❑	232 Nick Regilio SR	1.00	.40
❑	233 Orlando Rodriguez SR	1.00	.40
❑	234 Phil Stockman SR	1.00	.40
❑	235 Ramon Ramirez SR	1.00	.40
❑	236 Roberto Novoa SR	1.00	.40
❑	237 Dioner Navarro SR	1.00	.40
❑	238 Tim Bausher SR	1.00	.40
❑	239 Logan Kensing SR	1.00	.40
❑	240 Andy Green SR	1.00	.40
❑	241 Brad Halsey SR	1.00	.40
❑	242 Charles Thomas SR	1.00	.40
❑	243 George Sherrill SR	1.00	.40
❑	244 Jesse Crain SR	1.00	.40
❑	245 Jimmy Serrano SR	1.00	.40
❑	246 Joe Horgan SR	1.00	.40
❑	247 Chris Young SR	1.00	.40
❑	248 Joey Gathright SR	1.00	.40
❑	249 Gavin Floyd SR	1.00	.40
❑	250 Ryan Howard SR	5.00	2.00
❑	251 Lance Cormier SR	1.00	.40
❑	252 Matt Treanor SR	1.00	.40
❑	253 Jeff Francis SR	1.00	.40
❑	254 Nick Swisher SR	1.00	.40
❑	255 Scott Atchison SR	1.00	.40
❑	256 Travis Blackley SR	1.00	.40
❑	257 Travis Smith SR	1.00	.40
❑	258 Yadier Molina SR	1.00	.40
❑	259 Jeff Keppinger SR	1.00	.40
❑	260 Scott Kazmir SR	1.00	.40
❑	261 G.Anderson/V.Guerrero TL	.50	.20
❑	262 L.Gonzalez/R.Johnson TL	.50	.20
❑	263 A.Jones/C.Jones TL	.50	.20
❑	264 M.Tejada/R.Palmeiro TL	.30	.10
❑	265 C.Schilling/M.Ramirez TL	.50	.20
❑	266 M.Prior/S.Sosa TL	.50	.20
❑	267 F.Thomas/M.Ordonez TL	.50	.20
❑	268 B.Larkin/K.Griffey Jr. TL	.75	.30

	No.	Card		
❑	269	C.Sabathia/V.Martinez TL	.30	.10
❑	270	J.Burnitz/T.Helton TL	.30	.10
❑	271	D.Young/I.Rodriguez TL	.30	.10
❑	272	J.Beckett/M.Cabrera TL	.30	.10
❑	273	J.Bagwell/R.Clemens TL	.75	.30
❑	274	K.Harvey/M.Sweeney TL	.30	.10
❑	275	A.Beltre/E.Gagne TL	.30	.10
❑	276	B.Sheets/G.Jenkins TL	.30	.10
❑	277	J.Mauer/T.Hunter TL	.50	.20
❑	278	J.Vidro/L.Hernandez TL	.30	.10
❑	279	K.Matsui/M.Piazza TL	.50	.20
❑	280	A.Rodriguez/D.Jeter TL	1.50	.60
❑	281	E.Chavez/T.Hudson TL	.30	.10
❑	282	B.Abreu/J.Thome TL	.30	.10
❑	283	C.Wilson/J.Kendall TL	.30	.10
❑	284	B.Giles/P.Nevin TL	.30	.10
❑	285	A.Pierzynski/J.Schmidt TL	.30	.10
❑	286	B.Boone/I.Suzuki TL	.75	.30
❑	287	A.Pujols/S.Rolen TL	.75	.30
❑	288	A.Huff/T.Martinez TL	.30	.10
❑	289	H.Blalock/M.Teixeira TL	.30	.10
❑	290	C.Delgado/R.Halladay TL	.30	.10
❑	291	Vladimir Guerrero PR	.50	.20
❑	292	Curt Schilling PR	.30	.10
❑	293	Mark Prior PR	.50	.20
❑	294	Josh Beckett PR	.30	.10
❑	295	Roger Clemens PR	.75	.30
❑	296	Derek Jeter PR	.75	.30
❑	297	Eric Chavez PR	.30	.10
❑	298	Jim Thome PR	.30	.10
❑	299	Albert Pujols PR	.75	.30
❑	300	Hank Blalock PR	.30	.10
❑	301	Bartolo Colon	.30	.10
❑	302	Darin Erstad	.30	.10
❑	303	Garret Anderson	.30	.10
❑	304	Orlando Cabrera	.30	.10
❑	305	Steve Finley	.30	.10
❑	306	Javier Vazquez	.30	.10
❑	307	Russ Ortiz	.30	.10
❑	308	Chipper Jones	.75	.30
❑	309	Marcus Giles	.30	.10
❑	310	Raul Mondesi	.30	.10
❑	311	B.J. Ryan	.30	.10
❑	312	Luis Matos	.30	.10
❑	313	Sidney Ponson	.30	.10
❑	314	Bill Mueller	.30	.10
❑	315	David Ortiz	.75	.30
❑	316	Johnny Damon	.50	.20
❑	317	Keith Foulke	.30	.10
❑	318	Mark Bellhorn	.30	.10
❑	319	Wade Miller	.30	.10
❑	320	Aramis Ramirez	.30	.10
❑	321	Carlos Zambrano	.30	.10
❑	322	Greg Maddux	1.25	.50
❑	323	Kerry Wood	.30	.10
❑	324	Nomar Garciaparra	.75	.30
❑	325	Todd Walker	.30	.10
❑	326	Frank Thomas	.75	.30
❑	327	Freddy Garcia	.30	.10
❑	328	Joe Crede	.30	.10
❑	329	Jose Contreras	.30	.10
❑	330	Orlando Hernandez	.30	.10
❑	331	Shingo Takatsu	.30	.10
❑	332	Austin Kearns	.30	.10
❑	333	Eric Milton	.30	.10
❑	334	Ken Griffey Jr.	1.25	.50
❑	335	Aaron Boone	.30	.10
❑	336	David Riske	.30	.10
❑	337	Jake Westbrook	.30	.10
❑	338	Kevin Millwood	.30	.10
❑	339	Travis Hafner	.30	.10
❑	340	Aaron Miles	.30	.10
❑	341	Jeff Baker	.30	.10
❑	342	Todd Helton	.50	.20
❑	343	Garrett Atkins	.30	.10
❑	344	Carlos Pena	.30	.10
❑	345	Ivan Rodriguez	.50	.20
❑	346	Rondell White	.30	.10
❑	347	Troy Percival	.30	.10
❑	348	A.J. Burnett	.30	.10
❑	349	Carlos Delgado	.30	.10
❑	350	Guillermo Mota	.30	.10
❑	351	Paul Lo Duca	.30	.10
❑	352	Jason Lane	.30	.10
❑	353	Lance Berkman	.30	.10
❑	354	Angel Berroa	.30	.10
❑	355	David DeJesus	.30	.10
❑	356	Ruben Gotay	.30	.10
❑	357	Jose Lima	.30	.10
❑	358	Brad Penny	.30	.10
❑	359	J.D. Drew	.30	.10
❑	360	Jayson Werth	.30	.10
❑	361	Jeff Kent	.30	.10
❑	362	Odalis Perez	.30	.10
❑	363	Brady Clark	.30	.10
❑	364	Junior Spivey	.30	.10
❑	365	Rickie Weeks	.30	.10
❑	366	Jacque Jones	.30	.10
❑	367	Joe Nathan	.30	.10
❑	368	Nick Punto	.30	.10
❑	369	Shannon Stewart	.30	.10
❑	370	Doug Mientkiewicz	.30	.10
❑	371	Kris Benson	.30	.10
❑	372	Tom Glavine	.50	.20
❑	373	Victor Zambrano	.30	.10
❑	374	Bernie Williams	.50	.20
❑	375	Carl Pavano	.30	.10
❑	376	Jaret Wright	.30	.10
❑	377	Kevin Brown	.30	.10
❑	378	Mariano Rivera	.75	.30
❑	379	Danny Haren	.30	.10
❑	380	Eric Byrnes	.30	.10
❑	381	Erubiel Durazo	.30	.10
❑	382	Rich Harden	.30	.10
❑	383	Brett Myers	.30	.10
❑	384	Chase Utley	.50	.20
❑	385	Marlon Byrd	.30	.10
❑	386	Pat Burrell	.30	.10
❑	387	Placido Polanco	.30	.10
❑	388	Freddy Sanchez	.30	.10
❑	389	Jason Bay	.30	.10
❑	390	Josh Fogg	.30	.10
❑	391	Adam Eaton	.30	.10
❑	392	Jake Peavy	.30	.10
❑	393	Khalil Greene	.50	.20
❑	394	Mark Loretta	.30	.10
❑	395	Phil Nevin	.30	.10
❑	396	Ramon Hernandez	.30	.10
❑	397	Woody Williams	.30	.10
❑	398	Armando Benitez	.30	.10
❑	399	Edgardo Alfonzo	.30	.10
❑	400	Marquis Grissom	.30	.10
❑	401	Mike Matheny	.30	.10
❑	402	Richie Sexson	.30	.10
❑	403	Bret Boone	.30	.10
❑	404	Gil Meche	.30	.10
❑	405	Chris Carpenter	.30	.10
❑	406	Jeff Suppan	.30	.10
❑	407	Larry Walker	.50	.20
❑	408	Mark Grudzielanek	.30	.10
❑	409	Mark Mulder	.30	.10
❑	410	Scott Rolen	.50	.20
❑	411	Josh Phelps	.30	.10
❑	412	Jonny Gomes	.30	.10
❑	413	Francisco Cordero	.30	.10
❑	414	Kenny Rogers	.30	.10
❑	415	Richard Hidalgo	.30	.10
❑	416	Dave Bush	.30	.10
❑	417	Frank Catalanotto	.30	.10
❑	418	Gabe Gross	.30	.10
❑	419	Guillermo Quiroz	.30	.10
❑	420	Reed Johnson	.30	.10
❑	421	Cristian Guzman	.30	.10
❑	422	Esteban Loaiza	.30	.10
❑	423	Jose Guillen	.30	.10
❑	424	Nick Johnson	.30	.10
❑	425	Vinny Castilla	.30	.10
❑	426	Pete Orr SR RC	1.00	.40
❑	427	Tadahito Iguchi SR RC	2.50	1.00
❑	428	Jeff Baker SR	1.00	.40
❑	429	Marcos Carvajal SR RC	1.00	.40
❑	430	Justin Verlander SR RC	5.00	2.00
❑	431	Luke Scott SR RC	3.00	1.25
❑	432	Willy Taveras SR	1.00	.40
❑	433	Ambiorix Burgos SR RC	1.00	.40
❑	434	Andy Sisco SR	1.00	.40
❑	435	Denny Bautista SR	1.00	.40
❑	436	Mark Teahen SR	1.00	.40
❑	437	Ervin Santana SR	1.00	.40
❑	438	Dennis Houlton SR RC	1.00	.40
❑	439	Philip Humber SR RC	1.50	.60
❑	440	Steve Schmoll SR RC	1.00	.40
❑	441	J.J. Hardy SR	1.00	.40
❑	442	Ambiorix Concepcion SR RC	1.00	.40
❑	443	Dae-Sung Koo SR RC	1.00	.40
❑	444	Andy Phillips SR	1.00	.40
❑	445	Dan Meyer SR	1.00	.40
❑	446	Huston Street SR	1.50	.60
❑	447	Keiichi Yabu SR RC	1.00	.40
❑	448	Jeff Niemann SR RC	1.50	.60
❑	449	Jeremy Reed SR	1.00	.40
❑	450	Tony Blanco SR	1.00	.40
❑	451	Albert Pujols BG	.75	.30
❑	452	Alex Rodriguez BG	.75	.30
❑	453	Curt Schilling BG	.30	.10
❑	454	Derek Jeter BG	.75	.30
❑	455	Greg Maddux BG	.75	.30
❑	456	Ichiro Suzuki BG	.75	.30
❑	457	Ivan Rodriguez BG	.30	.10
❑	458	Jeff Bagwell BG	.30	.10
❑	459	Jim Thome BG	.30	.10
❑	460	Ken Griffey Jr. BG	.75	.30
❑	461	Manny Ramirez BG	.50	.20
❑	462	Mike Mussina BG	.30	.10
❑	463	Mike Piazza BG	.50	.20
❑	464	Pedro Martinez BG	.30	.10
❑	465	Rafael Palmeiro BG	.30	.10
❑	466	Randy Johnson BG	.50	.20
❑	467	Roger Clemens BG	.75	.30
❑	468	Sammy Sosa BG	.50	.20
❑	469	Todd Helton BG	.30	.10
❑	470	Vladimir Guerrero BG	.50	.20
❑	471	Vladimir Guerrero TC	.50	.20
❑	472	Shawn Green TC	.30	.10
❑	473	John Smoltz TC	.30	.10
❑	474	Miguel Tejada TC	.30	.10
❑	475	Curt Schilling TC	.30	.10
❑	476	Mark Prior TC	.30	.10
❑	477	Frank Thomas TC	.50	.20
❑	478	Ken Griffey Jr. TC	.75	.30
❑	479	C.C. Sabathia TC	.30	.10
❑	480	Todd Helton TC	.30	.10
❑	481	Ivan Rodriguez TC	.30	.10
❑	482	Miguel Cabrera TC	.30	.10
❑	483	Roger Clemens TC	.75	.30
❑	484	Mike Sweeney TC	.30	.10
❑	485	Eric Gagne TC	.30	.10
❑	486	Ben Sheets TC	.30	.10
❑	487	Johan Santana TC	.30	.10
❑	488	Mike Piazza TC	.50	.20
❑	489	Derek Jeter TC	.75	.30
❑	490	Eric Chavez TC	.30	.10
❑	491	Jim Thome TC	.30	.10
❑	492	Craig Wilson TC	.30	.10
❑	493	Jake Peavy TC	.30	.10
❑	494	Jason Schmidt TC	.30	.10
❑	495	Ichiro Suzuki TC	.75	.30
❑	496	Albert Pujols TC	.75	.30
❑	497	Carl Crawford TC	.30	.10
❑	498	Mark Teixeira TC	.30	.10
❑	499	Vernon Wells TC	.30	.10
❑	500	Jose Vidro TC	.30	.10

2006 Upper Deck

❑	COMPLETE SET (1250)	600.00	375.00
❑	COMPLETE SERIES 1 (500)	200.00	125.00
❑	COMPLETE SERIES 2 (500)	200.00	125.00
❑	COMPLETE UPDATE (250)	200.00	125.00
❑	COMP.UPDATE w/o SP's (200)	50.00	30.00
❑	COMMON CARD (1-1250)	.40	.15

❑ 1-500 ISSUED IN SERIES 1 PACKS
❑ 501-1000 ISSUED IN SERIES 2 PACKS
❑ 1001-1250 ISSUED IN UPDATE PACKS
❑ BAKER , REPKO BOTH CARD 283
❑ 1001-1250 SP STATED ODDS 1:2
❑ SP CL: 1005/1013/1021/1037/1045/1061/1069
❑ SP CL: 1077/1093/1101/1117/1125/1133/1149
❑ SP CL: 1157/1173/1181/1189/1205/1213
❑ SP CL: 1221-1250
❑ 4 MATCHED PLATES 1:2 SER.2 HOBBY CASES
❑ PLATE PRINT RUN 1 SET PER COLOR
❑ BLACK-CYAN-MAGENTA-YELLOW ISSUED
❑ NO PLATE PRICING DUE TO SCARCITY
❑ EXQUISITE EXCH 1 PER SER.2 HOBBY CASE
❑ EXQUISITE EXCH RANDOM IN UPD.CASES
❑ EXQUISITE EXCH DEADLINE 07/27/07
❑ 1 Adam Kennedy .40 .15
❑ 2 Bartolo Colon .40 .15
❑ 3 Bengie Molina .40 .15
❑ 4 Casey Kotchman .40 .15
❑ 5 Chone Figgins .40 .15
❑ 6 Dallas McPherson .40 .15
❑ 7 Darin Erstad .40 .15
❑ 8 Ervin Santana .40 .15
❑ 9 Francisco Rodriguez .40 .15
❑ 10 Garret Anderson .40 .15
❑ 11 Jarrod Washburn .40 .15
❑ 12 John Lackey .40 .15
❑ 13 Juan Rivera .40 .15
❑ 14 Orlando Cabrera .40 .15
❑ 15 Paul Byrd .40 .15
❑ 16 Steve Finley .40 .15
❑ 17 Vladimir Guerrero 1.00 .40
❑ 18 Alex Cintron .40 .15
❑ 19 Brandon Lyon .40 .15
❑ 20 Brandon Webb .40 .15
❑ 21 Chad Tracy .40 .15
❑ 22 Chris Snyder .40 .15
❑ 23 Claudio Vargas .40 .15
❑ 24 Conor Jackson .60 .25
❑ 25 Craig Counsell .40 .15
❑ 26 Javier Vazquez .40 .15
❑ 27 Jose Valverde .40 .15
❑ 28 Luis Gonzalez .40 .15
❑ 29 Royce Clayton .40 .15
❑ 30 Russ Ortiz .40 .15
❑ 31 Shawn Green .40 .15
❑ 32 Dustin Nippert (RC) .75 .30
❑ 33 Tony Clark .40 .15
❑ 34 Troy Glaus .40 .15
❑ 35 Adam LaRoche .40 .15
❑ 36 Andruw Jones .60 .25
❑ 37 Craig Hansen RC 3.00 1.25
❑ 38 Chipper Jones 1.00 .40
❑ 39 Horacio Ramirez .40 .15
❑ 40 Jeff Francoeur 1.00 .40
❑ 41 John Smoltz .60 .25
❑ 42 Joey Devine RC .75 .30
❑ 43 Johnny Estrada .40 .15
❑ 44 Anthony Lerew (RC) .75 .30
❑ 45 Julio Franco .40 .15
❑ 46 Kyle Farnsworth .40 .15
❑ 47 Marcus Giles .40 .15
❑ 48 Mike Hampton .40 .15
❑ 49 Rafael Furcal .40 .15
❑ 50 Chuck James (RC) 1.25 .50
❑ 51 Tim Hudson .40 .15
❑ 52 B.J. Ryan .40 .15
❑ 53 Bernie Castro (RC) .75 .30
❑ 54 Brian Roberts .40 .15
❑ 55 Walter Young (RC) .75 .30
❑ 56 Daniel Cabrera .40 .15
❑ 57 Eric Byrnes .40 .15
❑ 58 Alejandro Freire RC .75 .30
❑ 59 Erik Bedard .40 .15
❑ 60 Javy Lopez .40 .15
❑ 61 Jay Gibbons .40 .15
❑ 62 Jorge Julio .40 .15
❑ 63 Luis Matos .40 .15
❑ 64 Melvin Mora .40 .15
❑ 65 Miguel Tejada .40 .15
❑ 66 Rafael Palmeiro .60 .25
❑ 67 Rodrigo Lopez .40 .15
❑ 68 Sammy Sosa 1.00 .40
❑ 69 Alejandro Machado (RC) .75 .30
❑ 70 Bill Mueller .40 .15
❑ 71 Bronson Arroyo .40 .15
❑ 72 Curt Schilling .60 .25
❑ 73 David Ortiz 1.00 .40
❑ 74 David Wells .40 .15
❑ 75 Edgar Renteria .40 .15
❑ 76 Ryan Jorgensen RC .75 .30
❑ 77 Jason Varitek 1.00 .40
❑ 78 Johnny Damon .60 .25
❑ 79 Keith Foulke .40 .15
❑ 80 Kevin Youkilis .40 .15
❑ 81 Manny Ramirez .60 .25
❑ 82 Matt Clement .40 .15
❑ 83 Hanley Ramirez (RC) 2.00 .75
❑ 84 Tim Wakefield .40 .15
❑ 85 Trot Nixon .40 .15
❑ 86 Wade Miller .40 .15
❑ 87 Aramis Ramirez .40 .15
❑ 88 Carlos Zambrano .40 .15
❑ 89 Corey Patterson .40 .15
❑ 90 Derrek Lee .40 .15
❑ 91 Geovany Soto (RC) .75 .30
❑ 92 Greg Maddux 1.50 .60
❑ 93 Jeromy Burnitz .40 .15
❑ 94 Jerry Hairston .40 .15
❑ 95 Kerry Wood .40 .15
❑ 96 Mark Prior .60 .25
❑ 97 Matt Murton .40 .15
❑ 98 Michael Barrett .40 .15
❑ 99 Neifi Perez .40 .15
❑ 100 Nomar Garciaparra 1.00 .40
❑ 101 Rich Hill .40 .15
❑ 102 Ryan Dempster .40 .15
❑ 103 Todd Walker .40 .15
❑ 104 A.J. Pierzynski .40 .15
❑ 105 Aaron Rowand .40 .15
❑ 106 Bobby Jenks .40 .15
❑ 107 Carl Everett .40 .15
❑ 108 Dustin Hermanson .40 .15
❑ 109 Frank Thomas 1.00 .40
❑ 110 Freddy Garcia .40 .15
❑ 111 Jermaine Dye .40 .15
❑ 112 Joe Crede .40 .15
❑ 113 Jon Garland .40 .15
❑ 114 Jose Contreras .40 .15
❑ 115 Juan Uribe .40 .15
❑ 116 Mark Buehrle .40 .15
❑ 117 Orlando Hernandez .40 .15
❑ 118 Paul Konerko .40 .15
❑ 119 Scott Podsednik .40 .15
❑ 120 Tadahito Iguchi .40 .15
❑ 121 Aaron Harang .40 .15
❑ 122 Adam Dunn .40 .15
❑ 123 Austin Kearns .40 .15
❑ 124 Brandon Claussen .40 .15
❑ 125 Chris Denorfia (RC) .75 .30
❑ 126 Edwin Encarnacion .40 .15
❑ 127 Miguel Perez (RC) .75 .30
❑ 128 Felipe Lopez .40 .15
❑ 129 Jason LaRue .40 .15
❑ 130 Ken Griffey Jr. 1.50 .60
❑ 131 Chris Booker (RC) .75 .30
❑ 132 Luke Hudson .40 .15
❑ 133 Jason Bergmann RC .75 .30
❑ 134 Ryan Freel .40 .15
❑ 135 Sean Casey .40 .15
❑ 136 Wily Mo Pena .40 .15
❑ 137 Aaron Boone .40 .15
❑ 138 Ben Broussard .40 .15
❑ 139 Ryan Garko (RC) .75 .30
❑ 140 C.C. Sabathia .40 .15
❑ 141 Casey Blake .40 .15
❑ 142 Cliff Lee .40 .15
❑ 143 Coco Crisp .40 .15
❑ 144 David Riske .40 .15
❑ 145 Grady Sizemore .60 .25
❑ 146 Jake Westbrook .40 .15
❑ 147 Jhonny Peralta .40 .15
❑ 148 Josh Bard .40 .15
❑ 149 Kevin Millwood .40 .15
❑ 150 Ronnie Belliard .40 .15
❑ 151 Scott Elarton .40 .15
❑ 152 Travis Hafner .40 .15
❑ 153 Victor Martinez .40 .15
❑ 154 Aaron Cook .40 .15
❑ 155 Aaron Miles .40 .15
❑ 156 Brad Hawpe .40 .15
❑ 157 Mike Esposito (RC) .75 .30
❑ 158 Chin-Hui Tsao .40 .15
❑ 159 Clint Barmes .40 .15
❑ 160 Cory Sullivan .40 .15
❑ 161 Garrett Atkins .40 .15
❑ 162 J.D. Closser .40 .15
❑ 163 Jason Jennings .40 .15
❑ 164 Jeff Baker .40 .15
❑ 165 Jeff Francis .40 .15
❑ 166 Luis A. Gonzalez .40 .15
❑ 167 Matt Holliday 1.00 .40
❑ 168 Todd Helton .60 .25
❑ 169 Bradon Inge .40 .15
❑ 170 Carlos Guillen .40 .15
❑ 171 Carlos Pena .40 .15
❑ 172 Chris Shelton .40 .15
❑ 173 Craig Monroe .40 .15
❑ 174 Curtis Granderson .40 .15
❑ 175 Dmitri Young .40 .15
❑ 176 Ivan Rodriguez .60 .25
❑ 177 Jason Johnson .40 .15
❑ 178 Jeremy Bonderman .40 .15
❑ 179 Magglio Ordonez .40 .15
❑ 180 Mark Woodyard (RC) .75 .30
❑ 181 Nook Logan .40 .15
❑ 182 Omar Infante .40 .15
❑ 183 Placido Polanco .40 .15
❑ 184 Chris Heintz RC .75 .30
❑ 185 A.J. Burnett .40 .15
❑ 186 Alex Gonzalez .40 .15
❑ 187 Josh Johnson (RC) .75 .30
❑ 188 Carlos Delgado .40 .15
❑ 189 Dontrelle Willis .40 .15
❑ 190 Josh Wilson (RC) .75 .30
❑ 191 Jason Vargas .40 .15
❑ 192 Jeff Conine .40 .15
❑ 193 Jeremy Hermida .40 .15
❑ 194 Josh Beckett .40 .15
❑ 195 Juan Encarnacion .40 .15
❑ 196 Juan Pierre .40 .15
❑ 197 Luis Castillo .40 .15
❑ 198 Miguel Cabrera .60 .25
❑ 199 Mike Lowell .40 .15
❑ 200 Paul Lo Duca .40 .15
❑ 201 Todd Jones .40 .15
❑ 202 Adam Everett .40 .15
❑ 203 Andy Pettitte .60 .25
❑ 204 Brad Ausmus .40 .15
❑ 205 Brad Lidge .40 .15
❑ 206 Brandon Backe .40 .15
❑ 207 Charlton Jimerson (RC) .75 .30
❑ 208 Chris Burke .40 .15
❑ 209 Craig Biggio .60 .25
❑ 210 Dan Wheeler .40 .15
❑ 211 Jason Lane .40 .15
❑ 212 Jeff Bagwell .60 .25
❑ 213 Lance Berkman .40 .15
❑ 214 Luke Scott .40 .15
❑ 215 Morgan Ensberg .40 .15
❑ 216 Roger Clemens 2.00 .75
❑ 217 Roy Oswalt .40 .15
❑ 218 Willy Taveras .40 .15
❑ 219 Andres Blanco .40 .15
❑ 220 Angel Berroa .40 .15
❑ 221 Ruben Gotay .40 .15
❑ 222 David DeJesus .40 .15
❑ 223 Emil Brown .40 .15
❑ 224 J.P. Howell .40 .15
❑ 225 Jeremy Affeldt .40 .15
❑ 226 Jimmy Gobble .40 .15
❑ 227 John Buck .40 .15
❑ 228 Jose Lima .40 .15
❑ 229 Mark Teahen .40 .15
❑ 230 Matt Stairs .40 .15
❑ 231 Mike MacDougal .40 .15
❑ 232 Mike Sweeney .40 .15
❑ 233 Runelvys Hernandez .40 .15
❑ 234 Terrence Long .40 .15
❑ 235 Zack Greinke .40 .15
❑ 236 Ron Flores RC .75 .30
❑ 237 Brad Penny .40 .15
❑ 238 Cesar Izturis .40 .15
❑ 239 D.J. Houlton .40 .15
❑ 240 Derek Lowe .40 .15
❑ 241 Eric Gagne .40 .15
❑ 242 Hee Seop Choi .40 .15

❑	243	J.D. Drew	.40	.15
❑	244	Jason Phillips	.40	.15
❑	245	Jason Repko	.40	.15
❑	246	Jayson Werth	.40	.15
❑	247	Jeff Kent	.40	.15
❑	248	Jeff Weaver	.40	.15
❑	249	Milton Bradley	.40	.15
❑	250	Odalis Perez	.40	.15
❑	251	Hong-Chih Kuo (RC)	2.00	.75
❑	252	Oscar Robles	.40	.15
❑	253	Ben Sheets	.40	.15
❑	254	Bill Hall	.40	.15
❑	255	Brady Clark	.40	.15
❑	256	Carlos Lee	.40	.15
❑	257	Chris Capuano	.40	.15
❑	258	Nelson Cruz (RC)	.75	.30
❑	259	Derrick Turnbow	.40	.15
❑	260	Doug Davis	.40	.15
❑	261	Geoff Jenkins	.40	.15
❑	262	J.J. Hardy	.40	.15
❑	263	Lyle Overbay	.40	.15
❑	264	Prince Fielder	1.50	.60
❑	265	Rickie Weeks	.40	.15
❑	266	Russell Branyan	.40	.15
❑	267	Tomo Ohka	.40	.15
❑	268	Jonah Bayliss (RC)	.75	.30
❑	269	Brad Radke	.40	.15
❑	270	Carlos Silva	.40	.15
❑	271	Francisco Liriano (RC)	4.00	1.50
❑	272	Jacque Jones	.40	.15
❑	273	Joe Mauer	.60	.25
❑	274	Travis Bowyer (RC)	.75	.30
❑	275	Joe Nathan	.40	.15
❑	276	Johan Santana	.60	.25
❑	277	Justin Morneau	.40	.15
❑	278	Kyle Lohse	.40	.15
❑	279	Lew Ford	.40	.15
❑	280	Matt LeCroy	.40	.15
❑	281	Michael Cuddyer	.40	.15
❑	282	Nick Punto	.40	.15
❑	283a	Scott Baker	.40	.15
❑	283b	Jason Repko UER	.40	.15
❑	284	Shannon Stewart	.40	.15
❑	285	Torii Hunter	.40	.15
❑	286	Braden Looper	.40	.15
❑	287	Carlos Beltran	.40	.15
❑	288	Cliff Floyd	.40	.15
❑	289	David Wright	1.50	.60
❑	290	Doug Mientkiewicz	.40	.15
❑	291	Anderson Hernandez (RC)	.75	.30
❑	292	Jose Reyes	1.00	.40
❑	293	Kazuo Matsui	.40	.15
❑	294	Kris Benson	.40	.15
❑	295	Miguel Cairo	.40	.15
❑	296	Mike Cameron	.40	.15
❑	297	Robert Andino RC	.75	.30
❑	298	Mike Piazza	1.00	.40
❑	299	Pedro Martinez	.60	.25
❑	300	Tom Glavine	.60	.25
❑	301	Victor Diaz	.40	.15
❑	302	Tim Hamulack (RC)	.75	.30
❑	303	Alex Rodriguez	1.50	.60
❑	304	Bernie Williams	.60	.25
❑	305	Carl Pavano	.40	.15
❑	306	Chien-Ming Wang	1.50	.60
❑	307	Derek Jeter	2.50	1.00
❑	308	Gary Sheffield	.40	.15
❑	309	Hideki Matsui	1.00	.40
❑	310	Jason Giambi	.40	.15
❑	311	Jorge Posada	.60	.25
❑	312	Kevin Brown	.40	.15
❑	313	Mariano Rivera	1.00	.40
❑	314	Matt Lawton	.40	.15
❑	315	Mike Mussina	.60	.25
❑	316	Randy Johnson	1.00	.40
❑	317	Robinson Cano	.60	.25
❑	318	Mike Vento (RC)	.75	.30
❑	319	Tino Martinez	.40	.15
❑	320	Tony Womack	.40	.15
❑	321	Barry Zito	.40	.15
❑	322	Bobby Crosby	.40	.15
❑	323	Bobby Kielty	.40	.15
❑	324	Dan Johnson	.40	.15
❑	325	Danny Haren	.40	.15
❑	326	Eric Chavez	.40	.15
❑	327	Erubiel Durazo	.40	.15
❑	328	Huston Street	.40	.15
❑	329	Jason Kendall	.40	.15
❑	330	Jay Payton	.40	.15
❑	331	Joe Blanton	.40	.15
❑	332	Joe Kennedy	.40	.15
❑	333	Kirk Saarloos	.40	.15
❑	334	Mark Kotsay	.40	.15
❑	335	Nick Swisher	.40	.15
❑	336	Rich Harden	.40	.15
❑	337	Scott Hatteberg	.40	.15
❑	338	Billy Wagner	.40	.15
❑	339	Bobby Abreu	.40	.15
❑	340	Brett Myers	.40	.15
❑	341	Chase Utley	1.00	.40
❑	342	Danny Sandoval RC	.75	.30
❑	343	David Bell	.40	.15
❑	344	Gavin Floyd	.40	.15
❑	345	Jim Thome	.60	.25
❑	346	Jimmy Rollins	.40	.15
❑	347	Jon Lieber	.40	.15
❑	348	Kenny Lofton	.40	.15
❑	349	Mike Lieberthal	.40	.15
❑	350	Pat Burrell	.40	.15
❑	351	Randy Wolf	.40	.15
❑	352	Ryan Howard	1.50	.60
❑	353	Vicente Padilla	.40	.15
❑	354	Bryan Bullington (RC)	.75	.30
❑	355	J.J. Furmaniak (RC)	.75	.30
❑	356	Craig Wilson	.40	.15
❑	357	Matt Capps (RC)	.75	.30
❑	358	Tom Gorzelanny (RC)	.75	.30
❑	359	Jack Wilson	.40	.15
❑	360	Jason Bay	.40	.15
❑	361	Jose Mesa	.40	.15
❑	362	Josh Fogg	.40	.15
❑	363	Kip Wells	.40	.15
❑	364	Steve Stemle RC	.75	.30
❑	365	Oliver Perez	.40	.15
❑	366	Rob Mackowiak	.40	.15
❑	367	Ronny Paulino (RC)	.75	.30
❑	368	Tike Redman	.40	.15
❑	369	Zach Duke	.40	.15
❑	370	Adam Eaton	.40	.15
❑	371	Scott Feldman RC	.75	.30
❑	372	Brian Giles	.40	.15
❑	373	Brian Lawrence	.40	.15
❑	374	Damian Jackson	.40	.15
❑	375	Dave Roberts	.40	.15
❑	376	Jake Peavy	.40	.15
❑	377	Joe Randa	.40	.15
❑	378	Khalil Greene	.60	.25
❑	379	Mark Loretta	.40	.15
❑	380	Ramon Hernandez	.40	.15
❑	381	Robert Fick	.40	.15
❑	382	Ryan Klesko	.40	.15
❑	383	Trevor Hoffman	.40	.15
❑	384	Woody Williams	.40	.15
❑	385	Xavier Nady	.40	.15
❑	386	Armando Benitez	.40	.15
❑	387	Brad Hennessey	.40	.15
❑	388	Brian Myrow RC	.75	.30
❑	389	Edgardo Alfonzo	.40	.15
❑	390	J.T. Snow	.40	.15
❑	391	Jeremy Accardo RC	.75	.30
❑	392	Jason Schmidt	.40	.15
❑	393	Lance Niekro	.40	.15
❑	394	Matt Cain	.60	.25
❑	395	Dan Ortmeier (RC)	.75	.30
❑	396	Moises Alou	.40	.15
❑	397	Doug Clark (RC)	.75	.30
❑	398	Omar Vizquel	.60	.25
❑	399	Pedro Feliz	.40	.15
❑	400	Randy Winn	.40	.15
❑	401	Ray Durham	.40	.15
❑	402	Adrian Beltre	.40	.15
❑	403	Eddie Guardado	.40	.15
❑	404	Felix Hernandez	.60	.25
❑	405	Gil Meche	.40	.15
❑	406	Ichiro Suzuki	1.50	.60
❑	407	Jamie Moyer	.40	.15
❑	408	Jeff Nelson	.40	.15
❑	409	Jeremy Reed	.40	.15
❑	410	Joel Pineiro	.40	.15
❑	411	Jaime Bubela (RC)	.75	.30
❑	412	Raul Ibanez	.40	.15
❑	413	Rickie Sexson	.40	.15
❑	414	Ryan Franklin	.40	.15
❑	415	Willie Bloomquist	.40	.15
❑	416	Yorvit Torrealba	.40	.15
❑	417	Yuniesky Betancourt	.40	.15
❑	418	Jeff Harris RC	.75	.30
❑	419	Albert Pujols	2.00	.75
❑	420	Chris Carpenter	.40	.15
❑	421	David Eckstein	.40	.15
❑	422	Jason Isringhausen	.40	.15
❑	423	Jason Marquis	.40	.15
❑	424	Adam Wainwright (RC)	.75	.30
❑	425	Jim Edmonds	.60	.25
❑	426	Ryan Theriot RC	.75	.30
❑	427	Chris Duncan (RC)	.75	.30
❑	428	Mark Grudzielanek	.40	.15
❑	429	Mark Mulder	.40	.15
❑	430	Matt Morris	.40	.15
❑	431	Reggie Sanders	.40	.15
❑	432	Scott Rolen	.60	.25
❑	433	Tyler Johnson (RC)	.75	.30
❑	434	Yadier Molina	.40	.15
❑	435	Alex S. Gonzalez	.40	.15
❑	436	Aubrey Huff	.40	.15
❑	437	Tim Corcoran RC	.75	.30
❑	438	Carl Crawford	.40	.15
❑	439	Casey Fossum	.40	.15
❑	440	Danys Baez	.40	.15
❑	441	Edwin Jackson	.40	.15
❑	442	Joey Gathright	.40	.15
❑	443	Jonny Gomes	.40	.15
❑	444	Jorge Cantu	.40	.15
❑	445	Julio Lugo	.40	.15
❑	446	Nick Green	.40	.15
❑	447	Rocco Baldelli	.40	.15
❑	448	Scott Kazmir	.60	.25
❑	449	Seth McClung	.40	.15
❑	450	Toby Hall	.40	.15
❑	451	Travis Lee	.40	.15
❑	452	Craig Breslow RC	.75	.30
❑	453	Alfonso Soriano	.40	.15
❑	454	Chris R. Young	.40	.15
❑	455	David Dellucci	.40	.15
❑	456	Francisco Cordero	.40	.15
❑	457	Gary Matthews	.40	.15
❑	458	Hank Blalock	.40	.15
❑	459	Juan Dominguez	.40	.15
❑	460	Josh Rupe (RC)	.75	.30
❑	461	Kenny Rogers	.40	.15
❑	462	Kevin Mench	.40	.15
❑	463	Laynce Nix	.40	.15
❑	464	Mark Teixeira	.60	.25
❑	465	Michael Young	.40	.15
❑	466	Richard Hidalgo	.40	.15
❑	467	Jason Botts (RC)	.75	.30
❑	468	Aaron Hill	.40	.15
❑	469	Alex Rios	.40	.15
❑	470	Corey Koskie	.40	.15
❑	471	Chris Demaria RC	.75	.30
❑	472	Eric Hinske	.40	.15
❑	473	Frank Catalanotto	.40	.15
❑	474	John-Ford Griffin (RC)	.75	.30
❑	475	Gustavo Chacin	.40	.15
❑	476	Josh Towers	.40	.15
❑	477	Miguel Batista	.40	.15
❑	478	Orlando Hudson	.40	.15
❑	479	Reed Johnson	.40	.15
❑	480	Roy Halladay	.40	.15
❑	481	Shaun Marcum (RC)	.75	.30
❑	482	Shea Hillenbrand	.40	.15
❑	483	Ted Lilly	.40	.15
❑	484	Vernon Wells	.40	.15
❑	485	Brad Wilkerson	.40	.15
❑	486	Darrell Rasner (RC)	.75	.30
❑	487	Chad Cordero	.40	.15
❑	488	Cristian Guzman	.40	.15
❑	489	Esteban Loaiza	.40	.15
❑	490	John Patterson	.40	.15
❑	491	Jose Guillen	.40	.15
❑	492	Jose Vidro	.40	.15
❑	493	Livan Hernandez	.40	.15
❑	494	Marlon Byrd	.40	.15
❑	495	Nick Johnson	.40	.15
❑	496	Preston Wilson	.40	.15
❑	497	Ryan Church	.40	.15
❑	498	Ryan Zimmerman (RC)	5.00	2.00
❑	499	Tony Armas Jr.	.40	.15

❑ 500 Vinny Castilla	.40	.15
❑ 501 Andy Green	.40	.15
❑ 502 Damion Easley	.40	.15
❑ 503 Eric Byrnes	.40	.15
❑ 504 Jason Grimsley	.40	.15
❑ 505 Jeff DaVanon	.40	.15
❑ 506 Johnny Estrada	.40	.15
❑ 507 Luis Vizcaino	.40	.15
❑ 508 Miguel Batista	.40	.15
❑ 509 Orlando Hernandez	.40	.15
❑ 510 Orlando Hudson	.40	.15
❑ 511 Terry Mulholland	.40	.15
❑ 512 Chris Reitsma	.40	.15
❑ 513 Edgar Renteria	.40	.15
❑ 514 John Thomson	.40	.15
❑ 515 Jorge Sosa	.40	.15
❑ 516 Oscar Villarreal	.40	.15
❑ 517 Pete Orr	.40	.15
❑ 518 Ryan Langerhans	.40	.15
❑ 519 Todd Pratt	.40	.15
❑ 520 Wilson Betemit	.40	.15
❑ 521 Brian Jordan	.40	.15
❑ 522 Lance Cormier	.40	.15
❑ 523 Matt Diaz	.40	.15
❑ 524 Mike Remlinger	.40	.15
❑ 525 Bruce Chen	.40	.15
❑ 526 Chris Gomez	.40	.15
❑ 527 Chris Ray	.40	.15
❑ 528 Corey Patterson	.40	.15
❑ 529 David Newhan	.40	.15
❑ 530 Ed Rogers (RC)	.75	.30
❑ 531 John Halama	.40	.15
❑ 532 Kris Benson	.40	.15
❑ 533 LaTroy Hawkins	.40	.15
❑ 534 Raul Chavez	.40	.15
❑ 535 Alex Cora	.40	.15
❑ 536 Alex Gonzalez	.40	.15
❑ 537 Coco Crisp	.40	.15
❑ 538 David Riske	.40	.15
❑ 539 Doug Mirabelli	.40	.15
❑ 540 Josh Beckett	.40	.15
❑ 541 J.T. Snow	.40	.15
❑ 542 Mike Timlin	.40	.15
❑ 543 Julian Tavarez	.40	.15
❑ 544 Rudy Seanez	.40	.15
❑ 545 Wily Mo Pena	.40	.15
❑ 546 Bob Howry	.40	.15
❑ 547 Glendon Rusch	.40	.15
❑ 548 Henry Blanco	.40	.15
❑ 549 Jacque Jones	.40	.15
❑ 550 Jerome Williams	.40	.15
❑ 551 John Mabry	.40	.15
❑ 552 Juan Pierre	.40	.15
❑ 553 Scott Eyre	.40	.15
❑ 554 Scott Williamson	.40	.15
❑ 555 Wade Miller	.40	.15
❑ 556 Will Ohman	.40	.15
❑ 557 Alex Cintron	.40	.15
❑ 558 Rob Mackowiak	.40	.15
❑ 559 Brandon McCarthy	.40	.15
❑ 560 Chris Widger	.40	.15
❑ 561 Cliff Politte	.40	.15
❑ 562 Javier Vazquez	.40	.15
❑ 563 Jim Thome	.60	.25
❑ 564 Matt Thornton	.40	.15
❑ 565 Neal Cotts	.40	.15
❑ 566 Pablo Ozuna	.40	.15
❑ 567 Ross Gload	.40	.15
❑ 568 Brandon Phillips	.40	.15
❑ 569 Bronson Arroyo	.40	.15
❑ 570 Dave Williams	.40	.15
❑ 571 David Ross	.40	.15
❑ 572 David Weathers	.40	.15
❑ 573 Eric Milton	.40	.15
❑ 574 Javier Valentin	.40	.15
❑ 575 Kent Mercker	.40	.15
❑ 576 Matt Belisle	.40	.15
❑ 577 Paul Wilson	.40	.15
❑ 578 Rich Aurilia	.40	.15
❑ 579 Rick White	.40	.15
❑ 580 Scott Hatteberg	.40	.15
❑ 581 Todd Coffey	.40	.15
❑ 582 Bob Wickman	.40	.15
❑ 583 Danny Graves	.40	.15
❑ 584 Eduardo Perez	.40	.15
❑ 585 Guillermo Mota	.40	.15
❑ 586 Jason Davis	.40	.15
❑ 587 Jason Johnson	.40	.15
❑ 588 Jason Michaels	.40	.15
❑ 589 Rafael Betancourt	.40	.15
❑ 590 Ramon Vazquez	.40	.15
❑ 591 Scott Sauerbeck	.40	.15
❑ 592 Todd Hollandsworth	.40	.15
❑ 593 Brian Fuentes	.40	.15
❑ 594 Danny Ardoin	.40	.15
❑ 595 David Cortes	.40	.15
❑ 596 Eli Marrero	.40	.15
❑ 597 Jamey Carroll	.40	.15
❑ 598 Jason Smith	.40	.15
❑ 599 Josh Fogg	.40	.15
❑ 600 Miguel Ojeda	.40	.15
❑ 601 Mike DeJean	.40	.15
❑ 602 Ray King	.40	.15
❑ 603 Omar Quintanilla (RC)	.75	.30
❑ 604 Zach Day	.40	.15
❑ 605 Fernando Rodney	.40	.15
❑ 606 Kenny Rogers	.40	.15
❑ 607 Mike Maroth	.40	.15
❑ 608 Nate Robertson	.40	.15
❑ 609 Todd Jones	.40	.15
❑ 610 Vance Wilson	.40	.15
❑ 611 Bobby Seay	.40	.15
❑ 612 Chris Spurling	.40	.15
❑ 613 Roman Colon	.40	.15
❑ 614 Jason Grilli	.40	.15
❑ 615 Marcus Thames	.40	.15
❑ 616 Ramon Santiago	.40	.15
❑ 617 Alfredo Amezaga	.40	.15
❑ 618 Brian Moehler	.40	.15
❑ 619 Chris Aguila	.40	.15
❑ 620 Franklyn German	.40	.15
❑ 621 Joe Borowski	.40	.15
❑ 622 Logan Kensing (RC)	.75	.30
❑ 623 Matt Treanor	.40	.15
❑ 624 Miguel Olivo	.40	.15
❑ 625 Sergio Mitre	.40	.15
❑ 626 Todd Wellemeyer	.40	.15
❑ 627 Wes Helms	.40	.15
❑ 628 Chad Qualls	.40	.15
❑ 629 Eric Bruntlett	.40	.15
❑ 630 Mike Gallo	.40	.15
❑ 631 Mike Lamb	.40	.15
❑ 632 Orlando Palmeiro	.40	.15
❑ 633 Russ Springer	.40	.15
❑ 634 Dan Wheeler	.40	.15
❑ 635 Eric Munson	.40	.15
❑ 636 Preston Wilson	.40	.15
❑ 637 Trever Miller	.40	.15
❑ 638 Ambiorix Burgos	.40	.15
❑ 639 Andy Sisco	.40	.15
❑ 640 Denny Bautista	.40	.15
❑ 641 Doug Mientkiewicz	.40	.15
❑ 642 Elmer Dessens	.40	.15
❑ 643 Esteban German	.40	.15
❑ 644 Joe Nelson (RC)	.75	.30
❑ 645 Mark Grudzielanek	.40	.15
❑ 646 Mark Redman	.40	.15
❑ 647 Mike Wood	.40	.15
❑ 648 Paul Bako	.40	.15
❑ 649 Reggie Sanders	.40	.15
❑ 650 Scott Elarton	.40	.15
❑ 651 Shane Costa	.40	.15
❑ 652 Tony Graffanino	.40	.15
❑ 653 Jason Bulger (RC)	.75	.30
❑ 654 Chris Bootcheck (RC)	.75	.30
❑ 655 Esteban Yan	.40	.15
❑ 656 Hector Carrasco	.40	.15
❑ 657 J.C. Romero	.40	.15
❑ 658 Jeff Weaver	.40	.15
❑ 659 Jose Molina	.40	.15
❑ 660 Kelvim Escobar	.40	.15
❑ 661 Maicer Izturis	.40	.15
❑ 662 Robb Quinlan	.40	.15
❑ 663 Scot Shields	.40	.15
❑ 664 Tim Salmon	.40	.15
❑ 665 Bill Mueller	.40	.15
❑ 666 Brett Tomko	.40	.15
❑ 667 Dioner Navarro	.40	.15
❑ 668 Jae Seo	.40	.15
❑ 669 Jose Cruz Jr.	.40	.15
❑ 670 Kenny Lofton	.40	.15
❑ 671 Lance Carter	.40	.15
❑ 672 Nomar Garciaparra	1.00	.40
❑ 673 Olmedo Saenz	.40	.15
❑ 674 Rafael Furcal	.40	.15
❑ 675 Ramon Martinez	.40	.15
❑ 676 Ricky Ledee	.40	.15
❑ 677 Sandy Alomar Jr.	.40	.15
❑ 678 Yhency Brazoban	.40	.15
❑ 679 Corey Koskie	.40	.15
❑ 680 Dan Kolb	.40	.15
❑ 681 Gabe Gross	.40	.15
❑ 682 Jeff Cirillo	.40	.15
❑ 683 Matt Wise	.40	.15
❑ 684 Rick Helling	.40	.15
❑ 685 Chad Moeller	.40	.15
❑ 686 Dave Bush	.40	.15
❑ 687 Jorge De La Rosa	.40	.15
❑ 688 Justin Lehr	.40	.15
❑ 689 Jason Bartlett	.40	.15
❑ 690 Jesse Crain	.40	.15
❑ 691 Juan Rincon	.40	.15
❑ 692 Luis Castillo	.40	.15
❑ 693 Mike Redmond	.40	.15
❑ 694 Rondell White	.40	.15
❑ 695 Tony Batista	.40	.15
❑ 696 Juan Castro	.40	.15
❑ 697 Luis Rodriguez	.40	.15
❑ 698 Matt Guerrier	.40	.15
❑ 699 Willie Eyre (RC)	.75	.30
❑ 700 Aaron Heilman	.40	.15
❑ 701 Billy Wagner	.40	.15
❑ 702 Carlos Delgado	.40	.15
❑ 703 Chad Bradford	.40	.15
❑ 704 Chris Woodward	.40	.15
❑ 705 Darren Oliver	.40	.15
❑ 706 Duaner Sanchez	.40	.15
❑ 707 Endy Chavez	.40	.15
❑ 708 Jorge Julio	.40	.15
❑ 709 Jose Valentin	.40	.15
❑ 710 Julio Franco	.40	.15
❑ 711 Paul Lo Duca	.40	.15
❑ 712 Ramon Castro	.40	.15
❑ 713 Steve Trachsel	.40	.15
❑ 714 Victor Zambrano	.40	.15
❑ 715 Xavier Nady	.40	.15
❑ 716 Andy Phillips	.40	.15
❑ 717 Bubba Crosby	.40	.15
❑ 718 Jaret Wright	.40	.15
❑ 719 Kelly Stinnett	.40	.15
❑ 720 Kyle Farnsworth	.40	.15
❑ 721 Mike Myers	.40	.15
❑ 722 Octavio Dotel	.40	.15
❑ 723 Ron Villone	.40	.15
❑ 724 Scott Proctor	.40	.15
❑ 725 Shawn Chacon	.40	.15
❑ 726 Tanyon Sturtze	.40	.15
❑ 727 Adam Melhuse	.40	.15
❑ 728 Brad Halsey	.40	.15
❑ 729 Esteban Loaiza	.40	.15
❑ 730 Frank Thomas	1.00	.40
❑ 731 Jay Witasick	.40	.15
❑ 732 Justin Duchscherer	.40	.15
❑ 733 Kiko Calero	.40	.15
❑ 734 Marco Scutaro	.40	.15
❑ 735 Mark Ellis	.40	.15
❑ 736 Milton Bradley	.40	.15
❑ 737 Aaron Fultz	.40	.15
❑ 738 Aaron Rowand	.40	.15
❑ 739 Geoff Geary	.40	.15
❑ 740 Arthur Rhodes	.40	.15
❑ 741 Chris Coste RC	.75	.30
❑ 742 Rheal Cormier	.40	.15
❑ 743 Ryan Franklin	.40	.15
❑ 744 Ryan Madson	.40	.15
❑ 745 Sal Fasano	.40	.15
❑ 746 Tom Gordon	.40	.15
❑ 747 Abraham Nunez	.40	.15
❑ 748 David Dellucci	.40	.15
❑ 749 Julio Santana	.40	.15
❑ 750 Shane Victorino	.40	.15
❑ 751 Damaso Marte	.40	.15
❑ 752 Freddy Sanchez	.40	.15
❑ 753 Humberto Cota	.40	.15
❑ 754 Jeromy Burnitz	.40	.15
❑ 755 Joe Randa	.40	.15
❑ 756 Jose Castillo	.40	.15
❑ 757 Mike Gonzalez	.40	.15

758	Ryan Doumit	.40	.15
759	Sean Burnett	.40	.15
760	Sean Casey	.40	.15
761	Ian Snell	.40	.15
762	John Grabow	.40	.15
763	Jose Hernandez	.40	.15
764	Roberto Hernandez	.40	.15
765	Ryan Vogelsong	.40	.15
766	Victor Santos	.40	.15
767	Adrian Gonzalez	.40	.15
768	Alan Embree	.40	.15
769	Brian Sweeney (RC)	.75	.30
770	Chan Ho Park	.40	.15
771	Clay Hensley	.40	.15
772	Dewon Brazelton	.40	.15
773	Doug Brocail	.40	.15
774	Eric Young	.40	.15
775	Geoff Blum	.40	.15
776	Josh Bard	.40	.15
777	Mark Bellhorn	.40	.15
778	Mike Cameron	.40	.15
779	Mike Piazza	1.00	.40
780	Rob Bowen	.40	.15
781	Scott Cassidy	.40	.15
782	Scott Linebrink	.40	.15
783	Shawn Estes	.40	.15
784	Termel Sledge	.40	.15
785	Vinny Castilla	.40	.15
786	Jeff Fassero	.40	.15
787	Jose Vizcaino	.40	.15
788	Mark Sweeney	.40	.15
789	Matt Morris	.40	.15
790	Steve Finley	.40	.15
791	Tim Worrell	.40	.15
792	Jamey Wright	.40	.15
793	Jason Ellison	.40	.15
794	Noah Lowry	.40	.15
795	Steve Kline	.40	.15
796	Todd Greene	.40	.15
797	Carl Everett	.40	.15
798	George Sherrill	.40	.15
799	J.J. Putz	.40	.15
800	Jake Woods	.40	.15
801	Jose Lopez	.40	.15
802	Julio Mateo	.40	.15
803	Mike Morse	.40	.15
804	Rafael Soriano	.40	.15
805	Roberto Petagine	.40	.15
806	Aaron Miles	.40	.15
807	Braden Looper	.40	.15
808	Gary Bennett	.40	.15
809	Hector Luna	.40	.15
810	Jeff Suppan	.40	.15
811	John Rodriguez	.40	.15
812	Josh Hancock	.40	.15
813	Juan Encarnacion	.40	.15
814	Larry Bigbie	.40	.15
815	Scott Spiezio	.40	.15
816	Sidney Ponson	.40	.15
817	So Taguchi	.40	.15
818	Brian Meadows	.40	.15
819	Damon Hollins	.40	.15
820	Dan Miceli	.40	.15
821	Doug Waechter	.40	.15
822	Jason Childers RC	.75	.30
823	Josh Paul	.40	.15
824	Julio Lugo	.40	.15
825	Mark Hendrickson	.40	.15
826	Sean Burroughs	.40	.15
827	Shawn Camp	.40	.15
828	Travis Harper	.40	.15
829	Ty Wigginton	.40	.15
830	Adam Eaton	.40	.15
831	Adrian Brown	.40	.15
832	Akinori Otsuka	.40	.15
833	Antonio Alfonseca	.40	.15
834	Brad Wilkerson	.40	.15
835	D'Angelo Jimenez	.40	.15
836	Gerald Laird	.40	.15
837	Joaquin Benoit	.40	.15
838	Kameron Loe	.40	.15
839	Kevin Millwood	.40	.15
840	Mark DeRosa	.40	.15
841	Phil Nevin	.40	.15
842	Rod Barajas	.40	.15
843	Vicente Padilla	.40	.15
844	A.J. Burnett	.40	.15
845	Bengie Molina	.40	.15
846	Gregg Zaun	.40	.15
847	John McDonald	.40	.15
848	Lyle Overbay	.40	.15
849	Russ Adams	.40	.15
850	Troy Glaus	.40	.15
851	Vinny Chulk	.40	.15
852	B.J. Ryan	.40	.15
853	Justin Speier	.40	.15
854	Pete Walker	.40	.15
855	Scott Downs	.40	.15
856	Scott Schoeneweis	.40	.15
857	Alfonso Soriano	.40	.15
858	Brian Schneider	.40	.15
859	Daryle Ward	.40	.15
860	Felix Rodriguez	.40	.15
861	Gary Majewski	.40	.15
862	Joey Eischen	.40	.15
863	Jon Rauch	.40	.15
864	Marlon Anderson	.40	.15
865	Matt LeCroy	.40	.15
866	Mike Stanton	.40	.15
867	Ramon Ortiz	.40	.15
868	Robert Fick	.40	.15
869	Royce Clayton	.40	.15
870	Ryan Drese	.40	.15
871	Vladimir Guerrero CL	1.00	.40
872	Craig Biggio CL	.60	.25
873	Barry Zito CL	.40	.15
874	Vernon Wells CL	.40	.15
875	Chipper Jones CL	1.00	.40
876	Prince Fielder CL	1.50	.60
877	Albert Pujols CL	2.00	.75
878	Greg Maddux CL	1.50	.60
879	Carl Crawford CL	.40	.15
880	Brandon Webb CL	.40	.15
881	J.D. Drew CL	.40	.15
882	Jason Schmidt CL	.40	.15
883	Victor Martinez CL	.40	.15
884	Ichiro Suzuki CL	1.50	.60
885	Miguel Cabrera CL	.60	.25
886	David Wright CL	1.50	.60
887	Alfonso Soriano CL	.40	.15
888	Miguel Tejada CL	.40	.15
889	Khalil Greene CL	.60	.25
890	Ryan Howard CL	1.50	.60
891	Jason Bay CL	.40	.15
892	Mark Teixeira CL	.60	.25
893	Manny Ramirez CL	.60	.25
894	Ken Griffey Jr. CL	1.50	.60
895	Todd Helton CL	.60	.25
896	Angel Berroa CL	.40	.15
897	Ivan Rodriguez CL	.60	.25
898	Johan Santana CL	.60	.25
899	Paul Konerko CL	.40	.15
900	Derek Jeter CL	2.50	1.00
901	Macay McBride (RC)	.75	.30
902	Tony Pena (RC)	.75	.30
903	Peter Moylan RC	.75	.30
904	Aaron Rakers (RC)	.75	.30
905	Chris Britton RC	.75	.30
906	Nick Markakis (RC)	1.25	.50
907	Sendy Rleal RC	.75	.30
908	Val Majewski (RC)	.75	.30
909	Jermaine Van Buren (RC)	.75	.30
910	Jonathan Papelbon (RC)	4.00	1.50
911	Angel Pagan (RC)	.75	.30
912	David Aardsma (RC)	.75	.30
913	Sean Marshall (RC)	.75	.30
914	Brian Anderson (RC)	.75	.30
915	Freddie Bynum (RC)	.75	.30
916	Fausto Carmona (RC)	.75	.30
917	Kelly Shoppach (RC)	.75	.30
918	Choo Freeman (RC)	.75	.30
919	Ryan Shealy (RC)	.75	.30
920	Joel Zumaya (RC)	2.00	.75
921	Jordan Tata RC	.75	.30
922	Justin Verlander (RC)	3.00	1.25
923	Carlos Martinez RC	.75	.30
924	Chris Resop (RC)	.75	.30
925	Dan Uggla (RC)	2.00	.75
926	Eric Reed (RC)	.75	.30
927	Hanley Ramirez (RC)	2.00	.75
928	Yusmeiro Petit (RC)	.75	.30
929	Josh Willingham (RC)	.75	.30
930	Mike Jacobs (RC)	.75	.30
931	Reggie Abercrombie (RC)	.75	.30
932	Ricky Nolasco (RC)	.75	.30
933	Scott Olsen (RC)	.75	.30
934	Fernando Nieve (RC)	.75	.30
935	Taylor Buchholz (RC)	1.25	.50
936	Cody Ross (RC)	.75	.30
937	James Loney (RC)	1.25	.50
938	Takashi Saito RC	1.25	.50
939	Tim Hamulack (RC)	.75	.30
940	Chris Demaria RC	.75	.30
941	Jose Capellan (RC)	.75	.30
942	David Gassner (RC)	.75	.30
943	Jason Kubel (RC)	.75	.30
944	Brian Bannister (RC)	.75	.30
945	Mike Thompson RC	.75	.30
946	Cole Hamels (RC)	2.00	.75
947	Paul Maholm (RC)	.75	.30
948	John Van Benschoten (RC)	.75	.30
949	Nate McLouth (RC)	.75	.30
950	Ben Johnson (RC)	.75	.30
951	Josh Barfield (RC)	.75	.30
952	Travis Ishikawa (RC)	.75	.30
953	Jack Taschner (RC)	.75	.30
954	Kenji Johjima RC	4.00	1.50
955	Skip Schumaker (RC)	.75	.30
956	Ruddy Lugo (RC)	.75	.30
957	Jason Hammel (RC)	.75	.30
958	Chris Roberson (RC)	.75	.30
959	Fabio Castro RC	.75	.30
960	Ian Kinsler (RC)	1.25	.50
961	John Koronka (RC)	.75	.30
962	Brandon Watson (RC)	.75	.30
963	Jon Lester RC	2.50	1.00
964	Ben Hendrickson (RC)	.75	.30
965	Martin Prado (RC)	.75	.30
966	Erick Aybar (RC)	.75	.30
967	Bobby Livingston (RC)	.75	.30
968	Ryan Spilborghs (RC)	1.25	.50
969	Tommy Murphy (RC)	.75	.30
970	Howie Kendrick (RC)	4.00	1.50
971	Casey Janssen RC	.75	.30
972	Michael O'Connor RC	.75	.30
973	Conor Jackson (RC)	1.25	.50
974	Jeremy Hermida (RC)	.75	.30
975	Renyel Pinto (RC)	.75	.30
976	Prince Fielder (RC)	3.00	1.25
977	Kevin Frandsen (RC)	1.25	.50
978	Ty Taubenheim RC	1.25	.50
979	Rich Hill (RC)	.75	.30
980	Jonathan Broxton (RC)	.75	.30
981	Jamie Shields RC	.75	.30
982	Carlos Villanueva RC	.75	.30
983	Boone Logan RC	.75	.30
984	Brian Wilson RC	.75	.30
985	Andre Ethier (RC)	2.00	.75
986	Mike Napoli RC	2.00	.75
987	Agustin Montero (RC)	.75	.30
988	Jack Hannahan RC	.75	.30
989	Boof Bonser (RC)	.75	.30
990	Carlos Ruiz (RC)	.75	.30
991	Jason Botts (RC)	.75	.30
992	Kendry Morales (RC)	2.00	.75
993	Alay Soler RC	.75	.30
994	Santiago Ramirez (RC)	.75	.30
995	Saul Rivera (RC)	.75	.30
996	Anthony Reyes (RC)	.75	.30
997	Matt Kemp (RC)	1.25	.50
998	Jae Kuk Ryu RC	.75	.30
999	Lastings Milledge (RC)	1.25	.50
NNO	Exquisite Redemption	200.00	125.00
1000	Jered Weaver (RC)	4.00	1.50
1001	Stephen Drew (RC)	2.00	.75
1002	Carlos Quentin (RC)	1.25	.50
1003	Livan Hernandez	.40	.15
1004	Chris B. Young (RC)	.75	.30
1005	Alberto Callaspo SP (RC)	8.00	3.00
1006	Enrique Gonzalez (RC)	.75	.30
1007	Tony Pena (RC)	.75	.30
1008	Bob Melvin MG	.40	.15
1009	Fernando Tatis	.40	.15
1010	Willy Aybar (RC)	.75	.30
1011	Ken Ray (RC)	.75	.30
1012	Scott Thorman (RC)	.75	.30
1013	Eric Hinske SP	8.00	3.00
1014	Kevin Barry (RC)	.75	.30

❑	1015	Bobby Cox MG	.40	.15
❑	1016	Phil Stockman (RC)	.75	.30
❑	1017	Brayan Pena (RC)	.75	.30
❑	1018	Adam Loewen (RC)	1.25	.50
❑	1019	Brandon Fahey RC	.75	.30
❑	1020	Jim Hoey RC	.75	.30
❑	1021	Kurt Birkins SP RC	8.00	3.00
❑	1022	Jim Johnson RC	.75	.30
❑	1023	Sam Perlozzo MG	.40	.15
❑	1024	Cory Morris RC	.75	.30
❑	1025	Hayden Penn (RC)	.75	.30
❑	1026	Javy Lopez	.40	.15
❑	1027	Dustin Pedroia (RC)	8.00	3.00
❑	1028	Kason Gabbard (RC)	.75	.30
❑	1029	David Pauley (RC)	.75	.30
❑	1030	Kyle Snyder	.40	.15
❑	1031	Terry Francona MG	.40	.15
❑	1032	Craig Breslow RC	.75	.30
❑	1033	Bryan Corey (RC)	.75	.30
❑	1034	Manny Delcarmen (RC)	.75	.30
❑	1035	Carlos Marmol RC	.75	.30
❑	1036	Buck Coats (RC)	.75	.30
❑	1037	Ryan O'Malley SP RC	8.00	3.00
❑	1038	Angel Guzman (RC)	.75	.30
❑	1039	Ronny Cedeno	.40	.15
❑	1040	Juan Mateo RC	.75	.30
❑	1041	Cesar Izturis	.40	.15
❑	1042	Les Walrond (RC)	.75	.30
❑	1043	Geovany Soto (RC)	.75	.30
❑	1044	Sean Tracey (RC)	.75	.30
❑	1045	Ozzie Guillen MG SP	8.00	3.00
❑	1046	Royce Clayton	.40	.15
❑	1047	Norris Hopper RC	.75	.30
❑	1048	Bill Bray (RC)	.75	.30
❑	1049	Jerry Narron MG	.40	.15
❑	1050	Brendan Harris (RC)	.75	.30
❑	1051	Brian Shackelford	.40	.15
❑	1052	Jeremy Sowers (RC)	.75	.30
❑	1053	Joe Inglett RC	.75	.30
❑	1054	Brian Slocum (RC)	.75	.30
❑	1055	Andrew Brown (RC)	.75	.30
❑	1056	Rafael Perez RC	.75	.30
❑	1057	Edward Mujica RC	.75	.30
❑	1058	Andy Marte (RC)	.75	.30
❑	1059	Shin-Soo Choo (RC)	.75	.30
❑	1060	Jeremy Guthrie (RC)	.75	.30
❑	1061	Franklin Gutierrez SP (RC)	8.00	3.00
❑	1062	Kazuo Matsui	.40	.15
❑	1063	Chris Iannetta RC	.75	.30
❑	1064	Manny Corpas RC	.75	.30
❑	1065	Clint Hurdle MG	.40	.15
❑	1066	Ramon Ramirez (RC)	.75	.30
❑	1067	Sean Casey	.40	.15
❑	1068	Zach Miner (RC)	.75	.30
❑	1069	Brent Clevlen SP (RC)	8.00	3.00
❑	1070	Bob Wickman	.40	.15
❑	1071	Jim Leyland MG	.40	.15
❑	1072	Alexis Gomez (RC)	.75	.30
❑	1073	Anibal Sanchez (RC)	1.25	.50
❑	1074	Taylor Tankersley (RC)	.75	.30
❑	1075	Eric Wedge MG	.40	.15
❑	1076	Jonah Bayliss RC	.75	.30
❑	1077	Paul Hoover SP (RC)	8.00	3.00
❑	1078	Eddie Guardado	.40	.15
❑	1079	Cody Ross (RC)	.75	.30
❑	1080	Aubrey Huff	.40	.15
❑	1081	Jason Hirsh (RC)	.75	.30
❑	1082	Brandon League	.40	.15
❑	1083	Matt Albers (RC)	.75	.30
❑	1084	Chris Sampson RC	.75	.30
❑	1085	Phil Garner MG	.40	.15
❑	1086	J.R. House (RC)	.75	.30
❑	1087	Ryan Shealy (RC)	.75	.30
❑	1088	Stephen Andrade (RC)	.75	.30
❑	1089	Bob Keppel (RC)	.75	.30
❑	1090	Buddy Bell MG	.40	.15
❑	1091	Justin Huber (RC)	.75	.30
❑	1092	Paul Phillips (RC)	.75	.30
❑	1093	Greg Jones SP (RC)	8.00	3.00
❑	1094	Jeff Mathis (RC)	.75	.30
❑	1095	Dustin Moseley (RC)	.75	.30
❑	1096	Joe Saunders (RC)	.75	.30
❑	1097	Reggie Willits RC	1.25	.50
❑	1098	Mike Scioscia MG	.40	.15
❑	1099	Greg Maddux	1.50	.60
❑	1100	Wilson Betemit	.40	.15
❑	1101	Chad Billingsley SP (RC)	8.00	3.00
❑	1102	Russell Martin (RC)	1.25	.50
❑	1103	Grady Little MG	.40	.15
❑	1104	David Bell	.40	.15
❑	1105	Kevin Mench	.40	.15
❑	1106	Laynce Nix	.40	.15
❑	1107	Chris Barnwell RC	.75	.30
❑	1108	Tony Gwynn Jr. (RC)	.75	.30
❑	1109	Corey Hart (RC)	.75	.30
❑	1110	Zach Jackson (RC)	.75	.30
❑	1111	Francisco Cordero	.40	.15
❑	1112	Joe Winkelsas (RC)	.75	.30
❑	1113	Ned Yost MG	.40	.15
❑	1114	Matt Garza (RC)	.75	.30
❑	1115	Chris Heintz	.40	.15
❑	1116	Pat Neshek RC	8.00	3.00
❑	1117	Josh Rabe SP RC	20.00	8.00
❑	1118	Mike Rivera	.40	.15
❑	1119	Ron Gardenhire MG	.40	.15
❑	1120	Shawn Green	.40	.15
❑	1121	Oliver Perez	.40	.15
❑	1122	Heath Bell	.40	.15
❑	1123	Bartolome Fortunato (RC)	.75	.30
❑	1124	Anderson Garcia RC	.75	.30
❑	1125	John Maine SP (RC)	8.00	3.00
❑	1126	Henry Owens RC	1.25	.50
❑	1127	Mike Pelfrey RC	3.00	1.25
❑	1128	Royce Ring (RC)	.75	.30
❑	1129	Willie Randolph MG	.40	.15
❑	1130	Bobby Abreu	.40	.15
❑	1131	Craig Wilson	.40	.15
❑	1132	T.J. Beam (RC)	.75	.30
❑	1133	Colter Bean SP (RC)	8.00	3.00
❑	1134	Melky Cabrera (RC)	1.25	.50
❑	1135	Mitch Jones (RC)	.75	.30
❑	1136	Jeffrey Karstens RC	2.00	.75
❑	1137	Wil Nieves (RC)	.75	.30
❑	1138	Kevin Reese (RC)	1.25	.50
❑	1139	Kevin Thompson (RC)	.75	.30
❑	1140	Jose Veras RC	.75	.30
❑	1141	Joe Torre MG	.60	.25
❑	1142	Jeremy Brown (RC)	.75	.30
❑	1143	Santiago Casilla (RC)	.75	.30
❑	1144	Shane Komine RC	1.25	.50
❑	1145	Mike Rouse (RC)	.75	.30
❑	1146	Jason Windsor (RC)	.75	.30
❑	1147	Ken Macha MG	.40	.15
❑	1148	Jamie Moyer	.40	.15
❑	1149	Phil Nevin SP	8.00	3.00
❑	1150	Eude Brito (RC)	.75	.30
❑	1151	Fabio Castro	.40	.15
❑	1152	Jeff Conine	.40	.15
❑	1153	Scott Mathieson (RC)	.75	.30
❑	1154	Brian Sanches (RC)	.75	.30
❑	1155	Matt Smith RC	.75	.30
❑	1156	Joe Thurston (RC)	.75	.30
❑	1157	Marlon Anderson SP	8.00	3.00
❑	1158	Xavier Nady	.40	.15
❑	1159	Shawn Chacon	.40	.15
❑	1160	Rajai Davis (RC)	.75	.30
❑	1161	Yurendell DeCaster (RC)	.75	.30
❑	1162	Marty McLeary (RC)	.75	.30
❑	1163	Chris Duffy	.40	.15
❑	1164	Josh Sharpless RC	.75	.30
❑	1165	Jim Tracy MG	.40	.15
❑	1166	David Wells	.40	.15
❑	1167	Russell Branyan	.40	.15
❑	1168	Todd Walker	.40	.15
❑	1169	Paul McAnulty (RC)	.75	.30
❑	1170	Bruce Bochy MG	.40	.15
❑	1171	Shea Hillenbrand	.40	.15
❑	1172	Eliezer Alfonzo RC	.75	.30
❑	1173	Justin Knoedler SP (RC)	8.00	3.00
❑	1174	Jonathan Sanchez (RC)	.75	.30
❑	1175	Travis Smith (RC)	.75	.30
❑	1176	Cha-Seung Baek	.40	.15
❑	1177	T.J. Bohn (RC)	.75	.30
❑	1178	Emiliano Fruto RC	.75	.30
❑	1179	Sean Green RC	.75	.30
❑	1180	Jon Huber RC	.75	.30
❑	1182	Mark Lowe (RC)	.75	.30
❑	1183	Eric O'Flaherty RC	.75	.30
❑	1184	Preston Wilson	.40	.15
❑	1185	Mike Hargrove MG	.40	.15
❑	1186	Jeff Weaver	.40	.15
❑	1187	Ronnie Belliard	.40	.15
❑	1188	John Gall (RC)	.75	.30
❑	1189	Josh Kinney SP RC	8.00	3.00
❑	1190	Tony LaRussa MG	.40	.15
❑	1191	Scott Dunn (RC)	.75	.30
❑	1192	B.J. Upton	.40	.15
❑	1193	Jon Switzer (RC)	.75	.30
❑	1194	Ben Zobrist (RC)	1.25	.50
❑	1195	Joe Maddon	.40	.15
❑	1196	Carlos Lee	.40	.15
❑	1197	Matt Stairs	.40	.15
❑	1198	Nick Masset (RC)	.75	.30
❑	1199	Nelson Cruz (RC)	.75	.30
❑	1200	Francisco Rosario (RC)	.75	.30
❑	1201	Wes Littleton (RC)	.75	.30
❑	1202	Drew Meyer (RC)	.75	.30
❑	1203	John Rheinecker (RC)	.75	.30
❑	1204	Robinson Tejeda	.40	.15
❑	1205	Jeremy Accardo SP	8.00	3.00
❑	1206	Luis Figueroa RC	.75	.30
❑	1207	John Hattig (RC)	.75	.30
❑	1208	Dustin McGowan (RC)	.75	.30
❑	1209	Ryan Roberts RC	.75	.30
❑	1210	Davis Romero (RC)	.75	.30
❑	1211	Ty Taubenheim	1.25	.50
❑	1212	John Gibbons MG	.40	.15
❑	1213	Shawn Hill SP (RC)	8.00	3.00
❑	1214	Brandon Harper RC	.75	.30
❑	1215	Travis Hughes (RC)	.75	.30
❑	1216	Chris Schroder RC	.75	.30
❑	1217	Austin Kearns	.40	.15
❑	1218	Felipe Lopez	.40	.15
❑	1219	Roy Corcoran RC	.75	.30
❑	1220	Melvin Dorta RC	.75	.30
❑	1221	Brandon Webb CL SP	5.00	2.00
❑	1222	Andruw Jones CL SP	5.00	2.00
❑	1223	Miguel Tejada CL SP	5.00	2.00
❑	1224	David Ortiz CL SP	5.00	2.00
❑	1225	Derrek Lee CL SP	5.00	2.00
❑	1226	Jim Thome CL SP	5.00	2.00
❑	1227	Ken Griffey Jr. CL SP	8.00	3.00
❑	1228	Travis Hafner CL SP	5.00	2.00
❑	1229	Todd Helton CL SP	5.00	2.00
❑	1230	Magglio Ordonez CL SP	5.00	2.00
❑	1231	Miguel Cabrera CL SP	5.00	2.00
❑	1232	Lance Berkman CL SP	5.00	2.00
❑	1233	Mike Sweeney CL SP	5.00	2.00
❑	1234	Vladimir Guerrero CL SP	5.00	2.00
❑	1235	Nomar Garciaparra CL SP	5.00	2.00
❑	1236	Prince Fielder CL SP	5.00	2.00
❑	1237	Johan Santana CL SP	5.00	2.00
❑	1238	Pedro Martinez CL SP	5.00	2.00
❑	1239	Derek Jeter CL SP	10.00	4.00
❑	1240	Barry Zito CL SP	5.00	2.00
❑	1241	Ryan Howard CL SP	8.00	3.00
❑	1242	Jason Bay CL SP	5.00	2.00
❑	1243	Trevor Hoffman CL SP	5.00	2.00
❑	1244	Jason Schmidt CL SP	5.00	2.00
❑	1245	Ichiro Suzuki CL SP	8.00	3.00
❑	1246	Albert Pujols CL SP	8.00	3.00
❑	1247	Carl Crawford CL SP	5.00	2.00
❑	1248	Mark Teixeira CL SP	5.00	2.00
❑	1249	Vernon Wells CL SP	5.00	2.00
❑	1250	Alfonso Soriano CL SP	5.00	2.00

2007 Upper Deck

❑ COMPLETE SET (1020) 300.00 200.00
❑ COMP.SET w/o RC EXCH (1000) 200.00 120.00
❑ COMP.SER.1 w/o RC EXCH (500) 80.00 40.00
❑ COMP.SER.2 w/o RC EXCH (500) 120.00 80.00
❑ COMMON CARD (1-1020) .40 .15
❑ COMMON ROOKIE .75 .30
❑ COMMON ROOKIE (501-520) 2.50 1.00
❑ 1-500 ISSUED IN SERIES 1 PACKS
❑ 501-1020 ISSUED IN SERIES 2 PACKS
❑ MATSUZAKA JSY RANDOMLY INSERTED
❑ NO MATSUZAKA JSY PRICING AVAILABLE
❑ OVERALL PLATE SER.1 ODDS 1:192 H
❑ OVERALL PLATE SER.2 ODDS 1:96 H
❑ PLATE PRINT RUN 1 SET PER COLOR
❑ BLACK-CYAN-MAGENTA-YELLOW ISSUED
❑ NO PLATE PRICING DUE TO SCARCITY
❑ ROOKIE EXCH APPX. 1-2 PER CASE
❑ ROOKIE EXCH DEADLINE 02/27/2010
❑ 1 Doug Slaten RC .75 .30
❑ 2 Miguel Montero (RC) .75 .30
❑ 3 Brian Burres (RC) .75 .30
❑ 4 Devern Hansack RC .75 .30
❑ 5 David Murphy (RC) .75 .30
❑ 6 Jose Reyes RC .75 .30
❑ 7 Scott Moore (RC) .75 .30
❑ 8 Josh Fields (RC) .75 .30
❑ 9 Chris Stewart RC .75 .30
❑ 10 Jerry Owens (RC) .75 .30
❑ 11 Ryan Sweeney (RC) .75 .30
❑ 12 Kevin Kouzmanoff (RC) .75 .30
❑ 13 Jeff Baker (RC) .75 .30
❑ 14 Justin Hampson (RC) .75 .30
❑ 15 Jeff Salazar (RC) .75 .30
❑ 16 Alvin Colina RC .75 .30
❑ 17 Troy Tulowitzki (RC) 2.00 .75
❑ 18 Andrew Miller RC 5.00 2.00
❑ 19 Mike Rabelo RC .75 .30
❑ 20 Jose Diaz (RC) .75 .30
❑ 21 Angel Sanchez RC .75 .30
❑ 22 Ryan Braun RC .75 .30
❑ 23 Delwyn Young (RC) .75 .30
❑ 24 Drew Anderson RC .75 .30
❑ 25 Dennis Sarfate (RC) .75 .30
❑ 26 Vinny Rottino (RC) .75 .30
❑ 27 Glen Perkins (RC) .75 .30
❑ 28 Alexi Casilla RC 1.25 .50
❑ 29 Philip Humber (RC) .75 .30
❑ 30 Andy Cannizaro RC .75 .30
❑ 31 Jeremy Brown .40 .15
❑ 32 Sean Henn (RC) .75 .30
❑ 33 Brian Rogers .40 .15
❑ 34 Carlos Maldonado (RC) .75 .30
❑ 35 Juan Morillo (RC) .75 .30
❑ 36 Fred Lewis (RC) .75 .30
❑ 37 Patrick Misch (RC) .75 .30
❑ 38 Billy Sadler (RC) .75 .30
❑ 39 Ryan Feierabend (RC) .75 .30
❑ 40 Cesar Jimenez RC .75 .30
❑ 41 Oswaldo Navarro RC .75 .30
❑ 42 Travis Chick (RC) .75 .30
❑ 43 Delmon Young (RC) 2.00 .75
❑ 44 Shawn Riggans (RC) .75 .30
❑ 45 Brian Stokes (RC) .75 .30
❑ 46 Juan Salas (RC) .75 .30
❑ 47 Joaquin Arias (RC) .75 .30
❑ 48 Adam Lind (RC) .75 .30
❑ 49 Beltran Perez (RC) .75 .30
❑ 50 Brett Campbell RC .75 .30
❑ 51 Brian Roberts .40 .15
❑ 52 Miguel Tejada .40 .15
❑ 53 Brandon Fahey .40 .15
❑ 54 Jay Gibbons .40 .15
❑ 55 Corey Patterson .40 .15
❑ 56 Nick Markakis .60 .25
❑ 57 Ramon Hernandez .40 .15
❑ 58 Kris Benson .40 .15
❑ 59 Adam Loewen .40 .15
❑ 60 Erik Bedard .40 .15
❑ 61 Chris Ray .40 .15
❑ 62 Chris Britton .40 .15
❑ 63 Daniel Cabrera .40 .15
❑ 64 Sendy Rleal .40 .15
❑ 65 Manny Ramirez .60 .25
❑ 66 David Ortiz 1.00 .40
❑ 67 Gabe Kapler .40 .15
❑ 68 Alex Cora .40 .15
❑ 69 Dustin Pedroia .40 .15
❑ 70 Trot Nixon .40 .15
❑ 71 Doug Mirabelli .40 .15
❑ 72 Mark Loretta .40 .15
❑ 73 Curt Schilling .60 .25
❑ 74 Jonathan Papelbon 1.00 .40
❑ 75 Tim Wakefield .40 .15
❑ 76 Jon Lester .60 .25
❑ 77 Craig Hansen .40 .15
❑ 78 Keith Foulke .40 .15
❑ 79 Jermaine Dye .40 .15
❑ 80 Jim Thome .60 .25
❑ 81 Tadahito Iguchi .40 .15
❑ 82 Rob Mackowiak .40 .15
❑ 83 Brian Anderson .40 .15
❑ 84 Juan Uribe .40 .15
❑ 85 A.J. Pierzynski .40 .15
❑ 86 Alex Cintron .40 .15
❑ 87 Jon Garland .40 .15
❑ 88 Jose Contreras .40 .15
❑ 89 Neal Cotts .40 .15
❑ 90 Bobby Jenks .40 .15
❑ 91 Mike MacDougal .40 .15
❑ 92 Javier Vazquez .40 .15
❑ 93 Travis Hafner .40 .15
❑ 94 Jhonny Peralta .40 .15
❑ 95 Ryan Garko .40 .15
❑ 96 Victor Martinez .40 .15
❑ 97 Hector Luna .40 .15
❑ 98 Casey Blake .40 .15
❑ 99 Jason Michaels .40 .15
❑ 100 Shin-Soo Choo .60 .25
❑ 101 C.C. Sabathia .40 .15
❑ 102 Paul Byrd .40 .15
❑ 103 Jeremy Sowers .40 .15
❑ 104 Cliff Lee .40 .15
❑ 105 Rafael Betancourt .40 .15
❑ 106 Francisco Cruceta .40 .15
❑ 107 Sean Casey .40 .15
❑ 108 Brandon Inge .40 .15
❑ 109 Placido Polanco .40 .15
❑ 110 Omar Infante .40 .15
❑ 111 Ivan Rodriguez .60 .25
❑ 112 Magglio Ordonez .40 .15
❑ 113 Craig Monroe .40 .15
❑ 114 Marcus Thames .40 .15
❑ 115 Justin Verlander 1.00 .40
❑ 116 Todd Jones .40 .15
❑ 117 Kenny Rogers .40 .15
❑ 118 Joel Zumaya .60 .25
❑ 119 Jeremy Bonderman .40 .15
❑ 120 Nate Robertson .40 .15
❑ 121 Mark Teahen .40 .15
❑ 122 Ryan Shealy .40 .15
❑ 123 Mitch Maier RC .75 .30
❑ 124 Doug Mientkiewicz .40 .15
❑ 125 Mark Grudzielanek .40 .15
❑ 126 Shane Costa .40 .15
❑ 127 John Buck .40 .15
❑ 128 Reggie Sanders .40 .15
❑ 129 Mike Sweeney .40 .15
❑ 130 Mark Redman .40 .15
❑ 131 Todd Wellemeyer .40 .15
❑ 132 Scott Elarton .40 .15
❑ 133 Ambiorix Burgos .40 .15
❑ 134 Joe Nelson .40 .15
❑ 135 Howie Kendrick .40 .15
❑ 136 Chone Figgins .40 .15
❑ 137 Orlando Cabrera .40 .15
❑ 138 Maicer Izturis .40 .15
❑ 139 Jose Molina .40 .15
❑ 140 Vladimir Guerrero 1.00 .40
❑ 141 Darin Erstad .40 .15
❑ 142 Juan Rivera .40 .15
❑ 143 Jered Weaver .60 .25
❑ 144 John Lackey .40 .15
❑ 145 Joe Saunders .40 .15
❑ 146 Bartolo Colon .40 .15
❑ 147 Scot Shields .40 .15
❑ 148 Francisco Rodriguez .40 .15
❑ 149 Justin Morneau .40 .15
❑ 150 Jason Bartlett .40 .15
❑ 151 Luis Castillo .40 .15
❑ 152 Nick Punto .40 .15
❑ 153 Shannon Stewart .40 .15
❑ 154 Michael Cuddyer .40 .15
❑ 155 Jason Kubel .40 .15
❑ 156 Joe Mauer .60 .25
❑ 157 Francisco Liriano 1.00 .40
❑ 158 Joe Nathan .40 .15
❑ 159 Dennys Reyes .40 .15
❑ 160 Brad Radke .40 .15
❑ 161 Boof Bonser .40 .15
❑ 162 Juan Rincon .40 .15
❑ 163 Derek Jeter 2.50 1.00
❑ 164 Jason Giambi .40 .15
❑ 165 Robinson Cano .60 .25
❑ 166 Andy Phillips .40 .15
❑ 167 Bobby Abreu .40 .15
❑ 168 Gary Sheffield .40 .15
❑ 169 Bernie Williams .60 .25
❑ 170 Melky Cabrera .40 .15
❑ 171 Mike Mussina .60 .25
❑ 172 Chien-Ming Wang 1.50 .60
❑ 173 Mariano Rivera 1.00 .40
❑ 174 Scott Proctor .40 .15
❑ 175 Jaret Wright .40 .15
❑ 176 Kyle Farnsworth .40 .15
❑ 177 Eric Chavez .40 .15
❑ 178 Bobby Crosby .40 .15
❑ 179 Frank Thomas 1.00 .40
❑ 180 Dan Johnson .40 .15
❑ 181 Marco Scutaro .40 .15
❑ 182 Nick Swisher .40 .15
❑ 183 Milton Bradley .40 .15
❑ 184 Jay Payton .40 .15
❑ 185 Joe Blanton .40 .15
❑ 186 Barry Zito .40 .15
❑ 187 Rich Harden .40 .15
❑ 188 Esteban Loaiza .40 .15
❑ 189 Huston Street .40 .15
❑ 190 Chad Gaudin .40 .15
❑ 191 Richie Sexson .40 .15
❑ 192 Yuniesky Betancourt .40 .15
❑ 193 Willie Bloomquist .40 .15
❑ 194 Ben Broussard .40 .15
❑ 195 Kenji Johjima 1.00 .40
❑ 196 Ichiro Suzuki 1.50 .60
❑ 197 Raul Ibanez .40 .15
❑ 198 Chris Snelling .40 .15
❑ 199 Felix Hernandez .60 .25
❑ 200 Cha-Seung Baek .40 .15
❑ 201 Joel Pineiro .40 .15
❑ 202 Julio Mateo .40 .15
❑ 203 J.J. Putz .40 .15
❑ 204 Rafael Soriano .40 .15
❑ 205 Jorge Cantu .40 .15
❑ 206 B.J. Upton .40 .15
❑ 207 Ty Wigginton .40 .15
❑ 208 Greg Norton .40 .15
❑ 209 Dioner Navarro .40 .15
❑ 210 Carl Crawford .40 .15
❑ 211 Jonny Gomes .40 .15
❑ 212 Damon Hollins .40 .15
❑ 213 Scott Kazmir .60 .25
❑ 214 Casey Fossum .40 .15
❑ 215 Ruddy Lugo .40 .15
❑ 216 James Shields .40 .15
❑ 217 Tyler Walker .40 .15
❑ 218 Shawn Camp .40 .15
❑ 219 Mark Teixeira .60 .25
❑ 220 Hank Blalock .40 .15
❑ 221 Ian Kinsler .40 .15
❑ 222 Jerry Hairston Jr. .40 .15
❑ 223 Gerald Laird .40 .15
❑ 224 Carlos Lee .40 .15
❑ 225 Gary Matthews .40 .15
❑ 226 Mark DeRosa .40 .15
❑ 227 Kip Wells .40 .15
❑ 228 Akinori Otsuka .40 .15
❑ 229 Vicente Padilla .40 .15
❑ 230 John Koronka .40 .15
❑ 231 Kevin Millwood .40 .15
❑ 232 Wes Littleton .40 .15
❑ 233 Troy Glaus .40 .15
❑ 234 Lyle Overbay .40 .15

❑ 235 Aaron Hill .40 .15
❑ 236 John McDonald .40 .15
❑ 237 Bengie Molina .40 .15
❑ 238 Vernon Wells .40 .15
❑ 239 Reed Johnson .40 .15
❑ 240 Frank Catalanotto .40 .15
❑ 241 Roy Halladay .40 .15
❑ 242 B.J. Ryan .40 .15
❑ 243 Gustavo Chacin .40 .15
❑ 244 Scott Downs .40 .15
❑ 245 Casey Janssen .40 .15
❑ 246 Justin Speier .40 .15
❑ 247 Stephen Drew .60 .25
❑ 248 Conor Jackson .40 .15
❑ 249 Orlando Hudson .40 .15
❑ 250 Chad Tracy .40 .15
❑ 251 Johnny Estrada .40 .15
❑ 252 Luis Gonzalez .40 .15
❑ 253 Eric Byrnes .40 .15
❑ 254 Carlos Quentin .40 .15
❑ 255 Brandon Webb .40 .15
❑ 256 Claudio Vargas .40 .15
❑ 257 Juan Cruz .40 .15
❑ 258 Jorge Julio .40 .15
❑ 259 Luis Vizcaino .40 .15
❑ 260 Livan Hernandez .40 .15
❑ 261 Chipper Jones 1.00 .40
❑ 262 Edgar Renteria .40 .15
❑ 263 Adam LaRoche .40 .15
❑ 264 Willy Aybar .40 .15
❑ 265 Brian McCann .40 .15
❑ 266 Ryan Langerhans .40 .15
❑ 267 Jeff Francoeur 1.00 .40
❑ 268 Matt Diaz .40 .15
❑ 269 Tim Hudson .40 .15
❑ 270 John Smoltz .60 .25
❑ 271 Oscar Villarreal .40 .15
❑ 272 Horacio Ramirez .40 .15
❑ 273 Bob Wickman .40 .15
❑ 274 Chad Paronto .40 .15
❑ 275 Derrek Lee .40 .15
❑ 276 Ryan Theriot .40 .15
❑ 277 Cesar Izturis .40 .15
❑ 278 Ronny Cedeno .40 .15
❑ 279 Michael Barrett .40 .15
❑ 280 Juan Pierre .40 .15
❑ 281 Jacque Jones .40 .15
❑ 282 Matt Murton .40 .15
❑ 283 Carlos Zambrano .40 .15
❑ 284 Mark Prior .60 .25
❑ 285 Rich Hill .40 .15
❑ 286 Sean Marshall .40 .15
❑ 287 Ryan Dempster .40 .15
❑ 288 Ryan O'Malley .40 .15
❑ 289 Scott Hatteberg .40 .15
❑ 290 Brandon Phillips .40 .15
❑ 291 Edwin Encarnacion .40 .15
❑ 292 Rich Aurilia .40 .15
❑ 293 David Ross .40 .15
❑ 294 Ken Griffey Jr. 1.50 .60
❑ 295 Ryan Freel .40 .15
❑ 296 Chris Denorfia .40 .15
❑ 297 Bronson Arroyo .40 .15
❑ 298 Aaron Harang .40 .15
❑ 299 Brandon Claussen .40 .15
❑ 300 Todd Coffey .40 .15
❑ 301 David Weathers .40 .15
❑ 302 Eric Milton .40 .15
❑ 303 Todd Helton .60 .25
❑ 304 Clint Barmes .40 .15
❑ 305 Kazuo Matsui .40 .15
❑ 306 Jamey Carroll .40 .15
❑ 307 Yorvit Torrealba .40 .15
❑ 308 Matt Holliday 1.00 .40
❑ 309 Choo Freeman .40 .15
❑ 310 Brad Hawpe .40 .15
❑ 311 Jason Jennings .40 .15
❑ 312 Jeff Francis .40 .15
❑ 313 Josh Fogg .40 .15
❑ 314 Aaron Cook .40 .15
❑ 315 Ubaldo Jimenez (RC) .75 .30
❑ 316 Manny Corpas .40 .15
❑ 317 Miguel Cabrera .60 .25
❑ 318 Dan Uggla .60 .25
❑ 319 Hanley Ramirez .60 .25
❑ 320 Wes Helms .40 .15
❑ 321 Miguel Olivo .40 .15
❑ 322 Jeremy Hermida .40 .15
❑ 323 Cody Ross .40 .15
❑ 324 Josh Willingham .40 .15
❑ 325 Dontrelle Willis .40 .15
❑ 326 Anibal Sanchez .40 .15
❑ 327 Josh Johnson .40 .15
❑ 328 Jose Garcia RC .75 .30
❑ 329 Joe Borowski .40 .15
❑ 330 Taylor Tankersley .40 .15
❑ 331 Lance Berkman .40 .15
❑ 332 Craig Biggio .60 .25
❑ 333 Aubrey Huff .40 .15
❑ 334 Adam Everett .40 .15
❑ 335 Brad Ausmus .40 .15
❑ 336 Willy Taveras .40 .15
❑ 337 Luke Scott .40 .15
❑ 338 Chris Burke .40 .15
❑ 339 Roger Clemens 2.00 .75
❑ 340 Andy Pettitte .60 .25
❑ 341 Brandon Backe .40 .15
❑ 342 Hector Gimenez (RC) .75 .30
❑ 343 Brad Lidge .40 .15
❑ 344 Dan Wheeler .40 .15
❑ 345 Nomar Garciaparra 1.00 .40
❑ 346 Rafael Furcal .40 .15
❑ 347 Wilson Betemit .40 .15
❑ 348 Julio Lugo .40 .15
❑ 349 Russell Martin .40 .15
❑ 350 Andre Ethier .60 .25
❑ 351 Matt Kemp .40 .15
❑ 352 Kenny Lofton .40 .15
❑ 353 Brad Penny .40 .15
❑ 354 Derek Lowe .40 .15
❑ 355 Chad Billingsley .40 .15
❑ 356 Greg Maddux 1.50 .60
❑ 357 Takashi Saito .40 .15
❑ 358 Jonathan Broxton .40 .15
❑ 359 Prince Fielder 1.00 .40
❑ 360 Rickie Weeks .40 .15
❑ 361 Bill Hall .40 .15
❑ 362 J.J. Hardy .40 .15
❑ 363 Jeff Cirillo .40 .15
❑ 364 Tony Gwynn Jr. .40 .15
❑ 365 Corey Hart .40 .15
❑ 366 Laynce Nix .40 .15
❑ 367 Doug Davis .40 .15
❑ 368 Ben Sheets .40 .15
❑ 369 Chris Capuano .40 .15
❑ 370 Dave Bush .40 .15
❑ 371 Derrick Turnbow .40 .15
❑ 372 Francisco Cordero .40 .15
❑ 373 Jose Reyes .40 .15
❑ 374 Carlos Delgado .40 .15
❑ 375 Julio Franco .40 .15
❑ 376 Jose Valentin .40 .15
❑ 377 Paul LoDuca .40 .15
❑ 378 Carlos Beltran .40 .15
❑ 379 Shawn Green .40 .15
❑ 380 Lastings Milledge .60 .25
❑ 381 Endy Chavez .40 .15
❑ 382 Pedro Martinez .60 .25
❑ 383 John Maine .40 .15
❑ 384 Orlando Hernandez .40 .15
❑ 385 Steve Trachsel .40 .15
❑ 386 Billy Wagner .40 .15
❑ 387 Ryan Howard 1.50 .60
❑ 388 Chase Utley 1.00 .40
❑ 389 Jimmy Rollins .40 .15
❑ 390 Chris Coste .40 .15
❑ 391 Jeff Conine .40 .15
❑ 392 Aaron Rowand .40 .15
❑ 393 Shane Victorino .40 .15
❑ 394 David Dellucci .40 .15
❑ 395 Cole Hamels .60 .25
❑ 396 Jamie Moyer .40 .15
❑ 397 Ryan Madson .40 .15
❑ 398 Brett Myers .40 .15
❑ 399 Tom Gordon .40 .15
❑ 400 Geoff Geary .40 .15
❑ 401 Freddy Sanchez .40 .15
❑ 402 Xavier Nady .40 .15
❑ 403 Jose Castillo .40 .15
❑ 404 Joe Randa .40 .15
❑ 405 Jason Bay .40 .15
❑ 406 Chris Duffy .40 .15
❑ 407 Jose Bautista .40 .15
❑ 408 Ronny Paulino .40 .15
❑ 409 Ian Snell .40 .15
❑ 410 Zach Duke .40 .15
❑ 411 Tom Gorzelanny .40 .15
❑ 412 Shane Youman RC .75 .30
❑ 413 Mike Gonzalez .40 .15
❑ 414 Matt Capps .40 .15
❑ 415 Adrian Gonzalez .40 .15
❑ 416 Josh Barfield .40 .15
❑ 417 Todd Walker .40 .15
❑ 418 Khalil Greene .60 .25
❑ 419 Mike Piazza 1.00 .40
❑ 420 Dave Roberts .40 .15
❑ 421 Mike Cameron .40 .15
❑ 422 Geoff Blum .40 .15
❑ 423 Jake Peavy .40 .15
❑ 424 Chris R. Young .40 .15
❑ 425 Woody Williams .40 .15
❑ 426 Clay Hensley .40 .15
❑ 427 Cla Meredith .40 .15
❑ 428 Trevor Hoffman .40 .15
❑ 429 Shea Hillenbrand .40 .15
❑ 430 Pedro Feliz .40 .15
❑ 431 Ray Durham .40 .15
❑ 432 Mark Sweeney .40 .15
❑ 433 Eliezer Alfonzo .40 .15
❑ 434 Moises Alou .40 .15
❑ 435 Steve Finley .40 .15
❑ 436 Todd Linden .40 .15
❑ 437 Jason Schmidt .40 .15
❑ 438 Matt Cain .60 .25
❑ 439 Noah Lowry .40 .15
❑ 440 Brad Hennessey .40 .15
❑ 441 Armando Benitez .40 .15
❑ 442 Jonathan Sanchez .40 .15
❑ 443 Albert Pujols 2.00 .75
❑ 444 Ronnie Belliard .40 .15
❑ 445 David Eckstein .40 .15
❑ 446 Aaron Miles .40 .15
❑ 447 Yadier Molina .40 .15
❑ 448 Jim Edmonds .60 .25
❑ 449 Chris Duncan .40 .15
❑ 450 Juan Encarnacion .40 .15
❑ 451 Chris Carpenter .40 .15
❑ 452 Jeff Suppan .40 .15
❑ 453 Jason Marquis .40 .15
❑ 454 Jeff Weaver .40 .15
❑ 455 Jason Isringhausen .40 .15
❑ 456 Braden Looper .40 .15
❑ 457 Ryan Zimmerman 1.00 .40
❑ 458 Nick Johnson .40 .15
❑ 459 Felipe Lopez .40 .15
❑ 460 Brian Schneider .40 .15
❑ 461 Alfonso Soriano .40 .15
❑ 462 Austin Kearns .40 .15
❑ 463 Ryan Church .40 .15
❑ 464 Alex Escobar .40 .15
❑ 465 Ramon Ortiz .40 .15
❑ 466 Tony Armas .40 .15
❑ 467 Michael O'Connor .40 .15
❑ 468 Chad Cordero .40 .15
❑ 469 Jon Rauch .40 .15
❑ 470 Pedro Astacio .40 .15
❑ 471 Miguel Tejada CL .40 .15
❑ 472 David Ortiz CL 1.00 .40
❑ 473 Jermaine Dye CL .40 .15
❑ 474 Travis Hafner CL .40 .15
❑ 475 Magglio Ordonez CL .40 .15
❑ 476 Mark Teahen CL .40 .15
❑ 477 Vladimir Guerrero CL 1.00 .40
❑ 478 Justin Morneau CL .40 .15
❑ 479 Derek Jeter CL 2.50 1.00
❑ 480 Nick Swisher CL .40 .15
❑ 481 Ichiro Suzuki CL 1.50 .60
❑ 482 Scott Kazmir CL .60 .25
❑ 483 Mark Teixeira CL .60 .25
❑ 484 Vernon Wells CL .40 .15
❑ 485 Brandon Webb CL .40 .15
❑ 486 Andruw Jones CL .60 .25

❑ 487	Carlos Zambrano CL	.40	.15
❑ 488	Adam Dunn CL	.40	.15
❑ 489	Matt Holliday CL	1.00	.40
❑ 490	Miguel Cabrera CL	.60	.25
❑ 491	Lance Berkman CL	.40	.15
❑ 492	Nomar Garciaparra CL	1.00	.40
❑ 493	Prince Fielder CL	1.00	.40
❑ 494	Carlos Beltran CL	.40	.15
❑ 495	Ryan Howard CL	1.50	.60
❑ 496	Jason Bay CL	.40	.15
❑ 497	Adrian Gonzalez CL	.40	.15
❑ 498	Matt Cain CL	.60	.25
❑ 499	Albert Pujols CL	2.00	.75
❑ 500	Ryan Zimmerman CL	1.00	.40
❑ 501a	D.Matsuzaka Suit RC	60.00	30.00
❑ 501b	D.Matsuzaka Throwing RC	15.00	6.00
❑ 501c	Daisuke Matsuzaka Jsy/100		
❑ 501d	Daisuke Matsuzaka Ball/150		
❑ 502	Kei Igawa RC	4.00	1.50
❑ 503	Akinori Iwamura RC	6.00	2.50
❑ 504	Alex Gordon RC	25.00	10.00
❑ 505	Matt Chico (RC)	2.50	1.00
❑ 506	John Danks RC	2.50	1.00
❑ 507	Elijah Dukes RC	2.50	1.00
❑ 508	Gustavo Molina RC	2.50	1.00
❑ 509	Joakim Soria RC	6.00	2.50
❑ 510	Jay Marshall RC	6.00	2.50
❑ 511	Travis Buck (RC)	2.50	1.00
❑ 512	Brandon Wood (RC)	2.50	1.00
❑ 513	Kevin Cameron RC	2.50	1.00
❑ 514	Jared Burton RC	6.00	2.50
❑ 515	Kory Casto (RC)	2.50	1.00
❑ 516	Joe Smith RC	2.50	1.00
❑ 517	Jose Garcia RC	2.50	1.00
❑ 518	Hunter Pence (RC)	20.00	8.00
❑ 519	Felix Pie (RC)	2.50	1.00
❑ 520	Zach Segovia (RC)	2.50	1.00
❑ 521	Randy Johnson	1.00	.40
❑ 522	Brandon Lyon	.40	.15
❑ 523	Robby Hammock	.40	.15
❑ 524	Micah Owings (RC)	.75	.30
❑ 525	Doug Davis	.40	.15
❑ 526	Brian Barden RC	.75	.30
❑ 527	Alberto Callaspo	.40	.15
❑ 528	Stephen Drew	.60	.25
❑ 529	Chris Young	.40	.15
❑ 530	Edgar Gonzalez	.40	.15
❑ 531	Brandon Medders	.40	.15
❑ 532	Tony Pena	.40	.15
❑ 533	Jose Valverde	.40	.15
❑ 534	Chris Snyder	.40	.15
❑ 535	Tony Clark	.40	.15
❑ 536	Scott Hairston	.40	.15
❑ 537	Jeff DaVanon	.40	.15
❑ 538	Randy Johnson CL	1.00	.40
❑ 539	Mark Redman	.40	.15
❑ 540	Andruw Jones	.60	.25
❑ 541	Rafael Soriano	.40	.15
❑ 542	Scott Thorman	.40	.15
❑ 543	Chipper Jones	1.00	.40
❑ 544	Mike Gonzalez	.40	.15
❑ 545	Lance Cormier	.40	.15
❑ 546	Kyle Davies	.40	.15
❑ 547	Mike Hampton	.40	.15
❑ 548	Chuck James	.40	.15
❑ 549	Macay McBride	.40	.15
❑ 550	Tanyon Sturtze	.40	.15
❑ 551	Tyler Yates	.40	.15
❑ 552	Pete Orr	.40	.15
❑ 553	Craig Wilson	.40	.15
❑ 554	Chris Woodward	.40	.15
❑ 555	Kelly Johnson	.40	.15
❑ 556	Chipper Jones CL	1.00	.40
❑ 557	Chad Bradford	.40	.15
❑ 558	John Parrish	.40	.15
❑ 559	Jeremy Guthrie	.40	.15
❑ 560	Steve Trachsel	.40	.15
❑ 561	Scott Williamson	.40	.15
❑ 562	Jaret Wright	.40	.15
❑ 563	Paul Bako	.40	.15
❑ 564	Chris Gomez	.40	.15
❑ 565	Melvin Mora	.40	.15
❑ 566	Freddie Bynum	.40	.15
❑ 567	Aubrey Huff	.40	.15
❑ 568	Jay Payton	.40	.15
❑ 569	Miguel Tejada	.40	.15
❑ 570	Kurt Birkins	.40	.15
❑ 571	Danys Baez	.40	.15
❑ 572	Brian Roberts CL	.40	.15
❑ 573	Josh Beckett	.60	.25
❑ 574	Matt Clement	.40	.15
❑ 575	Hideki Okajima RC	5.00	2.00
❑ 576	Javier Lopez	.40	.15
❑ 577	Joel Pineiro	.40	.15
❑ 578	J.C. Romero	.40	.15
❑ 579	Kyle Snyder	.40	.15
❑ 580	Julian Tavarez	.40	.15
❑ 581	Mike Timlin	.40	.15
❑ 582	Jason Varitek	1.00	.40
❑ 583	Mike Lowell	.40	.15
❑ 584	Kevin Youkilis	.40	.15
❑ 585	Coco Crisp	.40	.15
❑ 586	J.D. Drew	.40	.15
❑ 587	Eric Hinske	.40	.15
❑ 588	Wily Mo Pena	.40	.15
❑ 589	Julio Lugo	.40	.15
❑ 590	David Ortiz	1.00	.40
❑ 591	Manny Ramirez	.60	.25
❑ 592	Daisuke Matsuzaka CL	4.00	1.50
❑ 593	Scott Eyre	.40	.15
❑ 594	Angel Guzman	.40	.15
❑ 595	Bob Howry	.40	.15
❑ 596	Ted Lilly	.40	.15
❑ 597	Juan Mateo	.40	.15
❑ 598	Wade Miller	.40	.15
❑ 599	Carlos Zambrano	.40	.15
❑ 600	Will Ohman	.40	.15
❑ 601	Michael Wuertz	.40	.15
❑ 602	Henry Blanco	.40	.15
❑ 603	Aramis Ramirez	.40	.15
❑ 604	Cliff Floyd	.40	.15
❑ 605	Kerry Wood	.40	.15
❑ 606	Alfonso Soriano	.40	.15
❑ 607	Daryle Ward	.40	.15
❑ 608	Jason Marquis	.40	.15
❑ 609	Mark DeRosa	.40	.15
❑ 610	Neal Cotts	.40	.15
❑ 611	Derrek Lee	.40	.15
❑ 612	Aramis Ramirez CL	.40	.15
❑ 613	David Aardsma	.40	.15
❑ 614	Mark Buehrle	.40	.15
❑ 615	Nick Masset	.40	.15
❑ 616	Andrew Sisco	.40	.15
❑ 617	Matt Thornton	.40	.15
❑ 618	Toby Hall	.40	.15
❑ 619	Joe Crede	.40	.15
❑ 620	Paul Konerko	.40	.15
❑ 621	Darin Erstad	.40	.15
❑ 622	Pablo Ozuna	.40	.15
❑ 623	Scott Podsednik	.40	.15
❑ 624	Jim Thome	.60	.25
❑ 625	Jermaine Dye	.40	.15
❑ 626	Jim Thome CL	.60	.25
❑ 627	Adam Dunn	.40	.15
❑ 628	Bill Bray	.40	.15
❑ 629	Alex Gonzalez	.40	.15
❑ 630	Josh Hamilton (RC)	5.00	2.00
❑ 631	Matt Belisle	.40	.15
❑ 632	Rheal Cormier	.40	.15
❑ 633	Kyle Lohse	.40	.15
❑ 634	Eric Milton	.40	.15
❑ 635	Kirk Saarloos	.40	.15
❑ 636	Mike Stanton	.40	.15
❑ 637	Javier Valentin	.40	.15
❑ 638	Juan Castro	.40	.15
❑ 639	Jeff Conine	.40	.15
❑ 640	Jon Coutlangus (RC)	.75	.30
❑ 641	Ken Griffey Jr.	1.50	.60
❑ 642	Ken Griffey Jr. CL	1.50	.60
❑ 643	Fernando Cabrera	.40	.15
❑ 644	Fausto Carmona	.40	.15
❑ 645	Jason Davis	.40	.15
❑ 646	Aaron Fultz	.40	.15
❑ 647	Roberto Hernandez	.40	.15
❑ 648	Jake Westbrook	.40	.15
❑ 649	Kelly Shoppach	.40	.15
❑ 650	Josh Barfield	.40	.15
❑ 651	Andy Marte	.40	.15
❑ 652	Joe Inglett	.40	.15
❑ 653	David Dellucci	.40	.15
❑ 654	Joe Borowski	.40	.15
❑ 655	Franklin Gutierrez	.40	.15
❑ 656	Trot Nixon	.40	.15
❑ 657	Grady Sizemore	.60	.25
❑ 658	Mike Rouse	.40	.15
❑ 659	Travis Hafner	.40	.15
❑ 660	Victor Martinez	.40	.15
❑ 661	C.C. Sabathia	.40	.15
❑ 662	Grady Sizemore CL	.60	.25
❑ 663	Jeremy Affeldt	.40	.15
❑ 664	Taylor Buchholz	.40	.15
❑ 665	Brian Fuentes	.40	.15
❑ 666	Latroy Hawkins	.40	.15
❑ 667	Byung-Hyun Kim	.40	.15
❑ 668	Brian Lawrence	.40	.15
❑ 669	Rodrigo Lopez	.40	.15
❑ 670	Jeff Francis	.40	.15
❑ 671	Chris Ianetta	.40	.15
❑ 672	Garrett Atkins	.40	.15
❑ 673	Todd Helton	.60	.25
❑ 674	Steve Finley	.40	.15
❑ 675	John Mabry	.40	.15
❑ 676	Willy Taveras	.40	.15
❑ 677	Jason Hirsh	.40	.15
❑ 678	Ramon Ramirez	.40	.15
❑ 679	Matt Holliday	1.00	.40
❑ 680	Todd Helton CL	.60	.25
❑ 681	Roman Colon	.40	.15
❑ 682	Chad Durbin	.40	.15
❑ 683	Jason Grilli	.40	.15
❑ 684	Wilfredo Ledezma	.40	.15
❑ 685	Mike Maroth	.40	.15
❑ 686	Jose Mesa	.40	.15
❑ 687	Justin Verlander	1.00	.40
❑ 688	Fernando Rodney	.40	.15
❑ 689	Vance Wilson	.40	.15
❑ 690	Carlos Guillen	.40	.15
❑ 691	Neifi Perez	.40	.15
❑ 692	Curtis Granderson	.40	.15
❑ 693	Gary Sheffield	.40	.15
❑ 694	Justin Verlander CL	1.00	.40
❑ 695	Kevin Gregg	.40	.15
❑ 696	Logan Kensing	.40	.15
❑ 697	Randy Messenger	.40	.15
❑ 698	Sergio Mitre	.40	.15
❑ 699	Ricky Nolasco	.40	.15
❑ 700	Scott Olsen	.40	.15
❑ 701	Renyel Pinto	.40	.15
❑ 702	Matt Treanor	.40	.15
❑ 703	Alfredo Amezaga	.40	.15
❑ 704	Aaron Boone	.40	.15
❑ 705	Mike Jacobs	.40	.15
❑ 706	Miguel Cabrera	.60	.25
❑ 707	Joe Borchard	.40	.15
❑ 708	Jorge Julio	.40	.15
❑ 709	Rick Vanden Hurk RC	1.25	.50
❑ 710	Lee Gardner (RC)	.75	.30
❑ 711	Matt Lindstrom (RC)	.75	.30
❑ 712	Henry Owens	.40	.15
❑ 713	Hanley Ramirez	.60	.25
❑ 714	Alejandro De Aza RC	.75	.30
❑ 715	Hanley Ramirez CL	.60	.25
❑ 716	Dave Borkowski	.40	.15
❑ 717	Jason Jennings	.40	.15
❑ 718	Trever Miller	.40	.15
❑ 719	Roy Oswalt	.40	.15
❑ 720	Wandy Rodriguez	.40	.15
❑ 721	Humberto Quintero	.40	.15
❑ 722	Morgan Ensberg	.40	.15
❑ 723	Mike Lamb	.40	.15
❑ 724	Mark Loretta	.40	.15
❑ 725	Jason Lane	.40	.15
❑ 726	Carlos Lee	.40	.15
❑ 727	Orlando Palmeiro	.40	.15
❑ 728	Woody Williams	.40	.15
❑ 729	Chad Qualls	.40	.15
❑ 730	Lance Berkman	.40	.15
❑ 731	Rick White	.40	.15
❑ 732	Chris Sampson	.40	.15
❑ 733	Carlos Lee CL	.40	.15
❑ 734	Jorge De La Rosa	.40	.15
❑ 735	Octavio Dotel	.40	.15

❑ 736 Jimmy Gobble .40 .15
❑ 737 Zack Greinke .40 .15
❑ 738 Luke Hudson .40 .15
❑ 739 Gil Meche .40 .15
❑ 740 Joel Peralta .40 .15
❑ 741 Odalis Perez .40 .15
❑ 742 David Riske .40 .15
❑ 743 Jason LaRue .40 .15
❑ 744 Tony Pena .40 .15
❑ 745 Esteban German .40 .15
❑ 746 Ross Gload .40 .15
❑ 747 Emil Brown .40 .15
❑ 748 David DeJesus .40 .15
❑ 749 Brandon Duckworth .40 .15
❑ 750 Alex Gordon CL 2.50 1.00
❑ 751 Jered Weaver .60 .25
❑ 752 Vladimir Guerrero 1.00 .40
❑ 753 Hector Carrasco .40 .15
❑ 754 Kelvim Escobar .40 .15
❑ 755 Darren Oliver .40 .15
❑ 756 Dustin Moseley .40 .15
❑ 757 Ervin Santana .40 .15
❑ 758 Mike Napoli .40 .15
❑ 759 Shea Hillenbrand .40 .15
❑ 760 Casey Kotchman .40 .15
❑ 761 Reggie Willits .40 .15
❑ 762 Robb Quinlan .40 .15
❑ 763 Garret Anderson .40 .15
❑ 764 Gary Matthews .40 .15
❑ 765 Justin Speier .40 .15
❑ 766 Jered Weaver CL .60 .25
❑ 767 Joe Beimel .40 .15
❑ 768 Yhency Brazoban .40 .15
❑ 769 Elmer Dessens .40 .15
❑ 770 Mark Hendrickson .40 .15
❑ 771 Hong-Chih Kuo .40 .15
❑ 772 Jason Schmidt .40 .15
❑ 773 Brett Tomko .40 .15
❑ 774 Randy Wolf .40 .15
❑ 775 Mike Lieberthal .40 .15
❑ 776 Marlon Anderson .40 .15
❑ 777 Jeff Kent .40 .15
❑ 778 Ramon Martinez .40 .15
❑ 779 Olmedo Saenz .40 .15
❑ 780 Luis Gonzalez .40 .15
❑ 781 Juan Pierre .40 .15
❑ 782 Jason Repko .40 .15
❑ 783 Nomar Garciaparra 1.00 .40
❑ 784 Wilson Valdez .40 .15
❑ 785 Jason Schmidt CL .40 .15
❑ 786 Greg Aquino .40 .15
❑ 787 Brian Shouse .40 .15
❑ 788 Jeff Suppan .40 .15
❑ 789 Carlos Villanueva .40 .15
❑ 790 Matt Wise .40 .15
❑ 791 Johnny Estrada .40 .15
❑ 792 Craig Counsell .40 .15
❑ 793 Tony Graffanino .40 .15
❑ 794 Corey Koskie .40 .15
❑ 795 Claudio Vargas .40 .15
❑ 796 Brady Clark .40 .15
❑ 797 Gabe Gross .40 .15
❑ 798 Geoff Jenkins .40 .15
❑ 799 Kevin Mench .40 .15
❑ 800 Bill Hall CL .40 .15
❑ 801 Sidney Ponson .40 .15
❑ 802 Jesse Crain .40 .15
❑ 803 Matt Guerrier .40 .15
❑ 804 Pat Neshek .60 .25
❑ 805 Ramon Ortiz .40 .15
❑ 806 Johan Santana .60 .25
❑ 807 Carlos Silva .40 .15
❑ 808 Mike Redmond .40 .15
❑ 809 Jeff Cirillo .40 .15
❑ 810 Luis Rodriguez .40 .15
❑ 811 Lew Ford .40 .15
❑ 812 Torii Hunter .40 .15
❑ 813 Jason Tyner .40 .15
❑ 814 Rondell White .40 .15
❑ 815 Justin Morneau .40 .15
❑ 816 Joe Mauer .60 .25
❑ 817 Johan Santana CL .60 .25
❑ 818 David Newhan .40 .15
❑ 819 Aaron Sele .40 .15
❑ 820 Ambiorix Burgos .40 .15
❑ 821 Pedro Feliciano .40 .15
❑ 822 Tom Glavine .60 .25
❑ 823 Aaron Heilman .40 .15
❑ 824 Guillermo Mota .40 .15
❑ 825 Jose Reyes .40 .15
❑ 826 Oliver Perez .40 .15
❑ 827 Duaner Sanchez .40 .15
❑ 828 Scott Schoeneweis .40 .15
❑ 829 Ramon Castro .40 .15
❑ 830 Damion Easley .40 .15
❑ 831 David Wright 1.50 .60
❑ 832 Moises Alou .40 .15
❑ 833 Carlos Beltran .40 .15
❑ 834 Dave Williams .40 .15
❑ 835 David Wright CL 1.50 .60
❑ 836 Brian Bruney .40 .15
❑ 837 Mike Myers .40 .15
❑ 838 Carl Pavano .40 .15
❑ 839 Andy Pettitte .60 .25
❑ 840 Luis Vizcaino .40 .15
❑ 841 Jorge Posada .60 .25
❑ 842 Miguel Cairo .40 .15
❑ 843 Doug Mientkiewicz .40 .15
❑ 844 Derek Jeter 2.50 1.00
❑ 845 Alex Rodriguez 1.50 .60
❑ 846 Johnny Damon .60 .25
❑ 847 Hideki Matsui 1.00 .40
❑ 848 Josh Phelps .40 .15
❑ 849 Phil Hughes (RC) 4.00 1.50
❑ 850 Roger Clemens 2.00 .75
❑ 851 Jason Giambi CL .40 .15
❑ 852 Kiko Calero .40 .15
❑ 853 Justin Duchscherer .40 .15
❑ 854 Alan Embree .40 .15
❑ 855 Todd Walker .40 .15
❑ 856 Rich Harden .40 .15
❑ 857 Dan Haren .40 .15
❑ 858 Joe Kennedy .40 .15
❑ 859 Jason Kendall .40 .15
❑ 860 Adam Melhuse .40 .15
❑ 861 Mark Ellis .40 .15
❑ 862 Bobby Kielty .40 .15
❑ 863 Mark Kotsay .40 .15
❑ 864 Shannon Stewart .40 .15
❑ 865 Mike Piazza 1.00 .40
❑ 866 Mike Piazza CL 1.00 .40
❑ 867 Antonio Alfonseca .40 .15
❑ 868 Carlos Ruiz .40 .15
❑ 869 Adam Eaton .40 .15
❑ 870 Freddy Garcia .40 .15
❑ 871 Jon Lieber .40 .15
❑ 872 Matt Smith .40 .15
❑ 873 Rod Barajas .40 .15
❑ 874 Wes Helms .40 .15
❑ 875 Abraham Nunez .40 .15
❑ 876 Pat Burrell .40 .15
❑ 877 Jayson Werth .40 .15
❑ 878 Greg Dobbs .40 .15
❑ 879 Joseph Bisenius RC .75 .30
❑ 880 Michael Bourn (RC) .75 .30
❑ 881 Chase Utley 1.00 .40
❑ 882 Ryan Howard 1.50 .60
❑ 883 Chase Utley CL 1.00 .40
❑ 884 Tony Armas .40 .15
❑ 885 Shawn Chacon .40 .15
❑ 886 John Grabow .40 .15
❑ 887 Paul Maholm .40 .15
❑ 888 Damaso Marte .40 .15
❑ 889 Salomon Torres .40 .15
❑ 890 Humberto Cota .40 .15
❑ 891 Ryan Doumit .40 .15
❑ 892 Adam LaRoche .40 .15
❑ 893 Jack Wilson .40 .15
❑ 894 Nate McLouth .40 .15
❑ 895 Brad Eldred .40 .15
❑ 896 Jonah Bayliss .40 .15
❑ 897 Juan Perez RC .75 .30
❑ 898 Jason Bay .40 .15
❑ 899 Adam LaRoche CL .40 .15
❑ 900 Doug Brocail .40 .15
❑ 901 Scott Cassidy .40 .15
❑ 902 Scott Linebrink .40 .15
❑ 903 Greg Maddux 1.50 .60
❑ 904 Jake Peavy .40 .15
❑ 905 Mike Thompson .40 .15
❑ 906 David Wells .40 .15
❑ 907 Josh Bard .40 .15
❑ 908 Rob Bowen .40 .15
❑ 909 Marcus Giles .40 .15
❑ 910 Russell Branyan .40 .15
❑ 911 Jose Cruz .40 .15
❑ 912 Terrmel Sledge .40 .15
❑ 913 Trevor Hoffman .40 .15
❑ 914 Brian Giles .40 .15
❑ 915 Trevor Hoffman CL .40 .15
❑ 916 Vinnie Chulk .40 .15
❑ 917 Kevin Correia .40 .15
❑ 918 Tim Lincecum RC 20.00 8.00
❑ 919 Matt Morris .40 .15
❑ 920 Russ Ortiz .40 .15
❑ 921 Barry Zito .40 .15
❑ 922 Bengie Molina .40 .15
❑ 923 Rich Aurilia .40 .15
❑ 924 Omar Vizquel .60 .25
❑ 925 Jason Ellison .40 .15
❑ 926 Ryan Klesko .40 .15
❑ 927 Dave Roberts .40 .15
❑ 928 Randy Winn .40 .15
❑ 929 Barry Zito CL .40 .15
❑ 930 Miguel Batista .40 .15
❑ 931 Horacio Ramirez .40 .15
❑ 932 Chris Reitsma .40 .15
❑ 933 George Sherrill .40 .15
❑ 934 Jarrod Washburn .40 .15
❑ 935 Jeff Weaver .40 .15
❑ 936 Jake Woods .40 .15
❑ 937 Adrian Beltre .40 .15
❑ 938 Jose Lopez .40 .15
❑ 939 Ichiro Suzuki 1.50 .60
❑ 940 Jose Vidro .40 .15
❑ 941 Jose Guillen .40 .15
❑ 942 Sean White RC .75 .30
❑ 943 Brandon Morrow RC .75 .30
❑ 944 Felix Hernandez .60 .25
❑ 945 Felix Hernandez CL .60 .25
❑ 946 Randy Flores .40 .15
❑ 947 Ryan Franklin .40 .15
❑ 948 Kelvin Jimenez RC .75 .30
❑ 949 Tyler Johnson .40 .15
❑ 950 Mark Mulder .40 .15
❑ 951 Anthony Reyes .40 .15
❑ 952 Russ Springer .40 .15
❑ 953 Brad Thompson .40 .15
❑ 954 Adam Wainwright .40 .15
❑ 955 Kip Wells .40 .15
❑ 956 Gary Bennett .40 .15
❑ 957 Adam Kennedy .40 .15
❑ 958 Scott Rolen .60 .25
❑ 959 Scott Spiezio .40 .15
❑ 960 So Taguchi .40 .15
❑ 961 Preston Wilson .40 .15
❑ 962 Skip Schumaker .40 .15
❑ 963 Albert Pujols 2.00 .75
❑ 964 Chris Carpenter .40 .15
❑ 965 Chris Carpenter CL .40 .15
❑ 966 Edwin Jackson .40 .15
❑ 967 Jae Kuk Ryu .40 .15
❑ 968 Jae Seo .40 .15
❑ 969 Jon Switzer .40 .15
❑ 970 Josh Paul .40 .15
❑ 971 Ben Zobrist .40 .15
❑ 972 Rocco Baldelli .40 .15
❑ 973 Scott Kazmir .60 .25
❑ 974 Carl Crawford .40 .15
❑ 975 Delmon Young CL .60 .25
❑ 976 Bruce Chen .40 .15
❑ 977 Joaquin Benoit .40 .15
❑ 978 Scott Feldman .40 .15
❑ 979 Eric Gagne .40 .15
❑ 980 Kameron Loe .40 .15
❑ 981 Brandon McCarthy .40 .15
❑ 982 Robinson Tejeda .40 .15
❑ 983 C.J. Wilson .40 .15
❑ 984 Mark Teixeira .60 .25
❑ 985 Michael Young .40 .15
❑ 986 Kenny Lofton .40 .15
❑ 987 Brad Wilkerson .40 .15

Card		
❑ 988 Nelson Cruz	.40	.15
❑ 989 Sammy Sosa	1.00	.40
❑ 990 Michael Young CL	.40	.15
❑ 991 Vernon Wells	.40	.15
❑ 992 Matt Stairs	.40	.15
❑ 993 Jeremy Accardo	.40	.15
❑ 994 A.J. Burnett	.40	.15
❑ 995 Jason Frasor	.40	.15
❑ 996 Roy Halladay	.40	.15
❑ 997 Shaun Marcum	.40	.15
❑ 998 Tomo Ohka	.40	.15
❑ 999 Josh Towers	.40	.15
❑ 1000 Gregg Zaun	.40	.15
❑ 1001 Royce Clayton	.40	.15
❑ 1002 Jason Smith	.40	.15
❑ 1003 Alex Rios	.40	.15
❑ 1004 Frank Thomas	1.00	.40
❑ 1005 Roy Halladay CL	.40	.15
❑ 1006 Jesus Flores RC	.75	.30
❑ 1007 Dmitri Young	.40	.15
❑ 1008 Ray King	.40	.15
❑ 1009 Micah Bowie	.40	.15
❑ 1010 Shawn Hill	.40	.15
❑ 1011 John Patterson	.40	.15
❑ 1012 Levale Speigner RC	.75	.30
❑ 1013 Ryan Wagner	.40	.15
❑ 1014 Jerome Williams	.40	.15
❑ 1015 Ryan Zimmerman	1.00	.40
❑ 1016 Cristian Guzman	.40	.15
❑ 1017 Nook Logan	.40	.15
❑ 1018 Chris Snelling	.40	.15
❑ 1019 Ronnie Belliard	.40	.15
❑ 1020 Nick Johnson CL	.40	.15
❑ NNO Rookie EXCH	60.00	30.00

2007 Upper Deck Elements

❑ COMMON CARD .75 .30
❑ CARDS 1-42 FOUND IN GRIFFEY PACKS
❑ CARDS 43-84 FOUND IN RIPKEN PACKS
❑ CARDS 85-126 FOUND IN JETER PACKS
❑ ALL VETERAN VERSIONS EQUAL VALUE
❑ COMMON RC (127-168) 2.00 .75
❑ RC 127-168 FOUND IN GRIFFEY PACKS
❑ RC 169-210 FOUND IN RIPKEN PACKS
❑ COMMON RC (211-252) 2.50 1.00
❑ RC 211-252 FOUND IN JETER PACKS
❑ ROOKIE PRINT RUN 550 SER.#'d SETS
❑ PRINTING PLATES RANDOMLY INSERTED
❑ PLATE PRINT RUN 1 SET PER COLOR
❑ BLACK-CYAN-MAGENTA-YELLOW ISSUED
❑ NO PLATE PRICING DUE TO SCARCITY
❑ GIFT EXCH ODDS 1 PER CASE
❑ GIFT EXCH DEADLINE 9/30/2007

Card		
❑ 1 Stephen Drew	1.25	.50
❑ 2 Andruw Jones	1.25	.50
❑ 3 Chipper Jones	2.00	.75
❑ 4 Miguel Tejada	.75	.30
❑ 5 David Ortiz	2.00	.75
❑ 6 Manny Ramirez	1.25	.50
❑ 7 Derrek Lee	.75	.30
❑ 8 Alfonso Soriano	.75	.30
❑ 9 Jermaine Dye	.75	.30
❑ 10 Jim Thome	1.25	.50
❑ 11 Ken Griffey Jr.	3.00	1.25
❑ 12 Adam Dunn	.75	.30
❑ 13 Travis Hafner	.75	.30
❑ 14 Grady Sizemore	1.25	.50
❑ 15 Todd Helton	1.25	.50
❑ 16 Gary Sheffield	.75	.30
❑ 17 Miguel Cabrera	1.25	.50
❑ 18 Lance Berkman	.75	.30
❑ 19 Mark Teahen	.75	.30
❑ 20 Vladimir Guerrero	2.00	.75
❑ 21 Jered Weaver	1.25	.50
❑ 22 Rafael Furcal	.75	.30
❑ 23 Prince Fielder	2.00	.75
❑ 24 Justin Morneau	.75	.30
❑ 25 Johan Santana	1.25	.50
❑ 26 David Wright	3.00	1.25
❑ 27 Jose Reyes	2.00	.75
❑ 28 Derek Jeter	5.00	2.00
❑ 29 Alex Rodriguez	3.00	1.25
❑ 30 Nick Swisher	.75	.30
❑ 31 Ryan Howard	3.00	1.25
❑ 32 Jason Bay	.75	.30
❑ 33 Adrian Gonzalez	.75	.30
❑ 34 Ray Durham	.75	.30
❑ 35 Ichiro Suzuki	3.00	1.25
❑ 36 Albert Pujols	4.00	1.50
❑ 37 Scott Rolen	1.25	.50
❑ 38 Carl Crawford	.75	.30
❑ 39 Mark Teixeira	1.25	.50
❑ 40 Michael Young	.75	.30
❑ 41 Vernon Wells	.75	.30
❑ 42 Ryan Zimmerman	2.00	.75
❑ 43 Stephen Drew	1.25	.50
❑ 44 Andruw Jones	1.25	.50
❑ 45 Chipper Jones	2.00	.75
❑ 46 Miguel Tejada	.75	.30
❑ 47 David Ortiz	2.00	.75
❑ 48 Manny Ramirez	1.25	.50
❑ 49 Derrek Lee	.75	.30
❑ 50 Alfonso Soriano	.75	.30
❑ 51 Jermaine Dye	.75	.30
❑ 52 Jim Thome	1.25	.50
❑ 53 Ken Griffey Jr.	3.00	1.25
❑ 54 Adam Dunn	.75	.30
❑ 55 Travis Hafner	.75	.30
❑ 56 Grady Sizemore	1.25	.50
❑ 57 Todd Helton	1.25	.50
❑ 58 Gary Sheffield	.75	.30
❑ 59 Miguel Cabrera	1.25	.50
❑ 60 Lance Berkman	.75	.30
❑ 61 Mark Teahen	.75	.30
❑ 62 Vladimir Guerrero	2.00	.75
❑ 63 Jered Weaver	1.25	.50
❑ 64 Rafael Furcal	.75	.30
❑ 65 Prince Fielder	2.00	.75
❑ 66 Justin Morneau	.75	.30
❑ 67 Johan Santana	1.25	.50
❑ 68 David Wright	3.00	1.25
❑ 69 Jose Reyes	2.00	.75
❑ 70 Derek Jeter	5.00	2.00
❑ 71 Alex Rodriguez	3.00	1.25
❑ 72 Nick Swisher	.75	.30
❑ 73 Ryan Howard	3.00	1.25
❑ 74 Jason Bay	.75	.30
❑ 75 Adrian Gonzalez	.75	.30
❑ 76 Ray Durham	.75	.30
❑ 77 Ichiro Suzuki	3.00	1.25
❑ 78 Albert Pujols	4.00	1.50
❑ 79 Scott Rolen	1.25	.50
❑ 80 Carl Crawford	.75	.30
❑ 81 Mark Teixeira	1.25	.50
❑ 82 Michael Young	.75	.30
❑ 83 Vernon Wells	.75	.30
❑ 84 Ryan Zimmerman	2.00	.75
❑ 85 Stephen Drew	1.25	.50
❑ 86 Andruw Jones	1.25	.50
❑ 87 Chipper Jones	2.00	.75
❑ 88 Miguel Tejada	.75	.30
❑ 89 David Ortiz	2.00	.75
❑ 90 Manny Ramirez	1.25	.50
❑ 91 Derrek Lee	.75	.30
❑ 92 Alfonso Soriano	.75	.30
❑ 93 Jermaine Dye	.75	.30
❑ 94 Jim Thome	1.25	.50
❑ 95 Ken Griffey Jr.	3.00	1.25
❑ 96 Adam Dunn	.75	.30
❑ 97 Travis Hafner	.75	.30
❑ 98 Grady Sizemore	1.25	.50
❑ 99 Todd Helton	1.25	.50
❑ 100 Gary Sheffield	.75	.30
❑ 101 Miguel Cabrera	1.25	.50
❑ 102 Lance Berkman	.75	.30
❑ 103 Mark Teahen	.75	.30
❑ 104 Vladimir Guerrero	2.00	.75
❑ 105 Jered Weaver	1.25	.50
❑ 106 Rafael Furcal	.75	.30
❑ 107 Prince Fielder	2.00	.75
❑ 108 Justin Morneau	.75	.30
❑ 109 Johan Santana	1.25	.50
❑ 110 David Wright	3.00	1.25
❑ 111 Jose Reyes	2.00	.75
❑ 112 Derek Jeter	5.00	2.00
❑ 113 Alex Rodriguez	3.00	1.25
❑ 114 Nick Swisher	.75	.30
❑ 115 Ryan Howard	3.00	1.25
❑ 116 Jason Bay	.75	.30
❑ 117 Adrian Gonzalez	.75	.30
❑ 118 Ray Durham	.75	.30
❑ 119 Ichiro Suzuki	3.00	1.25
❑ 120 Albert Pujols	4.00	1.50
❑ 121 Scott Rolen	1.25	.50
❑ 122 Carl Crawford	.75	.30
❑ 123 Mark Teixeira	1.25	.50
❑ 124 Michael Young	.75	.30
❑ 125 Vernon Wells	.75	.30
❑ 126 Ryan Zimmerman	2.00	.75
❑ 127 Miguel Montero (RC)	2.00	.75
❑ 128 Doug Slaten RC	2.00	.75
❑ 129 Hunter Pence (RC)	25.00	10.00
❑ 130 Brian Burres (RC)	2.00	.75
❑ 131 Daisuke Matsuzaka RC	15.00	6.00
❑ 132 Hideki Okajima RC	8.00	3.00
❑ 133 Devern Hansack RC	2.00	.75
❑ 134 Felix Pie (RC)	5.00	2.00
❑ 135 Ryan Sweeney (RC)	2.00	.75
❑ 136 Chris Stewart RC	3.00	1.25
❑ 137 Jarrod Saltalamacchia (RC)	3.00	1.25
❑ 138 John Danks RC	3.00	1.25
❑ 139 Travis Buck (RC)	2.00	.75
❑ 140 Troy Tulowitzki (RC)	8.00	3.00
❑ 141 Chase Wright RC	3.00	1.25
❑ 142 Matt DeSalvo (RC)	3.00	1.25
❑ 143 Micah Owings (RC)	2.00	.75
❑ 144 Jeff Baker (RC)	2.00	.75
❑ 145 Andy LaRoche (RC)	2.00	.75
❑ 146 Billy Butler (RC)	8.00	3.00
❑ 147 Jose Garcia RC	2.00	.75
❑ 148 Angel Sanchez RC	2.00	.75
❑ 149 Alex Gordon RC	15.00	6.00
❑ 150 Glen Perkins (RC)	2.00	.75
❑ 151 Alexi Casilla RC	3.00	1.25
❑ 152 Joe Smith RC	2.00	.75
❑ 153 Kei Igawa RC	8.00	3.00
❑ 154 Sean Henn (RC)	5.00	2.00
❑ 155 Phil Hughes (RC)	15.00	6.00
❑ 156 Michael Bourn (RC)	2.00	.75
❑ 157 Josh Hamilton (RC)	8.00	3.00
❑ 158 Kevin Kouzmanoff (RC)	2.00	.75
❑ 159 Tim Lincecum RC	60.00	30.00
❑ 160 Brandon Morrow RC	3.00	1.25
❑ 161 Brandon Wood (RC)	2.00	.75
❑ 162 Akinori Iwamura RC	5.00	2.00
❑ 163 Delmon Young (RC)	3.00	1.25
❑ 164 Juan Salas (RC)	2.00	.75
❑ 165 Elijah Dukes RC	3.00	1.25
❑ 166 Joaquin Arias (RC)	2.00	.75
❑ 167 Adam Lind (RC)	2.00	.75
❑ 168 Matt Chico (RC)	2.00	.75
❑ 169 Miguel Montero (RC)	2.00	.75
❑ 170 Doug Slaten RC	2.00	.75
❑ 171 Hunter Pence (RC)	25.00	10.00
❑ 172 Brian Burres (RC)	2.00	.75
❑ 173 Daisuke Matsuzaka RC	15.00	6.00

❑ 174 Hideki Okajima RC	8.00	3.00
❑ 175 Devern Hansack RC	2.00	.75
❑ 176 Felix Pie (RC)	5.00	2.00
❑ 177 Ryan Sweeney (RC)	2.00	.75
❑ 178 Chris Stewart RC	3.00	1.25
❑ 179 Jarrod Saltalamacchia (RC)	3.00	1.25
❑ 180 John Danks RC	3.00	1.25
❑ 181 Travis Buck (RC)	2.00	.75
❑ 182 Troy Tulowitzki (RC)	8.00	3.00
❑ 183 Chase Wright RC	3.00	1.25
❑ 184 Matt DeSalvo (RC)	3.00	1.25
❑ 185 Micah Owings (RC)	2.00	.75
❑ 186 Jeff Baker (RC)	2.00	.75
❑ 187 Andy LaRoche (RC)	2.00	.75
❑ 188 Billy Butler (RC)	8.00	3.00
❑ 189 Jose Garcia RC	2.00	.75
❑ 190 Angel Sanchez RC	2.00	.75
❑ 191 Alex Gordon RC	15.00	6.00
❑ 192 Glen Perkins (RC)	2.00	.75
❑ 193 Alexi Casilla RC	3.00	1.25
❑ 194 Joe Smith RC	2.00	.75
❑ 195 Kei Igawa RC	8.00	3.00
❑ 196 Sean Henn (RC)	5.00	2.00
❑ 197 Phil Hughes (RC)	15.00	6.00
❑ 198 Michael Bourn (RC)	2.00	.75
❑ 199 Josh Hamilton (RC)	8.00	3.00
❑ 200 Kevin Kouzmanoff (RC)	2.00	.75
❑ 201 Tim Lincecum RC	60.00	30.00
❑ 202 Brandon Morrow RC	3.00	1.25
❑ 203 Brandon Wood (RC)	2.00	.75
❑ 204 Akinori Iwamura RC	5.00	2.00
❑ 205 Delmon Young (RC)	3.00	1.25
❑ 206 Juan Salas (RC)	2.00	.75
❑ 207 Elijah Dukes RC	3.00	1.25
❑ 208 Joaquin Arias (RC)	2.00	.75
❑ 209 Adam Lind (RC)	2.00	.75
❑ 210 Matt Chico (RC)	2.00	.75
❑ 211 Miguel Montero (RC)	2.50	1.00
❑ 212 Doug Slaten RC	2.50	1.00
❑ 213 Hunter Pence (RC)	25.00	10.00
❑ 214 Brian Burres (RC)	2.50	1.00
❑ 215 Daisuke Matsuzaka RC	25.00	10.00
❑ 216 Hideki Okajima RC	10.00	4.00
❑ 217 Devern Hansack RC	2.50	1.00
❑ 218 Felix Pie (RC)	6.00	2.50
❑ 219 Ryan Sweeney (RC)	2.50	1.00
❑ 220 Chris Stewart RC	4.00	1.50
❑ 221 Jarrod Saltalamacchia (RC)	4.00	1.50
❑ 222 John Danks RC	4.00	1.50
❑ 223 Travis Buck (RC)	2.50	1.00
❑ 224 Troy Tulowitzki (RC)	10.00	4.00
❑ 225 Chase Wright RC	4.00	1.50
❑ 226 Matt DeSalvo (RC)	4.00	1.50
❑ 227 Micah Owings (RC)	2.50	1.00
❑ 228 Jeff Baker (RC)	2.50	1.00
❑ 229 Andy LaRoche (RC)	2.50	1.00
❑ 230 Billy Butler (RC)	10.00	4.00
❑ 231 Jose Garcia RC	2.50	1.00
❑ 232 Angel Sanchez RC	2.50	1.00
❑ 233 Alex Gordon RC	20.00	8.00
❑ 234 Glen Perkins (RC)	2.50	1.00
❑ 235 Alexi Casilla RC	4.00	1.50
❑ 236 Joe Smith RC	2.50	1.00
❑ 237 Kei Igawa RC	10.00	4.00
❑ 238 Sean Henn (RC)	6.00	2.50
❑ 239 Phil Hughes (RC)	15.00	6.00
❑ 240 Michael Bourn (RC)	2.50	1.00
❑ 241 Josh Hamilton (RC)	10.00	4.00
❑ 242 Kevin Kouzmanoff (RC)	2.50	1.00
❑ 243 Tim Lincecum RC	50.00	25.00
❑ 244 Brandon Morrow RC	4.00	1.50
❑ 245 Brandon Wood (RC)	2.50	1.00
❑ 246 Akinori Iwamura RC	6.00	2.50
❑ 247 Delmon Young (RC)	4.00	1.50
❑ 248 Juan Salas (RC)	2.50	1.00
❑ 249 Elijah Dukes RC	4.00	1.50
❑ 250 Joaquin Arias (RC)	2.50	1.00
❑ 251 Adam Lind (RC)	2.50	1.00
❑ 252 Matt Chico (RC)	2.50	1.00
❑ NNO Gift EXCH	150.00	90.00

2006 Upper Deck Epic

❑ COMMON CARD (1-300)	5.00	2.00
❑ COMMON ROOKIE	5.00	2.00
❑ STATED PRINT RUN 450 SERIAL #'d SETS		
❑ 1 Conor Jackson (RC)	8.00	3.00
❑ 2 Brandon Webb	5.00	2.00
❑ 3 Craig Counsell	5.00	2.00
❑ 4 Luis Gonzalez	5.00	2.00
❑ 5 Miguel Batista	5.00	2.00
❑ 6 Orlando Hudson	5.00	2.00
❑ 7 Russ Ortiz	5.00	2.00
❑ 8 Shawn Green	5.00	2.00
❑ 9 Andruw Jones	8.00	3.00
❑ 10 Chipper Jones	8.00	3.00
❑ 11 Edgar Renteria	5.00	2.00
❑ 12 Jeff Francoeur	8.00	3.00
❑ 13 John Smoltz	8.00	3.00
❑ 14 Marcus Giles	5.00	2.00
❑ 15 Mike Hampton	5.00	2.00
❑ 16 Tim Hudson	5.00	2.00
❑ 17 Erik Bedard	5.00	2.00
❑ 18 Brian Roberts	5.00	2.00
❑ 19 Javy Lopez	5.00	2.00
❑ 20 Jay Gibbons	5.00	2.00
❑ 21 Jeff Conine	5.00	2.00
❑ 22 Melvin Mora	5.00	2.00
❑ 23 Miguel Tejada	5.00	2.00
❑ 24 Daniel Cabrera	5.00	2.00
❑ 25 Rodrigo Lopez	5.00	2.00
❑ 26 Ramon Hernandez	5.00	2.00
❑ 27 Bronson Arroyo	5.00	2.00
❑ 28 Curt Schilling	8.00	3.00
❑ 29 David Ortiz	8.00	3.00
❑ 30 David Wells	5.00	2.00
❑ 31 Jason Varitek	8.00	3.00
❑ 32 Josh Beckett	5.00	2.00
❑ 33 Kevin Youkilis	5.00	2.00
❑ 34 Manny Ramirez	8.00	3.00
❑ 35 Matt Clement	5.00	2.00
❑ 36 Mike Lowell	5.00	2.00
❑ 37 Tim Wakefield	5.00	2.00
❑ 38 Trot Nixon	5.00	2.00
❑ 39 Aramis Ramirez	5.00	2.00
❑ 40 Carlos Zambrano	5.00	2.00
❑ 41 Derrek Lee	5.00	2.00
❑ 42 Greg Maddux	12.00	5.00
❑ 43 Juan Pierre	5.00	2.00
❑ 44 Kerry Wood	5.00	2.00
❑ 45 Mark Prior	8.00	3.00
❑ 46 Michael Barrett	5.00	2.00
❑ 47 Ryan Dempster	5.00	2.00
❑ 48 Todd Walker	5.00	2.00
❑ 49 Wade Miller	5.00	2.00
❑ 50 A.J. Pierzynski	5.00	2.00
❑ 51 Brian Anderson (RC)	5.00	2.00
❑ 52 Frank Thomas	8.00	3.00
❑ 53 Javier Vazquez	5.00	2.00
❑ 54 Jim Thome	8.00	3.00
❑ 55 Joe Crede	5.00	2.00
❑ 56 Jon Garland	5.00	2.00
❑ 57 Juan Uribe	5.00	2.00
❑ 58 Mark Buehrle	5.00	2.00
❑ 59 Paul Konerko	5.00	2.00
❑ 60 Scott Podsednik	5.00	2.00
❑ 61 Tadahito Iguchi	5.00	2.00
❑ 62 Aaron Harang	5.00	2.00

❑ 63 Adam Dunn	5.00	2.00
❑ 64 Austin Kearns	5.00	2.00
❑ 65 Edwin Encarnacion	5.00	2.00
❑ 66 Eric Milton	5.00	2.00
❑ 67 Felipe Lopez	5.00	2.00
❑ 68 Jason LaRue	5.00	2.00
❑ 69 Ken Griffey Jr.	12.00	5.00
❑ 70 Wily Mo Pena	5.00	2.00
❑ 71 Aaron Boone	5.00	2.00
❑ 72 Ben Broussard	5.00	2.00
❑ 73 C.C. Sabathia	5.00	2.00
❑ 74 Casey Blake	5.00	2.00
❑ 75 Cliff Lee	5.00	2.00
❑ 76 Grady Sizemore	8.00	3.00
❑ 77 Jake Westbrook	5.00	2.00
❑ 78 Josh Bard	5.00	2.00
❑ 79 Travis Hafner	5.00	2.00
❑ 80 Victor Martinez	5.00	2.00
❑ 81 Chin-hui Tsao	5.00	2.00
❑ 82 Clint Barmes	5.00	2.00
❑ 83 Garrett Atkins	5.00	2.00
❑ 84 Josh Wilson (RC)	5.00	2.00
❑ 85 Luis Gonzalez	5.00	2.00
❑ 86 Matt Holliday	6.00	2.50
❑ 87 Todd Helton	8.00	3.00
❑ 88 Brandon Inge	5.00	2.00
❑ 89 Carlos Guillen	5.00	2.00
❑ 90 Chris Shelton	5.00	2.00
❑ 91 Craig Monroe	5.00	2.00
❑ 92 Dmitri Young	5.00	2.00
❑ 93 Ivan Rodriguez	8.00	3.00
❑ 94 Jeremy Bonderman	5.00	2.00
❑ 95 Magglio Ordonez	5.00	2.00
❑ 96 Alex Gonzalez	5.00	2.00
❑ 97 Brian Moehler	5.00	2.00
❑ 98 Dontrelle Willis	5.00	2.00
❑ 99 Jeremy Hermida (RC)	8.00	3.00
❑ 100 Jason Vargas	5.00	2.00
❑ 101 Miguel Cabrera	8.00	3.00
❑ 102 Adam Everett	5.00	2.00
❑ 103 Andy Pettitte	5.00	2.00
❑ 104 Brad Ausmus	5.00	2.00
❑ 105 Brad Lidge	5.00	2.00
❑ 106 Craig Biggio	8.00	3.00
❑ 107 Dan Wheeler	5.00	2.00
❑ 108 Jeff Bagwell	8.00	3.00
❑ 109 Lance Berkman	5.00	2.00
❑ 110 Morgan Ensberg	5.00	2.00
❑ 111 Preston Wilson	5.00	2.00
❑ 112 Roger Clemens	15.00	6.00
❑ 113 Roy Oswalt	5.00	2.00
❑ 114 Dave Gassner (RC)	5.00	2.00
❑ 115 Angel Berroa	5.00	2.00
❑ 116 Doug Mientkiewicz	5.00	2.00
❑ 117 Joe Mays	5.00	2.00
❑ 118 Mark Grudzielanek	5.00	2.00
❑ 119 Mike Sweeney	5.00	2.00
❑ 120 Reggie Sanders	5.00	2.00
❑ 121 Runelvys Hernandez	5.00	2.00
❑ 122 Scott Elarton	5.00	2.00
❑ 123 Brandon Watson (RC)	5.00	2.00
❑ 124 Zack Greinke	5.00	2.00
❑ 125 Brad Penny	5.00	2.00
❑ 126 Derek Lowe	5.00	2.00
❑ 127 Eric Gagne	5.00	2.00
❑ 128 J.D. Drew	5.00	2.00
❑ 129 Jayson Werth	5.00	2.00
❑ 130 Jeff Kent	5.00	2.00
❑ 131 Nomar Garciaparra	8.00	3.00
❑ 132 Olmedo Saenz	5.00	2.00
❑ 133 Rafael Furcal	5.00	2.00
❑ 134 Ben Sheets	5.00	2.00
❑ 135 Bill Hall	5.00	2.00
❑ 136 Carlos Lee	5.00	2.00
❑ 137 Geoff Jenkins	5.00	2.00
❑ 138 Prince Fielder (RC)	15.00	6.00
❑ 139 Rickie Weeks	5.00	2.00
❑ 140 Jose Capellan (RC)	5.00	2.00
❑ 141 Brad Radke	5.00	2.00
❑ 142 Joe Mauer	8.00	3.00
❑ 143 Joe Nathan	5.00	2.00
❑ 144 Johan Santana	8.00	3.00
❑ 145 Justin Morneau	5.00	2.00
❑ 146 Kyle Lohse	5.00	2.00

❑ 147	Lew Ford	5.00	2.00
❑ 148	Luis Castillo	5.00	2.00
❑ 149	Matt LeCroy	5.00	2.00
❑ 150	Michael Cuddyer	5.00	2.00
❑ 151	Shannon Stewart	5.00	2.00
❑ 152	Torii Hunter	5.00	2.00
❑ 153	Billy Wagner	5.00	2.00
❑ 154	Carlos Beltran	5.00	2.00
❑ 155	Carlos Delgado	5.00	2.00
❑ 156	Cliff Floyd	5.00	2.00
❑ 157	David Wright	12.00	5.00
❑ 158	Jose Reyes	5.00	2.00
❑ 159	Kazuo Matsui	5.00	2.00
❑ 160	Mike Piazza	8.00	3.00
❑ 161	Paul Lo Duca	5.00	2.00
❑ 162	Pedro Martinez	8.00	3.00
❑ 163	Tom Glavine	8.00	3.00
❑ 164	Victor Diaz	5.00	2.00
❑ 165	Alex Rodriguez	12.00	5.00
❑ 166	Bernie Williams	8.00	3.00
❑ 167	Carl Pavano	5.00	2.00
❑ 168	Chien-Ming Wang	12.00	5.00
❑ 169	Derek Jeter	20.00	8.00
❑ 170	Gary Sheffield	5.00	2.00
❑ 171	Hideki Matsui	8.00	3.00
❑ 172	Jason Giambi	5.00	2.00
❑ 173	Johnny Damon	8.00	3.00
❑ 174	Jorge Posada	8.00	3.00
❑ 175	Robinson Cano	8.00	3.00
❑ 176	Mariano Rivera	8.00	3.00
❑ 177	Mike Mussina	8.00	3.00
❑ 178	Randy Johnson	8.00	3.00
❑ 179	Miguel Cairo	5.00	2.00
❑ 180	Barry Zito	5.00	2.00
❑ 181	Bobby Crosby	5.00	2.00
❑ 182	Bobby Kielty	5.00	2.00
❑ 183	Eric Chavez	5.00	2.00
❑ 184	Josh Barfield (RC)	5.00	2.00
❑ 185	Esteban Loaiza	5.00	2.00
❑ 186	Huston Street	5.00	2.00
❑ 187	Jason Kendall	5.00	2.00
❑ 188	Nick Swisher	5.00	2.00
❑ 189	Aaron Rowand	5.00	2.00
❑ 190	Bobby Abreu	5.00	2.00
❑ 191	Chase Utley	8.00	3.00
❑ 192	Gavin Floyd	5.00	2.00
❑ 193	Jimmy Rollins	5.00	2.00
❑ 194	Mike Lieberthal	5.00	2.00
❑ 195	Pat Burrell	5.00	2.00
❑ 196	Ryan Howard	10.00	4.00
❑ 197	Craig Wilson	5.00	2.00
❑ 198	Jack Wilson	5.00	2.00
❑ 199	Jason Bay	5.00	2.00
❑ 200	Joe Randa	5.00	2.00
❑ 201	Josh Fogg	5.00	2.00
❑ 202	Kip Wells	5.00	2.00
❑ 203	Sean Casey	5.00	2.00
❑ 204	Zach Duke	5.00	2.00
❑ 205	Brian Giles	5.00	2.00
❑ 206	Dave Roberts	5.00	2.00
❑ 207	Jake Peavy	5.00	2.00
❑ 208	Khalil Greene	8.00	3.00
❑ 209	Mike Cameron	5.00	2.00
❑ 210	Ryan Klesko	5.00	2.00
❑ 211	Trevor Hoffman	5.00	2.00
❑ 212	Vinny Castilla	5.00	2.00
❑ 213	Armando Benitez	5.00	2.00
❑ 214	Jason Schmidt	5.00	2.00
❑ 215	Matt Morris	5.00	2.00
❑ 216	Moises Alou	5.00	2.00
❑ 217	Omar Vizquel	8.00	3.00
❑ 218	Ray Durham	5.00	2.00
❑ 219	Adrian Beltre	5.00	2.00
❑ 220	Carl Everett	5.00	2.00
❑ 221	Kenji Johjima RC	15.00	6.00
❑ 222	Felix Hernandez	8.00	3.00
❑ 223	Ichiro Suzuki	12.00	5.00

❑ 224	Jamie Moyer	5.00	2.00
❑ 225	Jeremy Reed	5.00	2.00
❑ 226	Joel Pineiro	5.00	2.00
❑ 227	Raul Ibanez	5.00	2.00
❑ 228	Richie Sexson	5.00	2.00
❑ 229	Albert Pujols	15.00	6.00
❑ 230	Chris Carpenter	5.00	2.00
❑ 231	David Eckstein	5.00	2.00
❑ 232	Jason Marquis	5.00	2.00
❑ 233	Jeff Suppan	5.00	2.00
❑ 234	Jim Edmonds	8.00	3.00
❑ 235	Yadier Molina	5.00	2.00
❑ 236	Mark Mulder	5.00	2.00
❑ 237	Scott Rolen	8.00	3.00
❑ 238	Alex Scott Gonzalez	5.00	2.00
❑ 239	Aubrey Huff	5.00	2.00
❑ 240	Carl Crawford	5.00	2.00
❑ 241	Casey Fossum	5.00	2.00
❑ 242	Joey Gathright	5.00	2.00
❑ 243	Scott Kazmir	5.00	2.00
❑ 244	Toby Hall	5.00	2.00
❑ 245	Travis Lee	5.00	2.00
❑ 246	Adam Eaton	5.00	2.00
❑ 247	Francisco Cordero	5.00	2.00
❑ 248	Hank Blalock	5.00	2.00
❑ 249	Kevin Mench	5.00	2.00
❑ 250	Kevin Millwood	5.00	2.00
❑ 251	Laynce Nix	5.00	2.00
❑ 252	Mark Teixeira	8.00	3.00
❑ 253	Michael Young	5.00	2.00
❑ 254	A.J. Burnett	5.00	2.00
❑ 255	Alex Rios	5.00	2.00
❑ 256	B.J. Ryan	5.00	2.00
❑ 257	Corey Koskie	5.00	2.00
❑ 258	Josh Towers	5.00	2.00
❑ 259	Lyle Overbay	5.00	2.00
❑ 260	Reed Johnson	5.00	2.00
❑ 261	Roy Halladay	5.00	2.00
❑ 262	Russ Adams	5.00	2.00
❑ 263	Troy Glaus	5.00	2.00
❑ 264	Vernon Wells	5.00	2.00
❑ 265	Alfonso Soriano	5.00	2.00
❑ 266	John Patterson	5.00	2.00
❑ 267	Damian Jackson	5.00	2.00
❑ 268	Jose Guillen	5.00	2.00
❑ 269	Jose Vidro	5.00	2.00
❑ 270	Livan Hernandez	5.00	2.00
❑ 271	Adam Kennedy	5.00	2.00
❑ 272	Bartolo Colon	5.00	2.00
❑ 273	Bengie Molina	5.00	2.00
❑ 274	Casey Kotchman	5.00	2.00
❑ 275	Chone Figgins	5.00	2.00
❑ 276	Matt Cain (RC)	8.00	3.00
❑ 277	Darin Erstad	5.00	2.00
❑ 278	Edgardo Alfonzo	5.00	2.00
❑ 279	Francisco Rodriguez	5.00	2.00
❑ 280	Garret Anderson	5.00	2.00
❑ 281	Vladimir Guerrero	8.00	3.00
❑ 282	Chris Denorfia (RC)	5.00	2.00
❑ 283	Joey Devine RC	5.00	2.00
❑ 284	Justin Verlander (RC)	15.00	6.00
❑ 285	Scott Feldman RC	5.00	2.00
❑ 286	Jason Bergmann RC	5.00	2.00
❑ 287	Jeremy Accardo RC	5.00	2.00
❑ 288	Adam Wainwright (RC)	8.00	3.00
❑ 289	Hanley Ramirez (RC)	6.00	2.50
❑ 290	Josh Johnson (RC)	8.00	3.00
❑ 291	Ryan Zimmerman (RC)	25.00	10.00
❑ 292	Anderson Hernandez (RC)	5.00	2.00
❑ 293	Francisco Liriano (RC)	20.00	8.00
❑ 294	Josh Willingham (RC)	5.00	2.00
❑ 295	Hong-Chih Kuo (RC)	10.00	4.00
❑ 296	Steve Stemle RC	5.00	2.00
❑ 297	Jeff Harris RC	5.00	2.00
❑ 298	John Van Benschoten (RC)	5.00	2.00
❑ 299	Jonathan Papelbon (RC)	20.00	8.00
❑ 300	Jason Kubel (RC)	5.00	2.00

2007 Upper Deck First Edition

❑	COMPLETE SET (300)	50.00	20.00
❑	COMMON CARD (1-300)	.30	.12
❑	COMMON ROOKIE (1-300)	.40	.15
❑	PRINTING PLATE ODDS 1 PER CASE		
❑	PLATE PRINT RUN 1 SET PER COLOR		
❑	BLACK-CYAN-MAGENTA-YELLOW ISSUED		
❑	NO PLATE PRICING DUE TO SCARCITY		
❑ 1	Doug Slaten RC	.40	.15
❑ 2	Miguel Montero (RC)	.40	.15
❑ 3	Brian Burres (RC)	.40	.15
❑ 4	Devern Hansack RC	.40	.15
❑ 5	David Murphy (RC)	.40	.15
❑ 6	Jose Reyes RC	.40	.15
❑ 7	Scott Moore (RC)	.40	.15
❑ 8	Josh Fields (RC)	.40	.15
❑ 9	Chris Stewart RC	.40	.15
❑ 10	Jerry Owens (RC)	.40	.15
❑ 11	Ryan Sweeney (RC)	.40	.15
❑ 12	Kevin Kouzmanoff (RC)	.40	.15
❑ 13	Jeff Baker (RC)	.40	.15
❑ 14	Justin Hampson (RC)	.40	.15
❑ 15	Jeff Salazar (RC)	.40	.15
❑ 16	Alvin Colina RC	.40	.15
❑ 17	Troy Tulowitzki (RC)	1.00	.40
❑ 18	Andrew Miller RC	2.50	1.00
❑ 19	Mike Rabelo RC	.40	.15
❑ 20	Jose Diaz (RC)	.40	.15
❑ 21	Angel Sanchez RC	.40	.15
❑ 22	Ryan Braun RC	.40	.15
❑ 23	Delwyn Young (RC)	.40	.15
❑ 24	Drew Anderson RC	.40	.15
❑ 25	Dennis Sarfate (RC)	.40	.15
❑ 26	Vinny Rottino (RC)	.40	.15
❑ 27	Glen Perkins (RC)	.40	.15
❑ 28	Alexi Casilla RC	.60	.25
❑ 29	Philip Humber (RC)	.60	.25
❑ 30	Andy Cannizaro RC	.40	.15
❑ 31	Jeremy Brown	.30	.12
❑ 32	Sean Henn (RC)	.40	.15
❑ 33	Brian Rogers (RC)	.40	.15
❑ 34	Carlos Maldonado (RC)	.40	.15
❑ 35	Juan Morillo (RC)	.40	.15
❑ 36	Fred Lewis (RC)	.40	.15
❑ 37	Patrick Misch (RC)	.40	.15
❑ 38	Billy Sadler (RC)	.40	.15
❑ 39	Ryan Feierabend (RC)	.40	.15
❑ 40	Cesar Jimenez RC	.40	.15
❑ 41	Oswaldo Navarro RC	.40	.15
❑ 42	Travis Chick (RC)	.40	.15
❑ 43	Delmon Young (RC)	1.00	.40
❑ 44	Shawn Riggans (RC)	.40	.15
❑ 45	Brian Stokes (RC)	.40	.15
❑ 46	Juan Salas (RC)	.40	.15
❑ 47	Joaquin Arias (RC)	.40	.15
❑ 48	Adam Lind (RC)	.40	.15
❑ 49	Beltran Perez (RC)	.40	.15
❑ 50	Brett Campbell RC	.40	.15
❑ 51	Miguel Tejada	.30	.12
❑ 52	Brandon Fahey	.30	.12
❑ 53	Jay Gibbons	.30	.12
❑ 54	Nick Markakis	.50	.20
❑ 55	Kris Benson	.30	.12
❑ 56	Erik Bedard	.30	.12
❑ 57	Chris Ray	.30	.12

❑ 58 Chris Britton .30 .12
❑ 59 Manny Ramirez .50 .20
❑ 60 David Ortiz .75 .30
❑ 61 Alex Cora .30 .12
❑ 62 Trot Nixon .30 .12
❑ 63 Doug Mirabelli .30 .12
❑ 64 Curt Schilling .50 .20
❑ 65 Jonathan Papelbon .75 .30
❑ 66 Craig Hansen .30 .12
❑ 67 Jermaine Dye .30 .12
❑ 68 Jim Thome .50 .20
❑ 69 Rob Mackowiak .30 .12
❑ 70 Brian Anderson .30 .12
❑ 71 A.J. Pierzynski .30 .12
❑ 72 Alex Cintron .30 .12
❑ 73 Jose Contreras .30 .12
❑ 74 Bobby Jenks .30 .12
❑ 75 Mike MacDougal .30 .12
❑ 76 Travis Hafner .30 .12
❑ 77 Ryan Garko .30 .12
❑ 78 Victor Martinez .30 .12
❑ 79 Casey Blake .30 .12
❑ 80 Shin-Soo Choo .50 .20
❑ 81 Paul Byrd .30 .12
❑ 82 Jeremy Sowers .30 .12
❑ 83 Cliff Lee .30 .12
❑ 84 Sean Casey .30 .12
❑ 85 Brandon Inge .30 .12
❑ 86 Omar Infante .30 .12
❑ 87 Magglio Ordonez .30 .12
❑ 88 Marcus Thames .30 .12
❑ 89 Justin Verlander .75 .30
❑ 90 Todd Jones .30 .12
❑ 91 Joel Zumaya .50 .20
❑ 92 Nate Robertson .30 .12
❑ 93 Mark Teahen .30 .12
❑ 94 Ryan Shealy .30 .12
❑ 95 Mark Grudzielanek .30 .12
❑ 96 Shane Costa .30 .12
❑ 97 Reggie Sanders .30 .12
❑ 98 Mark Redman .30 .12
❑ 99 Todd Wellemeyer .30 .12
❑ 100 Ambiorix Burgos .30 .12
❑ 101 Joe Nelson .30 .12
❑ 102 Orlando Cabrera .30 .12
❑ 103 Maicer Izturis .30 .12
❑ 104 Vladimir Guerrero .75 .30
❑ 105 Juan Rivera .30 .12
❑ 106 Jered Weaver .50 .20
❑ 107 Joe Saunders .30 .12
❑ 108 Bartolo Colon .30 .12
❑ 109 Francisco Rodriguez .30 .12
❑ 110 Justin Morneau .30 .12
❑ 111 Luis Castillo .30 .12
❑ 112 Michael Cuddyer .30 .12
❑ 113 Joe Mauer .50 .20
❑ 114 Francisco Liriano .75 .30
❑ 115 Joe Nathan .30 .12
❑ 116 Brad Radke .30 .12
❑ 117 Juan Rincon .30 .12
❑ 118 Derek Jeter 2.00 .75
❑ 119 Jason Giambi .30 .12
❑ 120 Bobby Abreu .30 .12
❑ 121 Gary Sheffield .30 .12
❑ 122 Melky Cabrera .30 .12
❑ 123 Chien-Ming Wang 1.25 .50
❑ 124 Mariano Rivera .75 .30
❑ 125 Jaret Wright .30 .12
❑ 126 Kyle Farnsworth .30 .12
❑ 127 Frank Thomas .75 .30
❑ 128 Dan Johnson .30 .12
❑ 129 Marco Scutaro .30 .12
❑ 130 Jay Payton .30 .12
❑ 131 Joe Blanton .30 .12
❑ 132 Rich Harden .30 .12
❑ 133 Esteban Loaiza .30 .12
❑ 134 Chad Gaudin .30 .12
❑ 135 Yuniesky Betancourt .30 .12
❑ 136 Willie Bloomquist .30 .12
❑ 137 Ichiro Suzuki 1.25 .50
❑ 138 Raul Ibanez .30 .12
❑ 139 Chris Snelling .30 .12
❑ 140 Cha-Seung Baek .30 .12
❑ 141 Julio Mateo .30 .12
❑ 142 Rafael Soriano .30 .12
❑ 143 Jorge Cantu .30 .12
❑ 144 B.J. Upton .30 .12
❑ 145 Dioner Navarro .30 .12
❑ 146 Carl Crawford .30 .12
❑ 147 Damon Hollins .30 .12
❑ 148 Casey Fossum .30 .12
❑ 149 Ruddy Lugo .30 .12
❑ 150 Tyler Walker .30 .12
❑ 151 Shawn Camp .30 .12
❑ 152 Ian Kinsler .30 .12
❑ 153 Jerry Hairston Jr. .30 .12
❑ 154 Gerald Laird .30 .12
❑ 155 Mark DeRosa .30 .12
❑ 156 Kip Wells .30 .12
❑ 157 Vicente Padilla .30 .12
❑ 158 John Koronka .30 .12
❑ 159 Wes Littleton .30 .12
❑ 160 Lyle Overbay .30 .12
❑ 161 Aaron Hill .30 .12
❑ 162 John McDonald .30 .12
❑ 163 Vernon Wells .30 .12
❑ 164 Frank Catalanotto .30 .12
❑ 165 Roy Halladay .30 .12
❑ 166 B.J. Ryan .30 .12
❑ 167 Casey Janssen .30 .12
❑ 168 Stephen Drew .50 .20
❑ 169 Conor Jackson .30 .12
❑ 170 Chad Tracy .30 .12
❑ 171 Johnny Estrada .30 .12
❑ 172 Eric Byrnes .30 .12
❑ 173 Carlos Quentin .30 .12
❑ 174 Brandon Webb .30 .12
❑ 175 Jorge Julio .30 .12
❑ 176 Luis Vizcaino .30 .12
❑ 177 Chipper Jones .75 .30
❑ 178 Adam LaRoche .30 .12
❑ 179 Brian McCann .30 .12
❑ 180 Ryan Langerhans .30 .12
❑ 181 Matt Diaz .30 .12
❑ 182 John Smoltz .50 .20
❑ 183 Oscar Villarreal .30 .12
❑ 184 Chad Paronto .30 .12
❑ 185 Derrek Lee .30 .12
❑ 186 Ryan Theriot .30 .12
❑ 187 Ronny Cedeno .30 .12
❑ 188 Juan Pierre .30 .12
❑ 189 Matt Murton .30 .12
❑ 190 Carlos Zambrano .30 .12
❑ 191 Mark Prior .50 .20
❑ 192 Ryan Dempster .30 .12
❑ 193 Ryan O'Malley .30 .12
❑ 194 Brandon Phillips .30 .12
❑ 195 Rich Aurilia .30 .12
❑ 196 Ken Griffey Jr. 1.25 .50
❑ 197 Ryan Freel .30 .12
❑ 198 Aaron Harang .30 .12
❑ 199 Brandon Claussen .30 .12
❑ 200 David Weathers .30 .12
❑ 201 Eric Milton .30 .12
❑ 202 Kazuo Matsui .30 .12
❑ 203 Jamey Carroll .30 .12
❑ 204 Matt Holliday .75 .30
❑ 205 Brad Hawpe .30 .12
❑ 206 Jason Jennings .30 .12
❑ 207 Josh Fogg .30 .12
❑ 208 Aaron Cook .30 .12
❑ 209 Miguel Cabrera .50 .20
❑ 210 Dan Uggla .50 .20
❑ 211 Hanley Ramirez .50 .20
❑ 212 Jeremy Hermida .30 .12
❑ 213 Cody Ross .30 .12
❑ 214 Josh Willingham .30 .12
❑ 215 Anibal Sanchez .30 .12
❑ 216 Jose Garcia RC .40 .15
❑ 217 Taylor Tankersley .30 .12
❑ 218 Lance Berkman .30 .12
❑ 219 Craig Biggio .50 .20
❑ 220 Brad Ausmus .30 .12
❑ 221 Willy Taveras .30 .12
❑ 222 Chris Burke .30 .12
❑ 223 Roger Clemens 1.50 .60
❑ 224 Brandon Backe .30 .12
❑ 225 Brad Lidge .30 .12
❑ 226 Dan Wheeler .30 .12
❑ 227 Wilson Betemit .30 .12
❑ 228 Julio Lugo .30 .12
❑ 229 Russell Martin .30 .12
❑ 230 Kenny Lofton .30 .12
❑ 231 Brad Penny .30 .12
❑ 232 Chad Billingsley .30 .12
❑ 233 Greg Maddux 1.25 .50
❑ 234 Jonathan Broxton .30 .12
❑ 235 Rickie Weeks .30 .12
❑ 236 Bill Hall .30 .12
❑ 237 Tony Gwynn Jr. .30 .12
❑ 238 Corey Hart .30 .12
❑ 239 Laynce Nix .30 .12
❑ 240 Ben Sheets .30 .12
❑ 241 Dave Bush .30 .12
❑ 242 Francisco Cordero .30 .12
❑ 243 Jose Reyes .30 .12
❑ 244 Carlos Delgado .30 .12
❑ 245 Paul Lo Duca .30 .12
❑ 246 Carlos Beltran .30 .12
❑ 247 Lastings Milledge .50 .20
❑ 248 Pedro Martinez .50 .20
❑ 249 John Maine .30 .12
❑ 250 Steve Trachsel .30 .12
❑ 251 Ryan Howard 1.25 .50
❑ 252 Jimmy Rollins .30 .12
❑ 253 Chris Coste .30 .12
❑ 254 Jeff Conine .30 .12
❑ 255 David Dellucci .30 .12
❑ 256 Cole Hamels .50 .20
❑ 257 Ryan Madson .30 .12
❑ 258 Brett Myers .30 .12
❑ 259 Freddy Sanchez .30 .12
❑ 260 Xavier Nady .30 .12
❑ 261 Jose Castillo .30 .12
❑ 262 Jason Bay .30 .12
❑ 263 Jose Bautista .30 .12
❑ 264 Ronny Paulino .30 .12
❑ 265 Zach Duke .30 .12
❑ 266 Shane Youman RC .40 .15
❑ 267 Matt Capps .30 .12
❑ 268 Adrian Gonzalez .30 .12
❑ 269 Josh Barfield .30 .12
❑ 270 Mike Piazza .75 .30
❑ 271 Dave Roberts .30 .12
❑ 272 Geoff Blum .30 .12
❑ 273 Chris Young .30 .12
❑ 274 Woody Williams .30 .12
❑ 275 Cla Meredith .30 .12
❑ 276 Trevor Hoffman .30 .12
❑ 277 Ray Durham .30 .12
❑ 278 Mark Sweeney .30 .12
❑ 279 Eliezer Alfonzo .30 .12
❑ 280 Todd Linden .30 .12
❑ 281 Jason Schmidt .30 .12
❑ 282 Noah Lowry .30 .12
❑ 283 Brad Hennessey .30 .12
❑ 284 Jonathan Sanchez .30 .12
❑ 285 Albert Pujols 1.50 .60
❑ 286 David Eckstein .30 .12
❑ 287 Jim Edmonds .50 .20
❑ 288 Chris Duncan .30 .12
❑ 289 Juan Encarnacion .30 .12
❑ 290 Jeff Suppan .30 .12
❑ 291 Jeff Weaver .30 .12
❑ 292 Braden Looper .30 .12
❑ 293 Ryan Zimmerman .75 .30
❑ 294 Nick Johnson .30 .12
❑ 295 Alfonso Soriano .30 .12
❑ 296 Austin Kearns .30 .12
❑ 297 Alex Escobar .30 .12
❑ 298 Tony Armas .30 .12
❑ 299 Chad Cordero .30 .12
❑ 300 Jon Rauch .30 .12

2006 Upper Deck First Pitch

❑ COMPLETE SET (220)	50.00	20.00
❑ 1 Chad Tracy	.30	.10
❑ 2 Conor Jackson	.30	.10
❑ 3 Craig Counsell	.30	.10
❑ 4 Javier Vazquez	.30	.10
❑ 5 Luis Gonzalez	.30	.10
❑ 6 Shawn Green	.30	.10
❑ 7 Troy Glaus	.30	.10
❑ 8 Joey Devine RC	.50	.20
❑ 9 Andruw Jones	.50	.20
❑ 10 Chipper Jones	.75	.30
❑ 11 John Smoltz	.50	.20
❑ 12 Marcus Giles	.30	.10
❑ 13 Jeff Francoeur	.75	.30
❑ 14 Tim Hudson	.30	.10
❑ 15 Brian Roberts	.30	.10
❑ 16 Erik Bedard	.30	.10
❑ 17 Javy Lopez	.30	.10
❑ 18 Melvin Mora	.30	.10
❑ 19 Miguel Tejada	.30	.10
❑ 20 Alejandro Freire RC	.50	.20
❑ 21 Sammy Sosa	.75	.30
❑ 22 Craig Hansen RC	3.00	1.25
❑ 23 Curt Schilling	.50	.20
❑ 24 David Ortiz	.75	.30
❑ 25 Edgar Renteria	.30	.10
❑ 26 Johnny Damon	.50	.20
❑ 27 Manny Ramirez	.50	.20
❑ 28 Matt Clement	.30	.10
❑ 29 Trot Nixon	.30	.10
❑ 30 Aramis Ramirez	.30	.10
❑ 31 Carlos Zambrano	.30	.10
❑ 32 Derrek Lee	.50	.20
❑ 33 Greg Maddux	1.25	.50
❑ 34 Jeromy Burnitz	.30	.10
❑ 35 Kerry Wood	.30	.10
❑ 36 Mark Prior	.50	.20
❑ 37 Nomar Garciaparra	.75	.30
❑ 38 Aaron Rowand	.30	.10
❑ 39 Chris DeMaria RC	.50	.20
❑ 40 Jon Garland	.30	.10
❑ 41 Mark Buehrle	.30	.10
❑ 42 Paul Konerko	.30	.10
❑ 43 Scott Podsednik	.30	.10
❑ 44 Tadahito Iguchi	.30	.10
❑ 45 Adam Dunn	.30	.10
❑ 46 Austin Kearns	.30	.10
❑ 47 Felipe Lopez	.30	.10
❑ 48 Ken Griffey Jr.	1.25	.50
❑ 49 Ryan Freel	.30	.10
❑ 50 Sean Casey	.30	.10
❑ 51 Wily Mo Pena	.30	.10
❑ 52 C.C. Sabathia	.30	.10
❑ 53 Cliff Lee	.30	.10
❑ 54 Coco Crisp	.30	.10
❑ 55 Grady Sizemore	.50	.20
❑ 56 Jake Westbrook	.30	.10
❑ 57 Travis Hafner	.30	.10
❑ 58 Victor Martinez	.30	.10
❑ 59 Aaron Miles	.30	.10
❑ 60 Clint Barmes	.30	.10
❑ 61 Garrett Atkins	.30	.10
❑ 62 Jeff Baker	.30	.10
❑ 63 Jeff Francis	.30	.10
❑ 64 Matt Holliday	.40	.15
❑ 65 Todd Helton	.50	.20
❑ 66 Carlos Guillen	.30	.10
❑ 67 Chris Shelton	.30	.10
❑ 68 Dmitri Young	.30	.10
❑ 69 Ivan Rodriguez	.50	.20
❑ 70 Jeremy Bonderman	.30	.10
❑ 71 Magglio Ordonez	.30	.10
❑ 72 Placido Polanco	.30	.10
❑ 73 A.J. Burnett	.30	.10
❑ 74 Carlos Delgado	.30	.10
❑ 75 Dontrelle Willis	.30	.10
❑ 76 Josh Beckett	.30	.10
❑ 77 Juan Pierre	.30	.10
❑ 78 Ryan Jorgensen RC	.50	.20
❑ 79 Miguel Cabrera	.50	.20
❑ 80 Robert Andino RC	.50	.20
❑ 81 Andy Pettitte	.50	.20
❑ 82 Brad Lidge	.30	.10
❑ 83 Craig Biggio	.50	.20
❑ 84 Jeff Bagwell	.50	.20
❑ 85 Lance Berkman	.30	.10
❑ 86 Morgan Ensberg	.30	.10
❑ 87 Roger Clemens	1.50	.60
❑ 88 Roy Oswalt	.30	.10
❑ 89 Angel Berroa	.30	.10
❑ 90 David DeJesus	.30	.10
❑ 91 Steve Stemle RC	.30	.10
❑ 92 Jonah Bayliss RC	.30	.10
❑ 93 Mike Sweeney	.30	.10
❑ 94 Ryan Theriot RC	.50	.20
❑ 95 Zack Greinke	.30	.10
❑ 96 Brad Penny	.30	.10
❑ 97 Cesar Izturis	.30	.10
❑ 98 Brian Myrow RC	.30	.10
❑ 99 Eric Gagne	.30	.10
❑ 100 J.D. Drew	.30	.10
❑ 101 Jeff Kent	.30	.10
❑ 102 Milton Bradley	.30	.10
❑ 103 Odalis Perez	.30	.10
❑ 104 Ben Sheets	.30	.10
❑ 105 Brady Clark	.30	.10
❑ 106 Carlos Lee	.30	.10
❑ 107 Geoff Jenkins	.30	.10
❑ 108 Lyle Overbay	.30	.10
❑ 109 Prince Fielder	.75	.30
❑ 110 Rickie Weeks	.30	.10
❑ 111 Jacque Jones	.30	.10
❑ 112 Joe Mauer	.75	.30
❑ 113 Joe Nathan	.30	.10
❑ 114 Johan Santana	.75	.30
❑ 115 Justin Morneau	.30	.10
❑ 116 Chris Heintz RC	.30	.10
❑ 117 Torii Hunter	.30	.10
❑ 118 Carlos Beltran	.30	.10
❑ 119 Cliff Floyd	.30	.10
❑ 120 David Wright	.75	.30
❑ 121 Jose Reyes	.30	.10
❑ 122 Mike Cameron	.30	.10
❑ 123 Mike Piazza	.75	.30
❑ 124 Pedro Martinez	.50	.20
❑ 125 Tom Glavine	.50	.20
❑ 126 Alex Rodriguez	1.25	.50
❑ 127 Derek Jeter	2.00	.75
❑ 128 Gary Sheffield	.30	.10
❑ 129 Hideki Matsui	.75	.30
❑ 130 Jason Giambi	.30	.10
❑ 131 Jorge Posada	.50	.20
❑ 132 Mariano Rivera	.75	.30
❑ 133 Mike Mussina	.50	.20
❑ 134 Randy Johnson	.75	.30
❑ 135 Barry Zito	.30	.10
❑ 136 Bobby Crosby	.30	.10
❑ 137 Danny Haren	.30	.10
❑ 138 Eric Chavez	.30	.10
❑ 139 Huston Street	.30	.10
❑ 140 Ron Flores RC	.50	.20
❑ 141 Nick Swisher	.30	.10
❑ 142 Rich Harden	.30	.10
❑ 143 Bobby Abreu	.30	.10
❑ 144 Danny Sandoval RC	.50	.20
❑ 145 Chase Utley	.50	.20
❑ 146 Jim Thome	.50	.20
❑ 147 Jimmy Rollins	.30	.10
❑ 148 Pat Burrell	.30	.10
❑ 149 Ryan Howard	1.25	.50
❑ 150 Craig Wilson	.30	.10
❑ 151 Jack Wilson	.30	.10
❑ 152 Jason Bay	.30	.10
❑ 153 Matt Lawton	.30	.10
❑ 154 Oliver Perez	.30	.10
❑ 155 Rob Mackowiak	.30	.10
❑ 156 Zach Duke	.50	.20
❑ 157 Brian Giles	.30	.10
❑ 158 Jake Peavy	.30	.10
❑ 159 Craig Breslow RC	.50	.20
❑ 160 Khalil Greene	.50	.20
❑ 161 Mark Loretta	.30	.10
❑ 162 Ryan Klesko	.30	.10
❑ 163 Trevor Hoffman	.30	.10
❑ 164 J.T. Snow	.30	.10
❑ 165 Jason Schmidt	.30	.10
❑ 166 Marquis Grissom	.30	.10
❑ 167 Moises Alou	.30	.10
❑ 168 Omar Vizquel	.50	.20
❑ 169 Pedro Feliz	.30	.10
❑ 170 Jeremy Accardo RC	.50	.20
❑ 171 Adrian Beltre	.30	.10
❑ 172 Ichiro Suzuki	1.25	.50
❑ 173 Felix Hernandez	.50	.20
❑ 174 Jeff Harris RC	.30	.10
❑ 175 Randy Winn	.30	.10
❑ 176 Raul Ibanez	.30	.10
❑ 177 Richie Sexson	.30	.10
❑ 178 Albert Pujols	1.50	.60
❑ 179 Chris Carpenter	.30	.10
❑ 180 David Eckstein	.30	.10
❑ 181 Jim Edmonds	.30	.10
❑ 182 Larry Walker	.50	.20
❑ 183 Matt Morris	.30	.10
❑ 184 Reggie Sanders	.30	.10
❑ 185 Scott Rolen	.50	.20
❑ 186 Aubrey Huff	.30	.10
❑ 187 Jonny Gomes	.30	.10
❑ 188 Carl Crawford	.30	.10
❑ 189 Tim Corcoran RC	.50	.20
❑ 190 Julio Lugo	.30	.10
❑ 191 Rocco Baldelli	.30	.10
❑ 192 Scott Kazmir	.30	.10
❑ 193 Alfonso Soriano	.30	.10
❑ 194 Hank Blalock	.30	.10
❑ 195 Kenny Rogers	.30	.10
❑ 196 Scott Feldman RC	.30	.10
❑ 197 Laynce Nix	.30	.10
❑ 198 Mark Teixeira	.50	.20
❑ 199 Michael Young	.30	.10
❑ 200 Aaron Hill	.30	.10
❑ 201 Alex Rios	.30	.10
❑ 202 Eric Hinske	.30	.10
❑ 203 Gustavo Chacin	.30	.10
❑ 204 Roy Halladay	.30	.10
❑ 205 Shea Hillenbrand	.30	.10
❑ 206 Vernon Wells	.30	.10
❑ 207 Brad Wilkerson	.30	.10
❑ 208 Chad Cordero	.30	.10
❑ 209 Jose Guillen	.30	.10
❑ 210 Jose Vidro	.30	.10
❑ 211 Livan Hernandez	.30	.10
❑ 212 Preston Wilson	.30	.10
❑ 213 Jason Bergmann RC	.30	.10
❑ 214 Bartolo Colon	.30	.10
❑ 215 Chone Figgins	.30	.10
❑ 216 Darin Erstad	.30	.10
❑ 217 Francisco Rodriguez	.30	.10
❑ 218 Garret Anderson	.30	.10
❑ 219 Steve Finley	.30	.10
❑ 220 Vladimir Guerrero	.75	.30

2006 Upper Deck Future Stars

Item	Hi	Lo
❑ COMP.SET w/o AU's (75)	25.00	10.00
❑ COMMON CARD (1-75)	.40	.15
❑ COMMON AU RC (76-159)	8.00	3.00
❑ FIVE AU RC PER BOX ON AVERAGE		
❑ NO SP PRICING DUE TO SCARCITY		
❑ PRINTING PLATE ODDS 1:2 CASES		
❑ PLATE PRINT RUN 1 SET PER COLOR		
❑ BLACK-CYAN-MAGENTA-YELLOW ISSUED		
❑ NO PLATE PRICING DUE TO SCARCITY		
❑ 1 Miguel Tejada	.40	.15
❑ 2 Brian Roberts	.40	.15
❑ 3 Brandon Webb	.40	.15
❑ 4 Luis Gonzalez	.40	.15
❑ 5 Andruw Jones	.60	.25
❑ 6 Chipper Jones	1.00	.40
❑ 7 John Smoltz	.60	.25
❑ 8 Curt Schilling	.60	.25
❑ 9 Josh Beckett	.40	.15
❑ 10 David Ortiz	1.00	.40
❑ 11 Manny Ramirez	.60	.25
❑ 12 Jim Thome	.60	.25
❑ 13 Paul Konerko	.40	.15
❑ 14 Jermaine Dye	.40	.15
❑ 15 Derrek Lee	.40	.15
❑ 16 Greg Maddux	1.50	.60
❑ 17 Ken Griffey Jr.	1.50	.60
❑ 18 Adam Dunn	.40	.15
❑ 19 Felipe Lopez	.40	.15
❑ 20 Travis Hafner	.40	.15
❑ 21 Victor Martinez	.40	.15
❑ 22 Grady Sizemore	.60	.25
❑ 23 Todd Helton	.60	.25
❑ 24 Matt Holliday	1.00	.40
❑ 25 Jeremy Bonderman	.40	.15
❑ 26 Ivan Rodriguez	.60	.25
❑ 27 Miguel Cabrera	.60	.25
❑ 28 Dontrelle Willis	.40	.15
❑ 29 Roger Clemens	2.00	.75
❑ 30 Roy Oswalt	.40	.15
❑ 31 Lance Berkman	.40	.15
❑ 32 Reggie Sanders	.40	.15
❑ 33 Vladimir Guerrero	1.00	.40
❑ 34 Chone Figgins	.40	.15
❑ 35 Jeff Kent	.40	.15
❑ 36 Eric Gagne	.40	.15
❑ 37 Carlos Lee	.40	.15
❑ 38 Rickie Weeks	.40	.15
❑ 39 Johan Santana	.60	.25
❑ 40 Torii Hunter	.40	.15
❑ 41 Alex Rodriguez	1.50	.60
❑ 42 Derek Jeter	2.50	1.00
❑ 43 Randy Johnson	1.00	.40
❑ 44 Hideki Matsui	1.00	.40
❑ 45 Johnny Damon	.60	.25
❑ 46 Pedro Martinez	.60	.25
❑ 47 David Wright	1.50	.60
❑ 48 Carlos Beltran	.40	.15
❑ 49 Rich Harden	.40	.15
❑ 50 Eric Chavez	.40	.15
❑ 51 Huston Street	.40	.15
❑ 52 Ryan Howard	1.50	.60
❑ 53 Bobby Abreu	.40	.15
❑ 54 Chase Utley	1.00	.40
❑ 55 Jason Bay	.40	.15
❑ 56 Jake Peavy	.40	.15
❑ 57 Brian Giles	.40	.15
❑ 58 Trevor Hoffman	.40	.15
❑ 59 Jason Schmidt	.40	.15
❑ 60 Randy Winn	.40	.15
❑ 61 Kenji Johjima RC	2.00	.75
❑ 62 Ichiro Suzuki	1.50	.60
❑ 63 Felix Hernandez	.60	.25
❑ 64 Albert Pujols	2.00	.75
❑ 65 Chris Carpenter	.40	.15
❑ 66 Jim Edmonds	.60	.25
❑ 67 Carl Crawford	.40	.15
❑ 68 Scott Kazmir	.60	.25
❑ 69 Jonny Gomes	.40	.15
❑ 70 Mark Teixeira	.60	.25
❑ 71 Michael Young	.40	.15
❑ 72 Vernon Wells	.40	.15
❑ 73 Roy Halladay	.40	.15
❑ 74 Nick Johnson	.40	.15
❑ 75 Alfonso Soriano	.40	.15
❑ 76 A.Wainwright AU (RC)	20.00	8.00
❑ 77 A.Hernandez AU (RC)	8.00	3.00
❑ 78 A.Ethier AU SP (RC)	25.00	10.00
❑ 79 Colter Bean AU SP (RC)	10.00	4.00
❑ 80 Ben Johnson AU (RC)	8.00	3.00
❑ 81 Boof Bonser AU SP (RC)	12.00	5.00
❑ 82 Boone Logan AU RC	8.00	3.00
❑ 83 Brian Anderson AU (RC)	8.00	3.00
❑ 84 B.Bannister AU (RC)	8.00	3.00
❑ 85 C.Denorfia AU SP (RC)	10.00	4.00
❑ 86 C.Billingsley AU SP (RC)	20.00	8.00
❑ 87 Cody Ross AU (RC)	8.00	3.00
❑ 88 Cole Hamels AU SP (RC)	40.00	15.00
❑ 89 Conor Jackson AU (RC)	12.00	5.00
❑ 90 Dan Uggla AU SP (RC)		
❑ 91 D.Gassner AU SP (RC)	8.00	3.00
❑ 92 Jordan Tata AU RC	8.00	3.00
❑ 93 Eric Reed AU (RC)	8.00	3.00
❑ 94 Fausto Carmona AU (RC)	25.00	10.00
❑ 95 Luis Figueroa AU SP RC		
❑ 96 F.Liriano AU SP (RC)	25.00	10.00
❑ 97 Freddie Bynum AU (RC)	8.00	3.00
❑ 98 H.Ramirez AU SP (RC)	40.00	15.00
❑ 99 H.Kuo AU SP (RC)	60.00	30.00
❑ 100 Ian Kinsler AU (RC)	20.00	8.00
❑ 101 N.Cruz AU SP (RC)	8.00	3.00
❑ 102 Ruddy Lugo AU (RC)	8.00	3.00
❑ 103 J.Kubel AU SP (RC)	8.00	3.00
❑ 104 Jeff Harris AU RC	8.00	3.00
❑ 105 S.Ramirez AU (RC)	8.00	3.00
❑ 106 Jer.Weaver AU SP (RC)	50.00	20.00
❑ 107 J.Accardo AU SP RC	15.00	6.00
❑ 108 J.Willingham AU SP (RC)	8.00	3.00
❑ 109 J.Zumaya AU SP (RC)	25.00	10.00
❑ 110 Joey Devine AU RC	8.00	3.00
❑ 111 John Koronka AU (RC)	8.00	3.00
❑ 112 J.Papelbon AU (RC)	40.00	15.00
❑ 113 Jose Capellan AU (RC)	8.00	3.00
❑ 114 Josh Johnson AU (RC)	12.00	5.00
❑ 115 Josh Rupe AU SP (RC)	8.00	3.00
❑ 116 J.Hermida AU SP (RC)	8.00	3.00
❑ 117 Josh Wilson AU (RC)	8.00	3.00
❑ 118 J.Verlander AU SP (RC)		
❑ 119 K.Shoppach AU (RC)	8.00	3.00
❑ 120 K.Morales AU (RC)	12.00	5.00
❑ 121 Sean Tracey AU (RC)	8.00	3.00
❑ 122 Macay McBride AU (RC)	8.00	3.00
❑ 123 M.Prado AU SP (RC)		
❑ 124 Matt Cain AU (RC)	12.00	5.00
❑ 125 R.Martin AU (RC)	12.00	5.00
❑ 126 T.Hamulack AU SP (RC)	8.00	3.00
❑ 127 Mike Jacobs AU (RC)	8.00	3.00
❑ 128 B.Hendrickson AU (RC)	8.00	3.00
❑ 129 Jack Taschner AU (RC)	8.00	3.00
❑ 130 Nate McLouth AU (RC)	8.00	3.00
❑ 131 J.Sowers AU SP (RC)	20.00	8.00
❑ 132 Paul Maholm AU (RC)	8.00	3.00
❑ 133 S.Drew AU SP (RC)		
❑ 134 Jason Bergmann AU RC	8.00	3.00
❑ 135 Rich Hill AU SP (RC)	30.00	12.50
❑ 136 M.Cabrera AU SP (RC)		
❑ 137 Scott Dunn AU (RC)	8.00	3.00
❑ 138 R.Zimmerman AU (RC)	50.00	20.00
❑ 139 A.Sanchez AU (RC)	12.00	5.00
❑ 140 Sean Marshall AU (RC)	12.00	5.00
❑ 141 T.Saito AU SP RC		
❑ 142 T.Buchholz AU (RC)	8.00	3.00
❑ 143 C.Quentin AU SP (RC)	8.00	3.00
❑ 144 Matt Garza AU (RC)	12.00	5.00
❑ 145 Wil Nieves AU (RC)	8.00	3.00
❑ 146 Jamie Shields AU RC	8.00	3.00
❑ 147 Jon Lester AU SP RC		
❑ 148 Craig Hansen AU SP RC		
❑ 149 Aaron Rakers AU (RC)	8.00	3.00
❑ 150 B.Livingston AU (RC)	8.00	3.00
❑ 151 B.Harris AU (RC)	8.00	3.00
❑ 152 Alay Soler AU SP RC	8.00	3.00
❑ 153 Chris Britton AU RC	8.00	3.00
❑ 154 H.Kendrick AU SP (RC)	40.00	15.00
❑ 155 J.Van Buren AU (RC)	8.00	3.00
❑ 156 C.Freeman AU SP (RC)	8.00	3.00
❑ 157 Matt Capps AU (RC)	8.00	3.00
❑ 158 Peter Moylan AU RC	8.00	3.00
❑ 159 Ty Taubenheim AU RC	12.00	5.00

2007 Upper Deck Future Stars

Item	Hi	Lo
❑ COMP.SET w/o AU's (100)	25.00	10.00
❑ COMMON CARD (1-100)	.40	.15
❑ COMMON AU RC (101-190)	8.00	3.00
❑ 101-190 ODDS 1:6 HOB,1:24 RET,1:350 WALMART		
❑ EXCHANGE DEADLINE 9/5/2009		
❑ 1 Brandon Webb	.40	.15
❑ 2 Conor Jackson	.40	.15
❑ 3 Stephen Drew	.60	.25
❑ 4 Chipper Jones	1.00	.40
❑ 5 Andruw Jones	.60	.25
❑ 6 Jeff Francoeur	1.00	.40
❑ 7 John Smoltz	.60	.25
❑ 8 Miguel Tejada	.40	.15
❑ 9 Nick Markakis	.60	.25
❑ 10 Brian Roberts	.40	.15
❑ 11 David Ortiz	1.00	.40
❑ 12 Manny Ramirez	.60	.25
❑ 13 Josh Beckett	.40	.15
❑ 14 Curt Schilling	.60	.25
❑ 15 Derrek Lee	.40	.15
❑ 16 Aramis Ramirez	.40	.15
❑ 17 Carlos Zambrano	.40	.15
❑ 18 Alfonso Soriano	.40	.15
❑ 19 Jim Thome	.60	.25
❑ 20 Paul Konerko	.40	.15
❑ 21 Jon Garland	.40	.15
❑ 22 Ken Griffey Jr.	1.50	.60
❑ 23 Adam Dunn	.40	.15
❑ 24 Aaron Harang	.40	.15
❑ 25 Travis Hafner	.40	.15

❑ 26 Victor Martinez	.40	.15
❑ 27 Grady Sizemore	.60	.25
❑ 28 C.C. Sabathia	.40	.15
❑ 29 Todd Helton	.60	.25
❑ 30 Matt Holliday	.50	.20
❑ 31 Garrett Atkins	.40	.15
❑ 32 Ivan Rodriguez	.60	.25
❑ 33 Magglio Ordonez	.40	.15
❑ 34 Gary Sheffield	.40	.15
❑ 35 Justin Verlander	1.00	.40
❑ 36 Miguel Cabrera	.60	.25
❑ 37 Hanley Ramirez	.60	.25
❑ 38 Dontrelle Willis	.40	.15
❑ 39 Lance Berkman	.40	.15
❑ 40 Roy Oswalt	.40	.15
❑ 41 Carlos Lee	.40	.15
❑ 42 Gil Meche	.40	.15
❑ 43 Emil Brown	.40	.15
❑ 44 Mark Teahen	.40	.15
❑ 45 Vladimir Guerrero	1.00	.40
❑ 46 Jered Weaver	.60	.25
❑ 47 Howie Kendrick	.40	.15
❑ 48 Juan Pierre	.40	.15
❑ 49 Nomar Garciaparra	1.00	.40
❑ 50 Rafael Furcal	.40	.15
❑ 51 Jeff Kent	.40	.15
❑ 52 Prince Fielder	1.00	.40
❑ 53 Ben Sheets	.40	.15
❑ 54 Rickie Weeks	.40	.15
❑ 55 Justin Morneau	.40	.15
❑ 56 Joe Mauer	.60	.25
❑ 57 Torii Hunter	.40	.15
❑ 58 Johan Santana	.60	.25
❑ 59 Jose Reyes	1.00	.40
❑ 60 David Wright	1.50	.60
❑ 61 Carlos Delgado	.40	.15
❑ 62 Carlos Beltran	.40	.15
❑ 63 Derek Jeter	2.50	1.00
❑ 64 Alex Rodriguez	1.50	.60
❑ 65 Johnny Damon	.60	.25
❑ 66 Jason Giambi	.40	.15
❑ 67 Bobby Abreu	.40	.15
❑ 68 Mike Piazza	1.00	.40
❑ 69 Nick Swisher	.40	.15
❑ 70 Eric Chavez	.40	.15
❑ 71 Ryan Howard	1.50	.60
❑ 72 Chase Utley	1.00	.40
❑ 73 Jimmy Rollins	.40	.15
❑ 74 Jason Bay	.40	.15
❑ 75 Freddy Sanchez	.40	.15
❑ 76 Zach Duke	.40	.15
❑ 77 Greg Maddux	1.50	.60
❑ 78 Adrian Gonzalez	.40	.15
❑ 79 Jake Peavy	.40	.15
❑ 80 Ray Durham	.40	.15
❑ 81 Barry Zito	.40	.15
❑ 82 Matt Cain	.60	.25
❑ 83 Ichiro Suzuki	1.50	.60
❑ 84 Felix Hernandez	.60	.25
❑ 85 Richie Sexson	.40	.15
❑ 86 Albert Pujols	2.00	.75
❑ 87 Scott Rolen	.60	.25
❑ 88 Chris Carpenter	.40	.15
❑ 89 Chris Duncan	.40	.15
❑ 90 Carl Crawford	.40	.15
❑ 91 Rocco Baldelli	.40	.15
❑ 92 Scott Kazmir	.60	.25
❑ 93 Michael Young	.40	.15
❑ 94 Mark Teixeira	.60	.25
❑ 95 Ian Kinsler	.40	.15
❑ 96 Troy Glaus	.40	.15
❑ 97 Vernon Wells	.40	.15
❑ 98 Roy Halladay	.40	.15
❑ 99 Ryan Zimmerman	1.00	.40
❑ 100 Nick Johnson	.40	.15
❑ 101 Zack Segovia AU (RC)	8.00	3.00
❑ 102 Joaquin Arias AU (RC)	8.00	3.00
❑ 103 T.Tulowitzki AU SP (RC)		
❑ 104 Travis Buck AU (RC)	10.00	4.00

❑ 105 Mike Schultz AU RC	8.00	3.00
❑ 106 Sean White AU SP RC		
❑ 107 Sean Henn AU (RC)	8.00	3.00
❑ 108 Ryan Z. Braun AU RC	15.00	6.00
❑ 109 Rick Vanden Hurk AU RC	8.00	3.00
❑ 110 Carlos Gomez AU SP RC		
❑ 111 Mike Rabelo AU RC	10.00	4.00
❑ 112 Felix Pie AU (RC)	10.00	4.00
❑ 113 Miguel Montero AU (RC)	10.00	4.00
❑ 114 Michael Bourn AU (RC)	10.00	4.00
❑ 115 M.Owings AU SP (RC) EXCH		
❑ 116 Matt Lindstrom AU (RC)	8.00	3.00
❑ 117 Matt Chico AU (RC)	8.00	3.00
❑ 118 Levale Speigner AU RC	8.00	3.00
❑ 119 Lee Gardner AU (RC)	8.00	3.00
❑ 120 Kory Casto AU (RC)	10.00	4.00
❑ 121 Kevin Kouzmanoff AU (RC)	10.00	4.00
❑ 122 Kevin Cameron AU RC	8.00	3.00
❑ 123 Kei Igawa AU SP RC		
❑ 124 Tyler Clippard AU (RC)	15.00	6.00
❑ 125 Juan Perez AU RC	8.00	3.00
❑ 126 Josh Hamilton AU SP (RC)	15.00	6.00
❑ 127 Joseph Bisenius AU RC	8.00	3.00
❑ 128 Jose Luis Garcia AU RC	8.00	3.00
❑ 129 Jon Knott AU RC	8.00	3.00
❑ 130 Jon Coutlangus AU (RC)	10.00	4.00
❑ 131 John Danks AU RC	8.00	3.00
❑ 132 Joe Smith AU RC	8.00	3.00
❑ 133 Matt Brown AU RC	8.00	3.00
❑ 134 Joakim Soria AU RC	15.00	6.00
❑ 135 Jesus Flores AU RC	15.00	6.00
❑ 136 Jeff Baker AU (RC)	8.00	3.00
❑ 137 Jay Marshall AU RC	8.00	3.00
❑ 138 Jared Burton AU RC	10.00	4.00
❑ 139 Jamie Vermilyea AU RC	10.00	4.00
❑ 140 Jamie Burke AU (RC)	10.00	4.00
❑ 141 Ryan Rowland-Smith AU RC	10.00	4.00
❑ 142 Connor Robertson AU RC	8.00	3.00
❑ 143 Hector Gimenez AU (RC)	8.00	3.00
❑ 144 Gustavo Molina AU RC	10.00	4.00
❑ 145 Glen Perkins AU (RC)	8.00	3.00
❑ 146 J.Chamberlain AU SP RC EXCH	200.00	150.00
❑ 147 Doug Slaten AU RC	8.00	3.00
❑ 148 Ryan Braun AU (RC)	60.00	30.00
❑ 149 Delmon Young AU SP (RC)		
❑ 150 Garrett Jones AU (RC)	8.00	3.00
❑ 151 Chris Stewart AU SP RC		
❑ 152 Cesar Jimenez AU RC	10.00	4.00
❑ 153 Brian Stokes AU (RC)	8.00	3.00
❑ 154 Brian Burres AU (RC)	10.00	4.00
❑ 155 Brian Barden AU SP RC		
❑ 156 Kyle Kendrick AU RC	30.00	12.50
❑ 157 Andrew Miller AU RC	20.00	8.00
❑ 158 Alexi Casilla AU RC	8.00	3.00
❑ 159 Alex Gordon AU SP RC	70.00	35.00
❑ 160 A.J. Murray AU RC	10.00	4.00
❑ 161 A.Iwamura AU SP RC		
❑ 162 Adam Lind AU (RC)	10.00	4.00
❑ 163 Chase Wright AU RC	12.00	5.00
❑ 164 Dallas Braden AU RC	8.00	3.00
❑ 165 Rocky Cherry AU RC	12.00	5.00
❑ 166 Andy Gonzalez AU RC	8.00	3.00
❑ 167 Neal Musser AU RC	8.00	3.00
❑ 168 Mark Reynolds AU RC	20.00	8.00
❑ 169 Dennis Dove AU (RC)	8.00	3.00
❑ 170 Justin Hampson AU (RC)	10.00	4.00
❑ 171 Phil Hughes AU SP (RC)		
❑ 172 Kelvin Jimenez AU RC	8.00	3.00
❑ 173 Hunter Pence AU SP (RC)		
❑ 174 Brad Salmon AU RC	15.00	6.00
❑ 175 Ryan Sweeney AU (RC)	8.00	3.00
❑ 176 Brandon Wood AU (RC)	15.00	6.00
❑ 177 Billy Butler AU SP (RC)		
❑ 178 Ben Francisco AU (RC)	8.00	3.00
❑ 179 Devern Hansack AU SP RC		
❑ 180 Yoel Hernandez AU RC	8.00	3.00
❑ 181 Tim Lincecum AU SP RC		
❑ 182 Danny Putnam AU (RC)	12.00	5.00

❑ 183 J.Salta AU SP (RC)	15.00	6.00
❑ 184 Andy LaRoche AU SP (RC)		
❑ 185 Matt DeSalvo AU (RC)	12.00	5.00
❑ 186 Fred Lewis AU (RC)	8.00	3.00
❑ 187 Anthony Lerew AU (RC)	8.00	3.00
❑ 188 Jesse Litsch AU RC	10.00	4.00
❑ 189a Daisuke Matsuzaka RC		
❑ 189b Daisuke Matsuzaka AU SP EXCH	300.00	250.00

2007 Upper Deck Goudey

❑ COMP.SET w/o SPs (200)	50.00	20.00
❑ COMMON CARD (1-200)	.50	.20
❑ COMMON ROOKIE (1-200)	.75	.30
❑ COMMON SP (201-240)	5.00	2.00
❑ SP ODDS 1:6 HOBBY,1:6 RETAIL		
❑ 1933 ORIGINALS ODDS TWO PER CASE		
❑ SEE 1933 GOUDEY PRICING FOR ORIGINALS		
❑ 1 A.J. Burnett	.50	.20
❑ 2 Aaron Boone	.50	.20
❑ 3 Aaron Rowand	.50	.20
❑ 4 Adam Dunn	.50	.20
❑ 5 Adrian Beltre	.50	.20
❑ 6 Albert Pujols	2.50	1.00
❑ 7 Ivan Rodriguez	.75	.30
❑ 8 Alfonso Soriano	.50	.20
❑ 9 Andruw Jones	.75	.30
❑ 10 Andy Pettitte	.75	.30
❑ 11 Aramis Ramirez	.50	.20
❑ 12 B.J. Upton	.50	.20
❑ 13 Barry Zito	.50	.20
❑ 14 Bartolo Colon	.50	.20
❑ 15 Ben Sheets	.50	.20
❑ 16 Bobby Abreu	.50	.20
❑ 17 Bobby Crosby	.50	.20
❑ 18 Brian Giles	.50	.20
❑ 19 Brian Roberts	.50	.20
❑ 20 C.C. Sabathia	.50	.20
❑ 21 Carlos Beltran	.50	.20
❑ 22 Carlos Delgado	.50	.20
❑ 23 Carlos Lee	.50	.20
❑ 24 Carlos Zambrano	.50	.20
❑ 25 Chad Cordero	.50	.20
❑ 26 Chad Tracy	.50	.20
❑ 27 Chipper Jones	1.25	.50
❑ 28 Craig Biggio	.75	.30
❑ 29 Curt Schilling	.75	.30
❑ 30 Danny Haren	.50	.20
❑ 31 Darin Erstad	.50	.20
❑ 32 David Ortiz	1.25	.50
❑ 33 Billy Wagner	.50	.20
❑ 34 Derek Jeter	3.00	1.25
❑ 35 Derek Lee	.50	.20
❑ 36 Dontrelle Willis	.50	.20
❑ 37 Edgar Renteria	.50	.20
❑ 38 Eric Chavez	.50	.20
❑ 39 Felix Hernandez	.75	.30
❑ 40 Garret Anderson	.50	.20
❑ 41 Garrett Atkins	.50	.20
❑ 42 Gary Sheffield	.50	.20
❑ 43 Grady Sizemore	.75	.30
❑ 44 Greg Maddux	2.00	.75
❑ 45 Hank Blalock	.50	.20
❑ 46 Hanley Ramirez	.75	.30
❑ 47 J.D. Drew	.50	.20

❑ 48 Jacque Jones .50 .20
❑ 49 Jake Peavy .50 .20
❑ 50 Jake Westbrook .50 .20
❑ 51 Jason Bay .50 .20
❑ 52 Jason Giambi .50 .20
❑ 53 Jason Schmidt .50 .20
❑ 54 Jason Varitek 1.25 .50
❑ 55 Troy Tulowitzki (RC) 2.00 .75
❑ 56 Jeff Francoeur 1.25 .50
❑ 57 Jeff Kent .50 .20
❑ 58 Jeremy Bonderman .50 .20
❑ 59 Jim Edmonds .75 .30
❑ 60 Jim Thome .75 .30
❑ 61 Jimmy Rollins .50 .20
❑ 62 Joe Mauer .75 .30
❑ 63 Johan Santana .75 .30
❑ 64 John Smoltz .75 .30
❑ 65 Johnny Damon .75 .30
❑ 66 Jose Reyes 1.25 .50
❑ 67 Josh Beckett .75 .30
❑ 68 Justin Morneau .50 .20
❑ 69 Ken Griffey Jr. 2.00 .75
❑ 70 Kerry Wood .50 .20
❑ 71 Khalil Greene .75 .30
❑ 72 Lance Berkman .50 .20
❑ 73 Livan Hernandez .50 .20
❑ 74 Manny Ramirez .75 .30
❑ 75 Mark Mulder .50 .20
❑ 76 Chase Utley 1.25 .50
❑ 77 Mark Teixeira .75 .30
❑ 78 Miguel Tejada .50 .20
❑ 79 Miguel Cabrera .75 .30
❑ 80 Mike Piazza 1.25 .50
❑ 81 Pat Burrell .50 .20
❑ 82 Paul LoDuca .50 .20
❑ 83 Pedro Martinez .75 .30
❑ 84 Prince Fielder 1.25 .50
❑ 85 Rafael Furcal .50 .20
❑ 86 Randy Johnson 1.25 .50
❑ 87 Richie Sexson .50 .20
❑ 88 Robinson Cano .75 .30
❑ 89 Roy Halladay .50 .20
❑ 90 Roy Oswalt .50 .20
❑ 91 Scott Rolen .75 .30
❑ 92 Tim Hudson .50 .20
❑ 93 Todd Helton .75 .30
❑ 94 Tom Glavine .75 .30
❑ 95 Torii Hunter .50 .20
❑ 96 Travis Hafner .50 .20
❑ 97 Trevor Hoffman .50 .20
❑ 98 Vernon Wells .50 .20
❑ 99 Vladimir Guerrero 1.25 .50
❑ 100 Zach Duke .50 .20
❑ 101 Alex Rodriguez 2.00 .75
❑ 102 Ryan Howard 2.00 .75
❑ 103 Michael Barrett .50 .20
❑ 104 Ichiro Suzuki 2.00 .75
❑ 105 Hideki Matsui 1.25 .50
❑ 106 Jered Weaver .75 .30
❑ 107 Dan Uggla .75 .30
❑ 108 Ryan Freel .50 .20
❑ 109 Bill Hall .50 .20
❑ 110 Ray Durham .50 .20
❑ 111 Morgan Ensberg .50 .20
❑ 112 Shawn Green .50 .20
❑ 113 Brandon Webb .50 .20
❑ 114 Frank Thomas 1.25 .50
❑ 115 Corey Patterson .50 .20
❑ 116 Edwin Encarnacion .50 .20
❑ 117 Mike Cameron .50 .20
❑ 118 Matt Holliday 1.25 .50
❑ 119 Jhonny Peralta .50 .20
❑ 120 Nick Swisher .50 .20
❑ 121 Brad Penny .50 .20
❑ 122 Kenji Johjima 1.25 .50
❑ 123 Francisco Rodriguez .50 .20
❑ 124 Mark Teahen .50 .20
❑ 125 Jonathan Papelbon 1.25 .50
❑ 126 Carlos Guillen .50 .20
❑ 127 Freddy Sanchez .50 .20
❑ 128 Chien-Ming Wang 2.00 .75
❑ 129 Andre Ethier .75 .30
❑ 130 Matt Cain .75 .30
❑ 131 Austin Kearns .50 .20
❑ 132 Ramon Hernandez .50 .20
❑ 133 Chris Carpenter .50 .20
❑ 134 Michael Cuddyer .50 .20
❑ 135 Stephen Drew .75 .30
❑ 136 David Wright 2.00 .75
❑ 137 David DeJesus .50 .20
❑ 138 Gary Matthews .50 .20
❑ 139 Brandon Phillips .50 .20
❑ 140 Josh Barfield .50 .20
❑ 141 Alex Gordon RC 4.00 1.50
❑ 142 Scott Kazmir .75 .30
❑ 143 Luis Gonzalez .50 .20
❑ 144 Mike Sweeney .50 .20
❑ 145 Luis Castillo .50 .20
❑ 146 Huston Street .50 .20
❑ 147 Phil Hughes (RC) 4.00 1.50
❑ 148 Adrian Gonzalez .50 .20
❑ 149 Raul Ibanez .50 .20
❑ 150 Joe Crede .50 .20
❑ 151 Mark Loretta .50 .20
❑ 152 Adam LaRoche (RC) .75 .30
❑ 153 Troy Glaus .50 .20
❑ 154 Conor Jackson .50 .20
❑ 155 Michael Young .50 .20
❑ 156 Scott Podsednik .50 .20
❑ 157 David Eckstein .50 .20
❑ 158 Mike Jacobs .50 .20
❑ 159 Nomar Garciaparra 1.25 .50
❑ 160 Mariano Rivera 1.25 .50
❑ 161 Pedro Feliz .50 .20
❑ 162 Josh Hamilton (RC) 2.00 .75
❑ 163 Ryan Langerhans .50 .20
❑ 164 Willy Taveras .50 .20
❑ 165 Carl Crawford .50 .20
❑ 166 Melvin Mora .50 .20
❑ 167 Francisco Liriano 1.25 .50
❑ 168 Orlando Cabrera .50 .20
❑ 169 Chris Duncan .50 .20
❑ 170 Johnny Estrada .50 .20
❑ 171 Ryan Zimmerman 1.25 .50
❑ 172 Rickie Weeks .50 .20
❑ 173 Paul Konerko .50 .20
❑ 174 Jack Wilson .50 .20
❑ 175 Jorge Posada .75 .30
❑ 176 Magglio Ordonez .50 .20
❑ 177 Nick Johnson .50 .20
❑ 178 Geoff Jenkins .50 .20
❑ 179 Reggie Sanders .50 .20
❑ 180 Moises Alou .50 .20
❑ 181 Glen Perkins (RC) .75 .30
❑ 182 Brad Lidge .50 .20
❑ 183 Kevin Kouzmanoff (RC) .75 .30
❑ 184 Jorge Cantu .50 .20
❑ 185 Carlos Quentin .50 .20
❑ 186 Rich Harden .50 .20
❑ 187 Jose Vidro .50 .20
❑ 188 Aaron Harang .50 .20
❑ 189 Noah Lowry .50 .20
❑ 190 Jermaine Dye .50 .20
❑ 191 Victor Martinez .50 .20
❑ 192 Chone Figgins .50 .20
❑ 193 Aubrey Huff .50 .20
❑ 194 Jason Isringhausen .50 .20
❑ 195 Brian McCann .50 .20
❑ 196 Juan Pierre .50 .20
❑ 197 Delmon Young (RC) 1.25 .50
❑ 198 Felipe Lopez .50 .20
❑ 199 Brad Hawpe .50 .20
❑ 200 Justin Verlander 1.25 .50
❑ 201 Mike Schmidt SP 10.00 4.00
❑ 202 Nolan Ryan SP 12.00 5.00
❑ 203 Cal Ripken Jr. SP 10.00 4.00
❑ 204 Harmon Killebrew SP 6.00 2.50
❑ 205 Reggie Jackson SP 6.00 2.50
❑ 206 Johnny Bench SP 6.00 2.50
❑ 207 Carlton Fisk SP 6.00 2.50
❑ 208 Yogi Berra SP 6.00 2.50
❑ 209 Al Kaline SP 6.00 2.50
❑ 210 Alan Trammell SP 5.00 2.00
❑ 211 Bill Mazeroski SP 6.00 2.50
❑ 212 Bob Gibson SP 6.00 2.50
❑ 213 Brooks Robinson SP 6.00 2.50
❑ 214 Carl Yastrzemski SP 8.00 3.00
❑ 215 Don Mattingly SP 12.00 5.00
❑ 216 Fergie Jenkins SP 5.00 2.00
❑ 217 Jim Rice SP 5.00 2.00
❑ 218 Lou Brock SP 6.00 2.50
❑ 219 Rod Carew SP 6.00 2.50
❑ 220 Stan Musial SP 8.00 3.00
❑ 221 Tom Seaver SP 6.00 2.50
❑ 222 Tony Gwynn SP 6.00 2.50
❑ 223 Wade Boggs SP 6.00 2.50
❑ 224 Alex Rodriguez SP 8.00 3.00
❑ 225 David Wright SP 8.00 3.00
❑ 226 Ryan Howard SP 8.00 3.00
❑ 227 Ichiro Suzuki SP 8.00 3.00
❑ 228 Ken Griffey Jr. SP 8.00 3.00
❑ 229 Daisuke Matsuzaka SP RC 10.00 4.00
❑ 230 Kei Igawa SP RC 6.00 2.50
❑ 231 Akinori Iwamura SP RC 8.00 3.00
❑ 232 Derek Jeter SP 10.00 4.00
❑ 233 Albert Pujols SP 10.00 4.00
❑ 234 Greg Maddux SP 8.00 3.00
❑ 235 David Ortiz SP 6.00 2.50
❑ 236 Manny Ramirez SP 6.00 2.50
❑ 237 Johan Santana SP 6.00 2.50
❑ 238 Pedro Martinez SP 6.00 2.50
❑ 239 Roger Clemens SP 10.00 4.00
❑ 240 Vladimir Guerrero SP 6.00 2.50

2001 Upper Deck Ovation

❑ COMP.SET w/o SP'S (60) 20.00 8.00
❑ COMMON CARD (1-60) .40 .15
❑ COMMON WP (61-90) 5.00 2.00
❑ 1 Troy Glaus .40 .15
❑ 2 Darin Erstad .40 .15
❑ 3 Jason Giambi .40 .15
❑ 4 Tim Hudson .40 .15
❑ 5 Eric Chavez .40 .15
❑ 6 Carlos Delgado .40 .15
❑ 7 David Wells .40 .15
❑ 8 Greg Vaughn .40 .15
❑ 9 Omar Vizquel UER .60 .25
❑ 10 Jim Thome .60 .25
❑ 11 Roberto Alomar .60 .25

Card		
❑ 12 John Olerud	.40	.15
❑ 13 Edgar Martinez	.60	.25
❑ 14 Cal Ripken	3.00	1.25
❑ 15 Alex Rodriguez	1.50	.60
❑ 16 Ivan Rodriguez	.60	.25
❑ 17 Manny Ramirez Sox	.60	.25
❑ 18 Nomar Garciaparra	1.50	.60
❑ 19 Pedro Martinez	.60	.25
❑ 20 Jermaine Dye	.40	.15
❑ 21 Juan Gonzalez	.40	.15
❑ 22 Matt Lawton	.40	.15
❑ 23 Frank Thomas	1.00	.40
❑ 24 Magglio Ordonez	.40	.15
❑ 25 Bernie Williams	.60	.25
❑ 26 Derek Jeter	2.50	1.00
❑ 27 Roger Clemens	2.00	.75
❑ 28 Jeff Bagwell	.60	.25
❑ 29 Richard Hidalgo	.40	.15
❑ 30 Chipper Jones	1.00	.40
❑ 31 Greg Maddux	1.50	.60
❑ 32 Andruw Jones	.60	.25
❑ 33 Jeromy Burnitz	.40	.15
❑ 34 Mark McGwire	2.50	1.00
❑ 35 Jim Edmonds	.40	.15
❑ 36 Sammy Sosa	1.00	.40
❑ 37 Kerry Wood	.40	.15
❑ 38 Randy Johnson	1.00	.40
❑ 39 Steve Finley	.40	.15
❑ 40 Gary Sheffield	.40	.15
❑ 41 Kevin Brown	.40	.15
❑ 42 Shawn Green	.40	.15
❑ 43 Vladimir Guerrero	1.00	.40
❑ 44 Jose Vidro	.40	.15
❑ 45 Barry Bonds	2.50	1.00
❑ 46 Jeff Kent	.40	.15
❑ 47 Preston Wilson	.40	.15
❑ 48 Luis Castillo	.40	.15
❑ 49 Mike Piazza	1.50	.60
❑ 50 Edgardo Alfonzo	.40	.15
❑ 51 Tony Gwynn	1.25	.50
❑ 52 Ryan Klesko	.40	.15
❑ 53 Scott Rolen	.60	.25
❑ 54 Bob Abreu	.40	.15
❑ 55 Jason Kendall	.40	.15
❑ 56 Brian Giles	.40	.15
❑ 57 Ken Griffey Jr.	1.50	.60
❑ 58 Barry Larkin	.60	.25
❑ 59 Todd Helton	.60	.25
❑ 60 Mike Hampton	.40	.15
❑ 61 Corey Patterson WP	5.00	2.00
❑ 62 Timo Perez WP	5.00	2.00
❑ 63 Toby Hall WP	5.00	2.00
❑ 64 Brandon Inge WP	5.00	2.00
❑ 65 Joe Crede WP	8.00	3.00
❑ 66 Xavier Nady WP	5.00	2.00
❑ 67 Adam Pettyjohn WP RC	5.00	2.00
❑ 68 Keith Ginter WP	5.00	2.00
❑ 69 Brian Cole WP	5.00	2.00
❑ 70 Tyler Walker WP RC	5.00	2.00
❑ 71 Juan Uribe WP RC	5.00	2.00
❑ 72 Alex Hernandez WP	5.00	2.00
❑ 73 Leo Estrella WP	5.00	2.00
❑ 74 Joey Nation WP	5.00	2.00
❑ 75 Aubrey Huff WP	5.00	2.00
❑ 76 Ichiro Suzuki WP RC	50.00	25.00
❑ 77 Jay Spurgeon WP	5.00	2.00
❑ 78 Sun Woo Kim WP	5.00	2.00
❑ 79 Pedro Feliz WP	5.00	2.00
❑ 80 Pablo Ozuna WP	5.00	2.00
❑ 81 Hiram Bocachica WP	5.00	2.00
❑ 82 Brad Wilkerson WP	5.00	2.00
❑ 83 Rocky Biddle WP	5.00	2.00
❑ 84 Aaron McNeal WP	5.00	2.00
❑ 85 Adam Bernero WP	5.00	2.00
❑ 86 Danys Baez WP	5.00	2.00
❑ 87 Dee Brown WP	5.00	2.00
❑ 88 Jimmy Rollins WP	5.00	2.00
❑ 89 Jason Hart WP	5.00	2.00
❑ 90 Ross Gload WP	5.00	2.00

2006 Upper Deck Ovation

Card		
❑ COMP.SET w/o RC's (84)	25.00	10.00
❑ COMMON CARD (1-84)	.50	.20
❑ COMMON ROOKIE (85-126)	5.00	2.00
❑ 85-126 STATED ODDS 1:18		
❑ 85-126 PRINT RUN 999 SERIAL #'d SETS		
❑ EXQUISITE EXCH ODDS 1:144		
❑ EXQUISITE EXCH DEADLINE 07/27/07		
❑ 1 Vladimir Guerrero	1.25	.50
❑ 2 Bartolo Colon	.50	.20
❑ 3 Chone Figgins	.50	.20
❑ 4 Lance Berkman	.50	.20
❑ 5 Roy Oswalt	.50	.20
❑ 6 Craig Biggio	.75	.30
❑ 7 Rich Harden	.50	.20
❑ 8 Eric Chavez	.50	.20
❑ 9 Huston Street	.50	.20
❑ 10 Vernon Wells	.50	.20
❑ 11 Roy Halladay	.50	.20
❑ 12 Troy Glaus	.50	.20
❑ 13 Andruw Jones	.75	.30
❑ 14 Chipper Jones	1.25	.50
❑ 15 John Smoltz	.75	.30
❑ 16 Carlos Lee	.50	.20
❑ 17 Rickie Weeks	.50	.20
❑ 18 J.J. Hardy	.50	.20
❑ 19 Albert Pujols	2.50	1.00
❑ 20 Chris Carpenter	.50	.20
❑ 21 Scott Rolen	.75	.30
❑ 22 Derrek Lee	.50	.20
❑ 23 Mark Prior	.75	.30
❑ 24 Aramis Ramirez	.50	.20
❑ 25 Carl Crawford	.50	.20
❑ 26 Scott Kazmir	.75	.30
❑ 27 Luis Gonzalez	.50	.20
❑ 28 Brandon Webb	.50	.20
❑ 29 Chad Tracy	.50	.20
❑ 30 Jeff Kent	.50	.20
❑ 31 J.D. Drew	.50	.20
❑ 32 Jason Schmidt	.50	.20
❑ 33 Randy Winn	.50	.20
❑ 34 Travis Hafner	.50	.20
❑ 35 Victor Martinez	.50	.20
❑ 36 Grady Sizemore	.75	.30
❑ 37 Ichiro Suzuki	2.00	.75
❑ 38 Felix Hernandez	.75	.30
❑ 39 Adrian Beltre	.50	.20
❑ 40 Miguel Cabrera	.75	.30
❑ 41 Dontrelle Willis	.50	.20
❑ 42 David Wright	2.00	.75
❑ 43 Jose Reyes	1.25	.50
❑ 44 Pedro Martinez	.75	.30
❑ 45 Carlos Beltran	.50	.20
❑ 46 Alfonso Soriano	.50	.20
❑ 47 Livan Hernandez	.50	.20
❑ 48 Jose Guillen	.50	.20
❑ 49 Miguel Tejada	.50	.20
❑ 50 Brian Roberts	.50	.20
❑ 51 Melvin Mora	.50	.20
❑ 52 Jake Peavy	.50	.20
❑ 53 Brian Giles	.50	.20
❑ 54 Khalil Greene	.75	.30
❑ 55 Bobby Abreu	.50	.20
❑ 56 Ryan Howard	2.00	.75
❑ 57 Chase Utley	1.25	.50
❑ 58 Jason Bay	.50	.20
❑ 59 Sean Casey	.50	.20
❑ 60 Mark Teixeira	.75	.30
❑ 61 Michael Young	.50	.20
❑ 62 Hank Blalock	.50	.20
❑ 63 Manny Ramirez	.75	.30
❑ 64 David Ortiz	1.25	.50
❑ 65 Josh Beckett	.50	.20
❑ 66 Jason Varitek	1.25	.50
❑ 67 Ken Griffey Jr.	2.00	.75
❑ 68 Adam Dunn	.50	.20
❑ 69 Todd Helton	.75	.30
❑ 70 Garrett Atkins	.50	.20
❑ 71 Reggie Sanders	.50	.20
❑ 72 Mike Sweeney	.50	.20
❑ 73 Chris Shelton	.50	.20
❑ 74 Ivan Rodriguez	.75	.30
❑ 75 Johan Santana	.75	.30
❑ 76 Torii Hunter	.50	.20
❑ 77 Justin Morneau	.50	.20
❑ 78 Jim Thome	.75	.30
❑ 79 Paul Konerko	.50	.20
❑ 80 Scott Podsednik	.50	.20
❑ 81 Derek Jeter	3.00	1.25
❑ 82 Hideki Matsui	1.25	.50
❑ 83 Johnny Damon	.75	.30
❑ 84 Alex Rodriguez	2.00	.75
❑ 85 Conor Jackson (RC)	8.00	3.00
❑ 86 Joey Devine RC	5.00	2.00
❑ 87 Jonathan Papelbon (RC)	15.00	6.00
❑ 88 Freddie Bynum (RC)	5.00	2.00
❑ 89 Chris Denorfia (RC)	5.00	2.00
❑ 90 Ryan Shealy (RC)	5.00	2.00
❑ 91 Josh Wilson (RC)	8.00	3.00
❑ 92 Brian Anderson (RC)	5.00	2.00
❑ 93 Justin Verlander (RC)	12.00	5.00
❑ 94 Jeremy Hermida (RC)	8.00	3.00
❑ 95 Mike Jacobs (RC)	5.00	2.00
❑ 96 Josh Johnson (RC)	8.00	3.00
❑ 97 Hanley Ramirez (RC)	10.00	4.00
❑ 98 Josh Willingham (RC)	5.00	2.00
❑ 99 Cole Hamels (RC)	10.00	4.00
❑ 100 Hong-Chih Kuo (RC)	15.00	6.00
❑ 101 Cody Ross (RC)	5.00	2.00
❑ 102 Jose Capellan (RC)	5.00	2.00
❑ 103 Prince Fielder (RC)	12.00	5.00
❑ 104 David Gassner (RC)	5.00	2.00
❑ 105 Jason Kubel (RC)	5.00	2.00
❑ 106 Francisco Liriano (RC)	15.00	6.00
❑ 107 Anderson Hernandez (RC)	5.00	2.00
❑ 108 Boof Bonser (RC)	5.00	2.00
❑ 109 Jered Weaver (RC)	15.00	6.00
❑ 110 Ben Johnson (RC)	5.00	2.00
❑ 111 Jeff Harris RC	5.00	2.00
❑ 112 Stephen Drew (RC)	10.00	4.00
❑ 113 Matt Cain (RC)	8.00	3.00
❑ 114 Skip Schumaker (RC)	5.00	2.00
❑ 115 Adam Wainwright (RC)	8.00	3.00
❑ 116 Jeremy Sowers (RC)	5.00	2.00
❑ 117 Jason Bergmann RC	5.00	2.00
❑ 118 Chad Billingsley (RC)	15.00	6.00
❑ 119 Ryan Zimmerman (RC)	20.00	8.00
❑ 120 Macay McBride (RC)	5.00	2.00
❑ 121 Aaron Rakers (RC)	5.00	2.00
❑ 122 Alay Soler RC	5.00	2.00
❑ 123 Melky Cabrera (RC)	15.00	6.00
❑ 124 Tim Hamulack (RC)	5.00	2.00
❑ 125 Andre Ethier (RC)	12.00	5.00
❑ 126 Kenji Johjima RC	15.00	6.00
❑ NNO Exquisite Redemption	200.00	125.00

2007 Upper Deck Premier

❑ COMMON CARD (1-200) 5.00 2.00
❑ BASE CARD ODDS ONE PER PACK
❑ 1-200 STATED PRINT RUN 99 SER.#'d SETS
❑ COMMON ROOKIE (201-244) 5.00 2.00
❑ RC ODDS ONE PER PACK
❑ 201-244 STATED PRINT RUN 199 SER.#'d SETS
❑ PRINT.PLATES RANDOM INSERTS IN PACKS
❑ PLATE PRINT RUN 1 SET PER COLOR
❑ BLACK-CYAN-MAGENTA-YELLOW ISSUED
❑ NO PLATE PRICING DUE TO SCARCITY

❑	1 Roy Campanella	10.00	4.00
❑	2 Ty Cobb	12.00	5.00
❑	3 Mickey Cochrane	5.00	2.00
❑	4 Dizzy Dean	8.00	3.00
❑	5 Don Drysdale	8.00	3.00
❑	6 Jimmie Foxx	10.00	4.00
❑	7 Lou Gehrig	15.00	6.00
❑	8 Lefty Grove	5.00	2.00
❑	9 Rogers Hornsby	10.00	4.00
❑	10 Walter Johnson	10.00	4.00
❑	11 Eddie Mathews	10.00	4.00
❑	12 Christy Mathewson	10.00	4.00
❑	13 Johnny Mize	8.00	3.00
❑	14 Thurman Munson	12.00	5.00
❑	15 Mel Ott	8.00	3.00
❑	16 Satchel Paige	10.00	4.00
❑	17 Jackie Robinson	12.00	5.00
❑	18 Babe Ruth	20.00	8.00
❑	19 George Sisler	5.00	2.00
❑	20 Honus Wagner	10.00	4.00
❑	21 Cy Young	10.00	4.00
❑	22 Luis Aparicio	5.00	2.00
❑	23 Johnny Bench	10.00	4.00
❑	24 Yogi Berra	10.00	4.00
❑	25 Rod Carew	8.00	3.00
❑	26 Orlando Cepeda	5.00	2.00
❑	27 Bob Feller	8.00	3.00
❑	28 Carlton Fisk	8.00	3.00
❑	29 Bob Gibson	8.00	3.00
❑	30 Catfish Hunter	5.00	2.00
❑	31 Reggie Jackson	8.00	3.00
❑	32 Al Kaline	10.00	4.00
❑	33 Harmon Killebrew	10.00	4.00
❑	34 Buck Leonard	5.00	2.00
❑	35 Juan Marichal	5.00	2.00
❑	36 Bill Mazeroski	8.00	3.00
❑	37 Willie McCovey	8.00	3.00
❑	38 Joe Morgan	8.00	3.00
❑	39 Eddie Murray	10.00	4.00
❑	40 Jim Palmer	8.00	3.00
❑	41 Tony Perez	8.00	3.00
❑	42 Pee Wee Reese	8.00	3.00
❑	43 Brooks Robinson	10.00	4.00
❑	44 Nolan Ryan	20.00	8.00
❑	45 Mike Schmidt	10.00	4.00
❑	46 Tom Seaver	8.00	3.00
❑	47 Enos Slaughter	5.00	2.00
❑	48 Willie Stargell	8.00	3.00
❑	49 Early Wynn	5.00	2.00
❑	50 Robin Yount	10.00	4.00
❑	51 Tony Gwynn	10.00	4.00
❑	52 Cal Ripken Jr.	25.00	10.00
❑	53 Ernie Banks	10.00	4.00
❑	54 Wade Boggs	8.00	3.00
❑	55 Steve Carlton	5.00	2.00
❑	56 Will Clark	8.00	3.00
❑	57 Fergie Jenkins	5.00	2.00
❑	58 Bo Jackson	10.00	4.00
❑	59 Don Mattingly	15.00	6.00
❑	60 Stan Musial	12.00	5.00
❑	61 Frank Robinson	5.00	2.00
❑	62 Ryne Sandberg	12.00	5.00
❑	63 Ozzie Smith	15.00	6.00
❑	64 Carl Yastrzemski	12.00	5.00
❑	65 Dave Winfield	8.00	3.00
❑	66 Paul Molitor	5.00	2.00
❑	67 Jason Bay	5.00	2.00
❑	68 Freddy Sanchez	5.00	2.00
❑	69 Josh Beckett	5.00	2.00
❑	70 Carlos Beltran	5.00	2.00
❑	71 Craig Biggio	10.00	4.00
❑	72 Matt Holliday	6.00	2.50
❑	73 A.J. Burnett	5.00	2.00
❑	74 Miguel Cabrera	8.00	3.00
❑	75 Dontrelle Willis	5.00	2.00
❑	76 Chris Carpenter	8.00	3.00
❑	77 Roger Clemens	15.00	6.00
❑	78 Johnny Damon	8.00	3.00
❑	79 Jermaine Dye	5.00	2.00
❑	80 Jim Thome	8.00	3.00
❑	81 Vladimir Guerrero	10.00	4.00
❑	82 Travis Hafner	5.00	2.00
❑	83 Victor Martinez	5.00	2.00
❑	84 Trevor Hoffman	5.00	2.00
❑	85 Derek Jeter	20.00	8.00
❑	86 Ken Griffey Jr.	12.00	5.00
❑	87 Randy Johnson	10.00	4.00
❑	88 Andruw Jones	8.00	3.00
❑	89 Derrek Lee	5.00	2.00
❑	90 Greg Maddux	12.00	5.00
❑	91 Magglio Ordonez	8.00	3.00
❑	92 David Ortiz	10.00	4.00
❑	93 Jake Peavy	5.00	2.00
❑	94 Roy Oswalt	5.00	2.00
❑	95 Mike Piazza	10.00	4.00
❑	96 Jose Reyes	10.00	4.00
❑	97 Ivan Rodriguez	10.00	4.00
❑	98 Johan Santana	8.00	3.00
❑	99 Scott Rolen	8.00	3.00
❑	100 Curt Schilling	8.00	3.00
❑	101 John Smoltz	8.00	3.00
❑	102 Alfonso Soriano	5.00	2.00
❑	103 Miguel Tejada	8.00	3.00
❑	104 Frank Thomas	12.00	5.00
❑	105 Chase Utley	10.00	4.00
❑	106 Joe Mauer	8.00	3.00
❑	107 Alex Rodriguez	15.00	6.00
❑	108 Alex Rios	8.00	3.00
❑	109 Justin Verlander	10.00	4.00
❑	110 Ryan Howard	12.00	5.00
❑	111 Jered Weaver	8.00	3.00
❑	112 Francisco Liriano	10.00	4.00
❑	113 David Wright	12.00	5.00
❑	114 Felix Hernandez	8.00	3.00
❑	115 Jeremy Sowers	8.00	3.00
❑	116 Cole Hamels	8.00	3.00
❑	117 B.J. Upton	5.00	2.00
❑	118 Chien-Ming Wang	50.00	20.00
❑	119 Justin Morneau	8.00	3.00
❑	120 Jonny Gomes	5.00	2.00
❑	121 Adrian Gonzalez	5.00	2.00
❑	122 Bill Hall	8.00	3.00
❑	123 Rich Harden	8.00	3.00
❑	124 Rich Hill	5.00	2.00
❑	125 Tadahito Iguchi	5.00	2.00
❑	126 Scott Kazmir	8.00	3.00
❑	127 Howie Kendrick	5.00	2.00
❑	128 Dan Uggla	8.00	3.00
❑	129 Hanley Ramirez	8.00	3.00
❑	130 Josh Willingham	5.00	2.00
❑	131 Nick Markakis	8.00	3.00
❑	132 Grady Sizemore	10.00	4.00
❑	133 Ian Kinsler	8.00	3.00
❑	134 Jonathan Papelbon	12.00	5.00
❑	135 Ryan Zimmerman	10.00	4.00
❑	136 Stephen Drew	8.00	3.00
❑	137 Adam Wainwright	5.00	2.00
❑	138 Joel Zumaya	8.00	3.00
❑	139 Prince Fielder	10.00	4.00
❑	140 Carl Crawford	8.00	3.00
❑	141 Huston Street	5.00	2.00
❑	142 Matt Cain	8.00	3.00
❑	143 Andre Ethier	8.00	3.00
❑	144 Brian McCann	8.00	3.00
❑	145 Josh Barfield	5.00	2.00
❑	146 Anibal Sanchez	5.00	2.00
❑	147 Brian Roberts	8.00	3.00
❑	148 Brandon Webb	5.00	2.00
❑	149 Chipper Jones	10.00	4.00
❑	150 Tim Hudson	8.00	3.00
❑	151 Adam LaRoche	5.00	2.00
❑	152 Jeff Francoeur	10.00	4.00
❑	153 Marcus Giles	5.00	2.00
❑	154 Jason Varitek	12.00	5.00
❑	155 Coco Crisp	8.00	3.00
❑	156 Manny Ramirez	8.00	3.00
❑	157 Trot Nixon	8.00	3.00
❑	158 Carlos Zambrano	5.00	2.00
❑	159 Mark Prior	8.00	3.00
❑	160 Aramis Ramirez	5.00	2.00
❑	161 Mark Buehrle	5.00	2.00
❑	162 Paul Konerko	5.00	2.00
❑	163 Adam Dunn	8.00	3.00
❑	164 C.C. Sabathia	5.00	2.00
❑	165 Todd Helton	8.00	3.00
❑	166 Garrett Atkins	8.00	3.00
❑	167 Jeremy Bonderman	10.00	4.00
❑	168 Curtis Granderson	8.00	3.00
❑	169 Sean Casey	8.00	3.00
❑	170 Lance Berkman	8.00	3.00
❑	171 Brad Lidge	5.00	2.00
❑	172 Reggie Sanders	5.00	2.00
❑	173 Brad Penny	5.00	2.00
❑	174 Nomar Garciaparra	12.00	5.00
❑	175 Jeff Kent	8.00	3.00
❑	176 Chone Figgins	5.00	2.00
❑	177 Ben Sheets	8.00	3.00
❑	178 Rickie Weeks	8.00	3.00
❑	179 Joe Nathan	8.00	3.00
❑	180 Torii Hunter	8.00	3.00
❑	181 Carlos Delgado	8.00	3.00
❑	182 Tom Glavine	10.00	4.00
❑	183 Paul Lo Duca	5.00	2.00
❑	184 Mariano Rivera	12.00	5.00
❑	185 Robinson Cano	10.00	4.00
❑	186 Bobby Abreu	8.00	3.00
❑	187 Hideki Matsui	12.00	5.00
❑	188 Barry Zito	5.00	2.00
❑	189 Eric Chavez	8.00	3.00
❑	190 Jimmy Rollins	8.00	3.00
❑	191 Khalil Greene	10.00	4.00
❑	192 Brian Giles	5.00	2.00
❑	193 Jason Schmidt	5.00	2.00
❑	194 Ichiro Suzuki	30.00	12.50
❑	195 David Eckstein	10.00	4.00
❑	196 Jim Edmonds	8.00	3.00
❑	197 Mark Teixeira	8.00	3.00
❑	198 Michael Young	5.00	2.00
❑	199 Vernon Wells	8.00	3.00
❑	200 Roy Halladay	8.00	3.00
❑	201 Delmon Young (RC)	8.00	3.00
❑	202 Andrew Miller RC	20.00	8.00
❑	203 Troy Tulowitzki (RC)	8.00	3.00
❑	204 Jeff Fiorentino (RC)	5.00	2.00
❑	205 David Murphy (RC)	5.00	2.00
❑	206 Jeff Baker (RC)	5.00	2.00
❑	207 Kevin Hooper (RC)	5.00	2.00
❑	208 Kevin Kouzmanoff (RC)	5.00	2.00
❑	209 Adam Lind (RC)	8.00	3.00

❑ 210 Mike Rabelo RC	8.00	3.00
❑ 211 John Nelson (RC)	5.00	2.00
❑ 212 Mitch Maier RC	5.00	2.00
❑ 213 Ryan Braun RC	5.00	2.00
❑ 214 Vinny Rottino (RC)	5.00	2.00
❑ 215 Drew Anderson RC	5.00	2.00
❑ 216 Alexi Casilla RC	8.00	3.00
❑ 217 Glen Perkins (RC)	5.00	2.00
❑ 218 Cesar Jimenez RC	5.00	2.00
❑ 219 Tim Gradoville RC	5.00	2.00
❑ 220 Shane Youman RC	5.00	2.00
❑ 221 Billy Sadler (RC)	5.00	2.00
❑ 222 Patrick Misch (RC)	5.00	2.00
❑ 223 Juan Salas (RC)	5.00	2.00
❑ 224 Beltran Perez (RC)	5.00	2.00
❑ 225 Hector Gimenez (RC)	5.00	2.00
❑ 226 Philip Humber (RC)	8.00	3.00
❑ 227 Eric Stults RC	5.00	2.00
❑ 228 Dennis Sarfate (RC)	5.00	2.00
❑ 229 Andy Cannizaro RC	8.00	3.00
❑ 230 Juan Morillo (RC)	5.00	2.00
❑ 231 Fred Lewis (RC)	5.00	2.00
❑ 232 Ryan Sweeney (RC)	5.00	2.00
❑ 233 Chris Narveson (RC)	5.00	2.00
❑ 234 Michael Bourn (RC)	5.00	2.00
❑ 235 Joaquin Arias (RC)	5.00	2.00
❑ 236 Carlos Maldonado (RC)	5.00	2.00
❑ 237 Alvin Colina RC	5.00	2.00
❑ 238 Jon Knott (RC)	5.00	2.00
❑ 239 Justin Hampson (RC)	5.00	2.00
❑ 240 Jeff Salazar (RC)	5.00	2.00
❑ 241 Josh Fields (RC)	5.00	2.00
❑ 242 Delwyn Young (RC)	5.00	2.00
❑ 243 Daisuke Matsuzaka RC	100.00	50.00
❑ 244 Kei Igawa RC	20.00	8.00

2001 Upper Deck Prospect Premieres

❑ COMP.SET w/o SP's (90)	80.00	50.00
❑ COMMON CARD (1-90)	.40	.15
❑ COMMON AUTO (91-102)	15.00	6.00
❑ 1 Jeff Mathis XRC	.50	.20
❑ 2 Jake Woods XRC	.40	.15
❑ 3 Dallas McPherson XRC	1.00	.40
❑ 4 Steven Shell XRC	.40	.15
❑ 5 Ryan Budde XRC	.40	.15
❑ 6 Kirk Saarloos XRC	.40	.15
❑ 7 Ryan Stegall XRC	.40	.15
❑ 8 Bobby Crosby XRC	3.00	1.25
❑ 9 J.T. Stotts XRC	.40	.15
❑ 10 Neal Cotts XRC	1.00	.40
❑ 11 Jeremy Bonderman XRC	4.00	1.50
❑ 12 Brandon League XRC	.40	.15
❑ 13 Tyrell Godwin XRC	.40	.15
❑ 14 Gabe Gross XRC	.50	.20
❑ 15 Chris Neylan XRC	.40	.15
❑ 16 Macay McBride XRC	.75	.30
❑ 17 Josh Burrus XRC	.40	.15
❑ 18 Adam Stern XRC	.40	.15
❑ 19 Richard Lewis XRC	.40	.15
❑ 20 Cole Barthel XRC	.40	.15
❑ 21 Mike Jones XRC	.50	.20
❑ 22 J.J. Hardy XRC	6.00	2.50
❑ 23 Jon Steitz XRC	.40	.15
❑ 24 Brad Nelson XRC	.40	.15
❑ 25 Justin Pope XRC	.40	.15
❑ 26 Dan Haren XRC	2.00	.75
❑ 27 Andy Sisco XRC	.40	.15
❑ 28 Ryan Theriot XRC	3.00	1.25
❑ 29 Ricky Nolasco XRC	2.00	.75
❑ 30 Jon Switzer XRC	.40	.15
❑ 31 Justin Wechsler XRC	.40	.15
❑ 32 Mike Gosling XRC	.40	.15
❑ 33 Scott Hairston XRC	.50	.20
❑ 34 Brian Pilkington XRC	.40	.15
❑ 35 Kole Strayhorn XRC	.40	.15
❑ 36 David Taylor XRC	.40	.15
❑ 37 Donald Levinski XRC	.40	.15
❑ 38 Mike Hinckley XRC	.50	.20
❑ 39 Nick Long XRC	.40	.15
❑ 40 Brad Hennessey XRC	.50	.20
❑ 41 Noah Lowry XRC	2.00	.75
❑ 42 Josh Cram XRC	.40	.15
❑ 43 Jesse Foppert XRC	.50	.20
❑ 44 Julian Benavidez XRC	.40	.15
❑ 45 Dan Denham XRC	.40	.15
❑ 46 Travis Foley XRC	.40	.15
❑ 47 Mike Conroy XRC	.40	.15
❑ 48 Jake Dittler XRC	.40	.15
❑ 49 Rene Rivera XRC	.40	.15
❑ 50 John Cole XRC	.40	.15
❑ 51 Lazaro Abreu XRC	.40	.15
❑ 52 David Wright XRC	40.00	15.00
❑ 53 Aaron Heilman XRC	.50	.20
❑ 54 Len DiNardo XRC	.40	.15
❑ 55 Alhaji Turay XRC	.40	.15
❑ 56 Chris Smith XRC	.40	.15
❑ 57 Rommie Lewis XRC	.40	.15
❑ 58 Bryan Bass XRC	.40	.15
❑ 59 David Crouthers XRC	.40	.15
❑ 60 Josh Barfield XRC	3.00	1.25
❑ 61 Jake Peavy XRC	5.00	2.00
❑ 62 Ryan Howard XRC	40.00	15.00
❑ 63 Gavin Floyd XRC	1.00	.40
❑ 64 Michael Floyd XRC	.40	.15
❑ 65 Stefan Bailie XRC	.40	.15
❑ 66 Jon DeVries XRC	.40	.15
❑ 67 Steve Kelly XRC	.40	.15
❑ 68 Alan Moye XRC	.40	.15
❑ 69 Justin Gillman XRC	.40	.15
❑ 70 Jayson Nix XRC	.40	.15
❑ 71 John Draper XRC	.40	.15
❑ 72 Kenny Baugh XRC	.40	.15
❑ 73 Michael Woods XRC	.40	.15
❑ 74 Preston Larrison XRC	.50	.20
❑ 75 Matt Coenen XRC	.40	.15
❑ 76 Scott Tyler XRC	.50	.20
❑ 77 Jose Morales XRC	.40	.15
❑ 78 Corwin Malone XRC	.40	.15
❑ 79 Dennis Ulacia XRC	.40	.15
❑ 80 Andy Gonzalez XRC	.40	.15
❑ 81 Kris Honel XRC	.40	.15
❑ 82 Wyatt Allen XRC	.40	.15
❑ 83 Ryan Wing XRC	.40	.15
❑ 84 Sean Henn XRC	.40	.15
❑ 85 John-Ford Griffin XRC	.40	.15
❑ 86 Bronson Sardinha XRC	.40	.15
❑ 87 Jon Skaggs XRC	.40	.15
❑ 88 Shelley Duncan XRC	4.00	1.50
❑ 89 Jason Arnold XRC	.40	.15
❑ 90 Aaron Rifkin XRC	.40	.15
❑ 91 Colt Griffin AU XRC	15.00	6.00
❑ 92 J.D. Martin AU XRC	15.00	6.00
❑ 93 Justin Wayne AU XRC	15.00	6.00
❑ 94 J.VanBenschoten AU XRC	15.00	6.00
❑ 95 Chris Burke AU XRC	25.00	10.00
❑ 96 Casey Kotchman AU XRC	50.00	20.00
❑ 97 Michael Garciaparra AU XRC	15.00	6.00
❑ 98 Jake Gautreau AU XRC	15.00	6.00
❑ 99 Jerome Williams AU XRC	15.00	6.00
❑ 100 Toe Nash AU XRC	15.00	6.00
❑ 101 Joe Borchard AU XRC	15.00	6.00
❑ 102 Mark Prior AU XRC	60.00	35.00

2002 Upper Deck Prospect Premieres

❑ COMP.SET w/o SP's (72)	40.00	25.00
❑ COMMON CARD (1-60)	.40	.15
❑ COMMON CARD (61-85)	5.00	2.00
❑ COMMON CARD (86-97)	8.00	3.00
❑ COMMON RIPKEN (98-99)	2.00	.75
❑ COMMON MCGWIRE (100-105)	2.00	.75
❑ COMMON DIMAGGIO (106-109)	1.50	.60
❑ PENDER COR AVAIL.VIA MAIL EXCHANGE		
❑ 1 Josh Rupe XRC	.40	.15
❑ 2 Blair Johnson XRC	.40	.15
❑ 3 Jason Pridie XRC	.40	.15
❑ 4 Tim Gilhooly XRC	.40	.15
❑ 5 Kennard Jones XRC	.40	.15
❑ 6 Darrell Rasner XRC	.40	.15
❑ 7 Adam Donachie XRC	.40	.15
❑ 8 Josh Murray XRC	.40	.15
❑ 9 Brian Dopirak XRC	1.00	.40
❑ 10 Jason Cooper XRC	.40	.15
❑ 11 Zach Hammes XRC	.40	.15
❑ 12 Jon Lester XRC	20.00	8.00
❑ 13 Kevin Jepsen XRC	.50	.20
❑ 14 Curtis Granderson XRC	4.00	1.50
❑ 15 David Bush XRC	1.00	.40
❑ 16 Joel Guzman	.75	.30
❑ 17A M.Pender UER Granderson	1.50	.60
❑ 17B Matt Pender COR		
❑ 18 Derick Grigsby XRC	.40	.15
❑ 19 Jeremy Reed XRC	1.00	.40
❑ 20 Jonathan Broxton XRC	1.00	.40
❑ 21 Jesse Crain XRC	.75	.30
❑ 22 Justin Jones XRC	.50	.20
❑ 23 Brian Slocum XRC	.40	.15
❑ 24 Brian McCann XRC	8.00	3.00
❑ 25 Francisco Liriano XRC	8.00	3.00
❑ 26 Fred Lewis XRC	.40	.15
❑ 27 Steve Stanley XRC	.40	.15
❑ 28 Chris Snyder XRC	.50	.20
❑ 29 Dan Cevette XRC	.40	.15
❑ 30 Kiel Fisher XRC	.50	.20
❑ 31 Brandon Weeden XRC	.40	.15
❑ 32 Pat Osborn XRC	.40	.15
❑ 33 Taber Lee XRC	.40	.15
❑ 34 Dan Ortmeier XRC	.50	.20
❑ 35 Josh Johnson XRC	4.00	1.50
❑ 36 Val Majewski XRC	.40	.15
❑ 37 Larry Broadway XRC	.40	.15
❑ 38 Joey Gomes XRC	.40	.15
❑ 39 Eric Thomas XRC	.40	.15
❑ 40 James Loney XRC	5.00	2.00
❑ 41 Charlie Morton XRC	.40	.15
❑ 42 Mark McLemore XRC	.40	.15
❑ 43 Matt Craig XRC	.50	.20
❑ 44 Ryan Rodriguez XRC	.40	.15
❑ 45 Rich Hill XRC	3.00	1.25
❑ 46 Bob Malek XRC	.40	.15
❑ 47 Justin Maureau XRC	.40	.15
❑ 48 Randy Braun XRC	.40	.15
❑ 49 Brian Grant XRC	.40	.15
❑ 50 Tyler Davidson XRC	.50	.20
❑ 51 Travis Hanson XRC	.50	.20
❑ 52 Kyle Boyer XRC	.40	.15
❑ 53 James Holcomb XRC	.40	.15

❑ 54 Ryan Williams XRC	.40	.15
❑ 55 Ben Crockett XRC	.40	.15
❑ 56 Adam Greenberg XRC	.75	.30
❑ 57 John Baker XRC	.40	.15
❑ 58 Matt Carson XRC	.40	.15
❑ 59 Jonathan George XRC	.40	.15
❑ 60 David Jensen XRC	.40	.15
❑ 61 Nick Swisher JSY XRC	15.00	6.00
❑ 62 Brent Clevlen JSY UER XRC	12.00	5.00
❑ 63 Royce Ring JSY XRC	5.00	2.00
❑ 64 Mike Nixon JSY XRC	5.00	2.00
❑ 65 Ricky Barrett JSY XRC	5.00	2.00
❑ 66 Russ Adams JSY XRC	5.00	2.00
❑ 67 Joe Mauer JSY XRC	25.00	10.00
❑ 68 Jeff Francoeur JSY XRC	30.00	15.00
❑ 69 Joe Blanton JSY XRC	8.00	3.00
❑ 70 Micah Schilling JSY XRC	5.00	2.00
❑ 71 John McCurdy JSY XRC	5.00	2.00
❑ 72 Sergio Santos JSY XRC	8.00	3.00
❑ 73 Josh Womack JSY XRC	5.00	2.00
❑ 74 Jared Doyle JSY XRC	5.00	2.00
❑ 75 Ben Fritz JSY XRC	5.00	2.00
❑ 76 Greg Miller JSY XRC	5.00	2.00
❑ 77 Luke Hagerty JSY XRC	5.00	2.00
❑ 78 Matt Whitney JSY XRC	5.00	2.00
❑ 79 Dan Meyer JSY XRC	8.00	3.00
❑ 80 Bill Murphy JSY XRC	5.00	2.00
❑ 81 Zach Segovia JSY XRC	5.00	2.00
❑ 82 Steve Obenchain JSY XRC	5.00	2.00
❑ 83 Matt Clanton JSY XRC	5.00	2.00
❑ 84 Mark Teahen JSY XRC	8.00	3.00
❑ 85 Kyle Pawelczyk JSY XRC	5.00	2.00
❑ 86 Khalil Greene AU XRC	40.00	20.00
❑ 87 Joe Saunders AU XRC	20.00	8.00
❑ 88 Jeremy Hermida AU XRC	50.00	30.00
❑ 89 Drew Meyer AU XRC	8.00	3.00
❑ 90 Jeff Francis AU XRC	30.00	12.50
❑ 91 Scott Moore AU XRC	8.00	3.00
❑ 92 Prince Fielder AU XRC	200.00	125.00
❑ 93 Zack Greinke AU XRC	25.00	10.00
❑ 94 Chris Gruler AU XRC	8.00	3.00
❑ 95 Scott Kazmir AU XRC	80.00	40.00
❑ 96 B.J. Upton AU XRC	60.00	30.00
❑ 97 Clint Everts AU XRC	8.00	3.00
❑ 98 Cal Ripken TRIB	2.00	.75
❑ 99 Cal Ripken TRIB	2.00	.75
❑ 100 Mark McGwire TRIB	2.00	.75
❑ 101 Mark McGwire TRIB	2.00	.75
❑ 102 Mark McGwire TRIB	2.00	.75
❑ 103 Mark McGwire TRIB	2.00	.75
❑ 104 Mark McGwire TRIB	2.00	.75
❑ 105 Joe DiMaggio TRIB	1.50	.60
❑ 106 Joe DiMaggio TRIB	1.50	.60
❑ 107 Joe DiMaggio TRIB	1.50	.60
❑ 108 Joe DiMaggio TRIB	1.50	.60
❑ 109 Joe DiMaggio TRIB	1.50	.60

2003 Upper Deck Prospect Premieres

❑ COMPLETE SET (90)	40.00	20.00
❑ 1 Bryan Opdyke XRC	.40	.15
❑ 2 Gabriel Sosa XRC	.40	.15
❑ 3 Tila Reynolds XRC	.40	.15
❑ 4 Aaron Hill XRC	1.00	.40
❑ 5 Aaron Marsden XRC	.50	.20
❑ 6 Abe Alvarez XRC	.50	.20
❑ 7 Adam Jones XRC	5.00	2.00
❑ 8 Adam Miller XRC	3.00	1.25
❑ 9 Andre Ethier XRC	8.00	3.00
❑ 10 Anthony Gwynn XRC	1.25	.50
❑ 11 Brad Snyder XRC	.75	.30
❑ 12 Brad Sullivan XRC	.50	.20
❑ 13 Brian Anderson XRC	2.00	.75
❑ 14 Brian Buscher XRC	.40	.15
❑ 15 Brian Snyder XRC	.50	.20
❑ 16 Carlos Quentin XRC	3.00	1.25
❑ 17 Chad Billingsley XRC	4.00	1.50
❑ 18 Fraser Dizard XRC	.40	.15
❑ 19 Chris Durbin XRC	.40	.15
❑ 20 Chris Ray XRC	1.00	.40
❑ 21 Conor Jackson XRC	3.00	1.25
❑ 22 Kory Casto XRC	.50	.20
❑ 23 Craig Whitaker XRC	.50	.20
❑ 24 Daniel Moore XRC	.40	.15
❑ 25 Daric Barton XRC	3.00	1.25
❑ 26 Darin Downs XRC	.50	.20
❑ 27 David Murphy XRC	.75	.30
❑ 28 Dustin Majewski XRC	.50	.20
❑ 29 Edgardo Baez XRC	.50	.20
❑ 30 Jake Fox XRC	.75	.30
❑ 31 Jake Stevens XRC	.50	.20
❑ 32 Jamie D'Antona XRC	.75	.30
❑ 33 James Houser XRC	.50	.20
❑ 34 Jarrod Saltalamacchia XRC	5.00	2.00
❑ 35 Jason Hirsh XRC	2.00	.75
❑ 36 Javi Herrera XRC	.50	.20
❑ 37 Jeff Allison XRC	.40	.15
❑ 38 John Hudgins XRC	.40	.15
❑ 39 Jo Jo Reyes XRC	1.00	.40
❑ 40 Justin James XRC	.40	.15
❑ 41 Kurt Isenberg XRC	.40	.15
❑ 42 Kyle Boyer XRC	.40	.15
❑ 43 Lastings Milledge XRC	5.00	2.00
❑ 44 Luis Atilano XRC	.40	.15
❑ 45 Matt Murton XRC	2.00	.75
❑ 46 Matt Moses XRC	.75	.30
❑ 47 Matt Harrison XRC	.75	.30
❑ 48 Michael Bourn XRC	.75	.30
❑ 49 Miguel Vega XRC	.40	.15
❑ 50 Mitch Maier XRC	.50	.20
❑ 51 Omar Quintanilla XRC	.50	.20
❑ 52 Ryan Sweeney XRC	2.00	.75
❑ 53 Scott Baker XRC	1.00	.40
❑ 54 Sean Rodriguez XRC	2.00	.75
❑ 55 Steve Lerud XRC	.50	.20
❑ 56 Thomas Pauly XRC	.40	.15
❑ 57 Tom Gorzelanny XRC	1.50	.60
❑ 58 Tim Moss XRC	.40	.15
❑ 59 Robbie Wooley XRC	.50	.20
❑ 60 Trey Webb XRC	.40	.15
❑ 61 Wes Littleton XRC	.50	.20
❑ 62 Beau Vaughan XRC	.50	.20
❑ 63 Willy Jo Ronda XRC	.50	.20
❑ 64 Chris Lubanski XRC	1.25	.50
❑ 65 Ian Stewart XRC	5.00	2.00
❑ 66 John Danks XRC	3.00	1.25
❑ 67 Kyle Sleeth XRC	.50	.20
❑ 68 Michael Aubrey XRC	.75	.30
❑ 69 Kevin Kouzmanoff XRC	5.00	2.00
❑ 70 Ryan Harvey XRC	2.00	.75
❑ 71 Tim Stauffer XRC	.75	.30
❑ 72 Tony Richie XRC	.40	.15
❑ 73 Brandon Wood XRC	8.00	3.00
❑ 74 David Aardsma XRC	.50	.20
❑ 75 David Shinskie XRC	.40	.15
❑ 76 Dennis Dove XRC	.50	.20
❑ 77 Eric Sultemeier XRC	.40	.15
❑ 78 Jay Sborz XRC	.40	.15
❑ 79 Jimmy Barthmaier XRC	.40	.15
❑ 80 Josh Whitesell XRC	.40	.15
❑ 81 Josh Anderson XRC	.50	.20
❑ 82 Kenny Lewis XRC	.50	.20
❑ 83 Mateo Miramontes XRC	.40	.15
❑ 84 Nick Markakis XRC	5.00	2.00
❑ 85 Paul Bacot XRC	.50	.20
❑ 86 Peter Stonard XRC	.40	.15
❑ 87 Reggie Willits XRC	2.50	1.00
❑ 88 Shane Costa XRC	.40	.15
❑ 89 Billy Sadler XRC	.40	.15
❑ 90 Delmon Young XRC	8.00	3.00

2007 Upper Deck SP Rookie Edition

❑ COMP.SET w/o RC's (100)	15.00	6.00
❑ COMMON CARD (1-100)	.30	.12
❑ COMMON RC (101-142)	.60	.25
❑ COMMON SP (143-234)	1.00	.40
❑ SP ODDS 1:2		
❑ COMMON CARD (235-284)	.30	.12
❑ 1 Chipper Jones	.75	.30
❑ 2 Andruw Jones	.50	.20
❑ 3 Jeff Francoeur	.75	.30
❑ 4 Stephen Drew	.50	.20
❑ 5 Randy Johnson	.75	.30
❑ 6 Brandon Webb	.30	.12
❑ 7 Alfonso Soriano	.30	.12
❑ 8 Derrek Lee	.30	.12
❑ 9 Aramis Ramirez	.30	.12
❑ 10 Carlos Zambrano	.30	.12
❑ 11 Ken Griffey Jr.	1.25	.50
❑ 12 Adam Dunn	.30	.12
❑ 13 Bronson Arroyo	.30	.12
❑ 14 Todd Helton	.50	.20
❑ 15 Jeff Francis	.30	.12
❑ 16 Matt Holliday	.75	.30
❑ 17 Hanley Ramirez	.50	.20
❑ 18 Dontrelle Willis	.30	.12
❑ 19 Miguel Cabrera	.50	.20
❑ 20 Lance Berkman	.30	.12
❑ 21 Roy Oswalt	.30	.12
❑ 22 Carlos Lee	.30	.12
❑ 23 Nomar Garciaparra	.75	.30
❑ 24 Jason Schmidt	.30	.12
❑ 25 Juan Pierre	.30	.12
❑ 26 Rafael Furcal	.30	.12
❑ 27 Rickie Weeks	.30	.12
❑ 28 Prince Fielder	.75	.30
❑ 29 Ben Sheets	.30	.12
❑ 30 David Wright	1.25	.50
❑ 31 Jose Reyes	.75	.30
❑ 32 Pedro Martinez	.50	.20
❑ 33 Carlos Beltran	.30	.12
❑ 34 Cole Hamels	.50	.20
❑ 35 Jimmy Rollins	.30	.12
❑ 36 Ryan Howard	1.25	.50
❑ 37 Jason Bay	.30	.12
❑ 38 Freddy Sanchez	.30	.12
❑ 39 Zach Duke	.30	.12
❑ 40 Jake Peavy	.30	.12
❑ 41 Greg Maddux	1.25	.50
❑ 42 Trevor Hoffman	.30	.12
❑ 43 Matt Cain	.50	.20
❑ 44 Barry Zito	.30	.12
❑ 45 Omar Vizquel	.50	.20
❑ 46 Albert Pujols	1.50	.60
❑ 47 Chris Carpenter	.30	.12
❑ 48 Jim Edmonds	.50	.20
❑ 49 Scott Rolen	.50	.20
❑ 50 Ryan Zimmerman	.75	.30
❑ 51 Felipe Lopez	.30	.12
❑ 52 Austin Kearns	.30	.12
❑ 53 Miguel Tejada	.30	.12

❑ 54 Erik Bedard .30 .12
❑ 55 Chris Ray .30 .12
❑ 56 David Ortiz .75 .30
❑ 57 Curt Schilling .50 .20
❑ 58 Manny Ramirez .50 .20
❑ 59 Jonathan Papelbon .75 .30
❑ 60 Jim Thome .50 .20
❑ 61 Paul Konerko .30 .12
❑ 62 Bobby Jenks .30 .12
❑ 63 Grady Sizemore .50 .20
❑ 64 Victor Martinez .30 .12
❑ 65 C.C. Sabathia .30 .12
❑ 66 Ivan Rodriguez .50 .20
❑ 67 Justin Verlander .75 .30
❑ 68 Joel Zumaya .50 .20
❑ 69 Jeremy Bonderman .30 .12
❑ 70 Gil Meche .30 .12
❑ 71 Mike Sweeney .30 .12
❑ 72 Mark Teahen .30 .12
❑ 73 Vladimir Guerrero .75 .30
❑ 74 Howie Kendrick .30 .12
❑ 75 Francisco Rodriguez .30 .12
❑ 76 Johan Santana .50 .20
❑ 77 Justin Morneau .30 .12
❑ 78 Joe Mauer .50 .20
❑ 79 Joe Nathan .30 .12
❑ 80 Alex Rodriguez 1.25 .50
❑ 81 Derek Jeter 2.00 .75
❑ 82 Johnny Damon .50 .20
❑ 83 Mariano Rivera .75 .30
❑ 84 Rich Harden .30 .12
❑ 85 Mike Piazza .75 .30
❑ 86 Nick Swisher .30 .12
❑ 87 Ichiro Suzuki 1.25 .50
❑ 88 Felix Hernandez .50 .20
❑ 89 Kenji Johjima .75 .30
❑ 90 Richie Sexson .30 .12
❑ 91 Carl Crawford .30 .12
❑ 92 Scott Kazmir .50 .20
❑ 93 B.J. Upton .30 .12
❑ 94 Michael Young .30 .12
❑ 95 Mark Teixeira .50 .20
❑ 96 Eric Gagne .30 .12
❑ 97 Hank Blalock .30 .12
❑ 98 Vernon Wells .30 .12
❑ 99 Roy Halladay .30 .12
❑ 100 Frank Thomas .75 .30
❑ 101 Joaquin Arias (RC) .60 .25
❑ 102 Jeff Baker (RC) .60 .25
❑ 103 Brian Barden RC .60 .25
❑ 104 Michael Bourn (RC) .60 .25
❑ 105 Kevin Slowey (RC) 1.50 .60
❑ 106 Chase Wright RC 1.50 .60
❑ 107 Kory Casto (RC) .60 .25
❑ 108 Matt Chico (RC) .60 .25
❑ 109 Matt DeSalvo (RC) .60 .25
❑ 110 Homer Bailey (RC) 1.00 .40
❑ 111 Ryan Braun (RC) 4.00 1.50
❑ 112 Felix Pie (RC) .60 .25
❑ 113 Jesus Flores RC .60 .25
❑ 114 Ryan Sweeney (RC) .60 .25
❑ 115 Ryan Z. Braun RC .60 .25
❑ 116 Alex Gordon RC 3.00 1.25
❑ 117 Josh Hamilton (RC) 1.50 .60
❑ 118 Sean Henn (RC) .60 .25
❑ 119 Kei Igawa RC 1.50 .60
❑ 120 Akinori Iwamura RC 1.50 .60
❑ 121 Andy LaRoche (RC) .60 .25
❑ 122 Kevin Kouzmanoff (RC) .60 .25
❑ 123 Matt Lindstrom (RC) .60 .25
❑ 124 Tim Lincecum RC 6.00 2.50
❑ 125 Daisuke Matsuzaka RC 6.00 2.50
❑ 126 Gustavo Molina RC .60 .25
❑ 127 Miguel Montero (RC) .60 .25
❑ 128 Brandon Morrow RC 1.00 .40
❑ 129 Hideki Okajima RC 3.00 1.25
❑ 130 Adam Lind (RC) .60 .25
❑ 131 Mike Rabelo RC .60 .25
❑ 132 Micah Owings (RC) .60 .25
❑ 133 Brandon Wood (RC) .60 .25
❑ 134 Alexi Casilla RC 1.00 .40
❑ 135 Joe Smith RC .60 .25
❑ 136 Hunter Pence (RC) 4.00 1.50
❑ 137 Glen Perkins (RC) .60 .25
❑ 138 Chris Stewart RC .60 .25
❑ 139 Troy Tulowitzki (RC) 1.50 .60
❑ 140 Billy Butler (RC) 1.00 .40
❑ 141 Delmon Young (RC) 1.00 .40
❑ 142 Phil Hughes (RC) 3.00 1.25
❑ 143 Joaquin Arias 95 1.00 .40
❑ 144 Jeff Baker 95 1.00 .40
❑ 145 Brian Barden 95 1.00 .40
❑ 146 Michael Bourn 95 1.00 .40
❑ 147 Kevin Slowey 95 2.50 1.00
❑ 148 Chase Wright 95 2.50 1.00
❑ 149 Kory Casto 95 1.00 .40
❑ 150 Matt Chico 95 1.00 .40
❑ 151 Shawn Riggans 95 1.00 .40
❑ 152 Juan Salas 95 1.00 .40
❑ 153 Ryan Braun 95 6.00 2.50
❑ 154 Felix Pie 95 1.00 .40
❑ 155 Jesus Flores 95 1.00 .40
❑ 156 Ryan Sweeney 95 1.00 .40
❑ 157 Ryan Z. Braun 95 1.00 .40
❑ 158 Alex Gordon 95 5.00 2.00
❑ 159 Josh Hamilton 95 2.50 1.00
❑ 160 Sean Henn 95 1.00 .40
❑ 161 Kei Igawa 95 2.50 1.00
❑ 162 Akinori Iwamura 95 2.50 1.00
❑ 163 Andy LaRoche 95 1.00 .40
❑ 164 Kevin Kouzmanoff 95 1.00 .40
❑ 165 Matt Lindstrom 95 1.00 .40
❑ 166 Tim Lincecum 95 8.00 3.00
❑ 167 Daisuke Matsuzaka 95 10.00 4.00
❑ 168 Gustavo Molina 95 1.00 .40
❑ 169 Miguel Montero 95 1.00 .40
❑ 170 Brandon Morrow 95 1.50 .60
❑ 171 Hideki Okajima 95 5.00 2.00
❑ 172 Adam Lind 95 1.00 .40
❑ 173 Mike Rabelo 95 1.00 .40
❑ 174 Micah Owings 95 1.00 .40
❑ 175 Brandon Wood 95 1.00 .40
❑ 176 Alexi Casilla 95 1.50 .60
❑ 177 Joe Smith 95 1.00 .40
❑ 178 Hunter Pence 95 6.00 2.50
❑ 179 Glen Perkins 95 1.00 .40
❑ 180 Chris Stewart 95 1.00 .40
❑ 181 Troy Tulowitzki 95 2.50 1.00
❑ 182 Billy Butler 95 1.50 .60
❑ 183 Delmon Young 95 1.50 .60
❑ 184 Phil Hughes 95 5.00 2.00
❑ 185 Joaquin Arias 93 1.00 .40
❑ 186 Jeff Baker 93 1.00 .40
❑ 187 Mark Reynolds 93 2.50 1.00
❑ 188 Joseph Bisenius 93 1.00 .40
❑ 189 Michael Bourn 93 1.00 .40
❑ 190 Zack Segovia 93 1.00 .40
❑ 191 Kevin Slowey 93 2.50 1.00
❑ 192 Chase Wright 93 2.50 1.00
❑ 193 Rocky Cherry 93 2.50 1.00
❑ 194 Danny Putnam 93 1.00 .40
❑ 195 Kory Casto 93 1.00 .40
❑ 196 Matt Chico 93 1.00 .40
❑ 197 John Danks 93 1.00 .40
❑ 198 Homer Bailey 93 1.50 .60
❑ 199 Ryan Braun 93 6.00 2.50
❑ 200 Felix Pie 93 1.00 .40
❑ 201 Jesus Flores 93 1.00 .40
❑ 202 Andy Gonzalez 93 1.00 .40
❑ 203 Ryan Sweeney 93 1.00 .40
❑ 204 Jarrod Saltalamacchia 93 1.50 .60
❑ 205 Alex Gordon 93 5.00 2.00
❑ 206 Josh Hamilton 93 2.50 1.00
❑ 207 Sean Henn 93 1.00 .40
❑ 208 Kei Igawa 93 2.50 1.00
❑ 209 Akinori Iwamura 93 2.50 1.00
❑ 210 Andy LaRoche 93 1.00 .40
❑ 211 Rick Vanden Hurk 93 1.50 .60
❑ 212 Kevin Kouzmanoff 93 1.00 .40
❑ 213 Matt Lindstrom 93 1.00 .40
❑ 214 Tim Lincecum 93 8.00 3.00
❑ 215 Daisuke Matsuzaka 93 10.00 4.00
❑ 216 Gustavo Molina 93 1.00 .40
❑ 217 Miguel Montero 93 1.00 .40
❑ 218 Brandon Morrow 93 1.50 .60
❑ 219 Hideki Okajima 93 5.00 2.00
❑ 220 Adam Lind 93 1.00 .40
❑ 221 Mike Rabelo 93 1.00 .40
❑ 222 Brian Burres 93 1.00 .40
❑ 223 Micah Owings 93 1.00 .40
❑ 224 Brandon Wood 93 1.00 .40
❑ 225 Alexi Casilla 93 1.50 .60
❑ 226 Joe Smith 93 1.00 .40
❑ 227 Hunter Pence 93 6.00 2.50
❑ 228 Glen Perkins 93 1.00 .40
❑ 229 Chris Stewart 93 1.00 .40
❑ 230 Ben Francisco 93 1.00 .40
❑ 231 Troy Tulowitzki 93 2.50 1.00
❑ 232 Billy Butler 93 1.50 .60
❑ 233 Delmon Young 93 1.50 .60
❑ 234 Phil Hughes 93 5.00 2.00
❑ 235 Joaquin Arias 96 .60 .25
❑ 236 Jeff Baker 96 .60 .25
❑ 237 Mark Reynolds 96 1.50 .60
❑ 238 Joseph Bisenius 96 .60 .25
❑ 239 Michael Bourn 96 .60 .25
❑ 240 Zack Segovia 96 .60 .25
❑ 241 Travis Buck 96 .60 .25
❑ 242 Chase Wright 96 1.50 .60
❑ 243 Rocky Cherry 96 1.50 .60
❑ 244 Danny Putnam 96 .60 .25
❑ 245 Kory Casto 96 .60 .25
❑ 246 Matt Chico 96 .60 .25
❑ 247 John Danks 96 .60 .25
❑ 248 Juan Salas 96 .60 .25
❑ 249 Ryan Braun 96 4.00 1.50
❑ 250 Felix Pie 96 .60 .25
❑ 251 Jesus Flores 96 .60 .25
❑ 252 Andy Gonzalez 96 .60 .25
❑ 253 Ryan Sweeney 96 .60 .25
❑ 254 Jarrod Saltalamacchia 96 1.00 .40
❑ 255 Alex Gordon 96 3.00 1.25
❑ 256 Josh Hamilton 96 1.50 .60
❑ 257 Sean Henn 96 .60 .25
❑ 258 Kei Igawa 96 1.50 .60
❑ 259 Akinori Iwamura 96 1.50 .60
❑ 260 Andy LaRoche 96 .60 .25
❑ 261 Rick Vanden Hurk 96 1.00 .40
❑ 262 Kevin Kouzmanoff 96 .60 .25
❑ 263 Matt Lindstrom 96 .60 .25
❑ 264 Tim Lincecum 96 5.00 2.00
❑ 265 Daisuke Matsuzaka 96 6.00 2.50
❑ 266 Gustavo Molina 96 .60 .25
❑ 267 Miguel Montero 96 .60 .25
❑ 268 Brandon Morrow 96 1.00 .40
❑ 269 Hideki Okajima 96 3.00 1.25
❑ 270 Adam Lind 96 .60 .25
❑ 271 Mike Rabelo 96 .60 .25
❑ 272 Brian Burres 96 .60 .25
❑ 273 Micah Owings 96 .60 .25
❑ 274 Brandon Wood 96 .60 .25
❑ 275 Alexi Casilla 96 1.00 .40
❑ 276 Joe Smith 96 .60 .25
❑ 277 Hunter Pence 96 4.00 1.50
❑ 278 Glen Perkins 96 .60 .25
❑ 279 Chris Stewart 96 .60 .25
❑ 280 Ben Francisco 96 .60 .25
❑ 281 Troy Tulowitzki 96 1.50 .60
❑ 282 Billy Butler 96 1.00 .40
❑ 283 Delmon Young 96 1.00 .40
❑ 284 Phil Hughes 96 3.00 1.25

2006 Upper Deck Special F/X

❑ COMMON CARD (1-900) .75 .30
❑ COMMON RC (901-1025) 1.25 .50
❑ 1 Adam Kennedy .75 .30
❑ 2 Bartolo Colon .75 .30
❑ 3 Bengie Molina .75 .30
❑ 4 Casey Kotchman .75 .30
❑ 5 Chone Figgins .75 .30
❑ 6 Dallas McPherson .75 .30
❑ 7 Darin Erstad .75 .30
❑ 8 Ervin Santana .75 .30
❑ 9 Francisco Rodriguez .75 .30
❑ 10 Garret Anderson .75 .30
❑ 11 Jarrod Washburn .75 .30
❑ 12 John Lackey .75 .30

❑ 13	Juan Rivera	.75	.30
❑ 14	Orlando Cabrera	.75	.30
❑ 15	Paul Byrd	.75	.30
❑ 16	Steve Finley	.75	.30
❑ 17	Vladimir Guerrero	2.00	.75
❑ 18	Alex Cintron	.75	.30
❑ 19	Brandon Lyon	.75	.30
❑ 20	Brandon Webb	.75	.30
❑ 21	Chad Tracy	.75	.30
❑ 22	Chris Snyder	.75	.30
❑ 23	Claudio Vargas	.75	.30
❑ 24	Conor Jackson	1.25	.50
❑ 25	Craig Counsell	.75	.30
❑ 26	Javier Vazquez	.75	.30
❑ 27	Jose Valverde	.75	.30
❑ 28	Luis Gonzalez	.75	.30
❑ 29	Royce Clayton	.75	.30
❑ 30	Russ Ortiz	.75	.30
❑ 31	Shawn Green	.75	.30
❑ 32	Dustin Nippert (RC)	1.25	.50
❑ 33	Tony Clark	.75	.30
❑ 34	Troy Glaus	.75	.30
❑ 35	Adam LaRoche	.75	.30
❑ 36	Andruw Jones	1.25	.50
❑ 37	Craig Hansen RC	5.00	2.00
❑ 38	Chipper Jones	2.00	.75
❑ 39	Horacio Ramirez	.75	.30
❑ 40	Jeff Francoeur	2.00	.75
❑ 41	John Smoltz	1.25	.50
❑ 42	Joey Devine RC	1.25	.50
❑ 43	Johnny Estrada	.75	.30
❑ 44	Anthony Lerew (RC)	1.25	.50
❑ 45	Julio Franco	.75	.30
❑ 46	Kyle Farnsworth	.75	.30
❑ 47	Marcus Giles	.75	.30
❑ 48	Mike Hampton	.75	.30
❑ 49	Rafael Furcal	.75	.30
❑ 50	Chuck James (RC)	2.00	.75
❑ 51	Tim Hudson	.75	.30
❑ 52	B.J. Ryan	.75	.30
❑ 53	Bernie Castro (RC)	1.25	.50
❑ 54	Brian Roberts	.75	.30
❑ 55	Walter Young (RC)	1.25	.50
❑ 56	Daniel Cabrera	.75	.30
❑ 57	Eric Byrnes	.75	.30
❑ 58	Alejandro Freire RC	1.25	.50
❑ 59	Erik Bedard	.75	.30
❑ 60	Javy Lopez	.75	.30
❑ 61	Jay Gibbons	.75	.30
❑ 62	Jorge Julio	.75	.30
❑ 63	Luis Matos	.75	.30
❑ 64	Melvin Mora	.75	.30
❑ 65	Miguel Tejada	.75	.30
❑ 66	Rafael Palmeiro	1.25	.50
❑ 67	Rodrigo Lopez	.75	.30
❑ 68	Sammy Sosa	2.00	.75
❑ 69	Alejandro Machado (RC)	1.25	.50
❑ 70	Bill Mueller	.75	.30
❑ 71	Bronson Arroyo	.75	.30
❑ 72	Curt Schilling	1.25	.50
❑ 73	David Ortiz	2.00	.75
❑ 74	David Wells	.75	.30
❑ 75	Edgar Renteria	.75	.30
❑ 76	Ryan Jorgensen RC	1.25	.50
❑ 77	Jason Varitek	2.00	.75
❑ 78	Johnny Damon	1.25	.50
❑ 79	Keith Foulke	.75	.30
❑ 80	Kevin Youkilis	.75	.30
❑ 81	Manny Ramirez	1.25	.50
❑ 82	Matt Clement	.75	.30
❑ 83	Hanley Ramirez (RC)	3.00	1.25
❑ 84	Tim Wakefield	.75	.30
❑ 85	Trot Nixon	.75	.30
❑ 86	Wade Miller	.75	.30
❑ 87	Aramis Ramirez	.75	.30
❑ 88	Carlos Zambrano	.75	.30
❑ 89	Corey Patterson	.75	.30
❑ 90	Derrek Lee	.75	.30
❑ 91	Geovany Soto (RC)	1.25	.50
❑ 92	Greg Maddux	3.00	1.25
❑ 93	Jeromy Burnitz	.75	.30
❑ 94	Jerry Hairston Jr.	.75	.30
❑ 95	Kerry Wood	.75	.30
❑ 96	Mark Prior	1.25	.50
❑ 97	Matt Murton	.75	.30
❑ 98	Michael Barrett	.75	.30
❑ 99	Neifi Perez	.75	.30
❑ 100	Nomar Garciaparra	2.00	.75
❑ 101	Rich Hill	.75	.30
❑ 102	Ryan Dempster	.75	.30
❑ 103	Todd Walker	.75	.30
❑ 104	A.J. Pierzynski	.75	.30
❑ 105	Aaron Rowand	.75	.30
❑ 106	Bobby Jenks	.75	.30
❑ 107	Carl Everett	.75	.30
❑ 108	Dustin Hermanson	.75	.30
❑ 109	Frank Thomas	2.00	.75
❑ 110	Freddy Garcia	.75	.30
❑ 111	Jermaine Dye	.75	.30
❑ 112	Joe Crede	.75	.30
❑ 113	Jon Garland	.75	.30
❑ 114	Jose Contreras	.75	.30
❑ 115	Juan Uribe	.75	.30
❑ 116	Mark Buehrle	.75	.30
❑ 117	Orlando Hernandez	.75	.30
❑ 118	Paul Konerko	.75	.30
❑ 119	Scott Podsednik	.75	.30
❑ 120	Tadahito Iguchi	.75	.30
❑ 121	Aaron Harang	.75	.30
❑ 122	Adam Dunn	.75	.30
❑ 123	Austin Kearns	.75	.30
❑ 124	Brandon Claussen	.75	.30
❑ 125	Chris Denorfia (RC)	1.25	.50
❑ 126	Edwin Encarnacion	.75	.30
❑ 127	Miguel Perez (RC)	1.25	.50
❑ 128	Felipe Lopez	.75	.30
❑ 129	Jason LaRue	.75	.30
❑ 130	Ken Griffey Jr.	3.00	1.25
❑ 131	Chris Booker (RC)	1.25	.50
❑ 132	Luke Hudson	.75	.30
❑ 133	Jason Bergmann RC	1.25	.50
❑ 134	Ryan Freel	.75	.30
❑ 135	Sean Casey	.75	.30
❑ 136	Wily Mo Pena	.75	.30
❑ 137	Aaron Boone	.75	.30
❑ 138	Ben Broussard	.75	.30
❑ 139	Ryan Garko (RC)	1.25	.50
❑ 140	C.C. Sabathia	.75	.30
❑ 141	Casey Blake	.75	.30
❑ 142	Cliff Lee	.75	.30
❑ 143	Coco Crisp	.75	.30
❑ 144	David Riske	.75	.30
❑ 145	Grady Sizemore	1.25	.50
❑ 146	Jake Westbrook	.75	.30
❑ 147	Jhonny Peralta	.75	.30
❑ 148	Josh Bard	.75	.30
❑ 149	Kevin Millwood	.75	.30
❑ 150	Ronnie Belliard	.75	.30
❑ 151	Scott Elarton	.75	.30
❑ 152	Travis Hafner	.75	.30
❑ 153	Victor Martinez	.75	.30
❑ 154	Aaron Cook	.75	.30
❑ 155	Aaron Miles	.75	.30
❑ 156	Brad Hawpe	.75	.30
❑ 157	Mike Esposito (RC)	1.25	.50
❑ 158	Chin-Hui Tsao	.75	.30
❑ 159	Clint Barmes	.75	.30
❑ 160	Cory Sullivan	.75	.30
❑ 161	Garrett Atkins	.75	.30
❑ 162	J.D. Closser	.75	.30
❑ 163	Jason Jennings	.75	.30
❑ 164	Jeff Baker	.75	.30
❑ 165	Jeff Francis	.75	.30
❑ 166	Luis Gonzalez	.75	.30
❑ 167	Matt Holliday	1.00	.40
❑ 168	Todd Helton	1.25	.50
❑ 169	Brandon Inge	.75	.30
❑ 170	Carlos Guillen	.75	.30
❑ 171	Carlos Pena	.75	.30
❑ 172	Chris Shelton	.75	.30
❑ 173	Craig Monroe	.75	.30
❑ 174	Curtis Granderson	.75	.30
❑ 175	Dmitri Young	.75	.30
❑ 176	Ivan Rodriguez	1.25	.50
❑ 177	Jason Johnson	.75	.30
❑ 178	Jeremy Bonderman	.75	.30
❑ 179	Magglio Ordonez	.75	.30
❑ 180	Mark Woodyard (RC)	1.25	.50
❑ 181	Nook Logan	.75	.30
❑ 182	Omar Infante	.75	.30
❑ 183	Placido Polanco	.75	.30
❑ 184	Chris Heintz RC	1.25	.50
❑ 185	A.J. Burnett	.75	.30
❑ 186	Alex Gonzalez	.75	.30
❑ 187	Josh Johnson (RC)	2.00	.75
❑ 188	Carlos Delgado	.75	.30
❑ 189	Dontrelle Willis	.75	.30
❑ 190	Josh Wilson (RC)	1.25	.50
❑ 191	Jason Vargas	.75	.30
❑ 192	Jeff Conine	.75	.30
❑ 193	Jeremy Hermida	.75	.30
❑ 194	Josh Beckett	.75	.30
❑ 195	Juan Encarnacion	.75	.30
❑ 196	Juan Pierre	.75	.30
❑ 197	Luis Castillo	.75	.30
❑ 198	Miguel Cabrera	1.25	.50
❑ 199	Mike Lowell	.75	.30
❑ 200	Paul Lo Duca	.75	.30
❑ 201	Todd Jones	.75	.30
❑ 202	Adam Everett	.75	.30
❑ 203	Andy Pettitte	.75	.30
❑ 204	Brad Ausmus	.75	.30
❑ 205	Brad Lidge	.75	.30
❑ 206	Brandon Backe	.75	.30
❑ 207	Charlton Jimerson (RC)	1.25	.50
❑ 208	Chris Burke	.75	.30
❑ 209	Craig Biggio	1.25	.50
❑ 210	Dan Wheeler	.75	.30
❑ 211	Jason Lane	.75	.30
❑ 212	Jeff Bagwell	1.25	.50
❑ 213	Lance Berkman	.75	.30
❑ 214	Luke Scott	.75	.30
❑ 215	Morgan Ensberg	.75	.30
❑ 216	Roger Clemens	4.00	1.50
❑ 217	Roy Oswalt	.75	.30
❑ 218	Willy Taveras	.75	.30
❑ 219	Andres Blanco	.75	.30
❑ 220	Angel Berroa	.75	.30
❑ 221	Ruben Gotay	.75	.30
❑ 222	David DeJesus	.75	.30
❑ 223	Emil Brown	.75	.30
❑ 224	J.P. Howell	.75	.30
❑ 225	Jeremy Affeldt	.75	.30
❑ 226	Jimmy Gobble	.75	.30
❑ 227	John Buck	.75	.30
❑ 228	Jose Lima	.75	.30
❑ 229	Mark Teahen	.75	.30
❑ 230	Matt Stairs	.75	.30
❑ 231	Mike MacDougal	.75	.30
❑ 232	Mike Sweeney	.75	.30
❑ 233	Runelvys Hernandez	.75	.30
❑ 234	Terrence Long	.75	.30
❑ 235	Zack Greinke	.75	.30
❑ 236	Ron Flores RC	1.25	.50
❑ 237	Brad Penny	.75	.30
❑ 238	Cesar Izturis	.75	.30
❑ 239	D.J. Houlton	.75	.30
❑ 240	Derek Lowe	.75	.30
❑ 241	Eric Gagne	.75	.30
❑ 242	Hee Seop Choi	.75	.30

❑ 243 J.D. Drew .75 .30
❑ 244 Jason Phillips .75 .30
❑ 245 Jason Repko .75 .30
❑ 246 Jayson Werth .75 .30
❑ 247 Jeff Kent .75 .30
❑ 248 Jeff Weaver .75 .30
❑ 249 Milton Bradley .75 .30
❑ 250 Odalis Perez .75 .30
❑ 251 Hong-Chih Kuo (RC) 3.00 1.25
❑ 252 Oscar Robles .75 .30
❑ 253 Ben Sheets .75 .30
❑ 254 Bill Hall .75 .30
❑ 255 Brady Clark .75 .30
❑ 256 Carlos Lee .75 .30
❑ 257 Chris Capuano .75 .30
❑ 258 Nelson Cruz (RC) 1.25 .50
❑ 259 Derrick Turnbow .75 .30
❑ 260 Doug Davis .75 .30
❑ 261 Geoff Jenkins .75 .30
❑ 262 J.J. Hardy .75 .30
❑ 263 Lyle Overbay .75 .30
❑ 264 Prince Fielder 3.00 1.25
❑ 265 Rickie Weeks .75 .30
❑ 266 Russell Branyan .75 .30
❑ 267 Tomo Ohka .75 .30
❑ 268 Jonah Bayliss (RC) 1.25 .50
❑ 269 Brad Radke .75 .30
❑ 270 Carlos Silva .75 .30
❑ 271 Francisco Liriano (RC) 6.00 2.50
❑ 272 Jacque Jones .75 .30
❑ 273 Joe Mauer 1.25 .50
❑ 274 Travis Bowyer (RC) 1.25 .50
❑ 275 Joe Nathan .75 .30
❑ 276 Johan Santana 1.25 .50
❑ 277 Justin Morneau .75 .30
❑ 278 Kyle Lohse .75 .30
❑ 279 Lew Ford .75 .30
❑ 280 Matthew LeCroy .75 .30
❑ 281 Michael Cuddyer .75 .30
❑ 282 Nick Punto .75 .30
❑ 283 Scott Baker .75 .30
❑ 284 Shannon Stewart .75 .30
❑ 285 Torii Hunter .75 .30
❑ 286 Braden Looper .75 .30
❑ 287 Carlos Beltran .75 .30
❑ 288 Cliff Floyd .75 .30
❑ 289 David Wright 3.00 1.25
❑ 290 Doug Mientkiewicz .75 .30
❑ 291 Anderson Hernandez (RC) 1.25 .50
❑ 292 Jose Reyes .75 .30
❑ 293 Kazuo Matsui .75 .30
❑ 294 Kris Benson .75 .30
❑ 295 Miguel Cairo .75 .30
❑ 296 Mike Cameron .75 .30
❑ 297 Robert Andino RC 1.25 .50
❑ 298 Mike Piazza 2.00 .75
❑ 299 Pedro Martinez 1.25 .50
❑ 300 Tom Glavine 1.25 .50
❑ 301 Victor Diaz .75 .30
❑ 302 Tim Hamulack (RC) 1.25 .50
❑ 303 Alex Rodriguez 3.00 1.25
❑ 304 Bernie Williams 1.25 .50
❑ 305 Carl Pavano .75 .30
❑ 306 Chien-Ming Wang 3.00 1.25
❑ 307 Derek Jeter 5.00 2.00
❑ 308 Gary Sheffield .75 .30
❑ 309 Hideki Matsui 2.00 .75
❑ 310 Jason Giambi .75 .30
❑ 311 Jorge Posada 1.25 .50
❑ 312 Kevin Brown .75 .30
❑ 313 Mariano Rivera 2.00 .75
❑ 314 Matt Lawton .75 .30
❑ 315 Mike Mussina 1.25 .50
❑ 316 Randy Johnson 2.00 .75
❑ 317 Robinson Cano 1.25 .50
❑ 318 Mike Vento (RC) 1.25 .50
❑ 319 Tino Martinez .75 .30
❑ 320 Tony Womack .75 .30
❑ 321 Barry Zito .75 .30
❑ 322 Bobby Crosby .75 .30
❑ 323 Bobby Kielty .75 .30
❑ 324 Dan Johnson .75 .30
❑ 325 Danny Haren .75 .30
❑ 326 Eric Chavez .75 .30
❑ 327 Erubiel Durazo .75 .30
❑ 328 Huston Street .75 .30
❑ 329 Jason Kendall .75 .30
❑ 330 Jay Payton .75 .30
❑ 331 Joe Blanton .75 .30
❑ 332 Joe Kennedy .75 .30
❑ 333 Kirk Saarloos .75 .30
❑ 334 Mark Kotsay .75 .30
❑ 335 Nick Swisher .75 .30
❑ 336 Rich Harden .75 .30
❑ 337 Scott Hatteberg .75 .30
❑ 338 Billy Wagner .75 .30
❑ 339 Bobby Abreu .75 .30
❑ 340 Brett Myers .75 .30
❑ 341 Chase Utley 2.00 .75
❑ 342 Danny Sandoval RC 1.25 .50
❑ 343 David Bell .75 .30
❑ 344 Gavin Floyd .75 .30
❑ 345 Jim Thome 1.25 .50
❑ 346 Jimmy Rollins .75 .30
❑ 347 Jon Lieber .75 .30
❑ 348 Kenny Lofton .75 .30
❑ 349 Mike Lieberthal .75 .30
❑ 350 Pat Burrell .75 .30
❑ 351 Randy Wolf .75 .30
❑ 352 Ryan Howard 3.00 1.25
❑ 353 Vicente Padilla .75 .30
❑ 354 Bryan Bullington (RC) 1.25 .50
❑ 355 J.J. Furmaniak (RC) 1.25 .50
❑ 356 Craig Wilson .75 .30
❑ 357 Matt Capps (RC) 1.25 .50
❑ 358 Tom Gorzelanny (RC) 1.25 .50
❑ 359 Jack Wilson .75 .30
❑ 360 Jason Bay .75 .30
❑ 361 Jose Mesa .75 .30
❑ 362 Josh Fogg .75 .30
❑ 363 Kip Wells .75 .30
❑ 364 Steve Stemle RC 1.25 .50
❑ 365 Oliver Perez .75 .30
❑ 366 Rob Mackowiak .75 .30
❑ 367 Ronny Paulino (RC) 1.25 .50
❑ 368 Tike Redman .75 .30
❑ 369 Zach Duke .75 .30
❑ 370 Adam Eaton .75 .30
❑ 371 Scott Feldman (RC) 1.25 .50
❑ 372 Brian Giles .75 .30
❑ 373 Brian Lawrence .75 .30
❑ 374 Damian Jackson .75 .30
❑ 375 Dave Roberts .75 .30
❑ 376 Jake Peavy .75 .30
❑ 377 Joe Randa .75 .30
❑ 378 Khalil Greene 1.25 .50
❑ 379 Mark Loretta .75 .30
❑ 380 Ramon Hernandez .75 .30
❑ 381 Robert Fick .75 .30
❑ 382 Ryan Klesko .75 .30
❑ 383 Trevor Hoffman .75 .30
❑ 384 Woody Williams .75 .30
❑ 385 Xavier Nady .75 .30
❑ 386 Armando Benitez .75 .30
❑ 387 Brad Hennessey .75 .30
❑ 388 Brian Myrow RC 1.25 .50
❑ 389 Edgardo Alfonzo .75 .30
❑ 390 J.T. Snow .75 .30
❑ 391 Jeremy Accardo RC 1.25 .50
❑ 392 Jason Schmidt .75 .30
❑ 393 Lance Niekro .75 .30
❑ 394 Matt Cain 1.25 .50
❑ 395 Daniel Ortmeier (RC) 1.25 .50
❑ 396 Moises Alou .75 .30
❑ 397 Doug Clark (RC) 1.25 .50
❑ 398 Omar Vizquel 1.25 .50
❑ 399 Pedro Feliz .75 .30
❑ 400 Randy Winn .75 .30
❑ 401 Ray Durham .75 .30
❑ 402 Adrian Beltre .75 .30
❑ 403 Eddie Guardado .75 .30
❑ 404 Felix Hernandez 1.25 .50
❑ 405 Gil Meche .75 .30
❑ 406 Ichiro Suzuki 3.00 1.25
❑ 407 Jamie Moyer .75 .30
❑ 408 Jeff Nelson .75 .30
❑ 409 Jeremy Reed .75 .30
❑ 410 Joel Pineiro .75 .30
❑ 411 Jaime Bubela (RC) 1.25 .50
❑ 412 Raul Ibanez .75 .30
❑ 413 Richie Sexson .75 .30
❑ 414 Ryan Franklin .75 .30
❑ 415 Willie Bloomquist .75 .30
❑ 416 Yorvit Torrealba .75 .30
❑ 417 Yuniesky Betancourt .75 .30
❑ 418 Jeff Harris RC 1.25 .50
❑ 419 Albert Pujols 4.00 1.50
❑ 420 Chris Carpenter .75 .30
❑ 421 David Eckstein .75 .30
❑ 422 Jason Isringhausen .75 .30
❑ 423 Jason Marquis .75 .30
❑ 424 Adam Wainwright (RC) 1.25 .50
❑ 425 Jim Edmonds 1.25 .50
❑ 426 Ryan Theriot RC 1.25 .50
❑ 427 Chris Duncan (RC) 2.00 .75
❑ 428 Mark Grudzielanek .75 .30
❑ 429 Mark Mulder .75 .30
❑ 430 Matt Morris .75 .30
❑ 431 Reggie Sanders .75 .30
❑ 432 Scott Rolen 1.25 .50
❑ 433 Tyler Johnson (RC) 1.25 .50
❑ 434 Yadier Molina .75 .30
❑ 435 Alex Gonzalez .75 .30
❑ 436 Aubrey Huff .75 .30
❑ 437 Tim Corcoran RC 1.25 .50
❑ 438 Carl Crawford .75 .30
❑ 439 Casey Fossum .75 .30
❑ 440 Danys Baez .75 .30
❑ 441 Edwin Jackson .75 .30
❑ 442 Joey Gathright .75 .30
❑ 443 Jonny Gomes .75 .30
❑ 444 Jorge Cantu .75 .30
❑ 445 Julio Lugo .75 .30
❑ 446 Nick Green .75 .30
❑ 447 Rocco Baldelli .75 .30
❑ 448 Scott Kazmir 1.25 .50
❑ 449 Seth McClung .75 .30
❑ 450 Toby Hall .75 .30
❑ 451 Travis Lee .75 .30
❑ 452 Craig Breslow RC 1.25 .50
❑ 453 Alfonso Soriano .75 .30
❑ 454 Chris R. Young .75 .30
❑ 455 David Dellucci .75 .30
❑ 456 Francisco Cordero .75 .30
❑ 457 Gary Matthews .75 .30
❑ 458 Hank Blalock .75 .30
❑ 459 Juan Dominguez .75 .30
❑ 460 Josh Rupe (RC) 1.25 .50
❑ 461 Kenny Rogers .75 .30
❑ 462 Kevin Mench .75 .30
❑ 463 Laynce Nix .75 .30
❑ 464 Mark Teixeira 1.25 .50
❑ 465 Michael Young .75 .30
❑ 466 Richard Hidalgo .75 .30
❑ 467 Jason Botts (RC) 1.25 .50
❑ 468 Aaron Hill .75 .30
❑ 469 Alex Rios .75 .30
❑ 470 Corey Koskie .75 .30
❑ 471 Chris Demaria RC 1.25 .50
❑ 472 Eric Hinske .75 .30
❑ 473 Frank Catalanotto .75 .30
❑ 474 John-Ford Griffin (RC) 1.25 .50
❑ 475 Gustavo Chacin .75 .30
❑ 476 Josh Towers .75 .30
❑ 477 Miguel Batista .75 .30
❑ 478 Orlando Hudson .75 .30
❑ 479 Reed Johnson .75 .30
❑ 480 Roy Halladay .75 .30
❑ 481 Shaun Marcum (RC) 1.25 .50
❑ 482 Shea Hillenbrand .75 .30
❑ 483 Ted Lilly .75 .30
❑ 484 Vernon Wells .75 .30
❑ 485 Brad Wilkerson .75 .30
❑ 486 Darrell Rasner (RC) 1.25 .50
❑ 487 Chad Cordero .75 .30